2020
Harris
Michigan
Industrial Directory

Published February 2020 next update February 2021

WARNING: Purchasers and users of this directory may not use this directory to compile mailing lists, other marketing aids and other types of data, which are sold or otherwise provided to third parties. Such use is wrongful, illegal and a violation of the federal copyright laws.

CAUTION: Because of the many thousands of establishment listings contained in this directory and the possibilities of both human and mechanical error in processing this information, Harris InfoSource cannot assume liability for the correctness of the listings or information on which they are based. Hence, no information contained in this work should be relied upon in any instance where there is a possibility of any loss or damage as a consequence of any error or omission in this volume.

Publisher

Mergent Inc.
444 Madison Ave
New York, NY 10022

©Mergent Inc All Rights Reserved
2020 Mergent Business Press
ISSN 1080-2614
ISBN 978-1-64141-621-4

TABLE OF CONTENTS

Summary of Contents & Explanatory Notes 4
User's Guide to Listings 6

Geographic Section
County/City Cross-Reference Index 9
Firms Listed by Location 13

Standard Industrial Classification (SIC) Section
SIC Alphabetical Index 689
SIC Numerical Index 691
Firms Listed by SIC 695

Alphabetic Section
Firms Listed by Firm Name 881

Product Section
Product Index 1115
Firms Listed by Product Category 1139

SUMMARY OF CONTENTS

Number of Companies 18,203
Number of Decision Makers 37,763
Minimum Number of Employees 3

EXPLANATORY NOTES

How to Cross-Reference in This Directory

Sequential Entry Numbers. Each establishment in the Geographic Section is numbered sequentially (G-0000). The number assigned to each establishment is referred to as its "entry number." To make cross-referencing easier, each listing in the Geographic, SIC, Alphabetic and Product Sections includes the establishment's entry number. To facilitate locating an entry in the Geographic Section, the entry numbers for the first listing on the left page and the last listing on the right page are printed at the top of the page next to the city name.

Source Suggestions Welcome

Although all known sources were used to compile this directory, it is possible that companies were inadvertently omitted. Your assistance in calling attention to such omissions would be greatly appreciated. A special form on the facing page will help you in the reporting process.

Analysis

Every effort has been made to contact all firms to verify their information. The one exception to this rule is the annual sales figure, which is considered by many companies to be confidential information. Therefore, estimated sales have been calculated by multiplying the nationwide average sales per employee for the firm's major SIC/NAICS code by the firm's number of employees. Nationwide averages for sales per employee by SIC/NAICS codes are provided by the U.S. Department of Commerce and are updated annually. All sales—sales (est)—have been estimated by this method. The exceptions are parent companies (PA), division headquarters (DH) and headquarter locations (HQ) which may include an actual corporate sales figure—sales (corporate-wide) if available.

Types of Companies

Descriptive and statistical data are included for companies in the entire state. These comprise manufacturers, machine shops, fabricators, assemblers and printers. Also identified are corporate offices in the state.

Employment Data

The employment figure shown in the Geographic Section includes male and female employees and embraces all levels of the company: administrative, clerical, sales and maintenance. This figure is for the facility listed and does not include other plants or offices. It should be recognized that these figures represent an approximate year-round average. These employment figures are broken into codes A through G and used in the Product and SIC Sections to further help you in qualifying a company. Be sure to check the footnotes on the bottom of pages for the code breakdowns.

Standard Industrial Classification (SIC)

The Standard Industrial Classification (SIC) system used in this directory was developed by the federal government for use in classifying establishments by the type of activity they are engaged in. The SIC classifications used in this directory are from the 1987 edition published by the U.S. Government's Office of Management and Budget. The SIC system separates all activities into broad industrial divisions (e.g., manufacturing, mining, retail trade). It further subdivides each division. The range of manufacturing industry classes extends from two-digit codes (major industry group) to four-digit codes (product).

For example:

Industry Breakdown	Code	Industry, Product, etc.
*Major industry group	20	Food and kindred products
Industry group	203	Canned and frozen foods
*Industry	2033	Fruits and vegetables, etc.

*Classifications used in this directory

Only two-digit and four-digit codes are used in this directory.

Arrangement

1. The **Geographic Section** contains complete in-depth corporate data. This section is sorted by cities listed in alphabetical order and companies listed alphabetically within each city. A County/City Index for referencing cities within counties precedes this section.

> IMPORTANT NOTICE: It is a violation of both federal and state law to transmit an unsolicited advertisement to a facsimile machine. Any user of this product that violates such laws may be subject to civil and criminal penalties, which may exceed $500 for each transmission of an unsolicited facsimile. Harris InfoSource provides fax numbers for lawful purposes only and expressly forbids the use of these numbers in any unlawful manner.

2. The **Standard Industrial Classification (SIC) Section** lists companies under approximately 500 four-digit SIC codes. An alphabetical and a numerical index precedes this section. A company can be listed under several codes. The codes are in numerical order with companies listed alphabetically under each code.

3. The **Alphabetic Section** lists all companies with their full physical or mailing addresses and telephone number.

4. The **Product Section** lists companies under unique Harris categories. An index preceding this section lists all product categories in alphabetical order. Companies can be listed under several categories.

USER'S GUIDE TO LISTINGS

GEOGRAPHIC SECTION

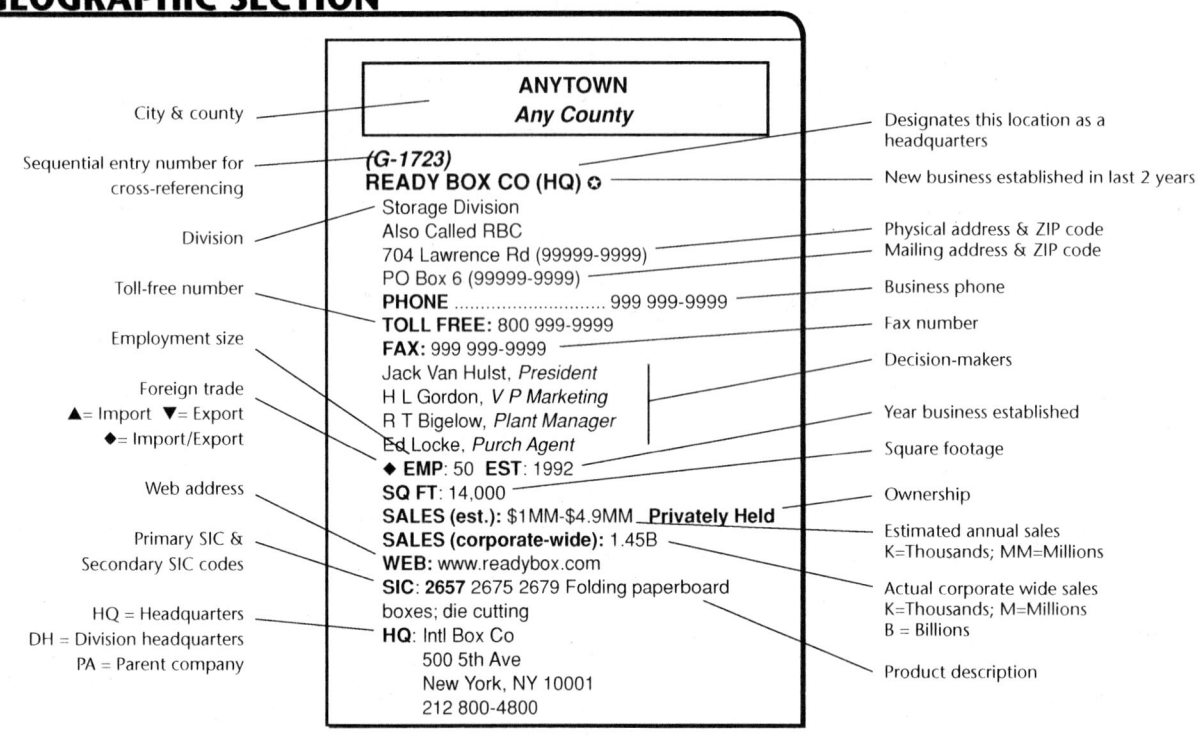

SIC SECTION

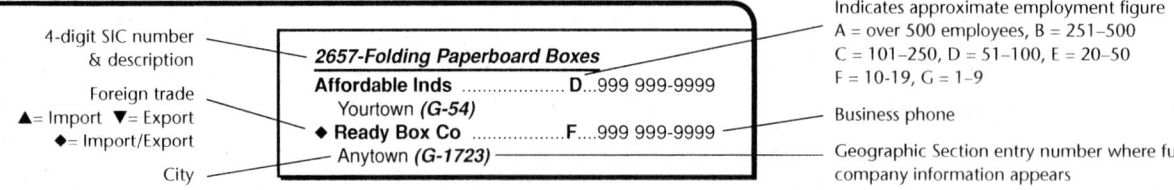

ALPHABETIC SECTION

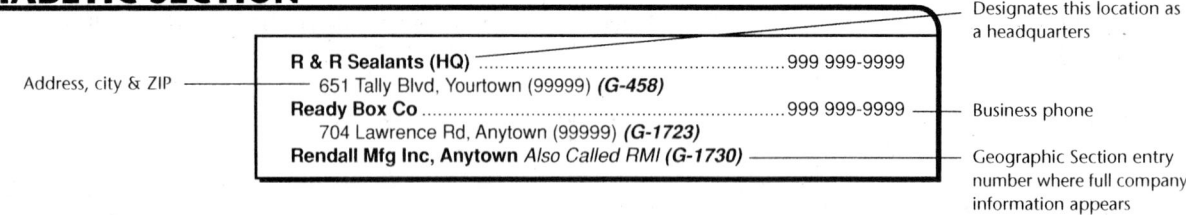

PRODUCT SECTION

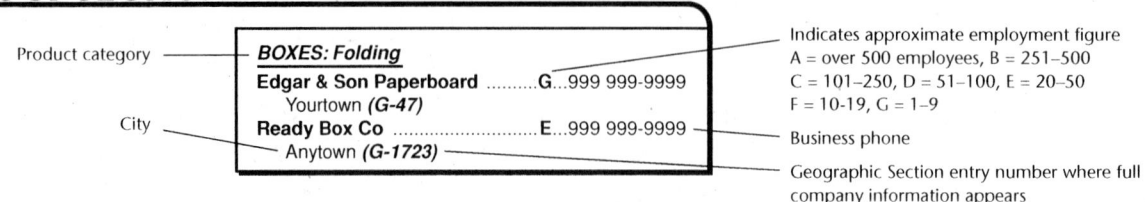

GEOGRAPHIC SECTION
Companies sorted by city in alphabetical order
In-depth company data listed

STANDARD INDUSTRIAL CLASSIFICATIONS
Alphabetical index of classifcation descriptions
Numerical index of classifcation descriptions
Companies sorted by SIC product groupings

ALPHABETIC SECTION
Company listings in alphabetical order

PRODUCT INDEX
Product categories listed in alphabetical order

PRODUCT SECTION
Companies sorted by product and manufacturing service classifications

COUNTY/CITY CROSS-REFERENCE INDEX

Alcona
City	Entry #
Curran	(G-3617)
Glennie	(G-5942)
Greenbush	(G-7120)
Harrisville	(G-7361)
Lincoln	(G-9561)
Spruce	(G-15213)

Alger
City	Entry #
Chatham	(G-2675)
Eben Junction	(G-4740)
Grand Marais	(G-6118)
Munising	(G-11243)
Trenary	(G-16149)
Wetmore	(G-17615)

Allegan
City	Entry #
Allegan	(G-146)
Burnips	(G-2133)
Dorr	(G-4523)
Douglas	(G-4530)
Fennville	(G-5169)
Hamilton	(G-7228)
Hopkins	(G-7959)
Martin	(G-10594)
Moline	(G-11010)
Otsego	(G-12235)
Plainwell	(G-12516)
Pullman	(G-13087)
Saugatuck	(G-14458)
Wayland	(G-17396)

Alpena
City	Entry #
Alpena	(G-271)
Herron	(G-7470)
Hubbard Lake	(G-8125)
Lachine	(G-9075)
Ossineke	(G-12230)

Antrim
City	Entry #
Alba	(G-112)
Alden	(G-137)
Bellaire	(G-1434)
Central Lake	(G-2588)
Eastport	(G-4714)
Elk Rapids	(G-4774)
Ellsworth	(G-4787)
Kewadin	(G-9037)
Mancelona	(G-10384)

Arenac
City	Entry #
Alger	(G-138)
Au Gres	(G-740)
Omer	(G-12144)
Standish	(G-15215)
Sterling	(G-15242)
Turner	(G-16708)

Baraga
City	Entry #
Baraga	(G-1096)
Covington	(G-3593)
Keweenaw Bay	(G-9041)
Lanse	(G-9188)
Watton	(G-17395)

Barry
City	Entry #
Delton	(G-3815)
Dowling	(G-4564)
Freeport	(G-5763)
Hastings	(G-7401)
Middleville	(G-10796)
Nashville	(G-11458)
Woodland	(G-17943)

Bay
City	Entry #
Auburn	(G-748)
Bay City	(G-1269)
Bentley	(G-1477)
Essexville	(G-4867)
Kawkawlin	(G-8969)
Linwood	(G-9598)
Munger	(G-11241)
Pinconning	(G-12506)

Benzie
City	Entry #
Benzonia	(G-1573)
Beulah	(G-1608)
Frankfort	(G-5598)
Honor	(G-7952)
Lake Ann	(G-9083)

Berrien
City	Entry #
Baroda	(G-1123)
Benton Harbor	(G-1478)
Berrien Center	(G-1590)
Berrien Springs	(G-1591)
Bridgman	(G-1859)
Buchanan	(G-2108)
Coloma	(G-3353)
Eau Claire	(G-4737)
Galien	(G-5817)
New Buffalo	(G-11514)
New Troy	(G-11560)
Niles	(G-11592)
Riverside	(G-13285)
Saint Joseph	(G-14300)
Sawyer	(G-14481)
Sodus	(G-14745)
Stevensville	(G-15551)
Three Oaks	(G-15848)
Union Pier	(G-16737)
Watervliet	(G-17390)

Branch
City	Entry #
Bronson	(G-2022)
Coldwater	(G-3286)
Montgomery	(G-11100)
Quincy	(G-13088)
Sherwood	(G-14737)
Union City	(G-16731)

Calhoun
City	Entry #
Albion	(G-113)
Athens	(G-729)
Battle Creek	(G-1137)
Burlington	(G-2132)
Ceresco	(G-2601)
East Leroy	(G-4684)
Homer	(G-7936)
Marshall	(G-10562)
Springfield	(G-15187)
Tekonsha	(G-15817)

Cass
City	Entry #
Cassopolis	(G-2526)
Dowagiac	(G-4533)
Edwardsburg	(G-4756)
Jones	(G-8651)
Marcellus	(G-10464)
Union	(G-16727)
Vandalia	(G-16799)

Charlevoix
City	Entry #
Beaver Island	(G-1381)
Boyne City	(G-1815)
Boyne Falls	(G-1839)
Charlevoix	(G-2604)
East Jordan	(G-4626)

Cheboygan
City	Entry #
Afton	(G-105)
Cheboygan	(G-2676)
Indian River	(G-8217)
Mackinaw City	(G-10098)
Wolverine	(G-17934)

Chippewa
City	Entry #
Barbeau	(G-1117)
Brimley	(G-2013)
Dafter	(G-3620)
De Tour Village	(G-3667)
Drummond Island	(G-4565)
Kincheloe	(G-9050)
Paradise	(G-12382)
Pickford	(G-12481)
Rudyard	(G-13983)
Sault Sainte Marie	(G-14461)

Clare
City	Entry #
Clare	(G-2863)
Farwell	(G-5157)
Harrison	(G-7307)
Lake	(G-9082)

Clinton
City	Entry #
Bath	(G-1134)
Dewitt	(G-4459)
Eagle	(G-4616)
Elsie	(G-4795)
Fowler	(G-5553)
Lansing	(G-9201)
Ovid	(G-12271)
Saint Johns	(G-14280)
Westphalia	(G-17614)

Crawford
City	Entry #
Frederic	(G-5750)
Grayling	(G-7101)

Delta
City	Entry #
Bark River	(G-1118)
Cornell	(G-3575)
Escanaba	(G-4811)
Gladstone	(G-5906)
Rapid River	(G-13111)
Rock	(G-13552)

Dickinson
City	Entry #
Channing	(G-2603)
Felch	(G-5167)
Iron Mountain	(G-8274)
Kingsford	(G-9054)
Norway	(G-11816)
Quinnesec	(G-13101)
Sagola	(G-14186)
Vulcan	(G-16846)

Eaton
City	Entry #
Bellevue	(G-1453)
Charlotte	(G-2636)
Dimondale	(G-4519)
Eaton Rapids	(G-4715)
Grand Ledge	(G-6099)
Lansing	(G-9272)
Mulliken	(G-11238)
Olivet	(G-12141)
Potterville	(G-13072)
Sunfield	(G-15644)
Vermontville	(G-16821)

Emmet
City	Entry #
Alanson	(G-110)
Harbor Springs	(G-7272)
Levering	(G-9546)
Pellston	(G-12425)
Petoskey	(G-12439)

Genesee
City	Entry #
Burton	(G-2142)
Clio	(G-3266)
Davison	(G-3640)
Fenton	(G-5180)
Flint	(G-5366)
Flushing	(G-5530)
Gaines	(G-5804)
Goodrich	(G-5951)
Grand Blanc	(G-5958)
Lennon	(G-9518)
Linden	(G-9590)
Montrose	(G-11101)
Mount Morris	(G-11155)
Otisville	(G-12232)
Swartz Creek	(G-15659)

Gladwin
City	Entry #
Beaverton	(G-1382)
Gladwin	(G-5922)

Gogebic
City	Entry #
Bessemer	(G-1603)
Ironwood	(G-8323)
Wakefield	(G-16848)
Watersmeet	(G-17389)

Grand Traverse
City	Entry #
Acme	(G-1)
Grawn	(G-7096)
Interlochen	(G-8236)
Kingsley	(G-9069)
Traverse City	(G-15886)
Williamsburg	(G-17710)

Gratiot
City	Entry #
Alma	(G-231)
Ashley	(G-726)
Breckenridge	(G-1843)
Elwell	(G-4797)
Ithaca	(G-8355)
Middleton	(G-10793)
North Star	(G-11667)
Perrinton	(G-12432)
Riverdale	(G-13284)
Saint Louis	(G-14357)
Sumner	(G-15642)
Wheeler	(G-17617)

Hillsdale
City	Entry #
Allen	(G-193)
Camden	(G-2338)
Hillsdale	(G-7512)
Jonesville	(G-8653)
Litchfield	(G-9600)
North Adams	(G-11654)
Osseo	(G-12226)
Pittsford	(G-12515)
Reading	(G-13136)
Waldron	(G-16857)

Houghton
City	Entry #
Atlantic Mine	(G-735)
Calumet	(G-2324)
Chassell	(G-2671)
Dollar Bay	(G-4521)
Hancock	(G-7247)
Houghton	(G-7971)
Hubbell	(G-8126)
Lake Linden	(G-9107)
Laurium	(G-9502)
Pelkie	(G-12421)
South Range	(G-14817)
Toivola	(G-15885)

Huron
City	Entry #
Bad Axe	(G-1056)
Bay Port	(G-1372)
Caseville	(G-2505)
Elkton	(G-4782)
Filion	(G-5346)
Harbor Beach	(G-7263)
Pigeon	(G-12485)
Port Austin	(G-12878)
Ruth	(G-13987)
Sebewaing	(G-14514)
Ubly	(G-16716)

Ingham
City	Entry #
East Lansing	(G-4649)
Haslett	(G-7396)
Holt	(G-7904)
Lansing	(G-9330)
Leslie	(G-9540)
Mason	(G-10628)
Okemos	(G-12112)
Stockbridge	(G-15588)
Webberville	(G-17446)
Williamston	(G-17725)

Ionia
City	Entry #
Belding	(G-1396)
Clarksville	(G-2966)
Ionia	(G-8247)
Lake Odessa	(G-9110)
Lyons	(G-10094)
Muir	(G-11237)
Pewamo	(G-12478)
Portland	(G-13060)
Saranac	(G-14452)

Iosco
City	Entry #
East Tawas	(G-4686)
Hale	(G-7224)
National City	(G-11464)
Oscoda	(G-12205)
Tawas City	(G-15675)
Whittemore	(G-17709)

Iron
City	Entry #
Amasa	(G-330)
Caspian	(G-2509)

COUNTY/CITY CROSS-REFERENCE

	ENTRY #		ENTRY #		ENTRY #		ENTRY #		ENTRY #
Crystal Falls	(G-3608)	Attica	(G-739)	Ray	(G-13131)	Erie	(G-4800)	Huntington Woods	(G-8188)
Iron River	(G-8307)	Clifford	(G-3009)	Richmond	(G-13257)	Ida	(G-8193)	Keego Harbor	(G-8978)
Isabella		Columbiaville	(G-3376)	Romeo	(G-13623)	La Salle	(G-9074)	Lake Orion	(G-9121)
Blanchard	(G-1711)	Dryden	(G-4567)	Roseville	(G-13766)	Lambertville	(G-9181)	Lakeville	(G-9177)
Mount Pleasant	(G-11168)	Imlay City	(G-8195)	Saint Clair Shores	(G-14238)	Maybee	(G-10672)	Lathrup Village	(G-9497)
Rosebush	(G-13765)	Lapeer	(G-9439)	Shelby Township	(G-14538)	Milan	(G-10931)	Leonard	(G-9526)
Shepherd	(G-14726)	Lum	(G-10090)	Sterling Heights	(G-15245)	Monroe	(G-11012)	Madison Heights	(G-10175)
Weidman	(G-17456)	Metamora	(G-10772)	Sterling Hts	(G-15549)	Newport	(G-11587)	Milford	(G-10952)
Winn	(G-17746)	North Branch	(G-11657)	Utica	(G-16740)	Ottawa Lake	(G-12259)	New Hudson	(G-11530)
Jackson		**Leelanau**		Warren	(G-16905)	Petersburg	(G-12434)	Novi	(G-11822)
Brooklyn	(G-2036)	Cedar	(G-2539)	Washington	(G-17302)	South Rockwood	(G-14820)	Oak Park	(G-12047)
Clarklake	(G-2893)	Glen Arbor	(G-5940)	Washington Township (G-17320)		Temperance	(G-15822)	Oakland	(G-12106)
Concord	(G-3523)	Lake Leelanau	(G-9098)	**Manistee**		**Montcalm**		Oakland Township	(G-12110)
Grass Lake	(G-7083)	Maple City	(G-10460)	Bear Lake	(G-1376)	Carson City	(G-2488)	Orchard Lake	(G-12164)
Hanover	(G-7260)	Northport	(G-11670)	Brethren	(G-1847)	Coral	(G-3574)	Orion	(G-12172)
Horton	(G-7963)	Suttons Bay	(G-15649)	Copemish	(G-3572)	Crystal	(G-3607)	Ortonville	(G-12193)
Jackson	(G-8368)	**Lenawee**		Filer City	(G-5345)	Edmore	(G-4749)	Oxford	(G-12332)
Michigan Center	(G-10783)	Addison	(G-36)	Kaleva	(G-8930)	Greenville	(G-7122)	Pleasant Ridge	(G-12555)
Munith	(G-11252)	Adrian	(G-41)	Manistee	(G-10413)	Howard City	(G-8000)	Pontiac	(G-12797)
Parma	(G-12387)	Blissfield	(G-1712)	Onekama	(G-12151)	Lakeview	(G-9171)	Rochester	(G-13311)
Pleasant Lake	(G-12552)	Britton	(G-2018)	Wellston	(G-17463)	Pierson	(G-12484)	Rochester Hills	(G-13357)
Rives Junction	(G-13308)	Cement City	(G-2574)	**Marquette**		Sheridan	(G-14732)	Royal Oak	(G-13897)
Spring Arbor	(G-15118)	Clayton	(G-3006)	Arnold	(G-725)	Sidney	(G-14738)	Sidney	(G-14739)
Springport	(G-15208)	Clinton	(G-3015)	Champion	(G-2602)	Six Lakes	(G-14740)	South Lyon	(G-14785)
Kalamazoo		Deerfield	(G-3811)	Gwinn	(G-7215)	Stanton	(G-15227)	Southfield	(G-14823)
Augusta	(G-1052)	Hudson	(G-8127)	Ishpeming	(G-8342)	Vestaburg	(G-16825)	Sylvan Lake	(G-15671)
Climax	(G-3012)	Manitou Beach	(G-10448)	Marquette	(G-10517)	**Montmorency**		Troy	(G-16164)
Galesburg	(G-5805)	Morenci	(G-11109)	Negaunee	(G-11466)	Atlanta	(G-730)	Walled Lake	(G-16889)
Kalamazoo	(G-8670)	Onsted	(G-12152)	Palmer	(G-12381)	Hillman	(G-7508)	Waterford	(G-17321)
Portage	(G-12980)	Tecumseh	(G-15784)	Republic	(G-13244)	Lewiston	(G-9547)	West Bloomfield	(G-17464)
Richland	(G-13248)	Tipton	(G-15884)	**Mason**		**Muskegon**		White Lake	(G-17628)
Schoolcraft	(G-14489)	Weston	(G-17613)	Ludington	(G-10047)	Bailey	(G-1077)	Wixom	(G-17748)
Scotts	(G-14503)	**Livingston**		Scottville	(G-14508)	Brunswick	(G-2107)	Wolverine Lake	(G-17935)
Vicksburg	(G-16830)	Brighton	(G-1875)	**Mecosta**		Casnovia	(G-2507)	**Oceana**	
Kalkaska		Fowlerville	(G-5557)	Big Rapids	(G-1622)	Fruitport	(G-5787)	Hart	(G-7370)
Fife Lake	(G-5339)	Gregory	(G-7164)	Mecosta	(G-10687)	Holton	(G-7932)	Hesperia	(G-7477)
Kalkaska	(G-8935)	Hamburg	(G-7225)	Morley	(G-11117)	Montague	(G-11089)	Mears	(G-10686)
Rapid City	(G-13109)	Hartland	(G-7388)	Paris	(G-12383)	Muskegon	(G-11255)	New ERA	(G-11519)
South Boardman	(G-14748)	Howell	(G-8008)	Remus	(G-13237)	Norton Shores	(G-11737)	Pentwater	(G-12428)
Kent		Pinckney	(G-12495)	Rodney	(G-13612)	Ravenna	(G-13118)	Rothbury	(G-13894)
Ada	(G-3)	**Luce**		Stanwood	(G-15231)	Twin Lake	(G-16712)	Shelby	(G-14523)
Alto	(G-322)	Mc Millan	(G-10685)	**Menominee**		Whitehall	(G-17660)	Walkerville	(G-16884)
Belmont	(G-1455)	Newberry	(G-11579)	Carney	(G-2463)	**Newaygo**		**Ogemaw**	
Byron Center	(G-2175)	**Mackinac**		Daggett	(G-3621)	Bitely	(G-1710)	Lupton	(G-10091)
Caledonia	(G-2287)	Cedarville	(G-2566)	Hermansville	(G-7466)	Fremont	(G-5768)	Prescott	(G-13080)
Cedar Springs	(G-2544)	Curtis	(G-3619)	Ingalls	(G-8224)	Grant	(G-7077)	Rose City	(G-13756)
Comstock Park	(G-3458)	Engadine	(G-4798)	Menominee	(G-10721)	Newaygo	(G-11563)	South Branch	(G-14749)
Grand Rapids	(G-6119)	Hessel	(G-7481)	Powers	(G-13076)	White Cloud	(G-17618)	West Branch	(G-17505)
Grandville	(G-7015)	Mackinac Island	(G-10097)	Spalding	(G-15086)	**Oakland**		**Ontonagon**	
Kent City	(G-8986)	Moran	(G-11107)	Stephenson	(G-15235)	Auburn Hills	(G-759)	Kenton	(G-8995)
Kentwood	(G-8997)	Naubinway	(G-11465)	Wallace	(G-16885)	Berkley	(G-1577)	Mass City	(G-10661)
Lowell	(G-10022)	Saint Ignace	(G-14279)	**Midland**		Beverly Hills	(G-1613)	Ontonagon	(G-12158)
Rockford	(G-13555)	**Macomb**		Coleman	(G-3342)	Bingham Farms	(G-1648)	Trout Creek	(G-16162)
Sand Lake	(G-14423)	Armada	(G-714)	Edenville	(G-4748)	Birmingham	(G-1674)	White Pine	(G-17658)
Sparta	(G-15088)	Bruce Twp	(G-2077)	Hope	(G-7954)	Bloomfield	(G-1731)	**Osceola**	
Walker	(G-16861)	Center Line	(G-2576)	Midland	(G-10812)	Bloomfield Hills	(G-1738)	Evart	(G-4877)
Wyoming	(G-17983)	Chesterfield	(G-2730)	Sanford	(G-14448)	Clarkston	(G-2903)	Hersey	(G-7471)
Keweenaw		Clinton Township	(G-3026)	**Missaukee**		Clawson	(G-2968)	Leroy	(G-9529)
Ahmeek	(G-108)	Eastpointe	(G-4697)	Falmouth	(G-4891)	Commerce Township	(G-3384)	Marion	(G-10489)
Eagle Harbor	(G-4618)	Fraser	(G-5610)	Lake City	(G-9085)	Davisburg	(G-3624)	Reed City	(G-13210)
Lake		Harrison Township	(G-7317)	Mc Bain	(G-10677)	Detroit	(G-3821)	Sears	(G-14512)
Baldwin	(G-1081)	Harrison Twp	(G-7360)	Merritt	(G-10763)	Farmington	(G-4894)	Tustin	(G-16709)
Irons	(G-8322)	Lenox	(G-9520)	**Monroe**		Farmington Hills	(G-4917)	**Oscoda**	
Luther	(G-10093)	Macomb	(G-10102)	Carleton	(G-2451)	Ferndale	(G-5251)	Comins	(G-3383)
Lapeer		Mount Clemens	(G-11122)	Dundee	(G-4574)	Franklin	(G-5608)	Fairview	(G-4889)
Almont	(G-250)	New Baltimore	(G-11479)			Hazel Park	(G-7432)	Mio	(G-11002)
		New Haven	(G-11522)			Highland	(G-7483)		
						Holly	(G-7868)		

2020 Harris Michigan Industrial Directory

COUNTY/CITY CROSS-REFERENCE

Otsego
City	Entry #
Elmira	(G-4790)
Gaylord	(G-5847)
Johannesburg	(G-8649)
Vanderbilt	(G-16803)

Ottawa
City	Entry #
Allendale	(G-214)
Conklin	(G-3528)
Coopersville	(G-3547)
Ferrysburg	(G-5332)
Grand Haven	(G-5990)
Holland	(G-7544)
Hudsonville	(G-8143)
Jenison	(G-8616)
Macatawa	(G-10096)
Marne	(G-10503)
Norton Shores	(G-11806)
Nunica	(G-12031)
Spring Lake	(G-15130)
West Olive	(G-17531)
Zeeland	(G-18109)

Presque Isle
City	Entry #
Hawks	(G-7430)
Millersburg	(G-10991)
Onaway	(G-12145)
Posen	(G-13069)
Presque Isle	(G-13082)
Rogers City	(G-13613)

Roscommon
City	Entry #
Higgins Lake	(G-7482)
Houghton Lake	(G-7987)
Prudenville	(G-13084)
Roscommon	(G-13747)
Saint Helen	(G-14278)

Saginaw
City	Entry #
Birch Run	(G-1663)
Bridgeport	(G-1848)
Burt	(G-2139)
Carrollton	(G-2484)
Chesaning	(G-2722)
Frankenmuth	(G-5582)
Freeland	(G-5752)
Hemlock	(G-7459)
Merrill	(G-10760)
Oakley	(G-12111)
Saginaw	(G-13990)
Saint Charles	(G-14189)

Sanilac
City	Entry #
Applegate	(G-712)
Argyle	(G-713)
Brown City	(G-2044)
Carsonville	(G-2497)
Croswell	(G-3595)
Deckerville	(G-3807)
Lexington	(G-9556)
Marlette	(G-10494)
Melvin	(G-10691)
Minden City	(G-11000)
Peck	(G-12418)
Sandusky	(G-14428)
Snover	(G-14741)

Schoolcraft
City	Entry #
Cooks	(G-3546)
Germfask	(G-5901)
Gulliver	(G-7211)
Manistique	(G-10438)
Seney	(G-14522)

Shiawassee
City	Entry #
Bancroft	(G-1087)
Byron	(G-2171)
Corunna	(G-3577)
Durand	(G-4604)
Henderson	(G-7465)
Laingsburg	(G-9080)
Morrice	(G-11119)
Owosso	(G-12275)
Perry	(G-12433)

St. Clair
City	Entry #
Algonac	(G-141)
Allenton	(G-228)
Anchorville	(G-331)
Brockway	(G-2019)
Burtchville	(G-2140)
Capac	(G-2447)
Casco	(G-2498)
China	(G-2858)
Clay	(G-2991)
Clyde	(G-3282)
Columbus	(G-3377)
Cottrellville	(G-3587)
East China	(G-4619)
Fort Gratiot	(G-5547)
Greenwood	(G-7163)
Harsens Island	(G-7368)
Ira	(G-8255)
Kenockee	(G-8984)
Kimball	(G-9042)
Marine City	(G-10470)
Marysville	(G-10598)
Memphis	(G-10709)
Mussey	(G-11457)
North Street	(G-11668)
Port Huron	(G-12879)
Riley	(G-13273)
Saint Clair	(G-14204)
Wales	(G-16859)
Yale	(G-18045)

St. Joseph
City	Entry #
Burr Oak	(G-2134)
Centreville	(G-2593)
Colon	(G-3369)
Constantine	(G-3532)
Mendon	(G-10711)
Sturgis	(G-15594)
Three Rivers	(G-15853)
White Pigeon	(G-17643)

Tuscola
City	Entry #
Akron	(G-109)
Caro	(G-2465)
Cass City	(G-2510)
Fostoria	(G-5552)
Gagetown	(G-5801)
Kingston	(G-9073)
Mayville	(G-10675)
Millington	(G-10993)
Reese	(G-13228)
Vassar	(G-16810)

Van Buren
City	Entry #
Bangor	(G-1088)
Bloomingdale	(G-1812)
Covert	(G-3591)
Decatur	(G-3802)
Gobles	(G-5946)
Grand Junction	(G-6098)
Hartford	(G-7381)
Kendall	(G-8983)
Lawrence	(G-9504)
Lawton	(G-9510)
Mattawan	(G-10662)
Paw Paw	(G-12396)
South Haven	(G-14751)

Washtenaw
City	Entry #
Ann Arbor	(G-332)
Chelsea	(G-2698)
Dexter	(G-4470)
Manchester	(G-10401)
Saline	(G-14371)
Superior Township	(G-15647)
Whitmore Lake	(G-17683)
Willis	(G-17744)
Ypsilanti	(G-18049)

Wayne
City	Entry #
Allen Park	(G-194)
Belleville	(G-1439)
Brownstown	(G-2058)
Brownstown Township	(G-2069)
Brownstown Twp	(G-2071)
Canton	(G-2342)
Dearborn	(G-3669)
Dearborn Heights	(G-3777)
Detroit	(G-3823)
Ecorse	(G-4741)
Flat Rock	(G-5347)
Garden City	(G-5820)
Gibraltar	(G-5904)
Grosse Ile	(G-7167)
Grosse Pointe	(G-7178)
Grosse Pointe Farms	(G-7185)
Grosse Pointe Park	(G-7189)
Grosse Pointe Shores	(G-7198)
Grosse Pointe Woods	(G-7201)
Hamtramck	(G-7243)
Harper Woods	(G-7299)
Highland Park	(G-7502)
Inkster	(G-8225)
Lincoln Park	(G-9572)
Livonia	(G-9614)
Melvindale	(G-10692)
New Boston	(G-11496)
Northville	(G-11674)
Plymouth	(G-12557)
Redford	(G-13140)
River Rouge	(G-13274)
Riverview	(G-13288)
Rockwood	(G-13603)
Romulus	(G-13644)
Southgate	(G-15071)
Taylor	(G-15685)
Trenton	(G-16152)
Van Buren Twp	(G-16745)
Wayne	(G-17421)
Westland	(G-17537)
Woodhaven	(G-17937)
Wyandotte	(G-17944)

Wexford
City	Entry #
Buckley	(G-2128)
Cadillac	(G-2219)
Manton	(G-10450)
Mesick	(G-10766)

GEOGRAPHIC SECTION

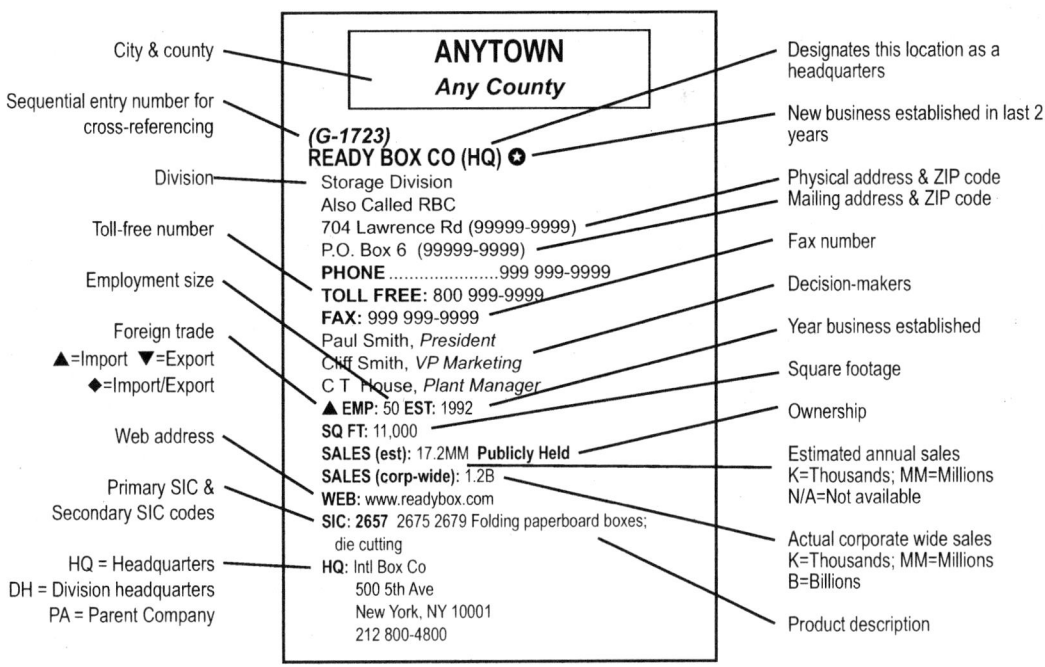

See footnotes for symbols and codes identification.
- This section is in alphabetical order by city.
- Companies are sorted alphabetically under their respective cities.
- To locate cities within a county refer to the County/City Cross Reference Index.

IMPORTANT NOTICE: It is a violation of both federal and state law to transmit an unsolicited advertisement to a facsimile machine. Any user of this product that violates such laws may be subject to civil and criminal penalties which may exceed $500 for each transmission of an unsolicited facsimile. Harris InfoSource provides fax numbers for lawful purposes only and expressly forbids the use of these numbers in any unlawful manner.

Acme
Grand Traverse County

(G-1)
ACME TOOL & DIE CO
5181 S Lautner Rd (49610)
P.O. Box 208 (49610-0208)
PHONE..................................231 938-1260
Lewis C Griffith, *Owner*
EMP: 4
SALES: 160K **Privately Held**
SIC: 3469 3585 3312 3544 Metal stampings; ice making machinery; tool & die steel; special dies, tools, jigs & fixtures; sheet metalwork

(G-2)
ADVANCED INC
5474 Em 72 (49610)
P.O. Box 157 (49610-0157)
PHONE..................................231 938-2233
Christopher Stoppel, *President*
Lois Stoppel, *Vice Pres*
EMP: 6
SQ FT: 3,000
SALES (est): 784.6K **Privately Held**
SIC: 5999 2394 Awnings; canvas & related products

Ada
Kent County

(G-3)
ACCESS BUSINESS GROUP LLC (DH)
7575 Fulton St E (49355-0001)
P.O. Box 513 (49301-0513)
PHONE..................................616 787-6000
Allen Senninger, *Superintendent*
Jamie Francis, *Business Mgr*
Lisa Smith, *Counsel*
Jeff Hazy, *Project Mgr*
Tim Marvel, *Project Mgr*
▲ **EMP:** 277
SQ FT: 3,200,000
SALES (est): 974.6MM
SALES (corp-wide): 8.7B **Privately Held**
SIC: 2842 5122 2833 5136 Specialty cleaning, polishes & sanitation goods; drugs, proprietaries & sundries; toiletries; cosmetics, perfumes & hair products; vitamins, natural or synthetic: bulk, uncompounded; men's & boys' clothing; women's & children's clothing; detergents & soaps, except specialty cleaning
HQ: Alticor Inc.
7575 Fulton St E
Ada MI 49355
616 787-1000

(G-4)
ADA GAGE INC
9450 Grand River Dr Se (49301-9246)
PHONE..................................616 676-3338
David Theule Jr, *President*
Kim Tubergen, *Opers Dir*
EMP: 6
SALES (est): 678.9K **Privately Held**
WEB: www.adagage.com
SIC: 3544 Special dies & tools

(G-5)
ALTICOR GLOBAL HOLDINGS INC (PA)
7575 Fulton St E (49301)
PHONE..................................616 787-1000
Doug Devos, *President*
Joseph Heindlmeyer, *Principal*
Lindsay Rappold, *Regional Mgr*
Jay Ertl, *Vice Pres*
Mike Horrigan, *Vice Pres*
EMP: 10
SQ FT: 3,200,000
SALES (est): 8.7B **Privately Held**
SIC: 5963 2833 5136 5137 Direct selling establishments; food services, direct sales; beverage services, direct sales; vitamins, natural or synthetic: bulk, uncompounded; men's & boys' clothing; women's & children's clothing; furniture; detergents & soaps, except specialty cleaning

(G-6)
ALTICOR INC (DH)
Also Called: Amway
7575 Fulton St E (49355-0001)
PHONE..................................616 787-1000
Scott Balfour, *President*
Doug Devos, *President*
Richard M Devos Sr, *President*
Steve Van Andel, *Chairman*
Brad Rick, *COO*
◆ **EMP:** 120 **EST:** 1949
SQ FT: 3,200,000
SALES (est): 8.7B
SALES (corp-wide): 8.7B **Privately Held**
WEB: www.alticor.com
SIC: 5963 2833 5136 5137 Direct selling establishments; food services, direct sales; beverage services, direct sales; vitamins, natural or synthetic: bulk, uncompounded; men's & boys' clothing; women's & children's clothing; furniture; detergents & soaps, except specialty cleaning
HQ: Solstice Holdings Inc.
7575 Fulton St E
Ada MI 49355
616 787-1000

(G-7)
AMWAY INTERNATIONAL INC (DH)
7575 Fulton St E (49355-0001)
PHONE..................................616 787-1000
Douglas Devos, *President*
Jerry Cunningham, *Vice Pres*
Edward Van Dam, *Vice Pres*
Amir Amirfazli, *Project Mgr*
Allen Scnninger, *Engineer*
◆ **EMP:** 27
SQ FT: 2,800,000
SALES (est): 929.4MM
SALES (corp-wide): 8.7B **Privately Held**
SIC: 5963 5122 5099 5199 Direct selling establishments; toiletries; cosmetics; vitamins & minerals; child restraint seats, automotive; video & audio equipment; gifts & novelties; fabrics, yarns & knit goods; food preparations; canned specialties
HQ: Alticor Inc.
7575 Fulton St E
Ada MI 49355
616 787-1000

Ada - Kent County (G-8)

(G-8)
AMWAY INTERNATIONAL DEV INC (DH)
7575 Fulton St E (49301)
PHONE..................................616 787-6000
Lynn J Lyall, *Principal*
Bill Roth, *Treasurer*
EMP: 10
SALES (est): 2.4MM
SALES (corp-wide): 8.7B **Privately Held**
SIC: 2844 2841 Toilet preparations; soap & other detergents
HQ: Amway International, Inc
  7575 Fulton St E
  Ada MI 49355
  616 787-1000

(G-9)
ARCTUITION LLC
8011 Thornapple Clb Dr Se (49301-9415)
PHONE..................................616 635-9959
Pei Zhan, *CEO*
Charles Nivison,
EMP: 6
SALES (est): 169.7K **Privately Held**
SIC: 7372 Application computer software

(G-10)
BAKER BOOK HOUSE COMPANY (PA)
Also Called: Baker Publishing Group
6030 Fulton St E (49301-9156)
P.O. Box 6287, Grand Rapids (49516-6287)
PHONE..................................616 676-9185
Dwight Baker, *CEO*
Brian Thomasson, *Editor*
Richard Baker, *Chairman*
Jack Kuhatschek, *Exec VP*
Daniel Baker, *Vice Pres*
▲ **EMP:** 148
SQ FT: 90,000
SALES: 59.8MM **Privately Held**
WEB: www.brazospress.com
SIC: 2731 5942 Books: publishing only; book stores; books, religious

(G-11)
BPG INTERNATIONAL FIN CO LLC (PA)
Also Called: Burke Porter Group
4760 Fulton St E Ste 201 (49301-9097)
PHONE..................................616 855-1480
Daniel Webber,
EMP: 1 **EST:** 2017
SALES (est): 32.8MM **Privately Held**
SIC: 3552 8711 7363 Opening machinery & equipment; engineering services; industrial engineers; engineering help service

(G-12)
DAILY DE-LISH
1235 Thrnpple River Dr Se (49301-7574)
PHONE..................................616 450-9562
Molly Dawson, *Principal*
EMP: 5
SALES (est): 256.1K **Privately Held**
SIC: 2711 Newspapers, publishing & printing

(G-13)
DIE THERM ENGINEERING LLC
5387 Hartfield Ct Se (49301-7727)
PHONE..................................616 915-6975
Greg Jacobs, *CFO*
Scott Kirkman, *Mng Member*
EMP: 3
SALES (est): 344K **Privately Held**
SIC: 3599 Machine shop, jobbing & repair

(G-14)
DRILL TECHNOLOGY
Also Called: Willmar
399 Greentree Ln Ne (49301-9796)
P.O. Box 456 (49301-0456)
PHONE..................................616 676-1287
William Ogrady, *Owner*
William O'Grady, *Owner*
EMP: 3
SQ FT: 10,000
SALES (est): 300.2K **Privately Held**
WEB: www.drilltechnology.com
SIC: 3545 7389 Drills (machine tool accessories); shaping tools (machine tool accessories); hand tool designers

(G-15)
FALCON PRINTING INC
Also Called: Falcon Promotional Tools
6360 Fulton St E (49301-9038)
P.O. Box 280 (49301-0280)
PHONE..................................616 676-3737
Juergen Lohrke, *President*
Kathy Cross, *Vice Pres*
Tom Kerkstra, *Vice Pres*
EMP: 20
SQ FT: 23,000
SALES (est): 3.7MM **Privately Held**
WEB: www.falconprinting.com
SIC: 2752 Commercial printing, offset

(G-16)
GENERAL ELECTRIC COMPANY
7575 Fulton St E 74-1a (49355-0001)
P.O. Box 767 (49301-0767)
PHONE..................................616 676-0870
Michael Mazowita, *Partner*
Buck Surratt, *Manager*
EMP: 10
SALES (corp-wide): 121.6B **Publicly Held**
SIC: 3569 Assembly machines, non-metalworking
PA: General Electric Company
  41 Farnsworth St
  Boston MA 02210
  617 443-3000

(G-17)
GUDHO USA INC
138 Deer Run Dr Ne (49301-9541)
PHONE..................................616 682-7814
Karin Deutschler, *President*
EMP: 12
SALES (est): 778.9K **Privately Held**
SIC: 3553 Woodworking machinery

(G-18)
HUBBLE ENTERPRISES INC
7807 Ashwood Dr Se (49301-8542)
PHONE..................................616 676-4485
Julie Hubble, *President*
EMP: 3
SALES (est): 361.7K **Privately Held**
SIC: 3089 Plastics products

(G-19)
JOSTENS INC
4670 Fulton St E Ste 202 (49301-8409)
PHONE..................................734 308-3879
EMP: 4
SALES (corp-wide): 1.4B **Privately Held**
SIC: 5944 3915 Jewelry, precious stones & precious metals; jewelers' materials & lapidary work
HQ: Jostens, Inc.
  7760 France Ave S Ste 400
  Minneapolis MN 55435
  952 830-3300

(G-20)
K S B PROMOTIONS INC
55 Honey Creek Ave Ne (49301-8209)
PHONE..................................616 676-0758
Kate Bandos, *President*
Doug Bandos, *Vice Pres*
EMP: 3
SALES: 95K **Privately Held**
WEB: www.ksbpromotions.com
SIC: 8743 2731 Public relations & publicity; promotion service; book publishing

(G-21)
KEM ENTERPRISES INC
579 Roundtree Dr Ne (49301-9707)
PHONE..................................616 676-0213
Kellie Laine, *Principal*
EMP: 3
SALES (est): 236K **Privately Held**
WEB: www.kemonline.com
SIC: 3089 Injection molded finished plastic products

(G-22)
M-INDUSTRIES LLC
6352 Fulton St E (49301-9038)
PHONE..................................616 682-4642
Jack McNally, *Marketing Staff*
Karlis Mateus, *Mng Member*
EMP: 12
SALES (est): 2.2MM **Privately Held**
SIC: 2631 Container, packaging & boxboard

(G-23)
MERCHANDISING PRODUCTIONS
7575 Fulton St E (49356-0001)
PHONE..................................616 676-6000
Jay Van Andel, *Ch of Bd*
Richard De Vos, *President*
Lawrence M Call, *Treasurer*
EMP: 38
SALES (est): 4.3MM
SALES (corp-wide): 8.7B **Privately Held**
WEB: www.alticor.com
SIC: 2844 Cosmetic preparations
HQ: Alticor Inc.
  7575 Fulton St E
  Ada MI 49355
  616 787-1000

(G-24)
MICHIGAN MED INNOVATIONS LLC
481 Pettis Ave Se (49301-9540)
PHONE..................................616 682-4848
Robert C Shaver, *Mng Member*
EMP: 5 **EST:** 2008
SALES (est): 389.4K **Privately Held**
SIC: 3841 Diagnostic apparatus, medical

(G-25)
NOBLE FILMS CORPORATION
967 Spaulding Ave Se B1 (49301-3700)
PHONE..................................616 977-3770
Christine Nicoletti, *President*
▲ **EMP:** 9
SALES (est): 1.3MM **Privately Held**
SIC: 2671 Packaging paper & plastics film, coated & laminated

(G-26)
PENIN OIL & GAS COMPAN MICHIGA
555 Ada Dr Se (49301-9024)
P.O. Box 96 (49301-0096)
PHONE..................................616 676-2090
Gary McAleenan, *Partner*
EMP: 5
SALES (est): 364.7K **Privately Held**
WEB: www.pent.com
SIC: 1382 1389 Oil & gas exploration services; oil field services

(G-27)
PENINSULAR TECHNOLOGIES LLC
555 Ada Dr Se (49301-9024)
P.O. Box 728 (49301-0728)
PHONE..................................616 676-9811
Laurie Hans, *Manager*
Jamie Taggart, *CTO*
Gary F McAleenan,
EMP: 14
SALES (est): 1.2MM **Privately Held**
SIC: 7372 Prepackaged software

(G-28)
PERFORATED TUBES INC
4850 Fulton St E (49301-9062)
PHONE..................................616 942-4550
Alan C Doezema Jr, *President*
David B Doezema, *Vice Pres*
Bruce Daniels, *Purch Mgr*
Scott Hillyer, *Asst Controller*
EMP: 30 **EST:** 1954
SQ FT: 36,000
SALES (est): 9.3MM **Privately Held**
WEB: www.perftubes.com
SIC: 3317 Tubes, seamless steel

(G-29)
SB3 LLC
967 Spaulding Ave Se B (49301-3700)
PHONE..................................877 978-6286
Thomas Rinks, *President*
Rene Canetti, *Vice Pres*
Brian Van Dommelen, *Vice Pres*
▲ **EMP:** 3
SALES (est): 343.5K **Privately Held**
SIC: 2844 2253 Suntan lotions & oils; beachwear, knit

(G-30)
TELOCYTE LLC
9464 Conservation St Ne (49301-9752)
PHONE..................................616 570-4515
Michael Fossel,
Mark Hodges,
Peter Rayson,
EMP: 3
SQ FT: 123
SALES (est): 164K **Privately Held**
SIC: 2834 Solutions, pharmaceutical

(G-31)
TIP TOP GRAVEL CO INC
9741 Fulton St E (49301-8915)
PHONE..................................616 897-8342
John Mathews, *President*
June Mathews, *Vice Pres*
EMP: 7 **EST:** 1966
SQ FT: 500
SALES (est): 1.9MM **Privately Held**
SIC: 1442 1794 Gravel mining; excavation work

(G-32)
TITANIUM OPERATIONS LLC
5199 Mountain Ridge Dr Ne (49301-9557)
PHONE..................................616 717-0218
Jacob Lueder, *Principal*
EMP: 6 **EST:** 2011
SALES (est): 618.1K **Privately Held**
SIC: 3356 Titanium

(G-33)
WALTZ-HOLST BLOW PIPE COMPANY
230 Alta Dale Ave Se (49301-9113)
PHONE..................................616 676-8119
Karl Paganelli, *President*
James D Holst, *Treasurer*
Donald Lang, *Controller*
Matt Paganelli, *Sales Engr*
EMP: 40
SQ FT: 33,500
SALES: 16.1MM **Privately Held**
WEB: www.waltzholst.com
SIC: 3444 3564 1796 3443 Sheet metalwork; air cleaning systems; installing building equipment; fabricated plate work (boiler shop)

(G-34)
WEST MICHIGAN PRINTING INC
Also Called: Grand Rapids Legal News
513 Pine Land Dr Se (49301-9119)
PHONE..................................616 676-2190
EMP: 5 **EST:** 1935
SQ FT: 13,500
SALES (est): 410K **Privately Held**
SIC: 2752 2721 Lithographic Commercial Printing Periodicals-Publishing/Printing

(G-35)
WMC SALES LLC
4455 Tiffany Ave Ne (49301-8216)
PHONE..................................616 813-7237
Mark Putnam, *President*
EMP: 3
SALES (est): 277.9K **Privately Held**
SIC: 3531 Cranes

Addison
Lenawee County

(G-36)
DARBY READY MIX CONCRETE CO
Also Called: Darbyreadymix.com
U.S 12 & Herold Hwy (49220)
PHONE..................................517 547-7004
Randy Darby, *President*
Mike Comstock, *Vice Pres*
EMP: 22
SQ FT: 2,500
SALES (est): 3.8MM **Privately Held**
SIC: 3273 3272 Ready-mixed concrete; concrete products

▲ = Import ▼ = Export
◆ = Import/Export

GEOGRAPHIC SECTION
Adrian - Lenawee County (G-64)

(G-37)
NEXT SPECIALTY RESINS INC
215 N Talbot St (49220-1100)
P.O. Box 365 (49220-0365)
PHONE..................................419 843-4600
Shirish Naik, *Plant Mgr*
Shirish M Naik, *Administration*
EMP: 15
SALES (est): 2.7MM **Privately Held**
SIC: 2821 Molding compounds, plastics
PA: Next Specialty Resins, Inc.
  3315 Centennial Rd Ste J
  Sylvania OH 43560

(G-38)
ROUND LAKE SAND & GRAVEL INC
8707 Round Lake Hwy (49220-9736)
P.O. Box 90, West Millgrove OH (43467-0090)
PHONE..................................517 467-4458
Tim Cottrill, *Opers-Prdtn-Mfg*
EMP: 7
SQ FT: 500
SALES (corp-wide): 2.6MM **Privately Held**
SIC: 1442 Common sand mining; gravel mining
PA: Round Lake Sand & Gravel, Inc.
  6126 S Main St
  West Millgrove OH
  419 288-2790

(G-39)
SEAGATE PLASTICS COMPANY
320 S Steer St (49220-9632)
PHONE..................................517 547-8123
Eric Harbaugh, *Branch Mgr*
EMP: 20
SQ FT: 8,500
SALES (corp-wide): 11.9MM **Privately Held**
WEB: www.seagateplastics.com
SIC: 3089 Injection molding of plastics; plastic processing
PA: Seagate Plastics Company
  1110 Disher Dr
  Waterville OH 43566
  419 878-5010

(G-40)
US 223 INLAND MARINE LLC
17250 Us Highway 223 (49220-9541)
PHONE..................................517 547-2628
Mark Olford,
Mark Qlford,
EMP: 4
SALES (est): 275.5K **Privately Held**
SIC: 3799 Boat trailers

Adrian
Lenawee County

(G-41)
A TIME TO REMEMBER
4450 W Carleton Rd (49221-9770)
PHONE..................................517 263-1960
Kerri Daniels, *Owner*
EMP: 3
SALES (est): 96K **Privately Held**
SIC: 2732 Books: printing & binding

(G-42)
ACE DRILL CORPORATION
2600 E Maumee St (49221-3533)
P.O. Box 160 (49221-0160)
PHONE..................................517 265-5184
Alfred J Brown, *CEO*
Joan Brown, *Corp Secy*
Alfred J Brown III, *Vice Pres*
EMP: 6
SQ FT: 50,000
SALES (est): 3.5MM **Privately Held**
SIC: 5051 3545 3546 Steel; drills (machine tool accessories); reamers, machine tool; drills & drilling tools

(G-43)
ADRIAN COATINGS COMPANY
3202 Northmor Dr W (49221-9135)
PHONE..................................517 438-8699
Erik Skampo, *Principal*
EMP: 22
SALES (est): 2.6MM **Privately Held**
SIC: 3479 Metal coating & allied service

(G-44)
ADRIAN LVA BIOFUEL LLC
Also Called: W2fuel Adrian
1571 W Beecher Rd (49221-8754)
PHONE..................................517 920-4863
Paul Orentas,
EMP: 16
SALES (est): 2MM **Privately Held**
SIC: 2869 Fuels

(G-45)
ADRIAN PRECISION MACHINING LLC
605 Industrial Dr (49221-8767)
PHONE..................................517 263-4564
Derek Frey, *Office Mgr*
Jason Fisher,
EMP: 20
SQ FT: 800
SALES (est): 2.8MM **Privately Held**
SIC: 3544 Special dies & tools

(G-46)
ADRIAN STEEL COMPANY (PA)
906 James St (49221-3996)
PHONE..................................517 265-6194
Harley J Westfall, *Ch of Bd*
David E Pilmore, *President*
Steve Patterson, *Vice Pres*
Randy Marks, *Prdtn Mgr*
Barry Barnhart, *Production*
▼ **EMP:** 375 **EST:** 1953
SQ FT: 165,000
SALES (est): 125MM **Privately Held**
SIC: 3496 3469 Shelving, made from purchased wire; boxes: tool, lunch, mail, etc.: stamped metal

(G-47)
ADRIAN TEAM LLC
795 Richlyn Dr (49221-9297)
PHONE..................................517 264-6148
J P McDevitt, *Principal*
EMP: 3
SALES (est): 143.4K **Privately Held**
SIC: 2711 Newspapers

(G-48)
ADRIAN TOOL CORPORATION
1441 Enterprise Ave (49221-8789)
PHONE..................................517 263-6530
G Steven Pickle, *President*
Todd Renner, *Sales Mgr*
Keith Behm, *Manager*
EMP: 23
SQ FT: 20,000
SALES (est): 5.5MM **Privately Held**
WEB: www.adrian-tool.com
SIC: 3441 3544 Fabricated structural metal; special dies, tools, jigs & fixtures

(G-49)
ANDERSON DEVELOPMENT COMPANY
Also Called: ADC
1415 E Michigan St (49221-3499)
PHONE..................................517 263-2121
Mark Kramer, *President*
Joseph Greulich, *President*
Naoya Sakamoto, *Exec VP*
Jay Nollman, *Engineer*
Barry E Swartz, *CFO*
◆ **EMP:** 115 **EST:** 1965
SQ FT: 183,000
SALES (est): 47.8MM **Privately Held**
WEB: www.andersondevelopment.com
SIC: 2821 Plastics materials & resins
HQ: Mitsui Chemicals America, Inc.
  800 Westchester Ave N607
  Rye Brook NY 10573
  914 253-0777

(G-50)
AUTO TRIM NORTHWEST OHIO IN
2294 Porter Hwy (49221-9782)
PHONE..................................517 265-3202
Robert O'Leary, *Owner*
EMP: 3
SALES (est): 306.3K **Privately Held**
SIC: 3993 Signs & advertising specialties

(G-51)
BRAZEWAY INC (PA)
2711 E Maumee St (49221-3586)
PHONE..................................517 265-2121
Stephen L Hickman, *Ch of Bd*
Stephanie Hickman Boyse, *President*
Michael Adams, *Vice Pres*
John P Benzing, *Vice Pres*
Emory M Schmidt, *Vice Pres*
▲ **EMP:** 100
SQ FT: 102,000
SALES (est): 218MM **Privately Held**
WEB: www.brazeway.com
SIC: 3354 3353 Tube, extruded or drawn, aluminum; aluminum sheet, plate & foil

(G-52)
C & J PALLETS INC
2368 E Us Highway 223 (49221-9251)
PHONE..................................517 263-7415
Edd Keck, *President*
Nancy Keck, *Vice Pres*
EMP: 6
SQ FT: 3,000
SALES (est): 725.6K **Privately Held**
SIC: 2448 Pallets, wood & wood with metal

(G-53)
CARTER INDUSTRIES INC
906 James St (49221-3914)
PHONE..................................510 324-6700
David Pilmore, *President*
Joe Emens, *Vice Pres*
Joseph E Emens, *CFO*
Harley Westfall, *Treasurer*
EMP: 30
SQ FT: 62,000
SALES (est): 3.9MM
SALES (corp-wide): 125MM **Privately Held**
WEB: www.carterind.com
SIC: 3713 5531 5013 3714 Truck & bus bodies; truck equipment & parts; motor vehicle supplies & new parts; motor vehicle parts & accessories
PA: Adrian Steel Company
  906 James St
  Adrian MI 49221
  517 265-6194

(G-54)
CASTALLOY CORPORATION
414 Addison St (49221-2401)
PHONE..................................517 265-2452
Ernest McDonnell, *President*
EMP: 6
SALES (est): 677.4K **Privately Held**
SIC: 3365 Aluminum foundries

(G-55)
CENTRAL LENAWEE SEWAGE PLANT
4350 Deerfield Rd (49221-9604)
PHONE..................................517 263-0955
Steven May, *Manager*
EMP: 4
SALES (est): 273.6K **Privately Held**
SIC: 3589 Sewage & water treatment equipment

(G-56)
D K PRODUCTS INC
2370 E Us Highway 223 (49221-9251)
P.O. Box 187 (49221-0187)
PHONE..................................517 263-3025
William B Brown, *President*
EMP: 3
SQ FT: 7,000
SALES (est): 300K **Privately Held**
WEB: www.dkproducts.com
SIC: 3549 Metalworking machinery

(G-57)
DAIRY FARMERS AMERICA INC
1336 E Maumee St (49221-3444)
PHONE..................................517 265-5045
Dan Hofbauer, *Prdtn Mgr*
Mark Keller, *Branch Mgr*
EMP: 30
SQ FT: 15,000
SALES (corp-wide): 13.6B **Privately Held**
WEB: www.dfamilk.com
SIC: 2023 2026 Dry, condensed, evaporated dairy products; fluid milk
PA: Dairy Farmers Of America, Inc.
  1405 N 98th St
  Kansas City KS 66111
  816 801-6455

(G-58)
DAVID A MOHR JR
Also Called: Gyro Enterprises
4153 Carson Hwy (49221-9509)
PHONE..................................517 266-2694
David A Mohr Jr, *Owner*
EMP: 3
SALES (est): 235.1K **Privately Held**
SIC: 3599 3441 3541 7539 Machine & other job shop work; machine shop, jobbing & repair; crankshafts & camshafts, machining; fabricated structural metal; home workshop machine tools, metalworking; machine shop, automotive; automotive welding

(G-59)
DEPIERRE INDUSTRIES INC
Also Called: Aget Manufacturing Company
1408 E Church St (49221-3437)
PHONE..................................517 263-5781
Robert Depierre, *President*
Timothy Kirkendall, *CFO*
EMP: 25 **EST:** 2016
SQ FT: 45,000
SALES: 5MM **Privately Held**
SIC: 3564 Purification & dust collection equipment

(G-60)
EAGLE PRESS REPAIRS & SER
2025 E Gier Rd (49221-9667)
PHONE..................................419 539-7206
Chuck Collins, *President*
EMP: 13
SALES (est): 2MM **Privately Held**
SIC: 3555 Printing presses

(G-61)
EESCO INC
125 N Tecumseh St (49221-2849)
PHONE..................................517 265-5148
Dwayne Detgen, *Branch Mgr*
EMP: 3 **Publicly Held**
SIC: 5063 3699 3634 Electrical supplies; electrical equipment & supplies; electric housewares & fans
HQ: Eesco, Inc.
  2401 Internationale Pkwy C
  Woodridge IL 60517
  800 333-0011

(G-62)
ERVIN INDUSTRIES INC
Ervin Amasteel Div Ervin Inds
915 Tabor St (49221-3995)
PHONE..................................517 265-6118
James C Lemon, *Opers-Prdtn-Mfg*
Jennifer Gatt, *Purchasing*
Richard Payne, *Plant Engr*
Sheri Weasel, *Credit Staff*
Philip Waser, *Sales Engr*
EMP: 100
SALES (corp-wide): 200MM **Privately Held**
WEB: www.ervinindustries.com
SIC: 3291 Steel shot abrasive
PA: Ervin Industries, Inc.
  3893 Research Park Dr
  Ann Arbor MI 48108
  734 769-4600

(G-63)
EVERGREEN GREASE SERVICE INC
4382 3rd St (49221-1033)
P.O. Box 1484 (49221-7484)
PHONE..................................517 264-9913
Neil T Liston, *President*
Diana Liston, *Admin Sec*
EMP: 5
SALES (est): 616.2K **Privately Held**
WEB: www.evergreengrease.com
SIC: 2077 Animal & marine fats & oils

(G-64)
FALVEY LIMITED
3456 N Adrian Hwy (49221-1140)
PHONE..................................517 263-2699
Travis Poore, *Principal*
Schultz Kristen, *Vice Pres*

Adrian - Lenawee County (G-65)

Isabelle Therrien, *Vice Pres*
Sheila Springer, *Executive Asst*
EMP: 3
SALES: 10K **Privately Held**
SIC: 3519 7538 Gas engine rebuilding; engine rebuilding: automotive

(G-65)
FLYING OTTER WINERY LLC
3402 Chase Rd (49221-8305)
PHONE 517 424-7107
Robert Utter,
EMP: 4
SALES: 1K **Privately Held**
SIC: 2084 Wines

(G-66)
GATEHOUSE MEDIA LLC
Also Called: Daily Telegram, The
133 N Winter St (49221-2042)
P.O. Box 647 (49221-0647)
PHONE 517 265-5111
Paul Heidbrder, *Manager*
EMP: 17
SALES (corp-wide): 1.5B **Privately Held**
WEB: www.gatehousemedia.com
SIC: 2711 Newspapers, publishing & printing; newspapers: publishing only, not printed on site
HQ: Gatehouse Media, Llc
175 Sullys Trl Fl 3
Pittsford NY 14534
585 598-0030

(G-67)
HOLLIS SEWER & PLUMBING SVC
311 E Hunt St (49221-2229)
PHONE 517 263-8151
EMP: 3
SALES (est): 196.7K **Privately Held**
SIC: 3589 Mfg Service Industry Machinery

(G-68)
II ADRIAN LLC W2FUEL
Also Called: W2fuel Adrian II
1571 W Beecher Rd (49221-8754)
PHONE 517 920-4863
Graham Towerton, *CEO*
EMP: 30 **EST:** 2012
SALES (est): 6.4MM **Privately Held**
SIC: 2869 Fuels

(G-69)
INTEVA PRODUCTS LLC
Also Called: Inteva Adrian
1450 E Beecher St (49221-3562)
PHONE 517 266-8030
Rebecca Farless, *Plant Mgr*
Ann Smokoska, *Mfg Mgr*
Scott Baumgartner, *Engineer*
Dale Brockert, *Engineer*
Jason Lee, *Engineer*
EMP: 300
SALES (corp-wide): 4.1B **Privately Held**
SIC: 3089 Injection molding of plastics
HQ: Inteva Products, Llc
1401 Crooks Rd
Troy MI 48084

(G-70)
J & M PRODUCTS AND SERVICE LLC
615 N Scott St (49221-1338)
PHONE 517 263-3082
Marcia Mikuski, *Owner*
Jack Mikuski, *Owner*
EMP: 6 **EST:** 1999
SALES (est): 567.8K **Privately Held**
SIC: 3648 Lighting equipment

(G-71)
JACK WEAVER CORP
343 Lawrence Ave (49221-3340)
PHONE 517 263-6500
Alfred J Brown, *President*
Terry L Tornow, *Vice Pres*
William Brown, *Admin Sec*
EMP: 9
SQ FT: 30,000
SALES (est): 1.7MM **Privately Held**
SIC: 3569 Jacks, hydraulic

(G-72)
JD PLASTICS INC
1305 Railroad Ave (49221-3419)
PHONE 517 264-6858
David Edwards, *President*
Jack Terlesky, *Vice Pres*
Rida Edwards, *Treasurer*
Jill Terlesky, *Admin Sec*
EMP: 3
SQ FT: 7,000
SALES (est): 507.9K **Privately Held**
SIC: 3089 Automotive parts, plastic; molding primary plastic

(G-73)
KING TOOL & DIE INC
971 Division St (49221-4097)
PHONE 517 265-2741
Larry King, *President*
Kevin King, *Treasurer*
David L King, *Shareholder*
▲ **EMP:** 15 **EST:** 1965
SQ FT: 31,000
SALES (est): 3MM **Privately Held**
SIC: 3599 Custom machinery

(G-74)
KUHLMAN CONCRETE INC
240 W Maple Ave (49221-1647)
P.O. Box 714, Toledo OH (43697-0714)
PHONE 517 265-2722
Timothy L Goligoski, *President*
Terrance D Schaefer, *Corp Secy*
James D Gilmore, *Vice Pres*
EMP: 9
SQ FT: 3,000
SALES: 3.6MM
SALES (corp-wide): 53.5MM **Privately Held**
WEB: www.kuhlman-corp.com
SIC: 3273 Ready-mixed concrete
PA: Kuhlman Corporation
1845 Indian Wood Cir
Maumee OH 43537
419 897-6000

(G-75)
MACHINED SOLUTIONS
360 Mulzer Ave (49221-3953)
PHONE 517 759-4075
Isaac Snead, *Principal*
EMP: 3
SALES (est): 250.4K **Privately Held**
SIC: 3599 Machine shop, jobbing & repair

(G-76)
MADISON MACHINE COMPANY
2815 Sharp Rd (49221-8660)
PHONE 517 265-8532
Gregory M Betz, *President*
Jeff Pelham, *General Mgr*
Gail Betz, *Corp Secy*
EMP: 8 **EST:** 1951
SQ FT: 17,000
SALES (est): 243.3K **Privately Held**
SIC: 3544 Industrial molds

(G-77)
MADISON STREET HOLDINGS LLC
Also Called: Aget Manufacturing Company
1408 E Church St (49221-3437)
P.O. Box 248 (49221-0248)
PHONE 517 252-2031
Lauren Cato, *CEO*
John Mitchem, *COO*
Timothy Kirkendall, *Vice Pres*
Steph Hoagland, *Traffic Mgr*
Cheyenne Lulham, *Engineer*
EMP: 25
SQ FT: 45,000
SALES (est): 9.1MM **Privately Held**
WEB: www.agetmfg.com
SIC: 3564 5084 Dust or fume collecting equipment, industrial; precipitators, electrostatic; purification & dust collection equipment; industrial machinery & equipment

(G-78)
MASCO CABINETRY LLC
5353 W Us Highway 223 (49221-8901)
PHONE 517 263-0771
Karen Strauss, *Branch Mgr*
EMP: 110
SALES (corp-wide): 8.3B **Publicly Held**
SIC: 2434 Vanities, bathroom: wood
HQ: Masco Cabinetry Llc
4600 Arrowhead Dr
Ann Arbor MI 48105
734 205-4600

(G-79)
MERILLAT INDUSTRIES LLC
5353 W Us Highway 223 (49221-8901)
P.O. Box 1946 (49221-7946)
PHONE 517 263-0269
Shane Taylor, *Production*
EMP: 5
SALES (est): 153.6K **Privately Held**
SIC: 2434 Wood kitchen cabinets

(G-80)
MERILLAT LP (DH)
5353 W Us Highway 223 (49221-8901)
P.O. Box 1946 (49221-7946)
PHONE 517 263-0771
Eugene A Gargaro Jr, *Partner*
Warren J Potter, *Partner*
Clay Kiefaber, *General Ptnr*
▲ **EMP:** 110
SQ FT: 63,000
SALES (est): 199.7MM
SALES (corp-wide): 8.3B **Publicly Held**
SIC: 2434 Wood kitchen cabinets
HQ: Masco Cabinetry Llc
4600 Arrowhead Dr
Ann Arbor MI 48105
734 205-4600

(G-81)
MEYERS BOAT COMPANY INC
343 Lawrence Ave (49221-3340)
PHONE 517 265-9821
Alfred James Brown, *President*
William Brown, *Vice Pres*
EMP: 12
SQ FT: 2,000
SALES (est): 1MM **Privately Held**
WEB: www.meyersboats.com
SIC: 3089 3732 Boats, nonrigid: plastic; boat building & repairing

(G-82)
MITCHELL WELDING CO LLC
2708 E Maumee St (49221-3535)
P.O. Box 191 (49221-0191)
PHONE 517 265-8105
Jason Roe,
EMP: 3 **EST:** 1946
SQ FT: 10,000
SALES: 500K **Privately Held**
SIC: 3441 Fabricated structural metal

(G-83)
OLIVER OF ADRIAN INC
1111 E Beecher St (49221-4017)
P.O. Box 189 (49221-0189)
PHONE 517 263-2132
Neal E Garrison Jr, *President*
Dale E Thielan, *Vice Pres*
Michael Borton, *Treasurer*
EMP: 9 **EST:** 1913
SQ FT: 50,000
SALES (est): 1MM **Privately Held**
WEB: www.oliverinstrument.com
SIC: 3541 5084 Machine tools, metal cutting type; industrial machinery & equipment

(G-84)
PLANEWAVE INSTRUMENTS INC
1375 N Main St (49221)
PHONE 310 639-1662
Richard Hedrick, *President*
Joseph Haberman, *Vice Pres*
Shelby Stubbe, *Engineer*
David Rowe, *Officer*
Jason Fourier, *Admin Sec*
EMP: 4 **EST:** 2006
SALES: 4MM **Privately Held**
SIC: 3827 Telescopes: elbow, panoramic, sighting, fire control, etc.

(G-85)
PLASTIC OMNIUM AUTO INERGY
1549 W Beecher Rd (49221-8754)
PHONE 517 265-1100
Ross Johnson, *Director*
Vincent Torres, *Technician*
EMP: 242
SALES (corp-wide): 10.4MM **Privately Held**
SIC: 3089 3714 Blow molded finished plastic products; motor vehicle parts & accessories
HQ: Plastic Omnium Auto Inergy (Usa) Llc
2710 Bellingham Dr
Troy MI 48083
248 743-5700

(G-86)
PPG INDUSTRIES INC
Also Called: Coatings & Resins Division
961 Division St (49221-4023)
PHONE 517 263-7831
Raymond F Schappert, *Enginr/R&D Mgr*
EMP: 45
SQ FT: 10,000
SALES (corp-wide): 15.3B **Publicly Held**
WEB: www.ppg.com
SIC: 2891 2851 Adhesives; paints & paint additives
PA: Ppg Industries, Inc.
1 Ppg Pl
Pittsburgh PA 15272
412 434-3131

(G-87)
PRIMORE INC (PA)
Also Called: Sedco Division Primore
2300 W Beecher Rd (49221-9769)
P.O. Box 605 (49221-0605)
PHONE 517 263-2220
Robert E Price, *President*
Richard Hutt, *Vice Pres*
EMP: 14 **EST:** 1946
SQ FT: 9,500
SALES (est): 10MM **Privately Held**
WEB: www.primore.com
SIC: 3491 3563 Valves, automatic control; air & gas compressors

(G-88)
PRIMORE INC
Sedco Primore
2304 W Beecher Rd (49221-9769)
P.O. Box 624 (49221-0624)
PHONE 517 263-2220
Mark Roberts, *Manager*
EMP: 40
SALES (est): 3.8MM
SALES (corp-wide): 10MM **Privately Held**
WEB: www.primore.com
SIC: 3494 5085 3491 Valves & pipe fittings; industrial supplies; industrial valves
PA: Primore Inc
2300 W Beecher Rd
Adrian MI 49221
517 263-2220

(G-89)
QUICKPRINT OF ADRIAN INC
Also Called: Quick Print
142 N Main St (49221-2745)
PHONE 517 263-2290
Dennis Swartzlander, *President*
Duane Swartzlander, *Corp Secy*
Gary Swartzlander, *Vice Pres*
EMP: 10
SQ FT: 7,000
SALES (est): 1.2MM **Privately Held**
WEB: www.quickprintofadrian.com
SIC: 2752 7334 Commercial printing, offset; photocopying & duplicating services

(G-90)
RILEY ENTERPRISES LLC
1703 E Gier Rd (49221-9666)
P.O. Box 236 (49221-0236)
PHONE 517 263-9115
Robert Willet, *President*
Joseph T Adams, *Principal*
Mary L Willet, *Principal*
EMP: 3
SALES (est): 394K **Privately Held**
WEB: www.rileyent.com
SIC: 3644 Noncurrent-carrying wiring services

(G-91)
ROBOGISTICS LLC
100 Industrial Dr (49221-9767)
PHONE 409 234-1033

GEOGRAPHIC SECTION

Albion - Calhoun County (G-115)

Kerry Powell, *Branch Mgr*
EMP: 18
SQ FT: 1,200
SALES (corp-wide): 5.8MM **Privately Held**
SIC: 3646 Commercial indusl & institutional electric lighting fixtures
PA: Robogistics Llc
363 N Sam Houston Pkwy E # 1100
Houston TX 77060
409 234-1033

(G-92)
ROTO-PLASTICS CORPORATION
Also Called: Tuff Body Padding Company
1001 Division St (49221-4023)
P.O. Box 779 (49221-0779)
PHONE 517 263-8981
David Mulligan, *President*
Clyne W Durst Jr, *Corp Secy*
Joe Cabello, *Vice Pres*
Barry Kafer, *Plant Mgr*
Mark Reilly, *Warehouse Mgr*
EMP: 55
SQ FT: 62,000
SALES (est): 8.8MM **Privately Held**
WEB: www.rotoplastics.com
SIC: 3089 Injection molding of plastics

(G-93)
SCHAFERS ELEVATOR CO
4105 Country Club Rd (49221-9216)
PHONE 517 263-7202
Keith Schafer, *Partner*
Ralph Schafer, *Corp Secy*
Alan Schafer, *Vice Pres*
EMP: 4
SQ FT: 19,000
SALES (est): 310K **Privately Held**
SIC: 3534 5153 Elevators & equipment; grains

(G-94)
SCIENTEMP CORP
3565 S Adrian Hwy (49221-9293)
PHONE 517 263-6020
Howard J Tenniswood, *President*
Steve Tenniswood, *Vice Pres*
Steven Tenniswood, *Vice Pres*
EMP: 20
SQ FT: 10,000
SALES (est): 4.3MM **Privately Held**
WEB: www.scientemp.com
SIC: 3585 5064 3632 Refrigeration & heating equipment; electrical appliances, television & radio; household refrigerators & freezers

(G-95)
SEDCO INC
2304 W Beecher Rd (49221-9769)
P.O. Box 624 (49221-0624)
PHONE 517 263-2220
Robert E Price, *President*
Larry Ansthuetz, *President*
Bob Curly, *Vice Pres*
Richard D Hutt, *Vice Pres*
▼ **EMP:** 44 **EST:** 1956
SQ FT: 25,000
SALES: 10MM **Privately Held**
SIC: 3491 Industrial valves
PA: Primore Inc
2300 W Beecher Rd
Adrian MI 49221
517 263-2220

(G-96)
SERVICE TECTONICS INC
2827 Treat St (49221-4499)
PHONE 517 263-0758
Stephen J Dalton, *President*
Jon Dalton, *Vice Pres*
Shirly Dalton, *Treasurer*
▲ **EMP:** 15
SQ FT: 15,000
SALES (est): 39.8K **Privately Held**
WEB: www.padprinting.net
SIC: 3569 Assembly machines, non-metalworking

(G-97)
SPOTTED COW
1336 N Main St Ste 1 (49221-1773)
PHONE 517 265-6188
Don Barron, *Principal*
EMP: 30

SALES (est): 3.4MM **Privately Held**
SIC: 3556 Ice cream manufacturing machinery

(G-98)
TOMS WORLD OF WOOD
105 Sand Creek Hwy (49221-9130)
PHONE 517 264-2836
EMP: 4
SQ FT: 2,560
SALES: 150K **Privately Held**
SIC: 2499 5945 5251 Custom Woodworking Ret Arts & Crafts & Woodworking Tools

(G-99)
VENCHURS INC
Also Called: Nuestro
800 Tabor St (49221-3969)
PHONE 517 263-1206
Jeffery M Wyatt, *Branch Mgr*
EMP: 45
SALES (est): 6.2MM **Privately Held**
WEB: www.venchurs.com
SIC: 2671 3714 Paper coated or laminated for packaging; motor vehicle parts & accessories

(G-100)
VENCHURS INC
Also Called: Nuestro
751 S Center St (49221-3912)
PHONE 517 263-8937
Ron Reeves, *Branch Mgr*
EMP: 10
SALES (est): 1.1MM **Privately Held**
WEB: www.venchurs.com
SIC: 2671 3523 3714 Paper coated or laminated for packaging; planting, haying, harvesting & processing machinery; motor vehicle parts & accessories

(G-101)
W2FUEL LLC (PA)
Also Called: W2fuel Keokuk I
1571 W Beecher Rd (49221-8754)
PHONE 517 920-4868
Graham Towerton, *CEO*
Roy Strom, *CFO*
EMP: 24
SALES (est): 8.8MM **Privately Held**
SIC: 2911 Diesel fuels

(G-102)
WACKER BIOCHEM CORPORATION
3301 Sutton Rd (49221-9335)
PHONE 517 264-8500
Ingo Kavor, *President*
▲ **EMP:** 500
SALES (est): 71.6MM
SALES (corp-wide): 5.7B **Privately Held**
WEB: www.wackerchemicalcorporation.com
SIC: 2899 Chemical preparations
HQ: Wacker Chemical Corporation
3301 Sutton Rd
Adrian MI 49221
517 264-8500

(G-103)
WACKER CHEMICAL CORPORATION (DH)
3301 Sutton Rd (49221-9335)
PHONE 517 264-8500
David Wilhoit, *President*
Rolf Hirsenkorn, *Vice Pres*
Thomas Koini, *Vice Pres*
John Tacca, *Vice Pres*
Tim Corbin, *Purch Agent*
◆ **EMP:** 525
SQ FT: 1,000,000
SALES: 2.9B
SALES (corp-wide): 5.7B **Privately Held**
WEB: www.wackerchemicalcorporation.com
SIC: 2869 5169 Silicones; industrial chemicals
HQ: Wacker Chemie Ag
Hanns-Seidel-Platz 4
Munchen 81737
896 279-0

(G-104)
WORKFORCE PAYHUB INC
104 E Maumee St (49221-2704)
PHONE 517 759-4026
Eric Jones, *President*
Rachel Dochstader, *Associate*
EMP: 7
SQ FT: 4,400
SALES (est): 246K **Privately Held**
SIC: 8721 7372 Payroll accounting service; business oriented computer software

Afton
Cheboygan County

(G-105)
ARROWHEAD INDUSTRIES INC
1715 E M 68 Hwy (49705-9715)
PHONE 231 238-9366
Thomas J Redman, *President*
EMP: 45
SALES: 1,000K **Privately Held**
SIC: 3499 Fabricated metal products

(G-106)
ROMAN ENGINEERING
1715 E M 68 Hwy (49705-9715)
PHONE 231 238-7644
Thomas Radman, *President*
Robert Radman, *Chairman*
EMP: 100
SALES (est): 5.9MM **Privately Held**
SIC: 5014 3498 3317 8711 Tires & tubes; fabricated pipe & fittings; steel pipe & tubes; engineering services

(G-107)
TUBE FAB/ROMAN ENGRG CO INC
1715 Michigan 68 Afton (49705)
PHONE 231 238-9366
Thomas J Redman, *President*
Robert J Redman, *Chairman*
Cynthia A Redman, *Corp Secy*
Marc Brach, *Engineer*
Matt Morton, *Engineer*
EMP: 136
SQ FT: 190,000
SALES (est): 41.5MM **Privately Held**
WEB: www.tubefab.org
SIC: 3498 Tube fabricating (contract bending & shaping)

Ahmeek
Keweenaw County

(G-108)
NEUVOKAS CORPORATION
32066 Rd (49901)
P.O. Box 220 (49901-0220)
PHONE 906 934-2661
Erik Kiilunen, *CEO*
Steve Eskola, *Sales Staff*
Tara Kiilunen, *Sales Staff*
EMP: 5
SALES (est): 792.1K **Privately Held**
SIC: 3299 Mica products

Akron
Tuscola County

(G-109)
WISNER MACHINE WORKS LLC
7800 M 25 (48701-9773)
PHONE 989 274-7690
Tyler Gledhill, *Manager*
EMP: 3
SALES: 10K **Privately Held**
SIC: 3441 Fabricated structural metal

Alanson
Emmet County

(G-110)
HALE MANUFACTURING INC
6235 Cupp Rd (49706-9512)
PHONE 231 529-6271
Wayne Hunter, *President*
EMP: 9 **EST:** 1963
SQ FT: 5,000
SALES: 1MM **Privately Held**
WEB: www.haleman.com
SIC: 3825 Electrical power measuring equipment

(G-111)
K & J ENTERPRISES INC
Also Called: Team Spankys
7566 S Us Highway 31 (49706-8528)
P.O. Box 443 (49706-0443)
PHONE 231 548-5222
Karen Kovacs, *Owner*
Jerry Kovacs, *General Mgr*
EMP: 3
SALES (est): 452.5K **Privately Held**
SIC: 3799 Snowmobiles

Alba
Antrim County

(G-112)
C & R TOOL DIE
4643 Alba Hwy (49611)
P.O. Box 148 (49611-0148)
PHONE 231 584-3588
Calvin Hoogerhyde, *Owner*
EMP: 4
SQ FT: 4,000
SALES (est): 100K **Privately Held**
SIC: 3544 7692 Special dies & tools; welding repair

Albion
Calhoun County

(G-113)
ALBION INDUSTRIES LLC (PA)
800 N Clark St (49224-1455)
PHONE 800 835-8911
Ron Nousain, *Regional Mgr*
Terri Rush, *Buyer*
Anna Thompson, *Buyer*
Shawn Collyer, *Engineer*
Dennis Byrd, *Treasurer*
▲ **EMP:** 145
SQ FT: 70,000
SALES (est): 30.2MM **Privately Held**
WEB: www.albioninc.com
SIC: 3429 5084 Manufactured hardware (general); materials handling machinery

(G-114)
ALBION MACHINE AND TOOL LLC
1001 Industrial Blvd (49224-8551)
PHONE 517 629-8838
William Dobbins, *Manager*
EMP: 14
SALES (est): 600.3K **Privately Held**
SIC: 3544 Special dies, tools, jigs & fixtures

(G-115)
ALL CHROME LLC
512 N Clark St (49224-1913)
PHONE 517 554-1649
Corey Conley,
EMP: 3
SQ FT: 3,500
SALES (est): 121.6K **Privately Held**
SIC: 3471 7699 Plating of metals or formed products; anodizing (plating) of metals or formed products; decorative plating & finishing of formed products; gold plating; replating shop, except silverware

Albion - Calhoun County (G-116)

GEOGRAPHIC SECTION

(G-116)
CALHOUN COMMUNICATIONS INC (PA)
Also Called: Albion Recorder
125 E Cass St (49224-1726)
PHONE.....................517 629-0041
Richard Milliman II, *President*
Teresa Fitzwater, *Publisher*
EMP: 15
SQ FT: 30,000
SALES (est): 1MM **Privately Held**
SIC: 2711 Commercial printing & newspaper publishing combined

(G-117)
CARR BROTHERS AND SONS INC
14555 Elm Row Rd (49224-9646)
PHONE.....................517 629-3549
Michelle Moulton, *Manager*
EMP: 30
SALES (corp-wide): 10.4MM **Privately Held**
SIC: 1442 1794 Gravel mining; excavation work
PA: Carr Brothers And Sons, Inc.
   13613 E Erie Rd
   Albion MI 49224
   517 531-3358

(G-118)
CARR BROTHERS AND SONS INC (PA)
13613 E Erie Rd (49224-9620)
PHONE.....................517 531-3358
John R Carr Jr, *Vice Pres*
William B Carr III, *Treasurer*
EMP: 10
SQ FT: 5,000
SALES (est): 10.4MM **Privately Held**
SIC: 1442 1794 Gravel mining; excavation work

(G-119)
CASTER CONCEPTS INC
Also Called: Machine Center, The
214 E Michigan Ave (49224-1738)
PHONE.....................517 629-2456
Charles James, *Branch Mgr*
EMP: 4
SALES (corp-wide): 10.4MM **Privately Held**
WEB: www.themachinecenter.com
SIC: 3429 Manufactured hardware (general)
PA: Caster Concepts, Inc.
   16000 E Michigan Ave
   Albion MI 49224
   888 781-1470

(G-120)
CLARIANT PLAS COATINGS USA LLC
Masterbatch Division
926 Elliott St (49224-9506)
PHONE.....................517 629-9101
Dinesh Pandya, *Opers-Prdtn-Mfg*
Jerry Willis, *QC Mgr*
Gary Ott, *Supervisor*
EMP: 78
SQ FT: 52,000
SALES (corp-wide): 6.6B **Privately Held**
WEB: www.myclariant.com
SIC: 2869 Industrial organic chemicals
HQ: Clariant Plastics & Coatings Usa Llc
   4000 Monroe Rd
   Charlotte NC 28205
   704 331-7000

(G-121)
COMPLETE ELECTRIC
1670 E Michigan Ave (49224-9203)
PHONE.....................517 629-9267
Daniel Hoch, *Owner*
EMP: 3 **EST:** 1965
SQ FT: 5,000
SALES: 57K **Privately Held**
SIC: 7694 Electric motor repair

(G-122)
DECKER MANUFACTURING CORP (PA)
703 N Clark St (49224-1456)
PHONE.....................517 629-3955
Steve Konkle, *President*
Bernard L Konkle, *Chairman*
Henry R Konkle, *Chairman*
Bernard L Konkle II, *COO*
John C Hagy, *Exec VP*
▲ **EMP:** 93
SQ FT: 130,000
SALES: 38.7MM **Privately Held**
WEB: www.deckernut.com
SIC: 3452 3432 Bolts, nuts, rivets & washers; plumbing fixture fittings & trim

(G-123)
ERNIE ROMANCO
Also Called: Co2 Central
661 N Concord Rd (49224-9647)
PHONE.....................517 531-3686
Ernest Romanco, *Owner*
EMP: 25
SQ FT: 10,000
SALES: 4MM **Privately Held**
SIC: 8748 2899 8711 7381 Business consulting; fire extinguisher charges; engineering services; detective & armored car services

(G-124)
GREAT LAKES WATERJET LASER LLC
1101 Industrial Blvd (49224-9515)
PHONE.....................517 629-9900
Matt Canfield, *General Mgr*
Kathleen N Johnson, *Mng Member*
Howard Johnson,
EMP: 6
SQ FT: 12,000
SALES: 180K **Privately Held**
WEB: www.greatlakeswaterjetandlaser.com
SIC: 3541 Machine tool replacement & repair parts, metal cutting types

(G-125)
GUARDIAN INDUSTRIES LLC
1000 E North St (49224-1440)
PHONE.....................517 629-9464
Duane Faulkner, *Branch Mgr*
EMP: 10
SALES (corp-wide): 40.6B **Privately Held**
WEB: www.guardian.com
SIC: 3211 Flat glass
HQ: Guardian Industries, Llc
   2300 Harmon Rd
   Auburn Hills MI 48326
   248 340-1800

(G-126)
K & S WELDING
Also Called: K&S Welding & Fabricating
17200 24 Mile Rd (49224-9557)
PHONE.....................517 629-7842
Vanessa Keson, *Owner*
EMP: 3
SALES (est): 197.1K **Privately Held**
SIC: 7692 1799 Welding repair; welding on site

(G-127)
KNAUF INSULATION INC
Also Called: Guardian Fiberglass
1000 E North St (49224-1440)
PHONE.....................517 630-2000
Tom Campion, *Manager*
EMP: 126
SALES (corp-wide): 8.2B **Privately Held**
SIC: 3296 1742 Fiberglass insulation; insulation, buildings
HQ: Knauf Insulation, Inc.
   1 Knauf Dr
   Shelbyville IN 46176
   317 398-4434

(G-128)
PATRIOT SOLAR GROUP LLC
708 Valhalla Dr (49224-9402)
PHONE.....................517 629-9292
Josh Mathie, *Sales Staff*
Jeffrey Mathie, *Mng Member*
▲ **EMP:** 27
SALES: 12MM **Privately Held**
SIC: 3674 4911 Solar cells;

(G-129)
PREMIER CORRUGATED INC
916 Burstein Dr (49224-4011)
PHONE.....................517 629-5700
Jack Schwarz, *President*
EMP: 50
SALES (est): 8.6MM
SALES (corp-wide): 40.6B **Privately Held**
SIC: 2653 Boxes, corrugated: made from purchased materials
HQ: Georgia-Pacific Corrugated Iii Llc
   5645 W 82nd St
   Indianapolis IN 46278

(G-130)
SHAFER BROS INC
29150 C Dr N (49224-9410)
PHONE.....................517 629-4800
Gerald C Shafer, *President*
Ester W Shafer, *Admin Sec*
EMP: 4
SALES (est): 301.4K **Privately Held**
SIC: 3273 Ready-mixed concrete

(G-131)
SHAFER REDI-MIX INC (PA)
Also Called: Shafer Brothers
29150 C Dr N (49224-9410)
P.O. Box 178 (49224-0178)
PHONE.....................517 629-4800
Gerald C Shafer, *President*
Doug Shafer, *Vice Pres*
EMP: 65 **EST:** 1982
SQ FT: 2,000
SALES (est): 22.1MM **Privately Held**
WEB: www.shaferbros.com
SIC: 3273 Ready-mixed concrete

(G-132)
SPARTANNASH COMPANY
Also Called: Felpausch Food Center 1992
1406 N Eaton St (49224-9470)
P.O. Box 869 (49224-0869)
PHONE.....................517 629-6313
Joe Waid, *Branch Mgr*
John Beyer, *Director*
EMP: 110
SALES (corp-wide): 8B **Publicly Held**
WEB: www.spartanstores.com
SIC: 5411 5921 5912 2051 Grocery stores, independent; liquor stores; drug stores & proprietary stores; bread, cake & related products; bakeries
PA: Spartannash Company
   850 76th St Sw
   Byron Center MI 49315
   616 878-2000

(G-133)
TETRA PAK INC
1104 Industrial Blvd (49224-9515)
PHONE.....................517 629-2163
Fax: 517 629-2166
EMP: 3
SQ FT: 20,000
SALES (corp-wide): 7.9B **Privately Held**
SIC: 3565 Mfg Packaging Machinery
HQ: Tetra Pak Inc
   3300 Airport Rd
   Denton TX 76207
   940 565-8800

(G-134)
VELOCITY MANUFACTURING LLC
921 Elliott St (49224-9506)
P.O. Box 236 (49224-0236)
PHONE.....................517 630-0408
Meghan McGuigan, *Vice Pres*
Jamie Cruz,
▲ **EMP:** 3
SQ FT: 7,500
SALES (est): 379.6K **Privately Held**
WEB: www.velocitymfg.com
SIC: 3544 Special dies & tools

(G-135)
VERITAS VINEYARD LLC
2199 N Concord Rd (49224-9645)
PHONE.....................517 474-9026
John A Burtka Jr, *Principal*
EMP: 8
SALES (corp-wide): 2MM **Privately Held**
SIC: 2084 Wines, brandy & brandy spirits
PA: Veritas Vineyard Llc
   117 W Louis Glick Hwy
   Jackson MI 49201
   517 962-2427

(G-136)
WORLD CORRUGATED CONTAINER INC
930 Elliott St (49224-9506)
P.O. Box 840 (49224-0840)
PHONE.....................517 629-9400
Connie Reuther, *Ch of Bd*
Charles Reuther, *President*
EMP: 40
SQ FT: 106,000
SALES (est): 14MM **Privately Held**
WEB: www.worldcorrugated.com
SIC: 2653 Boxes, corrugated: made from purchased materials

Alden
Antrim County

(G-137)
TRI COUNTY SAND AND STONE INC
Also Called: Tri County Sand & Stone Shop
5318 Bebb Rd (49612)
P.O. Box 268 (49612-0268)
PHONE.....................231 331-6549
Larry McCulloch, *President*
Joann McCulloch, *Corp Secy*
Greg McCulloch, *Vice Pres*
Rick McCulloch, *Vice Pres*
EMP: 4
SALES (est): 537.9K **Privately Held**
SIC: 1442 Common sand mining

Alger
Arenac County

(G-138)
DOWD BROTHERS FORESTRY
Also Called: Dowd Brothers Forest Products
2718 School Rd (48610-9652)
PHONE.....................989 345-7459
EMP: 4 **EST:** 1984
SALES: 150K **Privately Held**
SIC: 2421 Sawmill/Planing Mill

(G-139)
MTM TRANSPORT
2173 Roseburgh Rd (48610-9719)
PHONE.....................989 709-0475
Thomas Sheneman, *Owner*
Amanda Sheneman, *Owner*
EMP: 3
SALES (est): 148.5K **Privately Held**
SIC: 3715 Truck trailers

(G-140)
ZK ENTERPRISES INC (PA)
Also Called: PSI Satellite
2382 M 33 (48610-9439)
PHONE.....................989 728-4439
Rick Kalosis, *President*
Gerard Zajechowski, *Treasurer*
EMP: 4
SQ FT: 6,250
SALES: 450K **Privately Held**
SIC: 3993 Electric signs

Algonac
St. Clair County

(G-141)
ANCHOR BAY CANV AND UPHOLSTERY
2001 Pointe Tremble Rd (48001-1613)
PHONE.....................810 512-4325
Scott Hanel,
EMP: 3 **EST:** 2012
SALES (est): 190.3K **Privately Held**
SIC: 2394 Canvas & related products

(G-142)
CANVAS CONCEPTS INC
2001 Pointe Tremble Rd (48001-1613)
PHONE.....................810 794-3305
Russell Grose, *President*
EMP: 1

GEOGRAPHIC SECTION

Allegan - Allegan County (G-170)

SALES: 1.2MM **Privately Held**
SIC: **2394** 5091 Canvas & related products; boat accessories & parts

(G-143)
FANNON PRODUCTS LLC (PA)
5318 Pointe Tremble Rd (48001-4367)
PHONE..................................810 794-2000
David P Fannon, *Managing Prtnr*
David Fannon, *Technology*
Keith Fannon,
▲ EMP: 18
SQ FT: 800
SALES: 3.3MM **Privately Held**
WEB: www.fannoninfrared.com
SIC: **3823** Industrial instrmnts msrmnt display/control process variable

(G-144)
FORMULA ONE TOOL & ENGINEERING
6052 Pointe Tremble Rd (48001-4296)
PHONE..................................810 794-3617
Carl W Reams, *President*
EMP: 6
SQ FT: 2,800
SALES: 250K **Privately Held**
SIC: **3545** Machine tool accessories

(G-145)
OCEAN EXPRESS POWERBOATS INC
9483 Smith St (48001)
PHONE..................................810 794-5551
Ross Focht, *President*
Marsha M Focht, *Vice Pres*
EMP: 3
SQ FT: 35,000
SALES (est): 440.8K **Privately Held**
WEB: www.oceanexpress.com
SIC: **3732** Boats, fiberglass: building & repairing; motorized boat, building & repairing

Allegan
Allegan County

(G-146)
AGGREGATE AND DEVELOPING LLC
1108 Lincoln Rd (49010-9075)
PHONE..................................269 217-5492
Bill W Smith,
EMP: 5
SALES (est): 691.9K **Privately Held**
SIC: **1422** Crushed & broken limestone

(G-147)
ALL-FAB CORPORATION
1235 Lincoln Rd Unit 1235 # 1235 (49010-9706)
PHONE..................................269 673-6572
Jim Plesnicar, *President*
Joe Plesnicar, *Vice Pres*
▲ EMP: 8
SQ FT: 12,000
SALES (est): 3MM **Privately Held**
WEB: www.allfabcorp.com
SIC: **5084** 1799 3548 Machine tools & accessories; welding on site; welding apparatus

(G-148)
ALLEGAN METAL FINISHING C
1274 Lincoln Rd (49010-9172)
P.O. Box 217 (49010-0217)
PHONE..................................269 673-6604
EMP: 3
SALES (est): 150K **Privately Held**
SIC: **3471** Plating/Polishing Service

(G-149)
ALLEGAN TUBULAR PRODUCTS INC
1276 Lincoln Rd (49010-9172)
P.O. Box 217 (49010-0217)
PHONE..................................269 673-6636
Bernard Sosnowski, *President*
Ed Sosnowski, *Principal*
Ja Dalm, *Vice Pres*
J Verdonk, *Treasurer*
Teresa Erickson, *Human Res Dir*

EMP: 65 EST: 1962
SQ FT: 45,000
SALES (est): 13MM **Privately Held**
WEB: www.allegantube.com
SIC: **3498** 3714 Tube fabricating (contract bending & shaping); motor vehicle parts & accessories; industrial furnaces & ovens

(G-150)
B & G CUSTOM WORKS INC
Also Called: Advanced Conveyor Systems
2830 113th Ave (49010-9096)
PHONE..................................269 686-9420
Jennifer Edson, *President*
John Hare, *Admin Sec*
EMP: 44
SQ FT: 70,000
SALES (est): 6.8MM **Privately Held**
WEB: www.bgcustomworks.com
SIC: **7692** 3441 Welding repair; fabricated structural metal

(G-151)
B AND L METAL FINISHING LLC
755 Airway Dr (49010-8507)
PHONE..................................269 767-2225
Kim Collins, *Principal*
EMP: 3
SALES (est): 162.6K **Privately Held**
SIC: **3471** Plating & polishing

(G-152)
CHRISTIAN OIL COMPANY
2589 30th St (49010-9268)
PHONE..................................269 673-2218
Aaron Hartman, *President*
Pamela Hartman, *Admin Sec*
EMP: 10
SQ FT: 10,000
SALES (est): 2.2MM **Privately Held**
SIC: **1311** Crude petroleum production; natural gas production

(G-153)
CVM SERVICES LLC
Also Called: Independent Tool and Mfg
665 44th St (49010-9331)
PHONE..................................269 521-4811
Linda L Muenzer, *Director*
EMP: 25
SALES (est): 1.3MM **Privately Held**
SIC: **3441** Fabricated structural metal

(G-154)
CYRUS FOREST PRODUCTS
4234 127th Ave (49010-9434)
PHONE..................................269 751-6535
Fax: 269 751-6535
EMP: 6
SALES: 130K **Privately Held**
SIC: **2421** Sawmill/Planing Mill

(G-155)
DDR HEATING INC (PA)
Also Called: Electro-Heat
700 Grand St (49010-8012)
P.O. Box 190 (49010-0190)
PHONE..................................269 673-2145
Randy Hunziker, *President*
David Blair, *Treasurer*
▲ EMP: 25 EST: 2011
SQ FT: 44,000
SALES: 4.1MM **Privately Held**
SIC: **3567** Heating units & devices, industrial: electric

(G-156)
DDR HEATING INC
2870 116th Ave (49010-9004)
PHONE..................................269 673-2145
Randy Hunziker, *President*
Anita Dominique, *Purch Mgr*
EMP: 3
SALES (corp-wide): 4.1MM **Privately Held**
SIC: **3567** Heating units & devices, industrial: electric
PA: Ddr Heating, Inc.
 700 Grand St
 Allegan MI 49010
 269 673-2145

(G-157)
DIGITAL IMAGING GROUP INC
Also Called: Jh Packaging
504 Eastern Ave (49010-9070)
PHONE..................................269 686-8744
Tim Shultz, *President*
Herb Dekoff, *Technical Mgr*
Heidi Schrott, *Manager*
Jeff Wille, *Info Tech Dir*
EMP: 125
SALES (est): 14MM
SALES (corp-wide): 16.2B **Publicly Held**
WEB: www.jhpackaging.com
SIC: **2752** 2759 Business form & card printing, lithographic; commercial printing
HQ: Mps Holdco, Inc.
 5800 W Grand River Ave
 Lansing MI 48906

(G-158)
DONALD GLEASON
Also Called: Gleason's Plating
3480 125th Ave (49010-9221)
PHONE..................................269 673-6802
Donald Gleason, *Owner*
EMP: 3
SQ FT: 2,400
SALES: 300K **Privately Held**
SIC: **2448** 2441 Wood pallets & skids; nailed wood boxes & shook

(G-159)
E H INC
2870 116th Ave (49010-9004)
PHONE..................................269 673-6456
David Wade, *Ch of Bd*
▲ EMP: 20
SQ FT: 25,000
SALES (est): 2.2MM **Privately Held**
WEB: www.electroheatinc.com
SIC: **3567** 3634 Heating units & devices, industrial: electric; electric housewares & fans

(G-160)
FABRICATED COMPONENTS & ASSEMB
Also Called: F C & A
603 N Eastern Ave (49010-9593)
PHONE..................................269 673-7100
Brian Hicks, *President*
Chris Hicks, *Vice Pres*
EMP: 10
SQ FT: 12,000
SALES (est): 2.2MM **Privately Held**
SIC: **3441** Fabricated structural metal

(G-161)
FINISH LINE FABRICATING LLC
779 38th St (49010-9131)
PHONE..................................269 686-8400
Tim Curry, *Mng Member*
Judy Curry, *Mng Member*
EMP: 5 EST: 1996
SALES (est): 824.9K **Privately Held**
SIC: **3711** Automobile assembly, including specialty automobiles

(G-162)
FLASHES PUBLISHERS INC
Also Called: Allegan Flashes
595 Jenner Dr (49010-1567)
PHONE..................................269 673-2141
John P Morgan, *President*
Hendrik G Meijer, *Treasurer*
EMP: 180
SQ FT: 40,000
SALES (est): 26.3MM **Privately Held**
WEB: www.flashespublishers.com
SIC: **2752** 2741 Commercial printing, offset; shopping news: publishing & printing; directories, telephone: publishing & printing

(G-163)
FRONTIER TECHNOLOGY INC
2489 118th Ave (49010-9552)
PHONE..................................269 673-9464
Sandra Anderson, *President*
▲ EMP: 8
SQ FT: 14,000
SALES: 1.4MM **Privately Held**
SIC: **3556** 3559 Food products machinery; chemical machinery & equipment

(G-164)
HANSE ENVIRONMENTAL INC (PA)
235 Hubbard St (49010-1320)
PHONE..................................269 673-8638
John K Hanse, *President*
John C Hanse, *Corp Secy*
Peter Hanse, *Vice Pres*
Lydia Hanse,
▲ EMP: 10
SQ FT: 5,000
SALES (est): 1.5MM **Privately Held**
WEB: www.hanseenv.com
SIC: **3826** Environmental testing equipment

(G-165)
INDEPENDENT TOOL AND MFG CO
661 44th St (49010-9382)
PHONE..................................269 521-4811
James Muenzer, *President*
Linda Muenzer, *Corp Secy*
EMP: 35 EST: 1971
SQ FT: 60,000
SALES (est): 6.2MM **Privately Held**
SIC: **3469** 3544 Stamping metal for the trade; special dies, tools, jigs & fixtures

(G-166)
J & J FABRICATIONS INC
611 N Eastern Ave (49010-9593)
P.O. Box 266 (49010-0266)
PHONE..................................269 673-5488
Ryan Venderkamp, *President*
EMP: 8
SQ FT: 13,000
SALES (est): 1MM **Privately Held**
SIC: **3441** Fabricated structural metal

(G-167)
JENNCO INDUSTRIES LLC
Also Called: Lotus Spa & Salon
3145 Babylon Rd (49010-9205)
PHONE..................................269 290-3145
Jennifer S Dunlop,
EMP: 3
SALES (est): 135.8K **Privately Held**
SIC: **3999** Manufacturing industries

(G-168)
KAECHELE PUBLICATIONS INC
Also Called: Allegan News & Gazette
241 Hubbard St (49010-1320)
P.O. Box 189 (49010-0189)
PHONE..................................269 673-5534
Cheryl Kaechele, *President*
Walter Kaechele, *Vice Pres*
EMP: 25
SALES (est): 1.4MM **Privately Held**
WEB: www.allegannews.com
SIC: **2711** Newspapers: publishing only, not printed on site

(G-169)
KEY GAS COMPONENTS INC
Also Called: Crescent Div Key Gas Cmponents
1303 Lincoln Rd (49010-9701)
PHONE..................................269 673-2151
John Blount, *Plant Mgr*
Lloyd Esterline, *Branch Mgr*
EMP: 46
SALES (corp-wide): 12.1MM **Privately Held**
SIC: **3491** 3498 3432 3564 Gas valves & parts, industrial; manifolds, pipe: fabricated from purchased pipe; plumbing fixture fittings & trim; blowers & fans; valves & pipe fittings
PA: Key Gas Components, Inc.
 160 Clay St
 Marion NC 28752
 828 655-1700

(G-170)
L PERRIGO COMPANY (DH)
515 Eastern Ave (49010-9070)
PHONE..................................269 673-8451
Joseph Papa, *CEO*
David Gibbons, *Ch of Bd*
Arthur J Shannon, *Principal*
Richard Hansen, *Vice Pres*
Daniel Matias, *Engineer*
◆ EMP: 1800 EST: 1887

Allegan - Allegan County (G-171)

GEOGRAPHIC SECTION

SALES (est): 1.6B **Privately Held**
SIC: 2834 Pharmaceutical preparations
HQ: Perrigo Company
   515 Eastern Ave
   Allegan MI 49010
   269 673-8451

(G-171)
L PERRIGO COMPANY
300 Water St (49010-1308)
PHONE.................................269 673-7962
Sinjan De, *Research*
Brent Burtrum, *Engineer*
Comer Skinner, *Branch Mgr*
Larry Areaux, *Manager*
Michael Maule, *Manager*
EMP: 5 **Privately Held**
SIC: 2834 Adrenal pharmaceutical preparations
HQ: L Perrigo Company
   515 Eastern Ave
   Allegan MI 49010
   269 673-8451

(G-172)
L PERRIGO COMPANY
809 Airway Dr (49010-8516)
PHONE.................................269 673-7962
EMP: 4 **Privately Held**
SIC: 2834 Pharmaceutical preparations
HQ: L Perrigo Company
   515 Eastern Ave
   Allegan MI 49010
   269 673-8451

(G-173)
L PERRIGO COMPANY
500 Eastern Ave (49010-9070)
PHONE.................................269 673-1608
Michael Heimann, *Prdtn Mgr*
Nathan Tate, *Engineer*
Mary Rusk, *Manager*
Norman Lenhart, *Supervisor*
EMP: 78 **Privately Held**
SIC: 2834 Pharmaceutical preparations
HQ: L Perrigo Company
   515 Eastern Ave
   Allegan MI 49010
   269 673-8451

(G-174)
LAKESIDE MECHANICAL CONTRS
1741 Forest Cove Trl (49010-8407)
P.O. Box 610, Douglas (49406-0610)
PHONE.................................616 786-0211
Bruce Visser, *President*
EMP: 25
SQ FT: 4,800
SALES (est): 2.9MM **Privately Held**
WEB: www.lakesidemechanical.com
SIC: 7692 1799 Welding repair; welding on site

(G-175)
LANE SOFT WATER
132 Grand St (49010-1196)
PHONE.................................269 673-3272
Terry W Johnson, *Partner*
Pamela Johnson, *Partner*
EMP: 6
SALES: 500K **Privately Held**
SIC: 3589 7389 Water filters & softeners, household type; water softener service

(G-176)
MATERIAL TRANSFER AND STOR INC
1214 Lincoln Rd (49010-9077)
P.O. Box 218 (49010-0218)
PHONE.................................800 836-7068
Scott Nyhof, *President*
Brenda Nyhof, *Corp Secy*
Tom Hofman, *Vice Pres*
EMP: 20
SQ FT: 250,000
SALES (est): 4.8MM **Privately Held**
WEB: www.materialtransfer.com
SIC: 3535 Conveyors & conveying equipment

(G-177)
MORRIS COMMUNICATIONS CORP
Also Called: Kalamazoo Express
595 Jenner Dr M40 (49010-1516)
PHONE.................................269 673-2141
Jerry Rabb, *Manager*
Darlene Kollar, *Info Tech Mgr*
EMP: 130 **Privately Held**
WEB: www.morris.com
SIC: 2721 2741 2791 2752 Periodicals; shopping news: publishing & printing; directories, telephone: publishing & printing; typesetting; commercial printing, lithographic; newspapers
HQ: Morris Communications Company Llc
   725 Broad St
   Augusta GA 30901
   706 724-0851

(G-178)
NASH CAR TRAILER CORPORATION
1305 Lincoln Rd (49010-9169)
P.O. Box 44 (49010-0044)
PHONE.................................269 673-5776
Monty Sailer, *President*
Daven Hansen, *Vice Pres*
Kris Nash, *Treasurer*
EMP: 12
SALES (est): 105.7K **Privately Held**
SIC: 3799 Trailers & trailer equipment

(G-179)
P J PRINTING
633 114th Ave Ste 5 (49010-9061)
P.O. Box 278 (49010-0278)
PHONE.................................269 673-3372
Douglas Ernst, *President*
EMP: 5
SALES (est): 538.9K **Privately Held**
SIC: 2752 Commercial printing, offset

(G-180)
PBM NUTRITIONALS LLC
515 Eastern Ave (49010-9070)
PHONE.................................269 673-8451
Joseph C Papa, *Ch of Bd*
Judy L Brown, *Vice Pres*
John T Hendrickson, *Vice Pres*
Art Shannon, *Vice Pres*
Matt Nolin, *Engineer*
EMP: 11
SALES (est): 1.4MM **Privately Held**
SIC: 2834 Pharmaceutical preparations
HQ: Perrigo Company
   515 Eastern Ave
   Allegan MI 49010
   269 673-8451

(G-181)
PERRIGO COMPANY
Also Called: Perrigo Logistics Center
900 Industrial Dr (49010-8544)
PHONE.................................269 686-1973
Gary Tenney, *Credit Mgr*
Nathan Hoffman, *Branch Mgr*
Gary Ezinga, *Supervisor*
Lacy Myers, *Administration*
Julie Sosnowski, *Assistant*
EMP: 15 **Privately Held**
SIC: 2834 Pharmaceutical preparations
HQ: Perrigo Company
   515 Eastern Ave
   Allegan MI 49010
   269 673-8451

(G-182)
PERRIGO COMPANY (HQ)
515 Eastern Ave (49010-9070)
PHONE.................................269 673-8451
Uve Roehrhoff, *CEO*
Joseph C Papa, *Ch of Bd*
Svend Andersen, *President*
Douglas S Boothe, *President*
Sharon Kochan, *President*
◆ **EMP:** 4400
SALES (est): 4.3B **Privately Held**
WEB: www.perrigo.com
SIC: 2834 Analgesics

(G-183)
PERRIGO COMPANY
515 Eastern Ave (49010-9070)
PHONE.................................269 673-7962
EMP: 12 **Privately Held**
SIC: 2834 Mfg Pharmaceutical Preparations
HQ: Perrigo Company
   515 Eastern Ave
   Allegan MI 49010
   269 673-8451

(G-184)
PERRIGO PHARMACEUTICALS CO
515 Eastern Ave (49010-9070)
PHONE.................................269 673-8451
Murray S Kessler, *President*
Leticia Remo, *Opers Staff*
Timothy Williams, *Senior Mgr*
EMP: 10
SALES (est): 867.3K **Privately Held**
SIC: 2834 Pharmaceutical preparations
HQ: Perrigo Company
   515 Eastern Ave
   Allegan MI 49010
   269 673-8451

(G-185)
PMI BRANDED PHARMACEUTICALS
Also Called: Perrigo Brnded Phrmcticals Inc
515 Eastern Ave (49010-9070)
PHONE.................................269 673-8451
Murray S Kessler, *President*
EMP: 10
SALES (est): 623.9K **Privately Held**
SIC: 2834 Pharmaceutical preparations
HQ: Perrigo Company
   515 Eastern Ave
   Allegan MI 49010
   269 673-8451

(G-186)
RAPA ELECTRIC INC
1173 Lincoln Rd (49010-9077)
PHONE.................................269 673-3157
Ronnie E Rapa, *President*
Dominik Bergner, *VP Opers*
William Wall, *Purch Mgr*
Misty Jackson, *Buyer*
Shannon Walcott, *Treasurer*
EMP: 25 **EST:** 1966
SQ FT: 15,000
SALES: 6MM **Privately Held**
WEB: www.rapaelectric.com
SIC: 5063 7694 Motors, electric; electric motor repair

(G-187)
RIVER VALLEY MACHINE INC
600 N Eastern Ave (49010-9592)
PHONE.................................269 673-8070
Lyle Kollar, *President*
Gale Kollar, *Admin Sec*
EMP: 22
SALES (est): 3.2MM **Privately Held**
SIC: 3312 3498 3494 3433 Tubes, steel & iron; fabricated pipe & fittings; valves & pipe fittings; heating equipment, except electric; manufactured hardware (general)

(G-188)
SOUTHWEST GRAVEL INC
Also Called: R Smith and Sons
3641 108th Ave (49010-8111)
PHONE.................................269 673-4665
Roger A Smith, *President*
EMP: 6
SALES (est): 1.1MM **Privately Held**
SIC: 1442 Construction sand mining; gravel mining

(G-189)
STUDTMANS STUFF (PA)
422 N Cedar St (49010-1206)
PHONE.................................269 673-3126
EMP: 4
SALES: 40K **Privately Held**
SIC: 3999 5999 Mfg Misc Products Ret Misc Merchandise

(G-190)
WAANDERS CONCRETE CO
3169 Babylon Rd (49010-9205)
PHONE.................................269 673-6352
Mark Waanders, *President*
Chuck Waanders, *Vice Pres*
Irene Waanders, *Treasurer*
EMP: 20 **EST:** 1935
SALES (est): 3.4MM **Privately Held**
SIC: 3273 3271 1442 1422 Ready-mixed concrete; concrete block & brick; construction sand & gravel; crushed & broken limestone

(G-191)
WEST MICHIGAN MEDICAL
595 Jenner Dr (49010-1516)
PHONE.................................269 673-2141
Debbie Sloan, *Editor*
Bill Carlson, *Manager*
EMP: 3
SALES (est): 74.9K **Privately Held**
SIC: 2711 Newspapers

(G-192)
WEST MICHIGAN METALS LLC
1168 33rd St (49010-8302)
PHONE.................................269 978-7021
Gerard H Bierling,
EMP: 5
SALES (est): 626K **Privately Held**
SIC: 1751 1791 3441 Lightweight steel framing (metal stud) installation; building front installation metal; fabricated structural metal

Allen
Hillsdale County

(G-193)
QUALITY TOOL COMPANY INC
6577 W Chicago Rd (49227-9716)
PHONE.................................517 869-2490
John E Watts, *President*
EMP: 3
SQ FT: 1,800
SALES: 100K **Privately Held**
SIC: 3541 Grinding machines, metalworking; milling machines

Allen Park
Wayne County

(G-194)
AEES POWER SYSTEMS LTD PARTNR (DH)
Also Called: Engineered Plastic Components
999 Republic Dr (48101-3668)
PHONE.................................248 489-4900
Frank Sovis, *Mng Member*
Walter E Frankiewicz,
▲ **EMP:** 80
SALES (est): 912.1MM
SALES (corp-wide): 1B **Privately Held**
SIC: 3694 Harness wiring sets, internal combustion engines

(G-195)
COLLECTIVE INDUSTRIES CORP
Also Called: Collective Industries Group
14835 Mclain Ave (48101-1816)
P.O. Box 886 (48101-0886)
PHONE.................................313 879-1080
Teresa Feijoo, *Principal*
Terrence C Scott, *Director*
EMP: 4
SALES (est): 213.6K **Privately Held**
SIC: 3999 Manufacturing industries

(G-196)
CULTIVATION STN - DETROIT INC
6540 Allen Rd (48101-2002)
PHONE.................................313 383-1766
Jeffrey Shahady, *Branch Mgr*
EMP: 9
SALES (corp-wide): 7.5MM **Privately Held**
SIC: 3999 Hydroponic equipment
PA: The Cultivation Station - Detroit Inc
   2518 Market St
   Detroit MI 48207
   313 394-0441

GEOGRAPHIC SECTION

Allendale - Ottawa County (G-223)

(G-197)
DOWNRIVER CREATIVE WOODWORKING
4631 Parkside Blvd (48101-3205)
PHONE.................................313 274-4090
Stephen Nikodemski, *Principal*
Scott Berels, *Technical Staff*
EMP: 4
SALES (est): 385.9K **Privately Held**
SIC: 2431 Millwork

(G-198)
FORD MOTOR COMPANY
1555 Fairlane Dr Ste 100 (48101-3629)
PHONE.................................313 594-4090
Karen Fisher, *Opers Staff*
Suzie Furton, *Manager*
Fay Watts, *Technical Staff*
Michael Gagnon, *Network Enginr*
EMP: 1353
SALES (corp-wide): 160.3B **Publicly Held**
SIC: 5511 3714 Automobiles, new & used; motor vehicle parts & accessories
PA: Ford Motor Company
   1 American Rd
   Dearborn MI 48126
   313 322-3000

(G-199)
JOBS INC
14829 Philomene Blvd (48101-2123)
PHONE.................................810 714-0522
Marco Livelli, *President*
Michael Oldham, *Administration*
▲ EMP: 3
SALES (est): 606.3K **Privately Held**
WEB: www.jobs.it
SIC: 3599 Custom machinery
HQ: Jobs Automazione Spa
   Via Emilia Parmense 164
   Piacenza PC 29122

(G-200)
LISA BAIN
9636 Chatham Ave (48101-1361)
PHONE.................................313 389-9661
Lisa Bain, *Principal*
EMP: 4
SALES (est): 300.7K **Privately Held**
SIC: 2674 Cement bags: made from purchased materials

(G-201)
M J DAY MACHINE TOOL COMPANY
19231 Van Born Rd (48101-2814)
PHONE.................................313 730-1200
Mitchell Day, *President*
EMP: 6
SALES: 700K **Privately Held**
SIC: 3449 Miscellaneous metalwork

(G-202)
MARTEL TOOL CORPORATION
5831 Pelham Rd (48101-2899)
PHONE.................................313 278-2420
Steven Martel, *CEO*
David Martel, *President*
Don Hass, *Principal*
Joseph Slifka, *Vice Pres*
Denise Clark, *Treasurer*
EMP: 11 EST: 1958
SQ FT: 10,000
SALES: 1.5MM **Privately Held**
WEB: www.marteltool.com
SIC: 3829 3545 3823 Measuring & controlling devices; gauges (machine tool accessories); industrial instrmnts msrmnt display/control process variable

(G-203)
ONESIAN ENTERPRISES INC
10520 Balfour Ave (48101-1143)
PHONE.................................313 382-5875
Charles Onesian, *President*
EMP: 4 EST: 1997
SALES (est): 200.1K **Privately Held**
SIC: 2711 Newspapers

(G-204)
PERMACOAT INC
14868 Champaign Rd (48101-1619)
PHONE.................................313 388 7798
Robert Lahousse, *CEO*
Shane La Housse, *President*
EMP: 17
SQ FT: 2,000
SALES (est): 1.2MM **Privately Held**
SIC: 3479 Aluminum coating of metal products

(G-205)
RED ROCK INDUSTRIES INC
16705 Ecorse Rd (48101-2447)
PHONE.................................734 992-3522
EMP: 3
SALES (est): 136.3K **Privately Held**
SIC: 3999 Manufacturing industries

(G-206)
RIVIERA INDUSTRIES INC
Also Called: Major Products
16038 Southfield Rd (48101-2563)
PHONE.................................313 381-5500
Donald Riviera, *President*
Hal Matthews, *Office Mgr*
EMP: 7
SQ FT: 4,000
SALES: 400K **Privately Held**
WEB: www.rivieratech.com
SIC: 3545 Boring machine attachments (machine tool accessories)

(G-207)
ROUSH ENTERPRISES INC
16630 Southfield Rd (48101-2555)
PHONE.................................313 294-8200
Dan Powerson, *Director*
EMP: 27 **Privately Held**
SIC: 3714 3711 Motor vehicle parts & accessories; motor vehicles & car bodies
PA: Roush Enterprises, Inc.
   34300 W 9 Mile Rd
   Farmington MI 48335

(G-208)
SIEMENS PRODUCT LIFE MGMT SFTW
1555 Fairlane Dr Ste 300 (48101-2869)
PHONE.................................313 317-6100
Barbara Havard, *Manager*
Christopher Koliba, *Consultant*
EMP: 30
SALES (corp-wide): 95B **Privately Held**
WEB: www.ugs.com
SIC: 7372 Business oriented computer software
HQ: Siemens Industry Software Inc.
   5800 Granite Pkwy Ste 600
   Plano TX 75024
   972 987-3000

(G-209)
SIGN SPECIALTIES CO INC
17140 Ecorse Rd (48101-2454)
PHONE.................................313 928-4230
William Spicer, *President*
Ivy Wilson, *Manager*
EMP: 3
SALES (est): 243.7K **Privately Held**
SIC: 3993 Signs, not made in custom sign painting shops

(G-210)
STEEL MILL COMPONENTS INC (PA)
17000 Ecorse Rd (48101-2452)
PHONE.................................313 386-0893
Andrew B Pellegrino, *CEO*
Chris Klompstra, *CFO*
EMP: 20
SQ FT: 40,000
SALES (est): 6.1MM **Privately Held**
SIC: 3441 Building components, structural steel

(G-211)
TERADYNE INC
Also Called: Teradyne Diagnostic Solutions
1800 Fairlane Dr Ste 200 (48101-2777)
PHONE.................................313 425-3900
Mark Lindauer, *Project Mgr*
EMP: 140
SALES (corp-wide): 2.1B **Publicly Held**
SIC: 3825 3643 3829 3678 Semiconductor test equipment; connectors & terminals for electrical devices; measuring & controlling devices; electronic connectors; semiconductors & related devices
PA: Teradyne, Inc.
   600 Riverpark Dr
   North Reading MA 01864
   978 370-2700

(G-212)
VENTCON INC
500 Enterprise Dr (48101-3091)
PHONE.................................313 336-4000
Sammy Speen, *Vice Ch Bd*
Dennis Berger, *Vice Ch Bd*
Todd W Hill, *President*
Ray Sliwinski, *Exec VP*
Dennis T Monaghan, *Vice Pres*
EMP: 120
SQ FT: 32,000
SALES (est): 36.2MM **Privately Held**
WEB: www.ventcon-mi.com
SIC: 3444 Sheet metalwork

(G-213)
WHIPPLE PRINTING INC
17140 Ecorse Rd (48101-2454)
PHONE.................................313 382-8033
Joe Hirsch, *President*
EMP: 4
SALES (est): 367K **Privately Held**
SIC: 2759 2752 Letterpress printing; commercial printing, offset

Allendale
Ottawa County

(G-214)
ALUWAX DENTAL PRODUCTS CO INC
5260 Edgewater Dr (49401-8401)
P.O. Box 87 (49401-0087)
PHONE.................................616 895-4385
Patrick Gemmen, *President*
EMP: 5
SQ FT: 2,190
SALES (est): 681,7K **Privately Held**
WEB: www.aluwaxdental.com
SIC: 3843 Impression material, dental; wax, dental

(G-215)
CONSTRUCTIVE SHEET METAL INC
Also Called: C S M
11670 46th Ave (49401-8834)
PHONE.................................616 245-5306
Terry Lantz, *President*
Carl Vrooman, *Project Mgr*
Michele Sunde, *Human Res Mgr*
Tab Jonge, *Sales Executive*
EMP: 34
SQ FT: 36,000
SALES (est): 7.3MM **Privately Held**
WEB: www.constructivesheetmetal.com
SIC: 3444 1796 3564 3535 Ducts, sheet metal; installing building equipment; blowers & fans; conveyors & conveying equipment; miscellaneous fabricated wire products; fabricated plate work (boiler shop)

(G-216)
ELITE INDUSTRIAL MFG LLC
9967 68th Ave (49401-9316)
P.O. Box 300 (49401-0300)
PHONE.................................616 895-1873
Bradley Grooters, *Purchasing*
Adam Vanderwal,
EMP: 8 EST: 2010
SALES (est): 1.1MM **Privately Held**
SIC: 3621 Phase or rotary converters (electrical equipment)

(G-217)
FRANDALE SUB SHOP
11250 Kistler Dr Unit 5 (49401-8070)
PHONE.................................616 446-6311
Sonya Bolks, *President*
EMP: 10 EST: 1976
SALES (est): 800.4K **Privately Held**
SIC: 2099 2038 Sandwiches, assembled & packaged: for wholesale market; pizza, frozen

(G-218)
GREAT LAKES LASER DYNAMICS INC
Also Called: Laser-Dynamics
4881 Allen Park Dr (49401-8625)
PHONE.................................616 892-7070
William Herberg, *President*
Ken Koster, *Vice Pres*
Paula Crawford, *Purchasing*
Andrew Rozema, *Engineer*
EMP: 60
SQ FT: 48,000
SALES (est): 18.3MM **Privately Held**
SIC: 3443 3499 Fabricated plate work (boiler shop); machine bases, metal; metal household articles

(G-219)
JIMDI PLASTICS INC
5375 Edgeway Dr (49401-8476)
PHONE.................................616 895-7766
Richard Schrotenboer, *President*
David L Gerdeman, *Vice Pres*
Jay Dewitt, *CFO*
Gary Stroven, *Financial Exec*
Mike McDaniel, *Info Tech Dir*
▲ EMP: 30
SQ FT: 25,000
SALES (est): 9.5MM **Privately Held**
WEB: www.jimdiplastics.com
SIC: 3544 3089 Special dies, tools, jigs & fixtures; injection molding of plastics

(G-220)
LAW ENFORCEMENT SUPPLY INC
10920 64th Ave (49401-8065)
P.O. Box 85 (49401-0085)
PHONE.................................616 895-7875
Gerald Carter Sr, *President*
Rod Bosker, *Vice Pres*
Sheryle Boscar, *Treasurer*
Roberta Boeve, *Admin Sec*
EMP: 4 EST: 1973
SQ FT: 2,184
SALES (est): 570.7K **Privately Held**
WEB: www.porta-clip.com
SIC: 3496 Clips & fasteners, made from purchased wire

(G-221)
LEPRINO FOODS COMPANY
4700 Rich St (49401-9237)
PHONE.................................616 895-5800
Steven Burchett, *Safety Dir*
Seth Berghorst, *Human Res Mgr*
Nick Opper, *Branch Mgr*
Dale Draper, *Manager*
Mark Lilly, *Manager*
EMP: 160
SALES (corp-wide): 1.7B **Privately Held**
WEB: www.leprinofoods.com
SIC: 2022 Natural cheese
PA: Leprino Foods Company
   1830 W 38th Ave
   Denver CO 80211
   303 480-2600

(G-222)
METTEK LLC
11480 53rd Ave Ste B (49401-8502)
PHONE.................................616 895-2033
Dave Munkres, *Cust Mgr*
Mark Ensink,
Doug Ensink,
Sandy Ensink,
Tracy Ensink,
EMP: 4
SQ FT: 8,300
SALES (est): 425K **Privately Held**
WEB: www.mettekllc.com
SIC: 2759 Screen printing

(G-223)
MORREN MOLD & MACHINE INC
10345 60th Ave (49401-8355)
PHONE.................................616 892-7474
David Morren, *President*
Sandra Morren, *Vice Pres*
EMP: 7
SQ FT: 12,500
SALES: 500K **Privately Held**
SIC: 3089 3599 Injection molding of plastics; machine & other job shop work

Allendale - Ottawa County (G-224)

(G-224)
MORREN PLASTIC MOLDING INC
7677 Fillmore St (49401-9627)
PHONE..................................616 997-7474
Nelson Morren, *President*
Julie Cornelius, *Vice Pres*
Sharon Morren, *Vice Pres*
EMP: 10 **EST:** 1999
SQ FT: 50,000
SALES (est): 1.7MM **Privately Held**
SIC: 3089 Molding primary plastic; injection molding of plastics

(G-225)
MUG SHOTS BURGERS AND BREWS
4633 Lake Michigan Dr (49401-9529)
PHONE..................................616 895-2337
Michael Sirotko, *Principal*
EMP: 4 **EST:** 2015
SALES (est): 231.1K **Privately Held**
SIC: 2082 Malt beverages

(G-226)
SUPERIOR WOOD PRODUCTS INC
7584 Warner St (49401-8759)
PHONE..................................616 453-4100
Kenneth Stevens, *President*
EMP: 12
SALES (est): 2.3MM **Privately Held**
WEB: www.superiorwoodproducts.com
SIC: 2431 Moldings, wood: unfinished & prefinished

(G-227)
WEST SHORE SERVICES INC (PA)
6620 Lake Michigan Dr (49401-9257)
P.O. Box 188 (49401-0188)
PHONE..................................616 895-4347
Jeff Dupilka, *President*
Dan Stollings, *Project Mgr*
Ken Council, *Human Res Dir*
Brian McDowell, *Manager*
Marty Rousseau, *Manager*
EMP: 24
SQ FT: 13,100
SALES (est): 5.2MM **Privately Held**
WEB: www.westshoreservices.com
SIC: 3669 1799 2521 Sirens, electric: vehicle, marine, industrial & air raid; building mover, including houses; wood office furniture

Allenton
St. Clair County

(G-228)
A S K MACHINING SERVICES
14919 Hough Rd (48002-3711)
P.O. Box 7 (48002-0007)
PHONE..................................810 650-0019
Andrew T Klos, *President*
EMP: 3
SALES (est): 287.3K **Privately Held**
SIC: 3599 Machine shop, jobbing & repair

(G-229)
MCCALLUM FABRICATING LLC
13927 Hough Rd (48002-3913)
PHONE..................................586 784-5555
Donald Mc Callum, *Owner*
EMP: 10 **EST:** 1948
SQ FT: 7,200
SALES (est): 510K **Privately Held**
SIC: 3914 Stainless steel ware

(G-230)
TIDE RINGS LLC
14150 Hough Rd (48002-3809)
PHONE..................................586 206-3142
Kevin M Lutz, *Principal*
EMP: 4
SALES: 250K **Privately Held**
SIC: 3999 Manufacturing industries

Alma
Gratiot County

(G-231)
ADW INDUSTRIES INC
130 Woodworth Ave (48801-2441)
P.O. Box 878 (48801-0878)
PHONE..................................989 466-4742
Thomas C Adle, *President*
EMP: 35 **EST:** 1982
SQ FT: 10,000
SALES (est): 7.9MM **Privately Held**
SIC: 3535 3714 3441 Conveyors & conveying equipment; motor vehicle parts & accessories; fabricated structural metal

(G-232)
ALMA CONCRETE PRODUCTS COMPANY (PA)
1277 Bridge Rd (48801-9700)
P.O. Box 389, Mount Pleasant (48804-0389)
PHONE..................................989 463-5476
Ralph J Fisher Jr, *President*
James O Fisher, *Corp Secy*
Arthur J Fisher, *Vice Pres*
Kyle White, *Manager*
EMP: 3
SALES (est): 1.3MM **Privately Held**
SIC: 3273 Ready-mixed concrete

(G-233)
ALMA CONTAINER CORPORATION
1000 Charles Ave (48801-9603)
P.O. Box 98 (48801-0098)
PHONE..................................989 463-2106
Michael D Maybank, *President*
Don Weaver, *Site Mgr*
Susan Maybank, *Treasurer*
Kathy Legene, *Admin Sec*
EMP: 15 **EST:** 1962
SQ FT: 52,000
SALES: 2MM **Privately Held**
WEB: www.almacontainer.com
SIC: 2653 Boxes, corrugated: made from purchased materials

(G-234)
ALMA PRODUCTS COMPANY
150 N Court Ave (48801-1910)
PHONE..................................989 463-1151
Brad Broucher, *Manager*
EMP: 4 **Privately Held**
SIC: 3566 Torque converters, except automotive
HQ: Alma Products I Llc
2000 Michigan Ave
Alma MI 48801
989 463-0290

(G-235)
ALMA PRODUCTS I LLC (DH)
2000 Michigan Ave (48801-9796)
PHONE..................................989 463-0290
Alan Galtan, *CEO*
Thomas H Quinn, *Ch of Bd*
Michael Flint, *President*
Andy Gasser, *CFO*
Matthew W Hanson, *Controller*
◆ **EMP:** 176
SQ FT: 180,000
SALES (est): 29.2MM **Privately Held**
WEB: www.almaproducts.com
SIC: 3714 Motor vehicle parts & accessories

(G-236)
AVALON & TAHOE MFG INC
903 Michigan Ave (48801-1933)
P.O. Box 698 (48801-0698)
PHONE..................................989 463-2112
Jim Wolf, *President*
Gregg Knight, *Exec VP*
Brian Richards, *Vice Pres*
Kelly Trevino, *Purch Agent*
Duane Dinninger, *Engineer*
EMP: 130
SQ FT: 150,000
SALES (est): 57.9MM **Privately Held**
SIC: 3732 Pontoons, except aircraft & inflatable

(G-237)
ETX HOLDINGS INC (DH)
2000 Michigan Ave (48801-9703)
PHONE..................................989 463-1151
Thomas H Quinn, *Ch of Bd*
Alan Gatlin, *President*
Andy Gasser, *CFO*
▼ **EMP:** 3
SALES (est): 148.3MM **Privately Held**
SIC: 3585 3621 3714 5013 Compressors for refrigeration & air conditioning equipment; motors & generators; motor vehicle parts & accessories; automotive supplies & parts; fittings for pipe, plastic
HQ: Transtar Industries, Inc.
7350 Young Dr
Cleveland OH 44146
440 232-5100

(G-238)
INTERNATIONAL AUTOMOTIVE COMPO
1965 Williams Rd (48801-2086)
PHONE..................................989 620-7649
Susan Gardner, *Manager*
Tammy Wright, *Manager*
David Dickey, *Technology*
EMP: 283 **Privately Held**
SIC: 3714 Motor vehicle parts & accessories
HQ: International Automotive Components Group North America, Inc.
28333 Telegraph Rd
Southfield MI 48034

(G-239)
MARYKAY SOFTWARE INC
5142 N State Rd (48801-9713)
PHONE..................................989 463-4385
Mary Kathryn Geopfert, *President*
EMP: 5
SALES (est): 283.4K **Privately Held**
SIC: 7372 Business oriented computer software

(G-240)
MERRILL INSTITUTE INC
520 Republic Ave (48801-2049)
PHONE..................................989 462-0330
Mark Johnston, *Director*
EMP: 6
SALES (est): 591.6K **Privately Held**
SIC: 3441 Fabricated structural metal

(G-241)
MERRILL TECHNOLOGIES GROUP INC
Also Called: Merrill Fabricators
520 Republic Ave (48801-2049)
PHONE..................................989 462-0330
Robert Yackel, *CEO*
Jeff Yackel, *COO*
Brian Blackmer, *Purchasing*
EMP: 123
SALES (corp-wide): 60MM **Privately Held**
SIC: 3533 3443 3446 Oil & gas field machinery; tanks, standard or custom fabricated: metal plate; architectural metalwork
PA: Merrill Technologies Group, Inc.
400 Florence St
Saginaw MI 48602
989 791-6676

(G-242)
MICHIGAN PAVING AND MTLS CO
1950 Williams Rd (48801-2085)
PHONE..................................989 463-1323
James Monroe, *Division Mgr*
EMP: 14
SALES (corp-wide): 30.6B **Privately Held**
SIC: 1771 2951 Blacktop (asphalt) work; asphalt paving mixtures & blocks
HQ: Michigan Paving And Materials Company
2575 S Haggerty Rd # 100
Canton MI 48188
734 397-2050

(G-243)
MORNING STAR PUBLISHING CO
Also Called: Alma Reminder
311 E Superior St Ste A (48801-1832)
PHONE..................................989 463-6071
Tamaera Fischer, *General Mgr*
EMP: 10
SALES (corp-wide): 697.5MM **Privately Held**
SIC: 2711 2741 Newspapers, publishing & printing; miscellaneous publishing
HQ: Morning Star Publishing Company
311 E Superior St Ste A
Alma MI 48801
989 779-6000

(G-244)
MORNING STAR PUBLISHING CO (DH)
311 E Superior St Ste A (48801-1832)
PHONE..................................989 779-6000
Bill McHugh, *President*
Jason Sharp, *CTO*
EMP: 150
SQ FT: 60,000
SALES (est): 32.8MM
SALES (corp-wide): 697.5MM **Privately Held**
SIC: 2711 Newspapers, publishing & printing
HQ: 21st Century Newspapers, Inc.
19176 Hall Rd Ste 200
Clinton Township MI 48038
586 469-4510

(G-245)
MORNING STAR PUBLISHING CO
Also Called: St Johns Reminder
311 E Superior St Ste A (48801-1832)
P.O. Box 473, Saint Johns (48879-0473)
PHONE..................................989 779-6000
Bonnie Fyvie, *Manager*
EMP: 5
SALES (corp-wide): 697.5MM **Privately Held**
SIC: 2711 7313 2741 Newspapers, publishing & printing; newspaper advertising representative; shopping news: publishing & printing
HQ: Morning Star Publishing Company
311 E Superior St Ste A
Alma MI 48801
989 779-6000

(G-246)
OERLIKON BLZERS CATING USA INC
7800 N Alger Rd (48801-9321)
PHONE..................................989 463-6268
Robert Smith, *Principal*
EMP: 8
SALES (corp-wide): 2.6B **Privately Held**
SIC: 3479 Painting, coating & hot dipping
HQ: Oerlikon Balzers Coating Usa Inc.
1700 E Golf Rd Ste 200
Schaumburg IL 60173
847 619-5541

(G-247)
PRODUCTION MACHINING OF ALMA
6595 N Jerome Rd (48801-9706)
PHONE..................................989 463-1495
Raymond Cull, *President*
Dennis Cull, *Vice Pres*
Ray Cull, *Vice Pres*
James Fedor, *QC Mgr*
Cull Raymond Jr, *Manager*
▲ **EMP:** 26
SQ FT: 33,000
SALES (est): 3.7MM **Privately Held**
SIC: 3599 Machine shop, jobbing & repair

(G-248)
REBEATS (PA)
219 Prospect Ave (48801-2262)
P.O. Box 6 (48801-0006)
PHONE..................................989 463-4757
George Robert Cook, *Owner*
EMP: 11
SQ FT: 2,000

SALES: 100K **Privately Held**
WEB: www.rebeats.com
SIC: **3931** 5736 5731 Drums, parts & accessories (musical instruments); drums & related percussion instruments; high fidelity stereo equipment

(G-249)
SHILOH INDUSTRIES INC
250 Adams St (48801-2517)
PHONE.................................989 463-6166
Dustin McDonald, *Plant Mgr*
EMP: 90 **Publicly Held**
SIC: **3363** 3714 Aluminum die-castings; motor vehicle parts & accessories
PA: Shiloh Industries, Inc.
  880 Steel Dr
  Valley City OH 44280

Almont
Lapeer County

(G-250)
AFGCO SAND & GRAVEL CO INC
5171 Sandhill Rd (48003-9735)
PHONE.................................810 798-3293
Ken Measel, *President*
EMP: 5
SQ FT: 2,500
SALES (est): 423.7K **Privately Held**
SIC: **1442** Construction sand & gravel

(G-251)
ALDEZ NORTH AMERICA LLC
4260 Van Dyke Rd Ste 109 (48003-8546)
PHONE.................................810 577-3891
Michael J Byrne, *Mng Member*
Jeffrey Copak,
EMP: 5
SALES: 1.5MM **Privately Held**
SIC: **2653** 7538 7389 4214 Corrugated & solid fiber boxes; general automotive repair shops; industrial & commercial equipment inspection service; local trucking with storage

(G-252)
ASSOCIATED BROACH CORPORATION
7481 Research Dr (48003-8513)
PHONE.................................810 798-9112
Fax: 810 798-2270
EMP: 24
SQ FT: 10,000
SALES (est): 1.6MM **Privately Held**
SIC: **3545** Mfg Broaches

(G-253)
C T & G ENTERPRISES INC (PA)
79415 Scottish Hills Dr (48003)
P.O. Box 180233, Utica (48318-0233)
PHONE.................................810 798-8661
Carl T Mullins, *President*
EMP: 5
SALES: 1.7MM **Privately Held**
SIC: **3535** Conveyors & conveying equipment

(G-254)
CONCORDANT PUBLISHING CONCERN
6800 Hough Rd (48003-9710)
P.O. Box 449 (48003-0449)
PHONE.................................810 798-3563
James Coram, *President*
EMP: 7
SALES: 236.2K **Privately Held**
SIC: **2741** Miscellaneous publishing

(G-255)
D & D FABRICATIONS INC
8005 Tiffany Dr (48003-8642)
PHONE.................................810 798-2491
Allan Lagrou, *President*
Karen S Lagrou, *Co-Owner*
EMP: 4
SALES (est): 407.4K **Privately Held**
WEB: www.aluminumv8.com
SIC: **5015** 3449 Automotive parts & supplies, used; bars, concrete reinforcing; fabricated steel

(G-256)
ELMONT DISTRICT LIBRARY
Also Called: Henry Stephens Memorial Lib
213 W Saint Clair St (48003-8476)
P.O. Box 517 (48003-0517)
PHONE.................................810 798-3100
Maybelle Smith, *Chairman*
Kay Hurd, *Director*
EMP: 8
SALES (est): 439K **Privately Held**
WEB: www.adlmi.org
SIC: **8231** 2731 Public library; book publishing

(G-257)
GEAR MASTER INC
7481 Research Dr (48003-8513)
PHONE.................................810 798-9254
Gerald Stroud, *President*
Melissa Garner, *Accounting Mgr*
EMP: 10
SQ FT: 2,400
SALES (est): 1.3MM **Privately Held**
WEB: www.gears-manufacturers.com
SIC: **7389** 3728 Grinding, precision: commercial or industrial; gears, aircraft power transmission

(G-258)
INPLAST INTERIOR TECH LLC
Also Called: Trims Unlimited
3863 Van Dyke Rd (48003-8049)
PHONE.................................810 724-3500
Bill Welch, *Plant Mgr*
William Welch,
EMP: 3
SALES (est): 310K **Privately Held**
SIC: **2396** 5091 2392 7389 Automotive trimmings, fabric; fitness equipment & supplies; boat cushions; sewing contractor; plastic boats & other marine equipment

(G-259)
INTER-POWER CORPORATION (PA)
Also Called: Tarifa
3578 Van Dyke Rd (48003-8045)
PHONE.................................810 798-7050
Gary Gariglio, *President*
▲ EMP: 27
SQ FT: 60,000
SALES (est): 19.4MM **Privately Held**
WEB: www.interpwr.com
SIC: **3567** Induction heating equipment

(G-260)
KEN MEASEL SUPPLY INC
6343 Hayfield Ln (48003-9706)
PHONE.................................810 798-3293
Ken Measel, *President*
EMP: 5
SALES (est): 1.3MM **Privately Held**
SIC: **1442** Sand mining

(G-261)
LIGON HELICOPTER CORPORATION
Also Called: Trim Star Warehouse
3776 Van Dyke Rd (48003-8047)
P.O. Box 482 (48003-0482)
PHONE.................................810 706-1885
James T Ligon Jr, *President*
EMP: 3
SALES: 350K **Privately Held**
SIC: **3089** Automotive parts, plastic

(G-262)
MASTER ROBOTICS LLC
7300 Danielle Dr (48003-8065)
PHONE.................................586 484-7710
Mike Riley,
EMP: 3
SALES (est): 684.1K **Privately Held**
SIC: **3569** Robots, assembly line: industrial & commercial

(G-263)
MERC-O-TRONIC INSTRUMENTS CORP
215 Branch St (48003-1004)
P.O. Box 488 (48003-0488)
PHONE.................................586 894-9529
Arthur W Schafer Jr, *President*
Dane A Schafer, *Treasurer*
EMP: 11 EST: 1955
SQ FT: 5,000
SALES (est): 1.5MM **Privately Held**
WEB: www.mercotronic.com
SIC: **3825** Instruments to measure electricity

(G-264)
MIG MOLDING LLC
3778 Van Dyke Rd (48003-8043)
PHONE.................................810 660-8435
EMP: 9 EST: 2014
SALES (est): 1.1MM **Privately Held**
SIC: **3089** Molding primary plastic

(G-265)
SEEWALD INDUSTRIES
6960 Hollow Corners Rd (48003-7907)
PHONE.................................586 322-1042
Kenneth L Seewald, *Principal*
EMP: 3 EST: 2018
SALES (est): 163.9K **Privately Held**
SIC: **3999** Manufacturing industries

(G-266)
SHOWCASE CABINETRY INC
4005 Van Dyke Rd (48003-8514)
PHONE.................................810 798-9966
Ken Daugherty, *President*
EMP: 3
SALES (est): 383.8K **Privately Held**
SIC: **2434** Wood kitchen cabinets

(G-267)
SPRING DYNAMICS INC
7378 Research Dr (48003-8512)
PHONE.................................810 798-2622
Thomas Boles, *President*
▲ EMP: 45
SQ FT: 33,000
SALES (est): 13.9MM **Privately Held**
WEB: www.springdynamics.com
SIC: **3495** Wire springs

(G-268)
SUMMERS ROAD GRAVEL & DEV LLC
Also Called: Summers Rd Gravel
3620 Van Dyke Rd (48003-8041)
PHONE.................................810 798-8533
EMP: 3
SALES (est): 162K **Privately Held**
SIC: **1442** Construction sand & gravel

(G-269)
VICTORA USA INC
3776 Van Dyke Rd (48003-8047)
PHONE.................................810 798-0253
James T Ligon, *COO*
Deepak Kumar, *Manager*
▲ EMP: 7 EST: 2013
SALES (est): 1.2MM **Privately Held**
SIC: **3714** Camshafts, motor vehicle
PA: Victora Auto Private Limited
  Scf - 24, Sector-11d, Huda Market,
  Faridabad HR 12100

(G-270)
WEATHER PANE INC
6209 Bordman Rd (48003-9704)
PHONE.................................810 798-8695
Richard Keller, *President*
Barbara Keller, *Corp Secy*
EMP: 5
SQ FT: 8,000
SALES: 270K **Privately Held**
SIC: **3089** Windows, plastic

Alpena
Alpena County

(G-271)
ADMIRAL
2520 Us Highway 23 S (49707-4618)
PHONE.................................989 356-6419
G Kendzirorski, *Manager*
Gary Kendzirorski, *Manager*
EMP: 6 EST: 2011
SALES (est): 558.3K **Privately Held**
SIC: **5541** 5411 3589 Gasoline service stations; convenience stores; car washing machinery

(G-272)
AIR DEVICES CO
2723 Pearl Rd (49707-4623)
P.O. Box 888 (49707-0888)
PHONE.................................989 354-5740
Randy Patterson, *Managing Prtnr*
EMP: 3
SQ FT: 500
SALES (est): 240K **Privately Held**
WEB: www.airdevices.com
SIC: **3593** Fluid power cylinders, hydraulic or pneumatic

(G-273)
ALPENA AGGREGATE INC
7590 Weiss Rd (49707-8963)
PHONE.................................989 595-2511
Earl R Dubey, *President*
EMP: 12
SQ FT: 300,000
SALES (est): 2.2MM **Privately Held**
SIC: **1442** Common sand mining; gravel mining

(G-274)
ALPENA BIOREFINERY
412 Ford Ave (49707-2346)
PHONE.................................989 340-1190
Mark Szczepanik, *Administration*
EMP: 3
SALES (est): 167.3K **Privately Held**
SIC: **2493** Reconstituted wood products

(G-275)
ALPENA ELECTRIC MOTOR SERVICE
1581 M 32 W (49707-8193)
P.O. Box 565 (49707-0565)
PHONE.................................989 354-8780
James E Vivian II, *President*
Judith K Vivian, *Admin Sec*
EMP: 6
SQ FT: 15,000
SALES (est): 1.2MM **Privately Held**
WEB: www.alpena.com
SIC: **7694** 5063 Rebuilding motors, except automotive; rewinding services; motors, electric

(G-276)
AMOS MFG INC
3490 Us Highway 23 N (49707-6910)
P.O. Box 177 (49707-0177)
PHONE.................................989 358-7187
Debra J Winter, *President*
EMP: 33
SALES (est): 7.3MM **Privately Held**
SIC: **3589** Shredders, industrial & commercial

(G-277)
ATLANTIS TECH CORP
706 Island View Dr (49707-1325)
P.O. Box 205 (49707-0205)
PHONE.................................989 356-6954
Paul Diamond, *Principal*
EMP: 3 EST: 2007
SALES (est): 405K **Privately Held**
SIC: **3312** Stainless steel

(G-278)
AUNT MILLIES BAKERIES
3450 Us Highway 23 S (49707-4840)
PHONE.................................989 356-6688
Fax: 989 354-3212
EMP: 7
SALES (est): 411.5K **Privately Held**
SIC: **2051** Mfg Bread/Related Products

(G-279)
AUSTIN BROTHERS BEER CO LLC
821 W Miller St (49707-1825)
PHONE.................................909 213-4194
Dana Austin, *CEO*
Blake Austin, *CFO*
Brant Austin, *Manager*
EMP: 3
SALES (est): 257.1K **Privately Held**
SIC: **2082** Near beer

(G-280)
BAKER ENTERPRISES INC (HQ)
801 Johnson St (49707-1870)
PHONE.................................989 354-2189

Alpena - Alpena County (G-281)

Gary Stevens, *President*
EMP: 30 **EST:** 1929
SQ FT: 45,000
SALES (est): 5.1MM
SALES (corp-wide): 243.4MM **Privately Held**
WEB: www.besser.com
SIC: 3564 3443 3537 3441 Dust or fume collecting equipment, industrial; fabricated plate work (boiler shop); industrial trucks & tractors; fabricated structural metal
PA: Besser Company
801 Johnson St
Alpena MI 49707
989 354-4111

(G-281)
BAY MANUFACTURING CORPORATION
3750 Us Highway 23 N (49707-7949)
P.O. Box 205 (49707-0205)
PHONE..................989 358-7198
Gregory Winter, *President*
Debra Winter, *Treasurer*
EMP: 49
SALES (est): 6.5MM **Privately Held**
SIC: 3469 3535 Machine parts, stamped or pressed metal; conveyors & conveying equipment

(G-282)
BESSER COMPANY (PA)
801 Johnson St (49707-1897)
PHONE..................989 354-4111
Kevin L Curtis, *CEO*
Chandramouli Nagarajan, *Engineer*
Juli S Musch, *CFO*
◆ **EMP:** 350 **EST:** 1897
SQ FT: 500,000
SALES (est): 243.4MM **Privately Held**
SIC: 3531 3559 3564 3443 Concrete plants; concrete products machinery; dust or fume collecting equipment, industrial; fabricated plate work (boiler shop)

(G-283)
CLAY & GRAHAM INC
Also Called: Thunder Bay Concrete Products
4770 Werth Rd (49707-9551)
PHONE..................989 354-5292
Norma Clay, *President*
EMP: 8
SQ FT: 5,000
SALES (est): 1.1MM **Privately Held**
WEB: www.newobjectivity.com
SIC: 3271 5211 Blocks, concrete or cinder: standard; masonry materials & supplies

(G-284)
CORR-FAC CORPORATION
Also Called: Rack Engineering Division
4040 Us Highway 23 N (49707-7944)
P.O. Box 205 (49707-0205)
PHONE..................989 358-7050
Gregory C Winter, *President*
Debra J Winter, *Corp Secy*
EMP: 4
SALES (est): 678.9K **Privately Held**
WEB: www.rack-eng.com
SIC: 3559 5084 Foundry machinery & equipment; conveyor systems

(G-285)
DECORATIVE PANELS INTL INC
416 Ford Ave (49707-2346)
PHONE..................989 354-2121
Len Werda, *Plant Mgr*
Lloyd Springer, *Manager*
EMP: 50 **Privately Held**
WEB: www.decorativepanelsinternational.com
SIC: 2421 Building & structural materials, wood
HQ: Decorative Panels International, Inc.
2900 Hill Ave
Toledo OH 43607
419 535-5921

(G-286)
EAGLE ENGINEERING & SUPPLY CO
101 N Industrial Hwy (49707-8167)
PHONE..................989 356-4526
Curtis D Eagle, *President*
Joan Eagle, *Corp Secy*

Bradley Eagle, *Vice Pres*
EMP: 20
SQ FT: 15,000
SALES (est): 6.4MM **Privately Held**
WEB: www.eaglecompanies.com
SIC: 5063 3823 3535 3613 Motors, electric; motor controls, starters & relays: electric; panelboard indicators, recorders & controllers: receiver; conveyors & conveying equipment; switchgear & switchboard apparatus

(G-287)
ENDURA-VEYOR INC
3490 Us Highway 23 N (49707-6910)
P.O. Box 205 (49707-0205)
PHONE..................989 358-7060
Gregory C Winter, *Principal*
▼ **EMP:** 16
SALES (est): 4.2MM **Privately Held**
WEB: www.endura-veyor.com
SIC: 3535 Conveyors & conveying equipment

(G-288)
FALCON CONSULTING SERVICES LLC
112 1/2 W Chisholm St A (49707-2446)
PHONE..................989 262-9325
Lori Fields,
EMP: 4
SALES (est): 139.1K **Privately Held**
SIC: 3599 7371 8742 Machine & other job shop work; custom computer programming services; materials mgmt. (purchasing, handling, inventory) consultant

(G-289)
FIBER-CHAR CORPORATION
3336 Piper Rd (49707-4751)
P.O. Box 307 (49707-0307)
PHONE..................989 356-5501
Dennis A Schultz, *President*
Patricia Schultz, *Corp Secy*
Mitch Schuch, *Prdtn Mgr*
Adam Zeeman, *Sales Staff*
Ryan Martin, *Sales Associate*
▼ **EMP:** 20 **EST:** 1978
SQ FT: 30,000
SALES (est): 3.2MM **Privately Held**
SIC: 2431 Moldings, wood: unfinished & prefinished; trim, wood

(G-290)
FRAMON MFG CO INC (PA)
1201 W Chisholm St (49707-1619)
PHONE..................989 356-6296
Frank Michael Aguis, *President*
Ann McConnell, *Principal*
Ann Aguis, *Corp Secy*
Phil Aguis, *Vice Pres*
EMP: 7
SQ FT: 2,000
SALES (est): 1.2MM **Privately Held**
WEB: www.framon.com
SIC: 3541 Machine tools, metal cutting type

(G-291)
GARANTS OFFICE SUPS & PRTG INC
117 W Washington Ave (49707-2757)
PHONE..................989 356-3930
Ronald Garant, *President*
Darlene Garant, *Admin Sec*
EMP: 5 **EST:** 1984
SALES (est): 600K **Privately Held**
SIC: 5943 2752 5712 Office forms & supplies; commercial printing, offset; office furniture

(G-292)
GILDNERS CONCRETE
Also Called: Gildner's Concrete Products
400 Commerce Dr (49707-1952)
PHONE..................989 356-5156
Greg Gildner, *Owner*
Michael Gildner, *Owner*
Ernie Gildner, *Co-Owner*
EMP: 4
SALES (est): 368.4K **Privately Held**
SIC: 5211 5999 1771 3273 Concrete & cinder block; concrete products, pre-cast; concrete work; ready-mixed concrete

(G-293)
INGLIS FARMS INC
Also Called: F & T Fur Harvesters Trdg Post
10681 Bushey Rd (49707-9205)
PHONE..................989 727-8727
Ralph Inglis, *President*
Shawn Inglis, *Vice Pres*
EMP: 3
SQ FT: 8,650
SALES (est): 280K **Privately Held**
SIC: 3999 0191 Furs; general farms, primarily crop

(G-294)
L & S TRANSIT MIX CONCRETE CO
500 Tuttle St (49707-2733)
PHONE..................989 354-5363
Gerold Lancaster, *President*
Tim Lancaster, *Vice Pres*
Evelyn Lancaster, *Treasurer*
▲ **EMP:** 15
SALES (est): 2.2MM **Privately Held**
SIC: 3273 5211 Ready-mixed concrete; masonry materials & supplies

(G-295)
LAFARGE NORTH AMERICA INC
1435 Ford Ave (49707-2100)
P.O. Box 396 (49707-0396)
PHONE..................989 354-4171
Paul Rogers, *Plant Mgr*
George Kistler, *Enginr/R&D Mgr*
Thomas Ward, *Technician*
Randy Hartman, *Maintence Staff*
Klay Wagner, *Maintence Staff*
EMP: 8
SALES (corp-wide): 27.6B **Privately Held**
WEB: www.lafargenorthamerica.com
SIC: 3241 5032 Portland cement; cement
HQ: Lafarge North America Inc.
8700 W Bryn Mawr Ave
Chicago IL 60631
773 372-1000

(G-296)
MANIGG ENTERPRISES INC (PA)
1010 Us Highway 23 N (49707-1250)
P.O. Box 678 (49707-0678)
PHONE..................989 356-4986
Roger Glawe, *President*
Jeff Weiland, *Corp Secy*
Gary Glawe, *Vice Pres*
EMP: 17
SQ FT: 2,500
SALES (est): 7.1MM **Privately Held**
SIC: 1794 2411 1411 4213 Excavation work; wood chips, produced in the field; limestone, dimension-quarrying; trucking, except local

(G-297)
MAX ENDURA INC
Also Called: Endura-Veyor
3490 Us Highway 23 S (49707-4841)
P.O. Box 205 (49707-0205)
PHONE..................989 356-1593
Gregory C Winter, *President*
Debra J Winter, *Corp Secy*
EMP: 25
SALES (est): 3.4MM **Privately Held**
SIC: 3589 3535 Shredders, industrial & commercial; conveyors & conveying equipment

(G-298)
MICHAEL NADEAU CABINET MAKING
4357 M 32 W (49707-8133)
PHONE..................989 356-0229
Michael Nadeau, *Owner*
EMP: 3
SQ FT: 5,200
SALES: 148K **Privately Held**
SIC: 2431 2541 2499 Interior & ornamental woodwork & trim; trim, wood; woodwork, interior & ornamental; table or counter tops, plastic laminated; decorative wood & woodwork

(G-299)
MICHIGAN EAST SIDE SALES LLC
4220 Us Highway 23 S (49707-5140)
PHONE..................989 354-6867
Kiley Selden, *General Mgr*
Robert Papin, *Mng Member*
EMP: 3
SALES: 1.5MM **Privately Held**
WEB: www.michiganeastsidesales.com
SIC: 5012 3792 6531 5511 Recreational vehicles, motor homes & trailers; house trailers, except as permanent dwellings; real estate leasing & rentals; new & used car dealers

(G-300)
MID-WEST INNOVATORS INC
Also Called: Mid-West Mfg.
3810 Us Highway 23 N (49707-7925)
P.O. Box 115 (49707-0115)
PHONE..................989 358-7147
Gregory C Winter, *President*
Deborah J Winter, *Treasurer*
EMP: 19
SALES (est): 3.4MM **Privately Held**
SIC: 3441 Fabricated structural metal

(G-301)
MODEL PRINTING SERVICE INC
Also Called: Allegra Alpena
829 W Chisholm St (49707-1717)
PHONE..................989 356-0834
Edward Klimczak, *President*
Lori Ann Klimzzak, *Bookkeeper*
EMP: 12
SQ FT: 4,500
SALES (est): 2.3MM **Privately Held**
WEB: www.modelprintingservice.com
SIC: 2752 Commercial printing, offset

(G-302)
MOTIVATION IDEAS INC
Also Called: Alpena Print Master
1101 Dow Dr (49707-1203)
PHONE..................989 356-1817
Jim Baker, *President*
EMP: 3 **EST:** 1975
SQ FT: 2,000
SALES (est): 356.2K **Privately Held**
SIC: 2752 Commercial printing, offset

(G-303)
NOVA-TRON CONTROLS CORP
111 S Second Ave (49707-2813)
P.O. Box 103 (49707-0103)
PHONE..................989 358-6126
EMP: 8
SALES (est): 1MM **Privately Held**
SIC: 3679 Electronic circuits

(G-304)
OMNI METALCRAFT CORP (PA)
4040 Us Highway 23 N (49707-7923)
P.O. Box 352 (49707-0352)
PHONE..................989 354-4075
Ronald W Winter, *Chairman*
Gregory C Winter, *COO*
Paul L Diamond, *Vice Pres*
William C Kaschner, *Vice Pres*
Debra J Winter, *CFO*
▲ **EMP:** 35
SQ FT: 7,200
SALES (est): 8.4MM **Privately Held**
SIC: 3535 5084 Conveyors & conveying equipment; industrial machinery & equipment

(G-305)
OVERHEAD DOOR COMPANY ALPENA
Also Called: Thermo-Shield Window Mfg
2550 Us Highway 23 S (49707-4618)
PHONE..................989 354-8316
John G Adams, *President*
Norma Adams, *Corp Secy*
Steven Adams, *Vice Pres*
EMP: 5
SQ FT: 8,600
SALES (est): 940.4K **Privately Held**
SIC: 5211 1521 3089 Garage doors, sale & installation; doors, wood or metal, except storm; doors, storm: wood or metal; general remodeling, single-family houses; windows, plastic

GEOGRAPHIC SECTION

Ann Arbor - Washtenaw County (G-332)

(G-306)
PANEL PROCESSING OREGON INC (HQ)
Also Called: Thermo Pressed Laminates
120 N Industrial Hwy (49707-7729)
PHONE.................................989 356-9007
Charles T Smith, *Principal*
EMP: 23 EST: 1971
SALES (est): 2.4MM
SALES (corp-wide): 95.4MM **Privately Held**
SIC: 2541 3442 Store fixtures, wood; metal doors, sash & trim
PA: Panel Processing, Inc.
120 N Industrial Hwy
Alpena MI 49707
800 433-7142

(G-307)
PCI PROCAL INC
3810 Us Highway 23 N (49707-7925)
P.O. Box 115 (49707-0115)
PHONE.................................989 358-7070
Maureen Bolda, *Principal*
Tina Friedman, *Controller*
Nancy Pomish, *Human Res Dir*
EMP: 18 EST: 2001
SALES (est): 3.5MM **Privately Held**
SIC: 3571 3714 3568 3537 Electronic computers; motor vehicle parts & accessories; power transmission equipment; industrial trucks & tractors; conveyors & conveying equipment

(G-308)
PRO-BUILT MFG
820 Long Lake Ave (49707-1855)
P.O. Box 115 (49707-0115)
PHONE.................................989 354-1321
EMP: 3 EST: 2010
SALES (est): 288.8K **Privately Held**
SIC: 3999 Manufacturing industries

(G-309)
PUNCHING CONCEPTS INC
Also Called: Procal
3810 Us Highway 23 N (49707-7925)
P.O. Box 115 (49707-0115)
PHONE.................................989 358-7070
Gregory C Winter, *President*
Debra J Winter, *Corp Secy*
EMP: 15
SALES (est): 2.6MM **Privately Held**
WEB: www.pcimfg.com
SIC: 3469 Metal stampings

(G-310)
QSR OUTDOOR PRODUCTS INC
600 W Campbell St (49707-3004)
PHONE.................................989 354-0777
EMP: 5
SALES (est): 256.5K **Privately Held**
SIC: 3949 Sporting & athletic goods

(G-311)
RAND L INDUSTRIES INC
2046 Partridge St (49707-8990)
PHONE.................................989 657-5175
Randy Benoit, *Principal*
EMP: 3
SALES (est): 321.9K **Privately Held**
SIC: 3131 Rands

(G-312)
SMIGELSKI PROPERTIES LLC
712 N Second Ave (49707-2230)
PHONE.................................989 255-6252
Andrew Smigelski,
EMP: 5 EST: 2010
SALES (est): 304.4K **Privately Held**
SIC: 2013 Prepared beef products from purchased beef

(G-313)
STANDARD PROVISION LLC
1505 Greenhaven Ln (49707-4257)
PHONE.................................989 354-4975
Vicki Shooks, *Principal*
EMP: 6
SALES (est): 442.2K **Privately Held**
SIC: 2011 Meat packing plants

(G-314)
STEEL CRAFT INC
1086 Hamilton Rd (49707)
P.O. Box 205 (49707-0205)
PHONE.................................989 358-7196
Gregory Winter, *President*
Debra Winter, *Corp Secy*
EMP: 24
SQ FT: 20,000
SALES (est): 3.6MM **Privately Held**
SIC: 3535 3441 Conveyors & conveying equipment; fabricated structural metal

(G-315)
STEVENS CUSTOM FABRICATION
928 Lockwood St (49707-1744)
PHONE.................................989 340-1184
Scott Stevens, *Owner*
EMP: 4
SALES (est): 384.8K **Privately Held**
SIC: 3441 3599 Fabricated structural metal; machine shop, jobbing & repair

(G-316)
STEVENS CUSTOM FABRICATION
615 W Campbell St (49707-3003)
PHONE.................................989 340-1184
Scott Stevens,
Todd Briton,
Will Rensberry,
Ann Sherman,
Trent Sherman,
EMP: 5 EST: 2013
SALES: 600K **Privately Held**
SIC: 3441 Fabricated structural metal

(G-317)
STONEY ACRES WINERY
4268 Truckey Rd (49707-9701)
PHONE.................................989 356-1041
Jim Grochowski, *Partner*
Helen Grochowski, *Partner*
EMP: 5
SALES (est): 257.3K **Privately Held**
WEB: www.stoneyacreswinery.com
SIC: 2084 Wine cellars, bonded: engaged in blending wines; wines

(G-318)
SUPERIOR FABRICATING INC
320 N Eleventh Ave (49707-1716)
P.O. Box 501 (49707-0501)
PHONE.................................989 354-8877
Robert Westenbarger, *President*
Diedre Westenbarger, *Treasurer*
EMP: 10 EST: 1975
SQ FT: 6,000
SALES (est): 1.3MM **Privately Held**
SIC: 3449 Bars, concrete reinforcing: fabricated steel

(G-319)
W G BENJEY INC (PA)
2293 Werth Rd (49707-4652)
PHONE.................................989 356-0016
Michael Ableidinger, *President*
Dave Seifferlein, *Manager*
EMP: 15 EST: 1960
SQ FT: 4,000
SALES (est): 5.2MM **Privately Held**
WEB: www.benjey.com
SIC: 3559 8711 Automotive related machinery; consulting engineer

(G-320)
W G BENJEY INC
Also Called: W G Benjey North
108 E Herman St (49707-2140)
PHONE.................................989 356-0027
Wayne Bates, *Manager*
EMP: 5
SALES (corp-wide): 5.2MM **Privately Held**
WEB: www.benjey.com
SIC: 3452 5084 Screws, metal; conveyor systems
PA: W. G. Benjey, Inc.
2293 Werth Rd
Alpena MI 49707
989 356-0016

(G-321)
YUKON MANUFACTURING
167 N Industrial Hwy (49707-8153)
PHONE.................................989 358-6248
Ed Bowerman, *Principal*
EMP: 10
SALES (est): 1.1MM **Privately Held**
SIC: 3999 Manufacturing industries

Alto
Kent County

(G-322)
ALTO MEAT PROCESSING
12605 60th St Se (49302-9689)
PHONE.................................616 868-6080
Brian Peterson, *Owner*
EMP: 3
SALES (est): 217.8K **Privately Held**
SIC: 2011 Meat packing plants

(G-323)
BV TECHNOLOGY LLC
7855 Sandy Hollow Dr Se (49302-9796)
PHONE.................................616 558-1746
Robert Briody, *CEO*
Richard Anthony Marquis, *Principal*
Bobby Neal Wilmoth Jr, *Principal*
Yen-Oahn Thi Vo, *Manager*
EMP: 4
SALES (est): 206K **Privately Held**
SIC: 2899 7389 Rifle bore cleaning compounds;

(G-324)
CALEDONIA CMNTY SAWMILL LLC
8298 96th St Se (49302-9598)
PHONE.................................616 891-8561
Matthew Brown, *Principal*
EMP: 3
SALES (est): 180.5K **Privately Held**
SIC: 2421 Sawmills & planing mills, general

(G-325)
CASCADE METAL WORKS INC
6098 Alden Nash Ave Se (49302-9762)
PHONE.................................616 868-0668
Michael Alderink, *President*
EMP: 15
SQ FT: 15,560
SALES (est): 2.3MM **Privately Held**
SIC: 3544 Special dies & tools

(G-326)
CORAL CORPORATION
Also Called: Thermal Trends
8358 68th St Se (49302-9532)
PHONE.................................616 868-6295
Louis Braun, *President*
Al Johnson, *Vice Pres*
EMP: 3
SQ FT: 2,800
SALES (est): 240K **Privately Held**
SIC: 3089 3081 Injection molding of plastics; vinyl film & sheet

(G-327)
JAMES D FRISBIE
Also Called: Fris-T
8989 66th St Se (49302-9646)
P.O. Box 302 (49302-0302)
PHONE.................................616 868-0092
James D Frisbie, *Owner*
Kyle Fate, *General Mgr*
EMP: 12
SQ FT: 3,500
SALES (est): 723.2K **Privately Held**
SIC: 3993 3949 Signs & advertising specialties; golf equipment

(G-328)
MAGNA MIRRORS AMERICA INC
Also Called: Magna Mirros Lowell
6151 Bancroft Ave Se (49302-9313)
PHONE.................................616 868-6122
Joey Miller, *Vice Pres*
Mark Werner, *Engineer*
Robert Cecutti, *Controller*
Liliana Oprea, *Controller*
Don Walker, *Branch Mgr*
EMP: 200
SALES (corp-wide): 40.8B **Privately Held**
WEB: www.donnelly.com
SIC: 3231 Products of purchased glass
HQ: Magna Mirrors Of America, Inc.
5085 Kraft Ave Se
Grand Rapids MI 49512
616 786-5120

(G-329)
MAGNA MIRRORS NORTH AMER LLC (HQ)
Also Called: Lowell Engineering
6151 Bancroft Ave Se (49302-9313)
P.O. Box 96 (49302-0096)
PHONE.................................616 868-6122
Carlos Mazzorin, *President*
Rhonda McNally, *Vice Pres*
Hussam Azar, *Manager*
Brian Fisher,
▲ **EMP:** 650
SQ FT: 172,000
SALES (est): 316.3MM
SALES (corp-wide): 40.8B **Privately Held**
SIC: 3231 3442 Mirrors, truck & automobile: made from purchased glass; metal doors, sash & trim
PA: Magna International Inc
337 Magna Dr
Aurora ON L4G 7
905 726-2462

Amasa
Iron County

(G-330)
CONNOR SPORTS FLOORING CORP
251 Industrial Park Rd (49903)
P.O. Box 246 (49903-0246)
PHONE.................................906 822-7311
Conred Stromberg, *Manager*
EMP: 10
SALES (corp-wide): 533.7K **Privately Held**
WEB: www.connorfloor.com
SIC: 2426 Flooring, hardwood
HQ: Connor Sports Flooring, Llc
1830 Howard St Ste F
Elk Grove Village IL 60007

Anchorville
St. Clair County

(G-331)
INSTASET PLASTICS COMPANY LLC
10101 Marine City Hwy (48004)
PHONE.................................586 725-0229
Christopher Goetz, *Mng Member*
Peggy Lang, *Executive*
▲ **EMP:** 302
SALES (est): 12.1MM **Privately Held**
SIC: 3089 Injection molded finished plastic products; thermoformed finished plastic products
PA: Wgs Global Services, L.C.
6350 Taylor Dr
Flint MI 48507

Ann Arbor
Washtenaw County

(G-332)
826 MICHIGAN
115 E Liberty St (48104-2109)
PHONE.................................734 761-3463
Amanda Uhle, *Exec Dir*
Nancy Sizer, *Director*
Amy Sumerton, *Program Dir*
EMP: 3
SALES: 467K **Privately Held**
SIC: 3999 Education aids, devices & supplies

Ann Arbor - Washtenaw County (G-333)

(G-333)
A&D TECHNOLOGY INC
4622 Runway Blvd (48108-9555)
PHONE 734 973-1111
Teru Moriya, *CEO*
Dale Block, *Vice Pres*
Akio Suzuki, *Treasurer*
Satoshi Fucukawa, *Admin Sec*
▲ **EMP:** 90
SQ FT: 61,000
SALES: 15.6MM **Privately Held**
WEB: www.aanddtech.com
SIC: 3823 3825 3829 Industrial instrmnts msrmnt display/control process variable; instruments to measure electricity; measuring & controlling devices
PA: A&D Company, Limited
1-243, Asahi
Kitamoto STM 364-0

(G-334)
A&T MACHINING CO INC
240 Parkland Plz (48103-6201)
PHONE 734 761-6006
Thomas Graber, *President*
EMP: 3
SQ FT: 3,000
SALES: 900K **Privately Held**
WEB: www.atmachining.com
SIC: 3599 Machine shop, jobbing & repair; machine & other job shop work

(G-335)
A-1 SCREENPRINTING LLC (PA)
Also Called: Underground Printing
260 Metty Dr Ste G (48103-9154)
PHONE 734 665-2692
Ryan Greg, *Managing Dir*
Emily Bolley, *Store Mgr*
Kathleen Byrne, *Human Resources*
Nick Demarchi, *Regl Sales Mgr*
Kim Shea, *Sales Staff*
EMP: 70
SQ FT: 33,000
SALES (est): 18.8MM **Privately Held**
WEB: www.undergroundshirts.com
SIC: 2759 Screen printing

(G-336)
A2 MOTUS LLC
3575 Stanton Ct (48105-3032)
PHONE 734 780-7334
Mark Moldwin, *CEO*
Perry Samson, *Co-Owner*
Lauro Ojeda, *Chief Engr*
Arie Sheinker, *Development*
EMP: 4
SALES (est): 206.2K **Privately Held**
SIC: 3812 Search & navigation equipment

(G-337)
AAPHARMASYN LLC
3985 Res Pk Dr Ste 500 (48108)
PHONE 734 213-2123
Helen T Lee, *Mng Member*
Gary L Bolton,
Xue Min Cheng,
EMP: 10
SQ FT: 4,000
SALES (est): 680K **Privately Held**
SIC: 2869 2899 2833 Industrial organic chemicals; chemical preparations; medicinals & botanicals

(G-338)
ABRACADABRA JEWELRY
Also Called: Gem Gallery
205 E Liberty St (48104-2120)
PHONE 734 994-4848
Katherine Lesse, *Owner*
EMP: 8 **EST:** 1973
SQ FT: 2,000
SALES: 500K **Privately Held**
WEB: www.abracadabrajewelry.com
SIC: 3911 5944 7631 Jewelry apparel; jewelry, precious stones & precious metals; jewelry repair services

(G-339)
ABSOLUTE NANO LLC
303 S Main St Apt 304 (48104-2194)
PHONE 617 319-9617
John Hart, *Partner*
EMP: 3
SALES: 75K **Privately Held**
SIC: 3821 Laboratory apparatus & furniture

(G-340)
ACCURI CYTOMETERS INC
173 Parkland Plz (48103-6299)
P.O. Box 1388 (48106-1388)
PHONE 734 994-8000
Jeffrey S Williams, *CEO*
Collin Rich, *Vice Pres*
Steven Calef, *Treasurer*
EMP: 50
SALES (est): 13.5MM
SALES (corp-wide): 15.9B **Publicly Held**
WEB: www.accuricytometers.com
SIC: 3821 Laboratory apparatus, except heating & measuring
PA: Becton, Dickinson And Company
1 Becton Dr
Franklin Lakes NJ 07417
201 847-6800

(G-341)
ACCUTHERM SYSTEMS INC
41 Enterprise Dr (48103-9503)
PHONE 734 930-0461
Marilyn Katz-Pek, *CEO*
EMP: 4
SALES (est): 282K **Privately Held**
SIC: 3845 Surgical support systems: heart-lung machine, exc. iron lung

(G-342)
ADANA VOLTAICS LLC
5776 Cedar Ridge Dr (48103-9098)
PHONE 734 622-0193
Ibrahim Oraiqat, *President*
Cagliyan Kurdak, *Manager*
EMP: 6
SALES (est): 361.8K **Privately Held**
SIC: 3691 Batteries, rechargeable

(G-343)
ADCAA LLC
Also Called: Apex Dental Milling
3110 W Liberty Rd Ste B (48103-8000)
PHONE 734 623-4236
Dave Molnar, *Accounts Mgr*
John Farah,
John Powers,
EMP: 7
SQ FT: 3,000
SALES (est): 640K **Privately Held**
SIC: 3466 Crowns & closures

(G-344)
ADJUNCT ADVOCATE CORPORATION
817 Brookside Dr (48105-1162)
PHONE 734 930-6854
P Lesko, *President*
Patricia Lesko, *Publisher*
EMP: 3
SALES (est): 269.7K **Privately Held**
WEB: www.adjunctnation.com
SIC: 2721 Magazines: publishing & printing

(G-345)
ADVANCE PRINT & GRAPHICS INC
Also Called: Advance Specialties
4553 Concourse Dr (48108-9631)
PHONE 734 663-6816
Gary Hambell, *President*
Bill Christie, *Vice Pres*
Sheila Worton, *Director*
EMP: 20
SQ FT: 12,000
SALES (est): 3.2MM **Privately Held**
WEB: www.advprint.com
SIC: 2752 Commercial printing, offset

(G-346)
ADVANCED PHOTONIX INC (PA)
2925 Boardwalk St (48104-6765)
PHONE 734 864-5647
Dominic Schneider, *Manager*
Richard D Kurtz, *Administration*
EMP: 8
SALES (est): 1MM **Privately Held**
SIC: 3674 Semiconductors & related devices

(G-347)
ADVANTAGE TRUCK ACC INC
5400 S State Rd (48108-9754)
PHONE 800 773-3110
William Reminder, *President*
Jeff Fink, *General Mgr*
Kelly Kneifl, *COO*
Jim Bresingham, *CFO*
Maria Zwas, *Admin Sec*
▼ **EMP:** 45
SQ FT: 50,000
SALES (est): 7MM
SALES (corp-wide): 255.3MM **Privately Held**
WEB: www.advantagetruckaccessories.com
SIC: 3714 Motor vehicle parts & accessories
HQ: Tectum Holdings, Inc.
5400 Data Ct
Ann Arbor MI 48108
734 677-0444

(G-348)
AFFINIA GROUP INC
1101 Technology Dr (48108-8921)
P.O. Box 1967, Gastonia NC (28053-1967)
PHONE 734 827-5400
Terry McCormack, *CEO*
EMP: 28
SALES (est): 5.3MM **Privately Held**
SIC: 3714 Motor vehicle parts & accessories

(G-349)
AK REWARDS LLC
Also Called: Stridepost
2723 S State St Ste 150 (48104-6188)
PHONE 734 272-7078
EMP: 6
SALES (est): 215K **Privately Held**
SIC: 7372 Prepackaged Software Services

(G-350)
AKORN INC
Also Called: Akorn Consumer Health
2929 Plymouth Rd (48105-3206)
PHONE 800 579-8327
Scott Chapman, *Vice Pres*
Tom Arens, *Marketing Staff*
EMP: 38
SALES (corp-wide): 694MM **Publicly Held**
SIC: 2834 Pharmaceutical preparations
PA: Akorn, Inc.
1925 W Field Ct Ste 300
Lake Forest IL 60045
847 279-6100

(G-351)
ALF ENTERPRISES INC
Also Called: Alf Studios
1342 N Main St Ste 11a (48104-1008)
PHONE 734 665-2012
Gregg Alf, *President*
EMP: 4
SQ FT: 2,700
SALES (est): 539.9K **Privately Held**
WEB: www.alfstudios.com
SIC: 3931 5736 Violins & parts; string instruments

(G-352)
AMERICAN MATHEMATICAL SOCIETY
Mathematical Reviews
416 4th St (48103-4816)
P.O. Box 8604 (48107-8604)
PHONE 734 996-5250
Jane Kister, *Principal*
EMP: 90
SALES (corp-wide): 33.9MM **Privately Held**
SIC: 2741 Miscellaneous publishing
PA: American Mathematical Society Inc
201 Charles St
Providence RI 02904
401 455-4000

(G-353)
AMF-NANO CORPORATION
320 Miller Ave Ste 140 (48103-3385)
PHONE 734 726-0148
G Krishna Kumar, *CEO*
Rakesh Katragadda, *COO*
Salim Momin, *Senior VP*
Joseph Chalil, *Vice Pres*
Nishit Choksi, *Vice Pres*
EMP: 3
SALES (est): 318.8K **Privately Held**
SIC: 3674 3822 7373 7389 Semiconductors & related devices; thermostats & other environmental sensors; computer integrated systems design;

(G-354)
AMONG FRIENDS LLC
Also Called: Among Friends Baking Mixes
191 Orchard Hills Ct (48104-1826)
PHONE 734 997-9720
EMP: 11
SALES (est): 1.3MM **Privately Held**
SIC: 2052 2099 Mfg Cookies/Crackers Mfg Food Preparations

(G-355)
ANA FUEL INC
2759 Seminole Rd (48108-1324)
PHONE 810 422-5659
EMP: 2
SALES (est): 338.4K **Privately Held**
SIC: 2869 Mfg Industrial Organic Chemicals

(G-356)
ANN ARBOR CHRONICLE
330 Mulholland Ave (48103-4357)
PHONE 734 645-2633
Mary Morgan, *Principal*
EMP: 3
SALES (est): 159.2K **Privately Held**
SIC: 2711 Newspapers

(G-357)
ANN ARBOR DISTILLING CO
220 Felch St (48103-3392)
PHONE 734 769-6075
EMP: 7
SALES (est): 633.5K **Privately Held**
SIC: 2085 Distilled & blended liquors

(G-358)
ANN ARBOR OBSERVER COMPANY
2390 Winewood Ave (48103-1400)
PHONE 734 769-3175
Patricia M Garcia, *Partner*
John Hilton, *Partner*
EMP: 28 **EST:** 1976
SQ FT: 5,000
SALES (est): 3.8MM **Privately Held**
WEB: www.annarborobserver.com
SIC: 2721 2711 Magazines: publishing only, not printed on site; newspapers

(G-359)
ANSYS INC
2805 S Industrial Hwy # 100 (48104-6791)
PHONE 248 613-2677
Bil Cody, *Principal*
EMP: 6
SALES (corp-wide): 1.2B **Publicly Held**
SIC: 7372 Prepackaged software
PA: Ansys, Inc.
2600 Ansys Dr
Canonsburg PA 15317
884 462-6797

(G-360)
API / INMET INC
300 Dino Dr (48103-9502)
PHONE 734 426-5553
Jill Kale, *President*
Jon Carlson, *Corp Secy*
Eric Gettel, *Accounting Mgr*
Lynn McLean, *Cust Mgr*
EMP: 104
SQ FT: 25,000
SALES (est): 25.1MM **Privately Held**
SIC: 3825 Microwave test equipment
PA: Api Technologies Corp.
400 Nickerson Rd Ste 1
Marlborough MA 01752

(G-361)
API TECHNOLOGIES CORP
Also Called: Weinschel An API Technolo
300 Dino Dr (48103-9502)
PHONE 301 846-9222
EMP: 3 **Privately Held**
SIC: 3674 Semiconductors & related devices
PA: Api Technologies Corp.
400 Nickerson Rd Ste 1
Marlborough MA 01752

GEOGRAPHIC SECTION
Ann Arbor - Washtenaw County (G-389)

(G-362)
ARBOR ASSAYS INC
1514 Eisenhower Pl (48108-3284)
PHONE.................................734 677-1774
Barbara Scheuer, *CEO*
Russell Hart, *Principal*
Bobbi O'Hara, *Director*
EMP: 11 **EST:** 2017
SALES (est): 1.1MM **Privately Held**
SIC: 2836 Veterinary biological products

(G-363)
ARBOR INTERNATIONAL INC
143 Enterprise Dr (48103-9561)
PHONE.................................734 761-5200
George Yoanides, *President*
Evelyn Yoanides, *Treasurer*
EMP: 4
SQ FT: 8,000
SALES (est): 508.1K **Privately Held**
SIC: 3569 Jacks, hydraulic

(G-364)
ARBOR KITCHEN LLC
124 W Summit St Ste B (48103-3208)
PHONE.................................248 921-4602
EMP: 3
SALES (est): 180.3K **Privately Held**
SIC: 3999 5812 ; eating places

(G-365)
ARBOR SPRINGS WATER COMPANY (PA)
1440 Plymouth Rd (48105-1702)
PHONE.................................734 668-8270
William J Davis Jr, *President*
Judith Davis, *Corp Secy*
EMP: 24
SQ FT: 22,500
SALES (est): 2.9MM **Privately Held**
WEB: www.arborspringswater.com
SIC: 5499 2086 Water: distilled mineral or spring; pasteurized & mineral waters, bottled & canned

(G-366)
ARBORMETRIX INC
339 E Liberty St Ste 210 (48104-2258)
PHONE.................................734 661-7944
Brett Furst, *CEO*
Christian Birkmeyer, *COO*
Denis Dudzinski, *VP Sales*
Galaan Dafa, *Accounts Mgr*
John Birkmeyer, *Officer*
EMP: 11 **EST:** 2011
SQ FT: 3,500
SALES (est): 1.6MM **Privately Held**
SIC: 7372 Application computer software

(G-367)
ARNETS INC (PA)
Also Called: Arnet's Memorials
5060 Jackson Rd Ste H (48103-1894)
PHONE.................................734 665-3650
Martha Moomey, *Treasurer*
Stephen T Arnet, *Shareholder*
Jimmey Moomey, *Admin Sec*
▲ **EMP:** 13 **EST:** 1904
SQ FT: 8,000
SALES (est): 1.9MM **Privately Held**
WEB: www.ampetmemorials.com
SIC: 5999 7261 3272 3993 Monuments, finished to custom order; crematory; grave markers, tombstones / monuments, concrete; signs, not made in custom sign painting shops

(G-368)
AROTECH CORPORATION (PA)
1229 Oak Valley Dr (48108-9675)
PHONE.................................800 281-0356
Jon B Kutler, *Ch of Bd*
Dean M Krutty, *President*
Kelli L Kellar, *CFO*
Kenneth Cappell, *Bd of Directors*
EMP: 30
SQ FT: 17,300
SALES: 96.6MM **Publicly Held**
WEB: www.arotech.com
SIC: 3691 3694 Batteries, rechargeable; battery charging alternators & generators; battery charging generators, automobile & aircraft

(G-369)
ASCOTT CORPORATION
1202 N Main St (48104-1091)
PHONE.................................734 663-2023
Andrew S Crawford, *President*
EMP: 5 **EST:** 1974
SQ FT: 6,800
SALES (est): 486.8K **Privately Held**
SIC: 2396 Screen printing on fabric articles

(G-370)
ASSAY DESIGNS INC
5777 Hines Dr (48108-7901)
P.O. Box 3909 (48106-3909)
PHONE.................................734 214-0923
Daniel Calvo, *President*
EMP: 38
SQ FT: 14,000
SALES (est): 5.1MM
SALES (corp-wide): 81.1MM **Publicly Held**
WEB: www.assaydesigns.com
SIC: 3829 2819 Medical diagnostic systems, nuclear; industrial inorganic chemicals
PA: Enzo Biochem, Inc.
527 Madison Ave Rm 901
New York NY 10022
212 583-0100

(G-371)
ASSOCIATED METALS INC
Also Called: National Discount X-Ray Supply
6235 Jackson Rd Ste B (48103-9933)
PHONE.................................734 369-3851
Kenneth W Fil, *CEO*
EMP: 5
SQ FT: 6,000
SALES (est): 711.8K **Privately Held**
WEB: www.amifilmbin.com
SIC: 3412 5047 5085 5113 Metal barrels, drums & pails; X-ray film & supplies; commercial containers; industrial & personal service paper

(G-372)
ATTEROCOR INC
301 N Main St Ste 100 (48104-1296)
PHONE.................................734 845-9300
Julia C Owens, *CEO*
Keri Mattox, *Principal*
Jeffery M Brinza, *Senior VP*
Jessica Reed, *Director*
Stephen Hunt, *Officer*
EMP: 6
SALES (est): 800.3K **Privately Held**
SIC: 2834 Adrenal pharmaceutical preparations

(G-373)
AUTO ENGINEERING LAB
1231 Beal Ave (48109-2133)
PHONE.................................734 764-4254
Dennis Assanis, *Director*
EMP: 50
SALES (est): 2.2MM **Privately Held**
SIC: 3842 Surgical appliances & supplies

(G-374)
AUTOMOTIVE INFO SYSTEMS INC
315 E Eisenhower Pkwy # 211 (48108-3350)
PHONE.................................734 332-1970
Troy Ontko, *President*
Shelly Luckett, *Manager*
EMP: 6
SALES (est): 565.8K
SALES (corp-wide): 32.3B **Privately Held**
WEB: www.autodealerhelp.com
SIC: 2741 Newsletter publishing
HQ: Autotrader Group, Inc.
3003 Summit Blvd
Brookhaven GA 30319
404 568-8000

(G-375)
AVEN INC
Also Called: Aven Tools
4330 Varsity Dr (48108-2241)
PHONE.................................734 973-0099
Mike Shahpurwala, *President*
Bakir Kanpurwala, *CFO*
▲ **EMP:** 10
SQ FT: 12,000
SALES (est): 1.8MM **Privately Held**
WEB: www.aveninc.com
SIC: 3423 Hand & edge tools

(G-376)
AVFLIGHT CORPORATION (HQ)
47 W Ellsworth Rd (48108-2206)
P.O. Box 1387 (48106-1387)
PHONE.................................734 663-6466
Carl Muhs, *Manager*
EMP: 1
SALES (est): 31.3MM
SALES (corp-wide): 329.1MM **Privately Held**
SIC: 2911 Jet fuels
PA: Crs Acquisition Corporation
47 W Ellsworth Rd
Ann Arbor MI
734 663-6466

(G-377)
AVOMEEN LLC
Also Called: Avomeen Analytical Services
4840 Venture Dr (48108-9559)
PHONE.................................734 222-1090
Mark Harvill, *CEO*
Andrew Zolbert, *President*
Jiangyin Bao, *Project Dir*
Ying Long, *Project Dir*
Spenser Staebler, *Marketing Staff*
EMP: 50
SQ FT: 25,000
SALES: 11.2MM **Privately Held**
SIC: 8734 2834 Testing laboratories; pharmaceutical preparations

(G-378)
AXIOBIONICS
6111 Jackson Rd Ste 200 (48103-9167)
PHONE.................................734 327-2946
Philip E Muccio, *Principal*
EMP: 4
SALES (est): 490.4K **Privately Held**
SIC: 3842 Prosthetic appliances

(G-379)
B & B HEARTWOODS INC
5444 Whitmore Lake Rd (48105-9635)
PHONE.................................734 332-9525
William J Geschwender, *President*
Bonnie J Geschwender, *Vice Pres*
EMP: 4
SQ FT: 3,000
SALES: 250K **Privately Held**
SIC: 2426 5211 Hardwood dimension & flooring mills; lumber products

(G-380)
BANGGAMEUS
2590 Cook Creek Dr (48103-8971)
PHONE.................................734 904-1916
Chris Lin, *Principal*
EMP: 8
SALES (est): 360.1K **Privately Held**
SIC: 2731 Book publishing

(G-381)
BEAD GALLERY
311 E Liberty St (48104-2276)
PHONE.................................734 663-6800
Julie Van Dyke, *Owner*
EMP: 10
SQ FT: 1,200
SALES (est): 835.3K **Privately Held**
WEB: www.beadgalleryannarbor.com
SIC: 5944 3961 Jewelry stores; jewelry apparel, non-precious metals; costume jewelry, ex. precious metal & semi-precious stones

(G-382)
BENCHMARK COATING SYSTEMS LLC
2075 W Stadium Blvd (48106-7700)
PHONE.................................517 782-4061
Terry Kelly, *Principal*
EMP: 3
SALES (est): 237.5K **Privately Held**
SIC: 2851 Paints & paint additives

(G-383)
BESSENBERG BINDERY CORPORATION
215 N 5th Ave (48104-1407)
P.O. Box 7970 (48107-7970)
PHONE.................................734 996-9696
Fax: 734 996-1445
EMP: 4
SQ FT: 3,000
SALES: 250K **Privately Held**
SIC: 2789 Book Binding & Restoration Services

(G-384)
BIOFLEX INC
6111 Jackson Rd Ste 200 (48103-9167)
PHONE.................................734 327-2946
Philip Muccio, *President*
EMP: 5
SALES (est): 563.1K **Privately Held**
SIC: 2389 Apparel for handicapped

(G-385)
BOARD FOR STUDENT PUBLICATIONS
420 Maynard St (48109-1327)
PHONE.................................734 418-4115
Mark Bealafeld, *General Mgr*
Amrutha Sivakumar, *Editor*
Jacob Axelrad, *Chief*
EMP: 300
SALES: 2MM **Privately Held**
SIC: 2711 Newspapers, publishing & printing

(G-386)
BOROPHARM INC
2800 Plymouth Rd Bldg 40 (48109-2800)
PHONE.................................517 455-7847
Paul Herrinton, *Vice Pres*
EMP: 20
SALES (corp-wide): 12MM **Privately Held**
SIC: 2869 Laboratory chemicals, organic
PA: Boropharm, Inc.
39555 Orchard Hill Pl # 600
Novi MI 48375
248 348-5776

(G-387)
BOROPHARM INC
600 S Wagner Rd (48103-9002)
PHONE.................................734 585-0601
EMP: 3
SALES (corp-wide): 12MM **Privately Held**
SIC: 2819 Boron compounds, not from mines
PA: Boropharm, Inc.
39555 Orchard Hill Pl # 600
Novi MI 48375
248 348-5776

(G-388)
BORRIES MKG SYSTEMS PARTNR
3744 Plaza Dr Ste 1c (48108-1665)
PHONE.................................734 761-9549
Lothar Von Arnin, *Partner*
Donald Hubchik, *General Mgr*
L Von Arnin, *Ltd Ptnr*
Anna Kistner, *Sales Staff*
Udo Spindler, *Manager*
EMP: 5
SQ FT: 3,200
SALES (est): 479.5K **Privately Held**
SIC: 3953 Marking devices
HQ: Borries Markier-Systeme Gmbh
Siemensstr. 3
Pliezhausen 72124
712 797-970

(G-389)
BPI HOLDINGS INTERNATIONAL INC
1101 Technology Dr (48108-8921)
PHONE.................................815 363-9000
EMP: 5
SALES (corp-wide): 2.9B **Privately Held**
SIC: 3714 Motor vehicle brake systems & parts
HQ: Bpi Holdings International, Inc.
4400 Prime Pkwy
Mchenry IL 60050
815 363-9000

Ann Arbor - Washtenaw County (G-390) GEOGRAPHIC SECTION

(G-390)
BRIO DEVICE LLC
2104 Georgetown Blvd (48105-1535)
PHONE....................734 945-5728
Laura L Walz,
Hannah Hensel,
Laura McCormick,
Douglas Mullen,
Sabina Siddiqui,
EMP: 4
SALES (est): 279.7K **Privately Held**
SIC: 3841 Surgical & medical instruments

(G-391)
BUDGET EUROPE TRAVEL SERVICE
2557 Meade Ct (48105-1304)
PHONE....................734 668-0529
Robert L Brown, *President*
Linda Pogreba, *Vice Pres*
EMP: 5
SALES: 880K **Privately Held**
WEB: www.budgeteuropetravel.com
SIC: 4724 4725 2711 Tourist agency arranging transport, lodging & car rental; tour operators; newspapers: publishing only, not printed on site

(G-392)
BULLDOG FABRICATING CORP
50 Enterprise Dr (48103-9503)
P.O. Box 106, Dexter (48130-0106)
PHONE....................734 761-3111
Steven C Kern, *President*
EMP: 5
SQ FT: 10,000
SALES: 1.2MM **Privately Held**
SIC: 5085 3569 Filters, industrial; filter elements, fluid, hydraulic line

(G-393)
BUYERS DEVELOPMENT GROUP LLC (PA)
Also Called: Grow Show, The
4095 Stone School Rd (48108-9723)
PHONE....................734 677-0009
Cayman Hartigan,
EMP: 12
SQ FT: 4,800
SALES (est): 1.2MM **Privately Held**
SIC: 3524 Lawn & garden equipment

(G-394)
CASTLE REMEDIES INC
2345 S Huron Pkwy Ste 1 (48104-5124)
PHONE....................734 973-8990
Edward Linkner MD, *President*
Marian Smith, *General Mgr*
Cindy Klement, *Consultant*
Mary Tillinghast, *Instructor*
EMP: 11
SALES (est): 800K **Privately Held**
SIC: 2023 Dietary supplements, dairy & non-dairy based

(G-395)
CAYMAN CHEMICAL COMPANY INC (PA)
1180 E Ellsworth Rd (48108-2419)
PHONE....................734 971-3335
Kirk M Maxey, *President*
Gregory W Endres, *Vice Pres*
Jeffrey K Johnson, *Vice Pres*
Craig Maxey, *Vice Pres*
Barbara J Rice, *Vice Pres*
EMP: 100
SQ FT: 80,000
SALES (est): 28.9MM **Privately Held**
WEB: www.caymanchem.com
SIC: 2834 2899 Pharmaceutical preparations; chemical preparations

(G-396)
CBM LLC
Also Called: Sleeping Bear Press
2395 S Huron Pkwy Ste 200 (48104-5170)
PHONE....................800 487-2323
Ben Mondloch, *Branch Mgr*
EMP: 13
SALES (est): 1.2MM **Privately Held**
SIC: 2731 Book publishing
PA: Cbm, Llc
1750 Northway Dr Ste 101
North Mankato MN 56003

(G-397)
CELSEE DIAGNOSTICS INC (PA)
100 Phoenix Dr Ste 321 (48108-2600)
PHONE....................866 748-1448
Priyadarshini Gogoi, *Principal*
John Stark, *Director*
EMP: 43
SALES: 693.6K **Privately Held**
SIC: 3826 Environmental testing equipment

(G-398)
CENTRUM FORCE FABRICATION LLC
3425 Stone School Rd (48108-2305)
PHONE....................517 857-4774
Thomas B Monahan,
Greg Turcotte,
EMP: 4
SALES (est): 569.8K **Privately Held**
SIC: 3569 Centrifuges, industrial

(G-399)
CHOUTEAU FUELS COMPANY LLC
414 S Main St Ste 600 (48104-2398)
PHONE....................734 302-4800
EMP: 4 **EST:** 2011
SALES (est): 336.9K **Privately Held**
SIC: 2869 Fuels

(G-400)
CLEAR IMAGE DEVICES LLC
3930 N Michael Rd (48103-9344)
PHONE....................734 645-6459
John L Stinson, *President*
EMP: 6
SALES: 967.6K **Privately Held**
WEB: www.clearimagedevices.com
SIC: 3841 Surgical & medical instruments

(G-401)
CLIFF KEEN WRESTLING PDTS INC
Also Called: Cliff Keen Athletic
4480 Varsity Dr Ste B (48108-5007)
P.O. Box 1447 (48106-1447)
PHONE....................734 975-8800
James C Keen, *President*
Mark Churella Sr, *Corp Secy*
Barry Bellaire, *Vice Pres*
Ryan Churella, *Vice Pres*
Chad Clark, *Vice Pres*
▲ **EMP:** 45
SQ FT: 25,000
SALES (est): 6.9MM **Privately Held**
WEB: www.cliffkeen.com
SIC: 2329 2339 Men's & boys' athletic uniforms; men's & boys' sportswear & athletic clothing; women's & misses' athletic clothing & sportswear

(G-402)
COBALT FRICTION TECHNOLOGIES
4595 Platt Rd (48108-9726)
PHONE....................734 274-3030
Ernest G Bocchino, *President*
Headley G Lee, *Vice Pres*
Cleve A Bispott, *Admin Sec*
EMP: 10
SALES (est): 1.2MM **Privately Held**
SIC: 3292 Asbestos friction materials

(G-403)
COBHAM MCRLCTRNIC SLUTIONS INC (DH)
310 Dino Dr (48103-9502)
PHONE....................734 426-1230
Jill Kale, *CEO*
Jon E Carlson, *CFO*
EMP: 9
SQ FT: 4,000
SALES: 35.9MM
SALES (corp-wide): 2.3B **Privately Held**
WEB: www.mcecompanies.com
SIC: 3679 3825 Microwave components; microwave test equipment

(G-404)
CONTROL GAGING INC
847 Avis Dr (48108-9615)
PHONE....................734 668-6750
David Hayes, *President*
Jody Scott, *Vice Pres*
▲ **EMP:** 32
SQ FT: 24,000
SALES (est): 6.7MM
SALES (corp-wide): 988.5K **Privately Held**
WEB: www.controlgaging.com
SIC: 3545 Precision measuring tools
HQ: Marposs Spa
Via Saliceto 13
Bentivoglio BO 40010
051 899-111

(G-405)
COPAGEN LLC
5528 Gallery Park Dr (48103-5054)
PHONE....................734 904-0365
Daniel Rhodes,
EMP: 4
SALES (est): 222.6K **Privately Held**
SIC: 2834 Pharmaceutical preparations

(G-406)
COVALENT MEDICAL INC
4750 S State Rd (48108-9719)
PHONE....................734 604-0688
Bruno Lowinger, *President*
Johan Lowinger, *General Mgr*
EMP: 4
SQ FT: 4,000
SALES (est): 2.5MM **Privately Held**
SIC: 2891 Adhesives; glue

(G-407)
COVARON INC
4401 Varsity Dr Ste A (48108-5003)
PHONE....................480 298-9433
Dave Hattfield, *CEO*
Bill Yaklin, *Principal*
Cameron Smith, *CFO*
Vince Alessi, *Security Dir*
EMP: 3
SALES (est): 473.2K **Privately Held**
SIC: 8711 2899 Engineering services; chemical preparations

(G-408)
CREATIVE ENGINEERING INC
Also Called: Creative Health Products
7621 E Joy Rd (48105-9682)
PHONE....................734 996-5900
Marlene Donoghue, *President*
Wallace Donoghue, *Vice Pres*
EMP: 8
SALES: 1.6MM **Privately Held**
WEB: www.chponline.com
SIC: 5047 5999 3829 Hospital equipment & furniture; alarm & safety equipment stores; aircraft & motor vehicle measurement equipment

(G-409)
CUSHING-MALLOY INC
Also Called: CM Book
1350 N Main St (48104-1045)
P.O. Box 8632 (48107-8632)
PHONE....................734 663-8554
Tom Cushing, *Ch of Bd*
Thomas Weber, *President*
Connie Cushing, *Treasurer*
Laurie Jean, *Office Mgr*
EMP: 50 **EST:** 1948
SQ FT: 40,000
SALES (est): 7.3MM **Privately Held**
WEB: www.cushing-malloy.com
SIC: 2732 2752 2789 Books: printing only; commercial printing, lithographic; bookbinding & related work

(G-410)
D & C INVESTMENT GROUP INC (PA)
Also Called: Nematron
5840 Interface Dr (48103-9176)
PHONE....................734 994-0591
Gregory Chandler, *President*
Craig Richter, *Technical Mgr*
Russ Rehak, *Sales Mgr*
Dave Stratford, *Marketing Staff*
EMP: 15
SQ FT: 51,000
SALES (est): 3.3MM **Privately Held**
WEB: www.nematron.com
SIC: 3823 Computer interface equipment for industrial process control

(G-411)
DAILY GARDENER LLC
5211 Pontiac Trl (48105-9238)
PHONE....................734 754-6527
Doris Hill, *Principal*
EMP: 3
SALES (est): 85.7K **Privately Held**
SIC: 2711 Newspapers, publishing & printing

(G-412)
DANMAR PRODUCTS INC (PA)
221 Jackson Industrial Dr (48103-9104)
PHONE....................734 761-1990
Karen Lindner, *CEO*
Daniel Russo, *President*
Hidie Bowman, *COO*
Tim Mullins, *Engineer*
EMP: 25 **EST:** 1967
SQ FT: 9,000
SALES (est): 3.7MM **Privately Held**
WEB: www.danmarproducts.com
SIC: 3842 Surgical appliances & supplies

(G-413)
DEGRASYN BIOSCIENCES LLC
4476 Boulder Pond Dr (48108-8601)
PHONE....................713 582-3395
Nicholas Donato,
EMP: 5
SALES (est): 229.7K **Privately Held**
SIC: 2833 Medicinal chemicals

(G-414)
DELMAS TYPESETTING
461 Hilldale Dr (48105-1120)
PHONE....................734 662-8899
William Kalvin, *President*
EMP: 8
SALES: 180K **Privately Held**
WEB: www.delmastype.com
SIC: 2791 Typesetting

(G-415)
DENTAL CONSULTANTS INC
3100 W Liberty Rd (48108-3724)
PHONE....................734 663-6777
John W Farah, *President*
John M Powers, *Treasurer*
Chris Voigtman, *Sales Staff*
Stanley T Mendenhall, *Admin Sec*
EMP: 20
SQ FT: 1,000
SALES (est): 2.1MM **Privately Held**
WEB: www.dentaladvisor.com
SIC: 2721 Trade journals: publishing only, not printed on site

(G-416)
DESIGN & TEST TECHNOLOGY INC (PA)
3744 Plaza Dr Ste 2 (48108-1651)
P.O. Box 1526 (48106-1526)
PHONE....................734 665-4316
Michael Murphy, *President*
Nancy Murphy, *Vice Pres*
Linda Taylor, *Senior Buyer*
EMP: 10
SQ FT: 6,000
SALES: 1MM **Privately Held**
WEB: www.designtest.com
SIC: 3825 7373 Test equipment for electronic & electric measurement; computer systems analysis & design

(G-417)
DETROIT FUDGE COMPANY INC
2251 W Liberty St (48103-4405)
PHONE....................734 369-8573
EMP: 7 **EST:** 2018
SALES (est): 463.4K **Privately Held**
SIC: 2064 Fudge (candy)

(G-418)
DETROIT LEGAL NEWS PUBG LLC
Also Called: Washtenaw Legal News
2301 Platt Rd Ste 300 (48104-5149)
P.O. Box 1367 (48106-1367)
PHONE....................734 477-0201
Brad Thompson, *President*
Bradley L Thompson II,
EMP: 4

GEOGRAPHIC SECTION
Ann Arbor - Washtenaw County (G-447)

SALES (est): 260.4K **Privately Held**
SIC: 2711 Newspapers: publishing only, not printed on site

(G-419)
DIAMOND ELECTRIC
455 E Eisenhower Pkwy # 200 (48108-3323)
PHONE..................734 995-5525
EMP: 4
SALES (est): 133.8K **Privately Held**
SIC: 4911 3699 Electric Services Mfg Electrical Equipment/Supplies

(G-420)
DIAMOND ELECTRIC MFG CORP
455 E Eisenhower Pkwy # 200 (48108-3356)
P.O. Box 830, Eleanor WV (25070-0830)
PHONE..................734 995-5525
Dan Sheehan, *Branch Mgr*
EMP: 15 **Privately Held**
WEB: www.diaelec.com
SIC: 3694 3621 Ignition coils, automotive; motors & generators
HQ: Diamond Electric Mfg Corp
  State Rt 62 Elnor Indus P
  Eleanor WV 25070
  304 586-0070

(G-421)
DIAPIN THERAPEUTICS LLC
1600 Huron Pkwy B520 (48109-5001)
PHONE..................734 764-9123
Bruce Markham, *Mng Member*
Zongmin MA,
EMP: 3
SALES (est): 251.5K **Privately Held**
SIC: 2834 Pharmaceutical preparations

(G-422)
DNA SOFTWARE INC
334 E Washington St (48104-2010)
PHONE..................734 222-9080
John Santalucia, *CEO*
Norm Watkins, *COO*
Joseph A Johnson, *Vice Pres*
EMP: 10
SALES (est): 996.9K **Privately Held**
SIC: 7372 Business oriented computer software

(G-423)
DOG MIGHT LLC
303 Metty Dr (48103-8330)
PHONE..................734 679-0646
EMP: 17
SALES (est): 398.5K **Privately Held**
SIC: 5199 5945 3944 Wood carvings; toys & games; board games, puzzles & models, except electronic

(G-424)
DOMINOS PIZZA LLC (HQ)
30 Frank Lloyd Wright Dr (48105-9757)
P.O. Box 997 (48106-0997)
PHONE..................734 930-3030
Michael Lawton, *Exec VP*
Stan Gage, *Vice Pres*
Jeffrey Musser, *Opers Staff*
Peter Saucier, *Business Anlyst*
Hughes John, *Marketing Staff*
▲ EMP: 150
SQ FT: 320,000
SALES (est): 567.8MM
SALES (corp-wide): 3.4B **Publicly Held**
WEB: www.dominos.com
SIC: 5812 6794 5046 5149 Pizzeria, chain; franchises, selling or leasing; restaurant equipment & supplies; pizza supplies; management services; prepared flour mixes & doughs
PA: Domino's Pizza, Inc.
  30 Frank Lloyd Wright Dr
  Ann Arbor MI 48105
  734 930-3030

(G-425)
DREW TECHNOLOGIES INC
3915 Res Pk Dr Ste A10 (48108)
PHONE..................734 222-5228
Michael Drew, *President*
Andrew Lipp, *Engineer*
Cliff Koch, *Senior Engr*
Hugh Atkins, *Sales Mgr*
Glen Eaton, *Manager*
▲ EMP: 9
SQ FT: 4,500
SALES (est): 2.5MM **Privately Held**
WEB: www.drewtech.com
SIC: 3559 Automotive maintenance equipment
PA: Opus Inspection, Inc.
  7 Kripes Rd
  East Granby CT 06026

(G-426)
DTE ENERGY RESOURCES INC (HQ)
414 S Main St Ste 600 (48104-2398)
PHONE..................734 302-4800
Lillian Bauder, *Vice Pres*
▼ EMP: 100
SALES (est): 210.3MM **Publicly Held**
SIC: 4911 1389 Electric services; gas field services

(G-427)
DUO SECURITY INC (HQ)
123 N Ashley St Ste 200 (48104-1316)
PHONE..................734 330-2673
Douglas Song, *CEO*
William Welch, *President*
Aaron Melear, *Partner*
George Vasey, *Partner*
Michael Hanley, *General Mgr*
EMP: 200
SALES: 6MM
SALES (corp-wide): 51.9B **Publicly Held**
SIC: 7372 Prepackaged software
PA: Cisco Systems, Inc.
  170 W Tasman Dr
  San Jose CA 95134
  408 526-4000

(G-428)
DYNICS INC
620 Technology Dr (48108-8937)
PHONE..................734 677-6100
Edward Gatt, *President*
Kimberly Dornes, *Purch Agent*
Kimberly Herrst, *Purch Agent*
Brandon Mirto, *Electrical Engi*
Mark Kozlowski, *Controller*
EMP: 75
SQ FT: 18,000
SALES: 16.1MM **Privately Held**
WEB: www.dynics.com
SIC: 3575 5734 Computer terminals, monitors & components; software, business & non-game

(G-429)
DZANC BOOKS INC
2702 Lillian Rd (48104-5300)
PHONE..................734 756-5701
Dan Wickett, *Exec Dir*
EMP: 3
SALES: 50K **Privately Held**
SIC: 2731 Book publishing

(G-430)
EATON CORPORATION
4743 Venture Dr (48108-9560)
PHONE..................517 787-8121
Becca Gorman, *Principal*
Bill Lopez, *Principal*
John Perkin, *Engineer*
Rex Robb, *Manager*
EMP: 13 **Privately Held**
WEB: www.eaton.com
SIC: 8711 3812 Engineering services; search & navigation equipment
HQ: Eaton Corporation
  1000 Eaton Blvd
  Cleveland OH 44122
  440 523-5000

(G-431)
EATON INDUSTRIES INC (PA)
254 S Wagner Rd (48103-1940)
P.O. Box 669, Manchester (48158-0669)
PHONE..................734 428-0000
Eric Babbitt, *Ch of Bd*
Paul P Kluwe, *President*
Sam Ascher, *Vice Pres*
Jason Gauss, *Engineer*
Karl F Kluwe, *Treasurer*
EMP: 8
SALES (est): 3.3MM **Privately Held**
SIC: 3845 Cardiographs

(G-432)
ECO SIGN SOLUTIONS LLC
37 Enterprise Dr (48103-9503)
PHONE..................734 276-8585
Dave Small, *Owner*
EMP: 6
SALES (est): 627K **Privately Held**
SIC: 3993 Electric signs

(G-433)
ECOVIA RENEWABLES INC
600 Suth Wagner Rd Ste 15 (48103)
PHONE..................248 953-0594
Jeremy Minty,
Xiaoxia Lin,
EMP: 3
SALES (est): 335.8K **Privately Held**
SIC: 2869 7389 Industrial organic chemicals;

(G-434)
EDWARD AND COLE INC
Also Called: Dotmine Day Planners
5540 Tanglewood Dr (48105-9549)
PHONE..................734 996-9074
EMP: 4
SALES (est): 471.1K **Privately Held**
SIC: 2678 Mfg Stationery Products

(G-435)
EDWARD BROTHERS MALLOY
5949 Jackson Rd (48103-9573)
PHONE..................734 665-6113
EMP: 4
SALES (est): 380.6K **Privately Held**
SIC: 2732 Book printing

(G-436)
EDWARDS BROTHERS INC (HQ)
Also Called: Edwards Brothers Malloy
5411 Jackson Rd (48103-1861)
PHONE..................800 722-3231
John Edwards, *President*
William Upton, *CFO*
Bill Ralph, *Sales Staff*
Anne Maier, *Supervisor*
Pete Shima, *Director*
▲ EMP: 240 EST: 1893
SQ FT: 188,000
SALES: 233.5MM
SALES (corp-wide): 388.7MM **Privately Held**
WEB: www.edwardsbrothers.com
SIC: 2732 2789 Books: printing & binding; bookbinding & related work
PA: Edwards Brothers Malloy, Inc.
  5411 Jackson Rd
  Ann Arbor MI 48103
  734 665-6113

(G-437)
EDWARDS BROTHERS MALLOY INC (PA)
5411 Jackson Rd (48103-1861)
PHONE..................734 665-6113
John Edwards, *President*
William Upton, *CFO*
Jennifer Stewart, *Human Res Mgr*
Terri Salisbury, *Executive Asst*
Jay Moore, *Administration*
EMP: 400
SQ FT: 188,000
SALES (est): 388.7MM **Privately Held**
SIC: 2732 Books: printing only

(G-438)
EJUSTICE SOLUTIONS LLC
3600 Green Ct Ste 780 (48105-1570)
PHONE..................248 232-0509
Dave Hawkins, *CFO*
Mike McGarry, *CTO*
Larry Beach,
Dennis Blanchette,
EMP: 25
SALES (est): 1.2MM **Privately Held**
SIC: 7372 Prepackaged software

(G-439)
ELECTRIC EYE CAFE
811 N Main St (48104-1032)
PHONE..................734 369-6904
Rachel Pell, *Principal*
EMP: 4

SALES (est): 64.3K **Privately Held**
SIC: 5812 3699 Cafe; electrical equipment & supplies

(G-440)
ELEGUS EPS LLC
1600 Huron Pkwy Rm 2345 (48109-5001)
PHONE..................734 224-9900
John Hennessy,
Long Qian,
Siuon Tung,
EMP: 3
SALES (est): 146.9K **Privately Held**
SIC: 2621 Specialty papers

(G-441)
ELMO MANUFACTURING CO INC
98 Valhalla Dr 950 (48103-5847)
P.O. Box 1312 (48106-1312)
PHONE..................734 995-5966
Ellen Pesko, *President*
Robert Pesko, *Vice Pres*
EMP: 6
SQ FT: 1,000
SALES (est): 623.2K **Privately Held**
SIC: 3546 Saws & sawing equipment

(G-442)
EMAG TECHNOLOGIES INC
775 Technology Dr Ste 300 (48108-8948)
PHONE..................734 996-3624
Kazem F Sabet, *President*
EMP: 10
SQ FT: 8,000
SALES (est): 1.8MM **Privately Held**
WEB: www.emagtechnologies.com
SIC: 8732 3663 Business research service; radio & TV communications equipment

(G-443)
EMPOWER FINANCIALS INC
4343 Concourse Dr Ste 140 (48108-8672)
PHONE..................734 747-9393
Robert Murray, *President*
EMP: 11
SQ FT: 1,800
SALES (est): 737.5K **Privately Held**
WEB: www.empowerfin.com
SIC: 7371 7372 Computer software development; prepackaged software

(G-444)
ENDECTRA LLC
1600 Huron Pkwy Bldg 520 (48109-5001)
PHONE..................734 476-9381
Nicholas Cucinelli, *CEO*
Roy Clarke, *Principal*
Norman Rapino,
EMP: 3
SALES (est): 225.3K **Privately Held**
SIC: 3829 Personnel dosimetry devices

(G-445)
ENDRA LIFE SCIENCES INC
3600 Green Ct Ste 350 (48105-2440)
PHONE..................734 255-0242
Francois Michelon, *President*
Anthony Digiandomenico, *Treasurer*
Mark Baum, *Director*
Dr Sanjiv Sam Gambhir, *Director*
Alexander Tokman, *Director*
EMP: 9
SQ FT: 3,500
SALES: 6.1K **Privately Held**
SIC: 3845 Ultrasonic scanning devices, medical

(G-446)
EOTECH INC
1201 E Ellsworth Rd (48108-2420)
PHONE..................734 741-8868
Rick Berger, *President*
EMP: 6
SALES (est): 1MM **Privately Held**
SIC: 3827 Optical instruments & lenses

(G-447)
ERVIN INDUSTRIES INC (PA)
Also Called: Ervin Amasteel
3893 Research Park Dr (48108-2267)
P.O. Box 1168 (48106-1168)
PHONE..................734 769-4600
John E Pearson, *President*
James Trent Pearson, *Exec VP*
Bill Rhodaberger, *Vice Pres*

Ann Arbor - Washtenaw County (G-448) GEOGRAPHIC SECTION

Kenneth R Prior, *VP Mfg*
Michael Fleeger, *Plant Supt*
◆ **EMP:** 50 **EST:** 1920
SQ FT: 40,000
SALES: 200MM **Privately Held**
WEB: www.ervinindustries.com
SIC: 3291 6159 Steel shot abrasive; grit, steel; machinery & equipment finance leasing

(G-448)
ESPERION THERAPEUTICS INC
3891 Ranchero Dr Ste 150 (48108-2837)
PHONE.................................734 887-3903
Tim M Mayleben, *President*
Narendra D Lalwani, *COO*
Richard B Bartram, *CFO*
Dov Goldstein, *Bd of Directors*
Mark Glickman, *Officer*
EMP: 57
SQ FT: 7,900
SALES: 1K **Privately Held**
WEB: www.esperion.com
SIC: 2834 Pharmaceutical preparations

(G-449)
ESSEN INSTRUMENTS INC (HQ)
Also Called: Essen Bioscience
300 W Morgan Rd (48108-9108)
PHONE.................................734 769-1600
Brett Williams, *CEO*
Bruno Brun, *VP Opers*
Brad Neagle, *VP Engrg*
Doug Kalis, *QA Dir*
Ashley Moseby, *Sales Staff*
EMP: 75
SQ FT: 25,000
SALES: 22.8MM
SALES (corp-wide): 1.7B **Privately Held**
WEB: www.essen-instruments.com
SIC: 3826 Analytical instruments
PA: Sartorius Ag
   Otto-Brenner-Str. 20
   Gottingen   37079
   551 308-0

(G-450)
EVERIST GENOMICS INC (PA)
455 E Eisenhower Pkwy # 200
(48108-3323)
PHONE.................................734 929-9475
Stephen Everist, *CEO*
Thomas Everist, *CEO*
Prasad Sunkara, *President*
John Freshley, *Principal*
John Stchur, *CFO*
EMP: 10
SALES (est): 1.3MM **Privately Held**
SIC: 2835 In vitro & in vivo diagnostic substances

(G-451)
EXPO KITCHEN & BATH LTD
2459 W Stadium Blvd (48103-3809)
PHONE.................................734 741-5888
Rebecca Gregory, *President*
EMP: 3
SALES (est): 336.2K **Privately Held**
SIC: 2434 Wood kitchen cabinets

(G-452)
EXPRESSIGN DESIGN
2239 W Liberty St (48103-4405)
PHONE.................................734 747-7444
Jim Fisher, *Owner*
EMP: 4
SALES: 300K **Privately Held**
SIC: 3993 Signs, not made in custom sign painting shops

(G-453)
EXSTO US INC
2723 S State St Ste 150 (48104-6235)
PHONE.................................734 834-7225
Nicolas Muller, *Principal*
EMP: 3
SALES (est): 239.1K **Privately Held**
SIC: 3089 Injection molding of plastics

(G-454)
EXTANG CORPORATION
5400 S State Rd (48108-9754)
PHONE.................................734 677-0444
William Reminder, *President*
Kelly Kneifl, *COO*
James Bresingham, *CFO*

Maria Zwas, *Admin Sec*
▲ **EMP:** 100
SQ FT: 56,900
SALES (est): 40.6MM
SALES (corp-wide): 255.3MM **Privately Held**
WEB: www.extang.com
SIC: 3714 Motor vehicle parts & accessories
HQ: Tectum Holdings, Inc.
   5400 Data Ct
   Ann Arbor MI 48108
   734 677-0444

(G-455)
FAAC INCORPORATED
1195 Oak Valley Dr (48108-9674)
PHONE.................................734 761-5836
EMP: 9 **Publicly Held**
SIC: 3699 Electrical equipment & supplies
HQ: Faac Incorporated
   1229 Oak Valley Dr
   Ann Arbor MI 48108
   734 761-5836

(G-456)
FAAC INCORPORATED (HQ)
Also Called: Ies Inter/Realtime Tech
1229 Oak Valley Dr (48108-9675)
PHONE.................................734 761-5836
Kurt A Flosky, *President*
Rob McCue, *General Mgr*
Todd Glenn, *COO*
Christopher J Caruana, *Exec VP*
Menashe Haim, *Vice Pres*
EMP: 103
SQ FT: 20,000
SALES (est): 46MM **Publicly Held**
WEB: www.faac.com
SIC: 8711 7372 Engineering services; business oriented computer software

(G-457)
FBH ARCHITECTURAL SECURITY INC
1080 Rosewood St (48104-6269)
PHONE.................................734 332-3740
Brent Rice, *Office Mgr*
EMP: 27
SALES (corp-wide): 16.7MM **Privately Held**
SIC: 3442 Metal doors
PA: Fbh Architectural Security, Inc.
   600 Bloor Ave
   Flint MI 48507
   810 239-9471

(G-458)
FEDERAL-MOGUL POWERTRAIN LLC
560 Avis Dr (48108-9767)
PHONE.................................734 930-1590
Keri Wesbrooke, *Director*
EMP: 35
SALES (corp-wide): 11.7B **Publicly Held**
SIC: 3764 3053 3592 3562 Engines & engine parts, guided missile; gaskets & sealing devices; pistons & piston rings; ball bearings & parts
HQ: Federal-Mogul Powertrain Llc
   27300 W 11 Mile Rd
   Southfield MI 48034

(G-459)
FEDEX OFFICE & PRINT SVCS INC
505 E Liberty St Ste 400 (48104-2465)
PHONE.................................734 761-4539
EMP: 10
SALES (corp-wide): 69.6B **Publicly Held**
WEB: www.kinkos.com
SIC: 7334 2791 2789 7338 Photocopying & duplicating services; typesetting; bookbinding & related work; secretarial & court reporting
HQ: Fedex Office And Print Services, Inc.
   7900 Legacy Dr
   Plano TX 75024
   800 463-3339

(G-460)
FEDEX OFFICE & PRINT SVCS INC
2609 Plymouth Rd Ste 7 (48105-2468)
PHONE.................................734 996-0050

EMP: 25
SALES (corp-wide): 69.6B **Publicly Held**
WEB: www.kinkos.com
SIC: 7334 2791 2759 7338 Photocopying & duplicating services; typesetting; commercial printing; secretarial & court reporting; signs & advertising specialties
HQ: Fedex Office And Print Services, Inc.
   7900 Legacy Dr
   Plano TX 75024
   800 463-3339

(G-461)
FENDT BUILDERS SUPPLY INC
3285 W Liberty Rd (48103-9795)
PHONE.................................734 663-4277
Alan Fendt, *Owner*
EMP: 15
SALES (corp-wide): 13.1MM **Privately Held**
WEB: www.fendtproducts.com
SIC: 3271 5211 Blocks, concrete or cinder: standard; lumber & other building materials
PA: Fendt Builders Supply Inc
   22005 Gill Rd
   Farmington Hills MI 48335
   248 474-3211

(G-462)
FLASHPLAYS LIVE LLC
412 Hamilton Pl (48104-2308)
PHONE.................................978 888-3935
Parth Valecha, *CEO*
EMP: 5
SALES (est): 117.2K **Privately Held**
SIC: 7372 7389 Application computer software;

(G-463)
FLOW EZY FILTERS INC
147 Enterprise Dr (48103-9282)
P.O. Box 1749 (48106-1749)
PHONE.................................734 665-8777
Theodore Fosdick, *President*
Tony Day, *Purch Mgr*
Dale Fosdick, *Treasurer*
Bill Crowell, *Manager*
Melinda Porter, *Web Dvlpr*
EMP: 18
SALES (est): 4.1MM **Privately Held**
WEB: www.flowezyfilters.com
SIC: 3569 5084 Filters, general line: industrial; industrial machinery & equipment

(G-464)
FORENSIC PRESS
2980 Provincial Dr (48104-4116)
PHONE.................................734 997-0256
Emmanuel Tanay, *Owner*
Emanuel Tanay, *Principal*
EMP: 3
SALES (est): 190.6K **Privately Held**
SIC: 2741 Miscellaneous publishing

(G-465)
FORESEE SESSION REPLAY INC
2500 Green Rd Ste 400 (48105-1573)
PHONE.................................800 621-2850
Bill Ruckelshaus, *President*
Jay Sinder, *Treasurer*
Eugene Davis, *Director*
Caleb Chill, *Admin Sec*
EMP: 4
SALES (est): 4.2MM **Publicly Held**
SIC: 7372 Prepackaged software
HQ: Foresee Results, Inc.
   2500 Green Rd Ste 400
   Ann Arbor MI 48105
   734 205-2600

(G-466)
FOURTH AVE BIRKENSTOCK
209 N 4th Ave (48104-1403)
PHONE.................................734 663-1644
Paul Tinkerhess, *Owner*
EMP: 7
SALES (est): 532.9K **Privately Held**
SIC: 5661 3944 Shoes, custom; games, toys & children's vehicles

(G-467)
FREEDOM IMAGING SYSTEMS
3600 Green Ct (48105-1570)
PHONE.................................734 327-5600

David Gillis, *President*
Michael Wesley, *Software Dev*
EMP: 30
SALES (est): 10MM **Privately Held**
WEB: www.freeimage.com
SIC: 7372 Prepackaged software

(G-468)
GAN SYSTEMS CORP
2723 S State St Ste 150 (48104-6188)
PHONE.................................248 609-7643
Larry Spaziani, *Vice Pres*
Paul Wiener, *Vice Pres*
Julian Styles, *Business Dir*
EMP: 6
SALES (est): 725K **Privately Held**
SIC: 3674 Semiconductors & related devices

(G-469)
GELMAN SCIENCES INC
Also Called: Pall Life Sciences
674 S Wagner Rd (48103-9793)
PHONE.................................734 665-0651
Eric Krasnoff, *Ch of Bd*
Don Stevens, *COO*
Lisa McDermott, *CFO*
Cynthia Haney, *Manager*
▲ **EMP:** 610 **EST:** 1980
SQ FT: 180,000
SALES (est): 93MM
SALES (corp-wide): 19.8B **Publicly Held**
SIC: 3821 3569 3564 3841 Laboratory apparatus, except heating & measuring; filters, general line: industrial; air purification equipment; surgical instruments & apparatus; electromedical apparatus; insect lamps, electric
HQ: Pall Corporation
   25 Harbor Park Dr
   Port Washington NY 11050
   516 484-5400

(G-470)
GENE CODES FORENSICS INC
525 Avis Dr Ste 8 (48108-9616)
PHONE.................................734 769-7249
Howard Cash, *CEO*
Natalie Kerns, *Accountant*
EMP: 18
SALES (est): 515.8K **Privately Held**
SIC: 7372 Application computer software

(G-471)
GENERAL SCIENTIFIC CORPORATION
77 Enterprise Dr (48103-9503)
PHONE.................................734 996-9200
Byung Jin Chang, *President*
Sharon Chang, *Vice Pres*
Henry Gretzinger, *Vice Pres*
Byung Chang, *Plant Mgr*
Dave Lavey, *Engineer*
▲ **EMP:** 45
SQ FT: 21,600
SALES (est): 14.4MM **Privately Held**
WEB: www.gscoptics.com
SIC: 3827 3851 3229 Lenses, optical: all types except ophthalmic; lupes magnifying instruments, optical; ophthalmic goods; pressed & blown glass

(G-472)
GFG INSTRUMENTATION INC
Also Called: Gfg Dynamation
1194 Oak Valley Dr Ste 20 (48108-8942)
PHONE.................................734 769-0573
Robert Henderson, *President*
Michael Fleck, *Purch Mgr*
Jeff Allsworth, *Engineer*
Francis Johnson, *Regl Sales Mgr*
EMP: 25
SQ FT: 13,000
SALES (est): 5.7MM **Privately Held**
WEB: www.gfg-mbh.com
SIC: 3829 Gas detectors

(G-473)
GLOBAL GREEN CORPORATION
5068 Plymouth Rd (48105-9520)
PHONE.................................734 560-1743
Doug Benit, *President*
EMP: 10

GEOGRAPHIC SECTION

Ann Arbor - Washtenaw County (G-501)

SALES (est): 568.4K **Privately Held**
SIC: 5063 1731 3646 3648 Lighting fixtures, commercial & industrial; energy management controls; lighting contractor; commercial indusl & institutional electric lighting fixtures; lighting equipment

(G-474)
GMI PACKAGING CO (PA)
1371 Centennial Ln (48103)
PHONE..................734 972-7389
Joyce Mueller, *President*
EMP: 5
SALES: 1.5MM **Privately Held**
SIC: 3535 Unit handling conveying systems

(G-475)
GPBC INC
Also Called: Grizzly Peak Brewing Company
120 W Washington St Ste 1 (48104-1356)
PHONE..................734 741-7325
Jon Carlson, *President*
Bery Haven, *President*
Scott Keller, *Manager*
EMP: 120
SQ FT: 6,000
SALES (est): 11.9MM **Privately Held**
WEB: www.gpbc.org
SIC: 2082 5813 5812 Beer (alcoholic beverage); tavern (drinking places); eating places

(G-476)
GRAFAKTRI INC
1200 N Main St (48104-1041)
PHONE..................734 665-0717
W A P John, *President*
Waldemar John, *President*
Julie Ritter, *Vice Pres*
EMP: 7
SQ FT: 10,000
SALES (est): 1MM **Privately Held**
WEB: www.grafaktri.com
SIC: 3993 2759 Displays & cutouts, window & lobby; screen printing; posters, including billboards: printing

(G-477)
GRAVIKOR INC
401 W Morgan Rd (48108-9109)
PHONE..................734 302-3200
Andrew Taylor, *President*
James Richter, *Principal*
EMP: 5
SQ FT: 500
SALES (est): 460K **Privately Held**
SIC: 3829 Medical diagnostic systems, nuclear

(G-478)
GREAT LAKES SPT PUBLICATIONS
3588 Plymouth Rd (48105-2603)
PHONE..................734 507-0241
Art McCafferty, *CEO*
Cheryl Clark, *CFO*
EMP: 5
SALES: 300K **Privately Held**
WEB: www.glsp.com
SIC: 2741 Miscellaneous publishing

(G-479)
GREENVIEW DATA INC
Also Called: Spamstopshere
8178 Jackson Rd Ste A (48103-9806)
PHONE..................734 426-7500
Theodore Green, *President*
EMP: 21
SQ FT: 5,000
SALES: 3.5MM
SALES (corp-wide): 70.4MM **Publicly Held**
SIC: 7372 Application computer software
PA: Zix Corporation
   2711 N Haskell Ave # 2300
   Dallas TX 75204
   214 370-2000

(G-480)
GUDEL INC
4881 Runway Blvd (48108-9558)
PHONE..................734 214-0000
Stefan Nilsson, *CEO*
Joe Campbell, *Vice Pres*
Brant Blasier, *Engineer*
Austin Joyce, *Engineer*
Chad Bhavsar, *Finance*
▲ **EMP:** 78 **EST:** 1995
SQ FT: 7,000
SALES (est): 28.3MM
SALES (corp-wide): 195.7MM **Privately Held**
WEB: www.gudel.com
SIC: 3535 Conveyors & conveying equipment
HQ: Gudel Group Ag
   C/O Gudel Ag
   Langenthal BE 4900
   629 169-191

(G-481)
HANNA INSTRUMENTS INC
3820 Packard St Ste 120 (48108-5016)
PHONE..................734 971-8160
John Martino, *Manager*
EMP: 6 **Privately Held**
WEB: www.hannainst.com
SIC: 3841 Surgical & medical instruments
PA: Hanna Instruments, Inc.
   584 Park East Dr
   Woonsocket RI 02895

(G-482)
HARLOW SHEET METAL LLC
5140 Park Rd (48103-9549)
PHONE..................734 996-1509
EMP: 4
SALES (est): 374.5K **Privately Held**
SIC: 3446 Mfg Architectural Metalwork

(G-483)
HARVARD SQUARE EDITIONS
2112 Brockman Blvd (48104-4530)
PHONE..................734 668-7523
Jocelyn Morin, *Owner*
EMP: 4
SALES (est): 185.4K **Privately Held**
SIC: 2731 Book publishing

(G-484)
HAWKINS INDUSTRIES INC
3660 Plaza Dr Ste 1b (48108-1668)
PHONE..................734 663-9889
William F Hawkins, *President*
EMP: 3
SQ FT: 1,600
SALES (est): 250K **Privately Held**
SIC: 3599 Machine shop, jobbing & repair

(G-485)
HEALTHCARE DME LLC
Also Called: Healthcare Medical Supply
2911 Carpenter Rd (48108-1163)
PHONE..................734 975-6668
Ashfaq Kadwani, *CEO*
Joseph Wucker, *Materials Mgr*
Aisha Ashfaq, *Treasurer*
Kristen Kiester, *Human Res Mgr*
Shahzeb Ashfaq, *Sales Mgr*
EMP: 8
SQ FT: 2,500
SALES: 252K **Privately Held**
SIC: 5047 5049 3841 3845 Medical equipment & supplies; laboratory equipment, except medical or dental; surgical & medical instruments; respiratory analysis equipment, electromedical

(G-486)
HEALTHPLUS SPCLTY PHARMA
4350 Jackson Rd 250 (48103-1890)
PHONE..................734 769-1300
Indu Joshi, *Principal*
EMP: 5
SALES (est): 420.3K **Privately Held**
SIC: 2834 Pharmaceutical preparations

(G-487)
HEARING HEALTH SCIENCE INC
Also Called: Hhsi
2723 S State St Ste 150 (48104-6188)
PHONE..................734 476-9490
Barry S Seifer, *CEO*
EMP: 7
SALES (est): 738.8K **Privately Held**
SIC: 2833 Medicinals & botanicals

(G-488)
HEART SYNC INC
4401 Varsity Dr Ste D (48108-5003)
PHONE..................734 213-5530
Stuart Shulman, *President*
Megan Kerns, *Opers Staff*
EMP: 14 **EST:** 2007
SALES: 2.2MM **Privately Held**
SIC: 3845 Electromedical apparatus

(G-489)
HERALD NEWSPAPERS COMPANY INC
Also Called: Ann Arbor News, The
704 Airport Blvd Ste 6 (48108-3607)
PHONE..................734 926-4510
Karl Metzgeer, *Branch Mgr*
EMP: 175
SALES (corp-wide): 5.5B **Privately Held**
WEB: www.post-standard.com
SIC: 2711 Newspapers, publishing & printing
HQ: The Herald Newspapers Company Inc
   220 S Warren St
   Syracuse NY 13202
   315 470-0011

(G-490)
HIGH-PO-CHLOR INC
Also Called: Hypo-Systems
1181 Freesia Ct (48105-1972)
PHONE..................734 942-1500
Michael Kenney, *President*
John Martin, *Vice Pres*
Marilee Slicker, *Vice Pres*
EMP: 6 **EST:** 1981
SQ FT: 1,800
SALES (est): 1.1MM **Privately Held**
SIC: 2842 2819 Bleaches, household: dry or liquid; industrial inorganic chemicals

(G-491)
HIGHLANDER GRAPHICS LLC
75 Aprill Dr (48103-1901)
PHONE..................734 449-9733
Brent Wall, *President*
Justin McLean, *General Mgr*
EMP: 4
SQ FT: 4,000
SALES (est): 243.2K **Privately Held**
SIC: 3993 Signs & advertising specialties

(G-492)
HINES INDUSTRIES INC (PA)
240 Metty Dr Ste A (48103-9498)
PHONE..................734 769-2300
Dawn Hines, *CEO*
Chelsea Gibbons, *Marketing Staff*
Beverly Monge, *Manager*
Dave Bauer, *Director*
Mavis Hines, *Admin Sec*
◆ **EMP:** 40
SQ FT: 40,000
SALES (est): 8.1MM **Privately Held**
WEB: www.hinesindustries.com
SIC: 3829 3823 Measuring & controlling devices; industrial instrmnts msrmnt display/control process variable

(G-493)
HISTOSONICS INC
3526 W Liberty Rd Ste 100 (48103-8872)
PHONE..................734 926-4630
Mike Blue, *President*
Thomas Davison, *Chairman*
Christine Gibbons, *COO*
Jim Bertolina, *Vice Pres*
EMP: 7
SQ FT: 2,600
SALES (est): 1.1MM **Privately Held**
SIC: 3845 Ultrasonic scanning devices, medical

(G-494)
HOME NICHES INC
2777 Mystic Dr (48103-8952)
PHONE..................734 330-9189
Robert Chen, *President*
Scott Chen, *Vice Pres*
▲ **EMP:** 7
SALES: 4MM **Privately Held**
WEB: www.homeniches.com
SIC: 5719 2499 Closet organizers & shelving units; hampers, laundry

(G-495)
HORIBA INSTRUMENTS INC
Automotive Systems Div
5900 Hines Dr (48108-7941)
PHONE..................734 213-6555
Ken Mitera, *Branch Mgr*
EMP: 85
SQ FT: 1,000 **Privately Held**
WEB: www.horibalab.com
SIC: 3823 3826 3829 3511 Industrial instrmnts msrmnt display/control process variable; analytical instruments; measuring & controlling devices; turbines & turbine generator sets; instruments to measure electricity
HQ: Horiba Instruments Incorporated
   9755 Research Dr
   Irvine CA 92618
   949 250-4811

(G-496)
HOSFORD & CO INC
1204 N Main St (48104-1041)
PHONE..................734 769-5660
Jonathan Hosford, *President*
EMP: 5
SQ FT: 11,000
SALES (est): 805K **Privately Held**
WEB: www.hosfordco.com
SIC: 3599 Machine shop, jobbing & repair

(G-497)
HURON VALLEY TELECOM
605 Argo Dr (48105-1650)
PHONE..................734 995-9780
John Lieberman, *President*
EMP: 3
SALES (est): 280K **Privately Held**
SIC: 4813 5999 3661 1731 Telephone communication, except radio; telephone equipment & systems; fiber optics communications equipment; computer installation

(G-498)
HYGRATEK LLC
1600 Huron Pkwy Fl 2 (48109-5001)
PHONE..................847 962-6180
Anish Tuteja, *Principal*
Michael Gurin, *Officer*
EMP: 3
SQ FT: 935
SALES (est): 271.4K **Privately Held**
SIC: 2851 8731 3589 Lacquers, varnishes, enamels & other coatings; commercial physical research; sewage & water treatment equipment

(G-499)
IDEATION INC
Also Called: All Things Made In America
3389 Breckland Ct (48108-9311)
PHONE..................734 761-4360
Thomas Ungrodt, *President*
Chris Gallup, *CFO*
Virginia Lum, *Treasurer*
EMP: 50
SQ FT: 18,000
SALES (est): 4.1MM **Privately Held**
WEB: www.ideationgifts.com
SIC: 2741 Catalogs: publishing only, not printed on site

(G-500)
IDRINK PRODUCTS INC
6109 Jackson Rd (48103-9140)
PHONE..................734 531-6324
Douglas Wang, *CEO*
EMP: 7
SALES: 716.3K **Privately Held**
SIC: 3089 Plastic kitchenware, tableware & houseware

(G-501)
IMAGEMASTER LLC (PA)
Also Called: Imagemaster Printing
1182 Oak Valley Dr (48108-9624)
PHONE..................734 821-2500
Jennifer Braun, *Production*
Daniel Rodriguez, *VP Sales*
Albert M Rodriguez, *Mng Member*
Bob Lees, *Director*
▲ **EMP:** 44
SQ FT: 20,000
SALES (est): 6.4MM **Privately Held**
SIC: 2759 Business forms: printing

Ann Arbor - Washtenaw County (G-502)   GEOGRAPHIC SECTION

(G-502)
IMAGEMASTER PRINTING LLC
1182 Oak Valley Dr (48108-9624)
PHONE...................................734 821-2511
Albert Rodriguez, *Manager*
EMP: 34
SQ FT: 17,000
SALES (est): 1.5MM **Privately Held**
SIC: 2732 Books: printing & binding

(G-503)
IMRA AMERICA INC (HQ)
1044 Woodridge Ave (48105-9774)
PHONE...................................734 669-7377
Takashi Omitsu, *President*
Christopher Sorel, *Technology*
Makoto Yoshida, *Admin Sec*
EMP: 45
SQ FT: 30,000
SALES: 40.7MM **Privately Held**
SIC: 8732 3699 Research services, except laboratory; laser systems & equipment

(G-504)
INDUSTRIAL OPTICAL MEASUREMENT
1349 King George Blvd (48108-3214)
PHONE...................................734 975-0436
Stephen Segall, *COO*
EMP: 3
SALES: 150K **Privately Held**
SIC: 3825 Test equipment for electronic & electric measurement

(G-505)
INGHAM TOOL LLC
6155 Jackson Rd Ste B (48108-9170)
PHONE...................................734 929-2390
Jeff Cheesman, *Mng Member*
EMP: 5 **EST:** 2013
SALES: 750K **Privately Held**
SIC: 3599 Machine shop, jobbing & repair

(G-506)
INORA TECHNOLOGIES INC (PA)
Also Called: Metronom US
333 Jackson Plz 1000 (48103-1922)
PHONE...................................734 302-7488
Ingobert Schmadel, *President*
Thomas Gendera, *Senior Engr*
Mary Jane Hourani, *Controller*
Mary Hourani, *Controller*
Monika Schneider, *Sales Mgr*
EMP: 11
SALES (est): 1.5MM **Privately Held**
WEB: www.metronomus.com
SIC: 8748 7372 3829 5049 Systems analysis & engineering consulting services; application computer software; aircraft & motor vehicle measurement equipment; scientific & engineering equipment & supplies

(G-507)
INTERFACE ASSOCIATES INC
1070 Rosewood St (48104-6250)
PHONE...................................734 327-9500
Michael Nadeau, *President*
EMP: 6
SALES (est): 550.4K **Privately Held**
WEB: www.rec-sports.com
SIC: 3577 7378 5045 4813 Computer peripheral equipment; computer peripheral equipment repair & maintenance; computers;

(G-508)
IX INNOVATIONS LLC
4488 Jackson Rd Ste 6 (48103-1812)
EMP: 4 **EST:** 2010
SALES: 20K **Privately Held**
SIC: 3825 Mfg Electrical Measuring Instruments

(G-509)
JACKHILL OIL COMPANY
305 E Eisenhower Pkwy # 300 (48108-3354)
PHONE...................................734 994-6599
David Dzierwa, *President*
Larry L French, *Treasurer*
Donald S Chisholm, *Admin Sec*
EMP: 3
SALES (est): 300K **Privately Held**
SIC: 1311 Natural gas production; crude petroleum production

(G-510)
JDA SOFTWARE GROUP INC
900 Victors Way Ste 360 (48108-2832)
PHONE...................................734 741-4205
Fax: 734 887-4555
EMP: 8
SALES (corp-wide): 1.3B **Privately Held**
SIC: 7372 Prepackaged Software Services
HQ: Jda Software Group, Inc.
   14400 N 87th St
   Scottsdale AZ 85254

(G-511)
JODON ENGINEERING ASSOC INC
62 Enterprise Dr (48103-9562)
PHONE...................................734 761-4044
Michael Gillespie, *President*
Mark Haddox, *Vice Pres*
John Werenski, *Opers Mgr*
Bruce Gray, *Purch Agent*
Curt Gifford, *Engineer*
EMP: 12
SQ FT: 15,000
SALES (est): 1.4MM **Privately Held**
WEB: www.jodon.com
SIC: 3826 3841 3825 Laser scientific & engineering instruments; analytical optical instruments; ophthalmic lasers; microwave test equipment; test equipment for electronic & electrical circuits

(G-512)
JOHN ALLEN ENTERPRISES
4281 Climbing Way (48103-9402)
PHONE...................................734 426-2507
John Towsley, *Principal*
▲ **EMP:** 8
SALES (est): 913.4K **Privately Held**
SIC: 3089 Plastics products

(G-513)
JOHNSON CONTROLS INC
1935 S Industrial Hwy (48104-4613)
PHONE...................................734 995-3016
Cara Luff, *Manager*
EMP: 8 **Privately Held**
SIC: 3691 Lead acid batteries (storage batteries)
HQ: Johnson Controls, Inc.
   5757 N Green Bay Ave
   Milwaukee WI 53209
   414 524-1200

(G-514)
K & S PRINTING CENTERS INC
Also Called: Qps Printing
4860 Greenway Ct (48103-9414)
PHONE...................................734 482-1680
Sherry Cradick, *President*
Kim Cradick, *Vice Pres*
EMP: 5
SQ FT: 1,800
SALES (est): 599.3K **Privately Held**
SIC: 2752 7334 Commercial printing, offset; photocopying & duplicating services

(G-515)
KAISER OPTICAL SYSTEMS INC (DH)
371 Parkland Plz (48103-6202)
PHONE...................................734 665-8083
Tim Harrison, *President*
Harry Owen, *Vice Pres*
Joe Slater, *Vice Pres*
Todd Mead, *CFO*
David Strachan, *Sales Staff*
▲ **EMP:** 75
SQ FT: 31,000
SALES (est): 14.1MM
SALES (corp-wide): 2.8B **Privately Held**
WEB: www.kosi.com
SIC: 3827 Optical test & inspection equipment; optical elements & assemblies, except ophthalmic
HQ: Endress + Hauser Messtechnik Gmbh + Co. Kg
   Colmarer Str. 6
   Weil Am Rhein 79576
   762 197-501

(G-516)
KAYDON CORPORATION (DH)
2723 S State St Ste 300 (48104-6188)
PHONE...................................734 747-7025
Timothy J Heasley, *President*
Les Miller, *President*
Peter C Dechants, *Senior VP*
Debra K Crane, *Vice Pres*
Laura Kowalchik, *Vice Pres*
◆ **EMP:** 277
SALES (est): 643.5MM
SALES (corp-wide): 9.5B **Privately Held**
WEB: www.kaydon.com
SIC: 3562 3569 3592 3053 Ball & roller bearings; ball bearings & parts; roller bearings & parts; filters, general line: industrial; pistons & piston rings; gaskets & sealing devices; sliprings, for motors or generators; electronic circuits

(G-517)
KOLOSSOS PRINTING INC (PA)
2055 W Stadium Blvd (48103-4570)
PHONE...................................734 994-5400
Nicholas Arhangelos, *President*
Kathleen Arhangelos, *Corp Secy*
EMP: 18
SQ FT: 7,500
SALES (est): 3.7MM **Privately Held**
WEB: www.kolossosprinting.com
SIC: 2752 7334 7389 4215 Commercial printing, offset; photocopying & duplicating services; sign painting & lettering shop; courier services, except by air; mailing service

(G-518)
KOLOSSOS PRINTING INC
301 E Liberty St (48104-2262)
PHONE...................................734 741-1600
Tony Arghenglos, *Branch Mgr*
EMP: 9
SALES (corp-wide): 3.7MM **Privately Held**
SIC: 2621 4731 Wrapping & packaging papers; freight transportation arrangement
PA: Kolossos Printing Inc
   2055 W Stadium Blvd
   Ann Arbor MI 48103
   734 994-5400

(G-519)
KORE GROUP INC (PA)
Also Called: Fastsigns
3500 Washtenaw Ave (48104-5244)
PHONE...................................734 677-1500
Roger Cunningham, *President*
Kevin Miller, *Vice Pres*
EMP: 8
SQ FT: 1,800
SALES: 900K **Privately Held**
WEB: www.koreinc.com
SIC: 3993 Signs & advertising specialties

(G-520)
KRAIG BIOCRAFT LABS INC
2723 S State St Ste 150 (48104-6188)
PHONE...................................734 619-8066
Kim Thompson, *President*
Jonathan R Rice, *COO*
EMP: 7
SALES: 401.6K **Privately Held**
SIC: 2823 Cellulosic manmade fibers

(G-521)
KUMANU INC
535 W William St Ste 4n (48103-4978)
PHONE...................................734 822-6673
Victor Strecher, *CEO*
David Gregorka, *COO*
Katherine Harding, *COO*
John Holmes, *Software Engr*
Mike Behnke, *Sr Software Eng*
EMP: 13
SQ FT: 5,000
SALES (est): 1.1MM **Privately Held**
SIC: 7372 Application computer software

(G-522)
L-3 COMMUNICATIONS EOTECH INC
1201 E Ellsworth Rd (48108-2420)
PHONE...................................734 741-8868
Paul Mangano, *President*
Kindig Rollin, *Business Dir*
EMP: 120
SQ FT: 35,000
SALES (est): 21.6MM
SALES (corp-wide): 6.8B **Publicly Held**
SIC: 3827 Sighting & fire control equipment, optical
HQ: L3 Technologies, Inc.
   600 3rd Ave Fl 34
   New York NY 10016
   212 697-1111

(G-523)
L3 TECHNOLOGIES INC
1201 E Ellsworth Rd (48108-2420)
PHONE...................................734 741-8868
Edward Schoppman, *Principal*
EMP: 208
SALES (corp-wide): 6.8B **Publicly Held**
SIC: 3663 Telemetering equipment, electronic
HQ: L3 Technologies, Inc.
   600 3rd Ave Fl 34
   New York NY 10016
   212 697-1111

(G-524)
LAKESIDE SOFTWARE INC
201 S Main St Ste 200 (48104-2153)
PHONE...................................248 686-1700
Michael Schumacher, *Branch Mgr*
EMP: 15
SALES (corp-wide): 9.8MM **Privately Held**
SIC: 7372 Prepackaged software
PA: Lakeside Software, Inc.
   40950 Woodward Ave # 200
   Bloomfield Hills MI 48304
   248 686-1700

(G-525)
LAMBERT INDUSTRIES INC
69 Enterprise Dr (48103-9503)
PHONE...................................734 668-6864
Robert Lambert, *President*
Rose Lambert, *Vice Pres*
EMP: 10
SQ FT: 6,500
SALES (est): 1.9MM **Privately Held**
SIC: 3599 3544 Machine shop, jobbing & repair; special dies & tools

(G-526)
LAURMARK ENTERPRISES INC
Also Called: Bak Industries
5400 Data Ct (48108-8961)
PHONE...................................818 365-9000
William Reminder, *President*
Kelly Kneifl, *COO*
Jesse Del Toro, *Vice Pres*
Jim Bresingham, *CFO*
Maria Zwas, *Admin Sec*
EMP: 35
SQ FT: 57,000
SALES: 14.2MM
SALES (corp-wide): 255.3MM **Privately Held**
WEB: www.bakliner.com
SIC: 3714 Motor vehicle parts & accessories
HQ: Tectum Holdings, Inc.
   5400 Data Ct
   Ann Arbor MI 48108
   734 677-0444

(G-527)
LEELANAU WINE CELLARS LTD
35 Research Dr Ste 300 (48103-2981)
P.O. Box 68, Omena (49674-0068)
PHONE...................................231 386-5201
Michael H Jacobson, *President*
Bob Jacobson, *Vice Pres*
▲ **EMP:** 5 **EST:** 1975
SQ FT: 8,000
SALES (est): 2.3MM **Privately Held**
SIC: 2084 Wines

(G-528)
LEON SPEAKERS INC (PA)
715 W Ellsworth Rd Ste A (48108-3386)
PHONE...................................734 213-2151
Noah Kaplan, *President*
Judith Sexton, *Vice Pres*
Bryan Lancaster, *Foreman/Supr*
Nancy Mathews, *Senior Buyer*
Yarro Ireland, *Engineer*
▲ **EMP:** 37

GEOGRAPHIC SECTION

Ann Arbor - Washtenaw County (G-555)

SALES (est): 4.6MM **Privately Held**
SIC: 3651 Speaker systems

(G-529)
LEXICOM PUBLISHING GROUP
1945 Pauline Blvd Ste 18 (48103-5047)
PHONE.................................734 994-8600
Diane Durance, *Principal*
EMP: 3
SALES (est): 185.9K **Privately Held**
WEB: www.lexpub.com
SIC: 2721 Magazines: publishing only, not printed on site

(G-530)
LIQUID MANUFACTURING LLC
305 Westwood Ave (48103-3550)
PHONE.................................810 220-2802
Peter W Paisley, *CEO*
▲ EMP: 110
SQ FT: 78,000
SALES (est): 13.4MM **Privately Held**
WEB: www.liquidmfg.com
SIC: 2085 2086 Rum (alcoholic beverage); vodka (alcoholic beverage); gin (alcoholic beverage); bottled & canned soft drinks

(G-531)
LIVER TRANSPLANT/UNIV OF MICH
1500 E Medical Center Dr (48109-5000)
PHONE.................................734 936-7670
Jeffery Punch, *Director*
Robert J Merion, *Director*
EMP: 6
SALES (est): 516.1K **Privately Held**
SIC: 3523 7363 8093 Transplanters; medical help service; specialty outpatient clinics

(G-532)
LNA SOLUTIONS INC
3924a Varsity Dr Ste A (48108-2226)
PHONE.................................734 677-2305
Terence Doran, *CEO*
Joseph Komaromi, *Sales Engr*
Terry Doran, *Manager*
Ed Stollenwerck, *Manager*
▲ EMP: 10
SALES (est): 1.6MM
SALES (corp-wide): 14.6B **Privately Held**
SIC: 3441 Building components, structural steel
HQ: Kee Safety, Inc.
100 Stradtman St Ste 6
Buffalo NY 14206
716 896-4949

(G-533)
LOGIC SOLUTIONS INC
2929 Plymouth Rd Ste 207b (48105-3206)
PHONE.................................734 930-0009
Grace Lee, *Branch Mgr*
EMP: 3 **Privately Held**
SIC: 7372 Application computer software
PA: Logic Solutions Inc
2929 Plymouth Rd Ste 207
Ann Arbor MI 48105

(G-534)
LOGICAL DIGITAL AUDIO VIDEO
Also Called: Silver Tortoise Sound Lab
4602 Central Blvd (48108-1346)
PHONE.................................734 572-0022
Jonas D Berzanskis, *Owner*
EMP: 4
SQ FT: 1,000
SALES: 150K **Privately Held**
WEB: www.stsproducts.com
SIC: 3651 Household audio & video equipment

(G-535)
LTEK INDUSTRIES INC
Also Called: ASAP Source
2298 S Industrial Hwy (48104-6124)
PHONE.................................734 747-6105
Edsel Roberts, *President*
Deborah Roberts, *Vice Pres*
EMP: 6
SQ FT: 14,000
SALES (est): 795.6K **Privately Held**
WEB: www.ltekindustries.com
SIC: 3599 5085 Machine shop, jobbing & repair; industrial supplies

(G-536)
M & M TYPEWRITER SERVICE INC
Also Called: Michigan Printer Service
251 Collingwood St (48103-3873)
PHONE.................................734 995-4033
John Mulcare, *President*
Claudia Nbee, *Treasurer*
Arlene Mulcare, *Admin Sec*
EMP: 5 EST: 1971
SQ FT: 4,710
SALES (est): 200K **Privately Held**
SIC: 3555 5087 7359 Copy holders, printers'; service establishment equipment; business machine & electronic equipment rental services

(G-537)
M DEN ON MAIN
3777 Plaza Dr Ste 5 (48108-3634)
PHONE.................................734 761-1030
Doug Horning, *Owner*
EMP: 6
SALES (est): 633.7K **Privately Held**
SIC: 2253 Bathing suits & swimwear, knit

(G-538)
M&B HOLDINGS LLC (PA)
Also Called: Gaging Solutions & Services
3035 Washtenaw Ave A322 (48104-5119)
PHONE.................................734 677-0454
Jay Mullick, *Mng Member*
Scott Burk,
EMP: 7
SALES: 3.5MM **Privately Held**
SIC: 3829 Measuring & controlling devices

(G-539)
M4 CIC LLC
719 W Ellsworth Rd Ste 1a (48108-1663)
PHONE.................................734 436-8507
EMP: 7 EST: 2015
SALES (est): 676.7K **Privately Held**
SIC: 2082 Malt beverages

(G-540)
MAGNETIC MICHIGAN
101 N Main St (48104-5507)
PHONE.................................734 922-7068
Drew Stirton, *Branch Mgr*
EMP: 72
SALES (corp-wide): 17.9MM **Privately Held**
SIC: 7372 Prepackaged software
PA: Magnetic Michigan
167 2nd Ave
San Mateo CA 94401
650 544-2400

(G-541)
MAHINDRA TRACTOR ASSEMBLY INC
Also Called: Mahindra Genze
1901 E Ellsworth Rd (48108-2804)
PHONE.................................734 274-2239
Vish Palekar, *CEO*
EMP: 25
SALES (corp-wide): 7.4B **Privately Held**
SIC: 3523 Tractors, farm
HQ: Mahindra Tractor Assembly, Inc.
48016 Fremont Blvd
Fremont CA 94538
650 779-5180

(G-542)
MALLOY INCORPORATED
Also Called: Edwards Brothers Malloy
5411 Jackson Rd (48103-1865)
PHONE.................................734 665-6113
John Edwards, *CEO*
William Upton, *CFO*
EMP: 600
SQ FT: 188,000
SALES (est): 85.2MM
SALES (corp-wide): 388.7MM **Privately Held**
WEB: www.malloy.com
SIC: 2732 2789 2752 Books: printing & binding; bookbinding & related work; commercial printing, lithographic
PA: Edwards Brothers Malloy, Inc.
5411 Jackson Rd
Ann Arbor MI 48103
734 665-6113

(G-543)
MARC SCHRREIBER & COMPANY INC
120 E Liberty St Ste 370 (48104-2130)
PHONE.................................734 222-9930
Marc Margolis,
EMP: 18
SALES (est): 807K **Privately Held**
SIC: 7372 Prepackaged software

(G-544)
MASCO CABINETRY LLC
4600 Arrowhead Dr (48105-2773)
PHONE.................................517 263-0771
Doug Jacot, *Branch Mgr*
EMP: 87
SALES (corp-wide): 8.3B **Publicly Held**
SIC: 2434 Wood kitchen cabinets
HQ: Masco Cabinetry Llc
4600 Arrowhead Dr
Ann Arbor MI 48105
734 205-4600

(G-545)
MASCO CABINETRY LLC
Also Called: Merillat Cabinets
4600 Arrowhead Dr (48105-2773)
PHONE.................................740 286-5033
John Lewis, *Branch Mgr*
EMP: 455
SQ FT: 104,000
SALES (corp-wide): 8.3B **Publicly Held**
SIC: 2434 Wood kitchen cabinets
HQ: Masco Cabinetry Llc
4600 Arrowhead Dr
Ann Arbor MI 48105
734 205-4600

(G-546)
MASCO CABINETRY LLC (HQ)
Also Called: Denova
4600 Arrowhead Dr (48105-2773)
PHONE.................................734 205-4600
Joe Gross, *President*
Chris Winans, *Vice Pres*
◆ EMP: 360
SQ FT: 150,000
SALES (est): 1.4B
SALES (corp-wide): 8.3B **Publicly Held**
SIC: 2434 Wood kitchen cabinets
PA: Masco Corporation
17450 College Pkwy
Livonia MI 48152
313 274-7400

(G-547)
MASCO CABINETRY LLC
4600 Arrowhead Dr (48105-2773)
PHONE.................................239 561-7266
Ken Olesen, *Branch Mgr*
EMP: 12
SALES (corp-wide): 8.3B **Publicly Held**
SIC: 2434 Wood kitchen cabinets
HQ: Masco Cabinetry Llc
4600 Arrowhead Dr
Ann Arbor MI 48105
734 205-4600

(G-548)
MASCO CABINETRY LLC
Also Called: Quality Cabinets
4600 Arrowhead Dr (48105-2773)
PHONE.................................407 857-4444
Albert Robinson, *Branch Mgr*
EMP: 6
SALES (corp-wide): 8.3B **Publicly Held**
SIC: 2434 Wood kitchen cabinets
HQ: Masco Cabinetry Llc
4600 Arrowhead Dr
Ann Arbor MI 48105
734 205-4600

(G-549)
MASCO CABINETRY LLC
4600 Arrowhead Dr (48105-2773)
PHONE.................................770 447-6363
John Winfree, *Branch Mgr*
EMP: 80
SALES (corp-wide): 8.3B **Publicly Held**
SIC: 2434 5211 Wood kitchen cabinets; cabinets, kitchen
HQ: Masco Cabinetry Llc
4600 Arrowhead Dr
Ann Arbor MI 48105
734 205-4600

(G-550)
MAY MOBILITY INC
650 Avis Dr Ste 100 (48108-9623)
PHONE.................................312 869-2711
Edwin Olson, *CEO*
Alisyn Malek, *COO*
Steve Vozar, *Treasurer*
Tammera Bollman, *Manager*
Alyssa Jernigan, *Executive Asst*
EMP: 10
SALES (est): 421.4K **Privately Held**
SIC: 4119 3711 Local passenger transportation; motor vehicles & car bodies

(G-551)
MEDIMAGE INC
331 Metty Dr Ste 1 (48103-9156)
PHONE.................................734 665-5400
Robert A Helton, *CEO*
Patricia Van Riper, *Corp Secy*
Tod Henderstein, *Sales Mgr*
Randy Pratt, *Manager*
EMP: 8
SQ FT: 2,000
SALES (est): 790K **Privately Held**
WEB: www.medimage.com
SIC: 7372 7379 Prepackaged software; computer related maintenance services

(G-552)
MENDENHALL ASSOCIATES INC
Also Called: Orthopedic Network News
1500 Cedar Bend Dr (48105-2305)
PHONE.................................734 741-4710
Stanley T Mendenhall, *President*
EMP: 6
SQ FT: 300
SALES (est): 129.9K
SALES (corp-wide): 2.2MM **Privately Held**
WEB: www.orthopedicnetworknews.com
SIC: 2731 7371 8742 Book publishing; computer software development; management consulting services
PA: Curvo Labs, Inc.
58 Adams Ave
Evansville IN 47713
619 316-1202

(G-553)
METEOR WEB MARKETING INC
Also Called: Us-Bingo.com
3438 E Ellsworth Rd Ste A (48108-2056)
PHONE.................................734 822-4999
Catherine Storie, *CEO*
Randy Storie, *Vice Pres*
EMP: 15
SQ FT: 55,000
SALES (est): 2.5MM **Privately Held**
WEB: www.us-bingo.com
SIC: 2759 3944 5961 Tickets: printing; bingo boards (games);

(G-554)
MICHIGAN DEVELOPMENT CORP
3520 Green Ct Ste 300 (48105-1566)
PHONE.................................734 302-4600
Kenneth R Baker, *President*
Mary V Knoell, *Vice Pres*
Philip Fazio, *Treasurer*
Douglas R Gilbert, *Asst Treas*
Walter E Vashak, *Admin Sec*
EMP: 250
SQ FT: 6,000
SALES (est): 6.9MM
SALES (corp-wide): 56.8MM **Privately Held**
WEB: www.eotech-inc.com
SIC: 8732 3827 Research services, except laboratory; optical instruments & lenses
PA: Altarum Institute
3520 Green Ct Ste 300
Ann Arbor MI 48105
734 302-4600

(G-555)
MICHIGAN LIVE INC
339 E Liberty St Ste 210 (48104-2258)
PHONE.................................734 997-7090
Mark Hauptschein, *CEO*
John Hiner, *Vice Pres*
Dale Glinz, *Accounts Exec*

(PA)=Parent Co (HQ)=Headquarters (DH)=Div Headquarters
◯ = New Business established in last 2 years

2020 Harris Michigan Industrial Directory

Ann Arbor - Washtenaw County (G-556)

Colleen Huff, *Sales Staff*
EMP: 17
SALES (est): 706.9K
SALES (corp-wide): 5.5B **Privately Held**
WEB: www.advance.net
SIC: 2711 Newspapers, publishing & printing
PA: Advance Publications, Inc.
1 World Trade Ctr Fl 43
New York NY 10007
718 981-1234

(G-556)
MICHIGAN SIGNS INC
5527 Gallery Park Dr (48103-5055)
P.O. Box 1162 (48106-1162)
PHONE.................................734 662-1503
Linda Braun, *President*
Harold Braun, *Vice Pres*
EMP: 7
SQ FT: 7,500
SALES (est): 765.5K **Privately Held**
WEB: www.michigansinsinc.com
SIC: 3993 1799 Electric signs; sign installation & maintenance

(G-557)
MID-TECH INC
175 Dino Dr (48103-9502)
PHONE.................................734 426-4327
Gerry Jedele, *President*
EMP: 9 **EST:** 1985
SQ FT: 7,200
SALES (est): 1.7MM **Privately Held**
SIC: 3469 3599 3732 3544 Stamping metal for the trade; machine shop, jobbing & repair; boat building & repairing; special dies & tools

(G-558)
MIGHTY LEGAL LLC
329 Burr Oak Dr (48103-2079)
PHONE.................................800 870-4605
Scott Thede, *Accounts Mgr*
Daniel Papajcik,
EMP: 8
SALES (est): 63.6K **Privately Held**
SIC: 7372 Application computer software

(G-559)
MILLENDO THERAPEUTICS INC (PA)
Also Called: OVASCIENCE
110 Miller Ave Ste 100 (48104-1305)
PHONE.................................734 845-9000
Julia Owens, *President*
Todd Applebaum, *Vice Pres*
Jonathan Gillis, *Finance*
Carole Nuechterlein, *Director*
Tamara Joseph, *General Counsel*
EMP: 24 **EST:** 2011
SQ FT: 25,200
SALES (est): 1.4MM **Publicly Held**
SIC: 2834 8731 Pharmaceutical preparations; medical research, commercial

(G-560)
MILLENDO TRANSACTIONSUB INC
301 N Main St Ste 100 (48104-1296)
PHONE.................................734 845-9300
Julia C Owens, *President*
Ryan Zeidan, *Senior VP*
Thomas Hoover, *Vice Pres*
Michael Yeh, *Vice Pres*
Louis Arcudi III, *CFO*
EMP: 8
SALES (est): 1.4MM **Publicly Held**
SIC: 2834 8731 Pharmaceutical preparations; medical research, commercial
PA: Millendo Therapeutics, Inc.
110 Miller Ave Ste 100
Ann Arbor MI 48104
734 845-9000

(G-561)
MODEL SHOP INC
4659 Freedom Dr (48108-9784)
PHONE.................................734 645-8290
Philip Krzyzaniak, *President*
EMP: 3
SQ FT: 3,200
SALES: 165K **Privately Held**
SIC: 3599 Machine shop, jobbing & repair

(G-562)
MOEHRLE INC
4305 Pontiac Trl (48105-9626)
PHONE.................................734 761-2000
EMP: 15 **EST:** 1945
SQ FT: 22,000
SALES (est): 2.5MM **Privately Held**
SIC: 3545 Mfg Machine Tool Accessories

(G-563)
MONROE FUEL COMPANY LLC
414 S Main St Ste 600 (48104-2398)
PHONE.................................734 302-4824
Dave Ruud, *President*
EMP: 4
SALES (est): 383K **Privately Held**
SIC: 2869 Fuels

(G-564)
MONTRONIX INC
4343 Concourse Dr Ste 370 (48108-8672)
PHONE.................................734 213-6500
Jeurg Vonwil, *CEO*
Sudhir Agarwal, *General Mgr*
Srinivasa Prasad, *Managing Dir*
Patricia Son, *Controller*
Dennis Turner, *Technology*
EMP: 9
SALES (est): 1.4MM **Privately Held**
WEB: www.montronix.com
SIC: 3829 5084 3699 Measuring & controlling devices; industrial machinery & equipment; electrical equipment & supplies

(G-565)
MOTAWI TILEWORKS INC
170 Enterprise Dr (48103-9158)
PHONE.................................734 213-0017
Nawal Motawi, *President*
EMP: 20
SQ FT: 12,000
SALES (est): 1.5MM **Privately Held**
WEB: www.motawi.com
SIC: 3253 5032 Ceramic wall & floor tile; brick, stone & related material

(G-566)
MOVELLUS CIRCUITS INC (PA)
220 E Huron St Ste 650 (48104-1991)
PHONE.................................877 321-7667
Muhammad Faisal, *CEO*
Julie Ledford, *Office Mgr*
EMP: 7
SALES (est): 1.2MM **Privately Held**
SIC: 3679 Electronic circuits

(G-567)
MSCSOFTWARE CORPORATION
201 Depot St Ste 100 (48104-1019)
PHONE.................................734 994-3800
Doug Sieman, *Branch Mgr*
Walter Schrauwen, *Technical Staff*
EMP: 200
SALES (corp-wide): 4.3B **Privately Held**
SIC: 7372 Business oriented computer software
HQ: Msc.Software Corporation
4675 Macarthur Ct Ste 900
Newport Beach CA 92660
714 540-8900

(G-568)
NAGEL PRECISION INC
288 Dino Dr (48103-9502)
PHONE.................................734 426-5650
Peter Nagel, *President*
Rolf Bochsler, *Vice Pres*
Willi Koch, *Vice Pres*
Wolf Nagel, *Vice Pres*
Rich Digue, *Project Mgr*
◆ **EMP:** 130 **EST:** 1987
SQ FT: 42,260
SALES (est): 33.9MM **Privately Held**
WEB: www.nagelusa.com
SIC: 3541 3545 Honing & lapping machines; honing heads

(G-569)
NANOCEROX INC (PA)
712 State Cir (48108-1648)
PHONE.................................734 741-9522
Gregory Quarles, *President*
Bin Zhao, *Engineer*
Kim Kochan, *Manager*
EMP: 19
SQ FT: 11,900
SALES (est): 3.7MM **Privately Held**
WEB: www.nanocerox.com
SIC: 2819 Industrial inorganic chemicals

(G-570)
NANOSYSTEMS INC
3588 Plymouth Rd (48105-2603)
PHONE.................................734 274-0020
John Nanos, *President*
▲ **EMP:** 15
SALES: 2MM **Privately Held**
SIC: 3086 2211 Padding, foamed plastic; bandages, gauzes & surgical fabrics, cotton

(G-571)
NATIONAL ADVANCED MOBILITY
3025 Boardwalk St Ste 225 (48108-3266)
PHONE.................................734 995-3098
Rick Jarman, *Ch of Bd*
Christopher Rohe, *President*
EMP: 1 **EST:** 2009
SALES (est): 103.3MM **Privately Held**
SIC: 3549 5084 Assembly machines, including robotic; robots, industrial

(G-572)
NAVITAS SYSTEMS LLC (HQ)
4880 Venture Dr (48108-9559)
PHONE.................................630 755-7920
Christopher E Pruitt, *President*
Jonathan Weisberg, *Opers Staff*
Peter Aurora, *Research*
Mohamad Hoteit, *Engineer*
Peter Dixon, *Technician*
▲ **EMP:** 10 **EST:** 2011
SQ FT: 14,000
SALES: 3.1MM
SALES (corp-wide): 2.8B **Privately Held**
SIC: 3691 Storage batteries
PA: East Penn Manufacturing Co.
102 Deka Rd
Lyon Station PA 19536
610 682-6361

(G-573)
NEURABLE LLC
2260 Fuller Ct Apt 5 (48105-2324)
PHONE.................................206 696-4469
Ramses Alcaide, *CEO*
Max Jacobson, *COO*
Tatyana Dobreva, *Chief Engr*
David Brown, *CFO*
EMP: 3 **EST:** 2015
SALES (est): 137.2K **Privately Held**
SIC: 7372 Application computer software

(G-574)
NIPGUARDS LLC
Also Called: Runguards
2232 S Main St Ste 361 (48103-6938)
PHONE.................................734 544-4490
Andrew C Hopper, *President*
EMP: 4
SALES (est): 564.6K **Privately Held**
SIC: 5091 3949 Athletic goods; sporting & athletic goods

(G-575)
NORCOLD INC
7101 Jackson Rd (48103-9506)
PHONE.................................734 769-6000
Michael Harris, *Branch Mgr*
EMP: 7
SALES (corp-wide): 482MM **Privately Held**
SIC: 3632 Refrigerators, mechanical & absorption; household
HQ: Norcold Inc.
600 S Kuther Rd
Sidney OH 45365

(G-576)
NOSTRUM ENERGY LLC
330 E Liberty St Fl 4 (48104-2238)
PHONE.................................734 548-6977
Kaushik Vyas, *CEO*
Nirmal Mulye, *President*
Naag Piduru, *Research*
Pallavi Rathod, *Finance*
▼ **EMP:** 13
SQ FT: 400
SALES: 100K **Privately Held**
SIC: 3714 Fuel systems & parts, motor vehicle

(G-577)
NSK AMERICAS INC (HQ)
4200 Goss Rd (48105-2799)
P.O. Box 134007 (48113-4007)
PHONE.................................734 913-7500
Brian Lindsay, *President*
Elli Kirschnick, *Vice Pres*
Brad Muston, *Transportation*
Angelo Zanoto, *Buyer*
Carrie Almquist, *Engineer*
▲ **EMP:** 214
SALES (est): 781MM **Privately Held**
SIC: 3714 5013 5085 Steering mechanisms, motor vehicle; automotive supplies & parts; industrial supplies

(G-578)
NSK STEERING SYSTEMS AMER INC (DH)
Also Called: Nssa Hq
4200 Goss Rd (48105-2799)
P.O. Box 134007 (48113-4007)
PHONE.................................734 913-7500
Michael Rivenburgh, *President*
Tsutomu Komori, *Exec VP*
Masahide Matsubara, *Exec VP*
Naoki Mitsue, *Exec VP*
Toshihiro Uchiyama, *Exec VP*
▲ **EMP:** 109
SQ FT: 175,000
SALES (est): 183MM **Privately Held**
WEB: www.nssa.nsk.com
SIC: 3714 Steering mechanisms, motor vehicle

(G-579)
NUSTEP LLC
5111 Venture Dr Ste 1 (48108-5928)
PHONE.................................734 769-3939
Steven Sarns, *Principal*
Richard Sarns, *Principal*
Alejandro Capetillo, *Vice Pres*
Dwayne Hyzak, *Vice Pres*
▲ **EMP:** 100
SQ FT: 68,000
SALES (est): 19.3MM **Privately Held**
WEB: www.nustep.com
SIC: 3949 Exercise equipment

(G-580)
OFF GRID LLC
2950 Trillium Ln (48103-8824)
PHONE.................................734 780-4434
Lindsey Newton, *CFO*
Barbara Wilson, *Executive*
James W McElroy,
Joseph W McElroy,
EMP: 3
SALES (est): 176.6K **Privately Held**
SIC: 3648 7389 Lighting equipment;

(G-581)
OG TECHNOLOGIES INC
4480 Varsity Dr Ste G (48108-5007)
PHONE.................................734 973-7500
Tzyy-Shuh Chang, *President*
Terence C Liddy, *Chairman*
▲ **EMP:** 15
SQ FT: 5,400
SALES: 5.9MM **Privately Held**
WEB: www.ogtechnology.com
SIC: 3829 Measuring & controlling devices

(G-582)
OLD XEMBEDDED LLC
3915 Res Pk Dr Ste A8 (48108)
PHONE.................................734 975-0577
Scott Kania, *Mng Member*
EMP: 9
SALES (est): 905.7K
SALES (corp-wide): 12.5MM **Privately Held**
WEB: www.monroeengineering.com
SIC: 3443 Process vessels, industrial: metal plate
PA: Acromag, Incorporated
30765 S Wixom Rd
Wixom MI 48393
248 624-1541

GEOGRAPHIC SECTION

Ann Arbor - Washtenaw County (G-611)

(G-583)
ONL THERAPEUTICS LLC
1600 Huron Pkwy (48109-5001)
PHONE.................................734 998-8339
John Freshley, *CEO*
David Zacks, *President*
Anna Schwendeman, *Vice Pres*
Andrew Kocab, *Manager*
EMP: 4
SALES (est): 315.7K **Privately Held**
SIC: 2834 8731 Pharmaceutical preparations; biological research

(G-584)
OPHIR CRAFTS LLC
Also Called: Ophir Yarn and Fiber
1522 N Maple Rd (48103-2412)
PHONE.................................734 794-7777
EMP: 3
SALES (est): 347.7K **Privately Held**
SIC: 2282 5945 Throwing/Winding Mill Ret Hobbies/Toys/Games

(G-585)
OPTEOS INC
775 Technology Dr Ste 200 (48108-8948)
PHONE.................................734 929-3333
Kyoung Yang, *President*
EMP: 5
SALES (est): 494.8K **Privately Held**
SIC: 3825 Test equipment for electronic & electric measurement

(G-586)
OVA SCIENCE INC
301 N Main St Ste 100 (48104-1296)
PHONE.................................617 758-8605
EMP: 3
SALES (est): 183.1K **Privately Held**
SIC: 2835 In vitro & in vivo diagnostic substances

(G-587)
OXFORD INSTRUMENTS AMERICA INC
120 Enterprise Dr (48103-9282)
PHONE.................................734 821-3003
EMP: 11
SALES (corp-wide): 429.1MM **Privately Held**
SIC: 3829 Medical diagnostic systems, nuclear
HQ: Oxford Instruments America, Inc.
300 Baker Ave Ste 150
Concord MA 01742
978 369-9933

(G-588)
PACIFIC INDUSTRIAL DEV CORP (PA)
4788 Runway Blvd (48108-9557)
PHONE.................................734 930-9292
WEI Wu, *CEO*
Gang Wu, *General Mgr*
Jeffery Lachapelle, *Vice Pres*
Jacob Wilson, *Facilities Mgr*
Lee Flake, *CFO*
▲ **EMP:** 80
SQ FT: 150,000
SALES (est): 19.9MM **Privately Held**
WEB: www.pidc.com
SIC: 2819 Industrial inorganic chemicals

(G-589)
PERCEPTION ANLYTICS RBTICS LLC
3239 Kilburn Park Cir (48105-4125)
PHONE.................................734 846-5650
Vineet Kamat,
Manu Akula,
Suyang Dong,
EMP: 3
SALES (est): 133.9K **Privately Held**
SIC: 7372 Application computer software

(G-590)
PERFECTION SPRINKLER COMPANY
Also Called: Sure-Flo Fittings
2077 S State St (48104-4607)
P.O. Box 1363 (48106-1363)
PHONE.................................734 761-5110
Thomas R Wilkins, *President*
Charles Wilkins, *Admin Sec*
EMP: 8 **EST:** 1933
SQ FT: 9,500
SALES (est): 1.6MM **Privately Held**
WEB: www.sure-flo.com
SIC: 3494 Pipe fittings

(G-591)
PERFORM3-D LLC
411 Huronview Blvd # 200 (48103-2973)
PHONE.................................734 604-4100
Timothy Lock,
EMP: 6
SALES (est): 538.7K **Privately Held**
SIC: 3827 Optical instruments & apparatus

(G-592)
PHOENIX SOUND SYSTEMS
3514 W Liberty Rd (48103-9013)
PHONE.................................734 662-6405
Robert Frushower, *President*
EMP: 3
SQ FT: 2,000
SALES (est): 422K **Privately Held**
WEB: www.phoenixsound.com
SIC: 3679 5945 Recording & playback apparatus, including phonograph; hobby, toy & game shops

(G-593)
PITTSFIELD PRODUCTS INC (PA)
Also Called: Pittsfield of Indiana
5741 Jackson Rd (48103-9199)
P.O. Box 1027 (48106-1027)
PHONE.................................734 665-3771
Theodore Fosdick, *President*
▲ **EMP:** 45
SQ FT: 15,000
SALES (est): 35.1MM **Privately Held**
WEB: www.pittsfieldproducts.com
SIC: 3569 3564 3496 3494 Filters, general line: industrial; blowers & fans; miscellaneous fabricated wire products; valves & pipe fittings

(G-594)
POLK GAS PRODUCER LLC
414 S Main St Ste 600 (48104-2398)
PHONE.................................734 913-2970
Mark Cousino, *Manager*
EMP: 4
SALES (est): 374.1K **Privately Held**
SIC: 3569 Gas producers, generators & other gas related equipment

(G-595)
POLYTORX LLC (DH)
Also Called: Helix Steel
2300 Washtenaw Ave # 200 (48104-4500)
PHONE.................................734 322-2114
Chris Doran, *CEO*
Luke Pinkerton, *President*
Kate Hanke, *Office Mgr*
Arkady Horak, *Director*
◆ **EMP:** 4
SQ FT: 1,000
SALES (est): 2.1MM
SALES (corp-wide): 2.4MM **Privately Held**
WEB: www.helixfiber.com
SIC: 3496 Concrete reinforcing mesh & wire

(G-596)
POSSIBILITIES FOR CHANGE LLC
674 S Wagner Rd (48103-9002)
P.O. Box 331, Brighton (48116-0331)
PHONE.................................810 333-1347
Jennifer Salerno, *CEO*
EMP: 4
SALES (est): 728.4K **Privately Held**
SIC: 7372 Educational computer software

(G-597)
POWER SPORTS ANN ARBOR LLC
Also Called: Nicholson's
4405 Jackson Rd (48103-1833)
PHONE.................................734 585-3300
Mary Gulliver, *Principal*
Charles Stephenson,
EMP: 13
SALES (est): 1.3MM **Privately Held**
SIC: 3799 All terrain vehicles (ATV); snowmobiles

(G-598)
PRECISE METAL COMPONENTS INC
91 Enterprise Dr Ste A (48103-9126)
PHONE.................................734 769-0790
James C Dickert, *President*
Andrea Stager, *Treasurer*
Gus Stager, *Admin Sec*
EMP: 6
SQ FT: 5,000
SALES: 1.2MM **Privately Held**
SIC: 7389 3599 Grinding, precision: commercial or industrial; machine shop, jobbing & repair

(G-599)
PRECISION CONTROLS COMPANY
107 Enterprise Dr (48103-9564)
PHONE.................................734 663-3104
William Olzack, *President*
Lawrence Murphy, *Admin Sec*
▲ **EMP:** 25 **EST:** 1955
SQ FT: 6,000
SALES (est): 3.8MM **Privately Held**
SIC: 3625 Relays & industrial controls

(G-600)
PRECISION MANUFACTURING SVCS
3738 W Liberty Rd (48103-9014)
PHONE.................................734 995-3505
Borje Rosaen, *President*
Denver Lewis, *Corp Secy*
Tricia Rosaen, *Vice Pres*
Dwight Morningstar, *Prdtn Mgr*
EMP: 9 **EST:** 1979
SQ FT: 7,000
SALES (est): 1.5MM **Privately Held**
WEB: www.precisionmanufacturingservices.com
SIC: 3599 Machine shop, jobbing & repair

(G-601)
PRECISION MEASUREMENT CO
885 Oakdale Rd (48105-1076)
P.O. Box 7676 (48107-7676)
PHONE.................................734 995-0041
Sam Clark, *President*
EMP: 25
SALES (est): 2.7MM **Privately Held**
WEB: www.pmctransducers.com
SIC: 3829 Pressure transducers

(G-602)
PREHAB TECHNOLOGIES LLC
Also Called: Prenovo
103 E Liberty St Ste 201 (48104-2136)
PHONE.................................734 368-9983
Lora Kerr, *CEO*
Siobhan Norman, *General Mgr*
June Sullivan, *Info Tech Mgr*
EMP: 9 **EST:** 2015
SQ FT: 700
SALES (est): 308.9K **Privately Held**
SIC: 7372 7371 Business oriented computer software; computer software development & applications

(G-603)
PRIBUSIN INC
3938 Trade Center Dr (48108-2072)
PHONE.................................734 677-0459
Victor Buhr, *President*
David Price, *Corp Secy*
Michael Gerstweiler, *Vice Pres*
EMP: 3
SQ FT: 480
SALES (est): 230.4K **Privately Held**
WEB: www.pribusin.com
SIC: 3679 Microwave components

(G-604)
PRINT-TECH INC
6800 Jackson Rd (48103-9565)
PHONE.................................734 996-2345
James Ceely, *President*
Margaret Loy, *Marketing Staff*
▲ **EMP:** 28
SQ FT: 15,000
SALES (est): 4.7MM **Privately Held**
WEB: www.printtechinc.com
SIC: 2752 2791 2789 Commercial printing, offset; typesetting; bookbinding & related work

(G-605)
PRO-FACE AMERICA LLC (HQ)
Also Called: Proface America
1050 Highland Dr Ste D (48108-2262)
PHONE.................................734 477-0600
Peter Klein, *Vice Pres*
Cindy Bunton, *Accountant*
Jeff Scallion, *Sales Staff*
Mike Yeager, *Sales Staff*
Russell Hawkins, *Marketing Staff*
▲ **EMP:** 48 **EST:** 1968
SQ FT: 108,000
SALES: 8.5MM
SALES (corp-wide): 177.9K **Privately Held**
WEB: www.xycom.com
SIC: 3575 3577 3571 Computer terminals; computer peripheral equipment; minicomputers
PA: Schneider Electric Se
35 Rue Joseph Monier
Rueil-Malmaison
146 046-982

(G-606)
PROQUEST OUTDOOR SOLUTIONS INC
789 E Eisenhower Pkwy (48108-3218)
PHONE.................................734 761-4700
Sandra Parr, *Publisher*
Bruce Rhoads, *Senior VP*
Simon Beale, *Vice Pres*
John Campbell, *Vice Pres*
Christopher Cowan, *Vice Pres*
EMP: 3
SALES (est): 19.7K
SALES (corp-wide): 29.5MM **Privately Held**
WEB: www.proquestcompany.com
SIC: 2741 Miscellaneous publishing
HQ: Voyager Learning Company
17855 Dallas Pkwy Ste 400
Dallas TX 75287
214 932-9500

(G-607)
PSI LABS
3970 Varsity Dr (48108-2226)
PHONE.................................734 369-6273
EMP: 5
SALES (est): 460.7K **Privately Held**
SIC: 3999 8734 ; testing laboratories

(G-608)
Q-PHOTONICS LLC
3830 Packard St Ste 170 (48108-2272)
PHONE.................................734 477-0133
George Loutts, *CEO*
Run Liu, *Engineer*
WEI Yang, *Sales Engr*
◆ **EMP:** 4 **EST:** 2000
SQ FT: 1,200
SALES (est): 900K **Privately Held**
WEB: www.qphotonics.com
SIC: 3826 Laser scientific & engineering instruments

(G-609)
QE TOOLS LLC
417 8th St (48103-4751)
PHONE.................................734 330-4707
Patrick Hammett, *President*
EMP: 3
SALES: 30K **Privately Held**
SIC: 7372 Business oriented computer software

(G-610)
QUAD CITY INNOVATIONS LLC
Also Called: Q C I
600 S Wagner Rd (48103-9002)
PHONE.................................513 200-6980
Ronald Jona, *Mng Member*
EMP: 5
SALES (est): 1MM **Privately Held**
SIC: 3699 Electrical equipment & supplies

(G-611)
QUALITY FILTERS INC
7215 Jackson Rd Ste 3 (48103-9536)
P.O. Box 129, Dexter (48130-0129)
PHONE.................................734 668-0211
George Spottswood, *CEO*
David M Husak, *President*
EMP: 13
SQ FT: 20,000

Ann Arbor - Washtenaw County (G-612)

SALES (est): 292.3K **Privately Held**
WEB: www.qualityfilters.com
SIC: 3569 3564 3496 3494 Filters, general line: industrial; filter elements, fluid, hydraulic line; blowers & fans; miscellaneous fabricated wire products; valves & pipe fittings

(G-612)
REBO LIGHTING & ELEC LLC
3990 Research Park Dr (48108-2220)
PHONE 734 213-4159
Yu Zhang, *Mng Member*
EMP: 17
SQ FT: 100,000
SALES (est): 748K
SALES (corp-wide): 17.8MM **Privately Held**
SIC: 3647 Automotive lighting fixtures
HQ: Chongqing Boao Industrial Co., Ltd.
No.2, Huixing Road, Beibu New Area
Chongqing 40112

(G-613)
RED TIN BOAT
4081 Thornoaks Dr (48104-4253)
PHONE 734 239-3796
Middy Matthews, *Principal*
EMP: 3
SALES (est): 206.5K **Privately Held**
SIC: 3356 Tin

(G-614)
REGENER-EYES LLC
330 E Liberty St Ll (48104-2274)
PHONE 248 207-4641
Ranjit Kommineni, *CEO*
Ann Arbor,
EMP: 4
SALES (est): 180K **Privately Held**
SIC: 3674 Solid state electronic devices

(G-615)
REGENTS OF THE UNIVERSITY MICH
Also Called: Printing & Auxiliary Services
1919 Green Rd (48109-2564)
PHONE 734 764-6230
Pat Squires, *Manager*
EMP: 50
SALES (corp-wide): 7.4B **Privately Held**
WEB: www.umich.edu
SIC: 2731 2759 2752 2396 Book publishing; commercial printing; commercial printing, lithographic; automotive & apparel trimmings
PA: Regents Of The University Of Michigan
503 Thompson St
Ann Arbor MI 48109
734 764-1817

(G-616)
REGENTS OF THE UNIVERSITY MICH
Also Called: University of Michigan Press
839 Greene St (48104-3209)
PHONE 734 764-4388
Gabriella Beres, *Manager*
EMP: 30
SALES (corp-wide): 7.4B **Privately Held**
WEB: www.umich.edu
SIC: 2731 8221 Book publishing; university
PA: Regents Of The University Of Michigan
503 Thompson St
Ann Arbor MI 48109
734 764-1817

(G-617)
REGENTS OF THE UNIVERSITY MICH
Also Called: University Michigan Software
3003 S State St Spc 1272 (48109-1272)
PHONE 734 936-0435
Kenneth Nisbet, *Director*
EMP: 18
SALES (corp-wide): 7.4B **Privately Held**
WEB: www.umich.edu
SIC: 7372 8221 Prepackaged software; university
PA: Regents Of The University Of Michigan
503 Thompson St
Ann Arbor MI 48109
734 764-1817

(G-618)
REGENTS OF THE UNIVERSITY MICH
Also Called: Orthotics & Prosthetics Center
2850 S Industrial Hwy # 400 (48104-6796)
PHONE 734 973-2400
Anita Limberman-Lampear, *Director*
EMP: 34
SALES (corp-wide): 7.4B **Privately Held**
WEB: www.umich.edu
SIC: 3842 8221 Surgical appliances & supplies; university
PA: Regents Of The University Of Michigan
503 Thompson St
Ann Arbor MI 48109
734 764-1817

(G-619)
RELEAF MICHIGAN INC
1100 N Main St Ste 105 (48104-1073)
PHONE 734 662-6350
Chris Pargoff, *President*
William Lawrence, *President*
Charles Honkala, *Treasurer*
Melinda Jones, *Exec Dir*
EMP: 3
SALES: 166.4K **Privately Held**
WEB: www.globalreleaf.org
SIC: 3822 Auto controls regulating residntl & coml environmt & applncs

(G-620)
RETROSENSE THERAPEUTICS LLC
330 E Liberty St Ll (48104-2274)
PHONE 734 369-9333
Sean Ainsworth, *CEO*
Steven Bramer, *Officer*
Peter Francis, *Officer*
CAM Gallagher, *Officer*
EMP: 4
SALES (est): 559.3K **Privately Held**
SIC: 2835 8731 In vitro & in vivo diagnostic substances; biotechnical research, commercial
PA: Allergan Holdings Unlimited Company
Clonshaugh Business & Technology Park
Dublin

(G-621)
RIPPLE SCIENCE CORPORATION
303 Detroit St Ste 100 (48104-1128)
PHONE 919 451-0241
Nestor Lopez-Duran, *President*
Jacob Bonenberger, *Co-Owner*
EMP: 5 EST: 2016
SALES (est): 195.3K **Privately Held**
SIC: 7372 Application computer software

(G-622)
ROBBIE DEAN PRESS LLC
2910 E Eisenhower Pkwy (48108-3222)
PHONE 734 973-9511
Dr Fairy C Hayes-Scott, *Mng Member*
Donald Cardinal, *Assoc Prof*
▲ EMP: 5
SALES (est): 364.4K **Privately Held**
WEB: www.robbiedeanpress.com
SIC: 2731 Books: publishing only

(G-623)
ROBERT BOSCH LLC
3021 Miller Rd (48103-2122)
PHONE 734 302-2000
EMP: 4
SALES (est): 271.3K **Privately Held**
SIC: 3565 Mfg Packaging Machinery

(G-624)
ROSEDALE PRODUCTS INC (PA)
3730 W Liberty Rd (48103-9763)
P.O. Box 1085 (48106-1085)
PHONE 734 665-8201
Nils N Rosaen, *President*
Denver Lewis, *Vice Pres*
Carl Gnath, *Materials Mgr*
Steve Cannaert, *Engineer*
Jeff Kerner, *Plant Engr*
◆ EMP: 62 EST: 1972
SQ FT: 35,000
SALES (est): 15.2MM **Privately Held**
WEB: www.rosedaleproducts.com
SIC: 3569 3564 3494 Filters, general line: industrial; blowers & fans; valves & pipe fittings

(G-625)
RSR SALES INC
Also Called: RSR Industries
232 Haeussler Ct (48103-6203)
P.O. Box 2741 (48106-2741)
PHONE 734 668-8166
Richard Cohen, *President*
▲ EMP: 20
SQ FT: 6,000
SALES (est): 5.1MM **Privately Held**
SIC: 5072 3429 Hardware; manufactured hardware (general)

(G-626)
S-3 ENGINEERING INC
95 Enterprise Dr (48103-9503)
PHONE 734 996-2303
Andrea Stager, *President*
Augustus P Stager III, *Vice Pres*
EMP: 10 EST: 1973
SQ FT: 10,000
SALES (est): 1.8MM **Privately Held**
WEB: www.s-three.com
SIC: 3599 Machine shop, jobbing & repair

(G-627)
SAAGARA LLC
709 W Ellsworth Rd # 200 (48108-3371)
PHONE 734 658-4693
Nagabhushanam Peddi, *CEO*
EMP: 10
SALES (est): 720.1K **Privately Held**
SIC: 7372 Application computer software

(G-628)
SENSIGMA LLC
3660 Plaza Dr (48108-1685)
PHONE 734 998-8328
Aparajita Mazumber, *Vice Pres*
Jyoti Mazumder, *Officer*
EMP: 6
SALES (est): 551.4K **Privately Held**
SIC: 3699 8731 Electrical equipment & supplies; electronic research

(G-629)
SHAREDBOOK INC
Also Called: Academicpub Xanedu
4750 Venture Dr Ste 400 (48108-9505)
PHONE 734 302-6500
Jason Plackowski, *CFO*
EMP: 20 EST: 2003
SALES (est): 465.3K **Privately Held**
SIC: 2741 Miscellaneous publishing

(G-630)
SHUTTERBOOTH
4972 S Ridgeside Cir (48105-9447)
PHONE 734 680-6067
Michael Robins, *Principal*
EMP: 3
SALES (est): 189.1K **Privately Held**
SIC: 3442 Shutters, door or window: metal

(G-631)
SIEMENS PRODUCT LIFE MGMT SFTW
2600 Green Rd Ste 100 (48105-4632)
PHONE 734 994-7300
Anna Newton, *Project Mgr*
Robert Haubrock, *Manager*
EMP: 75
SALES (corp-wide): 95B **Privately Held**
SIC: 7372 Business oriented computer software
HQ: Siemens Industry Software Inc.
5800 Granite Pkwy Ste 600
Plano TX 75024
972 987-3000

(G-632)
SIGNARAMA ANN ARBOR
4655 Washtenaw Ave (48108-1301)
PHONE 734 221-5141
Megan Yu, *Principal*
EMP: 3
SALES (est): 121.6K **Privately Held**
SIC: 3993 Signs, not made in custom sign painting shops

(G-633)
SIGNS BY TOMORROW
3965 Varsity Dr (48108-2225)
PHONE 734 822-0537
Joe Reynolds, *Principal*
EMP: 3
SALES (est): 321.4K **Privately Held**
SIC: 3993 Signs & advertising specialties

(G-634)
SIZZL LLC
721 S Forest Ave Apt 309 (48104-3157)
PHONE 201 454-1938
Atharva Talpade, *Mng Member*
Bhavisk Gummadi,
Ryan Helmlinger,
EMP: 10
SALES: 12K **Privately Held**
SIC: 7372 7389 Application computer software;

(G-635)
SKY PROMOTIONS
3990 Calgary Ct (48108-2797)
PHONE 248 613-1637
Bennett Borsuk, *Owner*
Mary Mills, *Advt Staff*
EMP: 12
SALES (est): 570K **Privately Held**
SIC: 3993 Signs & advertising specialties

(G-636)
SKYSYNC INC
Also Called: Portal Architects
801 W Ellsworth Rd # 200 (48108-3314)
PHONE 734 822-6858
Mark Brazeau, *CEO*
Garth Jackson, *Corp Secy*
Nicky Borcea, *Vice Pres*
EMP: 50 EST: 2012
SQ FT: 3,156
SALES (est): 12.2MM **Privately Held**
SIC: 7372 Prepackaged software

(G-637)
SNIFFER ROBOTICS LLC
330 E Liberty St (48104-2274)
PHONE 855 476-4333
Arthur Mohrm,
David Barron,
Bob Dentzman,
EMP: 4
SALES (est): 154.7K **Privately Held**
SIC: 3812 Search & navigation equipment

(G-638)
SOLAR TONIC LLC (PA)
2232 S Main St Ste 364 (48103-6938)
PHONE 734 368-0215
Brian Tell, *Managing Prtnr*
Harry Giles, *Managing Prtnr*
EMP: 8
SALES (est): 1.1MM **Privately Held**
SIC: 3648 Street lighting fixtures

(G-639)
SOLIDICA INC
5840 Interface Dr Ste 200 (48103-9176)
P.O. Box 4248 (48106-4248)
PHONE 734 222-4680
Ken Johnson, *CEO*
John Ford, *COO*
EMP: 15
SQ FT: 9,000
SALES: 2.1MM **Privately Held**
WEB: www.solidica.com
SIC: 3541 3822 Machine tools, metal cutting type; temperature sensors for motor windings

(G-640)
SOLOHILL ENGINEERING INC
4370 Varsity Dr Ste B (48108-2359)
PHONE 734 973-2956
Tim Solomon, *CEO*
David E Solomon, *Ch of Bd*
Mark Szczypka, *President*
Dr William J Hillegas, *Vice Pres*
Kris Conley, *CFO*
EMP: 30
SQ FT: 24,000
SALES (est): 2.3MM **Privately Held**
WEB: www.solohill.com
SIC: 2833 Medicinal chemicals

GEOGRAPHIC SECTION
Ann Arbor - Washtenaw County (G-665)

(G-641)
SONETICS ULTRASOUND INC
2890 Carptr Rd Ste 1800 (48108)
PHONE..................734 260-4800
Jennifer Baird, *CEO*
Cullen Rich, *Principal*
David Lemmerhilt, *Research*
EMP: 3
SALES (est): 276.3K **Privately Held**
SIC: 3841 Medical instruments & equipment, blood & bone work

(G-642)
SPOTTED DOG WINERY
5743 Ping Dr (48108-8580)
PHONE..................734 944-9463
John Olsen, *Principal*
EMP: 3
SALES (est): 217.7K **Privately Held**
SIC: 2084 Wines

(G-643)
SPRY PUBLISHING LLC
315 E Eisenhower Pkwy # 2 (48108-3329)
PHONE..................877 722-2264
James M Edwards, *Mng Member*
Jim Edwards, *Officer*
EMP: 8
SALES (est): 477.1K **Privately Held**
SIC: 2741 Miscellaneous publishing

(G-644)
STAMATOPOLOS & SONS
869 W Eisenhower Pkwy (48103-6641)
PHONE..................734 369-2995
EMP: 3
SALES (est): 137.9K **Privately Held**
SIC: 2079 Olive oil

(G-645)
STEL TECHNOLOGIES LLC
600 S Wagner Rd Ste 142 (48103-9002)
PHONE..................248 802-9457
Lisa Larkin,
Michael Smietana,
EMP: 3
SALES (est): 255.9K **Privately Held**
SIC: 2836 Veterinary biological products

(G-646)
STEVES CUSTOM SIGNS INC
4676 Freedom Dr (48108-9104)
P.O. Box 799, Saline (48176-0799)
PHONE..................734 662-5964
Steve Jedele, *President*
EMP: 12
SALES (est): 1.6MM **Privately Held**
SIC: 3993 Electric signs

(G-647)
STM POWER INC (PA)
275 Metty Dr (48103-9444)
PHONE..................734 214-1448
Dorrance J Noonan Jr, *President*
Mark Abbo, *Vice Pres*
EMP: 17
SQ FT: 19,000
SALES (est): 5MM **Privately Held**
WEB: www.stmpower.com
SIC: 3724 8731 Cooling systems, aircraft engine; industrial laboratory, except testing

(G-648)
STRATEGIC COMPUTER SOLUTIONS
Also Called: S C S
2625 Shefman Ter Ste 200 (48105-3441)
PHONE..................248 888-0666
Leeron Kopelman, *President*
Matthew Rindfleisch, *Vice Pres*
Josh Ballard, *Senior Engr*
EMP: 4
SQ FT: 1,550
SALES: 750K **Privately Held**
WEB: www.stratcom.com
SIC: 7379 5045 7371 7372 Computer related consulting services; computer hardware requirements analysis; computers, peripherals & software; computer software systems analysis & design, custom; prepackaged software

(G-649)
STRATOS TECHNOLOGIES INC
617 Detroit St (48104-1112)
PHONE..................248 808-2117
Thiago Olson, *CEO*
Chris Bartenstein, *President*
Henry Balanon, *Principal*
Craig Sprinkle, *CFO*
EMP: 3
SQ FT: 200
SALES: 800K **Privately Held**
SIC: 3571 5731 Computers, digital, analog or hybrid; consumer electronic equipment

(G-650)
SUNRISE SCREEN PRINTING INC
Also Called: Sunrise Printed Embroidered AP
5277 Jackson Rd Ste C (48103-1869)
PHONE..................734 769-3888
Gregory Bornschein, *President*
EMP: 3
SQ FT: 2,000
SALES: 600K **Privately Held**
WEB: www.sunrisescreenprints.com
SIC: 2759 Screen printing

(G-651)
SUNTECH INDUSTRIALS LLC
5137 Colonial Ct (48108-8651)
PHONE..................734 678-5922
Christina Luo, *Administration*
EMP: 3
SALES (est): 191.7K **Privately Held**
SIC: 3646 Commercial indusl & institutional electric lighting fixtures

(G-652)
SWIFT BIOSCIENCES INC
674 S Wagner Rd Ste 100 (48103-9002)
PHONE..................734 330-2568
David Olson, *President*
Vladimir Makarov, *Officer*
EMP: 4
SALES (est): 1.2MM **Privately Held**
SIC: 2835 In vitro & in vivo diagnostic substances

(G-653)
SYMOREX LTD
3728 Plaza Dr Ste 3 (48108-3625)
PHONE..................734 971-6000
Chris Erickson, *President*
EMP: 18
SQ FT: 6,000
SALES (est): 6.5MM **Privately Held**
WEB: www.symorex.com
SIC: 5085 3625 3536 3535 Industrial supplies; relays & industrial controls; hoists, cranes & monorails; conveyors & conveying equipment

(G-654)
TECAT PERFORMANCE SYSTEMS LLC
705 Technology Dr (48108)
PHONE..................248 615-9862
Ron Rath, *CEO*
Douglas Baker, *Principal*
Joseph Byker, *Principal*
Brenda Duquette, *Administration*
EMP: 11
SALES (est): 572.2K **Privately Held**
SIC: 8711 3829 Engineering services; stress, strain & flaw detecting/measuring equipment

(G-655)
TECTUM HOLDINGS INC (DH)
5400 Data Ct (48108-8961)
PHONE..................734 677-0444
William Reminder, *President*
Kelly Kneifl, *COO*
Mark Hickey, *Exec VP*
David Wells, *Exec VP*
Jim Bresingham, *CFO*
EMP: 23
SALES (est): 276.9MM
SALES (corp-wide): 255.3MM **Privately Held**
SIC: 3713 5013 Truck bodies & parts; truck parts & accessories

HQ: Truck Hero, Inc.
5400 Data Ct Ste 100
Ann Arbor MI 48108
877 875-4376

(G-656)
TECTUM HOLDINGS INC
Also Called: Truck Hero Ann Arbor
4670 Runway Blvd (48108-9557)
PHONE..................734 926-2362
William Reminder, *CEO*
EMP: 100
SALES (corp-wide): 255.3MM **Privately Held**
SIC: 8748 3714 Test development & evaluation service; pickup truck bed liners
HQ: Tectum Holdings, Inc.
5400 Data Ct
Ann Arbor MI 48108
734 677-0444

(G-657)
TECUMSEH COMPRESSOR CO LLC
5683 Hines Dr (48108-7901)
PHONE..................662 566-2231
Doug Murdock, *President*
Michael Bauersfeld, *President*
William Prete, *Technical Staff*
EMP: 4680 **EST:** 2002
SALES (est): 109.6MM **Privately Held**
SIC: 3585 Compressors for refrigeration & air conditioning equipment

(G-658)
TECUMSEH COMPRESSOR COMPANY
1136 Oak Valley Dr (48108-9624)
PHONE..................734 585-9500
Michael Noelke, *Vice Pres*
Janice Stipp, *Treasurer*
Roger Jackson, *Admin Sec*
▲ **EMP:** 8
SALES (est): 1.1MM
SALES (corp-wide): 876.5MM **Privately Held**
WEB: www.tecumseh.com
SIC: 3585 Compressors for refrigeration & air conditioning equipment
HQ: Tecumseh Products Company Llc
5683 Hines Dr
Ann Arbor MI 48108
734 585-9500

(G-659)
TECUMSEH PRODUCTS COMPANY
Applied Electronics
4220 Varsity Dr Ste C (48108-5006)
PHONE..................734 973-1359
Jim Doyle, *Manager*
EMP: 10
SALES (corp-wide): 876.5MM **Privately Held**
WEB: www.tecumseh.com
SIC: 3585 Parts for heating, cooling & refrigerating equipment
HQ: Tecumseh Products Company Llc
5683 Hines Dr
Ann Arbor MI 48108
734 585-9500

(G-660)
TECUMSEH PRODUCTS COMPANY
5683 Hines Dr (48108-7901)
PHONE..................734 769-0650
Gary L Cowger, *Branch Mgr*
EMP: 225
SALES (corp-wide): 876.5MM **Privately Held**
SIC: 3585 Parts for heating, cooling & refrigerating equipment
HQ: Tecumseh Products Company Llc
5683 Hines Dr
Ann Arbor MI 48108
734 585-9500

(G-661)
TECUMSEH PRODUCTS COMPANY LLC (HQ)
5683 Hines Dr (48108-7901)
PHONE..................734 585-9500
Harold M Karp, *President*
Ronald E Pratt, *President*

Eric L Stolzenberg, *President*
Jerry L Mosingo, *Exec VP*
Ryan Burns, *Engineer*
◆ **EMP:** 1100 **EST:** 1930
SQ FT: 49,500
SALES (est): 1.4B
SALES (corp-wide): 876.5MM **Privately Held**
WEB: www.tecumseh.com
SIC: 3585 3679 Parts for heating, cooling & refrigerating equipment; compressors for refrigeration & air conditioning equipment; condensers, refrigeration; hermetic seals for electronic equipment
PA: Tecumseh Products Holdings Llc
5683 Hines Dr
Ann Arbor MI 48108
734 585-9500

(G-662)
TECUMSEH PRODUCTS COMPANY LLC
Also Called: Cool Products Division
5683 Hines Dr (48108-7901)
PHONE..................734 585-9500
Michael Forman, *Branch Mgr*
EMP: 6
SALES (corp-wide): 876.5MM **Privately Held**
WEB: www.tecumseh.com
SIC: 3585 Parts for heating, cooling & refrigerating equipment
HQ: Tecumseh Products Company Llc
5683 Hines Dr
Ann Arbor MI 48108
734 585-9500

(G-663)
TECUMSEH PRODUCTS HOLDINGS LLC (PA)
5683 Hines Dr (48108-7901)
PHONE..................734 585-9500
Gregory L Christopher, *CEO*
EMP: 10
SALES (est): 876.5MM **Privately Held**
SIC: 3585 3679 6719 Parts for heating, cooling & refrigerating equipment; hermetic seals for electronic equipment; investment holding companies, except banks

(G-664)
TERAMETRIX LLC
2725 S Industrial Hwy # 100 (48104-6281)
PHONE..................540 769-8430
Ricahrd Kurtz, *CEO*
Scott Graeff, *President*
Robin Risser, *COO*
John Duquette, *Engineer*
Jeff Anderson, *CFO*
EMP: 120
SQ FT: 50,335
SALES (est): 7.9MM
SALES (est): 42.9MM **Publicly Held**
WEB: www.picometrix.com
SIC: 3674 4823 Semiconductors & related devices; industrial instrmnts msrmnt display/control process variable
HQ: Former Luna Subsidiary, Inc.

Camarillo CA 93012

(G-665)
TERUMO AMERICAS HOLDING INC
Also Called: Terumo Cardiovascular Systems
6200 Jackson Rd (48103-9586)
PHONE..................734 663-4145
John Briddon, *General Mgr*
Masao Hitotsuyanagi, *General Mgr*
Alain Grenier, *Plant Mgr*
Viralyne Lipps, *Mfg Staff*
Arnt Danielsen, *Buyer*
EMP: 400 **Privately Held**
WEB: www.terumomedical.com
SIC: 3841 Needles, suture
HQ: Terumo Americas Holding, Inc.
265 Davidson Ave Ste 320
Somerset NJ 08873
732 302-4900

Ann Arbor - Washtenaw County (G-666)   GEOGRAPHIC SECTION

(G-666)
TERUMO CRDVSCULAR SYSTEMS CORP (DH)
Also Called: T C V S
6200 Jackson Rd (48103-9586)
PHONE.................................734 663-4145
Robert Deryke, *President*
Chris Zarecki, *Vice Pres*
James Doherty, *Production*
Jeff Simone, *QC Mgr*
Keith Reiner, *Technical Mgr*
▲ **EMP:** 250
SQ FT: 400,000
SALES (est): 221.5MM **Privately Held**
WEB: www.terumo-us.com
SIC: 3845 3841 Electromedical equipment; surgical & medical instruments; needles, suture; catheters
HQ: Terumo Americas Holding, Inc.
265 Davidson Ave Ste 320
Somerset NJ 08873
732 302-4900

(G-667)
TGI DIRECT INC
Also Called: Grimbac Division
1225 Rosewood St (48104-6226)
PHONE.................................810 239-5553
Melinda Arnson, *Project Mgr*
Sharon Kirt, *Project Mgr*
Doughlas Bacon, *Manager*
Donn Peel, *Manager*
Renee Kowal, *Administration*
EMP: 15
SQ FT: 9,600
SALES (corp-wide): 12.7MM **Privately Held**
WEB: www.tgidirect.com
SIC: 7331 2791 2759 2752 Mailing service; typesetting; commercial printing; commercial printing, lithographic
PA: Tgi Direct, Inc.
5365 Hill 23 Dr
Flint MI 48507
810 239-5553

(G-668)
THALNER ELECTRONIC LABS INC
Also Called: T E L
7235 Jackson Rd (48103-9550)
PHONE.................................734 761-4506
Timothy Boggs, *President*
Chris Lindsay, *Opers Staff*
Tim Boggs, *Engineer*
Richard Schoenfeldt, *CFO*
EMP: 30 **EST:** 1965
SQ FT: 17,000
SALES: 14.7MM **Privately Held**
WEB: www.thalner.com
SIC: 1731 3663 5099 Closed circuit television installation; television closed circuit equipment; video & audio equipment

(G-669)
THERMO FISHER SCIENTIFIC INC
2868 W Delhi Rd (48103-9011)
PHONE.................................734 662-4117
Katie McMullen, *Sales Staff*
EMP: 14
SALES (corp-wide): 24.3B **Publicly Held**
WEB: www.thermo.com
SIC: 3826 Analytical instruments
PA: Thermo Fisher Scientific Inc.
168 3rd Ave
Waltham MA 02451
781 622-1000

(G-670)
THETFORD CORPORATION (DH)
7101 Jackson Rd (48103-9506)
P.O. Box 1285 (48106-1285)
PHONE.................................734 769-6000
Stephane Cordeille, *CEO*
Kevin Phillips, *President*
Barry Eckel, *Vice Pres*
Peter Struijs, *CFO*
▲ **EMP:** 217
SQ FT: 89,000
SALES (est): 107.1MM
SALES (corp-wide): 482MM **Privately Held**
WEB: www.thetford.com
SIC: 3632 3089 2842 2621 Refrigerators, mechanical & absorption: household; toilets, portable chemical: plastic; sanitation preparations; sanitary tissue paper; metal sanitary ware; chemical preparations
HQ: Dkm, Ltd.
2515 South Rd
Poughkeepsie NY 12601
212 661-4600

(G-671)
THOMAS-WARD SYSTEMS LLC
314 Pauline Blvd (48103-5565)
PHONE.................................734 929-0644
Alicia Frenette,
EMP: 4
SALES (est): 420.5K **Privately Held**
SIC: 3559 Automotive related machinery

(G-672)
THOMSON REUTERS CORPORATION
100 Phoenix Dr (48108-2635)
PHONE.................................734 913-3930
Aaron Snapke, *Principal*
EMP: 89
SALES (corp-wide): 10.6B **Publicly Held**
SIC: 2731 Books: publishing only
HQ: Thomson Reuters Corporation
3 Times Sq
New York NY 10036
646 223-4000

(G-673)
THORATEC CORPORATION
6190 Jackson Rd (48103-9140)
PHONE.................................734 827-7422
EMP: 147
SALES (corp-wide): 30.5B **Publicly Held**
SIC: 3845 3841 Electromedical equipment; surgical & medical instruments
HQ: Thoratec Llc
6035 Stoneridge Dr
Pleasanton CA 94588
925 847-8600

(G-674)
THREE CHAIRS CO
215 S Ashley St (48104-1350)
PHONE.................................734 665-2796
Susan Monroe, *Branch Mgr*
EMP: 5
SALES (corp-wide): 2.3MM **Privately Held**
WEB: www.threechairs.com
SIC: 2392 Household furnishings
PA: Three Chairs Co.
208 S Ashley St
Ann Arbor MI 48104
734 665-2314

(G-675)
TISSUE SEAL LLC
Also Called: Medical Product Manufacturer
4401 Varsity Dr Ste D (48108-5003)
PHONE.................................734 213-5530
Mike Perkaj, *Accounts Mgr*
Stephen Shulman, *Mng Member*
EMP: 10
SALES (est): 2.1MM **Privately Held**
SIC: 3069 Medical & laboratory rubber sundries & related products

(G-676)
TITANIA SOFTWARE LLC
2232 S Main St Ste 454 (48103-6938)
P.O. Box 428, Saline (48176-0428)
PHONE.................................734 786-8225
Timothy Allen, *President*
Scott Youngblom, *Corp Secy*
Scott Allen, *COO*
Stephanie Castillo, *Vice Pres*
Joseph Jenkins, *Vice Pres*
EMP: 7 **EST:** 2012
SQ FT: 2,000
SALES (est): 203.3K **Privately Held**
SIC: 7372 Business oriented computer software

(G-677)
TLS PRODUCTIONS INC
78 Jackson Plz (48103-1917)
PHONE.................................810 220-8577
William Ross, *President*
Kirt Bachiero, *Vice Pres*
Brad Hayes, *Vice Pres*
Sue McCloy, *Vice Pres*
Phil Stroud, *Opers Mgr*
EMP: 24
SQ FT: 41,126
SALES (est): 4.4MM **Privately Held**
WEB: www.tobinslake.com
SIC: 1799 3648 7922 Rigging, theatrical; stage lighting equipment; lighting, theatrical

(G-678)
TMC FURNITURE INC
119 E Ann St (48104-1414)
PHONE.................................734 622-0080
Blake Ratcliffe, *President*
Madison Rosneck, *Sales Staff*
Joy Johnsen, *Marketing Staff*
EMP: 7
SALES (corp-wide): 3.3MM **Privately Held**
WEB: www.tmcfurniture.com
SIC: 2531 Public building & related furniture
PA: Tmc Furniture, Inc.
4525 Airwest Dr Se
Kentwood MI 49512
734 622-0080

(G-679)
TOMUKUN NOODLE BAR
505 E Liberty St Ste 200 (48104-2465)
PHONE.................................734 995-8668
EMP: 8
SALES (est): 670.4K **Privately Held**
SIC: 2098 Noodles (e.g. egg, plain & water), dry

(G-680)
TRENTON CORPORATION (PA)
7700 Jackson Rd (48103-9545)
PHONE.................................734 424-3600
Charles Kennedy, *President*
Milton Weidmayer, *Treasurer*
Pete Gallus, *Sales Mgr*
David Snell, *Marketing Staff*
Merrilyn Akpapuna, *Consultant*
◆ **EMP:** 25 **EST:** 1949
SQ FT: 20,000
SALES (est): 13.9MM **Privately Held**
WEB: www.trentoncorp.com
SIC: 5169 2891 Anti-corrosion products; mucilage

(G-681)
TRUCK ACQUISITION INC (HQ)
5400 Data Ct (48108-8961)
PHONE.................................877 875-4376
William Reminder, *CEO*
EMP: 2
SALES: 255.3MM **Privately Held**
SIC: 3714 Pickup truck bed liners
PA: Truck Holdings Inc.
5400 Data Ct Ste 100
Ann Arbor MI 48108
877 875-4376

(G-682)
TRUCK HERO INC (DH)
5400 Data Ct Ste 100 (48108-8961)
PHONE.................................877 875-4376
William Reminder, *President*
Kelly Kneifl, *COO*
Ryan Herman, *Exec VP*
Robert Gaarder, *Vice Pres*
Jim Bresingham, *CFO*
EMP: 100 **EST:** 2015
SALES (est): 278.9MM
SALES (corp-wide): 255.3MM **Privately Held**
SIC: 3714 Pickup truck bed liners
HQ: Truck Acquisition Inc
5400 Data Ct
Ann Arbor MI 48108
877 875-4376

(G-683)
TRUCK HOLDINGS INC (PA)
5400 Data Ct Ste 100 (48108-8961)
PHONE.................................877 875-4376
William Reminder, *CEO*
EMP: 2
SALES: 255.3MM **Privately Held**
SIC: 3714 6719 Pickup truck bed liners; investment holding companies, except banks

(G-684)
TYLER TECHNOLOGIES INC
525 Avis Dr Ste 3 (48108-9616)
PHONE.................................734 677-0550
Marv McElzain, *Principal*
Michael Hitchcock, *Engineer*
Eric Burnson, *Executive*
EMP: 15
SALES (corp-wide): 935.2MM **Publicly Held**
SIC: 7371 7372 Computer software development; prepackaged software
PA: Tyler Technologies, Inc.
5101 Tennyson Pkwy
Plano TX 75024
972 713-3700

(G-685)
UBE MACHINERY INC
Also Called: Ube Industries
5700 S State Rd (48108-9634)
PHONE.................................734 741-7000
Mitsuhiro Kawamura, *President*
Yasuhiro Inoue, *Principal*
Pat Berry, *Plant Mgr*
Romica Vlad, *Engineer*
Satoshi Nishioka, *Treasurer*
▲ **EMP:** 60
SQ FT: 47,000
SALES (est): 18.8MM **Privately Held**
WEB: www.ubemachinery.com
SIC: 3559 5084 3363 3354 Plastics working machinery; clay working & tempering machines; industrial machinery & equipment; plastic products machinery; aluminum die-castings; aluminum extruded products
HQ: Ube Machinery Corporation,Ltd.
1980, Azaokinoyama, Kogushi
Ube YMG 755-0

(G-686)
ULTRAMOUSE LTD
1442 E Park Pl (48104-4347)
PHONE.................................734 761-1144
Ann Clinger, *President*
EMP: 3 **EST:** 1985
SALES (est): 244.1K **Privately Held**
SIC: 3999 5999 Pet supplies; pet supplies

(G-687)
UM ORTHOTICS PROS CNTR
2500 Green Rd Ste 100 (48105-1573)
PHONE.................................734 764-3100
EMP: 3
SALES (est): 107.6K **Privately Held**
SIC: 3842 Orthopedic appliances

(G-688)
UNIVERSITY PLASTICS INC
7150 Jackson Rd (48103-9552)
PHONE.................................734 668-8773
William C Trachet, *President*
Lydia Trachet, *Vice Pres*
EMP: 7 **EST:** 1975
SQ FT: 4,800
SALES: 700K **Privately Held**
SIC: 3089 Injection molded finished plastic products

(G-689)
UREFER INC
Also Called: Amplifinity
912 N Main St Ste 100 (48104-1055)
PHONE.................................734 585-5684
Bill Weissman, *CEO*
Susie Paisley, *Vice Pres*
Eric Jacobson, *CFO*
EMP: 7
SALES (est): 923.3K
SALES (corp-wide): 12.5MM **Privately Held**
SIC: 7372 Business oriented computer software
PA: Impartner, Inc.
10619 S Jordan Gtwy # 130
South Jordan UT 84095
801 501-7000

GEOGRAPHIC SECTION

Armada - Macomb County (G-716)

(G-690)
VAN BOVEN INCORPORATED
Also Called: Van Boven Clothing
326 S State St (48104-2412)
P.O. Box 4600 (48106-4600)
PHONE..................................734 665-7228
James A Orr, *President*
Tom Haney, *General Mgr*
Susan A Orr, *Vice Pres*
EMP: 7
SQ FT: 2,000
SALES (est): 1.1MM **Privately Held**
WEB: www.vanboven.com
SIC: 5611 2329 Suits, men's; clothing accessories: men's & boys'; men's & boys' sportswear & athletic clothing

(G-691)
VANROTH LLC
Also Called: Blue Lion Fitness
401 S Maple Rd (48103-3834)
PHONE..................................734 929-5268
Daniel Roth, *Mng Member*
Ryan Van Bergen,
EMP: 10 **EST:** 2015
SALES: 480K **Privately Held**
SIC: 7991 7372 Physical fitness facilities; application computer software

(G-692)
VIDATAK LLC
1327 Jones Dr Ste 203 (48105-1898)
PHONE..................................877 392-6273
Lance Patak,
Bryan Traughber,
◆ **EMP:** 4
SALES (est): 270K **Privately Held**
WEB: www.vidatak.com
SIC: 5047 3669 Medical equipment & supplies; intercommunication systems, electric

(G-693)
VISIUN INC
Also Called: Management Insight Analytics
3865 S Michael Rd (48103-9345)
PHONE..................................734 741-0356
Thomas Joseph, *President*
Denis Burke, *Co-Owner*
EMP: 7
SALES (est): 463.5K **Privately Held**
SIC: 7372 Application computer software

(G-694)
WANDRES CORPORATION
719 W Ellsworth Rd Ste 7 (48108-1663)
PHONE..................................734 214-9903
Justin Elsley, *Vice Pres*
Tom Longanbach, *Sales Mgr*
Stefan Schatz, *Sales Mgr*
Tarola Klingele, *Office Mgr*
▲ **EMP:** 10
SQ FT: 3,600
SALES (est): 1.7MM **Privately Held**
WEB: www.wandresusa.com
SIC: 3471 Cleaning, polishing & finishing

(G-695)
WARMILU LLC
8186 Jackson Rd Ste C (48103-9802)
PHONE..................................855 927-6458
Grace Hsia, *CEO*
Larrea Young, *COO*
Douglas Wolf, *Project Mgr*
Gerry Hanson, *Technical Staff*
EMP: 8 **EST:** 2012
SQ FT: 2,041
SALES: 47.5K **Privately Held**
SIC: 3841 Surgical & medical instruments

(G-696)
WASHTENAW COMMUNICATIONS INC
1510 Saunders Cres (48103-2534)
PHONE..................................734 662-7138
Kenneth L Aungst, *President*
EMP: 8
SALES: 125K **Privately Held**
SIC: 5731 7622 3663 Radios, two-way, citizens' band, weather, short-wave, etc.; radio repair & installation; radio broadcasting & communications equipment

(G-697)
WASHTENAW VOICE
4800 E Huron River Dr (48105-9481)
PHONE..................................734 677-5405
EMP: 3
SALES (est): 124.6K **Privately Held**
SIC: 2711 Newspapers, publishing & printing

(G-698)
WHITE LOTUS FARMS INC
7217 W Liberty Rd (48103-9381)
PHONE..................................734 904-1379
EMP: 7
SALES: 432.1K **Privately Held**
SIC: 0214 2051 0182 2022 Goat farm; buns, bread type: fresh or frozen; vegetable crops grown under cover; natural cheese

(G-699)
WHITE PINES CORPORATION
5204 Jackson Rd Ste 1 (48103-1866)
PHONE..................................734 761-2670
Martha Edwards, *President*
Bob Weber, *Sales Staff*
EMP: 30
SQ FT: 20,000
SALES (est): 4.8MM
SALES (corp-wide): 6.4MM **Privately Held**
SIC: 2752 Commercial printing, offset
PA: Foresight Group, Inc.
2822 N Martin Luther
Lansing MI 48906
517 485-5700

(G-700)
WOLVERINE GRINDING INC
160 N Staebler Rd Bldg B (48103-9755)
PHONE..................................734 769-4499
Roger Hamlin, *President*
EMP: 4
SQ FT: 4,000
SALES: 540K **Privately Held**
SIC: 3599 Machine shop, jobbing & repair

(G-701)
WOODWARD INC
331 Metty Dr Ste 4 (48103-9156)
PHONE..................................970 482-5811
EMP: 3
SALES (corp-wide): 2.3B **Publicly Held**
SIC: 3625 Industrial controls: push button, selector switches, pilot
PA: Woodward, Inc.
1081 Woodward Way
Fort Collins CO 80524
970 482-5811

(G-702)
WORD BARON INC
315 E Eisenhower Pkwy # 2 (48108-3350)
PHONE..................................248 471-4080
Cheryl E Baron, *President*
EMP: 10
SQ FT: 9,600
SALES (est): 837.1K **Privately Held**
WEB: www.thewordbaroninc.com
SIC: 7336 2752 Commercial art & graphic design; poster & decal printing, lithographic

(G-703)
XORAN HOLDINGS LLC (PA)
5210 S State Rd (48108-7936)
PHONE..................................734 418-5108
Jacqueline Vestevich,
EMP: 5
SALES (est): 24.8MM **Privately Held**
SIC: 3845 Ultrasonic scanning devices, medical

(G-704)
XORAN TECHNOLOGIES LLC
5210 S State Rd (48108-7936)
PHONE..................................734 663-7194
Jodie Haberkorn, *Controller*
EMP: 60 **EST:** 2015
SALES (est): 24.8MM **Privately Held**
SIC: 3845 Ultrasonic scanning devices, medical
PA: Xoran Holdings Llc
5210 S State Rd
Ann Arbor MI 48108
734 418-5108

(G-705)
XPO CNW INC (HQ)
2211 Old Earhart Rd (48105-2963)
PHONE..................................734 757-1444
Douglas W Stotlar, *President*
Stephen K Krull, *Exec VP*
Kevin S Coel, *Senior VP*
Leslie P Lundberg, *Senior VP*
Robert Musto, *Opers Staff*
EMP: 120
SALES (est): 6.1B
SALES (corp-wide): 17.2B **Publicly Held**
WEB: www.cnf.com
SIC: 4213 4731 3715 Contract haulers; less-than-truckload (LTL) transport; trailer or container on flat car (TOFC/COFC); domestic freight forwarding; foreign freight forwarding; customhouse brokers; truck trailers
PA: Xpo Logistics, Inc.
5 American Ln
Greenwich CT 06831
844 742-5976

(G-706)
ZCC USA INC
3622 W Liberty Rd (48103-9049)
PHONE..................................734 997-3811
Difei LI, *President*
Steve Ramirez, *Sales Staff*
▲ **EMP:** 17
SALES (est): 2.6MM
SALES (corp-wide): 181.2MM **Privately Held**
SIC: 3545 Machine tool accessories
PA: Zhuzhou Cemented Carbide Cutting Tools Co., Ltd.
Huanghe Nan Road, Tianyuan District,
Zhuzhou 41200
731 228-8946

(G-707)
ZIEL OPTICS INC
7167 Jackson Rd (48103-9506)
PHONE..................................734 994-9803
Eric Sieczka, *President*
Fred Collin, *Shareholder*
EMP: 7
SALES (est): 357.9K **Privately Held**
SIC: 3674 Solid state electronic devices

(G-708)
ZINGERMANS BAKEHOUSE INC
3711 Plaza Dr Ste 5 (48108-1680)
PHONE..................................734 761-2095
Frank Carollo, *President*
Amy Emberling, *Partner*
Paul Saginaw, *Corp Secy*
ARI Weinzweig, *Vice Pres*
Josh Pollock, *Project Mgr*
EMP: 60
SQ FT: 6,400
SALES (est): 12.7MM **Privately Held**
WEB: www.zingermansbakehouse.com
SIC: 2051 Bread, all types (white, wheat, rye, etc): fresh or frozen; pastries, e.g. danish: except frozen

(G-709)
ZINGERMANS CREAMERY LLC
3723 Plaza Dr Ste 2 (48108-3327)
PHONE..................................734 929-0500
John Loomis,
EMP: 12
SALES (est): 2MM **Privately Held**
SIC: 2022 Cheese, natural & processed

(G-710)
ZOMEDICA PHARMACEUTICAL INC
100 Phoenix Dr Ste 190 (48108-2636)
PHONE..................................734 369-2555
Gerald Solensky Jr, *Chairman*
EMP: 9
SALES (est): 212.3K
SALES (corp-wide): 1.8MM **Publicly Held**
SIC: 2834 Pharmaceutical preparations
PA: Zomedica Pharmaceuticals Corp.
100 Phoenix Dr Ste 190
Ann Arbor MI 48108
734 369-2555

(G-711)
ZOMEDICA PHARMACEUTICALS CORP (PA)
100 Phoenix Dr Ste 190 (48108-2636)
PHONE..................................734 369-2555
Stephanie Morley, *President*
Shameze Rampertab, *CFO*
Bruk Herbst, *Ch Credit Ofcr*
EMP: 18
SQ FT: 7,900
SALES (est): 1.8MM **Publicly Held**
SIC: 2834 Veterinary pharmaceutical preparations

Applegate
Sanilac County

(G-712)
MARTIN STRUCTURAL CONSULT
2300 Loree Rd (48401-9757)
PHONE..................................810 633-9111
Toll Free: ....888 -
Craig Martin, *President*
EMP: 8
SALES: 500K **Privately Held**
WEB: www.martinstructuralconsultants.com
SIC: 3272 Concrete stuctural support & building material

Argyle
Sanilac County

(G-713)
AVID INDUSTRIES INC
4887 Ubly Rd (48410)
PHONE..................................810 672-9100
William R Kroetsch, *President*
EMP: 4
SALES: 150K **Privately Held**
SIC: 3599 Machine shop, jobbing & repair

Armada
Macomb County

(G-714)
ARMADA GRAIN CO (PA)
73180 Fulton St (48005-4738)
P.O. Box 918 (48005-0918)
PHONE..................................586 784-5911
Lance Hollweg, *Owner*
Robert E Hollweg, *Vice Pres*
EMP: 35
SQ FT: 40,000
SALES (est): 16.4MM **Privately Held**
SIC: 5153 2048 Grains; feeds from meat & from meat & vegetable meals

(G-715)
ARMADA PRINTWEAR INC
Also Called: API Promotional Products
74135 Church St (48005-3334)
P.O. Box 518 (48005-0518)
PHONE..................................586 784-5553
Richard Mills, *President*
Paulina Mills, *Admin Sec*
EMP: 6
SQ FT: 9,000
SALES (est): 952.9K **Privately Held**
SIC: 2262 5199 Screen printing: man-made fiber & silk broadwoven fabrics; advertising specialties

(G-716)
ARMADA RUBBER MANUFACTURING CO
24586 Armada Ridge Rd (48005-4827)
P.O. Box 579 (48005-0579)
PHONE..................................586 784-9135
Lawrence Weymouth III, *President*
Lawrence Weymouth Jr, *President*
Dawn Weymouth, *Admin Sec*
EMP: 70 **EST:** 1947
SQ FT: 53,000

SALES: 21.6MM **Privately Held**
WEB: www.armadarubber.com
SIC: **3069** 3713 3643 3061 Rubber hardware; truck & bus bodies; current-carrying wiring devices; mechanical rubber goods; gaskets, packing & sealing devices; synthetic rubber

(G-717)
BLAKES ORCHARD INC (PA)
Also Called: Blake's Orchard & Cider Mill
17985 Armada Center Rd (48005-2323)
PHONE.................................586 784-5343
Peter Blake, *Owner*
Paul M Blake, *Treasurer*
EMP: 3 EST: 1946
SQ FT: 19,400
SALES (est): 1.9MM **Privately Held**
SIC: **0175** 2099 5148 0171 Apple orchard; cider, nonalcoholic; fruits; strawberry farm; canned fruits & specialties; vegetables & melons

(G-718)
DON YOHE ENTERPRISES INC
74054 Church St (48005-3332)
P.O. Box 250 (48005-0250)
PHONE.................................586 784-5556
Dan Yohe, *President*
Jodi Hansen, *Corp Secy*
Brad Yohe, *Vice Pres*
EMP: 11
SQ FT: 2,000
SALES (est): 2.1MM **Privately Held**
SIC: **1382** Oil & gas exploration services

(G-719)
EXPERIENCED CONCEPTS INC
15400 Chets Way St (48005-1160)
P.O. Box 556, Romeo (48065-0556)
PHONE.................................586 752-4200
Robert Wood, *President*
Destinee Doutry, *Admin Mgr*
EMP: 15
SQ FT: 18,000
SALES (est): 3.4MM **Privately Held**
WEB: www.expconcepts.com
SIC: **8711** 3544 3599 7539 Consulting engineer; jigs & fixtures; machine shop, jobbing & repair; air intake filters, internal combustion engine, except auto; machine shop, automotive; metalworking machinery

(G-720)
IAEC CORPORATION
21641 34 Mile Rd (48005-3102)
PHONE.................................586 354-5996
Chadwick Stayton, *CEO*
David White, *CTO*
▼ EMP: 65
SQ FT: 2,800
SALES: 4MM **Privately Held**
SIC: **3699** Electrical equipment & supplies

(G-721)
ORSCO INC
69900 Powell Rd (48005-4030)
PHONE.................................314 679-4200
Albert Adams, *Human Res Mgr*
Bob Borowski, *Manager*
▲ EMP: 5
SQ FT: 18,000
SALES (est): 1.2MM
SALES (corp-wide): 9.5B **Privately Held**
WEB: www.orsco.com
SIC: **3569** 5085 Lubricating equipment; industrial supplies
HQ: Lincoln Industrial Corporation
   5148 N Hanley Rd
   Saint Louis MO 63134
   314 679-4200

(G-722)
PATEREK MOLD & ENGINEERING
74081 Church St (48005-4710)
P.O. Box 519 (48005-0519)
PHONE.................................586 784-8030
John W Paterek, *President*
Annette Paterek, *Vice Pres*
EMP: 5
SQ FT: 5,400
SALES: 500K **Privately Held**
SIC: **3544** Special dies & tools

(G-723)
SKF MOTION TECHNOLOGIES LLC
Also Called: SKF Lnear Mtion Precision Tech
69900 Powell Rd (48005-4030)
PHONE.................................586 752-0060
Tarek Bugaighis, *President*
EMP: 46
SALES (corp-wide): 83.5K **Privately Held**
WEB: www.skfusa.com
SIC: **3562** Ball & roller bearings
HQ: Skf Motion Technologies, Llc
   890 Forty Foot Rd Ste 105
   Lansdale PA 19446
   267 436-6000

(G-724)
VAN PAEMELS EQUIPMENT COMPANY
Also Called: Van Paemel Mini-Storage
75357 North Ave (48005-2746)
PHONE.................................586 784-5295
Robert Vanpaemel, *President*
Robert Van Paemel, *President*
EMP: 3
SQ FT: 8,000
SALES (est): 758.1K **Privately Held**
SIC: **5083** 7699 3523 Farm implements; farm equipment parts & supplies; cesspool cleaning; farm machinery & equipment

Arnold
Marquette County

(G-725)
USHER LOGGING LLC
4423 Cty Rd 557 (49819)
P.O. Box 105 (49819-0105)
PHONE.................................906 238-4261
Terry W Usher, *Director*
Terry Usher, *Bd of Directors*
EMP: 6 EST: 2011
SALES (est): 549.8K **Privately Held**
SIC: **2411** Logging

Ashley
Gratiot County

(G-726)
BELLINGER PACKING
1557 E Wilson Rd (48806-9745)
PHONE.................................989 838-2274
Mike Bellinger, *Owner*
EMP: 14 EST: 1952
SQ FT: 10,680
SALES (est): 640K **Privately Held**
SIC: **0751** 5421 2011 Slaughtering: custom livestock services; meat markets, including freezer provisioners; meat packing plants

(G-727)
COG MARKETERS LTD
Also Called: Agro-Clture Liquid Fertilizers
302 W Sectionline Rd (48806-9354)
PHONE.................................434 455-3209
Gerrit Bancroft, *Site Mgr*
Colina Gillespie, *Opers Staff*
Tom Hoten, *Manager*
Bill Severns, *Supervisor*
Dennis Clark, *Assistant*
EMP: 10
SALES (corp-wide): 42.9MM **Privately Held**
SIC: **2875** Fertilizers, mixing only
PA: Cog Marketers, Ltd.
   3055 W M 21
   Saint Johns MI 48879
   989 227-3827

(G-728)
PLESKO SHEET METAL INC
8980 S Ransom Rd (48806-9307)
PHONE.................................989 847-3771
Edward Plesko, *President*
EMP: 3
SQ FT: 1,600
SALES (est): 313.4K **Privately Held**
SIC: **3444** Sheet metalwork

Athens
Calhoun County

(G-729)
TEACHOUT AND ASSOCIATES INC
Also Called: Rta Water Treatment
1887 M 66 (49011-9322)
P.O. Box 427 (49011-0427)
PHONE.................................269 729-4440
Rod Teachout, *President*
EMP: 6
SQ FT: 5,600
SALES (est): 300K **Privately Held**
SIC: **2899** Water treating compounds

Atlanta
Montmorency County

(G-730)
BRUNO WOJCIK
Also Called: Rogue Industrial Service
12270 E Shore (49709-9078)
PHONE.................................989 785-5555
Bruno Wojcik, *Owner*
EMP: 6
SQ FT: 2,400
SALES (est): 323.5K **Privately Held**
SIC: **1389** Oil field services

(G-731)
GENCO TOOL
12510 Park St (49709)
PHONE.................................989 785-5588
Gary Genco, *Owner*
EMP: 3 EST: 2001
SALES (est): 257.7K **Privately Held**
SIC: **3599** Machine shop, jobbing & repair

(G-732)
MONTMORENCY PRESS INC
Also Called: Montmorency County Tribune
12625 State 33 N (49709)
P.O. Box 186 (49709-0186)
PHONE.................................989 785-4214
William Pinson, *President*
Michelle Pinson, *Admin Sec*
EMP: 8 EST: 1886
SQ FT: 5,000
SALES: 650K **Privately Held**
SIC: **2711** Commercial printing & newspaper publishing combined

(G-733)
TRIAD INDUSTRIAL CORP
11656 Reimann Rd (49709)
PHONE.................................989 358-7191
Hugo Benjamin, *Principal*
▲ EMP: 15
SALES (est): 2.6MM **Privately Held**
SIC: **3535** Conveyors & conveying equipment

(G-734)
WOOD BROTHERS LOGGING
5915 Gamble Rd (49709-9123)
PHONE.................................989 350-6064
William Jeffery Wood, *Owner*
EMP: 3
SALES (est): 220.7K **Privately Held**
SIC: **2411** Logging camps & contractors

Atlantic Mine
Houghton County

(G-735)
EVERBLADES INC
46104 State Highway M26 (49905-9160)
PHONE.................................906 483-0174
Benjamin Halonen, *President*
EMP: 4
SALES: 400K **Privately Held**
SIC: **3714** Windshield wiper systems, motor vehicle

(G-736)
HALONEN MFG GROUP INC
Also Called: Silver Bear Manufacturing
46104 State Highway M26 (49905-9160)
PHONE.................................906 483-4077
Ben Halonen, *President*
Tim Halonen, *Vice Pres*
EMP: 3 EST: 1997
SQ FT: 2,500
SALES (est): 409.7K **Privately Held**
SIC: **3991** Brooms & brushes

(G-737)
LINDSAY NETTELL INC
47301 Janovosky Rd (49905-9015)
PHONE.................................906 482-3549
Lindsay Nettell, *President*
EMP: 4
SALES (est): 319.4K **Privately Held**
SIC: **2411** Logging

(G-738)
NDSAY NETTELL LOGGING
47301 Janovosky Rd (49905-9015)
PHONE.................................906 482-3549
Lindsay Nettell, *Principal*
EMP: 6
SALES (est): 582.5K **Privately Held**
SIC: **2411** Logging camps & contractors

Attica
Lapeer County

(G-739)
CARE2SHARE BAKING COMPANY
5512 Attica Rd (48412-9710)
PHONE.................................810 280-0307
EMP: 4
SALES (est): 225.2K **Privately Held**
SIC: **2051** Bread, cake & related products

Au Gres
Arenac County

(G-740)
AG HARVESTERS LLC
533 N Court St (48703-9204)
P.O. Box 647 (48703-0647)
PHONE.................................989 876-7161
Brandon Schnettler, *Principal*
Daniel Peterson, *Controller*
EMP: 25
SQ FT: 43,000
SALES (est): 1.4MM **Privately Held**
SIC: **3523** Planting, haying, harvesting & processing machinery

(G-741)
ATD ENGINEERING AND MCH LLC
533 N Court St (48703-9204)
P.O. Box 647 (48703-0647)
PHONE.................................989 876-7161
Daniel Minor, *Mng Member*
EMP: 35
SQ FT: 43,000
SALES (est): 6.8MM
SALES (corp-wide): 81.3MM **Privately Held**
SIC: **3599** Machine shop, jobbing & repair
PA: Cadillac Casting, Inc.
   1500 4th Ave
   Cadillac MI 49601
   231 779-9600

(G-742)
AU GRES SHEEP FACTORY
211 N Huron Rd (48703-9616)
P.O. Box 711 (48703-0711)
PHONE.................................989 876-8787
Fax: 989 876-2446
▲ EMP: 15
SALES: 492K **Privately Held**
SIC: **3944** Mfg Wool Craft Items

GEOGRAPHIC SECTION

Auburn Hills - Oakland County (G-766)

(G-743)
BESSINGER PICKLE CO INC
537 N Court St (48703-9204)
P.O. Box 396 (48703-0396)
PHONE..................989 876-8008
Craig R Carruthers, *President*
Ladeema Carruthers, *Corp Secy*
Caroline Carruthers, *Vice Pres*
EMP: 4
SQ FT: 28,940
SALES (est): 353.3K **Privately Held**
SIC: 2035 Pickled fruits & vegetables

(G-744)
BOPP-BUSCH MANUFACTURING CO (PA)
545 E Huron Rd (48703-9326)
P.O. Box 589 (48703-0589)
PHONE..................989 876-7121
Robert Busch, *CEO*
William Busch, *President*
Micheal Busch, *Vice Pres*
Terrie Dittenber, *Purch Mgr*
Michael Busch, *VP Sales*
▲ **EMP:** 50
SQ FT: 90,000
SALES (est): 17MM **Privately Held**
WEB: www.boppbusch.com
SIC: 3465 Body parts, automobile: stamped metal

(G-745)
BOPP-BUSCH MANUFACTURING CO
Also Called: Bopp-Busch Plant 2
205 N Mackinaw St (48703-9790)
P.O. Box 589 (48703-0589)
PHONE..................989 876-7924
Doug Moulton, *Manager*
Greg Vanderveen, *Manager*
EMP: 40
SALES (corp-wide): 17MM **Privately Held**
WEB: www.boppbusch.com
SIC: 3471 7692 3496 3469 Finishing, metals or formed products; welding repair; miscellaneous fabricated wire products; metal stampings; automotive stampings
PA: Bopp-Busch Manufacturing Co.
545 E Huron Rd
Au Gres MI 48703
989 876-7121

(G-746)
INTERNATIONAL TEMPERATURE CTRL
2415 E Huron Rd (48703)
P.O. Box 805 (48703-0805)
PHONE..................989 876-8075
Louis Perrot, *President*
EMP: 8
SQ FT: 6,500
SALES: 840K **Privately Held**
WEB: www.itc-controls.com
SIC: 3823 Temperature instruments: industrial process type

(G-747)
MODERN CRAFT WINERY LLC
211 E Huron Rd (48703-5000)
P.O. Box 393 (48703-0393)
PHONE..................989 876-4948
Tom Nixon, *Mng Member*
EMP: 7
SALES (est): 733.7K **Privately Held**
SIC: 2084 Wines

Auburn
Bay County

(G-748)
A AND D DESIGN ELECTRONICS
301 W Midland Rd (48611-9360)
P.O. Box 311 (48611-0311)
PHONE..................989 493-1884
Nicolas Jock, *Owner*
EMP: 2
SALES (est): 150K **Privately Held**
SIC: 7389 3672 7539 Design services; printed circuit boards; trailer repair

(G-749)
ANTIMICROBIAL SPECIALIST ASSOC
Also Called: Amsa
4714 Garfield Rd (48611-9434)
PHONE..................989 662-0377
Attila Relenyi, *President*
Cindy Wallick, *CFO*
Jerry Davis, *Officer*
▲ **EMP:** 12
SQ FT: 4,000
SALES (est): 2.3MM **Privately Held**
SIC: 2899 5084 Water treating compounds; pollution control equipment, water (environmental)

(G-750)
APPLIED GRAPHICS & FABRICATING
1994 W Midland Rd (48611-9514)
PHONE..................989 662-3334
Stanley Baryla Sr, *President*
Frances Renneberg, *Admin Sec*
EMP: 12 **EST:** 1960
SALES (est): 1.4MM **Privately Held**
SIC: 2759 2396 Screen printing; screen printing on fabric articles

(G-751)
DOW SILICONES CORPORATION (DH)
Also Called: Dow Corning
2200 W Salzburg Rd (48611-9517)
P.O. Box 994, Midland (48686-0001)
PHONE..................989 496-4000
Andrew Liveries, *CEO*
J Donald Sheets, *Exec VP*
Ganesh Kailasam, *Senior VP*
Sue K McDonnell, *Vice Pres*
Orf Ilyas, *Project Mgr*
◆ **EMP:** 900
SQ FT: 50,000
SALES (est): 2.3B
SALES (corp-wide): 61B **Publicly Held**
WEB: www.dowcorning.com
SIC: 2821 2869 Silicone resins; silicones
HQ: The Dow Chemical Company
2211 H H Dow Way
Midland MI 48642
989 636-1000

(G-752)
DOW SILICONES CORPORATION
5300 11 Mile Rd (48611-8555)
P.O. Box 994, Midland (48686-0001)
PHONE..................989 496-1306
Steve Dopp, *Mfg Staff*
Genine Ziegler, *Production*
Judy Gunderman, *Purchasing*
Shelly Livermore, *Purchasing*
Mike Balwinski, *Engineer*
EMP: 125
SALES (corp-wide): 61B **Publicly Held**
WEB: www.dowcorning.com
SIC: 2869 Silicones
HQ: Dow Silicones Corporation
2200 W Salzburg Rd
Auburn MI 48611
989 496-4000

(G-753)
ITTNER BEAN & GRAIN INC (PA)
Also Called: Er Simons
301 Park Ave (48611-9447)
P.O. Box 4 (48611-0004)
PHONE..................989 662-4461
Thomas Ittner, *President*
Jeanne Zielinski, *Treasurer*
Luella Ittner, *Admin Sec*
▲ **EMP:** 10 **EST:** 1968
SQ FT: 1,800
SALES (est): 8.1MM **Privately Held**
SIC: 5153 5191 2041 Field beans; grains; fertilizers & agricultural chemicals; flour & other grain mill products

(G-754)
J & R TOOL INC
4575 Garfield Rd (48611-9504)
PHONE..................989 662-0026
Robert Gray, *President*
Joseph Mapes, *Vice Pres*
EMP: 5
SQ FT: 3,500
SALES: 500K **Privately Held**
SIC: 3541 Lathes, metal cutting & polishing; milling machines

(G-755)
LASER CONNECTION LLC
947 W Midland Rd (48611-9406)
P.O. Box 46 (48611-0046)
PHONE..................989 662-4022
Dan E Meeker, *Mng Member*
Mike Assels, *Manager*
Stu Roy, *Manager*
EMP: 24
SQ FT: 7,000
SALES (est): 2.7MM **Privately Held**
WEB: www.laser-connection.com
SIC: 3861 Reproduction machines & equipment

(G-756)
MACHINERY PRTS SPECIALISTS LLC
4533d Garfield Rd (48611)
P.O. Box 391 (48611-0391)
PHONE..................989 662-7810
Steven D Clark,
EMP: 3
SALES (est): 204.7K **Privately Held**
SIC: 3714 Motor vehicle parts & accessories

(G-757)
MIKA TOOL & DIE INC
5127 Garfield Rd (48611-9555)
P.O. Box 116 (48611-0116)
PHONE..................989 662-6979
Richard L Mapes, *President*
EMP: 9
SQ FT: 4,859
SALES (est): 1.1MM **Privately Held**
SIC: 3599 Machine shop, jobbing & repair

(G-758)
WINFORD ENGINEERING LLC
4561 Garfield Rd (48611-9504)
PHONE..................989 671-9721
Ben Bright, *Mng Member*
John Bright, *Mng Member*
Philip Bright, *Mng Member*
EMP: 6
SALES (est): 600K **Privately Held**
WEB: www.winfordeng.com
SIC: 3678 3625 3629 7389 Electronic connectors; switches, electronic applications; power conversion units, a.c. to d.c.: static-electric;

Auburn Hills
Oakland County

(G-759)
ABA OF AMERICA INC (DH)
2430 E Walton Blvd (48326-1956)
PHONE..................815 332-5170
Nils Bergstrom, *Ch of Bd*
Arne R Stegvik, *President*
Annette Gustafson-Guenther, *Admin Sec*
◆ **EMP:** 19 **EST:** 1978
SQ FT: 25,000
SALES (est): 1.3MM
SALES (corp-wide): 1.2B **Privately Held**
WEB: www.abaofamerica.com
SIC: 3429 Clamps & couplings, hose
HQ: Norma Sweden Ab
Visirgatan 1
Anderstorp 334 3
865 414-00

(G-760)
ACME MANUFACTURING COMPANY (PA)
4240 N Atlantic Blvd (48326-1578)
PHONE..................248 393-7300
Glen Carlson III, *President*
Floyd Fishleigh, *Vice Pres*
Thomas Mc Kaig, *CFO*
◆ **EMP:** 80 **EST:** 1910
SQ FT: 47,000
SALES (est): 15.4MM **Privately Held**
WEB: www.acmemfg.com
SIC: 3541 Grinding, polishing, buffing, lapping & honing machines; buffing & polishing machines; brushing machines (metalworking machinery); deburring machines

(G-761)
AEGIS WELDING SUPPLY
1080 Centre Rd (48326-2681)
PHONE..................248 475-9860
Joan Cinquemani, *Administration*
EMP: 6
SALES (est): 44.4K **Privately Held**
SIC: 7692 Welding repair

(G-762)
AIR INTERNATIONAL (US) INC (DH)
Also Called: Air Intrntonal Thermal Systems
750 Standard Pkwy (48326-1448)
PHONE..................248 391-7970
Yongming Zhang, *Chairman*
Michael Repetto, *Corp Secy*
Joseph Cuniberti, *Engineer*
Wayne Wright, *Engineer*
Duanhui Wan, *CFO*
▲ **EMP:** 59
SQ FT: 57,000
SALES (est): 17.9MM
SALES (corp-wide): 177.9K **Privately Held**
WEB: www.aithermalsystems.com
SIC: 3585 Air conditioning, motor vehicle

(G-763)
AIRBOSS FLEXIBLE PRODUCTS CO
2600 Auburn Ct (48326-3201)
PHONE..................248 852-5500
Glenn Reid, *President*
Douglas L Reid, *Vice Pres*
Ronald J Dzierzawski, *Treasurer*
▲ **EMP:** 250
SQ FT: 135,000
SALES (est): 119.1MM
SALES (corp-wide): 316.6MM **Privately Held**
WEB: www.flexible-products.com
SIC: 3069 3714 Rubber automotive products; motor vehicle parts & accessories
PA: Airboss Of America Corp
16441 Yonge St
Newmarket ON L3X 2
905 751-1188

(G-764)
ALLEGRO MICROSYSTEMS LLC
691 N Squirrel Rd Ste 107 (48326-2868)
PHONE..................248 242-5044
Sean Burke, *Vice Pres*
Bob Fortin, *Vice Pres*
Philip Yates, *Sales Staff*
Jason Boudreau, *Marketing Mgr*
Dan Jacques, *Marketing Staff*
EMP: 4 **Privately Held**
SIC: 3674 Semiconductors & related devices
HQ: Allegro Microsystems, Llc
955 Perimeter Rd
Manchester NH 03103
603 626-2300

(G-765)
ALLIED METALS CORP
2668 Lapeer Rd (48326-1925)
PHONE..................248 680-2400
Gary L Wasserman, *CEO*
Mark Kroll, *President*
Mike Pivitt, *Opers Mgr*
Frank Kinney, *CFO*
◆ **EMP:** 25
SALES (est): 30.5MM **Privately Held**
WEB: www.alliedmet.com
SIC: 5051 3325 3341 Iron or steel flat products; steel foundries; secondary nonferrous metals

(G-766)
ALPINE ELECTRONICS AMERICA INC (HQ)
1500 Atlantic Blvd (48326-1500)
PHONE..................248 409-9444
Toshinori Kobayashi, *CEO*

Auburn Hills - Oakland County (G-767) **GEOGRAPHIC SECTION**

Isao Nagasako, *President*
Mike Wakefield, *Opers Mgr*
Peter Geddes, *Senior Buyer*
Tsubasa Kishi, *Purchasing*
◆ **EMP:** 200 **EST:** 1978
SQ FT: 120,000
SALES (est): 348.4MM **Privately Held**
WEB: www.alpine-usa.com
SIC: 5064 3651 3679 Radios, motor vehicle; household audio & video equipment; harness assemblies for electronic use: wire or cable

(G-767)
AM GENERAL LLC
1399 Pacific Dr (48326-1569)
PHONE 734 523-8098
Stephanie Tucker, *Principal*
Dan Chien, *Vice Pres*
Denise Vidusic, *Senior Buyer*
Keith Arndt, *Buyer*
Dave Caldwell, *Chief Engr*
EMP: 275 **Privately Held**
WEB: www.amgmil.com
SIC: 8711 3713 Engineering services; truck & bus bodies
HQ: Am General Llc
 105 N Niles Ave
 South Bend IN 46617
 574 237-6222

(G-768)
AME FOR AUTO DEALERS INC
1000 N Opdyke Rd Ste J (48326-2672)
PHONE 248 720-0245
David Easterbrook, *President*
Jerry Hall, *Vice Pres*
Bryan Talaga, *Vice Pres*
Ryan Kilgore, *Administration*
EMP: 5
SALES (est): 689.3K **Privately Held**
SIC: 2541 3531 3559 Cabinets, lockers & shelving; automobile wrecker hoists; wheel balancing equipment, automotive

(G-769)
AMERICAN AXLE & MFG INC
Also Called: Eng Advance Technology Dev Ctr
2007 Taylor Rd (48326-1772)
PHONE 248 276-2328
EMP: 18
SALES (corp-wide): 7.2B **Publicly Held**
SIC: 3714 Motor vehicle parts & accessories
HQ: American Axle & Manufacturing, Inc.
 1 Dauch Dr
 Detroit MI 48211

(G-770)
ANALYTICAL PROCESS SYSTEMS INC
Also Called: A P S
1771 Harmon Rd Ste 100 (48326-1587)
PHONE 248 393-0700
Brian Kundinger, *President*
John Leece, *CFO*
EMP: 25
SQ FT: 17,000
SALES (est): 10.5MM **Privately Held**
WEB: www.aps-mich.com
SIC: 5084 3829 Measuring & testing equipment, electrical; gas detectors; testing equipment: abrasion, shearing strength, etc.

(G-771)
ANDROID INDSTRS- SHREVEPORT LLC
2155 Executive Hills Dr (48326-2943)
PHONE 248 454-0500
David Donnay,
EMP: 200
SQ FT: 160,000
SALES (est): 17.4MM **Privately Held**
SIC: 3465 Body parts, automobile: stamped metal

(G-772)
ANDROID INDUSTRIES-WIXOM LLC (HQ)
4444 W Maple Dr (48326)
PHONE 248 732-0000
John Gregory, *CEO*
Kathryn Nichols, *Vice Pres*

Luke Brigmon, *Engineer*
Bruce Kelley, *Maintence Staff*
▲ **EMP:** 40
SALES (est): 10MM
SALES (corp-wide): 559.5MM **Privately Held**
SIC: 3714 Motor vehicle parts & accessories
PA: Android Industries, L.L.C.
 2155 Executive Hills Dr
 Auburn Hills MI 48326
 248 454-0500

(G-773)
ANJUN AMERICA INC
2735 Paldan Dr (48326-1827)
PHONE 248 680-8825
Josh Park, *Manager*
▲ **EMP:** 10 **EST:** 2009
SALES (est): 989.3K **Privately Held**
SIC: 3465 3714 Body parts, automobile: stamped metal; motor vehicle parts & accessories

(G-774)
ANROID INDUSTRIES INC
2155 Executive Hills Dr (48326-2943)
PHONE 248 732-0000
Kathryn Nicholas, *Vice Pres*
Wolfgang Imgartchen, *Vice Pres*
Keizo Kashimoto, *Vice Pres*
EMP: 34 **EST:** 2010
SALES (est): 7MM **Privately Held**
SIC: 3548 Welding apparatus

(G-775)
ANTOLIN INTERIORS USA INC (DH)
Also Called: Atreum
1700 Atlantic Blvd (48326-1504)
PHONE 248 373-1749
Pablo M Baroja, *President*
Ramsay Brindley, *QC Mgr*
Kevin Nagar, *Program Mgr*
Joe Ogrodnik, *Program Mgr*
Lori McDowell, *Manager*
▲ **EMP:** 300
SALES (est): 5.8MM
SALES (corp-wide): 33.3MM **Privately Held**
WEB: www.atreum.com
SIC: 3714 Motor vehicle parts & accessories
HQ: Grupo Antolin North America, Inc.
 1700 Atlantic Blvd
 Auburn Hills MI 48326
 248 373-1749

(G-776)
APOLLO AMERICA INC
Also Called: Air Products and Controls
25 Corporate Dr (48326-2919)
PHONE 248 332-3900
Tyler Newsom, *President*
Jerry Black, *Vice Pres*
Andrew Frost, *Vice Pres*
Daniel Gundlach, *Vice Pres*
Louise Laing, *Vice Pres*
▲ **EMP:** 67
SQ FT: 20,000
SALES (est): 18.8MM
SALES (corp-wide): 1.5B **Privately Held**
WEB: www.ap-c.com
SIC: 3669 3625 3829 Smoke detectors; relays & industrial controls; measuring & controlling devices
HQ: Halma Holdings Inc.
 11500 Northlake Dr # 306
 Cincinnati OH 45249
 513 772-5501

(G-777)
APTIV CORPORATION
Also Called: Delphi
2611 Superior Ct (48326-4313)
PHONE 248 724-5900
Rodney O'Neal, *President*
EMP: 5
SALES (corp-wide): 16.6B **Privately Held**
SIC: 3714 Motor vehicle parts & accessories
HQ: Aptiv Corporation
 5820 Innovation Dr
 Troy MI 48098

(G-778)
APTIV SERVICES US LLC
Also Called: Delphi
3000 University Dr (48326-2496)
PHONE 810 459-8809
Rodney O'Neal, *Branch Mgr*
EMP: 7
SALES (corp-wide): 16.6B **Privately Held**
SIC: 3714 Motor vehicle parts & accessories
HQ: Aptiv Services Us, Llc
 5725 Innovation Dr
 Troy MI 48098

(G-779)
APTIV SERVICES US LLC
2611 Superior Ct (48326-4313)
PHONE 248 724-5900
EMP: 81
SALES (corp-wide): 16.6B **Privately Held**
SIC: 3714 Motor vehicle parts & accessories
HQ: Aptiv Services Us, Llc
 5725 Innovation Dr
 Troy MI 48098

(G-780)
ART LASER INC
Also Called: Laser Dynamics
4141 N Atlantic Blvd (48326-1570)
PHONE 248 391-6600
Donald H Bailey, *President*
Ralph Weil, *General Mgr*
Jeanette Cooley, *Treasurer*
EMP: 13
SQ FT: 70,000
SALES (est): 2.1MM **Privately Held**
WEB: www.laserdco.com
SIC: 3545 3599 Machine tool accessories; machine & other job shop work

(G-781)
ATLAS COPCO IAS LLC
3301 Cross Creek Pkwy (48326-2839)
PHONE 248 377-9722
Anders Hoperg, *Mng Member*
Keri Everhart, *Program Mgr*
▲ **EMP:** 86
SALES (est): 10.9MM
SALES (corp-wide): 10.5B **Privately Held**
WEB: www.sca-usa.net
SIC: 3586 Measuring & dispensing pumps
HQ: Atlas Copco North America Llc
 6 Century Dr Ste 310
 Parsippany NJ 07054
 973 397-3400

(G-782)
AUBURN HILLS MANUFACTURING INC
1987 Taylor Rd (48326-1770)
PHONE 313 758-2000
Norman Willemse, *President*
EMP: 175
SQ FT: 76,000
SALES (est): 74.1MM
SALES (corp-wide): 7.2B **Publicly Held**
SIC: 3568 Pulleys, power transmission
HQ: American Axle & Manufacturing, Inc.
 1 Dauch Dr
 Detroit MI 48211

(G-783)
AUTO TEX
3686 S Shimmons Cir C (48326-3920)
PHONE 248 340-0844
Dan Bolen, *Owner*
EMP: 3
SALES (est): 199.8K **Privately Held**
SIC: 2299 Acoustic felts

(G-784)
AUTOLIV ASP INC
Also Called: Autoliv N Amer Technical Cntr
1320 Pacific Dr (48326-1569)
PHONE 248 475-9000
Dave Braeger, *Branch Mgr*
Enrique Gonzalez, *Manager*
EMP: 376
SALES (corp-wide): 8.6B **Publicly Held**
SIC: 3714 Motor vehicle parts & accessories
HQ: Autoliv Asp, Inc.
 1000 W 3300 S
 Ogden UT 84401
 248 475-9000

(G-785)
AUTOLIV HOLDING INC
1320 Pacific Dr (48326-1569)
PHONE 248 475-9000
Jan Carlson, *CEO*
Raj Valera, *Business Mgr*
Kim Kovac, *Vice Pres*
Srinivas Modi, *Vice Pres*
Franck Roussel, *Vice Pres*
EMP: 77
SALES (est): 50.9MM
SALES (corp-wide): 8.6B **Publicly Held**
WEB: www.autoliv.com
SIC: 3714 Motor vehicle parts & accessories
PA: Autoliv, Inc.
 3350 Airport Rd
 Ogden UT 84405
 801 629-9800

(G-786)
AUTOMATED SYSTEMS INC
2400 Commercial Dr (48326-2410)
PHONE 248 373-5600
Bruce Claycomb, *President*
Robert Yarmak, *Vice Pres*
◆ **EMP:** 32
SQ FT: 32,000
SALES (est): 9.9MM **Privately Held**
WEB: www.automatedsystems.com
SIC: 3535 3534 Conveyors & conveying equipment; elevators & moving stairways

(G-787)
AUTOMBILI LAMBORGHINI AMER LLC
Also Called: Volkswagen Group
3800 Hamlin Rd (48326-2829)
PHONE 866 681-6276
EMP: 4
SALES (corp-wide): 270B **Privately Held**
SIC: 3465 Body parts, automobile: stamped metal
HQ: Automobili Lamborghini America Llc
 2200 Ferdinand Porsche Dr
 Herndon VA 20171
 866 681-6276

(G-788)
AUTOMOTIVE EXTERIORS LLC (DH)
2800 High Meadow Cir (48326-2772)
PHONE 248 458-0702
Marc Cornet, *President*
EMP: 1
SALES (est): 19.8MM
SALES (corp-wide): 10.4MM **Privately Held**
SIC: 3714 Motor vehicle parts & accessories

(G-789)
AUTOMOTIVE LIGHTING LLC (DH)
Also Called: Automotive Lighting North Amer
3900 Automation Ave (48326-1788)
PHONE 248 418-3000
Matthieu Paillard, *Opers Staff*
Wendy Maldonado, *Purch Mgr*
John Bono, *Buyer*
Stacey Drake, *Buyer*
Kenzie Herd, *Buyer*
◆ **EMP:** 40 **EST:** 1998
SQ FT: 140,000
SALES (est): 167.1MM **Privately Held**
WEB: www.magnetimarelli.us
SIC: 8711 3647 Engineering services; headlights (fixtures), vehicular
HQ: Marelli Europe Spa
 Viale Aldo Borletti 61/63
 Corbetta MI 20011
 029 722-7111

(G-790)
BAE INDUSTRIES INC
1426 Pacific Dr (48326-1571)
PHONE 248 475-9600
Bill Hoepner, *Maint Spvr*
Jeff Creech, *Purchasing*
Eric Downs, *Buyer*
Joel Hudson, *Engineer*
Melynn Zylka, *CFO*
EMP: 16

GEOGRAPHIC SECTION
Auburn Hills - Oakland County (G-811)

SALES (corp-wide): 37MM **Privately Held**
SIC: 3465 3469 Body parts, automobile: stamped metal; metal stampings
HQ: Bae Industries, Inc.
26020 Sherwood Ave
Warren MI 48091
586 754-3000

(G-791)
BENTELER AUTOMOTIVE CORP
Also Called: Benteler Steel & Tube
2650 N Opdyke Rd Ste B (48326-1954)
PHONE.................................616 247-3936
Lawrence A Abbott, *President*
George Leonardos, *Vice Pres*
Scott Schantz, *Engineer*
Jeff Shaffer, *Engineer*
Patrick Whitfield, *Engineer*
EMP: 400
SQ FT: 135,000
SALES (corp-wide): 9.2B **Privately Held**
SIC: 3465 3544 3469 3444 Automotive stampings; special dies, tools, jigs & fixtures; metal stampings; sheet metalwork; steel pipe & tubes; blast furnaces & steel mills
HQ: Benteler Automotive Corporation
2650 N Opdyke Rd Ste B
Auburn Hills MI 48326
248 364-7190

(G-792)
BENTELER AUTOMOTIVE CORP (DH)
2650 N Opdyke Rd Ste B (48326-1954)
PHONE.................................248 364-7190
Joachim Perske, *President*
Martin Weidlich, *Exec VP*
Ulrike Hildebrand, *Vice Pres*
Guido Paffhausen, *Vice Pres*
Steve Bates, *Plant Mgr*
◆ EMP: 200
SALES (est): 845.1MM
SALES (corp-wide): 9.2B **Privately Held**
SIC: 3714 3465 3999 Manifolds, motor vehicle; automotive stampings; atomizers, toiletry
HQ: Benteler Business Services GmbH
Residenzstr. 1
Paderborn 33104
525 481-0

(G-793)
BENTELER DEFENSE CORP
2650 N Opdyke Rd Ste B (48326-1954)
PHONE.................................248 377-9999
Mark Savarese, *President*
Todd Schill, *Principal*
EMP: 7
SALES (est): 560.2K
SALES (corp-wide): 9.2B **Privately Held**
SIC: 3795 3469 3315 3312 Tanks & tank components; tile, floor or wall: stamped metal; cable, steel: insulated or armored; blast furnaces & steel mills
PA: Benteler International Aktiengesellschaft
SchillerstraBe 25
Salzburg 5020
662 228-30

(G-794)
BONSAL AMERICAN INC
Also Called: Surface Coatings Company
2280 Auburn Rd (48326-3102)
PHONE.................................248 338-0335
Lee Lowis, *Branch Mgr*
EMP: 10
SALES (corp-wide): 30.6B **Privately Held**
SIC: 3272 Concrete products
HQ: Bonsal American, Inc.
625 Griffith Rd Ste 100
Charlotte NC 28217
704 525-1621

(G-795)
BORG WARNER AUTOMOTIVE
3850 Hamlin Rd (48326-2872)
P.O. Box 214260 (48321-4260)
PHONE.................................248 754-9200
James R Verrier, *Principal*
James Verrier, *Vice Pres*
Kristi Williamson, *Vice Pres*
Ted Odom, *Buyer*
Glenn Harris, *Purchasing*
EMP: 32 EST: 2011
SALES (est): 7.9MM **Privately Held**
SIC: 3714 Motor vehicle parts & accessories

(G-796)
BORGWARNER EMISSIONS (HQ)
Also Called: Borgwrner Trbo Emssion Systems
3800 Automation Ave # 200 (48326-1781)
PHONE.................................248 754-9600
Roger J Wood, *President*
▲ EMP: 66
SQ FT: 176,000
SALES (est): 380.5MM
SALES (corp-wide): 10.5B **Publicly Held**
SIC: 3714 Transmissions, motor vehicle
PA: Borgwarner Inc.
3850 Hamlin Rd
Auburn Hills MI 48326
248 754-9200

(G-797)
BORGWARNER INC
3800 Automation Ave # 100 (48326-1781)
PHONE.................................248 371-0040
Susan Bass, *President*
Warner Borg, *Principal*
David Kaitschuck, *Vice Pres*
John McGill, *Vice Pres*
Adam Zolnierowicz, *Opers Spvr*
EMP: 5
SALES (corp-wide): 10.5B **Publicly Held**
SIC: 3714 Motor vehicle parts & accessories
PA: Borgwarner Inc.
3850 Hamlin Rd
Auburn Hills MI 48326
248 754-9200

(G-798)
BORGWARNER INC
3800 Automation Ave # 100 (48326-1781)
PHONE.................................248 754-9600
Frederic Lissalde, *Branch Mgr*
EMP: 5
SALES (corp-wide): 10.5B **Publicly Held**
SIC: 3714 Motor vehicle parts & accessories
PA: Borgwarner Inc.
3850 Hamlin Rd
Auburn Hills MI 48326
248 754-9200

(G-799)
BORGWARNER INC (PA)
3850 Hamlin Rd (48326-2872)
PHONE.................................248 754-9200
Frederic B Lissalde, *President*
Brady D Ericson, *Exec VP*
Anthony D Hensel, *Vice Pres*
Glenn Swanson, *Mfg Staff*
Dave Hotchkiss, *Purch Agent*
EMP: 277
SALES: 10.5B **Publicly Held**
WEB: www.borgwarner.com
SIC: 3714 Motor vehicle parts & accessories; transmissions, motor vehicle

(G-800)
BORGWARNER INC
Borgwarner Drivetrain Systems
3800 Automation Ave (48326-1781)
PHONE.................................248 754-9600
Steve Roskowski, *Principal*
Matthias Burmeister, *Chief Engr*
John C Hunt, *Engineer*
Thad Kopp, *Engineer*
Erik Marshall, *Engineer*
EMP: 30
SALES (corp-wide): 10.5B **Publicly Held**
SIC: 3714 Motor vehicle parts & accessories
PA: Borgwarner Inc.
3850 Hamlin Rd
Auburn Hills MI 48326
248 754-9200

(G-801)
BORGWARNER INC
Borgwarner Drivetrain Systems
3850 Hamlin Rd (48326-2872)
PHONE.................................248 754-9200
EMP: 30

SALES (corp-wide): 10.5B **Publicly Held**
SIC: 3714 Motor vehicle parts & accessories
PA: Borgwarner Inc.
3850 Hamlin Rd
Auburn Hills MI 48326
248 754-9200

(G-802)
BORGWARNER INV HOLDG INC (HQ)
3850 Hamlin Rd (48326-2872)
PHONE.................................248 754-9200
James R Verrier, *CEO*
Jan Carlson, *President*
EMP: 4
SALES (est): 2.6MM
SALES (corp-wide): 10.5B **Publicly Held**
SIC: 3714 Motor vehicle parts & accessories
PA: Borgwarner Inc.
3850 Hamlin Rd
Auburn Hills MI 48326
248 754-9200

(G-803)
BORGWARNER PDS (USA) INC (HQ)
3850 Hamlin Rd (48326-2872)
PHONE.................................248 754-9600
James R Verrier, *President*
Steve G Carlson, *Vice Pres*
Ronald T Hundzinski, *CFO*
Thomas J McGill, *Treasurer*
▲ EMP: 400 EST: 1994
SQ FT: 80,000
SALES (est): 305MM
SALES (corp-wide): 10.5B **Publicly Held**
SIC: 3714 Motor vehicle parts & accessories
PA: Borgwarner Inc.
3850 Hamlin Rd
Auburn Hills MI 48326
248 754-9200

(G-804)
BORGWARNER TRANSM SYSTEMS INC (HQ)
3800 Automation Ave # 500 (48326-1781)
PHONE.................................248 754-9200
Bob Welding, *President*
John G Sanderson, *President*
Michelle Collins, *Marketing Staff*
▲ EMP: 470
SQ FT: 120,000
SALES (est): 717.7MM
SALES (corp-wide): 10.5B **Publicly Held**
SIC: 3714 Transmissions, motor vehicle
PA: Borgwarner Inc.
3850 Hamlin Rd
Auburn Hills MI 48326
248 754-9200

(G-805)
BORGWRNER EMSSIONS SYSTEMS LLC (HQ)
3800 Automation Ave # 200 (48326-1781)
PHONE.................................248 754-9600
James R Verrier, *President*
▲ EMP: 1
SALES (est): 79.5MM
SALES (corp-wide): 10.5B **Publicly Held**
SIC: 3694 Ignition apparatus & distributors
PA: Borgwarner Inc.
3850 Hamlin Rd
Auburn Hills MI 48326
248 754-9200

(G-806)
BRC RUBBER & PLASTICS INC
Also Called: BRC Automotive Engrg & Sls Off
1091 Centre Rd Ste 210 (48326-2671)
PHONE.................................248 745-9200
Charles V Chaffee, *CEO*
Paul Parsons, *Draft/Design*
Michelle Quinn, *Accounting Mgr*
EMP: 6
SALES (corp-wide): 156.3MM **Privately Held**
SIC: 3061 Mechanical rubber goods
PA: Brc Rubber & Plastics, Inc.
1029a W State Blvd
Fort Wayne IN 46808
260 693-2171

(G-807)
BROSE NEW BOSTON INC
3933 Automation Ave (48326-1788)
PHONE.................................248 339-4000
Werner Appelmann, *President*
Katrin Haarer, *President*
Surinder Chauhan, *General Mgr*
Jinglong Wang, *Project Mgr*
Valerie Majewski, *Purchasing*
EMP: 7
SALES (corp-wide): 1.2B **Privately Held**
SIC: 3694 Automotive electrical equipment
HQ: Brose New Boston, Inc.
23400 Bell Rd
New Boston MI 48164

(G-808)
BROSE NORTH AMERICA INC (HQ)
3933 Automation Ave (48326-1788)
PHONE.................................248 339-4000
Jrgen Otto, *CEO*
Wilm Uhlenbecker, *President*
Scott Conrad, *Vice Pres*
Adriana Walker, *Buyer*
Jake Helmstetter, *Engineer*
▲ EMP: 250
SALES (est): 1.3B
SALES (corp-wide): 1.2B **Privately Held**
WEB: www.brose.net
SIC: 3714 Motor vehicle parts & accessories
PA: Brose Fahrzeugteile Gmbh & Co. Kg, Coburg
Max-Brose-Str. 1
Coburg 96450
956 121-0

(G-809)
CAPSONIC AUTOMOTIVE INC
3121 University Dr # 120 (48326-2385)
PHONE.................................248 754-1100
Seth Gutkowski, *President*
Thomas Bradley, *General Mgr*
Gloria Tripp, *Purchasing*
Sabino Alvarez, *QC Mgr*
EMP: 4 **Privately Held**
SIC: 3089 8748 8711 Automotive parts, plastic; testing services; engineering services
PA: Capsonic Automotive, Inc.
460 2nd St
Elgin IL 60123

(G-810)
CARDELL CORPORATION
Also Called: Cardell Automotive
2025 Taylor Rd (48326-1772)
PHONE.................................248 371-9700
Pete Krehbiel, *President*
David Prym, *President*
Louis Hecht, *Admin Sec*
EMP: 11
SQ FT: 86,000
SALES (est): 1.1MM
SALES (corp-wide): 40.6B **Privately Held**
WEB: www.molex.com
SIC: 3678 3679 3643 3357 Electronic connectors; electronic switches; electronic circuits; connectors & terminals for electrical devices; communication wire; fiber optic cable (insulated)
HQ: Molex, Llc
2222 Wellington Ct
Lisle IL 60532
630 969-4550

(G-811)
CCO HOLDINGS LLC
4000 Baldwin Rd (48326-1221)
PHONE.................................248 494-4550
EMP: 3
SALES (corp-wide): 43.6B **Publicly Held**
SIC: 5064 4841 3663 3651 Electrical appliances, television & radio; cable & other pay television services; radio & TV communications equipment; household audio & video equipment
HQ: Cco Holdings, Llc
400 Atlantic St
Stamford CT 06901
203 905-7801

Auburn Hills - Oakland County (G-812)

(G-812)
CHAMPION PLASTICS INC
1892 Taylor Rd (48326-1584)
PHONE.................................248 373-8995
Michael McDermott, *President*
Ken Vink, *General Mgr*
Mathew McDermott, *Vice Pres*
Bill Rohr, *QC Mgr*
EMP: 15 **EST:** 1981
SQ FT: 25,000
SALES (est): 3.1MM **Privately Held**
WEB: www.championplastics.com
SIC: 3089 5162 Injection molding of plastics; plastics products

(G-813)
CI LIGHTING LLC
2083 Pontiac Rd (48326-2485)
PHONE.................................248 997-4415
Donald Bernier Jr, *Mng Member*
EMP: 5
SQ FT: 6,000
SALES (est): 1.7MM **Privately Held**
SIC: 3672 3648 Printed circuit boards; lighting equipment

(G-814)
CLEANESE AMERICAS LLC
Also Called: Hoechst Celanese Corp
1195 Centre Rd (48326-2603)
PHONE.................................248 377-2700
David Vranesich, *Principal*
EMP: 4
SALES (corp-wide): 7.1B **Publicly Held**
SIC: 2821 Plastics materials & resins
HQ: Celanese Americas Llc
    222 Colinas Blvd W 900n
    Irving TX 75039
    972 443-4000

(G-815)
CLINTON RIVER MEDICAL PDTS LLC
1025 Doris Rd (48326-2614)
PHONE.................................248 289-1825
Tom Gitter, *CEO*
Murry Pierce, *Purchasing*
EMP: 6 **EST:** 2011
SALES (est): 746.9K **Privately Held**
SIC: 3842 Wheelchairs

(G-816)
CODE SYSTEMS INC
2365 Pontiac Rd Frnt (48326-2484)
PHONE.................................248 307-3884
Peter J Stouffer, *President*
Joseph Santavicca, *Vice Pres*
Michael Schroeder, *Vice Pres*
Joseph Dentamaro, *VP Sales*
EMP: 20 **EST:** 1979
SALES (est): 2.7MM
SALES (corp-wide): 446.8MM **Publicly Held**
SIC: 3679 Electronic circuits
PA: Voxx International Corporation
    2351 J Lawson Blvd
    Orlando FL 32824
    800 645-7750

(G-817)
CONCORDE INC
4200 N Atlantic Blvd (48326-1578)
PHONE.................................248 391-8177
EMP: 10
SALES (est): 1.2MM **Privately Held**
SIC: 3714 2674 Mfg Motor Vehicle Parts/Accessories Mfg Bags-Uncoated Paper

(G-818)
CONTINENTAL AUTO SYSTEMS INC
Emitec
2400 Executive Hills Dr (48326-2980)
PHONE.................................248 253-2969
Scott Brooks, *Vice Pres*
Chris Rinehart, *Project Mgr*
Bree Vanerp, *Purch Agent*
Robert Lavik, *QC Mgr*
Vyacheslav Birman, *Engineer*
EMP: 464
SQ FT: 164,422
SALES (corp-wide): 50.8B **Privately Held**
SIC: 3694 Engine electrical equipment
HQ: Continental Automotive Systems, Inc.
    1 Continental Dr
    Auburn Hills MI 48326
    248 393-5300

(G-819)
CONTINENTAL AUTO SYSTEMS INC (DH)
1 Continental Dr (48326-1581)
PHONE.................................248 393-5300
Elmar Degenhart, *CEO*
David Stout, *President*
Kathryn Blackwell, *Vice Pres*
Rocky Istavan, *Vice Pres*
Jennifer Wahnschaff, *Vice Pres*
◆ **EMP:** 605 **EST:** 1998
SQ FT: 24,000
SALES (est): 856MM
SALES (corp-wide): 50.8B **Privately Held**
SIC: 3714 Motor vehicle brake systems & parts

(G-820)
CONTINENTAL AUTO SYSTEMS INC
2400 Executive Hills Dr (48326-2980)
PHONE.................................248 209-4000
Mark Macdonald, *Engineer*
Pete Carozza, *Human Res Dir*
Carolyn Cerny, *Marketing Staff*
Eric Garza-Colvin, *Manager*
EMP: 324
SALES (corp-wide): 50.8B **Privately Held**
SIC: 3714 5013 3621 Fuel systems & parts, motor vehicle; automotive engines & engine parts; automotive supplies & parts; motors, electric
HQ: Continental Automotive Systems, Inc.
    1 Continental Dr
    Auburn Hills MI 48326
    248 393-5300

(G-821)
CONTINENTAL AUTO SYSTEMS INC
Also Called: VDO Automotive
2400 Executive Hills Dr (48326-2980)
PHONE.................................248 874-2597
Wolfgang Burkhardt, *Manager*
EMP: 1280
SALES (corp-wide): 50.8B **Privately Held**
SIC: 3694 Automotive electrical equipment
HQ: Continental Automotive Systems, Inc.
    1 Continental Dr
    Auburn Hills MI 48326
    248 393-5300

(G-822)
CONTINENTAL AUTO SYSTEMS INC
2400 Executive Hills Dr (48326-2980)
PHONE.................................248 874-1801
Ralf Cramer, *Director*
EMP: 325
SALES (corp-wide): 50.8B **Privately Held**
SIC: 3714 Fuel systems & parts, motor vehicle
HQ: Continental Automotive Systems, Inc.
    1 Continental Dr
    Auburn Hills MI 48326
    248 393-5300

(G-823)
CONTINENTAL STRL PLAS INC (DH)
255 Rex Blvd (48326-2954)
PHONE.................................248 237-7800
Steve Rooney, *CEO*
Eric Haiss, *Exec VP*
Brent Cagala, *Mfg Mgr*
Patty McFadden, *Materials Mgr*
Ted Henecke, *Opers Staff*
▲ **EMP:** 150
SALES (est): 798.8MM **Privately Held**
WEB: www.cs-plastics.com
SIC: 3089 Plastic processing
HQ: Csp Holding Corp.
    255 Rex Blvd
    Auburn Hills MI 48326
    248 237-7800

(G-824)
CONTINNTAL STRL PLAS HLDNGS CO (HQ)
255 Rex Blvd (48326-2954)
PHONE.................................248 237-7800
Steve Rooney, *President*
Eric Haiss, *Exec VP*
Frank Silvagi, *Vice Pres*
Joe Huggins, *Materials Mgr*
Rob Turner, *Opers Staff*
EMP: 150 **EST:** 2005
SALES (est): 823.9MM **Privately Held**
SIC: 3089 Plastic processing

(G-825)
COOPER-STANDARD AUTOMOTIVE INC
2110 Executive Hills Dr (48326-2947)
PHONE.................................248 836-9400
Joe Burrell, *Engineer*
Shoua Lee, *Engineer*
Alexis Hummel, *Hum Res Coord*
Larry Beard, *Branch Mgr*
Paul Spiers, *Manager*
EMP: 310
SALES (corp-wide): 3.6B **Publicly Held**
WEB: www.cooperstandard.com
SIC: 3443 Heat exchangers, condensers & components
HQ: Cooper-Standard Automotive Inc.
    39550 Orchard Hill Pl
    Novi MI 48375
    248 596-5900

(G-826)
COOPER-STANDARD AUTOMOTIVE INC
2545 N Opdyke Rd Ste 102 (48326-1970)
P.O. Box 615, Grand Blanc (48480-0615)
PHONE.................................248 630-7262
Matt Lang, *Accounts Mgr*
Mike Federle, *Branch Mgr*
EMP: 8
SQ FT: 2,600
SALES (corp-wide): 3.6B **Publicly Held**
SIC: 3465 Body parts, automobile: stamped metal
HQ: Cooper-Standard Automotive Inc.
    39550 Orchard Hill Pl
    Novi MI 48375
    248 596-5900

(G-827)
COOPER-STANDARD AUTOMOTIVE INC
2650 N Opdyke Rd Ste A (48326-1954)
P.O. Box 217009 (48321-7009)
PHONE.................................248 754-2000
Eugene Segal, *QC Mgr*
Larkin Leach, *Engineer*
Larry Beard, *Branch Mgr*
EMP: 240
SALES (corp-wide): 3.6B **Publicly Held**
WEB: www.cooperstandard.com
SIC: 3714 Motor vehicle parts & accessories
HQ: Cooper-Standard Automotive Inc.
    39550 Orchard Hill Pl
    Novi MI 48375
    248 596-5900

(G-828)
COVESTRO LLC
2401 E Walton Blvd (48326-1957)
PHONE.................................248 475-7700
Samuel Stewart, *Branch Mgr*
EMP: 30
SQ FT: 30,000
SALES (corp-wide): 16.7B **Privately Held**
SIC: 2822 2821 Synthetic rubber; plastics materials & resins
HQ: Covestro Llc
    1 Covestro Cir
    Pittsburgh PA 15205
    412 413-2000

(G-829)
CPI PRODUCTS INC (DH)
Also Called: De-Sta-Co Automotive Group
15 Corporate Dr (48326-2919)
PHONE.................................231 547-6064
Byron Paul, *President*
▲ **EMP:** 111
SQ FT: 54,000
SALES (est): 14.2MM
SALES (corp-wide): 6.9B **Publicly Held**
WEB: www.cpiproducts.com
SIC: 3535 Conveyors & conveying equipment
HQ: Dover Energy, Inc.
    691 N Squirrel Rd Ste 250
    Auburn Hills MI 48326
    248 836-6700

(G-830)
CSM PRODUCTS INC
1920 Opdyke Ct Ste 200 (48326-2479)
PHONE.................................248 836-4995
Paul Vanophem, *President*
EMP: 8
SALES (est): 1.4MM
SALES (corp-wide): 775.7K **Privately Held**
SIC: 3825 Instruments to measure electricity
HQ: Csm Computer-Systeme-Messtechnik Gmbh
    Raiffeisenstr. 36
    Filderstadt 70794
    711 779-640

(G-831)
CSP HOLDING CORP (DH)
255 Rex Blvd (48326-2954)
PHONE.................................248 237-7800
EMP: 12
SALES (est): 823.9MM **Privately Held**
SIC: 3089 Plastic processing
HQ: Continental Structural Plastics Holdings Corporation
    255 Rex Blvd
    Auburn Hills MI 48326
    248 237-7800

(G-832)
CSP HOLDING CORP
1200 Harmon Rd (48326-1550)
PHONE.................................248 724-4410
EMP: 4 **Privately Held**
SIC: 3089 Plastic processing
HQ: Csp Holding Corp.
    255 Rex Blvd
    Auburn Hills MI 48326
    248 237-7800

(G-833)
CUSTOM SERVICE & DESIGN INC (PA)
1259 Doris Rd Ste B (48326-2618)
P.O. Box 214923 (48321-4923)
PHONE.................................248 340-9005
Donald Saville, *President*
John Frosheiser, *Sales Mgr*
Megan Foster, *Admin Asst*
Lori Vawter, *Administration*
EMP: 20
SALES (est): 3.3MM **Privately Held**
WEB: www.customserviceanddesign.com
SIC: 3564 3589 Purification & dust collection equipment; commercial cleaning equipment

(G-834)
CZ INDUSTRIES INC
1929-1939 N (48326)
PHONE.................................248 475-4415
Petr Skrna,
EMP: 4
SQ FT: 5,600
SALES (est): 500K **Privately Held**
SIC: 3545 Machine tool accessories

(G-835)
DANA DRIVESHAFT MFG LLC
Dana Driveshaft Products
4440 N Atlantic Blvd (48326-1580)
PHONE.................................248 623-2185
Jeff Periat, *Manager*
EMP: 230 **Publicly Held**
SIC: 3714 Motor vehicle parts & accessories
HQ: Dana Driveshaft Manufacturing, Llc
    3939 Technology Dr
    Maumee OH 43537

(G-836)
DASSAULT SYSTEMES AMERICAS
900 N Squirrel Rd Ste 100 (48326-2789)
PHONE.................................248 267-9696

GEOGRAPHIC SECTION
Auburn Hills - Oakland County (G-860)

Pascal Daloz, *Exec VP*
Phil Borchard, *Vice Pres*
Mirela Manga, *Research*
EMP: 195
SALES (corp-wide): 1.8B **Privately Held**
SIC: 7372 Application computer software
HQ: Dassault Systemes Americas Corp.
    175 Wyman St
    Waltham MA 02451
    781 810-3000

(G-837)
DATA REPRODUCTIONS CORPORATION
4545 Glenmeade Ln (48326-1767)
PHONE 248 371-3700
Dennis M Kavanagh, *President*
Kimberly Kavanagh, *Sales Mgr*
Bonnie Kahler, *Cust Mgr*
Nick Janosi, *Sales Staff*
Ollie Fenwick, *Maintence Staff*
▼ **EMP:** 55
SQ FT: 100,000
SALES (est): 24.6MM **Privately Held**
WEB: www.datarepro.com
SIC: 2752 Commercial printing, offset

(G-838)
DE-STA-CO CYLINDERS INC
15 Corporate Dr (48326-2919)
P.O. Box 2800, Troy (48007-2800)
PHONE 248 836-6700
Patric Carol, *President*
Laura Grillo, *Finance Mgr*
▲ **EMP:** 400
SALES (est): 62.9MM
SALES (corp-wide): 6.9B **Publicly Held**
SIC: 3593 3495 Fluid power cylinders, hydraulic or pneumatic; precision springs
HQ: Dover Engineered Systems, Inc.
    3005 Highland Pkwy # 200
    Downers Grove IL 60515
    630 743-2505

(G-839)
DELPHI POWERTRAIN SYSTEMS LLC
3000 University Dr (48326-2496)
PHONE 248 813-2000
Kevin P Clark, *President*
EMP: 209
SALES (corp-wide): 1.5MM **Privately Held**
WEB: www.delphiauto.com
SIC: 3714 Motor vehicle parts & accessories
HQ: Delphi Powertrain Systems, Llc
    5825 Innovation Dr
    Troy MI 48098
    248 813-2000

(G-840)
DELUXE FRAME COMPANY INC
2275 N Opdyke Rd Ste D (48326-2469)
PHONE 248 373-8811
Paul Meloche, *President*
Colleen Carter, *Corp Secy*
Tom Stevenson, *Vice Pres*
EMP: 20
SALES (est): 3.1MM **Privately Held**
WEB: www.deluxeframe.com
SIC: 3089 Plastic hardware & building products

(G-841)
DM3D TECHNOLOGY LLC
2350 Pontiac Rd (48326-2461)
PHONE 248 409-7900
Roger D Parsons, *CEO*
Dr Bhaskar Dutta, *COO*
Arshad Harooni, *Engineer*
Mark Lewan, *Design Engr*
Johns M George, *CFO*
EMP: 12
SQ FT: 37,000
SALES (est): 2.2MM **Privately Held**
SIC: 3699 Electrical equipment & supplies

(G-842)
DOVER ENERGY INC
Also Called: Destaco Industries
15 Corporate Dr (48326-2919)
PHONE 248 836-6750
Brian Malolloy, *Controller*
Ray Pachuta, *Technical Staff*
EMP: 132
SALES (corp-wide): 6.9B **Publicly Held**
SIC: 3494 3495 Valves & pipe fittings; wire springs
HQ: Dover Energy, Inc.
    691 N Squirrel Rd Ste 250
    Auburn Hills MI 48326
    248 836-6700

(G-843)
DOVER ENERGY INC (HQ)
Also Called: De-Sta-Co
691 N Squirrel Rd Ste 250 (48326-2871)
PHONE 248 836-6700
Byron Paul, *President*
Bill Crusey, *Vice Pres*
Benjamin Smithson, *Project Mgr*
Jim Geary, *Research*
Gene Changnon, *Engineer*
▲ **EMP:** 111
SQ FT: 50,000
SALES (est): 168.5MM
SALES (corp-wide): 6.9B **Publicly Held**
SIC: 3429 Clamps, metal
PA: Dover Corporation
    3005 Highland Pkwy # 200
    Downers Grove IL 60515
    630 541-1540

(G-844)
DURA AUTO SYSTEMS CBLE OPRTONS
Also Called: Dura-Kentwood
1780 Pond Run (48326-2752)
PHONE 248 299-7500
Kevin Grady,
EMP: 9
SALES (est): 716.8K
SALES (corp-wide): 4.1B **Privately Held**
SIC: 3714 Motor vehicle brake systems & parts
HQ: Dura Operating, Llc
    1780 Pond Run
    Auburn Hills MI 48326
    248 299-7500

(G-845)
DURA AUTOMOTIVE SYSTEMS LLC (HQ)
1780 Pond Run (48326-2752)
PHONE 248 299-7500
Lynn Tilton, *CEO*
Jeffrey M Stafeil, *CEO*
Martin Becker, *COO*
David Pettyes, *Exec VP*
Fran Ois Stouvenot, *Exec VP*
◆ **EMP:** 125
SQ FT: 100,000
SALES (est): 2.9B
SALES (corp-wide): 4.1B **Privately Held**
SIC: 3714 Motor vehicle brake systems & parts
PA: Patriarch Partners, Llc
    1 Liberty Plz Rm 3500
    New York NY 10006
    212 825-0550

(G-846)
DURA OPERATING LLC (DH)
Also Called: Dura Automotive Systems
1780 Pond Run (48326-2752)
PHONE 248 299-7500
Lyn Tilton, *CEO*
Tyrone Michael Jordan, *President*
David Pettyes, *Exec VP*
Sanjay Singh, *Exec VP*
Kevin Grady, *CFO*
◆ **EMP:** 160
SQ FT: 64,150
SALES (est): 1.5B
SALES (corp-wide): 4.1B **Privately Held**
SIC: 3429 3714 Motor vehicle hardware; motor vehicle electrical equipment

(G-847)
DYNAMIC CORPORATION
Also Called: Dynamic Prototype Operations
2193 Executive Hills Dr (48326-2943)
PHONE 248 338-1100
Ray Atwood, *Manager*
EMP: 12
SALES (est): 1.7MM
SALES (corp-wide): 8.4MM **Privately Held**
WEB: www.ah.dynamicinc.com
SIC: 3711 Cars, electric, assembly of
PA: Dynamic Corporation
    2565 Van Ommen Dr
    Holland MI 49424
    616 399-9391

(G-848)
DYNAMIC ROBOTIC SOLUTIONS INC
Also Called: Shape Process Automation
1255 Harmon Rd (48326-1539)
PHONE 248 829-2800
Bruce Potts, *President*
Robert J Offer, *Vice Pres*
▲ **EMP:** 120
SQ FT: 93,000
SALES (est): 23.3MM
SALES (corp-wide): 162.7MM **Privately Held**
WEB: www.kmtgroup.com
SIC: 3541 Robots for drilling, cutting, grinding, polishing, etc.
HQ: Shape Technologies Group, Inc.
    23500 64th Ave S
    Kent WA 98032
    253 246-3200

(G-849)
E I DU PONT DE NEMOURS & CO
Also Called: Dupont Performance Materials
1250 Harmon Rd (48326-1550)
PHONE 302 999-6566
Janet M Sawgle, *Branch Mgr*
EMP: 50
SALES (corp-wide): 30.6B **Publicly Held**
WEB: www.dupont.com
SIC: 3541 Plastics materials & resins
HQ: E. I. Du Pont De Nemours And Company
    974 Centre Rd Bldg 735
    Wilmington DE 19805
    302 485-3000

(G-850)
E-PROCUREMENT SERVICES LLC
691 N Squirrel Rd Ste 220 (48326-2835)
PHONE 248 630-7200
David Saroli, *CEO*
EMP: 22
SALES (est): 2.9MM **Privately Held**
SIC: 7372 Business oriented computer software

(G-851)
EDW C LEVY CO
Clawson Concrete Division
2470 Auburn Rd (48326-3104)
PHONE 248 334-4302
EMP: 15
SALES (corp-wide): 376.1MM **Privately Held**
SIC: 3273 Mfg Ready-Mix Concrete
PA: Edw. C. Levy Co.
    9300 Dix
    Dearborn MI 48120
    313 429-2200

(G-852)
ELDEC LLC
3355 Bald Mountain Rd # 30 (48326-4312)
PHONE 248 364-4750
Jochen Arnold, *President*
Rick Bovensiep, *Engineer*
EMP: 16
SQ FT: 30,000
SALES (est): 3.2MM
SALES (corp-wide): 770.3MM **Privately Held**
WEB: www.eldec-usa.com
SIC: 3567 Induction heating equipment
HQ: Emag Systems Gmbh
    Austr. 24
    Salach 73084
    716 217-0

(G-853)
ELECTROHEAT TECHNOLOGIES LLC
691 N Squirrel Rd Ste 247 (48326-2871)
PHONE 810 798-2400
EMP: 28
SQ FT: 20,000
SALES (est): 4MM **Privately Held**
SIC: 3567 Mfg Industrial Furnaces/Ovens

(G-854)
ELLIOTT TAPE INC (PA)
Also Called: Elliott Group International
1882 Pond Run (48326-2768)
PHONE 248 475-2000
R Hugh Elliott, *President*
Charles Tafel, *Vice Pres*
Sherilyn Friend, *Accounts Exec*
▲ **EMP:** 26 **EST:** 1974
SQ FT: 28,000
SALES (est): 18.3MM **Privately Held**
WEB: www.egitape.com
SIC: 5113 2672 5013 Pressure sensitive tape; tape, pressure sensitive: made from purchased materials; motor vehicle supplies & new parts

(G-855)
EMABOND SOLUTIONS LLC
1797 Atlantic Blvd (48326-1505)
PHONE 201 767-7400
Chris Koenig, *Maint Spvr*
Jody Albin, *Purchasing*
Scott Tedrick, *Sales Dir*
Steve Chookazian, *Mng Member*
Drew Lamarca, *Mng Member*
EMP: 25
SALES (est): 5MM **Privately Held**
SIC: 3548 Welding apparatus

(G-856)
ESYS AUTOMATION LLC (DH)
1000 Brown Rd (48326-1506)
PHONE 248 754-1900
Christopher Marcus, *Co-President*
David Valentine, *Co-President*
Scott Claxton, *Vice Pres*
Darren Jackson, *Project Mgr*
Kevin Lipischak, *Mfg Mgr*
EMP: 76 **EST:** 1999
SALES (est): 24.4MM
SALES (corp-wide): 230.4MM **Privately Held**
WEB: www.esyscorp.com
SIC: 3549 3599 8711 8742 Assembly machines, including robotic; custom machinery; engineering services; automation & robotics consultant; robotic conveyors
HQ: J.R. Automation Technologies, Llc
    13365 Tyler St
    Holland MI 49424
    616 399-2168

(G-857)
EXCEL CIRCUITS LLC
2601 Lapeer Rd (48326-1926)
PHONE 248 373-0700
Tod Goslin, *Controller*
EMP: 10
SALES (est): 1.6MM **Privately Held**
SIC: 3672 Printed circuit boards

(G-858)
EXIDE TECHNOLOGIES
2750 Auburn Rd (48326-3114)
P.O. Box 214410 (48321-4410)
PHONE 248 853-5000
Carl Sickles, *Manager*
EMP: 12
SALES (corp-wide): 2.3B **Privately Held**
WEB: www.exideworld.com
SIC: 3691 3629 Storage batteries; battery chargers, rectifying or nonrotating
PA: Exide Technologies
    13000 Deerfield Pkwy # 200
    Milton GA 30004
    678 566-9000

(G-859)
FATA ALUMINUM LLC (PA)
2333 E Walton Blvd (48326-1955)
PHONE 248 724-7669
Martin Wright, *CEO*
▲ **EMP:** 13
SQ FT: 46,400
SALES (est): 5MM **Privately Held**
WEB: www.fataaluminum.com
SIC: 3559 5084 Foundry machinery & equipment; industrial machinery & equipment

(G-860)
FATA AUTOMATION INC (PA)
2333 E Walton Blvd (48326-1955)
PHONE 248 724-7660
Martin Wright, *President*

Auburn Hills - Oakland County (G-861)   **GEOGRAPHIC SECTION**

Ronald Benish, *Vice Pres*
Robert Smolinski, *Vice Pres*
Neil Abrahamson, *Plant Mgr*
Heather Fontecchio, *Engineer*
▲ **EMP:** 82
SQ FT: 46,800
SALES (est): 32MM **Privately Held**
WEB: www.fatainc.com
SIC: 3535 Conveyors & conveying equipment

(G-861)
FAURECIA INTERIOR SYSTEMS INC (DH)
Also Called: Faurecia North America
2500 Executive Hills Dr (48326-2983)
P.O. Box 214587 (48321-4587)
PHONE.................................248 724-5100
Donald Hampton, *President*
Eric Di Nisi, *Engineer*
Vincent Leroy, *CFO*
▲ **EMP:** 320
SALES (est): 862.7MM
SALES (corp-wide): 38.2MM **Privately Held**
SIC: 3999 5013 Atomizers, toiletry; automotive supplies & parts
HQ: Faurecia Usa Holdings, Inc.
2800 High Meadow Cir
Auburn Hills MI 48326
248 724-5100

(G-862)
FAURECIA INTERIOR SYSTEMS INC
2500 Executive Hills Dr (48326-2983)
PHONE.................................248 409-3500
Dan Lambert, *Branch Mgr*
Edward Dennis, *Manager*
EMP: 250
SALES (corp-wide): 38.2MM **Privately Held**
WEB: www.detroit.faurecia.com
SIC: 3465 Body parts, automobile: stamped metal
HQ: Faurecia Interior Systems, Inc.
2500 Executive Hills Dr
Auburn Hills MI 48326
248 724-5100

(G-863)
FAURECIA NORTH AMERICA INC
2800 High Meadow Cir (48326-2772)
PHONE.................................248 288-1000
Mark Stdham, *President*
Jean-Michel Renaudie, *Exec VP*
Jean-Pierre Sounillac, *Exec VP*
Hagen Wiesner, *Exec VP*
Michel Favre, *CFO*
EMP: 10
SALES (est): 1.2MM
SALES (corp-wide): 38.2MM **Privately Held**
SIC: 2399 5013 5012 Automotive covers, except seat & tire covers; automotive supplies & parts; automotive engines & engine parts; automotive supplies; automotive brokers
HQ: Faurecia Usa Holdings, Inc.
2800 High Meadow Cir
Auburn Hills MI 48326
248 724-5100

(G-864)
FAURECIA USA HOLDINGS INC (HQ)
2800 High Meadow Cir (48326-2772)
P.O. Box 214710 (48321-4710)
PHONE.................................248 724-5100
Mark Stidham, *President*
Eduard Hamidullin, *Plant Mgr*
Henda Rekik, *Plant Mgr*
Christine Sneden, *Buyer*
Michael Kingston, *Purchasing*
▲ **EMP:** 4
SALES (est): 3.2B
SALES (corp-wide): 38.2MM **Privately Held**
SIC: 3714 Mufflers (exhaust), motor vehicle
PA: Faurecia
23 27
Nanterre 92000
172 367-000

(G-865)
FCA INTRNTIONAL OPERATIONS LLC
1000 Chrysler Dr (48326-2766)
PHONE.................................800 334-9200
Sergio Marchionne, *CEO*
Michael Manley, *President*
Alfredo Altavilla, *Senior VP*
Holly E Leese, *Senior VP*
Giorgio Fossati, *Vice Pres*
◆ **EMP:** 20
SALES (est): 25.1MM
SALES (corp-wide): 126.4B **Privately Held**
SIC: 5012 3714 Automobiles & other motor vehicles; motor vehicle engines & parts
PA: Fiat Chrysler Automobiles N.V.
Onbekend Nederlands Adres
Onbekend
442 077-6603

(G-866)
FCA NORTH AMERICA HOLDINGS LLC (DH)
1000 Chrysler Dr (48326-2766)
PHONE.................................248 512-2950
Elaine Thompson, *Chief*
Heather Allen, *Purch Mgr*
Mark Tulczynski, *Senior Buyer*
Diwakar Reddy, *Chief Engr*
Timothy Atkins, *Engineer*
EMP: 46
SALES (est): 26.8B
SALES (corp-wide): 126.4B **Privately Held**
SIC: 3714 3711 Motor vehicle parts & accessories; motor vehicle engines & parts; automobile assembly, including specialty automobiles

(G-867)
FCA US LLC
Also Called: Chrysler Twinsburg Stamping
1000 Chrysler Dr (48326-2766)
PHONE.................................248 512-2950
David Partlow, *Chairman*
Matt Sjostrand, *Chief*
Davide Mele, *COO*
Jeremy Keating, *Plant Mgr*
Johnene Eggert, *Opers Staff*
EMP: 1850
SALES (corp-wide): 126.4B **Privately Held**
SIC: 3465 Automotive stampings
HQ: Fca Us Llc
1000 Chrysler Dr
Auburn Hills MI 48326

(G-868)
FCA US LLC
Also Called: Chrysler
800 Chrysler Dr (48326-2757)
P.O. Box 218004 (48321-8004)
PHONE.................................800 247-9753
Ralph Gilles, *Vice Pres*
Brian Harlow, *Vice Pres*
Jeffrey Kommor, *Vice Pres*
Teresa S Soave, *Vice Pres*
Mark Flowers, *Plant Mgr*
EMP: 2300
SALES (corp-wide): 126.4B **Privately Held**
SIC: 5511 3711 Automobiles, new & used; motor vehicles & car bodies
HQ: Fca Us Llc
1000 Chrysler Dr
Auburn Hills MI 48326

(G-869)
FCA US LLC (DH)
Also Called: Fiat Chrysler Automobiles
1000 Chrysler Dr (48326-2766)
P.O. Box 218004 (48321-8004)
PHONE.................................248 576-5741
Leslie Burley, *Chief*
Marjorie H Loeb, *Senior VP*
Alessandro Gili, *Vice Pres*
Thomas Lindquist, *Mfg Staff*
Thomas Czapski, *Engineer*
◆ **EMP:** 120
SALES (est): 26.8B
SALES (corp-wide): 126.4B **Privately Held**
SIC: 5511 3711 Automobiles, new & used; automobile assembly, including specialty automobiles

(G-870)
FEDEX OFFICE & PRINT SVCS INC
2785 University Dr (48326-2542)
PHONE.................................248 377-2222
EMP: 15
SALES (corp-wide): 69.6B **Publicly Held**
WEB: www.kinkos.com
SIC: 7334 5999 2791 2789 Photocopying & duplicating services; business machines & equipment; typesetting; bookbinding & related work
HQ: Fedex Office And Print Services, Inc.
7900 Legacy Dr
Plano TX 75024
800 463-3339

(G-871)
FEED - LEASE CORP
2750 Paldan Dr (48326-1826)
PHONE.................................248 377-0000
John Stretten, *President*
Martha J Stretten, *Corp Secy*
Bill Konieczny, *Engineer*
Jason Stretten, *Sales Executive*
▲ **EMP:** 25
SQ FT: 12,000
SALES (est): 6.2MM **Privately Held**
WEB: www.feedlease.com
SIC: 3621 3547 3545 3542 Motors & generators; rolling mill machinery; machine tool accessories; machine tools, metal forming type; coiling machinery

(G-872)
FEV TEST SYSTEMS INC
4554 Glenmeade Ln (48326-1766)
PHONE.................................248 373-6000
EMP: 5
SALES (est): 525.5K
SALES (corp-wide): 636MM **Privately Held**
SIC: 3519 8711 Mfg Internal Combustion Engines Engineering Services
HQ: Fev Europe Gmbh
Neuenhofstr. 181
Aachen 52078
241 568-90

(G-873)
FIELDTURF USA INC
903 N Opdyke Rd Ste A1 (48326-2693)
PHONE.................................706 625-6533
EMP: 3
SALES (est): 81.6K **Privately Held**
SIC: 3999 Grasses, artificial & preserved

(G-874)
FISCHER AMERICA INC
Also Called: Fischer Automotive Systems
1084 Doris Rd (48326-2613)
PHONE.................................248 276-1940
Klaus Fischer, *Owner*
John Fischer, *Principal*
Robert Anderson, *Vice Pres*
Peter Biske, *Vice Pres*
Mary Pankowski, *Purch Agent*
▲ **EMP:** 136
SQ FT: 60,773
SALES (est): 42.8MM
SALES (corp-wide): 397.8MM **Privately Held**
WEB: www.fischerus.com
SIC: 3089 Automotive parts, plastic
HQ: Fischer Automotive Systems Gmbh & Co. Kg
Industriestr. 103
Horb Am Neckar 72160
744 312-5500

(G-875)
FIVE STAR MANUFACTURING INC
2430 E Walton Blvd (48326-1956)
PHONE.................................815 723-2245
Mike McMorran, *President*
EMP: 35
SQ FT: 11,000
SALES (est): 5.5MM **Privately Held**
WEB: www.fivestarclamps.com
SIC: 3429 Clamps, metal

(G-876)
FLUID HUTCHINSON MANAGEMENT (DH)
Also Called: Hutchinson Fts, Inc.
3201 Cross Creek Pkwy (48326-2765)
PHONE.................................248 679-1327
Paul H Campbell, *CEO*
Sean Canty, *Vice Pres*
Walter Molitor, *Plant Mgr*
Jim Horn, *Manager*
▲ **EMP:** 90
SALES (est): 250MM
SALES (corp-wide): 8.4B **Publicly Held**
SIC: 3714 3061 3567 3492 Air conditioner parts, motor vehicle; mechanical rubber goods; industrial furnaces & ovens; fluid power valves & hose fittings; fabricated plate work (boiler shop); manufactured hardware (general)
HQ: Hutchinson Corporation
460 Fuller Ave Ne
Grand Rapids MI 49503
616 459-4541

(G-877)
FLUXTROL INC
1388 Atlantic Blvd (48326-1572)
PHONE.................................248 393-2000
Raoul Montgomery Jr, *President*
Riccardo Ruffini, *President*
EMP: 9
SQ FT: 8,000
SALES (est): 1.5MM **Privately Held**
WEB: www.fluxtrol.com
SIC: 3499 Magnetic shields, metal

(G-878)
FREMONT L DURA L C
1780 Pond Run (48326-2752)
PHONE.................................248 299-7500
Kevin Grady,
▲ **EMP:** 3
SALES (est): 18.3K
SALES (corp-wide): 4.1B **Privately Held**
SIC: 3714 Motor vehicle parts & accessories
HQ: Dura Operating, Llc
1780 Pond Run
Auburn Hills MI 48326
248 299-7500

(G-879)
G-III APPAREL GROUP LTD
Also Called: Dkny
4192 Baldwin Rd (48326-1266)
PHONE.................................248 332-4922
Karan Nschwarz, *Branch Mgr*
EMP: 157
SALES (corp-wide): 3B **Publicly Held**
SIC: 2335 Women's, juniors' & misses' dresses
PA: G-Iii Apparel Group, Ltd.
512 7th Ave Fl 35
New York NY 10018
212 403-0500

(G-880)
GEEP USA INC
Also Called: Geep Global
20 Corporate Dr (48326-2918)
PHONE.................................313 937-5350
Marilyn Alexander, *Officer*
▲ **EMP:** 25
SALES (est): 2.1MM **Privately Held**
SIC: 3559 Recycling machinery

(G-881)
GEMINI GROUP PLASTIC SALES
3250 University Dr # 110 (48326-2391)
PHONE.................................248 435-7991
EMP: 5
SALES (est): 503.4K **Privately Held**
SIC: 3089 Injection molding of plastics

(G-882)
GEMO HOPKINS USA INC
2900 Auburn Ct (48326-3204)
PHONE.................................734 330-1271
Richard Conlin, *General Mgr*
EMP: 9
SQ FT: 10,000

GEOGRAPHIC SECTION
Auburn Hills - Oakland County (G-902)

SALES (est): 403.2K
SALES (corp-wide): 54.6MM **Privately Held**
SIC: 3357 5015 Automotive wire & cable, except ignition sets: nonferrous; automotive accessories, used
PA: Gemo Gmbh & Co. Kg
Saalestr. 21
Krefeld 47800
215 144-160

(G-883)
GEORGE P JOHNSON COMPANY (HQ)
Also Called: Intaglio Associates In Design
3600 Giddings Rd (48326-1515)
PHONE..................................248 475-2500
Chris Meyer, *CEO*
Denise Wong, *President*
Tiffany Fong, *Partner*
Phyllis Teo, *General Mgr*
Paolo Zeppa, *General Mgr*
▲ **EMP:** 100 **EST:** 1914
SQ FT: 435,000
SALES (est): 196.9MM
SALES (corp-wide): 285.9MM **Privately Held**
SIC: 3993 7389 Signs & advertising specialties; advertising, promotional & trade show services
PA: Project Worldwide, Inc.
3600 Giddings Rd
Auburn Hills MI 48326
248 475-8863

(G-884)
GIFFIN INC
Also Called: Giffin, Inc. and Affiliates
1900 Brown Rd (48326-1701)
PHONE..................................248 494-9600
Donald J P Giffin, *President*
Steven Smith, *Vice Pres*
Randy Cleghorn, *Project Mgr*
Kevin Bone, *Opers Staff*
Brian Thom, *Purchasing*
▲ **EMP:** 100 **EST:** 1980
SQ FT: 125,000
SALES (est): 118.8MM **Privately Held**
WEB: www.giffinusa.com
SIC: 3559 Metal finishing equipment for plating, etc.

(G-885)
GKN DRIVELINE NORTH AMER INC (DH)
Also Called: GKN Automotive
2200 N Opdyke Rd (48326-2389)
PHONE..................................248 296-7000
Peter Molgg, *CEO*
Ramon Kuczera, *Senior VP*
Jesus Ley, *Production*
◆ **EMP:** 400 **EST:** 1977
SQ FT: 113,000
SALES (est): 640.1MM
SALES (corp-wide): 11B **Privately Held**
WEB: www.gknai.com
SIC: 3714 5013 Universal joints, motor vehicle; drive shafts, motor vehicle; automotive engines & engine parts
HQ: Gkn America Corp.
1180 Peachtree St Ne # 2450
Atlanta GA 30309
630 972-9300

(G-886)
GKN NORTH AMERICA INC
2200 N Opdyke Rd (48326-2389)
PHONE..................................248 296-7200
Robert Willig, *President*
EMP: 3295 **EST:** 1981
SQ FT: 110,000
SALES (est): 228.8MM
SALES (corp-wide): 11B **Privately Held**
SIC: 3714 5013 7359 Motor vehicle transmissions, drive assemblies & parts; transmissions, motor vehicle; universal joints, motor vehicle; drive shafts, motor vehicle; motor vehicle supplies & new parts; equipment rental & leasing
HQ: Gkn Holdings Limited
Ipsley House
Redditch WORCS
152 751-7715

(G-887)
GKN NORTH AMERICA SERVICES INC
3300 University Dr (48326-2362)
PHONE..................................248 377-1200
Pat Barky, *Manager*
EMP: 17
SALES (corp-wide): 11B **Privately Held**
SIC: 3714 Motor vehicle transmissions, drive assemblies & parts
HQ: Gkn North America Services, Inc.
1180 Peachtree St Ne # 2450
Atlanta GA 30309

(G-888)
GKN SINTER METALS LLC (DH)
1670 Opdyke Ct (48326)
PHONE..................................248 296-7832
Rich McCorry, *President*
Peter M Lgg, *Senior VP*
John Schlaack, *Vice Pres*
Paul Cook, *Opers Mgr*
Ryan Vollmert, *Purch Mgr*
◆ **EMP:** 3
SQ FT: 100,000
SALES (est): 507MM
SALES (corp-wide): 11B **Privately Held**
SIC: 3714 3568 3369 3366 Motor vehicle engines & parts; motor vehicle transmissions, drive assemblies & parts; gears, motor vehicle; bearings, motor vehicle; power transmission equipment; sprockets (power transmission equipment); bearings, plain; nonferrous foundries; copper foundries
HQ: Gkn Limited
Po Box 4128
Redditch WORCS
152 751-7715

(G-889)
GLOBAL AUTOMOTIVE SYSTEMS LLC (HQ)
Also Called: Dura Automotive - Global Fwdg
1780 Pond Run (48326-2752)
PHONE..................................248 299-7500
Lynn Tilton, *CEO*
Martin Becker, *COO*
Franois Stouvenot, *Exec VP*
Nizar Trigui, *Exec VP*
Christopher Gwisdala, *Engineer*
EMP: 38
SQ FT: 15,000
SALES (est): 291.7MM
SALES (corp-wide): 4.1B **Privately Held**
SIC: 3469 Metal stampings
PA: Patriarch Partners, Llc
1 Liberty Plz Rm 3500
New York NY 10006
212 825-0550

(G-890)
GOERTZ+SCHIELE CORPORATION
1750 Summit Dr (48326-1780)
PHONE..................................248 393-0414
Roland Schiele, *President*
Hans Jung, *Vice Pres*
Wolsgang Speck, *Vice Pres*
▲ **EMP:** 148
SQ FT: 60,000
SALES (est): 18.1MM **Privately Held**
WEB: www.goertz-schiele.com
SIC: 3462 Automotive forgings, ferrous: crankshaft, engine, axle, etc.

(G-891)
GRUPO ANTOLIN NORTH AMER INC (DH)
1700 Atlantic Blvd (48326-1504)
PHONE..................................248 373-1749
Jesus Pascual Santos, *CEO*
Pablo Munoz Baroja, *President*
Ernesto Antolin Arribas, *President*
Mark Kubat, *Vice Pres*
Mara Helena Antoln Raybaud, *Vice Pres*
▲ **EMP:** 200 **EST:** 1993
SQ FT: 38,700
SALES: 80MM
SALES (corp-wide): 33.3MM **Privately Held**
SIC: 3714 Motor vehicle engines & parts

HQ: Grupo Antolin Holdco Sa
Carretera Madrid-Irun (Burgos) (Km 244.8)
Burgos 09059
947 477-700

(G-892)
GUARDIAN FABRICATION LLC (PA)
2300 Harmon Rd (48326-1714)
PHONE..................................248 340-1800
Richard Zoulek, *President*
Eric Woodward, *Treasurer*
Thomas Pastore, *Admin Sec*
EMP: 4
SALES (est): 23.4MM **Privately Held**
SIC: 3211 3231 Plate glass, polished & rough; tempered glass; insulating glass, sealed units; products of purchased glass; mirrored glass

(G-893)
GUARDIAN FABRICATION INC
2300 Harmon Rd (48326-1714)
PHONE..................................248 340-1800
William Davidson, *President*
EMP: 625
SALES (est): 21.1MM
SALES (corp-wide): 40.6B **Privately Held**
WEB: www.guardian.com
SIC: 3211 Flat glass
HQ: Guardian Industries, Llc
2300 Harmon Rd
Auburn Hills MI 48326
248 340-1800

(G-894)
GUARDIAN INDUSTRIES LLC (HQ)
2300 Harmon Rd (48326-1714)
PHONE..................................248 340-1800
Ron Vaupel, *CEO*
Jerry Ray, *Partner*
Matt Hill, *Regional Mgr*
Kendra Mattison, *Counsel*
Elizabeth Page, *Vice Pres*
◆ **EMP:** 260 **EST:** 1968
SQ FT: 120,000
SALES (est): 3.5B
SALES (corp-wide): 40.6B **Privately Held**
WEB: www.guardian.com
SIC: 3211 Flat glass
PA: Koch Industries, Inc.
4111 E 37th St N
Wichita KS 67220
316 828-5500

(G-895)
HAOSEN AUTOMATION N AMER INC
691 N Squirrel Rd Ste 288 (48326-2846)
PHONE..................................248 556-6398
Yan Feng, *President*
EMP: 5 **EST:** 2016
SALES (est): 130K **Privately Held**
SIC: 3569 Assembly machines, non-metalworking; liquid automation machinery & equipment

(G-896)
HENNIGES AUTO HOLDINGS INC (HQ)
Also Called: Hennigs Automobiles
2750 High Meadow Cir (48326-2796)
PHONE..................................248 340-4100
Larry Williams, *President*
Lawrence Williams, *Vice Pres*
L Brooks Mallard, *CFO*
EMP: 263
SQ FT: 50,000
SALES (est): 964MM **Privately Held**
WEB: www.hennigesautomotive.com
SIC: 3069 2891 3714 Rubber automotive products; adhesives & sealants; motor vehicle electrical equipment

(G-897)
HENNIGES AUTO SLING SYSTEMS N (DH)
Also Called: Metzeler Auto Profile Systems
2750 High Meadow Cir (48326-2796)
PHONE..................................248 340-4100
Rob Depierre, *CEO*
Lorenze Williams, *President*
◆ **EMP:** 160

SQ FT: 60,000
SALES (est): 233.6MM **Privately Held**
WEB: www.gdxautomotive.com
SIC: 3053 2891 3714 Gaskets, packing & sealing devices; adhesives & sealants; motor vehicle parts & accessories

(G-898)
HENNIGES AUTOMOTIVE N AMERICA (DH)
Also Called: Automotive Operations
2750 High Meadow Cir (48326-2796)
PHONE..................................248 340-4100
Larry Williams, *President*
▲ **EMP:** 888
SQ FT: 21,000
SALES (est): 95.1MM **Privately Held**
SIC: 5013 3053 Automotive supplies & parts; automotive trim; gaskets, packing & sealing devices

(G-899)
HIROTEC AMERICA INC (DH)
3000 High Meadow Cir (48326-2796)
PHONE..................................248 836-5100
Katsutoshi Uno, *CEO*
Jim Toeniskoetter, *President*
Paul Demarco, *Exec VP*
Scott Abbate, *Vice Pres*
Sharon Beetham, *Vice Pres*
◆ **EMP:** 300
SQ FT: 215,000
SALES (est): 172.6MM **Privately Held**
WEB: www.hirotecamerica.com
SIC: 3569 Assembly machines, non-metalworking

(G-900)
HIRSCHMANN CAR COMM INC
Also Called: Hirschmann Electronics
1183 Centre Rd (48326-2603)
PHONE..................................248 373-7150
Oliver Neil, *President*
Chris Bala, *Vice Pres*
Bjoern Heimberger, *CFO*
Frank Homann, *Planning*
▲ **EMP:** 10
SQ FT: 7,050
SALES (est): 2.6MM
SALES (corp-wide): 13.9B **Privately Held**
WEB: www.hirschmann-car.com
SIC: 3679 Electronic circuits
HQ: Hirschmann Car Communication Gmbh
Stuttgarter Str. 45-51
Neckartenzlingen 72654
712 714-0

(G-901)
HUNTSMAN CORPORATION
2190 Exec Dr Blvd (48326)
PHONE..................................248 322-8682
Liz McDaniel, *Vice Pres*
Pete Panourgias, *Safety Mgr*
Terry Phillips, *Engineer*
Katie Skok, *Engineer*
Steve Wilaniskis, *Accounts Mgr*
EMP: 75
SALES (corp-wide): 9.3B **Publicly Held**
SIC: 2821 Polystyrene resins
PA: Huntsman Corporation
10003 Woodloch Forest Dr # 260
The Woodlands TX 77380
281 719-6000

(G-902)
HUNTSMAN-COOPER LLC
Also Called: Huntsman Polyurethanes
2190 Executive Hills Dr (48326-2947)
PHONE..................................248 322-7300
Michael Anderson, *Business Mgr*
Peter De Vries, *Plant Mgr*
Susan Hanrahan, *Human Res Mgr*
Frank Schietaert, *Sales Staff*
Keith Day, *Manager*
EMP: 90
SALES (corp-wide): 9.3B **Publicly Held**
SIC: 2821 Plastics materials & resins
HQ: Huntsman-Cooper, L.L.C.
500 S Huntsman Way
Salt Lake City UT 84108
801 584-5700

Auburn Hills - Oakland County (G-903)

(G-903)
HUTCHINSON SEAL CORPORATION
Also Called: Hutchinson Seal De Mexico
3201 Cross Creek Pkwy (48326-2765)
PHONE.................................248 375-4190
Cedric Duclos, *Principal*
Gene Harning, *Executive*
EMP: 3
SALES (corp-wide): 8.4B **Publicly Held**
SIC: 3069 Jar rings, rubber
HQ: Hutchinson Seal Corporation
11634 Patton Rd
Downey CA 90241

(G-904)
HUTCHINSON SEALING SYST
3201 Cross Creek Pkwy (48326-2765)
PHONE.................................248 375-3721
Robert C Hanson, *President*
Cedric Duclos, *CFO*
Michael F Kanan, *Treasurer*
EMP: 76
SQ FT: 26,000
SALES (est): 155.5K
SALES (corp-wide): 8.4B **Publicly Held**
SIC: 3069 3714 3444 Rubber automotive products; motor vehicle parts & accessories; sheet metalwork
HQ: Hutchinson Sealing Systems, Inc.
3201 Cross Creek Pkwy
Auburn Hills MI 48326
248 375-3720

(G-905)
HUTCHINSON SEALING SYSTEMS INC (DH)
Also Called: Hutchinson Sales
3201 Cross Creek Pkwy (48326-2765)
PHONE.................................248 375-3720
Robert C Hanson, *President*
Jeanine Goven, *Senior Buyer*
Pamela Burke, *Buyer*
John Attard, *Treasurer*
Nancy Clark, *Director*
▲ **EMP:** 76
SALES (est): 222MM
SALES (corp-wide): 8.4B **Publicly Held**
SIC: 3069 Rubber automotive products
HQ: Hutchinson Corporation
460 Fuller Ave Ne
Grand Rapids MI 49503
616 459-4541

(G-906)
HYDRA-ZORB COMPANY
1751 Summit Dr (48326-1780)
P.O. Box 214407 (48321-4407)
PHONE.................................248 373-5151
Orval A Opperthauser, *Ch of Bd*
Glen Opperthauser, *President*
Robert Dodge, *Vice Pres*
▲ **EMP:** 15
SQ FT: 22,200
SALES (est): 4.2MM **Privately Held**
WEB: www.hydra-zorb.com
SIC: 3429 Clamps, metal

(G-907)
IBC PRECISION INC
2715 Paldan Dr (48326-1827)
PHONE.................................248 373-8202
Berry Buschmann, *President*
EMP: 7
SQ FT: 8,800
SALES: 900K **Privately Held**
WEB: www.ibcprecision.com
SIC: 3599 3365 Machine shop, jobbing & repair; aluminum foundries

(G-908)
INALFA ROAD SYSTEM INC
1370 Pacific Dr (48326-1569)
PHONE.................................248 371-3060
Frederick L M Welschen, *President*
Mary S Drexler, *Corp Secy*
Mary Drexler, *Treasurer*
▲ **EMP:** 464
SALES (est): 35.7MM **Privately Held**
WEB: www.inalfa.com
SIC: 3714 3231 Sun roofs, motor vehicle; products of purchased glass

(G-909)
INALFA ROOF SYSTEMS INC (DH)
Also Called: Inalfa-Hollandia
1370 Pacific Dr (48326-1569)
PHONE.................................248 371-3060
Ton Hougen, *President*
David Fan, *General Mgr*
Cong He, *General Mgr*
Marek Kolarik, *General Mgr*
Gang Yang, *General Mgr*
◆ **EMP:** 409
SQ FT: 125,000
SALES (est): 364.4MM
SALES (corp-wide): 7.3MM **Privately Held**
SIC: 3714 Sun roofs, motor vehicle
HQ: Inalfa Roof Systems Group B.V.
De Amfoor 2
Oostrum Lb 5807
478 555-444

(G-910)
INCOE CORPORATION (PA)
2850 High Meadow Cir (48326-2772)
P.O. Box 485, Troy (48099-0485)
PHONE.................................248 616-0220
Eric J Seres Jr, *CEO*
Kurt Curtis, *General Mgr*
Laura Lettieri, *Purch Agent*
Donald Cavitt, *Engineer*
Mark Hibbert, *Engineer*
EMP: 110 **EST:** 1958
SALES (est): 36.8MM **Privately Held**
WEB: www.incoe.com
SIC: 3544 3823 3499 3625 Dies, plastics forming; temperature instruments: industrial process type; nozzles, spray: aerosol, paint or insecticide; relays & industrial controls; plumbing fixture fittings & trim; manufactured hardware (general)

(G-911)
INCOE INTERNATIONAL INC (HQ)
2850 High Meadow Cir (48326-2772)
PHONE.................................248 616-0220
Alex Seres, *Principal*
EMP: 4
SALES (est): 1.6MM
SALES (corp-wide): 36.8MM **Privately Held**
WEB: www.incoe.com
SIC: 3544 Dies, plastics forming
PA: Incoe Corporation
2850 High Meadow Cir
Auburn Hills MI 48326
248 616-0220

(G-912)
INDUSTRIAL EXPRMENTAL TECH LLC
Also Called: I E T
3199 Lapeer Rd (48326-1937)
PHONE.................................248 371-8000
Karl Snitchler, *QC Mgr*
James A Karchon, *Mng Member*
Chuck Ball, *Program Mgr*
EMP: 39
SQ FT: 13,000
SALES (est): 8MM **Privately Held**
SIC: 3469 Metal stampings

(G-913)
INDUSTRIAL MODEL INC
Also Called: IMI
2170 Pontiac Rd (48326-2455)
PHONE.................................586 254-0450
Peter H Koppi, *President*
Christian Koppi, *Vice Pres*
Agnes Koppi, *Treasurer*
EMP: 6
SALES: 1MM **Privately Held**
SIC: 3565 3543 Vacuum packaging machinery; industrial patterns

(G-914)
INTERNTIONAL CATALYST TECH INC (PA)
2347 Commercial Dr (48326-2408)
PHONE.................................248 340-1040
William Staron, *President*
Joerg Von Roden, *Corp Secy*
▲ **EMP:** 1

SALES (est): 2.1MM **Privately Held**
SIC: 3714 Exhaust systems & parts, motor vehicle

(G-915)
IQ MANUFACTURING LLC
1180 Centre Rd (48326-2602)
PHONE.................................586 634-7185
Kelly Vaught, *CEO*
Chris Braniecki, *Director*
EMP: 5 **EST:** 2015
SALES (est): 264.1K **Privately Held**
SIC: 3544 3599 Industrial molds; forms (molds), for foundry & plastics working machinery; dies & die holders for metal cutting, forming, die casting; crankshafts & camshafts, machining; electrical discharge machining (EDM)

(G-916)
JABIL CIRCUIT INC
3800 Giddings Rd (48326-1519)
PHONE.................................248 292-6000
Marc Leaman, *Principal*
Andrew Priestley, *Vice Pres*
Dave Flint, *QC Mgr*
David Anthus, *Engineer*
Ray Farrell, *Engineer*
EMP: 502
SQ FT: 173,976
SALES (corp-wide): 25.2B **Publicly Held**
WEB: www.jabil.com
SIC: 3672 Printed circuit boards
PA: Jabil Inc.
10560 Dr Mrtn Lther King
Saint Petersburg FL 33716
727 577-9749

(G-917)
JABIL CIRCUIT MICHIGAN INC
3800 Giddings Rd (48326-1519)
PHONE.................................248 292-6000
EMP: 25 **EST:** 1995
SALES (est): 5MM **Privately Held**
SIC: 3672 Printed circuit boards

(G-918)
JAMCO MANUFACTURING INC
2960 Auburn Ct (48326-3204)
PHONE.................................248 852-1988
Jon D Wolfenberg, *President*
EMP: 8
SQ FT: 17,400
SALES (est): 1.4MM **Privately Held**
SIC: 3451 3594 Screw machine products; motors, pneumatic; motors: hydraulic, fluid power or air

(G-919)
JO-DAN INTERNATIONAL INC (PA)
Also Called: Jdi Technologies
2704 Paldan Dr (48326-1826)
PHONE.................................248 340-0300
Henry Milan, *President*
Christine Milan, *Corp Secy*
▲ **EMP:** 7
SQ FT: 32,000
SALES (est): 3.3MM **Privately Held**
WEB: www.jditech.com
SIC: 5045 3577 5065 Computers, peripherals & software; computer peripheral equipment; input/output equipment, computer; electronic parts & equipment

(G-920)
JOHNSON CONTROLS INC
2875 High Meadow Cir (48326-2773)
PHONE.................................248 276-6000
Ray Cloutire, *Branch Mgr*
EMP: 65
SQ FT: 18,800 **Privately Held**
SIC: 3822 5084 Building services monitoring controls, automatic; industrial machinery & equipment
HQ: Johnson Controls, Inc.
5757 N Green Bay Ave
Milwaukee WI 53209
414 524-1200

(G-921)
JOYSON SAFETY SYSTEMS
2025 Harmon Rd (48326-1776)
PHONE.................................248 364-6023
Guido Durrer, *CEO*
EMP: 3

SALES (corp-wide): 8B **Privately Held**
SIC: 3714 Motor vehicle parts & accessories
HQ: Joyson Safety Systems Acquisition Llc
2500 Innovation Dr
Auburn Hills MI 48326
248 373-8040

(G-922)
JOYSON SAFETY SYSTEMS
Also Called: Restraint Systems Division
2500 Innovation Dr (48326-2611)
PHONE.................................248 373-8040
Timothy Healy, *President*
EMP: 400
SALES (corp-wide): 8B **Privately Held**
SIC: 3842 Personal safety equipment
HQ: Joyson Safety Systems Acquisition Llc
2500 Innovation Dr
Auburn Hills MI 48326
248 373-8040

(G-923)
JOYSON SFETY SYSTEMS ACQSTION (HQ)
2500 Innovation Dr (48326-2611)
PHONE.................................248 373-8040
Guido Durrer, *President*
Claus Rudolf, *COO*
Karen Hong, *CFO*
Bob Weiss, *General Counsel*
Kirk Morris, *Security Dir*
◆ **EMP:** 15
SALES (est): 3B
SALES (corp-wide): 8B **Privately Held**
SIC: 3714 Motor vehicle parts & accessories
PA: Ningbo Joyson Electronic Corp.
No.99, Qingyi Road, High-Tech Zone
Ningbo 31504
574 879-0700

(G-924)
KATCON USA INC
2965 Lapeer Rd (48326-1933)
PHONE.................................248 499-1500
Jose Denigris, *President*
Bob Houtschilt, *President*
Fernando Gonzalez, *General Mgr*
Vanessa Georges, *Engineer*
Sebastian Jarosinski, *Engineer*
▲ **EMP:** 80
SQ FT: 60,000
SALES (est): 8.4MM **Privately Held**
SIC: 3714 8711 Motor vehicle parts & accessories; engineering services

(G-925)
KEEN POINT INTERNATIONAL INC
1377 Atlantic Blvd (48326-1573)
PHONE.................................248 340-8732
Rob Mollenhauer, *President*
John Palmer, *Vice Pres*
Jim Prokopetz, *Vice Pres*
▲ **EMP:** 25
SQ FT: 5,000
SALES (est): 2.3MM **Privately Held**
SIC: 3471 Plating & polishing

(G-926)
KEY SAFETY SYSTEMS INC (DH)
Also Called: K S S
2025 Harmon Rd (48326-1776)
PHONE.................................586 726-3800
Wang Jianfeng, *Chairman*
Cindy Crow, *Accounts Mgr*
Mark Novak, *Mktg Dir*
Jenni Ellis, *Manager*
Maria Peruzzi, *Asst Secy*
▲ **EMP:** 200
SALES (est): 2.5B
SALES (corp-wide): 8B **Privately Held**
WEB: www.breedtech.com
SIC: 2399 3714 Seat belts, automobile & aircraft; motor vehicle steering systems & parts
HQ: Joyson Safety Systems Acquisition Llc
2500 Innovation Dr
Auburn Hills MI 48326
248 373-8040

GEOGRAPHIC SECTION

Auburn Hills - Oakland County (G-951)

(G-927)
KEY SFETY RSTRAINT SYSTEMS INC (DH)
Also Called: K S S
2025 Harmon Rd (48326-1776)
PHONE.................................586 726-3800
Manuel Cepeda, *Superintendent*
Joe Perkins, *Principal*
Jim Bayer, *Opers Spvr*
Rogelio Deleon, *Mfg Staff*
Jason Bustin, *Purchasing*
◆ **EMP:** 600
SALES (est): 255.8MM
SALES (corp-wide): 8B **Privately Held**
SIC: 3714 2399 Motor vehicle parts & accessories; instrument board assemblies, motor vehicle; seat belts, automobile & aircraft
HQ: Joyson Safety Systems Acquisition Llc
2500 Innovation Dr
Auburn Hills MI 48326
248 373-8040

(G-928)
KNIGHT INDUSTRIES INC
Also Called: Knight Global
2705 Commerce Pkwy (48326-1789)
PHONE.................................248 377-4950
EMP: 7 **EST:** 2014
SALES (est): 1.2MM **Privately Held**
SIC: 3559 Sewing machines & hat & zipper making machinery

(G-929)
LJ/HAH HOLDINGS CORPORATION (PA)
2750 High Meadow Cir (48326-2796)
PHONE.................................248 340-4100
Larry Williams, *CEO*
EMP: 5
SALES (est): 1B **Privately Held**
SIC: 2891 3714 Adhesives & sealants; motor vehicle parts & accessories

(G-930)
LOUCA MOLD ARSPC MACHINING INC (PA)
Also Called: Louca Mold & Arospc Machining
1925 Taylor Rd (48326-1770)
PHONE.................................248 391-1616
Kyriacos P Louca, *President*
Randal Bellestri, *President*
Kim Bellestri, *Vice Pres*
Mitch Leeman, *Program Mgr*
Dennis Dasilva, *Manager*
▲ **EMP:** 250
SQ FT: 225,000
SALES (est): 106.3MM **Privately Held**
SIC: 3544 Industrial molds

(G-931)
LXR BIOTECH LLC
4225 N Atlantic Blvd (48326-1578)
PHONE.................................248 860-4246
Andrew Krause, *CEO*
Debbie Lucas, *Opers Mgr*
John Lee, *CFO*
Dan Collins, *Sales Staff*
EMP: 25
SQ FT: 35,000
SALES: 5MM **Privately Held**
SIC: 2834 Vitamin, nutrient & hematinic preparations for human use

(G-932)
MAGNA CAR TOP SYSTEMS AMER INC (HQ)
2725 Commerce Pkwy (48326-1789)
PHONE.................................248 836-4500
Shawn Bentley, *General Mgr*
Austin Oneill, *Project Mgr*
Timothy Dawson, *Engineer*
Ruth Kell, *Finance Dir*
Jenny Rew, *Asst Controller*
▲ **EMP:** 62
SQ FT: 20,000
SALES (est): 117.6MM
SALES (corp-wide): 40.8B **Privately Held**
WEB: www.cartopsystems.com
SIC: 2394 Convertible tops, canvas or boat: from purchased materials
PA: Magna International Inc
337 Magna Dr
Aurora ON L4G 7
905 726-2462

(G-933)
MAGNA ELECTRONICS INC (DH)
2050 Auburn Rd (48326-3100)
PHONE.................................248 729-2643
Carlos Mazzorine, *President*
Dennis Hamilton, *Materials Mgr*
Bob Carmack, *Safety Mgr*
Paul Bender, *Senior Buyer*
Paul McKinney, *Buyer*
▲ **EMP:** 250
SQ FT: 35,000
SALES: 152.1MM
SALES (corp-wide): 40.8B **Privately Held**
WEB: www.magna.com
SIC: 3672 3714 Printed circuit boards; electronic circuits
HQ: Magna Mirrors Of America, Inc.
5085 Kraft Ave Se
Grand Rapids MI 49512
616 786-5120

(G-934)
MAGNA ELECTRONICS INC
Magna Elec Technical Ctr
2050 Auburn Rd (48326-3100)
PHONE.................................248 606-0606
John Lou, *Engineer*
Brian Brasier, *Engineer*
Frank Budzyn, *Engineer*
Jon Conger, *Engineer*
Alan Cordeiro, *Engineer*
EMP: 34
SALES (corp-wide): 40.8B **Privately Held**
SIC: 3679 Electronic circuits
HQ: Magna Electronics Inc.
2050 Auburn Rd
Auburn Hills MI 48326

(G-935)
MAGNA EXTERIORS AMERICA INC
2050 Auburn Rd (48326-3100)
PHONE.................................248 844-5446
Tamara Griffin, *Vice Pres*
EMP: 4
SALES (corp-wide): 40.8B **Privately Held**
SIC: 3714 Motor vehicle parts & accessories
HQ: Magna Exteriors Of America, Inc.
750 Tower Dr
Troy MI 48098
248 631-1100

(G-936)
MAGNA EXTERIORS AMERICA INC
Also Called: Specialty Vehicle Engineering
1750 Brown Rd (48326-1512)
PHONE.................................248 409-1817
Gaetano Melaragni, *Branch Mgr*
EMP: 290
SALES (corp-wide): 40.8B **Privately Held**
SIC: 3714 3544 8711 Motor vehicle parts & accessories; forms (molds), for foundry & plastics working machinery; engineering services
HQ: Magna Exteriors Of America, Inc.
750 Tower Dr
Troy MI 48098
248 631-1100

(G-937)
MAGNA SEATING AMERICA INC
Also Called: Magna Seating Auburn Hills
3800 Lapeer Rd (48326-1734)
PHONE.................................248 243-7158
Bob Sherman, *Manager*
EMP: 100
SALES (corp-wide): 40.8B **Privately Held**
SIC: 3714 Motor vehicle parts & accessories
HQ: Magna Seating Of America, Inc.
30020 Cabot Dr
Novi MI 48377

(G-938)
MAGNETI MARELLI HOLDG USA LLC (DH)
3900 Automation Ave (48326-1788)
PHONE.................................248 418-3000
E Razelli, *Ch of Bd*
Eugenio Razelli, *Ch of Bd*
James Rosseau, *President*
Tomas Szombathy, *Prdtn Mgr*
Thiago Frizoni, *Engineer*
EMP: 46
SALES (est): 2.6B **Privately Held**
SIC: 3714 Motor vehicle parts & accessories
HQ: Marelli Europe Spa
Viale Aldo Borletti 61/63
Corbetta MI 20011
029 722-7111

(G-939)
MAGNETI MARELLI NORTH AMER INC (DH)
3900 Automation Ave (48326-1788)
PHONE.................................248 418-3000
Edison Lino, *President*
Sebastian Nadal, *Chairman*
Jose Tavares, *Vice Pres*
Gianmaurizio Garrone, *Purchasing*
David Barron, *Engineer*
▲ **EMP:** 6
SALES (est): 38.2MM **Privately Held**
SIC: 5013 3714 Springs, shock absorbers & struts; motor vehicle body components & frame; shock absorbers, motor vehicle

(G-940)
MAHINDRA NORTH AMERICAN (DH)
Also Called: Mahindra Automotive N Amer Mfg
275 Rex Blvd (48326-2954)
PHONE.................................248 268-6600
Richard Haas, *President*
Mike Speck, *Design Engr*
Frederick Laws, *CFO*
Kristina Rudolph, *Analyst*
EMP: 130
SQ FT: 31,000
SALES: 50.5MM
SALES (corp-wide): 7.4B **Privately Held**
SIC: 3711 3713 8711 Automobile assembly, including specialty automobiles; specialty motor vehicle bodies; mechanical engineering
HQ: Mahindra Automotive North America Inc.
275 Rex Blvd
Auburn Hills MI 48326
248 268-6600

(G-941)
MAHINDRA VEHICLE MFRS LTD
Also Called: Mahindra N Amrcn Technical Ctr
275 Rex Blvd (48326-2954)
PHONE.................................248 268-6600
Richard Haas, *President*
Frederick Laws, *CFO*
Kristina Rudolph, *Analyst*
EMP: 150 **EST:** 2015
SALES: 67MM **Privately Held**
SIC: 3713 8711 3714 Specialty motor vehicle bodies; mechanical engineering; automobile assembly, including specialty automobiles

(G-942)
MARELLI TENNESSEE USA LLC
3900 Automation Ave (48326-1788)
PHONE.................................248 418-3000
Mario Corsi, *Branch Mgr*
EMP: 7 **Privately Held**
SIC: 3714 Shock absorbers, motor vehicle
HQ: Marelli Tennessee Usa Llc
181 Bennett Dr
Pulaski TN 38478

(G-943)
MARTINREA JONESVILLE LLC
Also Called: Martinrea Featherstone
2325 Featherstone Rd (48326-2808)
PHONE.................................248 630-7730
EMP: 6
SALES (corp-wide): 2.8B **Privately Held**
SIC: 3465 Mfg Automotive Stampings
HQ: Martinrea Jonesville Llc
260 Gaige St
Jonesville MI 49250

(G-944)
MAYCO INTERNATIONAL LLC
Also Called: Njt Enterprises LLC
1020 Doris Rd (48326-2613)
P.O. Box 180149, Utica (48318-0149)
PHONE.................................586 803-6000
Allen L Grajek, *CFO*
EMP: 30 **Privately Held**
SIC: 3089 Injection molding of plastics
PA: Mayco International Llc
42400 Merrill Rd
Sterling Heights MI 48314

(G-945)
MELLO MEATS INC (PA)
Also Called: Kubisch Sausage
270 Rex Blvd (48326-2953)
PHONE.................................800 852-5019
Micheal Delly, *Director*
EMP: 10 **EST:** 1931
SQ FT: 12,000
SALES (est): 1.2MM **Privately Held**
SIC: 2013 Sausages from purchased meat; smoked meats from purchased meat

(G-946)
MITCHELLS FABRICATION CO
2238 E Walton Blvd (48326-1952)
PHONE.................................248 373-2199
Leon Mitchell, *Owner*
EMP: 3
SQ FT: 5,000
SALES (est): 250K **Privately Held**
SIC: 3443 Weldments

(G-947)
MONTAPLAST NORTH AMERICA INC
1849 Pond Run (48326-2769)
PHONE.................................248 353-5553
David Burnett, *Vice Pres*
Mike Reed, *Opers Staff*
Rebecca Buchanan, *Buyer*
Ed Belanger, *Engineer*
Wolfgang Kern, *Engineer*
EMP: 10
SALES (corp-wide): 1.4B **Privately Held**
SIC: 3089 3714 Plastic processing; motor vehicle parts & accessories
HQ: Montaplast Of North America, Inc.
2011 Hoover Blvd
Frankfort KY 40601

(G-948)
MORGAN MACHINE LLC
2760 Auburn Rd (48326-3114)
PHONE.................................248 293-3277
Patricia Mobley,
EMP: 9
SALES (est): 1.4MM **Privately Held**
SIC: 3541 Numerically controlled metal cutting machine tools

(G-949)
MORRELL INCORPORATED (PA)
3333 Bald Mountain Rd (48326-1808)
PHONE.................................248 373-1600
Steven L Tallman, *President*
James E Cook, *Vice Pres*
Russ Martin, *Vice Pres*
Jeff McMinn, *Project Mgr*
Mike Hanzalik, *Opers Mgr*
◆ **EMP:** 100
SQ FT: 70,000
SALES (est): 96.6MM **Privately Held**
WEB: www.morrellinc.com
SIC: 5084 5065 3621 3643 Hydraulic systems equipment & supplies; electronic parts; motors & generators; power line cable; metal finishing equipment for plating, etc.; nonferrous wiredrawing & insulating

(G-950)
MUBEA INC
1701 Harmon Rd (48326-1549)
PHONE.................................248 393-9600
Thomas Muhr, *President*
Michael Lehmann, *Sales Executive*
EMP: 100
SALES (corp-wide): 2.5B **Privately Held**
SIC: 3089 Automotive parts, plastic
HQ: Mubea, Inc.
6800 Industrial Rd
Florence KY 41042
859 746-5300

(G-951)
MULTI-PRECISION DETAIL INC
Also Called: M P D
2635 Paldan Dr (48326-1825)
PHONE.................................248 373-3330
Jeffrey Dean, *CEO*

Auburn Hills - Oakland County (G-952)   GEOGRAPHIC SECTION

Michael Dean, *President*
Jack Douglas, *Sales Staff*
Mark Hetherington, *Manager*
Paul Chalker, *Director*
EMP: 25
SQ FT: 18,000
SALES (est): 5MM **Privately Held**
SIC: 3544 Special dies & tools

(G-952)
NATIONAL ORDANACE AUTO MFG LLC
2900 Auburn Ct (48326-3204)
PHONE....................248 853-8822
Christopher Boes, *Mng Member*
Chris Boes,
EMP: 6 **EST:** 2011
SALES (est): 532.7K **Privately Held**
SIC: 3441 Fabricated structural metal

(G-953)
NATIONAL ORDNANCE AUTO MFG LLC
2900 Auburn Ct (48326-3204)
PHONE....................248 853-8822
Chris Boes, *Mng Member*
EMP: 7 **EST:** 1979
SQ FT: 12,000
SALES (est): 40.2K **Privately Held**
SIC: 3444 3499 3714 Sheet metalwork; aerosol valves, metal; motor vehicle parts & accessories

(G-954)
NB COATINGS INC
2851 High Meadow Cir # 140 (48326-2794)
PHONE....................248 365-1100
Michael Dwyer, *Engineer*
Jim Carlisle, *Manager*
EMP: 9 **Privately Held**
WEB: www.nbcoatings.com
SIC: 2851 Paints & allied products
HQ: Nb Coatings, Inc.
  2701 E 170th St
  Lansing IL 60438
  800 323-3224

(G-955)
NEXTEER AUTOMOTIVE CORPORATION (HQ)
1272 Doris Rd (48326-2617)
PHONE....................248 340-8200
Guibin Zhao, *CEO*
Mike Richardson, *Senior VP*
Judie Harris, *Buyer*
Saad Jamoua, *Engrg Dir*
George Arlt, *Engineer*
◆ **EMP:** 3500
SALES (est): 2.8B **Privately Held**
SIC: 3714 Motor vehicle parts & accessories

(G-956)
NHT SALES INC
Also Called: Now Hear This
2142 Pontiac Rd Ste 201 (48326-2409)
PHONE....................248 623-6114
Andy Combs, *President*
Randy Smith, *Sales Staff*
Regina Wiseheart, *Manager*
EMP: 3
SALES (est): 141.3K **Privately Held**
SIC: 3663 Radio & TV communications equipment

(G-957)
NIDEC MOTORS & ACTUATORS (USA)
1800 Opdyke Ct (48326-2475)
PHONE....................248 340-9977
Benjamin You, *Project Mgr*
Robert Hans-Kalb, *Branch Mgr*
EMP: 25 **Privately Held**
SIC: 3621 Motors & generators
HQ: Nidec Motors & Actuators
  133 B Rue De L Universite
  Paris 7e Arrondissement
  153 579-236

(G-958)
NIKE RETAIL SERVICES INC
4000 Baldwin Rd (48326-1221)
PHONE....................248 858-9291
Brian Deali, *Branch Mgr*
EMP: 34
SALES (corp-wide): 39.1B **Publicly Held**
SIC: 3021 Rubber & plastics footwear
HQ: Nike Retail Services, Inc.
  1 Sw Bowerman Dr
  Beaverton OR 97005
  503 671-6453

(G-959)
NORMA MICHIGAN INC (HQ)
Also Called: Norma Americas
2430 E Walton Blvd (48326-1956)
PHONE....................248 373-4300
Werner Deggim, *CEO*
Timothy Jones, *President*
John Stephenson, *COO*
Clawson Cannon, *Vice Pres*
Aaron Lopas, *Vice Pres*
▲ **EMP:** 200
SQ FT: 4,000
SALES (est): 85.1MM
SALES (corp-wide): 1.2B **Privately Held**
WEB: www.torcausa.com
SIC: 3498 3714 3713 3429 Couplings, pipe: fabricated from purchased pipe; motor vehicle parts & accessories; truck & bus bodies; manufactured hardware (general)
PA: Norma Group Se
  Edisonstr. 4
  Maintal 63477
  618 140-30

(G-960)
NORTH AMERICAN ASSEMBLY LLC
4325 Giddings Rd (48326-1532)
PHONE....................248 335-6702
Kristen Kittell, *CFO*
Tom Schaenzer,
Aaron Hutyra, *Technician*
EMP: 50
SQ FT: 54,000
SALES: 8MM **Privately Held**
WEB: www.naassembly.com
SIC: 3089 Automotive parts, plastic

(G-961)
NORTH AMERICAN MOLD LLC (PA)
4345 Giddings Rd (48326-1532)
PHONE....................248 335-6702
Denise Schaenzer, *CEO*
Thomas Schaenzer,
EMP: 25
SQ FT: 14,000
SALES: 500K **Privately Held**
SIC: 3089 Automotive parts, plastic

(G-962)
NOVACEUTICALS LLC
3201 University Dr # 250 (48326-2394)
PHONE....................248 309-3402
Dawn Hanna,
EMP: 4
SQ FT: 1,000
SALES (est): 134.5K **Privately Held**
SIC: 3295 Minerals, ground or otherwise treated

(G-963)
NOVATION ANALYTICS LLC
2851 High Meadow Cir (48326-2792)
PHONE....................313 910-3280
Gregory M Pannone,
Heidi A Schroeder,
Michael F Shields,
EMP: 9
SALES: 900K **Privately Held**
SIC: 7372 7389 Application computer software; brokers' services

(G-964)
OJI INTERTECH INC
1091 Centre Rd Ste 110 (48326-2670)
PHONE....................248 373-7733
Aaron Highley, *Engineer*
John Fredrick, *Branch Mgr*
EMP: 7 **Privately Held**
SIC: 3552 Finishing machinery, textile
HQ: Oji Intertech, Inc.
  906 W Hanley Rd
  North Manchester IN 46962
  260 982-1544

(G-965)
OLD DURA INC (DH)
1780 Pond Run (48326-2752)
PHONE....................248 299-7500
Lynn Tilton, *CEO*
Martin Becker, *Exec VP*
Mario Buttino, *Exec VP*
Jim Gregory, *Exec VP*
Franois Stouvenot, *Exec VP*
▲ **EMP:** 3
SALES (est): 609.8K
SALES (corp-wide): 4.1B **Privately Held**
WEB: www.duraauto.com
SIC: 3714 Motor vehicle brake systems & parts

(G-966)
OPEO INC
Also Called: Opeo Automotive
2700 Auburn Ct (48326-3202)
PHONE....................248 299-4000
Dong Joo Youn, *President*
Sue Kwon, *Principal*
▲ **EMP:** 12
SQ FT: 5,000
SALES (est): 1.8MM **Privately Held**
SIC: 3061 3089 5013 5531 Automotive rubber goods (mechanical); automotive parts, plastic; automotive supplies & parts; automotive parts; rubber automotive products; motor vehicle brake systems & parts

(G-967)
ORION TEST SYSTEMS INC
Also Called: Orion Test Systems & Engrg
4260 Giddings Rd (48326-1529)
PHONE....................248 373-9097
Robert Pilat, *President*
▲ **EMP:** 53
SQ FT: 30,000
SALES (est): 15.6MM **Privately Held**
SIC: 3825 3861 Digital test equipment, electronic & electrical circuits; photo reconnaissance systems

(G-968)
OXUS AMERICA INC
2676 Paldan Dr (48326-1824)
PHONE....................248 475-0925
Gary Abusamra, *President*
Ryan Lenarcic, *QC Mgr*
Andy Voto, *Chief Engr*
▲ **EMP:** 8
SQ FT: 13,612
SALES (est): 3.2MM **Privately Held**
SIC: 3841 Surgical & medical instruments

(G-969)
PALO ALTO MANUFACTURING LLC
2700 Auburn Ct (48326-3202)
PHONE....................248 266-3669
Donald Tinsley,
EMP: 4
SALES (est): 161.9K **Privately Held**
SIC: 3999 Manufacturing industries

(G-970)
PARAVIS INDUSTRIES INC
Also Called: United Paravis Cnc
1597 Atlantic Blvd (48326-1501)
PHONE....................248 393-2300
Glenn M Charest, *President*
EMP: 40
SQ FT: 27,000
SALES: 5.5MM **Privately Held**
WEB: www.paravis1.com
SIC: 3599 3544 Machine shop, jobbing & repair; special dies, tools, jigs & fixtures; special dies & tools

(G-971)
PENINSULA PLASTICS COMPANY INC (PA)
2800 Auburn Ct (48326-3203)
PHONE....................248 852-3731
Ryan Victory, *President*
Richard Jositas, *Chairman*
Jessica Davis, *Production*
Mike Blanchard, *Sales Staff*
EMP: 85
SQ FT: 40,000
SALES: 15MM **Privately Held**
WEB: www.peninsulaplastics.com
SIC: 3089 Trays, plastic; plastic containers, except foam

(G-972)
PIERBURG PUMP TECH US LLC
975 S Opdyke Rd Ste 100 (48326-3437)
PHONE....................864 688-1322
Rene Gansauga, *Mng Member*
Stefano Fiorini, *Senior Mgr*
EMP: 3
SALES (corp-wide): 7B **Privately Held**
SIC: 3089 Automotive parts, plastic
HQ: Pierburg Pump Technology Us, Llc
  5 Southchase Ct
  Fountain Inn SC 29644

(G-973)
PIERBURG US LLC
975 S Opdyke Rd Ste 100 (48326-3437)
PHONE....................864 688-1322
Brandon Woltz, *Engineer*
Rene Gansauga, *Mng Member*
EMP: 12
SALES (corp-wide): 7B **Privately Held**
WEB: www.pierburginc.com
SIC: 3714 Motor vehicle engines & parts
HQ: Pierburg Us, Llc
  5 Southchase Ct
  Fountain Inn SC 29644

(G-974)
PLASTIC ENGRG TCHNCAL SVCS INC
Also Called: P E T S
4141 Luella Ln (48326-1576)
PHONE....................248 373-0800
Patrick A Tooman, *President*
Steve Hinderer, *Mktg Dir*
▲ **EMP:** 24
SQ FT: 42,000
SALES (est): 5.1MM **Privately Held**
WEB: www.petsinc.net
SIC: 3544 Industrial molds

(G-975)
PLASTICS PLUS INC (PA)
4237 N Atlantic Blvd (48326-1578)
PHONE....................800 975-8694
Roger Ziemba, *President*
▲ **EMP:** 22
SQ FT: 46,000
SALES (est): 4.4MM **Privately Held**
SIC: 2821 Plastics materials & resins

(G-976)
PONCRAFT DOOR CO INC
2005 Pontiac Rd (48326-2481)
PHONE....................248 373-6060
Kevin French, *President*
Dave Hughes, *General Mgr*
EMP: 15 **EST:** 1965
SQ FT: 30,000
SALES: 1.6MM **Privately Held**
WEB: www.poncraft.com
SIC: 3089 Doors, folding: plastic or plastic coated fabric

(G-977)
PR39 INDUSTRIES LLC
2005 Pontiac Rd (48326-2481)
PHONE....................248 481-8512
Brandon Whitney, *Principal*
EMP: 3
SALES (est): 143K **Privately Held**
SIC: 3563 Air & gas compressors

(G-978)
PRECISION BORING AND MACHINE
2238 E Walton Blvd (48326-1952)
PHONE....................248 371-9140
Robert Fuller, *President*
Lisa Fuller, *Vice Pres*
EMP: 7
SQ FT: 10,000
SALES (est): 1MM **Privately Held**
SIC: 3599 Machine shop, jobbing & repair

(G-979)
PRECISION MASTERS INC
Also Called: Maple Mold Technologies
2441 N Opdyke Rd (48326-2442)
PHONE....................248 648-8071

GEOGRAPHIC SECTION

Auburn Hills - Oakland County (G-1007)

Doug Bachan, *Branch Mgr*
EMP: 21
SALES (corp-wide): 12.8MM **Privately Held**
SIC: 3089 Injection molding of plastics
PA: Precision Masters Inc.
1985 Northfield Dr
Rochester Hills MI 48309
248 853-0308

(G-980)
PRESS PLAY LLC
2123 Willot Rd (48326-2669)
PHONE.....................248 802-3837
Eric Mendieta, *Principal*
EMP: 6 **EST:** 2010
SALES (est): 243.5K **Privately Held**
SIC: 2741 Miscellaneous publishing

(G-981)
PROTEAN ELECTRIC INC
1700 Harmon Rd Ste 3 (48326-1588)
PHONE.....................248 504-4940
EMP: 90 **EST:** 2010
SALES (est): 10.3MM **Privately Held**
SIC: 3694 Mfg In-Wheel Electric Drive System For Automobiles & Other Vehicles
PA: Protean Holdings Corp
1700 Harmon Rd Ste 3
Auburn Hills MI 48326

(G-982)
PROTEAN HOLDINGS CORP (PA)
1700 Harmon Rd Ste 3 (48326-1588)
PHONE.....................248 504-4940
EMP: 4
SALES (est): 10.3MM **Privately Held**
SIC: 3694 Mfg In-Wheel Electric Drive System For Automobiles & Other Vehicles

(G-983)
PUNATI CHEMICAL CORP
1160 N Opdyke Rd (48326-2645)
PHONE.....................248 276-0101
Bernard Shandler, *President*
Jeffrey J Shandler, *President*
▼ **EMP:** 19 **EST:** 1978
SQ FT: 36,000
SALES (est): 5.5MM **Privately Held**
SIC: 2842 Industrial plant disinfectants or deodorants; deodorants, nonpersonal

(G-984)
R G RAY CORPORATION
2430 E Walton Blvd (48326-1956)
PHONE.....................248 373-4300
Daniel J Mitrano, *President*
Tim Jones, *Vice Pres*
Durg Kumar, *Admin Sec*
▲ **EMP:** 12
SQ FT: 125,000
SALES (est): 2.1MM
SALES (corp-wide): 1.2B **Privately Held**
WEB: www.rgrayclamps.com
SIC: 3429 Clamps, metal
HQ: Norma Group Holding Gmbh
Edisonstr. 4
Maintal 63477
618 140-30

(G-985)
RALCO INDUSTRIES INC (PA)
2720 Auburn Ct (48326-3202)
PHONE.....................248 853-3200
Tom Gitter, *CEO*
Jim Piper, *President*
Matt Winowski, *QC Mgr*
Sarah Piper, *Engineer*
Ted Popa, *Engineer*
EMP: 88 **EST:** 1970
SQ FT: 58,000
SALES (est): 30.7MM **Privately Held**
WEB: www.ralcoind.com
SIC: 3714 3544 Motor vehicle parts & accessories; special dies & tools

(G-986)
RALCO INDUSTRIES INC
1025 Doris Rd (48326-2614)
PHONE.....................248 853-3200
Tom Gitter, *CEO*
EMP: 20

SALES (corp-wide): 30.7MM **Privately Held**
SIC: 3714 3544 Motor vehicle parts & accessories; special dies, tools, jigs & fixtures
PA: Ralco Industries, Inc.
2720 Auburn Ct
Auburn Hills MI 48326
248 853-3200

(G-987)
RALCO INDUSTRIES INC
2860 Auburn Ct (48326-3203)
PHONE.....................248 853-3200
Tom Gitter, *Branch Mgr*
EMP: 50
SALES (corp-wide): 30.7MM **Privately Held**
WEB: www.ralcoind.com
SIC: 3465 Automotive stampings
PA: Ralco Industries, Inc.
2720 Auburn Ct
Auburn Hills MI 48326
248 853-3200

(G-988)
RE-SOL LLC
1771 Harmon Rd Ste 150 (48326-1587)
PHONE.....................248 270-7777
John Vaughn, *VP Opers*
Peter Kaub, *Mng Member*
EMP: 12
SALES (est): 2.5MM **Privately Held**
WEB: www.re-sol.com
SIC: 3824 Fluid meters & counting devices

(G-989)
REPLY INC (DH)
691 N Squirrel Rd Ste 202 (48326-2871)
PHONE.....................248 686-2481
Gianluca Di Stefano, *President*
EMP: 14
SALES: 50MM
SALES (corp-wide): 647.8MM **Privately Held**
SIC: 8748 7373 3571 Business consulting; computer integrated systems design; computers, digital, analog or hybrid
HQ: Logistics Reply Srl
Via Castellanza 11
Milano MI 20151
025 357-61

(G-990)
RIDER REPORT MAGAZINE
3906 Baldwin Rd (48321-7700)
PHONE.....................248 854-8460
Mark Edward, *Owner*
EMP: 4
SALES (est): 193.5K **Privately Held**
SIC: 2721 Magazines: publishing only, not printed on site

(G-991)
RIGAKU INNOVATIVE TECH INC
1900 Taylor Rd (48326-1740)
PHONE.....................248 232-6400
John McGill, *President*
Licai Jiang, *Vice Pres*
Scott Bendle, *Opers Staff*
Wes L Hardenburg, *CFO*
Paul Pennartz, *Manager*
EMP: 200
SQ FT: 57,000
SALES (est): 32.3MM **Privately Held**
WEB: www.rigaku.com
SIC: 3826 Analytical instruments
HQ: Rigaku Americas Corporation
9009 New Trails Dr
The Woodlands TX 77381
281 362-2300

(G-992)
RITE MARK STAMP COMPANY
Also Called: Clean Cut Divison
4141 N Atlantic Blvd (48326-1570)
PHONE.....................248 391-7600
Donald H Bailey, *President*
EMP: 27 **EST:** 1965
SQ FT: 70,000
SALES: 1.7MM **Privately Held**
WEB: www.ritemark.com
SIC: 3953 3599 Marking devices; machine shop, jobbing & repair

(G-993)
ROCHESTER MLLS PROD BREWRY LLC
3275 Lapeer Rd W (48326-1723)
PHONE.....................248 377-3130
Jamie Mosshart,
EMP: 8
SALES (est): 848.8K **Privately Held**
SIC: 2082 Brewers' grain

(G-994)
RTR ALPHA INC
Also Called: Allegra Marketing Print Signs
2285 N Opdyke Rd Ste G (48326-2468)
PHONE.....................248 377-4060
Michael Wysocki, *President*
EMP: 3 **EST:** 2010
SALES (est): 194.2K **Privately Held**
SIC: 8742 7311 2752 Marketing consulting services; advertising agencies; commercial printing, offset

(G-995)
RUBBER & PLASTICS CO (PA)
3650 Lapeer Rd (48326-1730)
PHONE.....................248 370-0700
Lawrence V Harding, *President*
M E Harding, *Vice Pres*
EMP: 27
SQ FT: 15,000
SALES (est): 5.5MM **Privately Held**
SIC: 2821 Plastics materials & resins

(G-996)
SHANNON PRECISION FASTENER LLC
Purks Rd Mfg Plant
4425 Purks Rd (48326-1749)
PHONE.....................248 589-9670
Ed Lumm, *CEO*
EMP: 50
SALES (corp-wide): 100MM **Privately Held**
SIC: 3452 Bolts, nuts, rivets & washers
PA: Shannon Precision Fastener, Llc
31600 Stephenson Hwy
Madison Heights MI 48071
248 589-9670

(G-997)
SHIELD MATERIAL HANDLING INC
4280 N Atlantic Blvd (48326-1578)
PHONE.....................248 418-0986
Joseph Chin, *Director*
Lisa Jun, *Director*
EMP: 10
SALES: 1MM **Privately Held**
SIC: 3829 Measuring & controlling devices

(G-998)
SHURE STAR LLC
2498 Commercial Dr (48326-2410)
PHONE.....................248 365-4382
Bruce R Bacon, *Branch Mgr*
EMP: 27
SALES (corp-wide): 5MM **Privately Held**
SIC: 3442 Window & door frames
PA: Shure Star Llc
15200 Century Dr
Dearborn MI 48120
248 365-4382

(G-999)
SIERRA 3 DEFENSE LLC
2830 Tall Oaks Ct Apt 23 (48326-4156)
PHONE.....................248 343-1066
Donny Parker, *Principal*
EMP: 3
SALES (est): 173.2K **Privately Held**
SIC: 3812 Defense systems & equipment

(G-1000)
SL AMERICA CORPORATION
4375 Giddings Rd (48326-1532)
PHONE.....................586 731-8511
Jake Evans, *Purch Mgr*
Billy Frank, *Buyer*
Kevin Jones, *Buyer*
Wayne Embry, *Human Res Mgr*
Darin Duda, *Program Mgr*
EMP: 30 **Privately Held**
SIC: 3714 Motor vehicle parts & accessories

HQ: Sl America Corporation
312 Frank L Diggs Dr
Clinton TN 37716

(G-1001)
STACKPOLE PWRTRN INTL USA LLC
Also Called: Stackpole International
3201 University Dr # 350 (48326-2394)
PHONE.....................248 481-4600
Peter Ballantyne, *CEO*
Robert Mooy, *Vice Pres*
Alexis Zhu, *Buyer*
Doina Draganoiu, *Engineer*
Kelly Dickinson, *Manager*
EMP: 6
SALES (est): 598.3K **Privately Held**
SIC: 3714 Motor vehicle parts & accessories
HQ: Stackpole International
Avenue John F. Kennedy 46a
Luxembourg 1855
420 335-

(G-1002)
STATE CRUSHING INC
2260 Auburn Rd (48326-3102)
PHONE.....................248 332-6210
Manual Orozco, *President*
Raymond J Orozco, *Vice Pres*
Dorothy Laffrey, *Manager*
EMP: 7
SQ FT: 1,200
SALES (est): 2MM **Privately Held**
SIC: 1422 Cement rock, crushed & broken-quarrying

(G-1003)
STEGNER CONTROLS LLC
3333 Bald Mountain Rd (48326-1808)
PHONE.....................248 904-0400
EMP: 23
SALES (est): 4.9MM **Privately Held**
SIC: 3625 Control equipment, electric

(G-1004)
STRATTEC POWER ACCESS LLC (HQ)
2998 Dutton Rd (48326-1864)
PHONE.....................248 649-9742
Richard Messina, *Mng Member*
Curtis Braun, *Program Mgr*
Rainer Goelz,
Patrick J Hansen,
Harold M Stratton II,
▲ **EMP:** 18
SALES (est): 60.1MM **Publicly Held**
SIC: 2396 Automotive & apparel trimmings

(G-1005)
STRATTEC SECURITY CORPORATION
2998 Dutton Rd (48326-1864)
PHONE.....................248 649-9742
Dennis Kazmierski, *Manager*
EMP: 25 **Publicly Held**
WEB: www.strattec.com
SIC: 3429 3714 Locks or lock sets; keys & key blanks; motor vehicle parts & accessories
PA: Strattec Security Corporation
3333 W Good Hope Rd
Milwaukee WI 53209

(G-1006)
SURE SOLUTIONS CORPORATION
40 Corporate Dr (48326-2918)
PHONE.....................248 674-7210
Mary Buchzeiger, *CEO*
Karen Ryan, *Finance Mgr*
▲ **EMP:** 1
SQ FT: 3,500
SALES: 14.8MM **Privately Held**
SIC: 3559 Automotive related machinery

(G-1007)
SURPLUS STEEL INC
321 Collier Rd (48326-1407)
PHONE.....................248 338-0000
Robert Stepanian, *President*
Kevin Wood, *Engineer*
Paul McKune, *Manager*
EMP: 3
SQ FT: 5,000

Auburn Hills - Oakland County (G-1008)

SALES (est): 675.6K **Privately Held**
SIC: **5051** 3441 Steel; structural shapes, iron or steel; fabricated structural metal

(G-1008)
SWAROVSKI NORTH AMERICA LTD
4000 Baldwin Rd (48326-1221)
PHONE...................................248 874-0753
EMP: 36
SALES (corp-wide): 4.7B **Privately Held**
SIC: **3961** Costume jewelry
HQ: Swarovski North America Limited
1 Kenney Dr
Cranston RI 02920
401 463-6400

(G-1009)
SYNCREON ACQUISITION CORP (HQ)
2851 High Meadow Cir # 250 (48326-2791)
PHONE...................................248 377-4700
Brian Enright, *CEO*
EMP: 15
SALES (est): 20.1MM **Privately Held**
SIC: **3559** Automotive related machinery

(G-1010)
SYNCREONUS INC (HQ)
2851 High Meadow Cir # 250 (48326-2791)
PHONE...................................248 377-4700
Brian Enright, *CEO*
Michael Neumann, *President*
Galina Blokhina, *Counsel*
Annette Cyr, *Exec VP*
Niall Connolly, *Vice Pres*
▲ EMP: 75
SQ FT: 85,000
SALES (est): 40.9MM **Privately Held**
SIC: **3446** 3714 3231 2531 Architectural metalwork; motor vehicle parts & accessories; products of purchased glass; public building & related furniture

(G-1011)
TAJCO NORTH AMERICA INC
2851 High Meadow Cir # 190 (48326-2790)
PHONE...................................248 418-7550
Rolf Ebbesen, *CEO*
Jakob Bonde Jessen, *COO*
Kenneth Bergstrom Andersen, *CFO*
Steve Widdett, *Ch Credit Ofcr*
Henri Kirchof, *CTO*
▲ EMP: 7
SALES (est): 19.8MM
SALES (corp-wide): 135.8MM **Privately Held**
SIC: **3465** Body parts, automobile: stamped metal
HQ: Tajco A/S
Jens Ravns Vej 11a
Vejle 7100
753 214-11

(G-1012)
TAKATA AMERICAS (DH)
Also Called: Tk Holdings
2500 Takata Dr Ste 300 (48326-2636)
PHONE...................................336 547-1600
Jonathan Halas, *Partner*
Heiko Ruck, *Manager*
EMP: 29
SQ FT: 600
SALES (est): 1.3MM
SALES (corp-wide): 8B **Privately Held**
SIC: **2296** 2221 2399 2396 Cord for reinforcing rubber tires; automotive fabrics, manmade fiber; seat belts, automobile & aircraft; automotive trimmings, fabric; motor vehicle parts & accessories
HQ: Joyson Safety Systems Acquisition Llc
2500 Innovation Dr
Auburn Hills MI 48326
248 373-8040

(G-1013)
TALL CITY LLC
3386 Countryside Cir (48326-2218)
PHONE...................................248 854-0713
Dennis Kruse, *Vice Pres*
Angela Staples, *Vice Pres*
Gary Womack, *VP Opers*
Craig Hanagan, *Opers Staff*

Marlu Hiller, *Controller*
EMP: 7
SALES: 100K **Privately Held**
SIC: **2339** Women's & misses' outerwear

(G-1014)
TEC INTERNATIONAL II (PA)
Also Called: Matrix Metalcraft
68 S Squirrel Rd (48326-3282)
PHONE...................................248 724-1800
Anthony Carmen, *Partner*
Nicholas A Salvatore, *Partner*
EMP: 2
SALES: 5MM **Privately Held**
SIC: **7389** 1799 3479 7699 Metal cutting services; welding on site; coating of metals & formed products; industrial equipment services

(G-1015)
TECTONICS INDUSTRIES LLC (PA)
1681 Harmon Rd (48326-1547)
PHONE...................................248 597-1600
Lee Skandalaris, *Principal*
EMP: 4
SALES (est): 339.2K **Privately Held**
SIC: **2759** Commercial printing

(G-1016)
TEIJIN ADVAN COMPO AMERI INC
1200 Harmon Rd (48326-1550)
PHONE...................................248 365-6600
Jun Suzuki, *Principal*
Osamu Nishikawa, *Senior VP*
▲ EMP: 8
SQ FT: 47,460
SALES (est): 3.2MM **Privately Held**
SIC: **3089** Plastic processing
HQ: Teijin Holdings Usa Inc.
600 Lexington Ave Fl 27
New York NY 10022
212 308-8744

(G-1017)
TELESPECTOR CORPORATION
1460 N Opdyke Rd (48326-2651)
PHONE...................................248 373-5400
David Piccirilli, *President*
Daniel Piccirilli, *Vice Pres*
Theodora Zurbrick, *Purchasing*
EMP: 15
SQ FT: 6,500
SALES (est): 2.8MM **Privately Held**
WEB: www.telespector.com
SIC: **3589** Water treatment equipment, industrial

(G-1018)
THE POM GROUP INC
Also Called: Precision Optical Mfg
2350 Pontiac Rd (48326-2461)
PHONE...................................248 409-7900
Jyothi Mazumder, *President*
EMP: 17
SQ FT: 30,000
SALES (est): 3.8MM **Privately Held**
WEB: www.pomgroup.com
SIC: **3312** Tool & die steel & alloys

(G-1019)
THYSSENKRUPP SYSTEM ENGRG (DH)
901 Doris Rd (48326-2716)
P.O. Box 2440, Carol Stream IL (60132-2440)
PHONE...................................248 340-8000
Daniel Stiers, *President*
Caleb Upchurch, *Superintendent*
Tami Jakuboski, *COO*
Kevin McBain, *Project Mgr*
Jim Carter, *Opers Mgr*
▲ EMP: 150
SQ FT: 165,000

SALES (est): 53.4MM
SALES (corp-wide): 39.8B **Privately Held**
WEB: www.thyssenkruppsystemengineeringinc.com
SIC: **7699** 3548 3541 3569 Industrial machinery & equipment repair; welding apparatus; machine tools, metal cutting type; tapping machines; drilling machine tools (metal cutting); milling machines; robots, assembly line: industrial & commercial
HQ: Thyssenkrupp North America, Inc.
111 W Jackson Blvd # 2400
Chicago IL 60604
312 525-2800

(G-1020)
TI AUTOMOTIVE LLC (DH)
2020 Taylor Rd (48326-1771)
PHONE...................................248 494-5000
Paul Whittleston, *Managing Dir*
Anthony Shears, *Production*
Debra Geier, *Purch Agent*
Mark Botts, *Engineer*
Jim Harrison, *Engineer*
▲ EMP: 173
SALES (est): 1B
SALES (corp-wide): 3.9B **Privately Held**
SIC: **3317** 3312 3599 3052 Tubes, seamless steel; tubing, mechanical or hypodermic sizes: cold drawn stainless; tubes, steel & iron; amusement park equipment; plastic hose; filters: oil, fuel & air, motor vehicle; fuel systems & parts, motor vehicle; air conditioning equipment, complete

(G-1021)
TI AUTOMOTIVE LLC
Also Called: Millennium Machining & Asm
1700 Harmon Rd Ste 2 (48326-1588)
PHONE...................................248 393-4525
Gus Ploss, *Manager*
EMP: 6
SALES (corp-wide): 3.9B **Privately Held**
SIC: **3469** Metal stampings
HQ: Ti Automotive, L.L.C.
2020 Taylor Rd
Auburn Hills MI 48326
248 494-5000

(G-1022)
TI GROUP AUTO SYSTEMS LLC (DH)
2020 Taylor Rd (48326-1771)
PHONE...................................248 296-8000
William Kozyra, *CEO*
Bill Laule, *President*
Kwang-Joon Jeong, *Business Mgr*
Hans Dieltjens, *Exec VP*
David Murrell, *Exec VP*
◆ EMP: 300 EST: 1922
SALES (est): 1B
SALES (corp-wide): 3.9B **Privately Held**
WEB: www.tiautomotive.com
SIC: **3317** 3312 3599 3052 Tubes, seamless steel; tubing, mechanical or hypodermic sizes: cold drawn stainless; tubes, steel & iron; hose, flexible metallic; plastic hose; fuel systems & parts, motor vehicle; filters: oil, fuel & air, motor vehicle; refrigeration & heating equipment
HQ: Ti Automotive, L.L.C.
2020 Taylor Rd
Auburn Hills MI 48326
248 494-5000

(G-1023)
TI GROUP AUTO SYSTEMS LLC
Also Called: Bundy Tubing Division
2020 Taylor Rd (48326-1771)
PHONE...................................859 235-5420
Steve Foote, *Manager*
Mark Hill, *Manager*
EMP: 199
SALES (corp-wide): 3.9B **Privately Held**
WEB: www.tiautomotive.com
SIC: **3317** 3714 3498 Steel pipe & tubes; motor vehicle parts & accessories; fabricated pipe & fittings
HQ: Ti Group Automotive Systems, Llc
2020 Taylor Rd
Auburn Hills MI 48326
248 296-8000

(G-1024)
TI GROUP AUTO SYSTEMS LLC
Also Called: Hvac Group
1272 Doris Rd 100 (48326-2617)
PHONE...................................248 494-5000
Bill Kozyra, *President*
Brian Hildebrand, *Managing Dir*
Jim Brodie, *Plant Mgr*
Juvenal Manalo, *Opers Mgr*
David Enders, *QC Mgr*
EMP: 250
SALES (corp-wide): 3.9B **Privately Held**
WEB: www.tiautomotive.com
SIC: **3498** 3429 Tube fabricating (contract bending & shaping); manufactured hardware (general)
HQ: Ti Group Automotive Systems, Llc
2020 Taylor Rd
Auburn Hills MI 48326
248 296-8000

(G-1025)
TI GROUP AUTO SYSTEMS LLC
1227 Centre Rd (48326-2605)
PHONE...................................248 475-4663
Jim Allen, *Branch Mgr*
Dan Mingledorff, *Info Tech Mgr*
EMP: 500
SALES (corp-wide): 3.9B **Privately Held**
WEB: www.tiautomotive.com
SIC: **3317** 3714 Tubes, seamless steel; motor vehicle parts & accessories
HQ: Ti Group Automotive Systems, Llc
2020 Taylor Rd
Auburn Hills MI 48326
248 296-8000

(G-1026)
TICONA POLYMERS INC
2600 N Opdyke Rd (48326-1940)
PHONE...................................248 377-6868
Gayle Hinds, *Branch Mgr*
EMP: 100
SALES (corp-wide): 7.1B **Publicly Held**
SIC: **3087** Custom compound purchased resins
HQ: Ticona Polymers, Inc.
222 Las Colinas Blvd W 900n
Irving TX 75039
859 525-4740

(G-1027)
TITANIUM TECHNOLOGIES INC
4280 Giddings Rd (48326-1529)
PHONE...................................248 836-2100
John Dimovski, *CEO*
Kathleen Murray, *President*
Bill Keating, *Exec VP*
EMP: 3
SALES (est): 127.2K **Privately Held**
SIC: **3356** Titanium

(G-1028)
TK MEXICO INC
2500 Innovation Dr (48326-2611)
PHONE...................................248 373-8040
Ken Bowling, *Admin Sec*
EMP: 5
SALES (est): 1.1MM
SALES (corp-wide): 8B **Privately Held**
SIC: **2399** Seat covers, automobile
HQ: Joyson Safety Systems Acquisition Llc
2500 Innovation Dr
Auburn Hills MI 48326
248 373-8040

(G-1029)
TRACE ZERO INC
2740 Auburn Ct (48326-3202)
PHONE...................................248 289-1277
McGregor Neville, *President*
▲ EMP: 14
SALES (est): 2.6MM **Privately Held**
SIC: **2899** Acids

(G-1030)
TRANSGLOBAL DESIGN & MFG LLC (PA)
1020 Doris Rd (48326-2613)
PHONE...................................734 525-2651
Doug Nichol, *Vice Pres*
Tim Bradley, *Manager*
EMP: 75
SQ FT: 67,000

GEOGRAPHIC SECTION

Augusta - Kalamazoo County (G-1054)

SALES (est): 17.8MM **Privately Held**
WEB: www.tdmco.com
SIC: 3711 Motor vehicles & car bodies

(G-1031)
TRANSIGN LLC
281 Collier Rd (48326-1405)
P.O. Box 300005, Drayton Plains (48330-0005)
PHONE..................................248 623-6400
Joan Booth, *Manager*
Jan Griffioen,
Jill Youngblood,
EMP: 8 **EST**: 2011
SALES (est): 1.2MM **Privately Held**
SIC: 3993 Electric signs

(G-1032)
TSM CORPORATION
1175 N Opdyke Rd (48326-2685)
PHONE..................................248 276-4700
Thomas A Prior, *President*
David Woehlke, *Engineer*
Stephen Strunk, *Manager*
▲ **EMP**: 60
SQ FT: 85,000
SALES (est): 19.4MM **Privately Held**
SIC: 3599 Machine shop, jobbing & repair

(G-1033)
U S FARATHANE PORT HURON LLC
2700 High Meadow Cir (48326-2796)
PHONE..................................248 754-7000
Andrew Greenlee, *Principal*
EMP: 5
SALES (est): 505.8K **Privately Held**
SIC: 3089 Plastics products

(G-1034)
UNIQUE FABRICATING INC (PA)
800 Standard Pkwy (48326-1415)
PHONE..................................248 853-2333
Doug Cain, *CEO*
Richard L Baum Jr, *Ch of Bd*
Jim Lenning, *Maint Spvr*
Dris Taylor, *Opers Staff*
Mark Messman, *Engineer*
EMP: 28
SQ FT: 150,000
SALES: 174.9MM **Publicly Held**
SIC: 3714 3053 3086 3296 Motor vehicle parts & accessories; gaskets, all materials; plastics foam products; mineral wool; packaging paper & plastics film, coated & laminated

(G-1035)
UNIQUE FABRICATING NA INC (HQ)
800 Standard Pkwy (48326-1415)
PHONE..................................248 853-2333
Richard L Baum Jr, *Ch of Bd*
Thomas Tekiele, *CFO*
▲ **EMP**: 320 **EST**: 1975
SQ FT: 150,000
SALES: 175.2MM
SALES (corp-wide): 174.9MM **Publicly Held**
WEB: www.uniquefab.com
SIC: 3053 3086 3296 2671 Gaskets, all materials; plastics foam products; mineral wool; packaging paper & plastics film, coated & laminated
PA: Unique Fabricating, Inc.
800 Standard Pkwy
Auburn Hills MI 48326
248 853-2333

(G-1036)
UNIQUE-INTASCO USA INC
800 Standard Pkwy (48326-1415)
PHONE..................................810 982-3360
EMP: 9
SALES (est): 2.2MM
SALES (corp-wide): 175.2MM **Publicly Held**
SIC: 2752 3555 Lithographic Commercial Printing Manufacturing Printing Trades Machinery
HQ: Unique Fabricating Na, Inc.
800 Standard Pkwy
Auburn Hills MI 48326
248 853-2333

(G-1037)
US FARATHANE LLC
2700 High Meadow Cir (48326-2796)
PHONE..................................248 754-7000
Tony Drumm, *General Mgr*
Andrew Greenlee, *Mng Member*
EMP: 31 **EST**: 2013
SALES (est): 1.5MM
SALES (corp-wide): 876MM **Privately Held**
SIC: 3089 Battery cases, plastic or plastic combination
PA: U.S. Farathane Holdings Corp.
11650 Park Ct
Shelby Township MI 48315
586 726-1200

(G-1038)
US FARATHANE HOLDINGS CORP
1350 Harmon Rd (48326-1540)
PHONE..................................780 246-1034
Andy Greenlee, *President*
EMP: 115
SALES (corp-wide): 876MM **Privately Held**
WEB: www.deltatechgroup.com
SIC: 3089 Automotive parts, plastic
PA: U.S. Farathane Holdings Corp.
11650 Park Ct
Shelby Township MI 48315
586 726-1200

(G-1039)
US FARATHANE HOLDINGS CORP
2082 Brown Rd (48326-1702)
PHONE..................................248 391-6801
Bob Vamos, *Branch Mgr*
Peter Mozer,
EMP: 10
SALES (corp-wide): 876MM **Privately Held**
WEB: www.deltatechgroup.com
SIC: 3089 Automotive parts, plastic
PA: U.S. Farathane Holdings Corp.
11650 Park Ct
Shelby Township MI 48315
586 726-1200

(G-1040)
US FARATHANE HOLDINGS CORP
2700 High Meadow Cir (48326-2796)
PHONE..................................248 754-7000
Steve Maczko, *General Mgr*
EMP: 200
SALES (corp-wide): 876MM **Privately Held**
SIC: 3089 Injection molding of plastics
PA: U.S. Farathane Holdings Corp.
11650 Park Ct
Shelby Township MI 48315
586 726-1200

(G-1041)
USF DELTA TOOLING LLC (HQ)
Also Called: Delta Tooling Co.
1350 Harmon Rd (48326-1540)
PHONE..................................248 391-6800
Peter Mozer, *CEO*
Rudolf W Mozer, *Chairman*
Tibor Toreki, *COO*
Dennis Carroll, *Plant Mgr*
Tibor Torecke, *Engineer*
◆ **EMP**: 150 **EST**: 1953
SQ FT: 170,000
SALES (est): 26.8MM
SALES (corp-wide): 876MM **Privately Held**
WEB: www.deltatool.com
SIC: 3544 3999 Industrial molds; jigs & fixtures; models, general, except toy
PA: U.S. Farathane Holdings Corp.
11650 Park Ct
Shelby Township MI 48315
586 726-1200

(G-1042)
USF WESTLAND LLC
2700 High Meadow Cir (48326-2796)
PHONE..................................248 754-7000
EMP: 4 **EST**: 2016
SALES (est): 185.9K **Privately Held**
SIC: 3089 Plastics products

(G-1043)
VALEO NORTH AMERICA INC
Also Called: Valeo Inc Eng Coolg Auto Div
4100 N Atlantic Blvd (48326-1570)
PHONE..................................248 209-8253
Dave Cure, *Business Mgr*
Marcos Ferrari, *Project Mgr*
Jeff Roodbeen, *Opers Staff*
Connie Hollin, *Production*
Janet Cole, *Purch Mgr*
EMP: 150
SQ FT: 119,000
SALES (corp-wide): 177.9K **Privately Held**
WEB: www.valeoinc.com
SIC: 3714 Motor vehicle parts & accessories
HQ: Valeo North America, Inc.
150 Stephenson Hwy
Troy MI 48083

(G-1044)
VALEO RADAR SYSTEMS INC
3000 University Dr (48326-2356)
PHONE..................................248 340-3126
EMP: 21
SALES (est): 3.4MM **Privately Held**
SIC: 3812 Mfg Search/Navigation Equipment

(G-1045)
VISIONEERING INC (PA)
2055 Taylor Rd (48326-1772)
PHONE..................................248 622-5600
Brad Hallett, *President*
Tim Bellestri, *Vice Pres*
Tony Robinson, *Vice Pres*
Sofia Palushaj, *Purch Mgr*
Jeff Lytwyn, *QC Mgr*
▲ **EMP**: 259 **EST**: 1953
SQ FT: 183,000
SALES: 55.1MM **Privately Held**
SIC: 3544 Jigs & fixtures; industrial molds

(G-1046)
VITESCO TECHNOLOGIES
1 Continental Dr (48326-1581)
PHONE..................................704 442-8000
EMP: 3
SALES (corp-wide): 50.8B **Privately Held**
SIC: 3714 Motor vehicle parts & accessories
HQ: Vitesco Technologies Usa, Llc
2400 Executive Hills Dr
Auburn Hills MI 48326
248 209-4000

(G-1047)
VITESCO TECHNOLOGIES USA LLC (DH)
2400 Executive Hills Dr (48326-2980)
PHONE..................................248 209-4000
Alberto Jimenez, *Electrical Engi*
Andreas Wolf, *Mng Member*
EMP: 10
SALES (est): 455.8MM
SALES (corp-wide): 50.8B **Privately Held**
SIC: 3714 Motor vehicle parts & accessories
HQ: Continental Automotive Systems, Inc.
1 Continental Dr
Auburn Hills MI 48326
248 393-5300

(G-1048)
VOLKSWAGEN GROUP AMERICA INC
Also Called: Volkswagen Auto Securitization
3800 Hamlin Rd (48326-2829)
PHONE..................................248 754-5000
Wayne Killen, *General Mgr*
Dale Drury, *Sales Mgr*
Eric Nawrocki, *Marketing Staff*
Gerhard Riechel, *Branch Mgr*
Jean Sailland, *Manager*
EMP: 85
SALES (corp-wide): 270B **Privately Held**
WEB: www.vw.com
SIC: 3699 Security devices
HQ: Volkswagen Group Of America, Inc.
2200 Ferdinand Porsche Dr
Herndon VA 20171
703 364-7000

(G-1049)
WABCO HOLDINGS INC (PA)
1220 Pacific Dr (48326-1589)
PHONE..................................248 270-9300
Jacques Esculier, *Ch of Bd*
Jane McLeod, *President*
Nick Rens, *President*
Jorge Solis, *President*
Sean Deason, *Vice Pres*
▲ **EMP**: 107
SALES: 3.8B **Publicly Held**
SIC: 3714 Motor vehicle brake systems & parts; motor vehicle steering systems & parts; motor vehicle transmissions, drive assemblies & parts

(G-1050)
WEBER AUTOMOTIVE CORPORATION
1750 Summit Dr (48326-1780)
PHONE..................................248 393-5520
Dieter Albers, *COO*
Chip Quarrier, *Vice Pres*
Jonas Linke, *VP Opers*
Achim Lohner, *VP Opers*
Jeremy Kjorli, *Opers Staff*
▲ **EMP**: 226
SQ FT: 250,000
SALES: 58MM
SALES (corp-wide): 177K **Privately Held**
SIC: 3714 Motor vehicle engines & parts
HQ: Weber Automotive Gmbh
Otto-Lilienthal-Str. 5
Markdorf 88677
754 496-30

(G-1051)
YOKOHAMA INDS AMERICAS INC
2285 N Opdyke Rd Ste F (48326-2468)
PHONE..................................248 276-0480
John Schimelfanick, *Engineer*
EMP: 169 **Privately Held**
SIC: 3496 Conveyor belts
HQ: Yokohama Industries Americas Inc.
105 Industry Dr
Versailles KY 40383
859 873-2188

Augusta
Kalamazoo County

(G-1052)
COMMERCIAL ELECTRIC CO
7255 Pin Oak Cir (49012-8869)
PHONE..................................269 731-3350
Robert C Galen, *President*
EMP: 3 **EST**: 1936
SQ FT: 6,000
SALES (est): 200K **Privately Held**
SIC: 7694 Electric motor repair

(G-1053)
KNAPPEN MILLING COMPANY
110 S Water St (49012-9781)
P.O. Box 245 (49012-0245)
PHONE..................................269 731-4141
Emily Likens, *President*
Bob Likens, *Senior VP*
John Shouse, *Vice Pres*
Todd C Wright, *Vice Pres*
Darrell Roose, *Treasurer*
EMP: 37
SQ FT: 3,000
SALES (est): 8.5MM **Privately Held**
WEB: www.knappen.com
SIC: 2041 Flour; bran & middlings (except rice)

(G-1054)
SMITH METAL LLC
211 S Webster St (49012-9780)
PHONE..................................269 731-5211
David Sutton,
EMP: 8
SALES (est): 267.8K **Privately Held**
SIC: 3599 Machine shop, jobbing & repair

Augusta - Kalamazoo County (G-1055)

(G-1055)
SMITH METAL TURNING INC
Also Called: Smith Metal Turning Service
211 S Webster St (49012-9780)
P.O. Box 218 (49012-0218)
PHONE.................................269 731-5211
Robert Smith, *President*
Patricia Smith, *Treasurer*
EMP: 6 **EST:** 1969
SQ FT: 4,500
SALES (est): 939.5K **Privately Held**
SIC: 3599 Machine shop, jobbing & repair

Bad Axe
Huron County

(G-1056)
AMERICAN TCHNCAL FBRCATORS LLC
414 E Soper Rd (48413-9500)
PHONE.................................989 269-6262
Bryan Barwig, *Mng Member*
EMP: 27
SQ FT: 66,000
SALES (est): 5.3MM **Privately Held**
WEB: www.amtechfab.com
SIC: 3444 Sheet metalwork

(G-1057)
AXLY PRODUCTION MACHINING INC
Also Called: Axly-Briney Sales
700 E Soper Rd (48413-9497)
PHONE.................................989 269-2444
William Roberts, *President*
David Hyzer, *Vice Pres*
Clark Shuart Sr, *Treasurer*
Frank Peplinski, *Admin Sec*
EMP: 480
SQ FT: 52,500
SALES (est): 44.8MM **Privately Held**
SIC: 3541 3325 3366 Machine tools, metal cutting type; bushings, cast steel: except investment; copper foundries
PA: Gemini Group, Inc.
   175 Thompson Rd Ste A
   Bad Axe MI 48413

(G-1058)
BAD AXE FAMILY VISION CENTER
1266 Sand Beach Rd (48413-8817)
P.O. Box 249 (48413-0249)
PHONE.................................989 269-5393
Gregory Atkins, *Owner*
Rebecca J Atkins, *Office Mgr*
EMP: 3
SALES (est): 217.9K **Privately Held**
SIC: 8042 3851 Specialized optometrists; lenses, ophthalmic

(G-1059)
CLEMCO PRINTING INC
116 Scott St (48413-1212)
PHONE.................................989 269-8364
Terri Tschirhart, *President*
Gerald Tschirhart, *Corp Secy*
EMP: 6 **EST:** 1973
SQ FT: 1,500
SALES (est): 920.8K **Privately Held**
SIC: 2752 2759 Commercial printing, offset; letterpress printing

(G-1060)
ENTERPRISE TOOL AND GEAR INC (PA)
635 Liberty St (48413-9532)
PHONE.................................989 269-9797
Joel Dean, *President*
Neal Rogers, *Admin Sec*
EMP: 60
SQ FT: 60,000
SALES (est): 6.7MM **Privately Held**
SIC: 3544 3545 3462 3366 Jigs & fixtures; machine tool accessories; iron & steel forgings; copper foundries

(G-1061)
GAINORS MEAT PACKING INC
317 N Port Crescent St (48413-1221)
PHONE.................................989 269-8161
EMP: 8 **EST:** 1946
SQ FT: 2,000
SALES (est): 470K **Privately Held**
SIC: 2011 Beat Packing Plant

(G-1062)
GEMINI GROUP INC (PA)
175 Thompson Rd Ste A (48413-8274)
P.O. Box 100 (48413-0100)
PHONE.................................989 269-6272
David Hyzer, *Vice Pres*
Corey Terry, *Prdtn Mgr*
Dave Shepherd, *Safety Mgr*
Tammy Gwisdalla, *Production*
Wendy Barnes, *QC Mgr*
EMP: 12
SQ FT: 16,000
SALES (est): 379.4MM **Privately Held**
SIC: 8741 3089 Management services; extruded finished plastic products

(G-1063)
GEMINI GROUP SERVICES INC
175 Thompson Rd Ste A (48413-8274)
P.O. Box 100 (48413-0100)
PHONE.................................248 435-7271
Lynette Drake, *President*
EMP: 3 **EST:** 2016
SALES (est): 160.5K **Privately Held**
SIC: 3089 Injection molding of plastics

(G-1064)
GEMINI PRECISION MACHINING INC (HQ)
Also Called: Axly Production Machining
700 E Soper Rd (48413-9497)
PHONE.................................989 269-9702
Lynette Drake, *President*
David Hyzer, *Vice Pres*
Frank Peplinski, *Treasurer*
Jennifer Sosnoski, *Personnel*
Mark Tomlinson, *Sales Executive*
EMP: 124 **EST:** 1947
SALES (est): 23.7MM **Privately Held**
WEB: www.ckstool.com
SIC: 3544 Special dies, tools, jigs & fixtures

(G-1065)
GEMINI PRECISION MACHINING INC
Also Called: Briney Tooling Systems
700 E Soper Rd (48413-9497)
PHONE.................................989 269-9702
Evan Osantoski, *Engineer*
Tom Carrizeau, *Manager*
EMP: 85 **Privately Held**
WEB: www.ckstool.com
SIC: 3544 3567 3545 Special dies, jigs & fixtures; industrial furnaces & ovens; machine tool accessories
HQ: Gemini Precision Machining, Inc.
   700 E Soper Rd
   Bad Axe MI 48413
   989 269-9702

(G-1066)
GLOBAL LIFT CORP
684 N Port Crescent St C (48413-1275)
PHONE.................................989 269-5900
Lee Steinman, *President*
Josh Steinman, *Vice Pres*
Joshua Steinman, *Vice Pres*
Brian Essenmacher, *Design Engr*
EMP: 12
SALES (est): 2.2MM **Privately Held**
SIC: 3449 Bars, concrete reinforcing: fabricated steel

(G-1067)
HURON PUBLISHING COMPANY INC (HQ)
Also Called: Huron Daily Tribune, The
211 N Heisterman St (48413-1239)
PHONE.................................989 269-6461
Jan Stoeckle, *Publisher*
Jerry Gibbard, *Prdtn Mgr*
Gail Soper, *Financial Exec*
Rebecca Watson, *Adv Dir*
Vicki Yaroch, *Advt Staff*
EMP: 58
SQ FT: 5,000
SALES (est): 4MM
SALES (corp-wide): 8.3B **Privately Held**
WEB: www.michigansthumb.com
SIC: 2711 2752 Newspapers: publishing only, not printed on site; commercial printing, lithographic
PA: The Hearst Corporation
   300 W 57th St Fl 42
   New York NY 10019
   212 649-2000

(G-1068)
HURON TOOL & ENGINEERING CO (HQ)
635 Liberty St (48413-9532)
PHONE.................................989 269-9927
Neil Rogers, *President*
Aaron Darbee, *Opers Mgr*
Rod Mausolf, *Engineer*
▲ **EMP:** 50
SQ FT: 36,000
SALES (est): 9MM
SALES (corp-wide): 6.7MM **Privately Held**
WEB: www.huron-tool.com
SIC: 3541 3544 3545 3452 Machine tool replacement & repair parts, metal cutting types; special dies, tools, jigs & fixtures; machine tool accessories; bolts, nuts, rivets & washers; copper foundries
PA: Enterprise Tool And Gear Inc
   635 Liberty St
   Bad Axe MI 48413
   989 269-9797

(G-1069)
MINUTEMAN METAL WORKS INC
1600 Patterson St (48413-9479)
PHONE.................................989 269-8342
Gene Brade, *President*
EMP: 4
SQ FT: 6,500
SALES (est): 500K **Privately Held**
SIC: 3446 Architectural metalwork

(G-1070)
SIERRA PLASTICS INC
175 Thompson Rd Ste A (48413-8274)
P.O. Box 100 (48413-0100)
PHONE.................................989 269-6272
David Hyzer, *President*
EMP: 20 **EST:** 1998
SALES (est): 2.6MM **Privately Held**
SIC: 3465 Body parts, automobile: stamped metal
PA: Gemini Group, Inc.
   175 Thompson Rd Ste A
   Bad Axe MI 48413

(G-1071)
SRW INC (PA)
175 Thompson Rd Ste A (48413-8274)
P.O. Box 100 (48413-0100)
PHONE.................................989 269-8528
David Hyzer, *President*
William F Roberts, *Vice Pres*
Frank M Peplinski, *Treasurer*
Clark K Shaurt, *Admin Sec*
EMP: 10
SALES (est): 3.2MM **Privately Held**
SIC: 1381 1389 Drilling oil & gas wells; oil field services

(G-1072)
TALCO INDUSTRIES
705 E Woodworth St (48413-1548)
PHONE.................................989 269-6260
Eric Cook, *Owner*
EMP: 4
SQ FT: 14,000
SALES (est): 750K **Privately Held**
SIC: 3089 Molding primary plastic

(G-1073)
THUMB BLANKET
55 Westland Dr (48413-7741)
PHONE.................................989 269-9918
Jack Guza, *General Mgr*
Michele Dicus, *Manager*
EMP: 6
SALES (est): 492K
SALES (corp-wide): 697.5MM **Privately Held**
WEB: www.macombdaily.com
SIC: 2741 Shopping news: publishing only, not printed on site
HQ: 21st Century Newspapers, Inc.
   19176 Hall Rd Ste 200
   Clinton Township MI 48038
   586 469-4510

(G-1074)
THUMB PLASTICS INC
400 Liberty St (48413-9490)
PHONE.................................989 269-9791
William Roberts, *CEO*
David Hyzer, *CFO*
Clark Shuart Sr, *Treasurer*
Frank Peplinski, *Admin Sec*
EMP: 50
SQ FT: 27,000
SALES (est): 45.2MM **Privately Held**
WEB: www.geminigroup.net
SIC: 3089 Injection molded finished plastic products
HQ: Pepro Enterprises, Inc.
   4385 Garfield St
   Ubly MI 48475
   989 658-3200

(G-1075)
THUMB TOOL & ENGINEERING CO
354 Liberty St (48413-9302)
PHONE.................................989 269-9731
Jack Rochefort, *President*
Lynette Drake, *Principal*
Clark K Shuart, *Corp Secy*
Gerald Rochefort, *Assistant VP*
Jeffrey Rochefort, *Assistant VP*
▲ **EMP:** 250
SQ FT: 93,000
SALES (est): 42.2MM **Privately Held**
WEB: www.thumbtool.com
SIC: 3544 Special dies & tools; jigs & fixtures
PA: Gemini Group, Inc.
   175 Thompson Rd Ste A
   Bad Axe MI 48413

(G-1076)
VALLEY GEAR AND MACHINE INC
514 Chickory St (48413-1550)
PHONE.................................989 269-8177
Richard Booms, *President*
Ryan Booms, *Vice Pres*
Al Kleinknecht, *Sales Mgr*
EMP: 10
SQ FT: 4,800
SALES (est): 1.8MM **Privately Held**
WEB: www.valley-gear.com
SIC: 3566 3559 Speed changers, drives & gears; plastics working machinery

Bailey
Muskegon County

(G-1077)
BECMAR CORP
585 Canada Rd (49303-9731)
PHONE.................................616 675-7479
Arthur Proctor, *President*
Susan Proctor, *Vice Pres*
EMP: 7
SQ FT: 18,500
SALES (est): 580K **Privately Held**
WEB: www.becmar.com
SIC: 3552 Printing machinery, textile

(G-1078)
BONDFIRE COMPANY
1373 Newaygo Rd (49303-9757)
P.O. Box 106 (49303-0106)
PHONE.................................231 834-5696
Lawrence Bond, *President*
EMP: 18
SALES: 1.5MM **Privately Held**
WEB: www.dumpersunlimited.com
SIC: 3537 Hoppers, end dump

(G-1079)
GUERNE PRECISION MACHINING
13761 Bailey Rd (49303-9706)
PHONE.................................231 834-7417
Wayne Guerne, *President*
EMP: 5 **EST:** 1974
SQ FT: 2,400

GEOGRAPHIC SECTION

Baraga - Baraga County (G-1107)

SALES: 300K **Privately Held**
SIC: 3599 Machine shop, jobbing & repair

(G-1080)
MCNEES MANUFACTURING INC
750 Canada Rd (49303-9732)
PHONE.................................616 675-7480
Richard McNees, *President*
Ann Watkins, *Bookkeeper*
EMP: 12
SALES (est): 28.4K **Privately Held**
SIC: 3451 Screw machine products

Baldwin
Lake County

(G-1081)
ALTERNATIVE HEATING & FUEL
910 N M 37 (49304-9091)
PHONE.................................231 745-6110
Robert Panrock, *Owner*
EMP: 3
SALES (est): 289.1K **Privately Held**
SIC: 3993 Signs & advertising specialties

(G-1082)
AUSTIN TUBE PRODUCTS INC
5629 S Forman Rd (49304-8046)
P.O. Box 1120 (49304-1120)
PHONE.................................231 745-2741
Joe Day, *President*
Derrielene Day, *Admin Sec*
EMP: 20
SQ FT: 15,000
SALES (est): 3.9MM **Privately Held**
WEB: www.austintubeproducts.com
SIC: 3492 3498 3444 3441 Hose & tube fittings & assemblies, hydraulic/pneumatic; fabricated pipe & fittings; sheet metalwork; fabricated structural metal; aluminum extruded products; steel pipe & tubes

(G-1083)
JEROME MILLER LUMBER CO (PA)
7027 S James Rd (49304-7135)
PHONE.................................231 745-3694
Jerome Miller, *Owner*
Toni Miller, *Co-Owner*
Shelly Miller, *Manager*
EMP: 8
SALES: 990K **Privately Held**
SIC: 2421 Sawmills & planing mills, general

(G-1084)
JEROME MILLER LUMBER CO
Baldwin Rd (49304)
P.O. Box 60 (49304-0060)
PHONE.................................231 745-3694
Jerome Miller, *Owner*
EMP: 9
SALES (corp-wide): 990K **Privately Held**
SIC: 2421 2411 Sawmills & planing mills, general; logging
PA: Jerome Miller Lumber Co
7027 S James Rd
Baldwin MI 49304
231 745-3694

(G-1085)
PGI HOLDINGS INC
Also Called: Pioneer Publishing
851 Michigan Ave (49304-8140)
P.O. Box 399 (49304-0399)
PHONE.................................231 745-4635
Jim Bruskotter, *Systems Mgr*
EMP: 3
SALES (corp-wide): 8.3B **Privately Held**
WEB: www.bigrapidsnews.com
SIC: 2711 Newspapers: publishing only, not printed on site
HQ: Pgi Holdings, Inc.
115 N Michigan Ave
Big Rapids MI 49307
231 796-4831

(G-1086)
WHEELERS WOLF LAKE SAWMILL
195 N M 37 # 137 (49304-7896)
PHONE.................................231 745-7078
Patricia Wheeler, *President*
Rodney L Wheeler, *Admin Sec*
EMP: 8
SALES (est): 800K **Privately Held**
SIC: 2421 Sawmills & planing mills, general

Bancroft
Shiawassee County

(G-1087)
CEREPHEX CORPORATION
3001 Miller Rd (48414-9308)
PHONE.................................517 719-0414
Jeffrey B Hargrove, *CEO*
EMP: 5
SALES (est): 367.8K **Privately Held**
SIC: 3845 Electromedical equipment

Bangor
Van Buren County

(G-1088)
BANGOR PLASTICS INC
809 Washington St (49013-1155)
P.O. Box 99 (49013-0099)
PHONE.................................269 427-7971
Glenn F Wokeck, *President*
Barbara Kovell, *Manager*
EMP: 20 EST: 1944
SQ FT: 29,000
SALES (est): 3.6MM **Privately Held**
WEB: www.bangorplastics.com
SIC: 3089 3083 Injection molding of plastics; laminated plastics plate & sheet

(G-1089)
BARBER PACKAGING COMPANY
300 Industrial Park Rd (49013-1265)
PHONE.................................269 427-7995
David Barber, *President*
EMP: 45
SQ FT: 16,000
SALES (est): 7.5MM **Privately Held**
SIC: 3086 Packaging & shipping materials, foamed plastic

(G-1090)
DIE CAST PRESS MFG CO INC
46652 Sycamore Dr (49013-9510)
PHONE.................................269 427-5408
Casper Smidt, *Owner*
EMP: 7
SALES (corp-wide): 4.2MM **Privately Held**
WEB: www.diecastpress.com
SIC: 3542 Machine tools, metal forming type
PA: Die Cast Press Manufacturing Company, Inc.
56480 Kasper Dr
Paw Paw MI 49079
269 657-6060

(G-1091)
GREAT MEADHALL BREWING CO LLC
215 W Monroe St (49013-1330)
PHONE.................................269 427-0827
David J McCarty,
EMP: 3
SALES: 33K **Privately Held**
SIC: 2084 Wines

(G-1092)
LINK TECH INC
59648 M 43 (49013-9617)
PHONE.................................269 427-8297
Bruce Linker, *CEO*
Randy Perkinson, *President*
Linda Irwin, *Office Mgr*
◆ EMP: 5
SALES (est): 664.6K **Privately Held**
WEB: www.linktech-inc.com
SIC: 3081 8742 Packing materials, plastic sheet; productivity improvement consultant

(G-1093)
MARRONE MICHIGAN MANUFACTORING
700 Industrial Park Rd (49013-1266)
PHONE.................................269 427-0300
Jake Wahmoff, *Chairman*
EMP: 3
SALES (est): 292.5K **Privately Held**
SIC: 3999 Manufacturing industries

(G-1094)
REMINDER SHOPPING GUIDE INC
416 Railroad St (49013-1366)
P.O. Box 218 (49013-0218)
PHONE.................................269 427-7474
Kim Montoy, *Director*
EMP: 7
SALES (est): 459K **Privately Held**
SIC: 2711 Newspapers, publishing & printing

(G-1095)
SAGE ACOUSTICS LLC
55962 M 43 (49013-9566)
PHONE.................................269 861-5593
Michael Frank,
Joshua Barr,
Michael Butts,
EMP: 3 EST: 2015
SQ FT: 1,800
SALES: 700K **Privately Held**
SIC: 3679 Transducers, electrical

Baraga
Baraga County

(G-1096)
ALL-WOOD INC
101 Us Highway 41 S (49908-9789)
P.O. Box 489 (49908-0489)
PHONE.................................906 353-6642
Marie A Jacobson, *President*
EMP: 4 EST: 1965
SQ FT: 9,500
SALES (est): 469.2K **Privately Held**
SIC: 2421 Lumber: rough, sawed or planed

(G-1097)
BARAGA COUNTY CONCRETE COMPANY
468 N Superior Ave (49908)
PHONE.................................906 353-6595
Arthur D Barrett, *President*
EMP: 5
SALES (est): 716.9K **Privately Held**
SIC: 3273 Ready-mixed concrete

(G-1098)
BESSE FOREST PRODUCTS INC
Also Called: Baraga Lumber Division
16522 Westland Dr (49908-9211)
PHONE.................................906 353-7193
Don Rosenberger, *Manager*
Nancy McIntyre, *Technology*
EMP: 20
SALES (corp-wide): 117.9MM **Privately Held**
SIC: 5099 5031 2426 2421 Logs, hewn ties, posts & poles; lumber, plywood & millwork; veneer; hardwood dimension & flooring mills; sawmills & planing mills, general
PA: Forest Besse Products Inc
933 N 8th St
Gladstone MI 49837
906 428-3113

(G-1099)
CCI ARNHEIM INC
14935 Arnheim (49908)
P.O. Box 861 (49908-0861)
PHONE.................................906 353-6330
David Mattson, *President*
EMP: 4
SALES (est): 403.4K **Privately Held**
SIC: 2451 Mobile buildings: for commercial use

(G-1100)
CRAZY JOES ENTERPRISES LLC
13751 State Highway M38 (49908-9084)
PHONE.................................906 395-1522
Damien Waara, *COO*
Keith Herrala,
EMP: 3
SALES (est): 96.9K **Privately Held**
SIC: 5499 2035 2033 Gourmet food stores; pickles, sauces & salad dressings; vegetables & vegetable products in cans, jars, etc.

(G-1101)
DESROCHERS BROTHERS INC
107 3rd St (49908)
P.O. Box 524 (49908-0524)
PHONE.................................906 353-6346
Robert Desrochers, *President*
Jim Desrochers, *Vice Pres*
EMP: 15
SQ FT: 20,000
SALES (est): 1.9MM **Privately Held**
SIC: 3599 Machine shop, jobbing & repair

(G-1102)
EDWARDS OUTDOOR SCIENCE
Also Called: Edwards Outdoor Advertising
419 N Superior Ave (49908-9602)
PHONE.................................906 353-7375
EMP: 3
SALES: 100K **Privately Held**
SIC: 3993 7312 Manufactures Signs And Advertising Specialties

(G-1103)
HOMESTEAD GRAPHICS DESIGN INC
516 S Superior Ave (49908-9698)
P.O. Box 579 (49908-0579)
PHONE.................................906 353-6741
Joseph Kayramo, *President*
EMP: 7
SQ FT: 6,000
SALES (est): 714.3K **Privately Held**
WEB: www.homesteadgraphics.com
SIC: 2759 2752 Screen printing; commercial printing, lithographic

(G-1104)
KEWEENAW BAY INDIAN COMMUNITY
Also Called: American Made Tubcraft Plus
16429 Bear Town Rd (49908-9210)
PHONE.................................906 524-5757
Richard Shalifoe, *President*
Susan Lafernier, *Chairman*
Amy St Arnold, *Treasurer*
EMP: 10
SQ FT: 13,800
SALES (est): 100K **Privately Held**
SIC: 3229 Glass fiber products

(G-1105)
KOSKI WELDING INC
13529 Old 41 Rd (49908-9022)
PHONE.................................906 353-7588
EMP: 7
SQ FT: 4,800
SALES: 500K **Privately Held**
SIC: 3599 7692 Machine Shop

(G-1106)
LASER NORTH INC
455 N Superior Ave (49908-9602)
P.O. Box 845 (49908-0845)
PHONE.................................906 353-6090
Mark Niemela, *Owner*
EMP: 7
SALES: 928.7K **Privately Held**
SIC: 7389 7373 3448 Metal cutting services; computer-aided design (CAD) systems service; prefabricated metal components

(G-1107)
LASER NORTH INC
Also Called: Northern Tool & Engineering
442 N Superior Ave (49908-9602)
P.O. Box 845 (49908-0845)
PHONE.................................906 353-6090
Leo L Niemela, *President*
Mark Niemela, *General Mgr*
Carol Ketola, *Vice Pres*

EMP: 5 EST: 1974
SQ FT: 7,500
SALES (est): 783.6K **Privately Held**
SIC: 3449 3544 Bars, concrete reinforcing: fabricated steel; special dies, tools, jigs & fixtures

(G-1108)
LINDEMANN MACHINING & WELDING
14265 Lindemann Rd (49908-9169)
PHONE..................906 353-6424
Nick Lindemann, *President*
EMP: 3
SALES (est): 332.3K **Privately Held**
SIC: 3599 Machine shop, jobbing & repair

(G-1109)
MASSIE MFG INC
445 N Superior Ave (49908-9602)
P.O. Box 339 (49908-0339)
PHONE..................906 353-6381
Peter M Massie, *President*
Michael Hirzel, *General Mgr*
David Massie, *Vice Pres*
Siena Tober, *Admin Sec*
EMP: 20
SALES (est): 3.9MM **Privately Held**
SIC: 3443 Fabricated plate work (boiler shop)

(G-1110)
MORIN FIREWORKS
15781 Us Highway 41 N (49908-9200)
PHONE..................906 353-6650
Pete Morin, *Owner*
EMP: 3 EST: 1970
SALES (est): 150.1K **Privately Held**
SIC: 5999 2899 Fireworks; fireworks

(G-1111)
NORTHERN ORTHOTICS PROSTHETICS (PA)
509 S Superior Ave (49908-9698)
PHONE..................906 353-7161
Thomas R Penfold, *President*
Constance Penfold, *Vice Pres*
EMP: 4
SQ FT: 2,000
SALES (est): 384.7K **Privately Held**
SIC: 3842 5999 Limbs, artificial; orthopedic & prosthesis applications

(G-1112)
PENINSULA POWDER COATING INC
128 Hemlock St (49908-9675)
P.O. Box 609 (49908-0609)
PHONE..................906 353-7234
Brian Baccus, *President*
EMP: 24
SQ FT: 5,000
SALES: 3MM **Privately Held**
WEB: www.peninsulapowdercoating.com
SIC: 3479 Coating of metals & formed products

(G-1113)
PETTIBONE/TRAVERSE LIFT LLC (DH)
1100 S Superior Ave (49908-9629)
PHONE..................906 353-4800
Scott Raffaelli, *Vice Pres*
Jamie Menard, *Purch Mgr*
Kathryn Pirkola, *QC Mgr*
John Westman, *Project Engr*
Sandra Lytikainen, *Marketing Mgr*
▲ EMP: 37 EST: 1946
SQ FT: 50,000
SALES: 20MM
SALES (corp-wide): 1.2B **Privately Held**
SIC: 3537 Lift trucks, industrial: fork, platform, straddle, etc.
HQ: Pettibone L.L.C.
 27501 Bella Vista Pkwy
 Warrenville IL 60555
 630 353-5000

(G-1114)
PETTIBONE/TRAVERSE LIFT LLC
16243 Main St (49908-9217)
PHONE..................906 353-6668
Nick Linderman, *Manager*
EMP: 30

SALES (corp-wide): 1.2B **Privately Held**
WEB: www.pettiboneusa.com
SIC: 3537 Lift trucks, industrial: fork, platform, straddle, etc.
HQ: Pettibone/Traverse Lift, L.L.C.
 1100 S Superior Ave
 Baraga MI 49908
 906 353-4800

(G-1115)
SELKEY FABRICATORS LLC
13170 Lindblom Rd (49908-9150)
PHONE..................906 353-7104
Nicholas Lindemann, *General Mgr*
EMP: 12
SQ FT: 35,000
SALES (est): 669.3K **Privately Held**
SIC: 2899 Fluxes: brazing, soldering, galvanizing & welding

(G-1116)
VAN STRATEN BROTHERS INC
14908 Us Highway 41 (49908-9014)
PHONE..................906 353-6490
Peter Van Straten, *President*
George Van Straten, *Vice Pres*
EMP: 45
SQ FT: 12,000
SALES (est): 3.6MM **Privately Held**
SIC: 7692 Welding repair

Barbeau
Chippewa County

(G-1117)
SCHALLIPS INC
Also Called: Cookies Cubed
17592 S Simonsen Rd (49710-9416)
PHONE..................906 635-0941
Robert Schallip, *President*
Mary A Schallip, *Vice Pres*
EMP: 3
SALES (est): 257.3K **Privately Held**
WEB: www.cookiescubed.com
SIC: 3556 8711 7389 Biscuit cutters (machines); aviation &/or aeronautical engineering; marine engineering; inspection & testing services

Bark River
Delta County

(G-1118)
BARK RIVER CONCRETE PDTS CO (PA)
1397 Us Highway 2 41 (49807-8908)
P.O. Box 67 (49807-0067)
PHONE..................906 466-9940
Donald T Vanenkevort, *President*
James Vanenkevort, *Vice Pres*
Paul Vanenkevort, *Treasurer*
David Vanenkevort, *Admin Sec*
EMP: 10
SQ FT: 20,000
SALES (est): 1.9MM **Privately Held**
SIC: 3271 Blocks, concrete or cinder: standard

(G-1119)
FOR THE LOVE OF CUPCAKES
5835 F Rd (49807-9575)
PHONE..................906 399-3004
Kelli Vanginhoven, *Principal*
EMP: 3
SALES (est): 91.7K **Privately Held**
SIC: 2051 Bread, cake & related products

(G-1120)
LUCAS LOGGING
W1564 State Highway M69 (49807)
PHONE..................906 246-3629
Wayne Lucas, *Owner*
EMP: 6
SALES (est): 545K **Privately Held**
SIC: 2411 Logging camps & contractors

(G-1121)
MESSERSMITH MANUFACTURING INC
2612 F Rd (49807-9718)
PHONE..................906 466-9010
Gailyn Messersmith, *President*
Valerie Messersmith, *Corp Secy*
EMP: 7
SQ FT: 10,700
SALES (est): 1.1MM **Privately Held**
WEB: www.burnchips.com
SIC: 3433 Stokers, mechanical: domestic or industrial

(G-1122)
S & S MOWING INC
1460 15.5 Rd (49807-9529)
PHONE..................906 466-9009
Shelly Lippens, *President*
Gregory Knauf, *Vice Pres*
Scott Lippens, *Treasurer*
EMP: 4
SALES (est): 291.8K **Privately Held**
SIC: 3523 Grounds mowing equipment

Baroda
Berrien County

(G-1123)
DABLON VINEYARDS LLC
111 W Shawnee Rd (49101)
PHONE..................269 422-2846
Amy Hemphill, *Business Mgr*
EMP: 7
SALES (est): 627.4K **Privately Held**
SIC: 2084 Wines

(G-1124)
FRANK W SMALL MET FABRICATION
8961 First St (49101)
PHONE..................269 422-2001
Frank W Small, *Owner*
EMP: 3
SALES (est): 190K **Privately Held**
SIC: 3312 3444 Blast furnaces & steel mills; sheet metalwork

(G-1125)
GAST CABINET CO
8836 Stevensville Baroda (49101-9349)
PHONE..................269 422-1587
Robert R Gast, *Owner*
EMP: 30 EST: 1967
SALES (est): 935.9K **Privately Held**
WEB: www.invitrotech.com
SIC: 1751 5947 2541 2434 Cabinet & finish carpentry; gift shop; wood partitions & fixtures; vanities, bathroom: wood

(G-1126)
LAKESHORE DIE CAST INC
8829 Stvnsville Baroda Rd (49101-9301)
P.O. Box 96 (49101-0096)
PHONE..................269 422-1523
Fred Schaller, *President*
Adam Schaller, *Office Mgr*
EMP: 18 EST: 1959
SQ FT: 42,000
SALES (est): 3.6MM **Privately Held**
SIC: 3364 3363 Zinc & zinc-base alloy die-castings; aluminum die-castings

(G-1127)
MIDWEST DIE CORP
9220 First St (49101-8923)
P.O. Box 132 (49101-0132)
PHONE..................269 422-2171
Rodney Nitz, *President*
Richard Nitz, *Vice Pres*
Cindy Schroeder, *Manager*
EMP: 14
SQ FT: 9,000
SALES (est): 1.8MM **Privately Held**
SIC: 3544 Dies & die holders for metal cutting, forming, die casting

(G-1128)
ORONOKO IRON WORKS INC
9243 First St (49101-8923)
P.O. Box 313 (49101-0313)
PHONE..................269 326-7045
Rusty Riley, *President*
EMP: 6
SQ FT: 10,000
SALES (est): 366.2K **Privately Held**
SIC: 3499 Aerosol valves, metal

(G-1129)
Q M E INC
Also Called: Quality Mold and Engineering
9070 First St (49101-8924)
P.O. Box 285 (49101-0285)
PHONE..................269 422-2137
James T Florian, *President*
Patricia Florian, *Admin Sec*
▼ EMP: 45
SQ FT: 30,000
SALES (est): 4.4MM **Privately Held**
WEB: www.quality-molds.com
SIC: 3544 Industrial molds

(G-1130)
R C M S INC
Also Called: Heart of The Vnyrd Wnry/Bd/Brk
10981 Hills Rd (49101-8742)
PHONE..................269 422-1617
Richard C Moersch, *President*
Sherry Moersch, *Vice Pres*
EMP: 6
SALES (est): 1.3MM **Privately Held**
SIC: 5149 7011 2084 Wine makers' equipment & supplies; bed & breakfast inn; wines, brandy & brandy spirits

(G-1131)
SELECT TOOL AND DIE INC
9170 First St (49101-8927)
P.O. Box 247 (49101-0247)
PHONE..................269 422-2812
Michael J Conrad, *President*
Jamie Conrad, *Corp Secy*
EMP: 8
SQ FT: 5,000
SALES (est): 1.2MM **Privately Held**
SIC: 3544 Industrial molds; forms (molds), for foundry & plastics working machinery

(G-1132)
TIGMASTER CO
9283 First St (49101-8923)
P.O. Box 183 (49101-0183)
PHONE..................800 824-4830
Terry Schmaltz, *President*
Jeff Sukupchak, *President*
EMP: 40
SQ FT: 31,000
SALES: 5MM **Privately Held**
WEB: www.tigmaster.com
SIC: 3444 3496 7692 Sheet metalwork; miscellaneous fabricated wire products; welding repair

(G-1133)
WOLFGANG MONETA
Also Called: King Products
8903 Stvnsville Baroda Rd (49101-8755)
P.O. Box 146 (49101-0146)
PHONE..................269 422-2296
Wolfgang Moneta, *Owner*
EMP: 5 EST: 1975
SQ FT: 5,544
SALES (est): 494.8K **Privately Held**
SIC: 3444 3714 Sheet metalwork; motor vehicle parts & accessories

Bath
Clinton County

(G-1134)
FRONT PORCH PRESS
4733 Hawk Hollow Dr E (48808-8769)
PHONE..................888 484-1997
Suzette Tyler, *President*
Elizabeth Spaedt, *Manager*
EMP: 3
SALES: 400K **Privately Held**
WEB: www.frontporchpress.com
SIC: 2731 Books: publishing only

GEOGRAPHIC SECTION

Battle Creek - Calhoun County (G-1162)

(G-1135)
ORTHOTIC INSOLES LLC
12390 Center Rd (48808-8422)
PHONE.............................517 641-4166
EMP: 3 EST: 2010
SALES (est): 120K Privately Held
SIC: 3842 Mfg Surgical Appliances/Supplies

(G-1136)
SUMMERTIME CONCRETE INC (PA)
Also Called: Summertime Precast
15765 Chandler Rd (48808-9751)
PHONE.............................517 641-6966
Gar Martin, *President*
EMP: 4
SQ FT: 1,000
SALES: 500K Privately Held
SIC: 3273 Ready-mixed concrete

Battle Creek
Calhoun County

(G-1137)
ADAMS SHIRT SHACK INC
100 Beadle Lake Rd (49014-4502)
PHONE.............................269 964-3323
Jan Walton, *President*
Randle Walton, *Vice Pres*
EMP: 3
SALES (est): 241.7K Privately Held
SIC: 5699 2759 2395 T-shirts, custom printed; screen printing; embroidery products, except schiffli machine

(G-1138)
ADIENT US LLC
76 Armstrong Rd (49037-7315)
PHONE.............................269 968-3000
Todd Callis, *Controller*
Steve Johnson, *Manager*
EMP: 300 Privately Held
SIC: 3714 Motor vehicle parts & accessories
HQ: Adient Us Llc
 49200 Halyard Dr
 Plymouth MI 48170
 734 254-5000

(G-1139)
ADLIB GRAFIX & APPAREL
10 Van Armon Ave (49017-5448)
PHONE.............................269 964-2810
Theodore Lawrence, *Partner*
Lisa Lawrence, *Partner*
EMP: 5
SALES: 280K Privately Held
SIC: 7389 2759 2395 Textile & apparel services; screen printing; embroidery products, except schiffli machine

(G-1140)
ADVANCED PLASTIC MFG INC
5501 Wayne Rd (49037-7327)
PHONE.............................269 962-9697
Toshihiro Tsujimoto, *President*
▲ EMP: 1
SALES (est): 1.4MM Privately Held
SIC: 3089 Molding primary plastic

(G-1141)
ADVANCED SPECIAL TOOLS INC
320 Clark Rd (49037-7303)
PHONE.............................269 962-9697
Shigeyuki Fujiwara, *President*
Haruyasu Iida, *Vice Pres*
Hal Kato, *Engineer*
Stephanie Garcia, *Human Res Mgr*
▲ EMP: 110
SQ FT: 20,500
SALES (est): 18.7MM Privately Held
WEB: www.astbc.com
SIC: 3544 7692 3089 Forms (molds), for foundry & plastics working machinery; welding repair; molding primary plastic
PA: Katayama Corp.
 1-30, Himegaoka
 Kani GIF 509-0

(G-1142)
ADVANTAGE SINTERED METALS INC
60 Clark Rd (49037-7372)
PHONE.............................269 964-1212
Jet Perelli, *President*
Dale Sinclair, *General Mgr*
▲ EMP: 101
SALES (est): 23.5MM Privately Held
WEB: www.advantagesintered.com
SIC: 3399 Powder, metal

(G-1143)
AGGREGATE INDUSTRIES-WCR INC
18646 12 Mile Rd (49014-8421)
PHONE.............................269 963-7263
EMP: 3
SALES (corp-wide): 27.6B Privately Held
SIC: 3273 Ready-mixed concrete
HQ: Aggregate Industries-Wcr, Inc.
 1687 Cole Blvd Ste 300
 Lakewood CO 80401
 303 716-5200

(G-1144)
AKERS WOOD PRODUCTS INC (PA)
1124 River Rd W (49037-6101)
PHONE.............................269 962-3802
Toll Free:.............................888 -
Jerry Akers, *President*
Lydia Akers, *Corp Secy*
John Akers, *Vice Pres*
EMP: 6 EST: 1963
SQ FT: 6,000
SALES: 750K Privately Held
SIC: 2448 Pallets, wood

(G-1145)
ALLEN PATTERN OF MICHIGAN
202 Mcgrath Pl (49014-5859)
PHONE.............................269 963-4131
Gregory G Allen, *President*
David L Habenicht, *Vice Pres*
EMP: 14
SQ FT: 23,500
SALES (est): 2.2MM Privately Held
SIC: 3543 3599 3993 2542 Industrial patterns; machine shop, jobbing & repair; signs & advertising specialties; partitions & fixtures, except wood

(G-1146)
ANATECH LTD
1020 Harts Lake Rd (49037-7365)
PHONE.............................269 964-6450
Ada Feldman, *CEO*
Elizabeth Dapson, *Vice Pres*
Art Nunley, *Vice Pres*
Delia Wolfe, *CFO*
Rachel Fowler, *Treasurer*
EMP: 10
SQ FT: 10,000
SALES: 871.3K Privately Held
WEB: www.anatechltdusa.com
SIC: 2835 In vitro diagnostics

(G-1147)
ARCHER-DANIELS-MIDLAND COMPANY
Also Called: ADM
436 Porter St Unit F2 (49014-6806)
PHONE.............................269 968-2900
Bill Carr, *Branch Mgr*
EMP: 112
SALES (corp-wide): 64.3B Publicly Held
SIC: 2041 Flour & other grain mill products
PA: Archer-Daniels-Midland Company
 77 W Wacker Dr Ste 4600
 Chicago IL 60601
 312 634-8100

(G-1148)
B & M IMAGING INC
Also Called: Allegra Battle Creek
1514 Columbia Ave W (49015-2838)
PHONE.............................269 968-2403
Eric Bird, *President*
EMP: 6
SQ FT: 5,400
SALES (est): 978.4K Privately Held
WEB: www.allegrabattlecreek.com
SIC: 2752 Commercial printing, offset

(G-1149)
BAHAMA SOUVENIRS INC (PA)
20260 North Ave (49017-9700)
PHONE.............................269 964-8275
Larry G Poley, *President*
Diane Polsey, *Vice Pres*
EMP: 7
SALES: 1MM Privately Held
SIC: 6513 5099 5094 2353 Apartment building operators; souvenirs; jewelry; hats & caps

(G-1150)
BARKER MANUFACTURING CO (PA)
Also Called: Braund Manufacturing Co
1125 Watkins Rd (49015-8605)
P.O. Box 460 (49016-0460)
PHONE.............................269 965-2371
Norma Barker, *President*
Jack Budrow, *Vice Pres*
Susan Stansverry, *Purch Mgr*
Tom Hancock, *CFO*
EMP: 27
SQ FT: 7,500
SALES (est): 6.6MM Privately Held
WEB: www.brakeroller.com
SIC: 3714 Motor vehicle parts & accessories

(G-1151)
BARKER MANUFACTURING CO
781 Watkins Rd (49015-8695)
P.O. Box 460 (49016-0460)
PHONE.............................269 965-2371
Mike Walters, *Branch Mgr*
EMP: 25
SALES (est): 3MM
SALES (corp-wide): 6.6MM Privately Held
WEB: www.brakeroller.com
SIC: 3714 Motor vehicle parts & accessories
PA: Barker Manufacturing Co.
 1125 Watkins Rd
 Battle Creek MI 49015
 269 965-2371

(G-1152)
BATTLE CREEK TENT & AWNING CO
110 Taylor Ave (49037-1458)
PHONE.............................269 964-1824
David J Duval, *President*
Dennis M Duval, *Vice Pres*
EMP: 3
SQ FT: 6,200
SALES (est): 23.5K Privately Held
SIC: 2394 7699 5999 Awnings, fabric: made from purchased materials; liners & covers, fabric: made from purchased materials; tent repair shop; awning repair shop; flags

(G-1153)
BENJAMIN PRESS
380 Van Buren St W (49037-2322)
PHONE.............................269 964-7562
Robert Benjamin, *Owner*
EMP: 3
SQ FT: 2,060
SALES (est): 247.9K Privately Held
SIC: 2752 Commercial printing, offset

(G-1154)
BIG GREEN TOMATO LLC
478 Main St (49014-5136)
P.O. Box 770 (49016-0770)
PHONE.............................269 282-1593
David Michael Bye,
EMP: 5
SALES (est): 366.7K Privately Held
SIC: 3524 Lawn & garden equipment

(G-1155)
BLEISTAHL N AMER LTD PARTNR
190 Clark Rd (49037-7393)
PHONE.............................269 719-8585
Thomas Glas, *President*
Duane Spurling, *Mfg Staff*
Jon Garavalia, *Purchasing*
Dan Coffman, *Engineer*
Solomon Gaddam, *Engineer*
EMP: 35
SALES (est): 68.6K
SALES (corp-wide): 181.8MM Privately Held
SIC: 3714 Cylinder heads, motor vehicle
HQ: Bleistahl Ltd.
 43311 Joy Rd Pmb 427
 Canton MI 48187
 248 202-1277

(G-1156)
BRAETEC INC
346 E Michigan Ave (49014-4944)
PHONE.............................269 968-4711
Charles Norton, *President*
EMP: 6
SQ FT: 3,700
SALES: 1MM Privately Held
SIC: 3743 3714 Brakes, air & vacuum: railway; motor vehicle brake systems & parts

(G-1157)
BRAKE ROLLER CO INC
Also Called: BRC
1125 Watkins Rd (49015-8605)
P.O. Box 460 (49016-0460)
PHONE.............................269 965-2371
Jack Budrow, *President*
Norma Barker, *Vice Pres*
EMP: 42
SQ FT: 7,500
SALES (est): 3.2MM Privately Held
SIC: 3542 3312 Brakes, metal forming; blast furnaces & steel mills

(G-1158)
BROTHERS MEAD 3 LLC
19915 Capital Ave Ne # 208 (49017-8124)
PHONE.............................269 883-6241
Austin Mead,
EMP: 6 EST: 2013
SALES (est): 884.2K Privately Held
SIC: 3825 Test equipment for electronic & electrical circuits

(G-1159)
BRUTSCHE CONCRETE PRODUCTS CO (PA)
15150 6 1/2 Mile Rd (49014)
P.O. Box 1031 (49016-1031)
PHONE.............................269 963-1554
Timothy J Brutsche, *President*
Katherine L Brutsche, *Vice Pres*
EMP: 32
SQ FT: 40,000
SALES (est): 4.9MM Privately Held
SIC: 3272 Burial vaults, concrete or precast terrazzo; building materials, except block or brick: concrete

(G-1160)
BURR ENGINEERING & DEV CO (PA)
730 Michigan Ave E (49014-6200)
P.O. Box 460 (49016-0460)
PHONE.............................269 965-2371
Jack Budrow, *President*
Norma Barker, *Vice Pres*
Martha Mc Millan, *Admin Sec*
EMP: 3 EST: 1960
SALES (est): 6.3MM Privately Held
WEB: www.burractuators.com
SIC: 3625 3714 Actuators, industrial; motor vehicle parts & accessories

(G-1161)
C S SYSTEMS INC
1405 Michigan Ave W (49037-1920)
PHONE.............................269 962-8434
Michael Markusic, *President*
William Bopp, *Treasurer*
EMP: 3
SQ FT: 7,500
SALES (est): 202.9K Privately Held
SIC: 7372 Application computer software

(G-1162)
CALHOUN COUNTY MED CARE FCILTY
1150 Michigan Ave E (49014-6113)
PHONE.............................269 962-5458
Donna Mahoney, *CFO*
Karen Adams, *Administration*
EMP: 20

Battle Creek - Calhoun County (G-1163)

SALES: 15.8MM **Privately Held**
SIC: 3829 Measuring & controlling devices

(G-1163)
CARIBBEAN ADVENTURE LLC
Also Called: Freshwater Communications
5420 Beckley Rd Ste 244 (49015-5719)
PHONE.....................269 441-5675
EMP: 10
SALES (est): 680K **Privately Held**
SIC: 2721 Periodicals-Publishing/Printing

(G-1164)
CELLO-FOIL PRODUCTS INC (DH)
155 Brook St (49037-3031)
PHONE.....................229 435-4777
Kenneth M Lesiow, *Ch of Bd*
Carol Rhodes, *Vice Pres*
John E Thomas, *CFO*
Cynthia Bauman, *Admin Sec*
EMP: 200 **EST:** 1949
SQ FT: 140,000
SALES (est): 23.4MM
SALES (corp-wide): 1.6B **Privately Held**
WEB: www.cello-foil.com
SIC: 2671 Packaging paper & plastics film, coated & laminated
HQ: Transcontinental Us Llc
8600 W Br Mw Ave 800n
Chicago IL 60631
773 877-3300

(G-1165)
CENTRAL MICHIGAN CREMATORY
151506 One Half Mile Rd (49014)
P.O. Box 1031 (49016-1031)
PHONE.....................269 963-1554
Timothy Brutsche, *President*
Katherine L Brutsche, *Vice Pres*
EMP: 28
SALES: 579.5K **Privately Held**
SIC: 3272 Burial vaults, concrete or pre-cast terrazzo

(G-1166)
CHANDLER RICCHIO PUBG LLC
890 Wattles Rd N (49014-7812)
PHONE.....................269 660-0840
David Bye,
EMP: 3
SALES (est): 193K **Privately Held**
SIC: 2731 Book publishing

(G-1167)
CLASSIC GLASS BATTLE CREEK INC
21472 Bedford Rd N (49017-8035)
PHONE.....................269 968-2791
Sharon Van Nortwick, *President*
Ronald Voelker, *Vice Pres*
Phillip A Voelker, *Admin Sec*
EMP: 18
SQ FT: 9,000
SALES (est): 1.7MM **Privately Held**
WEB: www.battlecreekglass.com
SIC: 3231 Insulating glass: made from purchased glass

(G-1168)
CLYDE UNION (HOLDINGS) INC
4625 Beckley Rd (49015-7948)
PHONE.....................269 966-4600
EMP: 321
SALES (est): 2.5MM
SALES (corp-wide): 2B **Publicly Held**
SIC: 3561 5084 Industrial pumps & parts; pumps & pumping equipment
PA: Spx Flow, Inc.
13320 Balntyn Corp Pl
Charlotte NC 28277
704 752-4400

(G-1169)
COVERIS
155 Brook St (49037-3031)
PHONE.....................269 964-1130
Berry Fulpomer, *General Mgr*
EMP: 31
SALES (est): 9.4MM
SALES (corp-wide): 1.6B **Privately Held**
SIC: 2673 2631 Bags: plastic, laminated & coated; paperboard mills

HQ: Transcontinental Holding Corp.
8600 W Bryn Mawr Ave
Chicago IL 60631
773 877-3300

(G-1170)
CSE MORSE INC
Also Called: Honeywell Authorized Dealer
17 Race Ct (49017-4181)
P.O. Box 669 (49016-0669)
PHONE.....................269 962-5548
Bruce A Boyer, *President*
Stan N Zygadlo, *Treasurer*
Nicholas Zygadlo, *Admin Sec*
EMP: 65
SQ FT: 25,000
SALES (est): 11.1MM **Privately Held**
SIC: 3444 Sheet metal specialties, not stamped

(G-1171)
DENSO AIR SYSTEMS MICHIGAN INC (DH)
300 Fritz Keiper Blvd (49037-5607)
PHONE.....................269 962-9676
Katsuaki Kawai, *Vice Pres*
Cindy Collins, *Production*
Charlie Mack, *Production*
Mike Reniger, *Production*
Gabriela Sanchez, *Buyer*
▲ **EMP:** 84
SQ FT: 167,000
SALES (est): 64.7MM **Privately Held**
WEB: www.koyocorporation.com
SIC: 3714 3498 Air conditioner parts, motor vehicle; fabricated pipe & fittings

(G-1172)
DENSO MANUFACTURING NC INC
500 Fritz Keiper Blvd (49037-7306)
PHONE.....................269 441-2040
Masanori Iyama, *President*
EMP: 700 **Privately Held**
SIC: 3621 3089 Motors, electric; plastic & fiberglass tanks
HQ: Denso Manufacturing North Carolina, Inc.
470 Crawford Rd
Statesville NC 28625

(G-1173)
DENSO SALES MICHIGAN INC
1 Denso Rd (49037-7313)
PHONE.....................269 965-3322
James O'Dowd, *Principal*
Mike Winkler, *Marketing Staff*
Bob Powell, *Manager*
Russ Cox, *Supervisor*
Chris Withers, *Supervisor*
▼ **EMP:** 49
SALES (est): 9.9MM **Privately Held**
SIC: 3714 Motor vehicle parts & accessories

(G-1174)
DIEOMATIC INCORPORATED
Also Called: Cosma Casting Michigan
10 Clark Rd (49037-7302)
PHONE.....................269 966-4900
Steve Flannery, *General Mgr*
EMP: 12
SALES (corp-wide): 40.8B **Privately Held**
SIC: 3714 Motor vehicle parts & accessories
HQ: Dieomatic Incorporated
750 Tower Dr Mail 7000 Mail Code
Troy MI 48098

(G-1175)
DLA DOCUMENT SERVICES
74 Washington Ave N 2a12 (49037-3085)
PHONE.....................269 961-4895
Betty McAdow, *Principal*
EMP: 3 **Publicly Held**
SIC: 2752 9711 Commercial printing, lithographic; national security;
HQ: Dla Document Services
5450 Carlisle Pike Bldg 9
Mechanicsburg PA 17050
717 605-2362

(G-1176)
DUNN BEVERAGE INTL LLC
95 Minges Rd N (49015-7909)
PHONE.....................269 420-1547

Sara Durkee, *Manager*
EMP: 4 **EST:** 2010
SALES (est): 347.1K **Privately Held**
SIC: 2084 Wines

(G-1177)
ENDRES PROCESSING MICHIGAN LLC
170 Angell St (49037-8273)
P.O. Box 1413 (49016-1413)
PHONE.....................269 965-0427
Glen Voetverg, *Mng Member*
EMP: 11
SALES (est): 2.3MM **Privately Held**
WEB: www.endresprocessing.com
SIC: 2048 Prepared feeds
PA: Endres Processing, L.L.C.
13420 Court House Blvd
Rosemount MN 55068

(G-1178)
ENVIRON MANUFACTURING INC
972 Graham Lake Ter (49014-8309)
PHONE.....................616 644-6846
James Trent, *CEO*
EMP: 7 **EST:** 2018
SALES (est): 43.6K **Privately Held**
SIC: 3559 Electronic component making machinery

(G-1179)
EPI PRINTERS INC (PA)
Also Called: Epi Marketing Services
5404 Wayne Rd (49037-7300)
P.O. Box 1025 (49016-1025)
PHONE.....................800 562-9733
William Guzy, *President*
Dennis Bridges, *General Mgr*
Pat Kolodziejczak, *General Mgr*
Mitch Mauer, *Vice Pres*
Ivan Mellema, *Vice Pres*
◆ **EMP:** 40 **EST:** 1959
SQ FT: 30,000
SALES (est): 198.2MM **Privately Held**
WEB: www.epiinc.com
SIC: 2752 Commercial printing, offset

(G-1180)
EPI PRINTERS INC
61 Clark Rd (49037-7364)
P.O. Box 1025 (49016-1025)
PHONE.....................269 968-2221
Jeff Adams, *Manager*
EMP: 120
SALES (corp-wide): 198.2MM **Privately Held**
WEB: www.epiinc.com
SIC: 2752 7389 Commercial printing, offset; coupon redemption service
PA: Epi Printers, Inc.
5404 Wayne Rd
Battle Creek MI 49037
800 562-9733

(G-1181)
EPI PRINTERS INC
Also Called: Epi Market
5350 W Dickman Rd (49037-7312)
P.O. Box 1025 (49016-1025)
PHONE.....................269 968-2221
William Guzy, *President*
Jeff Brown, *Opers Mgr*
Julie Guzy, *Accounts Mgr*
Paul Bajorek, *Sales Staff*
Rich Fitch, *CIO*
EMP: 96
SALES (corp-wide): 198.2MM **Privately Held**
WEB: www.epiinc.com
SIC: 2752 Commercial printing, offset
PA: Epi Printers, Inc.
5404 Wayne Rd
Battle Creek MI 49037
800 562-9733

(G-1182)
EPI PRINTERS INC
Also Called: Arm Fulfillment
4956 Wayne Rd (49037-7332)
P.O. Box 1025 (49016-1025)
PHONE.....................269 964-4600
Rich Fitch, *Vice Pres*
EMP: 50

SALES (corp-wide): 198.2MM **Privately Held**
WEB: www.epiinc.com
SIC: 7389 2752 Coupon redemption service; commercial printing, lithographic
PA: Epi Printers, Inc.
5404 Wayne Rd
Battle Creek MI 49037
800 562-9733

(G-1183)
EPI PRINTERS INC
Also Called: Epi Marketing Services
65 Clark Rd (49037-7364)
PHONE.....................269 964-6744
Duane Lantis, *Branch Mgr*
EMP: 53
SALES (corp-wide): 198.2MM **Privately Held**
WEB: www.epiinc.com
SIC: 2752 Commercial printing, offset
PA: Epi Printers, Inc.
5404 Wayne Rd
Battle Creek MI 49037
800 562-9733

(G-1184)
FAMILY FARE LLC
294 Highland Ave (49015-3373)
PHONE.....................269 965-5631
Eddie Garcia, *Branch Mgr*
EMP: 4
SALES (corp-wide): 5.5MM **Privately Held**
SIC: 3578 Automatic teller machines (ATM)
PA: Family Fare, Llc
1406 N Eaton St
Albion MI 49224
517 629-6313

(G-1185)
FAST CASH
641 Capital Ave Sw (49015-5002)
PHONE.....................269 966-0079
Don Quada, *Manager*
EMP: 4
SALES (est): 402.7K **Privately Held**
SIC: 3651 Audio electronic systems

(G-1186)
FEDERATED PUBLICATIONS INC (HQ)
Also Called: Lansing State Journal
155 Van Buren St W (49017-3002)
P.O. Box 677313, Dallas TX (75267-7313)
PHONE.....................269 962-5394
Ellen M Leifeld, *President*
Kelly Carr, *Editor*
Larry F Miller, *Treasurer*
David Davies, *Controller*
Thomas L Chapple, *Admin Sec*
EMP: 131 **EST:** 1928
SQ FT: 150,000
SALES (est): 29.8MM
SALES (corp-wide): 2.9B **Publicly Held**
SIC: 2711 Newspapers, publishing & printing
PA: Gannett Co., Inc.
7950 Jones Branch Dr
Mc Lean VA 22102
703 854-6000

(G-1187)
FERREES TOOLS INC
1477 Michigan Ave E (49014-7974)
PHONE.....................269 965-0511
Clifford M Ferree, *President*
Katherine Neeley, *Vice Pres*
EMP: 28 **EST:** 1946
SQ FT: 3,600
SALES (est): 1.3MM **Privately Held**
WEB: www.ferreestools.com
SIC: 3931 3423 Musical instruments; hand & edge tools

(G-1188)
FIVE-WAY SWITCH MUSIC
9478 Huntington Rd (49017-9731)
PHONE.....................269 425-2843
Matt Kirkland, *Principal*
EMP: 4
SALES (est): 224.6K **Privately Held**
SIC: 3679 Electronic switches

GEOGRAPHIC SECTION

Battle Creek - Calhoun County (G-1212)

(G-1189)
FLEX-N-GATE BATTLE CREEK LLC
10250 F Dr N (49014-8237)
PHONE.................................269 962-2982
Chris Meloche, *General Mgr*
Jim Burgie, *Controller*
Nancy Davis, *Human Res Mgr*
Jill Dowell, *Human Resources*
Shahid Khan, *Mng Member*
▲ **EMP:** 185
SALES (est): 81MM
SALES (corp-wide): 3.3B **Privately Held**
WEB: www.flex-n-gate.com
SIC: 3714 Motor vehicle parts & accessories
PA: Flex-N-Gate Llc
  1306 E University Ave
  Urbana IL 61802
  217 384-6600

(G-1190)
FRANKLIN IRON & METAL CO INC (PA)
Also Called: Franklin Plastics
120 South Ave (49014-4136)
P.O. Box 664 (49016-0664)
PHONE.................................269 968-6111
Susan Franklin Behnke, *President*
Sonya Hart, *Assistant*
EMP: 45
SQ FT: 15,000
SALES (est): 16.6MM **Privately Held**
WEB: www.franklin-scrap.com
SIC: 5093 3341 Ferrous metal scrap & waste; nonferrous metals scrap; plastics scrap; secondary nonferrous metals

(G-1191)
GANNETT CO INC
Also Called: Battle Creek Enquirer
34 Jackson St W Ste 3b (49017-3542)
PHONE.................................269 964-7161
Ellen Leitfeld, *Manager*
EMP: 200
SALES (corp-wide): 2.9B **Publicly Held**
WEB: www.gannett.com
SIC: 2711 2752 Newspapers, publishing & printing; commercial printing, lithographic
PA: Gannett Co., Inc.
  7950 Jones Branch Dr
  Mc Lean VA 22102
  703 854-6000

(G-1192)
GEISLINGER CORPORATION
200 Geislinger Dr (49037-5622)
PHONE.................................269 441-7000
Michael Krenn, *President*
Sabine Mosdorfer, *CFO*
Mike Gapp, *Accountant*
Alex Winchester, *Sales Mgr*
Alex Hemmila, *Sales Engr*
▲ **EMP:** 14
SQ FT: 40,000
SALES (est): 3.8MM
SALES (corp-wide): 19.5MM **Privately Held**
WEB: www.geislinger.com
SIC: 3568 3519 Power transmission equipment; internal combustion engines
PA: Ellergon Antriebstechnik Gmbh
  Hallwanger LandesstraBe 3
  Hallwang 5300
  662 669-990

(G-1193)
GOTTCH-YA GRAPHIX USA
5875 B Dr S (49014-8314)
PHONE.................................269 979-7587
Mary Dayhuff, *Owner*
EMP: 3
SALES (est): 198.1K **Privately Held**
WEB: www.gg-usa.com
SIC: 2396 7375 Screen printing on fabric articles; information retrieval services

(G-1194)
GRAPHIC PACKAGING INTL LLC
70 Michigan Ave W Ste 500 (49017-3627)
PHONE.................................269 969-7446
John Cleveland, *Manager*
Chad Longcore, *Technical Staff*
EMP: 74 **Publicly Held**
SIC: 2657 Folding paperboard boxes
HQ: Graphic Packaging International, Llc
  1500 Riveredge Pkwy # 100
  Atlanta GA 30328

(G-1195)
GRAPHIC PACKAGING INTL LLC
79 Fountain St E (49017-4130)
PHONE.................................269 963-6135
Ron Fox, *Opers Mgr*
William Welling, *Purch Agent*
Alan Ackley, *Engineer*
Rae Badgley, *Hum Res Coord*
Mark Reed, *Branch Mgr*
EMP: 200 **Publicly Held**
SIC: 2631 Container board
HQ: Graphic Packaging International, Llc
  1500 Riveredge Pkwy # 100
  Atlanta GA 30328

(G-1196)
GRAPHIX 2 GO INC
7200 Tower Rd (49014-7529)
PHONE.................................269 969-7321
Denise Jones, *President*
Kim Harrington, *Vice Pres*
Jolene Nagy, *Opers Mgr*
Amy Howard, *Sales Staff*
EMP: 8
SQ FT: 5,000
SALES (est): 1.4MM **Privately Held**
SIC: 7389 2759 Advertising, promotional & trade show services; commercial printing; promotional printing; advertising literature: printing

(G-1197)
HDN F&A INC
Also Called: F & A Fabricating
104 Arbor St (49015-3026)
P.O. Box 102 (49016-0102)
PHONE.................................269 965-3268
Hiep D Nguyen, *President*
EMP: 30
SQ FT: 24,000
SALES (est): 5MM **Privately Held**
WEB: www.fa-fabricating.com
SIC: 3444 Sheet metal specialties, not stamped

(G-1198)
HI-LEX AMERICA INCORPORATED (DH)
5200 Wayne Rd (49037-7392)
PHONE.................................269 968-0781
Katsuaki Shima, *Ch of Bd*
Tom Strictland, *President*
▲ **EMP:** 323
SQ FT: 175,000
SALES (est): 152.2MM **Privately Held**
WEB: www.hci.hi-lex.com
SIC: 3496 3357 Cable, uninsulated wire: made from purchased wire; nonferrous wiredrawing & insulating
HQ: Tsk Of America, Inc.
  152 Simpson Dr
  Litchfield MI 49252
  517 542-2955

(G-1199)
II STANLEY CO INC
1500 Hill Brady Rd (49037-7320)
PHONE.................................269 660-7777
Seiichi Fujii, *President*
James Huberty, *Exec VP*
Mike Isham, *Exec VP*
Shinishiro Kojima, *Exec VP*
Shoji Ichikawa, *Treasurer*
▲ **EMP:** 747
SQ FT: 360,000
SALES (est): 20.6MM **Privately Held**
WEB: www.iistanleybc.com
SIC: 3647 Automotive lighting fixtures
HQ: Stanley Electric Us Co Inc
  420 E High St
  London OH 43140
  740 852-5200

(G-1200)
INSULATION WHOLESALE SUPPLY
Also Called: Wheeler Insulation
11280 Michigan Ave E (49014-8904)
PHONE.................................269 968-9746
Janet Wakenight, *Ch of Bd*
Ramar Wakenight, *President*
Loren Mills, *Vice Pres*
Richard Wakenight, *Treasurer*
Franklin Hill, *Admin Sec*
EMP: 6
SQ FT: 9,000
SALES (est): 429.9K **Privately Held**
SIC: 5211 3699 1742 Insulation material, building; electrical equipment & supplies; insulation, buildings

(G-1201)
J J STEEL INC
2000 Ottawa Trl (49037-8282)
PHONE.................................269 964-0474
Gert Jensen, *President*
▲ **EMP:** 21
SQ FT: 13,000
SALES (est): 4.6MM **Privately Held**
WEB: www.jjsteel.net
SIC: 3556 Dairy & milk machinery

(G-1202)
J-AD GRAPHICS INC
Battle Creek Shopper News
1001 Columbia Ave E (49014-4401)
P.O. Box 163 (49016-0163)
PHONE.................................269 965-3955
Fred Jacobs, *Publisher*
Donna Hazel, *General Mgr*
Shelly Sulser, *Editor*
EMP: 21
SALES (corp-wide): 15.3MM **Privately Held**
WEB: www.j-adgraphics.com
SIC: 2741 2711 2789 2752 Shopping news: publishing & printing; newspapers, publishing & printing; bookbinding & related work; commercial printing, lithographic
PA: J-Ad Graphics, Inc.
  1351 N M 43 Hwy
  Hastings MI 49058
  800 870-7085

(G-1203)
JETCO SIGNS
302 Capital Ave Sw (49037-8680)
PHONE.................................269 420-0202
Tim Conlogue, *Principal*
EMP: 4 **EST:** 2008
SALES (est): 300.2K **Privately Held**
SIC: 3993 Signs & advertising specialties

(G-1204)
JETECH INC
555 Industrial Park Dr (49037-7446)
PHONE.................................269 965-6311
Bin Qi, *CEO*
Jacob Harmon, *COO*
John Vanoostendorp, *CFO*
◆ **EMP:** 31
SQ FT: 1,600
SALES (est): 7.1MM **Privately Held**
WEB: www.jetech.com
SIC: 3561 5084 3599 7359 Industrial pumps & parts; industrial machinery & equipment; machine shop, jobbing & repair; equipment rental & leasing

(G-1205)
K & L SHEET METAL LLC
131 Grand Trunk Ave C (49037-8442)
PHONE.................................269 965-0027
Kurt Hansen, *Mng Member*
EMP: 8
SALES (est): 1.3MM **Privately Held**
SIC: 3441 5051 Fabricated structural metal; steel

(G-1206)
K-TWO INC
1 Kellogg Sq (49017-3534)
P.O. Box 3599 (49016-3599)
PHONE.................................269 961-2000
Carlo Guthierrez, *President*
◆ **EMP:** 19
SALES (est): 3MM
SALES (corp-wide): 13.5B **Publicly Held**
WEB: www.kelloggs.com
SIC: 2043 Cereal breakfast foods
PA: Kellogg Company
  1 Kellogg Sq
  Battle Creek MI 49017
  269 961-2000

(G-1207)
KEEBLER COMPANY (HQ)
1 Kellogg Sq (49017-3534)
PHONE.................................269 961-2000
David McKay, *President*
David A Fedko, *Purchasing*
Janet Di Iorio, *Manager*
◆ **EMP:** 500
SQ FT: 115,000
SALES (est): 2.1B
SALES (corp-wide): 13.5B **Publicly Held**
WEB: www.keebler.com
SIC: 2052 2051 Cookies; crackers, dry; cones, ice cream; pretzels; bread, cake & related products
PA: Kellogg Company
  1 Kellogg Sq
  Battle Creek MI 49017
  269 961-2000

(G-1208)
KELLOGG (THAILAND) LIMITED
1 Kellogg Sq (49017-3534)
PHONE.................................269 969-8937
James M Jenness, *CEO*
EMP: 3
SALES (est): 122K
SALES (corp-wide): 13.5B **Publicly Held**
WEB: www.kellog.com
SIC: 2043 Cereal breakfast foods
PA: Kellogg Company
  1 Kellogg Sq
  Battle Creek MI 49017
  269 961-2000

(G-1209)
KELLOGG CHILE INC
1 Kellogg Sq (49017-3534)
PHONE.................................269 961-2000
EMP: 4
SALES (est): 313.3K
SALES (corp-wide): 13.5B **Publicly Held**
WEB: www.kelloggs.com
SIC: 2043 Cereal breakfast foods
PA: Kellogg Company
  1 Kellogg Sq
  Battle Creek MI 49017
  269 961-2000

(G-1210)
KELLOGG COMPANY
Also Called: W.K. Kellogg Institute
2 Hamblin Ave E (49017-3560)
PHONE.................................269 961-2000
Yuvraj Arora, *Vice Pres*
Viswas Ghorpade, *Engineer*
Eric Lewandowski, *Engineer*
Nancy Marks, *Engineer*
Kathy Casey, *Mktg Dir*
EMP: 385
SALES (corp-wide): 13.5B **Publicly Held**
WEB: www.kelloggs.com
SIC: 2043 8733 Cereal breakfast foods; research institute
PA: Kellogg Company
  1 Kellogg Sq
  Battle Creek MI 49017
  269 961-2000

(G-1211)
KELLOGG COMPANY (PA)
1 Kellogg Sq (49017-3534)
P.O. Box 3599 (49016-3599)
PHONE.................................269 961-2000
Alistair D Hirst, *Senior VP*
Melissa A Howell, *Senior VP*
Cydney Kilduff, *Senior VP*
Nelson Almeida, *Vice Pres*
Kurt Forche, *Vice Pres*
◆ **EMP:** 600 **EST:** 1906
SALES: 13.5B **Publicly Held**
WEB: www.kelloggs.com
SIC: 2041 2052 2051 2038 Flour & other grain mill products; cookies; crackers, dry; pastries, e.g. danish: except frozen; waffles, frozen; corn flakes: prepared as cereal breakfast food

(G-1212)
KELLOGG COMPANY
70 Michigan Ave W Ste 750 (49017-3666)
PHONE.................................269 964-8525
Kevin Shelton, *Opers Staff*
Shey Oconnor, *Manager*
Daniel Powell, *Director*
EMP: 385

Battle Creek - Calhoun County (G-1213)   GEOGRAPHIC SECTION

SALES (corp-wide): 13.5B **Publicly Held**
SIC: **2043** Cereal breakfast foods
PA: Kellogg Company
1 Kellogg Sq
Battle Creek MI 49017
269 961-2000

(G-1213)
KELLOGG COMPANY
235 Porter St (49014-6210)
PHONE..................269 969-8107
EMP: 6
SALES (corp-wide): 12.9B **Publicly Held**
SIC: **2043** Mfg Cereal Breakfast Food
PA: Kellogg Company
1 Kellogg Sq
Battle Creek MI 49017
269 961-2000

(G-1214)
KELLOGG COMPANY
1 Kellogg Sq (49017-3534)
PHONE..................901 373-6115
Glen Carich, *Manager*
EMP: 385
SALES (corp-wide): 13.5B **Publicly Held**
WEB: www.kelloggs.com
SIC: **2043** Cereal breakfast foods
PA: Kellogg Company
1 Kellogg Sq
Battle Creek MI 49017
269 961-2000

(G-1215)
KELLOGG COMPANY
2 E Hammond Ave (49014)
P.O. Box 1988 (49016-1988)
PHONE..................269 961-2000
EMP: 91
SALES (corp-wide): 13.5B **Publicly Held**
WEB: www.kelloggs.com
SIC: **8733 2043** Noncommercial research organizations; cereal breakfast foods
PA: Kellogg Company
1 Kellogg Sq
Battle Creek MI 49017
269 961-2000

(G-1216)
KELLOGG COMPANY
Financial Service Ctr (49014)
PHONE..................269 961-6693
EMP: 703
SALES (corp-wide): 13.5B **Publicly Held**
WEB: www.kelloggs.com
SIC: **2043** Corn flakes: prepared as cereal breakfast food
PA: Kellogg Company
1 Kellogg Sq
Battle Creek MI 49017
269 961-2000

(G-1217)
KELLOGG COMPANY
425 Porter St (49014-6800)
PHONE..................269 961-2000
Linda Pell, *Owner*
EMP: 176
SALES (corp-wide): 13.5B **Publicly Held**
SIC: **2043** Cereal breakfast foods
HQ: Kellogg Usa Inc.
1 Kellogg Sq
Battle Creek MI 49017

(G-1218)
KELLOGG NORTH AMERICA COMPANY
1 Kellogg Sq (49017-3534)
PHONE..................269 961-2000
David McKay, *President*
Jeffrey Delonis, *Marketing Staff*
EMP: 4459
SALES (est): 182.7MM
SALES (corp-wide): 13.5B **Publicly Held**
SIC: **2052** Cookies
HQ: Keebler Company
1 Kellogg Sq
Battle Creek MI 49017
269 961-2000

(G-1219)
KELLOGG USA INC (HQ)
1 Kellogg Sq (49017-3534)
P.O. Box 3599 (49016-3599)
PHONE..................269 961-2000
David Pfanzelter, *Principal*

▼ EMP: 200
SALES: 934.3MM
SALES (corp-wide): 13.5B **Publicly Held**
SIC: **2043** Cereal breakfast foods
PA: Kellogg Company
1 Kellogg Sq
Battle Creek MI 49017
269 961-2000

(G-1220)
KMI CLEANING SOLUTIONS INC
Also Called: K M I
157 Beadle Lake Rd (49014-4504)
P.O. Box 2535 (49016-2535)
PHONE..................269 964-2557
Russel Bloch, *President*
David Lafler, *Vice Pres*
EMP: 10
SQ FT: 4,600
SALES (est): 6.3MM **Privately Held**
SIC: **5084 5169 2842** Cleaning equipment, high pressure, sand or steam; detergents & soaps, except specialty cleaning; specialty cleaning, polishes & sanitation goods

(G-1221)
KNOEDLER MANUFACTURERS INC
7185 Tower Rd (49014-8522)
PHONE..................269 969-7722
Wilhelm Sturhan, *President*
▲ EMP: 10
SALES: 4MM **Privately Held**
WEB: www.knoedler.com
SIC: **3714 2531** Motor vehicle parts & accessories; public building & related furniture

(G-1222)
LAWSON PRINTERS INC
685 Columbia Ave W (49015-3070)
PHONE..................269 965-0525
Betty Rankin, *President*
Dennis Rankin, *Vice Pres*
EMP: 30 EST: 1932
SQ FT: 18,100
SALES (est): 5.8MM **Privately Held**
WEB: www.lawsonprinters.com
SIC: **2752 2759 2672** Commercial printing, offset; commercial printing; coated & laminated paper

(G-1223)
LOTTE USA INCORPORATED
Also Called: Lotte U S A
5243 Wayne Rd (49037-7323)
PHONE..................269 963-6664
Takeo Shigemitsu, *President*
Hiroyuki Shigemitsu, *Vice Pres*
▲ EMP: 11 EST: 1978
SQ FT: 93,000
SALES (est): 2.3MM **Privately Held**
WEB: www.lotteusainc.com
SIC: **2064 2052 2067** Candy & other confectionery products; cookies; chewing gum base
PA: Lotte Holdings Co., Ltd.
3-20-1, Nishishinjuku
Shinjuku-Ku TKY 160-0

(G-1224)
LS PRECISION TOOL & DIE INC
140 Jacaranda Dr (49015-8663)
PHONE..................269 963-9910
Gerhard Loewe, *President*
Volker Schwarz, *Vice Pres*
Terri Loewe, *Admin Sec*
EMP: 7 EST: 1997
SQ FT: 6,000
SALES (est): 480K **Privately Held**
SIC: **3544** Special dies, tools, jigs & fixtures

(G-1225)
MANNETRON
Also Called: Mannetron Animatronics
74 Leonard Wood Rd (49037-7309)
PHONE..................269 962-3475
Michael Clark, *Owner*
EMP: 22
SQ FT: 100,000
SALES: 1.5MM **Privately Held**
SIC: **3999 5099** Puppets & marionettes; robots, service or novelty

(G-1226)
MARLEY PRECISION INC (HQ)
455 Fritz Keiper Blvd (49037-7374)
PHONE..................269 963-7374
Shigemitsu Takagi, *President*
Hiro Kitagawa, *President*
Kenji Takagi, *Exec VP*
Todd Greer, *Vice Pres*
Beth Brown, *Human Res Mgr*
EMP: 50
SQ FT: 14,000
SALES (est): 28.7MM **Privately Held**
SIC: **3714** Motor vehicle parts & accessories

(G-1227)
METZGER SAWMILL
3100 W Halbert Rd (49017-8078)
PHONE..................269 963-3022
Ronald Metzger, *Owner*
Gayla Metzger, *Co-Owner*
EMP: 4
SALES: 360K **Privately Held**
SIC: **2448** Pallets, wood; skids, wood

(G-1228)
MICHIGAN CARTON PAPER BOY
79 Fountain St E (49017-4130)
PHONE..................269 963-4004
David Scheible, *Principal*
EMP: 5
SALES (est): 428.9K **Privately Held**
SIC: **2657** Folding paperboard boxes

(G-1229)
MODERN MACHINING INC
415 Upton Ave (49037-8382)
PHONE..................269 964-4415
Patrick Ballinger, *President*
EMP: 4
SQ FT: 5,000
SALES: 280K **Privately Held**
SIC: **3599** Machine shop, jobbing & repair

(G-1230)
MUSASHI AUTO PARTS MICH INC
Also Called: Technical Auto Parts
195 Brydges Dr (49037-7340)
PHONE..................269 965-0057
Mr Takayuki Miyata, *President*
Lonnie Bennett, *Engineer*
Brian Davis, *Manager*
▲ EMP: 330
SQ FT: 97,000
SALES (est): 78.3MM **Privately Held**
WEB: www.mapmi.com
SIC: **3714** Motor vehicle transmissions, drive assemblies & parts
PA: Musashi Seimitsu Industry Co., Ltd.
39-5, Daizen, Uetacho
Toyohashi AIC 441-8

(G-1231)
NATIONAL SIGN & SIGNAL CO
301 Armstrong Rd (49037-7374)
PHONE..................269 963-2817
Ronald E Scherer, *CEO*
John Cairns, *President*
David B Thompson, *Corp Secy*
EMP: 32
SQ FT: 28,000
SALES (est): 6.1MM **Privately Held**
WEB: www.nationalssc.com
SIC: **3669 3993** Traffic signals, electric; signs, not made in custom sign painting shops

(G-1232)
NEW MOON NOODLE INCORPORATED
Also Called: Kowloon Noodle Company
909 Stanley Dr (49037-7370)
PHONE..................269 962-8820
Lee Lum, *President*
Lillian Lum, *Corp Secy*
EMP: 20
SQ FT: 20,000
SALES (est): 3.2MM **Privately Held**
SIC: **5149 2099 0182** Groceries & related products; noodles, fried (Chinese); bean sprouts grown under cover

(G-1233)
NEXTHERMAL CORPORATION
1045 Harts Lake Rd (49037-7357)
P.O. Box 2404 (49016-2404)
PHONE..................269 964-0271
Srekumar Bandyopadhyay, *President*
▲ EMP: 95
SQ FT: 25,000
SALES (est): 25.9MM **Privately Held**
WEB: www.hotset.com
SIC: **3567** Heating units & devices, industrial: electric
PA: Nexthermal Manufacturing India Private Limited
No 3b
Bengaluru KA 56007

(G-1234)
OTTERS OASIS
36 Grand Blvd (49015-5027)
PHONE..................269 788-9987
Dennis Marshall, *Principal*
EMP: 4
SALES (est): 339.4K **Privately Held**
SIC: **3911** Cigar & cigarette accessories

(G-1235)
PALMER ENVELOPE CO
309 Fritz Keiper Blvd (49037-7305)
P.O. Box 428 (49016-0428)
PHONE..................269 965-1336
Charles A Stevenson, *President*
Shirley Stevenson, *Corp Secy*
EMP: 20 EST: 1939
SQ FT: 30,000
SALES (est): 2MM **Privately Held**
SIC: **2752** Commercial printing, offset

(G-1236)
POST FOODS LLC
275 Cliff St (49014-6354)
PHONE..................269 966-1000
Kevin Hunt, *CEO*
Jennifer Hutchinson, *General Mgr*
Caitlin Clancy, *Project Mgr*
Ron Denig, *Project Mgr*
Ted Krenkel, *Safety Mgr*
EMP: 202
SALES (est): 75MM **Publicly Held**
SIC: **2043** Cereal breakfast foods
PA: Post Holdings, Inc.
2503 S Hanley Rd
Saint Louis MO 63144

(G-1237)
PRINTLINK SHORT RUN
309 Fritz Keiper Blvd (49037-7305)
PHONE..................269 965-1336
Paul E Punnett, *President*
Debra Punnett, *Vice Pres*
▲ EMP: 10
SQ FT: 7,500
SALES (est): 1.5MM **Privately Held**
SIC: **2759** Commercial printing

(G-1238)
PROGRESSIVE PRTG & GRAPHICS
148 Columbia Ave E (49015-3735)
PHONE..................269 965-8909
Daniel Egan, *Owner*
▼ EMP: 4
SQ FT: 4,000
SALES (est): 377.7K **Privately Held**
WEB: www.progressiveprinting.net
SIC: **2752 5621 2791** Commercial printing, offset; bridal shops; typesetting

(G-1239)
R B CHRISTIAN INC (PA)
525 24th St N (49037-7807)
PHONE..................269 963-9327
Richard Christian, *President*
EMP: 6 EST: 1952
SALES (est): 1MM **Privately Held**
WEB: www.rbchristian.com
SIC: **3446 5211** Architectural metalwork; lumber & other building materials; concrete & cinder block

(G-1240)
RECYCLING FLUID TECHNOLOGIES
4039 Columbia Ave W (49015-9606)
PHONE..................269 788-0488

GEOGRAPHIC SECTION
Battle Creek - Calhoun County (G-1266)

Malcolm Hikok, *President*
Patricia Hikok, *Vice Pres*
EMP: 10 **EST:** 1992
SALES: 3.7MM **Privately Held**
SIC: 5169 2899 Chemicals & allied products; antifreeze compounds

(G-1241)
RIVERSIDE SCREW MCH PDTS INC
52 Edison St S (49014-5795)
P.O. Box 486 (49016-0486)
PHONE 269 962-5449
Mitchell Smith, *President*
▲ **EMP:** 18
SQ FT: 21,000
SALES (est): 2.6MM **Privately Held**
SIC: 3451 Screw machine products

(G-1242)
ROSLER METAL FINISHING USA LLC (PA)
1551 Denso Rd (49037-7390)
PHONE 269 441-3000
Nicole Spooner, *Project Mgr*
Leslie Nessel, *Production*
Nick Nieto, *Production*
Heather Roe, *Production*
Pam Bussler, *Purchasing*
▲ **EMP:** 75
SQ FT: 300,000
SALES (est): 20.9MM **Privately Held**
WEB: www.roslerusa.com
SIC: 2821 3559 Plastics materials & resins; ; metal finishing equipment for plating, etc.

(G-1243)
RX OPTICAL LABORATORIES INC
65 Columbia Ave E (49015-3705)
PHONE 269 965-5106
Gena Durt, *Manager*
EMP: 4
SALES (corp-wide): 43.3MM **Privately Held**
WEB: www.rxoptical.com
SIC: 5995 3851 Opticians; ophthalmic goods
PA: Rx Optical Laboratories, Inc
1825 S Park St
Kalamazoo MI 49001
269 342-5958

(G-1244)
SCOOTERS REFUSE SERVICE INC
1185 Raymond Rd N (49014-5847)
PHONE 269 962-2201
Mike McLain, *Manager*
EMP: 9
SALES (est): 1MM **Privately Held**
SIC: 3083 3089 4212 4953 Laminated plastics plate & sheet; thermoformed finished plastic products; garbage collection & transport, no disposal; refuse collection & disposal services

(G-1245)
SGK LLC
Also Called: Schawk
70 Michigan Ave W Ste 400 (49017-3620)
PHONE 269 381-3820
Ainjon Cook, *General Mgr*
EMP: 100
SALES (corp-wide): 1.6B **Publicly Held**
WEB: www.schawk.com
SIC: 3555 2796 Printing trades machinery; platemaking services
HQ: Sgk, Llc
1695 S River Rd
Des Plaines IL 60018
847 827-9494

(G-1246)
SHIRTS N MORE INC
Also Called: Ad-Mission
131 Grand Trunk Ave (49037-8442)
PHONE 269 963-3266
Diane Kendall, *CEO*
Tim Kendall, *President*
EMP: 15
SQ FT: 12,400
SALES (est): 1MM **Privately Held**
WEB: www.shirtsnmore.com
SIC: 2395 2396 5199 Embroidery products, except schiffli machine; screen printing on fabric articles; advertising specialties

(G-1247)
SHOULDICE INDUS MFRS CNTRS INC
182 Elm St (49014-4000)
PHONE 269 962-5579
David R Vanmiddlesworth, *President*
David J Shouldice, *Vice Pres*
Dan Vanmiddlesworth, *Vice Pres*
Randy Sample, *Project Mgr*
Eric Monaweck, *Manager*
EMP: 75 **EST:** 1919
SQ FT: 14,982
SALES (est): 18.6MM **Privately Held**
WEB: www.shouldicebrothers.com
SIC: 3444 1761 Sheet metal specialties, not stamped; sheet metalwork

(G-1248)
SILENT OBSERVER
Also Called: Battle Creek Chamber Commerce
20 Division St N (49014-4004)
PHONE 269 966-3550
James Boss, *Vice Pres*
EMP: 4
SALES (est): 184.2K **Privately Held**
SIC: 2711 Newspapers, publishing & printing

(G-1249)
SINOSCAN INC
965 Capital Ave Sw (49015-3818)
PHONE 269 966-0932
Ole B Andersen, *President*
▲ **EMP:** 3
SALES: 500K **Privately Held**
WEB: www.sinoscan.com
SIC: 3462 Iron & steel forgings

(G-1250)
SMITH WELL & PUMP
499 E Shore Dr (49017)
PHONE 269 721-3118
Michael J Smith, *Partner*
Dorene Smith, *Partner*
EMP: 4
SALES (est): 233.8K **Privately Held**
SIC: 1381 Drilling water intake wells

(G-1251)
SNACKWERKS OF MICHIGAN LLC
Also Called: Jpg Resources Food Mfg
180 Goodale Ave E (49037-2728)
PHONE 269 719-8282
Jeff Grogg, *Managing Dir*
Jeffrey P Grogg,
Pete Borozan,
EMP: 13
SALES (est): 2MM **Privately Held**
SIC: 2043 Cereal breakfast foods

(G-1252)
STAIR SPECIALIST INC
2257 Columbia Ave W (49015-8639)
PHONE 269 964-2351
Ted Goff, *President*
EMP: 4
SQ FT: 4,000
SALES (est): 437.7K **Privately Held**
WEB: www.stairspecialistinc.com
SIC: 2431 Staircases & stairs, wood

(G-1253)
STEWART INDUSTRIES LLC
150 Mcquiston Dr (49037-7376)
PHONE 269 660-9290
Joseph Stewart, *CEO*
Erick Stewart, *President*
Steve Bishop, *Vice Pres*
Edward Devito, *Vice Pres*
EMP: 60 **EST:** 2000
SQ FT: 60,000
SALES (est): 8.6MM **Privately Held**
WEB: www.stewartindustries.com
SIC: 3714 Air conditioner parts, motor vehicle

(G-1254)
STEWART METROLOGY LLC
150 Mcquiston Dr (49037-7376)
PHONE 269 660-9290
Erick Stewart,
EMP: 3
SQ FT: 3,000
SALES (est): 73.4K **Privately Held**
SIC: 7389 3823 Check validation service; industrial process measurement equipment

(G-1255)
STUDIO ONE MIDWEST INC
74 Leonard Wood Rd (49037-7309)
PHONE 269 962-3475
Michael D Clark, *President*
EMP: 10
SQ FT: 20,000
SALES (est): 950K **Privately Held**
WEB: www.mannetron.com
SIC: 3999 3842 Figures, wax; models, anatomical

(G-1256)
SWEETWATERS DONUT MILL
2807 Capital Ave Sw (49015-4105)
PHONE 269 979-1944
Harold Hell, *Manager*
Linda Bradshaw, *Manager*
EMP: 15
SALES (est): 627.6K **Privately Held**
SIC: 5461 2051 Doughnuts; doughnuts, except frozen

(G-1257)
SYSTEX PRODUCTS CORPORATION (DH)
Also Called: Pyper Products Corporation
300 Buckner Rd (49037-5602)
PHONE 269 964-8800
Tamotsu Inoue, *Ch of Bd*
Naohisa Miyashita, *President*
Jason Bailey, *Prdtn Mgr*
Alejandro Ramos, *Engineer*
Makoto Saito, *Treasurer*
▲ **EMP:** 98
SQ FT: 106,000
SALES (est): 84.1MM **Privately Held**
WEB: www.systexproducts.com
SIC: 3089 Injection molded finished plastic products

(G-1258)
TODA AMERICA INCORPORATED
4750 W Dickman Rd (49037-7391)
PHONE 269 962-0353
Jun Nakano, *President*
Hiroyasu Watanabe, *Technical Mgr*
Yoshiharu Aizawa, *Engineer*
Timothy Delong, *Accountant*
▲ **EMP:** 5 **EST:** 1996
SQ FT: 3,000
SALES (est): 1.3MM **Privately Held**
SIC: 2899 Magnetic inspection oil or powder
PA: Toda Kogyo Corp.
1-23, Kyobashicho, Minami-Ku
Hiroshima HIR 732-0

(G-1259)
TRANSCONTINENTAL US LLC
155 Brook St (49037-3031)
PHONE 269 964-7137
Todd Maguire, *Branch Mgr*
EMP: 53
SALES (corp-wide): 1.6B **Privately Held**
SIC: 2673 Bags: plastic, laminated & coated
HQ: Transcontinental Us Llc
8600 W Br Mw Ave 800n
Chicago IL 60631
773 877-3300

(G-1260)
TREEHOUSE PRIVATE BRANDS INC
Also Called: Ralston Foods
150 Mccamly St S (49017-3522)
P.O. Box 197 (49016-0197)
PHONE 269 968-6181
Benjamin Bronson, *Warehouse Mgr*
Michelle Hull, *Human Res Mgr*
Joe Orolin, *Branch Mgr*
Theresa Johnson, *Supervisor*
EMP: 144
SALES (corp-wide): 5.8B **Publicly Held**
SIC: 2043 Cereal breakfast foods
HQ: Treehouse Private Brands, Inc.
2021 Spring Rd Ste 600
Oak Brook IL 60523

(G-1261)
TRMI INC
Also Called: Tokai Rika Group
100 Hill Brady Rd (49037-7301)
PHONE 269 966-0800
Ken Noguchi, *President*
Keith Eyre, *Engineer*
Lee Lim, *Senior Mgr*
Ben Potter, *IT/INT Sup*
▲ **EMP:** 550
SQ FT: 205,000
SALES (est): 145.6MM **Privately Held**
SIC: 3714 3643 Motor vehicle electrical equipment; electric switches
HQ: Tram, Inc.
47200 Port St
Plymouth MI 48170
734 254-8500

(G-1262)
UNCLE EDS OIL SHOPPES INC
2050 Columbia Ave W (49015-2846)
PHONE 269 962-0999
Eric Gibbs, *Manager*
EMP: 4 **Privately Held**
SIC: 1389 Oil field services
PA: Uncle Ed's Oil Shoppes, Inc
2515 Capital Ave Sw
Battle Creek MI 49015

(G-1263)
UPSTON ASSOCIATES INC
5 Minges Ln (49015-7921)
PHONE 269 349-2782
Dwight Upston, *President*
Deborah Upston, *Vice Pres*
EMP: 7
SQ FT: 1,200
SALES (est): 450K **Privately Held**
SIC: 2721 Periodicals: publishing & printing

(G-1264)
W W THAYNE ADVERTISING CONS
Also Called: Thayne Art Mart
4642 Capital Ave Sw (49015-9305)
PHONE 269 979-1411
Richard F De Ruiter, *President*
Rick Deruiter, *Publisher*
Sherii Sherban, *Editor*
Shirley De Ruiter, *Vice Pres*
EMP: 10 **EST:** 1971
SQ FT: 2,800
SALES (est): 1.3MM **Privately Held**
WEB: www.wwthayne.com
SIC: 7311 2721 Advertising consultant; magazines: publishing only, not printed on site

(G-1265)
WACO CLASSIC AIRCRAFT CORP
15955 South Airport Rd (49015-7608)
PHONE 269 565-1000
Peter Bowers, *President*
Julie Bunday, *Controller*
Carl Dye, *Manager*
EMP: 30
SQ FT: 40,000
SALES (est): 5.2MM **Privately Held**
WEB: www.wacoclassic.com
SIC: 3721 Airplanes, fixed or rotary wing

(G-1266)
WALTERS PLUMBING COMPANY
Also Called: Walters Plumbing & Htg Sups
189 20th St N (49015-1799)
PHONE 269 962-6253
Mark Saunders, *President*
EMP: 15
SQ FT: 15,000
SALES (est): 1.3MM **Privately Held**
SIC: 1711 1381 5074 Plumbing contractors; warm air heating & air conditioning contractor; drilling water intake wells; plumbing & hydronic heating supplies

Battle Creek - Calhoun County (G-1267)

GEOGRAPHIC SECTION

(G-1267)
WESTROCK RKT LLC
177 Angell St (49037-8274)
PHONE.................................269 963-5511
Tim Hagenbach, *Branch Mgr*
Robert Bob Slater, *Info Tech Dir*
EMP: 161
SALES (corp-wide): 16.2B **Publicly Held**
WEB: www.rocktenn.com
SIC: 2653 Corrugated & solid fiber boxes
HQ: Westrock Rkt, Llc
1000 Abernathy Rd Ste 125
Atlanta GA 30328
770 448-2193

(G-1268)
WRKCO INC
Westrock Box On Demand
4075 Columbia Ave W (49015-9606)
PHONE.................................269 964-7181
Chris Hansen, *Principal*
Kevin McKnight, *Manager*
EMP: 30
SQ FT: 145,000
SALES (corp-wide): 16.2B **Publicly Held**
WEB: www.plymouth-packaging.com
SIC: 2653 2657 5113 Boxes, corrugated: made from purchased materials; folding paperboard boxes; corrugated & solid fiber boxes
HQ: Wrkco Inc.
1000 Abernathy Rd
Atlanta GA 30328
770 448-2193

Bay City
Bay County

(G-1269)
A & B DISPLAY SYSTEMS INC
Also Called: Mill Town Woodworks
1111 S Henry St (48706-5061)
PHONE.................................989 893-6642
James Belanger, *President*
Gregory Lundquist, *Treasurer*
Laure Belanger, *Admin Sec*
EMP: 11
SQ FT: 40,000
SALES (est): 1.3MM **Privately Held**
WEB: www.abdisplays.com
SIC: 3999 7319 5211 1751 Advertising display products; display advertising service; cabinets, kitchen; cabinet & finish carpentry; products of purchased glass; adhesives & sealants

(G-1270)
ACKERMAN BROTHERS INC
200 S Linn St (48706-4943)
PHONE.................................989 892-4122
Richard T Swantek Jr, *President*
Cynthia Auger, *Manager*
EMP: 6 **EST:** 1933
SQ FT: 5,000
SALES: 550K **Privately Held**
SIC: 3444 7692 Sheet metalwork; welding repair

(G-1271)
ACRA CAST INC
1837 1st St (48708-6298)
PHONE.................................989 893-3961
Richard Singer IV, *President*
▼ **EMP:** 22 **EST:** 1966
SQ FT: 9,130
SALES: 1.2MM **Privately Held**
WEB: www.acracast.com
SIC: 3365 3369 3324 Aluminum foundries; castings, except die-castings, precision; steel investment foundries

(G-1272)
ADVANCED TEX SCREEN PRINTING
Also Called: Advanced Tex Screenprinting
4177 3 Mile Rd (48706-9607)
PHONE.................................989 643-7288
Dennis V Barthel, *President*
Kendall Bader, *Sales Staff*
Jerrod Gillman, *Director*
Julie A Barthel, *Admin Sec*
▼ **EMP:** 20
SQ FT: 15,000
SALES (est): 2.4MM **Privately Held**
WEB: www.atsprinting.com
SIC: 2759 Screen printing

(G-1273)
AEROSPACE AMERICA INC
900 Harry S Truman Pkwy (48706-4114)
P.O. Box 189 (48707-0189)
PHONE.................................989 684-2121
Arthur P Dore, *Ch of Bd*
Mike Alley, *President*
Murray Sutherland, *President*
EMP: 20 **EST:** 1962
SQ FT: 80,000
SALES (est): 5.2MM **Privately Held**
WEB: www.aerospaceamerica.com
SIC: 3589 3714 3949 3484 Asbestos removal equipment; radiators & radiator shells & cores, motor vehicle; hunting equipment; small arms; machine guns or machine gun parts, 30 mm. & below; test equipment for electronic & electrical circuits

(G-1274)
ALRO STEEL CORPORATION
3125 N Water St (48708-5455)
PHONE.................................989 893-9553
Mark Oliver, *Division Mgr*
Robert Wendland, *Finance Mgr*
EMP: 18
SQ FT: 40,000
SALES (corp-wide): 2.2B **Privately Held**
WEB: www.alro.com
SIC: 5051 3498 3446 Steel; tube fabricating (contract bending & shaping); open flooring & grating for construction
PA: Alro Steel Corporation
3100 E High St
Jackson MI 49203
517 787-5500

(G-1275)
AMERICAN PWR CNNECTION SYSTEMS
2460 Midland Rd (48706-9469)
PHONE.................................989 686-6302
Paul Wujek, *CEO*
Marcy Wujek, *President*
▲ **EMP:** 10
SQ FT: 8,000
SALES (est): 1MM **Privately Held**
WEB: www.american-power.com
SIC: 3643 Connectors & terminals for electrical devices

(G-1276)
ARNOLD & SAUTTER CO (PA)
408 N Euclid Ave (48706-2996)
P.O. Box 1121 (48706-0121)
PHONE.................................989 684-7557
James G Arnold, *President*
EMP: 15
SQ FT: 5,800
SALES (est): 3.4MM **Privately Held**
WEB: www.arnoldsales.com
SIC: 1521 3442 3446 3444 General remodeling, single-family houses; shutters, door or window: metal; storm doors or windows, metal; bank fixtures, ornamental metal; sheet metalwork; glass & glazing work; carpentry work

(G-1277)
ASIAN NOODLE LLC
200 Center Ave (48708-5636)
PHONE.................................989 316-2380
EMP: 5 **EST:** 2014
SALES (est): 224.2K **Privately Held**
SIC: 2098 Noodles (e.g. egg, plain & water), dry

(G-1278)
AURORA PRESERVED FLOWERS
7201 Westside Saginaw Rd # 5 (48706-8327)
PHONE.................................989 498-0290
Jane A Huegel, *Owner*
EMP: 7
SALES (est): 355.9K **Privately Held**
WEB: www.aurorapreservedflowers.com
SIC: 3999 Flowers, artificial & preserved

(G-1279)
BALDAUF ENTERPRISES INC (PA)
Also Called: Kerkau Manufacturing Company
1321 S Valley Center Dr (48706-9798)
PHONE.................................989 686-0350
Harold E Baldauf, *President*
Laura Horney, *Vice Pres*
Fred H May Jr, *Vice Pres*
Tom Nelson, *Vice Pres*
David Baldauf, *Treasurer*
▲ **EMP:** 82
SQ FT: 200,000
SALES (est): 21.2MM
SALES (corp-wide): 22.6MM **Privately Held**
SIC: 3444 3498 Sheet metalwork; fabricated pipe & fittings

(G-1280)
BALDAUF ENTERPRISES INC
Also Called: Kerkau Manufacturing
910 Harry S Truman Pkwy (48706-4171)
PHONE.................................989 686-0350
Harold E Baldauf, *Branch Mgr*
EMP: 26
SALES (corp-wide): 22.6MM **Privately Held**
SIC: 3542 Machine tools, metal forming type
PA: Baldauf Enterprises, Inc.
1321 S Valley Center Dr
Bay City MI 48706
989 686-0350

(G-1281)
BARNEYS BAKERY
421 S Van Buren St (48706-7379)
PHONE.................................989 895-5466
Daniel Zielinski, *Owner*
EMP: 6
SQ FT: 2,893
SALES (est): 199K **Privately Held**
SIC: 5461 2051 Doughnuts; bread, cake & related products

(G-1282)
BAY CARBON INC
800 Marquette St Ste 2 (48706-4098)
P.O. Box 205 (48707-0205)
PHONE.................................989 686-8090
William Clare, *President*
James Clare, *Vice Pres*
Michael Clare, *Vice Pres*
EMP: 26
SQ FT: 10,000
SALES (est): 4.7MM **Privately Held**
WEB: www.baycarbon.com
SIC: 3624 3674 Carbon & graphite products; semiconductor circuit networks

(G-1283)
BAY CAST INC
2611 Center Ave (48706-6396)
P.O. Box 126 (48707-0126)
PHONE.................................989 892-0511
Max D Holman, *President*
Jason J Holman, *Vice Pres*
Cynthia Hildinger, *Treasurer*
Max Holeman, *Manager*
Scott S Holman, *Director*
◆ **EMP:** 75
SQ FT: 500,000
SALES (est): 15MM **Privately Held**
WEB: www.baycastinc.com
SIC: 3325 Alloy steel castings, except investment

(G-1284)
BAY CAST TECHNOLOGIES INC
2611 Center Ave (48706-6396)
P.O. Box 126 (48707-0126)
PHONE.................................989 892-9500
Scott S Holman, *President*
Jason J Holman, *Vice Pres*
Cynthia Hildinger, *Treasurer*
Max D Holman, *Director*
Max Holman, *Admin Sec*
▼ **EMP:** 29
SQ FT: 300,000
SALES (est): 4.4MM **Privately Held**
WEB: www.baycasttech.com
SIC: 3599 Machine shop, jobbing & repair

(G-1285)
BAY CITY FIBERGLASS INC
Also Called: Bay City Fiberglass Repair
1809 S Water St (48708-7787)
PHONE.................................989 751-9622
Paul Witter, *President*
Joseph Childs, *Vice Pres*
EMP: 3
SQ FT: 20,000
SALES (est): 339.8K **Privately Held**
SIC: 3732 2221 7699 Boats, fiberglass: building & repairing; fiberglass fabrics; boat repair

(G-1286)
BAY CITY FIREWORKS FESTIVAL
3296 E Fisher Rd (48706-3226)
P.O. Box 873 (48707-0873)
PHONE.................................989 892-2264
EMP: 7
SALES: 273.5K **Privately Held**
SIC: 2899 Mfg Chemical Preparations

(G-1287)
BAY MACHINING AND SALES INC
4421 Ace Commercial Ct (48706-1974)
PHONE.................................989 316-1801
Ronald Seymour, *President*
Julie Seymour, *Vice Pres*
EMP: 12
SQ FT: 3,000
SALES (est): 1.7MM **Privately Held**
SIC: 3599 Machine shop, jobbing & repair

(G-1288)
BAY PLASTICS MACHINERY CO LLC
3494 N Euclid Ave (48706-1637)
PHONE.................................989 671-9630
Anthony Forgash, *CEO*
Jason Forgash, *President*
AG Fath, *Vice Pres*
Bob Hewitt, *Engineer*
Jeff Forgash, *VP Sales*
EMP: 50
SQ FT: 20,000
SALES: 8MM **Privately Held**
SIC: 5046 3549 Commercial equipment; cutting & slitting machinery

(G-1289)
BAY UNITED MOTORS INC
4353 Wilder Rd (48706-2297)
PHONE.................................989 684-3972
Joseph P Noonan, *President*
Patti Noonan, *Vice Pres*
EMP: 13
SQ FT: 11,000
SALES (est): 4.4MM **Privately Held**
SIC: 5063 7694 Motors, electric; electric motor repair

(G-1290)
BGT AEROSPACE LLC
4412 Ace Commercial Ct (48706-1973)
PHONE.................................989 225-5812
Garrett O'Brien,
Terry Clemens,
Ben Davis,
EMP: 3
SQ FT: 5,500
SALES (est): 165.2K **Privately Held**
SIC: 3728 Aircraft parts & equipment

(G-1291)
BIMBO BAKERIES USA INC
3801 Wilder Rd (48706-2301)
PHONE.................................989 667-0551
EMP: 24 **Privately Held**
SIC: 2051 Bread, cake & related products
HQ: Bimbo Bakeries Usa, Inc
255 Business Center Dr # 200
Horsham PA 19044
215 347-5500

(G-1292)
BORDENER ENGNRED LAMINATES INC
Also Called: Bordener Engineered Surfaces
106 S Walnut St Ste 1 (48706-4990)
PHONE.................................989 835-6881
Robert Bordener, *CEO*
Mark McKinley, *Chairman*

▲ = Import ▼ =Export
◆ =Import/Export

GEOGRAPHIC SECTION
Bay City - Bay County (G-1317)

Mark Kochavar, *Treasurer*
James Milhench, *Admin Sec*
EMP: 5
SALES (est): 434.8K **Privately Held**
SIC: 3083 Laminated plastics plate & sheet

(G-1293)
CAMBRON ENGINEERING INC
3800 Wilder Rd (48706-2196)
PHONE.................................989 684-5890
Stephen D Sheppard, *President*
David A Ferrio, *Vice Pres*
Renee Riddle, *Plant Mgr*
Cathy Chappel, *Manager*
Brian Christilaw, *Info Tech Mgr*
EMP: 44
SQ FT: 30,500
SALES: 7.9MM **Privately Held**
WEB: www.cambronengineering.com
SIC: 3544 Special dies & tools

(G-1294)
CARBONE OF AMERICA
900 Harrison St (48708-8299)
PHONE.................................989 894-2911
Kirk Keihly, *Office Mgr*
EMP: 15
SALES (est): 2.9MM **Privately Held**
SIC: 3624 Carbon & graphite products

(G-1295)
CLAMPTECH LLC
106 S Walnut St Ste 1 (48706-4990)
PHONE.................................989 832-8027
Stacy Pastein,
EMP: 7
SALES: 300K **Privately Held**
SIC: 3429 Manufactured hardware (general)

(G-1296)
COCA-COLA REFRESHMENTS USA INC
2500 Broadway St (48708-8402)
PHONE.................................989 895-8537
Russ Marvin, *Manager*
EMP: 60
SQ FT: 40,000
SALES (corp-wide): 31.8B **Publicly Held**
WEB: www.cokecce.com
SIC: 2086 Bottled & canned soft drinks
HQ: Coca-Cola Refreshments Usa, Inc.
 2500 Windy Ridge Pkwy Se
 Atlanta GA 30339
 770 989-3000

(G-1297)
COMPUTER OPERATED MFG
1710 Lewis St (48706-1133)
PHONE.................................989 686-1333
Doug Rechsteiner, *President*
Gary Rechsteiner, *Principal*
EMP: 20
SQ FT: 20,000
SALES (est): 3MM **Privately Held**
WEB: www.comcncmachining.com
SIC: 3599 3498 3494 3462 Machine shop, jobbing & repair; fabricated pipe & fittings; valves & pipe fittings; iron & steel forgings; nonferrous foundries

(G-1298)
CONNIES CLUTTER
3361 Fairway Dr (48706-3329)
PHONE.................................517 684-7291
Connie Robetoy, *Administration*
EMP: 3
SALES (est): 88K **Privately Held**
SIC: 2835 In vitro & in vivo diagnostic substances

(G-1299)
DELTA CONTAINERS INC (PA)
Also Called: Flint Packaging Systems Div
1400 Eddy St (48708-6179)
P.O. Box 623 (48707-0623)
PHONE.................................810 742-2730
Virginia R Landaal, *Ch of Bd*
Stephen Landaal, *Exec VP*
Martha Jeanne Stetson, *Treasurer*
Nichole Salzano, *Marketing Staff*
James Trembley, *Admin Sec*
▲ **EMP:** 225
SQ FT: 325,000
SALES (est): 58MM **Privately Held**
WEB: www.landaal.com
SIC: 2653 4783 2675 2671 Boxes, corrugated: made from purchased materials; boxes, solid fiber: made from purchased materials; containerization of goods for shipping; crating goods for shipping; packing goods for shipping; die-cut paper & board; packaging paper & plastics film, coated & laminated; wood pallets & skids

(G-1300)
DELTA CONTAINERS INC
Also Called: Landaal Packaging Systems
1400 Eddy St (48708-6179)
PHONE.................................810 742-2730
Stephen Landaal, *Vice Pres*
Diane McDonald, *Purch Mgr*
EMP: 50
SALES (corp-wide): 58MM **Privately Held**
SIC: 5113 2653 7389 5199 Corrugated & solid fiber boxes; corrugated & solid fiber boxes; packaging & labeling services; packaging materials; corrugated paper: made from purchased material
PA: Delta Containers, Inc.
 1400 Eddy St
 Bay City MI 48708
 810 742-2730

(G-1301)
DICE CORPORATION
1410 S Valley Center Dr (48706-9754)
PHONE.................................989 891-2800
Clifford V Dice, *President*
Myra Thomas, *Editor*
Victoria Dice, *Vice Pres*
Dean Martin, *Facilities Mgr*
Lori Jezowski, *CFO*
EMP: 50
SQ FT: 30,000
SALES: 7.6MM **Privately Held**
WEB: www.dicecorp.com
SIC: 3699 1731 5063 7382 Security control equipment & systems; fire detection & burglar alarm systems specialization; alarm systems; security systems services

(G-1302)
DIE STAMPCO INC
1301 N Lincoln St (48708-6172)
PHONE.................................989 893-7790
Clyde Hart, *President*
Robbin Hart, *Vice Pres*
Jason Hart, *Production*
EMP: 11
SQ FT: 2,400
SALES (est): 2.3MM **Privately Held**
WEB: www.diestampco.com
SIC: 3449 3061 3089 Miscellaneous metalwork; mechanical rubber goods; molding primary plastic

(G-1303)
DINO S DUMPSTERS LLC
900 Harry S Truman Pkwy (48706-4171)
PHONE.................................989 225-5635
Dennis Dore, *Principal*
EMP: 3
SALES (est): 147.8K **Privately Held**
SIC: 3443 Dumpsters, garbage

(G-1304)
DOBSON INDUSTRIAL INC (PA)
Also Called: Dobson Heavy Haul Inc Division
3660 N Euclid Ave (48706-2026)
P.O. Box 1368 (48706-0368)
PHONE.................................800 298-6063
Dale Bash, *Chairman*
Jim Dobson, *Shareholder*
▲ **EMP:** 50
SQ FT: 39,000
SALES (est): 8.8MM **Privately Held**
WEB: www.dobsonindustrial.com
SIC: 1799 1791 3441 5031 Rigging & scaffolding; structural steel erection; fabricated structural metal; doors; materials handling machinery

(G-1305)
DOUG WIRT ENTERPRISES INC
Also Called: Wirt Stone Dock
400 Martin St (48706-4121)
PHONE.................................989 684-5777
Doug Wirt, *Manager*
EMP: 6
SALES (est): 580.8K
SALES (corp-wide): 1.5MM **Privately Held**
SIC: 1411 4212 5083 5032 Limestone & marble dimension stone; dump truck haulage; landscaping equipment; limestone
PA: Wirt Doug Enterprises Inc
 4700 Crow Island Rd
 Saginaw MI 48601
 989 753-6404

(G-1306)
DOW SILICONES CORPORATION
1 E Main St (48708-7495)
PHONE.................................989 895-3397
Lacey Cameron, *Branch Mgr*
EMP: 400
SALES (corp-wide): 61B **Publicly Held**
SIC: 2869 Industrial organic chemicals
HQ: Dow Silicones Corporation
 2200 W Salzburg Rd
 Auburn MI 48611
 989 496-4000

(G-1307)
E J M BALL SCREW LLC
209 Morton St (48706-5348)
PHONE.................................989 893-7674
Ernest Machelski, *Mng Member*
Michael Machelski,
EMP: 15
SQ FT: 12,000
SALES: 750K **Privately Held**
WEB: www.ejmballscrew.com
SIC: 3452 3593 Screws, metal; fluid power cylinders & actuators

(G-1308)
EMCOR INC
5154 Alliance Dr (48706-8709)
PHONE.................................989 667-0652
John P O'Brien, *President*
John P O Brien, *President*
Ann M O Brien, *Treasurer*
EMP: 18 **EST:** 1982
SQ FT: 18,000
SALES (est): 3.4MM **Privately Held**
WEB: www.emcorinc.net
SIC: 3541 3544 Machine tool replacement & repair parts, metal cutting types; special dies & tools

(G-1309)
EUCLID COATING SYSTEMS INC
3494 N Euclid Ave (48706-1637)
PHONE.................................989 922-4789
Scott A Seymour, *President*
EMP: 15
SQ FT: 2,000
SALES: 350K **Privately Held**
WEB: www.euclidlabcoater.com
SIC: 3554 3559 Coating & finishing machinery, paper; fiber optics strand coating machinery

(G-1310)
EUCLID INDUSTRIES INC (PA)
1655 Tech Dr (48706-9792)
PHONE.................................989 686-8920
Ronald Beebe, *President*
Carmen Gueli, *Vice Pres*
Bob Kietzman, *Engineer*
Holly Martin, *Engineer*
Paul Piotrowski, *Supervisor*
▲ **EMP:** 160
SQ FT: 117,000
SALES (est): 33.9MM **Privately Held**
SIC: 3599 7389 3714 2431 Machine shop, jobbing & repair; packaging & labeling services; motor vehicle parts & accessories; millwork

(G-1311)
EVERGREEN WINERY LLC
Also Called: Cadillac Winery
3835 Huszan Dr (48706-2221)
PHONE.................................989 392-2044
Jean Charbonneau, *Co-Owner*
EMP: 5 **EST:** 2017
SALES (est): 169.2K **Privately Held**
SIC: 2084 Wine cellars, bonded: engaged in blending wines

(G-1312)
F P HORAK COMPANY (PA)
Also Called: Horak Company, The
1311 Straits Dr (48706-8708)
P.O. Box 925 (48707-0925)
PHONE.................................989 892-6505
Frederick Horak, *Ch of Bd*
Marisa Horak Belotti, *President*
Timothy Dust, *President*
Darrin Demott, *COO*
Guy Jeffrey, *Vice Pres*
EMP: 162
SQ FT: 147,000
SALES (est): 50.4MM **Privately Held**
WEB: www.fphorak.com
SIC: 2752 2761 2791 2789 Commercial printing, offset; continuous forms, office & business; computer forms, manifold or continuous; typesetting; bookbinding & related work; commercial printing

(G-1313)
FABIANO BROS DEV - WSCNSIN LLC
1885 Bevanda Ct (48706-8720)
PHONE.................................989 509-0200
Joseph Fabiano, *Principal*
Joseph R Fabiano, *Principal*
EMP: 4
SALES (est): 230.4K **Privately Held**
SIC: 2082 Beer (alcoholic beverage)

(G-1314)
FBE ASSOCIATES INC
513 N Madison Ave Ste 101 (48708-6460)
PHONE.................................989 894-2785
Patrick Race, *President*
Tom Goodman, *Corp Secy*
EMP: 5
SALES: 250K **Privately Held**
WEB: www.fbe-inc.com
SIC: 7372 Educational computer software

(G-1315)
GENERAL MOTORS LLC
1001 Woodside Ave (48708-5470)
PHONE.................................989 894-7210
Jonathan Kelch, *Project Mgr*
Shane Bremer, *Engineer*
Dennis Hawley, *Engineer*
John Wing, *Engineer*
Joe Mazzeo, *Branch Mgr*
EMP: 450 **Publicly Held**
SIC: 5511 3714 3592 3561 Automobiles, new & used; motor vehicle parts & accessories; carburetors, pistons, rings, valves; pumps & pumping equipment; bolts, nuts, rivets & washers; fabricated structural metal
HQ: General Motors Llc
 300 Renaissance Ctr L1
 Detroit MI 48243

(G-1316)
GENERAL PARTS INC
Also Called: Carquest Auto Parts
3616 Wilder Rd (48706-2126)
PHONE.................................989 686-3114
Terry Schlager, *Manager*
EMP: 22
SALES (corp-wide): 9.5B **Publicly Held**
WEB: www.carquest.com
SIC: 5013 5531 3599 7539 Automotive supplies & parts; automotive parts; machine shop, jobbing & repair; machine shop, automotive
HQ: General Parts, Inc.
 2635 E Millbrook Rd Ste C
 Raleigh NC 27604
 919 573-3000

(G-1317)
GOUGEON HOLDING CO (PA)
100 Patterson Ave (48706-4136)
P.O. Box 908 (48707-0908)
PHONE.................................989 684-7286
Robert H Monroe, *President*
Meade Gougeon, *Chairman*
Joanne R Gradowsky, *Corp Secy*
Grant W Urband, *Vice Pres*
EMP: 3
SQ FT: 27,000
SALES (est): 34.7MM **Privately Held**
SIC: 2851 Epoxy coatings

Bay City - Bay County (G-1318)

(G-1318)
GRAPHICS PLUS INC
2011 Columbus Ave (48708-6832)
PHONE.................989 893-0651
Dick Waldbauer, *President*
Doris Waldbauer, *Corp Secy*
EMP: 4
SQ FT: 3,000
SALES: 200K **Privately Held**
SIC: 2752 Commercial printing, offset

(G-1319)
GRAPHITE ELECTRODES LTD
Also Called: GENERAL GRAPHITES
1311 N Sherman St (48708-6070)
PHONE.................989 893-3635
Patrick Martin, *President*
Michelle L Martin, *Director*
EMP: 14 **EST:** 1961
SQ FT: 22,000
SALES: 3.4MM **Privately Held**
SIC: 3599 3624 Machine shop, jobbing & repair; carbon & graphite products

(G-1320)
HIGHLAND INDUSTRIAL INC
Also Called: Caseway Industrial Products
3487 Highland Dr (48706-2414)
PHONE.................989 391-9992
Willis Wells, *President*
Suzanne Wells, *Vice Pres*
EMP: 6
SALES (est): 460K **Privately Held**
SIC: 2891 Adhesives, plastic

(G-1321)
IDEAL TOOL INC
1707 Marquette St (48706-4170)
P.O. Box 8 (48707-0008)
PHONE.................989 893-8336
Jack Covieo, *President*
Robert Spegel, *Vice Pres*
Robbin Spegel, *Admin Sec*
EMP: 11
SQ FT: 6,000
SALES (est): 1.4MM **Privately Held**
SIC: 3599 3541 3549 Machine shop, jobbing & repair; machine tools, metal cutting type; assembly machines, including robotic

(G-1322)
INNOVATION UNLIMITED LLC
1409 4th St (48708-6133)
PHONE.................574 635-1064
Michael Westenburg, *Mng Member*
EMP: 8
SALES (est): 429.7K **Privately Held**
SIC: 5015 3571 Automotive supplies, used; electronic computers

(G-1323)
J M KUSCH INC
3530 Wheeler Rd (48706-1711)
P.O. Box 1337 (48706-0337)
PHONE.................989 684-8820
Carole S Kusch, *President*
Wendy L Kusch, *Vice Pres*
EMP: 24
SALES (est): 3.8MM **Privately Held**
SIC: 3544 Special dies & tools

(G-1324)
K-R METAL ENGINEERS CORP
815 S Henry St (48706-4989)
PHONE.................989 892-1901
Susan Leitelt, *President*
Mark H Beyer, *Corp Secy*
Gary L Linda, *Admin Sec*
EMP: 15 **EST:** 1938
SQ FT: 12,200
SALES: 3.5MM **Privately Held**
WEB: www.krmetal.com
SIC: 3441 Fabricated structural metal

(G-1325)
KOKALY SPORTS
509 N Johnson St (48708-6726)
PHONE.................989 671-7412
Isaac Kokaly, *Owner*
EMP: 3
SALES: 94K **Privately Held**
SIC: 3949 7389 Sporting & athletic goods;

(G-1326)
KRZYSIAK FAMILY RESTAURANT
Also Called: Krzysiak's House
1605 Michigan Ave (48708-8454)
PHONE.................989 894-5531
Donald J Krzysiak, *President*
Lois Krzysiak, *Vice Pres*
EMP: 60 **EST:** 1965
SQ FT: 1,500
SALES: 3MM **Privately Held**
WEB: www.krzysiaks.com
SIC: 5812 2098 2013 Restaurant; family: independent; noodles (e.g. egg, plain & water), dry; sausages from purchased meat

(G-1327)
MARK 7 MACHINE INC
535 S Tuscola Rd (48708-9632)
PHONE.................989 922-7335
Mark Walkowiak, *President*
Mary Walkowiak, *Treasurer*
EMP: 9
SQ FT: 4,940
SALES: 586K **Privately Held**
SIC: 3549 7549 Wiredrawing & fabricating machinery & equipment, ex. die; lubrication service, automotive

(G-1328)
MCG PLASTICS INC
3661 N Euclid Ave (48706-2041)
PHONE.................989 667-4349
Mario C Garza, *President*
Annette Garza, *Admin Sec*
EMP: 21
SQ FT: 10,000
SALES (est): 1.4MM **Privately Held**
SIC: 3089 Injection molded finished plastic products; injection molding of plastics

(G-1329)
MERSEN
900 Harrison St (48708-8244)
PHONE.................989 894-2911
Sohail Qamar, *Principal*
Don Guelzo, *Sales Staff*
Maryann Spyhalski, *Manager*
Michael Colony, *Info Tech Mgr*
John Hartnagle, *Info Tech Mgr*
EMP: 15
SALES (est): 3.9MM **Privately Held**
SIC: 3624 Carbon & graphite products

(G-1330)
MERSEN USA BAY CITY-MI LLC
900 Harrison St (48708-8244)
PHONE.................989 894-2911
Joseph Tracey, *Principal*
Michael Colony, *Manager*
EMP: 120 **EST:** 2014
SQ FT: 104,000
SALES: 25MM
SALES (corp-wide): 2MM **Privately Held**
SIC: 3295 Graphite, natural: ground, pulverized, refined or blended
HQ: Mersen Usa Ptt Corp.
400 Myrtle Ave
Boonton NJ 07005
973 334-0700

(G-1331)
METAL SALES MANUFACTURING CORP
5209 Mackinaw Rd (48708-9700)
PHONE.................989 686-5879
Chris Vanwormer, *Branch Mgr*
EMP: 32
SALES (corp-wide): 390.6MM **Privately Held**
SIC: 3444 Roof deck, sheet metal; siding, sheet metal
HQ: Metal Sales Manufacturing Corporation
545 S 3rd St Ste 200
Louisville KY 40202
502 855-4300

(G-1332)
METRO-FABRICATING LLC
1650 Tech Dr (48706-9792)
PHONE.................989 667-8100
Amy Lyday, *President*
Russ Charbonneau, *Mfg Spvr*
Amy Cunningham, *Purch Mgr*
Scott Vachon, *CFO*
Dave Voss, *Manager*
EMP: 75
SQ FT: 56,000
SALES: 6.6MM **Privately Held**
WEB: www.metrofab.com
SIC: 3444 3613 Laundry hampers, sheet metal; control panels, electric

(G-1333)
MICHIGAN SUGAR COMPANY (PA)
Also Called: Michigan Sugar Beet Growers
122 Uptown Dr Unit 300 (48708-5627)
P.O. Box 673089, Detroit (48267-3089)
PHONE.................989 686-0161
Mark Flegenheimer, *President*
Richard Gerstenberger, *Chairman*
Charles Bauer, *Vice Pres*
Jerry Coleman, *Vice Pres*
Pedro L Figueroa, *Vice Pres*
▲ **EMP:** 65
SALES: 600MM **Privately Held**
SIC: 2063 Beet sugar

(G-1334)
MODERN MACHINE CO
1111 S Water St (48708-7097)
PHONE.................989 895-8563
Gary Emede, *President*
Julia Emede, *Corp Secy*
EMP: 27 **EST:** 1956
SQ FT: 19,000
SALES (est): 4.5MM **Privately Held**
WEB: www.modernmachine.com
SIC: 3599 Machine shop, jobbing & repair

(G-1335)
MORIN BOATS
377 State Park Dr (48708-1339)
PHONE.................989 686-7353
Douglas Morin, *Manager*
EMP: 6
SALES (est): 700.9K **Privately Held**
SIC: 3732 Boat building & repairing

(G-1336)
NEETZ PRINTING INC
700 S Euclid Ave (48706-3304)
PHONE.................989 684-4620
Rick Neetz, *President*
Larry Neetz II, *President*
Sharon Neetz, *Admin Sec*
EMP: 4
SQ FT: 5,000
SALES (est): 560.5K **Privately Held**
SIC: 2752 Commercial printing, lithographic

(G-1337)
NEW CENTURY HEATERS LTD
4432 Ace Commercial Ct (48706-1973)
PHONE.................989 671-1994
Dean Van Derjagt, *President*
Dean Vander Jagt, *President*
EMP: 3
SALES (est): 280K **Privately Held**
WEB: www.newcenturyheaters.com
SIC: 3634 Immersion heaters, electric: household

(G-1338)
NORTHERN CONCRETE PIPE INC (PA)
401 Kelton St (48706-5395)
PHONE.................989 892-3545
William Washabaugh Jr, *President*
Paula Washabaugh, *Vice Pres*
Tim Phillips, *Safety Dir*
John Overset, *Maint Spvr*
Gary Frie, *Purchasing*
EMP: 40 **EST:** 1958
SQ FT: 1,600
SALES (est): 21.3MM **Privately Held**
WEB: www.ncp-inc.com
SIC: 3272 3441 Pipe, concrete or lined with concrete; fabricated structural metal

(G-1339)
OAKLAND ORTHOPEDIC APPLS INC (PA)
515 Mulholland St (48708-7644)
PHONE.................989 893-7544
Richard L Smith, *President*
Vivian J Smith, *Vice Pres*
Jennifer Draves, *Info Tech Mgr*
EMP: 64
SQ FT: 2,500
SALES (est): 6.8MM **Privately Held**
SIC: 3842 5999 Braces, orthopedic; orthopedic & prosthesis applications

(G-1340)
PLASTIC TAG & TRADE CHECK CO
252 Killarney Beach Rd (48706-8109)
P.O. Box 40, Essexville (48732-0040)
PHONE.................989 892-7913
Earl J Mast, *President*
John R Regan, *Admin Sec*
EMP: 10
SALES (est): 1.2MM **Privately Held**
SIC: 3089 Injection molding of plastics

(G-1341)
PLY-FORMS INCORPORATED
4684 Fraser Rd (48706-9423)
P.O. Box 136, Auburn (48611-0136)
PHONE.................989 686-5681
Bob Williams, *President*
EMP: 16
SQ FT: 30,000
SALES (est): 2.3MM **Privately Held**
SIC: 2436 2435 Softwood veneer & plywood; hardwood veneer & plywood

(G-1342)
PONDER INDUSTRIAL INCORPORATED
287 S River Rd (48708-9601)
PHONE.................989 684-9841
Dale A Bash, *President*
Barb J Bash, *Corp Secy*
Mike Campbell, *Manager*
EMP: 40
SQ FT: 30,000
SALES (est): 10.2MM **Privately Held**
WEB: www.imm.net
SIC: 3441 Fabricated structural metal

(G-1343)
PYRAMID PAVING AND CONTG CO (PA)
Also Called: Pyramid Paving Co
600 N Jefferson St (48708-6456)
PHONE.................989 895-5861
Bruce Weiss, *President*
Kurt Kloha, *Vice Pres*
John Freed, *Treasurer*
EMP: 44
SQ FT: 22,000
SALES (est): 10.1MM **Privately Held**
WEB: www.pyramidpaving.com
SIC: 1611 2951 1771 Resurfacing contractor; asphalt paving mixtures & blocks; concrete work

(G-1344)
QUALITY TRANSPARENT BAG INC (PA)
110 Mcgraw St (48708-8276)
P.O. Box 486 (48707-0486)
PHONE.................989 893-3561
Stephen Kessler, *President*
Marry Carey, *Manager*
EMP: 10 **EST:** 1955
SQ FT: 56,000
SALES (est): 14.1MM **Privately Held**
WEB: www.qualitybag.com
SIC: 2673 2671 3081 Plastic bags: made from purchased materials; plastic film, coated or laminated for packaging; unsupported plastics film & sheet

(G-1345)
QUANTUM COMPOSITES INC
1310 S Valley Center Dr (48706-9798)
PHONE.................989 922-3863
Terry Morgan, *CEO*
Bill Kennedy, *President*
Ganesh RAO, *President*
▲ **EMP:** 14
SQ FT: 50,000
SALES (est): 6.1MM
SALES (corp-wide): 39.1B **Privately Held**
WEB: www.premix.com
SIC: 2821 Molding compounds, plastics

GEOGRAPHIC SECTION

Bay Port - Huron County (G-1374)

HQ: Premix, Inc.
3365 E Center St
North Kingsville OH 44068
440 224-2181

(G-1346)
R & R READY-MIX INC
1601 W Youngs Ditch Rd (48708-9173)
PHONE..................989 892-9313
EMP: 4
SALES (corp-wide): 3.3MM **Privately Held**
SIC: 5211 3273 Ret Lumber/Building Materials Mfg Ready-Mixed Concrete
PA: R & R Ready-Mix, Inc.
6050 Melbourne Rd
Saginaw MI 48604
989 753-3862

(G-1347)
RANE INNOVATION LLC
2016 Crescent Dr (48706-9406)
PHONE..................419 577-2126
Pranav Rane,
EMP: 3
SALES (est): 71.1K **Privately Held**
SIC: 7372 Application computer software

(G-1348)
RAP PRODUCTS INC
500 Germania St (48706-5049)
P.O. Box 459 (48707-0459)
PHONE..................989 893-5583
Kelly D McDonald, *President*
EMP: 5 EST: 1950
SQ FT: 120,000
SALES (est): 924.1K **Privately Held**
SIC: 2851 2992 3412 2869 Paint removers; oils & greases, blending & compounding; barrels, shipping: metal; industrial organic chemicals; industrial inorganic chemicals

(G-1349)
REAL FLAVORS LLC
135 Washington Ave (48708-5845)
P.O. Box 380, Freeland (48623-0380)
PHONE..................855 443-9685
Oliver Yu, *Manager*
Taylor Small, *Administration*
EMP: 16
SQ FT: 2,100
SALES (est): 2.9MM **Privately Held**
SIC: 2869 2087 Perfumes, flavorings & food additives; flavors or flavoring materials, synthetic; flavoring extracts & syrups; extracts, flavoring; syrups, flavoring (except drink)

(G-1350)
RICHMAN COMPANY PRODUCTS INC
3474 W Pressler Dr (48706-3214)
PHONE..................989 686-6251
Dixie Gunther, *President*
EMP: 3
SALES (est): 159.8K **Privately Held**
SIC: 3993 2679 Signs & advertising specialties; tags & labels, paper

(G-1351)
RUSH STATIONERS PRINTERS INC
1310 N Johnson St (48708-6258)
PHONE..................989 891-9305
Mary L Bleau, *President*
EMP: 15 EST: 1929
SQ FT: 10,500
SALES: 1.9MM **Privately Held**
SIC: 5943 5021 2752 5999 Office forms & supplies; office furniture; commercial printing, offset; rubber stamps

(G-1352)
RWC INC (PA)
2105 S Euclid Ave (48706-3409)
P.O. Box 920 (48707-0920)
PHONE..................989 684-4030
William Perlberg, *President*
Rebecca Wynn, *General Mgr*
Tom Navarre, *Project Mgr*
Pat Fassezke, *Purch Agent*
Pat Fazzeske, *Purch Agent*
EMP: 80 EST: 1945
SQ FT: 123,160

SALES: 14MM **Privately Held**
WEB: www.rwcinc.com
SIC: 3541 Machine tools, metal cutting type

(G-1353)
S AND S ENTERPRISE LLC
Also Called: S and S Enterprises
123 Webster St (48708-7788)
PHONE..................989 894-7002
Dennis Strefling,
Sue Strefling,
EMP: 3
SQ FT: 5,000
SALES (est): 476.6K **Privately Held**
SIC: 3825 Shunts, electrical

(G-1354)
S C JOHNSON & SON INC
Also Called: S C Johnson Wax
4867 Wilder Rd (48706-1942)
PHONE..................989 667-0211
Paul Bilello, *Branch Mgr*
EMP: 150
SALES (corp-wide): 3.6B **Privately Held**
WEB: www.scjohnson.com
SIC: 2842 Floor waxes
PA: S. C. Johnson & Son, Inc.
1525 Howe St
Racine WI 53403
262 260-2000

(G-1355)
SANDLOT SPORTS (PA)
600 N Euclid Ave (48706-2950)
PHONE..................989 391-9684
Adam McCauley, *Owner*
Ryan Dost, *Co-Owner*
EMP: 15
SALES (est): 919.8K **Privately Held**
SIC: 2759 Screen printing

(G-1356)
SC JOHNSON & SON
4867 Wilder Rd (48706-1942)
PHONE..................989 667-0235
Tom Wood, *Engineer*
Toni Garcia, *Marketing Staff*
David Schultz, *Technical Staff*
EMP: 6
SALES (est): 747.2K **Privately Held**
SIC: 2842 Specialty cleaning, polishes & sanitation goods

(G-1357)
SHELTI INC
3020 N Water St (48708-5454)
PHONE..................989 893-1739
Randy Eigner, *President*
Dave Straw, *President*
Bruce Allen, *Engineer*
Diane Skinner, *Accounts Mgr*
Tina Grocholski, *Office Mgr*
◆ EMP: 27
SALES (est): 3.8MM **Privately Held**
WEB: www.shelti.com
SIC: 3944 Games, toys & children's vehicles

(G-1358)
SNYDER PLASTICS INC
1707 Lewis St (48706-1100)
PHONE..................989 684-8355
Jeffrey L Preston, *President*
Christina M Preston, *Admin Sec*
EMP: 20
SQ FT: 8,400
SALES (est): 2.6MM **Privately Held**
WEB: www.snyderplastics.com
SIC: 3339 3053 Silicon, pure; gaskets, packing & sealing devices

(G-1359)
SOLI-BOND INC (PA)
2377 2 Mile Rd (48706-8130)
PHONE..................989 684-9611
Dwight Hartley, *President*
Gary Draeger, *Vice Pres*
William Solan, *Vice Pres*
EMP: 8
SQ FT: 5,000
SALES (est): 34.8MM **Privately Held**
SIC: 1389 Oil field services

(G-1360)
ST LAURENT BROTHERS INC
Also Called: Saint Laurent Brothers
1101 N Water St (48708-5625)
P.O. Box 117 (48707-0117)
PHONE..................989 893-7522
Keith Whitney, *President*
Steve Frye, *Vice Pres*
EMP: 30
SQ FT: 35,000
SALES (est): 4.2MM **Privately Held**
WEB: www.stlaurentbrothers.com
SIC: 2099 5441 2068 Peanut butter; candy, nut & confectionery stores; salted & roasted nuts & seeds

(G-1361)
STRAITS CORPORATION
Also Called: Bay City Div
4804 Wilder Rd (48706-2245)
PHONE..................989 684-3584
Dave Nethers, *Manager*
EMP: 13
SALES (corp-wide): 21.7MM **Privately Held**
SIC: 2491 Preserving (creosoting) of wood
PA: The Straits Corporation
616 Oak St
Tawas City MI 48763
989 684-5088

(G-1362)
SUMMIT PRINTING & GRAPHICS
205 4th St (48708-5608)
PHONE..................989 892-2267
Beth Rodenborg, *President*
EMP: 2
SALES: 200K **Privately Held**
SIC: 2752 Commercial printing, offset

(G-1363)
TRANSIT SOLUTIONS LLC
1322 Washington Ave (48708-5711)
PHONE..................989 893-3230
Allison Short, *Mng Member*
EMP: 7 EST: 2005
SALES (est): 419.6K **Privately Held**
SIC: 3695 Computer software tape & disks: blank, rigid & floppy

(G-1364)
TUSCOLA ENERGY
920 N Water St Ste 204 (48708-5689)
PHONE..................989 894-5815
Carl Adler, *Principal*
EMP: 6
SALES (est): 555K **Privately Held**
SIC: 1389 Oil field services

(G-1365)
TWM TECHNOLOGY LLC
Also Called: Rotational Levitation Levi
3490 E North Union Rd (48706-2533)
PHONE..................989 684-7050
Henry Johnson,
EMP: 10
SALES: 100K **Privately Held**
SIC: 3621 Motors & generators

(G-1366)
UNIT STEP COMPANY INC
3788 S Huron Rd (48706-2065)
PHONE..................989 684-9361
Robert Koehler, *President*
EMP: 4 EST: 1954
SQ FT: 5,600
SALES (est): 320K **Privately Held**
SIC: 3272 Steps, prefabricated concrete

(G-1367)
UNIVERSAL PRINT
2758 E Fisher Rd (48706-3020)
PHONE..................989 525-5055
Andrew Budd, *Principal*
EMP: 4
SALES (est): 409.2K **Privately Held**
SIC: 2752 Commercial printing, lithographic

(G-1368)
UNIVERSAL PRINTING COMPANY INC
1200 Woodside Ave (48708-5000)
PHONE..................989 671-9409
Richard Budd, *Manager*

EMP: 15
SALES (est): 2.1MM **Privately Held**
SIC: 2752 Commercial printing, lithographic

(G-1369)
VALLEY PUBLISHING
5215 Mackinaw Rd (48706-9700)
PHONE..................989 671-1200
David Roberts, *Branch Mgr*
EMP: 140
SALES (est): 7.7MM **Privately Held**
SIC: 2741 Miscellaneous publishing

(G-1370)
WEST SYSTEM INC
102 Patterson Ave (48706-4136)
P.O. Box 665 (48707-0665)
PHONE..................989 684-7286
Robert Monroe, *President*
EMP: 45
SALES (est): 3.5MM
SALES (corp-wide): 34.7MM **Privately Held**
WEB: www.westsystem.com
SIC: 2851 2891 Epoxy coatings; epoxy adhesives
PA: Gougeon Holding Co.
100 Patterson Ave
Bay City MI 48706
989 684-7286

(G-1371)
YORK ELECTRIC INC (PA)
Also Called: York Servo Motor Repair
611 Andre St (48706-4195)
PHONE..................989 684-7460
Franklin K York, *CEO*
Kevin Krupp, *President*
Danielle Krupp, *Treasurer*
Christine Cathcart, *Controller*
Jade York, *Marketing Staff*
EMP: 71
SQ FT: 80,000
SALES (est): 16.4MM **Privately Held**
SIC: 7694 5063 Electric motor repair; motors, electric

Bay Port
Huron County

(G-1372)
BERKLEY INDUSTRIES INC (PA)
9938 Pigeon Rd (48720-9702)
P.O. Box 207 (48720-0207)
PHONE..................989 656-2171
Steven Pyykkonen, *President*
EMP: 18
SALES (est): 2.1MM **Privately Held**
WEB: www.berkleyindustries.com
SIC: 3498 3317 Tube fabricating (contract bending & shaping); steel pipe & tubes

(G-1373)
FALCON TRUCKING COMPANY
Also Called: Wallace Stone Plant
8785 Ribble Rd (48720-9739)
PHONE..................989 656-2831
Ralph D Bronson, *Manager*
EMP: 21
SQ FT: 20,000
SALES (corp-wide): 17.1MM **Privately Held**
WEB: www.levyco.net
SIC: 1442 1422 Sand mining; crushed & broken limestone
PA: Falcon Trucking Company
9300 Dix
Dearborn MI 48120
313 843-7200

(G-1374)
RICHMOND BROS FABRICATION LLC
7911 Murdoch Rd (48720-9763)
PHONE..................989 551-1996
Mike Richmond, *Partner*
Carrie Damm, *Manager*
EMP: 5
SALES (est): 522K **Privately Held**
SIC: 3444 Sheet metalwork

Bay Port - Huron County (G-1375) — GEOGRAPHIC SECTION

(G-1375)
S & S TUBE INC
9938 Pigeon Rd (48720-9702)
P.O. Box 207 (48720-0207)
PHONE...................989 656-7211
Tim Sears, *President*
Dennis Carter, *QC Mgr*
EMP: 18
SQ FT: 21,000
SALES (est): 3.6MM **Privately Held**
SIC: 3714 3498 3317 Motor vehicle brake systems & parts; transmission housings or parts, motor vehicle; gas tanks, motor vehicle; fabricated pipe & fittings; steel pipe & tubes

Bear Lake
Manistee County

(G-1376)
BLARNEY CASTLE INC (PA)
Also Called: Blarney Castle Oil
12218 West St (49614-9453)
P.O. Box 246 (49614-0246)
PHONE...................231 864-3111
Dennis E Mc Carthy, *President*
Dennis B Mc Carthy, *President*
EMP: 3 **EST:** 1941
SQ FT: 5,000
SALES (est): 10.4MM **Privately Held**
SIC: 5541 1311 Gasoline service stations; crude petroleum production

(G-1377)
CORNILLIE ACQUISITIONS LLC
17443 Pleasanton Hwy (49614-9634)
PHONE...................231 946-5600
Robert Cherry, *Branch Mgr*
EMP: 3
SALES (est): 166.8K
SALES (corp-wide): 2.5MM **Privately Held**
SIC: 3273 Ready-mixed concrete
PA: Cornillie Acquisitions, Llc
805 W 13th St
Cadillac MI 49601
231 946-5600

(G-1378)
CORRECT COMPRESSION INC
11903 Chippewa Hwy (49614-9424)
PHONE...................231 864-2101
Tony Merrill, *President*
Reilly Merrill, *Opers Mgr*
Angela Eisenlohr, *Office Mgr*
Mathew Saxton, *Supervisor*
Fred Blankenship, *Technician*
EMP: 6
SALES (est): 1.1MM **Privately Held**
SIC: 3563 7699 Air & gas compressors including vacuum pumps; compressor repair

(G-1379)
NORTHVIEW WINDOW & DOOR
9844 Milarch Rd (49614-9714)
PHONE...................231 889-4565
Ron C Payette, *President*
Alison Payette, *Corp Secy*
EMP: 5
SQ FT: 2,500
SALES (est): 750K **Privately Held**
SIC: 2431 Louver windows, glass, wood frame

(G-1380)
PIONEER PRESS PRINTING (PA)
12326 Virginia St (49614-5100)
PHONE...................231 864-2404
Larry L Marek, *Owner*
EMP: 5
SQ FT: 1,000
SALES (est): 460.6K **Privately Held**
SIC: 2752 2759 7311 Commercial printing, offset; letterpress printing; advertising agencies

Beaver Island
Charlevoix County

(G-1381)
EAGER BEAVER CLEAN & STORE
27220 Barneys Lake Rd N (49782-9789)
P.O. Box 254 (49782-0254)
PHONE...................231 448-2476
Jeff Cashman, *Branch Mgr*
EMP: 4
SQ FT: 300
SALES (est): 198.9K
SALES (corp-wide): 84.4K **Privately Held**
SIC: 2711 Newspapers, publishing & printing
PA: Eager Beaver Clean & Store
36586 Kings Hwy
Beaver Island MI 49782
231 448-2050

Beaverton
Gladwin County

(G-1382)
ADVANCE ENGINEERING COMPANY
3982 Terry Dianne St (48612-9126)
P.O. Box 564 (48612-0564)
PHONE...................989 435-3641
Pete Vining, *Manager*
EMP: 40
SALES (corp-wide): 54.3MM **Privately Held**
WEB: www.adveng.net
SIC: 3089 3086 2671 Thermoformed finished plastic products; plastics foam products; packaging paper & plastics film, coated & laminated
PA: Advance Engineering Company
7505 Baron Dr
Canton MI 48187
313 537-3500

(G-1383)
BROWN LLC (DH)
330 N Ross St (48612-8165)
P.O. Box 434 (48612-0434)
PHONE...................989 435-7741
Bryan Redman, *President*
Jim Block, *Vice Pres*
Brian Keeley, *Vice Pres*
Ron Lejman, *Vice Pres*
Kay McCandless, *CFO*
◆ **EMP:** 210 **EST:** 1998
SQ FT: 140,000
SALES (est): 61.3MM **Privately Held**
SIC: 3555 3559 Printing trades machinery; plastics working machinery
HQ: Thermoforming Technology Group Llc
330 N Ross St
Beaverton MI 48612
989 435-7741

(G-1384)
DOW CHEMICAL COMPANY
2922 Mcculloch Rd (48612-9769)
PHONE...................989 638-6571
EMP: 30
SALES (corp-wide): 61B **Publicly Held**
WEB: www.dow.com
SIC: 2869 Industrial organic chemicals
HQ: The Dow Chemical Company
2211 H H Dow Way
Midland MI 48642
989 636-1000

(G-1385)
HOWE RACING ENTERPRISES INC
3195 Lyle Rd (48612-8617)
PHONE...................989 435-7080
Charles E Howe, *President*
Charles K Howe, *President*
Dina Howe, *Corp Secy*
Mark Koboldt, *Facilities Mgr*
Dan Myers, *Purchasing*
EMP: 18 **EST:** 1973
SQ FT: 6,570
SALES (est): 3.3MM **Privately Held**
WEB: www.howeracing.com
SIC: 5531 3714 Automotive parts; motor vehicle parts & accessories

(G-1386)
KILN KREATIONS
5366 M 18 (48612-9118)
PHONE...................989 435-3296
Edda Yost, *Principal*
EMP: 3 **EST:** 2008
SALES (est): 208.5K **Privately Held**
SIC: 3559 Kilns

(G-1387)
LANG TOOL COMPANY
2520 Glidden Rd (48612-9209)
PHONE...................989 435-9864
William J Lang, *President*
Nancy Lang, *Mktg Dir*
▲ **EMP:** 4 **EST:** 1991
SQ FT: 12,000
SALES (est): 2.2MM **Privately Held**
WEB: www.langtool.com
SIC: 3531 Backhoe mounted, hydraulically powered attachments

(G-1388)
LYLE INDUSTRIES
4144 Lyle Rd (48612-8603)
P.O. Box 434 (48612-0434)
PHONE...................989 435-7717
Brian Redmond, *President*
Brian Crawford, *Vice Pres*
Sandra Schwartz, *Vice Pres*
Kirk Haines, *Plant Mgr*
Gil Lautzenhiser, *Buyer*
▲ **EMP:** 56
SQ FT: 80,000
SALES (est): 20.5MM **Privately Held**
WEB: www.lyleindustries.com
SIC: 3559 Plastics working machinery
PA: Tenex Capital Management, L.P.
60 E 42nd St Rm 5230
New York NY 10165

(G-1389)
MID STATE SEAWALL INC
4418 Jones Rd (48612-8714)
PHONE...................989 435-3887
Floyd McDonald Jr, *President*
Sonya McDonald, *Vice Pres*
EMP: 3
SALES (est): 406.6K **Privately Held**
SIC: 3531 Construction machinery

(G-1390)
RIVERSIDE TOOL & MOLD INC
5819 Calhoun Rd (48612-9719)
PHONE...................989 435-9142
Fred Athey, *President*
Patricia Athey, *Vice Pres*
Debra Williams, *Admin Sec*
EMP: 3
SQ FT: 2,000
SALES: 150K **Privately Held**
SIC: 3469 3544 Machine parts, stamped or pressed metal; forms (molds), for foundry & plastics working machinery

(G-1391)
SAINT-GOBAIN PRFMCE PLAS CORP
3910 Terry Dianne St (48612-9126)
PHONE...................989 435-9533
Todd Cunning, *Branch Mgr*
EMP: 100
SALES (corp-wide): 215.9MM **Privately Held**
SIC: 2821 Plastics materials & resins
HQ: Saint-Gobain Performance Plastics Corporation
31500 Solon Rd
Solon OH 44139
440 836-6900

(G-1392)
SAINT-GOBAIN PRFMCE PLAS CORP
3910 Industrial Dr (48612)
PHONE...................989 435-9533
Tod Kundinger, *Manager*
EMP: 75
SALES (corp-wide): 215.9MM **Privately Held**
SIC: 3089 2822 Synthetic resin finished products; synthetic rubber
HQ: Saint-Gobain Performance Plastics Corporation
31500 Solon Rd
Solon OH 44139
440 836-6900

(G-1393)
SIMMYS EDM LLC
3018 Crockett Rd (48612-9757)
PHONE...................989 802-2516
Brenda Simpson,
EMP: 3
SALES (est): 318.5K **Privately Held**
SIC: 3599 7389 Electrical discharge machining (EDM);

(G-1394)
THERMFRMER PARTS SUPPLIERS LLC
Also Called: Tps
3818 Terry Dianne St (48612-8652)
P.O. Box 485 (48612-0485)
PHONE...................989 435-3800
John Beebe, *President*
Chuck Fanslow, *Vice Pres*
Brad Moore, *Vice Pres*
Randy Grieser, *Sales Staff*
EMP: 5
SQ FT: 3,520
SALES (est): 978.9K **Privately Held**
SIC: 3559 3599 Plastics working machinery; machine shop, jobbing & repair

(G-1395)
THERMOFORMING TECH GROUP LLC (HQ)
330 N Ross St (48612-8165)
PHONE...................989 435-7741
Ron Lejman, *CEO*
Kay McCandless, *Vice Pres*
Bryan Redman, *Vice Pres*
EMP: 3 **EST:** 2013
SALES (est): 61.3MM **Privately Held**
SIC: 3555 3559 Printing trades machinery; plastics working machinery

Belding
Ionia County

(G-1396)
ACE TOOL & ENGINEERING INC
500 Reed St (48809-1532)
PHONE...................616 361-4800
Eugene Pratt, *President*
EMP: 7
SQ FT: 4,000
SALES: 450K **Privately Held**
WEB: www.acetoolengineering.com
SIC: 3599 Machine shop, jobbing & repair

(G-1397)
B & O SAWS INC
825 Reed St (48809-1576)
P.O. Box 26 (48809-0026)
PHONE...................616 794-7297
Jason Kohn, *President*
John Kohn, *Vice Pres*
EMP: 28
SQ FT: 29,550
SALES (est): 7MM **Privately Held**
WEB: www.bosaws.com
SIC: 3541 Saws & sawing machines

(G-1398)
BAKER ROAD UPHOLSTERY INC
Also Called: Baker Rd Seating & Restoration
1122 S Bridge St (48809-9703)
PHONE...................616 794-3027
EMP: 9
SQ FT: 30,000
SALES (est): 1.4MM **Privately Held**
SIC: 2531 Manufacture Auditorium Seating

(G-1399)
BELCO INDUSTRIES INC
Also Called: Paint Finishing Div
9138 W Belding Rd (48809-1768)
PHONE...................616 794-0410
Charles Kitchel, *President*

GEOGRAPHIC SECTION

Belding - Ionia County (G-1425)

EMP: 125
SALES (corp-wide): 87MM **Privately Held**
WEB: www.belcoind.com
SIC: 3567 3563 3541 3535 Industrial furnaces & ovens; air & gas compressors; machine tools, metal cutting type; conveyors & conveying equipment; sheet metalwork
PA: Belco Industries, Inc.
9138 W Belding Rd
Belding MI 48809
616 794-0410

(G-1400)
BELCO INDUSTRIES INC (PA)
9138 W Belding Rd (48809-1768)
PHONE.................................616 794-0410
Thomas F Kohn, *CEO*
Mike Kohn, *President*
Larry Mercer, *Purchasing*
Rod Anderson, *Engineer*
Dan Krajewski, *Engineer*
▲ **EMP:** 20
SQ FT: 15,000
SALES (est): 87MM **Privately Held**
WEB: www.belcoind.com
SIC: 3567 5084 3541 3535 Paint baking & drying ovens; industrial machinery & equipment; machine tools, metal cutting type; conveyors & conveying equipment; sheet metalwork

(G-1401)
BELDING QUICKLUBE PLUS
9299 W Belding Rd (48809-9201)
PHONE.................................616 794-9548
Don E Cupp, *Owner*
EMP: 3
SALES (est): 360K **Privately Held**
SIC: 2911 Oils, lubricating

(G-1402)
BELDING TOOL ACQUISITION LLC (PA)
Also Called: Belding Tool and Machine
1114 S Bridge St (48809-9703)
P.O. Box 235 (48809-0235)
PHONE.................................586 816-4450
Jason Markham, *Principal*
EMP: 15
SQ FT: 11,000
SALES (est): 1.7MM **Privately Held**
SIC: 3599 Custom machinery; machine shop, jobbing & repair

(G-1403)
BELDING TOOL ACQUISITION LLC
Also Called: Belding Tool and Machine
1114 S Bridge St (48809-9703)
PHONE.................................616 794-0100
Jason Markham, *President*
EMP: 3
SALES (corp-wide): 1.7MM **Privately Held**
SIC: 3599 Custom machinery; machine shop, jobbing & repair
PA: Belding Tool Acquisition, Llc
1114 S Bridge St
Belding MI 48809
586 816-4450

(G-1404)
BTM NATIONAL HOLDINGS LLC
Also Called: Belding Tool and Machine
1114 S Bridge St (48809-9703)
PHONE.................................616 794-0100
Peter K Tur,
Jason Markham,
EMP: 15 **EST:** 2016
SALES (est): 543.1K **Privately Held**
SIC: 3544 Special dies, tools, jigs & fixtures

(G-1405)
BTMC HOLDINGS INC (PA)
1114 S Bridge St (48809-9703)
P.O. Box 235 (48809-0235)
PHONE.................................616 794-0100
Michael J Petersen, *President*
Jason Markham, *President*
EMP: 8
SQ FT: 10,000

SALES (est): 3.4MM **Privately Held**
WEB: www.beldingtool.com
SIC: 3544 Special dies & tools

(G-1406)
CCO HOLDINGS LLC
301 W Main St (48809-1675)
PHONE.................................616 244-2071
EMP: 3
SALES (corp-wide): 43.6B **Publicly Held**
SIC: 5064 4841 3663 3651 Electrical appliances, television & radio; cable & other pay television services; radio & TV communications equipment; household audio & video equipment
HQ: Cco Holdings, Llc
400 Atlantic St
Stamford CT 06901
203 905-7801

(G-1407)
CLARK GRANCO INC
7298 Storey Rd (48809-9360)
PHONE.................................616 794-2600
Jeffrey Ferman, *President*
Lynn Austin, *Engineer*
Scott Buiten, *Engineer*
Kevin Nink, *Engineer*
Robert Frostic, *CFO*
▲ **EMP:** 65
SQ FT: 60,000
SALES (est): 15.7MM **Privately Held**
WEB: www.grancoclark.com
SIC: 3542 3567 Extruding machines (machine tools), metal; industrial furnaces & ovens

(G-1408)
D & R FABRICATION INC
Also Called: Belding Tank Technologies
200 Gooding St (48809-1865)
P.O. Box 160 (48809-0160)
PHONE.................................616 794-1130
Daniel Blunt Jr, *CEO*
Daniel W Blunt Sr, *President*
EMP: 65
SQ FT: 25,000
SALES (est): 23MM **Privately Held**
SIC: 2519 Fiberglass & plastic furniture

(G-1409)
DIGITAL FABRICATION INC
7251 Whites Bridge Rd (48809-9404)
PHONE.................................616 794-2848
Richard Hebert, *President*
Tom Hebert, *Vice Pres*
▲ **EMP:** 10 **EST:** 1998
SQ FT: 18,000
SALES (est): 2MM **Privately Held**
SIC: 3444 Sheet metalwork

(G-1410)
DRIVEN DESIGNS INC
1135 S Bridge St (48809-9703)
PHONE.................................616 794-9977
Gordon Lanting, *President*
▲ **EMP:** 5
SALES (est): 580K **Privately Held**
WEB: www.drivendesigns.com
SIC: 8711 3651 Designing: ship, boat, machine & product; electronic kits for home assembly: radio, TV, phonograph

(G-1411)
DS MOLD LLC
807 Edna St (48809-2431)
PHONE.................................616 794-1639
Douglas Stearins, *Owner*
Mark Nordgren, *Project Engr*
EMP: 22
SQ FT: 70,000
SALES (est): 2MM **Privately Held**
SIC: 3544 Industrial molds

(G-1412)
ENGINEERED AUTOMATION SYSTEMS
95 Whites Bridge Rd (48809-9785)
PHONE.................................616 897-0920
Robert Schafer, *President*
EMP: 2
SALES (est): 1.2MM **Privately Held**
SIC: 3569 Robots, assembly line: industrial & commercial

(G-1413)
EXTRUDED ALUMINUM CORPORATION
7200 Industrial Dr (48809-9259)
PHONE.................................616 794-0300
Edward Rahe, *CEO*
Charlie Hall, *President*
Todd Myers, *Vice Pres*
Tony Caterino, *Buyer*
Jeremy Baylis, *Engineer*
EMP: 12
SQ FT: 180,000
SALES (est): 3.4MM **Privately Held**
WEB: www.extrudedaluminum.com
SIC: 3354 Aluminum extruded products
PA: Btmc Holdings, Inc.
1114 S Bridge St
Belding MI 48809
616 794-0100

(G-1414)
EXTRUDED METALS INC
Also Called: Mueller Brass
302 Ashfield St (48809-1594)
PHONE.................................616 794-4851
George Dykhuizen, *President*
Laura Shears, *Principal*
Joseph Napolitian, *Vice Pres*
▲ **EMP:** 150
SQ FT: 275,000
SALES (est): 23.8MM
SALES (corp-wide): 2.5B **Publicly Held**
WEB: www.extrudedmetals.com
SIC: 3354 Aluminum rod & bar
HQ: Mueller Brass Co.
8285 Tournament Dr # 150
Memphis TN 38125
901 753-3200

(G-1415)
FINISHING TECHNOLOGIES INC
Also Called: Fintech
7125 Whites Bridge Rd (48809-9404)
PHONE.................................616 794-4001
Robert J Greenland, *President*
Tom Barnes, *Sales Staff*
Kelly Cox, *Sales Executive*
Donna Greenland, *Admin Sec*
▲ **EMP:** 17
SQ FT: 16,000
SALES (est): 4.1MM **Privately Held**
WEB: www.finishingtechnologies.com
SIC: 5085 3291 Abrasives; abrasive products

(G-1416)
GERREF INDUSTRIES INC
206 N York St (48809-1834)
PHONE.................................616 794-3110
Harold Rich, *President*
Mark Rich, *President*
James Jones, *Vice Pres*
Adam Udell, *Engineer*
Joanne Strobel, *CFO*
EMP: 25
SQ FT: 24,500
SALES (est): 6.8MM **Privately Held**
WEB: www.gerref.com
SIC: 3567 3441 Industrial furnaces & ovens; fabricated structural metal

(G-1417)
HILLS CRATE MILL INC
3851 Hoyt Rd (48809-9508)
PHONE.................................616 761-3555
Burton Hill Jr, *President*
EMP: 8
SQ FT: 5,600
SALES (est): 969.3K **Privately Held**
SIC: 2448 Pallets, wood; cargo containers, wood

(G-1418)
HUNT HOPPOUGH CUSTOM CRAFTED
Also Called: Thomas Construction
700 Reed St (48809-1578)
PHONE.................................616 794-3455
James J Hunt, *President*
Todd Hoppough, *Vice Pres*
Cathy Hoppough, *Treasurer*
Kelly Hunt, *Admin Sec*
EMP: 30
SQ FT: 4,100

SALES (est): 3.2MM **Privately Held**
SIC: 2452 Modular homes, prefabricated, wood

(G-1419)
INDUSTRIAL ENGINEERING SERVICE
Also Called: Industrial Engnrng Service
215 E High St (48809-1500)
P.O. Box 415 (48809-0415)
PHONE.................................616 794-1330
David M Laux, *President*
EMP: 10
SQ FT: 20,000
SALES (est): 1.5MM **Privately Held**
WEB: www.indeng.com
SIC: 3469 3312 Stamping metal for the trade; tool & die steel & alloys

(G-1420)
JICE PHARMACEUTICALS CO INC
6895 Belding Rd (48809-8504)
PHONE.................................616 897-5910
John Dunn, *President*
EMP: 6
SQ FT: 3,500
SALES (est): 500K **Privately Held**
SIC: 2834 Veterinary pharmaceutical preparations

(G-1421)
JORDAN MANUFACTURING COMPANY
308 Reed St (48809-1528)
P.O. Box 130 (48809-0130)
PHONE.................................616 794-0900
Steven Johnson, *President*
Karlene Johnson, *Vice Pres*
EMP: 20
SQ FT: 25,000
SALES (est): 4.6MM **Privately Held**
WEB: www.jordanmfg.com
SIC: 3469 3544 Metal stampings; special dies, tools, jigs & fixtures

(G-1422)
K&P DISCOUNT PALLETS INC
7165 Whites Bridge Rd (48809-9404)
PHONE.................................616 835-1661
EMP: 3
SALES (est): 246.2K **Privately Held**
SIC: 2448 7389 Mfg Wood Pallets/Skids Business Services At Non-Commercial Site

(G-1423)
KASSOUNI MANUFACTURING INC
Also Called: Kmi
815 S Front St (48809-2235)
PHONE.................................616 794-0989
Van Kassouni, *President*
Tom O'Malley, *Vice Pres*
Bob Hams, *Sales Mgr*
▲ **EMP:** 48
SQ FT: 90,000
SALES (est): 13.6MM **Privately Held**
SIC: 2834 2812 Chlorination tablets & kits (water purification); chlorine, compressed or liquefied

(G-1424)
LAKE DESIGN AND MFG CO
7280 Storey Rd (48809-9360)
PHONE.................................616 794-0290
Ernest Hallas, *President*
John Elliott, *Vice Pres*
EMP: 8
SQ FT: 14,000
SALES (est): 1.7MM **Privately Held**
SIC: 3544 Special dies & tools

(G-1425)
MIZKAN AMERICA INC
Also Called: Indian Summer
700 Kiddville St (48809)
PHONE.................................616 794-0226
Michelle Jones, *Manager*
EMP: 12 **Privately Held**
SIC: 2099 2033 Cider, nonalcoholic; vinegar; fruit juices: fresh

Belding - Ionia County (G-1426)

HQ: Mizkan America, Inc.
1661 Feehanville Dr # 200
Mount Prospect IL 60056
847 590-0059

(G-1426)
MUELLER BRASS CO
Also Called: Mueller Brass Products
302 Ashfield St (48809-1524)
PHONE.................................616 794-1200
Joseph Napolitan, *President*
▲ **EMP:** 26
SALES (est): 6.2MM **Privately Held**
SIC: 3399 Brads: aluminum, brass or other nonferrous metal or wire

(G-1427)
NELSON RAPIDS CO INC
11834 Old Belding Rd Ne (48809-9389)
PHONE.................................616 691-8041
Gerald J Duncan, *President*
EMP: 4 **EST:** 1953
SQ FT: 10,000
SALES (est): 500K **Privately Held**
SIC: 2298 Cordage: abaca, sisal, henequen, hemp, jute or other fiber

(G-1428)
ROBROY ENCLOSURES INC
Also Called: Stahlin Enclosures
505 W Maple St (48809-1936)
PHONE.................................616 794-0700
Craig Mitchell, *President*
Roger Schroder, *Engineer*
Cameron Delet, *Marketing Staff*
EMP: 215 **EST:** 1905
SALES (est): 27MM
SALES (corp-wide): 70.2MM **Privately Held**
SIC: 3229 Glass fiber products
PA: Robroy Industries, Inc.
10 River Rd
Verona PA 15147
412 828-2100

(G-1429)
ROBROY INDUSTRIES INC
Also Called: Stahlin Division
505 W Maple St (48809-1999)
PHONE.................................616 794-0700
Alexander Calvi, *Engineer*
Brian Knoerl, *Engineer*
Jeffrey Seagle, *Branch Mgr*
EMP: 95
SALES (corp-wide): 70.2MM **Privately Held**
SIC: 3089 3699 Injection molding of plastics; electrical equipment & supplies
PA: Robroy Industries, Inc.
10 River Rd
Verona PA 15147
412 828-2100

(G-1430)
UNIQUE PRODUCTS
7205 Whites Bridge Rd (48809-9404)
PHONE.................................616 794-3800
James Anderson, *Owner*
EMP: 3
SQ FT: 1,750
SALES (est): 334K **Privately Held**
SIC: 3469 3544 Machine parts, stamped or pressed metal; dies & die holders for metal cutting, forming, die casting

(G-1431)
WEST MICH AUTO STL & ENGRG INC
Also Called: Hillside Finishing
550 E Ellis Ave (48809-1522)
PHONE.................................616 560-8198
Herman C Siegel Jr, *President*
Herman C Siegel III, *Vice Pres*
EMP: 20
SQ FT: 18,000
SALES (est): 3.4MM **Privately Held**
SIC: 3469 1796 3499 3714 Machine parts, stamped or pressed metal; machinery installation; welding tips, heat resistant: metal; motor vehicle parts & accessories; blowers & fans

(G-1432)
WEST MICHIGAN FAB CORP
321 Root St 3ph (48809-1561)
P.O. Box 296 (48809-0296)
PHONE.................................616 794-3750
Tony Walcutt, *President*
John Schofield, *Principal*
EMP: 4
SQ FT: 30,000
SALES: 1MM **Privately Held**
SIC: 3498 Tube fabricating (contract bending & shaping)

(G-1433)
WIESEN EDM INC
8630 Storey Rd (48809-9427)
PHONE.................................616 794-9870
Jeff Wiesen, *President*
Scott Gladding, *Engineer*
EMP: 20
SQ FT: 11,580
SALES: 900K **Privately Held**
WEB: www.wiesen.com
SIC: 3312 Tool & die steel

Bellaire
Antrim County

(G-1434)
ANCHOR LAMINA AMERICA INC
Lamina Bronze Products
3650 S Derenzy Rd (49615-9699)
P.O. Box 250 (49615-0250)
PHONE.................................231 533-8646
Larry Johnson, *Engineer*
Steve Osborn, *Engineer*
Sharon Mendoza, *Marketing Staff*
Joe Lerman, *Branch Mgr*
Zach Brown, *Manager*
EMP: 115
SQ FT: 95,000 **Privately Held**
WEB: www.anchorlamina.com
SIC: 3366 3545 3546 3452 Copper foundries; machine tool accessories; power-driven handtools; bolts, nuts, rivets & washers; nonferrous rolling & drawing; copper rolling & drawing
HQ: Anchor Lamina America, Inc.
39830 Grand River Ave B-2
Novi MI 48375
248 489-9122

(G-1435)
BELLAIRE LOG HOMES INDUS HM
6633 Bellaire Hwy (49615-9610)
PHONE.................................231 533-6669
Jim Barnard, *Principal*
EMP: 3
SALES (est): 299.3K **Privately Held**
SIC: 3398 Metal heat treating

(G-1436)
BP PACK INC
5332 Alpenhorn Ct (49615-9644)
PHONE.................................612 594-0839
Betsy Poupard, *Principal*
EMP: 3
SALES (est): 216.7K **Privately Held**
SIC: 3565 Packaging machinery

(G-1437)
DAYTON LAMINA CORP
3650 S Derenzy Rd (49615-9699)
PHONE.................................231 533-8646
Scott Jones, *General Mgr*
Sawato Hayashi, *Chairman*
Andrew Chandler, *Buyer*
EMP: 3 **EST:** 2017
SALES (est): 150K **Privately Held**
SIC: 3544 Special dies, tools, jigs & fixtures

(G-1438)
KENYON TJ & ASSOCIATES INC
902 Green Acres St (49615-9418)
PHONE.................................231 544-1144
Tom J Kenyon, *Owner*
Ken Schiffer, *Engineer*
Chuck Bultman, *Director*
EMP: 30
SALES (est): 2.1MM **Privately Held**
SIC: 3999 Manufacturing industries

Belleville
Wayne County

(G-1439)
ACTION AD NEWSPAPERS INC
Also Called: View, The
45223 Wear Rd (48111-9685)
PHONE.................................734 740-6966
Sharron Russell, *President*
Clarence Russell, *Treasurer*
EMP: 5
SQ FT: 800
SALES: 100K **Privately Held**
SIC: 2711 Newspapers: publishing only, not printed on site

(G-1440)
AHEARN SIGNS AND PRINTING
290 Industrial Park Dr (48111-4937)
PHONE.................................734 699-3777
Dominic Ahearn, *Owner*
Eric Bosman, *Graphic Designe*
EMP: 3
SALES (est): 247.1K **Privately Held**
SIC: 2741 5043 2752 Miscellaneous publishing; printing apparatus, photographic; commercial printing, lithographic

(G-1441)
BELLEVILLE AREA INDEPENDENT
152 Main St Ste 9 (48111-3911)
PHONE.................................734 699-9020
Rosemarie Otzman, *President*
Rosemary Otzman, *Principal*
EMP: 4 **EST:** 1998
SALES (est): 253.6K **Privately Held**
WEB: www.bellevilleareaindependent.com
SIC: 2711 Newspapers: publishing only, not printed on site

(G-1442)
BLACKMORE CO INC
10800 Blackmore Ave (48111-2500)
PHONE.................................734 483-8661
Fred N Blackmore Jr, *CEO*
Scott Blackmore, *President*
Steve Meadows, *Plant Engr*
Bruce Hudson, *CFO*
◆ **EMP:** 52
SQ FT: 47,000
SALES: 25.4MM **Privately Held**
WEB: www.blackmoreco.com
SIC: 3089 Planters, plastic

(G-1443)
COCA-COLA COMPANY
100 Coca Cola Dr (48111-1633)
PHONE.................................734 397-2700
Doug Gullette, *Branch Mgr*
EMP: 150
SALES (corp-wide): 31.8B **Publicly Held**
WEB: www.cocacola.com
SIC: 2086 Bottled & canned soft drinks
PA: The Coca-Cola Company
1 Coca Cola Plz Nw
Atlanta GA 30313
404 676-2121

(G-1444)
EBERBACH CORPORATION
5900 Schooner St (48111-5371)
P.O. Box 1024, Ann Arbor (48106-1024)
PHONE.................................734 665-8877
Ralph O Boehnke Jr, *President*
EMP: 25 **EST:** 1843
SQ FT: 30,000
SALES (est): 5.3MM **Privately Held**
WEB: www.eberbachlabtools.com
SIC: 3821 Laboratory equipment: fume hoods, distillation racks, etc.

(G-1445)
GENERAL SCOREBOARD SERVICES
21099 Clark Rd (48111-9606)
PHONE.................................734 753-5652
Greg Lucas, *Manager*
EMP: 3
SALES (est): 242K **Privately Held**
SIC: 3993 Scoreboards, electric

(G-1446)
KELLERS FARM BAKERY
23888 Haggerty Rd (48111-9660)
PHONE.................................734 753-4360
Danny Joe Keller, *Owner*
EMP: 3
SALES (est): 178.9K **Privately Held**
SIC: 2051 5461 Bread, cake & related products; bakeries

(G-1447)
KELTROL ENTERPRISES INC
35 Main St Ste 102 (48111-3287)
PHONE.................................734 697-3011
Dr Carol Moynihan DDS, *President*
EMP: 4 **EST:** 1976
SQ FT: 1,800
SALES (est): 320K **Privately Held**
SIC: 3089 Plastic processing

(G-1448)
MIKES GARAGE
20080 Sumpter Rd (48111-8965)
PHONE.................................734 779-7383
Mike Sliwa, *Mng Member*
EMP: 3
SALES (est): 351K **Privately Held**
SIC: 3547 Rod mills (rolling mill equipment)

(G-1449)
NEXT TOOL LLC
41200 Coca Cola Dr (48111-1640)
PHONE.................................734 405-7079
Nicholas Baise,
EMP: 10
SQ FT: 18,060
SALES (est): 1.3MM **Privately Held**
SIC: 3544 Special dies & tools

(G-1450)
QUARTER MANIA
22080 Elwell Rd (48111-9358)
PHONE.................................734 368-2765
Stacy Edwards, *Principal*
EMP: 3
SALES (est): 310.7K **Privately Held**
SIC: 3131 Quarters

(G-1451)
VERY BEST STEEL LLC
Also Called: Van Buren Steel
327 Davis St (48111-2911)
P.O. Box 954 (48112-0954)
PHONE.................................734 697-8609
Matthew Sorna, *Opers Mgr*
David Costa, *Mng Member*
EMP: 7
SQ FT: 35,000
SALES (est): 4.3MM **Privately Held**
SIC: 5051 3441 Steel; building components, structural steel

(G-1452)
VIEW NEWSPAPER
Also Called: Heritage Newspaper
159 Main St (48111-2737)
PHONE.................................734 697-8255
Fax: 734 697-4610
EMP: 4 **EST:** 1997
SALES (est): 170K **Privately Held**
SIC: 2711 Newspaper Publishing And Printing

Bellevue
Eaton County

(G-1453)
CUSTOM CRAFTERS
7889 S Ionia Rd (49021-9470)
P.O. Box 97 (49021-0097)
PHONE.................................269 763-9180
James Treat, *Owner*
EMP: 4
SALES (est): 290K **Privately Held**
SIC: 2541 2521 1751 Counter & sink tops; cabinets, lockers & shelving; wood office furniture; cabinet & finish carpentry

(G-1454)
F G CHENEY LIMESTONE CO
9400 Sand Rd (49021-9720)
PHONE.................................269 763-9541

GEOGRAPHIC SECTION

Benton Harbor - Berrien County (G-1480)

William T Cheney, *President*
William S Cheney, *President*
Ronald Vogt, *Corp Secy*
EMP: 4
SQ FT: 4,200
SALES (est): 341.6K **Privately Held**
WEB: www.cheneylimestone.com
SIC: 1422 Crushed & broken limestone

Belmont
Kent County

(G-1455)
ALTERNATIVE ENGINEERING INC
5670 West River Dr Ne (49306-9739)
PHONE.................616 785-7200
D Robert Rodriguez, *President*
Sharon E Rodriguez, *Vice Pres*
Shaun Brigham, *Purchasing*
Mike Panik, *Engineer*
EMP: 24
SQ FT: 44,000
SALES: 4MM **Privately Held**
WEB: www.alternativeengineering.com
SIC: 3535 Bulk handling conveyor systems

(G-1456)
AVASURE HOLDINGS INC (PA)
5801 Safety Dr Ne (49306-8832)
PHONE.................616 301-0129
Brad Playford, *CEO*
Kyle Pett, *COO*
Troy Van Hooren, *Design Engr*
Heather Fisher, *Controller*
Dirk Boomstra, *Executive*
EMP: 50
SQ FT: 4,000
SALES (est): 20MM **Privately Held**
SIC: 3842 Orthopedic appliances

(G-1457)
BELMONT ENGINEERED PLAS LLC
5801 Safety Dr Ne (49306-8832)
P.O. Box 52250, Knoxville TN (37950-2250)
PHONE.................616 785-6279
Stephen King, *President*
Jody Craig, *Vice Pres*
David Schmid, *Vice Pres*
Chris Yerger, *Vice Pres*
Asa Briggs, *Maint Spvr*
▲ **EMP:** 55
SQ FT: 149,000
SALES: 14.9MM **Privately Held**
SIC: 3089 Injection molding of plastics

(G-1458)
BELMONT PLASTICS SOLUTIONS LLC
8211 Graphic Dr Ne (49306-8934)
PHONE.................616 340-3147
Greg Mumford, *Executive*
John Bouwhuis, *Executive*
EMP: 7
SALES (est): 1.2MM **Privately Held**
SIC: 3082 Tubes, unsupported plastic

(G-1459)
BOOKCOMP INC
6124 Belmont Ave Ne (49306-9609)
PHONE.................616 774-9700
Jon Dertien, *President*
Carol Bifulco, *Prdtn Mgr*
EMP: 12
SALES (est): 1.4MM **Privately Held**
WEB: www.bookcomp.com
SIC: 2791 Typesetting

(G-1460)
CARDS OF WOOD INC
7754 Pine Island Ct Ne (49306-9720)
PHONE.................616 887-8680
Tate Lenderink, *President*
Sally Ann Lenderink, *Corp Secy*
◆ **EMP:** 8
SQ FT: 2,500
SALES (est): 560K **Privately Held**
WEB: www.cardsofwood.com
SIC: 2499 Decorative wood & woodwork

(G-1461)
ELTEK INC
6688 Wildwood Creek Dr Ne (49306-9325)
PHONE.................616 363-6397
EMP: 6
SQ FT: 4,000
SALES: 1.1MM **Privately Held**
SIC: 3621 Mfg Electronic Controls

(G-1462)
GRAND RAPIDS GRAVEL COMPANY
3800 7 Mile Rd Ne (49306)
P.O. Box 9160, Grand Rapids (49509-0160)
PHONE.................616 538-9000
Gary Myers, *Manager*
EMP: 14
SALES (corp-wide): 26.5MM **Privately Held**
WEB: www.grgravel.com
SIC: 3273 1442 Ready-mixed concrete; construction sand & gravel
PA: Grand Rapids Gravel Company
2700 28th St Sw
Grand Rapids MI 49519
616 538-9000

(G-1463)
JANT GROUP LLC
Also Called: Retail Sign Systems
8111 Belmont Ave Ne (49306-8823)
PHONE.................616 863-6600
Patrick Szymczak,
EMP: 9
SALES (est): 1.8MM **Privately Held**
SIC: 3577 Graphic displays, except graphic terminals

(G-1464)
KB STAMPING INC
8110 Graphic Dr Ne (49306-9448)
PHONE.................616 866-5917
Gary Kurtz, *President*
Rick Kurtz, *Vice Pres*
EMP: 10
SQ FT: 10,000
SALES (est): 1.2MM **Privately Held**
SIC: 3469 Patterns on metal

(G-1465)
LBV SALES LLC
5669 Rolling Highlands Dr (49306)
PHONE.................616 874-9390
Michael Wavra, *Mng Member*
EMP: 7
SQ FT: 2,000
SALES: 6MM **Privately Held**
SIC: 2673 Plastic bags; made from purchased materials

(G-1466)
LENDERINK INC
Also Called: Lenderink Family Tree Farms
1267 House St Ne (49306-9203)
PHONE.................616 887-8257
Thomas A Lenderink, *President*
Tracey Devries, *Director*
Sallyanne Lenderink, *Director*
EMP: 10
SQ FT: 7,000
SALES: 3MM **Privately Held**
SIC: 8732 2891 2899 Research services, except laboratory; adhesives; fire retardant chemicals

(G-1467)
LOGOSPOT
8200 Graphic Dr Ne (49306-8934)
PHONE.................616 785-7170
Phil Roode, *Principal*
EMP: 7 EST: 2015
SALES (est): 767.7K **Privately Held**
SIC: 2752 2395 Commercial printing, lithographic; embroidery products, except schiffli machine

(G-1468)
MAHLE BEHR INDUSTY AMERICA LP
5858 Safety Dr Ne (49306-9788)
P.O. Box 2840, Farmington Hills (48333-2840)
PHONE.................616 647-3490
Micheal Goerg, *Partner*
Lidia Constantin, *Manager*
Mona Genrich, *Info Tech Mgr*
▲ **EMP:** 99 EST: 2000
SQ FT: 60,000
SALES: 23.8MM
SALES (corp-wide): 504.6K **Privately Held**
SIC: 3585 Refrigeration & heating equipment
HQ: Mahle Industrial Thermal Systems Gmbh & Co. Kg
Heilbronner Str. 380
Stuttgart 70469
711 501-4210

(G-1469)
OHIO TRANSMISSION CORPORATION
Also Called: Filter and Coating
5706 West River Dr Ne (49306-9206)
P.O. Box 2287, Grand Rapids (49501-2287)
PHONE.................616 784-3228
Steve Workman, *Branch Mgr*
EMP: 21
SALES (corp-wide): 469.4MM **Privately Held**
SIC: 3569 Filters
PA: Ohio Transmission Corporation
1900 Jetway Blvd
Columbus OH 43219
614 342-6247

(G-1470)
SSI ELECTRONICS INC
8080 Graphic Dr Ne (49306-9448)
PHONE.................616 866-8880
Daniel Anderson, *President*
John B Miller, *Chairman*
Shirley Grice, *Corp Secy*
Scott Miller, *Vice Pres*
Melissa White, *Sales Staff*
▲ **EMP:** 36
SQ FT: 19,200
SALES (est): 6.4MM **Privately Held**
SIC: 3679 3643 3613 Electronic switches; current-carrying wiring devices; switchgear & switchboard apparatus

(G-1471)
STEEL CRAFT TECHNOLOGIES INC
8057 Graphic Dr Ne (49306-9448)
PHONE.................616 866-4400
Drew Boersma, *President*
EMP: 120
SALES (est): 24.7MM **Privately Held**
SIC: 3545 Precision tools, machinists'

(G-1472)
TECHNICAL AIR PRODUCTS LLC
8069 Belmont Ave Ne (49306-8877)
PHONE.................616 863-9115
Joseph Morgan, *Mng Member*
EMP: 14
SQ FT: 22,800
SALES (est): 1.9MM **Privately Held**
WEB: www.technicalairproducts.com
SIC: 3564 Air cleaning systems

(G-1473)
TRADEMARK DIE & ENGINEERING
8060 Graphic Dr Ne Unit 1 (49306-9448)
PHONE.................616 863-6660
Michael O'Keefe, *President*
EMP: 30
SQ FT: 21,000
SALES (est): 5.4MM **Privately Held**
WEB: www.tmde.net
SIC: 3544 Special dies & tools

(G-1474)
WILLIAMS FORM ENGINEERING CORP (PA)
8165 Graphic Dr Ne (49306-9448)
PHONE.................616 866-0815
Ronald R Williams Sr, *Ch of Bd*
Ronald Townsend, *President*
Bruce Jensen, *Exec VP*
Rich Leverett, *Exec VP*
Jon Roelofs, *Vice Pres*
◆ **EMP:** 75 EST: 1937
SQ FT: 15,000
SALES (est): 65.2MM
SALES (corp-wide): 71.7MM **Privately Held**
WEB: www.williamsform.com
SIC: 3559 3452 Concrete products machinery; bolts, nuts, rivets & washers; bolts, metal

(G-1475)
WOLVERINE TOOL & ENGRG CO
5641 West River Dr Ne (49306-9739)
PHONE.................616 785-9796
Michael Fish, *Corp Secy*
EMP: 35
SQ FT: 18,500
SALES (est): 5.4MM **Privately Held**
SIC: 3544 Die sets for metal stamping (presses)

(G-1476)
WYNALDA LITHO INC (PA)
Also Called: Wynalda Packaging
8221 Graphic Dr Ne (49306-8934)
P.O. Box 370 (49306-0370)
PHONE.................616 866-1561
Robert M Wynalda Sr, *Ch of Bd*
Robert M Wynalda Jr, *President*
Janet Davis, *Controller*
Connie Wynalda, *Admin Sec*
▲ **EMP:** 130
SQ FT: 150,000
SALES (est): 39.3MM **Privately Held**
WEB: www.wynalda.com
SIC: 2752 2657 Commercial printing, offset; folding paperboard boxes

Bentley
Bay County

(G-1477)
HOBYS CONTRACTING
Also Called: Hoby's Sewer Cleaning
2463 Whitefeather Rd (48613-9645)
PHONE.................989 631-4263
Hobert Bailey, *President*
EMP: 3
SALES (est): 509.3K **Privately Held**
SIC: 1389 Excavating slush pits & cellars

Benton Harbor
Berrien County

(G-1478)
ABC PRECISION MACHINING INC
2077 Yore Ave (49022-9674)
PHONE.................269 926-6322
Al Kasewurm, *President*
Doris Kasewurm, *Corp Secy*
EMP: 4 EST: 1962
SQ FT: 5,600
SALES (est): 601.5K **Privately Held**
WEB: www.abcprecision.com
SIC: 3541 3714 Machine tool replacement & repair parts, metal cutting types; filters: oil, fuel & air, motor vehicle

(G-1479)
ACUBAR INC (PA)
Also Called: Kelm Acubar
1055 N Shore Dr (49022-3516)
PHONE.................269 927-3000
EMP: 2
SQ FT: 4,800
SALES (est): 1.1MM **Privately Held**
SIC: 3599 Mfg Machine Shop

(G-1480)
ADVANCE PRODUCTS CORPORATION
2527 N M 63 (49022-2599)
PHONE.................269 849-1000
David Kraklau, *President*
John Piehl, *Purch Agent*
Dorthy Kraklau, *Shareholder*
Joan Kraklau, *Admin Sec*
▲ **EMP:** 40 EST: 1948
SQ FT: 25,000

Benton Harbor - Berrien County (G-1481) — GEOGRAPHIC SECTION

SALES (est): 6.9MM **Privately Held**
WEB: www.advanceproductscorp.com
SIC: **3545** 3569 3542 3564 Machine tool attachments & accessories; lubrication machinery, automatic; die casting machines; blowers & fans

(G-1481)
ANBREN INC
Also Called: Spartan Industries
1025 Point O Woods Dr (49022-9356)
P.O. Box 476, Coloma (49038-0476)
PHONE..................................269 944-5066
Andrew Baldwin, *President*
Brenda Baldwin, *Corp Secy*
EMP: 7
SQ FT: 10,000
SALES (est): 886.9K **Privately Held**
WEB: www.anbren.com
SIC: **2448** 2441 Pallets, wood; cargo containers, wood; nailed wood boxes & shook

(G-1482)
ARNT ASPHALT SEALING INC (PA)
Also Called: Great Lakes Coating
1240 S Crystal Ave (49022-1808)
PHONE..................................269 927-1532
Stanley L Arnt, *CEO*
Eric Anderson, *President*
Garson Bisnett, *Principal*
Jeffery Michels, *Principal*
Phil Ameling, *Vice Pres*
EMP: 66 EST: 1970
SQ FT: 15,000
SALES (est): 11.2MM **Privately Held**
WEB: www.arntasphaltco.com
SIC: **1771** 2952 Blacktop (asphalt) work; asphalt felts & coatings

(G-1483)
ART & IMAGE
582 E Napier Ave (49022-5816)
PHONE..................................800 566-4162
Scott Schonschack, *Owner*
EMP: 3
SALES (est): 332.6K **Privately Held**
SIC: **3993** Signs & advertising specialties

(G-1484)
BATSON PRINTING INC
195 Michigan St (49022-4598)
PHONE..................................269 926-6011
William Batson, *CEO*
Todd Batson, *Director*
▲ EMP: 65 EST: 1969
SQ FT: 30,000
SALES (est): 10.2MM **Privately Held**
WEB: www.batsonprinting.com
SIC: **2752** Commercial printing, offset

(G-1485)
BENTON HARBOR AWNING & TENT
Also Called: B H Awning & Tent
2275 M 139 (49022-6190)
PHONE..................................800 272-2187
Charles Dill, *President*
Marilyn Dill, *Vice Pres*
EMP: 20
SQ FT: 16,000
SALES (est): 2.1MM **Privately Held**
WEB: www.bhawning.com
SIC: **2394** 2391 Awnings, fabric: made from purchased materials; tents: made from purchased materials; liners & covers, fabric: made from purchased materials; tarpaulins, fabric: made from purchased materials; curtains & draperies; draperies, plastic & textile: from purchased materials

(G-1486)
BENTON HARBOR LLC
Also Called: Benton Harbor Heat Treating
800 S Fair Ave (49022-3821)
PHONE..................................269 925-6581
EMP: 4
SALES (est): 3.7MM **Privately Held**
SIC: **3398** Metal heat treating
HQ: Bwt Llc
201 Brookfield Pkwy
Greenville SC 29607

(G-1487)
BLOSSOMLAND CONTAINER CORP
1652 E Empire Ave (49022-2094)
P.O. Box 963 (49023-0963)
PHONE..................................269 926-8206
Dan McCumber, *President*
Dan Cumber, *President*
Dan Mc Cumber, *Exec VP*
John S Beall, *Producer*
EMP: 13 EST: 1966
SQ FT: 33,000
SALES (est): 2.5MM **Privately Held**
SIC: **2653** Boxes, corrugated: made from purchased materials; corrugated boxes, partitions, display items, sheets & pad

(G-1488)
BULK AG INNOVATIONS LLC
Also Called: West Michigan Tool & Die
1007 Nickerson Ave (49022-2405)
PHONE..................................269 925-0900
Victor Mowatt, *CEO*
▲ EMP: 14
SALES (est): 243.1K **Privately Held**
SIC: **7699** 3541 3451 Industrial equipment services; machine tools, metal cutting type; vertical turning & boring machines (metalworking); screw machine products

(G-1489)
CHAMPLAIN SPECIALTY METALS INC
2235 Dewey Ave (49022-9604)
PHONE..................................269 926-7241
Tess Robinson, *General Mgr*
EMP: 25
SALES (est): 5MM
SALES (corp-wide): 1B **Privately Held**
SIC: **3312** Rails, steel or iron
PA: American Industrial Acquisition Corporation
1 Harbor Point Rd # 1700
Stamford CT 06902
203 952-9212

(G-1490)
COLONIAL MANUFACTURING LLC
Also Called: Empire Molded Plastics
1246 E Empire Ave (49022-3834)
PHONE..................................269 926-1000
Patrick Bb, *Vice Pres*
Patrick Beebe, *Manager*
Mark Bainbridge,
▲ EMP: 12
SQ FT: 17,500
SALES (est): 1.9MM
SALES (corp-wide): 3.3MM **Privately Held**
WEB: www.colonialengineering.com
SIC: **3089** Injection molding of plastics
PA: Colonial Engineering, Inc.
6400 Corporate Ave
Portage MI 49002
269 323-2495

(G-1491)
CONNECTION SERVICE COMPANY
1377 M 139 (49022-5741)
P.O. Box 8728 (49023-8728)
PHONE..................................269 926-2658
Susan Adent, *President*
Melissa Henry, *Purch Mgr*
▲ EMP: 13
SQ FT: 6,500
SALES (est): 4.5MM **Privately Held**
SIC: **5072** 3452 7389 Bolts; bolts, metal; packaging & labeling services

(G-1492)
DAWSON MANUFACTURING COMPANY (PA)
1042 N Crystal Ave (49022-9266)
PHONE..................................269 925-0100
Bob Trivedi, *President*
Mike Burk, *General Mgr*
Kevin Fosnaugh, *Vice Pres*
Sue Morgan, *Purch Mgr*
Janette Hendrix, *CFO*
▲ EMP: 160
SQ FT: 78,000

SALES (est): 59.9MM **Privately Held**
SIC: **3061** Automotive rubber goods (mechanical)

(G-1493)
DAWSON MANUFACTURING COMPANY
1042 N Crystal Ave (49022-9266)
P.O. Box 603 (49023-0603)
PHONE..................................269 925-0100
Bob Trivedi, *Manager*
EMP: 125
SQ FT: 50,000
SALES (corp-wide): 59.9MM **Privately Held**
SIC: **3061** 3714 2822 Mechanical rubber goods; motor vehicle parts & accessories; synthetic rubber
PA: Dawson Manufacturing Company
1042 N Crystal Ave
Benton Harbor MI 49022
269 925-0100

(G-1494)
DGH ENTERPRISES INC (PA)
Also Called: K-O Products Company
1225 Milton St (49022-4029)
PHONE..................................269 925-0657
Barbara J Herrold, *President*
Dennis G Herrold, *Admin Sec*
▼ EMP: 23
SQ FT: 150,000
SALES (est): 3MM **Privately Held**
WEB: www.koproducts.com
SIC: **3469** 3465 3714 3999 Stamping metal for the trade; automotive stampings; motor vehicle parts & accessories; custom pulverizing & grinding of plastic materials; hardware

(G-1495)
DGH ENTERPRISES INC
Also Called: Ko Products
1225 Milton St (49022-4029)
PHONE..................................269 925-0657
Barbara Herrold, *President*
EMP: 5
SALES (corp-wide): 3MM **Privately Held**
WEB: www.koproducts.com
SIC: **3429** 3469 Manufactured hardware (general); stamping metal for the trade
PA: Dgh Enterprises, Inc.
1225 Milton St
Benton Harbor MI 49022
269 925-0657

(G-1496)
ELECTRIC EQUIPMENT COMPANY
401 Klock Rd (49022-3648)
P.O. Box 32, Riverside (49084-0032)
PHONE..................................269 925-3266
Donald P Boerma, *President*
Georgia Boerma, *Vice Pres*
EMP: 4 EST: 1955
SALES (est): 277.6K **Privately Held**
SIC: **7694** 5063 Electric motor repair; motors, electric

(G-1497)
FAIRMOUNT SANTROL INC
400 Riverview Dr Ste 302 (49022-5071)
PHONE..................................800 255-7263
Jose Luis Perez Flor, *General Mgr*
Pedro Ochoa, *Terminal Mgr*
Kody Upchurch, *Manager*
EMP: 22
SALES (corp-wide): 142.6MM **Publicly Held**
SIC: **1446** Foundry sand mining
HQ: Fairmount Santrol Inc.
3 Summit Park Dr Ste 700
Independence OH 44131
440 214-3200

(G-1498)
FORTRESS MANUFACTURING INC
2255 Pipestone Rd (49022-2425)
PHONE..................................269 925-1336
Fred Huff, *President*
EMP: 12
SQ FT: 8,000

SALES (est): 2MM **Privately Held**
SIC: **3444** 3469 Sheet metal specialties, not stamped; metal stampings

(G-1499)
FRESH STRT TRANSITIONAL LIVING
400 S Fair Ave (49022-7212)
PHONE..................................269 757-5195
EMP: 3 EST: 2008
SALES (est): 120K **Privately Held**
SIC: **3131** Mfg Footwear Cut Stock

(G-1500)
G M BRASS & ALUM FNDRY INC
200 W Wall St (49022-4739)
P.O. Box 486 (49023-0486)
PHONE..................................269 926-6366
Joan Smith, *President*
Elizabeth Griesbaum, *Corp Secy*
Erich Smith, *Vice Pres*
EMP: 10 EST: 1935
SQ FT: 40,000
SALES (est): 1.6MM **Privately Held**
SIC: **3325** 3366 3365 Steel foundries; brass foundry; castings (except die); aluminum & aluminum-based alloy castings

(G-1501)
GAISHIN MANUFACTURING INC
240 Urbandale Ave (49022-1943)
PHONE..................................269 934-9340
Mike Gaishin Sr, *President*
Rudy Gaishin, *CFO*
EMP: 24
SQ FT: 6,000
SALES (est): 5.9MM **Privately Held**
SIC: **3599** Machine shop, jobbing & repair

(G-1502)
GAMS INC
Also Called: Graphic Services Co
549 Nickerson Ave (49022-6313)
PHONE..................................269 926-6765
Leonard E Menchinger, *President*
Geraldine Menchinger, *Vice Pres*
EMP: 3
SQ FT: 2,000
SALES (est): 202.9K **Privately Held**
SIC: **2791** Typesetting

(G-1503)
GAST MANUFACTURING INC (HQ)
2300 M 139 (49022-6114)
P.O. Box 97 (49023-0097)
PHONE..................................269 926-6171
Eric Ashelman, *President*
Kimberly Fields, *Principal*
Frank J Notaro, *Principal*
Drew Covert, *Engineer*
◆ EMP: 320 EST: 1921
SQ FT: 196,000
SALES (est): 104.9MM
SALES (corp-wide): 2.4B **Publicly Held**
WEB: www.gasthk.com
SIC: **3563** 3594 3621 3566 Vacuum pumps, except laboratory; air & gas compressors including vacuum pumps; motors, hydraulic, fluid power or air; motors & generators; speed changers, drives & gears; pumps & pumping equipment
PA: Idex Corporation
1925 W Field Ct Ste 200
Lake Forest IL 60045
847 498-7070

(G-1504)
GAST MANUFACTURING INC
775 Nickerson Ave (49022-6317)
PHONE..................................269 926-6171
Kim Fields, *President*
EMP: 300
SALES (corp-wide): 2.4B **Publicly Held**
SIC: **3563** Vacuum pumps, except laboratory
HQ: Gast Manufacturing, Inc.
2300 M 139
Benton Harbor MI 49022
269 926-6171

(G-1505)
GAST MANUFACTURING INC
2550 Meadowbrook Rd (49022-9609)
P.O. Box 97 (49023-0097)
PHONE..................................269 926-6171

▲ = Import ▼ = Export
◆ = Import/Export

GEOGRAPHIC SECTION

Benton Harbor - Berrien County (G-1533)

Dennis Kugle, *Vice Pres*
EMP: 80
SALES (corp-wide): 2.4B **Publicly Held**
WEB: www.gasthk.com
SIC: 3563 Air & gas compressors including vacuum pumps
HQ: Gast Manufacturing, Inc.
2300 M 139
Benton Harbor MI 49022
269 926-6171

(G-1506)
H & T SKIDMORE ASPHALT
Also Called: H & T Asphalt
720 S Bainbridge Ctr Rd (49022-9353)
PHONE 269 468-3530
Hurley Skidmore, *Partner*
Tom Skimore, *Partner*
EMP: 4
SALES (est): 568.9K **Privately Held**
SIC: 2951 Asphalt paving mixtures & blocks

(G-1507)
HARBOR GREEN SOLUTIONS LLC
900 Davis Dr (49022-2767)
P.O. Box 8711, Grand Rapids (49518-8711)
PHONE 269 352-0265
Anthony Reeves II,
Robert Taylor,
EMP: 5
SALES (est): 324.8K **Privately Held**
SIC: 3089 2821 5162 5093 Plastic processing; plastics materials & resins; plastics materials & basic shapes; plastics resins; plastics scrap

(G-1508)
HARBOR SCREW MACHINE PRODUCTS
430 Cass St (49022-4402)
PHONE 269 925-5855
Jerry Tomaszewki, *President*
Ken Bates, *Vice Pres*
EMP: 4
SQ FT: 5,400
SALES (est): 535K **Privately Held**
SIC: 3451 Screw machine products

(G-1509)
HI-SPEED BUSINESS FORMS INC
1586 Paw Paw Ave (49022-2732)
PHONE 269 927-3191
Shirley Gorzynski, *President*
Richard Gorzynski, *Vice Pres*
Robert Gorzynski, *Vice Pres*
EMP: 7
SQ FT: 14,250
SALES: 463.3K **Privately Held**
SIC: 2761 Manifold business forms

(G-1510)
HIGH GRADE MATERIALS COMPANY
1915 Yore Ave (49022-9674)
PHONE 269 926-6900
Matt Craig, *Manager*
EMP: 14
SALES (corp-wide): 28.3MM **Privately Held**
SIC: 3273 Ready-mixed concrete
PA: High Grade Materials Company
9266 Snows Lake Rd
Greenville MI 48838
616 754-5545

(G-1511)
HOVERTECHNICS LLC
1520 Townline Rd Bldg A (49022-9656)
PHONE 269 461-3934
Chris Fitzgerald, *Mng Member*
EMP: 7
SQ FT: 25,000
SALES (est): 1MM **Privately Held**
WEB: www.hovertechnics.com
SIC: 3713 Specialty motor vehicle bodies

(G-1512)
IAN DAVIDSON & ASSOC INC
240 W Britain Ave (49022-7438)
PHONE 269 925-7552
Ian Davidson, *Principal*

Sara Cessna, *Sales Staff*
EMP: 7
SALES (est): 572.6K **Privately Held**
SIC: 3443 Liners, industrial: metal plate

(G-1513)
INNOVATIVE WOODWORKING
2227 Plaza Dr (49022-2215)
PHONE 269 926-9663
Jim Strouse,
Kenneth Wenger,
EMP: 8
SALES: 500K **Privately Held**
SIC: 2431 Millwork

(G-1514)
J B DOUGH CO
5600 E Napier Ave (49022-8619)
P.O. Box 557, Saint Joseph (49085-0557)
PHONE 269 944-4160
John Dwan, *Partner*
Beverlee Dwan, *Partner*
EMP: 6
SALES (est): 558.7K **Privately Held**
WEB: www.jbdough.com
SIC: 2099 Food preparations

(G-1515)
JOMAR INC
Also Called: Harbor Packaging
1090 S Crystal Ave (49022-1632)
P.O. Box 156 (49023-0156)
PHONE 269 925-2222
Joseph Mazzucco Jr, *President*
Marc Deising, *Vice Pres*
Loucetta Crosse, *Treasurer*
Patricia E Mazzucco, *Admin Sec*
EMP: 11
SQ FT: 24,000
SALES (est): 1.8MM **Privately Held**
SIC: 2759 Commercial printing

(G-1516)
KELM ACUBAR LC (PA)
Also Called: Kelm Acubar Company
1055 N Shore Dr (49022-3516)
PHONE 269 927-3000
Tim Kill, *Plant Mgr*
Melissa Saltzman, *Engineer*
Annette Woodfin, *Bookkeeper*
Kathy Kissane, *Office Mgr*
Pat Strzyzykowski, *Supervisor*
▲ **EMP:** 16
SQ FT: 40,000
SALES (est): 3.8MM **Privately Held**
WEB: www.kelmacubar.com
SIC: 3541 Machine tools, metal cutting type

(G-1517)
KELM ACUBAR LC
1055 N Shore Dr (49022-3516)
PHONE 269 925-2007
Andrew Bodnar, *President*
EMP: 8
SALES (corp-wide): 3.8MM **Privately Held**
WEB: www.acubar.com
SIC: 3599 Machine shop, jobbing & repair
PA: Kelm Acubar Lc
1055 N Shore Dr
Benton Harbor MI 49022
269 927-3000

(G-1518)
KISER INDUSTRIAL MFG CO
1860 Yore Ave (49022-9674)
PHONE 269 934-9220
Brian Kiser, *President*
Pam Kiser, *Admin Sec*
EMP: 13
SQ FT: 17,500
SALES (est): 2.2MM **Privately Held**
SIC: 3599 Machine shop, jobbing & repair

(G-1519)
KITCHENAID
553 Benson Rd (49022-2664)
PHONE 800 541-6390
Melissa Husmann, *Accounts Mgr*
Marci Wark, *Marketing Mgr*
Jeff Galyan, *Manager*
Patrick McLarnon, *Manager*
Loren Patterson, *Manager*
EMP: 3 EST: 2010

SALES (est): 247.9K **Privately Held**
SIC: 3556 Cutting, chopping, grinding, mixing & similar machinery

(G-1520)
KIWOTO INC
1130 E Empire Ave (49022-3832)
P.O. Box 1526 (49023-1526)
PHONE 269 944-1552
C David Tober, *President*
Donna Tober, *Corp Secy*
EMP: 3 EST: 1982
SQ FT: 3,000
SALES (est): 429.5K **Privately Held**
SIC: 3548 Electric welding equipment; electrode holders, for electric welding apparatus

(G-1521)
KOEHLER INDUSTRIES INC
1520 Townline Rd (49022-9656)
PHONE 269 934-9670
Mike Koehler, *Owner*
EMP: 9
SALES (est): 1MM **Privately Held**
SIC: 3599 Industrial machinery

(G-1522)
LAZER GRAPHICS
1101 Pipestone Rd (49022-4018)
PHONE 269 926-1066
Dennis Barker, *President*
Debbie Barker, *Vice Pres*
EMP: 22
SQ FT: 15,000
SALES (est): 2.2MM **Privately Held**
WEB: www.lazergraphicsinc.com
SIC: 5699 7336 2396 2395 Customized clothing & apparel; commercial art & graphic design; automotive & apparel trimmings; pleating & stitching

(G-1523)
M T S CHENAULT LLC
665 Pipestone St (49022-4151)
PHONE 269 861-0053
William Macgoodwin, *CEO*
EMP: 5
SALES (est): 352.3K **Privately Held**
SIC: 3672 Printed circuit boards

(G-1524)
MACH MOLD INCORPORATED
360 Urbandale Ave (49022-1944)
PHONE 269 925-2044
William Mach, *President*
Vicki Mach, *Vice Pres*
EMP: 41
SQ FT: 30,000
SALES (est): 9.4MM **Privately Held**
WEB: www.machmold.com
SIC: 3544 Industrial molds; forms (molds), for foundry & plastics working machinery

(G-1525)
MARTIN BROS MILL FNDRY SUP CO
Also Called: Meltex
289 Hinkley St (49022-3603)
P.O. Box 246 (49023-0246)
PHONE 269 927-1355
Ilene Martin, *President*
Stephen Martin, *Admin Sec*
EMP: 40 EST: 1930
SQ FT: 6,000
SALES (est): 7.1MM **Privately Held**
SIC: 5093 3341 Ferrous metal scrap & waste; secondary nonferrous metals

(G-1526)
MAX 3 LLC
360 Urbandale Ave (49022-1944)
PHONE 269 925-2044
David Lagrow,
EMP: 44 EST: 2017
SQ FT: 30,000
SALES (est): 1.4MM **Privately Held**
SIC: 3544 Special dies, tools, jigs & fixtures

(G-1527)
MAX CASTING COMPANY INC
116 Paw Paw Ave (49022-4416)
P.O. Box 1326 (49023-1326)
PHONE 269 925-8081
Richard T Graebel Jr, *President*

Jean Graebel, *Corp Secy*
EMP: 11
SQ FT: 8,000
SALES: 650K **Privately Held**
WEB: www.exelnet.net
SIC: 3365 Aluminum & aluminum-based alloy castings

(G-1528)
MAXIMUM MOLD INC
1440 Territorial Rd (49022-1959)
PHONE 269 468-6291
Dave Lagrow, *Principal*
Todd Crumley, *Buyer*
Nathan Mukavetz, *QC Mgr*
▲ **EMP:** 5
SALES (est): 658.3K **Privately Held**
SIC: 5085 3599 Industrial supplies; machine shop, jobbing & repair

(G-1529)
MAYTAG CORPORATION (HQ)
Also Called: Maytag Appliances
2000 N M 63 (49022-2632)
PHONE 269 923-5000
Jeff M Fettig, *Ch of Bd*
William L Beer, *President*
Thomas A Briatico, *President*
Arthur B Learmonth, *President*
David R McConnaughey, *President*
◆ **EMP:** 181 EST: 1893
SQ FT: 500,000
SALES (est): 3.8B
SALES (corp-wide): 21B **Publicly Held**
WEB: www.maytagcorp.com
SIC: 3631 3632 3639 3635 Gas ranges, domestic; electric ranges, domestic; household refrigerators & freezers; dishwashing machines, household; garbage disposal units, household; household vacuum cleaners; automatic vending machines; laundry dryers, household or coin-operated
PA: Whirlpool Corporation
2000 N M 63
Benton Harbor MI 49022
269 923-5000

(G-1530)
MIDWEST TIMER SERVICE INC
Also Called: MTS
4815 M63 N (49022)
P.O. Box 126 (49023-0126)
PHONE 269 849-2800
James R Chapman Jr, *President*
Bruce Chapman, *Owner*
Jason McDonnough, *Prdtn Mgr*
Leroy Perry, *Info Tech Mgr*
Keith A Chapman, *Admin Sec*
▲ **EMP:** 70
SQ FT: 60,000
SALES: 10MM **Privately Held**
SIC: 3823 Time cycle & program controllers, industrial process type

(G-1531)
MODINEER COATINGS DIVISION
2200 E Empire Ave (49022-1647)
PHONE 269 925-0702
EMP: 7
SALES (est): 876.1K **Privately Held**
SIC: 3479 Metal coating & allied service

(G-1532)
MONO CERAMICS INC
2235 Pipestone Rd (49022-2425)
PHONE 269 925-0212
Mukesh Rawal, *President*
Ashok Kedia, *VP Finance*
▲ **EMP:** 45
SQ FT: 20,000
SALES (est): 6MM
SALES (corp-wide): 352.2K **Privately Held**
WEB: www.monoceramics.com
SIC: 3255 Castable refractories, clay
HQ: Monocon International Refractories Limited
Davy Road, Denaby Lane
Doncaster DN12
170 986-4848

(G-1533)
MOTION INDUSTRIES INC
2450 M 139 Ste B (49022-6445)
PHONE 269 926-7216

Benton Harbor - Berrien County (G-1534)   **GEOGRAPHIC SECTION**

Brian Martiniak, *Purchasing*
Jeff Guyton, *Manager*
EMP: 5
SALES (corp-wide): 18.7B **Publicly Held**
WEB: www.motion-ind.com
SIC: 3569 Robots, assembly line: industrial & commercial
HQ: Motion Industries, Inc.
    1605 Alton Rd
    Birmingham AL 35210
    205 956-1122

(G-1534)
MPC COMPANY INC
Also Called: Midwest Fruit Package Co.
1891 Territorial Rd (49022-8035)
PHONE 269 927-3371
Sam Monde, *Owner*
EMP: 4
SALES (corp-wide): 15.2MM **Privately Held**
SIC: 2033 5148 5921 Fruits: packaged in cans, jars, etc.; fruits; liquor stores
PA: Mpc Company, Inc.
    3752 Riverside Rd
    Riverside MI 49084

(G-1535)
NATIONAL ZINC PROCESSORS INC
1256 Milton St (49022-4030)
PHONE 269 926-1161
Dennis Rook, *President*
Bruce Sokol, *Principal*
EMP: 15
SQ FT: 100,000
SALES (est): 1.5MM **Privately Held**
SIC: 4953 3341 3643 3471 Recycling, waste materials; zinc smelting & refining (secondary); current-carrying wiring devices; plating & polishing; lead & zinc ores

(G-1536)
OLD EUROPE CHEESE INC
1330 E Empire Ave (49022-2000)
PHONE 269 925-5003
Francisco Rodrigues Garcia, *CEO*
Francois Capt, *Vice Pres*
◆ **EMP:** 90
SQ FT: 60,000
SALES (est): 18.1MM **Privately Held**
WEB: www.oldeuropecheese.com
SIC: 2026 Fermented & cultured milk products

(G-1537)
OVERSTREET PROPERTY MGT CO
Also Called: Overstreet Management
1852 Commonwealth Rd (49022-7010)
P.O. Box 8629 (49023-8629)
PHONE 269 252-1560
Nicholas R Overstreet, *Property Mgr*
Nicholas Overstreet, *Manager*
EMP: 5
SALES (est): 163.1K **Privately Held**
SIC: 6519 7349 7299 0782 Real property lessors; building maintenance services; home improvement & renovation contractor agency; mowing services, lawn; grounds mowing equipment

(G-1538)
PRAXAIR INC
2320 Meadowbrook Rd (49022-9605)
PHONE 269 926-8296
Phil Larsen, *Branch Mgr*
EMP: 20 **Privately Held**
SIC: 2813 Industrial gases
HQ: Praxair, Inc.
    10 Riverview Dr
    Danbury CT 06810
    203 837-2000

(G-1539)
PRIMETALS TECHNOLOGIES USA LLC
470 Paw Paw Ave (49022-3447)
PHONE 269 927-3591
▲ **EMP:** 7
SALES (est): 417.8K **Privately Held**
SIC: 3312 Bars, iron: made in steel mills

(G-1540)
PROTO SPEC
1419 Townline Rd (49022-8621)
PHONE 269 934-8615
Jon Schiff, *Owner*
EMP: 3
SALES (est): 417.3K **Privately Held**
SIC: 3944 Board games, puzzles & models, except electronic

(G-1541)
R BETKER & ASSOCIATES
1400 Territorial Rd (49022-1946)
PHONE 269 927-3233
Roland Betker, *President*
EMP: 7
SALES: 800K **Privately Held**
SIC: 3441 Building components, structural steel

(G-1542)
R W PATTERSON PRINTING CO
1550 Territorial Rd (49022-1937)
PHONE 269 925-2177
Leroy Patterson, *President*
Greg Patterson, *Treasurer*
Angela Sonnenberg, *EMP:* 80 EST: 1948
SQ FT: 65,000
SALES (est): 17.4MM **Privately Held**
WEB: www.patterson-printing.com
SIC: 2752 2789 2732 Commercial printing, offset; bookbinding & related work; book printing

(G-1543)
RAPID GRAPHICS INC
Also Called: Rapid Printing
2185 M 139 (49022-6109)
PHONE 269 925-7087
James Rice, *President*
Jennifer Dumont, *Vice Pres*
Jeff Rice, *Vice Pres*
Judith Rice, *Admin Sec*
EMP: 8
SQ FT: 4,000
SALES: 390K **Privately Held**
SIC: 2752 Commercial printing, offset

(G-1544)
ROSTA USA CORP
797 Ferguson Dr (49022-6401)
PHONE 269 841-5448
Jeremy Thiele, *President*
EMP: 12
SQ FT: 10,000
SALES: 2MM **Privately Held**
SIC: 3061 8711 Mechanical rubber goods; engineering services

(G-1545)
SANDVIK INC
Also Called: Sanvik Materials Technology
2235 Dewey Ave (49022-9604)
PHONE 269 926-7241
Peter Frosini, *General Mgr*
EMP: 50
SALES (corp-wide): 11.1B **Privately Held**
SIC: 3312 5051 3444 3316 Plate, sheet & strip, except coated products; metals service centers & offices; sheet metalwork; cold finishing of steel shapes
HQ: Sandvik, Inc.
    17-02 Nevins Rd
    Fair Lawn NJ 07410
    201 794-5000

(G-1546)
SHORELINE MOLD & ENGRG LLC
1530 Townline Rd (49022-9656)
PHONE 269 926-2223
Tom Fillwock, *Finance*
Pam Fillwock, *Mng Member*
EMP: 5
SQ FT: 8,100
SALES (est): 747.8K **Privately Held**
SIC: 3544 3089 Dies, plastics forming; molding primary plastic

(G-1547)
SIEMENS INDUSTRY INC
Also Called: Metals Division
470 Paw Paw Ave (49022-3447)
PHONE 269 927-3591
Phillip W Schingel, *Branch Mgr*
EMP: 81
SALES (corp-wide): 95B **Privately Held**
SIC: 3822 Air conditioning & refrigeration controls; thermostats & other environmental sensors
HQ: Siemens Industry, Inc.
    1000 Deerfield Pkwy
    Buffalo Grove IL 60089
    847 215-1000

(G-1548)
SIEMENS VAI SERVICES LLC
Also Called: Mri-PA
470 Paw Paw Ave (49022-3447)
PHONE 269 927-3591
Phillip W Schingel, *Principal*
▲ **EMP:** 10
SALES (est): 1MM **Privately Held**
SIC: 3471 Electroplating of metals or formed products

(G-1549)
SMITH MANUFACTURING CO INC
1636 Red Arrow Hwy (49022-1916)
PHONE 269 925-8155
Scott Smith, *President*
Robin Smith, *Treasurer*
Theresa Smith, *Admin Sec*
EMP: 15
SQ FT: 34,000
SALES: 2.5MM **Privately Held**
WEB: www.smithmanufacturing.com
SIC: 2499 Decorative wood & woodwork

(G-1550)
SOUTH SHORE TOOL & DIE INC
2460 Meadowbrook Rd (49022-9605)
P.O. Box 235, Baroda (49101-0235)
PHONE 269 925-9660
Larry Keene, *President*
Doug Medlin, *Vice Pres*
EMP: 42
SQ FT: 24,000
SALES (est): 6.8MM **Privately Held**
WEB: www.sstd.net
SIC: 3599 Machine shop, jobbing & repair

(G-1551)
ST JOE VALLEY GRINDING INC
396 E Main St (49022-4443)
P.O. Box 206, Berrien Springs (49103-0206)
PHONE 269 925-0709
Mike Melton, *President*
EMP: 3
SALES (est): 291.4K **Privately Held**
SIC: 3599 Grinding castings for the trade

(G-1552)
STATE TOOL & MANUFACTURING CO (PA)
1650 E Empire Ave (49022-2024)
PHONE 269 927-3153
Manroe Raschke, *President*
Mary Ann Raschke, *Vice Pres*
Doug Christy, *VP Sales*
EMP: 80
SQ FT: 25,000
SALES (est): 10.6MM **Privately Held**
SIC: 3643 Sockets, electric

(G-1553)
TECHNICKEL INC
1200 S Crystal Ave (49022-1808)
P.O. Box 1264 (49023-1264)
PHONE 269 926-8505
Dave Vogl, *CEO*
Cynthia Zuhl, *Vice Pres*
EMP: 15
SQ FT: 45,000
SALES: 3MM **Privately Held**
WEB: www.technickel.com
SIC: 3471 Electroplating of metals or formed products

(G-1554)
TECHNISAND INC
400 Riverview Dr Ste 300 (49022-5009)
P.O. Box 400, Bridgman (49106-0400)
PHONE 269 465-5833
Lee Stachurski, *Branch Mgr*
EMP: 57
SALES (corp-wide): 142.6MM **Publicly Held**
SIC: 1442 Sand mining
HQ: Technisand, Inc.
    11833 Ravenna Rd
    Chardon OH 44024

(G-1555)
TOWER TAG & LABEL LLC
1300 E Empire Ave (49022-2018)
PHONE 269 927-1065
Thomas Miller, *President*
▼ **EMP:** 10
SQ FT: 60,000
SALES (est): 1.7MM **Privately Held**
WEB: www.towertag.com
SIC: 3089 Clothes hangers, plastic

(G-1556)
TRELLBORG SLING SLTIONS US INC
1042 N Crystal Ave (49022-9266)
PHONE 269 639-4217
Conny Torstensson, *Vice Pres*
Gary Madewell, *VP Mfg*
Jonas Kling, *Human Res Dir*
Jan Pettersson, *Branch Mgr*
Dave Cummings, *Manager*
EMP: 3
SALES (corp-wide): 3.7B **Privately Held**
SIC: 3089 Plastic processing
HQ: Trelleborg Sealing Solutions Us, Inc.
    2531 Bremer Rd
    Fort Wayne IN 46803
    260 749-9631

(G-1557)
UNIVERSAL INDUCTION INC
352 W Britain Ave (49022-5002)
P.O. Box 516, Saint Joseph (49085-0516)
PHONE 269 925-9890
Manuel A Jack, *President*
EMP: 9
SQ FT: 20,000
SALES (est): 1.4MM **Privately Held**
SIC: 3398 Metal heat treating

(G-1558)
UNIVERSAL STAMPING INC
1570 Townline Rd (49022-9656)
PHONE 269 925-5300
Richard C Jackson, *President*
Janet Jackson, *Vice Pres*
EMP: 25
SQ FT: 26,000
SALES (est): 5MM **Privately Held**
WEB: www.universalstamping.com
SIC: 3469 Stamping metal for the trade

(G-1559)
US JACK COMPANY
1125 Industrial Ct (49022-1879)
P.O. Box 8826 (49023-8826)
PHONE 269 925-7777
Dennis Housewortth, *President*
EMP: 8
SQ FT: 8,500
SALES: 3.1MM **Privately Held**
WEB: www.usjack.com
SIC: 3569 Jacks, hydraulic

(G-1560)
VENT-RITE VALVE CORP
Also Called: Skidmore
1875 Dewey Ave (49022-9608)
PHONE 269 925-8812
David P Van Houten, *Vice Pres*
Larry Carlson, *Project Engr*
Mark Hendrix, *VP Sales*
EMP: 40
SQ FT: 60,000
SALES (corp-wide): 5.4MM **Privately Held**
WEB: www.skidmorepump.com
SIC: 3561 3443 Pumps, domestic: water or sump; fabricated plate work (boiler shop)
PA: Vent-Rite Valve Corp.
    300 Pond St
    Randolph MA 02368
    781 986-2000

(G-1561)
VINEYARD 2121 LLC
2121 Kerlikowske Rd (49022-9218)
PHONE 269 429-0555

▲ = Import ▼ = Export   ◆ = Import/Export

Deborah Pallas,
EMP: 10
SQ FT: 3,700
SALES (est): 717K **Privately Held**
SIC: 2084 Wine cellars, bonded: engaged in blending wines

(G-1562)
VOMELA SPECIALTY COMPANY
Also Called: Harbor Graphics
375 Urbandale Ave (49022-1942)
PHONE 269 927-6500
Larry Graefen, *Manager*
EMP: 35
SALES (corp-wide): 128.5MM **Privately Held**
SIC: 7336 2396 Graphic arts & related design; automotive & apparel trimmings
PA: Vomela Specialty Company
    845 Minnehaha Ave E
    Saint Paul MN 55106
    651 228-2200

(G-1563)
W VBH
78 W Wall St (49022-4735)
PHONE 269 927-1527
Charles Kelly, *Owner*
EMP: 3
SALES (est): 129.7K **Privately Held**
SIC: 2711 Newspapers, publishing & printing

(G-1564)
WEST MICHIGAN TOOL & DIE CO
Also Called: Ark Industrial
1007 Nickerson Ave (49022-2405)
PHONE 269 925-0900
Jerry W Jackson, *President*
Laura Jackson, *Accounting Mgr*
Fred Layton, *Sales Mgr*
EMP: 22
SQ FT: 8,800
SALES (est): 4.5MM **Privately Held**
WEB: www.wmtd.com
SIC: 3544 Special dies & tools

(G-1565)
WHIRLPOOL CORPORATION (PA)
2000 N M 63 (49022-2692)
PHONE 269 923-5000
Marc R Bitzer, *Ch of Bd*
Joao C Brega, *Exec VP*
Joseph T Liotine, *Exec VP*
Shengpo Wu, *Exec VP*
Shahzad Akhtar, *Vice Pres*
▼ **EMP:** 2200
SALES: 21B **Publicly Held**
WEB: www.whirlpoolcorp.com
SIC: 3633 3585 3632 3635 Household laundry equipment; air conditioning units, complete: domestic or industrial; refrigerators, mechanical & absorption: household; freezers, home & farm; household vacuum cleaners

(G-1566)
WHIRLPOOL CORPORATION
600 W Main St (49022-3618)
PHONE 269 923-5000
Michelle Obenour, *Human Res Mgr*
Phyllis Caro, *Manager*
Monica Clark, *Manager*
Hari Pasupathy, *Manager*
Megan Hibler, *Asst Mgr*
EMP: 7
SALES (corp-wide): 21B **Publicly Held**
SIC: 3633 3585 3632 3635 Household laundry equipment; air conditioning units, complete: domestic or industrial; refrigerators, mechanical & absorption: household; freezers, home & farm; household vacuum cleaners
PA: Whirlpool Corporation
    2000 N M 63
    Benton Harbor MI 49022
    269 923-5000

(G-1567)
WHIRLPOOL CORPORATION
1800 Paw Paw Ave (49022-2648)
PHONE 269 923-7400
James Kuhn, *Safety Dir*
Jim Mann, *Project Mgr*
Antwan Taylor, *Opers Mgr*
Angela Seger, *Purch Agent*
David Provost, *Purchasing*
EMP: 125
SALES (corp-wide): 21B **Publicly Held**
WEB: www.whirlpoolcorp.com
SIC: 3633 3632 Household laundry equipment; household refrigerators & freezers
PA: Whirlpool Corporation
    2000 N M 63
    Benton Harbor MI 49022
    269 923-5000

(G-1568)
WHIRLPOOL CORPORATION
750 Monte Rd (49022-2600)
PHONE 269 923-5000
Phillip Pejovich, *Vice Pres*
Christopher Carlson, *Engineer*
David Goshgarian, *Engineer*
Martin Lewis, *Engineer*
Yingqin Yuan, *Engineer*
EMP: 80
SALES (corp-wide): 21B **Publicly Held**
WEB: www.whirlpoolcorp.com
SIC: 3633 Household laundry equipment
PA: Whirlpool Corporation
    2000 N M 63
    Benton Harbor MI 49022
    269 923-5000

(G-1569)
WHIRLPOOL CORPORATION
151 Riverview Dr (49022-3619)
PHONE 269 923-6486
Timothy Mayberry, *Engineer*
Amanda Schilling, *Accountant*
Jim Spicer, *Manager*
Jagdish Mukka, *Manager*
Cherie Shane, *Manager*
EMP: 300
SALES (corp-wide): 21B **Publicly Held**
WEB: www.whirlpoolcorp.com
SIC: 3633 Household laundry equipment
PA: Whirlpool Corporation
    2000 N M 63
    Benton Harbor MI 49022
    269 923-5000

(G-1570)
WHIRLPOOL CORPORATION
2000 N M 63 (49022-2692)
PHONE 269 923-5000
Tom Egan, *Vice Pres*
Nephti Patron, *Engineer*
EMP: 350
SALES (corp-wide): 21B **Publicly Held**
WEB: www.whirlpoolcorp.com
SIC: 3585 3632 3639 3635 Air conditioning units, complete: domestic or industrial; refrigerators, mechanical & absorption: household; freezers, home & farm; dishwashing machines, household; garbage disposal units, household; trash compactors, household; household vacuum cleaners; gas ranges, domestic; electric ranges, domestic; microwave ovens, including portable: household; washing machines, household: including coin-operated
PA: Whirlpool Corporation
    2000 N M 63
    Benton Harbor MI 49022
    269 923-5000

(G-1571)
WHIRLPOOL CORPORATION
150 Hilltop Rd Mldrop7590 7590 Maildrop (49022)
PHONE 269 923-3009
Kevin Steinke, *Principal*
Charles Stenchfield, *Vice Pres*
Narendra Carambiah, *Manager*
Gabe Bernhard, *Senior Mgr*
EMP: 175
SALES (corp-wide): 21B **Publicly Held**
SIC: 3633 3585 3632 3639 Household laundry machines, including coin-operated; washing machines, household: including coin-operated; laundry dryers, household or coin-operated; air conditioning units, complete: domestic or industrial; freezers, home & farm; refrigerators, mechanical & absorption: household; dishwashing machines, household; garbage disposal units, household; trash compactors, household
PA: Whirlpool Corporation
    2000 N M 63
    Benton Harbor MI 49022
    269 923-5000

(G-1572)
WORTHINGTON ARMSTRONG VENTURE
Also Called: Wave
745 Enterprise Way (49022-2773)
PHONE 269 934-6200
Ron Badger, *Manager*
EMP: 10 **Privately Held**
SIC: 3446 8051 3449 3444 Architectural metalwork; skilled nursing care facilities; miscellaneous metalwork; sheet metal work
PA: Worthington Armstrong Venture
    101 Lindenwood Dr Ste 350
    Malvern PA 19355

Benzonia
Benzie County

(G-1573)
BEE DAZZLED CANDLE WORKS
6289 River Rd (49616-9713)
PHONE 231 882-7765
Sharon Jones, *Owner*
EMP: 4
SALES (est): 10K **Privately Held**
WEB: www.beedazzled.com
SIC: 3999 Candles

(G-1574)
CHERRY HUT PRODUCTS LLC (PA)
1046 Michigan Ave (49616-8661)
P.O. Box 333 (49616-0333)
PHONE 231 882-4431
Andrew Case, *Sales Executive*
Leonard L Case,
EMP: 2
SQ FT: 2,400
SALES (est): 1.4MM **Privately Held**
WEB: www.cherryhutproducts.com
SIC: 5812 2033 Eating places; jams, including imitation: packaged in cans, jars, etc.; jellies, edible, including imitation: in cans, jars, etc.

(G-1575)
GILLISONS VAR FABRICATION INC (PA)
3033 Benzie Hwy (49616-8616)
PHONE 231 882-5921
Ronald Gillison, *President*
Dianne Gillison, *Corp Secy*
◆ **EMP:** 28
SQ FT: 5,760
SALES: 8.3MM **Privately Held**
SIC: 5999 3523 3599 Farm machinery; farm machinery & equipment; machine shop, jobbing & repair

(G-1576)
PRESSCRAFT PAPERS INC
Also Called: Gwen Frostic Prints
5140 River Rd (49616-8703)
P.O. Box 300 (49616-0300)
PHONE 231 882-5505
Pamela Lorenz, *President*
EMP: 30
SQ FT: 7,500
SALES (est): 3.9MM **Privately Held**
WEB: www.gwenfrostic.com
SIC: 2752 2759 2678 Cards, lithographed; commercial printing; stationery products

Berkley
Oakland County

(G-1577)
A & E AGG INC
3500 11 Mile Rd Ste D (48072-1225)
PHONE 248 547-4711
Ben Fyke, *President*
EMP: 12
SQ FT: 2,000
SALES (est): 2.8MM **Privately Held**
SIC: 1442 Construction sand & gravel

(G-1578)
ACME TUBE BENDING COMPANY
3180 W 11 Mile Rd (48072-1207)
P.O. Box 888, Royal Oak (48068-0888)
PHONE 248 545-8500
Chris Lyons, *President*
◆ **EMP:** 8
SQ FT: 7,500
SALES: 800K **Privately Held**
WEB: www.acmetubebending.com
SIC: 3498 Tube fabricating (contract bending & shaping)

(G-1579)
AMERICAN & EFIRD LLC
1919 Coolidge Hwy (48072-1543)
PHONE 248 399-1166
Kathy Will, *Marketing Staff*
Rich Bowman, *Manager*
EMP: 12
SALES (corp-wide): 1B **Privately Held**
WEB: www.amefird.com
SIC: 2284 Thread from natural fibers
HQ: American & Efird Llc
    22 American St
    Mount Holly NC 28120
    704 827-4311

(G-1580)
AU ENTERPRISES INC
3916 11 Mile Rd (48072-1005)
PHONE 248 544-9700
Linus L Drogs III, *President*
Thelma Kester, *Director*
EMP: 14
SQ FT: 2,400
SALES (est): 1.3MM **Privately Held**
SIC: 3915 Jewelers' castings

(G-1581)
BERKLEY FROSTY FREEZE INC
2415 Coolidge Hwy (48072-1571)
PHONE 248 336-2634
Emily Tong, *Manager*
EMP: 3
SALES (est): 139.6K **Privately Held**
SIC: 2024 Ice cream, bulk

(G-1582)
CORNELIUS SYSTEMS INC (PA)
3966 11 Mile Rd (48072-1005)
PHONE 248 545-5558
Michael A Cornelius, *CEO*
Michael T Cornelius, *President*
Anna I Cornelius, *Admin Sec*
EMP: 47 **EST:** 1973
SQ FT: 6,000
SALES (est): 6.8MM **Privately Held**
WEB: www.corneliussystems.com
SIC: 7629 3578 1731 7382 Business machine repair, electric; automatic teller machines (ATM); access control systems specialization; banking machine installation & service; security systems services

(G-1583)
FYKE WASHED SAND GRAVEL
3500 11 Mile Rd Ste D (48072-1225)
PHONE 248 547-4714
Barb Edwards, *Manager*
EMP: 3
SALES (est): 162.1K **Privately Held**
SIC: 1442 Construction sand & gravel

(G-1584)
INDUSTRIAL PACKAGING CORP (PA)
3060 11 Mile Rd (48072-1206)
PHONE 248 677-0084
John B Mager Sr, *CEO*
John Mager Jr, *President*
Sandra Donia, *Treasurer*
EMP: 10
SQ FT: 15,000
SALES (est): 1.8MM **Privately Held**
SIC: 2448 2653 Pallets, wood; boxes, corrugated: made from purchased materials

Berkley - Oakland County (G-1585) GEOGRAPHIC SECTION

(G-1585)
INNOVATEC LLC
3972 Thomas Ave (48072-3166)
PHONE.................813 545-6818
Robert Weber, *President*
EMP: 3
SALES (est): 148.9K **Privately Held**
SIC: 2821 Molding compounds, plastics

(G-1586)
INTELLIFORM INC
3918 12 Mile Rd (48072-3175)
PHONE.................248 541-4000
Gregg Archambault, *President*
Laura Archambault, *Vice Pres*
EMP: 3
SQ FT: 400
SALES: 1.5MM **Privately Held**
WEB: www.intelliform.org
SIC: 2752 Business form & card printing, lithographic

(G-1587)
MICHIGAN PLAQUES & AWARDS INC
Also Called: Michigan Graphics & Awards
3742 12 Mile Rd (48072-1114)
PHONE.................248 398-6400
Michael Hood, *President*
R Michael Hood, *President*
Toni G Hood, *Corp Secy*
Toni Hood, *Human Res Dir*
▲ **EMP:** 24
SQ FT: 7,500
SALES (est): 3.6MM **Privately Held**
WEB: www.michiganplaques.com
SIC: 3993 3914 Signs, not made in custom sign painting shops; name plates: except engraved, etched, etc.: metal; displays & cutouts, window & lobby; trophies

(G-1588)
NOISEMETERS INC
3233 Coolidge Hwy (48072-1633)
PHONE.................248 840-6559
Andrew Snell, *President*
Louise Snell, *Vice Pres*
EMP: 5
SALES (est): 481K **Privately Held**
SIC: 3625 Noise control equipment

(G-1589)
SWEET ESSENTIALS LLC
Also Called: Sydney Bogg's Sweet Essentials
3233 12 Mile Rd (48072-1341)
PHONE.................248 398-7933
Lisa Peasley,
Gary Schlicker,
EMP: 4
SALES (est): 466.2K **Privately Held**
SIC: 2064 Candy & other confectionery products

Berrien Center
Berrien County

(G-1590)
CHILD EVNGELISM FELLOWSHIP INC
7463 Elm St (49102-9745)
P.O. Box 64 (49102)
PHONE.................269 461-6953
Larry Depue, *Principal*
EMP: 41
SALES (corp-wide): 24.4MM **Privately Held**
SIC: 2752 Commercial printing, lithographic
PA: Child Evangelism Fellowship Incorporated
17482 Highway M
Warrenton MO 63383
636 456-4321

Berrien Springs
Berrien County

(G-1591)
ALL ABOUT QUILTING AND DESIGN
Also Called: Marie Louise Moon
4683 E Hillcrest Dr (49103-9582)
PHONE.................269 471-7359
Marie Moon, *Owner*
Robert Moon, *Co-Owner*
EMP: 3
SALES (est): 118.8K **Privately Held**
SIC: 7389 2395 Design services; quilting & quilting supplies

(G-1592)
APPLE VALLEY NATURAL FOODS (PA)
9067 Us Highway 31 Ofc A (49103-1806)
PHONE.................269 471-3234
Kevin Benfield, *President*
George Schmidt, *Manager*
EMP: 124
SALES (est): 31.1MM **Privately Held**
WEB: www.avnf.com
SIC: 5499 5411 2051 Health foods; grocery stores; bread, cake & related products

(G-1593)
BERRIEN CUSTOM CABINET INC
Also Called: Berrien Custom Cab & Design
4231 E Snow Rd (49103-9223)
PHONE.................269 473-3404
Bradley Osborn, *President*
EMP: 6
SQ FT: 6,000
SALES (est): 453K **Privately Held**
SIC: 2434 Wood kitchen cabinets

(G-1594)
FAB-N-WELD SHEETMETAL
4445 E Shawnee Rd (49103-9769)
PHONE.................269 471-7453
Michael F Huspen, *Owner*
EMP: 5
SQ FT: 40,000
SALES (est): 615.6K **Privately Held**
SIC: 7692 Welding repair

(G-1595)
FAIRVIEW FARMS
Also Called: Radtke Farms
6735 S Scottdale Rd (49103-9707)
PHONE.................269 449-0500
Yvonne Radtke, *President*
David Radtke, *Vice Pres*
EMP: 5
SALES: 50K **Privately Held**
SIC: 2033 0191 Jams, including imitation: packaged in cans, jars, etc.; jellies, edible, including imitation: in cans, jars, etc.; general farms, primarily crop

(G-1596)
FAULKNER FABRICATORS INC
10106 N Tudor Rd (49103-9634)
PHONE.................269 473-3073
Thomas A Faulkner, *President*
Ann Christensen, *Corp Secy*
Ed Faulkner, *Vice Pres*
▲ **EMP:** 12
SQ FT: 24,000
SALES (est): 2.3MM **Privately Held**
SIC: 2499 Spools, wood; spools, reels & pulleys: wood

(G-1597)
LEMON CREEK WINERY LTD (PA)
Also Called: Lemon Creek Farm
533 E Lemon Creek Rd (49103-9714)
PHONE.................269 471-1321
Tim Lemon, *President*
Jeffrey Lemon, *Vice Pres*
EMP: 25
SQ FT: 5,200
SALES (est): 3.2MM **Privately Held**
WEB: www.lemoncreekwinery.com
SIC: 2084 5921 Wines; wine

(G-1598)
LITHOTECH
Also Called: Anders University Lithotech
212 Harrigan Hall (49104-0001)
PHONE.................269 471-6027
Rod Church, *Manager*
EMP: 12
SALES (est): 1.2MM **Privately Held**
SIC: 2759 Commercial printing

(G-1599)
MILTONS CABINET SHOP INC
10331 Us Highway 31 (49103-9528)
PHONE.................269 473-2743
Milton Jenks, *President*
Michael Jenks, *Vice Pres*
EMP: 5
SQ FT: 5,500
SALES (est): 481K **Privately Held**
SIC: 2434 Wood kitchen cabinets

(G-1600)
RAYS WELDING CO INC
8469 Hollywood Rd (49103-9788)
PHONE.................269 473-1140
Charles Kinnison, *President*
EMP: 3
SQ FT: 6,000
SALES: 550K **Privately Held**
SIC: 7692 Welding repair

(G-1601)
TAFCOR INC
9918 N Tudor Rd (49103-9681)
P.O. Box 222 (49103-0222)
PHONE.................269 471-2351
Edward Faulkner, *President*
Karen Faulkner, *Shareholder*
Laura Faulkner, *Shareholder*
▼ **EMP:** 16
SQ FT: 55,000
SALES: 1.9MM **Privately Held**
WEB: www.tafcor.com
SIC: 2431 Moldings, wood: unfinished & prefinished

(G-1602)
ZICKS SPECIALTY MEATS INC
Also Called: Zick's Meats
215 N Mechanic St (49103-1150)
PHONE.................269 471-7121
Gary Zick, *President*
Patricia Zick, *Vice Pres*
EMP: 9
SQ FT: 8,000
SALES (est): 1.3MM **Privately Held**
SIC: 2013 Snack sticks, including jerky: from purchased meat

Bessemer
Gogebic County

(G-1603)
BREAD OF LIFE BAKERY & CAFE
105 N Sophie St (49911-1150)
PHONE.................906 663-4005
Robert Samson, *Owner*
EMP: 10
SQ FT: 3,750
SALES: 150K **Privately Held**
SIC: 2051 5812 Bread, all types (white, wheat, rye, etc): fresh or frozen; cafe

(G-1604)
DECOTIES INC
807 Spring St (49911-1638)
PHONE.................906 285-1286
Oscar Buselli, *President*
EMP: 4
SQ FT: 700
SALES (est): 264.2K **Privately Held**
SIC: 3965 Fasteners

(G-1605)
FOREST CORULLO PRODUCTS CORP
300 S Massie Ave (49911-1329)
PHONE.................906 667-0275
Raymond J Corullo, *President*
EMP: 26
SALES (est): 4.3MM **Privately Held**
SIC: 2421 2611 2436 2435 Sawmills & planing mills, general; pulp mills; softwood veneer & plywood; hardwood veneer & plywood

(G-1606)
R AND JS GRAVEL
108 N Cedar Ave (49911-1266)
PHONE.................906 663-4571
Roger Colgin, *Principal*
EMP: 3
SALES (est): 146.4K **Privately Held**
SIC: 1442 Construction sand & gravel

(G-1607)
STEIGERS TIMBER OPERATIONS
401 S Tamarack Ave (49911-1259)
P.O. Box 112 (49911-0112)
PHONE.................906 667-0266
Patrick Steiger, *Owner*
EMP: 4
SALES (est): 501.3K **Privately Held**
SIC: 2411 Logging camps & contractors

Beulah
Benzie County

(G-1608)
AURIC ENTERPRISES INC
Also Called: Diack
7755 Narrow Gauge Rd (49617-9792)
PHONE.................231 882-7251
Robert Brown, *President*
EMP: 4
SALES (est): 594.2K **Privately Held**
WEB: www.thornsmithlabs.com
SIC: 3826 3829 3842 3825 Analytical instruments; measuring & controlling devices; surgical appliances & supplies; instruments to measure electricity; industrial instrmnts msrmnt display/control process variable

(G-1609)
CLASSIC DOCK & LIFT LLC
8862 Us Highway 31 (49617-9729)
P.O. Box 1151, Frankfort (49635-1151)
PHONE.................231 882-4374
Dean Michael,
Edith Michael, *Shareholder*
EMP: 8
SALES: 300K **Privately Held**
SIC: 3448 Docks: prefabricated metal

(G-1610)
LEROY WORDEN
Also Called: Worden Farms
1944 N Marshall Rd (49617-8542)
PHONE.................231 325-3837
Leroy Worden, *Owner*
EMP: 4
SALES (est): 141.1K **Privately Held**
SIC: 2087 Flavoring extracts & syrups

(G-1611)
NIPPA SAUNA STOVES LLC
8862 Us Highway 31 (49617-9729)
P.O. Box 1151, Frankfort (49635-1151)
PHONE.................231 882-7707
Dean Michael,
EMP: 8
SQ FT: 12,000
SALES: 250K **Privately Held**
SIC: 3634 Sauna heaters, electric

(G-1612)
SLEEPING BEAR APIARIES LTD
Also Called: Sleeping Bear Farms
971 S Pioneer Rd (49617-9778)
PHONE.................231 882-4456
Kirk Jones, *President*
Dave Nesky, *Vice Pres*
Susan Kile, *CFO*
Sharon Jones, *Treasurer*
Mike Williams, *Admin Sec*
EMP: 10
SALES (est): 1.2MM **Privately Held**
WEB: www.sleepingbearfarms.com
SIC: 2099 5947 Honey, strained & bottled; gift, novelty & souvenir shop

GEOGRAPHIC SECTION

Big Rapids - Mecosta County (G-1639)

Beverly Hills
Oakland County

(G-1613)
ARC PRINT SOLUTIONS LLC
19101 Saxon Dr (48025-2930)
PHONE....................248 917-7052
James Steven Chapman, *President*
Giri Gondi, *CIO*
▼ **EMP:** 10 **EST:** 2009
SALES: 1.2MM **Privately Held**
SIC: 2759 Commercial printing

(G-1614)
BAYLUME INC
31255 Downing Pl (48025-5236)
PHONE....................877 881-3641
EMP: 4
SALES (est): 370K **Privately Held**
SIC: 3645 Mfg Residential Lighting Fixtures

(G-1615)
CAMERON INTERNATIONAL CORP
32440 Evergreen Rd (48025-2808)
PHONE....................248 646-6743
Gary Cameron, *Branch Mgr*
EMP: 54 **Publicly Held**
SIC: 3533 Oil field machinery & equipment
HQ: Cameron International Corporation
4646 W Sam Houston Pkwy N
Houston TX 77041

(G-1616)
DRIVE SYSTEM INTEGRATION INC
32600 Westlady Dr (48025-2747)
PHONE....................248 568-7750
Dare Sommer, *President*
Paul Wire, *Vice Pres*
EMP: 4
SALES (est): 230K **Privately Held**
SIC: 3544 Special dies, tools, jigs & fixtures

(G-1617)
J & E APPLIANCE COMPANY INC
30170 Stellamar St (48025-4925)
PHONE....................248 642-9191
Eric Kopsch, *President*
EMP: 5
SALES (est): 627.7K **Privately Held**
SIC: 3639 Major kitchen appliances, except refrigerators & stoves

(G-1618)
METAL MATES INC (PA)
20135 Elwood St (48025-5015)
PHONE....................248 646-9831
A Clarence Karbum, *President*
Curt A Karbum, *Vice Pres*
Keith M Karbum, *Vice Pres*
Catherine J Karbum, *Admin Sec*
EMP: 2
SQ FT: 10,000
SALES: 2MM **Privately Held**
WEB: www.metalmates.com
SIC: 2869 Industrial organic chemicals

(G-1619)
MICHIGAN BEER GROWLER COMPANY
31221 Southfield Rd (48025-5455)
PHONE....................248 385-3773
Janae Condit, *Administration*
EMP: 5
SALES (est): 299.4K **Privately Held**
SIC: 2082 Malt beverages

(G-1620)
MICROFORMS INC
Also Called: Safran Group, The
30706 Georgetown Dr (48025-4735)
PHONE....................586 939-7900
James A Safran, *President*
Cory Ward, *Buyer*
Betty Pickett, *Purchasing*
Veronica Klein, *Manager*
Wes Tribble, *Technical Staff*
EMP: 60
SQ FT: 20,400
SALES (est): 6.8MM **Privately Held**
WEB: www.microforms.com
SIC: 2752 2796 2791 2782 Commercial printing, offset; platemaking services; typesetting; blankbooks & looseleaf binders; manifold business forms; commercial printing

(G-1621)
SAFRAN PRINTING COMPANY INC
30706 Georgetown Dr (48025-4735)
PHONE....................586 939-7600
James Safran, *President*
Brian Mehrshahi, *Purch Mgr*
Eric Kline, *Engineer*
Lisa Dudley, *Accountant*
Sandra Conley, *Human Res Mgr*
EMP: 20
SQ FT: 20,000
SALES (est): 1.7MM **Privately Held**
SIC: 2754 7338 2796 2791 Commercial printing, gravure; secretarial & court reporting; platemaking services; typesetting; commercial printing, lithographic

Big Rapids
Mecosta County

(G-1622)
BIG RAPIDS PRODUCTS INC (PA)
Also Called: Big Rapids Tool & Engineering
1313 Maple St (49307-1654)
PHONE....................231 796-3593
John Chaput, *CEO*
Tom Tacia, *Plant Mgr*
Kent Brooks, *Engineer*
Kimberly Preston, *Engineer*
Sandra Doyle, *CFO*
EMP: 65 **EST:** 1975
SALES (est): 26.8MM **Privately Held**
WEB: www.brproducts.com
SIC: 3469 Stamping metal for the trade

(G-1623)
CAL PARK LOGGING LLC
17130 15 Mile Rd (49307-9526)
PHONE....................231 796-4662
Calvin Park, *Principal*
EMP: 3
SALES (est): 213.8K **Privately Held**
SIC: 2411 Logging

(G-1624)
CHRIS UNDERHILL
Also Called: Underhill Logging
22772 18 Mile Rd (49307-9709)
PHONE....................231 349-5228
Chris Underhill, *Principal*
EMP: 3
SALES (est): 152.2K **Privately Held**
SIC: 2411 Logging

(G-1625)
COOKS BLACKSMITH WELDING INC
402 Bjornson St (49307-1202)
PHONE....................231 796-6819
Robert Cook, *President*
EMP: 7
SALES (est): 973.7K **Privately Held**
SIC: 7699 7692 Blacksmith shop; welding repair

(G-1626)
FEDERAL SCREW WORKS
Also Called: Boyne City Division
400 N Dekraft Ave (49307-1273)
PHONE....................734 941-4211
William Harness, *President*
Jeffrey Harness, *Vice Pres*
Aaron Zurschmiede, *Vice Pres*
Daimien Lynch, *Mfg Mgr*
Christian Bersano, *Engineer*
EMP: 25
SALES (corp-wide): 2.4K **Privately Held**
WEB: www.federalscrew.com
SIC: 3451 3592 3452 Screw machine products; carburetors, pistons, rings, valves; bolts, nuts, rivets & washers
PA: Federal Screw Works
34846 Goddard Rd
Romulus MI 48174
734 941-4211

(G-1627)
FEDERAL SCREW WORKS
Big Rapids Division
400 N Dekraft Ave (49307-1273)
PHONE....................231 796-7664
Carman Bean, *Branch Mgr*
EMP: 147
SALES (corp-wide): 2.4K **Privately Held**
WEB: www.federalscrew.com
SIC: 3452 3714 Bolts, metal; motor vehicle parts & accessories
PA: Federal Screw Works
34846 Goddard Rd
Romulus MI 48174
734 941-4211

(G-1628)
FLUID ROUTING SOLUTIONS INC
600 N Dekraft Ave (49307-1272)
PHONE....................231 592-1700
Richard Davis, *Branch Mgr*
EMP: 33
SQ FT: 100,000
SALES (corp-wide): 1.6B **Publicly Held**
WEB: www.daycoinc.com
SIC: 3312 3714 3498 Tubes, steel & iron; motor vehicle parts & accessories; fabricated pipe & fittings
HQ: Fluid Routing Solutions, Llc
30000 Stephenson Hwy B
Madison Heights MI 48071
248 228-8900

(G-1629)
FLUID ROUTING SOLUTIONS INC
123 N Dekraft Ave (49307-1280)
PHONE....................231 796-4489
Brian Reeves, *Branch Mgr*
EMP: 25
SALES (corp-wide): 1.6B **Publicly Held**
WEB: www.daycoinc.com
SIC: 3714 Fuel systems & parts, motor vehicle
HQ: Fluid Routing Solutions, Llc
30000 Stephenson Hwy B
Madison Heights MI 48071
248 228-8900

(G-1630)
GENERAL WOOD PRODUCTS CO
Also Called: Big Rapids Box Company
403 Bjornson St Ste 403 # 403 (49307-1201)
P.O. Box 1869, Birmingham (48012-1869)
PHONE....................248 221-0214
Louis A Braun Jr, *President*
Delphine Defever, *Teacher*
EMP: 10 **EST:** 1977
SALES: 1MM **Privately Held**
SIC: 2448 2653 Pallets, wood; skids, wood; boxes, solid fiber; made from purchased materials

(G-1631)
HAMTECH INC
1916 Industrial Dr N (49307-9011)
PHONE....................231 796-3917
David Hamelund, *President*
EMP: 4
SALES (est): 340K **Privately Held**
WEB: www.hamtechinc.com
SIC: 3599 Machine shop, jobbing & repair

(G-1632)
HANCHETT MANUFACTURING INC
20000 19 Mile Rd (49307-9737)
PHONE....................231 796-7678
Don Selfridge, *President*
Brian Sauntman, *Vice Pres*
Mark Renne, *Purch Mgr*
Ken Shefferly, *Controller*
EMP: 110
SQ FT: 95,000
SALES (est): 19.1MM **Privately Held**
WEB: www.hanchett.com
SIC: 3545 3596 3423 Shaping tools (machine tool accessories); balancing machines (machine tool accessories); scales & balances, except laboratory; hand & edge tools

(G-1633)
HAWORTH INC
Also Called: Big Rapids Components
300 N Bronson Ave (49307-8681)
PHONE....................231 796-1400
Tom Roberts, *Mfg Staff*
Victor Laing, *Manager*
EMP: 300
SALES (corp-wide): 1.8B **Privately Held**
WEB: www.haworth-furn.com
SIC: 2522 2521 Office furniture, except wood; wood office furniture
HQ: Haworth, Inc.
1 Haworth Ctr
Holland MI 49423
616 393-3000

(G-1634)
HELP-U-SELL RE BIG RAPIDS
412 S State St Ofc A (49307-1963)
PHONE....................231 796-3966
Claira Shwabb, *Owner*
EMP: 10
SALES (est): 368.6K **Privately Held**
WEB: www.helpusellbr.com
SIC: 6531 2759 Real estate agents & managers; advertising literature: printing

(G-1635)
KELLYS CATERING
Also Called: Kellys Catering and Deer Proc
19077 12 Mile Rd (49307-8802)
PHONE....................231 796-5414
Colin Kelly, *Owner*
EMP: 3
SALES (est): 414.8K **Privately Held**
SIC: 5147 5812 2013 2011 Meats & meat products; caterers; sausages & other prepared meats; meat packing plants

(G-1636)
KMK MACHINING
10842 Northland Dr (49307-9294)
PHONE....................231 629-8068
Kevin G Wells, *Manager*
EMP: 11 **EST:** 2012
SALES (est): 1.5MM **Privately Held**
SIC: 3599 Machine shop, jobbing & repair

(G-1637)
KURT DUBOWSKI
14472 Mckinley Rd (49307-9537)
PHONE....................231 796-0055
Kurt Dubowski, *Principal*
EMP: 3
SALES (est): 240.8K **Privately Held**
SIC: 3089 Plastics products

(G-1638)
LC MATERIALS
15151 Old Millpond Rd (49307-9502)
PHONE....................231 796-8685
Phil Potvin, *Manager*
EMP: 8
SALES (corp-wide): 8MM **Privately Held**
SIC: 3273 Ready-mixed concrete
PA: Lc Materials
805 W 13th St
Cadillac MI 49601
231 825-2473

(G-1639)
ORIGINAL FOOTWEAR COMPANY
1005 Baldwin St (49307-1119)
PHONE....................231 796-5828
David Warren, *Branch Mgr*
Becky Stanton, *Manager*
EMP: 400
SALES (corp-wide): 13.9MM **Privately Held**
SIC: 3172 3021 3143 Personal leather goods; rubber & plastics footwear; boots, dress or casual; men's
PA: The Original Footwear Company Inc
5968 Commerce Blvd
Morristown TN 37814
423 254-8022

Big Rapids - Mecosta County (G-1640)

(G-1640)
PGI HOLDINGS INC (DH)
Also Called: Pioneer Group, Inc., The
115 N Michigan Ave (49307-1401)
PHONE.....................................231 796-4831
Mark Aldam, *President*
John Norton, *General Mgr*
Tom McHugh, *CFO*
Judy Hale, *Advt Staff*
Laura Waltz, *Manager*
EMP: 25
SQ FT: 20,000
SALES (est): 25.6MM
SALES (corp-wide): 8.3B **Privately Held**
WEB: www.bigrapidsnews.com
SIC: 2752 2711 Commercial printing, lithographic; commercial printing & newspaper publishing combined
HQ: Hearst Communications, Inc.
300 W 57th St
New York NY 10019
212 649-2000

(G-1641)
PGI HOLDINGS INC
Also Called: River Valley Shopper
115 N Michigan Ave (49307-1401)
PHONE.....................................231 937-4740
John Batdorff III, *Manager*
EMP: 4
SALES (corp-wide): 8.3B **Privately Held**
WEB: www.bigrapidsnews.com
SIC: 2711 2741 Commercial printing & newspaper publishing combined; shopping news: publishing only, not printed on site
HQ: Pgi Holdings, Inc.
115 N Michigan Ave
Big Rapids MI 49307
231 796-4831

(G-1642)
PIONEER PRESS (PA)
Also Called: Pioneer Group
22405 18 Mile Rd (49307-9720)
PHONE.....................................231 796-8072
Jack Batdorss, *Owner*
John Norton, *General Mgr*
Scott Yoshonis, *Editor*
Chris Squires, *Credit Staff*
Aaron Dekuiper, *Manager*
EMP: 12 **EST:** 1972
SALES (est): 4.8MM **Privately Held**
SIC: 2752 Commercial printing, offset

(G-1643)
PRIMO TOOL & MANUFACTURING
20070 19 Mile Rd (49307-9737)
PHONE.....................................231 592-5262
David Grveles, *President*
Holly Grveles, *Vice Pres*
EMP: 5
SQ FT: 5,000
SALES (est): 325K **Privately Held**
SIC: 3599 Machine shop, jobbing & repair

(G-1644)
RODNEY E HARTER
12880 190th Ave (49307-9060)
PHONE.....................................231 796-6734
Rodney E Harter, *Principal*
EMP: 6
SALES (est): 567.5K **Privately Held**
SIC: 2411 Logging

(G-1645)
SIMONDS INTERNATIONAL LLC
Also Called: Simonds Industries
120 E Pere Marquette St (49307-1159)
PHONE.....................................231 527-2322
Dave Campbell, *Branch Mgr*
EMP: 70
SALES (corp-wide): 174.1MM **Privately Held**
WEB: www.simondsinternational.com
SIC: 3545 Cutting tools for machine tools
HQ: Simonds International L.L.C.
135 Intervale Rd
Fitchburg MA 01420
978 424-0100

(G-1646)
WHITE CLOUD MANUFACTURING CO (PA)
123 N Dekraft Ave (49307-1280)
P.O. Box 1117 (49307-0307)
PHONE.....................................231 796-8603
Jack Benedict, *President*
Tom Benedict, *Vice Pres*
EMP: 38
SQ FT: 30,000
SALES (est): 4MM **Privately Held**
SIC: 3369 Nonferrous foundries

(G-1647)
WOODVILLE HEIGHTS ENTERPRISES
7147 6 Mile Rd (49307-9147)
PHONE.....................................231 629-7750
Alice Gerst, *President*
EMP: 10
SALES (est): 532.4K **Privately Held**
SIC: 3599 Industrial machinery

Bingham Farms
Oakland County

(G-1648)
ARDEN COMPANIES LLC (PA)
30400 Telg Rd Ste 200 (48025)
PHONE.....................................248 415-8500
Robert S Sachs, *CEO*
Cecil Kearse, *President*
John F Connell, *Exec VP*
Charles Thompson, *Senior VP*
Sreedhar Bandaru, *Vice Pres*
▲ **EMP:** 50 **EST:** 1964
SQ FT: 15,000
SALES (est): 140.9MM **Privately Held**
WEB: www.ardencompanies.com
SIC: 2392 Cushions & pillows

(G-1649)
AUTHENTIC 3D
30800 Telg Rd Ste 4775 (48025)
PHONE.....................................248 469-8809
Jorey Chernett, *CEO*
John David, *Engineer*
Alexander Kappaz, *Accounts Mgr*
EMP: 4
SALES (est): 605.1K **Privately Held**
SIC: 3826 Magnetic resonance imaging apparatus

(G-1650)
CHALDEAN NEWS LLC
30850 Telg Rd Ste 220 (48025)
PHONE.....................................248 996-8360
Martin Manna, *Owner*
EMP: 11
SALES (est): 598.5K **Privately Held**
SIC: 2711 Newspapers, publishing & printing

(G-1651)
DETROIT TECHNOLOGIES INC (PA)
Also Called: Conform Group
32500 Telg Rd Ste 207 (48025)
PHONE.....................................248 647-0400
Steven Phillips, *CEO*
William Vaughn, *Exec VP*
Gary M Stanis, *CFO*
John Mastin, *Admin Sec*
▲ **EMP:** 15
SQ FT: 4,000
SALES (est): 312.3MM **Privately Held**
SIC: 3714 Motor vehicle parts & accessories

(G-1652)
DTI MOLDED PRODUCTS INC (HQ)
Also Called: Conform Automotive
32500 Telg Rd Ste 207 (48025)
PHONE.....................................248 647-0400
Steve Phillips, *CEO*
Gary Stanis, *CFO*
Denise Arnold, *Finance*
EMP: 10 **EST:** 1999
SQ FT: 4,500
SALES (est): 18.8MM **Privately Held**
SIC: 3465 3069 Moldings or trim, automobile: stamped metal; molded rubber products

(G-1653)
FORD GLOBAL TECHNOLOGIES LLC (HQ)
30600 Telg Rd Ste 2345 (48025)
PHONE.....................................313 312-3000
Rebecca Burtless-Creps, *Asst Sec*
EMP: 14 **EST:** 2002
SALES (est): 13.1MM
SALES (corp-wide): 160.3B **Publicly Held**
SIC: 3465 Body parts, automobile: stamped metal
PA: Ford Motor Company
1 American Rd
Dearborn MI 48126
313 322-3000

(G-1654)
INTRINSIC4D LLC (PA)
Also Called: Legal Art Works
30800 Telg Rd Ste 4775 (48025)
PHONE.....................................248 469-8811
Jorey Chernett, *CEO*
Marjorie McKenzie, *Vice Pres*
EMP: 10
SALES (est): 1.5MM **Privately Held**
SIC: 7372 8099 Application computer software; medical services organization

(G-1655)
KRAMS ENTERPRISES INC
Also Called: Arden-Benhar Mills
30400 Telg Rd Ste 200 (48025)
PHONE.....................................248 415-8500
Bob Sachs, *President*
Robert S Sachs, *President*
Kenneth Sachs, *Corp Secy*
John F Connell, *Exec VP*
Ronald P Zemenak, *Exec VP*
▲ **EMP:** 887
SQ FT: 5,500
SALES (est): 78MM **Privately Held**
SIC: 2392 Cushions & pillows

(G-1656)
MASTER DATA CENTER INC
Also Called: Mdc
30200 Telg Rd Ste 300 (48025)
PHONE.....................................248 352-5810
Orlee Chamblin, *Buyer*
Hemant Gandhi, *Treasurer*
Michael Perez, *Director*
EMP: 98
SQ FT: 12,000
SALES (est): 13MM
SALES (corp-wide): 328.1K **Privately Held**
WEB: www.informationholdings.com
SIC: 6794 7374 7372 Patent buying, licensing, leasing; data processing service; prepackaged software
HQ: Information Holdings Inc.
1500 Spring Garden St # 4
Philadelphia PA 19130
215 386-0100

(G-1657)
MICHIGAN INTERACTIVE LLC
30600 Telg Rd Ste 2345 (48025)
PHONE.....................................517 241-4341
David Freund, *President*
Stephen M Kovzan, *Treasurer*
William V Asselt, *Admin Sec*
William Van Asselt, *Admin Sec*
EMP: 9
SQ FT: 1,500
SALES (est): 321.9K
SALES (corp-wide): 344.9MM **Publicly Held**
SIC: 7372 Business oriented computer software
HQ: Nicusa, Inc.
25501 W Valley Pkwy # 300
Olathe KS 66061

(G-1658)
PRESSED PAPERBOARD TECH LLC
Also Called: Papertech
30400 Telg Rd Ste 386 (48025)
PHONE.....................................248 646-6500
Larry Epstein, *Mng Member*
EMP: 100
SALES (est): 49.8MM **Privately Held**
SIC: 2679 Food dishes & utensils, from pressed & molded pulp

(G-1659)
REUTTER LLC (DH)
30150 Telg Rd Ste 172 (48025)
PHONE.....................................248 621-9220
Frank Horlacher, *CEO*
Johannes Wienands, *Director*
◆ **EMP:** 5
SQ FT: 3,000
SALES: 5MM
SALES (corp-wide): 401.9K **Privately Held**
SIC: 3089 3795 Closures, plastic; tanks & tank components
HQ: Reutter Gmbh
Hans-Paul-Kaysser-Str. 10
Leutenbach 71397
719 595-9870

(G-1660)
STREMA SALES CORP
Also Called: Wayne Wire Cloths
31000 Telg Rd Ste 240 (48025)
PHONE.....................................248 645-0626
Michael G Brown, *President*
Newell Confer, *Manager*
EMP: 4
SALES: 40MM **Privately Held**
SIC: 3496 Miscellaneous fabricated wire products

(G-1661)
TAXTIME USA INC
30800 Telegraph Rd (48025-4542)
PHONE.....................................248 642-7070
Michael Schwartz, *President*
EMP: 3
SALES (est): 247.2K **Privately Held**
SIC: 7372 8721 Business oriented computer software; accounting, auditing & bookkeeping

(G-1662)
TRILLACORPE/BK LLC
Also Called: Trillacorpe Construction
30100 Telg Rd Ste 366 (48025)
PHONE.....................................248 433-0585
Larry Goss,
EMP: 8
SALES: 20MM **Privately Held**
SIC: 1442 Construction sand & gravel

Birch Run
Saginaw County

(G-1663)
AVKO EDUCTL RES FOUNDATION
3084 Willard Rd (48415-9404)
PHONE.....................................810 686-9283
Devorah Wolf, *President*
Elmer Waley, *Vice Pres*
Donald Mc Cabe, *Research*
Aaron Miller, *Treasurer*
Daniel Dolan, *Admin Sec*
EMP: 13
SQ FT: 1,200
SALES: 56.7K **Privately Held**
SIC: 2731 8732 Books: publishing only; educational research

(G-1664)
KRISELER WELDING INC
11877 Maple Rd (48415-8207)
PHONE.....................................989 624-9266
David Bowns, *President*
Barbara Bowns, *Treasurer*
EMP: 6
SQ FT: 6,000
SALES: 300K **Privately Held**
SIC: 3599 7692 3544 3471 Machine shop, jobbing & repair; welding repair; special dies, tools, jigs & fixtures; plating & polishing

GEOGRAPHIC SECTION — Birmingham - Oakland County (G-1694)

(G-1665)
LUXOTTICA OF AMERICA INC
Also Called: Sunglass Hut 4711
8825 Market Place Dr # 340 (48415-8344)
PHONE..................989 624-8958
Lori Dillon, *Manager*
EMP: 3
SALES (corp-wide): 1.4MM **Privately Held**
SIC: 3231 Products of purchased glass
HQ: Luxottica Of America Inc.
4000 Luxottica Pl
Mason OH 45040

(G-1666)
MID-MICHIGAN SCREEN PRINTING
Also Called: Mmsp
11917 Conquest St (48415-9294)
P.O. Box 333 (48415-0333)
PHONE..................989 624-9827
Floyd McClintock, *Owner*
EMP: 4
SQ FT: 1,600
SALES (est): 407.8K **Privately Held**
SIC: 2752 Commercial printing, lithographic

(G-1667)
PVH CORP
8925 Market Place Dr # 450 (48415-8346)
PHONE..................989 624-5575
EMP: 33
SALES (corp-wide): 8.2B **Publicly Held**
SIC: 2339 Mfg Clothing
PA: Pvh Corp.
200 Madison Ave Bsmt 1
New York NY 10016
212 381-3500

(G-1668)
PVH CORP
Also Called: Van Heusen
12245 S Beyer Rd Ste A060 (48415-8318)
PHONE..................989 624-5651
EMP: 5
SALES (corp-wide): 8.2B **Publicly Held**
SIC: 2321 Mfg Men's/Boy's Furnishings
PA: Pvh Corp.
200 Madison Ave Bsmt 1
New York NY 10016
212 381-3500

(G-1669)
ROCKY MTN CHOCLAT FCTRY INC
8825 Market Place Dr # 425 (48415-8345)
PHONE..................989 624-4784
Jerilynn Daenzer, *Manager*
EMP: 4
SALES (corp-wide): 34.5MM **Publicly Held**
WEB: www.rmcfusa.com
SIC: 5441 2066 Candy; chocolate
HQ: Rocky Mountain Chocolate Factory, Inc.
265 Turner Dr
Durango CO 81303
970 259-0554

(G-1670)
RUNWAY LIQUIDATION LLC
12150 S Beyer Rd (48415-9494)
PHONE..................989 624-4756
Sirena Crawford, *President*
EMP: 8
SALES (corp-wide): 570.1MM **Privately Held**
WEB: www.bcbg.com
SIC: 2335 Women's, juniors' & misses' dresses
HQ: Runway Liquidation, Llc
2761 Fruitland Ave
Vernon CA 90058
323 589-2224

(G-1671)
SGS INC
11195 Dixie Hwy (48415-9751)
PHONE..................989 239-1726
Debrah Rothgeb, *President*
EMP: 3
SALES (est): 250K **Privately Held**
SIC: 1761 3494 Gutter & downspout contractor; sprinkler systems, field

(G-1672)
SKECHERS USA INC
Also Called: Skechers Factory Outlet 235
12240 S Beyer Rd (48415-9401)
PHONE..................989 624-9336
Sarah Snyder, *General Mgr*
EMP: 10 **Publicly Held**
SIC: 5661 2252 Footwear, athletic; socks
PA: Skechers U.S.A., Inc.
228 Manhattan Beach Blvd # 200
Manhattan Beach CA 90266

(G-1673)
SPRING SAGINAW COMPANY
11008 Dixie Hwy (48415-9745)
P.O. Box 328 (48415-0328)
PHONE..................989 624-9333
Fern Wheeler, *President*
EMP: 4
SQ FT: 3,500
SALES (est): 531.1K **Privately Held**
SIC: 3495 Wire springs

Birmingham
Oakland County

(G-1674)
ALPHA DATA BUSINESS FORMS INC
Also Called: Graywolf Printing
757 S Eton St Ste D (48009-6841)
PHONE..................248 540-5930
Max Grayvold, *President*
Marc Grayvold, *Vice Pres*
EMP: 5
SQ FT: 800
SALES (est): 640K **Privately Held**
WEB: www.graywolfprinting.com
SIC: 5112 2761 2759 2752 Business forms; manifold business forms; commercial printing; commercial printing, lithographic; coated & laminated paper; packaging paper & plastics film, coated & laminated

(G-1675)
CANTRICK KIP CO
999 S Adams Rd (48009-7039)
PHONE..................248 644-7622
George A Cantrick Jr, *President*
EMP: 4
SQ FT: 1,478
SALES (est): 375.7K **Privately Held**
WEB: www.kipcantrickcompany.com
SIC: 3086 Packaging & shipping materials, foamed plastic

(G-1676)
CHERRY GROWERS INC (PA)
401 S Old Woodward Ave # 340 (48009-6621)
PHONE..................231 276-9241
Ed Send, *Vice Ch Bd*
Brian Mitchell, *President*
Dan Winowiecki, *Finance Dir*
John Gallaher Jr, *Admin Sec*
Eric Macleod, *Asst Sec*
◆ EMP: 125 EST: 1939
SALES (est): 16.2MM **Privately Held**
WEB: www.cherrygrowers.net
SIC: 2037 2033 Fruits, quick frozen & cold pack (frozen); fruits: packaged in cans, jars, etc.

(G-1677)
COLE WAGNER CABINETRY
735 Forest Ave (48009-6429)
PHONE..................248 642-5330
EMP: 3 EST: 2010
SALES (est): 283.2K **Privately Held**
SIC: 2434 Wood kitchen cabinets

(G-1678)
CONCEPT TECHNOLOGY INC (PA)
144 Wimbleton Dr (48009-5633)
PHONE..................248 765-0100
Thomas F Hornung, *President*
Susan A Hornung, *Admin Sec*
EMP: 24 EST: 1971
SQ FT: 2,000
SALES (est): 3.7MM **Privately Held**
SIC: 3825 Engine electrical test equipment

(G-1679)
CRUSE HARDWOOD LUMBER INC
2499 Cole St (48009-7084)
PHONE..................517 688-4891
Robert H Cruse, *President*
Gladys Anne Cruse, *Corp Secy*
EMP: 7
SALES (est): 840.2K **Privately Held**
SIC: 2421 Sawmills & planing mills, general

(G-1680)
DART ENERGY CENTER
260 E Brown St Ste 200 (48009-6231)
PHONE..................248 203-2924
EMP: 3
SALES (est): 155.6K **Privately Held**
SIC: 3494 Plumbing & heating valves

(G-1681)
DAVID WACHLER & SONS INC
Also Called: Wachler, David & Sons Jewelers
112 S Old Woodward Ave (48009-6101)
PHONE..................248 540-4622
Buzz Wachler, *President*
Leonard Wachler, *Principal*
Gary Wachler, *Vice Pres*
Lincoln Wachler, *Vice Pres*
EMP: 15
SQ FT: 2,500
SALES (est): 2.3MM **Privately Held**
WEB: www.wachlerjewelers.com
SIC: 3911 Jewelry, precious metal

(G-1682)
E-CON LLC
Also Called: Econ Global Services
320 Martin St Ste 60 (48009-1486)
PHONE..................248 766-9000
Djeamourty Ramkumar,
EMP: 50
SQ FT: 2,000
SALES (est): 4.4MM **Privately Held**
SIC: 7379 7376 7371 7363 Computer related consulting services; computer facilities management; computer software development; labor resource services; business oriented computer software

(G-1683)
ERNST BENZ COMPANY LLC
177 S Old Woodward Ave (48009-6102)
PHONE..................248 203-2323
Efim Khankin,
▼ EMP: 6
SALES (est): 576.8K **Privately Held**
SIC: 3873 Watches, clocks, watchcases & parts

(G-1684)
GACO SOURCING LLC
2254 Cole St (48009-7072)
PHONE..................248 633-2656
Stephanie Wineman, *CEO*
Lisa Norton, *General Mgr*
Ted Farah, *CFO*
Cindy Gibbs, *Accountant*
Jessica Kwartowitz, *Accounts Mgr*
▲ EMP: 5 EST: 2011
SALES (est): 1.1MM **Privately Held**
SIC: 3069 Balloons, advertising & toy: rubber

(G-1685)
GREENBACK INC
Also Called: Greenback.com
600 Suffield Ave (48009-4627)
PHONE..................313 443-4272
Joseph Lauer, *CEO*
EMP: 3
SALES (est): 84.5K **Privately Held**
SIC: 7371 7372 Computer software development & applications; business oriented computer software

(G-1686)
HORIZON INTL GROUP LLC
1411 Westboro (48009-5862)
PHONE..................734 341-9336
Heather Gardner, *CEO*
EMP: 51
SQ FT: 39,000
SALES (est): 3.1MM **Privately Held**
SIC: 8742 5013 3714 Management consulting services; automotive supplies & parts; motor vehicle parts & accessories

(G-1687)
KEVIN S MACADDINO
380 N Old Woodward Ave # 300 (48009-5347)
PHONE..................248 642-0333
Kevin Macaddino, *Principal*
EMP: 3
SALES (est): 170K **Privately Held**
SIC: 3291 Abrasive products

(G-1688)
LITTLE SILVER CORP
725 S Adams Rd Ste 250 (48009-6982)
PHONE..................248 642-0860
Allen Ross, *CEO*
▲ EMP: 3
SALES (est): 489.7K **Privately Held**
WEB: www.slifter.com
SIC: 2833 Animal based products

(G-1689)
M & M IRISH ENTERPRISES INC
Also Called: Batteries Plus
34164 Woodward Ave (48009-0920)
PHONE..................248 644-0666
Barry Murphy, *Principal*
EMP: 7
SQ FT: 1,650
SALES (est): 980K **Privately Held**
SIC: 3691 5531 5063 Storage batteries; batteries, automotive & truck; light bulbs & related supplies

(G-1690)
MAGNI GROUP INC (PA)
390 Park St Ste 300 (48009-3400)
PHONE..................248 647-4500
David E Berry, *Chairman*
Jack Benson, *Vice Pres*
Kirk Weaver, *Vice Pres*
Bradley Nance, *Purchasing*
Tom McIntosh, *VP Sales*
▲ EMP: 14
SQ FT: 8,000
SALES (est): 80.5MM **Privately Held**
WEB: www.themagnigroup.com
SIC: 2899 3479 Rust resisting compounds; coating, rust preventive

(G-1691)
MARK ADLER HOMES
401 S Old Woodward Ave # 3 (48009-6611)
PHONE..................586 850-0630
Mark Adler, *Administration*
EMP: 4
SALES (est): 334.4K **Privately Held**
SIC: 3448 Buildings, portable: prefabricated metal

(G-1692)
MATTHEWS SOFTWARE INC
145 Larchlea Dr (48009-1516)
PHONE..................248 593-6999
EMP: 5
SALES (est): 244.2K **Privately Held**
SIC: 7372 Prepackaged software

(G-1693)
MILLS PHRM & APOTHECARY LLC
Also Called: Epicure By Mills, The
1740 W Maple Rd (48009-1545)
PHONE..................248 633-2872
Pierre Pourtos, *Mng Member*
EMP: 3
SALES (est): 206.1K **Privately Held**
SIC: 2834 Pharmaceutical preparations

(G-1694)
MOUNT-N-REPAIR
Also Called: Mount-N-Repair Silver Jewelry
205 Pierce St Ste 101 (48009-6014)
PHONE..................248 647-8670
Joel Kaber, *Owner*
EMP: 4
SALES (est): 195.3K **Privately Held**
SIC: 3911 5944 Jewelry, precious metal; jewelry stores

Birmingham - Oakland County (G-1695)

(G-1695)
NEXTCAT INC
2344 Fairway Dr (48009-1813)
PHONE..................................248 514-6742
Charles A Salley Jr, *President*
EMP: 3
SALES (est): 264.4K **Privately Held**
SIC: 2819 Industrial inorganic chemicals

(G-1696)
NORTHERN TRADING GROUP LLC
284 W Maple Rd (48009-3336)
P.O. Box 131008, Ann Arbor (48113-1008)
PHONE..................................248 885-8750
Sandy Graham, *Branch Mgr*
EMP: 5
SALES (est): 414.7K
SALES (corp-wide): 1.2MM **Privately Held**
SIC: 3949 Camping equipment & supplies
PA: Northern Trading Group, Llc
227 E Front St
Traverse City MI 49684
231 946-1339

(G-1697)
PERMAWICK COMPANY INC (PA)
255 E Brown St Ste 100 (48009-6207)
PHONE..................................248 433-3500
Martin L Abel, *President*
Joseph M Lane, *Treasurer*
Mark Nabors, *Manager*
▲ **EMP:** 2 **EST:** 1956
SALES (est): 2MM **Privately Held**
WEB: www.permawick.com
SIC: 2992 3569 Lubricating oils; lubricating equipment

(G-1698)
PIONEER MEATS LLC
915 E Maple Rd (48009-6410)
PHONE..................................248 862-1988
Robert S File, *President*
Bob Capoccia, *Controller*
Steven Malek, *Controller*
Robert George,
EMP: 10
SALES (est): 1MM **Privately Held**
SIC: 2013 Cooked meats from purchased meat

(G-1699)
QUESTOR PARTNERS FUND II LP (PA)
101 Southfield Rd 2 (48009-1601)
PHONE..................................248 593-1930
Jay Alix, *Managing Prtnr*
Robert Shields, *Partner*
Robert D Denious, *Director*
Wallace Reuckel, *Director*
Mary Ellen Sanko, *Administration*
EMP: 3 **EST:** 1995
SALES (est): 533.3MM **Privately Held**
SIC: 8742 2099 Management consulting services; ready-to-eat meals, salads & sandwiches

(G-1700)
R J S TOOL & GAGE CO
Also Called: R J S
1081 S Eton St (48009-7133)
PHONE..................................248 642-8620
Deborah S Stamp, *President*
Richard J Stamp Jr, *President*
Richard Stamp III, *Vice Pres*
John Mittelstaedt, *Sales Mgr*
EMP: 25
SQ FT: 6,000
SALES (est): 4.3MM **Privately Held**
WEB: www.rjstool.com
SIC: 3545 3423 Tools & accessories for machine tools; gauges (machine tool accessories); hand & edge tools

(G-1701)
S & W HOLDINGS LTD (PA)
114 S Old Woodward Ave (48009-6107)
PHONE..................................248 723-2870
Paul Steffanutti, *President*
EMP: 1
SQ FT: 1,000
SALES: 10MM **Privately Held**
SIC: 3714 3554 Transmission housings or parts, motor vehicle; die cutting & stamping machinery, paper converting; coating & finishing machinery, paper

(G-1702)
SHWAYDER COMPANY
2335 E Lincoln St (48009-7124)
PHONE..................................248 645-9511
Mark Shwayder, *President*
EMP: 5 **EST:** 1954
SQ FT: 15,000
SALES (est): 758.2K **Privately Held**
SIC: 3429 3545 Keys, locks & related hardware; machine tool accessories

(G-1703)
T R S FIELDBUS SYSTEMS INC
666 Baldwin Ct (48009-3863)
P.O. Box 4210, Troy (48099-4210)
PHONE..................................586 826-9696
Karl Sachs, *President*
Adelheid Seidensticker, *Vice Pres*
EMP: 4
SALES (est): 500K **Privately Held**
SIC: 3357 Fiber optic cable (insulated)

(G-1704)
TESSONICS CORP
2019 Hazel St (48009-6825)
PHONE..................................248 885-8335
Roman Maev, *President*
Joe Udzbinac, *CFO*
EMP: 6
SALES (est): 600K **Privately Held**
WEB: www.tessonics.com
SIC: 3829 Measuring & controlling devices

(G-1705)
TITAN GLOBAL OIL SERVICES INC
401 S Old Woodward Ave # 308 (48009-6612)
PHONE..................................248 594-5983
Jeffrey Groen, *Principal*
Kelly M Hayes, *Principal*
Edward Shehab, *Principal*
EMP: 11
SALES (est): 1.1MM **Privately Held**
SIC: 3533 Oil & gas field machinery

(G-1706)
TOTLE INC
260 E Brown St Ste 200 (48009-6231)
PHONE..................................248 645-1111
David Bleznak, *CEO*
EMP: 9 **EST:** 2017
SALES: 7.2MM **Privately Held**
SIC: 7389 7372 Financial services; application computer software

(G-1707)
U S DISTRIBUTING INC
Also Called: Sundog Construction Heaters
2333 Cole St (48009-7031)
PHONE..................................248 646-0550
William E Beattie Jr, *President*
Jeff Lewis, *Sales Staff*
Bill Pearre, *Manager*
EMP: 20
SQ FT: 10,000
SALES (est): 3.7MM **Privately Held**
SIC: 3433 3585 7359 Room heaters, gas; air conditioning units, complete: domestic or industrial; propane equipment rental

(G-1708)
WELLSENSE USA INC
199 W Brown St Ste 110 (48009-6005)
PHONE..................................888 335-0995
Eitan Machover, *CEO*
▲ **EMP:** 4 **EST:** 2011
SALES (est): 465K **Privately Held**
SIC: 3829 Measuring & controlling devices

(G-1709)
WOOLLY & CO LLC
Also Called: Woolly and Co
575 Stanley Blvd (48009-1401)
PHONE..................................248 480-4354
Aviva Susser, *Mng Member*
▲ **EMP:** 6
SALES (est): 545.4K **Privately Held**
SIC: 2281 5199 Crochet yarn, spun; embroidery yarn, spun; knitting yarn, spun; spinning yarn; yarns

Bitely
Newaygo County

(G-1710)
DARRELL A CURTICE
669 E Roosevelt Rd (49309-9677)
PHONE..................................231 745-9890
Darrell Curtice, *Principal*
EMP: 3
SALES (est): 263.3K **Privately Held**
SIC: 2411 Logging

Blanchard
Isabella County

(G-1711)
NOBLE FORESTRY INC
Also Called: Thomas Dale Noble & Noble
5012 Taylor Rd (49310-9718)
PHONE..................................989 866-6495
Tom Nobel, *President*
EMP: 5
SALES (est): 390K **Privately Held**
SIC: 2411 Logging

Blissfield
Lenawee County

(G-1712)
AIRGAS USA LLC
7031 Silberhorn Hwy (49228-9587)
PHONE..................................517 673-0997
EMP: 11
SALES (corp-wide): 125.9MM **Privately Held**
SIC: 5169 5084 5085 2813 Industrial gases; gases, compressed & liquefied; carbon dioxide; dry ice; welding machinery & equipment; safety equipment; welding supplies; industrial gases; carbon dioxide; nitrous oxide; dry ice, carbon dioxide (solid); industrial inorganic chemicals; calcium carbide
HQ: Airgas Usa, Llc
259 N Radnor Chester Rd
Radnor PA 19087
610 687-5253

(G-1713)
BLISSFIELD MANUFACTURING CO (PA)
626 Depot St (49228-1358)
PHONE..................................517 486-2121
Patrick Farver, *CEO*
Patrick D Farver, *COO*
Nancy Schiffer, *Exec VP*
Pat Howard, *Vice Pres*
Brian Miller, *Plant Mgr*
▲ **EMP:** 342 **EST:** 1946
SQ FT: 250,000
SALES (est): 79.1MM **Privately Held**
WEB: www.blissfield.com
SIC: 3498 3599 3629 3585 Fabricated pipe & fittings; tubing, flexible metallic; condensers, for motors or generators; refrigeration & heating equipment; air & gas compressors

(G-1714)
BMC GLOBAL LLC
Also Called: Blissfield
626 Depot St (49228-1358)
PHONE..................................517 486-2121
Peter Kos, *CEO*
Greg Wales, *CFO*
EMP: 52
SALES: 3.3MM **Privately Held**
SIC: 3443 Heat exchangers, condensers & components

(G-1715)
CRESCENT MANUFACTURING COMPANY
368 Sherman St (49228-1174)
PHONE..................................517 486-2670
Frank Wojick, *Owner*
EMP: 27
SALES (corp-wide): 16.1MM **Privately Held**
SIC: 3999 Barber & beauty shop equipment
PA: Crescent Manufacturing Company
1310 Majestic Dr
Fremont OH 43420
419 332-6484

(G-1716)
K AND J ABSORBENT PRODUCTS LLC
10009 E Us Highway 223 (49228-9566)
P.O. Box 45 (49228-0045)
PHONE..................................517 486-3110
Janet Street,
Ken Street,
EMP: 7
SALES (est): 735.7K **Privately Held**
SIC: 2392 3569 Dust cloths: made from purchased materials; filters, general line: industrial

(G-1717)
L & W INC
Also Called: Plant 4
11505 E Us Highway 223 (49228-9527)
P.O. Box 59 (49228-0059)
PHONE..................................517 486-6321
Clair Stewart, *Manager*
EMP: 201
SALES (corp-wide): 2.2B **Privately Held**
SIC: 3465 3469 Automotive stampings; stamping metal for the trade
HQ: L & W, Inc.
17757 Woodland Dr
New Boston MI 48164
734 397-6300

(G-1718)
M FORCHE FARMS INC
1080 S Piotter Hwy (49228-9541)
PHONE..................................517 447-3488
Michael Forche, *President*
Darlene Forche, *Principal*
Kathleen Forche, *Principal*
Leo Forche, *Principal*
EMP: 12
SALES (est): 1.3MM **Privately Held**
SIC: 2033 0139 Tomato products: packaged in cans, jars, etc.; food crops

(G-1719)
MAXITROL COMPANY
Also Called: Blissfield Div
235 Sugar St (49228-1367)
PHONE..................................517 486-2820
Paul Friess, *QA Mgr*
Lovina Clipfell, *Controller*
Donald R Bohlka, *Branch Mgr*
Robert Taylor, *Manager*
EMP: 40
SQ FT: 7,000
SALES (corp-wide): 54.8MM **Privately Held**
WEB: www.maxitrol.com
SIC: 3621 3823 3625 3494 Motors & generators; industrial instrmnts msrmnt display/control process variable; relays & industrial controls; valves & pipe fittings
PA: Maxitrol Company
23555 Telegraph Rd
Southfield MI 48033
248 356-1400

(G-1720)
MIDWEST PANEL SYSTEMS INC
Also Called: Great Lakes Insulspan
9012 E Us Highway 223 (49228-9665)
PHONE..................................517 486-4844
Frank B Baker, *President*
EMP: 40
SQ FT: 32,000

SALES (est): 4.4MM Privately Held
WEB: www.insulspan.com
SIC: 2452 1521 2439 2435 Panels & sections, prefabricated, wood; single-family housing construction; structural wood members; hardwood veneer & plywood

(G-1721)
NORTON EQUIPMENT CORPORATION (PA)
203 E Adrian St (49228-1301)
P.O. Box 68 (49228-0068)
PHONE.................517 486-2113
Steven D Cantrell, *President*
H Dwayne Cantrell, *Chairman*
C Sue Cantrell, *Corp Secy*
Scott Cantrell, *Vice Pres*
EMP: 11 EST: 1935
SQ FT: 22,000
SALES (est): 1.9MM Privately Held
SIC: 3356 Magnesium & magnesium alloy bars, sheets, shapes, etc.

(G-1722)
PEARSON PRECAST CONCRETE PDTS
7951 E Us Highway 223 (49228-9664)
PHONE.................517 486-4060
Jamie Pearson, *President*
Dawn Pearson, *Corp Secy*
EMP: 5
SALES: 750K Privately Held
SIC: 3281 3272 Burial vaults, stone; concrete products

(G-1723)
PFB MANUFACTURING LLC
Also Called: Insulspan
9012 E Us Highway 223 (49228-9665)
P.O. Box 38 (49228-0038)
PHONE.................517 486-4844
Kym Hurst, *Admin Sec*
EMP: 24 EST: 2004
SALES: 6MM
SALES (corp-wide): 17.1MM Privately Held
SIC: 2899 5085 Insulating compounds; plastic pallets
PA: Pfb America Corporation
 711 E Broadway Ave
 Meridian ID 83642
 208 887-1020

(G-1724)
RESCAR INC
11440 Cemetery Rd (49228)
P.O. Box 12, Riga (49276-0012)
PHONE.................517 486-3130
EMP: 4
SALES (est): 361K Privately Held
SIC: 3743 Railroad equipment

(G-1725)
RIVER RAISIN PUBLICATIONS
Also Called: Advance Publishing & Printing
121 Newspaper St (49228-1248)
PHONE.................517 486-2400
Marcia Loder, *President*
EMP: 9
SALES (est): 1MM Privately Held
SIC: 2711 Newspapers

(G-1726)
RIVERBEND TIMBER FRAMING INC
9012 E Us Highway 223 (49228-9665)
P.O. Box 26 (49228-0026)
PHONE.................517 486-3629
Frank B Baker, *CEO*
EMP: 75 EST: 1980
SQ FT: 14,500
SALES (est): 7.8MM
SALES (corp-wide): 133.3MM Privately Held
WEB: www.riverbendtf.com
SIC: 2452 1521 2439 2421 Log cabins, prefabricated, wood; single-family housing construction; structural wood members; sawmills & planing mills, general
PA: Plasti-Fab Ltd
 300-2891 Sunridge Way Ne
 Calgary AB T1Y 7
 403 569-4300

(G-1727)
TEC-OPTION INC
334 Sherman St (49228-1174)
PHONE.................517 486-6055
Bryan W Domschot, *President*
John Hildebrandt, *General Mgr*
Kirk Chwialkowski, *QC Mgr*
Shelley Keller-Merillat, *Office Mgr*
Jason Wegner, *Manager*
▲ **EMP:** 11
SQ FT: 6,800
SALES (est): 2.4MM Privately Held
WEB: www.tec-option.com
SIC: 7692 3599 Welding repair; amusement park equipment

(G-1728)
THERMALFAB PRODUCTS INC
10005 E Us Highway 223 (49228-9528)
P.O. Box 157 (49228-0157)
PHONE.................517 486-2073
Bill Bernard, *President*
EMP: 12
SALES (est): 2.7MM Privately Held
SIC: 3567 Industrial furnaces & ovens

(G-1729)
UCKELE HEALTH AND NUTRITION (PA)
Also Called: Uckele Health & Nutrition
5600 Silberhorn Hwy (49228-9529)
P.O. Box 160 (49228-0160)
PHONE.................800 248-0330
Mike Uckele, *CEO*
Caroline Brewer, *Vice Pres*
Kevin Isley, *VP Sales*
Leann Cupp, *Accounts Mgr*
Del Collins, *Officer*
◆ **EMP:** 28
SQ FT: 14,000
SALES (est): 5.5MM Privately Held
WEB: www.uckele.com
SIC: 2834 Pharmaceutical preparations

(G-1730)
VALERO RENEWABLE FUELS CO LLC
Also Called: Valero Riga Ethanol Plant
7025 Silberhorn Hwy (49228-9587)
P.O. Box 12, Riga (49276-0012)
PHONE.................517 486-6190
Bill Welever, *Manager*
EMP: 46
SALES (corp-wide): 117B Publicly Held
SIC: 2869 Ethyl alcohol, ethanol
HQ: Valero Renewable Fuels Company, Llc
 1 Valero Way
 San Antonio TX 78249

Bloomfield
Oakland County

(G-1731)
AAA LANGUAGE SERVICES
Also Called: Iterotext
1573 S Telegraph Rd (48302-0048)
PHONE.................248 239-1138
EMP: 12 EST: 1973
SQ FT: 3,000
SALES: 1.5MM Privately Held
SIC: 7389 2791 Business Services Typesetting Services

(G-1732)
BEDNARSH MRRIS JWLY DESIGN MFG
Also Called: M B Jewelry Design & Mfg
6600 Telegraph Rd (48301-3012)
PHONE.................248 671-0087
Morris Bednarsh, *President*
Anthony Ferrari, *Vice Pres*
Christopher Schornack, *Vice Pres*
Marcia Bednarsh, *Treasurer*
EMP: 13
SQ FT: 2,100
SALES (est): 2.2MM Privately Held
SIC: 5944 3911 Jewelry, precious stones & precious metals; jewelry apparel

(G-1733)
ECOLOGY COATINGS
35980 Woodward Ave # 200 (48304-0903)
PHONE.................248 723-2223
Richard Stromback, *Principal*
EMP: 3
SALES (est): 144.5K Privately Held
SIC: 2869 8732 Industrial organic chemicals; market analysis or research

(G-1734)
KAYAYAN HAYK JEWELRY MFG CO (PA)
Also Called: J.L. McHael Hayk Kyyan Jwelers
869 W Long Lake Rd (48302-2011)
PHONE.................248 626-3060
Hayk Kayayan, *President*
Harriet Kayayan, *Corp Secy*
EMP: 26 EST: 1970
SQ FT: 5,400
SALES (est): 2.5MM Privately Held
SIC: 3911 7631 5944 Jewelry, precious metal; jewelry repair services; jewelry, precious stones & precious metals

(G-1735)
REZOOP LLC
1270 Romney Rd (48304-1537)
PHONE.................248 952-8070
Rohit Singla,
Roli Rani Agrawal,
EMP: 4
SQ FT: 2,000
SALES (est): 234.3K Privately Held
SIC: 7372 Application computer software

(G-1736)
SPECIFICATIONS SERVICE COMPANY
Also Called: Specs Office Supply
5444 Saint Martins Ct (48302-2549)
PHONE.................248 353-0244
Richard Apakarien, *Owner*
Aruther Apaskarien, *Vice Pres*
EMP: 15 EST: 1938
SQ FT: 7,000
SALES (est): 1.2MM Privately Held
SIC: 5943 7334 2752 Office forms & supplies; photocopying & duplicating services; blueprinting service; commercial printing, offset

(G-1737)
WARD-WILLISTON COMPANY (PA)
36700 Woodward Ave # 101 (48304-0929)
PHONE.................248 594-6622
Thomas Cunnington, *CEO*
James Con, *President*
Mr Laurie Cunnington, *President*
Nathan Conway, *COO*
Mr Rodney Conway, *Vice Pres*
EMP: 16
SALES: 156.7K Privately Held
SIC: 1382 Oil & gas exploration services

Bloomfield Hills
Oakland County

(G-1738)
313 CERTIFIED LLC
Also Called: 313certified
6379 Muirfield Dr (48301-1571)
PHONE.................248 915-8419
EMP: 4 EST: 2013
SALES (est): 238.8K Privately Held
SIC: 7372 Prepackaged Software Services

(G-1739)
A PLUS ASPHALT LLC
41000 Woodward Ave (48304-5130)
PHONE.................888 754-1125
Edward Phillips, *CEO*
EMP: 28
SALES: 1.4MM Privately Held
SIC: 2951 Asphalt paving mixtures & blocks

(G-1740)
ACCESSIBLE INFORMATION LLC
124 N Berkshire Rd (48302-0402)
PHONE.................248 338-4928
Daniel Mc Clure, *Principal*
EMP: 4
SALES (est): 236K Privately Held
SIC: 7372 Prepackaged software

(G-1741)
ACME MILLS COMPANY
Also Called: Great Lakes Filter
33 Bloomfield Hills Pkwy (48304-2944)
PHONE.................800 521-8585
David Terry, *Manager*
EMP: 5
SALES (corp-wide): 83.5MM Privately Held
SIC: 3569 Filters
PA: Acme Mills Company
 33 Bloomfield Hills Pkwy
 Bloomfield Hills MI 48304
 248 203-2000

(G-1742)
ADJUSTABLE LOCKING TECH LLC
Also Called: Alt
6632 Telegraph Rd Ste 298 (48301-3012)
PHONE.................248 443-9664
John K Scheer Sr, *CEO*
Bill Sbordon, *President*
EMP: 90 EST: 1997
SALES (est): 8.1MM Privately Held
WEB: www.adjustablelockingtech.com
SIC: 3429 Locks or lock sets

(G-1743)
AJM PACKAGING CORPORATION (PA)
Also Called: A J M
E-4111 Andover Rd (48302)
PHONE.................248 901-0040
Robert Epstein, *President*
Joan Epstein, *Partner*
Linda Manrique, *Vice Pres*
Greg Gilliam, *Project Mgr*
Gary Desjardins, *Prdtn Mgr*
▲ **EMP:** 60
SQ FT: 12,000
SALES (est): 351.1MM Privately Held
WEB: www.ajmpack.com
SIC: 2656 2674 Plates, paper: made from purchased material; paper bags: made from purchased materials

(G-1744)
AMERICAN MUS ENVIRONMENTS INC
1133 W Long Lake Rd # 200 (48302-1983)
PHONE.................248 646-2020
Tom Krikorian, *President*
Deborah Krikorian, *Admin Sec*
EMP: 16
SQ FT: 150,000
SALES (est): 2.9MM Privately Held
WEB: www.amemusic.com
SIC: 3651 Music distribution apparatus

(G-1745)
AMT SOFTWARE LLC
21 E Long Lake Rd Ste 225 (48304-2399)
PHONE.................248 458-0359
Victor Bovey, *Manager*
EMP: 3
SALES (est): 266.1K Privately Held
SIC: 7372 Prepackaged software

(G-1746)
ANN WILLIAMS GROUP LLC
784 Industrial Ct (48302-0380)
PHONE.................248 731-8588
Sheila A Wright, *President*
Dan Wright, *Vice Pres*
EMP: 7
SALES: 2MM Privately Held
SIC: 3944 Games, toys & children's vehicles

Bloomfield Hills - Oakland County (G-1747)

(G-1747)
ARCH GLOBAL PRECISION LLC (HQ)
2600 S Telg Rd Ste 180 (48302)
PHONE.................................734 266-6900
Eli Crotzer, *President*
Timothy Smith, *Vice Pres*
Don Piper, *CFO*
EMP: 10 **EST:** 2011
SALES (est): 96MM
SALES (corp-wide): 724.3MM **Privately Held**
SIC: 5049 3399 Precision tools; metal fasteners
PA: The Jordan Company L P
399 Park Ave Fl 30
New York NY 10022
212 572-0800

(G-1748)
AUTOMOTIVE ELECTRONIC SPC
Also Called: Aesi
2930 Turtle Pond Ct (48302-0720)
PHONE.................................248 335-3229
E Richard Mc Intyre, *President*
James Arholt, *Vice Pres*
Jeanne Mc Intyre, *Admin Sec*
EMP: 20
SQ FT: 3,100
SALES: 1.5MM **Privately Held**
SIC: 3679 5065 Electronic circuits; electronic parts & equipment

(G-1749)
B4 SPORTS INC
Also Called: National Flag Football
2055 Franklin Rd (48302-0327)
PHONE.................................248 454-9700
Kathleen Forsyth, *Principal*
Matt Kosek, *Marketing Mgr*
EMP: 3 **EST:** 2014
SALES (est): 202.9K **Privately Held**
SIC: 3949 Balls: baseball, football, basketball, etc.

(G-1750)
BBCM INC
1015 Golf Dr (48302-0108)
PHONE.................................248 410-2528
William Massie, *President*
EMP: 4 **EST:** 2006
SALES (est): 271.1K **Privately Held**
SIC: 7389 3577 Design services; computer peripheral equipment

(G-1751)
BLACK COBRA FINANCIAL SVCS LLC
41000 Woodward Ave # 350 (48304-5092)
PHONE.................................248 298-9368
Rhonda Hollaway,
EMP: 3
SALES (est): 86.5K **Privately Held**
SIC: 2741 2731 ; books: publishing only

(G-1752)
BOB ALLISON ENTERPRISES
Also Called: Ask Your Neighbor
6560 Red Maple Ln (48301-3224)
PHONE.................................248 540-8467
Robert A Allasee, *President*
Margaret Allesee, *Admin Sec*
EMP: 5
SALES (est): 64K **Privately Held**
SIC: 3663 7389 4832 2721 Radio & TV communications equipment; promoters of shows & exhibitions; radio broadcasting stations; periodicals

(G-1753)
BOEING COMPANY
6001 N Adams Rd Ste 105 (48304-1575)
PHONE.................................248 258-7191
Lewis Seno, *Manager*
EMP: 4
SALES (corp-wide): 101.1B **Publicly Held**
SIC: 3721 Aircraft
PA: The Boeing Company
100 N Riverside Plz
Chicago IL 60606
312 544-2000

(G-1754)
COEUS LLC
1605 S Telegraph Rd (48302-0044)
PHONE.................................248 564-1958
Brian Slaght, *Principal*
EMP: 10
SALES (est): 217.5K **Privately Held**
SIC: 7371 7372 Computer software development & applications; business oriented computer software

(G-1755)
COLEMAN BOWMAN & ASSOCIATES
Also Called: Coleman Specialty Products
3535 Wooddale Ct (48301-2460)
PHONE.................................248 642-8221
Gordon Coleman, *President*
Catherine Coleman, *Treasurer*
Richard Poling, *Admin Sec*
EMP: 6
SQ FT: 1,500
SALES: 5MM **Privately Held**
SIC: 5085 3565 Industrial supplies; packaging machinery

(G-1756)
CONCORD INDUSTRIAL CORPORATION
36400 Woodward Ave # 110 (48304-0912)
P.O. Box 217, Birmingham (48012-0217)
PHONE.................................248 646-9225
EMP: 4
SQ FT: 1,000
SALES (est): 390K **Privately Held**
SIC: 3089 Mfg Plastic Products

(G-1757)
DELOREAN ASSOCIATES INC
Also Called: Home & Garden Concepts
2779 Amberly Rd (48301-2658)
PHONE.................................248 646-1930
Jack De Lorean, *President*
Jack Z De Lorean, *Agent*
EMP: 6
SQ FT: 3,400
SALES (est): 530K **Privately Held**
WEB: www.toolcorner.net
SIC: 8711 3631 Designing: ship, boat, machine & product; household cooking equipment

(G-1758)
DIGITAL SYSTEMS ADIO VIDEO LLC
1668 S Telg Rd Ste L130 (48302)
PHONE.................................248 454-0387
Reginald Walker,
Debbie Wolf,
EMP: 5
SALES (est): 750K **Privately Held**
WEB: www.davs.com
SIC: 3651 Household audio & video equipment

(G-1759)
DIMENSION MACHINE TECH LLC
18815 Kelly Ct (48304)
PHONE.................................586 649-4747
Steve Davis,
James Russell,
EMP: 13
SQ FT: 10,000
SALES: 1.5MM **Privately Held**
SIC: 7699 3451 3599 3535 Industrial machinery & equipment repair; screw machine products; machine shop, jobbing & repair; robotic conveyors

(G-1760)
DOLL FACE CHEF LLC
41000 Woodward Ave # 350 (48304-5130)
P.O. Box 811, Royal Oak (48068-0811)
PHONE.................................248 495-8280
Lashawne Richmond-Tyler, *Mng Member*
EMP: 5
SALES (est): 229.5K **Privately Held**
SIC: 2051 Cakes, pies & pastries

(G-1761)
DS BIOTECH LLC
1665 Dell Rose Dr (48302-0111)
PHONE.................................248 894-1474
Ghassan Saed, *President*
EMP: 3 **EST:** 2010
SQ FT: 2,000
SALES (est): 186.9K **Privately Held**
SIC: 2834 Druggists' preparations (pharmaceuticals)

(G-1762)
DUPEARL TECHNOLOGY LLC
120 Hadsell Dr (48302-0408)
PHONE.................................248 390-9609
Theresa Varickattu, *CEO*
James George, *Chairman*
John Vari, *Vice Pres*
EMP: 89
SALES: 28.4MM **Privately Held**
WEB: www.dupearltechnology.com
SIC: 3679 5084 7371 3089 Harness assemblies for electronic use: wire or cable; industrial machinery & equipment; computer software systems analysis & design, custom; automotive parts, plastic; printed circuit boards

(G-1763)
ELITE BUSINESS SERVICES & EXEC
Also Called: Alure International
2510 S Telg Rd Ste L280 (48302)
PHONE.................................734 956-4550
Caree J Eason, *CEO*
EMP: 75
SQ FT: 1,800
SALES: 185K **Privately Held**
SIC: 4812 5999 7389 2759 Cellular telephone services; mobile telephones & equipment; telephone services; commercial printing

(G-1764)
ERVINS GROUP LLC (PA)
550 Hulet Dr Ste 103 (48302-0322)
PHONE.................................248 203-2000
Karol Ervins, *President*
EMP: 5
SQ FT: 30,000
SALES (est): 2.2MM **Privately Held**
SIC: 8742 3714 3429 Management consulting services; motor vehicle parts & accessories; manufactured hardware (general)

(G-1765)
EUTECTIC ENGINEERING CO INC
817 Rock Spring Rd (48304-3141)
PHONE.................................313 892-2248
Charles E Baer, *President*
Michael Eberle, *Vice Pres*
Maryanne Pruss, *Plant Mgr*
Dennis Arwood, *QC Mgr*
Donna Fuga, *CFO*
EMP: 32 **EST:** 1961
SQ FT: 50,000
SALES (est): 6.4MM **Privately Held**
SIC: 3341 3324 Secondary nonferrous metals; steel investment foundries

(G-1766)
FORTIS ENERGY SERVICES INC
36700 Woodward Ave # 107 (48304-0929)
PHONE.................................231 258-4596
George Molski, *Branch Mgr*
EMP: 32
SALES (corp-wide): 45.6MM **Privately Held**
SIC: 1381 3625 3621 Drilling oil & gas wells; noise control equipment; motors & generators
PA: Fortis Energy Services, Inc.
3001 W Big Beaver Rd # 525
Troy MI 48084
248 283-7100

(G-1767)
GEOFABRICA INC
1490 Lakewood Rd (48302-2751)
PHONE.................................810 728-2468
George Caravias, *Principal*
EMP: 4
SALES (est): 181.3K **Privately Held**
SIC: 3569 General industrial machinery

(G-1768)
GEORGIA WALKER & ASSOC INC
2306 Eastways Rd (48304-2400)
P.O. Box 2657, Birmingham (48012-2657)
PHONE.................................248 594-6447
Donald Graves III, *Principal*
EMP: 3
SALES (est): 170K **Privately Held**
SIC: 3842 Walkers

(G-1769)
GLAXOSMITHKLINE LLC
721 Parkman Dr (48304-2449)
PHONE.................................248 561-3022
EMP: 27
SALES (corp-wide): 39.5B **Privately Held**
SIC: 2834 Pharmaceutical preparations
HQ: Glaxosmithkline Llc
5 Crescent Dr
Philadelphia PA 19112
215 751-4000

(G-1770)
GLOBAL ELECTRONICS LIMITED
2075 Franklin Rd (48302-0303)
PHONE.................................248 353-0100
Michael M Bahn, *CEO*
Mary C Bahn, *President*
Robert Wiebe, *Vice Pres*
EMP: 39 **EST:** 1997
SALES (est): 7.7MM **Privately Held**
WEB: www.geltd.net
SIC: 3569 3825 Robots, assembly line: industrial & commercial; instruments to measure electricity

(G-1771)
HAARTZ CORPORATION
40950 Woodward Ave # 150 (48304-5125)
PHONE.................................248 646-8200
Tim Jackson, *Manager*
EMP: 6
SALES (corp-wide): 112MM **Privately Held**
WEB: www.haartz.com
SIC: 2295 5131 Resin or plastic coated fabrics; piece goods & notions
PA: The Haartz Corporation
87 Hayward Rd
Acton MA 01720
978 264-2600

(G-1772)
HAROLD G SCHAEVITZ INDS LLC
Also Called: Sensor Connection, The
42690 Woodward Ave # 200 (48304-5062)
PHONE.................................248 636-1515
Neill Murphy, *Technical Staff*
Harold Schaevitz,
EMP: 6
SALES (est): 468.5K **Privately Held**
SIC: 3699 Electrical equipment & supplies

(G-1773)
HIS & HER SELF DEFENSE
1945 Lone Pine Rd (48302-2522)
PHONE.................................248 767-9085
EMP: 3
SALES (est): 150.8K **Privately Held**
SIC: 3812 Defense systems & equipment

(G-1774)
HOUSE OF HERO LLC
7335 Deep Run Apt 513 (48301-3831)
PHONE.................................248 260-8300
Keith Young,
EMP: 5
SALES: 100K **Privately Held**
SIC: 2741 Miscellaneous publishing

(G-1775)
INTERNATIONAL BRANDS INC
3371 W Maple Rd (48301-3368)
PHONE.................................248 644-2701
Kevin Pattah, *Owner*
EMP: 3
SALES (est): 99.6K **Privately Held**
SIC: 2024 Ice cream & frozen desserts

GEOGRAPHIC SECTION
Bloomfield Hills - Oakland County (G-1806)

(G-1776)
LAKESIDE SOFTWARE INC (PA)
40950 Woodward Ave # 200 (48304-5127)
PHONE..................................248 686-1700
Michael Schumacher, *CEO*
Mike Klingbeil, *Engineer*
Benjamin Murphy, *Engineer*
David Donaldson, *Manager*
EMP: 30
SQ FT: 15,000
SALES (est): 9.8MM **Privately Held**
SIC: 7372 Business oriented computer software

(G-1777)
LIGHT METAL FORMING CORP
4397 Stony River Dr (48301-3652)
PHONE..................................248 851-3984
EMP: 17
SALES (est): 1.7MM **Privately Held**
SIC: 3086 Mfg Plastic Foam Products

(G-1778)
LOGAN MARKETING GROUP LLC
Also Called: Maestro Media Print Solutions
44 E Long Lake Rd Ste 400 (48304-2321)
PHONE..................................248 731-7650
Shaun Buss, *Administration*
EMP: 12
SALES (corp-wide): 45MM **Privately Held**
SIC: 7389 7331 2721 Printers' services: folding, collating; direct mail advertising services; mailing service; periodicals: periodicals: publishing & printing; magazines: publishing & printing
PA: Logan Marketing Group, Llc
  431 Yerkes Rd
  King Of Prussia PA 19406
  610 265-8210

(G-1779)
LSD INVESTMENTS INC
2350 Franklin Rd Ste 115 (48302-0337)
PHONE..................................248 333-9085
Chris Caswell, *Branch Mgr*
Marvin Schexnider, *Manager*
EMP: 4
SALES (corp-wide): 4MM **Privately Held**
SIC: 5211 2431 1751 Doors, storm: wood or metal; doors & door parts & trim, wood; window & door (prefabricated) installation
PA: Lsd Investments, Inc.
  3605 S Huron Rd
  Bay City MI
  989 684-9811

(G-1780)
MANN + HUMMEL USA INC
2285 Franklin Rd Ste 200 (48302-0325)
PHONE..................................248 857-8500
Rick Dishaw, *Branch Mgr*
EMP: 17
SALES (corp-wide): 4.5B **Privately Held**
SIC: 3089 3714 Injection molding of plastics; motor vehicle parts & accessories
HQ: Mann + Hummel Usa, Inc.
  6400 S Sprinkle Rd
  Portage MI 49002
  269 329-3900

(G-1781)
MEDICAL INFRMTICS SLUTIONS LLC
7285 Cathedral Dr (48301-3733)
PHONE..................................248 851-3124
Gerald W Brouhard, *President*
EMP: 4
SALES (est): 484.8K **Privately Held**
SIC: 8742 3825 Hospital & health services consultant; network analyzers

(G-1782)
MENDOZA ENTERPRISES
6905 Telegraph Rd Ste 117 (48301-3158)
P.O. Box 123, Northville (48167-0123)
PHONE..................................248 792-9120
Lisa Mendoza, *Owner*
EMP: 4
SALES (est): 482.1K **Privately Held**
SIC: 2752 Commercial printing, lithographic

(G-1783)
MICROMET CORP
3790 Burning Tree Dr (48302-1533)
PHONE..................................231 885-1047
Fax: 231 761-7106
EMP: 5
SQ FT: 2,000
SALES (est): 470K **Privately Held**
SIC: 3812 Mfg Search/Navigation Equipment

(G-1784)
MOORE FLAME CUTTING CO
1022 Top View Rd (48304-3160)
PHONE..................................586 978-1090
Gary Nadlicki, *President*
M Kathryn Finkbeiner-Nadlicki, *Corp Secy*
EMP: 57
SQ FT: 29,000
SALES (est): 7.5MM **Privately Held**
SIC: 3443 3441 Plate work for the metalworking trade; fabricated structural metal

(G-1785)
MUSEUM APPAREL
40750 Woodward Ave Unit 3 (48304-5113)
PHONE..................................248 644-2303
Renee Lalonde, *Principal*
EMP: 4
SALES (est): 286.8K **Privately Held**
SIC: 2389 Apparel & accessories

(G-1786)
N A VISSCHER-CARAVELLE INC
2525 S Telg Rd Ste 302 (48302)
PHONE..................................248 851-9800
Robert Meek, *President*
▲ **EMP:** 9
SALES: 13MM
SALES (corp-wide): 183.7K **Privately Held**
WEB: www.rdmeekco.com
SIC: 2273 Mats & matting
HQ: Visscher Caravelle Holding B.V.
  Sisalstraat 85
  Genemuiden 8281
  383 855-015

(G-1787)
O2/SPECIALTY MFG HOLDINGS LLC (PA)
40900 Woodward Ave # 130 (48304-5115)
PHONE..................................248 554-4228
EMP: 5
SALES (est): 15.9MM **Privately Held**
SIC: 3494 Holding Company For Valve Manufacturing Business

(G-1788)
PENSKE COMPANY LLC (HQ)
2555 S Telegraph Rd (48302-0974)
PHONE..................................248 648-2000
Jim Parsons, *General Mgr*
Roger S Penske, *Mng Member*
Terrie King, *Clerk*
▲ **EMP:** 1 **EST:** 2000
SALES: 246.9MM
SALES (corp-wide): 11.1B **Privately Held**
SIC: 3647 Vehicular lighting equipment
PA: Penske Corporation
  2555 S Telegraph Rd
  Bloomfield Hills MI 48302
  248 648-2000

(G-1789)
PENZO AMERICA INC
6335 Thorncrest Dr (48301-1710)
PHONE..................................248 723-0802
Penelope A Vincent, *President*
Gerardus B Norrdanus, *Vice Pres*
EMP: 4
SALES (est): 315.1K **Privately Held**
SIC: 3269 5023 Art & ornamental ware, pottery; pottery

(G-1790)
PERFECT EXPRESSIONS
3643 W Maple Rd (48301-3376)
PHONE..................................248 640-1287
Brian Klayman, *Principal*
EMP: 4
SALES (est): 402.2K **Privately Held**
SIC: 3949 Camping equipment & supplies

(G-1791)
PHYSICIANS COMPOUNDING PHRM
1900 S Telg Rd Ste 102 (48302)
PHONE..................................248 758-9100
Debbie Vinuya, *President*
Jerrin Raehtz, *Vice Pres*
EMP: 4
SALES (est): 750K **Privately Held**
SIC: 2834 Druggists' preparations (pharmaceuticals)

(G-1792)
PROTEIN PROCUREMENT SVCS INC (PA)
1750 S Telg Rd Ste 310 (48302)
PHONE..................................248 738-7970
Keith Jahnke, *CEO*
Claudia Hershey, *President*
Galina Martin, *Manager*
EMP: 5
SQ FT: 4,800
SALES (est): 43MM **Privately Held**
SIC: 2824 5147 Protein fibers; meats & meat products

(G-1793)
REKO INTERNATIONAL HOLDINGS (HQ)
6001 N Adams Rd Ste 251 (48304-1547)
PHONE..................................519 737-6974
Diane St John, *President*
EMP: 2
SALES (est): 8.7MM
SALES (corp-wide): 31.7MM **Privately Held**
SIC: 5084 3465 Industrial machinery & equipment; automotive stampings
PA: Reko International Group Inc
  469 Silver Creek Industrial Dr
  Windsor ON N8N 4
  519 727-3287

(G-1794)
RGI BRANDS LLC (PA)
Also Called: Dragon Bleu USA
3950 Wabeek Lake Dr E (48302-1262)
PHONE..................................312 253-7400
Jared Rapp, *Mng Member*
▲ **EMP:** 10
SQ FT: 14,000
SALES (est): 250K **Privately Held**
SIC: 2085 5182 Bourbon whiskey; vodka (alcoholic beverage); cocktails, alcoholic: premixed

(G-1795)
RIEKE-ARMINAK CORP
39400 Woodward Ave # 130 (48304-5150)
PHONE..................................248 631-5450
EMP: 7
SALES (est): 510K
SALES (corp-wide): 877.1MM **Publicly Held**
SIC: 3799 3714 Trailer hitches; motor vehicle parts & accessories
PA: Trimas Corporation
  38505 Woodward Ave # 200
  Bloomfield Hills MI 48304
  248 631-5450

(G-1796)
ROCK INDUSTRIES INC (PA)
Also Called: Rock Construction
6125 Old Orchard Dr (48301-1472)
PHONE..................................248 338-2800
Robert Bruza, *President*
EMP: 28
SQ FT: 15,000
SALES (est): 20MM **Privately Held**
WEB: www.rockconstruction.net
SIC: 1389 1799 5085 8741 Construction, repair & dismantling services; coating, caulking & weather, water & fireproofing; industrial supplies; construction management: institutional building construction

(G-1797)
SCHWARTZ PRECISION GEAR CO
38525 Woodward Ave # 2000 (48304-5011)
PHONE..................................586 754-4600
Jeffrey Myers, *Manager*
EMP: 21

SALES (est): 2.7MM **Privately Held**
SIC: 3462 Iron & steel forgings

(G-1798)
STAMPING GROUNDS INC (PA)
Also Called: Image Encore
6827 Crestway Dr (48301-2810)
PHONE..................................248 851-6764
Dorothy L Baccari, *President*
EMP: 3
SALES (est): 511.7K **Privately Held**
SIC: 3953 5999 Marking devices; rubber stamps

(G-1799)
SUGAR BUSH PRINTING INC
Also Called: Digital Media Solutions
281 Enterprise Ct Ste 100 (48302-0310)
PHONE..................................248 373-8888
Mark C Parent, *President*
EMP: 8
SQ FT: 6,400
SALES (est): 1.3MM **Privately Held**
WEB: www.sugarbushprinting.com
SIC: 2752 Commercial printing, offset

(G-1800)
SUPERIOR POLYOLEFIN FILMS INC
465 Fox River Dr (48304-1009)
PHONE..................................248 334-8074
Frank Baker Jr, *Partner*
Francis E Baker Sr, *Partner*
EMP: 5
SALES (est): 720K **Privately Held**
SIC: 2673 Plastic & pliofilm bags

(G-1801)
TEMPERFORM CORP
1975 Tuckaway Dr (48302-1779)
PHONE..................................248 851-9611
A Bartoletto, *Principal*
EMP: 4
SALES (est): 109.9K **Privately Held**
SIC: 3325 Steel foundries

(G-1802)
TESLIR LLC
100 W Long Lake Rd # 102 (48304-2772)
PHONE..................................248 644-5500
Paul Nine,
Douglas Miller,
EMP: 5 **EST:** 2012
SALES (est): 359.2K **Privately Held**
SIC: 3812 3674 Infrared object detection equipment; infrared sensors, solid state

(G-1803)
THIRD VAULT INC
7300 Deep Run Apt 1613 (48301-3822)
PHONE..................................248 353-5555
Gilbert Borman, *President*
EMP: 3
SALES (est): 130.5K **Privately Held**
SIC: 3571 Computers, digital, analog or hybrid

(G-1804)
TORENZO INC
6632 Telegraph Rd Ste 122 (48301-3012)
PHONE..................................313 732-7874
EMP: 10 **EST:** 2015
SQ FT: 600
SALES (est): 263.2K **Privately Held**
SIC: 7371 7372 7379 8748 Computer Programming Svc Prepackaged Software Svc Computer Related Svcs Business Consulting Svcs

(G-1805)
TOTAL TENNIS LLC
2519 W Maple Rd (48301-2750)
PHONE..................................248 594-1749
Karl Philip Woods, *Mng Member*
EMP: 6
SALES: 300K **Privately Held**
SIC: 3949 Strings, tennis racket

(G-1806)
TRIMAS COMPANY LLC (HQ)
39400 Woodward Ave # 130 (48304-5151)
PHONE..................................248 631-5450
Terry Collins, *President*
EMP: 15

Bloomfield Hills - Oakland County (G-1807)   GEOGRAPHIC SECTION

SALES (est): 8.3MM
SALES (corp-wide): 877.1MM **Publicly Held**
SIC: 3715 Truck trailers
PA: Trimas Corporation
38505 Woodward Ave # 200
Bloomfield Hills MI 48304
248 631-5450

(G-1807)
TRIMAS CORPORATION (PA)
38505 Woodward Ave # 200 (48304-5096)
PHONE................................248 631-5450
Samuel Valenti III, *Ch of Bd*
Thomas A Amanto, *President*
Paul A Swart, *Vice Pres*
Jan Van Dijk, *Vice Pres*
William Dickey, *VP Opers*
◆ EMP: 30
SALES: 877.1MM **Publicly Held**
WEB: www.trimascorp.com
SIC: 3799 3714 3443 2672 Trailer hitches; motor vehicle parts & accessories; trailer hitches, motor vehicle; fabricated plate work (boiler shop); drums, knockout (reflux, etc.): metal plate; cylinders, pressure: metal plate; tape, pressure sensitive: made from purchased materials; bolts, nuts, rivets & washers; bolts, metal; screws, metal; machine tool accessories; drills (machine tool accessories); milling cutters

(G-1808)
TRUSS DEVELOPMENT
1573 S Telegraph Rd (48302-0048)
PHONE................................248 624-8100
Basil Bacall, *Principal*
EMP: 6 EST: 2010
SALES (est): 764.6K **Privately Held**
SIC: 2439 Structural wood members

(G-1809)
UNGAR FROZEN FOOD PRODUCT
Also Called: Doctor Prager Sensible Foods
1556 Lone Pine Rd (48302-2639)
PHONE................................248 626-3148
Eva Freed, *Owner*
EMP: 3
SALES: 70K **Privately Held**
SIC: 5142 3497 Frozen vegetables & fruit products; foil containers for bakery goods & frozen foods

(G-1810)
WHEELHOUSE GRAPHIX LLC
445 Enterprise Ct (48302-0339)
PHONE................................800 732-0815
Shauna Ryder, *President*
EMP: 17
SQ FT: 9,057
SALES: 1,000K **Privately Held**
SIC: 3993 Signs, not made in custom sign painting shops

(G-1811)
WINDSONG MOBILE HOME
1750 S Telg Rd Ste 106 (48302)
PHONE................................248 758-2140
EMP: 3
SALES (est): 293.2K **Privately Held**
SIC: 2451 Mfg Mobile Homes

Bloomingdale
Van Buren County

(G-1812)
NATHAN SHETLER
Also Called: Northern Building Components
44815 County Rd Ste 388 (49026)
PHONE................................269 521-4554
Nathan Shetler, *Owner*
EMP: 10
SALES: 3MM **Privately Held**
SIC: 3448 Prefabricated metal buildings

(G-1813)
PATHWAY PUBLISHING CORPORATION (DH)
Also Called: Pathway Publishers
43632 County Road 390 (49026-8755)
PHONE................................269 521-3025
Lewis Lambright, *General Mgr*
Sarah Lambright, *Asst Mgr*
EMP: 4
SQ FT: 1,500
SALES: 332.7K
SALES (corp-wide): 646.8K **Privately Held**
SIC: 5963 5192 2721 Newspapers, home delivery, not by printers or publishers; books, periodicals & newspapers; comic books: publishing & printing
HQ: Pcm
P C M Pcm Pumps Delasco Foodys
Levallois-Perret 92300
177 683-100

(G-1814)
SOUTHWESTERN MICH DUST CTRL
110 E Spring St (49026-5109)
P.O. Box 152 (49026-0152)
PHONE................................269 521-7638
Lew Baron Page, *President*
Carrol Page, *Vice Pres*
EMP: 13
SQ FT: 1,800
SALES (est): 1.6MM **Privately Held**
WEB: www.lakesandcountry.com
SIC: 1611 1311 Highway & street maintenance; crude petroleum production

Boyne City
Charlevoix County

(G-1815)
ARETE INDUSTRIES INC
1 Altair Dr (49712-9618)
PHONE................................231 582-4470
Leon Tupper, *CEO*
Tom Monley, *President*
Michael Lange, *Vice Pres*
EMP: 10
SQ FT: 67,000
SALES (est): 1.4MM **Privately Held**
WEB: www.aretenorth.com
SIC: 3714 Motor vehicle parts & accessories

(G-1816)
BOYNE AREA WLDG & FABRICATION
1095 Dam Rd (49712-9613)
PHONE................................231 582-6078
Mike Markiewicz, *President*
EMP: 11
SALES (est): 220K **Privately Held**
SIC: 7692 Welding repair

(G-1817)
BOYNE CITY GAZETTE
5 W Main St Unit 7 (49712-3700)
PHONE................................231 582-2799
Chris Faulknor, *Principal*
EMP: 7
SALES (est): 485.7K **Privately Held**
SIC: 2711 Newspapers, publishing & printing

(G-1818)
BULMANN ENTERPRISES INC
Also Called: Bulmann Dock & Lift
175 Magnet Dr (49712-8117)
PHONE................................231 549-5020
Stephen Bulmann, *President*
Rebecca Bulmann, *Admin Sec*
EMP: 28 EST: 1998
SQ FT: 22,000
SALES: 2.5MM **Privately Held**
WEB: www.bulmanndock.com
SIC: 3536 Boat lifts

(G-1819)
CHRIS FAULKNOR
5 W Main St Unit 7 (49712-3700)
PHONE................................231 645-1970
Chris Faulknor, *Principal*
EMP: 3
SALES (est): 99.2K **Privately Held**
SIC: 2711 Newspapers

(G-1820)
CLASSIC INSTRUMENTS INC
826 Moll Dr (49712-8112)
P.O. Box 411 (49712-0411)
PHONE................................231 582-0461
Mike Stowe, *President*
John McLeod III, *General Mgr*
Devin Butterbrodt, *Engineer*
Jason Knight, *Engineer*
Bill Mullins, *Natl Sales Mgr*
▲ EMP: 9
SALES (est): 1.6MM **Privately Held**
WEB: www.classicinstruments.com
SIC: 3825 Instruments to measure electricity

(G-1821)
HARBOR HOUSE PUBLISHERS INC
221 Water St (49712-1801)
PHONE................................231 582-2814
Michelle Cortright, *President*
Diane Gemmell, *Accounts Mgr*
Pam Withorn, *Accounts Mgr*
Cassidy Shankleton, *Manager*
Leif Hanson, *Info Tech Dir*
EMP: 12
SALES (est): 1.5MM **Privately Held**
WEB: www.harborhouse.com
SIC: 2731 2721 Books: publishing only; magazines: publishing & printing; trade journals: publishing & printing

(G-1822)
HONEYWELL INTERNATIONAL INC
375 N Lake St (49712-1101)
PHONE................................231 582-5686
John Martenson, *Manager*
Rajani Gudipudi, *Senior Mgr*
EMP: 200
SALES (corp-wide): 41.8B **Publicly Held**
WEB: www.honeywell.com
SIC: 3728 3825 3823 3812 Aircraft parts & equipment; instruments to measure electricity; industrial instrmnts msrmnt display/control process variable; search & navigation equipment
PA: Honeywell International Inc.
300 S Tryon St
Charlotte NC 28202
973 455-2000

(G-1823)
INDUSTRIAL MAGNETICS INC (PA)
1385 S M 75 (49712-9689)
PHONE................................231 582-3100
Walter J Shear III, *CEO*
Robin Stanley, *CFO*
▲ EMP: 72 EST: 1961
SQ FT: 38,000
SALES (est): 28.1MM **Privately Held**
WEB: www.magnetics.com
SIC: 3499 Magnets, permanent: metallic

(G-1824)
J & J TRANSPORT LLC
4556 Lakeshore Rd (49712-9677)
PHONE................................231 582-6083
Joyce Raveau,
James Raveau,
EMP: 5
SALES: 327K **Privately Held**
SIC: 3537 Trucks: freight, baggage, etc.: industrial, except mining

(G-1825)
JERVIS B WEBB COMPANY
1254 Boyne Ave (49712-9699)
PHONE................................231 582-6558
Jim Izzard, *Branch Mgr*
EMP: 60
SQ FT: 73,600 **Privately Held**
WEB: www.jervisbwebb.com
SIC: 3444 3699 3535 Sheet metalwork; electrical equipment & supplies; conveyors & conveying equipment
HQ: Jervis B. Webb Company
30100 Cabot Dr
Novi MI 48377
248 553-1000

(G-1826)
KIRTLAND PRODUCTS LLC
1 Altair Dr (49712-9618)
PHONE................................231 582-7505
Leon Tupper, *Mng Member*
EMP: 12
SALES (est): 2MM **Privately Held**
SIC: 3484 Pellet & BB guns

(G-1827)
LEXAMAR CORPORATION
100 Lexamar Dr (49712-9799)
PHONE................................231 582-3163
Al Powers, *President*
Cheryl Savoix, *Traffic Mgr*
Sheila Bellant, *Buyer*
Craig Avery, *Engineer*
Rob Neumann, *Engineer*
EMP: 325
SQ FT: 85,000
SALES (est): 130MM
SALES (corp-wide): 40.8B **Privately Held**
WEB: www.lexamar.com
SIC: 3089 Injection molded finished plastic products
HQ: Magna Exteriors Of America, Inc.
750 Tower Dr
Troy MI 48098
248 631-1100

(G-1828)
MAGNETIC SYSTEMS INTL INC
Also Called: MSI
1095 Dam Rd (49712-9613)
PHONE................................231 582-9600
Michael Markiewicz, *President*
▲ EMP: 15
SQ FT: 27,000
SALES (est): 3.3MM **Privately Held**
SIC: 3499 Magnets, permanent: metallic

(G-1829)
MITCHELL COATES
5293 Korthase Rd (49712-9507)
PHONE................................231 582-5878
EMP: 52
SALES (est): 3.1MM **Privately Held**
SIC: 3949 Mfg Sporting/Athletic Goods

(G-1830)
MOUNT MFG LLC
200 Air Industrial Pk Dr (49712-9616)
PHONE................................231 487-2118
John Sanchez, *Principal*
Eric Lintula, *Principal*
EMP: 6
SALES (est): 240.2K **Privately Held**
SIC: 3999 Manufacturing industries

(G-1831)
OUTLINE INDUSTRIES LLC
Also Called: Torque-Tight
100 Industrial Parkway Dr (49712-9745)
PHONE................................303 632-6782
Jonathon Thompson, *Mng Member*
EMP: 3 EST: 2010
SALES: 275K **Privately Held**
SIC: 3531 Paving breakers

(G-1832)
PAINE PRESS LLC
209 S Lake St (49712-1398)
PHONE................................231 645-1970
Faulknor Christopher, *Principal*
EMP: 3
SALES (est): 263.8K **Privately Held**
SIC: 2741 Miscellaneous publishing

(G-1833)
PRECISION EDGE SRGCAL PDTS LLC
1448 Lexamar Dr (49712-9751)
PHONE................................231 459-4304
John Truckey, *President*
EMP: 127 **Privately Held**
SIC: 3841 Surgical & medical instruments
PA: Precision Edge Surgical Products Company Llc
415 W 12th Ave
Sault Sainte Marie MI 49783

(G-1834)
R B I MECHANICAL INC
204 Industrial Parkway Dr (49712-9616)
PHONE................................231 582-2970

▲ = Import ▼ = Export
◆ = Import/Export

GEOGRAPHIC SECTION

Dan Atkinson, *President*
Edward Robinson, *Vice Pres*
EMP: 20 **EST:** 1981
SQ FT: 3,000
SALES (est): 1.7MM **Privately Held**
WEB: www.uunet.com
SIC: 1711 3444 Ventilation & duct work contractor; sheet metalwork

(G-1835)
TEMPREL INC
206 Industrial Parkway Dr (49712-9616)
PHONE..................................231 582-6585
John R Bertsch, *President*
Steve Habitz, *Manager*
EMP: 25
SQ FT: 4,000
SALES (est): 4.6MM **Privately Held**
WEB: www.temprel.com
SIC: 3829 3823 3357 Thermocouples; industrial instrmnts msrmnt display/control process variable; nonferrous wiredrawing & insulating

(G-1836)
TRI-STATE CAST TECHNOLOGIES CO (PA)
926 N Lake St (49712-1185)
P.O. Box 230 (49712-0230)
PHONE..................................231 582-0452
J Andrew Darien, *President*
John Darien, *CFO*
EMP: 4 **EST:** 1978
SQ FT: 2,700
SALES: 3MM **Privately Held**
SIC: 3365 3599 Aluminum foundries; machine shop, jobbing & repair

(G-1837)
VAN DAM MARINE CO
Also Called: Van Dam Wood Craft
970 E Division St (49712-9609)
PHONE..................................231 582-2323
Stephen Van Dam, *President*
Jean Van Dam, *Treasurer*
Chad James, *Manager*
James Van Dam, *Admin Sec*
▲ **EMP:** 19
SQ FT: 96,000
SALES: 1.1MM **Privately Held**
SIC: 3732 4493 Boat building & repairing; boat yards, storage & incidental repair

(G-1838)
WOOD SHOP INC
111 N East St (49712-1213)
PHONE..................................231 582-9835
Bruce Janssen, *President*
EMP: 5
SALES (est): 420K **Privately Held**
SIC: 2499 Signboards, wood

Boyne Falls
Charlevoix County

(G-1839)
HEARTWOOD MILLS LLC
4740 Skop Rd Ste A (49713-9791)
PHONE..................................888 829-5909
Brad Baird, *Mng Member*
William Tudor,
▼ **EMP:** 12 **EST:** 2015
SALES: 1.7MM **Privately Held**
SIC: 2431 Millwork

(G-1840)
LOGGING LONG BRANCH
377 Swaybury Ln (49713-9785)
PHONE..................................231 549-3031
Rex Bannister, *Principal*
EMP: 3
SALES (est): 179K **Privately Held**
SIC: 2411 Logging camps & contractors

(G-1841)
MATELSKI LUMBER COMPANY
2617 M 75 S (49713-9793)
PHONE..................................231 549-2780
Edward Matelski Jr, *President*
George Matelski, *Treasurer*
Marjorie Matelski, *Admin Sec*
EMP: 45
SQ FT: 1,200

SALES (est): 6.6MM **Privately Held**
SIC: 2426 2448 Furniture dimension stock, hardwood; pallets, wood

(G-1842)
TOWN & COUNTRY CEDAR HOMES
Also Called: Town & Country Log Homes Mill
4740 Skop Rd (49713-9791)
PHONE..................................231 347-4360
Allen Maffey, *President*
EMP: 8
SALES (corp-wide): 17.2MM **Privately Held**
WEB: www.cedarhomes.net
SIC: 2421 3444 2431 Sawmills & planing mills, general; sheet metalwork; millwork
PA: Town & Country Cedar Homes Inc
4772 Us Highway 131
Petoskey MI
231 347-4360

Breckenridge
Gratiot County

(G-1843)
INTEGRITY FAB & MACHINE INC
150 Enterprise Dr (48615-8724)
P.O. Box 456 (48615-0456)
PHONE..................................989 481-3200
Kirk Smith, *President*
Leo Kennedy, *Engineer*
Tyler Gulick, *Sales Associate*
Brent Calkins, *Supervisor*
Jessica Colthorp, *Clerk*
EMP: 11 **EST:** 2007
SQ FT: 15,000
SALES (est): 2.9MM **Privately Held**
SIC: 7692 3544 Welding repair; special dies, tools, jigs & fixtures

(G-1844)
NUTRIEN AG SOLUTIONS INC
8263 N Ransom Rd (48615)
P.O. Box 157 (48615-0157)
PHONE..................................989 842-1185
Jeff Schulz, *Manager*
EMP: 9 **Privately Held**
WEB: www.cropproductionservices.com
SIC: 2875 4221 4813 Fertilizers, mixing only; bean elevator; grain elevator, storage only;
HQ: Nutrien Ag Solutions, Inc.
3005 Rocky Mountain Ave
Loveland CO 80538
970 685-3300

(G-1845)
ORACLE BREWING COMPANY LLC
1411 W Pine River Rd (48615-9622)
PHONE..................................989 401-7446
Christopher Younk,
EMP: 4
SALES (est): 106.5K **Privately Held**
SIC: 5813 2082 5921 5181 Bars & lounges; ale (alcoholic beverage); beer (alcoholic beverage); beer (packaged); beer & ale

(G-1846)
SAGINAW VALLEY SHOPPER INC
221 E Saginaw St (48615-2511)
P.O. Box 185 (48615-0185)
PHONE..................................989 842-3164
Edward L Belles, *President*
Edward Belles, *President*
Gloria Belles, *Corp Secy*
EMP: 3 **EST:** 1948
SQ FT: 3,200
SALES (est): 290.5K **Privately Held**
SIC: 2741 Shopping news: publishing & printing

Brethren
Manistee County

(G-1847)
TRACY WILK
Also Called: Northwoods Products
15840 Dickson Rd (49619-9739)
PHONE..................................231 477-5135
Tracy Wilks, *Owner*
Clyde Wilks, *Project Mgr*
EMP: 3
SQ FT: 700
SALES (est): 343.6K **Privately Held**
SIC: 3449 Miscellaneous metalwork

Bridgeport
Saginaw County

(G-1848)
AMIGO MOBILITY INTL INC (PA)
6693 Dixie Hwy (48722-9725)
PHONE..................................989 777-0910
Beth L Thieme, *CEO*
Tim Drumhiller, *President*
Al Thieme, *Chairman*
Jess Butler, *Purchasing*
Mike Henris, *Engineer*
◆ **EMP:** 66
SQ FT: 62,700
SALES (est): 15MM **Privately Held**
WEB: www.amigoscooters.com
SIC: 3842 3441 Wheelchairs; fabricated structural metal

(G-1849)
AREA CYCLE INC
7482 Dixie Hwy (48722-9716)
PHONE..................................989 777-0850
Kenneth Leaym, *President*
Larry Leaym, *Treasurer*
Williams Sims, *Manager*
EMP: 3
SQ FT: 4,000
SALES (est): 270K **Privately Held**
SIC: 5571 7699 7513 5261 Motorcycle parts & accessories; motorcycle repair service; truck rental & leasing, no drivers; lawnmowers & tractors; engines, gasoline; saws & sawing equipment

(G-1850)
BRIDGEPORT MANUFACTURING INC
6689 Dixie Hwy (48722-9725)
PHONE..................................989 777-4314
Mel Shepard, *President*
Nancy Shepard, *Vice Pres*
Benjamin Bussinger, *Manager*
EMP: 4
SQ FT: 2,200
SALES (est): 572.8K **Privately Held**
WEB: www.myamigo.com
SIC: 3441 3599 Fabricated structural metal; machine shop, jobbing & repair

(G-1851)
COOPER GLOVE AND SAFETY LLC
6100 Onyx Rd (48722-9518)
PHONE..................................706 512-0486
Traci Loy, *Principal*
EMP: 4
SALES (est): 350.9K **Privately Held**
SIC: 3842 Gloves, safety

(G-1852)
GREAT LAKES GAUGE COMPANY
6950 Junction Rd (48722-9776)
PHONE..................................989 652-6136
Clint Bucholz, *General Mgr*
EMP: 16
SALES (est): 3.1MM **Privately Held**
SIC: 3443 Cooling towers, metal plate

(G-1853)
MCLEOD WOOD AND CHRISTMAS PDTS
6794 Dixie Hwy (48722-9701)
PHONE..................................989 777-4800
Charles G McLeod, *President*
Michaelene McLeod, *Vice Pres*
EMP: 3
SQ FT: 5,000
SALES (est): 321.2K **Privately Held**
SIC: 2426 3999 5999 Flooring, hardwood; novelties, bric-a-brac & hobby kits; Christmas lights & decorations

(G-1854)
NORTHFIELD BLOCK COMPANY
6045 Dixie Hwy (48722-9507)
PHONE..................................989 777-2575
Dan Meiser, *Branch Mgr*
EMP: 5
SALES (corp-wide): 30.6B **Privately Held**
SIC: 3272 Concrete products
HQ: Northfield Block Company
1 Hunt Ct
Mundelein IL 60060
847 816-9000

(G-1855)
ORCHID ORTHPD SOLUTIONS LLC
6688 Dixie Hwy (48722-9725)
PHONE..................................989 746-0780
Mike Barker, *Project Mgr*
Brenda Wood, *Controller*
Kim Brabant, *Sales Staff*
Barry Torrey, *Manager*
Allison Monroe, *Consultant*
EMP: 16
SALES (corp-wide): 319MM **Privately Held**
SIC: 3841 Surgical & medical instruments
HQ: Orchid Orthopedic Solutions Llc
1489 Cedar St
Holt MI 48842
517 694-2300

(G-1856)
SIGNATURE SIGNS INC
6578 Dixie Hwy (48722-9622)
PHONE..................................989 777-8701
Angela Thayer, *President*
EMP: 4
SALES (est): 275K **Privately Held**
SIC: 3993 Signs & advertising specialties

(G-1857)
SPX CORPORATION
6950 Junction Rd (48722-9776)
PHONE..................................989 652-6136
Gerald M Yuba, *Manager*
EMP: 65
SALES (corp-wide): 1.5B **Publicly Held**
WEB: www.spx.com
SIC: 3443 Cooling towers, metal plate
PA: Spx Corporation
13320a Balntyn Corp Pl
Charlotte NC 28277
980 474-3700

(G-1858)
STONEY CREST REGRIND SERVICE
6243 Dixie Hwy (48722-9513)
PHONE..................................989 777-7190
George Clauss III, *President*
EMP: 10
SQ FT: 4,800
SALES (est): 1.4MM **Privately Held**
WEB: www.stoneycrest.com
SIC: 3545 3599 3541 Cutting tools for machine tools; machine shop, jobbing & repair; machine tools, metal cutting type

Bridgman
Berrien County

(G-1859)
APOLLO SEIKO LTD
3969 Lemon Creek Rd (49106-9503)
PHONE..................................269 465-3400
Rick G Schiffer, *CEO*
EMP: 12

Bridgman - Berrien County (G-1860)

SALES (est): 2.3MM **Privately Held**
WEB: www.apolloseiko.com
SIC: 3549 Assembly machines, including robotic

(G-1860)
ART/FX SIGN CO
9751 Red Arrow Hwy (49106-9710)
P.O. Box 695 (49106-0695)
PHONE.................................269 465-5706
Doyle Rogers, *Owner*
EMP: 4
SALES (est): 373.1K **Privately Held**
SIC: 3993 Signs, not made in custom sign painting shops

(G-1861)
CHI CO/TABOR HILL WINERY
Also Called: Tabor Hill Champagne Cellar
10243 Red Arrow Hwy (49106)
PHONE.................................269 465-6566
David Upton, *President*
EMP: 3
SALES (corp-wide): 6.3MM **Privately Held**
WEB: www.taborhill.com
SIC: 2084 Wines
PA: Chi Co/Tabor Hill Winery
　　185 Mount Tabor Rd
　　Buchanan MI 49107
　　269 422-1161

(G-1862)
D & F MOLD LLC
8088 Jericho Rd (49106-9519)
PHONE.................................269 465-6633
Gary Zech, *Design Engr*
Ed Lowe, *Sales Engr*
Richard Lockman,
EMP: 15
SQ FT: 10,000
SALES: 1MM **Privately Held**
SIC: 3544 Special dies & tools

(G-1863)
GAL GAGE CO
2953 Hinchman Rd (49106-9501)
P.O. Box 218, Stevensville (49127-0218)
PHONE.................................269 465-5750
Goodwin A Lycan, *President*
Isabella Valadez, *Principal*
Mark Raines, *VP Admin*
Dieter Timm, *Vice Pres*
Sue Wolfram, *Sales Executive*
EMP: 20 EST: 1975
SQ FT: 5,000
SALES (est): 3.5MM **Privately Held**
WEB: www.galgage.com
SIC: 3545 3548 3429 3325 Gauges (machine tool accessories); welding & cutting apparatus & accessories; manufactured hardware (general); steel foundries

(G-1864)
GREAT LAKES METAL STAMPING INC
4607 Rambo Rd (49106-8700)
PHONE.................................269 465-4415
Keith Hettig, *President*
Tim Eisengruber, *Plant Mgr*
Scott Ross, *Opers Staff*
Ben McGarvey, *Production*
Jim Porch, *Purch Dir*
▲ EMP: 26
SQ FT: 38,000
SALES (est): 10.1MM **Privately Held**
SIC: 3469 Stamping metal for the trade

(G-1865)
GREAT LAKES STAIR & CASE CO
9155 Gast Rd (49106-9378)
PHONE.................................269 465-3777
Howard Klotz, *President*
Jim Woodsen, *Admin Sec*
EMP: 7
SQ FT: 7,500
SALES: 400K **Privately Held**
SIC: 2431 Staircases & stairs, wood; doors, wood

(G-1866)
HANSON SYSTEMS LLC
Also Called: EAGLE TECHNOLOGIES GROUP
9850 Red Arrow Hwy (49106-9000)
PHONE.................................269 465-6986
Michael Koziel, *President*
Jason Cleveland, *President*
Dan Kuntz, *General Mgr*
Jay Craig, *Exec VP*
Brandon Fuller, *Senior VP*
▲ EMP: 250
SQ FT: 255,000
SALES: 80.9MM **Privately Held**
WEB: www.weldun.com
SIC: 3569 Assembly machines, non-metalworking

(G-1867)
INDUSTRIAL FABRICATION LLC
9550 Mathieu St (49106-9575)
P.O. Box 458 (49106-0458)
PHONE.................................269 465-5960
Rodney Ross, *Purchasing*
Ronald Mikesell,
Jason Ross,
EMP: 35
SQ FT: 50,000
SALES (est): 7.6MM **Privately Held**
SIC: 3441 Fabricated structural metal

(G-1868)
KATAI MACHINE SHOP
8632 Jericho Rd (49106-9518)
PHONE.................................269 465-6051
EMP: 15 EST: 1967
SQ FT: 1,200
SALES (est): 1.2MM **Privately Held**
SIC: 3544 Mfg Dies/Tools/Jigs/Fixtures

(G-1869)
KRUGER PLASTIC PRODUCTS LLC (PA)
Also Called: Springboard Manufacturing
4015 Lemon Creek Rd (49106-9503)
P.O. Box 895 (49106-0895)
PHONE.................................269 465-6404
Douglas Constable, *President*
Louis Manetti, *CFO*
EMP: 2
SALES: 10.1MM **Privately Held**
SIC: 3089 Injection molding of plastics

(G-1870)
LAZY BALLERINA WINERY LLC
4209 Lake St (49106-9113)
PHONE.................................269 759-8486
Melanie Owen, *Branch Mgr*
EMP: 12
SALES (corp-wide): 1MM **Privately Held**
SIC: 2084 Wines
PA: Lazy Ballerina Winery Llc
　　315 State St
　　Saint Joseph MI 49085
　　269 363-6218

(G-1871)
M & M DIE CAST INC
8556 Gast Rd (49106-9504)
P.O. Box 751 (49106-0751)
PHONE.................................269 465-6206
Rita Jones, *President*
Michael R Jones, *Vice Pres*
Michael Oman, *Vice Pres*
Jody Fairchild, *Office Mgr*
▼ EMP: 28
SQ FT: 30,000
SALES (est): 3.5MM **Privately Held**
SIC: 3363 Aluminum die-castings

(G-1872)
PRATT INDUSTRIES INC
11365 Red Arrow Hwy (49106-9757)
PHONE.................................269 465-7676
Brian McPheely, *CEO*
Anthony Pratt, *Ch of Bd*
William F Pratt, *President*
David Dennis, *COO*
Cathy Foley, *Vice Pres*
▲ EMP: 60
SQ FT: 1,500
SALES (est): 21.3MM **Privately Held**
WEB: www.prattindustries.net
SIC: 3715 Truck trailer chassis

(G-1873)
ROBERT BOSCH LLC
Bosch Packing Technology Div
9890 Red Arrow Hwy (49106-9001)
P.O. Box 579 (49106-0579)
PHONE.................................616 466-4063
Jones Paruch, *Branch Mgr*
EMP: 75
SALES (corp-wide): 294.8MM **Privately Held**
WEB: www.boschservice.com
SIC: 3565 Packaging machinery
HQ: Robert Bosch Llc
　　2800 S 25th Ave
　　Broadview IL 60155
　　248 876-1000

(G-1874)
ST JOE TOOL CO
11521 Red Arrow Hwy (49106)
P.O. Box 158, Sawyer (49125-0158)
PHONE.................................269 426-4300
Henry Braddock, *President*
Rose Braddock, *Vice Pres*
Portia Haber, *CFO*
EMP: 27
SQ FT: 25,000
SALES (est): 6MM **Privately Held**
SIC: 3451 Screw machine products

Brighton
Livingston County

(G-1875)
A-1 ENGRAVING & SIGNS INC
397 Washington St Ste A (48116-1482)
PHONE.................................810 231-2227
Geoff Boltach, *President*
Trevor McElroy, *Vice Pres*
EMP: 4
SQ FT: 1,200
SALES (est): 389.7K **Privately Held**
SIC: 2796 3993 Engraving on copper, steel, wood or rubber: printing plates; signs & advertising specialties

(G-1876)
AACCESS ENTERTAINMENT
11552 Eagle Way (48114-9019)
PHONE.................................734 260-1002
Brub Zamarron, *Owner*
EMP: 4
SALES (est): 252.1K **Privately Held**
SIC: 3669 Communications equipment

(G-1877)
ACTION TOOL & MACHINE INC
5976 Ford Ct (48116-8511)
PHONE.................................810 229-6300
San Miyamoto, *President*
Debra Cubr, *Controller*
Debra Eddie, *Officer*
EMP: 28
SQ FT: 14,000
SALES (est): 5.6MM **Privately Held**
WEB: www.actiontoolmachine.com
SIC: 3544 3545 3599 Special dies & tools; cutting tools for machine tools; machine shop, jobbing & repair

(G-1878)
AEROSPOKE INCORPORATED
5034 Walnut Hills Dr (48116-8880)
PHONE.................................248 685-9009
EMP: 6
SQ FT: 8,400
SALES (est): 1MM **Privately Held**
SIC: 3751 5941 Motorcycles, Bicycles, And Parts, Nsk

(G-1879)
AFTERMARKET INDUSTRIES LLC
315 E Main St (48116-1613)
PHONE.................................810 229-3200
Dana Kraft, *Vice Pres*
Scott Kraft, *Mng Member*
EMP: 8
SALES (est): 1.1MM **Privately Held**
SIC: 3999 Atomizers, toiletry

(G-1880)
AIRMAN INC
6150 Whitmore Lake Rd (48116-1926)
PHONE.................................248 960-1354
Stephen Burke, *President*
Jeremy O'Neil, *Vice Pres*
EMP: 36
SQ FT: 17,000
SALES (est): 11.3MM **Privately Held**
WEB: www.airmaninc.com
SIC: 3999 3492 Atomizers, toiletry; control valves, aircraft: hydraulic & pneumatic

(G-1881)
AIRMAN PRODUCTS LLC
6150 Whitmore Lake Rd (48116-1926)
PHONE.................................248 960-1354
Krissa Corkins,
▲ EMP: 45
SALES (est): 3.3MM **Privately Held**
SIC: 3492 3593 Control valves, fluid power: hydraulic & pneumatic; fluid power actuators, hydraulic or pneumatic

(G-1882)
AJAX MATERIALS CORPORATION
Also Called: Ajax Paving Industries
7329 Kensington Rd (48116)
PHONE.................................248 244-3445
Craig Turnupceed, *Manager*
EMP: 12
SQ FT: 720
SALES (corp-wide): 301.7MM **Privately Held**
SIC: 2951 3531 Asphalt & asphaltic paving mixtures (not from refineries); asphalt plant, including gravel-mix type
HQ: Ajax Materials Corporation
　　1957 Crooks Rd A
　　Troy MI 48084
　　248 244-3300

(G-1883)
ALLOR MANUFACTURING INC
Also Called: Plesh Industries
12534 Emerson Dr (48116-8437)
P.O. Box 1540 (48116-5340)
PHONE.................................248 486-4500
Frederick M Allor, *President*
James J Newbold, *Corp Secy*
Bernard J Wendt, *Vice Pres*
▲ EMP: 100 EST: 1972
SQ FT: 25,000
SALES (est): 28.6MM **Privately Held**
WEB: www.allor.com
SIC: 3462 3568 3535 3444 Chains, forged steel; power transmission equipment; conveyors & conveying equipment; sheet metalwork; fabricated structural metal

(G-1884)
AMERICAN COMPOUNDING SPC LLC
Also Called: ACS
9984 Borderline Dr (48116-2082)
PHONE.................................810 227-3500
Dave Donie, *Mng Member*
EMP: 60
SALES (est): 5.4MM
SALES (corp-wide): 1.9MM **Privately Held**
SIC: 2821 Thermoplastic materials
HQ: Ravago Americas Llc
　　1900 Summit Tower Blvd
　　Orlando FL 32810
　　407 875-9595

(G-1885)
AMPHENOL T&M ANTENNAS INC
Also Called: Amphenol Saa
7117 Fieldcrest Dr (48116-8607)
PHONE.................................847 478-5600
Craig Lampo, *CFO*
EMP: 5
SALES (corp-wide): 8.2B **Publicly Held**
SIC: 3663 Antennas, transmitting & communications
HQ: Amphenol T&M Antennas, Inc.
　　100 Tri State Intl # 255
　　Lincolnshire IL 60069
　　847 478-5600

(G-1886)
APPLIED INSTRUMENTS COMPANY
Also Called: Plasti-Co Equipment Co
37 Summit St (48116-1834)
PHONE.................................810 227-5510
Robert W Limbright, *President*
Carol Limbright, *Corp Secy*
Wayne Limbright, *Vice Pres*
Mike Ervin, *Sales Mgr*
Abby Collett, *Sales Staff*
▲ **EMP:** 26 **EST:** 1974
SQ FT: 11,000
SALES (est): 5.9MM **Privately Held**
WEB: www.aicequipment.com
SIC: 7699 5084 3559 3452 Professional instrument repair services; controlling instruments & accessories; plastics working machinery; bolts, nuts, rivets & washers

(G-1887)
ASPEN TECHNOLOGIES INC (PA)
7963 Lochlin Dr (48116-8329)
PHONE.................................248 446-1485
Kyle Richardson, *Principal*
Dan Knezevich, *Principal*
Sam Provencher, *Info Tech Dir*
▲ **EMP:** 63
SALES (est): 18MM **Privately Held**
SIC: 3086 Plastics foam products

(G-1888)
BALOGH TAG INC
3637 S Old Us Highway 23 (48114-7668)
PHONE.................................248 486-7343
Joseph Tomashik, *CEO*
Etienne Balogh, *CEO*
EMP: 5
SQ FT: 8,400
SALES (est): 4.3MM **Privately Held**
SIC: 5084 5063 3625 Instruments & control equipment; time switches; electric controls & control accessories, industrial

(G-1889)
BEST SELF STORAGE
7286 Grand River Rd (48114-7329)
PHONE.................................810 227-7050
Steve Krause, *Branch Mgr*
EMP: 6 **Privately Held**
WEB: www.beststorageintown.com
SIC: 2511 Storage chests, household: wood
PA: Best Self Storage
700 N Old Us Highway 23
Brighton MI 48114

(G-1890)
BRIGHTON LABORATORIES INC
11871 Grand River Rd (48116-9618)
PHONE.................................810 225-9520
Gregory Yates, *President*
Casey Yates, *Materials Mgr*
Denny Baker, *Engineer*
EMP: 10
SQ FT: 35,000
SALES (est): 5MM **Privately Held**
WEB: www.brightonlabs.com
SIC: 2899 Chemical preparations

(G-1891)
BUY BEST MANUFACTURING LLC
988 Rickett Rd Ste B (48116-1828)
PHONE.................................248 875-2491
Clifton Mahathey,
EMP: 10
SALES: 500K **Privately Held**
SIC: 3444 Sheet metalwork

(G-1892)
BWI CHASSIS DYNAMICS NA INC (DH)
12501 Grand River Rd (48116-8389)
PHONE.................................937 455-5308
Zijian Zhao, *Admin Sec*
EMP: 2
SALES (est): 8.1MM
SALES (corp-wide): 7.3MM **Privately Held**
SIC: 3714 Motor vehicle parts & accessories
HQ: Bwi (Shanghai) Co., Ltd.
No.68, Debao Road, Pudong New Area
Shanghai 20013
215 057-4610

(G-1893)
BWI NORTH AMERICA INC
Also Called: Brighton Technical Center
12501 Grand River Rd (48116-8389)
PHONE.................................810 494-4584
Matt Henry, *Principal*
John Pepple, *Accounts Mgr*
EMP: 130
SALES (corp-wide): 7.3MM **Privately Held**
SIC: 3714 8734 8731 Motor vehicle parts & accessories; testing laboratories; commercial physical research
HQ: Bwi North America Inc.
3100 Res Blvd Ste 240
Kettering OH 45420

(G-1894)
C & B MACHINERY COMPANY
7771 Lochlin Dr (48116-8329)
PHONE.................................734 462-0600
Joseph C Parker, *CEO*
Jeffrey Allen, *President*
Jason White, *Project Mgr*
Bruce Mazurowski, *Mfg Mgr*
Matt Warstler, *Engineer*
▲ **EMP:** 33
SQ FT: 30,000
SALES: 12MM **Privately Held**
SIC: 3541 7699 7629 3531 Grinding machines, metalworking; industrial machinery & equipment repair; electrical repair shops; crushers, grinders & similar equipment

(G-1895)
C & C SPORTS INC
8090 Grand River Rd (48114-9372)
PHONE.................................810 227-7068
William Piggins, *President*
EMP: 27
SQ FT: 9,000
SALES (est): 8.2MM **Privately Held**
WEB: www.ccsport.com
SIC: 5571 5599 5261 5551 Motorcycles; motorcycle parts & accessories; snowmobiles; lawnmowers & tractors; motor boat dealers; motorcycle repair service; snowmobile repair; lawn mower repair shop; boat repair; boat building & repairing

(G-1896)
CAILLAU USA INC
7000 Kensington Rd (48116-8334)
PHONE.................................248 446-1900
Pierre Andre Fernandez, *President*
Martine Boucton, *Vice Pres*
Laurent Chapdelaine, *Vice Pres*
EMP: 6
SQ FT: 6,000
SALES: 2MM
SALES (corp-wide): 83.5K **Privately Held**
SIC: 3429 Metal fasteners
HQ: Caillau
Etablissements Caillau Ets Caillau
Issy-Les-Moulineaux 92130
145 299-300

(G-1897)
CARL ZEISS INDUS METROLOGY LLC
6826 Kensington Rd (48116-8513)
PHONE.................................248 486-2670
Jeff O'Brien, *Facilities Mgr*
Brett Labadie, *Manager*
EMP: 40
SALES (corp-wide): 449.3K **Privately Held**
SIC: 3827 Optical instruments & lenses
HQ: Carl Zeiss Industrial Metrology, Llc
6250 Sycamore Ln N
Maple Grove MN 55369

(G-1898)
CARL ZEISS MICROSCOPY LLC
6826 Kensington Rd (48116-8513)
PHONE.................................248 486-7600
Madhav Jha, *Sales Mgr*
Bill Bell, *Branch Mgr*
Phadhavee Chiakchai, *Manager*
Michael Kambeitz, *Manager*
EMP: 11
SALES (corp-wide): 449.3K **Privately Held**
SIC: 3826 Microscopes, electron & proton
HQ: Carl Zeiss Nts, Llc
1 Corporate Pl Ste 3
Peabody MA 01960

(G-1899)
CE II HOLDINGS INC
12866 Sutherland Rd (48116-8515)
PHONE.................................248 305-7700
Robert H Edwards, *President*
Joseph C Cherup, *Vice Pres*
▲ **EMP:** 15
SQ FT: 7,800
SALES (est): 3.5MM **Privately Held**
WEB: www.custom-electric.com
SIC: 3567 Industrial furnaces & ovens

(G-1900)
COMBAT ACTION LLC
4124 Deeside Dr (48116-8000)
PHONE.................................810 772-3758
Jon Ford, *Manager*
EMP: 3
SALES (est): 217.6K **Privately Held**
SIC: 3484 3699 Small arms; electronic training devices

(G-1901)
CONATUS INC
9933 Weber St Ste B (48116-1900)
PHONE.................................810 494-6210
Daniel Confer, *President*
Debra Confer, *Shareholder*
▲ **EMP:** 3
SQ FT: 3,300
SALES (est): 100K **Privately Held**
WEB: www.conatus-inc.com
SIC: 3589 5013 Automotive parts, plastic; automotive supplies

(G-1902)
COR-MET INC
12500 Grand River Rd (48116-8326)
PHONE.................................810 227-0004
J Peter Kiilunen, *President*
David Kiilunen, *Vice Pres*
Mary Kiilunen, *Treasurer*
Scott Frasso, *Sales Staff*
◆ **EMP:** 35
SQ FT: 111,000
SALES (est): 9.1MM **Privately Held**
WEB: www.cor-met.com
SIC: 3496 3548 Miscellaneous fabricated wire products; welding wire, bare & coated

(G-1903)
CORNELL PUBLICATIONS LLC
11075 Shadywood Dr (48114-9248)
PHONE.................................810 225-3075
Abigail Mouat, *Principal*
EMP: 4 **EST:** 2009
SALES (est): 262.9K **Privately Held**
SIC: 2741 Miscellaneous publishing

(G-1904)
CORRIGAN ENTERPRISES INC
775 N 2nd St (48116-1218)
PHONE.................................810 229-6323
Michael B Corrigan, *CEO*
EMP: 50
SALES (est): 1.8MM **Privately Held**
SIC: 2911 Oils, fuel

(G-1905)
CORTAR LASER AND FAB LLC
12828 Emerson Dr (48116-8560)
PHONE.................................248 446-1110
Livia Walker,
Robert Boroniec,
EMP: 4
SQ FT: 16,000
SALES (est): 619.7K **Privately Held**
SIC: 3699 Laser systems & equipment

(G-1906)
COXEN ENTERPRISES INC
12785 Emerson Dr (48116-8562)
PHONE.................................248 486-3800
Mike Lamarra, *President*
◆ **EMP:** 90 **EST:** 1937
SQ FT: 140,000
SALES (est): 49.6MM
SALES (corp-wide): 255MM **Privately Held**
WEB: www.excelda.com
SIC: 2992 7389 2842 Lubricating oils & greases; packaging & labeling services; specialty cleaning, polishes & sanitation goods
PA: Kem Krest Llc
3221 Magnum Dr
Elkhart IN 46516
574 389-2650

(G-1907)
CRAIG C ASKINS
Also Called: Lane Gainer Sports Co
6172 Winans Dr (48116-5122)
P.O. Box 130462, Ann Arbor (48113-0462)
PHONE.................................810 231-4340
Craig C Askins, *Owner*
EMP: 3
SALES (est): 181.2K **Privately Held**
WEB: www.lanegainer.com
SIC: 3949 Water sports equipment

(G-1908)
DAKKOTA INTEGRATED SYSTEMS LLC (PA)
123 Brighton Lake Rd # 202 (48116-6773)
PHONE.................................517 694-6500
Andra Rush, *Chairman*
David Wojie, *Business Mgr*
Peter Goguen, *COO*
Mark McCauley, *COO*
Mark Kelly, *Plant Mgr*
▲ **EMP:** 297
SALES (est): 242.2MM **Privately Held**
SIC: 3711 Automobile assembly, including specialty automobiles

(G-1909)
DATA ACQUISITION CTRL SYSTEMS
7965 Kensington Ct Ste A2 (48116-6808)
PHONE.................................248 437-6096
Peter Collins, *President*
Pete Collins, *Owner*
EMP: 12
SQ FT: 5,000
SALES (est): 2MM **Privately Held**
SIC: 8711 3625 Consulting engineer; electric controls & control accessories, industrial

(G-1910)
DE LUXE DIE SET INC
5939 Ford Ct (48116-8511)
PHONE.................................810 227-2556
Bill L Andersen, *President*
Eileen K Andersen, *Vice Pres*
EMP: 6
SQ FT: 20,000
SALES (est): 839K **Privately Held**
SIC: 3544 3312 Die sets for metal stamping (presses); plate, steel

(G-1911)
DISPENSE TECHNOLOGIES LLC
7036 Kensington Rd (48116-8334)
P.O. Box 1108 (48116-2708)
PHONE.................................248 486-6244
Mark D Perry, *Mng Member*
Michelle Perry,
EMP: 8
SQ FT: 10,000
SALES (est): 1.6MM **Privately Held**
WEB: www.dispensetech.com
SIC: 3586 3569 Measuring & dispensing pumps; liquid automation machinery & equipment

(G-1912)
DR SCHNEIDER AUTO SYSTEMS INC
716 Advance St Ste A (48116-2925)
PHONE.................................270 858-5400
EMP: 4
SALES (corp-wide): 524MM **Privately Held**
SIC: 3089 Mfg Plastic Products
HQ: Dr. Schneider Automotive Systems, Inc.
223 Progress Dr
Russell Springs KY 42642
270 858-5400

Brighton - Livingston County (G-1913) GEOGRAPHIC SECTION

(G-1913)
DUNNAGE ENGINEERING INC (PA)
721 Advance St (48116-1292)
PHONE.....................................810 229-9501
David Joseph, *President*
Richard Amatucci, *Purchasing*
Janet A Joseph, *Treasurer*
Jim Banish, *Manager*
▲ EMP: 50
SQ FT: 36,000
SALES (est): 9MM **Privately Held**
WEB: www.dunnage-eng.com
SIC: 3089 3479 3441 Injection molding of plastics; coating of metals with plastic or resins; fabricated structural metal

(G-1914)
E B I INC
10454 Grand River Rd (48116-6524)
PHONE.....................................810 227-8180
John C Rogers, *President*
James E Rogers, *Vice Pres*
Robert Rogers, *Vice Pres*
William C Rogers, *Treasurer*
EMP: 5
SALES (est): 492.9K **Privately Held**
SIC: 2452 Modular homes, prefabricated, wood

(G-1915)
EBERSPAECHER NORTH AMERICA INC
2035 Orndorf Dr (48116-2398)
PHONE.....................................810 225-4582
Dennis Berry, *Branch Mgr*
EMP: 240
SALES (corp-wide): 5.2B **Privately Held**
WEB: www.eberspacher.com
SIC: 3559 Automotive related machinery
HQ: Eberspaecher North America, Inc.
29101 Haggerty Rd
Novi MI 48377
248 994-7010

(G-1916)
EBERSPECHER CONTRLS N AMER INC
2035 Charles Orndorf Dr (48116)
PHONE.....................................248 994-7010
Massimo Venturi, *President*
EMP: 3
SQ FT: 200
SALES (est): 120.4K
SALES (corp-wide): 5.2B **Privately Held**
SIC: 3714 8711 Motor vehicle electrical equipment; electrical or electronic engineering
HQ: Eberspacher Climate Control Systems Gmbh & Co. Kg
Eberspacherstr. 24
Esslingen Am Neckar 73730
711 939-00

(G-1917)
EBINGER MANUFACTURING COMPANY
Also Called: Jets Glove Manufacturing
7869 Kensington Rd (48116)
PHONE.....................................248 486-8880
Janny Lu, *President*
◆ EMP: 15
SQ FT: 42,000
SALES: 22MM **Privately Held**
WEB: www.ebinger-mfg.com
SIC: 3965 3999 5084 Fasteners, glove; atomizers, toiletry; machine tools & accessories

(G-1918)
ENER2 LLC
7685 Athlone Dr (48116-8847)
PHONE.....................................248 842-2662
George Moser,
EMP: 12
SALES (est): 1.1MM **Privately Held**
SIC: 3511 Turbines & turbine generator sets

(G-1919)
ENGRAVERS JOURNAL
10087 Spencer Rd (48114-7524)
P.O. Box 318 (48116-0318)
PHONE.....................................810 229-5725
James J Farrell, *President*

Michael J Davis, *President*
Michael Davis, *Treasurer*
EMP: 3 EST: 1975
SALES (est): 260K **Privately Held**
WEB: www.engraversjournal.com
SIC: 2721 Trade journals: publishing & printing

(G-1920)
EXPORT CORPORATION
6060 Whitmore Lake Rd (48116-1941)
PHONE.....................................810 227-6153
Donald Peitz, *President*
David Peitz, *Vice Pres*
Tim Spickler, *Vice Pres*
Robert McLane, *VP Opers*
Jeff Rauch, *Purch Mgr*
▲ EMP: 51 EST: 1972
SQ FT: 175,000
SALES (est): 26.3MM **Privately Held**
WEB: www.exportcorporation.com
SIC: 2441 4783 Nailed wood boxes & shook; packing goods for shipping

(G-1921)
FARR & FARON ASSOCIATES INC
136 E Grand River Ave 3 (48116-1510)
PHONE.....................................810 229-7730
Walter J Faron, *CEO*
Ryan Faron, *Vice Pres*
EMP: 3 EST: 1980
SALES: 3MM **Privately Held**
SIC: 3699 Electronic training devices

(G-1922)
FEDERAL SCREW WORKS
Also Called: Novex Tool Division
77 Advance St (48116)
PHONE.....................................810 227-7712
Jeffrey Harness, *Sales & Mktg St*
EMP: 45
SALES (corp-wide): 2.4K **Privately Held**
WEB: www.federalscrew.com
SIC: 3451 3544 Screw machine products; special dies, tools, jigs & fixtures
PA: Federal Screw Works
34846 Goddard Rd
Romulus MI 48174
734 941-4211

(G-1923)
FLARETITE INC
7723 Kensington Ct (48116-8391)
P.O. Box 130, Fenton (48430-0130)
PHONE.....................................810 750-4140
Norm Mathers, *President*
Kirk Smith, *Marketing Staff*
EMP: 8
SQ FT: 2,500
SALES: 1MM **Privately Held**
SIC: 3491 5085 Industrial valves; gaskets & seals
PA: Flaretite Pty Ltd
4 Forte Ct
Bridgeman Downs QLD

(G-1924)
FLEXDEX INC
10421 Citation Dr Ste 900 (48116-6558)
PHONE.....................................810 522-9009
Clark Barousse, *President*
Randall Sullivan, *COO*
Kin Cheung, *Vice Pres*
Eugene Thomas, *Sales Staff*
Gregory Bowles, *Chief Mktg Ofcr*
EMP: 12
SALES (est): 382.9K **Privately Held**
SIC: 3841 Surgical & medical instruments

(G-1925)
FORTECH PRODUCTS INC
7600 Kensington Ct (48116-8392)
PHONE.....................................248 446-9500
Creighton E Forester, *President*
Luis Madeleno, *COO*
Jim McCrate, *Opers Mgr*
Debbie Roberts, *Manager*
▲ EMP: 30
SQ FT: 40,000
SALES (est): 11.8MM **Privately Held**
WEB: www.fortechproducts.com
SIC: 2992 2911 Lubricating oils & greases; fuel additives; fractionation products of crude petroleum, hydrocarbons

(G-1926)
FREEDOM TECHNOLOGIES CORP (PA)
10559 Citation Dr Ste 205 (48116-6546)
PHONE.....................................810 227-3737
Rodney Aldrich, *CEO*
Brad Aldrich, *Ch of Bd*
Rick Scorey, *President*
Sue Aldrich,
EMP: 30
SQ FT: 6,400
SALES (est): 4.9MM **Privately Held**
WEB: www.freedomcorp.com
SIC: 7373 3575 5045 Computer integrated systems design; computer terminals, monitors & components; computers, peripherals & software

(G-1927)
GARBAGE MAN LLC
5441 Ethel St (48116-1907)
P.O. Box 573 (48116-0573)
PHONE.....................................810 225-3001
Josh Tinsley, *Mng Member*
EMP: 4
SALES (est): 200K **Privately Held**
SIC: 3589 7389 Garbage disposers & compactors, commercial;

(G-1928)
GD ENTERPRISES LLC
7974 Lochlin Dr Ste B4 (48116-1664)
PHONE.....................................248 486-9800
Ron Gardner,
EMP: 6
SALES (est): 1MM **Privately Held**
SIC: 3559 Automotive related machinery

(G-1929)
GENERAL CHEMICAL CORPORATION
12336 Emerson Dr (48116-8343)
PHONE.....................................248 587-5600
Manesh Shah, *CEO*
Mehul Shah, *Vice Pres*
Kim Boyer,
◆ EMP: 9
SQ FT: 98,000
SALES (est): 2.8MM **Privately Held**
WEB: www.generalchem.com
SIC: 2851 2899 Paint removers; metal treating compounds; fluxes: brazing, soldering, galvanizing & welding; rust resisting compounds

(G-1930)
GENERAL MACHINE & BORING INC
5983 Ford Ct (48116-8511)
PHONE.....................................810 220-1203
Allen Kastl Jr, *President*
Jerry Brown, *Manager*
EMP: 9
SALES (est): 1.1MM **Privately Held**
SIC: 3599 Machine shop, jobbing & repair

(G-1931)
GKI FOODS LLC
Also Called: Granola Kitchens
7926 Lochlin Dr (48116-8329)
PHONE.....................................248 486-0055
Manny Zapata, *President*
Carl Myers, *Corp Secy*
Chris Keating, *Vice Pres*
Michelle Smith, *Sales Mgr*
EMP: 100 EST: 1974
SQ FT: 65,000
SALES (est): 27.8MM **Privately Held**
WEB: www.gkifoods.com
SIC: 2064 Candy & other confectionery products
PA: Central Investment Llc
7265 Kenwood Rd Ste 240
Cincinnati OH 45236

(G-1932)
GOOD SENSE COFFEE LLC
7931 State St (48116-1346)
PHONE.....................................810 355-2349
Ian Boyle,
EMP: 7

SALES (est): 118.2K **Privately Held**
SIC: 5812 2095 5149 Coffee shop; coffee roasting (except by wholesale grocers); coffee, green or roasted

(G-1933)
GRAPHIC ART SERVICE & SUPPLY
Also Called: Graphics Arts Service & Supply
1343 Rickett Rd (48116-1879)
PHONE.....................................810 229-4700
Steve Tubergen, *President*
EMP: 5
SALES (corp-wide): 4.5MM **Privately Held**
WEB: www.gasupply.com
SIC: 5084 3554 7699 Printing trades machinery, equipment & supplies; cutting machines, paper; knife, saw & tool sharpening & repair
PA: Graphic Arts Service And Supply, Inc.
3933 S Greenbrooke Dr Se
Grand Rapids MI 49512
616 698-9300

(G-1934)
GREEN OAK TOOL AND SVCS INC
9449 Maltby Rd (48116-1665)
PHONE.....................................586 531-2255
Henry W Dodson III, *Principal*
EMP: 4
SALES (est): 330.3K **Privately Held**
SIC: 3542 3545 Arbor presses; presses: forming, stamping, punching, sizing (machine tools); die casting machines; machine tool accessories; machine tool attachments & accessories; tools & accessories for machine tools

(G-1935)
GUIDOBONO CONCRETE INC
7474 Whitmore Lake Rd (48116-8536)
PHONE.....................................810 229-2666
John Guidobono II, *President*
John Anthony Guidobono Jr, *Vice Pres*
EMP: 14
SQ FT: 3,000
SALES (est): 1.9MM **Privately Held**
SIC: 3273 5211 Ready-mixed concrete; concrete & cinder block

(G-1936)
GUYS TIMING INC
Also Called: Schill U.S.
7044 Winding Trl (48116-9163)
PHONE.....................................517 404-3746
James E Karnes, *President*
▲ EMP: 3
SALES (est): 576K **Privately Held**
SIC: 5088 3949 Ships; team sports equipment

(G-1937)
H H BARNUM CO
12865 Silver Lake Rd (48116-8516)
PHONE.....................................248 486-5982
EMP: 5
SALES (corp-wide): 72.8MM **Privately Held**
SIC: 3613 Regulators, power
PA: H. H. Barnum Co.
7915 Lochlin Dr
Brighton MI 48116
248 486-7300

(G-1938)
HELLNER & ASSOCIATES INC
2233 Euler Rd (48114-7411)
PHONE.....................................810 220-3472
Robert Hellner, *President*
Linda Hellner, *Business Mgr*
EMP: 7
SQ FT: 3,000
SALES: 700K **Privately Held**
SIC: 3842 Prosthetic appliances

(G-1939)
HOFFMANN FILTER CORPORATION (PA)
7627 Kensington Ct (48116-8392)
PHONE.....................................248 486-8430
Georg Hoffmann, *CEO*
Detlef Mieth, *President*
Anna Mieth, *Regional Mgr*

GEOGRAPHIC SECTION   Brighton - Livingston County (G-1967)

Bianca Gansler, *Project Mgr*
Alex Herrera, *Manager*
▲ **EMP:** 15
SQ FT: 30,000
SALES (est): 2.8MM **Privately Held**
WEB: www.hoffmanfilter.com
SIC: 3569 5084 Filters, general line: industrial; industrial machinery & equipment

(G-1940)
HORN CORP
Also Called: Eclipse Tanning
2169 Corlett Rd (48114-8100)
PHONE..................................248 358-8883
Matthew Horn, *President*
EMP: 4
SALES (est): 151.3K **Privately Held**
SIC: 7299 3111 Tanning salon; leather tanning & finishing

(G-1941)
HOWELL MACHINE PRODUCTS INC
6265 Grand River Rd # 100 (48114-5303)
PHONE..................................517 546-0580
Irene C Vogt, *President*
Robert Vogt Jr, *Corp Secy*
Ronald Vogt, *Vice Pres*
EMP: 16
SQ FT: 1,000
SALES (est): 1.4MM **Privately Held**
WEB: www.hmpinc.com
SIC: 3599 Machine shop, jobbing & repair

(G-1942)
HUG-A-PLUG INC
2332 Pine Hollow Trl (48114-4900)
P.O. Box 2190 (48116-5990)
PHONE..................................810 626-1224
Robert Green, *President*
Carol Green, *Manager*
EMP: 5
SALES (est): 300K **Privately Held**
SIC: 3643 7389 Plugs, electric;

(G-1943)
INNOVATIVE PHARMACEUTICALS
2250 Genoa Business Park (48114-7371)
PHONE..................................248 789-0999
Xhesika Tasi, *Principal*
EMP: 7
SALES (est): 1.1MM **Privately Held**
SIC: 2834 Pharmaceutical preparations

(G-1944)
J & J LAMINATE CONNECTION INC
10603 Grand River Rd (48114-9609)
PHONE..................................810 227-1824
Jim Roy, *President*
John Roy, *Vice Pres*
EMP: 4
SQ FT: 1,200
SALES (est): 200K **Privately Held**
SIC: 2541 1799 Counter & sink tops; kitchen & bathroom remodeling

(G-1945)
KADIA INC
8020 Kensington Ct (48116-8520)
PHONE..................................248 446-1970
Gerhard Klein, *President*
Dennis L Tanis, *Vice Pres*
▲ **EMP:** 2
SALES (est): 5.8MM
SALES (corp-wide): 2.6MM **Privately Held**
SIC: 3541 Machine tools, metal cutting type
HQ: Kadia Produktion GmbH + Co.
Fabrikstr. 2
Nurtingen 72622
702 260-060

(G-1946)
KARMS LLC
1279 Rickett Rd (48116-1832)
PHONE..................................810 229-0829
Bruce Lavalley,
Steven E March,
EMP: 3
SALES (est): 153.9K **Privately Held**
WEB: www.marchcoatings.com
SIC: 2269 Finishing plants

(G-1947)
L & J PRODUCTS K HUNTINGTON
9954 Weber St (48116-1939)
PHONE..................................810 919-3550
Kim Huntington, *Owner*
EMP: 3 **EST:** 2011
SALES (est): 196.9K **Privately Held**
SIC: 2099 Food preparations

(G-1948)
L A BURNHART INC (PA)
2095 Euler Rd (48114-6816)
PHONE..................................810 227-4567
Gar Boling, *President*
EMP: 2
SQ FT: 14,000
SALES (est): 2MM **Privately Held**
SIC: 3498 3599 Tube fabricating (contract bending & shaping); boiler tube cleaners

(G-1949)
LA GOLD MINE INC
Also Called: Continental Diamond
425 W Main St (48116-1484)
PHONE..................................517 540-1050
Andre Duscio, *President*
EMP: 5
SQ FT: 1,600
SALES (est): 437.9K **Privately Held**
SIC: 5944 3911 Jewelry, precious stones & precious metals; jewelry apparel

(G-1950)
LADDERTECH LLC
7081 Dan Mcguire Dr (48116-8532)
PHONE..................................248 437-7100
Anette Gaines, *President*
EMP: 10
SALES (est): 1.2MM **Privately Held**
SIC: 3499 Metal ladders

(G-1951)
LIVINGSTON COUNTY CONCRETE INC
550 N Old Us Highway 23 (48114-7632)
PHONE..................................810 632-3030
Mike Horan, *President*
Ron Lammy, *Vice Pres*
Eric Taylor, *Manager*
EMP: 14
SQ FT: 7,500
SALES (est): 2.8MM **Privately Held**
SIC: 3273 3271 Ready-mixed concrete; blocks, concrete: landscape or retaining wall

(G-1952)
LOWRY HOLDING COMPANY INC (PA)
Also Called: Lowry Solutions
9420 Maltby Rd (48116-8801)
PHONE..................................810 229-7200
Michael Lowry, *CEO*
Steven R Lowry, *Exec VP*
Denis Bishop, *Vice Pres*
Jeffrey Polly, *Vice Pres*
Kathe Copeland, *Opers Staff*
◆ **EMP:** 135
SALES (est): 107.5MM **Privately Held**
WEB: www.lowrycomputer.com
SIC: 5045 2672 8742 7373 Computers, peripherals & software; coated & laminated paper; management consulting services; systems integration services; office equipment; computer & software stores

(G-1953)
MARCH COATINGS INC (PA)
160 Summit St (48116-2413)
PHONE..................................810 229-6464
Steven E March, *CEO*
Bruce La Valley, *President*
Janie Thayer, *Human Res Mgr*
EMP: 80
SQ FT: 93,000
SALES (est): 12.3MM **Privately Held**
SIC: 3479 7389 Painting of metal products; packaging & labeling services

(G-1954)
MARCIE ELECTRIC INC
8190 Boardwalk Rd Ste B (48116-8100)
PHONE..................................248 486-1200

Mark Marcie, *President*
EMP: 5
SQ FT: 3,600
SALES (est): 1.1MM **Privately Held**
SIC: 3612 Control transformers

(G-1955)
MATRIX ENGINEERING INC
8830 Whitmore Lake Rd (48116-8325)
PHONE..................................810 231-0212
Ralph Nalepa, *Treasurer*
EMP: 9
SQ FT: 5,600
SALES (est): 490K **Privately Held**
SIC: 3544 Special dies & tools

(G-1956)
MAXIM INTEGRATED PRODUCTS INC
10355 Citation Dr Ste 100 (48116-6578)
PHONE..................................408 601-1000
Dale Schacht, *Branch Mgr*
EMP: 5
SALES (corp-wide): 2.3B **Publicly Held**
WEB: www.maxim-ic.com
SIC: 3674 Microcircuits, integrated (semiconductor)
PA: Maxim Integrated Products, Inc.
160 Rio Robles
San Jose CA 95134
408 601-1000

(G-1957)
MC GUIRE SPRING CORPORATION
6135 Grand River Rd (48114-9329)
PHONE..................................517 546-7311
Robert Puste, *President*
Andrea Puste, *Vice Pres*
Aaren Schwanitz, *Admin Sec*
EMP: 6
SALES (est): 905K **Privately Held**
SIC: 3495 Wire springs

(G-1958)
MCS CONSULTANTS INC
1347 Rickett Rd (48116-1879)
PHONE..................................810 229-4222
Dale Swystun, *President*
Buell Cash, *Vice Pres*
EMP: 13
SQ FT: 7,650
SALES (est): 1.4MM **Privately Held**
WEB: www.medicalcomfort.com
SIC: 3069 5047 Medical sundries, rubber; medical & hospital equipment

(G-1959)
MICHIGAN DEBURRING TOOL LLC
2155 Pless Dr Ste B (48114-5306)
PHONE..................................810 227-1000
Brandon Dix, *Plant Mgr*
Jim Robinson,
EMP: 3 **EST:** 2012
SALES (est): 362.6K **Privately Held**
SIC: 3546 Power-driven handtools

(G-1960)
MICRO GAUGE INC
7350 Kensington Rd (48116-8354)
PHONE..................................248 446-3720
Jim Rourke, *Principal*
EMP: 190
SQ FT: 8,700
SALES (est): 20.6MM
SALES (corp-wide): 2.5B **Publicly Held**
SIC: 3599 Machine shop, jobbing & repair
HQ: Mueller Brass Co.
8285 Tournament Dr # 150
Memphis TN 38125
901 753-3200

(G-1961)
MICROGAUGE MACHINING INC
7350 Kensington Rd (48116-8354)
PHONE..................................248 446-3720
James Skivington, *President*
EMP: 140
SQ FT: 10,000
SALES (est): 12.5MM
SALES (corp-wide): 2.5B **Publicly Held**
WEB: www.muellerbrass.com
SIC: 3465 Body parts, automobile: stamped metal

HQ: Mueller Brass Co.
8285 Tournament Dr # 150
Memphis TN 38125
901 753-3200

(G-1962)
MID AMERICAN AEL LLC
1375 Rickett Rd (48116-2227)
PHONE..................................810 229-5483
Craig Trojan,
EMP: 6
SALES (est): 721.4K **Privately Held**
SIC: 3647 Vehicular lighting equipment

(G-1963)
MOHR ENGINEERING INC
1351 Rickett Rd (48116-2227)
P.O. Box 779 (48116-0779)
PHONE..................................810 227-4598
David R McDowell, *President*
Glen Howard, *Vice Pres*
EMP: 25
SQ FT: 30,000
SALES (est): 6.3MM **Privately Held**
SIC: 3089 3451 Injection molded finished plastic products; screw machine products

(G-1964)
MUELLER INDUSTRIES INC
7350 Kensington Rd (48116-8354)
PHONE..................................248 446-3720
Lisa Lee, *Manager*
EMP: 64
SALES (corp-wide): 2.5B **Publicly Held**
SIC: 3351 3463 3494 3089 Copper & copper alloy pipe & tube; pipe, brass & bronze; tubing, copper & copper alloy; extruded shapes, copper & copper alloy; nonferrous forgings; aluminum forgings; valves & pipe fittings; plumbing & heating valves; fittings for pipe, plastic
PA: Mueller Industries, Inc.
150 Schilling Blvd # 100
Collierville TN 38017
901 753-3200

(G-1965)
N C BRIGHTON MACHINE CORP
7300 Whitmore Lake Rd (48116-8558)
PHONE..................................810 227-6190
Jack Clausnitzer, *President*
Bill Barton, *Principal*
Karl Barton, *Principal*
Tim Clausnitzer, *Principal*
Shirley Barton, *CFO*
▲ **EMP:** 140 **EST:** 1965
SQ FT: 200,000
SALES (est): 30.8MM **Privately Held**
WEB: www.brightonnc.com
SIC: 3599 Machine shop, jobbing & repair

(G-1966)
NATIONAL ELEMENT INC
7939 Lochlin Dr (48116-8329)
PHONE..................................248 486-1810
Lauren S Best, *President*
Jim Vance, *Purch Mgr*
Robert J Stevenson, *Treasurer*
Brian Aubert, *Info Tech Dir*
Patricia Best, *Director*
EMP: 30
SQ FT: 30,000
SALES (est): 7.2MM **Privately Held**
WEB: www.nationalelement.com
SIC: 3567 3568 3535 8748 Heating units & devices, industrial: electric; drives, chains & sprockets; drives: belt, cable or rope; belt conveyor systems, general industrial use; systems analysis or design; electric housewares & fans

(G-1967)
NEW ECHELON DIRECT MKTG LLC
Also Called: Ne - Direct
9825 Lyon Dr (48114-7556)
PHONE..................................248 809-2485
Michael C Arnold,
Yvonne Arnold,
EMP: 3
SALES: 2.2MM **Privately Held**
SIC: 7331 2759 7389 7374 Mailing service; commercial printing; design services; data processing service

Brighton - Livingston County (G-1968) — GEOGRAPHIC SECTION

(G-1968)
NIKON METROLOGY INC (DH)
12701 Grand River Rd (48116-8506)
PHONE.................810 220-4360
Kenji Yoshikawa, *CEO*
Ken Waterfield, *General Mgr*
Hideaki Okamoto, *Managing Dir*
Alex Lucas, *Business Mgr*
Sarah Jagenow, *Buyer*
◆ **EMP:** 166
SQ FT: 100,000
SALES (est): 28.4MM **Privately Held**
SIC: 3829 Meteorological instruments
HQ: Nikon Metrology
Geldenaaksebaan 329
Leuven 3001
167 401-01

(G-1969)
NIKON METROLOGY INC
12589 Grand River Rd (48116-8390)
PHONE.................810 220-4347
EMP: 3 **Privately Held**
SIC: 3829 Measuring & controlling devices
HQ: Nikon Metrology, Inc.
12701 Grand River Rd
Brighton MI 48116
810 220-4360

(G-1970)
NOVI PRECISION PRODUCTS INC
11777 Grand River Rd (48116-9617)
PHONE.................810 227-1024
Ronald Karaisz II, *President*
John Goit, *President*
James Reichel, *Vice Pres*
Jim Nagle, *Plant Mgr*
Tim Hohl, *Project Mgr*
▲ **EMP:** 24
SQ FT: 36,000
SALES (est): 6.7MM **Privately Held**
WEB: www.noviprecision.com
SIC: 3549 3544 Assembly machines, including robotic; special dies, tools, jigs & fixtures

(G-1971)
NOVI SPRING INC
7735 Boardwalk Rd (48116-8521)
PHONE.................248 486-4220
Jason Johnson, *President*
Sean Johnson, *President*
Kevin Howkins, *Vice Pres*
Kevin Hawkins, *Mfg Mgr*
Monica Darin, *Purchasing*
▲ **EMP:** 17
SQ FT: 30,000
SALES (est): 4.1MM **Privately Held**
WEB: www.novispring.com
SIC: 3493 Steel springs, except wire

(G-1972)
PACKAGE DESIGN & MFG INC (PA)
Also Called: PDM
12424 Emerson Dr (48116-8343)
P.O. Box 596, Whitmore Lake (48189-0596)
PHONE.................248 486-4390
David Rosser, *President*
Brian Pazolka, *Production*
Nick Ruitenberg, *CFO*
Dan Brown, *Controller*
Kevin Dabrowski, *Manager*
EMP: 50
SQ FT: 26,000
SALES (est): 11.8MM **Privately Held**
WEB: www.packdm.com
SIC: 2621 3053 3086 2821 Wrapping & packaging papers; packing materials; plastics foam products; plastics materials & resins

(G-1973)
PACKAGING ENGINEERING LLC
Also Called: Packaging Engineering-Brighton
7138 Kensington Rd (48116-8335)
PHONE.................248 437-9444
James Rittmueller,
Jim Lantis,
Andy Wowianko,
EMP: 7

SALES (est): 1.5MM **Privately Held**
WEB: www.performpack.com
SIC: 3086 Packaging & shipping materials, foamed plastic

(G-1974)
PATRICK WYMAN
Also Called: Freedom Dental
7892 Winfield Dr (48116-1791)
PHONE.................810 227-2199
EMP: 3 **EST:** 1997
SQ FT: 1,250
SALES: 595K **Privately Held**
SIC: 3843 Dental Equipment And Supplies

(G-1975)
PDQ INK INC
Also Called: Big PDQ
7475 Grand River Rd (48114-9374)
PHONE.................810 229-2989
Kirt Albrecht, *President*
Tammy Albrecht, *Owner*
James McKechnie, *Graphic Designe*
EMP: 12
SQ FT: 7,000
SALES (est): 2MM **Privately Held**
WEB: www.bigpdq.com
SIC: 2752 7334 Commercial printing, offset; blueprinting service

(G-1976)
PEAKER SERVICES INC
8080 Kensington Ct (48116-8591)
PHONE.................248 437-4174
Ian Bradbury, *President*
Richard R Steele, *Chairman*
William Craft, *Vice Pres*
Rose Mary Stornes, *Manager*
Richard Marsh, *Admin Sec*
▲ **EMP:** 72
SQ FT: 37,000
SALES (est): 332.1K
SALES (corp-wide): 11.4MM **Privately Held**
WEB: www.peaker.com
SIC: 7699 3519 3743 3823 Engine repair & replacement, non-automotive; diesel engine rebuilding; streetcars & car equipment; industrial instrmnts msrmnt display/control process variable; relays & industrial controls
PA: Psi Holding Company
8080 Kensington Ct
Brighton MI 48116
248 437-4174

(G-1977)
PENCHURA LLC
889 S Old Us 23 (48114-7684)
PHONE.................810 229-6245
Leslie Stempek, *Bookkeeper*
Jennifer Kopplin, *Marketing Mgr*
Eric Sheffer, *Mng Member*
EMP: 10
SQ FT: 2,000
SALES: 5MM **Privately Held**
SIC: 5941 3949 Playground equipment; playground equipment

(G-1978)
PETERSEN PRODUCTS INC
7915 Kensington Ct (48116-8597)
PHONE.................248 446-0500
Peter Lyders, *President*
EMP: 11
SQ FT: 10,500
SALES (est): 2MM **Privately Held**
SIC: 3089 Injection molded finished plastic products; boxes, plastic

(G-1979)
PLESH INDUSTRIES INC (PA)
12534 Emerson Dr (48116-8437)
PHONE.................716 873-4916
Ronald Plesh, *President*
EMP: 10 **EST:** 1969
SQ FT: 130,000
SALES (est): 2.8MM **Privately Held**
WEB: www.plesh.com
SIC: 3462 3599 3443 Chains, forged steel; machine shop, jobbing & repair; liners/lining

(G-1980)
PRO LIGHTING GROUP INC
Also Called: Prolighting
716 Advance St Ste A (48116-2925)
PHONE.................810 229-5600
Paul Kluska, *President*
Gary Bonk, *VP Sales*
▼ **EMP:** 7
SALES: 4MM **Privately Held**
SIC: 3646 Commercial indusl & institutional electric lighting fixtures

(G-1981)
PROMESS INC (PA)
Also Called: Promess Dimensions
11429 Grand River Rd (48116-9615)
P.O. Box 748 (48116-0748)
PHONE.................810 229-9334
Larry E Stockline, *CEO*
Glenn Nausley, *Vice Pres*
Scott Spencer, *Engineer*
Andy Joseph, *Director*
Kurt Delanoy, *Administration*
EMP: 124
SQ FT: 50,000
SALES (est): 25.2MM **Privately Held**
WEB: www.promessinc.com
SIC: 3829 Fatigue testing machines, industrial: mechanical

(G-1982)
PSI HOLDING COMPANY (PA)
Also Called: Peaker Services
8080 Kensington Ct (48116-8520)
PHONE.................248 437-4174
Richard R Steele, *CEO*
Kurt Ulbick, *Sales Mgr*
Ben Wagner, *Technician*
▲ **EMP:** 75
SQ FT: 45,500
SALES (est): 11.4MM **Privately Held**
SIC: 7699 3519 Engine repair & replacement, non-automotive; diesel engine rebuilding

(G-1983)
R F M INCORPORATED
2001 Orndorf Dr (48116-2398)
PHONE.................810 229-4567
Motoharu Yamamoto, *President*
Rudolf F Meffert, *Vice Pres*
▲ **EMP:** 15
SQ FT: 8,000
SALES (est): 3MM **Privately Held**
SIC: 3541 3599 Machine tools, metal cutting type; machine shop, jobbing & repair
HQ: Mitsubishi Materials Usa Corp
11250 Slater Ave
Fountain Valley CA 92708
714 352-6100

(G-1984)
RECYCLEDLPS COM
6320 Superior Dr (48116-9584)
PHONE.................810 623-4498
Wendy Roberts, *Administration*
EMP: 3 **EST:** 2010
SALES (est): 165.8K **Privately Held**
SIC: 3999 Framed artwork

(G-1985)
REFRIGERATION RESEARCH INC (PA)
Also Called: Solar Research Division
525 N 5th St (48116-1293)
P.O. Box 869 (48116-0869)
PHONE.................810 227-1151
Edward Bottum Jr, *President*
Tim Abramson, *Vice Pres*
Gladys L Bottum, *Vice Pres*
Mike Ramalia, *Vice Pres*
Nancy B Ramalia, *Vice Pres*
EMP: 80 **EST:** 1944
SQ FT: 60,000
SALES (est): 11.6MM **Privately Held**
WEB: www.refresearch.com
SIC: 3433 3585 3443 Solar heaters & collectors; refrigeration equipment, complete; heat pumps, electric; fabricated plate work (boiler shop)

(G-1986)
ROBERTSON-STEWART INC
1351 Rickett Rd (48116-2227)
P.O. Box 690 (48116-0690)
PHONE.................810 227-4500

Glenn Howard, *President*
David R Mc Dowell, *Vice Pres*
EMP: 15
SQ FT: 11,000
SALES (est): 2MM **Privately Held**
SIC: 3714 Motor vehicle parts & accessories

(G-1987)
RYSON TUBE INC
2095 Euler Rd (48114-6816)
PHONE.................810 227-4567
Gar Boling, *President*
EMP: 10
SQ FT: 15,000
SALES: 1MM
SALES (corp-wide): 2MM **Privately Held**
SIC: 3498 7692 Tube fabricating (contract bending & shaping); welding repair
PA: L A Burnhart Inc
2095 Euler Rd
Brighton MI 48114
810 227-4567

(G-1988)
SERMA COAT LLC
1279 Rickett Rd (48116-1832)
PHONE.................810 229-0829
Steve March, *Mng Member*
▲ **EMP:** 10
SQ FT: 25,000
SALES (est): 1.4MM **Privately Held**
SIC: 3479 Coating of metals & formed products

(G-1989)
SHARP INDUSTRIES INCORPORATED
5975 Ford Ct (48116-8511)
PHONE.................810 229-6305
Dennis Robson, *President*
EMP: 7
SQ FT: 1,500
SALES: 500K **Privately Held**
SIC: 3469 Machine parts, stamped or pressed metal

(G-1990)
SIGN A RAMA INC
Also Called: Sign-A-Rama
5050 S Old Us Highway 23 # 200 (48114-7801)
PHONE.................810 494-7446
Kailee Marcom, *Manager*
EMP: 5
SALES (corp-wide): 39.4MM **Privately Held**
SIC: 3993 Signs & advertising specialties
HQ: Sign A Rama Inc.
2121 Vista Pkwy
West Palm Beach FL 33411
561 640-5570

(G-1991)
SIGNS BY TOMORROW
2150 Pless Dr Ste 3a (48114-9401)
PHONE.................810 225-7446
John Nagel, *Owner*
EMP: 3 **EST:** 2010
SALES (est): 331K **Privately Held**
SIC: 3993 Signs & advertising specialties

(G-1992)
SPIRAL-MATIC INC
7772 Park Pl (48116-8387)
PHONE.................248 486-5080
Daniel T Mc Phail, *President*
EMP: 9
SQ FT: 20,000
SALES (est): 1.7MM **Privately Held**
WEB: www.spiralmatic.com
SIC: 3556 Food products machinery

(G-1993)
SUNAIRE WINDOW MANUFACTURING
7936 Boardwalk Rd (48116-8312)
PHONE.................248 437-5870
Mark Fowkes, *President*
Linda Fowkes, *Treasurer*
EMP: 3
SQ FT: 2,500
SALES: 300K **Privately Held**
WEB: www.kirsch.com
SIC: 3089 Window frames & sash, plastic

(G-1994)
SURCLEAN INC
7974 Lochlin Dr Ste B1 (48116-1664)
PHONE...................248 791-2226
Susan Sprentall, *President*
Michael Nardozzi, *COO*
Beverly Wall, *Treasurer*
Michael Malloure, *Director*
Donald Sprentall, *Director*
EMP: 5 **EST:** 2015
SALES (est): 256.1K **Privately Held**
SIC: 8711 7699 3569 Designing: ship, boat, machine & product; industrial machinery & equipment repair; assembly machines, non-metalworking

(G-1995)
TECHNACRAFT CORP
Also Called: Sunchime Company
2635 Pady Ln (48114-8600)
PHONE...................810 227-8281
Ed Tury, *President*
EMP: 3
SQ FT: 3,000
SALES: 225K **Privately Held**
SIC: 3999 Bleaching & dyeing of sponges

(G-1996)
TEMCOR SYSTEMS INC
1341 Rickett Rd (48116-1879)
PHONE...................810 229-0006
Joseph Kelly, *President*
EMP: 8
SQ FT: 4,500
SALES (est): 1.3MM **Privately Held**
SIC: 3625 Relays & industrial controls

(G-1997)
TG FLUID SYSTEMS USA CORP
Also Called: Tg North America
100 Brighton Interior Dr (48116-7469)
PHONE...................810 220-6161
Bryan Soddrill, *President*
Steven Holley, *Prdtn Mgr*
Harley Scribner, *Engineer*
Mark Allen, *Finance*
Shellie Shrm, *Human Resources*
◆ **EMP:** 350
SQ FT: 70,000
SALES: 85MM **Privately Held**
WEB: www.toyoda-gosei.co.jp
SIC: 3082 3089 Unsupported plastics profile shapes; plastic processing
PA: Toyoda Gosei Co., Ltd.
1, Nagahata, Haruhi
Kiyosu AIC 452-0

(G-1998)
THOMPSON ART GLASS INC
6815 Grand River Rd (48114-9345)
PHONE...................810 225-8766
Dirk Thompson III, *President*
Dirk J Thompson, *Corp Secy*
EMP: 6
SQ FT: 5,000
SALES: 285K **Privately Held**
WEB: www.thompsonartglass.com
SIC: 3231 2499 Stained glass: made from purchased glass; decorative wood & woodwork

(G-1999)
TRANSTAR AUTOBODY TECH LLC
Also Called: Transtar Autobody Tech Inc
2040 Heiserman Dr (48114-8969)
PHONE...................810 220-3000
Monte Ahuja, *Ch of Bd*
Charles E Fuqua, *President*
Rick Coy, *Maint Spvr*
Connie Bully, *Production*
Julie Dewitt, *Technical Mgr*
◆ **EMP:** 120
SQ FT: 71,000
SALES (est): 14.7MM **Privately Held**
WEB: www.tat-co.com
SIC: 7213 2891 2899 2819 Coat supply: adhesives & sealants; chemical preparations; industrial inorganic chemicals; specialty cleaning, polishes & sanitation goods
HQ: Transtar Group, Inc
7350 Young Dr
Walton Hills OH

(G-2000)
TUBE WRIGHT INC
2111 Euler Rd (48114-7411)
PHONE...................810 227-4567
Earl M Lemley, *President*
EMP: 28
SQ FT: 40,000
SALES: 2.9MM **Privately Held**
SIC: 3498 Tube fabricating (contract bending & shaping)

(G-2001)
U K EDM LTD
8192 Boardwalk Rd (48116-8312)
PHONE...................248 437-9500
Austin Hirschhorn, *President*
EMP: 3
SALES (est): 242.4K **Privately Held**
SIC: 3544 Special dies & tools

(G-2002)
UNIFLEX INC
7830 Lochlin Dr (48116-8329)
PHONE...................248 486-6000
Robert D Judge, *President*
Arthur J Bucki, *Vice Pres*
Lance Mitchell, *Purchasing*
EMP: 9
SQ FT: 2,000
SALES (est): 1.5MM **Privately Held**
SIC: 3069 3089 5162 8711 Molded rubber products; injection molding of plastics; plastics products; engineering services; mechanical rubber goods; gaskets, packing & sealing devices

(G-2003)
UNILOCK MICHIGAN INC
12591 Emerson Dr (48116-8562)
PHONE...................248 437-1380
Edward Bryant, *President*
Tony Hooper, *Vice Pres*
Joseph C Kerr, *Vice Pres*
▲ **EMP:** 25
SALES (est): 3.5MM **Privately Held**
SIC: 3281 Paving blocks, cut stone

(G-2004)
UNITED SYSTEMS GROUP LLC (PA)
2111 Euler Rd (48114-7411)
PHONE...................810 227-4567
Earl Lemley,
Douglas Beck,
EMP: 8
SQ FT: 25,000
SALES (est): 2.8MM **Privately Held**
SIC: 3714 Radiators & radiator shells & cores, motor vehicle

(G-2005)
VECTECH PHARMACEUTICAL CONS (PA)
12501 Grand River Rd (48116-8389)
PHONE...................248 478-5820
Allan F Pfitzenmaier, *President*
EMP: 10
SQ FT: 13,000
SALES (est): 3.3MM **Privately Held**
WEB: www.devlan.com
SIC: 2834 6512 7363 Pharmaceutical preparations; commercial & industrial building operation; temporary help service

(G-2006)
VECTORALL MANUFACTURING INC
7675 Lochlin Dr (48116-8329)
PHONE...................248 486-4570
Brian Ledford, *President*
Nate Ladd, *Purchasing*
Dave Ringer, *Department Mgr*
EMP: 30
SQ FT: 35,000
SALES (est): 4.5MM **Privately Held**
SIC: 3599 7389 5013 3462 Machine shop, jobbing & repair; inspection & testing services; automotive supplies & parts; iron & steel forgings

(G-2007)
VIKING SALES INC
169 Summit St (48116-1834)
P.O. Box 639 (48116-0639)
PHONE...................810 227-2222
John Spitler, *Principal*
Kathleen Kramer, *Corp Secy*
Elizabeth H Spitler, *Vice Pres*
▲ **EMP:** 15
SQ FT: 12,000
SALES (est): 2.6MM **Privately Held**
SIC: 3799 Trailers & trailer equipment

(G-2008)
WELK-KO FABRICATORS INC
Also Called: Kar Enterprises
11777 Grand River Rd (48116-9617)
PHONE...................810 227-7500
Ron Karaisz, *President*
EMP: 4
SALES (corp-wide): 3.7MM **Privately Held**
WEB: www.kar-ent.com
SIC: 3444 5013 Sheet metal specialties, not stamped; motor vehicle supplies & new parts
PA: Welk-Ko Fabricators, Inc.
11885 Mayfield St
Livonia MI 48150
734 425-6840

(G-2009)
WHITE DRESS THE LLC
209 W Main St Ste 101 (48116-1523)
PHONE...................810 588-6147
Kristy Koryzno,
EMP: 6
SALES (est): 427.6K **Privately Held**
SIC: 2335 Wedding gowns & dresses

(G-2010)
WMT PROPERTIES INC
7771 Kensington Ct (48116-8391)
PHONE...................248 486-6400
John Yaros, *President*
Brian S Dzmelyk, *Vice Pres*
Ronald J Lezotte Jr, *Vice Pres*
Elizabeth K Johnston, *Treasurer*
Beth Johnston, *Controller*
EMP: 19
SQ FT: 12,000
SALES (est): 3.7MM **Privately Held**
SIC: 3599 Machine shop, jobbing & repair

(G-2011)
WYMAN-GORDON FORGINGS INC
7250 Whitmore Lake Rd (48116-8558)
PHONE...................810 229-9550
James Mulvihill, *Manager*
EMP: 33
SALES (corp-wide): 225.3B **Publicly Held**
SIC: 3462 Iron & steel forgings
HQ: Wyman-Gordon Forgings, Inc.
10825 Telge Rd
Houston TX 77095
281 856-9900

(G-2012)
ZKS SALES
10315 Grand River Rd # 303 (48116-9586)
PHONE...................810 360-0682
Geoff Witte, *Owner*
EMP: 3
SALES (est): 228.1K **Privately Held**
SIC: 3499 Reels, cable: metal

Brimley
Chippewa County

(G-2013)
BOURQUE H JAMES & ASSOC INC
3060 W M 28 (49715)
P.O. Box 292, Sault Sainte Marie (49783-0292)
PHONE...................906 635-9191
H James Bourque, *President*
EMP: 5
SALES (est): 402.2K **Privately Held**
SIC: 1481 Mine development, nonmetallic minerals

(G-2014)
CG LOGGING
11375 W Irish Line Rd (49715-9384)
PHONE...................906 322-1018
Traverse Carole Joan, *Owner*
EMP: 3 **EST:** 2015
SALES (est): 106.5K **Privately Held**
SIC: 2411 Logging

(G-2015)
CONTINENTAL AUTO SYSTEMS INC
9301 S M 221 (49715-9218)
PHONE...................906 248-6700
Ryan Alastan, *Manager*
EMP: 15
SALES (corp-wide): 50.8B **Privately Held**
SIC: 3714 Motor vehicle parts & accessories
HQ: Continental Automotive Systems, Inc.
1 Continental Dr
Auburn Hills MI 48326
248 393-5300

(G-2016)
LAKE SUPERIOR LOGGING
8453 Old Brimley Grade Rd (49715-9434)
P.O. Box 186 (49715-0186)
PHONE...................906 440-3567
EMP: 3
SALES (est): 98.8K **Privately Held**
SIC: 2411 Logging

(G-2017)
ZF ACTIVE SAFETY US INC
21105 W M 28 Bldg 6 (49715-9126)
PHONE...................906 248-3882
EMP: 3
SALES (corp-wide): 216.2K **Privately Held**
SIC: 3714 Motor vehicle parts & accessories
HQ: Zf Active Safety Us Inc.
12001 Tech Center Dr
Livonia MI 48150
734 812-6979

Britton
Lenawee County

(G-2018)
JS WELDING INC
8400 Shaw Hwy (49229-8512)
PHONE...................517 451-2098
James D Stromski, *President*
James J Stomski, *Shareholder*
EMP: 3
SALES (est): 133.1K **Privately Held**
SIC: 3441 7692 1799 Fabricated structural metal; welding repair; welding on site

Brockway
St. Clair County

(G-2019)
CENTER LINE GAGE INC
110 Commerce Dr (48097-3460)
PHONE...................810 387-4300
Matt Jurcak, *CEO*
EMP: 7
SQ FT: 8,500
SALES: 500K **Privately Held**
WEB: www.clgage.com
SIC: 3545 3544 8711 Machine tool accessories; special dies, tools, jigs & fixtures; machine tool design

(G-2020)
PRESSING POINT
8870 Arendt Rd (48097-2302)
PHONE...................810 387-3441
Dale Turner, *Principal*
EMP: 3
SALES (est): 209.7K **Privately Held**
SIC: 3582 Ironers, commercial laundry & drycleaning

(G-2021)
YALE STEEL INC
13334 Jeddo Rd (48097-2309)
PHONE...................810 387-2567
Shane W Tesluck, *President*
Robert J Tesluck, *Vice Pres*
Thomas R Tesluck, *Treasurer*

EMP: 8
SQ FT: 9,408
SALES (est): 670K Privately Held
WEB: www.yalesteel.com
SIC: 5211 3443 Lumber & other building materials; fabricated plate work (boiler shop)

Bronson
Branch County

(G-2022)
D & L TOOLING INC
502 N Matteson St (49028-1153)
P.O. Box 172 (49028-0172)
PHONE..................................517 369-5655
Lynn Scott, *President*
Donald S Carpenter, *Vice Pres*
Shawn Scott, *Treasurer*
Margarette Scott, *Admin Sec*
EMP: 7
SQ FT: 5,000
SALES (est): 1MM Privately Held
SIC: 3544 Forms (molds), for foundry & plastics working machinery

(G-2023)
DAVIS LOGGING
857 Herl Rd (49028-9242)
PHONE..................................517 617-4550
Dale Davis, *Principal*
EMP: 3
SALES (est): 204.6K Privately Held
SIC: 2411 Logging camps & contractors

(G-2024)
DK TOOL & MACHINE INC
703 Gilead Shores Dr (49028-8736)
PHONE..................................517 369-1401
EMP: 3 **EST:** 1990
SQ FT: 2,400
SALES: 250K Privately Held
SIC: 3544 Mfg Dies/Tools/Jigs/Fixtures

(G-2025)
DOUGLAS AUTOTECH CORPORATION (HQ)
300 Albers Rd (49028-1239)
PHONE..................................517 369-2315
Etsutaka Ogusu, *CEO*
◆ **EMP:** 50
SQ FT: 125,000
SALES (est): 82.3MM Privately Held
WEB: www.douglasautotech.com
SIC: 3714 7361 Steering mechanisms, motor vehicle; employment agencies

(G-2026)
G & W DISPLAY FIXTURES INC
300 Mill St (49028-1018)
P.O. Box 6 (49028-0006)
PHONE..................................517 369-7110
EMP: 30
SALES (corp-wide): 7.1MM Privately Held
SIC: 2542 3993 2541 5046 Partitions And Fixtures, Except Wood, Nsk
PA: G & W Display Fixtures, Inc.
804 N Matteson St
Bronson MI 49028
517 369-7341

(G-2027)
GEIGER EDM INC
898 W Chicago Rd (49028-9426)
P.O. Box 185 (49028-0185)
PHONE..................................517 369-9752
Rick Outwater, *President*
Kelly Outwater, *Treasurer*
EMP: 12
SQ FT: 5,000
SALES (est): 1.4MM Privately Held
WEB: www.geigeredm.com
SIC: 3599 Machine shop, jobbing & repair; electrical discharge machining (EDM)

(G-2028)
H G GEIGER MANUFACTURING CO
416 Mill St (49028-1098)
PHONE..................................517 369-7357
Hubert G Geiger, *President*
Julie Geiger, *Corp Secy*
EMP: 15
SQ FT: 20,000
SALES (est): 800K Privately Held
SIC: 3451 2542 3599 Screw machine products; fixtures: display, office or store: except wood; machine shop, jobbing & repair

(G-2029)
HICE AND SUMMEY INC (PA)
Also Called: Protective Coating Associates
404 Union St (49028-1037)
PHONE..................................269 651-6217
John Summey, *President*
Mike Brown, *Vice Pres*
Ruth Summey, *Vice Pres*
EMP: 14
SQ FT: 19,000
SALES (est): 2MM Privately Held
SIC: 3479 Painting, coating & hot dipping; coating of metals & formed products; coating of metals with plastic or resins

(G-2030)
HICE AND SUMMEY INC
Also Called: Protective Coating & Assoc
404 Union St (49028-1037)
PHONE..................................269 651-6217
John Summey, *President*
EMP: 15
SALES (est): 911.2K
SALES (corp-wide): 2MM Privately Held
SIC: 3479 Coating of metals & formed products
PA: Hice And Summey, Inc.
404 Union St
Bronson MI 49028
269 651-6217

(G-2031)
K & W MANUFACTURING CO INC
555 W Chicago Rd (49028-9282)
P.O. Box 97 (49028-0097)
PHONE..................................517 369-9708
Korinna Burke, *President*
Korinna Kehoe, *Vice Pres*
Wendy Kehoe, *Vice Pres*
Hank Burke, *Manager*
Jeanette Kehoe, *Admin Sec*
EMP: 12
SQ FT: 4,900
SALES (est): 2.4MM Privately Held
WEB: www.customtoolboxes.com
SIC: 3599 3444 3443 3429 Machine shop, jobbing & repair; sheet metalwork; fabricated plate work (boiler shop); manufactured hardware (general)

(G-2032)
MADDOX INDUSTRIES INC
900 W Chicago Rd (49028-9426)
P.O. Box 190 (49028-0190)
PHONE..................................517 369-8665
Steve Maddox, *President*
Shelly Maddox, *Admin Sec*
EMP: 20
SQ FT: 13,000
SALES (est): 3.4MM Privately Held
SIC: 3544 Special dies & tools

(G-2033)
MSC BLINDS & SHADES INC
1241 W Chicago Rd (49028-9739)
PHONE..................................269 489-5188
EMP: 4
SQ FT: 3,200
SALES (est): 380K Privately Held
SIC: 2591 Commercial Installations / Mfg Vertical Blinds

(G-2034)
VAN PEETE ENTERPRISES
897 W Chicago Rd (49028-9426)
P.O. Box 117 (49028-0117)
PHONE..................................517 369-2123
William Peterhim, *Owner*
EMP: 4
SQ FT: 6,000
SALES: 500K Privately Held
SIC: 2511 5712 Children's wood furniture; juvenile furniture

(G-2035)
WICKEY CUSTOM CABINETS
807 N Matteson St (49028-1132)
PHONE..................................517 858-1119
Sam Wickey, *Principal*
EMP: 3 **EST:** 2010
SALES (est): 255.5K Privately Held
SIC: 2434 Wood kitchen cabinets

Brooklyn
Jackson County

(G-2036)
BROOKLYN PRODUCTS INTL
171 Wamplers Lake Rd (49230-9585)
PHONE..................................517 592-2185
Bob Linenfelser, *Principal*
Lisa Bascom, *Vice Pres*
Cindy Lewandowski, *Opers Mgr*
Bob Reed, *Engineer*
Todd Wanty, *Accounts Mgr*
◆ **EMP:** 25
SQ FT: 70,000
SALES (est): 4.7MM Privately Held
WEB: www.brooklynproducts.com
SIC: 3086 Padding, foamed plastic

(G-2037)
GOETZ CRAFT PRINTERS INC
121 Paula Dr (49230-9707)
PHONE..................................734 973-7604
J Larry Goetz, *President*
Britton L Goetz, *Vice Pres*
Tasha Goetz, *Sales Staff*
Paulette Goetz, *Admin Sec*
EMP: 16
SQ FT: 12,000
SALES (est): 2.5MM Privately Held
WEB: www.goetzcraft.com
SIC: 2752 Commercial printing, offset

(G-2038)
HOGLE SALES & MFG LLC
208 Irwin St (49230-9282)
P.O. Box 478 (49230-0478)
PHONE..................................517 592-1980
Gregory M Hogle,
EMP: 5
SQ FT: 500
SALES (est): 793.9K Privately Held
SIC: 3544 Special dies, tools, jigs & fixtures

(G-2039)
MAXABLE INC
202 Sherman St (49230-9261)
PHONE..................................517 592-5638
Anton Eichmuller, *President*
▲ **EMP:** 48
SQ FT: 25,000
SALES (est): 6.1MM Privately Held
WEB: www.maxableinc.com
SIC: 3714 7692 Motor vehicle parts & accessories; welding repair

(G-2040)
MID-AMERICA MACHINING INC
11530 Brooklyn Rd (49230-8486)
PHONE..................................517 592-4945
Robert Berry, *President*
Cheryl Berry, *Corp Secy*
Peter Lobbestael, *Vice Pres*
Crystal Page, *Controller*
Jenna Berry, *Human Res Dir*
EMP: 75
SQ FT: 55,000
SALES (est): 14.9MM Privately Held
WEB: www.mid-americamachining.com
SIC: 3599 Machine shop, jobbing & repair

(G-2041)
PLATFORMSH INC
106 S Main St Ste 4 (49230-8588)
P.O. Box 536 (49230-0536)
PHONE..................................734 707-9124
Frederic Plais, *CEO*
Erin Austin, *Office Mgr*
Matt Glaman, *Consultant*
Ryan Szrama, *CTO*
EMP: 13
SQ FT: 400
SALES (est): 1.4MM
SALES (corp-wide): 1.6MM Privately Held
SIC: 7372 Business oriented computer software
PA: Platform.Sh Sas
131 Boulevard De Sebastopol
Paris 2e Arrondissement 75002
140 093-000

(G-2042)
SCHEPELER CORPORATION
Also Called: Exponent, The
160 S Main St (49230-8588)
PHONE..................................517 592-6811
Kris D Schepeler, *Principal*
Matthew B Schepeler, *Corp Secy*
EMP: 15
SQ FT: 3,600
SALES (est): 1.2MM Privately Held
WEB: www.theexponent.com
SIC: 2711 2752 Newspapers: publishing only, not printed on site; commercial printing, offset

(G-2043)
VERITAS VINEYARD LLC
11000 Silver Lake Hwy (49230-8618)
PHONE..................................517 592-4663
John Burtka,
EMP: 8
SALES (corp-wide): 2MM Privately Held
SIC: 2084 Wines
PA: Veritas Vineyard Llc
117 W Louis Glick Hwy
Jackson MI 49201
517 962-2427

Brown City
Sanilac County

(G-2044)
AQUA SYSTEMS INC
7070 Enterprise Dr (48416-9002)
PHONE..................................810 346-2525
Jack Dempsey, *Vice Pres*
EMP: 6
SALES (corp-wide): 2MM Privately Held
WEB: www.aquasystemsinc.com
SIC: 3443 5999 Heat exchangers, condensers & components; aquarium supplies
PA: Aqua Systems, Inc.
289 Exeter Rd
Hampton Falls NH 03844
603 778-8796

(G-2045)
AUTOMATED TECHNIQUES LLC
7105 Enterprise Dr (48416-9084)
PHONE..................................810 346-4670
Raymond L Billig,
EMP: 7
SALES (est): 1MM Privately Held
WEB: www.automatedtechniques.com
SIC: 3599 Custom machinery

(G-2046)
BECHTEL SAND & GRAVEL
5278 Churchill Rd (48416-9669)
PHONE..................................810 346-2041
Paul Bechtel, *Owner*
EMP: 8
SALES (est): 591.4K Privately Held
SIC: 1442 Gravel mining

(G-2047)
BROWN CITY BANNER INC
Also Called: Banner The
4241 Main St (48416-7715)
P.O. Box 250 (48416-0250)
PHONE..................................810 346-2753
Fax: 810 346-2579
EMP: 3
SALES (est): 140K Privately Held
SIC: 2711 Newspapers-Publishing/Printing

(G-2048)
BROWN CITY MACHINE PDTS LLC (PA)
3989 Burnsline Rd (48416-8473)
PHONE..................................810 346-3070
Kevin Brehmer,

EMP: 5
SQ FT: 14,150
SALES: 700K **Privately Held**
SIC: 3451 Screw machine products

(G-2049)
DEMPSEY MANUFACTURING CO
4835 Van Dyke Rd (48416-9682)
PHONE..................810 346-2273
Jack Dempsey, *Owner*
EMP: 3
SALES (est): 219K **Privately Held**
SIC: 3433 Heating equipment, except electric

(G-2050)
EMMIE DIE AND ENGINEERING CORP
7254 Maple Valley Rd (48416-8247)
P.O. Box 66 (48416-0066)
PHONE..................810 346-2914
George A Emmie, *President*
Joseph Kipper, *Vice Pres*
Dawn Considine, *Office Mgr*
EMP: 8 EST: 1977
SQ FT: 34,000
SALES (est): 760K **Privately Held**
SIC: 3544 Special dies & tools; die sets for metal stamping (presses); jigs & fixtures

(G-2051)
FRANK INDUSTRIES INC
Also Called: Xplorer Motor Home Division
4467 Vine St (48416-8657)
P.O. Box 130 (48416-0130)
PHONE..................810 346-3234
David Bockstanz, *Ch of Bd*
Joseph Murray, *Senior VP*
EMP: 35
SQ FT: 50,000
SALES: 1.7MM **Privately Held**
WEB: www.xplorermotorhome.com
SIC: 3711 3792 3714 3716 Motor vehicles & car bodies; travel trailers & campers; motor vehicle parts & accessories; recreational van conversion (self-propelled), factory basis

(G-2052)
J T EXPRESS LTD
4200 Van Dyke Rd (48416-9473)
P.O. Box 204, Imlay City (48444-0204)
PHONE..................810 724-6471
Joyce Ann Treash, *President*
EMP: 6
SALES: 600K **Privately Held**
SIC: 1442 4214 Construction sand & gravel; local trucking with storage

(G-2053)
KADEST INDUSTRIES
4300 Churchill Rd (48416-9407)
PHONE..................810 614-5362
William Mulliniks, *President*
EMP: 3
SQ FT: 3,600
SALES (est): 124.7K **Privately Held**
WEB: www.kardel.com
SIC: 3465 Automotive stampings

(G-2054)
LLINK TECHNOLOGIES LLC
3953 Burnsline Rd (48416-8473)
PHONE..................586 336-9370
Jeff Goulet,
Joe Gamache,
Richard Knill,
Lisa Spencer,
▲ **EMP:** 44
SQ FT: 40,000
SALES (est): 9.6MM **Privately Held**
SIC: 3442 3444 3449 3465 Metal doors, sash & trim; sheet metalwork; miscellaneous metalwork; automotive stampings; metal stampings; steel springs, except wire

(G-2055)
MAPLE VALLEY PLASTICS LLC
4119 Main St (48416-7713)
P.O. Box 130 (48416-0130)
PHONE..................810 346-3040
Bill Woodall, *Mng Member*
EMP: 47
SALES: 11.7MM **Privately Held**
SIC: 3089 Injection molding of plastics

(G-2056)
RAYS GAME
Also Called: Ray's Big Game Processing
4101 Maple St (48416-8012)
PHONE..................810 346-2628
Ray Dupuie, *Owner*
Linda Dupuie, *Owner*
EMP: 4
SALES (est): 84.7K **Privately Held**
SIC: 2011 Meat packing plants

(G-2057)
SALVO TOOL & ENGINEERING CO (PA)
3948 Burnsline Rd (48416-8473)
P.O. Box 129 (48416-0129)
PHONE..................810 346-2727
Sheri Robbins, *President*
Bruce Bedker, *President*
Beverly Zobay, *Vice Pres*
EMP: 29 EST: 1947
SALES (est): 4.5MM **Privately Held**
WEB: www.salvotool.com
SIC: 3542 Thread rolling machines

Brownstown
Wayne County

(G-2058)
AMERICAN INDUS TRAINING INC
32715 Groat Blvd (48173-8636)
PHONE..................734 752-2451
Kristy Stapula, *President*
Lynn Espinoza, *Vice Pres*
EMP: 3
SALES (est): 207.3K **Privately Held**
SIC: 3496 Slings, lifting: made from purchased wire

(G-2059)
BEST CONCRETE & SUPPLY INC
17200 Dix Toledo Hwy (48193-8415)
PHONE..................734 283-7055
Gary Pachota, *President*
Richard Pachota, *Vice Pres*
EMP: 7
SQ FT: 2,500
SALES: 1.2MM **Privately Held**
SIC: 3273 5032 Ready-mixed concrete; concrete building products; building blocks; sand, construction; stone, crushed or broken

(G-2060)
BUTCHER ENGINEERING ENTPS
20501 Pennsylvania Rd # 150 (48193-8472)
PHONE..................734 246-7700
David Butcher, *Vice Pres*
EMP: 100
SALES (corp-wide): 158.1MM **Privately Held**
SIC: 3565 Packaging machinery
PA: Butcher Engineering Enterprises Limited, The
2755 Lauzon Pky
Windsor ON N8T 3
519 944-9200

(G-2061)
CONTRACT FURN SOLUTIONS INC
25069 Pine Ridge Dr (48134-9085)
PHONE..................734 941-2750
Helen Wages-Duggan, *CEO*
EMP: 50
SALES (est): 1.2MM **Privately Held**
SIC: 2511 Kitchen & dining room furniture; wood bedroom furniture

(G-2062)
FORD MOTOR COMPANY
24999 Pennsylvania Rd (48174)
PHONE..................734 942-6248
EMP: 1516
SALES (corp-wide): 160.3B **Publicly Held**
SIC: 5511 3713 3714 6153 Automobiles, new & used; truck & bus bodies; motor vehicle parts & accessories; financing of dealers by motor vehicle manufacturers organ.; buying of installment notes; passenger car leasing
PA: Ford Motor Company
1 American Rd
Dearborn MI 48126
313 322-3000

(G-2063)
GENERAL MOTORS COMPANY
20001 Brownstown Ctr Dr (48183-1679)
PHONE..................248 249-6347
EMP: 18 **Publicly Held**
SIC: 5511 3714 Automobiles, new & used; motor vehicle parts & accessories
PA: General Motors Company
300 Renaissance Ctr L1
Detroit MI 48243

(G-2064)
GREENFIELD HOLDINGS LLC (PA)
19881 Brownstown Ctr Dr (48183-1680)
PHONE..................734 530-5600
James Comer, *Mng Member*
Lear Corporation,
Comer Holdings LLC,
EMP: 10
SALES (est): 32.4MM **Privately Held**
SIC: 2531 Seats, automobile

(G-2065)
HYDRO-ZONE INC
17800 Telegraph Rd (48174-9545)
PHONE..................734 247-4488
Dave Hill, *President*
John Desmaretz, *Manager*
Laura Johns, *Manager*
Andi Coil, *Executive*
EMP: 5
SQ FT: 2,000
SALES (est): 1MM **Privately Held**
SIC: 2819 Industrial inorganic chemicals

(G-2066)
KENNY G MFG & SLS LLC
27275 Ritter Blvd (48134-0709)
PHONE..................313 218-6297
Kenneth Cox,
EMP: 4
SALES (est): 218.3K **Privately Held**
SIC: 3999 Manufacturing industries

(G-2067)
LINCOLN PARK DIE & TOOL CO
Also Called: Lincoln Forge
18325 Dix Toledo Hwy (48193-8406)
PHONE..................734 285-1680
Roger Magnusson, *President*
Bruce R Magnusson, *Vice Pres*
Monica Magnusson, *Vice Pres*
Patricia Magnusson, *Treasurer*
Leisa Wilson, *Human Resources*
▼ **EMP:** 40 EST: 1962
SQ FT: 39,000
SALES (est): 12.2MM **Privately Held**
WEB: www.lincolnforge.com
SIC: 3462 3463 3544 Horseshoes; aluminum forgings; special dies & tools

(G-2068)
THERAPYLINE TECHNOLOGIES INC
21635 Adams Dr (48193-4575)
PHONE..................734 407-9626
Faisal Khan, *President*
EMP: 20
SALES (est): 382.7K **Privately Held**
SIC: 7372 8322 8011 Application computer software; telephone counseling service; psychiatrist

Brownstown Township
Wayne County

(G-2069)
FUEL CELL SYSTEM MFG LLC
20001 Brownstown Ctr Dr (48183-1679)
PHONE..................313 319-5571
Suhed Haq, *President*
EMP: 3
SALES (est): 99K **Privately Held**
SIC: 3674 Fuel cells, solid state

(G-2070)
MTU AMERICA INCORPORATED
19771 Brownstown Ctr (48183-1684)
PHONE..................734 561-2040
Thomas Koenig, *President*
Kimberly Rowe, *Branch Mgr*
EMP: 150
SALES (corp-wide): 20.2B **Privately Held**
SIC: 3519 Diesel, semi-diesel or duel-fuel engines, including marine
HQ: Mtu America Inc.
39525 Mackenzie Dr
Novi MI 48377
248 560-8000

Brownstown Twp
Wayne County

(G-2071)
CERCO INC (PA)
Also Called: Northern Rfractories Insul Div
27301 Fort St (48183-4973)
PHONE..................734 362-8664
Carl Rigg, *President*
EMP: 20
SQ FT: 12,000
SALES (est): 3.4MM **Privately Held**
SIC: 1741 3441 3297 2899 Foundation building; bricklaying; concrete block masonry laying; refractory or acid brick masonry; fabricated structural metal; nonclay refractories; chemical preparations

(G-2072)
STEEL TOOL & ENGINEERING CO
28005 Fort St (48183-4909)
PHONE..................734 692-8580
Peter C La Fond, *President*
Roy W Rapp III, *Chairman*
Eugene Calderone, *Mfg Spvr*
Christopher McDonald, *Mfg Spvr*
Jennifer Smith, *Purchasing*
EMP: 70 EST: 1959
SQ FT: 17,200
SALES (est): 18.7MM
SALES (corp-wide): 11.8MM **Privately Held**
WEB: www.steeltool.com
SIC: 3724 3511 Aircraft engines & engine parts; turbines & turbine generator sets
PA: Rapp & Son, Inc.
3767 11th St
Wyandotte MI 48192
734 283-1000

(G-2073)
SUBURBAN INDUSTRIES INC
28093 Fort St (48183-4900)
PHONE..................734 676-6141
William James Wilson, *President*
Gregory Wilson, *Vice Pres*
EMP: 10 EST: 1962
SQ FT: 36,000
SALES (est): 1.6MM **Privately Held**
SIC: 3544 Special dies & tools

(G-2074)
SYSTRAND MANUFACTURING CORP (PA)
19050 Allen Rd (48183-1002)
PHONE..................734 479-8100
Sharon A Cannarsa, *President*
Anthony Cannarsa, *Vice Pres*
Michael Cannarsa, *VP Mfg*
Luis Flores, *Production*
Anthony Kuczek, *VP Engrg*
▲ **EMP:** 159

Brownstown Twp - Wayne County (G-2075)

SQ FT: 200,000
SALES (est): 34.3MM **Privately Held**
SIC: 3714 8742 Motor vehicle transmissions, drive assemblies & parts; motor vehicle body components & frame; management consulting services

(G-2075)
SYSTRAND PRSTA ENG SYSTEMS LLC
19050 Allen Rd Ste 200 (48183-1002)
PHONE..................................734 479-8100
Sharon Cannarsa, *CEO*
Rob Lidster, *Exec VP*
Carlos Dias, *Vice Pres*
EMP: 15
SQ FT: 400
SALES (est): 1.3MM **Privately Held**
WEB: www.systrand.com
SIC: 3599 Crankshafts & camshafts, machining

(G-2076)
VAMP SCREW PRODUCTS COMPANY
Also Called: Vamp Company
28055 Fort St (48183-4909)
PHONE..................................734 676-8020
David Topolewski, *President*
Allan Topolewski, *Vice Pres*
▲ EMP: 24 EST: 1946
SQ FT: 18,500
SALES: 6.4MM **Privately Held**
SIC: 3452 Nuts, metal

Bruce Twp
Macomb County

(G-2077)
ALL SEASONS AGENCY INC
Also Called: All Seasons Communications
5455 34 Mile Rd (48065-2903)
P.O. Box 100, Romeo (48065-0100)
PHONE..................................586 752-6381
Kenneth Monicatti, *President*
Beth Monicatti, *Vice Pres*
Linda Monicatti, *Admin Sec*
EMP: 6
SQ FT: 1,600
SALES: 200K **Privately Held**
WEB: www.allseasonscommunications.com
SIC: 8743 2721 7311 Public relations & publicity; magazines: publishing only, not printed on site; advertising agencies

(G-2078)
AUTO CONNECTION
75903 Peters Dr (48065-2525)
PHONE..................................586 752-6371
Nick Batsikouras, *Owner*
EMP: 4
SALES: 600K **Privately Held**
SIC: 2721 Magazines: publishing only, not printed on site

(G-2079)
CHIEF EDM
9703 Cranbrook Ct (48065-3737)
PHONE..................................586 752-5078
Gregory D Blondeau, *President*
EMP: 3
SQ FT: 2,000
SALES (est): 261.8K **Privately Held**
SIC: 3599 Electrical discharge machining (EDM)

(G-2080)
CUSTOM BIOGENIC SYSTEMS INC
Also Called: C B S
74100 Van Dyke Rd (48065-3215)
PHONE..................................586 331-2600
John Brothers, *President*
▲ EMP: 35
SQ FT: 47,000
SALES (est): 9MM **Privately Held**
WEB: www.custombiogenics.com
SIC: 3443 Cryogenic tanks, for liquids & gases

(G-2081)
CUSTOM BLEND FEEDS INC
77500 Brown Rd (48065-2103)
PHONE..................................810 798-3265
Robert Harrow, *President*
Sidney Williams, *Treasurer*
EMP: 6
SQ FT: 10,000
SALES (est): 539.7K **Privately Held**
SIC: 2048 5191 Prepared feeds; animal feeds

(G-2082)
DECLARKS LANDSCAPING INC
13800 33 Mile Rd (48065-3901)
PHONE..................................586 752-7200
Mike Declark, *President*
Bryan Lingeman, *General Mgr*
Annette Declark, *Treasurer*
EMP: 50
SALES (est): 3.2MM **Privately Held**
WEB: www.declarkslandscaping.com
SIC: 0781 3271 0782 Landscape services; landscape architects; blocks, concrete: landscape or retaining wall; fertilizing services, lawn; mowing services, lawn; mulching services, lawn; landscape contractors

(G-2083)
HARD MILLING SOLUTIONS INC
107 Peyerk Ct (48065-4921)
PHONE..................................586 286-2300
Corey Greenwald, *President*
EMP: 6
SQ FT: 5,000
SALES (est): 1.3MM **Privately Held**
SIC: 3544 Special dies & tools

(G-2084)
INNOVATION FAB INC
77909 Pearl Dr (48065-1610)
PHONE..................................586 752-3092
Melvin McCartt, *President*
Eugene McKee, *Sales Mgr*
Sandie McCartt, *Manager*
EMP: 12
SALES (est): 980K **Privately Held**
SIC: 3469 Electronic enclosures, stamped or pressed metal

(G-2085)
JOMAT INDUSTRIES LTD
131 Mclean (48065-4919)
PHONE..................................586 336-1801
Catherine Taylor, *CEO*
Blake Taylor, *President*
Kristine Demink, *Purch Mgr*
EMP: 10
SQ FT: 20,000
SALES (est): 2.3MM **Privately Held**
WEB: www.jomat.com
SIC: 3829 5084 5085 Measuring & controlling devices; industrial machine parts; industrial tools

(G-2086)
KORTEN QUALITY INC
69069 Powell Rd (48065-4920)
P.O. Box 120, Romeo (48065-0120)
PHONE..................................586 752-6255
Chester Zochowski, *President*
◆ EMP: 110
SQ FT: 5,000
SALES: 5MM
SALES (corp-wide): 19.5B **Privately Held**
SIC: 3565 4225 Packaging machinery; general warehousing & storage
HQ: Day & Ross Inc
398 Main St
Hartland NB E7P 1
506 375-4401

(G-2087)
L & L PRODUCTS INC (HQ)
160 Mclean (48065-4919)
PHONE..................................586 336-1600
John Ligon, *CEO*
Tom Klieno, *President*
Larry R Schmidt, *Chairman*
Robert M Ligon, *Treasurer*
Wilbur E Lane, *Admin Sec*
◆ EMP: 775
SQ FT: 207,000
SALES (est): 228.8MM **Privately Held**
WEB: www.llproducts.com
SIC: 3053 Gaskets & sealing devices; gaskets, all materials

(G-2088)
L & L PRODUCTS INC
Also Called: Romeo North
160 Mclean (48065-4919)
PHONE..................................586 752-6681
Claude Dembey, *President*
EMP: 304
SQ FT: 87,000 **Privately Held**
SIC: 3053 2891 Gaskets, packing & sealing devices; adhesives & sealants
HQ: L & L Products, Inc.
160 Mclean
Bruce Twp MI 48065
586 336-1600

(G-2089)
L & L PRODUCTS INC
Also Called: Romeo South
159 Mclean (48065-4919)
PHONE..................................586 336-1600
Susan Deeb, *Branch Mgr*
EMP: 500 **Privately Held**
WEB: www.llproducts.com
SIC: 3053 Gaskets & sealing devices; gaskets, all materials
HQ: L & L Products, Inc.
160 Mclean
Bruce Twp MI 48065
586 336-1600

(G-2090)
LANZEN INCORPORATED (PA)
Also Called: Lanzen Fabricating
100 Peyerk Ct (48065-4921)
PHONE..................................586 771-7070
Terry K Lanzen, *President*
Archie Coffman, *Exec VP*
Scott Cooper, *Vice Pres*
Anne Nicolazzo, *Vice Pres*
▲ EMP: 56
SQ FT: 32,000
SALES (est): 28.8MM **Privately Held**
WEB: www.lanzenfab.com
SIC: 3444 3489 2531 Sheet metal specialties, not stamped; metal housings, enclosures, casings & other containers; ordnance & accessories; vehicle furniture

(G-2091)
MAC-MOLD BASE INC
14921 32 Mile Rd (48065-4914)
PHONE..................................586 752-1956
Michael Gustavus, *President*
EMP: 26
SQ FT: 16,000
SALES (est): 5.2MM **Privately Held**
WEB: www.macmold.com
SIC: 3544 Industrial molds

(G-2092)
PLASCO FORMULATING DIVISION
14951 32 Mile Rd (48065-4914)
PHONE..................................586 281-3714
EMP: 3
SALES (est): 750K **Privately Held**
SIC: 2891 Expoxy Tooling

(G-2093)
R C M INC
Also Called: Reliable Concepts Management
14901 32 Mile Rd (48065-4914)
PHONE..................................586 336-1237
Robert Quinn, *President*
EMP: 8
SQ FT: 15,000
SALES (est): 1.2MM **Privately Held**
SIC: 3544 Special dies & tools

(G-2094)
ROMEO MOLD TECHNOLOGIES INC
121 Mclean (48065-4919)
PHONE..................................586 336-1245
Mark Suddon, *President*
Michael Fillo, *Corp Secy*
Bob Pulliam, *Vice Pres*
Geoffrey Watz, *Manager*
EMP: 19
SQ FT: 15,000
SALES (est): 3MM **Privately Held**
SIC: 3544 Industrial molds

(G-2095)
ROMEO TECHNOLOGIES INC
101 Mclean (48065-4919)
PHONE..................................586 336-5015
Mark Suddon, *President*
Craig Carpenter, *Project Mgr*
Scott Hunter, *Project Mgr*
Peter Ellis, *Opers Mgr*
Sal Gelardi, *Mfg Spvr*
EMP: 60
SQ FT: 50,000
SALES (est): 11.4MM **Privately Held**
WEB: www.romeotech.com
SIC: 3544 8711 Industrial molds; engineering services

(G-2096)
ROMEO-RIM INC
Also Called: RR
74000 Van Dyke Rd (48065-3208)
PHONE..................................586 336-5800
Chris Morin, *CEO*
Tim Emmitt, *President*
Paul Condeelis, *Vice Pres*
R Mark Hamlin Jr, *Vice Pres*
Phil Whisman, *Vice Pres*
▲ EMP: 240
SQ FT: 151,000
SALES (est): 88.6MM **Privately Held**
WEB: www.romeorim.com
SIC: 3089 Blow molded finished plastic products; injection molding of plastics

(G-2097)
RONALD R WELLINGTON
Also Called: Bernal Products
141 Mclean (48065-4919)
PHONE..................................586 488-3087
Ronald R Wellington, *Administration*
EMP: 10
SALES (est): 1MM **Privately Held**
SIC: 3544 Special dies, tools, jigs & fixtures

(G-2098)
SBN ENTERPRISES LLC
Also Called: Black Ops Gunsmithing
72901 Sorrel Dr (48065-3934)
PHONE..................................586 839-4782
Nicholas Black, *Principal*
EMP: 3 EST: 2011
SALES (est): 193.2K **Privately Held**
SIC: 3484 Guns (firearms) or gun parts, 30 mm. & below

(G-2099)
SCHIENKE PRODUCTS INC
Also Called: Schienke Electric & Mch Svcs I
120 Mclean (48065-4919)
PHONE..................................586 752-5454
David Schienke, *President*
Fred Schienke, *Admin Sec*
EMP: 8
SQ FT: 13,000
SALES (est): 1.1MM **Privately Held**
WEB: www.schienkeproducts.com
SIC: 3541 Numerically controlled metal cutting machine tools

(G-2100)
SHAMROCK PRINTING
109 Peyerk Ct (48065-4921)
PHONE..................................586 752-8580
Eileen Shaughnessy, *Principal*
EMP: 4
SALES (est): 486.3K **Privately Held**
SIC: 2752 Commercial printing, offset

(G-2101)
SHARP MODEL CO (PA)
Also Called: Sharp Tooling Solutions
70745 Powell Rd (48065-4918)
PHONE..................................586 752-3099
Roger P Walker, *President*
EMP: 61
SQ FT: 3,000
SALES (est): 12.4MM **Privately Held**
WEB: www.sharpmodel.com
SIC: 3544 3714 Special dies & tools; motor vehicle parts & accessories

(G-2102)
SMART DIET SCALE LLC
75903 Peters Dr (48065-2525)
PHONE..................................586 383-6734
Nick Batsikouras,
EMP: 5
SALES (est): 260.3K **Privately Held**
SIC: 7371 3569 7389 Computer software development & applications; blast cleaning equipment, dustless;

(G-2103)
SPARTAN POLYMERS LLC
11186 Chapman Ct (48065-3735)
P.O. Box 146, Romeo (48065-0146)
PHONE..................................586 255-5644
Michael Kirtley,
EMP: 1
SALES (est): 1MM **Privately Held**
SIC: 2821 Acrylic resins

(G-2104)
TOOL & DIE FUTURES INITIATIVE
14901 32 Mile Rd (48065-4914)
PHONE..................................586 336-1237
Bob Quinn, *President*
EMP: 7
SALES (est): 450K **Privately Held**
SIC: 3544 Special dies, tools, jigs & fixtures

(G-2105)
ULTRAFORM INDUSTRIES INC
150 Peyerk Ct (48065-4921)
PHONE..................................586 752-4508
Donald Frattaroli, *President*
Sheryl Frattaroli, *Principal*
Debra Westbrook, *Principal*
Mike Rosenmund, *QC Dir*
Kevin Archambault, *Engineer*
EMP: 66 **EST:** 1960
SQ FT: 29,000
SALES (est): 13.8MM **Privately Held**
SIC: 3496 3469 Clips & fasteners, made from purchased wire; metal stampings

(G-2106)
ZEPHYROS INC (PA)
Also Called: L&L Products
160 Mclean (48065-4919)
P.O. Box 308, Romeo (48065-0308)
PHONE..................................586 336-1600
John Ligon, *CEO*
Claude Z Demby, *President*
Larry R Schmidt, *Chairman*
Robert M Ligon, *Treasurer*
Wilbur E Lane, *Admin Sec*
EMP: 775
SQ FT: 207,000
SALES (est): 38.7MM **Privately Held**
SIC: 3053 Gaskets & sealing devices; gaskets, all materials

Brunswick
Muskegon County

(G-2107)
CYGEIRTS SAWMILL
6875 Marvin Rd (49425-8519)
P.O. Box 402, Holton (49425-0402)
PHONE..................................231 821-0083
Mike Cygeirt, *Owner*
EMP: 3
SALES (est): 257.1K **Privately Held**
SIC: 2421 Sawmills & planing mills, general

Buchanan
Berrien County

(G-2108)
AEROSPACE MFG SVCS INC
Also Called: AMS
206 Main St Ste 2 (49107-1376)
PHONE..................................269 697-4800
EMP: 3
SALES (corp-wide): 807K **Privately Held**
SIC: 3812 Mfg Defense Systems & Equipment

PA: Aerospace Manufacturing Services, Inc.
1035 Pearl St
Boulder CO
303 810-6886

(G-2109)
B C P PRINTING
Also Called: Berrien County Printing
206 Days Ave (49107-1612)
P.O. Box 236 (49107-0236)
PHONE..................................269 695-3877
Elizabeth Christie, *Owner*
EMP: 4
SQ FT: 10,000
SALES (est): 246.9K **Privately Held**
SIC: 2759 Commercial printing

(G-2110)
BERRIEN METAL PRODUCTS INC
460 Post Rd Ste A (49107-1070)
PHONE..................................269 695-5000
Larry Barrett, *President*
Valore Barrett, *Vice Pres*
Joel S Barrett, *Plant Mgr*
EMP: 18
SQ FT: 46,000
SALES (est): 4.3MM **Privately Held**
WEB: www.metalstamp.com
SIC: 3443 Fabricated plate work (boiler shop)

(G-2111)
BUCHANAN METAL FORMING INC (PA)
Also Called: B M F
103 W Smith St (49107-1548)
PHONE..................................269 695-3836
Richard Tapper, *Ch of Bd*
▲ **EMP:** 35
SQ FT: 30,000
SALES (est): 6.2MM **Privately Held**
WEB: www.bmfcorp.com
SIC: 3462 Iron & steel forgings

(G-2112)
C & S MACHINE PRODUCTS INC
248 Post Rd (49107)
PHONE..................................269 695-6859
Joe Saratoge, *Branch Mgr*
EMP: 45
SALES (corp-wide): 11.4MM **Privately Held**
WEB: www.candsmachine.com
SIC: 3599 Machine shop, jobbing & repair
PA: C & S Machine Products, Inc.
2929 Saratore Dr
Niles MI 49120
269 695-6859

(G-2113)
CHI CO/TABOR HILL WINERY (PA)
Also Called: Tabor Hill Winery & Restaurant
185 Mount Tabor Rd (49107-8326)
PHONE..................................269 422-1161
Linda Upton, *President*
▲ **EMP:** 70
SALES (est): 6.3MM **Privately Held**
WEB: www.taborhill.com
SIC: 2084 5812 Wines; American restaurant

(G-2114)
COLE POLYMER TECHNOLOGIES INC
15512 Walton Rd (49107-9110)
PHONE..................................269 695-6275
Russel Cole, *CEO*
Melinda Cole, *Treasurer*
EMP: 4
SALES (est): 433.1K **Privately Held**
SIC: 2821 Plastics materials & resins

(G-2115)
FAPCO INC
926 Terre Coupe St (49107-1037)
PHONE..................................269 695-6889
EMP: 3
SALES (corp-wide): 17.1MM **Privately Held**
SIC: 3086 Packaging & shipping materials, foamed plastic

PA: Fapco, Inc.
216 Post Rd
Buchanan MI 49107
269 695-6889

(G-2116)
FINE ARTS
108 W Roe St (49107-1514)
PHONE..................................269 695-6263
Karen Falkenstein, *President*
EMP: 20
SALES (est): 1.5MM **Privately Held**
SIC: 3356 Tin

(G-2117)
FRAME PRODUCTS INC
206 Main St Ste B (49107-1376)
PHONE..................................269 695-5884
Jeremy Frame, *President*
EMP: 3
SALES (est): 336.2K **Privately Held**
SIC: 3599 Machine shop, jobbing & repair

(G-2118)
G P MANUFACTURING INC
16689 Bakertown Rd (49107-9201)
PHONE..................................269 695-1202
Brenda L Payton, *President*
Brenda Payton, *President*
Gordon L Payton, *Vice Pres*
EMP: 7
SALES (est): 490K **Privately Held**
SIC: 3599 Machine shop, jobbing & repair

(G-2119)
GENERAL MACHINE SERVICES
Also Called: Gms Industries
807 W 4th St (49107)
P.O. Box 167 (49107-0167)
PHONE..................................269 695-2244
Gerald M Smedley, *President*
Michael Smedley, *Vice Pres*
▲ **EMP:** 5
SQ FT: 12,750
SALES (est): 663.9K **Privately Held**
WEB: www.genmachine.com
SIC: 3532 3533 3599 Mining machinery; oil field machinery & equipment; machine shop, jobbing & repair

(G-2120)
HICKORY CREEK WINERY LLC
750 Browntown Rd (49107-8336)
PHONE..................................269 422-1100
Eric Wagner, *President*
▲ **EMP:** 3
SALES (est): 217.7K **Privately Held**
SIC: 2084 Wines

(G-2121)
JACK-POST CORPORATION
800 E 3rd St (49107-1803)
PHONE..................................269 695-7000
John T Bycraft, *President*
Charles M Pomeroy III, *Treasurer*
Ronald J Jaicomo, *Admin Sec*
▲ **EMP:** 14
SQ FT: 260,000
SALES (est): 2.6MM **Privately Held**
SIC: 2514 3446 2511 Metal lawn & garden furniture; architectural metalwork; flagpoles, metal; fences or posts, ornamental iron or steel; ornamental metalwork; wood household furniture

(G-2122)
K&S CONSULTANTS LLC
Also Called: Kilgore Industries
404 River St (49107-1483)
PHONE..................................269 240-7767
Brian Kilgore, *Partner*
EMP: 4
SQ FT: 58,000
SALES: 60K **Privately Held**
SIC: 3541 3548 3536 Machine tool replacement & repair parts, metal cutting types; electric welding equipment; hoisting slings

(G-2123)
LEAN FACTORY AMERICA LLC
816 E 3rd St (49107-1468)
PHONE..................................513 297-3086
Kurt Greissinger, *Vice Pres*
Keith Chabut,
▲ **EMP:** 5

SALES (est): 778.6K
SALES (corp-wide): 10.9MM **Privately Held**
SIC: 3442 Window & door frames
PA: Orgatex Gmbh & Co. Kg
Albert-Einstein-Str. 19
Langenfeld (Rheinland) 40764
217 310-640

(G-2124)
OPTIMYSTIC ENTERPRISES INC
Also Called: Electric Steam Generator
600 S Oak St (49107-1564)
P.O. Box 21 (49107-0021)
PHONE..................................269 695-7741
Carol L Roussin, *President*
F Thomas Roussin, *Vice Pres*
Mark C Lee, *Treasurer*
Caroline J Murphy, *Admin Sec*
EMP: 5 **EST:** 1946
SQ FT: 8,000
SALES (est): 961.2K **Privately Held**
WEB: www.esgcorp.com
SIC: 3629 Mercury arc rectifiers (electrical apparatus)

(G-2125)
PRECISION PLUMBING - T (PA)
Also Called: Benjamin Franklin Plumbing
317 Post Rd (49107-1049)
PHONE..................................269 695-2402
Leslie Roundy,
William Roundy,
EMP: 4
SQ FT: 6,000
SALES (est): 329.6K **Privately Held**
SIC: 1711 3259 Plumbing contractors; clay sewer & drainage pipe & tile

(G-2126)
RAMER PRODUCTS INC
400 Post Rd (49107-1052)
P.O. Box 1027, Niles (49120-1027)
PHONE..................................269 409-8583
Andrew Racine, *President*
EMP: 5
SQ FT: 8,000
SALES (est): 869.1K **Privately Held**
WEB: www.ramerproducts.com
SIC: 3829 Measuring & controlling devices

(G-2127)
REDBUD ROOTS LAB I LLC
215 Post Rd (49107-1020)
PHONE..................................312 656-3823
Alexander Leonowicz, *Principal*
EMP: 4
SALES (est): 326.5K **Privately Held**
SIC: 3999

Buckley
Wexford County

(G-2128)
AMERICAN DIE AND MOLD INC
141 S Industrial Dr (49620-9732)
PHONE..................................231 269-3788
Scott Flees, *President*
EMP: 6
SALES: 250K **Privately Held**
SIC: 3544 Industrial molds

(G-2129)
BRIDGE TOOL AND DIE LLC
125 S Industrial Dr (49620-9732)
PHONE..................................231 269-3200
Greg Mort, *Business Mgr*
Brent Bridgman, *Research*
Glenn Bridgman, *Mng Member*
EMP: 8
SALES (est): 1.4MM **Privately Held**
SIC: 3544 Special dies & tools

(G-2130)
MIDWEST TRACTOR & EQUIPMENT CO
10736 N M 37 (49620-9468)
P.O. Box 66 (49620-0066)
PHONE..................................231 269-4100
James Jurik, *President*
Larry Cade, *Treasurer*
EMP: 12
SQ FT: 10,200

SALES (est): 2.5MM **Privately Held**
WEB: www.midwesttractor.com
SIC: 3537 5511 7538 Industrial trucks & tractors; trucks, tractors & trailers: new & used; truck engine repair, except industrial

(G-2131)
SEAL RIGHT SERVICES INC
141 W Wexford Ave (49620-8600)
PHONE..................................231 357-5595
Theodore Allen, *Principal*
EMP: 3
SALES (est): 142.2K **Privately Held**
SIC: 1389 Oil field services

Burlington
Calhoun County

(G-2132)
HAMPTON COMPANY INC
12709 M 60 E (49029-9777)
PHONE..................................517 765-2222
Terry Hampton, *President*
EMP: 8
SQ FT: 22,000
SALES (est): 1MM **Privately Held**
SIC: 3944 Electronic game machines, except coin-operated

Burnips
Allegan County

(G-2133)
OLDCASTLE BUILDINGENVELOPE INC
4257 30th St (49314)
PHONE..................................616 896-8341
Brent Moomey, *Manager*
Kathryn Hutchins, *Executive*
EMP: 32
SALES (corp-wide): 30.6B **Privately Held**
WEB: www.oldcastleglass.com
SIC: 5039 5013 3231 Glass construction materials; automobile glass; products of purchased glass
HQ: Oldcastle Buildingenvelope, Inc.
  5005 Lndn B Jnsn Fwy 10
  Dallas TX 75244
  214 273-3400

Burr Oak
St. Joseph County

(G-2134)
C E B TOOLING INC
335 S 2nd St (49030-5142)
P.O. Box 12 (49030-0012)
PHONE..................................269 489-2251
Carl Baumeister, *President*
EMP: 5
SQ FT: 4,900
SALES (est): 785.2K **Privately Held**
SIC: 3089 Injection molding of plastics

(G-2135)
DO-MOR PRODUCTS
29435 Hackman Rd (49030-9779)
PHONE..................................269 651-7362
John L Miller, *Partner*
David Miller, *Partner*
EMP: 3
SALES (est): 459.4K **Privately Held**
SIC: 3523 Barn, silo, poultry, dairy & livestock machinery

(G-2136)
LEEANN PLASTICS INC
300 Halfway Rd (49030-9792)
PHONE..................................269 489-5035
Gary L Kirtley, *President*
Sharry Kirtley, *Corp Secy*
EMP: 16 EST: 1979
SQ FT: 10,500
SALES (est): 2.7MM **Privately Held**
SIC: 3089 Injection molding of plastics

(G-2137)
SCHULER TOOL & DIE COMPANY
319 S 2nd St (49030-5142)
P.O. Box 285 (49030-0285)
PHONE..................................269 489-2900
Andrew Schuler, *President*
Kimberly Keagle, *Corp Secy*
William J Schuler, *Vice Pres*
EMP: 3
SQ FT: 3,600
SALES (est): 220K **Privately Held**
SIC: 3544 3599 Dies & die holders for metal cutting, forming, die casting; machine shop, jobbing & repair

(G-2138)
VICTOR SCREW PRODUCTS CO
235 S 4th St (49030-5109)
P.O. Box 274 (49030-0274)
PHONE..................................269 489-2760
Fax: 269 489-2940
EMP: 4 EST: 1937
SQ FT: 7,500
SALES: 172.8K **Privately Held**
SIC: 3451 Mfg Screw Machine Products

Burt
Saginaw County

(G-2139)
VILLANUEVO SOLEDAD
Also Called: El Acapulco Tamales
2855 E Burt Rd (48417-2341)
P.O. Box 128 (48417-0128)
PHONE..................................989 770-4309
Soledad Villanuevo, *Owner*
Annette Graves, *Exec Dir*
EMP: 21
SALES (est): 1.2MM **Privately Held**
SIC: 2099 Food preparations

Burtchville
St. Clair County

(G-2140)
COLUMBUS OIL & GAS LLC
6436 Lakeshore Rd (48059-2557)
P.O. Box 610158, Port Huron (48061-0158)
PHONE..................................810 385-9140
At Kuhns III, *COO*
Charles Lawrence,
EMP: 4
SALES (est): 1.7MM **Privately Held**
SIC: 1389 1311 Gas field services; oil field services; crude petroleum & natural gas production; crude petroleum production

(G-2141)
TOASTMASTERS INTERNATIONAL
6415 State Rd (48059-2411)
PHONE..................................810 385-5477
Rick Stone,
EMP: 11
SALES (corp-wide): 31.3MM **Privately Held**
WEB: www.d70toastmasters.org
SIC: 8299 2721 Educational service, non-degree granting: continuing educ.; magazines: publishing only, not printed on site
PA: Toastmasters International
  9127 S Jamaica St Ste 400
  Englewood CO 80112
  949 858-8255

Burton
Genesee County

(G-2142)
ADAPTIVE MFG SOLUTIONS LLC
4206 S Saginaw St (48529)
PHONE..................................810 743-1600
Laurie Moncrieff, *General Mgr*
Laurie S Moncrieff,
EMP: 3

SQ FT: 21,000
SALES (est): 472.5K **Privately Held**
SIC: 3544 Special dies, tools, jigs & fixtures

(G-2143)
AMERICAN ELECTRIC MOTOR CORP (PA)
4102 Davison Rd (48509-1455)
PHONE..................................810 743-6080
Mark Lippincott, *President*
EMP: 13
SQ FT: 17,000
SALES (est): 2MM **Privately Held**
SIC: 7694 7699 Electric motor repair; hydraulic equipment repair

(G-2144)
ANTCLIFF WINDOWS & DOORS INC
2417 E Judd Rd (48529-2456)
PHONE..................................810 742-5963
Patti Zizka, *President*
John Zizka, *Vice Pres*
Matthew Giddings, *Sales Staff*
EMP: 19
SQ FT: 60,000
SALES (est): 4MM **Privately Held**
SIC: 3089 5031 5039 Windows, plastic; doors & windows; windows; doors, sliding

(G-2145)
BNB WELDING & FABRICATION INC
3162 E Hemphill Rd (48529-1456)
PHONE..................................810 820-1508
Jason Brewer, *President*
EMP: 8
SALES (est): 236.7K **Privately Held**
SIC: 7692 1799 3312 Welding repair; welding on site; structural shapes & pilings, steel

(G-2146)
BUCKS CEMENT INC
4299 Fenton Rd (48529)
PHONE..................................810 233-4141
Napoleon Groleau, *President*
Joyce Groleau, *Vice Pres*
EMP: 6
SALES (est): 598.9K **Privately Held**
SIC: 3713 Cement mixer bodies

(G-2147)
C & D ENTERPRISES INC
G4349 S Dort Hwy (48529-1805)
PHONE..................................248 373-0011
Charles Farley, *President*
Craig Hefner, *Vice Pres*
EMP: 18
SQ FT: 15,400
SALES (est): 3.5MM **Privately Held**
SIC: 2821 3543 Plastics materials & resins; industrial patterns

(G-2148)
C/W SOUTH INC
1220 N Center Rd (48509-1427)
PHONE..................................810 767-2806
Robert Sibilsky, *President*
EMP: 20
SQ FT: 70,000
SALES (est): 2.7MM **Privately Held**
SIC: 2653 Boxes, corrugated: made from purchased materials

(G-2149)
COLBERG RADIATOR & WELDING
4114 Davison Rd (48509-1455)
PHONE..................................810 742-0028
James Coleman, *President*
EMP: 3
SALES (est): 550.3K **Privately Held**
WEB: www.colbergradiator.com
SIC: 7539 7692 Radiator repair shop, automotive; welding repair

(G-2150)
COMMERCIAL GRAPHICS OF MICH
1453 Walli Strasse Dr (48509-1798)
PHONE..................................810 744-2102
Michael Rogers, *President*
▲ EMP: 3

SQ FT: 3,500
SALES: 600K **Privately Held**
SIC: 2752 3993 7336 2791 Commercial printing, offset; signs, not made in custom sign painting shops; graphic arts & related design; typesetting; bookbinding & related work

(G-2151)
COMPAK INC (PA)
1220 N Center Rd (48509-1427)
PHONE..................................810 767-2806
William E Martin, *Ch of Bd*
Joe Goggins, *Director*
Joel Liggett, *Director*
Mark E Martin, *Director*
EMP: 9
SQ FT: 6,000
SALES (est): 1.8MM **Privately Held**
WEB: www.compakinc.com
SIC: 2653 Display items, corrugated: made from purchased materials

(G-2152)
COMPAK INC
Also Called: Compac
1220 N Center Rd (48509-1427)
PHONE..................................989 288-3199
Clarence Koan, *Manager*
EMP: 5
SALES (est): 749.6K
SALES (corp-wide): 1.8MM **Privately Held**
WEB: www.compakinc.com
SIC: 2653 5113 Display items, corrugated: made from purchased materials; corrugated & solid fiber boxes
PA: Compak, Inc.
  1220 N Center Rd
  Burton MI 48509
  810 767-2806

(G-2153)
CUSTOM COMPONENTS TRUSS CO
Also Called: Custom Wood Products
3109 E Bristol Rd (48529-1411)
PHONE..................................810 744-0771
Peter Bomireto, *President*
Patricia Bomireto, *Vice Pres*
EMP: 50
SALES (est): 7.4MM **Privately Held**
SIC: 2439 Trusses, wooden roof

(G-2154)
FLINT BOXMAKERS INC
Also Called: Landahl Packaging Systems
G 2490 E Bristol Rd (48529)
P.O. Box 41, Flint (48501-0041)
PHONE..................................810 743-0400
Virginia R Landaal, *Ch of Bd*
Thomas Landaal, *President*
Stephen Landaal, *Exec VP*
Martha Jeanne Stetson, *Treasurer*
James Trembley, *Admin Sec*
EMP: 40
SQ FT: 86,000
SALES (est): 6.3MM
SALES (corp-wide): 58MM **Privately Held**
SIC: 2653 Boxes, corrugated: made from purchased materials; boxes, solid fiber: made from purchased materials
PA: Delta Containers, Inc.
  1400 Eddy St
  Bay City MI 48708
  810 742-2730

(G-2155)
GENOAK MATERIALS INC
Also Called: Tri City Aggregates
3251 E Bristol Rd (48529-1411)
P.O. Box 182, Holly (48442-0182)
PHONE..................................810 742-0050
Bernhard Rumbold, *Branch Mgr*
EMP: 4
SALES (est): 275K **Privately Held**
SIC: 1442 Gravel & pebble mining
PA: Genoak Materials Inc
  14300 Shields Rd
  Holly MI 48442

Byron Center - Kent County (G-2184)

(G-2156)
HOLLANDER MACHINE CO INC
Also Called: Precision USA Mfg
G3333 S Dort Hwy (48529-1446)
PHONE..................810 742-1660
Mathew Moses, *President*
EMP: 6 **EST:** 1973
SQ FT: 3,000
SALES: 500K **Privately Held**
SIC: 3541 3451 Screw machines, automatic; screw machine products

(G-2157)
KIRBY METAL CORPORATION
Also Called: Kirby Steel
4072 Flint Asphalt Dr (48529-1857)
PHONE..................810 743-3360
James R Kirby, *President*
Michael Kirby, *Vice Pres*
EMP: 20
SQ FT: 42,000
SALES (est): 5.9MM **Privately Held**
SIC: 3441 Fabricated structural metal

(G-2158)
MID WEST PALLET
2206 E Parkwood Ave (48529-1768)
PHONE..................810 919-3072
Marcus Ellis, *Principal*
EMP: 4
SALES (est): 263.5K **Privately Held**
SIC: 2448 Pallets, wood & wood with metal

(G-2159)
MJ MFG CO
2441 E Bristol Rd (48529-1304)
PHONE..................810 744-3840
Edward P Arends, *President*
Dawn Mueller, *Buyer*
Zanita Arends, *Admin Sec*
EMP: 7
SQ FT: 62,000
SALES (est): 1.2MM **Privately Held**
SIC: 3714 Motor vehicle parts & accessories

(G-2160)
OMARA SPRUNG FLOORS INC
3130 Eugene St (48519-1655)
PHONE..................810 743-8281
Edward J Omara, *President*
Mary Omara, *Vice Pres*
Ariel Omara, *Marketing Staff*
EMP: 7
SQ FT: 5,000
SALES (est): 1.2MM **Privately Held**
WEB: www.sprungfloors.com
SIC: 2426 Flooring, hardwood

(G-2161)
PRO-TECH MACHINE INC
3085 Joyce St (48529-1421)
PHONE..................810 743-1854
David Currie, *President*
Scott Kamieniecki, *Controller*
EMP: 25
SQ FT: 17,000
SALES (est): 6.4MM **Privately Held**
WEB: www.protechmachine.net
SIC: 3549 3544 Assembly machines, including robotic; special dies, tools, jigs & fixtures

(G-2162)
QUINLAN LUMBER CO
2470 E Bristol Rd (48529-1325)
PHONE..................810 743-0700
Edward J Quinlan, *President*
EMP: 8 **EST:** 1942
SQ FT: 20,000
SALES (est): 818.9K **Privately Held**
SIC: 2449 Wood containers

(G-2163)
SCHMALD TOOL & DIE INC (PA)
G4206 S Saginaw St (48529-1695)
PHONE..................810 743-1600
Laurie S Moncrieff, *President*
EMP: 15 **EST:** 1948
SQ FT: 30,000
SALES: 3.4MM **Privately Held**
WEB: www.schmald.com
SIC: 3544 Special dies & tools; dies & die holders for metal cutting, forming, die casting; forms (molds), for foundry & plastics working machinery

(G-2164)
SGP TECHNOLOGIES
2097 Amy St (48519-1105)
PHONE..................810 744-1715
Tim Carver, *Owner*
EMP: 5
SQ FT: 10,000
SALES: 600K **Privately Held**
WEB: www.sgptechnologies.com
SIC: 3089 Plastic processing

(G-2165)
SHAMROCK FABRICATING INC
2347 E Bristol Rd (48529-1304)
PHONE..................810 744-0677
George Gilliam Jr, *President*
Tina Tomaszewski, *Corp Secy*
EMP: 14
SQ FT: 5,800
SALES: 266K **Privately Held**
SIC: 3412 Pails, shipping: metal

(G-2166)
SOROC PRODUCTS INC
4349 S Dort Hwy (48529)
PHONE..................810 743-2660
Dennis Cox, *CEO*
EMP: 49 **EST:** 1973
SQ FT: 24,000
SALES (est): 9.8MM **Privately Held**
WEB: www.sorocproducts.com
SIC: 3089 Molding primary plastic

(G-2167)
STONE SPECIALISTS INC
4231 Davison Rd (48509-1405)
P.O. Box 90322 (48509-0322)
PHONE..................810 744-2278
Jason Treichel, *President*
▲ **EMP:** 15 **EST:** 1996
SQ FT: 30,000
SALES (est): 2.1MM **Privately Held**
WEB: www.stonespecialists.net
SIC: 3281 Curbing, granite or stone

(G-2168)
TYRONE TOOL COMPANY INC
Also Called: J T Products
3336 Associates Dr (48529-1302)
PHONE..................810 742-4762
Dennis Conklin, *President*
Karen Conklin, *President*
EMP: 4
SQ FT: 2,400
SALES: 50K **Privately Held**
SIC: 3599 Machine shop, jobbing & repair

(G-2169)
VANITY FUR
1184 S Belsay Rd Ste B (48509-1921)
PHONE..................810 744-3000
Janice M Fletcher, *Principal*
EMP: 3
SALES (est): 190.9K **Privately Held**
SIC: 3999 Furs

(G-2170)
WEBCOR PACKAGING CORPORATION (PA)
1220 N Center Rd (48509-1427)
PHONE..................810 767-2806
William Martin, *Ch of Bd*
Mark Blackburn, *Manager*
John Goggins, *Shareholder*
▲ **EMP:** 70
SQ FT: 70,000
SALES (est): 24.5MM **Privately Held**
WEB: www.comwebinc.com
SIC: 2653 Boxes, corrugated: made from purchased materials

Byron
Shiawassee County

(G-2171)
FORSYTH MILLWORK AND FARMS
15315 Duffield Rd (48418-9543)
PHONE..................810 266-4000
Michael Forsyth, *Owner*
EMP: 5
SQ FT: 6,500
SALES: 1.2MM **Privately Held**
SIC: 2431 Millwork

(G-2172)
GUILE & SON INC
11951 Rathbon Rd (48418-9614)
PHONE..................517 376-2116
Ted Guile, *President*
EMP: 5
SALES (est): 150K **Privately Held**
SIC: 3446 Architectural metalwork

(G-2173)
JOSHS FROGS
11629 Glen Mary Dr (48418-9670)
PHONE..................517 648-0260
Joshua Willard, *Executive*
EMP: 3 **EST:** 2005
SALES (est): 206.1K **Privately Held**
SIC: 3999 Pet supplies

(G-2174)
ON THE SIDE SIGN DSIGN GRPHICS
15216 Murray Rd (48418-9006)
PHONE..................810 266-7446
Dan Rozboril, *Owner*
Steve Fairman, *Partner*
EMP: 4
SQ FT: 5,500
SALES (est): 296.2K **Privately Held**
SIC: 3993 7532 3479 3353 Signs & advertising specialties; customizing services, non-factory basis; etching & engraving; aluminum sheet, plate & foil; products of purchased glass; commercial printing, lithographic

Byron Center
Kent County

(G-2175)
ALAN BRUCE ENTERPRISES
4590 28th St Sw (49315-9609)
PHONE..................616 262-4609
Bruce Breuker, *President*
EMP: 6
SALES: 900K **Privately Held**
SIC: 3312 Light oil crude from chemical recovery coke ovens

(G-2176)
AMPLIFIED LIFE NETWORK LLC
7791 Byron Center Ave Sw (49315-8412)
PHONE..................800 453-7733
Lyle Labardee, *General Mgr*
EMP: 3 **EST:** 2012
SALES (est): 248.5K **Privately Held**
SIC: 8322 2731 2741 General counseling services; pamphlets: publishing only, not printed on site; art copy & poster publishing; newsletter publishing

(G-2177)
ATLAS ROOFING CORPORATION
Atlas Eps
8240 Byron Center Ave Sw (49315-8866)
PHONE..................616 878-1568
Bob Butkus, *General Mgr*
Greg Larson, *Engineer*
Jennifer Ryan, *Accounts Exec*
Amber Spray, *Accounts Exec*
Corinne Mitrzyk, *Mktg Coord*
EMP: 200 **Privately Held**
WEB: www.atlasroofing.com
SIC: 3086 Insulation or cushioning material, foamed plastic
HQ: Atlas Roofing Corporation
  802 Highway 19 N Ste 190
  Meridian MS 39307
  601 484-8900

(G-2178)
AVOCADOUGH LLC
494 Oldfield Dr Se (49315-8076)
PHONE..................908 596-1437
Ian Rugg, *Mng Member*
EMP: 4
SALES (est): 98.3K **Privately Held**
SIC: 7372 Application computer software

(G-2179)
BENNETT FUNERAL COACHES INC
584 76th St Sw B (49315-8307)
PHONE..................616 538-8100
Rex Troost, *President*
W Rance Bennett, *Vice Pres*
EMP: 8
SQ FT: 7,000
SALES (est): 760K **Privately Held**
SIC: 3711 Hearses (motor vehicles), assembly of

(G-2180)
BPV LLC
Also Called: Bpv Environmental
511 76th St Sw (49315-8306)
PHONE..................616 281-4502
Laureen Hiscock, *Accounting Mgr*
Jody Black, *Mng Member*
Nicole Spain, *Manager*
Jeff Vanderweide, *Maintence Staff*
EMP: 50
SALES: 10MM
SALES (corp-wide): 40.8MM **Privately Held**
WEB: www.bpv.net
SIC: 2611 Pulp manufactured from waste or recycled paper
HQ: Pestell Pet Products Inc
  141 Hamilton Rd Suite 794
  New Hamburg ON N3A 2
  519 662-2877

(G-2181)
COMPOSITE TECHNIQUES INC
7850 Clyde Park Ave Sw (49315-9390)
PHONE..................616 878-9795
Jeff Cable, *President*
EMP: 10
SQ FT: 7,000
SALES (est): 1.7MM **Privately Held**
SIC: 3089 8711 Injection molding of plastics; structural engineering; industrial engineers

(G-2182)
CONSUMERS CONCRETE CORPORATION
8257 S Division Ave (49315-9031)
PHONE..................616 827-0063
Gregg Ferguson, *Manager*
EMP: 8
SALES (corp-wide): 102.9MM **Privately Held**
WEB: www.consumersconcrete.com
SIC: 3273 Ready-mixed concrete
PA: Consumers Concrete Corporation
  3508 S Sprinkle Rd
  Kalamazoo MI 49001
  269 342-0136

(G-2183)
CONTROL SOLUTIONS INC
8535 Byron Commerce Dr Sw A (49315-9129)
PHONE..................616 247-9422
Ryan E Kauffman, *President*
Michael D Heavner, *Vice Pres*
Liz Pearson, *CFO*
EMP: 75
SQ FT: 3,600
SALES (est): 3.3MM **Privately Held**
SIC: 3822 Temperature controls, automatic

(G-2184)
CORVAC COMPOSITES LLC (HQ)
104 84th St Sw (49315-9305)
PHONE..................616 281-4026
James Fitzell, *President*
Rich Jordan, *President*
John Humphrey, *Principal*
Christine Black, *Controller*
Paul J Dieterle, *Human Res Dir*
◆ **EMP:** 30
SALES (est): 132.5MM
SALES (corp-wide): 171MM **Privately Held**
SIC: 3559 Automotive related machinery
PA: Humphrey Companies Llc
  2851 Prairie St Sw
  Grandville MI 49418
  616 530-1717

Byron Center - Kent County (G-2185)

(G-2185)
CUSTOM CRUSHING & RECYCLE INC
978 64th St Sw (49315-8685)
PHONE.................................616 249-3329
Mark Fennema, *Owner*
EMP: 3
SALES (est): 646.3K **Privately Held**
SIC: 2611 Pulp manufactured from waste or recycled paper

(G-2186)
CUSTOM DOOR PARTS
8177 Clyde Park Ave Sw (49315-9332)
PHONE.................................616 949-5000
John H Brinkert Sr, *President*
EMP: 3 **EST:** 2017
SALES (est): 50.2K **Privately Held**
SIC: 2499 Laundry products, wood

(G-2187)
DIOCESAN PUBLICATIONS (PA)
1050 74th St Sw (49315-8166)
P.O. Box 2461, Grand Rapids (49501-2461)
PHONE.................................616 878-5200
Robert Zielke, *Ch of Bd*
Carl Galant, *President*
Kevin Stapleton, *Exec VP*
Richard Wilterdink, *Vice Pres*
Fabio Espinosa, *Sales Staff*
EMP: 40 **EST:** 1960
SQ FT: 11,000
SALES (est): 6.7MM **Privately Held**
WEB: www.diocesanpublications.com
SIC: 2741 Business service newsletters: publishing & printing

(G-2188)
EDWARD D JONES & CO LP
2465 Byron Station Dr Sw E (49315-7982)
PHONE.................................616 583-0387
Jay Zahran, *Branch Mgr*
EMP: 5
SALES (corp-wide): 8.5B **Privately Held**
SIC: 3674 Semiconductors & related devices
HQ: Edward D. Jones & Co., L.P.
12555 Manchester Rd
Saint Louis MO 63131
314 515-2000

(G-2189)
ENDRES PROCESSING LLC
8557 Piedmont Ind Dr Sw (49315-9356)
PHONE.................................616 878-4230
Glen Voetborg, *Branch Mgr*
EMP: 61 **Privately Held**
WEB: www.endresprocessing.com
SIC: 2048 Prepared feeds
PA: Endres Processing, L.L.C.
13420 Court House Blvd
Rosemount MN 55068

(G-2190)
FABTEC ENTERPRISES INC
8538 Centre Indus Dr Sw (49315-9291)
PHONE.................................616 878-9288
Tim Stevens, *President*
Mitch Dalman, *Vice Pres*
EMP: 12
SALES (est): 3MM **Privately Held**
SIC: 3316 Cold finishing of steel shapes

(G-2191)
FLOW-RITE CONTROLS LTD
960 74th St Sw (49315-7914)
PHONE.................................616 583-1700
Robert Burnetter, *CEO*
Dan Campau, *President*
Rick Mavrakis, *Exec VP*
Ken Denman, *Buyer*
Cindy Honea, *Buyer*
EMP: 35
SQ FT: 25,000
SALES (est): 11.4MM **Privately Held**
SIC: 3494 3594 3728 3823 Valves & pipe fittings; fluid power pumps & motors; aircraft parts & equipment; industrial instrmnts msrmnt display/control process variable

(G-2192)
G & T INDUSTRIES INC (PA)
1001 76th St Sw (49315-7956)
PHONE.................................616 452-8611
Roland Grit, *President*
Drew Schramm, *Managing Prtnr*
David Boggiano, *General Mgr*
John Bosch, *General Mgr*
Kevin Kolesar, *Exec VP*
▲ **EMP:** 90
SQ FT: 205,000
SALES (est): 46.1MM **Privately Held**
WEB: www.gtindustries.com
SIC: 3086 5072 Insulation or cushioning material, foamed plastic; packaging & shipping materials, foamed plastic; hardware

(G-2193)
GRABBER INC
365 84th St Sw Ste 4 (49315-7936)
PHONE.................................616 940-1914
John Bradley Wagner Jr, *President*
Gary Gerds, *Vice Pres*
John Weathers, *Treasurer*
Joe Vergona, *Director*
Takafumi Sakaguchi, *Admin Sec*
EMP: 32
SALES (est): 3.3MM **Privately Held**
SIC: 2392 5023 Blankets, comforters & beddings; blankets

(G-2194)
GRAND RAPIDS CHAIR COMPANY
1250 84th St Sw (49315-8048)
PHONE.................................616 774-0561
Dave Miller, *CEO*
Geoffrey Miller, *Vice Pres*
Tom Southwell, *Vice Pres*
Greg Bremer, *CFO*
▲ **EMP:** 120
SQ FT: 150,000
SALES (est): 26.5MM **Privately Held**
WEB: www.grandrapidschair.com
SIC: 2511 Wood household furniture

(G-2195)
INGLASS USA INC
Also Called: Hrsflow
920 74th St Sw (49315-7914)
PHONE.................................616 228-6900
Maurizio Bazzo, *Principal*
Andrea Zigante, *Plant Mgr*
Tammy Baker, *Human Res Mgr*
Steve Eddy, *Accounts Mgr*
Tim Bruin, *Cust Mgr*
▲ **EMP:** 10
SALES (est): 860.9K
SALES (corp-wide): 57.2K **Privately Held**
SIC: 3544 Industrial molds
HQ: Inglass Spa
Via Piave 4
San Polo Di Piave TV 31020
042 275-0111

(G-2196)
LAMON GROUP INC
Also Called: 3dx Tech
889 76th St Sw Unit 1 (49315-8400)
PHONE.................................616 710-3169
Matthew Howlett, *President*
▲ **EMP:** 20
SALES (est): 1.1MM **Privately Held**
SIC: 2759 Commercial printing

(G-2197)
MAYVILLE ENGINEERING CO INC
990 84th St Sw (49315-9301)
PHONE.................................616 878-5235
Robert D Kamphuis, *CEO*
Chad Belbeck, *Design Engr*
Kris Rafalski, *Manager*
EMP: 296
SALES (corp-wide): 354.5MM **Publicly Held**
SIC: 3469 Stamping metal for the trade
PA: Mayville Engineering Co Inc
715 South St
Mayville WI 53050
920 387-4500

(G-2198)
MCDONALD ACQUISITIONS LLC
Also Called: Proficient Machine & Tool
8074 Clyde Park Ave Sw (49315-9332)
PHONE.................................616 878-7800
Thomas McDonald, *President*
EMP: 40
SQ FT: 7,000
SALES (est): 15MM **Privately Held**
SIC: 3599 Custom machinery

(G-2199)
MCM DISPOSAL LLC
978 64th St Sw (49315-8685)
PHONE.................................616 656-4049
Dan Strock,
Chad Arp,
EMP: 5
SQ FT: 10,000
SALES (est): 396.6K **Privately Held**
SIC: 3443 4953 Dumpsters, garbage; recycling, waste materials; refuse collection & disposal services; rubbish collection & disposal; ashes, collection & disposal

(G-2200)
MICRO ENGINEERING INC
Also Called: Micro Belmont
257 Sorrento Dr Se (49315-9315)
PHONE.................................616 534-9681
James Jolliffe, *President*
EMP: 30
SALES (est): 4.3MM **Privately Held**
WEB: www.microbelmont.com
SIC: 3842 3599 5012 5599 Traction apparatus; machine shop, jobbing & repair; snowmobiles; snowmobiles; special dies, tools, jigs & fixtures; hand & edge tools

(G-2201)
MIDWEST DIRECT TRANSPORT INC
1144 73rd St Sw Ste A (49315-6924)
PHONE.................................616 698-8900
David B Welsch, *President*
David Eninga, *President*
EMP: 15
SALES (est): 2.9MM **Privately Held**
SIC: 3799 Trailers & trailer equipment

(G-2202)
MITTEX GROUP
8936 Conifer Ridge Dr Sw (49315-8443)
PHONE.................................616 878-4090
Brett M Deacon, *President*
Michelle Deacon, *Accountant*
EMP: 3
SALES (est): 374K **Privately Held**
SIC: 3469 Metal stampings

(G-2203)
MIX MASTERS INC
530 76th St Sw Ste 400 (49315-8042)
PHONE.................................616 490-8520
Christopher Davey, *Principal*
EMP: 5
SALES (est): 458.6K **Privately Held**
SIC: 3273 Ready-mixed concrete

(G-2204)
MODEL PATTERN COMPANY INC
Also Called: Mp Components
8499 Centre Indus Dr Sw (49315-9292)
PHONE.................................616 878-9710
Joseph Schlatter, *President*
Otto Schlatter, *Chairman*
John Schlatter, *Vice Pres*
EMP: 40
SQ FT: 32,000
SALES (est): 8.2MM **Privately Held**
WEB: www.mpcomponents-inc.com
SIC: 3543 Industrial patterns

(G-2205)
OFLOW-RITE CONTROLS LTD
960 74th St Sw (49315-7914)
PHONE.................................616 583-1700
Kimberly Chiodini, *Materials Mgr*
Mike Semm, *Opers Staff*
EMP: 55
SALES (est): 5.6MM **Privately Held**
WEB: www.flow-rite.com
SIC: 3823 Industrial instrmnts msrmnt display/control process variable

(G-2206)
P S MONOGRAMS
160 84th St Sw Ste 4 (49315-7301)
PHONE.................................616 698-1177
Dave Hood, *Owner*
EMP: 3
SQ FT: 400
SALES (est): 233.8K **Privately Held**
SIC: 2395 Embroidery & art needlework

(G-2207)
PHILLIPS-MEDISIZE LLC
8140 Cool Ridge Dr Sw (49315-8466)
PHONE.................................616 878-5030
Mike Stevenson, *Branch Mgr*
EMP: 176
SALES (corp-wide): 40.6B **Privately Held**
SIC: 3089 Injection molding of plastics
HQ: Pantheon Topco, Inc.
7 Long Lake Dr
Phillips WI 54555
715 386-4320

(G-2208)
PIONEER STEEL CORPORATION
Also Called: Pioneer Die Sets
8700 Byron Commerce Dr Sw (49315-8125)
PHONE.................................616 878-5800
Greg Tapper, *Site Mgr*
Gil Hoard, *Branch Mgr*
EMP: 30
SALES (corp-wide): 29.7MM **Privately Held**
WEB: www.pioneersteel.us
SIC: 3544 Die sets for metal stamping (presses)
PA: Pioneer Steel Corporation
7447 Intervale St
Detroit MI 48238
313 933-9400

(G-2209)
PRO-VISION SOLUTIONS LLC
Also Called: Pro-Vision Video Systems
8625b Byron Cmmerce Dr Sw (49315-8249)
P.O. Box 8821, Kentwood (49518-8821)
PHONE.................................616 583-1520
Stephen Peacock, *President*
▲ **EMP:** 20
SQ FT: 5,400
SALES (est): 6.1MM **Privately Held**
WEB: www.pro-visions.com
SIC: 3651 Household audio & video equipment

(G-2210)
QUARRY RIDGE STONE INC
555 Ste B Sw (49315)
PHONE.................................616 827-8244
Daniel W Fox, *President*
Joe Fox, *Manager*
EMP: 15
SALES (est): 1.2MM **Privately Held**
SIC: 3281 Stone, quarrying & processing of own stone products

(G-2211)
SHOP MAKARIOS LLC
4390 104th St Sw (49315-9713)
PHONE.................................800 479-0032
Maxwell Kolend, *President*
Airika Kolenda, *Vice Pres*
EMP: 3 **EST:** 2014
SALES (est): 187.5K **Privately Held**
SIC: 5999 3993 7299 2511 Art & architectural supplies; signs, not made in custom sign painting shops; stitching, custom; wood household furniture; bedding (sheets, blankets, spreads & pillows)

(G-2212)
TG MANUFACTURING LLC (PA)
Also Called: Dorr Industries
8197 Clyde Park Ave Sw (49315-9332)
PHONE.................................616 935-7575
Richard Actenberg,
EMP: 30
SQ FT: 30,000
SALES (est): 10.2MM **Privately Held**
SIC: 3498 3441 3469 Tube fabricating (contract bending & shaping); fabricated structural metal; metal stampings

GEOGRAPHIC SECTION

Cadillac - Wexford County (G-2238)

(G-2213)
USHER TOOL & DIE INC
1015 84th St Sw (49315-9301)
PHONE................................616 583-9160
Jay Usher, *President*
Kyle Hofman, *President*
EMP: 12 **EST:** 1975
SQ FT: 10,000
SALES (est): 1.3MM **Privately Held**
WEB: www.usher-td.com
SIC: 3469 3544 Metal stampings; jigs & fixtures

(G-2214)
VAN BEEKS CUSTOM WOOD PRODUCTS
7950 Clyde Park Ave Sw (49315-7912)
PHONE................................616 583-9002
Kevin Van Volkinburg, *President*
EMP: 15
SQ FT: 8,500
SALES: 900K **Privately Held**
WEB: www.vanbeekscwp.com
SIC: 2431 Doors, wood

(G-2215)
VISUAL WORKPLACE LLC
1300 Richfield Ct Sw (49315-9493)
PHONE................................616 583-9400
Rhonda Kovera, *Principal*
▲ **EMP:** 11
SALES (est): 1.1MM **Privately Held**
SIC: 3993 Signs & advertising specialties

(G-2216)
WARMERSCOM
365 84th St Sw Ste 4 (49315-7936)
PHONE................................800 518-0938
EMP: 3
SALES (est): 156K **Privately Held**
SIC: 2252 Tights & leg warmers

(G-2217)
WOOD TECH INC
670 76th St Sw (49315-6959)
PHONE................................616 455-0800
Mike Staples, *President*
EMP: 30
SQ FT: 22,000
SALES (est): 4.9MM **Privately Held**
SIC: 2439 Trusses, except roof: laminated lumber; trusses, wooden roof

(G-2218)
WYSER INNOVATIVE PRODUCTS LLC
8560 Centre Indstrl Dr E (49315)
PHONE................................616 583-9225
John Kyser,
EMP: 8
SALES (est): 1.5MM **Privately Held**
WEB: www.wyserproducts.com
SIC: 3545 8748 Cutting tools for machine tools; business consulting

Cadillac
Wexford County

(G-2219)
AAR CORP
10732 Pine Shore Dr (49601-8257)
PHONE................................231 779-4859
David Barber, *Principal*
Jean Langmesser, *Manager*
Stacie Tropf, *Manager*
Clarence Martenies, *Info Tech Dir*
EMP: 10
SALES (corp-wide): 2B **Publicly Held**
SIC: 3724 Aircraft engines & engine parts
PA: Aar Corp.
1100 N Wood Dale Rd
Wood Dale IL 60191
630 227-2000

(G-2220)
AAR MANUFACTURING INC
Also Called: AAR Mobility Systems
201 Haynes St (49601-1803)
P.O. Box 550 (49601-0550)
PHONE................................231 779-8800
Mark McDonald, *Vice Pres*
Ryan Kennedy, *Purch Dir*
Mike Eardley, *Buyer*
Renee Kroes, *Buyer*
Therese Longstreet, *Buyer*
EMP: 48
SALES (corp-wide): 2B **Publicly Held**
SIC: 2448 2449 3537 3411 Wood pallets & skids; wood containers; industrial trucks & tractors; metal cans; aluminum rolling & drawing
HQ: Aar Manufacturing, Inc.
1100 N Wood Dale Rd
Wood Dale IL 60191
630 227-2000

(G-2221)
ABLE HTNG CLNG & PLMBNG
9542 Peterson Dr (49601-9758)
PHONE................................231 779-5430
James Huston, *Principal*
EMP: 4
SALES (est): 143K **Privately Held**
SIC: 3567 Industrial furnaces & ovens

(G-2222)
ADVANCED RUBBER TECH INC
10640 W Cadillac Rd (49601-9415)
PHONE................................231 775-3112
Philip West, *President*
Robert Stanhope, *Owner*
Erica Szegda, *General Mgr*
Thomas Boughner, *Maintence Staff*
EMP: 19
SQ FT: 15,000
SALES (est): 2.3MM **Privately Held**
WEB: www.ast-paving.com
SIC: 3069 Molded rubber products; rubber automotive products

(G-2223)
AKWEL CADILLAC USA INC (DH)
Also Called: Avon Automotive-Orizaba
603 7th St (49601-1344)
PHONE................................231 876-8020
Leland J Richards, *President*
William C Dircks, *CFO*
Scott Maresh, *Treasurer*
Roger Abrahamson, *Controller*
Joseph Wojciechowski, *Director*
▲ **EMP:** 280
SQ FT: 6,000
SALES (est): 102.4MM **Privately Held**
WEB: www.avonauto.com
SIC: 3061 3089 Mechanical rubber goods; injection molded finished plastic products

(G-2224)
AKWEL CADILLAC USA INC
Also Called: Avon Automotive Orizaba
603 7th St (49601-1344)
PHONE................................231 775-6571
Chuck Strickland, *Branch Mgr*
EMP: 146 **Privately Held**
WEB: www.avonauto.com
SIC: 3061 Automotive rubber goods (mechanical)
HQ: Akwel Cadillac Usa, Inc
603 7th St
Cadillac MI 49601
231 876-8020

(G-2225)
AKWEL CADILLAC USA INC
Also Called: Avon Automotive Holdings
603 7th St (49601-1344)
PHONE................................231 876-1361
EMP: 5 **Privately Held**
SIC: 3052 Rubber hose
HQ: Akwel Cadillac Usa, Inc
603 7th St
Cadillac MI 49601
231 876-8020

(G-2226)
AKWEL USA INC
Also Called: Avon Automotive
603 7th St (49601-1344)
PHONE................................231 775-6571
Chuck Strickland, *Branch Mgr*
EMP: 150 **Privately Held**
SIC: 3061 Mechanical rubber goods
HQ: Akwel Usa, Inc.
603 7th St
Cadillac MI 49601

(G-2227)
AMERICAN BOTTLING COMPANY
Also Called: 7 Up Bottling Co
1481 Potthoff St (49601-9671)
PHONE................................231 775-7393
Charlie Kelly, *Principal*
Tom Soltis, *Manager*
EMP: 40 **Publicly Held**
WEB: www.cs-americas.com
SIC: 2086 Soft drinks: packaged in cans, bottles, etc.
HQ: The American Bottling Company
5301 Legacy Dr
Plano TX 75024

(G-2228)
ARVCO CONTAINER CORPORATION
1355 Marty Paul St (49601-8244)
PHONE................................231 876-0935
Mike Gordon, *Branch Mgr*
EMP: 15
SALES (est): 2.9MM
SALES (corp-wide): 58.8MM **Privately Held**
WEB: www.arvco.com
SIC: 2653 Boxes, corrugated: made from purchased materials
PA: Arvco Container Corporation
845 Gibson St
Kalamazoo MI 49001
269 381-0900

(G-2229)
AUSABLE UPHOLSTERY
131 1/2 Evart St (49601-2307)
PHONE................................989 366-5219
Doreen Brandt, *Partner*
Arthur Brandt, *Partner*
EMP: 3
SALES (est): 229.3K **Privately Held**
SIC: 2499 7641 Decorative wood & woodwork; furniture repair & maintenance

(G-2230)
AVON PROTECTION SYSTEMS INC (DH)
503 8th St (49601-1370)
PHONE................................231 779-6200
Michael Hamner, *President*
Scott Jesweak, *President*
John Kime, *COO*
Bruce Schorer, *Vice Pres*
Renee Kroes, *Senior Buyer*
◆ **EMP:** 182
SALES (est): 43.8MM
SALES (corp-wide): 211MM **Privately Held**
WEB: www.avon-protection.com
SIC: 3842 Gas masks
HQ: Avon Rubber & Plastics, Inc.
503 8th St
Cadillac MI 49601
231 779-6290

(G-2231)
BIG FOOT MANUFACTURING CO
1480 Potthoff St (49601-9671)
PHONE................................231 775-5588
R Lyle Matteson, *President*
Bernie Geers, *Treasurer*
EMP: 11
SQ FT: 29,500
SALES (est): 1.3MM **Privately Held**
WEB: www.bigfootmfg.com
SIC: 3531 3523 3498 3496 Wellpoint systems; farm machinery & equipment; fabricated pipe & fittings; miscellaneous fabricated wire products

(G-2232)
BORGWARNER INC
1100 Wright St (49601-9278)
PHONE................................231 779-7500
Mark Reese, *Engineer*
Brad Soules, *Engineer*
Vince Tembreull, *Engineer*
Ken Mulder, *Controller*
John Raasio, *Marketing Staff*
EMP: 30
SALES (corp-wide): 10.5B **Publicly Held**
SIC: 3714 Motor vehicle parts & accessories
PA: Borgwarner Inc.
3850 Hamlin Rd
Auburn Hills MI 48326
248 754-9200

(G-2233)
BORGWARNER THERMAL SYSTEMS INC
Also Called: Borg Warner Automotive
1100 Wright St (49601-9278)
PHONE................................231 779-7500
Todd Bennington, *Manager*
EMP: 29
SALES (corp-wide): 10.5B **Publicly Held**
SIC: 3625 3568 3713 3564 Control equipment, electric; power transmission equipment; truck & bus bodies; blowers & fans
HQ: Borgwarner Thermal Systems Inc.
1507 S Kalamazoo Ave
Marshall MI 49068
269 781-1228

(G-2234)
BROOKS & PERKINS INC
Also Called: B & P Manufacturing
8051 E 34 Rd (49601-9013)
PHONE................................231 775-2229
Keith Merchant, *CEO*
Jeff Olson, *President*
Erik Warner, *Design Engr*
Gale Merchant, *CFO*
Pay Mys, *Marketing Staff*
▲ **EMP:** 66
SQ FT: 6,000
SALES (est): 18.4MM **Privately Held**
WEB: www.bpmfg.com
SIC: 3355 Aluminum rail & structural shapes

(G-2235)
CADILLAC CASTING INC (PA)
1500 4th Ave (49601-9062)
PHONE................................231 779-9600
John Hass, *President*
John Haas, *President*
Alex Boosalis, *Vice Pres*
Donald Grage, *Production*
Don Hiltz, *Engineer*
EMP: 97
SQ FT: 280,000
SALES (est): 81.3MM **Privately Held**
WEB: www.cadillaccasting.com
SIC: 3321 Gray & ductile iron foundries

(G-2236)
CADILLAC CULVERT INC
5305 M 115 (49601-9610)
PHONE................................231 775-3761
Chuck Thomas, *President*
Don Aldrich, *Vice Pres*
EMP: 12
SALES (est): 2.2MM **Privately Held**
SIC: 3498 Fabricated pipe & fittings

(G-2237)
CADILLAC ENGINEERED PLAS INC
Also Called: Fiamm Technologies
1550 Leeson Ave (49601-8975)
PHONE................................231 775-2900
Stefano Roselini, *President*
▲ **EMP:** 14
SQ FT: 16,000
SALES (est): 2.3MM
SALES (corp-wide): 1.3MM **Privately Held**
WEB: www.fiammamerica.com
SIC: 3089 Injection molded finished plastic products
HQ: Fiamm Technologies, L.L.C.
23880 Industrial Park Dr
Farmington Hills MI 48335

(G-2238)
CADILLAC FABRICATION INC (PA)
Also Called: Yard King
1340 Marty Paul St (49601-8244)
PHONE................................231 775-7386
Thomas D Bosscher, *President*
Susan Smith, *Human Res Mgr*
Dave Vanhouten, *Supervisor*
Cindy Bazuin, *IT/INT Sup*
EMP: 38

Cadillac - Wexford County (G-2239)

SQ FT: 10,800
SALES (est): 9.8MM **Privately Held**
WEB: www.cadfab.com
SIC: 3441 Fabricated structural metal

(G-2239)
CADILLAC PRINTING COMPANY
214 S Mitchell St (49601-2140)
P.O. Box 157 (49601-0157)
PHONE..................................231 775-2488
Orren Tate, *President*
EMP: 10 EST: 1926
SQ FT: 15,000
SALES (est): 1.6MM **Privately Held**
SIC: 2752 5943 Commercial printing, offset; office forms & supplies

(G-2240)
CADILLAC TOOL AND DIE INC
1011 6th St (49601-9264)
PHONE..................................231 775-9007
Brian Ward, *President*
EMP: 8
SQ FT: 1,000
SALES (est): 1.1MM **Privately Held**
SIC: 3544 Special dies & tools

(G-2241)
CHAS LEVY CIRCULATING CO
Also Called: Charles Levy Circulating
1125 1st Ave (49601-1307)
PHONE..................................231 779-8940
Robert Fisher, *Manager*
EMP: 8
SALES (corp-wide): 105.5MM **Privately Held**
WEB: www.nationwidemidwest.com
SIC: 2721 5192 Magazines: publishing & printing; books, periodicals & newspapers
PA: Chas. Levy Circulating Co.
    1930 George St Ste 4
    Melrose Park IL 60160
    708 356-3600

(G-2242)
CORNILLIE ACQUISITIONS LLC (PA)
Also Called: Cornillie Concrete
805 W 13th St (49601-9281)
PHONE..................................231 946-5600
Richard Deneweth, *Partner*
Robert Cherry, *Partner*
Joe Cornilie, *Partner*
EMP: 17
SALES (est): 2.5MM **Privately Held**
SIC: 3273 Ready-mixed concrete

(G-2243)
CRANDALL PRECISION INC
460 5th St (49601-1329)
P.O. Box 224 (49601-0224)
PHONE..................................231 775-7101
Lloyd Crandall, *President*
EMP: 5 EST: 1977
SQ FT: 6,500
SALES (est): 460K **Privately Held**
SIC: 3599 Machine shop, jobbing & repair

(G-2244)
DONALD FRANCIS STRZYNSKI
Also Called: Strzynski Signs
1010 1st Ave (49601-1306)
PHONE..................................231 929-7443
Donald Strzynski, *Owner*
EMP: 5
SALES (est): 49.1K **Privately Held**
SIC: 3993 Signs & advertising specialties

(G-2245)
DUMBARTON TOOL INC
151 Clay Dr (49601-8614)
PHONE..................................231 775-4342
Daniel Gray, *President*
Dan Gray, *Owner*
Robert King, *Vice Pres*
Paul Warner, *Treasurer*
EMP: 12
SQ FT: 8,000
SALES (est): 2MM **Privately Held**
WEB: www.dumbartontool.com
SIC: 3545 Cutting tools for machine tools

(G-2246)
FAUBLES PRTG & SPECIALITIES
611 Seneca Pl (49601-9254)
PHONE..................................231 775-4973
Michael D Faubles, *Owner*
EMP: 3
SALES: 100K **Privately Held**
SIC: 5199 7338 2752 Advertising specialties; secretarial & court reporting; commercial printing, lithographic

(G-2247)
FIAMM TECHNOLOGIES LLC
Also Called: Research & Developement
1550 Leeson Ave (49601-8975)
PHONE..................................231 775-2900
Ben Beale, *Branch Mgr*
EMP: 12
SALES (corp-wide): 1.3MM **Privately Held**
SIC: 3714 Horns, motor vehicle
HQ: Fiamm Technologies, L.L.C.
    23880 Industrial Park Dr
    Farmington Hills MI 48335

(G-2248)
FRANKE SALISBURY VIRGINIA
Also Called: Franke Septic Tank Service
11894 S Mackinaw Trl (49601-9082)
PHONE..................................231 775-7014
Virginia Franke Salisbury, *Owner*
EMP: 4 EST: 1947
SQ FT: 4,000
SALES (est): 347.3K **Privately Held**
SIC: 1794 3272 4212 7699 Excavation work; septic tanks, concrete; dump truck haulage; septic tank cleaning service; sewer cleaning & rodding

(G-2249)
GLASTRON LLC
925 Frisbie St (49601-9259)
PHONE..................................800 354-3141
Mary Neu, *Purch Mgr*
Mary Frerich, *Personnel*
Roch Lambert, *Mng Member*
Al Kuebelbeck, *Mng Member*
▼ EMP: 450
SALES (est): 23.7MM
SALES (corp-wide): 1.1MM **Privately Held**
SIC: 3732 Boat building & repairing
HQ: Rec Boat Holdings, Llc
    925 Frisbie St
    Cadillac MI 49601

(G-2250)
GOODWILL INDS NTHRN MICH INC
Also Called: Goodwill Cadillac Transition H
901 N Mitchell St Ste 15 (49601-1254)
PHONE..................................231 779-1311
Todd Salisbury, *Manager*
EMP: 4
SALES (corp-wide): 15.9MM **Privately Held**
SIC: 5932 8331 2431 8322 Clothing, secondhand; sheltered workshop; millwork; meal delivery program; settlement house
PA: Goodwill Industries Of Northern Michigan, Inc.
    2279 S Airport Rd W
    Traverse City MI 49684
    231 922-4805

(G-2251)
GOODWILL INDS NTHRN MICH INC
Also Called: Goodwill Resale Store
610 S Mitchell St (49601-2510)
PHONE..................................231 779-1361
Ruth Blick, *Branch Mgr*
EMP: 6
SALES (corp-wide): 15.9MM **Privately Held**
SIC: 5932 8331 8322 2431 Used merchandise stores; sheltered workshop; meal delivery program; settlement house; millwork
PA: Goodwill Industries Of Northern Michigan, Inc.
    2279 S Airport Rd W
    Traverse City MI 49684
    231 922-4805

(G-2252)
HOPE NETWORK WEST MICHIGAN
Also Called: N O C Industries
1610 Corwin St (49601-8139)
PHONE..................................231 775-3425
Carol Wood, *Branch Mgr*
EMP: 25
SALES (corp-wide): 124.7MM **Privately Held**
SIC: 3469 Metal stampings
HQ: Hope Network West Michigan
    795 36th St Se
    Grand Rapids MI 49548
    616 248-5900

(G-2253)
HOSTESS CAKE ITT CONTNTL BKG
Also Called: Wonder Hostess Thrift Store
838 N Mitchell St (49601-1472)
PHONE..................................231 775-4629
EMP: 9
SALES (est): 48.5K **Privately Held**
SIC: 2051 Mfg Bread/Related Products

(G-2254)
HUTCHINSON ANTIVIBRATION
Also Called: Paulstra C R C-Cadillac Div
600 7th St (49601-1345)
P.O. Box 209 (49601-0209)
PHONE..................................231 775-9737
Thomas Kelley, *Plant Mgr*
Jane Bigham, *Human Res Mgr*
Tom Kelley, *Manager*
EMP: 138
SALES (corp-wide): 8.4B **Publicly Held**
SIC: 3069 3061 Molded rubber products; mechanical rubber goods
HQ: Hutchinson Antivibration Systems, Inc.
    460 Fuller Ave Ne
    Grand Rapids MI 49503
    616 459-4541

(G-2255)
INLAND LAKES MACHINE INC
314 Haynes St (49601-1806)
PHONE..................................231 775-6543
Carl Kuhn, *President*
Richard C Kuhn, *Corp Secy*
Rich Kuhn, *Vice Pres*
Trent Kuhn, *Production*
EMP: 25 EST: 1945
SQ FT: 60,000
SALES (est): 5.6MM **Privately Held**
WEB: www.inlandlakes.com
SIC: 3599 3541 3451 3369 Machine shop, jobbing & repair; machine tools, metal cutting type; screw machine products; nonferrous foundries

(G-2256)
JANET KELLY
Also Called: Kel Graphics
110 W River St (49601-1816)
PHONE..................................231 775-2313
Janet Kelly, *Owner*
Travis Butkovich, *Manager*
EMP: 10
SQ FT: 6,000
SALES (est): 1.3MM **Privately Held**
SIC: 2261 2395 3993 2752 Finishing plants, cotton; embroidery products, except schiffli machine; signs & advertising specialties; commercial printing, lithographic; automotive & apparel trimmings

(G-2257)
KEURIG DR PEPPER INC
Also Called: Dr Pepper Snapple Group
1481 Potthoff St (49601-9671)
PHONE..................................231 775-7393
Tom Soltis, *Branch Mgr*
EMP: 6 **Publicly Held**
SIC: 2086 Soft drinks: packaged in cans, bottles, etc.
PA: Keurig Dr Pepper Inc.
    5301 Legacy Dr
    Plano TX 01803

(G-2258)
KIDDER MACHINE COMPANY
702 8th St (49601)
P.O. Box 507 (49601-0507)
PHONE..................................231 775-9271
Dean L Kidder, *President*
Michael Wylie, *Vice Pres*
Charles Kilpatrick, *Site Mgr*
Douglas Hansen, *Manager*
Philip Klintworth, *Manager*
EMP: 4
SQ FT: 6,200
SALES: 339.3K **Privately Held**
SIC: 3544 Industrial molds

(G-2259)
KYSOR INDUSTRIAL CORPORATION
Kysor Cadillac Division
1100 Wright St (49601-8275)
PHONE..................................231 779-7500
Patrick Laine, *Branch Mgr*
EMP: 214
SALES (corp-wide): 1.5B **Publicly Held**
SIC: 3714 Motor vehicle parts & accessories
HQ: Kysor Industrial Corporation
    2227 Welbilt Blvd
    Trinity FL 34655
    727 376-8600

(G-2260)
LC MATERIALS (PA)
Also Called: Lc Ready Mix
805 W 13th St (49601-9281)
PHONE..................................231 825-2473
David E Gilde, *President*
Philip Gilde, *Vice Pres*
Kenneth Gilde Jr, *Treasurer*
EMP: 8
SQ FT: 5,000
SALES (est): 8MM **Privately Held**
SIC: 3273 1442 Ready-mixed concrete; construction sand mining; gravel mining

(G-2261)
LC MATERIALS
8183 E 34 Rd (49601-9013)
PHONE..................................231 775-9301
Dave Gilde, *President*
EMP: 8
SALES (corp-wide): 8MM **Privately Held**
SIC: 3273 Ready-mixed concrete
PA: Lc Materials
    805 W 13th St
    Cadillac MI 49601
    231 825-2473

(G-2262)
MAHNKE MACHINE INC
1551 Filmore Ave Ste A (49601-1163)
PHONE..................................231 775-0581
Bonnie Mahnke, *President*
Michael Mahnke, *Vice Pres*
EMP: 4
SALES (est): 53.2K **Privately Held**
SIC: 3599 Machine shop, jobbing & repair

(G-2263)
MATTESON MANUFACTURING INC
1480 Potthoff St (49601-9671)
PHONE..................................231 779-2898
R Lyle Matteson, *President*
EMP: 6
SQ FT: 5,000
SALES: 270K **Privately Held**
SIC: 3599 7692 Machine shop, jobbing & repair; welding repair

(G-2264)
METAL PUNCH CORPORATION
907 Saunders St (49601-9270)
PHONE..................................231 775-8391
Irvin J Swider, *CEO*
Larry Roderick, *Vice Pres*
Chuck Cooper, *Engineer*
EMP: 37
SQ FT: 20,000
SALES: 5MM **Privately Held**
SIC: 3544 3545 Punches, forming & stamping; special dies & tools; machine tool accessories

(G-2265)
MI NEWS 26
320 W 13th St (49601-8114)
PHONE..................................231 577-1844
Eric Wotila, *Principal*
EMP: 5

GEOGRAPHIC SECTION

Caledonia - Kent County (G-2292)

SALES (est): 322.4K **Privately Held**
SIC: 2711 Newspapers

(G-2266)
MILITARY & VETERANS AFFAIRS
Army National Guard
415 Haynes St (49601-1807)
PHONE.....................231 775-7222
Brian Lince, *Branch Mgr*
EMP: 90 **Privately Held**
WEB: www.mi.ngb.army.mil
SIC: 3728 Military aircraft equipment & armament
HQ: Michigan Department Of Military And Veterans Affairs
3411 N Martin Luther King
Lansing MI 48906

(G-2267)
MIRROR IMAGE
10797 Pine Shore Dr (49601-8257)
PHONE.....................231 775-2939
Timothy Anderson, *Owner*
EMP: 3
SALES (est): 224.8K **Privately Held**
WEB: www.scantek.com
SIC: 3577 Computer peripheral equipment

(G-2268)
NORTHLAND
Also Called: Northland Trailers
903 N Mitchell St (49601-1254)
PHONE.....................231 775-3101
Everett Rowe, *Partner*
Michael Rowe, *Partner*
Nancy Rowe, *Partner*
EMP: 3
SQ FT: 2,800
SALES (est): 456.7K **Privately Held**
SIC: 5561 3792 5731 Recreational vehicle parts & accessories; campers, for mounting on trucks; television sets; high fidelity stereo equipment; consumer electronic equipment

(G-2269)
PERFECTION BAKERIES INC
Also Called: Aunt Millie's Bakeries
7701 E 34 Rd (49601-8839)
PHONE.....................231 779-5365
David Lijewski, *Manager*
EMP: 14
SALES (corp-wide): 535.8MM **Privately Held**
SIC: 2051 Bread, cake & related products
PA: Perfection Bakeries, Inc.
350 Pearl St
Fort Wayne IN 46802
260 424-8245

(G-2270)
PERFECTION INDUSTRIES INC
218 Hanthorn St (49601-1020)
PHONE.....................231 779-5325
Lawrence Coles, *Manager*
EMP: 3
SALES (corp-wide): 2.2MM **Privately Held**
WEB: www.perfectionindustries.com
SIC: 3999 Barber & beauty shop equipment
PA: Perfection Industries Inc
18571 Weaver St
Detroit MI 48228
313 272-4040

(G-2271)
PIRANHA HOSE PRODUCTS INC
2500 Weigel St (49601-8106)
PHONE.....................231 779-4390
Thomas Hanyok, *President*
Dan Miller, *Engineer*
▲ EMP: 30
SQ FT: 38,000
SALES (est): 8.7MM **Privately Held**
WEB: www.piranhahose.com
SIC: 3052 Plastic hose
HQ: Kuriyama Of America, Inc.
360 E State Pkwy
Schaumburg IL 60173
847 755-0360

(G-2272)
PROCTOR LOGGING INC
298 Bramblewood (49601-8178)
PHONE.....................231 775-3820

Kevin Proctor, *Principal*
EMP: 6
SALES (est): 400.9K **Privately Held**
SIC: 2411 Logging

(G-2273)
REC BOAT HOLDINGS LLC (DH)
925 Frisbie St (49601-9259)
PHONE.....................231 775-1351
Christophe Lavigne, *President*
Rick Videan, *Vice Pres*
Joe Perrin, *Plant Mgr*
Dan Prince, *Warehouse Mgr*
Melinda Hannula, *Purchasing*
◆ EMP: 97
SALES (est): 71.2MM
SALES (corp-wide): 1.1MM **Privately Held**
SIC: 3732 Boat building & repairing

(G-2274)
REMPCO ACQUISITION INC
251 Bell Ave (49601-1103)
P.O. Box 1020 (49601-6020)
PHONE.....................231 775-0108
Lawrence Lajoie, *President*
Willard Lajoie, *Vice Pres*
Jeff Johnson, *Sales Mgr*
Eric Johnson, *Accounts Mgr*
Susan Martin, *Office Mgr*
EMP: 28
SQ FT: 19,500
SALES (est): 2.6MM **Privately Held**
WEB: www.rempco.com
SIC: 3451 3542 5084 Screw machine products; machine tools, metal forming type; industrial machinery & equipment

(G-2275)
SABER TOOL COMPANY INC
1553 N Mitchell St (49601-1130)
PHONE.....................231 779-4340
Kenneth Bollman, *President*
EMP: 15
SQ FT: 10,000
SALES (est): 2.2MM **Privately Held**
WEB: www.sabertool.com
SIC: 3599 Machine shop, jobbing & repair

(G-2276)
SHELLY MEEHOF
Also Called: Creative Embroidery
1156 Plett Rd Ste 1 (49601-1292)
PHONE.....................231 775-3065
Shelly Meehof, *Owner*
EMP: 3 EST: 1990
SALES: 75K **Privately Held**
SIC: 2395 Embroidery products, except schiffli machine

(G-2277)
SOUTHWEST BROACH
311 E Harris St (49601-2126)
PHONE.....................714 356-2967
Michael Ochs, *Principal*
EMP: 5 EST: 2013
SALES (est): 421.8K **Privately Held**
SIC: 3545 Cutting tools for machine tools

(G-2278)
SPEEDWAY LLC
Also Called: Speedway Superamerica 3570
2010 N Mitchell St (49601-1138)
PHONE.....................231 775-8101
EMP: 10
SALES (corp-wide): 100.2B **Publicly Held**
SIC: 1311 Crude Petroleum/Natural Gas Production
HQ: Speedway Llc
500 Speedway Dr
Enon OH 45323
937 864-3000

(G-2279)
SPENCER PLASTICS INC
2300 Gary E Schwach St (49601-8309)
PHONE.....................231 942-7100
Thomas Spencer, *CEO*
Shannon Abraham, *Vice Pres*
Cindy May, *Materials Mgr*
EMP: 25
SQ FT: 45,000

SALES: 6.7MM **Privately Held**
WEB: www.spencerplastics.com
SIC: 3089 Injection molding of plastics; molding primary plastic

(G-2280)
STAGG MACHINE PRODUCTS INC
11711 W Cadillac Rd (49601-9412)
PHONE.....................231 775-2355
Phillip Stagg, *President*
Cynthia Stagg, *Corp Secy*
EMP: 8
SQ FT: 23,500
SALES (est): 1.2MM **Privately Held**
WEB: www.staggmachine.com
SIC: 3451 Screw machine products

(G-2281)
TALLULAHS SATCHELS
615 White Pine Dr (49601-8515)
PHONE.....................231 775-4082
Christine Samardich, *Administration*
EMP: 3
SALES (est): 219.6K **Privately Held**
SIC: 3161 Satchels

(G-2282)
TETER ORTHOTICS & PROSTHETICS
8865 Professional Dr C (49601-8424)
PHONE.....................231 779-8022
Robin Goodenow, *Branch Mgr*
EMP: 3
SALES (corp-wide): 12.2MM **Privately Held**
WEB: www.teterop.com
SIC: 3842 Orthopedic appliances; prosthetic appliances
PA: Teter Orthotics And Prosthetics Inc
1225 W Front St Ste A
Traverse City MI 49684
231 947-5701

(G-2283)
TRAININGMASK LLC
1140 Plett Rd (49601-1212)
PHONE.....................888 407-7555
Casey Danford, *Principal*
Toby Danford, *Opers Staff*
Michael Gennusa, *Info Tech Mgr*
EMP: 13
SALES (est): 1.5MM **Privately Held**
SIC: 3949 Masks: hockey, baseball, football, etc.

(G-2284)
WEDIN INTERNATIONAL INC (PA)
1111 6th Ave (49601-9276)
PHONE.....................231 779-8650
Jack N Rabun, *President*
Jack Rabun, *Principal*
Jack N Rabun Jr, *Vice Pres*
Vickie Templeton, *Admin Asst*
EMP: 52
SQ FT: 47,000
SALES (est): 9.2MM **Privately Held**
WEB: www.wedin.com
SIC: 3452 3545 3535 3462 Screws, metal; rivets, metal; machine tool accessories; conveyors & conveying equipment; iron & steel forgings

(G-2285)
WEXFORD WOOD WORKINGS LLC
407 Goode Ave (49601-1007)
PHONE.....................231 876-9663
Mary Stark,
EMP: 5
SALES (est): 478.1K **Privately Held**
WEB: www.wexfordwoodworkings.com
SIC: 2431 Ornamental woodwork: cornices, mantels, etc.

(G-2286)
WILLIAM C FOX ENTERPRISES INC
Also Called: Printmasters
1215 N Mitchell St (49601-1260)
PHONE.....................231 775-2732
William C Fox, *President*
EMP: 22
SQ FT: 9,000

SALES (est): 2.8MM **Privately Held**
SIC: 2752 Commercial printing, offset

Caledonia
Kent County

(G-2287)
ACTION PACKAGING LLC
6995 Southbelt Dr Se (49316-7664)
PHONE.....................616 871-5200
Kevin Manor, *President*
Eric Stepnitz, *General Mgr*
Ralph B Stoner, *Principal*
Mike Seifert, *Vice Pres*
Doug Stoner, *Plant Mgr*
EMP: 40 EST: 1987
SQ FT: 80,000
SALES (est): 20.3MM **Privately Held**
WEB: www.actionpackaging.com
SIC: 2653 2655 Partitions, corrugated: made from purchased materials; partitions, solid fiber: made from purchased materials; boxes, corrugated: made from purchased materials; boxes, solid fiber: made from purchased materials; fiber shipping & mailing containers
PA: Safeway Packaging, Inc.
300 White Mountain Dr
New Bremen OH 45869
419 629-3200

(G-2288)
ACTIVE PLASTICS INC
125 Mill Ave Se (49316-9440)
PHONE.....................616 813-5109
Jeff Kusmierz, *President*
EMP: 10
SALES (est): 298K **Privately Held**
WEB: www.activeplastics.com
SIC: 3999 3089 Models, general, except toy; plastic processing

(G-2289)
BIG O SMOKEHOUSE
9740 Cherry Valley Ave Se (49316-9521)
P.O. Box 182 (49316-0182)
PHONE.....................616 891-5555
Keith Osterhaven, *Owner*
EMP: 12
SQ FT: 35,000
SALES (est): 532.4K **Privately Held**
SIC: 2013 2091 Smoked meats from purchased meat; fish, smoked

(G-2290)
BLACK BOX CORPORATION
8180 Broadmoor Ave Se A (49316-8526)
PHONE.....................616 246-1320
EMP: 11
SALES (corp-wide): 855.7MM **Publicly Held**
SIC: 3577 Mfg Computer Peripheral Equipment
PA: Black Box Corporation
1000 Park Dr
Lawrence PA 15055
724 746-5500

(G-2291)
BOAT CUSTOMS TRAILERS LLC
3678 68th St Se (49316-9130)
PHONE.....................517 712-3512
Chris Mills, *Principal*
EMP: 3
SALES (est): 123.6K **Privately Held**
SIC: 3799 Boat trailers

(G-2292)
BOB-O-LINK ASSOCIATES LLC (PA)
4668 2nd St (49316-9211)
PHONE.....................616 891-6939
David Maas,
Daniel Timmer,
EMP: 4
SQ FT: 1,100
SALES (est): 561.6K **Privately Held**
SIC: 3531 Asphalt plant, including gravel-mix type

Caledonia - Kent County (G-2293)

(G-2293)
BUDDINGH WEEDER CO
7015 Hammond Ave Se (49316-8352)
PHONE..................616 698-8613
Ruth Sarver, *Owner*
Phil Sarver, *Principal*
EMP: 3 **EST:** 1946
SQ FT: 7,000
SALES: 300K **Privately Held**
WEB: www.buddinghweeder.com
SIC: 3523 Weeding machines, agricultural

(G-2294)
CIG JAN PRODUCTS LTD
3300 Hanna Lk Indus Dr Se (49316)
PHONE..................616 698-9070
Jerome A Janssen, *President*
Richard Tolan, *Vice Pres*
EMP: 15
SQ FT: 30,000
SALES (est): 2.8MM **Privately Held**
WEB: www.cigjan.com
SIC: 3281 Cut stone & stone products

(G-2295)
CLEARFORM
5220 68th St Se Ste 8 (49316-7406)
PHONE..................616 656-5359
Michael Bieker, *Principal*
EMP: 6
SALES (est): 573.9K **Privately Held**
SIC: 3089 Plastic processing

(G-2296)
GR X MANUFACTURING
7000 Dtton Indus Pk Dr Se (49316-8385)
PHONE..................616 541-7420
EMP: 7
SALES (est): 93.5K **Privately Held**
SIC: 3999 Manufacturing industries

(G-2297)
HELEN INC
Also Called: Chemical Specialties
6450 Hanna Lake Ave Se (49316-8365)
PHONE..................616 698-8102
Michael McAllister, *President*
Mihir Shah, *Info Tech Dir*
▼ **EMP:** 16
SQ FT: 55,000
SALES (est): 5.8MM **Privately Held**
WEB: www.enviropowder.com
SIC: 2851 Paints: oil or alkyd vehicle or water thinned; lacquers, varnishes, enamels & other coatings; enamels; varnishes

(G-2298)
HERITAGE RESOURCES INC
6490 68th St Se (49316-8964)
PHONE..................616 554-9888
Kirk Velting, *President*
EMP: 8
SQ FT: 200
SALES (est): 2.5MM **Privately Held**
SIC: 1442 Construction sand & gravel

(G-2299)
HIGH GRADE MATERIALS COMPANY
6869 E Paris Ave Se (49316-7630)
PHONE..................616 554-8828
Stu Africa, *Manager*
EMP: 25
SALES (corp-wide): 28.3MM **Privately Held**
SIC: 3273 Ready-mixed concrete
PA: High Grade Materials Company
9266 Snows Lake Rd
Greenville MI 48838
616 754-5545

(G-2300)
HILCO PLASTIC PRODUCTS CO
3260 Hanna Lake Ind Park (49316-9190)
PHONE..................616 554-8833
Matthew Holwerda, *Branch Mgr*
EMP: 50
SALES (corp-wide): 23.7MM **Privately Held**
SIC: 3089 8711 Molding primary plastic; designing: ship, boat, machine & product
PA: Hilco Industrial Plastics, Llc
4172 Danvers Ct Se
Grand Rapids MI 49512
616 957-1081

(G-2301)
HYDRO-CHEM SYSTEMS INC
6605 Broadmoor Ave Se (49316-9511)
PHONE..................616 531-6420
Dave Presley, *President*
Jim Teague, *Principal*
June Heyn, *Vice Pres*
John Teague, *Vice Pres*
Ginger Travis, *Admin Sec*
EMP: 28
SQ FT: 20,000
SALES: 3.1MM **Privately Held**
WEB: www.hcsclean.com
SIC: 2841 2842 Soap & other detergents; cleaning or polishing preparations

(G-2302)
J & J ENGINEERING AND MACHINE
3265 68th St Se (49316-7419)
PHONE..................616 554-3302
Mark Scott, *President*
EMP: 7
SQ FT: 3,000
SALES: 1MM **Privately Held**
WEB: www.jandjengandmach.com
SIC: 3599 Machine shop, jobbing & repair

(G-2303)
JELD-WEN INC
Also Called: Karona
4100 Korona Ct Se (49316-8419)
PHONE..................616 554-3551
Matt Waite, *Engineer*
Lee Donaldson, *Sales Staff*
Brent Wagner, *Director*
EMP: 150 **Publicly Held**
SIC: 2431 Doors, wood
HQ: Jeld-Wen, Inc.
2645 Silver Crescent Dr
Charlotte NC 28273
800 535-3936

(G-2304)
JOHNSON SYSTEMS INC
7835 100th St Se (49316-9548)
PHONE..................616 455-1900
John J Johnson, *President*
Loretta Johnson, *Corp Secy*
EMP: 5
SQ FT: 8,000
SALES: 425K **Privately Held**
SIC: 3499 1711 Machine bases, metal; mechanical contractor

(G-2305)
KOOIKER TOOL & DIE INC
3259 68th St Se (49316-8425)
PHONE..................616 554-3630
Jason O'Krangley, *President*
Marci Peterson, *Vice Pres*
EMP: 11
SQ FT: 1,200
SALES: 1MM **Privately Held**
SIC: 3545 Precision tools, machinists'

(G-2306)
MARKETLAB INC
5220 68th St Se (49316-7405)
PHONE..................616 656-5359
Michael Bieker, *President*
EMP: 11
SALES (est): 1.3MM **Privately Held**
SIC: 2821 Acrylic resins

(G-2307)
MARKETLAB INC
6850 Southbelt Dr Se (49316-7680)
PHONE..................866 237-3722
Mike Bieker, *CEO*
Steve Bosio, *President*
Bob Schmidt, *CFO*
David Conn, *Marketing Staff*
Phill Llyod, *CIO*
EMP: 95
SQ FT: 100,000
SALES (est): 43.6MM
SALES (corp-wide): 330.2MM **Privately Held**
WEB: www.marketlabinc.com
SIC: 5047 3841 3821 Medical laboratory equipment; medical instruments & equipment, blood & bone work; laboratory apparatus & furniture
PA: Water Street Healthcare Partners Llc
444 W Lake St Ste 1800
Chicago IL 60606
312 506-2900

(G-2308)
MCCANN
6187 Wild Currant Way Se (49316-7559)
PHONE..................734 429-2781
J McCann, *Principal*
EMP: 3
SALES (est): 232.7K **Privately Held**
SIC: 3272 Concrete products

(G-2309)
MICRO MANUFACTURING INC
6900 Dtton Indus Pk Dr Se (49316-7323)
PHONE..................616 554-9200
Donald Jolliffe, *President*
EMP: 25
SQ FT: 45,000
SALES (est): 4.9MM **Privately Held**
WEB: www.micromfg.com
SIC: 3599 Machine shop, jobbing & repair

(G-2310)
NATIONAL PLASTEK INC
7050 Dtton Indus Pk Dr Se (49316-8900)
PHONE..................616 698-9559
Mike Klein, *President*
Brad Whalen, *General Mgr*
Dan Murphy, *Plant Mgr*
Helen Wittenbach, *CFO*
Hellen Wittenbach, *Controller*
EMP: 27
SQ FT: 60,000
SALES (est): 5.2MM **Privately Held**
SIC: 3081 Polyethylene film

(G-2311)
R AND T WEST MICHIGAN INC
6955 E Paris Indus Ct Se (49316-7784)
PHONE..................616 698-9931
Robert Wiegand, *President*
Thomas Wolfgang, *Vice Pres*
EMP: 22
SQ FT: 20,000
SALES (est): 4.7MM **Privately Held**
SIC: 3542 Machine tools, metal forming type

(G-2312)
RATTUNDE CORPORATION (PA)
5080 Beltway Dr Se (49316-7465)
PHONE..................616 940-3340
Ulrich Rattunde, *Principal*
▲ **EMP:** 4
SALES (est): 677.1K **Privately Held**
SIC: 3541 Saws & sawing machines

(G-2313)
RESORT + RECREATION MAGAZINE
9820 Ravine Rdg Se (49316-8235)
P.O. Box 378 (49316-0378)
PHONE..................616 891-5747
Ronald Anger, *Principal*
EMP: 5
SALES (est): 440.6K **Privately Held**
SIC: 2721 Periodicals

(G-2314)
RKP CONSULTING INC
Also Called: Industrial Powder Coating
3286 Hnna Lk Ind Pk Dr Se (49316-9190)
PHONE..................616 698-0300
Robert E Price, *President*
Sam Boeshart, *Data Proc Staff*
▲ **EMP:** 31
SQ FT: 30,000
SALES (est): 10.4MM **Privately Held**
WEB: www.priceindustriesinc.com
SIC: 3441 Fabricated structural metal

(G-2315)
SILICONATURE CORPORATION
4255 68th St Se (49316-9191)
PHONE..................312 987-1848
David Arado, *President*
EMP: 25
SALES: 25MM **Privately Held**
SIC: 2671 Packaging paper & plastics film, coated & laminated

(G-2316)
SPECIALTY METAL FABRICATORS
6975 Dtton Indus Pk Dr Se (49316-9146)
PHONE..................616 698-9020
James Harris, *Principal*
EMP: 7
SALES (est): 1.3MM **Privately Held**
SIC: 3499 Fabricated metal products

(G-2317)
STEFFENS ENTERPRISES INC
Also Called: Fold A Cover
4045 Korona Ct Se (49316-8428)
PHONE..................616 656-6886
Charles Steffens, *President*
▼ **EMP:** 45
SQ FT: 40,000
SALES (est): 10.9MM **Privately Held**
SIC: 3713 3792 Truck bodies & parts; travel trailers & campers

(G-2318)
SUITE SPA MANUFACTURING LLC
464 Stanton Farms Dr (49316-9226)
PHONE..................616 560-2713
Vickie Bennett, *CEO*
Victor Bennett, *CEO*
EMP: 5
SALES (est): 229.7K **Privately Held**
SIC: 2869 Perfumes, flavorings & food additives

(G-2319)
TILE BY BILL & SONDRA
6873 Rosecrest Dr Se (49316-9073)
PHONE..................616 554-5413
William Vandergeld, *President*
EMP: 3
SALES (est): 225.8K **Privately Held**
SIC: 3993 Signs & advertising specialties

(G-2320)
US BIO CARBON LLC
435 N Lake Dr (49316-9625)
PHONE..................616 334-9862
Patrick Mohney, *Mng Member*
EMP: 3
SALES: 250K **Privately Held**
SIC: 2819 Charcoal (carbon), activated

(G-2321)
VAN DELLEN STEEL INC
6945 Dtton Indus Pk Dr Se (49316-9148)
PHONE..................616 698-9950
Corey Van Dellen, *CEO*
James Devries, *President*
Sharon Van Dellen, *Owner*
Corey Dellen, *COO*
Joel Bruin-Slot, *Plant Mgr*
EMP: 30
SQ FT: 50,000
SALES (est): 7.5MM **Privately Held**
WEB: www.vandellensteel.com
SIC: 3441 Building components, structural steel

(G-2322)
VIKING GROUP INC (DH)
5150 Beltway Dr Se (49316-7447)
PHONE..................616 432-6800
Kevin Ortyl, *President*
Janice Oshinski, *CFO*
Paul Evangelista, *Manager*
EMP: 8
SALES (est): 235.7MM **Privately Held**
SIC: 3569 5961 Sprinkler systems, fire: automatic; mail order house
HQ: Minimax Viking Gmbh
Industriestr. 10/
Bad Oldesloe 23843
453 180-30

(G-2323)
XL ENGINEERING LLC
6960 Hammond Ave Se (49316-8351)
PHONE..................616 656-0324
Kevin Swiderski, *Mng Member*
EMP: 9
SQ FT: 3,000
SALES (est): 2.4MM **Privately Held**
SIC: 3565 Bottling & canning machinery

GEOGRAPHIC SECTION   Canton - Wayne County (G-2350)

Calumet
Houghton County

(G-2324)
BAY MACHINE INC
53167 Golf Course Rd (49913-9332)
P.O. Box 143 (49913-0143)
PHONE..................................906 250-0458
Richard Wiita, *President*
EMP: 3
SALES: 400K **Privately Held**
SIC: 3599 Machine shop, jobbing & repair

(G-2325)
BEAN COUNTER INC
25963 Cedar St (49913-1249)
PHONE..................................906 523-5027
Deborah Bean, *Principal*
EMP: 3
SALES (est): 268.8K **Privately Held**
SIC: 3131 Counters

(G-2326)
COPPER ISLAND PRTG GRPHIC SVCS
Also Called: Greenlee Printing Company
423 Pine St (49913-1463)
PHONE..................................906 337-1300
Toll Free:............................888 -
Marc J Norton, *President*
Gary Lubinski, *Finance*
EMP: 3
SQ FT: 4,000
SALES (est): 339.8K **Privately Held**
SIC: 2752 Commercial printing, offset

(G-2327)
DOUG ANDERSON LOGGING
54586 Oikarinen Rd (49913-9207)
PHONE..................................906 337-3707
Doug Anderson, *Owner*
Rebecca Anderson, *Co-Owner*
EMP: 5
SALES (est): 350K **Privately Held**
SIC: 2411 Logging camps & contractors

(G-2328)
KIILUNEN MFG GROUP INC
Also Called: Superior Polymer Products
25280 Renaissance Rd (49913-2701)
PHONE..................................906 337-2433
Erik Kiilunen, *President*
Kurt Johnson, *General Mgr*
▲ **EMP:** 7
SQ FT: 6,000
SALES (est): 1.2MM **Privately Held**
WEB: www.superiorpolymer.com
SIC: 2891 Adhesives & sealants

(G-2329)
LEONARD J HILL LOGGING CO
30980 Woodbush Rd (49913-9542)
PHONE..................................906 337-3435
Leonard Hill, *Owner*
EMP: 10
SALES (est): 813K **Privately Held**
SIC: 2411 Logging

(G-2330)
MQ OPERATING COMPANY
Also Called: Calumet Machine
416 6th St (49913-1412)
PHONE..................................906 337-1515
Eugene Londo, *President*
Nancy Londo, *Office Mgr*
EMP: 21 **EST:** 1972
SQ FT: 16,000
SALES (est): 7.1MM **Privately Held**
WEB: www.calumetmachine.com
SIC: 5084 7699 7629 3568 Machine tools & accessories; welding machinery & equipment; industrial machinery & equipment repair; electrical repair shops; power transmission equipment; mining machinery

(G-2331)
PAUL J BARONI CO
512 6th St (49913-1414)
P.O. Box 84 (49913-0084)
PHONE..................................906 337-3920
Timothy Baroni, *President*
Nancy Baroni, *Vice Pres*
EMP: 4 **EST:** 1935
SQ FT: 12,000
SALES: 50K **Privately Held**
WEB: www.baronis.com
SIC: 2032 2038 Italian foods: packaged in cans, jars, etc.; pizza, frozen; ethnic foods, frozen

(G-2332)
REL MACHINE INC
57640 11th St (49913-3118)
PHONE..................................906 337-3018
Josh Loukus, *President*
Robert E Loukus, *Vice Pres*
Kitti Loukus, *Info Tech Mgr*
Zach Erkkila, *Software Dev*
EMP: 2
SQ FT: 12,000
SALES (est): 3.2MM **Privately Held**
WEB: www.relmachine.com
SIC: 3599 3469 Machine shop, jobbing & repair; machine parts, stamped or pressed metal

(G-2333)
RIPPA PRODUCTS INC
25256 Renaissance Rd (49913-2701)
PHONE..................................906 337-0010
Robert Rippa, *President*
Chris Johnson, *Vice Pres*
EMP: 20
SQ FT: 7,200
SALES (est): 1.5MM **Privately Held**
SIC: 3452 Nuts, metal

(G-2334)
UP OFFICEEXPRESS LLC
Also Called: Doxxpress
53091 Dover Rd (49913-9329)
PHONE..................................906 281-0089
John Ham, *Mng Member*
Dallas Bond, *Mng Member*
EMP: 3
SALES (est): 170K **Privately Held**
SIC: 2522 8748 7389 Office furniture, except wood; business consulting;

(G-2335)
VOCATIONAL STRATEGIES INC
23390 Airpark Blvd (49913-9233)
PHONE..................................906 482-6142
Kevin Store, *Exec Dir*
EMP: 25 **EST:** 1970
SQ FT: 20,000
SALES: 670.6K **Privately Held**
WEB: www.vocstrat.org
SIC: 8331 3993 2448 2426 Sheltered workshop; signs & advertising specialties; wood pallets & skids; hardwood dimension & flooring mills

(G-2336)
WANDAS BARIUM COOKIE LLC
25770 Elm St (49913-1220)
P.O. Box 294 (49913-0294)
PHONE..................................906 281-1788
EMP: 5
SALES (est): 546.2K **Privately Held**
SIC: 2834 Proprietary drug products

(G-2337)
WARM RAIN CORPORATION (PA)
51675 Industrial Dr (49913-9235)
P.O. Box 600, Hancock (49930-0600)
PHONE..................................906 482-3750
George Kronschnabel, *President*
Jack Laux, *General Mgr*
Brian Mayworm, *General Mgr*
Ted Kronschnabel, *Vice Pres*
Jack Resnick, *CFO*
EMP: 52
SQ FT: 55,000
SALES (est): 5.4MM **Privately Held**
WEB: www.warmrain.com
SIC: 3088 Tubs (bath, shower & laundry), plastic; hot tubs, plastic or fiberglass; shower stalls, fiberglass & plastic

Camden
Hillsdale County

(G-2338)
CAMPUB INC (HQ)
Also Called: Camden Publications
331 E Bell St (49232-9613)
P.O. Box 130 (49232-0130)
PHONE..................................517 368-0365
Julia Hite, *General Mgr*
Ken Ungar, *Vice Pres*
EMP: 10
SQ FT: 9,000
SALES (est): 6.7MM
SALES (corp-wide): 2.9B **Publicly Held**
SIC: 2711 2741 Newspapers: publishing only, not printed on site; art copy: publishing & printing
PA: Gannett Co., Inc.
7950 Jones Branch Dr
Mc Lean VA 22102
703 854-6000

(G-2339)
CURTIS COUNTRY CONNECTION LLC
338 E Bell St (49232-9613)
PHONE..................................517 368-5542
Dave Curtis, *CEO*
David Curtis, *General Mgr*
Steve Sanders, *Engineer*
EMP: 14
SALES: 1MM **Privately Held**
SIC: 2448 Wood pallets & skids

(G-2340)
D P EQUIPMENT CO
10700 S Edon Rd (49232-9011)
P.O. Box 159 (49232-0159)
PHONE..................................517 368-5266
Dale R Pushee, *President*
Patricia D Pushee, *Corp Secy*
Sharon Gillen, *Office Mgr*
EMP: 11 **EST:** 1968
SQ FT: 11,000
SALES: 2MM **Privately Held**
WEB: www.dpequipment.com
SIC: 3531 7353 5261 7699 Construction machinery; earth moving equipment, rental or leasing; lawnmowers & tractors; lawn mower repair shop

(G-2341)
DIGITAL DIMENSIONS INC
4300 E Territorial Rd (49232-9748)
PHONE..................................419 630-4343
Craig Kidston, *President*
EMP: 3
SQ FT: 4,000
SALES (est): 195.3K **Privately Held**
SIC: 3694 Distributors, motor vehicle engine

Canton
Wayne County

(G-2342)
3R INFO LLC
5840 N Canton Center Rd # 295 (48187-2684)
PHONE..................................201 221-6133
S Raju Nadimpalli, *Mng Member*
EMP: 19
SALES (est): 849.9K **Privately Held**
SIC: 7371 7372 7379 Computer software systems analysis & design, custom; prepackaged software; computer related consulting services

(G-2343)
A S A P MACHINE COMPANY
8575 Ronda Dr (48187-2003)
PHONE..................................734 459-2447
Mark Swain, *President*
EMP: 5
SQ FT: 2,500
SALES (est): 428K **Privately Held**
SIC: 3599 Machine shop, jobbing & repair

(G-2344)
ADVANCE ENGINEERING COMPANY (PA)
Also Called: Advance Engineering Co Mich
7505 Baron Dr (48187-2494)
PHONE..................................313 537-3500
George Helms, *President*
Joe Stupnicki, *Executive*
EMP: 95
SALES (est): 54.3MM **Privately Held**
WEB: www.adveng.net
SIC: 3465 3469 3823 Automotive stampings; metal stampings; thermal conductivity instruments, industrial process type

(G-2345)
ADVANCED MAGNET SOURCE CORP
5033 Belleville Rd (48188-2407)
PHONE..................................734 398-7188
▲ **EMP:** 7
SALES: 2MM **Privately Held**
SIC: 3499 Mfg Permanent Magnet

(G-2346)
AIRHUG LLC
47960 Red Run Dr (48187-5461)
PHONE..................................734 262-0431
Wayne Fung, *Partner*
Kam Lee, *Partner*
EMP: 4
SALES (est): 244.6K **Privately Held**
SIC: 2221 3564 Broadwoven fabric mills, manmade; purification & dust collection equipment

(G-2347)
AMERICAN LABEL & TAG INC
41878 Koppernick Rd (48187-2409)
P.O. Box 85488, Westland (48185-0488)
PHONE..................................734 454-7600
Tim Gleason, *President*
Eric Marschner, *Shareholder*
EMP: 28
SQ FT: 52,000
SALES (est): 6.9MM **Privately Held**
WEB: www.americanlabel.com
SIC: 2672 3993 2789 2671 Labels (unprinted), gummed: made from purchased materials; name plates: except engraved, etched, etc.: metal; bookbinding & related work; packaging paper & plastics film, coated & laminated

(G-2348)
ANTECH TOOL INC
7553 Baron Dr (48187-2494)
PHONE..................................734 207-3622
Anthony Szafraniec, *President*
Linda Szafraniec, *Treasurer*
Dennis Perry, *Supervisor*
EMP: 15
SQ FT: 13,000
SALES (est): 4.1MM **Privately Held**
WEB: www.antechtool.com
SIC: 5084 3541 Machine tools & accessories; drilling & boring machines

(G-2349)
ATG PRECISION PRODUCTS LLC
7545 N Haggerty Rd (48187-2435)
PHONE..................................586 247-5400
Esad Kaknjo, *President*
Randy Link, *QC Mgr*
Robert Janus, *Engineer*
Frank Bacheldor, *Sales Associate*
Mike Strube, *Business Dir*
EMP: 35 **EST:** 1942
SQ FT: 78,000
SALES (est): 7.7MM
SALES (corp-wide): 21.1MM **Privately Held**
WEB: www.dirksenscrew.com
SIC: 3451 Screw machine products
PA: Dirksen Screw Products Co.
14490 23 Mile Rd
Shelby Township MI 48315
586 247-5400

(G-2350)
BCC DISTRIBUTION INC
7529 Baron Dr (48187-2494)
PHONE..................................734 737-9300
Jon Newman, *President*

Lisa Fritz, *Sales Staff*
Donna Newman, *Technology*
Donna Allbritten, *Sr Software Eng*
EMP: 12
SQ FT: 3,500
SALES (est): 2.9MM **Privately Held**
WEB: www.bccdistribution.com
SIC: 3577 Bar code (magnetic ink) printers

(G-2351)
BERKSHIRE & ASSOCIATES INC
5840 N Canton Center Rd (48187-2684)
PHONE......................734 719-1822
Anthony Morris, *President*
EMP: 10 **EST:** 2011
SALES: 355K **Privately Held**
SIC: 8741 3577 Management services; data conversion equipment, media-to-media: computer

(G-2352)
BIO SOURCE NATURALS LLC
47887 Michigan Ave # 203 (48188-2239)
PHONE......................734 335-6798
Lezlie Cebulski, *President*
EMP: 4
SALES (est): 347.1K **Privately Held**
SIC: 2844 2899 Cosmetic preparations; essential oils

(G-2353)
BODYCOTE THERMAL PROC INC
8468 Ronda Dr (48187-2002)
PHONE......................734 459-8514
Brett Burns, *Plant Mgr*
Steve Richardson, *Branch Mgr*
Ahmad Hammoud, *Manager*
EMP: 50
SALES (corp-wide): 935.8MM **Privately Held**
SIC: 3398 Metal heat treating
HQ: Bodycote Thermal Processing, Inc.
  12700 Park Central Dr # 700
  Dallas TX 75251
  214 904-2420

(G-2354)
BODYCOTE THERMAL PROC INC
8580 N Haggerty Rd (48187-2095)
PHONE......................734 451-0338
Michael Harrison, *General Mgr*
EMP: 30
SALES (corp-wide): 935.8MM **Privately Held**
SIC: 3398 Brazing (hardening) of metal
HQ: Bodycote Thermal Processing, Inc.
  12700 Park Central Dr # 700
  Dallas TX 75251
  214 904-2420

(G-2355)
BOYERS MEAT PROCESSING INC
4125 Barr Rd (48188-2103)
PHONE......................734 495-1342
Robert Boyer, *President*
EMP: 4
SQ FT: 7,200
SALES: 140K **Privately Held**
SIC: 2011 Meat packing plants

(G-2356)
CADILLAC ASPHALT LLC (PA)
2575 S Haggerty Rd # 100 (48188-2673)
PHONE......................734 397-2050
John Peters, *General Mgr*
Gregg Campbell, *CFO*
Greg Campbell, *CFO*
EMP: 52
SQ FT: 12,000
SALES (est): 47.3MM **Privately Held**
WEB: www.cadillacasphalt.com
SIC: 2951 Asphalt paving mixtures & blocks

(G-2357)
CARRIGAN GRAPHICS INC
Also Called: AlphaGraphics 336
7994 N Lilley Rd (48187-2432)
PHONE......................734 455-6550
Robert Carrigan, *President*
Mark Carrigan, *Vice Pres*
EMP: 7
SQ FT: 3,350
SALES (est): 1.2MM **Privately Held**
SIC: 2752 Commercial printing, lithographic

(G-2358)
CASUAL PTIO FURN RFNISHING INC
7851 Haverhill Ct N (48187-1047)
PHONE......................586 254-1900
Michael Maloney, *President*
Ronald Lippard, *Vice Pres*
EMP: 7
SQ FT: 10,000
SALES: 1MM **Privately Held**
SIC: 3645 5021 Garden, patio, walkway & yard lighting fixtures: electric; furniture

(G-2359)
CENTER MASS INC
6845 Woonsocket St (48187-2749)
PHONE......................734 207-8934
Jeff Felts, *President*
▼ **EMP:** 7
SALES: 1MM **Privately Held**
WEB: www.centermassinc.com
SIC: 3496 7389 Slings, lifting: made from purchased wire;

(G-2360)
CHAMPAGNE GRINDING & MFG CO
8600 Ronda Dr (48187-2005)
PHONE......................734 459-1759
Leo E Champagne, *President*
Mark B Champagne, *Vice Pres*
Gernith Champagne, *Admin Sec*
EMP: 18
SQ FT: 9,600
SALES (est): 2.6MM **Privately Held**
SIC: 3545 Tools & accessories for machine tools; gauges (machine tool accessories)

(G-2361)
CHROMATECH INC (PA)
7723 Market Dr (48187-2445)
PHONE......................734 451-1230
Roy Perlove, *President*
Paul Stema, *Accountant*
◆ **EMP:** 14
SQ FT: 39,000
SALES: 3.7MM
SALES (corp-wide): 4MM **Privately Held**
WEB: www.chromatechcolors.com
SIC: 2865 5198 Color pigments, organic; colors & pigments

(G-2362)
CLEAN AIR TECHNOLOGY INC
41105 Capital Dr (48187-2444)
PHONE......................734 459-6320
Jeffrey L Waller, *President*
Beverly A Favor, *Corp Secy*
Casey J Bell, *Vice Pres*
Daniel Sanders, *Project Mgr*
Bryan White, *Engineer*
EMP: 24 **EST:** 1980
SQ FT: 18,400
SALES (est): 9.6MM **Privately Held**
WEB: www.cleanairtechnology.com
SIC: 1542 8711 3564 Nonresidential construction; engineering services; blowers & fans

(G-2363)
D & L WATER CONTROL INC
7534 Baron Dr (48187-2493)
PHONE......................734 455-6982
Douglas Day, *President*
Lilli Day, *Vice Pres*
Pete Weiland, *Opers Staff*
Thomas Poole, *Engineer*
Tomas Wysocki, *Engineer*
▲ **EMP:** 12
SQ FT: 13,000
SALES (est): 2.8MM **Privately Held**
WEB: www.dlwater.com
SIC: 3589 Water treatment equipment, industrial

(G-2364)
DETROIT MARKING PRODUCTS CORP
8201 Ronda Dr (48187-2078)
PHONE......................313 838-9760
William Foerg, *President*
Joseph R Foerg, *Vice Pres*
Thomas S Foerg, *Vice Pres*
EMP: 11 **EST:** 1918
SQ FT: 10,000
SALES (est): 1.7MM **Privately Held**
WEB: www.detroitmarking.com
SIC: 3993 3953 Signs & advertising specialties; embossing seals & hand stamps

(G-2365)
DIRECTIONAL REGULATED SYSTEMS
Also Called: Landsculpt
8491 Ronda Dr (48187-2001)
PHONE......................734 451-1416
Danny R Stirsman, *President*
Sheila Stirsman, *Corp Secy*
EMP: 7
SQ FT: 5,200
SALES: 1.2MM **Privately Held**
WEB: www.drsystemsinc.net
SIC: 3599 Custom machinery

(G-2366)
DOWNRIVER PLASTICS INC
8349 Ronda Dr (48187-2079)
PHONE......................734 246-3031
Charles E Haynes, *President*
EMP: 3
SQ FT: 1,200
SALES: 600K **Privately Held**
SIC: 3089 Injection molding of plastics; plastic processing

(G-2367)
DUO-GARD INDUSTRIES INC
40442 Koppernick Rd (48187-4279)
PHONE......................734 207-9700
Albert S Miller, *CEO*
David M Miller, *President*
Michael Arvidson, *Vice Pres*
Fred Hankes, *Opers Staff*
Greg Dehetre, *QC Mgr*
▼ **EMP:** 68
SQ FT: 24,000
SALES: 11.5MM **Privately Held**
WEB: www.duo-gard.com
SIC: 3089 3083 3448 3444 Windows, plastic; laminated plastics plate & sheet; prefabricated metal buildings; sheet metalwork: metal doors, sash & trim; products of purchased glass

(G-2368)
DYNAMIC MTAL TREATING INTL INC
Also Called: Dynamic Surface Technologies
7784 Ronda Dr (48187-2447)
PHONE......................734 459-8022
Loren J Epler, *President*
Jack Dewan, *Accounts Mgr*
Alex Koprivica, *Regl Sales Mgr*
Richard Leal, *Sales Staff*
▲ **EMP:** 25
SALES: 2MM **Privately Held**
WEB: www.dynablue.com
SIC: 3398 Metal heat treating

(G-2369)
E3 DIAGNOSTICS INC
Also Called: E3 Gordon Stowe
5918 N Lilley Rd Ste 3 (48187-3688)
PHONE......................734 981-3655
Tom Switalski, *General Mgr*
Christine Koss, *Admin Sec*
EMP: 7
SALES (corp-wide): 1.2MM **Privately Held**
SIC: 3845 Audiological equipment, electromedical
HQ: E3 Diagnostics, Inc.
  3333 N Kennicott Ave
  Arlington Heights IL 60004
  847 459-1770

(G-2370)
EDI EXPERTS LLC
700 Pinehurst Dr (48188-1094)
P.O. Box 87131 (48187-0131)
PHONE......................734 844-7016
Glades Adams, *CEO*
EMP: 3 **EST:** 2015

SALES (est): 122.1K **Privately Held**
SIC: 7371 7372 7373 7379 Computer software systems analysis & design, custom; computer software development & applications; prepackaged software; value-added resellers, computer systems; computer related consulting services;

(G-2371)
ENGTECHNIK INC (PA)
40615 Koppernick Rd # 2 (48187-4280)
PHONE......................734 667-4237
Jose Aldo Francioli, *CEO*
Mackenzie Wilson, *Manager*
EMP: 3
SALES: 1.2MM **Privately Held**
SIC: 3089 7371 4911 Injection molding of plastics; software programming applications; electric services

(G-2372)
EP MAGNETS & COMPONENTS LLC
5055 Belleville Rd (48188-2407)
PHONE......................734 398-7188
EMP: 1 **EST:** 2013
SALES: 1MM **Privately Held**
SIC: 3559 Mfg Misc Industry Machinery

(G-2373)
EXECUTIVE OPERATIONS LLC
2340 Leigh Ct (48188-3232)
PHONE......................313 312-0653
David Trader, *CEO*
EMP: 25 **EST:** 2016
SALES (est): 629.8K **Privately Held**
SIC: 8721 7382 1731 4119 Accounting, auditing & bookkeeping; protective devices, security; safety & security specialization; local rental transportation; semitrailers for missile transportation

(G-2374)
FAIRLANE GEAR INC
8182 N Canton Center Rd (48187-1305)
PHONE......................734 459-2440
John Ptak, *President*
Stanley Z Ptak, *President*
Michael Ptak, *General Mgr*
Lydia Ptak, *Prdtn Mgr*
Barbara Bidwell, *Info Tech Mgr*
EMP: 9
SQ FT: 21,000
SALES: 1.1MM **Privately Held**
SIC: 3566 Gears, power transmission, except automotive

(G-2375)
FARO SCREEN PROCESS INC
41805 Koppernick Rd (48187-2416)
PHONE......................734 207-8400
Edward M Brown, *President*
Jack Brown, *Vice Pres*
Jackson Brown, *Vice Pres*
Mike Brown, *Human Res Dir*
Steven Graf, *VP Sales*
EMP: 19
SQ FT: 31,000
SALES (est): 2.5MM **Privately Held**
WEB: www.faroscreen.com
SIC: 2759 Screen printing

(G-2376)
FASTUBE LLC
41714 Haggerty Cir S (48188-2227)
PHONE......................734 398-0474
Steve Nichols, *President*
▼ **EMP:** 15
SQ FT: 30,000
SALES (est): 2.8MM **Privately Held**
WEB: www.fastube.com
SIC: 3011 Industrial inner tubes

(G-2377)
GIL-MAR MANUFACTURING CO (PA)
Also Called: GM
7925 Ronda Dr (48187-2456)
PHONE......................248 640-4303
Gildo Ruicci, *President*
William L Martin, *Vice Pres*
Joseph Ruicci, *Vice Pres*
Joy Gutowski, *Production*
Steve Harsch, *Plant Engr*
◆ **EMP:** 70
SQ FT: 50,000

GEOGRAPHIC SECTION

Canton - Wayne County (G-2403)

SALES (est): 24.4MM **Privately Held**
WEB: www.gil-mar.com
SIC: 3599 Machine shop, jobbing & repair

(G-2378)
GLADIATOR QUALITY SORTING LLC
43220 Oakbrook Ct (48187-2034)
PHONE.................734 578-1950
Mary T Hulett, *President*
EMP: 6
SQ FT: 800
SALES (est): 494.9K **Privately Held**
SIC: 3312 Pipes & tubes

(G-2379)
GREENFIELD DIE & MFG CORP
Also Called: Canton Manufacturing
7295 N Haggerty Rd Rf (48187-2452)
PHONE.................734 454-4000
Ramzi Hermiz, *CEO*
James Fanello, *President*
EMP: 250 EST: 1955
SALES (est): 32.4MM **Publicly Held**
SIC: 3544 3469 Special dies & tools; metal stampings
PA: Shiloh Industries, Inc.
   880 Steel Dr
   Valley City OH 44280

(G-2380)
GROSSE POINTE NEWS
1167 Longfellow Dr (48187-5024)
PHONE.................734 674-0131
Debra A Pascoe, *Principal*
EMP: 3 EST: 2011
SALES (est): 135.8K **Privately Held**
SIC: 2711 Newspapers, publishing & printing

(G-2381)
GRUPO ANTOLIN PRIMERA AUTO SYS (DH)
Also Called: Grupo Antolin Wayne
47440 Mi Ave Ste 150 (48188-2215)
PHONE.................734 495-9180
William Pickard, *President*
▲ EMP: 85
SQ FT: 170,000
SALES (est): 40.4MM
SALES (corp-wide): 33.3MM **Privately Held**
SIC: 3714 Motor vehicle body components & frame
HQ: Grupo Antolin-Irausa Sa
   Carretera Madrid-Irun (Burgos) (- Km 244,8)
   Burgos 09007
   947 477-700

(G-2382)
H W MOTOR HOMES INC
5390 Belleville Rd (48188-2424)
PHONE.................734 394-2000
Toll Free:.................888 -
Forest H White, *President*
Daniel White, *Vice Pres*
Jeff White, *Manager*
EMP: 8
SQ FT: 3,000
SALES (est): 1.3MM **Privately Held**
WEB: www.hwmotorhomes.com
SIC: 3799 Recreational vehicles

(G-2383)
HGKS INDUSTRIAL CLAY TOOL CO I
1911 Scenic Dr (48188-1416)
P.O. Box 871181 (48187-6181)
PHONE.................734 340-5500
Herbert Gaschler, *Owner*
Denise Gaschler, *Admin Sec*
EMP: 4
SALES (est): 546.8K **Privately Held**
SIC: 3423 3999 Hand & edge tools; models, except toy

(G-2384)
INDUSTRIAL TEMPERATURE CONTROL (PA)
7282 N Haggerty Rd (48187-2436)
PHONE.................734 451-8740
Dale Robenault, *President*
EMP: 6 EST: 1952
SQ FT: 3,000
SALES: 700K **Privately Held**
SIC: 5075 3823 8734 3822 Warm air heating equipment & supplies; thermocouples, industrial process type; temperature instruments: industrial process type; testing laboratories; auto controls regulating residntl & coml environmt & applncs; relays & industrial controls; industrial furnaces & ovens

(G-2385)
INLAND VAPOR OF MICHIGAN LLC
125 N Haggerty Rd (48187-3901)
PHONE.................734 738-6312
EMP: 5
SALES (est): 387.7K
SALES (corp-wide): 2.5MM **Privately Held**
SIC: 3641 Electric lamps
PA: Inland Vapor Of Michigan Llc
   33447 Ford Rd
   Garden City MI 48135
   734 237-4389

(G-2386)
INNKEEPER LLC
4902 Dewitt Rd Ste 104 (48188-2451)
PHONE.................734 743-1707
Kevin Kretschmann, *Mng Member*
Christie Peters, *Manager*
EMP: 4
SALES (est): 746.1K **Privately Held**
WEB: www.innkeeperllc.com
SIC: 3829 Testing equipment: abrasion, shearing strength, etc.

(G-2387)
INNOVATIVE SOLUTIONS TECH INC
Also Called: Starlite Coatings
41158 Koppernick Rd (48187-2405)
PHONE.................734 335-6665
Danny J Werner, *President*
Gordon Brooks, *Vice Pres*
Timothy G Williams, *CFO*
EMP: 9 EST: 2008
SQ FT: 20,000
SALES (est): 2.4MM **Privately Held**
SIC: 2851 Paints & allied products

(G-2388)
INTERNATIONAL DOOR INC
Also Called: American Industrial Door
8001 Ronda Dr (48187-2090)
PHONE.................248 547-7240
John Kaounas, *President*
Colin Hepker, *Chief Engr*
Ron Barnett, *Engineer*
Devar Sateesh, *Engineer*
Ervin Zejnati, *Electrical Engi*
EMP: 30
SQ FT: 27,000
SALES (est): 9.7MM **Privately Held**
WEB: www.international-door.com
SIC: 3442 3613 Metal doors; hangar doors, metal; switchgear & switchboard apparatus

(G-2389)
JEP INDUSTRIES LLC
1965 Oakview Dr (48187-3140)
PHONE.................734 844-3506
James Parks III, *Mng Member*
Lori Parks,
EMP: 4
SALES (est): 34.7K **Privately Held**
WEB: www.mazdausa.com
SIC: 3498 Piping systems for pulp paper & chemical industries

(G-2390)
K & Y MANUFACTURING INC
41880 Koppernick Rd (48187-2409)
PHONE.................734 414-7000
Andrew Istvan, *President*
Mark Saker, *Opers Mgr*
Kimberly Istvan, *Controller*
Diana Istvan, *Shareholder*
▲ EMP: 35 EST: 1948
SQ FT: 29,000
SALES (est): 13.8MM **Privately Held**
WEB: www.kymfg.com
SIC: 3451 Screw machine products

(G-2391)
KRISTA MESSER
50619 Colchester Ct (48187-4464)
PHONE.................734 459-1952
Krista Messer, *Principal*
EMP: 3
SALES (est): 275K **Privately Held**
SIC: 3443 Fabricated plate work (boiler shop)

(G-2392)
LINDE GAS NORTH AMERICA LLC
5001 Dewitt Rd (48188-2411)
PHONE.................734 397-7373
Jeff Matheny, *Branch Mgr*
EMP: 3 **Privately Held**
SIC: 2813 Oxygen, compressed or liquefied
HQ: Linde Gas North America Llc
   200 Somerset Corp Blvd # 7000
   Bridgewater NJ 08807

(G-2393)
LIVONIA MAGNETICS LLC
44005 Michigan Ave (48188-2552)
PHONE.................734 397-8844
Larry Farr, *President*
Glenn R Stork, *Vice Pres*
Glenn Stork, *Sales Staff*
Virginia Pattee, *Sales Executive*
EMP: 19
SQ FT: 18,360
SALES (est): 5.5MM **Privately Held**
SIC: 3535 Belt conveyor systems, general industrial use

(G-2394)
LOTUS INTERNATIONAL COMPANY
6880 Commerce Blvd (48187-4457)
PHONE.................734 245-0140
Madan M Sharma, *President*
Geralyn Venkat, *Human Res Mgr*
Prasad Koppolu, *Sales Executive*
Al Lukas, *IT/INT Sup*
Amar Paul, *Director*
◆ EMP: 520
SQ FT: 295,000
SALES: 387.5MM **Privately Held**
WEB: www.licus.com
SIC: 8711 3651 1221 Consulting engineer; television receiving sets; bituminous coal & lignite-surface mining

(G-2395)
LYON MANUFACTURING INC
7121 N Haggerty Rd (48187-2452)
PHONE.................734 359-3000
John Lyon, *President*
Sean Fineran, *Opers Mgr*
James Lyon, *Treasurer*
EMP: 50
SQ FT: 35,500
SALES (est): 9.8MM **Privately Held**
WEB: www.lyonmfg.com
SIC: 3451 Screw machine products

(G-2396)
MARIAS ITALIAN BAKERY INC
115 N Haggerty Rd (48187-3901)
PHONE.................734 981-1200
Peter Koza, *President*
Jerome Mc Donald, *General Mgr*
Sam Abdal, *Vice Pres*
EMP: 12 EST: 1972
SQ FT: 11,000
SALES (est): 1.3MM **Privately Held**
SIC: 5411 5921 2052 2051 Grocery stores, independent; beer (packaged); wine; hard liquor; cookies & crackers; bread, cake & related products; eating places

(G-2397)
MARIMBA AUTO LLC
41150 Van Born Rd (48188-2745)
PHONE.................734 398-9000
Anurag Bajaj, *Mng Member*
▲ EMP: 60
SQ FT: 50,000
SALES (est): 9.9MM **Privately Held**
WEB: www.marimbaauto.com
SIC: 3714 Motor vehicle engines & parts

(G-2398)
MATERIAL SCIENCES CORPORATION (PA)
6855 Commerce Blvd (48187-4458)
PHONE.................734 207-4444
Patrick Murley, *CEO*
Michael Noble, *Vice Pres*
Michael R Wilson, *Vice Pres*
James Todd, *CFO*
▲ EMP: 10
SQ FT: 205,000
SALES (est): 131.2MM **Privately Held**
WEB: www.matsci.com
SIC: 3479 3471 Painting of metal products; coating of metals & formed products; coating, rust preventive; electroplating of metals or formed products

(G-2399)
MATRIX ENGINEERING AND SLS INC
44330 Duchess Dr (48187-3244)
PHONE.................734 981-7321
EMP: 5
SALES: 500K **Privately Held**
SIC: 3357 Automotive wire & cable, except ignition sets: nonferrous

(G-2400)
MEDTEST DX INC
5449 Research Dr (48188-2261)
PHONE.................866 540-2715
Hanjoon Ryu, *CEO*
Randy Daniel, *Chairman*
Ronald Jamison, *Vice Pres*
Willie Retana, *Vice Pres*
Maricel Roberts, *Vice Pres*
EMP: 51
SALES: 3.9MM **Privately Held**
SIC: 2869 Laboratory chemicals, organic

(G-2401)
MERCHANTS AUTOMATIC PDTS INC
Also Called: Mapco Manufacturing
5740 S Beck Rd (48188-2262)
PHONE.................734 829-0020
George Merchant Jr, *President*
Tina Baditoi, *Sls & Mktg Exec*
Nicole Pinter, *Marketing Staff*
▲ EMP: 38
SQ FT: 30,000
SALES (est): 8.3MM **Privately Held**
WEB: www.mapcomfg.com
SIC: 3452 3451 3599 Dowel pins, metal; screw machine products; machine & other job shop work

(G-2402)
MERCHANTS INDUSTRIES INC
Also Called: L & R Grinding
5715 S Sheldon Rd (48188-2534)
PHONE.................734 397-3031
George H Merchant Sr, *CEO*
George Merchant Jr, *President*
EMP: 6 EST: 1980
SQ FT: 4,400
SALES (est): 562.1K **Privately Held**
SIC: 3599 Machine shop, jobbing & repair

(G-2403)
MERIT TECH WORLDWIDE LLC (HQ)
7261 Commerce Blvd (48187-4287)
PHONE.................734 927-9520
Moon-Gyu Kong, *President*
Elie Mordavanaki, *Vice Pres*
Jacek Sznaza, *Vice Pres*
Jack Chaudill, *Controller*
▲ EMP: 20
SQ FT: 116,000
SALES (est): 8.2MM
SALES (corp-wide): 83.5MM **Privately Held**
SIC: 3465 Body parts, automobile: stamped metal
PA: Gns North America, Inc.
   13341 Quincy St
   Holland MI 49424
   616 796-0433

Canton - Wayne County (G-2404)   GEOGRAPHIC SECTION

(G-2404)
METALTEC STEEL ABRASIVE CO (HQ)
41155 Joy Rd (48187-2094)
PHONE................................734 459-7900
Gary Stevers, *President*
Gary Wood, *Treasurer*
◆ **EMP:** 36
SALES (est): 11.1MM
SALES (corp-wide): 284.4MM **Privately Held**
WEB: www.metaltecsteel.com
SIC: 3291 Steel shot abrasive
PA: Corinthian Capital Group, Llc
    601 Lexington Ave Rm 5901
    New York NY 10022
    212 920-2300

(G-2405)
MICHIGAN PAVING AND MTLS CO (DH)
2575 S Haggerty Rd # 100 (48188-2673)
PHONE................................734 397-2050
Dennis Rickard, *President*
Mike Jackson, *Division Mgr*
Nick Ricketts, *Area Mgr*
Ben Schmittling, *Area Mgr*
Jason Vanpatten, *Area Mgr*
▲ **EMP:** 30
SQ FT: 12,000
SALES (est): 252.4MM
SALES (corp-wide): 30.6B **Privately Held**
SIC: 1522 1541 2911 Residential construction; industrial buildings, new construction; asphalt or asphaltic materials, made in refineries

(G-2406)
MOBILITY TRNSP SVCS INC
Also Called: Mobilitytrans
42000 Koppernick Rd A3 (48187-4282)
PHONE................................734 453-6452
David Brown, *President*
Geralyn Brown, *Vice Pres*
EMP: 38
SQ FT: 25,000
SALES: 28.5MM **Privately Held**
WEB: www.mobilitytrans.com
SIC: 7532 3713 Van conversion; van bodies

(G-2407)
MOBILITYTRANS LLC
42000 Koppernick Rd A3 (48187-4282)
PHONE................................734 453-6452
David Brown, *Principal*
Geralyn Brown, *Principal*
Nicholas Brown, *Principal*
EMP: 45
SALES (est): 32.9K **Privately Held**
SIC: 7532 3713 Van conversion; van bodies

(G-2408)
MORNING STAR LAND COMPANY LLC
Also Called: Dynamic Metal Treating
7857 Ronda Dr (48187-2456)
PHONE................................734 459-8022
Lauren Epler,
EMP: 40
SALES (est): 700K **Privately Held**
SIC: 2899 Metal treating compounds

(G-2409)
MSC PRE FINISH METALS EGV INC
6855 Commerce Blvd (48187-4458)
PHONE................................734 207-4400
EMP: 3
SALES (corp-wide): 131.2MM **Privately Held**
SIC: 3479 Coating of metals & formed products
HQ: Msc Pre Finish Metals (Egv) Inc.
    2250 Pratt Blvd
    Elk Grove Village IL 60007
    847 439-2210

(G-2410)
MULTI-SYNC POWER LLC
47561 Lindenhurst Blvd (48188-3300)
PHONE................................734 658-3384
Vrinda Mahishi,
EMP: 3
SALES: 150K **Privately Held**
SIC: 3511 Turbines & turbine generator sets

(G-2411)
NATIONAL FUELS INC
40401 Michigan Ave (48188-2915)
PHONE................................734 895-7836
Abbas Nasser, *Principal*
EMP: 5
SALES (est): 388.8K **Privately Held**
SIC: 2869 Fuels

(G-2412)
NSS TECHNOLOGIES INC (DH)
Also Called: N S S Industries
8680 N Haggerty Rd (48187-2098)
PHONE................................734 459-9500
Mark Donegan, *CEO*
◆ **EMP:** 40 **EST:** 1970
SQ FT: 45,000
SALES (est): 42MM
SALES (corp-wide): 225.3B **Publicly Held**
SIC: 3452 3316 Bolts, metal; nuts, metal; screws, metal; cold finishing of steel shapes
HQ: Sps Technologies, Llc
    301 Highland Ave
    Jenkintown PA 19046
    215 572-3000

(G-2413)
NSS TECHNOLOGIES INC
8101 Ronda Dr (48187-2093)
PHONE................................734 459-9500
Mark Donegan, *CEO*
EMP: 40
SALES (corp-wide): 225.3B **Publicly Held**
SIC: 3452 Bolts, metal
HQ: Nss Technologies, Inc.
    8680 N Haggerty Rd
    Canton MI 48187
    734 459-9500

(G-2414)
PC TECHS ON WHEELS
8418 Brooke Park Dr # 111 (48187-5123)
PHONE................................734 262-4424
Craig Livingston, *Partner*
EMP: 4
SALES (est): 181.6K **Privately Held**
WEB: www.pctechsonwheels.com
SIC: 3571 Electronic computers

(G-2415)
PERENNIAL SOFTWARE
45185 Joy Rd Ste 102 (48187-1729)
PHONE................................734 414-0760
Michael Marks, *Owner*
Erick Steckel, *Accounts Exec*
John Doyle, *Manager*
Lisa Gambatese, *Training Spec*
EMP: 10
SALES (est): 586.3K **Privately Held**
SIC: 7372 Prepackaged software

(G-2416)
POCO INC
4850 S Sheldon Rd (48188-2527)
PHONE................................313 220-6752
Martin Powelson, *President*
Murray Powelson, *Vice Pres*
EMP: 30
SALES (est): 4.3MM **Privately Held**
SIC: 3499 7359 3993 Barricades, metal; sign rental; signs & advertising specialties

(G-2417)
POINTE SCIENTIFIC INC
5449 Research Dr (48188-2261)
P.O. Box 87188 (48187-0188)
PHONE................................734 487-8300
Wayne Brinster, *CEO*
Randy Daniel, *Chairman*
Ronald Jamison, *Vice Pres*
Willie Retana, *Vice Pres*
Rhonda Bloomfield, *Office Mgr*
▲ **EMP:** 30
SQ FT: 24,000
SALES (est): 5.8MM **Privately Held**
WEB: www.pointescientific.com
SIC: 3841 Diagnostic apparatus, medical

(G-2418)
PRIME WHEEL CORPORATION
6250 N Haggerty Rd (48187-3605)
PHONE................................248 207-4739
Joseph Atwell, *Engineer*
Mike Dailey, *Manager*
EMP: 5
SALES (corp-wide): 331.7MM **Privately Held**
SIC: 3312 Wheels
PA: Prime Wheel Corporation
    17705 S Main St
    Gardena CA 90248
    310 516-9126

(G-2419)
PRIORITY ONE EMERGENCY INC
5755 Belleville Rd (48188-2425)
PHONE................................734 398-5900
Sarah Nolan, *President*
EMP: 5 **EST:** 1999
SQ FT: 5,000
SALES (est): 880K **Privately Held**
WEB: www.priority1emergency.com
SIC: 7549 2311 2399 Automotive customizing services, non-factory basis; firemen's uniforms: made from purchased materials; policemen's uniforms: made from purchased materials; emblems, badges & insignia

(G-2420)
PRITECH CORPORATION
46036 Michigan Ave # 188 (48188-2304)
PHONE................................248 488-9120
Warren Jiang, *President*
◆ **EMP:** 5
SALES (est): 489.9K **Privately Held**
SIC: 3751 3714 Motorcycles & related parts; frames, motor vehicle

(G-2421)
PROSYS INDUSTRIES INC
7666 Market Dr (48187-2441)
PHONE................................734 207-3710
Phillipe Dupessey, *CEO*
Xaver Tomaszewski, *General Mgr*
Jim Brant, *Engineer*
EMP: 20
SQ FT: 20,000
SALES: 3.7MM
SALES (corp-wide): 355.8K **Privately Held**
WEB: www.prosys-industries.com
SIC: 3549 3677 Assembly machines, including robotic; coil windings, electronic
HQ: Prosys Sa
    Zae Defindrol
    Fillinges 74250

(G-2422)
RILAS & ROGERS LLC
44440 Meadowcreek Ln (48187-2471)
PHONE................................937 901-4228
Henry Washington, *President*
P F Thomas III, *CFO*
EMP: 10
SALES (est): 750K **Privately Held**
SIC: 3999 Manufacturing industries

(G-2423)
RND ENGINEERING LLC
46036 Michigan Ave # 201 (48188-2304)
PHONE................................734 328-8277
Richalin Dique, *President*
Richalin K Digue,
EMP: 8
SQ FT: 8,500
SALES (est): 1.3MM **Privately Held**
SIC: 3541 Machine tools, metal cutting type

(G-2424)
S & N GRAPHIC SOLUTIONS LLC
1818 Stonebridge Way (48188-3273)
PHONE................................734 495-3314
Greg Jahn,
EMP: 7
SQ FT: 8,000
SALES: 780K **Privately Held**
SIC: 2752 Commercial printing, offset

(G-2425)
SCHULER INCORPORATED (DH)
Also Called: Schuler Hydroforming
7145 Commerce Blvd (48187-4288)
PHONE................................734 207-7200
Stefan Klebert, *CEO*
Klaus Hertell, *General Mgr*
Peter Jost, *COO*
Tim Quinn, *Vice Pres*
Robert Rich, *Vice Pres*
◆ **EMP:** 85 **EST:** 1961
SQ FT: 53,160
SALES (est): 81.3MM
SALES (corp-wide): 6.9B **Privately Held**
WEB: www.schulerinc.com
SIC: 5084 3444 3599 Industrial machinery & equipment; sheet metal specialties, not stamped; custom machinery
HQ: Schuler Ag
    Schuler-Platz 1
    Goppingen 73033
    716 166-0

(G-2426)
SHILOH INDUSTRIES INC
Also Called: Canton Manufacturing
7295 N Haggerty Rd (48187-2452)
PHONE................................734 454-4000
Kathy Henneman, *Plant Mgr*
EMP: 77 **Publicly Held**
SIC: 3469 Metal stampings
PA: Shiloh Industries, Inc.
    880 Steel Dr
    Valley City OH 44280

(G-2427)
SPHEROS NORTH AMERICA INC
5536 Research Dr (48188-2261)
P.O. Box 1905, Elkhart IN (46515-1905)
PHONE................................734 218-7350
Krzysztof Kulaga, *Principal*
▲ **EMP:** 8
SALES (est): 3.4MM
SALES (corp-wide): 177.9K **Privately Held**
SIC: 5074 5075 3465 Plumbing & hydronic heating supplies; air conditioning & ventilation equipment & supplies; body parts, automobile: stamped metal
HQ: Valeo Thermal Commercial Vehicles Germany Gmbh
    Friedrichshafener Str. 7
    Gilching 82205
    810 577-210

(G-2428)
SPORTSWEAR SPECIALTIES INC
7930 N Lilley Rd (48187-2432)
PHONE................................734 416-9941
Brad Craig, *President*
EMP: 7
SQ FT: 1,600
SALES (est): 727.7K **Privately Held**
SIC: 2395 Embroidery & art needlework

(G-2429)
STAR RINGMASTER
1261 S Lotz Rd (48188-1345)
PHONE................................734 641-7147
Brian McElfresh, *Owner*
EMP: 5
SALES (est): 354.9K **Privately Held**
WEB: www.starringmaster.com
SIC: 3545 Machine tool accessories

(G-2430)
STYLECRAFT PRINTING CO (PA)
Also Called: Stylecraft Printing & Graphics
8472 Ronda Dr (48187-2087)
PHONE................................734 455-5500
Richard A Pesci, *President*
Tim Chytry, *Production*
▲ **EMP:** 75
SQ FT: 25,000
SALES (est): 11.1MM **Privately Held**
WEB: www.stylecraftprinting.com
SIC: 2752 Commercial printing, offset; business forms, lithographed

GEOGRAPHIC SECTION

(G-2431)
SWISS AMERICAN SCREW PDTS INC
5740 S Sheldon Rd (48188-2507)
PHONE..................734 397-1600
Roland Leist, *President*
Mary Leist, *Corp Secy*
Robert Leist, *Vice Pres*
Lisa Rowe, *Director*
EMP: 18 **EST:** 1962
SQ FT: 8,200
SALES (est): 2.4MM **Privately Held**
WEB: www.sasp.biz
SIC: 3451 3769 3714 Screw machine products; guided missile & space vehicle parts & auxiliary equipment; motor vehicle parts & accessories

(G-2432)
TECHNICAL ILLUSTRATION CORP
Also Called: Ticglobal
46177 Windridge Ln (48188-6226)
PHONE..................313 982-9660
Peter Kapas, *President*
Anthony Kapas, *Vice Pres*
Colleen Kapas, *Treasurer*
Helen Kapas, *Admin Sec*
EMP: 18
SQ FT: 3,800
SALES (est): 1.3MM **Privately Held**
WEB: www.ticglobal.com
SIC: 2741 Technical manuals: publishing only, not printed on site

(G-2433)
TECHNOLOGY PLUS TRAILERS INC
7780 Ronda Dr (48187-2447)
PHONE..................734 928-0001
Emory Buttermore, *President*
EMP: 10
SQ FT: 22,000
SALES (est): 1.4MM **Privately Held**
SIC: 3792 5561 3715 Camping trailers & chassis; travel trailers: automobile, new & used; truck trailers

(G-2434)
TEKNICOLORS INC
43319 Joy Rd (48187-2075)
PHONE..................734 414-9900
John Ewart, *Branch Mgr*
EMP: 4
SALES (corp-wide): 2.5MM **Privately Held**
SIC: 5231 3479 Paint & painting supplies; painting, coating & hot dipping
PA: Teknicolors, Inc.
101 1/2 N Saginaw St
Pontiac MI 48342
248 745-9400

(G-2435)
TEKNIKUT CORPORATION
46036 Michigan Ave (48188-2304)
PHONE..................586 778-7150
Sean McNeilly, *President*
EMP: 5
SQ FT: 2,000
SALES: 1MM **Privately Held**
SIC: 3545 5084 Cutting tools for machine tools; machine tools & accessories

(G-2436)
TRINITY SEVEN ENTERPRISES INC
4398 Pond Run (48188-2175)
PHONE..................216 906-0984
Raphael Maduako, *CEO*
EMP: 3
SALES (est): 249.9K **Privately Held**
SIC: 2841 Soap & other detergents

(G-2437)
UNIVERSAL IMPEX INC
1619 Mclaine St (48188-8024)
PHONE..................734 306-6684
Saif Schareef, *CEO*
EMP: 3
SALES (est): 247.1K **Privately Held**
SIC: 3596 Industrial scales

(G-2438)
VERSATILE SYSTEMS LLC
8347 Ronda Dr (48188-2079)
PHONE..................734 397-3957
EMP: 16
SQ FT: 2,400
SALES (est): 3MM **Privately Held**
SIC: 3625 Mfg Relays/Industrial Controls

(G-2439)
VISIBLE INK PRESS LLC
43311 Joy Rd 414 (48187-2075)
PHONE..................734 667-3211
Roger Janecke, *Principal*
Martin Connors,
▲ **EMP:** 3
SALES (est): 2MM **Privately Held**
WEB: www.visibleink.com
SIC: 2741 Miscellaneous publishing

(G-2440)
VISTEON CORPORATION
45004 Lothrop Ct (48188-1077)
PHONE..................734 718-8927
EMP: 83
SALES (corp-wide): 7.5B **Publicly Held**
SIC: 3714 Mfg Motor Vehicle Parts/Accessories
PA: Visteon Corporation
1 Village Center Dr
Van Buren Twp MI 48111
800 847-8366

(G-2441)
VITAL SIGNS INC (PA)
Also Called: VSI Archtectural Signs Systems
6753 Kings Mill Dr (48187-5478)
PHONE..................313 491-2010
Francis A Schmitt, *President*
EMP: 6
SALES: 390K **Privately Held**
SIC: 3993 Signs, not made in custom sign painting shops

(G-2442)
VOXELJET AMERICA INC
41430 Haggerty Cir S (48188-2227)
PHONE..................734 709-8237
Ingo Ederer, *CEO*
David Tait, *Managing Dir*
Rudolf Franz, *COO*
▲ **EMP:** 13
SQ FT: 50,000
SALES (est): 1.7MM
SALES (corp-wide): 29.7MM **Privately Held**
SIC: 3555 Printing presses
PA: Voxeljet Ag
Paul-Lenz-Str. 1a
Friedberg 86316
821 748-3100

(G-2443)
WATER MASTER INC
Also Called: Master Pump Service
41747 Joy Rd (48187-2062)
PHONE..................313 255-3930
Stephen B Fritz, *Principal*
Wayne E Fritz, *Corp Secy*
Wayne Fritz, *Treasurer*
EMP: 3
SALES (est): 486.6K **Privately Held**
SIC: 3561 1711 Pumps & pumping equipment; irrigation sprinkler system installation

(G-2444)
WORTHINGTON INDUSTRIES INC
5260 S Haggerty Rd (48188-2775)
PHONE..................734 397-6187
Michael Maggard, *Branch Mgr*
EMP: 4
SALES (corp-wide): 3.7B **Publicly Held**
SIC: 3316 Cold finishing of steel shapes
PA: Worthington Industries, Inc.
200 W Wlson Bridge Rd
Worthington OH 43085
614 438-3210

(G-2445)
YAZAKI INTERNATIONAL CORP (HQ)
6801 N Haggerty Rd 4707e (48187-3538)
PHONE..................734 983-1000
Yutaka Inagaki, *Principal*
Kim Ward, *Counsel*
Takashige Miyashita, *Exec VP*
Jim Romine, *Exec VP*
Richard Tajer, *Vice Pres*
◆ **EMP:** 9
SALES (est): 1.8B **Privately Held**
SIC: 5013 3643 Automotive supplies & parts; current-carrying wiring devices

(G-2446)
ZSI-FOSTER INC (DH)
45065 Michigan Ave (48188-2441)
PHONE..................734 844-0055
Rick Stepien, *CEO*
◆ **EMP:** 56
SALES (est): 12.4MM
SALES (corp-wide): 1.2MM **Privately Held**
SIC: 3429 Clamps, metal
HQ: Ideal Tridon Holdings, Inc.
8100 Tridon Dr
Smyrna TN 37167
615 459-5800

Capac
St. Clair County

(G-2447)
CELANI PRINTING CO
126 N Main St (48014-3142)
PHONE..................810 395-1609
Daniel Celani, *Principal*
EMP: 3
SALES (est): 289.8K **Privately Held**
SIC: 2752 Commercial printing, lithographic

(G-2448)
IMLAY CITY HIGH PRESSURE
Also Called: Newark High Pressure
113 S Glassford St (48014-3607)
P.O. Box 366 (48014-0366)
PHONE..................810 395-7459
Gerald I Schwartzkopf, *Owner*
EMP: 3
SALES (est): 120K **Privately Held**
SIC: 7542 2097 Carwash, self-service; ice cubes

(G-2449)
MILLER BROACH INC
Also Called: MB
14510 Bryce Rd (48014-3179)
P.O. Box 99 (48014-0099)
PHONE..................810 395-8810
Jeffrey Miller, *President*
Ken Nemec, *Vice Pres*
John Robert, *Prdtn Mgr*
Chad Palmer, *Opers Staff*
Laura McKay, *Controller*
EMP: 80
SQ FT: 58,000
SALES (est): 6MM **Privately Held**
WEB: www.millerbroach.com
SIC: 3545 3541 Broaches (machine tool accessories); machine tools, metal cutting type

(G-2450)
MILLER PROD & MACHINING INC
14510 Bryce Rd (48014-3179)
P.O. Box 99 (48014-0099)
PHONE..................810 395-8810
Krista Starna-Miller, *CEO*
Jeffrey Miller, *President*
EMP: 20 **EST:** 2016
SQ FT: 20,000
SALES (est): 1MM **Privately Held**
SIC: 3599 Machine shop, jobbing & repair

Carleton
Monroe County

(G-2451)
A & L METAL PRODUCTS
Also Called: Detroit Mini Safe Co
11984 Telegraph Rd (48117-9045)
P.O. Box 135 (48117-0135)
PHONE..................734 654-8990
Fax: 734 654-0045
EMP: 5
SQ FT: 12,000
SALES (est): 520.6K **Privately Held**
SIC: 3613 3499 5072 Mfg Switchgear/Switchboards & Deposit Safes & Whol Security Hardware

(G-2452)
D AND G GLASS INC
3355 Carleton Rockwood Rd (48117-9760)
PHONE..................734 341-0038
Darell Williams, *President*
Shawn Williams, *Vice Pres*
EMP: 3
SALES: 230K **Privately Held**
SIC: 3088 Shower stalls, fiberglass & plastic

(G-2453)
DAILY RECYCLING OF MICHIGAN
201 Matlin Rd (48117)
PHONE..................734 654-9800
Nick Straub, *Manager*
EMP: 3
SALES (est): 125.9K **Privately Held**
SIC: 2711 4953 Newspapers, publishing & printing; refuse systems

(G-2454)
FCX PERFORMANCE INC (PA)
Also Called: Renew Valve & Machine Co.
845 Monroe St (48117-9077)
PHONE..................734 654-2201
JB Rorick, *Mng Member*
Glenn Goodnight, *Technical Staff*
EMP: 30
SALES (est): 3.5MM **Privately Held**
SIC: 7699 3491 Valve repair, industrial; industrial valves

(G-2455)
GREEN FUELS LLC
715 Indian Trail Rd (48117-9315)
PHONE..................734 735-6802
Lauren L Smith, *Administration*
EMP: 4
SALES (est): 278K **Privately Held**
SIC: 2869 Fuels

(G-2456)
GUARDIAN INDUSTRIES LLC
14600 Romine Rd (48117-9257)
PHONE..................734 654-4285
Mike Boucher, *Project Mgr*
Gerry Hool, *Opers-Prdtn-Mfg*
D Rogers, *Buyer*
Conrad Sobania, *QC Mgr*
Charles Buiocchi, *Manager*
EMP: 500
SALES (corp-wide): 40.6B **Privately Held**
WEB: www.guardian.com
SIC: 3211 3231 3229 Flat glass; products of purchased glass; pressed & blown glass
HQ: Guardian Industries, Llc
2300 Harmon Rd
Auburn Hills MI 48326
248 340-1800

(G-2457)
GUARDIAN INDUSTRIES LLC
Also Called: Guardian Science & Tech Ctr
14511 Romine Rd (48117-9647)
PHONE..................734 654-1111
Scott Thompson, *Branch Mgr*
EMP: 85
SALES (corp-wide): 40.6B **Privately Held**
WEB: www.guardian.com
SIC: 3211 Flat glass
HQ: Guardian Industries, Llc
2300 Harmon Rd
Auburn Hills MI 48326
248 340-1800

(G-2458)
KACE LOGISTICS LLC (PA)
862 Will Carleton Rd (48117-9704)
PHONE..................734 946-8600
Kenyon S Calender, *CEO*
Joseph Parin, *President*
Jeff Carroll, *Vice Pres*
Paul Pavelich, *Vice Pres*
EMP: 60

Carleton - Monroe County (G-2459)

SALES (est): 24.1MM **Privately Held**
SIC: **4731** 3577 Truck transportation brokers; bar code (magnetic ink) printers

(G-2459)
LAKEWOOD MACHINE PRODUCTS CO
12429 Maxwell Rd (48117-8800)
P.O. Box 388 (48117-0388)
PHONE..................734 654-6677
Martin Lisowski, *President*
Howard J Morrin, *Vice Pres*
Lois Schafer Lisowski, *Treasurer*
Elizabeth Duvall, *Admin Sec*
EMP: 30
SQ FT: 22,000
SALES (est): 9.7MM **Privately Held**
SIC: **3537** Platforms, stands, tables, pallets & similar equipment

(G-2460)
LV METALS INC
2094 Ready Rd (48117-9778)
PHONE..................734 654-8081
EMP: 5
SQ FT: 20,000
SALES (est): 346.1K **Privately Held**
SIC: **7389** 5051 3444 Business Services Metals Service Center Mfg Sheet Metalwork

(G-2461)
REVEALED ENGINEERING LLC
13177 Briar Hill Rd (48117-9202)
PHONE..................734 642-5551
Candace Baxter,
Jeffrey Baxter,
EMP: 3
SALES (est): 201K **Privately Held**
SIC: **8711** 3621 Mechanical engineering; frequency converters (electric generators)

(G-2462)
RVM COMPANY OF TOLEDO
Also Called: Dayton Precision Services
845 Monroe St (48117-9077)
PHONE..................734 654-2201
Tim Rorick, *President*
EMP: 40
SQ FT: 30,000
SALES (est): 1.5MM
SALES (corp-wide): 3.5MM **Privately Held**
WEB: www.renewvalve.com
SIC: **7699** 5085 3599 Valve repair, industrial; valves & fittings; machine shop, jobbing & repair
PA: Fcx Performance Inc
845 Monroe St
Carleton MI 48117
734 654-2201

Carney
Menominee County

(G-2463)
JASPERS SUGAR BUSH LLC
W1867 County Road 374 (49812-9333)
PHONE..................906 639-2588
Gail Clark, *Materials Mgr*
Bob Casperson, *Engineer*
Mark Jasper, *Mng Member*
Angie Krause, *Manager*
David Nemetz, *Manager*
EMP: 6
SALES (est): 90K **Privately Held**
WEB: www.jaspermaple.com
SIC: **2099** Sugar, industrial maple; maple syrup

(G-2464)
SUPERIOR CEDAR PRODUCTS INC
101 Fence Factory Rd (49812)
P.O. Box 38 (49812-0038)
PHONE..................906 639-2132
Dwaine Mellen, *President*
Timothy Bruce, *Vice Pres*
Charles Olson, *Vice Pres*
Charles Dornfeld, *Treasurer*
EMP: 40 **EST:** 1998

SALES (est): 10MM **Privately Held**
WEB: www.superiorcedar.com
SIC: **3524** Lawn & garden equipment

Caro
Tuscola County

(G-2465)
ANDOOR CRAFTMASTER
3521 Lobdell Rd (48723-9552)
PHONE..................989 672-2020
Tracy Mazur, *Owner*
EMP: 7
SALES (est): 399.3K **Privately Held**
SIC: **2431** 3442 Doors, wood; metal doors, sash & trim

(G-2466)
CAROL PACKING HOUSE
1131 Weeden Rd (48723-9583)
PHONE..................989 673-2688
Dan Maurer, *Partner*
EMP: 6 **EST:** 1947
SQ FT: 5,000
SALES (est): 661.5K **Privately Held**
SIC: **2011** Meat packing plants

(G-2467)
CARRY MANUFACTURING INC
Also Called: Carry Pump Co.
1360 Prospect Ave (48723-9288)
PHONE..................989 672-2779
Del Nichols, *CEO*
James Nichols, *President*
Delmar Nichiols, *Vice Pres*
Gene Nichols, *Treasurer*
Jeanie Nichols, *Treasurer*
EMP: 3
SQ FT: 11,000
SALES (est): 3.8MM **Privately Held**
WEB: www.carrymfg.com
SIC: **3312** 3914 Stainless steel; stainless steel ware

(G-2468)
ENGINEERED TOOLS CORP
2710 W Caro Rd (48723-9609)
P.O. Box 209 (48723-0209)
PHONE..................989 673-8733
Glen Perkins, *President*
Ross Deneau, *Engineer*
Richard Perkins, *Mktg Dir*
Patricia Perkins, *Admin Sec*
EMP: 52
SQ FT: 24,500
SALES (est): 9.3MM **Privately Held**
WEB: www.engineeredtools.com
SIC: **3545** 8711 Cutting tools for machine tools; engineering services

(G-2469)
GREAT LAKES LIFT INC
1382 E Caro Rd (48723-9306)
PHONE..................989 673-2109
David J Sturtevant, *President*
Brenda Stein, *Admin Sec*
EMP: 4
SQ FT: 10,000
SALES (est): 750.9K **Privately Held**
WEB: www.greatlakeslift.com
SIC: **3536** 3448 3799 Boat lifts; docks: prefabricated metal; trailers & trailer equipment

(G-2470)
LASER MARKING TECHNOLOGIES LLC
1101 W Sanilac Rd (48723-9539)
PHONE..................989 673-6690
Gary Lester, *Engineer*
Ty Brock, *Electrical Engi*
Staci Meyer, *Office Mgr*
Samuel Palmeter,
▲ **EMP:** 13
SALES (est): 3MM **Privately Held**
SIC: **3699** Laser systems & equipment

(G-2471)
MICHIGAN ETHANOL LLC
Also Called: Poet Biorefining- Caro 25200
1551 Empire Dr (48723-8804)
PHONE..................989 672-1222
David Gloer, *General Mgr*

Jeffrey Broin, *Chairman*
EMP: 41
SALES (est): 9.1MM **Privately Held**
SIC: **2869** Ethyl alcohol, ethanol
PA: Poet, Llc
4615 N Lewis Ave
Sioux Falls SD 57104

(G-2472)
MICHIGAN SUGAR COMPANY
725 S Almer St (48723-1812)
P.O. Box 107 (48723-0107)
PHONE..................989 673-3126
William Gough, *Manager*
EMP: 150
SALES (corp-wide): 600MM **Privately Held**
SIC: **2063** 2062 Beet sugar from beet sugar refinery; cane sugar refining
PA: Michigan Sugar Company
122 Uptown Dr Unit 300
Bay City MI 48708
989 686-0161

(G-2473)
MICHIGAN SUGAR COMPANY
819 Peninsular St (48723)
P.O. Box 107 (48723-0107)
PHONE..................989 673-2223
Daniel Mashue, *Branch Mgr*
EMP: 70
SALES (corp-wide): 600MM **Privately Held**
SIC: **5149** 2063 2061 Sugar, honey, molasses & syrups; beet sugar; raw cane sugar
PA: Michigan Sugar Company
122 Uptown Dr Unit 300
Bay City MI 48708
989 686-0161

(G-2474)
MIDWEST BUILD CENTER LLC
1750 Speirs Rd (48723-8211)
PHONE..................989 673-1388
Henry Rice, *Mng Member*
EMP: 7 **EST:** 2017
SALES (est): 395.6K **Privately Held**
SIC: **3721** Airplanes, fixed or rotary wing

(G-2475)
PRECISION CONCEPTS INC
1220 W Sanilac Rd (48723-9594)
PHONE..................989 673-8555
John Stoick, *President*
Joel Stoick, *Vice Pres*
EMP: 1
SQ FT: 10,000
SALES: 1MM **Privately Held**
WEB: www.precisionconceptsinc.com
SIC: **3799** Automobile trailer chassis

(G-2476)
R & S TOOL & DIE INC
545 Columbia St Ste B (48723-8935)
PHONE..................989 673-8511
Robert H Cotton Sr, *President*
Ruth Cotton, *Corp Secy*
Stephen Cotton, *Manager*
EMP: 9
SQ FT: 5,000
SALES (est): 1.6MM **Privately Held**
SIC: **3559** 3549 3545 3544 Plastics working machinery; metalworking machinery; gauges (machine tool accessories); die sets for metal stamping (presses); machine shop, jobbing & repair

(G-2477)
TI GROUP AUTO SYSTEMS LLC
Also Called: Caro Test Center
630 Columbia St (48723-9502)
PHONE..................989 672-1200
Kurt Nickel, *Agent*
Kurt Mickel, *Agent*
EMP: 300
SALES (corp-wide): 3.9B **Privately Held**
WEB: www.tiautomotive.com
SIC: **3714** Motor vehicle parts & accessories
HQ: Ti Group Automotive Systems, Llc
2020 Taylor Rd
Auburn Hills MI 48326
248 296-8000

(G-2478)
TI GROUP AUTO SYSTEMS LLC
630 Columbia St (48723-9502)
PHONE..................989 673-7727
Roger Affeldt, *Branch Mgr*
EMP: 97
SALES (corp-wide): 3.9B **Privately Held**
WEB: www.tiautomotive.com
SIC: **3714** Motor vehicle parts & accessories
HQ: Ti Group Automotive Systems, Llc
2020 Taylor Rd
Auburn Hills MI 48326
248 296-8000

(G-2479)
TUSCOLA COUNTY ADVERTISER INC (PA)
344 N State St (48723-1538)
P.O. Box 106 (48723-0106)
PHONE..................989 673-3181
Bob Edwards, *President*
Tim Murphy, *Publisher*
Joyce Edwards, *Corp Secy*
Jerry Edwards, *Vice Pres*
Steve Edwards, *Vice Pres*
EMP: 35 **EST:** 1868
SQ FT: 9,000
SALES (est): 40.6MM **Privately Held**
WEB: www.tcadvertiser.com
SIC: **2711** 2741 Newspapers: publishing only, not printed on site; miscellaneous publishing

(G-2480)
TUSCOLA COUNTY ADVERTISER INC
Also Called: Heritage Press
344 N State St (48723-1538)
PHONE..................517 673-3181
EMP: 438
SALES (corp-wide): 40.6MM **Privately Held**
SIC: **2759** Commercial printing
PA: Tuscola County Advertiser, Inc.
344 N State St
Caro MI 48723
989 673-3181

(G-2481)
VARSITY MONTHLY THUMB
251 N State St (48723-1560)
PHONE..................810 404-5297
EMP: 3
SALES (est): 118.5K **Privately Held**
SIC: **2721** Magazines: publishing only, not printed on site

(G-2482)
WOW PLASTICS LLC
3394 Carmel Mtn Rd 250 (48723)
PHONE..................760 827-7800
Glen White, *CEO*
Sue Bonsky, *QC Mgr*
John Armstrong, *Maintence Staff*
David Allen,
EMP: 1 **EST:** 2014
SALES (est): 2.1MM **Privately Held**
SIC: **3089** 7373 Automotive parts, plastic; systems software development services

(G-2483)
WOW PRODUCTS USA
1111 S Colling Rd (48723-9238)
PHONE..................989 672-1300
EMP: 4
SALES (est): 346.7K **Privately Held**
SIC: **3089** Injection molding of plastics

Carrollton
Saginaw County

(G-2484)
CUSTOM DESIGN & MANUFACTURING
3673 Carrollton Rd (48724-5004)
P.O. Box 190 (48724-0190)
PHONE..................989 754-9962
James Nuerminger, *President*
Dan Vesterfelt, *Vice Pres*
EMP: 15
SQ FT: 5,000

GEOGRAPHIC SECTION

SALES: 1.2MM **Privately Held**
SIC: **3441** 7692 3444 1799 Fabricated structural metal; welding repair; sheet metalwork; welding on site

(G-2485)
DARLING INGREDIENTS INC
340 Tyler St (48724-5061)
P.O. Box 181 (48724-0181)
PHONE.................................989 752-4340
Sam Immel, *Manager*
EMP: 10
SALES (corp-wide): 3.3B **Publicly Held**
WEB: www.darlingii.com
SIC: **2077** 4212 Tallow rendering, inedible; local trucking, without storage
PA: Darling Ingredients Inc.
  5601 N Macarthur Blvd
  Irving TX 75038
  972 717-0300

(G-2486)
ROCK REDI-MIX INC
Also Called: Rock Products, The
2820 Carrollton Rd (48724)
P.O. Box 39 (48724-0039)
PHONE.................................989 752-0795
Dan Henson, *Manager*
EMP: 9
SALES (est): 1.2MM **Privately Held**
SIC: **3273** Ready-mixed concrete

(G-2487)
SAGINAW ASPHALT PAVING CO
2981 Carrollton Rd (48724)
PHONE.................................989 755-8147
Edward Levy, *President*
▲ **EMP:** 100 **EST:** 1952
SQ FT: 18,000
SALES (est): 15.4MM
SALES (corp-wide): 368.1MM **Privately Held**
SIC: **1611** 8741 2951 Highway & street paving contractor; construction management; asphalt & asphaltic paving mixtures (not from refineries)
PA: Edw. C. Levy Co.
  9300 Dix
  Dearborn MI 48120
  313 429-2200

Carson City
Montcalm County

(G-2488)
DUTCHMANS WELDING & REPAIR
6161 County Line Rd (48811)
PHONE.................................989 584-6861
Harvey Imhoff, *Owner*
Ruth Imhoff, *Co-Owner*
EMP: 4
SALES: 100K **Privately Held**
SIC: **7692** Welding repair

(G-2489)
GRANDVIEW FOOT & ANKLE
423 E Main St Ste C (48811-9741)
P.O. Box 430, Greenville (48838-0430)
PHONE.................................989 584-3916
Stacy A Uebele, *Owner*
Stacey A Eubele, *Owner*
EMP: 5 **EST:** 2007
SALES (est): 460.8K **Privately Held**
SIC: **2252** Anklets (hosiery)

(G-2490)
GREAT LAKES SNOW & ICE INC
7123 S Garlock Rd (48811-8529)
PHONE.................................989 584-1211
Bill Hubler, *President*
Wendy Hubler, *Vice Pres*
EMP: 2
SQ FT: 5,000
SALES (est): 1.1MM **Privately Held**
SIC: **3531** 5083 Blades for graders, scrapers, dozers & snow plows; mowers, power

(G-2491)
HIGH GRADE MATERIALS COMPANY
10101 E Carson City Rd (48811)
P.O. Box 112 (48811-0112)
PHONE.................................989 584-6004
Bill Hall, *Branch Mgr*
EMP: 3
SALES (corp-wide): 28.3MM **Privately Held**
SIC: **3273** Ready-mixed concrete
PA: High Grade Materials Company
  9266 Snows Lake Rd
  Greenville MI 48838
  616 754-5545

(G-2492)
MARTIN ELECTRIC MTRS SLS & SVC
Also Called: Martin Electric Mtr Sls & Svc
10116 Cleveland Rd (48811-9421)
PHONE.................................989 584-3850
Dean Martin, *Owner*
Mark Martin, *Partner*
EMP: 3
SALES: 240K **Privately Held**
SIC: **7694** 5084 Electric motor repair; engines & transportation equipment

(G-2493)
MIDTOWN BAR
116 W Main (48811)
PHONE.................................989 584-6212
Scott Chamberlain, *Owner*
EMP: 4
SALES (est): 345.4K **Privately Held**
SIC: **2599** Bar, restaurant & cafeteria furniture

(G-2494)
NEUCADIA LLC
404 S 2nd St (48811-5101)
P.O. Box 189 (48811-0189)
PHONE.................................989 572-0324
Grady McCrackin, *President*
Michael McCrackin,
Frank Rosenbaum,
EMP: 5
SALES (est): 261.7K **Privately Held**
SIC: **3499** Machine bases, metal

(G-2495)
PADDLE KING INC
7110 S Crystal Rd (48811-8503)
PHONE.................................989 235-6776
Mark Brusskoter, *President*
EMP: 11
SALES (est): 3MM **Privately Held**
WEB: www.paddleking.com
SIC: **3732** 2394 2499 Non-motorized boat, building & repairing; canvas & related products; floating docks, wood; ladders, wood

(G-2496)
PLASTICO INDUSTRIES INC (PA)
320 W Main St (48811-5116)
P.O. Box 325, Springville CA (93265-0325)
PHONE.................................616 304-6289
EMP: 13
SQ FT: 30,000
SALES (est): 1MM **Privately Held**
SIC: **3089** Mfg Injection Molded Plastic Point-Of-Purchase Displays

Carsonville
Sanilac County

(G-2497)
NATURES BEST TOP SOIL COMPOST
640 Old 51 (48419-9427)
PHONE.................................810 657-9528
Michael Davis, *Owner*
EMP: 5
SALES (est): 367.5K **Privately Held**
WEB: www.naturesbestlandscape.com
SIC: **2875** Compost

Casco
St. Clair County

(G-2498)
AFTERSHOCK MOTORSPORTS
5831 Church Rd (48064-4207)
PHONE.................................586 273-1333
Ruby Bishop, *Owner*
EMP: 5
SQ FT: 7,200
SALES: 120K **Privately Held**
WEB: www.aftershockmotorsports.com
SIC: **3711** 5571 Automobile assembly, including specialty automobiles; motorcycle parts & accessories

(G-2499)
CCI DRIVELINE LLC
9568 Marine City Hwy (48064-4109)
PHONE.................................586 716-1160
Michael Cameron,
EMP: 3
SQ FT: 10,000
SALES (est): 403.9K **Privately Held**
SIC: **3714** 5013 Axle housings & shafts, motor vehicle; axles, motor vehicle; automotive supplies & parts

(G-2500)
INDIAN SUMMER RECYCLING INC
5877 Bethuy Rd (48064-4106)
PHONE.................................586 725-1340
Fred Thompson, *President*
Robert Brooks, *Admin Sec*
EMP: 3
SQ FT: 3,000
SALES (est): 1MM **Privately Held**
SIC: **2875** Compost

(G-2501)
INNOVATED PORTABLE WELDIN
5221 Lois Ct (48064-4663)
PHONE.................................586 322-4442
EMP: 3
SALES (est): 42K **Privately Held**
SIC: **7692** Welding repair

(G-2502)
MAGNETIC CHUCK SERVICES CO INC
Also Called: Industrial System Services
9391 Lindsey Rd (48064-2412)
PHONE.................................586 822-9441
James Ewald, *President*
EMP: 6
SQ FT: 2,500
SALES: 80K **Privately Held**
SIC: **7699** 3545 Industrial machinery & equipment repair; chucks: drill, lathe or magnetic (machine tool accessories)

(G-2503)
NEW LFE CPPR & BRSS MAINT FREE
Also Called: All Metal Finishing
9984 Marine City Hwy (48064-4108)
PHONE.................................586 725-3286
Ken Hancock, *Mng Member*
EMP: 6
SALES: 150K **Privately Held**
SIC: **5051** 3471 Copper products; finishing, metals or formed products

(G-2504)
PACE SOFTWARE SYSTEMS INC
5345 Meldrum Rd (48064-3703)
P.O. Box 458, Fraser (48026-0458)
PHONE.................................586 727-3189
Roger Pace, *President*
EMP: 10
SALES (est): 435.5K **Privately Held**
WEB: www.pacesoftwaresystems.com
SIC: **7372** Prepackaged software

Caseville
Huron County

(G-2505)
EVENHEAT KILN INC
6949 Legion Rd (48725-9575)
P.O. Box 399 (48725-0399)
PHONE.................................989 856-2281
John D Watson, *President*
Susan Siver, *Office Mgr*
EMP: 12 **EST:** 1948
SQ FT: 20,000
SALES (est): 2MM **Privately Held**
WEB: www.evenheat-kiln.com
SIC: **3567** Ceramic kilns & furnaces

(G-2506)
STEADFAST TOOL & MACHINE INC
6601 Limerick Rd (48725-9724)
PHONE.................................989 856-8127
Chad Bohn, *President*
EMP: 4 **EST:** 1997
SALES: 500K **Privately Held**
SIC: **3541** Brushing machines (metalworking machinery)

Casnovia
Muskegon County

(G-2507)
DANMARK GRAPHICS LLC
153 N Main St (49318-8704)
P.O. Box 96 (49318-0096)
PHONE.................................616 675-7499
Mark Vanderzanden, *Principal*
EMP: 7
SALES (est): 540.8K **Privately Held**
SIC: **7336** 2759 5999 Commercial art & graphic design; letterpress & screen printing; banners, flags, decals & posters

(G-2508)
RIDGEVIEW METALS INCORPORATED
71 S Main St (49318-9719)
PHONE.................................850 259-1808
Scott Barscewski, *President*
EMP: 3 **EST:** 2012
SALES (est): 323.9K **Privately Held**
SIC: **3448** Prefabricated metal components

Caspian
Iron County

(G-2509)
NORTHEASTERN PRODUCTS CORP
85 Brady Ave (49915-5115)
P.O. Box 467 (49915-0467)
PHONE.................................906 265-6241
Mark Stauber, *Manager*
EMP: 22
SALES (corp-wide): 11MM **Privately Held**
WEB: www.nep-co.com
SIC: **2493** Reconstituted wood products
PA: Northeastern Products Corp.
  115 Sweet Rd
  Warrensburg NY 12885
  518 623-3161

Cass City
Tuscola County

(G-2510)
AMI INDUSTRIES INC
Also Called: AM Industries
6285 Garfield Ave (48726-1341)
PHONE.................................989 872-8823
Ryan Thorpe, *Branch Mgr*
EMP: 15
SALES (corp-wide): 35.6MM **Privately Held**
SIC: **3559** Automotive related machinery

Cass City - Tuscola County (G-2511)   GEOGRAPHIC SECTION

PA: Ami Industries, Inc.
5093 N Red Oak Rd
Lewiston MI 49756
989 786-3755

(G-2511)
ANROD SCREEN CYLINDER COMPANY
6160 Garfield Ave (48726-1309)
P.O. Box 117 (48726-0117)
PHONE.................989 872-2101
Gregory A Biddinger, *President*
Richard Biddinger, *Corp Secy*
EMP: 44 **EST:** 1950
SQ FT: 32,000
SALES (est): 8.5MM **Privately Held**
WEB: www.anrodscreen.com
SIC: 3496 3714 3564 3494 Cylinder wire cloth; motor vehicle parts & accessories; blowers & fans; valves & pipe fittings; metal stampings

(G-2512)
CASS CITY CHRONICLE INC
6550 Main St (48726-1561)
P.O. Box 115 (48726-0115)
PHONE.................989 872-2010
Clarke Haire, *President*
John Haire, *Vice Pres*
EMP: 9
SALES (est): 616.7K **Privately Held**
WEB: www.ccchronicle.net
SIC: 2711 Newspapers: publishing only, not printed on site

(G-2513)
COLE CARBIDE INDUSTRIES INC
6880 Cass City Rd (48726-9642)
PHONE.................989 872-4348
Scott Kelly, *General Mgr*
Dennis Kessler, *Site Mgr*
Scott Kelley, *Marketing Staff*
EMP: 63
SQ FT: 17,000
SALES (corp-wide): 14.3MM **Privately Held**
SIC: 3545 Cutting tools for machine tools
PA: Cole Carbide Industries, Inc.
4930 S Lapeer Rd
Lake Orion MI 48359
248 276-1278

(G-2514)
ERLAS INC
Also Called: Erla's Food Center
6233 Church St (48726-1111)
PHONE.................989 872-2191
EMP: 100 **EST:** 1953
SQ FT: 30,000
SALES (est): 21.6MM **Privately Held**
SIC: 5147 5411 2013 2011 Whol Meats/Products Ret Groceries Mfg Prepared Meats Meat Packing Plant

(G-2515)
IDA D BYLER
4169 Moore Rd (48726-9506)
PHONE.................810 672-9355
Ida D Byler, *Principal*
EMP: 3
SALES (est): 196.6K **Privately Held**
SIC: 2421 Sawmills & planing mills, general

(G-2516)
KAPPEN SAW MILL
4518 Hurds Corner Rd (48726-9473)
PHONE.................989 872-4410
Wallace Kappen, *Owner*
EMP: 4
SALES (est): 273.8K **Privately Held**
SIC: 2421 Sawmills & planing mills, general

(G-2517)
LAFAVE HYDRAULICS & METAL
Also Called: Lafave Hydrlics Met Fbrication
8260 Van Dyke Rd (48726-9636)
PHONE.................989 872-2163
Kevin R Krueger, *Mng Member*
Kevin Krueger,
EMP: 4
SALES (est): 422.1K **Privately Held**
SIC: 3499 Fabricated metal products

(G-2518)
LAGOS FARMS & MACHINING
1040 Plain Rd (48726-9396)
PHONE.................989 872-4895
EMP: 3
SALES (est): 20.4K **Privately Held**
SIC: 3599 Mfg Industrial Machinery

(G-2519)
MI-TECH TOOLING INC
6215 Garfield Ave (48726-1341)
PHONE.................989 912-2440
Joseph Langenburg, *President*
EMP: 26
SQ FT: 7,500
SALES: 2.1MM **Privately Held**
WEB: www.mi-techtool.com
SIC: 3541 Home workshop machine tools, metalworking

(G-2520)
MICRO EDM CO LLC
6172 Main St (48726-1106)
PHONE.................989 872-4306
Robert Bredemeyer,
EMP: 6
SALES (est): 1.2MM **Privately Held**
WEB: www.microedm.com
SIC: 3599 5084 Electrical discharge machining (EDM); machine tools & metalworking machinery

(G-2521)
MILLENNIUM STEERING LLC
6285 Garfield Ave (48726-1341)
PHONE.................989 872-8823
Gary Vollmar,
▲ **EMP:** 75
SQ FT: 5,000
SALES (est): 14.3MM **Privately Held**
SIC: 3714 Motor vehicle engines & parts

(G-2522)
STAR OF WEST MILLING COMPANY
4073 N Cemetery Rd (48726-9377)
PHONE.................989 872-5847
Mike Wellman, *Manager*
EMP: 12
SALES (corp-wide): 380.1MM **Privately Held**
SIC: 2041 Flour & other grain mill products
PA: Star Of The West Milling Company
121 E Tuscola St
Frankenmuth MI 48734
989 652-9971

(G-2523)
TUCKEY CONCRETE PRODUCTS
6062 Cass City Rd (48726-9301)
PHONE.................989 872-4779
Scott Wissner, *Principal*
EMP: 3
SALES (est): 305.3K **Privately Held**
SIC: 3273 Ready-mixed concrete

(G-2524)
WALBRO LLC
6242 Garfield Ave (48726-1325)
PHONE.................989 872-2131
Dave McNaughton, *General Mgr*
Judy Gardner, *Business Mgr*
Edward Duplaga, *Vice Pres*
Ron Roche, *Vice Pres*
Jorge Gastelum, *Opers Mgr*
EMP: 240 **Privately Held**
SIC: 3592 3714 3694 3561 Carburetors; motor vehicle parts & accessories; engine electrical equipment; pumps & pumping equipment; fabricated plate work (boiler shop)
HQ: Walbro Llc
2015 W River Rd Ste 202
Tucson AZ 85704

(G-2525)
WHITTAKER TIMBER CORPORATION
3623 Elmwood Rd (48726-9476)
PHONE.................989 872-3065
David A Whittaker, *President*
EMP: 4
SALES (est): 451.2K **Privately Held**
SIC: 2411 Logging

Cassopolis
Cass County

(G-2526)
ALONZO PRODUCTS INC
Also Called: ICM Arizona
805 Wolfe Ave (49031-9777)
PHONE.................269 445-0847
Kenneth E Charboneau, *President*
Donna J Charboneau, *Corp Secy*
EMP: 11 **EST:** 1989
SALES (est): 762K **Privately Held**
SIC: 2819 Silica compounds

(G-2527)
AMERI-KART(MI) CORP
19300 Grange St (49031-9501)
PHONE.................269 641-5811
Mike O'Brien, *General Mgr*
Lee Karn, *Plant Mgr*
Cindy Schneider, *Sales Staff*
Randy Shelton, *Maintence Staff*
▲ **EMP:** 140 **EST:** 1969
SQ FT: 200,000
SALES: 20.2MM
SALES (corp-wide): 566.7MM **Publicly Held**
WEB: www.po.amerikart.com
SIC: 3089 Injection molding of plastics; plastic processing
PA: Myers Industries, Inc.
1293 S Main St
Akron OH 44301
330 253-5592

(G-2528)
DW ALUMINUM LLC
Also Called: Postle Extrusions
201 N Edwards St (49031-9348)
PHONE.................269 445-5601
Dennis D Woods,
EMP: 50
SALES (est): 10.9MM **Privately Held**
SIC: 3355 Extrusion ingot, aluminum: made in rolling mills

(G-2529)
ECO SMART COATINGS LLC
67178 Lamb Rd (49031-9571)
PHONE.................574 370-5708
Randall Herring, *Principal*
EMP: 3
SALES (est): 289.6K **Privately Held**
SIC: 2851 Paints & allied products

(G-2530)
ENGINEERED CONCEPTS INC
67990 Milmc Ln (49031-7547)
PHONE.................574 333-9110
John McColley, *President*
EMP: 10 **EST:** 2010
SALES (est): 392.4K **Privately Held**
SIC: 3599 Custom machinery

(G-2531)
ICM PRODUCTS INC (DH)
805 Wolfe Ave (49031-9777)
PHONE.................269 445-0847
Levi Cottington, *CEO*
Tom Gawlik, *CFO*
Kenneth Charboneau, *CTO*
▲ **EMP:** 31 **EST:** 2012
SQ FT: 75,000
SALES: 21.3MM
SALES (corp-wide): 144.1K **Privately Held**
SIC: 2819 2822 Chemicals, high purity: refined from technical grade; silicone rubbers
HQ: Cht Germany Gmbh
Bismarckstr. 102
Tubingen 72072
707 115-40

(G-2532)
ICMP INC
805 Wolfe Ave (49031-9777)
PHONE.................269 445-0847
Kenneth Charboneau, *President*
Bobbi Post, *Principal*
Donna Charboneau, *Corp Secy*
Kent Charboneau, *Accountant*
Dana Baker, *Marketing Staff*
▲ **EMP:** 38
SQ FT: 75,000
SALES (est): 12.3MM
SALES (corp-wide): 144.1K **Privately Held**
SIC: 2819 Industrial inorganic chemicals
HQ: Cht Germany Gmbh
Bismarckstr. 102
Tubingen 72072
707 115-40

(G-2533)
K & M MACHINE-FABRICATING INC
20745 M 60 (49031-9431)
P.O. Box 218 (49031-0218)
PHONE.................269 445-2495
Michael McLoughlin, *President*
▲ **EMP:** 250 **EST:** 1951
SQ FT: 335,000
SALES (est): 61.5MM **Privately Held**
WEB: www.k-mm.com
SIC: 3599 Machine shop, jobbing & repair

(G-2534)
MORGOLD INC
18409 Quaker St (49031-9482)
P.O. Box 26 (49031-0026)
PHONE.................269 445-3844
Robert Morgan, *President*
Phyllis Morgan, *Corp Secy*
EMP: 6
SQ FT: 4,800
SALES: 1.3MM **Privately Held**
WEB: www.morgold.com
SIC: 3491 5085 Industrial valves; pistons & valves

(G-2535)
SCHWINTEK INC
Also Called: Pwr-Arm
310 Ranger Dr (49031-9810)
PHONE.................269 445-9999
▲ **EMP:** 6
SQ FT: 13,000
SALES: 1.5MM **Privately Held**
WEB: www.schwintek.com
SIC: 3089 Automotive parts, plastic

(G-2536)
STEPHEN A JAMES
Also Called: Industrial Extrusion Belting
68730 Calvin Center Rd (49031-9570)
PHONE.................269 641-5879
Stephen A James, *Owner*
EMP: 5
SQ FT: 8,000
SALES: 450K **Privately Held**
SIC: 3052 Rubber belting

(G-2537)
UNIVERSAL CASKET CO
17664 Chain Lake St (49031-9538)
PHONE.................269 476-2163
Charles Jones, *President*
Edward Jones, *Vice Pres*
Ej Jones, *Vice Pres*
▲ **EMP:** 26
SQ FT: 7,000
SALES (est): 3.9MM **Privately Held**
SIC: 3995 Burial caskets

(G-2538)
VIN-LEE-RON MEAT PACKING LLC
54501 Griffis Rd (49031-9759)
PHONE.................574 353-1386
Randy Cuthpert, *President*
Ron M Buncich, *President*
Vincent R Buncich, *Treasurer*
EMP: 50
SALES: 18MM **Privately Held**
SIC: 2011 Meat packing plants

Cedar
Leelanau County

(G-2539)
BULLETIN OF CONCERNED ASI
3693 S Bay Bluffs Dr (49621-9434)
PHONE.................231 228-7116
Martha K Winnacker, *Owner*

GEOGRAPHIC SECTION

Cedarville - Mackinac County (G-2567)

EMP: 4
SALES: 106.1K **Privately Held**
SIC: **2711** Newspapers, publishing & printing

(G-2540)
CHERRY BEND TOOL & DIE
Hoxie Rd (49621)
P.O. Box 27 (49621-0027)
PHONE..................................231 947-3046
Harold Lautmer, *Owner*
Harold Lautmer, *Owner*
EMP: 4
SALES (est): 315K **Privately Held**
SIC: **3599** Machine shop, jobbing & repair

(G-2541)
FARMER MUSICAL INSTRUMENTS
8568 E Lincoln Rd (49621-9453)
PHONE..................................206 412-5379
Pete Farmer, *Principal*
EMP: 3
SALES (est): 190.2K **Privately Held**
SIC: **3931** Musical instruments

(G-2542)
STACHNIK LOGGING LLC
5664 S Townline Rd (49621-9757)
P.O. Box 235, Interlochen (49643-0235)
PHONE..................................231 275-7641
Marjorie Stachnik, *Principal*
EMP: 3
SALES (est): 243.4K **Privately Held**
SIC: **2411** Logging

(G-2543)
WEATHERVANE VINYARDS INC
Also Called: Bel Lago
6530 S Lake Shore Dr (49621-9615)
PHONE..................................231 228-4800
Charlie Charles Edson, *President*
Charles Edson, *President*
Amy F Iezzoni, *Treasurer*
Kathy Calcutt, *Manager*
EMP: 8 EST: 1996
SALES (est): 540.5K **Privately Held**
WEB: www.bellago.com
SIC: **2084** 0762 Wines; vineyard management & maintenance services

Cedar Springs
Kent County

(G-2544)
AB WEAPONS DIVISION INC
Also Called: Applied Ballistics Weapons Div
25 S Main 2 (49319-5103)
P.O. Box 195 (49319-0195)
PHONE..................................616 696-2008
Bryan Litz, *President*
Kathy Barnhart, *Principal*
Mitchell Fitzpatrick, *Principal*
EMP: 3
SALES (est): 148.8K **Privately Held**
SIC: **3484** Guns (firearms) or gun parts, 30 mm. & below

(G-2545)
ATWOOD FOREST PRODUCTS INC
1177 17 Mile Rd Ne (49319-7817)
P.O. Box 548 (49319-0548)
PHONE..................................616 696-0081
Ronald Atwood, *President*
Karen Atwood, *Vice Pres*
▼ EMP: 50
SALES (est): 15.6MM **Privately Held**
WEB: www.lakestateslumber.com
SIC: **2411** 2421 2426 Logging camps & contractors; sawmills & planing mills, general; hardwood dimension & flooring mills

(G-2546)
CEDAR MOBILE HOME SERVICE INC
4720 Russell St (49319-9111)
PHONE..................................616 696-1580
EMP: 6
SQ FT: 2,500
SALES: 475K **Privately Held**
SIC: **7699** 4213 2451 5561 Repair Services Truck Operator-Nonlocal Mfg Mobile Homes Ret Recreational Vhcls

(G-2547)
CEDAR SPRINGS POST INC
Also Called: Cedar Springs Post Newspaper
36 E Maple (49319-5143)
P.O. Box 370 (49319-0370)
PHONE..................................616 696-3655
Lois Allen, *President*
Roger Allen, *Treasurer*
EMP: 8
SALES (est): 475.5K **Privately Held**
WEB: www.cedarspringspost.com
SIC: **2711** Newspapers: publishing only, not printed on site

(G-2548)
CEDAR SPRINGS SALES LLC
Also Called: Cedar Springs Sales & Graphix
2571 20 Mile Rd Ne (49319-9615)
PHONE..................................616 696-2111
Mark Vanlangen, *Partner*
Gregg Vanlangen, *Partner*
Denise Vanlangen, *Office Mgr*
EMP: 6
SQ FT: 4,000
SALES: 750K **Privately Held**
WEB: www.cedarspringssales.com
SIC: **2396** 2759 Fabric printing & stamping; printing & embossing on plastics fabric articles; letterpress & screen printing

(G-2549)
COPIES PLUS PRINTING CO LLC
111 S Main (49319-5104)
P.O. Box 42 (49319-0042)
PHONE..................................616 696-1288
Dan Spitsbergen, *Mng Member*
EMP: 3
SALES (est): 353.8K **Privately Held**
WEB: www.copiesplusofcedar.com
SIC: **2752** Commercial printing, offset

(G-2550)
COPYRIGHT TRAVELER S TRUNK P
15071 Hanna Ave Ne (49319-9698)
PHONE..................................937 903-9233
Amanda Litz,
EMP: 3 EST: 2011
SALES: 20K **Privately Held**
SIC: **2741** Miscellaneous publishing

(G-2551)
CS MANUFACTURING INC
299 W Cherry St (49319-8678)
PHONE..................................616 696-2772
Tim Mabie, *President*
Brendan Fitzgerald, *Vice Pres*
Jason Ballard, *Project Engr*
Laura Cunningham, *Controller*
◆ EMP: 105
SQ FT: 82,000
SALES (est): 40.7MM **Privately Held**
WEB: www.csmanufacturing.com
SIC: **3089** Injection molding of plastics

(G-2552)
CS TOOL ENGINEERING INC
251 W Cherry St (49319-8678)
P.O. Box K210 (49319-0910)
PHONE..................................616 696-0940
Don Mabie, *President*
Thomas Mabie, *Principal*
Jim Steenwyk, *Purchasing*
Lee Snider, *Engineer*
Cindy Humphrey, *CFO*
EMP: 50 EST: 1967
SQ FT: 43,000
SALES (est): 8.3MM **Privately Held**
WEB: www.cste.com
SIC: **3544** Industrial molds

(G-2553)
DISPLAY PACK INC (PA)
650 West St (49319-9699)
PHONE..................................616 451-3061
Victor Hansen, *President*
Jim Woodcock, *President*
Brian Pankratz, *Business Mgr*
Jason Rose, *Mfg Dir*
Shannon Moorman, *Production*
EMP: 250
SQ FT: 375,000
SALES (est): 132.3MM **Privately Held**
WEB: www.displaypack.com
SIC: **3089** 2759 7389 Plastic processing; commercial printing; packaging & labeling services

(G-2554)
DISPLAY PACK DISC INC
650 West St (49319-9699)
PHONE..................................616 451-3061
EMP: 3
SALES (est): 282.8K **Privately Held**
SIC: **2631** Packaging board

(G-2555)
DISPLAY PACK DISC VDH INC
650 West St (49319-9699)
PHONE..................................616 451-3061
EMP: 3
SALES (est): 162.3K **Privately Held**
SIC: **2631** Packaging board

(G-2556)
FLAUNT IT SPORTSWEAR
34 N Main Ste B (49319-5102)
P.O. Box 294 (49319-0294)
PHONE..................................616 696-9084
Karen Sudhoss, *Partner*
EMP: 8
SALES (est): 1MM **Privately Held**
SIC: **2396** Screen printing on fabric articles

(G-2557)
MACKARYNN INC
12175 Northland Dr (49319-8455)
PHONE..................................616 263-9743
EMP: 20
SALES (est): 2.7MM **Privately Held**
SIC: **2211** Bed tickings, cotton

(G-2558)
MICHIGAN PROTEIN INC
15030 Stout Ave Ne (49319-9727)
PHONE..................................616 696-7854
Dirk Longstrth, *President*
Joe Castine, *Senior VP*
Ramone Castine, *Vice Pres*
EMP: 4
SALES (est): 350.6K **Privately Held**
SIC: **2077** Grease rendering, inedible

(G-2559)
PRACTICAL PAPER INC
Also Called: Print Metro
98 E Division St Sparta (49319)
P.O. Box 125, Sparta (49345-0125)
PHONE..................................616 887-1723
Thomas Owen, *President*
EMP: 10
SQ FT: 14,000
SALES: 1.5MM **Privately Held**
SIC: **5113** 2732 Paper & products, wrapping or coarse; book printing

(G-2560)
PRECISION JIG & FIXTURE INC
4030 Cedar Coml Dr Ne (49319)
PHONE..................................616 696-2595
Tom Oshinski, *Plant Mgr*
Rob Conner, *QC Mgr*
David Schuiling, *Administration*
EMP: 45 **Privately Held**
SIC: **3544** Jigs: inspection, gauging & checking
PA: Peterson Jig & Fixture, Inc.
    301 Rockford Park Dr Ne
    Rockford MI 49341

(G-2561)
QUALITY GUEST PUBLISHING INC
Also Called: Heaven Is My Home
12920 Algoma Ave Ne (49319-9428)
P.O. Box 333, Rockford (49341-0333)
PHONE..................................616 894-1111
Gary Meyers, *Owner*
EMP: 10
SALES: 250K **Privately Held**
SIC: **2741** Miscellaneous publishing

(G-2562)
STEEL 21 LLC
11786 White Creek Ave Ne (49319-9417)
PHONE..................................616 884-2121
Kimm E Slater, *President*
Kevin Nozkowski, *General Mgr*
Andy Couturier, *Engineer*
Jessica Slater, *Admin Asst*
EMP: 26 EST: 2014
SQ FT: 30,000
SALES: 6MM **Privately Held**
SIC: **3312** Plate, steel

(G-2563)
STEELTECH LTD
Also Called: Cedar Springs Castings
69 Maple (49319)
PHONE..................................616 696-1130
John Becker, *Branch Mgr*
EMP: 18
SALES (corp-wide): 19.1MM **Privately Held**
WEB: www.steeltechltd.com
SIC: **3325** 3321 Alloy steel castings, except investment; gray & ductile iron foundries
PA: Steeltech, Ltd.
    1251 Phillips Ave Sw
    Grand Rapids MI 49507
    616 243-7920

(G-2564)
TARGET CONSTRUCTION INC
3850 Russell St (49319)
PHONE..................................616 866-7728
Kenneth Newman, *President*
EMP: 60
SALES (est): 10.5MM **Privately Held**
SIC: **3444** Sheet metalwork

(G-2565)
WEFA CEDAR INC
104 W Beech St (49319-8679)
P.O. Box K209 (49319-0909)
PHONE..................................616 696-0873
Jon Veenstra, *President*
EMP: 13
SQ FT: 40,000
SALES (est): 2.7MM
SALES (corp-wide): 8.7MM **Privately Held**
SIC: **3544** Extrusion dies
PA: Wefa Singen Gmbh
    Rudolf-Diesel-Str. 11
    Singen (Hohentwiel) 78224
    773 183-900

Cedarville
Mackinac County

(G-2566)
CARMEUSE LIME INC
5093 E M 134 (49719-9511)
PHONE..................................906 484-2201
Todd Nyberg, *Branch Mgr*
Kursten G Walton, *Manager*
EMP: 49
SALES (corp-wide): 177.9K **Privately Held**
SIC: **1422** Crushed & broken limestone
HQ: Carmeuse Lime, Inc.
    11 Stanwix St Fl 21
    Pittsburgh PA 15222
    412 995-5500

(G-2567)
FLOATATION DOCKING INC (PA)
Also Called: CEDARVILLE MARINE
160 Hodeck St (49719)
P.O. Box 178 (49719-0178)
PHONE..................................906 484-3422
Cody Carmichael, *Owner*
Teresa Carmichael, *Office Mgr*
EMP: 35
SQ FT: 25,000
SALES: 6.4MM **Privately Held**
SIC: **3731** 5599 4493 Drydocks, floating; snowmobiles; marinas

Cedarville - Mackinac County (G-2568)

GEOGRAPHIC SECTION

(G-2568)
LES CHENEAUX DISTILLERS INC
508 E Grove St (49719-9436)
P.O. Box 126 (49719-0126)
PHONE..................906 748-0505
Jason D Bowlby, *Administration*
EMP: 5
SALES (est): 377.2K **Privately Held**
SIC: 2085 Distilled & blended liquors

(G-2569)
O N MINERALS
5093 E M 134 (49719-9511)
PHONE..................906 484-2201
Michael Lundin, *Principal*
EMP: 5
SALES (est): 324.6K **Privately Held**
SIC: 1422 Crushed & broken limestone

(G-2570)
O-N MINERALS MICHIGAN COMPANY
Also Called: Aggregate
5093 E M 134 134 M (49719-9511)
PHONE..................906 484-2201
Raymond Leclair, *Manager*
EMP: 100
SALES (corp-wide): 58.1MM **Privately Held**
SIC: 1422 Limestones, ground
PA: O-N Minerals (Michigan) Company
   1035 Calcite Rd
   Rogers City MI 49779
   989 734-2131

(G-2571)
O-N MINERALS MICHIGAN COMPANY
Also Called: Carmeuse Lime & Stone
5093 E M 134 (49719-9511)
PHONE..................906 484-2201
EMP: 5
SALES (corp-wide): 177.9K **Privately Held**
SIC: 1422 Crushed & broken limestone
HQ: O-N Minerals (Michigan) Company
   11 Stanwix St Fl 21
   Pittsburgh PA 15222
   412 995-5500

(G-2572)
TASSIER BOAT WORKS INC
1011 S Islington Rd (49719-9744)
PHONE..................906 484-2573
James Hart, *President*
Alice Smith, *Principal*
Martha Hart, *Corp Secy*
Dan Smith, *Vice Pres*
EMP: 7
SQ FT: 1,200
SALES (est): 462.6K **Privately Held**
WEB: www.tassierboatworks.com
SIC: 7699 5551 3732 Boat repair; marine supplies & equipment; boat building & repairing

(G-2573)
VIKING BOAT HARBOR INC
1121 S Islington Rd (49719-9744)
PHONE..................906 484-3303
Joanne Honnila, *President*
Steve Honnila, *Corp Secy*
Linda M Sudol, *Office Mgr*
Steven Honnila, *Manager*
David Sudol, *Commissioner*
EMP: 10 EST: 1947
SQ FT: 34,100
SALES (est): 1.2MM **Privately Held**
WEB: www.vikingboatharbor.com
SIC: 3732 Boat building & repairing

Cement City
Lenawee County

(G-2574)
ABRASIVE SOLUTIONS LLC
12875 Mack Ave (49233-9791)
PHONE..................517 592-2668
Nathan Baumann,
EMP: 5 EST: 2011
SQ FT: 3,800
SALES: 500K **Privately Held**
SIC: 1721 3471 Commercial painting; sand blasting of metal parts

(G-2575)
ROSS DESIGN & ENGINEERING INC (PA)
14445 E Chicago Rd (49233-9677)
PHONE..................517 547-6033
Jack Plate, *President*
EMP: 20
SQ FT: 31,000
SALES (est): 13.7MM **Privately Held**
WEB: www.rossdesign.net
SIC: 3544 8711 Special dies, tools, jigs & fixtures; engineering services

Center Line
Macomb County

(G-2576)
AIRSERVE LLC
26770 Liberal (48015-1237)
P.O. Box 510, Warren (48090-0510)
PHONE..................586 427-5349
Ken Fasse, *President*
EMP: 4
SQ FT: 2,000
SALES (est): 558.8K **Privately Held**
SIC: 2813 Oxygen, compressed or liquefied

(G-2577)
ALL-COTE COATINGS COMPANY LLC
23896 Sherwood (48015-2011)
PHONE..................586 427-0062
George Shrock,
EMP: 6
SALES (est): 988.1K **Privately Held**
SIC: 2851 Paints & allied products

(G-2578)
AMERICAN DUMPSTER SERVICES LLC
6490 E 10 Mile Rd (48015-1144)
PHONE..................586 501-3600
Gary Smith,
EMP: 8
SALES (est): 311.7K **Privately Held**
SIC: 3443 Dumpsters, garbage

(G-2579)
BINSON-BECKER INC
Also Called: Binsons Orthtic Prsthtics Svcs
26834 Lawrence (48015-1262)
PHONE..................888 246-7667
James Binson, *President*
Craig Boyles, *President*
Loretta Miller, *Admin Sec*
EMP: 10
SQ FT: 5,000
SALES: 820K **Privately Held**
SIC: 5999 3842 Orthopedic & prosthesis applications; prosthetic appliances

(G-2580)
LASER PRODUCT DEVELOPMENT LLC
24340 Sherwood (48015-1061)
PHONE..................800 765-4424
EMP: 4 EST: 2006
SALES (est): 310K **Privately Held**
SIC: 3699 Mfg Electrical Equipment/Supplies

(G-2581)
PALLET PROS LLC
8233 Sterling (48015-1715)
PHONE..................586 864-3353
Phillip Eddins, *Principal*
EMP: 4
SALES (est): 243.4K **Privately Held**
SIC: 2448 Pallets, wood & wood with metal

(G-2582)
PRIMA TECHNOLOGIES INC
24837 Sherwood (48015-1058)
PHONE..................586 759-0250
Arturo Desantes Jr, *President*
Richard Vansteenkiste, *General Mgr*
Richard Van Steenkiste, *Corp Secy*
EMP: 14
SQ FT: 15,000
SALES (est): 2MM **Privately Held**
WEB: www.prima-tec.com
SIC: 3544 Dies, plastics forming

(G-2583)
SODECIA AUTO DETROIT CORP
Sodecia North America
23993 Sherwood (48015)
PHONE..................586 759-2200
EMP: 163 **Privately Held**
SIC: 3465 Body parts, automobile: stamped metal
HQ: Sodecia Automotive Detroit Corp.
   969 Chicago Rd
   Troy MI 48083
   586 759-2200

(G-2584)
SOPHIAS TEXTILES & FURN INC
24170 Sherwood (48015-2027)
PHONE..................586 759-6231
Sofia Yousif, *Principal*
▲ EMP: 17
SALES (est): 934.2K **Privately Held**
SIC: 2591 Blinds vertical; venetian blinds; window shades

(G-2585)
TRIANON INDUSTRIES CORPORATION
24331 Sherwood (48015-1060)
P.O. Box 3067 (48015-0067)
PHONE..................586 759-2200
Francis Barge, *President*
Jean-Claude Garolla, *CFO*
EMP: 3141
SALES (est): 23.7K **Privately Held**
SIC: 3465 3544 Automotive stampings; special dies & tools; jigs & fixtures

(G-2586)
WHITLAM GROUP INC (PA)
24800 Sherwood (48015-1059)
PHONE..................586 757-5100
Richard Shaieb, *President*
James Shaieb, *Vice Pres*
John Paul Shaieb, *Vice Pres*
Jim Shaieb, *VP Opers*
Bruce Crofts, *QC Mgr*
EMP: 121 EST: 1969
SQ FT: 125,000
SALES (est): 26.7MM **Privately Held**
WEB: www.whitlam.com
SIC: 2759 Flexographic printing

(G-2587)
WICO METAL PRODUCTS COMPANY
24400 Sherwood (48015-2023)
PHONE..................586 755-9600
Brodie Richard, *Branch Mgr*
EMP: 13
SALES (est): 1.8MM
SALES (corp-wide): 42.8MM **Privately Held**
SIC: 3544 Special dies & tools
PA: Wico Metal Products Company Inc
   23500 Sherwood Ave
   Warren MI 48091
   586 755-9600

Central Lake
Antrim County

(G-2588)
CENTRAL LAKE ARMOR EXPRESS INC
7915 Cameron St (49622-9458)
P.O. Box 516 (49622-0516)
PHONE..................231 544-6090
Matthew Davis, *President*
Lushana Offutt, *Senior VP*
Rick Dressler, *Vice Pres*
Thomas Thebes Jr, *CFO*
Frank Cappo, *VP Sales*
◆ EMP: 105
SQ FT: 15,000
SALES (est): 43.9MM
SALES (corp-wide): 11.2MM **Privately Held**
WEB: www.armorexpress.com
SIC: 3312 3842 Armor plate; bulletproof vests
PA: Praesidium Spa
   Via Della Giustizia 10/A
   Milano MI 20125
   023 030-971

(G-2589)
CREATIVE CHARACTERS INC
7924 Cameron St (49622-9458)
P.O. Box 699 (49622-0699)
PHONE..................231 544-6084
Jack Bodis, *President*
EMP: 5 EST: 1989
SQ FT: 3,000
SALES (est): 166.3K **Privately Held**
SIC: 2752 2731 Commercial printing, offset; books: publishing & printing

(G-2590)
DEFOREST & BLOOM SEPTIC TANKS
7994 Houghton Rd (49622-9558)
PHONE..................231 544-3599
Victor Bloom, *Owner*
EMP: 4
SALES: 69K **Privately Held**
SIC: 3272 1711 Septic tanks, concrete; septic system construction

(G-2591)
ECHO QUALITY GRINDING INC
3166 Muckle Rd (49622-9526)
PHONE..................231 544-6637
James Kowal, *President*
EMP: 18
SQ FT: 14,200
SALES (est): 2.6MM **Privately Held**
SIC: 3599 3469 Grinding castings for the trade; machine parts, stamped or pressed metal

(G-2592)
MAMMOTH DISTILLING LLC
1554 N East Torch Lake Dr (49622-9631)
P.O. Box 459 (49622-0459)
PHONE..................773 841-4242
Chad Munger, *Mng Member*
EMP: 5
SALES (est): 270.3K **Privately Held**
SIC: 2085 Applejack (alcoholic beverage)

Centreville
St. Joseph County

(G-2593)
BIRKHOLD PATTERN COMPANY INC
22921 S River Rd (49032-9757)
PHONE..................269 467-8705
EMP: 7 EST: 1936
SQ FT: 15,000
SALES (est): 62.5K **Privately Held**
SIC: 3365 Aluminum Foundry

(G-2594)
FOREST RIVER INC
Viking Recreational Vehicle
580 W Burr Oak St (49032-9592)
PHONE..................269 471-6321
Gar Warlick, *Branch Mgr*
EMP: 70
SALES (corp-wide): 225.3B **Publicly Held**
WEB: www.forestriverinc.com
SIC: 3792 Truck campers (slide-in)
HQ: Forest River, Inc.
   900 County Road 1 N
   Elkhart IN 46514

(G-2595)
HOCHSTETLER SAWMILL
24700 Walters Rd (49032-9760)
PHONE..................269 467-7018
Vernon Hochstetler, *Principal*
EMP: 3
SALES (est): 219.3K **Privately Held**
SIC: 2421 Sawmills & planing mills, general

GEOGRAPHIC SECTION

Charlevoix - Charlevoix County (G-2620)

(G-2596)
MAGIC CITY HEATING & COOLING
27290 Marvin Rd (49032-8720)
PHONE..................................269 467-6406
Jack A Stauffer, *Owner*
EMP: 3 **EST:** 1982
SALES (est): 184.8K **Privately Held**
SIC: 1711 3444 Plumbing, heating, air-conditioning contractors; ducts, sheet metal

(G-2597)
SUPERIOR RECEIPT BOOK CO INC
215 S Clark St (49032-5133)
P.O. Box 326 (49032-0326)
PHONE..................................269 467-8265
Cheryl Gilbert, *President*
Barbara J Taggart, *Vice Pres*
EMP: 26 **EST:** 1946
SQ FT: 2,400
SALES (est): 4.2MM **Privately Held**
WEB: www.receipts.com
SIC: 2782 Receipt books

(G-2598)
VAN EMON BRUCE
Also Called: A A A Machine
501 S Clark St (49032)
P.O. Box 19 (49032-0019)
PHONE..................................269 467-7803
Bruce Van Emon, *Owner*
EMP: 4
SQ FT: 1,200
SALES (est): 252.8K **Privately Held**
WEB: www.aaamachine.com
SIC: 3545 3544 3316 Machine tool attachments & accessories; special dies, tools, jigs & fixtures; cold finishing of steel shapes

(G-2599)
WALDRONS ANTIQUE EXHAUST
Also Called: Waldron's Exhaust
208 W Main St (49032-9534)
P.O. Box 99 (49032-0099)
PHONE..................................269 467-7185
Joseph Tonetto, *President*
EMP: 5 **EST:** 1963
SQ FT: 2,400
SALES (est): 919.1K **Privately Held**
SIC: 3714 Motor vehicle parts & accessories

(G-2600)
WAYNE ALLEN LAMBERT
Also Called: Lambert Industries
231 N Clark St (49032-9590)
PHONE..................................269 467-4624
Wayne Lambert, *Owner*
EMP: 5
SALES (est): 200K **Privately Held**
WEB: www.lambertindustries.com
SIC: 3544 Special dies, tools, jigs & fixtures

Ceresco
Calhoun County

(G-2601)
BEAR CREEK LOGGING
123 Court St (49033-9659)
PHONE..................................269 317-7475
Gary L Bauer, *Principal*
EMP: 6
SALES (est): 452.5K **Privately Held**
SIC: 2411 Logging

Champion
Marquette County

(G-2602)
EAGLE MINE LLC
4547 County Road 601 (49814-9475)
PHONE..................................906 339-7000
Ben Rose, *CFO*
Derrick Kleckner, *Technology*
EMP: 300
SALES (est): 57.6MM
SALES (corp-wide): 1.7B **Privately Held**
SIC: 1021 Copper ore milling & preparation
PA: Lundin Mining Corporation
150 King St W Suite 1500
Toronto ON M5H 1
416 342-5560

Channing
Dickinson County

(G-2603)
J CAREY LOGGING INC
Sawyer Lake Rd (49815)
PHONE..................................906 542-3420
James R Carey, *President*
Anita Leeman, *Bookkeeper*
Ryan Carey, *Train & Dev Mgr*
EMP: 12
SQ FT: 5,000
SALES (est): 2.1MM **Privately Held**
SIC: 2411 Logging camps & contractors

Charlevoix
Charlevoix County

(G-2604)
A M MANUFACTURING LLC
6300 Us Highway 31 S (49720-8915)
PHONE..................................231 437-3377
Alex Mitchell,
EMP: 5
SQ FT: 6,500
SALES (est): 670.1K **Privately Held**
SIC: 3599 Custom machinery

(G-2605)
ACAT GLOBAL LLC (PA)
5339 M 66 N (49720-9511)
PHONE..................................231 330-2553
Joseph Moch, *CEO*
Jim Lentz, *Controller*
Chelsea Meeder, *Assistant*
EMP: 10
SALES (est): 2.4MM **Privately Held**
SIC: 3714 Exhaust systems & parts, motor vehicle

(G-2606)
ALP LIGHTING CEILING PDTS INC
Also Called: Lexalite
10163 Us Highway 31 N (49720-9649)
PHONE..................................231 547-6584
Al B Brunner, *Plant Mgr*
Tom Barnes, *Manager*
EMP: 58
SALES (corp-wide): 167.2MM **Privately Held**
SIC: 3089 Injection molding of plastics; extruded finished plastic products
PA: Alp Lighting & Ceiling Products, Inc.
6333 W Gross Point Rd
Niles IL 60714
773 774-9550

(G-2607)
B & G ENTERPRISES
10400 Burnett Rd (49720-9183)
PHONE..................................231 348-2705
George Barbour, *Principal*
EMP: 4
SALES (est): 502.4K **Privately Held**
SIC: 2851 Removers & cleaners

(G-2608)
BALDWIN PRECISION INC
Also Called: Oliver Racing Parts
5339 M 66 N (49720-9511)
PHONE..................................231 237-4515
Bruce B Baldwin, *President*
EMP: 49
SQ FT: 102,000
SALES (est): 3MM **Privately Held**
WEB: www.oliver-rods.com
SIC: 3714 Connecting rods, motor vehicle engine

(G-2609)
BDK GROUP NORTHERN MICH INC
Also Called: Hodgkiss & Douma
6795 Us Highway 31 N (49720-9416)
PHONE..................................574 875-5183
Thomas R Irwin, *President*
EMP: 25 **EST:** 1938
SQ FT: 8,000
SALES (est): 2.3MM **Privately Held**
SIC: 1611 1442 1794 1623 General contractor, highway & street construction; highway & street paving contractor; construction sand mining; gravel mining; excavation & grading, building construction; sewer line construction; water main construction; concrete work; curb construction; blacktop (asphalt) work; asphalt paving mixtures & blocks

(G-2610)
CEMEX CEMENT INC
1600 Bells Bay Rd (49720)
P.O. Box 367 (49720-0367)
PHONE..................................231 547-9971
John Laney, *Manager*
EMP: 220 **Privately Held**
SIC: 3273 Ready-mixed concrete
HQ: Cemex Cement, Inc.
10100 Katy Fwy Ste 300
Houston TX 77043
713 650-6200

(G-2611)
CHARLEVOIX MACHINE PRODUCTS
15164 Ferry Rd (49720-9579)
PHONE..................................231 547-2697
James Bearss, *Owner*
Angel Bearss, *Partner*
EMP: 3
SQ FT: 6,500
SALES (est): 150K **Privately Held**
SIC: 3599 Machine shop, jobbing & repair

(G-2612)
CHARLEVOIX SCREEN MASTERS INC
12512 Taylor Rd (49720-1022)
PHONE..................................231 547-5111
Roger Nesburg, *President*
Annette Nesburg, *Treasurer*
Angela Behling, *Admin Sec*
EMP: 7
SQ FT: 7,000
SALES (est): 550K **Privately Held**
SIC: 2261 2395 Screen printing of cotton broadwoven fabrics; embroidery products, except schiffli machine

(G-2613)
DCL INC (PA)
Also Called: Dust Control & Loading Systems
8660 Ance Rd (49720-2055)
P.O. Box 125 (49720-0125)
PHONE..................................231 547-5600
Tim English, *President*
Reinhard Matye, *President*
Werner Egger, *Vice Pres*
Kurt Danforth, *Electrical Engi*
▼ **EMP:** 130
SQ FT: 45,000
SALES (est): 34.5MM **Privately Held**
WEB: www.dclinc.com
SIC: 3535 5084 3564 3494 Conveyors & conveying equipment; industrial machinery & equipment; blowers & fans; valves & pipe fittings

(G-2614)
FOX CHARLEVOIX FORD MODEM
6725 Us Highway 31 N (49720-9701)
PHONE..................................231 547-4401
Craig Wierda, *Principal*
EMP: 7
SALES (est): 958.3K **Privately Held**
SIC: 3661 Modems

(G-2615)
GERBERS HOME MADE SWEETS
8218 Pincherry Rd (49720-9413)
PHONE..................................231 348-3743
Jerry J Gerber, *Owner*
EMP: 4
SALES (est): 277.1K **Privately Held**
SIC: 2064 Candy & other confectionery products

(G-2616)
GIC LLC
Also Called: Gic Thermo Dynamics
12575 Us Highway 31 N (49720-1101)
PHONE..................................231 237-7000
Thomas Ray, *President*
Linda Clements, *General Mgr*
Timothy Reeves, *Executive*
EMP: 12
SALES (est): 950K **Privately Held**
SIC: 3823 3829 Industrial instrmnts msrmnt display/control process variable; measuring & controlling devices

(G-2617)
HARBOR INDUSTRIES INC
100 Harbor View Ln (49720-1294)
P.O. Box 228 (49720-0228)
PHONE..................................231 547-3280
Al Corp, *QC Dir*
Tammie Deschermeir, *Sales Staff*
William Olstrom, *Manager*
EMP: 300
SQ FT: 65,000
SALES (corp-wide): 159.9MM **Privately Held**
WEB: www.harborind.com
SIC: 3993 2542 2541 Displays & cutouts, window & lobby; partitions & fixtures, except wood; wood partitions & fixtures
PA: Harbor Industries, Inc.
14130 172nd Ave
Grand Haven MI 49417
616 842-5330

(G-2618)
HARBOR INDUSTRIES INC
107 Airport Dr (49720-8904)
PHONE..................................616 842-5330
EMP: 60
SALES (corp-wide): 159.9MM **Privately Held**
SIC: 2541 Display fixtures, wood
PA: Harbor Industries, Inc.
14130 172nd Ave
Grand Haven MI 49417
616 842-5330

(G-2619)
IRISH BOAT SHOP INC
13000 Stover Rd (49720-9500)
PHONE..................................231 547-9967
Michael Esposito, *President*
Cliff Biddick, *Vice Pres*
John Hodge, *Vice Pres*
Jack Hodge, *Branch Mgr*
EMP: 25
SALES (corp-wide): 12.6MM **Privately Held**
WEB: www.irishboatshop.com
SIC: 4493 5551 5561 4226 Boat yards, storage & incidental repair; boat dealers; recreational vehicle dealers; special warehousing & storage; boat building & repairing
PA: Irish Boat Shop, Inc.
400 E Bay St
Harbor Springs MI 49740
231 526-6225

(G-2620)
MICHIGAN SCIENTIFIC CORP
8500 Ance Rd (49720-2033)
PHONE..................................231 547-5511
Robert Popovczak, *Engineer*
John Suomi, *Engineer*
Randal Schnackenberg, *Sales Mgr*
Mike Castiglione, *Manager*
Kent Larsen, *Administration*
EMP: 65
SQ FT: 15,000
SALES (corp-wide): 16.7MM **Privately Held**
WEB: www.michsci.com
SIC: 3829 8734 3825 3469 Testing equipment: abrasion, shearing strength, etc.; testing laboratories; instruments to measure electricity; metal stampings

Charlevoix - Charlevoix County (G-2621)

PA: Michigan Scientific Corporation
321 E Huron St
Milford MI 48381
248 685-3939

(G-2621)
MIDWEST INTL STD PDTS INC
105 Stover Rd (49720-1756)
P.O. Box 438 (49720-0438)
PHONE.................................231 547-4073
Ron Pair, *CEO*
Kevin Crellin, *Fire Chief*
Walter Pair, *Chief Mktg Ofcr*
Brandon Wood, *Supervisor*
▼ **EMP:** 8
SALES (est): 2.1MM **Privately Held**
SIC: 3564 Blowers & fans

(G-2622)
NORTHERN SAWMILLS INC
7250 Dalton Rd (49720-9470)
PHONE.................................231 547-9452
Dennis Golovich, *President*
EMP: 3
SALES (est): 180K **Privately Held**
SIC: 2421 Custom sawmill

(G-2623)
NU-CORE INC
8833 Gibbons Dr (49720-2056)
PHONE.................................231 547-2600
Bob Grove, *President*
Jesse Grove, *Engineer*
▲ **EMP:** 8
SALES (est): 1.5MM **Privately Held**
SIC: 3599 Machine shop, jobbing & repair

(G-2624)
OPTIC EDGE CORPORATION
6279 Us Highway 31 S (49720-8916)
P.O. Box 503 (49720-0503)
PHONE.................................231 547-6090
Dan Yenglin, *President*
EMP: 5
SQ FT: 5,000
SALES: 500K **Privately Held**
WEB: www.mktec.com
SIC: 3641 Electric lamps & parts for generalized applications
PA: Market Technologies, Inc.
6279 Us Highway 31 S
Charlevoix MI

(G-2625)
PARSONS CENTENNIAL FARM LLC
Also Called: Harwood Hritg Gold Maple Syrup
61 Parsons Rd (49720-8910)
PHONE.................................231 547-2038
David W Parsons, *Principal*
EMP: 4
SALES (est): 253.2K **Privately Held**
SIC: 2099 0831 Maple syrup; maple sap gathering

(G-2626)
PINE RIVER INC
5339 M 66 N (49720-9511)
PHONE.................................231 758-3400
Michael Way, *President*
EMP: 14
SQ FT: 35,000
SALES: 1MM **Privately Held**
SIC: 2952 Siding materials

(G-2627)
PRECISION PALLET LLC
17195 Beck Rd (49720-9736)
PHONE.................................252 943-5193
EMP: 3
SALES (est): 160K **Privately Held**
SIC: 2448 Pallets, wood & wood with metal

(G-2628)
RK WOJAN INC
6336 Us Highway 31 N (49720-9416)
P.O. Box 189 (49720-0189)
PHONE.................................231 347-1160
Robert Wojan, *President*
Keri Wojan, *Vice Pres*
EMP: 40 **EST:** 1965
SQ FT: 45,000
SALES (est): 6.7MM **Privately Held**
WEB: www.bayshoresteel.com
SIC: 3535 3443 Bulk handling conveyor systems; fabricated plate work (boiler shop)

(G-2629)
RON PAIR ENTERPRISES INC
105 Stover Rd (49720-1756)
P.O. Box 438 (49720-0438)
PHONE.................................231 547-4000
Ronald Pair, *President*
EMP: 35 **EST:** 1965
SQ FT: 21,000
SALES (est): 5.9MM **Privately Held**
WEB: www.midwestmagic.com
SIC: 3564 Dust or fume collecting equipment, industrial

(G-2630)
SEELYE EQUIPMENT SPECIALIST
Also Called: S E S
1217 State St (49720-1683)
PHONE.................................231 547-9430
Donald Seelye, *Owner*
EMP: 3
SQ FT: 3,600
SALES (est): 329.2K **Privately Held**
WEB: www.flexcharge.com
SIC: 3674 5063 3822 3625 Solar cells; electrical apparatus & equipment; auto controls regulating residntl & coml environmt & applncs; relays & industrial controls; heating equipment, except electric

(G-2631)
ST MARYS CEMENT US LLC
16000 Bells Bay Rd (49720-8707)
P.O. Box 367 (49720-0367)
PHONE.................................231 547-9971
Edmond Gary Drew, *Manager*
EMP: 27
SALES (corp-wide): 1.1MM **Privately Held**
SIC: 3241 Masonry cement
HQ: St. Marys Cement U.S. Llc
9333 Dearborn St
Detroit MI 48209
313 842-4600

(G-2632)
STEVEN CRANDELL
10436 Burnett Rd (49720-9183)
PHONE.................................231 582-7445
Steven Crandell, *Principal*
EMP: 3
SALES (est): 263K **Privately Held**
SIC: 2411 Logging

(G-2633)
THAT FRENCH PLACE
212 Bridge St (49720-1404)
PHONE.................................231 437-6037
Brian Freund, *Owner*
EMP: 10
SALES (est): 682.8K **Privately Held**
SIC: 2024 Ice cream & frozen desserts

(G-2634)
VILLAGE GRAPHICS INC
Also Called: Kwikie Duplicating Center
111 Antrim St (49720-1305)
PHONE.................................231 547-4172
Paul Casciani, *President*
EMP: 4 **EST:** 1973
SQ FT: 1,500
SALES (est): 457.7K **Privately Held**
SIC: 2752 Commercial printing, offset

(G-2635)
WOJAN ALUMINUM PRODUCTS CORP (PA)
Also Called: Wojan Window & Door
217 Stover Rd (49720-9580)
P.O. Box 95 (49720-0095)
PHONE.................................231 547-2931
Dennis Wojan, *President*
Steve Kur, *Vice Pres*
Jeff Wright, *Vice Pres*
Ralph Ignasky, *Engineer*
Keith Demeuse, *CFO*
EMP: 95
SQ FT: 144,000
SALES (est): 27.2MM **Privately Held**
WEB: www.wojan.com
SIC: 3442 Storm doors or windows, metal

Charlotte
Eaton County

(G-2636)
CASS POLYMERS (HQ)
Also Called: Ad-Tech Plastics Systems
815 W Shepherd St Ste 2 (48813-2037)
PHONE.................................517 543-7510
Richard Bullock, *CEO*
Doug Frans, *President*
B J Goodrich, *Manager*
EMP: 44
SQ FT: 6,400
SALES (est): 4.3MM
SALES (corp-wide): 11.5MM **Privately Held**
WEB: www.adtechplastics.com
SIC: 2821 3087 2891 2851 Epoxy resins; polyesters; custom compound purchased resins; adhesives & sealants; paints & allied products
PA: Cass Polymers, Inc.
311 Nw 122nd St Ste 100
Oklahoma City OK 73114
405 755-8448

(G-2637)
CATI ARMOR LLC
435 Packard Hwy Ste C (48813-7748)
PHONE.................................269 788-4322
Brian Moore, *President*
EMP: 5
SALES (est): 591.2K **Privately Held**
SIC: 3711 Cars, armored, assembly of

(G-2638)
CHARLOTTE ANODIZING PDTS INC
591 Packard Hwy (48813-9701)
PHONE.................................517 543-1911
Ronald Mc Diarmid, *President*
EMP: 65
SQ FT: 20,000
SALES (est): 8.7MM **Privately Held**
WEB: www.charlotte-anodizing.com
SIC: 3471 Anodizing (plating) of metals or formed products

(G-2639)
CHARLOTTE CABINETS INC
629 W Seminary St (48813-1883)
P.O. Box 132 (48813-0132)
PHONE.................................517 543-1522
John S Little, *President*
EMP: 6
SQ FT: 8,000
SALES (est): 797.1K **Privately Held**
SIC: 2434 2511 5211 1751 Wood kitchen cabinets; wood household furniture; cabinets, kitchen; cabinet & finish carpentry

(G-2640)
CITIZENS LLC
421 N Cochran Ave (48813-1125)
P.O. Box F (48813-0523)
PHONE.................................517 541-1449
Sam Hudnutt, *Owner*
EMP: 8
SALES (corp-wide): 91.2MM **Privately Held**
SIC: 5153 2041 Grains; flour & other grain mill products
PA: Citizens L.L.C.
870 S Main St
Vermontville MI 49096
517 726-0514

(G-2641)
CNI PLASTICS LLC
Also Called: Futuris Automotive
400 Parkland Dr (48813-8799)
PHONE.................................517 541-4960
Merv Dunn, *CEO*
William Peterson, *CFO*
EMP: 50
SALES (est): 7.5MM **Privately Held**
SIC: 3089 Injection molding of plastics

HQ: Cni Enterprises, Inc.
1451 E Lincoln Ave
Madison Heights MI 48071
248 586-3300

(G-2642)
COUNTRY MILL FARMS LLC
4648 Otto Rd (48813-9723)
PHONE.................................517 543-1019
Bernard Tennes,
Steve Tennes,
EMP: 30
SQ FT: 10,000
SALES (est): 991.6K **Privately Held**
WEB: www.countrymill.com
SIC: 0175 2051 2033 5947 Apple orchard; bread, cake & related products; canned fruits & specialties; gift, novelty & souvenir shop; eating places

(G-2643)
COUNTY JOURNAL INC
Also Called: Flashes Advertising & News
241 S Cochran Ave Ste 1 (48813-1584)
PHONE.................................517 543-1099
Cindy Gaedert, *Administration*
EMP: 11
SALES (est): 809K **Privately Held**
WEB: www.county-journal.com
SIC: 2711 Commercial printing & newspaper publishing combined; newspapers, publishing & printing

(G-2644)
CRANDELL BROS TRUCKING CO
800 Island Hwy (48813-9359)
P.O. Box 370 (48813-0370)
PHONE.................................517 543-2930
Randolph A Crandell, *President*
Daniel Crandell, *Vice Pres*
EMP: 40 **EST:** 1955
SQ FT: 7,200
SALES (est): 6.1MM **Privately Held**
SIC: 4212 1442 Dump truck haulage; construction sand mining

(G-2645)
DORNBOS SIGN INC
619 W Harris St (48813-1466)
PHONE.................................517 543-4000
Robert Dornbos, *President*
Jeff Dornbos, *Vice Pres*
Andrea Johnston, *Office Mgr*
Pete Lahr, *Supervisor*
EMP: 14 **EST:** 1954
SQ FT: 10,000
SALES (est): 3.7MM **Privately Held**
WEB: www.dornbossign.com
SIC: 3993 Signs & advertising specialties

(G-2646)
ENOVAPREMIER LLC
403 Parkland Dr (48813-7733)
PHONE.................................517 541-3200
George Gunlock, *Engineer*
EMP: 4 **Privately Held**
WEB: www.enovapremier.com
SIC: 3089 3714 Automotive parts, plastic; motor vehicle parts & accessories
PA: Enovapremier Llc
1630 Lyndon Farm Ct # 100
Louisville KY 40223

(G-2647)
FAMILY TRDTONS TREE STANDS LLC
202 Morrell St (48813-1136)
PHONE.................................517 543-3926
Jack Turner,
EMP: 9
SALES: 1MM **Privately Held**
WEB: www.familytraditiontreestands.com
SIC: 3949 Hunting equipment

(G-2648)
FARMERS EGG COOPERATIVE
Also Called: Grazing Fields
1300 W Mount Hope Hwy (48813-8631)
PHONE.................................517 649-8957
Jane Bush, *CEO*
Sam Catey, *Director*
EMP: 7
SALES: 300K **Privately Held**
SIC: 0252 2015 Chicken eggs; egg processing

GEOGRAPHIC SECTION

Chatham - Alger County (G-2675)

(G-2649)
FLASHES SHOPPERS GUIDE & NEWS
241 S Cochran Ave Ste 1 (48813-1584)
P.O. Box 156, Eaton Rapids (48827-0156)
PHONE.....................517 663-2361
Rod Mc Laughlin, *Owner*
EMP: 8
SALES (est): 470.1K **Privately Held**
SIC: 2741 2752 Shopping news: publishing only, not printed on site; commercial printing, lithographic

(G-2650)
G-FORCE TOOLING LLC (PA)
1325 Island Hwy (48813-9358)
PHONE.....................517 541-2747
Julie Cotter, *Principal*
Todd Cotter, *Engineer*
EMP: 5
SALES (est): 626.5K **Privately Held**
SIC: 3721 Helicopters

(G-2651)
GALE BRIGGS INC (PA)
311 State St (48813-1735)
PHONE.....................517 543-1320
Steve Briggs, *President*
Gale Lee Briggs, *President*
Betty Briggs, *Corp Secy*
EMP: 9
SQ FT: 16,900
SALES (est): 1.6MM **Privately Held**
SIC: 3273 1442 Ready-mixed concrete; sand mining; gravel mining

(G-2652)
GO CAT FEATHER TOYS
605 W Lovett St (48813-1427)
PHONE.....................517 543-7519
Harriet Morier, *President*
▲ **EMP:** 4
SALES (est): 437.4K **Privately Held**
WEB: www.go-cat.com
SIC: 5999 5199 3069 Pet supplies; cats; toys, rubber

(G-2653)
GRANTS WOODSHOP INC
3802 N Chester Rd (48813-8813)
PHONE.....................517 543-1116
Don Grant, *President*
Marcia Grant, *Corp Secy*
EMP: 3
SQ FT: 12,000
SALES (est): 300K **Privately Held**
WEB: www.grantswoodshop.com
SIC: 2499 2426 Handles, poles, dowels & stakes: wood; hardwood dimension & flooring mills

(G-2654)
HOME SHOP
406 E Broadway Hwy (48813-8561)
PHONE.....................517 543-5325
John Wilson, *Partner*
John Kellogg, *Partner*
Eric Pintar, *Manager*
EMP: 3
SALES: 200K **Privately Held**
WEB: www.shakerovalbox.com
SIC: 2441 2511 Boxes, wood; novelty furniture: wood

(G-2655)
J & D LOGGING
1212 N Chester Rd (48813-8866)
PHONE.....................517 543-3873
James E Wright, *Principal*
EMP: 3
SALES (est): 267.2K **Privately Held**
SIC: 2411 Logging camps & contractors

(G-2656)
J-AD GRAPHICS INC
Also Called: Charlotte Lithograph
144 S Cochran Ave (48813-1510)
PHONE.....................517 543-4041
Brian Rayner, *Manager*
EMP: 4
SALES (corp-wide): 15.3MM **Privately Held**
WEB: www.j-adgraphics.com
SIC: 2741 8611 2752 Guides: publishing & printing; business associations; commercial printing, offset
PA: J-Ad Graphics, Inc.
    1351 N M 43 Hwy
    Hastings MI 49058
    800 870-7085

(G-2657)
K-TEL CORPORATION
Also Called: Universal Brick System
518 W Lovett St Ste 1 (48813-1774)
PHONE.....................517 543-6174
EMP: 10
SQ FT: 2,000
SALES (est): 1.2MM **Privately Held**
SIC: 3271 5039 Mfg Concrete Block/Brick Whol Construction Materials Ret Lumber/Building Materials

(G-2658)
LINDE INC
500 Packard Hwy (48813-9701)
PHONE.....................517 541-2473
Robert Hill, *Principal*
EMP: 3 **EST:** 2008
SALES (est): 183.1K **Privately Held**
SIC: 2813 Industrial gases

(G-2659)
MEREDITH LEA SAND GRAVEL
6703 Lansing Rd (48813-9328)
PHONE.....................517 930-3662
Meredith Smith, *Principal*
EMP: 6 **EST:** 2015
SALES (est): 418.2K **Privately Held**
SIC: 3273 Ready-mixed concrete

(G-2660)
MICHIGAN PALLET INC
1100 Packard Hwy (48813-9779)
PHONE.....................517 543-0606
EMP: 15
SALES (est): 617.2K
SALES (corp-wide): 2.8MM **Privately Held**
SIC: 2448 Pallets, wood
PA: Michigan Pallet, Inc.
    1225 N Saginaw St
    Saint Charles MI 48655
    989 865-9915

(G-2661)
MURPHY USA INC
Also Called: Murphy USA 7601
1686 Packard Hwy (48813-9717)
PHONE.....................517 541-0502
EMP: 13 **Publicly Held**
SIC: 5541 2911 Gasoline service stations; petroleum refining
PA: Murphy Usa Inc.
    200 E Peach St
    El Dorado AR 71730

(G-2662)
NORTHERN CONCRETE PIPE INC
5281 Lansing Rd (48813-9374)
PHONE.....................517 645-2777
John Washabaugh, *Sales Staff*
Bob Washabaugh, *Manager*
Robert Washabaugh, *Executive*
EMP: 60
SALES (est): 8.6MM
SALES (corp-wide): 21.3MM **Privately Held**
WEB: www.ncp-inc.com
SIC: 3272 5032 Pipe, concrete or lined with concrete; sewer pipe, clay
PA: Northern Concrete Pipe, Inc.
    401 Kelton St
    Bay City MI 48706
    989 892-3545

(G-2663)
S P KISH INDUSTRIES INC
600 W Seminary St (48813-1876)
P.O. Box C (48813-0802)
PHONE.....................517 543-2650
Robert Kish, *President*
Robert Kendregan, *Sales Executive*
Mike Desai, *Director*
▼ **EMP:** 25
SQ FT: 100,000
SALES (est): 4MM **Privately Held**
WEB: www.kishindustries.com
SIC: 2851 Paints & allied products

(G-2664)
SILK SCREENSTUFF
2860 S Cochran Rd (48813-9177)
PHONE.....................517 543-7716
Kevin Bowen, *Owner*
EMP: 4
SQ FT: 1,400
SALES: 100K **Privately Held**
WEB: www.silkscreenstuff.com
SIC: 2396 2759 2395 Screen printing on fabric articles; screen printing; embroidery products, except schiffli machine

(G-2665)
SPARTAN MOTORS INC (PA)
1541 Reynolds Rd (48813-2099)
PHONE.....................517 543-6400
James A Sharman, *Ch of Bd*
Daryl M Adams, *President*
Todd Fierro, *President*
Stephen K Guillaume, *President*
John W Slawson, *President*
◆ **EMP:** 570
SQ FT: 12,000
SALES (est): 816.1MM **Publicly Held**
SIC: 3711 3714 7519 Chassis, motor vehicle; fire department vehicles (motor vehicles), assembly of; ambulances (motor vehicles), assembly of; motor vehicle parts & accessories; utility trailer rental

(G-2666)
SPARTAN MOTORS CHASSIS INC
Also Called: Spartan Chassis
1541 Reynolds Rd (48813-2099)
PHONE.....................517 543-6400
John E Sztykiel, *CEO*
Daryl M Adams, *COO*
Thomas T Kivell, *Vice Pres*
Steven Heidtke, *Opers Mgr*
Lori L Wade, *CFO*
▼ **EMP:** 943
SALES (est): 330.7MM
SALES (corp-wide): 816.1MM **Publicly Held**
SIC: 3711 Chassis, motor vehicle
PA: Spartan Motors, Inc.
    1541 Reynolds Rd
    Charlotte MI 48813
    517 543-6400

(G-2667)
SPARTAN MOTORS USA INC (HQ)
Also Called: Spartan Erv
1541 Reynolds Rd (48813-2099)
PHONE.....................517 543-6400
Daryl M Adams, *CEO*
John Slawson, *President*
Frederick Sohm, *Treasurer*
Chris Davis, *Manager*
Thomas W Gorman, *Director*
◆ **EMP:** 100
SQ FT: 100,000
SALES (est): 6.5B
SALES (corp-wide): 816.1MM **Publicly Held**
SIC: 3711 Fire department vehicles (motor vehicles), assembly of
PA: Spartan Motors, Inc.
    1541 Reynolds Rd
    Charlotte MI 48813
    517 543-6400

(G-2668)
ST REGIS CULVERT INC (PA)
202 Morrell St (48813-1198)
PHONE.....................517 543-3430
John R Mooney, *President*
Christopher Mooney, *Vice Pres*
Charlie Alley, *Engineer*
Brian Caldwell, *Sales Staff*
Brian Reed, *Sales Staff*
EMP: 15
SQ FT: 20,000
SALES (est): 4.3MM **Privately Held**
WEB: www.stregisculvert.com
SIC: 3498 Fabricated pipe & fittings

(G-2669)
T S MANUFACTURING & DESIGN
2250 Otto Rd (48813-7760)
P.O. Box 261 (48813-0261)
PHONE.....................517 543-5368
Tom Southworth, *President*
EMP: 3
SALES: 70K **Privately Held**
SIC: 3599 7389 Custom machinery; design, commercial & industrial

(G-2670)
WALMART INC
1680 Packard Hwy (48813-9773)
PHONE.....................517 541-1481
Terry Lantz, *Manager*
Dorothy Schroeder, *Executive*
EMP: 300
SQ FT: 189,173
SALES (corp-wide): 514.4B **Publicly Held**
WEB: www.walmartstores.com
SIC: 5311 5411 5812 5531 Department stores, discount; supermarkets, hypermarket; eating places; automotive & home supply stores; bread, cake & related products; drug stores & proprietary stores
PA: Walmart Inc.
    702 Sw 8th St
    Bentonville AR 72716
    479 273-4000

Chassell
Houghton County

(G-2671)
ANDERSON WELDING & MFG INC
41315 Us 41 (49916)
P.O. Box 262 (49916-0262)
PHONE.....................906 523-4661
Ron Anderson, *CEO*
EMP: 14
SQ FT: 10,000
SALES: 1.3MM **Privately Held**
SIC: 3715 3443 3444 5083 Truck trailers; weldments; sheet metalwork; livestock equipment; machine shop, jobbing & repair; welding on site

(G-2672)
BODA CORPORATION
Us 41 (49916)
PHONE.....................906 353-7320
Allen M Boda, *President*
EMP: 5
SQ FT: 1,800
SALES (est): 320K **Privately Held**
SIC: 3544 Special dies & tools

(G-2673)
ERICKSON LOGGING INC
40734 Lower Pike Rd (49916-9497)
PHONE.....................906 523-4049
Travis L Erickson, *Principal*
Michelle Erickson, *Admin Sec*
EMP: 5
SALES (est): 530.1K **Privately Held**
SIC: 2411 Logging camps & contractors

(G-2674)
NIEMELA
39466 Tapiola Rd (49916-9411)
PHONE.....................906 523-4362
Benjamin Niemela, *Principal*
EMP: 3
SALES (est): 254.9K **Privately Held**
SIC: 3999 Manufacturing industries

Chatham
Alger County

(G-2675)
PORCUPINE PRESS INC
Also Called: Porky Press
3720 Munising St E (49816)
P.O. Box 200 (49816-0200)
PHONE.....................906 439-5111
Michael Van Denbranden, *President*

Michael Vandenbranden, *President*
Jeremy Williams, *Principal*
Robin Lindinberg, *Vice Pres*
EMP: 8
SALES: 750K **Privately Held**
WEB: www.upmag.net
SIC: 2711 Newspapers: publishing only, not printed on site

Cheboygan
Cheboygan County

(G-2676)
CHAMBERS OTTAWA INC
2064 Campbell Rd (49721-9305)
P.O. Box 173 (49721-0173)
PHONE.................................231 238-2122
Curtis Chambers,
EMP: 4
SALES: 250K **Privately Held**
SIC: 2676 Sanitary paper products

(G-2677)
CHEBOYGAN CEMENT PRODUCTS INC (PA)
702 Lafayette Ave (49721-2199)
PHONE.................................231 627-5631
Ernest Gildner, *President*
Veronica Gildner, *Corp Secy*
Michael Gildner, *Vice Pres*
Ashley Ptasnik, *Treasurer*
EMP: 50 **EST:** 1946
SALES (est): 8.6MM **Privately Held**
SIC: 3273 3271 3272 1442 Ready-mixed concrete; blocks, concrete or cinder: standard; septic tanks, concrete; burial vaults, concrete or precast terrazzo; dry mixture concrete; construction sand & gravel

(G-2678)
CHEBOYGAN GOLF AND COUNTRY CLB
Also Called: Cheboygan Golf Club Pro Shop
1431 Old Mackinaw Rd (49721-9303)
PHONE.................................231 627-4264
Jim Ingram, *Manager*
EMP: 20
SALES (est): 1.4MM **Privately Held**
SIC: 3949 Shafts, golf club

(G-2679)
CHEBOYGAN HOUSING COMMISSION
Also Called: Mi030
659 Cuyler St (49721-2201)
P.O. Box 5069 (49721-5069)
PHONE.................................231 627-7189
Dorene Stempky, *Exec Dir*
EMP: 3
SALES: 708K **Privately Held**
SIC: 3812 Heads-up display systems (HUD), aeronautical

(G-2680)
GREAT LAKES TISSUE COMPANY
437 S Main St (49721-1999)
PHONE.................................231 627-0200
Clarence Roznowski, *CEO*
EMP: 100
SQ FT: 450,000
SALES (est): 25MM **Privately Held**
SIC: 2621 Towels, tissues & napkins: paper & stock

(G-2681)
INVERNESS DAIRY INC
1631 Woiderski Rd (49721-8969)
PHONE.................................231 627-4655
EMP: 20 **EST:** 1922
SQ FT: 10,000
SALES (est): 213.8K **Privately Held**
SIC: 2026 2021 Mfg Fluid Milk Mfg Creamery Butter

(G-2682)
J B LUNDS & SONS INC
Also Called: Cheboygan Harbor Marine
707 Cleveland Ave (49721-2049)
P.O. Box 370 (49721-0370)
PHONE.................................231 627-9070
George E Lund, *Vice Pres*

Clayton Lund, *Treasurer*
Richard Lund, *Admin Sec*
EMP: 4 **EST:** 1902
SQ FT: 5,000
SALES (est): 355.9K **Privately Held**
SIC: 3599 5051 Machine shop, jobbing & repair; steel

(G-2683)
JOHNSON CLEANING & PAINTING
Also Called: Johnson Home Decorating Ctr
425 Dresser St (49721-1509)
PHONE.................................231 627-2211
Roger Johnson, *Owner*
Sheila Johnson, *Co-Owner*
EMP: 3
SALES (est): 99.3K **Privately Held**
SIC: 3479 Painting, coating & hot dipping

(G-2684)
KEEBLER COMPANY
10364 Neuman Rd (49721-8914)
PHONE.................................231 445-0335
Peter Chasse, *Principal*
EMP: 69
SALES (corp-wide): 13.5B **Publicly Held**
SIC: 2052 Cookies
HQ: Keebler Company
1 Kellogg Sq
Battle Creek MI 49017
269 961-2000

(G-2685)
KELLY ST AMOUR
2834 Olson Rd (49721-9128)
PHONE.................................231 625-9789
Kelly S Amour, *Principal*
EMP: 3
SALES (est): 281K **Privately Held**
SIC: 2411 Logging camps & contractors

(G-2686)
LIEBNER ENTERPRISES LLC
Also Called: United States Ski Pole Company
1160 E State St Unit C (49721-2166)
PHONE.................................231 331-3076
Andrew Liebner, *Mng Member*
Roger Liebner, *Mng Member*
EMP: 5
SALES: 575K **Privately Held**
SIC: 3949 Sporting & athletic goods

(G-2687)
NICHOLASS BLACK RIVER VINEYAR (PA)
Also Called: Nicholas Wine Sampling Room
6209 N Black River Rd (49721-9457)
PHONE.................................231 625-9060
Nick J Koklanaris, *President*
▲ **EMP:** 5
SALES (est): 318.1K **Privately Held**
SIC: 2084 Wines

(G-2688)
NORTHERN MICH MMRALS MONUMENTS
2754 Old Mackinaw Rd (49721-9311)
PHONE.................................231 290-2333
Matthew Redmond, *Principal*
EMP: 3 **EST:** 2015
SALES (est): 128.2K **Privately Held**
SIC: 2435 Hardwood veneer & plywood

(G-2689)
NORTHPORT NATURALS
8627 N Straits Hwy (49721-9011)
P.O. Box 6003 (49721-6003)
PHONE.................................231 420-9448
Thomas Good, *Founder*
EMP: 3 **EST:** 2016
SALES (est): 168.4K **Privately Held**
SIC: 2844 Toilet preparations

(G-2690)
PEPSI
Also Called: Pepsico
6303 N Straits Hwy (49721-9048)
PHONE.................................231 627-2290
Richard Sikorski, *Principal*
EMP: 4
SALES (est): 139.6K **Privately Held**
SIC: 2086 Carbonated soft drinks, bottled & canned

(G-2691)
PRECISION THREADING CORP
Also Called: North Attleboro Taps
1306 Higgins Dr (49721-1061)
PHONE.................................231 627-3133
Arthur C Heintel, *President*
Paul Scheer, *Vice Pres*
Mike Kelly, *Engineer*
Amy L Deeter, *CFO*
Amy Deeter, *CFO*
▲ **EMP:** 7
SQ FT: 28,000
SALES (est): 934K **Privately Held**
WEB: www.cheboygantap.com
SIC: 3545 Machine tool accessories

(G-2692)
R K C CORPORATION
600 Riggs Dr (49721-1066)
PHONE.................................231 627-9131
Reinhardt Jahn, *President*
C Reinhardt Jahn, *President*
EMP: 8
SQ FT: 40,000
SALES (est): 800.5K **Privately Held**
SIC: 3599 Custom machinery

(G-2693)
ROBERT A NELSON
11118 N Straits Hwy (49721-9090)
PHONE.................................231 597-9225
Robert A Nelson, *Principal*
Robert Nelson, *Principal*
EMP: 3
SALES (est): 264.2K **Privately Held**
SIC: 3841 Veterinarians' instruments & apparatus

(G-2694)
SCHWARTZ BOILER SHOP INC
Also Called: Schwartz Blast & Paint
850 Lahaie Rd (49721-1810)
P.O. Box 312 (49721-0312)
PHONE.................................231 627-2556
Jade Hunt, *President*
Roger A Schwartz, *Vice Pres*
Diane Schwartz, *Admin Sec*
EMP: 9
SQ FT: 8,000
SALES (est): 1.1MM **Privately Held**
SIC: 7699 3471 7353 Nautical repair services; ship boiler & tank cleaning & repair, contractors; sand blasting of metal parts; cranes & aerial lift equipment, rental or leasing

(G-2695)
SHOPPERS FAIR INC
Also Called: Cheboygan Tribune
308 N Main St (49721-1545)
PHONE.................................231 627-7144
Gary Lambert, *President*
Janis Coryell, *Bookkeeper*
Renee Glass, *Manager*
EMP: 29
SALES (est): 934K **Privately Held**
WEB: www.shoppersfair.com
SIC: 2711 Commercial printing & newspaper publishing combined; newspapers, publishing & printing

(G-2696)
STRAITS AREA PRINTING CORP
313 Lafayette Ave (49721-2154)
P.O. Box 11 (49721-0011)
PHONE.................................231 627-5647
Charles Beard, *President*
Sandra Beard, *Treasurer*
Michelle White, *Graphic Designe*
EMP: 9
SQ FT: 2,100
SALES (est): 700K **Privately Held**
SIC: 2752 2759 Commercial printing, offset; letterpress printing

(G-2697)
WELD TECH UNLIMITED INC
10983 Townline Rd (49721-9701)
PHONE.................................231 627-7531
Marc Brach, *President*
EMP: 3
SALES (est): 197.3K **Privately Held**
SIC: 7692 Welding repair

Chelsea
Washtenaw County

(G-2698)
ABRASIVE FINISHING INC
Also Called: Burr Bench
11770 Dexter Chelsea Rd (48118-9539)
PHONE.................................734 433-9236
William Ackley, *Owner*
◆ **EMP:** 6
SALES (est): 1.1MM **Privately Held**
SIC: 3291 Abrasive products

(G-2699)
ADVANCED INDUSTRIES INC
Also Called: Koolblast
3955 S Fletcher Rd (48118-9207)
PHONE.................................734 433-1800
Kevin Beckington, *President*
Jason Beckington, *VP Bus Dvlpt*
EMP: 24
SQ FT: 15,000
SALES (est): 4.3MM **Privately Held**
WEB: www.advancedindustriesinc.com
SIC: 3599 Machine shop, jobbing & repair

(G-2700)
AFI ENTERPRISES INC
11770 Dexter Chelsea Rd (48118-9539)
PHONE.................................734 475-9111
William A Ackley, *President*
◆ **EMP:** 20 **EST:** 1954
SQ FT: 80,000
SALES (est): 1.8MM **Privately Held**
SIC: 3291 Grinding balls, ceramic; stones, abrasive

(G-2701)
AL CORP
Also Called: Phoenix Color
525 Glazier Rd (48118-9779)
PHONE.................................734 475-7357
EMP: 15
SALES (est): 941K **Privately Held**
SIC: 2759 2796 2791 Commercial Printing Platemaking Services Typesetting Services
PA: Access Bidco Incorporated
200 N Washington Sq # 440
Lansing MI 48933

(G-2702)
ALLOY INDUSTRIES CORPORATION
13500 Luick Dr (48118-9587)
PHONE.................................734 433-1112
Carl E Perry, *President*
EMP: 8
SQ FT: 8,500
SALES (est): 1.1MM **Privately Held**
SIC: 3599 Machine shop, jobbing & repair

(G-2703)
CHELSEA GRAIN LLC
11800 Dexter Chelsea Rd (48118-9539)
PHONE.................................734 475-1386
Klaus Bachmann, *Mng Member*
EMP: 3 **EST:** 1999
SALES (est): 4.9MM **Privately Held**
SIC: 3534 4221 Elevators & equipment; farm product warehousing & storage

(G-2704)
CHELSEA MILLING COMPANY (PA)
201 W North St (48118-1297)
P.O. Box 460 (48118-0460)
PHONE.................................734 475-1361
Howdy S Holmes, *President*
Doug Garriga, *Business Mgr*
John Kennedy, *Vice Pres*
Russ Denies, *Opers Mgr*
Ashley Ogden-Holden, *Opers Mgr*
EMP: 300
SQ FT: 350,000
SALES (est): 86.6MM **Privately Held**
WEB: www.jiffymix.com
SIC: 2041 Flour: blended, prepared or self-rising

GEOGRAPHIC SECTION

Chesterfield - Macomb County (G-2731)

(G-2705)
CHELSEA TOOL INC
20401 W Old Us Highway 12 # 4 (48118-2300)
P.O. Box 178 (48118-0178)
PHONE..................734 475-9679
Dennis Boos, *President*
EMP: 5
SQ FT: 4,000
SALES: 230K **Privately Held**
SIC: 3599 Machine shop, jobbing & repair

(G-2706)
DETROIT ABRASIVES COMPANY (PA)
11910 Dexter Chelsea Rd (48118-9539)
PHONE..................734 475-1651
Richard G Wallace, *President*
Katherine A Wallace, *Corp Secy*
▲ **EMP:** 5
SQ FT: 10,000
SALES (est): 953.2K **Privately Held**
SIC: 3291 Aluminum oxide (fused) abrasives

(G-2707)
DEXTER CIDER MILL INC
4885 Kalmbach Rd (48118-9701)
PHONE..................734 475-6419
EMP: 3
SALES (est): 127.3K **Privately Held**
SIC: 2099 Cider, nonalcoholic

(G-2708)
DEXTER MANUFACTURING INC
20401 W Old Us Highway 12 # 1 (48118-2300)
P.O. Box 114 (48118-0114)
PHONE..................734 475-8046
Bill J Mikkelson, *President*
EMP: 5
SQ FT: 3,500
SALES: 550K **Privately Held**
SIC: 3599 Machine shop, jobbing & repair

(G-2709)
ELITE ARMS INC
Also Called: Elite Defense
18600 W Old Us Highway 12 (48118-9645)
PHONE..................734 424-9955
Dennis Finnegan, *President*
Sherry Elling, *Warehouse Mgr*
Theresa Helm, *Export Mgr*
Brittany Westcott, *Sales Staff*
Jack Ulrich, *Director*
EMP: 14 **EST:** 2007
SALES (est): 2.2MM **Privately Held**
SIC: 3949 5091 5136 Shooting equipment & supplies, general; firearms, sporting; uniforms, men's & boys'

(G-2710)
FILTER PLUS INC
2442 Mckinley Rd (48118-9512)
PHONE..................734 475-7403
John Temple, *President*
EMP: 15
SALES: 1MM **Privately Held**
WEB: www.filterplus.com
SIC: 3841 Surgical & medical instruments

(G-2711)
GESTAMP WASHTENAW LLC
5800 Sibley Rd (48118-1262)
PHONE..................248 251-3004
Jeffrey Wilson, *President*
EMP: 30
SALES (est): 1.1MM **Privately Held**
SIC: 3465 Body parts, automobile: stamped metal

(G-2712)
GREENE MANUFACTURING INC
Also Called: GMI
3985 S Fletcher Rd (48118-9653)
PHONE..................734 428-8304
Bruce Greene, *President*
Julie Greene, *Controller*
Charles Gale, *Graphic Designe*
EMP: 23 **EST:** 1969
SQ FT: 15,000
SALES: 5.5MM **Privately Held**
WEB: www.greenemfg.com
SIC: 3444 2531 Sheet metalwork; school furniture

(G-2713)
HATCH STAMPING COMPANY LLC
570 Cleveland St (48118-1303)
PHONE..................734 433-1903
Rick Potham, *Manager*
EMP: 150
SALES (corp-wide): 863.9MM **Privately Held**
WEB: www.hatchstamping.com
SIC: 3465 Body parts, automobile: stamped metal
HQ: Hatch Stamping Company Llc
635 E Industrial Dr
Chelsea MI 48118
734 475-8628

(G-2714)
JAYTEC LLC
5800 Sibley Rd (48118-1262)
PHONE..................734 397-6300
Darryl Macneil, *General Mgr*
Robert Koss, *Vice Pres*
EMP: 10
SALES (corp-wide): 2.2B **Privately Held**
SIC: 3465 Automotive stampings
HQ: Jaytec, Llc
17757 Woodland Dr
New Boston MI 48164
517 451-8272

(G-2715)
KERN AUTO SALES AND SVC LLC
1630 S Main St (48118-1411)
PHONE..................734 475-2722
Thomas D Kern,
Vickie Kern,
EMP: 14 **EST:** 2007
SALES (est): 2.1MM **Privately Held**
SIC: 5521 7539 2869 5411 Automobiles, used cars only; automotive repair shops; fuels; convenience stores

(G-2716)
MANLY INNOVATIONS LLC
19735 Deerfield Ct (48118-9316)
PHONE..................734 548-0200
Joseph Manly,
EMP: 4
SALES (est): 284.1K **Privately Held**
SIC: 3484 Guns (firearms) or gun parts, 30 mm. & below

(G-2717)
PLOW POINT BREWING CO
6447 Stillwater Dr (48118-9166)
PHONE..................734 562-9102
Don Smith, *Principal*
EMP: 3
SALES (est): 68.6K **Privately Held**
SIC: 2082 Malt beverages

(G-2718)
PRECISION HRDWOOD RSOURCES INC
Also Called: Hardwood Solutions Inc
680 E Industrial Dr (48118-1285)
PHONE..................734 475-0144
Jeffrey Hardcastle, *President*
Bob Mendoza, *Vice Pres*
Debra Hardcastle, *Treasurer*
Linda Parker, *Admin Asst*
◆ **EMP:** 15
SQ FT: 42,000
SALES (est): 3.4MM **Privately Held**
WEB: www.hardwoodsolutions.net
SIC: 2421 Sawmills & planing mills, general

(G-2719)
SHERIDAN BOOKS INC (DH)
613 E Industrial Dr (48118-1536)
P.O. Box 370 (48118-0370)
PHONE..................734 475-9145
Robert Moore, *President*
Michal Seagram, *President*
Jim Weaks, *Facilities Mgr*
Jessica Ansorge, *Sales Staff*
◆ **EMP:** 197
SALES (est): 233.4MM
SALES (corp-wide): 536.1MM **Privately Held**
WEB: www.sheridanbooks.com
SIC: 2752 Commercial printing, offset
HQ: The Sheridan Group Inc
450 Fame Ave
Hanover PA 17331
717 632-3535

(G-2720)
W A THOMAS COMPANY
446 Congdon St (48118-1598)
PHONE..................734 475-8626
Wayne Meyer, *Principal*
EMP: 3
SALES (est): 226.7K **Privately Held**
SIC: 3451 Screw machine products

(G-2721)
WATCHDOG QUARTERLY INC
19 Chestnut Dr (48118-9416)
PHONE..................734 593-7039
EMP: 3
SALES: 3.3K **Privately Held**
SIC: 2731 Books-Publishing/Printing

Chesaning
Saginaw County

(G-2722)
CHARLIES WOOD SHOP
Also Called: Puzzleman Toys, The
603 S Main St (48616-1709)
P.O. Box 187 (48616-0187)
PHONE..................989 845-2632
Charles H W Hall, *Owner*
Charles Hall, *Finance*
EMP: 14
SQ FT: 3,900
SALES: 1.8MM **Privately Held**
WEB: www.charlieswoodshop.com
SIC: 3944 3993 3544 3172 Games, toys & children's vehicles; signs & advertising specialties; special dies, tools, jigs & fixtures; personal leather goods; wood household furniture; nailed wood boxes & shook

(G-2723)
DESIGNS BY BEAN
233 W Broad St (48616-1204)
PHONE..................989 845-4371
Michael Greenfelder, *Partner*
EMP: 8
SQ FT: 2,000
SALES (est): 787.4K **Privately Held**
SIC: 2396 2395 2759 Screen printing on fabric articles; embroidery products, except schiffli machine; screen printing

(G-2724)
INTEGRATED BUILDING SOLUTIONS
13609 Larner Rd (48616-9445)
PHONE..................616 889-3070
Kevin Damic, *Owner*
EMP: 10
SQ FT: 3,000
SALES: 2.5MM **Privately Held**
SIC: 3822 Building services monitoring controls, automatic

(G-2725)
LIPPERT COMPONENTS MFG INC
Also Called: Hehr Michigan Division
1103 Pearl St (48616-1007)
P.O. Box 217 (48616-0217)
PHONE..................989 845-3061
Douglas Gerding, *Branch Mgr*
EMP: 130
SALES (corp-wide): 2.4B **Publicly Held**
WEB: www.hehrintl.com
SIC: 3231 3714 3442 3354 Windshields, glass: made from purchased glass; motor vehicle parts & accessories; metal doors, sash & trim; aluminum extruded products; van conversion; doors & windows
HQ: Lippert Components Manufacturing, Inc.
3501 County Road 6 E
Elkhart IN 46514
574 535-1125

(G-2726)
LIPPERT COMPONENTS MFG INC
Hehr Glass
200 S 1st St (48616-1035)
P.O. Box 388 (48616-0388)
PHONE..................323 663-1261
Bob Wagner, *Sales/Mktg Mgr*
Dawn Adams, *Persnl Dir*
EMP: 137
SALES (corp-wide): 2.4B **Publicly Held**
WEB: www.hehrintl.com
SIC: 3211 3231 Tempered glass; products of purchased glass
HQ: Lippert Components Manufacturing, Inc.
3501 County Road 6 E
Elkhart IN 46514
574 535-1125

(G-2727)
LORENCZ CONSTRUCTION CO
812 E Liberty St (48616-1745)
PHONE..................989 798-3151
Daniel Lorencz, *Owner*
EMP: 4
SALES (est): 323K **Privately Held**
SIC: 1521 2452 General remodeling, single-family houses; log cabins, prefabricated, wood

(G-2728)
SWARTZMILLER LUMBER COMPANY (PA)
802 W Broad St (48616-1002)
P.O. Box 126 (48616-0126)
PHONE..................989 845-6625
Donald Swartzmiller, *Ch of Bd*
Annette Swartzmiller, *President*
Christopher Theily, *Vice Pres*
EMP: 6
SQ FT: 40,000
SALES (est): 1.3MM **Privately Held**
SIC: 5211 3271 3273 5961 Home centers; lumber products; concrete block & brick; ready-mixed concrete; catalog & mail-order houses; truck rental, without drivers

(G-2729)
VB CHESANING LLC
624 Brady St (48616-1155)
PHONE..................989 323-2333
EMP: 3
SALES (est): 291.1K **Privately Held**
SIC: 3999

Chesterfield
Macomb County

(G-2730)
1271 ASSOCIATES INC (PA)
Also Called: Welders and Presses
27295 Luckino Dr (48047-5229)
PHONE..................586 948-4300
Robert Kohler, *President*
David Kohler, *Exec VP*
EMP: 65
SQ FT: 42,000
SALES (est): 12.5MM **Privately Held**
SIC: 3548 5085 7699 Resistance welders, electric; welding supplies; industrial machinery & equipment repair

(G-2731)
ACHATZS HAND MADE PIE CO (PA)
30301 Commerce Blvd (48051-1243)
PHONE..................586 749-2882
David Achatz, *Owner*
Joann Austin, *Opers Mgr*
Renee Brown, *Human Res Mgr*
Sarah Achatz, *Office Mgr*
Sarah Jacques, *Manager*
EMP: 51
SQ FT: 4,500
SALES (est): 12MM **Privately Held**
WEB: www.achatzpies.com
SIC: 2038 2051 5141 Frozen specialties; bread, cake & related products; groceries, general line

Chesterfield - Macomb County (G-2732)

(G-2732)
ADVANCED BORING AND TOOL CO
26950 23 Mile Rd Lowr (48051-3400)
PHONE..................586 598-9300
Thomas J Carter, *Ch of Bd*
Stefan Wanczyk, *President*
EMP: 80
SALES: 12MM
SALES (corp-wide): 565.7MM **Privately Held**
WEB: www.advancedboring.com
SIC: 3599 Machine shop, jobbing & repair
PA: Utica Enterprises, Inc.
5750 New King Dr Ste 200
Troy MI 48098
586 726-4300

(G-2733)
ADVANCED INTEG TOOLING SOLNS
Also Called: Advanced Integration Tech Mich
29700 Commerce Blvd (48051-1244)
PHONE..................586 749-5525
Edward J Chalupa, *Partner*
▲ **EMP:** 230
SALES (est): 75.3MM
SALES (corp-wide): 88.5MM **Privately Held**
SIC: 3544 Industrial molds
PA: Advanced Integration Technology, Lp
2805 E Plano Pkwy Ste 300
Plano TX 75074
972 423-8354

(G-2734)
ADVANCED INTEGRATION TECH LP
Also Called: Ait Tooling
29700 Commerce Blvd (48051-1244)
PHONE..................586 749-5525
William Pallante, *Manager*
EMP: 5
SALES (corp-wide): 88.5MM **Privately Held**
SIC: 3728 8711 Aircraft parts & equipment; machine tool design
PA: Advanced Integration Technology, Lp
2805 E Plano Pkwy Ste 300
Plano TX 75074
972 423-8354

(G-2735)
ADVANCED MACHINING LTD
25425 Terra Industrial Dr (48051-2733)
PHONE..................586 465-2220
Slobodan Nikolich, *President*
EMP: 10
SQ FT: 12,500
SALES (est): 1.6MM **Privately Held**
WEB: www.advanced-company.com
SIC: 3599 Machine shop, jobbing & repair

(G-2736)
AMERICAN BRAKE AND CLUTCH INC
Also Called: Superior Waterjet Service
50631 E Russell Schmidt (48051-2454)
PHONE..................586 948-3730
Daniel C Breazeale, *President*
EMP: 10
SQ FT: 55,000
SALES (est): 1.3MM **Privately Held**
WEB: www.americanbrake.com
SIC: 3625 3542 Electromagnetic clutches or brakes; plasma jet spray metal forming machines

(G-2737)
ANCHOR BAY MANUFACTURING CORP (PA)
30905 23 Mile Rd (48047-5702)
PHONE..................586 949-4040
Victoria Pierno, *Principal*
Robert Kebblish, *Design Engr*
EMP: 8
SALES (est): 907.6K **Privately Held**
SIC: 2621 Paper mills

(G-2738)
ANCHOR BAY PACKAGING CORP (PA)
Also Called: Phoenix Packaging Corporation
30905 23 Mile Rd (48047-5702)
PHONE..................586 949-4040
Victoria L Pierno, *President*
Chris Hastings, *Principal*
Collin Tripp, *Principal*
Philip Taravella, *Vice Pres*
Mark Mets, *QC Mgr*
▲ **EMP:** 27 EST: 1985
SQ FT: 40,000
SALES (est): 20.8MM **Privately Held**
WEB: www.anchorbaypackaging.com
SIC: 2653 8734 3565 Boxes, corrugated: made from purchased materials; testing laboratories; packaging machinery

(G-2739)
ANCHOR BAY PACKAGING CORP
30871 23 Mile Rd (48047-1894)
PHONE..................586 949-1500
EMP: 50
SALES (corp-wide): 20.8MM **Privately Held**
WEB: www.anchorbaypackaging.com
SIC: 2653 2671 2631 Boxes, corrugated: made from purchased materials; packaging paper & plastics film, coated & laminated; paperboard mills
PA: Anchor Bay Packaging Corporation
30905 23 Mile Rd
Chesterfield MI 48047
586 949-4040

(G-2740)
ANKARA INDUSTRIES INCORPORATED
56359 N Bay Dr (48051-3738)
PHONE..................586 749-1190
Richard B Moore, *President*
EMP: 15
SQ FT: 35,000
SALES (est): 3.1MM **Privately Held**
WEB: www.ankaraindustries.com
SIC: 3452 3465 Nuts, metal; automotive stampings

(G-2741)
ARNOLD TOOL & DIE CO (PA)
48800 Structural Dr (48051)
PHONE..................586 598-0099
Thomas A McKay, *President*
Margaret McKay, *Vice Pres*
Jeff McKay, *Plant Mgr*
Gary Schultz, *Program Mgr*
EMP: 50
SALES (est): 8.9MM **Privately Held**
WEB: www.arnoldtool.com
SIC: 3599 3544 3469 Machine shop, jobbing & repair; special dies, tools, jigs & fixtures; metal stampings

(G-2742)
ARO WELDING TECHNOLOGIES INC
Also Called: Savair
48500 Structural Dr (48051-2673)
PHONE..................586 949-9353
Pierre Barthelemy, *President*
Jean- Yves David, *President*
Albert Roland, *Principal*
Carl Paschall, *Project Mgr*
Thomas Hendershot, *Purch Mgr*
▲ **EMP:** 99 EST: 1986
SQ FT: 80,000
SALES (est): 23.5MM
SALES (corp-wide): 971.2MM **Privately Held**
WEB: www.savairinc.com
SIC: 3548 Electric welding equipment
PA: Langley Holdings Plc
Enterprise Park
Retford NOTTS DN22
162 351-8350

(G-2743)
AUTHORITY FLAME HARDENING & ST
49803 Leona Dr (48051-2480)
PHONE..................586 598-5887
David Decook,
Darlene Decook,
Matthew Decook,
EMP: 11
SQ FT: 11,000
SALES (est): 2.1MM **Privately Held**
WEB: www.authorityflame.com
SIC: 3398 Metal heat treating

(G-2744)
AUTO BUILDERS INC
46571 Continental Dr (48047-5207)
P.O. Box 180726, Utica (48318-0726)
PHONE..................586 948-3780
EMP: 25 EST: 2003
SALES (est): 3.7MM **Privately Held**
SIC: 3599 Mfg Industrial Machinery

(G-2745)
BERG TOOL INC
56253 Precision Dr (48051-3736)
PHONE..................586 646-7100
Michael B Bergmann, *President*
Glenn Burmeister, *Supervisor*
EMP: 19
SQ FT: 14,000
SALES (est): 3.6MM **Privately Held**
SIC: 3541 3544 Machine tools, metal cutting type; special dies, tools, jigs & fixtures

(G-2746)
BRICO WELDING & FAB INC
27057 Morelli Dr (48051-2033)
PHONE..................586 948-8881
Brian W Coons, *President*
Bradford W Coons, *Vice Pres*
EMP: 22
SQ FT: 27,500
SALES (est): 4.3MM **Privately Held**
WEB: www.bricowelding.com
SIC: 7692 Welding repair

(G-2747)
BRIGGS INDUSTRIES INC
54145 Bates Rd (48051-1617)
P.O. Box 160, New Baltimore (48047-0160)
PHONE..................586 749-5191
Elmer Lee Briggs, *President*
Cynthia J Rogers, *Corp Secy*
EMP: 30
SQ FT: 17,000
SALES (est): 6MM **Privately Held**
SIC: 3545 3543 3544 3086 Tools & accessories for machine tools; industrial patterns; special dies, tools, jigs & fixtures; plastics foam products

(G-2748)
BROACHING INDUSTRIES INC
25755 Dhondt Ct (48051-2601)
PHONE..................586 949-3775
Michael E Priehs Sr, *President*
EMP: 40
SQ FT: 6,200
SALES (est): 1.2MM **Privately Held**
SIC: 8711 3469 3452 3545 Engineering services; metal stampings; bolts, nuts, rivets & washers; machine tool accessories; blast furnaces & steel mills; machine tools, metal cutting type

(G-2749)
BURTEK ENTERPRISES INC
50325 Patricia St (48051-3803)
PHONE..................586 421-8000
Jeff Daniel, *President*
Michael Cass, *Vice Pres*
Gregory Gallagher, *Vice Pres*
Pat McAleer, *Vice Pres*
Kevin Schrage, *Vice Pres*
▼ **EMP:** 130 EST: 2012
SQ FT: 250,000
SALES (est): 47.7MM
SALES (corp-wide): 121.3MM **Privately Held**
SIC: 3812 Defense systems & equipment
PA: Burtek Holdings Inc.
50325 Patricia St
Chesterfield MI

(G-2750)
C & M MANUFACTURING CORP INC
30207 Commerce Blvd (48051-1241)
PHONE..................586 749-3455
Mat Warren, *President*
Linda Warren, *Vice Pres*
Troy Warren, *Plant Mgr*
Jim Smolinski, *Purch Mgr*
EMP: 40
SQ FT: 50,000
SALES (est): 6.8MM **Privately Held**
WEB: www.candmmfg.com
SIC: 3465 3312 Automotive stampings; tool & die steel

(G-2751)
CAMRYN FABRICATION LLC
Also Called: Pro-Weld
50625 Richard W Blvd (48051-2493)
PHONE..................586 949-0818
Steve Remstad, *President*
Rhonda Wendland, *Manager*
Jim Comer,
Les Stansbery,
EMP: 115
SALES: 24MM **Privately Held**
SIC: 3441 Fabricated structural metal

(G-2752)
CHAINSAW MAN OF MICHIGAN
28312 Katie Rd (48047-6406)
P.O. Box 486, Almont (48003-0486)
PHONE..................586 977-7856
Dr Emil Szkipala, *President*
EMP: 3
SALES (est): 146.1K **Privately Held**
WEB: www.treecarvings.com
SIC: 2499 Carved & turned wood

(G-2753)
CHESTERFIELD ENGINES INC
Also Called: Chesterfield Engines Nic
52420 Gratiot Ave (48051-2024)
PHONE..................586 949-5777
Gerald Barylski, *President*
EMP: 6
SALES (est): 1MM **Privately Held**
SIC: 7538 7699 7539 5084 Engine rebuilding: automotive; boat repair; machine shop, automotive; engines & parts, diesel; machine shop, jobbing & repair

(G-2754)
COLUMBIA MARKING TOOLS INC
27430 Luckino Dr (48047-5270)
PHONE..................586 949-8400
Michelle Krembel, *President*
Andrew Habedank, *Engineer*
Jim Skalny, *Engineer*
Brian Barbara, *Regl Sales Mgr*
Jeff Curtis, *Sales Staff*
EMP: 40
SQ FT: 30,000
SALES (est): 9.6MM **Privately Held**
WEB: www.columbiamt.com
SIC: 3549 3953 3544 3542 Marking machines, metalworking; marking devices; special dies, tools, jigs & fixtures; machine tools, metal forming type; commercial printing

(G-2755)
COSTELLO MACHINE LLC
56358 Precision Dr (48051-3737)
PHONE..................586 749-0136
Frank Keena, *Managing Dir*
Victor A Costello, *Mng Member*
Ezekiel Costello, *Manager*
Thomas Orban, *Information Mgr*
◆ **EMP:** 27
SQ FT: 35,000
SALES (est): 4.3MM **Privately Held**
SIC: 3545 Comparators (machinists' precision tools); precision tools, machinists'

(G-2756)
COX INDUSTRIES INC (PA)
30800 26 Mile Rd (48051-1234)
P.O. Box 480366, New Haven (48048-0366)
PHONE..................586 749-6650
Alice Cox, *President*
Charles Cox, *Vice Pres*
Corey Makar, *Plant Mgr*
Richard Ventura, *Sales Mgr*
EMP: 15
SALES (est): 1.5MM **Privately Held**
SIC: 3399 Metal fasteners

GEOGRAPHIC SECTION — Chesterfield - Macomb County

(G-2757)
CUSOLAR INDUSTRIES INC
28161 Kehrig St (48047-5218)
PHONE.................586 949-3880
Thomas W Cusack, *President*
Nadine Cusack, *Vice Pres*
EMP: 30 **EST:** 1979
SQ FT: 12,000
SALES: 1.2MM **Privately Held**
SIC: 3672 3714 3677 3694 Printed circuit boards; filters: oil, fuel & air, motor vehicle; coil windings, electronic; engine electrical equipment; brakes, electromagnetic; molding primary plastic

(G-2758)
D & B METAL FINISHING
34537 Shorewood St (48047-4412)
PHONE.................586 725-6056
Deana Ulman, *Owner*
Bruce Ulman, *Co-Owner*
EMP: 6
SALES: 400K **Privately Held**
SIC: 3471 Plating of metals or formed products; electroplating of metals or formed products

(G-2759)
DAJACO IND INC
49715 Leona Dr (48051-2478)
PHONE.................586 949-1590
Denise Hardy, *Principal*
EMP: 5
SALES (est): 397.2K **Privately Held**
SIC: 3469 Metal stampings

(G-2760)
DAJACO INDUSTRIES INC
49715 Leona Dr (48051-2478)
PHONE.................586 949-1590
James M Ureel, *President*
James Ureel Jr, *President*
Jeffery Ureel, *Vice Pres*
Susan Sheaver, *Controller*
George Wittbrodt, *Sales Mgr*
EMP: 56
SQ FT: 55,000
SALES (est): 12.6MM **Privately Held**
SIC: 3469 3465 Stamping metal for the trade; body parts, automobile: stamped metal

(G-2761)
DANLYN CONTROLS INC
25090 Terra Industrial Dr (48051-2739)
P.O. Box 711, Mount Clemens (48046-0711)
PHONE.................586 773-6797
James Zimmerman, *President*
EMP: 5
SQ FT: 10,000
SALES: 400K **Privately Held**
SIC: 3613 Control panels, electric

(G-2762)
DAVALOR MOLD COMPANY LLC
46480 Continental Dr (48047-5206)
PHONE.................586 598-0100
Don Rospierski, *Plant Mgr*
Cheryl Crandall, *Buyer*
John Wnuk, *Engineer*
Williams Werling, *CFO*
Bill Werling, *Controller*
EMP: 155
SALES (est): 25MM **Privately Held**
SIC: 3089 Injection molding of plastics

(G-2763)
DEGELE MANUFACTURING INC
25700 Dhondt Ct (48051-2600)
PHONE.................586 949-3550
John Degele, *President*
Mary Louise Degele, *Vice Pres*
EMP: 20
SQ FT: 34,000
SALES (est): 3.2MM **Privately Held**
SIC: 3469 Metal stampings

(G-2764)
DEMAG CRANES & COMPONENTS CORP
46545 Continental Dr (48047-5207)
PHONE.................586 954-1000
Bill Carney, *Controller*
James Satow, *Manager*
EMP: 57
SALES (corp-wide): 3.6B **Privately Held**
WEB: www.demag-us.com
SIC: 3536 Hoists, cranes & monorails
HQ: Demag Cranes & Components Corp.
6675 Parkland Blvd # 200
Solon OH 44139
440 248-2400

(G-2765)
DESIGN SERVICES UNLIMITED INC
Also Called: DSU
25754 Dhondt Ct (48051-2600)
PHONE.................586 463-3225
Craig Marsack, *President*
EMP: 6
SALES (est): 1MM **Privately Held**
SIC: 3541 Machine tools, metal cutting type

(G-2766)
DICO MANUFACTURING LLC
48605 Structural Dr (48051-2666)
PHONE.................586 731-3008
Diane L Centofanti,
EMP: 4
SALES: 830K **Privately Held**
SIC: 2891 Laminating compounds

(G-2767)
DIE HEAT SYSTEMS INC
Also Called: D H S
54145 Bates Rd (48051-1617)
P.O. Box 160, New Baltimore (48047-0160)
PHONE.................586 749-9756
Michael Martin, *President*
EMP: 3
SALES (est): 392.5K **Privately Held**
WEB: www.dieheatsystems.com
SIC: 3398 3613 Metal heat treating; control panels, electric

(G-2768)
DYNAMIC PLASTICS INC
29831 Commerce Blvd (48051-1245)
PHONE.................586 749-6100
Joe Doss, *President*
James Connell, *Vice Pres*
EMP: 23
SQ FT: 13,500
SALES (est): 4.8MM **Privately Held**
SIC: 3544 Industrial molds

(G-2769)
E M P MANUFACTURING CORP
28190 23 Mile Rd (48051-2318)
PHONE.................586 949-8277
Randy Harm, *President*
Kris McClintock, *CFO*
EMP: 10
SQ FT: 14,000
SALES: 3MM **Privately Held**
SIC: 3452 Bolts, metal; nuts, metal; screws, metal

(G-2770)
EAGLE MARBLE & GRANITE
49763 Leona Dr (48051-2478)
PHONE.................586 421-1912
Pjerin Brucaj, *Managing Prtnr*
▲ **EMP:** 5
SQ FT: 7,600
SALES: 500K **Privately Held**
SIC: 2541 Counter & sink tops

(G-2771)
ECLIPSE MOLD INCORPORATED
50320 Patricia St (48051-3802)
PHONE.................586 792-3320
EMP: 104
SALES (corp-wide): 33.5MM **Privately Held**
SIC: 3089 Injection molding of plastics
PA: Eclipse Mold Incorporated
23155 15 Mile Rd
Clinton Township MI 48035
586 792-3320

(G-2772)
ELLSWORTH CUTTING TOOLS LLC
25190 Terra Industrial Dr (48051-2728)
PHONE.................586 598-6040
Doug Ellsworth, *Partner*
Ellsworth Miller,
EMP: 15
SALES (est): 3.5MM **Privately Held**
SIC: 3545 7699 Cutting tools for machine tools; knife, saw & tool sharpening & repair

(G-2773)
EMHART TEKNOLOGIES LLC
Also Called: Emhart Industries
50501 E Russell Schmidt B (48051-2452)
P.O. Box 868, Mount Clemens (48046-0868)
PHONE.................586 949-0440
Daniel Lebeau, *Branch Mgr*
EMP: 10
SALES (corp-wide): 13.9B **Publicly Held**
WEB: www.helicoil.com
SIC: 3541 Machine tools, metal cutting type
HQ: Emhart Teknologies Llc
480 Myrtle St
New Britain CT 06053
800 783-6427

(G-2774)
EXCO EXTRUSION DIES INC
Also Called: Ets Exco Tooling Solutions
56617 N Bay Dr (48051-3746)
PHONE.................586 749-5400
Bryan Robbins, *CEO*
Bonnie Cartwright, *President*
Mathew Robbins, *COO*
Randy Hoover, *Safety Mgr*
Marilynne Moroni, *Controller*
▲ **EMP:** 127
SQ FT: 8,000
SALES (est): 38.7MM **Privately Held**
SIC: 3544 Dies, steel rule; special dies & tools

(G-2775)
FISHER KELLERING CO
30500 Commerce Blvd (48051-1212)
PHONE.................586 749-6616
Fax: 586 749-9424
◆ **EMP:** 6
SQ FT: 18,500
SALES: 500K **Privately Held**
SIC: 3544 Mfg Progressive Dies

(G-2776)
FLAGLER CORPORATION
56513 Precision Dr (48051-3736)
PHONE.................586 749-6300
Harley J Flagler, *President*
Ken Gasko, *Manager*
Mary Lou Flagler, *Admin Sec*
EMP: 20 **EST:** 1949
SQ FT: 22,000
SALES (est): 4.1MM **Privately Held**
WEB: www.flaglercorp.com
SIC: 3542 3544 3549 Sheet metalworking machines; special dies, tools, jigs & fixtures; metalworking machinery

(G-2777)
FLINT HYDROSTATICS INC (HQ)
48175 Gratiot Ave (48051-2604)
PHONE.................901 794-2462
Shirish Pareek, *CEO*
David Kelley, *VP Opers*
Timm Flint, *CFO*
◆ **EMP:** 10 **EST:** 1977
SALES (est): 8.7MM **Privately Held**
WEB: www.flinthydrostatics.com
SIC: 3594 3621 5084 Hydrostatic drives (transmissions); motors & generators; industrial machinery & equipment

(G-2778)
FORMA-KOOL MANUFACTURING INC
46880 Continental Dr (48047-5269)
PHONE.................586 949-4813
Deanna Males, *President*
EMP: 24
SQ FT: 18,000
SALES (est): 3.6MM **Privately Held**
WEB: www.formakool.com
SIC: 3585 3442 5078 3564 Refrigeration equipment, complete; metal doors, sash & trim; refrigerators, commercial (reach-in & walk-in); blowers & fans; household refrigerators & freezers

(G-2779)
FOURSLIDES INC
50801 E Russell Schmidt (48051-2457)
PHONE.................313 564-5600
George Kofmeister, *President*
EMP: 15
SQ FT: 44,800
SALES (est): 2.3MM **Privately Held**
WEB: www.4slides.net
SIC: 3965 Fasteners

(G-2780)
FREAL FUEL INC
28230 23 Mile Rd (48051-2317)
PHONE.................248 790-7202
Husam Sami, *Principal*
EMP: 4
SALES (est): 299K **Privately Held**
SIC: 2869 Fuels

(G-2781)
GLOBAL ADVANCED PRODUCTS LLC
30707 Commerce Blvd (48051-1231)
PHONE.................586 749-6800
Ravinder Sandhu, *President*
Bruce Havel,
▲ **EMP:** 100
SQ FT: 90,000
SALES (est): 653.8K
SALES (corp-wide): 15.4MM **Privately Held**
WEB: www.coreplug.com
SIC: 3469 Metal stampings
PA: Advanced Assembly Products, Inc.
1300 E 9 Mile Rd
Hazel Park MI 48030
248 543-2427

(G-2782)
GLOBAL ENTERPRISE LIMITED
Also Called: Global Chesterfield
50450 E Rssell Schmidt Bl (48051-2449)
P.O. Box 328, Taylor (48180-0328)
PHONE.................586 948-4100
Irving Thompson, *Principal*
EMP: 5
SALES (est): 1.5MM **Privately Held**
SIC: 3089 Plastic containers, except foam

(G-2783)
GRACE PRODUCTION SERVICES LLC
Also Called: Global Plastic Systems
52100 Sierra Dr (48047-1309)
PHONE.................810 643-8070
Gracemary Allen, *CEO*
Leeann Hamilton, *Manager*
EMP: 6 **EST:** 2013
SQ FT: 10,000
SALES (est): 451.7K **Privately Held**
SIC: 3089 Injection molding of plastics

(G-2784)
HERITAGE MFG INC
49787 Leona Dr (48051-2478)
PHONE.................586 949-7446
Fax: 586 949-6143
EMP: 4
SQ FT: 6,250
SALES: 800K **Privately Held**
SIC: 3599 2821 Mfg Industrial Machinery Mfg Plastic Materials/Resins

(G-2785)
HUB TOOL AND MACHINE INC
53770 Hubs Ln (48051-1772)
PHONE.................586 772-7866
Fax: 586 772-7867
EMP: 3
SQ FT: 4,500
SALES: 100K **Privately Held**
SIC: 3544 Mfg Dies/Tools/Jigs/Fixtures

(G-2786)
HYDRAULEX INTL HOLDINGS INC (PA)
Also Called: Hydraulex Global
48175 Gratiot Ave (48051-2604)
PHONE.................914 682-2700
Shirish Pareek, *CEO*
Jerry Kolb, *Purchasing*
David Perry, *CFO*
Matt Clark, *Sales Mgr*
Steve Hurst, *Sales Mgr*

(PA)=Parent Co (HQ)=Headquarters (DH)=Div Headquarters
✪ = New Business established in last 2 years

Chesterfield - Macomb County (G-2787)

EMP: 27
SALES (est): 91.3MM **Privately Held**
SIC: 3594 3621 5084 Hydrostatic drives (transmissions); motors & generators; industrial machinery & equipment

(G-2787)
INDEXABLE CUTTER ENGINEERING
Also Called: Ice Tools
50525 Metzen Dr (48051-3137)
PHONE..................586 598-1540
Bob Lotz, *President*
Wade Dougherty, *Chairman*
EMP: 6
SQ FT: 3,000
SALES (est): 1.1MM **Privately Held**
WEB: www.icetools.com
SIC: 3545 Cutting tools for machine tools

(G-2788)
INDUSTRIES UNLIMITED INC
49739 Leona Dr (48051-2478)
PHONE..................586 949-4300
Scott Atchison, *President*
EMP: 20
SQ FT: 6,500
SALES (est): 3.2MM **Privately Held**
SIC: 3496 3089 Clips & fasteners, made from purchased wire; injection molding of plastics

(G-2789)
INNOVATIVE TOOL INC
28195 Kehrig St (48047-5218)
PHONE..................586 329-4922
Jeffrey S Rambow, *CEO*
Brian A Rambow, *President*
Sharon McCone, *General Mgr*
Erik Koch, *Manager*
EMP: 28
SQ FT: 20,000
SALES (est): 5.5MM **Privately Held**
SIC: 3599 Machine shop, jobbing & repair

(G-2790)
INNOVATIVE WORKS INC
28323 Anchor Dr (48047-5300)
PHONE..................586 231-1960
Wendy Moran, *President*
▼ **EMP:** 4
SALES (est): 706.2K **Privately Held**
SIC: 3599 Machine shop, jobbing & repair

(G-2791)
INOVISION SFTWR SOLUTIONS INC (PA)
50561 Chesterfield Rd (48051-3119)
PHONE..................586 598-8750
David Treadwell, *President*
Curtis Goff, *President*
EMP: 6
SQ FT: 1,400
SALES (est): 3MM **Privately Held**
WEB: www.inovision.net
SIC: 7373 7372 7371 Computer integrated systems design; application computer software; computer software development

(G-2792)
J SOLUTIONS LLC
25215 Terra Industrial Dr (48051-2729)
PHONE..................586 477-0127
Jan Jorgensen, *Mng Member*
EMP: 5
SALES (est): 131.7K **Privately Held**
SIC: 3499 Fabricated metal products

(G-2793)
KALB & ASSOCIATES INC
Also Called: Applied Tech Industries
50271 E Russell Schm (48051-2446)
PHONE..................586 949-2735
David Kalb, *President*
EMP: 40
SQ FT: 50,000
SALES: 4MM **Privately Held**
SIC: 3479 Coating of metals & formed products

(G-2794)
KEEPING YOU IN STITCHES
46545 Continental Dr (48047-5207)
PHONE..................586 421-9509
Lori Tessmar, *Owner*
EMP: 3
SALES (est): 135.3K **Privately Held**
SIC: 2395 Embroidery products, except schiffli machine

(G-2795)
KENA CORPORATION
45832 Edgewater St (48047-5321)
PHONE..................586 873-4761
Glen J Nayes, *President*
Kevin S Nayes, *Vice Pres*
EMP: 3
SQ FT: 3,500
SALES: 400K **Privately Held**
SIC: 3316 3313 3312 Cold-rolled strip or wire; ferrotitanium; tool & die steel & alloys

(G-2796)
KENT TOOL AND DIE INC
50605 Richard W Blvd (48051-2493)
P.O. Box 580, New Baltimore (48047-0580)
PHONE..................586 949-6600
Steve Ellis, *President*
Joseph Duffey, *Corp Secy*
Neil Haske, *Vice Pres*
Patricia Graf, *CTO*
EMP: 17 **EST:** 1966
SQ FT: 34,000
SALES (est): 2.3MM **Privately Held**
WEB: www.kentdie.com
SIC: 3544 Special dies & tools

(G-2797)
KIMASTLE CORPORATION
Also Called: Dager Systems
28291 Kehrig St (48047-5248)
PHONE..................586 949-2355
Kirk Gilewski, *President*
EMP: 82
SQ FT: 17,000
SALES (est): 27.1MM **Privately Held**
SIC: 3559 3544 Degreasing machines, automotive & industrial; special dies, tools, jigs & fixtures

(G-2798)
KNIGHT CARBIDE INC
48665 Structural Dr (48051-2666)
PHONE..................586 598-4888
Bruce Kyle, *President*
Chris Kyle, *Vice Pres*
Teresa Rylee, *Human Resources*
John Hoh, *Sales Staff*
EMP: 46
SQ FT: 24,000
SALES (est): 9.6MM **Privately Held**
WEB: www.knightcarbide.com
SIC: 3545 Tools & accessories for machine tools; cutting tools for machine tools

(G-2799)
KRAFTS & THINGZ
51382 Village Edge N (48047-3518)
PHONE..................810 689-2457
EMP: 4
SALES (est): 226.5K **Privately Held**
SIC: 2022 Mfg Cheese

(G-2800)
M & W MANUFACTURING CO LLC
Also Called: M & W Tubing
46409 Continental Dr (48047-5251)
PHONE..................586 741-8897
Jon Misch, *Vice Pres*
Robin Misch, *Vice Pres*
EMP: 8
SALES (est): 876K **Privately Held**
SIC: 3317 Steel pipe & tubes

(G-2801)
MARQUIS JEWELERS LTD
34748 23 Mile Rd (48047-4437)
PHONE..................586 725-3990
Matthew Gates, *President*
EMP: 5 **EST:** 1977
SQ FT: 1,750
SALES (est): 520K **Privately Held**
WEB: www.goldart.net
SIC: 3911 Jewelry, precious metal

(G-2802)
MAYNARD L MACLEAN L C
50855 E Russell Schmidt (48051-2457)
PHONE..................586 949-0471
Tom Wenzel, *Engineer*
Mark Brown, *Info Tech Mgr*
Tim Taylor,
Greg Lasonde,
Robert B Loebs,
◆ **EMP:** 77
SQ FT: 52,000
SALES (est): 14MM
SALES (corp-wide): 1.2B **Privately Held**
WEB: www.maclean-fogg.com
SIC: 3452 3451 Screws, metal; bolts, metal; nuts, metal; screw machine products
PA: Mac Lean-Fogg Company
1000 Allanson Rd
Mundelein IL 60060
847 566-0010

(G-2803)
METAL FORMING TECHNOLOGY INC
48630 Structural Dr (48051-2665)
PHONE..................586 949-4586
Fred Guimaraes, *CEO*
▲ **EMP:** 10
SQ FT: 30,000
SALES (est): 1.4MM
SALES (corp-wide): 133.5MM **Privately Held**
SIC: 3494 Plumbing & heating valves
PA: Gnutti Cirillo Spa
Via Ruca 96
Lumezzane BS 25065

(G-2804)
METALBUILT LLC
50171 E Russell Schmdt Bl (48051-2444)
PHONE..................586 786-9106
Ronald McCormick, *Mng Member*
EMP: 30
SALES (est): 7.2MM **Privately Held**
SIC: 3441 Fabricated structural metal

(G-2805)
METARIS HYDRAULICS
48175 Gratiot Ave (48051-2604)
PHONE..................586 949-4240
EMP: 3
SALES (est): 212.4K **Privately Held**
SIC: 3594 5084 Fluid power pumps & motors; industrial machinery & equipment

(G-2806)
MICHIGAN METAL TECH INC
50250 E Russell Schmidt (48051-2445)
P.O. Box 85367, Westland (48185-0367)
PHONE..................586 598-7800
EMP: 23
SALES (corp-wide): 4.5MM **Privately Held**
SIC: 3544 Mfg Industrial Metal Molds
PA: Michigan Metal Technologies, Inc.
50320 E Russell Schmdt Bl
Chesterfield MI

(G-2807)
MODULATED METALS INC
56409 Precision Dr (48051-3736)
PHONE..................586 749-8400
James C Stelzer, *President*
Frank S Campo, *Vice Pres*
Jacqueline M Campo, *Treasurer*
Geraldine G Stelzer, *Admin Sec*
EMP: 15
SQ FT: 13,400
SALES (est): 2.7MM **Privately Held**
WEB: www.modulatedmetals.com
SIC: 3444 Sheet metal specialties, not stamped

(G-2808)
MOTOR CITY STAMPINGS INC (PA)
47783 Gratiot Ave (48051-2721)
PHONE..................586 949-8420
Judith Kucway, *President*
Roger Kucway, *Vice Pres*
Bob Ritter, *Plant Mgr*
Steve Saunders, *Plant Mgr*
Beverly Hinton, *Opers Mgr*
▲ **EMP:** 330
SQ FT: 225,000
SALES (est): 64.9MM **Privately Held**
WEB: www.mcstamp.com
SIC: 3465 3544 Body parts, automobile: stamped metal; special dies, tools, jigs & fixtures

(G-2809)
MOTOR CITY STAMPINGS INC
Also Called: Plant 2
47781 Gratiot Ave (48051-2721)
PHONE..................586 949-8420
Roger Kucway, *President*
EMP: 123
SALES (corp-wide): 64.9MM **Privately Held**
WEB: www.mcstamp.com
SIC: 3465 3544 Body parts, automobile: stamped metal; special dies, tools, jigs & fixtures
PA: Motor City Stampings, Inc.
47783 Gratiot Ave
Chesterfield MI 48051
586 949-8420

(G-2810)
OFF SITE MFG TECH INC (PA)
50350 E Russell Sch (48051)
PHONE..................586 598-3110
Michael C Wallace, *President*
▲ **EMP:** 68
SALES (est): 8.7MM **Privately Held**
WEB: www.offsitemfg.com
SIC: 3713 Truck bodies & parts

(G-2811)
OFFSITE MANUFACTURING INC
Also Called: Off Site Manufacturing Tech
750 Structural Dr (48051)
PHONE..................586 598-8850
Michael C Wallace, *President*
EMP: 7 **Privately Held**
WEB: www.offsitemfg.com
SIC: 3714 Motor vehicle parts & accessories
PA: Off Site Manufacturing Technologies, Inc.
50350 E Russell Sch
Chesterfield MI 48051

(G-2812)
OGURA CORPORATION
55025 Gratiot Ave (48051-1249)
PHONE..................586 749-1900
Yasahiro Ogura, *Ch of Bd*
Masayoshi Takahashi, *Vice Ch Bd*
Steve Chrisopoulos, *Prdtn Mgr*
Andrew Shippy, *Production*
Keith Bentler, *Purchasing*
▲ **EMP:** 105
SQ FT: 111,000
SALES (est): 25.9MM **Privately Held**
SIC: 3714 5013 Clutches, motor vehicle; clutches
PA: Ogura Clutch Co., Ltd.
2-678, Aioicho
Kiryu GNM 376-0

(G-2813)
OTH CONSULTANTS INC
Also Called: Davalor Mold
46480 Continental Dr (48047-5206)
PHONE..................586 598-0100
James Puscas, *CEO*
Orman L Bernhardt, *Treasurer*
EMP: 200
SQ FT: 100,000
SALES (est): 43.2MM **Privately Held**
WEB: www.davalor.com
SIC: 3089 Injection molding of plastics

(G-2814)
P D E SYSTEMS INC
37230 26 Mile Rd (48047-2909)
PHONE..................586 725-3330
Paul Painter, *President*
Donna M Painter, *Treasurer*
EMP: 20 **EST:** 2012
SALES (est): 1.2MM **Privately Held**
SIC: 3599 Custom machinery

(G-2815)
PEDRI MOLD INC
46429 Continental Dr (48047-5251)
PHONE..................586 598-0882
Ernest Pedri, *President*

GEOGRAPHIC SECTION   Chesterfield - Macomb County (G-2846)

Ernest Pedri Jr, *Vice Pres*
Raymond Pedri, *Vice Pres*
EMP: 8
SQ FT: 5,300
SALES (est): 887.9K **Privately Held**
SIC: 3544 Industrial molds

(G-2816)
PFG ENTERPRISES INC (PA)
Also Called: Bellevue Processing
50271 E Rssell Smith Blvd (48051)
PHONE..................................586 755-1053
Kenneth Pape, *CEO*
Fred Pape, *President*
Sandra Pape, *Admin Sec*
EMP: 40
SQ FT: 50,000
SALES (est): 33.8MM **Privately Held**
SIC: 3471 Cleaning, polishing & finishing

(G-2817)
PIN POINT WELDING INC
50505 Metzen Dr (48051-3137)
PHONE..................................586 598-7382
Terry Yadon, *President*
Kim Yadon, *Corp Secy*
EMP: 4
SQ FT: 2,400
SALES (est): 240K **Privately Held**
SIC: 7692 Welding repair

(G-2818)
PLASTICS TECHNOLOGY CO
48325 Gratiot Ave (48051-2607)
PHONE..................................586 421-0479
Jimmie Williams, *Owner*
Denise Williams, *Co-Owner*
EMP: 3
SQ FT: 5,000
SALES (est): 307.6K **Privately Held**
SIC: 3089 Molding primary plastic

(G-2819)
POSEIDON INDUSTRIES INC
25700 Dhondt Ct (48051-2600)
PHONE..................................586 949-3550
John Degele, *President*
Mary Degele, *Treasurer*
EMP: 7
SQ FT: 12,000
SALES (est): 716.7K **Privately Held**
SIC: 3544 Special dies, tools, jigs & fixtures

(G-2820)
POWDER IT INC
46070 Edgewater St (48047-5325)
PHONE..................................586 949-0395
Michael Ursem, *President*
EMP: 5
SALES (est): 208.3K **Privately Held**
SIC: 2399 Powder puffs & mitts

(G-2821)
PRISM PLASTICS INC (DH)
52111 Sierra Dr (48047-1309)
PHONE..................................810 292-6300
Rodney Bricker, *President*
Jeff Wolf, *Treasurer*
EMP: 12
SQ FT: 28,000
SALES: 28MM
SALES (corp-wide): 225.3B **Publicly Held**
SIC: 3089 Automotive parts, plastic; injection molding of plastics
HQ: Marmon Engineered Components Company
181 W Madison St Fl 26
Chicago IL 60602
312 372-9500

(G-2822)
PROBE-TEC
48454 Harbor Dr (48047-3469)
PHONE..................................765 252-0257
Tom Houck, *Principal*
EMP: 4
SALES: 300K **Privately Held**
SIC: 3429 Manufactured hardware (general)

(G-2823)
PROFILE EDM LLC
50571 E Rssll Schmdt Blvd (48051-2452)
PHONE..................................586 949-4586

Ken Neiman,
EMP: 3 **EST:** 2008
SALES (est): 170.3K **Privately Held**
SIC: 3999 Manufacturing industries

(G-2824)
PROFILE MFG INC
50790 Richard W Blvd (48051-2496)
PHONE..................................586 598-0007
James Gall, *President*
EMP: 30
SQ FT: 30,000
SALES (est): 5.3MM **Privately Held**
WEB: www.profilemfg.com
SIC: 3714 Motor vehicle parts & accessories

(G-2825)
PROGRESSIVE FINISHING INC
50800 E Russell S (48051)
PHONE..................................586 949-6961
Paul R Hinderliter, *President*
Paul Hinderliter, *President*
Mike Stornant, *Mfg Mgr*
Sandy Scott, *QC Mgr*
Clint Meyering, *Treasurer*
EMP: 20
SQ FT: 42,000
SALES (est): 3.3MM **Privately Held**
SIC: 3599 Machine shop, jobbing & repair

(G-2826)
PROTOTECH LASER INC
Also Called: Plant 2
46340 Continental Dr (48047-5255)
PHONE..................................586 948-3032
Mike Williams, *Branch Mgr*
EMP: 12
SALES (corp-wide): 7.9MM **Privately Held**
SIC: 3714 Motor vehicle parts & accessories
PA: Prototech Laser, Inc.
46340 Continental Dr
Chesterfield MI 48047
586 598-6900

(G-2827)
PROTOTECH LASER INC (PA)
46340 Continental Dr (48047-5255)
PHONE..................................586 598-6900
Ed Genord, *President*
Donna Sharp, *Sales Staff*
Dave Mayle, *Manager*
Larry Hallesy, *Supervisor*
EMP: 30
SQ FT: 47,000
SALES (est): 7.9MM **Privately Held**
WEB: www.ptlaser.com
SIC: 3599 3444 3499 Machine & other job shop work; forming machine work, sheet metal; machine bases, metal

(G-2828)
QUALITY LUBE EXPRESS INC
50900 Donner Rd (48047-1753)
PHONE..................................586 421-0600
Prab Putta, *Principal*
EMP: 3
SALES (est): 259.9K **Privately Held**
SIC: 2992 Lubricating oils

(G-2829)
R C GRINDING AND TOOL COMPANY
49669 Leona Dr (48051-2476)
PHONE..................................586 949-4373
Robert E Collinge, *President*
EMP: 6 **EST:** 1973
SQ FT: 6,000
SALES: 260K **Privately Held**
SIC: 3599 Machine shop, jobbing & repair

(G-2830)
RAINBOW WRAP
46440 Jefferson Ave (48047-5365)
PHONE..................................586 949-3976
Thomas Svoboda, *Owner*
EMP: 10
SALES (est): 599.4K **Privately Held**
SIC: 2754 Wrapper & seal printing, gravure

(G-2831)
RICHMOND STEEL INC
50570 E Russell Schmidt (48051-2451)
PHONE..................................586 948-4700

Christopher M Austin, *President*
EMP: 26
SQ FT: 28,000
SALES (est): 5.6MM **Privately Held**
WEB: www.richmondsteel.biz
SIC: 3353 Aluminum sheet, plate & foil

(G-2832)
ROCKTECH SYSTEMS LLC
50250 E Russell Schmidt (48051-2445)
PHONE..................................586 330-9031
Rhyan Adamson, *Project Engr*
Steve Pierik, *Mng Member*
EMP: 50
SALES: 10MM **Privately Held**
SIC: 3089 Automotive parts, plastic

(G-2833)
ROYAL ALUMINUM AND STEEL INC
51401 Chesterfield Rd (48051-2002)
PHONE..................................586 421-0057
Roy Esposito, *President*
Lisa Esposito, *Vice Pres*
EMP: 10
SQ FT: 26,000
SALES: 1.8MM **Privately Held**
WEB: www.royalaluminum.com
SIC: 3496 Fencing, made from purchased wire

(G-2834)
S A S
33614 Lakeview St (48047-3486)
PHONE..................................586 725-6381
Thomas Yaschen, *Principal*
EMP: 4
SALES (est): 281.5K **Privately Held**
SIC: 3131 Footwear cut stock

(G-2835)
SABRE-TEC INC
48705 Structural Dr (48051-2664)
PHONE..................................586 949-5386
Jose Villalobos, *President*
David Gault, *Vice Pres*
EMP: 15 **EST:** 1980
SQ FT: 16,000
SALES (est): 2.4MM **Privately Held**
SIC: 3541 Numerically controlled metal cutting machine tools

(G-2836)
SAFIE SPECIALTY FOODS CO INC
25565 Terra Industrial Dr (48051-2734)
P.O. Box 46333, Mount Clemens (48046-6333)
PHONE..................................586 598-8282
Mary D Safie, *President*
EMP: 50
SQ FT: 22,000
SALES (est): 8.9MM **Privately Held**
WEB: www.safiespecialtyfoods.com
SIC: 2099 Food preparations

(G-2837)
SCHALLER CORPORATION (PA)
49495 Gratiot Ave (48051-2523)
PHONE..................................586 949-6000
Robert Schaller, *President*
Michael Evans, *General Mgr*
Albert Schaller, *Chairman*
Roger L Schaller, *Exec VP*
Arv Pikunas, *Plant Mgr*
EMP: 110
SQ FT: 92,000
SALES (est): 23.4MM **Privately Held**
SIC: 3469 Machine parts, stamped or pressed metal

(G-2838)
SCHALLER TOOL & DIE CO
49505 Gratiot Ave (48051-2525)
PHONE..................................586 949-5500
Steven G Shaller, *President*
Steven Schaller, *President*
Albert L Schaller, *Vice Pres*
Brian Torey, *Prdtn Mgr*
Roger L Schaller, *Treasurer*
EMP: 25
SQ FT: 28,000
SALES (est): 3.6MM **Privately Held**
SIC: 3544 3599 3545 Special dies & tools; jigs & fixtures; custom machinery; machine tool accessories

(G-2839)
SHARK TOOL & DIE INC
29500 25 Mile Rd (48051-1240)
PHONE..................................586 749-7400
David Gryspeerd, *President*
EMP: 6
SQ FT: 8,000
SALES (est): 807.5K **Privately Held**
SIC: 3544 3429 Special dies & tools; metal fasteners

(G-2840)
SHARP SCREW PRODUCTS INC
49650 Leona Dr (48051-2475)
PHONE..................................586 598-0440
Stephen A Burson, *President*
Susan Trottier, *Admin Sec*
EMP: 5
SQ FT: 8,300
SALES (est): 725.8K **Privately Held**
SIC: 3451 Screw machine products

(G-2841)
SL HOLDINGS INC
Also Called: Protective Land & Sea Systems
50625 Richard W Blvd (48051-2493)
PHONE..................................586 949-0818
Rhonda Wendland, *President*
EMP: 4
SALES (est): 417.3K **Privately Held**
SIC: 3441 Fabricated structural metal

(G-2842)
SONRIZE LLC
48051 Book Ct (48047-2252)
PHONE..................................586 329-3225
Charles Pope, *President*
EMP: 4
SALES (est): 302K **Privately Held**
SIC: 3648 Lighting equipment

(G-2843)
STELMATIC INDUSTRIES INC
50575 Richard W Blvd (48051-2487)
PHONE..................................586 949-0160
Edward K Stelzer, *President*
Marjorie Stelzer, *Corp Secy*
EMP: 10 **EST:** 1962
SQ FT: 20,000
SALES (est): 1.7MM **Privately Held**
SIC: 3444 Sheet metal specialties, not stamped

(G-2844)
SUR-FORM LLC
50320 E Russell Schmidt (48051-2447)
PHONE..................................586 221-1950
Edward Stacey, *President*
Robert Wolfbauer, *Admin Sec*
EMP: 41 **EST:** 2015
SQ FT: 30,000
SALES (est): 1.9MM **Privately Held**
SIC: 3089 Plastic containers, except foam
HQ: Big 3 Precision Products, Inc.
2923 S Wabash Ave
Centralia IL 62801
618 533-3251

(G-2845)
TACHYON CORPORATION
48705 Gratiot Ave (48051-2614)
PHONE..................................586 598-4320
David Nicholas, *President*
Gregory Mitchell, *Vice Pres*
Kenneth Young, *Treasurer*
Barry Thorp, *Admin Sec*
EMP: 50
SQ FT: 3,000
SALES: 4MM **Privately Held**
WEB: www.tachyoncorporation.com
SIC: 1796 3625 Machinery installation; electric controls & control accessories, industrial

(G-2846)
TECHNICAL STAMPING INC
50600 E Russell Schmidt (48051-2453)
PHONE..................................586 948-3285
Timothy Schaffner, *President*
Larry Laporte, *Vice Pres*
EMP: 5
SQ FT: 7,000
SALES (est): 683.6K **Privately Held**
SIC: 3469 Stamping metal for the trade

Chesterfield - Macomb County (G-2847)

(G-2847)
THEUT PRODUCTS INC
47875 Gratiot Ave (48051-2722)
PHONE.....................586 949-1300
Eric Theut, *Manager*
EMP: 45
SALES (corp-wide): 15.4MM **Privately Held**
WEB: www.theutproducts.com
SIC: 3273 Ready-mixed concrete
PA: Theut Products, Inc.
73408 Van Dyke Rd
Bruce Twp MI 48065
586 752-4541

(G-2848)
TI GROUP AUTO SYSTEMS LLC
Also Called: TI Automotive Systems
30600 Commerce Blvd (48051-1228)
PHONE.....................586 948-6006
Charlie Cronenworth, *Manager*
EMP: 115
SALES (corp-wide): 3.9B **Privately Held**
WEB: www.tiautomotive.com
SIC: 3714 3643 3429 Motor vehicle parts & accessories; current-carrying wiring devices; manufactured hardware (general)
HQ: Ti Group Automotive Systems, Llc
2020 Taylor Rd
Auburn Hills MI 48326
248 296-8000

(G-2849)
TOOL COMPANY INC
48707 Gratiot Ave (48051-2614)
PHONE.....................586 598-1519
Don Artman, *President*
EMP: 6
SQ FT: 5,000
SALES (est): 558.5K **Privately Held**
SIC: 3544 Special dies & tools

(G-2850)
TRI-TOOL BORING MACHINE CO
46440 Continental Dr (48047-5206)
PHONE.....................586 598-0036
Salvatore Riera, *President*
EMP: 15
SQ FT: 8,500
SALES (est): 2.3MM **Privately Held**
WEB: www.tri-tool.com
SIC: 3599 Machine shop, jobbing & repair

(G-2851)
TROY TUBE & MANUFACTURING CO
50100 E Russell Schmidt B (48051-2443)
P.O. Box 696, New Baltimore (48047-0696)
PHONE.....................586 949-8700
John Maniaci, *President*
EMP: 100 **EST:** 1978
SQ FT: 70,000
SALES: 22.4MM **Privately Held**
WEB: www.troytube.com
SIC: 3498 7692 Tube fabricating (contract bending & shaping); welding repair

(G-2852)
UTICA AEROSPACE INC
26950 23 Mile Rd (48051-1999)
PHONE.....................586 598-9300
Kathy Phillips, *Principal*
EMP: 10
SALES (est): 528.9K **Privately Held**
SIC: 3812 Acceleration indicators & systems components, aerospace

(G-2853)
UTICA STEEL INC
48000 Structural Dr (48051-2629)
PHONE.....................586 949-1900
David Kraemer, *President*
Charles Lafontaine, *Vice Pres*
Ray Mach, *Vice Pres*
Chuck Lafontaine, *Plant Mgr*
Sherry Dawson, *Treasurer*
EMP: 75
SQ FT: 75,000
SALES (est): 28.9MM **Privately Held**
WEB: www.uticasteel.com
SIC: 3441 Fabricated structural metal

(G-2854)
VERSTAR GROUP INC (PA)
Also Called: Accurate Welding
50305 Patricia St (48051-3803)
PHONE.....................586 465-5033
Derek Starks, *President*
Tom Vertin, *Vice Pres*
Tony Vincent, *Vice Pres*
EMP: 17
SALES (est): 3.7MM **Privately Held**
SIC: 3599 Machine shop, jobbing & repair

(G-2855)
VISIONCRAFT
28161 Kehrig St (48047-5218)
PHONE.....................586 949-6540
Nick Sorvala, *Administration*
EMP: 5
SALES (est): 374.6K **Privately Held**
SIC: 5048 3827 Optometric equipment & supplies; optical instruments & lenses

(G-2856)
WELDERS & PRESSES INC
27295 Luckino Dr (48047-5229)
PHONE.....................586 948-4300
EMP: 5
SALES (est): 264.5K **Privately Held**
SIC: 7692 Welding Repair

(G-2857)
Z MOLD & ENGINEERING INC
46390 Continental Dr (48047-5255)
PHONE.....................586 948-5000
Konrad Zuschlag, *President*
Sheryl Zuschlag, *Vice Pres*
EMP: 8
SQ FT: 7,500
SALES (est): 605K **Privately Held**
WEB: www.zmold.com
SIC: 3544 Industrial molds

China
St. Clair County

(G-2858)
ANTOLIN INTERIORS USA INC
Also Called: Mitc St Clair
4662 Puttygut Rd (48054-2109)
PHONE.....................810 329-1045
Joe McCluskey, *General Mgr*
EMP: 600
SALES (corp-wide): 33.3MM **Privately Held**
SIC: 3714 Motor vehicle body components & frame
HQ: Antolin Interiors Usa, Inc.
1700 Atlantic Blvd
Auburn Hills MI 48326
248 373-1749

(G-2859)
DIE & SLIDE TECHNOLOGIES INC
6630 Belle River Rd (48054-2401)
PHONE.....................810 326-0986
Steven G Reeves, *President*
EMP: 3
SALES: 1MM **Privately Held**
SIC: 3544 Special dies & tools

(G-2860)
HEWTECH ELECTRONICS
5691 Starville Rd (48054-4207)
PHONE.....................810 765-0820
Scott Hewelt, *Owner*
EMP: 3
SALES (est): 140K **Privately Held**
WEB: www.hewtechelect.com
SIC: 3672 3674 3625 Printed circuit boards; hybrid integrated circuits; control equipment, electric

(G-2861)
J G WELDING & MAINTENANCE INC
7059 Lindsey Rd (48054-2304)
PHONE.....................586 758-0150
Julius Gaffke, *President*
EMP: 4
SQ FT: 6,000
SALES: 600K **Privately Held**
SIC: 7692 Welding repair

(G-2862)
THREE D PRECISION TOOL
5405 Starville Rd (48054-3612)
PHONE.....................810 765-9418
Dale Lindow, *Owner*
EMP: 3
SALES (est): 160.5K **Privately Held**
SIC: 3639 Household appliances

Clare
Clare County

(G-2863)
ADVANCED BATTERY CONCEPTS LLC
8 Consumes Energy Pkwy (48617)
PHONE.....................989 424-6645
Edward O Shaffer II, *CEO*
Ronald Beebe, *Vice Chairman*
Michael Everett, *COO*
Gerald Mullis, *COO*
Jon Joslin, *CFO*
▲ **EMP:** 22
SALES (est): 4.8MM **Privately Held**
SIC: 3691 Storage batteries

(G-2864)
ATHEY PRECISION INC
2021 S Athey Ave (48617-9776)
PHONE.....................989 386-4523
John Pirosko, *President*
Regina Pirosko, *Admin Sec*
EMP: 9
SQ FT: 6,000
SALES (est): 487.8K **Privately Held**
SIC: 3544 Special dies & tools

(G-2865)
BURNRITE PELLET CORPORATION
2495 E Rock Rd (48617-9424)
PHONE.....................989 429-1067
James Swan, *President*
Mark Ghile, *Vice Pres*
Jim Eckman, *Treasurer*
Tim Walker, *Shareholder*
EMP: 5
SQ FT: 800
SALES: 500K **Privately Held**
SIC: 2448 Pallets, wood

(G-2866)
CLARE COUNTY REVIEW
105 W 4th St Ste 1 (48617-1458)
PHONE.....................989 386-4414
Patricia Maurer, *Owner*
Sherry Landon, *Graphic Designe*
EMP: 5
SALES: 300K **Privately Held**
WEB: www.clarecountyreview.com
SIC: 2711 Newspapers: publishing only, not printed on site

(G-2867)
CLARE PRINT & PULP
409 N Mcewan St (48617-1402)
PHONE.....................989 386-3497
Pete Montini, *Owner*
EMP: 4 **EST:** 1975
SQ FT: 1,600
SALES (est): 230K **Privately Held**
SIC: 5943 2752 5044 Office forms & supplies; lithographing on metal; office equipment

(G-2868)
DYNA- BIGNELL PRODUCTS LLC
201 W 3rd St (48617-1408)
PHONE.....................989 418-5050
EMP: 4
SALES (est): 508.8K **Privately Held**
SIC: 3541 Machine tools, metal cutting type

(G-2869)
E & M CORES INC
Also Called: E and M Cores
9805 S Athey Ave (48617-9688)
PHONE.....................989 386-9223
Jeff Thomski, *Owner*
EMP: 4
SALES (est): 280.1K **Privately Held**
SIC: 2655 3321 3272 Fiber cans, drums & similar products; gray & ductile iron foundries; concrete products

(G-2870)
FILCON INC
528 Pioneer Pkwy (48617-8812)
PHONE.....................989 386-2986
O David Rogers, *CEO*
Brian Johnson, *President*
Richard I Rogers, *Vice Pres*
Wesley E Parker, *Treasurer*
▲ **EMP:** 10
SALES (est): 2.6MM
SALES (corp-wide): 5.3MM **Privately Held**
WEB: www.filcon.com
SIC: 2671 3089 3081 Plastic film, coated or laminated for packaging; plastic processing; unsupported plastics film & sheet
PA: Rogers Group, Inc.
528 Pioneer Pkwy
Clare MI 48617
989 386-7393

(G-2871)
GREEN GABLES SAW MILL
5605 E Surrey Rd (48617-9793)
PHONE.....................989 386-7846
Andrew Byler, *Principal*
EMP: 3
SALES (est): 160.4K **Privately Held**
SIC: 2421 Sawmills & planing mills, general

(G-2872)
INTEGRITY MACHINE SERVICES
Also Called: IMS
5615 S Clare Ave (48617-8608)
PHONE.....................989 386-0216
Larry Kleinhardt, *President*
Judy Kleinhardt, *Admin Sec*
EMP: 7
SALES (est): 590K **Privately Held**
WEB: www.imsmachines.net
SIC: 3599 Machine shop, jobbing & repair

(G-2873)
JD METALWORKS INC
635 Industrial Dr (48617-9225)
PHONE.....................989 386-3231
Duane Gottsclark, *President*
John Miller, *Vice Pres*
Matt Alexander, *Plant Mgr*
Jennifer Crystal, *Human Resources*
EMP: 70
SQ FT: 30,000
SALES (est): 17.4MM **Privately Held**
WEB: www.jdmetalworks.com
SIC: 3449 Miscellaneous metalwork

(G-2874)
JT BAKERS
127 W 4th St Ste 2 (48617-1410)
PHONE.....................989 424-5102
EMP: 3
SALES (est): 179.4K **Privately Held**
SIC: 2051 Bakery: wholesale or wholesale/retail combined

(G-2875)
KTR PRINTING INC
Also Called: Integrity Printing
801 Industrial Dr (48617-9140)
P.O. Box 809 (48617-0809)
PHONE.....................989 386-9740
Dale Smith, *President*
Kirk Smith, *Vice Pres*
Scott Richards, *Executive*
▲ **EMP:** 15
SQ FT: 29,000
SALES: 4MM **Privately Held**
WEB: www.integrityprinting.com
SIC: 2759 Commercial printing

(G-2876)
LETHERER TRUSS INC (PA)
851 Industrial Dr (48617-9140)
PHONE.................................989 386-4999
Steven C Letherer, *President*
Bernard C Letherer, *Corp Secy*
Jeffrey Letherer, *VP Opers*
Steve Letherer, *Marketing Staff*
Christena Gotts, *Admin Sec*
EMP: 37
SQ FT: 19,600
SALES (est): 7.2MM **Privately Held**
SIC: 2439 Trusses, except roof: laminated lumber; trusses, wooden roof

(G-2877)
MID-MICHIGAN INDUSTRIES INC
Also Called: Mid Michigan Industries
790 Industrial Dr (48617-9224)
PHONE.................................989 386-7707
Chris Zeigler, *Manager*
EMP: 24
SALES (corp-wide): 5.9MM **Privately Held**
WEB: www.mmionline.com
SIC: 8331 3471 2396 Vocational training agency; plating & polishing; automotive & apparel trimmings
PA: Mid-Michigan Industries, Inc.
    2426 Parkway Dr
    Mount Pleasant MI 48858
    989 773-6918

(G-2878)
MILLERS WOODWORKING
3378 E Beaverton Rd (48617-9430)
PHONE.................................989 386-8110
Mettie Miller, *Owner*
EMP: 6
SALES (est): 600K **Privately Held**
SIC: 2449 Wood containers

(G-2879)
NEVILL SUPPLY INCORPORATED
8415 S Eberhart Ave (48617-9736)
PHONE.................................989 386-4522
Donald Nevill, *President*
Andrew Nevill, *Vice Pres*
EMP: 9
SQ FT: 5,000
SALES: 2.3MM **Privately Held**
SIC: 5211 1799 2499 Fencing; fence construction; snow fence, wood

(G-2880)
NORTHERN EXTRUSION INC
4915 E Colonville Rd (48617-8920)
PHONE.................................989 386-7556
Steven Schunk, *President*
EMP: 3
SALES (est): 99.9K **Privately Held**
SIC: 3355 Extrusion ingot, aluminum: made in rolling mills

(G-2881)
NORTHERN LOGISTICS LLC
805 Industrial Dr (48617-9140)
PHONE.................................989 386-2389
Ron Kunse,
Tom Kunse,
Steve Stark,
EMP: 36
SQ FT: 10,000
SALES (est): 6MM **Privately Held**
WEB: www.northernlogisticsinc.com
SIC: 3089 4213 Plastic processing; trucking, except local

(G-2882)
NORTHERN PALLET
4915 E Colonville Rd (48617-8920)
P.O. Box 650 (48617-0650)
PHONE.................................989 386-7556
Steven Schunk, *Executive*
EMP: 4 **EST:** 2008
SALES (est): 406.9K **Privately Held**
SIC: 2448 Pallets, wood

(G-2883)
PACKARD FARMS LLC
6584 S Brand Ave (48617-9645)
PHONE.................................989 386-3816
Roger Packard, *President*
EMP: 30

SQ FT: 3,500
SALES (est): 3.1MM **Privately Held**
SIC: 3523 Barn, silo, poultry, dairy & livestock machinery

(G-2884)
PIONEER POLE BUILDINGS N INC
7400 S Clare Ave (48617-8619)
PHONE.................................989 386-2570
Robert Griffor, *President*
Joan Griffor, *Vice Pres*
EMP: 20
SALES (est): 3.8MM **Privately Held**
SIC: 1542 3448 2452 7389 Farm building construction; prefabricated metal buildings; prefabricated wood buildings;

(G-2885)
ROBMAR PLASTICS INC
1385 E Maple Rd (48617-9455)
P.O. Box 326 (48617-0326)
PHONE.................................989 386-9600
Robert D Ohler, *President*
Martha Ohler, *Admin Sec*
EMP: 5
SQ FT: 10,000
SALES (est): 920.2K **Privately Held**
WEB: www.robmarplastics.com
SIC: 3089 Plastic processing

(G-2886)
ROBOTIC WELDED PARTS INC
314 E 4th St (48617-1500)
P.O. Box 298 (48617-0298)
PHONE.................................989 386-5376
Scott Carter, *President*
Robbie A Maie, *Treasurer*
Gary Cotter, *Manager*
▲ **EMP:** 30
SALES (est): 4.2MM **Privately Held**
WEB: www.lincolnelectric.coop
SIC: 7692 Welding repair

(G-2887)
ROGERS ATHLETIC
495 Pioneer Pkwy (48617-8813)
P.O. Box 208 (48617-0208)
PHONE.................................989 386-7393
EMP: 8
SALES (est): 199.7K **Privately Held**
SIC: 3949 Sporting & athletic goods

(G-2888)
SHARPCO WLDG & FABRICATION LLC
26 Consumers Energy Pkwy (48617-9540)
PHONE.................................989 915-0556
Seth Sharp, *Mng Member*
EMP: 4
SALES (est): 356.7K **Privately Held**
SIC: 7692 Welding repair

(G-2889)
SOUND PRODUCTIONS ENTRMT
Also Called: Soundcase
1601 E Maple Rd (48617-8806)
P.O. Box 236 (48617-0236)
PHONE.................................989 386-2221
James Paetschow, *President*
Ashley Bellmer, *Sales Staff*
EMP: 25
SQ FT: 15,000
SALES (est): 3.5MM **Privately Held**
SIC: 3648 3161 7929 3663 Lighting equipment; cases, carrying; disc jockey service; radio & TV communications equipment; commercial indusl & institutional electric lighting fixtures

(G-2890)
STAGERIGHT CORPORATION (PA)
Also Called: Stage Right
495 Pioneer Pkwy (48617-8813)
PHONE.................................989 386-7393
David Rogers, *President*
Tim Hockemeyer, *Engineer*
Wes Parker, *Controller*
Judy Fargher, *Sales Staff*
Kate Nicefield, *Sales Staff*
◆ **EMP:** 180
SQ FT: 150,000

SALES (est): 43.3MM **Privately Held**
WEB: www.stageright.com
SIC: 3999 3444 Stage hardware & equipment, except lighting; sheet metalwork

(G-2891)
TRANQUIL SYSTEMS INTL LLC
528 Pioneer Pkwy (48617-8812)
PHONE.................................800 631-0212
Kevin Beavers, *President*
Tim Moore, *Manager*
EMP: 10
SQ FT: 15,000
SALES (est): 716.4K
SALES (corp-wide): 5.3MM **Privately Held**
SIC: 2521 Wood office furniture
PA: Rogers Group, Inc.
    528 Pioneer Pkwy
    Clare MI 48617
    989 386-7393

(G-2892)
WHITE PALLET CHAIR
4961 E Colonville Rd (48617-8920)
PHONE.................................989 424-8771
Tammi L Beckley, *Principal*
EMP: 3
SALES (est): 150K **Privately Held**
SIC: 2448 Pallets, wood & wood with metal

Clarklake
Jackson County

(G-2893)
ADVANCED ELECTRIC
10300 Hayes Dr (49234-9750)
PHONE.................................517 529-9050
Andrew Slabey, *President*
EMP: 3
SALES (est): 263.3K **Privately Held**
SIC: 1731 3599 5063 Electrical work; industrial machinery; switchboards

(G-2894)
AIRMASTER FAN COMPANY
Also Called: Autumaire Fan Co.
9229 S Meridian Rd (49234-9613)
PHONE.................................517 764-2300
Dick Stone, *CEO*
Lawrence L Bullen, *Vice Pres*
Ronald Johnson, *CFO*
Robert La Zebnik, *Treasurer*
Megan Stevens, *Manager*
▲ **EMP:** 60
SQ FT: 400,000
SALES: 13MM
SALES (corp-wide): 102.6MM **Privately Held**
WEB: www.airmasterfan.com
SIC: 3564 Ventilating fans: industrial or commercial
HQ: Maico Elektroapparate-Fabrik Gesellschaft Mit Beschrankter Haftung
    Steinbeisstr. 20
    Villingen-Schwenningen 78056
    772 069-40

(G-2895)
CLARKLAKE MACHINE INCORPORATED
9451 S Meridian Rd (49234-9613)
PHONE.................................517 529-9454
Michael P De Karske, *President*
Mark H De Karske, *Vice Pres*
Matt Dekarske, *Engineer*
EMP: 25 **EST:** 1968
SQ FT: 20,000
SALES (est): 3.3MM **Privately Held**
WEB: www.clarklakemachine.com
SIC: 3599 Machine shop, jobbing & repair

(G-2896)
CLEARWATER TREATMENT SYSTEMS
4700 Industrial Dr (49234-9636)
PHONE.................................517 688-9316
Paul Gietek, *CEO*
EMP: 4
SALES (est): 276.7K **Privately Held**
SIC: 2899 Water treating compounds

(G-2897)
NU-ICE AGE INC
9700 Myers Rd (49234-9642)
PHONE.................................517 990-0665
Edward L Cooper, *President*
EMP: 10
SALES (est): 750K **Privately Held**
SIC: 3569 Ice crushers (machinery)

(G-2898)
PRODUCTION SAW & MACHINE CO
9091 S Meridian Rd (49234-9613)
PHONE.................................517 529-4014
James M Vancalbergh, *CEO*
David C Bevier, *President*
Greg Vancalbergh, *Exec VP*
Terry Maynard, *Vice Pres*
Steve Shong, *Engineer*
EMP: 55
SQ FT: 113,000
SALES (est): 12.2MM **Privately Held**
WEB: www.productionsaw.com
SIC: 3599 Machine shop, jobbing & repair

(G-2899)
RUHLMAN RACE CARS
2132 Jefferson Rd (49234-9675)
PHONE.................................517 529-4661
Brian G Ruhlman, *Owner*
EMP: 3
SALES (est): 405.6K **Privately Held**
SIC: 3711 Automobile assembly, including specialty automobiles

(G-2900)
SPEC CORPORATION
4701 Industrial Dr (49234-9636)
P.O. Box 333 (49234-0333)
PHONE.................................517 529-4105
Ronald Miller, *President*
Bonita Miller, *Admin Sec*
EMP: 5 **EST:** 1972
SQ FT: 7,000
SALES (est): 506.2K **Privately Held**
SIC: 8711 3613 Electrical or electronic engineering; control panels, electric

(G-2901)
STONECRAFTERS INC
4807 Industrial Dr (49234-9636)
PHONE.................................517 529-4990
Hunter Andrews, *President*
Kath Rhodes, *Admin Sec*
EMP: 13
SALES (est): 1.2MM **Privately Held**
SIC: 3281 2821 Table tops, marble; granite, cut & shaped; plastics materials & resins

(G-2902)
YOUR HOME TOWN USA INC
Also Called: Platemate
9301 Hyde Rd (49234-9023)
P.O. Box 335 (49234-0335)
PHONE.................................517 529-9421
Sharon Jones, *President*
EMP: 25
SQ FT: 2,400
SALES (est): 3.9MM **Privately Held**
SIC: 7311 2759 2721 Advertising agencies; commercial printing; periodicals: publishing only

Clarkston
Oakland County

(G-2903)
ACME GROOVING TOOL CO
7409 S Village Dr (48346-5000)
PHONE.................................800 633-8828
EMP: 17 **EST:** 1953
SQ FT: 9,000
SALES: 1.1MM **Privately Held**
SIC: 3545 Mfg Machine Tool Accessories

(G-2904)
ADE INC
8949 Dixie Hwy (48348-4246)
P.O. Box 660 (48347-0660)
PHONE.................................248 625-7200
Bryan Ellis, *President*
Jim Haggerty, *Opers Staff*

Clarkston - Oakland County (G-2905)
GEOGRAPHIC SECTION

Bridget McEvilly, *Marketing Mgr*
Penny Ward, *Office Mgr*
EMP: 7
SQ FT: 1,200
SALES (est): 1MM **Privately Held**
WEB: www.adeincorp.com
SIC: 3695 Computer software tape & disks: blank, rigid & floppy

(G-2905)
ADVANCED DEF VHCL SYSTEMS CORP
Also Called: Advs
6716 Ridgeview Dr (48346-4461)
PHONE 248 391-3200
James Leblanc Jr, *President*
Richard Leblanc, *Exec VP*
EMP: 35
SALES (est): 5.8MM **Privately Held**
SIC: 3711 Motor vehicles & car bodies

(G-2906)
ADVANCED POLYMERS COMPOSITES
7111 Dixie Hwy 110 (48346-2077)
PHONE 248 766-1507
Robert Bogart, *Principal*
EMP: 3
SALES (est): 261.2K **Privately Held**
SIC: 2821 Thermosetting materials

(G-2907)
ANSCO PATTERN & MACHINE CO
7945 Perry Lake Rd (48348-4646)
PHONE 248 625-1362
Brian Anderson, *Owner*
EMP: 4
SALES: 750K **Privately Held**
SIC: 3089 Injection molded finished plastic products

(G-2908)
AUTOMOTIVE LIGHTING LLC
5600 Bow Pointe Dr (48346-3115)
PHONE 248 418-3000
EMP: 3 **Privately Held**
SIC: 3647 Headlights (fixtures), vehicular
HQ: Automotive Lighting Llc
3900 Automation Ave
Auburn Hills MI 48326
248 418-3000

(G-2909)
C & B GLASS INC
3960 S Ortonville Rd (48346-1246)
PHONE 248 625-4376
Donald Short Jr, *CEO*
EMP: 3
SALES (est): 157.8K **Privately Held**
SIC: 3231 Products of purchased glass

(G-2910)
CABINET ONE INC
4571 White Lake Ct (48346-2549)
PHONE 248 625-9440
Joseph D Delude, *President*
Caroline Frericks, *Vice Pres*
EMP: 4
SQ FT: 10,440
SALES: 190K **Privately Held**
SIC: 2434 Vanities, bathroom: wood

(G-2911)
CLARKSON SMOOTHIE INC
7150 Sashabaw Rd (48346-4738)
PHONE 248 620-8005
EMP: 3
SALES (est): 147.9K **Privately Held**
SIC: 2037 Frozen fruits & vegetables

(G-2912)
CLARKSTON CONTROL PRODUCTS
4809 Crestview Dr (48348-3946)
PHONE 248 394-1430
Richard E Kopicko, *President*
Diana Kopicko, *Treasurer*
EMP: 6
SQ FT: 2,250
SALES (est): 643.5K **Privately Held**
WEB: www.clarkstoncontrols.com
SIC: 8711 3613 7699 Industrial engineers; control panels, electric; industrial equipment services

(G-2913)
CLARKSTON COURTS LLC
Also Called: Parker's Hilltop Brewery
6110 Dixie Hwy (48346-3409)
PHONE 248 383-8444
Dave Parker, *President*
Nico Campbell, *Corp Secy*
Heather Karl, *Opers Mgr*
EMP: 200
SALES (est): 12.4MM **Privately Held**
SIC: 5181 2082 Beer & ale; ale (alcoholic beverage)

(G-2914)
CLAWSON TANK COMPANY (PA)
4701 White Lake Rd (48346-2554)
PHONE 248 625-8700
Terrance Groh, *President*
Robert Harding, *Buyer*
Dick Harding, *Treasurer*
Richard T Harding, *Treasurer*
Edward Moskwa, *Regl Sales Mgr*
EMP: 45 **EST:** 1953
SQ FT: 100,000
SALES (est): 9.9MM **Privately Held**
WEB: www.clawsontank.com
SIC: 3443 Tanks, standard or custom fabricated: metal plate; containers, shipping (bombs, etc.): metal plate; process vessels, industrial: metal plate

(G-2915)
COMPLEX TOOL & MACHINE INC
Also Called: J W Briney Products
6460 Sashabaw Rd (48346-2262)
PHONE 248 625-0664
John H Bender, *President*
Patricia A Bender, *Corp Secy*
Rachel Toole, *Manager*
EMP: 5
SQ FT: 11,000
SALES (est): 575.5K **Privately Held**
WEB: www.complexmachine.ca
SIC: 3599 3545 Machine shop, jobbing & repair; machine tool accessories

(G-2916)
DEKES CONCRETE INC
6653 Andersonville Rd (48346-2701)
PHONE 810 686-5570
Sam Dekalita, *President*
EMP: 20
SQ FT: 9,250
SALES (est): 2MM **Privately Held**
SIC: 3273 Ready-mixed concrete

(G-2917)
E D C O PUBLISHING INC
Also Called: Edco Media
990 S Baldwin Rd (48346-3608)
PHONE 248 690-9184
Edna Stephens, *President*
EMP: 7
SQ FT: 2,500
SALES (est): 541.9K **Privately Held**
WEB: www.edcopublishing.com
SIC: 2741 2731 Miscellaneous publishing; book publishing

(G-2918)
ENDOSCOPIC SOLUTIONS
5701 Bow Pointe Dr # 370 (48346-3198)
PHONE 248 625-4055
M Veslav Stecevic, *Principal*
EMP: 8
SALES (est): 619.8K **Privately Held**
SIC: 3845 Endoscopic equipment, electromedical

(G-2919)
EXPORT SERVICE INTERNATIONAL
Also Called: RDM Associates
8098 Caribou Lake Ln (48346-1981)
PHONE 248 620-7100
Cynthia Sikina, *CEO*
Richard Miller, *President*
EMP: 3
SALES (est): 230K **Privately Held**
SIC: 7379 7372 7373 Computer related consulting services; business oriented computer software; computer systems analysis & design

(G-2920)
EYEWEAR DETROIT COMPANY
6466 Shappie Rd (48348-1960)
PHONE 248 396-2214
EMP: 3 **EST:** 2018
SALES (est): 232K **Privately Held**
SIC: 3827 Optical instruments & lenses

(G-2921)
FLOTRONICS INC
Also Called: M A T
7214 Gateway Park Dr (48346-2574)
PHONE 248 620-1820
Thomas Miller, *Engineer*
John Murphy, *Engineer*
Michael Schmaltz, *Manager*
EMP: 9
SALES (corp-wide): 12.1MM **Privately Held**
WEB: www.flotronicsinc.com
SIC: 3354 Aluminum extruded products
PA: Flotronics, Inc.
10435 Ortonville Rd Ste A
Clarkston MI 48348
248 627-4556

(G-2922)
FLOW COATINGS LLC
4866 White Lake Rd (48346-2555)
PHONE 248 625-3052
Andrew Suman, *Mng Member*
EMP: 3
SALES (est): 501.1K **Privately Held**
SIC: 2851 Paints & allied products

(G-2923)
G & G METAL PRODUCTS INC
9575 Rattalee Lake Rd (48346-1531)
PHONE 248 625-8099
Gerald Rumph, *President*
Jerry Rumph, *General Mgr*
EMP: 4
SALES: 200K **Privately Held**
SIC: 3599 Machine shop, jobbing & repair

(G-2924)
G G & D INC
Also Called: Print Shop, The
5911 Dixie Hwy (48346-3361)
PHONE 248 623-1212
Eugene Metzger, *President*
EMP: 8
SQ FT: 1,800
SALES (est): 1MM **Privately Held**
SIC: 2752 Commercial printing, offset

(G-2925)
HD SELCATING PAV SOLUTIONS LLC
8205 Valleyview Dr (48348-4042)
PHONE 248 241-6526
Alyssa Retsel,
David Retsel,
EMP: 2
SALES: 1MM **Privately Held**
SIC: 2951 1611 1771 1799 Asphalt paving mixtures & blocks; surfacing & paving; resurfacing contractor; driveway, parking lot & blacktop contractors; parking lot maintenance

(G-2926)
HOLLOW METAL SERVICES LLC
5311 Whipple Lake Rd (48348-3056)
PHONE 248 394-0233
Randall McLaughlin, *Principal*
EMP: 3
SALES (est): 144.3K **Privately Held**
SIC: 5963 3442 7641 Direct selling establishments; metal doors, sash & trim; reupholstery & furniture repair

(G-2927)
I B P INC
Also Called: Industrial Building Panels
9295 Allen Rd (48348-2726)
PHONE 248 588-4710
Clarence E Johns, *President*
EMP: 20
SQ FT: 25,000
SALES (est): 3.5MM **Privately Held**
WEB: www.ibp.com
SIC: 3448 Panels for prefabricated metal buildings

(G-2928)
I S MY DEPARTMENT INC
711 Dixie Hwy 366 (48346)
PHONE 248 622-0622
EMP: 3
SALES (est): 221.2K **Privately Held**
SIC: 3571 Mfg Electronic Computers

(G-2929)
IBC NORTH AMERICA INC (HQ)
4545 Clawson Tank Dr (48346-2581)
PHONE 248 625-8700
Richard Harding, *President*
Dick Harding, *President*
Micheal Harding, *Exec VP*
Robert Harding Jr, *Treasurer*
Terrance Groh, *Admin Sec*
▲ **EMP:** 41
SALES (est): 10.9MM **Privately Held**
WEB: www.ibcna.com
SIC: 2631 Container, packaging & boxboard

(G-2930)
IBC NORTH AMERICA INC
4750 Clawson Tank Dr (48346-0001)
P.O. Box 1050 (48347-1050)
PHONE 248 625-8700
Lee Gearig, *Principal*
EMP: 13 **Privately Held**
WEB: www.ibcna.com
SIC: 2631 Container, packaging & boxboard
HQ: Ibc North America, Inc.
4545 Clawson Tank Dr
Clarkston MI 48346
248 625-8700

(G-2931)
INSTANT MARINE INC
5020 White Lake Rd (48346-2641)
PHONE 248 398-1011
Rick Hambrick, *President*
Margaret Hambrick, *Admin Sec*
▲ **EMP:** 7
SQ FT: 3,500
SALES (est): 1.4MM **Privately Held**
WEB: www.instantmarinedocks.com
SIC: 3448 Docks: prefabricated metal

(G-2932)
INTEGRATED PROGRAM MGT LLC
5904 Warbler Dr (48346-2974)
PHONE 248 241-9257
Rick Heys, *Managing Prtnr*
Rick Heyes, *Mng Member*
Paul Bazely,
EMP: 2
SALES: 2.5MM **Privately Held**
WEB: www.integrated-pm.com
SIC: 8742 3465 3714 8741 Marketing consulting services; automotive stampings; motor vehicle parts & accessories; business management;

(G-2933)
KIMBERLY LIGHTING LLC
Also Called: Kimberly Led Lighting
5827 Terex (48346-1717)
PHONE 888 480-0070
Laura Squier, *Mng Member*
Kim Jenkins, *Agent*
▲ **EMP:** 38
SQ FT: 50,000
SALES (est): 815.6K **Privately Held**
SIC: 3674 Light emitting diodes

(G-2934)
LAWRENCE PLASTICS LLC (PA)
6338 Sashabaw Rd (48346-2260)
PHONE 248 475-0186
Pruitt Pendergrass, *Materials Mgr*
Mike Bloomfield, *Engineer*
Laura McKay, *Controller*
Matthew Cotter, *Mng Member*
Michael Bloomfield,
▼ **EMP:** 100
SQ FT: 60,000
SALES (est): 27.5MM **Privately Held**
SIC: 3089 Injection molding of plastics

Clarkston - Oakland County (G-2964)

(G-2935)
MACHINING TECHNOLOGIES LLC
9635 Davisburg Rd (48348-4135)
PHONE..................248 379-4201
Todd Horner, *Mng Member*
EMP: 4
SQ FT: 6,500
SALES: 1.2MM **Privately Held**
SIC: 3545 Precision tools, machinists'

(G-2936)
MAUSER
4750 Clawson Tank Dr (48346-0001)
PHONE..................248 795-2330
▲ EMP: 9
SALES (est): 1.7MM **Privately Held**
SIC: 3412 2655 Barrels, shipping: metal; fiber cans, drums & containers

(G-2937)
MEYERS METAL FAB INC
Also Called: Meyers Metal Fabrications Co
9665 Northwest Ct (48346-1744)
PHONE..................248 620-5411
Ron Meyers, *President*
EMP: 3
SALES: 280K **Privately Held**
SIC: 3312 Blast furnaces & steel mills

(G-2938)
MICHAELENES INC
Also Called: Michaelene's Gourmet Granola
7415 Deer Forest Ct (48348-2734)
PHONE..................248 625-0156
Michaelene Hearn, *President*
Lawrence Hearn, *Vice Pres*
EMP: 5
SQ FT: 1,200
SALES (est): 297.8K **Privately Held**
WEB: www.gourmetgranola.com
SIC: 2043 Cereal breakfast foods

(G-2939)
MIDWEST NATIONAL LLC
Also Called: Midwest Lift Trucks
9951 Norman Rd (48348-2441)
PHONE..................260 894-0963
Rodney Dean,
EMP: 3
SALES (est): 253.3K **Privately Held**
SIC: 3537 Lift trucks, industrial: fork, platform, straddle, etc.

(G-2940)
MOBILE KNOWLEGE GROUP SERVICES (PA)
Also Called: Mkg
5750 Bella Rosa Blvd # 100 (48348-4780)
PHONE..................248 625-3327
Craig S Miller, *President*
Steve C Buchholz, *Principal*
EMP: 5
SQ FT: 2,200
SALES: 3.5MM **Privately Held**
WEB: www.mkgsoft.com
SIC: 3679 3575 5084 Antennas, receiving; computer terminals; industrial machinery & equipment

(G-2941)
OBLUT LTD
Also Called: Unique Shape Fabricating
7111 Dixie Hwy (48346-2077)
PHONE..................248 645-9130
EMP: 12
SALES (est): 950.2K **Privately Held**
SIC: 3465 Manufacturer Of Low Volume Prototype Automobile Parts

(G-2942)
OLDCASTLE MATERIALS INC
4751 White Lake Rd (48346-2554)
PHONE..................248 625-5891
Richard Brilhirt, *Manager*
EMP: 57
SALES (corp-wide): 30.6B **Privately Held**
WEB: www.oldcastlematerials.com
SIC: 2951 1611 Asphalt & asphaltic paving mixtures (not from refineries); highway & street paving contractor
HQ: Oldcastle Materials, Inc.
900 Ashwood Pkwy Ste 700
Atlanta GA 30338

(G-2943)
OSCAR W LARSON COMPANY
10080 Dixie Hwy (48348-2412)
PHONE..................248 575-0320
Jim Lintol, *Branch Mgr*
EMP: 3
SALES (corp-wide): 82.9MM **Privately Held**
SIC: 3714 7549 Fuel systems & parts, motor vehicle; fuel system conversion, automotive
PA: The Oscar W Larson Company
10100 Dixie Hwy
Clarkston MI 48348
248 620-0070

(G-2944)
PFIZER INC
7064 Oak Meadows Dr (48348-4254)
PHONE..................248 867-9067
Josh Wiggins, *Principal*
EMP: 225
SALES (corp-wide): 53.6B **Publicly Held**
SIC: 2834 Pharmaceutical preparations
PA: Pfizer Inc.
235 E 42nd St
New York NY 10017
212 733-2323

(G-2945)
PINNACLE ENERGY LLC
5071 Timber Ridge Trl (48346-3850)
PHONE..................248 623-6091
Jeffrey Crampton, *Vice Pres*
Howard Crampton,
EMP: 4
SALES: 200K **Privately Held**
SIC: 1382 Oil & gas exploration services

(G-2946)
PLAYER PRINTS LLC
5904 Warbler Dr (48346-2974)
PHONE..................844 774-7773
Thomas Willhite,
EMP: 3
SALES: 120K **Privately Held**
SIC: 2396 Screen printing on fabric articles

(G-2947)
PONTIAC COIL INC (PA)
5800 Moody Dr (48346-4768)
PHONE..................248 922-1100
Nick Najmolhoda, *CEO*
John Moody, *President*
Michael T Gidley, *Exec VP*
Mike Gidley, *Exec VP*
Jeff Reddy, *Exec VP*
▲ EMP: 196 EST: 1958
SQ FT: 77,000
SALES (est): 67.6MM **Privately Held**
WEB: www.pontiaccoil.com
SIC: 3498 3621 3677 3714 Fabricated pipe & fittings; motors & generators; coil windings, electronic; motor vehicle parts & accessories

(G-2948)
PPG INDUSTRIES INC
Also Called: PPG 5637
5860 Sashabaw Rd (48346-3152)
PHONE..................248 625-7282
EMP: 24
SALES (corp-wide): 15.3B **Publicly Held**
WEB: www.ppg.com
SIC: 2851 Paints & allied products
PA: Ppg Industries, Inc.
1 Ppg Pl
Pittsburgh PA 15272
412 434-3131

(G-2949)
RANDY L PALMER
9915 Reese Rd (48348-1855)
PHONE..................586 298-7629
Randy Palmer, *Owner*
EMP: 3
SALES: 48K **Privately Held**
SIC: 3648 Lighting equipment

(G-2950)
RANGE CARDS
5680 Golf Pointe Dr (48348-5148)
PHONE..................248 880-8444
Michael Ashley, *Owner*
EMP: 3
SALES: 250K **Privately Held**
SIC: 3089 Plastics products

(G-2951)
RECTICEL FOAM CORPORATION (HQ)
5600 Bow Pointe Dr (48346-3115)
P.O. Box 8985, Wilmington DE (19899-8985)
PHONE..................248 241-9100
Olivier Chapelle, *CEO*
◆ EMP: 2
SALES (est): 14.9MM
SALES (corp-wide): 305.9MM **Privately Held**
SIC: 2515 Mattresses, containing felt, foam rubber, urethane, etc.
PA: Recticel
Avenue Des Olympiades 2
Bruxelles 1140
277 518-11

(G-2952)
REILLY & ASSOCIATES INC
7754 Parkcrest Cir (48348-2967)
PHONE..................248 605-9393
Daniel Reilly, *President*
EMP: 16
SALES: 5MM **Privately Held**
SIC: 7372 Prepackaged software

(G-2953)
SAFE N SIMPLE LLC
5827 Terex (48346-1717)
PHONE..................248 875-0840
Tyler Sajan, *Opers Staff*
Elizabet Sajan,
▲ EMP: 17
SALES (est): 2.7MM **Privately Held**
SIC: 2834 Pharmaceutical preparations

(G-2954)
SHEFFLER MANUFACTURING LLC
6338 Sashabaw Rd (48346-2260)
PHONE..................248 409-0966
John Sheffler, *Principal*
▲ EMP: 18
SALES: 6MM **Privately Held**
SIC: 2499 Kitchen, bathroom & household ware: wood

(G-2955)
SHERMAN PUBLICATIONS INC
Also Called: Clarkston News
5 S Main St Ste 1 (48346-1597)
PHONE..................248 625-3370
Cynthia Burroughs, *Manager*
EMP: 9
SQ FT: 7,528
SALES (est): 373.4K
SALES (corp-wide): 5.5MM **Privately Held**
WEB: www.oxfordleader.com
SIC: 2711 Newspapers: publishing only, not printed on site
PA: Sherman Publications Inc
666 S Lapeer Rd
Oxford MI 48371
248 628-4801

(G-2956)
SKG INTERNATIONAL INC
7550 Deerhill Dr (48346-1236)
P.O. Box 1962 (48347-1962)
PHONE..................248 620-4139
Tony Kayyod, *CEO*
Steven Tarino, *Director*
EMP: 10
SALES (est): 1.1MM **Privately Held**
SIC: 3714 Air conditioner parts, motor vehicle

(G-2957)
SPECTRUM PRINTING
4758 Clarkston Rd (48348-3558)
PHONE..................248 625-5014
Dale Lage, *Owner*
EMP: 3
SQ FT: 1,200
SALES (est): 303.8K **Privately Held**
SIC: 2752 Commercial printing, offset

(G-2958)
ST PIERRE INC
9649 Northwest Ct (48346-1744)
PHONE..................248 620-2755
James C St Pierre, *President*
Joseph S Pierre, *Treasurer*
Joseph St Pierre, *Treasurer*
William J St Pierre, *Admin Sec*
EMP: 6
SQ FT: 6,000
SALES (est): 660K **Privately Held**
WEB: www.stpierre.com
SIC: 3599 Machine shop, jobbing & repair

(G-2959)
STEEL TANK & FABRICATING CO (PA)
Also Called: Clawson Tank
4701 White Lake Rd (48346-2554)
PHONE..................248 625-8700
Richard T Harding II, *Engineer*
Robert E Harding Jr, *Treasurer*
◆ EMP: 75
SQ FT: 15,000
SALES (est): 14.1MM **Privately Held**
SIC: 3443 Tanks, standard or custom fabricated: metal plate

(G-2960)
SUBWAY RESTAURANT
7743 Sashabaw Rd Ste B (48348-4775)
PHONE..................248 625-5739
Joe Grant, *Manager*
EMP: 9 EST: 2008
SALES (est): 204.7K **Privately Held**
SIC: 5812 2099 Sandwiches & submarines shop; salads, fresh or refrigerated

(G-2961)
TLC PRINTING
7826 High Ridge Ct (48348-2971)
PHONE..................248 620-3228
Lou Diantonio, *Principal*
EMP: 3
SALES (est): 282.4K **Privately Held**
SIC: 2752 Commercial printing, lithographic

(G-2962)
TST TOOLING SOFTWARE TECH LLC (PA)
6547 Dixie Hwy (48346-5500)
PHONE..................248 922-9293
Anthony Watson, *Principal*
Patty Poma, *Info Tech Mgr*
James Kesteloot,
Debra Kesteloot,
EMP: 11
SALES: 950K **Privately Held**
SIC: 7372 Prepackaged software

(G-2963)
UNION COMMISSARY LLC
Also Called: Union Kitchen
64 S Main St (48346-5303)
PHONE..................248 795-2483
Curt Catallo, *Mng Member*
EMP: 10
SALES (est): 342.9K
SALES (corp-wide): 3.8MM **Privately Held**
SIC: 2099 Food preparations
PA: Union Joints, Llc
90 N Main St
Clarkston MI 48346
248 795-2483

(G-2964)
WEBER ULTRASONICS AMERICA LLC
7478 Gateway Park Dr (48346-2574)
P.O. Box 840 (48347-0840)
PHONE..................248 620-5142
Britton Diver, *Mng Member*
▲ EMP: 3
SALES (est): 285K **Privately Held**
WEB: www.weber-ultrasonics.us
SIC: 3699 Cleaning equipment, ultrasonic, except medical & dental

(G-2965)
WELDING & JOINING TECH LLC
Also Called: Weldpower
5439 Bristol Parke Dr (48348-4801)
PHONE..................................248 625-3045
Stephen Boergert, *Managing Dir*
EMP: 4
SQ FT: 10,000
SALES (est): 335.2K **Privately Held**
SIC: 8742 8999 8748 7692 Management consulting services; scientific consulting; business consulting; welding repair; fabricated plate work (boiler shop)

Clarksville
Ionia County

(G-2966)
BLOUGH HARDWOODS INC
9975 W Clarksville Rd (48815-9604)
PHONE..................................616 693-2174
Marvin Blough, *President*
EMP: 8
SQ FT: 3,200
SALES (est): 1.5MM **Privately Held**
SIC: 2421 Sawmills & planing mills, general

(G-2967)
WEST MICHIGAN SAWMILL
7760 Nash Hwy (48815-9715)
PHONE..................................616 693-0044
Jim Bough, *Owner*
EMP: 11 **EST:** 2007
SALES (est): 1.7MM **Privately Held**
SIC: 2421 Lumber: rough, sawed or planed

Clawson
Oakland County

(G-2968)
ACCESSORIES BY GIGI LLC
452 E Elmwood Ave Apt 103 (48017-1645)
PHONE..................................248 242-0036
Mari Byrd, *CEO*
EMP: 3
SALES (est): 121.7K **Privately Held**
SIC: 3171 Women's handbags & purses

(G-2969)
ACOUFELT LLC
1238 Anderson Rd Fl 2 (48017-1002)
PHONE..................................800 966-8557
Jessica Grace, *Sales Staff*
Sarah Myers, *Office Mgr*
Ben Grace, *Mng Member*
Janelle Truan, *Associate*
EMP: 7 **EST:** 2018
SALES (est): 729.4K **Privately Held**
SIC: 2299 Acoustic felts

(G-2970)
ADAPTABLE TOOL SUPPLY LLC
309 N Chocolay Ave (48017-1379)
P.O. Box 120 (48017-0120)
PHONE..................................248 439-0866
Libertee Chamberlin, *Mng Member*
EMP: 10
SQ FT: 4,000
SALES: 1MM **Privately Held**
SIC: 3545 5084 Cutting tools for machine tools; machine tools & accessories

(G-2971)
AMERICAN ARROW CORP INC
105 Kinross Ave (48017-1417)
PHONE..................................248 435-6115
Donald W Sommer, *President*
EMP: 8 **EST:** 1964
SQ FT: 4,000
SALES (est): 1.2MM **Privately Held**
WEB: www.donsommer.com
SIC: 3429 Motor vehicle hardware

(G-2972)
AMERICAN FLAG & BANNER COMPANY
28 S Main St (48017-2088)
PHONE..................................248 288-3010
William S Miles, *President*
Jane Miles, *Vice Pres*
EMP: 8
SQ FT: 8,500
SALES: 900K **Privately Held**
SIC: 2399 5999 Flags, fabric; banners, made from fabric; flags; posters

(G-2973)
AMERICAN REPROGRAPHICS CO LLC
Also Called: Entire Rprdction Imging Sltion
1009 W Maple Rd (48017-1058)
PHONE..................................248 299-8900
Dick Ricky, *Manager*
EMP: 45
SALES (corp-wide): 400.7MM **Publicly Held**
WEB: www.e-arc.com
SIC: 7336 2791 2759 7334 Commercial art & graphic design; typesetting; commercial printing; blueprinting service
HQ: American Reprographics Company, L.L.C.
1981 N Broadway Ste 385
Walnut Creek CA 94596
925 949-5100

(G-2974)
CARLET TOOL INC
926 W 14 Mile Rd (48017-1406)
PHONE..................................248 435-0319
Robert Baran, *President*
Hydie Baran, *Admin Sec*
EMP: 3 **EST:** 1968
SQ FT: 2,000
SALES (est): 315.1K **Privately Held**
SIC: 3544 Special dies & tools

(G-2975)
CREATIVE SOLUTIONS GROUP INC (PA)
1250 N Crooks Rd (48017-1047)
PHONE..................................248 288-9700
Thomas Valentine, *President*
Dave Sherman, *COO*
James Bailey, *Vice Pres*
Brian Christy, *Vice Pres*
Mark Wolf, *Traffic Mgr*
EMP: 97 **EST:** 1998
SQ FT: 86,000
SALES (est): 30.2MM **Privately Held**
WEB: www.csgnow.com
SIC: 7389 2542 Advertising, promotional & trade show services; partitions & fixtures, except wood

(G-2976)
D & S ENGINE SPECIALIST INC
875 N Rochester Rd (48017-1731)
PHONE..................................248 583-9240
Michael N Henderson, *President*
EMP: 10
SALES (est): 2MM **Privately Held**
SIC: 5084 3519 7538 Engines & parts, air-cooled; gas engine rebuilding; engine rebuilding: automotive

(G-2977)
E & E MANUFACTURING CO INC
701 S Main St (48017-2017)
PHONE..................................248 616-1300
Matt Mills, *Branch Mgr*
EMP: 18
SALES (corp-wide): 100.9MM **Privately Held**
WEB: www.eemfg.com
SIC: 3714 3465 3469 3452 Motor vehicle parts & accessories; automotive stampings; metal stampings; bolts, nuts, rivets & washers
PA: E & E Manufacturing Company, Inc.
300 400 Indus Drv Plymouth
Plymouth MI 48170
734 451-7600

(G-2978)
FOUR WAY INDUSTRIES INC
855 N Rochester Rd (48017-1731)
PHONE..................................248 588-5421
David Tye, *President*
Aaron T Tye, *Manager*
EMP: 10
SALES (est): 1.4MM **Privately Held**
SIC: 3469 Patterns on metal

(G-2979)
G R INVESTMENT GROUP LTD
839 N Rochester Rd (48017-1731)
PHONE..................................248 588-3946
Richard McDermott, *Partner*
Kim Belanger, *Office Mgr*
EMP: 3
SALES (est): 415.8K **Privately Held**
WEB: www.grinvest.com
SIC: 3463 Automotive forgings, nonferrous

(G-2980)
GJ PREY COML & INDUS PNTG COV
710 N Crooks Rd (48017-1399)
PHONE..................................248 250-4792
Gary Prey, *Owner*
EMP: 5 **EST:** 1997
SALES: 175K **Privately Held**
SIC: 1721 3471 Commercial painting; industrial painting; plating & polishing

(G-2981)
JULIAN BROTHERS INC
540 S Rochester Rd (48017-2124)
PHONE..................................248 588-0280
Richard P Julian, *President*
EMP: 26 **EST:** 1971
SQ FT: 3,000
SALES: 1.6MM **Privately Held**
WEB: www.julianbrothers.com
SIC: 5461 2051 2053 Bread; bread, cake & related products; cakes, bakery: frozen

(G-2982)
ND INDUSTRIES INC (PA)
Also Called: ND Technologies
1000 N Crooks Rd (48017-1003)
PHONE..................................248 288-0000
Richard Wallace, *President*
Tim Cross, *General Mgr*
Tracy Haase, *Principal*
Michael Garofalo, *Exec VP*
Jim Barr, *Vice Pres*
▲ **EMP:** 120
SALES (est): 81.5MM **Privately Held**
WEB: www.ndindustries.com
SIC: 3452 5072 3479 2891 Bolts, nuts, rivets & washers; miscellaneous fasteners; coating of metals & formed products; adhesives & sealants; paints & allied products

(G-2983)
PATRIOT SENSORS & CONTRLS CORP (HQ)
Also Called: Ametek-APT
1080 N Crooks Rd (48017-1003)
PHONE..................................248 435-0700
Bob Soeder, *Vice Pres*
Ron Jayroe, *Controller*
Heidemarie Lelowicz, *Manager*
◆ **EMP:** 95
SQ FT: 60,000
SALES (est): 67.8MM
SALES (corp-wide): 4.8B **Publicly Held**
WEB: www.patriotsensors.com
SIC: 3823 3829 3643 3621 Controllers for process variables, all types; accelerometers; pressure transducers; current-carrying wiring devices; motors & generators; switchgear & switchboard apparatus; switches, electronic applications
PA: Ametek, Inc.
1100 Cassatt Rd
Berwyn PA 19312
610 647-2121

(G-2984)
PEAKTRONICS INC
1363 Anderson Rd Ste A (48017-1051)
PHONE..................................248 542-5640
Jack M Leason, *President*
Peter W Mueller, *Exec VP*
Peter Mueller, *Exec VP*
Marion Spurlock, *Mfg Mgr*
◆ **EMP:** 8
SQ FT: 10,000
SALES (est): 3.6MM **Privately Held**
WEB: www.peaktronics.com
SIC: 3823 Industrial instrmnts msrmnt display/control process variable

(G-2985)
PROFORMA PLTNUM PRTG PRMOTIONS
143 W Tacoma St (48017-1983)
PHONE..................................248 341-3814
Suzanne Ashcraft, *Owner*
EMP: 4
SALES (est): 398.2K **Privately Held**
SIC: 2752 Commercial printing, lithographic

(G-2986)
STIRNEMANN TOOL & MCH CO INC
1457 N Main St (48017-1199)
PHONE..................................248 435-4040
James Stirnemann, *President*
EMP: 5 **EST:** 1946
SQ FT: 5,000
SALES: 700K **Privately Held**
SIC: 7699 3599 Industrial equipment services; machine shop, jobbing & repair

(G-2987)
TRIPLE THREAD
25 W 14 Mile Rd (48017-1922)
PHONE..................................248 321-7757
Ken Weeks, *Partner*
EMP: 3
SALES (est): 256.6K **Privately Held**
SIC: 2759 Screen printing

(G-2988)
UNCLE EDS OIL SHOPPES INC
1116 W 14 Mile Rd (48017-1493)
PHONE..................................248 288-4738
Dale Lifton, *Manager*
EMP: 5
SQ FT: 1,962 **Privately Held**
SIC: 3714 Filters: oil, fuel & air, motor vehicle
PA: Uncle Ed's Oil Shoppes, Inc
2515 Capital Ave Sw
Battle Creek MI 49015

(G-2989)
WILSON TECHNOLOGIES INC
Also Called: Oplogic
851 W Maple Rd (48017-1185)
PHONE..................................248 655-0005
John Parent, *President*
EMP: 9
SALES (est): 644.2K **Privately Held**
SIC: 7372 Business oriented computer software

(G-2990)
WORLD INDUSTRIES INC (PA)
1000 N Crooks Rd (48017-1003)
P.O. Box 1770, Troy (48099-1770)
PHONE..................................248 288-0000
EMP: 6
SALES (est): 799.2K **Privately Held**
SIC: 3999 Manufacturing industries

Clay
St. Clair County

(G-2991)
ADVANCED AUTOMOTIVE GROUP LLC
8784 Folkert Rd (48001-3700)
PHONE..................................586 206-2478
Steven Bartolomucci, *President*
EMP: 10
SQ FT: 8,000
SALES (est): 452.9K **Privately Held**
SIC: 3599 Machine & other job shop work

(G-2992)
ALGONAC MARINE CAST LLC
9300 Stone Rd (48001-4436)
PHONE..................................810 794-9391
John Pugh,
EMP: 12
SQ FT: 48,000
SALES (est): 5.8MM **Privately Held**
WEB: www.algonaccast.com
SIC: 3365 3369 Aluminum & aluminum-based alloy castings; nonferrous foundries

GEOGRAPHIC SECTION

(G-2993) AMERICAN DIE CORPORATION
6860 Holland Rd (48001-3722)
PHONE..................................810 794-4080
Steve Bartolomucci, *President*
EMP: 25
SALES (est): 2.6MM **Privately Held**
WEB: www.americandie.com
SIC: 3544 Special dies & tools

(G-2994) AUTO CRAFT TOOL & DIE CO
Also Called: Eckhart USA
1800 Fruit St (48001-4503)
PHONE..................................810 794-4929
Michael Duvernay, *President*
David Du Vernay, *Vice Pres*
David Duvernay, *Vice Pres*
Travis Duvernay, *Opers Mgr*
Christopher Rodman, *Engineer*
▲ EMP: 35 EST: 1958
SQ FT: 57,250
SALES (est): 15.7MM
SALES (corp-wide): 3.6MM **Privately Held**
WEB: www.auto-craft.com
SIC: 3544 Special dies, tools, jigs & fixtures
HQ: Eckhart Holdings, Inc.
 16185 National Pkwy
 Lansing MI 48906
 517 321-7700

(G-2995) AUTO CRAFT TOOL & DIE CO
1800 Fruit St (48001-4503)
PHONE..................................810 794-4929
EMP: 25
SALES (corp-wide): 17.2MM **Privately Held**
SIC: 3544 Mfg Dies/Tools/Jigs/Fixtures
PA: Auto Craft Tool & Die Co.
 1800 Fruit St
 Clay MI 48001
 810 794-4929

(G-2996) D MICHAEL SERVICES
Also Called: Northland Die Engineering
8855 Stone Rd (48001-3821)
PHONE..................................810 794-2407
Dave Pawlak, *President*
EMP: 4
SQ FT: 5,000
SALES: 500K **Privately Held**
SIC: 3599 1521 Ferris wheels; single-family home remodeling, additions & repairs

(G-2997) H AND H ELECTRONICS
7357 Bealane Rd (48001-3006)
PHONE..................................586 725-5412
Vincent C Hohnsbein, *Owner*
EMP: 3
SALES: 60K **Privately Held**
SIC: 3679 7629 Electronic circuits; electronic equipment repair

(G-2998) J CILLUFFO SON STUDIO
Also Called: Cilluffo Son Studio & Gallery
8397 Starville Rd (48001-3207)
PHONE..................................810 794-2911
Joe Cilluffo, *Owner*
EMP: 3
SALES (est): 127.3K **Privately Held**
SIC: 3952 Water colors, artists'

(G-2999) METAL WORXS INC
7374 Flamingo St (48001-4132)
PHONE..................................586 484-9355
Robert Hamilton, *Principal*
EMP: 5
SALES (est): 602.2K **Privately Held**
SIC: 7692 Welding repair

(G-3000) NU-ERA HOLDINGS INC (PA)
Also Called: Monnier
2034 Fruit St (48001)
P.O. Box 409, Algonac (48001-0409)
PHONE..................................810 794-4935
Patrick Nichols, *President*
EMP: 43
SQ FT: 29,000
SALES (est): 8.6MM **Privately Held**
WEB: www.monnier.com
SIC: 3569 Filters, general line: industrial; lubricating equipment

(G-3001) PRINTING SERVICE INC
7257 Parklane Dr (48001-4223)
PHONE..................................586 718-4103
Deno Loupes, *President*
Dino Loupes, *President*
Barbara Loupes, *Vice Pres*
EMP: 3
SALES (est): 165K **Privately Held**
SIC: 2752 Commercial printing, offset

(G-3002) SCAFF-ALL INC
Also Called: Scott-Systems
7269 Cardinal St (48001-4107)
PHONE..................................888 204-9990
Daniel Zempel, *Treasurer*
William Bowser, *Director*
Kimberly Bowser, *Director*
Elliott Clark, *Director*
Anthony Dayble, *Director*
EMP: 5
SALES (est): 218K **Privately Held**
SIC: 3429 Manufactured hardware (general)

(G-3003) SUNSATION PRODUCTS INC
Also Called: Sunsation Boats
9666 Kretz Dr (48001-4622)
PHONE..................................810 794-4888
Wayne Schaldenbrand, *President*
Joseph Schaldenbrand, *Vice Pres*
EMP: 38
SQ FT: 12,000
SALES (est): 6.6MM **Privately Held**
SIC: 3732 Boats, fiberglass: building & repairing

(G-3004) THUMBPRINT NEWS
8061 Marsh Rd (48001-3401)
PHONE..................................810 794-2300
Scott Zimmer, *Manager*
EMP: 5
SALES (est): 179.2K **Privately Held**
SIC: 2711 Commercial printing & newspaper publishing combined; newspapers, publishing & printing

(G-3005) ULTRA-TEMP CORPORATION
7270 Flamingo St (48001-4130)
P.O. Box 230035, Fair Haven (48023-0035)
PHONE..................................810 794-4709
Thomas C Kershaw, *President*
Roy Lueth, *Vice Pres*
EMP: 9
SALES (est): 1.1MM **Privately Held**
SIC: 3567 Industrial furnaces & ovens

Clayton
Lenawee County

(G-3006) DEMLOW PRODUCTS INC
7404 Tomer Rd (49235-8602)
PHONE..................................517 436-3529
James A Demlow, *President*
Joan Demlow, *Vice Pres*
EMP: 12
SQ FT: 10,000
SALES (est): 2MM **Privately Held**
WEB: www.demlowproducts.com
SIC: 3495 3496 Wire springs; miscellaneous fabricated wire products

(G-3007) FISCHELL MACHINERY LLC
6122 Whaley Hwy (49235-9632)
PHONE..................................517 445-2828
James Fischer,
EMP: 7
SALES (est): 829.6K **Privately Held**
SIC: 3599 Custom machinery

(G-3008) JEFF BROWN SAND & GRAVEL
6894 Morey Hwy (49235-9724)
PHONE..................................517 445-2700
Jeff Brown, *Owner*
EMP: 3
SALES (est): 170.9K **Privately Held**
SIC: 1442 Construction sand & gravel

Clifford
Lapeer County

(G-3009) ADVANCED DRAINAGE SYSTEMS INC
4800 Marlette Rd (48727-9743)
PHONE..................................989 761-7610
Larry Butcher, *Prdtn Mgr*
Roger Corkins, *Branch Mgr*
EMP: 9
SALES (corp-wide): 1.3B **Publicly Held**
SIC: 3084 Plastics pipe
PA: Advanced Drainage Systems, Inc.
 4640 Trueman Blvd
 Hilliard OH 43026
 614 658-0050

(G-3010) DECO ENGINEERING INC
Also Called: Newcor, Deco Division
9900 Main St (48727-9550)
PHONE..................................989 761-7521
David S Segal, *Ch of Bd*
James Connor, *President*
EMP: 150
SALES (est): 20MM
SALES (corp-wide): 118.8MM **Privately Held**
WEB: www.decoengineering.com
SIC: 3599 Machine shop, jobbing & repair
HQ: Newcor, Inc.
 1021 N Shiawassee St
 Corunna MI 48817
 248 537-0014

(G-3011) ROCHESTER GEAR INC (DH)
9900 Main St (48727-9550)
PHONE..................................989 659-2899
David Siegel, *President*
EMP: 60 EST: 1944
SQ FT: 45,000
SALES (est): 20.1MM
SALES (corp-wide): 118.8MM **Privately Held**
SIC: 3714 Gears, motor vehicle
HQ: Newcor, Inc.
 1021 N Shiawassee St
 Corunna MI 48817
 248 537-0014

Climax
Kalamazoo County

(G-3012) BETZ CONTRACTING INC
Also Called: Betz Contracting and Machining
320 N Main St (49034-9502)
P.O. Box 156 (49034-0156)
PHONE..................................269 746-3320
Sean Betz, *President*
Carol Ann Betz, *Corp Secy*
Rodney Betz, *Vice Pres*
EMP: 6
SALES (est): 660K **Privately Held**
WEB: www.betzmachine.com
SIC: 3544 Special dies & tools

(G-3013) BURKETT SIGNS CORP
15886 E Michigan Ave (49034-9710)
PHONE..................................269 746-4285
Robb Perrin, *President*
Paul Gault, *Controller*
Jodie Harrison, *Office Mgr*
Sean Perrin, *Admin Sec*
EMP: 16
SQ FT: 2,400
SALES: 1.5MM **Privately Held**
WEB: www.burkettsigns.com
SIC: 3993 Signs & advertising specialties

(G-3014) WOODHAMS ENTERPRISES INC
Also Called: International Minute Press
11546 W County Line Rd (49034-8801)
PHONE..................................269 383-0600
James Woodhams, *President*
Margaret Woodhams, *Vice Pres*
EMP: 3
SQ FT: 1,400
SALES: 250K **Privately Held**
SIC: 2752 2791 2789 Commercial printing, offset; typesetting; bookbinding & related work

Clinton
Lenawee County

(G-3015) C M E PLASTIC COMPANY
3820 E Michigan Ave (49236-9576)
P.O. Box 649 (49236-0649)
PHONE..................................517 456-7722
Helmut Linsgeseder, *President*
EMP: 5
SQ FT: 7,000
SALES: 500K **Privately Held**
WEB: www.cmeplastics.com
SIC: 3559 3089 Plastics working machinery; caps, plastic

(G-3016) CASING INNOVATIONS LLC
19739 15 Mill Rd (49236)
PHONE..................................248 939-0821
Diana Rancilio, *Mng Member*
EMP: 3
SALES (est): 300.4K **Privately Held**
SIC: 2431 Millwork

(G-3017) CLINTON MACHINE TOOL INC
4003 W Us Highway 12 (49236-9761)
PHONE..................................517 456-4810
Joseph D Butcko, *President*
EMP: 15
SQ FT: 8,000
SALES: 1.2MM **Privately Held**
SIC: 3599 Machine shop, jobbing & repair

(G-3018) DST INDUSTRIES INC
11900 Tecumseh Clinton Rd (49236-9439)
PHONE..................................734 941-0300
Dan Ulrich, *Manager*
EMP: 10
SQ FT: 174,000
SALES (corp-wide): 31.1MM **Privately Held**
WEB: www.dstindustries.com
SIC: 3714 Motor vehicle parts & accessories
HQ: Dst Industries, Inc.
 34364 Goddard Rd
 Romulus MI 48174
 734 941-0300

(G-3019) EDEN FOODS INC (PA)
Also Called: NEW MERIDIAN
701 Tecumseh Rd (49236-9599)
PHONE..................................517 456-7424
Michael Potter, *Ch of Bd*
John Ardrey, *General Mgr*
Nicholas Cannon, *General Mgr*
Lucas McCabe, *Production*
Racine Spencer, *Production*
◆ EMP: 140
SQ FT: 40,000
SALES: 42.7MM **Privately Held**
WEB: www.edenfoods.com
SIC: 2099 Food preparations

(G-3020) FORESTRY MANAGEMENT SVCS INC
Also Called: Hardwoods of Michigan
430 Division St (49236-9702)
P.O. Box 620 (49236-0620)
PHONE..................................517 456-7431

Clinton - Lenawee County (G-3021)

Bob Vogel, *President*
Richard L Service, *Chairman*
Jeff Mercy, *Vice Pres*
Ron Steele, *Safety Mgr*
Mike Schlegel, *Purch Agent*
◆ **EMP**: 140
SQ FT: 3,000
SALES (est): 977.7K **Privately Held**
WEB: www.hmilumber.com
SIC: 2421 2426 Kiln drying of lumber; furniture stock & parts, hardwood

(G-3021)
FRYE PRINTING COMPANY INC (PA)
11801 Tecumseh Clinton Rd (49236-9676)
PHONE.................517 456-4124
John R Frye, *President*
EMP: 15
SQ FT: 10,700
SALES (est): 1.8MM **Privately Held**
WEB: www.fryeprinting.com
SIC: 2752 2789 2761 2759 Commercial printing, offset; bookbinding & related work; manifold business forms; commercial printing

(G-3022)
HAVERS HERITAGE
7500 Clinton Macon Rd (49236-9564)
PHONE.................517 423-3455
Sharon Haver, *Owner*
EMP: 5
SALES (est): 324.8K **Privately Held**
SIC: 3999 Potpourri

(G-3023)
HMI HARDWOODS LLC
Also Called: Tri-County Logging
430 Division St (49236-9702)
P.O. Box 620 (49236-0620)
PHONE.................517 456-7431
Robert Vogel, *President*
John Binegar, *Vice Pres*
Jeffrey Mercy, *Vice Pres*
Laura Gebhardt, *CFO*
EMP: 100
SALES (est): 301.7K
SALES (corp-wide): 859.8MM **Privately Held**
SIC: 2421 Sawmills & planing mills, general
PA: Hardwoods Distribution Inc
  9440 202 St Unit 306
  Langley BC V1M 4
  604 881-1988

(G-3024)
JAD PRODUCTS INC
4003 W Us Highway 12 (49236-9761)
PHONE.................517 456-4810
David Giles, *President*
EMP: 4
SQ FT: 10,000
SALES (est): 579.9K **Privately Held**
WEB: www.jadcnc.com
SIC: 3469 8711 Machine parts, stamped or pressed metal; consulting engineer

(G-3025)
STANSLEY MINERAL RESOURCES INC
Also Called: Adrian Sand & Stone
13500 Allen Rd (49236-9652)
PHONE.................517 456-6310
Dan White, *Manager*
EMP: 7
SALES (corp-wide): 15MM **Privately Held**
SIC: 1442 Construction sand & gravel
PA: Stansley Mineral Resources, Inc.
  3793 Silica Rd B
  Sylvania OH 43560
  419 843-2813

Clinton Township
Macomb County

(G-3026)
21ST CENTURY NEWSPAPERS INC (HQ)
Also Called: Macomb Daily
19176 Hall Rd Ste 200 (48038-6914)
PHONE.................586 469-4510
Bob Jelenic, *CEO*
Robert M Jelenic, *Principal*
Scott Wright, *Senior VP*
EMP: 200 **EST**: 1995
SALES (est): 109.9MM
SALES (corp-wide): 697.5MM **Privately Held**
WEB: www.macombdaily.com
SIC: 2711 Newspapers, publishing & printing

(G-3027)
A & M INDUSTRIES INC
35590 Groesbeck Hwy (48035-2519)
PHONE.................586 791-5610
Frank Migliaczo, *President*
Royce C Sam, *General Mgr*
Shane Duda, *Project Mgr*
EMP: 45
SQ FT: 12,000
SALES (est): 6.3MM **Privately Held**
SIC: 3599 Machine shop, jobbing & repair

(G-3028)
A M T WELDING INC
21446 Carlo Dr (48038-1512)
PHONE.................586 463-7030
Joseph Ouimet, *President*
EMP: 8
SQ FT: 5,000
SALES (est): 1.5MM **Privately Held**
SIC: 7692 Welding repair

(G-3029)
A S A P TOOL INC
35660 Groesbeck Hwy (48035-2561)
PHONE.................586 790-6550
Thomas Smits, *President*
EMP: 4
SQ FT: 6,400
SALES (est): 596.2K **Privately Held**
SIC: 3544 Special dies & tools

(G-3030)
A S PLUS INDUSTRIES INC
34728 Centaur Dr (48035-3701)
PHONE.................586 741-0400
Sarita Hingorani, *President*
Arun Hingorani, *Vice Pres*
EMP: 7
SQ FT: 8,300
SALES: 430K **Privately Held**
SIC: 3089 Molding primary plastic

(G-3031)
AARON INCORPORATED
33674 Kelly Rd (48035-4844)
PHONE.................586 791-0320
Thomas A Dempsey, *President*
EMP: 8
SQ FT: 8,000
SALES (est): 775.9K **Privately Held**
WEB: www.triphero.com
SIC: 3465 Body parts, automobile: stamped metal

(G-3032)
AARONS FABRICATION OF STEEL
21427 Carlo Dr (48038-1513)
PHONE.................586 883-0652
Sue Bursteinowicz, *President*
EMP: 7 **EST**: 2014
SALES (est): 208.8K **Privately Held**
SIC: 3449 7359 Miscellaneous metalwork; home appliance, furniture & entertainment rental services

(G-3033)
ACCURATE INJECTION MOLDS INC
Also Called: A I M I
22264 Starks Dr (48036-1199)
PHONE.................586 954-2553
James P Jarrett, *President*
EMP: 17
SQ FT: 12,000
SALES (est): 2.6MM **Privately Held**
SIC: 3089 Injection molding of plastics

(G-3034)
ACHIEVE INDUSTRIES LLC
44421 N Groesbeck Hwy (48036-1117)
PHONE.................586 493-9780
Dave McGoffin,
EMP: 7 **EST**: 2011
SALES (est): 1.1MM **Privately Held**
SIC: 3999 Manufacturing industries

(G-3035)
ACME GEAR COMPANY INC
23402 Reynolds Ct (48036-1240)
PHONE.................586 465-7740
David P Kelly, *President*
Scott Kelly, *Vice Pres*
Jeffrey Kelly, *Treasurer*
EMP: 13 **EST**: 1960
SQ FT: 10,000
SALES (est): 1.8MM **Privately Held**
SIC: 3599 Machine shop, jobbing & repair

(G-3036)
ACTION WOOD TECHNOLOGIES INC
Also Called: Action Wood 360
44500 Reynolds Dr (48036-1246)
PHONE.................586 468-2300
Christopher A Grobbel, *CEO*
▲ **EMP**: 25
SQ FT: 31,000
SALES (est): 5.4MM **Privately Held**
WEB: www.actionwoodtech.com
SIC: 2449 4783 Rectangular boxes & crates, wood; packing & crating

(G-3037)
ADMIRAL BROACH COMPANY INC
21391 Carlo Dr (48038-1511)
PHONE.................586 468-8411
Patrick W Considine, *President*
Will Smith, *Vice Pres*
William Smith, *Vice Pres*
Debra Considine, *Office Mgr*
▲ **EMP**: 20 **EST**: 1976
SQ FT: 12,200
SALES (est): 4.5MM **Privately Held**
WEB: www.admiralbroach.com
SIC: 3545 Broaches (machine tool accessories)

(G-3038)
ADVANCED MOLD SOLUTIONS
43682 N Gratiot Ave (48036-3330)
PHONE.................586 468-6883
David Forner, *Owner*
EMP: 4
SALES (est): 312.8K **Privately Held**
WEB: www.advancedmold.net
SIC: 3544 Industrial molds

(G-3039)
ADVANTAGE DESIGN & TOOL INC
22760 Macomb Indus Dr (48036-1137)
PHONE.................586 463-2800
Michele Kerner, *President*
Joe Torre, *Vice Pres*
EMP: 7
SALES (est): 963.2K **Privately Held**
WEB: www.advantagedesign.com
SIC: 3544 Special dies & tools

(G-3040)
AIM PLASTICS INC
22264 Starks Dr (48036-1199)
PHONE.................586 954-2553
Craig Fisher, *President*
Gaetano Aprea, *Marketing Mgr*
James Jarrett, *Admin Sec*
EMP: 35
SQ FT: 4,000
SALES (est): 7.6MM
SALES (corp-wide): 18.5MM **Privately Held**
SIC: 3089 Injection molding of plastics
PA: Medbio, Inc.
  5346 36th St Se
  Grand Rapids MI 49512
  616 245-0214

(G-3041)
ALLAGRA PRINT AND IMAGING
Also Called: American Speedy Printing
42120 Garfield Rd (48038-1645)
PHONE.................586 263-0060
Lee Karvola, *President*
Mark J Fecht, *Owner*
Anna L Fecht, *Partner*
Leslie R Fecht, *Partner*
EMP: 3
SQ FT: 1,200
SALES (est): 230K **Privately Held**
SIC: 2752 Commercial printing, offset

(G-3042)
ALLEGIANCE PACKAGING LLC
23361 Quinn Rd (48035-3732)
PHONE.................586 846-2453
John C Bommarito, *CEO*
Salvatore Bommarito, *CFO*
EMP: 4 **EST**: 2002
SQ FT: 30,000
SALES (est): 898.7K **Privately Held**
WEB: www.allegiance-packaging.com
SIC: 2679 Corrugated paper: made from purchased material

(G-3043)
ALLIED SIGNS INC
33650 Giftos Dr (48035-4241)
PHONE.................586 791-7900
Randy Schmitt, *President*
Carrie Howe, *Opers Staff*
Art Conley, *Sales Staff*
EMP: 10
SALES (est): 1.4MM **Privately Held**
WEB: www.alliedsignsinc.com
SIC: 3993 Signs & advertising specialties

(G-3044)
AME INTERNATIONAL LLC
21481 Carlo Dr (48038-1513)
P.O. Box 182010, Shelby Township (48318-2010)
PHONE.................586 532-8981
EMP: 30
SALES: 950K **Privately Held**
SIC: 3999 Mfg Misc Products

(G-3045)
AMERICA INK PRINT
33812 Groesbeck Hwy (48035-3970)
PHONE.................586 790-2555
Karen Vaughn, *Owner*
EMP: 3
SALES (est): 341.5K **Privately Held**
SIC: 2752 Commercial printing, lithographic

(G-3046)
AMERICAN AIRCRAFT PARTS MFG CO
44801 Centre Ct E (48038-5512)
PHONE.................586 294-3300
Michael Thomas, *President*
James Tigani, *Vice Pres*
EMP: 26 **EST**: 1952
SQ FT: 33,267
SALES (est): 5.3MM **Privately Held**
SIC: 3728 Aircraft parts & equipment

(G-3047)
AMERICAN INK USA PRNTG & GRPHC
33812 Groesbeck Hwy (48035-3970)
PHONE.................586 790-2555
Karen Vaughn, *President*
Shannon Vaughn, *Controller*
EMP: 5 **EST**: 1999
SQ FT: 2,500
SALES (est): 782.4K **Privately Held**
WEB: www.americanink.biz
SIC: 2752 Commercial printing, offset

GEOGRAPHIC SECTION
Clinton Township - Macomb County (G-3077)

(G-3048)
AMERICAN LAZER CENTERS
16010 19 Mile Rd Ste 100 (48038-1141)
PHONE..................................248 798-6552
Karen Harris, *Manager*
EMP: 4
SALES (est): 331.7K **Privately Held**
SIC: 3845 Laser systems & equipment, medical

(G-3049)
AMOUR YOUR BODY LLC
Also Called: Ayb
16518 Festian Dr (48035-2229)
PHONE..................................586 846-3100
Canetha Porter, *Mng Member*
EMP: 4
SALES: 100K **Privately Held**
SIC: 7389 2844 ; lotions, shaving

(G-3050)
AMPHENOL CORPORATION
Also Called: Amphenol Sine Systems
44724 Morley Dr (48036-1357)
PHONE..................................586 465-3131
Alma Vancamp, *Owner*
Don Hunsucker, *Manager*
Richard Zaleuke, *Manager*
Rene Curry, *Director*
EMP: 345
SALES (corp-wide): 8.2B **Publicly Held**
SIC: 3678 Electronic connectors
PA: Amphenol Corporation
  358 Hall Ave
  Wallingford CT 06492
  203 265-8900

(G-3051)
AMTEX INC
34680 Nova Dr (48035-3716)
PHONE..................................586 792-7888
Daniel Cowie, *President*
Steven Schutz, *Vice Pres*
EMP: 7
SQ FT: 5,000
SALES (est): 1MM **Privately Held**
WEB: www.amtex-inc.com
SIC: 3625 8711 Electric controls & control accessories, industrial; engineering services

(G-3052)
ANBO TOOL & MANUFACTURING INC
22785 Macomb Indus Dr (48036-1181)
PHONE..................................586 465-7610
Andrew Music, *President*
Bobby Ray Wiley, *Admin Sec*
EMP: 5
SQ FT: 2,400
SALES: 534.7K **Privately Held**
SIC: 3545 Precision tools, machinists'

(G-3053)
ANDERSON-COOK INC (PA)
Also Called: L M Gear Company Division
44785 Macomb Indus Dr (48036-1147)
PHONE..................................586 954-0700
Dennis Neagher, *CEO*
Kim Anderson, *Ch of Bd*
Mark Schmidt, *COO*
Scott McViegh, *CFO*
Dave Swineford, *Manager*
▲ **EMP:** 55 **EST:** 1970
SALES (est): 65.9MM **Privately Held**
WEB: www.andersoncook.com
SIC: 3542 3714 3599 3549 Spline rolling machines; gears, motor vehicle; machine shop, jobbing & repair; metalworking machinery; machine tool accessories

(G-3054)
ANDERSON-COOK INC
Mra Industries
44785 Macomb Indus Dr (48036-1147)
PHONE..................................586 954-0700
Bob Russ, *Branch Mgr*
Matthew Richey, *IT/INT Sup*
EMP: 50
SALES (corp-wide): 65.9MM **Privately Held**
WEB: www.andersoncook.com
SIC: 3542 3714 Spline rolling machines; gears, motor vehicle

PA: Anderson-Cook, Inc.
  44785 Macomb Indus Dr
  Clinton Township MI 48036
  586 954-0700

(G-3055)
API POLYMERS INC
34654 Nova Dr (48035-3716)
PHONE..................................855 274-7659
Dave Hogan, *President*
EMP: 3 **EST:** 2008
SALES (est): 395.7K **Privately Held**
SIC: 2821 Plastics materials & resins

(G-3056)
ARC SERVICES OF MACOMB INC
44050 N Gratiot Ave (48036-1308)
PHONE..................................586 469-1600
Lisa Lepine, *President*
Renee Hartman, *Bookkeeper*
Marie Bommarito, *Finance*
Deborah Shirkey, *Human Resources*
Ron Kimball, *Exec Dir*
EMP: 39
SQ FT: 20,000
SALES: 3.4MM **Privately Held**
SIC: 8331 3471 Sheltered workshop; plating & polishing

(G-3057)
ATLANTIC TOOL INC
22826 Patmore Dr (48036-1191)
PHONE..................................586 954-9268
Walter J Hoeckl, *President*
EMP: 6
SALES: 750K **Privately Held**
WEB: www.cablesonline.net
SIC: 3544 Special dies & tools

(G-3058)
AUDIA WOODWORKING & FINE FURN
16627 Millar Rd (48035-1639)
PHONE..................................586 296-6330
Salvatore Audia, *President*
EMP: 15 **EST:** 1955
SQ FT: 30,000
SALES (est): 1.5MM **Privately Held**
SIC: 2511 2431 Tables, household: wood; chairs, household, except upholstered: wood; desks, household: wood; millwork

(G-3059)
AUDIONET AMERICA INC
33900 Harper Ave Ste 101 (48035-4258)
PHONE..................................586 944-0043
Colleen Shefferly, *Principal*
Dana Miriani, *Manager*
EMP: 6
SALES (est): 153.5K **Privately Held**
SIC: 3842 Hearing aids

(G-3060)
AUTOMOTIVE PROTOTYPE STAMPING
17207 Millar Rd (48036-2071)
PHONE..................................586 445-6792
Keith Larose, *President*
EMP: 8
SALES (est): 1.1MM **Privately Held**
WEB: www.automotiveprototypestampings.com
SIC: 3469 Metal stampings

(G-3061)
AXALTA COATING SYSTEMS LLC
45000 River Ridge Dr # 200 (48038-5582)
PHONE..................................586 846-4160
Michael Magdich, *Vice Pres*
EMP: 7
SALES (corp-wide): 4.7B **Publicly Held**
SIC: 2851 Paints & allied products
HQ: Axalta Coating Systems, Llc
  2001 Market St Ste 3600
  Philadelphia PA 19103
  215 255-4347

(G-3062)
B & S MANUFACTURING INC
39159 Cadborough Dr (48038-2744)
PHONE..................................586 939-5130
Lawrence W Bisby, *President*
Wayne A Bisby, *Treasurer*

EMP: 9
SQ FT: 13,500
SALES (est): 1.4MM **Privately Held**
WEB: www.bsmanufacturing.com
SIC: 3452 Bolts, metal

(G-3063)
BECK INDUSTRIES INC
24454 Sorrentino Ct (48035-3258)
PHONE..................................586 790-4060
Mike Beck, *President*
Mary Beck, *Vice Pres*
EMP: 5
SQ FT: 8,500
SALES (est): 750K **Privately Held**
SIC: 3599 Machine shop, jobbing & repair; machine & other job shop work

(G-3064)
BELL FORKLIFTS
4660 Centaur Ave (48035)
PHONE..................................586 469-7979
EMP: 4
SALES (est): 379.2K **Privately Held**
SIC: 3537 Forklift

(G-3065)
BENCHWORK INC
Also Called: Bench Works
34100 Kelly Rd (48035-3369)
PHONE..................................586 464-6699
Joseph L Janis, *President*
Craig Janis, *Principal*
Jason Janis, *Principal*
EMP: 4
SQ FT: 4,000
SALES (est): 584.2K **Privately Held**
SIC: 2599 Work benches, factory

(G-3066)
BEST TOOL & ENGINEERING CO
34730 Nova Dr (48035-3717)
PHONE..................................586 792-4119
Jean Cherluck, *President*
Joe Cherluck, *Principal*
EMP: 12
SALES (est): 2MM **Privately Held**
SIC: 3544 Industrial molds

(G-3067)
BIG BOY RESTAURANTS INTL LLC
16880 Hall Rd (48038-1205)
PHONE..................................586 263-6220
Dave Newcomb, *Branch Mgr*
EMP: 90
SALES (corp-wide): 81.9MM **Privately Held**
SIC: 5812 2051 5461 Restaurant, family: chain; bread, cake & related products; bakeries
PA: Big Boy Restaurants International L.L.C.
  4199 Marcy St
  Warren MI 48091
  586 759-6000

(G-3068)
BOB G MACHINING LLC
44345 N Groesbeck Hwy (48036-1116)
PHONE..................................586 285-1400
Bob Gjerovski, *Mng Member*
Jasmina Gjerovski,
EMP: 7 **EST:** 2010
SQ FT: 3,000
SALES: 650K **Privately Held**
SIC: 3541 3545 Vertical turning & boring machines (metalworking); milling machine attachments (machine tool accessories)

(G-3069)
BRAVO MACHINE AND TOOL INC
16453 Chatham Dr (48035-1121)
PHONE..................................586 790-3463
John P Vogler, *President*
EMP: 10 **EST:** 1978
SQ FT: 6,000
SALES: 800K **Privately Held**
SIC: 3544 Special dies & tools

(G-3070)
BURKARD INDUSTRIES INC
35300 Kelly Rd (48035-2446)
PHONE..................................586 791-6520

John A Burkard, *CEO*
Jay Burkard, *President*
Patricia Moore, *Plant Mgr*
Cyndi Stahl, *Supervisor*
▲ **EMP:** 104
SQ FT: 70,000
SALES (est): 21.4MM **Privately Held**
WEB: www.burkardind.com
SIC: 3479 Coating of metals & formed products

(G-3071)
C & J FABRICATION INC
34885 Groesbeck Hwy (48035-3366)
PHONE..................................586 791-6269
Dan Cole, *President*
EMP: 6
SALES (est): 894.2K **Privately Held**
SIC: 2221 3441 Automotive fabrics, man-made fiber; fabricated structural metal

(G-3072)
C & S MILLWORK INC
44163 N Groesbeck Hwy (48036-1179)
PHONE..................................586 465-6470
Christopher Griebe, *Owner*
Steven Griebe, *Corp Secy*
EMP: 10
SQ FT: 3,000
SALES (est): 1.4MM **Privately Held**
SIC: 2431 Millwork

(G-3073)
CAL TOLLIVER
Aiso Called: Cals Welding Co
36429 Groesbeck Hwy (48035-1551)
PHONE..................................586 790-1610
Cal Tolliver, *Owner*
EMP: 3
SQ FT: 3,000
SALES: 100K **Privately Held**
SIC: 7692 Welding repair

(G-3074)
CALIBER INDUSTRIES LLC
Also Called: Pneumatic Feed Service
19000 15 Mile Rd (48035-2506)
PHONE..................................586 774-6775
Eric Werner, *President*
EMP: 15 **EST:** 2016
SALES: 1MM **Privately Held**
SIC: 3535 Conveyors & conveying equipment

(G-3075)
CARBIDE SURFACE COMPANY (PA)
44336 Reynolds Dr (48036-1242)
PHONE..................................586 465-6110
Hugh Vestal, *President*
Mary Vestal, *Vice Pres*
EMP: 7
SQ FT: 8,000
SALES: 1.7MM **Privately Held**
SIC: 3479 3545 Coating of metals & formed products; drill bushings (drilling jig)

(G-3076)
CCM MODERNIZATION CO
41580 Janet Cir (48038-2054)
PHONE..................................586 231-0396
Joseph Cilluffo, *President*
EMP: 3
SALES (est): 256.5K **Privately Held**
SIC: 2434 1521 Wood kitchen cabinets; general remodeling, single-family houses

(G-3077)
CERTIFIED METAL PRODUCTS INC
22802 Morelli Dr (48036-1176)
PHONE..................................586 598-1000
Paul Steinmetz, *President*
Paul Subbio, *Sales Staff*
EMP: 10
SQ FT: 6,500
SALES (est): 1.3MM **Privately Held**
WEB: www.cwbgroup.com
SIC: 3544 Special dies & tools

Clinton Township - Macomb County (G-3078)

(G-3078)
CHOICE CORPORATION
Also Called: Choice Mold Components
44383 Reynolds Dr (48036-1243)
PHONE..................................586 783-5600
James W Humes, *President*
EMP: 25
SALES (est): 3.5MM **Privately Held**
SIC: 3544 Industrial molds

(G-3079)
CHOICE MOLD COMPONENTS INC
44383 Reynolds Dr (48036-1243)
PHONE..................................586 783-5600
James W Humes, *President*
Kathryn Humes, *Vice Pres*
▲ EMP: 24
SALES (est): 4.2MM **Privately Held**
WEB: www.choicemold.com
SIC: 3544 Industrial molds

(G-3080)
CIGNET LLC (PA)
24601 Capital Blvd (48036-1345)
PHONE..................................586 307-3790
Patrick Green, *CEO*
Tom Davidson, *COO*
Will Lianos, *CFO*
Richard S Crawford, *Manager*
Crawford Group LLC,
EMP: 40
SQ FT: 1,500
SALES (est): 23.4MM **Privately Held**
SIC: 3694 Engine electrical equipment

(G-3081)
CIRCLES WAY TO GO AROUND INC
43508 Rivergate Dr (48038-1350)
PHONE..................................313 384-1193
EMP: 10
SALES (est): 450K **Privately Held**
SIC: 2397 Mfg Schiffli Embroideries

(G-3082)
COLONIAL BUSHINGS INC
44336 Reynolds Dr (48036-1242)
PHONE..................................586 954-3880
Hugh Vestal, *President*
Mary Vestal, *Vice Pres*
EMP: 17 EST: 1946
SQ FT: 8,000
SALES: 1.5MM
SALES (corp-wide): 1.7MM **Privately Held**
WEB: www.colonialbushings.com
SIC: 3545 3568 Drill bushings (drilling jig); power transmission equipment
PA: Carbide Surface Company
44336 Reynolds Dr
Clinton Township MI 48036
586 465-6110

(G-3083)
COLONIAL MOLD INC
Also Called: Colonial Group
44479 Reynolds Dr (48036-1245)
PHONE..................................586 469-4944
Cathy Roberts, *CEO*
Richard J Roberts, *President*
Rich Blasutig, *Plant Mgr*
Scott Burnham, *Engineer*
Richard Roberts, *Administration*
EMP: 35
SQ FT: 45,000
SALES (est): 7.6MM **Privately Held**
SIC: 3544 Industrial molds

(G-3084)
COLT - 7 CORPORATION
34859 Groesbeck Hwy (48035-3366)
PHONE..................................586 792-9050
Craig Bubka, *President*
EMP: 15
SQ FT: 10,000
SALES (est): 1.7MM **Privately Held**
WEB: www.colt7corp.com
SIC: 3599 Machine shop, jobbing & repair

(G-3085)
COMPLETE PROTOTYPE SVCS INC (PA)
Also Called: C P S
44783 Morley Dr (48036-1357)
PHONE..................................586 690-8897
Chris Michayluk, *President*
EMP: 280
SQ FT: 24,000
SALES (est): 71.1MM **Privately Held**
SIC: 3543 3714 Industrial patterns; motor vehicle body components & frame

(G-3086)
COMPLETE SURFACE TECHNOLOGIES
21338 Carlo Dr (48038-1510)
PHONE..................................586 493-5800
Peter Ruggirello, *CEO*
Gordon Pinger, *President*
Debbie Hagedorn, *Administration*
EMP: 29 EST: 1999
SQ FT: 42,000
SALES: 5MM **Privately Held**
SIC: 3544 Dies, plastics forming; forms (molds), for foundry & plastics working machinery

(G-3087)
CONNER ENGINEERING LLC
21200 Carlo Dr (48038-1508)
PHONE..................................586 465-9590
Bill Middletown,
EMP: 20
SQ FT: 22,000
SALES (est): 3.4MM **Privately Held**
SIC: 3599 Machine shop, jobbing & repair

(G-3088)
CONSTRUCTION RETAIL SVCS INC
Also Called: Llowds Retail Construction
38555 Moravian Dr (48036-1958)
PHONE..................................586 469-2289
Gregory Oakwood, *President*
Timothy Ozment, *Vice Pres*
Robert Moore, *Treasurer*
EMP: 6
SALES: 630K **Privately Held**
SIC: 2542 7389 Fixtures, store: except wood;

(G-3089)
CONSUMER ADVNTAGE RFERENCE SVC
Also Called: Longshot Golf
43830 N Groesbeck Hwy (48036-1106)
PHONE..................................586 783-1806
James Krause, *CEO*
Kathleen Krause, *Exec VP*
EMP: 6
SQ FT: 7,000
SALES: 500K **Privately Held**
WEB: www.longshotgolf.com
SIC: 5091 3949 Golf equipment; golf equipment

(G-3090)
CONTINENTAL CARBIDE LTD INC
23545 Reynolds Ct (48036-1269)
PHONE..................................586 463-9577
Terrence Mc Quade, *President*
Karola Mc Quade, *Corp Secy*
Karola McQuade, *Treasurer*
EMP: 11 EST: 1982
SQ FT: 20,000
SALES (est): 1.8MM **Privately Held**
WEB: www.continental-carbide.com
SIC: 2819 5085 Carbides; industrial supplies

(G-3091)
COUGAR CUTTING TOOLS INC
23529 Reynolds Ct (48036-1269)
PHONE..................................586 469-1310
Vasko Stefanoski, *President*
Sue Stefanoski, *Vice Pres*
Andrew Stefanoski, *Opers Mgr*
Andrew Stefanowski, *Opers Mgr*
Mike Premo, *QC Mgr*
EMP: 19
SQ FT: 10,000
SALES (est): 3.1MM **Privately Held**
WEB: www.cougarct.com
SIC: 3545 Cutting tools for machine tools

(G-3092)
CREATIVE SURFACES INC
20500 Hall Rd (48038-5326)
PHONE..................................586 226-2950
Stella M Giannini, *President*
EMP: 10
SALES (est): 2MM **Privately Held**
SIC: 3531 2851 Surfacers, concrete grinding; epoxy coatings

(G-3093)
CREMATION SERVICE OF MICHIGAN
44481 N Groesbeck Hwy (48036-1190)
PHONE..................................586 465-1700
Gina Kapler, *Mng Member*
EMP: 5
SALES (est): 475.4K **Privately Held**
SIC: 3272 Burial vaults, concrete or precast terrazzo

(G-3094)
CTS MANUFACTURING INC
44760 Trinity Dr (48038-1553)
PHONE..................................586 465-4594
Steven Sterrett, *President*
Kim Sterrett, *Vice Pres*
EMP: 8
SQ FT: 5,000
SALES (est): 983.1K **Privately Held**
WEB: www.ctsmanufacturinginc.com
SIC: 3544 Special dies & tools

(G-3095)
CUMMINS INC
43575 N Gratiot Ave (48036-3327)
PHONE..................................586 469-2010
Susan Lake, *Manager*
EMP: 19
SALES (corp-wide): 23.7B **Publicly Held**
WEB: www.bridgewaypower.com
SIC: 5084 3519 Engines & parts, diesel; internal combustion engines
PA: Cummins Inc.
500 Jackson St
Columbus IN 47201
812 377-5000

(G-3096)
CUSTOM ROYALTEES
37537 Brynford Dr (48036-4436)
PHONE..................................586 943-9849
Maggie Dawson, *Principal*
EMP: 3
SALES (est): 149.5K **Privately Held**
SIC: 2759 Screen printing

(G-3097)
D & T SMOKE LLC
41964 Hayes Rd (48038-1877)
PHONE..................................586 263-6888
EMP: 3 EST: 2012
SALES (est): 210K **Privately Held**
SIC: 2131 Mfg Chewing/Smoking Tobacco

(G-3098)
D-N-S INDUSTRIES INC
Also Called: American Roll Manufacturing
44805 Trinity Dr (48038-1557)
PHONE..................................586 465-2444
Dennis R Mc Quade, *President*
Carol Mc Quade, *Vice Pres*
EMP: 15
SQ FT: 20,000
SALES (est): 2.3MM **Privately Held**
WEB: www.dnsindustries.com
SIC: 3599 3547 Machine shop, jobbing & repair; steel rolling machinery

(G-3099)
DATUM PRECISION MACHINE INC
35235 Automation Dr (48035-3115)
PHONE..................................586 790-1120
Raymond Alarie, *President*
Bonnie Alarie, *Vice Pres*
EMP: 7
SQ FT: 8,000
SALES: 500K **Privately Held**
SIC: 3599 Machine shop, jobbing & repair

(G-3100)
DEPEX PRINT SERVICES
19751 15 Mile Rd (48035-3407)
PHONE..................................586 465-6820
Douglas Gostomski, *Executive*
EMP: 3
SALES (est): 318.8K **Privately Held**
SIC: 2752 Commercial printing, offset

(G-3101)
DETROIT FLAME HARDENING CO
43554 Riverbend Blvd (48038-2479)
PHONE..................................586 484-1726
Allen Leach, *Principal*
EMP: 9
SALES (corp-wide): 3.2MM **Privately Held**
SIC: 3398 Brazing (hardening) of metal
PA: Detroit Flame Hardening Company Inc
17644 Mount Elliott St
Detroit MI
313 891-2936

(G-3102)
DIAMOND DIE AND MOLD COMPANY
Also Called: DDM
35401 Groesbeck Hwy (48035-2518)
PHONE..................................586 791-0700
Joann Hinds, *President*
Sharon Baldyga, *Vice Pres*
Patricia Quackenbush, *Treasurer*
EMP: 15 EST: 1956
SQ FT: 17,200
SALES: 2MM **Privately Held**
WEB: www.diamond-die.com
SIC: 3544 Special dies & tools

(G-3103)
DIAMOND RACING PRODUCTS INC
23003 Diamond Dr (48035-3126)
PHONE..................................586 792-6620
Vincent J Cavallaro, *President*
EMP: 15
SALES (est): 2MM **Privately Held**
SIC: 3599 Machine shop, jobbing & repair

(G-3104)
DIVERSIFIED FABRICATORS INC
Also Called: DFI
21482 Carlo Dr (48038-1512)
PHONE..................................586 868-1000
Robert Landuyt, *President*
EMP: 18 EST: 1981
SQ FT: 14,600
SALES (est): 6.2MM **Privately Held**
WEB: www.diversifiedfab.com
SIC: 3441 3444 Fabricated structural metal; housings for business machines, sheet metal; vats, sheet metal

(G-3105)
DRAKE ENTERPRISES INC
24800 Capital Blvd (48036-1351)
PHONE..................................586 783-3009
Leroy Stemple, *President*
Richard Stemple, *Vice Pres*
Joseph Sharp, *Engineer*
Kevin Cran, *Info Tech Mgr*
▲ EMP: 45
SQ FT: 38,000
SALES (est): 11.7MM **Privately Held**
WEB: www.drakeent.com
SIC: 3714 Motor vehicle body components & frame; steering mechanisms, motor vehicle

(G-3106)
E D M SHUTTLE INC
44695 Enterprise Dr (48038-1533)
PHONE..................................586 468-9880
Daniel Bruck, *President*
Jacqueline Bruck, *Manager*
EMP: 6
SQ FT: 5,600
SALES (est): 625.5K **Privately Held**
SIC: 3599 Electrical discharge machining (EDM)

GEOGRAPHIC SECTION

Clinton Township - Macomb County (G-3135)

(G-3107)
E I DU PONT DE NEMOURS & CO
15350 Renshaw Dr (48038-2654)
PHONE.................586 263-0258
Gregory Dknox, *Branch Mgr*
EMP: 339
SALES (corp-wide): 30.6B **Publicly Held**
SIC: 2879 Agricultural chemicals
HQ: E. I. Du Pont De Nemours And Company
  974 Centre Rd Bldg 735
  Wilmington DE 19805
  302 485-3000

(G-3108)
EATON CORPORATION
19700 Hall Rd Ste B (48038-4451)
PHONE.................586 228-2029
Cheryl Breza, *Principal*
EMP: 217 **Privately Held**
SIC: 3625 Relays & industrial controls
HQ: Eaton Corporation
  1000 Eaton Blvd
  Cleveland OH 44122
  440 523-5000

(G-3109)
ELECTROPLATING INDUSTRIES INC
Also Called: E P I
21410 Carlo Dr (48038-1512)
PHONE.................586 469-2390
Jeffrey Curtis, *President*
EMP: 15
SQ FT: 19,400
SALES (est): 2MM **Privately Held**
WEB: www.epiplating.com
SIC: 3471 Electroplating of metals or formed products; plating of metals or formed products

(G-3110)
EXCEPTIONAL PRODUCT SALES LLC
16010 19 Mile Rd Ste 103 (48038-1141)
PHONE.................586 286-3240
Michael Kovacs, *Mng Member*
Brent Solek,
EMP: 15
SQ FT: 2,000
SALES: 12MM **Privately Held**
SIC: 3317 Steel pipe & tubes

(G-3111)
FAB CONCEPTS
22791 Macomb Indus Dr (48036-1181)
PHONE.................586 466-6411
James Szczesny, *President*
Lisa Szczesny, *Office Mgr*
EMP: 4 **EST:** 1997
SQ FT: 9,400
SALES (est): 578K **Privately Held**
WEB: www.fabconceptsinc.com
SIC: 3312 1751 Structural shapes & pilings, steel; store fixture installation

(G-3112)
FAB-JET SERVICES LLC
44335 Macomb Indus Dr (48036-1143)
PHONE.................586 463-9622
Jason Glezman,
EMP: 5
SALES: 500K **Privately Held**
WEB: www.fab-jet.com
SIC: 3496 3545 Miscellaneous fabricated wire products; cutting tools for machine tools

(G-3113)
FALCON INDUSTRY INC
44660 Macomb Indus Dr (48036-1185)
PHONE.................586 468-7010
Joe Azzopardi, *President*
Joseph Azzopardi, *President*
Erik Azzopardi, *Engineer*
George Montgomery, *Software Dev*
EMP: 14
SALES (est): 3.2MM **Privately Held**
WEB: www.falconindustry.com
SIC: 3544 Special dies & tools

(G-3114)
FEGA TOOL & GAGE COMPANY
44837 Macomb Indus Dr (48036-1140)
PHONE.................586 469-4400
Roy Usteski, *President*
Martha Ann Usteski, *Treasurer*
EMP: 15 **EST:** 1952
SQ FT: 11,000
SALES (est): 2.2MM **Privately Held**
SIC: 3544 7389 3545 3599 Dies & die holders for metal cutting, forming, die casting; grinding, precision: commercial or industrial; machine tool attachments & accessories; gauges (machine tool accessories); machine shop, jobbing & repair

(G-3115)
FERRO FAB LLC
Also Called: Abz Steel Systems
23309 Quinn Rd (48035-3732)
PHONE.................586 791-3561
Gina Wolf, *CEO*
EMP: 10
SALES (est): 2MM **Privately Held**
SIC: 5051 2296 3441 Steel; steel tire cords & tire cord fabrics; fabricated structural metal

(G-3116)
FIDO ENTERPRISES INC
34692 Nova Dr (48035-3716)
PHONE.................586 790-8200
Philip L Edwards, *President*
Brenda Nemens, *Plant Mgr*
▲ **EMP:** 9
SQ FT: 7,500
SALES (est): 1.4MM **Privately Held**
WEB: www.petaction.com
SIC: 3089 Injection molded finished plastic products

(G-3117)
FINAZZO MANUFACTURING CO INC
34654 Nova Dr (48035-3716)
PHONE.................586 757-3955
Phillip Finazzo, *President*
EMP: 3
SQ FT: 800
SALES: 100K **Privately Held**
SIC: 3599 Machine shop, jobbing & repair

(G-3118)
FINISHING SPECIALTIES INC
44100 N Groesbeck Hwy (48036-1109)
PHONE.................586 954-1338
Renee Mc Laughlin, *President*
Brian McLaughlin, *Business Mgr*
EMP: 8
SQ FT: 13,000
SALES (est): 750K **Privately Held**
SIC: 3479 Painting of metal products

(G-3119)
FIRST IMPRSSONS CSTM PRINTWEAR
44432 Reynolds Dr (48036-1244)
PHONE.................586 783-5210
EMP: 10 **EST:** 1994
SQ FT: 3,800
SALES (est): 996.6K **Privately Held**
WEB: www.firstimpressionscorp.com
SIC: 2759 Screen printing

(G-3120)
FIVE LAKES MANUFACTURING INC
Also Called: F L M
24400 Capital Blvd (48036-1342)
PHONE.................586 463-4123
Roger Eger Jr, *CEO*
Patricia Tischbein, *President*
EMP: 50
SQ FT: 40,000
SALES (est): 11.3MM **Privately Held**
WEB: www.fivelakesmfg.com
SIC: 2431 Doors, wood

(G-3121)
FLAMINGO LABEL CO
21428 Carlo Dr (48038-1512)
PHONE.................586 469-9587
Brian Klauss, *President*
Jason Ford, *Sales Staff*
Matt Collier, *Manager*
EMP: 17
SALES (est): 3.9MM **Privately Held**
WEB: www.flamingolabel.com
SIC: 2672 Labels (unprinted), gummed: made from purchased materials

(G-3122)
FLEX MANUFACTURING INC
44805 Trinity Dr (48038-1557)
PHONE.................586 469-1076
David Gleason, *President*
Quin Gleason, *Vice Pres*
EMP: 15
SQ FT: 4,000
SALES: 850K **Privately Held**
WEB: www.flexmfginc.com
SIC: 3545 Precision tools, machinists'

(G-3123)
FLUID SYSTEMS ENGINEERING INC
18855 E 14 Mile Rd (48035-3901)
PHONE.................586 790-8880
Mark T Steiner, *President*
John Doll, *Vice Pres*
Paul Lipiec, *Foreman/Supr*
Michelle Hopkins, *Purchasing*
Joseph A Baker, *Treasurer*
EMP: 27
SQ FT: 19,700
SALES: 15.8MM
SALES (corp-wide): 77.7MM **Privately Held**
WEB: www.fluidsystemseng.com
SIC: 5085 3561 5084 Valves & fittings; industrial pumps & parts; machine tools & accessories
HQ: Motion & Control Enterprises Llc
  100 Williams Dr
  Zelienople PA 16063
  724 452-6000

(G-3124)
FREER TOOL & DIE INC
Also Called: Freer Tool and Supply
44675 Morley Dr (48036-1358)
PHONE.................586 463-3200
John Fulton, *President*
Bruce Hammons, *Plant Mgr*
▲ **EMP:** 31
SQ FT: 22,280
SALES (est): 5.3MM **Privately Held**
WEB: www.freertool.com
SIC: 3544 Special dies & tools

(G-3125)
FREER TOOL & DIE INC
Also Called: Freer Tool & Supply
44675 Morley Dr (48036-1358)
PHONE.................586 741-5274
John Fulton, *Principal*
EMP: 7
SALES (est): 1.3MM **Privately Held**
SIC: 3544 Special dies & tools

(G-3126)
FRICTION COATING CORPORATION
44833 Centre Ct (48038-1316)
PHONE.................586 731-0990
Charles Neff, *President*
Seachrist Frank, *Sales Engr*
EMP: 34
SALES (est): 7.7MM **Privately Held**
WEB: www.frictioncoating.com
SIC: 3599 Machine shop, jobbing & repair

(G-3127)
FRICTION CONTROL LLC
35360 Forton Ct (48035-5626)
PHONE.................586 741-8493
John Bireescu, *Mng Member*
Susan Bireescu,
EMP: 5
SQ FT: 5,288
SALES (est): 927K **Privately Held**
WEB: www.frictioncontrol.com
SIC: 3568 Clutches, except vehicular

(G-3128)
GAGE BILT INC
44766 Centre Ct (48038-1315)
PHONE.................586 226-1500
Bruce Godfrey, *President*
EMP: 35
SQ FT: 25,005
SALES: 4.2MM **Privately Held**
WEB: www.gagebilt.com
SIC: 3452 Rivets, metal; bolts, metal

(G-3129)
GREAT LAKES AVIAITON SVCS LLC
Also Called: Glas
41358 Lore Dr (48038-2089)
PHONE.................586 770-3450
Benjamin Zawodni, *Vice Pres*
David Garijo, *Vice Pres*
EMP: 3
SALES (est): 243.5K **Privately Held**
SIC: 3721 Airplanes, fixed or rotary wing

(G-3130)
GREENE METAL PRODUCTS INC (PA)
24500 Capital Blvd (48036-1348)
PHONE.................586 465-6800
Bruce Wilden, *President*
Tina Smith, *General Mgr*
Robert Wilden, *Chairman*
Jamie Schneider, *CFO*
Ann Smith, *Receptionist*
▲ **EMP:** 49
SQ FT: 60,000
SALES: 11.2MM **Privately Held**
WEB: www.greenemetal.com
SIC: 3444 3443 3441 Sheet metalwork; fabricated plate work (boiler shop); fabricated structural metal

(G-3131)
GREENE METAL PRODUCTS INC
24500 Capital Blvd (48036-1348)
PHONE.................586 465-6800
Paul Kutchen, *Manager*
EMP: 15
SALES (corp-wide): 11.2MM **Privately Held**
WEB: www.greenemetal.com
SIC: 3444 Sheet metalwork
PA: Greene Metal Products, Inc.
  24500 Capital Blvd
  Clinton Township MI 48036
  586 465-6800

(G-3132)
GRIND-ALL PRECISION TOOL CO
21300 Carlo Dr (48038-1510)
PHONE.................586 954-3430
M Dean McCreadie, *President*
EMP: 10
SQ FT: 12,000
SALES: 1.3MM **Privately Held**
SIC: 3545 3599 Precision tools, machinists'; grinding castings for the trade

(G-3133)
HANDY BINDERY CO INC
23170 Giacoma Ct (48036-4608)
PHONE.................586 469-2240
Suzanne Canu, *President*
EMP: 22
SQ FT: 8,000
SALES (est): 2.4MM **Privately Held**
SIC: 2759 2789 Letterpress printing; bookbinding & related work

(G-3134)
HARRY MAJOR MACHINE & TOOL CO (PA)
24801 Capital Blvd (48036-1347)
PHONE.................586 783-7030
H Curtis Major, *President*
Robert Lester, *General Mgr*
Fred Achatz, *Manager*
▲ **EMP:** 75
SQ FT: 100,000
SALES (est): 19.7MM **Privately Held**
WEB: www.harrymajormachine.com
SIC: 3535 Conveyors & conveying equipment

(G-3135)
HEATING INDUCTION SERVICES INC
24483 Sorrentino Ct (48035-3240)
PHONE.................586 791-3160
Ernest W Taylor, *President*

Clinton Township - Macomb County (G-3136)

Shirley Taylor, *Admin Sec*
EMP: 9
SQ FT: 12,400
SALES (est): 1.9MM **Privately Held**
SIC: 3567 7699 Induction heating equipment; industrial machinery & equipment repair

(G-3136)
HUSITE ENGINEERING CO INC
44831 N Groesbeck Hwy (48036-1124)
PHONE..................248 588-0337
Larry Huston, *President*
Jack T Huston, *Vice Pres*
EMP: 26 **EST:** 1957
SALES (est): 4.1MM **Privately Held**
SIC: 3543 3369 3363 Industrial patterns; nonferrous foundries; aluminum die-castings

(G-3137)
HYLITE TOOL & MACHINE INC
44685 Macomb Indus Dr (48036-1148)
PHONE..................586 465-7878
Holger Joost, *President*
Gary Romatz, *Vice Pres*
Harold Joost, *Treasurer*
EMP: 7
SQ FT: 12,000
SALES: 750K **Privately Held**
SIC: 3599 Machine shop, jobbing & repair

(G-3138)
HYPER ALLOYS INC
17001 19 Mile Rd Ste 1 (48038-4867)
PHONE..................586 772-0571
Harold Fletcher, *President*
Pamela Neumann-Liedke, *President*
Ronald J Liedke, *Vice Pres*
Monika Mathy, *Admin Sec*
EMP: 25 **EST:** 1958
SQ FT: 22,000
SALES: 6.8MM **Privately Held**
WEB: www.hyperalloys.com
SIC: 3499 Boxes for packing & shipping, metal

(G-3139)
IDC INDUSTRIES INC
18901 15 Mile Rd (48035-2504)
PHONE..................586 427-4321
Jamie Pangborn, *President*
Michael Pangborn, *Vice Pres*
Andrew Janies, *Treasurer*
EMP: 42
SQ FT: 50,000
SALES (est): 12.6MM **Privately Held**
WEB: www.idcind.com
SIC: 3568 5085 Power transmission equipment; power transmission equipment & apparatus

(G-3140)
INFINITY RECYCLING LLC
Also Called: Infinity Transportation
44057 N Groesbeck Hwy (48036-1123)
PHONE..................248 939-2563
Peter Corrado, *Vice Pres*
EMP: 10
SALES (est): 743.6K **Privately Held**
SIC: 2611 Pulp manufactured from waste or recycled paper

(G-3141)
INTEGRATED INDUSTRIES INC
33670 Lipke St (48035-3617)
PHONE..................586 790-1550
Paul T Newman, *President*
EMP: 70
SQ FT: 25,000
SALES (est): 6.8MM **Privately Held**
SIC: 3444 Ducts, sheet metal

(G-3142)
INTERNATIONAL MOLD CORPORATION
44370 N Groesbeck Hwy (48036-1110)
PHONE..................586 801-2314
EMP: 9
SALES (corp-wide): 23MM **Privately Held**
SIC: 3544 Special dies, tools, jigs & fixtures

PA: International Mold Corporation
23224 Giacoma Ct
Clinton Township MI 48036
586 783-6890

(G-3143)
INTERNATIONAL MOLD CORPORATION (PA)
23224 Giacoma Ct (48036-4608)
PHONE..................586 783-6890
James H Pelcher, *President*
Michael Lilla, *Treasurer*
Tim Cook, *Program Mgr*
Tim Malloy, *Program Mgr*
Tom Pfropper, *Program Mgr*
▲ **EMP:** 82
SQ FT: 12,000
SALES (est): 23MM **Privately Held**
WEB: www.internationalmold.net
SIC: 3544 Industrial molds

(G-3144)
INTL GIUSEPPES OILS & VINEGARS
17330 Hall Rd (48038-4869)
PHONE..................586 263-4200
Joseph Cucinello, *Principal*
EMP: 3 **EST:** 2011
SALES (est): 237.9K **Privately Held**
SIC: 2099 Vinegar

(G-3145)
IRON TOOL & DIE INC
35531 Groesbeck Hwy (48035-2520)
PHONE..................586 791-1389
Carl Reneski, *President*
EMP: 3
SQ FT: 3,600
SALES (est): 450K **Privately Held**
SIC: 3544 Special dies, tools, jigs & fixtures

(G-3146)
J & J METAL PRODUCTS INC
Also Called: J & J Sheet Metal
34145 Groesbeck Hwy (48035-3355)
PHONE..................586 792-2680
Robert J Kehoe, *President*
Robert Kehole, *President*
EMP: 4 **EST:** 1945
SQ FT: 3,800
SALES (est): 732.7K **Privately Held**
SIC: 3444 Ducts, sheet metal

(G-3147)
JAM TIRE INC
36031 Groesbeck Hwy (48035-1542)
PHONE..................586 772-2900
Kenny Weber, *Branch Mgr*
EMP: 61
SALES (corp-wide): 49.5MM **Privately Held**
SIC: 7534 5531 5014 3011 Tire retreading & repair shops; automotive tires; tires & tubes; tires & inner tubes
PA: Jam Tire Inc
6202 Fairfield Dr
Northwood OH 43619
419 661-1800

(G-3148)
JEFFERY TOOL & MFG CO
44371 Macomb Indus Dr (48036-1143)
PHONE..................586 307-8846
Kenneth Grasl, *President*
Ronald Grasl, *Treasurer*
Harley Grasl, *Admin Sec*
EMP: 12
SQ FT: 15,000
SALES (est): 1.8MM **Privately Held**
WEB: www.jefferytool.com
SIC: 3544 Special dies & tools

(G-3149)
JEM COMPUTERS INC
Also Called: Jem Tech Group
23537 Lakepointe Dr (48036-3323)
PHONE..................586 783-3400
James Miller, *CEO*
Jami M Moore, *President*
EMP: 14
SQ FT: 6,500

SALES (est): 10.2MM **Privately Held**
SIC: 5045 3629 3577 2522 Computer peripheral equipment; computer software; electronic generation equipment; power conversion units, a.c. to d.c.: static-electric; computer peripheral equipment; printers, computer; office furniture, except wood; computer peripheral equipment

(G-3150)
JOGGLE TOOL & DIE CO INC
24424 Kolleen Ln (48035-5438)
PHONE..................586 792-7477
Thomas Platte, *President*
Frank Hiegel, *Vice Pres*
Terry Jelineck, *Admin Sec*
EMP: 4
SQ FT: 6,000
SALES: 400K **Privately Held**
SIC: 3544 Special dies & tools

(G-3151)
JVIS - USA LLC
Also Called: Jvis USA LLC - Harper
34501 Harper Ave (48035-3708)
P.O. Box 530, Mount Clemens (48046-0530)
PHONE..................586 803-6056
Michael Alexander, *Vice Pres*
EMP: 400
SALES (corp-wide): 381.6MM **Privately Held**
SIC: 3559 Automotive related machinery
PA: Jvis - Usa, Llc
52048 Shelby Pkwy
Shelby Township MI 48315
586 884-5700

(G-3152)
K AND K MACHINE TOOLS INC
22393 Starks Dr (48036-1197)
PHONE..................586 463-1177
Moritz C Cunha, *President*
Mark Cunha, *Vice Pres*
Susan Cunha, *Admin Sec*
EMP: 5
SQ FT: 6,000
SALES: 490K **Privately Held**
SIC: 3561 3544 Industrial pumps & parts; special dies, tools, jigs & fixtures

(G-3153)
KATECH INC
Also Called: Katech Performance
24324 Sorrentino Ct (48035-3238)
PHONE..................586 791-4120
Tony Mannarino, *CEO*
EMP: 43 **EST:** 2014
SALES (est): 8MM **Privately Held**
SIC: 3519 Parts & accessories, internal combustion engines

(G-3154)
KENNEDY SALES INC
19683 Tanglewood Cir (48038-4964)
PHONE..................586 228-9390
James D Kennedy, *President*
Constance Kennedy, *Vice Pres*
EMP: 2
SALES (est): 2.1MM **Privately Held**
SIC: 3949 Playground equipment

(G-3155)
KMJ BORING CO INC
42965 Biland Dr (48035-5630)
PHONE..................586 465-8771
Ron Bryce, *President*
Doug Lowell, *Corp Secy*
EMP: 3 **EST:** 1997
SQ FT: 3,500
SALES (est): 500K **Privately Held**
SIC: 3559 Automotive related machinery

(G-3156)
L F M ENTERPRISES INC
Also Called: Laporte Industries
33256 Kelly Rd (48035-3982)
PHONE..................586 792-7220
Dennis Laporte, *President*
Diane Hanson, *Corp Secy*
Tom Laporte, *Foreman/Supr*
EMP: 30
SQ FT: 20,000
SALES (est): 5.7MM **Privately Held**
WEB: www.800laporte.com
SIC: 3599 Machine shop, jobbing & repair

(G-3157)
L T C ROLL & ENGINEERING CO (PA)
Also Called: L. T. C Roll & Engineering Co
23500 John Gorsuch Dr (48036-1215)
PHONE..................586 465-1023
Andrew Ligda, *President*
Ned M Cavallaro, *Vice Pres*
Ned Cavallaro, *Vice Pres*
Amy Garrett, *QC Mgr*
Steve Ackerman, *Design Engr*
▲ **EMP:** 28
SQ FT: 100,000
SALES (est): 27.7MM **Privately Held**
WEB: www.ltcroll.com
SIC: 3469 Metal stampings

(G-3158)
L&L PRINTING INC
Also Called: American Speedy Printing
42120 Garfield Rd (48038-1645)
PHONE..................586 263-0060
Loren K Maurina, *President*
EMP: 6
SQ FT: 1,600
SALES (est): 832.7K **Privately Held**
SIC: 2752 Commercial printing, offset

(G-3159)
LAKESIDE BORING INC
16627 Terra Bella St (48038-4080)
PHONE..................586 286-8883
Ray Marah Sr, *President*
EMP: 3
SQ FT: 3,200
SALES (est): 190K **Privately Held**
SIC: 3599 Machine & other job shop work

(G-3160)
LEE PRINTING COMPANY
21222 Cass Ave (48036-1403)
P.O. Box 832, Mount Clemens (48046-0832)
PHONE..................586 463-1564
Keith Lesperance, *President*
Beverly Lesperance, *Shareholder*
EMP: 10 **EST:** 1964
SQ FT: 4,800
SALES: 1MM **Privately Held**
WEB: www.leeprint.com
SIC: 2752 Commercial printing, offset

(G-3161)
M S MANUFACTURING INC
44431 Reynolds Dr (48036-1245)
PHONE..................586 463-2788
Craig S Walworth, *President*
Terry Walworth, *Vice Pres*
EMP: 10 **EST:** 2010
SQ FT: 20,000
SALES (est): 146.4K **Privately Held**
SIC: 3714 Motor vehicle body components & frame

(G-3162)
MACOMB BUSINESS FORMS INC
Also Called: American Graphics Printing
34895 Groesbeck Hwy (48035-3366)
PHONE..................586 790-8500
Robert A Hindman, *President*
Michael Grix, *General Mgr*
Virginia Hindman, *Vice Pres*
Mary Typurski, *Office Mgr*
EMP: 16 **EST:** 1975
SQ FT: 10,000
SALES (est): 2.5MM **Privately Held**
SIC: 2752 Commercial printing, offset

(G-3163)
MACOMB PRINTING INC
Also Called: Macomb Marketing Media
44272 N Groesbeck Hwy (48036-1188)
PHONE..................586 463-2301
Ronald Bracali, *President*
Pam Bracali, *Vice Pres*
EMP: 33
SQ FT: 35,000
SALES (est): 6.9MM **Privately Held**
WEB: www.macombprinting.com
SIC: 2752 2791 2789 Commercial printing, offset; typesetting; bookbinding & related work

Clinton Township - Macomb County (G-3194)

(G-3164)
MACOMB SHEET METAL INC
35195 Forton Ct (48035-3132)
PHONE..................586 790-4600
Richard Opatik, *President*
Kathy Opatik, *Vice Pres*
EMP: 27
SQ FT: 20,000
SALES (est): 6.7MM **Privately Held**
WEB: www.msmetal.com
SIC: 3699 Laser welding, drilling & cutting equipment

(G-3165)
MAJIK GRAPHICS INC
19751 15 Mile Rd (48035-3407)
PHONE..................586 792-8055
Marcetta Hurst, *President*
EMP: 9
SQ FT: 4,000
SALES (est): 575K **Privately Held**
WEB: www.majikgraphics.com
SIC: 3993 Signs & advertising specialties

(G-3166)
MANOR INDUSTRIES INC
24400 Maplehurst Dr (48036-1323)
PHONE..................586 463-4604
Ray Tokarczyk, *President*
Jerald Decker, *President*
Richard Decker, *Vice Pres*
Neal Hamel, *Sales Executive*
EMP: 16
SQ FT: 33,000
SALES: 1.5MM **Privately Held**
WEB: www.manorindustries.com
SIC: 3599 Machine shop, jobbing & repair

(G-3167)
MANOS AUTHENTIC LLC
22599 15 Mile Rd (48035-6020)
PHONE..................800 242-2796
EMP: 5
SALES (est): 255.4K **Privately Held**
SIC: 2096 Potato chips & similar snacks

(G-3168)
MARINE MACHINING AND MFG
33475 Giftos Dr (48035-4242)
PHONE..................586 791-8800
Brian A Jenich, *Owner*
Val Jenich, *Co-Owner*
▼ EMP: 6
SQ FT: 1,000
SALES (est): 548.1K **Privately Held**
SIC: 3599 Machine shop, jobbing & repair

(G-3169)
MASTER MACHINE & TOOL CO INC
23414 Reynolds Ct (48036-1240)
PHONE..................586 469-4243
Tom Mireau, *CEO*
Natalie Mireau, *President*
EMP: 8 EST: 1954
SQ FT: 8,900
SALES: 1MM **Privately Held**
WEB: www.mastermachineandtool.com
SIC: 3544 3545 Jigs & fixtures; precision tools, machinists'

(G-3170)
MATRIX TOOL CO
40577 Sunfield Ct (48038-4171)
PHONE..................586 296-6010
Kenneth J Kraft, *President*
Daniel Kraft, *Vice Pres*
EMP: 20
SALES (est): 1.2MM **Privately Held**
SIC: 3544 3444 Special dies & tools; sheet metalwork

(G-3171)
MAYCO INTERNATIONAL LLC
Also Called: Njt Enterprises LLC
34501 Harper Ave (48035-3708)
P.O. Box 180149, Utica (48318-0149)
PHONE..................586 803-6000
Allen L Grajek, *CFO*
EMP: 210 **Privately Held**
SIC: 3089 Injection molding of plastics
PA: Mayco International Llc
42400 Merrill Rd
Sterling Heights MI 48314

(G-3172)
MECCOM INDUSTRIAL PRODUCTS CO
Also Called: Pebco Sales
22797 Morelli Dr (48036-1187)
PHONE..................586 463-2828
Paul Baltzer Jr, *CEO*
Philip Bearance, *President*
Glenn Ortez, *Vice Pres*
EMP: 14
SQ FT: 12,000
SALES: 3MM
SALES (corp-wide): 5MM **Privately Held**
WEB: www.meccomindustrial.com
SIC: 5085 3069 Valves & fittings; rubber goods, mechanical; expansion joints, rubber
PA: Pebco Sales, Inc
22797 Morelli Dr
Clinton Township MI 48036
586 463-7850

(G-3173)
METRO SIGN FABRICATORS INC
43984 N Groesbeck Hwy (48036-1107)
PHONE..................586 493-0502
Timothy White, *President*
EMP: 5
SALES (est): 570.3K **Privately Held**
SIC: 3993 Signs & advertising specialties

(G-3174)
MIDSTATES INDUSTRIAL GROUP INC
21299 Carlo Dr (48038-1509)
PHONE..................586 307-3414
Arnold D Jones, *President*
Dean Jones, *Purchasing*
Frank Soullier, *Engineer*
Barbara Hopkins, *Bookkeeper*
EMP: 24 EST: 1999
SQ FT: 18,500
SALES (est): 5.5MM **Privately Held**
WEB: www.midstatesind.com
SIC: 3465 3711 8711 Automotive stampings; automobile assembly, including specialty automobiles; engineering services

(G-3175)
MIDWEST PRESS AND AUTOMTN LLC
20417 Calumet Dr (48038-1465)
PHONE..................586 212-1937
Lori Stone, *Branch Mgr*
EMP: 3 **Privately Held**
SIC: 2741 Miscellaneous publishing
PA: Midwest Press And Automation, Llc
2904 Snow Rd
Lansing MI 48917

(G-3176)
MILES CAKE CANDY SUPPLIES
Also Called: Miles Cake Decorating Supply
44885 Morley Dr (48036-1359)
PHONE..................586 783-9252
Christina Orquino, *Owner*
EMP: 3
SALES (est): 229.2K **Privately Held**
SIC: 2051 Bread, cake & related products

(G-3177)
MILLENNIUM MOLD & TOOL INC
35225 Automation Dr (48035-3115)
PHONE..................586 791-1711
Michelle Fournier, *President*
Joseph R Fournier, *Vice Pres*
EMP: 4
SQ FT: 4,200
SALES (est): 530.1K **Privately Held**
WEB: www.millmold.com
SIC: 3544 Special dies & tools

(G-3178)
MINI-MIX INC
33600 Kelly Rd (48035-4844)
PHONE..................586 792-2260
Joe Latorre, *President*
Sam Latorre, *Vice Pres*
EMP: 40
SQ FT: 3,000
SALES (est): 1.3MM **Privately Held**
SIC: 3273 Ready-mixed concrete

(G-3179)
MJC TOOL & MACHINE CO INC
35806 Groesbeck Hwy (48035-2524)
PHONE..................586 790-4766
Laura Clarkston, *CEO*
Michael Clarkston, *Admin Sec*
EMP: 7
SQ FT: 5,000
SALES: 320K **Privately Held**
SIC: 7699 3545 7539 Industrial machinery & equipment repair; machine tool accessories; machine shop, automotive

(G-3180)
MORLEY BRANDS LLC
23770 Hall Rd (48036-1275)
PHONE..................586 468-4300
Ronald W Rapson, *Mng Member*
EMP: 100
SALES: 12MM
SALES (corp-wide): 178.7MM **Privately Held**
WEB: www.morleycandy.com
SIC: 2064 5441 Candy & other confectionery products; candy
HQ: Sanders Candy, Llc
23770 Hall Rd
Clinton Township MI 48036
800 651-7263

(G-3181)
MOUNT CLEMENS ORTHOPEDIC APPLS
Also Called: Mount Clmens Orthopaedic Appls
24432 Crocker Blvd (48036-3215)
PHONE..................586 463-3600
Rolf Schroeter, *President*
Werner Schroeter, *President*
EMP: 5
SALES (est): 796.4K **Privately Held**
SIC: 3842 5999 Orthopedic appliances; orthopedic & prosthesis applications

(G-3182)
MT CLEMENS GLASS & MIRROR CO
1231 S Gratiot Ave (48036-3595)
PHONE..................586 465-1733
David Egge, *President*
EMP: 16
SQ FT: 7,800
SALES: 2.3MM **Privately Held**
SIC: 1793 3442 Glass & glazing work; window & door frames

(G-3183)
NOELCO INC
22303 Starks Dr (48036-1197)
PHONE..................586 846-4955
Robert J Noel, *President*
David R Osborn, *Vice Pres*
EMP: 2
SALES: 1.5MM **Privately Held**
SIC: 3625 Relays & industrial controls

(G-3184)
NORRIS GRAPHICS INC
Also Called: Signs By Tomorrow
33251 S Gratiot Ave (48035-4039)
PHONE..................586 447-0646
Fax: 586 447-0650
EMP: 4
SALES (est): 260K **Privately Held**
SIC: 3993 Signsadv Specs

(G-3185)
NORTH AMERICAN TOOL INC
43933 N Groesbeck Hwy (48036-1113)
PHONE..................586 463-1746
Craig Hawkins, *President*
EMP: 3
SALES (est): 972K **Privately Held**
SIC: 3599 Machine shop, jobbing & repair

(G-3186)
NORTH-EAST GAGE INC
33398 Kelly Rd (48035-3983)
PHONE..................586 792-6790
Harry James Freer, *President*
EMP: 7
SALES (est): 750K **Privately Held**
SIC: 3545 Gauges (machine tool accessories)

(G-3187)
OAKLEY INDUSTRIES INC (PA)
35166 Automation Dr (48035-3113)
PHONE..................586 791-3194
Ronald Oakley, *CEO*
Michael Oakley, *President*
Brenda Oakley, *Corp Secy*
Dennis Barbier, *QC Mgr*
EMP: 30
SQ FT: 8,800
SALES (est): 18.5MM **Privately Held**
WEB: www.oakley-ind.com
SIC: 3465 3089 Automotive stampings; injection molding of plastics

(G-3188)
OAKLEY INDUSTRIES INC
35224 Automation Dr (48035-3114)
PHONE..................586 792-1261
Ronald Oakley, *Manager*
EMP: 40
SALES (corp-wide): 18.5MM **Privately Held**
WEB: www.oakley-ind.com
SIC: 3465 Automotive stampings
PA: Oakley Industries, Inc.
35166 Automation Dr
Clinton Township MI 48035
586 791-3194

(G-3189)
ODYSSEY TOOL LLC
22373 Starks Dr (48036-1197)
PHONE..................586 468-6696
Carol Harris, *Manager*
George Tilli,
EMP: 12
SALES (est): 2.4MM **Privately Held**
SIC: 3544 Special dies & tools

(G-3190)
OMEGA PLASTICS INC
24401 Capital Blvd (48036-1343)
PHONE..................586 954-2100
Jeffrey Kaczperski, *President*
Brian Dimuzio, *Maint Spvr*
EMP: 70
SALES (est): 22MM **Privately Held**
WEB: www.opinc.com
SIC: 3089 3544 Injection molded finished plastic products; industrial molds

(G-3191)
OXYGENPLUS LLC
15760 19 Mile Rd Ste E (48038-6319)
PHONE..................586 221-9112
Robert Rudowski, *Mng Member*
EMP: 5 EST: 2007
SALES (est): 619.8K **Privately Held**
SIC: 3841 Medical instruments & equipment, blood & bone work

(G-3192)
PCT SECURITY INC
34668 Nova Dr (48035-3716)
PHONE..................888 567-3287
Dave Janicki, *President*
Richard Shaffer, *General Mgr*
Chris Dowden, *Project Mgr*
Kevin Buchanan, *Opers Staff*
Tracy Lawrence, *Controller*
EMP: 4
SALES (est): 979.7K **Privately Held**
SIC: 5065 7382 3699 Security control equipment & systems; security systems services; security devices

(G-3193)
PERFORMANCE SAILING INC
Also Called: U K Sailmakers
24227 Sorrentino Ct (48035-3237)
PHONE..................586 790-7500
Alex J Declercq, *President*
EMP: 19
SQ FT: 12,000
SALES (est): 2.1MM **Privately Held**
SIC: 2394 2221 Sails: made from purchased materials; broadwoven fabric mills, manmade

(G-3194)
PLAST-O-FOAM LLC
24601 Capital Blvd (48036-1345)
PHONE..................586 307-3790
Lisa Antosh, *Accountant*
Andy Watts, *Marketing Mgr*

Clinton Township - Macomb County (G-3195) — GEOGRAPHIC SECTION

Jeremy Tom, *Program Mgr*
Thomas Davidson,
Jenny Cantrell, *Admin Asst*
▲ **EMP:** 74
SQ FT: 110,000
SALES (est): 23.3MM
SALES (corp-wide): 23.4MM **Privately Held**
WEB: www.cignet.net
SIC: 3089 Injection molded finished plastic products; pallets, plastic
PA: Cignet, L.L.C.
24601 Capital Blvd
Clinton Township MI 48036
586 307-3790

(G-3195)
PLASTICOS INC
21445 Carlo Dr Ste B (48038-1513)
PHONE 586 493-1908
Marcelino Ramirez III, *President*
Steve Anderson, *President*
EMP: 4
SQ FT: 20,000
SALES (est): 2MM **Privately Held**
SIC: 2821 Plastics materials & resins

(G-3196)
PLATINUM SKIN CARE INC
20556 Hall Rd (48038-5326)
PHONE 586 598-6075
Jennifer Tilney, *President*
▲ **EMP:** 9
SQ FT: 2,800
SALES (est): 1.7MM **Privately Held**
SIC: 2844 Toilet preparations

(G-3197)
POTATOE BALL LLC
42160 Lochmoor St (48038-1772)
PHONE 313 483-0901
Jonathone Johnson, *Mng Member*
EMP: 3
SALES: 10K
SALES (corp-wide): 791K **Privately Held**
SIC: 2037 Potato products, quick frozen & cold pack
PA: Inspired By Mom Food And Specialty Industries Inc.
42160 Lochmoor St
Clinton Township MI 48038
586 215-5172

(G-3198)
PRECISION BORING COMPANY
24400 Maplehurst Dr (48036-1323)
PHONE 586 463-3900
Gerald R Decker, *President*
David Decker, *General Mgr*
Richard Decker Jr, *Vice Pres*
Dolf Burnham, *Foreman/Supr*
Jason Chumbler, *Manager*
▲ **EMP:** 42
SQ FT: 35,000
SALES (est): 7.5MM **Privately Held**
WEB: www.precisionboring.com
SIC: 3599 Machine shop, jobbing & repair

(G-3199)
PRECISION DIE CAST INC
44396 Reynolds Dr (48036-1242)
PHONE 586 463-1800
Craig La Pierre, *CEO*
EMP: 8
SQ FT: 6,800
SALES: 2.5MM **Privately Held**
WEB: www.precisiondiecast.com
SIC: 3363 Aluminum die-castings

(G-3200)
PRECISIONCRAFT CO
44395 Reynolds Dr (48036-1243)
PHONE 586 954-9510
Gary R Hartigan, *President*
Doug Hartigan, *Vice Pres*
Jack Hartigan, *Vice Pres*
Jim Hartigan, *Vice Pres*
EMP: 14 **EST:** 1964
SQ FT: 13,850
SALES: 2.2MM **Privately Held**
SIC: 3599 Machine shop, jobbing & repair

(G-3201)
PRESS-WAY INC
19101 15 Mile Rd (48035-2508)
PHONE 586 790-3324
Robert Grant, *President*
Steven Grant, *Vice Pres*
EMP: 90 **EST:** 1961
SALES (est): 11.7MM
SALES (corp-wide): 16.5MM **Privately Held**
WEB: www.grantgrp.com
SIC: 3465 3469 Body parts, automobile: stamped metal; metal stampings
PA: Grant Industries, Incorporated
33415 Groesbeck Hwy
Fraser MI 48026
586 293-9200

(G-3202)
PRESTIGE ENGRG RSRCES TECH INC (PA)
24700 Capital Blvd (48036-1350)
PHONE 586 573-3070
William G Fritts, *President*
Michael Wilson, *Controller*
Tom Nichols, *Manager*
Cindy Seguin, *Admin Asst*
EMP: 17 **EST:** 1998
SALES (est): 13.9MM **Privately Held**
WEB: www.prestigeeng.com
SIC: 3599 3714 Amusement park equipment; motor vehicle engines & parts

(G-3203)
PRIME MOLD LLC
44645 Macomb Indus Dr (48036-1148)
PHONE 586 221-2512
Tim Whitmore, *Sales Mgr*
Timothy Whitmore,
EMP: 15
SALES (est): 100.6K **Privately Held**
SIC: 3544 Industrial molds

(G-3204)
PRINTING CYLINDERS INC
22045 Olson St (48035-1758)
PHONE 586 791-5231
John R Vallad, *President*
Timothy Vallad, *Vice Pres*
EMP: 3 **EST:** 1978
SQ FT: 3,600
SALES (est): 432.7K **Privately Held**
SIC: 3443 Cylinders, pressure: metal plate

(G-3205)
PRIORITY WASTE LLC
42822 Garfield Rd (48038-1656)
PHONE 586 228-1200
Pauline R Stamper,
EMP: 20
SALES (est): 405.8K **Privately Held**
SIC: 4212 3443 Dump truck haulage; dumpsters, garbage

(G-3206)
PRO - TECH GRAPHICS LTD
34851 Groesbeck Hwy (48035-3366)
PHONE 586 791-6363
David Hoffman, *President*
▲ **EMP:** 11
SQ FT: 5,600
SALES (est): 1.3MM **Privately Held**
SIC: 3479 Etching & engraving

(G-3207)
REEF TOOL & GAGE CO
44800 Macomb Indus Dr (48036-1146)
PHONE 586 468-3000
E Robert Langtry Jr, *President*
EMP: 15
SALES (est): 2.5MM **Privately Held**
SIC: 3544 3545 Special dies & tools; jigs: inspection, gauging & checking; gauges (machine tool accessories)

(G-3208)
REGENCY CONSTRUCTION CORP
Also Called: Regency Dki
35240 Forton Ct (48035-3131)
PHONE 586 741-8000
Scott Stamper, *President*
EMP: 30
SQ FT: 3,000
SALES (est): 1.8MM **Privately Held**
WEB: www.regencydki.com
SIC: 7349 1521 8744 8748 Janitorial service, contract basis; general remodeling, single-family houses; ; business consulting; manufactured hardware (general)

(G-3209)
RELIABLE REASONABLE TL SVC LLC
21356 Carlo Dr (48038-1510)
PHONE 586 630-6016
Jason Rhodes, *CEO*
Ronald Rhodes,
EMP: 16
SQ FT: 16,000
SALES: 1.4MM **Privately Held**
SIC: 3089 Injection molded finished plastic products

(G-3210)
RETURNABLE PACKAGING CORP
1917 S Riverehill Dr (48038)
PHONE 586 206-8050
Bruce Steffens, *President*
EMP: 16
SALES (est): 3MM **Privately Held**
SIC: 3443 Trash racks, metal plate

(G-3211)
RICHMOND INSTRS & SYSTEMS INC
21392 Carlo Dr (48038-1510)
PHONE 586 954-3770
Dennis Mach, *President*
Marilyn Mach, *Corp Secy*
Mike Mach, *Vice Pres*
EMP: 15
SQ FT: 11,500
SALES (est): 4.1MM **Privately Held**
WEB: www.risi1.com
SIC: 3829 Measuring & controlling devices

(G-3212)
RITE MACHINE PRODUCTS INC
44795 Enterprise Dr (48038-1535)
PHONE 586 465-9393
Gregory Hall, *CEO*
Regina Hall, *Corp Secy*
Kenneth Hall, *Vice Pres*
Michael Hall, *Vice Pres*
Cheryl Mc Guire, *Vice Pres*
EMP: 19
SQ FT: 20,200
SALES (est): 3.9MM **Privately Held**
WEB: www.ritemachine.com
SIC: 3451 Screw machine products

(G-3213)
RJL SCIENCES INC
Also Called: Rjl Systems
33939 Harper Ave (48035-4218)
PHONE 800 528-4513
Rudolph J Liedtke, *President*
EMP: 10
SQ FT: 10,000
SALES (est): 1.6MM **Privately Held**
WEB: www.rjlsystems.com
SIC: 3841 Surgical & medical instruments

(G-3214)
ROSATI SPECIALTIES LLC
24300 Capital Blvd (48036-1340)
PHONE 586 783-3866
Donald R Rosati,
EMP: 3
SALES (est): 681.1K **Privately Held**
WEB: www.rosatispecialties.com
SIC: 2431 2435 Moldings, wood: unfinished & prefinished; panel work, wood; hardwood plywood, prefinished

(G-3215)
ROTH-WILLIAMS INDUSTRIES INC
Also Called: Lunar Industries
34335 Groesbeck Hwy (48035-3359)
PHONE 586 792-0090
Patricia Williams, *President*
Tony Horner, *General Mgr*
Roger Roth, *Chairman*
Gordon Clor, *Plant Mgr*
Kerry Shier, *QC Mgr*
EMP: 16
SQ FT: 18,000
SALES: 2.7MM **Privately Held**
WEB: www.lunarind.com
SIC: 3544 3545 Special dies & tools; industrial molds; machine tool accessories

(G-3216)
ROURA ACQUISITION INC (PA)
Also Called: Roura Material Handling
35355 Forton Ct (48035-3133)
PHONE 586 790-6100
Mike Genter, *President*
▲ **EMP:** 14 **EST:** 1915
SQ FT: 25,000
SALES (est): 4.9MM **Privately Held**
WEB: www.rourahn.com
SIC: 3444 Metal housings, enclosures, casings & other containers

(G-3217)
RTS CUTTING TOOLS INC
24100 Capital Blvd (48036-1338)
PHONE 586 954-1900
Michael Disser, *President*
Greg Berentt, *Owner*
Carl R Garbarino, *Vice Pres*
Daniel Hulgrave, *Treasurer*
EMP: 35 **EST:** 1939
SALES (est): 6.5MM **Privately Held**
WEB: www.rtscut.com
SIC: 3545 3546 3541 3423 Cutting tools for machine tools; power-driven hand-tools; machine tools, metal cutting type; hand & edge tools

(G-3218)
RUSSOS BAKERY INC
35160 Forton Ct (48035-3130)
PHONE 586 791-7320
Andjelko Stamevski, *President*
▲ **EMP:** 18
SQ FT: 10,000
SALES (est): 3.6MM **Privately Held**
SIC: 2051 Bakery: wholesale or wholesale/retail combined

(G-3219)
RYDIN AND ASSOCIATES INC
Also Called: Rydin & Associates
44604 Macomb Indus Dr (48036-1185)
PHONE 586 783-9772
Bruce Rydin, *President*
David Peck, *Vice Pres*
EMP: 12
SALES (est): 1.6MM **Privately Held**
WEB: www.rydinassociates.com
SIC: 3699 Laser welding, drilling & cutting equipment

(G-3220)
SALDET SALES AND SERVICES INC
44810 Vic Wertz Dr (48036-1250)
PHONE 586 469-4312
Larry Sylvester, *President*
Fred Parker, *Owner*
EMP: 20
SQ FT: 12,500
SALES (est): 2.2MM **Privately Held**
SIC: 3679 Harness assemblies for electronic use: wire or cable

(G-3221)
SANDERS CANDY LLC (HQ)
23770 Hall Rd (48036-1275)
PHONE 800 651-7263
Ronald Rapson, *President*
Jennifer Szubelak, *Purch Agent*
Ann Koch, *Sales Staff*
▲ **EMP:** 100 **EST:** 1919
SQ FT: 70,000
SALES (est): 47.3MM
SALES (corp-wide): 178.7MM **Privately Held**
WEB: www.morleycandy.com
SIC: 2064 2066 5441 Candy & other confectionery products; chocolate & cocoa products; candy
PA: Knpc Holdco, Llc
1200 E 14 Mile Rd
Madison Heights MI 48071
248 588-1903

(G-3222)
SENSTRONIC INC
44990 Vic Wertz Dr Ste A (48036-1251)
PHONE 586 466-4108
Remy Kirchdoerffer, *President*
EMP: 200
SQ FT: 3,000

SALES (est): 483.1K **Privately Held**
SIC: 3559 Electronic component making machinery

(G-3223)
SEQUOIA TOOL INC
44831 N Groesbeck Hwy (48036-1124)
PHONE..................586 463-4400
Joseph Coates, *CEO*
Joe Coates, *President*
James Coates, *General Mgr*
Frank Coates, *Vice Pres*
Craig Walworgh, *Vice Pres*
EMP: 82
SQ FT: 14,000
SALES (est): 43MM **Privately Held**
WEB: www.sequoiatool.net
SIC: 3444 Sheet metalwork

(G-3224)
SHARPE FABRICATING INC
44049 N Groesbeck Hwy (48036-1123)
P.O. Box 27, Richmond (48062-0027)
PHONE..................586 465-4468
Ken Watson, *President*
EMP: 4
SQ FT: 4,000
SALES (est): 512.2K **Privately Held**
SIC: 3441 Fabricated structural metal

(G-3225)
SHORECREST ENTERPRISES INC
Also Called: Signs By Tomorrow
33251 S Gratiot Ave (48035-4039)
PHONE..................586 948-9226
Bruce Slezak, *President*
Kenneth Slezak, *Vice Pres*
EMP: 5
SALES (est): 502.7K **Privately Held**
SIC: 3993 Signs & advertising specialties

(G-3226)
SHORES ENGINEERING CO INC
34632 Nova Dr (48035-3716)
PHONE..................586 792-2748
Brian Quinlan, *President*
EMP: 15
SQ FT: 2,400
SALES (est): 1.5MM **Privately Held**
SIC: 3544 Special dies, tools, jigs & fixtures

(G-3227)
SIGMA TOOL MFG INC
35280 Forton Ct (48035-3131)
PHONE..................586 792-3300
Wolfgang Pfahl, *Owner*
EMP: 5
SALES (est): 729.8K **Privately Held**
WEB: www.sigmatoolmfg.com
SIC: 3544 Special dies & tools

(G-3228)
SIGN-A-RAMA
36886 Harper Ave (48035-2014)
PHONE..................586 792-7446
Bryan Duquet, *Owner*
EMP: 4
SALES (est): 388.4K **Privately Held**
WEB: www.teamsignarama.com
SIC: 3993 Signs & advertising specialties

(G-3229)
SIMS SOFTWARE II INC
44668 Morley Dr (48036-1358)
PHONE..................586 491-0058
Matthew Trompeter, *President*
EMP: 5
SALES (est): 610K **Privately Held**
SIC: 7372 Prepackaged software

(G-3230)
SINE SYSTEMS CORPORATION (HQ)
44724 Morley Dr (48036-1357)
P.O. Box Caller 2336, Mount Clemens (48046)
PHONE..................586 465-3131
R Adam Norwit, *CEO*
Wayne Spence, *Business Mgr*
John Blood, *Info Tech Mgr*
▲ **EMP:** 200
SQ FT: 70,000
SALES (est): 65.9MM
SALES (corp-wide): 8.2B **Publicly Held**
WEB: www.sineco.com
SIC: 3643 3678 3357 3625 Connectors & terminals for electrical devices; electronic connectors; nonferrous wiredrawing & insulating; control circuit relays, industrial
PA: Amphenol Corporation
358 Hall Ave
Wallingford CT 06492
203 265-8900

(G-3231)
SLATER TOOLS INC
44725 Trinity Dr (48038-1554)
PHONE..................586 465-5000
John R Scaduto Jr, *President*
Kris Renner, *Sales Staff*
EMP: 25 **EST:** 1951
SQ FT: 22,000
SALES (est): 3.5MM **Privately Held**
WEB: www.slatertool.com
SIC: 3544 3451 Special dies, tools, jigs & fixtures; screw machine products

(G-3232)
SPARTAN PALLET LLC
22387 Starks Dr (48036-1197)
PHONE..................586 291-8898
Mike Rubino, *Principal*
EMP: 4
SALES (est): 376K **Privately Held**
SIC: 2448 Pallets, wood & wood with metal

(G-3233)
SRS MANUFACTURING INC
Also Called: Framar
18840 Kelly Ct (48035-3980)
PHONE..................586 792-5693
Scott Stay, *President*
EMP: 11 **EST:** 1996
SQ FT: 10,000
SALES (est): 1.8MM **Privately Held**
SIC: 3599 Machine shop, jobbing & repair

(G-3234)
STATE SCREW PRODUCTS CORP
44605 Macomb Indus Dr (48036-1148)
PHONE..................586 463-3892
William Graessle, *President*
EMP: 13
SALES (est): 2.1MM **Privately Held**
SIC: 3451 Screw machine products

(G-3235)
STATISTICAL PROCESSED PRODUCTS (PA)
35409 Groesbeck Hwy (48035-2518)
PHONE..................586 792-6900
Ernest Young, *President*
EMP: 20
SALES (est): 1.7MM **Privately Held**
SIC: 2851 3465 3089 Paints & allied products; automotive stampings; blow molded finished plastic products

(G-3236)
SUNLITE MARKET INC
34705 S Gratiot Ave (48035-3543)
PHONE..................586 792-9870
Amin Wahbi, *President*
EMP: 3
SALES (est): 353.1K **Privately Held**
SIC: 5921 5411 2085 Beer (packaged); wine; grocery stores, independent; distilled & blended liquors

(G-3237)
SUPERIOR HEAT TREAT LLC
36125 Groesbeck Hwy (48035-1544)
PHONE..................586 792-9500
Lue Bertha Brown, *Office Mgr*
Ralph J Kaiser Sr,
Mark Kaiser,
EMP: 25
SQ FT: 17,300
SALES (est): 6MM **Privately Held**
WEB: www.superiorheattreat.com
SIC: 3398 Metal heat treating

(G-3238)
SUPERIOR NON-FERROUS INC
35475 Forton Ct (48035-5624)
PHONE..................586 791-7988
Johnny Smith, *President*
Dana Smith, *Admin Sec*
EMP: 3
SQ FT: 7,000
SALES: 150K **Privately Held**
SIC: 3365 3364 Aluminum & aluminum-based alloy castings; zinc & zinc-base alloy die-castings

(G-3239)
SUPREME MEDIA BLASTING AND POW
36427 Groesbeck Hwy (48035-1551)
PHONE..................586 792-7705
John Feldpausch, *CEO*
Todd Nowak, *Director*
EMP: 4
SQ FT: 11,500
SALES (est): 162K **Privately Held**
SIC: 3471 2851 Sand blasting of metal parts; epoxy coatings

(G-3240)
SUPREME WELDING INC
34727 Nova Dr (48035-3718)
PHONE..................586 791-8860
Bernard J Nowak Jr, *President*
Tom Nowak, *Vice Pres*
EMP: 3
SALES (est): 271.7K **Privately Held**
SIC: 7692 Welding repair

(G-3241)
SYNERGY ADDITIVE MFG LLC (HQ)
Also Called: Sam
22792 Macomb Indus Dr (48036-1137)
PHONE..................248 719-2194
Marcus Stackpoole,
Kunal Varma,
EMP: 4
SALES (est): 647.3K
SALES (corp-wide): 2.9MM **Privately Held**
SIC: 3441 Fabricated structural metal
PA: Synergy Prototype Stamping Llc
22778 Macomb Indus Dr
Clinton Township MI 48036
586 961-6109

(G-3242)
SYNERGY PROTOTYPE STAMPING LLC (PA)
22778 Macomb Indus Dr (48036-1137)
PHONE..................586 961-6109
Marcus Stackpoole,
EMP: 30
SQ FT: 2,000
SALES: 2.9MM **Privately Held**
SIC: 3469 Stamping metal for the trade

(G-3243)
TAPER-LINE INC (PA)
23426 Reynolds Ct (48036-1240)
PHONE..................586 775-5960
James Finn, *President*
Pamela Montay, *Corp Secy*
EMP: 8
SQ FT: 12,000
SALES: 1MM **Privately Held**
WEB: www.taperline.com
SIC: 3452 Nuts, metal

(G-3244)
TEMO INC
Also Called: Temo Sunrooms
20400 Hall Rd (48038-1480)
PHONE..................800 344-8366
Giovanni Vitale, *CEO*
James Hall, *President*
Angela Fowler, *Corp Secy*
Kevin Kahl, *Vice Pres*
Tony Maltese, *Engineer*
▲ **EMP:** 160
SQ FT: 93,000
SALES (est): 52.8MM **Privately Held**
WEB: www.oikos.com
SIC: 3448 Prefabricated metal buildings

(G-3245)
TENIBAC-GRAPHION INC (HQ)
35155 Automation Dr (48036-3116)
PHONE..................586 792-0150
Jim Deliz, *CEO*
James Deliz, *General Mgr*
EMP: 75 **EST:** 1969
SQ FT: 45,000
SALES (est): 9.9MM
SALES (corp-wide): 791.5MM **Publicly Held**
WEB: www.tenibac.com
SIC: 3469 Patterns on metal
PA: Standex International Corporation
11 Keewaydin Dr Ste 300
Salem NH 03079
603 893-9701

(G-3246)
THUNDER BAY PATTERN WORKS INC
44345 Macomb Indus Dr (48036-1143)
PHONE..................586 783-1126
Dorothy La Fleche, *CEO*
James Flom, *President*
George La Fleche, *Chairman*
Bruce La Fleche, *Vice Pres*
Georgene Hildebrand, *Treasurer*
EMP: 21
SQ FT: 30,000
SALES (est): 4.8MM **Privately Held**
WEB: www.thunderbaypatternworks.com
SIC: 3089 Automotive parts, plastic

(G-3247)
TIJER INC
44326 Macomb Indus Dr (48036-1142)
PHONE..................586 741-0308
Tim Taylor, *President*
Jerry Auclair, *Vice Pres*
EMP: 4
SALES: 700K **Privately Held**
WEB: www.tijerlilyco.com
SIC: 3544 Special dies, tools, jigs & fixtures

(G-3248)
TOP CRAFT TOOL INC
33674 Giftos Dr (48035-4241)
PHONE..................586 461-4600
Gary Kimmen, *President*
Kelley Kimmen, *Opers Staff*
Lloyd Kimmen, *Treasurer*
EMP: 24 **EST:** 1968
SQ FT: 10,000
SALES: 2.9MM **Privately Held**
WEB: www.topcrafttool.com
SIC: 3599 3544 Machine shop, jobbing & repair; special dies & tools

(G-3249)
TOP DECK SYSTEMS INC
44753 Centre Ct (48038-1317)
PHONE..................586 263-1550
Robert Jankowski, *President*
Magda O'Hanlon, *Vice Pres*
Joe Guastella, *Draft/Design*
▲ **EMP:** 8
SQ FT: 18,500
SALES (est): 1.7MM **Privately Held**
WEB: www.alusett.com
SIC: 3993 Displays & cutouts, window & lobby

(G-3250)
TOWER AUTOMOTIVE OPERATIONS I
44850 N Groesbeck Hwy (48036-1121)
PHONE..................586 465-5158
Joe Amann, *Engineer*
Timothy Bottorff, *Engineer*
Marie Ventimiglia, *Human Resources*
Jim Ruzzin, *Manager*
Mike Deshais, *Analyst*
EMP: 351
SALES (corp-wide): 2.2B **Privately Held**
SIC: 3465 Automotive stampings
HQ: Tower Automotive Operations Usa I, Llc
17672 N Laurel Park Dr 400e
Livonia MI 48152

(G-3251)
TREND PERFORMANCE PRODUCTS
Also Called: Diamond Racing Products Co
23003 Diamond Dr (48035-3126)
PHONE..................586 792-6620
Robert Fox, *President*
EMP: 30

Clinton Township - Macomb County (G-3252)

SALES (est): 4.1MM
SALES (corp-wide): 8.2MM **Privately Held**
WEB: www.trendperform.com
SIC: 3599 3714 3592 3519 Machine & other job shop work; motor vehicle parts & accessories; carburetors, pistons, rings, valves; internal combustion engines
PA: Trend Performance Products Inc
23444 Schoenherr Rd
Warren MI 48089
586 447-0400

(G-3252)
TWEDDLE GROUP INC (PA)
24700 Maplehurst Dr (48036-1336)
PHONE 586 307-3700
Patrick Aubry, *CEO*
Tina Stuart, *COO*
Atul Kishore, *Exec VP*
Geral Chapman, *Vice Pres*
Laura Klimaski, *Vice Pres*
▲ **EMP:** 250 **EST:** 1954
SQ FT: 120,000
SALES (est): 186MM **Privately Held**
SIC: 2732 2791 2752 2759 Book printing; photocomposition, for the printing trade; typesetting, computer controlled; commercial printing, lithographic; commercial printing; technical manual & paper publishing; computer software development & applications

(G-3253)
ULTRA-SONIC EXTRUSION DIES INC
34863 Groesbeck Hwy (48035-3366)
PHONE 586 791-8550
David Schoenegge, *President*
Al Gwozdz, *Corp Secy*
Jim Delmotte, *Design Engr*
David Nicholas, *Director*
EMP: 30
SQ FT: 10,000
SALES (est): 3.5MM **Privately Held**
WEB: www.usedies.com
SIC: 3544 Extrusion dies

(G-3254)
UNIVERSAL MANUFACTURING CO
43900 N Groesbeck Hwy (48036-1107)
PHONE 586 463-2560
Sandra Kedzierski, *CEO*
William Kedzierski, *President*
Roy Seelbinder, *Treasurer*
▼ **EMP:** 11
SQ FT: 18,000
SALES (est): 1.9MM **Privately Held**
SIC: 3648 3441 Lighting fixtures, except electric: residential; tower sections, radio & television transmission

(G-3255)
VERSA-CRAFT INC
35117 Automation Dr (48035-3116)
PHONE 586 465-5999
Don Johnson, *President*
Karen Johnson, *Admin Sec*
EMP: 8
SQ FT: 13,000
SALES (est): 1.4MM **Privately Held**
SIC: 3535 Belt conveyor systems, general industrial use

(G-3256)
VINCO TOOL INC
44616 Macomb Indus Dr (48036-1185)
PHONE 586 465-1961
Vincent Mc Dermott, *President*
EMP: 3
SQ FT: 2,400
SALES: 219K **Privately Held**
SIC: 3544 Special dies, tools, jigs & fixtures

(G-3257)
VOICE COMMUNICATIONS CORP (PA)
Also Called: Voice Newspapers, The
19176 Hall Rd Ste 200 (48038-6914)
PHONE 586 716-8100
Debbie Loggins, *General Mgr*
Jim McCormick, *Principal*
Katelyn Larese, *Director*

EMP: 25
SQ FT: 2,800
SALES (est): 1.4MM **Privately Held**
WEB: www.voicenews.com
SIC: 2711 Newspapers: publishing only, not printed on site

(G-3258)
WARREN INDUSTRIAL WELDING CO
44441 N Groesbeck Hwy (48036-1117)
PHONE 586 463-6600
Greg Lee, *Manager*
EMP: 4
SQ FT: 3,500
SALES (corp-wide): 2MM **Privately Held**
WEB: www.warrenindustrial.com
SIC: 7692 Welding repair
PA: Warren Industrial Welding Company Inc
24275 Hoover Rd
Warren MI 48089
586 756-0230

(G-3259)
WARREN INDUSTRIES INC (PA)
22805 Interstate Dr (48035-3742)
PHONE 586 741-0420
Douglas Udicki, *President*
Stevan Udicki, *Vice Pres*
Michael Lassila, *Project Mgr*
Michael Bachan, *Prdtn Mgr*
Vladimir Samoila, *Chief Engr*
EMP: 96
SQ FT: 95,000
SALES (est): 35.9MM **Privately Held**
SIC: 3541 Numerically controlled metal cutting machine tools; drilling & boring machines

(G-3260)
WARTROM MACHINE SYSTEMS
22786 Patmore Dr (48036-1191)
PHONE 586 469-1915
Terry A Ward, *CEO*
Martha L Ward, *Vice Pres*
Kevin Caperton, *Mfg Staff*
Jeff Mosko, *Production*
Janet Husovsky, *Purchasing*
EMP: 35
SQ FT: 21,000
SALES: 6.3MM **Privately Held**
WEB: www.wartrom.com
SIC: 3569 3544 Assembly machines, non-metalworking; special dies, tools, jigs & fixtures

(G-3261)
WOLVERINE PRODUCTS INC
35220 Groesbeck Hwy (48035-2513)
PHONE 586 792-3740
Matthew Chase, *President*
David Chase, *Vice Pres*
EMP: 12
SQ FT: 23,000
SALES (est): 1.9MM **Privately Held**
WEB: www.wolverineproductsinc.com
SIC: 3544 3543 Industrial molds; jigs & fixtures; industrial patterns

(G-3262)
XCENTRIC MOLD & ENGRG INC
24541 Maplehurst Dr (48036-1352)
PHONE 586 598-4636
Brendan Weaver, *President*
Damon Weaver, *Treasurer*
Tyler Laperriere, *Accounts Mgr*
Paula Williams, *Manager*
EMP: 16
SQ FT: 13,500
SALES (est): 4.9MM **Privately Held**
WEB: www.xcentricmold.com
SIC: 3544 Industrial molds

(G-3263)
YOE INDUSTRIES INC
24451 Sorrentino Ct (48035-3240)
PHONE 586 791-7660
Henry F Yoe, *President*
EMP: 5
SQ FT: 10,000
SALES (est): 350K **Privately Held**
SIC: 7699 3561 Hydraulic equipment repair; cylinders, pump

(G-3264)
ZAJAC INDUSTRIES INC
Also Called: Zajac Packaging
21319 Carlo Dr (48038-1511)
PHONE 586 489-6746
Bob Zajac, *President*
EMP: 15 **EST:** 1994
SALES (est): 3.2MM **Privately Held**
SIC: 2671 Paper coated or laminated for packaging

(G-3265)
ZUNAIRAH FUELS INC
37109 Harper Ave (48036-3013)
PHONE 647 405-1606
Asher Ahmed, *Principal*
EMP: 3 **EST:** 2014
SALES (est): 184.1K **Privately Held**
SIC: 2869 Fuels

Clio
Genesee County

(G-3266)
CAR AUDIO OUTLET LLC
11581 N Saginaw Rd (48420-1635)
PHONE 810 686-3300
Ammar Hadid,
EMP: 3
SALES (est): 130.9K **Privately Held**
SIC: 5731 3621 7549 Sound equipment, automotive; starters, for motors; glass tinting, automotive

(G-3267)
CARDINAL MACHINE CO
860 Tacoma Ct (48420-1581)
PHONE 810 686-1190
Brian Pennington, *President*
Linda Pennington, *Corp Secy*
Jeremy Clontz, *Engineer*
Dan Mills, *Engineer*
Brent Koester, *Design Engr*
EMP: 27
SQ FT: 24,000
SALES (est): 6MM **Privately Held**
WEB: www.cardinalmachine.com
SIC: 3549 3545 Metalworking machinery; machine tool attachments & accessories

(G-3268)
CMG AMERICA INC
11424 N Saginaw Rd (48420-1679)
P.O. Box 178, Frankenmuth (48734-0178)
PHONE 810 686-3064
Vittiorio Martei, *President*
Stephen Myers, *Vice Pres*
▲ **EMP:** 6
SQ FT: 14,000
SALES: 400K **Privately Held**
SIC: 3821 Granulators, laboratory

(G-3269)
DEMMEM ENTERPRISES LLC
Also Called: Perfect Fit Brdal Tuxedos Prom
4268 W Vienna Rd (48420-9454)
PHONE 810 564-9500
Daniel McKay,
EMP: 10
SALES (est): 250.7K **Privately Held**
SIC: 7299 2335 7219 Tuxedo rental; wedding gowns & dresses; garment making, alteration & repair

(G-3270)
DODGE WEST JOE NICKEL
2219 E Farrand Rd (48420-9188)
PHONE 810 691-2133
Joseph Nickels, *Principal*
EMP: 4 **EST:** 2009
SALES (est): 382.3K **Privately Held**
SIC: 3356 Nickel

(G-3271)
FIRST CLASS TIRE SHREDDERS INC
7302 W Vienna Rd (48420-9448)
PHONE 810 639-5888
Fax: 810 639-3125
EMP: 15
SALES (est): 1.4MM **Privately Held**
SIC: 3069 Mfg Fabricated Rubber Products

(G-3272)
GENESEE COUNTY HERALD INC
Also Called: Bridal Nook
10098 N Dort Hwy (48420-1670)
P.O. Box 127, Mount Morris (48458-0127)
PHONE 810 686-3840
Michael Harrington, *President*
EMP: 17 **EST:** 1967
SALES (est): 1.2MM **Privately Held**
WEB: www.geneseeny.org
SIC: 2711 5621 3993 2791 Job printing & newspaper publishing combined; bridal shops; signs & advertising specialties; typesetting; commercial printing; commercial printing, lithographic

(G-3273)
KENS REDI MIX INC
14406 N Saginaw Rd (48420-8864)
PHONE 810 687-6000
Jeff Bailey, *President*
EMP: 10
SALES (est): 879.6K **Privately Held**
SALES (corp-wide): 3.7MM **Privately Held**
SIC: 3273 Ready-mixed concrete
PA: Ken's Redi Mix, Inc.
8016 S State Rd
Goodrich MI 48438
810 238-4931

(G-3274)
KENYON SPECIALTIES INC
1153 Liberty St (48420)
P.O. Box 160, Mount Morris (48458-0160)
PHONE 810 686-3190
Peggy Duford, *President*
Margaret A Duford, *President*
Norman O Duford General, *Manager*
EMP: 8
SQ FT: 14,600
SALES (est): 530K **Privately Held**
SIC: 3544 Special dies & tools

(G-3275)
MARQUEE ENGRAVING INC
600 S Mill St Ste A (48420-2317)
PHONE 810 686-7550
Jennifer Rendue, *President*
EMP: 4
SALES: 125K **Privately Held**
SIC: 2759 5999 Engraving; trophies & plaques

(G-3276)
MICHIGAN SCREEN PRINTING
204 S Railway St (48420-1340)
PHONE 810 687-5550
Paul Gustafson, *Owner*
EMP: 5
SALES (est): 306K **Privately Held**
WEB: www.michiganbizsearch.com
SIC: 2759 Screen printing

(G-3277)
MILLENNIUM MACHINE INC
2232 Hayward St (48420-1838)
PHONE 810 687-0671
Dave Clark, *President*
Julie Clark, *Vice Pres*
EMP: 3 **EST:** 1999
SQ FT: 4,000
SALES (est): 254.5K **Privately Held**
WEB: www.millenniummachine.net
SIC: 3599 Machine shop, jobbing & repair

(G-3278)
MONTAGUE LATCH COMPANY
Also Called: Montague Tool
2000 W Dodge Rd (48420-1657)
PHONE 810 687-4242
Joel Stinedurf, *President*
▲ **EMP:** 18
SQ FT: 10,000
SALES: 3.3MM **Privately Held**
WEB: www.montaguelatch.com
SIC: 3823 Industrial instrmnts msrmnt display/control process variable

(G-3279)
MONTAGUE TOOL AND MFG CO
Also Called: Paws Workholding
11533 Liberty St Ste 3 (48420-1493)
PHONE 810 686-0000
Jim Montague, *CEO*
John Montague, *President*

GEOGRAPHIC SECTION

Coldwater - Branch County (G-3304)

Joel Montague, *Vice Pres*
Lois Montague, *Treasurer*
EMP: 35 **EST:** 1943
SQ FT: 20,000
SALES (est): 7.9MM **Privately Held**
WEB: www.montaguetool.com
SIC: 3599 3545 Machine shop, jobbing & repair; machine tool accessories

(G-3280)
R & R READY-MIX INC
14151 N Saginaw Rd (48420-8802)
PHONE 810 686-5570
Jeff Parent, *Owner*
EMP: 7
SALES (corp-wide): 4MM **Privately Held**
SIC: 3273 Ready-mixed concrete
PA: R & R Ready-Mix, Inc.
 6050 Melbourne Rd
 Saginaw MI 48604
 989 753-3862

(G-3281)
RUNYAN POTTERY SUPPLY INC
820 Tacoma Ct (48420-1581)
PHONE 810 687-4500
Paul Runyan, *Owner*
Mary Runyan, *Co-Owner*
EMP: 3
SALES (est): 257K **Privately Held**
WEB: www.runyanpotterysupply.com
SIC: 5945 5199 3295 Arts & crafts supplies; art goods; clay, ground or otherwise treated

Clyde
St. Clair County

(G-3282)
DOW CHEMICAL COMPANY
3381 Woodview (48049-4330)
PHONE 810 966-9816
EMP: 68
SALES (corp-wide): 48.1B **Publicly Held**
SIC: 2821 Mfg Plastic Materials/Resins
PA: The Dow Chemical Company
 2030 Dow Ctr
 Midland MI 48642
 989 636-1000

(G-3283)
HESS ASPHALT PAV SAND CNSTR CO
6330 Lapeer Rd (48049-4221)
PHONE 810 984-4466
Frederick T Hess, *President*
Thomas J Hess, *Treasurer*
Gloria Hess, *Admin Sec*
EMP: 12
SQ FT: 3,200
SALES (est): 1.7MM **Privately Held**
SIC: 1611 2951 Highway & street paving contractor; resurfacing contractor; asphalt & asphaltic paving mixtures (not from refineries)

(G-3284)
REDLINE FABRICATIONS
4752 Walker Rd (48049-3939)
PHONE 810 984-5621
Barrie Rusch, *Owner*
EMP: 4
SALES: 124.3K **Privately Held**
WEB: www.redlinefabrications.com
SIC: 3711 Automobile assembly, including specialty automobiles

(G-3285)
ZOBL QUARTER HORSES
4065 Abbottsford Rd (48049-3001)
PHONE 810 479-9534
Joleen Zobl, *Manager*
EMP: 3 **EST:** 2014
SALES (est): 97.9K **Privately Held**
SIC: 3131 Quarters

Coldwater
Branch County

(G-3286)
4EVER ALUMINUM PRODUCTS INC
628 Pebblestone Dr (49036-7551)
PHONE 517 368-0000
James Starr, *President*
Kevin Bowers, *General Mgr*
EMP: 15
SQ FT: 14,000
SALES: 1.7MM **Privately Held**
SIC: 5084 3448 Lift trucks & parts; docks: prefabricated metal

(G-3287)
ALERIS INTERNATIONAL INC
368 W Garfield Ave (49036-9711)
P.O. Box 338 (49036-0338)
PHONE 517 279-9596
Steven J Demetriou, *CEO*
Roeland Baan, *Exec VP*
Christopher R Clegg, *Exec VP*
Sean M Stack, *Exec VP*
Scott A McKinley, *Senior VP*
EMP: 21
SALES (est): 5.1MM **Privately Held**
SIC: 3334 Primary aluminum

(G-3288)
ANITOM AUTOMATION LLC
349 S Clay St (49036-2139)
P.O. Box 10 (49036-0010)
PHONE 517 278-6205
Thomas G Waller, *Co-Owner*
Rick F Morris, *Co-Owner*
EMP: 20
SQ FT: 8,000
SALES (est): 4.2MM **Privately Held**
SIC: 3544 Special dies & tools; jigs & fixtures

(G-3289)
ASAMA COLDWATER MFG INC
Also Called: Acm
180 Asama Pkwy (49036-1590)
PHONE 517 279-1090
Masao Yamaura, *President*
Frank Draper, *Buyer*
Tim Arey, *Purchasing*
Jack Stevens, *Purchasing*
Dannie Larder, *Engineer*
▲ **EMP:** 340
SQ FT: 400,000
SALES (est): 107.4MM **Privately Held**
WEB: www.asamacm.com
SIC: 3714 Motor vehicle steering systems & parts
HQ: Asama Giken Co.,Ltd.
 450, Azaushihara, Oazamimitori
 Komoro NAG 384-0

(G-3290)
AUSTIN MACHINE & TOOL LLC
237 N Angola Rd (49036-8576)
PHONE 517 278-1717
Richard Austin, *Principal*
Scott Austin, *Principal*
EMP: 7
SALES: 980K **Privately Held**
SIC: 3599 Machine shop, jobbing & repair

(G-3291)
BDS COMPANY INC
491 W Garfield Ave (49036-8000)
PHONE 517 279-2135
Lonnie Avra, *CEO*
Steve Olmsted, *President*
▲ **EMP:** 30
SQ FT: 60,000
SALES: 7.5MM **Privately Held**
SIC: 3568 3713 3714 3711 Power transmission equipment; truck bodies & parts; motor vehicle parts & accessories; motor vehicles & car bodies; bolts, nuts, rivets & washers; manufactured hardware (general)

(G-3292)
BURNHAM & NORTHERN INC
169 Industrial Ave (49036-2168)
P.O. Box 481 (49036-0481)
PHONE 517 279-7501
Leslie Northern, *President*
Connie Voice, *Chairman*
Candace Northern, *Vice Pres*
EMP: 6
SQ FT: 10,000
SALES: 350K **Privately Held**
SIC: 3444 3498 3441 3312 Sheet metalwork; fabricated pipe & fittings; fabricated structural metal; blast furnaces & steel mills

(G-3293)
C & M MANUFACTURING INC
129 Industrial Ave (49036-2178)
PHONE 517 279-0013
Carl Albert, *President*
Michelle Albert, *Vice Pres*
EMP: 20
SQ FT: 40,000
SALES (est): 4.2MM **Privately Held**
SIC: 3441 Fabricated structural metal

(G-3294)
CASE WELDING & FABRICATION INC
235 N Angola Rd (49036-8575)
PHONE 517 278-2729
Wayne Case, *President*
EMP: 4
SQ FT: 3,000
SALES (est): 440K **Privately Held**
SIC: 7692 1799 Welding repair; welding on site

(G-3295)
CLEMENS FOOD GROUP LLC
572 Newton Rd (49036-9465)
PHONE 517 278-2500
EMP: 3
SALES (corp-wide): 705.7MM **Privately Held**
SIC: 2011 2013 Pork products from pork slaughtered on site; sausages & other prepared meats
HQ: Clemens Food Group, Llc
 2700 Clemens Rd
 Hatfield PA 19440
 215 368-2500

(G-3296)
CLEMENS WELCOME CENTER
285 N Michigan Ave (49036-1528)
PHONE 517 278-2500
EMP: 3
SALES (est): 163.2K **Privately Held**
SIC: 2011 Meat packing plants

(G-3297)
COLDWATER VENEER INC (PA)
548 Race St (49036-2122)
PHONE 517 278-5676
Dean Calhoun, *CEO*
Dave Counterman, *President*
Sandy Calhoun, *Vice Pres*
Ali Tanade, *CFO*
Brad Hickok, *Human Resources*
◆ **EMP:** 160 **EST:** 2015
SALES: 40MM **Privately Held**
SIC: 2435 Hardwood veneer & plywood

(G-3298)
COLDWTER SINTERED MET PDTS INC
300 Race St (49036-2120)
PHONE 517 278-8750
Kenneth Bible, *President*
Michael Lange, *Vice Pres*
Sharolyn Brainard, *Admin Sec*
EMP: 30
SQ FT: 68,000
SALES (est): 5.9MM **Privately Held**
SIC: 3399 Powder, metal

(G-3299)
COMMERCIAL GRAPHICS COMPANY
205 W Garfield Ave (49036-9711)
PHONE 517 278-2159
Michael Liechty, *President*
Lynne Liechty, *Vice Pres*
EMP: 5
SQ FT: 5,400
SALES (est): 569K **Privately Held**
WEB: www.commercialgraphics.net
SIC: 2752 7313 7336 Commercial printing, offset; printed media advertising representatives; graphic arts & related design

(G-3300)
DAILY REPORTER
Also Called: Gatehouse Publishing
15 W Pearl St (49036-1912)
PHONE 517 278-2318
Dan Pollefson, *President*
Lisa Vickers, *Advt Staff*
Karen Allard, *Manager*
Carla Ludwick, *Manager*
EMP: 40
SALES (est): 2.2MM **Privately Held**
WEB: www.thedailyreporter.com
SIC: 2711 2752 Newspapers: publishing only, not printed on site; commercial printing, lithographic

(G-3301)
DARLING INGREDIENTS INC
600 Jay St (49036-2153)
PHONE 517 279-9731
Bill Fritz, *General Mgr*
Jim Roth, *Manager*
EMP: 106
SALES (corp-wide): 3.3B **Publicly Held**
WEB: www.darlingii.com
SIC: 2077 2048 Grease rendering, inedible; prepared feeds
PA: Darling Ingredients Inc.
 5601 N Macarthur Blvd
 Irving TX 75038
 972 717-0300

(G-3302)
ENVIROLITE LLC
421 Race St (49036-2119)
PHONE 888 222-2191
Vatche Tazian,
EMP: 60
SALES (corp-wide): 24.2MM **Privately Held**
SIC: 3086 5999 5199 Plastics foam products; foam & foam products; foams & rubber
PA: Envirolite, Llc
 1700 W Big Beaver Rd # 150
 Troy MI 48084
 248 792-3184

(G-3303)
EXO-S US LLC
Also Called: Coldwater Plant
25 Concept Dr (49036-1585)
PHONE 517 278-8567
Craige Mohney, *Branch Mgr*
EMP: 80
SALES (corp-wide): 115.9MM **Privately Held**
SIC: 3089 Injection molding of plastics
HQ: Exo-S Us Llc
 6505 N State Road 9
 Howe IN 46746
 260 562-4100

(G-3304)
GATEHOUSE MEDIA MICH HOLDINGS
Also Called: Evening News The
15 W Pearl St (49036-1912)
PHONE 585 598-0030
Howard Kaiser, *Publisher*
Scott Brand, *Editor*
Tami Miller, *Sales Staff*
Cathy Kaiser, *Manager*
Garrett J Cummings,
EMP: 55
SQ FT: 25,000
SALES (est): 8.2MM
SALES (corp-wide): 1.5B **Privately Held**
WEB: www.sooeveningnews.com
SIC: 2711 Commercial printing & newspaper publishing combined
PA: New Media Investment Group Inc.
 1345 Avenue Of The Americ
 New York NY 10105
 212 479-3160

Coldwater - Branch County (G-3305)

(G-3305)
GOKOH COLDWATER INCORPORATED
Also Called: GCI
100 Concept Dr (49036-1588)
PHONE..................517 279-1080
Kenji Iwato, *President*
EMP: 15
SQ FT: 34,000
SALES (est): 6.4MM **Privately Held**
WEB: www.tellthat.com
SIC: 3559 3471 3444 3369 Foundry, smelting, refining & similar machinery; foundry machinery & equipment; plating & polishing; sheet metalwork; nonferrous foundries
HQ: Gokoh Corporation
1280 Archer Dr
Troy OH 45373
937 339-4977

(G-3306)
GRAPHICS 3 INC
205 W Garfield Ave (49036-8001)
PHONE..................517 278-2159
Larry Iverson, *President*
Michael Iverson, *Vice Pres*
Terry Garn, *Prdtn Mgr*
Jacquelyn Iverson, *Treasurer*
EMP: 11
SQ FT: 11,900
SALES (est): 1.9MM **Privately Held**
WEB: www.g-three.com
SIC: 2752 Commercial printing, offset

(G-3307)
GROHOLSKI MFG SOLUTIONS LLC
Also Called: G M S
127 Industrial Ave (49036-2168)
P.O. Box 428 (49036-0428)
PHONE..................517 278-9339
Tom Crampton, *Sales Engr*
Steven C Groholski,
EMP: 20
SQ FT: 12,000
SALES (est): 5.1MM **Privately Held**
SIC: 3552 3545 Dyeing, drying & finishing machinery & equipment; tools & accessories for machine tools

(G-3308)
HAROLD K SCHULTZ
Also Called: Shopper's Guide
57 S Monroe St (49036-1928)
PHONE..................517 279-9764
Harold K Schultz, *Owner*
EMP: 12 EST: 1954
SQ FT: 9,000
SALES (est): 498.1K **Privately Held**
SIC: 2711 2752 Newspapers: publishing only, not printed on site; commercial printing, offset

(G-3309)
HC STARCK INC
Also Called: H.C. Starck Group
460 Jay St (49036-2181)
PHONE..................517 279-9511
Andreas Meier, *CEO*
Uwe Salzer, *President*
Ludger Heuberg, *CFO*
Matthias Schmitz, *CFO*
▲ EMP: 43
SALES (est): 7.7MM
SALES (corp-wide): 177.9K **Privately Held**
SIC: 3299 3441 Ceramic fiber; fabricated structural metal
HQ: H.C. Starck Gmbh
Im Schleeke 78-91
Goslar 38642
532 175-10

(G-3310)
INTERNTONAL HARDWOODS MICHIANA
600 1/2 W Chicago Rd (49036)
PHONE..................517 278-8446
Jim Fansler, *Owner*
EMP: 3
SQ FT: 62,000
SALES (est): 250K **Privately Held**
SIC: 2431 5031 2426 Moldings & baseboards, ornamental & trim; lumber: rough, dressed & finished; flooring, hardwood

(G-3311)
KNAPP MANUFACTURING INC
555 Hillside Dr (49036-9787)
PHONE..................517 279-9538
Chris Knapp, *President*
Joyce Knapp, *Corp Secy*
EMP: 12 EST: 1973
SQ FT: 13,200
SALES (est): 1.9MM **Privately Held**
WEB: www.knappmanufacturing.com
SIC: 3599 Machine & other job shop work

(G-3312)
KNAPP MANUFACTURING LLC
555 Hillside Dr (49036-9787)
PHONE..................517 279-9538
Wade Thompson, *Mng Member*
EMP: 3
SALES (est): 83.9K **Privately Held**
SIC: 3999 Manufacturing industries

(G-3313)
L & S PRODUCTS LLC
294 Block Rd (49036-9757)
PHONE..................517 238-4645
▲ EMP: 3 EST: 1954
SQ FT: 168,000
SALES (est): 1MM **Privately Held**
SIC: 5199 2542 Whol Nondurable Goods Mfg Partitions/Fixtures-Nonwood

(G-3314)
LONGSTREET GROUP LLC
Also Called: LONGSTREET LIVING
720 E Chicago Rd (49036-9404)
PHONE..................517 278-4487
EMP: 16 EST: 2007
SALES (est): 4.1MM **Privately Held**
SIC: 3444 5712 Metal flooring & siding; beds & accessories

(G-3315)
MICHIGAN GRAPHIC ARTS
131 N Angola Rd (49036-8573)
PHONE..................517 278-4120
James Knisely, *Owner*
EMP: 5
SQ FT: 8,000
SALES: 675K **Privately Held**
SIC: 3993 2395 Signs & advertising specialties; embroidery products, except schiffli machine

(G-3316)
P-T STAMPING CO LTD
460 Race St (49036-2177)
PHONE..................517 278-5961
Mark Yearling, *President*
EMP: 3
SQ FT: 11,800
SALES (est): 430.6K **Privately Held**
WEB: www.chinametalstampings.com
SIC: 3469 Machine parts, stamped or pressed metal

(G-3317)
PANEL PROCESSING INC
Also Called: Panel Processing of Coldwater
681 Race St (49036-2121)
PHONE..................517 279-8051
Brent Belcher, *Opers Mgr*
Debbie Griffin, *Accounts Mgr*
Chuck Stevens, *Accounts Mgr*
Brian Sexton, *Branch Mgr*
EMP: 40
SALES (corp-wide): 95.4MM **Privately Held**
SIC: 2541 Wood partitions & fixtures
PA: Panel Processing, Inc.
120 N Industrial Hwy
Alpena MI 49707
800 433-7142

(G-3318)
PEPSI-COLA METRO BTLG CO INC
101 Treat Dr (49036-9709)
PHONE..................517 279-8436
Brian Farmer, *Manager*
EMP: 30
SALES (corp-wide): 64.6B **Publicly Held**
WEB: www.joy-of-cola.com
SIC: 2086 5149 Soft drinks: packaged in cans, bottles, etc.; groceries & related products
HQ: Pepsi-Cola Metropolitan Bottling Company, Inc.
1111 Westchester Ave
White Plains NY 10604
914 767-6000

(G-3319)
PERFECTION BAKERIES INC
Also Called: Coldwater Bakery
189 W Garfield Ave (49036-9704)
PHONE..................517 278-2370
Ron Georgi, *Manager*
EMP: 60
SALES (corp-wide): 535.8MM **Privately Held**
WEB: www.perfectionpastries.com
SIC: 2051 Bread, all types (white, wheat, rye, etc): fresh or frozen; buns, bread type: fresh or frozen
PA: Perfection Bakeries, Inc.
350 Pearl St
Fort Wayne IN 46802
260 424-8245

(G-3320)
POLY-GREEN FOAM LLC
325 Jay St (49036-2176)
P.O. Box 513, Lamar MO (64759-0513)
PHONE..................517 279-8019
Danny Little, *Mng Member*
Chris Scripsick,
Ron Scripsick,
EMP: 20
SALES (est): 1.2MM **Privately Held**
SIC: 2298 Insulator pads, cordage

(G-3321)
PROTO SHAPES INC
125 Industrial Ave (49036-2168)
P.O. Box 143 (49036-0143)
PHONE..................517 278-3947
Robert C Small, *President*
Elaine Gray, *Office Mgr*
Donita Small, *Office Mgr*
▲ EMP: 15
SQ FT: 10,000
SALES (est): 2.2MM **Privately Held**
WEB: www.protoshapes.com
SIC: 3089 5162 Injection molding of plastics; plastics products

(G-3322)
PUTNAM MACHINE PRODUCTS INC
35 Cecil Dr (49036-9155)
PHONE..................517 278-2364
Glenna R Bartholomew, *CEO*
Rob Putnam, *General Mgr*
James Putnam, *Materials Mgr*
Paul Quiter, *Engineer*
Cecil Putnam III, *Treasurer*
EMP: 36
SQ FT: 38,000
SALES (est): 5.5MM **Privately Held**
WEB: www.putnammachine.com
SIC: 3599 Machine shop, jobbing & repair

(G-3323)
QUALITY SPRING/TOGO INC
Also Called: Qsti
355 Jay St (49036-2176)
PHONE..................517 278-2391
Kazuyoshi Murase, *CEO*
Mineo Muto, *President*
Jason Wittenmyer, *Sales Staff*
Dawn Stephens, *Office Mgr*
◆ EMP: 104
SQ FT: 125,445
SALES (est): 15.2MM **Privately Held**
WEB: www.qsti.com
SIC: 3493 3714 5013 3495 Steel springs, except wire; motor vehicle parts & accessories; automotive supplies & parts; mechanical springs, precision
HQ: Togo Seisakusyo Corporation
1, Azahiruike, Haruki, Togocho
Aichi-Gun AIC 470-0

(G-3324)
REAL ALLOY RECYCLING LLC
267 N Fillmore Rd (49036-9784)
PHONE..................517 279-9596
Richard Kerr, *Manager*
EMP: 90
SALES (corp-wide): 103.9MM **Privately Held**
SIC: 4953 3341 Recycling, waste materials; secondary nonferrous metals
HQ: Real Alloy Recycling, Llc
3700 Park East Dr Ste 300
Beachwood OH 44122
216 755-8900

(G-3325)
REAL ALLOY RECYCLING LLC
Also Called: Aleris
368 W Garfield Ave (49036-9711)
PHONE..................517 279-9596
Doug Bryant, *Plant Mgr*
Clint Lane, *Opers Mgr*
Brady Myers, *Manager*
EMP: 130
SQ FT: 118,000
SALES (corp-wide): 103.9MM **Privately Held**
SIC: 3334 3341 Pigs, aluminum; aluminum smelting & refining (secondary)
HQ: Real Alloy Recycling, Llc
3700 Park East Dr Ste 300
Beachwood OH 44122
216 755-8900

(G-3326)
REHRIG PACIFIC COMPANY
500 Jonesville Rd (49036-9648)
PHONE..................517 278-9808
EMP: 3 **Privately Held**
SIC: 3089 Air mattresses, plastic
HQ: Rehrig Pacific Company
4010 E 26th St
Vernon CA 90058
323 262-5145

(G-3327)
REMNANT PUBLICATIONS INC
649 E Chicago Rd Ste B (49036-8444)
PHONE..................517 279-1304
Dwight Hall, *CEO*
David Berthiaume, *Manager*
Dan Hall, *Admin Sec*
▲ EMP: 20
SQ FT: 20,000
SALES (est): 6.7MM **Privately Held**
SIC: 2731 8011 Textbooks: publishing & printing; offices & clinics of medical doctors

(G-3328)
RWS & ASSOCIATES LLC
Also Called: Excell Paving Plus
305 W Chicago Rd (49036-9334)
PHONE..................517 278-3134
Randy Sell, *Manager*
EMP: 11
SQ FT: 400
SALES (est): 1.6MM **Privately Held**
SIC: 2951 1771 1611 Asphalt paving mixtures & blocks; blacktop (asphalt) work; surfacing & paving

(G-3329)
SCHAFER PRODUCTS CO (PA)
714 S Angola Rd (49036-9591)
PHONE..................517 238-2266
Charles Davis, *Owner*
Ann Davis, *Partner*
EMP: 3
SQ FT: 1,200
SALES (est): 309.7K **Privately Held**
SIC: 3965 Collar/cuff buttons, except precious & semiprecious

(G-3330)
SCHMITZ FOAM PRODUCTS LLC
188 Treat Dr (49036-9709)
PHONE..................517 781-6615
Erguen Oezcan, *CEO*
Allen Hubbard, *Natl Sales Mgr*
EMP: 25
SALES: 4.5MM
SALES (corp-wide): 242.1K **Privately Held**
SIC: 3086 Padding, foamed plastic

GEOGRAPHIC SECTION

Coloma - Berrien County (G-3356)

HQ: Schmitz Foam Products B.V.
Produktieweg 6
Roermond 6045
475 370-270

(G-3331)
SEKISUI AMERICA CORPORATION
Voltek Division
17 Allen Ave (49036-2101)
PHONE..................517 279-7587
Heath Gillette, *QC Mgr*
Joe Hughes, *Manager*
EMP: 180 **Privately Held**
SIC: 3086 2821 Plastics foam products; plastics materials & resins
HQ: Sekisui America Corporation
333 Meadowlands Pkwy
Secaucus NJ 07094
201 423-7960

(G-3332)
SEKISUI VOLTEK LLC
17 Allen Ave (49036-2101)
PHONE..................517 279-7587
Anna Monetza, *Project Mgr*
Rob Knapp, *Purch Dir*
Donald Myers, *Engineer*
Keiji Wakayama, *Engineer*
Joseph Hughes, *Branch Mgr*
EMP: 180 **Privately Held**
SIC: 3086 Plastics foam products
HQ: Sekisui Voltek, Llc
100 Shepard St
Lawrence MA 01843

(G-3333)
SPARTANNASH COMPANY
Also Called: Felpausch Food Center 1955
410 Marshall St (49036-1139)
P.O. Box 187 (49036-0187)
PHONE..................517 278-8963
Ken Smoker, *Manager*
EMP: 85
SALES (corp-wide): 8B **Publicly Held**
WEB: www.spartanstores.com
SIC: 5411 5992 5912 5735 Supermarkets; florists; drug stores & proprietary stores; record & prerecorded tape stores; bakeries; bread, cake & related products
PA: Spartannash Company
850 76th St Sw
Byron Center MI 49315
616 878-2000

(G-3334)
ST USA HOLDING CORP (PA)
491 W Garfield Ave (49036-8000)
PHONE..................517 278-7144
Mark Meldrum, *President*
EMP: 100
SALES: 70MM **Privately Held**
SIC: 3446 Acoustical suspension systems, metal

(G-3335)
ST USA HOLDING CORP
575 Race St (49036-2121)
PHONE..................800 637-3303
EMP: 170
SALES (corp-wide): 70MM **Privately Held**
SIC: 3446 Acoustical suspension systems, metal
PA: St Usa Holding Corp.
491 W Garfield Ave
Coldwater MI 49036
517 278-7144

(G-3336)
SYSTEMS UNLIMITED INC
300 Jay St (49036-2110)
P.O. Box 529 (49036-0529)
PHONE..................517 279-8407
David Eyre, *President*
Matthew Watkins, *Treasurer*
Mitch Miller, *Manager*
Richard Austin, *Admin Sec*
David McGrath, *Admin Sec*
EMP: 28 **EST:** 1975
SQ FT: 48,000

SALES (est): 5.9MM **Privately Held**
WEB: www.systemsui.com
SIC: 3541 3535 7692 3537 Drilling & boring machines; milling machines; unit handling conveying systems; robotic conveyors; welding repair; industrial trucks & tractors

(G-3337)
TJ RAMPIT USA INC
338 Bidwell Rd (49036-9238)
PHONE..................517 278-9015
Cody Herendeen, *CEO*
EMP: 45
SQ FT: 6,000
SALES (est): 1.9MM **Privately Held**
SIC: 3448 Ramps: prefabricated metal

(G-3338)
TRI STATE OPTICAL INC
350 Marshall St Ste B (49036-1176)
PHONE..................517 279-2701
Michael Sussex, *President*
Daniel J Casey, *President*
Robert Heath, *Vice Pres*
EMP: 8
SQ FT: 750
SALES (est): 1.2MM **Privately Held**
SIC: 5048 3851 5047 Ophthalmic goods; ophthalmic goods; medical equipment & supplies

(G-3339)
UNION PALLET & CONT CO INC
161 Race St (49036-2114)
PHONE..................517 279-4888
Jonathan Slack, *President*
Twyla Slack, *Treasurer*
EMP: 40
SQ FT: 36,000
SALES (est): 7.5MM **Privately Held**
SIC: 2449 2448 Wood containers; pallets, wood & wood with metal

(G-3340)
VACHON INDUSTRIES INC (PA)
Also Called: Koltec Div
580 Race St (49036-2122)
P.O. Box 383 (49036-0383)
PHONE..................517 278-2354
Douglas Mc Michael, *Vice Pres*
▲ **EMP:** 18
SQ FT: 35,000
SALES (est): 2.3MM **Privately Held**
WEB: www.abrasiveproducts.net
SIC: 3291 5085 Abrasive wheels & grindstones, not artificial; buffing or polishing wheels, abrasive or nonabrasive; wheels, abrasive; abrasives; abrasives & adhesives

(G-3341)
WARNER OIL COMPANY
Also Called: Roost Oil Company
400 Race St (49036-2177)
P.O. Box 367 (49036-0367)
PHONE..................517 278-5844
Mark Loveberry, *President*
Mike Swallows, *Sales Staff*
EMP: 14
SQ FT: 17,500
SALES: 12MM **Privately Held**
SIC: 2992 5172 Lubricating oils; petroleum products; fuel oil; diesel fuel; gasoline

Coleman
Midland County

(G-3342)
CHEMLOC INC
4996 N Dickenson Rd (48618-9643)
P.O. Box 169 (48618-0169)
PHONE..................989 465-6541
Ryan Roman, *President*
Tim Roman, *Vice Pres*
Jan Roman, *Treasurer*
EMP: 4
SQ FT: 1,970
SALES: 200K **Privately Held**
SIC: 2842 Cleaning or polishing preparations

(G-3343)
HOMESTEAD PRODUCTS INC
2618 Coolidge Rd (48618-9402)
PHONE..................989 465-6182
Ben Robinson, *President*
Tim Ewert, *Plant Mgr*
Dan Wood, *Manager*
EMP: 15
SQ FT: 2,400
SALES (est): 2.5MM **Privately Held**
SIC: 3089 Plastic processing

(G-3344)
HOMESTEAD TOOL AND MACHINE
Also Called: Homestead Foundry
2618 Coolidge Rd (48618-9402)
PHONE..................989 465-6182
Bernard L Robinson, *President*
Jenny Ewert, *Finance*
Kim Brown, *Office Mgr*
Dan Wood, *Info Tech Mgr*
EMP: 50 **EST:** 1976
SQ FT: 2,400
SALES (est): 7.1MM **Privately Held**
SIC: 3544 3543 3363 Special dies & tools; dies, plastics forming; forms (molds), for foundry & plastics working machinery; industrial patterns; aluminum die-castings

(G-3345)
HUHTAMAKI INC
5700 W Shaffer Rd (48618-9706)
PHONE..................989 465-9046
Ross Harms, *General Mgr*
Ross Farm, *Branch Mgr*
EMP: 250
SALES (corp-wide): 3.5B **Privately Held**
SIC: 3089 Plastic containers, except foam
HQ: Huhtamaki, Inc.
9201 Packaging Dr
De Soto KS 66018
913 583-3025

(G-3346)
HUHTAMAKI INC
Also Called: Huhtamaki Plastics
5760 W Shaffer Rd (48618-9706)
PHONE..................989 633-8900
Michael Gross, *Branch Mgr*
EMP: 300
SALES (corp-wide): 3.5B **Privately Held**
SIC: 3089 2656 Pallets, plastic; sanitary food containers
HQ: Huhtamaki, Inc.
9201 Packaging Dr
De Soto KS 66018
913 583-3025

(G-3347)
LP PRODUCTS (PA)
6680 M 18 (48618-8543)
PHONE..................989 465-0287
Larry Peters, *Owner*
EMP: 11
SALES (est): 1.4MM **Privately Held**
SIC: 3544 Special dies & tools

(G-3348)
LP PRODUCTS
4363 Us 10 (48618-8930)
PHONE..................989 465-1485
Larry Peters, *Owner*
EMP: 4
SALES (corp-wide): 1.4MM **Privately Held**
SIC: 3544 Special dies & tools
PA: Lp Products
6680 M 18
Coleman MI 48618
989 465-0287

(G-3349)
MURPHYS CUSTOM CRAFTSMEN INC
4125 W Shearer Rd (48618-9354)
PHONE..................989 205-7305
Randy Murphy, *President*
EMP: 3
SQ FT: 3,000
SALES (est): 158.5K **Privately Held**
SIC: 2434 Wood kitchen cabinets

(G-3350)
ROBINSON INDUSTRIES INC
3051 W Curtis Rd (48618-8549)
PHONE..................989 465-6111
Inez Kaleto, *CEO*
Bernard Robinson, *President*
Treva Robinson, *Corp Secy*
▼ **EMP:** 190 **EST:** 1949
SQ FT: 78,300
SALES (est): 39.4MM **Privately Held**
WEB: www.robinsonind.com
SIC: 3089 Injection molded finished plastic products; pallets, plastic

(G-3351)
TIGNER PRINTING INC
221 E Railway St (48618-9799)
P.O. Box 289 (48618-0289)
PHONE..................989 465-6916
Jack Tigner, *President*
EMP: 5
SQ FT: 3,000
SALES (est): 678.4K **Privately Held**
SIC: 2752 Commercial printing, offset

(G-3352)
TOUGHBUOY CO
3051 W Curtis Rd (48618-9568)
PHONE..................989 465-6111
Ardis V Robinson, *President*
Bernard L Robinson, *Vice Pres*
Inez J Kaleto, *Treasurer*
Ardis V Foster, *Admin Sec*
EMP: 5
SALES: 66.8K **Privately Held**
SIC: 3499 Metal household articles

Coloma
Berrien County

(G-3353)
AMHAWK LLC
236 N West St (49038-8407)
PHONE..................269 468-4141
Regi Kurien, *Branch Mgr*
EMP: 10
SALES (corp-wide): 6.9MM **Privately Held**
SIC: 3441 Fabricated structural metal
PA: Amhawk, Llc
200 Dunbar St
Hartford MI 49057
269 468-4177

(G-3354)
BOS CONCRETE INC
6902 Paw Paw Lake Rd (49038-9800)
P.O. Box 367 (49038-0367)
PHONE..................269 468-7267
Mark Bos, *Principal*
Mike Bos, *Vice Pres*
EMP: 10
SALES (est): 1.5MM **Privately Held**
SIC: 3273 Ready-mixed concrete

(G-3355)
CCO HOLDINGS LLC
1850 Friday Rd (49038-8920)
PHONE..................269 202-3286
EMP: 3
SALES (corp-wide): 43.6B **Publicly Held**
SIC: 5064 4841 3663 3651 Electrical appliances, television & radio; cable & other pay television services; radio & TV communications equipment; household audio & video equipment
HQ: Cco Holdings, Llc
400 Atlantic St
Stamford CT 06901
203 905-7801

(G-3356)
COLOMA FROZEN FOODS INC (PA)
4145 Coloma Rd (49038-8967)
PHONE..................269 849-0500
Bradley Wendzel, *President*
Alton Wendzel, *Chairman*
Rodney Winkel, *Vice Pres*
Pauline Wendzel, *Sales Staff*
Tom Czuba, *Manager*
EMP: 80
SQ FT: 52,000

Coloma - Berrien County (G-3357)

SALES (est): 44MM **Privately Held**
WEB: www.colomafrozen.com
SIC: 2037 Frozen fruits & vegetables; fruits, quick frozen & cold pack (frozen); vegetables, quick frozen & cold pack, excl. potato products

(G-3357)
JOHNS GLASS
Also Called: John's Glass & Windows
271 N Paw Paw St (49038-9589)
P.O. Box 762 (49038-0762)
PHONE...................................269 468-4227
John Demis, *Owner*
EMP: 3
SALES (est): 384.2K **Privately Held**
SIC: 3089 7699 Window frames & sash, plastic; miscellaneous building item repair services

(G-3358)
M&I MACHINE INC
5040 M 63 N (49038-9139)
PHONE...................................269 849-3624
Mark Coons, *President*
EMP: 10
SALES (est): 1.4MM **Privately Held**
SIC: 3599 Machine shop, jobbing & repair

(G-3359)
M&M POLISHING INC
320 Park St (49038-9485)
PHONE...................................269 468-4407
Brian G Bittner, *Principal*
EMP: 15
SALES (est): 1.8MM **Privately Held**
SIC: 3471 Polishing, metals or formed products

(G-3360)
MAX2 LLC
320 Park St (49038-9485)
P.O. Box 152 (49038-0152)
PHONE...................................269 468-3452
Tom Buttars, *Treasurer*
David A Lagrow, *Mng Member*
EMP: 10
SQ FT: 400
SALES (est): 654K **Privately Held**
SIC: 3541 3469 Milling machines; electrochemical milling machines; machine parts, stamped or pressed metal

(G-3361)
MENASHA PACKAGING COMPANY LLC
238 N West St (49038-8407)
P.O. Box 490 (49038-0490)
PHONE...................................800 253-1526
EMP: 19
SALES (corp-wide): 1.8B **Privately Held**
SIC: 2653 Boxes, corrugated: made from purchased materials
HQ: Menasha Packaging Company, Llc
1645 Bergstrom Rd
Neenah WI 54956
920 751-1000

(G-3362)
MICHIGAN MOLD INC
320 Park St (49038-9485)
P.O. Box 705 (49038-0705)
PHONE...................................269 468-3346
Larry Bittner, *President*
Brian Bittner, *Vice Pres*
Rosanne Bittner, *Director*
EMP: 40
SQ FT: 20,000
SALES (est): 4.7MM **Privately Held**
WEB: www.michmold.com
SIC: 3544 Industrial molds

(G-3363)
NORTH SHORE MFG CORP
4706 M 63 N (49038-9140)
PHONE...................................269 849-2551
Mark Frank, *President*
Christine Frank, *Vice Pres*
▲ EMP: 30
SQ FT: 20,000
SALES (est): 4.9MM **Privately Held**
WEB: www.nshoremfg.com
SIC: 3363 3364 Aluminum die-castings; lead & zinc die-castings; zinc & zinc-base alloy die-castings

(G-3364)
REGAL FINISHING CO INC
3927 Bessemer Rd (49038-8979)
PHONE...................................269 849-2963
Jim Kodis, *President*
Nancy Kodis, *Vice Pres*
Richard Hildebrand, *Production*
Eli Reybuck, *Sales Mgr*
Sharon Wallis, *Sales Mgr*
EMP: 60 EST: 1966
SQ FT: 40,000
SALES (est): 9.6MM **Privately Held**
WEB: www.regalfinishing.com
SIC: 3089 Injection molding of plastics

(G-3365)
SPI BLOW MOLDING LLC
3930 Bessemer Rd (49038-8979)
P.O. Box 359 (49038-0359)
PHONE...................................269 849-3200
John Doster Sr, *President*
Susan Doster,
EMP: 31
SQ FT: 46,000
SALES (est): 4.7MM **Privately Held**
SIC: 3089 Blow molded finished plastic products

(G-3366)
VINEYARDS GOURMET
6841 High St (49038-9678)
PHONE...................................269 468-4778
Brenda Fulton, *Principal*
EMP: 5
SALES (est): 196.5K **Privately Held**
SIC: 2064 Candy & other confectionery products

(G-3367)
WHIRLPOOL CORPORATION
3694 Kerlikowske Rd (49038-9473)
PHONE...................................269 849-0907
EMP: 175
SALES (corp-wide): 20.8B **Publicly Held**
SIC: 3633 3585 3632 Mfg Washing Machines Refrigerators Air Conditionin Units Dishwashers Vacuum Cleaners & Cooking Ranges
PA: Whirlpool Corporation
2000 N M 63
Benton Harbor MI 49022
269 923-5000

(G-3368)
WITCHCRAFT TAPE PRODUCTS INC (PA)
Also Called: W T P
100 Klitchman Dr (49038-8749)
P.O. Box 937 (49038-0937)
PHONE...................................269 468-3399
Henry Klitchman, *President*
Dave Pentridge, *Info Tech Mgr*
EMP: 61
SQ FT: 16,000
SALES (est): 5.7MM **Privately Held**
WEB: www.wtp-inc.com
SIC: 2295 3949 2672 Tape, varnished: plastic & other coated (except magnetic); sporting & athletic goods; coated & laminated paper

Colon
St. Joseph County

(G-3369)
ABBOTTS MAGIC MANUFACTURING CO
Also Called: Abbott Magic
124 S Saint Joseph St (49040-9342)
PHONE...................................269 432-3235
Greg W Bordner, *President*
Martin Bordner, *Treasurer*
EMP: 5 EST: 1934
SQ FT: 6,500
SALES (est): 442.4K **Privately Held**
SIC: 5945 3999 3944 Hobby, toy & game shops; magic equipment, supplies & props; games, toys & children's vehicles

(G-3370)
CCO HOLDINGS LLC
643 E State St (49040-9311)
PHONE...................................269 432-0052
EMP: 3
SALES (corp-wide): 43.6B **Publicly Held**
SIC: 5064 4841 3663 3651 Electrical appliances, television & radio; cable & other pay television services; radio & TV communications equipment; household audio & video equipment
HQ: Cco Holdings, Llc
400 Atlantic St
Stamford CT 06901
203 905-7801

(G-3371)
COLES POLISHING
33230 Oak Leaf Trl (49040-9233)
PHONE...................................269 625-2542
EMP: 3
SALES (est): 110K **Privately Held**
SIC: 3471 Plating/Polishing Service

(G-3372)
FRISBIE SAND & GRAVEL
644 E State St (49040-9311)
PHONE...................................269 432-3379
Duane Frisbie, *Principal*
EMP: 3 EST: 2009
SALES (est): 137K **Privately Held**
SIC: 1442 Construction sand & gravel

(G-3373)
FULL SPECTRUM STAINED GL INC
31323 W Colon Rd (49040-9512)
PHONE...................................269 432-2610
John McCartney, *President*
Valerie McCartney, *Vice Pres*
EMP: 8
SALES (est): 322.1K **Privately Held**
WEB: www.churchwindows.net
SIC: 3231 5231 Stained glass: made from purchased glass; glass, leaded or stained

(G-3374)
MAXITROL COMPANY
1000 E State St (49040-9420)
PHONE...................................269 432-3291
EMP: 170
SQ FT: 51,000
SALES (est): 54.8MM **Privately Held**
WEB: www.maxitrol.com
SIC: 3822 3625 Gas burner, automatic controls; relays & industrial controls
PA: Maxitrol Company
23555 Telegraph Rd
Southfield MI 48033
248 356-1400

(G-3375)
RIVERSIDE VANS INC
57951 Farrand Rd (49040-9513)
P.O. Box 44 (49040-0044)
PHONE...................................269 432-3212
Ann Gilchrist, *President*
Harold Hemel, *Corp Secy*
EMP: 10
SQ FT: 9,000
SALES (est): 1.2MM **Privately Held**
SIC: 3716 Recreational van conversion (self-propelled), factory basis

Columbiaville
Lapeer County

(G-3376)
CCO HOLDINGS LLC
4680 Water St (48421-9162)
PHONE...................................810 545-4020
EMP: 3
SALES (corp-wide): 43.6B **Publicly Held**
SIC: 5064 4841 3663 3651 Electrical appliances, television & radio; cable & other pay television services; radio & TV communications equipment; household audio & video equipment
HQ: Cco Holdings, Llc
400 Atlantic St
Stamford CT 06901
203 905-7801

Columbus
St. Clair County

(G-3377)
BLUEWATER CANVAS LLC
2022 Bauman Rd (48063-3600)
PHONE...................................586 727-5345
Diana Fortuna, *Mng Member*
Robert Fortuna,
EMP: 3
SALES (est): 164.5K **Privately Held**
SIC: 2394 Canvas & related products

(G-3378)
DUANE YOUNG & SON LUMBER
Also Called: Young, W & Son Lumber
8760 Big Hand Rd (48063-3101)
PHONE...................................586 727-1470
Duane Young,
EMP: 4
SALES (est): 100K **Privately Held**
SIC: 2421 5211 2431 2426 Lumber: rough, sawed or planed; planing mill products & lumber; millwork; hardwood dimension & flooring mills; logging

(G-3379)
JOHN T STOLIKER ENTERPRISES
9353 Gratiot Ave (48063-3611)
PHONE...................................586 727-1402
John T Stoliker, *Owner*
EMP: 3
SALES (est): 198.9K **Privately Held**
SIC: 1382 Oil & gas exploration services

(G-3380)
KGF ENTERPRISE INC
2141 Werner Rd (48063-3729)
PHONE...................................586 430-4182
Kerry Fleury, *President*
Debra Fleury, *Treasurer*
EMP: 4
SALES (est): 453.1K **Privately Held**
SIC: 3844 5047 X-ray apparatus & tubes; medical equipment & supplies

(G-3381)
PROTO-FORM ENGINEERING INC
10312 Gratiot Ave (48063-4007)
P.O. Box 174, Richmond (48062-0174)
PHONE...................................586 727-9803
Frederick G Weeks, *President*
EMP: 395
SQ FT: 6,000
SALES (est): 31.7MM **Privately Held**
SIC: 3442 Metal doors, sash & trim

(G-3382)
RACERS INC
9627 Crawford Rd (48063-2307)
PHONE...................................586 727-4069
John Grigg, *President*
Jennifer Grigg, *Treasurer*
EMP: 3
SQ FT: 1,500
SALES (est): 486.7K **Privately Held**
SIC: 3711 Automobile assembly, including specialty automobiles

Comins
Oscoda County

(G-3383)
MICHIGAN LUMBER & WOOD FIBER I
4776 N Abbe Rd (48619-9730)
P.O. Box 97 (48619-0097)
PHONE...................................989 848-2100
Jessika Bills, *Asst Controller*
EMP: 21
SALES (est): 3.6MM **Privately Held**
SIC: 2421 Sawmills & planing mills, general

Commerce Township
Oakland County

(G-3384)
ACCELL TECHNOLOGIES INC
4143 Pioneer Dr (48390-1355)
PHONE..................................248 360-3762
Daniel R Helland, *President*
EMP: 5
SQ FT: 5,200
SALES (est): 300K **Privately Held**
SIC: 3545 Gauges (machine tool accessories)

(G-3385)
ACE FILTRATION INC
Also Called: Ace Purification
4123 Pioneer Dr (48390-1355)
PHONE..................................248 624-6300
Robert McKay, *President*
◆ EMP: 8
SQ FT: 3,000
SALES (est): 1MM **Privately Held**
SIC: 3699 Generators, ultrasonic

(G-3386)
ALADDIN PRINTING
1546 Union Lake Rd (48382-2238)
PHONE..................................248 360-2842
Matt Mac Dermaid, *Owner*
EMP: 4
SALES (est): 320K **Privately Held**
WEB: www.aladdin-printing.com
SIC: 2752 2791 2789 Commercial printing, offset; typesetting; bookbinding & related work

(G-3387)
ALL ABOUT DRAINAGE LLC
1940 Alton Cir (48390-2605)
PHONE..................................248 921-0766
Keith Swan, *Partner*
Kody Swan, *Partner*
EMP: 7
SALES: 500K **Privately Held**
SIC: 3272 1771 Concrete products used to facilitate drainage; concrete repair

(G-3388)
ALLIED WELDING INCORPORATED
8240 Goldie St (48390-4108)
PHONE..................................248 360-1122
Randy Horstmann, *President*
EMP: 4
SALES (est): 278.4K **Privately Held**
SIC: 7692 7699 Welding repair; marine propeller repair

(G-3389)
AMERICAN MFG INNOVATORS INC
Also Called: A M I
1840 W West Maple Rd (48390-2951)
PHONE..................................248 669-5990
Conrad Lindstrom, *President*
Elizabeth Lindstrom, *Controller*
EMP: 11
SQ FT: 15,000
SALES (est): 3.2MM **Privately Held**
SIC: 3599 Machine shop, jobbing & repair

(G-3390)
ARBOC LTD (PA)
3504 Car Dr (48382-1603)
PHONE..................................248 684-2895
James Bartel, *President*
Corrine Bartel, *Treasurer*
EMP: 7
SALES (est): 1.1MM **Privately Held**
WEB: www.arboc.com
SIC: 8711 3715 Consulting engineer; truck trailer chassis

(G-3391)
ARMALY SPONGE COMPANY (PA)
Also Called: Armaly Brands
1900 Easy St (48390-3220)
P.O. Box 611, Walled Lake (48390-0611)
PHONE..................................248 669-2100
John W Armaly Jr, *President*
Annmarie Armaly, *Corp Secy*
Gilbert C Armaly, *Vice Pres*
Kristine Armaly, *Natl Sales Mgr*
Ann M Armaly, *CIO*
◆ EMP: 40
SQ FT: 69,000
SALES (est): 8.2MM **Privately Held**
WEB: www.armalybrands.com
SIC: 3089 3086 5199 Sponges, plastic; plastics foam products; sponges (animal)

(G-3392)
AUGUSTINE INNOVATIONS LLC
2900 Union Lake Rd # 214 (48382-3526)
PHONE..................................248 686-1822
Alivia Arabo,
EMP: 3
SQ FT: 1,100
SALES (est): 146.4K **Privately Held**
SIC: 2299 Pillow fillings: curled hair, cotton waste, moss, hemp tow

(G-3393)
BASC MANUFACTURING INC
4325 Martin Rd (48390-4121)
PHONE..................................248 360-2272
Michael J Burskey, *President*
Stephen Fricke, *COO*
EMP: 5
SALES (est): 791.2K **Privately Held**
WEB: www.bascmfg.com
SIC: 2542 Shelving, office & store: except wood

(G-3394)
CHAMPION GASKET & RUBBER INC
3225 Haggerty Hwy (48390-1725)
PHONE..................................248 624-6140
Robin C Dubuc, *President*
Nathan Dubuc, *Vice Pres*
EMP: 30 EST: 1971
SQ FT: 40,000
SALES (est): 6MM **Privately Held**
WEB: www.championgasket.com
SIC: 3053 Gaskets, all materials

(G-3395)
CORPORATE AV SERVICES LLC
8508 Buffalo Dr Ste B (48382-3406)
PHONE..................................248 939-0900
Mike Bowers, *President*
EMP: 3
SQ FT: 3,500
SALES: 1MM **Privately Held**
SIC: 8748 7373 5999 5065 Systems analysis or design; systems integration services; audio-visual equipment & supplies; video equipment, electronic; video & audio equipment; audio electronic systems

(G-3396)
CRANKSHAFT CRAFTSMAN INC
1960 W West Maple Rd (48390-2950)
PHONE..................................313 366-0140
Russell Taylor, *President*
Susan P Taylor, *Corp Secy*
Timothy Taylor, *Vice Pres*
EMP: 4 EST: 1962
SQ FT: 17,500
SALES: 300K **Privately Held**
SIC: 3599 Machine shop, jobbing & repair

(G-3397)
D G GRINDING INC
1711 Traditional Dr (48390-2975)
PHONE..................................248 624-7280
Richard Meyers, *President*
Joe Bromm, *Corp Secy*
Craig Meyers, *Vice Pres*
EMP: 3
SQ FT: 3,600
SALES: 250K **Privately Held**
SIC: 3599 Machine shop, jobbing & repair

(G-3398)
DAVIS IRON WORKS INC
1166 Benstein Rd (48390-2926)
P.O. Box 900, Walled Lake (48390-0900)
PHONE..................................248 624-5960
Frank G Nehr Sr, *President*
Frank G Nehr Jr, *Exec VP*
Debra Hartman, *Manager*
Elizabeth J Nehr, *Admin Sec*
EMP: 30
SQ FT: 20,000
SALES (est): 5.7MM **Privately Held**
WEB: www.davisironworksinc.com
SIC: 1791 3446 Structural steel erection; architectural metalwork

(G-3399)
DIAMONDBACK CORP
Also Called: Diamondback Abrasive Co
3141 Old Farm Ln (48390-1655)
PHONE..................................248 960-8260
Douglas Menzies, *President*
EMP: 20
SQ FT: 2,500
SALES (est): 2.3MM **Privately Held**
SIC: 3291 Wheels, grinding: artificial

(G-3400)
DIRECT CONNECT SYSTEMS LLC
8246 Goldie St (48390-4108)
PHONE..................................248 694-0130
Stacey Wissner, *Buyer*
Dan Wissner, *Mng Member*
EMP: 25
SALES (est): 4.3MM **Privately Held**
WEB: www.directconnectsystems.com
SIC: 3679 Harness assemblies for electronic use: wire or cable

(G-3401)
DKO INTL
39550 W 14 Mile Rd (48390-3908)
PHONE..................................248 926-9115
Dennis Kiraga, *Owner*
EMP: 10 EST: 1993
SALES (est): 793.3K **Privately Held**
SIC: 2499 Picture frame molding, finished

(G-3402)
E-LIGHT LLC
3144 Martin Rd (48390-1627)
PHONE..................................734 427-0600
EMP: 4
SALES (est): 197.9K **Privately Held**
SIC: 3646 Mfg Commercial Lighting Fixtures

(G-3403)
ECA EDUCATIONAL SERVICES INC
Also Called: Eca Educational Services Div
1981 Dallavo Dr (48390-1683)
PHONE..................................248 669-7170
Dennis J Harlan, *President*
Claudia Harlan, *Vice Pres*
Nancy Perkins, *Bookkeeper*
EMP: 47
SALES (est): 7.7MM **Privately Held**
WEB: www.sciencekitwarehouse.com
SIC: 3944 7372 Science kits: microscopes, chemistry sets, etc.; educational computer software

(G-3404)
EMBASSY DISTRIBUTING COMPANY
Also Called: Embassy Bakery
39560 W 14 Mile Rd (48390-3908)
PHONE..................................248 926-0590
Steven Lagas, *President*
Cindy Lagas, *Treasurer*
EMP: 6
SALES (est): 440K **Privately Held**
SIC: 2051 Bread, all types (white, wheat, rye, etc): fresh or frozen

(G-3405)
FITZ-RITE PRODUCTS INC
Also Called: Special Tooling Service, Inc.
4228 Pioneer Dr (48390-1353)
PHONE..................................248 360-3730
Dean Fitzpatrick, *President*
EMP: 7
SALES (est): 36K **Privately Held**
SIC: 3541 Machine tools, metal cutting type

(G-3406)
FKA DISTRIBUTING CO LLC (PA)
Also Called: Homedics
3000 N Pontiac Trl (48390-2720)
PHONE..................................248 863-3000
Gergely Molnar, *Vice Pres*
Jim Blovet, *Facilities Mgr*
Monica Roberts, *Production*
Ben Dvir, *Purchasing*
Janene Sesti, *Purchasing*
◆ EMP: 277
SQ FT: 400,000
SALES (est): 120.2MM **Privately Held**
WEB: www.homedics.com
SIC: 3679 3634 Headphones, radio; massage machines, electric, except for beauty/barber shops

(G-3407)
FOUR STAR RUBBER INC
3185 Old Farm Ln (48390-1655)
PHONE..................................810 632-3335
Rosemary Voros, *President*
Dan Voros, *Treasurer*
EMP: 8
SQ FT: 5,200
SALES (est): 1.3MM **Privately Held**
WEB: www.fourstarrubber.com
SIC: 3061 5085 Mechanical rubber goods; rubber goods, mechanical

(G-3408)
GOVRO-NELSON CO
1132 Ladd Rd (48390-3032)
PHONE..................................810 329-4727
Ann Schmidt, *President*
Roger Keylon, *General Mgr*
EMP: 5
SALES: 1MM **Privately Held**
WEB: www.govro.com
SIC: 3541 Drilling machine tools (metal cutting); tapping machines

(G-3409)
H-O-H WATER TECHNOLOGY INC
1013 Rig St (48390-2265)
PHONE..................................248 669-6667
Thomas Brown, *Branch Mgr*
David Hallilwell, *Manager*
EMP: 11
SALES (corp-wide): 34.4MM **Privately Held**
SIC: 2899 3589 Water treating compounds; water treatment equipment, industrial
PA: H-O-H Water Technology, Inc.
500 S Vermont St
Palatine IL 60067
847 358-7400

(G-3410)
HEINZMANN D TOOL & DIE INC
Also Called: D H Tool & Die
4335 Pineview Dr (48390-4129)
PHONE..................................248 363-5115
Dieter Heinzmann, *President*
Joanne Heinzmann, *Corp Secy*
EMP: 10
SQ FT: 8,000
SALES (est): 960K **Privately Held**
SIC: 3544 3469 Special dies & tools; jigs & fixtures; metal stampings

(G-3411)
HERKULES EQUIPMENT CORPORATION
2760 Ridgeway Ct (48390-1662)
PHONE..................................248 960-7100
Todd Bacon, *President*
Don Hunt, *Site Mgr*
Jenny Achenbach, *Purch Mgr*
Kevin Taylor, *Purch Agent*
Elaine Wakley, *Engineer*
▲ EMP: 25
SQ FT: 32,000
SALES (est): 19.5MM **Privately Held**
WEB: www.herkules.us
SIC: 5084 3535 Paint spray equipment, industrial; conveyors & conveying equipment

(G-3412)
HIGHLAND MACHINE DESIGN INC
Also Called: Wojo Associates
3125 Old Farm Ln (48390-1655)
PHONE..................................248 669-6150
Ian Joyce, *President*
EMP: 6
SQ FT: 2,000

Commerce Township - Oakland County (G-3413)   GEOGRAPHIC SECTION

SALES: 400K **Privately Held**
SIC: **8711** 3541 Machine tool design; machine tools, metal cutting type

(G-3413)
HOLD IT PRODUCTS CORPORATION
1900 Easy St (48390-3220)
P.O. Box 731, Walled Lake (48390-0731)
PHONE..................................248 624-1195
John W Armaly Jr, *President*
Annette Brown, *Director*
▼ EMP: 5
SQ FT: 3,000
SALES (est): 759.1K **Privately Held**
WEB: www.holditproducts.com
SIC: **3089** Plastic containers, except foam

(G-3414)
HOMEDICS USA LLC (HQ)
Also Called: Homedics Group Canada
3000 N Pontiac Trl (48390-2720)
PHONE..................................248 863-3000
Anthony Koperski, *Vice Pres*
Mark Cohrs, *Engineer*
Joann Berg, *Benefits Mgr*
Debi Gearhart, *Nat'l Sales Mgr*
Alon Kaufman, *Mng Member*
◆ EMP: 300
SALES (est): 95.2MM
SALES (corp-wide): 120.2MM **Privately Held**
SIC: **2844** 5047 5961 Toilet preparations; medical equipment & supplies; fitness & sporting goods, mail order
PA: Fka Distributing Co., Llc
    3000 N Pontiac Trl
    Commerce Township MI 48390
    248 863-3000

(G-3415)
HOUSE OF MARLEY LLC
Also Called: House of Marley Canada
3000 N Pontiac Trl (48390-2720)
PHONE..................................248 863-3000
Alon Kaufman, *CEO*
Roman Ferber, *President*
Sam Vanderveer, *Senior VP*
▲ EMP: 5
SALES (est): 766.6K
SALES (corp-wide): 120.2MM **Privately Held**
SIC: **3679** Headphones, radio
PA: Fka Distributing Co., Llc
    3000 N Pontiac Trl
    Commerce Township MI 48390
    248 863-3000

(G-3416)
INKPRESSIONS LLC
3175 Martin Rd (48390-1628)
PHONE..................................248 461-2555
Tracey Chase,
EMP: 20
SALES (est): 414.6K **Privately Held**
SIC: **2395** 2261 Emblems, embroidered; printing of cotton broadwoven fabrics

(G-3417)
IRENE INDUSTRIES LLC
866 Grandview Dr (48390-5932)
PHONE..................................757 696-3969
Kelly Rankin, *Principal*
EMP: 3
SALES (est): 318.6K **Privately Held**
SIC: **3999** Manufacturing industries

(G-3418)
K&S FUEL VENTURES
519 W Commerce Rd (48382-3924)
PHONE..................................248 360-0055
EMP: 4
SALES (est): 383.6K **Privately Held**
SIC: **2869** Fuels

(G-3419)
LANCAST URETHANE INC
1132 Ladd Rd (48390-3032)
PHONE..................................517 485-6070
Dan Eckert, *President*
EMP: 5
SALES: 315K **Privately Held**
SIC: **2851** Polyurethane coatings

(G-3420)
LETTY MANUFACTURING INC
4576 Driftwood Dr (48382-1313)
PHONE..................................248 461-6604
Tina Harma, *President*
EMP: 3
SALES (est): 115.8K **Privately Held**
SIC: **3599** Machine & other job shop work; machine shop, jobbing & repair

(G-3421)
LINCOLN-REMI GROUP LLC
Also Called: Propur USA
1200 Benstein Rd (48390-2200)
PHONE..................................248 255-0200
Steve Steinway, *CEO*
▲ EMP: 3
SQ FT: 3,800
SALES (est): 476.3K **Privately Held**
SIC: **3589** Water filters & softeners, household type

(G-3422)
LIQUID OTC LLC
Also Called: Lol
3250 Old Farm Ln Ste 1 (48390-1602)
P.O. Box 1351, Walled Lake (48390-5351)
PHONE..................................248 214-7771
Thomas F Morse,
Alina Morse,
EMP: 6
SQ FT: 3,000
SALES (est): 737.3K **Privately Held**
SIC: **2064** 3843 Lollipops & other hard candy; dental equipment & supplies

(G-3423)
LOST HORIZONS INC
232 Oriole St (48382-4047)
PHONE..................................248 366-6858
Peter Hendrickson, *President*
EMP: 3
SALES (est): 514.2K **Privately Held**
WEB: www.losthorizons.com
SIC: **5192** 3944 Books; board games, children's & adults'

(G-3424)
M C PRODUCTS
3105 Old Farm Ln (48390-1655)
PHONE..................................248 960-0590
Jack Carter, *Owner*
EMP: 3
SALES (est): 191.4K **Privately Held**
SIC: **2499** Food handling & processing products, wood

(G-3425)
MACAIR INC
3940 Loch Bend Dr (48382-4341)
PHONE..................................248 242-6860
Robert McKay, *President*
▲ EMP: 4
SALES (est): 886.2K **Privately Held**
SIC: **3567** Driers & redriers, industrial process

(G-3426)
MANUFCTRING SOLUTIONS TECH LLC
Also Called: Vitullo & Associates
1975 Alpha St (48382-2302)
PHONE..................................734 744-5050
David Townsend, *Mng Member*
Chris Jones,
EMP: 8
SQ FT: 16,100
SALES (est): 1MM **Privately Held**
WEB: www.vitulloinc.com
SIC: **3549** 3544 Metalworking machinery; special dies, tools, jigs & fixtures

(G-3427)
MARBLE DELUXE A C
1820 W West Maple Rd (48390-2951)
PHONE..................................248 668-8200
Michael Dimitrievski, *Principal*
Vladimir Dimitrievski, *Vice Pres*
EMP: 8
SALES (est): 756.5K **Privately Held**
SIC: **3281** Marble, building: cut & shaped

(G-3428)
MAVERICK BUILDING SYSTEMS LLC
3190 Walnut Lake Rd (48390-1743)
PHONE..................................248 366-9410
Brian Dittenber, *Sales Staff*
Kevin A Maguire,
Glenn Johnson,
EMP: 17
SQ FT: 25,000
SALES (est): 2.5MM **Privately Held**
WEB: www.mavbldgsys.com
SIC: **2439** 5031 Trusses, wooden roof; lumber, plywood & millwork

(G-3429)
MECHANICAL AIR SYSTEM INC
1994 Dorchester Dr (48390-2990)
PHONE..................................248 346-7995
Kamal Shamoun, *Manager*
EMP: 3
SALES (est): 312.9K **Privately Held**
SIC: **3585** Heating & air conditioning combination units

(G-3430)
MEGA MANIA DIVERSIONS LLC
Also Called: Snap-Back Shuffleboard
3747 Loch Bend Dr (48382-4337)
P.O. Box 21, Walled Lake (48390-0021)
PHONE..................................888 322-9076
Donald C Campion,
▲ EMP: 6 EST: 2005
SALES (est): 65K **Privately Held**
WEB: www.megamaniadiversions.com
SIC: **2511** 7389 Wood game room furniture;

(G-3431)
MERIDIAN CONTG & EXCVTG LLC
Also Called: Meridian Reclamation
5520 Huron Hills Dr (48390-4819)
PHONE..................................734 476-5933
Robert Reichenbach, *General Mgr*
EMP: 3
SALES: 250K **Privately Held**
SIC: **1389** 7389 Excavating slush pits & cellars;

(G-3432)
MICHIGAN MATTRESS LIMITED LLC
3168 Welch Rd (48390-1566)
PHONE..................................248 669-6345
Jylord Rowe, *Sales Staff*
EMP: 3
SALES (est): 12.1K **Privately Held**
SIC: **2515** Mattresses & bedsprings

(G-3433)
MICHIGAN ROLL FORM INC (PA)
Also Called: American Eagle Systems
1132 Ladd Rd (48390-3032)
PHONE..................................248 669-3700
Steven M Arens, *President*
EMP: 36 EST: 1986
SQ FT: 28,600
SALES (est): 3.9MM **Privately Held**
WEB: www.mrf-inc.com
SIC: **3542** 3559 Spinning, spline rolling & winding machines; plastics working machinery

(G-3434)
OLD SAWMILL WOODWORKING CO
4552 Newcroft St (48382-3820)
PHONE..................................248 366-6245
Robert Milkowski, *Manager*
EMP: 6 EST: 1991
SALES (est): 653.3K **Privately Held**
SIC: **2421** Sawmills & planing mills, general

(G-3435)
ONIEL METAL FORMING INC
1098 Rig St (48390-2264)
PHONE..................................248 960-1804
Jeffery O'Neill, *President*
Collen Muszynski, *Administration*
EMP: 6
SQ FT: 8,700
SALES (est): 69.1K **Privately Held**
SIC: **3441** Fabricated structural metal

(G-3436)
OPTIONS CABINETRY INC
2121 Easy St (48390-3225)
PHONE..................................248 669-0000
Alan Edelson, *President*
EMP: 14
SQ FT: 24,600
SALES: 3.6MM **Privately Held**
SIC: **3429** Cabinet hardware

(G-3437)
PACE MACHINE TOOL INC
1144 Rig St (48390-2266)
PHONE..................................248 960-9903
Linda Hobbel, *President*
Raymond Hobble, *Vice Pres*
EMP: 20
SQ FT: 11,000
SALES (est): 3.7MM **Privately Held**
WEB: www.pacemachinetool.com
SIC: **3599** Machine shop, jobbing & repair

(G-3438)
PETERSON AMERICAN CORPORATION
K P American Division
3285 Martin Rd Ste N106 (48390-1601)
PHONE..................................248 799-5410
Carl Atwater, *Manager*
EMP: 6
SALES (corp-wide): 290.5MM **Privately Held**
WEB: www.pspring.com
SIC: **3495** Wire springs
PA: Peterson American Corporation
    21200 Telegraph Rd
    Southfield MI 48033
    248 799-5400

(G-3439)
PHOENIX TRAILER & BODY COMPANY
4751 Juniper Dr (48382-1512)
PHONE..................................248 360-7184
Emory Buttermore, *President*
EMP: 10
SALES: 90K **Privately Held**
WEB: www.phoenixtrailer.com
SIC: **3799** 7389 Trailers & trailer equipment; design services

(G-3440)
PRECISION COATINGS INC (PA)
8120 Goldie St (48390-4107)
PHONE..................................248 363-8361
Andrew W Rich, *President*
Robin Vantilburg, *COO*
Norman Sweet, *Vice Pres*
Jason Smith, *Production*
Robert F Wider, *CFO*
EMP: 95 EST: 1970
SQ FT: 50,000
SALES (est): 18.8MM **Privately Held**
WEB: www.pcicoatings.com
SIC: **3479** Coating of metals & formed products

(G-3441)
PREFERRED PRODUCTS INC
Also Called: Preferred Screen Printing
1200 Benstein Rd (48390-2200)
PHONE..................................248 255-0200
Steve Steinway, *President*
Debra Steinway, *Vice Pres*
EMP: 22
SQ FT: 10,600
SALES (est): 3.5MM **Privately Held**
SIC: **3842** 2392 Orthopedic appliances; household furnishings

(G-3442)
PRESTWICK GROUP LLP
4057 Pioneer Dr (48390-1365)
PHONE..................................248 360-6113
Martin Ballen, *Partner*
EMP: 3
SALES (est): 270K **Privately Held**
SIC: **2273** Carpets & rugs

(G-3443)
QUANENERGY SYSTEMS INC
2655 E Oakley Park Rd # 105 (48390-1684)
PHONE..................................248 859-5587
EMP: 3

SALES (est): 213.8K **Privately Held**
SIC: **3812** Search & navigation equipment

(G-3444)
QUARTERS VENDING LLC
3174 Old Farm Ln (48390-1633)
PHONE..................................313 510-5555
EMP: 4
SALES (est): 336.1K **Privately Held**
SIC: **3131** Quarters

(G-3445)
R & J MANUFACTURING COMPANY
3200 Martin Rd (48390-1629)
PHONE..................................248 669-2460
Anabella Richardi, *President*
EMP: 20
SQ FT: 25,000
SALES (est): 3.5MM **Privately Held**
WEB: www.rjman.com
SIC: **3053** 3829 3061 Gaskets & sealing devices; testing equipment: abrasion, shearing strength, etc.; mechanical rubber goods

(G-3446)
REAL ESTATE ONE INC
Also Called: Real Estate One Licensing Co
3100 Old Farm Ln Ste 10 (48390-1652)
PHONE..................................248 851-2600
Jeff Dixon, *Branch Mgr*
EMP: 4
SALES (corp-wide): 106.9MM **Privately Held**
WEB: www.personalperks.net
SIC: **2752** Promotional printing, lithographic
PA: Real Estate One, Inc.
  25800 Northwestern Hwy # 100
  Southfield MI 48075
  248 208-2900

(G-3447)
REAL GREEN SYSTEMS INC (PA)
4375 Pineview Dr (48390-4129)
PHONE..................................888 345-2154
Donald F Brown, *CEO*
Peter Brown, *Vice Pres*
Steve Katz, *Vice Pres*
Joseph McPhail, *Vice Pres*
Bryan Brown, *Production*
EMP: 60
SQ FT: 18,000
SALES (est): 15.6MM **Privately Held**
WEB: www.realgreen.com
SIC: **7331** 2396 7371 0782 Direct mail advertising services; printing & embossing on plastics fabric articles; software programming applications; lawn & garden services; landscape services; carpet & rug cleaning & repairing plant

(G-3448)
REX RUSH INC
4330 Cooley Lake Rd (48382-1105)
PHONE..................................248 684-0221
Rex Rush, *President*
EMP: 3
SALES (est): 230K **Privately Held**
SIC: **2411** Logging

(G-3449)
ROBERTSON TOOL & ENGINEERING
1054 Rig St (48390-2264)
PHONE..................................248 624-3838
Robert W Robertson Jr, *President*
Robert W Robertson Sr, *Vice Pres*
Beverly Robertson, *Treasurer*
Richard Lavolette, *Admin Sec*
EMP: 5
SQ FT: 2,000
SALES: 150K **Privately Held**
SIC: **3599** Machine shop, jobbing & repair

(G-3450)
RODAN TOOL & MOLD LLC
3185 Old Farm Ln (48390-1655)
PHONE..................................248 926-9200
Dan Voros, *Mng Member*
EMP: 5
SALES (est): 539.5K **Privately Held**
SIC: **3545** Tools & accessories for machine tools

(G-3451)
ROPP ORTHOPEDIC CLINIC LLC
2075 E West Maple Rd B207 (48390-3816)
PHONE..................................248 669-9222
Jeffrey Ropp,
EMP: 3
SALES: 200K **Privately Held**
SIC: **3842** Limbs, artificial

(G-3452)
SKINNY KID RACE CARS
3170 E Oakley Park Rd A (48390-1661)
PHONE..................................248 668-1040
Keith Engling, *Owner*
EMP: 5
SALES (est): 921.8K **Privately Held**
SIC: **3711** Automobile assembly, including specialty automobiles

(G-3453)
TECLA COMPANY INC (PA)
Also Called: Resco Pet Products
1250 Ladd Rd (48390-3067)
P.O. Box 1177, Walled Lake (48390-5177)
PHONE..................................248 624-8200
Richard N Clark, *President*
Jeffrey L Clark, *Corp Secy*
Robert W Clark, *Vice Pres*
▲ EMP: 24 EST: 1897
SQ FT: 23,000
SALES: 3.8MM **Privately Held**
WEB: www.teclausa.com
SIC: **3429** 3999 3089 Marine hardware; pet supplies; plastic processing

(G-3454)
THREE M TOOL & MACHINE INC
Also Called: Ultra-Grip International Div
8135 Richardson Rd (48390-4131)
PHONE..................................248 363-0982
Sharon Medwid, *Manager*
EMP: 20
SALES (corp-wide): 9.5MM **Privately Held**
WEB: www.three-m.com
SIC: **3599** Machine shop, jobbing & repair
PA: Three M Tool & Machine, Inc.
  8155 Richardson Rd
  Commerce Township MI 48390
  248 363-1555

(G-3455)
TS CARBIDE INC
3131 Ruler Dr (48390-1675)
PHONE..................................248 486-8330
Todd Temple, *Manager*
EMP: 5
SALES (est): 582.6K **Privately Held**
SIC: **3545** Cutting tools for machine tools

(G-3456)
VISION-CRAFT INC
3285 Martin Rd Ste 110 (48390-1601)
PHONE..................................248 669-1130
Jason L Mansuy, *Vice Pres*
Jason Mansuy, *Vice Pres*
EMP: 27
SQ FT: 9,800
SALES (est): 4.1MM
SALES (corp-wide): 1.4MM **Privately Held**
WEB: www.vcmich.com
SIC: **3851** Lenses, ophthalmic
HQ: Essilor Laboratories Of America, Inc.
  13515 N Stemmons Fwy
  Dallas TX 75234
  972 241-4141

(G-3457)
WOLVERINE ORTHOTICS INC
2028 Applebrook Dr (48382-1576)
PHONE..................................248 360-3736
Melissa Bastian, *Principal*
EMP: 3
SALES (est): 292.2K **Privately Held**
SIC: **3842** Orthopedic appliances

Comstock Park
Kent County

(G-3458)
ABC PACKAGING EQUIPMENT & MTLS
544 7 Mile Rd Nw (49321-8254)
P.O. Box 435 (49321-0435)
PHONE..................................616 784-2330
Frank Peltz, *Owner*
Robert Brechting, *Co-Owner*
EMP: 11
SALES (est): 1.4MM **Privately Held**
SIC: **3089** 5113 Plastics products; industrial & personal service paper

(G-3459)
ADVANCED TOOLING SYSTEMS INC (HQ)
Also Called: Tsg Tooling Systems Group
1166 7 Mile Rd Nw (49321-9783)
PHONE..................................616 784-7513
Drew Boresma, *President*
▼ EMP: 12
SQ FT: 48,000
SALES (est): 4.3MM **Privately Held**
SIC: **3544** Special dies & tools

(G-3460)
ASELTINE CIDER COMPANY INC
533 Lamoreaux Dr Nw (49321-9204)
PHONE..................................616 784-7676
John Klamt, *President*
Ronald Klamt, *Corp Secy*
EMP: 4
SQ FT: 4,000
SALES (est): 441K **Privately Held**
SIC: **2099** Cider, nonalcoholic

(G-3461)
B W MANUFACTURING INC
3706 Mill Creek Dr Ne (49321-9043)
PHONE..................................616 447-9076
Bruce Williams, *President*
Darrel Miller, *Opers Mgr*
▲ EMP: 3
SALES (est): 669.1K **Privately Held**
SIC: **2842** Specialty cleaning, polishes & sanitation goods

(G-3462)
BAUBLE PATCH INC
5228 Alpine Ave Nw Ste A (49321-7802)
PHONE..................................616 785-1100
Richard Kerkau, *President*
EMP: 7
SQ FT: 1,200
SALES (est): 1MM **Privately Held**
WEB: www.motherrings.com
SIC: **5944** 7631 5094 3911 Jewelry, precious stones & precious metals; jewelry repair services; jewelry; jewelry, precious metal; jewelry mountings & trimmings

(G-3463)
BIBLE DOCTRINES TO LIVE BY INC
Also Called: Bible Doctrines Publications
895 W River Center Dr Ne (49321-8955)
P.O. Box 564 (49321-0564)
PHONE..................................616 453-0493
Joel McGarvey, *CEO*
S Lee Homoki, *President*
Darlene Homoki, *Corp Secy*
EMP: 6
SQ FT: 1,000
SALES: 100K **Privately Held**
SIC: **2759** 1761 Periodicals: printing; roofing, siding & sheet metal work

(G-3464)
BIER BARREL DISTILLERY LLC
5295 West River Dr Ne # 200 (49321-8030)
PHONE..................................616 633-8601
Joel Bierling, *Administration*
EMP: 8
SALES (est): 723.3K **Privately Held**
SIC: **2085** Distilled & blended liquors

(G-3465)
BUILDERS IRON INC
5900 Comstock Park Dr Nw (49321-8256)
PHONE..................................616 887-9127
Tom Hopping, *Owner*
Tim Hopping, *Vice Pres*
EMP: 25
SQ FT: 7,500
SALES (est): 6.6MM **Privately Held**
SIC: **3441** Fabricated structural metal

(G-3466)
CENTERLINE ENGINEERING INC
940 7 Mile Rd Nw (49321-7918)
P.O. Box 2 (49321-0002)
PHONE..................................616 735-2506
Bob Haadsma, *CEO*
Dan Hansen, *President*
EMP: 91
SQ FT: 6,600
SALES (est): 8.7MM **Privately Held**
WEB: www.centerlineeng.com
SIC: **3544** Special dies, tools, jigs & fixtures

(G-3467)
CG AUTOMATION & FIXTURE INC
5352 Rusche Dr Nw (49321-9551)
PHONE..................................616 785-5400
Douglas Alan Bouwman, *CEO*
EMP: 24
SQ FT: 24,000
SALES (est): 6MM **Privately Held**
SIC: **3544** Special dies & tools

(G-3468)
CG PLASTICS INC
5349 Rusche Dr Nw (49321-9551)
PHONE..................................616 785-1900
Jane A Bulkowski Bouwman, *President*
EMP: 7
SQ FT: 18,000
SALES (est): 1.3MM **Privately Held**
SIC: **3089** Injection molding of plastics

(G-3469)
CHAMPION DIE INCORPORATED
5510 West River Dr Ne (49321-8914)
PHONE..................................616 784-2397
Robert G Champion, *President*
Linda Champion, *Vice Pres*
EMP: 25
SALES (est): 3.6MM **Privately Held**
WEB: www.championdie.com
SIC: **3544** Dies, steel rule; special dies & tools

(G-3470)
COMMERCIAL TOOL & DIE INC
Also Called: Commercial Tool Group
5351 Rusche Dr Nw (49321-9551)
PHONE..................................616 785-8100
Doug Bouwman, *CEO*
Chris Ostosh, *President*
Dave Ketelaar, *General Mgr*
Keith Foster, *Vice Pres*
Jeff Castle, *Project Mgr*
▲ EMP: 141
SQ FT: 47,000
SALES (est): 30.6MM **Privately Held**
WEB: www.commercialtool.com
SIC: **3599** Machine shop, jobbing & repair

(G-3471)
CONCEPT METAL MACHINING LLC
5320 6 Mile Ct Nw (49321-9634)
PHONE..................................616 647-9200
Robert Baker, *President*
Rick Williams, *General Mgr*
EMP: 45
SQ FT: 25,000
SALES (est): 1.3MM **Privately Held**
SIC: **3599** Machine shop, jobbing & repair
PA: Concept Metal Products, Inc.
  16928 148th Ave
  Spring Lake MI 49456

(G-3472)
CPJ COMPANY INC
3739 Laramie Dr Ne (49321-8973)
PHONE..................................616 784-6355
Charles Brickey, *President*

Comstock Park - Kent County (G-3473)

Pamela Brickey, *Vice Pres*
Peter Schamel, *Vice Pres*
Steve Hendricks, *Plant Mgr*
Roery Maclean, *Regl Sales Mgr*
EMP: 36
SQ FT: 18,000
SALES (est): 8.8MM **Privately Held**
WEB: www.dubric.com
SIC: 3561 7699 7629 3593 Pumps & pumping equipment; hydraulic equipment repair; pumps & pumping equipment repair; electrical repair shops; fluid power cylinders & actuators; gaskets, packing & sealing devices

(G-3473)
CRETE DRY-MIX & SUPPLY CO
20 N Park St (49321)
PHONE..................616 784-5790
Hilda Roede, *Ch of Bd*
Ronald R Roede, *President*
Mary Nixon, *Vice Pres*
EMP: 10 **EST:** 1952
SQ FT: 20,000
SALES (est): 1.3MM **Privately Held**
SIC: 3273 Ready-mixed concrete

(G-3474)
D&M METAL PRODUCTS COMPANY
4994 West River Dr Ne (49321-8521)
PHONE..................616 784-0601
Robert Buist, *President*
Russ Deviries, *Vice Pres*
EMP: 50 **EST:** 1977
SQ FT: 60,000
SALES (est): 11.2MM **Privately Held**
WEB: www.dmmetalproducts.com
SIC: 3444 Sheet metal specialties, not stamped

(G-3475)
DADCO INC
848 W River Center Dr Ne C (49321-8010)
PHONE..................616 785-2888
Michael Diebolt, *Owner*
EMP: 5
SALES (corp-wide): 32.5MM **Privately Held**
SIC: 3593 Fluid power cylinders & actuators
PA: Dadco, Inc.
43850 Plymouth Oaks Blvd
Plymouth MI 48170
734 207-1100

(G-3476)
DESIGN MANUFACTURING LLC
950 Vitality Dr Nw Ste B (49321-7807)
PHONE..................616 647-2229
Brad Graham,
Brian Cole,
Bob Graham,
EMP: 20
SALES (est): 4.6MM **Privately Held**
SIC: 3999 Advertising display products

(G-3477)
DH2 INC
87 10 Mile Rd Ne (49321-9657)
P.O. Box 456, Sparta (49345-0456)
PHONE..................616 887-2700
Karen Dehaan, *President*
EMP: 3
SQ FT: 512
SALES (est): 427.8K **Privately Held**
WEB: www.dh2.com
SIC: 2621 Building & roofing paper, felts & insulation siding

(G-3478)
DIVERSIFIED MECH SVCS INC
844 W River Center Dr Ne (49321-8955)
PHONE..................616 785-2735
EMP: 10
SQ FT: 6,000
SALES (est): 1.4MM **Privately Held**
SIC: 1711 3443 Plumbing/Heating/Air Cond Contractor Mfg Fabricated Plate Work

(G-3479)
DRAG FINISHING TECH LLC (PA)
Also Called: Advanced Finishing Tech
835 W River Center Dr Ne # 2 (49321-8016)
PHONE..................616 785-0400
Brandon Karst, *Sales Staff*
Tim Dyer,
Terry Dyer,
▲ **EMP:** 4
SQ FT: 100
SALES (est): 3MM **Privately Held**
SIC: 3531 Finishers & spreaders (construction equipment)

(G-3480)
DUBOIS PRODUCTION SERVICES INC
30 N Park St Ne (49321)
P.O. Box 209 (49321-0209)
PHONE..................616 785-0088
Kathleen Dubois, *President*
EMP: 25
SQ FT: 70,000
SALES (est): 2.1MM **Privately Held**
WEB: www.duboisproduction.com
SIC: 7692 3599 3544 3444 Welding repair; machine shop, jobbing & repair; special dies, tools, jigs & fixtures; sheet metalwork

(G-3481)
EAGLE INDUSTRIAL GROUP INC
847 W River Center Dr Ne (49321-8955)
PHONE..................616 647-9904
Chad Boersma, *President*
EMP: 30
SALES (est): 8.3MM **Privately Held**
SIC: 5082 3728 5084 General construction machinery & equipment; military aircraft equipment & armament; tool & die makers' equipment

(G-3482)
GLS ENTERPRISES INC
Also Called: GLS Promotional Specialties
960 W River Center Dr Ne G (49321-8570)
PHONE..................616 243-2574
Steve Williams, *President*
EMP: 4
SQ FT: 3,200
SALES (est): 1MM **Privately Held**
WEB: www.glsenter.com
SIC: 5199 2389 Advertising specialties; handkerchiefs, except paper

(G-3483)
GREAT LAKES LABEL LLC
910 Metzgar Dr Nw (49321-9728)
PHONE..................616 647-9880
John A Cook, *President*
Clark Miles, *Purchasing*
Ross Scholma, *Engineer*
Dan Basilius, *Controller*
Sallly Odonnel, *Human Resources*
EMP: 38
SALES: 9MM **Privately Held**
SIC: 2759 Labels & seals: printing

(G-3484)
GREAT LAKES PRECAST SYSTEMS
Also Called: Great Lakes Precast Products
5830 Comstock Park Dr Nw (49321-9593)
P.O. Box 453 (49321-0453)
PHONE..................616 784-5900
Larry Roelofs, *President*
Harriet Roelofs, *Admin Sec*
EMP: 3
SQ FT: 2,500
SALES (est): 304.6K **Privately Held**
SIC: 3272 Concrete products, precast

(G-3485)
INDUSTRIAL FINISHING CO LLC
3620 Mill Creek Dr Ne (49321-9042)
PHONE..................616 784-5737
Daniel Welch, *Mng Member*
EMP: 3
SQ FT: 8,000
SALES: 400K **Privately Held**
SIC: 7389 2851 3471 Furniture finishing; paints & allied products; plating & polishing

(G-3486)
INTERLOCK DESIGN
5830 Comstock Park Dr Nw (49321-9593)
P.O. Box 453 (49321-0453)
PHONE..................616 784-5901
Larry Roelofs, *President*
EMP: 10
SALES (est): 1.4MM **Privately Held**
SIC: 3271 Concrete block & brick

(G-3487)
JAVA MANUFACTURING INC
4760 West River Dr Ne (49321-8927)
P.O. Box 546 (49321-0546)
PHONE..................616 784-3873
Norine Smulders, *President*
EMP: 7
SQ FT: 4,500
SALES (est): 1.2MM **Privately Held**
WEB: www.javacontrolsmfg.com
SIC: 3613 Panelboards & distribution boards, electric

(G-3488)
KEN RODENHOUSE DOOR & WINDOW
Also Called: Rodenhouse Door & Window
5120 West River Dr Ne (49321-8522)
PHONE..................616 784-3365
Fax: 616 784-7663
EMP: 10
SQ FT: 15,000
SALES: 900K **Privately Held**
SIC: 3442 Mfg Metal Doors/Sash/Trim

(G-3489)
KENTWATER TOOL & MFG CO
5516 West River Dr Ne (49321-8914)
PHONE..................616 784-7171
Frank T Marek, *President*
Dave Marek, *Vice Pres*
Thomas Merek, *Admin Sec*
EMP: 9 **EST:** 1964
SQ FT: 13,000
SALES: 750K **Privately Held**
SIC: 3544 3599 Special dies & tools; custom machinery

(G-3490)
KIMBOW INC
901 Metzgar Dr Nw (49321-9728)
PHONE..................616 774-4680
Tim Schelhaas, *President*
EMP: 12 **EST:** 1996
SALES (est): 1MM **Privately Held**
SIC: 3444 Sheet metal specialties, not stamped

(G-3491)
KORE INC
5263 6 Mile Ct Nw (49321-9635)
PHONE..................616 785-5900
Karl J Burdick, *President*
Dan Jones, *General Mgr*
Lindsey Myers, *Buyer*
▲ **EMP:** 20
SQ FT: 12,000
SALES: 2MM **Privately Held**
SIC: 3699 8731 Electrical equipment & supplies; electronic research

(G-3492)
KSB DUBRIC INC
3737 Laramie Dr Ne (49321-8973)
P.O. Box 43 (49321-0043)
PHONE..................616 784-6355
Jeffrey Koeper, *CEO*
EMP: 35
SALES (est): 811.9K **Privately Held**
SIC: 5085 3561 7699 7629 Seals, industrial; packing, industrial; pumps & pumping equipment; hydraulic equipment repair; pumps & pumping equipment repair; electrical repair shops; fluid power cylinders & actuators; gaskets, packing & sealing devices

(G-3493)
LAKELAND ELEC MTR SVCS INC
3810 Mill Creek Dr Ne (49321-9044)
PHONE..................616 647-0331
Steve Rokos, *President*
EMP: 29

SALES (est): 6.4MM **Privately Held**
SIC: 3548 Electric welding equipment

(G-3494)
M & J ENTP GRND RAPIDS LLC
5304 Alpine Ave Nw (49321-9708)
PHONE..................616 485-9775
Michael Granger,
EMP: 10
SQ FT: 58,000
SALES: 50K **Privately Held**
SIC: 2631 Cardboard

(G-3495)
MAGNUM POWDER COATING INC
5500 West River Dr Ne (49321-8914)
PHONE..................616 785-3155
Nancy Couturier, *President*
Steve Couturier, *Opers Staff*
EMP: 8
SQ FT: 6,000
SALES: 1.3MM **Privately Held**
WEB: www.magnumpowdercoating.com
SIC: 3479 Coating of metals & formed products; painting, coating & hot dipping

(G-3496)
MARKETING COMMUNICATIONS INC
Also Called: Sightline Display
950 Vitality Dr Nw Ste A (49321-7807)
PHONE..................616 784-4488
Steve Cole, *CEO*
Brian S Cole, *President*
▲ **EMP:** 7
SQ FT: 2,800
SALES (est): 4MM **Privately Held**
SIC: 3578 Point-of-sale devices

(G-3497)
MAYCO TOOL
5880 Comstock Park Dr Nw (49321-9593)
PHONE..................616 785-7350
Kurt May, *Owner*
EMP: 5
SALES (est): 651K **Privately Held**
SIC: 3544 Special dies, tools, jigs & fixtures

(G-3498)
MBA PRINTING INC
Also Called: M B A Printing
90 Windflower St Ne (49321-8235)
PHONE..................616 243-1600
Jerry Hofman, *President*
EMP: 9
SALES (est): 700.6K **Privately Held**
SIC: 2759 Thermography

(G-3499)
MEGA WALL INC
5340 6 Mile Ct Nw (49321-9634)
PHONE..................616 647-4190
David McGinnis, *President*
Brad McGinnis, *CFO*
Mark McGinnis, *Manager*
▲ **EMP:** 17
SQ FT: 41,000
SALES (est): 3.8MM **Privately Held**
WEB: www.megawall.com
SIC: 2542 Fixtures, store: except wood

(G-3500)
META4MAT LLC
320 Dodge Rd Ne Ste B (49321-8045)
PHONE..................616 214-7418
Grant Cooper, *Principal*
Dan Norman, *Principal*
Brian Krueger, *Prdtn Mgr*
Ashley Rozeveld, *Production*
EMP: 8 **EST:** 2012
SALES (est): 1.3MM **Privately Held**
SIC: 2759 Commercial printing

(G-3501)
NBHX TRIM USA CORPORATION (DH)
1020 7 Mile Rd Nw (49321-9542)
PHONE..................616 785-9400
Stefan Clemens, *President*
Michael Homrich, *Vice Pres*
Pete Walenta, *Vice Pres*
Debra Crocker, *Production*
Nick Bailey, *Engineer*

GEOGRAPHIC SECTION

Concord - Jackson County (G-3527)

▲ **EMP:** 115
SQ FT: 125,000
SALES (est): 96.1MM
SALES (corp-wide): 2.1B **Privately Held**
WEB: www.nbhx-trim.com
SIC: 3714 Motor vehicle parts & accessories
HQ: Nbhx Trim Gmbh
Gutenbergstr. 30-32
Heilsbronn 91560
987 280-2280

(G-3502)
NORTH WOODS INDUSTRIAL
3644 Mill Creek Dr Ne (49321-9042)
P.O. Box 141006, Grand Rapids (49514-1006)
PHONE..............................616 784-2840
David L Vandermolen, *President*
Carol Vandermolen, *Corp Secy*
David Vandermolen Jr, *Vice Pres*
EMP: 8
SQ FT: 13,000
SALES: 2.5MM **Privately Held**
SIC: 3567 3535 3444 Industrial furnaces & ovens; conveyors & conveying equipment; sheet metalwork

(G-3503)
NUCRAFT FURNITURE COMPANY
5151 West River Dr Ne (49321-8938)
PHONE..............................616 784-6016
Bob Bockheim, *President*
Timothy Schad, *Chairman*
James Doletzky, *Vice Pres*
Lori Stokes, *Materials Mgr*
Mike Turley, *Production*
▼ **EMP:** 60
SQ FT: 200,000
SALES (est): 13.6MM **Privately Held**
WEB: www.nucraft.com
SIC: 2521 Wood office furniture

(G-3504)
OVER TOP STEEL COATING LLC
931 W River Center Dr Ne B (49321-8008)
PHONE..............................616 647-9140
Jason Hoek, *Mng Member*
EMP: 7
SALES (est): 661.7K **Privately Held**
WEB: www.overthetopsealcoating.com
SIC: 2952 Asphalt felts & coatings

(G-3505)
PARKER EXCVTG GRAV & RECYCLE
295 Hayes Rd Nw (49321-9712)
PHONE..............................616 784-1681
Russell G Parker, *President*
Carolyn Parker, *Corp Secy*
Kevin Parker, *Vice Pres*
Ross Parker, *Vice Pres*
EMP: 13
SQ FT: 3,376
SALES (est): 1.1MM **Privately Held**
SIC: 5032 1442 Gravel; gravel mining

(G-3506)
PATTEN MONUMENT COMPANY (PA)
Also Called: Pattern Monument
3980 West River Dr Ne (49321-8997)
P.O. Box 427 (49321-0427)
PHONE..............................616 785-4141
Eric Ericksen, *President*
Andy Bolt, *Corp Secy*
Chris Fortosis, *Vice Pres*
Alex Fortosis, *Sales Staff*
Brandy Hawley, *Office Mgr*
EMP: 60
SQ FT: 55,000
SALES (est): 15.6MM **Privately Held**
WEB: www.pattenmonument.com
SIC: 5099 5999 3281 Monuments & grave markers; monuments & tombstones; cut stone & stone products

(G-3507)
PERRIN SCREEN PRINTING INC
5320 Rusche Dr Nw (49321-9551)
PHONE..............................616 785-9900
Randy Perrin, *President*
EMP: 60
SQ FT: 39,000
SALES (est): 5.4MM **Privately Held**
WEB: www.perrinwear.com
SIC: 2396 2261 Screen printing on fabric articles; screen printing of cotton broadwoven fabrics

(G-3508)
PERRIN SOUVENIR DISTRS INC
5320 Rusche Dr Nw (49321-9551)
PHONE..............................616 785-9700
Mitch Heiman, *President*
Randy Perrin, *President*
Rick Koster, *CFO*
Brooke Emrich, *Merchandising*
▲ **EMP:** 300 **EST:** 1977
SQ FT: 120,000
SALES (est): 33.9MM **Privately Held**
SIC: 2759 2396 2395 7389 Labels & seals; printing; automotive & apparel trimmings; pleating & stitching; decoration service for special events

(G-3509)
PREFERRED TOOL & DIE CO INC
Also Called: Diebotics
5400 West River Dr Ne (49321-8925)
P.O. Box 386 (49321-0386)
PHONE..............................616 784-6789
Timothy R Launiere, *President*
Robert E Launiere, *Admin Sec*
▲ **EMP:** 30 **EST:** 1966
SQ FT: 20,000
SALES: 5MM **Privately Held**
WEB: www.diebotics.com
SIC: 3544 Special dies & tools; jigs & fixtures

(G-3510)
PUMMILL PRINT SERVICES LC
960 W River Center Dr Ne (49321-8570)
P.O. Box 140108, Grand Rapids (49514-0108)
PHONE..............................616 785-7960
David R Pummill,
EMP: 4
SALES (est): 950K **Privately Held**
SIC: 2752 Commercial printing, offset

(G-3511)
QUALITY LIQUID FEEDS INC
5715 Comstock Park Dr Nw (49321-7200)
PHONE..............................616 784-2930
Kevin Pratt, *Branch Mgr*
EMP: 5
SALES (corp-wide): 148.2MM **Privately Held**
SIC: 2048 Feed supplements
PA: Quality Liquid Feeds, Inc.
3586 State Road 23
Dodgeville WI 53533
608 935-2345

(G-3512)
R N B MACHINE & TOOL INC
5200 West River Dr Ne (49321-8523)
PHONE..............................616 784-6868
David Bogardus, *President*
Kenneth Bogardus, *Vice Pres*
Jady Bogardus, *Treasurer*
Ed Bogardus, *Admin Sec*
EMP: 5
SQ FT: 6,600
SALES: 500K **Privately Held**
SIC: 3599 Machine shop, jobbing & repair

(G-3513)
RAPID ENGINEERING LLC (PA)
1100 7 Mile Rd Nw (49321-9782)
PHONE..............................616 784-0500
Bruce Bellamy, *Vice Pres*
Christina Hulstrand, *Purch Mgr*
Robert Gordon,
▲ **EMP:** 65
SQ FT: 85,000
SALES: 14MM **Privately Held**
WEB: www.rapidengineering.com
SIC: 3585 3567 Heating equipment, complete; paint baking & drying ovens

(G-3514)
REFRIGERATION CONCEPTS INC
5959 Comstock Park Dr Nw (49321-8258)
PHONE..............................616 785-7335
Tom Cooper, *President*
Todd McCoy, *Engineer*
Robert Swem, *Treasurer*
Mike Rikkers, *IT Specialist*
Roger Bainbridge, *Officer*
EMP: 22
SQ FT: 7,000
SALES (est): 3.9MM **Privately Held**
WEB: www.rcicold.com
SIC: 7389 1711 7623 3498 Design, commercial & industrial; refrigeration contractor; refrigeration repair service; piping systems for pulp paper & chemical industries

(G-3515)
SERVICE EXTRUSION DIE CO INC
3648 Mill Creek Dr Ne (49321-9042)
P.O. Box 44 (49321-0044)
PHONE..............................616 784-6933
Robert Warnes, *President*
EMP: 6
SQ FT: 7,200
SALES (est): 1MM **Privately Held**
SIC: 3544 Extrusion dies

(G-3516)
SIGNATURE CNSTR SVCS LLC
Also Called: Signature Stone Tops
3704 Mill Creek Dr Ne (49321-9043)
PHONE..............................616 451-0549
Daniel Stein, *Owner*
Daniel J Stein,
EMP: 8
SALES: 280K **Privately Held**
SIC: 3272 Monuments & grave markers, except terrazo

(G-3517)
SUGAR FREE SPECIALTIES LLC (PA)
Also Called: Dr. John's Candies
5320 West River Dr Ne (49321-8524)
PHONE..............................616 734-6999
Debra L Bruinsma, *VP Sales*
Michael McDonald, *Mng Member*
EMP: 16
SALES (est): 1.8MM **Privately Held**
SIC: 2064 2066 Candy & other confectionery products; chocolate & cocoa products

(G-3518)
TOTAL TOOLING CONCEPTS INC
4870 West River Dr Ne A (49321-8942)
PHONE..............................616 785-8402
David Walejewski, *President*
Ken Scholl, *General Mgr*
EMP: 7 **EST:** 2001
SQ FT: 6,300
SALES (est): 1.6MM **Privately Held**
WEB: www.totaltooling.net
SIC: 3545 Machine tool accessories

(G-3519)
VALLEY CITY SIGN COMPANY
5009 West River Dr Ne (49321-8961)
PHONE..............................616 784-5711
Judson L Kovalak Jr, *CEO*
Randy Czubko, *President*
Dave Jerrils, *General Mgr*
Susan Sear, *Production*
Lynn Kiel, *CFO*
EMP: 50 **EST:** 1948
SQ FT: 75,000
SALES (est): 8.1MM **Privately Held**
WEB: www.valleycitysign.com
SIC: 3993 3446 Electric signs; architectural metalwork

(G-3520)
WEATHER-RITE LLC
1100 7 Mile Rd Nw (49321-9727)
PHONE..............................612 338-1401
Patrick Stone, *Mng Member*
▼ **EMP:** 65
SQ FT: 85,000
SALES (est): 16.3MM **Privately Held**
WEB: www.weather-rite.com
SIC: 3585 3357 Heating equipment, complete; air conditioning equipment, complete; magnet wire, nonferrous

(G-3521)
WOODLAND PAVING CO (PA)
3566 Mill Creek Dr Ne (49321-9041)
P.O. Box 309 (49321-0309)
PHONE..............................616 784-5220
Toni Reyburn, *Office Mgr*
Old Castle,
EMP: 47 **EST:** 1969
SQ FT: 2,000
SALES (est): 4.3MM **Privately Held**
SIC: 1611 1771 2951 Surfacing & paving; parking lot construction; asphalt & asphaltic paving mixtures (not from refineries)

(G-3522)
YELLOWSTONE PRODUCTS INC
310 Dodge Rd Ne Ste C (49321-8043)
PHONE..............................616 299-7855
Michael Olman, *President*
Mike Olman, *Administration*
EMP: 6
SALES: 1MM **Privately Held**
SIC: 3281 Granite, cut & shaped

Concord
Jackson County

(G-3523)
BELGIAN SCREW MACHINE PDTS INC
600 Homer Rd (49237-9528)
P.O. Box 637 (49237-0637)
PHONE..............................517 524-8825
Camiel E Thorrez, *President*
Theresa J Stevens, *Vice Pres*
Jeffrey Thorrez, *Vice Pres*
Donald L Wheeler, *Vice Pres*
Michael Thorrez, *Treasurer*
EMP: 9
SQ FT: 5,000
SALES (est): 82.7K **Privately Held**
WEB: www.belgiancorp.com
SIC: 3451 Screw machine products

(G-3524)
SALESMAN INC
Also Called: Salesman Publications
102 S Main St (49237)
PHONE..............................517 563-8860
Bettie J Watson, *Branch Mgr*
Kathryn I Palon, *Admin Sec*
EMP: 12 **Privately Held**
SIC: 2741 Shopping news: publishing only, not printed on site
PA: The Salesman Inc
1101 Greenwood Ave
Jackson MI 49203

(G-3525)
SPRY SIGN & GRAPHICS CO LLC
12123 Spring Arbor Rd (49237-9722)
P.O. Box 603 (49237-0603)
PHONE..............................517 524-7685
Kim Spry,
EMP: 4
SALES (est): 240K **Privately Held**
SIC: 3993 Signs & advertising specialties

(G-3526)
UNIQUE FABRICATING NA INC
13221 Allman Rd (49237-9813)
PHONE..............................517 524-9010
EMP: 135
SALES (corp-wide): 174.9MM **Publicly Held**
SIC: 3053 Gaskets, all materials
HQ: Unique Fabricating Na, Inc.
800 Standard Pkwy
Auburn Hills MI 48326
248 853-2333

(G-3527)
UNIQUE MOLDED FOAM TECH INC
13221 Allman Rd (49237-9813)
PHONE..............................517 524-9010
Tim Pecker, *General Mgr*
EMP: 115 **EST:** 2015

SALES (est): 5.9MM
SALES (corp-wide): 174.9MM **Publicly Held**
SIC: 3086 Plastics foam products
HQ: Unique Fabricating Na, Inc.
800 Standard Pkwy
Auburn Hills MI 48326
248 853-2333

Conklin
Ottawa County

(G-3528)
APPLE QUEST INC
1380 Coolidge St (49403-8707)
PHONE..................................616 299-4834
Bruce E Rasch, *President*
EMP: 130
SALES (est): 15.6MM **Privately Held**
SIC: 2034 Dehydrated fruits, vegetables, soups

(G-3529)
CAVEMAN PALLETS LLC
2382 Van Dyke St (49403-9596)
P.O. Box 116, Casnovia (49318-0116)
PHONE..................................616 675-7270
Tina E Rooks, *Mng Member*
EMP: 13
SALES: 1.5MM **Privately Held**
SIC: 2448 Pallets, wood

(G-3530)
MICHIGAN ORNAMENTAL IR & FABG
219 Roosevelt St (49403-9715)
P.O. Box 67 (49403-0067)
PHONE..................................616 899-2441
Mary Kay Menn, *President*
Stephen A Menn, *Principal*
EMP: 10
SQ FT: 8,500
SALES: 840K **Privately Held**
SIC: 3446 Ornamental metalwork

(G-3531)
PHIL BROWN WELDING CORPORATION
4689 8 Mile Rd (49403-9604)
PHONE..................................616 784-3046
Phillip A Brown, *President*
Dorothy Brown, *Vice Pres*
▲ EMP: 15
SQ FT: 15,000
SALES (est): 3.1MM **Privately Held**
SIC: 3523 7692 Farm machinery & equipment; welding repair

Constantine
St. Joseph County

(G-3532)
BERRY GLOBAL INC
700 Centreville St (49042-1273)
P.O. Box 187 (49042-0187)
PHONE..................................269 435-2425
Gayle Sears, *Branch Mgr*
EMP: 127 **Publicly Held**
SIC: 3089 3081 Bottle caps, molded plastic; unsupported plastics film & sheet
HQ: Berry Global, Inc.
101 Oakley St
Evansville IN 47710
812 424-2904

(G-3533)
DENARCO INC
301 Industrial Park Dr (49042-9702)
PHONE..................................269 435-8404
Dennis G Harr, *President*
Scott Karle, *Prdtn Mgr*
EMP: 6
SQ FT: 20,000
SALES (est): 879.2K **Privately Held**
SIC: 2891 Sealants

(G-3534)
E L NICKELL CO
Also Called: Alnco
385 Centreville St (49042-1201)
P.O. Box 97 (49042-0097)
PHONE..................................269 435-2475
Shelby Nickell, *President*
Martin Eltzroth, *Professor*
EMP: 10 EST: 1944
SQ FT: 35,000
SALES: 7MM **Privately Held**
SIC: 3443 Industrial vessels, tanks & containers

(G-3535)
FIBRE CONVERTERS INC (PA)
1 Industrial Park Dr (49042-8735)
P.O. Box 130 (49042-0130)
PHONE..................................269 279-1700
James D Stuck, *CEO*
Stephen N Reed, *Vice Pres*
EMP: 48 EST: 1949
SQ FT: 160,000
SALES (est): 12.1MM **Privately Held**
WEB: www.fibreconverters.com
SIC: 2671 2631 2396 Packaging paper & plastics film, coated & laminated; paperboard mills; automotive & apparel trimmings

(G-3536)
HELPING HEARTS HELPING HANDS
285 Mill St (49042-1025)
PHONE..................................248 980-5090
Nancy Sebring-Cale, *Principal*
EMP: 3 EST: 2010
SALES: 55.9K **Privately Held**
SIC: 2515 Foundations & platforms

(G-3537)
HIG RECOVERY FUND INC
485 Florence Rd (49042-1261)
P.O. Box 188 (49042-0188)
PHONE..................................269 435-8414
Angela Pollard, *Principal*
EMP: 4
SALES (est): 366.8K **Privately Held**
SIC: 2295 Resin or plastic coated fabrics

(G-3538)
MARCON TECHNOLOGIES LLC
1 Industrial Park Dr (49042-8735)
P.O. Box 130 (49042-0130)
PHONE..................................269 279-1701
Jim Stuck, *Mng Member*
▲ EMP: 20
SQ FT: 25,000
SALES (est): 3.2MM
SALES (corp-wide): 12.1MM **Privately Held**
WEB: www.marcontechnologies.com
SIC: 3089 Extruded finished plastic products
PA: Fibre Converters, Inc.
1 Industrial Park Dr
Constantine MI 49042
269 279-1700

(G-3539)
MICHIGAN MILK PRODUCERS ASSN
Constantine Plant
125 Depot St (49042-1066)
P.O. Box 158 (49042-0158)
PHONE..................................269 435-2835
Thomas Carpenter, *Manager*
EMP: 30
SQ FT: 10,000
SALES (corp-wide): 854MM **Privately Held**
WEB: www.mimilk.com
SIC: 2021 2026 2023 Creamery butter; milk processing (pasteurizing, homogenizing, bottling); dry, condensed, evaporated dairy products
PA: Michigan Milk Producers Association
41310 Bridge St
Novi MI 48375
248 474-6672

(G-3540)
MONSANTO COMPANY
67760 Us 31 (49042)
PHONE..................................269 483-1300
Countess Price, *Counsel*
Amit Thukral, *Counsel*
Tom D Hartley, *Vice Pres*
Ibrahim E Menschawi, *Vice Pres*
Fred N Perlak, *Vice Pres*
EMP: 25
SALES (corp-wide): 45.3B **Privately Held**
WEB: www.monsanto.com
SIC: 2879 Agricultural chemicals
HQ: Monsanto Company
800 N Lindbergh Blvd
Saint Louis MO 63167
314 694-1000

(G-3541)
OWENS-BROCKWAY GLASS CONT INC
Also Called: Rexam Plastic Containers
950 Industrial Park Dr (49042-9763)
PHONE..................................269 435-2535
Les Hurtline, *Manager*
EMP: 3
SALES (corp-wide): 6.8B **Publicly Held**
SIC: 3221 Glass containers
HQ: Owens-Brockway Glass Container Inc.
1 Michael Owens Way
Perrysburg OH 43551
567 336-8449

(G-3542)
OX ENGINEERED PRODUCTS LLC
700 Centreville St (49042-1273)
PHONE..................................269 435-2425
EMP: 83
SALES (corp-wide): 1.4MM **Privately Held**
SIC: 2493 Wall tile, fiberboard
PA: Ox Engineered Products, Llc
22260 Haggerty Rd Ste 365
Northville MI 48167
248 289-9950

(G-3543)
OX PAPERBOARD MICHIGAN LLC
700 Centreville St (49042-1273)
PHONE..................................800 345-8881
Kevin Hayward, *CEO*
Mike Davis, *General Mgr*
Timothy Michaels, *General Mgr*
Matthew Sullivan, *Vice Pres*
Mark Wallace, *VP Opers*
EMP: 80 EST: 2012
SALES (est): 34.7MM **Privately Held**
SIC: 2631 Coated paperboard

(G-3544)
RETRO ENTERPRISES INC
1045 Parkview St (49042-1278)
PHONE..................................269 435-8583
Ron Wetstone, *President*
EMP: 5
SALES (est): 733.2K **Privately Held**
SIC: 3089 Plastic containers, except foam

(G-3545)
VAUPELL MOLDING & TOOLING INC
485 Florence Rd (49042-1261)
PHONE..................................269 435-8414
EMP: 55 **Privately Held**
SIC: 3089 Injection molding of plastics
HQ: Vaupell Molding & Tooling, Inc.
1144 Nw 53rd St
Seattle WA 98107

Cooks
Schoolcraft County

(G-3546)
GARDEN BAY WINERY LLC (PA)
11858 Hwy Us 2 (49817)
PHONE..................................906 361-0318
Gloria Anderson, *Mng Member*
John Lucas, *Manager*
EMP: 4 EST: 2012
SQ FT: 6,000
SALES: 189K **Privately Held**
SIC: 5182 2084 Wine; wines

Coopersville
Ottawa County

(G-3547)
AGGRESSIVE TOOL & DIE INC
728 Main St (49404-1363)
PHONE..................................616 837-1983
Gregory Wiersma, *President*
Tom Zuidema, *Vice Pres*
Jeff Kubiak, *Project Mgr*
Cody Kalman, *Engineer*
James Smith, *Engineer*
EMP: 45
SQ FT: 12,500
SALES: 4.5MM **Privately Held**
WEB: www.aggressivetooldie.com
SIC: 3544 Special dies, tools, jigs & fixtures

(G-3548)
BAKKER WELDING & MECHANICS LLC (PA)
Also Called: BAKKER METAL FABRICATION
15031 84th Ave (49404-9787)
PHONE..................................616 828-8664
Sid Bakker,
EMP: 6
SALES (est): 627K **Privately Held**
SIC: 7692 Welding repair

(G-3549)
BRONCO CONNECTION INC
305 Main St (49404-1232)
PHONE..................................616 997-2263
Pat Harig, *Principal*
EMP: 4
SALES (est): 321K **Privately Held**
SIC: 3949 Sporting & athletic goods

(G-3550)
BROOKFIELD INC
8041 Leonard St (49404-9794)
PHONE..................................616 997-9663
Les Yoder, *President*
EMP: 6
SQ FT: 10,000
SALES: 770K **Privately Held**
WEB: www.brookfieldcase.com
SIC: 2493 Reconstituted wood products

(G-3551)
CCO HOLDINGS LLC
327 Main St (49404-1232)
PHONE..................................616 384-2060
EMP: 3
SALES (corp-wide): 43.6B **Publicly Held**
SIC: 5064 4841 3663 3651 Electrical appliances, television & radio; cable & other pay television services; radio & TV communications equipment; household audio & video equipment
HQ: Cco Holdings, Llc
400 Atlantic St
Stamford CT 06901
203 905-7801

(G-3552)
CONTINENTAL DAR FACILITIES LLC
999 W Randall St (49404-1311)
PHONE..................................616 837-7641
Steve Cooper, *COO*
Dustin Sarber, *Manager*
▲ EMP: 65 EST: 2008
SALES (est): 34.3MM **Privately Held**
SIC: 2023 Dry, condensed, evaporated dairy products

(G-3553)
CONVEYOR CONCEPTS MICHIGAN LLC
743 Main St (49404-1362)
PHONE..................................616 997-5200
Mary Alice Brown, *Prgrmr*
James Malda,
Doug Stapley,
EMP: 12
SQ FT: 20,000
SALES (est): 3.9MM **Privately Held**
WEB: www.ccmich.com
SIC: 3535 Conveyors & conveying equipment

GEOGRAPHIC SECTION

(G-3554)
COOPERSVILLE OBSERVER INC
1374 W Randall St (49404-9701)
P.O. Box 111 (49404-0111)
PHONE..................................616 997-5049
Kerri Snowdin, *President*
EMP: 4
SALES: 100K **Privately Held**
WEB: www.coopersvilleobserver.com
SIC: 2711 Newspapers, publishing & printing

(G-3555)
DE MEESTER SAW MILL
15519 32nd Ave (49404-9636)
PHONE..................................616 677-3144
Daniel De Meester Jr, *Partner*
Shelley J Braden, *CPA*
EMP: 9 EST: 1955
SQ FT: 6,860
SALES: 650K **Privately Held**
SIC: 2426 Furniture stock & parts, hardwood; frames for upholstered furniture, wood

(G-3556)
DEMEESTER WOOD PRODUCTS INC
15527 32nd Ave (49404-9636)
PHONE..................................616 677-5995
Daniel D Meester, *Owner*
EMP: 12
SALES (est): 1.8MM **Privately Held**
SIC: 2426 2449 2448 2441 Furniture stock & parts, hardwood; frames for upholstered furniture, wood; wood containers; wood pallets & skids; nailed wood boxes & shook

(G-3557)
DIE-VERSE SOLUTIONS LLC
15630 68th Ave (49404-9705)
PHONE..................................616 384-3550
John Sturm, *Mng Member*
John Dejonge,
EMP: 13
SALES (est): 341.3K **Privately Held**
SIC: 3544 3469 7389 7699 Dies & die holders for metal cutting, forming, die casting; metal stampings; metal cutting services; metal reshaping & replating services

(G-3558)
FLEXTRONICS INTL USA INC
323 Skeels St (49404-1326)
PHONE..................................616 837-9711
Hamid Najmolhoda, *General Mgr*
John Cruden, *Mfg Mgr*
Ralph Verburg, *Design Engr*
Tom Versas, *Branch Mgr*
David Phillips, *IT/INT Sup*
EMP: 270
SALES (corp-wide): 26.2B **Privately Held**
WEB: www.saturnee.com
SIC: 3672 3625 8711 3714 Printed circuit boards; control circuit relays, industrial; solenoid switches (industrial controls); switches, electronic applications; electrical or electronic engineering; motor vehicle parts & accessories; current-carrying wiring devices; manufactured hardware (general)
HQ: Flextronics International Usa, Inc.
6201 America Center Dr
San Jose CA 95002

(G-3559)
GEM WOOD PRODUCTS INC
350 Skeels St Ste A (49404-1386)
PHONE..................................616 384-3460
Jason Tuttle, *President*
Steven Tuttle, *Vice Pres*
EMP: 6
SQ FT: 20,000
SALES (est): 68.5K **Privately Held**
SIC: 2426 Carvings, furniture: wood

(G-3560)
HANGERS PLUS LLC
411 64th Ave N Ste B (49404-1070)
PHONE..................................616 997-4264
James G Hansen, *President*
Chris Chan, *Sales Staff*
▲ EMP: 3
SQ FT: 1,000
SALES (est): 433.3K **Privately Held**
SIC: 2499 3089 3315 Garment hangers, wood; clothes hangers, plastic; hangers (garment), wire

(G-3561)
HEATH MANUFACTURING COMPANY (HQ)
Also Called: Heath Ultra Products
140 Mill St Ste A (49404-1269)
PHONE..................................616 997-8181
Jim Campbell, *President*
Jenna Burke, *Treasurer*
Andris Chapin, *Director*
▲ EMP: 53 EST: 1947
SQ FT: 82,500
SALES (est): 12.2MM
SALES (corp-wide): 50.1MM **Privately Held**
WEB: www.heathmfg.com
SIC: 2048 2499 3499 3523 Bird food, prepared; fencing, docks & other outdoor wood structural products; metal household articles; farm machinery & equipment
PA: Chapin Manufacturing, Inc
700 Ellicott St Ste 3
Batavia NY 14020
585 343-3140

(G-3562)
KINNEY TOOL AND DIE INC
Also Called: Ranger Die
1300 W Randall St (49404-9701)
PHONE..................................616 997-0901
Leo Raap, *President*
Joseph Raap, *Vice Pres*
Stephen Raap, *Vice Pres*
EMP: 100 EST: 1955
SQ FT: 105,000
SALES: 17.5MM **Privately Held**
WEB: www.rangerdie.com
SIC: 3544 3469 Special dies & tools; metal stampings

(G-3563)
LAKELAND PALLETS INC
50 64th Ave S (49404-1391)
PHONE..................................616 997-4441
Fax: 616 997-4442
EMP: 3 EST: 2010
SALES (est): 130K **Privately Held**
SIC: 2448 Mfg Wood Pallets/Skids

(G-3564)
MARK-PACK INC (PA)
Also Called: Accord Paper and Packaging
776 Main St (49404-1363)
P.O. Box 305 (49404-0305)
PHONE..................................616 837-5400
David Nielsen, *CEO*
Michael Marine, *President*
David Martel, *Vice Pres*
Donnis Pastor, *Purch Mgr*
Denise Bragg, *Accounts Mgr*
EMP: 25
SQ FT: 31,000
SALES (est): 6.2MM **Privately Held**
WEB: www.markpackinc.com
SIC: 3953 5084 5113 Marking devices; processing & packaging equipment; industrial & personal service paper

(G-3565)
MIDWEST MACHINING INC
Also Called: Self Lube
526 Omalley Dr (49404-1372)
PHONE..................................616 837-0165
Phillip Allor, *President*
Greg Kirchhoff, *Sales Mgr*
Jennifer Anderson, *Office Mgr*
EMP: 25
SQ FT: 26,000
SALES (est): 4.4MM **Privately Held**
WEB: www.selflube.com
SIC: 3544 Special dies & tools

(G-3566)
NIEBOERS PIT STOP
288 Main St (49404-1233)
PHONE..................................616 997-2026
Gregg Nieboer, *Partner*
EMP: 4
SALES (est): 226K **Privately Held**
SIC: 2541 Store & office display cases & fixtures

(G-3567)
OMLOR ENTERPRISES INC
Also Called: Accucam/Pmc
135 Mason Dr (49404-1361)
PHONE..................................616 837-6361
Ted Omlor, *President*
EMP: 15
SALES (est): 1.7MM **Privately Held**
SIC: 3451 Screw machine products

(G-3568)
PHILIPS MACHINING COMPANY
80 Mason Dr (49404-1354)
PHONE..................................616 997-7777
James Pleune, *President*
Randy Mosher, *General Mgr*
Tanner Hilbrand, *Draft/Design*
EMP: 10
SQ FT: 7,000
SALES (est): 1.7MM **Privately Held**
SIC: 3545 3315 3544 Machine tool accessories; steel wire & related products; special dies, tools, jigs & fixtures

(G-3569)
REEVES PLASTICS LLC
507 Omalley Dr (49404-1373)
PHONE..................................616 997-0777
David A Reeves, *President*
Sharon L Reeves, *Corp Secy*
Mark Lempke, *Vice Pres*
Kimberlee Lempke, *Office Mgr*
EMP: 25
SQ FT: 20,000
SALES (est): 5.2MM **Privately Held**
WEB: www.plastic-injection-molder.com
SIC: 3089 3544 Molding primary plastic; special dies, tools, jigs & fixtures

(G-3570)
STRAITOPLANE INC
7193 Arthur St (49404-9757)
PHONE..................................616 997-2211
Richard Fink, *President*
Steven Fink, *Vice Pres*
Theresa Fink, *Admin Sec*
EMP: 6
SALES: 400K **Privately Held**
SIC: 3553 Planers, woodworking machines

(G-3571)
SURFACE BLASTING SYSTEMS LLC
90 Mason Dr (49404-1354)
PHONE..................................616 384-3351
Mike Kraft, *Bookkeeper*
David Gufendach, *Mng Member*
EMP: 8
SALES: 800K **Privately Held**
WEB: www.surface-blasting.com
SIC: 3559 Automotive related machinery

Copemish
Manistee County

(G-3572)
JOHN BARNES
Also Called: Barnes and Sons Logging
11783 W 8 Rd (49625-9634)
PHONE..................................231 885-1561
EMP: 3 EST: 2012
SALES (est): 130K **Privately Held**
SIC: 2411 Logging

(G-3573)
M-R PRODUCTS INC (PA)
Also Called: Mr Chain
16612 Russo Dr (49625-8503)
P.O. Box 128 (49625-0128)
PHONE..................................231 378-2251
Mary Mulvoy, *President*
Ryan Schultz, *Controller*
EMP: 5 EST: 1960
SQ FT: 2,220
SALES (est): 4.8MM **Privately Held**
WEB: www.plasticchain.com
SIC: 3089 Injection molded finished plastic products

Coral
Montcalm County

(G-3574)
JNS SAWMILL
4991 N Satterlee Rd (49322-9744)
PHONE..................................989 352-5430
John Hershberger, *Principal*
EMP: 3 EST: 2014
SALES (est): 233.4K **Privately Held**
SIC: 2411 7389 Saw logs;

Cornell
Delta County

(G-3575)
MARVIN NELSON FOREST PRODUCTS
9868 County 426 E Rd (49818-9348)
PHONE..................................906 384-6700
Marvin Nelson, *President*
Donna Nelson, *Vice Pres*
Brian Nelson, *Treasurer*
David Nelson, *Admin Sec*
EMP: 17
SALES: 1.2MM **Privately Held**
SIC: 2411 4212 Logging camps & contractors; timber trucking, local

(G-3576)
USHER LOGGING LLC
14443 Sa Rd 426 Sa (49818-9442)
PHONE..................................906 238-4261
Denise Usher,
Terry W Usher,
EMP: 4
SALES: 444K **Privately Held**
SIC: 2411 Logging camps & contractors

Corunna
Shiawassee County

(G-3577)
ADVANCED AIR TECHNOLOGIES INC
300 Sleeseman Dr (48817-1078)
PHONE..................................989 743-5544
Jerry A Dedic, *President*
Stefanie Childers, *Accounting Mgr*
▲ EMP: 8
SQ FT: 9,500
SALES (est): 1.6MM **Privately Held**
SIC: 3564 Air purification equipment

(G-3578)
BOURNE INDUSTRIES INC
491 S Comstock St (48817-1799)
PHONE..................................989 743-3461
Jeffrey Walters, *President*
Kim Rathburn, *Finance Mgr*
EMP: 22 EST: 1977
SQ FT: 57,000
SALES (est): 3.9MM **Privately Held**
WEB: www.bourneindustries.com
SIC: 2521 2531 2493 2541 Wood office furniture; school furniture; particleboard, plastic laminated; store & office display cases & fixtures; display fixtures, wood; cabinets, lockers & shelving

(G-3579)
CITY ANIMATION CO
Also Called: Neway Manufacturing
1013 N Shiawassee St (48817-1151)
P.O. Box 188 (48817-0188)
PHONE..................................989 743-3458
James D Schultz, *Branch Mgr*
EMP: 10
SALES (corp-wide): 11.2MM **Privately Held**
WEB: www.cityanimation.com
SIC: 5099 3993 7359 7812 Video & audio equipment; signs & advertising specialties; audio-visual equipment & supply rental; video tape production; machine tools, metal cutting type

Corunna - Shiawassee County (G-3580) — GEOGRAPHIC SECTION

PA: City Animation Co.
57 Park Dr
Troy MI 48083
248 589-0600

(G-3580)
CORUNNA MILLS FEED LLC
417 S Shiawassee St (48817-1643)
PHONE.................989 743-3110
Chris Demerly, *Mng Member*
Dick Demerly,
Jamie Demerly,
EMP: 7
SQ FT: 20,000
SALES: 490K **Privately Held**
SIC: 5999 2048 5261 5153 Feed & farm supply; feed premixes; fertilizer; grains

(G-3581)
MACHINE TOOL & GEAR INC (DH)
Also Called: Mtg
1021 N Shiawassee St (48817-1151)
PHONE.................989 743-3936
David Segal, *Ch of Bd*
EMP: 78
SQ FT: 300,000
SALES: 150K
SALES (corp-wide): 118.8MM **Privately Held**
WEB: www.machinetoolgear.com
SIC: 3714 5051 3089 Motor vehicle parts & accessories; iron or steel flat products; automotive parts, plastic
HQ: Newcor, Inc.
1021 N Shiawassee St
Corunna MI 48817
248 537-0014

(G-3582)
MONOGRAM ETC
231 N Shiawassee St (48817-1457)
PHONE.................989 743-5999
Jeffery Bodary, *Owner*
Patricia Bodary, *Co-Owner*
EMP: 4
SALES (est): 200K **Privately Held**
SIC: 2395 Embroidery products, except schiffli machine; embroidery & art needlework

(G-3583)
NEWAY MANUFACTURING INC
1013 N Shiawassee St (48817-1151)
P.O. Box 188 (48817-0188)
PHONE.................989 743-3458
James D Schultz, *President*
Mary Eickholt, *Vice Pres*
▼ EMP: 5 EST: 1973
SALES: 845.6K **Privately Held**
SIC: 3541 Machine tools, metal cutting type

(G-3584)
NEWCOR INC (HQ)
Also Called: Bay City Division
1021 N Shiawassee St (48817-1151)
PHONE.................248 537-0014
David Segal, *CEO*
Scott Wright, *Admin Sec*
EMP: 150 EST: 1969
SQ FT: 210,000
SALES (est): 116.6MM
SALES (corp-wide): 118.8MM **Privately Held**
WEB: www.newcor.com
SIC: 3714 Motor vehicle transmissions, drive assemblies & parts; gears, motor vehicle; drive shafts, motor vehicle; transmission housings or parts, motor vehicle
PA: Cie Automotive, Sa
Alameda Mazarredo, 69 - Piso 8o
Bilbao 48009
944 255-108

(G-3585)
STRAUSS TOOL INC
410 S Shiawassee St (48817-1644)
PHONE.................989 743-4741
Joseph Strauss, *President*
Joseph M Strauss Jr, *Vice Pres*
EMP: 4
SQ FT: 6,000
SALES: 600K **Privately Held**
SIC: 3599 Machine shop, jobbing & repair

(G-3586)
WINANS INC
Also Called: Winans Electric Motor Repair
494 S Comstock St (48817-1726)
P.O. Box 233 (48817-0233)
PHONE.................810 744-1240
Barry Catrell, *President*
▼ EMP: 7 EST: 1980
SQ FT: 11,800
SALES: 4MM **Privately Held**
WEB: www.electricmotorwarehouse.com
SIC: 7694 5063 Electric motor repair; motors, electric

Cottrellville
St. Clair County

(G-3587)
HOWELL ENGINE DEVELOPMENTS INC
6201 Industrial Way (48039-1326)
PHONE.................810 765-5100
Matthew Howell, *President*
Jennifer Siegel Tallman, *Office Mgr*
EMP: 14
SQ FT: 7,000
SALES (est): 2.2MM **Privately Held**
WEB: www.howell-efi.com
SIC: 3714 7539 Automotive wiring harness sets; fuel system repair, motor vehicle

(G-3588)
INDUSTRIAL MTAL FBRICATORS LLC
Also Called: I M F
2700 Plank Rd (48039-1461)
PHONE.................810 765-8960
Kenneth Teneyck,
EMP: 12
SQ FT: 10,000
SALES (est): 2.4MM **Privately Held**
SIC: 3444 Sheet metalwork

(G-3589)
IROQUOIS INDUSTRIES INC
7177 Marine City Hwy (48039-1008)
PHONE.................586 465-1023
Beth Malek, *Administration*
EMP: 31
SALES (corp-wide): 56.8MM **Privately Held**
SIC: 3465 Automotive stampings
PA: Iroquois Industries, Inc.
24400 Hoover Rd
Warren MI 48089
586 771-5734

(G-3590)
L R OLIVER AND COMPANY INC
Also Called: Oliver Carbide Products
7445 Mayer Rd (48039-2410)
PHONE.................810 765-1000
Rex Oliver, *President*
Steven Simasko, *Principal*
Kris Grumbling, *Treasurer*
▲ EMP: 46
SALES (est): 6.3MM **Privately Held**
WEB: www.olivercorp.com
SIC: 3291 Abrasive products

Covert
Van Buren County

(G-3591)
SWING-LO SUSPENDED SCAFFOLD CO
Also Called: Swing-Lo System
75609 County Road 376 (49043-9794)
P.O. Box 128 (49043-0128)
PHONE.................269 764-8989
George Saleeby, *CEO*
Stephen Leonard, *President*
EMP: 18 EST: 1955
SQ FT: 31,000
SALES (est): 3.3MM **Privately Held**
WEB: www.swing-lo.com
SIC: 3446 Scaffolds, mobile or stationary: metal

(G-3592)
WEST MICH FLCKING ASSEMBLY LLC
78277 County Road 378 (49043-9521)
PHONE.................269 639-1634
Melvin Fox, *President*
Alexander Fergus,
EMP: 55 EST: 1977
SQ FT: 95,000
SALES (est): 6.5MM **Privately Held**
SIC: 3999 3569 Flocking metal products; assembly machines, non-metalworking

Covington
Baraga County

(G-3593)
YOUNGGREN FARM & FOREST INC
34392 Younggren Rd (49919-9021)
PHONE.................906 355-2272
Francis Younggren, *President*
EMP: 8
SQ FT: 2,000
SALES (est): 570K **Privately Held**
SIC: 2411 Logging camps & contractors

(G-3594)
YOUNGGREN TIMBER COMPANY
34392 Younggren Rd (49919-9021)
PHONE.................906 355-2272
Greg Younggren, *Partner*
Daniel Younggren, *Partner*
Paul Younggren, *Partner*
EMP: 7
SALES: 950K **Privately Held**
SIC: 2411 Logging

Croswell
Sanilac County

(G-3595)
BEADEN SCREEN INC
305 Melvin St (48422-1027)
P.O. Box 199 (48422-0199)
PHONE.................810 679-3119
William O'Connor, *President*
Steven O'Connor, *Vice Pres*
Steve Oconnor, *Vice Pres*
Matthew Spana,
EMP: 30 EST: 1961
SQ FT: 11,100
SALES (est): 5.6MM **Privately Held**
WEB: www.beadenscreen.com
SIC: 3496 3494 Cylinder wire cloth; valves & pipe fittings

(G-3596)
FLEMINGS MEAT PROCESSING
Also Called: Fleming's Processing
4200 Old M 51 (48422-9465)
PHONE.................810 679-3668
Eason Fleming, *Owner*
Joulian Miok, *Principal*
EMP: 3
SALES (est): 110.5K **Privately Held**
SIC: 7299 2011 5421 0751 Butcher service, processing only; meat packing plants; meat markets, including freezer provisioners; slaughtering: custom livestock services

(G-3597)
HAZLOC INDUSTRIES LLC
Paramount Industries
304 N Howard Ave (48422-1011)
PHONE.................810 679-2551
Glenn Garbowicz, *President*
Steve Matthews, *Engineer*
Lucas Robbins, *Engineer*
EMP: 40 **Privately Held**
SIC: 3646 Commercial indusl & institutional electric lighting fixtures
HQ: Hazloc Industries Llc
304 N Howard Ave
Croswell MI 48422
810 679-2551

(G-3598)
JAY & KAY MANUFACTURING LLC (PA)
72 Louise St (48422-1043)
PHONE.................810 679-2333
James Essad, *Vice Pres*
Mark Boone,
Joseph Heider,
▼ EMP: 38
SQ FT: 58,000
SALES (est): 7.4MM **Privately Held**
WEB: www.jaykaymfg.com
SIC: 3429 3714 Marine hardware; motor vehicle parts & accessories

(G-3599)
JAY & KAY MANUFACTURING LLC
141 E Sanborn Ave (48422-1404)
PHONE.................810 679-3079
EMP: 5
SALES (est): 308.5K
SALES (corp-wide): 10.2MM **Privately Held**
SIC: 3429 3714 Mfg Hardware Mfg Motor Vehicle Parts/Accessories
PA: Jay & Kay Manufacturing, Llc
72 Louise St
Croswell MI 48422
810 679-2333

(G-3600)
MATERIAL CONTROL INC (PA)
Also Called: Conveyor Components Co Div
130 Seltzer Rd (48422-9180)
PHONE.................630 892-4274
Clinton F Stimpson III, *President*
Keith Clayton, *Admin Sec*
▼ EMP: 3
SALES (est): 82.6MM **Privately Held**
WEB: www.cotterman.com
SIC: 3535 Bucket type conveyor systems

(G-3601)
MICHIGAN SUGAR COMPANY
159 S Howard Ave (48422-1398)
PHONE.................810 679-2241
Wanita Junga, *General Mgr*
Gregory Soule, *Branch Mgr*
EMP: 80
SALES (corp-wide): 600MM **Privately Held**
SIC: 2063 Beet sugar from beet sugar refinery
PA: Michigan Sugar Company
122 Uptown Dr Unit 300
Bay City MI 48708
989 686-0161

(G-3602)
PEDMIC CONVERTING INC
7241 Wildcat Rd (48422-9012)
P.O. Box 226 (48422-0226)
PHONE.................810 679-9600
Dennis Pedler, *Ch of Bd*
William I Mc Comb, *President*
EMP: 20
SQ FT: 30,000
SALES (est): 2.4MM **Privately Held**
WEB: www.pedmic.com
SIC: 3086 Packaging & shipping materials, foamed plastic

(G-3603)
SUPERIOR PRODUCTS MFG INC
124 Louise St (48422-1050)
PHONE.................810 679-4479
Jeffrey Stringer, *President*
Donna Stringer, *Corp Secy*
EMP: 5
SALES (est): 810.7K **Privately Held**
SIC: 3544 3599 Special dies, tools, jigs & fixtures; machine shop, jobbing & repair

(G-3604)
THEUT CONCRETE PRODUCTS INC
138 E Harrington Rd (48422-1121)
PHONE.................810 679-3376
EMP: 13 EST: 1920
SQ FT: 10,000
SALES (est): 126.8K **Privately Held**
SIC: 3271 5032 3273 Mfg Concrete Block/Brick Whol Brick/Stone Matrls Mfg Ready-Mixed Concrete

GEOGRAPHIC SECTION

(G-3605)
VAN S FABRICATIONS INC
Also Called: Van's Fabrications
4446 Peck Rd (48422-9620)
PHONE..................810 679-2115
Gerrit Van Der Maas, *President*
EMP: 5
SQ FT: 3,000
SALES (est): 598.6K **Privately Held**
SIC: 3599 7389 3469 5984 Machine shop, jobbing & repair; metal slitting & shearing; stamping metal for the trade; propane gas, bottled; welding on site

(G-3606)
WINDMILL HILL FARM LLC
1686 Sheridan Line Rd (48422-8763)
PHONE..................810 378-5972
Don Ragan,
EMP: 3
SALES (est): 333.6K **Privately Held**
WEB: www.windmillhillfarm.com
SIC: 2099 5149 7389 Honey, strained & bottled; honey;

Crystal
Montcalm County

(G-3607)
ACCESSORIES & SPECIALTIES INC
121 E Park St (48818)
P.O. Box 91 (48818-0091)
PHONE..................989 235-3331
Fax: 989 235-3859
EMP: 6
SALES (est): 310K **Privately Held**
SIC: 3949 Mfg Sporting/Athletic Goods

Crystal Falls
Iron County

(G-3608)
CRYSTAL FALLS SPRINGS INC
Also Called: Cool Artesian Water
346 Rock Crusher Rd (49920-9041)
PHONE..................906 875-3191
Debra Rose, *President*
Brian Rose, *Vice Pres*
Dennis Rose, *VP Sales*
EMP: 5
SQ FT: 10,000
SALES: 500K **Privately Held**
SIC: 2086 Water, pasteurized: packaged in cans, bottles, etc.

(G-3609)
DJW ENTERPRISES INC
324 N Light Lake Rd (49920-9607)
PHONE..................262 251-9500
Deborah J Bristoll, *President*
EMP: 65
SQ FT: 28,000
SALES (est): 14.2MM
SALES (corp-wide): 1.2B **Privately Held**
WEB: www.engineered-plastics.com
SIC: 3089 Injection molded finished plastic products
HQ: Maclean-Fogg Component Solutions, L.L.C
1000 Allanson Rd
Mundelein IL 60060
248 853-2525

(G-3610)
J B LOG HOMES INC
207 Fisher Rd (49920-9797)
PHONE..................906 875-6581
John Bruce, *President*
Bonnie Bruce, *COO*
EMP: 3
SALES (est): 192.8K **Privately Held**
SIC: 2452 Log cabins, prefabricated, wood

(G-3611)
MAGIGLIDE INC
Also Called: Land Quilts
257 Industrial Park Rd (49920-9643)
PHONE..................906 822-7321
Dennis Box, *President*
Leann Davis, *Manager*
EMP: 15
SALES (est): 2.2MM **Privately Held**
WEB: www.magiglide.com
SIC: 2431 Doors, wood

(G-3612)
PRIME ASSEMBLIES INC
2525 Us Highway 2 (49920-9109)
P.O. Box 445, Iron Mountain (49801-0445)
PHONE..................906 875-6420
Cynthia Rahoi, *President*
Joseph Rahoi, *Vice Pres*
EMP: 12
SALES: 300K **Privately Held**
SIC: 3643 Current-carrying wiring devices

(G-3613)
R J MANUFACTURING INCORPORATED
110 Forest Gtwy (49920-8856)
P.O. Box 886, Iron Mountain (49801-0886)
PHONE..................906 779-9151
James W Flood, *President*
Joan Flood, *Corp Secy*
EMP: 9
SALES (est): 1.8MM **Privately Held**
SIC: 3567 3991 Paint baking & drying ovens; brooms & brushes

(G-3614)
SUPERIOR SUPPLIERS NETWORK LLC
1307 Harrison Ave (49920-1022)
PHONE..................906 284-1561
Jim Bottomly, *President*
EMP: 15
SALES: 950K **Privately Held**
SIC: 3441 Fabricated structural metal

(G-3615)
WILLIAMS REDDI MIX INC
1345 Us Highway 2 (49920-1048)
PHONE..................906 875-6952
Dennis Williams, *President*
EMP: 8 **EST:** 1973
SQ FT: 2,800
SALES: 750K **Privately Held**
SIC: 3273 Ready-mixed concrete

(G-3616)
WILLIAMS REDI MIX
170 Williams Rd (49920-9412)
PHONE..................906 875-6839
Dennis Williams, *Principal*
EMP: 6 **EST:** 2009
SALES (est): 778.9K **Privately Held**
SIC: 3273 Ready-mixed concrete

Curran
Alcona County

(G-3617)
WELCH LAND & TIMBER INC
2708 N Reeves Rd (48728-9775)
PHONE..................989 848-5197
EMP: 6
SALES (est): 480K **Privately Held**
SIC: 2411 Logging

(G-3618)
YODER FOREST PRODUCTS L L C
7310 W M 72 (48728-9765)
PHONE..................989 848-2437
William Leroy Yoder, *Principal*
Corey Yoder,
Duane Yoder,
EMP: 3
SALES (est): 443.7K **Privately Held**
SIC: 2411 Wooden logs

Curtis
Mackinac County

(G-3619)
DUBERVILLE LOGGING
W16683 Sandtown Rd (49820-9606)
PHONE..................906 586-6267
Jake Duberville, *Principal*
EMP: 3
SALES (est): 271.6K **Privately Held**
SIC: 2411 Logging camps & contractors

Dafter
Chippewa County

(G-3620)
REID CONTRACTORS INC
11969 S Mackinac Trl (49724-9543)
PHONE..................906 632-2936
Art Reid, *President*
EMP: 3
SALES: 200K **Privately Held**
SIC: 1795 1389 Demolition, buildings & other structures; excavating slush pits & cellars

Daggett
Menominee County

(G-3621)
JOHN SIVULA LOGGING & CNSTR
N13300 Sivula Lane T 1 (49821-9342)
PHONE..................906 639-2714
Matt Sivula, *Principal*
EMP: 3 **EST:** 2001
SALES (est): 377.9K **Privately Held**
SIC: 2411 Logging camps & contractors

(G-3622)
MOTTO CEDAR PRODUCTS INC
Us Hwy 41 & County Rd 360 (49821)
P.O. Box 56 (49821-0056)
PHONE..................906 753-4892
Gary Motto, *President*
Garland Motto, *Vice Pres*
Jody Motto, *Vice Pres*
Larry Motto, *Treasurer*
EMP: 4 **EST:** 1958
SALES (est): 651.2K **Privately Held**
WEB: www.mottocedar.com
SIC: 2411 2426 5211 Posts, wood: hewn, round or split; furniture stock & parts, hardwood; lumber & other building materials

(G-3623)
US PRINTERS
W4763 Okwood Rd 30 (49821-9543)
PHONE..................906 639-3100
EMP: 3
SALES (est): 107.2K **Privately Held**
SIC: 2752 Commercial printing, offset

Davisburg
Oakland County

(G-3624)
ALPHA DIRECTIONAL BORING
11910 Scott Rd (48350-3018)
PHONE..................586 405-0171
Kevin Pattison, *Principal*
EMP: 4
SALES (est): 512.3K **Privately Held**
SIC: 1381 Directional drilling oil & gas wells

(G-3625)
AUTOMTION MDLAR COMPONENTS INC (PA)
Also Called: AMC
10301 Enterprise Dr (48350-1312)
PHONE..................248 922-4740
Richard A Shore Sr, *CEO*
D Ick Shore, *President*
Jeff Barrett, *Plant Mgr*
Gary Ballard, *Project Mgr*
Thomas Baumaster, *Project Mgr*
▲ **EMP:** 83
SQ FT: 63,000
SALES (est): 27.2MM **Privately Held**
WEB: www.amcautomation.com
SIC: 3535 Conveyors & conveying equipment

(G-3626)
AWD ASSOCIATES INC
10560 Enterprise Dr Ste A (48350-1346)
P.O. Box 99, Clarkston (48347-0099)
PHONE..................248 922-9898
Larry Littleson, *President*
Sharon Littleson, *Vice Pres*
EMP: 12
SQ FT: 8,000
SALES: 700K **Privately Held**
WEB: www.awddrills.com
SIC: 3599 Machine shop, jobbing & repair

(G-3627)
BCS CREATIVE LLC
10012 Old Farm Trl (48350-2235)
PHONE..................248 917-1660
Candice Layton,
EMP: 4
SALES (est): 240.5K **Privately Held**
SIC: 3993 7389 Signs, not made in custom sign painting shops;

(G-3628)
C & D TOOL & DIE COMPANY INC
12395 Shaffer Rd (48350-3714)
PHONE..................248 922-5937
Mike Bender, *President*
Pat Endres, *Vice Pres*
EMP: 25 **EST:** 1968
SQ FT: 15,000
SALES: 6.3MM **Privately Held**
SIC: 3544 Special dies, tools, jigs & fixtures

(G-3629)
CARBIDE FORM MASTER INC
10565 Dixie Hwy (48350-1309)
PHONE..................248 625-9373
James L Stoglin, *President*
Richard Coburn, *Vice Pres*
Penny A Stoglin, *Admin Sec*
EMP: 8
SQ FT: 6,280
SALES: 721.7K **Privately Held**
SIC: 3545 Cutting tools for machine tools

(G-3630)
COLOMBO SALES & ENGRG INC
Also Called: Colombo Beverage Chase Systems
10421 Enterprise Dr Ste A (48350-1345)
PHONE..................248 547-2820
Harry Colombo, *President*
EMP: 10 **EST:** 1970
SQ FT: 9,500
SALES: 2MM **Privately Held**
WEB: www.colombpts.com
SIC: 3535 7699 Pneumatic tube conveyor systems; miscellaneous building item repair services

(G-3631)
EDW C LEVY CO
16255 Tindall Rd (48350-1035)
PHONE..................248 634-0879
Rick Will, *Manager*
EMP: 5
SALES (corp-wide): 368.1MM **Privately Held**
WEB: www.edwclevy.com
SIC: 2951 Asphalt & asphaltic paving mixtures (not from refineries)
PA: Edw. C. Levy Co.
9300 Dix
Dearborn MI 48120
313 429-2200

(G-3632)
FABRICATION SPECIALTIES INC
9600 Melissa Ln (48350-1200)
PHONE..................313 891-7181
Denise Mc Clain, *President*
Maryanne Mazzenga, *Admin Sec*
EMP: 5
SALES: 750K **Privately Held**
WEB: www.fabricationspecialties.net
SIC: 3444 Sheet metalwork

(G-3633)
FALCON TRUCKING COMPANY
Also Called: Holly Sand & Gravel
16240 Tindall Rd (48350-1034)
PHONE..................248 634-9471

Davisburg - Oakland County (G-3634)

Scott Bandkau, *Manager*
EMP: 12
SALES (corp-wide): 17.1MM **Privately Held**
WEB: www.levyco.net
SIC: 1442 5032 Sand mining; gravel mining; paving materials
PA: Falcon Trucking Company
9300 Dix
Dearborn MI 48120
313 843-7200

(G-3634)
GENERAL INSPECTION LLC
10585 Enterprise Dr (48350-1338)
P.O. Box 189002, Utica (48318-9002)
PHONE 248 625-0529
Lisa Carpenter, *Prdtn Mgr*
Laura Poletti, *Mktg Coord*
Kyle Harmer, *Manager*
Kelly Peter, *Manager*
Mike Nygaard,
EMP: 12
SALES: 3.6MM **Privately Held**
WEB: www.geninsp.com
SIC: 3829 Measuring & controlling devices

(G-3635)
GLOBAL SUPPLY INTEGRATOR LLC
10145 Creekwood Trl (48350-2059)
PHONE 586 484-0734
Randy Leach,
EMP: 6
SQ FT: 4,000
SALES: 3.2MM **Privately Held**
WEB: www.globalgsi.com
SIC: 3089 8711 7371 Injection molded finished plastic products; engineering services; computer software development

(G-3636)
J W HARRIS CO INC
6774 Country Lane Dr (48350-2936)
PHONE 248 634-0737
Bob Henson, *Principal*
EMP: 4
SALES (corp-wide): 3B **Publicly Held**
SIC: 3599 Machine shop, jobbing & repair
HQ: J. W. Harris Co., Inc.
4501 Quality Pl
Mason OH 45040
513 754-2000

(G-3637)
PITNEY BOWES INC
9915 Boulder Ct (48350-2053)
PHONE 248 625-1666
Bryan Bonnici, *Branch Mgr*
EMP: 61
SALES (corp-wide): 3.5B **Publicly Held**
SIC: 3579 Postage meters
PA: Pitney Bowes Inc.
3001 Summer St Ste 3
Stamford CT 06905
203 356-5000

(G-3638)
PRECISION RACE SERVICES INC
16749 Dixie Hwy Ste 9 (48350-1051)
PHONE 248 634-4010
James P Kelly, *President*
David L Decker, *Vice Pres*
EMP: 9
SQ FT: 5,000
SALES (est): 1.2MM **Privately Held**
WEB: www.p-r-s.com
SIC: 7539 3714 Electrical services; automotive wiring harness sets

(G-3639)
QUALITY FIRST SYSTEMS INC
10301 Enterprise Dr (48350-1312)
PHONE 248 922-4780
John Welch, *Vice Pres*
John N Welch, *Vice Pres*
Richard Shore Jr, *CFO*
Jere Hill, *Manager*
Dave Onions, *Manager*
◆ **EMP:** 18
SQ FT: 62,000
SALES (est): 3.8MM **Privately Held**
SIC: 3829 Fatigue testing machines, industrial: mechanical

Davison
Genesee County

(G-3640)
BRISTOL MANUFACTURING INC
4416 N State Rd (48423-8538)
PHONE 810 658-9510
Victor Moody, *President*
Raymond Oliver, *Vice Pres*
EMP: 23
SQ FT: 6,000
SALES (est): 4.8MM **Privately Held**
WEB: www.bristolmanufacturing.com
SIC: 7353 3537 Cranes & aerial lift equipment, rental or leasing; forklift trucks

(G-3641)
BRISTOL STEEL & CONVEYOR CORP
4416 N State Rd (48423-8538)
PHONE 810 658-9510
Raymond D Oliver, *President*
Michelle June, *Purch Agent*
Terry J Oliver, *Admin Sec*
EMP: 50
SQ FT: 2,800
SALES (est): 16MM **Privately Held**
SIC: 3441 3449 1791 3535 Building components, structural steel; miscellaneous metalwork; iron work, structural; conveyors & conveying equipment; sheet metalwork

(G-3642)
COLES MACHINE SERVICE INC
201 W Rising St (48423-1537)
PHONE 810 658-5373
Kenneth Cole, *President*
Cora Cole, *Corp Secy*
Keith Cole, *Vice Pres*
Kyle Cole, *Manager*
EMP: 20 **EST:** 1967
SQ FT: 14,000
SALES (est): 4.3MM **Privately Held**
WEB: www.colesmachine.com
SIC: 3544 3545 3599 Special dies & tools; machine tool accessories; custom machinery

(G-3643)
CONQUEST SCENTS
8399 E Bristol Rd (48423-8767)
PHONE 810 653-2759
Karen Roberts, *Principal*
EMP: 22
SALES (est): 4.4MM **Privately Held**
SIC: 2844 Toilet preparations

(G-3644)
CORNER CONE
5515 N Irish Rd (48423-8949)
PHONE 810 412-4433
Leslee Cone, *Principal*
EMP: 5 **EST:** 2010
SALES (est): 353K **Privately Held**
SIC: 2024 Ice cream, bulk

(G-3645)
D & W AWNING AND WINDOW CO
8068 E Court St (48423-2503)
PHONE 810 742-0340
David Wood, *President*
Mark Wood, *Vice Pres*
EMP: 50 **EST:** 1959
SQ FT: 70,000
SALES (est): 10.9MM **Privately Held**
SIC: 3089 3444 3354 Window frames & sash, plastic; awnings & canopies; aluminum extruded products

(G-3646)
DAVISON TOOL SERVICE INC
Also Called: D T S
236 Mill St (48423-1442)
P.O. Box 160 (48423-0160)
PHONE 810 653-6920
John Frazier, *President*
EMP: 3 **EST:** 1967
SQ FT: 1,050
SALES: 275K **Privately Held**
SIC: 7699 3542 Tool repair services; riveting machines

(G-3647)
FERGUSON BLOCK CO INC
5430 N State Rd (48423-8596)
PHONE 810 653-2812
Lillian Diehl, *President*
Robert Ferguson, *Admin Sec*
EMP: 14 **EST:** 1927
SQ FT: 1,600
SALES (est): 4MM **Privately Held**
SIC: 3271 3273 5211 Blocks, concrete or cinder: standard; ready-mixed concrete; concrete & cinder block

(G-3648)
FERNCO INC (PA)
Also Called: Fernco Joint Sealer Company
300 S Dayton St (48423-1564)
PHONE 810 503-9000
Chris Cooper, *CEO*
Mark Cooper, *President*
Darrell Cooper, *Chairman*
Glenn P Ginther, *Corp Secy*
Steve Moore, *Production*
◆ **EMP:** 140
SQ FT: 75,000
SALES (est): 37.9MM **Privately Held**
WEB: www.fernco.com
SIC: 3432 3498 Plastic plumbing fixture fittings, assembly; fabricated pipe & fittings

(G-3649)
FILTRATION MACHINE
10049 N Hunt Ct (48423-3511)
PHONE 810 845-0536
Michael Ovadek, *Principal*
EMP: 3
SALES (est): 146.9K **Privately Held**
SIC: 3724 Aircraft engines & engine parts

(G-3650)
GENOVA PRODUCTS INC (PA)
Also Called: Delve Communications
7034 E Court St (48423-2504)
P.O. Box 309 (48423-0309)
PHONE 810 744-4500
Robert M Williams, *Ch of Bd*
Michael S Deboer, *President*
Jeanette M Kollias, *Vice Pres*
Don Dinkgrave, *VP Opers*
Todd Ambroz, *Plant Supt*
◆ **EMP:** 60 **EST:** 1962
SALES (est): 206.7MM **Privately Held**
WEB: www.genovaproducts.com
SIC: 3089 2891 2911 3494 Gutters (glass fiber reinforced), fiberglass or plastic; downspouts, plastic; fittings for pipe, plastic; glue; solvents; plumbing & heating valves; plastics pipe; asphalt felts & coatings

(G-3651)
GENOVA-MINNESOTA INC
7034 E Court St (48423-2504)
PHONE 810 744-4500
Robert M Williams, *President*
▼ **EMP:** 100
SALES (est): 17.7MM
SALES (corp-wide): 206.7MM **Privately Held**
WEB: www.genovaproducts.com
SIC: 3089 Plastic containers, except foam
PA: Genova Products, Inc
7034 E Court St
Davison MI 48423
810 744-4500

(G-3652)
GLOBAL PUMP COMPANY LLC (PA)
10162 E Coldwater Rd (48423-8598)
PHONE 810 653-4828
Rod Mersino Jr,
David Tersignio,
◆ **EMP:** 5
SQ FT: 70,000
SALES (est): 2.6MM **Privately Held**
WEB: www.globalpump.com
SIC: 7699 7359 5084 3561 Pumps & pumping equipment repair; equipment rental & leasing; pumps & pumping equipment; industrial pumps & parts

(G-3653)
HENSLEY MFG INC
1097 S State Rd Ste 3 (48423-1934)
PHONE 810 653-3226
Colin Connell, *President*
▲ **EMP:** 14
SQ FT: 1,200
SALES: 2.6MM **Privately Held**
WEB: www.hensleymfg.com
SIC: 3799 3231 Trailer hitches; mirrored glass

(G-3654)
HILTON SCREENERS INC
210 N Main St (48423-1432)
PHONE 810 653-0711
Kent Elliott, *President*
Kim Elliott, *Vice Pres*
EMP: 7
SQ FT: 1,600
SALES: 325K **Privately Held**
SIC: 2261 2759 Screen printing of cotton broadwoven fabrics; screen printing

(G-3655)
KELLOGG COMPANY
2166 Oak Shade Dr (48423-2105)
PHONE 810 653-5625
Robin Kellogg, *Principal*
EMP: 385
SALES (corp-wide): 13.5B **Publicly Held**
SIC: 2043 Cereal breakfast foods
PA: Kellogg Company
1 Kellogg Sq
Battle Creek MI 49017
269 961-2000

(G-3656)
MURPHY WATER WELL BITS (PA)
3340 S State Rd (48423-8755)
PHONE 810 658-1554
Larry Murphy, *Owner*
◆ **EMP:** 6
SALES: 420K **Privately Held**
SIC: 3533 Water well drilling equipment

(G-3657)
PARISEAUS PRINTING INC
218 Mill St (48423-1442)
PHONE 810 653-8420
Alan Pariseau, *President*
Stephen Pariseau, *President*
EMP: 5
SQ FT: 2,500
SALES: 225K **Privately Held**
WEB: www.pariseausprinting.com
SIC: 2752 Commercial printing, offset

(G-3658)
PERFECTION BAKERIES INC
3330 S State Rd (48423-8755)
PHONE 810 653-2378
EMP: 57
SALES (corp-wide): 535.8MM **Privately Held**
SIC: 2051 Bread, all types (white, wheat, rye, etc): fresh or frozen
PA: Perfection Bakeries, Inc.
350 Pearl St
Fort Wayne IN 46802
260 424-8245

(G-3659)
PIONEER CABINETRY INC
301 W Rising St Ste 2 (48423-1571)
P.O. Box 280 (48423-0280)
PHONE 810 658-2075
Lawrence E Fox, *President*
Karen S Dixon, *Treasurer*
EMP: 100
SQ FT: 74,000
SALES: 7MM **Privately Held**
WEB: www.pioneercabinetry.net
SIC: 2434 Vanities, bathroom: wood

(G-3660)
R J MANUFACTURING
4196 S Irish Rd (48423-8737)
PHONE 810 610-0205
Richard Steel, *Owner*
EMP: 5
SQ FT: 3,800
SALES (est): 180K **Privately Held**
SIC: 3999 Manufacturing industries

GEOGRAPHIC SECTION

(G-3661)
RIEGLE PRESS INC (PA)
Also Called: Frankenmuth Printing
1282 N Gale Rd (48423-2552)
P.O. Box 207, Flint (48501-0207)
PHONE..............................810 653-9631
Gerald R Carmody, *President*
Chester Parish, *Vice Pres*
David Young, *Vice Pres*
Candi Franzel, *Sales Staff*
EMP: 35 **EST:** 1962
SQ FT: 40,000
SALES (est): 9MM **Privately Held**
WEB: www.rieglepress.com
SIC: 2752 2759 2789 2761 Commercial printing, offset; business forms, lithographed; commercial printing; bookbinding & related work; manifold business forms

(G-3662)
SPARE TIME STUDIOS
2310 N State Rd (48423-1137)
PHONE..............................810 653-2337
William Wonka, *Owner*
EMP: 3 **EST:** 2006
SALES (est): 125.2K **Privately Held**
WEB: www.sparetimeevents.com
SIC: 3299 Architectural sculptures: gypsum, clay, papier mache, etc.

(G-3663)
SPECIAL T CUSTOM PRODUCTS
1492 Newcastle Dr (48423-8371)
PHONE..............................810 654-9602
John McCrea, *Owner*
Terri McCrea, *Co-Owner*
EMP: 4
SQ FT: 500
SALES (est): 162.2K **Privately Held**
WEB: www.specialtembroidery.com
SIC: 2395 Embroidery & art needlework

(G-3664)
UNIVERSAL SFTWR SOLUTIONS INC
1334 S Irish Rd (48423-8313)
PHONE..............................810 653-5000
Christopher Dobiesz, *President*
Dave Golen, *Vice Pres*
Michelle Dobiesz, *Treasurer*
EMP: 14
SQ FT: 5,000
SALES: 750K **Privately Held**
WEB: www.universalss.com
SIC: 7372 Prepackaged software

(G-3665)
VEIT TOOL & GAGE INC
303 S Dayton St (48423-1501)
PHONE..............................810 658-4949
Duane Veit, *President*
EMP: 15
SQ FT: 7,000
SALES (est): 2.9MM **Privately Held**
SIC: 3544 3599 Special dies & tools; custom machinery

(G-3666)
WILLIAMS GUN SIGHT COMPANY
7389 Lapeer Rd (48423-2509)
P.O. Box 329 (48423-0329)
PHONE..............................800 530-9028
Thomas Wright, *President*
Brian Wright, *COO*
Cary Morin, *Purchasing*
Diane Parker, *CFO*
▼ **EMP:** 67 **EST:** 1951
SQ FT: 78,500
SALES (est): 10.9MM **Privately Held**
WEB: www.williamsgunsight.com
SIC: 5941 3827 Firearms; gun sights, optical

De Tour Village
Chippewa County

(G-3667)
CEDAR MILL LLC
1501 S Caribou Lake Rd (49725)
PHONE..............................906 297-2318
Larry Lucy,
EMP: 3
SALES (est): 256.7K **Privately Held**
SIC: 2421 Sawmills & planing mills, general

(G-3668)
NETTLETON WOOD PRODUCTS INC
34882 S Mcadams Rd (49725-9586)
PHONE..............................906 297-5791
Gerald Nettleton, *President*
Diane Nettleton, *Vice Pres*
EMP: 4
SALES (est): 500.4K **Privately Held**
WEB: www.nettletonwoodproducts.com
SIC: 2421 2426 Lumber: rough, sawed or planed; hardwood dimension & flooring mills

Dearborn
Wayne County

(G-3669)
1ST QUALITY LLC
6700 Wyoming St Ste A (48126-2345)
P.O. Box 519, Garden City (48136-0519)
PHONE..............................313 908-4864
Dennis Lane, *Mng Member*
EMP: 5
SQ FT: 1,500
SALES (est): 235.8K **Privately Held**
SIC: 3714 Transmissions, motor vehicle

(G-3670)
A E G M INC
Also Called: Artistic European Granich MBL
335 S Telegraph Rd (48124-1478)
PHONE..............................313 304-5279
John Borota, *President*
EMP: 7
SALES: 1MM **Privately Held**
SIC: 3281 Furniture, cut stone

(G-3671)
ACTIVE SOLUTIONS GROUP INC
Also Called: Data Center
4 Parklane Blvd Ste 170 (48126-4215)
PHONE..............................313 278-4522
Frank Kadaf, *President*
EMP: 5 **EST:** 2003
SQ FT: 1,900
SALES (est): 376K **Privately Held**
WEB: www.activesolutionsmi.com
SIC: 7378 7373 5045 3357 Computer maintenance & repair; computer integrated systems design; computers, peripherals & software; nonferrous wiredrawing & insulating

(G-3672)
AK STEEL CORPORATION
Also Called: Dearborn Works
14661 Rotunda Dr (48120-1256)
P.O. Box 1699 (48121-1699)
PHONE..............................313 317-8900
Scott Gosselin, *General Mgr*
Mike Lewandowski, *General Mgr*
Denise Johnson, *Vice Pres*
David Pray, *Safety Mgr*
Bashar Alzihery, *Engineer*
EMP: 500 **Publicly Held**
SIC: 3312 Blast furnaces & steel mills
HQ: Ak Steel Corporation
9227 Centre Pointe Dr
West Chester OH 45069
513 425-4200

(G-3673)
AK STEEL CORPORATION
Also Called: Severstal Dearborn
4001 Miller Rd (48120-1461)
P.O. Box 8750, West Chester OH (45071-8750)
PHONE..............................800 532-8857
Bruce Black, *Branch Mgr*
Sid Haymour, *Department Mgr*
EMP: 1600 **Publicly Held**
SIC: 3312 Stainless steel; sheet or strip, steel, cold-rolled: own hot-rolled
HQ: Ak Steel Corporation
9227 Centre Pointe Dr
West Chester OH 45069
513 425-4200

(G-3674)
ALBASARA FUEL LLC
10419 Ford Rd (48126-3334)
PHONE..............................313 443-6581
Al Mursalan, *Principal*
EMP: 3
SALES (est): 172.6K **Privately Held**
SIC: 2869 Fuels

(G-3675)
AMERICO CORPORATION
25120 Trowbridge St (48124-2443)
PHONE..............................313 565-6550
Lillian Wozniak, *President*
E Lillian Wozniak, *President*
John Carey, *Vice Pres*
Stan Lukasik, *Vice Pres*
EMP: 9 **EST:** 1963
SQ FT: 12,000
SALES (est): 1.6MM **Privately Held**
SIC: 3089 3069 Plastic processing; hard rubber & molded rubber products

(G-3676)
ANCHOR CONVEYOR PRODUCTS INC
6830 Kingsley St (48126-1941)
PHONE..............................313 582-5045
William Farmer, *Owner*
▲ **EMP:** 5
SALES (est): 1.2MM **Privately Held**
WEB: www.anchorconveyor.com
SIC: 3535 Conveyors & conveying equipment

(G-3677)
APTIV SERVICES US LLC
Also Called: Delphi
15021 S Commerce Dr # 100 (48120-1238)
PHONE..............................313 322-6845
Frank Magda, *Manager*
EMP: 6
SALES (corp-wide): 16.6B **Privately Held**
SIC: 3714 Motor vehicle parts & accessories
HQ: Aptiv Services Us, Llc
5725 Innovation Dr
Troy MI 48098

(G-3678)
ARAB AMERICAN NEWS INC
5706 Chase Rd (48126-2102)
PHONE..............................313 582-4888
Oussama Siblani, *President*
EMP: 9
SALES: 360K **Privately Held**
WEB: www.arabamericannews.com
SIC: 2711 Newspapers, publishing & printing

(G-3679)
ARCTURIAN LLC
3319 Greenfield Rd 423 (48120-1212)
PHONE..............................313 643-5326
Kevin Starks, *Managing Prtnr*
Anthony Evans, *Managing Prtnr*
Kim Rivers, *Managing Prtnr*
Neal Starks, *Managing Prtnr*
EMP: 4
SALES: 250K **Privately Held**
SIC: 3465 Body parts, automobile: stamped metal

(G-3680)
BALLARD POWER SYSTEMS CORP
15001 N Commerce Dr (48120-1226)
PHONE..............................313 583-5980
John Sheridan, *CEO*
▲ **EMP:** 1100
SQ FT: 38,400
SALES (est): 104.2MM
SALES (corp-wide): 2B **Privately Held**
WEB: www.ballard.com
SIC: 3621 Electric motor & generator parts
PA: Superior Plus Corp
200 Wellington St W Suite 401
Toronto ON M5V 3
416 345-8050

(G-3681)
BENMAR COMMUNICATIONS LLC
1 Parklane Blvd Ste 1105e (48126-4256)
PHONE..............................313 593-0690
Samuel A Dawson,
Lawrence Jackson,
Lawrence B Jackson,
EMP: 15
SQ FT: 6,800
SALES (est): 1.4MM **Privately Held**
SIC: 3555 Printing trades machinery

(G-3682)
BIG 3 PRECISION PRODUCTS INC
Also Called: Industrial Dsign Innvtions Div
10611 Haggerty St (48126-1908)
PHONE..............................313 846-6601
Chuck McHugh, *Branch Mgr*
EMP: 36 **Privately Held**
SIC: 3544 Special dies & tools
HQ: Big 3 Precision Products, Inc.
2923 S Wabash Ave
Centralia IL 62801
618 533-3251

(G-3683)
CAFFINA COFFEE CO
7520 Greenfield Rd (48126-1363)
PHONE..............................313 584-3584
Allen Bakri, *President*
EMP: 5
SQ FT: 1,000
SALES (est): 438.8K **Privately Held**
SIC: 2095 Coffee, ground: mixed with grain or chicory

(G-3684)
CAMMENGA & ASSOCIATES LLC
2011 Bailey St (48124-2404)
PHONE..............................313 914-7160
Christopher Karchon, *Principal*
Michael A Alexander,
EMP: 20
SQ FT: 15,000
SALES: 1.3MM **Privately Held**
WEB: www.cammenga.com
SIC: 3829 5084 Measuring & controlling devices; controlling instruments & accessories

(G-3685)
CAMMENGA COMPANY LLC
2011 Bailey St (48124-2404)
PHONE..............................313 914-7160
Michael Alexander,
EMP: 3
SQ FT: 15,000
SALES (est): 474.3K **Privately Held**
SIC: 3812 Compasses & accessories

(G-3686)
CARHARTT INC (PA)
5750 Mercury Dr (48126-4167)
P.O. Box 600 (48121-0600)
PHONE..............................313 271-8460
Mark Valade, *CEO*
Linda P Hubbard, *President*
Tony Ambroza, *Vice Pres*
Glenda Arnold, *Vice Pres*
Jennifer Piscopink, *Vice Pres*
◆ **EMP:** 450 **EST:** 1889
SQ FT: 56,000
SALES (est): 1.9B **Privately Held**
WEB: www.carhartt.com
SIC: 2326 2325 2329 Overalls & coveralls; dungarees: men's, youths' & boys'; jeans: men's, youths' & boys'; men's & boys' leather, wool & down-filled outerwear; coats (oiled fabric, leatherette, etc.): men's & boys'; hunting coats & vests, men's

(G-3687)
CHANDAS ENGINEERING INC
4800 Curtis St (48126-4125)
P.O. Box 1583 (48121-1583)
PHONE..............................313 582-8666
Philip Pettyjohn, *President*
EMP: 10
SALES (est): 985.5K **Privately Held**
SIC: 3519 8711 Internal combustion engines; aviation &/or aeronautical engineering

Dearborn - Wayne County (G-3688)

(G-3688)
CUMMINS INC
3760 Wyoming St (48120-1419)
PHONE.................313 843-6200
Craig Henrikson, *Manager*
EMP: 30
SALES (corp-wide): 23.7B **Publicly Held**
WEB: www.bridgewaypower.com
SIC: 7538 3519 Diesel engine repair: automotive; internal combustion engines
PA: Cummins Inc.
500 Jackson St
Columbus IN 47201
812 377-5000

(G-3689)
DEARBORN IMAGING GROUP LLC
1946 Monroe St (48124-2917)
PHONE.................313 561-1173
Mark Mendoza,
EMP: 3
SALES: 750K **Privately Held**
SIC: 2759 Commercial printing

(G-3690)
DEARBORN OFFSET PRINTING INC
1946 Monroe St (48124-2917)
PHONE.................313 561-1173
Tim Cote, *President*
Margaret Cote, *Admin Sec*
EMP: 6 **EST:** 1952
SQ FT: 2,500
SALES: 150K **Privately Held**
SIC: 2752 Commercial printing, offset

(G-3691)
DEARBORN SIGNS & AWNINGS
8700 Brandt St (48126-4708)
PHONE.................313 584-8828
Hayffam Boussi, *President*
EMP: 3
SALES (est): 258.8K **Privately Held**
SIC: 3993 Signs & advertising specialties

(G-3692)
DELACO STEEL CORPORATION (PA)
8111 Tireman Ave Ste 1 (48126-1789)
PHONE.................313 491-1200
Gerald F Diez, *President*
Chris Currie, *Vice Pres*
Jim Jaggers, *Plant Mgr*
Joseph Jezioro, *Plant Mgr*
Glenn Hejna, *Facilities Mgr*
EMP: 72
SQ FT: 200,000
SALES: 45.1MM **Privately Held**
SIC: 5051 3465 3312 Steel; automotive stampings; blast furnaces & steel mills

(G-3693)
DIE-MOLD-AUTOMATION COMPONENT
Also Called: N Forcer
14300 Henn St Ste A (48126-4521)
PHONE.................313 581-6510
Jessica Martin, *President*
Paul J Martin, *Vice Pres*
EMP: 5
SQ FT: 19,000
SALES (est): 390K **Privately Held**
WEB: www.n-forcer.com
SIC: 3544 3443 Special dies & tools; fabricated plate work (boiler shop)

(G-3694)
DOUBLE EAGLE DEFENSE LLC (PA)
25205 Trowbridge St (48124-2414)
PHONE.................313 562-5550
EMP: 3
SALES (est): 1.8MM **Privately Held**
SIC: 3599 Supplier Of Production Prototype Metal Components And Assemblies

(G-3695)
DOUBLE EAGLE STEEL COATING CO
3000 Miller Rd (48120-1400)
PHONE.................313 203-9800
Bill Boege, *President*
EMP: 140
SQ FT: 300,000
SALES (est): 19.7MM **Privately Held**
SIC: 3479 Galvanizing of iron, steel or end-formed products

(G-3696)
E C MOORE COMPANY (PA)
Also Called: Challenge Packaging Division
13325 Leonard St (48126-3633)
P.O. Box 353 (48121-0353)
PHONE.................313 581-7878
George G Aho, *President*
Dan Noble, *Opers Mgr*
▲ **EMP:** 78 **EST:** 1894
SQ FT: 5,100
SALES (est): 9.3MM **Privately Held**
WEB: www.ecmoore.com
SIC: 3291 3843 Abrasive products; abrasive points, wheels & disks, dental

(G-3697)
E C MOORE COMPANY
13249 Leonard St (48126-3631)
P.O. Box 353 (48121-0353)
PHONE.................313 581-7878
Dale Williams, *Manager*
EMP: 30
SQ FT: 5,100
SALES (corp-wide): 9.3MM **Privately Held**
WEB: www.ecmoore.com
SIC: 3843 Abrasive points, wheels & disks, dental; cement, dental
PA: E C Moore Company
13325 Leonard St
Dearborn MI 48126
313 581-7878

(G-3698)
EDDIES QUICK STOP INC
5517 Middlesex St (48126-5021)
PHONE.................313 712-1818
Daher Faraj, *Principal*
EMP: 11 **EST:** 2013
SQ FT: 3,000
SALES (est): 782.6K **Privately Held**
SIC: 3715 Truck trailers

(G-3699)
EDENS POLITICAL
360 Devonshire St (48124-1084)
PHONE.................313 277-0700
David Eden, *Owner*
Arlene Eden, *Co-Owner*
EMP: 4
SQ FT: 1,000
SALES (est): 191.4K **Privately Held**
WEB: www.edencompanies.com
SIC: 2759 Screen printing

(G-3700)
EDW C LEVY CO (PA)
Also Called: Ace Asphalt Products Company
9300 Dix (48120-1528)
PHONE.................313 429-2200
Edward C Levy Jr, *President*
Robert Scholz, *Vice Pres*
S E Weiner, *Vice Pres*
Michelle Barnett, *Manager*
Alan Pawlik, *Technology*
▲ **EMP:** 357 **EST:** 1946
SQ FT: 7,500
SALES (est): 368.1MM **Privately Held**
WEB: www.edwclevy.com
SIC: 5032 2951 3295 Aggregate; asphalt & asphaltic paving mixtures (not from refineries); blast furnace slag

(G-3701)
ENERGY DEVELOPMENT ASSOC LLC
15201 Century Dr (48120-1232)
PHONE.................313 354-2644
Kent Harmon, *CEO*
Anil Tulandhar, *CTO*
Neil Tuldhar, *CTO*
EMP: 8
SALES (est): 929.7K **Privately Held**
SIC: 8711 3822 Electrical or electronic engineering; energy cutoff controls, residential or commercial types

(G-3702)
ENVISIONTEC INC
15162 S Commerce Dr (48120-1237)
PHONE.................313 436-4300
Ali El Siblani, *CEO*
Zena Makki, *Opers Staff*
Christian Tauber, *Engineer*
Michael Gasparovich, *Accountant*
Richard Scherer, *Sales Mgr*
EMP: 65
SALES (est): 25.6MM **Privately Held**
SIC: 3577 2821 3544 7699 Plotters, computer; printers, computer; data conversion equipment, media-to-media: computer; plastics materials & resins; forms (molds), for foundry & plastics working machinery; professional instrument repair services

(G-3703)
EPPINGER MFG CO
6340 Schaefer Rd (48126-2285)
PHONE.................313 582-3205
Karen Eppinger, *President*
Jennifer Buftamante, *Admin Sec*
EMP: 18 **EST:** 1906
SQ FT: 9,000
SALES: 1.5MM **Privately Held**
SIC: 3949 Fishing tackle, general

(G-3704)
FALCON TRUCKING COMPANY (PA)
9300 Dix (48120-1528)
PHONE.................313 843-7200
S Evan Weiner, *President*
Robert Flucker, *Treasurer*
EMP: 8 **EST:** 1967
SQ FT: 10,000
SALES (est): 17.1MM **Privately Held**
WEB: www.levyco.net
SIC: 1442 4212 Sand mining; gravel mining; local trucking, without storage

(G-3705)
FEDEX OFFICE & PRINT SVCS INC
23400 Michigan Ave # 145 (48124-1924)
PHONE.................313 359-3124
EMP: 17
SALES (corp-wide): 69.6B **Publicly Held**
WEB: www.kinkos.com
SIC: 7334 3993 2789 2759 Photocopying & duplicating services; signs & advertising specialties; bookbinding & related work; commercial printing; coated & laminated paper
HQ: Fedex Office And Print Services, Inc.
7900 Legacy Dr
Plano TX 75024
800 463-3339

(G-3706)
FEDEX OFFICE & PRINT SVCS INC
15851 Ford Rd (48126-4151)
PHONE.................313 271-8877
EMP: 17
SALES (corp-wide): 69.6B **Publicly Held**
WEB: www.kinkos.com
SIC: 7334 2791 2789 7338 Photocopying & duplicating services; typesetting; bookbinding & related work; secretarial & court reporting
HQ: Fedex Office And Print Services, Inc.
7900 Legacy Dr
Plano TX 75024
800 463-3339

(G-3707)
FIRST RESPONSE MED SUPS LLC
2020 N Lafayette St (48128-1148)
PHONE.................313 731-2554
Mirza Salmaci, *President*
EMP: 10
SALES (est): 500.6K **Privately Held**
SIC: 5661 3842 Shoes, orthopedic; foot appliances, orthopedic

(G-3708)
FORD GLOBAL TREASURY INC
1 American Rd (48126-2701)
PHONE.................313 322-3000
James P Hackett, *President*
EMP: 4

SALES (est): 17K
SALES (corp-wide): 160.3B **Publicly Held**
SIC: 3711 Motor vehicles & car bodies
PA: Ford Motor Company
1 American Rd
Dearborn MI 48126
313 322-3000

(G-3709)
FORD MOTOR COMPANY (PA)
1 American Rd (48126-2701)
P.O. Box 685 (48121-0685)
PHONE.................313 322-3000
William Clay Ford Jr, *Ch of Bd*
James P Hackett, *President*
Rebecca Burtless-Creps, *Counsel*
Ray Day, *Vice Pres*
Bruce Hettle, *Vice Pres*
EMP: 277 **EST:** 1903
SALES: 160.3B **Publicly Held**
WEB: www.ford.com
SIC: 3711 3713 3714 6153 Automobile assembly, including specialty automobiles; truck & bus bodies; motor vehicle parts & accessories; financing of dealers by motor vehicle manufacturers organ.; buying of installment notes; financing: automobiles, furniture, etc., not a deposit bank; automobile loans, including insurance; passenger car leasing

(G-3710)
FORD MOTOR COMPANY
3001 Miller Rd (48120-1496)
PHONE.................313 594-0050
Jim Padilla, *President*
Fnu Brinda, *Engineer*
Jeff Pizzo, *Supervisor*
Tom Morrison, *Prgrmr*
Richard Chapman, *Representative*
EMP: 1297
SQ FT: 2,100,000
SALES (corp-wide): 160.3B **Publicly Held**
WEB: www.ford.com
SIC: 3714 Motor vehicle parts & accessories
PA: Ford Motor Company
1 American Rd
Dearborn MI 48126
313 322-3000

(G-3711)
FORD MOTOR COMPANY
21175 Oakwood Blvd (48124-4079)
P.O. Box 1899 (48121-1899)
PHONE.................313 322-7715
Noori Pandit, *Engineer*
Patrick Witkowski, *Manager*
Jay Moore, *Supervisor*
Chad Jolly, *Technology*
Michele Katynski, *Technology*
EMP: 2600
SALES (corp-wide): 160.3B **Publicly Held**
WEB: www.ford.com
SIC: 3711 3713 Motor vehicles & car bodies; truck & bus bodies
PA: Ford Motor Company
1 American Rd
Dearborn MI 48126
313 322-3000

(G-3712)
FORD MOTOR COMPANY
20100 Rotunda Dr (48124-3997)
PHONE.................313 805-5938
Rinku Patel, *Engineer*
Alexander Mizzi, *Technology*
Aishwarya Vasu, *Software Engr*
Jaafar Abbass, *Technical Staff*
EMP: 22
SALES (corp-wide): 160.3B **Publicly Held**
SIC: 3568 8711 Power transmission equipment; mechanical engineering
PA: Ford Motor Company
1 American Rd
Dearborn MI 48126
313 322-3000

(G-3713)
FORUM AND LINK INC
12740 W Wrren Ave Ste 100 (48126)
PHONE.................313 945-5465

GEOGRAPHIC SECTION

Muhannad Haimour, *CEO*
EMP: 8
SALES (est): 408.2K **Privately Held**
WEB: www.forumandlink.com
SIC: 2711 8748 Newspapers, publishing & printing; communications consulting

(G-3714)
GERRY GOSTENIK
2745 Academy St (48124-4511)
PHONE...................313 319-0100
Gerry Gostenik, *Owner*
EMP: 3
SALES (est): 132.8K **Privately Held**
SIC: 2399 Fishing nets

(G-3715)
GLASS RECYCLERS LTD
6465 Wyoming St (48126-2341)
PHONE...................313 584-3434
Robert S Rahaim, *President*
Daniel Easterly, *Vice Pres*
Douglas Rahaim, *Vice Pres*
Frank Meli, *Supervisor*
EMP: 80
SQ FT: 35,000
SALES (est): 11.3MM **Privately Held**
SIC: 3231 4953 Products of purchased glass; recycling, waste materials

(G-3716)
GLOBAL RESTAURANT GROUP INC
13250 Rotunda Dr (48120-1230)
PHONE...................313 271-2777
Ahmad Hodroj, *President*
EMP: 12 **EST:** 2007
SALES (est): 1.1MM **Privately Held**
SIC: 2032 2086 5141 5149 Ethnic foods: canned, jarred, etc.; carbonated beverages, nonalcoholic: bottled & canned; food brokers; beverages, except coffee & tea; soft drinks

(G-3717)
GREAT LAKES MECHANICAL CORP (PA)
Also Called: Great Lakes Heating, Coolng
3800 Maple St (48126-3672)
PHONE...................313 581-1400
Mark Perpich, *President*
Harold J Perpich, *Chairman*
George Perpich II, *Vice Pres*
EMP: 150 **EST:** 1955
SQ FT: 50,000
SALES (est): 28.8MM **Privately Held**
SIC: 1711 3444 Mechanical contractor; sheet metalwork

(G-3718)
HARRY MILLER FLOWERS INC
1832 Grindley Park St (48124-2504)
PHONE...................313 581-2328
Jim Matlock, *President*
EMP: 3
SALES (est): 180K **Privately Held**
SIC: 5992 5947 3089 Flowers, fresh; plants, potted; gift shop; greeting cards; flower pots, plastic

(G-3719)
HATTERAS INC
Also Called: Focus 1
12801 Prospect St (48126-3651)
PHONE...................734 525-5500
Claudia Nesbitt, *President*
Rebecca McFarlane, *Corp Secy*
James Nesbitt, *Vice Pres*
Tonia Lake, *Accountant*
John Orlando, *VP Sales*
EMP: 35
SQ FT: 35,000
SALES (est): 10MM **Privately Held**
WEB: www.4hatteras.com
SIC: 2752 2791 2789 Commercial printing, offset; typesetting; bookbinding & related work

(G-3720)
HOLLINGSWORTH CONTAINER LLC
14225 W Warren Ave (48126-1456)
PHONE...................313 768-1400
Steven Barr,
Charles Angell,
Mike McNamara,
Mark Renfer,
David Sandor,
EMP: 4 **EST:** 1997
SALES: 6MM **Privately Held**
SIC: 3499 Boxes for packing & shipping, metal
PA: Hollingsworth, Inc.
14225 W Warren Ave
Dearborn MI 48126

(G-3721)
HOWDEN NORTH AMERICA INC
8111 Tireman Ave (48126-1789)
PHONE...................313 931-4000
EMP: 3
SALES (corp-wide): 224.5MM **Privately Held**
SIC: 3564 Blowers & fans
PA: Howden North America Inc.
2475 George Urban Blvd # 120
Depew NY 14043
330 867-8540

(G-3722)
HT COMPUTING SERVICES
23253 Edward St (48128-1357)
PHONE...................313 563-0087
J Dove, *Manager*
EMP: 4
SALES (est): 373.8K **Privately Held**
SIC: 7372 Prepackaged software

(G-3723)
IBIDLTD-BLUE GREEN ENERGY (PA)
6659 Schaefer Rd Ste 110 (48126-1812)
PHONE...................909 547-5160
Kelley Elisabeth, *Principal*
EMP: 3
SALES (est): 1.6MM **Privately Held**
SIC: 2869 Fuels

(G-3724)
ILLUSION SIGNS & GRAPHICS INC
14241 Michigan Ave (48126-3524)
PHONE...................313 581-4376
Shehad Harazi, *President*
EMP: 9
SALES (est): 1.2MM **Privately Held**
SIC: 3993 Signs, not made in custom sign painting shops

(G-3725)
INTELLIGENT DYNAMICS LLC
456 Berkley St (48124-1397)
PHONE...................313 727-9920
Michael A Staszel, *Mng Member*
EMP: 10
SALES: 250K **Privately Held**
SIC: 3829 Measuring & controlling devices

(G-3726)
INTERIOR RESOURCE SUPPLY INC
9335 Saint Stephens St (48126-3801)
PHONE...................313 584-4399
Kim J Anderson, *President*
EMP: 2
SALES: 1MM **Privately Held**
SIC: 3469 Tile, floor or wall: stamped metal

(G-3727)
IRIS DESIGN & PRINT INC
24730 Michigan Ave (48124-1750)
PHONE...................313 277-0505
EMP: 8
SQ FT: 5,600
SALES (est): 700K **Privately Held**
SIC: 2752 7336 2731 7389 Lithographic Coml Print Coml Art/Graphic Design Book-Publishing/Printing Business Services

(G-3728)
JIT STEEL CORP
8111 Tireman Ave Ste 1 (48126-1789)
PHONE...................313 491-3212
Gerald F Diez, *President*
Gerald Diez, *Personnel*
EMP: 150
SALES (est): 18.5MM
SALES (corp-wide): 45.1MM **Privately Held**
SIC: 5051 3312 Steel; blast furnaces & steel mills
PA: Delaco Steel Corporation
8111 Tireman Ave Ste 1
Dearborn MI 48126
313 491-1200

(G-3729)
KENWAL PICKLING LLC
8223 W Warren Ave (48126-1615)
PHONE...................313 739-1040
Kenneth Eisenberg,
EMP: 50
SQ FT: 130,000
SALES (est): 5.4MM **Privately Held**
SIC: 3471 Plating & polishing

(G-3730)
KLANN
1439 S Telegraph Rd (48124-1808)
PHONE...................313 565-4135
Kennith Klann, *Principal*
EMP: 3
SALES (est): 186.6K **Privately Held**
SIC: 3089 Injection molding of plastics

(G-3731)
KRASITYS MED SURGICAL SUP INC
1825 Bailey St (48124-2488)
PHONE...................313 274-2210
Eric Krasity, *President*
John Krasity, *Chairman*
Eric J Krasity, *Corp Secy*
Joe Marvin, *Opers Mgr*
Travis Hell, *Marketing Staff*
EMP: 12
SQ FT: 13,000
SALES (est): 9MM **Privately Held**
WEB: www.krasitys.com
SIC: 3841 Surgical & medical instruments

(G-3732)
L A MARTIN COMPANY
14400 Henn St (48126-1887)
PHONE...................313 581-3444
Paul J Martin, *President*
Laura Martin, *Corp Secy*
EMP: 35 **EST:** 1928
SQ FT: 22,000
SALES (est): 5.4MM **Privately Held**
WEB: www.lamartincompany.com
SIC: 3451 Screw machine products

(G-3733)
LEVY INDIANA SLAG CO (PA)
Also Called: Ashland Slag Company
9300 Dix (48126-1528)
PHONE...................313 843-7200
S Evan Weiner, *President*
Edward C Levy Jr, *Chairman*
Robert P Scholz, *CFO*
▲ **EMP:** 13
SALES (est): 12.6MM **Privately Held**
SIC: 1411 Limestone, dimension-quarrying

(G-3734)
LYON SAND & GRAVEL CO (PA)
Also Called: Oakland Sand & Gravel
9300 Dix (48126-1528)
PHONE...................313 843-7200
S Evan Weiner, *President*
Robert Flucker, *Vice Pres*
Edward C Levy Jr, *Vice Pres*
Scott Carson, *Opers Mgr*
EMP: 3
SQ FT: 5,000
SALES (est): 4.4MM **Privately Held**
WEB: www.edwclevy.net
SIC: 1442 Gravel mining

(G-3735)
MACOMB SMOKED MEATS LLC
2450 Wyoming St (48120-1518)
PHONE...................313 842-2375
Clifford T Meier, *Mng Member*
Justin Havlick,
Michael K Kosch,
EMP: 80
SQ FT: 30,000
SALES (est): 16.6MM **Privately Held**
SIC: 2013 Sausages from purchased meat

(G-3736)
MAGNETIC VENTURES LLC
445 Nightingale St (48128-1561)
PHONE...................313 670-3036
Nicholas Clay,
EMP: 3
SALES (est): 222.5K **Privately Held**
SIC: 3842 Surgical appliances & supplies

(G-3737)
MD HILLER CORP
2021 Monroe St Ste 103 (48124-2926)
PHONE...................877 751-9010
EMP: 5
SALES (est): 336.4K **Privately Held**
SIC: 2834 Vitamin, nutrient & hematinic preparations for human use

(G-3738)
MED SHARE INC
1039 Washington St (48124-2016)
PHONE...................888 266-3567
Deepa Shah, *Manager*
EMP: 10
SALES (corp-wide): 22.1MM **Privately Held**
WEB: www.med-share.com
SIC: 2835 2834 In vitro & in vivo diagnostic substances; pharmaceutical preparations
PA: Med Share, Inc.
26222 Telg Rd Ste 100
Southfield MI 48033
248 827-7200

(G-3739)
METAL PREP TECHNOLOGY INC
621 Nightingale St (48128-1562)
PHONE...................313 843-2890
Stanley S Luckow, *President*
Al Miller, *Vice Pres*
EMP: 13
SQ FT: 34,000
SALES (est): 884.4K **Privately Held**
SIC: 3471 3398 Finishing, metals or formed products; shot peening (treating steel to reduce fatigue)

(G-3740)
METALFAB INC (PA)
6900 Chase Rd (48126-4504)
PHONE...................313 381-7579
James C Pinkney, *President*
EMP: 7
SQ FT: 4,000
SALES (est): 2.6MM **Privately Held**
SIC: 3441 Fabricated structural metal

(G-3741)
MICHELS INC (PA)
Also Called: M J Diamonds
18900 Michigan Ave K103 (48126-3929)
PHONE...................313 441-3620
Michael Ansara, *President*
Hilda Ansara, *Admin Sec*
▲ **EMP:** 5 **EST:** 1976
SQ FT: 2,400
SALES (est): 1.9MM **Privately Held**
SIC: 5944 3911 Jewelry, precious stones & precious metals; jewelry apparel

(G-3742)
MILLER DESIGNWORKS LLC
Also Called: Spectrum Signs & Designs
3001 S Gulley Rd Ste D (48124-4534)
PHONE...................313 562-4000
Roger L Miller,
EMP: 8
SALES: 650K **Privately Held**
WEB: www.spectrumsignsanddesigns.com
SIC: 3993 Signs, not made in custom sign painting shops

(G-3743)
NATION WIDE FUEL INC
6341 Barrie St (48126-2033)
PHONE...................734 721-7110
Ali Aboutaam, *Principal*
EMP: 4
SALES (est): 221.6K **Privately Held**
SIC: 2869 Fuels

Dearborn - Wayne County (G-3744)

GEOGRAPHIC SECTION

(G-3744)
NEW YASMEEN DETROIT INC
Also Called: New Yasmeen Bakery
13900 W Warren Ave (48126-1455)
PHONE..................313 582-6035
Mohamed Seblini, *President*
Hussain Seblini, *Corp Secy*
Ahmad Seblini, *Vice Pres*
EMP: 45
SQ FT: 10,000
SALES (est): 2.4MM **Privately Held**
SIC: 5461 5149 2051 Bread; bakery products; bread, cake & related products

(G-3745)
OAKWOOD CUSTOM COATING INC
1100 Oakwood Blvd (48124-2820)
PHONE..................313 561-7740
Laurence Morey, *Branch Mgr*
Jonathan Black, *Program Mgr*
EMP: 19
SALES (corp-wide): 178.3MM **Privately Held**
SIC: 3479 3544 3441 3089 Painting, coating & hot dipping; special dies & tools; fabricated structural metal; injection molded finished plastic products
HQ: Oakwood Energy Management, Inc.
9755 Inkster Rd
Taylor MI 48180
734 947-7700

(G-3746)
OAKWOOD METAL FABRICATING CO (PA)
Also Called: Oakwood Group, The
1100 Oakwood Blvd (48124-2820)
PHONE..................313 561-7740
Richard Audi, *President*
Phil Biondi, *Business Mgr*
John Gentis, *Engineer*
Simon Michalik, *Engineer*
Tom Perkins, *Controller*
▲ **EMP:** 390
SQ FT: 17,000
SALES (est): 178.3MM **Privately Held**
SIC: 3441 3714 3089 Fabricated structural metal; motor vehicle engines & parts; injection molded finished plastic products; injection molding of plastics

(G-3747)
PEAK INDUSTRIES CO INC
5320 Oakman Blvd (48126-3394)
PHONE..................313 846-8666
James Kostaroff, *CEO*
Timothy Kostaroff, *President*
EMP: 52 **EST:** 1965
SQ FT: 50,000
SALES (est): 8.2MM **Privately Held**
WEB: www.peakindustries.com
SIC: 3544 3535 3548 3822 Jigs & fixtures; conveyors & conveying equipment; welding apparatus; auto controls regulating residntl & coml environmt & applncs; relays & industrial controls; machine tool accessories

(G-3748)
PINETREE TRADING LLC
10540 W Warren Ave (48126-1539)
PHONE..................313 584-2700
Hassan Khalife,
EMP: 10
SALES: 1.5MM **Privately Held**
SIC: 2599 Factory furniture & fixtures

(G-3749)
PLASTECH HOLDING CORP
21551 Cherry Hill St (48124-1151)
PHONE..................313 565-5927
Julie N Brown, *CEO*
EMP: 15
SALES: 999K **Privately Held**
SIC: 3531 Construction machinery

(G-3750)
PRAXAIR INC
5825 Wyoming St (48126-2355)
PHONE..................313 319-6220
EMP: 3 **Privately Held**
SIC: 2813 Industrial gases

HQ: Praxair, Inc.
10 Riverview Dr
Danbury CT 06810
203 837-2000

(G-3751)
PRINTXPRESS INC
7120 Chase Rd (48126-4505)
PHONE..................313 846-1644
Ali Ashkar, *CEO*
EMP: 4
SALES (est): 565.2K **Privately Held**
SIC: 7336 2759 Graphic arts & related design; commercial printing; promotional printing

(G-3752)
QUICK DRAW TARPAULIN SYSTEMS (PA)
10200 Ford Rd (48126-3333)
PHONE..................313 945-0766
Walt Demonte, *President*
Sheri Le Blanc, *Vice Pres*
Sheri Leblanc, *Vice Pres*
Alan Schieffer, *Branch Mgr*
▲ **EMP:** 15
SQ FT: 20,000
SALES (est): 12.7MM **Privately Held**
WEB: www.quickdrawtarps.com
SIC: 2394 Tarpaulins, fabric: made from purchased materials

(G-3753)
RHOMBUS ENERGY SOLUTIONS INC
15201 Century Dr (48120-1232)
PHONE..................313 406-3292
Kent Harmin, *Branch Mgr*
EMP: 7
SALES (corp-wide): 600K **Privately Held**
SIC: 8711 3822 Engineering services; energy cutoff controls, residential or commercial types
PA: Rhombus Energy Solutions, Inc
10915 Technology Pl
San Diego CA
858 353-1002

(G-3754)
S & A FUEL LLC
10005 W Warren Ave (48126-1653)
PHONE..................313 945-6555
Iman Zreik, *Principal*
EMP: 4
SALES (est): 350.9K **Privately Held**
SIC: 2862 Fuels

(G-3755)
SAB AMERICA INC
10800 W Wrren Ave Ste 260 (48126)
PHONE..................313 363-3392
Amir Beydoun, *President*
Ayman Beydoun, *Manager*
Youssef Beydoun, *Manager*
EMP: 3
SALES: 100K **Privately Held**
SIC: 2782 Scrapbooks, albums & diaries

(G-3756)
SECURE CROSSING RES & DEV INC
1122 Mason St (48124-2801)
PHONE..................248 535-3800
Robert G Lorente, *President*
Randall E Reeves, *CTO*
EMP: 18
SALES: 700K **Privately Held**
WEB: www.securecrossing.com
SIC: 3699 Security devices

(G-3757)
SERVICES TO ENHANCE POTENTIAL (PA)
Also Called: Step
2941 S Gulley Rd (48124-3160)
PHONE..................313 278-3040
Brent Mikulski, *President*
Timothy Kachmarik, *Mfg Staff*
Douglas Rousell, *CFO*
Cheryl Fregolle, *Director*
Tamaria White, *Director*
EMP: 8
SQ FT: 20,000

SALES (est): 18.2MM **Privately Held**
WEB: www.stepcentral.org
SIC: 3999 5932 7349 8322 Bric-a-brac; used merchandise stores; building & office cleaning services; adult day care center; job training & vocational rehabilitation services

(G-3758)
SHATILA FOOD PRODUCTS INC (PA)
8505 W Warren Ave (48126-1617)
PHONE..................313 934-1520
Riad Shatila, *President*
▲ **EMP:** 50
SQ FT: 48,000
SALES (est): 36.1MM **Privately Held**
WEB: www.shatila.com
SIC: 5149 5461 2052 2051 Bakery products; bakeries; cookies & crackers; bread, cake & related products

(G-3759)
SHELFACTORY LLC
1750 N Gulley Rd (48128-1041)
PHONE..................734 709-3615
James Bustamante, *Administration*
EMP: 3
SALES (est): 275.4K **Privately Held**
SIC: 2499 Wood products

(G-3760)
SHURE STAR LLC (PA)
15200 Century Dr (48120-1254)
PHONE..................248 365-4382
Bruce R Bacon,
EMP: 3 **EST:** 2011
SALES: 5MM **Privately Held**
SIC: 3442 Window & door frames

(G-3761)
SND MANUFACTURING LLC
23000 Arlington St (48128-1806)
PHONE..................313 996-5088
Neil Shuell, *Mng Member*
EMP: 6
SQ FT: 3,000
SALES: 400K **Privately Held**
SIC: 2431 Doors & door parts & trim, wood

(G-3762)
SOUTH PARK SALES & MFG INC
6900 Chase Rd (48126-4504)
PHONE..................313 381-7579
James Pinkney, *President*
Antoinette Pinkney, *Corp Secy*
EMP: 5
SQ FT: 2,000
SALES (est): 731K **Privately Held**
WEB: www.southparksales.com
SIC: 5084 3498 3451 3441 Machine tools & accessories; tube fabricating (contract bending & shaping); screw machine products; fabricated structural metal; paperboard mills

(G-3763)
STEVES BACKROOM LLC
13250 Rotunda Dr (48120-1230)
PHONE..................313 527-7240
Andre Dixon, *General Mgr*
EMP: 10
SQ FT: 7,000
SALES (est): 450K **Privately Held**
SIC: 2099 Ready-to-eat meals, salads & sandwiches

(G-3764)
THERMO ARL US INC
15300 Rotunda Dr Ste 301 (48120-1239)
PHONE..................313 336-3901
EMP: 12
SALES (corp-wide): 5.6MM **Privately Held**
SIC: 3826 3823 Mfg Analytical Instruments Mfg Process Control Instruments
PA: Thermo Arl U.S. Inc.
1400 Northpoint Pkwy # 50
West Palm Beach FL 33407
800 532-4752

(G-3765)
THINK NORTH AMERICA INC (PA)
Also Called: Think NA
22226 Garrison St (48124-2208)
PHONE..................313 565-6781
Barry Engle, *CEO*
Richard Canny, *Chairman*
EMP: 20
SALES (est): 3.9MM **Privately Held**
SIC: 3711 Motor vehicles & car bodies

(G-3766)
THOMAS INDUSTRIAL ROLLS INC
8526 Brandt St (48126-2330)
PHONE..................313 584-9696
Dennis Simpson, *President*
Debbie Simpson, *Vice Pres*
▲ **EMP:** 15
SQ FT: 20,000
SALES (est): 3.3MM **Privately Held**
WEB: www.tirinc.com
SIC: 3469 Metal stampings

(G-3767)
UNIVESITY MICHIGAN-DEARBORN
Also Called: Michigan Journal, The
4901 Evergreen Rd # 2130 (48128-2406)
PHONE..................313 593-5428
Domenico Grasso, *Chancellor*
Kristina Calvird, *Manager*
EMP: 11
SALES (corp-wide): 7.4B **Privately Held**
SIC: 2711 8221 Newspapers, publishing & printing; university
HQ: Univesity Of Michigan-Dearborn
4901 Evergreen Rd
Dearborn MI 48128
313 593-5000

(G-3768)
VISTEON SYSTEMS LLC
5500 Auto Club Dr (48126-2779)
PHONE..................313 755-9500
Rich Wood, *Engineer*
Kevin Singer,
Kathy Burris, *Executive Asst*
▲ **EMP:** 150
SALES (est): 53.6MM
SALES (corp-wide): 2.9B **Publicly Held**
SIC: 3711 Motor vehicles & car bodies
PA: Visteon Corporation
1 Village Center Dr
Van Buren Twp MI 48111
800 847-8366

(G-3769)
VITESCO TECHNOLOGIES
15001 N Commerce Dr (48120-1226)
PHONE..................313 583-5980
Gregory Razook, *Engineer*
EMP: 107
SALES (corp-wide): 50.8B **Privately Held**
SIC: 3714 Motor vehicle parts & accessories
HQ: Vitesco Technologies Usa, Llc
2400 Executive Hills Dr
Auburn Hills MI 48326
248 209-4000

(G-3770)
VORTECH PHARMACEUTICAL LTD
6851 Chase Rd (48126-1748)
P.O. Box 189 (48121-0189)
PHONE..................313 584-4088
John A Macneil, *President*
Viberta Macneil, *Vice Pres*
EMP: 15
SQ FT: 12,000
SALES (est): 2.8MM **Privately Held**
SIC: 2834 Pharmaceutical preparations

(G-3771)
W W WILLIAMS COMPANY LLC
4000 Stecker St (48126-3803)
PHONE..................313 584-6150
Alan Gatlin, *CEO*
L Ed McIntyre, *Manager*
EMP: 45
SALES (corp-wide): 5.7B **Privately Held**
WEB: www.williamsdistribution.com
SIC: 3519 Internal combustion engines

GEOGRAPHIC SECTION

Decatur - Van Buren County (G-3802)

HQ: The W W Williams Company Llc
5025 Bradenton Ave # 130
Dublin OH 43017
614 228-5000

(G-3772)
WARREN CITY FUEL
134 N Silvery Ln (48128-1536)
PHONE.................................586 759-4759
Hussein Beydoun, *Principal*
EMP: 3 **EST:** 2010
SALES (est): 460K **Privately Held**
SIC: 2869 Fuels

(G-3773)
WATER DEPARTMENT
Also Called: Dearborn Water Department
2951 Greenfield Rd (48120-1318)
PHONE.................................313 943-2307
Samuel Smalley, *Manager*
EMP: 40
SALES (est): 2.1MM **Privately Held**
SIC: 3561 Pumps, domestic: water or sump

(G-3774)
WOLVERINE ADVANCED MTLS LLC (DH)
5850 Mercury Dr Ste 250 (48126-2980)
PHONE.................................313 749-6100
Grant Beard, *CEO*
Remi Riou, *General Mgr*
Peter Knittig, *Managing Dir*
Marcelo Teixeira, *Opers Staff*
Doug Smock, *Production*
▲ **EMP:** 50
SALES (est): 173.4MM
SALES (corp-wide): 2.7B **Publicly Held**
SIC: 3559 3694 Automotive related machinery; automotive electrical equipment
HQ: Itt Llc
1133 Westchester Ave N-100
White Plains NY 10604
914 641-2000

(G-3775)
YOGURTOWN INC
22231 Watsonia St (48128-1415)
PHONE.................................313 908-9376
Mahmoud Nasser, *Principal*
EMP: 7
SALES (est): 531.7K **Privately Held**
SIC: 2026 Yogurt

(G-3776)
ZAKRON USA INC
3319 Greenfield Rd 365 (48120-1212)
PHONE.................................313 582-0462
Roman Zakrajsek, *President*
Viktor Zakrajsek, *Vice Pres*
Wanda Zakrajsek, *Treasurer*
EMP: 10
SQ FT: 24,000
SALES: 1MM **Privately Held**
SIC: 3545 Gauge blocks

Dearborn Heights
Wayne County

(G-3777)
ABC GRINDING INC
26950 Van Born Rd (48125-1206)
PHONE.................................313 295-1060
Mike Resetar, *Principal*
EMP: 3
SALES (est): 336.5K **Privately Held**
SIC: 3599 Grinding castings for the trade

(G-3778)
AOM ENGINEERING SOLUTIONS LLC (PA)
26300 Ford Rd Ste 315 (48127-2854)
PHONE.................................313 406-8130
John Micheli, *President*
EMP: 4
SQ FT: 5,000
SALES: 1.4MM **Privately Held**
WEB: www.aomengineering.com
SIC: 3711 8711 Military motor vehicle assembly; engineering services

(G-3779)
ARMORED GROUP LLC
2727 S Beech Daly St (48125-1156)
PHONE.................................602 840-2271
Robert Pazderka, *CEO*
Jeff Carnicom, *COOL*
Jacque Hughes, *Vice Pres*
Mike Toth, *QC Mgr*
◆ **EMP:** 50
SQ FT: 144,000
SALES (est): 15.9MM **Privately Held**
SIC: 3711 Cars, armored, assembly of

(G-3780)
AUGUST COMMUNICATIONS INC
Also Called: Allegra DH API 382
22250 Ford Rd (48127-2420)
PHONE.................................313 561-8000
Michael Hurite, *President*
EMP: 6 **EST:** 2008
SALES (est): 576.5K **Privately Held**
SIC: 2752 7334 Commercial printing, lithographic; photocopying & duplicating services

(G-3781)
DEARBORN TOTAL AUTO SVC CTR
23416 Van Born Rd (48125-2353)
PHONE.................................313 291-6300
George Ascione, *President*
EMP: 10
SALES (est): 286.9K **Privately Held**
SIC: 7533 5531 7539 7538 Muffler shop, sale or repair & installation; automotive parts; electrical services; general automotive repair shops; motor vehicle parts & accessories

(G-3782)
DIVINE DESSERT
25930 Ford Rd (48127-2936)
PHONE.................................313 278-3322
Ayman Akrouch, *Principal*
EMP: 8
SALES (est): 685.2K **Privately Held**
SIC: 2051 Cakes, pies & pastries

(G-3783)
EASTERN POWER AND LIGHTING
5758 Hubbell St (48127-2444)
PHONE.................................248 739-0908
EMP: 3
SALES (est): 238.1K **Privately Held**
SIC: 3612 Transformers, except electric

(G-3784)
ELSTON ENTERPRISES INC
22250 Ford Rd (48127-2420)
PHONE.................................313 561-8000
David Elston, *President*
Nancy Kimberlin, *Graphic Designe*
EMP: 10
SQ FT: 2,000
SALES (est): 922.2K **Privately Held**
SIC: 7334 2752 Photocopying & duplicating services; commercial printing, lithographic

(G-3785)
FIRE SAFETY DISPLAYS CO
20422 Van Born Rd (48125-3051)
PHONE.................................313 274-7888
David C Cox, *President*
Mary Ann Cox, *Treasurer*
EMP: 9
SQ FT: 5,000
SALES (est): 1.1MM **Privately Held**
WEB: www.firesafetydisplays.com
SIC: 7389 3993 Fire protection service other than forestry or public; electric signs

(G-3786)
GRAPHICS & PRINTING LLC
7208 Hillside Dr (48127-1666)
PHONE.................................313 942-2022
Dounia El Hayani,
EMP: 3
SALES (est): 98.2K **Privately Held**
SIC: 2759 Commercial printing

(G-3787)
INITIAL ARTISTRY
25450 Ford Rd (48127-3020)
PHONE.................................313 277-6300
Marilyn Beardsley, *President*
Rufus Beardsley, *Owner*
EMP: 3
SQ FT: 1,000
SALES (est): 156.3K **Privately Held**
SIC: 2395 Embroidery products, except schiffli machine; decorative & novelty stitching, for the trade

(G-3788)
LEADER PRINTING AND DESIGN INC
25034 W Warren St (48127-2145)
PHONE.................................313 565-0061
Stephen P Henry, *President*
EMP: 10
SALES: 600K **Privately Held**
SIC: 2752 Commercial printing, offset

(G-3789)
M & R MACHINE COMPANY
5900 N Telegraph Rd (48127-3221)
PHONE.................................313 277-1570
Blazija Resetar, *President*
Ray Resetar, *Treasurer*
EMP: 6 **EST:** 1973
SQ FT: 12,000
SALES (est): 887.1K **Privately Held**
SIC: 3599 Machine shop, jobbing & repair

(G-3790)
MR EDS SEWER CLEANING SERVICE
5673 Mckinley Ct (48125-2581)
PHONE.................................313 565-2740
Ed Allred, *Owner*
EMP: 3
SALES (est): 231.2K **Privately Held**
SIC: 2842 1711 Drain pipe solvents or cleaners; plumbing contractors

(G-3791)
MURRAY GRINDING INC
5441 Sylvia St (48125-1230)
PHONE.................................313 295-6030
Maurice Wrobleski, *President*
▲ **EMP:** 15 **EST:** 1952
SQ FT: 14,500
SALES: 1MM **Privately Held**
WEB: www.murraygrinding.com
SIC: 3599 Machine shop, jobbing & repair; grinding castings for the trade

(G-3792)
NB CEMENT CO
4203 Merrick St (48125-2849)
PHONE.................................313 278-8299
John Bossio, *Partner*
Mario Naccarito, *Partner*
EMP: 4
SALES (est): 282.6K **Privately Held**
SIC: 3241 Cement, hydraulic

(G-3793)
PATRIOT TOOL INC
5310 Bayham St (48125-1300)
PHONE.................................313 299-1400
Randal A Manny, *President*
Ryan Teichmiller, *Vice Pres*
EMP: 5
SQ FT: 14,000
SALES (est): 733.7K **Privately Held**
WEB: www.patriottool.com
SIC: 3599 Machine shop, jobbing & repair

(G-3794)
RESETAR EQUIPMENT INC
26950 Van Born Rd (48125-1206)
PHONE.................................313 291-0500
Balzija Resetar, *President*
Blazija Resetar, *President*
EMP: 5
SALES (est): 1.1MM **Privately Held**
SIC: 3599 3312 Machine shop, jobbing & repair; blast furnaces & steel mills

(G-3795)
RHEMA PRODUCTS INC
24141 Ann Arbor Trl Ste 5 (48127-1797)
PHONE.................................313 561-6800
Katherine M Lee, *President*
EMP: 5
SALES (est): 656.9K **Privately Held**
WEB: www.rhemafoundation.com
SIC: 2841 Detergents, synthetic organic or inorganic alkaline

(G-3796)
SHEBA PROFESSIONAL NAIL PDTS
5681 S Beech Daly St (48125-1713)
PHONE.................................313 291-8010
Sheila Bargas, *President*
EMP: 5
SQ FT: 2,500
SALES (est): 465.1K **Privately Held**
WEB: www.shebanails.com
SIC: 3999 Fingernails, artificial

(G-3797)
SPARTAN FORMS INC
24215 Ann Arbor Trl (48127-1712)
PHONE.................................313 278-6960
John Martin, *President*
EMP: 3
SQ FT: 1,700
SALES (est): 388.8K **Privately Held**
WEB: www.spartanforms.com
SIC: 2759 Commercial printing

(G-3798)
TAIZ FUEL INC
4630 S Beech Daly St (48125-1571)
PHONE.................................313 485-2972
Gamila Kaid, *Principal*
EMP: 3
SALES (est): 153.8K **Privately Held**
SIC: 2869 Fuels

(G-3799)
TUMBLWEED WELD/FAB
3904 Campbell St (48125-2719)
PHONE.................................313 277-6860
James Banks, *Owner*
EMP: 5
SALES (est): 124.4K **Privately Held**
SIC: 7692 Welding repair

(G-3800)
UNITED PRECISION PDTS CO INC
25040 Van Born Rd (48125-2008)
PHONE.................................313 292-0100
Gary M Winkler, *President*
Brian Chichila, *Plant Supt*
Jennifer Hamilton, *Controller*
EMP: 36 **EST:** 1947
SQ FT: 16,000
SALES (est): 7.4MM **Privately Held**
WEB: www.uppci.com
SIC: 3728 3724 3452 3451 Aircraft parts & equipment; aircraft engines & engine parts; bolts, nuts, rivets & washers; screw machine products

(G-3801)
WERNER ELECTRIC CO
20520 Van Born Rd (48125-3054)
PHONE.................................313 561-0854
Matthew Mattern, *President*
Mary C Mattern, *Corp Secy*
EMP: 3 **EST:** 1960
SQ FT: 1,600
SALES (est): 324.2K **Privately Held**
SIC: 7694 5063 Electric motor repair; motors, electric

Decatur
Van Buren County

(G-3802)
DECATUR WOOD PRODUCTS INC
79201 M 51 (49045-8209)
P.O. Box 85, Paw Paw (49079-0085)
PHONE.................................269 657-6041
John Tapper Jr, *President*
▲ **EMP:** 30
SQ FT: 42,000
SALES: 1.7MM **Privately Held**
SIC: 2435 2431 2421 Plywood, hardwood or hardwood faced; millwork; sawmills & planing mills, general

Decatur - Van Buren County (G-3803)

(G-3803)
DOLE PACKAGED FOODS LLC
Also Called: Dole Packaged Food Company
101 W Bronson St (49045-1259)
PHONE..................................269 423-6375
Kurt Wiese, *Manager*
EMP: 50 **Privately Held**
WEB: www.jrwood.com
SIC: 2037 Fruits, quick frozen & cold pack (frozen); vegetables, quick frozen & cold pack, excl. potato products
HQ: Dole Packaged Foods, Llc
3059 Townsgate Rd Ste 400
Westlake Village CA 91361
805 601-5500

(G-3804)
KWK INDUSTRIES INC
56040 Territorial Rd (49045-9022)
PHONE..................................269 423-6213
Robert Weber, *President*
Kurt Weber, *Vice Pres*
Irene Weber, *Treasurer*
EMP: 5
SQ FT: 5,000
SALES: 380K **Privately Held**
SIC: 3544 Dies & die holders for metal cutting, forming, die casting

(G-3805)
MOORMANN PRINTING INC
Also Called: Decatur Republican
121 S Phelps St (49045-1117)
P.O. Box 36 (49045-0036)
PHONE..................................269 423-2411
David D Moormann, *Owner*
EMP: 7
SALES (corp-wide): 660.5K **Privately Held**
WEB: www.marcellusnews.com
SIC: 2711 2791 2759 2752 Newspapers, publishing & printing; typesetting; commercial printing; commercial printing, lithographic
PA: Moormann Printing Inc
149 W Main St
Marcellus MI 49067
269 646-2101

(G-3806)
SPECIAL-LITE INC
860 S Williams St (49045-1258)
P.O. Box 6 (49045-0006)
PHONE..................................800 821-6531
Henry L Upjohn II, *Ch of Bd*
Kevin J Hanley, *President*
W Dow Ruch, *Vice Pres*
Cathy Ericksen, *CFO*
EMP: 120 **EST:** 1971
SQ FT: 150,000
SALES (est): 38.4MM **Privately Held**
WEB: www.special-lite.com
SIC: 3089 3354 3442 Doors, folding: plastic or plastic coated fabric; aluminum extruded products; metal doors

Deckerville
Sanilac County

(G-3807)
DESTINY PLASTICS INCORPORATED
2121 Stoutenberg (48427)
P.O. Box 7 (48427-0007)
PHONE..................................810 622-0018
Todd Cristy, *President*
EMP: 15
SQ FT: 25,000
SALES (est): 3.3MM **Privately Held**
WEB: www.destiny-plastics.com
SIC: 3089 Plastic processing

(G-3808)
FLOWERS BY KEVIN
2486 Black River St (48427-9425)
P.O. Box 277 (48427-0277)
PHONE..................................810 376-4600
Kevin Kubacki, *Owner*
EMP: 4
SQ FT: 2,100
SALES (est): 167K **Privately Held**
SIC: 5992 3999 Flowers, fresh; artificial flower arrangements

(G-3809)
MIDWEST RUBBER COMPANY (PA)
3525 Range Line Rd (48427-9420)
P.O. Box 98 (48427-0098)
PHONE..................................810 376-2085
Kenneth L Jehle, *President*
Donald E Rose, *Vice Pres*
EMP: 61
SQ FT: 88,000
SALES (est): 23.4MM **Privately Held**
WEB: www.mwrco.com
SIC: 3061 Mechanical rubber goods

(G-3810)
PROTO CRAFTS INC (PA)
4740 Shabbona Rd (48427-9364)
P.O. Box 36 (48427-0036)
PHONE..................................810 376-3665
Lowell Manley, *President*
Faith Manley, *Corp Secy*
EMP: 51
SQ FT: 4,500
SALES (est): 5.6MM **Privately Held**
SIC: 3089 Injection molding of plastics

Deerfield
Lenawee County

(G-3811)
DECOCKERS INC
1502 Bucholtz Hwy (49238-9506)
PHONE..................................517 447-3635
Jim Decocker, *President*
John Decocker, *Assistant VP*
Jeanne Decocker, *Admin Sec*
EMP: 3
SALES (est): 357.2K **Privately Held**
SIC: 3599 4212 Machine shop, jobbing & repair; local trucking, without storage

(G-3812)
LIMO-REID INC
420 Carey St (49238-9741)
P.O. Box 355 (49238-0355)
PHONE..................................517 447-4164
James O'Brien II, *CEO*
EMP: 8
SALES (est): 686.7K **Privately Held**
WEB: www.hybra-drive.com
SIC: 8711 3594 Engineering services; motors: hydraulic, fluid power or air; pumps, hydraulic power transfer

(G-3813)
MERIDIAN MECHATRONICS LLC
120 W Keegan St (49238-9612)
PHONE..................................517 447-4587
Kevin Iott, *Owner*
EMP: 3
SALES (est): 309.6K **Privately Held**
SIC: 3827 Telescopes: elbow, panoramic, sighting, fire control, etc.

(G-3814)
OBRIEN ENGINEERED PRODUCTS
Also Called: Obep
420 Carey St (49238-9741)
P.O. Box 164 (49238-0164)
PHONE..................................517 447-3602
James A O'Brien II, *President*
Sharon A O'Brien, *Vice Pres*
EMP: 12
SQ FT: 3,500
SALES (est): 715K **Privately Held**
SIC: 3429 Door locks, bolts & checks

Delton
Barry County

(G-3815)
ALLIED MACHINE & TOOL INC
3590 Hope Industry Dr (49046-9812)
PHONE..................................269 623-7295
Rodney Morris, *President*
Troy Norris, *Vice Pres*
Gail H Houglan, *Manager*
EMP: 10
SQ FT: 12,000
SALES: 1.3MM **Privately Held**
WEB: www.allied-machine.com
SIC: 3599 Machine shop, jobbing & repair

(G-3816)
BOURDO LOGGING
5794 Mullen Ridge Dr (49046-8100)
PHONE..................................269 623-4981
Gordon Bourdo, *Principal*
EMP: 3
SALES (est): 258.2K **Privately Held**
SIC: 2411 Logging

(G-3817)
LAWS & PONIES LOGGING SHOW
6805 Pine Lake Rd (49046-8495)
PHONE..................................269 838-3942
Cheryl L Laws, *President*
EMP: 3 **EST:** 2013
SALES (est): 160K **Privately Held**
SIC: 2411 Logging

(G-3818)
M R D INDUSTRIES
9755 Kingsbury Rd (49046-9528)
PHONE..................................269 623-8452
Dale Payne, *Partner*
Todd Payne, *Partner*
EMP: 3 **EST:** 1970
SQ FT: 4,500
SALES: 150K **Privately Held**
SIC: 3599 5172 7538 5983 Machine shop, jobbing & repair; petroleum products; truck engine repair, except industrial; fuel oil dealers

(G-3819)
MARSHALL CLAYTON & SONS LOG
8101 Keller Rd (49046-8723)
PHONE..................................269 623-8898
Clayton Marshall, *Partner*
Brad Marshall, *Partner*
Eddie Marshall, *Partner*
EMP: 3
SALES (est): 210.9K **Privately Held**
SIC: 2411 0191 Logging camps & contractors; general farms, primarily crop

(G-3820)
SCRAPALOO
6590 S M 43 Hwy (49046-9627)
PHONE..................................269 623-7310
John Carpenter, *Owner*
EMP: 4
SALES (est): 255.6K **Privately Held**
SIC: 2782 Scrapbooks

Detroit
Oakland County

(G-3821)
REB RESEARCH & CONSULTING CO (PA)
Also Called: Mr. Hydrogen
25451 Gardner St (48237-1348)
PHONE..................................248 547-7942
Robert Buxbaum, *President*
EMP: 3
SALES: 235K **Privately Held**
SIC: 3569 Filters

(G-3822)
WRIGHT & FILIPPIS INC
23520 Woodward Ave (48220-1346)
PHONE..................................248 336-8460
Kurt Schlau, *Manager*
EMP: 30
SALES (corp-wide): 51.4MM **Privately Held**
WEB: www.firsttoserve.com
SIC: 5999 7352 3842 3841 Hospital equipment & supplies; invalid supplies rental; surgical appliances & supplies; surgical & medical instruments
PA: Wright & Filippis, Inc.
2845 Crooks Rd
Rochester Hills MI 48309
248 829-8292

Detroit
Wayne County

(G-3823)
3-D DESIGNS LLC
5566 Radnor St (48224-4309)
PHONE..................................313 658-1249
Deleshia Dawson, *Mng Member*
EMP: 3
SALES: 10K **Privately Held**
SIC: 2299 7389 Linen fabrics;

(G-3824)
3M COMPANY
11900 E 8 Mile Rd (48205-1048)
P.O. Box 5130 (48205-0130)
PHONE..................................313 372-4200
Donald Hess, *Personnel*
Wendell Smith, *Sales Mgr*
Paul Tamanaha, *Branch Mgr*
Kurt Archer, *Maintence Staff*
EMP: 30
SALES (corp-wide): 32.7B **Publicly Held**
WEB: www.mmm.com
SIC: 3291 Abrasive products
PA: 3m Company
3m Center
Saint Paul MN 55144
651 733-1110

(G-3825)
5 MILE BREWING COMPANY LLC (PA)
Also Called: Eastern Market Brewing
2515 Riopelle St (48207-4526)
PHONE..................................313 348-1628
Dayne Bartscht, *Mng Member*
Paul Hoskin,
Dave Keyte,
Bradley Silverman,
EMP: 6
SALES (est): 1.8MM **Privately Held**
SIC: 2082 Beer (alcoholic beverage)

(G-3826)
A & R SPECIALTY SERVICES CORP
Also Called: United Metal Products
8101 Lyndon St (48238-2452)
PHONE..................................313 933-8750
Fax: 313 933-1001
EMP: 24
SALES (est): 5.3MM **Privately Held**
SIC: 3469 Mfg Metal Stampings

(G-3827)
A K SERVICES INC
1604 Clay St Ste 137 (48211-1903)
PHONE..................................313 972-1010
Alan Kaniarz, *President*
EMP: 4
SQ FT: 6,600
SALES: 250K **Privately Held**
SIC: 2434 2511 3231 7699 Wood kitchen cabinets; wood household furniture; ornamental glass: cut, engraved or otherwise decorated; antique repair & restoration, except furniture, automobiles; antiques

(G-3828)
A N L SPRING MANUFACTURING
18307 Weaver St (48228-1153)
PHONE..................................313 837-0200
Anthony Luna, *President*
Dave Cheedie, *Vice Pres*
EMP: 5
SQ FT: 3,200
SALES (est): 741.2K **Privately Held**
SIC: 3493 3495 Steel springs, except wire; wire springs

(G-3829)
A&M ASSEMBLY AND MACHINING LLC
6400 E Hildale St (48234-2594)
PHONE..................................313 369-9475
William Baker, *Prdtn Mgr*
Scott McAslan,
Angela Bove,
Cling Cerny,
Mark J Diponio,
EMP: 43

GEOGRAPHIC SECTION

Detroit - Wayne County (G-3855)

SQ FT: 50,000
SALES (est): 8.7MM **Privately Held**
SIC: 3714 Motor vehicle parts & accessories

(G-3830)
A-LINE PRODUCTS CORPORATION
2955 Bellevue St (48207-3502)
PHONE..................313 571-8300
Alger Laura, *CEO*
Kevin E Laura, *President*
Dave Laura, *Accounts Mgr*
EMP: 15
SQ FT: 73,000
SALES (est): 3.7MM **Privately Held**
WEB: www.a-line.com
SIC: 2851 2822 2899 Lacquers, varnishes, enamels & other coatings; butyl rubber, isobutylene-isoprene rubbers; rust resisting compounds

(G-3831)
AAM INTERNATIONAL HOLDINGS INC (DH)
1 Dauch Dr (48211-1115)
PHONE..................313 758-2000
Richard E Dauch, *Ch of Bd*
EMP: 27
SALES (est): 129.6MM
SALES (corp-wide): 7.2B **Publicly Held**
SIC: 3463 Automotive forgings, nonferrous

(G-3832)
AAM WHOLESALE CARPET CORP (PA)
9504 Whittier St (48224-1810)
PHONE..................313 898-5101
Abdulmalek Aldalaly, *President*
Odai Mohammad, *Principal*
Greg Miller, *Engineer*
EMP: 4
SALES: 375K **Privately Held**
SIC: 5713 5021 2434 Carpets; furniture; wood kitchen cabinets

(G-3833)
AAPICO DETROIT LLC (PA)
6401 W Fort St (48209-1271)
PHONE..................313 652-5254
Mark Simpson, *Mng Member*
EMP: 2
SALES: 121MM **Privately Held**
SIC: 3711 Automobile assembly, including specialty automobiles

(G-3834)
AAPICO DETROIT LLC
6401 W Fort St Bldg 2 (48209-1271)
PHONE..................313 551-6001
Mark Simpson, *Branch Mgr*
EMP: 307
SALES (corp-wide): 121MM **Privately Held**
SIC: 3711 Automobile assembly, including specialty automobiles
PA: Aapico Detroit Llc
   6401 W Fort St
   Detroit MI 48209
   313 652-5254

(G-3835)
AAPICO DETROIT LLC
100 American Way St (48209-2955)
PHONE..................313 551-6001
Mark Simpson, *Branch Mgr*
EMP: 100
SALES (corp-wide): 121MM **Privately Held**
SIC: 3714 5013 5531 Motor vehicle parts & accessories; automotive supplies & parts; automotive parts
PA: Aapico Detroit Llc
   6401 W Fort St
   Detroit MI 48209
   313 652-5254

(G-3836)
ABB ENTERPRISE SOFTWARE INC
16503 Manor St (48221-2825)
PHONE..................313 863-1909
Bernice Early, *Branch Mgr*
EMP: 3

SALES (corp-wide): 36.4B **Privately Held**
SIC: 3674 Microcircuits, integrated (semiconductor)
HQ: Abb Inc.
   305 Gregson Dr
   Cary NC 27511

(G-3837)
ABB ENTERPRISE SOFTWARE INC
65 Cadillac Sq (48226-2844)
PHONE..................313 965-8900
George Helwagen, *Branch Mgr*
EMP: 100
SALES (corp-wide): 36.4B **Privately Held**
WEB: www.elsterelectricity.com
SIC: 3823 Industrial instrmnts msrmnt display/control process variable
HQ: Abb Inc.
   305 Gregson Dr
   Cary NC 27511

(G-3838)
ACCUFORM PRTG & GRAPHICS INC
7231 Southfield Fwy (48228-3598)
PHONE..................313 271-5600
Helen Konczal, *President*
Gail Konczal, *Treasurer*
EMP: 19
SQ FT: 5,500
SALES: 3MM **Privately Held**
WEB: www.accuform.net
SIC: 7389 3861 5112 Printers' services: folding, collating; photographic equipment & supplies; stationery & office supplies

(G-3839)
ACE-TEX ENTERPRISES INC (PA)
Also Called: Ace Wiping Cloth
7601 Central St (48210-1038)
PHONE..................313 834-4000
Martin Laker, *President*
Irving Laker, *President*
Daniel Chupinsky, *Corp Secy*
▲ EMP: 40
SQ FT: 122,000
SALES: 20.3MM **Privately Held**
WEB: www.ace-tex.com
SIC: 2621 2211 Toweling tissue, paper; scrub cloths

(G-3840)
ACME PLATING INC
18636 Fitzpatrick St (48228-1493)
PHONE..................313 838-3870
Kenneth J Jurban, *President*
Nancy Jurban, *Vice Pres*
EMP: 7
SQ FT: 9,800
SALES (est): 1MM **Privately Held**
WEB: www.acmeplating.com
SIC: 3471 Plating of metals or formed products

(G-3841)
ACME WIRE & IRON WORKS LLC
3527 E Canfield St (48207-1701)
PHONE..................313 923-7555
Robert A Galster, *President*
Barbara Galster, *General Mgr*
Marvin E Galster, *Vice Pres*
Una C Galster, *Admin Sec*
EMP: 12 EST: 1899
SQ FT: 50,000
SALES (est): 2.1MM **Privately Held**
WEB: www.acmewireandironworks.com
SIC: 3496 Miscellaneous fabricated wire products

(G-3842)
ADGRAVERS INC
269 Walker St (48207-4258)
PHONE..................313 259-3780
John T Flanagan, *President*
Kurt Flanagan, *Vice Pres*
EMP: 40
SQ FT: 16,000
SALES (est): 3.2MM **Privately Held**
WEB: www.adgravers.com
SIC: 2796 2791 Lithographic plates, positives or negatives; typesetting

(G-3843)
ADHESIVE SYSTEMS INC
15477 Woodrow Wilson St (48238-1586)
PHONE..................313 865-4448
George H Hill, *President*
Arnold F Joseff, *Vice Pres*
Paul Borkosh, *CFO*
▲ EMP: 50
SQ FT: 85,000
SALES (est): 15.3MM
SALES (corp-wide): 92.6MM **Privately Held**
WEB: www.diversifiedchemicalinc.com
SIC: 2891 Glue
PA: Diversified Chemical Technologies, Inc.
   15477 Woodrow Wilson St
   Detroit MI 48238
   313 867-5444

(G-3844)
ADVANCED URETHANES INC
Also Called: Aldoa Company
12727 Westwood St (48223-3433)
PHONE..................313 273-5705
Irfan Raza, *President*
Mahmood Farooqi, *Vice Pres*
Laura Mitchell, *Bookkeeper*
▲ EMP: 7 EST: 1957
SQ FT: 15,000
SALES (est): 1.6MM **Privately Held**
WEB: www.aldoaco.com
SIC: 2869 8731 Industrial organic chemicals; chemical laboratory, except testing

(G-3845)
AFT
16555 Shaftsbury Ave (48219-4011)
PHONE..................313 320-0218
EMP: 3
SALES (est): 115.3K **Privately Held**
SIC: 3471 Plating & polishing

(G-3846)
AGS PUBLISHING
7312 2nd Ave (48202-2711)
PHONE..................313 494-1000
David Snead, *Principal*
Zachary Sweet, *Teacher*
EMP: 3
SALES (est): 45.4K **Privately Held**
SIC: 2741 Miscellaneous publishing

(G-3847)
AIR PRODUCTS AND CHEMICALS INC
1025 Oakwood Blvd (48217)
PHONE..................313 297-2006
EMP: 48
SALES (corp-wide): 8.9B **Publicly Held**
SIC: 2813 Industrial gases
PA: Air Products And Chemicals, Inc.
   7201 Hamilton Blvd
   Allentown PA 18195
   610 481-4911

(G-3848)
AIR TIGHT SOLUTIONS LLC
18677 Robson St (48235-2808)
PHONE..................248 629-0461
Frank Usher,
EMP: 5
SALES: 120K **Privately Held**
SIC: 3559 Recycling machinery

(G-3849)
AIRTEC CORPORATION
17565 Walter P Chrysler (48203-2366)
PHONE..................313 892-7800
James F Boettcher, *CEO*
Christopher Boettcher, *President*
Barbara Boettcher, *Corp Secy*
EMP: 8 EST: 1936
SQ FT: 16,000
SALES (est): 4MM **Privately Held**
WEB: www.airteccorp.net
SIC: 3339 Babbitt metal (primary)

(G-3850)
AJAX METAL PROCESSING INC (PA)
4651 Bellevue St (48207-1713)
PHONE..................313 267-2100
Derek J Stevens, *Ch of Bd*
Frank Buono, *President*
Gregory Wronkowicz, *Vice Pres*

Daniel L Morrell, *CFO*
▲ EMP: 7
SQ FT: 281,780
SALES (est): 30.3MM **Privately Held**
WEB: www.ajaxmetal.com
SIC: 3471 3398 3479 4783 Plating of metals or formed products; metal heat treating; annealing of metal; coating of metals & formed products; packing goods for shipping

(G-3851)
AJM PACKAGING CORPORATION
6910 Dix St (48209-1269)
PHONE..................313 842-7530
Keith Stillson, *Manager*
EMP: 200
SALES (corp-wide): 351.1MM **Privately Held**
WEB: www.ajmpack.com
SIC: 2656 2674 2676 Plates, paper: made from purchased material; paper bags: made from purchased materials; sanitary paper products
PA: A.J.M. Packaging Corporation
   E-4111 Andover Rd
   Bloomfield Hills MI 48302
   248 901-0040

(G-3852)
ALBION AUTOMOTIVE LIMITED
1 Dauch Dr (48211-1115)
PHONE..................313 758-2000
David C Dauch, *CEO*
EMP: 496 EST: 2015
SALES (est): 87.6K
SALES (corp-wide): 7.2B **Publicly Held**
SIC: 3714 Motor vehicle parts & accessories
PA: American Axle & Manufacturing Holdings, Inc.
   1 Dauch Dr
   Detroit MI 48211
   313 758-2000

(G-3853)
ALCO PRODUCTS LLC
580 Saint Jean St (48214-3476)
PHONE..................313 823-7500
Neil Jackson, *President*
David Martin, *General Mgr*
Edward Karpinski, *Mng Member*
Lee Vandermyde,
EMP: 20 EST: 2009
SQ FT: 100,000
SALES (est): 8.4MM **Privately Held**
WEB: www.alconvc.com
SIC: 2952 3441 3255 2951 Roofing felts, cements or coatings; coating compounds, tar; fabricated structural metal; clay refractories; asphalt paving mixtures & blocks; adhesives & sealants

(G-3854)
ALGO ESPECIAL VARIETY STR INC
2628 Bagley St (48216-1722)
PHONE..................313 963-9013
Raul Hernandez, *President*
Martha Hernandez, *Vice Pres*
EMP: 3
SALES (est): 249.1K **Privately Held**
WEB: www.algoespecial.com
SIC: 5942 2711 5411 5735 Books, foreign; newspapers; grocery stores, independent; records; audio tapes, prerecorded

(G-3855)
ALINOSI FRENCH ICE CREAM CO
Also Called: Alinosi Ice Cream Co.
12748 E Mcnichols Rd (48205-3353)
PHONE..................313 527-3195
Steven Di Maggio, *President*
Joseph Di Maggio, *Corp Secy*
Steve Di Maggio, *Human Res Dir*
EMP: 5 EST: 1921
SQ FT: 4,000
SALES (est): 459.5K **Privately Held**
SIC: 2024 2066 5451 5441 Ice cream, bulk; ice cream, packaged: molded, on sticks, etc.; chocolate candy, solid; ice cream (packaged); candy

Detroit - Wayne County (G-3856)

(G-3856)
ALL AMERICAN WHSE & COLD STOR
14401 Dexter Ave (48238-2633)
P.O. Box 38368 (48238-0368)
PHONE...................313 865-3870
Sophie Tatarian Nemeth, *President*
EMP: 30
SQ FT: 80,000
SALES (est): 4.5MM **Privately Held**
SIC: 4222 2037 Warehousing, cold storage or refrigerated; frozen fruits & vegetables

(G-3857)
ALL-CHEM CORPORATION
15120 3rd St (48203-3724)
P.O. Box 6273, Plymouth (48170-0273)
PHONE...................313 865-3600
James S Lear, *President*
EMP: 5
SQ FT: 50,000
SALES (est): 735K **Privately Held**
SIC: 2842 Cleaning or polishing preparations

(G-3858)
ALLIANCE ENGNRED SLTONS NA LTD
18615 Sherwood St (48234-2813)
PHONE...................586 291-3694
Sekou Shorter, *Vice Pres*
EMP: 200 **EST:** 2012
SQ FT: 125,000
SALES (est): 41.5K **Privately Held**
SIC: 3442 Rolling doors for industrial buildings or warehouses, metal

(G-3859)
ALLY SERVICING LLC (HQ)
Also Called: Semperian Collection Center
500 Woodward Ave Fl 1 (48226-3416)
PHONE...................248 948-7702
Evan Noulas, *President*
Lee G McCarty, *Exec VP*
William C Ploog, *Exec VP*
Cathy L Quenneville, *Admin Sec*
EMP: 19
SQ FT: 20,486
SALES (est): 171.5MM
SALES (corp-wide): 10.4B **Publicly Held**
WEB: www.accutelinc.com
SIC: 1389 Roustabout service
PA: Ally Financial Inc.
500 Woodward Ave Fl 10
Detroit MI 48226
866 710-4623

(G-3860)
ALO LLC
Also Called: Workshop Detroit
3011 W Grand Blvd Ste 105 (48202-3068)
PHONE...................313 318-9029
Kevin Borsay,
EMP: 6
SALES (est): 264.2K **Privately Held**
SIC: 2511 Wood household furniture

(G-3861)
ALPHA RESINS LLC
17350 Ryan Rd (48212-1116)
PHONE...................313 366-9300
Jenniffer Deckard,
EMP: 4
SALES (est): 194.4K
SALES (corp-wide): 142.6MM **Publicly Held**
SIC: 3087 Custom compound purchased resins
HQ: Covia Holdings Corporation
3 Summit Park Dr Ste 700
Independence OH 44131
440 214-3284

(G-3862)
ALUMINUM ARCHITECTURAL MET CO
8711 Epworth St (48204-2957)
PHONE...................313 895-2555
Frank J Mueth Jr, *President*
EMP: 12 **EST:** 1920
SQ FT: 20,500
SALES: 3MM
SALES (corp-wide): 6MM **Privately Held**
WEB: www.sconcepts.com
SIC: 3446 Architectural metalwork
PA: Dumas Concepts In Building, Inc.
8711 Epworth St
Detroit MI

(G-3863)
ALUMINUM SUPPLY COMPANY INC
14359 Meyers Rd (48227-3923)
PHONE...................313 491-5040
Nancy Marshall, *President*
Brian Pollak, *Accounts Mgr*
Eric Noe, *Sales Staff*
Lucas Zoll, *Marketing Staff*
Brenda Moua,
EMP: 28 **EST:** 1948
SQ FT: 15,000
SALES (est): 5.9MM **Privately Held**
WEB: www.aluminumsupply.com
SIC: 3446 5051 Architectural metalwork; miscellaneous nonferrous products

(G-3864)
AMBASSADOR MAGAZINE
151 W Congress St 306 (48226-3204)
PHONE...................313 965-6789
EMP: 5
SALES (est): 340K **Privately Held**
SIC: 2721 Periodicals-Publishing/Printing

(G-3865)
AMERICAN AXLE & MFG INC (HQ)
Also Called: AAMCO Transmissions
1 Dauch Dr (48211-1198)
PHONE...................313 758-3600
Yogendra N Rahangdale, *Vice Ch Bd*
Tolga Oal, *President*
Katy Severson, *General Mgr*
John J Bellanti, *Exec VP*
Timothy E Bowes, *Senior VP*
▲ **EMP:** 325
SALES (est): 1.1B
SALES (corp-wide): 7.2B **Publicly Held**
WEB: www.aam.com
SIC: 3714 Rear axle housings, motor vehicle
PA: American Axle & Manufacturing Holdings, Inc.
1 Dauch Dr
Detroit MI 48211
313 758-2000

(G-3866)
AMERICAN AXLE MFG HOLDINGS INC (PA)
Also Called: AAM
1 Dauch Dr (48211-1198)
PHONE...................313 758-2000
David C Dauch, *Ch of Bd*
Michael K Simonte, *President*
Chaitanya Apte, *Vice Pres*
Michael Bly, *Vice Pres*
David M Buckley, *Vice Pres*
EMP: 160 **EST:** 1994
SALES: 7.2B **Publicly Held**
SIC: 3714 3711 Axles, motor vehicle; axle housings & shafts, motor vehicle; chassis, motor vehicle

(G-3867)
AMERICAN METALLURGICAL SVCS
Also Called: Can-AM Metallurgical
2731 Jerome St (48212-1545)
PHONE...................313 893-8328
Rod Woodworth, *President*
Patty Woodworth, *Treasurer*
EMP: 10
SQ FT: 17,000
SALES (est): 1.2MM **Privately Held**
SIC: 3398 Metal heat treating

(G-3868)
AMRICAN PETRO INC
Also Called: Allstate
9210 Freeland St (48228-2309)
PHONE...................313 520-8404
Malak Tarhini, *President*
Ali Tarhini, *Principal*
Ahmad Abadi, *Vice Pres*
EMP: 7
SALES (est): 613.4K **Privately Held**
SIC: 2911 7389 Gases & liquefied petroleum gases;

(G-3869)
ANAYAS PALLETS & TRANSPORT INC
163 Morrell St (48209-3129)
PHONE...................313 843-6570
Zeferino Anaya, *CEO*
Eli Galarza, *General Mgr*
EMP: 40
SQ FT: 60,000
SALES (est): 4.8MM **Privately Held**
WEB: www.anaya.com
SIC: 2448 Pallets, wood & wood with metal

(G-3870)
ANCHOR WIPING CLOTH INC
3855 E Outer Dr (48234-2936)
PHONE...................313 892-4000
Scott L Baskin, *President*
Marc Baskin, *Principal*
▲ **EMP:** 65
SQ FT: 80,000
SALES (est): 10.6MM **Privately Held**
WEB: www.anchorwipingcloth.com
SIC: 2392 2842 Household furnishings; dusting cloths, chemically treated

(G-3871)
ANEW LF PRSTHTICS ORTHTICS LLC
6438 Woodward Ave (48202-3216)
PHONE...................313 870-9610
Christopher Casteel, *Mng Member*
EMP: 5
SALES (est): 758.8K **Privately Held**
SIC: 3842 Prosthetic appliances

(G-3872)
ANWAR ATWA PRISM AUTOBODY
15800 Tireman St (48228-3798)
PHONE...................313 655-0000
EMP: 10
SALES (est): 421.5K **Privately Held**
SIC: 3559 Automotive related machinery; automotive maintenance equipment; degreasing machines, automotive & industrial

(G-3873)
ARCELORMITTAL TAILORED BLANKS
8650 Mount Elliott St (48211-1722)
PHONE...................313 332-5300
Todd Baker, *President*
Brian Aranaha, *Director*
Paul Liebenson, *Admin Sec*
EMP: 300
SALES: 60MM **Privately Held**
SIC: 7692 Automotive welding

(G-3874)
ARCELORMITTAL USA LLC
8650 Mount Elliott St (48211-1722)
PHONE...................313 332-5600
EMP: 11 **Privately Held**
SIC: 3317 Welded pipe & tubes
HQ: Arcelormittal Usa Llc
1 S Dearborn St Ste 1800
Chicago IL 60603
312 346-0300

(G-3875)
ARCHER RECORD PRESSING CO
7401 E Davison St (48212-1912)
PHONE...................313 365-9545
Michael Archer, *Corp Secy*
Richard J Archer, *Manager*
EMP: 6
SQ FT: 4,800
SALES: 380K **Privately Held**
WEB: www.archerrecordpressing.com
SIC: 3652 5735 7389 Phonograph record blanks; records; music & broadcasting services

(G-3876)
ARCO ALLOYS CORP
1891 Trombly St (48211-2195)
PHONE...................313 871-2680
David S Aronow, *Principal*
Adria Aronow, *Vice Pres*
Roslyn Aronow, *Treasurer*
EMP: 30 **EST:** 1938
SALES (est): 7.5MM **Privately Held**
WEB: www.arcoalloys.com
SIC: 3339 3341 Zinc smelting (primary), including zinc residue; zinc smelting & refining (secondary)

(G-3877)
ARLINGTON DISPLAY INDS INC
19303 W Davison St (48223-3418)
PHONE...................313 837-1212
Fax: 313 837-3425
EMP: 8 **EST:** 1947
SQ FT: 37,500
SALES (est): 690K **Privately Held**
SIC: 3993 2542 Mfg Signs/Ad Specialties Mfg Nonwd Partition/Fixt

(G-3878)
ARPLAS USA LLC
1928 Marston St (48211-1316)
PHONE...................888 527-5553
Karel Pieterman, *Mng Member*
EMP: 4
SQ FT: 12,000
SALES: 674.7K **Privately Held**
SIC: 3548 Resistance welders, electric

(G-3879)
ARROW CHEMICAL PRODUCTS INC
2067 Sainte Anne St (48216-1501)
PHONE...................313 237-0277
Cynthia Schroeder, *President*
Caroline Brown, *Principal*
Nanci Wallace, *Vice Pres*
Nancy Wallace, *Vice Pres*
Lynda Harris, *Marketing Mgr*
EMP: 25 **EST:** 1928
SQ FT: 20,000
SALES (est): 6.4MM **Privately Held**
WEB: www.arrowchemicalproducts.com
SIC: 2842 Disinfectants, household or industrial plant; sanitation preparations, disinfectants & deodorants

(G-3880)
ARTED CHROME PLATING INC
38 Piquette St (48202-3512)
PHONE...................313 871-3331
Ronald F Borawski, *President*
Frank Borawski, *Vice Pres*
EMP: 12 **EST:** 1946
SQ FT: 9,000
SALES (est): 1MM **Privately Held**
WEB: www.artedchrome.com
SIC: 3471 Plating of metals or formed products

(G-3881)
ARTJEN COMPLEXUS USA LLC
440 Burroughs St Ste 250 (48202-3429)
PHONE...................519 919-0814
Joseph Artiss, *Mng Member*
K-L Catherin Jen,
▼ **EMP:** 6
SQ FT: 1,500
SALES (est): 291.9K **Privately Held**
SIC: 2023 Dietary supplements, dairy & non-dairy based

(G-3882)
ASP GREDE INTRMDATE HLDNGS LLC (DH)
1 Dauch Dr (48211-1115)
PHONE...................313 758-2000
David C Dauch, *Ch of Bd*
EMP: 2344
SALES (est): 560.2MM
SALES (corp-wide): 7.2B **Publicly Held**
SIC: 3711 3714 Motor vehicles & car bodies; motor vehicle parts & accessories

(G-3883)
ASP HHI ACQUISITION CO INC (DH)
1 Dauch Dr (48211-1115)
PHONE...................313 758-2000
David C Dauch, *Ch of Bd*
Patricia Boomer, *Finance Mgr*
EMP: 5

GEOGRAPHIC SECTION

Detroit - Wayne County (G-3911)

SALES (est): 328.8MM
SALES (corp-wide): 7.2B **Publicly Held**
SIC: 3714 3711 Motor vehicle parts & accessories; motor vehicles & car bodies
HQ: Asp Hhi Intermediate Holdings Ii, Inc.
  1 Towne Sq Ste 550
  Southfield MI 48076
  248 727-1800

(G-3884)
AUTOMATED BOOKKEEPING INC
1555 Broadway St (48226-2160)
PHONE 866 617-3122
Steve Robert, *CEO*
Aaron Schmid, *COO*
EMP: 9
SQ FT: 10,000
SALES: 200K **Privately Held**
SIC: 7372 Business oriented computer software

(G-3885)
AUTOMOTIVE TUMBLING CO INC
3125 Meldrum St (48207-2404)
PHONE 313 925-7450
Dale Webster, *President*
EMP: 8 **EST:** 1963
SQ FT: 6,000
SALES: 920K **Privately Held**
SIC: 3471 Tumbling (cleaning & polishing) of machine parts; finishing, metals or formed products

(G-3886)
AVANTI PRESS INC (PA)
Also Called: Avanti Greeting Cards
155 W Congress St Ste 200 (48226-3261)
PHONE 800 228-2684
Frederic G Ruffner III, *President*
Calvin Kerr, *Vice Pres*
Michael Quackenbush, *Vice Pres*
Scott Singelyn, *Vice Pres*
Aubrey Stalnaker, *Director*
EMP: 45
SALES (est): 14.2MM **Privately Held**
WEB: www.avantipress.com
SIC: 2771 2741 Greeting cards; miscellaneous publishing

(G-3887)
AWCOA INC
17210 Gable St (48212-1369)
PHONE 313 892-4100
Randy Sandys, *President*
Monika Sandys, *Vice Pres*
EMP: 7
SQ FT: 14,000
SALES (est): 1.4MM **Privately Held**
WEB: www.awcoa.com
SIC: 3496 Miscellaneous fabricated wire products

(G-3888)
AXLE OF DEARBORN INC
20446 W Warren Ave (48228-3242)
PHONE 313 581-3300
Mouhamed Musheinesh, *President*
EMP: 5
SALES (corp-wide): 67.7MM **Privately Held**
SIC: 3711 7539 Cars, electric, assembly of; frame & front end repair services
PA: Axle Of Dearborn, Inc.
  2000 W 8 Mile Rd
  Ferndale MI 48220
  248 543-5995

(G-3889)
AZZ ON FIRE LLC
Also Called: Azz On Fire Salsas and Spices
6055 Southfield Fwy Apt 2 (48228-3899)
PHONE 248 470-3742
Valerie Boston, *Principal*
EMP: 3
SALES: 20K **Privately Held**
SIC: 2099 Seasonings & spices

(G-3890)
B & B ENTPS PRTG CNVRTING INC
17800 Filer St (48212-1408)
PHONE 313 891-9840
Tim Barnett, *President*

Brian Barnett, *Vice Pres*
EMP: 9
SQ FT: 40,000
SALES (est): 350K **Privately Held**
SIC: 2679 Book covers, paper

(G-3891)
B & B PRODUCTION LLC
10103 Kercheval St (48214-3118)
PHONE 586 822-9960
Deane Benetti,
EMP: 7 **EST:** 1998
SQ FT: 24,000
SALES (est): 749.3K **Privately Held**
WEB: www.bbproduction.net
SIC: 3599 Machine shop, jobbing & repair

(G-3892)
B & J ENMELING INC A MICH CORP
6827 E Davison St (48212-1909)
PHONE 313 365-6620
Judy Barkus, *President*
EMP: 18
SQ FT: 13,000
SALES: 1.3MM **Privately Held**
SIC: 3479 Enameling, including porcelain, of metal products

(G-3893)
BAZZI TIRE & WHEELS
8001 Schaefer Hwy (48228-2744)
PHONE 313 846-8888
Nick Bazzi, *Owner*
EMP: 4
SALES (est): 440.7K **Privately Held**
SIC: 3312 Wheels

(G-3894)
BD DIAGNOSTIC SYSTEMS
920 Henry St (48201-2532)
PHONE 313 442-8800
Lee Bowling, *Director*
EMP: 50
SALES (est): 4.9MM **Privately Held**
SIC: 3841 Diagnostic apparatus, medical

(G-3895)
BEARD BALM LLC
1951 Temple St (48216-1279)
PHONE 313 451-3653
Nadine Beydoun, *Marketing Staff*
Jonathan Koller,
EMP: 8 **EST:** 2012
SALES (est): 968.5K **Privately Held**
SIC: 2844 Shampoos, rinses, conditioners: hair

(G-3896)
BEARING HOLDINGS LLC (DH)
1 Dauch Dr (48211-1115)
PHONE 313 758-2000
David C Dauch, *Ch of Bd*
EMP: 3
SALES (est): 1.5MM
SALES (corp-wide): 7.2B **Publicly Held**
SIC: 3711 3714 Motor vehicles & car bodies; motor vehicle parts & accessories
HQ: Hhi Holdings, Llc
  1 Dauch Dr
  Detroit MI 48211
  313 758-2000

(G-3897)
BECHARAS BROS COFFEE CO
14501 Hamilton Ave (48203-3788)
PHONE 313 869-4700
Dean Becharas, *Ch of Bd*
Nicholas Becharas, *President*
Stephanie Becharas, *Corp Secy*
Telmer Constan, *Vice Pres*
John Parks, *Vice Pres*
EMP: 20 **EST:** 1914
SQ FT: 20,000
SALES (est): 5.3MM **Privately Held**
SIC: 5149 2095 Coffee, green or roasted; roasted coffee

(G-3898)
BECTON DICKINSON AND COMPANY
Also Called: Becton Dcknson Dagnstc Systems
920 Henry St (48201-2532)
PHONE 313 442-8700

Deb Strandquist, *Manager*
EMP: 49
SALES (corp-wide): 15.9B **Publicly Held**
SIC: 3841 Diagnostic apparatus, medical
PA: Becton, Dickinson And Company
  1 Becton Dr
  Franklin Lakes NJ 07417
  201 847-6800

(G-3899)
BELL FORK LIFT INC
13700 Mellon St (48217-1307)
PHONE 313 841-1220
Mike Berger, *Branch Mgr*
EMP: 16
SQ FT: 2,500
SALES (corp-wide): 70.8MM **Privately Held**
WEB: www.bellforklift.com
SIC: 7699 3537 Industrial machinery & equipment repair; forklift trucks
PA: Bell Fork Lift, Inc.
  34660 Centaur Dr
  Clinton Township MI 48035
  586 469-7979

(G-3900)
BELLEVUE PROC MET PREP INC
Also Called: Parts Finishing Group
5143 Bellevue St (48211-3211)
PHONE 313 921-1931
Kenneth Pape, *CEO*
Fred Pape, *President*
EMP: 30
SQ FT: 47,000
SALES: 2.1MM
SALES (corp-wide): 33.8MM **Privately Held**
SIC: 3471 3398 Finishing, metals or formed products; metal heat treating
PA: Pfg Enterprises, Inc.
  50271 E Rssell Smith Blvd
  Chesterfield MI 48051
  586 755-1053

(G-3901)
BERRY & SONS-RABABEH
2496 Orleans St (48207-4521)
PHONE 313 259-6925
Salah Rababeh, *President*
Yasseen Rababeh, *Treasurer*
EMP: 5
SQ FT: 11,000
SALES: 250K **Privately Held**
SIC: 5159 0214 2011 Skins, raw; sheep & goats; lamb products from lamb slaughtered on site

(G-3902)
BETTER MADE SNACK FOODS INC
Also Called: Better Made Potato Chips
10148 Gratiot Ave (48213-3211)
PHONE 313 925-4774
Robert Marracino, *President*
Isidore Cipriano, *Vice Pres*
Salvatore Cipriano, *Vice Pres*
Michael Schena, *Mfg Staff*
Doug Christensen, *VP Finance*
EMP: 152
SQ FT: 34,000
SALES (est): 32.5MM **Privately Held**
SIC: 2099 2096 Food preparations; potato chips & other potato-based snacks

(G-3903)
BIG COLOR PRINTING CENTER
20400 Freeland St (48235-1517)
PHONE 313 933-9290
Richard Field, *Owner*
EMP: 3
SALES: 140K **Privately Held**
SIC: 2759 Commercial printing

(G-3904)
BIRKS WORKS ENVIRONMENTAL LLC
19719 Mount Elliott St (48234-2726)
PHONE 313 891-1310
Jeffrey Heard, *President*
EMP: 6
SQ FT: 2,000

SALES (est): 1.8MM **Privately Held**
SIC: 8744 3589 ; vacuum cleaners & sweepers, electric: industrial

(G-3905)
BLACK BOTTOM BREWING CO INC
1055 Trumbull St (48216-1938)
PHONE 313 205-5493
Sean Murphy, *CEO*
EMP: 3 **EST:** 2016
SALES (est): 115.1K **Privately Held**
SIC: 2082 Beer (alcoholic beverage)

(G-3906)
BMC EAST LLC
Detroit Panel Systems
1401 Rosa Parks Blvd (48216-1953)
PHONE 313 963-2044
Timothy Oliver, *Manager*
EMP: 30
SQ FT: 40,000 **Publicly Held**
WEB: www.stockbuildingsupply.com
SIC: 2431 Millwork
HQ: Bmc East, Llc
  8020 Arco Corp Dr Ste 400
  Raleigh NC 27617
  919 431-1000

(G-3907)
BOLDEN INDUSTRIES INC
19231 Bretton Dr (48223-1363)
PHONE 248 387-9489
Kenneth Bolden II, *Principal*
Sakina Bolden, *Principal*
EMP: 10 **EST:** 2016
SALES (est): 408.2K **Privately Held**
SIC: 3999 Manufacturing industries

(G-3908)
BOND BAILEY AND SMITH COMPANY
Also Called: Bond, Bailey & Smith Machining
2707 W Fort St (48216-2000)
PHONE 313 496-0177
David D Smith, *President*
Dudley Smith, *President*
EMP: 7
SALES (est): 692.4K **Privately Held**
SIC: 3599 7692 7629 Machine shop, jobbing & repair; welding repair; electrical repair shops

(G-3909)
BOND MANUFACTURING LLC
17910 Van Dyke St (48234-3954)
PHONE 313 671-0799
Arthur Cartwright,
EMP: 5
SALES (est): 203.2K **Privately Held**
SIC: 3131 2389 Boot & shoe accessories; apparel & accessories

(G-3910)
BOOMER COMPANY (PA)
Also Called: Boomer Construction Materials
1940 E Forest Ave (48207-1119)
P.O. Box 07039 (48207-0039)
PHONE 313 832-5050
Robert Boomr, *Ch of Bd*
George Gill, *President*
Ed Basile, *Vice Pres*
John Formentin, *Vice Pres*
Anne Milligan, *Treasurer*
▲ **EMP:** 38 **EST:** 1903
SQ FT: 5,200
SALES (est): 8.3MM **Privately Held**
WEB: www.boomermaterials.com
SIC: 3441 7359 5082 5032 Building components, structural steel; equipment rental & leasing; general construction machinery & equipment; brick, except refractory

(G-3911)
BOULDING FILTRATION CO LLC
11900 E Mcnichols Rd (48205-3357)
PHONE 313 300-2388
Mercedes Boulding, *Principal*
EMP: 4
SALES (est): 231K **Privately Held**
SIC: 3569 Filters

Detroit - Wayne County (G-3912) GEOGRAPHIC SECTION

(G-3912)
BRAIQ INC
2000 Brush St Ste 201 (48226-2269)
PHONE.................................858 729-4116
Sameer Saproo, *President*
Paul Sajda, *Bd of Directors*
Victor Shih, *Bd of Directors*
EMP: 4
SQ FT: 5,000
SALES (est): 89.7K **Privately Held**
SIC: 7371 7372 8748 Computer software development; application computer software; systems engineering consultant, ex. computer or professional

(G-3913)
BRAMIN ENTERPRISES
2218 Ford St (48238-2934)
PHONE.................................313 960-1528
Thomas Hanifin, *Owner*
EMP: 5 **EST:** 2015
SALES (est): 220K **Privately Held**
SIC: 2741 7389 ;

(G-3914)
BREDE INC
19000 Glendale (48223-3424)
PHONE.................................313 273-1079
Michael Brede, *President*
EMP: 6 **EST:** 1923
SQ FT: 12,000
SALES (est): 974.2K **Privately Held**
SIC: 2035 Horseradish, prepared

(G-3915)
BREW DETROIT LLC
1401 Abbott St (48216-1946)
PHONE.................................313 974-7366
Jerry Kocak, *CEO*
EMP: 12
SALES (est): 1.5MM **Privately Held**
SIC: 2082 5921 Beer (alcoholic beverage); beer (packaged)

(G-3916)
BRIDGEWATER INTERIORS LLC (DH)
4617 W Fort St (48209-3208)
PHONE.................................313 842-3300
Ron Hall, *President*
Cassandra Alston-Childs, *COO*
Carrie Elaine Tingle, *Exec VP*
Ronald Hall, *Vice Pres*
John Cloud, *CFO*
▲ **EMP:** 200 **EST:** 1998
SQ FT: 155,871
SALES (est): 300.1MM **Privately Held**
SIC: 5013 2531 Motor vehicle supplies & new parts; public building & related furniture
HQ: Adient Us Llc
49200 Halyard Dr
Plymouth MI 48170
734 254-5000

(G-3917)
BRIGHT STAR SIGN INC
13300 Foley St (48227-3592)
PHONE.................................313 933-4460
Ibrihim McAimech, *President*
EMP: 6
SQ FT: 8,000
SALES (est): 800K **Privately Held**
WEB: www.brightstarsign.com
SIC: 3993 Neon signs

(G-3918)
BRINTLEY ENTERPRISES
Also Called: Original Stay Cool Cap, The
8660 Rosemont Ave (48228-3139)
PHONE.................................248 991-4086
Carmen Brintley, *Principal*
Angelique Mathis, *Principal*
Monique Mathis, *Principal*
Temica Slay, *Principal*
EMP: 4
SALES (est): 257.5K **Privately Held**
SIC: 5137 5131 5632 2339 Women's & children's clothing; hair accessories; apparel accessories; women's & misses' accessories

(G-3919)
BROPHY ENGRAVING CO INC
626 Harper Ave (48202-3540)
PHONE.................................313 871-2333
Howard Brophy, *President*
Darcie Grubba, *Controller*
Michael Sturtz, *Sales Dir*
Greg Carr, *Manager*
Scott Susalla, *Director*
EMP: 30 **EST:** 1939
SQ FT: 18,000
SALES (est): 4.3MM **Privately Held**
WEB: www.brophy.com
SIC: 2796 2791 2759 2752 Photoengraving plates, linecuts or halftones; typesetting; commercial printing; commercial printing, lithographic

(G-3920)
BURHANI LABS INC
18254 Livernois Ave (48221-4214)
PHONE.................................313 212-3842
Taher Patrawala, *President*
EMP: 4
SALES (est): 326.5K **Privately Held**
SIC: 2869 Laboratory chemicals, organic

(G-3921)
BUSTED BRA SHOP LLC
15 E Kirby St Ste A (48202-4047)
PHONE.................................313 288-0449
Lee Padgett, *Mng Member*
EMP: 5
SQ FT: 1,400
SALES: 14K **Privately Held**
SIC: 2342 Brassieres

(G-3922)
BUTLER MILL SERVICE COMPANY
Also Called: Whitesville Mill Service Co
8800 Dix St (48209-1093)
PHONE.................................313 429-2486
S Evan Weiner, *Principal*
EMP: 107 **Privately Held**
SIC: 3449 Miscellaneous metalwork
PA: Butler Mill Service Company
9300 Dix
Dearborn MI 48120

(G-3923)
C & A WHOLESALE INC
18942 Hayes St (48205-2960)
PHONE.................................248 302-3555
Ceaser Yaldo, *CEO*
EMP: 5
SALES: 950K **Privately Held**
SIC: 3663 Radio & TV communications equipment

(G-3924)
C & A WOOD PRODUCTS INC
17434 Cliff St (48212-1902)
PHONE.................................313 365-8400
Archie Price, *President*
Vicky Price, *Vice Pres*
EMP: 10
SQ FT: 10,600
SALES (est): 1.3MM **Privately Held**
SIC: 2431 Millwork

(G-3925)
C F BURGER CREAMERY CO
Also Called: Twin Pines
8101 Greenfield Rd (48228-2296)
PHONE.................................313 584-4040
Lawrence Angott, *Ch of Bd*
Thomas V Angott Sr, *Ch of Bd*
Dean Angott, *Vice Pres*
Laura Sawchuk, *Vice Pres*
Barbara Reark, *Treasurer*
▲ **EMP:** 57 **EST:** 1928
SQ FT: 100,000
SALES (est): 33.9MM **Privately Held**
WEB: www.twinpines.com
SIC: 5143 2026 5149 Dairy products, except dried or canned; milk processing (pasteurizing; homogenizing, bottling); half & half; cream, whipped; beverages, except coffee & tea

(G-3926)
CADILLAC OIL COMPANY
13650 Helen St (48212-2096)
PHONE.................................313 365-6200
Roger Piceu, *President*
Austin Tilotti, *Technical Staff*
▼ **EMP:** 18
SQ FT: 42,000
SALES (est): 7.2MM **Privately Held**
WEB: www.cadillacoil.com
SIC: 3479 2992 Coating, rust preventive; lubricating oils

(G-3927)
CAMRYN INDUSTRIES LLC
1401 Abbott St (48216-1946)
PHONE.................................248 663-5900
EMP: 40
SALES (corp-wide): 35.5K **Privately Held**
SIC: 2821 Molding compounds, plastics
HQ: Camryn Industries, Llc
21624 Melrose Ave
Southfield MI 48075

(G-3928)
CARACO PHARMA INC
1150 Elijah Mccoy Dr (48202-3344)
PHONE.................................313 871-8400
Jitendra N Doshi, *President*
G P Singh, *Senior VP*
Mukul Rathi, *CFO*
▲ **EMP:** 3
SALES (est): 602.8K
SALES (corp-wide): 1.3B **Privately Held**
SIC: 2834 Pharmaceutical preparations
HQ: Sun Pharmaceutical Industries, Inc.
270 Prospect Plains Rd
Cranbury NJ 08512
609 495-2800

(G-3929)
CARAVAN TECHNOLOGIES INC
3033 Bourke St (48238-2170)
P.O. Box 2067, Dearborn (48123-2067)
PHONE.................................313 341-2551
Robert Charleston, *Principal*
EMP: 12
SQ FT: 2,000
SALES (est): 1.8MM **Privately Held**
SIC: 2841 2899 2869 2842 Soap & other detergents; chemical preparations; industrial organic chemicals; specialty cleaning, polishes & sanitation goods; industrial inorganic chemicals

(G-3930)
CARCO INC
Also Called: Mike Haas
10333 Shoemaker St (48213-3313)
P.O. Box 13859 (48213-0859)
PHONE.................................313 925-1053
Harvey Gordon, *President*
Mike Haas, *Corp Secy*
David Gordon, *Vice Pres*
EMP: 15
SQ FT: 14,000
SALES (est): 2.6MM **Privately Held**
WEB: www.carcousa.com
SIC: 3953 2899 3951 Marking devices; ink or writing fluids; markers, soft tip (felt, fabric, plastic, etc.)

(G-3931)
CBP FABRICATION INC
12700 Mansfield St (48227-4901)
PHONE.................................313 653-4220
Joseph Calcaterra, *President*
Robert Black, *Treasurer*
Michelle Calcaterra, *Controller*
EMP: 45
SQ FT: 35,000
SALES (est): 14.8MM **Privately Held**
SIC: 3441 Fabricated structural metal

(G-3932)
CHEMICAL COMPANY OF AMERICA
Also Called: Chemcoa
8951 Freeland St (48228-2306)
PHONE.................................313 272-4310
Harper H Cunningham, *President*
Catherine Auerbach, *Safety Mgr*
Thomas F Valkoff, *Treasurer*
Lesa Venticinque, *Sales Staff*
EMP: 5
SQ FT: 14,000
SALES (est): 941.4K **Privately Held**
WEB: www.chemcoa.com
SIC: 2842 Specialty cleaning, polishes & sanitation goods

(G-3933)
CHEMTRADE CHEMICALS US LLC
800 Marion Ave (48218-1689)
PHONE.................................313 842-5222
Ken Hayes, *Executive*
EMP: 4
SALES (corp-wide): 1.2B **Privately Held**
SIC: 2819 Industrial inorganic chemicals
HQ: Chemtrade Chemicals Us Llc
90 E Halsey Rd
Parsippany NJ 07054

(G-3934)
CHEWYS GOURMET KITCHEN LLC
2939 Russell St (48207-4825)
PHONE.................................313 757-2595
Bertha Bowles, *Principal*
EMP: 4
SQ FT: 3,000
SALES (est): 122.8K **Privately Held**
SIC: 2051 2052 Bakery: wholesale or wholesale/retail combined; bakery products, dry

(G-3935)
CHIIPSS
10229 Joseph Campau St (48212-3223)
PHONE.................................248 345-6112
Patrick Miller, *Owner*
EMP: 4
SALES (est): 258.2K **Privately Held**
SIC: 3949 Skateboards

(G-3936)
CHRYSLER & KOPPIN COMPANY
7000 Intervale St (48238-2498)
PHONE.................................313 491-7100
Douglas Koppin, *President*
Dale Koppin, *Vice Pres*
Karen Oakley, *CFO*
Donna Hutton, *Admin Sec*
EMP: 12 **EST:** 1883
SQ FT: 38,000
SALES (est): 2.5MM **Privately Held**
WEB: www.chryslerkoppin.com
SIC: 3585 Refrigeration equipment, complete

(G-3937)
CISCO SYSTEMS INC
200 Renaissance Ctr (48243-1300)
PHONE.................................800 553-6387
Tom Myers, *Partner*
Monte Huber, *General Mgr*
Patrick Romzek, *Vice Pres*
Frank Misak, *Engineer*
Kelle Likly, *Accounts Mgr*
EMP: 678
SALES (corp-wide): 51.9B **Publicly Held**
SIC: 3577 Data conversion equipment, media-to-media: computer
PA: Cisco Systems, Inc.
170 W Tasman Dr
San Jose CA 95134
408 526-4000

(G-3938)
CLAIR EVANS-ST INC
Also Called: Evan's Industries
200 Rnmiance Ctr Ste 3150 (48243)
PHONE.................................313 259-2266
Robert B Evans Jr, *Ch of Bd*
EMP: 3
SALES (est): 310.5K
SALES (corp-wide): 43.7MM **Privately Held**
WEB: www.eiihq.com
SIC: 3069 2891 Molded rubber products; adhesives
HQ: Evans Industries, Inc.
200 Renaissance Ctr # 3150
Detroit MI 48243
313 259-2266

(G-3939)
CLARITY CBD LLC
1401 W Fort St (48232-7701)
PHONE.................................248 251-6991
Jacob Gants,
EMP: 4 **EST:** 2017
SALES (est): 125.1K **Privately Held**
SIC: 3999

GEOGRAPHIC SECTION
Detroit - Wayne County (G-3965)

(G-3940)
CLOYES GEAR HOLDINGS LLC (DH)
1 Dauch Dr (48211-1115)
PHONE.................................313 758-2000
David C Dauch, *Ch of Bd*
EMP: 3
SALES (est): 254.7MM
SALES (corp-wide): 7.2B **Publicly Held**
SIC: 3714 3711 Motor vehicle parts & accessories; motor vehicles & car bodies
HQ: Gearing Holdings, Llc
1 Dauch Dr
Detroit MI 48211
313 758-2000

(G-3941)
COAT IT INC OF DETROIT
15400 Woodrow Wilson St (48238-1564)
PHONE.................................313 869-8500
Arnold Joseff, *President*
EMP: 4
SALES (est): 238.8K **Privately Held**
SIC: 2851 Paints: oil or alkyd vehicle or water thinned

(G-3942)
COCA-COLA REFRESHMENTS USA INC
5981 W Warren Ave (48210-1116)
PHONE.................................313 897-2176
Paul Creech, *Vice Pres*
EMP: 170
SQ FT: 217,716
SALES (corp-wide): 31.8B **Publicly Held**
WEB: www.cokecce.com
SIC: 2086 Bottled & canned soft drinks
HQ: Coca-Cola Refreshments Usa, Inc.
2500 Windy Ridge Pkwy Se
Atlanta GA 30339
770 989-3000

(G-3943)
COLE KING FOODS
40 Clairmount St (48202-1507)
PHONE.................................313 872-0220
Amir Bashir, *Owner*
EMP: 20
SALES (est): 1.2MM **Privately Held**
SIC: 2038 Ethnic foods, frozen

(G-3944)
COMPOSITE FORGINGS LTD PARTNR
Also Called: Finkl Steel- Composite
2300 W Jefferson Ave (48216-2055)
P.O. Box 441457 (48244-1457)
PHONE.................................313 496-1226
Charles Brian Hopper, *Partner*
Paul Budd, *Vice Pres*
Jerry McDonald, *Safety Mgr*
Michael John Hammerly, *VP Finance*
▲ EMP: 76
SQ FT: 100,000
SALES (est): 15.1MM
SALES (corp-wide): 3.7B **Privately Held**
WEB: www.compforge.com
SIC: 3462 Iron & steel forgings
HQ: A. Finkl & Sons Co.
1355 E 93rd St
Chicago IL 60619
773 975-2510

(G-3945)
COMPUWARE CORPORATION (DH)
1 Campus Martius Fl 4 (48226-5099)
PHONE.................................313 227-7300
Chris O'Malley, *President*
Ken Baldwin, *President*
Christopher Omalley, *President*
Tommi White, *President*
Jim Langston, *Principal*
▲ EMP: 148
SQ FT: 1,100,000
SALES (est): 225.9MM **Privately Held**
WEB: www.compuware.com
SIC: 7371 7372 Computer software development; software programming applications; prepackaged software
HQ: Compuware Holdings, Llc
1 Campus Martius
Detroit MI 48226
313 227-7300

(G-3946)
CONANT GARDENERS
18621 San Juan Dr (48221-2173)
P.O. Box 21663 (48221-0663)
PHONE.................................313 863-2624
Clyde Hopkins, *Ch of Bd*
Orlin Jones, *Vice Pres*
Ray Chaney, *Treasurer*
Carol Carringdon, *Admin Sec*
EMP: 6
SALES: 300K **Privately Held**
SIC: 2731 Book publishing

(G-3947)
CONTRACTORS FENCE SERVICE
14900 Telegraph Rd (48239-3457)
PHONE.................................313 592-1300
Michael Novik, *CEO*
EMP: 35 EST: 1967
SQ FT: 12,000
SALES (est): 3.6MM **Privately Held**
WEB: www.contractorsfence.com
SIC: 1799 5211 2499 Fence construction; fencing; fencing, wood

(G-3948)
COOPERATIVE OPTICAL SERVICES (PA)
Also Called: Co Optical Service
2424 E 8 Mile Rd (48234-1010)
PHONE.................................313 366-5100
Jackee Smith, *President*
Charles Benson, *Senior VP*
Ben Edwards, *Vice Pres*
EMP: 68
SQ FT: 19,000
SALES (est): 15.7MM **Privately Held**
WEB: www.coopoptical.com
SIC: 5995 3851 Optical goods stores; frames, lenses & parts, eyeglass & spectacle

(G-3949)
COTTON CONCEPTS PRINTING LLC
1220 Longfellow St (48202-1545)
PHONE.................................313 444-3857
Ken Lemon,
EMP: 4
SALES: 46K **Privately Held**
SIC: 8099 3993 Health screening service; signs & advertising specialties

(G-3950)
CRAIN COMMUNICATIONS INC (PA)
Also Called: Genomeweb
1155 Gratiot Ave (48207-2732)
PHONE.................................313 446-6000
Keith E Crain, *CEO*
Rance E Crain, *President*
William Bisson, *Publisher*
Mary Kramer, *Publisher*
Karen Rentschler, *Publisher*
EMP: 310 EST: 1916
SQ FT: 100,000
SALES: 225MM **Privately Held**
WEB: www.crainsnewyork.com
SIC: 2721 2711 Magazines: publishing only, not printed on site; newspapers, publishing & printing

(G-3951)
CRAIN COMMUNICATIONS INC
Also Called: Crain's Chicago Business
1155 Gratiot Ave (48207-2732)
PHONE.................................313 446-6000
Keith E Crain, *Ch of Bd*
Kathleen Ligocki, *President*
Kurlander Brisky, *Partner*
Ferrazzano Kirschbaum, *Partner*
Alison V Mikula, *Partner*
EMP: 300
SALES (corp-wide): 225MM **Privately Held**
WEB: www.crainsnewyork.com
SIC: 2721 5521 2711 Magazines: publishing only, not printed on site; used car dealers; newspapers
PA: Crain Communications, Inc.
1155 Gratiot Ave
Detroit MI 48207
313 446-6000

(G-3952)
CRAIN COMMUNICATIONS INC
Also Called: Advertising Age Magazine
1155 Gratiot Ave (48207-2732)
PHONE.................................313 446-6000
David May, *Editor*
Keith Crain, *Chairman*
Nettie Boivin, *Corp Comm Staff*
EMP: 300
SALES (corp-wide): 225MM **Privately Held**
WEB: www.crainsnewyork.com
SIC: 2721 Periodicals: publishing & printing
PA: Crain Communications, Inc.
1155 Gratiot Ave
Detroit MI 48207
313 446-6000

(G-3953)
CRC INDUSTRIES INC
Also Called: Weld-Aid Products
14650 Dequindre St (48212-1504)
PHONE.................................313 883-6977
EMP: 25
SALES (corp-wide): 2.9B **Privately Held**
SIC: 2899 Fluxes: brazing, soldering, galvanizing & welding
HQ: Crc Industries, Inc.
800 Enterprise Rd Ste 103
Horsham PA 19044
215 674-4300

(G-3954)
CREATIVE POWER SYSTEMS INC
Also Called: Power Without Wires
1921 10th St (48216-1518)
PHONE.................................313 961-2460
Murray Davis, *CEO*
EMP: 20
SQ FT: 8,000
SALES: 500K **Privately Held**
SIC: 3825 7539 Power measuring equipment, electrical; electrical services

(G-3955)
CROWN HEATING INC
24521 W Mcnichols Rd (48219-3654)
PHONE.................................248 352-1688
Floyd Caver, *President*
EMP: 4
SALES (est): 545.1K **Privately Held**
SIC: 1542 1721 3585 1711 Commercial & office building contractors; residential wallcovering contractor; heating & air conditioning combination units; heating systems repair & maintenance; heating & air conditioning contractors; warm air heating & air conditioning contractor; boilers, low-pressure heating: steam or hot water

(G-3956)
CTE PUBLISHING LLC
18451 Rosemont Ave (48219-2919)
PHONE.................................313 338-4335
Clarence Terrell, *President*
EMP: 5
SALES (est): 360K **Privately Held**
SIC: 2721 Magazines: publishing & printing

(G-3957)
CUMMINGS-MOORE GRAPHITE CO
1646 N Green St (48209-2093)
PHONE.................................313 841-1615
Michael Mares, *President*
Debra L Nowacki, *General Mgr*
William T Meglaughlin, *Treasurer*
H Marvin Riddle III, *Admin Sec*
▲ EMP: 24 EST: 1916
SALES (est): 6.1MM
SALES (corp-wide): 126.7MM **Privately Held**
SIC: 3624 2992 2899 Carbon & graphite products; lubricating oils & greases; chemical preparations
PA: Asbury Carbons, Inc.
405 Old Main St
Asbury NJ 08802
908 537-2155

(G-3958)
CUSTO ARCH SHEE META
Also Called: Cass
5641 Conner St (48213-3407)
PHONE.................................313 571-2277
Glen Parvin, *President*
Ed Wloszek, *Project Mgr*
Greg Gietek, *Administration*
EMP: 15
SQ FT: 12,000
SALES (est): 2.5MM **Privately Held**
WEB: www.casssheetmetal.com
SIC: 1761 3444 Architectural sheet metal work; sheet metalwork

(G-3959)
D & W SQUARE LLC
8932 Coyle St (48228-2359)
PHONE.................................313 493-4970
Willie Pitts,
Dennis Bright,
EMP: 5
SALES: 60K **Privately Held**
SIC: 3612 Voltage regulators, transmission & distribution

(G-3960)
DAC INC
2930 S Dartmouth St (48217-1019)
PHONE.................................313 388-4342
Douglas Crouther, *President*
EMP: 50
SALES (est): 1MM **Privately Held**
SIC: 2731 Book publishing

(G-3961)
DAUGHTERY GROUP INC
16892 Parkside St (48221-3155)
PHONE.................................313 452-7918
Robert L Daughtery, *President*
EMP: 4
SALES: 3K **Privately Held**
SIC: 3449 Bars, concrete reinforcing: fabricated steel

(G-3962)
DCR SERVICES & CNSTR INC (PA)
828 S Dix St (48217-1304)
PHONE.................................313 297-6544
Dwight Belyue, *CEO*
EMP: 12
SALES (est): 700K **Privately Held**
SIC: 1541 0782 8748 0781 Industrial buildings & warehouses; lawn & garden services; business consulting; landscape counseling & planning; oil & gas exploration services; surveying services

(G-3963)
DE WITT PRODUCTS CO
5860 Plumer St (48209-1398)
PHONE.................................313 554-0575
Donald D McClellan, *President*
Jack McClellan, *Exec VP*
Ed Rader, *Vice Pres*
Jack D McClellan Jr, *CFO*
▲ EMP: 22 EST: 1931
SQ FT: 60,000
SALES (est): 6.2MM **Privately Held**
WEB: www.dewittproducts.com
SIC: 2952 Roofing felts, cements or coatings

(G-3964)
DEADLINE DETROIT
66 Winder St Apt 443 (48201-3131)
PHONE.................................248 219-5985
Allan Lengel, *Administration*
EMP: 3
SALES (est): 146.7K **Privately Held**
SIC: 2711 Newspapers, publishing & printing

(G-3965)
DEALER AID ENTERPRISES
Also Called: A-Day Badge Co
8200 E Jefferson Ave # 604 (48214-3974)
PHONE.................................313 331-5800
Geraldine Tigner, *Owner*
EMP: 4
SQ FT: 3,800
SALES: 500K **Privately Held**
SIC: 3999 5199 Badges, metal: policemen, firemen, etc.; advertising specialties

Detroit - Wayne County (G-3966)

GEOGRAPHIC SECTION

(G-3966)
DEARBORN MID WEST CONVEYOR CO
19440 Glendale St (48223-3426)
PHONE....................313 273-2804
Johnny Lindeman, *Principal*
▲ **EMP:** 6
SALES (est): 625.4K **Privately Held**
SIC: 3535 Conveyors & conveying equipment

(G-3967)
DELTA IRON WORKS INC
1801 Meldrum St (48207-3497)
PHONE....................313 579-1445
Chris Manor, *President*
Lorraine L Manos, *President*
Kathy Manor, *Vice Pres*
Chris Manos, *Vice Pres*
Kathy Manos, *Vice Pres*
EMP: 13
SQ FT: 32,000
SALES (est): 2MM **Privately Held**
SIC: 3444 3443 Sheet metalwork; fabricated plate work (boiler shop)

(G-3968)
DESLATAE
5522 Bluehill St (48224-2109)
PHONE....................313 820-4321
Laura Bragg, *Principal*
EMP: 5
SALES (est): 193.2K **Privately Held**
SIC: 2741 Miscellaneous publishing

(G-3969)
DETMAR CORPORATION
2001 W Alexandrine St (48208-2605)
P.O. Box 8098 (48208-0098)
PHONE....................313 831-1155
George A Wrigley, *President*
Dean Henkel, *Controller*
▲ **EMP:** 15 **EST:** 1958
SQ FT: 70,000
SALES (est): 2.9MM **Privately Held**
WEB: www.detmarcorp.com
SIC: 3429 Marine hardware; motor vehicle hardware

(G-3970)
DETROIT ART COLLECTION LLC
1074 Woodward Ave (48226-1906)
PHONE....................313 373-7689
Jennifer Gilbert, *Mng Member*
EMP: 3 **EST:** 2016
SALES: 53K **Privately Held**
SIC: 3993 7372 Advertising artwork; application computer software

(G-3971)
DETROIT BIKES LLC (PA)
13639 Elmira St (48227-3015)
PHONE....................313 646-4109
Tina Johnson, *Human Res Mgr*
Vak Pashak, *Mng Member*
Stephen Cuomo, *Manager*
Kathie Marlin, *Manager*
▲ **EMP:** 9
SQ FT: 50,000
SALES (est): 800K **Privately Held**
SIC: 3751 5941 Bicycles & related parts; bicycle & bicycle parts

(G-3972)
DETROIT BOILER COMPANY (PA)
2931 Beaufait St (48207-3401)
PHONE....................313 921-7060
Ronald Johnson, *President*
Chris Lanzon, *President*
Craig Lanzon, *Superintendent*
EMP: 15
SQ FT: 23,000
SALES: 4MM **Privately Held**
SIC: 1711 3443 Boiler maintenance contractor; boiler setting contractor; fabricated plate work (boiler shop)

(G-3973)
DETROIT BUYERS CLUB LLC
18914 Stoepel St (48221-2253)
PHONE....................248 871-7827
Demetrius Frank, *Principal*
EMP: 3

SALES: 50K **Privately Held**
SIC: 3634 Vaporizers, electric: household

(G-3974)
DETROIT CHASSIS LLC
6501 Lynch Rd (48234-4140)
PHONE....................313 571-2100
Michael J Guthrie, *Mng Member*
Joseph W Gause, *Mng Member*
Carlton Guthrie, *Mng Member*
Linda Ratliff, *Manager*
▲ **EMP:** 4
SQ FT: 218,000
SALES (est): 25.6MM
SALES (corp-wide): 21.8MM **Privately Held**
WEB: www.detroitchassis.com
SIC: 3711 Chassis, motor vehicle
PA: Spectra Lmp, Llc
    6501 Lynch Rd
    Detroit MI 48234
    313 571-2100

(G-3975)
DETROIT CHILI CO INC
11575 Harper Ave (48213-1632)
PHONE....................313 521-6323
Tim Keros, *Manager*
EMP: 3
SALES (corp-wide): 451.8K **Privately Held**
SIC: 2032 Chili with or without meat: packaged in cans, jars, etc.
PA: Detroit Chili Co Inc
    21400 Telegraph Rd
    Southfield MI 48033
    248 440-5933

(G-3976)
DETROIT CHROME INC
Also Called: DCI Aerotech
7515 Lyndon St (48238-2481)
PHONE....................313 341-9478
Ronald N Nichols Sr, *President*
Bruce Nichols, *Vice Pres*
Bryan Nichols, *Vice Pres*
Ronald Nichols II, *Vice Pres*
Matthew J Howell CPA, *CFO*
EMP: 48
SQ FT: 100,000
SALES (est): 8MM **Privately Held**
WEB: www.detroitchrome.com
SIC: 3471 7389 Electroplating of metals or formed products; plating of metals or formed products; finishing, metals or formed products; grinding, precision: commercial or industrial

(G-3977)
DETROIT CITY DISTILLERY LLC
Also Called: Spirits of Detroit, The
2462 Riopelle St (48207-4525)
PHONE....................313 338-3760
John Paul Jerone,
EMP: 11
SALES (est): 1.7MM **Privately Held**
SIC: 2085 Distilled & blended liquors

(G-3978)
DETROIT CUSTOM CHASSIS LLC
6501 Lynch Rd (48234-4140)
PHONE....................313 571-2100
Anderson L Dobbins, *Vice Pres*
Anderson Dobbins, *VP Opers*
Joseph Gause, *CFO*
Michael J Guthrie, *Mng Member*
Carlton Guthrie, *Mng Member*
EMP: 225
SQ FT: 200,000
SALES (est): 15.4MM
SALES (corp-wide): 21.8MM **Privately Held**
SIC: 3711 Chassis, motor vehicle
PA: Spectra Lmp, Llc
    6501 Lynch Rd
    Detroit MI 48234
    313 571-2100

(G-3979)
DETROIT DENIM LLC
1401 Vermont St Ste 164 (48216-1884)
PHONE....................313 626-9216
EMP: 3
SALES (est): 62K **Privately Held**
SIC: 2211 Denims

(G-3980)
DETROIT DIESEL CORPORATION (HQ)
Also Called: Detroit Diesel USA
13400 W Outer Dr (48239-1309)
PHONE....................313 592-5000
Eckhard Cordes, *Ch of Bd*
Jeffrey Latkiewicz, *General Mgr*
Sandeep Singh, *General Mgr*
Keith Vaugn, *Area Mgr*
Roman Laczkovich, *Vice Pres*
◆ **EMP:** 3500
SQ FT: 3,000,000
SALES (est): 2.1B
SALES (corp-wide): 191.6B **Privately Held**
WEB: www.detroitdeisel.com
SIC: 3519 3714 7538 Engines, diesel & semi-diesel or dual-fuel; diesel engine rebuilding; motor vehicle engines & parts; diesel engine repair: automotive
PA: Daimler Ag
    Mercedesstr. 120
    Stuttgart 70372
    711 170-

(G-3981)
DETROIT DIRT LLC
2503 22nd St (48216-1076)
PHONE....................616 260-4383
Pashon Murray, *President*
EMP: 3 **EST:** 2016
SALES (est): 149.1K **Privately Held**
SIC: 2873 Fertilizers: natural (organic), except compost

(G-3982)
DETROIT DUMPSTER INC
8701 Grinnell St (48213-1152)
PHONE....................313 466-3174
EMP: 9
SALES (est): 1.2MM **Privately Held**
SIC: 3443 Dumpsters, garbage

(G-3983)
DETROIT EDGE TOOL COMPANY (PA)
Also Called: Michigan Flame Hardening
6570 E Nevada St (48234-2866)
PHONE....................313 366-4120
Raymond R Ebbing, *Ch of Bd*
Karen Hayes, *COO*
John Ebbing, *Vice Pres*
Jerome Madynski, *Vice Pres*
▲ **EMP:** 100
SQ FT: 35,000
SALES (est): 34.1MM **Privately Held**
WEB: www.detroitedge.com
SIC: 3599 3545 3423 Machine & other job shop work; machine knives, metalworking; hand & edge tools

(G-3984)
DETROIT FD ENTRPRNRSHIP ACDEMY
Also Called: DETROIT FOOD ACADEMY
4444 2nd Ave (48201-1216)
PHONE....................248 894-8941
Jacob Schoenknecht, *Opers Staff*
Jen Rusciano, *Exec Dir*
Angela Abiodun, *Program Dir*
EMP: 13
SALES: 529.5K **Privately Held**
SIC: 8211 8299 2064 Academy; cooking school; granola & muesli, bars & clusters

(G-3985)
DETROIT FRNDS POTATO CHIPS LLC
8230 E Forest Ave (48214-1156)
PHONE....................313 924-0085
Michael Wimberley,
EMP: 6
SALES: 5K **Privately Held**
SIC: 2096 Potato chips & other potato-based snacks

(G-3986)
DETROIT IMPRESSION COMPANY INC
1111 Bellevue St Unit 100 (48207-3675)
PHONE....................313 921-9077
Edward W Godsalve, *President*
EMP: 3

SALES (est): 219.3K **Privately Held**
SIC: 2759 Screen printing

(G-3987)
DETROIT LEGAL NEWS COMPANY (PA)
Also Called: Inland Press
2001 W Lafayette Blvd (48216-1880)
PHONE....................313 961-6000
Bradley L Thompson II, *President*
Michael Mc Masters, *Vice Pres*
Andy Thompson, *Engineer*
Steve Fowler, *CFO*
Marsha Johnson, *Bookkeeper*
▲ **EMP:** 60 **EST:** 1895
SQ FT: 65,000
SALES (est): 7.9MM **Privately Held**
WEB: www.inlandpress.com
SIC: 2711 2721 Commercial printing & newspaper publishing combined; periodicals: publishing & printing

(G-3988)
DETROIT LITHO INC
8200 W Outer Dr (48219-3580)
PHONE....................313 993-6186
Rick McCarty, *President*
EMP: 4
SQ FT: 3,000
SALES: 600K **Privately Held**
WEB: www.net-fusion.com
SIC: 2752 Commercial printing, lithographic

(G-3989)
DETROIT MFG SYSTEMS LLC (PA)
12701 Suthfield Rd Bldg A (48223)
PHONE....................313 243-0700
Andra M Rush, *CEO*
Tony Pashigian, *Vice Pres*
Charles R Pear, *CFO*
Michael Rutkowski, *Treasurer*
John White, *Accounting Mgr*
EMP: 60 **EST:** 2011
SQ FT: 480,000
SALES (est): 19.8MM **Privately Held**
SIC: 3711 Automobile bodies, passenger car, not including engine, etc.

(G-3990)
DETROIT NEWS INC
Also Called: Detroit News, The
600 W Fort St (48226-3138)
PHONE....................313 222-6400
Joyce Jenereaux, *President*
Kevin Bull, *Editor*
John Gallagher, *Editor*
Brian Manzullo, *Editor*
Rose McKean, *Editor*
EMP: 290 **EST:** 1840
SALES (est): 44.7MM
SALES (corp-wide): 2.9B **Publicly Held**
SIC: 2711 Newspapers: publishing only, not printed on site
PA: Gannett Co., Inc.
    7950 Jones Branch Dr
    Mc Lean VA 22102
    703 854-6000

(G-3991)
DETROIT NEWS INC (DH)
Also Called: Detroit News, The
160 W Fort St (48226-3700)
PHONE....................313 222-2300
Jona Thanwolman, *Editor*
David J Butler, *Editor*
Kelly Root, *Manager*
Drew Vantongeren, *Director*
EMP: 290 **EST:** 1970
SQ FT: 300,000
SALES (est): 52.3MM
SALES (corp-wide): 4.2B **Privately Held**
SIC: 2711 4833 Newspapers, publishing & printing; television broadcasting stations

(G-3992)
DETROIT NEWS INC
Also Called: Detroit News, The
3801 W Jefferson Ave (48216-1610)
PHONE....................313 223-4500
Raymond Freeman, *Director*
EMP: 3
SALES (corp-wide): 4.2B **Privately Held**
SIC: 2711 Newspapers

GEOGRAPHIC SECTION
Detroit - Wayne County (G-4018)

HQ: The Detroit News Inc
160 W Fort St
Detroit MI 48226
313 222-2300

(G-3993)
DETROIT NEWS INC
Also Called: Detroit News, The
615 W Lafayette Blvd (48226-3124)
PHONE...................313 222-6400
Kelly Root, *Manager*
EMP: 6
SALES (corp-wide): 4.2B **Privately Held**
SIC: 2711 Newspapers
HQ: The Detroit News Inc
160 W Fort St
Detroit MI 48226
313 222-2300

(G-3994)
DETROIT NEWSPAPER PARTNR LP (HQ)
Also Called: Detroit Media Partnership
160 W Fort St (48226-3700)
PHONE...................313 222-2300
Dean Krajewski, *President*
Joyce Jenereaux, *Partner*
Tracey M Medley, *Partner*
Mark J Brown, *Vice Pres*
Karen Carpenter, *Accountant*
EMP: 700
SQ FT: 300,000
SALES (est): 387.7MM
SALES (corp-wide): 2.9B **Publicly Held**
WEB: www.dnps.com
SIC: 2711 Newspapers: publishing only; not printed on site; newspapers, publishing & printing
PA: Gannett Co., Inc.
7950 Jones Branch Dr
Mc Lean VA 22102
703 854-6000

(G-3995)
DETROIT NEWSPAPER PARTNR LP
600 W Fort St (48226-3138)
PHONE...................313 222-6400
Frank J Vega, *President*
EMP: 503
SALES (corp-wide): 2.9B **Publicly Held**
WEB: www.dnps.com
SIC: 2711 Newspapers, publishing & printing
HQ: Detroit Newspaper Partnership, L.P.
160 W Fort St
Detroit MI 48226
313 222-2300

(G-3996)
DETROIT NIPPLE WORKS INC (PA)
Also Called: Taylor Supply Company, The
6530 Beaubien St (48202-3226)
PHONE...................313 872-6370
Richard I Larsen, *President*
Michael Larsen, *Vice Pres*
Nancy Larsen, *Treasurer*
EMP: 13 **EST:** 1934
SQ FT: 41,000
SALES (est): 6.5MM **Privately Held**
SIC: 5085 3498 Valves & fittings; fabricated pipe & fittings

(G-3997)
DETROIT PLATE FABRICATORS INC
2931 Beaufait St (48207-3401)
PHONE...................313 921-7020
Amante C Lanzon, *President*
EMP: 8
SQ FT: 23,000
SALES (est): 861.9K
SALES (corp-wide): 4MM **Privately Held**
SIC: 3443 Fabricated plate work (boiler shop)
PA: Detroit Boiler Company
2931 Beaufait St
Detroit MI 48207
313 921-7060

(G-3998)
DETROIT READY MIX CONCRETE
9189 Central St (48204-4323)
PHONE...................313 931-7043
Shel Wheatley, *President*
Shelby Wheatley, *Manager*
EMP: 12
SALES (est): 2.4MM **Privately Held**
SIC: 3273 4212 Ready-mixed concrete; delivery service, vehicular

(G-3999)
DETROIT RENEWABLE ENERGY LLC
5700 Russell St (48211-2545)
PHONE...................313 972-5700
Steven A White, *CEO*
Eric Vanhouten, *Director*
James Royce, *Officer*
EMP: 151
SALES (est): 28.5MM **Privately Held**
SIC: 3612 5211 Power & distribution transformers; energy conservation products

(G-4000)
DETROIT RIVERTWN BREWING CO LL
Also Called: Atwater Brewery
237 Joseph Campau St (48207-4107)
PHONE...................313 877-9205
Mark Rieth, *Mng Member*
Mark Rieth, *Mng Member*
EMP: 150 **EST:** 2004
SALES (est): 17.1MM **Privately Held**
SIC: 2082 5812 Malt beverages; American restaurant

(G-4001)
DETROIT SALT COMPANY LC (HQ)
12841 Sanders St (48217-1407)
PHONE...................313 554-0456
Janette Ferrantino, *President*
EMP: 40
SALES (est): 41.6MM
SALES (corp-wide): 5MM **Privately Held**
SIC: 1481 Nonmetallic mineral services
PA: Kissner Group Holdings Lp
148 Manitou Dr Suite 301
Kitchener ON N2C 1
519 279-4860

(G-4002)
DETROIT SAUSAGE CO INC
2715 Saint Aubin St (48207-2107)
PHONE...................313 259-0555
Anthony Peters, *President*
Charles Peters, *Corp Secy*
Phillip Peters Jr, *Vice Pres*
EMP: 10
SQ FT: 8,000
SALES (est): 1.3MM **Privately Held**
WEB: www.detroitsausage.com
SIC: 2013 Sausages from purchased meat

(G-4003)
DETROIT TUBE PRODUCTS LLC
300 S Junction St (48209-3192)
PHONE...................313 841-0300
M Therese Bellaimey,
EMP: 25 **EST:** 1911
SQ FT: 37,000
SALES (est): 5.4MM **Privately Held**
SIC: 3498 Tube fabricating (contract bending & shaping)

(G-4004)
DETROIT TUBING MILL INC
12301 Hubbell St (48227-3900)
PHONE...................313 491-8823
Kenneth Kokko, *President*
Rudolph Taylor, *President*
Peter G Corriveau, *Vice Pres*
Jimmie R Edwards, *Vice Pres*
EMP: 28 **EST:** 1978
SQ FT: 100,000
SALES (est): 9.1MM **Privately Held**
SIC: 3317 Tubes, wrought: welded or lock joint

(G-4005)
DETROIT WRECKER SALES LLC
19303 W Davison St (48223-3418)
PHONE...................313 835-8700
Mike Farrell, *CEO*
Rick Farrell, *Mng Member*
EMP: 6
SQ FT: 12,100
SALES (est): 1.2MM **Privately Held**
WEB: www.detroitwrecker.com
SIC: 3799 5511 Towing bars & systems; pickups, new & used

(G-4006)
DEVELOPMENTAL SERVICES INC
13621 Park Grove St (48205-2838)
PHONE...................313 653-1185
Johnnie Bennett, *Principal*
Miranda Sanders, *Principal*
Rhonda Sanders, *Agent*
EMP: 4
SALES (est): 50K **Privately Held**
SIC: 2731 6531 7389 Books: publishing only; real estate brokers & agents; music recording producer

(G-4007)
DHS INC
1925 Elsmere St (48209-1436)
PHONE...................313 724-6566
EMP: 4
SALES (est): 240K **Privately Held**
SIC: 3543 Mfg Industrial Patterns

(G-4008)
DIETERT FOUNDRY TESTING EQP (PA)
9190 Roselawn St (48204-5903)
PHONE...................313 491-4680
David Miller, *President*
David E Miller, *President*
Raymond R Booth, *Treasurer*
Darlene T Miller, *Admin Sec*
EMP: 5
SQ FT: 7,359
SALES (est): 1.1MM **Privately Held**
WEB: www.dietertlab.com
SIC: 3829 Testing equipment: abrasion, shearing strength, etc.

(G-4009)
DIGITAL INFORMATION SVCS LLC
19954 Conant St Ste B (48234-1595)
P.O. Box 19058 (48219-0058)
PHONE...................313 365-7299
George Williams, *President*
Katina Bryant,
EMP: 3
SQ FT: 2,976
SALES (est): 100.5K **Privately Held**
SIC: 3993 Signs & advertising specialties

(G-4010)
DIVERSIFIED CHEM TECHNOLOGIES
15477 Woodrow Wilson St (48238-1586)
PHONE...................313 867-5444
George H Hill, *President*
Arnold F Joseff, *Vice Pres*
Fawzi Tomey, *Vice Pres*
EMP: 200
SQ FT: 51,000
SALES: 16.3MM
SALES (corp-wide): 92.6MM **Privately Held**
WEB: www.dchem.com
SIC: 2865 Cyclic crudes & intermediates
PA: Diversified Chemical Technologies, Inc.
15477 Woodrow Wilson St
Detroit MI 48238
313 867-5444

(G-4011)
DIVERSIFIED CHEMICAL TECH INC (PA)
15477 Woodrow Wilson St (48238-1586)
PHONE...................313 867-5444
George H Hill, *President*
Arnold F Joseff, *Vice Pres*
EMP: 170 **EST:** 1971
SQ FT: 51,000
SALES (est): 92.6MM **Privately Held**
WEB: www.diversifiedchemicalinc.com
SIC: 2891 2992 2899 2842 Sealing compounds, synthetic rubber or plastic; glue; epoxy adhesives; lubricating oils & greases; chemical preparations; specialty cleaning, polishes & sanitation goods; soap & other detergents

(G-4012)
DIVERSITAK INC
15477 Woodrow Wilson St (48238-1586)
PHONE...................313 869-8500
Pam Newton, *Manager*
▲ **EMP:** 50
SALES: 13.3MM **Privately Held**
SIC: 2891 Adhesives

(G-4013)
DLH WORLD LLC
2517 Hazelwood St (48206-2291)
PHONE...................313 915-0274
Derek Higgins, *President*
EMP: 4 **EST:** 2016
SALES (est): 189.9K **Privately Held**
SIC: 3272 Sills, concrete

(G-4014)
DO-ALL PLASTIC INC
1265 Terminal St (48214-3444)
PHONE...................313 824-6565
Gary Laduke, *President*
Gary La Duke, *President*
Melinda Stine, *QC Dir*
EMP: 11 **EST:** 1953
SQ FT: 20,000
SALES (est): 1.6MM **Privately Held**
SIC: 3089 Injection molding of plastics

(G-4015)
DORDEN & COMPANY INC
Also Called: Dorden Squeegees
7446 Central St (48210-1037)
P.O. Box 10247 (48210-0247)
PHONE...................313 834-7910
Bruce Gale, *President*
▲ **EMP:** 7
SQ FT: 10,000
SALES (est): 810.3K **Privately Held**
WEB: www.dordensqueegee.com
SIC: 3999 Window squeegees

(G-4016)
DOUTHITT CORPORATION (PA)
245 Adair St (48207-4287)
PHONE...................313 259-1565
Robert J Diehl, *Ch of Bd*
Douglas Diehl, *Co-President*
John Diehl, *Co-President*
Mark Diehl, *Co-President*
James Haggerty Jr, *Co-President*
▲ **EMP:** 40
SQ FT: 26,000
SALES (est): 5.6MM **Privately Held**
WEB: www.douthittcorp.com
SIC: 3861 3555 Printing equipment, photographic; printing trades machinery

(G-4017)
DOUTHITT CORPORATION
277 Adair St (48207-4246)
PHONE...................313 259-1565
Robert J Diehl, *Branch Mgr*
EMP: 10
SALES (corp-wide): 5.6MM **Privately Held**
WEB: www.douthittcorp.com
SIC: 3861 Printing equipment, photographic
PA: Douthitt Corporation
245 Adair St
Detroit MI 48207
313 259-1565

(G-4018)
DSW HOLDINGS INC (PA)
400 Renaissance Ctr Lbby (48243-1607)
PHONE...................313 567-4500
Daniel S Weiss, *President*
Chris Fitch, *Vice Pres*
Jim Hart, *Vice Pres*
Mayank Batra, *Consultant*
EMP: 1
SQ FT: 3,000

Detroit - Wayne County (G-4019) GEOGRAPHIC SECTION

SALES (est): 8.8MM **Privately Held**
WEB: www.dswholdings.com
SIC: 2899 Water treating compounds

(G-4019)
DTE ENERGY COMPANY (PA)
1 Energy Plz (48226-1221)
PHONE..................313 235-4000
Barry Matherly, *CEO*
Jerry Norcia, *President*
Christy Wicke, *General Mgr*
Karen Weiss, *Principal*
Peter Dietrich, *Senior VP*
▼ EMP: 20
SALES: 14.2B **Publicly Held**
WEB: www.dteenergy.com
SIC: 4911 4923 1311 ; generation, electric power; transmission, electric power; ; gas transmission & distribution; crude petroleum & natural gas

(G-4020)
DTE ENERGY RESOURCES INC
Also Called: Ees Coke Battery
1400 Zug Island Rd (48209-2892)
P.O. Box 18309 (48218-0309)
PHONE..................313 297-4203
Gary Gross, *Manager*
EMP: 137 **Publicly Held**
SIC: 4911 1389 Electric services; gas field services
HQ: Dte Energy Resources, Inc.
414 S Main St Ste 600
Ann Arbor MI 48104

(G-4021)
DTE ENERGY TRUST II
2000 2nd Ave (48226-1279)
PHONE..................313 235-8822
Michael A McNalley, *President*
Steve Hare, *Engineer*
EMP: 1
SALES: 22.3MM **Publicly Held**
WEB: www.dteenergy.com
SIC: 4911 4923 1311 ; gas transmission & distribution; crude petroleum & natural gas
PA: Dte Energy Company
1 Energy Plz
Detroit MI 48226

(G-4022)
DYNATRACE LLC
Also Called: Smartscape
2000 Brush St Ste 501 (48226-2266)
PHONE..................313 227-7300
Shawn White, *Vice Pres*
Kevin Burns, *CFO*
Mark Bunch, *Accounting Mgr*
Mary Lee, *Finance*
Mike Maciag, *Chief Mktg Ofcr*
EMP: 76
SALES (corp-wide): 430.9MM **Publicly Held**
SIC: 7372 Application computer software
HQ: Dynatrace Holdings Llc
1601 Trapelo Rd Ste 116
Waltham MA 02451
781 530-1000

(G-4023)
EAST CENTRAL MACHINE INC
5718 Saint Jean St (48213-3415)
PHONE..................313 579-2315
Jozef Jablonski, *President*
EMP: 8
SQ FT: 5,000
SALES (est): 487.4K **Privately Held**
SIC: 3599 Machine shop, jobbing & repair

(G-4024)
EASTSIDE PHARMACY INC
Also Called: Health Mart
4673 Conner St (48215-2028)
PHONE..................313 579-1755
Raef Hamaed, *President*
EMP: 11
SALES (est): 1.4MM **Privately Held**
SIC: 2834 Pharmaceutical preparations

(G-4025)
EATON DETROIT SPRING SVC CO
1555 Michigan Ave (48216-1325)
PHONE..................313 963-3839
Michael M Eaton, *President*
Kim Mitchell, *Vice Pres*
Sandy Eaton, *Office Mgr*
EMP: 10 EST: 1937
SQ FT: 8,200
SALES (est): 1.4MM **Privately Held**
WEB: www.eatonsprings.com
SIC: 3493 Leaf springs: automobile, locomotive, etc.

(G-4026)
ECLECTIC METAL ARTS LLC
20225 Livernois Ave (48221-1283)
PHONE..................248 251-5924
Dennis Graham, *CEO*
EMP: 8
SALES (est): 323.9K **Privately Held**
SIC: 3339 Primary nonferrous metals

(G-4027)
EDEN FOODS INC
Also Called: Eden Organic Pasta Company
9104 Culver St (48213-2237)
PHONE..................313 921-2053
Steven Swaney, *Manager*
EMP: 12
SALES (corp-wide): 42.7MM **Privately Held**
WEB: www.edenfoods.com
SIC: 2098 Noodles (e.g. egg, plain & water), dry
PA: Eden Foods, Inc.
701 Tecumseh Rd
Clinton MI 49236
517 456-7424

(G-4028)
EDW C LEVY CO
Also Called: Milford Sand & Gravel
8800 Dix St (48209-1093)
PHONE..................313 843-7200
Edward C Levy Jr, *President*
EMP: 100
SALES (corp-wide): 368.1MM **Privately Held**
WEB: www.edwclevy.com
SIC: 3273 3295 5032 2951 Ready-mixed concrete; minerals, ground or treated; aggregate; asphalt & asphaltic paving mixtures (not from refineries); highway & street paving contractor
PA: Edw. C. Levy Co.
9300 Dix
Dearborn MI 48120
313 429-2200

(G-4029)
EDWARDS BUILDING & HM SUP INC
Also Called: Edward's Kitchen & Bath
30 E 8 Mile Rd (48203-1124)
PHONE..................313 368-9120
Marianthe Joanides, *President*
Alex Joanides, *Admin Sec*
EMP: 8
SQ FT: 9,000
SALES (est): 1MM **Privately Held**
SIC: 2434 Wood kitchen cabinets

(G-4030)
EHC INC (PA)
Also Called: Evans Holding Company
200 Renaissance Ctr # 3150 (48243-1300)
PHONE..................313 259-2266
Robert B Evans Jr, *Ch of Bd*
▲ EMP: 8
SALES (est): 43.7MM **Privately Held**
SIC: 3366 3365 3519 3621 Brass foundry; aluminum foundries; marine engines; motors & generators; injection molded finished plastic products; hard rubber & molded rubber products

(G-4031)
ELECTRIC MOTOR & CONTG CO
1133 W Baltimore St (48202-2905)
PHONE..................313 871-3775
Patricia Farris, *President*
David Jager, *Vice Pres*
Pat Farris, *Manager*
EMP: 10
SQ FT: 6,000
SALES: 758.8K **Privately Held**
SIC: 7694 7699 Electric motor repair; industrial machinery & equipment repair

(G-4032)
ELITE FUELS LLC
1140 Clay St (48211-1941)
PHONE..................313 871-6308
Ismail Sayied, *Principal*
EMP: 3 EST: 2011
SALES (est): 172.2K **Privately Held**
SIC: 2869 Fuels

(G-4033)
ELLIS INFINITY LLC
1545 Clay St Unit 6 (48211-1911)
PHONE..................313 570-0840
Nailah Ellis- Brown, *Mng Member*
EMP: 9
SQ FT: 4,000
SALES: 105K **Privately Held**
SIC: 2086 5149 Iced tea & fruit drinks, bottled & canned; tea

(G-4034)
ELMWOOD MANUFACTURING COMPANY
3925 Beaufait St (48207-1861)
PHONE..................313 571-1777
Felix Zagumny, *President*
EMP: 4
SQ FT: 2,000
SALES (est): 330.1K **Privately Held**
SIC: 3714 Motor vehicle parts & accessories

(G-4035)
EMBERS BALLSCREW REPAIR
10200 Grinnell St (48213-1167)
PHONE..................586 216-8444
Ernie Williams, *Owner*
EMP: 12
SQ FT: 6,000
SALES (est): 500K **Privately Held**
WEB: www.embersballscrewrepair.com
SIC: 3451 Screw machine products

(G-4036)
EMCO CHEMICAL INC
4470 Lawton St (48208-2198)
PHONE..................313 894-7650
Emrys Davies, *President*
EMP: 12 EST: 1962
SQ FT: 21,000
SALES: 7MM **Privately Held**
SIC: 2899 Rust resisting compounds; metal treating compounds

(G-4037)
EMERSON PROCESS MANAGEMENT
3031 W Grand Blvd Ste 423 (48202-3008)
PHONE..................313 874-0860
EMP: 206
SALES (corp-wide): 17.4B **Publicly Held**
SIC: 3823 Industrial instrmnts msrmnt display/control process variable
HQ: Emerson Process Management Power & Water Solutions, Inc.
200 Beta Dr
Pittsburgh PA 15238
412 963-4000

(G-4038)
ENGINEERING REPRODUCTION INC (PA)
13550 Conant St (48212-1602)
PHONE..................313 366-3390
Shawna Cornish, *President*
Jonathan Shuert, *General Mgr*
EMP: 13 EST: 1942
SQ FT: 8,700
SALES (est): 2.3MM **Privately Held**
WEB: www.eng-repro.com
SIC: 7334 7389 2399 3993 Blueprinting service; laminating service; banners, made from fabric; advertising novelties

(G-4039)
ENVIRODRONE INC
440 Burroughs St (48202-3429)
PHONE..................226 344-5614
Ryan Cant, *CEO*
EMP: 5
SALES (est): 203.2K **Privately Held**
SIC: 3861 Aerial cameras

(G-4040)
EPIC 4D LLC
98 Hague St (48202-2119)
PHONE..................800 470-8948
Melvin Claxton, *Mng Member*
EMP: 5 EST: 2014
SQ FT: 1,000
SALES (est): 239.1K **Privately Held**
SIC: 7372 Educational computer software

(G-4041)
ESPINOZA BROS
2397 Stair St (48209-1209)
PHONE..................313 468-7775
Enrique Espinoza, *Principal*
EMP: 3
SALES (est): 282.2K **Privately Held**
SIC: 3272 Fireplace & chimney material: concrete

(G-4042)
ESSENTIAL SCREEN PRINTING LLC
Also Called: ESP
2630 Orleans St (48207-4507)
PHONE..................313 300-6411
Scott Michalski, *Principal*
EMP: 4
SQ FT: 1,300
SALES: 360K **Privately Held**
SIC: 2759 Screen printing

(G-4043)
EUCLID MANUFACTURING CO INC
1500 E Euclid St (48211-1310)
PHONE..................734 397-6300
Scott Jones, *President*
Bob Koss, *CFO*
EMP: 20
SALES: 4MM
SALES (corp-wide): 2.2B **Privately Held**
SIC: 3469 Metal stampings
HQ: L & W, Inc.
17757 Woodland Dr
New Boston MI 48164
734 397-6300

(G-4044)
EV ANYWHERE LLC
3011 W Grand Blvd # 1800 (48202-3096)
PHONE..................313 653-9870
Kwabena Johnson, *Principal*
EMP: 3
SALES (est): 176.3K **Privately Held**
SIC: 3621 Generators for gas-electric or oil-electric vehicles

(G-4045)
EVANS INDUSTRIES INC (HQ)
Also Called: Great Lakes Plastics Division
200 Renaissance Ctr # 3150 (48243-1303)
PHONE..................313 259-2266
Robert Beverly Evans, *Ch of Bd*
Jeff Johnson, *Vice Pres*
William Martin, *Director*
▲ EMP: 3
SQ FT: 8,000
SALES (est): 43.7MM **Privately Held**
WEB: www.eiihq.com
SIC: 6726 3363 3364 3089 Investment offices; aluminum die-castings; brass & bronze die-castings; injection molding of plastics; rubber automotive products
PA: Ehc, Inc.
200 Renaissance Ctr # 3150
Detroit MI 48243
313 259-2266

(G-4046)
EVANS INDUSTRIES INC
Darnell Rose Div
12402 Hubbell St (48227-2757)
PHONE..................313 272-8200
John Wood, *Enginr/R&D Mgr*
EMP: 5
SQ FT: 37,000
SALES (corp-wide): 43.7MM **Privately Held**
WEB: www.eiihq.com
SIC: 3562 3568 3429 Casters; couplings, shaft: rigid, flexible, universal joint, etc.; manufactured hardware (general)

GEOGRAPHIC SECTION
Detroit - Wayne County (G-4071)

HQ: Evans Industries, Inc.
200 Renaissance Ctr # 3150
Detroit MI 48243
313 259-2266

(G-4047)
EXQUISE INC
Also Called: Fire and Safety
2512 W Grand Blvd (48208-1239)
PHONE..................248 220-9048
Gerald W Parker, *President*
Jessica Parker, *Vice Pres*
Wilbert Parker, *Admin Sec*
Alice Knight,
Beverly Parker,
EMP: 5
SALES (est): 351K **Privately Held**
SIC: 3829 1711 5099 3999 Fire detector systems, non-electric; fire sprinkler system installation; fire extinguishers; fire extinguishers, portable; fire extinguishers; electric alarms & signaling equipment

(G-4048)
F M ENVELOPE INC
5938 Linsdale St (48204-3591)
PHONE..................313 899-4065
Thomas Mucker, *President*
Thomas D Mucker, *President*
Norma Mucker, *Corp Secy*
EMP: 40 **EST:** 1966
SQ FT: 60,000
SALES: 4.5MM **Privately Held**
WEB: www.fmenvelope.com
SIC: 2677 Envelopes

(G-4049)
FABRICATIONS UNLIMITED INC
4651 Beaufait St (48207-1711)
PHONE..................313 567-9616
Lee Perrell, *President*
EMP: 5
SALES (corp-wide): 1.2MM **Privately Held**
SIC: 3443 Fabricated plate work (boiler shop)
PA: Fabrications Unlimited Inc
45757 Cornwall St
Shelby Township MI 48317
313 567-9616

(G-4050)
FAIRMONT SIGN COMPANY (PA)
3750 E Outer Dr (48234-2900)
PHONE..................313 368-4000
David Haddad, *President*
Phil Farhood, *General Mgr*
Salim Haddad, *Chairman*
Nick Hanna, *VP Mfg*
Alicia Deneau, *Project Mgr*
EMP: 45 **EST:** 1979
SQ FT: 176,000
SALES (est): 7.2MM **Privately Held**
WEB: www.fairmontsign.com
SIC: 3993 Signs, not made in custom sign painting shops

(G-4051)
FAIRMOUNT SANTROL INC
17350 Ryan Rd (48212-1116)
PHONE..................440 279-0204
EMP: 6
SALES (corp-wide): 142.6MM **Publicly Held**
SIC: 2891 Adhesives
HQ: Fairmount Santrol Inc.
3 Summit Park Dr Ste 700
Independence OH 44131
440 214-3200

(G-4052)
FAYGO BEVERAGES INC (DH)
3579 Gratiot Ave (48207-1892)
PHONE..................313 925-1600
Nick A Caporella, *Ch of Bd*
Alan Chittaro, *President*
Stanley M Sheridan, *President*
David Piontkowski, *Vice Pres*
Orlando Woods, *Vice Pres*
EMP: 375 **EST:** 1907
SQ FT: 400,000
SALES (est): 351.8MM
SALES (corp-wide): 1B **Publicly Held**
WEB: www.wisconsin-cheeseman.com
SIC: 2086 Soft drinks: packaged in cans, bottles, etc.; mineral water, carbonated: packaged in cans, bottles, etc.

(G-4053)
FCA US LLC
Mt Elliott Tool & Die
3675 E Outer Dr (48234-2659)
PHONE..................313 369-7312
Robert Vulaj, *Opers Mgr*
Ray Waelchli, *Branch Mgr*
Paul Bryant, *Manager*
Ken Eaton, *Manager*
EMP: 1500
SALES (corp-wide): 126.4B **Privately Held**
SIC: 3544 Special dies, tools, jigs & fixtures
HQ: Fca Us Llc
1000 Chrysler Dr
Auburn Hills MI 48326

(G-4054)
FCA US LLC
Also Called: Chrysler Engine Plant 2
4500 Saint Jean St (48214-4719)
PHONE..................313 957-7000
Mike Lutsch, *Manager*
EMP: 130
SALES (corp-wide): 126.4B **Privately Held**
SIC: 3519 Engines, diesel & semi-diesel or dual-fuel
HQ: Fca Us Llc
1000 Chrysler Dr
Auburn Hills MI 48326

(G-4055)
FCA US LLC
Also Called: Detroit Office & Warehouse
12501 Chrysler Dr (48203-3506)
PHONE..................313 956-6460
Richard Steinberg, *Manager*
EMP: 100
SALES (corp-wide): 126.4B **Privately Held**
SIC: 3711 Motor vehicles & car bodies
HQ: Fca Us Llc
1000 Chrysler Dr
Auburn Hills MI 48326

(G-4056)
FERRANTE MANUFACTURING CO
6626 Gratiot Ave (48207-1912)
PHONE..................313 571-1111
Sante Ferrante, *President*
Daniel Friedel, *Vice Pres*
Dave Costa, *Engineer*
William Bonnell, *Treasurer*
Tony Costa, *Manager*
EMP: 50 **EST:** 1946
SQ FT: 60,000
SALES (est): 8MM **Privately Held**
WEB: www.ferrantemfg.com
SIC: 2541 2542 Bar fixtures, wood; partitions & fixtures, except wood

(G-4057)
FIDELIS CONTRACTING LLC
5640 Saint Jean St (48213-3415)
PHONE..................313 361-1000
Robert Nast, *President*
EMP: 3 **EST:** 2014
SALES (est): 117K **Privately Held**
SIC: 1442 1542 1611 1629 Construction sand & gravel; commercial & office building contractors; commercial & office buildings, renovation & repair; general contractor, highway & street construction; athletic & recreation facilities construction

(G-4058)
FIFE PEARCE ELECTRIC COMPANY
20201 Sherwood St (48234-2926)
PHONE..................313 369-2560
Roger N Pearce, *President*
John Fracassa, *Vice Pres*
Debbi Hamlin, *Controller*
Chuck Jones, *Manager*
Betsy Pearce, *Admin Sec*
EMP: 19 **EST:** 1923
SQ FT: 40,000
SALES (est): 5.6MM **Privately Held**
WEB: www.fifepearce.com
SIC: 7694 Electric motor repair

(G-4059)
FIRE EQUIPMENT COMPANY
Also Called: Michigan Fire Estinguishers
20100 John R St (48203-1138)
PHONE..................313 891-3164
Mark Agar, *President*
Jim McMillan, *General Mgr*
Willis C Beard, *Chairman*
James McMillan, *Corp Secy*
Ronald Laplante, *Vice Pres*
EMP: 28
SQ FT: 14,000
SALES: 3.2MM **Privately Held**
SIC: 3699 7389 Fire control or bombing equipment, electronic; fire extinguisher servicing

(G-4060)
FIRE-RITE INC
13801 Lyndon St (48227-3146)
P.O. Box 219, Davisburg (48350-0219)
PHONE..................313 273-3730
Richard D Yovich, *President*
▲ **EMP:** 40 **EST:** 1975
SQ FT: 50,000
SALES (est): 10.2MM **Privately Held**
SIC: 3398 7389 3471 Metal heat treating; metal cutting services; plating & polishing

(G-4061)
FITZGERALD FINISHING LLC
17450 Filer St (48212-1908)
PHONE..................313 368-3630
Aaron Gant, *Plant Mgr*
Thomas Melita, *Mng Member*
Derrell Bracy, *Manager*
Sharon Halnyi,
EMP: 90
SQ FT: 80,000
SALES (est): 11MM **Privately Held**
SIC: 3471 Electroplating of metals or formed products

(G-4062)
FLEXIBLE CONTROLS CORPORATION
Also Called: Fitzgerald Finishing
17450 Filer St (48212-1908)
PHONE..................313 368-3630
Thomas Melita, *President*
Larry Gutowsky, *Vice Pres*
James R Gitre, *Treasurer*
Sharon Halnyj, *Controller*
EMP: 90
SQ FT: 107,000
SALES (est): 6.7MM **Privately Held**
WEB: www.fitzgeraldfinishing.com
SIC: 3471 Decorative plating & finishing of formed products

(G-4063)
FLINT GROUP US LLC
Also Called: Flint Ink North America Div
25111 Glendale (48239-2646)
PHONE..................313 538-0479
Magenta Zheng, *General Mgr*
Kathy Marx, *Principal*
EMP: 4
SALES (corp-wide): 177.9K **Privately Held**
WEB: www.flintink.com
SIC: 2893 Printing ink
HQ: Flint Group Us Llc
17177 N Laurel Park Dr # 300
Livonia MI 48152
734 781-4600

(G-4064)
FLINT LIME INDUSTRIES INC
327 S Fordson St (48217-1314)
P.O. Box 133, Allen Park (48101-0133)
PHONE..................313 843-6050
Greg Sartor, *President*
EMP: 6
SALES (est): 352.8K **Privately Held**
SIC: 1422 Crushed & broken limestone

(G-4065)
FMMB LLC
Also Called: Stanek Rack Company
4786 Bellevue St (48207-1302)
P.O. Box 7280 (48207-0280)
PHONE..................313 372-7420
Joe McClelland, *General Mgr*
Mark McClelland,
EMP: 20 **EST:** 1960
SQ FT: 20,000
SALES (est): 3.3MM **Privately Held**
SIC: 2542 Racks, merchandise display or storage: except wood

(G-4066)
FONTANA FOREST PRODUCTS
1910 Trombly St (48211-2130)
PHONE..................313 841-8950
Carl Fontana, *President*
EMP: 30
SQ FT: 40,000
SALES (est): 3.6MM
SALES (corp-wide): 13.6MM **Privately Held**
WEB: www.michiganbox.com
SIC: 2448 Pallets, wood
PA: Michigan Box Company
1910 Trombly St
Detroit MI 48211
313 873-9500

(G-4067)
FORD MOTOR COMPANY
300 Renaissance Ctr (48243-1402)
PHONE..................313 446-5945
Pamela Stogiera, *Purchasing*
Mr Bob Reilly, *Manager*
Sanjay Abhyankar, *Technical Staff*
Joe Sellinger, *Software Dev*
Amy Pellegrini, *Executive*
EMP: 1500
SALES (corp-wide): 160.3B **Publicly Held**
WEB: www.ford.com
SIC: 3211 8734 Window glass, clear & colored; product testing laboratory, safety or performance
PA: Ford Motor Company
1 American Rd
Dearborn MI 48126
313 322-3000

(G-4068)
FORGED TUBULAR
9339 W Fort St (48209-2555)
PHONE..................313 843-4870
Richard Bekolay, *Owner*
EMP: 3
SALES (est): 170.1K **Privately Held**
SIC: 3465 Body parts, automobile: stamped metal

(G-4069)
FORGED TUBULAR PRODUCTS INC (PA)
Also Called: B & H Machine Sales
9339 W Fort St (48209-2555)
PHONE..................313 843-6720
Richard Tm Bekolay, *President*
EMP: 9
SALES (est): 1.2MM **Privately Held**
SIC: 3317 Seamless pipes & tubes

(G-4070)
FORGING HOLDINGS LLC (DH)
1 Dauch Dr (48211-1115)
PHONE..................313 758-2000
David C Dauch, *Ch of Bd*
Catherine Hansen, *Sales Staff*
EMP: 5
SALES (est): 284.9MM
SALES (corp-wide): 7.2B **Publicly Held**
SIC: 3711 3714 Motor vehicles & car bodies; motor vehicle parts & accessories
HQ: Hhi Holdings, Llc
1 Dauch Dr
Detroit MI 48211
313 758-2000

(G-4071)
FPT SCHLAFER
Also Called: Schlafer Iron & Steel Co
1950 Medbury St (48211-2626)
PHONE..................313 925-8200
Barry Briskin, *President*
Anthony Benacquisto, *Corp Secy*

Detroit - Wayne County (G-4072)

GEOGRAPHIC SECTION

Steven Benacquisto, *Vice Pres*
▲ **EMP:** 50
SQ FT: 38,000
SALES (est): 9MM **Privately Held**
SIC: 5093 3341 Ferrous metal scrap & waste; secondary nonferrous metals

(G-4072)
FRANK SMITH
Also Called: Frank's Oil King
13021 Harper Ave (48213)
PHONE..................313 443-8882
Frank Smith, *Owner*
EMP: 3
SALES (est): 91.3K **Privately Held**
SIC: 2079 Edible fats & oils

(G-4073)
FRITZ ENTERPRISES
Also Called: Fritz Products
255 Marion Ave (48218-1695)
PHONE..................313 841-9460
Al Seguin, *Safety Dir*
EMP: 34
SALES (corp-wide): 72MM **Privately Held**
WEB: www.fritzinc.com
SIC: 3567 3334 Smelting ovens; primary aluminum
HQ: Fritz Enterprises
  1650 W Jefferson Ave
  Trenton MI 48183
  734 283-7272

(G-4074)
G A MACHINE COMPANY INC
8851 Mark Twain St (48228-2310)
PHONE..................313 836-5646
Steven Kiss, *President*
Betty J Kiss, *Vice Pres*
EMP: 7 **EST:** 1946
SQ FT: 3,200
SALES: 400K **Privately Held**
SIC: 3544 3545 Special dies & tools; sockets (machine tool accessories)

(G-4075)
GADGET LOCKER LLC
11260 Somerset Ave (48224-1129)
P.O. Box 241668 (48224-5668)
PHONE..................702 901-1440
Ashley Stewart, *CEO*
EMP: 3
SALES (est): 176.2K **Privately Held**
SIC: 2676 3679 Toilet paper: made from purchased paper; headphones, radio

(G-4076)
GANAS LLC
7511 Intervale St (48238-2401)
PHONE..................734 748-0434
Richard Ganas, *Principal*
EMP: 10
SALES (est): 1.1MM **Privately Held**
SIC: 3999 Manufacturing industries

(G-4077)
GANNETT STLLITE INFO NTWRK INC
Also Called: USA Today
601 Rogell Dr (48242-1103)
PHONE..................734 229-1150
EMP: 117
SALES (corp-wide): 3.1B **Publicly Held**
SIC: 2711 Newspapers-Publishing/Printing
HQ: Gannett Satellite Information Network, Llc
  7950 Jones Branch Dr
  Mc Lean VA 22102
  703 854-6000

(G-4078)
GEARING HOLDINGS LLC (DH)
1 Dauch Dr (48211-1115)
PHONE..................313 758-2000
David C Dauch, *Ch of Bd*
EMP: 3
SALES (est): 254.7MM
SALES (corp-wide): 7.2B **Publicly Held**
SIC: 3714 3711 Motor vehicle parts & accessories; motor vehicles & car bodies
HQ: Hhi Holdings, Llc
  1 Dauch Dr
  Detroit MI 48211
  313 758-2000

(G-4079)
GEEKS OF DETROIT LLC
282 Newport St Ste 1a (48215-3170)
PHONE..................734 576-2363
Donnie Hall,
Tamara Canty,
Deshoun Smith,
EMP: 4
SQ FT: 2,000
SALES (est): 348.9K **Privately Held**
SIC: 3575 7378 Computer terminals; computer maintenance & repair

(G-4080)
GENERAL HARDWOOD COMPANY (PA)
Also Called: All Overhead Door Operator Co
7201 E Mcnichols Rd (48212-2050)
PHONE..................313 365-7733
Ronald Ellerbrock, *President*
Mark Ellerbrock, *Vice Pres*
EMP: 16
SQ FT: 3,200
SALES (est): 5.4MM **Privately Held**
SIC: 5031 2431 Lumber: rough, dressed & finished; millwork

(G-4081)
GENERAL MOTORS CHINA INC (DH)
300 Renaissance Ctr L1 (48243-1403)
PHONE..................313 556-5000
Lillian Orth, *CEO*
Matthew Tsien, *Exec VP*
EMP: 53
SALES (est): 37.7MM **Publicly Held**
SIC: 3714 Motor vehicle parts & accessories

(G-4082)
GENERAL MOTORS COMPANY (PA)
300 Renaissance Ctr L1 (48243-1403)
PHONE..................313 667-1500
Mary T Barra, *Ch of Bd*
EMP: 277
SALES (est): 147B **Publicly Held**
SIC: 3711 3714 Motor vehicles & car bodies; motor vehicle parts & accessories

(G-4083)
GENERAL MOTORS HOLDINGS LLC (HQ)
300 Renaissance Ctr L1 (48243-1403)
PHONE..................313 556-5000
Robert A Lutz, *CEO*
Thomas G Stephens, *Vice Ch Bd*
Jaime Ardila, *Exec VP*
Mary T Barra, *Exec VP*
Michael P Millikin, *Exec VP*
▲ **EMP:** 26
SALES (est): 14B **Publicly Held**
SIC: 5511 3714 Automobiles, new & used; motor vehicle parts & accessories

(G-4084)
GENERAL MOTORS LLC
2500 E Grand Blvd (48211-2006)
PHONE..................313 972-6000
EMP: 2000 **Publicly Held**
SIC: 3711 3714 6153 6141 Mfg Assemble And Sale Motor Vehicles Related Parts And Accessories Auto Financing Leasing Insur And Mtg Banking And Investmen
HQ: General Motors Llc
  300 Renaissance Ctr L1
  Detroit MI 48243

(G-4085)
GENERAL MOTORS LLC (HQ)
300 Renaissance Ctr L1 (48243-1403)
PHONE..................313 410-2704
Mary T Barra, *CEO*
Dan Ammann, *President*
Cathy Ehgotz, *General Mgr*
David Stillwell, *General Mgr*
Trevor Winch, *General Mgr*
▼ **EMP:** 120
SALES (est): 1.5B **Publicly Held**
SIC: 5511 3714 Automobiles, new & used; motor vehicle parts & accessories

(G-4086)
GENERAL MOTORS LLC
2500 E Grand Blvd (48211-2006)
PHONE..................313 972-6000
Troy Clarke, *Manager*
EMP: 2000 **Publicly Held**
SIC: 3711 Motor vehicles & car bodies
HQ: General Motors Llc
  300 Renaissance Ctr L1
  Detroit MI 48243

(G-4087)
GENERAL MOTORS LLC
2500 E Grand Motors Blvd (48211)
PHONE..................313 556-5000
EMP: 2028 **Publicly Held**
SIC: 3711 3714 Mfg Motor Vehicle/Car Bodies Mfg Motor Vehicle Parts/Accessories
HQ: General Motors Llc
  300 Renaissance Ctr L1
  Detroit MI 48243

(G-4088)
GENOA HEALTHCARE LLC
5716 Michigan Ave (48210-3039)
PHONE..................313 989-0536
EMP: 5
SALES (corp-wide): 226.2B **Publicly Held**
SIC: 2834 Pharmaceutical preparations
HQ: Genoa Healthcare Llc
  707 S Grady Way Ste 700
  Renton WA 98057

(G-4089)
GERALD HARRIS
Also Called: Domnmar Manufacturing Group
14846 Dexter Ave (48238-2123)
PHONE..................985 774-0261
Gerald Harris, *Owner*
EMP: 4
SALES: 10K **Privately Held**
SIC: 3541 Machine tools, metal cutting type

(G-4090)
GIFT BIKES 4 KIDS
3166 S Bassett St (48217-1517)
PHONE..................313 573-5619
Aloysous W Carter, *Principal*
EMP: 3
SALES (est): 150K **Privately Held**
SIC: 3751 Motorcycles, bicycles & parts

(G-4091)
GINKGOTREE INC
1555 Broadway St Ste 300 (48226-2159)
PHONE..................734 707-7191
Lida Hasbrouck, *CEO*
Scott Hasbrouck, *CEO*
Andrew Colchagoff, *Chief Engr*
EMP: 4 **EST:** 2012
SALES (est): 313.7K **Privately Held**
SIC: 7379 7371 7372 ; computer software development & applications; educational computer software

(G-4092)
GM COMPONENTS HOLDINGS LLC (DH)
Also Called: General Mtrs Cmpnents Holdings
300 Renaissance Ctr (48243-1402)
PHONE..................313 665-4707
Daniel Milot, *District Mgr*
Niharika Taskar Ramdev, *Vice Pres*
David Bartoy, *Opers Mgr*
Jason Cummings, *Maint Spvr*
Emery Tinson, *Opers Staff*
▲ **EMP:** 120
SALES (est): 430.3MM **Publicly Held**
SIC: 5511 3714 Automobiles, new & used; motor vehicle parts & accessories

(G-4093)
GM LAAM HOLDINGS LLC (DH)
300 Renaissance Ctr (48243-1402)
PHONE..................313 556-5000
EMP: 5
SALES (est): 5.4MM **Publicly Held**
SIC: 3711 3714 Automobile assembly, including specialty automobiles; truck & tractor truck assembly; military motor vehicle assembly; motor vehicle parts & accessories

(G-4094)
GO FRAC LLC
Also Called: Gofrac
7000 Calmont Ave Ste 310 (48207)
PHONE..................817 731-0301
Richard Crawford, *CEO*
Buddy Petersen, *COO*
Harlan Foster, *Vice Pres*
Kevin McGlinch, *CFO*
EMP: 30
SALES (est): 7.2MM **Privately Held**
SIC: 1389 Oil field services

(G-4095)
GODS CHILDREN IN UNITY INTL M
19325 Barlow St (48205-2164)
PHONE..................313 528-8285
Elizabeth Beasley, *Director*
EMP: 3
SALES (est): 98.2K **Privately Held**
SIC: 2759 Music sheet: printing

(G-4096)
GOLDEN POINTE INC
Also Called: Golden Pointe Awning & Sign Co
16050 W Warren Ave (48228-3740)
PHONE..................313 581-8284
Nouhad Elhajj, *President*
EMP: 7
SQ FT: 3,200
SALES (est): 943.3K **Privately Held**
WEB: www.goldenpt.com
SIC: 3993 3089 Signs & advertising specialties; awnings, fiberglass & plastic combination

(G-4097)
GONZALEZ PROD SYSTEMS INC
2555 Clark St (48209-9704)
PHONE..................313 297-6682
Terry Henderson, *President*
EMP: 86
SALES (corp-wide): 57.7MM **Privately Held**
WEB: www.gonzalez-group.com
SIC: 7363 2542 7389 Engineering help service; partitions & fixtures, except wood; design services
PA: Gonzalez Production Systems, Inc.
  1670 Highwood E
  Pontiac MI 48340
  248 548-6010

(G-4098)
GRAHAMS PRINTING COMPANY INC
8620 Gratiot Ave (48213-2931)
PHONE..................313 925-1188
Cecil Graham, *President*
Juanita Graham, *Vice Pres*
EMP: 4
SQ FT: 3,000
SALES (est): 370K **Privately Held**
SIC: 2752 Commercial printing, offset

(G-4099)
GRANDPAPAS INC
6500 E Davison St (48212-1422)
PHONE..................313 891-6830
Mike Robin, *President*
▼ **EMP:** 25 **EST:** 1996
SQ FT: 45,000
SALES (est): 5.2MM **Privately Held**
WEB: www.grandpapas.com
SIC: 2096 Pork rinds

(G-4100)
GREAT LAKES DOCK & DOOR LLC
19345 John R St (48203-1660)
P.O. Box 128, Hazel Park (48030-0128)
PHONE..................313 368-6300
C J Ruffing,
EMP: 20
SALES: 8MM **Privately Held**
SIC: 3537 Loading docks: portable, adjustable & hydraulic

GEOGRAPHIC SECTION
Detroit - Wayne County (G-4126)

(G-4101)
GREAT LAKES WOODWORKING CO INC
11345 Mound Rd (48212-2556)
PHONE..................313 892-8500
Michael J Mancinelli, *President*
Tony Gatliff, *Partner*
Chris Dee, *Vice Pres*
Paul La Croix, *Vice Pres*
Camille Thornton, *Project Mgr*
EMP: 50
SQ FT: 42,000
SALES: 5MM **Privately Held**
WEB: www.g-l-w.com
SIC: 2541 Display fixtures, wood

(G-4102)
GREEN POLYMERIC MATERIALS INC
6031 Joy Rd (48204-2909)
PHONE..................313 933-7390
Yogesh Goel, *President*
Lov Goel, *Vice Pres*
EMP: 50
SQ FT: 70,000
SALES: 5MM **Privately Held**
SIC: 3069 3053 3086 Reclaimed rubber (reworked by manufacturing processes); packing materials; plastics foam products; insulation or cushioning material, foamed plastic; padding, foamed plastic

(G-4103)
GREENFIELD NOODLE SPECIALTY CO
Also Called: Greenfeld Homemade Egg Noodles
600 Custer St (48202-3128)
PHONE..................313 873-2212
Kenneth Michaels, *President*
Mary Michaels, *Vice Pres*
EMP: 12 **EST:** 1947
SQ FT: 13,000
SALES (est): 1.8MM **Privately Held**
SIC: 2098 5149 Noodles (e.g. egg, plain & water), dry; groceries & related products

(G-4104)
GREENING INCORPORATED (PA)
19465 Mount Elliott St (48234-2742)
PHONE..................313 366-7160
Charles W Greening Sr, *CEO*
Charles W Greening Jr, *President*
Brent D Greening, *Vice Pres*
Marilyn F Greening, *Admin Sec*
▲ **EMP:** 2
SQ FT: 21,000
SALES (est): 7.2MM **Privately Held**
SIC: 3829 8734 Dynamometer instruments; product testing laboratory, safety or performance

(G-4105)
GREENING ASSOCIATES INC
Also Called: Greening Testing Laboratories
19465 Mount Elliott St (48234-2742)
PHONE..................313 366-7160
Charles W Greening Sr, *Ch of Bd*
Brent D Greening, *President*
Charles W Greening Jr, *Vice Pres*
Niki Bidinger, *Purch Mgr*
Ron Kaake, *Design Engr*
▲ **EMP:** 25
SQ FT: 22,000
SALES (est): 5.7MM
SALES (corp-wide): 7.2MM **Privately Held**
WEB: www.greeninginc.com
SIC: 3825 3829 Instruments to measure electricity; dynamometer instruments
PA: Greening, Incorporated
19465 Mount Elliott St
Detroit MI 48234
313 366-7160

(G-4106)
GRIGG BOX CO INC
18900 Fitzpatrick St (48228-1496)
PHONE..................313 273-9000
Rocco F Franco, *President*
Gary Turnbull, *General Mgr*
EMP: 25
SQ FT: 40,000
SALES (est): 4.5MM **Privately Held**
WEB: www.griggbox.com
SIC: 2441 Boxes, wood

(G-4107)
GROUP 7500 INC
Also Called: Red Door Digital
7500 Oakland St (48211-1350)
PHONE..................313 875-9026
Roger Robinson, *President*
EMP: 18
SALES (est): 2.1MM **Privately Held**
WEB: www.group7500.com
SIC: 2759 Commercial printing

(G-4108)
GUIDING OUR DESTINY MINISTRY
14811 Greenfield Rd A4 (48227-2263)
PHONE..................313 212-9063
Elmira Robinson, *Exec Dir*
EMP: 5
SALES (est): 317.3K **Privately Held**
SIC: 3799 Transportation equipment

(G-4109)
H M PRODUCTS INC
1435 E Milwaukee St (48211-2009)
PHONE..................313 875-5148
Harry S Radcliff, *President*
Mitchell Radcliff, *Vice Pres*
EMP: 6
SQ FT: 750
SALES (est): 624.6K **Privately Held**
SIC: 3914 2899 Silverware & plated ware; chemical preparations

(G-4110)
HACIENDA MEXICAN FOODS LLC (PA)
6100 Buchanan St (48210-2400)
P.O. Box 10678 (48210-0678)
PHONE..................313 895-8823
Lydia Guttuierrez, *President*
EMP: 80
SQ FT: 33,000
SALES (est): 16.5MM **Privately Held**
WEB: www.mexicantown.org
SIC: 2096 5149 Tortilla chips; diet foods

(G-4111)
HACIENDA MEXICAN FOODS LLC
6016 W Vernor Hwy (48209-2060)
PHONE..................313 843-7007
Lydia Gutierrez, *Manager*
EMP: 10
SALES (corp-wide): 16.5MM **Privately Held**
WEB: www.mexicantown.org
SIC: 2096 2099 Tortilla chips; tortillas, fresh or refrigerated
PA: Hacienda Mexican Foods, Llc
6100 Buchanan St
Detroit MI 48210
313 895-8823

(G-4112)
HACKETT BRASS FOUNDRY CO (PA)
1200 Lillibridge St (48214-3295)
PHONE..................313 822-1214
Alan L Wright, *President*
Lucas Wright, *Vice Pres*
EMP: 20
SQ FT: 25,000
SALES (est): 2.6MM **Privately Held**
WEB: www.hackettbrass.com
SIC: 3364 3363 Copper & copper alloy die-castings; aluminum die-castings

(G-4113)
HACKETT BRASS FOUNDRY CO
Also Called: Centro Division
45 Saint Jean St (48214-3491)
PHONE..................313 331-6005
Lucas Wright, *Manager*
EMP: 25
SQ FT: 22,729
SALES (corp-wide): 2.6MM **Privately Held**
WEB: www.hackettbrass.com
SIC: 3365 3369 3366 3325 Aluminum & aluminum-based alloy castings; nonferrous foundries; copper foundries; steel foundries
PA: Hackett Brass Foundry Co.
1200 Lillibridge St
Detroit MI 48214
313 822-1214

(G-4114)
HALLER INTERNATIONAL TECH INC
Also Called: Acro-Feed Industries
609 Old St Jean (48214)
PHONE..................313 821-0809
Dennis A Haller, *President*
Joseph Haller, *Vice Pres*
Jack Accardo, *CFO*
EMP: 8 **EST:** 1955
SQ FT: 16,000
SALES (est): 4.4MM **Privately Held**
WEB: www.acrofeed.com
SIC: 5084 3545 Industrial machinery & equipment; machine tool attachments & accessories

(G-4115)
HAMTRAMCK REVIEW INC
3020 Caniff St (48212-3019)
PHONE..................313 874-2100
John Ulaj, *President*
EMP: 6
SALES (est): 352.7K **Privately Held**
SIC: 2711 Newspapers: publishing only, not printed on site

(G-4116)
HAPPY HOWIES INC
15510 Dale St (48223-1038)
P.O. Box 231837 (48223-8037)
PHONE..................313 537-7200
Stan Dickson, *President*
David Collado, *Vice Pres*
Wayne Whitney, *Natl Sales Mgr*
▲ **EMP:** 10
SQ FT: 600,000
SALES: 700K **Privately Held**
WEB: www.happyhowies.com
SIC: 2047 Dog food

(G-4117)
HARPER ARRINGTON PUBG LLC
18701 Grand River Ave # 105 (48223-2214)
PHONE..................313 282-6751
Michael Harper,
Jay Arrington,
EMP: 4
SALES: 442K **Privately Held**
SIC: 7372 2731 Publishers' computer software; books: publishing only

(G-4118)
HATTIEGIRL ICE CREAM FOODS LLC
16159 Wyoming St (48221-2846)
PHONE..................877 444-3738
James D Render, *Principal*
EMP: 6
SQ FT: 1,000
SALES (est): 293.5K **Privately Held**
SIC: 2024 Ice cream & frozen desserts

(G-4119)
HEALTHCURE LLC
6501 Lynch Rd (48234-4140)
PHONE..................313 743-2331
John McIntyre, *President*
Carlton Guthrie, *Chairman*
Joseph Gause, *Vice Pres*
Darlene Lanoye, *Administration*
Mark Arizmendi,
EMP: 10
SALES (est): 760K **Privately Held**
SIC: 2842 Sanitation preparations

(G-4120)
HECKETT MULTISERVE
7819 W Jefferson Ave (48209-2857)
PHONE..................313 842-2120
Troy Partin, *Principal*
EMP: 3
SALES (est): 231.5K **Privately Held**
SIC: 3325 Steel foundries

(G-4121)
HHI FORMTECH LLC (DH)
1 Dauch Dr (48211-1115)
PHONE..................313 758-2000
David C Dauch, *Ch of Bd*
EMP: 282
SALES (est): 7.3MM
SALES (corp-wide): 7.2B **Publicly Held**
SIC: 3714 3711 Motor vehicle parts & accessories; motor vehicles & car bodies
HQ: Hhi Formtech Holdings Llc
1 Dauch Dr
Detroit MI 48211
313 758-2000

(G-4122)
HHI FORMTECH HOLDINGS LLC (DH)
1 Dauch Dr (48211-1115)
PHONE..................313 758-2000
David C Dauch, *Ch of Bd*
EMP: 3
SALES (est): 14.4MM
SALES (corp-wide): 7.2B **Publicly Held**
SIC: 3711 3714 Motor vehicles & car bodies; motor vehicle parts & accessories
HQ: Hephaestus Holdings, Llc
39475 W 13 Mile Rd # 105
Novi MI 48377
248 479-2700

(G-4123)
HHI FUNDING II LLC
1 Dauch Dr (48211-1115)
PHONE..................313 758-2000
David C Dauch, *Ch of Bd*
EMP: 214
SALES (est): 5.6MM
SALES (corp-wide): 7.2B **Publicly Held**
SIC: 3714 3711 Motor vehicle parts & accessories; motor vehicles & car bodies
HQ: Hephaestus Holdings, Llc
39475 W 13 Mile Rd # 105
Novi MI 48377
248 479-2700

(G-4124)
HHI HOLDINGS LLC (DH)
1 Dauch Dr (48211-1115)
PHONE..................313 758-2000
David C Dauch, *Ch of Bd*
EMP: 3
SALES (est): 530.3MM
SALES (corp-wide): 7.2B **Publicly Held**
SIC: 3714 3711 Motor vehicle parts & accessories; motor vehicles & car bodies
HQ: Asp Hhi Acquisition Co., Inc.
1 Dauch Dr
Detroit MI 48211
313 758-2000

(G-4125)
HMW CONTRACTING LLC
Also Called: H M White
12855 Burt Rd (48223-3316)
PHONE..................313 531-8477
Jonathon B Ricker, *President*
Jon Ricker, *Engineer*
Domenico E Colone, *Treasurer*
William White, *Mng Member*
Jennifer Zimmer, *Director*
EMP: 150
SQ FT: 35,000
SALES: 47.4MM **Privately Held**
SIC: 3444 Metal ventilating equipment

(G-4126)
HOME STYLE FOODS INC
5163 Edwin St (48212-3377)
PHONE..................313 874-3250
Micheal Kowliski, *President*
EMP: 14 **EST:** 1953
SQ FT: 5,000
SALES (est): 5.5MM **Privately Held**
WEB: www.homestylefoods.com
SIC: 5148 5149 2099 Vegetables; groceries & related products; macaroni; ready-to-eat meals, salads & sandwiches

(PA)=Parent Co (HQ)=Headquarters (DH)=Div Headquarters
◯ = New Business established in last 2 years

Detroit - Wayne County (G-4127)   **GEOGRAPHIC SECTION**

(G-4127)
HOOVER TREATED WOOD PDTS INC
7500 E Davison St (48212-1925)
PHONE..................................313 365-4200
Thomas Spiekhout, *Manager*
EMP: 45
SALES (corp-wide): 2.7B **Publicly Held**
WEB: www.hooverfrtw.com
SIC: 2491 Structural lumber & timber, treated wood
HQ: Hoover Treated Wood Products, Inc.
154 Wire Rd
Thomson GA 30824
706 595-5058

(G-4128)
HOPE FOCUS
Also Called: Focus Hope Mfg
1200 Oakman Blvd (48238-2998)
PHONE..................................313 494-4500
Carlton M Faison, *Vice Pres*
Elliot Forsyth, *Vice Pres*
Burt Jordan, *Vice Pres*
Daryl Hurley, *CFO*
Robert L Watson, *Asst Treas*
EMP: 35
SALES (corp-wide): 38.4MM **Privately Held**
SIC: 3714 Motor vehicle parts & accessories
PA: Hope Focus
1355 Oakman Blvd
Detroit MI 48238
313 494-5500

(G-4129)
HOPE FOCUS (PA)
1355 Oakman Blvd (48238-2849)
PHONE..................................313 494-5500
Vernice Davis Anthony, *CEO*
Timothy M Duperron, *COO*
Annette Vanover, *Treasurer*
Yolanda Crain, *Manager*
Edna Jackson, *Manager*
EMP: 192 **EST:** 1968
SQ FT: 16,000
SALES: 38.4MM **Privately Held**
SIC: 8399 3714 8249 8299 Neighborhood development group; motor vehicle parts & accessories; vocational schools; educational services

(G-4130)
HOPE FOCUS COMPANIES INC (HQ)
Also Called: Focus Hope Logistics
1200 Oakman Blvd (48238-2998)
PHONE..................................313 494-4500
Timothy Duperron, *CEO*
Martha Schultz, *Treasurer*
Kenneth Kudek, *Admin Sec*
▲ **EMP:** 20
SALES: 29.3MM
SALES (corp-wide): 38.4MM **Privately Held**
SIC: 3545 Precision tools, machinists'
PA: Hope Focus
1355 Oakman Blvd
Detroit MI 48238
313 494-5500

(G-4131)
HOUGHTON INTERNATIONAL INC
Also Called: D.A. Stuart Company
9100 Freeland St (48228-2309)
PHONE..................................313 273-7374
Paul Kaucher, *Purch Mgr*
Regan Seymur, *Manager*
EMP: 80
SALES (corp-wide): 867.5MM **Publicly Held**
WEB: www.d-a-stuart.com
SIC: 2992 Cutting oils, blending: made from purchased materials; re-refining lubricating oils & greases
HQ: Houghton International Inc.
945 Madison Ave
Norristown PA 19403
888 459-9844

(G-4132)
HYDE SPRING AND WIRE COMPANY
14341 Schaefer Hwy (48227-5603)
PHONE..................................313 272-2201
John M Hyde, *Owner*
Bonnie Hyde, *Vice Pres*
Leona Lear, *Office Mgr*
Moe Hernadez, *Manager*
EMP: 10
SQ FT: 22,000
SALES: 500K **Privately Held**
WEB: www.hydespring.com
SIC: 3495 Mechanical springs, precision

(G-4133)
IDEAL SHIELD LLC
2525 Clark St (48209-1337)
PHONE..................................866 825-8659
Richard Grove, *Sales Staff*
Ashley Kozlowski, *Sales Staff*
Frank Venegas,
Jesse Venegas,
Linzie Venegas,
▼ **EMP:** 50
SQ FT: 67,000
SALES: 19.8MM
SALES (corp-wide): 268.6MM **Privately Held**
SIC: 3089 3449 Plastic processing; miscellaneous metalwork
PA: The Ideal Group Inc
2525 Clark St
Detroit MI 48209
313 849-0000

(G-4134)
IDEAL STEEL & BLDRS SUPS LLC
2525 Clark St (48209-9703)
PHONE..................................313 849-0000
Frank Venegas, *CEO*
Rachel Johnson, *CFO*
EMP: 22
SALES (est): 985.2K **Privately Held**
SIC: 3441 Fabricated structural metal

(G-4135)
IDEAL WROUGHT IRON
7839 Greenfield Rd (48228-3603)
PHONE..................................313 581-1324
Larry Krench, *President*
Greg Krench, *President*
Laurie Waring, *Admin Sec*
EMP: 3
SQ FT: 3,000
SALES (est): 457.8K **Privately Held**
SIC: 3446 Gates, ornamental metal; railings, bannisters, guards, etc.: made from metal pipe

(G-4136)
IHC INC
Also Called: International Hardcoat
12400 Burt Rd (48228-5500)
PHONE..................................313 535-3210
Jeffrey R Pernick, *President*
Joel Peltier, *General Mgr*
Joe Peltier, *Vice Pres*
James D Weil, *Vice Pres*
Al Harrell, *Prdtn Mgr*
EMP: 115
SQ FT: 100,000
SALES (est): 16.7MM **Privately Held**
WEB: www.ihccorp.com
SIC: 3471 Anodizing (plating) of metals or formed products

(G-4137)
IMPACT FORGE HOLDINGS LLC (DH)
1 Dauch Dr (48211-1115)
PHONE..................................313 758-2000
David C Dauch, *Ch of Bd*
EMP: 3
SALES (est): 145MM
SALES (corp-wide): 7.2B **Publicly Held**
SIC: 3714 3711 Motor vehicle parts & accessories; motor vehicles & car bodies
HQ: Hhi Forging, Llc
2727 W 14 Mile Rd
Royal Oak MI 48073
248 284-2900

(G-4138)
INDUSTRIAL CONTAINER INC
6671 French Rd (48213-3277)
PHONE..................................313 923-8778
David Tito, *CEO*
Douglas Tito, *President*
Mark Higgins, *Buyer*
Rick Fogarty, *Sales Staff*
Victoria Sumner, *Manager*
EMP: 18
SQ FT: 36,000
SALES (est): 5.8MM **Privately Held**
SIC: 3443 Containers, shipping (bombs, etc.): metal plate

(G-4139)
INDUSTRIAL ELC CO DETROIT INC
Also Called: I.E. Communications
275 E Milwaukee St (48202-3233)
PHONE..................................313 872-1133
William M Darish, *President*
John T Darish, *Corp Secy*
Thomas R Darish, *Vice Pres*
Tom Darish, *Project Mgr*
Jeff Myny, *Foreman/Supr*
EMP: 55
SQ FT: 5,500
SALES (est): 10MM **Privately Held**
WEB: www.industrialelectric.net
SIC: 1731 7694 General electrical contractor; armature rewinding shops

(G-4140)
INLAND MANAGEMENT INC (HQ)
4086 Michigan Ave (48210-3261)
PHONE..................................313 899-3014
Jeffery Stark, *President*
Claude Kubrak, *President*
Dan Ford, *Vice Pres*
Andrea Stier, *Opers Mgr*
Tom Gray, *Sls & Mktg Exec*
▼ **EMP:** 2
SQ FT: 43,000
SALES (est): 29.1MM **Privately Held**
SIC: 3589 Sewer cleaning equipment, power

(G-4141)
INNOVATIVE MATERIAL HANDLING
18820 Woodward Ave (48203-1901)
PHONE..................................586 291-3694
Gregory Armstrong, *CEO*
EMP: 12
SALES (est): 496K **Privately Held**
SIC: 2396 Automotive & apparel trimmings

(G-4142)
INTEGRATED CMNTY COMMERCE LLC
200 Mount Elliott St # 105 (48207-4466)
PHONE..................................313 220-2253
Jim Morgan, *Manager*
EMP: 3
SALES (est): 152.3K **Privately Held**
SIC: 2676 Sanitary paper products

(G-4143)
INTEGRATED MFG & ASSEMBLY LLC
Also Called: Ima Service Center - Detroit
12601 Southfield Fwy C (48223-3473)
PHONE..................................313 267-2634
Tony Tucker, *Branch Mgr*
EMP: 29 **Privately Held**
SIC: 2531 Seats, automobile
PA: Integrated Manufacturing & Assembly, Llc
6501 E Nevada St
Detroit MI 48234

(G-4144)
INTEGRATED MFG & ASSEMBLY LLC (PA)
Also Called: I M A
6501 E Nevada St (48234-2833)
PHONE..................................734 530-5600
James Comer,
Andrea Puchalsky,
▲ **EMP:** 350
SQ FT: 40,000
SALES (est): 180.8MM **Privately Held**
SIC: 2531 Seats, automobile

(G-4145)
INTELLIBEE INC
400 Renaissance Ctr # 2600 (48243-1502)
PHONE..................................313 586-4122
Prasad Beesabathuni, *President*
EMP: 3
SALES (est): 176.4K **Privately Held**
SIC: 7379 7373 7371 7372 Computer related consulting services; computer integrated systems design; custom computer programming services; computer software development & applications; application computer software; minicomputers

(G-4146)
INTRAMODE LLC
1420 Brdwy St (48226)
PHONE..................................313 964-6990
Maureen Kraemer, *Principal*
Robert Kraemer,
EMP: 6
SQ FT: 10,000
SALES (est): 1.4MM **Privately Held**
WEB: www.intramode.com
SIC: 2392 Household furnishings

(G-4147)
INVENT DETROIT R&D COLLABORATI
440 Burroughs St (48202-3429)
PHONE..................................313 451-2658
Chelsea Kelly, *Program Mgr*
John Howard,
EMP: 3
SALES (est): 141.9K **Privately Held**
SIC: 3429 3498 7389 0851 Clamps, couplings, nozzles & other metal hose fittings; nozzles, fire fighting; couplings, pipe: fabricated from purchased pipe; fire protection service other than forestry or public; fire fighting services, forest

(G-4148)
INVENTEV LLC
440 Burroughs St Ste 661 (48202-3475)
PHONE..................................248 535-0477
David Stenson, *Partner*
Mark Abbo, *Partner*
EMP: 6 **EST:** 2011
SALES (est): 460K **Privately Held**
SIC: 3711 7389 Automobile assembly, including specialty automobiles;

(G-4149)
IPAX ATLANTIC LLC
8301 Lyndon St (48238-2444)
PHONE..................................313 933-4211
Ledion Curi, *Accounting Mgr*
EMP: 10
SQ FT: 50,000
SALES (est): 1.9MM **Privately Held**
SIC: 2842 2843 2841 Cleaning or polishing preparations; degreasing solvent; surface active agents; textile soap

(G-4150)
IPAX CLEANOGEL INC
8301 Lyndon St (48238-2444)
PHONE..................................313 933-4211
Alla Katz, *President*
Igor Berger, *Vice Pres*
Paul Katz, *Vice Pres*
▼ **EMP:** 8
SQ FT: 30,000
SALES: 1.2MM **Privately Held**
WEB: www.ipax.com
SIC: 2842 Cleaning or polishing preparations

(G-4151)
IRON CLAD SECURITY INC
Also Called: Iron Clad Security Products
15047 Schaefer Hwy (48227-3641)
PHONE..................................313 837-0390
Ian McGibbon, *President*
Ian Mc Gibbon, *President*
Elise Mc Gibbon, *Admin Sec*
EMP: 3
SQ FT: 2,300
SALES (est): 240K **Privately Held**
SIC: 3312 Hot-rolled iron & steel products

GEOGRAPHIC SECTION
Detroit - Wayne County (G-4180)

(G-4152)
ITALIAN BTR BREAD STICKS BKY
4241 E Mcnichols Rd (48212-1717)
PHONE 313 893-4945
Veljko Djuric, *Partner*
Kosara Djuric, *Partner*
EMP: 4
SQ FT: 3,000
SALES (est): 418.2K **Privately Held**
SIC: 2051 Bread, all types (white, wheat, rye, etc): fresh or frozen

(G-4153)
IVAN DOVERSPIKE
Also Called: E-Course Machinery
9501 Conner St (48213-1241)
PHONE 313 579-3000
Ivan D Doverspike, *President*
Judith Doverspike, *Vice Pres*
Gary Ede, *Safety Mgr*
Jill Doverspike Neal, *Treasurer*
Jill Neal, *Treasurer*
EMP: 20
SQ FT: 4,000
SALES (est): 2.8MM **Privately Held**
SIC: 3312 5084 3541 Rods, iron & steel: made in steel mills; industrial machinery & equipment; machine tools, metal cutting type

(G-4154)
J & G PALLETS INC
2971 Bellevue St (48207-3502)
PHONE 313 921-0222
Geraldine Wooten, *President*
EMP: 7
SALES (est): 887.2K **Privately Held**
SIC: 2448 Pallets, wood & wood with metal
PA: J & G Pallets Inc.
2971 Bellevue St
Detroit MI 48207

(G-4155)
J & G PALLETS INC (PA)
2971 Bellevue St (48207-3502)
PHONE 313 921-0222
Geraldine Givahen, *President*
EMP: 8
SALES (est): 1.3MM **Privately Held**
SIC: 2448 Pallets, wood

(G-4156)
JAM ENTERPRISES
16349 E Warren Ave (48224-2715)
PHONE 313 417-9200
James Antwine, *Owner*
EMP: 4
SQ FT: 1,400
SALES (est): 312.8K **Privately Held**
SIC: 2396 Screen printing on fabric articles

(G-4157)
JANUTOL PRINTING CO INC
9920 Conner St (48213-1245)
PHONE 313 526-6196
Peter Janutol, *President*
Charles Janutol, *Corp Secy*
Eleanor Janutol, *Vice Pres*
EMP: 5 **EST:** 1956
SQ FT: 9,000
SALES: 500K **Privately Held**
WEB: www.janutolprinting.com
SIC: 2752 Commercial printing, offset

(G-4158)
JAR-ME LLC
16801 Grand River Ave # 2 (48227-1421)
PHONE 313 319-7765
Bryanna Reed,
EMP: 4
SALES (est): 116.1K **Privately Held**
SIC: 2037 Frozen fruits & vegetables

(G-4159)
JASCO INTERNATIONAL LLC (PA)
7140 W Fort St (48209-2917)
PHONE 313 841-5000
Louis James, *President*
Pat Dennis, *CFO*
Eiichi Seto, *Treasurer*
EMP: 14

SALES (est): 5.2MM **Privately Held**
SIC: 3711 4213 4214 7389 Automobile assembly, including specialty automobiles; trucking, except local; local trucking with storage; inventory stocking service

(G-4160)
JEDI MACHINING CORP
18564 Fitzpatrick St (48228-1450)
PHONE 313 272-9500
Shelia Capler, *President*
Jeff Capler, *Vice Pres*
EMP: 3
SALES (est): 349.6K **Privately Held**
SIC: 3599 Machine shop, jobbing & repair

(G-4161)
JERNBERG HOLDINGS LLC (DH)
1 Dauch Dr (48211-1115)
PHONE 313 758-2000
David C Dauch, *Ch of Bd*
EMP: 3
SALES (est): 108.9MM
SALES (corp-wide): 7.2B **Publicly Held**
SIC: 3714 3711 Motor vehicle parts & accessories; motor vehicles & car bodies
HQ: Hhi Forging, Llc
2727 W 14 Mile Rd
Royal Oak MI 48073
248 284-2900

(G-4162)
JO-MAR ENTERPRISES INC
7489 E Davison St (48212-1912)
PHONE 313 365-9200
Joseph R Joye, *President*
EMP: 6 **EST:** 1955
SQ FT: 3,600
SALES: 430K **Privately Held**
SIC: 3471 Chromium plating of metals or formed products

(G-4163)
JOGUE INC
6349 E Palmer St (48211-3201)
PHONE 313 921-4802
Dr Warren McKlenden, *Principal*
Mike Letourneau, *Manager*
EMP: 6
SALES (corp-wide): 12.2MM **Privately Held**
WEB: www.jogue.com
SIC: 2087 2844 Extracts, flavoring; toilet preparations
PA: Jogue, Inc.
14731 Helm Ct
Plymouth MI 48170
734 207-0100

(G-4164)
JOHNICO LLC
Also Called: America's Green Line
400 Monroe St Ste 480 (48226-2960)
PHONE 248 895-7820
Nico Gatzaros,
John Economy,
EMP: 25 **EST:** 2014
SALES (est): 3.9MM **Privately Held**
SIC: 3641 3646 3648 Tubes, electric light; commercial indusl & institutional electric lighting fixtures; public lighting fixtures; street lighting fixtures

(G-4165)
JOHNSON CONTROLS INC
4617 W Fort St (48209-3208)
PHONE 313 842-3300
Denise Stinson, *Manager*
EMP: 230 **Privately Held**
SIC: 3714 Motor vehicle parts & accessories
HQ: Johnson Controls, Inc.
5757 N Green Bay Ave
Milwaukee WI 53209
414 524-1200

(G-4166)
JR LARRY DUDLEY
Also Called: If Walls Could Talk Prof Svcs
7701 Forrer St (48228-3615)
PHONE 313 721-3600
Larry Dudley Jr, *Owner*
EMP: 3

SALES (est): 81.4K **Privately Held**
SIC: 1389 7389 Construction, repair & dismantling services;

(G-4167)
JSP INTERNATIONAL LLC
13889 W Chicago St (48228-2525)
PHONE 313 834-0612
Stan Purnsley, *Manager*
EMP: 20 **Privately Held**
SIC: 3081 Polyethylene film
HQ: Jsp International Llc
1285 Drummers Ln Ste 301
Wayne PA 19087
610 651-8600

(G-4168)
K AND A PUBLISHING CO LLC
18085 Forrer St (48235-3114)
PHONE 734 743-1541
Kalio White,
EMP: 6
SALES (est): 219.1K **Privately Held**
SIC: 2721 Magazines: publishing & printing

(G-4169)
K G S SCREEN PROCESS INC
12650 Burt Rd (48223-3315)
PHONE 313 794-2777
Glenn J King, *President*
Donna King, *Vice Pres*
EMP: 5
SQ FT: 15,000
SALES: 500K **Privately Held**
SIC: 2759 Screen printing

(G-4170)
KAMPS INC
Also Called: Kamps Pallets
19001 Glendale St (48223-3423)
PHONE 313 381-2681
Clifton Cheek, *Manager*
EMP: 33
SALES (corp-wide): 157.4MM **Privately Held**
SIC: 2448 2499 Pallets, wood; mulch, wood & bark
PA: Kamps, Inc.
2900 Peach Ridge Ave Nw
Grand Rapids MI 49534
616 453-9676

(G-4171)
KAR-BONES INC
8350 John Kronk St (48210-2101)
PHONE 313 582-5551
Hussain Al-Nassari, *Mng Member*
EMP: 7 **EST:** 2016
SALES (est): 609.8K **Privately Held**
SIC: 3714 Motor vehicle parts & accessories

(G-4172)
KAUL GLOVE AND MFG CO (PA)
Also Called: Choctaw-Kaul Distribution Co
3540 Vinewood St (48208-2363)
PHONE 313 894-9494
Kenny Tubby, *CEO*
Anthony C Naso, *Vice Pres*
Stephen Kovats, *Purch Agent*
Teresa Aaron, *Purchasing*
Michael G Conniff Jr, *CFO*
EMP: 30
SQ FT: 110,000
SALES (est): 50.1MM **Privately Held**
WEB: www.choctawkaul.com
SIC: 2381 3151 5136 Fabric dress & work gloves; gloves, leather: work; work clothing, men's & boys'

(G-4173)
KAUTEX INC
Also Called: Kautex Detroit
2627 Clark St (48210-3265)
PHONE 313 633-2254
EMP: 280
SALES (corp-wide): 13.9B **Publicly Held**
SIC: 3089 Plastic containers, except foam; automotive parts, plastic
HQ: Kautex Inc.
750 Stephenson Hwy # 200
Troy MI 48083
248 616-5100

(G-4174)
KELLYS RECYCLING SERVICE INC
14800 Castleton St (48227-2422)
PHONE 313 389-7870
Bert Kelly, *Principal*
EMP: 5
SALES (est): 337K **Privately Held**
WEB: www.kellegous.com
SIC: 2077 Tallow rendering, inedible

(G-4175)
KERRY INC
4444 52nd St (48210-2728)
PHONE 616 871-9940
EMP: 65 **Privately Held**
SIC: 2023 Dry, condensed, evaporated dairy products
HQ: Kerry Inc.
3400 Millington Rd
Beloit WI 53511
608 363-1200

(G-4176)
KEURIG DR PEPPER INC
Also Called: Seven-Up of Detroit
12201 Beech Daly Rd (48239-2431)
PHONE 313 937-3500
Michael Nelson, *Branch Mgr*
EMP: 99 **Publicly Held**
SIC: 2086 Soft drinks: packaged in cans, bottles, etc.
PA: Keurig Dr Pepper Inc.
53 South Ave
Burlington MA 01803

(G-4177)
KEYSTONE CABLE CORPORATION
8200 Lynch Rd (48234-4143)
PHONE 313 924-9720
Thomas A Scott, *President*
Marijore Scott, *Corp Secy*
Timothy Scott, *Vice Pres*
Margorir Scott, *Treasurer*
EMP: 6
SQ FT: 13,000
SALES: 1.3MM **Privately Held**
WEB: www.keystonecable.net
SIC: 3694 Battery cable wiring sets for internal combustion engines

(G-4178)
KIMS MART INC
Also Called: Beauty Spot
20240 W 7 Mile Rd (48219-3469)
PHONE 313 592-4929
Hungwoo Kim, *Principal*
EMP: 4
SALES (est): 311.5K **Privately Held**
SIC: 3999 Barber & beauty shop equipment

(G-4179)
KIRKS AUTOMOTIVE INCORPORATED (PA)
Also Called: R K Parts
9330 Roselawn St (48204-2749)
PHONE 313 933-7030
Robert E Kirkman, *President*
Stephen Allen Benish, *Vice Pres*
Micheal Kirkman, *Vice Pres*
▲ **EMP:** 35 **EST:** 1946
SQ FT: 52,000
SALES (est): 11.2MM **Privately Held**
WEB: www.kirksauto.com
SIC: 5013 3694 Automotive supplies & parts; engine electrical equipment

(G-4180)
KOLENE CORPORATION
12890 Westwood St (48223-3436)
PHONE 313 273-9220
Roger L Shoemaker, *CEO*
W Scott Schilling, *President*
Tom Strickland, *General Mgr*
Dennis J McCardle, *Exec VP*
Michael Axline, *Vice Pres*
▼ **EMP:** 35 **EST:** 1939
SQ FT: 38,800
SALES (est): 11.2MM **Privately Held**
WEB: www.kolene.com
SIC: 2899 3567 Metal treating compounds; fuel-fired furnaces & ovens

Detroit - Wayne County (G-4181) **GEOGRAPHIC SECTION**

(G-4181)
KONNECTIONS BLOG
400 Renaissance Ctr # 26001425 (48243-1502)
PHONE.................................888 921-1114
Kimberly E Paris,
EMP: 3
SALES: 700K **Privately Held**
SIC: 2741

(G-4182)
KOWALSKI COMPANIES INC (PA)
2270 Holbrook St (48212-3445)
PHONE.................................313 873-8200
Michael Kowalski, *President*
George Dragisity, *COO*
Shawn Cinco, *Plant Mgr*
Crystal Towery, *Opers Mgr*
Ulrich Eggert, *Treasurer*
EMP: 116 EST: 1946
SQ FT: 60,000
SALES (est): 42.6MM **Privately Held**
WEB: www.kowality.com
SIC: 2013 5421 Sausages from purchased meat; bacon, side & sliced: from purchased meat; meat extracts from purchased meat; meat & fish markets

(G-4183)
KREATIONS INC
15340 Dale St (48223-1036)
PHONE.................................313 255-1230
Elias Madi, *President*
Imad Madi, *Vice Pres*
EMP: 10
SQ FT: 4,500
SALES (est): 580.8K **Privately Held**
SIC: 2541 8712 Cabinets, except refrigerated: show, display, etc.: wood; architectural services

(G-4184)
KRUMBSNATCHER ENTERPRISES LLC
Also Called: Krumbsnatcher Cookies
11000 W Mcnic (48235)
PHONE.................................313 408-6802
Daryll Gray, *Mng Member*
Christine Gray,
Tonya Gray,
Tina Poole,
EMP: 10
SALES: 500K **Privately Held**
SIC: 2052 7389 Cookies;

(G-4185)
KUHLMAN CASTING CO INC
20415 Woodingham Dr (48221-1288)
PHONE.................................248 853-2382
Neal Norgrove, *President*
Thomas F Hanrahan, *Corp Secy*
Richard Hanrahan, *Vice Pres*
EMP: 11 EST: 1949
SQ FT: 6,900
SALES: 1MM **Privately Held**
SIC: 3369 Machinery castings, nonferrous: ex. alum., copper, die, etc.

(G-4186)
KYKLOS HOLDINGS INC (DH)
1 Dauch Dr (48211-1115)
PHONE.................................313 758-2000
David C Dauch, *Ch of Bd*
EMP: 3
SALES (est): 1.2MM
SALES (corp-wide): 7.2B **Publicly Held**
SIC: 3711 3714 Motor vehicles & car bodies; motor vehicle parts & accessories
HQ: Bearing Holdings, Llc
1 Dauch Dr
Detroit MI 48211
313 758-2000

(G-4187)
LA ROSA REFRIGERATION & EQP CO
19191 Filer St (48234-2883)
PHONE.................................313 368-6620
Sebastiano Grillo, *President*
Jerry Grillo, *Vice Pres*
EMP: 20
SQ FT: 30,000
SALES (est): 5.3MM **Privately Held**
WEB: www.larosaequip.com
SIC: 3585 2599 Refrigeration equipment, complete; restaurant furniture, wood or metal

(G-4188)
LA SOLUCION CORP
19930 Conner St (48234-3227)
PHONE.................................313 893-9760
Patricia Maria Leon, *President*
Pat Leon, *Manager*
◆ EMP: 5 EST: 1999
SALES (est): 644.2K **Privately Held**
SIC: 3677 Filtration devices, electronic

(G-4189)
LABOR EDUCATION AND RES PRJ
Also Called: Labor Notes
7435 Michigan Ave (48210-2227)
PHONE.................................313 842-6262
Mark Brenner, *Director*
Theresa El Amin, *Bd of Directors*
EMP: 9
SALES (est): 1.1MM **Privately Held**
WEB: www.labornotes.org
SIC: 2759 Publication printing

(G-4190)
LABTECH CORPORATION
7707 Lyndon St (48238-2465)
PHONE.................................313 862-1737
Corey Bryce, *President*
EMP: 11
SQ FT: 75,000
SALES (est): 2.9MM **Privately Held**
SIC: 2842 Cleaning or polishing preparations

(G-4191)
LAFARGE NORTH AMERICA INC
1301 Springwells Ct (48209-4608)
PHONE.................................313 842-9258
Jodie Weiss, *Manager*
EMP: 6
SALES (corp-wide): 27.6B **Privately Held**
WEB: www.lafargenorthamerica.com
SIC: 3273 Ready-mixed concrete
HQ: Lafarge North America Inc.
8700 W Bryn Mawr Ave
Chicago IL 60631
773 372-1000

(G-4192)
LAKESIDE BUILDING PRODUCTS
9189 Central St (48204-4323)
P.O. Box 2900, Farmington Hills (48333-2900)
PHONE.................................248 349-3500
EMP: 4
SALES (est): 367.8K **Privately Held**
SIC: 3273 Mfg Ready-Mixed Concrete

(G-4193)
LAND STAR INC
Also Called: Michigan Masonry Materials
14284 Meyers Rd (48227-3922)
PHONE.................................313 834-2366
Fred Warstler, *President*
EMP: 4
SALES (est): 534.9K **Privately Held**
SIC: 5211 3273 Lumber & other building materials; ready-mixed concrete

(G-4194)
LATINO PRESS INC
6301 Michigan Ave (48210-2954)
PHONE.................................313 361-3000
Elias Gutierrez, *President*
EMP: 7
SQ FT: 4,000
SALES: 480K **Privately Held**
SIC: 2711 Newspapers, publishing & printing

(G-4195)
LAUGHABITS LLC
9301 Dwight St (48214-2903)
PHONE.................................248 990-3011
Greg Robinson, *Mng Member*
EMP: 5
SALES (est): 260.1K **Privately Held**
SIC: 3993 Advertising artwork

(G-4196)
LEAR AUTOMOTIVE MFG LLC
6555 E Davison St (48212-1455)
PHONE.................................248 447-1603
EMP: 11
SALES (est): 556.8K
SALES (corp-wide): 20.4B **Publicly Held**
SIC: 3714 7532 Mfg Of Aftermarket Auto Parts And Leather Goods
PA: Lear Corporation
21557 Telegraph Rd
Southfield MI 48033
248 447-1500

(G-4197)
LEAR AUTOMOTIVE MFG LLC
6555 E Davidson St (48212)
PHONE.................................248 447-1603
Barney Theisen, *Vice Pres*
EMP: 11
SALES (est): 19.4K
SALES (corp-wide): 21.1B **Publicly Held**
SIC: 3714 7532 Motor vehicle electrical equipment; instrument board assemblies, motor vehicle; automotive wiring harness sets; motor vehicle body components & frame; upholstery & trim shop, automotive
PA: Lear Corporation
21557 Telegraph Rd
Southfield MI 48033
248 447-1500

(G-4198)
LEMICA CORPORATION
11201 Manning St (48234-3538)
PHONE.................................313 839-2150
Gary L Brown, *CEO*
EMP: 15
SQ FT: 28,000
SALES (est): 2.2MM **Privately Held**
SIC: 2431 Doors, wood; moldings, wood: unfinished & prefinished

(G-4199)
LEONARD FOUNTAIN SPC INC
Also Called: Leonard's Syrups
4601 Nancy St (48212-1213)
PHONE.................................313 891-4141
Leonard Bugajewski, *President*
Leonard Bugajewski III, *Vice Pres*
Sherri Bugajewski, *Admin Sec*
EMP: 54
SQ FT: 75,000
SALES (est): 12MM **Privately Held**
SIC: 7359 2087 Equipment rental & leasing; syrups, drink

(G-4200)
LETTS INDUSTRIES INC (PA)
1111 Bellevue St (48207-3683)
PHONE.................................313 579-1100
Charles E Letts Jr, *President*
Craig Pickard, *Treasurer*
Sandy N Phillip, *Manager*
Sandy Phillip, *Manager*
▲ EMP: 4 EST: 1909
SQ FT: 83,000
SALES (est): 722.9K **Privately Held**
WEB: www.letts.com
SIC: 3714 3462 5084 Steering mechanisms, motor vehicle; automotive forgings, ferrous: crankshaft, engine, axle, etc.; machine tools & metalworking machinery; materials handling machinery

(G-4201)
LEVEL ELEVEN LLC
1520 Woodward Ave Fl 3 (48226-2040)
PHONE.................................313 662-2000
Robert Marsh, *CEO*
Bill Johnson, *COO*
David Leinweber, *Vice Pres*
Justin Soullier, *Sales Staff*
Jake Zott, *Sales Staff*
EMP: 28 EST: 2012
SALES (est): 2.4MM **Privately Held**
SIC: 7372 Business oriented computer software

(G-4202)
LGC GLOBAL INC
Also Called: Lakeshore Global Corporation
7310 Woodward Ave 500a (48202-3165)
PHONE.................................313 989-4141
Avinash Rachmale, *CEO*
Fred Feliciano, *VP Bus Dvlpt*
EMP: 42
SQ FT: 20,000
SALES (est): 16.1MM **Privately Held**
WEB: www.lakeshoretech.com
SIC: 8711 1623 1389 4931 Construction & civil engineering; water, sewer & utility lines; construction, repair & dismantling services; electric & other services combined; environmental consultant

(G-4203)
LIBERTY BURNISHING CO
18401 Sherwood St (48234-2832)
PHONE.................................313 366-7878
Jeffrey Davis, *President*
Rodney Pett, *Corp Secy*
Laura Davis, *Vice Pres*
Julie Pett, *Vice Pres*
EMP: 5
SQ FT: 6,500
SALES (est): 639K **Privately Held**
SIC: 3471 Tumbling (cleaning & polishing) of machine parts; finishing, metals or formed products

(G-4204)
LIGHTHOUSE DIRECT BUY LLC
Also Called: Lighthouse Cards and Gifts
16143 Wyoming St (48221-2846)
P.O. Box 21637 (48221-0637)
PHONE.................................313 340-1850
Jack Taylor Jones, *Mng Member*
Claudy E Jones,
Claudy Jones,
EMP: 5
SQ FT: 3,100
SALES (est): 121K **Privately Held**
SIC: 5947 5999 5942 2752 Gift shop; religious goods; book stores; photolithographic printing; clothing accessories: men's & boys'; gifts & novelties

(G-4205)
LIGHTING ENTERPRISES INC
Also Called: Universal Led
16706 Telegraph Rd (48219-3729)
PHONE.................................313 693-9504
Mohammed Abueida, *CEO*
Khaled Abueida, *Principal*
John Bruton, *Vice Pres*
Linda Kaiser, *Regl Sales Mgr*
▲ EMP: 8
SALES (est): 1.8MM **Privately Held**
WEB: www.lightingenterprises.com
SIC: 3645 Table lamps; floor lamps

(G-4206)
LIN ADAM FUEL INC
13330 Linwood St (48238-3448)
PHONE.................................313 733-6631
EMP: 6 EST: 2012
SALES (est): 874.9K **Privately Held**
SIC: 2869 Fuels

(G-4207)
LIVE TRACK PRODUCTIONS INC
848 Manistique St (48215-2974)
PHONE.................................313 704-2224
Robert Kelsey, *President*
EMP: 5
SALES: 117K **Privately Held**
SIC: 2741 7389 Music book & sheet music publishing;

(G-4208)
LOCAL MEDIA GROUP INC
9 Alger Pl (48230-1908)
PHONE.................................313 885-2612
EMP: 69
SALES (corp-wide): 1.5B **Privately Held**
WEB: www.ottaway.com
SIC: 2711 Newspapers; publishing only, not printed on site
HQ: Local Media Group, Inc.
40 Mulberry St
Middletown NY 10940
845 341-1100

(G-4209)
LOPEZ REPRODUCTIONS INC
645 Griswold St Ste 27 (48226-4013)
P.O. Box 94, Allen Park (48101-0094)
PHONE.................................313 386-4526
Leonard Lopez, *President*
Ronald Lopez, *Vice Pres*

GEOGRAPHIC SECTION

Detroit - Wayne County (G-4238)

EMP: 7
SQ FT: 1,000
SALES (est): 410K **Privately Held**
SIC: 2752 7334 Commercial printing, offset; photocopying & duplicating services

(G-4210)
LORENZO WHITE
Also Called: Quality Lock & Door
20029 Cooley St (48219-1208)
PHONE.................................313 943-3667
Lorenzo White, *Owner*
EMP: 4
SALES (est): 348.3K **Privately Held**
SIC: 3442 Metal doors, sash & trim

(G-4211)
LOYALTY 1977 INK
18528 Margareta St (48219-2932)
PHONE.................................313 759-1006
Brandon Cunningham, *Partner*
EMP: 4 **EST:** 2011
SALES (est): 279.6K **Privately Held**
SIC: 2396 Fabric printing & stamping

(G-4212)
LYNDON FABRICATORS INC
12478 Beech Daly Rd (48239-2400)
PHONE.................................313 937-3640
John Largent, *President*
EMP: 6 **EST:** 1946
SQ FT: 4,500
SALES (est): 1MM **Privately Held**
SIC: 3444 Sheet metal specialties, not stamped

(G-4213)
M AND A FUELS
13601 Plymouth Rd (48227-3026)
PHONE.................................313 397-7141
Mohammed Al, *Administration*
EMP: 3
SALES (est): 194.1K **Privately Held**
SIC: 2869 Fuels

(G-4214)
MAGNA INTERNATIONAL AMER INC
Also Called: Magna Seating Detroit
12800 Oakland Pkwy (48203-3587)
PHONE.................................313 422-6000
Laura Bryant, *HR Admin*
Simon Kew, *Branch Mgr*
EMP: 420
SALES (corp-wide): 40.8B **Privately Held**
SIC: 3714 Motor vehicle parts & accessories
HQ: Magna International Of America, Inc.
750 Tower Dr 7000
Troy MI 48098

(G-4215)
MAGNI-INDUSTRIES INC (HQ)
2771 Hammond St (48209-1239)
PHONE.................................313 843-7855
David E Berry, *Ch of Bd*
Colette Walsh, *Research*
Warren Knape, *Executive*
▲ **EMP:** 38 **EST:** 1978
SQ FT: 4,200
SALES (est): 29.7MM
SALES (corp-wide): 80.5MM **Privately Held**
SIC: 2899 Rust resisting compounds
PA: The Magni Group Inc
390 Park St Ste 300
Birmingham MI 48009
248 647-4500

(G-4216)
MAJESTIC PATTERN COMPANY INC
20400 Sherwood St (48234-2986)
PHONE.................................313 892-5800
Wallace G Harper, *President*
Tony Atherholt, *Foreman/Supr*
EMP: 7 **EST:** 1929
SQ FT: 7,000
SALES (est): 700K **Privately Held**
WEB: www.majesticpattern.com
SIC: 3543 Industrial patterns

(G-4217)
MAKAVELI CNSTR & ASSOC INC
20131 James (48235)
PHONE.................................810 892-3412
Dawn Montgomery, *CEO*
EMP: 3 **EST:** 2018
SALES (est): 94.1K **Privately Held**
SIC: 1521 1771 1081 1761 Single-family housing construction; stucco, gunite & grouting contractors; metal mining exploration & development services; gutter & downspout contractor; painting & paper hanging; plastering, drywall & insulation

(G-4218)
MARAND PRODUCTS COMPANY INC
17243 Filer St (48212-2040)
PHONE.................................313 369-2000
Andrew Kulikowski, *President*
Mary Defranzoi, *Admin Sec*
EMP: 4
SQ FT: 11,000
SALES: 600K **Privately Held**
SIC: 2992 Oils & greases, blending & compounding

(G-4219)
MARTAK CULTURED MARBLE
18841 John R St (48203-2004)
PHONE.................................313 891-5400
Takis Nomides, *President*
Ernest Nomides, *Vice Pres*
Ted Gregorio, *Treasurer*
EMP: 4
SQ FT: 21,927
SALES (est): 512.9K **Privately Held**
SIC: 2299 Tops, manmade fiber

(G-4220)
MAVEN DRIVE LLC
300 Renaissance Ctr (48243-1402)
PHONE.................................313 667-1541
Julia Steyn, *CEO*
EMP: 90
SALES: 14MM **Publicly Held**
SIC: 3711 Motor vehicles & car bodies
HQ: General Motors Llc
300 Renaissance Ctr L1
Detroit MI 48243

(G-4221)
MCCLURES PICKLES LLC
8201 Saint Aubin St (48211-1301)
PHONE.................................248 837-9323
Joseph McClure, *Mng Member*
Robert McClure,
▼ **EMP:** 24
SQ FT: 20,000
SALES (est): 5.4MM **Privately Held**
SIC: 2099 2033 Food preparations; canned fruits & specialties

(G-4222)
MCDONALD WHOLESALE DISTRIBUTOR
19536 W Davison St (48223-3422)
PHONE.................................313 273-2870
Patricia McDonald, *President*
George McDonald, *Vice Pres*
EMP: 4
SQ FT: 4,800
SALES: 520K **Privately Held**
SIC: 5023 2591 Window furnishings; window shades

(G-4223)
MCNIC OIL & GAS PROPERTIES
2000 2nd Ave (48226-1203)
PHONE.................................313 256-5500
Rai P K Bhargava, *Ch of Bd*
Joseph T Williams, *President*
Daniel L Schiffer, *Vice Pres*
EMP: 3
SALES (est): 240K **Privately Held**
SIC: 1311 Natural gas production

(G-4224)
MECCOM CORPORATION
5945 Martin St (48210-1650)
PHONE.................................313 895-4900
James Steele, *President*
EMP: 8
SQ FT: 25,000
SALES (est): 654.9K **Privately Held**
SIC: 7692 3498 3441 Welding repair; fabricated pipe & fittings; expansion joints (structural shapes), iron or steel

(G-4225)
MEDIA SOLUTIONS INC
4715 Woodward Ave Fl 2 (48201-1307)
PHONE.................................313 831-3152
Lila Abraham, *President*
Odette Jones, *Vice Pres*
EMP: 4
SQ FT: 1,500
SALES (est): 437.5K **Privately Held**
SIC: 7336 3993 Graphic arts & related design; signs & advertising specialties

(G-4226)
MERIDIANRX LLC
1 Campus Martius Ste 750 (48226-5013)
PHONE.................................855 323-4580
Jon Cotton, *President*
Rene Acker, *COO*
Steve Raymond, *Vice Pres*
Justin Bookmeier, *Opers Mgr*
Joseph Andreoli, *Sales Staff*
EMP: 65
SALES (est): 6.7MM
SALES (corp-wide): 20.4B **Publicly Held**
SIC: 2834 Pharmaceutical preparations
HQ: The Wellcare Management Group Inc
280 Broadway Ste 3
Newburgh NY
845 440-2400

(G-4227)
METAL TECH PRODUCTS INC
15720 Dale St (48223-1040)
PHONE.................................313 533-5277
Richard Mollick, *President*
Letitia Gordon, *Vice Pres*
EMP: 22
SQ FT: 39,000
SALES (est): 5.7MM **Privately Held**
WEB: www.metaltechproducts.com
SIC: 3443 Weldments

(G-4228)
METALDYNE LLC (DH)
1 Dauch Dr (48211-1115)
PHONE.................................734 207-6200
David Dauch, *President*
Thomas V Chambers, *COO*
Robert Defauw, *Vice Pres*
Doug Grimm, *Vice Pres*
Christoph Guhe, *Vice Pres*
EMP: 150
SALES: 1.3B
SALES (corp-wide): 7.2B **Publicly Held**
SIC: 3714 Motor vehicle parts & accessories

(G-4229)
METALDYNE PWRTRAIN CMPNNTS INC (DH)
1 Dauch Dr (48211-1115)
PHONE.................................313 758-2000
Thomas A Amato, *CEO*
▲ **EMP:** 170
SQ FT: 30,000
SALES (est): 60MM
SALES (corp-wide): 7.2B **Publicly Held**
WEB: www.metaldyne.com
SIC: 3519 Parts & accessories, internal combustion engines

(G-4230)
METRIC TOOL COMPANY INC
17144 Mount Elliott St (48212-1361)
PHONE.................................313 369-9610
Peter Hayda, *President*
EMP: 10
SQ FT: 32,000
SALES (est): 1.5MM **Privately Held**
SIC: 3599 Machine shop, jobbing & repair

(G-4231)
METRO PIPING INC
1500b Trombly St (48211-2126)
PHONE.................................313 872-4330
Steven H Lowe, *President*
John Morrison, *Vice Pres*
EMP: 18 **EST:** 2000
SQ FT: 32,000
SALES (est): 6MM **Privately Held**
WEB: www.lhcc.org
SIC: 3494 Pipe fittings

(G-4232)
METRO WBE ASSOCIATES INC
18353 W Mcnichols Rd (48219-4199)
PHONE.................................248 504-7563
Stephanie Corona, *President*
Paula Holt, *Treasurer*
EMP: 3 **EST:** 2010
SALES (est): 273.9K **Privately Held**
SIC: 3841 8748 8721 Surgical & medical instruments; business consulting; accounting, auditing & bookkeeping

(G-4233)
METROPOLITAN ALLOYS CORP
17385 Ryan Rd (48212-1196)
PHONE.................................313 366-4443
Murray Spilman, *President*
EMP: 20
SQ FT: 18,000
SALES (est): 13.5MM
SALES (corp-wide): 34.3MM **Privately Held**
WEB: www.metroalloys.com
SIC: 5051 3643 3341 3339 Zinc; anode metal; current-carrying wiring devices; secondary nonferrous metals; primary nonferrous metals
PA: Mac Group International Incorporated
17385 Ryan Rd
Detroit MI 48212
313 366-4444

(G-4234)
METROPOLITAN BAKING COMPANY
Also Called: Michigan Baking Co.
8579 Lumpkin St (48212-3622)
PHONE.................................313 875-7246
James G Kordas, *President*
Mike Zrimec, *General Mgr*
David Bushbaker, *Controller*
EMP: 65 **EST:** 1945
SQ FT: 75,000
SALES: 15.8MM **Privately Held**
SIC: 2051 Bread, all types (white, wheat, rye, etc): fresh or frozen

(G-4235)
MEXICO EXPRESS
7611 W Vernor Hwy (48209-1513)
PHONE.................................313 843-6717
Francisco Leon, *President*
EMP: 10
SALES (est): 606.7K **Privately Held**
SIC: 3111 4822 Leather tanning & finishing; telegraph & other communications

(G-4236)
MICHIGAN AMMO LLC
4680 High St (48229-1406)
PHONE.................................313 383-4430
Michael Patrick, *President*
EMP: 4
SQ FT: 4,600
SALES (est): 489.6K **Privately Held**
SIC: 3482 Small arms ammunition

(G-4237)
MICHIGAN BOX COMPANY (PA)
Also Called: Fontana Forest Products
1910 Trombly St (48211-2130)
PHONE.................................313 873-9500
Carl Fontana, *President*
Elaine Fontana, *President*
Louis Fontana, *Vice Pres*
Phil Petro, *Transptn Dir*
Greg White, *Purch Mgr*
▼ **EMP:** 55
SQ FT: 160,000
SALES (est): 13.6MM **Privately Held**
WEB: www.michiganbox.com
SIC: 2441 2652 2653 Boxes, wood; filing boxes, paperboard: made from purchased materials; boxes, corrugated: made from purchased materials

(G-4238)
MICHIGAN BRUSH MFG CO
7446 Central St (48210-1037)
P.O. Box 10247 (48210-0247)
PHONE.................................313 834-1070
Bruce Gale, *President*

Detroit - Wayne County (G-4239)

EMP: 20 **EST:** 1917
SQ FT: 55,000
SALES (est): 3.2MM **Privately Held**
WEB: www.mi-brush.com
SIC: 3991 Brushes, household or industrial; brooms; paint rollers

(G-4239)
MICHIGAN BTLG & CSTM PACK CO
13940 Tireman St (48228-2718)
PHONE 313 846-1717
Sal Landa, *President*
Chaker Aoun, *COO*
▲ **EMP:** 65
SQ FT: 40,000
SALES (est): 9.4MM **Privately Held**
SIC: 2086 Bottled & canned soft drinks

(G-4240)
MICHIGAN CHRONICLE PUBG CO
1452 Randolph St Ste 400 (48226-2284)
PHONE 313 963-5522
Haram Jackson, *President*
EMP: 50 **EST:** 1936
SQ FT: 30,000
SALES: 4MM **Privately Held**
WEB: www.michronicle.com
SIC: 2711 Newspapers, publishing & printing

(G-4241)
MICHIGAN FRONT PAGE LLC
479 Ledyard St (48201-2641)
PHONE 313 963-5522
Sam Logan, *Publisher*
EMP: 8
SALES (est): 307.9K
SALES (corp-wide): 7.2MM **Privately Held**
SIC: 2711 Newspapers: publishing only, not printed on site
PA: Real Times Ii Llc
4445 S Dr Mrtn Lther King Martin Luther King
Chicago IL 60653
312 225-2400

(G-4242)
MICHIGAN PAPER DIE INC
632 Harper Ave (48202-3540)
PHONE 313 873-0404
Mark Megie, *President*
Nick Bommarito, *Treasurer*
EMP: 16
SQ FT: 10,000
SALES (est): 1.4MM **Privately Held**
SIC: 2675 Die-cut paper & board

(G-4243)
MICHIGAN STEEL FINISHING CO
Also Called: MICHIGAN STEEL SPRING COMPANY
12850 Mansfield St (48227-1240)
PHONE 313 838-3925
John S Haine, *President*
Roger L Abram, *Vice Pres*
EMP: 13 **EST:** 1976
SQ FT: 18,000
SALES (est): 2.2MM **Privately Held**
SIC: 3452 3495 Washers; wire springs

(G-4244)
MICHIGAN TILE AND MARBLE CO (PA)
9317 Freeland St (48228-2300)
PHONE 313 931-1700
Maryann Brady, *President*
Michele Kelly, *Business Mgr*
Katherine Vitto, *Treasurer*
James Broquet, *VP Human Res*
James Lanzetta, *Admin Sec*
▲ **EMP:** 50 **EST:** 1943
SQ FT: 3,000
SALES (est): 4.3MM **Privately Held**
SIC: 3281 1411 Cut stone & stone products; dimension stone

(G-4245)
MICRO PLATERS SALES INC
Also Called: Hajjar Plating
221 Victor St (48203-3131)
PHONE 313 865-2293
Howard Hicks, *President*
Tammy T Packer, *Vice Pres*
John Hicks, *Treasurer*
▲ **EMP:** 32
SALES (est): 4MM **Privately Held**
SIC: 3471 Plating of metals or formed products; polishing, metals or formed products

(G-4246)
MICRO RIM CORPORATION
221 Victor St (48203-3131)
PHONE 313 865-1090
Tammy Parker, *President*
Howard T Hicks II, *Vice Pres*
Donna De Michael, *Manager*
▲ **EMP:** 10
SQ FT: 125,000
SALES (est): 1.2MM **Privately Held**
SIC: 3714 Bumpers & bumperettes, motor vehicle

(G-4247)
MID-WEST TRUCK ACCESSORIES
26425 Grand River Ave (48240-1504)
PHONE 313 592-1788
EMP: 3
SALES (corp-wide): 3.9MM **Privately Held**
SIC: 7532 3711 Van conversion; trucks, pickup, assembly of
PA: Mid-West Truck Accessories, Inc
18610 Fort St
Riverview MI 48193
734 283-9650

(G-4248)
MIDWEST STEEL INC (PA)
2525 E Grand Blvd (48211-2001)
PHONE 313 873-2220
Gary R Broad, *President*
Mark Dungan, *Superintendent*
Kenny Kerr, *Superintendent*
Tom Sherrill, *Superintendent*
Bob Vellmure, *Superintendent*
EMP: 50
SQ FT: 30,000
SALES: 130MM **Privately Held**
SIC: 3441 1791 Fabricated structural metal; structural steel erection

(G-4249)
MILANO BAKERY INC
3500 Russell St (48207-2030)
PHONE 313 833-3500
Dragoslav Janevski, *President*
EMP: 30 **EST:** 1978
SQ FT: 6,000
SALES (est): 4.8MM **Privately Held**
WEB: www.milanobakeryinc.com
SIC: 2051 Bread, all types (white, wheat, rye, etc): fresh or frozen

(G-4250)
MILTON MANUFACTURING INC
Also Called: Wayne Stmping Intrntnal- Sbsid
301 E Grixdale (48203-2073)
PHONE 313 366-2450
Shelly L Green, *President*
Jeff Benton, *General Mgr*
Lisa Grover, *General Mgr*
Jim Green Jr, *Vice Pres*
Frank Sheckell, *Vice Pres*
EMP: 50 **EST:** 1945
SQ FT: 350,000
SALES (est): 17.4MM **Privately Held**
WEB: www.miltonmfg.com
SIC: 3444 3496 3441 3429 Sheet metal specialties, not stamped; miscellaneous fabricated wire products; fabricated structural metal; manufactured hardware (general)

(G-4251)
MJC INDUSTRIES INC
Also Called: Hy-Vac Technologies
15701 Glendale St (48227-1708)
PHONE 313 838-2800
Kevan Johnston, *President*
Jim McClelland, *Vice Pres*
EMP: 12 **EST:** 1983
SQ FT: 20,000
SALES (est): 2.1MM **Privately Held**
WEB: www.mjcindustries.com
SIC: 3398 Annealing of metal; brazing (hardening) of metal

(G-4252)
MLH SERVICES LLC
11310 Kenmoor St (48205-3284)
PHONE 313 768-4403
Stacey Horn,
Keith Horn,
EMP: 4
SALES (est): 212.5K **Privately Held**
SIC: 3953 Seal presses, notary & hand

(G-4253)
MODIFIED GEAR AND SPLINE INC
18300 Mount Elliott St (48234-2735)
PHONE 313 893-3511
Randall Dulecki, *President*
EMP: 10
SQ FT: 12,000
SALES: 600K **Privately Held**
SIC: 3599 Grinding castings for the trade

(G-4254)
MOOSE MFG & MACHINING LLC
440 Burroughs St Ste 692 (48202-3476)
PHONE 586 765-4686
Vladimir Yasnogorodskiy,
EMP: 4
SALES (est): 162.4K **Privately Held**
SIC: 3728 Aircraft parts & equipment

(G-4255)
MOTOR CITY BENDING & ROLLING
17655 Filer St (48212-1495)
PHONE 313 368-4400
James Vanderjagt, *President*
James Vander Jagt, *President*
EMP: 8 **EST:** 1961
SQ FT: 9,600
SALES (est): 1.5MM **Privately Held**
SIC: 3498 3599 Fabricated pipe & fittings; machine shop, jobbing & repair

(G-4256)
MOTOR CITY ELECTRIC TECH INC
9440 Grinnell St (48213-1151)
PHONE 313 921-5300
Dale M Wieczorek, *President*
Denise Hodgins, *Vice Pres*
Walter Szpulak, *Project Mgr*
Justin Nelson, *Technician*
EMP: 95
SQ FT: 60,000
SALES (est): 22.2MM
SALES (corp-wide): 133.5MM **Privately Held**
WEB: www.mceco.com
SIC: 3613 8711 Control panels, electric; engineering services
PA: Motor City Electric Co.
9440 Grinnell St
Detroit MI 48213
313 567-5300

(G-4257)
MOTOR CITY SEWING
1651 Church St (48216-1524)
PHONE 313 595-5275
Sarah Lapinski, *Principal*
EMP: 3
SALES (est): 152.8K **Privately Held**
SIC: 2337 Women's & misses' suits & coats

(G-4258)
MR MCGOOZ PRODUCTS INC
18911 W 7 Mile Rd (48219-2764)
PHONE 313 693-4003
Ronald Husdon, *Principal*
EMP: 3
SALES (est): 171.3K **Privately Held**
SIC: 3999 Manufacturing industries

(G-4259)
MRM IDA PRODUCTS CO INC
8385 Lyndon St (48238-2444)
PHONE 313 834-0200
Sanford Moser, *President*
EMP: 8 **EST:** 1974
SQ FT: 8,500
SALES (est): 1.1MM **Privately Held**
SIC: 5211 5031 3589 Windows, storm: wood or metal; sash, wood or metal; windows; metal doors, sash & trim; garbage disposers & compactors, commercial

(G-4260)
MSMAC DESIGNS LLC
11069 Nashville St (48205-3232)
PHONE 313 521-6289
Patrice Kathleen McDonald, *CEO*
EMP: 8
SALES (est): 301.7K **Privately Held**
SIC: 3999 Manufacturing industries

(G-4261)
MYLOCKERCOM LLC
Also Called: Customcat
1300 Rosa Parks Blvd (48216-1952)
PHONE 877 898-3366
Paul Domke, *Controller*
Jesse Mason, *Marketing Staff*
Alex Phillips, *Marketing Staff*
Robert Hake, *Mng Member*
Mike Trevino, *Info Tech Mgr*
▲ **EMP:** 280
SQ FT: 126,000
SALES (est): 40MM **Privately Held**
SIC: 2759 Letterpress & screen printing

(G-4262)
NATIONAL BAKERY
736 E State Fair (48203-1115)
PHONE 313 891-7803
Chris Cvhokodki, *Owner*
EMP: 7
SALES (est): 685.8K **Privately Held**
SIC: 2051 Bakery: wholesale or wholesale/retail combined

(G-4263)
NATIONAL FLEET SERVICE LLC
10100 Grinnell St (48213-1142)
PHONE 313 923-1799
Timothy Lariviere, *Mng Member*
▲ **EMP:** 50
SALES (est): 6.3MM **Privately Held**
WEB: www.magnefine.com
SIC: 3714 Motor vehicle parts & accessories

(G-4264)
NAVARRE INC
Also Called: Michigan Motor Exchange
3500 E 8 Mile Rd (48234-1005)
PHONE 313 892-7300
Kenneth Navarre, *President*
EMP: 21
SALES (corp-wide): 2.2MM **Privately Held**
WEB: www.michiganmotorexchange.com
SIC: 3714 3519 Rebuilding engines & transmissions, factory basis; internal combustion engines
PA: Navarre Inc
6497 Highland Rd Ste B
Waterford MI

(G-4265)
NEIGHBORHOOD ARTISANS INC
85 Oakman Blvd (48203-3051)
PHONE 313 865-5373
Mary Jane Karsinski, *Director*
EMP: 6
SQ FT: 10,000
SALES: 79K **Privately Held**
WEB: www.neighborhoodartisans.com
SIC: 8399 2396 Community development groups; automotive & apparel trimmings

(G-4266)
NELSON IRON WORKS INC
6350 Benham St (48211-1899)
PHONE 313 925-5355
John N Knill Jr, *President*
Sara Havlik, *Human Res Dir*
EMP: 9 **EST:** 1947
SQ FT: 10,000
SALES (est): 1.9MM **Privately Held**
SIC: 3441 Fabricated structural metal

(G-4267)
NEW CENTER STAMPING INC
950 E Milwaukee St (48211-2008)
PHONE 313 872-3500
Ronald Hall, *CEO*

GEOGRAPHIC SECTION
Detroit - Wayne County (G-4297)

Greg Smith, *COO*
Don Stein, *Vice Pres*
Chris Garvey, *CFO*
Doug Braun, *Director*
EMP: 110
SQ FT: 200,000
SALES (est): 34MM **Privately Held**
WEB: www.newcenter.net
SIC: 3469 Metal stampings

(G-4268)
NEW MARTHA WASHINGTON BAKERY
10335 Joseph Campau St (48212-3259)
PHONE..................313 872-1988
Petar Petrovic, *Owner*
EMP: 7
SALES (est): 430.3K **Privately Held**
SIC: 2051 5461 Bakery: wholesale or wholesale/retail combined; bakeries

(G-4269)
NEXTEK POWER SYSTEMS INC (PA)
461 Burroughs St (48202-3419)
PHONE..................313 887-1321
Paul Savage, *President*
Wayne Gutschow, *President*
Brian Noble, *CFO*
Ben Hartman, *CTO*
▲ **EMP:** 20
SQ FT: 5,000
SALES (est): 4.8MM **Privately Held**
WEB: www.nextekpower.com
SIC: 3612 8711 5063 Fluorescent ballasts; electrical or electronic engineering; lighting fixtures

(G-4270)
NICOLE ACARTER LLC
Also Called: Medusa's Antidote
551 Newport St (48215-3245)
PHONE..................248 251-2800
Nicole Carter,
EMP: 3
SALES (est): 147.3K **Privately Held**
SIC: 3171 7389 Women's handbags & purses; artists' agents & brokers; styling of fashions, apparel, furniture, textiles, etc.; textile & apparel services

(G-4271)
NICRO FINISHING LLC
6431 E Palmer St (48211-3201)
PHONE..................313 924-0661
James R Gay, *Mng Member*
EMP: 10
SQ FT: 25,000
SALES: 2MM **Privately Held**
SIC: 3471 Electroplating & plating

(G-4272)
NIKIS FOOD CO INC
Also Called: Niki's Warehouse
8844 Gratiot Ave (48213-2907)
PHONE..................313 925-0876
Dennis Kesallinis, *President*
EMP: 3
SALES (est): 224.1K **Privately Held**
SIC: 3639 Major kitchen appliances, except refrigerators & stoves

(G-4273)
NJE ENTERPRISES LLC
Also Called: Allegra Print Imaging Detroit
400 Renaissance Ctr Lbby (48216-1607)
PHONE..................313 963-3600
N Eschenburg, *Mng Member*
Norma Eschenburg,
EMP: 5
SQ FT: 2,700
SALES: 650K **Privately Held**
SIC: 2752 2759 Commercial printing, offset; commercial printing

(G-4274)
NO LIMIT WIRELESS-MICHIGAN INC
6236 Michigan Ave (48210-2953)
PHONE..................313 285-8402
EMP: 3 **EST:** 2009
SALES (est): 223.7K **Privately Held**
SIC: 4812 3679 8748 Cellular telephone services; headphones, radio; telecommunications consultant

(G-4275)
NORBROOK PLATING INC
19230 Mount Elliott St (48234-2723)
PHONE..................313 369-9304
Gerald Plodzick, *Manager*
EMP: 8
SALES (est): 490K **Privately Held**
SIC: 3471 Plating of metals or formed products

(G-4276)
NORTHERN MILLWORK CO
Also Called: General Hardwood Co
7201 E Mcnichols Rd (48212-2050)
PHONE..................313 365-7733
Ronald Ellerbrock, *President*
Mark Ellerbrock, *Vice Pres*
EMP: 10
SQ FT: 16,000
SALES (est): 945.5K
SALES (corp-wide): 5.4MM **Privately Held**
SIC: 2431 Millwork
PA: General Hardwood Company
7201 E Mcnichols Rd
Detroit MI 48212
313 365-7733

(G-4277)
NORTRONIC COMPANY
20210 Sherwood St (48234-2952)
PHONE..................313 893-3730
Timothy Butts, *President*
Alfred Krause, *Treasurer*
Maryann Arquette, *Admin Sec*
▲ **EMP:** 6 **EST:** 1964
SQ FT: 22,000
SALES: 990K **Privately Held**
SIC: 5084 3548 7699 Welding machinery & equipment; welding & cutting apparatus & accessories; welding equipment repair

(G-4278)
NOTES FROM MAN CAVE LLC
3680 Seminole St (48214-1124)
PHONE..................586 604-1997
Theresa Zuber, *CEO*
Arika Ewell, *CFO*
EMP: 4 **EST:** 2016
SALES (est): 150.5K **Privately Held**
SIC: 2771 Greeting cards

(G-4279)
NU-FOLD INC
4444 Lawton St (48208-2162)
PHONE..................313 898-4695
Steven Finkbiner, *President*
EMP: 17
SQ FT: 3,000
SALES (est): 1MM **Privately Held**
SIC: 2675 Folders, filing, die-cut: made from purchased materials

(G-4280)
NUTCO INC (PA)
Also Called: Germack Nut Co
2140 Wilkins St (48207-2123)
PHONE..................800 872-4006
Bill Gierman, *President*
Frank Germack III, *Corp Secy*
Wally Szul, *Plant Mgr*
Robin Edwards, *Bookkeeper*
Suzanne Germack, *Shareholder*
EMP: 30
SALES (est): 12.8MM **Privately Held**
WEB: www.germack.com
SIC: 5145 2068 5441 Nuts, salted or roasted; salted & roasted nuts & seeds; nuts

(G-4281)
O E M PARTS SUPPLY INC
16583 Greenview Ave (48219-4121)
PHONE..................313 729-4283
Dave Smith, *President*
EMP: 3
SALES: 200K **Privately Held**
SIC: 3713 Truck bodies & parts

(G-4282)
OAKLAND BOLT & NUT CO LLC
8977 Lyndon St (48238)
PHONE..................313 659-1677
Henry Wojcik II, *President*
Keith Williamson, *Treasurer*
David Lavoie, *Manager*
EMP: 4
SQ FT: 15,000
SALES (est): 432.5K **Privately Held**
SIC: 3452 Bolts, nuts, rivets & washers

(G-4283)
OAKLAND STAMPING LLC (HQ)
1200 Woodland St (48211-1071)
PHONE..................734 397-6300
Scott Jones, *President*
Robert Koss, *Treasurer*
▲ **EMP:** 250
SALES (est): 49.3MM **Privately Held**
SIC: 3469 Stamping metal for the trade

(G-4284)
OMAHA AUTOMATION INC
8301 Saint Aubin St (48211-1330)
PHONE..................313 557-3565
Phillip M Cifuentes, *President*
Ronald Scott Muschong, *Vice Pres*
EMP: 7
SQ FT: 10,000
SALES (est): 1.3MM **Privately Held**
SIC: 8711 3711 Engineering services; automobile assembly, including specialty automobiles

(G-4285)
OSBERN RACING
16751 Riverview St (48219-3723)
PHONE..................313 538-8933
William Osbern Jr, *Owner*
EMP: 3
SALES (est): 219.1K **Privately Held**
SIC: 3711 Automobile assembly, including specialty automobiles

(G-4286)
PAINEX CORPORATION
Also Called: Ringmaster Robin Oil
18307 James Couzens Fwy (48235-2504)
P.O. Box 35936 (48235-0936)
PHONE..................313 863-1200
Frank Sewell, *CEO*
Douglas Sewell, *President*
Darrcel Anderson, *Principal*
EMP: 4
SQ FT: 7,500
SALES (est): 266.8K **Privately Held**
WEB: www.ringmasternow.com
SIC: 2834 Pharmaceutical preparations

(G-4287)
PAINEXX CORPORATION
18307 James Couzens Fwy (48235-2504)
P.O. Box 35936 (48235-0936)
PHONE..................313 863-1200
Nicole Weldon, *CEO*
Douglas Sewell, *Chairman*
EMP: 6
SALES: 100K **Privately Held**
SIC: 2834 Pharmaceutical preparations

(G-4288)
PANTER COMPANY INC
26029 W 8 Mile Rd (48240-1135)
PHONE..................313 537-5700
Marlene Lyons, *President*
EMP: 11
SQ FT: 8,000
SALES (est): 1.7MM **Privately Held**
WEB: www.labelholders.com
SIC: 3399 Metal powders, pastes & flakes

(G-4289)
PAPPAS CUTLERY-GRINDING INC
575 E Milwaukee St (48202-3237)
PHONE..................800 521-0888
John C Pappas, *President*
David La Motte, *Vice Pres*
EMP: 6
SQ FT: 7,200
SALES (est): 1.1MM **Privately Held**
WEB: www.pappasinc.com
SIC: 3556 5084 Grinders, commercial, food; food industry machinery

(G-4290)
PARJANA DISTRIBUTION LLC
1274 Library St Ste 600 (48226-2283)
PHONE..................313 915-5406
Gregory McPartlin,
EMP: 7
SQ FT: 1,200

SALES (est): 1.1MM **Privately Held**
SIC: 3823 Water quality monitoring & control systems

(G-4291)
PAUL TOUSLEY INC
131 S Military St (48209-3032)
PHONE..................313 841-5400
Brian Thom, *Branch Mgr*
EMP: 13
SALES (corp-wide): 4.4MM **Privately Held**
WEB: www.peerlessmetal.com
SIC: 3399 Powder, metal
PA: Peerless Metal Powders & Abrasive, Llc
124 S Military St
Detroit MI 48209
313 841-5400

(G-4292)
PCM US STEERING HOLDING LLC (HQ)
300 Renaissance Ctr (48243-1402)
PHONE..................313 556-5000
EMP: 4
SALES (est): 147.1MM **Privately Held**
SIC: 3711 3714 Motor vehicles & car bodies; motor vehicle parts & accessories

(G-4293)
PEERLESS METAL POWDERS
6307 W Fort St (48209-2940)
PHONE..................313 841-5400
Paul Tousley, *President*
EMP: 13
SALES (corp-wide): 4.4MM **Privately Held**
WEB: www.peerlessmetal.com
SIC: 3399 Powder, metal
PA: Peerless Metal Powders & Abrasive, Llc
124 S Military St
Detroit MI 48209
313 841-5400

(G-4294)
PEERLESS QUALITY PRODUCTS
7707 Lyndon St (48238-2465)
P.O. Box 480, Grand Blanc (48480-0480)
PHONE..................313 933-7525
EMP: 11
SQ FT: 27,000
SALES (est): 2MM **Privately Held**
SIC: 2842 Mfg Polish/Sanitation Goods

(G-4295)
PEGASUS TOOL LLC
12680 Farley (48239-2643)
PHONE..................313 255-5900
Arthur Scharr Sr,
EMP: 4
SALES (est): 352.6K **Privately Held**
WEB: www.pegasustool.com
SIC: 3069 3089 Molded rubber products; injection molding of plastics

(G-4296)
PEPSI-COLA METRO BTLG CO INC
1555 Mack Ave (48207-4719)
PHONE..................313 832-0910
Clarence Gabriel, *Manager*
Dani Raether, *Supervisor*
EMP: 20
SQ FT: 365,694
SALES (corp-wide): 64.6B **Publicly Held**
WEB: www.joy-of-cola.com
SIC: 2086 Carbonated soft drinks, bottled & canned
HQ: Pepsi-Cola Metropolitan Bottling Company, Inc.
1111 Westchester Ave
White Plains NY 10604
914 767-6000

(G-4297)
PERFECTION INDUSTRIES INC (PA)
18571 Weaver St (48228-1187)
PHONE..................313 272-4040
Arthur G Ryan, *President*
EMP: 20
SQ FT: 13,000

Detroit - Wayne County (G-4298)

GEOGRAPHIC SECTION

SALES (est): 2.2MM **Privately Held**
WEB: www.perfectionindustries.com
SIC: 3471 Electroplating of metals or formed products

(G-4298)
PERIGEE MANUFACTURING CO INC
7519 Intervale St (48238-2401)
PHONE.................................313 933-4420
Michael F Topolewski, *President*
EMP: 12 EST: 1964
SQ FT: 20,000
SALES (est): 1.8MM **Privately Held**
SIC: 3452 Nuts, metal

(G-4299)
PETE PULLUM COMPANY INC
15330 Castleton St (48227-2016)
PHONE.................................313 837-9440
John R Pullum Jr, *President*
EMP: 4 EST: 1940
SQ FT: 52,800
SALES (est): 750.4K **Privately Held**
SIC: 2431 5031 Windows & window parts & trim, wood; door frames, wood; windows

(G-4300)
PEWABIC SOCIETY INC
Also Called: Pewabic Pottery
10125 E Jefferson Ave (48214-3138)
PHONE.................................313 626-2000
Amanda Rogers, *Marketing Staff*
Whitney Kenniburg, *Manager*
Mario Lopez, *Technical Staff*
Steve McBride, *Exec Dir*
Christina Devlin, *Director*
EMP: 35
SQ FT: 10,500
SALES: 2.6MM **Privately Held**
WEB: www.pewabic.org
SIC: 3255 8412 8299 Tile, clay refractory; museum; art gallery, noncommercial; arts & crafts schools

(G-4301)
PIMS CO
300 Renaissance Ctr (48243-1402)
PHONE.................................313 665-8837
Philippe De Schryver, *Director*
Cyril Rauscher, *Director*
Timothy R Miller, *Admin Sec*
EMP: 3
SALES (est): 125.5K **Publicly Held**
SIC: 3711 3714 Motor vehicles & car bodies; motor vehicle parts & accessories
PA: General Motors Company
300 Renaissance Ctr L1
Detroit MI 48243

(G-4302)
PINGREE MFG L3C
Also Called: Pingree Detroit
6438 Woodward Ave (48202-3216)
PHONE.................................313 444-8428
Jarret Schlaff, *CEO*
EMP: 4
SALES (est): 193.1K **Privately Held**
SIC: 3999 Manufacturing industries

(G-4303)
PIONEER STEEL CORPORATION (PA)
7447 Intervale St (48238-2401)
PHONE.................................313 933-9400
Donald R Sazama, *President*
Gil Hoard, *General Mgr*
Donald Seavey, *COO*
Michael R Small, *Vice Pres*
Mike Houghton, *Plant Mgr*
EMP: 43
SQ FT: 38,000
SALES (est): 29.7MM **Privately Held**
WEB: www.pioneersteel.us
SIC: 5051 3544 Plates, metal; bars, metal; die sets for metal stamping (presses)

(G-4304)
PISTON AUTOMOTIVE LLC
4015 Michigan Ave (48210-3266)
PHONE.................................313 541-8789
Robert Ajersch, *Branch Mgr*
EMP: 30
SALES (corp-wide): 1.6B **Privately Held**
SIC: 3714 Motor vehicle parts & accessories
HQ: Piston Automotive, L.L.C.
12723 Telegraph Rd Ste 1
Redford MI 48239
313 541-8674

(G-4305)
PLASTECH WELD
2364 17th St (48216-1505)
PHONE.................................313 963-3194
Bonnie Desiro, *Principal*
EMP: 3
SALES (est): 214.5K **Privately Held**
SIC: 3089 Automotive parts, plastic

(G-4306)
POLISH DAILY NEWS INC
Also Called: Polish Weekly
11903 Joseph Campau St (48212-3004)
P.O. Box 80790, Rochester (48308-0790)
PHONE.................................313 365-1990
Bruno Nowicki, *President*
Michael Szymanski, *Chairman*
EMP: 3
SALES (est): 197.8K **Privately Held**
SIC: 2711 Commercial printing & newspaper publishing combined

(G-4307)
PPG COATING SERVICES
Also Called: Crown Group Detroit Plant
6334 Lynch Rd (48234-4119)
PHONE.................................313 922-8433
James Keena, *General Mgr*
Vince Mulrenin, *Vice Pres*
Joan Odonnell, *Admin Mgr*
EMP: 75
SALES (corp-wide): 15.3B **Publicly Held**
SIC: 3479 Painting of metal products
HQ: Ppg Coating Services
5875 New King Ct
Troy MI 48098
586 575-9800

(G-4308)
PRAXAIR DISTRIBUTION INC
12820 Evergreen Rd (48223-3439)
PHONE.................................313 778-7085
Ramona Owens, *Principal*
Mike Barras, *Plant Mgr*
Derick Searle, *Plant Mgr*
EMP: 43 **Privately Held**
SIC: 5999 2813 Welding supplies; carbon dioxide
HQ: Praxair Distribution, Inc.
10 Riverview Dr
Danbury CT 06810
203 837-2000

(G-4309)
PRECISION HONE & TOOL INC
13600 Evergreen Rd (48223-3441)
PHONE.................................313 493-9760
Mark Behr, *President*
EMP: 3 EST: 2000
SALES (est): 394.9K **Privately Held**
SIC: 3599 Machine shop, jobbing & repair

(G-4310)
PRESSURE VESSEL SERVICE INC (PA)
Also Called: PVS Chemicals
10900 Harper Ave (48213-3364)
PHONE.................................313 921-1200
James B Nicholson, *President*
Patrick Collins, *Business Mgr*
Lauren Kovaleski, *Exec VP*
David A Nicholson, *Vice Pres*
James M Nicholson, *Vice Pres*
◆ EMP: 45 EST: 1945
SQ FT: 187,000
SALES (est): 558.5MM **Privately Held**
WEB: www.1pvs.ca
SIC: 5169 2819 2899 4953 Acids; industrial chemicals; sulfuric acid, oleum; water treating compounds; acid waste, collection & disposal; conveyors & conveying equipment

(G-4311)
PRODUCTION ACCESSORIES CO
123 E Golden Gate (48203-2053)
PHONE.................................313 366-1500
John Else, *President*
William Else, *Manager*
EMP: 8 EST: 1940
SQ FT: 15,000
SALES: 850K **Privately Held**
SIC: 3535 Unit handling conveying systems

(G-4312)
PRODUCTION TUBE COMPANY INC
481 Beaufait St (48207-4303)
PHONE.................................313 259-3990
EMP: 8
SQ FT: 21,000
SALES (est): 750K **Privately Held**
SIC: 3498 3471 3444 3398 Mfg Fabrctd Pipe/Fitting Plating/Polishing Svcs Mfg Sheet Metalwork Metal Heat Treating Copper Foundry

(G-4313)
PROFILES MAGAZINE
18250 Redfern St (48219-2357)
P.O. Box 19767 (48219-0767)
PHONE.................................313 531-9041
EMP: 3 EST: 2003
SALES (est): 150K **Privately Held**
SIC: 2721 Periodicals-Publishing/Printing

(G-4314)
PROP ART STUDIO INC
112 E Grand Blvd (48207-3713)
PHONE.................................313 824-2200
Michael Stapleton, *President*
Denise Connolly, *Vice Pres*
EMP: 6
SQ FT: 7,200
SALES: 125K **Privately Held**
WEB: www.propartstudio.com
SIC: 1799 2759 Float (parade) construction; prop, set or scenery construction, theatrical; posters, including billboards: printing

(G-4315)
PSC INDUSTRIAL OUTSOURCING LP
Also Called: Hydrochempsc
515 Lycaste St (48214-3473)
PHONE.................................313 824-5859
Steve Snider, *Manager*
EMP: 100
SALES (corp-wide): 607.5MM **Privately Held**
SIC: 3443 Vessels, process or storage (from boiler shops): metal plate; reactor containment vessels, metal plate; heat exchangers: coolers (after, inter), condensers, etc.; columns (fractioning, etc.): metal plate
PA: Psc Industrial Outsourcing, Lp
900 Georgia Ave
Deer Park TX 77536
713 393-5600

(G-4316)
PULL OUR OWN WEIGHT
12811 Ardmore St (48227-3103)
PHONE.................................313 686-4685
Andre Williams Jr,
EMP: 3
SALES (est): 120K **Privately Held**
SIC: 2731 5961 7819 7922 Book music: publishing & printing; record &/or tape (music or video) club, mail order; sound (effects & music production), motion picture; entertainment promotion; popular music groups or artists;

(G-4317)
PUNKIN DSIGN SEDS ORGNLITY LLC
633 Burlingame St (48202-1004)
PHONE.................................313 347-8488
Susan Y Jones,
EMP: 7
SALES: 144K **Privately Held**
SIC: 2711 Newspapers

(G-4318)
PVS CHEMICAL SOLUTIONS INC (HQ)
Also Called: PVS Chemicals, Inc. Illinois
10900 Harper Ave (48213-1247)
PHONE.................................313 921-1200
Dean H Larson, *President*
Allan Schlumberger, *Vice Pres*
Bill Militello, *Sales Staff*
Ron Gray, *Manager*
Johnathan S Taub, *Admin Sec*
EMP: 5
SALES (est): 31.5MM
SALES (corp-wide): 558.5MM **Privately Held**
SIC: 2819 Industrial inorganic chemicals
PA: Pressure Vessel Service, Inc.
10900 Harper Ave
Detroit MI 48213
313 921-1200

(G-4319)
PVS HOLDINGS INC (HQ)
10900 Harper Ave (48213-3364)
PHONE.................................313 921-1200
Don Sosnoski, *President*
▲ EMP: 3
SALES: 30MM
SALES (corp-wide): 558.5MM **Privately Held**
WEB: www.pvsholdings.com
SIC: 3535 Conveyors & conveying equipment
PA: Pressure Vessel Service, Inc.
10900 Harper Ave
Detroit MI 48213
313 921-1200

(G-4320)
PVS-NOLWOOD CHEMICALS INC (HQ)
10900 Harper Ave (48213-3364)
PHONE.................................313 921-1200
James B Nicholson, *CEO*
Richard Peacock, *President*
Robert Couch, *Opers Dir*
Candee Saferian, *CFO*
James Devleeschouwer, *Controller*
◆ EMP: 30 EST: 1987
SQ FT: 225,000
SALES: 168.6MM
SALES (corp-wide): 558.5MM **Privately Held**
WEB: www.pvschemicals.com
SIC: 2819 Industrial inorganic chemicals
PA: Pressure Vessel Service, Inc.
10900 Harper Ave
Detroit MI 48213
313 921-1200

(G-4321)
QUAKER CHEMICAL CORPORATION
14301 Birwood St (48238-2207)
PHONE.................................313 931-6910
Chris Taylor, *Manager*
EMP: 68
SQ FT: 80,000
SALES (corp-wide): 867.5MM **Publicly Held**
WEB: www.quakerchem.com
SIC: 2899 Chemical preparations
PA: Quaker Chemical Corporation
1 Quaker Park
Conshohocken PA 19428
610 832-4000

(G-4322)
QUALITY BENDING THREADING INC
5100 Stanton St (48208-2064)
PHONE.................................313 898-5100
Matthew J Seely, *President*
EMP: 10
SQ FT: 35,000
SALES (est): 1.6MM **Privately Held**
WEB: www.qualitybending.com
SIC: 3599 Machine shop, jobbing & repair

(G-4323)
QUESTRON PACKAGING LLC
7650 W Chicago (48204-2862)
PHONE.................................313 657-1630
Aiman Kawas, *President*
EMP: 8 EST: 2014

GEOGRAPHIC SECTION
Detroit - Wayne County (G-4350)

SQ FT: 50,000
SALES: 200K **Privately Held**
SIC: 2899 Fuel tank or engine cleaning chemicals

(G-4324)
R & L COLOR GRAPHICS INC
18709 Meyers Rd (48235-1310)
PHONE....................313 345-3838
Linda Davis, *Owner*
Richard Jackson, *Vice Pres*
EMP: 5
SQ FT: 3,000
SALES (est): 846.4K **Privately Held**
SIC: 2752 Commercial printing, lithographic

(G-4325)
R B L PLASTICS INCORPORATED
Also Called: Kwik Paint Products
6040 Russell St (48211-2120)
PHONE....................313 873-8800
Ronald B Lipson, *President*
Brian K Lipson, *Vice Pres*
Rosalie Lipson, *Treasurer*
Tim Mclsaac, *Sales Staff*
Joni Lipson, *Admin Sec*
▲ EMP: 40
SQ FT: 50,000
SALES (est): 4.8MM **Privately Held**
WEB: www.kwikpaint.com
SIC: 3089 Injection molded finished plastic products; thermoformed finished plastic products

(G-4326)
R N E BUSINESS ENTERPRISES (PA)
Also Called: American Speedy Printing
400 Renaissance Ctr Lbby (48243-1607)
PHONE....................313 963-3600
Norma Eschenberg, *President*
Kurt Eschenberg, *Vice Pres*
EMP: 6
SQ FT: 2,500
SALES (est): 913.8K **Privately Held**
SIC: 2752 Commercial printing, offset

(G-4327)
R R DONNELLEY & SONS COMPANY
Also Called: Bowne Financial Print
3031 W Grand Blvd Ste 400 (48202-3038)
PHONE....................313 964-1330
Mark Kwicinski, *Principal*
Laura Buchanan, *Production*
Charlotte Grain, *Dir Ops-Prd-Mfg*
EMP: 75
SQ FT: 1,200
SALES (corp-wide): 6.8B **Publicly Held**
SIC: 2752 2791 Commercial printing, offset; typesetting
PA: R. R. Donnelley & Sons Company
35 W Wacker Dr
Chicago IL 60601
312 326-8000

(G-4328)
RADIANT ELECTRIC SIGN CORP
14500 Schoolcraft St (48227-2874)
PHONE....................313 835-1400
Marty Weinstock, *President*
Paul Weinsock, *Vice Pres*
EMP: 6
SQ FT: 5,000
SALES: 800K **Privately Held**
SIC: 3993 Neon signs

(G-4329)
RANDLIS MANUFACTURING CO
Also Called: Ranger Products
19669 John R St (48203-1662)
P.O. Box 8189, Calabasas CA (91372-8189)
PHONE....................313 368-0220
David Golde, *President*
▲ EMP: 5 EST: 1988
SQ FT: 30,000
SALES (est): 697.8K **Privately Held**
SIC: 2399 3949 Fishing nets; hooks, fishing; fishing equipment

(G-4330)
RBC ENTERPRISES INC (PA)
12301 Hubbell St (48227-2777)
P.O. Box 28159 (48228-0159)
PHONE....................313 491-3350
Rudy Taylor, *President*
EMP: 20
SALES: 6MM **Privately Held**
SIC: 3317 Steel pipe & tubes

(G-4331)
RBL PRODUCTS INC
6040 Russell St (48211-2120)
PHONE....................313 873-8806
Ronald P Lipson, *President*
▲ EMP: 14
SQ FT: 49,610
SALES (est): 1.4MM **Privately Held**
SIC: 3089 Aquarium accessories, plastic

(G-4332)
REBEL NELL L3C
4731 Grand River Ave (48208-2250)
PHONE....................716 640-4267
Emily Peterson, *President*
EMP: 7
SALES: 300K **Privately Held**
SIC: 3911 Jewelry, precious metal

(G-4333)
RECARO NORTH AMERICA INC
4617 W Fort St (48209-3208)
PHONE....................313 842-3479
Jerald Davis, *Branch Mgr*
EMP: 500 **Privately Held**
SIC: 2531 Public building & related furniture
HQ: Recaro North America, Inc.
49200 Halyard Dr
Plymouth MI 48170
734 254-5000

(G-4334)
RECYCLED PAPERBOARD PDTS CORP
10400 Devine St (48213-3225)
PHONE....................313 579-6608
Joy Martinek, *President*
EMP: 6
SQ FT: 18,000
SALES (est): 923.5K **Privately Held**
SIC: 2653 Sheets, solid fiber: made from purchased materials

(G-4335)
RECYCLED POLYMETRIC MATERIALS
15477 Woodrow Wilson St (48238-1586)
PHONE....................313 957-6373
EMP: 5
SALES (est): 654.8K **Privately Held**
SIC: 2821 5169 Polyurethane resins; polyurethane products

(G-4336)
REED SPORTSWEAR MFG CO (PA)
1601 W Lafayette Blvd (48216-1927)
PHONE....................313 963-7980
Mark Silver, *Owner*
Eda Reed, *Vice Pres*
Roseann Silver, *Admin Sec*
▲ EMP: 50 EST: 1950
SQ FT: 37,000
SALES: 5MM **Privately Held**
WEB: www.reedsportswear.com
SIC: 2386 5136 Coats & jackets, leather & sheep-lined; leather & sheep lined clothing, men's & boys'

(G-4337)
REED SPORTSWEAR MFG CO
Also Called: Leather Unlimited
1601 W Lafayette Blvd (48216-1927)
PHONE....................313 963-7980
Rosco Mihajlovic, *Manager*
EMP: 6
SQ FT: 2,500
SALES (est): 534.6K
SALES (corp-wide): 5MM **Privately Held**
WEB: www.reedsportswear.com
SIC: 5611 5621 2339 Men's & boys' clothing stores; women's clothing stores; women's & misses' athletic clothing & sportswear

PA: Reed Sportswear Manufacturing Co.
1652 W Fort St
Detroit MI 48216
313 963-7980

(G-4338)
REILLY CRAFT CREAMERY LLC
4731 Bellevue St (48207-1301)
PHONE....................313 300-9859
Christopher Reilly,
Andrea Mahoney,
Timothy Mahoney,
EMP: 3
SQ FT: 500
SALES (est): 100.5K **Privately Held**
SIC: 2022 2024 Natural cheese; sherbets, dairy based

(G-4339)
RELIABLE GLASS COMPANY
Also Called: Reliable Architectural Mtls Co
9751 Erwin St (48213-1103)
PHONE....................313 924-9750
Douglas F Tarrance, *Owner*
Zach Havrilla, *QC Mgr*
Karen Havrilla, *Admin Sec*
EMP: 35 EST: 1960
SQ FT: 32,500
SALES: 7.9MM **Privately Held**
WEB: www.ramcometals.com
SIC: 5039 5031 3442 Structural assemblies, prefabricated: non-wood; glass construction materials; building materials, interior; metal doors; window & door frames

(G-4340)
RELIGIOUS COMMUNICATIONS LLC
5590 Coplin St (48213-3706)
PHONE....................313 822-3361
Kathleen Humprey, *Manager*
EMP: 5
SALES (est): 141.5K
SALES (corp-wide): 1.7MM **Privately Held**
SIC: 5049 2759 7374 7319 Religious supplies; commercial printing; computer graphics service; display advertising service
PA: Religious Communications Llc
2 Sun Ct Ste 300
Norcross GA

(G-4341)
REMACON COMPRESSORS INC
7939 Mcgraw St (48210-2156)
PHONE....................313 842-8219
Raymond G Mickiewicz, *President*
Laurie M Mickiewicz, *Corp Secy*
Charles J Mickiewicz, *Vice Pres*
EMP: 5
SQ FT: 9,800
SALES (est): 728.8K **Privately Held**
SIC: 3585 Compressors for refrigeration & air conditioning equipment

(G-4342)
REO HYDRAULIC & MFG INC
18475 Sherwood St (48234-2832)
PHONE....................313 891-2244
Robert E Obrecht, *President*
David Obrecht, *Vice Pres*
Rudy Vandenbroeck, *Engineer*
Chris Utah, *Director*
Raymond E Obrecht, *Admin Sec*
EMP: 20
SALES (est): 5.1MM **Privately Held**
SIC: 5084 3594 Pneumatic tools & equipment; fluid power pumps & motors

(G-4343)
REO HYDRO-PIERCE INC
18475 Sherwood St (48234-2832)
PHONE....................313 891-2244
Robert Obrecht, *President*
Catherine Seely, *Office Mgr*
▲ EMP: 30
SQ FT: 32,000
SALES (est): 2.2MM **Privately Held**
SIC: 3599 Machine shop, jobbing & repair

(G-4344)
REPAIR INDUSTRIES MICHIGAN INC
Also Called: Rim Custom Racks
6501 E Mcnichols Rd (48212-2027)
P.O. Box 290, Saint Clair Shores (48080-0290)
PHONE....................313 365-5300
Todd A Schorer, *President*
Michael Bahr, *Business Mgr*
Glenn Evans, *Draft/Design*
Howard Schorer, *Manager*
Anthony Schorer, *Technology*
EMP: 110
SQ FT: 156,000
SALES (est): 75.9MM **Privately Held**
WEB: www.repair-industries.com
SIC: 5021 3412 3312 Racks; metal barrels, drums & pails; blast furnaces & steel mills

(G-4345)
RICHARD BENNETT & ASSOCIATES
470 Brainard St (48201-1718)
PHONE....................313 831-4262
Richard Bennett, *President*
Betty Bennett, *Vice Pres*
EMP: 4
SQ FT: 28,500
SALES: 300K **Privately Held**
SIC: 3441 Fabricated structural metal

(G-4346)
RIVORE METALS LLC
7900 Dix St (48209-1173)
PHONE....................248 397-8724
Kosta Marselis, *Branch Mgr*
EMP: 22
SALES (corp-wide): 21.5MM **Privately Held**
SIC: 3914 Silverware & plated ware
PA: Rivore Metals Llc
850 Stephenson Hwy # 200
Troy MI 48083
800 248-1250

(G-4347)
RONALD M DAVIS CO INC
Also Called: Acrylic Specialties
16260 Meyers Rd (48235-4164)
PHONE....................313 864-5588
Ronald M Davis, *President*
EMP: 3
SQ FT: 2,000
SALES (est): 388.3K **Privately Held**
SIC: 3083 Laminated plastics plate & sheet

(G-4348)
ROWSEY CONSTRUCTION & DEV LLC
607 Shelby St Ste 722 (48226-3282)
PHONE....................313 675-2464
Clyde Rowsey, *President*
EMP: 5
SALES (est): 228K **Privately Held**
SIC: 1799 1389 1742 1771 Waterproofing; oil field services; stucco work, interior; stucco, gunite & grouting contractors

(G-4349)
RTLF-HOPE LLC
Also Called: Hope Global of Detroit
1401 Abbott St (48216-1946)
PHONE....................313 538-1700
John Luca, *Vice Pres*
Robert L Ferdinand,
Cheryl Merchant,
EMP: 36
SQ FT: 19,000
SALES (est): 3.4MM **Privately Held**
SIC: 2396 Automotive & apparel trimmings

(G-4350)
S B C HOLDINGS INC
300 River Place Dr # 5000 (48207-5068)
PHONE....................313 446-2000
John W Stroh III, *Chairman*
George E Kuehn, *Exec VP*
Mark Tuttle, *Vice Pres*
EMP: 15 EST: 1850
SQ FT: 17,000

Detroit - Wayne County (G-4351)

SALES (est): 167.9K
SALES (corp-wide): 2.8MM **Privately Held**
SIC: 2082 2086 Beer (alcoholic beverage); malt liquors; near beer; fruit drinks (less than 100% juice): packaged in cans, etc.; tea, iced: packaged in cans, bottles, etc.
PA: The Stroh Companies Inc
300 River Place Dr # 5000
Detroit MI 48207
313 446-2000

(G-4351)
SAA TECH INC
7420 Intervale St (48238-2460)
PHONE 313 933-4960
Scott Apkarian, *President*
EMP: 9
SALES: 2MM **Privately Held**
WEB: www.saatech.com
SIC: 3556 Meat processing machinery

(G-4352)
SALEM/SAVARD INDUSTRIES LLC
8561 W Chicago (48204-2623)
PHONE 313 931-6880
John A Savard,
EMP: 20
SQ FT: 25,000
SALES (est): 2.5MM **Privately Held**
SIC: 3564 3567 3444 Blowers & fans; industrial furnaces & ovens; sheet metalwork

(G-4353)
SAVARD CORPORATION
8561 W Chicago (48204-2623)
PHONE 313 931-6880
John Savard, *President*
Charles Savard, *Vice Pres*
Chris Savard, *Vice Pres*
Frank Savard, *Vice Pres*
EMP: 15
SQ FT: 20,000
SALES (est): 1.4MM **Privately Held**
SIC: 3549 Metalworking machinery

(G-4354)
SAVS WELDING SERVICES INC
11811 Pleasant St (48217-1619)
P.O. Box 18417, River Rouge (48218-0417)
PHONE 313 841-3430
Thomas Saville, *President*
Robert F Benso, *Vice Pres*
EMP: 2
SQ FT: 4,000
SALES: 3.1MM **Privately Held**
SIC: 7692 3441 Welding repair; fabricated structural metal

(G-4355)
SCHAD BOILER SETTING COMPANY
Also Called: Schad Refractory Cnstr Co
15240 Castleton St (48227-2092)
PHONE 313 273-2235
Richard Lee, *CEO*
James R Choate, *Vice Pres*
EMP: 60 **EST:** 1942
SQ FT: 50,000
SALES (est): 16.4MM **Privately Held**
WEB: www.schadrefractory.com
SIC: 3255 3443 Tile & brick refractories, except plastic; fabricated plate work (boiler shop)

(G-4356)
SCOTTEN STEEL PROCESSING INC
Also Called: C & J Steel Processing
3545 Scotten St (48210-3159)
PHONE 313 897-8837
Warren Chappel, *President*
Al Jones, *Vice Pres*
Alan Jones, *Vice Pres*
EMP: 12
SQ FT: 65,000
SALES: 1MM **Privately Held**
SIC: 7389 5051 3444 Scrap steel cutting; metals service centers & offices; sheet metalwork

(G-4357)
SEA FARE FOODS INC
2127 Brewster St (48207-2103)
P.O. Box 7587 (48207-0587)
PHONE 313 568-0223
S A Lincoln Sack, *President*
Phillip Sack, *Vice Pres*
Dorothy Sack, *Treasurer*
EMP: 20
SQ FT: 22,000
SALES (est): 2.5MM **Privately Held**
SIC: 2091 2092 Herring, cured; fresh or frozen packaged fish

(G-4358)
SET DUCT MANUFACTURING LLC
Also Called: Set Duct Manufacturing, Inc.
7800 Intervale St (48238-2463)
PHONE 313 491-4380
Victor Edozien,
EMP: 50
SALES (est): 7.1MM
SALES (corp-wide): 69.7MM **Privately Held**
SIC: 3444 Sheet metalwork
PA: Set Enterprises, Inc.
38600 Van Dy
Sterling Heights MI 48312
586 573-3600

(G-4359)
SHAW & SLAVSKY INC (PA)
Also Called: Shaw Design Group
13821 Elmira St (48227-3099)
PHONE 313 834-3990
Thomas G Smith, *President*
Reynaldo J Linares, *Vice Pres*
John J Debono, *CFO*
▲ **EMP:** 20
SQ FT: 100,000
SALES (est): 11MM **Privately Held**
SIC: 2542 3993 Office & store showcases & display fixtures; signs & advertising specialties

(G-4360)
SHAW & SLAVSKY INC
Also Called: Shaw Design
13639 Elmira St (48227-3015)
PHONE 313 834-3990
Tom Smith, *Manager*
EMP: 35
SALES (corp-wide): 11MM **Privately Held**
SIC: 2542 Stands, merchandise display: except wood
PA: Shaw & Slavsky, Inc.
13821 Elmira St
Detroit MI 48227
313 834-3990

(G-4361)
SHINOLA/DETROIT LLC (PA)
485 W Milwaukee St (48202-3220)
PHONE 888 304-2534
Tom Lewand, *CEO*
Jacques Panis, *President*
Shannon Washburn, *President*
Tim Barkume, *Production*
Jonathan Hughes, *Treasurer*
▲ **EMP:** 250 **EST:** 2011
SQ FT: 100,000
SALES: 95MM **Privately Held**
SIC: 3751 5094 3651 3199 Bicycles & related parts; clocks, watches & parts; watches & parts; household audio equipment; straps, leather; watches, clocks, watchcases & parts; bicycles

(G-4362)
SIGNAL-RETURN INC
1345 Division St Ste 102 (48207-2639)
PHONE 313 567-8970
Lynne Avadenka, *Director*
Jane Hoehner, *Director*
EMP: 5
SALES: 192.9K **Privately Held**
SIC: 2759 Letterpress printing

(G-4363)
SIMPLY SUZANNE LLC
200 River Place Dr Apt 10 (48207-4397)
PHONE 917 364-4549
EMP: 8
SALES (est): 567.3K **Privately Held**
SIC: 2064 Mfg Candy/Confectionery

(G-4364)
SKIN BAR VII LLC
18951 Livernois Ave (48221-2258)
PHONE 313 701-7958
EMP: 5
SQ FT: 1,500
SALES (est): 205.1K **Privately Held**
SIC: 3999 7231 Mfg Misc Products Beauty Shop

(G-4365)
SLEDGEHAMMER CONSTRUCTION INC
17706 Greenview Ave (48219-3587)
PHONE 313 478-5648
Anthony Sledge, *President*
EMP: 3
SALES (est): 124.1K **Privately Held**
SIC: 1389 Construction, repair & dismantling services

(G-4366)
SMITH WA INC
Also Called: Brite Products
14650 Dequindre St (48212-1504)
PHONE 313 883-6977
Steven Smith, *President*
Tony Zaccagni, *VP Sales*
Sherry Sprks, *Manager*
EMP: 43 **EST:** 1958
SQ FT: 12,000
SALES (est): 11.4MM **Privately Held**
WEB: www.weldaid.com
SIC: 2899 Chemical preparations

(G-4367)
SOPHIAS BAKERY INC
Also Called: Lebanon Baking Company
8421 Michigan Ave (48210-2076)
PHONE 313 582-6992
Lazaros Kircos, *President*
David Depoy, *Vice Pres*
Clide Manion, *Vice Pres*
Paula Kircos, *Treasurer*
EMP: 17
SQ FT: 22,000
SALES: 1MM **Privately Held**
SIC: 2051 Breads, rolls & buns

(G-4368)
SOUTHFIELD MACHINING INC
1831 Clay St (48211-1913)
PHONE 313 871-8200
Keith Worden, *President*
Darrell Johnson, *Vice Pres*
EMP: 4
SQ FT: 15,000
SALES (est): 505.5K **Privately Held**
SIC: 3599 3443 Machine shop, jobbing & repair; weldments

(G-4369)
SOUTHWEST METALS INCORPORATED
8122 W Fort St (48209-2774)
PHONE 313 842-2700
Steven Fawaz, *Principal*
EMP: 3 **EST:** 2010
SALES (est): 331.4K **Privately Held**
SIC: 3446 Ornamental metalwork

(G-4370)
SPECTRA LMP LLC (PA)
6501 Lynch Rd (48234-4140)
PHONE 313 571-2100
Michael Guthrie, *Mng Member*
Carlton Guthrie, *Mng Member*
EMP: 232
SALES: 21.8MM **Privately Held**
SIC: 3711 Chassis, motor vehicle

(G-4371)
SPECTRUM NEON COMPANY
3750 E Outer Dr (48234-2946)
PHONE 313 366-7333
John Haddad, *President*
EMP: 6
SQ FT: 5,000
SALES (est): 936.8K **Privately Held**
WEB: www.spectrumneon.com
SIC: 3993 Neon signs

(G-4372)
ST JOHN
4100 John R St (48201-2013)
PHONE 313 576-8212
Chris Fontichiaro, *Principal*
EMP: 5
SALES (est): 219.9K **Privately Held**
SIC: 2339 Sportswear, women's

(G-4373)
STAN SAX CORP (PA)
10900 Harper Ave (48213-3364)
PHONE 248 683-9199
David Sax, *President*
Barry Weber, *CFO*
EMP: 15
SQ FT: 25,000
SALES (est): 1.5MM **Privately Held**
WEB: www.stansaxcorp.com
SIC: 3291 Abrasive products

(G-4374)
STANDARD SCALE & SUPPLY CO (PA)
25421 Glendale (48239-4511)
P.O. Box 40720, Redford (48240-0720)
PHONE 313 255-6700
Clarence W Bowman Jr, *President*
John Bowman, *General Mgr*
Bill Bowman, *Vice Pres*
Suzanne A Bowman, *Treasurer*
EMP: 8
SQ FT: 12,000
SALES (est): 1.5MM **Privately Held**
WEB: www.standardscale.com
SIC: 5046 7699 3596 Scales, except laboratory; scale repair service; industrial scales

(G-4375)
STAR PAPER CONVERTERS INC
Also Called: Star Paper Products
1717 17th St (48216-1889)
P.O. Box 379, Allen Park (48101-0379)
PHONE 313 963-5200
Richard A Nawrocki, *President*
Helen Jenks, *Vice Pres*
Mark Laske, *Vice Pres*
Janet G Nawrocki, *Admin Sec*
EMP: 10
SQ FT: 50,000
SALES (est): 1.3MM **Privately Held**
WEB: www.star-paper.com
SIC: 2655 Fiber cans, drums & similar products

(G-4376)
STARLITE TOOL & DIE WELDING
12091 Woodbine (48239-2417)
PHONE 313 533-3462
Walter Milewski, *President*
EMP: 4
SQ FT: 1,900
SALES (est): 263.5K **Privately Held**
SIC: 7692 Welding repair

(G-4377)
STELLAR PLASTICS CORPORATION
14121 Gratiot Ave (48205-2865)
PHONE 313 527-7337
William Bletch, *President*
Bradford Franciosi, *Vice Pres*
EMP: 3 **EST:** 1949
SQ FT: 8,000
SALES: 200K **Privately Held**
WEB: www.stellarplastics.com
SIC: 3089 Plastic processing

(G-4378)
STELLAR PLASTICS FABG LLC
14121 Gratiot Ave (48205-2865)
PHONE 313 527-7337
Brad Franciosi,
EMP: 3
SALES (est): 212K **Privately Held**
SIC: 3089 Plastic processing

(G-4379)
STREET DENIM & CO
15530 Grand River Ave (48227-2223)
PHONE 313 837-1200
EMP: 4
SALES (est): 431.8K **Privately Held**
SIC: 2211 Cotton Broadwoven Fabric Mill

GEOGRAPHIC SECTION
Detroit - Wayne County (G-4410)

(G-4380)
STROH COMPANIES INC (PA)
300 River Place Dr # 5000 (48207-5068)
PHONE..................313 446-2000
John W Stroh III, *Chairman*
Mark K Tuttle, *CFO*
George E Kuehn, *Admin Sec*
EMP: 16
SQ FT: 508,000
SALES (est): 2.8MM **Privately Held**
SIC: 2082 2086 6552 6531 Beer (alcoholic beverage); malt liquors; near beer; fruit drinks (less than 100% juice); packaged in cans, etc.; tea, iced: packaged in cans, bottles, etc.; subdividers & developers; land subdividers & developers, commercial; real estate managers

(G-4381)
STRONG STEEL PRODUCTS LLC
6464 Strong St (48211-1862)
PHONE..................313 267-3300
Jeffrey N Cole, *President*
EMP: 25
SALES (est): 4.9MM **Privately Held**
SIC: 5093 3341 4953 3312 Ferrous metal scrap & waste; secondary nonferrous metals; refuse systems; blast furnaces & steel mills

(G-4382)
SUITE 600 T-SHIRTS LLC
277 Gratiot Ave Ste 600 (48226-2211)
PHONE..................866 712-7749
Ricardo Copeland, *Principal*
EMP: 5
SALES (est): 156.7K **Privately Held**
SIC: 2396 Fabric printing & stamping

(G-4383)
SULLIVAN REPRODUCTIONS INC
241 W Congress St (48226-3231)
PHONE..................313 965-3666
Pat Sullivan, *President*
Jane Sullivan, *Corp Secy*
Michael Sullivan, *Vice Pres*
EMP: 20
SALES (est): 218.9K **Privately Held**
SIC: 2752 Commercial printing, lithographic

(G-4384)
SUN PHARMACEUTICAL INDS INC
1150 Elijah Mccoy Dr (48202-3344)
PHONE..................609 495-2800
Subramanian Kalyanasundaram, *CEO*
Aimee Albanese, *Manager*
Robert Kurkiewicz, *Manager*
Ippan Ralati, *Info Tech Mgr*
EMP: 40
SALES (corp-wide): 1.3B **Privately Held**
SIC: 2834 Pharmaceutical preparations
HQ: Sun Pharmaceutical Industries, Inc.
270 Prospect Plains Rd
Cranbury NJ 08512
609 495-2800

(G-4385)
SUN TOOL COMPANY
18505 Weaver St (48228-1158)
PHONE..................313 837-2442
EMP: 4
SALES (est): 260K **Privately Held**
SIC: 3599 Mfg Industrial Machinery

(G-4386)
SUPER FLUIDS LLC
Also Called: Good Juice
8838 3rd St (48202-1706)
P.O. Box 2334 (48202-0334)
PHONE..................313 409-6522
EMP: 4
SALES (est): 127.7K **Privately Held**
SIC: 2037 Fruit juices

(G-4387)
SUPERIOR MATERIALS INC
20565 Hoover St (48205-1075)
PHONE..................888 988-4400
John Warner, *Branch Mgr*
EMP: 17
SQ FT: 26,077
SALES (corp-wide): 5MM **Privately Held**
SIC: 3273 Ready-mixed concrete
PA: Superior Materials Inc.
585 Stewart Ave
Farmington Hills MI 48333
248 788-8000

(G-4388)
SUPERIOR MTAL FINSHG RUSTPROOF
3510 E Mcnichols Rd (48212-1619)
PHONE..................313 893-1050
Dan Smith, *Vice Pres*
Robin Petty, *Treasurer*
EMP: 15 **EST:** 1967
SALES (est): 1.9MM **Privately Held**
SIC: 3479 3471 Coating of metals & formed products; plating & polishing

(G-4389)
SUPREME BAKING COMPANY
5401 Proctor St (48210-2221)
PHONE..................313 894-0222
Dusko Filipovich, *Partner*
Stojko Filipovich, *Partner*
EMP: 22
SQ FT: 8,000
SALES (est): 796K **Privately Held**
SIC: 5461 5411 5149 2051 Bakeries; grocery stores, independent; bakery products; bread, cake & related products; cookies & crackers

(G-4390)
SUSTAINABLE INDUSTRIES LLC
16800 Plainview Ave (48219-3363)
PHONE..................248 213-6599
Edward McShan,
EMP: 3
SALES (est): 287.2K **Privately Held**
SIC: 3999 Manufacturing industries

(G-4391)
SWEET POTATO SENSATIONS INC
17337 Lahser Rd (48219-2333)
PHONE..................313 532-7996
Casandra Thomas, *President*
Cassandra Thomas, *Treasurer*
EMP: 3
SQ FT: 700
SALES (est): 393.7K **Privately Held**
WEB: www.sweetpotatosensations.com
SIC: 2052 2051 Cookies & crackers; cakes, pies & pastries

(G-4392)
SWEETHEART BAKERY INC (PA)
19200 Kelly Rd (48225-1902)
PHONE..................313 839-6330
Michael Gralewski, *President*
Amelia Gralewski, *Vice Pres*
EMP: 58 **EST:** 1950
SQ FT: 9,000
SALES (est): 2.1MM **Privately Held**
WEB: www.sweetheartbakery.com
SIC: 5461 2051 Bakeries; bread, cake & related products

(G-4393)
T S M FOODS LLC
1241 Woodward Ave (48226-2006)
PHONE..................313 262-6556
EMP: 3
SALES (est): 314.1K **Privately Held**
SIC: 3421 Table & food cutlery, including butchers'

(G-4394)
T WIGLEY INC
1537 Hale St (48207-2008)
PHONE..................313 831-6881
Tom Wigley, *President*
EMP: 17 **EST:** 1999
SQ FT: 4,500
SALES: 7.2MM **Privately Held**
SIC: 5147 2013 Meats & meat products; corned beef from purchased meat

(G-4395)
TALON LLC
350 Talon Centre Dr (48207)
PHONE..................313 392-1000
Randolph J Agley, *Ch of Bd*
Michael T Timmis, *Vice Ch Bd*
Paul Sieloff, *CFO*
EMP: 64 **EST:** 1973
SALES (est): 319.4K **Privately Held**
SIC: 3544 8741 Industrial molds; business management; financial management for business; administrative management

(G-4396)
TEAM BREADWINNER LLC
14414 Mansfield St (48227-4907)
PHONE..................313 460-0152
Bruce J Spearman,
EMP: 5
SQ FT: 4,800
SALES (est): 198.3K **Privately Held**
SIC: 2731 Book publishing

(G-4397)
TECH TOOL COMPANY INC
18235 Weaver St (48228-1193)
PHONE..................313 836-4131
Jeff Emerson, *President*
EMP: 6
SQ FT: 8,880
SALES (est): 1.2MM **Privately Held**
WEB: www.techtoolinc.com
SIC: 3462 Gear & chain forgings

(G-4398)
TECHNO URBAN 3D LLC
20299 Greenview Ave (48219-1529)
PHONE..................313 740-8110
Glenn Walters,
EMP: 10
SALES (est): 334.8K **Privately Held**
SIC: 2759 8299 Commercial printing; educational services

(G-4399)
THREE DOGS ONE CAT
2472 Riopelle St (48207-4525)
PHONE..................313 285-8371
Rita Nelson, *Owner*
EMP: 3
SALES (est): 184.2K **Privately Held**
SIC: 2047 Dog & cat food

(G-4400)
TIPALOY INC
1435 E Milwaukee St (48211-2009)
PHONE..................313 875-5145
Harry S Radcliff Jr, *President*
Mitchell Radcliff, *Vice Pres*
Elizabeth C Radcliff, *Admin Sec*
▲ **EMP:** 11 **EST:** 1941
SQ FT: 13,500
SALES (est): 2.7MM **Privately Held**
WEB: www.tipaloy.com
SIC: 3548 Electrodes, electric welding

(G-4401)
TITAN SALES INTERNATIONAL LLC
Also Called: Titan Coatings International
1497 E Grand Blvd (48211-3451)
PHONE..................313 469-7105
Sean Kelly, *President*
EMP: 4
SALES (est): 699.6K **Privately Held**
SIC: 2851 Shellac (protective coating)

(G-4402)
TOLERANCE TOOL & ENGINEERING
20541 Glendale St (48223-3324)
PHONE..................313 592-4011
Gerard J Fiorentino, *President*
Dave Bruckman, *Vice Pres*
Gerard Fiorentino, *Director*
Sheryl Fiorentino, *Admin Sec*
EMP: 20
SQ FT: 14,000
SALES (est): 4.5MM **Privately Held**
WEB: www.toltool.com
SIC: 3544 3545 Special dies & tools; machine tool accessories

(G-4403)
TOMPKINS PRODUCTS INC (PA)
1040 W Grand Blvd (48208-2337)
PHONE..................313 894-2222
Charles S Tompkins III, *President*
Joseph B Tompkins, *Vice Pres*
Steve Berger, *Engineer*
Steven Zaborowski, *Engineer*
Katie McSkimming, *Human Res Mgr*
◆ **EMP:** 95 **EST:** 1939
SQ FT: 40,000
SALES (est): 36.4MM **Privately Held**
WEB: www.tompkinsproducts.com
SIC: 3451 Screw machine products

(G-4404)
TORCH STEEL PROCESSING LLC
8103 Lynch Rd (48234-4142)
PHONE..................313 571-7000
Kristine Bishop, *Office Mgr*
Edward Bishop,
▲ **EMP:** 35
SQ FT: 80,000
SALES (est): 6.4MM **Privately Held**
SIC: 3325 Steel foundries

(G-4405)
TPA INC
1360 Oakman Blvd (48238-4243)
P.O. Box 38778 (48238-0778)
PHONE..................248 302-9131
James J Padilla Jr, *President*
EMP: 5
SALES (est): 590K **Privately Held**
SIC: 2869 High purity grade chemicals, organic

(G-4406)
TRANOR INDUSTRIES LLC
19365 Sherwood St (48234-2820)
PHONE..................313 733-4888
Sam Fodale,
Gregory E Burcz,
▲ **EMP:** 12
SALES (est): 2.6MM **Privately Held**
SIC: 3544 Special dies & tools

(G-4407)
TRI-VISION LLC (PA)
Also Called: Pic-Turn
12326 E Mcnichols Rd (48205-3328)
PHONE..................313 526-6020
Paul Werner, *Mng Member*
Sean Powell, *Manager*
EMP: 10 **EST:** 1936
SQ FT: 5,000
SALES: 500K **Privately Held**
WEB: www.trivision.com
SIC: 3444 Sheet metalwork

(G-4408)
TRIANGLE BROACH COMPANY
18404 Fitzpatrick St (48228-1420)
PHONE..................313 838-2150
Gary Hanton, *President*
Carter Elton, *Vice Pres*
EMP: 14 **EST:** 1946
SQ FT: 8,000
SALES: 1.6MM **Privately Held**
WEB: www.trianglebroach.com
SIC: 3545 3544 3829 3541 Broaches (machine tool accessories); gauges (machine tool accessories); jigs & fixtures; measuring & controlling devices; machine tools, metal cutting type

(G-4409)
TRU POINT CORPORATION
6707 W Warren Ave (48210-1135)
PHONE..................313 897-9100
Michael Mainsinger, *President*
Valerie Mainsinger, *Treasurer*
EMP: 4
SQ FT: 4,600
SALES: 250K **Privately Held**
SIC: 3544 3545 Jigs & fixtures; collets (machine tool accessories)

(G-4410)
TWEDDLE GROUP INC
2111 Woodward Ave 8f (48201-3421)
PHONE..................586 840-3275
Paul Wilbur, *Manager*
EMP: 30
SALES (corp-wide): 186MM **Privately Held**
SIC: 7372 Prepackaged software
PA: Tweddle Group, Inc.
24780 Maplehurst Dr
Clinton Township MI 48036
586 307-3700

Detroit - Wayne County (G-4411)

(G-4411)
TWO JAMES SPIRITS LLC
2445 Michigan Ave (48216-1366)
PHONE.................................313 964-4800
David Landrum, Mng Member
Loretta Lucas, Director
▲ EMP: 9
SALES (est): 549.3K **Privately Held**
SIC: **5921** 2085 Liquor stores; distilled & blended liquors

(G-4412)
U S ICE CORP
10625 W 8 Mile Rd (48221-1032)
PHONE.................................313 862-3344
Saad Abbo, President
Fida Abbo, Admin Sec
EMP: 20
SQ FT: 9,000
SALES (est): 3.7MM **Privately Held**
SIC: **2097** Ice cubes

(G-4413)
UNCLE RAYS LLC
14300 Ilene St (48238-2216)
PHONE.................................313 739-6035
EMP: 3
SALES (corp-wide): 1.6B **Privately Held**
SIC: **2096** Potato chips & other potato-based snacks
HQ: Uncle Rays, Llc
   14245 Birwood St
   Detroit MI 48238

(G-4414)
UNCLE RAYS LLC (HQ)
14245 Birwood St (48238-2207)
PHONE.................................313 834-0800
Raymond Jenkins, President
Dennis Dapra, Vice Pres
Jennifer Jenkins, Vice Pres
Margaret Jackson, Human Res Mgr
Nathan Crankshaw, Manager
▲ EMP: 100
SQ FT: 75,000
SALES (est): 41.1MM
SALES (corp-wide): 1.6B **Privately Held**
WEB: www.unclerays.com
SIC: **2096** Potato chips & other potato-based snacks
PA: The H T Hackney Co
   502 S Gay St Ste 300
   Knoxville TN 37902
   865 546-1291

(G-4415)
UNITED STATES GYPSUM COMPANY
10090 W Jefferson Ave (48218-1363)
PHONE.................................313 842-4455
Matt Craig, Branch Mgr
EMP: 116
SALES (corp-wide): 8.2B **Privately Held**
WEB: www.usg.com
SIC: **3275** Gypsum products
HQ: United States Gypsum Company
   550 W Adams St Ste 1300
   Chicago IL 60661
   312 606-4000

(G-4416)
UNIVERSAL TIRE RECYCLING INC (PA)
19106 Livernois Ave (48221-1716)
PHONE.................................313 429-1212
Shanesia Fox, President
Joseph Fox, COO
EMP: 11
SQ FT: 4,000
SALES: 384K **Privately Held**
SIC: **3559** Tire shredding machinery

(G-4417)
US WIRE ROPE SUPPLY INC
Also Called: U.S. Wire & Rope
6555 Sherwood St (48211-2475)
PHONE.................................313 925-0444
James R Dagostino, President
Claudia R Dagostino, Finance
▲ EMP: 23 EST: 1971
SQ FT: 40,000
SALES (est): 4MM **Privately Held**
SIC: **3496** Grocery carts, made from purchased wire

(G-4418)
USHER ENTERPRISES INC
Also Called: Usher Oil Company
9000 Roselawn St (48204-2747)
PHONE.................................313 834-7055
Matthew Usher, President
Lori Anne Usher, Vice Pres
Richard Folsom, Accounts Exec
Mark Swirczek, Accounts Exec
Andrew Usher, Sales Associate
EMP: 35
SALES (est): 17.8MM **Privately Held**
WEB: www.usheroil.com
SIC: **5093** 3559 Oil, waste; recycling machinery

(G-4419)
UTICA WASHERS
3105 Beaufait St (48207-2401)
PHONE.................................313 571-1568
Bruce Jay, Plant Mgr
EMP: 4 EST: 2004
SALES (est): 254.2K **Privately Held**
SIC: **3452** Washers

(G-4420)
V&R ENTERPRIZE
Also Called: B&B T-Shirt Factory
16011 W Mcnichols Rd (48235-3547)
PHONE.................................313 837-5545
Reginald Lester, Owner
▲ EMP: 3
SQ FT: 1,500
SALES: 100K **Privately Held**
SIC: **2759** 2396 Commercial printing; automotive & apparel trimmings

(G-4421)
VALEO NORTH AMERICA INC
Valeo Front End Module
12240 Oakland Pkwy (48203-3543)
PHONE.................................313 883-8850
EMP: 215
SALES (corp-wide): 177.9K **Privately Held**
SIC: **3714** Radiators & radiator shells & cores, motor vehicle
HQ: Valeo North America, Inc.
   150 Stephenson Hwy
   Troy MI 48083

(G-4422)
VAN PELT CORPORATION
Also Called: Service Steel Co - Detroit
13700 Sherwood St Ste 1 (48212-2060)
PHONE.................................313 365-6500
Edward Masar, Branch Mgr
EMP: 13
SALES (corp-wide): 30.5MM **Privately Held**
WEB: www.servicesteel.com
SIC: **3317** 3441 Tubes, seamless steel; fabricated structural metal
PA: Van Pelt Corporation
   36155 Mound Rd
   Sterling Heights MI 48310
   313 365-3600

(G-4423)
VAUGHAN INDUSTRIES INC
8490 Lyndon St (48238-2446)
PHONE.................................313 935-2040
Lawrence J Balash, President
Nancy J Balash, Corp Secy
Eric Ashley, Manager
EMP: 15 EST: 1977
SQ FT: 25,000
SALES (est): 3.9MM **Privately Held**
SIC: **2841** 5084 2992 Soap & other detergents; meters, consumption registering; cutting oils, blending: made from purchased materials

(G-4424)
VENTURE LABEL INC
3380 Baseline Rd (48231)
PHONE.................................313 928-2545
EMP: 4
SALES (corp-wide): 2MM **Privately Held**
SIC: **2679** Labels, paper: made from purchased material
PA: Venture Labels
   2120 Fasan Dr
   Oldcastle ON N0R 1
   519 966-9580

(G-4425)
VERDUYN TARPS DETROIT INC
19231 W Davison St (48223-3416)
PHONE.................................313 270-4890
Lloyd Verduyn, President
▲ EMP: 8
SQ FT: 50,000
SALES (est): 1.2MM **Privately Held**
WEB: www.verduyntarps.com
SIC: **2399** 5199 Automotive covers, except seat & tire covers; tarpaulins

(G-4426)
VERNDALE PRODUCTS INC
8445 Lyndon St (48238-2483)
PHONE.................................313 834-4190
Laverne E Johnson, President
Dale Johnson, President
Fred Kreger, Vice Pres
Bradley Schleicher, Plant Supt
Rich Perry, Plant Mgr
EMP: 40 EST: 1958
SQ FT: 59,000
SALES (est): 15.6MM **Privately Held**
WEB: www.verndaleproducts.com
SIC: **2023** Powdered milk

(G-4427)
VERSA HANDLING CO (PA)
Also Called: Cleveland Tramrail Systems
12995 Hillview St (48227-4000)
PHONE.................................313 491-0500
James F McKean, President
Lisa McKean, Manager
EMP: 9
SQ FT: 70,000
SALES (est): 3.4MM **Privately Held**
WEB: www.versahandling.com
SIC: **3535** 3536 Conveyors & conveying equipment; cranes, overhead traveling

(G-4428)
VERSA HANDLING CO
Also Called: Grey Hub Trolley Wheel Company
17265 Gable St (48212-1321)
PHONE.................................313 891-1420
Diane Garvin, Manager
EMP: 3
SQ FT: 6,000
SALES (corp-wide): 3.4MM **Privately Held**
WEB: www.versahandling.com
SIC: **3535** Conveyors & conveying equipment
PA: Versa Handling Co.
   12995 Hillview St
   Detroit MI 48227
   313 491-0500

(G-4429)
VIPERS DEN WINERY LLC
3228 W Philadelphia St (48206-2351)
PHONE.................................734 644-0213
Dustin Vanderburg,
EMP: 3
SALES (est): 100.5K **Privately Held**
SIC: **2084** Wines, brandy & brandy spirits

(G-4430)
VIRTEC MANUFACTURING LLC
17565 W P Chrysler Fwy (48203)
PHONE.................................313 369-4858
EMP: 3
SALES: 950K **Privately Held**
SIC: **3499** Mfg Misc Fabricated Metal Products

(G-4431)
VIRTUOSO CUSTOM CREATIONS LLC
1111 Bellevue St Unit 201 (48207-3687)
PHONE.................................313 332-1299
Mark Klimkowski,
EMP: 8
SALES (est): 293.5K **Privately Held**
SIC: **2431** Millwork

(G-4432)
VISIONIT SUPPLIES AND SVCS INC
3031 W Grand Blvd Ste 600 (48202-3014)
PHONE.................................313 664-5650
David H Segura, CEO
EMP: 1000
SQ FT: 5,000
SALES (est): 86.2MM **Privately Held**
WEB: www.visionitinc.com
SIC: **3577** 3955 5734 Printers, computer; print cartridges for laser & other computer printers; printers & plotters: computers

(G-4433)
VITEC LLC
2801 Clark St (48210-9716)
PHONE.................................313 633-2254
William F Pickard, CEO
Lawrence Crawford,
Joseph Macneil,
Bruce E Thompson,
▲ EMP: 290
SQ FT: 150,000
SALES (est): 71.1MM **Privately Held**
WEB: www.vitec-usa.com
SIC: **3089** Plastic & fiberglass tanks; automotive parts, plastic

(G-4434)
VITESCO TECHNOLOGIES
18615 Sherwood St (48234-2813)
PHONE.................................248 393-5880
Cathy Thomas, Branch Mgr
EMP: 3
SALES (corp-wide): 50.8B **Privately Held**
SIC: **3714** Motor vehicle parts & accessories
HQ: Vitesco Technologies Usa, Llc
   2400 Executive Hills Dr
   Auburn Hills MI 48326
   248 209-4000

(G-4435)
WALL STREET JOURNAL GATE A 20
1 Detroit Metro Airport (48242-1004)
PHONE.................................734 941-4139
Tim Stibers, General Mgr
EMP: 3 EST: 2013
SALES (est): 133.9K **Privately Held**
SIC: **2711** Newspapers, publishing & printing

(G-4436)
WATERMAN AND SONS PRTG CO INC
17134 Wyoming St (48221-2452)
PHONE.................................313 864-5562
Homer E Waterman, President
Marie Waterman, Corp Secy
William O Waterman, Vice Pres
EMP: 3 EST: 1947
SQ FT: 1,800
SALES (est): 422.7K **Privately Held**
SIC: **2752** 2759 Commercial printing, offset; letterpress printing

(G-4437)
WESTCOTT DISPLAYS INC (PA)
Also Called: Westcott Paper Products
450 Amsterdam St (48202-3408)
PHONE.................................313 872-1200
Allan G Campbell III, President
Greg Campbell, President
George Chirillo, Exec VP
George A Chirillo, Vice Pres
Robert Schwanitz, Vice Pres
▲ EMP: 50
SQ FT: 100,000
SALES: 8.8MM **Privately Held**
WEB: www.westcottdisplays.com
SIC: **3993** Displays & cutouts, window & lobby

(G-4438)
WEYHING BROS MANUFACTURING CO
3040 Gratiot Ave (48207-2334)
PHONE.................................313 567-0600
Joseph Garofalo, President
Shirley A Garofalo, Vice Pres
EMP: 10
SQ FT: 8,000
SALES (est): 1MM **Privately Held**
SIC: **3911** 5944 Jewelry, precious metal; jewelry stores

(G-4439)
WHIMSICAL FUSIONS LLC
2326 E 7 Mile Rd (48234-1304)
PHONE.................................248 956-0952

GEOGRAPHIC SECTION

Angela Thornton,
EMP: 4
SALES: 25K **Privately Held**
SIC: 2844 Toilet preparations

(G-4440)
WHITESIDE CONSULTING GROUP LLC
Also Called: Wcg Design
19341 Stansbury St (48235-1733)
P.O. Box 35174 (48235-0174)
PHONE.................................313 288-6598
Ronald Whiteside,
Candice Whiteside,
Rashard Whiteside,
Tanisha Whiteside,
EMP: 5 **EST:** 2012
SALES (est): 205.2K **Privately Held**
SIC: 7374 7336 8742 2791 Computer graphics service; commercial art & graphic design; business consultant; typesetting, computer controlled; office computer automation systems integration;

(G-4441)
WHOLESALE WEAVE INC
3130 E 8 Mile Rd (48234-1019)
PHONE.................................800 762-2037
Shonny Beavers, *Vice Pres*
EMP: 10 **EST:** 2013
SALES (est): 342.6K **Privately Held**
SIC: 3999 7334 Doll wigs (hair); photocopying & duplicating services

(G-4442)
WILLIAM COSGRIFF ELECTRC
4761 Avery St (48208-2205)
PHONE.................................313 832-6958
William L Cosgriff, *Owner*
EMP: 3 **EST:** 1967
SALES: 400K **Privately Held**
SIC: 5084 3589 Sewing machines, industrial; sewer cleaning equipment, power

(G-4443)
WIRE FAB INC
18055 Sherwood St (48234-2812)
PHONE.................................313 893-8816
Michael Wehner, *President*
Annkaethe Wehner, *Corp Secy*
Richard Wehner, *Manager*
EMP: 10 **EST:** 1962
SQ FT: 11,500
SALES: 550K **Privately Held**
SIC: 3496 3545 Miscellaneous fabricated wire products; tools & accessories for machine tools

(G-4444)
WIRELESS 4 LESS INC
9660 Greenfield Rd (48227-2034)
PHONE.................................313 653-3345
Osama Zumot, *Principal*
EMP: 3
SALES (est): 228.6K **Privately Held**
SIC: 3661 Headsets, telephone

(G-4445)
WOLVERINE CONCRETE PRODUCTS
9189 Central St (48204-4323)
PHONE.................................313 931-7189
Shel Wheatley, *President*
EMP: 4
SQ FT: 15,000
SALES (est): 549K **Privately Held**
SIC: 3272 4212 Concrete products, precast; delivery service, vehicular

(G-4446)
WOLVERINE PACKING CO (PA)
2535 Rivard St (48207-2621)
PHONE.................................313 259-7500
A James Bonahoom, *President*
Jim Bonahoom, *Vice Pres*
Roger P Bonahoom, *Vice Pres*
Marvin Coleman, *Plant Mgr*
Jakeb Brooks, *Project Mgr*
◆ **EMP:** 100 **EST:** 1934
SQ FT: 55,000
SALES (est): 210.9MM **Privately Held**
WEB: www.wolverinepacking.com
SIC: 5147 2011 5142 Meats, fresh; veal from meat slaughtered on site; lamb products from lamb slaughtered on site; meat, frozen: packaged; poultry, frozen: packaged

(G-4447)
WOLVERING FUR
2937 Russell St (48207-4825)
PHONE.................................313 961-0620
Paul Petcoff, *President*
Clay Campbell, *Vice Pres*
Michael Van Buren, *Vice Pres*
EMP: 7
SALES (est): 416.4K **Privately Held**
SIC: 5632 2371 Furriers; apparel, fur

(G-4448)
WOODWARD ENERGY SOLUTIONS LLC
719 Griswold St Ste 720 (48226-3300)
PHONE.................................888 967-4533
Brandon Boudreau, *Co-Owner*
Jack Macintosh, *Legal Staff*
EMP: 15
SALES (est): 646.4K **Privately Held**
SIC: 3646 Commercial indusl & institutional electric lighting fixtures

(G-4449)
WORLD OF PALLETS AND TRUCKING
3420 Lovett St (48210-3135)
PHONE.................................313 899-2000
Fernando Anaya, *President*
Soledad Anaya, *Vice Pres*
EMP: 6
SALES (est): 250.5K **Privately Held**
SIC: 2448 4731 Wood pallets & skids; freight transportation arrangement

(G-4450)
WRIGHT & FILIPPIS INC
4201 Saint Antoine St (48201-2153)
PHONE.................................313 832-5020
Dale Ferguson, *Manager*
EMP: 6
SALES (corp-wide): 51.4MM **Privately Held**
WEB: www.firsttoserve.com
SIC: 3842 Prosthetic appliances
PA: Wright & Filippis, Inc.
2845 Crooks Rd
Rochester Hills MI 48309
248 829-8292

(G-4451)
WS MOLNAR CO
Also Called: Slipnot Metal Safety Flooring
2545 Beaufait St (48207-3467)
PHONE.................................313 923-0400
Marie Molnar, *President*
Jeff Baker, *General Mgr*
Christina Metrose, *General Mgr*
Christina Molnar, *Vice Pres*
Michael Schulte, *Project Mgr*
EMP: 30
SQ FT: 35,500
SALES (est): 13.8MM **Privately Held**
SIC: 3399 3479 Metal powders, pastes & flakes; etching & engraving

(G-4452)
XENITH LLC
1201 Woodward Ave Fl 5 (48226-2039)
PHONE.................................866 888-2322
John Duerden, *CEO*
Richard Burton, *Regl Sales Mgr*
Chris Simms, *Sales Staff*
Vin Ferrara, *Med Doctor*
Dean Baker, *Manager*
▲ **EMP:** 28 **EST:** 2007
SQ FT: 25,000
SALES (est): 6.1MM
SALES (corp-wide): 1.7B **Privately Held**
SIC: 3949 Helmets, athletic
HQ: Rock Ventures Llc
1074 Woodward Ave
Detroit MI 48226

(G-4453)
XYTEK INDUSTRIES INC
19431 W Davison St (48223-3419)
PHONE.................................313 838-6961
Bob W Shipton, *President*
Carl T Lizut, *Vice Pres*
Bert Shim, *Engineer*
EMP: 15
SQ FT: 7,500
SALES: 2MM **Privately Held**
SIC: 8711 8734 3694 Electrical or electronic engineering; testing laboratories; automotive electrical equipment

(G-4454)
YANFENG US AUTOMOTIVE
Also Called: Plastech
2931 E Jefferson Ave (48207-4288)
PHONE.................................313 259-3226
EMP: 218
SALES (corp-wide): 55MM **Privately Held**
SIC: 3089 Injection molded finished plastic products
HQ: Yanfeng Us Automotive Interior Systems I Llc
41935 W 12 Mile Rd
Novi MI 48377
248 319-7333

(G-4455)
YOUNG SUPPLY COMPANY
Also Called: Johnson Contrls Authorized Dlr
1177 W Baltimore St (48202-2905)
PHONE.................................313 875-3280
Ronald Vallan, *Owner*
Joe Bobzin, *Treasurer*
Bob Laho, *Sales Staff*
Richard Dunn, *Branch Mgr*
Jeffrey Beyer, *Manager*
▲ **EMP:** 20
SQ FT: 18,337
SALES (est): 2.8MM **Privately Held**
SIC: 3585 5078 5075 5074 Parts for heating, cooling & refrigerating equipment; refrigeration equipment & supplies; warm air heating & air conditioning; plumbing & hydronic heating supplies

(G-4456)
ZAK BROTHERS PRINTING LLC
Also Called: Palmer Printing Co
5480 Cass Ave (48202-3614)
PHONE.................................313 831-3216
William P Ganzak,
James J Ganzak,
EMP: 4 **EST:** 1938
SQ FT: 6,500
SALES (est): 440K **Privately Held**
SIC: 2752 2759 Commercial printing, offset; letterpress printing

(G-4457)
ZEMIS 5 LLC
Also Called: Snake Island
13207 Santa Clara St (48235-2613)
Drawer 195 29488, Royal Oak (48073)
PHONE.................................317 946-7015
Emmanuel El-Amin, *Principal*
Isaac El-Amin El-Amin, *Principal*
Maurice El-Amin, *Principal*
Stanley El-Amin, *Principal*
Zachary El-Amin, *Principal*
EMP: 5
SALES (est): 195.6K **Privately Held**
SIC: 2426 2321 Carvings, furniture: wood; sport shirts, men's & boys': from purchased materials

(G-4458)
ZURN INDUSTRIES LLC
7431 W 8 Mile Rd (48221-1262)
P.O. Box 37317, Oak Park (48237-0317)
PHONE.................................313 864-2800
George Johnston, *Branch Mgr*
EMP: 10 **Publicly Held**
WEB: www.zurn.com
SIC: 5074 3431 Plumbing & hydronic heating supplies; sinks: enameled iron, cast iron or pressed metal
HQ: Zurn Industries, Llc
1801 Pittsburgh Ave
Erie PA 16502
814 455-0921

Dewitt
Clinton County

(G-4459)
BLTS WEARABLE ART INC
1541 W Round Lake Rd (48820-9799)
PHONE.................................517 669-9659
Ronald Baumgardner, *Partner*
Tammy Baumgardner, *Treasurer*
EMP: 7
SQ FT: 3,000
SALES: 320K **Privately Held**
SIC: 2759 2396 Screen printing; automotive & apparel trimmings

(G-4460)
CAPITAL EQUIPMENT CLARE LLC (PA)
12263 S Us Highway 27 (48820-8374)
PHONE.................................517 669-5533
Gary Holt, *Principal*
EMP: 12
SALES (est): 766.2K **Privately Held**
SIC: 7353 3531 Heavy construction equipment rental; tractors, construction

(G-4461)
CARHARTT INC
128 Spring Meadows Ln (48820-9598)
PHONE.................................517 282-4193
EMP: 3
SALES (corp-wide): 1.9B **Privately Held**
SIC: 2326 Men's & boys' work clothing
PA: Carhartt, Inc.
5750 Mercury Dr
Dearborn MI 48126
313 271-8460

(G-4462)
H & R ELECTRICAL CONTRS LLC
10588 S Us Highway 27 (48820-8428)
P.O. Box 467 (48820-0467)
PHONE.................................517 669-2102
Amy C Rusnell, *Mng Member*
Todd Rusnell,
EMP: 4
SALES: 1MM **Privately Held**
SIC: 1731 3589 5063 General electrical contractor; commercial cooking & food-warming equipment; lighting fixtures, commercial & industrial

(G-4463)
LOGAN BROTHERS PRINTING INC
13544 Blackwood Dr (48820-8106)
PHONE.................................517 485-3771
Ronald A Maiers, *President*
Ron Maiers, *Mktg Dir*
Ron Bollinger, *Representative*
EMP: 16 **EST:** 1951
SQ FT: 7,000
SALES: 1.8MM **Privately Held**
WEB: www.loganbrothersprinting.com
SIC: 2752 2789 Commercial printing, offset; bookbinding & related work

(G-4464)
MAHONEY & ASSOCIATES INC
12750 Escanaba Dr Ste 1 (48820-8687)
PHONE.................................517 669-4300
Daria Mahoney, *President*
EMP: 8
SALES (est): 1.5MM **Privately Held**
WEB: www.mahoneypromo.com
SIC: 5199 2759 Advertising specialties; commercial printing

(G-4465)
MIDWEST WALL COMPANY LLC
13753 Cottonwood Dr (48820-8500)
PHONE.................................517 881-3701
Dean Bourdon, *Mng Member*
EMP: 10
SALES (est): 1.2MM **Privately Held**
SIC: 3444 Sheet metalwork

(G-4466)
SWEETIE PIE PANTRY (PA)
108 N Bridge St (48820-8900)
PHONE.................................517 669-9300

Dewitt - Clinton County (G-4467)

GEOGRAPHIC SECTION

Linda Hundt, *Mng Member*
EMP: 3
SALES (est): 1.2MM **Privately Held**
WEB: www.sweetie-licious.com
SIC: 2052 Bakery products, dry

(G-4467)
TIN CAN DEWITT
13175 Schavey Rd (48820-9000)
PHONE.................................517 624-2078
EMP: 3 **EST:** 2012
SALES (est): 236.5K **Privately Held**
SIC: 3411 Tin cans

(G-4468)
TOUCHSTONE DISTRIBUTING INC
Also Called: Touchstone Pottery
103 S Bridge St Ste B (48820-8840)
PHONE.................................517 669-8200
Paul Hartleib, *President*
▲ **EMP:** 6
SQ FT: 4,200
SALES: 515K **Privately Held**
SIC: 3911 Jewelry, precious metal

(G-4469)
TOWERLINE SOFTWARE LLC
240 S Bridge St Ste 110 (48820-8825)
PHONE.................................517 669-8112
Thomas A Adams,
EMP: 3
SALES (est): 295.6K **Privately Held**
SIC: 7372 Prepackaged software

Dexter
Washtenaw County

(G-4470)
AA EDM CORPORATION
7455 Newman Blvd (48130-1558)
PHONE.................................734 253-2784
John Macgregor, *President*
George Barbulescu, *Vice Pres*
Nicky Borcea, *Vice Pres*
Carl Naudi, *Sales Mgr*
EMP: 16
SALES (est): 3.2MM **Privately Held**
SIC: 3599 Electrical discharge machining (EDM)

(G-4471)
ABLETECH INDUSTRIES LLC
8383 Millview Ct (48130-9475)
PHONE.................................734 677-2420
Michael Olson, *CEO*
EMP: 9
SALES (est): 556.5K **Privately Held**
SIC: 3999 3829 Manufacturing industries; geophysical & meteorological testing equipment

(G-4472)
ADAIR PRINTING COMPANY (PA)
7850 2nd St (48130-1238)
PHONE.................................734 426-2822
Dennis Adair, *President*
Alisa Jenks, *Vice Pres*
Debbie Adair, *Marketing Staff*
Lawrence Govaere, *Manager*
Jane Padala, *Manager*
EMP: 30 **EST:** 1928
SQ FT: 150,000
SALES (est): 11.3MM **Privately Held**
WEB: www.adairprinting.com
SIC: 2759 2752 8742 7371 Catalogs: printing; commercial printing, lithographic; marketing consulting services; software programming applications

(G-4473)
AEROSTATICA INC
Also Called: Cameron Balloons - U.S.
7399 Newman Blvd (48130-1558)
P.O. Box 3672, Ann Arbor (48106-3672)
PHONE.................................734 426-5525
Tucker Comstock, *President*
EMP: 15 **EST:** 1970
SQ FT: 13,500
SALES (est): 2.9MM **Privately Held**
WEB: www.cameronballoons.com
SIC: 3721 3728 Balloons, hot air (aircraft); aircraft parts & equipment

(G-4474)
ALCO MANUFACTURING CORP
8763 Dexter Chelsea Rd (48130-9782)
PHONE.................................734 426-3941
Christopher Morgan,
EMP: 50
SQ FT: 25,000
SALES (est): 9.1MM **Privately Held**
SIC: 3492 3451 Fluid power valves & hose fittings; screw machine products
PA: Alco Manufacturing Corporation Llc
10584 Middle Ave
Elyria OH 44035

(G-4475)
ALPHA METAL FINISHING CO
8155 Huron St (48130-1026)
PHONE.................................734 426-2855
Robert E Wood, *President*
Greg Wood, *COO*
Bob Wood, *Plant Mgr*
Jamie Barrus, *QC Mgr*
Beverly Vieta, *Office Mgr*
EMP: 12 **EST:** 1966
SQ FT: 20,000
SALES (est): 2MM **Privately Held**
WEB: www.alphametal.com
SIC: 3471 Finishing, metals or formed products; anodizing (plating) of metals or formed products; chromium plating of metals or formed products

(G-4476)
BELJAN LTD INC
4635 Mcguiness Rd (48130-9546)
PHONE.................................734 426-3503
Faith Krug, *President*
Robin Janiszewski, *Vice Pres*
EMP: 10
SQ FT: 2,500
SALES (est): 537.3K **Privately Held**
WEB: www.beljan.com
SIC: 7374 2791 Data processing & preparation; typesetting

(G-4477)
BERNER SCIENTIFIC INC
7275 Joy Rd Ste C (48130-9268)
PHONE.................................248 253-0077
Richard Berner, *President*
EMP: 3
SALES (corp-wide): 384.7K **Privately Held**
WEB: www.bernerscientific.com
SIC: 3827 Optical instruments & apparatus
PA: Berner Scientific Inc
927 Minnesota Dr
Troy MI
248 253-0077

(G-4478)
BERRY & ASSOCIATES INC
2434 Bishop Cir E (48130-1570)
PHONE.................................734 426-3787
David Berry, *President*
Lana Berry, *Vice Pres*
Nancy Barta, *Opers Staff*
Joe Repine, *Research*
Julie Olson, *Finance*
EMP: 10
SQ FT: 7,500
SALES (est): 6MM **Privately Held**
SIC: 2869 Industrial organic chemicals
HQ: Lgc Limited
Old Perth Road
Inverness IV2 5

(G-4479)
BTI MEASUREMENT TSTG SVCS LLC
2800 Zeeb Rd Dockk (48130-2204)
PHONE.................................734 769-2100
Stephen Simon, *Manager*
EMP: 4
SALES (corp-wide): 1.1MM **Privately Held**
SIC: 3829 Testing equipment: abrasion, shearing strength, etc.
PA: Bti Measurement & Testing Services Llc
7035 Jomar Dr
Whitmore Lake MI 48189
734 769-2100

(G-4480)
BURLY OAK BUILDERS INC
9980 Dexter Chelsea Rd (48130-9777)
PHONE.................................734 368-4912
Richard Parr, *President*
EMP: 6
SALES: 700K **Privately Held**
SIC: 1521 3523 New construction, single-family houses; barn, silo, poultry, dairy & livestock machinery

(G-4481)
CLARK-MXR INC
7300 Huron River Dr Ste 1 (48130-1209)
PHONE.................................734 426-2803
William Clark, *President*
Taune De Bolt, *Admin Asst*
EMP: 20
SQ FT: 10,000
SALES (est): 3.6MM **Privately Held**
WEB: www.cmxr.com
SIC: 3826 3827 8731 Laser scientific & engineering instruments; optical instruments & apparatus; medical research, commercial

(G-4482)
CLEAN CLOTHES INC
Also Called: Maggie's Organics
7852 2nd St (48130-1238)
PHONE.................................734 482-4000
Bena Burda, *President*
Ronald Burda, *Vice Pres*
▲ **EMP:** 7
SQ FT: 1,500
SALES (est): 1.3MM **Privately Held**
WEB: www.organicclothes.com
SIC: 2339 Women's & misses' outerwear

(G-4483)
COMPLETE DSIGN AUTOMTN SYSTEMS (PA)
2117 Bishop Cir E (48130-1565)
PHONE.................................734 424-2789
EMP: 7
SQ FT: 10,000
SALES (est): 1.7MM **Privately Held**
SIC: 8711 3625 Engineering Services Mfg Relays/Industrial Controls

(G-4484)
DESIGN & TEST TECHNOLOGY INC
2430 Scio Rd (48130-9716)
P.O. Box 1526, Ann Arbor (48106-1526)
PHONE.................................734 665-4111
Michael Murphy, *President*
EMP: 8
SALES (corp-wide): 1MM **Privately Held**
WEB: www.designtest.com
SIC: 7373 3825 Computer systems analysis & design; test equipment for electronic & electric measurement
PA: Design & Test Technology, Inc
3744 Plaza Dr Ste 2
Ann Arbor MI 48108
734 665-4316

(G-4485)
DEXTER AUTOMATIC PRODUCTS CO
Also Called: Dapco Industries
2500 Bishop Cir E (48130-1566)
PHONE.................................734 426-8900
Willis E Tupper, *Ch of Bd*
Ronald E Tupper, *President*
Kevin Pequet, *Business Mgr*
Randy Arnett, *VP Opers*
Robert Spiess, *Buyer*
EMP: 180 **EST:** 1952
SQ FT: 80,000
SALES (est): 40.4MM **Privately Held**
WEB: www.dapcoind.com
SIC: 3592 3564 3544 3494 Valves, engine; blowers & fans; special dies, tools, jigs & fixtures; valves & pipe fittings; screw machine products

(G-4486)
DEXTER FASTENER TECH INC (PA)
Also Called: Dextech
2110 Bishop Cir E (48130-1594)
PHONE.................................734 426-0311
J Sakatoa, *Ch of Bd*

Mike Frazier, *President*
Don Semones, *Safety Mgr*
Dan White, *Purchasing*
Pete King, *QA Dir*
▲ **EMP:** 230
SQ FT: 350,000
SALES (est): 44.9MM **Privately Held**
WEB: www.dextech.com
SIC: 3452 Bolts, metal

(G-4487)
DEXTER FASTENER TECH INC
2103 Bishop Cir W (48130-1561)
PHONE.................................734 426-5200
Mike Frazier, *CEO*
EMP: 50
SALES (corp-wide): 44.9MM **Privately Held**
WEB: www.dextech.com
SIC: 3452 Bolts, nuts, rivets & washers
PA: Dexter Fastener Technologies, Inc.
2110 Bishop Cir E
Dexter MI 48130
734 426-0311

(G-4488)
DEXTER RESEARCH CENTER INC
7300 Huron River Dr Ste 2 (48130-1086)
PHONE.................................734 426-3921
Robert S Toth Jr, *President*
Kurt Hochrein, *COO*
Sheri Penar, *Engineer*
EMP: 55 **EST:** 1977
SQ FT: 21,680
SALES: 7MM **Privately Held**
WEB: www.dexterresearch.com
SIC: 3823 Infrared instruments, industrial process type

(G-4489)
DIECUTTING SERVICE INC
2415 Bishop Cir W (48130-1563)
P.O. Box 471 (48130-0471)
PHONE.................................734 426-0290
Les Baxter, *President*
Scott Baxter, *Vice Pres*
EMP: 14
SQ FT: 11,250
SALES: 1MM **Privately Held**
WEB: www.diecuttingserv.com
SIC: 2675 Paper die-cutting

(G-4490)
ELASTIZELL CORPORATION AMERICA
7900 2nd St (48130-1258)
PHONE.................................734 426-6076
EMP: 5
SALES (est): 566.2K
SALES (corp-wide): 1.5MM **Privately Held**
SIC: 3272 Concrete products
PA: Elastizell Corporation Of America
7900 2nd St
Dexter MI 48130
734 761-6900

(G-4491)
ELECTRO ARC MANUFACTURING CO
2055 N Lima Center Rd A (48130-9515)
PHONE.................................734 483-4233
Harold W Stark Jr, *President*
Stan Pylar, *VP Sales*
EMP: 20 **EST:** 1926
SALES (est): 4.7MM **Privately Held**
WEB: www.electroarc.com
SIC: 3829 5084 3541 Hardness testing equipment; industrial machine parts; machine tools, metal cutting: exotic (explosive, etc.)

(G-4492)
FABRICARI LLC
7100 Huron River Dr (48130-1066)
PHONE.................................734 972-2042
Leena Palmer,
EMP: 3
SALES (est): 151.7K **Privately Held**
SIC: 3498 4783 Tube fabricating (contract bending & shaping); containerization of goods for shipping

GEOGRAPHIC SECTION
Dexter - Washtenaw County (G-4517)

(G-4493)
GENESIS SERVICE ASSOCIATES LLC
3255 Central St Apt 1 (48130-1157)
PHONE.................734 994-3900
Michael Mason,
EMP: 5
SALES (est): 782.9K Privately Held
SIC: 2752 7336 Commercial printing, lithographic; graphic arts & related design

(G-4494)
INTELLIGENT VISION SYSTEMS LLC
7300 Huron River Dr Ste 4 (48130-1213)
PHONE.................734 426-3921
Robert Toth, CEO
Kurt Hochrein, COO
Nilton Renno, Officer
EMP: 3
SALES (est): 128K Privately Held
SIC: 3829 Meteorological instruments

(G-4495)
INTUITIVE TECHNOLOGY INC
3223 Boulder Ct (48130-9396)
PHONE.................602 249-5750
Chris Jones, CEO
Jason Marble, Software Engr
Geoff Oslund, Director
EMP: 5
SQ FT: 900
SALES: 1MM Privately Held
SIC: 3999 5087 5999 Barber & beauty shop equipment; service establishment equipment; alarm & safety equipment stores

(G-4496)
JOLLY PUMPKIN ARTISAN ALES LLC (PA)
3115 Broad St Ste A (48130-1137)
PHONE.................734 426-4962
Ronald S Jeffries,
Jerry Carlson,
Randy Reichwage,
EMP: 5
SALES: 200K Privately Held
SIC: 2082 Beer (alcoholic beverage)

(G-4497)
K-SPACE ASSOCIATES INC
2182 Bishop Cir E (48130-1564)
PHONE.................734 426-7977
Roy Clarke, President
Darryl Barlett, Exec VP
EMP: 20
SQ FT: 2,780
SALES: 5.3MM Privately Held
WEB: www.k-space.com
SIC: 3829 Stress, strain & flaw detecting/measuring equipment

(G-4498)
MERLIN SIMULATION INC
2135 Bishop Cir E Ste 6 (48130-1602)
P.O. Box 6110, Falls Church VA (22040-6110)
PHONE.................703 560-7203
Kenneth A Zimmerman, President
▲ EMP: 12 EST: 1996
SALES (est): 846.8K Privately Held
WEB: www.merlinsimulation.com
SIC: 3845 Transcutaneous electrical nerve stimulators (TENS)

(G-4499)
MICHIGAN MOVIE MAGAZINE LLC
9040 N Territorial Rd (48130-9607)
PHONE.................734 726-5299
Christopher Aliapoulios,
EMP: 3
SALES (est): 186.3K Privately Held
SIC: 2721 7389 Magazines: publishing & printing;

(G-4500)
MIDWEST GRAPHICS & AWARDS INC
2135 Bishop Cir E Ste 8 (48130-1602)
PHONE.................734 424-3700
Kevin Crouch, President
Jamie Punky, General Mgr
Mary Didonato, Vice Pres
Adam Hernandez, Opers Staff
Abbie Buhr, Manager
EMP: 4
SQ FT: 2,200
SALES (est): 492.4K Privately Held
SIC: 2759 5999 5094 Screen printing; decals: printing; trophies & plaques; coins, medals & trophies; trophies

(G-4501)
NULL TAPHOUSE
2319 Bishop Cir E (48130-1567)
PHONE.................734 792-9124
EMP: 3 EST: 2015
SALES (est): 197.7K Privately Held
SIC: 2082 Malt beverages

(G-4502)
PALADIN BRANDS GROUP INC (DH)
Also Called: Paladin Attachments
2800 Zeeb Rd (48130-2204)
PHONE.................319 378-3696
Steve Andrews, CEO
Matt Roney, President
Bob Ferguson, Vice Pres
Wendell Moss, Vice Pres
Dan Schmidt, Vice Pres
◆ EMP: 17
SALES (est): 394.1MM
SALES (corp-wide): 1.9B Privately Held
SIC: 3531 Finishers & spreaders (construction equipment); subgraders (construction equipment); drags, road (construction & road maintenance equipment)
HQ: International Equipment Solutions, Llc
2211 York Rd Ste 320
Oak Brook IL 60523
630 570-6880

(G-4503)
PHOTO SYSTEMS INC (PA)
7200 Huron River Dr Ste B (48130-1099)
PHONE.................734 424-9625
Alan Fischer, President
◆ EMP: 20
SQ FT: 42,000
SALES: 707.7K Privately Held
SIC: 5043 2899 Photographic equipment & supplies; chemical preparations

(G-4504)
PREDXION BIO INC
7455 Dexter Ann Arbor Rd (48130)
PHONE.................734 353-0191
Walker McHugh, CEO
EMP: 3
SALES (est): 95.3K Privately Held
SIC: 3841 Diagnostic apparatus, medical

(G-4505)
PROTOMATIC INC
2125 Bishop Cir W (48130)
PHONE.................734 426-3655
Rita Jean Wetzel, President
Douglas Wetzel, Vice Pres
Brian Heldt, Finance Mgr
David Wetzel, Sales Mgr
Mark Novitsch, Sales Staff
EMP: 42
SQ FT: 30,500
SALES (est): 3.7MM Privately Held
WEB: www.protomatic.com
SIC: 3841 Surgical & medical instruments

(G-4506)
QED ENVMTL SYSTEMS INC
2355 Bishop Cir W (48130-1592)
P.O. Box 3726, Ann Arbor (48106-3726)
PHONE.................734 995-2547
Timothy R White, President
Mark Weinberger, President
Lee Weil, Supervisor
▲ EMP: 80
SQ FT: 50,000
SALES (est): 41.1MM
SALES (corp-wide): 1.6B Publicly Held
WEB: www.qedenv.com
SIC: 3561 3823 3826 Industrial pumps & parts; controllers for process variables, all types; water testing apparatus

PA: Graco Inc.
88 11th Ave Ne
Minneapolis MN 55413
612 623-6000

(G-4507)
RICK OWEN & JASON VOGEL PARTNR
10475 N Territorial Rd (48130-8547)
PHONE.................734 417-3401
Rick Owen, Owner
EMP: 3
SALES (est): 188.3K Privately Held
SIC: 3088 Plastics plumbing fixtures

(G-4508)
ROSE CORPORATION
Also Called: Doors & Drawers
2467 Bishop Cir E (48130-1567)
PHONE.................734 426-0005
Charles J Manitz, President
Rosemary L Manitz, Vice Pres
Dave Bennett, Prdtn Mgr
Brian Manitz, Warehouse Mgr
EMP: 25
SQ FT: 10,000
SALES: 2.3MM Privately Held
SIC: 5712 5211 2521 2434 Cabinet work, custom; counter tops; wood office furniture; wood kitchen cabinets

(G-4509)
SIKO PRODUCTS INC
Also Called: Jim Schnabelt
2155 Bishop Cir E (48130-1565)
P.O. Box 279 (48130-0279)
PHONE.................734 426-3476
Darrell Davey, President
Ben King, Manager
▲ EMP: 9
SQ FT: 6,000
SALES: 2.6MM
SALES (corp-wide): 39.1MM Privately Held
WEB: www.sikoproducts.com
SIC: 3829 Measuring & controlling devices
PA: Siko Gmbh
Weihermattenweg 2
Buchenbach 79256
766 139-40

(G-4510)
SIMPLY GREEN OUTDOOR SVCS LLC
1535 Baker Rd (48130-1601)
PHONE.................734 385-6190
Richard E Olberg Jr,
EMP: 5
SALES: 750K Privately Held
SIC: 0721 1771 3271 0782 Planting services; concrete work; blocks, concrete: landscape or retaining wall; lawn care services

(G-4511)
SOHNER PLASTICS LLC
Also Called: Ipr Automation Sohner Plastic
7275 Joy Rd Ste D (48130-9268)
PHONE.................734 222-4847
Steve Flam, Sales Mgr
Laurie Loria, Office Mgr
Nicky Borcea, Mng Member
▲ EMP: 18
SQ FT: 10,400
SALES (est): 3.8MM Privately Held
WEB: www.borcea.com
SIC: 3089 Trays, plastic

(G-4512)
SWEEPSTER ATTACHMENTS LLC
Also Called: Harley Attachments
2800 Zeeb Rd (48130-2204)
PHONE.................734 996-9116
Matt Roney, Principal
Steve Brancheau, Export Mgr
Rodney Hill, Manager
Christian Jarzab, Manager
Allen Perko, Manager
▼ EMP: 1300
SQ FT: 465,000
SALES (est): 228.8MM
SALES (corp-wide): 1.9B Privately Held
WEB: www.sweepster.com
SIC: 3589 3991 Dirt sweeping units, industrial; brooms; street sweeping brooms, hand or machine; brushes, household or industrial
HQ: Paladin Brands Group, Inc.
2800 Zeeb Rd
Dexter MI 48130
319 378-3696

(G-4513)
THETFORD CORPORATION
800 Baker Rd (48130-1596)
P.O. Box 1285, Ann Arbor (48106-1285)
PHONE.................734 769-6000
Doug Shirley, Opers-Prdtn-Mfg
EMP: 80
SALES (corp-wide): 482MM Privately Held
WEB: www.thetford.com
SIC: 3431 2842 Metal sanitary ware; specialty cleaning, polishes & sanitation goods
HQ: Thetford Corporation
7101 Jackson Rd
Ann Arbor MI 48103
734 769-6000

(G-4514)
THOMSON-SHORE INC
7300 Joy Rd (48130-9492)
PHONE.................734 426-3939
Peter Shima, President
Kevin Spall, President
Thomson Shore, Principal
Terri Barlow, Vice Pres
◆ EMP: 200
SQ FT: 144,000
SALES (est): 56.5MM
SALES (corp-wide): 536.1MM Privately Held
WEB: www.tshore.com
SIC: 2741 Miscellaneous publishing
PA: Cjk Group, Inc.
3323 Oak St
Brainerd MN 56401
218 829-2877

(G-4515)
TRUCENT INC (PA)
7400 Newman Blvd (48130-1557)
PHONE.................734 426-9015
Tom Czartoski, CEO
Roger Wilson, General Mgr
Steve Hayes, Project Mgr
Tommy Hudson, Facilities Mgr
Richard N Ross, Facilities Mgr
EMP: 1
SALES (est): 35MM Privately Held
SIC: 8742 3677 5084 4953 Industrial consultant; filtration devices, electronic; industrial machinery & equipment; recycling, waste materials; refuse collection & disposal services

(G-4516)
TRUCENT SEPARATION TECH LLC
7400 Newman Blvd (48130-1557)
PHONE.................734 426-9015
Tom Czartoski, President
Matthew Grey, General Mgr
Monie Young, Business Mgr
Gary Snow, Plant Mgr
Jonah Corley, Sales Staff
EMP: 75
SQ FT: 12,000
SALES (est): 14.2MM Privately Held
WEB: www.solutionrecovery.com
SIC: 8742 3677 Industrial consultant; filtration devices, electronic
PA: Trucent, Inc.
7400 Newman Blvd
Dexter MI 48130

(G-4517)
VARIETY DIE & STAMPING CO
2221 Bishop Cir E (48130-1595)
PHONE.................734 426-4488
Kevin G Woods, Principal
Jonathan Woods, Corp Secy
Michael A Vernon, Vice Pres
Mike Vernon, Vice Pres
James Jarchow, QC Mgr

Dexter - Washtenaw County (G-4518)

▲ **EMP:** 75
SQ FT: 50,000
SALES (est): 17.8MM **Privately Held**
WEB: www.varietydie.com
SIC: 3465 3469 Automotive stampings; metal stampings

(G-4518)
WAHOO COMPOSITES LLC
7190 Huron River Dr (48130-1066)
PHONE 734 424-0966
Anne Parker, *CEO*
EMP: 10
SALES (est): 730K **Privately Held**
SIC: 3624 Carbon & graphite products

Dimondale
Eaton County

(G-4519)
PROSTHETIC CENTER INC
7343 Dupre Ave (48821-9547)
PHONE 517 372-7007
Toll Free: 877
EMP: 4
SQ FT: 2,200
SALES (est): 440.4K **Privately Held**
SIC: 3842 5999 Mfg Surgical Appliances/Supplies Ret Misc Merchandise

(G-4520)
TRIKALA INC
Also Called: Mackellar Screenworks
11546 Ransom Hwy (48821-8730)
PHONE 517 646-8188
Kirk Mackellar, *President*
EMP: 4
SALES: 370K **Privately Held**
WEB: www.mackellarscreenworks.com
SIC: 2759 Screen printing

Dollar Bay
Houghton County

(G-4521)
HORNER FLOORING COMPANY INC
23400 Hellman Ave (49922-9740)
PHONE 906 482-1180
Douglas Hamar, *CEO*
▼ **EMP:** 75
SALES (est): 12MM **Privately Held**
WEB: www.hornerflooring.com
SIC: 2426 Flooring, hardwood

(G-4522)
YOUNG MANUFACTURING INC
Also Called: Central Vac International
23455 Hellman Ave (49922)
P.O. Box 259 (49922-0259)
PHONE 906 483-3851
Mark Young, *President*
EMP: 5 **EST:** 2008
SALES (est): 1.4MM **Privately Held**
SIC: 3999 1761 Chairs, hydraulic, barber & beauty shop; sheet metalwork

Dorr
Allegan County

(G-4523)
DORR INDUSTRIES INC
1840 142nd Ave (49323-5104)
P.O. Box 308 (49323-0308)
PHONE 616 681-9440
Earl Parmelee, *President*
David Stebleton, *Principal*
EMP: 17
SQ FT: 20,000
SALES (est): 3.1MM **Privately Held**
WEB: www.dorrindinc.com
SIC: 3599 3469 Machine & other job shop work; machine shop, jobbing & repair; metal stampings
PA: Tg Manufacturing, Llc
  8197 Clyde Park Ave Sw
  Byron Center MI 49315

(G-4524)
INTEGRITY DOOR LLC
3010 143rd Ave (49323-9715)
PHONE 616 896-8077
Jared Dishinger,
EMP: 4
SALES (est): 253.5K **Privately Held**
SIC: 3442 Garage doors, overhead: metal

(G-4525)
PDS PLASTICS INC
3297 140th Ave (49323-9530)
PHONE 616 896-1109
Stacy Demaray, *President*
EMP: 17 **EST:** 1995
SALES (est): 3MM **Privately Held**
WEB: www.pdsplastics.com
SIC: 3089 2759 Injection molding of plastics; commercial printing

(G-4526)
REPAIR RITE MACHINE INC
1946 142nd Ave (49323-9593)
PHONE 616 681-9711
Jeffrey Schaeffer, *President*
Donna Schaeffer, *Admin Sec*
EMP: 3
SQ FT: 2,000
SALES (est): 100K **Privately Held**
SIC: 3531 Construction machinery

(G-4527)
S & S MACHINE TOOL REPAIR LLC
Also Called: S & S Specialties
1664 144th Ave (49323-9777)
P.O. Box 61, Wayland (49348-0061)
PHONE 616 877-4930
Scott Ellens,
Doug Cook,
EMP: 4
SALES (est): 516.8K **Privately Held**
SIC: 3541 Machine tool replacement & repair parts, metal cutting types

(G-4528)
SENNEKER ENTERPRISES INC
Also Called: Senneker Excavating
1585 142nd Ave (49323-9402)
P.O. Box 121 (49323-0121)
PHONE 616 877-4440
Robert Senneker, *President*
Patricia A Senneker, *Treasurer*
EMP: 3
SQ FT: 5,400
SALES (est): 248.8K **Privately Held**
SIC: 7539 7692 1794 Machine shop, automotive; welding repair; excavation work

(G-4529)
WILLIAMS TOOLING & MFG
1856 142nd Ave (49323-9501)
P.O. Box 7 (49323-0007)
PHONE 616 681-2093
Jerry Williams, *Owner*
Rebecca Davis, *Vice Pres*
Pat Wells, *Supervisor*
Lorie Williams, *Admin Sec*
EMP: 16
SQ FT: 4,000
SALES (est): 1.3MM **Privately Held**
WEB: www.williamstooling.com
SIC: 3544 Die sets for metal stamping (presses)

Douglas
Allegan County

(G-4530)
DOUGLAS MARINE CORPORATION
Also Called: Skater Boats
6780 Enterprise Dr (49406-5136)
P.O. Box 819 (49406-0819)
PHONE 269 857-1764
Peter C Hledin, *President*
▼ **EMP:** 28 **EST:** 1978
SQ FT: 51,000
SALES (est): 6.8MM **Privately Held**
SIC: 3732 Motorboats, inboard or outboard: building & repairing

(G-4531)
ENTERPRISE HINGE INC
6779 Enterprise Dr (49406-5211)
P.O. Box 397 (49406-0397)
PHONE 269 857-2111
Brian Pearson, *President*
David Pearson, *President*
▲ **EMP:** 8 **EST:** 1946
SQ FT: 15,500
SALES: 1.5MM **Privately Held**
WEB: www.enterprisehinge.com
SIC: 3429 Builders' hardware

(G-4532)
SAUGATUCK BREWING CO INC
2948 Blue Star Hwy (49406-5195)
P.O. Box 856 (49406-0856)
PHONE 269 857-7222
Barry Johnson, *President*
Tiffany Barton, *General Mgr*
Robert Klute, *General Ptnr*
Kerry O'Donohue, *Vice Pres*
Cathy Gillette, *Controller*
EMP: 50
SALES (est): 9MM **Privately Held**
SIC: 2082 Beer (alcoholic beverage)

Dowagiac
Cass County

(G-4533)
AUTOCAM CORPORATION
Also Called: Autocam-Pax
201 Percy St (49047-1500)
PHONE 269 782-5186
Charles Laue, *CEO*
Jason Geurink, *Mfg Staff*
Verlin Bush, *Enginr/R&D Mgr*
EMP: 125
SALES (corp-wide): 770.6MM **Publicly Held**
SIC: 3714 Motor vehicle engines & parts
HQ: Autocam Corporation
  4180 40th St Se
  Kentwood MI 49512
  616 698-0707

(G-4534)
AUTOCAM-PAX INC
201 Percy St (49047-1500)
PHONE 269 782-5186
John C Kennedy, *Ch of Bd*
Warren A Veltman, *CFO*
▲ **EMP:** 35
SQ FT: 35,000
SALES (est): 5.3MM
SALES (corp-wide): 770.6MM **Publicly Held**
WEB: www.autocam.com
SIC: 3451 3592 3494 3398 Screw machine products; valves; valves & pipe fittings; metal heat treating; nonferrous rolling & drawing; blast furnaces & steel mills
HQ: Autocam Corporation
  4180 40th St Se
  Kentwood MI 49512
  616 698-0707

(G-4535)
BAKERS RHAPSODY
144 S Front St (49047-1716)
PHONE 269 767-1368
Jordan A Anderson, *Principal*
EMP: 4
SALES (est): 246.7K **Privately Held**
SIC: 2053 Frozen bakery products, except bread

(G-4536)
COMMERCIAL WELDING COMPANY INC
316 Cass Ave (49047-2146)
P.O. Box 505 (49047-0505)
PHONE 269 782-5252
Mark Smith, *President*
David Smith, *Vice Pres*
EMP: 4 **EST:** 1946
SQ FT: 11,000
SALES (est): 623.2K **Privately Held**
WEB: www.commercialwelding.com
SIC: 3443 5084 Tanks, standard or custom fabricated: metal plate; pumps & pumping equipment

(G-4537)
CREATIVE FOAM CORPORATION
55210 Rudy Rd (49047-9641)
P.O. Box 238 (49047-0238)
PHONE 269 782-3483
Don Young, *Branch Mgr*
Kari Watson, *Supervisor*
Jennifer Martin, *Info Tech Mgr*
EMP: 150
SALES (corp-wide): 180.2MM **Privately Held**
SIC: 3086 Packaging & shipping materials, foamed plastic
PA: Creative Foam Corporation
  300 N Alloy Dr
  Fenton MI 48430
  810 629-4149

(G-4538)
CREATIVE VINYL
Also Called: Creative Vinyl Sign
54950 M 51 N (49047-9663)
PHONE 269 782-2833
Pam Spivey, *President*
EMP: 3
SALES: 200K **Privately Held**
SIC: 3993 Signs, not made in custom sign painting shops

(G-4539)
CYCLONE MANUFACTURING INC
56850 Woodhouse Dr (49047-7735)
P.O. Box 815 (49047-0815)
PHONE 269 782-9670
Dennis Day, *CEO*
EMP: 7
SALES (est): 1.3MM **Privately Held**
SIC: 3471 Plating & polishing

(G-4540)
DOREL HOME FURNISHINGS INC
202 Spaulding St (49047-1452)
PHONE 269 782-8661
Michele Stephens, *Senior Buyer*
Charles Foley, *Manager*
EMP: 400
SALES (corp-wide): 2.6B **Privately Held**
WEB: www.dorel.com
SIC: 2511 2493 Console tables: wood; coffee tables: wood; tea wagons: wood; reconstituted wood products
HQ: Dorel Home Furnishings, Inc.
  410 E 1st St S
  Wright City MO 63390
  636 745-3351

(G-4541)
DOWSETT SPRING COMPANY
27071 Marcellus Hwy (49047-7465)
PHONE 269 782-2138
Fax: 269 782-6283
EMP: 9
SQ FT: 15,000
SALES: 800.1K **Privately Held**
SIC: 3495 Mfg Wire Springs

(G-4542)
ENJOYMENT IMAGE PUBLICATIONS
111 W Prairie Ronde St (49047-1125)
PHONE 269 782-8259
Polli Smith-Ryder, *Owner*
EMP: 3
SALES (est): 200K **Privately Held**
SIC: 2752 Newspapers, lithographed only

(G-4543)
INNOVATIVE FAB INC
29160 Middle Crossing Rd (49047-8200)
PHONE 269 782-9154
Marty Mottweiler, *President*
EMP: 5
SALES (est): 490K **Privately Held**
SIC: 3599 Machine shop, jobbing & repair

GEOGRAPHIC SECTION
Dryden - Lapeer County (G-4571)

(G-4544)
JAC CUSTOM POUCHES INC
56525 Woodhouse Dr (49047-7710)
P.O. Box 29 (49047-0029)
PHONE.....................269 782-3190
Kimberly Sirovica, *President*
Steven Coleman, *Vice Pres*
George Bauer, *Shareholder*
Jean Bauer, *Shareholder*
Harry E Coleman, *Shareholder*
EMP: 27
SQ FT: 2,300
SALES (est): 3.4MM **Privately Held**
WEB: www.jaccustompouches.com
SIC: 2393 2394 2221 Bags & containers, except sleeping bags: textile; canvas & related products; broadwoven fabric mills, manmade

(G-4545)
JERZ MACHINE TOOL CORPORATION
415 E Prairie Ronde St (49047-1348)
PHONE.....................269 782-3535
Fax: 269 782-1998
EMP: 8
SQ FT: 5,500
SALES (est): 1MM **Privately Held**
SIC: 3599 7692 Mfg Industrial Machinery Welding Repair

(G-4546)
L&J PACKAGING
Also Called: L & J Meat Packaging
30838 Middle Crossing Rd (49047-9268)
PHONE.....................269 782-2628
Les Herter, *Owner*
Ruth Herter, *Co-Owner*
EMP: 3
SALES (est): 218.4K **Privately Held**
SIC: 2011 2013 Meat packing plants; sausages & other prepared meats

(G-4547)
LAYLIN WELDING INC
501 E Prairie Ronde St (49047-1545)
PHONE.....................269 782-2910
Gale Laylin, *President*
Shirley Laylin, *Corp Secy*
EMP: 4
SQ FT: 6,000
SALES (est): 125K **Privately Held**
SIC: 7692 Welding repair

(G-4548)
LYONS INDUSTRIES INC (PA)
30000 M 62 W (49047-9348)
P.O. Box 88 (49047-0088)
PHONE.....................269 782-3404
Donald D Lyons, *Ch of Bd*
Lance Lyons, *President*
Debbie Wright, *Vice Pres*
Richard Xouris, *CFO*
Toby Yuhas, *Assistant*
▼ **EMP:** 115
SQ FT: 96,000
SALES (est): 35.5MM **Privately Held**
SIC: 3088 Bathroom fixtures, plastic

(G-4549)
LYONS INDUSTRIES INC
Also Called: Headen Plant
414 West St (49047-1045)
PHONE.....................269 782-9516
Lance Lyons, *President*
EMP: 3
SALES (corp-wide): 35.5MM **Privately Held**
SIC: 3088 Plastics plumbing fixtures
PA: Lyons Industries, Inc.
30000 M 62 W
Dowagiac MI 49047
269 782-3404

(G-4550)
MENNEL MILLING CO OF MICH INC
301 S Mill St (49047-1473)
PHONE.....................269 782-5175
Don Mennel, *President*
Frank Herbes, *General Mgr*
Bud Wehrly, *Maintence Staff*
EMP: 200
SQ FT: 9,000
SALES (est): 21.4MM
SALES (corp-wide): 119.2MM **Privately Held**
WEB: www.troyelevator.com
SIC: 2041 Wheat flour
PA: The Mennel Milling Company
319 S Vine St
Fostoria OH 44830
419 435-8151

(G-4551)
MICHIGAN DIE CASTING LLC
51241 M 51 N (49047-9626)
PHONE.....................269 471-7715
Phil Munforde Jr, *President*
EMP: 60
SALES (est): 6.9MM **Privately Held**
SIC: 3363 Aluminum die-castings

(G-4552)
MICHIGAN PRECISION TL & ENGRG
Also Called: Michigan Precision Tl & Engrg
613 Rudy Rd (49047-9668)
PHONE.....................269 783-1300
Tony Karasch, *President*
Edwin Karasch Jr, *Corp Secy*
Henry D Karasch, *Vice Pres*
Terri Karasch, *Office Mgr*
EMP: 20
SQ FT: 17,000
SALES (est): 1MM **Privately Held**
SIC: 3544 Special dies & tools

(G-4553)
MOORE PRODUCTS INC
58151 Park Pl (49047-8327)
P.O. Box 695 (49047-0695)
PHONE.....................269 782-3957
Paul Moore, *President*
Mary T Moore, *Vice Pres*
EMP: 4
SQ FT: 1,920
SALES (est): 320K **Privately Held**
SIC: 2431 Doors, wood

(G-4554)
MV METAL PDTS & SOLUTIONS LLC
51241 M 51 N (49047-9626)
PHONE.....................269 462-4010
Virgil Dale, *Branch Mgr*
EMP: 60
SALES (est): 17.5MM
SALES (corp-wide): 131.5MM **Privately Held**
SIC: 3364 3363 Zinc & zinc-base alloy die-castings; aluminum die-castings
PA: Mv Metal Products & Solutions, Llc
3585 Bellflower Dr
Portage MI 49024
269 471-7715

(G-4555)
NASH SERVICES
57229 M 51 S (49047-9765)
PHONE.....................269 782-2016
EMP: 3
SQ FT: 3,000
SALES (est): 190K **Privately Held**
SIC: 7538 7539 7692 General Auto Repair Automotive Repair Welding Repair

(G-4556)
NATE RONALD
50317 W Lakeshore Dr (49047-8873)
PHONE.....................269 424-3777
Ronald Nate, *Owner*
EMP: 20
SALES (est): 1.7MM **Privately Held**
SIC: 2084 Wines

(G-4557)
PREFERRED PRINTING INC (PA)
304 E Division St (49047-1425)
PHONE.....................269 782-5488
Rich Mc Cormick, *President*
Sue Mc Cormick, *Vice Pres*
EMP: 14
SQ FT: 3,500
SALES: 1.1MM **Privately Held**
WEB: www.preferredprinting.com
SIC: 2752 Commercial printing, offset

(G-4558)
ROSPATCH JESSCO CORPORATION
Also Called: Ameriwood Furniture
202 Spaulding St (49047-1452)
PHONE.....................269 782-8661
Rick Jackson, *President*
◆ **EMP:** 350
SALES (est): 21.7MM **Privately Held**
SIC: 2511 2493 Wood household furniture; particleboard products

(G-4559)
ROTO-FEEDERS INC
28691 Middle Crossing Rd (49047-8207)
P.O. Box 27 (49047-0027)
PHONE.....................269 782-2456
John S Russom, *President*
Kathy Russom, *Corp Secy*
Thomas Russom, *Vice Pres*
EMP: 3
SQ FT: 4,000
SALES: 160K **Privately Held**
SIC: 3523 Barn, silo, poultry, dairy & livestock machinery

(G-4560)
SCHOTT SAW CO
54813 M 51 N (49047-9679)
P.O. Box 513 (49047-0513)
PHONE.....................269 782-3203
Ronnie Pond, *President*
EMP: 6 **EST:** 1960
SQ FT: 4,700
SALES (est): 456.2K **Privately Held**
SIC: 7699 3425 Knife, saw & tool sharpening & repair; saw blades & handsaws

(G-4561)
SECURIT METAL PRODUCTS CO
55905 92nd Ave (49047-9505)
PHONE.....................269 782-7076
Clayton A Wiker, *President*
Shirley M Wiker, *Corp Secy*
Craig A Wiker, *Vice Pres*
▼ **EMP:** 24 **EST:** 1952
SQ FT: 45,000
SALES (est): 3.4MM **Privately Held**
SIC: 3452 Rivets, metal

(G-4562)
STEINBAUER PERFORMANCE LLC
22790 Fosdick St (49047-7463)
PHONE.....................704 587-0856
Sherie Jones, *Pub Rel Mgr*
Herbert Steinbauer, *Mng Member*
Matt Ausen, *Technician*
Diesel Performance Australia,
▲ **EMP:** 9
SQ FT: 4,200
SALES (est): 1.4MM **Privately Held**
SIC: 3714 Motor vehicle parts & accessories

(G-4563)
SYMONDS MACHINE CO INC
414 West St (49047-1045)
P.O. Box 268 (49047-0268)
PHONE.....................269 782-8051
Bob Symonds, *President*
Don Symonds, *Corp Secy*
John Symonds, *Vice Pres*
EMP: 7
SALES (est): 780K **Privately Held**
SIC: 3599 Machine shop, jobbing & repair

Dowling
Barry County

(G-4564)
TNR MACHINE INC
2050 W Dowling Rd (49050-9714)
PHONE.....................269 623-2827
Norman Watson, *President*
Ronald Watson, *Vice Pres*
Thomas Watson, *Treasurer*
EMP: 20
SQ FT: 7,800
SALES (est): 2MM **Privately Held**
WEB: www.tnrmachine.com
SIC: 3544 Special dies & tools

Drummond Island
Chippewa County

(G-4565)
MANUFACTURERS SERVICES INDS (PA)
Also Called: MSI
40014 S Cream City Pt Rd (49726-8600)
PHONE.....................906 493-6685
David E Williams, *President*
EMP: 4
SQ FT: 23,000
SALES (est): 450.1K **Privately Held**
SIC: 3089 Plastic processing

(G-4566)
OSBORNE MATERIALS COMPANY
Also Called: Drummond Dolemite
23311 E Haul Rd (49726-9492)
PHONE.....................906 493-5211
Gilbert Aikey, *Manager*
EMP: 40 **Privately Held**
SIC: 1422 Travertine, crushed & brokenquarrying
PA: Osborne Materials Company
1 Williams St
Grand River OH 44045

Dryden
Lapeer County

(G-4567)
ADVANCE SCRAPING COMPANY
5063 Hollow Corners Rd (48428-9723)
PHONE.....................810 796-2676
Raymond Phillips, *Owner*
EMP: 3
SALES (est): 223.1K **Privately Held**
SIC: 3599 Machine shop, jobbing & repair

(G-4568)
CCO HOLDINGS LLC
5121 Dryden Rd (48428-9713)
PHONE.....................810 375-7020
EMP: 3
SALES (corp-wide): 43.6B **Publicly Held**
SIC: 5064 4841 3663 3651 Electrical appliances, television & radio; cable & other pay television services; radio & TV communications equipment; household audio & video equipment
HQ: Cco Holdings, Llc
400 Atlantic St
Stamford CT 06901
203 905-7801

(G-4569)
DRYDEN STEEL LLC
5585 North St Bldg D (48428-7723)
PHONE.....................586 777-7600
Michael Oddo,
EMP: 7
SALES (est): 214.5K **Privately Held**
SIC: 3291 Abrasive metal & steel products

(G-4570)
NEWARK GRAVEL COMPANY
4290 Calkins Rd (48428-9608)
PHONE.....................810 796-3072
EMP: 10
SQ FT: 2,400
SALES (est): 447.9K **Privately Held**
SIC: 1442 5032 Construction Sand/Gravel Whol Brick/Stone Material

(G-4571)
QUANTUM MACHINING INC (PA)
5573 North St (48428-7723)
P.O. Box 213 (48428-0213)
PHONE.....................810 796-2035
Keith Calkins, *President*
Gerri Doleckie, *Admin Sec*
EMP: 3
SALES (est): 553K **Privately Held**
WEB: www.quantummachining.com
SIC: 3599 3566 Machine shop, jobbing & repair; speed changers, drives & gears

(G-4572)
UNYTREX INC
5901 Dryden Rd (48428-9619)
PHONE..................810 796-9074
Gene Siemen, *President*
Cindy Stephens, *Treasurer*
Kathy Siemen, *Admin Sec*
EMP: 14
SQ FT: 16,000
SALES (est): 1.9MM **Privately Held**
WEB: www.unytrex.com
SIC: 3544 Industrial molds

(G-4573)
WIGTON PIPE ORGANS INC
4848 General Squier Rd (48428-9622)
PHONE..................810 796-3311
EMP: 3
SALES: 81.9K **Privately Held**
WEB: www.wigtonpipeorgans.com
SIC: 3931 7699 Pipes, organ; organ tuning & repair

Dundee
Monroe County

(G-4574)
AGGREGATE INDUSTRIES - MWR INC
6211 N Ann Arbor Rd (48131-9527)
PHONE..................734 529-5876
Tony Graham, *Prdtn Mgr*
Paul Simon, *Site Mgr*
Helvenstein Fabien, *Production*
Wahyu Dwicahyo, *Engineer*
Scott Letzter, *Sales Staff*
EMP: 21
SALES (corp-wide): 27.6B **Privately Held**
SIC: 3273 Ready-mixed concrete
HQ: Aggregate Industries - Mwr, Inc.
  2815 Dodd Rd
  Eagan MN 55121
  651 683-0600

(G-4575)
AMBROSIA INC
Also Called: Swan Creek Candle
129 Riley St (48131-1025)
PHONE..................734 529-7174
Erica Morrison, *Manager*
EMP: 6
SALES (corp-wide): 5.5MM **Privately Held**
SIC: 3999 Candles
PA: Ambrosia, Inc.
  395 W Airport Hwy
  Swanton OH 43558
  419 825-1151

(G-4576)
BARDON INC
Also Called: Aggregate Industries
6211 N Ann Arbor Rd (48131-9527)
PHONE..................734 529-5876
EMP: 48
SALES (corp-wide): 27.6B **Privately Held**
SIC: 3273 Ready-mixed concrete
HQ: Aggregate Industries - Mwr, Inc.
  2815 Dodd Rd
  Eagan MN 55121
  651 683-0600

(G-4577)
CLEAN TECH INC
500 Dunham St (48131-1159)
PHONE..................734 529-2475
EMP: 50
SALES (corp-wide): 1.3B **Privately Held**
SIC: 4953 3087 Recycling, waste materials; custom compound purchased resins
HQ: Clean Tech, Inc.
  41605 Ann Arbor Rd E
  Plymouth MI 48170

(G-4578)
DARBY READY MIX-DUNDEE LLC
7801 N Ann Arbor Rd (48131-9587)
PHONE..................734 529-7100
Joseph M Comstock,
EMP: 11

SALES: 950K **Privately Held**
SIC: 5211 3273 Cement; ready-mixed concrete

(G-4579)
DUNDEE CASTINGS COMPANY
500 Ypsilanti St (48131-1197)
PHONE..................734 529-2455
Edgar Crawley, *President*
Patricia Bradley, *Corp Secy*
Tim Maki, *Vice Pres*
Robert C Crawley, *Plant Supt*
Pat Bradley, *Controller*
▲ **EMP:** 95 **EST:** 1946
SQ FT: 13,200
SALES (est): 18.6MM **Privately Held**
WEB: www.dundeecastings.com
SIC: 3365 3369 Aluminum foundries; non-ferrous foundries

(G-4580)
DUNDEE MANUFACTURING CO INC
107 Fairchild Dr (48131-9585)
P.O. Box 143 (48131-0143)
PHONE..................734 529-2540
Peter Davis, *President*
Dale Davis, *Vice Pres*
EMP: 35
SQ FT: 32,000
SALES (est): 10.5MM **Privately Held**
WEB: www.dundeemfgco.com
SIC: 3429 Builders' hardware

(G-4581)
DUNDEE PRODUCTS COMPANY
14490 Stowell Rd (48131-9516)
PHONE..................734 529-2441
Lori Monagin, *President*
Mark Maschino, *Plant Mgr*
Brian Yensch, *Prdtn Mgr*
Theresa Van Buskirk, *IT/INT Sup*
Marjorie Monagin, *Admin Sec*
EMP: 24
SQ FT: 48,000
SALES (est): 6.3MM **Privately Held**
WEB: www.dundeeproducts.com
SIC: 3317 Steel pipe & tubes

(G-4582)
FCA US LLC
5800 N Ann Arbor Rd (48131-9772)
PHONE..................734 478-5658
Tania Young, *Plant Mgr*
Martin Sanders, *Engineer*
David Caballero, *Maintence Staff*
EMP: 500
SALES (corp-wide): 126.4B **Privately Held**
SIC: 3714 Motor vehicle parts & accessories
HQ: Fca Us Llc
  1000 Chrysler Dr
  Auburn Hills MI 48326

(G-4583)
FCAUS DUNDEE ENGINE PLANT
5800 N Ann Arbor Rd (48131-9772)
PHONE..................734 529-9256
Tanya Young, *Branch Mgr*
EMP: 720
SALES (corp-wide): 126.4B **Privately Held**
SIC: 3714 Motor vehicle parts & accessories
PA: Fiat Chrysler Automobiles N.V.
  Onbekend Nederlands Adres
  Onbekend
  442 077-6603

(G-4584)
GAZELLE PUBLISHING
Also Called: Independent Newspapers, The
112 Park Pl Ste 3 (48131-1016)
P.O. Box 98 (48131-0098)
PHONE..................734 529-2688
Sean McClellan, *Partner*
EMP: 8
SQ FT: 6,000
SALES (est): 552.5K **Privately Held**
WEB: www.dundeeonline.com
SIC: 2711 5943 Commercial printing & newspaper publishing combined; office forms & supplies

(G-4585)
GLOBAL ENGINE MFG ALIANCE LLC
Also Called: Gema
5800 N Ann Arbor Rd (48131-9772)
PHONE..................734 529-9888
Bruce Baumbach, *Plant Mgr*
EMP: 7
SALES (est): 1.1MM **Privately Held**
SIC: 3462 Automotive & internal combustion engine forgings

(G-4586)
HEINZERLING ENTERPRISES INC
Also Called: Beef Jerky Unlimited
438 Tecumseh St (48131-1052)
PHONE..................734 529-9100
Thomas Delago, *Principal*
Rachel Delago, *Principal*
EMP: 3
SALES (est): 210K **Privately Held**
SIC: 2013 Snack sticks, including jerky: from purchased meat

(G-4587)
HOLCIM (US) INC
6211 N Ann Arbor Rd (48131-9527)
P.O. Box 122 (48131-0122)
PHONE..................734 529-2411
Paul A Yhouse, *President*
Chuck Counts, *Superintendent*
Borislav Iskrenov, *Project Mgr*
Scott Poaps, *QC Mgr*
Arthur Hamm, *Engineer*
EMP: 100
SALES (corp-wide): 27.6B **Privately Held**
WEB: www.holcim.com/us
SIC: 3241 5032 Portland cement; brick, stone & related material
HQ: Holcim (Us) Inc.
  8700 W Bryn Mawr Ave
  Chicago IL 60631
  773 372-1000

(G-4588)
HOLCIM (US) INC
Also Called: Dundee Plant
15215 Day Rd (48131-9586)
P.O. Box 122 (48131-0122)
PHONE..................734 529-4600
Julija Skoro, *Marketing Staff*
Don Everett, *Manager*
Michele Donna, *Manager*
EMP: 140
SALES (corp-wide): 27.6B **Privately Held**
WEB: www.holcim.com/us
SIC: 3241 3272 Portland cement; concrete products
HQ: Holcim (Us) Inc.
  8700 W Bryn Mawr Ave
  Chicago IL 60631
  773 372-1000

(G-4589)
HYDROGEN ASSIST DEVELOPMENT
669 Strawberry St (48131-1040)
PHONE..................734 823-4969
Sean Drazin, *Administration*
EMP: 3
SALES (est): 141.2K **Privately Held**
SIC: 2813 Hydrogen

(G-4590)
L & W INC
Also Called: Axis Engineering Div
5461 Circle Seven Dr (48131-9561)
PHONE..................734 529-7290
Wayne D Jones, *Manager*
EMP: 10
SALES (corp-wide): 2.2B **Privately Held**
SIC: 3465 3469 Automotive stampings; stamping metal for the trade
HQ: L & W, Inc.
  17757 Woodland Dr
  New Boston MI 48164
  734 397-6300

(G-4591)
LAFARGE NORTH AMERICA INC
6211 N Ann Arbor Rd (48131-9527)
PHONE..................703 480-3600
Keith Howell, *Manager*
EMP: 19

SALES (corp-wide): 27.6B **Privately Held**
SIC: 3273 3272 3271 1442 Ready-mixed concrete; concrete products; precast terrazo or concrete products; prestressed concrete products; cylinder pipe, prestressed or pretensioned concrete; blocks, concrete or cinder: standard; construction sand & gravel; construction sand mining; gravel mining; asphalt paving mixtures & blocks; paving mixtures; asphalt & asphaltic paving mixtures (not from refineries); portland cement
HQ: Lafarge North America Inc.
  8700 W Bryn Mawr Ave
  Chicago IL 60631
  773 372-1000

(G-4592)
LAFARGE NORTH AMERICA INC ◆
6211 N Ann Arbor Rd (48131-9527)
PHONE..................703 480-3649
Misha Freimann, *Principal*
EMP: 12 **EST:** 2019
SALES (est): 1.9MM **Privately Held**
SIC: 3241 Cement, hydraulic

(G-4593)
LATTIMORE MATERIAL
6211 N Ann Arbor Rd (48131-9527)
PHONE..................972 837-2462
Anthony Bond, *President*
EMP: 3
SALES (est): 286.5K **Privately Held**
SIC: 3273 Ready-mixed concrete

(G-4594)
MAC VALVES INC
5555 N Ann Arbor Rd (48131-9201)
PHONE..................734 529-5099
Dory Wevyke, *Manager*
EMP: 20
SALES (corp-wide): 175.1MM **Privately Held**
WEB: www.macvalves.com
SIC: 5085 3494 3491 Valves & fittings; valves & pipe fittings; industrial valves
PA: Mac Valves, Inc.
  30569 Beck Rd
  Wixom MI 48393
  248 624-7700

(G-4595)
MATT AND DAVE LLC
Also Called: Schultz Motors
4706 N Ann Arbor Rd (48131-9684)
PHONE..................734 439-1988
Duane A Schultz,
EMP: 3
SALES (est): 161.7K **Privately Held**
SIC: 3594 Motors, pneumatic; motors: hydraulic, fluid power or air

(G-4596)
MITCHELL EQUIPMENT CORPORATION
Also Called: Mitchell Rail Gear
5275 N Ann Arbor Rd (48131-9201)
PHONE..................734 529-3400
Estel Lovitt Jr, *President*
Dana Fischer, *Technology*
▼ **EMP:** 25 **EST:** 1978
SQ FT: 44,000
SALES: 4MM **Privately Held**
WEB: www.mitchell-railgear.com
SIC: 3743 Railroad equipment

(G-4597)
PLASTIPAK PACKAGING INC
500 Dunham St (48131-1159)
PHONE..................734 529-2475
Clarice Hampson, *Accountant*
David Glover, *Manager*
EMP: 3
SALES (est): 254.3K **Privately Held**
SIC: 3089 Plastics products

(G-4598)
REAU MANUFACTURING CO
100 Research Pkwy (48131-9777)
PHONE..................734 823-5603
Dawn Reau, *President*
Adam Purser, *Engineer*
EMP: 3

GEOGRAPHIC SECTION

East Jordan - Charlevoix County (G-4626)

SALES (est): 528.6K **Privately Held**
SIC: **3699** 3599 1799 Laser welding, drilling & cutting equipment; machine shop, jobbing & repair; welding on site

(G-4599)
SALENBIEN WELDING SERVICE INC
460 Roosevelt St (48131-9557)
P.O. Box 134 (48131-0134)
PHONE..................................734 529-3280
George J Salenbien, *President*
EMP: 10
SQ FT: 10,000
SALES (est): 2.2MM **Privately Held**
SIC: **7692** Welding repair

(G-4600)
SCOTT ENTERPRISES
3000 Petersburg Rd (48131-9671)
PHONE..................................734 279-2078
Durell Scott, *Owner*
EMP: 3
SALES (est): 260K **Privately Held**
SIC: **3715** 1541 Truck trailers; steel building construction

(G-4601)
ST JULIAN WINE COMPANY INC
700 Freedom Ct (48131-9572)
PHONE..................................734 529-3700
David Baraganini, *Branch Mgr*
EMP: 15
SALES (corp-wide): 10.9MM **Privately Held**
SIC: **2084** Wines
PA: St. Julian Wine Company, Incorporated
716 S Kalamazoo St
Paw Paw MI 49079
269 657-5568

(G-4602)
TITANIUM SPORTS LLC
13705 Stowell Rd (48131-9735)
PHONE..................................734 818-0904
Richard M Williams, *Administration*
EMP: 3
SALES (est): 192.9K **Privately Held**
SIC: **3356** Titanium

(G-4603)
WHISPER CREATIVE PRODUCTS INC (PA)
1585 Wells Rd (48131-9519)
PHONE..................................734 529-2734
Dolores Rodriguez, *President*
Michelle M Crum, *Admin Sec*
EMP: 3
SALES: 200K **Privately Held**
SIC: **3086** 2679 2752 2499 Plastics foam products; cardboard products, except die-cut; cardboard: pasted, laminated, lined, or surface coated; transfers, decalcomania or dry: lithographed; laundry products, wood; wire & fabricated wire products

Durand
Shiawassee County

(G-4604)
2ND CHANCE WOOD COMPANY
7505 E M 71 Ste B (48429-9800)
PHONE..................................989 472-4488
▲ EMP: 6
SALES (est): 430K **Privately Held**
SIC: **2491** Structural lumber & timber, treated wood

(G-4605)
B & M MACHINE & TOOL COMPANY
Also Called: Co-Op Machine & Tool
7665 E M 71 (48429-9776)
PHONE..................................989 288-2934
Daniel L Brown, *President*
Jim Mahrle, *Vice Pres*
EMP: 6
SQ FT: 13,500
SALES: 450K **Privately Held**
SIC: **3544** 3599 Special dies & tools; jigs & fixtures; machine shop, jobbing & repair

(G-4606)
BEECHCRAFT PRODUCTS INC
1100 N Saginaw St (48429-1215)
PHONE..................................989 288-2606
Richard D Misner, *President*
Dorothy Misner, *Corp Secy*
Tom Misner, *Vice Pres*
EMP: 30
SQ FT: 40,000
SALES (est): 2.2MM **Privately Held**
WEB: www.beechcraftproducts.com
SIC: **3089** 3442 3211 2431 Plastic hardware & building products; metal doors, sash & trim; flat glass; louver doors, wood

(G-4607)
DELUX MONOGRAMMING SCREEN PRTG
Also Called: De Lux Sportswear
9070 E Lansing Rd (48429-1002)
PHONE..................................989 288-5321
Leonard Karwczyk, *President*
David L Johnson, *Vice Pres*
EMP: 9
SQ FT: 3,000
SALES (est): 1.5MM **Privately Held**
SIC: **5136** 5137 5611 5699 Sportswear, men's & boys'; sportswear, women's & children's; clothing, sportswear, men's & boys'; sports apparel; fabric printing & stamping; signs & advertising specialties

(G-4608)
EMPIRE MACHINE & CONVEYORS INC
5111 S Durand Rd (48429-1267)
PHONE..................................989 541-2060
Harry Oumedian, *President*
EMP: 11
SQ FT: 22,000
SALES: 1.4MM **Privately Held**
SIC: **3535** 3441 1791 Conveyors & conveying equipment; trolley conveyors; overhead conveyor systems; fabricated structural metal; building components, structural steel; iron work, structural

(G-4609)
MICHIGAN REEF DEVELOPMENT
8252 E Lansing Rd (48429-1059)
PHONE..................................989 288-2172
Harry Mohney, *President*
EMP: 7
SQ FT: 1,000
SALES (est): 378.3K **Privately Held**
SIC: **1311** Crude petroleum & natural gas

(G-4610)
MY-CAN LLC
989 N Saginaw St (48429-1265)
PHONE..................................989 288-7779
Connie Leedle,
EMP: 4
SALES (est): 388.7K **Privately Held**
SIC: **3949** Camping equipment & supplies

(G-4611)
PANCHECK LLC
Also Called: Shaw's Pharmacy
221 N Saginaw St (48429-1165)
PHONE..................................989 288-6886
Mark Pancheck,
EMP: 14
SALES (est): 691.9K **Privately Held**
SIC: **2834** 5122 Pharmaceutical preparations; drugs, proprietaries & sundries

(G-4612)
POWERSCREEN USA LLC
Also Called: Terex Simplicity
212 S Oak St (48429-1621)
PHONE..................................989 288-3121
EMP: 9
SALES (corp-wide): 5.1B **Publicly Held**
WEB: www.simplicityengineering.com
SIC: **3535** Conveyors & conveying equipment
HQ: Powerscreen Usa Llc
11001 Electron Dr
Louisville KY 40299
502 736-5200

(G-4613)
QUALITY FABG & ERECTION CO
8531 S Reed Rd (48429-9141)
PHONE..................................989 288-5210
Kenneth J Hodges, *Owner*
EMP: 3
SQ FT: 3,500
SALES: 150K **Privately Held**
SIC: **3441** 1796 Fabricated structural metal; machine moving & rigging

(G-4614)
TEREX CORPORATION
Also Called: Terex Canica
212 S Oak St (48429-1621)
PHONE..................................360 993-0515
Josh Ellis, *Design Engr*
Phr Gust, *Human Resources*
Mike Schultz, *Manager*
EMP: 7
SALES (corp-wide): 5.1B **Publicly Held**
WEB: www.terex.com
SIC: **3531** Cranes
PA: Terex Corporation
200 Nyala Farms Rd Ste 2
Westport CT 06880
203 222-7170

(G-4615)
WIESKE TOOL INC
202 S Hagle St (48429-1700)
P.O. Box 335 (48429-0335)
PHONE..................................989 288-2648
Dan Wieske, *President*
Roger Wieske, *Vice Pres*
EMP: 4
SQ FT: 5,500
SALES (est): 647.6K **Privately Held**
SIC: **3544** Special dies & tools

Eagle
Clinton County

(G-4616)
C&D PALLETS INC
13777 S Jones Rd (48822-9609)
PHONE..................................517 285-5228
Dean Gross, *Principal*
EMP: 4
SALES (est): 250.7K **Privately Held**
SIC: **2448** Pallets, wood & wood with metal

(G-4617)
TRUE BUILT WOODWORKING (PA)
11672 W Herbison Rd (48822-9745)
PHONE..................................517 626-6482
Charles H Truesdell, *Owner*
EMP: 3
SALES: 400K **Privately Held**
SIC: **2431** Trim, wood

Eagle Harbor
Keweenaw County

(G-4618)
SOCIETY OF SAINT JOHN INC
Also Called: Jampot
6559 State Highway M26 (49950-9642)
PHONE..................................906 289-4484
Fr Nicholas Glenn, *President*
Fr Basil Paris, *Admin Sec*
EMP: 6
SALES (est): 361.4K **Privately Held**
WEB: www.societystjohn.com
SIC: **8661** 2033 Monastery; jams, jellies & preserves: packaged in cans, jars, etc.

East China
St. Clair County

(G-4619)
A M R INC
671 Hathaway St (48054-1539)
PHONE..................................810 329-9049
Mark A Achatz, *President*
Mark J Achatz, *Vice Pres*
EMP: 9

SALES: 1MM **Privately Held**
WEB: www.actmachinery.com
SIC: **3089** Injection molding of plastics

(G-4620)
ADVANCED STAGE TOOLING LLC
4317 River Rd (48054-2913)
PHONE..................................810 444-9807
Jerry Eschenburg,
EMP: 7
SALES (est): 272.8K **Privately Held**
SIC: **3541** Machine tools, metal cutting type

(G-4621)
BLOOMBERRY
6189 Pleasant St (48054-4726)
PHONE..................................586 212-9510
Jim Numbers, *Principal*
EMP: 3
SALES (est): 180.9K **Privately Held**
SIC: **2026** Yogurt

(G-4622)
ILOWSKI SAUSAGE COMPANY INC
6650 Saint Clair Hwy (48054-1109)
PHONE..................................810 329-9117
Joe Ilowski, *President*
EMP: 3
SQ FT: 5,000
SALES: 300K **Privately Held**
SIC: **2013** 5421 Sausages & other prepared meats; meat markets, including freezer provisioners

(G-4623)
J & L TURNING INC
Also Called: Alliance Broach and Tool
5664 River Rd (48054-4176)
PHONE..................................810 765-5755
Helen Johnson, *President*
EMP: 10
SQ FT: 28,000
SALES (est): 1.5MM **Privately Held**
WEB: www.alliancebroach.com
SIC: **3599** 3545 Machine shop, jobbing & repair; broaches (machine tool accessories)

(G-4624)
KKSP PRECISION MACHINING LLC
650 Hathaway St (48054-1533)
PHONE..................................810 329-4731
John Mulqueen, *Sales Staff*
Thomas Ganly, *Manager*
EMP: 50
SALES (corp-wide): 43.7MM **Privately Held**
WEB: www.kksp.com
SIC: **3599** Machine shop, jobbing & repair
PA: Kksp Precision Machining, Llc
1688 Glen Ellyn Rd
Glendale Heights IL 60139
630 260-1735

(G-4625)
TRP ENTERPRISES INC
Also Called: Trp Sand & Gravel
6267 Saint Clair Hwy (48054-1209)
PHONE..................................810 329-4027
James Pieprzak, *President*
Terry Pieprazk, *Vice Pres*
EMP: 5
SALES (est): 369.8K **Privately Held**
SIC: **1442** 2875 Construction sand & gravel; potting soil, mixed

East Jordan
Charlevoix County

(G-4626)
BURNETTE FOODS INC
200 State St (49727-9799)
P.O. Box 887 (49727-0887)
PHONE..................................231 536-2284
Ted Sherman Jr, *Plant Mgr*
Jeff Hammond, *Branch Mgr*
Lynne Herrmann, *Executive*
EMP: 43

East Jordan - Charlevoix County (G-4627)

SALES (corp-wide): 92.7MM **Privately Held**
WEB: www.burnettefoods.com
SIC: 2033 Fruits: packaged in cans, jars, etc.; vegetables: packaged in cans, jars, etc.
PA: Burnette Foods, Inc.
701 S Us Highway 31
Elk Rapids MI 49629
231 264-8116

(G-4627)
CITY OF EAST JORDAN
218 N Lake St (49727-8823)
PHONE.................................231 536-2561
Troy Thomas, *Superintendent*
Tom Cannon, *Commissioner*
EMP: 9
SALES (est): 1MM **Privately Held**
SIC: 3321 Manhole covers, metal

(G-4628)
DOUBLE GUN JOURNAL
5014 Rockery School Rd (49727-9636)
P.O. Box 550 (49727-0550)
PHONE.................................231 536-7439
Daniel Cote, *Partner*
Joanna Cote, *Partner*
EMP: 5
SALES: 1MM **Privately Held**
SIC: 2721 Magazines: publishing only, not printed on site

(G-4629)
EJ AMERICAS LLC (HQ)
301 Spring St (49727-5128)
P.O. Box 439 (49727-0439)
PHONE.................................231 536-2261
Lori Willis, *Principal*
EMP: 0
SALES (est): 98.8MM **Privately Held**
SIC: 6719 3321 Investment holding companies, except banks; manhole covers, metal

(G-4630)
EJ ARDMORE INC
301 Spring St (49727-5128)
P.O. Box 477 (49727-0477)
PHONE.................................231 536-2261
Jack Poindexter, *CFO*
William Lorne, *Admin Sec*
EMP: 200
SALES (est): 16.3MM **Privately Held**
SIC: 3272 Manhole covers or frames, concrete

(G-4631)
EJ ASIA-PACIFIC INC
301 Spring St (49727-5128)
PHONE.................................231 536-2261
William Lorne, *Principal*
EMP: 4
SALES (est): 458.2K **Privately Held**
SIC: 3321 Manhole covers, metal
PA: Ej Group, Inc.
301 Spring St
East Jordan MI 49727

(G-4632)
EJ CO
5000 Airport Rd (49727-9094)
P.O. Box 439 (49727-0439)
PHONE.................................231 536-4527
Adam Morgan, *Mfg Mgr*
Marty Swanson, *Purch Agent*
Scott Hoogerhyde, *Electrical Engi*
Steve Youmans, *Human Res Mgr*
Jodi Kirkpatrick, *Marketing Staff*
EMP: 29 EST: 2013
SALES (est): 7.2MM **Privately Held**
SIC: 3321 Gray & ductile iron foundries

(G-4633)
EJ EUROPE LLC (HQ)
301 Spring St (49727-5128)
PHONE.................................231 536-2261
William Lorne, *Principal*
EMP: 4 EST: 2009
SALES (est): 2.1MM **Privately Held**
SIC: 3321 Manhole covers, metal

(G-4634)
EJ GROUP INC (PA)
301 Spring St (49727-5128)
P.O. Box 439 (49727-0439)
PHONE.................................231 536-2261
Tracey K Malpass, *CEO*
Simon Bottomley, *General Mgr*
Pete Dehaan, *District Mgr*
Brian Newman, *Counsel*
Andrew Malpass, *Vice Pres*
EMP: 25
SALES: 320.1MM **Privately Held**
SIC: 3321 Manhole covers, metal

(G-4635)
EJ TIMBER PRODUCERS INC
972 Toby Rd (49727-9252)
PHONE.................................231 544-9866
Virgil Lavanway, *President*
EMP: 11
SALES (est): 1.6MM **Privately Held**
SIC: 2411 Logging

(G-4636)
EJ USA INC (DH)
301 Spring St (49727-5128)
P.O. Box 477 (49727-0477)
PHONE.................................800 874-4100
Fred Malpass, *President*
Mike McGuane, *Regional Mgr*
Andy Long, *Facilities Mgr*
Bob Bowser, *Maint Spvr*
John Snyder, *Engineer*
▼ EMP: 500
SQ FT: 360,000
SALES (est): 248.1MM **Privately Held**
WEB: www.ejiw.com
SIC: 3321 Gray iron castings

(G-4637)
JORDAN VALLEY CONCRETE SERVICE
Also Called: North Land Septic Tank Service
126 Garner Rd (49727-8734)
PHONE.................................231 536-7701
EMP: 10
SQ FT: 600
SALES (est): 1.1MM **Privately Held**
SIC: 3273 3272 1794 Septic Tanks & Excavating Contractor

(G-4638)
JORDAN VALLEY GLASSWORKS
209 State St (49727-9799)
P.O. Box 362 (49727-0362)
PHONE.................................231 536-0539
Shelly Bavers, *President*
Jay Bavers, *Vice Pres*
Glenna Haney, *Vice Pres*
EMP: 4 EST: 1992
SALES (est): 421K **Privately Held**
WEB: www.jordanvalleyglassworks.com
SIC: 3231 3229 Stained glass: made from purchased glass; glassware, art or decorative

(G-4639)
MCCULLYS WLDG FABRICATION LLC
3916 E Old State Rd (49727-8713)
PHONE.................................231 499-3842
Mark McCully, *Principal*
EMP: 6
SALES (est): 107.3K **Privately Held**
SIC: 7692 Welding repair

(G-4640)
NORTHERN WOODS FINISHING LLC
2425 M 32 (49727-9116)
PHONE.................................231 536-9640
Craig Howard, *Principal*
EMP: 3
SALES (est): 417.8K **Privately Held**
SIC: 2431 Millwork

(G-4641)
NORTHWEST FABRICATION INC
Also Called: East Jordan Sandblasting
450 Griffin Rd (49727-5133)
P.O. Box 1148 (49727-1148)
PHONE.................................231 536-3229
Brian Stanek, *President*
Karen Stanek, *Treasurer*
EMP: 4 EST: 1998
SQ FT: 12,000
SALES (est): 275K **Privately Held**
SIC: 3441 3471 3444 3443 Fabricated structural metal; sand blasting of metal parts; sheet metalwork; fabricated plate work (boiler shop)

(G-4642)
PHOENIX TRAILERS LLC
6165 M 32 (49727-5142)
P.O. Box 498 (49727-0498)
PHONE.................................231 536-9760
Frank E Schwein III,
EMP: 9
SALES: 1.3MM **Privately Held**
SIC: 3799 Boat trailers

(G-4643)
PINNEYS LOGGING INC
4226 Healey Rd (49727-9002)
PHONE.................................231 536-7730
Keith E Pinney, *Principal*
EMP: 3
SALES (est): 387.7K **Privately Held**
SIC: 2411 Logging

(G-4644)
SIGNS LETTERS & GRAPHICS INC
4095 Jonathon Dr (49727-9637)
P.O. Box 832 (49727-0832)
PHONE.................................231 536-7929
Mark K Postma, *President*
EMP: 4
SALES (est): 331.4K **Privately Held**
SIC: 3993 Signs & advertising specialties

(G-4645)
SOCKS KICK LLC
117 S Lake St (49727-9375)
P.O. Box 587 (49727-0587)
PHONE.................................231 222-2402
EMP: 3
SALES (est): 88.8K **Privately Held**
SIC: 2252 Socks

(G-4646)
STONEHEDGE FARM
2246 Pesek Rd (49727-8817)
PHONE.................................231 536-2779
Debra Mc Dermott, *Owner*
EMP: 8
SALES (est): 749.2K **Privately Held**
WEB: www.stonehedgefibermill.com
SIC: 2231 Broadwoven fabric mills, wool

(G-4647)
WES CORP
5900 Airport Rd (49727-9071)
PHONE.................................231 536-2500
Richard Gotts, *Principal*
EMP: 4
SALES (est): 570K **Privately Held**
SIC: 3399 Primary metal products

(G-4648)
WIT-SON CARBIDE TOOL INC
6490 Rogers Rd (49727-5140)
P.O. Box 339 (49727-0339)
PHONE.................................231 536-2247
Douglas Barrett, *President*
Ron Peck, *Sales Staff*
EMP: 33 EST: 1959
SQ FT: 12,000
SALES (est): 5.9MM **Privately Held**
WEB: www.wit-son.com
SIC: 3545 Cutting tools for machine tools

East Lansing
Ingham County

(G-4649)
AALPHA TINADAWN INC
Also Called: Budget Printing Center
974 Trowbridge Rd (48823-5218)
P.O. Box 1331 (48826-1331)
PHONE.................................517 351-1200
Mina Saboury, *President*
EMP: 7
SQ FT: 1,050
SALES (est): 630K **Privately Held**
SIC: 2752 Commercial printing, lithographic

(G-4650)
ARTEMIS TECHNOLOGIES INC
2501 Coolidge Rd Ste 503 (48823-6352)
P.O. Box 4948 (48826-4948)
PHONE.................................517 336-9915
John W Gilkey III, *President*
Olubunmi Akinyemiju, *Vice Pres*
Kevin Mailand, *Software Dev*
EMP: 32
SQ FT: 2,756
SALES (est): 4MM **Privately Held**
SIC: 3571 Electronic computers

(G-4651)
BIOELECTRICA INC
325 E Grand River Ave (48823-4384)
PHONE.................................517 884-4542
Andrew McColm, *President*
Gemma Reguera, *Admin Sec*
EMP: 3
SALES (est): 123.2K **Privately Held**
SIC: 8731 2869 Commercial physical research; biotechnical research, commercial; high purity grade chemicals, organic

(G-4652)
BIOPOLYMER INNOVATIONS LLC
16647 Chandler Rd (48823-6111)
PHONE.................................517 432-3044
Laura Fisher,
Ramani Narayan,
EMP: 5
SALES (est): 320.6K **Privately Held**
WEB: www.biopolymerinnovations.com
SIC: 2834 Pharmaceutical preparations

(G-4653)
CAPITAL SOFTWARE INC MICHIGAN
4660 S Hagadorn Rd # 115 (48823-5353)
PHONE.................................517 324-9100
Chris Nelson, *President*
EMP: 5
SQ FT: 1,000
SALES (est): 408.4K **Privately Held**
WEB: www.capitalrating.com
SIC: 7372 Application computer software

(G-4654)
CHARLES WALTON
Also Called: Walton Electronics
810 Roxburgh Ave (48823-3129)
PHONE.................................517 332-1842
Charles Walton, *Owner*
EMP: 3
SALES: 100K **Privately Held**
SIC: 3812 Search & detection systems & instruments

(G-4655)
DETECTIR INC
325 E Grand River Ave # 355 (48823-4384)
PHONE.................................724 681-0975
Andrew E Tomaswick, *President*
EMP: 3
SALES (est): 164.2K **Privately Held**
SIC: 3679 Electronic switches

(G-4656)
FBE CORP
Also Called: Mayard Professional Center De
3510 West Rd (48823-7311)
PHONE.................................517 333-2605
Don Manard, *President*
▲ EMP: 7
SALES (est): 989.5K **Privately Held**
WEB: www.fbecorp.com
SIC: 3559 Plastics working machinery

(G-4657)
FEDEX OFFICE & PRINT SVCS INC
626 Michigan Ave (48823-4219)
PHONE.................................517 332-5855
EMP: 6

GEOGRAPHIC SECTION

East Tawas - Iosco County (G-4686)

SALES (corp-wide): 69.6B **Publicly Held**
WEB: www.kinkos.com
SIC: 7334 2791 2789 Photocopying & duplicating services; typesetting; bookbinding & related work
HQ: Fedex Office And Print Services, Inc.
7900 Legacy Dr
Plano TX 75024
800 463-3339

(G-4658)
FIT FUEL BY KT LLC
16400 Upton Rd Lot 227 (48823-9306)
PHONE..................................517 643-8827
Kaitlyn Kelly,
EMP: 5
SALES (est): 504.1K **Privately Held**
SIC: 2869 Fuels

(G-4659)
GOURMET KITCHEN QIUYANG LLC
2843 E Grand River Ave # 180 (48823-6722)
PHONE..................................517 332-8866
Yang Xiong, *Owner*
EMP: 3
SALES (est): 165.9K **Privately Held**
SIC: 2099 Food preparations

(G-4660)
HELIX DEVICES LLC
325 E Grand River Ave (48823-4384)
PHONE..................................724 681-0975
Andrew Tomaswick, *CEO*
EMP: 3
SALES (est): 117.4K **Privately Held**
SIC: 3841 Surgical & medical instruments

(G-4661)
HIGGINS ELECTRIC SIGN CO
4100 Hunsaker Dr Ste A (48823-6128)
PHONE..................................517 351-5255
Jamie Higgins, *President*
EMP: 3
SQ FT: 3,000
SALES (est): 414.6K **Privately Held**
SIC: 3993 Electric signs

(G-4662)
HUNTSMAN ADVANCED MATERIALS AM
4917 Dawn Ave (48823-5605)
PHONE..................................517 351-5900
Greg Benedict, *Project Engr*
Larry Klusack, *Manager*
Mark Diamond, *Telecom Exec*
EMP: 220
SALES (corp-wide): 9.3B **Publicly Held**
SIC: 2821 Plastics materials & resins
HQ: Huntsman Advanced Materials Americas Llc
10003 Woodloch Forest Dr # 260
The Woodlands TX 77380
281 719-6000

(G-4663)
INPORE TECHNOLOGIES INC
Also Called: Claytec
5901 E Sleepy Hollow Ln (48823-9706)
PHONE..................................517 481-2270
Gerald Roston, *CEO*
Thomas Pinnavaia, *Vice Pres*
Michael Rathke, *Professor*
Dana Spence, *Professor*
EMP: 6
SQ FT: 2,000
SALES (est): 606.1K **Privately Held**
SIC: 2819 Silica compounds

(G-4664)
INTEGRITY SLTONS FELD SVCS INC
Also Called: Is Field Services
411 W Lake Lansing Rd (48823-8445)
PHONE..................................303 263-9522
Josh Brewer, *Director*
EMP: 17
SALES: 3.4MM **Privately Held**
SIC: 1389 7389 Servicing oil & gas wells;

(G-4665)
INTERNATIONAL BUS MCHS CORP
Also Called: IBM
196 Crescent Rd (48823-5707)
PHONE..................................517 391-5248
Jason Gibson, *COO*
EMP: 400
SALES (corp-wide): 79.5B **Publicly Held**
SIC: 7379 7371 3571 3572 Computer related consulting services; computer software development; software programming applications; minicomputers; mainframe computers; personal computers (microcomputers); computer storage devices; disk drives, computer; tape storage units, computer; semiconductors & related devices; microcircuits, integrated (semiconductor)
PA: International Business Machines Corporation
1 New Orchard Rd Ste 1 # 1
Armonk NY 10504
914 499-1900

(G-4666)
ISENSIUM
325 E Grand River Ave (48823-4384)
PHONE..................................517 580-9022
EMP: 3 EST: 2014
SALES (est): 179.3K **Privately Held**
SIC: 2835 3841 3845 Diagnostic Substances, Nsk

(G-4667)
KARLE PBLCTIONS COMMUNICATIONS
1500 Kendale Blvd Ste 207 (48823-2073)
PHONE..................................517 351-2791
Ronald F Karle, *President*
EMP: 3
SALES (est): 235.4K **Privately Held**
SIC: 2721 Periodicals: publishing only

(G-4668)
LUHU LLC
540 Glenmoor Rd (48823-3999)
PHONE..................................320 469-3162
Rueben Hewitt, *Mng Member*
Zwede Hewitt,
EMP: 6
SALES (est): 135.3K **Privately Held**
SIC: 7372 7389 Application computer software;

(G-4669)
MICHIGAN SOFT WATER OF CENTR
Also Called: Wolverine Water Trtmnt Systems
2075 E M 78 (48823-9783)
PHONE..................................517 339-0722
Paul Mahaney, *President*
EMP: 100
SQ FT: 10,000
SALES (est): 14.8MM **Privately Held**
WEB: www.wolverinewatersystems.com
SIC: 3589 5074 5999 1711 Water filters & softeners, household type; water treatment equipment, industrial; water purification equipment, household type; water softeners, water heaters & purification equipment; water purification equipment; plumbing, heating, air-conditioning contractors

(G-4670)
MICHIGAN STATE MEDICAL SOCIETY (PA)
Also Called: Michigan Medical Society
120 W Saginaw St (48823-2605)
PHONE..................................517 337-1351
Julie L Novak, *CEO*
Paula Richardson, *CFO*
Dara J Barrera, *Manager*
EMP: 50
SQ FT: 32,000
SALES (est): 5.1MM **Privately Held**
SIC: 8621 2752 Health association; commercial printing, offset

(G-4671)
MICHIGAN STATE UNIV PRESS
Manly Miles Building (48823)
PHONE..................................517 355-9543
Anastasia Wraight, *Editor*

Gabriel M Dotto, *Director*
Claudia Holzman, *Program Dir*
EMP: 12
SALES (est): 928.1K
SALES (corp-wide): 1.9B **Privately Held**
SIC: 2731 Book publishing
PA: Michigan State University
426 Auditorium Rd
East Lansing MI 48824
517 355-1855

(G-4672)
NUWAVE TECHNOLOGY PARTNERS LLC
2501 Coolidge Rd (48823-6352)
PHONE..................................517 336-9915
Chuck Elenbaas, *VP Opers*
B Dreyfus, *Branch Mgr*
EMP: 3 **Privately Held**
SIC: 3661 Telephone & telegraph apparatus
PA: Nuwave Technology Partners, Llc
5268 Azo Dr
Kalamazoo MI 49048

(G-4673)
O AND P SPARTON
2947 Eyde Pkwy (48823-5373)
PHONE..................................517 220-4960
Dean Woolcock, *Principal*
EMP: 3 EST: 2016
SALES (est): 339K **Privately Held**
SIC: 3842 Orthopedic appliances

(G-4674)
PIEZONIX LLC
325 E Grand River Ave (48823-4384)
PHONE..................................517 231-9586
Shantanu Chakrabartty, *Vice Pres*
Yang Liu,
EMP: 3
SALES (est): 247.8K **Privately Held**
SIC: 3674 Infrared sensors, solid state

(G-4675)
SIZE REDUCTION SPECIALISTS
3510 West Rd (48823-7311)
PHONE..................................517 333-2605
Don Maynard, *CEO*
EMP: 6
SQ FT: 10,000
SALES (est): 982.2K **Privately Held**
WEB: www.srscorp.com
SIC: 3559 Plastics working machinery

(G-4676)
STATE NEWS INC
Also Called: Michigan State University Pape
435 E Grand River Ave # 100 (48823-4498)
PHONE..................................517 295-1680
Travis Ricks, *Opers Staff*
Precious Usuomon, *Adv Mgr*
Marty Sprigg, *Manager*
EMP: 130
SALES: 1.2MM **Privately Held**
SIC: 2711 Newspapers: publishing only, not printed on site

(G-4677)
STUDENT BOOK STORE INC
Also Called: Spartan Corner
103 E Grand River Ave (48823-4322)
PHONE..................................517 351-6768
Connie Harper, *Manager*
EMP: 7
SALES (corp-wide): 5.9MM **Privately Held**
WEB: www.sbsmsu.com
SIC: 5942 2395 College book stores; embroidery products, except schiffli machine
PA: Student Book Store, Inc.
421 E Grand River Ave
East Lansing MI 48823
517 351-4210

(G-4678)
SUPERIOR BRASS & ALUM CAST CO
4893 Dawn Ave (48823-5694)
PHONE..................................517 351-7534
Chris W Edwards, *President*
Sally Edwards, *Vice Pres*
EMP: 18 EST: 1956
SQ FT: 20,000

SALES: 5.5MM **Privately Held**
SIC: 3369 Nonferrous foundries

(G-4679)
SUPPORTED INTELLIGENCE LLC
1555 Watertower Pl # 300 (48823-6394)
PHONE..................................517 908-4420
Matthew Irey, *CEO*
EMP: 5
SALES (est): 255K **Privately Held**
SIC: 7372 Application computer software

(G-4680)
TRANSOLOGY ASSOCIATES
2915 Crestwood Dr (48823-2371)
PHONE..................................517 694-8645
John Darlington, *Partner*
Leo Defrain, *Partner*
EMP: 5
SALES: 420K **Privately Held**
SIC: 3823 Industrial process measurement equipment

(G-4681)
UNIGRAPHICS
Also Called: Unigraphics Print & Copy
6049 Skyline Dr (48823-1603)
PHONE..................................517 337-9316
Dennis Campbell, *Partner*
Lanita Campbell, *Partner*
EMP: 3
SQ FT: 2,100
SALES: 265K **Privately Held**
WEB: www.unigraphs.com
SIC: 2752 Commercial printing, offset

(G-4682)
WINE CELLAR VISIONS LLC
500 Kedzie St (48823-3534)
PHONE..................................517 332-1026
James Cash,
EMP: 3
SALES (est): 155.4K **Privately Held**
SIC: 2084 Wine cellars, bonded: engaged in blending wines

(G-4683)
WORKING BUGS LLC
2000 Merritt Rd (48823-2921)
PHONE..................................517 203-4744
Kylash Sivakumar, *Engineer*
Kris Berglund, *Mng Member*
EMP: 3
SALES: 55K **Privately Held**
SIC: 2869 Industrial organic chemicals

East Leroy
Calhoun County

(G-4684)
BEAR CREEK BALLISTICS CO
4199 D Dr S (49051-9749)
PHONE..................................269 806-2020
Marrit Shiery, *Principal*
EMP: 3
SALES (est): 234.6K **Privately Held**
SIC: 3761 Ballistic missiles, complete

(G-4685)
VAN MACHINE CO
131 2nd St (49051-5100)
P.O. Box 185 (49051-0185)
PHONE..................................269 729-9540
Steven Van Middlesworth, *Partner*
Robert Van Middlesworth, *Partner*
EMP: 6
SQ FT: 2,100
SALES: 700K **Privately Held**
SIC: 3599 Machine shop, jobbing & repair

East Tawas
Iosco County

(G-4686)
ALEXANDER DIRECTIONAL BORING
2395 Robinet Dr (48730)
P.O. Box 254 (48730-0254)
PHONE..................................989 362-9506

East Tawas - Iosco County (G-4687)

Randall Alexander, *President*
EMP: 6
SALES (est): 1MM **Privately Held**
SIC: 1381 Directional drilling oil & gas wells

(G-4687)
COOPER-STANDARD AUTOMOTIVE INC
645 Aulerich Rd (48730-9339)
PHONE.................989 362-5631
Tom Cagua, *Branch Mgr*
EMP: 80
SALES (corp-wide): 3.6B **Publicly Held**
WEB: www.cooperstandard.com
SIC: 3443 Heat exchangers, condensers & components
HQ: Cooper-Standard Automotive Inc.
39550 Orchard Hill Pl
Novi MI 48375
248 596-5900

(G-4688)
ELECTROMECH SERVICE CORP
1111 E Washington St (48730-1658)
PHONE.................989 362-6066
Geoffrey Hinman, *Principal*
EMP: 3
SALES (est): 218K **Privately Held**
SIC: 3625 Industrial electrical relays & switches

(G-4689)
IOSCO NEWS PRESS PUBLISHING CO
Also Called: Iosco News County Herald
110 W State St (48730-1229)
P.O. Box 72 (48730-0072)
PHONE.................989 362-3456
Natalie Rigg, *Bookkeeper*
EMP: 12 **Privately Held**
WEB: www.oscodapress.com
SIC: 2711 Newspapers, publishing & printing
HQ: Iosco News Press Publishing Co
311 S State St
Oscoda MI 48750
989 739-2054

(G-4690)
LOS CUARTO AMIGOS
1626 E Us 23 (48730-9351)
PHONE.................989 984-0200
EMP: 7 **Privately Held**
SIC: 3421 Mfg Cutlery
PA: Los Cuarto Amigos
4570 Bay Rd
Saginaw MI 48604

(G-4691)
OERLIKON BLZERS CATING USA INC
980 Aulerich Rd (48730-9565)
PHONE.................989 362-3515
Patrick Riesen, *Manager*
George Patterson, *Executive*
EMP: 7
SALES (corp-wide): 2.6B **Privately Held**
SIC: 3479 Coating of metals & formed products
HQ: Oerlikon Balzers Coating Usa Inc.
1700 E Golf Rd Ste 200
Schaumburg IL 60173
847 619-5541

(G-4692)
PLASTIC TRIM INTERNATIONAL INC (DH)
935 Aulerich Rd (48730-9565)
PHONE.................248 259-7468
Howard Boyer, *CEO*
Kathleen Burgess, *Vice Pres*
▲ **EMP:** 31
SQ FT: 11,500
SALES (est): 150MM **Privately Held**
WEB: www.ptrim.com
SIC: 3465 Body parts, automobile: stamped metal

(G-4693)
PLASTIC TRIM INTERNATIONAL INC
Starboard Industries
935 Aulerich Rd (48730-9565)
P.O. Box 32 (48730-0032)
PHONE.................989 362-4419
Paul Koroly, *Principal*
EMP: 175 **Privately Held**
WEB: www.ptrim.com
SIC: 3089 Extruded finished plastic products
HQ: Plastic Trim International, Inc.
935 Aulerich Rd
East Tawas MI 48730
248 259-7468

(G-4694)
PRINT N GO
1769 E Us 23 (48730-9393)
PHONE.................989 362-6041
Larry D Stimson, *Partner*
Robin D Pelton, *Partner*
Larry Stimson, *Partner*
EMP: 5
SQ FT: 2,800
SALES: 210K **Privately Held**
SIC: 2752 5943 Photo-offset printing; office forms & supplies

(G-4695)
TAWAS TOOL CO INC (HQ)
756 Aulerich Rd (48730-9568)
PHONE.................989 362-6121
Brad Lawton, *President*
Bradley L Lawton, *President*
Jeffrey Lawton, *Vice Pres*
Mark Timreck, *Plant Mgr*
Denise Hisscock, *Purch Agent*
▲ **EMP:** 60
SQ FT: 4,500
SALES (est): 12.8MM
SALES (corp-wide): 224.7MM **Privately Held**
SIC: 3545 Hobs
PA: Star Cutter Co.
23461 Industrial Park Dr
Farmington Hills MI 48335
248 474-8200

(G-4696)
TAWAS TOOL CO INC
Also Called: Tawas Tools Plant 2
980 Aulerich Rd (48730-9566)
PHONE.................989 362-0414
Jim Santorum, *Manager*
EMP: 60
SALES (corp-wide): 224.7MM **Privately Held**
SIC: 3545 3541 Hobs; machine tools, metal cutting type
HQ: Tawas Tool Co Inc
756 Aulerich Rd
East Tawas MI 48730
989 362-6121

Eastpointe
Macomb County

(G-4697)
A-W CUSTOM CHROME INC
17726 E 9 Mile Rd (48021-2565)
PHONE.................586 775-2040
Russ Brian Box, *President*
Steve Box, *Vice Pres*
Janet Box, *Treasurer*
EMP: 6
SQ FT: 2,000
SALES (est): 775.8K **Privately Held**
SIC: 3471 Buffing for the trade; chromium plating of metals or formed products; polishing, metals or formed products

(G-4698)
CONTROLLER SYSTEMS CORPORATION
Also Called: Controller Security Systems
21363 Gratiot Ave (48021-2886)
PHONE.................586 772-6100
Henry J Luks, *President*
Daniel Luks, *Vice Pres*
EMP: 26
SQ FT: 12,000
SALES (est): 4.3MM **Privately Held**
SIC: 3669 Burglar alarm apparatus, electric; fire alarm apparatus, electric

(G-4699)
CRK LTD
Also Called: UPS Stores, The
23205 Gratiot Ave (48021-1641)
PHONE.................586 779-5240
Joseph Solomon, *President*
EMP: 5
SQ FT: 1,000
SALES (est): 588.5K **Privately Held**
SIC: 7389 3053 Mailbox rental & related service; packing materials

(G-4700)
E X P SCREEN PRINTERS
18228 E 9 Mile Rd (48021-1948)
P.O. Box 294 (48021-0294)
PHONE.................586 772-6660
Norm Quast, *Owner*
EMP: 3
SALES (est): 194.8K **Privately Held**
SIC: 2759 Screen printing

(G-4701)
EASTPOINTE LUBE EXPRESS
17375 E 8 Mile Rd (48021-3111)
PHONE.................586 775-3234
Mohamed F Charara, *Administration*
EMP: 3
SALES (est): 311.4K **Privately Held**
SIC: 2992 Lubricating oils

(G-4702)
HADD ENTERPRISES
Also Called: Express Printer
15026 E 9 Mile Rd (48021-2140)
PHONE.................586 773-4260
Harold Schrade, *Owner*
EMP: 5 **EST:** 1964
SQ FT: 2,000
SALES: 256K **Privately Held**
SIC: 2752 5945 2759 Commercial printing, offset; hobbies; letterpress printing

(G-4703)
HERFERT SOFTWARE
Also Called: Herfert Chiropractic Software
15700 E 9 Mile Rd (48021-3905)
PHONE.................586 776-2880
Richard Herfert, *Owner*
EMP: 5
SALES (est): 372.5K **Privately Held**
WEB: www.herfertsoftware.com
SIC: 7372 Prepackaged software

(G-4704)
INDUSTRIAL IMPRNTNG & DIE CTNG
15291 E 10 Mile Rd (48021-1009)
PHONE.................586 778-9470
Ronald Baluch, *Owner*
EMP: 4
SQ FT: 3,300
SALES: 365K **Privately Held**
WEB: www.industrialimprinting.com
SIC: 7389 2752 2796 2759 Printers' services: folding, collating; commercial printing, lithographic; platemaking services; commercial printing; die-cut paper & board

(G-4705)
JS ORIGINAL SILKSCREENS LLC
18132 E 10 Mile Rd (48021-1345)
PHONE.................586 779-5456
Julia Cadotte-Capps, *Owner*
Mike Salvatore, *Manager*
EMP: 7
SQ FT: 2,450
SALES (est): 629.7K **Privately Held**
WEB: www.rhinoprint.com
SIC: 2396 5699 Screen printing on fabric articles; customized clothing & apparel; belts, apparel: custom

(G-4706)
LITHO PRINTING SERVICE INC
21541 Gratiot Ave (48021-2892)
PHONE.................586 772-6067
Dale Heid, *President*
Carole C Heid, *Admin Sec*
EMP: 9
SQ FT: 5,000
SALES (est): 2MM **Privately Held**
SIC: 2752 Commercial printing, offset

(G-4707)
MUNRO PRINTING
16145 E 10 Mile Rd (48021-1131)
PHONE.................586 773-9579
John Laforest, *Owner*
EMP: 4
SQ FT: 1,600
SALES (est): 417K **Privately Held**
SIC: 2752 Commercial printing, offset

(G-4708)
P & D UNIFORMS AND ACC INC
20936 Kelly Rd (48021-3129)
PHONE.................313 881-3881
Lula Sears, *President*
Delano Walton, *Vice Pres*
▲ **EMP:** 3
SQ FT: 2,000
SALES: 170K **Privately Held**
SIC: 5699 2311 2326 Uniforms; men's & boys' uniforms; work uniforms; medical & hospital uniforms, men's

(G-4709)
SCS FASTENERS LLC
23205 Gratiot Ave (48021-1641)
PHONE.................586 563-0865
Shirley Warne, *Administration*
EMP: 6 **EST:** 2016
SALES (est): 388.4K **Privately Held**
SIC: 3965 Fasteners

(G-4710)
VALADE PRECISION MACHINING INC
Also Called: V.P.M.
17155 Stephens Dr (48021-1767)
PHONE.................586 771-7705
EMP: 5
SQ FT: 5,000
SALES (est): 320.7K **Privately Held**
SIC: 3599 Mfg Machining Service

(G-4711)
VISUAL CHIMERA
Also Called: Golden Dental Solutions
23082 Saxony Ave (48021-1846)
PHONE.................586 585-1210
Michael Pavlak, *Owner*
EMP: 10
SALES (est): 713.5K **Privately Held**
SIC: 3843 Dental equipment & supplies

(G-4712)
WATKINS PRODUCTS
15734 Camden Ave (48021-1604)
PHONE.................586 774-3187
Douglas Knopf, *Principal*
EMP: 3
SALES (est): 184.6K **Privately Held**
SIC: 2087 Extracts, flavoring

(G-4713)
WINTER SAUSAGE MFG CO INC
22011 Gratiot Ave (48021-2294)
PHONE.................586 777-9080
Rosemary Wuerz, *President*
Ron Eckert, *Vice Pres*
EMP: 40
SQ FT: 26,000
SALES (est): 5.7MM **Privately Held**
WEB: www.wintersausage.com
SIC: 2013 Sausages from purchased meat

Eastport
Antrim County

(G-4714)
BROWNWOOD ACRES FOODS INC
4819 Us 31 (49627)
P.O. Box 486 (49627-0486)
PHONE.................231 599-3101
Stephen Detar, *President*
Dana Detar, *Treasurer*
EMP: 10
SQ FT: 8,000

GEOGRAPHIC SECTION

Ecorse - Wayne County (G-4742)

SALES (est): 1MM **Privately Held**
WEB: www.brownwoodacres.com
SIC: 2033 5411 Canned fruits & specialties; grocery stores

Eaton Rapids
Eaton County

(G-4715)
ADTEK GRAPHICS INC
Also Called: Crg Directories
228 1/2 S Main St (48827-1256)
P.O. Box 305 (48827-0305)
PHONE..................................517 663-2460
D Ed Shotwell, *President*
Jane Degrow, *Vice Pres*
EMP: 10
SQ FT: 1,200
SALES (est): 1.2MM **Privately Held**
WEB: www.eatonrapidsmi.net
SIC: 2741 Directories, telephone: publishing only, not printed on site

(G-4716)
ASTRAEUS WIND ENERGY INC
503 Marilin Ave (48827-1843)
PHONE..................................517 663-5455
Jeff Metts, *President*
John Truscott, *Vice Pres*
EMP: 3
SALES (est): 217.6K **Privately Held**
SIC: 3599 Industrial machinery

(G-4717)
AUTOMATED PRECISION EQP LLC
770 Jackson St Ste A (48827-1872)
PHONE..................................517 481-2414
Kurt Norgaard, *CEO*
EMP: 6
SALES (est): 400K **Privately Held**
SIC: 3553 7389 Woodworking machinery; grinding, precision: commercial or industrial

(G-4718)
AXSON TECH US INC
1611 Hults Dr (48827-9500)
PHONE..................................517 663-8191
Charles Churet, *Principal*
EMP: 18
SALES (corp-wide): 7.1B **Privately Held**
SIC: 2851 Lacquers, varnishes, enamels & other coatings
HQ: Sika Automotive Eaton Rapids, Inc.
    30800 Stephenson Hwy
    Madison Heights MI 48071
    248 588-2270

(G-4719)
BRIAN M FOWLER PIPE ORGANS
Also Called: Fowler Organ Co
215 Dexter Rd (48827-1129)
PHONE..................................517 485-3748
Brian M Fowler, *Owner*
EMP: 6 EST: 1978
SALES: 500K **Privately Held**
WEB: www.fowlerorgan.com
SIC: 7699 3931 Organ tuning & repair; organs, all types: pipe, reed, hand, electronic, etc.

(G-4720)
DOWDING INDUSTRIES INC (PA)
449 Marilin Ave (48827-1841)
PHONE..................................517 663-5455
G Christine Dowding, *President*
Jeff Metts, *President*
Maurice H Dowding, *Chairman*
Mike Gonser, *Exec VP*
Jason Ruiz, *IT/INT Sup*
▲ EMP: 20
SQ FT: 160,000
SALES: 24MM **Privately Held**
WEB: www.dowdingindustries.com
SIC: 3429 3441 3444 3449 Manufactured hardware (general); fabricated structural metal; sheet metalwork; miscellaneous metalwork; machine & other job shop work

(G-4721)
DOWDING MACHINING LLC
503 Marilin Ave (48827-1843)
PHONE..................................517 663-5455
Chris Dowding,
Maurice H Dowding,
Jeff Metts,
▲ EMP: 10
SALES: 18MM **Privately Held**
SIC: 3545 3511 Machine tool accessories; turbines & turbine generator set units, complete

(G-4722)
EDGEWATER APARTMENTS
223 N Main St (48827-1280)
PHONE..................................517 663-8123
Merri Domer, *Manager*
Kristine Jackson, *Manager*
EMP: 5 EST: 1999
SALES (est): 377.8K **Privately Held**
WEB: www.edgewaterapartments.com
SIC: 6513 2675 Apartment building operators; die-cut paper & board

(G-4723)
FELICITY FOUNTAINS
411 S River St (48827-1538)
PHONE..................................517 663-1324
Jeffrey J Scott, *Principal*
EMP: 3
SALES (est): 156.5K **Privately Held**
SIC: 3272 Fountains, concrete

(G-4724)
G & F TOOL PRODUCTS
7127 E 5 Point Hwy (48827-9053)
PHONE..................................517 663-3646
George Goodnoe Jr, *Owner*
Bill St Andrew, *QC Mgr*
EMP: 30
SQ FT: 35,000
SALES (est): 2.8MM **Privately Held**
SIC: 3544 Special dies & tools

(G-4725)
GSE MCHINING FABRICATION INC
330 Hamman Dr (48827-9596)
PHONE..................................517 663-9500
Tammy Emfield, *President*
Jacob Masteller, *Manager*
EMP: 12
SALES (est): 2.7MM **Privately Held**
SIC: 3599 Machine shop, jobbing & repair

(G-4726)
HOAG & SONS BOOK BINDERY INC
Also Called: Media Tecnologies
145 N Main St (48827-1225)
PHONE..................................517 857-2033
Dave Wiltus, *President*
Dorci Franks, *Manager*
EMP: 10 EST: 1893
SALES (est): 953.2K **Privately Held**
SIC: 2789 Binding only: books, pamphlets, magazines, etc.

(G-4727)
KEMCO INC
5820 W Plains Rd (48827-9653)
PHONE..................................517 543-2888
Brent Ballard, *President*
EMP: 7 EST: 1963
SALES (est): 854.9K **Privately Held**
WEB: www.kemcogaging.com
SIC: 3544 Special dies, tools, jigs & fixtures

(G-4728)
MAGNESIUM PRODUCTS AMERICA INC
2001 Industrial Dr (48827-8210)
PHONE..................................517 663-2700
Walt Aldrich, *Branch Mgr*
EMP: 4
SALES (est): 409.4K
SALES (corp-wide): 138.8MM **Privately Held**
SIC: 3364 Nonferrous die-castings except aluminum
HQ: Magnesium Products Of America Inc.
    47805 Galleon Dr
    Plymouth MI 48170

(G-4729)
PRECISION PROTOTYPE & MFG INC
500 Marilin Ave (48827-1844)
PHONE..................................517 663-4114
Ronald Taylor, *President*
Jason Beeler, *Safety Mgr*
EMP: 15
SQ FT: 6,500
SALES (est): 4.1MM **Privately Held**
WEB: www.precisionprototype.com
SIC: 3469 3444 Metal stampings; sheet metalwork

(G-4730)
PRO FLOOR SERVICE
11636 Columbia Hwy (48827-9278)
PHONE..................................517 663-5012
Tony Williams, *Owner*
EMP: 4
SALES (est): 490K **Privately Held**
SIC: 3996 Hard surface floor coverings

(G-4731)
RANCH LIFE PLASTICS INC
5260 S Clinton Trl (48827-8901)
P.O. Box 503 (48827-0503)
PHONE..................................517 663-2350
C Wayne Peek, *President*
EMP: 14
SQ FT: 12,000
SALES (est): 1.7MM **Privately Held**
WEB: www.ranchlifeplastics.com
SIC: 3496 1799 1521 Miscellaneous fabricated wire products; fence construction; patio & deck construction & repair

(G-4732)
RAPIDS TOOL & ENGINEERING
Also Called: Rapids Tool & Engnrng
10618 Petrieville Hwy (48827-9205)
PHONE..................................517 663-8721
Ronald Goodnoe, *Owner*
EMP: 8
SQ FT: 12,000
SALES (est): 430.9K **Privately Held**
SIC: 3544 Special dies & tools; dies & die holders for metal cutting, forming, die casting

(G-4733)
RICKS MEAT PROCESSING LLC
Also Called: Rick's Deer Processing
3320 Onondaga Rd (48827-9608)
PHONE..................................517 628-2263
EMP: 4
SALES (est): 170K **Privately Held**
SIC: 2011 Meat Packing Plant

(G-4734)
TETRA CORPORATION
1606 Hults Dr (48827-8955)
P.O. Box 10 (48827-0010)
PHONE..................................401 529-1630
George Cioe, *President*
Katherine Reincke, *Sales Staff*
EMP: 13
SALES (est): 1.9MM **Privately Held**
SIC: 5999 2834 Cosmetics; emulsions, pharmaceutical; solutions, pharmaceutical

(G-4735)
TOTAL LOCAL ACQUISITIONS LLC
Also Called: Crg Directories
117 E Knight St (48827-1219)
PHONE..................................517 663-2405
Teresa Miller, *Mng Member*
EMP: 7
SALES: 760K **Privately Held**
SIC: 7311 2741 Advertising agencies; telephone & other directory publishing

(G-4736)
VON WEISE LLC (DH)
402 Haven St Ste H (48827-1870)
PHONE..................................517 618-9763
Scott Abright, *Purchasing*
Alan Signer, *Engineer*
Kevin Hein, *CFO*
Beth Allen, *Sales Staff*
▲ EMP: 10
SALES (est): 3MM
SALES (corp-wide): 49.2MM **Privately Held**
SIC: 3714 3625 Gears, motor vehicle; actuators, industrial
HQ: Maradyne Corporation
    4540 W 160th St
    Cleveland OH 44135
    216 362-0755

Eau Claire
Berrien County

(G-4737)
ADEPT TOOL & MOLD INC
6892 E Main St (49111-9530)
PHONE..................................269 461-3765
Fax: 269 461-3765
EMP: 3
SQ FT: 2,000
SALES (est): 180K **Privately Held**
SIC: 3544 Mfg Industrial Molds & Dies

(G-4738)
ENGINEERED POLYMER PRODUCTS
7988 W Eureka Rd (49111-9691)
PHONE..................................269 461-6955
Robert Dorstewitz, *Owner*
Ashley Lawson, *Office Mgr*
EMP: 50
SQ FT: 21,000
SALES (est): 5.8MM **Privately Held**
SIC: 3089 Injection molding of plastics

(G-4739)
FLAMM PICKLE AND PACKAGING CO
4502 Hipps Hollow Rd (49111-9781)
P.O. Box 500 (49111-0500)
PHONE..................................269 461-6916
Gina D Flamm, *President*
Dorothy Munao, *General Mgr*
EMP: 15 EST: 1924
SQ FT: 38,000
SALES: 4MM **Privately Held**
SIC: 2035 Relishes, fruit & vegetable

Eben Junction
Alger County

(G-4740)
HALLSTROM COMPANY
M-94 W (49825)
P.O. Box 185 (49825-0185)
PHONE..................................906 439-5439
Edward Hallstrom, *President*
Ruth Hallstrom, *Vice Pres*
EMP: 7 EST: 1965
SQ FT: 3,500
SALES: 100K **Privately Held**
SIC: 3599 Machine shop, jobbing & repair

Ecorse
Wayne County

(G-4741)
A & S REEL & TACKLE INC
4420 High St (48229-1582)
PHONE..................................313 928-1667
Paul Rakecky, *President*
EMP: 5
SQ FT: 1,500
SALES (est): 336.6K **Privately Held**
SIC: 3469 Metal stampings

(G-4742)
BLACKBERRY PUBLICATIONS
3915 11th St (48229-1303)
PHONE..................................313 627-1520
Darlene Runnels, *Owner*
EMP: 20 EST: 2007
SALES: 25K **Privately Held**
SIC: 2741 Miscellaneous publishing

(G-4743)
DETROIT SMOKE HOUSE LLC
355 Visger Rd (48229-1647)
PHONE...................313 622-9714
Jeffery Watts, *CEO*
EMP: 3
SALES (est): 108.1K **Privately Held**
SIC: 2015 Poultry, processed: smoked

(G-4744)
PAK-RITE INDUSTRIES INC
4270 High St (48229-1572)
PHONE...................313 388-6400
Rory Renaud, *CEO*
Charles Lefler, *President*
Mike Lefler, *Corp Secy*
Joseph W Lefler, *Vice Pres*
Chris Rutchik, *Supervisor*
EMP: 80 **EST:** 1949
SQ FT: 3,000
SALES: 28MM **Privately Held**
SIC: 4783 2674 Packing goods for shipping; crating goods for shipping; shipping bags or sacks, including multiwall & heavy duty

(G-4745)
SECORD SOLUTIONS LLC
240 Southfield Rd (48229-1130)
P.O. Box 456, Grosse Ile (48138-0456)
PHONE...................734 363-8887
Alexandria Sroca, *Mng Member*
EMP: 5
SALES: 200K **Privately Held**
SIC: 8748 8711 3571 Systems engineering consultant, ex. computer or professional; consulting engineer; electronic computers

(G-4746)
TMS INTERNATIONAL LLC
1 Quality Dr (48229-1819)
P.O. Box 29190 (48229-0190)
PHONE...................313 378-6502
Aaron Plitt, *Branch Mgr*
EMP: 6 **Privately Held**
WEB: www.tubecity.com
SIC: 3312 Blast furnaces & steel mills
HQ: Tms International, Llc
2835 E Carson St Fl 3
Pittsburgh PA 15203
412 678-6141

(G-4747)
UNITED STATES STEEL CORP
Great Lakes Divison
1 Quality Dr (48229-1819)
P.O. Box 29811 (48229-0811)
PHONE...................313 749-2100
Wendell Amica, *Area Mgr*
Tom Errer, *Area Mgr*
David Runner, *Area Mgr*
Charles V Decaria, *Vice Pres*
Mid Aman, *Foreman/Supr*
EMP: 200
SALES (corp-wide): 14.1B **Publicly Held**
SIC: 3312 Sheet or strip, steel, hot-rolled
PA: United States Steel Corp
600 Grant St Ste 468
Pittsburgh PA 15219
412 433-1121

Edenville
Midland County

(G-4748)
SYNEX WOLVERINE LLC
6000 S M 30 (48620)
PHONE...................989 689-3161
Greg Sunell, *President*
EMP: 4
SALES (est): 201.1K **Privately Held**
SIC: 2046 Hydrol

Edmore
Montcalm County

(G-4749)
CAMPBELL INDUSTRIAL FORCE LLC
Also Called: C I F
1380 Industrial Park Dr (48829-8399)
PHONE...................989 427-0011
Rick Campbell, *Mng Member*
EMP: 23
SALES: 500K **Privately Held**
SIC: 2631 Boxboard

(G-4750)
EDMORE TOOL & GRINDING INC
Also Called: Cannon Vibrator Div
4255 E Hward Cy Edmore Rd (48829-9758)
PHONE...................989 427-3790
Vic Johnson, *President*
EMP: 30 **EST:** 1978
SQ FT: 18,000
SALES (est): 3.9MM **Privately Held**
SIC: 3599 3451 3822 Grinding castings for the trade; screw machine products; pneumatic relays, air-conditioning type

(G-4751)
HARRISON PACKING CO INC
394 E Deaner Rd (48829-8365)
PHONE...................989 427-5535
Gary Hadder, *Opers-Prdtn-Mfg*
Lisa Hellenga, *Office Mgr*
Kim Harrison, *Admin Asst*
EMP: 3
SALES (corp-wide): 2.1MM **Privately Held**
WEB: www.harrisonpacking.com
SIC: 2035 Cucumbers, pickles & pickle salting; pickles, vinegar
PA: Harrison Packing Co Inc
3420 Stadium Pkwy
Kalamazoo MI 49009
269 381-3837

(G-4752)
LAKELAND MILLS INC
1 Lakeland Pl (48829-8404)
PHONE...................989 427-5133
Jason Hunt, *Vice Pres*
Teresa Hunt, *Finance Mgr*
Calvin Hunt, *Chief Mktg Ofcr*
▼ **EMP:** 49
SQ FT: 113,000
SALES: 3.4MM **Privately Held**
WEB: www.lakelandmills.com
SIC: 3423 2511 Hand & edge tools; wood lawn & garden furniture

(G-4753)
PACKAGING CORPORATION AMERICA
Also Called: PCA/Edmore 321a
1106 Industrial Park Dr (48829-8396)
PHONE...................231 947-2220
Alan Garner, *Branch Mgr*
EMP: 8
SALES (corp-wide): 7B **Publicly Held**
WEB: www.packagingcorp.com
SIC: 2653 Boxes, corrugated: made from purchased materials
PA: Packaging Corporation Of America
1 N Field Ct
Lake Forest IL 60045
847 482-3000

(G-4754)
PACKAGING CORPORATION AMERICA
Also Called: PCA/Edmore 321
1106 Industrial Park Dr (48829-8396)
P.O. Box 80 (48829-0080)
PHONE...................989 427-5129
Michael Tusing, *General Mgr*
Al Garner, *Engineer*
EMP: 75
SALES (corp-wide): 7B **Publicly Held**
WEB: www.packagingcorp.com
SIC: 2653 Boxes, corrugated: made from purchased materials
PA: Packaging Corporation Of America
1 N Field Ct
Lake Forest IL 60045
847 482-3000

(G-4755)
RYANS EQUIPMENT INC
111 Quicksilver Ln (48829-7306)
P.O. Box 387 (48829-0387)
PHONE...................989 427-2829
Don Ryan, *President*
Jill Ryan, *Vice Pres*
Greg Saxton, *Technology*
◆ **EMP:** 25
SQ FT: 20,400
SALES: 3.7MM **Privately Held**
WEB: www.ryansequip.com
SIC: 3531 Construction machinery attachments

Edwardsburg
Cass County

(G-4756)
AB CUSTOM FABRICATING LLC
27531 May St (49112-9632)
PHONE...................269 663-8100
Mike Brumitt,
EMP: 28
SQ FT: 5,600
SALES (est): 3.3MM **Privately Held**
SIC: 3479 3441 Coating of metals & formed products; fabricated structural metal

(G-4757)
AIR CRAFT INDUSTRIES INC
27328 May St (49112-8681)
PHONE...................269 663-8544
Walter Smiles, *CEO*
Susan Klemm, *President*
EMP: 3
SQ FT: 5,000
SALES (est): 187K **Privately Held**
SIC: 3728 Oxygen systems, aircraft

(G-4758)
BENTZER ENTERPRISES
26601 May St (49112-9652)
PHONE...................269 663-2289
Karl Bentzer, *Principal*
EMP: 3
SALES (est): 352.6K **Privately Held**
SIC: 2295 Resin or plastic coated fabrics

(G-4759)
BENTZER INCORPORATED
69953 Section St (49112-8655)
PHONE...................269 663-3649
Karl Bentzer, *President*
Ryan Bentzer, *Officer*
EMP: 21
SALES (est): 4MM **Privately Held**
SIC: 3089 Injection molding of plastics

(G-4760)
BOURNE SPECIALTIES
68989 Cass St (49112)
PHONE...................269 663-2187
James E Bourne, *Owner*
EMP: 3
SALES: 315K **Privately Held**
SIC: 2431 Mantels, wood

(G-4761)
BROTHERS BAKING COMPANY
27260 Max St (49112-7615)
P.O. Box 680 (49112-0680)
PHONE...................269 663-8591
Donald Wegner, *President*
Thomas Wegner, *Vice Pres*
EMP: 45
SQ FT: 30,000
SALES (est): 15.4MM **Privately Held**
SIC: 2051 Cakes, bakery: except frozen; doughnuts, except frozen

(G-4762)
CHARLES BRIDENSTINE
21716 Channel Pkwy (49112-9764)
PHONE...................269 699-5170
Charles Bridenstine, *Manager*
EMP: 4
SALES (est): 247.8K **Privately Held**
SIC: 2834 Vitamin, nutrient & hematinic preparations for human use

(G-4763)
CHRISTIANSON INDUSTRIES INC
27328 May St (49112-8681)
P.O. Box 549 (49112-0723)
PHONE...................269 663-8502
Walter Smiles, *President*
Susan Klemm, *President*
EMP: 20
SQ FT: 15,000
SALES (est): 8MM **Privately Held**
SIC: 3353 Tubes, welded, aluminum

(G-4764)
DANCORP INC
27496 Max St (49112-9664)
PHONE...................269 663-5566
Dan Daniels, *President*
Lisa Lopez, *Principal*
Rose Cameron, *Office Mgr*
EMP: 12 **EST:** 1991
SQ FT: 14,000
SALES (est): 3.3MM **Privately Held**
SIC: 3589 Water treatment equipment, industrial

(G-4765)
DUO-FORM ACQUISITION CORP
Also Called: Duo-Form Plastics
69836 Kraus Rd (49112-9692)
PHONE...................269 663-8525
George G Thomas, *President*
Glenn L Duncan, *Principal*
EMP: 151
SQ FT: 5,000
SALES (est): 27.1MM **Privately Held**
WEB: www.duoformplastics.com
SIC: 3088 Tubs (bath, shower & laundry), plastic

(G-4766)
MERCURY DISPLACEMENT INDS INC
Also Called: M D I
25028 Us 12 E (49112)
P.O. Box 710 (49112-0711)
PHONE...................269 663-8574
Randy Brewers, *President*
▲ **EMP:** 75 **EST:** 1975
SQ FT: 25,500
SALES (est): 17.2MM **Privately Held**
WEB: www.mdius.com
SIC: 3625 3822 3643 Relays, for electronic use; float controls, residential or commercial types; current-carrying wiring devices

(G-4767)
MIDWEST TIMBER INC
190 Kraus Rd (49112)
P.O. Box 599 (49112-0579)
PHONE...................269 663-5315
Edwin C Finley, *President*
Richard L Opperman, *Vice Pres*
EMP: 50
SALES (est): 13.5MM **Privately Held**
WEB: www.midwesttimber.com
SIC: 2491 Bridges & trestles, treated wood; millwork, treated wood

(G-4768)
MINLAND MACHINE INC
19801 Old 205 (49112-9756)
PHONE...................269 641-7998
Fax: 269 641-7793
EMP: 8
SALES: 900K **Privately Held**
SIC: 3599 3559 Mfg Industrial Machinery Mfg Misc Industry Machinery

(G-4769)
NORTH AMERICAN FOREST PRODUCTS (HQ)
27263 May St (49112-8680)
P.O. Box 600 (49112-0580)
PHONE...................269 663-8500
Jonh Robert Wiley II, *President*
Bob Wiley, *President*
Andrew Clark, *COO*
Mike Chaffee, *Safety Mgr*
Doug Belardinella, *Manager*

GEOGRAPHIC SECTION

▲ **EMP:** 214 **EST:** 1989
SQ FT: 130,000
SALES (est): 65.6MM
SALES (corp-wide): 2.2B **Publicly Held**
SIC: 2421 5031 Resawing lumber into smaller dimensions; lumber: rough, sawed or planed; building & structural materials, wood; lumber: rough, dressed & finished
PA: Patrick Industries, Inc.
107 W Franklin St
Elkhart IN 46516
574 294-7511

(G-4770)
NORTH AMERICAN FOREST PRODUCTS
69708 Kraus Rd (49112-8474)
PHONE 269 663-8500
Chad Bosscher, *Managing Dir*
Robert Wiley, *Manager*
EMP: 6
SALES (corp-wide): 2.2B **Publicly Held**
SIC: 2421 2439 2431 2426 Sawmills & planing mills, general; structural wood members; millwork; hardwood dimension & flooring mills
HQ: North American Forest Products Liquidation, Inc.
27263 May St
Edwardsburg MI 49112
269 663-8500

(G-4771)
NORTH AMRCN MLDING LQDTION LLC (DH)
Also Called: North Amrcn Frest Pdts Lqdtion
70151 April St (49112-8485)
P.O. Box 600 (49112-0580)
PHONE 269 663-5300
Brett Lamont,
▲ **EMP:** 21
SQ FT: 91,000
SALES (est): 10.8MM
SALES (corp-wide): 2.2B **Publicly Held**
SIC: 2431 Moldings, wood: unfinished & prefinished
HQ: North American Forest Products Liquidation, Inc.
27263 May St
Edwardsburg MI 49112
269 663-8500

(G-4772)
ST EVANS INC
27383 May St (49112-8681)
PHONE 269 663-6100
Ronald Evans, *President*
EMP: 8
SQ FT: 6,400
SALES (est): 840K **Privately Held**
WEB: www.fireworksplus.com
SIC: 5092 2899 Toys & games; toy novelties & amusements; fireworks; fireworks

(G-4773)
VILLAGE AUTOMATICS INC
69576 Section St (49112-8607)
P.O. Box 617 (49112-0617)
PHONE 269 663-8521
Kenneth Strickland, *President*
Patty Strickland, *Treasurer*
EMP: 12
SQ FT: 14,000
SALES (est): 1.4MM **Privately Held**
SIC: 3599 Machine shop, jobbing & repair

Elk Rapids
Antrim County

(G-4774)
ALLUSION STAR INC
Also Called: Nelles Studios
11672 S Us Hwy 31 (49629)
P.O. Box 428 (49629-0428)
PHONE 231 264-5858
Scott Nelles, *President*
Mary Meier, *Office Mgr*
EMP: 3 **EST:** 1975
SQ FT: 4,000
SALES (est): 175K **Privately Held**
WEB: www.nellesstudios.com
SIC: 3366 Castings (except die): brass

(G-4775)
BOKHARA PET CARE CENTERS (PA)
Also Called: Bokhara's Grooming
11535 S Elk Lake Rd (49629)
P.O. Box 175 (49629-0175)
PHONE 231 264-6667
Richard Smith, *Owner*
Shen Smith, *Co-Owner*
EMP: 11
SQ FT: 15,000
SALES (est): 500K **Privately Held**
WEB: www.bokhara.com
SIC: 0752 7372 Boarding services, kennels; grooming services, pet & animal specialties; application computer software

(G-4776)
BURNETTE FOODS INC (PA)
701 S Us Highway 31 (49629-9525)
P.O. Box 128 (49629-0128)
PHONE 231 264-8116
William R Sherman, *President*
William Sherman, *General Mgr*
Theodore Sherman, *Corp Secy*
John Pelizzari, *COO*
Theresa Bott, *Vice Pres*
◆ **EMP:** 60
SALES (est): 92.7MM **Privately Held**
WEB: www.burnettefoods.com
SIC: 2033 Fruit juices: packaged in cans, jars, etc.; fruits: packaged in cans, jars, etc.; vegetables: packaged in cans, jars, etc.

(G-4777)
ELK LAKE TOOL CO
203 Ec Loomis Dr (49629-9501)
P.O. Box 79 (49629-0079)
PHONE 231 264-5616
Jerald C Rives, *President*
Sharon Rives, *Admin Sec*
EMP: 21 **EST:** 1965
SQ FT: 7,500
SALES (est): 3.2MM **Privately Held**
WEB: www.elklaketool.com
SIC: 3545 3555 Cutting tools for machine tools; printing trades machinery

(G-4778)
ELK RAPIDS ENGINEERING INC
210 Industrial Park Dr (49629-9452)
P.O. Box 728 (49629-0728)
PHONE 231 264-5661
Bradley Lawton, *President*
Martin Woodhouse, *Vice Pres*
John Stretlien, *Purchasing*
EMP: 34 **EST:** 1969
SQ FT: 25,000
SALES (est): 6.6MM
SALES (corp-wide): 224.7MM **Privately Held**
WEB: www.star-su.com
SIC: 3541 Machine tools, metal cutting type
PA: Star Cutter Co.
23461 Industrial Park Dr
Farmington Hills MI 48335
248 474-8200

(G-4779)
MICHIGAN MAPS INC
104 Dexter St (49629-5102)
P.O. Box 885 (49629-0885)
PHONE 231 264-6800
Mark Stone, *Principal*
EMP: 5
SALES (est): 270.6K **Privately Held**
SIC: 2711 Newspapers, publishing & printing

(G-4780)
SHORTS BREWING COMPANY LLC (PA)
211 Industrial Park Dr (49629-9452)
PHONE 231 498-2300
Joseph Short, *CEO*
Scott Newman Bale, *Vice Pres*
Emily Torrence, *Project Mgr*
Aaron Smith, *Opers Mgr*
Brian Beckwith, *CFO*
EMP: 90
SQ FT: 42,000
SALES (est): 25.9MM **Privately Held**
SIC: 2082 Malt beverages

(G-4781)
TRAVERSE BAY MANUFACTURING INC
8980 Cairn Hwy (49629-9453)
P.O. Box 548 (49629-0548)
PHONE 231 264-8111
Mark Toteff, *President*
Chad Toteff, *Exec VP*
Jo Nauman, *VP Opers*
EMP: 79
SQ FT: 16,000
SALES (est): 7.8MM **Privately Held**
SIC: 2326 2329 2339 Men's & boys' work clothing; men's & boys' sportswear & athletic clothing; men's & boys' leather, wool & down-filled outerwear; women's & misses' outerwear

Elkton
Huron County

(G-4782)
PAT MCARDLE
Also Called: Progressive Tool Machinery
60 Mullen St (48731-5123)
PHONE 989 375-4321
Pat McArdle, *Owner*
EMP: 3
SQ FT: 700
SALES (est): 540K **Privately Held**
SIC: 3312 Tool & die steel

(G-4783)
SCHUETTE FARMS
2679 N Elkton Rd (48731-9730)
PHONE 989 550-0563
Dale Schuette,
EMP: 9
SALES (est): 696K **Privately Held**
SIC: 3523 2063 2051 2046 Planting, haying, harvesting & processing machinery; granulated sugar from sugar beets; bread, all types (white, wheat, rye, etc): fresh or frozen; wet corn milling; soybeans

(G-4784)
TOWER AUTOMOTIVE OPERATIONS I
81 Drettman St (48731-5109)
P.O. Box 67 (48731-0067)
PHONE 989 375-2201
Scott Polega, *Engineer*
Aaron Sweeney, *Plant Engr*
Ellen Moorman, *Branch Mgr*
Len Nowicki, *Technology*
EMP: 389
SQ FT: 500,000
SALES (corp-wide): 2.2B **Publicly Held**
SIC: 3465 Automotive stampings
HQ: Tower Automotive Operations Usa I, Llc
17672 N Laurel Park Dr 400e
Livonia MI 48152

(G-4785)
TOWER INTERNATIONAL INC
81 Drettman St (48731-5109)
PHONE 989 623-2174
Tom Vestergaard, *Opers Mgr*
Bob Fegley, *Engineer*
Anita Schoonover, *Human Res Mgr*
Mark Autio, *Director*
Dennis N Oja, *Executive*
EMP: 4
SALES (corp-wide): 2.2B **Publicly Held**
SIC: 3465 Automotive stampings
HQ: Tower International, Inc.
17672 N Laurel Park Dr
Livonia MI 48152

(G-4786)
WELDALL CORPORATION
2295 Hartsell Rd (48731-9601)
PHONE 989 375-2251
Gary Gardner, *President*
James Neurath, *Treasurer*
Ellis Gardner, *Admin Sec*
EMP: 9
SQ FT: 9,000
SALES (est): 268K **Privately Held**
SIC: 3356 Nonferrous rolling & drawing

Ellsworth
Antrim County

(G-4787)
DTS ENTERPRISES INC
Also Called: Time Machines Unlimited
9910 N Us Highway 31 (49729-9720)
PHONE 231 599-3123
David L Draper, *President*
EMP: 38 **EST:** 1989
SALES (est): 4.9MM **Privately Held**
SIC: 7538 8711 3499 3444 General automotive repair shops; marine engineering; marine horns, compressed air or steam; restaurant sheet metalwork; upholstery & trim shop, automotive

(G-4788)
GRAND TRAVERSE ASSEMBLY INC
Also Called: Grand Traverse Pallet
7161 Essex Rd (49729-9713)
PHONE 231 588-2406
Michael Rottman, *President*
EMP: 22
SQ FT: 20,000
SALES: 1.8MM **Privately Held**
SIC: 2421 Sawmills & planing mills, general

(G-4789)
THOMAS COOPER
Also Called: Rocky Top Farm's
11486 Essex Rd (49729-9650)
PHONE 231 599-2251
Thomas Cooper, *Owner*
EMP: 4
SQ FT: 5,000
SALES (est): 313.9K **Privately Held**
WEB: www.rockytopfarms.com
SIC: 5961 2033 0171 0175 Fruit, mail order; preserves, including imitation: in cans, jars, etc.; blackberry farm; raspberry farm; cherry orchard; peach orchard

Elmira
Otsego County

(G-4790)
BEISHLAG WELDING LLC
3935 Buell Rd (49730-9734)
PHONE 231 881-5023
Garret Beishlag, *Principal*
EMP: 8
SALES (est): 88.7K **Privately Held**
SIC: 7692 Welding repair

(G-4791)
MAXIMUM OILFIELD SERVICE INC
7929 Alba Hwy (49730-8767)
PHONE 989 731-0099
Randy Odell, *President*
EMP: 40 **EST:** 1996
SALES (est): 6.1MM **Privately Held**
SIC: 1389 Oil field services

(G-4792)
PARIS NORTH HARDWOOD LUMBER
Also Called: Silvery Sawmill
542 Tobias Rd (49730-8234)
PHONE 231 584-2500
William Lenau, *President*
EMP: 27
SQ FT: 35,000
SALES: 7MM **Privately Held**
SIC: 2421 2491 2426 Lumber: rough, sawed or planed; wood preserving; hardwood dimension & flooring mills

(G-4793)
SILVER LEAF SAWMILL
542 Tobias Rd (49730-8234)
PHONE 231 584-2003
David Walston, *Principal*
EMP: 3 **EST:** 2012
SALES (est): 451.9K **Privately Held**
SIC: 2421 Sawmills & planing mills, general

Elmira - Otsego County (G-4794)

(G-4794)
VINNIES MACHINING TOOL DIE
3507 Buell Rd (49730-9734)
PHONE....................231 546-3290
Vincent Jaroneski, *Owner*
EMP: 3
SALES (est): 253.6K **Privately Held**
SIC: 3599 Machine shop, jobbing & repair

Elsie
Clinton County

(G-4795)
BNM TRAILERS SALES INC
7577 N Hollister Rd (48831-9627)
PHONE....................989 862-5252
Bill Jones, *President*
EMP: 30
SQ FT: 2,000
SALES (est): 4.2MM **Privately Held**
WEB: www.bnmtrailersalesinc.com
SIC: 3792 Travel trailers & campers

(G-4796)
H & N HAULING
7662 E S Gratiot Line Rd (48831-9632)
PHONE....................989 640-3847
Chad Hufnagel, *Principal*
EMP: 3
SALES (est): 151.3K **Privately Held**
SIC: 2411 Logging

Elwell
Gratiot County

(G-4797)
NELSON FARMS
7530 Madison Rd (48832-9732)
PHONE....................989 560-1303
Thomas R Nelson, *Owner*
EMP: 12
SALES: 100K **Privately Held**
SIC: 3523 Driers (farm): grain, hay & seed

Engadine
Mackinac County

(G-4798)
FERGIN & ASSOCIATES INC
Pk N9263 Kraus Rd (49827)
PHONE....................906 477-0040
Glenn E Fergin, *President*
Earl G Fergin, *Vice Pres*
Dorothy J Burgett, *Treasurer*
Ruth A Fergin, *Admin Sec*
EMP: 4
SALES (est): 300K **Privately Held**
SIC: 3569 Filters

(G-4799)
VIC FREED LOGGING
W13745 Hahn Rd (49827-9556)
PHONE....................906 477-9933
Victor Freed, *Owner*
EMP: 3
SALES (est): 296.7K **Privately Held**
SIC: 2411 Logging

Erie
Monroe County

(G-4800)
AUTOMATIC HANDLING INTL INC
360 La Voy Rd (48133-9436)
PHONE....................734 847-0633
David J Pienta, *President*
Lee Brockman, *Exec VP*
Andy Pienta, *Vice Pres*
Paul Payne, *Project Mgr*
Dana Pienta, *Purchasing*
▲ EMP: 75 EST: 2000
SQ FT: 100,000
SALES (est): 23.7MM **Privately Held**
WEB: www.automatichandling.com
SIC: 3535 Conveyors & conveying equipment

(G-4801)
BEDFORD MACHINERY INC
9899 Telegraph Rd (48133-9750)
PHONE....................734 848-4980
Vincent Fuleky, *President*
Donna Fuleky, *Corp Secy*
EMP: 5
SQ FT: 2,000
SALES: 280K **Privately Held**
SIC: 3799 3599 Trailers & trailer equipment; automobile trailer chassis; boat trailers; machine shop, jobbing & repair

(G-4802)
CONCENTRIC INDUSTRIES INC
Also Called: R D Tool & Mfg
720 La Voy Rd (48133-9665)
PHONE....................734 848-5133
Thomas Lingle, *President*
Michael Penn, *Vice Pres*
Mark Lingle, *Maintence Staff*
EMP: 22
SQ FT: 36,000
SALES: 3MM **Privately Held**
WEB: www.concentricindustries.com
SIC: 3599 Machine shop, jobbing & repair

(G-4803)
HEIDTMAN STEEL PRODUCTS INC
640 La Voy Rd (48133-9665)
PHONE....................734 848-2115
John Bates, *Manager*
EMP: 65
SALES (corp-wide): 271.7MM **Privately Held**
WEB: www.heidtman.com
SIC: 3549 3316 5051 3471 Coiling machinery; cold-rolled strip or wire; metal wires, ties, cables & screening; electroplating & plating
HQ: Heidtman Steel Products, Inc.
2401 Front St
Toledo OH 43605
419 691-4646

(G-4804)
INSTACOTE INC
160 La Voy Rd Ste C (48133-9412)
PHONE....................734 847-5260
Tom Nachtman, *President*
EMP: 4
SALES (est): 412.6K **Privately Held**
WEB: www.instacote.com
SIC: 3479 Coating of metals with plastic or resins

(G-4805)
LIEDEL POWER CLEANING
2850 Luna Pier Rd (48133)
PHONE....................734 848-2827
Brad Liedel, *Owner*
Beth Liedel, *Co-Owner*
EMP: 12
SALES (est): 370K **Privately Held**
SIC: 2842 7349 8999 Specialty cleaning preparations; cleaning service, industrial or commercial; artists & artists' studios

(G-4806)
M & F MACHINE & TOOL INC
6555 S Dixie Hwy (48133-9691)
PHONE....................734 847-0571
Mark D Milano, *President*
Robert J Milano, *Corp Secy*
Michael A Milano, *Vice Pres*
EMP: 26
SQ FT: 40,000
SALES (est): 3.7MM **Privately Held**
WEB: www.mfmachine.com
SIC: 3599 3544 3549 Custom machinery; special dies, tools, jigs & fixtures; metalworking machinery

(G-4807)
ORT TOOL & DIE CORPORATION (PA)
Also Called: O R T
6555 S Dixie Hwy (48133-9691)
P.O. Box 5008, Toledo OH (43611-0008)
PHONE....................419 242-9553
Jim Shock, *CEO*
Angelo J Milano, *Ch of Bd*
Robert Milano, *President*
Michael A Milano, *Vice Pres*
Nick Brigode, *QC Mgr*
EMP: 70 EST: 1958
SQ FT: 100,000
SALES (est): 34.2MM **Privately Held**
WEB: www.orttool.com
SIC: 8711 3544 3469 Machine tool design; industrial engineers; special dies, tools, jigs & fixtures; machine parts, stamped or pressed metal

(G-4808)
PRECISION MASKING INC
721 La Voy Rd (48133-9665)
PHONE....................734 848-4200
Mary F Waters, *Corp Secy*
Richard D Waters, *Vice Pres*
EMP: 20
SQ FT: 9,600
SALES (est): 4.1MM **Privately Held**
WEB: www.precisionmasking.com
SIC: 3544 3563 Special dies & tools; spraying & dusting equipment

(G-4809)
PROSERVICE MACHINE LTD
10835 Telegraph Rd (48133-9749)
PHONE....................734 317-7266
James Francis, *Owner*
Brandon Bihn,
EMP: 20
SQ FT: 2,600
SALES (est): 3.8MM **Privately Held**
SIC: 3312 Tool & die steel & alloys

(G-4810)
R J MARSHALL COMPANY
1740 E Erie Rd (48133-9500)
P.O. Box 278 (48133-0278)
PHONE....................734 848-5325
Dennis Lominac, *Manager*
EMP: 25
SALES (corp-wide): 20.3MM **Privately Held**
WEB: www.rjmarshallco.com
SIC: 3295 2899 Minerals, ground or treated; chemical preparations
PA: The R J Marshall Company
26776 W 12 Mile Rd # 201
Southfield MI 48034
248 353-4100

Escanaba
Delta County

(G-4811)
ANDEX INDUSTRIES INC (PA)
1911 4th Ave N (49829-1435)
P.O. Box 887 (49829-0887)
PHONE....................800 338-9882
John Anthony, *President*
David L Anthony, *Treasurer*
Laurie Sovey, *HR Admin*
Tom Uelmen, *Manager*
Sue Frisk, *MIS Dir*
EMP: 70
SQ FT: 130,000
SALES: 12MM **Privately Held**
WEB: www.andex.net
SIC: 2671 Packaging paper & plastics film, coated & laminated

(G-4812)
ANDEX INDUSTRIES INC
Also Called: Andex Printing Division
2300 20th Ave N (49829-9317)
PHONE....................906 786-7588
Tom Uelmen, *Branch Mgr*
Becky O'Brien, *Representative*
EMP: 45
SALES (est): 6.3MM
SALES (corp-wide): 12MM **Privately Held**
WEB: www.andex.net
SIC: 2752 2671 Commercial printing, offset; packaging paper & plastics film, coated & laminated
PA: Andex Industries, Inc.
1911 4th Ave N
Escanaba MI 49829
800 338-9882

(G-4813)
ANTHONY AND COMPANY
1503 N 23rd St (49829-1848)
P.O. Box 887 (49829-0887)
PHONE....................906 786-7573
David Anthony, *President*
Mary A Sherman, *Shareholder*
Eileen Vocke, *Shareholder*
John T Anthony, *Admin Sec*
▲ EMP: 15
SQ FT: 22,349
SALES: 1.5MM **Privately Held**
WEB: www.anthonyco.com
SIC: 2499 Paint sticks, wood; yard sticks, wood

(G-4814)
APS MACHINE LLC
2501 Danforth Rd (49829-2566)
PHONE....................906 212-5600
Christopher Doyle, *President*
Sarah Doyle, *Sales Staff*
EMP: 10 EST: 2012
SQ FT: 10,000
SALES (est): 718.8K **Privately Held**
SIC: 2295 Metallizing of fabrics

(G-4815)
BACH MOBILITIES INC
1617 N 28th St (49829-2513)
PHONE....................906 789-9490
Donald Fehrenbach, *President*
Bernice Fehrenbach, *Corp Secy*
EMP: 4
SALES (est): 300K **Privately Held**
WEB: www.bachmobilities.com
SIC: 3999 Wheelchair lifts

(G-4816)
BELLS BREWERY INC
3525 Airport Rd (49829-1096)
PHONE....................906 233-5000
EMP: 3
SALES (est): 55.2K **Privately Held**
SIC: 5813 5812 2082 Bar (drinking places); grills (eating places); malt beverages

(G-4817)
BELTONE SKORIC HEARNG AID CNTR
3600 Ludington St (49829-4220)
PHONE....................906 553-4660
EMP: 7
SALES (est): 94.1K **Privately Held**
SIC: 7629 3842 Lamp repair & mounting; absorbent cotton, sterilized

(G-4818)
BICHLER GRAVEL & CONCRETE CO
6851 County 426 M.5 Rd (49829-9559)
P.O. Box 263 (49829-0263)
PHONE....................906 786-0343
Thomas L Brayak, *President*
Terry Brayak, *Vice Pres*
Karen Meiers, *Admin Sec*
EMP: 10
SALES: 3.4MM **Privately Held**
WEB: www.bichlerconcrete.com
SIC: 3273 5032 Ready-mixed concrete; stone, crushed or broken; sand, construction; gravel

(G-4819)
BIMBO BAKERIES USA INC
1924 Ludington St (49829-2741)
PHONE....................906 786-4042
EMP: 24 **Privately Held**
SIC: 2051 Bakery: wholesale or wholesale/retail combined
HQ: Bimbo Bakeries Usa, Inc
255 Business Center Dr # 200
Horsham PA 19044
215 347-5500

(G-4820)
BINKS COCA-COLA BOTTLING CO (PA)
3001 Danforth Rd (49829-2576)
PHONE....................906 786-4144
Robert N Bink, *President*
Mildred Bink, *Corp Secy*
Nicolas Bink, *Corp Secy*
Sally Sarasin, *Office Mgr*

GEOGRAPHIC SECTION

Escanaba - Delta County (G-4848)

EMP: 23 EST: 1903
SQ FT: 45,000
SALES (est): 7.4MM **Privately Held**
SIC: 2086 Bottled & canned soft drinks

(G-4821)
CAL GRINDING INC (PA)
1401 N 26th St Stop 16 (49829-2500)
PHONE..................906 786-8749
Marc Calouette, *President*
Fred Caluhette, *Vice Pres*
Mike Calouette, *Treasurer*
EMP: 32
SQ FT: 50,000
SALES (est): 2.9MM **Privately Held**
WEB: www.calvalves.com
SIC: 3592 3494 3471 Valves, engine; valves & pipe fittings; plating & polishing

(G-4822)
CLARE BEDDING MFG CO
433 Stephenson Ave (49829-2733)
P.O. Box 528 (49829-0528)
PHONE..................906 789-9902
Donald Balsavich, *President*
Tim Angsten, *Corp Secy*
Mike Angsten, *Vice Pres*
Evelyn St Ours, *Manager*
EMP: 33
SQ FT: 49,000
SALES (est): 5.6MM **Privately Held**
SIC: 2515 Mattresses, innerspring or box spring; furniture springs

(G-4823)
D B A RICHARDS BOATWORKS MAR
4085 15th Rd (49829-9761)
PHONE..................906 789-4168
Steven Richards, *Owner*
EMP: 3 EST: 2015
SALES (est): 137.2K **Privately Held**
SIC: 3732 Boat building & repairing

(G-4824)
EMP ADVANCED DEVELOPMENT LLC
Also Called: Research and Development Off
2701 N 30th St (49829-9318)
PHONE..................906 789-7497
Brian Larche,
David Allen,
Paul Harvey,
EMP: 65
SALES (est): 7.2MM **Privately Held**
WEB: www.emp-corp.com
SIC: 8711 3561 Engineering services; pumps & pumping equipment
PA: Engineered Machined Products, Inc.
3111 N 28th St
Escanaba MI 49829

(G-4825)
EMP RACING INC
Also Called: Stewart Components
2701 N 30th St (49829-9318)
P.O. Box 1246 (49829-6246)
PHONE..................906 786-8404
Brian Larche, *Ch of Bd*
▲ EMP: 6
SALES (est): 746.6K **Privately Held**
WEB: www.waterpumps.com
SIC: 3519 3694 Internal combustion engines; ignition systems, high frequency

(G-4826)
ENGINEERED MACHINED PDTS INC (PA)
Also Called: E M P
3111 N 28th St (49829-9324)
P.O. Box 1246 (49829-6246)
PHONE..................906 786-8404
Brian K Larche, *CEO*
Mark Bader, *Vice Pres*
Jerry Guindon, *Vice Pres*
Ray Lanarche, *CFO*
Paul Harvey, *Admin Sec*
◆ EMP: 420
SQ FT: 250,000
SALES (est): 9MM **Privately Held**
WEB: www.emp-corp.com
SIC: 3519 3714 3568 3599 Internal combustion engines; water pump, motor vehicle; pulleys, power transmission; air intake filters, internal combustion engine, except auto; pumps & pumping equipment

(G-4827)
ENGINEERED MACHINED PDTS INC
2701 N 30th St (49829-9318)
PHONE..................906 789-7497
Brian Larche, *CEO*
EMP: 25
SALES (est): 2.3MM **Privately Held**
WEB: www.emp-corp.com
SIC: 3561 3714 Pumps & pumping equipment; motor vehicle parts & accessories
PA: Engineered Machined Products, Inc.
3111 N 28th St
Escanaba MI 49829

(G-4828)
ESCANABA AND LK SUPERIOR RR CO
Also Called: Car Shop
1401 N 26th St Bldg 20 (49829-2500)
PHONE..................906 786-9399
Mike Pratt, *Manager*
EMP: 9
SALES (corp-wide): 12.5MM **Privately Held**
WEB: www.elsrr.com
SIC: 4789 7692 Railroad car repair; welding repair
PA: Escanaba And Lake Superior Railroad Company
1 Larkin Plz
Wells MI 49894
906 786-0693

(G-4829)
EXPRESS WELDING INC
2525 14th Ave N (49829-1776)
PHONE..................906 786-8808
Duane Scheuren, *President*
Patricia Scheuren, *Corp Secy*
EMP: 4
SQ FT: 44,000
SALES (est): 599.7K **Privately Held**
SIC: 7692 3715 3523 Welding repair; truck trailers; farm machinery & equipment

(G-4830)
GENDZWILL CO
1600 16th Ave S (49829-2005)
PHONE..................906 786-9321
Sandra Beauchamp, *President*
Joann L Weingarten, *Corp Secy*
Warren Weingarten, *Vice Pres*
EMP: 3
SALES (est): 192.9K **Privately Held**
SIC: 2411 Logging camps & contractors

(G-4831)
GENESIS GRAPHICS INC
1823 7th Ave N (49829-1421)
P.O. Box 622 (49829-0622)
PHONE..................906 786-4913
Michael Olsen, *President*
Kim Perron, *Manager*
EMP: 7
SQ FT: 2,500
SALES (est): 400K **Privately Held**
WEB: www.genesisgraphics.com
SIC: 2759 Screen printing

(G-4832)
GIGUERE LOGGING INC
3200 5th Ave S (49829-4324)
PHONE..................906 786-3975
Edward Giguere, *President*
EMP: 8
SALES (est): 813.7K **Privately Held**
SIC: 2411 Logging camps & contractors

(G-4833)
HJ MANUFACTURING INC
Also Called: Delta Manufacturing
3707 19th Ave N (49829-2525)
PHONE..................906 233-1500
Harold Ross, *CEO*
Jean R Ross, *President*
▲ EMP: 11
SALES (est): 3MM **Privately Held**
SIC: 5088 3743 3479 8711 Railroad equipment & supplies; railroad equipment; painting of metal products; engineering services

(G-4834)
HURLEY MARINE INC
2717 N Lincoln Rd (49829-9569)
PHONE..................906 553-6249
Todd R Hurley, *President*
Leslie Walch, *Principal*
EMP: 4
SALES (est): 900K **Privately Held**
SIC: 3429 Marine hardware

(G-4835)
HYTEC EQUIPMENT
6614 N.75 Dr (49829-9325)
P.O. Box 916 (49829-0916)
PHONE..................906 789-5811
Dale Wieciech, *Owner*
EMP: 6
SQ FT: 18,000
SALES (est): 2.5MM **Privately Held**
WEB: www.hytecmfg.com
SIC: 2411 Timber, cut at logging camp

(G-4836)
INDEPENDENT MACHINE CO INC
Also Called: IMC
2501 Danforth Rd (49829-2566)
PHONE..................906 428-4524
Chris Doyle, *President*
Jim Calouette, *Vice Pres*
Mark Wyman,
EMP: 30
SQ FT: 50,000
SALES (est): 8.3MM **Privately Held**
SIC: 3537 3531 3599 Pallets, metal; railroad related equipment; machine & other job shop work

(G-4837)
JOHNSTON PRINTING & OFFSET
711 Ludington St (49829-3802)
PHONE..................906 786-1493
James Mc Donough, *President*
Bonnie Mc Donough, *Corp Secy*
EMP: 4
SQ FT: 2,400
SALES (est): 400K **Privately Held**
SIC: 2752 Commercial printing, offset

(G-4838)
LAKESTATE INDUSTRIES INC
Also Called: RUSTIC ROOM
1831 N 21st St (49829-9586)
P.O. Box 279 (49829-0279)
PHONE..................906 786-9212
Lisa Cloutier, *Office Mgr*
Cheryl Ohman, *Exec Dir*
Jennifer Mac Laren, *Exec Dir*
EMP: 32 EST: 1953
SQ FT: 17,000
SALES (est): 2.3MM **Privately Held**
WEB: www.lakestateindustries.org
SIC: 2499 8331 4953 Surveyors' stakes, wood; vocational rehabilitation agency; recycling, waste materials

(G-4839)
LEIGHS GARDEN WINERY INC
209 S 12th St (49829-3427)
PHONE..................906 553-7799
Leigh Schmidt, *Principal*
EMP: 5
SALES (est): 370K **Privately Held**
SIC: 2084 Wines

(G-4840)
LLOYD JOHNSON LIVESTOCK INC
3697 18th Rd (49829-9715)
PHONE..................906 786-4878
Lloyd Johnson, *President*
EMP: 3
SALES (est): 139.6K **Privately Held**
SIC: 2011 Meat packing plants

(G-4841)
MEAD WESTVACO PAPER DIV
1800 20th Ave N (49829-9500)
P.O. Box 757 (49829-0757)
PHONE..................906 233-2362
Keith Vanscotter, *President*
EMP: 6 EST: 1987
SALES (est): 832.8K **Privately Held**
SIC: 2672 Coated & laminated paper

(G-4842)
MECHANICAL SUPPLY A DIVISION
1701 N 26th St (49829-2558)
PHONE..................906 789-0355
John Liss, *President*
EMP: 30 EST: 1981
SQ FT: 2,200
SALES (est): 3.2MM **Privately Held**
WEB: www.northernmachining.com
SIC: 5085 7692 Seals, industrial; packing, industrial; welding repair

(G-4843)
MEIERS SIGNS INC
1717 N Lincoln Rd (49829-2504)
P.O. Box 441 (49829-0441)
PHONE..................906 786-3424
Joseph Twa, *Owner*
Karen Twa, *Partner*
EMP: 6
SQ FT: 5,000
SALES (est): 400K **Privately Held**
SIC: 3993 1731 7389 1799 Electrical work; sign painting & lettering shop; sign installation & maintenance; electric signs

(G-4844)
MERCHANT HOLDINGS INC
440 N 10th St (49829-3837)
PHONE..................906 786-7120
Terrie Peters, *Exec Dir*
EMP: 5
SALES (est): 331.9K **Privately Held**
SIC: 3731 Shipbuilding & repairing

(G-4845)
MICHIGAN MEAT PROCESSING
1120 S Lincoln Rd (49829-2147)
PHONE..................906 786-7010
William Newport, *Owner*
EMP: 10
SALES (est): 368K **Privately Held**
SIC: 2011 Meat packing plants

(G-4846)
NK DOCKSIDE SERVICE & REPAIR
1014 8th Ave S (49829-3214)
PHONE..................906 420-0777
Nicholas Kobasic, *Partner*
EMP: 6 EST: 2012
SALES (est): 457.3K **Privately Held**
SIC: 3731 Shipbuilding & repairing

(G-4847)
NORTHERN MACHINING & REPR INC
1701 N 26th St (49829-2558)
PHONE..................906 786-0526
Jon Liss, *President*
Melisa Johnson, *Controller*
EMP: 39
SQ FT: 40,000
SALES (est): 7.9MM **Privately Held**
SIC: 3599 3443 7692 3444 Machine shop, jobbing & repair; fabricated plate work (boiler shop); welding repair; sheet metalwork; fabricated structural metal

(G-4848)
NORTHERN SCREEN PRINTING & EMB
1001 Ludington St (49829-3501)
PHONE..................906 786-0373
Frank Bink, *Partner*
EMP: 5
SALES (est): 467.2K **Privately Held**
WEB: www.northernscreen.com
SIC: 5699 2759 Miscellaneous apparel & accessories; screen printing

Escanaba - Delta County (G-4849)

(G-4849)
OGDEN NEWSPAPERS INC
Also Called: Daily Press
600 Ludington St (49829-3830)
P.O. Box 828 (49829-0828)
PHONE...................906 786-2021
Tari Calouette, *Manager*
Sarah Maki, *Admin Sec*
EMP: 80 **Privately Held**
WEB: www.miningjournal.net
SIC: 2711 Newspapers: publishing only, not printed on site
HQ: The Ogden Newspapers Inc
1500 Main St
Wheeling WV 26003
304 233-0100

(G-4850)
OGDEN NEWSPAPERS INC
Also Called: U.P. Action News
600 2 Ludington St (49829)
P.O. Box 828 (49829-0828)
PHONE...................906 789-9122
Terrie Belongie, *Manager*
EMP: 5 **Privately Held**
WEB: www.upaction.com
SIC: 2711 Newspapers: publishing only, not printed on site
HQ: The Ogden Newspapers Inc
1500 Main St
Wheeling WV 26003
304 233-0100

(G-4851)
PHOTO OFFSET INC
Also Called: Photo-Offset Printing
109 S Lincoln Rd (49829-1339)
P.O. Box 128 (49829-0128)
PHONE...................906 786-5800
EMP: 5 **EST:** 1951
SQ FT: 1,200
SALES (est): 490K **Privately Held**
SIC: 2752 Offset Printer

(G-4852)
PLUM CREEK TIMBER COMPANY INC
Also Called: Nepko Lake Nursery
2831 N Lincoln Rd (49829-9569)
PHONE...................715 453-7952
EMP: 6
SALES (corp-wide): 1.4B **Publicly Held**
SIC: 5099 2411 Whol Durable Goods Logging
PA: Plum Creek Timber Company Inc
601 Union St Ste 3100
Seattle WA 98101
206 467-3600

(G-4853)
PRECISION PLUS
6911 County 426 M.5 Rd (49829-8500)
PHONE...................906 553-7900
Travis Gogfrey, *Owner*
EMP: 14
SALES (est): 1.6MM **Privately Held**
SIC: 3549 Metalworking machinery

(G-4854)
QUARRYSTONE INC
6851 County 426 M.5 Rd (49829-9559)
PHONE...................906 786-0343
Leonora Doonan, *President*
Cory Pangborn, *President*
EMP: 21
SALES (est): 1MM **Privately Held**
SIC: 3273 Ready-mixed concrete

(G-4855)
RACE RAMPS LLC
Also Called: Brute Industries
2003 23rd Ave N Ste 2533)
PHONE...................866 464-2788
David Buslee, *CFO*
EMP: 4
SALES (est): 371.7K **Privately Held**
SIC: 3559 Automotive related machinery

(G-4856)
RICHARDS PRINTING
718 Ludington St (49829-3829)
PHONE...................906 786-3540
Bette L Richards, *Owner*
EMP: 4
SQ FT: 1,900
SALES (est): 425.4K **Privately Held**
SIC: 2752 Commercial printing, offset

(G-4857)
RNJ SERVICES INC
2003 23rd Ave N Ste A (49829-2533)
PHONE...................906 786-0585
Richard Heinz, *President*
Eric Lucas, *Technology*
EMP: 16
SALES (est): 3.6MM **Privately Held**
SIC: 3559 Automotive maintenance equipment

(G-4858)
RT MANUFACTURING INC
2522 14th Ave N (49829-1792)
PHONE...................906 233-9158
Robert Triest, *President*
EMP: 10
SQ FT: 35,000
SALES (est): 4.9MM **Privately Held**
SIC: 3441 Fabricated structural metal

(G-4859)
SHESKI LOGGING
2875 18th Rd (49829-9737)
PHONE...................906 786-1886
John Sheski, *Principal*
EMP: 3
SALES (est): 292.6K **Privately Held**
SIC: 2411 Logging

(G-4860)
SIGN UP INC
Also Called: Sign Up Schumann Outdoor Arts
1300 Ludington St (49829-2844)
PHONE...................906 789-7446
Peggy Schumann, *President*
Terry Schumann, *Vice Pres*
EMP: 5 **EST:** 1986
SALES: 125K **Privately Held**
SIC: 3993 Signs, not made in custom sign painting shops

(G-4861)
STEWART KNIVES LLC
6911 County 426 M.5 Rd (49829-8500)
PHONE...................906 789-1801
Lesley Stewart, *Mng Member*
Mike Stewart, *Mng Member*
Jackilyn Stewart,
James Stewart,
EMP: 40 **EST:** 2008
SQ FT: 17,000
SALES: 4MM **Privately Held**
SIC: 3421 5091 Knives: butchers', hunting, pocket, etc.; hunting equipment & supplies

(G-4862)
T D VINETTE COMPANY
Also Called: Vinette Boatworks
1212 N 19th St (49829-1630)
P.O. Box 416 (49829-0416)
PHONE...................906 786-1884
Dan Branson, *President*
EMP: 6 **EST:** 1947
SQ FT: 26,500
SALES (est): 380K **Privately Held**
SIC: 3732 4493 Boat building & repairing; boat yards, storage & incidental repair

(G-4863)
UPPER PENINSULA CON PIPE CO (PA)
Also Called: U P Concrete Pipe
6480 Us Hwy 2 (49829)
P.O. Box 313 (49829-0313)
PHONE...................906 786-0934
John G Kloet Jr, *President*
Harland Courllard, *Vice Pres*
David Ross, *Office Mgr*
EMP: 15 **EST:** 1950
SQ FT: 110,800
SALES (est): 3.5MM **Privately Held**
WEB: www.upconcretepipe.net
SIC: 3272 Sewer pipe, concrete; culvert pipe, concrete

(G-4864)
UPPER PENINSULA RUBBER CO INC
Also Called: Tunnel Vision Pipeline Svcs
2101 N 19th St Bldg B (49829-9573)
P.O. Box 541 (49829-0541)
PHONE...................906 786-0460
John Kloet, *President*
James Laughbaum, *General Mgr*
Harland Coulliard, *Vice Pres*
Steven Delaire, *Engineer*
Steve Delaire, *Treasurer*
EMP: 5
SALES: 500K
SALES (corp-wide): 3.5MM **Privately Held**
WEB: www.upconcretepipe.net
SIC: 3053 Gasket materials; gaskets, all materials
PA: Upper Peninsula Concrete Pipe Co
6480 Us Hwy 2
Escanaba MI 49829
906 786-0934

(G-4865)
VERSO CORPORATION
Also Called: Escanaba Paper Company
7100 County 426 M.5 Rd (49829-8501)
P.O. Box 757 (49829-0757)
PHONE...................906 786-1660
Adrihan John, *Safety Mgr*
Sherri Peterson, *Human Res Dir*
Matt Archambeau, *Branch Mgr*
EMP: 1165 **Publicly Held**
SIC: 2621 Paper mills
PA: Verso Corporation
8540 Gander Creek Dr
Miamisburg OH 45342

(G-4866)
VIAUS SUPER MARKET
1519 Sheridan Rd (49829-1826)
PHONE...................906 786-1950
Wallace Viau, *President*
Jeanette Viau, *Corp Secy*
EMP: 8 **EST:** 1926
SQ FT: 6,100
SALES (est): 583.9K **Privately Held**
SIC: 5421 2013 5411 Meat markets, including freezer provisioners; sausages from purchased meat; smoked meats from purchased meat; grocery stores, independent

Essexville
Bay County

(G-4867)
AMERICAN GOURMET SNACKS LLC
1211 Woodside Ave (48732-1269)
PHONE...................989 892-4856
Robert Jaenicke, *Mng Member*
EMP: 9
SALES: 500K **Privately Held**
SIC: 2064 5461 5441 Candy & other confectionery products; pretzels; popcorn, including caramel corn

(G-4868)
BAY ARCHERY SALES CO
2713 Center Ave (48732-1749)
PHONE...................989 894-5800
Jere Brunette, *President*
James Brunette, *Vice Pres*
EMP: 7
SQ FT: 4,200
SALES (est): 690K **Privately Held**
SIC: 5941 3999 Archery supplies; backpacking equipment; camping equipment; wind chimes

(G-4869)
BAY COMPOSITES INC
1801 Jarman Rd (48732-9800)
PHONE...................989 891-9159
Glen Sonza, *President*
▲ **EMP:** 12 **EST:** 2008
SALES (est): 2.6MM **Privately Held**
SIC: 3624 Carbon & graphite products

(G-4870)
BAY MACHINE TOOL CO INC
110 Woodside Ave (48732-1110)
P.O. Box 78 (48732-0078)
PHONE...................989 894-2863
William R Voigt, *President*
John R Lash, *Corp Secy*
EMP: 20
SQ FT: 10,000
SALES (est): 1.3MM **Privately Held**
SIC: 3599 Machine shop, jobbing & repair

(G-4871)
BAY TOOL INC
110 Woodside Ave (48732-1110)
P.O. Box 78 (48732-0078)
PHONE...................989 894-2863
William Clark, *Vice Pres*
EMP: 7
SQ FT: 10,000
SALES (est): 634.8K **Privately Held**
SIC: 3599 Industrial machinery

(G-4872)
EBERHARD AND FATHER SIGNWORKS
108 Woodside Ave (48732-1110)
PHONE...................989 892-5566
Kathy Washabaugh, *Partner*
Greg Brown, *Partner*
EMP: 6 **EST:** 1957
SQ FT: 5,000
SALES (est): 471.9K **Privately Held**
SIC: 3993 Signs, not made in custom sign painting shops

(G-4873)
JCS TOOL & MFG CO INC
Also Called: J C S
193 N Powell Rd (48732-1714)
PHONE...................989 892-8975
Roger Felske, *President*
Roger Fleske, *Principal*
Kevin Socier, *Vice Pres*
Allan Badour, *Treasurer*
EMP: 22
SQ FT: 40,000
SALES (est): 3.9MM **Privately Held**
WEB: www.jcstool.com
SIC: 3544 3498 Special dies & tools; fabricated pipe & fittings

(G-4874)
K-C WELDING SUPPLY INC
1309 Main St (48732-1251)
PHONE...................989 893-6509
Keith Carolan II, *President*
Maureen A Carolan, *Treasurer*
Patrick Carolan, *Manager*
EMP: 14 **EST:** 1954
SQ FT: 12,000
SALES (est): 2.2MM **Privately Held**
SIC: 7692 5084 5085 Welding repair; welding machinery & equipment; industrial supplies

(G-4875)
LAFARGE NORTH AMERICA INC
Also Called: Lafargeholcim
1500 Main St (48732-1292)
PHONE...................989 894-0157
EMP: 7
SALES (corp-wide): 27.6B **Privately Held**
SIC: 3241 Cement, hydraulic
HQ: Lafarge North America Inc.
8700 W Bryn Mawr Ave
Chicago IL 60631
773 372-1000

(G-4876)
LAFARGE NORTH AMERICA INC
1500 Main St (48732-1292)
PHONE...................216 566-0545
EMP: 27
SALES (corp-wide): 27.6B **Privately Held**
SIC: 3241 Cement, hydraulic
HQ: Lafarge North America Inc.
8700 W Bryn Mawr Ave
Chicago IL 60631
773 372-1000

GEOGRAPHIC SECTION

Evart
Osceola County

(G-4877)
A1 UTILITY CONTRACTOR INC
8399 Evergreen Rd (49631-9605)
PHONE..................................989 324-8581
Troy Lyons, *President*
EMP: 56 **EST:** 2012
SALES: 7.5MM **Privately Held**
SIC: 1623 1311 Electric power line construction; natural gas production

(G-4878)
AMALGAMATED UAW
Also Called: Amalgamated Uaw Local 2270
601 W 7th St (49631-9408)
P.O. Box 1037 (49631-1037)
PHONE..................................231 734-9286
Dana Sible, *President*
EMP: 9
SALES: 204.4K **Privately Held**
SIC: 8631 3714 Labor unions & similar labor organizations; motor vehicle parts & accessories

(G-4879)
BENNETT SAWMILL
4161 90th Ave (49631)
PHONE..................................231 734-5733
Kenneth Bennett, *Partner*
Kevin Bennett, *Partner*
Mark Bennett, *Partner*
EMP: 7
SALES: 731.3K **Privately Held**
SIC: 2421 2411 Sawmills & planing mills, general; logging

(G-4880)
CHERRY CREEK POST LLC
Also Called: Cherry Creek Post Co
5882 7 Mile Rd (49631-8270)
PHONE..................................231 734-2466
Omer Miller, *Partner*
Dewayne Miller, *Partner*
EMP: 6
SALES: 2.8MM **Privately Held**
SIC: 5031 2499 Fencing, wood; fencing, wood

(G-4881)
FLOWTEK INC
8586 9 Mile Rd (49631-8214)
P.O. Box 1310, Kalkaska (49646-1310)
PHONE..................................231 734-3415
Jeffrey Vincent, *President*
EMP: 16 **EST:** 2008
SALES (est): 3.1MM **Privately Held**
SIC: 3491 Industrial valves

(G-4882)
HUFF MACHINE & TOOL CO INC
5469 85th Ave (49631-8763)
P.O. Box 638 (49631-0638)
PHONE..................................231 734-3291
Fax: 231 734-5833
EMP: 12
SQ FT: 1,200
SALES (est): 1.5MM **Privately Held**
SIC: 3599 Job Machine Shop

(G-4883)
INDUSTRIAL MACHINE & TOOL
743 W 7th St (49631-9429)
PHONE..................................231 734-2794
Joyce Bailey, *Owner*
Bruce Bailey, *Owner*
EMP: 3
SQ FT: 17,000
SALES (est): 230.2K **Privately Held**
SIC: 3441 Fabricated structural metal

(G-4884)
INTERNATIONAL AUTOMOTIVE COMPO
601 W 7th St (49631-9408)
PHONE..................................231 734-9000
JD Smith, *QA Dir*
Steve Tipton, *Program Mgr*
EMP: 80 **Privately Held**
WEB: www.iaaawards.com
SIC: 3647 Automotive lighting fixtures

HQ: International Automotive Components Group North America, Inc.
28333 Telegraph Rd
Southfield MI 48034

(G-4885)
LIBERTY DAIRY COMPANY
302 N River St (49631-9359)
PHONE..................................800 632-5552
Fax: 231 734-3880
EMP: 125
SALES (est): 13.3MM **Publicly Held**
SIC: 2026 2022 Mfg Fluid Milk Mfg Cheese
HQ: Dean Holding Company
2711 N Haskell Ave
Dallas TX 75204
214 303-3400

(G-4886)
RKAA BUSINESS LLC
Also Called: Chippewa Plastics
5843 100th Ave (49631-8421)
PHONE..................................231 734-5517
Albert Rohe, *President*
John Holmes, *Vice Pres*
▲ **EMP:** 35
SQ FT: 75,000
SALES (est): 7.6MM **Privately Held**
SIC: 3089 3544 Injection molding of plastics; special dies & tools

(G-4887)
TRIPLE DDD FIREWOOD
9533 90th Ave (49631-8321)
P.O. Box 1163 (49631-1163)
PHONE..................................231 734-5215
EMP: 3
SALES (est): 109.4K **Privately Held**
SIC: 5099 2411 Whol Durable Goods Logging

(G-4888)
VENTRA EVART LLC
601 W 7th St (49631-9468)
PHONE..................................231 734-9000
Amy Kellogg, *President*
Harold Stieber,
▲ **EMP:** 2
SALES (est): 1.3MM **Privately Held**
SIC: 3089 5531 Injection molding of plastics; automobile & truck equipment & parts

Fairview
Oscoda County

(G-4889)
COOPER-STANDARD AUTOMOTIVE INC
2799 E Miller Rd (48621-9802)
P.O. Box 219 (48621-0219)
PHONE..................................989 848-2272
Larry Wasnock, *Branch Mgr*
EMP: 112
SALES (corp-wide): 3.6B **Publicly Held**
WEB: www.cooperstandard.com
SIC: 3714 Power steering equipment, motor vehicle
HQ: Cooper-Standard Automotive Inc.
39550 Orchard Hill Pl
Novi MI 48375
248 596-5900

(G-4890)
FAIRVIEW SAWMILL INC
1901 Kneeland Rd (48621-9737)
PHONE..................................989 848-5238
Dallas Hendrich, *Partner*
Dawson Oaks, *Partner*
EMP: 5
SALES (est): 320K **Privately Held**
SIC: 2421 Sawmills & planing mills, general

Falmouth
Missaukee County

(G-4891)
ADVANCED MANUFACTURING LLC
311 E Prosper Rd (49632-9528)
PHONE..................................231 826-3859
Gary Gladu, *CEO*
EMP: 4
SALES (est): 314.8K **Privately Held**
SIC: 3061 Mechanical rubber goods

(G-4892)
EBELS HARDWARE INC
490 E Prosper Rd (49632-9521)
P.O. Box 100 (49632-0100)
PHONE..................................231 826-3334
Dave Ebels, *President*
Paul Ebels, *Vice Pres*
Gayle Ebels, *Treasurer*
Vicki Ebels, *Admin Sec*
EMP: 15
SALES (est): 1MM **Privately Held**
SIC: 5251 3546 3523 3524 Hardware; chain saws, portable; tractors, farm; grass catchers, lawn mower; lawnmowers & tractors; lawn mower repair shop

(G-4893)
GRANDPA HANKS MAPLE SYRUP LLC
2431 E Workman Rd (49632-9748)
PHONE..................................231 826-4494
Keith Dick, *Principal*
EMP: 3
SALES (est): 146.6K **Privately Held**
SIC: 2099 Maple syrup

Farmington
Oakland County

(G-4894)
AMERICAN STEEL FABRICATORS
34150 W 9 Mile Rd (48335-4716)
P.O. Box 2177, Windermere FL (34786-2177)
PHONE..................................248 476-8433
Marvin L Patrick, *President*
Scott K Patrick, *Vice Pres*
Rosemary Patrick, *Admin Sec*
EMP: 15
SALES (est): 3MM **Privately Held**
WEB: www.americansteelfabricators.com
SIC: 3441 Fabricated structural metal

(G-4895)
CASTINE COMMUNICATIONS INC
Also Called: Hockey Weekly
22658 Brookdale St (48336-4118)
PHONE..................................248 477-1600
John Castine, *President*
EMP: 4
SALES (est): 487.3K **Privately Held**
WEB: www.hockeyweekly.com
SIC: 2721 Magazines: publishing only, not printed on site

(G-4896)
CLARION CORPORATION AMERICA
Also Called: Clarion Group
34500 Grand River Ave (48335-3310)
PHONE..................................248 991-3100
Paul Lachner, *Branch Mgr*
EMP: 47 **Privately Held**
SIC: 5064 3651 Radios, motor vehicle; household audio equipment
HQ: Clarion Corporation Of America
6200 Gateway Dr
Cypress CA 90630
310 327-9100

(G-4897)
DETROIT MATERIALS INC
Also Called: Wayne Steel Tech
33225 Grand River Ave (48336-3123)
PHONE..................................248 924-5436
Pedro Guillen, *CEO*
Nick Moroz, *CTO*
EMP: 4 **EST:** 2013
SALES (est): 109.9K **Privately Held**
SIC: 3325 8742 Steel foundries; management engineering

(G-4898)
E & D MACHINE COMPANY INC
32777 Chesley Dr (48336-5115)
PHONE..................................248 473-0255
Edward E Mirabitur, *President*
EMP: 12
SQ FT: 2,500
SALES (est): 1.5MM **Privately Held**
SIC: 3599 Machine shop, jobbing & repair

(G-4899)
FARMINGTON BAKERY
33250 Grand River Ave (48336-3122)
PHONE..................................248 442-2360
Becky Burns, *Owner*
EMP: 5
SQ FT: 1,500
SALES (est): 314.5K **Privately Held**
SIC: 2051 Bread, cake & related products

(G-4900)
HTI USA INC
Also Called: Hi-Tech Industries, Inc.
33106 W 8 Mile Rd (48336-5400)
PHONE..................................248 358-5533
Herschel S Wright, *President*
▲ **EMP:** 26 **EST:** 1985
SQ FT: 40,000
SALES (est): 4MM
SALES (corp-wide): 180.7MM **Privately Held**
WEB: www.hi-techindustries.com
SIC: 3826 Analytical instruments
HQ: Sam Brown Sales, Llc
33106 W 8 Mile Rd
Farmington MI 48336
248 358-2626

(G-4901)
JAY CEE SALES & RIVET INC
32861 Chesley Dr (48336-5117)
P.O. Box 1150 (48332-1150)
PHONE..................................248 478-2150
Michael Clinton, *President*
Allan Weitzman, *Principal*
Greg Weitzman, *Principal*
Cary B Weitzman, *Vice Pres*
Tina Pierzynski, *Admin Sec*
▲ **EMP:** 18
SQ FT: 32,740
SALES (est): 10MM **Privately Held**
WEB: www.rivetnuts.com
SIC: 5072 3429 5085 Rivets; metal fasteners; abrasives & adhesives

(G-4902)
JUST JEWELERS
23105 Power Rd (48336-3185)
PHONE..................................248 476-9011
Bruce Campbell, *Owner*
EMP: 3
SQ FT: 625
SALES: 400K **Privately Held**
SIC: 3911 5944 Jewelry, precious metal; jewelry, precious stones & precious metals

(G-4903)
LIFT AID INC
33962 Moore Dr (48335-4151)
PHONE..................................248 345-5110
Guido Capaldi, *President*
EMP: 3
SALES (est): 236.6K **Privately Held**
SIC: 3842 8099 Technical aids for the handicapped; health & allied services

(G-4904)
MAHLE AFTERMARKET INC (DH)
23030 Mahle Dr (48335-2606)
PHONE..................................248 347-9700
Arnd Franz, *Ch of Bd*
Prof Dr LNG Heinz K Junker, *Chairman*
Ted Hughes, *Marketing Staff*

Farmington - Oakland County (G-4905)

GEOGRAPHIC SECTION

William O Foutch Jr, *Admin Sec*
▲ **EMP:** 196
SALES (est): 53.3MM
SALES (corp-wide): 504.6K **Privately Held**
SIC: 3714 Motor vehicle parts & accessories
HQ: Mahle Industries, Incorporated
  23030 Mahle Dr
  Farmington Hills MI 48335
  248 305-8200

(G-4905)
MOORE PRODUCTION TOOL SPC
Also Called: Moore Production Tool Spc
37531 Grand River Ave (48335-2879)
PHONE..................248 476-1200
Richard E Moore, *CEO*
Durk Moore, *President*
Jack Newcombe, *Treasurer*
EMP: 30
SQ FT: 40,000
SALES (est): 5MM **Privately Held**
SIC: 3541 3542 Machine tools, metal cutting type; machine tools, metal forming type

(G-4906)
PANNELL S-ERYNN
Also Called: Geeks Gmes Brains Stem Fun Ctr
31831 Grand River Ave (48336-4137)
PHONE..................248 692-3192
S Erynn Pannell, *Owner*
EMP: 3
SALES (est): 130K **Privately Held**
SIC: 7993 3944 Mechanical games, coin-operated; electronic games & toys

(G-4907)
PHOENIX IMAGING INC
36853 Heatherton Dr (48335-2925)
PHONE..................248 476-4578
Loren Krawec, *Manager*
EMP: 3 **Privately Held**
WEB: www.phoeniximaging.com
SIC: 3827 Optical test & inspection equipment
PA: Phoenix Imaging Inc
  29865 6 Mile Rd
  Livonia MI 48152

(G-4908)
PLUSKATE BOARDING COMPANY
33335 Grand River Ave (48336-3194)
PHONE..................248 426-0899
Robert Woelkers, *Principal*
EMP: 4
SALES (est): 450.1K **Privately Held**
SIC: 3949 Skateboards

(G-4909)
ROUSH ENTERPRISES INC (PA)
34300 W 9 Mile Rd (48335-4706)
PHONE..................734 805-4400
Evan Lyall, *CEO*
Geoffrey Smith, *President*
Jack Roush, *Chairman*
Doug Smith, *COO*
Andy Wozniacki, *CFO*
EMP: 125
SQ FT: 67,000
SALES (est): 428MM **Privately Held**
WEB: www.roushind.com
SIC: 8711 3714 7948 8734 Consulting engineer; motor vehicle engines & parts; race car owners; automobile proving & testing ground

(G-4910)
ROUSH MANUFACTURING INC
Also Called: Rouch Enterprises
34300 W 9 Mile Rd (48335-4706)
PHONE..................734 805-4400
Mark Slack, *Branch Mgr*
EMP: 70 **Privately Held**
SIC: 3714 Motor vehicle parts & accessories
HQ: Roush Manufacturing, Inc.
  12447 Levan Rd
  Livonia MI 48150
  734 779-7006

(G-4911)
SAM BROWN SALES LLC (DH)
Also Called: Hi-Tech Industries
33106 W 8 Mile Rd (48336-5400)
PHONE..................248 358-2626
Herschel S Wright, *President*
Hyman Brown, *Treasurer*
▲ **EMP:** 26
SQ FT: 44,000
SALES (est): 10.9MM
SALES (corp-wide): 180.7MM **Privately Held**
WEB: www.sambrownsales.com
SIC: 5087 5013 3714 3291 Carwash equipment & supplies; motor vehicle supplies & new parts; motor vehicle parts & accessories; abrasive products
HQ: Niteo Products, Llc
  5949 Sherry Ln Ste 540
  Dallas TX 75225
  214 245-5000

(G-4912)
SEIFERT CITY-WIDE PRINTING CO
30789 Shiawassee Rd # 12 (48336-4372)
PHONE..................248 477-9525
George Kourtakis, *President*
Demetrios Kourtakis, *Vice Pres*
Audrey Kourtakis, *Admin Sec*
EMP: 4
SQ FT: 10,000
SALES (est): 452.1K **Privately Held**
SIC: 2752 Commercial printing, offset

(G-4913)
SUPERFLY MANUFACTURING CO
31505 Grand River Ave 7c (48336-4231)
PHONE..................313 454-1492
Justin Draplin, *President*
▲ **EMP:** 10
SALES: 950K **Privately Held**
SIC: 2389 Apparel & accessories

(G-4914)
TEKSID INC (DH)
36524 Grand River Ave B-1 (48335-3011)
PHONE..................734 846-5897
Rogerio Silva, *President*
Colm Ohiggins, *CFO*
Karen McKinnon, *Admin Sec*
◆ **EMP:** 10
SQ FT: 7,400
SALES (est): 2.8MM
SALES (corp-wide): 126.4B **Privately Held**
SIC: 3714 3322 5051 Motor vehicle parts & accessories; malleable iron foundries; castings, rough: iron or steel
HQ: Teksid Spa
  Via Umberto Ii 5
  Carmagnola TO 10022
  011 979-4111

(G-4915)
WEATHER KING WINDOWS DOORS INC (PA)
Also Called: Weather King of Indiana
20775 Chesley Dr (48336-5111)
PHONE..................313 933-1234
William Earl King, *President*
Elizabeth Oliver, *Vice Pres*
Barry Breshgold, *Accounting Mgr*
Beth King, *Credit Mgr*
▲ **EMP:** 75
SQ FT: 90,215
SALES (est): 10.5MM **Privately Held**
WEB: www.weatherkingdoors.com
SIC: 3089 3442 Window frames & sash, plastic; storm doors or windows, metal; metal doors

(G-4916)
WEATHER KING WINDOWS DOORS INC
20775 Chesley Dr (48336-5111)
PHONE..................248 478-7788
George Apostol, *Manager*
EMP: 48
SQ FT: 46,300

SALES (corp-wide): 10.5MM **Privately Held**
WEB: www.weatherkingdoors.com
SIC: 3089 3442 Windows, plastic; boot or shoe products, plastic; storm doors or windows, metal; metal doors
PA: Weather King Windows And Doors, Inc.
  20775 Chesley Dr
  Farmington MI 48336
  313 933-1234

Farmington Hills
Oakland County

(G-4917)
ABB ENTERPRISE SOFTWARE INC
23629 Industrial Park Dr (48335-2857)
PHONE..................248 471-0888
Tom Wilson, *Branch Mgr*
EMP: 97
SALES (corp-wide): 36.4B **Privately Held**
WEB: www.elsterelectricity.com
SIC: 3823 Controllers for process variables, all types
HQ: Abb Inc.
  305 Gregson Dr
  Cary NC 27511

(G-4918)
ACCURATE MFG SOLUTIONS LLC
28232 Schroeder St (48331-3175)
PHONE..................248 553-2225
Philip Turner, *Principal*
EMP: 3
SALES (est): 227.7K **Privately Held**
SIC: 3999 Manufacturing industries

(G-4919)
ACE CONTROLS INC (DH)
23435 Industrial Park Dr (48335-2855)
PHONE..................248 476-0213
David Raguckas, *President*
Pete Satkowiak, *Safety Mgr*
Debbie Popp, *Purchasing*
Darryl Carlson, *QC Dir*
Robert Mitera, *QC Mgr*
◆ **EMP:** 150 **EST:** 1962
SQ FT: 85,000
SALES (est): 24.6MM
SALES (corp-wide): 428.8K **Privately Held**
WEB: www.acecontrols.com
SIC: 3594 3714 3593 3559 Fluid power pumps; motor vehicle engines & parts; fluid power cylinders, hydraulic or pneumatic; sewing machines & hat & zipper making machinery; anodizing equipment; fire- or burglary-resistive products; stabilizing bars (cargo), metal
HQ: Stabilus Gmbh
  Wallersheimer Weg 100
  Koblenz 56070
  261 890-00

(G-4920)
AEES INC (DH)
Also Called: Pkc Group
36555 Corp Dr Ste 300 (48331)
PHONE..................248 489-4700
Frank Sovis, *President*
Cortney Wilson, *Engineer*
Rico Mutone, *VP Sls/Mktg*
Sebastian Leung, *Program Mgr*
EMP: 277
SALES (est): 4.5B
SALES (corp-wide): 1B **Privately Held**
WEB: www.aeesinc.com
SIC: 3679 Electronic loads & power supplies
HQ: Pkc Group Usa Inc.
  36555 Corp Dr Ste 300
  Farmington Hills MI 48334
  248 489-4700

(G-4921)
AEES POWER SYSTEMS LTD PARTNR
Also Called: Engineered Plastic Components
36555 Corp Dr Ste 300 (48331)
PHONE..................269 668-4429
Chris Wooten, *Branch Mgr*

EMP: 14
SALES (corp-wide): 1B **Privately Held**
SIC: 3089 3841 3694 3678 Injection molding of plastics; injection molded finished plastic products; automotive parts, plastic; surgical & medical instruments; engine electrical equipment; electronic connectors; current-carrying wiring devices
HQ: Aees Power Systems Limited Partnership
  999 Republic Dr
  Allen Park MI 48101
  248 489-4900

(G-4922)
AGELESSMAGE FCIAL ASTHTICS LLC
28499 Orchard Lake Rd (48334-3702)
PHONE..................269 998-5547
McKenzie Zientek,
EMP: 3 **EST:** 2012
SALES (est): 146.9K **Privately Held**
SIC: 3842 Cosmetic restorations

(G-4923)
AGM AUTOMOTIVE LLC (HQ)
27755 Stansbury Blvd # 300 (48334-3837)
PHONE..................248 776-0600
Robert M Blinstrub, *President*
Richard Cook, *General Mgr*
Scott Smith, *COO*
Robert Grananta, *Exec VP*
Venkat Koneru, *Buyer*
▲ **EMP:** 90
SQ FT: 45,000
SALES (est): 45.1MM
SALES (corp-wide): 26.2B **Privately Held**
WEB: www.agmautomotive.com
SIC: 2399 3357 2396 Automotive covers, except seat & tire covers; automotive wire & cable, except ignition sets: nonferrous; automotive trimmings, fabric
PA: Flex Ltd.
  2 Changi South Lane
  Singapore 48612
  629 988-88

(G-4924)
AGM AUTOMOTIVE MEXICO LLC (DH)
27755 Stansbury Blvd # 300 (48334-3837)
PHONE..................248 925-4152
Chris O'Connell, *Mng Member*
EMP: 6 **EST:** 2015
SALES (est): 3.5MM
SALES (corp-wide): 26.2B **Privately Held**
SIC: 3714 Motor vehicle parts & accessories
HQ: Agm Automotive, Llc
  27755 Stansbury Blvd # 300
  Farmington Hills MI 48334
  248 776-0600

(G-4925)
AKEBONO BRAKE CORPORATION (HQ)
34385 W 12 Mile Rd (48331-3375)
PHONE..................248 489-7400
Wilm Uhlenbecker, *President*
William Gleeson, *Treasurer*
Brandon Kessinger, *Admin Sec*
◆ **EMP:** 123
SQ FT: 12,000
SALES (est): 847.4MM **Privately Held**
WEB: www.akebonobrake.net
SIC: 3714 Air brakes, motor vehicle

(G-4926)
AKWEL CADILLAC USA INC
Also Called: Detroit Sls & Engrg Ctr Div of
39205 Country Clb Ste C16 (48331-3497)
PHONE..................248 848-9599
Birgig Villeminey, *Branch Mgr*
EMP: 40 **Privately Held**
WEB: www.avonauto.com
SIC: 3089 3052 Battery cases, plastic or plastic combination; rubber & plastics hose & beltings
HQ: Akwel Cadillac Usa, Inc
  603 7th St
  Cadillac MI 49601
  231 876-8020

GEOGRAPHIC SECTION
Farmington Hills - Oakland County (G-4954)

(G-4927)
ALCOA AUTOMOTIVE- INDIANA (HQ)
37000 W 12 Mile Rd # 115 (48331-3055)
PHONE..................................248 489-4900
Jacques Vanier, *President*
Joe Kerkhove, *President*
Graeme Bottger, *Vice Pres*
John Kenna, *Vice Pres*
Sue Zemba, *Vice Pres*
▲ **EMP**: 370
SQ FT: 150,000
SALES (est): 26.4MM
SALES (corp-wide): 14B **Publicly Held**
SIC: 3353 Aluminum sheet, plate & foil
PA: Arconic Inc.
  201 Isabella St Ste 200
  New York NY 15212
  412 553-1950

(G-4928)
ALLGRAPHICS CORP
28960 E King William Dr (48331-2578)
PHONE..................................248 994-7373
Frank Alspector, *President*
EMP: 4
SQ FT: 3,000
SALES (est): 396.8K **Privately Held**
SIC: 2261 2759 Screen printing of cotton broadwoven fabrics; screen printing

(G-4929)
AMERICAN LASER CENTERS LLC
24555 Hallwood Ct (48335-1667)
PHONE..................................248 426-8250
Gregory Segall, *President*
EMP: 1529
SALES (est): 355.8K
SALES (corp-wide): 868MM **Privately Held**
SIC: 3999 3841 Hair & hair-based products; skin grafting equipment; cannulae
PA: Versa Capital Management, Llc
  2929 Arch St Ste 1650
  Philadelphia PA 19104
  215 609-3400

(G-4930)
AMERICAN SILK SCREEN & EMB
Also Called: Sportcap
24601 Hallwood Ct (48335-1604)
PHONE..................................248 474-1000
Michael R Lamb, *President*
Diana Lamb, *Vice Pres*
Todd Lamb, *Vice Pres*
EMP: 30
SQ FT: 42,000
SALES (est): 3.2MM **Privately Held**
WEB: www.theathleticsupporterltd.com
SIC: 2396 5136 5137 Screen printing on fabric articles; sportswear, men's & boys'; sportswear, women's & children's

(G-4931)
AMERICAN STANDARD WINDOWS
30281 Pipers Ln (48334-4731)
PHONE..................................734 788-2261
Martin Szelag, *President*
EMP: 12
SQ FT: 24,000
SALES (est): 1.5MM **Privately Held**
SIC: 3089 Windows, plastic

(G-4932)
ARCONIC INC
Also Called: Alcoa
37000 W 12 Mile Rd # 115 (48331-3032)
PHONE..................................248 489-4900
Misha Pesic, *Engineer*
Cynthia Birk, *Sales Associate*
Michel Murphy, *Branch Mgr*
John Blazevski, *Manager*
Brandon Landino, *Technical Staff*
EMP: 45
SALES (corp-wide): 14B **Publicly Held**
SIC: 3354 Aluminum extruded products
PA: Arconic Inc.
  201 Isabella St Ste 200
  New York NY 15212
  412 553-1950

(G-4933)
ASCO POWER TECHNOLOGIES LP
27280 Haggerty Rd C-16 (48331-5711)
PHONE..................................248 957-9050
Kevin Chmielewskri, *Manager*
EMP: 7
SALES (corp-wide): 177.9K **Privately Held**
SIC: 3699 Electrical equipment & supplies
HQ: Asco Power Technologies, L.P.
  160 Park Ave
  Florham Park NJ 07932

(G-4934)
ASW AMERCA INC
24762 Crestview Ct (48335-1506)
PHONE..................................248 957-9638
Markus Weber, *President*
Severin Beck, *Manager*
EMP: 4
SALES (est): 564K **Privately Held**
SIC: 3569 5962 Assembly machines, non-metalworking; merchandising machine operators

(G-4935)
ATLAS THREAD GAGE INC
30990 W 8 Mile Rd (48336-5323)
PHONE..................................248 477-3230
Doug Hamer, *President*
Cary Hamer, *Vice Pres*
Nancy Hamer, *Treasurer*
EMP: 9
SQ FT: 4,000
SALES (est): 1.1MM **Privately Held**
WEB: www.atlasthreadgage.com
SIC: 3545 Machine tool accessories

(G-4936)
AUTONEUM NORTH AMERICA INC
38555 Hills Tech Dr (48331-3423)
PHONE..................................248 848-0100
Bob Hornbuckle, *Branch Mgr*
EMP: 80
SALES (corp-wide): 2.3B **Privately Held**
WEB: www.rieter.com
SIC: 8748 3489 3296 Business consulting; ordnance & accessories; mineral wool
HQ: Autoneum North America, Inc.
  29293 Haggerty Rd
  Novi MI 48377
  248 848-0100

(G-4937)
AUTOWARES INC
23240 Industrial Park Dr (48335-2850)
PHONE..................................248 473-0928
EMP: 4
SALES (est): 298.9K **Privately Held**
SIC: 3465 Mfg Automotive Stampings

(G-4938)
AVANZADO LLC
25330 Interchange Ct (48335-1022)
P.O. Box 3435 (48333-3435)
PHONE..................................248 615-0538
Craig Frye, *CEO*
Leocadio J Padilla, *Ch of Bd*
Cathy Ferrel, *Exec VP*
Peter Ransome, *Exec VP*
Gregg Gabbana, *Vice Pres*
▲ **EMP**: 39
SQ FT: 28,000
SALES (est): 7.6MM **Privately Held**
SIC: 2752 Promotional printing, lithographic; color lithography

(G-4939)
AVIV GLOBAL LLC
32430 Northwestern Hwy (48334-1400)
PHONE..................................248 737-5777
Christopher Edwards, *Manager*
▲ **EMP**: 4
SALES (est): 295.2K **Privately Held**
SIC: 3431 Bathroom fixtures, including sinks

(G-4940)
BEHCO INC
32613 Folsom Rd (48336-4424)
PHONE..................................248 478-6336
Claudia Brady, *Principal*
EMP: 3
SALES (est): 118.7K **Privately Held**
SIC: 3511 Turbines & turbine generator sets

(G-4941)
BIRDSALL TOOL & GAGE CO
24735 Crestview Ct (48335-1507)
PHONE..................................248 474-5150
David Birdsall, *President*
Kurt Baron, *Treasurer*
Marge Goward, *Controller*
John Robson, *Sales Staff*
▼ **EMP**: 30
SQ FT: 13,700
SALES (est): 3.1MM **Privately Held**
WEB: www.birdsalltool.com
SIC: 3674 3542 Strain gages, solid state; machine tools, metal forming type

(G-4942)
BLANCO CANVAS COMPANY INC
23857 Industrial Park Dr (48335-2860)
PHONE..................................313 963-7787
Noel Scicluna, *President*
EMP: 3
SALES (est): 275K **Privately Held**
SIC: 2394 Canvas & related products

(G-4943)
BLUEWATER TECH GROUP INC
37900 Interchange Dr (48335-1034)
PHONE..................................248 356-4399
EMP: 4
SALES (corp-wide): 35.9MM **Privately Held**
SIC: 3669 3651 Visual communication systems; audio electronic systems
PA: Bluewater Technologies Group, Inc.
  24050 Northwestern Hwy
  Southfield MI 48075
  248 356-4399

(G-4944)
BMC SOFTWARE INC
27555 Executive Dr # 155 (48331-3568)
PHONE..................................248 888-4600
EMP: 11
SALES (corp-wide): 1.3B **Privately Held**
SIC: 7372 Prepackaged Software Services
HQ: Bmc Software, Inc.
  2103 Citywest Blvd # 2100
  Houston TX 77042
  713 918-8800

(G-4945)
BODY CONTOUR VENTURES LLC
Also Called: Light-Rx
34405 W 12 Mile Rd # 200 (48331-3391)
PHONE..................................248 579-6772
Richard C Morgan,
EMP: 5 **EST**: 2014
SALES (est): 223K **Privately Held**
SIC: 7991 3999 Spas; massage machines, electric: barber & beauty shops

(G-4946)
BRATTEN ENTERPRISES INC (PA)
Also Called: Hydromation Company
23900 Haggerty Rd (48335-2618)
PHONE..................................248 427-9090
Jack R Bratten, *President*
▲ **EMP**: 60 **EST**: 1979
SALES (est): 34.4MM **Privately Held**
WEB: www.filtrasystems.com
SIC: 3569 Filters

(G-4947)
BROTHERS INDUSTRIALS INC
38844 Steeple Chase # 27101 (48331-4935)
PHONE..................................248 794-5080
Atheer Ibrahim, *Principal*
▲ **EMP**: 3
SALES (est): 291.2K **Privately Held**
SIC: 3559 Special industry machinery

(G-4948)
BRUCE KANE ENTERPRISES LLC (PA)
Also Called: Passport Health of Michigan
28200 Orchard Lake Rd # 107 (48334-3761)
PHONE..................................410 727-0637
Kristy Robison, *Project Mgr*
Robert Rader, *Executive*
Bruce Kane,
EMP: 6
SALES (est): 608.2K **Privately Held**
SIC: 2836 Vaccines & other immunizing products

(G-4949)
BURST LED
29412 Windmill Ct (48334-3110)
PHONE..................................248 321-6262
Gary Gozmamian, *Manager*
EMP: 4 **EST**: 2016
SALES (est): 339.5K **Privately Held**
SIC: 3646 Commercial indusl & institutional electric lighting fixtures

(G-4950)
BWB LLC
Also Called: Cornillie Concrete
33469 W 14 Mile Rd (48331-1521)
P.O. Box 2900 (48333-2900)
PHONE..................................231 439-9200
Nathan Sommer, *Principal*
Karen Giles, *Corp Secy*
EMP: 70
SALES: 950K **Privately Held**
SIC: 3273 Ready-mixed concrete

(G-4951)
C L DESIGN INC
Also Called: Craig EDM
20739 Sunnydale St (48336-5254)
PHONE..................................248 474-4220
Marc J Craig, *President*
EMP: 4
SQ FT: 6,400
SALES (est): 540.8K **Privately Held**
SIC: 3613 3599 Control panels, electric; electrical discharge machining (EDM)

(G-4952)
C S M MANUFACTURING CORP (PA)
Also Called: CSM Cold Heading
24650 N Industrial Dr (48335-1553)
PHONE..................................248 471-0700
William A Fleury, *President*
Gail A Fleury, *Vice Pres*
EMP: 80
SALES (est): 23.3MM **Privately Held**
WEB: www.csm-mfg.com
SIC: 3451 3599 Screw machine products; machine shop, jobbing & repair

(G-4953)
CADFEM AMERICAS INC
27600 Farmington Rd # 209 (48334-3348)
PHONE..................................248 919-8410
Massood Omrani, *CEO*
EMP: 3
SALES (est): 78.2K **Privately Held**
SIC: 7372 Prepackaged software

(G-4954)
CAMACO LLC (HQ)
37000 W 12 Mile Rd # 105 (48331-3055)
PHONE..................................248 442-6800
Arvind Pradhan, *CEO*
Daphne Nelson, *Buyer*
Sanjay Vakil, *Chief Engr*
Delano Farmer, *Engineer*
David Williams, *Engineer*
▲ **EMP**: 25 **EST**: 1998
SQ FT: 5,000
SALES (est): 267.5MM
SALES (corp-wide): 549.3MM **Privately Held**
WEB: www.camaco.com
SIC: 3565 3499 Packaging machinery; automobile seat frames, metal
PA: P & C Group I, Inc.
  37000 W 12 Mile Rd
  Farmington Hills MI 48331
  248 442-6800

Farmington Hills - Oakland County (G-4955)

(G-4955)
CAPITAL BILLING SYSTEMS INC
33533 W 12 Mile Rd # 131 (48331-5634)
PHONE.....................248 478-7298
Diane Amendt, *President*
EMP: 7
SALES (est): 425K **Privately Held**
SIC: 7372 Prepackaged software

(G-4956)
CAPITAL STAMPING & MACHINE INC (PA)
24650 N Industrial Dr (48335-1553)
PHONE.....................248 471-0700
William A Fleury, *President*
Gail A Fleury, *Admin Sec*
EMP: 42
SQ FT: 35,000
SALES (est): 6.4MM **Privately Held**
WEB: www.csm-group.net
SIC: 3465 Automotive stampings

(G-4957)
CARLESIMO PRODUCTS INC
29800 W 8 Mile Rd (48336-5506)
PHONE.....................248 474-0415
John Carlesimo, *President*
Elizabeth Carlesimo, *Vice Pres*
EMP: 28 **EST:** 1923
SQ FT: 3,200
SALES (est): 4.7MM **Privately Held**
SIC: 3272 3271 Pipe, concrete or lined with concrete; manhole covers or frames, concrete; concrete block & brick

(G-4958)
CARRIER & GABLE INC (PA)
24110 Research Dr (48335-2633)
PHONE.....................248 477-8700
Dan Carrier, *President*
Gerald W Carrier, *Chairman*
Sally Carrier, *Vice Pres*
Geri M Schmidt, *Vice Pres*
Tim Dewitt, *Treasurer*
EMP: 30
SQ FT: 16,000
SALES: 10.4MM **Privately Held**
WEB: www.carriergable.com
SIC: 5063 5099 3993 Signaling equipment, electrical; reflective road markers; signs & advertising specialties

(G-4959)
CASPER CORPORATION
24081 Research Dr (48335-2632)
PHONE.....................248 442-9000
Jim Casper Jr, *President*
EMP: 12
SALES (corp-wide): 5.2MM **Privately Held**
WEB: www.caspercorp.com
SIC: 2542 Shelving, office & store: except wood
PA: The Casper Corporation
24081 Research Dr
Farmington Hills MI
248 442-9000

(G-4960)
CG & D GROUP
Also Called: CG&d Consulting
23700 Paddock Dr (48336-2226)
PHONE.....................248 310-9166
Cheryl Glenn, *President*
EMP: 3
SALES (est): 114K **Privately Held**
SIC: 8748 8742 3465 3069 Business consulting; management consulting services; automotive stampings; reclaimed rubber (reworked by manufacturing processes)

(G-4961)
CHAMPION TOOL COMPANY
24060 Orchard Lake Rd (48336-2554)
PHONE.....................248 474-6200
Ann M Cline, *President*
William Cline, *Vice Pres*
Marcia D Cline, *Treasurer*
EMP: 7 **EST:** 1950
SQ FT: 2,400
SALES (est): 879.1K **Privately Held**
SIC: 3545 Cutting tools for machine tools

(G-4962)
CHASSIS BRAKES INTL USA (PA)
27260 Haggerty Rd Ste A8 (48331-3400)
PHONE.....................248 957-9997
Dennis Berry, *President*
EMP: 9
SALES: 4.8MM **Privately Held**
SIC: 3714 Motor vehicle brake systems & parts

(G-4963)
CINCINNATI TIME SYSTEMS INC
23399 Commerce Dr Ste B3 (48335-2763)
PHONE.....................248 615-8300
Mark Dykstra, *President*
EMP: 15
SQ FT: 6,400
SALES (est): 4.3MM **Privately Held**
WEB: www.cintimesys.com
SIC: 5065 5072 7521 3559 Communication equipment; security control equipment & systems; security devices, locks; automobile parking; parking facility equipment & supplies

(G-4964)
COCA-COLA REFRESHMENTS USA INC
26777 Halsted Rd (48331-3577)
PHONE.....................313 897-5000
Stephen Orselli, *Branch Mgr*
EMP: 200
SALES (corp-wide): 31.8B **Publicly Held**
WEB: www.cokecce.com
SIC: 2086 Bottled & canned soft drinks
HQ: Coca-Cola Refreshments Usa, Inc.
2500 Windy Ridge Pkwy Se
Atlanta GA 30339
770 989-3000

(G-4965)
COMPTEK INC
37450 Enterprise Ct (48331-3437)
PHONE.....................248 477-5215
Richard B Gentry, *President*
William Wisniewski, *VP Sales*
EMP: 12
SQ FT: 15,000
SALES: 1.3MM **Privately Held**
SIC: 7373 3699 3625 3577 Turnkey vendors, computer systems; electrical equipment & supplies; relays & industrial controls; computer peripheral equipment

(G-4966)
CONTEMPORARY INDUSTRIES INC (PA)
24025 Research Dr (48335-2632)
PHONE.....................248 478-8850
Michael Wilczewski, *President*
Josh Pawlovich, *General Mgr*
Leslie Wilczewski, *Vice Pres*
EMP: 7
SQ FT: 3,200
SALES (est): 1.2MM **Privately Held**
SIC: 3499 8742 Trophies, metal, except silver; marketing consulting services

(G-4967)
COVENANT CPITL INVESTMENTS INC
Also Called: CCI Companies
24772 Crestview Ct (48335-1506)
PHONE.....................248 477-4230
David Setsuda, *President*
EMP: 10
SQ FT: 14,000
SALES (est): 1.2MM **Privately Held**
SIC: 3469 8741 5085 Machine parts, stamped or pressed metal; management services; industrial supplies

(G-4968)
DAL-TILE CORPORATION
24640 Drake Rd (48335-2504)
PHONE.....................248 471-7150
Jeff Glazier, *Manager*
EMP: 10
SQ FT: 1,500
SALES (corp-wide): 9.9B **Publicly Held**
WEB: www.mohawk.com
SIC: 2824 5032 Organic fibers, noncellulosic; ceramic wall & floor tile
HQ: Dal-Tile Corporation
7834 C F Hawn Fwy
Dallas TX 75217
214 398-1411

(G-4969)
DAMM COMPANY INC
24061 Research Dr (48335-2632)
PHONE.....................248 427-9060
Dan Damm, *President*
EMP: 3
SALES (est): 352.5K **Privately Held**
SIC: 3599 Electrical discharge machining (EDM); machine shop, jobbing & repair

(G-4970)
DEFENSE COMPONENTS AMERICA LLC
30955 Northwestern Hwy (48334-2580)
PHONE.....................248 789-1578
James Carlton, *President*
EMP: 6
SALES (est): 231.7K **Privately Held**
SIC: 3599 Machine shop, jobbing & repair

(G-4971)
DIAMOND MOBA AMERICAS INC
Also Called: Diamond Systems
23400 Haggerty Rd (48335-2613)
PHONE.....................248 476-7100
Richard Litman, *Vice Pres*
Bianca Stoner, *Buyer*
Lori Hass, *Purchasing*
Cort Murdock, *Engineer*
Jeff Day, *CFO*
◆ **EMP:** 135
SQ FT: 150,000
SALES: 39.4MM
SALES (corp-wide): 1.7MM **Privately Held**
WEB: www.diamondsystem.com
SIC: 3523 Farm machinery & equipment
HQ: Moba Group B.V.
Stationsweg 117
Barneveld 3771
342 455-655

(G-4972)
DIFFERENT BY DESIGN INC
38611 Cedarbrook Ct (48331-2919)
PHONE.....................248 588-4840
Yvette M Mortz, *President*
EMP: 22
SALES (est): 2MM **Privately Held**
SIC: 2791 7336 Typesetting; graphic arts & related design

(G-4973)
DIGESTED ORGANICS LLC
23745 Research Dr (48335-2625)
P.O. Box 3386, Ann Arbor (48106-3386)
PHONE.....................844 934-4378
Robert Levine, *CEO*
Ian Charles, *Ch of Bd*
Chris Maloney, *COO*
EMP: 3
SALES (est): 180.9K **Privately Held**
SIC: 1629 3589 Waste water & sewage treatment plant construction; water treatment equipment, industrial

(G-4974)
DMG DUMPSTERS INC
21339 Orchard Lake Rd (48336-4730)
PHONE.....................313 610-3476
Richard Tobacco, *Principal*
EMP: 3
SALES (est): 163.7K **Privately Held**
SIC: 3443 Dumpsters, garbage

(G-4975)
DOLPHIN DUMPSTERS LLC
30650 River Gln (48336-4739)
PHONE.....................734 272-8981
Douglas Wischmeyer, *Principal*
EMP: 3
SALES (est): 205.3K **Privately Held**
SIC: 3443 Dumpsters, garbage

(G-4976)
DYNAMIC COLOR PUBLICATIONS
Also Called: Real Estate Book
32905 W 12 Mile Rd # 210 (48334-3344)
PHONE.....................248 553-3115
Tom Hartman, *President*
Tobie Hartman, *Admin Sec*
EMP: 5
SALES (est): 390K **Privately Held**
SIC: 2721 Periodicals: publishing only

(G-4977)
E Z LOGIC DATA SYSTEMS INC
Also Called: EZ Logic
31455 Northwestern Hwy (48334-2574)
PHONE.....................248 817-8800
Ali Koumaiha, *President*
Omar Azrag, *COO*
EMP: 30
SALES: 2MM **Privately Held**
SIC: 7371 7372 Computer software systems analysis & design, custom; computer software development & applications; application computer software; business oriented computer software

(G-4978)
EGR INCORPORATED
27280 Haggerty Rd C-18 (48331-5711)
PHONE.....................248 848-1411
John Whitten, *Manager*
EMP: 5 **Privately Held**
SIC: 3714 Motor vehicle parts & accessories
HQ: Egr, Incorporated
4000 Greystone Dr
Ontario CA 91761

(G-4979)
ELECTRO-MATIC INTEGRATED INC
23410 Industrial Park Ct (48335-2848)
PHONE.....................248 478-1182
Mario Barraco, *President*
▲ **EMP:** 4
SQ FT: 23,180
SALES (est): 528.9K **Privately Held**
SIC: 3679 Harness assemblies for electronic use: wire or cable

(G-4980)
ELECTRO-MATIC PRODUCTS INC (HQ)
Also Called: Electro-Matic Company
23409 Industrial Park Ct (48335-2849)
PHONE.....................248 478-1182
Richar Laramee, *President*
Derek Klanke, *Accounts Mgr*
Scott Nuyttens, *Accounts Mgr*
Greg Toennies, *Accounts Mgr*
Mark Hayman, *Sales Staff*
EMP: 1
SALES (est): 5.1MM
SALES (corp-wide): 136.8MM **Privately Held**
SIC: 3694 5063 Distributors, motor vehicle engine; electrical apparatus & equipment
PA: Electro-Matic Ventures, Inc.
23409 Industrial Park Ct
Farmington Hills MI 48335
248 478-1182

(G-4981)
ELECTRO-MATIC VENTURES INC (PA)
Also Called: Electro-Matic, Inc.
23409 Industrial Park Ct (48335-2849)
PHONE.....................248 478-1182
James C Baker Jr, *President*
David Scaglione, *Treasurer*
Richard Laramee, *Admin Sec*
▲ **EMP:** 100
SQ FT: 42,000
SALES: 136.8MM **Privately Held**
WEB: www.electro-matic.com
SIC: 5063 3674 Electrical supplies; semiconductors & related devices

(G-4982)
ELECTRO-MATIC VISUAL INC
23409 Industrial Park Ct (48335-2849)
PHONE.....................248 478-1182
Jim Baker, *CEO*

Rich Laramee, *President*
EMP: 6
SALES (est): 534.5K **Privately Held**
SIC: 3699 Cleaning equipment, ultrasonic, except medical & dental

(G-4983)
EMAG LLC (DH)
38800 Grand River Ave (48335-1526)
PHONE..................248 477-7440
M Hessbrueggen,
▲ **EMP:** 48
SQ FT: 46,000
SALES (est): 10.1MM
SALES (corp-wide): 770.3MM **Privately Held**
WEB: www.emag-usa.com
SIC: 3541 3999 Grinding machines, metalworking; atomizers, toiletry
HQ: Emag Systems Gmbh
 Austr. 24
 Salach 73084
 716 217-0

(G-4984)
EMC CORPORATION
36555 Corporate Dr # 200 (48331-3567)
PHONE..................248 957-5800
Richard Milton, *Engineer*
Tony McCoy, *Branch Mgr*
Glenn Graber, *Director*
Sajan Sadanandan, *Sr Consultant*
EMP: 245
SALES (corp-wide): 90.6B **Publicly Held**
WEB: www.emc.com
SIC: 3572 7372 Computer storage devices; prepackaged software
HQ: Emc Corporation
 176 South St
 Hopkinton MA 01748
 508 435-1000

(G-4985)
EMM INC
23409 Industrial Park Ct (48335-2849)
PHONE..................248 478-1182
James C Baker Jr, *President*
Raymond J Persia, *Founder*
Robert Waldie, *Vice Pres*
Thomas C Moore, *Treasurer*
EMP: 9
SQ FT: 42,000
SALES (est): 1.3MM **Privately Held**
SIC: 3643 Connectors & terminals for electrical devices

(G-4986)
ENCORE COMMERCIAL PRODUCTS INC
Also Called: Postguard
37525 Interchange Dr (48335-1027)
PHONE..................248 354-4090
Bruce Liebowitz, *President*
Stuart Bernstein, *Vice Pres*
Ronald Klein, *Vice Pres*
▲ **EMP:** 12
SQ FT: 2,500
SALES (est): 2.9MM **Privately Held**
WEB: www.postguard.com
SIC: 3081 Unsupported plastics film & sheet

(G-4987)
ENCORE IMPRESSION LLC
20774 Orchard Lake Rd (48336-5221)
PHONE..................248 478-1221
Christine Cuthbert,
EMP: 3 EST: 2008
SQ FT: 2,500
SALES (est): 291.3K **Privately Held**
SIC: 2752 Commercial printing, offset

(G-4988)
ENERTROLS INC
Also Called: Boretti Div
23435 Industrial Park Dr (48335-2855)
PHONE..................734 595-4500
EMP: 40 EST: 1974
SQ FT: 10,000
SALES: 4MM **Privately Held**
SIC: 3714 Mfg Industrial Shock Absorbers

(G-4989)
ERAE AMS USA LLC
27150 Hills Tech Ct (48331-5724)
PHONE..................419 386-8876

James Kim, *President*
EMP: 17
SALES (est): 717.2K **Privately Held**
SIC: 3559 Automotive related machinery

(G-4990)
ETERNAL IMAGE INC
28800 Orchard Lake Rd (48334-2981)
PHONE..................248 932-3333
Clint Mytych, *CEO*
Donna Shatter, *Treasurer*
Wallace Popravsky, *VP Sales*
EMP: 3
SQ FT: 2,000
SALES (est): 347.4K **Privately Held**
WEB: www.eternalimage.net
SIC: 3281 3995 Urns, cut stone; burial vaults, fiberglass

(G-4991)
ETERON INC
23944 Freeway Park Dr (48335-2816)
PHONE..................248 478-2900
John C Kim II, *President*
EMP: 25
SALES (est): 6.4MM **Privately Held**
WEB: www.eteroninc.com
SIC: 2655 Drums, fiber: made from purchased material

(G-4992)
EUKO DESIGN-SIGNS INC
Also Called: Euko Signs
24849 Hathaway St (48335-1552)
PHONE..................248 478-1330
Eugene Diachenko, *President*
Andrea Diachenko, *Vice Pres*
EMP: 4
SQ FT: 4,500
SALES (est): 599.9K **Privately Held**
SIC: 3993 Electric signs; neon signs; advertising artwork

(G-4993)
EVEREST MANUFACTURING INC
23800 Research Dr (48335-2627)
P.O. Box 51951, Livonia (48151-5951)
PHONE..................313 401-2608
Mark Hendrickson, *President*
Mike Miller, *Vice Pres*
Steve Miller, *Treasurer*
Dave Morehead, *Sales Staff*
EMP: 12 EST: 2009
SALES: 1.2MM **Privately Held**
SIC: 2679 3086 Building, insulating & packaging paper; insulation or cushioning material, foamed plastic

(G-4994)
EVERLAST CONCRETE TECH LLC
31876 Northwestern Hwy (48334-1628)
PHONE..................248 894-1900
Anil Sanne,
EMP: 5
SALES: 1MM **Privately Held**
SIC: 3272 Building materials, except block or brick: concrete

(G-4995)
EVIEW 360 CORP
39255 Country Club Dr B1 (48331-3486)
PHONE..................248 306-5191
Wael Berrached, *CEO*
Pete Saules, *Program Mgr*
Anas Jame, *Software Dev*
EMP: 34
SQ FT: 2,000
SALES (est): 3.6MM **Privately Held**
SIC: 7372 7374 Application computer software; computer graphics service

(G-4996)
EXOTIC RUBBER & PLASTICS CORP (PA)
Also Called: Exotic Automation & Supply
34700 Grand River Ave (48335-3375)
PHONE..................248 477-2122
Thomas M Marino, *CEO*
Steve Orlando, *Vice Pres*
Kari Ryan, *Buyer*
Russell D Smaston, *CFO*
Justin Connor, *Accountant*
EMP: 100 EST: 1962

SQ FT: 85,000
SALES (est): 48.2MM **Privately Held**
WEB: www.erpc.com
SIC: 3089 3069 5085 5162 Injection molded finished plastic products; molded rubber products; hose, belting & packing; industrial fittings; plastics sheets & rods; rubber, crude; synthetic rubber

(G-4997)
FASTSIGNS
27853 Orchard Lake Rd (48334-3732)
PHONE..................248 488-9010
Gregory C Woelfel, *President*
Sue Woelfel, *Treasurer*
EMP: 7
SQ FT: 1,800
SALES (est): 800K **Privately Held**
SIC: 3993 Signs & advertising specialties

(G-4998)
FEDEX OFFICE & PRINT SVCS INC
29306 Orchard Lake Rd (48334-2967)
PHONE..................248 932-3373
Carrie Mudge, *Supervisor*
EMP: 15
SALES (corp-wide): 69.6B **Publicly Held**
WEB: www.kinkos.com
SIC: 7334 2791 2789 2759 Photocopying & duplicating services; typesetting; bookbinding & related work; commercial printing
HQ: Fedex Office And Print Services, Inc.
 7900 Legacy Dr
 Plano TX 75024
 800 463-3339

(G-4999)
FENDT BUILDERS SUPPLY INC (PA)
22005 Gill Rd (48335-4646)
P.O. Box 418 (48332-0418)
PHONE..................248 474-3211
Alan D Fendt, *President*
Junior L Fendt, *Chairman*
Bill Killen, *Sales Staff*
Ron Haller, *Manager*
Sharon Fendt, *Admin Sec*
EMP: 35
SQ FT: 42,000
SALES (est): 13.1MM **Privately Held**
WEB: www.fendtproducts.com
SIC: 5211 3271 3272 2951 Masonry materials & supplies; blocks, concrete or cinder: standard; paving blocks, concrete; blocks, concrete: landscape or retaining wall; concrete products; asphalt paving mixtures & blocks

(G-5000)
FIAMM TECHNOLOGIES LLC (HQ)
23880 Industrial Park Dr (48335-2871)
PHONE..................248 427-3200
John Defrances, *CEO*
Steve Lee, *Director*
Benjamin Beale,
◆ **EMP:** 175
SQ FT: 80,000
SALES (est): 50.3MM
SALES (corp-wide): 1.3MM **Privately Held**
SIC: 3714 Horns, motor vehicle
PA: Elettra 1938 Spa
 Galleria Del Pozzo Rosso 13
 Vicenza VI 36100
 044 423-3711

(G-5001)
FILTRA-SYSTEMS COMPANY LLC (PA)
23900 Haggerty Rd (48335-2618)
PHONE..................248 427-9090
Scott Bratten, *CEO*
Logan Wright, *Project Mgr*
Jamae Johnson, *Administration*
EMP: 14 EST: 2016
SALES (est): 16.9MM **Privately Held**
SIC: 3569 Filters

(G-5002)
FIVES CINETIC CORP (DH)
23400 Halsted Rd (48335-2840)
PHONE..................248 477-0800

Michael Dimichele, *President*
Barry Hawkins, *Purchasing*
Jeffrey Ritz, *Admin Sec*
Kenn Wyrobek,
EMP: 61
SALES (est): 32.9MM
SALES (corp-wide): 871.2K **Privately Held**
SIC: 3549 Assembly machines, including robotic
HQ: Fives Inc.
 23400 Halsted Rd
 Farmington Hills MI 48335
 248 477-0800

(G-5003)
FLEXI DISPLAY MARKETING INC
Also Called: Awarenessideas.com
34119 W 12 Mile Rd # 203 (48331-3300)
PHONE..................800 875-1725
Marvin Weisenthal, *President*
◆ **EMP:** 6
SQ FT: 7,600
SALES: 800K **Privately Held**
WEB: www.flexidisplay.com
SIC: 3999 Advertising display products

(G-5004)
FORGE DIE & TOOL CORP
31800 W 8 Mile Rd (48336-5210)
PHONE..................248 477-0020
Eric Kchikian, *President*
Van Kchikian, *President*
EMP: 45 EST: 1968
SQ FT: 35,000
SALES (est): 7.9MM **Privately Held**
WEB: www.forgeprecision.com
SIC: 3544 Dies & die holders for metal cutting, forming, die casting; special dies & tools

(G-5005)
FORGE PRECISION COMPANY
31800 W 8 Mile Rd (48336-5210)
PHONE..................248 477-0020
Van Kchikian, *President*
Eric Kchikian, *Treasurer*
EMP: 30
SQ FT: 20,000
SALES (est): 3.9MM **Privately Held**
SIC: 3599 Machine shop, jobbing & repair

(G-5006)
FUJIKURA AUTOMOTIVE AMER LLC (DH)
Also Called: F A A
27555 Executive Dr # 150 (48331-3554)
PHONE..................248 957-0130
Marina Gray, *Buyer*
Rose Goll, *Design Engr*
Justin Schemanske, *Accounts Mgr*
Kirk McCardell, *Mng Member*
▲ **EMP:** 20
SQ FT: 5,100
SALES (est): 13MM **Privately Held**
SIC: 3714 Motor vehicle parts & accessories
HQ: America Fujikura Ltd
 170 Ridgeview Cir
 Duncan SC 29334
 800 235-3423

(G-5007)
GABRIEL RIDE CONTROL LLC
39300 Country Club Dr (48331-3473)
PHONE..................248 247-7600
Lisa Bahash,
EMP: 65
SALES (est): 6.5MM **Privately Held**
SIC: 3714 Motor vehicle parts & accessories
HQ: Ride Control, Llc
 39300 Country Club Dr
 Farmington Hills MI 48331
 248 247-7600

(G-5008)
GEHRING CORPORATION
24800 Drake Rd (48335-2506)
PHONE..................248 478-8060
Robert Van Dermolen, *President*
Moreen Durkin, *Principal*
Heinz Gehring, *Chairman*
Dorothy Stein, *Chairman*
Tom Newbrough, *Materials Mgr*

Farmington Hills - Oakland County (G-5009)

EMP: 81
SQ FT: 43,500
SALES (est): 13MM **Privately Held**
WEB: www.gehring-lp.com
SIC: 6512 3541 Nonresidential building operators; machine tools, metal cutting type

(G-5009)
GLEASON WORKS
Also Called: Technical Center
39255 Country Club Dr B8 (48331-3486)
PHONE..................................248 522-0305
John Hartford, *Manager*
EMP: 12
SALES (corp-wide): 825.5MM **Privately Held**
WEB: www.gleason.com
SIC: 3714 Gears, motor vehicle
HQ: The Gleason Works
   1000 University Ave
   Rochester NY 14607
   585 473-1000

(G-5010)
GLOBAL HOSES & FITTINGS LLC (PA)
Also Called: Global Imported Fittings
30370 Fox Club Dr (48331-6006)
PHONE..................................248 219-9581
Brij Gujral,
EMP: 3
SALES (est): 348.8K **Privately Held**
WEB: www.globalfittings.com
SIC: 3569 5085 Assembly machines, non-metalworking; industrial fittings

(G-5011)
GLOBAL TECHNOLOGY VENTURES INC
Also Called: Globaltech Ventures
37408 Hills Tech Dr (48331-3414)
PHONE..................................248 324-3707
Steven Willis, *President*
John Reider, *Representative*
EMP: 8
SQ FT: 2,500
SALES (est): 2.2MM **Privately Held**
WEB: www.gtvinc.com
SIC: 8711 3089 3321 Designing; ship, boat, machine & product; casting of plastic; ductile iron castings

(G-5012)
GM BASSETT PATTERN INC
31162 W 8 Mile Rd (48336-5201)
PHONE..................................248 477-6454
Gerald Bassett, *President*
Scott Defrank, *Principal*
EMP: 5 EST: 1962
SQ FT: 3,200
SALES: 500K **Privately Held**
WEB: www.gmbassettpattern.com
SIC: 3543 Industrial patterns

(G-5013)
GRAPHIC VISIONS INC
23936 Industrial Park Dr (48335-2861)
PHONE..................................248 347-3355
Susan Dillon, *President*
Mike Dillon, *Vice Pres*
Jeff Wild, *Creative Dir*
EMP: 12
SALES (est): 1.8MM **Privately Held**
WEB: www.graphicvisionary.com
SIC: 3993 7336 Signs & advertising specialties; graphic arts & related design

(G-5014)
GRASSHOPPER SIGNS GRAPHICS LLC
Also Called: Identicom
24655 Halsted Rd (48335)
PHONE..................................248 946-8475
Giovanni Dinunzio, *Mng Member*
EMP: 13
SALES (est): 439.4K **Privately Held**
SIC: 3993 Signs & advertising specialties

(G-5015)
GREEN ROOM MICHIGAN LLC
32000 Northwestern Hwy (48334-1565)
PHONE..................................248 289-3288
Joseph Rogewitz,
EMP: 10

SALES: 250K **Privately Held**
SIC: 2023 Dietary supplements, dairy & non-dairy based

(G-5016)
HARMAN BECKER AUTO SYSTEMS INC
26500 Haggerty Rd (48331-3492)
PHONE..................................248 848-0393
EMP: 86
SALES (corp-wide): 6.1B **Publicly Held**
SIC: 3651 Mfg Home Audio/Video Equipment
HQ: Harman Becker Automotive Systems, Inc.
   30001 Cabot Dr
   Novi MI 48377
   248 848-9972

(G-5017)
HARMONIE INTERNATIONAL LLC
30201 Orchard Lake Rd (48334-2235)
PHONE..................................248 737-9933
William Donahue,
EMP: 20
SALES (est): 559.3K **Privately Held**
SIC: 1389 Gas field services

(G-5018)
HEXON CORPORATION
26050 Orchard Lake Rd # 100 (48334-4407)
PHONE..................................248 585-7585
Abdullah Zubi, *President*
EMP: 12
SQ FT: 40,000
SALES (est): 2.3MM **Privately Held**
WEB: www.hexoncorp.com
SIC: 2675 7389 2782 3993 Die-cut paper & board; printers' services: folding, collating; looseleaf binders & devices; signs & advertising specialties; automotive & apparel trimmings

(G-5019)
HIGH IMPACT SOLUTIONS INC
20793 Farmington Rd # 13 (48336-5182)
PHONE..................................248 473-9804
Bill Strobridge, *President*
EMP: 3
SQ FT: 800
SALES: 1MM **Privately Held**
WEB: www.prographics1.com
SIC: 2754 7389 8742 Commercial printing, gravure; product endorsement service; marketing consulting services

(G-5020)
HILLS MANUFACTURING LLC
26700 Haggerty Rd (48331-5714)
PHONE..................................248 536-3307
EMP: 3
SALES (est): 205.3K **Privately Held**
SIC: 3999 Manufacturing industries

(G-5021)
HITACHI AMERICA LTD
Farmington Hills Technical
34500 Grand River Ave (48335-3373)
PHONE..................................248 477-5400
Osumu Abe, *General Mgr*
Harsha Badarinarayan, *Director*
EMP: 30 **Privately Held**
WEB: www.hitachi.com
SIC: 5082 5065 5063 5084 Construction & mining machinery; electronic parts & equipment; electrical apparatus & equipment; industrial machinery & equipment; motor vehicle parts & accessories; petroleum refining
HQ: Hitachi America Ltd
   50 Prospect Ave
   Tarrytown NY 10591
   914 332-5800

(G-5022)
HUF NORTH AMERICA AUTOMOTI
24860 Hathaway St (48335-1513)
PHONE..................................248 213-4605
Randy Kingsley, *Branch Mgr*
Mike Mealoy, *Manager*
Michael Baker, *Recruiter*
EMP: 25

SALES (corp-wide): 2.6MM **Privately Held**
SIC: 3714 Motor vehicle parts & accessories
HQ: Huf North America Automotive Parts Manufacturing, Corp.
   395 T Elmer Cox Rd
   Greeneville TN 37743

(G-5023)
HUMANTICS INNVTIVE SLTIONS INC (PA)
Also Called: First Technology Safety System
23300 Haggerty Rd (48335-2603)
PHONE..................................734 451-7878
Christopher O'Connor, *President*
Lin Pan, *General Mgr*
Jim Davis, *Vice Pres*
Michael Jarouche, *Vice Pres*
Mike Van Horn, *VP Opers*
◆ EMP: 140
SQ FT: 34,000
SALES (est): 44.8MM **Privately Held**
SIC: 3829 Testing equipment: abrasion, shearing strength, etc.

(G-5024)
IBG NBT SYSTEMS CORP
20793 Farmington Rd Ste 8 (48336-5182)
PHONE..................................248 478-9490
Bill Buschur, *President*
Herbert Baumgartner, *President*
EMP: 3
SQ FT: 1,000
SALES (est): 456.9K
SALES (corp-wide): 8MM **Privately Held**
WEB: www.ibgndt.com
SIC: 3829 Measuring & controlling devices
PA: Ibg Prufcomputer Gmbh
   Pretzfelder Str. 27
   Ebermannstadt 91320
   919 473-840

(G-5025)
IDEATION INTERNATIONAL INC
32000 Northwestern Hwy # 145 (48334-1565)
PHONE..................................248 737-8854
Zion Bar-El, *Ch of Bd*
Boris Zlotin, *Exec VP*
EMP: 15
SQ FT: 1,500
SALES (est): 1.3MM **Privately Held**
WEB: www.ideationtriz.com
SIC: 7371 8742 7372 Computer software development & applications; business consultant; prepackaged software

(G-5026)
IDENTICOM SIGN SOLUTIONS LLC
24657 Halsted Rd (48335-1611)
PHONE..................................248 344-9590
John Dinunzio, *Principal*
EMP: 5 EST: 2011
SALES (est): 538K **Privately Held**
SIC: 3993 Electric signs

(G-5027)
INNOVATIVE SURFACE WORKS
23206 Commerce Dr (48335-2724)
PHONE..................................734 261-3010
Gary Bohr, *Owner*
Kim Bentti, *Sales Mgr*
EMP: 18
SALES (est): 3.4MM **Privately Held**
SIC: 3996 Hard surface floor coverings

(G-5028)
INOAC INTERIOR SYSTEMS LLC
Also Called: Inoac Automotive
22670 Haggerty Rd Ste 150 (48335-2637)
PHONE..................................248 488-7610
John Showalter, *Chief Engr*
Roger Dawes, *Mng Member*
Anthony Femminineo,
EMP: 44 EST: 2014
SALES (est): 24.7MM
SALES (corp-wide): 342.6MM **Privately Held**
SIC: 3069 3089 8711 Rubber automotive products; automotive parts, plastic; engineering services

PA: Inoac Usa, Inc.
   1515 Equity Dr Ste 200
   Troy MI 48084
   248 619-7031

(G-5029)
INTERNATIONAL WHEEL & TIRE INC (PA)
23255 Commerce Dr (48335-2705)
PHONE..................................248 298-0207
Richard Kerwin, *President*
Kevin Kerwin, *Vice Pres*
▼ EMP: 23
SALES (est): 909.9K **Privately Held**
SIC: 3559 Wheel balancing equipment, automotive

(G-5030)
IRISO USA INC (HQ)
34405 W 12 Mile Rd # 237 (48331-5627)
PHONE..................................248 324-9780
Akihiko Ohira, *CEO*
Keiko Iijima, *Admin Mgr*
▲ EMP: 27
SQ FT: 10,281
SALES: 66.5MM **Privately Held**
SIC: 3678 Electronic connectors

(G-5031)
JATCO USA INC
38700 Country Club Dr # 100 (48331-3404)
PHONE..................................248 306-9390
Shigeo Ishida, *Ch of Bd*
Tsuneaki Machida, *President*
John Nydam, *Exec VP*
Takashi Okamura, *Exec VP*
◆ EMP: 75
SQ FT: 76,000
SALES (est): 17.8MM **Privately Held**
WEB: www.jatco-usa.com
SIC: 3568 Power transmission equipment
HQ: Jatco Ltd .
   700-1, Imaizumi
   Fuji SZO 417-0

(G-5032)
JERVIS B WEBB COMPANY
Also Called: Worldwide Company
34375 W 12 Mile Rd (48331-3375)
PHONE..................................248 553-1222
John Doychich, *Vice Pres*
Terry Brosch, *Production*
Mel Edwards, *Chief Engr*
Michael Malaga, *Engineer*
Kenneth Hill, *Accountant*
EMP: 500 **Privately Held**
WEB: www.jervisbwebb.com
SIC: 3535 Conveyors & conveying equipment
HQ: Jervis B. Webb Company
   30100 Cabot Dr
   Novi MI 48377
   248 553-1000

(G-5033)
JOMARK INC
Also Called: Greenman's Printing & Imaging
30650 W 8 Mile Rd (48336-5302)
PHONE..................................248 478-2600
William Greenman, *President*
EMP: 11 EST: 1978
SQ FT: 3,600
SALES (est): 2MM **Privately Held**
WEB: www.gpidirect.com
SIC: 2752 7338 2791 2759 Commercial printing, offset; secretarial & court reporting; typesetting; commercial printing

(G-5034)
JST SALES AMERICA INC
37879 Interchange Dr (48335-1024)
PHONE..................................248 324-1957
Nishi Moto, *President*
▲ EMP: 43
SALES (est): 5.3MM **Privately Held**
SIC: 3643 Electric connectors

(G-5035)
JUST RITE BRACKET
21565 Verdun St (48336-6070)
PHONE..................................248 477-0592
Gary Justice, *Owner*
EMP: 6 EST: 1989
SALES (est): 536.3K **Privately Held**
SIC: 3861 Cameras & related equipment

GEOGRAPHIC SECTION
Farmington Hills - Oakland County (G-5059)

(G-5036)
JVIS FH LLC
23944 Freeway Park Dr (48335-2816)
PHONE.................................248 478-2900
Michael Alexander, *VP Finance*
EMP: 30
SQ FT: 40,000
SALES: 5MM
SALES (corp-wide): 381.6MM **Privately Held**
SIC: 3089 Automotive parts, plastic
PA: Jvis - Usa, Llc
52048 Shelby Pkwy
Shelby Township MI 48315
586 884-5700

(G-5037)
KERN-LIEBERS PIERON INC
24505 Indoplex Cir (48335-9991)
PHONE.................................248 427-1100
Frank Foernbacher, *President*
EMP: 20 **EST:** 1998
SQ FT: 15,000
SALES (est): 3.3MM
SALES (corp-wide): 878.4MM **Privately Held**
WEB: www.bohnert-springs.com
SIC: 3446 Architectural metalwork
PA: Hugo Kern Und Liebers Gmbh & Co.
Kg Platinen- Und Federnfabrik
Dr.-Kurt-Steim-Str. 35
Schramberg 78713
742 251-10

(G-5038)
KINGSTON EDUCATIONAL SOFTWARE
38452 Lynwood Ct (48331-3749)
PHONE.................................248 895-4803
Elan Benford, *President*
Sheila Wrightbenford, *General Mgr*
EMP: 5
SALES (est): 156.6K **Privately Held**
SIC: 7372 7371 Prepackaged software; computer software development & applications

(G-5039)
KURABE AMERICA CORPORATION
37735 Interchange Dr (48335-1030)
PHONE.................................248 939-5803
Yasuto Kanazawa, *CEO*
Takenobu Kanazawa, *President*
▲ **EMP:** 1100
SQ FT: 13,800
SALES (est): 110.9MM **Privately Held**
SIC: 3357 5531 3714 Automotive wire & cable, except ignition sets: nonferrous; automotive parts; heaters, motor vehicle

(G-5040)
KURTZ GRAVEL COMPANY INC (HQ)
33469 W 14 Mile Rd # 100 (48331-1521)
PHONE.................................810 787-6543
Jeff Sparr, *Principal*
EMP: 40 **EST:** 1920
SQ FT: 3,500
SALES (est): 9.2MM
SALES (corp-wide): 21.8MM **Privately Held**
WEB: www.kurtzgravelco.com
SIC: 3273 1442 3272 3271 Ready-mixed concrete; gravel mining; concrete products; concrete block & brick
PA: Superior Materials Inc.
585 Stewart Ave
Farmington Hills MI 48333
248 788-8000

(G-5041)
LA JALISCIENSE INC (PA)
31048 Applewood Ln (48331-1211)
PHONE.................................313 237-0008
Sergio Abundis, *President*
Gloria Cavarell, *Vice Pres*
Myrna Alge, *Treasurer*
Norma Abundes, *Admin Sec*
EMP: 15 **EST:** 1946
SQ FT: 6,000
SALES: 1MM **Privately Held**
WEB: www.tortillamundo.com
SIC: 2099 Tortillas, fresh or refrigerated

(G-5042)
LAMINA INC
Also Called: Anchor Danly
38505 Country Club Dr # 100 (48331-3403)
P.O. Box 2540 (48333-2540)
PHONE.................................248 489-9122
Roy Verstraete, *President*
Todd Castile, *Vice Pres*
John Christy, *Engineer*
Steve Zerio, *CFO*
Craig Swoish, *Treasurer*
EMP: 212 **EST:** 1992
SQ FT: 130,000
SALES (est): 29.3MM **Privately Held**
WEB: www.lamina.com
SIC: 3545 3546 Machine tool attachments & accessories; drills, portable, except rock: electric or pneumatic
HQ: Anchor Lamina America, Inc.
39830 Grand River Ave B-2
Novi MI 48375
248 489-9122

(G-5043)
LENNON FLUID SYSTEMS LLC
Also Called: Swagelok Michigan Toledo
23920 Freeway Park Dr (48335-2816)
PHONE.................................248 474-6624
Jill Whelan, *Principal*
Aaron Sexton,
EMP: 36 **EST:** 2017
SALES: 15MM **Privately Held**
SIC: 3494 Valves & pipe fittings

(G-5044)
LINE PRECISION INC
31666 W 8 Mile Rd (48336-5207)
PHONE.................................248 474-5280
Stanley R Clarke, *President*
Dave Mertz, *Vice Pres*
EMP: 39 **EST:** 1966
SQ FT: 28,000
SALES (est): 6.9MM **Privately Held**
WEB: www.lineprecision.com
SIC: 3599 3545 3544 3369 Grinding castings for the trade; precision tools, machinists'; special dies, tools, jigs & fixtures; nonferrous foundries; aluminum foundries

(G-5045)
LINTECH GLOBAL INC
34119 W 12 Mile Rd # 200 (48331-3300)
PHONE.................................248 553-8033
Michael Lin, *President*
Liza Lin, *Vice Pres*
Andy Hilbun, *Technical Staff*
Van Milne, *Director*
Paul Patillo, *Director*
EMP: 100
SQ FT: 2,000
SALES (est): 14.4MM **Privately Held**
WEB: www.lintechglobal.com
SIC: 7371 7372 7373 Computer software systems analysis & design, custom; prepackaged software; systems software development services

(G-5046)
LSPEDIA LLC
30201 Orchard Lake Rd # 108 (48334-2277)
PHONE.................................248 320-1909
Riya Cao, *Mng Member*
EMP: 8
SALES (est): 891.7K **Privately Held**
SIC: 7372 7371 Prepackaged software; application computer software; computer software development & applications

(G-5047)
LUMECON LLC
23107 Commerce Dr (48335-2723)
PHONE.................................248 505-1090
Daniel W Carrier,
▲ **EMP:** 3
SALES: 10.4MM **Privately Held**
SIC: 3229 5063 Bulbs for electric lights; light bulbs & related supplies; lighting fixtures, commercial & industrial
PA: Carrier & Gable, Inc.
24110 Research Dr
Farmington Hills MI 48335
248 477-8700

(G-5048)
MAGAZINES IN MOTION INC
35451 Valley Crk (48335-3947)
PHONE.................................248 310-7647
Thomas Ledermann, *Principal*
EMP: 3
SALES (est): 264.1K **Privately Held**
SIC: 2721 Periodicals

(G-5049)
MAGNECOR AUSTRALIA LIMITED
24581 Crestview Ct (48335-1503)
PHONE.................................248 471-9505
Richard J Cocks, *President*
Steve Brown, *Sales Mgr*
EMP: 10
SQ FT: 20,000
SALES (est): 1.4MM **Privately Held**
WEB: www.magnecor.com
SIC: 3694 Engine electrical equipment

(G-5050)
MAHLE INC
23030 Mahle Dr (48335-2606)
PHONE.................................248 305-8200
Jon Douglas, *General Mgr*
Lawrence Finner, *Principal*
Bruce Engleman, *Business Mgr*
Katherine Kedzior, *Business Mgr*
Brian Heckman, *Engineer*
EMP: 37 **EST:** 2011
SALES (est): 10.1MM **Privately Held**
SIC: 3714 Motor vehicle parts & accessories

(G-5051)
MAHLE ENG COMPONENTS USA INC
23030 Haggerty Rd (48335)
PHONE.................................248 305-8200
Marcio Coenca, *Engineer*
Robert Walters, *Sales Mgr*
Bill McKnight, *Marketing Staff*
Michelle Moehle, *Manager*
EMP: 16
SALES (corp-wide): 504.6K **Privately Held**
WEB: www.mahlemotorsports.com
SIC: 3592 3443 Pistons & piston rings; cylinders, pressure: metal plate
HQ: Mahle Engine Components Usa, Inc.
1 Mahle Dr
Morristown TN 37815
423 581-6603

(G-5052)
MAHLE INDUSTRIES INCORPORATED (DH)
23030 Mahle Dr (48335-2606)
PHONE.................................248 305-8200
EMP: 50
SQ FT: 100,000
SALES (est): 11.9MM **Privately Held**
SIC: 3714 7699 Mfg Motor Vehicle Parts/Accessories Repair Services
HQ: Mahle Gmbh
Pragstr. 26-46
Stuttgart 70376
711 501-0

(G-5053)
MAHLE INDUSTRIES INCORPORATED (DH)
23030 Mahle Dr (48335-2606)
P.O. Box 748, Morristown TN (37815-0748)
PHONE.................................248 305-8200
Prof Dr Heinz Junker, *Ch of Bd*
Scott Ferriman, *President*
Stephanie Smith, *Human Res Mgr*
Fabrizio Ruggiero, *Director*
▲ **EMP:** 1
SALES (est): 96.1MM
SALES (corp-wide): 504.6K **Privately Held**
SIC: 3714 Motor vehicle parts & accessories
HQ: Mahle Gmbh
Pragstr. 26-46
Stuttgart 70376
711 501-0

(G-5054)
MAHLE MANUFACTURING MGT INC
23030 Mahle Dr (48335-2606)
PHONE.................................248 735-3623
Chris Kaczmarek, *IT/INT Sup*
Wilm Uhlenbecker, *Bd of Directors*
Sandra Mulvaney, *Administration*
EMP: 5
SALES (est): 450.7K **Privately Held**
SIC: 3714 Motor vehicle parts & accessories

(G-5055)
MAHLE POWERTRAIN
23030 Haggerty Rd (48335)
PHONE.................................248 473-6511
Wolfgang Rein, *Principal*
EMP: 28
SALES (est): 5.4MM **Privately Held**
SIC: 3569 Filters

(G-5056)
MAHLE POWERTRAIN LLC (DH)
23030 Mahle Dr (48335-2606)
PHONE.................................248 305-8200
Paul Windisch, *Engineer*
Sumit Bhargava, *Manager*
Kathy Kedzior, *Manager*
Duncan Sheppard, *Technical Staff*
EMP: 90
SQ FT: 36,500
SALES (est): 31.4MM
SALES (corp-wide): 504.6K **Privately Held**
WEB: www.mahle-powertrain.com
SIC: 8711 3825 3823 3625 Engineering services; engine electrical test equipment; industrial instrmnts msrmnt display/control process variable; relays & industrial controls
HQ: Mahle Industries, Incorporated
23030 Mahle Dr
Farmington Hills MI 48335
248 305-8200

(G-5057)
MARELLI NORTH AMERICA INC
27000 Hills Tech Ct # 100 (48331-3447)
PHONE.................................248 848-4800
Masaya Goto, *Vice Pres*
Dave Keeney, *Manager*
Aaron Kleinow, *Manager*
Romi Shah, *Director*
EMP: 150 **Publicly Held**
WEB: www.calsonic.com
SIC: 3585 8734 8711 5162 Air conditioning, motor vehicle; testing laboratories; engineering services; plastics materials & basic shapes; warm air heating & air conditioning
HQ: Marelli North America, Inc.
1 Calsonic Way
Shelbyville TN 37160
931 684-4490

(G-5058)
MARKETING DISPLAYS INC
Also Called: Marketing Displays Intl
38271 W 12 Mile Rd (48331-3041)
P.O. Box 576, Farmington (48332-0576)
PHONE.................................248 553-1900
Lisa Sarkisian, *President*
John Sarkisian, *Vice Pres*
Jim Nash, *Production*
Keith Richardson, *Purch Agent*
Christopher Kluesner, *Treasurer*
◆ **EMP:** 165
SQ FT: 87,500
SALES (est): 36.4MM
SALES (corp-wide): 2.1MM **Privately Held**
WEB: www.mdiworldwide.com
SIC: 3993 3354 2396 Signs, not made in custom sign painting shops; aluminum extruded products; automotive & apparel trimmings
PA: Mdi France
Parc Icade Immeuble Paprika
Rungis 94150
155 531-630

(G-5059)
MASTERS MILLWORK LLC
37644 Hills Tech Dr (48331-5727)
PHONE.................................248 987-4511

Andy Kubiak,
EMP: 10 **EST:** 2013
SQ FT: 8,000
SALES (est): 1.1MM **Privately Held**
SIC: 2431 Millwork

(G-5060)
MAYA JIG GRINDING & GAGE CO
Also Called: Maya Gage Co.
20770 Parker St (48336-5150)
PHONE..................................248 471-0820
Kim S Beier, *President*
Tony Cucci, *Purch Mgr*
Steve Yeager, *QC Mgr*
Vic Adams, *Engineer*
EMP: 16
SQ FT: 7,000
SALES (est): 3.1MM **Privately Held**
WEB: www.mayagage.com
SIC: 3544 Special dies & tools

(G-5061)
MEDICAL SYSTEMS RESOURCE GROUP
26105 Orchard Lake Rd (48334-4576)
PHONE..................................248 476-5400
Raymond Malover, *Sales Staff*
Roger Avie,
EMP: 7
SALES (est): 378.6K **Privately Held**
SIC: 7372 7373 7378 Application computer software; business oriented computer software; systems integration services; turnkey vendors, computer systems; computer maintenance & repair

(G-5062)
MEDSKER ELECTRIC INC
28650 Grand River Ave (48336-5824)
PHONE..................................248 855-3383
Robert P Medsker, *President*
EMP: 27
SQ FT: 38,000
SALES (est): 838.3K **Privately Held**
SIC: 7694 5084 8734 Electric motor repair; instruments & control equipment; testing laboratories

(G-5063)
MERCEDES-BENZ EXTRA LLC
36455 Corp Dr Ste 175 (48331)
PHONE..................................205 747-8006
Bernhard Mader, *CFO*
EMP: 35
SALES (est): 1.1MM **Privately Held**
SIC: 3423 Hand & edge tools

(G-5064)
METER DEVICES COMPANY INC
23847 Industrial Park Dr (48335-2860)
PHONE..................................330 455-0301
Jack Roessner, *President*
John T Hanft, *Vice Pres*
▲ **EMP:** 612
SQ FT: 70,000
SALES (est): 52.9MM
SALES (corp-wide): 444.9MM **Privately Held**
WEB: www.meter-devices.com
SIC: 3625 3644 3643 3444 Switches, electric power; noncurrent-carrying wiring services; current-carrying wiring devices; sheet metalwork
HQ: E.J. Brooks Company
409 Hoosier Dr
Angola IN 46703
800 348-4777

(G-5065)
MICHIGAN INDUSTRIAL FINISHES
Also Called: Mif Custom Coatings
29463 Shenandoah Dr (48331-2464)
PHONE..................................248 553-7014
Norman Solomon, *President*
Sandra Felisiak, *Purch Agent*
EMP: 24 **EST:** 1949
SQ FT: 40,000
SALES (est): 2.2MM **Privately Held**
SIC: 2851 Paints & paint additives

(G-5066)
MICHIGAN WHOLESALE PRTG INC
24653 Halsted Rd (48335-1611)
PHONE..................................248 350-8230
Andrew Petty, *President*
EMP: 8
SQ FT: 5,500
SALES (est): 1.4MM **Privately Held**
WEB: www.mwprinting.com
SIC: 2752 Commercial printing, offset

(G-5067)
MICROTEMP FLUID SYSTEMS LLC
23900 Haggerty Rd (48335-2618)
PHONE..................................248 703-5056
Robert Schoenfeldt,
EMP: 7
SALES (est): 1.6MM **Privately Held**
SIC: 3585 Refrigeration & heating equipment

(G-5068)
MILLENNIUM PLANET LLC
Also Called: Millennium Filters
27300 Haggerty Rd Ste F28 (48331-5704)
PHONE..................................248 835-2331
Robert Oneill, *Principal*
EMP: 6 **EST:** 2013
SALES (est): 831.2K **Privately Held**
SIC: 3569 3533 3563 5085 Filters; filters, general line: industrial; oil field machinery & equipment; air & gas compressors; filters, industrial

(G-5069)
MILLENNM-THE INSIDE SLTION INC
Also Called: Futuristic Furnishings
24748 Crestview Ct (48335-1506)
PHONE..................................248 645-9005
Andrew Sallan, *President*
EMP: 32
SQ FT: 20,000
SALES (est): 303.4K **Privately Held**
WEB: www.millenniumcabinetry.com
SIC: 2517 2541 2511 2434 Home entertainment unit cabinets, wood; wood partitions & fixtures; wood household furniture; wood kitchen cabinets

(G-5070)
MLS AUTOMOTIVE INCORPORATED
27280 Haggerty Rd Ste C-9 (48331-3433)
PHONE..................................844 453-3669
Ahmad Sameh Jwania, *President*
Ghath Joueniah, *Controller*
EMP: 10
SALES (est): 1.8MM **Privately Held**
SIC: 3647 Automotive lighting fixtures

(G-5071)
MODA MANUFACTURING LLC
39255 Country Club Dr B1 (48331-3489)
PHONE..................................586 204-5120
EMP: 8
SALES (est): 894.4K **Privately Held**
SIC: 3553 5712 Cabinet makers' machinery; cabinet work, custom

(G-5072)
MOLDEX3D NORTHERN AMERICA INC (HQ)
27725 Stansbury Blvd (48334-3807)
PHONE..................................248 946-4570
Anthony Yang, *President*
Michael Dai, *President*
Prabhakar Vallury, *Vice Pres*
Michael Roth, *Accountant*
Kiki Kratzer, *Sales Staff*
EMP: 14 **EST:** 2011
SALES (est): 1.5MM **Privately Held**
SIC: 3089 8742 Injection molding of plastics; industry specialist consultants

(G-5073)
MPS TRADING GROUP LLC
38755 Hills Tech Dr (48331-3408)
PHONE..................................313 841-7588
Edward L Schwartz, *Principal*
EMP: 4

SALES (est): 459.2K **Privately Held**
SIC: 2851 Paint removers

(G-5074)
MUSLIM OBSERVER
29004 W 8 Mile Rd (48336-5910)
PHONE..................................248 426-7777
A R Nakader, *Owner*
EMP: 8
SQ FT: 3,111
SALES (est): 346.6K **Privately Held**
WEB: www.muslimobserver.com
SIC: 2711 Newspapers, publishing & printing

(G-5075)
NADEX OF AMERICA CORPORATION (PA)
Also Called: W T C
24775 Crestview Ct (48335-1507)
PHONE..................................248 477-3900
Durrell G Miller, *President*
David Androvich, *Vice Pres*
Steve Connors, *Vice Pres*
▲ **EMP:** 34 **EST:** 1939
SQ FT: 33,000
SALES (est): 21.2MM **Privately Held**
WEB: www.weltronic.com
SIC: 3625 3825 8711 3548 Control equipment, electric; current measuring equipment; electrical & electronic engineering; welding apparatus

(G-5076)
NARENS ASSOCIATES INC
30903 Northwestern Hwy # 22 (48334-2556)
PHONE..................................248 304-0300
Edward Narens, *President*
EMP: 3
SALES (est): 286.3K **Privately Held**
SIC: 3231 Mirrors, truck & automobile: made from purchased glass

(G-5077)
NATIONWIDE LASER TECHNOLOGIES
Also Called: Nationwide Toner Cartridge
27600 Farmington Rd B1 (48334-3363)
PHONE..................................248 488-0155
Omar Tame, *Owner*
EMP: 4
SALES (est): 150K **Privately Held**
SIC: 3861 7699 Toners, prepared photographic (not made in chemical plants); photocopy machine repair

(G-5078)
NDEX
31440 Northwestern Hwy (48334-5418)
PHONE..................................248 432-9000
Scott Goldstein, *CEO*
John Smith, *COO*
EMP: 11
SALES (est): 652.1K **Privately Held**
SIC: 2711 Newspapers, publishing & printing

(G-5079)
NEAPCO HOLDINGS LLC (DH)
38900 Hills Tech Dr (48331-3430)
PHONE..................................248 699-6500
Kenneth Hopkins, *CEO*
Steve Jensen, *Production*
Gary Rogers, *Purch Mgr*
Taner Bosnali, *Engineer*
David Krstich, *Engineer*
◆ **EMP:** 200
SQ FT: 350,000
SALES (est): 691MM
SALES (corp-wide): 2.9B **Privately Held**
SIC: 3568 3714 Power transmission equipment; motor vehicle parts & accessories

(G-5080)
NORMAN A LEWIS
Also Called: Global Auditing Solutions
27268 Pembridge Ln (48331-3671)
PHONE..................................248 219-5736
Norman A Lewis, *Owner*
EMP: 5
SALES (est): 229.7K **Privately Held**
SIC: 2834 Pharmaceutical preparations

(G-5081)
NORTH AMERICAN LIGHTING INC
36600 Corporate Dr (48331-3546)
PHONE..................................248 553-6408
Jack Keller, *General Mgr*
Tom Poorman, *General Mgr*
Kishore Ahuja, *Engineer*
Jeffrey Antoun, *Engineer*
Mark Ehrhardt, *Engineer*
EMP: 100 **Privately Held**
WEB: www.nal.com
SIC: 3647 Automotive lighting fixtures
HQ: North American Lighting, Inc.
2275 S Main St
Paris IL 61944
217 465-6600

(G-5082)
NORTHWEST PATTERN COMPANY
29473 Medbury St (48336-2124)
P.O. Box 403 (48332-0403)
PHONE..................................248 477-7070
John H Dutton, *President*
EMP: 6
SQ FT: 7,500
SALES (est): 450K **Privately Held**
SIC: 3553 3469 Pattern makers' machinery, woodworking; patterns on metal

(G-5083)
NPI
23910 Freeway Park Dr (48335-2816)
PHONE..................................248 478-0010
Michael K Hamzey, *President*
EMP: 5 **EST:** 1976
SQ FT: 4,000
SALES (est): 335K
SALES (corp-wide): 12MM **Privately Held**
WEB: www.rmwrightco.com
SIC: 7699 3594 3593 3494 Hydraulic equipment repair; fluid power pumps & motors; fluid power cylinders & actuators; valves & pipe fittings
PA: The R M Wright Company Inc
23910 Freeway Park Dr
Farmington Hills MI 48335
248 476-9800

(G-5084)
NU-ERA HOLDINGS INC
32613 Folsom Rd (48336-4424)
PHONE..................................248 477-2288
Pete Coulter, *Branch Mgr*
EMP: 15
SALES (corp-wide): 8.6MM **Privately Held**
SIC: 3593 Fluid power cylinders, hydraulic or pneumatic
PA: Nu-Era Holdings, Inc.
2034 Fruit St
Clay MI 48001
810 794-4935

(G-5085)
NUANCE COMMUNICATIONS INC
39255 Country Club Dr (48331-3486)
PHONE..................................248 919-7700
EMP: 4 **Publicly Held**
SIC: 7372 Prepackaged software
PA: Nuance Communications, Inc.
1 Wayside Rd
Burlington MA 01803

(G-5086)
OFFICE CONNECTION INC (PA)
37676 Enterprise Ct (48331-3440)
PHONE..................................248 871-2003
Karen Minc, *CEO*
Joseph Minc, *President*
Mike Eberle, *Sales Mgr*
EMP: 29
SQ FT: 15,100
SALES (est): 26.3MM **Privately Held**
WEB: www.offconn.com
SIC: 5112 5021 2752 Office supplies; office furniture; commercial printing, offset

Farmington Hills - Oakland County (G-5114)

(G-5087)
P & C GROUP I INC (PA)
Also Called: Chemical
37000 W 12 Mile Rd (48331-3032)
PHONE..................................248 442-6800
Arvind Pradhan, *President*
Vishal Pradhan, *Purchasing*
Jake Strawhecker, *Engineer*
▲ **EMP:** 35
SQ FT: 3,000
SALES (est): 549.3MM **Privately Held**
SIC: 3465 3499 Automotive stampings; automobile seat frames, metal

(G-5088)
PARAMETER DRIVEN SOFTWARE INC (PA)
32605 W 12 Mile Rd # 275 (48334-3337)
PHONE..................................248 553-6410
Patrick K Comeaux, *President*
Linda Comeaux, *Admin Sec*
EMP: 10
SQ FT: 1,700
SALES (est): 1.4MM **Privately Held**
WEB: www.pdswhq.com
SIC: 7373 7372 Local area network (LAN) systems integrator; business oriented computer software

(G-5089)
PCB LOAD & TORQUE INC
24350 Indoplex Cir (48335-2524)
PHONE..................................248 471-0065
Mike Lally, *President*
EMP: 20
SALES (est): 2.8MM
SALES (corp-wide): 778MM **Publicly Held**
SIC: 3829 Physical property testing equipment
HQ: Pcb Piezotronics, Inc.
3425 Walden Ave
Depew NY 14043
716 684-0001

(G-5090)
PCB PIEZOTRONICS INC
24350 Indoplex Cir (48335-2524)
PHONE..................................716 684-0001
Kirk Hinkins, *Administration*
EMP: 8
SALES (corp-wide): 778MM **Publicly Held**
SIC: 3829 Measuring & controlling devices
HQ: Pcb Piezotronics, Inc.
3425 Walden Ave
Depew NY 14043
716 684-0001

(G-5091)
PERFECT IMPRESSIONS INC
24580 N Industrial Dr (48335-1502)
PHONE..................................248 478-2644
Ratna Pasricha, *President*
EMP: 3
SQ FT: 2,600
SALES (est): 220K **Privately Held**
WEB: www.signsbypi.com
SIC: 3993 2752 Signs & advertising specialties; commercial printing, offset

(G-5092)
PHILIPS NORTH AMERICA LLC
Also Called: Philips Automotive Ltg N Amer
34119 W 12 Mile Rd # 102 (48331-3308)
PHONE..................................248 553-9080
Dennis Samsioippo, *Manager*
EMP: 40
SALES (corp-wide): 20.8B **Privately Held**
SIC: 3641 Electric lamps
HQ: Philips North America Llc
3000 Minuteman Rd Ms1203
Andover MA 01810
978 659-3000

(G-5093)
PIEDMONT CONCRETE INC
29934 W 8 Mile Rd (48336-5507)
PHONE..................................248 474-7740
David Guidobono, *President*
Anthony Guidobono, *Vice Pres*
EMP: 15 **EST:** 1959
SQ FT: 9,916
SALES (est): 2.2MM **Privately Held**
WEB: www.piedmontconcrete.com
SIC: 3273 Ready-mixed concrete

(G-5094)
PIONEER NORTH AMERICA INC
22630 Haggerty Rd (48335-2611)
PHONE..................................248 449-6799
Jenna Ashi, *Branch Mgr*
EMP: 20
SALES (corp-wide): 242.1K **Privately Held**
SIC: 3651 Household audio & video equipment
HQ: Pioneer North America, Inc.
2050 W 190th St Ste 100
Torrance CA 90504
310 952-2000

(G-5095)
PKC GROUP USA INC (DH)
36555 Corp Dr Ste 300 (48331)
PHONE..................................248 489-4700
Frank Sovis, *President*
Kieran Sheehy, *General Mgr*
Ivo Volkov, *General Mgr*
Jason Collins, *Production*
Marta Krakowiak, *Purchasing*
EMP: 11 **EST:** 1997
SALES (est): 4.5B
SALES (corp-wide): 1B **Privately Held**
SIC: 3679 Harness assemblies for electronic use: wire or cable
HQ: Pkc Wiring Systems Oy
Vihikari 10
Kempele 90440
201 752-111

(G-5096)
POLY FLEX PRODUCTS INC (PA)
23093 Commerce Dr (48335-2721)
PHONE..................................734 458-4194
Mark Kirchmer, *CEO*
Ken Bylo, *Vice Pres*
Ken Przbylowicz, *Vice Pres*
Bob Hatherley, *Plant Mgr*
Jeff Bosek, *Engineer*
◆ **EMP:** 50
SQ FT: 20,000
SALES (est): 9.3MM **Privately Held**
WEB: www.polyflexpro.com
SIC: 3089 Injection molding of plastics

(G-5097)
POSA-CUT CORPORATION
23600 Haggerty Rd (48335-2615)
PHONE..................................248 474-5620
Kevin B O Brien, *President*
Chris O Brien, *Vice Pres*
Donna O Brien, *Treasurer*
Ellen Obrien, *Office Mgr*
Jim Vecchio, *Manager*
EMP: 20
SQ FT: 12,000
SALES (est): 3.5MM **Privately Held**
WEB: www.posacut.com
SIC: 3541 3545 5084 Machine tools, metal cutting type; machine tool accessories; industrial machinery & equipment

(G-5098)
POWER CONTROLLERS LLC
23900 Freeway Park Dr (48335-2816)
PHONE..................................248 888-9896
David Backus, *CEO*
Mark Stanczak, *President*
EMP: 4
SALES (est): 154.1K **Privately Held**
SIC: 3613 3621 Power connectors, electric; power switching equipment; motors & generators; electric motor & generator parts; control equipment for electric buses & locomotives

(G-5099)
POWERGRID INC
28845 Inkster Rd (48334-5247)
PHONE..................................586 484-7185
Charles Minich, *Principal*
EMP: 3
SALES (est): 317.4K **Privately Held**
SIC: 3714 Motor vehicle parts & accessories

(G-5100)
PRINT HOUSE INC
23014 Commerce Dr (48335-2720)
PHONE..................................248 473-1414
Kenneth D Manko, *Vice Pres*
Barry J Melamed, *Vice Pres*
Marcia Reimer, *Graphic Designe*
EMP: 19 **EST:** 1975
SQ FT: 7,200
SALES (est): 3.4MM **Privately Held**
WEB: www.theprinthouse.com
SIC: 2752 7331 Commercial printing, offset; mailing service

(G-5101)
PRINTED IMPRESSIONS INC
32210 W 8 Mile Rd (48336-5100)
PHONE..................................248 473-5333
Thomas Mullen, *President*
Douglas Mullen, *Vice Pres*
Evelyn Mullen, *Treasurer*
EMP: 4
SQ FT: 2,500
SALES (est): 250K **Privately Held**
SIC: 2752 Commercial printing, offset

(G-5102)
PRO SEARCH
37761 Baywood Dr (48335-3609)
PHONE..................................248 553-7700
Charles Rush, *President*
Robert Eberline, *Managing Prtnr*
EMP: 3
SALES (est): 184.1K **Privately Held**
SIC: 7389 3952 Microfilm recording & developing service; boxes, sketching & paint

(G-5103)
PROSTHETIC & IMPLANT DENTISTRY
31954 Northwestern Hwy (48334-2534)
PHONE..................................248 254-3945
Furat George, *Principal*
EMP: 3 **EST:** 2018
SALES (est): 190.7K **Privately Held**
SIC: 3842 Prosthetic appliances

(G-5104)
PROTEGE CONCEPTS CORP
Also Called: Superior Water Screen Company
28230 Orchard Lake Rd # 204 (48334-3705)
P.O. Box 893, Alpena (49707-0893)
PHONE..................................248 419-5330
Matt Winter, *President*
EMP: 4
SQ FT: 350
SALES (est): 594K **Privately Held**
SIC: 3559 Anodizing equipment

(G-5105)
PROTO TOOL COMPANY
29660 W 9 Mile Rd (48336-4804)
PHONE..................................248 471-0577
Bruce A Pankow, *President*
EMP: 3 **EST:** 1980
SQ FT: 6,017
SALES (est): 450.9K **Privately Held**
WEB: www.prototoolco.com
SIC: 3599 Machine shop, jobbing & repair

(G-5106)
PTM-ELECTRONICS INC
39205 Country Club Dr C40 (48331-5701)
PHONE..................................248 987-4446
Jeffery Cohen, *President*
▲ **EMP:** 12
SQ FT: 6,000
SALES (est): 2.7MM
SALES (corp-wide): 17.6MM **Privately Held**
WEB: www.ptmelec.com
SIC: 3825 8711 Test equipment for electronic & electrical circuits; designing: ship, boat, machine & product
PA: Ahs & Js Limited
Cannock Wood Industrial Estate
Cannock STAFFS WS12
154 387-9788

(G-5107)
PUR E CLAT
27640 Gateway Dr E C106 (48334-4923)
PHONE..................................313 208-5763
Marlon Brantley, *Owner*
EMP: 3
SALES (est): 118.3K **Privately Held**
SIC: 2844 7389 Face creams or lotions;

(G-5108)
PUTNAM CABINETRY
29233 Scotten St (48336-5568)
PHONE..................................248 442-0118
Dennis Putnam, *Principal*
EMP: 4
SALES (est): 309.9K **Privately Held**
SIC: 2434 Wood kitchen cabinets

(G-5109)
QUIGLEY INDUSTRIES INC (HQ)
38880 Grand River Ave (48335-1526)
PHONE..................................248 426-8600
Carol C Quigley, *President*
Alice Flynn, *Vice Pres*
Shana Degroff, *Prdtn Mgr*
Rick Latack, *Materials Mgr*
Christine McCanham, *Bookkeeper*
EMP: 65
SQ FT: 42,000
SALES (est): 10.9MM
SALES (corp-wide): 18.7MM **Privately Held**
SIC: 3469 3465 3443 Stamping metal for the trade; automotive stampings; fabricated plate work (boiler shop)
PA: Quigley Manufacturing, Inc.
38880 Grand River Ave
Farmington Hills MI 48335
248 426-8600

(G-5110)
QUIGLEY MANUFACTURING INC (PA)
38880 Grand River Ave (48335-1526)
PHONE..................................248 426-8600
Carol C Quigley, *President*
Alice Flynn, *Vice Pres*
Robert A Moug, *Treasurer*
EMP: 200
SQ FT: 42,000
SALES (est): 18.7MM **Privately Held**
SIC: 3465 3469 3498 3829 Automotive stampings; metal stampings; tube fabricating (contract bending & shaping); gauges, motor vehicle: oil pressure, water temperature

(G-5111)
R M WRIGHT COMPANY INC (PA)
23910 Freeway Park Dr (48335-2816)
P.O. Box 382, Farmington (48332-0382)
PHONE..................................248 476-9800
Michael K Hamzey, *Principal*
EMP: 22
SQ FT: 15,000
SALES (est): 12MM **Privately Held**
WEB: www.rmwrightco.com
SIC: 5085 5084 3593 3494 Valves & fittings; industrial machinery & equipment; fluid power cylinders & actuators; valves & pipe fittings; manufactured hardware (general)

(G-5112)
RACELOGIC USA CORPORATION
27260 Haggerty Rd Ste A2 (48331-3400)
PHONE..................................248 994-9050
Reid Scott, *President*
EMP: 9
SALES (est): 806.3K **Privately Held**
SIC: 3825 Instruments to measure electricity

(G-5113)
READY MOLDS INC (PA)
Also Called: Ready Boring & Tooling
32645 Folsom Rd (48336-4424)
PHONE..................................248 474-4007
Lawrence P Nussio, *President*
EMP: 35
SQ FT: 9,000
SALES (est): 4.4MM **Privately Held**
WEB: www.readymold.com
SIC: 3544 Forms (molds), for foundry & plastics working machinery

(G-5114)
REYNOLDS WATER CONDITIONING CO
24545 Hathaway St (48335-1549)
PHONE..................................248 888-5000
James A Reynolds Sr, *President*

Farmington Hills - Oakland County (G-5115)

GEOGRAPHIC SECTION

April Woltman, *Project Engr*
Michelle Miller, *Office Mgr*
Elizabeth Reynolds, *Admin Sec*
▲ **EMP:** 15 **EST:** 1931
SQ FT: 10,000
SALES (est): 3.1MM **Privately Held**
WEB: www.reynoldswater.com
SIC: 3589 5999 Water treatment equipment, industrial; water filters & softeners, household type; water purification equipment

(G-5115)
RIDE CONTROL LLC (HQ)
Also Called: Gabriel Ride Control
39300 Country Club Dr (48331-3473)
PHONE.................................248 247-7600
Lisa J Bahash, *CEO*
Joseph Davis, *Engineer*
Spandana Sanne, *Engineer*
Nicholas Stafford, *Engineer*
James Neelley, *CFO*
◆ **EMP:** 100
SQ FT: 20,000
SALES: 171.4MM **Privately Held**
SIC: 3714 Shock absorbers, motor vehicle

(G-5116)
RODRIGUEZ PRINTING SERVICES (PA)
24649 Halsted Rd (48335-1611)
PHONE.................................248 651-7774
Raymond Rodriguez, *President*
EMP: 4 **EST:** 1997
SQ FT: 2,800
SALES: 400K **Privately Held**
WEB: www.rodriguezprinting.com
SIC: 2759 Commercial printing

(G-5117)
ROGER ZATKOFF COMPANY (PA)
Also Called: Zatkoff Seals & Packings
23230 Industrial Park Dr (48335-2850)
P.O. Box 486, Farmington (48332-0486)
PHONE.................................248 478-2400
Gary Zatkoff, *President*
Larry Cholody, *COO*
Hamilton Marques, *Vice Pres*
David Zatkoff, *Vice Pres*
Denise Stout, *Human Resources*
▲ **EMP:** 42
SQ FT: 25,000
SALES (est): 126.3MM **Privately Held**
WEB: www.zatkoff.com
SIC: 5085 5072 3053 Seals, industrial; hardware; gaskets & sealing devices; packing materials

(G-5118)
RS TECHNOLOGIES LTD
25286 Witherspoon St (48335-1369)
P.O. Box 2959 (48333-2959)
PHONE.................................248 888-8260
Ralph S Shoberg, *President*
Jo Ellen Prior, *Admin Asst*
EMP: 40
SALES (est): 6.3MM **Privately Held**
WEB: www.rstechltd.com
SIC: 3829 Physical property testing equipment

(G-5119)
SAFETY TECHNOLOGY HOLDINGS INC
23300 Haggerty Rd (48335-2603)
PHONE.................................415 983-2706
Christopher J Oconnor, *President*
Bryan J Brown, *Development*
James Habel, *CFO*
Janis E Major, *Human Resources*
EMP: 4
SALES (est): 172.7K **Privately Held**
SIC: 3829 Testing equipment: abrasion, shearing strength, etc.

(G-5120)
SATORI E-TECHNOLOGY INC
33533 W 12 Mile Rd # 305 (48331-5602)
PHONE.................................408 517-9130
Theodore J Roper, *Principal*
▲ **EMP:** 9
SALES (est): 1.2MM **Privately Held**
SIC: 3621 Motors, electric

(G-5121)
SBSI SOFTWARE INC (PA)
23570 Haggerty Rd (48335-2614)
PHONE.................................248 567-3044
Kristen Bye, *Principal*
EMP: 6
SALES (est): 440.5K **Privately Held**
SIC: 7372 Application computer software

(G-5122)
SFI ACQUISITION INC
Also Called: State Fabricators, Inc.
30550 W 8 Mile Rd (48336-5301)
PHONE.................................248 471-1500
Charles S Peltz, *CEO*
Matt Peltz, *President*
Robert Cureton, *Vice Pres*
Mark Ransley, *Supervisor*
EMP: 50
SQ FT: 25,000
SALES (est): 16MM **Privately Held**
WEB: www.statefab.com
SIC: 3537 2542 3443 3544 Pallets, metal; skids, metal; dollies (hand or power trucks), industrial except mining; pallet racks: except wood; weldments; special dies, tools, jigs & fixtures; sheet metalwork; wood pallets & skids

(G-5123)
SIGNATURE DESIGNS INC
24357 Indoplex Cir (48335-2525)
PHONE.................................248 426-9735
Robert Pietila, *President*
Bernard Hurwitz, *Vice Pres*
Rebecca Rakowski, *Admin Sec*
▲ **EMP:** 5
SQ FT: 3,600
SALES: 1.5MM **Privately Held**
WEB: www.signaturedesigns.net
SIC: 2591 2391 Window blinds; draperies, plastic & textile: from purchased materials

(G-5124)
SIGNTEXT INCORPORATED
Also Called: Signtext 2
24333 Indoplex Cir (48335-2525)
PHONE.................................248 442-9080
Michael Frasier, *President*
Jerry Feldman, *Accounts Mgr*
EMP: 24
SQ FT: 12,500
SALES: 3MM **Privately Held**
WEB: www.signtext.com
SIC: 3993 Signs, not made in custom sign painting shops; letters for signs, metal

(G-5125)
SIMNA SOLUTIONS LLC
31500 W 13 Mile Rd (48334-2164)
PHONE.................................313 442-7305
Smitha Cheruku, *Vice Pres*
Madhu Konduru, *Manager*
EMP: 3
SALES (est): 80.8K **Privately Held**
SIC: 7389 7371 7372 7373 ; custom computer programming services; prepackaged software; local area network (LAN) systems integrator; computer-aided manufacturing (CAM) systems service; computer-aided design (CAD) systems service

(G-5126)
SOFTWARE FINESSE LLC (PA)
31224 Mulfordton St # 200 (48334-1408)
P.O. Box 250673, West Bloomfield (48325-0673)
PHONE.................................248 737-8990
Ivan Avramov, *CEO*
Galia Avramov, *Principal*
EMP: 7
SALES (est): 925.8K **Privately Held**
SIC: 7371 7374 7372 Computer software systems analysis & design, custom; computer software writing services; optical scanning data service; prepackaged software; application computer software

(G-5127)
SPECIALTY STEEL TREATING INC
31610 W 8 Mile Rd (48336-5207)
PHONE.................................586 293-5355
Gary Parker, *Branch Mgr*
EMP: 45
SQ FT: 42,000
SALES (corp-wide): 49.4MM **Privately Held**
WEB: www.sstfraser.com
SIC: 3398 Metal heat treating
PA: Specialty Steel Treating, Inc.
34501 Commerce
Fraser MI 48026
586 293-5355

(G-5128)
SPRAYING SYSTEMS CO
30701 W 10 Mile Rd # 200 (48336-2634)
PHONE.................................248 473-1331
Richard Maxwell, *Manager*
EMP: 10
SALES (corp-wide): 241.1MM **Privately Held**
WEB: www.spray.com
SIC: 3499 Nozzles, spray: aerosol, paint or insecticide
PA: Spraying Systems Co.
200 W North Ave
Glendale Heights IL 60139
630 665-5000

(G-5129)
STAR CUTTER CO (PA)
Also Called: Star Cutter Company
23461 Industrial Park Dr (48335-2855)
P.O. Box 376, Farmington (48332-0376)
PHONE.................................248 474-8200
Bradley L Lawton, *President*
Julie Grimm, *Business Mgr*
Thomas Bel, *Vice Pres*
David W Goodfellow, *Vice Pres*
William Langendorfer, *Vice Pres*
▲ **EMP:** 30
SQ FT: 25,000
SALES (est): 224.7MM **Privately Held**
WEB: www.star-su.com
SIC: 3545 3479 3546 3541 Cutting tools for machine tools; hobs; reamers, machine tool; drilling machine attachments & accessories; painting, coating & hot dipping; power-driven handtools; machine tools, metal cutting type

(G-5130)
STAR SU COMPANY LLC
23461 Industrial Park Dr (48335-2855)
P.O. Box 376 (48332-0376)
PHONE.................................248 474-8200
Ron McCracken, *Regl Sales Mgr*
Brad Wilson, *Regl Sales Mgr*
Jim Caldwell, *Manager*
Brad Lawton,
EMP: 50
SALES (corp-wide): 180MM **Privately Held**
WEB: www.starsu.com
SIC: 3541 Machine tools, metal cutting type
PA: Star Su Company, Llc
5200 Prairie Stone Pkwy
Hoffman Estates IL 60192
847 649-1450

(G-5131)
STERLING MILLWORK INC
Also Called: Sterling Contracting
23350 Commerce Dr (48335-2726)
PHONE.................................248 427-1400
Mark A Bolitho, *President*
Nancy Bolitho, *Vice Pres*
EMP: 70
SQ FT: 30,000
SALES (est): 15MM **Privately Held**
WEB: www.sterlingmillwork.com
SIC: 2541 2431 1542 2517 Wood partitions & fixtures; millwork; commercial & office buildings, renovation & repair; commercial & office building, new construction; wood television & radio cabinets

(G-5132)
STEWART STEEL SPECIALTIES
20755 Whitlock St (48336-5169)
PHONE.................................248 477-0680
John C Stewart, *Partner*
Rick Stewart, *Partner*
EMP: 5 **EST:** 1911
SQ FT: 2,000
SALES (est): 330K **Privately Held**
SIC: 3444 Sheet metalwork

(G-5133)
SUBURBAN HOCKEY LLC (PA)
Also Called: Michigan Hockey
23995 Freeway Park Dr # 200 (48335-2829)
PHONE.................................248 478-1600
Thomas Anastos, *President*
EMP: 3
SQ FT: 3,300
SALES (est): 11.2MM **Privately Held**
SIC: 8748 2721 Business consulting; periodicals

(G-5134)
SUMIKA POLYMERS NORTH AMER LLC (DH)
27555 Executive Dr # 380 (48331-3554)
PHONE.................................248 284-4797
Brian K Weider, *President*
Osanu Sugasawa, *Vice Pres*
Joe Johnson, *CFO*
Scott Mitchell,
▲ **EMP:** 30 **EST:** 2011
SQ FT: 3,000
SALES (est): 7.8MM **Privately Held**
SIC: 2821 Polyoxymethylene resins
HQ: Sumitomo Chemical America, Inc.
150 E 42nd St Rm 701
New York NY 10017
212 572-8200

(G-5135)
SUN PHARMACEUTICAL INDS INC
29714 Orion Ct (48334-4114)
PHONE.................................248 346-7302
Jitendra Doshi, *Principal*
Jayesh Shah, *Project Mgr*
Greg Reed, *Manager*
EMP: 7
SALES (est): 721.3K **Privately Held**
SIC: 2834 Pharmaceutical preparations

(G-5136)
SUPERIOR MATERIALS LLC (PA)
30701 W 10 Mile Rd (48336-2617)
P.O. Box 2900 (48333-2900)
PHONE.................................248 788-8000
Jeff Spahr, *President*
EMP: 34 **EST:** 2007
SALES (est): 23.8MM **Privately Held**
SIC: 3273 Ready-mixed concrete

(G-5137)
SUPERIOR MATERIALS INC (PA)
585 Stewart Ave (48333)
P.O. Box 2900 (48333-2900)
PHONE.................................248 788-8000
Gary Lowell, *President*
EMP: 25
SALES (est): 21.8MM **Privately Held**
SIC: 3273 Ready-mixed concrete

(G-5138)
SUPERIOR MTLS HOLDINGS LLC
30701 W 10 Mile Rd (48336-2617)
P.O. Box 2900 (48333-2900)
PHONE.................................248 788-8000
Jeff Spahr, *President*
Karen Giles, *CFO*
EMP: 4
SALES (est): 244.3K **Privately Held**
SIC: 3273 Ready-mixed concrete

(G-5139)
TACHI-S ENGINEERING USA INC (HQ)
23227 Commerce Dr (48335-2705)
PHONE.................................248 478-5050
Kenji Kajihata, *President*
Craig Wisdom, *Production*
Mary Britton, *Senior Buyer*
Susan Serb, *Purch Agent*
Munjurul Hassan, *Engineer*
▲ **EMP:** 85
SQ FT: 57,400
SALES (est): 157.3MM **Privately Held**
WEB: www.tachi-s.com
SIC: 2531 Seats, automobile

GEOGRAPHIC SECTION

Farwell - Clare County (G-5166)

(G-5140)
THREAD GRINDING SERVICE INC
32420 W 8 Mile Rd (48336-5104)
PHONE..................248 474-5350
Donna Dancik, *President*
EMP: 8
SQ FT: 2,000
SALES (est): 678.1K **Privately Held**
WEB: www.threadcraft.com
SIC: 3599 Machine shop, jobbing & repair

(G-5141)
TITUS WELDING COMPANY
20750 Sunnydale St (48336-5251)
PHONE..................248 476-9366
Joseph F Cavanaugh, *President*
Paul E Centers, *Vice Pres*
EMP: 12
SQ FT: 7,000
SALES (est): 2.5MM **Privately Held**
WEB: www.tituswelding.com
SIC: 1791 7692 Structural steel erection; welding repair

(G-5142)
TMJ MANUFACTURING LLC
26842 Haggerty Rd (48331-5715)
PHONE..................248 987-7857
EMP: 20
SALES (est): 1.4MM **Privately Held**
SIC: 3841 Surgical & medical instruments

(G-5143)
TRW AUTOMOTIVE US LLC
23855 Research Dr (48335-2628)
PHONE..................248 426-3901
Fax: 248 426-3953
EMP: 45 **Privately Held**
SIC: 3469 Mfg Plastic Fastners
HQ: Trw Automotive U.S. Llc
12001 Tech Center Dr
Livonia MI 48150
734 855-2600

(G-5144)
TRYCO INC
23800 Research Dr (48335-2627)
P.O. Box 530188, Livonia, (48153-0188)
PHONE..................734 953-6800
Dave Moorehead, *President*
Sarah Ketelhut, *General Mgr*
Steve Miller, *Corp Secy*
Mark Henderickson, *Vice Pres*
Mark Hendrickson, *Info Tech Dir*
EMP: 14
SQ FT: 7,500
SALES (est): 4.5MM **Privately Held**
WEB: www.trycoinc.com
SIC: 2671 5169 5085 Paper coated or laminated for packaging; chemical additives; mill supplies

(G-5145)
VAL VALLEY INC
Also Called: International Minute Press
24409 Halsted Rd (48335-1669)
PHONE..................248 474-7335
Lynn Wattles, *President*
Sandy Pettit, *Vice Pres*
Dave Wattles, *Treasurer*
EMP: 3
SQ FT: 3,000
SALES (est): 426.9K **Privately Held**
WEB: www.impprinter.com
SIC: 2752 2791 2789 2759 Commercial printing, offset; typesetting; bookbinding & related work; commercial printing

(G-5146)
VAN-MARK PRODUCTS CORPORATION
24145 Industrial Park Dr (48335-2864)
PHONE..................248 478-1200
Jeff Van Cleave, *President*
Carol L Van Cleave, *Corp Secy*
Bryan Brillhart, *Sales Mgr*
Gary Weinert, *Sales Mgr*
Reine Gordon, *Office Mgr*
▼ **EMP:** 40
SQ FT: 26,000
SALES (est): 8.2MM **Privately Held**
SIC: 3549 3541 3542 Rotary slitters (metalworking machines); machine tools, metal cutting type; beaders, metal (machines)

(G-5147)
VERIMATION TECHNOLOGY INC
23883 Industrial Park Dr (48335-2860)
PHONE..................248 471-0000
Kenneth Law Sr, *Ch of Bd*
Bob Reuter, *Vice Pres*
EMP: 14 **EST:** 2002
SQ FT: 6,000
SALES (est): 3.4MM **Privately Held**
SIC: 3829 Gauging instruments, thickness ultrasonic

(G-5148)
VIBRACOUSTIC NORTH AMERICA LP
32605 W 12 Mile Rd # 350 (48334-3379)
PHONE..................248 410-5066
EMP: 3
SALES (est): 99K **Privately Held**
SIC: 2821 Plastics materials & resins

(G-5149)
VICOUNT INDUSTRIES INC
24704 Hathaway St (48335-1543)
PHONE..................248 471-5071
Philip D Padula, *President*
Jerry Sartor, *President*
Leonard Lavoy, *Vice Pres*
Gerard Sator, *Vice Pres*
Kevin Mann, *Project Mgr*
▲ **EMP:** 55
SQ FT: 30,000
SALES (est): 11.5MM **Privately Held**
WEB: www.vicount.net
SIC: 3544 3599 Special dies & tools; machine shop, jobbing & repair

(G-5150)
VOLK CORPORATION
Forbes Company
23936 Industrial Park Dr (48335-2861)
PHONE..................616 940-9900
Breck Foster, *Opers-Prdtn-Mfg*
EMP: 6
SQ FT: 10,000
SALES (corp-wide): 30.7MM **Privately Held**
WEB: www.volkcorp.com
SIC: 5113 3953 Shipping supplies; marking devices
PA: Volk Corporation
23936 Indl Pk Dr
Farmington Hills MI 48335
248 477-6700

(G-5151)
WELDING TECHNOLOGY CORP (HQ)
Also Called: W T C
24775 Crestview Ct (48335-1507)
PHONE..................248 477-3900
Durrell Miller, *Owner*
David Androvich, *Vice Pres*
Steve Connors, *Vice Pres*
◆ **EMP:** 10
SQ FT: 55,000
SALES (est): 6.5MM
SALES (corp-wide): 21.2MM **Privately Held**
WEB: www.weldtechcorp.com
SIC: 3548 3823 Welding & cutting apparatus & accessories; industrial instrmnts msrmnt display/control process variable
PA: Nadex Of America Corporation
24775 Crestview Ct
Farmington Hills MI 48335
248 477-3900

(G-5152)
WOODCRAFT CUSTOMS LLC
24790 Crestview Ct (48335-1506)
PHONE..................248 987-4473
Christopher Sentowski,
EMP: 6
SALES (est): 294.1K **Privately Held**
SIC: 2511 Wood household furniture

(G-5153)
WOOSHIN SAFETY SYSTEMS
23255 Commerce Dr (48335-2705)
PHONE..................248 615-4946
Chang Ho Lee, *Director*
EMP: 3 **EST:** 2016
SQ FT: 53,486
SALES (est): 100.3K **Privately Held**
SIC: 2399 Seat belts, automobile & aircraft

(G-5154)
ZF NORTH AMERICA INC
Also Called: ZF TRW Global Electronics
34605 W 12 Mile Rd (48331-3263)
PHONE..................248 478-7210
Chaity Math, *Supervisor*
EMP: 5
SALES (corp-wide): 216.2K **Privately Held**
SIC: 3469 Metal stampings
HQ: Zf North America, Inc.
15811 Centennial Dr 48
Northville MI 48168
734 416-6200

(G-5155)
ZF PASSIVE SAFETY
ZF TRW Automotive Electronics
24175 Research Dr (48335-2634)
PHONE..................248 478-7210
Darwin Mackew, *Senior Engr*
EMP: 339
SALES (corp-wide): 216.2K **Privately Held**
SIC: 3714 Motor vehicle parts & accessories
HQ: Zf Active Safety & Electronics Us Llc
12001 Tech Center Dr
Livonia MI 48150
734 855-2600

(G-5156)
ZUME IT INC
34405 W 12 Mile Rd # 137 (48331-5627)
PHONE..................248 522-6868
Sudhakar Nimmagadda, *President*
EMP: 5
SALES (est): 530.7K **Privately Held**
SIC: 7372 Prepackaged software

Farwell
Clare County

(G-5157)
ALLSTATE SIGN COMPANY INC
1291 E Surrey Rd (48622-8400)
PHONE..................989 386-4045
Michel Denoyer, *Owner*
EMP: 5
SALES (est): 537.8K **Privately Held**
SIC: 3993 Signs, not made in custom sign painting shops

(G-5158)
BOUCHEY AND SONS INC
750 Kapplinger Dr (48622-9478)
PHONE..................989 588-4118
Elizabeth Bouchey, *President*
Jack Bouchey, *Vice Pres*
Denise Bouchey, *Admin Sec*
EMP: 5
SALES (est): 898.5K **Privately Held**
SIC: 1794 1442 5211 4212 Excavation & grading, building construction; construction sand & gravel; sand & gravel; dump truck haulage; truck rental with drivers

(G-5159)
BUDD LOGGING LLC
3595 W Maple Grove Rd (48622-9782)
PHONE..................989 329-1578
James G Budd, *Principal*
EMP: 3 **EST:** 2010
SALES (est): 204.7K **Privately Held**
SIC: 2411 Logging

(G-5160)
CMC PLASTYK LLC
176 E Ludington Dr (48622-9447)
PHONE..................989 588-4468
Norman Myers,
Jeff Crandall,
Dave O'Dell,
EMP: 6
SQ FT: 18,000
SALES (est): 600K **Privately Held**
SIC: 2821 Molding compounds, plastics

(G-5161)
FUTURE MOLD CORPORATION
215 S Webber St (48622-8415)
PHONE..................989 588-9948
Melvin Otto, *President*
Marlene G Otto, *Vice Pres*
Michael Otto, *Vice Pres*
Don Trombley, *Plant Supt*
Joe Garvin, *Engineer*
EMP: 60 **EST:** 1970
SQ FT: 33,000
SALES (est): 10.5MM **Privately Held**
WEB: www.futuremoldcorp.com
SIC: 3544 Special dies, tools, jigs & fixtures

(G-5162)
JAMES JOY LLC
Also Called: Four Leaf Brewing
412 N Mcewan St (48622)
PHONE..................989 317-6629
Amy Shindorf, *Principal*
Brad Bellinger, *Principal*
EMP: 6 **EST:** 2014
SQ FT: 2,200
SALES (est): 460.7K **Privately Held**
SIC: 2082 Beer (alcoholic beverage)

(G-5163)
LEAR CORPORATION
Also Called: Renosol Seating
505 Hoover St (48622-9114)
P.O. Box 249 (48622-0249)
PHONE..................989 588-6181
Robert Webster, *Director*
EMP: 278
SALES (corp-wide): 21.1B **Publicly Held**
SIC: 3714 Motor vehicle electrical equipment
PA: Lear Corporation
21557 Telegraph Rd
Southfield MI 48033
248 447-1500

(G-5164)
MELLING PRODUCTS NORTH LLC
333 Grace St (48622-9772)
PHONE..................989 588-6147
Mark Melling, *Owner*
Thomas C Evanson, *Corp Secy*
David Dent, *Vice Pres*
Jennifer Struble, *Office Mgr*
EMP: 75
SQ FT: 44,000
SALES (est): 23.7MM
SALES (corp-wide): 265MM **Privately Held**
WEB: www.mellingproducts.com
SIC: 3498 3465 3714 Tube fabricating (contract bending & shaping); body parts, automobile; stamped metal; motor vehicle parts & accessories
PA: Melling Tool Co.
2620 Saradan Dr
Jackson MI 49202
517 787-8172

(G-5165)
ROGERS ATHLETIC COMPANY INC
3760 W Ludington Dr (48622-9795)
PHONE..................989 386-2950
David O Rogers, *President*
John Green, *Sales Dir*
Joel Brown, *Regl Sales Mgr*
Gabe Harrington, *Regl Sales Mgr*
Gary McMurry, *Regl Sales Mgr*
EMP: 10
SQ FT: 2,000
SALES (est): 6.3MM **Privately Held**
SIC: 3949 Football equipment & supplies, general

(G-5166)
SWAIN METER COMPANY
220 E Ludington Dr (48622-8413)
PHONE..................989 773-3700
Greg Gillespie, *CEO*
Brian Horanoff, *COO*
Tim Menjoulet, *Mfg Staff*

Felch - Dickinson County (G-5167)   GEOGRAPHIC SECTION

EMP: 5
SALES (est): 810.7K **Privately Held**
SIC: 3825 Ammeters

Felch
Dickinson County

(G-5167)
LE-Q FABRICATORS LTD
W4106 M 69 (49831)
P.O. Box 4, Niagara WI (54151-0004)
PHONE.................................906 246-3402
Mary Quick, *President*
Tim Quick, *Vice Pres*
EMP: 7 EST: 1972
SALES: 290K **Privately Held**
SIC: 3599 Machine shop, jobbing & repair

(G-5168)
M V A ENTERPRISES INC
N7721 Six Mile Lake Rd (49831-8878)
PHONE.................................906 282-6288
Mark Anderson, *President*
EMP: 3
SALES (est): 362.8K **Privately Held**
SIC: 2411 Logging camps & contractors

Fennville
Allegan County

(G-5169)
ABILITY MFG & ENGRG CO
Also Called: Ameco
1585 68th St (49408-9733)
P.O. Box 694, Saugatuck (49453-0694)
PHONE.................................269 227-3292
Jeff W Johnson, *President*
Elizabeth Johnson, *Vice Pres*
EMP: 19
SQ FT: 16,000
SALES (est): 2.2MM **Privately Held**
WEB: www.ameco.org
SIC: 7692 3441 3599 5084 Welding repair; fabricated structural metal; custom machinery; industrial machinery & equipment

(G-5170)
BIRDS EYE FOODS INC
100 Sherman Rd (49408)
P.O. Box 1050 (49408-1050)
PHONE.................................269 561-8211
Kim Baiers, *Branch Mgr*
EMP: 170
SALES (corp-wide): 9.5B **Publicly Held**
WEB: www.agrilinkfoods.com
SIC: 2033 Canned fruits & specialties
HQ: Birds Eye Foods, Inc.
   121 Woodcrest Rd
   Cherry Hill NJ 08003
   585 383-1850

(G-5171)
EVERGREEN LANE FARM LLC
1824 66th St (49408-9702)
PHONE.................................269 543-9900
Cathy Halinski, *President*
Tom Halinski, *CFO*
EMP: 3
SALES (est): 119.8K **Privately Held**
SIC: 0175 0139 2022 Apple orchard; food crops; herb or spice farm; cheese, natural & processed

(G-5172)
GREAT LAKES CANVAS CO
Also Called: Lakeside Canvas
2296 58th St (49408-8414)
PHONE.................................954 439-3090
Carl Miller, *President*
EMP: 3 EST: 2011
SALES: 100K **Privately Held**
SIC: 2211 Canvas

(G-5173)
HARRINGTON CONSTRUCTION CO
Also Called: Metal Fbrication Machining Div
6720 124th Ave (49408-9632)
PHONE.................................269 543-4251
Thomas L Harrington, *President*
Ed Miller, *Sales Executive*
EMP: 5 EST: 1942
SQ FT: 32,400
SALES (est): 1.3MM **Privately Held**
WEB: www.harringtonmarine.com
SIC: 3441 3599 Fabricated structural metal; machine shop, jobbing & repair

(G-5174)
HI TEC STAINLESS INC
6790 124th Ave (49408-9632)
PHONE.................................269 543-4205
Walter Radzinski, *President*
Gary Leonardis, *Vice Pres*
Lee Wagner, *Vice Pres*
EMP: 50
SALES (est): 7MM **Privately Held**
SIC: 3429 Marine hardware

(G-5175)
METALLURGICAL HIGH VACUUM CORP
6708 124th Ave (49408-9632)
PHONE.................................269 543-4291
Geoffrey Humberstone, *President*
Kristy Young, *Production*
Darel Roorda, *Engineer*
Deborah Humberstone, *Treasurer*
EMP: 17
SQ FT: 20,000
SALES (est): 3.5MM **Privately Held**
WEB: www.methivac.com
SIC: 3599 3563 Machine shop, jobbing & repair; air & gas compressors including vacuum pumps

(G-5176)
PGI OF SAUGATUCK INC
Also Called: Palazzolo's Gelato
413 3rd St (49408-8671)
PHONE.................................269 561-2000
Peter V Palazzolo, *President*
EMP: 30
SALES: 5MM **Privately Held**
WEB: www.4gelato.com
SIC: 2024 Ice cream, bulk

(G-5177)
SYSTEMS DESIGN & INSTALLATION
2091 66th St (49408-9779)
PHONE.................................269 543-4204
Paul Zehner, *President*
EMP: 4
SALES (est): 270K **Privately Held**
SIC: 1799 2522 Athletic & recreation facilities construction; office furniture, except wood

(G-5178)
TRANSPORT TRAILERS CO
2166 68th St (49408-8603)
PHONE.................................269 543-4405
Joel Johnson, *Owner*
EMP: 7
SQ FT: 8,000
SALES (est): 873K **Privately Held**
SIC: 3715 7539 Trailer bodies; trailer repair

(G-5179)
VIRTUE CIDER
2180 62nd St (49408-9407)
PHONE.................................269 455-0526
Gregory Hall, *Principal*
Michelle McDonnell, *Manager*
EMP: 7
SALES (est): 584.8K **Privately Held**
SIC: 2084 Wines

Fenton
Genesee County

(G-5180)
ALLIED INDUS SOLUTIONS LLC
Also Called: Ally Equipment Solutions
3061 W Thompson Rd Ste 1 (48430-9778)
PHONE.................................810 422-5093
Mark Kramer, *President*
David King, *General Mgr*
Kevin Kramer, *Controller*
EMP: 5 EST: 2017
SQ FT: 5,000
SALES (est): 339.3K **Privately Held**
SIC: 3535 Conveyors & conveying equipment

(G-5181)
ALLIED MAILING AND PRTG INC
Also Called: Allied Media.net
240 N Fenway Dr (48430-2699)
PHONE.................................810 750-8291
Christine Veit, *Project Mgr*
Richard Rockman Jr, *Admin Sec*
EMP: 20
SQ FT: 10,000
SALES (est): 4.3MM **Privately Held**
WEB: www.alliedmailing.net
SIC: 2752 Commercial printing, offset

(G-5182)
ALLY EQUIPMENT LLC
3061 W Thompson Rd (48430-9778)
PHONE.................................810 422-5093
Thomas Adams, *Mng Member*
David King,
EMP: 7
SQ FT: 5,000
SALES (est): 1.6MM **Privately Held**
WEB: www.allyequipmentsolutions.com
SIC: 3535 Conveyors & conveying equipment

(G-5183)
ATLAS TECHNOLOGIES LLC
Also Called: Material Cnversion Systems Div
3100 Copper Ave (48430-1778)
PHONE.................................810 714-2128
Samuel Seidman, *Chairman*
Kim Nation, *VP Finance*
▲ EMP: 55
SQ FT: 60,000
SALES: 12MM **Privately Held**
WEB: www.destacker.com
SIC: 3542 3549 3541 Sheet metalworking machines; assembly machines, including robotic; machine tools, metal cutting type
PA: Productivity Technologies Corp
   3100 Copper Ave
   Fenton MI 48430

(G-5184)
B & J TOOL CO
11289 Quality Dr (48430-9739)
PHONE.................................810 629-8577
Larry Shafer, *President*
Tim Le Cureux, *Vice Pres*
EMP: 12
SQ FT: 7,000
SALES (est): 2.1MM **Privately Held**
SIC: 3599 Machine shop, jobbing & repair

(G-5185)
B & J TOOL SERVICES INC
11289 Quality Way Dr (48430)
PHONE.................................810 629-8577
Michael Wagner, *President*
EMP: 4
SALES (est): 128.3K **Privately Held**
SIC: 3559 Automotive maintenance equipment

(G-5186)
BARGAIN BUSINESS SUPPLIES INC
1542 N Leroy St Ste 5 (48430-1972)
PHONE.................................810 750-0999
Jyoti Kapale, *CEO*
EMP: 3
SQ FT: 3,000
SALES (est): 120K **Privately Held**
SIC: 3692 Primary batteries, dry & wet

(G-5187)
BAY WOOD HOMES INC
1393 Eden Gardens Dr (48430-9623)
PHONE.................................989 245-4156
Richard W Haight, *President*
Bruce Holder, *Vice Pres*
EMP: 25
SQ FT: 14,000
SALES (est): 2.1MM **Privately Held**
SIC: 2452 3537 2541 2439 Prefabricated buildings, wood; industrial trucks & tractors; wood partitions & fixtures; structural wood members; hardwood veneer & plywood; millwork

(G-5188)
BENECOR INC
400 S Fenway Dr (48430-2667)
PHONE.................................248 437-4437
Brendan Foster, *President*
Corwin Foster, *Accounts Mgr*
▲ EMP: 14
SALES (est): 3.8MM **Privately Held**
SIC: 3561 Pumps & pumping equipment

(G-5189)
BENTLY SAND & GRAVEL
9220 Bennett Lake Rd (48430-9053)
PHONE.................................810 629-6172
Amma B Bentley, *Owner*
EMP: 4 EST: 1966
SALES: 200K **Privately Held**
SIC: 1442 5032 Gravel mining; gravel; sand, construction

(G-5190)
BOMAUR QUALITY PLASTICS INC
10388 Jayne Valley Ln (48430-3521)
PHONE.................................810 629-9701
Fax: 810 629-5183
EMP: 11
SQ FT: 9,000
SALES (est): 930K **Privately Held**
SIC: 3089 Plastic Injection Molding

(G-5191)
BREMEN CORP
300 N Alloy Dr (48430-2648)
PHONE.................................574 546-4238
David T Swallow, *President*
Steven Kelems, *Engineer*
Kaitlin Weaver, *Administration*
EMP: 3 EST: 2015
SALES (est): 287.5K **Privately Held**
SIC: 3086 Plastics foam products

(G-5192)
BURGAFLEX NORTH AMERICA LLC
Also Called: D & D Investments Equipment
1085 Grant St (48430-1715)
P.O. Box 435 (48430-0435)
PHONE.................................810 714-3285
Erik Roeren, *CEO*
David Kennedy, *President*
Jeremy Sheppard, *General Mgr*
Bob Siegwald, *Vice Pres*
Richard Reid, *Opers Staff*
▲ EMP: 32
SQ FT: 13,000
SALES (est): 17.3MM
SALES (corp-wide): 257.2K **Privately Held**
SIC: 3492 Hose & tube fittings & assemblies, hydraulic/pneumatic
HQ: Andre Bout Holding B.V.
   Mon Plaisir 112
   Etten-Leur

(G-5193)
CENTURY TOOL & GAGE LLC
200 S Alloy Dr (48430-1704)
PHONE.................................810 629-0784
Robert Rich, *President*
David Cummings, *Vice Pres*
Mike Swiecicki, *Purch Mgr*
Kevin Cummings, *Engineer*
Tim Cummings, *Engineer*
EMP: 75 EST: 1973
SQ FT: 72,000
SALES (est): 23.4MM
SALES (corp-wide): 48.7MM **Privately Held**
WEB: www.centurytool.com
SIC: 3544 Industrial molds; jigs & fixtures; special dies & tools
PA: Tooling Technology, Llc
   51223 Quadrate Dr
   Macomb MI 48042
   937 381-9211

(G-5194)
CLASSFCATION FLOTATION SYSTEMS
Also Called: C F S
235 Industrial Way (48430-1719)
PHONE.................................810 714-5200
Thomas Swaninger, *President*
EMP: 5

▲ = Import ▼ =Export
◆ =Import/Export

GEOGRAPHIC SECTION

Fenton - Genesee County (G-5223)

SALES (est): 1.1MM **Privately Held**
WEB: www.cfs-usa.com
SIC: 3532 Mining machinery

(G-5195)
CLIO SMOOTHIE LLC
1028 N Leroy St (48430-2756)
PHONE..................................810 691-9620
Craig Lemieux, *Principal*
EMP: 7
SALES (est): 608.2K **Privately Held**
SIC: 2037 Frozen fruits & vegetables

(G-5196)
CMI-SCHNEIBLE GROUP (HQ)
Also Called: C M I
3061 W Thompson Rd Ste 1 (48430-9778)
P.O. Box 155, Hartland (48353-0155)
PHONE..................................810 354-0404
William Goetz, *CEO*
Ray H Witt, *Director*
EMP: 39
SQ FT: 30,000
SALES (est): 4MM
SALES (corp-wide): 13.3MM **Privately Held**
WEB: www.cmischneible.com
SIC: 3443 Vessels, process or storage (from boiler shops): metal plate
PA: Cmi- Management Services Inc.
29580 Northwestern Hwy # 100
Southfield MI 48034
248 415-3950

(G-5197)
COMPATIBLE LASER PRODUCTS INC
1045 Grant St (48430-1715)
PHONE..................................810 629-0459
Susan Cave, *CEO*
Tony Cave, *President*
EMP: 12
SQ FT: 9,000
SALES: 1.1MM **Privately Held**
SIC: 3955 5943 3861 Print cartridges for laser & other computer printers; office forms & supplies; photographic equipment & supplies

(G-5198)
CREATIVE FOAM CORPORATION (PA)
Also Called: S P P D
300 N Alloy Dr (48430-2649)
PHONE..................................810 629-4149
Roger Morgan, *Ch of Bd*
Peter Swallow, *Vice Ch Bd*
Wayne Blessing, *President*
Bruce Graham, *Exec VP*
Dave Friend, *Vice Pres*
▲ EMP: 200
SQ FT: 102,500
SALES (est): 180.2MM **Privately Held**
SIC: 3061 3089 3053 3086 Mechanical rubber goods; injection molded finished plastic products; gaskets, packing & sealing devices; plastics foam products; foam rubber

(G-5199)
CREATIVE FOAM CORPORATION
Also Called: Fenway Business Unit
555 N Fenway Dr (48430-2636)
PHONE..................................810 714-0140
Greg Graham, *Engineer*
Paul Jonik, *Manager*
EMP: 90
SALES (corp-wide): 180.2MM **Privately Held**
SIC: 3089 3053 2671 3086 Injection molded finished plastic products; laminating of plastic; gaskets, packing & sealing devices; packaging paper & plastics film, coated & laminated; packaging & shipping materials, foamed plastic
PA: Creative Foam Corporation
300 N Alloy Dr
Fenton MI 48430
810 629-4149

(G-5200)
DOMICO MED-DEVICE LLC
14241 N Fenton Rd (48430-1541)
PHONE..................................810 750-5300
Michael Czop,
EMP: 84
SALES: 11MM **Privately Held**
SIC: 3841 Surgical & medical instruments

(G-5201)
EAGLE WELDING LLC
11413 Nora Dr (48430-8702)
PHONE..................................810 750-0772
Daniel Orzel, *Principal*
EMP: 7
SALES (est): 97K **Privately Held**
SIC: 7692 Welding repair

(G-5202)
ENERGY CONTROL SOLUTIONS INC
Also Called: Control Pak International
11494 Delmar Dr Ste 100 (48430-9018)
PHONE..................................810 735-2800
Timothy Glinke, *President*
EMP: 9
SQ FT: 8,000
SALES (est): 1.6MM **Privately Held**
WEB: www.controlpak.com
SIC: 3822 Thermostats & other environmental sensors

(G-5203)
ENIHCAM CORP
3061 W Thompson Rd Ste 1 (48430-9778)
P.O. Box 155, Hartland (48353-0155)
PHONE..................................810 354-0404
Brian Schram, *President*
EMP: 5
SALES (est): 276.7K **Privately Held**
SIC: 3541 Milling machines

(G-5204)
EPIC MACHINE INC
201 Industrial Way Ste A (48430-1793)
PHONE..................................810 629-9400
Mike Parker, *President*
Michael Parker, *President*
Nicholas Popa, *Chairman*
Daniel Whaley, *Vice Pres*
EMP: 20 EST: 1953
SALES (est): 4.1MM **Privately Held**
WEB: www.epicmachine.com
SIC: 3599 3544 Machine shop, jobbing & repair; special dies, tools, jigs & fixtures

(G-5205)
EXPOSURE UNLIMITED INC
4708 Brookside Rd (48430-9334)
PHONE..................................248 459-9104
Jacqueline Bailey, *President*
EMP: 4
SALES (est): 520K **Privately Held**
SIC: 5199 7389 2395 7336 Advertising specialties; advertising, promotional & trade show services; embroidery products, except schiffli machine; silk screen design

(G-5206)
EZBAKE TECHNOLOGIES LLC
Also Called: Bakery Ingredient Mfg
7244 Driftwood Dr (48430-4308)
P.O. Box 270527, Flower Mound TX (75027-0527)
PHONE..................................817 430-1621
Rita Tolvanen,
EMP: 3
SALES: 1.8MM **Privately Held**
SIC: 8742 7389 2045 Industry specialist consultants; ; prepared flour mixes & doughs

(G-5207)
FENTON CHAMBER COMMERCE
104 S Adelaide St (48430-2804)
PHONE..................................810 629-5447
Shelly Day, *President*
EMP: 3
SALES: 431.5K **Privately Held**
SIC: 8611 2711 Chamber of Commerce; newspapers

(G-5208)
FENTON CONCRETE INC
10513 Old Us 23 (48430-9385)
P.O. Box 497 (48430-0497)
PHONE..................................810 629-0783
Curtis M Schupbach, *President*
EMP: 7 EST: 1975
SQ FT: 4,800
SALES (est): 1.1MM **Privately Held**
SIC: 3273 5211 Ready-mixed concrete; lumber & other building materials

(G-5209)
FENTON CORPORATION (PA)
3236 Owen Rd (48430-1758)
PHONE..................................810 629-2858
Bobby D Butts, *President*
Brian Kelly, *Purchasing*
EMP: 6
SQ FT: 2,400
SALES (est): 3.2MM **Privately Held**
SIC: 6553 3272 5999 5099 Cemeteries, real estate operation; concrete products, precast; monuments & tombstones; monuments & grave markers

(G-5210)
FENTON MEMORIALS & VAULTS INC
3236 Owen Rd (48430-1758)
P.O. Box 289 (48430-0289)
PHONE..................................810 629-2858
Gregory Duberg, *President*
EMP: 18 EST: 1945
SQ FT: 1,800
SALES (est): 2.6MM
SALES (corp-wide): 3.2MM **Privately Held**
SIC: 3272 5099 5999 Burial vaults, concrete or precast terrazzo; monuments & grave markers; monuments & tombstones
PA: Fenton Corporation
3236 Owen Rd
Fenton MI 48430
810 629-2858

(G-5211)
FENTON PRINTING INC
14312 N Fenton Rd (48430-1544)
PHONE..................................810 750-9450
Mike Pearson, *President*
EMP: 3
SQ FT: 1,800
SALES (est): 497.6K **Privately Held**
WEB: www.fentonprinting.com
SIC: 2752 Commercial printing, offset

(G-5212)
FENTON RADIATOR & GARAGE INC
1542 N Leroy St Ste 4 (48430-1972)
PHONE..................................810 629-0923
Daniel Phalen, *President*
Tina Phalen, *Admin Sec*
EMP: 4
SQ FT: 4,000
SALES: 650K **Privately Held**
SIC: 7539 7538 5531 3599 Radiator repair shop, automotive; general automotive repair shops; automobile air conditioning equipment, sale, installation; flexible metal hose, tubing & bellows

(G-5213)
FENTON SAND & GRAVEL INC
11129 Delphinium Dr (48430-3530)
PHONE..................................810 750-4293
Carol Smith, *CEO*
EMP: 6
SALES (est): 570.6K **Privately Held**
SIC: 1442 Construction sand & gravel

(G-5214)
FENTON WINERY BREWERY
1545 N Leroy St Ste B (48430-1971)
PHONE..................................810 373-4194
Matt Sherrow, *Owner*
Jinny Sherrow, *Co-Owner*
EMP: 3
SALES (est): 297.9K **Privately Held**
SIC: 2084 Wines

(G-5215)
FOX FIRE GLASS LLC
3071 W Thompson Rd (48430-9705)
PHONE..................................248 332-2442
Donna Stiefel, *Mng Member*
EMP: 4
SALES (est): 421.2K **Privately Held**
SIC: 3231 Products of purchased glass

(G-5216)
GLOBAL FMI LLC
17195 Silver Pkwy Ste 111 (48430-3426)
PHONE..................................810 964-5555
Deane Nash, *Mng Member*
Tim Kruszka,
EMP: 70
SALES: 3MM **Privately Held**
SIC: 3463 3714 3465 3519 Nonferrous forgings; motor vehicle parts & accessories; automotive stampings; internal combustion engines

(G-5217)
GREAT LAKES TECH & MFG LLC
201 S Alloy Dr Ste C (48430-4435)
P.O. Box 550 (48430-0550)
PHONE..................................810 593-0257
Charles Rice,
EMP: 4
SALES: 900K **Privately Held**
SIC: 3535 Conveyors & conveying equipment

(G-5218)
H & H POWDERCOATING INC
300 S Fenway Dr (48430-2657)
PHONE..................................810 750-1800
Brett Hammond, *Principal*
EMP: 6 EST: 2005
SALES (est): 611.7K **Privately Held**
SIC: 3399 Powder, metal

(G-5219)
HARROUN ENTERPRISES INC
1111 Fenway Cir (48430-2644)
PHONE..................................810 629-9885
Hugh D Harroun, *President*
▲ EMP: 6
SQ FT: 30,000
SALES (est): 1.2MM **Privately Held**
WEB: www.harroun.com
SIC: 3545 Boring machine attachments (machine tool accessories); bits for use on lathes, planers, shapers, etc.; milling cutters

(G-5220)
HOLLY PLATING CO INC
1101 Copper Ave (48430-1770)
PHONE..................................810 714-9213
Paul Bubnar, *Manager*
EMP: 20
SALES (est): 1.6MM
SALES (corp-wide): 4.4MM **Privately Held**
SIC: 3471 Electroplating of metals or formed products
PA: Holly Plating Co. Inc.
111 Rosette St
Holly MI 48442
248 634-9361

(G-5221)
JENSEN INDUSTRIES INC. (PA)
3061 W Thompson Rd Ste 1 (48430-9778)
P.O. Box 325, Hartland (48353-0325)
PHONE..................................810 224-5005
EMP: 18
SALES (est): 3.4MM **Privately Held**
WEB: www.jensenind.com
SIC: 7699 3567 Industrial equipment services; radiant heating systems, industrial process

(G-5222)
KENEWELL GROUP
3031 W Thompson Rd (48430-9771)
PHONE..................................810 714-4290
Blair Kennewell, *Owner*
EMP: 8
SALES (est): 1MM **Privately Held**
WEB: www.kenewellgroup.com
SIC: 2759 7319 7334 7336 Commercial printing; advertising; photocopying & duplicating services; graphic arts & related design

(G-5223)
KOHLER CO
720 Grant St (48430-2059)
PHONE..................................810 208-0032
EMP: 48
SALES (corp-wide): 7.7B **Privately Held**
SIC: 3431 Plumbing fixtures: enameled iron cast iron or pressed metal

Fenton - Genesee County (G-5224)   GEOGRAPHIC SECTION

PA: Kohler Co.
444 Highland Dr
Kohler WI 53044
920 457-4441

(G-5224)
KUKA ASSEMBLY AND TEST CORP
255 S Fenway Dr (48430-2628)
P.O. Box 1968, Saginaw (48605-1968)
PHONE..................810 593-0350
John Guynn, *Mfg Staff*
Matt Shewell, *Engineer*
Scott Orendach, *Manager*
EMP: 85
SALES (corp-wide): 37.7B **Privately Held**
SIC: 3826 Environmental testing equipment
HQ: Kuka Assembly And Test Corp.
5675 Dixie Hwy
Saginaw MI 48601
989 220-3088

(G-5225)
LINEAR MEASUREMENT INSTRS CORP
Also Called: L M I
101 N Alloy Dr Ste B (48430-1794)
PHONE..................810 714-5811
Ernest Booker, *President*
Martha Knobler, *COO*
EMP: 21
SQ FT: 12,500
SALES (est): 3.1MM **Privately Held**
WEB: www.lmicorporation.com
SIC: 3599 Machine shop, jobbing & repair

(G-5226)
MOTT MEDIA LLC (PA)
Also Called: Living Hope Books & More
1130 Fenway Cir (48430-2641)
PHONE..................810 714-4280
William P Hoetger,
Jacqueline M Hoetger,
EMP: 15
SQ FT: 15,900
SALES (est): 1.4MM **Privately Held**
WEB: www.homeschoolingbooks.com
SIC: 2731 5192 Books: publishing only; books

(G-5227)
NORTHERN PROCESS SYSTEMS INC
235 Industrial Way (48430-1719)
PHONE..................810 714-5200
Thomas Swaninger, *President*
Tom Lippold, *Vice Pres*
EMP: 3
SALES (est): 377.2K **Privately Held**
SIC: 5084 3496 Screening machinery & equipment; wire cloth & woven wire products

(G-5228)
PARAGON MANUFACTURING CORP
2046 W Thompson Rd (48430-9798)
PHONE..................810 629-4100
Robert A Booher, *President*
EMP: 12
SQ FT: 8,000
SALES (est): 1.8MM **Privately Held**
SIC: 3599 Machine shop, jobbing & repair

(G-5229)
PARSHALLVILLE CIDER MILL
8507 Parshallville Rd (48430-9239)
P.O. Box 353, Clarkston (48347-0353)
PHONE..................810 629-9079
EMP: 6
SALES (est): 44.2K **Privately Held**
SIC: 2099 Mfg Food Preparations

(G-5230)
PHOENIX DENTAL INC
3452 W Thompson Rd (48430-9635)
PHONE..................810 750-2328
Jeffrey Cox, *President*
EMP: 5
SALES: 450K **Privately Held**
WEB: www.phoenixdental.com
SIC: 3843 Compounds, dental

(G-5231)
PRODUCTIVITY TECHNOLOGIES (PA)
3100 Copper Ave (48430-1778)
PHONE..................810 714-0200
Samuel N Seidman, *Ch of Bd*
Arthur Stupay, *Principal*
Michael D Austin, *Senior VP*
Jesse A Levine, *Vice Pres*
EMP: 160
SALES (est): 12.1MM **Privately Held**
WEB: www.productivitytech.com
SIC: 3542 3541 3545 Machine tools, metal forming type; machine tools, metal cutting type; machine tool accessories

(G-5232)
PUSHMAN MANUFACTURING CO INC
1044 Grant St (48430-1716)
PHONE..................810 629-9688
Michael D Pushman, *Ch of Bd*
Marie E Foguth, *Corp Secy*
Gerald Bidelman, *Vice Pres*
James W Pushman, *Vice Pres*
Jimi Pushman, *Project Mgr*
EMP: 25 **EST:** 1965
SQ FT: 18,000
SALES (est): 2.6MM **Privately Held**
SIC: 3599 7692 Machine shop, jobbing & repair; welding repair

(G-5233)
QUILTERS GARDEN INC
1347 Lake Valley Dr (48430-1244)
PHONE..................810 750-8104
Carolyn Nance, *President*
EMP: 3
SALES (est): 278.5K **Privately Held**
WEB: www.quiltersparadiseonline.com
SIC: 2395 5949 Quilted fabrics or cloth; quilting materials & supplies

(G-5234)
RING SCREW LLC
Fenton Operations
2480 Owen Rd (48430-1769)
PHONE..................810 629-6602
Jim O'Day, *Manager*
EMP: 112
SQ FT: 55,000
SALES (corp-wide): 30.9MM **Privately Held**
SIC: 3452 Bolts, nuts, rivets & washers
HQ: Ring Screw Llc
6125 18 Mile Rd
Sterling Heights MI 48314
586 997-5600

(G-5235)
ROCKMAN & SONS PUBLISHING LLC
240 N Fenway Dr (48430-2699)
PHONE..................810 750-6011
Mark Rockwood, *Info Tech Dir*
Craig Rockman,
Richard Rockman Jr,
EMP: 10
SQ FT: 5,500
SALES (est): 530K **Privately Held**
WEB: www.rockman-exe.com
SIC: 2711 2731 2721 Newspapers, publishing & printing; books: publishing only; periodicals

(G-5236)
ROCKMAN COMMUNICATIONS INC
Also Called: Tri-County Times
256 N Fenway Dr (48430-2699)
P.O. Box 1125 (48430-5125)
PHONE..................810 433-6800
John Evans, *Business Mgr*
Craig Rockman, *Vice Pres*
Jillian Banish, *Marketing Staff*
EMP: 35
SALES (est): 2.1MM **Privately Held**
WEB: www.rock7625site.com
SIC: 2711 4813 Newspapers;

(G-5237)
SANDYS CONTRACTING
10464 Circle J Ct (48430-9515)
PHONE..................810 629-2259
Sandy Meade, *Owner*
EMP: 5
SALES (est): 188.5K **Privately Held**
SIC: 1429 Crushed & broken stone

(G-5238)
SHOUSE TOOL INC
290 N Alloy Dr (48430-2645)
PHONE..................810 629-0391
Virgil Shouse, *President*
Haney Shouse, *Corp Secy*
Bill Shouse, *Vice Pres*
Mike Shouse, *VP Opers*
Kurt Mosher, *Sales Mgr*
EMP: 18
SALES (est): 2.4MM **Privately Held**
WEB: www.shousetool.com
SIC: 3545 Cutting tools for machine tools

(G-5239)
STANDALE SMOOTHIE LLC
1028 N Leroy St (48430-2756)
PHONE..................810 691-9625
Dianne Lemieux, *Principal*
EMP: 5 **EST:** 2015
SALES (est): 274.9K **Privately Held**
SIC: 2037 Frozen fruits & vegetables

(G-5240)
STONEBRDGE TECHNICAL ENTPS LTD
Also Called: Stonebridge Technical Services
14165 N Fenton Rd 102c (48430-1587)
PHONE..................810 750-0040
David Hense, *President*
Bill Rogner, *Opers Mgr*
Brad Austin, *Engineer*
EMP: 15
SALES (est): 1.2MM **Privately Held**
SIC: 8748 3492 3625 8711 Systems analysis or design; control valves, fluid power: hydraulic & pneumatic; electric controls & control accessories, industrial; machine tool design

(G-5241)
TELMAR MANUFACTURING COMPANY
2121 W Thompson Rd (48430-9704)
PHONE..................810 577-7050
Paul Martel, *Owner*
EMP: 6
SQ FT: 1,600
SALES: 420K **Privately Held**
SIC: 3714 Motor vehicle parts & accessories

(G-5242)
TELO
707 Hickory St (48430-1880)
PHONE..................810 845-8051
EMP: 5
SQ FT: 1,800
SALES (est): 162.6K **Privately Held**
SIC: 2051 Mfg Bread/Related Products

(G-5243)
THOMAS TOYS INC
2017 Bly Dr (48430-1486)
P.O. Box 405 (48430-0405)
PHONE..................810 629-8707
Julian R Thomas, *President*
Julie Thomas, *Principal*
Lorraine Thomas, *Corp Secy*
EMP: 3
SALES (est): 276.1K **Privately Held**
SIC: 3492 5945 Fluid power valves & hose fittings; toys & games

(G-5244)
TIG ENTITY LLC
Also Called: Thompson I.G.
3196 W Thompson Rd (48430-9799)
PHONE..................810 629-9558
Thomas Donovan, *Mng Member*
EMP: 3 **EST:** 2012
SALES (est): 48K **Privately Held**
SIC: 3229 Industrial-use glassware

(G-5245)
TOOL SALES & ENGINEERING
1045 Grant St (48430-1715)
PHONE..................810 714-5000
Charles L Marcotte, *Owner*
Diane Wedell, *Manager*
EMP: 3

SALES: 130K **Privately Held**
SIC: 3421 5251 Scissors, shears, clippers, snips & similar tools; tools

(G-5246)
TRI-TEC SEAL LLC (HQ)
Also Called: Tritec Performance Solutions
2111 W Thompson Rd (48430-9704)
PHONE..................810 655-3900
Steve Bentson, *CEO*
Marcus Pillion, *Mng Member*
▲ **EMP:** 33
SALES (est): 7MM
SALES (corp-wide): 79.6MM **Privately Held**
SIC: 3053 3566 Gaskets, all materials; gears, power transmission, except automotive
PA: Edgewater Capital Partners, L.P.
5005 Rockside Rd Ste 840
Independence OH 44131
216 292-3838

(G-5247)
TRUSTED TOOL MFG INC
8075 Old Us 23 (48430-9309)
PHONE..................810 750-6000
John K Martin, *President*
EMP: 7
SQ FT: 5,000
SALES (est): 1MM **Privately Held**
WEB: www.trustedtoolmfg.com
SIC: 3545 3599 Gauges (machine tool accessories); custom machinery

(G-5248)
VALMEC INC
12487 Thornbury Dr (48430-9558)
P.O. Box 1069 (48430-5069)
PHONE..................810 629-8750
Krystn Tatus, *CEO*
Bradley Van Leuven, *President*
Colin Van Leuven, *Vice Pres*
Larry Van Leuven, *Treasurer*
EMP: 6 **EST:** 1972
SALES: 1.5MM **Privately Held**
WEB: www.valmecinc.com
SIC: 5084 5199 3625 7389 Conveyor systems; packaging materials; electric controls & control accessories, industrial;

(G-5249)
ZANDER COLLOIDS LC (PA)
Also Called: Adcr
2040 W Thompson Rd (48430-9798)
P.O. Box 1095 (48430-5095)
PHONE..................810 714-1623
Doug Brumbill,
◆ **EMP:** 5
SQ FT: 3,400
SALES (est): 1.3MM **Privately Held**
SIC: 2821 Silicone resins

(G-5250)
ZF ACTIVE SAFETY US INC
9475 Center Rd (48430-9388)
PHONE..................810 750-1036
Bob Holman, *Manager*
EMP: 126
SALES (corp-wide): 216.2K **Privately Held**
SIC: 3714 Motor vehicle parts & accessories
HQ: Zf Active Safety Us Inc.
12001 Tech Center Dr
Livonia MI 48150
734 812-6979

Ferndale
Oakland County

(G-5251)
1395 JARVIS LLC
1395 Jarvis St (48220-2025)
PHONE..................248 545-6800
Ronald Desena, *President*
EMP: 3
SALES (est): 210.1K **Privately Held**
SIC: 3442 Metal doors

GEOGRAPHIC SECTION
Ferndale - Oakland County (G-5280)

(G-5252)
AEROBEE ELECTRIC INC
3030 Hilton Rd (48220-1019)
PHONE..................248 549-2044
Timothy Craddock, *President*
EMP: 9
SALES (est): 1.3MM **Privately Held**
WEB: www.aerobeeelectric.com
SIC: 1731 3699 General electrical contractor; electrical equipment & supplies

(G-5253)
AEROFAB COMPANY INC
2335 Goodrich St (48220-1440)
PHONE..................248 542-0051
Robert M Eckerman, *Ch of Bd*
Jules Bols III, *President*
EMP: 10 **EST:** 1991
SQ FT: 30,000
SALES (est): 1.7MM **Privately Held**
SIC: 3069 Molded rubber products

(G-5254)
AFRICAN AMERICAN PARENT PUBG
Also Called: Blac Detroit Magazine
22041 Woodward Ave (48220-2520)
PHONE..................248 398-3400
Alexis Bourkoulas, *Vice Pres*
Chantel Wright, *Director*
EMP: 7
SQ FT: 4,500
SALES (est): 249.1K **Privately Held**
SIC: 2721 Magazines: publishing only, not printed on site

(G-5255)
AIRGAS USA LLC
1200 Farrow St (48220-1960)
PHONE..................248 545-9353
Jim Borland, *Sales Staff*
Irving Sparage, *Branch Mgr*
EMP: 25
SALES (corp-wide): 125.9MM **Privately Held**
WEB: www.us.linde-gas.com
SIC: 5085 3548 Industrial supplies; welding apparatus
HQ: Airgas Usa, Llc
  259 N Radnor Chester Rd
  Radnor PA 19087
  610 687-5253

(G-5256)
ALL KIDS CONSIDERED PUBG GROUP
22041 Woodward Ave (48220-2520)
PHONE..................248 398-3400
Linda Holland, *Sales Staff*
Cornelius Fortune, *Assoc Editor*
Alyssa R Martina, *Administration*
EMP: 8
SALES (est): 796.9K **Privately Held**
SIC: 2741 Miscellaneous publishing

(G-5257)
ALL KIDS CONSIDERED PUBLISHING
Also Called: Metro Parent Media Group
22041 Woodward Ave (48220-2520)
PHONE..................248 398-3400
Alyssa R Martina, *President*
Stacey Mourtos, *Editor*
Stacey Winconek, *Editor*
Alexia Bourkoulas, *Vice Pres*
Chantel Maloney, *Opers Mgr*
EMP: 17
SALES (est): 2MM **Privately Held**
WEB: www.metroparent.com
SIC: 2721 Magazines: publishing only, not printed on site

(G-5258)
ALLENDER & COMPANY
615 Livernois St (48220-2303)
PHONE..................248 398-5776
Steven Allender, *Owner*
EMP: 3 **EST:** 1977
SQ FT: 4,200
SALES (est): 519.7K **Privately Held**
SIC: 5131 2211 Piece goods & other fabrics; shade cloth, window: cotton

(G-5259)
ALLIED PRINTING CO INC (PA)
Also Called: Allied Distribution
2035 Hilton Rd (48220-1574)
PHONE..................248 541-0551
Robert Straub, *CEO*
Paul Zimmer, *Ch of Bd*
David Bader, *President*
Tony Pelc - Vp, *Opers Staff*
Jim Sommerfeld, *Director*
EMP: 21
SQ FT: 255,000
SALES (est): 14.1MM **Privately Held**
WEB: www.allied-online.com
SIC: 2752 4212 Commercial printing, offset; mail carriers, contract

(G-5260)
ALLIED PRINTING CO INC
965 Wanda St (48220-2959)
PHONE..................248 514-7394
Joe Wegher, *Branch Mgr*
EMP: 50
SALES (corp-wide): 14.1MM **Privately Held**
SIC: 2752 4212 Commercial printing, offset; local trucking, without storage
PA: Allied Printing Co., Inc.
  2035 Hilton Rd
  Ferndale MI 48220
  248 541-0551

(G-5261)
ARC MIT
660 E 10 Mile Rd (48220-1036)
PHONE..................248 399-4800
EMP: 8
SALES (est): 671.6K **Privately Held**
SIC: 3312 Blast Furnace-Steel Works

(G-5262)
ARKIN AUTOMOTIVE INC
2600 Wolcott St (48220-1468)
PHONE..................248 542-1192
Frances Golden, *President*
Cherylinn Golden, *Corp Secy*
EMP: 3
SQ FT: 1,000
SALES (est): 289.6K **Privately Held**
SIC: 3699 Trouble lights

(G-5263)
AXLE OF DEARBORN INC (PA)
Also Called: Detroit Axle
2000 W 8 Mile Rd (48220-2215)
PHONE..................248 543-5995
Abdul Musheinesh, *President*
Mouhamad Musheinesh, *Vice Pres*
▲ **EMP:** 148
SQ FT: 175,000
SALES: 67.7MM **Privately Held**
SIC: 5013 5531 3312 Automotive hardware; automotive supplies; automotive parts; axles, rolled or forged: made in steel mills

(G-5264)
B NEKTAR LLC
Also Called: B Nektar Meadery
1505b Jarvis St (48220-2025)
PHONE..................313 999-5157
Brad Dahlhofer,
EMP: 4
SALES (est): 100K **Privately Held**
SIC: 2084 Wines

(G-5265)
CAMPBELL SOUP COMPANY
1220 E 9 Mile Rd (48220-1972)
PHONE..................248 336-8486
EMP: 90
SALES (corp-wide): 8.1B **Publicly Held**
SIC: 5461 2038 2033 2052 Bakeries; frozen specialties; canned fruits & specialties; cookies & crackers; bread, cake & related products; potato chips & similar snacks
PA: Campbell Soup Company
  1 Campbell Pl
  Camden NJ 08103
  856 342-4800

(G-5266)
CANDLE WICK
175 W 9 Mile Rd (48220-1730)
PHONE..................248 547-2987
Eric Paquette, *Owner*
EMP: 6
SALES (est): 476.3K **Privately Held**
SIC: 3999 Candles

(G-5267)
CONTEXT FURNITURE L L C
1054 W Lewiston Ave (48220-1286)
P.O. Box 2385, Sequim WA (98382-4341)
PHONE..................248 200-0724
Carrie Moore, *President*
Bryce Moore, *Vice Pres*
EMP: 4
SALES (est): 380.3K **Privately Held**
WEB: www.contextfurniture.com
SIC: 2511 Dining room furniture: wood

(G-5268)
COVENTRY CREATIONS INC (PA)
195 W 9 Mile Rd (48220-2914)
PHONE..................248 547-2987
EMP: 4
SALES (est): 511.7K **Privately Held**
SIC: 3999 Candles

(G-5269)
DARSON CORPORATION
10610 Galaxie Ave (48220-2171)
PHONE..................313 875-7781
Mary Ellen Darge, *President*
EMP: 10 **EST:** 1973
SQ FT: 15,000
SALES (est): 1.3MM **Privately Held**
SIC: 2759 Screen printing

(G-5270)
DAVID EPSTEIN INC
Also Called: Better-Form
1135 E 9 Mile Rd (48220-1936)
PHONE..................248 542-0802
David Epstein, *President*
▲ **EMP:** 10
SQ FT: 3,000
SALES (est): 1.5MM **Privately Held**
WEB: www.betterformfoot.com
SIC: 3842 3841 3131 Orthopedic appliances; surgical & medical instruments; footwear cut stock

(G-5271)
DETAIL PRECISION PRODUCTS INC
1480 E 9 Mile Rd (48220-2040)
PHONE..................248 544-3390
Michael W Fox, *President*
Linda J Fox, *Vice Pres*
EMP: 20
SQ FT: 12,000
SALES (est): 3.3MM **Privately Held**
WEB: www.detailprecision.com
SIC: 3728 3545 3462 Aircraft parts & equipment; machine tool accessories; iron & steel forgings

(G-5272)
DETAIL PRODUCTION COMPANY INC
1480 E 9 Mile Rd (48220-2040)
PHONE..................248 544-3390
Clifford J Seeger, *President*
Linda J Fox, *Corp Secy*
EMP: 15 **EST:** 1942
SQ FT: 12,000
SALES (est): 1.3MM **Privately Held**
SIC: 3714 Gears, motor vehicle

(G-5273)
DETROIT BUBBLE TEA COMPANY
22821 Woodward Ave (48220-1738)
PHONE..................248 239-1131
Lisa Beilstein, *Human Res Dir*
EMP: 7
SALES (est): 585.9K **Privately Held**
SIC: 2086 Tea, iced: packaged in cans, bottles, etc.

(G-5274)
DETROIT COIL CO
2435 Hilton Rd (48220-1599)
PHONE..................248 658-1543
Robert Dugan, *President*
David Gohlke, *CFO*
Kevin Browning, *Shareholder*
William Buban, *Shareholder*
Don Eichderger, *Shareholder*
▲ **EMP:** 45
SQ FT: 22,000
SALES (est): 7.4MM **Privately Held**
SIC: 3625 3728 3621 Solenoid switches (industrial controls); industrial controls: push button, selector switches, pilot; aircraft parts & equipment; motors & generators

(G-5275)
DETROIT CORNICE & SLATE CO INC
1315 Academy St (48220-2001)
PHONE..................248 398-7690
Doneen Hesse, *President*
Kurt Hesse, *Vice Pres*
Dawn Hesse, *Admin Sec*
EMP: 20 **EST:** 1888
SQ FT: 11,200
SALES (est): 5.6MM **Privately Held*
WEB: www.detroitcorniceandslate.com
SIC: 1761 3444 2952 Roofing contractor; sheet metalwork; sheet metalwork; asphalt felts & coatings

(G-5276)
DETROIT ELEVATOR COMPANY
2121 Burdette St Ste A (48220-1992)
PHONE..................248 591-7484
Donald Purdie, *President*
Sheri Depifanio, *Principal*
Don Purdie Jr, *Vice Pres*
Sheri Purdie, *Vice Pres*
Chris Frump, *Info Tech Mgr*
EMP: 50
SQ FT: 100,000
SALES (est): 7.9MM **Privately Held**
SIC: 1796 3534 7699 Elevator installation & conversion; elevators & equipment; elevators: inspection, service & repair

(G-5277)
DETROIT FINE PRODUCTS LLC
Also Called: Detroit Grooming Company LLC
2615 Wolcott St Ste E (48220-1422)
PHONE..................877 294-5826
Steve Henes, *Mng Member*
EMP: 12
SALES (est): 864.4K **Privately Held**
SIC: 2844 Hair preparations, including shampoos

(G-5278)
DETROIT NAME PLATE ETCHING INC
10610 Galaxie Ave (48220-2171)
PHONE..................248 543-5200
Gregory Rivard, *President*
Linda Sarp, *QC Mgr*
Chin Rivard, *Sales Staff*
David Rivard, *Manager*
John B Peabody, *Shareholder*
▲ **EMP:** 31 **EST:** 1986
SQ FT: 11,000
SALES (est): 5.2MM **Privately Held**
WEB: www.dnpe.com
SIC: 3479 2396 3993 Name plates: engraved, etched, etc.; automotive & apparel trimmings; signs & advertising specialties

(G-5279)
DISTINCTIVE CUSTOM FURNITURE
2425 Burdette St (48220-1445)
PHONE..................248 399-9175
Christopher Wilson, *President*
EMP: 3
SQ FT: 1,750
SALES (est): 270K **Privately Held**
WEB: www.dcffurniture.com
SIC: 2511 Kitchen & dining room furniture

(G-5280)
DIVERSFIED PRCUREMENT SVCS LLC
1530 Farrow St (48220-1907)
PHONE..................248 821-1147
Donald John O Connell,
EMP: 4

SALES (est): 330K **Privately Held**
SIC: 5047 3443 3469 3465 Medical equipment & supplies; metal parts; machine parts, stamped or pressed metal; automotive stampings; motor vehicle supplies & new parts; automotive supplies & parts

(G-5281)
DIVERSIFIED METAL FABRICATORS
2351 Hilton Rd (48220-1570)
PHONE..................................248 541-0500
Gary W Dulong, *President*
EMP: 23
SALES (est): 4.6MM **Privately Held**
SIC: 3444 Sheet metal specialties, not stamped

(G-5282)
ENGINEERED ALUM FABRICATORS CO
Also Called: Engineered Alum Fabricators
1530 Farrow St (48220-1907)
PHONE..................................248 582-3430
Donald John O'Connell, *President*
▲ EMP: 7
SALES: 500K **Privately Held**
SIC: 3441 Fabricated structural metal

(G-5283)
ENOVATE IT
1250 Woodward Hts (48220-1427)
PHONE..................................248 721-8104
Fred Calero, *COO*
EMP: 11
SALES (est): 1.8MM **Privately Held**
SIC: 3571 Electronic computers

(G-5284)
FERNDALE LABORATORIES INC (HQ)
Also Called: Ferndale Contract Mfg
780 W 8 Mile Rd (48220-2498)
PHONE..................................248 548-0900
James T McMillan II, *CEO*
Michael Burns, *President*
Scott Mason, *Vice Pres*
Lori Sloane, *VP Mfg*
Dean Gibson, *Project Mgr*
▲ EMP: 280 EST: 1897
SQ FT: 105,600
SALES: 78.9MM
SALES (corp-wide): 63.9MM **Privately Held**
WEB: www.ferndalelabs.com
SIC: 2834 Pharmaceutical preparations
PA: Ferndale Pharma Group, Inc.
 780 W 8 Mile Rd
 Ferndale MI 48220
 248 548-0900

(G-5285)
FERNDALE PHARMA GROUP INC (PA)
780 W 8 Mile Rd (48220-2422)
PHONE..................................248 548-0900
James McMillan, *CEO*
Michael Burns, *President*
Mark Diekman, *CFO*
Dave Stott, *Finance*
Kimberly Bedal, *Manager*
EMP: 280
SALES (est): 43.7MM
SALES (corp-wide): 63.9MM **Privately Held**
SIC: 2834 3841 Pharmaceutical preparations; surgical & medical instruments

(G-5286)
GAGE CORPORATION (PA)
821 Wanda St Ste 1 (48220-2944)
PHONE..................................248 541-3824
Michael J Gage, *Ch of Bd*
Donald R Dixon, *President*
Raymond D Gage III, *Director*
EMP: 10
SALES (est): 15.3MM **Privately Held**
SIC: 2869 Solvents, organic

(G-5287)
GAGE GLOBAL SERVICES INC (PA)
Also Called: Gage Products Company
821 Wanda St Ste 2 (48220-2944)
PHONE..................................248 541-3824
Donald Dixon, *President*
Anthony Morris, *Purch Mgr*
Dan Macgregor, *Controller*
Larry Messer, *Accounts Mgr*
Bob Rutovic, *Accounts Mgr*
EMP: 25
SALES (est): 8.6MM **Privately Held**
SIC: 2841 Scouring compounds

(G-5288)
GAGE PRODUCTS COMPANY
625 Wanda St (48220-2690)
PHONE..................................248 541-3824
EMP: 64
SALES (corp-wide): 15.3MM **Privately Held**
WEB: www.gageproducts.com
SIC: 2869 Industrial organic chemicals
HQ: Gage Products Company
 821 Wanda St
 Ferndale MI 48220
 248 541-3824

(G-5289)
GARDEN FRESH GOURMET LLC (HQ)
1220 E 9 Mile Rd (48220-1972)
PHONE..................................866 725-7239
EMP: 40 EST: 2015
SALES (est): 9.8MM
SALES (corp-wide): 8.1B **Publicly Held**
SIC: 2035 Pickles, sauces & salad dressings
PA: Campbell Soup Company
 1 Campbell Pl
 Camden NJ 08103
 856 342-4800

(G-5290)
GRATTAN FAMILY ENTERPRISES LLC
Also Called: UNI-Bond Brake
1350 Jarvis St (48220-2011)
PHONE..................................248 547-3870
Jim Langley, *Vice Pres*
Jenna Ratliff, *Controller*
Michael B Grattan,
▲ EMP: 55 EST: 2007
SQ FT: 102,000
SALES (est): 9.8MM **Privately Held**
SIC: 3714 3469 3446 Motor vehicle brake systems & parts; metal stampings; architectural metalwork

(G-5291)
GREAT LAKES ATM
701 Woodward Hts (48220-1492)
P.O. Box 547, New Baltimore (48047-0547)
PHONE..................................248 542-2613
Stuart Carter, *Principal*
EMP: 7
SALES (est): 705.8K **Privately Held**
SIC: 3578 Automatic teller machines (ATM)

(G-5292)
GREER INDUSTRIES INC
Also Called: Greer Steel Co
1520 E 9 Mile Rd (48220-2027)
PHONE..................................800 388-2868
John R Raes, *President*
EMP: 25
SQ FT: 38,328
SALES (corp-wide): 132MM **Privately Held**
WEB: www.greerlime.com
SIC: 4225 5051 3316 3312 General warehousing; metals service centers & offices; cold finishing of steel shapes; blast furnaces & steel mills
PA: Greer Industries, Inc.
 570 Canyon Rd
 Morgantown WV 26508
 304 296-2549

(G-5293)
I PARTH INC
Also Called: Midwest Circuits
2206 Burdette St (48220-1404)
PHONE..................................248 548-9722

Rajanber Patel, *President*
Jay Patel, *Vice Pres*
▲ EMP: 7
SQ FT: 14,000
SALES (est): 1MM **Privately Held**
SIC: 3672 3648 Printed circuit boards; lighting equipment

(G-5294)
IMAX PRINTING CO
756 Livernois St (48220-2307)
PHONE..................................248 629-9680
Jay Williams, *President*
EMP: 6
SQ FT: 3,800
SALES (est): 758.9K **Privately Held**
SIC: 2752 Commercial printing, offset

(G-5295)
JEFFERSON IRON WORKS INC
2441 Wolcott St (48220-1446)
PHONE..................................248 542-3554
Daniel Blake, *President*
EMP: 7
SQ FT: 18,000
SALES (est): 550K **Privately Held**
SIC: 3599 Machine shop, jobbing & repair

(G-5296)
K-TEC SYSTEMS INC (PA)
2615 Wolcott St (48220-1422)
PHONE..................................248 414-4100
Catherine Koch, *President*
Michael Martin, *Vice Pres*
EMP: 12
SALES (est): 3.9MM **Privately Held**
WEB: www.ktec-systems.com
SIC: 3823 Temperature instruments: industrial process type

(G-5297)
L BARGE & ASSOCIATES INC
Also Called: Midwest Diversified Products
1530 Farrow St (48220-1907)
PHONE..................................248 582-3430
Lloyd H Barge, *President*
Donald J O Connell, *Corp Secy*
EMP: 11
SQ FT: 30,000
SALES (est): 1.9MM **Privately Held**
WEB: www.lbarge.com
SIC: 3443 3469 3465 5013 Metal parts; machine parts, stamped or pressed metal; automotive stampings; motor vehicle supplies & new parts; automotive supplies & parts

(G-5298)
MACDERMID INCORPORATED
Also Called: Macdermid Ferndale Facility
1221 Farrow St (48220-1918)
PHONE..................................248 399-3553
David Bruce, *Director*
David Czapla, *Technician*
EMP: 38
SQ FT: 10,000
SALES (corp-wide): 1.9B **Publicly Held**
WEB: www.macdermid.com
SIC: 2899 Metal treating compounds
HQ: Macdermid, Incorporated
 245 Freight St
 Waterbury CT 06702
 203 575-5700

(G-5299)
MAYER ALLOYS CORPORATION (PA)
10711 Northend Ave (48220-2130)
PHONE..................................248 399-2233
Steven Ruzumna, *President*
Phyllis Mertins, *Manager*
EMP: 3
SQ FT: 2,400
SALES: 8MM **Privately Held**
WEB: www.mayeralloys.com
SIC: 3339 Lead smelting & refining (primary); tin-base alloys (primary)

(G-5300)
MAYER METALS CORPORATION
10711 Northend Ave (48220-2130)
PHONE..................................248 742-0077
Ilene Lubell, *President*
Phyllis Mertins, *Controller*
Steven Ruzumna, *Admin Sec*
EMP: 3

SQ FT: 500
SALES (est): 199.9K **Privately Held**
SIC: 3341 Lead smelting & refining (secondary)

(G-5301)
METRO TIMES INC
1200 Woodward Hts (48220-1427)
PHONE..................................313 961-4060
Lisa Rudy, *President*
George Lynett, *President*
EMP: 45 EST: 1980
SALES: 890K
SALES (corp-wide): 103MM **Privately Held**
WEB: www.scrantontimesefcu.com
SIC: 2711 7922 Newspapers, publishing & printing; theatrical producers & services
PA: The Scranton Times L P
 149 Penn Ave Ste 1
 Scranton PA 18503
 570 348-9100

(G-5302)
MOTOR CITY MANUFACTURING LTD
23440 Woodward Ave (48220-1344)
PHONE..................................586 731-1086
Fred Berg, *President*
Paul Berg, *Vice Pres*
EMP: 7
SALES (est): 620.8K **Privately Held**
SIC: 3993 Signs & advertising specialties

(G-5303)
NALCOR LLC (PA)
Also Called: Nalpac Enterprises
1365 Jarvis St (48220-2025)
PHONE..................................248 541-1140
Ralph S Caplan, *President*
Glenn Leboeuf, *Opers Staff*
Don Zerilli, *Senior Buyer*
Jane Kubiski, *Sales Staff*
Mike Cali, *Info Tech Mgr*
▲ EMP: 70 EST: 1971
SQ FT: 200,000
SALES (est): 39.1MM **Privately Held**
WEB: www.nalpac.com
SIC: 5199 5099 3993 2759 Gifts & novelties; advertising specialties; sunglasses; signs & advertising specialties; commercial printing; automotive & apparel trimmings

(G-5304)
NEW UNISON CORPORATION
1601 Wanda St (48220-2022)
PHONE..................................248 544-9500
David A Swider, *President*
◆ EMP: 30
SQ FT: 35,000
SALES (est): 6.4MM **Privately Held**
WEB: www.newunison.com
SIC: 3541 3549 Grinding machines, metalworking; metalworking machinery

(G-5305)
NEW YORK BAGEL BAKING CO (PA)
23316 Woodward Ave (48220-1302)
PHONE..................................248 548-2580
Harvey Goldsmith, *Partner*
Howard Goldsmith, *Partner*
EMP: 15
SQ FT: 5,000
SALES (est): 2.6MM **Privately Held**
SIC: 5461 5149 2051 Bagels; bakery products; bread, cake & related products

(G-5306)
NODEL-CO
2615 Wolcott St (48220-1422)
PHONE..................................248 543-1325
Norm Dell, *President*
Lynne Prudden, *Vice Pres*
EMP: 10
SALES (est): 918.4K **Privately Held**
SIC: 3999 3714 Cigarette filters; motor vehicle parts & accessories

(G-5307)
OVERHEAD CONVEYOR COMPANY (PA)
Also Called: OCC Systems
1330 Hilton Rd (48220-2898)
PHONE..................................248 547-3800
Tom Woodbeck, *President*
Mike Sherman, *Superintendent*
Glenn Toombs, *Superintendent*
Len Bochenek, *Project Mgr*
Grant Larose, *Site Mgr*
EMP: 40 **EST:** 1945
SALES: 53.4MM **Privately Held**
WEB: www.occ-conveyor.com
SIC: 3535 Conveyors & conveying equipment

(G-5308)
PC COMPLETE INC
Also Called: Pos Complete
742 Livernois St (48220-2307)
PHONE..................................248 545-4211
Marshall Miller, *President*
Jenifer Miller, *Corp Secy*
Jennifer Miller,
EMP: 9
SQ FT: 7,500
SALES (est): 880K **Privately Held**
WEB: www.pccomplete.com
SIC: 3578 Point-of-sale devices

(G-5309)
PERFORMANCE CRANKSHAFT INC
8829 Northend Ave (48220-2273)
PHONE..................................586 549-7557
Adney Brown, *President*
Penny Brown, *Admin Sec*
EMP: 3
SALES: 200K **Privately Held**
SIC: 3541 Crankshaft regrinding machines

(G-5310)
PK FABRICATING INC
1975 Hilton Rd (48220-1501)
PHONE..................................248 398-4500
Kathleen Kaiafas, *President*
Peter Kaiafas, *Vice Pres*
EMP: 12
SALES: 1MM **Privately Held**
SIC: 3441 Building components, structural steel

(G-5311)
PLASTI-FAB INC
2305 Hilton Rd (48220-1570)
PHONE..................................248 543-1415
Richard P Melin, *President*
Harold R Melin, *Corp Secy*
Phyllis Rowlands, *Asst Office Mgr*
EMP: 30
SQ FT: 15,000
SALES (est): 9MM **Privately Held**
WEB: www.plasti-fabinc.com
SIC: 3089 2672 2396 Plastic processing; coated & laminated paper; automotive & apparel trimmings

(G-5312)
POWERTRAN CORPORATION
1605 Bonner St (48220-1909)
PHONE..................................248 399-4300
Thomas M Schalk, *President*
Ramesh Naik, *Vice Pres*
EMP: 21
SQ FT: 10,000
SALES (est): 4.5MM **Privately Held**
WEB: www.powertran.com
SIC: 3677 Electronic transformers

(G-5313)
PRECISION SPINDLE SERVICE CO
836 Woodward Hts (48220-1431)
PHONE..................................248 544-0100
David Marschick, *President*
Bill Foy, *President*
EMP: 10
SQ FT: 6,000
SALES (est): 2.2MM **Privately Held**
WEB: www.spindlerebuilding.com
SIC: 3552 Spindles, textile

(G-5314)
PROGRESS CUSTOM SCREEN PRTG
Also Called: Progress Custom Screen Prtg
364 Hilton Rd (48220-2548)
PHONE..................................248 982-4247
Grant Gamlaski,
EMP: 5
SALES (est): 337.9K **Privately Held**
SIC: 2759 Screen printing

(G-5315)
REAL DETROIT WEEKLY LLC
1200 Woodward Hts (48220-1427)
PHONE..................................248 591-7325
John Badanhek,
Jerry Peterson,
Robert Del Valle, *Relations*
EMP: 16
SQ FT: 4,000
SALES (est): 1.1MM **Privately Held**
WEB: www.realdetroitweekly.com
SIC: 2711 Newspapers, publishing & printing

(G-5316)
ROSS SHEET METAL INC
2300 Hilton Rd (48220-1571)
PHONE..................................248 543-1170
David J Ross, *President*
Dorothy Horning, *Admin Sec*
Nancy Richter, *Admin Sec*
EMP: 5
SQ FT: 7,500
SALES: 350K **Privately Held**
WEB: www.rsmfab.com
SIC: 3448 Prefabricated metal components

(G-5317)
SCHRAMMS MEAD
327 W 9 Mile Rd (48220-1767)
PHONE..................................248 439-5000
EMP: 4
SALES (est): 324K **Privately Held**
SIC: 2084 Wines

(G-5318)
SEXTON ENTERPRIZE INC
2638 Hilton Rd (48220-1544)
PHONE..................................248 545-5880
Alexander Sexton, *President*
Darleen R Sexton, *Vice Pres*
EMP: 3
SQ FT: 3,000
SALES: 300K **Privately Held**
SIC: 1799 7692 3441 Welding on site; welding repair; fabricated structural metal

(G-5319)
SPRAYTEK INC (PA)
2535 Wolcott St (48220-1446)
PHONE..................................248 546-3551
Dave Berry, *President*
Marvin Hairston, *Vice Pres*
Darren Bossenberger, *Project Mgr*
Steven Ross, *Sales Mgr*
Laurie Alfonso, *Manager*
▲ **EMP:** 15
SALES (est): 2.1MM **Privately Held**
WEB: www.spraytek.com
SIC: 3479 Coating of metals & formed products

(G-5320)
STRUCTURAL EQUIPMENT CO
Also Called: Overhead Conveyer
1330 Hilton Rd (48220-2837)
PHONE..................................248 547-3800
Milford E Woodbeck Sr, *CEO*
Milford E Woodbeck Jr, *Vice Pres*
EMP: 50
SQ FT: 4,000
SALES (est): 6.7MM **Privately Held**
SIC: 3535 Conveyors & conveying equipment

(G-5321)
THERMAL WAVE IMAGING INC
Also Called: TWI
845 Livernois St (48220-2308)
PHONE..................................248 414-3730
Steven M Shepard, *Owner*
Yulin Hou, *Electrical Engi*
EMP: 12
SQ FT: 11,500
SALES: 5MM **Privately Held**
WEB: www.thermalwave.com
SIC: 8734 3829 Testing laboratories; testing equipment: abrasion, shearing strength, etc.

(G-5322)
TROY HAYGOOD
Also Called: Plush Apparel Cstm Impressions
2871 Hilton Rd (48220-1066)
PHONE..................................313 478-3308
Troy Haygood, *Owner*
EMP: 4
SALES: 40K **Privately Held**
SIC: 2759 Commercial printing

(G-5323)
TRU-THREAD CO INC
1600 Hilton Rd (48220-1911)
P.O. Box 20255 (48220-0255)
PHONE..................................248 399-0255
Milford Messer, *President*
Thomas Messer, *Vice Pres*
EMP: 8 **EST:** 1961
SQ FT: 14,000
SALES (est): 750K **Privately Held**
SIC: 3599 Machine shop, jobbing & repair

(G-5324)
TUBESOURCE MANUFACTURING INC
1600 E 9 Mile Rd (48220-2028)
PHONE..................................248 543-4746
James A Bery, *President*
Sandy Koelzer, *General Mgr*
▲ **EMP:** 15
SQ FT: 23,000
SALES (est): 3.2MM **Privately Held**
SIC: 3498 Tube fabricating (contract bending & shaping)

(G-5325)
UNI VUE INC
2424 Wolcott St (48220-1424)
P.O. Box 1558, Troy (48099-1558)
PHONE..................................248 545-0810
Chris Mytnik, *President*
Pamela Lee, *Marketing Staff*
▼ **EMP:** 20
SALES (est): 3MM **Privately Held**
WEB: www.uni-vue.com
SIC: 3465 Automotive stampings

(G-5326)
UNIVERSAL CONTAINER CORP
10750 Galaxie Ave (48220-2132)
PHONE..................................248 543-2788
Leonard W Horton II, *President*
J Anthony Mooter, *Corp Secy*
John Madigan, *Vice Pres*
Ron Roelofson, *Sales Mgr*
Brian Mathew, *Accounts Mgr*
EMP: 45 **EST:** 1975
SQ FT: 80,000
SALES (est): 10.8MM **Privately Held**
WEB: www.uni-con.com
SIC: 2653 Boxes, corrugated: made from purchased materials

(G-5327)
VALENTINE DISTILLING
161 Vester St (48220-1711)
PHONE..................................248 629-9951
Rifino Valentine, *Owner*
EMP: 8
SALES (est): 110.5K **Privately Held**
SIC: 2085 Vodka (alcoholic beverage)

(G-5328)
VALENTINE DISTILLING CO
965 Wanda St (48220-2959)
PHONE..................................646 286-2690
Rifino Valentine, *Owner*
EMP: 7
SALES (est): 582.5K **Privately Held**
SIC: 2085 Distilled & blended liquors

(G-5329)
VAN INDUSTRIES INC
1285 Wordsworth St (48220-2675)
PHONE..................................248 398-6990
Don La Flamboy, *President*
William H Howard, *Vice Pres*
Doug La Flamboy, *Vice Pres*
EMP: 10 **EST:** 1964
SQ FT: 13,000
SALES (est): 1.2MM **Privately Held**
SIC: 3291 Abrasive buffs, bricks, cloth, paper, stones, etc.

(G-5330)
WOODWARD AVENUE BREWERS
Also Called: Wab, The
22646 Woodward Ave (48220-1810)
PHONE..................................248 894-7665
Chris Johnston, *Partner*
Krista Johnston, *Partner*
EMP: 20
SALES (est): 2.2MM **Privately Held**
WEB: www.thewabsite.com
SIC: 2082 Beer (alcoholic beverage)

(G-5331)
ZOYES EAST INC
Also Called: Architectural Model Studios
1280 Hilton Rd (48220-2837)
PHONE..................................248 584-3300
Dean Zoyes, *President*
EMP: 5
SQ FT: 3,700
SALES (est): 505.4K **Privately Held**
SIC: 8712 3999 Architectural services; models, except toy

Ferrysburg
Ottawa County

(G-5332)
A M GRINDING
303 S 2nd St (49409)
P.O. Box 114 (49409-0114)
PHONE..................................616 847-8373
Alan McDonald, *Owner*
▲ **EMP:** 3
SALES: 112K **Privately Held**
SIC: 3599 Grinding castings for the trade

(G-5333)
ADVANCED SIGNS INCORPORATED
401 2nd St (49409-5133)
P.O. Box 67 (49409-0067)
PHONE..................................616 846-4667
Bernard Wade, *President*
EMP: 11
SQ FT: 12,500
SALES (est): 2.1MM **Privately Held**
WEB: www.adsigns.com
SIC: 3993 Signs, not made in custom sign painting shops; electric signs

(G-5334)
EPS INDUSTRIES INC
585 Second St (49409)
P.O. Box 502, Spring Lake (49456-0502)
PHONE..................................616 844-9220
Ed Summers, *President*
Ryan Elliston, *Vice Pres*
Elliston Ryan, *VP Opers*
Jon Kuipers, *Manager*
EMP: 25
SQ FT: 10,000
SALES (est): 2.9MM **Privately Held**
WEB: www.epsindustries.com
SIC: 3324 3366 3365 Aerospace investment castings, ferrous; commercial investment castings, ferrous; copper foundries; bronze foundry; aluminum foundries

(G-5335)
JOHNSTON BOILER COMPANY
300 Pine St (49409-5131)
P.O. Box 300 (49409-0300)
PHONE..................................616 842-5050
David Reinink, *President*
Leanna Haven, *Purch Agent*
Rick Slater, *Project Engr*
Mike Nienhuis, *Senior Engr*
Jon Mull, *Manager*
EMP: 45
SQ FT: 93,800
SALES: 10MM
SALES (corp-wide): 204.2MM **Privately Held**
WEB: www.johnstonboiler.com
SIC: 3443 Boilers: industrial, power, or marine

Ferrysburg - Ottawa County (G-5336)   GEOGRAPHIC SECTION

PA: Hines Corporation
1218 E Pontaluna Rd Ste B
Norton Shores MI 49456
231 799-6240

(G-5336)
NORTH SHORE MACHINE WORKS INC
595 W 2nd St (49409)
P.O. Box 37 (49409-0037)
PHONE..................................616 842-8360
Michael Olthof, *President*
Donald Olthof, *President*
Roger Olthof, *Vice Pres*
Annel Olthof, *Office Mgr*
EMP: 16
SQ FT: 29,600
SALES: 1.5MM **Privately Held**
SIC: 3451 3599 Screw machine products; machine shop, jobbing & repair

(G-5337)
PORTENGA MANUFACTURING COMPANY
220 5th St (49409)
P.O. Box 26 (49409-0026)
PHONE..................................616 846-2691
Chad Portenga, *President*
Jay Schuitema, *Vice Pres*
EMP: 7
SQ FT: 5,400
SALES: 350K **Privately Held**
WEB: www.portenga.com
SIC: 3543 Industrial patterns

(G-5338)
ST MARYS CEMENT INC (US)
555 W 2nd St (49409)
P.O. Box 142 (49409-0142)
PHONE..................................616 846-8553
Robert Vandyke, *Manager*
EMP: 3
SALES (corp-wide): 1.1MM **Privately Held**
SIC: 3273 3241 Ready-mixed concrete; cement, hydraulic
HQ: St. Marys Cement U.S. Llc
9333 Dearborn St
Detroit MI 48209
313 842-4600

Fife Lake
Kalkaska County

(G-5339)
DOLLARS SENSE
7850 Scotch Blf Sw (49633-8289)
PHONE..................................231 369-3610
EMP: 3 **EST:** 2010
SALES (est): 214.3K **Privately Held**
SIC: 3643 Outlets, electric: convenience

(G-5340)
FOREST BLAKE PRODUCTS INC
10723 Shippy Rd Sw (49633-9103)
PHONE..................................231 879-3913
Frank Blake, *President*
EMP: 9
SALES (est): 702.7K **Privately Held**
SIC: 2411 2611 4213 4212 Logging; pulp mills; trucking, except local; local trucking, without storage; sawmills & planing mills, general

(G-5341)
GUSTOS QUALITY SYSTEMS
11655 Gusto Dr (49633-9091)
PHONE..................................231 409-0219
John Gustafson, *Owner*
EMP: 8 **EST:** 2008
SALES (est): 255.7K **Privately Held**
SIC: 7692 7694 Automotive welding; hermetics repair

(G-5342)
HAYES MANUFACTURING INC
6875 Us Highway 131 (49633-9765)
P.O. Box 220 (49633-0220)
PHONE..................................231 879-3372
Holly Miller, *President*
Raymond J Hayes, *President*
Carol Ann Hayes, *Corp Secy*
Penny Challende, *Vice Pres*
Charles James Hayes, *Vice Pres*
▲ **EMP:** 30 **EST:** 1962
SQ FT: 24,000
SALES (est): 8.3MM **Privately Held**
WEB: www.hayescouplings.com
SIC: 3568 Couplings, shaft: rigid, flexible, universal joint, etc.

(G-5343)
TALLMAN INDUSTRIES INC
6592 Lund Rd Sw (49633-9112)
PHONE..................................231 879-4755
Andrew Tallman, *Principal*
EMP: 8
SALES (est): 753.6K **Privately Held**
SIC: 3999 Manufacturing industries

(G-5344)
WADE LOGGING
7108 W Sharon Rd Sw (49633-9208)
PHONE..................................231 463-0363
Jim Wade, *Owner*
EMP: 3
SALES (est): 189.9K **Privately Held**
SIC: 2411 Logging

Filer City
Manistee County

(G-5345)
PACKAGING CORPORATION AMERICA
Also Called: PCA/Filer City 640
2246 Udell St (49634-9801)
P.O. Box 5 (49634-0005)
PHONE..................................231 723-1442
Jill Schluter, *Opers Mgr*
Greg Fessenden, *Electrical Engi*
Colleen Kenny, *Finance Mgr*
Robert Peritin, *Branch Mgr*
Peter Caird, *Analyst*
EMP: 350
SALES (corp-wide): 7B **Publicly Held**
WEB: www.packagingcorp.com
SIC: 2653 Boxes, corrugated: made from purchased materials
PA: Packaging Corporation Of America
1 N Field Ct
Lake Forest IL 60045
847 482-3000

Filion
Huron County

(G-5346)
D R W SYSTEMS
4484 N Van Dyke Rd (48432-9727)
PHONE..................................989 874-4663
David Rushing, *Owner*
EMP: 4
SALES (est): 170K **Privately Held**
SIC: 3291 Synthetic abrasives

Flat Rock
Wayne County

(G-5347)
AUTO PALLETS-BOXES INC
27945 Cooke St (48134-1201)
PHONE..................................734 782-1110
EMP: 9
SALES (corp-wide): 6.9MM **Privately Held**
SIC: 2448 Mfg Wood Pallets/Skids
PA: Auto Pallets-Boxes, Inc.
28000 Southfield Rd Fl 2
Lathrup Village MI 48076
248 559-7744

(G-5348)
AUTOALLIANCE MANAGEMENT CO
1 International Dr (48134-9401)
PHONE..................................734 782-7800
Tim Young, *President*
Rodney Haynes, *CFO*
◆ **EMP:** 3200
SALES (est): 228.8MM **Privately Held**
SIC: 3711 Motor vehicles & car bodies

(G-5349)
BAR PROCESSING CORPORATION (HQ)
Also Called: Flat Rock
26601 W Huron River Dr (48134-1134)
P.O. Box 1090 (48134-2090)
PHONE..................................734 782-4454
Paul Lanzon, *CEO*
Brian Drozdowski, *General Mgr*
Jack Starkey, *Vice Pres*
Mike Maloney, *Plant Mgr*
Don Nash, *Plant Mgr*
▲ **EMP:** 200 **EST:** 1970
SALES (est): 39.9MM **Privately Held**
WEB: www.host2.frm.com
SIC: 3471 Finishing, metals or formed products; polishing, metals or formed products
PA: Shields Acquisition Company, Inc.
26601 W Huron River Dr
Flat Rock MI 48134
734 782-4454

(G-5350)
CANVAS SHOP
25188 Telegraph Rd (48134-1072)
PHONE..................................734 782-2222
Mike Thanasiu, *Manager*
EMP: 6
SALES (est): 318.6K **Privately Held**
SIC: 2394 Canvas & related products

(G-5351)
COUNTRY PRINTING
14850 Telegraph Rd (48134-9656)
PHONE..................................734 782-4044
EMP: 8
SQ FT: 11,000
SALES (est): 570K **Privately Held**
SIC: 2752 Offset Printing Company

(G-5352)
CUSTOM COATING TECHNOLOGIES
26601 W Huron River Dr (48134-1134)
PHONE..................................734 244-3610
EMP: 5
SALES (est): 429.7K **Privately Held**
SIC: 3479 Coating of metals & formed products

(G-5353)
FLAT ROCK METAL INC
Also Called: Flatrock Metal Bar and Proc
26601 W Huron River Dr (48134-1134)
P.O. Box 1090 (48134-2090)
PHONE..................................734 782-4454
Keith King, *CEO*
Paul Lanzon, *CEO*
Terry Moran, *President*
Fred Harrison, *Production*
John Silva, *Purch Mgr*
EMP: 200
SALES (est): 29.9MM **Privately Held**
SIC: 3471 3316 Plating & polishing; cold finishing of steel shapes

(G-5354)
FOUR WAY PALLET SERVICE
3988 Will Carleton Rd (48134-9659)
P.O. Box 304 (48134-0304)
PHONE..................................734 782-5914
Daniel E Gerhardi, *Owner*
EMP: 14
SQ FT: 6,000
SALES (est): 2MM **Privately Held**
SIC: 2448 Pallets, wood & wood with metal

(G-5355)
INDUSTRIAL REFLECTIONS INC
26601 W Huron River Dr (48134-1134)
PHONE..................................734 782-4454
Keith King, *President*
Terrance Moran, *CFO*
Terrance P Moran, *CFO*
EMP: 3
SALES (est): 151.2K **Privately Held**
SIC: 2514 Metal household furniture

(G-5356)
INNOVATIVE FABRICATION LLC
23851 Vreeland Rd (48134-9409)
PHONE..................................734 789-9099
Kristy Stapula,
EMP: 40
SALES (est): 899.4K **Privately Held**
SIC: 3999 Manufacturing industries

(G-5357)
MESSINA CONCRETE INC
14675 Telegraph Rd (48134-9655)
P.O. Box 1173 (48134-2173)
PHONE..................................734 783-1020
Vince Messina, *Manager*
EMP: 24
SALES (corp-wide): 5.8MM **Privately Held**
WEB: www.messinaconcrete.com
SIC: 3273 Ready-mixed concrete
PA: Messina Concrete, Inc.
725 N Dixie Hwy
Monroe MI
734 241-8380

(G-5358)
OT DYNAMICS LLC
27100 Hall Rd (48134-1195)
PHONE..................................734 984-7022
Bill Corbett, *Business Mgr*
EMP: 10
SQ FT: 30,000
SALES (est): 545K **Privately Held**
SIC: 2851 Paints & allied products

(G-5359)
QUALITY ALUM ACQUISITION LLC
14544 Telegraph Rd Ste 1 (48134-8910)
P.O. Box 269, Hastings (49058-0269)
PHONE..................................734 783-0990
Robert Clark, *CEO*
Corey Harrison, *CFO*
Craig Shumate, *Sales Executive*
EMP: 10
SALES (est): 1.1MM
SALES (corp-wide): 41MM **Privately Held**
WEB: www.qualityaluminum.com
SIC: 3444 3354 Sheet metalwork; aluminum extruded products
PA: Quality Aluminum Acquisition Llc
429 S Michigan Ave
Hastings MI 49058
800 550-1667

(G-5360)
QUALITY CLUTCHES INC
3966 Dauncy Rd (48134-9608)
PHONE..................................734 782-0783
Ricky Leigh Kargel, *President*
Judy Kargel, *Admin Sec*
EMP: 6
SQ FT: 4,000
SALES (est): 767.5K **Privately Held**
WEB: www.qualityclutches.com
SIC: 3714 Transmission housings or parts, motor vehicle

(G-5361)
RAAL INDUSTRIES INC
24802 Christian Dr (48134-9120)
PHONE..................................734 782-6216
Albert Catarino, *President*
EMP: 3 **EST:** 1965
SQ FT: 11,000
SALES: 500K **Privately Held**
SIC: 3545 Boring machine attachments (machine tool accessories)

(G-5362)
ROYAL ARC WELDING COMPANY (PA)
Also Called: Royal ARC Crane Service
23851 Vreeland Rd (48134-9409)
P.O. Box 419, Lincoln Park (48146-0419)
PHONE..................................734 789-9099
Robert Siemens, *President*
Hank Siemens, *Opers Mgr*
EMP: 35
SQ FT: 60,000

GEOGRAPHIC SECTION

Flint - Genesee County (G-5389)

SALES (est): 17MM **Privately Held**
SIC: 3536 3441 3412 8299 Cranes, industrial plant; fabricated structural metal; metal barrels, drums & pails; educational services; vocational schools

(G-5363)
SECOND NATURE SELF DEFENSE
25015 Meadows Ave (48134-1368)
PHONE 734 775-6257
Katie Marken, *Principal*
EMP: 3
SALES (est): 167.7K **Privately Held**
SIC: 3812 Defense systems & equipment

(G-5364)
SHIELDS ACQUISITION CO INC (PA)
26601 W Huron River Dr (48134-1134)
PHONE 734 782-4454
Keith S King, *President*
EMP: 2
SALES (est): 39.9MM **Privately Held**
SIC: 3471 Finishing, metals or formed products; polishing, metals or formed products

(G-5365)
SINGLE SOURCE INC
Also Called: C.P.
27100 Hall Rd (48134-1195)
PHONE 765 825-4111
Ernest Clark, *Sales Mgr*
Dan Boboltz, *Manager*
EMP: 6 **Privately Held**
SIC: 5013 2851 Automotive servicing equipment; paints & allied products
PA: Single Source, Inc.
4900 Fls Of Neuse Rd # 150
Raleigh NC 27609

Flint
Genesee County

(G-5366)
4D SYSTEMS LLC
4130 Market Pl (48507-3205)
PHONE 800 380-9165
Jean-Pierre Rasaiah, *President*
Fay Tanner, *Project Mgr*
Ryan Glogowski, *Design Engr*
Jeffrey Krieger, *VP Human Res*
Rohit Khanolkar, *Marketing Staff*
EMP: 25
SQ FT: 1,500
SALES (est): 5.8MM **Privately Held**
WEB: www.4dsysco.com
SIC: 7372 8711 Prepackaged software; engineering services

(G-5367)
A I FLINT LLC
4444 W Maple Ave (48507-3128)
PHONE 810 732-8760
Darrel Reece,
EMP: 1100 **EST:** 2000
SQ FT: 240,000
SALES (est): 114.6MM
SALES (corp-wide): 559.5MM **Privately Held**
SIC: 3714 Motor vehicle parts & accessories
PA: Android Industries, L.L.C.
2155 Executive Hills Dr
Auburn Hills MI 48326
248 454-0500

(G-5368)
ACCU-SHAPE DIE CUTTING INC
4050 Market Pl (48507-3203)
PHONE 810 230-2445
Preston D Means, *President*
Joe Brooks, *COO*
Emma Brooks, *CFO*
▲ **EMP:** 44
SQ FT: 45,000
SALES (est): 12.8MM **Privately Held**
WEB: www.accushape.com
SIC: 2675 3554 3544 Die-cut paper & board; paper industries machinery; special dies, tools, jigs & fixtures

(G-5369)
ACI PLASTICS INC (PA)
Also Called: A C I Plastics
2945 Davison Rd (48506-3928)
PHONE 810 767-3800
Mark Lieberman, *CEO*
Bill McCaffrey, *COO*
Scott Melton, *Vice Pres*
Justin Mann, *VP Opers*
◆ **EMP:** 50
SQ FT: 125,000
SALES (est): 67.2MM **Privately Held**
SIC: 4953 3087 5162 Recycling, waste materials; custom compound purchased resins; plastics resins

(G-5370)
ADVANCED FIBERGLASS SERVICES
Also Called: Fiberglass Specialists
3612 Circle Dr (48507-1886)
PHONE 810 785-7541
Daniel W Kryglowski, *President*
EMP: 4 **EST:** 1971
SQ FT: 5,000
SALES (est): 366.6K **Privately Held**
WEB: www.advancedfiberglassonline.com
SIC: 7699 5169 3732 Boat repair; specialty cleaning & sanitation preparations; boats, fiberglass: building & repairing

(G-5371)
ADVANCED MAINTENANCE TECH
3118 S Dye Rd (48507-1004)
PHONE 810 820-2554
Thomas Walker, *President*
EMP: 6
SALES (est): 484.7K **Privately Held**
SIC: 3541 Lathes

(G-5372)
AERO TRAIN CORP
5083 Miller Rd (48507-1075)
PHONE 810 230-8096
EMP: 3
SALES (est): 124.6K **Privately Held**
SIC: 3728 Aircraft parts & equipment

(G-5373)
AI-GENESEE LLC
4400 Matthew (48507-3152)
PHONE 810 720-4848
Larry Kip, *Director*
Darrel Reece,
Dave Donnay,
Marti Komer,
Keith Masserang,
EMP: 57
SQ FT: 280,000
SALES (est): 6.8MM **Privately Held**
SIC: 3711 Automobile assembly, including specialty automobiles

(G-5374)
ALDOS BAKERY INC
G5131 S Saginaw St (48507)
PHONE 810 744-9123
Lucy Salvati, *President*
Aldo Salvati, *Vice Pres*
EMP: 5 **EST:** 1974
SALES: 150K **Privately Held**
SIC: 2051 5461 Bread, all types (white, wheat, rye, etc): fresh or frozen; bakeries

(G-5375)
ALLIANCE AUTOMATION LLC
4072 Market Pl (48507-3203)
PHONE 810 953-9539
Bruce Cranston, *Founder*
Kevin Cranston, *Regl Sales Mgr*
Jason White, *Technical Staff*
▲ **EMP:** 5
SALES (est): 484.1K **Privately Held**
SIC: 5531 3463 3559 Automotive accessories; automotive forgings, nonferrous; automotive maintenance equipment

(G-5376)
AMERICAN COMMODITIES INC
2945 Davison Rd (48506-3928)
PHONE 810 767-3800
Mark Lieberman, *Manager*
EMP: 50

SALES (corp-wide): 67.2MM **Privately Held**
SIC: 4953 3087 5162 Recycling, waste materials; custom compound purchased resins; plastics resins
PA: Aci Plastics, Inc.
2945 Davison Rd
Flint MI 48506
810 767-3800

(G-5377)
ARROWHEAD SYSTEMS INC
3018 S Dye Rd (48507-1002)
PHONE 810 720-4770
Fax: 810 720-4773
EMP: 3
SALES (corp-wide): 70MM **Privately Held**
SIC: 3535 Mfg Conveyors
PA: Arrowhead Systems, Inc.
124 N Columbus St
Randolph WI 53956
920 326-3131

(G-5378)
ASSENMACHER LIGHTWEIGHT CYCLES
Also Called: Assemacher's Cycling Center
1272 W Hill Rd (48507-4762)
PHONE 810 232-2994
Lee Frantz, *Manager*
EMP: 5
SALES (corp-wide): 1MM **Privately Held**
WEB: www.assenmachers.com
SIC: 3949 5941 Exercising cycles; sporting goods & bicycle shops
PA: Assenmacher Lightweight Cycles
8053 Miller Rd
Swartz Creek MI 48473
810 635-7844

(G-5379)
ATTENTIVE INDUSTRIES INC
1301 Alabama Ave (48505-3985)
PHONE 810 233-7077
Brien Lord, *Branch Mgr*
EMP: 10 **Privately Held**
SIC: 3444 Sheet metalwork
PA: Attentive Industries, Inc.
502 Kelso St
Flint MI 48506

(G-5380)
ATTENTIVE INDUSTRIES INC (PA)
502 Kelso St (48506-4033)
PHONE 810 233-7077
Tom Brown, *President*
Brien Lord, *Vice Pres*
▲ **EMP:** 6
SQ FT: 7,500
SALES: 23MM **Privately Held**
SIC: 3444 Sheet metalwork

(G-5381)
AUTOMOTIVE PLASTICS RECYCLING
Also Called: American Commodities
2945 Davison Rd (48506-3928)
PHONE 810 767-3800
Mark Lieberman, *President*
M Scott Milton, *COO*
Scott Melton, *CFO*
EMP: 50
SQ FT: 45,000
SALES: 1MM **Privately Held**
SIC: 3089 4953 Plastic processing; refuse systems

(G-5382)
BANACOM INSTANT SIGNS
4463 Miller Rd (48507-1123)
PHONE 810 230-0233
Craig Hatch, *Owner*
EMP: 4
SALES (est): 260.4K **Privately Held**
SIC: 3993 Signs, not made in custom sign painting shops

(G-5383)
BARRETTE OUTDOOR LIVING INC
3200 Rbert T Longway Blvd (48506-4043)
PHONE 810 235-5400
Luke Cornell, *Engineer*

Christine McCann, *Human Res Mgr*
Lisa Miller, *Sales Staff*
Jill Barnette, *VP Mktg*
Mario Gaudreault, *Manager*
EMP: 25
SALES (corp-wide): 1.5MM **Privately Held**
SIC: 3315 Fence gates posts & fittings: steel
HQ: Barrette Outdoor Living, Inc.
7830 Freeway Cir
Middleburg Heights OH 44130
440 891-0790

(G-5384)
BARRYS SIGN COMPANY
Also Called: Benmark Advertising
3501 Blackington Ave (48503-4962)
PHONE 810 234-9919
Barry D Wiselogle, *President*
Sandra K Wiselogle, *Admin Sec*
EMP: 4
SQ FT: 6,000
SALES (est): 433.4K **Privately Held**
WEB: www.barrynickelsberg.net
SIC: 3993 Signs, not made in custom sign painting shops

(G-5385)
BAUMANS RUNNING CENTER INC
Also Called: Baumans Running & Walking Shop
1473 W Hill Rd (48507-4709)
PHONE 810 238-5981
Mark E Bauman, *President*
EMP: 8
SQ FT: 1,600
SALES: 1.4MM **Privately Held**
SIC: 5661 5699 2261 Footwear, athletic; sports apparel; screen printing of cotton broadwoven fabrics

(G-5386)
BEATTIE SPRING & WELDING SVC
2840 Rbert T Longway Blvd (48506-4038)
PHONE 810 239-9151
Matthew Beattie, *President*
EMP: 5
SALES (est): 477.3K **Privately Held**
SIC: 7539 7692 Automotive springs, rebuilding & repair; welding repair

(G-5387)
BENTLEY INDUSTRIES
1105 University Ave (48504-6223)
PHONE 810 625-0400
Steve Bentley, *Principal*
EMP: 3
SALES (est): 117.7K **Privately Held**
SIC: 3999 Manufacturing industries

(G-5388)
BESTWAY BUILDING SUPPLY CO
3021 S Dye Rd (48507-1084)
PHONE 810 732-6280
Harold Horton, *Owner*
EMP: 4
SQ FT: 6,320
SALES: 850K **Privately Held**
WEB: www.bestprojectonline.org
SIC: 1521 5211 3444 General remodeling, single-family houses; doors, storm: wood or metal; windows, storm: wood or metal; sheet metalwork

(G-5389)
BILL CARR SIGNS INC
719 W 12th St (48503-3851)
P.O. Box 7340 (48507-0340)
PHONE 810 232-1569
Jeremy Elfstrom, *President*
Ronald P Elfstrom, *President*
Mike Ellithorpe, *General Mgr*
Ken Hubbard, *Foreman/Supr*
Tya Tallieu, *Office Mgr*
EMP: 10
SQ FT: 16,000
SALES (est): 1.4MM **Privately Held**
WEB: www.billcarrsigns.com
SIC: 3993 7389 Signs, not made in custom sign painting shops; lettering & sign painting services

Flint - Genesee County (G-5390) — GEOGRAPHIC SECTION

(G-5390)
BIMBO BAKERIES USA INC
Also Called: Sara Lee Bakery Group
1356 W Hill Rd (48507-4737)
PHONE.................810 239-8070
Gary Bishoff, *Branch Mgr*
EMP: 35 **Privately Held**
SIC: 2051 5149 Bakery: wholesale or wholesale/retail combined; bakery products
HQ: Bimbo Bakeries Usa, Inc
255 Business Center Dr # 200
Horsham PA 19044
215 347-5500

(G-5391)
BLEVINS SCREW PRODUCTS INC
1838 Remell St (48503-4432)
PHONE.................810 744-1820
Bruce Blevins, *President*
Mark Blevins, *Vice Pres*
Larry Craney, *Prdtn Mgr*
Julie Sova, *QC Mgr*
Kathrine Perdue, *Office Mgr*
EMP: 21 **EST:** 1958
SQ FT: 9,000
SALES (est): 4.1MM **Privately Held**
SIC: 3599 Machine shop, jobbing & repair

(G-5392)
BOBIER TOOL SUPPLY INC
Also Called: Precision Metrology Inspection
G4163 Corunna Rd (48532-4360)
PHONE.................810 732-4030
Melville D Bobier, *President*
Devere Bobier Jr, *President*
Mary Bobier, *Vice Pres*
Kim Bobier, *Technology*
EMP: 15 **EST:** 1948
SQ FT: 12,000
SALES (est): 8.1MM **Privately Held**
WEB: www.bobiertool.com
SIC: 5084 3569 Industrial machinery & equipment; robots, assembly line: industrial & commercial

(G-5393)
BORNEMAN & PETERSON INC
1810 Remell St (48503-4432)
PHONE.................810 744-1890
Roger Blevins, *President*
Bruce Blevins, *Admin Sec*
EMP: 10
SQ FT: 12,500
SALES (est): 1.4MM **Privately Held**
WEB: www.bornemanandpeterson.com
SIC: 3451 3312 3599 1531 Screw machine products; blast furnaces & steel mills; machine shop, jobbing & repair; ; robots, assembly line: industrial & commercial

(G-5394)
BREMER PROSTHETIC DESIGN INC (PA)
3487 S Linden Rd Ste U (48507-3020)
PHONE.................810 733-3375
Thomas Bremer, *President*
Jackie Bremer, *Administration*
EMP: 5
SALES (est): 950K **Privately Held**
WEB: www.bremerprosthetics.com
SIC: 5999 3842 Orthopedic & prosthesis applications; prosthetic appliances

(G-5395)
CANVAS SHOPPE INC
3198 One Half S Dye Rd (48507)
PHONE.................810 733-1841
Michael Gargliano, *Owner*
EMP: 5
SQ FT: 2,600
SALES (est): 817.2K **Privately Held**
SIC: 2394 Liners & covers, fabric: made from purchased materials

(G-5396)
CASE ISLAND GLASS LLC
1120 Beach St (48502-1407)
PHONE.................810 252-1704
Suellen Parker, *Principal*
EMP: 3
SALES (est): 158.9K **Privately Held**
SIC: 3231 Products of purchased glass

(G-5397)
CHRISTIAN UNITY PRESS INC
5195 Exchange Dr Ste A (48507-2976)
PHONE.................402 362-5133
Kurt Heinze, *Director*
EMP: 5
SALES: 366.3K **Privately Held**
WEB: www.gemeindegottes.org
SIC: 2759 Commercial printing

(G-5398)
COCA-COLA REFRESHMENTS USA INC
2603 Lapeer Rd (48503-4352)
PHONE.................810 237-4000
Steve Sylzester, *Manager*
EMP: 100
SALES (corp-wide): 31.8B **Publicly Held**
WEB: www.cokecce.com
SIC: 2086 Bottled & canned soft drinks
HQ: Coca-Cola Refreshments Usa, Inc.
2500 Windy Ridge Pkwy Se
Atlanta GA 30339
770 989-3000

(G-5399)
COKE BOTTLE
2515 Lapeer Rd (48503-4350)
PHONE.................810 424-3352
Bryan Misenheimer, *Manager*
EMP: 7 **EST:** 2014
SALES (est): 563K **Privately Held**
SIC: 2086 Bottled & canned soft drinks

(G-5400)
COLORADO PAVERS & WALLS INC
3328 Torrey Rd (48507-3252)
PHONE.................517 881-1704
Chris Matthew Stalo, *Principal*
EMP: 3
SALES (est): 226.6K **Privately Held**
SIC: 2951 Asphalt paving mixtures & blocks

(G-5401)
COMPLETE HEALTH SYSTEM
5084 Vlla Lnde Pkwy Ste 7 (48532)
PHONE.................810 720-3891
Muhanad Jondy, *President*
EMP: 6
SALES (est): 797.6K **Privately Held**
SIC: 3841 Diagnostic apparatus, medical

(G-5402)
CONCRETE STEP CO
G5491 Clio Rd (48504-1238)
PHONE.................810 789 3061
Archie Gerstenberger, *President*
EMP: 5
SALES (est): 489K **Privately Held**
SIC: 3272 Concrete products, precast

(G-5403)
CORSAIR ENGINEERING INC (PA)
3020 Airpark Dr S (48507-3477)
PHONE.................810 233-0440
Howard W Campbell Jr, *President*
Todd Campbell, *Vice Pres*
EMP: 12
SQ FT: 30,000
SALES (est): 9.3MM **Privately Held**
WEB: www.richind.com
SIC: 7359 3496 Shipping container leasing; miscellaneous fabricated wire products

(G-5404)
CORSAIR ENGINEERING INC
2702 N Dort Hwy (48506-2958)
PHONE.................810 234-3664
Craig McLean, *Plant Mgr*
Richard Clark, *Manager*
EMP: 60
SALES (corp-wide): 9.3MM **Privately Held**
WEB: www.richind.com
SIC: 3496 3441 Miscellaneous fabricated wire products; fabricated structural metal
PA: Corsair Engineering Incorporated
3020 Airpark Dr S
Flint MI 48507
810 233-0440

(G-5405)
COUNTRY HOME CREATIONS INC
5132 Richfield Rd (48506-2121)
P.O. Box 126, Goodrich (48438-0126)
PHONE.................810 244-7348
Shirley Ann Kautman Jones, *President*
EMP: 30
SQ FT: 6,000
SALES (est): 4.3MM **Privately Held**
WEB: www.countryhomecreations.com
SIC: 2099 5499 5947 2022 Spices, including grinding; spices & herbs; gift shop; cheese, natural & processed

(G-5406)
COZART PRODUCERS
3130 Mcclure Ave (48506-2536)
PHONE.................810 736-1046
A C Cozart, *Owner*
EMP: 3
SALES (est): 169K **Privately Held**
SIC: 2079 Edible oil products, except corn oil

(G-5407)
CREATIVE PRINTING & GRAPHICS
430 S Dort Hwy (48503-2847)
PHONE.................810 235-8815
Cindy Barnes, *President*
Daniel Barnes, *Vice Pres*
EMP: 5
SQ FT: 2,000
SALES (est): 551.1K **Privately Held**
SIC: 2752 Commercial printing, offset

(G-5408)
CREATV FOAM CMPSITE SYSTMS
6401 Taylor Dr (48507-0500)
PHONE.................810 629-4149
David Swallow, *President*
Nark Shepler, *Vice Pres*
Terri Hamlet, *Controller*
EMP: 20
SALES (est): 1.1MM **Privately Held**
SIC: 3086 Plastics foam products

(G-5409)
CURBCO INC
3145 S Dye Rd (48507-1003)
P.O. Box 70, Swartz Creek (48473-0070)
PHONE.................810 232-2121
Keith Kirby, *President*
Carol Cruz, *Sales Staff*
EMP: 60
SALES (est): 8.7MM **Privately Held**
SIC: 7699 2952 8742 Fountain pen repair shop; asphalt felts & coatings; construction project management consultant

(G-5410)
CURTIS PRINTING INC
2171 Lodge Rd (48532-4949)
PHONE.................810 230-6711
Elaine Sass, *President*
Marilyn Alvord, *Corp Secy*
EMP: 5
SQ FT: 5,600
SALES (est): 200K **Privately Held**
SIC: 2752 Commercial printing, offset

(G-5411)
D & G SIGNS LLC
Also Called: Sign-A-Rama
4297 Miller Rd (48507-1227)
PHONE.................810 230-6445
Deana Wallace, *Mng Member*
EMP: 8
SQ FT: 1,200
SALES (est): 1MM **Privately Held**
SIC: 3993 Signs & advertising specialties

(G-5412)
D M J CORP
Also Called: One Stop Store 15
3910 Fenton Rd Ste 15 (48507-2469)
PHONE.................810 239-9071
Diane Wehby, *General Mgr*
EMP: 7
SALES (corp-wide): 44.8MM **Privately Held**
WEB: www.dmkdmk.com
SIC: 2869 5411 Fuels; convenience stores
PA: D M J Corp
710 N State Rd
Davison MI
810 658-2414

(G-5413)
DALLAS DESIGN INC
3432 S Saginaw St (48503-4146)
PHONE.................810 238-4546
Dallas Tiensivu, *President*
EMP: 5
SALES (est): 500K **Privately Held**
WEB: www.dallasdesign.com
SIC: 2541 5211 Cabinets, except refrigerated: show, display, etc.: wood; cabinets, kitchen

(G-5414)
DANA OFF-HGHWAY COMPONENTS LLC
3040 S Dye Rd (48507-1002)
PHONE.................586 467-1600
Jim Kamsickas, *CEO*
EMP: 29
SALES (est): 1MM **Publicly Held**
SIC: 3714 Rear axle housings, motor vehicle; steering mechanisms, motor vehicle; motor vehicle steering systems & parts
HQ: Dana Limited
3939 Technology Dr
Maumee OH 43537

(G-5415)
DAVISMADE INC
Also Called: Standing Dani
4400 S Saginaw St # 1470 (48507-2645)
PHONE.................810 743-5262
EMP: 10
SALES (est): 810K **Privately Held**
SIC: 3842 Mfg Orthopedic Appliances

(G-5416)
DELDUCAS WELDING & CO INC
Also Called: Delduca Welding & Service
4420 S Dort Hwy (48507)
PHONE.................810 743-1990
Don Delduca, *President*
EMP: 3
SALES (est): 213.5K **Privately Held**
SIC: 7692 3444 3441 Welding repair; sheet metalwork; fabricated structural metal

(G-5417)
DELTA PAVING INC
4186 Holiday Dr (48507-3513)
PHONE.................810 232-0220
Charles K Owens, *President*
Coyanne Owens, *Corp Secy*
Terry L Owens, *Vice Pres*
Mildred Jones, *Office Mgr*
EMP: 15
SQ FT: 4,000
SALES (est): 3.1MM **Privately Held**
SIC: 2951 1771 Asphalt paving mixtures & blocks; driveway contractor; parking lot construction

(G-5418)
DELTA TUBE & FABRICATING CORP
2610 N Dort Hwy (48506-2960)
PHONE.................810 239-0154
Howard W Campbell Jr, *Branch Mgr*
EMP: 180
SALES (corp-wide): 28.4MM **Privately Held**
SIC: 3446 Ornamental metalwork
PA: Delta Tube & Fabricating Corporation
4149 Grange Hall Rd
Holly MI 48442
248 634-8267

(G-5419)
DIPLOMAT SPCLTY PHRM FLINT LLC
4100 S Saginaw St (48507-2683)
PHONE.................810 768-9000
Phil Hagerman, *CEO*
Linda Rice, *Exec VP*
Jeanne Ann Stasny, *Vice Pres*
Michelle Schultz, *Finance Dir*
Jaime Zerka, *VP Sales*
EMP: 417 **EST:** 2005

GEOGRAPHIC SECTION

Flint - Genesee County (G-5447)

SALES (est): 19.9MM
SALES (corp-wide): 5.4B **Publicly Held**
SIC: 5912 5122 2834 Drug stores; pharmaceuticals; pharmaceutical preparations
PA: Diplomat Pharmacy, Inc.
4100 S Saginaw St
Flint MI 48507
888 720-4450

(G-5420)
EARL DAUP SIGNS
Also Called: EDS Enterprises
6060 Birch Rd (48507-4648)
PHONE...................810 767-2020
Gerald Daup, *President*
Daniel Daup, *Vice Pres*
EMP: 11
SQ FT: 18,000
SALES (est): 960K **Privately Held**
SIC: 3993 Electric signs; neon signs

(G-5421)
ECM MANUFACTURING INC
4301 Western Rd (48506-1805)
PHONE...................810 736-0299
Randy Wharram, *President*
EMP: 7
SALES (est): 309K **Privately Held**
SIC: 3999 Manufacturing industries

(G-5422)
ECM SPECIALTIES INC
4301 Western Rd (48506-1805)
PHONE...................810 736-0299
Randy Wharram, *President*
Gary Krueger, *Principal*
EMP: 7
SALES (est): 655.9K **Privately Held**
SIC: 3451 Screw machine products

(G-5423)
ED CUMINGS INC
2305 Branch Rd (48506-2910)
P.O. Box 90118, Burton (48509-0118)
PHONE...................810 736-0130
Jeffrey Powell, *President*
Richard Powell, *Admin Sec*
▲ EMP: 20
SQ FT: 28,000
SALES: 2.5MM **Privately Held**
WEB: www.cumingsnets.com
SIC: 2399 3949 Fishing nets; fishing equipment

(G-5424)
EMD WIRE TEK
4155 Holiday Dr (48507-3512)
PHONE...................810 235-5344
Paul E Schaeffer, *President*
Sandra Schaeffer, *Corp Secy*
EMP: 8
SQ FT: 6,700
SALES: 829.4K **Privately Held**
SIC: 3599 3544 Electrical discharge machining (EDM); special dies, tools, jigs & fixtures

(G-5425)
ENGINEERED PRODUCTS COMPANY (PA)
Also Called: Byron Manufacturing
601 Kelso St (48506-4034)
P.O. Box 108 (48501-0108)
PHONE...................810 767-2050
Treg Scott, *President*
Bill Mowl, *Technology*
▲ EMP: 24
SQ FT: 30,000
SALES (est): 3.5MM **Privately Held**
SIC: 3429 Builders' hardware; cabinet hardware; door opening & closing devices, except electrical

(G-5426)
EXACONNECT CORP
5141 Gateway Ctr Ste 400 (48507-3940)
PHONE...................810 232-1400
Gerald G Mansour, *President*
EMP: 8
SALES (est): 229.8K **Privately Held**
SIC: 3571 Electronic computers

(G-5427)
EXTREME PRECISION SCREW PDTS
1838 Remell St (48503-4499)
PHONE...................810 744-1980
Mark Blevins, *President*
Vicki Blevins, *Corp Secy*
EMP: 24 EST: 1965
SQ FT: 9,500
SALES (est): 4.1MM **Privately Held**
SIC: 3599 3728 3451 Machine shop, jobbing & repair; aircraft parts & equipment; screw machine products

(G-5428)
EZ FUEL INC
1330 E Atherton Rd (48507-2820)
PHONE...................810 744-4452
Aldabyani Dahan, *Manager*
EMP: 5 EST: 2012
SALES (est): 532.7K **Privately Held**
SIC: 2869 Fuels

(G-5429)
FLINT OPTICAL COMPANY INC
Also Called: Julie Opticians
518 S Saginaw St (48502-1804)
P.O. Box 819 (48501-0819)
PHONE...................810 235-4607
Julia Peachovich, *President*
EMP: 6
SQ FT: 4,800
SALES (est): 592.1K **Privately Held**
SIC: 5995 3851 Opticians; ophthalmic goods

(G-5430)
FLINT STOOL & CHAIR CO INC
1517 N Dort Hwy (48506-3915)
PHONE...................810 235-7001
Thomas Walter, *President*
Jeneffer Walter, *Admin Sec*
EMP: 4
SQ FT: 3,800
SALES: 500K **Privately Held**
SIC: 2531 Seats, miscellaneous public conveyances

(G-5431)
FLUSHING SAND AND GRAVEL
3502 W Mott Ave (48504-6953)
PHONE...................810 577-8260
Randy Osterman, *Principal*
EMP: 3
SALES (est): 180.4K **Privately Held**
SIC: 1442 Gravel mining

(G-5432)
GARRISONS HITCH CENTER INC
1050 Meida St (48532-5046)
PHONE...................810 239-5728
Jack R Johnson Jr, *President*
EMP: 4
SQ FT: 4,200
SALES: 200K **Privately Held**
SIC: 3714 7353 Trailer hitches, motor vehicle; heavy construction equipment rental

(G-5433)
GEI GLOBAL ENERGY CORP (PA)
4225 Miller Rd 269 (48507-1257)
PHONE...................810 610-2816
K Joel Berry, *Ch of Bd*
Jeff Berkowitz, *Vice Pres*
EMP: 3
SALES (est): 380.2K **Privately Held**
SIC: 3629 Electrochemical generators (fuel cells)

(G-5434)
GENERAL MOTORS LLC
G-2238 W Bristol Rd (48553-0001)
PHONE...................810 234-2710
Thomas V McLean, *Production*
Thomas Braun, *Engineer*
Don Mayton, *Branch Mgr*
EMP: 74 **Publicly Held**
SIC: 5511 3465 3444 Automobiles, new & used; automotive stampings; sheet metalwork
HQ: General Motors Llc
300 Renaissance Ctr L1
Detroit MI 48243

(G-5435)
GENERAL MOTORS LLC
2238 W Bristol Rd (48529)
PHONE...................810 234-2710
Don Mayton, *Branch Mgr*
Max Miller, *Manager*
EMP: 10 **Publicly Held**
SIC: 5511 3465 Automobiles, new & used; automotive stampings
HQ: General Motors Llc
300 Renaissance Ctr L1
Detroit MI 48243

(G-5436)
GENERAL MOTORS LLC
425 S Stevenson St (48503-1259)
P.O. Box 1730 (48501-1730)
PHONE...................810 236-1970
Tony Suggs, *Branch Mgr*
EMP: 325 **Publicly Held**
SIC: 3312 3544 3465 Tool & die steel; special dies, tools, jigs & fixtures; automotive stampings
HQ: General Motors Llc
300 Renaissance Ctr L1
Detroit MI 48243

(G-5437)
GENESEE CUT STONE & MARBLE CO (PA)
5276 S Saginaw Rd (48507-4493)
PHONE...................810 743-1800
David K Stites, *Managing Prtnr*
Richard J Bouck, *Partner*
Eva Hempel, *Partner*
Douglas Howes, *Partner*
Robert Paul, *Partner*
▲ EMP: 25
SQ FT: 35,600
SALES: 5MM **Privately Held**
WEB: www.gcsm.com
SIC: 5211 5032 3281 1423 Masonry materials & supplies; building stone; dimension stone for buildings; crushed & broken granite; crushed & broken limestone

(G-5438)
GENESEE FREE NET
1158 W Bristol Rd (48507-5518)
PHONE...................810 720-2880
Garry B Viele Jr, *Chairman*
EMP: 3 EST: 1993
SALES (est): 213.1K **Privately Held**
SIC: 7372 Application computer software

(G-5439)
GENESEE GROUP INC (PA)
Also Called: Genesee Packaging
2022 North St (48505-4544)
PHONE...................810 235-8041
Jane Worthing, *CEO*
Veronica Artis, *COO*
John Lindholm, *Admin Sec*
▲ EMP: 50
SQ FT: 109,000
SALES: 20.7MM **Privately Held**
SIC: 2653 Corrugated & solid fiber boxes

(G-5440)
GENESEE GROUP INC
Also Called: Genesee Packaging
1102 N Averill (48506)
PHONE...................810 235-6120
Jane Worthing, *CEO*
EMP: 80
SALES (corp-wide): 20.7MM **Privately Held**
SIC: 2653 Corrugated & solid fiber boxes
PA: The Genesee Group Inc
2022 North St
Flint MI 48505
810 235-8041

(G-5441)
GREAT LAKES AERO PRODUCTS
915 Kearsley Park Blvd (48503-4807)
PHONE...................810 235-1402
John A Zofko, *President*
John Zofko, *President*
Heather Z Bills, *Corp Secy*
Heather Zofko-Wiles, *Admin Sec*
EMP: 12 EST: 1973
SQ FT: 20,000
SALES: 500K **Privately Held**
WEB: www.glapinc.com
SIC: 3229 5599 5088 Pressed & blown glass; aircraft instruments, equipment or parts; aircraft equipment & supplies

(G-5442)
GREAT PUT ON INC
3240 W Pasadena Ave (48504-2330)
PHONE...................810 733-8021
Raji Salomon, *President*
Dennis Salim, *Vice Pres*
EMP: 9
SQ FT: 10,000
SALES: 1MM **Privately Held**
WEB: www.greatputon.com
SIC: 2261 7389 Screen printing of cotton broadwoven fabrics; textile & apparel services

(G-5443)
GROUND EFFECTS LLC (DH)
3302 Kent St (48503-4484)
PHONE...................810 250-5560
Jim Scott, *President*
Mark Kupko, *VP Finance*
EMP: 200
SALES (est): 344.2MM
SALES (corp-wide): 4.7B **Privately Held**
SIC: 3714 Motor vehicle parts & accessories
HQ: Ground Effects Ltd
4505 Rhodes Dr
Windsor ON N8W 5
519 944-3800

(G-5444)
HAAS GROUP INTERNATIONAL LLC
G3100 Van Slyke Rd (48551-0001)
PHONE...................810 236-0032
Lisa Perkette, *Branch Mgr*
EMP: 5 **Publicly Held**
SIC: 2899 Metal treating compounds; water treating compounds
HQ: Haas Group International, Llc
1475 Phoeni Pike Ste 101
West Chester PA 19380
484 564-4500

(G-5445)
HERALD NEWSPAPERS COMPANY INC
Also Called: Saginaw News
540 S Saginaw St Apt 403 (48502-1859)
PHONE...................989 752-7171
Paul Chafee, *Branch Mgr*
EMP: 200
SALES (corp-wide): 5.5B **Privately Held**
WEB: www.post-standard.com
SIC: 2711 7313 Newspapers, publishing & printing; newspaper advertising representative
HQ: The Herald Newspapers Company Inc
220 S Warren St
Syracuse NY 13202
315 470-0011

(G-5446)
HERALD NEWSPAPERS COMPANY INC
Also Called: Flint Journal, The
540 S Saginaw St Ste 101 (48502-1813)
PHONE...................810 766-6100
Matthew Sharp, *Publisher*
EMP: 100
SQ FT: 65,000
SALES (corp-wide): 5.5B **Privately Held**
WEB: www.post-standard.com
SIC: 2711 5192 Newspapers: publishing only, not printed on site; newspapers
HQ: The Herald Newspapers Company Inc
220 S Warren St
Syracuse NY 13202
315 470-0011

(G-5447)
HERALD NEWSPAPERS COMPANY INC
Also Called: Bay City Times
540 S Saginaw St Ste 101 (48502-1813)
PHONE...................989 895-8551
C K Dykema, *Publisher*
Matt Sharp, *Manager*
EMP: 50

Flint - Genesee County (G-5448)

SALES (corp-wide): 5.5B **Privately Held**
WEB: www.post-standard.com
SIC: 2711 7313 2759 Newspapers: publishing only, not printed on site; newspaper advertising representative; commercial printing
HQ: The Herald Newspapers Company Inc
220 S Warren St
Syracuse NY 13202
315 470-0011

(G-5448)
IRON MIKES WELDING& FABG
1535 N Dort Hwy (48506-3915)
PHONE..................................810 234-2996
Mike Corser, *Partner*
Linda Corser, *Partner*
EMP: 3 **EST:** 1970
SQ FT: 6,000
SALES (est): 65K **Privately Held**
SIC: 7692 Welding repair

(G-5449)
IRWIN ENTERPRISES INC
Also Called: Instant Copy Center
3030 W Pasadena Ave (48504-2365)
PHONE..................................810 732-0770
Larry J Irwin, *CEO*
EMP: 25
SQ FT: 2,000
SALES (est): 3.8MM **Privately Held**
SIC: 2752 2759 Commercial printing, offset; commercial printing

(G-5450)
ISLAND SUN TIMES INC
5152 Commerce Rd (48507-2939)
PHONE..................................810 230-1735
Vince Lorraine, *President*
Sherron Barden, *Editor*
Kim Davis, *Controller*
EMP: 15 **EST:** 1999
SQ FT: 10,000
SALES (est): 1MM **Privately Held**
WEB: www.islandsuntimes.com
SIC: 2711 Newspapers, publishing & printing

(G-5451)
J & K CANVAS PRODUCTS
8058 Corunna Rd (48532-5500)
PHONE..................................810 635-7711
Joann Carpenter, *Owner*
Kenneth A Carpenter, *Partner*
EMP: 3
SALES (est): 295.1K **Privately Held**
SIC: 2394 7699 7299 Awnings, fabric: made from purchased materials; general household repair services; rental of personal items, except for recreation & medical

(G-5452)
JAMES GLOVE & SUPPLY
3422 W Pasadena Ave (48504-2353)
PHONE..................................810 733-5780
Gail A McKone-Burns, *President*
Judith R McKone, *Treasurer*
EMP: 10 **EST:** 1972
SALES (est): 1MM **Privately Held**
SIC: 3842 5099 Personal safety equipment; gloves, safety; safety equipment & supplies

(G-5453)
KEARSLEY LAKE TERRACE LLC
3400 Benmark Pl Ofc (48506-1946)
PHONE..................................810 736-7000
Stanley Benmark,
EMP: 6
SALES (est): 363.8K **Privately Held**
SIC: 6515 3714 1522 5271 Mobile home site operators; motor vehicle parts & accessories; apartment building construction; mobile homes

(G-5454)
KENDALL & COMPANY INC
Also Called: Kendall Printing
1624 Lambden Rd (48532-4552)
PHONE..................................810 733-7330
Scott K Brown, *President*
EMP: 7
SQ FT: 2,800

SALES: 1MM **Privately Held**
WEB: www.printingbykendall.com
SIC: 2752 5112 7336 Commercial printing, offset; business forms; graphic arts & related design

(G-5455)
KICK IT AROUND SPORTS
3618 Fenton Rd (48507-1553)
PHONE..................................810 232-4986
Mary Siebernitz, *Owner*
EMP: 3
SQ FT: 5,400
SALES (est): 289.4K **Privately Held**
SIC: 5941 2759 Soccer supplies; imprinting

(G-5456)
KOEGEL MEATS INC (PA)
3400 W Bristol Rd (48507-3199)
PHONE..................................810 238-3685
John C Koegel, *President*
Kathryn Koegel, *Vice Pres*
Jim Lay, *Plant Mgr*
Albert J Koegel, *Treasurer*
Jonathon Jury, *Controller*
EMP: 109
SQ FT: 96,000
SALES (est): 34MM **Privately Held**
WEB: www.koegelmeats.com
SIC: 2013 5712 Frankfurters from purchased meat; bologna from purchased meat; luncheon meat from purchased meat; furniture stores

(G-5457)
LEAR CORPORATION
902 E Hamilton Ave (48550-0001)
PHONE..................................313 731-0833
EMP: 700
SALES (corp-wide): 21.1B **Publicly Held**
SIC: 3714 Motor vehicle electrical equipment; instrument board assemblies, motor vehicle; automotive wiring harness sets; motor vehicle body components & frame
PA: Lear Corporation
21557 Telegraph Rd
Southfield MI 48033
248 447-1500

(G-5458)
LIBERTY FABRICATORS INC
2229 W Hill Rd (48507-4654)
PHONE..................................810 877-7117
David Shemansky, *President*
Jack Hedrick, *Vice Pres*
EMP: 16
SQ FT: 45,000
SALES (est): 1.8MM **Privately Held**
WEB: www.libertyfab.com
SIC: 3559 3441 Automotive maintenance equipment; fabricated structural metal

(G-5459)
LOCKETT ENTERPRISES LLC
Also Called: Janitorial
607 E 2nd Ave Ste 30 (48502-2042)
P.O. Box 427 (48501-0427)
PHONE..................................810 407-6644
Corey Lockett, *CEO*
EMP: 5
SQ FT: 1,210
SALES (est): 390K **Privately Held**
SIC: 7349 5137 5136 5722 Janitorial service, contract basis; underwear: women's, children's & infants'; underwear, men's & boys'; household appliance stores; convection ovens, including portable: household

(G-5460)
LOGISTICS INSIGHT CORP
3311 Torrey Rd (48503-3251)
PHONE..................................810 424-0511
Mike Townley, *Principal*
EMP: 131
SALES (corp-wide): 1.4B **Publicly Held**
WEB: www.logisticsinsights.com
SIC: 3537 Tractors used in plants, docks, terminals, etc.: industrial
HQ: Logistics Insight Corp.
12755 E 9 Mile Rd
Warren MI 48089

(G-5461)
LOGOFIT LLC
3202 Lapeer Rd (48503-4424)
PHONE..................................810 715-1980
Jon Kraut,
Dave Kraut,
▲ **EMP:** 24 **EST:** 1992
SQ FT: 12,000
SALES (est): 1.8MM **Privately Held**
WEB: www.logofit.com
SIC: 2389 2396 Men's miscellaneous accessories; automotive & apparel trimmings

(G-5462)
LORBEC METALS - USA LTD
3415 Western Rd (48506-2327)
PHONE..................................810 736-0961
Jay Goldstein, *President*
Lawrence Leibov, *Corp Secy*
Lawrence Lifshitz, *Vice Pres*
▼ **EMP:** 47
SQ FT: 110,000
SALES (est): 16.3MM **Privately Held**
SIC: 5093 3341 Ferrous metal scrap & waste; secondary nonferrous metals

(G-5463)
MACHINING SPECIALISTS INC MICH
2712 N Saginaw St Ofc (48505-4408)
PHONE..................................517 881-2863
Duane Dahl, *President*
EMP: 5
SQ FT: 3,150
SALES (est): 430K **Privately Held**
SIC: 3599 Machine shop, jobbing & repair

(G-5464)
MAUREEN I MARTIN CASTER
2013 Ridgecliffe Dr (48532-3720)
PHONE..................................810 233-0484
EMP: 3
SALES (est): 254.7K **Privately Held**
SIC: 3562 Mfg Ball/Roller Bearings

(G-5465)
MICHIGAN HIGHWAY SIGNS INC (PA)
5182 S Saginaw Rd (48507-4470)
PHONE..................................810 695-7529
Timothy Peake, *President*
EMP: 9
SQ FT: 6,000
SALES (est): 2MM **Privately Held**
SIC: 3993 Signs, not made in custom sign painting shops

(G-5466)
MICHIGAN STEEL FABRICATORS INC
5225 Energy Dr (48505-1836)
PHONE..................................810 785-1478
Richard Webster, *President*
Chris Webster, *Vice Pres*
EMP: 20
SQ FT: 15,000
SALES (est): 5.1MM **Privately Held**
SIC: 3441 Fabricated structural metal

(G-5467)
MID-STATE PLATING CO INC
602 Kelso St (48506-4057)
PHONE..................................810 767-1622
Charles J Stokes, *CEO*
David Stokes, *President*
Tim Stokes, *Technician*
EMP: 30 **EST:** 1967
SQ FT: 30,000
SALES (est): 4.2MM **Privately Held**
WEB: www.midstateplating.com
SIC: 3471 Electroplating of metals or formed products

(G-5468)
MIDWEST FLEX SYSTEMS INC
415 Sb Chavez Dr (48503-1910)
PHONE..................................810 424-0060
Daniel Sternbergh, *President*
Jeff Moellering, *Manager*
EMP: 10
SQ FT: 4,000
SALES (est): 1.7MM **Privately Held**
WEB: www.midwestflex.com
SIC: 3829 Measuring & controlling devices

(G-5469)
MODERN INDUSTRIES INC
Also Called: Modern Concrete Products
3275 W Pasadena Ave (48504-2386)
PHONE..................................810 767-3330
Ronald D Lammy II, *President*
EMP: 20
SALES (est): 5.6MM **Privately Held**
SIC: 7353 3273 1442 Heavy construction equipment rental; ready-mixed concrete; construction sand & gravel

(G-5470)
MONROE TRUCK EQUIPMENT INC
Also Called: M T E
2400 Reo Dr (48507-6359)
PHONE..................................810 238-4603
David Quade, *President*
Tom Johnson, *CFO*
Donna Korpi, *Human Res Dir*
EMP: 50
SQ FT: 1,000
SALES (est): 9.7MM
SALES (corp-wide): 356.3MM **Privately Held**
WEB: www.monroetruckequipment.com
SIC: 3713 5013 Truck & bus bodies; truck parts & accessories
PA: Monroe Truck Equipment, Inc.
1051 W 7th St
Monroe WI 53566
608 328-8127

(G-5471)
MOORE BROTHERS ELECTRICAL CO
2602 Leith St (48506-2826)
P.O. Box 90062, Burton (48509-0062)
PHONE..................................810 232-2148
Rhex Moore, *President*
EMP: 5
SQ FT: 7,000
SALES (est): 1.4MM **Privately Held**
WEB: www.moorebrotherselectric.com
SIC: 5074 7694 Heating equipment (hydronic); electric motor repair

(G-5472)
NICKELS BOAT WORKS INC
1871 Tower St (48503-4435)
PHONE..................................810 767-4050
Hugh Armbruster, *President*
EMP: 10
SQ FT: 15,000
SALES: 1.4MM **Privately Held**
WEB: www.nickelsboats.com
SIC: 2221 2519 Dress fabrics, manmade fiber & silk; fiberglass furniture, household: padded or plain

(G-5473)
OAKLEY INDUSTRIES SUB ASSEMBLY (PA)
4333 Matthew (48507-3160)
PHONE..................................810 720-4444
Ronald Oakley, *President*
Arthur Meisels, *Principal*
Michael Oakley, *Corp Secy*
Moshe Kraus, *COO*
Robert O Trygstad, *Vice Pres*
EMP: 44
SQ FT: 80,000
SALES (est): 130.1MM **Privately Held**
SIC: 3714 Motor vehicle wheels & parts; motor vehicle body components & frame

(G-5474)
OAKLEY SUB ASSEMBLY INC
Also Called: Oakley Industries Saub Assembl
4333 Matthew (48507-3160)
PHONE..................................810 720-4444
Ronald Oakley, *President*
EMP: 35
SALES (est): 6.4MM
SALES (corp-wide): 130.1MM **Privately Held**
SIC: 3714 Motor vehicle wheels & parts
PA: Oakley Industries Sub Assembly Division, Inc.
4333 Matthew
Flint MI 48507
810 720-4444

GEOGRAPHIC SECTION

Flint - Genesee County (G-5501)

(G-5475)
OAKLEY SUB ASSEMBLY INTL INC
4333 Matthew (48507-3160)
PHONE..................................810 720-4444
Ronald Oakley, *President*
EMP: 3
SALES (est): 145.4K
SALES (corp-wide): 130.1MM **Privately Held**
SIC: 3714 Motor vehicle parts & accessories
PA: Oakley Industries Sub Assembly Division, Inc.
4333 Matthew
Flint MI 48507
810 720-4444

(G-5476)
OIL CHEM INC
711 W 12th St (48503-3851)
PHONE..................................810 235-3040
Robert Massey, *President*
Beverly Bryers, *Purch Agent*
Brandon Massey, *Manager*
Rachelle Palmateer, *Admin Asst*
EMP: 20
SQ FT: 61,272
SALES (est): 30.5MM **Privately Held**
WEB: www.oilcheminc.com
SIC: 5172 2841 2992 Lubricating oils & greases; detergents, synthetic organic or inorganic alkaline; lubricating oils & greases

(G-5477)
OMEGA SURGICAL INSTRUMENTS
1072 S Elms Rd Ste E (48532-3159)
PHONE..................................810 695-9800
Gary Adam, *President*
Dr Gary Weber, *Corp Secy*
David Miller, *Director*
EMP: 3
SALES (est): 381.4K **Privately Held**
WEB: www.omegasurgical.com
SIC: 3841 Surgical instruments & apparatus

(G-5478)
PANTER MASTER CONTROLS INC
3060 S Dye Rd Ste A (48507-1078)
PHONE..................................810 687-5600
Ronald Panter, *President*
Allen Panter, *Director*
EMP: 13
SALES (est): 1.7MM **Privately Held**
SIC: 3599 7371 Custom machinery; computer software development

(G-5479)
PEPSI-COLA METRO BTLG CO INC
6200g Taylor Dr (48507-4681)
PHONE..................................810 232-3925
John Ankey, *Manager*
Mark Levy, *Manager*
EMP: 100
SALES (corp-wide): 64.6B **Publicly Held**
WEB: www.joy-of-cola.com
SIC: 2086 5149 Soft drinks: packaged in cans, bottles, etc.; soft drinks
HQ: Pepsi-Cola Metropolitan Bottling Company, Inc.
1111 Westchester Ave
White Plains NY 10604
914 767-6000

(G-5480)
POSTAL SAVINGS DIRECT MKTG
Also Called: Postal Savers
1035 Ann Arbor St (48503-3603)
PHONE..................................810 238-8866
Charles J Koory, *President*
EMP: 10 **EST:** 1981
SQ FT: 3,000
SALES (est): 791.8K **Privately Held**
SIC: 7331 2752 Mailing list compilers; commercial printing, offset

(G-5481)
PPG INDUSTRIES INC
Also Called: PPG Automotive
3601 James P Cole Blvd (48505-3954)
PHONE..................................810 767-8030
John P Holewinski, *Branch Mgr*
EMP: 6
SALES (corp-wide): 15.3B **Publicly Held**
SIC: 2851 Paints & allied products
PA: Ppg Industries, Inc.
1 Ppg Pl
Pittsburgh PA 15272
412 434-3131

(G-5482)
PRECISION INDUSTRIES INC
3002 E Court St (48506-4093)
PHONE..................................810 239-5816
Jeffrey Swanson, *CEO*
Terri Daly, *CFO*
EMP: 15 **EST:** 1945
SQ FT: 10,500
SALES (est): 2MM **Privately Held**
WEB: www.precisionindinc.com
SIC: 3089 Injection molding of plastics

(G-5483)
PREMIERE PACKAGING INC (PA)
Also Called: Ppi
6220 Lehman Dr (48507-4678)
PHONE..................................810 239-7650
Mark Drolet, *President*
Kathy Elsworth, *Admin Sec*
▲ **EMP:** 75
SQ FT: 100,000
SALES (est): 45.7MM **Privately Held**
WEB: www.premierepkg.com
SIC: 2842 Polishing preparations & related products; waxes for wood, leather & other materials; automobile polish; stain removers

(G-5484)
PRINTCOMM INC (PA)
Also Called: Marketing Impact
2929 Davison Rd (48506-3992)
PHONE..................................810 239-5763
Kevin E Naughton, *President*
Gerald F Minarik, *President*
Eric Bauer, *Prdtn Mgr*
Scott Finendale, *Prdtn Mgr*
Deanna Schillag, *Accounting Mgr*
EMP: 51
SQ FT: 35,000
SALES (est): 30.9MM **Privately Held**
WEB: www.printcomm.com
SIC: 5112 2752 2791 2789 Business forms; commercial printing, offset; typesetting; bookbinding & related work; commercial printing

(G-5485)
PRINTING PERSPECTIVES LLC
1916 Owen St (48503-4361)
P.O. Box 260 (48501-0260)
PHONE..................................810 410-8186
Loyce Driskell,
Lewis Driskell,
Shannon Searcy,
EMP: 3 **EST:** 2013
SALES (est): 176.4K **Privately Held**
SIC: 2732 7389 Books: printing & binding;

(G-5486)
PYRAMID TUBULAR TECH INC
3214 S Dye Rd Ste C (48507-1088)
PHONE..................................810 732-6335
Tony Montalvo, *President*
Patrick Retsel, *VP Opers*
Heather Gross, *Project Mgr*
Jamie Retsel, *Manager*
EMP: 2
SALES (est): 2MM **Privately Held**
SIC: 3498 Fabricated pipe & fittings

(G-5487)
QFD RECYCLING
4450 Linden Creek Pkwy (48507-2943)
PHONE..................................810 733-2335
Douglas C Carlton,
Dr Anup Sud,
EMP: 12
SQ FT: 10,000

SALES (est): 211.5K **Privately Held**
WEB: www.pitcan.com
SIC: 3089 Plastic hardware & building products; downspouts, plastic

(G-5488)
QUALITY FIRST FIRE ALARM
4286 Pheasant Dr (48506-1742)
P.O. Box 618, Davison (48423-0618)
PHONE..................................810 736-4911
Greg Lauderbaugh, *Principal*
EMP: 3
SALES (est): 253K **Privately Held**
SIC: 3711 Fire department vehicles (motor vehicles), assembly of

(G-5489)
R & J ALMONDS INC
Also Called: Jonny Almond Nut Company
G4254 Fenton Rd (48507-3614)
PHONE..................................810 767-6887
Richard Krafsur, *President*
▲ **EMP:** 15
SALES (est): 2MM **Privately Held**
SIC: 2064 Nuts, candy covered

(G-5490)
RASSINI BRAKES LLC
4175 Pier North Blvd (48504-1386)
PHONE..................................810 780-4600
Robert Anderson, *Mng Member*
Gustavo Adolfo Aburto Campeas, *Manager*
EMP: 3 **EST:** 2013
SALES (est): 998.9K **Privately Held**
SIC: 3714 Vacuum brakes, motor vehicle
PA: Rassini, S.A.B. De C.V.
Pedregal No. 24, Piso 7
Ciudad De Mexico CDMX 11040

(G-5491)
RELIANCE ELECTRIC MACHINE CO
2601 Leith St (48506-2825)
PHONE..................................810 232-3355
Michael Gavroski, *President*
Olga Gavroski, *Vice Pres*
EMP: 12
SQ FT: 12,000
SALES (est): 633.8K **Privately Held**
SIC: 7694 5063 Electric motor repair; motors, electric

(G-5492)
RICHFIELD INDUSTRIES INC
3022 Airpark Dr S (48507-3477)
PHONE..................................810 233-0440
Howard W Campbell, *President*
Betty Campbell, *Corp Secy*
Howard Todd Campbell, *Vice Pres*
EMP: 16 **EST:** 1939
SQ FT: 12,000
SALES (est): 2.8MM **Privately Held**
SIC: 3315 3496 Baskets, steel wire; mesh, made from purchased wire

(G-5493)
RODZINA INDUSTRIES INC
Also Called: Ameriplastic Imprinting Co
3518 Fenton Rd (48507-1567)
PHONE..................................810 235-2341
Robert E Cross Jr, *President*
Ronald K Cross, *Vice Pres*
EMP: 4
SQ FT: 2,000
SALES: 500K **Privately Held**
SIC: 3953 3999 2759 3993 Embossing seals & hand stamps; identification badges & insignia; engraving; signs & advertising specialties; gaskets, packing & sealing devices

(G-5494)
ROGERS FOAM AUTOMOTIVE CORP (HQ)
501 W Kearsley St (48503-2647)
PHONE..................................810 820-6323
David P Marotta, *President*
▲ **EMP:** 50 **EST:** 2009
SALES (est): 19.2MM
SALES (corp-wide): 194.7MM **Privately Held**
SIC: 3086 Plastics foam products
PA: Rogers Foam Corporation
20 Vernon St Ste 1
Somerville MA 02145
617 623-3010

(G-5495)
ROHMANN IRON WORKS INC
201 Kelso St (48506-4087)
PHONE..................................810 233-5611
Jack Quinn, *President*
Jeff Quinn, *Vice Pres*
EMP: 15 **EST:** 1953
SQ FT: 16,000
SALES (est): 3.5MM **Privately Held**
WEB: www.rohmanniron.com
SIC: 3441 Building components, structural steel

(G-5496)
RPS BAR
533 Kelso St (48506-4032)
PHONE..................................810 235-8876
Reginal Prince, *Owner*
EMP: 3
SALES (est): 188.9K **Privately Held**
SIC: 2064 Candy bars, including chocolate covered bars

(G-5497)
SCHNEIDER ELECTRIC USA INC
4110 Pier North Blvd D (48504-1486)
PHONE..................................810 733-9400
EMP: 149
SALES (corp-wide): 177.9K **Privately Held**
WEB: www.squared.com
SIC: 3613 Switchgear & switchboard apparatus
HQ: Schneider Electric Usa, Inc.
201 Wshington St Ste 2700
Boston MA 02108
978 975-9600

(G-5498)
SEMTRON INC
6465 Corunna Rd (48532-5350)
PHONE..................................810 732-9080
Paul Semerad, *President*
Steve Lafon, *General Mgr*
G Ruth Semerad, *Vice Pres*
Audrey Henry, *Prdtn Mgr*
Katie Lafon, *Sales Staff*
▲ **EMP:** 12
SQ FT: 6,700
SALES (est): 1.8MM **Privately Held**
WEB: www.semtron.com
SIC: 3661 3643 Telephones & telephone apparatus; electric switches; connectors & terminals for electrical devices

(G-5499)
SIGN SCREEN INC
408 S Center Rd (48506-4128)
PHONE..................................810 239-1100
Gilbert L McCord, *President*
Gilbert McCord Jr, *Executive*
EMP: 7
SQ FT: 5,300
SALES (est): 1.1MM **Privately Held**
WEB: www.signscreen.com
SIC: 2759 7336 7389 3993 Screen printing; silk screen design; embroidering of advertising on shirts, etc.; signs & advertising specialties; automotive & apparel trimmings

(G-5500)
SIGNS BY CRANNIE INC (PA)
4145 Market Pl (48507-3204)
PHONE..................................810 487-0000
Daniel C Crannie Jr, *President*
EMP: 30
SQ FT: 17,000
SALES (est): 6.9MM **Privately Held**
WEB: www.signsbycrannie.com
SIC: 3993 Electric signs

(G-5501)
SPEN-TECH MACHINE ENGRG CORP
2851 James P Cole Blvd (48505-4500)
PHONE..................................810 275-6800
Troy S Spence, *CEO*
Dominic Costa, *Project Mgr*
Brendon Stokes, *Design Engr*
Glenn Grossbauer, *Executive*
EMP: 90
SQ FT: 165,000

Flint - Genesee County (G-5502)

SALES (est): 24.8MM **Privately Held**
WEB: www.spentechusa.com
SIC: 3549 8711 3599 Assembly machines, including robotic; consulting engineer; machine shop, jobbing & repair

(G-5502)
SPINFORM INC
1848 Tower St (48503-4436)
PHONE..................810 767-4660
Michael A Howells, *President*
EMP: 9
SQ FT: 7,500
SALES (est): 1.5MM **Privately Held**
SIC: 3444 3469 Sheet metalwork; metal stampings

(G-5503)
SPOILER WING KING
5042 Exchange Dr (48507-2906)
PHONE..................810 733-9464
Christina Burns, *Owner*
EMP: 5 EST: 2009
SALES (est): 416.5K **Privately Held**
SIC: 3465 Body parts, automobile: stamped metal

(G-5504)
STAINED GLASS AND GIFTS
4290 N Genesee Rd (48506-1504)
PHONE..................810 736-6766
Susan Godfrey, *Owner*
EMP: 4
SALES: 60K **Privately Held**
SIC: 3231 Products of purchased glass

(G-5505)
STANSLEY INDUSTRIES INC
4171 Holiday Dr (48507-3512)
PHONE..................810 515-1919
EMP: 3
SALES (est): 130.1K **Privately Held**
SIC: 3999 Manufacturing industries

(G-5506)
STOKES STEEL TREATING COMPANY
624 Kelso St (48506-4095)
PHONE..................810 235-3573
Robb Stokes, *President*
Ted Stokes, *Vice Pres*
Todd Stokes, *Vice Pres*
Wayne Stokes, *Shareholder*
EMP: 23
SQ FT: 8,000
SALES (est): 4.2MM **Privately Held**
SIC: 3398 Metal heat treating

(G-5507)
SUBTERRANEAN PRESS
913 Beard St (48503-5370)
P.O. Box 190106, Burton (48519-0106)
PHONE..................810 232-1489
Timothy K Holt, *Principal*
EMP: 9
SALES (est): 616.2K **Privately Held**
SIC: 2741 Miscellaneous publishing

(G-5508)
SUPERIOR GUN DRILLING
1830 Kelso St (48503-4418)
PHONE..................810 744-1112
Brian Aseltine, *Owner*
EMP: 3
SQ FT: 1,000
SALES (est): 289.6K **Privately Held**
SIC: 3599 Machine shop, jobbing & repair

(G-5509)
TGI DIRECT INC (PA)
5365 Hill 23 Dr (48507-3906)
P.O. Box 354 (48501-0354)
PHONE..................810 239-5553
Douglas Bacon, *President*
Joy Martinbianco, *Business Mgr*
Linda Bacon, *Corp Secy*
Deb Holbeck, *Vice Pres*
Deborah McKerracher, *Vice Pres*
▲ EMP: 40
SQ FT: 35,000
SALES (est): 12.7MM **Privately Held**
WEB: www.tgidirect.com
SIC: 2759 7389 7374 7331 Business forms: printing; packaging & labeling services; data processing service; mailing service

(G-5510)
THANGBOM LLC
336 W 1st St Ste 113 (48502-1382)
PHONE..................517 862-0144
Hien Nguyen,
Ryan Sadler,
EMP: 3
SALES (est): 170K **Privately Held**
SIC: 7372 7389 Application computer software; utility computer software;

(G-5511)
TRANE US INC
5335 Hill 23 Dr (48507-3906)
PHONE..................800 245-3964
EMP: 50 **Privately Held**
SIC: 3585 Mfg Refrigeration/Heating Equipment
HQ: Trane U.S. Inc.
    3600 Pammel Creek Rd
    La Crosse WI 54601
    608 787-2000

(G-5512)
TRANSPORTATION TECH GROUP INC (PA)
Also Called: Richfield Industries
3020 Airpark Dr S (48507-3477)
PHONE..................810 233-0440
Howard W Campbell, *President*
John Cuddeback, *General Mgr*
Al Rennert, *General Mgr*
Betty L Campell, *Corp Secy*
Ryan Pfeiffer, *Purch Agent*
EMP: 25
SQ FT: 12,000
SALES (est): 6.4MM **Privately Held**
SIC: 3315 3317 Baskets, steel wire; steel pipe & tubes

(G-5513)
TREASURE ENTERPRISE LLC
1161 N Ballenger Hwy # 7 (48504-7543)
PHONE..................810 233-7141
Larry Holley, *President*
EMP: 12
SALES (est): 823.1K **Privately Held**
SIC: 2711 Newspapers

(G-5514)
TRU CUSTOM BLENDS INC
2321 Branch Rd (48506-2910)
PHONE..................810 407-6207
Roland Urch, *CEO*
Timothy Urch, *COO*
EMP: 6
SALES (est): 653K **Privately Held**
SIC: 2851 Paints & allied products

(G-5515)
TURNER BUSINESS FORMS INC
Also Called: Tbf Graphics
1016 Professional Dr (48532-3635)
PHONE..................810 244-6980
Dan Maynard, *Branch Mgr*
EMP: 3
SALES (corp-wide): 2.9MM **Privately Held**
WEB: www.tbfgraphics.com
SIC: 2752 5112 Commercial printing, offset; business forms
PA: Turner Business Forms, Inc.
    19 Slatestone Dr
    Saginaw MI 48603
    989 752-5540

(G-5516)
U S SPEEDO INC
Also Called: Motor City Products
6050 Birch Rd (48507-4648)
PHONE..................810 244-0909
Terri Brink, *President*
Harry Brink, *Vice Pres*
Scott Ortega, *Sales Dir*
Carrie McCalpin, *Graphic Designe*
▲ EMP: 13
SQ FT: 15,000
SALES (est): 2.8MM **Privately Held**
WEB: www.usspeedo.com
SIC: 3824 Speedometers

(G-5517)
ULTIMATE TURF OF FLINT LLC
1054 W Schumacher Ave (48507-3633)
PHONE..................810 202-0203
EMP: 4
SALES (est): 520.3K **Privately Held**
SIC: 3523 Turf & grounds equipment

(G-5518)
UNIVERSAL COATING INC
5204 Energy Dr (48505-1837)
PHONE..................810 785-7555
Henry Johnson, *President*
Tim Johnson, *Treasurer*
Mary Ann Zaruba, *Manager*
Julie Tayler, *Data Proc Staff*
EMP: 55
SQ FT: 20,000
SALES (est): 7.9MM **Privately Held**
WEB: www.universalcoating.com
SIC: 3479 Coating of metals & formed products

(G-5519)
UPF INC
Also Called: UPF Group PLC
2851 James P Cole Blvd (48505-4500)
PHONE..................810 768-0001
David Wolgast, *CEO*
EMP: 100
SQ FT: 100,000
SALES: 10MM **Privately Held**
SIC: 3711 Chassis, motor vehicle

(G-5520)
VENTUOR LLC
336 W 1st St Ste 113 (48502-1382)
PHONE..................248 790-8700
Hesham Dean, *CEO*
EMP: 3
SALES (est): 80.9K **Privately Held**
SIC: 7371 7372 7389 Computer software development & applications; application computer software;

(G-5521)
VINYL SASH OF FLINT INC (PA)
5433 Fenton Rd G (48507-4022)
PHONE..................810 234-4831
Robert Bloss, *President*
Peggy J Bloss, *Admin Sec*
EMP: 45
SQ FT: 11,600
SALES (est): 4.5MM **Privately Held**
WEB: www.vinylsash.com
SIC: 1751 1521 1761 3442 Window & door (prefabricated) installation; patio & deck construction & repair; siding contractor; metal doors, sash & trim

(G-5522)
WESTROCK CP LLC
1409 E Pierson Rd (48505-3081)
PHONE..................810 787-6503
Bill Laimbeer, *Branch Mgr*
EMP: 17
SALES (corp-wide): 16.2B **Publicly Held**
WEB: www.sto.com
SIC: 2653 Boxes, corrugated: made from purchased materials
HQ: Westrock Cp, Llc
    1000 Abernathy Rd
    Atlanta GA 30328

(G-5523)
WGS GLOBAL SERVICES LC (PA)
6350 Taylor Dr (48507-4680)
PHONE..................810 239-4947
Adam Satkowiak, *Purchasing*
Ron Williams, *CFO*
Mary Haney, *Manager*
Ghaffan M Saab,
Susan Carnes,
▲ EMP: 65
SALES (est): 126.3MM **Privately Held**
SIC: 3711 Automobile assembly, including specialty automobiles

(G-5524)
WINSOL ELECTRONICS LLC
2000 N Saginaw St (48505-4770)
PHONE..................810 767-2987
EMP: 5
SALES: 63.5K **Privately Held**
SIC: 3999 Mfg Misc Products

(G-5525)
WOODWORTH INC
4201 Pier North Blvd (48504-1360)
PHONE..................810 820-6780
Matt Woodworth, *General Mgr*
EMP: 30
SALES (corp-wide): 15.1MM **Privately Held**
SIC: 3398 Metal heat treating
PA: Woodworth, Inc.
    500 Centerpoint Pkwy N
    Pontiac MI 48341
    248 481-2354

(G-5526)
WOOLEY INDUSTRIES INC
3034 S Ballenger Hwy (48507-1304)
PHONE..................810 341-8823
Dennis Allen, *Principal*
EMP: 8
SALES (est): 903K **Privately Held**
SIC: 3999 Manufacturing industries

(G-5527)
WPW INC
Also Called: Steel Fab
5225 Energy Dr (48505-1836)
PHONE..................810 785-1478
Chris Webster, *President*
Richard Webster, *President*
Brad Payne, *Vice Pres*
EMP: 15
SQ FT: 15,000
SALES (est): 1.5MM **Privately Held**
SIC: 3441 Fabricated structural metal

(G-5528)
X-TREME PRINTING INC
2638 Corunna Rd (48503-3316)
PHONE..................810 232-3232
Jean Benton, *President*
Gail Benedettini, *Vice Pres*
EMP: 5 EST: 1969
SQ FT: 2,300
SALES (est): 698.9K **Privately Held**
SIC: 2752 Commercial printing, offset

(G-5529)
ZYGOT OPERATIONS LIMITED
4301 Western Rd (48506-1805)
PHONE..................810 736-2900
Ronald D Wharram, *President*
EMP: 15
SQ FT: 25,000
SALES (est): 3.9MM **Privately Held**
WEB: www.michiganfasteners.com
SIC: 3451 3644 3469 Screw machine products; noncurrent-carrying wiring services; metal stampings

---

Flushing
Genesee County

(G-5530)
ADS PLUS PRINTING
767 E Main St (48433-2009)
PHONE..................810 659-7190
John Sanders, *Owner*
EMP: 5
SQ FT: 3,000
SALES (est): 446.7K **Privately Held**
SIC: 2759 7331 Screen printing; direct mail advertising services

(G-5531)
ALMAR ORCHARDS LLC
1431 Duffield Rd (48433-9764)
PHONE..................810 659-6568
James Koan,
Zachary Koan,
Monique Lapinski,
EMP: 20
SALES (est): 630K **Privately Held**
SIC: 0175 2051 2033 Apple orchard; bread, cake & related products; canned fruits & specialties

(G-5532)
CENTRAL CONCRETE PRODUCTS INC
4067 Commerce Dr (48433-2311)
PHONE..................810 659-7488
Rene Adkins, *President*

GEOGRAPHIC SECTION

Fowlerville - Livingston County (G-5558)

Larry C Adkins, *Treasurer*
EMP: 16
SQ FT: 10,000
SALES (est): 2.7MM **Privately Held**
SIC: 3273 Ready-mixed concrete

(G-5533)
COFFEE BEANERY LTD (HQ)
3429 Pierson Pl (48433-2498)
PHONE 810 733-1020
Joanne Shaw, *President*
Kevin Shaw, *President*
Julius Shaw, *Chairman*
Kurt Shaw, *Vice Pres*
Bret O'Brien, *Accountant*
▲ **EMP:** 48 **EST:** 1976
SQ FT: 45,000
SALES (est): 3.9MM
SALES (corp-wide): 16.9MM **Privately Held**
WEB: www.coffeebeanery.com
SIC: 5812 5149 6794 2099 Coffee shop; snow cone stand; coffee, green or roasted; tea; franchises, selling or licensing; food preparations; roasted coffee; flavoring extracts & syrups
PA: Shaw Coffee Company
3429 Pierson Pl
Flushing MI 48433
810 733-1020

(G-5534)
COLOR FACTORY
8034 N Mckinley Rd (48433-8801)
PHONE 810 577-2974
Diane Fondren, *Principal*
EMP: 4 **EST:** 2012
SALES (est): 257.6K **Privately Held**
SIC: 3479 Painting, coating & hot dipping

(G-5535)
FUEL TOBACCO STOP
Also Called: Marathon Oil
226 E Main St (48433-2026)
PHONE 810 487-2040
Shukri Abdulla, *Owner*
EMP: 4
SALES (est): 254K **Privately Held**
SIC: 2869 Fuels

(G-5536)
FUTURE TECHNOLOGIES GROUP LLC
6122 W Pierson Rd 10a (48433-3104)
P.O. Box 189 (48433-0189)
PHONE 810 733-3870
Matthew Catlin,
John E Davidek,
Stephen Davidek,
▲ **EMP:** 3
SQ FT: 4,500
SALES (est): 426.1K **Privately Held**
SIC: 3089 Injection molded finished plastic products

(G-5537)
JACOBS SIGNS
4182 Dillon Rd (48433-9705)
PHONE 810 659-2149
James Jacobs, *Partner*
EMP: 3
SALES: 170K **Privately Held**
SIC: 3993 Signs, not made in custom sign painting shops

(G-5538)
K & K TECHNOLOGY INC (PA)
3500 Woodridge Ct (48433-9795)
PHONE 989 399-9910
Russell Lafreniere, *President*
EMP: 3
SQ FT: 2,000
SALES: 700K **Privately Held**
SIC: 3559 8711 Automotive related machinery; engineering services

(G-5539)
KING PAR, LLC
Also Called: K P
5140 Flushing Rd (48433-2522)
PHONE 810 732-2470
▲ **EMP:** 54
SALES (est): 43.5MM **Privately Held**
WEB: www.kingparsuperstore.com
SIC: 5091 3949 Golf & skiing equipment & supplies; golf equipment

(G-5540)
MAT TEK INC
175 Industrial Dr Ste A (48433-1512)
P.O. Box 418 (48433-0418)
PHONE 810 659-0322
Matthew J Matus, *President*
EMP: 3
SQ FT: 1,000
SALES: 800K **Privately Held**
WEB: www.mat-tek.com
SIC: 3353 3462 3463 Aluminum sheet, plate & foil; iron & steel forgings; aluminum forgings

(G-5541)
MB LIQUIDATING CORPORATION
Also Called: Ultra-Dex Tooling Systems
7162 Sheridan Rd (48433-9610)
PHONE 810 638-5388
Pat Mulzahy, *President*
Dane Carnell, *Plant Mgr*
Jennifer Krupp, *Purch Mgr*
Meg Koos, *Human Res Mgr*
Dave Ives, *Manager*
EMP: 100
SQ FT: 12,000
SALES (est): 23.7MM **Privately Held**
WEB: www.ultradexusa.com
SIC: 3545 3541 Machine tool accessories; machine tools, metal cutting type

(G-5542)
STAR LINE COMMERCIAL PRINTING
6122 W Pierson Rd Unit 5 (48433-3104)
PHONE 810 733-1152
Cheryl Schultz, *Owner*
EMP: 12
SALES (est): 791.2K **Privately Held**
SIC: 2759 Post cards, picture: printing

(G-5543)
ULTRA-DEX USA LLC
7144 Sheridan Rd (48433-9610)
PHONE 810 638-5388
Eli Crotzer, *President*
Pat Mulcahy, *Vice Pres*
EMP: 5
SALES (est): 187.6K **Privately Held**
SIC: 3541 Machine tool replacement & repair parts, metal cutting types

(G-5544)
VETS ACCESS LLC
Also Called: Cor Health
1449 E Pierson Rd Ste B (48433-1885)
PHONE 810 639-2222
EMP: 8
SALES: 75K **Privately Held**
SIC: 3448 5047 7699 Mfg Prefab Metal Bldgs Whol Med/Hospital Equip Repairs Hospital Equipment

(G-5545)
WECO INTERNATIONAL INC
235 S Seymour Rd (48433-2618)
P.O. Box 189, Clio (48420-0189)
PHONE 810 686-7221
Brett Wehner, *President*
▲ **EMP:** 7
SALES (est): 1.3MM **Privately Held**
WEB: www.wecoproducts.com
SIC: 3634 Heating units, for electric appliances

(G-5546)
WILLIES WICKS
1315 Kapp Ct (48433-1403)
P.O. Box 16 (48433-0016)
PHONE 810 730-4176
William Francis Kumpon Jr, *Owner*
EMP: 3
SALES (est): 192.9K **Privately Held**
SIC: 3999 Candles

Fort Gratiot
St. Clair County

(G-5547)
C W ENTERPRISES INC
Also Called: Allegra Print Imging Port Hron
4137 24th Ave (48059-3802)
PHONE 810 385-9100
Chuck Warczynsky, *President*
Chris Warczinsky, *Admin Sec*
Cara Furness, *Representative*
EMP: 6
SQ FT: 2,500
SALES (est): 884.8K **Privately Held**
SIC: 2752 Commercial printing, offset

(G-5548)
CRESCENT CORPORATION
3720 Pine Grove Ave (48059-4250)
P.O. Box 610987, Port Huron (48061-0987)
PHONE 810 982-2784
Paul G Steinborn, *President*
EMP: 3
SQ FT: 2,000
SALES (est): 533.6K **Privately Held**
SIC: 3842 Walkers; canes, orthopedic

(G-5549)
FERGUSON STEEL INC
3755 N River Rd (48059-4146)
PHONE 810 984-3918
William White, *President*
EMP: 10
SQ FT: 18,000
SALES (est): 700K **Privately Held**
WEB: www.fergusonsteel.net
SIC: 3441 1791 Fabricated structural metal; structural steel erection

(G-5550)
NOBBY INC
Also Called: Forsports
3950 Pine Grove Ave (48059-4218)
PHONE 810 984-3300
Scott Forster, *President*
William Forster, *Vice Pres*
Sonya Dye, *Purch Mgr*
Carl Haas, *Treasurer*
Daniel Hartwick, *Manager*
EMP: 30
SQ FT: 16,000
SALES (est): 3.6MM **Privately Held**
WEB: www.fs4sports.com
SIC: 5999 5941 2396 2395 Trophies & plaques; sporting goods & bicycle shops; automotive & apparel trimmings; pleating & stitching

(G-5551)
PORT HURON MEDICAL ASSOC
3825 24th Ave (48059-4100)
PHONE 810 982-0100
Richard Covart, *Manager*
EMP: 5
SALES (est): 420K **Privately Held**
SIC: 2834 Medicines, capsuled or ampuled

Fostoria
Tuscola County

(G-5552)
NORTH BRANCH MACHINING & ENGRG
9318 Beech St (48435-7709)
P.O. Box 186 (48435-0186)
PHONE 989 795-2324
Michael P Grimes, *President*
Roxanne M Grimes, *Vice Pres*
EMP: 7
SQ FT: 3,000
SALES (est): 870.7K **Privately Held**
SIC: 3599 Machine shop, jobbing & repair

Fowler
Clinton County

(G-5553)
J J WOHLFERTS CUSTOM FURNITURE
10691 W M 21 (48835-5139)
PHONE 989 593-3283
Jerry J Wohlfert, *President*
Catherine Wohlfert, *Vice Pres*
EMP: 10 **EST:** 1980
SQ FT: 16,000
SALES (est): 1.3MM **Privately Held**
WEB: www.jjwohlferts.com
SIC: 2431 Millwork

(G-5554)
MILLERS REDI-MIX INC
6218 S Wright Rd (48835)
PHONE 989 587-6511
Joseph Miller, *President*
Dale Fedewa, *Vice Pres*
EMP: 18
SQ FT: 200
SALES (est): 3.2MM **Privately Held**
SIC: 3273 Ready-mixed concrete

(G-5555)
POHLS CUSTOM COUNTER TOPS
Also Called: Pohl's Cstm Cnter Tops Cbnetry
12185 W Colony Rd (48835-9760)
PHONE 989 593-2174
Russ Pohl, *Owner*
EMP: 4
SALES (est): 287.2K **Privately Held**
SIC: 2541 Counters or counter display cases, wood

(G-5556)
TRUE BUILT WOODWORKING
6140 S Wright Rd (48835)
PHONE 989 587-3041
Charles Truesdell, *Owner*
EMP: 3
SALES (corp-wide): 400K **Privately Held**
SIC: 2431 Trim, wood
PA: True Built Woodworking
11672 W Herbison Rd
Eagle MI 48822
517 626-6482

Fowlerville
Livingston County

(G-5557)
AMERICAN CHEMICAL TECH INC (PA)
485 E Van Riper Rd (48836-7931)
PHONE 517 223-0300
Kevin P Kovanda, *President*
James Kovanda, *Vice Pres*
Ross Kovanda, *Vice Pres*
Liz Jordan, *Project Mgr*
James Schultz, *Production*
▲ **EMP:** 24 **EST:** 1977
SQ FT: 65,000
SALES (est): 20.2MM **Privately Held**
WEB: www.americanchemtech.com
SIC: 5172 2869 Lubricating oils & greases; hydraulic fluids, synthetic base

(G-5558)
ARMOURED RSSTNCE MCHANISMS INC
Also Called: Armi
345 W Frank St (48836-7960)
P.O. Box 329 (48836-0329)
PHONE 517 223-7618
Susan Pretty, *President*
Steven Pretty, *Admin Sec*
EMP: 16
SQ FT: 12,600
SALES: 1.6MM **Privately Held**
WEB: www.banditproof.com
SIC: 3089 Flat panels, plastic

Fowlerville - Livingston County (G-5559)

(G-5559)
ASAHI KASEI PLAS N AMER INC (HQ)
1 Thermofil Way (48836-7936)
PHONE..................517 223-2000
John Moyer, *President*
Ramesh Iyer, *President*
Darrell Jackson, *Business Mgr*
Yuta Kume, *Corp Secy*
Fumihide Inada, *Senior VP*
◆ **EMP:** 119
SALES (est): 104.1MM **Privately Held**
SIC: 2821 Thermoplastic materials

(G-5560)
ASAHI KASEI PLASTICS AMER INC
1 Thermofil Way (48836-7936)
PHONE..................517 223-2000
Nobuyuki Shunaga, *President*
▲ **EMP:** 44
SQ FT: 150,000
SALES (est): 13.3MM **Privately Held**
SIC: 2821 Thermoplastic materials
PA: Asahi Kasei Corporation
1-1-2, Yurakucho
Chiyoda-Ku TKY 100-0

(G-5561)
BIGOS PRECAST
555 E Van Riper Rd (48836-7909)
PHONE..................517 223-5000
Dave Bigos, *Owner*
EMP: 5
SALES (est): 680.4K **Privately Held**
SIC: 3273 Ready-mixed concrete

(G-5562)
DEDOES INNOVATIVE MFG INC
925 Garden Ln (48836-9056)
PHONE..................517 223-2500
John Dedoes, *Owner*
Phyllis Dedoes, *Vice Pres*
Maria Woolford, *Human Resources*
EMP: 24
SALES (est): 6.1MM **Privately Held**
WEB: www.dedoesim.com
SIC: 3441 Boat & barge sections, prefabricated metal

(G-5563)
EXCELDA MFG HOLDG LLC
900 Garden Ln (48836-9053)
PHONE..................517 223-8000
Mike Mansfield, *Branch Mgr*
EMP: 10
SALES (corp-wide): 255MM **Privately Held**
WEB: www.excelda.com
SIC: 2992 7389 Lubricating oils & greases; packaging & labeling services
HQ: Excelda Manufacturing Holding, Llc
12785 Emerson Dr Bldg A
Brighton MI 48116
248 486-3800

(G-5564)
FLEX-N-GATE CORPORATION
8887 W Grand River Rd (48836-9208)
PHONE..................517 223-5900
EMP: 200
SALES (corp-wide): 3.3B **Privately Held**
WEB: www.meridianautosystems.com
SIC: 3465 Body parts, automobile: stamped metal
PA: Flex-N-Gate Llc
1306 E University Ave
Urbana IL 61802
217 384-6600

(G-5565)
FOWLERVILLE FEED & PET SUPS
120 Hale St (48836-9076)
P.O. Box 374 (48836-0374)
PHONE..................517 223-9115
Robert Esch, *President*
Duane Herbert, *Manager*
Richard Peckens, *Admin Sec*
EMP: 6
SALES (est): 622.1K **Privately Held**
SIC: 3999 Pet supplies; hair clippers for human use, hand & electric; hair driers, designed for beauty parlors

(G-5566)
FOWLERVILLE MACHINE TOOL INC
5010 W Grand River Rd (48836-8547)
PHONE..................517 223-8871
William David Mink, *President*
EMP: 9
SQ FT: 4,000
SALES (est): 605K **Privately Held**
SIC: 3544 Dies, steel rule

(G-5567)
FOWLERVILLE NEWS & VIEWS
Also Called: H & H Publications
731 S Grand Ave (48836-7914)
P.O. Box 937 (48836-0937)
PHONE..................517 223-8760
Steven Horton, *Partner*
Steve Horton, *Info Tech Mgr*
EMP: 4
SALES (est): 250K **Privately Held**
SIC: 2711 7313 Newspapers: publishing only, not printed on site; newspaper advertising representative

(G-5568)
GRANY GREENTHUMBS LLC
108 W Grand River Ave (48836)
PHONE..................517 223-1302
EMP: 3
SALES (est): 184.8K **Privately Held**
SIC: 3999 Hydroponic equipment

(G-5569)
HATCH STAMPING COMPANY LLC
901 Garden Ln (48836-9056)
PHONE..................517 223-1293
Marvin Lorenz, *Maint Spvr*
Ronald Hatch, *Mktg Dir*
Dan Craig, *Branch Mgr*
EMP: 60
SALES (corp-wide): 863.9MM **Privately Held**
WEB: www.hatchstamping.com
SIC: 3469 Metal stampings
HQ: Hatch Stamping Company Llc
635 E Industrial Dr
Chelsea MI 48118
734 475-8628

(G-5570)
INVENTION EVOLUTION COMP LLC
Also Called: IEC N.A.
144 National Park Dr (48836-9672)
PHONE..................517 219-0180
Michael B McLean,
EMP: 4
SALES (est): 88.8K **Privately Held**
SIC: 3465 Body parts, automobile: stamped metal

(G-5571)
J AMERICA LICENSED PDTS INC (PA)
Also Called: J America
445 E Van Riper Rd (48836-7931)
PHONE..................517 655-8800
Jeffrey Radway, *President*
Stacey Glemser, *Opers Mgr*
Tara Kirsch, *Production*
▲ **EMP:** 4
SALES (est): 500.5K **Privately Held**
SIC: 5949 5131 2221 Fabric stores piece goods; silk piece goods, woven; broadwoven fabric mills, manmade

(G-5572)
J N B MACHINERY LLC
175 National Park Dr (48836-9677)
P.O. Box 362 (48836-0362)
PHONE..................517 223-0711
Dennis Russ,
Brian Manson,
John Manson,
EMP: 1 **EST:** 2005
SQ FT: 30,000
SALES (est): 5.6MM **Privately Held**
SIC: 3699 Teaching machines & aids, electronic
PA: J.N.B. Machining Company, Inc.
9119 W Grand River Rd
Fowlerville MI 48836

(G-5573)
JNB MACHINING COMPANY INC (PA)
9119 W Grand River Rd (48836-9608)
P.O. Box 362 (48836-0362)
PHONE..................517 223-0725
John Manson, *President*
Brian Manson, *Vice Pres*
Evelyn Valeri, *Bookkeeper*
▲ **EMP:** 30
SQ FT: 17,000
SALES (est): 5.8MM **Privately Held**
WEB: www.jnbmach.com
SIC: 3599 Machine shop, jobbing & repair

(G-5574)
MAGNUS SOFTWARE INC
3883 Hogback Rd (48836-9543)
P.O. Box 358 (48836-0358)
PHONE..................517 294-0315
Shane Merem, *President*
EMP: 5 **EST:** 1994
SQ FT: 4,000
SALES (est): 365.4K **Privately Held**
SIC: 7372 Prepackaged software

(G-5575)
MEDICAL CMFORT SPECIALISTS LLC
919 Garden Ln (48836-9056)
PHONE..................810 229-4222
Douglas Sprague, *Mng Member*
EMP: 17
SALES (est): 3.3MM **Privately Held**
SIC: 3842 Surgical appliances & supplies

(G-5576)
MICHIGAN DIVERSIFIED METALS
144 Veterans Dr (48836-9050)
P.O. Box 508 (48836-0508)
PHONE..................517 223-7730
Dan Ordan, *President*
EMP: 7
SQ FT: 3,000
SALES (est): 134.7K **Privately Held**
SIC: 3441 Fabricated structural metal

(G-5577)
PROTECTIVE CTNGS EPOXY SYSTEMS
971 Arlene Ct (48836-9401)
PHONE..................517 223-1192
Mike Moran, *Owner*
EMP: 3
SALES (est): 120K **Privately Held**
SIC: 3479 Metal coating & allied service

(G-5578)
RDZ RACING INCORPORATED
9642 Sober Rd (48836-9394)
PHONE..................517 468-3254
Robert Earls, *Principal*
EMP: 4
SALES (est): 330.8K **Privately Held**
SIC: 3799 All terrain vehicles (ATV)

(G-5579)
RHE-TECH LLC
9201 W Grand River Rd (48836-9608)
PHONE..................517 223-4874
EMP: 8
SALES (corp-wide): 1.5B **Privately Held**
SIC: 3087 2821 Custom compound purchased resins; plastics materials & resins
HQ: Rhe-Tech, Llc
1500 E N Territorial Rd
Whitmore Lake MI 48189
734 769-0585

(G-5580)
TOTAL SECURITY SOLUTIONS INC
935 Garden Ln (48836-9056)
PHONE..................517 223-7807
John Richards, *President*
Jim Richards, *Vice Pres*
Travis Aumick, *Project Mgr*
Eric Malzahn, *Project Mgr*
Bob George, *Sales Mgr*
▼ **EMP:** 28
SALES (est): 6.2MM **Privately Held**
WEB: www.totalsecuritysolutionsinc.com
SIC: 3272 Concrete window & door components, sills & frames

(G-5581)
ZF ACTIVE SAFETY US INC
500 E Van Riper Rd (48836-7908)
PHONE..................517 223-8330
Kathy Grostelia, *Branch Mgr*
EMP: 111
SALES (corp-wide): 216.2K **Privately Held**
SIC: 3714 Motor vehicle parts & accessories
HQ: Zf Active Safety Us Inc.
12001 Tech Center Dr
Livonia MI 48150
734 812-6979

Frankenmuth
Saginaw County

(G-5582)
AMAZING ENGRAVING
9720 Junction Rd Ste B (48734-9526)
PHONE..................989 652-8503
James Hornfield, *Principal*
EMP: 3
SALES (est): 164.8K **Privately Held**
SIC: 5999 2759 Trophies & plaques; embossing on paper

(G-5583)
BERNTHAL PACKING INC
9378 Junction Rd (48734-9539)
PHONE..................989 652-2648
Herbert Bernthal, *CEO*
Philip Bernthal, *President*
Frances Bernthal, *Corp Secy*
EMP: 20 **EST:** 1966
SQ FT: 6,000
SALES (est): 1.4MM **Privately Held**
SIC: 5421 0751 2013 2011 Meat markets, including freezer provisioners; slaughtering: custom livestock services; sausages & other prepared meats; meat packing plants

(G-5584)
BRONNER DISPLAY SIGN ADVG INC
Also Called: Bronner Christmas Decorations
25 Christmas Ln (48734-1807)
P.O. Box 176 (48734-0176)
PHONE..................989 652-9931
Wayne Bronner, *President*
Carla Bronner Spletzer, *Vice Pres*
Maria Bronner Sutorik, *Vice Pres*
Lorene Bronner, *Buyer*
Jill Catterfeld, *CFO*
◆ **EMP:** 250
SQ FT: 320,000
SALES (est): 71.8MM **Privately Held**
WEB: www.bronners.com
SIC: 5999 5199 3699 Christmas lights & decorations; Christmas novelties; Christmas tree lighting sets, electric; Christmas tree ornaments, electric

(G-5585)
FRANKENMUTH BREWERY LLC
425 S Main St (48734-1615)
P.O. Box 226 (48734-0226)
PHONE..................989 262-8300
Clark Bien, *Treasurer*
Randall E Heine,
EMP: 140
SQ FT: 50,000
SALES: 20.9MM **Privately Held**
WEB: www.frankenmuthbrewery.com
SIC: 2082 Ale (alcoholic beverage)

(G-5586)
FRANKENMUTH BREWING COMPANY
Also Called: Frankenmuth Brewery
425 S Main St (48734-1615)
P.O. Box 226 (48734-0226)
PHONE..................989 262-8300
Anmar Sarafa, *President*
Haithem Sarafa, *General Mgr*
EMP: 60

GEOGRAPHIC SECTION

SALES: 4.8MM **Privately Held**
SIC: 5812 2082 Restaurant, family: independent; beer (alcoholic beverage)

(G-5587)
FRANKENMUTH INDUSTRIAL SVCS
310 List St (48734-1910)
P.O. Box 357 (48734-0357)
PHONE...................................989 652-3322
George Anscomb, *President*
George A Anscomb, *President*
Michelle L Anscomb, *Vice Pres*
EMP: 20
SQ FT: 20,000
SALES (est): 1MM **Privately Held**
SIC: 7692 3441 Welding repair; fabricated structural metal

(G-5588)
GLAXOSMITHKLINE LLC
1331 S Dehmel Rd (48734-9150)
PHONE...................................989 450-9859
EMP: 26
SALES (corp-wide): 39.5B **Privately Held**
SIC: 2834 Pharmaceutical preparations
HQ: Glaxosmithkline Llc
  5 Crescent Dr
  Philadelphia PA 19112
  215 751-4000

(G-5589)
GRASEL GRAPHICS INC
9710 Junction Rd (48734-9502)
P.O. Box 385 (48734-0385)
PHONE...................................989 652-5151
Steven Grasel, *President*
Amy Grasel, *Admin Sec*
EMP: 9
SQ FT: 5,500
SALES (est): 1.2MM **Privately Held**
WEB: www.graselgraphics.com
SIC: 2759 2395 Screen printing; embroidery products, except schiffli machine

(G-5590)
KERNS SAUSAGES INC
110 W Jefferson St (48734-1898)
PHONE...................................989 652-2684
Ronald Kern, *President*
Kevin Kern, *Vice Pres*
EMP: 20
SALES (est): 750K **Privately Held**
SIC: 5421 5411 2013 Meat markets, including freezer provisioners; grocery stores, independent; sausages & other prepared meats

(G-5591)
KGDH LLC
Also Called: Frankenmuth Sausage Company
316 S Main St (48734-1635)
PHONE...................................989 652-9041
Keith Gere,
Jackie Gere,
EMP: 3
SALES (est): 167.5K **Privately Held**
SIC: 2013 Sausages & other prepared meats

(G-5592)
KREMIN INC
235 Keystone Way (48734-9629)
PHONE...................................989 790-5147
Michael Kremin Jr, *President*
Gary Hiltz, *Production*
EMP: 27
SQ FT: 20,000
SALES (est): 5MM **Privately Held**
WEB: www.kremininc.com
SIC: 3599 3544 Machine shop, jobbing & repair; special dies, tools, jigs & fixtures

(G-5593)
MEMTRON TECHNOLOGIES CO
Also Called: Esterline Mmtron Input Cmpnnts
530 N Franklin St (48734-1000)
PHONE...................................989 652-2656
Denis Staver, *President*
▲ **EMP**: 82
SQ FT: 30,000
SALES (est): 21.1MM
SALES (corp-wide): 3.8B **Publicly Held**
WEB: www.memtron.com
SIC: 3679 Electronic circuits

HQ: Esterline Technologies Corp
  500 108th Ave Ne Ste 1500
  Bellevue WA 98004
  425 453-9400

(G-5594)
MILLER MOLD CO
690 Wren Rd (48734-9320)
PHONE...................................989 793-8881
Robert J Piesko, *President*
EMP: 35
SALES (est): 8.4MM **Privately Held**
WEB: www.millermold.com
SIC: 3559 3544 Plastics working machinery; special dies, tools, jigs & fixtures

(G-5595)
ST JULIAN WINE COMPANY INC
127 S Main St (48734-1611)
PHONE...................................989 652-3281
Gordon Lockhart, *Manager*
EMP: 7
SALES (corp-wide): 10.9MM **Privately Held**
SIC: 5921 2086 2084 Wine; bottled & canned soft drinks; wines, brandy & brandy spirits
PA: St. Julian Wine Company, Incorporated
  716 S Kalamazoo St
  Paw Paw MI 49079
  269 657-5568

(G-5596)
STAR OF WEST MILLING COMPANY (PA)
121 E Tuscola St (48734-1731)
P.O. Box 146 (48734-0146)
PHONE...................................989 652-9971
Gary Rummel, *Ch of Bd*
William A Zehnder III, *Vice Ch Bd*
Arthur A Loeffler, *President*
Michael Fassezke, *Vice Pres*
James Howe, *Vice Pres*
▼ **EMP**: 71 **EST**: 1870
SQ FT: 45,000
SALES: 380.1MM **Privately Held**
WEB: www.starofthewest.com
SIC: 2041 5153 5191 Flour; grains; beans, dry: bulk; fertilizer & fertilizer materials; seeds: field, garden & flower; feed

(G-5597)
ZEILINGER WOOL CO LLC
1130 Weiss St (48734-1995)
PHONE...................................989 652-2920
Kathy Zeilinger, *President*
Kathy Ann Zeilinger, *President*
Marilyn Faerber, *Manager*
EMP: 22
SQ FT: 7,000
SALES: 850K **Privately Held**
WEB: www.zwool.com
SIC: 7219 2299 5949 Reweaving textiles (mending service); batts & batting: cotton mill waste & related material; roves, flax & jute; sewing, needlework & piece goods

Frankfort
Benzie County

(G-5598)
BAYSIDE PRINTING INC
515 Main St (49635-9046)
P.O. Box 1124 (49635-1124)
PHONE...................................231 352-4440
Robert McNabb, *President*
EMP: 3
SALES (est): 273.7K **Privately Held**
WEB: www.baysideprintinginc.com
SIC: 2759 2752 2789 Letterpress printing; commercial printing, lithographic; bookbinding & related work

(G-5599)
BENZIE MANUFACTURING LLC
401 Parkview Ln (49635-9492)
PHONE...................................231 631-0498
Tami Scott,
Kevin Scott,
EMP: 3

SALES (est): 392.4K **Privately Held**
SIC: 3599 Machine & other job shop work; custom machinery; machine shop, jobbing & repair

(G-5600)
CONINE PUBLISHING INC
Also Called: Benzie County Record-Patriot
417 Main St (49635-9142)
P.O. Box 673 (49635-0673)
PHONE...................................231 352-9659
Roland Halliday, *Manager*
EMP: 4
SALES (corp-wide): 8.3B **Privately Held**
WEB: www.pioneergroup.net
SIC: 2711 Newspapers: publishing only, not printed on site
HQ: Conine Publishing Inc
  75 Maple St
  Manistee MI 49660
  231 723-3592

(G-5601)
FRANKFORT MANUFACTURING INC
1105 Main St (49635-9020)
P.O. Box 273 (49635-0273)
PHONE...................................231 352-7551
Donald Surber, *President*
EMP: 38
SQ FT: 15,000
SALES (est): 5.6MM **Privately Held**
SIC: 3544 Special dies & tools

(G-5602)
GRACELAND FRUIT INC
1123 Main St (49635-9341)
PHONE...................................231 352-7181
Alan Devore, *CEO*
Jeff Seeley, *President*
James Nugent, *Chairman*
Dan Engler, *COO*
Steve Nugent, *COO*
◆ **EMP**: 180 **EST**: 1973
SQ FT: 110,000
SALES (est): 83.2MM **Privately Held**
WEB: www.gracelandfruit.com
SIC: 2034 2037 Fruits, dried or dehydrated, except freeze-dried; fruits, quick frozen & cold pack (frozen)

(G-5603)
H W JENCKS INCORPORATED
Detroit Coil Company
1339 Elm St (49635-9674)
P.O. Box 1097 (49635-1097)
PHONE...................................231 352-4422
Fax: 231 352-4024
EMP: 35
SALES (corp-wide): 2.2MM **Privately Held**
SIC: 3677 3643 3621 Mfg Electronic Coils/Transformers Mfg Conductive Wiring Devices Mfg Motors/Generators
PA: H W Jencks Incorporated
  2435 Hilton Rd
  Ferndale MI

(G-5604)
OTSUKA AMERICA FOODS INC
1123 Main St (49635-9341)
PHONE...................................231 383-3124
Steve Nugent, *Principal*
EMP: 3 **Privately Held**
SIC: 2099 Food preparations
HQ: Otsuka America Foods, Inc.
  1 Embarcadero Ctr # 2020
  San Francisco CA 94111

(G-5605)
ROGER MIX STORAGE
1218 Elm St (49635-9338)
P.O. Box 2231 (49635-2231)
PHONE...................................231 352-9762
Roger Mix, *President*
EMP: 4
SALES (est): 212.3K **Privately Held**
SIC: 3273 4225 Ready-mixed concrete; general warehousing & storage

(G-5606)
SMELTZER COMPANIES INC
Also Called: Smeltzer Orchard Company
6032 Joyfield Rd (49635-9163)
PHONE...................................231 882-4421
Tim Brian, *President*

James H Brian, *Vice Pres*
Mike Henschell, *Vice Pres*
Clinton Brian, *Controller*
Clinton Smeltzer, *Director*
▼ **EMP**: 110
SQ FT: 106,150
SALES: 16MM **Privately Held**
WEB: www.smeltzerorchards.com
SIC: 2037 2034 Fruits, quick frozen & cold pack (frozen); vegetables, quick frozen & cold pack, excl. potato products; dehydrated fruits, vegetables, soups

(G-5607)
VITAL TECHNOLOGIES
Also Called: Vital Test
1152 Martin Dr (49635-9004)
PHONE...................................231 352-9364
Joseph P Simo, *Owner*
EMP: 3
SALES (est): 260.6K **Privately Held**
SIC: 3589 Water treatment equipment, industrial

Franklin
Oakland County

(G-5608)
PREMIER IMAGING CENTER
31500 Telg Rd Ste 225 (48025)
PHONE...................................248 594-3201
Anibal Drelichman, *Principal*
EMP: 3
SALES (est): 377.2K **Privately Held**
SIC: 3841 Diagnostic apparatus, medical

(G-5609)
TALBOT & ASSOCIATES INC
Also Called: Tai Consulting
30400 Telg Rd Ste 479 (48025)
PHONE...................................248 723-9700
Michael R Talbot, *President*
Michele Kandt, *Treasurer*
Linda Lavin, *Admin Sec*
EMP: 10
SALES (est): 1MM **Privately Held**
WEB: www.taiconsulting.com
SIC: 7372 Business oriented computer software

Fraser
Macomb County

(G-5610)
A B RUSGO INC (PA)
Also Called: Labor World
32064 Utica Rd (48026-2207)
PHONE...................................586 296-7714
Alan B Rusgo, *President*
Jacalyn Liebowitz, *Vice Pres*
EMP: 8
SQ FT: 2,800
SALES (est): 708.6K **Privately Held**
WEB: www.allegiancestaffing.com
SIC: 2711 Newspapers: publishing only, not printed on site

(G-5611)
A-1 STAMPINGS INC
33381 Kelly Rd (48026-1533)
PHONE...................................586 294-7790
Edmund Kirkman, *President*
EMP: 5 **EST**: 1962
SQ FT: 15,200
SALES (est): 610.2K **Privately Held**
SIC: 3469 3465 Stamping metal for the trade; automotive stampings

(G-5612)
ACCURATE BORING COMPANY INC
17420 Malyn Blvd (48026-1635)
PHONE...................................586 294-7555
Richard Smith, *President*
EMP: 15
SALES (est): 3MM
SALES (corp-wide): 18.2MM **Privately Held**
WEB: www.accurateboring.com
SIC: 3599 Machine shop, jobbing & repair

Fraser - Macomb County (G-5613)

PA: Wolverine Bronze Company
28178 Hayes Rd
Roseville MI 48066
586 776-8180

(G-5613)
ADVANCED INTEGRATED MFG
34673 Bennett (48026-3413)
PHONE...................................586 439-0300
Jeffrey R Siciliano, *President*
Michael W See, *Vice Pres*
EMP: 16
SQ FT: 5,000
SALES (est): 1.6MM **Privately Held**
WEB: www.aimcom.com
SIC: 3824 3823 3577 3571 Fluid meters & counting devices; industrial instrmnts msrmnt display/control process variable; computer peripheral equipment; electronic computers; systems software development services
PA: A S A P Computer Services, Inc
34673 Bennett
Fraser MI 48026

(G-5614)
AFFINITY ELECTRONICS INC
33710 Doreka (48026-3430)
PHONE...................................586 477-4920
John Hogan, *President*
EMP: 6
SQ FT: 5,000
SALES (est): 314.7K **Privately Held**
SIC: 3679 Loads, electronic

(G-5615)
AMBER MANUFACTURING INC
18320 Malyn Blvd (48026-3494)
PHONE...................................586 218-6080
Lyle J Atcton, *President*
Lyle J Acton, *President*
Janice Acton, *Vice Pres*
EMP: 7
SQ FT: 7,200
SALES (est): 1.1MM **Privately Held**
SIC: 3544 Special dies & tools

(G-5616)
AMERICAN AXLE & MFG INC
Also Called: AAM Fraser Mfg Fcilty
18450 15 Mile Rd (48026-3460)
PHONE...................................586 415-2000
EMP: 5
SALES (corp-wide): 7.2B **Publicly Held**
SIC: 3714 Motor vehicle engines & parts
HQ: American Axle & Manufacturing, Inc.
1 Dauch Dr
Detroit MI 48211

(G-5617)
AMERICAN PRIDE MACHINING INC
34062 James J Pompo Dr (48026-3408)
PHONE...................................586 294-6404
Susan Kolatski, *CEO*
EMP: 4
SALES: 1MM **Privately Held**
SIC: 7699 3541 Industrial machinery & equipment repair; machine tool replacement & repair parts, metal cutting types

(G-5618)
AMERICAS FINEST PRTG GRAPHICS (PA)
17060 Masonic Ste 101 (48026-2561)
PHONE...................................586 296-1312
Judy Hill, *President*
Joseph Hill, *Corp Secy*
Jason Hill, *Vice Pres*
EMP: 6
SQ FT: 1,200
SALES (est): 768.2K **Privately Held**
SIC: 2759 7338 2791 2789 Screen printing; secretarial & court reporting; typesetting; bookbinding & related work; commercial printing, lithographic

(G-5619)
AMERISTEEL INC
33900 Doreka (48026-1611)
PHONE...................................586 585-5250
Warren Damman, *President*
EMP: 11
SQ FT: 20,000
SALES (est): 8.7MM **Privately Held**
WEB: www.ameristeelonline.com
SIC: 5051 3714 Steel; motor vehicle parts & accessories

(G-5620)
ANDERSON-COOK INC
Also Called: Anderson Cook Machine Tool
17650 15 Mile Rd (48026-3450)
P.O. Box 26509 (48026-6509)
PHONE...................................586 293-0800
Brent Chartier, *Vice Pres*
Tom Thomas, *Vice Pres*
Ron Kurkowski, *Safety Mgr*
Jim Everlove, *Design Engr*
Michael Carmendy, *Sales Executive*
EMP: 60
SALES (corp-wide): 65.9MM **Privately Held**
WEB: www.andersoncook.com
SIC: 3542 3714 3599 3549 Spline rolling machines; gears, motor vehicle; machine shop, jobbing & repair; metalworking machinery; machine tool accessories
PA: Anderson-Cook, Inc.
44785 Macomb Indus Dr
Clinton Township MI 48036
586 954-0700

(G-5621)
ARENA PUBLISHING CO INC
Also Called: Movie Collectors World
15767 Kingston Dr (48026-2312)
P.O. Box 309 (48026-0309)
PHONE...................................586 296-5369
Brian Bukantis, *President*
Betty Bukantis, *Vice Pres*
EMP: 4
SQ FT: 1,400
SALES (est): 399.7K **Privately Held**
WEB: www.moviecollectorsworld.com
SIC: 2721 7338 Magazines: publishing & printing; secretarial & court reporting

(G-5622)
ARISTO-COTE INC
Also Called: Aristo Industries
32100 Groesbeck Hwy (48026-3144)
PHONE...................................586 447-9049
Matt Murray, *President*
EMP: 70 **Privately Held**
SIC: 3479 Coating of metals & formed products; coating of metals with plastic or resins; coating of metals with silicon; coating or wrapping steel pipe
PA: Aristo-Cote, Inc.
24951 Henry B Joy Blvd
Harrison Township MI 48045

(G-5623)
AUTO/CON CORP
33842 James J Pompo Dr (48026-3468)
PHONE...................................586 791-7474
Ronald R Matheson, *President*
Cheryl Cargill, *Corp Secy*
Daniel Hucul, *Vice Pres*
Gerald Stehlin, *Vice Pres*
EMP: 80
SQ FT: 70,900
SALES (est): 13.4MM **Privately Held**
SIC: 3549 Assembly machines, including robotic

(G-5624)
AUTO/CON SERVICES LLC
Also Called: ACS
33661 James J Pompo Dr (48026-3467)
PHONE...................................586 791-7474
Chris Michayluk, *CEO*
EMP: 25
SQ FT: 30,000
SALES (est): 1.6MM **Privately Held**
SIC: 7389 3569 3535 Design services; assembly machines, non-metalworking; robots, assembly line: industrial & commercial; overhead conveyor systems

(G-5625)
AUTOMATED PROD ASSEMBLIES
33957 Doreka (48026-1612)
PHONE...................................586 293-3990
Thomas Monroe, *President*
EMP: 13
SQ FT: 10,900

SALES: 3MM **Privately Held**
WEB: www.tapping.cc
SIC: 3599 Machine shop, jobbing & repair

(G-5626)
AW CARBIDE FABRICATORS INC
33891 Doreka (48026-3473)
PHONE...................................586 294-1850
Dennis A Wegner, *President*
James T Wegner, *Vice Pres*
EMP: 15 **EST:** 1961
SQ FT: 14,400
SALES (est): 2.5MM **Privately Held**
SIC: 3545 3544 3541 Cutting tools for machine tools; special dies, tools, jigs & fixtures; machine tools, metal cutting type

(G-5627)
BARNES GROUP INC
Also Called: Kaller Gas Springs
33280 Groesbeck Hwy (48026-1597)
PHONE...................................586 415-6677
Michael Ambrogio, *General Mgr*
EMP: 8
SALES (corp-wide): 1.5B **Publicly Held**
WEB: www.barnesgroupinc.com
SIC: 3495 3469 Wire springs; metal stampings
PA: Barnes Group Inc.
123 Main St
Bristol CT 06010
860 583-7070

(G-5628)
BAY PRODUCTS INC
17800 15 Mile Rd (48026-1601)
PHONE...................................586 296-7130
Thomas Bayagich, *Vice Pres*
EMP: 42
SQ FT: 18,000
SALES (est): 9.6MM **Privately Held**
WEB: www.bayproductsinc.com
SIC: 3544 Special dies & tools; jigs & fixtures

(G-5629)
BERMONT GAGE & AUTOMATION INC
Also Called: Bermont Technologies
34500 Klein Rd (48026-3022)
PHONE...................................586 296-1103
Vincent Dudek, *President*
Herg Langegger, *Vice Pres*
▼ **EMP:** 16
SQ FT: 24,000
SALES: 1.7MM **Privately Held**
WEB: www.bermontgage.com
SIC: 3599 Machine shop, jobbing & repair

(G-5630)
BMT AEROSPACE USA INC
Also Called: Orwood Precision Pdts Caratron
18559 Malyn Blvd (48026-1606)
PHONE...................................586 285-7700
Robert J Puckett, *President*
Michael S Wilson, *COO*
Muhammad Ali-Khan, *Engineer*
Kirby Hamilton, *Engineer*
John Klimaszewski, *Engineer*
◆ **EMP:** 100
SQ FT: 56,638
SALES (est): 28.1MM
SALES (corp-wide): 183.7K **Privately Held**
WEB: www.caratron.com
SIC: 3728 3541 Gears, aircraft power transmission; gear cutting & finishing machines
HQ: Bmt Aerospace International
Handelsstraat 6
Oostkamp 8020
502 490-00

(G-5631)
BOLYEA INDUSTRIES
33847 Doreka (48026-1646)
PHONE...................................586 293-8600
Rick Bolyea, *President*
James Bolyea, *Shareholder*
Joseph O'Brien, *Admin Sec*
EMP: 10
SQ FT: 15,000
SALES (est): 1.6MM **Privately Held**
SIC: 3479 Coating of metals & formed products

(G-5632)
BUDDIES FOODS LLC
Also Called: Chuck and Dave's Salsa
17445 Malyn Blvd (48026-1634)
PHONE...................................586 776-4036
Susan Maiorana, *Vice Pres*
Dave Kernya,
Cathy Kernya,
Vincent C Maiorana,
EMP: 35
SQ FT: 21,000
SALES: 6.5MM **Privately Held**
SIC: 2099 Sauces: gravy, dressing & dip mixes

(G-5633)
C & N MANUFACTURING INC
33722 James J Pompo Dr (48026-1645)
PHONE...................................586 293-9150
Gerald A Naski, *President*
Patricia Naski, *Vice Pres*
EMP: 20
SQ FT: 14,100
SALES (est): 3.9MM **Privately Held**
WEB: www.cnmfginc.com
SIC: 3599 3544 Machine shop, jobbing & repair; special dies, tools, jigs & fixtures

(G-5634)
CARBIDE TECHNOLOGIES INC
18101 Malyn Blvd (48026-3493)
PHONE...................................586 296-5200
Bernice Souris, *President*
Nicholas T Souris, *Vice Pres*
Theresa Monks, *Controller*
Efrain Oliva, *Director*
Kimberly A Souris, *Admin Sec*
EMP: 50
SQ FT: 70,000
SALES (est): 11.3MM **Privately Held**
WEB: www.carbidetechnologies.com
SIC: 3356 3545 3546 Tungsten, basic shapes; cutting tools for machine tools; reamers, machine tool; power-driven handtools

(G-5635)
CARDINAL CUSTOM DESIGNS INC
31469 Utica Rd (48026-2533)
PHONE...................................586 296-2060
Clarence Bury, *President*
EMP: 5
SQ FT: 3,800
SALES: 150K **Privately Held**
SIC: 2391 Draperies, plastic & textile: from purchased materials

(G-5636)
CDK ENTERPRISES LLC
Also Called: Apollo E.D.M. Company
16601 E 13 Mile Rd (48026-2554)
PHONE...................................586 296-9300
Christopher Kain,
EMP: 27
SQ FT: 15,000
SALES (est): 4.7MM **Privately Held**
WEB: www.apolloedm.com
SIC: 3599 Machine shop, jobbing & repair

(G-5637)
CENTURY TOOL WELDING INC
32873 Groesbeck Hwy (48026-3128)
PHONE...................................586 758-3330
Carl Wolschon, *President*
Stephen Wolschon, *Vice Pres*
Marilyn Wolschon, *Admin Sec*
EMP: 6
SALES (est): 330K **Privately Held**
SIC: 7692 Welding repair

(G-5638)
CONSOLDTED DCMENT SLUTIONS LLC
17601 Malyn Blvd (48026-3487)
P.O. Box 187 (48026-0187)
PHONE...................................586 293-8100
Rick Voss, *Sales Staff*
Charles Ftorm, *Mng Member*
EMP: 12 **EST:** 1989
SALES (est): 2.4MM **Privately Held**
WEB: www.cdocsolutions.com
SIC: 2759 5112 Business forms: printing; stationery & office supplies

GEOGRAPHIC SECTION

Fraser - Macomb County (G-5665)

(G-5639)
CONTINENTAL CRANE & SERVICE
33681 Groesbeck Hwy (48026-1542)
PHONE 586 294-7900
Edward Dungan Jr, *President*
Christian Dungan, *Vice Pres*
Joseph Dungan, *Vice Pres*
Susan Hood, *Treasurer*
Judy Hamilton, *Admin Sec*
EMP: 19 **EST:** 1973
SQ FT: 4,500
SALES (est): 3.8MM **Privately Held**
WEB: www.continentalcrane.com
SIC: 3535 7389 Conveyors & conveying equipment; crane & aerial lift service

(G-5640)
CW CREATIVE WELDING INC
33360 Groesbeck Hwy (48026-1545)
PHONE 586 294-1050
Rich Bursteinowicz, *President*
EMP: 5
SALES (est): 290.1K **Privately Held**
SIC: 7692 Welding repair

(G-5641)
DELTA PRECISION INC
33214 Janet (48026-4303)
PHONE 586 415-9005
Mark Detheridge, *President*
Donald Baross, *Vice Pres*
EMP: 4 **EST:** 1970
SQ FT: 3,000
SALES: 377.4K **Privately Held**
WEB: www.deltaprecision.com
SIC: 3544 Industrial molds

(G-5642)
DELUXE TECHNOLOGIES LLC
34537 Bennett (48026-1691)
P.O. Box 180149, Utica (48318-0149)
PHONE 586 294-2340
Nick Demiro, *President*
Patricia A Stephens, *Vice Pres*
EMP: 21
SQ FT: 40,000
SALES: 10MM **Privately Held**
SIC: 3999 Dock equipment & supplies, industrial

(G-5643)
DETROIT METALCRAFT FINISHING
34277 Doreka (48026-1660)
PHONE 586 415-7760
Enrique Vidal, *President*
EMP: 3
SALES: 300K **Privately Held**
SIC: 3471 Polishing, metals or formed products

(G-5644)
DORRIS COMPANY
17430 Malyn Blvd (48026-1635)
PHONE 586 293-5260
Robert Diez, *President*
Peter Osadczuk, *General Mgr*
EMP: 45
SQ FT: 70,000
SALES (est): 6.9MM
SALES (corp-wide): 7.3MM **Privately Held**
WEB: www.supremegear.com
SIC: 3566 3769 3724 3462 Speed changers, drives & gears; guided missile & space vehicle parts & auxiliary equipment; aircraft engines & engine parts; iron & steel forgings; sheet metalwork; gears, aircraft power transmission
PA: Supreme Gear Co.
17430 Malyn Bvld
Fraser MI 48026
586 775-6325

(G-5645)
DYTRON CORPORATION
17000 Masonic (48026-3948)
PHONE 586 296-9600
Richard C Donovan, *President*
Lois J Donovan, *Vice Pres*
EMP: 20
SQ FT: 8,000
SALES (est): 1.3MM **Privately Held**
SIC: 3548 5084 Welding wire, bare & coated; welding machinery & equipment

(G-5646)
EAGLE ASSEMBLIES INC
33275 Groesbeck Hwy (48026-4201)
PHONE 586 296-4836
Robert M Grant, *President*
Steven Grant, *Vice Pres*
Howard Fordree, *CFO*
EMP: 3
SALES (est): 367.4K **Privately Held**
SIC: 3714 3711 Motor vehicle parts & accessories; motor vehicles & car bodies

(G-5647)
EDRICH PRODUCTS INC
Also Called: Aquarich Water Treatment Pdts
33672 Doreka (48026-1609)
PHONE 586 296-3350
Howard A Smith, *President*
Dianna M Smith, *Corp Secy*
Debby Andy, *Vice Pres*
EMP: 12
SQ FT: 15,000
SALES (est): 3.5MM **Privately Held**
WEB: www.edrichproducts.com
SIC: 2992 Cutting oils, blending: made from purchased materials; rust arresting compounds, animal or vegetable oil base

(G-5648)
EIFEL MOLD & ENGINEERING INC
31071 Fraser Dr (48026-2504)
P.O. Box 190 (48026-0190)
PHONE 586 296-9640
Richard A Hecker, *President*
Gary Schulz, *Manager*
EMP: 20
SQ FT: 10,000
SALES (est): 3.9MM **Privately Held**
WEB: www.eifel-inc.com
SIC: 3544 Industrial molds; jigs & fixtures

(G-5649)
ELECTRO-WAY CO
17505 Helro (48026-2226)
P.O. Box 235 (48026-0235)
PHONE 586 771-9450
John Johnston, *President*
Nancy Johnston, *Admin Sec*
EMP: 4 **EST:** 1958
SQ FT: 3,000
SALES (est): 557.1K **Privately Held**
WEB: www.electro-way.com
SIC: 3599 Electrical discharge machining (EDM)

(G-5650)
ELECTROLABS INC
18503 E 14 Mile Rd (48026-1551)
P.O. Box 456 (48026-0456)
PHONE 586 294-4150
Dennis Suddon, *President*
Scott Sutton, *Vice Pres*
Robert Rein, *Treasurer*
Denise Dawson, *Admin Sec*
EMP: 10 **EST:** 1962
SQ FT: 7,500
SALES (est): 1.7MM **Privately Held**
WEB: www.electrolabs.com
SIC: 3444 Sheet metalwork

(G-5651)
ENMARK TOOL COMPANY
18100 Cross (48026-1666)
PHONE 586 293-2797
Gary M Enmark, *President*
John Enmark, *Vice Pres*
Michael Weidner, *Engineer*
Denny Garbula, *Manager*
Dolores Enmark, *Admin Sec*
EMP: 50
SQ FT: 46,000
SALES (est): 10.3MM **Privately Held**
WEB: www.enmarktool.com
SIC: 3544 3545 Special dies & tools; gauges (machine tool accessories)

(G-5652)
EPIC MATERIALS INC
33741 Groesbeck Hwy (48026-4207)
PHONE 586 294-0300
Howard A Smith, *President*
David Smith, *Manager*
EMP: 4
SALES: 250K **Privately Held**
WEB: www.epicmaterials.com
SIC: 3086 4783 Packaging & shipping materials, foamed plastic; packing goods for shipping

(G-5653)
FAIRLANE CO
33792 Doreka (48026-3430)
PHONE 586 294-6100
Justin Gordon, *CEO*
Wallace Duvall, *Info Tech Dir*
EMP: 33 **EST:** 2011
SALES (est): 6.3MM **Privately Held**
SIC: 3544 Special dies & tools

(G-5654)
FIXTUREWORKS LLC
33792 Doreka (48026-3430)
PHONE 586 294-6100
Delores Ferland, *Bookkeeper*
Tammy Labine, *Office Mgr*
Mark Gordon,
▲ **EMP:** 6
SQ FT: 12,000
SALES (est): 342K **Privately Held**
WEB: www.fixtureworks.net
SIC: 3544 5072 5085 Special dies, tools, jigs & fixtures; hardware; industrial fittings

(G-5655)
FRASER GRINDING CO (PA)
34235 Riviera (48026-1624)
PHONE 586 293-6060
Rudolf F Lipski, *President*
Marjory Lipski, *Vice Pres*
Kenneth York, *Vice Pres*
Thomas Schulte, *Sales Mgr*
EMP: 10
SQ FT: 90,000
SALES (est): 7.7MM **Privately Held**
SIC: 3599 Machine shop, jobbing & repair

(G-5656)
G F PROTO-TYPE PLASTER INC
Also Called: G & F Prototype Plaster
33670 Riviera (48026-1621)
PHONE 586 296-2750
William Hess, *President*
Gary Hess, *Vice Pres*
Jeff Hess, *Vice Pres*
EMP: 28 **EST:** 1966
SQ FT: 16,000
SALES (est): 4.7MM **Privately Held**
WEB: www.gfprototype.com
SIC: 3544 Special dies & tools; industrial molds

(G-5657)
GRANT INDUSTRIES INCORPORATED (PA)
33415 Groesbeck Hwy (48026-4203)
PHONE 586 293-9200
Robert Grant, *President*
Kathy Peterson, *Vice Pres*
Timothy Schley, *Vice Pres*
Kevin Pittenger, *Purchasing*
David Burley, *Design Engr*
EMP: 90
SQ FT: 82,000
SALES (est): 20.5MM **Privately Held**
WEB: www.grantgrp.com
SIC: 3465 3469 3452 3429 Body parts, automobile: stamped metal; metal stampings; bolts, nuts, rivets & washers; manufactured hardware (general); cold finishing of steel shapes; blast furnaces & steel mills

(G-5658)
GROSSEL TOOL CO
34190 Doreka (48026-3434)
PHONE 586 294-3660
Kurt Kowal, *President*
Laura Casano, *Human Resources*
Marilyn E Kowal, *Shareholder*
Dyana Jones, *Admin Sec*
EMP: 55
SQ FT: 20,000
SALES (est): 10.2MM **Privately Held**
WEB: www.grosseltool.com
SIC: 3548 3443 Welding apparatus; fabricated plate work (boiler shop)

(G-5659)
HAYNIE AND HESS REALTY CO LLC
33670 Riviera (48026-1621)
PHONE 586 296-2750
William Hess,
Gary Hess,
Jeff Hess,
EMP: 18
SQ FT: 23,500
SALES: 1MM **Privately Held**
SIC: 3555 Type casting, founding or melting machines

(G-5660)
HEALTHMARK INDUSTRIES CO INC
18600 Malyn Blvd (48026-3496)
PHONE 586 774-7600
Mark Basile, *President*
Ralph J Basile, *Vice Pres*
Suzanne Basile, *Vice Pres*
Kenny Costante, *Facilities Mgr*
Tina Monroe, *Purchasing*
▲ **EMP:** 167
SALES (est): 62.4MM **Privately Held**
WEB: www.hmark.com
SIC: 3841 Surgical & medical instruments

(G-5661)
HERCULES MACHINE TL & DIE LLC
33901 James J Pompo Dr (48026-3471)
PHONE 586 778-4120
EMP: 35 **Privately Held**
SIC: 3544 Special dies, tools, jigs & fixtures
HQ: Hercules Machine Tool & Die Llc
13920 E 10 Mile Rd
Warren MI 48089
586 778-4120

(G-5662)
HHI FORMTECH LLC
Also Called: Fraser Mfg Facility
18450 15 Mile Rd (48026-3460)
PHONE 586 415-2000
EMP: 40
SALES (corp-wide): 7.2B **Publicly Held**
WEB: www.formtech2.com
SIC: 3714 3544 3463 3462 Motor vehicle parts & accessories; special dies, tools, jigs & fixtures; nonferrous forgings; iron & steel forgings
HQ: Hhi Formtech, Llc
1 Dauch Dr
Detroit MI 48211
313 758-2000

(G-5663)
HI-CRAFT ENGINEERING INC
Also Called: Frost Division
33105 Kelly Rd Ste B (48026-4212)
PHONE 586 293-0551
Kevin Andre, *President*
Don Nemens, *Vice Pres*
Bill Duke, *CFO*
EMP: 60
SQ FT: 100,000
SALES: 10MM **Privately Held**
SIC: 3544 3089 Forms (molds), for foundry & plastics working machinery; injection molding of plastics

(G-5664)
HMR FABRICATION UNLIMITED INC
33830 Riviera (48026-4807)
PHONE 586 569-4288
Mark Blanchard, *President*
Samantha Klein, *Office Mgr*
EMP: 12
SALES: 3.5MM **Privately Held**
SIC: 3548 Welding & cutting apparatus & accessories

(G-5665)
HONEYWELL INTERNATIONAL INC
31807 Utica Rd (48026-3945)
PHONE 586 777-7870
EMP: 673
SALES (corp-wide): 41.8B **Publicly Held**
SIC: 3724 Aircraft engines & engine parts

Fraser - Macomb County (G-5666)

PA: Honeywell International Inc.
300 S Tryon St
Charlotte NC 28202
973 455-2000

(G-5666)
HOT TOOL CUTTER GRINDING CO
33545 Groesbeck Hwy (48026-4205)
PHONE..................................586 790-4867
George Juncaj, *Owner*
EMP: 21
SQ FT: 12,000
SALES (est): 2.4MM **Privately Held**
SIC: 3541 7699 Machine tools, metal cutting type; knife, saw & tool sharpening & repair

(G-5667)
IANNUZZI MILLWORK INC
33877 Doreka (48026-3473)
PHONE..................................586 285-1000
Dominic Iannuzzi, *President*
EMP: 13
SQ FT: 20,000
SALES (est): 1.8MM **Privately Held**
SIC: 2431 Interior & ornamental woodwork & trim

(G-5668)
ICM ENTERPRISES LLC
33451 James J Pompo Dr (48026-1625)
P.O. Box 26523 (48026-6523)
PHONE..................................586 415-2567
Fredrick Sladovich, *Mng Member*
EMP: 5
SALES: 200K **Privately Held**
SIC: 3089 Molding primary plastic

(G-5669)
IMAGE MACHINE & TOOL INC
34501 Bennett (48026-1691)
PHONE..................................586 466-3400
Kevin Kayne, *President*
EMP: 4
SALES (est): 242K **Privately Held**
SIC: 3545 Precision tools, machinists'

(G-5670)
INLINE TUBE
33783 Groesbeck Hwy (48026-4207)
PHONE..................................586 294-4093
James Kryta, *President*
EMP: 3
SALES (est): 199.1K **Privately Held**
SIC: 3317 Steel pipe & tubes

(G-5671)
INTER-LAKES BASES INC
17480 Malyn Blvd (48026-1671)
PHONE..................................586 294-8120
Barbara Kasper, *President*
David Moore, *Vice Pres*
EMP: 40
SQ FT: 40,000
SALES (est): 8.1MM **Privately Held**
WEB: www.interlakesbases.com
SIC: 3441 Fabricated structural metal

(G-5672)
INTERNATIONAL SEATING CO
31047 Fraser Dr (48026-2504)
PHONE..................................586 293-2201
William Gray, *President*
EMP: 3
SALES (est): 220K **Privately Held**
SIC: 2512 2599 Upholstered household furniture; bar, restaurant & cafeteria furniture

(G-5673)
INTERPOWER INDUCTION SVCS INC
34197 Doreka (48026-3435)
PHONE..................................586 296-7697
Gary M Gariglio, *CEO*
EMP: 9 **EST:** 1995
SALES (est): 209.3K **Privately Held**
SIC: 3567 Induction heating equipment

(G-5674)
JET GAGE & TOOL INC
31265 Kendall (48026-2590)
PHONE..................................586 294-3770
Annete C Braun, *President*
Annette C Braun, *President*
Irma Braun, *Corp Secy*
EMP: 4
SQ FT: 9,500
SALES: 517K **Privately Held**
SIC: 3544 Special dies & tools; jigs & fixtures

(G-5675)
JF HUBERT ENTERPRISES INC (PA)
Also Called: Sharp Tooling and Assembly
34480 Commerce (48026-1649)
PHONE..................................586 293-8660
Christopher J Hubertt, *CEO*
Christopher J Hubert, *President*
EMP: 14
SALES (est): 3.1MM **Privately Held**
SIC: 8711 3541 Machine tool design; machine tools, metal cutting type

(G-5676)
JPS MFG INC
17640 15 Mile Rd (48026-3450)
PHONE..................................586 415-8702
Joseph Szacon, *Principal*
EMP: 7
SALES (est): 1MM **Privately Held**
SIC: 3541 Machine tools, metal cutting type

(G-5677)
K & F ELECTRONIC INC
Also Called: K&F Electronics
33041 Groesbeck Hwy (48026-1514)
PHONE..................................586 294-8720
Richard Kincaid, *President*
Maria Pilarski, *General Mgr*
Mary Boik, *QC Mgr*
Susan McIlwain, *Bookkeeper*
Sean Kincaid, *Sales Mgr*
EMP: 25
SQ FT: 25,000
SALES (est): 4.6MM **Privately Held**
WEB: www.circuitboards.com
SIC: 3672 Circuit boards, television & radio printed

(G-5678)
KENDOR STEEL RULE DIE INC
31275 Fraser Dr (48026-2572)
PHONE..................................586 293-7111
Kenneth Dale Eltringham, *President*
Kathie McCarthy, *Office Mgr*
EMP: 36 **EST:** 1978
SQ FT: 30,000
SALES (est): 4MM **Privately Held**
WEB: www.kendor.com
SIC: 7389 3544 3469 3462 Metal cutting services; dies, steel rule; metal stampings; iron & steel forgings

(G-5679)
KOCH LIMITED
Also Called: K & K Tool & Die
34230 Riviera (48026-1623)
PHONE..................................586 296-3103
Joseph J Koch, *President*
Lea Timpf, *Controller*
EMP: 8
SQ FT: 5,000
SALES (est): 1.2MM **Privately Held**
SIC: 3541 3544 Machine tools, metal cutting type; special dies & tools

(G-5680)
KOUNTRY KEEPSAKES
31772 Forrest (48026-2623)
PHONE..................................586 294-4895
Laurie Ann Morrison, *Owner*
Harriet Pacholek, *Principal*
EMP: 3
SALES (est): 40K **Privately Held**
SIC: 2395 Decorative & novelty stitching, for the trade

(G-5681)
KURT MACHINE TOOL CO INC
33910 Riviera (48026-1627)
P.O. Box 68 (48026-0068)
PHONE..................................586 296-5070
Michael Phillips, *President*
Christine Phillips, *Corp Secy*
EMP: 10
SQ FT: 11,000
SALES (est): 1.8MM **Privately Held**
SIC: 3599 Machine shop, jobbing & repair

(G-5682)
L T C ROLL & ENGINEERING CO
31140 Kendall (48026)
PHONE..................................586 465-1023
Deborah Stephens, *Controller*
EMP: 10
SALES (corp-wide): 27.7MM **Privately Held**
SIC: 3714 Motor vehicle parts & accessories
PA: L. T. C. Roll & Engineering Co.
23500 John Gorsuch Dr
Clinton Township MI 48036
586 465-1023

(G-5683)
LASER FAB INC
33901 Riviera (48026-1614)
PHONE..................................586 415-8090
EMP: 4
SQ FT: 9,000
SALES (est): 480K **Privately Held**
SIC: 3699 3444 Mfg Electrical Equipment/Supplies Mfg Sheet Metalwork

(G-5684)
LEE BEAUTY & GEN MECHANDISE
16724 15 Mile Rd (48026-5011)
PHONE..................................586 294-4400
Sung Lee, *Principal*
EMP: 3
SALES (est): 136.7K **Privately Held**
SIC: 5999 3999 Cosmetics; barber & beauty shop equipment

(G-5685)
LUMBEE CUSTOM PAINTING LLC
31725 Fraser Dr (48026-2595)
PHONE..................................586 296-5083
Debra A Garrison,
EMP: 4
SALES (est): 259.2K **Privately Held**
SIC: 3559 Special industry machinery

(G-5686)
M & M TURNING CO
34480 Commerce (48026-1649)
PHONE..................................586 791-7188
Dennis Irwin, *CEO*
Charlie J Laforest, *President*
Debbie Nabor-Skidmore, *Office Admin*
EMP: 28
SALES (est): 5.4MM **Privately Held**
WEB: www.mmturning.com
SIC: 3542 Spinning lathes

(G-5687)
M & S SPRING COMPANY INC
34137 Doreka (48026-3435)
P.O. Box 388 (48026-0388)
PHONE..................................586 296-9850
W E Tillinger Sr, *President*
Joseph Tillinger, *Treasurer*
W E Tillinger Jr, *Shareholder*
EMP: 16
SQ FT: 15,000
SALES: 2.1MM **Privately Held**
WEB: www.msspring.com
SIC: 3493 3495 Flat springs, sheet or strip stock; instrument springs, precision

(G-5688)
M P PUMPS INC
34800 Bennett (48026-1694)
PHONE..................................586 293-8240
Greg Peabody, *President*
Robert Tolbert, *Supervisor*
▲ **EMP:** 90
SQ FT: 90,000
SALES (est): 37.8MM
SALES (est) (corp-wide): 2.6B **Publicly Held**
WEB: www.mppumps.com
SIC: 3594 3561 Fluid power pumps & motors; pumps & pumping equipment
PA: Gardner Denver Holdings, Inc.
222 E Erie St Ste 500
Milwaukee WI 53202
414 212-4700

(G-5689)
MADISON ELECTRIC COMPANY
Madison Electronics Division
17930 E 14 Mile Rd (48026-2291)
PHONE..................................586 294-8300
Scott Lemaster, *Principal*
Dave Garstecki, *Sales Staff*
Karen Lontorfos, *Manager*
EMP: 35
SALES (corp-wide): 158.4MM **Privately Held**
WEB: www.madisonelectric.com
SIC: 3355 3357 Aluminum wire & cable; nonferrous wiredrawing & insulating
PA: Madison Electric Company
31855 Van Dyke Ave
Warren MI 48093
586 825-0200

(G-5690)
MAGNUS PRECISION TOOL LLC
34082 James J Pompo Dr (48026-3409)
PHONE..................................586 285-2500
Christopher Alfastsen,
Pete Pizzimenti,
EMP: 4
SQ FT: 4,800
SALES (est): 394.2K **Privately Held**
SIC: 3599 Amusement park equipment

(G-5691)
MARTEN MODELS & MOLDS INC
18291 Mike C Ct (48026-1613)
PHONE..................................586 293-2260
Steve Marten, *President*
Tom Ruehlete, *Vice Pres*
EMP: 26
SQ FT: 17,000
SALES (est): 4.6MM **Privately Held**
SIC: 3544 3543 Industrial molds; industrial patterns

(G-5692)
MILLWORK INC
17420 15 Mile Rd (48026-3446)
PHONE..................................586 791-2330
Kenneth Albert Hazlett, *President*
EMP: 13
SQ FT: 10,000
SALES: 1.2MM **Privately Held**
SIC: 2434 Wood kitchen cabinets

(G-5693)
MILO BORING & MACHINING INC
34275 Riviera (48026-1624)
PHONE..................................586 293-8611
Ilija Milosavlevski, *President*
EMP: 4
SALES (est): 430.2K **Privately Held**
SIC: 3545 Machine tool accessories

(G-5694)
MODERN TOOL AND TAPPING INC
33517 Kelly Rd (48026-4231)
PHONE..................................586 777-5144
Cynthia Gohlke, *President*
EMP: 7
SALES: 500K **Privately Held**
WEB: www.moderntooltapping.com
SIC: 3549 Metalworking machinery

(G-5695)
MOLD-RITE LLC (PA)
33830 Riviera (48026-4807)
PHONE..................................586 296-3970
Mark Blanchard, *Mng Member*
Dave Blanchard, *Manager*
Patty Blanchard, *Manager*
EMP: 7 **EST:** 2009
SQ FT: 5,000
SALES (est): 861.4K **Privately Held**
SIC: 3089 Injection molding of plastics; molding primary plastic

(G-5696)
MTM MACHINE INC
34575 Commerce (48026-3419)
PHONE..................................586 443-5703
Glenn Middler, *President*
Peter Middler, *Vice Pres*
EMP: 8
SQ FT: 8,300

GEOGRAPHIC SECTION

Fraser - Macomb County (G-5725)

SALES (est): 780K **Privately Held**
SIC: **3599** 7539 Machine shop, jobbing & repair; machine shop, automotive

(G-5697)
NEW METHOD STEEL STAMPS INC
17801 Helro (48026-3818)
P.O. Box 338 (48026-0338)
PHONE..................586 293-0200
Charles Brown II, *President*
▼ EMP: 6 EST: 1931
SQ FT: 10,000
SALES (est): 1MM **Privately Held**
SIC: **3953** Embossing seals & hand stamps

(G-5698)
NEW WORLD ETCHING N AMER VE
Also Called: World Etching North America Ve
33870 Riviera (48026-4807)
PHONE..................586 296-8082
Vic Barbu,
EMP: 6
SALES (est): 671.1K **Privately Held**
SIC: **2759** Engraving

(G-5699)
NEW-MATIC INDUSTRIES INC
31256 Fraser Dr (48026-2571)
PHONE..................586 415-9801
Ronald Secord, *President*
Greg Karlichek, *Vice Pres*
EMP: 7
SQ FT: 8,000
SALES: 750K **Privately Held**
SIC: **3559** Automotive related machinery

(G-5700)
NOVA INDUSTRIES INC
34180 Klein Rd (48026-3020)
PHONE..................586 294-9182
Thomas Kruger, *CEO*
EMP: 38
SALES (est): 9.2MM **Privately Held**
SIC: **3089** Injection molding of plastics

(G-5701)
ORLANDI GEAR COMPANY INC
17755 Masonic (48026-3158)
PHONE..................586 285-9900
Michael Schiavi, *President*
Carlos Hernandez, *Plant Mgr*
Mark Berlin, *Mfg Staff*
Mike Kelmigian, *Treasurer*
Linda Baysdell, *Office Mgr*
EMP: 47 EST: 1944
SQ FT: 33,000
SALES (est): 11.8MM **Privately Held**
WEB: www.orlandigear.com
SIC: **3568** Shafts, flexible

(G-5702)
OSBORNE TRANSFORMER CORP
33258 Groesbeck Hwy (48026-1597)
P.O. Box 70 (48026-0070)
PHONE..................586 218-6900
James R Osborne, *President*
Susie Osborne, *General Mgr*
Suzanne Osborne, *Vice Pres*
EMP: 10 EST: 1932
SALES: 1MM **Privately Held**
WEB: www.osbornetransformer.com
SIC: **3612** 5063 3677 Power transformers, electric; electrical apparatus & equipment; electronic coils, transformers & other inductors

(G-5703)
PALMER DISTRIBUTORS INC
Also Called: Palmer Promotional Products
33525 Groesbeck Hwy (48026-4205)
PHONE..................586 772-4225
Jim Palmer, *President*
Al Vespa, *Purch Agent*
◆ EMP: 100 EST: 1953
SQ FT: 66,000
SALES (est): 31.5MM **Privately Held**
WEB: www.palmerpromos.com
SIC: **3089** 2821 Molding primary plastic; plastics materials & resins

(G-5704)
PARAGON MOLDS CORPORATION
33997 Riviera (48026-1670)
PHONE..................586 294-7630
Daniel V Smoger, *President*
David M Smoger, *Vice Pres*
EMP: 20
SQ FT: 15,200
SALES: 3.7MM **Privately Held**
WEB: www.paragonmolds.com
SIC: **3544** 3999 3543 Industrial molds; jigs & fixtures; models, general, except toy; industrial patterns

(G-5705)
PATMAI COMPANY INC
31425 Fraser Dr (48026-2584)
PHONE..................586 294-0370
Edwin S Maddox, *President*
James Defer, *Vice Pres*
Tamita Weigand, *Office Mgr*
▲ EMP: 26
SQ FT: 14,000
SALES: 875K **Privately Held**
SIC: **3471** Buffing for the trade; polishing, metals or formed products

(G-5706)
PCS COMPANY (DH)
34488 Doreka (48026-3438)
PHONE..................586 294-7780
Ed Mohrbach, *CEO*
Randy S Wissinger, *VP Finance*
Christian Papp, *Credit Mgr*
Bruce Konopinski, *Sales Mgr*
Joel Morse, *Manager*
▲ EMP: 94 EST: 1960
SQ FT: 40,000
SALES (est): 25.1MM **Privately Held**
WEB: www.pcs-company.com
SIC: **3544** Special dies, tools, jigs & fixtures
HQ: Dayton Progress Corporation
500 Progress Rd
Dayton OH 45449
937 859-5111

(G-5707)
POETRY FACTORY LTD
34028 James J Pompo Dr (48026-1643)
PHONE..................586 296-3125
Symella S Chengges, *President*
EMP: 5
SQ FT: 3,000
SALES (est): 60K **Privately Held**
SIC: **3499** Novelties & giftware, including trophies

(G-5708)
POLARIS ENGINEERING INC
17540 15 Mile Rd (48026-1603)
PHONE..................586 296-1603
Michael Burns, *President*
EMP: 10
SQ FT: 12,000
SALES (est): 1.6MM **Privately Held**
WEB: www.polarisenginc.com
SIC: **3599** Machine shop, jobbing & repair

(G-5709)
PRIMA WELDING & EXPERIMENTAL
31000 Fraser Dr (48026-2503)
PHONE..................586 415-8873
Dale Lohr, *President*
EMP: 7
SQ FT: 5,200
SALES: 500K **Privately Held**
WEB: www.primawelding.com
SIC: **7692** Welding repair

(G-5710)
PRODUCT AND TOOLING TECH INC
Also Called: P T T
33222 Groesbeck Hwy (48026-1597)
PHONE..................586 293-1810
Mark Fritz, *President*
Luke Fritz, *Vice Pres*
EMP: 40
SQ FT: 16,000
SALES (est): 8.7MM **Privately Held**
SIC: **3544** 3542 Special dies & tools; die casting & extruding machines

(G-5711)
PROTO DESIGN & MANUFACTURING
31140 Fraser Dr (48026-3947)
PHONE..................419 346-8416
Greg Durmeyer, *President*
EMP: 3
SALES (est): 370.2K **Privately Held**
SIC: **3545** Machine tool accessories

(G-5712)
PROTOJET LLC
17850 E 14 Mile Rd (48026-2271)
PHONE..................810 956-8000
Eric J Gunderson, *President*
Stephen Gunderson, *Mfg Dir*
EMP: 13
SQ FT: 9,000
SALES: 1.8MM **Privately Held**
WEB: www.protojet.com
SIC: **3089** 3999 Synthetic resin finished products; models, general, except toy

(G-5713)
PT TECH STAMPING INC
33222 Groesbeck Hwy (48026-1597)
PHONE..................586 293-1810
Mark Fritz, *CEO*
Jerry Swims, *President*
EMP: 25
SALES (est): 8.1MM **Privately Held**
WEB: www.pttech.us
SIC: **3465** 3542 Automotive stampings; machine tools, metal forming type

(G-5714)
QUALITY GRINDING INC
33950 Riviera (48026-1627)
PHONE..................586 293-3780
Fax: 586 293-3782
EMP: 4
SQ FT: 10,000
SALES (est): 320K **Privately Held**
SIC: **3599** Machine Shop

(G-5715)
R T GORDON INC
33792 Doreka (48026-3430)
PHONE..................586 294-6100
Mark Gordon, *Vice Pres*
EMP: 24 EST: 1975
SQ FT: 40,000
SALES (est): 2.8MM **Privately Held**
SIC: **3545** 3544 3429 Machine tool accessories; special dies, tools, jigs & fixtures; manufactured hardware (general)

(G-5716)
REGER MANUFACTURING COMPANY
31375 Fraser Dr (48026-2552)
PHONE..................586 293-5096
Gale English, *CEO*
Gale W English, *CEO*
Alfred English, *President*
Matthew English, *Vice Pres*
Dana Marino, *Office Mgr*
EMP: 9 EST: 1949
SALES (est): 1.7MM **Privately Held**
WEB: www.regermfg.com
SIC: **3544** 3549 Special dies & tools; jigs & fixtures; metalworking machinery

(G-5717)
REVERE PLASTICS SYSTEMS LLC
18401 Malyn Blvd (48026-1628)
PHONE..................586 415-4823
Kevin Stolzenfeld, *Director*
EMP: 200
SALES (corp-wide): 22.3MM **Privately Held**
WEB: www.sur-flo.com
SIC: **3089** Injection molding of plastics
HQ: Revere Plastics Systems, Llc
39555 Orchard Hill Pl # 362
Novi MI 48375

(G-5718)
RICHTER PRECISION INC
17741 Malyn Blvd (48026-1632)
PHONE..................586 465-0500
Brian Hornberger, *Design Engr*
Art Solkey, *Sls & Mktg Exec*
Randy Badger, *Regl Sales Mgr*
EMP: 30
SALES (corp-wide): 28.2MM **Privately Held**
WEB: www.richterprecision.com
SIC: **3479** 3398 2851 Coating of metals & formed products; metal heat treating; paints & allied products
PA: Richter Precision, Inc.
1021 Commercial Ave
East Petersburg PA 17520
717 560-9990

(G-5719)
RX-RITE OPTICAL CO
32925 Groesbeck Hwy (48026-3155)
PHONE..................586 294-8500
Anthony C Stefani, *President*
Corine Stefani, *Treasurer*
EMP: 30 EST: 1973
SQ FT: 1,500
SALES (est): 3.8MM **Privately Held**
SIC: **3851** 8042 Lens grinding, except prescription; ophthalmic; offices & clinics of optometrists

(G-5720)
RYDER AUTOMATIC & MFG
16636 Admiral (48026-3248)
PHONE..................586 293-2109
Reginald J Ryder, *President*
Theresa P Ryder, *Corp Secy*
EMP: 3
SQ FT: 3,500
SALES (est): 314.4K **Privately Held**
SIC: **3451** Screw machine products

(G-5721)
SAS AUTOMOTIVE USA INC
17801 E 14 Mile Rd (48026-2258)
PHONE..................248 606-1152
Daniel Guest, *Finance*
EMP: 4
SALES (corp-wide): 3.4B **Privately Held**
SIC: **3714** Motor vehicle parts & accessories
HQ: Sas Automotive Usa, Inc.
42555 Merrill Rd
Sterling Heights MI 48314

(G-5722)
SCORPION RELOADS LLC
34054 James J Pompo Dr (48026-3408)
PHONE..................586 214-3843
Jeff Doolin, *Principal*
EMP: 5 EST: 2010
SALES (est): 320.4K **Privately Held**
SIC: **3482** Cartridge cases for ammunition, 30 mm. & below; pellets & BB's, pistol & air rifle ammunition

(G-5723)
SGC INDUSTRIES INC
17430 Malyn Blvd (48026-1635)
PHONE..................586 293-5260
Robert Diez, *President*
EMP: 40
SALES (est): 3.2MM **Privately Held**
SIC: **3728** 3724 3711 3841 Gears, aircraft power transmission; aircraft engines & engine parts; universal carriers, military, assembly of; surgical & medical instruments; automotive related machinery; guided missile & space vehicle parts & auxiliary equipment

(G-5724)
SHARP DIE & MOLD CO
Also Called: Hubert Group
34480 Commerce (48026-1649)
PHONE..................586 293-8660
Josef Hubert, *President*
Brian Lorenz, *Corp Secy*
John Hubert, *Vice Pres*
EMP: 10 EST: 1967
SQ FT: 24,000
SALES (est): 680K **Privately Held**
SIC: **3544** 3549 Industrial molds; special dies & tools; metalworking machinery

(G-5725)
SMOKER BUTTS
34541 Utica Rd (48026-3576)
PHONE..................586 362-2451
EMP: 3 EST: 2007
SALES (est): 230K **Privately Held**
SIC: **2131** Mfg Chewing/Smoking Tobacco

(G-5726)
SOYAD BROTHERS TEXTILE CORP
Also Called: Quality Socks
34272 Doreka (48026-1659)
PHONE..........................586 755-5700
Toufic Soyad, *President*
Leba Soyad, *Vice Pres*
George Soyad, *Treasurer*
Joseph Soyad, *Admin Sec*
▲ **EMP:** 25
SQ FT: 26,000
SALES (est): 3.1MM **Privately Held**
WEB: www.soyadsocks.com
SIC: 2252 Socks

(G-5727)
SPARTAN CARBIDE INC
34110 Riviera (48026-4811)
PHONE..........................586 285-9786
Mark Maron, *President*
Thomas Haaberski, *Vice Pres*
Nanci Wishon, *Office Mgr*
EMP: 50
SQ FT: 20,000
SALES: 6.5MM **Privately Held**
WEB: www.spartancarbide.com
SIC: 3545 Cutting tools for machine tools

(G-5728)
SPECIAL TOOL & ENGINEERING INC (PA)
33910 James J Pompo Dr (48026-3470)
PHONE..........................586 285-5900
Andre F Special, *President*
Enrico Gualtieri, *Vice Pres*
Chris Laver, *Vice Pres*
Jason Smith, *Accounting Mgr*
EMP: 90
SQ FT: 43,000
SALES (est): 16.7MM **Privately Held**
SIC: 3544 Industrial molds

(G-5729)
SPECIALTY COATINGS INC (PA)
33835 Kelly Rd (48026-1503)
PHONE..........................586 294-8343
Dan Brownlee, *President*
Larry Alexander, *Sales Staff*
Anthony Citraro, *Administration*
▼ **EMP:** 10
SQ FT: 17,280
SALES (est): 1.3MM **Privately Held**
SIC: 2851 Epoxy coatings

(G-5730)
SPECIALTY STEEL TREATING INC (PA)
34501 Commerce (48026-1692)
PHONE..........................586 293-5355
Martha Parker, *CEO*
Harold Cox, *President*
Mary Verhelle, *President*
Anthony Richey, *General Mgr*
Brandon Couture, *Business Mgr*
EMP: 45 **EST:** 1956
SQ FT: 30,000
SALES (est): 49.4MM **Privately Held**
WEB: www.sstfraser.com
SIC: 5051 3423 3365 3339 Metals service centers & offices; hand & edge tools; aluminum foundries; primary nonferrous metals; primary copper; brazing (hardening) of metal

(G-5731)
SPECIALTY STEEL TREATING INC
17495 Malyn Blvd (48026-1634)
PHONE..........................586 415-8346
Mark Sosnowski, *Branch Mgr*
EMP: 16
SALES (corp-wide): 49.4MM **Privately Held**
SIC: 3398 Metal heat treating
PA: Specialty Steel Treating, Inc.
34501 Commerce
Fraser MI 48026
586 293-5355

(G-5732)
SPECIALTY STEEL TREATING INC
17555 Malyn Blvd (48026-3485)
PHONE..........................586 415-8346
Mark Sosnowski, *Branch Mgr*
EMP: 31
SALES (corp-wide): 49.4MM **Privately Held**
SIC: 3398 Metal heat treating
PA: Specialty Steel Treating, Inc.
34501 Commerce
Fraser MI 48026
586 293-5355

(G-5733)
SPECIALTY STEEL TREATING INC
17505 Malyn Blvd (48026)
PHONE..........................586 415-8346
Mark Sosnowski, *Branch Mgr*
EMP: 16
SALES (corp-wide): 49.4MM **Privately Held**
SIC: 3398 Metal heat treating
PA: Specialty Steel Treating, Inc.
34501 Commerce
Fraser MI 48026
586 293-5355

(G-5734)
SPLIT SECOND DEFENSE LLC
34024 James J Pompo Dr (48026-1643)
PHONE..........................586 709-1385
Jeff Doolin, *Principal*
EMP: 3
SALES (est): 175.7K **Privately Held**
SIC: 3812 Defense systems & equipment

(G-5735)
STANDEX INTERNATIONAL CORP
Also Called: Mold Tech Michigan
34497 Kelly Rd (48026-3404)
PHONE..........................586 296-5500
Omar Ahmed, *Research*
James McKinley, *Design Engr*
Robert Hamood, *Branch Mgr*
EMP: 45
SALES (corp-wide): 791.5MM **Publicly Held**
SIC: 2796 Engraving on copper, steel, wood or rubber: printing plates
PA: Standex International Corporation
11 Keewaydin Dr Ste 300
Salem NH 03079
603 893-9701

(G-5736)
SUPREME GEAR CO (PA)
17430 Malyn Blvd (48026)
PHONE..........................586 775-6325
Robert A Diez, *President*
Michelle Dombrowski, *Marketing Staff*
EMP: 45
SQ FT: 70,000
SALES (est): 7.3MM **Privately Held**
WEB: www.supremegear.com
SIC: 3724 3711 3795 3841 Aircraft engines & engine parts; motor vehicles & car bodies; tanks & tank components; surgical & medical instruments; power transmission equipment

(G-5737)
TAMSCO INC
17580 Helro (48026-2214)
PHONE..........................586 415-1500
Nancy Stachnik, *President*
EMP: 14
SQ FT: 7,000
SALES (est): 750K **Privately Held**
SIC: 7389 2448 Packaging & labeling services; cargo containers, wood & wood with metal

(G-5738)
TOOL SERVICE COMPANY INC
34150 Riviera (48026-4811)
PHONE..........................586 296-2500
Bruce Bellard, *President*
EMP: 8
SQ FT: 12,000
SALES: 1.6MM **Privately Held**
SIC: 3545 Cutting tools for machine tools

(G-5739)
TOP SHELF PAINTER INC
34400 Klein Rd (48026-3009)
PHONE..........................586 465-0867
Peter Rinaldi, *Principal*
EMP: 9 **EST:** 2014
SALES (est): 172.7K **Privately Held**
SIC: 1721 1389 1522 Residential painting; construction, repair & dismantling services; residential construction

(G-5740)
TRINITY INDUSTRIES INC
33910 James J Pompo Dr (48026-3470)
PHONE..........................586 285-1692
Lee Powers, *Superintendent*
Robert Chandler, *Warehouse Mgr*
Glenn Nichols, *Marketing Staff*
Skip Special, *Branch Mgr*
Mitch Hill, *Sr Ntwrk Engine*
EMP: 5
SALES (corp-wide): 2.5B **Publicly Held**
SIC: 3743 Freight cars & equipment
PA: Trinity Industries, Inc.
2525 N Stemmons Fwy
Dallas TX 75207
214 631-4420

(G-5741)
TRINITY TOOL CO
Also Called: Trinco
34600 Commerce (48026-1690)
P.O. Box 98 (48026-0098)
PHONE..........................586 296-5900
Katherine Boyle, *President*
William Boyle, *Vice Pres*
Karen Boyle, *Treasurer*
Kathy Boyle, *Executive*
▼ **EMP:** 25 **EST:** 1951
SQ FT: 44,000
SALES (est): 8.5MM **Privately Held**
WEB: www.trinco.com
SIC: 3569 3549 3291 Blast cleaning equipment, dustless; metalworking machinery; abrasive products

(G-5742)
TURN TECH INC
33901 Riviera (48026-1614)
PHONE..........................586 415-8090
Leonard Johnson, *President*
Jillian Harris, *Assistant*
EMP: 25
SQ FT: 9,000
SALES (est): 4.9MM **Privately Held**
SIC: 3599 Machine shop, jobbing & repair

(G-5743)
UNICOTE CORPORATION
33165 Groesbeck Hwy (48026-1596)
P.O. Box 426 (48026-0426)
PHONE..........................586 296-0700
Thomas G Kury, *President*
Adam Horetski, *Plant Mgr*
Chuck Gietzen, *Prdtn Mgr*
Ron Mattice, *QC Mgr*
Debbie Kury, *CFO*
EMP: 40
SQ FT: 35,000
SALES (est): 4.3MM **Privately Held**
WEB: www.unicotecorporation.com
SIC: 3479 Coating of metals & formed products

(G-5744)
UNITED STATES SOCKET (PA)
Also Called: United Dowel Pin Mfg Co
33675 Riviera (48026-1622)
PHONE..........................586 469-8811
Jac A Roth, *President*
Andrew Roth, *Vice Pres*
▲ **EMP:** 15
SQ FT: 23,800
SALES (est): 4MM **Privately Held**
WEB: www.ussocketscrew.com
SIC: 5072 3542 Screws; nuts (hardware); bolts; miscellaneous fasteners; punching & shearing machines

(G-5745)
VAN-DIES ENGINEERING INC
17525 Helro Ste A (48026-2252)
P.O. Box 408, Roseville (48066-0408)
PHONE..........................586 293-1430
Gary Vanhoorne, *President*
EMP: 20
SQ FT: 10,000
SALES (est): 2.5MM **Privately Held**
SIC: 3469 Stamping metal for the trade

(G-5746)
VISCOUNT EQUIPMENT CO INC
33743 Groesbeck Hwy (48026-4207)
PHONE..........................586 293-5900
James Warda, *President*
Kenneth J Warda, *Vice Pres*
Daniel J Warda, *Admin Sec*
EMP: 5
SQ FT: 10,000
SALES (est): 968.4K **Privately Held**
SIC: 5084 3541 Machine tools & accessories; drilling machine tools (metal cutting); tapping machines

(G-5747)
VISIONEERING INC
17085 Masonic (48026-3927)
PHONE..........................248 622-5600
Brad Hallett, *Branch Mgr*
EMP: 30
SALES (corp-wide): 55.1MM **Privately Held**
SIC: 3728 Aircraft assemblies, subassemblies & parts
PA: Visioneering, Inc.
2055 Taylor Rd
Auburn Hills MI 48326
248 622-5600

(G-5748)
WIRE DYNAMICS INC
18210 Malyn Blvd (48026-1631)
PHONE..........................586 879-0321
George Kozel, *President*
Jeff Kozel, *Vice Pres*
EMP: 5 **EST:** 1977
SQ FT: 2,400
SALES (est): 540K **Privately Held**
WEB: www.wirelessdynamics.com
SIC: 3544 Jigs & fixtures

(G-5749)
YARBROUGH PRECISION SCREWS LLC
17722 Rainbow (48026-2420)
PHONE..........................586 776-0752
EMP: 11
SALES (est): 2MM **Privately Held**
SIC: 3451 Mfg Precision Ball Screw

Frederic
Crawford County

(G-5750)
AUSABLE WOODWORKING CO INC
6677 Frederic St (49733-8761)
P.O. Box 108 (49733-0108)
PHONE..........................989 348-7086
EMP: 35
SALES: 1MM **Privately Held**
SIC: 2499 3993 3873 Mfg Wood Products Mfg Signs/Ad Specialties Mfg Watches/Clocks/Parts

(G-5751)
FLUIDTHERM CORP MICHIGAN
7730 Old 27 N (49733-9732)
PHONE..........................989 344-1500
Roger L Brummel, *President*
Brenda Brummel, *Admin Sec*
EMP: 4
SQ FT: 5,000
SALES: 260K **Privately Held**
SIC: 3567 Industrial furnaces & ovens

Freeland
Saginaw County

(G-5752)
BASTIAN BROTHERS & COMPANY
10240 Thor Dr Ste 1 (48623-8924)
P.O. Box 260 (48623-0260)
PHONE..........................989 239-5107
John R Waugh, *President*

GEOGRAPHIC SECTION

Jeffrey M Waugh, *Vice Pres*
EMP: 28 **EST:** 1893
SQ FT: 50,000
SALES (est): 2.5MM **Privately Held**
WEB: www.bastianbros.com
SIC: 2752 2759 2791 2789 Lithographing on metal; commercial printing, offset; letterpress printing; typesetting; bookbinding & related work

(G-5753)
BUSCH MACHINE TOOL SUPPLY LLC
7251 Midland Rd (48623-8760)
PHONE.................................989 798-4794
Greg Busch, *President*
EMP: 4 **EST:** 2007
SQ FT: 12,000
SALES: 500K **Privately Held**
SIC: 3999 5251 5085 Atomizers, toiletry; tools; tools

(G-5754)
DESIGNTECH CUSTOM INTERIORS
8570 Carter Rd (48623-9008)
PHONE.................................989 695-6306
Greg Awad, *Owner*
Joseph Rutkiewicz, *Vice Pres*
EMP: 4
SQ FT: 6,000
SALES: 500K **Privately Held**
SIC: 1751 2434 Cabinet building & installation; customized furniture & cabinets; vanities; bathroom: wood

(G-5755)
DOW CHEMICAL COMPANY
M B S Intl Hngr 5 (48623)
PHONE.................................989 695-2584
Dan Carroll, *Manager*
EMP: 75
SALES (corp-wide): 61B **Publicly Held**
WEB: www.dow.com
SIC: 2869 Industrial organic chemicals
HQ: The Dow Chemical Company
2211 H H Dow Way
Midland MI 48642
989 636-1000

(G-5756)
EGGERS EXCAVATING LLC
7832 Kochville Rd Ste 1 (48623-8003)
P.O. Box 5908, Saginaw (48603-0908)
PHONE.................................989 695-5205
Chadwick Eggers, *Mng Member*
Russell Eggers, *Mng Member*
EMP: 11
SALES (est): 912.4K **Privately Held**
SIC: 1794 6531 1499 1422 Excavation work; real estate leasing & rentals; asphalt mining & bituminous stone quarrying; crushed & broken limestone; industrial sand

(G-5757)
FRONT LINE SERVICES INC
Also Called: Slsi
8588 Carter Rd (48623-9008)
PHONE.................................989 695-6633
Jeffrey T Simon, *President*
Wendy Simon, *Vice Pres*
Devin Ream, *Sales Staff*
EMP: 13
SQ FT: 6,500
SALES (est): 2.2MM **Privately Held**
WEB: www.flsi.net
SIC: 7538 5087 5012 3569 General automotive repair shops; firefighting equipment; fire trucks; firefighting apparatus & related equipment

(G-5758)
R & M MACHINE TOOL INC
7920 Webster Rd (48623-8400)
P.O. Box 746 (48623-0746)
PHONE.................................989 695-6601
Ronald Miller Jr, *President*
EMP: 23
SQ FT: 7,000
SALES: 1.5MM **Privately Held**
SIC: 3599 Machine shop, jobbing & repair

(G-5759)
SAGINAW KNITTING MILLS INC
8788 Carter Rd (48623-8679)
P.O. Box 218 (48623-0218)
PHONE.................................989 695-2481
Terry W Grenell, *President*
Marie Grenell, *Vice Pres*
EMP: 15
SALES (est): 1.7MM **Privately Held**
SIC: 2396 2395 Screen printing on fabric articles; embroidery products, except schiffli machine

(G-5760)
TRI CITY BLINDS INC
10976 W Freeland Rd (48623-9523)
PHONE.................................989 695-5699
Timothy Apple, *President*
Dan Apple, *Vice Pres*
Andrea Apple, *Admin Sec*
EMP: 4
SALES (est): 350K **Privately Held**
SIC: 2591 5719 Window blinds; window shades

(G-5761)
WILLSIE LUMBER COMPANY
9770 Pierce Rd (48623-8101)
P.O. Box 603 (48623-0603)
PHONE.................................989 695-5094
Denny Willsie, *President*
EMP: 10
SQ FT: 20,000
SALES (est): 2.6MM **Privately Held**
SIC: 2421 Planing mills; furniture dimension stock, softwood

(G-5762)
WYSE GLASS SPECIALTIES INC
1100 Rockwell Dr (48623-9398)
PHONE.................................989 496-3510
Chris Sprague, *President*
Jane Sprague, *Treasurer*
EMP: 3
SQ FT: 2,520
SALES (est): 321.7K **Privately Held**
SIC: 3231 Industrial glassware: made from purchased glass

Freeport
Barry County

(G-5763)
BUSKIRK LUMBER COMPANY
319 Oak St (49325-9472)
P.O. Box 11 (49325-0011)
PHONE.................................616 765-5103
Paul Kamps, *Owner*
Ken Jones, *General Mgr*
Robert Zandstra, *Financial Exec*
EMP: 40
SALES (est): 5.7MM **Privately Held**
SIC: 2421 Sawmills & planing mills, general

(G-5764)
FREEPORT MILLING
223 Division St (49325-9757)
P.O. Box 1 (49325-0001)
PHONE.................................616 765-8421
Dan Fighter, *Principal*
EMP: 8
SALES (est): 1.2MM **Privately Held**
SIC: 2041 Flour & other grain mill products

(G-5765)
KETCHUM MACHINE CORPORATED
219 Oak St (49325-9471)
P.O. Box 26 (49325-0026)
PHONE.................................616 765-5101
Geoffrey G Ketchum, *President*
Duane Alerding, *Vice Pres*
Cynthia S Ketchum, *Treasurer*
Lucinda B Ketchum, *Admin Sec*
EMP: 18
SQ FT: 18,500
SALES (est): 734.7K **Privately Held**
SIC: 3544 3599 Special dies & tools; custom machinery

(G-5766)
MUNN MANUFACTURING COMPANY
312 County Line Rd (49325-5108)
P.O. Box 24 (49325-0024)
PHONE.................................616 765-3067
Steve Buehler, *President*
Wendy Buehler, *Treasurer*
EMP: 46
SQ FT: 12,500
SALES (est): 7.4MM **Privately Held**
WEB: www.munnman.com
SIC: 3599 3469 Machine shop, jobbing & repair; custom machinery; metal stampings

(G-5767)
PARAGON MODEL SHOP INC
10083 Thompson Rd (49325-9623)
PHONE.................................616 693-3224
Janet Mc Intyre, *President*
Randy McIntyre, *Vice Pres*
EMP: 4
SQ FT: 12,000
SALES (est): 685.9K **Privately Held**
SIC: 3599 Machine shop, jobbing & repair

Fremont
Newaygo County

(G-5768)
CONSUMERS CONCRETE CORPORATION
4550 W 72nd St (49412-7316)
PHONE.................................231 924-6131
Mike Woodward, *Director*
EMP: 12
SALES (corp-wide): 102.9MM **Privately Held**
WEB: www.consumersconcrete.com
SIC: 3273 Ready-mixed concrete
PA: Consumers Concrete Corporation
3508 S Sprinkle Rd
Kalamazoo MI 49001
269 342-0136

(G-5769)
CR FORGE LLC
1914 S Comstock Ave (49412-8034)
PHONE.................................231 924-2033
Christopher Ellesson, *Principal*
EMP: 3
SALES (est): 32.3K **Privately Held**
SIC: 3446 Architectural metalwork

(G-5770)
DURA OPERATING LLC
Also Called: Dura Automotive Systems
502 Connie Ave (49412-1812)
PHONE.................................231 924-0930
Tim Stevens, *Branch Mgr*
EMP: 500
SALES (corp-wide): 4.1B **Privately Held**
WEB: www.heywoodwilliamsusa.com
SIC: 3625 Relays & industrial controls
HQ: Dura Operating, Llc
1780 Pond Run
Auburn Hills MI 48326
248 299-7500

(G-5771)
FLAT-TO-FORM METAL SPC INC
9577 W 40th St (49412-8017)
PHONE.................................231 924-1288
Patrick Brown, *President*
Kevin Dummer, *Admin Sec*
EMP: 10
SQ FT: 9,000
SALES: 600K **Privately Held**
SIC: 3444 Sheet metal specialties, not stamped

(G-5772)
GERBER PRODUCTS COMPANY
405 State St (49412-1056)
PHONE.................................231 928-2076
Thomas Boerger, *Plant Mgr*
Jennifer Larkey, *Safety Mgr*
Seth Braafhart, *Train & Dev Mgr*
Craig Thompson, *Branch Mgr*
Trisha Shoemaker, *Director*
EMP: 20
SALES (corp-wide): 92B **Privately Held**
SIC: 2023 Dry, condensed, evaporated dairy products
HQ: Gerber Products Company
12 Vreeland Rd Fl 2
Florham Park NJ 07932
973 593-7500

(G-5773)
GERBER PRODUCTS COMPANY
Also Called: Nestle Infant Nutrition
445 State St (49413-0001)
PHONE.................................231 928-2000
Craig Thompson, *Branch Mgr*
EMP: 170
SALES (corp-wide): 92B **Privately Held**
SIC: 2023 Baby formulas
HQ: Gerber Products Company
12 Vreeland Rd Fl 2
Florham Park NJ 07932
973 593-7500

(G-5774)
GIBBIES DEER PROCESSING
215 Jerrette Ave (49412-1025)
PHONE.................................231 924-6042
Jeff Gibbie, *Owner*
EMP: 12
SALES (est): 887.3K **Privately Held**
SIC: 2011 Meat packing plants

(G-5775)
HI-LITES GRAPHIC INC (PA)
Also Called: Hi-Lites Shoppers Guide
1212 Locust St (49412-1858)
PHONE.................................231 924-0630
Jon Sovinski, *President*
Thomas Kowalski, *Treasurer*
Kelly Walker, *Sales Staff*
Julie Hagen, *Sales Executive*
Karen Baird, *Advt Staff*
EMP: 30
SQ FT: 15,000
SALES (est): 2.7MM **Privately Held**
WEB: www.hi-lites.com
SIC: 2752 2741 7336 2791 Commercial printing, offset; shopping news: publishing only, not printed on site; silk screen design; typesetting; bookbinding & related work

(G-5776)
HI-LITES GRAPHIC INC
Also Called: TS Silkscreen
1003 W Main St (49412-1488)
PHONE.................................231 924-4540
Tony Sovinsky, *Manager*
EMP: 3
SALES (corp-wide): 2.7MM **Privately Held**
WEB: www.hi-lites.com
SIC: 2752 3993 2396 Commercial printing, offset; signs & advertising specialties; automotive & apparel trimmings
PA: Hi-Lites Graphic Inc
1212 Locust St
Fremont MI 49412
231 924-0630

(G-5777)
K-MAR STRUCTURES LLC
Also Called: Mast Mini Barns
7960 Meinert Rd (49412-9162)
PHONE.................................231 924-3895
Alvin F Mast, *Purch Mgr*
Marvin Mast, *Mng Member*
Katie Mast, *Mng Member*
EMP: 10
SQ FT: 17,000
SALES (est): 950K **Privately Held**
SIC: 3272 5999 Solid containing units, concrete; sales barn

(G-5778)
M-B-M MANUFACTURING INC
9576 W 40th St (49412-8017)
PHONE.................................231 924-9614
William C Murphy, *President*
Jeffrey Murphy, *Vice Pres*
Troy Roberson, *Vice Pres*
David Murphy, *Treasurer*
Sandra Kilbourne, *Admin Sec*
EMP: 7
SQ FT: 5,000

Fremont - Newaygo County (G-5779)

GEOGRAPHIC SECTION

SALES (est): 709.4K **Privately Held**
SIC: **3949** 3569 Bowling pin machines, automatic; lubrication equipment, industrial

(G-5779)
NIEBOER ELECTRIC INC
502 E Main St (49412-9788)
PHONE.................................231 924-0960
Doug Nieboer, *President*
Douglas Nieboer, *Owner*
Nancy Nieboer, *Corp Secy*
Harry J Nieboer, *Vice Pres*
EMP: 12
SQ FT: 5,000
SALES: 1.4MM **Privately Held**
SIC: **1731** 5999 7694 General electrical contractor; motors, electric; electric motor repair

(G-5780)
OPCO LUBRICATION SYSTEMS INC
9569 W 40th St (49412-8017)
PHONE.................................231 924-6160
Patrick A Brown, *President*
▼ EMP: 8
SQ FT: 2,500
SALES: 400K **Privately Held**
SIC: **3569** Lubrication equipment, industrial

(G-5781)
PEARCE PLASTICS LLC
4898 W 80th St (49412-7321)
PHONE.................................231 519-5994
Mark Pearce, *Principal*
EMP: 5
SALES (est): 364.8K **Privately Held**
SIC: **3089** Injection molding of plastics

(G-5782)
PIONEER TECHNOLOGIES CORP
7998 W 90th St (49412-9164)
PHONE.................................702 806-3152
Michael Agin, *President*
Marta Agin, *Admin Sec*
EMP: 50 EST: 1997
SALES (est): 1.1MM **Privately Held**
SIC: **8711** 8748 3826 Aviation &/or aeronautical engineering; systems analysis & engineering consulting services; systems engineering consultant, ex. computer or professional; laser scientific & engineering instruments

(G-5783)
PROGRESSIVE MANUFACTURING LLC
425 Connie Ave (49412-1809)
PHONE.................................231 924-9975
Gordon Lucies,
Gordon Luchies,
John Lucus,
EMP: 4
SQ FT: 75,000
SALES: 500K **Privately Held**
SIC: **3444** Casings, sheet metal; ducts, sheet metal

(G-5784)
TIMES INDICATOR PUBLICATIONS
44 W Main St (49412-1176)
P.O. Box 7 (49412-0007)
PHONE.................................231 924-4400
Tony Komlance, *Owner*
EMP: 7
SALES (est): 311.1K **Privately Held**
WEB: www.timesindicator.com
SIC: **2711** Newspapers: publishing only, not printed on site

(G-5785)
TWO FEATHERS ENTERPRISE LLC
Also Called: Rj's Custom Plowing
1117 S Baldwin Ave (49412-9726)
PHONE.................................231 924-3612
Robin Jahr,
Bryan Jahr,
EMP: 3
SALES (est): 256.2K **Privately Held**
SIC: **2511** 7389 Stools, household: wood;

(G-5786)
WHITE RIVER KNIFE AND TOOL
Also Called: Reid Manufacturing
515 Industrial Dr (49412-1867)
PHONE.................................616 997-0026
Jeffery Cothery, *President*
EMP: 5
SALES (est): 641.3K **Privately Held**
WEB: www.reidmfg.com
SIC: **3544** Special dies, tools, jigs & fixtures

Fruitport
Muskegon County

(G-5787)
AUTOMATED INDUS MOTION INC
Also Called: Aim Mail Centers
5627 Airline Rd (49415-8753)
PHONE.................................231 865-1800
Kurt Witham, *President*
Floyd Howe, *Vice Pres*
Rocky Howe, *Vice Pres*
Karen Spoelma, *Manager*
Dick Lague, *Admin Sec*
EMP: 12
SQ FT: 10,000
SALES (est): 3.1MM **Privately Held**
WEB: www.aimcoil.com
SIC: **3542** 3599 Spinning, spline rolling & winding machines; custom machinery

(G-5788)
BASCH OLOVSON ENGINEERING CO
3438 E Mount Garfield Rd (49415-9209)
PHONE.................................231 865-2027
Roy Olovson Jr, *President*
Joni Olovson, *Vice Pres*
EMP: 6
SQ FT: 4,600
SALES (est): 916.3K **Privately Held**
SIC: **3452** Machine keys

(G-5789)
BK COMPUTING
5210 E Mount Garfield Rd (49415-9745)
PHONE.................................231 865-3558
William Rieger, *Owner*
EMP: 3 EST: 1993
SALES (est): 202.7K **Privately Held**
SIC: **3571** Mainframe computers

(G-5790)
BRALYN INC
Also Called: Ram Electronics
259 N 3rd Ave (49415-8843)
PHONE.................................231 865-3186
Robert Bradley Davis, *President*
Lynne Bosgraaf, *Vice Pres*
EMP: 15
SQ FT: 8,800
SALES (est): 616.7K **Privately Held**
SIC: **3672** Printed circuit boards

(G-5791)
COPIES & MORE INC
4491 Pontaluna Rd (49415-8718)
PHONE.................................231 865-6370
Ron Cooper, *President*
Mariann Cooper, *Manager*
EMP: 3
SALES (est): 125K **Privately Held**
SIC: **2752** Commercial printing, lithographic

(G-5792)
DYNAMIC FINISHING LLC (PA)
69 S 2nd Ave (49415-8936)
PHONE.................................231 737-8130
Steven Swanson, *Mng Member*
Alan Hayes,
EMP: 14
SQ FT: 1,300
SALES (est): 1.2MM **Privately Held**
SIC: **3471** Plating of metals or formed products

(G-5793)
INDUSTRIAL ASSEMBLIES INC
3130 Farr Rd (49415-8774)
PHONE.................................231 865-6500
Jerry Hanson, *CEO*
Scott Hanson, *President*
Marsha Hanson, *Corp Secy*
EMP: 18 EST: 1996
SQ FT: 80,000
SALES (est): 2.2MM **Privately Held**
SIC: **2541** Store & office display cases & fixtures

(G-5794)
KOLKEMA FABRICATING
6439 S Walker Rd (49415-8776)
PHONE.................................231 865-6380
Roger W Kolkema, *Owner*
EMP: 9
SQ FT: 5,000
SALES (est): 613.7K **Privately Held**
SIC: **3444** Sheet metalwork

(G-5795)
LEE MANUFACTURING INC
6406 Airline Rd (49415-8934)
PHONE.................................231 865-3359
Bruce Gaultney, *President*
Arloa Gaultney, *Vice Pres*
Cindy Gaultney, *Vice Pres*
EMP: 15
SQ FT: 12,000
SALES (est): 2.5MM **Privately Held**
SIC: **3599** Machine shop, jobbing & repair

(G-5796)
MARHAR SNOWBOARDS LLC
5693 Airline Rd (49415-8753)
PHONE.................................616 432-3104
Nathan Morse, *Partner*
Josh Skiles, *Partner*
EMP: 4
SALES (est): 422.5K **Privately Held**
SIC: **3949** Skateboards

(G-5797)
MODULAR SYSTEMS INC
169 Park St (49415-8896)
P.O. Box 399 (49415-0399)
PHONE.................................231 865-3167
Montgomery J Welch, *President*
James Knapp, *Vice Pres*
Harry Knudson, *Admin Sec*
▲ EMP: 8 EST: 1966
SQ FT: 50,000
SALES: 1.1MM **Privately Held**
WEB: www.mod-eez.com
SIC: **3452** 2541 Screws, metal; shelving, office & store, wood

(G-5798)
MOTION DYNAMICS CORPORATION
5621 Airline Rd (49415-8753)
PHONE.................................231 865-7400
Chris Witham, *President*
Paul Cooper, *Plant Mgr*
Norm Moss, *Opers Mgr*
Michael Erpenbeck, *Research*
EMP: 65
SQ FT: 12,000
SALES (est): 14.4MM **Privately Held**
WEB: www.motiondc.com
SIC: **3495** Precision springs

(G-5799)
RAM ELECTRONICS INC
259 N 3rd Ave (49415-8843)
PHONE.................................231 865-3186
Donald R Neidlinger, *President*
Teresa Vargo, *Purchasing*
Lynne Bosgraaf, *Engineer*
Shawn Gibson, *Shareholder*
EMP: 12
SQ FT: 8,800
SALES (est): 2.1MM **Privately Held**
WEB: www.ramelectronics.com
SIC: **8611** 3672 3699 Manufacturers' institute; printed circuit boards; electrical equipment & supplies

(G-5800)
SHIPSTON ALUM TECH MICH INC
Also Called: Busche Aluminum Technologies
14638 Apple Dr (49415-9511)
PHONE.................................616 842-3500
Nick Busche, *CEO*
Bethany Aebli, *Engineer*
David Bohlmann, *Engineer*
Tom Jennings, *Engineer*
Kristoffer Cole, *Program Mgr*
◆ EMP: 7
SQ FT: 230,000
SALES (est): 19MM
SALES (corp-wide): 360.5MM **Privately Held**
SIC: **3365** Aluminum foundries
HQ: Shipston Aluminum Technologies International, Inc.
1450 Commerce Pkwy
Franklin IN 46131

Gagetown
Tuscola County

(G-5801)
CHICAGO MFG & DIST CO
6592 Lincoln St (48735-5115)
P.O. Box 176 (48735-0176)
PHONE.................................989 665-2531
EMP: 3
SQ FT: 1,300
SALES: 198K **Privately Held**
SIC: **2992** Mfg Lube Oil Products

(G-5802)
JEFF R CABINETS LLC
4490 Elkton Rd (48735-9500)
PHONE.................................989 233-0976
Jeff Rajewski, *Mng Member*
EMP: 3
SALES: 150K **Privately Held**
SIC: **2434** Vanities, bathroom: wood

(G-5803)
VITA PLUS CORPORATION
Also Called: Vita Plus Gagetown
6506 Mill St (48735-9710)
P.O. Box 169 (48735-0169)
PHONE.................................989 665-0013
Don Jaster, *General Mgr*
Matt Wood, *Sales Mgr*
John Tilt, *Manager*
Jeff Herbers, *Manager*
EMP: 15
SALES (corp-wide): 126.8MM **Privately Held**
WEB: www.showinglivestock.com
SIC: **2047** 2048 5191 5153 Dog food; livestock feeds; feed premixes; animal feeds; grain elevators
HQ: Vita Plus Corporation
2514 Fish Hatchery Rd
Madison WI 53713
608 256-1988

Gaines
Genesee County

(G-5804)
GOLDEN NEEDLE AWNINGS LLC (PA)
8674 S County Line Rd (48436-8806)
PHONE.................................517 404-6219
William Thompson, *Owner*
EMP: 4
SALES: 175K **Privately Held**
SIC: **2394** Awnings, fabric: made from purchased materials

Galesburg
Kalamazoo County

(G-5805)
ALUMILITE CORPORATION
1458 S 35th St (49053-9679)
PHONE.................................269 488-4000

Mike Faupel, *President*
▲ **EMP:** 12
SALES (est): 2.6MM
SALES (corp-wide): 13.1MM **Privately Held**
SIC: 3089 3087 2821 Casting of plastic; custom compound purchased resins; plastics materials & resins
PA: Polytek Development Corp.
55 Hilton St
Easton PA 18042
610 559-8620

(G-5806)
BELLS BREWERY INC (PA)
8690 Krum Ave (49053-9555)
PHONE 269 382-2338
Laura Bell, *CEO*
Sharri Parks, *Corp Secy*
Angela Bell, *Vice Pres*
Tim Gossack, *Prdtn Mgr*
Ralph Stocker, *Facilities Mgr*
◆ **EMP:** 40
SQ FT: 30,000
SALES (est): 19MM **Privately Held**
SIC: 2082 Beer (alcoholic beverage)

(G-5807)
BENTELER AUTOMOTIVE CORP
9000 E Michigan Ave (49053-8509)
PHONE 269 665-4261
William Curtis, *Engineer*
David Dexter, *Design Engr*
Mike Glass, *Design Engr*
Bill Nieboer, *Branch Mgr*
EMP: 500
SALES (corp-wide): 9.2B **Privately Held**
SIC: 3714 Axles, motor vehicle
HQ: Benteler Automotive Corporation
2650 N Opdyke Rd Ste B
Auburn Hills MI 48326
248 364-7190

(G-5808)
BENTLER INDUSTRIES INC
9000 E Michigan Ave (49053-9772)
PHONE 269 665-4261
Rick Mayo, *Principal*
EMP: 3
SALES (est): 217.9K **Privately Held**
SIC: 5013 3714 Automotive supplies & parts; motor vehicle parts & accessories

(G-5809)
EATON CORPORATION
13100 E Michigan Ave (49053-9201)
PHONE 269 342-3000
Michael Sikorski, *Division Mgr*
Chand Tailor, *Exec VP*
Victor Demarco, *Vice Pres*
Ned Simon, *Vice Pres*
Michael Byrne, *Buyer*
EMP: 400 **Privately Held**
WEB: www.eaton.com
SIC: 3714 Motor vehicle transmissions, drive assemblies & parts
HQ: Eaton Corporation
1000 Eaton Blvd
Cleveland OH 44122
440 523-5000

(G-5810)
EATON CORPORATION
Also Called: Eaton Fuller Reman Center
13100 E Michigan Ave (49053-9201)
PHONE 269 342-3000
Gustavo Cruz, *Manager*
EMP: 135 **Privately Held**
WEB: www.eaton.com
SIC: 3714 Motor vehicle transmissions, drive assemblies & parts
HQ: Eaton Corporation
1000 Eaton Blvd
Cleveland OH 44122
440 523-5000

(G-5811)
IMPACT LABEL CORPORATION (PA)
Also Called: Vari-Data Co.
8875 Krum Ave (49053-9552)
PHONE 269 381-4280
Susan Fogleson, *President*
Jeff Cleveland, *Production*
Justin Paulton, *Sales Staff*
Geri Newell, *Director*
Julie Smith, *Associate*
EMP: 55
SQ FT: 35,000
SALES (est): 11.8MM **Privately Held**
WEB: www.impactlabel.com
SIC: 2759 3089 2672 2671 Labels & seals: printing; identification cards, plastic; coated & laminated paper; packaging paper & plastics film, coated & laminated; pleating & stitching

(G-5812)
ISRINGHAUSEN INC
1458 S 35th St (49053-9679)
PHONE 269 484-5333
Gary Slater, *General Mgr*
Tom Gucma, *Buyer*
Jay Chapman, *Manager*
▲ **EMP:** 130
SQ FT: 53,000
SALES (est): 9.3MM
SALES (corp-wide): 355.8K **Privately Held**
WEB: www.isringhausen.com
SIC: 2531 Seats, automobile
HQ: Isringhausen Gmbh & Co. Kg
Isringhausen-Ring 58
Lemgo 32657
526 121-00

(G-5813)
MICHIGAN GROWER PRODUCTS INC
251 Mccollum (49053-9509)
P.O. Box 373 (49053-0373)
PHONE 269 665-7071
Richard Derks, *President*
Dean Cramer, *Vice Pres*
Gregory D Bonnema, *Treasurer*
Gregory Bonnema, *Treasurer*
Lorence Wenke, *Admin Sec*
EMP: 15 **EST:** 1979
SQ FT: 43,000
SALES (est): 3MM **Privately Held**
SIC: 2875 Fertilizers, mixing only

(G-5814)
SMITHS MACHINE & GRINDING INC
203 E Battle Creek St (49053-9412)
PHONE 269 665-4231
Scott Ogden, *President*
John Wunderlin, *Purchasing*
Kate Geissel, *Receptionist*
◆ **EMP:** 34 **EST:** 1952
SQ FT: 24,000
SALES (est): 5.4MM **Privately Held**
SIC: 3599 Machine shop, jobbing & repair

(G-5815)
SOUPCAN INC
Also Called: Wet N Rugged Sports
9406 E K Ave Ste 5 (49053-8522)
PHONE 269 381-2101
EMP: 12
SQ FT: 2,800
SALES: 3MM **Privately Held**
SIC: 3949 Mfg Sporting/Athletic Goods

(G-5816)
TECNIQ INC
9100 E Michigan Ave (49053-8539)
PHONE 269 629-4440
Mark Pruss, *CEO*
Patrick Condon, *President*
John Vitek, *Vice Pres*
▲ **EMP:** 42
SALES (est): 11.5MM **Privately Held**
WEB: www.tecniqinc.com
SIC: 3647 Taillights, motor vehicle

Galien
Berrien County

(G-5817)
CAST COATINGS INC (PA)
203 W Southeastern St (49113-9688)
P.O. Box 385 (49113-0385)
PHONE 269 545-8373
Robert Anstey, *President*
Roxy Scheer, *Plant Mgr*
EMP: 25
SQ FT: 18,200
SALES (est): 4.2MM **Privately Held**
SIC: 3479 Coating of metals & formed products

(G-5818)
KRUGER PLASTICS PRODUCTS LLC
117 S Grant St (49113-5116)
P.O. Box 258 (49113-0258)
PHONE 269 545-3311
Pat Brandstatter, *Branch Mgr*
EMP: 35
SALES (corp-wide): 10.1MM **Privately Held**
SIC: 3089 Injection molding of plastics
PA: Kruger Plastic Products Llc
4015 Lemon Creek Rd
Bridgman MI 49106
269 465-6404

(G-5819)
PINECREST INDUSTRIES
Also Called: Pinecrest Farms
4355 Spring Creek Rd (49113-9621)
PHONE 269 545-8125
Richard Soper, *Owner*
EMP: 3
SALES (est): 176.3K **Privately Held**
SIC: 0811 0171 2899 Christmas tree farm; blueberry farm; chemical preparations

Garden City
Wayne County

(G-5820)
ALEXANDERS CUSTOM GL & MIRROR
29455 James St (48135-2047)
PHONE 734 513-5850
Eric Obsniuck, *President*
EMP: 3
SALES (est): 244.3K **Privately Held**
SIC: 3231 Mirrored glass

(G-5821)
CHILDS CARPENTRY
31585 Birchlawn St (48135-1937)
PHONE 734 425-8783
Timothy Childs, *Owner*
EMP: 3
SQ FT: 1,000
SALES (est): 210K **Privately Held**
SIC: 2542 Cabinets: show, display or storage: except wood

(G-5822)
DO RITE TOOL INC
32647 Parklane St (48135-1528)
PHONE 734 522-7510
David J Mc Donald, *President*
Lori Mc Donald, *Vice Pres*
EMP: 9
SQ FT: 4,800
SALES (est): 1.4MM **Privately Held**
SIC: 3544 Special dies & tools; jigs & fixtures

(G-5823)
E AND P FORM TOOL COMPANY INC
31759 Block St Ste A (48135-1538)
PHONE 734 261-3530
Joseph F Podzikowski, *President*
Mary J Podzikowski, *Treasurer*
EMP: 12
SQ FT: 7,000
SALES: 1.2MM **Privately Held**
SIC: 3451 Screw machine products

(G-5824)
FRANKLIN ELECTRIC CORPORATION
32606 Industrial Rd (48135-1523)
P.O. Box 12408, Detroit (48212-0408)
PHONE 248 442-8000
Russ D Gorden, *President*
EMP: 10
SALES: 1.2MM **Privately Held**
SIC: 7699 7629 7694 Industrial equipment services; electrical equipment repair, high voltage; electric motor repair

(G-5825)
GAIL PARKER
Also Called: P3 Vending
847 W Rose Ave (48135-3616)
PHONE 734 261-3842
Gail L Parker, *Owner*
EMP: 3
SALES (est): 229.2K **Privately Held**
WEB: www.gailparker.com
SIC: 3581 Automatic vending machines

(G-5826)
HITE TOOL CO INC
32127 Block St Ste 200 (48135-1537)
PHONE 734 422-1777
Jack Hite, *President*
Todd Hite, *Vice Pres*
EMP: 5
SQ FT: 3,200
SALES (est): 209.1K **Privately Held**
WEB: www.general-tool.com
SIC: 3544 Dies & die holders for metal cutting, forming, die casting

(G-5827)
INKORPORATE
6841 Middlebelt Rd (48135-2148)
PHONE 734 261-4657
Jim Neve, *Owner*
EMP: 6
SALES (est): 758.8K **Privately Held**
SIC: 2759 Screen printing

(G-5828)
INLAND VAPOR OF MICHIGAN LLC (PA)
33447 Ford Rd (48135-1154)
PHONE 734 237-4389
Ken Dobozy, *Manager*
Kenneth Dobozy, *Manager*
EMP: 13
SQ FT: 1,270
SALES (est): 2.5MM **Privately Held**
SIC: 3822 3641 Vapor heating controls; lamps, vapor

(G-5829)
INTEGRITY MARKETING PRODUCTS
5905 Middlebelt Rd (48135-2478)
P.O. Box 668, Dearborn Heights (48127-0668)
PHONE 734 522-5050
Daniel Seguin, *President*
EMP: 6
SQ FT: 4,600
SALES (est): 653.7K **Privately Held**
SIC: 2759 Screen printing

(G-5830)
INTERNATIONAL EXTRUSIONS INC (PA)
Also Called: Excrution Painting
5800 Venoy Rd (48135-1655)
PHONE 734 427-8700
Nicholas Noecker, *President*
George Gazepis, *CFO*
David Brokos, *Info Tech Dir*
Gregory Stangler, *Admin Sec*
EMP: 164 **EST:** 1971
SQ FT: 12,000
SALES (est): 36.3MM **Privately Held**
WEB: www.extrusion.net
SIC: 3354 3441 Aluminum extruded products; fabricated structural metal

(G-5831)
JAKES CAKES INC
418 Farmington Rd (48135-1017)
PHONE 734 522-2103
John Jones, *President*
EMP: 5
SALES (est): 261K **Privately Held**
SIC: 2053 Pastries (danish): frozen

(G-5832)
LARRYS BUTTON BOX
32641 Pierce St (48135-1273)
PHONE 734 425-4239
Larry Currie Sr, *Owner*
Dorothy Currie, *Co-Owner*
EMP: 3
SALES: 12K **Privately Held**
SIC: 3999 Buttons: Red Cross, union, identification

Garden City - Wayne County (G-5833)

(G-5833)
MATHESON TRI-GAS INC
5913 Middlebelt Rd (48135-2478)
PHONE.................734 425-8870
Gerald Hotero, *Branch Mgr*
EMP: 15 **Privately Held**
SIC: 2813 Industrial gases
HQ: Matheson Tri-Gas, Inc.
150 Allen Rd Ste 302
Basking Ridge NJ 07920
908 991-9200

(G-5834)
ORIN JEWELERS INC (PA)
29317 Ford Rd (48135-2887)
P.O. Box 549 (48136-0549)
PHONE.................734 422-7030
Orin J Mazzoni Jr, *President*
Megan Conner, *Sales Staff*
Joyce Pappas, *Sales Executive*
Matt Tatro, *Manager*
Allison Colby, *Consultant*
EMP: 17
SQ FT: 3,500
SALES (est): 3.5MM **Privately Held**
WEB: www.orinjewelers.com
SIC: 5944 7631 3911 Jewelry, precious stones & precious metals; watches; jewelry repair services; watch repair; jewelry, precious metal

(G-5835)
PUFF BABY LLC
6250 Middlebelt Rd (48135-2409)
PHONE.................734 620-9991
EMP: 3
SALES (est): 163.5K **Privately Held**
SIC: 3671 Gas or vapor tubes

(G-5836)
RICKS CUSTOM CYCLE LLP
31532 Ford Rd (48135-1874)
PHONE.................734 762-2077
Nicoll Levy, *Partner*
EMP: 3
SALES (est): 395.1K **Privately Held**
SIC: 2611 Pulp manufactured from waste or recycled paper

(G-5837)
SAF-AIR PRODUCTS INC
32839 Manor Park (48135-1526)
PHONE.................734 522-8360
Patricia Lescoe, *President*
Bob Lescoe, *Vice Pres*
EMP: 6
SQ FT: 5,000
SALES (est): 407K **Privately Held**
SIC: 3728 Aircraft parts & equipment

(G-5838)
SCHAEFER SCREW PRODUCTS CO
32832 Indl Rd (48135)
PHONE.................734 522-0020
Sanford Szalay, *President*
David McManus, *General Mgr*
Michael Szalay, *Vice Pres*
Brett Belda, *Human Res Mgr*
▲ **EMP:** 27
SQ FT: 16,000
SALES (est): 5.6MM **Privately Held**
WEB: www.schaeferscrew.com
SIC: 3599 Machine shop, jobbing & repair

(G-5839)
SGI MANUFACTURING INC
32832 Manor Park (48135-1545)
PHONE.................734 425-2680
Thomas Killion, *President*
EMP: 10
SQ FT: 5,000
SALES: 1MM **Privately Held**
SIC: 3599 Machine shop, jobbing & repair

(G-5840)
SHOMO TOOL COMPANY INC
28834 Cambridge St (48135-2173)
PHONE.................734 422-5588
Douglas A Shomo, *President*
EMP: 3
SQ FT: 3,000
SALES: 150K **Privately Held**
SIC: 3599 Machine shop, jobbing & repair

(G-5841)
SIDLEY DIAMOND TOOL COMPANY (PA)
32320 Ford Rd (48135-1507)
PHONE.................734 261-7970
Michael J Sidley, *President*
▲ **EMP:** 29 **EST:** 1956
SQ FT: 15,000
SALES (est): 3MM **Privately Held**
WEB: www.sidleydiamond.com
SIC: 3291 3545 Abrasive products; diamond cutting tools for turning, boring, burnishing, etc.; diamond dressing & wheel crushing attachments

(G-5842)
SIGN-A-RAMA INC
6641 Middlebelt Rd (48135-2146)
PHONE.................734 522-6661
Gregory Solovey, *CEO*
EMP: 5
SALES: 250K **Privately Held**
SIC: 3993 5099 Signs & advertising specialties; signs, except electric

(G-5843)
TEL-X CORPORATION
32400 Ford Rd (48135-1512)
PHONE.................734 425-2225
Gary Gillard, *President*
Keith Speck, *Vice Pres*
Jennifer Lauer, *Purch Mgr*
Tammy Carol, *Controller*
EMP: 31
SQ FT: 21,000
SALES (est): 7.8MM **Privately Held**
WEB: www.tel-xcorp.com
SIC: 3444 3465 Sheet metal specialties, not stamped; automotive stampings

(G-5844)
TRANS PARTS PLUS INC
32816 Manor Park (48135-1545)
P.O. Box 51655, Livonia (48151-5655)
PHONE.................734 427-6844
Bruce Zarbaugh, *President*
EMP: 5
SQ FT: 5,000
SALES (est): 630K **Privately Held**
WEB: www.trademile.com
SIC: 3714 Transmission housings or parts, motor vehicle

(G-5845)
US TRADE LLC
29145 Warren Rd (48135-2144)
PHONE.................800 676-0208
EMP: 4
SALES (est): 264.6K **Privately Held**
SIC: 3674 Light emitting diodes

(G-5846)
VIKING INDUSTRIES INC
6012 Hubbard St (48135-1520)
PHONE.................734 421-5416
Frank Klem, *President*
EMP: 10
SALES (est): 932.9K **Privately Held**
SIC: 3334 Primary aluminum

Gaylord
Otsego County

(G-5847)
AKSTON HUGHES INTL LLC
1865 Orourke Blvd Ste A (49735-8030)
PHONE.................989 448-2322
Daniel Walsh, *CEO*
EMP: 15
SALES (est): 1.3MM **Privately Held**
SIC: 2131 Smoking tobacco

(G-5848)
AMERICAN BOTTLING COMPANY
Also Called: 7-Up of Gaylord
1923 Orourke Blvd (49735-8029)
PHONE.................989 731-5392
EMP: 20 **Publicly Held**
SIC: 2086 Mfg Bottled/Canned Soft Drinks
HQ: The American Bottling Company
5301 Legacy Dr
Plano TX 75024

(G-5849)
BAKER HUGHES A GE COMPANY LLC
Unichem
526 Barnyard (49735)
PHONE.................989 732-2082
Gary Gallup, *Branch Mgr*
EMP: 6
SALES (corp-wide): 22.8B **Privately Held**
WEB: www.bjservices.com
SIC: 1389 Acidizing wells; oil field services
PA: Baker Hughes, A Ge Company Llc
17021 Aldine Westfield Rd
Houston TX 77073
713 439-8600

(G-5850)
BECKMAN PRODUCTION SVCS INC
M 32 E (49735)
PHONE.................989 732-9341
Robert Westfall, *Manager*
EMP: 22
SALES (corp-wide): 827.1MM **Publicly Held**
WEB: www.dartenergy.com
SIC: 1389 Oil field services
HQ: Beckman Production Services, Inc.
3786 Beebe Rd
Kalkaska MI 49646
231 258-9524

(G-5851)
BOZZER BROTHERS INC
1252 Krys Rd (49735-8211)
PHONE.................989 732-9684
Nelson Bozzer, *President*
Gino Bozzer, *Admin Sec*
EMP: 8 **EST:** 1974
SQ FT: 5,000
SALES (est): 1.1MM **Privately Held**
SIC: 3273 5211 Ready-mixed concrete; lumber & other building materials

(G-5852)
CHOICE PUBLICATIONS INC
112 E 6th St (49735-2015)
P.O. Box 382 (49734-0382)
PHONE.................989 732-8160
David Baragrey Sr, *President*
David G Baragrey Jr, *Shareholder*
Robert Eldredge, *Author*
EMP: 4
SQ FT: 10,000
SALES: 350K **Privately Held**
WEB: www.choicepublications.com
SIC: 2721 Magazines: publishing only, not printed on site

(G-5853)
CROSSROADS INDUSTRIES INC
2464 Silver Fox Trl (49735-7440)
P.O. Box 1337 (49734-5337)
PHONE.................989 732-1233
William Marshall, *CEO*
EMP: 75
SQ FT: 15,000
SALES (est): 488.7K **Privately Held**
SIC: 8331 2431 2441 Vocational rehabilitation agency; door frames, wood; boxes, wood

(G-5854)
CUMMINS INC
977 N Center Ave (49735-9375)
PHONE.................989 732-5055
Bryan Tromboy, *Mng Member*
EMP: 15
SALES (corp-wide): 23.7B **Publicly Held**
WEB: www.bridgewaypower.com
SIC: 7538 5063 3519 5999 Diesel engine repair: automotive; motors, electric; generators; motor controls, starters & relays; electric; internal combustion engines; engine & motor equipment & supplies; motors, electric
PA: Cummins Inc.
500 Jackson St
Columbus IN 47201
812 377-5000

(G-5855)
DEVONIAN ENERGY INC
132 N Otsego Ave (49735-1444)
P.O. Box 1094 (49734-5094)
PHONE.................989 732-9400
Scott Lampert, *President*
EMP: 3
SQ FT: 1,000
SALES (est): 257.6K **Privately Held**
SIC: 1311 Crude petroleum production; natural gas production

(G-5856)
DIVERSIFIED METAL PRODUCTS INC
1489 Oorouk Blvd (49735)
PHONE.................989 448-7120
Richard Ericson, *CEO*
Dennis Holden, *Admin Sec*
EMP: 20
SQ FT: 20,000
SALES: 4.1MM **Privately Held**
SIC: 3542 Die casting machines

(G-5857)
ELENZ INC
1455 Dickerson Rd (49735-7448)
PHONE.................989 732-7233
Edward Elenz, *President*
EMP: 10
SALES (corp-wide): 817.2K **Privately Held**
WEB: www.elenz.com
SIC: 2421 Wood chips, produced at mill
PA: Elenz, Inc
1829 Calkins Dr
Gaylord MI

(G-5858)
FORCE ENERGY INC
1680 Calkins Dr (49735-9501)
PHONE.................989 732-0724
Glenn E Forcier, *CEO*
Dan Forcier, *President*
Peter Forcier, *Vice Pres*
James Rawley, *Vice Pres*
EMP: 5
SQ FT: 6,000
SALES (est): 470K **Privately Held**
SIC: 1311 Crude petroleum production; natural gas production

(G-5859)
FORREST BROTHERS INC (PA)
1272 Millbocker Rd (49735-9507)
PHONE.................989 356-4011
Matthew Forrest, *President*
John Forrest, *Vice Pres*
EMP: 250
SQ FT: 62,000
SALES (est): 12.5MM **Privately Held**
SIC: 1796 3564 3823 Pollution control equipment installation; dust or fume collecting equipment, industrial; industrial instrmnts msrmnt display/control process variable

(G-5860)
GAYLORD MCH & FABRICATION LLC
2758 Dickerson Rd (49735-7453)
PHONE.................989 732-0817
Bob Pruitt,
EMP: 12
SQ FT: 8,400
SALES (est): 1MM **Privately Held**
SIC: 3599 Machine shop, jobbing & repair

(G-5861)
GREAT LKES TEX RESTORATION LLC
651 Expressway Ct (49735-8117)
P.O. Box 1821 (49734-5821)
PHONE.................989 448-8600
Douglas Bailey,
EMP: 5
SALES (est): 195.4K **Privately Held**
SIC: 2211 Laundry fabrics, cotton

(G-5862)
GROZDANOVSKI VASILKA
Also Called: Pando Leather Craft
4015 Hayes Tower Rd (49735-8885)
PHONE.................989 731-0723
Vasilka Grozdanovski, *Owner*

GEOGRAPHIC SECTION
Gaylord - Otsego County (G-5891)

EMP: 6
SALES: 82K **Privately Held**
WEB: www.pandoleather.com
SIC: 3199 Leather garments; holsters, leather

(G-5863)
GTM STEAMER SERVICE INC
647 Poplar Dr (49735-9406)
P.O. Box 171 (49734-0171)
PHONE.................................989 732-7678
Gary T Mayer, *President*
Ann Marie Mayer, *Vice Pres*
EMP: 4
SALES: 230K **Privately Held**
SIC: 1381 1799 4959 1389 Service well drilling; exterior cleaning, including sandblasting; snowplowing; oil field services

(G-5864)
H & S MOLD INC
1640 Orourke Blvd (49735-9565)
PHONE.................................989 732-3566
Douglas Hancock, *President*
Todd Hancock, *Corp Secy*
Dan Schirle, *Technology*
EMP: 10 **EST:** 1974
SQ FT: 10,000
SALES (est): 1.7MM **Privately Held**
SIC: 3544 Forms (molds), for foundry & plastics working machinery

(G-5865)
HRF EXPLORATION & PROD LLC
990 S Wisconsin Ave (49735-1781)
PHONE.................................989 732-6950
Harry Fruehauf, *Branch Mgr*
EMP: 18 **Privately Held**
SIC: 1382 Oil & gas exploration services
PA: Hrf Exploration & Production, L.L.C.
250 El Dorado Ln
Palm Beach FL 33480

(G-5866)
IMAGE FACTORY INC
870 N Center Ave (49735-1510)
P.O. Box 1234 (49734-5234)
PHONE.................................989 732-2712
Ronald Grendel, *President*
EMP: 5
SQ FT: 2,400
SALES (est): 792.2K **Privately Held**
SIC: 2752 5199 Commercial printing, offset; advertising specialties

(G-5867)
J R PRODUCTIONS INC
1522 Big Lake Rd (49735-8210)
PHONE.................................989 732-2905
Thomas P Burzynski, *President*
Barbara E Burzynski, *Treasurer*
EMP: 6
SALES (est): 394K **Privately Held**
SIC: 1382 Oil & gas exploration services

(G-5868)
JERRYS TOOL & DIE
5130 Alba Rd (49735-9235)
PHONE.................................989 732-4689
Gary Brandenberg, *Partner*
Brian Brandenberg, *Partner*
EMP: 3
SALES (est): 343.3K **Privately Held**
SIC: 3544 Special dies & tools

(G-5869)
JET SUBSURFACE ROD PUMPS CORP
450 Sides Dr (49735-7503)
P.O. Box 1866 (49734-5866)
PHONE.................................989 732-7513
Dave Findley, *President*
Randy Cherwinski, *General Mgr*
Lyle Benaway, *Purchasing*
EMP: 6
SQ FT: 5,600
SALES: 1MM **Privately Held**
SIC: 5251 1389 Pumps & pumping equipment; oil field services

(G-5870)
KASPER INDUSTRIES INC
356 Expressway Ct (49735-8111)
PHONE.................................989 705-1177
Tim Kasper, *President*
EMP: 25 **EST:** 1953
SQ FT: 26,000
SALES (est): 5MM **Privately Held**
SIC: 3599 Machine shop, jobbing & repair

(G-5871)
KEAYS FAMILY TRUCKIN
Also Called: Kft
1658 Ashley Ln (49735-8116)
PHONE.............................231 838-6430
Dannan Keays, *Principal*
EMP: 11
SALES (est): 833K **Privately Held**
SIC: 3523 4212 Driers (farm); grain, hay & seed; animal & farm product transportation services

(G-5872)
KRAFT POWER CORPORATION
2852 D And M Dr (49735-7417)
PHONE.................................989 748-4040
Tom Rogers, *Branch Mgr*
EMP: 19
SALES (corp-wide): 36.6MM **Privately Held**
SIC: 5084 3621 Engines & parts, diesel; industrial machine parts; power generators
PA: Kraft Power Corporation
199 Wildwood Ave
Woburn MA 01801
781 938-9100

(G-5873)
LAKEVIEW QUALITY TOOL INC
696 Alpine Rd (49735-9531)
PHONE.................................989 732-6417
Albert L Quaal, *President*
Jerry Cattaneo, *Vice Pres*
Regen Quaal, *Vice Pres*
Jerry C Cattaneo, *Manager*
EMP: 7
SQ FT: 5,500
SALES (est): 250K **Privately Held**
SIC: 3544 3599 Special dies & tools; jigs & fixtures; machine shop, jobbing & repair

(G-5874)
LAPPANS OF GAYLORD INC
Also Called: John Deere Authorized Dealer
4085 Old Us Highway 27 S (49735-9596)
PHONE.................................989 732-3274
James Lappan Sr, *President*
James A Lappan II, *Vice Pres*
Barbara Lappan, *Admin Sec*
EMP: 7
SQ FT: 2,000
SALES (est): 847K **Privately Held**
WEB: www.lappans.com
SIC: 3679 5082 Power supplies, all types: static; construction & mining machinery

(G-5875)
LOSHAW BROS INC
231 Meecher Rd (49735-9372)
P.O. Box 1761 (49734-5761)
PHONE.................................989 732-7263
Thomas Loshaw, *President*
Brenda Loshaw, *Vice Pres*
Stacy Loshaw, *Office Mgr*
EMP: 5
SQ FT: 2,000
SALES (est): 1.4MM **Privately Held**
SIC: 1389 7389 Oil field services; crane & aerial lift service

(G-5876)
MARBLE ERA PRODUCTS INC
2146 Deepwoods Dr (49735-9116)
PHONE.................................989 742-4513
David S Bickley, *President*
Sharon De Rossett, *Manager*
David Pbickley, *Manager*
Mel Wierzbicki, *Manager*
EMP: 20 **EST:** 1975
SQ FT: 14,000
SALES (est): 178.5K **Privately Held**
WEB: www.marbleera.com
SIC: 3281 Household articles, except furniture: cut stone; bathroom fixtures, cut stone

(G-5877)
MARK ONE CORPORATION
517 Alpine Rd (49735-9531)
PHONE.................................989 732-2427
Francis J Kestler, *President*
Mark Leighton, *Business Mgr*
Keith Crandall, *Vice Pres*
Jason Kniss, *Engineer*
Timothy Schmidt, *Design Engr*
EMP: 100
SQ FT: 50,000
SALES (est): 24.7MM **Privately Held**
WEB: www.markonecorp.com
SIC: 3549 3569 3535 Assembly machines, including robotic; lubricating equipment; conveyors & conveying equipment

(G-5878)
MAYFAIR ACCESSORIES INC
1639 Calkins Dr (49735-9501)
PHONE.................................989 732-8400
John Behnke, *President*
EMP: 4
SALES (est): 360.3K **Privately Held**
SIC: 2759 Imprinting

(G-5879)
MAYFAIR GOLF ACCESSORIES
1639 Calkins Dr (49735-9501)
PHONE.................................989 732-8400
Kevin Alread, *Owner*
John Benke, *Senior VP*
▲ **EMP:** 12
SALES (est): 945.1K **Privately Held**
SIC: 2396 3993 Printing & embossing on plastics fabric articles; signs & advertising specialties

(G-5880)
MAYFAIR PLASTICS INC
845 Dickerson Rd (49735-9204)
P.O. Box 995 (49734-0995)
PHONE.................................989 732-2441
Carl R Janssens, *CEO*
Scott Weir, *President*
Michelle Schwarz, *Vice Pres*
▲ **EMP:** 85
SQ FT: 40,000
SALES (est): 30.9MM **Privately Held**
WEB: www.mayfair.net
SIC: 3089 Injection molding of plastics

(G-5881)
MICHAEL R BURZYNSKI
1636 Big Lake Rd (49735-8210)
PHONE.................................989 732-1820
EMP: 3
SALES (est): 260K **Privately Held**
SIC: 1311 Crude Petroleum/Natural Gas Production

(G-5882)
MID NORTH PRINTING INC
316 W 2nd St (49735-1727)
PHONE.................................989 732-1313
Doug Johnson, *President*
EMP: 7
SALES (est): 816.4K **Privately Held**
SIC: 2752 Commercial printing, offset

(G-5883)
MID-STATES BOLT & SCREW CO
1069 Orourke Blvd (49735-9505)
PHONE.................................989 732-3265
Charles Schepperley, *Branch Mgr*
EMP: 12
SALES (corp-wide): 59MM **Privately Held**
WEB: www.midstatesbolt.com
SIC: 5072 3452 Miscellaneous fasteners; bolts, nuts, rivets & washers
PA: Mid-States Bolt & Screw Co.
4126 Somers Dr
Burton MI 48529
810 744-0123

(G-5884)
MUZYL OIL CORP
922 N Center Ave (49735-9375)
P.O. Box 673 (49734-0673)
PHONE.................................989 732-8100
William Muzyl, *President*
EMP: 3 **EST:** 1988
SQ FT: 3,000
SALES (est): 368.9K **Privately Held**
SIC: 1382 Oil & gas exploration services

(G-5885)
NORTHERN TANK TRUCK SERVICE
10764 Old Us Highway 27 S (49735)
P.O. Box 8, Waters (49797-0008)
PHONE.................................989 732-7531
Gary Courtright, *President*
Donald Nicewander, *President*
Dorothy Courtright, *Corp Secy*
EMP: 8
SALES: 650K **Privately Held**
SIC: 1389 1794 Oil field services; excavation work

(G-5886)
OTSEGO COUNTY HERALD TIMES
Also Called: Gaylord Herald Times
2058 S Otsego Ave (49735-9422)
PHONE.................................989 732-1111
Doug Caldwell, *President*
EMP: 14
SALES (est): 912.2K
SALES (corp-wide): 9.2MM **Privately Held**
WEB: www.heraldtimes.com
SIC: 2711 Newspapers: publishing only, not printed on site
PA: Northern Michigan Review, Inc.
319 State St
Petoskey MI 49770
231 547-6558

(G-5887)
P I W CORPORATION
Also Called: Waterjetplus
1492 Orourke Blvd (49735-9506)
PHONE.................................989 448-2501
Todd Shepherd, *President*
EMP: 8 **EST:** 1983
SALES (est): 377.2K **Privately Held**
SIC: 2221 3441 Fiberglass fabrics; fabricated structural metal

(G-5888)
PERFECTO INDUSTRIES INC (PA)
1567 Calkins Dr (49735-9501)
PHONE.................................989 732-2941
Kevin Roberts, *President*
Mike Skop, *Engineer*
◆ **EMP:** 45
SQ FT: 50,000
SALES (est): 12.9MM **Privately Held**
WEB: www.perfectoindustries.com
SIC: 3547 3549 3599 3537 Rolling mill machinery; coiling machinery; custom machinery; industrial trucks & tractors

(G-5889)
RLH INDUSTRIES INC
1574 Calkins Dr (49735-9501)
PHONE.................................989 732-0493
Robert Huta, *President*
Lisa Huta, *Vice Pres*
EMP: 10
SQ FT: 7,800
SALES (est): 907.5K **Privately Held**
WEB: www.chim-flex.com
SIC: 3433 3443 Heating equipment, except electric; liners/lining

(G-5890)
ROXBURY CREEK LLC
207 Arrowhead Trl (49735-9013)
PHONE.................................989 731-2062
Keithr R Martell Jr,
EMP: 4
SALES: 5K **Privately Held**
SIC: 2411 Logging

(G-5891)
RUSSELL R PETERS CO LLC
1370 Pineview St (49735-7400)
PHONE.................................989 732-0660
William T Peters,
EMP: 5 **EST:** 1930
SQ FT: 21,000

SALES (est): 3.3MM **Privately Held**
WEB: www.russellpeterspackaging.com
SIC: **2653** 3086 5113 2675 Corrugated boxes, partitions, display items, sheets & pad; packaging & shipping materials, foamed plastic; insulation or cushioning material, foamed plastic; padding, foamed plastic; corrugated & solid fiber boxes; containers, paper & disposable plastic; die-cut paper & board; fiber cans, drums & similar products

(G-5892)
SCENTMATCHERS LLC
514 Camp Ten Rd (49735-9229)
P.O. Box 1550 (49734-5550)
PHONE..................................800 859-9878
Adam Schultz, *President*
EMP: 4
SALES (est): 403.8K **Privately Held**
SIC: **2844** 7389 Perfumes & colognes;

(G-5893)
STELLAR COMPUTER SERVICES LLC
633 Crestwood Dr (49735-9141)
PHONE..................................989 732-7153
Robert Erat,
EMP: 4
SQ FT: 18,000
SALES (est): 206.9K **Privately Held**
SIC: **7378** 3571 Computer & data processing equipment repair/maintenance; computers, digital, analog or hybrid

(G-5894)
TANK TRUCK SERVICE & SALES INC
1981 Engel Ave (49735-7416)
PHONE..................................989 731-4887
Jeff Lawer, *Manager*
EMP: 5
SALES (corp-wide): 14.3MM **Privately Held**
SIC: **3541** Machine tools, metal cutting type
PA: Tank Truck Service & Sales, Inc.
25150 Dequindre Rd
Warren MI 48091
586 757-6500

(G-5895)
TIMBERLINE LOGGING INC
855 Dickerson Rd (49735-9204)
P.O. Box 395, Johannesburg (49751-0395)
PHONE..................................989 731-2794
James Payne Jr, *President*
EMP: 15
SQ FT: 1,000
SALES (est): 1.9MM **Privately Held**
SIC: **2411** Logging camps & contractors

(G-5896)
TNT WELL SERVICE LTD
6310 Ranger Lake Rd (49735-8574)
PHONE..................................989 939-7098
Tim Jennings, *Owner*
Debbie Jennings, *Co-Owner*
EMP: 3 EST: 1999
SALES (est): 376.5K **Privately Held**
SIC: **1389** Servicing oil & gas wells

(G-5897)
TOP OMICHIGAN RECLAIMERS INC
620 E Main St (49735-8519)
PHONE..................................989 705-7983
Philip J Mason, *President*
Henry Mason, *Vice Pres*
Lisa H Mason, *Treasurer*
Sarah Butler, *Admin Sec*
EMP: 4
SALES: 150K **Privately Held**
SIC: **1442** Gravel mining

(G-5898)
UPPER MICHIGAN NEWSPAPERS LLC
Also Called: Star Publication
1966 S Otsego Ave (49735-8489)
PHONE..................................989 732-5125
John Sherlock, *Controller*
◆ EMP: 15
SQ FT: 3,000
SALES (est): 590.2K **Privately Held**
SIC: **2741** Guides: publishing only, not printed on site

(G-5899)
W L SNOW ENTERPRISES INC
2017 Dickerson Rd (49735-7452)
PHONE..................................989 732-9501
William L Snow, *CEO*
W P Snow, *President*
Verna E Snow, *Corp Secy*
EMP: 3
SQ FT: 1,200
SALES (est): 430.3K **Privately Held**
SIC: **7261** 3272 Crematory; septic tanks, concrete; burial vaults, concrete or pre-cast terrazzo

(G-5900)
WODER CONSTRUCTION INC
3661 Nowak Rd (49735-9312)
P.O. Box 993 (49734-0993)
PHONE..................................989 731-6371
Timothy Woder, *President*
EMP: 27
SALES (est): 3.8MM **Privately Held**
SIC: **1389** Oil field services

Germfask
Schoolcraft County

(G-5901)
END OF ROAD WINERY LLC
6917 Burns Rd Unit 1 (49836-9036)
PHONE..................................906 450-1541
James Barker, *Principal*
EMP: 3
SALES (est): 72.6K **Privately Held**
SIC: **2084** Wines

(G-5902)
W J Z & SONS HARVESTING INC
481 Lustila Rd (49836-9041)
PHONE..................................906 586-6360
William Zellar, *President*
EMP: 27
SALES (est): 3.3MM **Privately Held**
SIC: **2411** Logging camps & contractors

(G-5903)
ZELLAR FOREST PRODUCTS
Also Called: John Zellar Jr Forest Products
462 Lustila Rd (49836-9041)
PHONE..................................906 586-9817
John Zellar Jr, *Owner*
EMP: 9
SALES (est): 831.7K **Privately Held**
SIC: **2411** 1794 Logging; excavation work

Gibraltar
Wayne County

(G-5904)
HYCAL CORP
Also Called: Ferrous Cal Co.
27800 W Jefferson Ave (48173-9796)
PHONE..................................216 671-6161
Eduardo Gonzalez, *President*
Reed McGivney, *Exec VP*
Anthony Potelicki, *Vice Pres*
David Hill, *CFO*
EMP: 15
SQ FT: 560,000
SALES (est): 1.5MM
SALES (corp-wide): 65.1MM **Privately Held**
SIC: **3398** Annealing of metal
PA: Ferragon Corporation
11103 Memphis Ave
Cleveland OH 44144
216 671-6161

(G-5905)
JB EQUIPMENT LLC
20200 Woodruff Rd (48173-9757)
PHONE..................................219 285-0668
Joshua Parsons, *Mng Member*
Wayne Parsons, *Mng Member*
EMP: 32
SQ FT: 20,000
SALES (est): 5.7MM **Privately Held**
SIC: **3443** Industrial vessels, tanks & containers

Gladstone
Delta County

(G-5906)
BAY DE NOC LURE COMPANY
810 Railway Ave (49837-1639)
P.O. Box 71 (49837-0071)
PHONE..................................906 428-1133
David Nyberg, *Partner*
Anders Nyberg, *Partner*
EMP: 10 EST: 1955
SQ FT: 4,000
SALES (est): 847.3K **Privately Held**
WEB: www.baydenoclure.com
SIC: **3949** Lures, fishing: artificial

(G-5907)
BRAMCO CONTAINERS INC
824 Clark Dr (49837-8966)
PHONE..................................906 428-2855
John O'Driscoll, *President*
Stephen O'Driscoll, *Vice Pres*
EMP: 8
SQ FT: 11,500
SALES: 800K **Privately Held**
WEB: www.bramcocontainers.com
SIC: **2653** Boxes, corrugated: made from purchased materials

(G-5908)
BUCKS SPORTS PRODUCTS INC
Also Called: Thesnowmobilestore.com
7721 Lake Bluff 19.4 Rd (49837-2448)
PHONE..................................763 229-1331
David Buckland, *President*
EMP: 5
SQ FT: 60
SALES: 500K **Privately Held**
SIC: **3949** Sporting & athletic goods

(G-5909)
BUGAY LOGGING
8409 N P.11 Dr (49837-2654)
PHONE..................................906 428-2125
Joe Bugay, *Principal*
EMP: 3 EST: 2013
SALES (est): 222K **Privately Held**
SIC: **2411** Logging

(G-5910)
CRL INC
Also Called: Marbels Outdoors
623 Rains Dr (49837-1156)
PHONE..................................906 428-3710
George Brinkley, *CEO*
Craig Lauerman, *President*
James Lauerman, *Vice Pres*
▲ EMP: 25 EST: 1964
SQ FT: 20,000
SALES (est): 3MM **Privately Held**
WEB: www.marblearms.com
SIC: **3484** 3949 3827 3421 Shotguns or shotgun parts, 30 mm. & below; sporting & athletic goods; optical instruments & lenses; cutlery

(G-5911)
DAVID HIRN CABINETS AND CONTG
1319 Delta Ave (49837-1315)
PHONE..................................906 428-1935
David Hirn, *President*
EMP: 5
SALES (est): 367.3K **Privately Held**
SIC: **2434** Wood kitchen cabinets

(G-5912)
DAWZYE EXCAVATION INC
7575 Rays M.7 Cir 7m (49837-9022)
PHONE..................................906 786-5276
Michael Bruce, *Principal*
EMP: 3
SALES (est): 231.6K **Privately Held**
SIC: **2411** Logging

(G-5913)
DELFAB INC
103 N 12th St (49837-1423)
P.O. Box 144 (49837-0144)
PHONE..................................906 428-9570
William Westlund, *President*
EMP: 23
SALES (est): 1MM **Privately Held**
WEB: www.delfab.com
SIC: **3548** Soldering equipment, except hand soldering irons

(G-5914)
K & M INDUSTRIAL LLC
80 Delta Ave (49837-1904)
PHONE..................................906 420-8770
Sarah Hoffmeyer, *CFO*
Josh King, *Info Tech Mgr*
EMP: 6
SALES: 200K **Privately Held**
SIC: **3561** 3441 2411 1629 Cylinders, pump; boat & barge sections, prefabricated metal; timber, cut at logging camp; dredging contractor; building construction consultant; industrial buildings, new construction

(G-5915)
LITTLE BAY CONCRETE PRODUCTS
119 N 9th St (49837-1644)
P.O. Box 342 (49837-0342)
PHONE..................................906 428-9859
John Kloet, *CEO*
Steve Delaire, *Treasurer*
Harlan Koulliard, *Admin Sec*
EMP: 6 EST: 1947
SQ FT: 1,000
SALES (est): 770.3K **Privately Held**
SIC: **3273** Ready-mixed concrete

(G-5916)
MARBLES GUN SIGHTS INC
Also Called: Marble Arms
420 Indl Pk Dr (49837)
P.O. Box 111 (49837-0111)
PHONE..................................906 428-3710
Craig R Lauerman, *CEO*
EMP: 5 EST: 2006
SALES (est): 165.5K **Privately Held**
SIC: **3484** Guns (firearms) or gun parts, 30 mm. & below

(G-5917)
NORTHERN MICHIGAN VENEERS INC
710 Rains Dr (49837-1129)
P.O. Box 352 (49837-0352)
PHONE..................................906 428-1082
John D Besse, *President*
Melissa Besse, *Treasurer*
Greg Besse, *Admin Sec*
▲ EMP: 65
SQ FT: 40,000
SALES: 25MM
SALES (corp-wide): 117.9MM **Privately Held**
SIC: **2435** Veneer stock, hardwood
PA: Forest Besse Products Inc
933 N 8th St
Gladstone MI 49837
906 428-3113

(G-5918)
PARDON INC
3510 State Highway M35 (49837-2652)
PHONE..................................906 428-3494
James Pardon, *President*
EMP: 40
SQ FT: 7,200
SALES (est): 7.1MM **Privately Held**
SIC: **3714** 3444 Hydraulic fluid power pumps for auto steering mechanism; cylinder heads, motor vehicle; sheet metalwork

(G-5919)
PISCES FISH MACHINERY INC (PA)
7036 Us Highway 2 41 M35 (49837-2503)
P.O. Box 189, Wells (49894-0189)
PHONE..................................906 789-1636
Trevor Wastell, *President*
Mathew Wastell, *Vice Pres*
▲ EMP: 22

SQ FT: 9,500
SALES: 3.3MM **Privately Held**
WEB: www.pisces-ind.com
SIC: 3556 Fish & shellfish processing machinery; poultry processing machinery

(G-5920)
SUPERIOR LUMBER INC
8000 County 426 M.5 Rd (49837-9107)
PHONE..................................906 786-1638
Robert Manninen, *President*
Laura Manninen, *Corp Secy*
EMP: 8
SALES (est): 540K **Privately Held**
SIC: 2421 Sawmills & planing mills, general

(G-5921)
VANAIRE INC
Also Called: Gladstone Metals
840 Clark Dr (49837-8966)
PHONE..................................906 428-4656
Steven Soderman, *CEO*
William Vandevusse, *President*
Beverly Vusse, *CFO*
EMP: 82
SQ FT: 48,000
SALES (est): 20.4MM **Privately Held**
WEB: www.gladstonemetals.com
SIC: 3589 Water treatment equipment, industrial

Gladwin
Gladwin County

(G-5922)
ACCURATE MACHINING & FABG INC
1650 S M 30 (48624-8474)
PHONE..................................989 426-5400
Marshall Grimmett, *CEO*
EMP: 4
SQ FT: 6,880
SALES (est): 316.1K **Privately Held**
SIC: 3599 Machine shop, jobbing & repair

(G-5923)
BOAT GUARD INC
3577 N West Branch Dr (48624-7933)
PHONE..................................989 424-1490
John Highfield, *President*
▲ EMP: 4 EST: 2010
SALES (est): 321.9K **Privately Held**
SIC: 2394 7389 Convertible tops, canvas or boat: from purchased materials;

(G-5924)
BOBCAT OIL & GAS INC (PA)
901 E Cedar Ave (48624-2252)
P.O. Box 483 (48624-0483)
PHONE..................................989 426-4375
Gordon Tuck, *President*
Joyce Tuck, *Admin Sec*
EMP: 6
SALES (est): 1.4MM **Privately Held**
SIC: 1382 Oil & gas exploration services

(G-5925)
CAM PACKAGING LLC
705 Weaver Ct (48624-1718)
PHONE..................................989 426-1200
Robert Oberloier, *President*
EMP: 12
SQ FT: 48,000
SALES: 2MM **Privately Held**
SIC: 2671 Packaging paper & plastics film, coated & laminated

(G-5926)
CAMERON KIRK FOREST PDTS INC
1467 S Shearer Rd (48624-9442)
PHONE..................................989 426-3439
Judy Cameron, *President*
Kirk Cameron, *Vice Pres*
EMP: 5
SALES: 200K **Privately Held**
SIC: 3713 Truck & bus bodies

(G-5927)
CHRIS MUMA FOREST PRODUCTS
1154 W 1st St (48624-1017)
P.O. Box 17 (48624-0017)
PHONE..................................989 426-5916
Chris Muma, *President*
Jamie Shell, *Admin Sec*
EMP: 17
SALES (est): 2.8MM **Privately Held**
SIC: 2411 Wood chips, produced in the field; logging camps & contractors

(G-5928)
D&W FINE PACK LLC
1191 Wolfson Ct (48624-7026)
PHONE..................................866 296-2020
EMP: 7
SALES (corp-wide): 614.5MM **Privately Held**
SIC: 3089 Plastic kitchenware, tableware & houseware
HQ: D&W Fine Pack Llc
777 Mark St
Wood Dale IL 60191

(G-5929)
E & D ENGINEERING SYSTEMS LLC
890 Industrial Dr (48624-1704)
PHONE..................................989 246-0770
Ed Wark, *Partner*
Debby Wark, *Partner*
▼ EMP: 4
SALES (est): 200K **Privately Held**
SIC: 3089 3599 Plastic processing; machine & other job shop work; custom machinery

(G-5930)
GLADWIN MACHINE INC
535 S M 18 (48624-9333)
PHONE..................................989 426-8753
Richard E Kinkela, *President*
Bunny Book, *CFO*
EMP: 8 EST: 1966
SQ FT: 6,000
SALES: 800K **Privately Held**
SIC: 3544 3599 Special dies & tools; machine shop, jobbing & repair

(G-5931)
GLADWIN METAL PROCESSING INC
795 E Maple St (48624-1717)
PHONE..................................989 426-9038
Lloyd R Bowen, *President*
Jean Bowen, *Vice Pres*
Carole Govitz, *Admin Sec*
EMP: 7
SQ FT: 16,000
SALES: 535K **Privately Held**
SIC: 3471 3479 Electroplating of metals or formed products; lacquering of metal products

(G-5932)
GLADWIN TANK MANUFACTURING INC
207 Industrial Park Ave (48624-1799)
PHONE..................................989 426-4768
Beverly Grove, *President*
Thane Grove, *Vice Pres*
EMP: 17
SQ FT: 28,500
SALES: 3.3MM **Privately Held**
WEB: www.gladwintank.com
SIC: 3443 3444 Tanks, standard or custom fabricated: metal plate; sheet metalwork

(G-5933)
LOOSE PLASTICS INC
1016 E 1st St (48624-1268)
PHONE..................................989 246-1880
Scott C Loose, *CEO*
Joshua Loose, *Vice Pres*
Mike Orr, *Vice Pres*
Jamie A Loose, *Treasurer*
EMP: 120
SQ FT: 144,000
SALES (est): 35.4MM **Privately Held**
SIC: 3081 Unsupported plastics film & sheet

(G-5934)
R V WOLVERINE
1088 N M 18 (48624-9202)
PHONE..................................989 426-9241
Howard Smith, *Owner*
EMP: 10
SALES (est): 656.7K **Privately Held**
SIC: 3792 3711 Campers, for mounting on trucks; motor homes, self-contained, assembly of

(G-5935)
ROLL RITE CORPORATION
650 Indl Pk Ave (48624)
PHONE..................................989 345-3434
Keith Searfoss, *Principal*
Rob Neering, *Principal*
Steve Hunter, *Vice Pres*
Jim Kenyon, *Vice Pres*
Scott Kartes, *Engineer*
▲ EMP: 46 EST: 1991
SQ FT: 53,000
SALES (est): 10.7MM **Privately Held**
WEB: www.rollrite.com
SIC: 3466 Closures, stamped metal

(G-5936)
ROLL-RITE LLC
Also Called: Roll Rite Group Holdings
650 Industrial Dr (48624-1708)
PHONE..................................989 345-3434
Brad Templeman, *CEO*
Keith Searfoss, *President*
Jim Kenyon, *Vice Pres*
Robert Neering, *CFO*
Jeremy Tennant, *Executive*
▲ EMP: 40
SALES (est): 1.2MM
SALES (corp-wide): 112.8MM **Privately Held**
SIC: 3466 Closures, stamped metal
HQ: Roll Rite Group Holdings Llc
650 Industrial Dr
Gladwin MI 48624
989 345-3434

(G-5937)
SHAWN MUMA
2315 Dassay Rd (48624-9761)
PHONE..................................989 426-9505
Shawn Muma, *Owner*
EMP: 3
SALES (est): 196.6K **Privately Held**
SIC: 2411 Logging

(G-5938)
SHAWN MUMA LOGGING
2315 Dassay Rd (48624-9761)
PHONE..................................989 426-6852
Shawn Muma, *Owner*
EMP: 8
SALES (est): 789.5K **Privately Held**
SIC: 2411 Logging camps & contractors

(G-5939)
WILLIAM R HALL KIMBERLY
Also Called: Hall Mat
4083 Cassidy Rd (48624-8900)
PHONE..................................989 426-4605
William R Hall, *Principal*
EMP: 4 EST: 2010
SALES (est): 445.1K **Privately Held**
SIC: 1311 Crude petroleum & natural gas

Glen Arbor
Leelanau County

(G-5940)
CHERRY REPUBLIC INC (PA)
6026 S Lake St (49636-5115)
P.O. Box 677 (49636-0677)
PHONE..................................231 334-3150
Robert Sutherland, *President*
Terry Hornbaker, *Prdtn Mgr*
Sara Budzik, *Research*
Nathaniel Gray, *Controller*
Jason Homa, *VP Sales*
EMP: 75
SALES (est): 12.7MM **Privately Held**
WEB: www.cherryrepublic.com
SIC: 2052 2033 5499 5812 Cookies; barbecue sauce: packaged in cans, jars, etc.; gourmet food stores; snack shop

(G-5941)
NORTHWODS PRPERTY HOLDINGS LLC
Also Called: Northwoods Hardware
6053 S Glen Lake Rd (49636-9771)
PHONE..................................231 334-3000
Jeff Gietzen, *General Mgr*
Kyle Lautner, *Mng Member*
EMP: 5
SALES: 1MM **Privately Held**
SIC: 5251 3559 7699 Hardware; glass cutting machinery; locksmith shop

Glennie
Alcona County

(G-5942)
GRIFF & SON TREE SERVICE INC
2921 Lakeshore Dr (48737-9396)
PHONE..................................989 735-5160
Gary Griffith, *President*
EMP: 5
SALES: 150K **Privately Held**
SIC: 0783 3531 Removal services, bush & tree; chippers: brush, limb & log

(G-5943)
INMAN FOREST PRODUCTS INC
4171 Fraser Rd (48737-9320)
PHONE..................................989 370-4473
Jack Inman, *President*
EMP: 3 EST: 1996
SALES (est): 425.8K **Privately Held**
SIC: 2411 Logging camps & contractors

(G-5944)
LONE WOLF CUSTOM BOWS
Also Called: Lone Wolf Archery
3893 Gray St (48737-9371)
PHONE..................................989 735-3358
Moira Maus, *Owner*
EMP: 4
SALES (est): 215.8K **Privately Held**
WEB: www.lonewolfcustombows.com
SIC: 3949 Bows, archery

(G-5945)
MC GUIRE MILL & LUMBER
4499 Ford Rd (48737-9749)
PHONE..................................989 735-3851
Richard Mc Guire, *Owner*
EMP: 4 EST: 1975
SALES (est): 395.1K **Privately Held**
SIC: 2421 5211 Sawmills & planing mills, general; lumber & other building materials

Gobles
Van Buren County

(G-5946)
ALLOY STEEL TREATING COMPANY
22138 M 40 (49055-8708)
P.O. Box 28 (49055-0028)
PHONE..................................269 628-2154
Scott Wesler, *President*
Cheryl Wesler, *Manager*
EMP: 16 EST: 1963
SQ FT: 15,000
SALES (est): 3.6MM **Privately Held**
SIC: 3398 Metal heat treating

(G-5947)
H & R WOOD SPECIALTIES INC
20783 County Road 653 (49055-9241)
PHONE..................................269 628-2181
Jim Hurst, *President*
Kevin McMahon, *General Mgr*
Robert Mercier, *Engineer*
Paul Haluch, *Project Engr*
Shane Harth, *Manager*
EMP: 20
SQ FT: 36,000
SALES (est): 3.6MM **Privately Held**
SIC: 3083 2426 2541 2431 Plastic finished products, laminated; furniture stock & parts, hardwood; display fixtures, wood; trim, wood

Gobles - Van Buren County (G-5948)

(G-5948)
PILLAR MANUFACTURING INC
35620 County Road 388 (49055-8618)
P.O. Box 414 (49055-0414)
PHONE..................................269 628-5605
Beth Pillar, *President*
Greg Pillar, *Vice Pres*
▲ **EMP:** 15
SQ FT: 12,000
SALES (est): 4.4MM **Privately Held**
WEB: www.pillarmfg.com
SIC: 3532 Mining machinery

(G-5949)
RENDON & SONS MACHINING INC
21870 M 40 (49055-8621)
PHONE..................................269 628-2200
Jesse Rendon, *President*
James Rendon, *Vice Pres*
EMP: 10
SQ FT: 7,000
SALES (est): 1.5MM **Privately Held**
SIC: 3599 3443 Machine shop, jobbing & repair; weldments

(G-5950)
WAHMHOFF FARMS LLC
11121 M 40 (49055-8639)
PHONE..................................269 628-4308
Ken Wahmoff, *Partner*
Dan Wahmhoff, *Partner*
Lorie Wahmhoff, *Manager*
EMP: 10
SQ FT: 600
SALES (est): 1.2MM **Privately Held**
WEB: www.mitrees.com
SIC: 0811 3441 0782 0181 Christmas tree farm; fabricated structural metal; lawn & garden services; ornamental nursery products; nurseries & garden centers; flowers & florists' supplies

Goodrich
Genesee County

(G-5951)
AZTEC AZPHALT TECHNOLOGY INC
12447 Kipp Rd (48438-9795)
PHONE..................................248 627-2120
Lawrence D Bond, *President*
EMP: 3 **EST:** 1985
SALES (est): 288.4K **Privately Held**
SIC: 2951 Asphalt paving mixtures & blocks

(G-5952)
BURKLAND INC (PA)
6520 S State Rd (48438-8710)
PHONE..................................810 636-2233
Scott P Nelson, *President*
David B Bronowski, *COO*
Wayne Morey, *Safety Mgr*
Mike McHugh, *Production*
Pat Thomas, *Engineer*
▲ **EMP:** 61 **EST:** 1961
SQ FT: 77,000
SALES (est): 33.6MM **Privately Held**
SIC: 3465 3469 3544 Automotive stampings; stamping metal for the trade; special dies, tools, jigs & fixtures

(G-5953)
FENTON SYSTEMS INC
7160 S State Rd Ste B (48438-8757)
PHONE..................................810 636-6318
James F Schembri, *President*
Kathy Thompson, *Prdtn Mgr*
James Crone, *Director*
Rick Rathke, *Director*
EMP: 7
SQ FT: 5,000
SALES: 987.1K **Privately Held**
WEB: www.fentonsystems.com
SIC: 3625 7373 Relays & industrial controls; systems integration services

(G-5954)
JANS SPORT SHOP INC
7285 S State Rd (48438-8860)
P.O. Box 266 (48438-0266)
PHONE..................................810 636-2241

Janet Hempton, *President*
EMP: 15
SQ FT: 10,000
SALES (est): 2.2MM **Privately Held**
WEB: www.janssports.com
SIC: 5551 3732 5699 Motor boat dealers; outboard motors; boat building & repairing; sports apparel

(G-5955)
KENS REDI MIX INC (PA)
8016 S State Rd (48438-8864)
P.O. Box 339 (48438-0339)
PHONE..................................810 238-4931
Jayme Simmonds, *Principal*
Jeff Bailey, *Comptroller*
EMP: 8
SQ FT: 1,500
SALES (est): 3.7MM **Privately Held**
SIC: 3273 Ready-mixed concrete

(G-5956)
PORTERS ORCHARDS FARM MARKET
12160 Hegel Rd (48438-9271)
PHONE..................................810 636-7156
Raymond Porter, *Owner*
Maxine Porter, *Co-Owner*
EMP: 15
SQ FT: 4,000
SALES (est): 429.6K **Privately Held**
SIC: 0175 2099 5431 Apple orchard; cider, nonalcoholic; fruit & vegetable markets

(G-5957)
SCHNEIDER NATIONAL INC
10316 Gale Rd (48438-9046)
PHONE..................................810 636-2220
Mark Schall, *Branch Mgr*
EMP: 10
SALES (corp-wide): 4.9B **Publicly Held**
SIC: 3559 Automotive related machinery
PA: Schneider National, Inc.
3101 Packerland Dr
Green Bay WI 54313
920 592-2000

Grand Blanc
Genesee County

(G-5958)
ALRO STEEL CORPORATION
3000 Tri Park Dr (48439-7020)
PHONE..................................810 695-7300
William McMurphy, *Manager*
EMP: 65
SQ FT: 70,000
SALES (corp-wide): 2.2B **Privately Held**
WEB: www.alro.com
SIC: 5051 3441 Steel; fabricated structural metal
PA: Alro Steel Corporation
3100 E High St
Jackson MI 49203
517 787-5500

(G-5959)
BARRON PRECISION INSTRUMENTS
8170 Embury Rd (48439-8192)
P.O. Box 973 (48480-0973)
PHONE..................................810 695-2080
Mark Barron, *President*
EMP: 28 **EST:** 1947
SALES (est): 4.4MM **Privately Held**
WEB: www.bpic.com
SIC: 3841 Skin grafting equipment

(G-5960)
BEHIND SHUTTER LLC
7070 Anna St (48439-8571)
PHONE..................................248 467-7237
Jessica Butterworth, *Principal*
EMP: 3
SALES (est): 139.7K **Privately Held**
SIC: 3442 Shutters, door or window: metal

(G-5961)
BURGAFLEX NORTH AMERICA INC
8186 Industrial Park Dr (48439-1865)
PHONE..................................810 584-7296

▼ **EMP:** 25
SALES (est): 5.1MM **Privately Held**
SIC: 3317 Steel pipe & tubes

(G-5962)
BURTRUM FURS
321 E Grand Blanc Rd (48439-1346)
P.O. Box 300528, Drayton Plains (48330-0528)
PHONE..................................810 771-4563
Amy Burtrum, *Principal*
EMP: 3
SALES (est): 158.6K **Privately Held**
SIC: 3999 Furs

(G-5963)
COMET INFORMATION SYSTEMS LLC
Also Called: Carefluence
8359 Office Park Dr (48439-2078)
PHONE..................................248 686-2600
Lloyd Williams, *COO*
Aditya Ayyagari, *CTO*
EMP: 15
SQ FT: 5,000
SALES (est): 305.2K **Privately Held**
SIC: 7372 Prepackaged software

(G-5964)
DAKOTA CUPCAKE FACTORY
10529 Village Ct (48439-9464)
PHONE..................................810 694-7198
Linda Burns, *Principal*
EMP: 4 **EST:** 2010
SALES (est): 208.4K **Privately Held**
SIC: 2051 Bread, cake & related products

(G-5965)
DOZY DOTES LLC
4493 Crimson Ct Ste 200 (48439-9056)
PHONE..................................866 870-1048
Richard Winkler, *Mng Member*
EMP: 3 **EST:** 2006
SQ FT: 7,000
SALES: 500K **Privately Held**
SIC: 2519 Household furniture, except wood or metal: upholstered

(G-5966)
GLOBAL IMPACT GROUP LLC
Also Called: Global Vehicle Works
9082 S Saginaw Rd (48439-9577)
PHONE..................................248 895-9900
Daniel Kocks,
EMP: 6
SALES (est): 1MM **Privately Held**
SIC: 8748 3711 Business consulting; automobile assembly, including specialty automobiles

(G-5967)
GRAND BLANC CEMENT PDTS INC (PA)
10709 Center Rd (48439-1032)
P.O. Box 585 (48480-0585)
PHONE..................................810 694-7500
Kenneth E Minnock, *Ch of Bd*
Norman A Nelson, *President*
Steven K Minnock, *Exec VP*
Michael J Hicks, *Vice Pres*
EMP: 45
SQ FT: 14,320
SALES (est): 9.9MM **Privately Held**
WEB: www.grandblanccement.com
SIC: 3271 5211 Blocks, concrete or cinder: standard; brick

(G-5968)
GRAND BLANC PRINTING INC
9449 Holly Rd (48439-8396)
PHONE..................................810 694-1155
Morton Stebbins, *President*
EMP: 37
SQ FT: 14,000
SALES (est): 6.5MM **Privately Held**
WEB: www.grandblancprinting.com
SIC: 2752 2759 2791 2789 Commercial printing, offset; newspapers: printing; typesetting; bookbinding & related work

(G-5969)
HERRMANN AEROSPACE
5202 Moceri Ln (48439-4330)
PHONE..................................810 695-1758
Robert Herrmann, *Principal*

EMP: 3
SALES (est): 165.6K **Privately Held**
SIC: 3812 Aircraft/aerospace flight instruments & guidance systems

(G-5970)
INFECTION PREVENTION TECH LLC
1245 E Grand Blanc Rd (48439-6325)
PHONE..................................248 340-8800
Mark Statham,
EMP: 8
SALES (est): 1.1MM **Privately Held**
SIC: 3648 Lighting equipment

(G-5971)
INNOVATIVE PROGRAMMING SYSTEMS
Also Called: Computer Assistanc
8210 S Saginaw St Ste 1 (48439-2463)
PHONE..................................810 695-9332
Duane Zimmer, *President*
EMP: 5
SALES (est): 607.1K **Privately Held**
WEB: www.ipsdev.com
SIC: 7372 7371 Prepackaged software; computer software systems analysis & design, custom

(G-5972)
KING STEEL CORPORATION (PA)
Also Called: American Rod Consumers
5225 E Cook Rd Ste K (48439-8388)
PHONE..................................800 638-2530
John King, *CEO*
Doug King, *Principal*
Dave Scribner, *Vice Pres*
Dennis Laga, *Inv Control Mgr*
Don Johnson, *CFO*
▲ **EMP:** 20 **EST:** 2010
SQ FT: 2,000
SALES (est): 24.2MM **Privately Held**
WEB: www.kingsteelcorp.com
SIC: 5051 3312 Steel; bar, rod & wire products

(G-5973)
LLOYD TOOL & MFG CORP
5505 Chatham Ln (48439-9742)
PHONE..................................810 694-3519
Richard R Lloyd, *President*
Tamara Garleff, *Corp Secy*
Edwin R Lloyd, *Vice Pres*
EMP: 29 **EST:** 1969
SQ FT: 21,000
SALES (est): 3.4MM **Privately Held**
WEB: www.lloydtool.com
SIC: 3542 3548 3544 3541 Presses: hydraulic & pneumatic, mechanical & manual; welding & cutting apparatus & accessories; special dies, tools, jigs & fixtures; machine tools, metal cutting type

(G-5974)
LOON LAKE PRECISION INC
Also Called: Dave Manson Precision Reamers
8200 Embury Rd Ste 4 (48439-7098)
PHONE..................................810 953-0732
David Manson, *President*
Ann Snyder-Manson, *Vice Pres*
Dara Stinger, *Office Mgr*
EMP: 3
SQ FT: 3,770
SALES (est): 199.6K **Privately Held**
WEB: www.mansonreamers.com
SIC: 3541 5251 Machine tools, metal cutting type; tools

(G-5975)
MACARTHUR CORP (PA)
3190 Tri Park Dr (48439-7088)
P.O. Box 10 (48480-0010)
PHONE..................................810 606-1777
Christie Wong, *CEO*
Tom Barrett, *President*
Michelle Oliver, *Business Mgr*
Angelo Martinez, *QC Mgr*
Omer Sanjay, *Engineer*
EMP: 49
SQ FT: 39,000

GEOGRAPHIC SECTION

Grand Haven - Ottawa County (G-6002)

SALES: 10MM **Privately Held**
WEB: www.macarthurcorp.com
SIC: **2672** 2679 2671 2675 Coated & laminated paper; labels, paper: made from purchased material; packaging paper & plastics film, coated & laminated; die-cut paper & board; commercial printing; gaskets, packing & sealing devices

(G-5976)
NEW TECHNOLOGIES TOOL & MFG
4380 E Baldwin Rd (48439)
P.O. Box 97 (48480-0097)
PHONE 810 694-5426
Andrew Bentley, *President*
John Lively, *Vice Pres*
Donald Schopieray, *Vice Pres*
Karen Bentley, *Financial Exec*
Bob Carbary, *Sales Staff*
EMP: 13
SQ FT: 15,000
SALES: 4.6MM **Privately Held**
SIC: **3599** 3535 Machine shop, jobbing & repair; conveyors & conveying equipment

(G-5977)
PINK PALLET LLC
4176 Knollwood Dr (48439-2025)
PHONE 586 873-2982
Suzanne Perreault, *Principal*
EMP: 4 EST: 2014
SALES (est): 207.4K **Privately Held**
SIC: **2448** Pallets, wood & wood with metal

(G-5978)
PROPRIDE INC
8538 Old Plank Rd (48439-2045)
PHONE 810 695-1127
Sean Woodruff, *Principal*
EMP: 5 EST: 2007
SALES (est): 658.1K **Privately Held**
SIC: **3714** Motor vehicle parts & accessories

(G-5979)
PURE WATER TECH OF MID-MI (PA)
8173 Embury Rd (48439-8192)
PHONE 888 310-9848
James Kasch, *Principal*
EMP: 3
SALES (est): 235.7K **Privately Held**
SIC: **2086** Pasteurized & mineral waters, bottled & canned

(G-5980)
RDC MACHINE INC
Also Called: Kuntz Tool & Die
7503 Fenton Rd (48439-8822)
PHONE 810 695-5587
Richard D Carr, *President*
Jerilynn Carr, *Corp Secy*
EMP: 4
SQ FT: 4,200
SALES (est): 200K **Privately Held**
SIC: **3599** 3544 Machine shop, jobbing & repair; special dies & tools

(G-5981)
ROCKY MTN CHOCLAT FCTRY INC
12821 S Saginaw St (48439-2457)
PHONE 810 606-8550
EMP: 59
SALES (corp-wide): 39.1MM **Publicly Held**
SIC: **2066** 2064 2026 6794 Mfg Chocolate/Cocoa Prdt Mfg Candy/Confectionery Mfg Fluid Milk Patent Owner/Lessor
PA: Rocky Mountain Chocolate Factory, Inc.
265 Turner Dr
Durango CO 81303
949 579-3000

(G-5982)
SASSY FABRICS INC (PA)
11805 S Saginaw St (48439-1311)
PHONE 810 694-0440
Karen Von Mach, *President*
EMP: 3 EST: 2003
SQ FT: 30,000
SALES (est): 978K **Privately Held**
WEB: www.sassysfabbys.com
SIC: **5131** 5949 7641 2391 Coated fabrics; upholstery fabrics, woven; fabric stores piece goods; reupholstery & furniture repair; curtains & draperies; broadwoven fabric mills, manmade

(G-5983)
SELMURO LTD
Also Called: Premier Tooling Systems
3111 Tri Park Dr (48439-7088)
PHONE 810 603-2117
Thomas Self, *CEO*
Richard Ouellette, *President*
Ben Vick, *Engineer*
Matthew Henion, *Design Engr*
Ryan Ouellette, *Sales Staff*
EMP: 27
SQ FT: 17,000
SALES (est): 5.4MM **Privately Held**
WEB: www.ptspremier.com
SIC: **3545** 3542 Cutting tools for machine tools; counterbores, metalworking; reamers, machine tool; die casting machines

(G-5984)
STEEL MASTER LLC
8018 Embury Rd Ste 1 (48439-8186)
PHONE 810 771-4943
James M Shook, *Mng Member*
Gus Andreopoulos, *Mng Member*
Gus Bisbikis, *Mng Member*
Charles Seitz,
EMP: 43
SQ FT: 52,000
SALES (est): 10.4MM **Privately Held**
WEB: www.steelmastertransfer.com
SIC: **3535** 3452 Unit handling conveying systems; washers

(G-5985)
SYCRON TECHNOLOGIES INC
8130 Industrial Park Dr (48439-1864)
PHONE 810 694-4007
Bradley A Thmpson, *President*
EMP: 3
SALES (est): 662.2K **Privately Held**
WEB: www.sycron.com
SIC: **5084** 7373 7371 3714 Machine tools & accessories; computer integrated systems design; computer software systems analysis & design, custom; motor vehicle parts & accessories; relays & industrial controls; metal stampings

(G-5986)
TECSTAR LP
Also Called: Tecstar Grand Blanc Facility
7075 Dort Hwy 600b (48439-8217)
PHONE 734 604-8962
Mike Hayes, *Director*
EMP: 56 **Privately Held**
SIC: **3711** Motor vehicles & car bodies
HQ: Tecstar, Lp
3033 Excelsior Blvd # 300
Minneapolis MN

(G-5987)
VISION SOLUTIONS INC
4417 Brighton Dr (48439-8086)
PHONE 810 695-9569
David Vanitvelt, *Owner*
EMP: 9 **Privately Held**
SIC: **2621** Printing paper
PA: Vision Solutions, Inc.
15300 Barranca Pkwy # 100
Irvine CA 92618

(G-5988)
W M ENTERPRISES
3487 Esson Dr (48439-7935)
PHONE 810 694-4384
Robert Harris, *Principal*
EMP: 3
SALES (est): 126.1K **Privately Held**
SIC: **3999** 5941 Pet supplies; bowling equipment & supplies

(G-5989)
WGS GLOBAL SERVICES LC
7075 Dort Hwy (48439-8217)
PHONE 810 694-3843
Anna Whippie, *Plant Mgr*
Pat Goetz, *Branch Mgr*
EMP: 80 **Privately Held**
SIC: **3711** Automobile assembly, including specialty automobiles
PA: Wgs Global Services, L.C.
6350 Taylor Dr
Flint MI 48507

Grand Haven
Ottawa County

(G-5990)
AGC GRAND HAVEN LLC
16750 Comstock St (49417-7949)
PHONE 616 842-1820
Yongping Gu, *Mng Member*
▲ EMP: 6 EST: 2007
SALES: 10MM **Privately Held**
SIC: **3559** 3463 Automotive maintenance equipment; pump, compressor, turbine & engine forgings, except auto

(G-5991)
ALTERNATE NUMBER FIVE INC (PA)
Also Called: Ultimate Highway Solutions
11095 W Olive Rd (49417-9682)
PHONE 616 842-2581
John Carlyle, *Ch of Bd*
Ronald Nienhouse, *President*
Leon Span, *President*
Ron Nienhouse, *VP Engrg*
Chad Sayen, *Sls & Mktg Exec*
EMP: 75 EST: 1988
SQ FT: 52,000
SALES (est): 21.4MM **Privately Held**
WEB: www.msslotting.net
SIC: **3469** Metal stampings

(G-5992)
ASP PLATING COMPANY
211 N Griffin St (49417-1125)
P.O. Box 227 (49417-0227)
PHONE 616 842-8080
Gary Rowe, *President*
EMP: 7
SALES (est): 873.4K **Privately Held**
SIC: **3471** Electroplating of metals or formed products

(G-5993)
ASSEM-TECH INC
1600 Kooiman St (49417-2529)
PHONE 616 846-3410
Michael Wilson, *President*
EMP: 50
SQ FT: 28,000
SALES (est): 10.6MM **Privately Held**
SIC: **3679** 3672 Harness assemblies for electronic use: wire or cable; printed circuit boards

(G-5994)
ATCOFLEX INC
Also Called: Atco Rubber Products
14261 172nd Ave (49417-9462)
P.O. Box 118 (49417-0118)
PHONE 616 842-4661
William H Tuggle, *President*
Darlene Graska, *Opers Mgr*
Jon E Graska, *Electrical Engi*
Scot Tuggle, *Sales Staff*
Mark Harder, *Admin Sec*
EMP: 13
SQ FT: 65,000
SALES (est): 2.3MM **Privately Held**
SIC: **3052** Rubber & plastics hose & beltings

(G-5995)
AUTOMATIC SPRING PRODUCTS CORP (PA)
803 Taylor Ave (49417-2159)
PHONE 616 842-2284
Steven Moreland, *President*
Pat Deshaw, *COO*
Michael Miller, *CFO*
EMP: 180 EST: 1950
SQ FT: 105,000
SALES (est): 51.7MM **Privately Held**
WEB: www.automaticspring.com
SIC: **3496** 3465 3469 3493 Clips & fasteners, made from purchased wire; automotive stampings; metal stampings; torsion bar springs

(G-5996)
BIGSIGNSCOM
22 S Harbor Dr Unit 101 (49417-1581)
PHONE 800 790-7611
Corey Leonard, *President*
Michelle R Alvarez, *Principal*
Paul Vandusen, *Project Mgr*
Mario Ferretti, *Natl Sales Mgr*
Tom Suszka, *Sales Staff*
EMP: 27
SALES (est): 3.2MM **Privately Held**
SIC: **3993** Signs, not made in custom sign painting shops

(G-5997)
BIOSOLUTIONS LLC
1800 Industrial Dr Ste F (49417-9496)
PHONE 616 846-1210
Dave Kittel, *Purchasing*
Gary Verplank,
Budd Brink,
Mark James Lackner,
Peter Sturrus,
EMP: 10
SQ FT: 10,000
SALES (est): 1.6MM **Privately Held**
WEB: www.biosolutionsllc.com
SIC: **2842** Specialty cleaning preparations

(G-5998)
BRILLIANCE PUBLISHING INC
Also Called: Brilliance Audio
1704 Eaton Dr (49417-2820)
P.O. Box 887 (49417-0887)
PHONE 616 846-5256
Jeffrey L Belle, *President*
Daniel Byrne, *Manager*
Eileen Hutton, *Admin Sec*
▲ EMP: 150
SQ FT: 40,000
SALES (est): 43.2MM **Publicly Held**
WEB: www.brillianceaudio.com
SIC: **3652** Magnetic tape (audio): prerecorded
PA: Amazon.Com, Inc.
410 Terry Ave N
Seattle WA 98109

(G-5999)
C & M COATINGS INC
1730 Airpark Dr Ste C (49417-8981)
PHONE 616 842-1925
David Van Portfliet, *President*
EMP: 13
SQ FT: 10,000
SALES (est): 2.1MM **Privately Held**
WEB: www.cmcoatings.com
SIC: **3479** Coating of metals with plastic or resins; coating of metals & formed products

(G-6000)
CARLON METER COMPANY INC
1710 Eaton Dr (49417-2820)
PHONE 616 842-0420
Raymond Pilch, *President*
▲ EMP: 9
SQ FT: 16,000
SALES (est): 1.6MM **Privately Held**
WEB: www.carlonmeter.com
SIC: **3824** Water meters; electromechanical counters

(G-6001)
CARTER MANUFACTURING CO INC
1725 Airpark Dr (49417-9424)
PHONE 616 842-8760
Jeff Berry, *President*
Harry Gruen, *Purchasing*
James Verduin, *Research*
Steve Williams, *Design Engr*
Mark Wesner, *Regl Sales Mgr*
EMP: 60 EST: 1945
SQ FT: 35,000
SALES (est): 17.2MM **Privately Held**
WEB: www.carterbearings.com
SIC: **3562** Ball & roller bearings

(G-6002)
CHADKO LLC
725 Taylor Ave Ste B (49417-2180)
P.O. Box 965 (49417-0965)
PHONE 616 402-9207
Carrie Frifeldt, *Mng Member*
EMP: 4

Grand Haven - Ottawa County (G-6003)

SQ FT: 4,500
SALES (est): 589.6K **Privately Held**
SIC: **3089** Organizers for closets, drawers, etc.: plastic

(G-6003)
CITY AUTO GLASS CO
Also Called: Glassource
295 N Beechtree St (49417-1158)
PHONE..................................616 842-3235
Jim Arnold, *President*
Rose Arnold, *Vice Pres*
Jim Arnolds, *Financial Exec*
Chloe Arnold, *Marketing Staff*
▲ EMP: 6
SALES (est): 147.9K **Privately Held**
SIC: **3229** 3231 Industrial-use glassware; doors, glass: made from purchased glass

(G-6004)
CLASSIC IMAGES EMBROIDERY
15774 Ronny Rd (49417-2946)
PHONE..................................616 844-1702
Barbara Lankes,
Michael Lankes,
EMP: 4
SALES (est): 266.5K **Privately Held**
SIC: **2395** 5199 Embroidery products, except schiffli machine; advertising specialties

(G-6005)
COMMERCIAL MFG & ASSEMBLY INC
17087 Hayes St (49417-8990)
PHONE..................................616 847-9980
John Geneva, *President*
Chris Geneva, *Principal*
Michael Voss, *Vice Pres*
Rick Cox, *Project Mgr*
Don Silvis, *Treasurer*
▲ EMP: 50
SQ FT: 65,000
SALES (est): 32.3MM **Privately Held**
WEB: www.callcma.com
SIC: **5085** 3544 7692 3469 Packing, industrial; punches, forming & stamping; welding repair; metal stampings; sheet metalwork

(G-6006)
CORLIN COMPANY
1640 Marion Ave (49417-2366)
P.O. Box 50, Spring Lake (49456-0050)
PHONE..................................616 842-7093
John Atherton, *Owner*
EMP: 7
SQ FT: 6,400
SALES (est): 560.5K **Privately Held**
SIC: **3479** Painting, coating & hot dipping

(G-6007)
CUSTOM WELDING SERVICE LLC
1700 Robbins Rd Lot 470 (49417-2869)
PHONE..................................616 402-6681
Barbara Sobolik,
Thomas Sobolik,
EMP: 13
SQ FT: 26,000
SALES: 540K **Privately Held**
SIC: **3441** Fabricated structural metal

(G-6008)
DAKE CORPORATION
724 Robbins Rd (49417-2690)
PHONE..................................616 842-7110
Jason Riemersma, *Principal*
Susan Brentana, *Buyer*
Eryn Leedy, *Mktg Coord*
Mark Nadolski, *Marketing Staff*
Alex Rltzema, *Manager*
▲ EMP: 58
SALES (est): 12.1MM
SALES (corp-wide): 550.2MM **Privately Held**
SIC: **3549** Metalworking machinery
PA: Jsj Corporation
    700 Robbins Rd
    Grand Haven MI 49417
    616 842-6350

(G-6009)
DEPOTTEY ACQUISITION INC
Also Called: Econoline Abrasive Products
401 N Griffin St (49417-1129)
P.O. Box 229 (49417-0229)
PHONE..................................616 846-4150
Daniel D Depottey, *President*
EMP: 24
SQ FT: 21,000
SALES: 4MM **Privately Held**
SIC: **3449** Miscellaneous metalwork

(G-6010)
DIMENSION PRODUCTS CORPORATION
13746 172nd Ave (49417-8909)
PHONE..................................616 842-6050
Ralph J Abraham, *President*
EMP: 10
SALES (est): 1.3MM **Privately Held**
SIC: **3829** Measuring & controlling devices

(G-6011)
ECON-O-LINE ABRASIVE PRODUCTS
401 N Griffin St (49417-1129)
P.O. Box 229 (49417-0229)
PHONE..................................616 846-4150
Dan Depottey, *President*
EMP: 22
SALES: 3.5MM **Privately Held**
WEB: www.sandblasting.com
SIC: **3449** Bars, concrete reinforcing: fabricated steel

(G-6012)
EFFIZIENT LLC
1500 S Beechtree St (49417-2846)
PHONE..................................616 935-3170
Ludwig Klaus Preidt, *President*
James Postma, *Exec VP*
Karl Ronald Chapel,
▲ EMP: 3 EST: 2011
SQ FT: 2,500
SALES (est): 627.4K **Privately Held**
SIC: **2599** 7699 Carts, restaurant equipment; shopping cart repair

(G-6013)
ELECTRICAL CONCEPTS INC
Also Called: Eci
12999 Wilderness Trl (49417-7639)
PHONE..................................616 847-0293
Chuck Vonesh, *President*
Ellen P Vonesh, *Vice Pres*
EMP: 22
SQ FT: 12,000
SALES (est): 2MM **Privately Held**
SIC: **3694** 3643 Harness wiring sets, internal combustion engines; current-carrying wiring devices

(G-6014)
EMERSON ELECTRIC CO
15399 Hofma Dr (49417-9678)
PHONE..................................616 846-3950
EMP: 49
SALES (corp-wide): 24.5B **Publicly Held**
SIC: **3823** Mfg Process Control Instruments
PA: Emerson Electric Co.
    8000 W Florissant Ave
    Saint Louis MO 63136
    314 553-2000

(G-6015)
ENGINE POWER COMPONENTS INC
Also Called: Engine Parts Grinding
1333 Fulton Ave (49417-1593)
P.O. Box 837 (49417-0837)
PHONE..................................616 846-0110
Mark Quigg, *President*
Duane L Quigg, *Chairman*
Peter Grose, *Vice Pres*
Rhonda Reed, *Purchasing*
Tony Daves, *Engineer*
▲ EMP: 300
SQ FT: 200,000
SALES (est): 69.8MM **Privately Held**
WEB: www.engpwr.com
SIC: **3714** Camshafts, motor vehicle

(G-6016)
ERVOTT TOOL CO LLC
13951 132nd Ave (49417-8722)
PHONE..................................616 842-3688
Rob Young, *Partner*
Robin Young,
Mike Ott,
EMP: 5
SQ FT: 2,000
SALES: 250K **Privately Held**
SIC: **3599** Machine shop, jobbing & repair

(G-6017)
FUTURE INDUSTRIES INC
1729 Airpark Dr (49417-9424)
P.O. Box 806 (49417-0806)
PHONE..................................616 844-0772
David Schultz, *President*
EMP: 24
SALES (est): 4.8MM **Privately Held**
SIC: **3469** 3498 Stamping metal for the trade; fabricated pipe & fittings

(G-6018)
GHSP INC (HQ)
Also Called: Convergence Technologies
1250 S Beechtree St (49417-2840)
PHONE..................................616 842-5500
Paul Doyle, *President*
Jeff Smith, *President*
Davy Ou, *General Mgr*
Jerry Scott, *Chairman*
Anil Mandala, *Business Mgr*
▲ EMP: 350
SQ FT: 200,000
SALES (est): 279.1MM
SALES (corp-wide): 550.2MM **Privately Held**
WEB: www.ghsp.com
SIC: **3714** Motor vehicle parts & accessories
PA: Jsj Corporation
    700 Robbins Rd
    Grand Haven MI 49417
    616 842-6350

(G-6019)
GHSP INC
Also Called: Kds Controls
1250 S Beechtree St (49417-2840)
PHONE..................................248 588-5095
Paul Doyle, *President*
Molly Snyder, *General Mgr*
EMP: 75
SALES (corp-wide): 550.2MM **Privately Held**
WEB: www.ghsp.com
SIC: **3714** 3625 Motor vehicle parts & accessories; electric controls & control accessories, industrial
HQ: Ghsp, Inc.
    1250 S Beechtree St
    Grand Haven MI 49417
    616 842-5500

(G-6020)
GRACE EXTENDED
714 Columbus Ave (49417-1549)
PHONE..................................616 502-2078
Kendra Higgins, *Vice Pres*
Barbara Lee, *Director*
Linda Bengstron, *Admin Sec*
EMP: 3 EST: 2015
SALES: 429.7K **Privately Held**
SIC: **8322** 2051 Social services for the handicapped; bakery: wholesale or wholesale/retail combined

(G-6021)
GRAND HAVEN CUSTOM MOLDING LLC
1500 S Beechtree St (49417-2846)
PHONE..................................616 935-3160
Karl R Chapel, *Principal*
Tanya Chapel, *Production*
Matt Whitney, *Purch Mgr*
Becky Mattson, *Accounting Mgr*
Charlene Johnson, *Clerk*
EMP: 48 EST: 2010
SALES (est): 17.6MM **Privately Held**
SIC: **3089** Injection molding of plastics

(G-6022)
GRAND HAVEN GASKET COMPANY
1701 Eaton Dr (49417-2824)
P.O. Box 671 (49417-0671)
PHONE..................................616 842-7682
Ruth Suchecki, *CEO*
Kent Suchecki, *President*
Bradley Suchecki, *Vice Pres*
Douglas Suchecki, *Vice Pres*
EMP: 16
SQ FT: 45,000
SALES (est): 4.2MM **Privately Held**
WEB: www.ghgc.com
SIC: **3053** Gaskets, all materials

(G-6023)
GRAND HAVEN POWDER COATING INC
Also Called: Ghpc
1710 Airpark Dr (49417-9476)
PHONE..................................616 850-8822
John Denhartigh, *President*
Sue Rollins, *Corp Secy*
Pete Denhartigh, *Vice Pres*
Deb Zellar, *Asst Mgr*
EMP: 30
SQ FT: 70,000
SALES (est): 3.9MM **Privately Held**
SIC: **3479** Coating of metals & formed products

(G-6024)
GRAND HAVEN PUBLISHING CORP
Also Called: Grand Haven Tribune
101 N 3rd St (49417-1209)
PHONE..................................616 842-6400
David Rau, *President*
Duncan Maclean, *Editor*
Alice W Rau, *Treasurer*
Alan Rowe, *Accounts Exec*
Kim Street, *Accounts Exec*
EMP: 50
SQ FT: 9,000
SALES (est): 3.2MM
SALES (corp-wide): 3.4MM **Privately Held**
WEB: www.grandhaventribune.com
SIC: **2711** 2752 Newspapers: publishing only, not printed on site; commercial printing, lithographic
PA: Herald Reflector Inc
    61 E Monroe St
    Norwalk OH 44857
    419 668-3771

(G-6025)
GRAND HAVEN STEEL PRODUCTS INC
Also Called: Dawson Grinding
1627 Marion Ave (49417-2365)
PHONE..................................616 842-2740
Barry King, *President*
EMP: 1
SALES (est): 9.7MM **Privately Held**
SIC: **3451** Screw machine products

(G-6026)
GRAND INDUSTRIES INC
1700 Airpark Dr (49417-9424)
P.O. Box 535 (49417-0535)
PHONE..................................616 846-7120
Brad Billinghurst, *President*
Mardy Carr, *General Mgr*
Dave Billinghurst, *Vice Pres*
Beth Norwick, *Manager*
EMP: 35
SQ FT: 55,000
SALES (est): 4.8MM **Privately Held**
SIC: **7389** 2448 Packaging & labeling services; cargo containers, wood

(G-6027)
GREAT LAKES CONTRACTING INC
14370 172nd Ave (49417-9000)
PHONE..................................616 846-8888
Raymond Buikema, *President*
Jane Kalavitz, *Business Mgr*
EMP: 18
SQ FT: 20,000
SALES: 4.6MM **Privately Held**
WEB: www.glccontracting.com
SIC: **3441** Fabricated structural metal

GEOGRAPHIC SECTION
Grand Haven - Ottawa County (G-6052)

(G-6028)
GTI LIQUIDATING INC (PA)
Also Called: Texas Transformer
1500 Marion Ave (49417-2368)
P.O. Box 799 (49417-0799)
PHONE..................................616 842-5430
Ed Smith, *COO*
EMP: 70 **EST:** 1951
SQ FT: 50,000
SALES (est): 20.2MM **Privately Held**
WEB: www.gtipower.com
SIC: 3612 Transformers, except electric

(G-6029)
GTI POWER ACQUISITION LLC (PA)
Also Called: Grand Power Systems
1500 Marion Ave (49417-2368)
P.O. Box 799 (49417-0799)
PHONE..................................616 842-5430
Ed Smith, *CEO*
James Baughman, *Technology*
EMP: 52
SALES (est): 39.7MM **Privately Held**
SIC: 3612 Autotransformers, electric (power transformers); control transformers; distribution transformers, electric

(G-6030)
GYRO POWDER COATING INC
1624 Marion Ave (49417-2366)
PHONE..................................616 846-2580
Peter Van Oordt, *President*
EMP: 12
SQ FT: 30,000
SALES (est): 1.3MM **Privately Held**
SIC: 3479 Coating of metals & formed products

(G-6031)
HAMILTON EQUINE PRODUCTS LLC
14057 108th Ave (49417-9755)
PHONE..................................616 842-2406
Thomas Hamilton, *Principal*
EMP: 3
SALES (est): 126.8K **Privately Held**
SIC: 2399 Horse & pet accessories, textile

(G-6032)
HARBOR INDUSTRIES INC (PA)
14130 172nd Ave (49417-9446)
PHONE..................................616 842-5330
Henry T Parker Jr, *President*
Timothy Parker, *President*
Susan Wright, *Principal*
Walter Miranda, *Exec VP*
Michael Detenber, *Vice Pres*
◆ **EMP:** 70 **EST:** 1950
SQ FT: 190,000
SALES (est): 159.9MM **Privately Held**
WEB: www.harborind.com
SIC: 2541 3993 Display fixtures, wood; signs & advertising specialties

(G-6033)
HARBOR INDUSTRIES INC
14170 172nd Ave (49417-9446)
PHONE..................................616 842-5330
Henry Parker Jr, *President*
EMP: 75
SALES (corp-wide): 159.9MM **Privately Held**
WEB: www.harborind.com
SIC: 2541 Wood partitions & fixtures
PA: Harbor Industries, Inc.
    14130 172nd Ave
    Grand Haven MI 49417
    616 842-5330

(G-6034)
HAVEN INNOVATION INC
1705 Eaton Dr (49417-2824)
PHONE..................................616 935-1040
Donald Wisner, *President*
Jacob Wisner, *CFO*
Sammie Baker, *Admin Asst*
▲ **EMP:** 25
SALES (est): 2.8MM **Privately Held**
SIC: 3569 Assembly machines, non-metalworking

(G-6035)
HAVEN MANUFACTURING COMPANY
13720 172nd Ave (49417-8909)
PHONE..................................616 842-1260
James Warners, *President*
Jim Warners, *Master*
EMP: 13 **EST:** 1966
SQ FT: 9,000
SALES (est): 1MM **Privately Held**
SIC: 3599 Machine shop, jobbing & repair

(G-6036)
HEYBOER TRANSFORMERS INC (PA)
17382 Hayes St (49417-9305)
PHONE..................................616 842-5830
Arlyn Arendson, *President*
Alden Arendson, *Principal*
Philip Dannenburg, *Vice Pres*
EMP: 24 **EST:** 1957
SQ FT: 13,200
SALES (est): 2MM **Privately Held**
WEB: www.heyboertransformers.com
SIC: 3612 Power transformers, electric

(G-6037)
HOLLAND PLASTICS CORPORATION (PA)
Also Called: Anderson Technologies, Inc.
14000 172nd Ave (49417-9431)
PHONE..................................616 844-2505
Glenn C Anderson, *President*
Jim Morren, *COO*
Steve Bosch, *Vice Pres*
Chuck Cell, *Engineer*
Dianne Hiles, *Controller*
▲ **EMP:** 50
SQ FT: 80,000
SALES (est): 16.6MM
SALES (corp-wide): 18.3MM **Privately Held**
WEB: www.andtec.com
SIC: 3089 3544 Injection molding of plastics; special dies, tools, jigs & fixtures; industrial molds; dies, plastics forming

(G-6038)
IZZY PLUS
Also Called: Izzy Better Together
700 Robbins Rd (49417-2603)
PHONE..................................574 821-1200
Chuck Saylor, *CEO*
▲ **EMP:** 9 **EST:** 2009
SALES (est): 1.2MM **Privately Held**
SIC: 2521 5712 Wood office furniture; furniture stores

(G-6039)
JOST INTERNATIONAL CORP (DH)
1770 Hayes St (49417-9428)
PHONE..................................616 846-7700
Lee Brace, *President*
Greg Laarman, *President*
Todd Vandermolen, *Regional Mgr*
Rich Carroll, *Vice Pres*
Richard Carroll, *Vice Pres*
◆ **EMP:** 227
SQ FT: 65,000
SALES (est): 112.5MM
SALES (corp-wide): 864.8MM **Privately Held**
WEB: www.jostinternational.com
SIC: 3714 Motor vehicle parts & accessories
HQ: Jost-Werke International Beteiligungsverwaltung Gmbh
    Siemensstr. 2
    Neu-Isenburg 63263
    610 229-50

(G-6040)
JOY-MAX INC
Also Called: Penzel Oil Quick Change
718 Elliott Ave (49417-1110)
PHONE..................................616 847-0990
Chuck Anderson, *General Mgr*
EMP: 6
SALES (corp-wide): 756.2K **Privately Held**
WEB: www.joy-max.com
SIC: 2911 Oils, lubricating

PA: Joy-Max Inc
    714 Elliott Ave
    Grand Haven MI 49417
    616 846-2341

(G-6041)
JSJ CORPORATION
Also Called: Ghsp
1250 S Beechtree St (49417-2840)
PHONE..................................616 842-5500
Joe Martella, *President*
Jerry Scott, *Branch Mgr*
EMP: 408
SQ FT: 160,000
SALES (corp-wide): 550.2MM **Privately Held**
SIC: 3469 Stamping metal for the trade
PA: Jsj Corporation
    700 Robbins Rd
    Grand Haven MI 49417
    616 842-6350

(G-6042)
JSJ CORPORATION (PA)
700 Robbins Rd (49417-2603)
PHONE..................................616 842-6350
Nelson Jacobson, *President*
Barry Lemay, *COO*
Thomas J Rizzi, *COO*
Erick P Johnson, *Exec VP*
Timothy Liang, *Vice Pres*
◆ **EMP:** 25 **EST:** 1919
SQ FT: 12,000
SALES (est): 550.2MM **Privately Held**
SIC: 3465 3469 3366 3089 Automotive stampings; metal stampings; stamping metal for the trade; castings (except die): brass; castings (except die): bronze; injection molded finished plastic products; plastics foam products; chairs, office: padded or plain, except wood; desks, office: except wood

(G-6043)
JSJ FURNITURE CORPORATION (HQ)
Also Called: Izzy
700 Robbins Rd (49417-2603)
PHONE..................................616 847-6534
Chuck Saylor, *CEO*
Nancy Dallinger, *President*
Rick Glasser, *President*
Gregg Masenthin, *President*
Joan Hill, *COO*
▲ **EMP:** 32
SALES (est): 121.3MM
SALES (corp-wide): 550.2MM **Privately Held**
WEB: www.izzydesign.com
SIC: 2521 Cabinets, office: wood
PA: Jsj Corporation
    700 Robbins Rd
    Grand Haven MI 49417
    616 842-6350

(G-6044)
L THOMPSON CO LLC
126 Lafayette Ave (49417-1342)
PHONE..................................616 844-1135
Lauren Thompson, *Mng Member*
EMP: 12
SALES (est): 1MM **Privately Held**
SIC: 6719 3824 Investment holding companies, except banks; electronic totalizing counters

(G-6045)
LAKESHORE AUTOMATIC PDTS INC
1810 Industrial Dr Ste D (49417-8930)
PHONE..................................616 846-4005
Albert R Hoffman, *President*
EMP: 6
SALES (est): 900.9K **Privately Held**
SIC: 3451 Screw machine products

(G-6046)
LAKESHORE CUSTOM POWDR COATING
411 N Griffin St (49417-1129)
PHONE..................................616 296-9330
Craig Pitts, *Owner*
EMP: 4
SALES (est): 556K **Privately Held**
SIC: 3399 Powder, metal

(G-6047)
LAKESHORE FITTINGS INC
Also Called: Cascade Manufacturing
1865 Industrial Park Dr (49417-7970)
PHONE..................................616 846-5090
Albert R Hoffman, *President*
Sheryl Porter, *Director*
Rebecca Hanes, *Executive*
EMP: 51
SQ FT: 40,000
SALES (est): 10.6MM **Privately Held**
WEB: www.lakeshore-automatic.com
SIC: 3451 Screw machine products
PA: Alco Manufacturing Corporation Llc
    10584 Middle Ave
    Elyria OH 44035

(G-6048)
LEMON CREEK WINERY LTD
327 N Beacon Blvd (49417-1108)
PHONE..................................616 844-1709
Tim Lemon, *Branch Mgr*
EMP: 5
SALES (est): 267.4K
SALES (corp-wide): 3.2MM **Privately Held**
SIC: 2084 Wines
PA: Lemon Creek Winery Ltd
    533 E Lemon Creek Rd
    Berrien Springs MI 49103
    269 471-1321

(G-6049)
LIGHT CORP INC (PA)
14800 172nd Ave (49417-8969)
PHONE..................................616 842-5100
Gary Verplank, *CEO*
Budd Brink, *Vice Pres*
Samantha Pertner, *Manager*
▲ **EMP:** 150
SQ FT: 100,000
SALES (est): 31.2MM **Privately Held**
WEB: www.lightcorp.com
SIC: 3646 Desk lamps, commercial

(G-6050)
LOFTIS ALUMI-TEC INC
13888 172nd Ave (49417-8910)
P.O. Box 753 (49417-0753)
PHONE..................................616 846-1990
James Loftis, *President*
EMP: 24
SQ FT: 13,000
SALES (est): 3MM **Privately Held**
WEB: www.alumitecmanifolds.com
SIC: 3498 3594 3494 3354 Manifolds, pipe: fabricated from purchased pipe; fluid power pumps & motors; valves & pipe fittings; aluminum extruded products

(G-6051)
LOFTIS MACHINE COMPANY
13888 172nd Ave (49417-8910)
P.O. Box 753 (49417-0753)
PHONE..................................616 846-1990
James Loftis, *President*
EMP: 25
SQ FT: 15,000
SALES (est): 3.5MM **Privately Held**
SIC: 3599 3444 Machine shop, jobbing & repair; sheet metalwork

(G-6052)
MAGNA MIRRORS AMERICA INC
Service Parts Division
1800 Hayes St (49417-9428)
PHONE..................................616 786-7000
Jeff Westbrook, *Engineer*
Terry Bekins, *Project Engr*
Scott Brownlie, *Senior Engr*
Darryl De Wind, *Design Engr*
Darin Loveland, *Electrical Engi*
EMP: 50
SQ FT: 50,000
SALES (corp-wide): 40.8B **Privately Held**
WEB: www.donnelly.com
SIC: 3231 Mirrored glass
HQ: Magna Mirrors Of America, Inc.
    5085 Kraft Ave Se
    Grand Rapids MI 49512
    616 786-5120

Grand Haven - Ottawa County (G-6053)

(G-6053) MAGNUM MACHINE AND TOOL INC
13744 172nd Ave (49417-8909)
PHONE..................616 844-1940
Rod Eitnieat, *President*
EMP: 3
SALES: 100K **Privately Held**
WEB: www.magnumtool.com
SIC: 3599 Machine shop, jobbing & repair

(G-6054) MAPLE LEAF PRESS INC
1215 S Beechtree St (49417-2839)
PHONE..................616 846-8844
Vicki Patterson, *President*
Doug Patterson, *Vice Pres*
EMP: 6 EST: 1975
SALES: 1MM **Privately Held**
WEB: www.mapleleafpress.com
SIC: 3555 Printing presses

(G-6055) MECA-SYSTEME USA INC
101 Washington Ave (49417-1302)
PHONE..................616 843-5566
William Butch, *Manager*
Alain Gatard, *Director*
▲ EMP: 5
SALES (est): 441.3K **Privately Held**
SIC: 3565 Packaging machinery

(G-6056) MOLDING SOLUTIONS INC
Also Called: Advanced Molding Solutions
1734 Airpark Dr Ste F (49417-8943)
PHONE..................616 847-6822
Robert Buresh, *Principal*
Brad Ahrens, *Principal*
▲ EMP: 20
SQ FT: 10,000
SALES (est): 3.7MM **Privately Held**
WEB: www.molding-solutions.com
SIC: 3089 Injection molding of plastics

(G-6057) MONTINA MANUFACTURING INC
13740 172nd Ave (49417-8909)
P.O. Box 505, Spring Lake (49456-0505)
PHONE..................616 846-1080
Gary Cobb, *President*
Dawn Cobb, *Treasurer*
EMP: 7
SQ FT: 7,000
SALES (est): 1.2MM **Privately Held**
SIC: 3599 Machine shop, jobbing & repair

(G-6058) NAUTICAL KNOTS
301 N Harbor Dr Ste 12 (49417-1078)
PHONE..................231 206-0400
Jeff Gundy, *Owner*
Connie Gundy, *Co-Owner*
EMP: 9
SALES (est): 574.6K **Privately Held**
SIC: 2052 Pretzels

(G-6059) NETSHAPE INTERNATIONAL LLC
1900 Hayes St (49417-8937)
PHONE..................616 846-8700
Gary Verplank, *Ch of Bd*
EMP: 129
SALES (est): 72.3K **Privately Held**
WEB: www.netshapecorp.com
SIC: 3449 Miscellaneous metalwork

(G-6060) PARKER PROPERTY DEV INC
Also Called: Stoneway Marble Granite & Tile
12589 104th Ave (49417-9732)
PHONE..................616 842-6118
G Kevin Parker, *President*
Karen Parker, *Vice Pres*
EMP: 11
SQ FT: 10,200
SALES (est): 1.5MM **Privately Held**
SIC: 3281 Cut stone & stone products

(G-6061) POLYPLY COMPOSITES LLC
1540 Marion Ave (49417-2368)
PHONE..................616 842-6330
Kip Downhour, *General Mgr*
Dan Lockard, *Director*
Thomas White,
EMP: 40
SQ FT: 70,000
SALES (est): 11.1MM **Privately Held**
WEB: www.polyplycomposites.com
SIC: 3083 3089 Laminated plastics plate & sheet; plastic processing

(G-6062) PPG INDUSTRIAL COATINGS
14295 172nd Ave (49417-9431)
PHONE..................616 844-4391
EMP: 3
SALES (est): 76K **Privately Held**
SIC: 2851 Paints & allied products

(G-6063) PPG INDUSTRIES INC
Also Called: I.V.C. Industrial
1855 Industrial Park Dr (49417-7970)
PHONE..................616 846-4400
Sonny Smith, *Plant Engr*
Shekhar Nanivadekar, *Manager*
EMP: 50
SALES (corp-wide): 15.3B **Publicly Held**
SIC: 2851 Paints & paint additives; enamels; varnishes; lacquer: bases, dopes, thinner
PA: Ppg Industries, Inc.
1 Ppg Pl
Pittsburgh PA 15272
412 434-3131

(G-6064) PRIORITY TOOL INC
1650 Marion Ave (49417-2366)
PHONE..................616 847-1337
Maurice Sterzer, *President*
Darryl Sterzer, *President*
EMP: 3
SQ FT: 3,420
SALES: 250K **Privately Held**
SIC: 3549 Metalworking machinery

(G-6065) PRO SOURCE MANUFACTURING INC
12880 N Cedar Dr Ste A (49417-8446)
PHONE..................616 607-2990
Kris Rillema, *President*
EMP: 3 EST: 2012
SALES (est): 230K **Privately Held**
SIC: 3599 Machine shop, jobbing & repair

(G-6066) PRO TOOL LLC
14714 Indian Trails Dr (49417-9126)
PHONE..................616 850-0556
Jeff Friedgen,
Julie Friedgen,
EMP: 8
SALES (est): 847K **Privately Held**
SIC: 3544 Special dies, tools, jigs & fixtures

(G-6067) R A MILLER INDUSTRIES INC
Also Called: Rami
14500 168th Ave (49417-9460)
P.O. Box 858 (49417-0858)
PHONE..................888 845-9450
Paul E Miller, *President*
Jillane Payne, *Vice Pres*
Travis Dahlman, *Buyer*
EMP: 120 EST: 1956
SQ FT: 110,000
SALES (est): 26.4MM **Privately Held**
WEB: www.rami.com
SIC: 3669 3663 3812 Intercommunication systems, electric; antennas, transmitting & communications; antennas, radar or communications

(G-6068) RAP ELECTRONICS & MACHINES
13353 Green St (49417-8720)
PHONE..................616 846-1437
Rex Pease, *Owner*
Janice Pease, *Treasurer*
EMP: 10
SALES: 60K **Privately Held**
SIC: 7378 3824 Computer maintenance & repair; controls, revolution & timing instruments

(G-6069) REED YACHT SALES LLC
1333 Madison St Blgd A St (49417)
P.O. Box 730 (49417-0730)
PHONE..................616 842-8899
EMP: 18
SALES (corp-wide): 4.5MM **Privately Held**
SIC: 3732 Yachts, building & repairing
PA: Reed Yacht Sales Llc
11840 Toledo Beach Rd
La Salle MI 48145
419 304-4405

(G-6070) REFAB LLC
1811 Hayes St Ste D (49417-9493)
PHONE..................616 842-9705
Joshua W Vink,
Michelle Perri- Vink,
EMP: 4
SQ FT: 6,000
SALES (est): 798.3K **Privately Held**
WEB: www.refab.com
SIC: 3312 Hot-rolled iron & steel products

(G-6071) RENUCELL
41 Washington Ave Ste 345 (49417-3303)
PHONE..................888 400-6032
EMP: 5
SALES (est): 411.8K **Privately Held**
SIC: 2834 Pharmaceutical preparations

(G-6072) RIDGID SLOTTING LLC
12046 120th Ave (49417-9621)
PHONE..................616 847-0332
Jim Bourque,
EMP: 12
SQ FT: 12,000
SALES: 1.3MM **Privately Held**
SIC: 3498 Tube fabricating (contract bending & shaping)

(G-6073) SEAVER FINISHING INC
Also Called: E Coat Division
16900 Hayes St (49417-8989)
PHONE..................616 844-4360
Craig Seaver, *President*
Kathy Meekhof, *Executive*
David L Seaver, *Shareholder*
EMP: 70
SQ FT: 45,000
SALES: 4.3MM **Privately Held**
SIC: 3479 Painting of metal products; painting, coating & hot dipping

(G-6074) SEAVER INDUSTRIAL FINISHING CO
1645 Marion Ave (49417-2365)
P.O. Box 857 (49417-0857)
PHONE..................616 842-8560
David L Seaver, *CEO*
Craig Seaver, *President*
EMP: 58
SQ FT: 33,000
SALES (est): 2.3MM
SALES (corp-wide): 14.3MM **Privately Held**
WEB: www.seaverfinishing.com
SIC: 3479 3471 Coating of metals & formed products; plating & polishing
PA: Seaver-Smith, Inc.
1645 Marion Ave
Grand Haven MI 49417
616 842-8560

(G-6075) SEAVER-SMITH INC (PA)
Also Called: Seaver Finishing
1645 Marion Ave (49417-2365)
P.O. Box 857 (49417-0857)
PHONE..................616 842-8560
David L Seaver, *CEO*
Craig Seaver, *President*
EMP: 50
SQ FT: 33,000
SALES (corp-wide): 14.3MM **Privately Held**
WEB: www.seaverfinishing.com
SIC: 3479 Painting of metal products

(G-6076) SHAPE CORP
14600 172nd Ave (49417-8904)
PHONE..................616 296-6300
Gary Breplank, *Owner*
EMP: 500
SALES (corp-wide): 565.6MM **Privately Held**
WEB: www.shape-corp.com
SIC: 3449 Miscellaneous metalwork
PA: Shape Corp.
1900 Hayes St
Grand Haven MI 49417
616 846-8700

(G-6077) SHAPE CORP (PA)
1900 Hayes St (49417-8937)
P.O. Box 369 (49417-0369)
PHONE..................616 846-8700
Gary Verplank, *Ch of Bd*
Mary Anderson, *Editor*
Bob Currier, *Vice Pres*
Sondra Hoffmeyer, *QC Mgr*
Roger Thomas, *Engineer*
◆ EMP: 300
SQ FT: 225,000
SALES (est): 565.6MM **Privately Held**
WEB: www.shape-corp.com
SIC: 3449 3089 Miscellaneous metalwork; molding primary plastic

(G-6078) SHAPE CORP
1825 Industrial Park Dr (49417-9429)
PHONE..................616 844-3215
Daniel Bloom, *Branch Mgr*
EMP: 30
SALES (corp-wide): 565.6MM **Privately Held**
SIC: 3449 3089 Miscellaneous metalwork; molding primary plastic
PA: Shape Corp.
1900 Hayes St
Grand Haven MI 49417
616 846-8700

(G-6079) SHAPE CORP
16344 Comstock St (49417-9423)
PHONE..................616 846-8700
EMP: 129
SALES (corp-wide): 425MM **Privately Held**
SIC: 3449 Mfg Misc Structural Metalwork
PA: Shape Corp.
1900 Hayes St
Grand Haven MI 49417
616 846-8700

(G-6080) SHAPE CORP
1835 Hayes St (49417-9428)
PHONE..................616 846-8700
David Heatherington, *Branch Mgr*
EMP: 133
SALES (corp-wide): 565.6MM **Privately Held**
WEB: www.shape-corp.com
SIC: 3449 Miscellaneous metalwork
PA: Shape Corp.
1900 Hayes St
Grand Haven MI 49417
616 846-8700

(G-6081) SOS ENGINEERING INC
1901 Hayes St (49417-8937)
PHONE..................616 846-5767
David Suchecki, *President*
Brett Suchecki, *Vice Pres*
EMP: 13 EST: 1973
SQ FT: 25,000
SALES (est): 2.5MM **Privately Held**
SIC: 3469 Metal stampings

(G-6082) STANCO METAL PRODUCTS INC (PA)
Also Called: Stanco Metal Products Company
2101 168th Ave (49417-9396)
PHONE..................616 842-5000
Gerald Slagel, *President*
Benjamin Slagel, *Vice Pres*
Dennis Bayle, *QC Mgr*
Corey Cowart, *QC Mgr*

▲ = Import ▼=Export
◆ =Import/Export

Steve Zimmer, *Engineer*
◆ **EMP:** 45
SQ FT: 135,000
SALES (est): 42.5MM **Privately Held**
WEB: www.stancometal.com
SIC: 3465 3469 Automotive stampings; stamping metal for the trade

(G-6083)
STANDARD SAND CORPORATION
14201 Lakeshore Dr (49417-8918)
PHONE..............................616 538-3667
David Sensibar, *President*
Albert Freund, *Treasurer*
Steven Davis, *Admin Sec*
EMP: 8 **EST:** 1930
SQ FT: 3,000
SALES (est): 327.1K
SALES (corp-wide): 142.6MM **Publicly Held**
SIC: 1446 Foundry sand mining
HQ: Fairmount Santrol Inc.
   3 Summit Park Dr Ste 700
   Independence OH 44131
   440 214-3200

(G-6084)
STAR BOARD MULTI MEDIA INC
Also Called: Star Board ATT Tev
41 Washington Ave Ste 395 (49417-3305)
PHONE..............................616 296-0823
Kevin Galbavi, *President*
EMP: 5
SALES (est): 585.2K **Privately Held**
SIC: 3674 7336 7374 7372 Read-only memory (ROM); graphic arts & related design; computer graphics service; application computer software

(G-6085)
STEADFAST ENGINEERED PDTS LLC
775 Woodlawn Ave (49417-2141)
PHONE..............................616 846-4747
Gary Ball, *Plant Mgr*
Allan J Westmaas II,
EMP: 11
SQ FT: 10,000
SALES: 3.5MM **Privately Held**
WEB: www.steadfastep.com
SIC: 3451 Screw machine products

(G-6086)
STEWART REED INC
Also Called: Econaway Abrasive Co
747 Grant Ave (49417-1840)
PHONE..............................616 846-2550
Darwin Stewart, *President*
Mike Reed, *Vice Pres*
EMP: 4
SQ FT: 4,500
SALES (est): 290K **Privately Held**
SIC: 3291 Cloth, abrasive: garnet, emery, aluminum oxide coated; paper, abrasive: garnet, emery, aluminum oxide coated

(G-6087)
SUPERIOR MONUMENTS CO
1003 S Beacon Blvd (49417-2585)
PHONE..............................616 844-1700
David Sietsema, *Branch Mgr*
EMP: 4
SALES (est): 156.4K
SALES (corp-wide): 782.1K **Privately Held**
SIC: 5999 5087 3281 Monuments, finished to custom order; cemetary supplies & equipment; cut stone & stone products
PA: Superior Monuments Co
   354 Ottawa St
   Muskegon MI 49442
   231 728-2211

(G-6088)
SWEET TMPTTONS ICE CREAM PRLOR
1003 S Beacon Blvd (49417-2585)
PHONE..............................616 842-8108
Ray Marine, *Owner*
EMP: 4 **EST:** 2001
SALES (est): 277.7K **Privately Held**
SIC: 2024 Ice cream & frozen desserts

(G-6089)
TRAINER METAL FORMING CO INC
Also Called: Steel Forming Systems
14080 172nd Ave (49417-9431)
P.O. Box 139 (49417-0139)
PHONE..............................616 844-9982
D J Trainer, *President*
Jeffrey W Harms, *Principal*
EMP: 23
SQ FT: 79,000
SALES (est): 4.4MM **Privately Held**
WEB: www.steelformingsystems.com
SIC: 3544 Forms (molds), for foundry & plastics working machinery

(G-6090)
TRANSFER TOOL SYSTEMS INC
Also Called: Transfer Tool Products
14444 168th Ave (49417-9454)
PHONE..............................616 846-8510
James Raterink, *President*
John M Fiore, *Vice Pres*
Heath Verstraete, *Opers Staff*
Kyle Viening, *Purch Agent*
Randy Barnhard, *Engineer*
EMP: 60
SQ FT: 45,000
SALES (est): 15.7MM **Privately Held**
WEB: www.transfertool.com
SIC: 3469 3541 3965 Stamping metal for the trade; machine tool replacement & repair parts, metal cutting types; fasteners, buttons, needles & pins

(G-6091)
UNISLAT LLC
13660 172nd Ave (49417-8908)
PHONE..............................616 844-4211
Jeff Berry,
EMP: 4
SQ FT: 5,000
SALES (est): 474.3K **Privately Held**
SIC: 2541 Display fixtures, wood

(G-6092)
UNIVERSAL COATING TECHNOLOGY
16891 Johnson St Ste A (49417-8461)
PHONE..............................616 847-6036
Timothy Widner, *Owner*
EMP: 6
SQ FT: 6,000
SALES (est): 650.9K **Privately Held**
SIC: 3479 Coating of metals & formed products

(G-6093)
V & V INC
Also Called: Harbor Deburring & Finshg Co
1703 Eaton Dr (49417-2824)
P.O. Box 547 (49417-0547)
PHONE..............................616 842-8611
Steven Vink, *President*
EMP: 11
SQ FT: 37,500
SALES (est): 1.4MM **Privately Held**
SIC: 3471 Finishing, metals or formed products; tumbling (cleaning & polishing) of machine parts

(G-6094)
VAN PELT INDUSTRIES LLC
720 Taylor Ave (49417-2158)
P.O. Box 541 (49417-0541)
PHONE..............................616 842-1200
Holly Bacon, *Principal*
Kevin Bacon,
EMP: 4 **EST:** 2011
SQ FT: 18,000
SALES (est): 278.4K **Privately Held**
SIC: 3498 Tube fabricating (contract bending & shaping)

(G-6095)
VER DUINS INC
623 Washington Ave (49417-1456)
P.O. Box 658 (49417-0658)
PHONE..............................616 842-0730
Robert Ver Duin, *President*
Michael Duin, *General Mgr*
EMP: 3
SQ FT: 9,000
SALES (est): 673.6K **Privately Held**
WEB: www.verduins.com
SIC: 5199 2752 Advertising specialties; commercial printing, offset

(G-6096)
WARNER INSTRUMENTS
Also Called: Fireright Controls
1320 Fulton Ave (49417-1534)
PHONE..............................616 843-5342
Gene L Warner, *Owner*
EMP: 7
SQ FT: 4,600
SALES: 510K **Privately Held**
WEB: www.fireright.com
SIC: 3823 3822 3625 Temperature instruments: industrial process type; auto controls regulating residntl & coml environmt & applncs; relays & industrial controls

(G-6097)
WEST MICHIGAN MOLDING INC
Also Called: Grand Haven Nursery Products
1425 Aerial View Dr (49417-9400)
PHONE..............................616 846-4950
Alan Chapel, *President*
Karl Chapel, *Vice Pres*
Ken Byrne, *QC Mgr*
Bruce Duff, *Controller*
Kevin Wierda, *Program Mgr*
▲ **EMP:** 103
SALES (est): 30.2MM **Privately Held**
WEB: www.ghplastics.com
SIC: 3089 Injection molded finished plastic products; injection molding of plastics

Grand Junction
Van Buren County

(G-6098)
SOLLMAN & SON MOLD & TOOL
Also Called: S & S Mold & Tool
254 58th St (49056-9534)
PHONE..............................269 236-6700
Todd Sollman, *President*
EMP: 4
SALES (est): 586.7K **Privately Held**
SIC: 3544 Special dies & tools

Grand Ledge
Eaton County

(G-6099)
AER
16574 S Bauer Rd (48837-9169)
PHONE..............................517 345-7272
Jason Smith, *Principal*
EMP: 4 **EST:** 2010
SALES (est): 357.9K **Privately Held**
SIC: 3714 Motor vehicle parts & accessories

(G-6100)
AMERICAN BOTTLING COMPANY
Also Called: 7 Up Lansing
1145 Comet Ln (48837-9363)
PHONE..............................517 622-8605
Jim Willett, *Manager*
EMP: 60 **Publicly Held**
WEB: www.cs-americas.com
SIC: 2086 5149 Bottled & canned soft drinks; groceries & related products
HQ: The American Bottling Company
   5301 Legacy Dr
   Plano TX 75024

(G-6101)
ARCHER-DANIELS-MIDLAND COMPANY
Also Called: ADM
16994 Wright Rd (48837-9258)
PHONE..............................517 627-4017
Don Seidl, *Branch Mgr*
EMP: 12
SALES (corp-wide): 64.3B **Publicly Held**
WEB: www.admworld.com
SIC: 2041 Flour & other grain mill products
PA: Archer-Daniels-Midland Company
   77 W Wacker Dr Ste 4600
   Chicago IL 60601
   312 634-8100

(G-6102)
BITZENBURGER MACHINE & TOOL
13060 Lawson Rd (48837-9701)
PHONE..............................517 627-8433
Jerry Anderson, *Owner*
Bill Anderson, *Manager*
EMP: 4 **EST:** 1996
SALES (est): 334.9K **Privately Held**
WEB: www.bitzenburger.com
SIC: 3949 Archery equipment, general

(G-6103)
CONTRACTORS PRINTING
10236 W Grand River Hwy (48837-9204)
PHONE..............................517 622-1888
Rick Washburn, *Owner*
EMP: 6
SALES (est): 288.5K **Privately Held**
SIC: 2759 Screen printing

(G-6104)
DANS CONCRETE LLC
9202 Riverside Dr (48837-9273)
PHONE..............................517 242-0754
Daniel Rahall,
EMP: 9
SALES (est): 250K **Privately Held**
SIC: 2951 Asphalt paving mixtures & blocks

(G-6105)
E-T-M ENTERPRISES I INC (PA)
920 N Clinton St (48837-1106)
PHONE..............................517 627-8461
David Mohnke, *President*
Ron Clewley, *Opers Staff*
Michael Buter, *Buyer*
Jack Brockhaus, *Technical Mgr*
Tony Fitzpatrick, *Engineer*
▲ **EMP:** 163 **EST:** 1970
SQ FT: 100,000
SALES (est): 35.6MM **Privately Held**
WEB: www.etmenterprises.com
SIC: 3544 3089 3714 3713 Special dies & tools; spouting, plastic & glass fiber reinforced; molding primary plastic; motor vehicle parts & accessories; truck & bus bodies

(G-6106)
ENERCO CORPORATION (PA)
317 N Bridge St (48837-1632)
PHONE..............................517 627-1669
Robert T Othmer, *President*
Cathy Gwilt, *General Mgr*
Jo Ann Cranson, *Vice Pres*
Jo Cranson, *Vice Pres*
Rudy Othmer, *Vice Pres*
EMP: 20 **EST:** 1977
SALES (est): 2.6MM **Privately Held**
WEB: www.enercocorp.com
SIC: 2899 Water treating compounds

(G-6107)
G-FORCE TOOLING LLC
425 Spring St (48837-1436)
PHONE..............................517 712-8177
Julie Cotter, *Branch Mgr*
EMP: 3
SALES (corp-wide): 626.5K **Privately Held**
SIC: 3721 Helicopters
PA: G-Force Tooling Llc
   1325 Island Hwy
   Charlotte MI 48813
   517 541-2747

(G-6108)
GREAT LAKES NEON
9861 W Grand River Hwy (48837-9259)
PHONE..............................517 582-7451
Sain Robert, *Principal*
EMP: 3
SALES (est): 123.2K **Privately Held**
SIC: 2813 Neon

(G-6109)
KEYSTONE PRINTING INC
3540 Jefferson Hwy (48837-9750)
PHONE..............................517 627-4078

Grand Ledge - Eaton County (G-6110)

Ann E Gienapp, *CEO*
Timothy A Clark, *President*
Mitch Macnamara, *Vice Pres*
EMP: 16
SQ FT: 10,000
SALES (est): 44.7K **Privately Held**
WEB: www.keyprintgroup.com
SIC: 2752 Commercial printing, offset

(G-6110)
L & W INC
Also Called: L & W, Engineering
13112 Oneida Rd (48837-9772)
PHONE..................................517 627-7333
EMP: 10
SALES (corp-wide): 2.2B **Privately Held**
SIC: 3469 Stamping metal for the trade
HQ: L & W, Inc.
  17757 Woodland Dr
  New Boston MI 48164
  734 397-6300

(G-6111)
MICHIGAN POLY PIPE INC
Also Called: Michigan Pipe Company
10242 W Grand River Hwy (48837-9204)
PHONE..................................517 709-8100
Chad Cadwell, *President*
EMP: 7
SQ FT: 3,000
SALES: 6MM **Privately Held**
SIC: 3321 Cast iron pipe & fittings

(G-6112)
MILLBROOK PRINTING CO
Also Called: Keystone Millbrook
3540 Jefferson Hwy (48837-9750)
PHONE..................................517 627-4078
Paul Doerfler, *President*
Laura Hall, *General Mgr*
Tim Clark, *Principal*
Ryan Schatzle, *Project Mgr*
Bill Devault, *Prdtn Mgr*
EMP: 45 **EST:** 1962
SQ FT: 24,600
SALES (est): 8.4MM **Privately Held**
WEB: www.millbrookprinting.com
SIC: 2752 2789 2791 Commercial printing, offset; bookbinding & related work; typesetting

(G-6113)
PITCHFORD BERTIE
Also Called: Pitchfords Auto Parts & Svc
7821 W Grand River Hwy (48837-8212)
PHONE..................................517 627-1151
Bertie Pitchford, *Owner*
David Pitchford, *Principal*
EMP: 6
SQ FT: 4,400
SALES (est): 370K **Privately Held**
SIC: 7538 7539 3546 General automotive repair shops; machine shop, automotive; saws & sawing equipment

(G-6114)
ROBERTS SINTO CORPORATION
Also Called: Systemation
150 Orchard St (48837-1210)
P.O. Box 39 (48837-0039)
PHONE..................................517 371-2471
Debbie Eckmeter, *Plant Mgr*
Debbie Ketchum, *Warehouse Mgr*
EMP: 100
SQ FT: 59,320 **Privately Held**
WEB: www.robertssinto.com
SIC: 3535 3537 Conveyors & conveying equipment; industrial trucks & tractors
HQ: Roberts Sinto Corporation
  3001 W Main St
  Lansing MI 48917
  517 371-2460

(G-6115)
RT SWANSON INC
1030 Tulip St (48837-2045)
PHONE..................................517 627-4955
Richard Swanson, *President*
EMP: 6
SALES (est): 380K **Privately Held**
SIC: 3931 Organ parts & materials

(G-6116)
SPECIALTY WELDING
12703 Melody Rd (48837-8940)
PHONE..................................517 627-5566
Jim Westwood, *Owner*
EMP: 6
SALES (est): 220K **Privately Held**
SIC: 7692 1799 Welding repair; welding on site

(G-6117)
ZION INDUSTRIES INC
1180 Comet Ln (48837-9362)
PHONE..................................517 622-3409
Steve Sandstedt, *Manager*
EMP: 10
SALES (corp-wide): 11MM **Privately Held**
SIC: 3398 Metal heat treating
PA: Zion Industries, Inc.
  6229 Grafton Rd
  Valley City OH 44280
  330 225-3246

Grand Marais
Alger County

(G-6118)
GREAT LAKES PILOT PUBG CO
E22029 Everett Ave (49839-5119)
P.O. Box 339 (49839-0339)
PHONE..................................906 494-2391
Enrico Capogrossa, *President*
Mary Capogrossa, *Admin Sec*
EMP: 3
SALES (est): 267.2K **Privately Held**
SIC: 2711 Newspapers: publishing only, not printed on site

Grand Rapids
Kent County

(G-6119)
3 D & A DISPLAY LLC
7377 Expressway Dr Sw (49548-7980)
PHONE..................................616 827-3323
Dave Fenske, *Owner*
▲ **EMP:** 3 **EST:** 2008
SALES (est): 312.9K **Privately Held**
SIC: 3993 Signs & advertising specialties

(G-6120)
3DM SOURCE INC
555 Plymouth Ave Ne (49505-6029)
PHONE..................................616 647-9513
Brian Huff, *President*
Drew Boersma, *Treasurer*
EMP: 13
SQ FT: 6,000
SALES (est): 1.3MM **Privately Held**
SIC: 3842 5999 Surgical appliances & supplies; business machines & equipment

(G-6121)
3DXTECH LLC
904 36th St Se Ste B (49508-2532)
PHONE..................................616 717-3811
Matthew Howlett, *President*
EMP: 7
SALES (est): 887.7K **Privately Held**
SIC: 3672 Printed circuit boards

(G-6122)
A & K FINISHING INC
4175 Danvers Ct Se (49512-4041)
P.O. Box 888159 (49588-8159)
PHONE..................................616 949-9100
Scott Hankamp, *Opers Mgr*
Jerry Posthumus, *Materials Mgr*
Don Bolt, *Manager*
Duane Osbun, *Manager*
EMP: 30
SALES (corp-wide): 8.4MM **Privately Held**
WEB: www.akfinishing.com
SIC: 3479 Etching & engraving; painting, coating & hot dipping
PA: A & K Finishing, Inc.
  4436 Donkers Ct Se
  Grand Rapids MI 49512
  616 949-9100

(G-6123)
A A A MAILING & PACKG SUPS LLC
Also Called: D N D Business Machines
3148 Plainfield Ave Ne # 258 (49525-3285)
PHONE..................................616 481-9120
Joe Feller, *Mng Member*
EMP: 4
SALES: 200K **Privately Held**
SIC: 3579 Mailing, letter handling & addressing machines

(G-6124)
A C MACHINING LLC
7490 Division Ave S (49548-7162)
PHONE..................................616 455-3870
Ann Timmer, *Principal*
Allen Timmer,
EMP: 5
SALES: 250K **Privately Held**
SIC: 3599 Machine shop, jobbing & repair

(G-6125)
A K OIL LLC DBA SPEEDY OIL AND
925 Leonard St Nw (49504-4153)
PHONE..................................616 233-9505
Alex Kanaan, *Principal*
EMP: 4
SALES (est): 313.6K **Privately Held**
SIC: 2992 Lubricating oils

(G-6126)
A-PAC MANUFACTURING COMPANY
2719 Courier Dr Nw (49534-1247)
PHONE..................................616 791-7222
Leonard J Fouty, *President*
David Kraai, *Corp Secy*
Tim Takken, *Plant Mgr*
Tim Harms, *CFO*
EMP: 48
SQ FT: 34,000
SALES (est): 8.9MM **Privately Held**
WEB: www.polybags.com
SIC: 3081 2673 Packing materials, plastic sheet; bags: plastic, laminated & coated

(G-6127)
A2Z COATING
200 Garden St Se (49507-1711)
PHONE..................................616 805-3281
EMP: 4
SALES (est): 381.4K **Privately Held**
SIC: 3479 Metal coating & allied service

(G-6128)
ABC COATING COMPANY INC
Also Called: ABC Coating Company Michigan
1503 Burlingame Ave Sw (49509-1001)
P.O. Box 9484 (49509-0484)
PHONE..................................616 245-4626
Marcella Acuna, *President*
EMP: 10
SALES (corp-wide): 7.4MM **Privately Held**
WEB: www.abccoating.com
SIC: 3312 Blast furnaces & steel mills
PA: Abc Coating Company, Inc.
  2236 S Yukon Ave
  Tulsa OK 74107
  918 585-2587

(G-6129)
ABC NAILS LLC
20 Monroe Center St Ne # 110 (49503-3276)
PHONE..................................616 776-6000
Charlie Vu, *Mng Member*
EMP: 4
SALES (est): 416.3K **Privately Held**
SIC: 2824 Anidex fibers

(G-6130)
ABLE MANUFACTURING INC
601 Crosby St Nw (49504-3104)
PHONE..................................616 235-3322
Russ Golemba, *President*
EMP: 17
SQ FT: 20,000
SALES (est): 2.8MM **Privately Held**
SIC: 3599 Grinding castings for the trade; machine shop, jobbing & repair

(G-6131)
ACCELERATED TOOLING LLC
2909 Buchanan Ave Sw (49548-1027)
PHONE..................................616 293-9612
Scott Oshinski, *Mng Member*
Chris Brooker,
EMP: 13
SALES: 2MM **Privately Held**
WEB: www.acceltool.com
SIC: 3599 Machine shop, jobbing & repair

(G-6132)
ACCUFORM INDUSTRIES INC (PA)
1701 Broadway Ave Nw (49504-2049)
PHONE..................................616 363-3801
Mark Holleman, *President*
EMP: 15
SQ FT: 20,000
SALES (est): 3.2MM **Privately Held**
WEB: www.accuform-fascias.com
SIC: 3444 Sheet metal specialties, not stamped

(G-6133)
ACCUFORM INDUSTRIES INC
Also Called: Accu-Form Metal Products
1701 Broadway Ave Nw (49504-2049)
PHONE..................................616 363-3801
Mark Holleman, *Manager*
EMP: 12
SALES (est): 1.3MM
SALES (corp-wide): 3.2MM **Privately Held**
WEB: www.accuform-fascias.com
SIC: 3444 Sheet metal specialties, not stamped
PA: Accuform Industries, Inc.
  1701 Broadway Ave Nw
  Grand Rapids MI 49504
  616 363-3801

(G-6134)
ACCURATE COATING INC
955 Godfrey Ave Sw (49503-5003)
P.O. Box 1214 (49501-1214)
PHONE..................................616 452-0016
Dave Kasper, *Principal*
EMP: 5
SALES (est): 402.6K **Privately Held**
SIC: 3471 Finishing, metals or formed products

(G-6135)
ACE VENDING SERVICE INC
Also Called: Kent Commerce Center
3417 R B Chaffee Memrl (49548)
PHONE..................................616 243-7983
Thomas Lileikis, *Vice Pres*
EMP: 33
SQ FT: 77,000
SALES: 4MM **Privately Held**
SIC: 5962 6512 5963 2099 Sandwich & hot food vending machines; commercial & industrial building operation; direct selling establishments; food preparations

(G-6136)
ACTION FABRICATORS INC
Also Called: Boyd
3760 East Paris Ave Se (49512-3903)
PHONE..................................616 957-2032
Matt Alferink, *President*
Don Armbrester, *Vice Pres*
Bruce Barthuly, *Plant Supt*
Robin Hay, *Purch Mgr*
Karen King, *Purch Mgr*
EMP: 150
SQ FT: 105,000
SALES: 52.7MM
SALES (corp-wide): 915.2MM **Privately Held**
WEB: www.actionfab.com
SIC: 3053 3086 2891 Gaskets & sealing devices; plastics foam products; adhesives
HQ: Boyd Corporation
  5960 Inglewood Dr Ste 115
  Pleasanton CA 94588
  209 236-1111

GEOGRAPHIC SECTION

Grand Rapids - Kent County (G-6162)

(G-6137)
ACTION MOLD & MACHINING INC
3120 Ken O Sha Ind Park S (49508-1360)
PHONE.................................616 452-1580
Michael P Fassbender, *Officer*
▲ **EMP:** 45
SALES (est): 9.4MM **Privately Held**
WEB: www.actionmold.net
SIC: 3544 Industrial molds

(G-6138)
ADAC AUTOMOTIVE TRIM INC (HQ)
5920 Tahoe Dr Se (49546-7123)
P.O. Box 888375 (49588-8375)
PHONE.................................616 957-0311
Kenneth G Hungerford, *CEO*
Jim Teets, *President*
▲ **EMP:** 27
SALES (est): 5.9MM
SALES (corp-wide): 263.6MM **Privately Held**
SIC: 3089 Injection molding of plastics
PA: Adac Plastics, Inc.
5920 Tahoe Dr Se
Grand Rapids MI 49546
616 957-0311

(G-6139)
ADAC DOOR COMPONENTS INC
Also Called: Adac Automotive
5920 Tahoe Dr Se (49546-7123)
P.O. Box 888375 (49588-8375)
PHONE.................................616 957-0311
▲ **EMP:** 1
SALES: 7.5MM
SALES (corp-wide): 263.6MM **Privately Held**
SIC: 3089 3711 Injection molding of plastics; motor vehicles & car bodies
PA: Adac Plastics, Inc.
5920 Tahoe Dr Se
Grand Rapids MI 49546
616 957-0311

(G-6140)
ADAC PLASTICS INC (PA)
Also Called: Adac Automotive
5920 Tahoe Dr Se (49546-7123)
P.O. Box 888375 (49588-8375)
PHONE.................................616 957-0311
Kenneth G Hungerford, *Ch of Bd*
Jim Teets, *President*
Adam Smith, *Business Mgr*
Carey Wentzloff, *Mfg Mgr*
Sue Fenicle, *Materials Mgr*
▲ **EMP:** 40
SQ FT: 13,000
SALES (est): 263.6MM **Privately Held**
WEB: www.adacplastics.com
SIC: 3089 Injection molding of plastics

(G-6141)
ADAC PLASTICS INC
Also Called: Adac Automotive
2929 32nd St Se (49512-1771)
PHONE.................................616 957-0311
David Lovelace, *Branch Mgr*
Mark McWilliams, *Manager*
EMP: 10
SALES (corp-wide): 263.6MM **Privately Held**
SIC: 3089 Injection molding of plastics
PA: Adac Plastics, Inc.
5920 Tahoe Dr Se
Grand Rapids MI 49546
616 957-0311

(G-6142)
ADAC PLASTICS INC
5670 Eagle Dr Se (49512-2057)
P.O. Box 888375 (49588-8375)
PHONE.................................616 957-0311
Jim Teets, *Branch Mgr*
EMP: 40
SALES (corp-wide): 263.6MM **Privately Held**
SIC: 3089 Injection molding of plastics
PA: Adac Plastics, Inc.
5920 Tahoe Dr Se
Grand Rapids MI 49546
616 957-0311

(G-6143)
ADCO SPECIALTIES INC
4331 E Beltline Ave Ne (49525-9784)
PHONE.................................616 452-6882
Matthew Coash, *President*
EMP: 7
SQ FT: 1,400
SALES (est): 1.4MM **Privately Held**
WEB: www.shopadco.com
SIC: 5199 7389 2261 Advertising specialties; embroidering of advertising on shirts, etc.; embossing cotton broadwoven fabrics

(G-6144)
ADVANCE BCI INC (PA)
Also Called: Advance Newspapers
3102 Walker Ridge Dr Nw (49544-9125)
PHONE.................................616 669-1366
Joel Holland, *Publisher*
Erin Sparks, *Manager*
Mike Winegarden, *Manager*
EMP: 75 **EST:** 1966
SQ FT: 12,000
SALES (est): 6.2MM **Privately Held**
WEB: www.advancenewspapers.com
SIC: 2741 2752 2711 Shopping news: publishing & printing; commercial printing, offset; newspapers

(G-6145)
ADVANCE BCI INC
Also Called: Jenison Printing
3102 Walker Ridge Dr Nw (49544-9125)
PHONE.................................616 669-5210
Marilynn Driesenga, *Manager*
EMP: 60
SALES (corp-wide): 6.2MM **Privately Held**
WEB: www.advancenewspapers.com
SIC: 2752 2791 2711 Commercial printing, offset; typesetting; newspapers
PA: Advance Bci Inc.
3102 Walker Ridge Dr Nw
Grand Rapids MI 49544
616 669-1366

(G-6146)
ADVANCE PACKAGING ACQUISITION (HQ)
Also Called: Colonial Packaging
4450 36th St Se (49512-1917)
P.O. Box 888311 (49588-8311)
PHONE.................................616 949-6610
Carol Hoyt, *CEO*
Donald W Crossley, *President*
▲ **EMP:** 80 **EST:** 2000
SALES (est): 5.1MM
SALES (corp-wide): 147MM **Privately Held**
SIC: 2653 Boxes, corrugated: made from purchased materials; sheets, corrugated: made from purchased materials
PA: Advance Packaging Corporation
4459 40th St Se
Grand Rapids MI 49512
616 949-6610

(G-6147)
ADVANCE PACKAGING CORPORATION (PA)
4459 40th St Se (49512-4036)
P.O. Box 888311 (49588-8311)
PHONE.................................616 949-6610
Carol Hoyt, *CEO*
Don Crossley, *President*
Sue Albrecht, *Vice Pres*
Jean Kennedy, *Buyer*
Cindy Mitchell, *Credit Mgr*
EMP: 185 **EST:** 1966
SQ FT: 170,700
SALES (est): 147MM **Privately Held**
WEB: www.advancepkg.com
SIC: 2653 3412 Boxes, corrugated: made from purchased materials; sheets, corrugated: made from purchased materials; metal barrels, drums & pails

(G-6148)
ADVANCED FOOD TECHNOLOGIES INC
1140 Butterworth St Sw (49504-6104)
P.O. Box 202 (49501-0202)
PHONE.................................616 574-4144
Robert Roskam, *CEO*
Jessica Lamp, *Purch Agent*
▲ **EMP:** 65
SQ FT: 70,000
SALES (est): 23.6MM **Privately Held**
SIC: 2045 2041 Prepared flour mixes & doughs; flour mixes

(G-6149)
ADVANCED SHEET METAL
320 Marion Ave Sw (49504-6107)
PHONE.................................616 301-3828
EMP: 7
SALES (est): 684K **Privately Held**
SIC: 3444 Sheet metalwork

(G-6150)
ADVANTAGE LABEL AND PACKG INC
Also Called: Advantage Label & Packg Pdts
5575 Executive Pkwy Se (49512-5509)
PHONE.................................616 656-1900
Brad Knoth, *President*
Todd Geglio, *Vice Pres*
Ray Deladurantaye, *Plant Mgr*
Debbie Tavolacci, *Purch Mgr*
Thomas J Long, *Treasurer*
EMP: 46
SQ FT: 14,000
SALES (est): 8MM **Privately Held**
WEB: www.advantagelabel.com
SIC: 2754 2759 Labels: gravure printing; commercial printing

(G-6151)
AFTECH INC
3056 Walker Ridge Dr Nw A (49544-9133)
PHONE.................................616 866-1650
EMP: 4
SALES (est): 499.4K **Privately Held**
SIC: 3714 Motor vehicle parts & accessories

(G-6152)
AGAPE PLASTICS INC
11474 1st Ave Nw (49534-3399)
PHONE.................................616 735-4091
Cynthia Alt, *CEO*
David Cornelius, *President*
Christopher Davis, *Engineer*
Stacey Drozd, *Project Engr*
Mike Krajewski, *Project Engr*
EMP: 175
SQ FT: 67,000
SALES (est): 54MM **Privately Held**
WEB: www.agapeplastics.com
SIC: 3089 Injection molded finished plastic products

(G-6153)
AGENDA 2020 INC
Also Called: La Familia Stop 'n' Shop
555 Cascade West Pkwy Se (49546-2105)
PHONE.................................616 581-6271
Jose Flores, *President*
EMP: 11
SALES (est): 1.4MM **Privately Held**
WEB: www.lavozmi.com
SIC: 5411 2721 Convenience stores; magazines: publishing only, not printed on site

(G-6154)
AGROPUR INC
Also Called: Parmalat Grand Rapids
5252 Clay Ave Sw (49548-5658)
PHONE.................................616 538-3822
Mark Sherman, *Branch Mgr*
EMP: 100
SALES (corp-wide): 4.5B **Privately Held**
WEB: www.farmlanddairies.com
SIC: 2022 Cheese, natural & processed
HQ: Agropur Inc.
3500 E Destination Dr # 200
Appleton WI 54915
920 944-0990

(G-6155)
AIS CONSTRUCTION EQP SVC CORP
4781 Clay Ave Sw (49548-3070)
PHONE.................................616 538-2400
Brandon Peter, *Branch Mgr*
EMP: 25
SALES (corp-wide): 176MM **Privately Held**
SIC: 3531 Construction machinery
PA: Ais Construction Equipment Service Corporation
600 44th St Sw
Grand Rapids MI 49548
616 538-2400

(G-6156)
ALEXANDER DODDS COMPANY
3000 Walkent Dr Nw (49544-1453)
PHONE.................................616 784-6000
Bernard Campbell, *CEO*
Bob Linner, *Director*
▲ **EMP:** 8
SQ FT: 27,600
SALES (est): 2MM **Privately Held**
WEB: www.dodds.com
SIC: 3553 Woodworking machinery

(G-6157)
ALGOMA PRODUCTS INC
4201 Brockton Dr Se (49512-4051)
PHONE.................................616 285-6440
Trevor Wolfe, *President*
EMP: 10
SQ FT: 23,000
SALES (est): 2MM **Privately Held**
SIC: 2819 Industrial inorganic chemicals

(G-6158)
ALL BENDING & TUBULAR PDTS LLC
430 Cummings Ave Nw Ste G (49534-7984)
PHONE.................................616 333-2364
Dave Willet, *Marketing Mgr*
Carol Willet, *Mng Member*
EMP: 12
SQ FT: 10,000
SALES (est): 200K **Privately Held**
SIC: 3317 Steel pipe & tubes

(G-6159)
ALL PHASE WELDING SERVICE INC
711 Ionia Ave Nw (49503-1414)
PHONE.................................616 235-6100
Dave Deweese, *President*
Jeffrey Vereeke, *Vice Pres*
EMP: 8
SQ FT: 15,000
SALES: 600K **Privately Held**
SIC: 7692 Welding repair

(G-6160)
ALLEGRA PRINT AND IMAGING
929 Alpine Commerce Park (49544-8232)
PHONE.................................616 784-6699
Eric Vetter, *Principal*
EMP: 9
SALES (est): 468.3K **Privately Held**
SIC: 8741 2752 Business management; commercial printing, offset

(G-6161)
ALLIANCE CNC LLC
Also Called: Alliance Cnc Ctter Grnding Svc
3987 Brockton Dr Se Ste A (49512-4070)
PHONE.................................616 971-4700
Richard Czarniecki, *President*
Fred Edmonson, *Prdtn Mgr*
Brent Dyke, *QC Mgr*
EMP: 14
SQ FT: 10,000
SALES (est): 2.2MM
SALES (corp-wide): 1MM **Privately Held**
WEB: www.alliancecnc.com
SIC: 3599 Machine shop, jobbing & repair
PA: Gws Tool Holdings, Llc
595 County Road 448
Tavares FL 32778
352 343-8778

(G-6162)
ALLIANT ENTERPRISES LLC
Also Called: Alliant Healthcare Products
333 Bridge St Nw Ste 1125 (49504-5367)
PHONE.................................269 629-0300
Bob Taylor, *Owner*
Mark McKinney, *Sales Staff*
▲ **EMP:** 26
SQ FT: 3,600
SALES (est): 9MM **Privately Held**
WEB: www.allianthealthcare.com
SIC: 3841 Surgical & medical instruments

Grand Rapids - Kent County (G-6163)

(G-6163)
ALLIED FINISHING INC
4100 Broadmoor Ave Se (49512-3933)
P.O. Box 3728 (49501-3728)
PHONE..................................616 698-7550
Bruce Stone, *President*
Jerry Vandersloot, *Materials Mgr*
Scott Alvesteffer, *Treasurer*
John Ruzic, *VP Sales*
Matt Lepzinski, *Program Mgr*
EMP: 145 **EST:** 1977
SQ FT: 96,000
SALES (est): 21.4MM **Privately Held**
WEB: www.alliedfinishinginc.com
SIC: 3471 Plating of metals or formed products; electroplating of metals or formed products

(G-6164)
ALLSALES ENTERPRISES INC
Also Called: Ag-Pro
1013 Country Gdns Nw (49534-7919)
PHONE..................................616 437-0639
Roger De Haan, *President*
Chad Morton, *Principal*
Todd Rose, *Principal*
David Vandervelde, *Principal*
Jean Dehaan, *CFO*
EMP: 10 **EST:** 1994
SQ FT: 1,200
SALES (est): 1.1MM **Privately Held**
WEB: www.rjksalesinc.com
SIC: 2671 5999 Packaging paper & plastics film, coated & laminated; packaging materials: boxes, padding, etc.

(G-6165)
AMERICAN COOLING SYSTEMS LLC
3099 Wilson Dr Nw (49534-7565)
PHONE..................................616 954-0280
John B Jahns,
▼ **EMP:** 38 **EST:** 1999
SALES (est): 8.7MM **Privately Held**
WEB: www.americancooling.com
SIC: 3564 Filters, air: furnaces, air conditioning equipment, etc.

(G-6166)
AMERICAN SEATING COMPANY (PA)
801 Broadway Ave Nw # 200 (49504-4463)
PHONE..................................616 732-6600
Edward J Clark, *CEO*
Thomas E Bush, *President*
Keith A McDowell, *Vice Pres*
David B McLaughlin, *Vice Pres*
Bruce R Weener, *Vice Pres*
◆ **EMP:** 425 **EST:** 1886
SQ FT: 640,000
SALES (est): 110.6MM **Privately Held**
WEB: www.amseco.com
SIC: 2522 2531 Office furniture, except wood; vehicle furniture; stadium seating

(G-6167)
AMERIKAM INC
1337 Judd Ave Sw (49509-1096)
PHONE..................................616 243-5833
Stephanie Leonardos, *Ch of Bd*
Roberta Warren, *General Mgr*
Dr Helen Popovich, *Corp Secy*
Michael Zolnierek, *Mfg Mgr*
Chau Nguyen, *Purch Mgr*
EMP: 90 **EST:** 1934
SQ FT: 55,000
SALES (est): 24.2MM **Privately Held**
WEB: www.amerikam.com
SIC: 3451 3441 Screw machine products; fabricated structural metal

(G-6168)
AMPHENOL BORISCH TECH INC (HQ)
Also Called: Borisch Mfg
4511 East Paris Ave Se (49512-5314)
PHONE..................................616 554-9820
Jonathan Borisch, *President*
Bill Callahan, *General Mgr*
Eric Johr, *General Mgr*
Ariel Koblenz, *Business Mgr*
Jacob Vriesman, *Purch Mgr*
▲ **EMP:** 115

SALES (est): 34.1MM
SALES (corp-wide): 8.2B **Publicly Held**
WEB: www.borisch.com
SIC: 3679 3599 Harness assemblies for electronic use: wire or cable; electronic circuits; machine shop, jobbing & repair
PA: Amphenol Corporation
  358 Hall Ave
  Wallingford CT 06492
  203 265-8900

(G-6169)
ANCHOR LAMINA AMERICA INC
4300 40th St Se (49512-4101)
PHONE..................................519 966-4431
Brian Russell, *Manager*
EMP: 43 **Privately Held**
WEB: www.anchorlamina.com
SIC: 3544 Special dies, tools, jigs & fixtures
HQ: Anchor Lamina America, Inc.
  39830 Grand River Ave B-2
  Novi MI 48375
  248 489-9122

(G-6170)
ANGSTROM ALUMINUM CASTINGS LLC
3559 Kraft Ave Se (49512-2033)
PHONE..................................616 309-1208
Lalitha Gadiraju, *Finance Dir*
Nagesh K Palakurthi,
EMP: 39
SALES (est): 2.4MM **Privately Held**
SIC: 3363 Aluminum die-castings
PA: Angstrom Automotive Group, Llc
  26980 Trolley Indus Dr
  Taylor MI 48180

(G-6171)
APEX SPRING & STAMPING CORP
11420 1st Ave Nw (49534-3399)
PHONE..................................616 453-5463
Dennis K Bhaskaran, *CEO*
Dennis Bhaskaran, *CEO*
Dave Monterusso, *Sales Engr*
David Holtrop, *Sales Staff*
EMP: 65
SQ FT: 78,000
SALES (est): 23.3MM **Privately Held**
WEB: www.apexspring.com
SIC: 3496 3469 3544 3495 Miscellaneous fabricated wire products; metal stampings; special dies, tools, jigs & fixtures; wire springs; bolts, nuts, rivets & washers; manufactured hardware (general)

(G-6172)
APOLLO TOOL & ENGINEERING INC
3020 Wilson Dr Nw (49534-7564)
PHONE..................................616 735-4934
Mike Hartley, *President*
Floyd Hoyt, *Corp Secy*
EMP: 17
SQ FT: 2,500
SALES (est): 3.2MM **Privately Held**
SIC: 3545 Cutting tools for machine tools

(G-6173)
APPLIED ANALYTICS INC
4767 Broadmoor Ave Se # 7 (49512-9397)
PHONE..................................616 285-7810
Frederick Clowney, *President*
EMP: 10
SQ FT: 10,000
SALES (est): 1.3MM **Privately Held**
WEB: www.appliedanalyticsinc.com
SIC: 3812 Navigational systems & instruments

(G-6174)
APPLIED MECHANICS CORPORATION
Also Called: Amcor
14122 Ironwood Dr Nw (49534-1034)
PHONE..................................616 677-1355
Theodore Vecchio, *President*
G M Minnhaar-Tomatis, *Vice Pres*
M Minnhaar Tomatis, *Purchasing*
EMP: 5
SQ FT: 5,500

SALES (est): 739K **Privately Held**
WEB: www.amcortooling.com
SIC: 3544 Special dies & tools

(G-6175)
APPROPOS LLC
Also Called: Appropos Digital
678 Front Ave Nw Ste 100 (49504-5323)
PHONE..................................844 462-7776
Jon Faber, *CEO*
Todd Slager, *Partner*
David Case, *Chief*
Brandon Merritt, *Officer*
EMP: 30
SQ FT: 9,000
SALES (est): 1MM **Privately Held**
SIC: 7372 7335 Business oriented computer software; commercial photography

(G-6176)
APTIV SERVICES US LLC
Also Called: Delphi
2100 Burlingame Ave Sw (49509-1753)
PHONE..................................616 246-2471
Fred Brown, *Branch Mgr*
EMP: 11
SALES (corp-wide): 16.6B **Privately Held**
SIC: 3714 Motor vehicle parts & accessories
HQ: Aptiv Services Us, Llc
  5725 Innovation Dr
  Troy MI 48098

(G-6177)
APV BAKER
3223 Kraft Ave Se (49512-2063)
PHONE..................................616 784-3111
John Cox, *Principal*
Baker Perkins, *Sales Staff*
Dawn Termeer, *Info Tech Mgr*
Brett Cutler, *Technical Staff*
EMP: 3
SALES (est): 367.2K **Privately Held**
SIC: 3556 Food products machinery

(G-6178)
ARBOR GAGE & TOOLING INC
2031 Calvin Ave Se (49507-3305)
PHONE..................................616 454-8266
Edward Heerema Jr, *President*
Ruth Heerema, *Vice Pres*
Jacob Verduin, *Project Mgr*
Thanh Nguyen, *Data Proc Dir*
EMP: 35
SQ FT: 37,000
SALES (est): 5.7MM **Privately Held**
WEB: www.arborgage.com
SIC: 2542 3544 3543 Office & store showcases & display fixtures; special dies, tools, jigs & fixtures; industrial patterns

(G-6179)
ARCHITECTURAL ELEMENTS INC
4707 40th St Se (49512-4076)
PHONE..................................616 241-6001
Kurg Bouna, *President*
EMP: 12
SALES (est): 1.1MM **Privately Held**
SIC: 2431 Millwork

(G-6180)
ARGUS TECHNOLOGIES LLC
Also Called: C2 Group The
560 5th St Nw Ste 100 (49504-5243)
PHONE..................................616 538-9895
Michael Kunzler, *Mng Member*
Brian Hill, *Project Leader*
Chris Harter, *Software Dev*
Brian Oliver, *Software Dev*
Jacob Pilkinton, *Software Dev*
EMP: 25
SALES (est): 734.8K **Privately Held**
SIC: 7372 Application computer software

(G-6181)
ARKEMA INC
Also Called: Arkema Coating Resins
1415 Steele Ave Sw (49507-1562)
PHONE..................................616 243-4578
Chuck Bennett, *CEO*
Jeff Mills, *Plant Mgr*
Scott Harris, *Manager*
EMP: 123

SALES (corp-wide): 98.4MM **Privately Held**
SIC: 2812 Chlorine, compressed or liquefied
HQ: Arkema Inc.
  900 First Ave
  King Of Prussia PA 19406
  610 205-7000

(G-6182)
ARMICK INC (PA)
1516 Blaine Ave Se (49507-2002)
PHONE..................................616 481-5882
Blair Heethuis,
Nick Jacques,
EMP: 4
SALES (est): 480K **Privately Held**
SIC: 3544 Industrial molds

(G-6183)
ART OPTICAL CONTACT LENS INC
3175 3 Mile Rd Nw (49534-1325)
P.O. Box 1848 (49501-1848)
PHONE..................................616 453-1888
Thomas Anastor, *President*
Sheryl Pine, *General Mgr*
Chad Boyce, *COO*
Jill Anastor, *Vice Pres*
Cheryl Parish, *Controller*
EMP: 110 **EST:** 1960
SQ FT: 30,000
SALES (est): 25.6MM **Privately Held**
WEB: www.artoptical.com
SIC: 3851 Contact lenses

(G-6184)
ARTESIAN DISTILLERS
955 Ken O Sha Ind Park (49508-8246)
P.O. Box 43, Burnips (49314-0043)
PHONE..................................616 252-1700
EMP: 5
SALES (est): 419.6K **Privately Held**
SIC: 2085 Mfg Distilled/Blended Liquor

(G-6185)
ARTIFLEX MANUFACTURING LLC
I T S
731 Broadway Ave Nw (49504-5247)
PHONE..................................616 459-8285
Dan Whitehouse, *Plant Supt*
Don Mekkes, *Plant Mgr*
John Schury, *Prdtn Mgr*
Jeff Dies, *Purch Agent*
Jennifer Elliott-Umlor, *Purchasing*
EMP: 160
SALES (corp-wide): 197MM **Privately Held**
SIC: 3544 Die sets for metal stamping (presses)
PA: Artiflex Manufacturing, Llc
  1425 E Bowman St
  Wooster OH 44691
  330 262-2015

(G-6186)
ARVRON INC
4720 Clay Ave Sw (49548-3071)
PHONE..................................616 530-1888
Marvin Wynalda, *President*
Doug Oostdyk, *Plant Mgr*
▲ **EMP:** 30
SQ FT: 63,000
SALES: 18.9MM **Privately Held**
SIC: 2821 Polyurethane resins

(G-6187)
ASSOCIATED RACK CORPORATION
4910 Kraft Ave Se (49512-9708)
PHONE..................................616 554-6004
W L Faulman, *President*
EMP: 5
SALES (corp-wide): 54.2MM **Privately Held**
SIC: 2542 Racks, merchandise display or storage: except wood
PA: Associated Rack Corporation
  70 Athens Dr
  Mount Juliet TN 37122
  615 288-4204

GEOGRAPHIC SECTION

Grand Rapids - Kent County (G-6216)

(G-6188)
ASTELLAS PHARMA US INC
5905 Kraft Ave Se (49512-9684)
PHONE..................616 698-8825
Arla Boot, *Owner*
EMP: 12 Privately Held
WEB: www.ambisome.com
SIC: 2834 Vitamin, nutrient & hematinic preparations for human use
HQ: Astellas Pharma Us, Inc.
1 Astellas Way
Northbrook IL 60062
800 888-7704

(G-6189)
AUSTEMPER INC
341 Grant St Sw (49503-4921)
PHONE..................616 458-7061
Lee Price, *Manager*
EMP: 30
SALES (corp-wide): 19.5MM Privately Held
WEB: www.austemperinc.com
SIC: 3398 Annealing of metal
HQ: Austemper, Inc.
30760 Century Dr
Wixom MI 48393
586 293-4554

(G-6190)
AUTO-MASTERS INC
6521 Division Ave S (49548-7891)
PHONE..................616 455-4510
Gordon Gillman, *President*
Ralph Bos, *Vice Pres*
EMP: 20
SQ FT: 16,000
SALES (est): 2.3MM Privately Held
SIC: 5531 5013 7538 3716 Automotive accessories; automotive parts; automotive supplies & parts; general automotive repair shops; motor homes

(G-6191)
AUTOCAM MEDICAL DEVICES LLC (HQ)
4152 East Paris Ave Se (49512-3911)
PHONE..................877 633-8080
John C Kennedy, *President*
Warren A Veltman, *CFO*
EMP: 25
SQ FT: 190,000
SALES (est): 35.5MM Privately Held
SIC: 3842 3841 Implants, surgical; surgical & medical instruments

(G-6192)
AUTODIE LLC
44 Coldbrook St Nw (49503-1046)
PHONE..................616 454-9361
David Crandall, *COO*
Mark Battle, *Vice Pres*
Charlie Murphy, *CFO*
Jam Bertsch, *Treasurer*
Rodney Brouwer, *Mng Member*
▲ EMP: 250
SALES (est): 51.1MM
SALES (corp-wide): 126.4B Privately Held
SIC: 3544 Special dies & tools
HQ: Fca Us Llc
1000 Chrysler Dr
Auburn Hills MI 48326

(G-6193)
AUTOEXEC INC
4477 East Paris Ave Se (49512-5312)
PHONE..................616 971-0080
Charles Lippert, *CEO*
David Lippert, *President*
Kevin Smallegan, *Manager*
Priscilla Carrick, *Director*
▲ EMP: 5 EST: 1993
SALES (est): 751.6K Privately Held
SIC: 2522 Office desks & tables; except wood

(G-6194)
AUVESY INC
146 Monroe Center St Nw # 1210 (49503-2821)
PHONE..................616 888-3770
Robert Glaser, *CEO*
Emma Baranowski, *Office Mgr*
EMP: 5
SALES (est): 117.2K Privately Held
SIC: 7372 Prepackaged software

(G-6195)
AVANTIS INC
5441 36th St Se (49512-2015)
PHONE..................616 285-8000
Douglas Oosterman, *Vice Pres*
Joe Brophy, *Manager*
▲ EMP: 5
SALES: 250K Privately Held
SIC: 2522 Office furniture, except wood

(G-6196)
AWARD CUTTER COMPANY INC
5577 Crippen Ave Sw (49548-5716)
PHONE..................616 531-0430
Mark Beilfuss, *President*
Brenda Vanreenens, *Vice Pres*
EMP: 10
SQ FT: 6,000
SALES (est): 1.4MM Privately Held
WEB: www.awardcutter.com
SIC: 3545 End mills

(G-6197)
AXIS DIGITAL INC
6532 Clay Ave Sw (49548-7832)
PHONE..................616 698-9890
Greg Lindhout, *President*
EMP: 20 EST: 1986
SALES (est): 1.1MM Privately Held
WEB: www.axisdigital.com
SIC: 2754 Photogravure printing

(G-6198)
B & G PRODUCTS INC
3631 44th St Se Ste E (49512-3971)
PHONE..................616 698-9050
Kathleen Geddes, *President*
Jacci Harding, *Vice Pres*
Caleb Woodwyk, *Engineer*
EMP: 17
SQ FT: 5,000
SALES (est): 4.8MM Privately Held
SIC: 3565 3443 Bottling machinery: filling, capping, labeling; bottling & canning machinery; metal parts

(G-6199)
B-QUICK INSTANT PRINTING
3120 Division Ave S (49548-1133)
PHONE..................616 243-6562
Gary Ball, *Owner*
EMP: 5 EST: 1974
SQ FT: 1,600
SALES: 250K Privately Held
SIC: 2752 Commercial printing, offset

(G-6200)
BAINBRIDGE MANUFACTURING INC
1931 Will Ave Nw Ste 1 (49504-2013)
PHONE..................616 447-7631
Eugene Bainbridge, *President*
Barbara Bainbridge, *Corp Secy*
William Bainbridge, *Vice Pres*
EMP: 7
SQ FT: 10,000
SALES (est): 301.8K Privately Held
SIC: 2499 Carved & turned wood

(G-6201)
BAKER BOOK HOUSE COMPANY
2768 East Paris Ave Se (49546-6139)
PHONE..................616 957-3110
Susan Smith, *Branch Mgr*
EMP: 30
SALES (corp-wide): 59.8MM Privately Held
WEB: www.brazospress.com
SIC: 2731 Books: publishing only
PA: Baker Book House Company
6030 Fulton St E
Ada MI 49301
616 676-9185

(G-6202)
BAKER PERKINS INC
3223 Kraft Ave Se (49512-2063)
PHONE..................616 784-3111
John Cowx, *Principal*
Alma Erickson, *Project Mgr*
Michael Kieliszewski, *Project Mgr*
Larry Tyron, *Buyer*
Andy Barker, *Engineer*
◆ EMP: 55
SQ FT: 25,000
SALES (est): 12.7MM
SALES (corp-wide): 74.7MM Privately Held
WEB: www.bakerperkinsgroup.com
SIC: 3556 Smokers, food processing equipment
HQ: Baker Perkins Limited
Manor Drive
Peterborough CAMBS PE4 7
173 328-3000

(G-6203)
BANTA FURNITURE COMPANY
Also Called: Banta Management Resources
3390 Broadmoor Ave Se A (49512-8181)
PHONE..................616 575-8180
Theodore Banta, *President*
EMP: 11
SQ FT: 13,500
SALES: 1.5MM Privately Held
WEB: www.softblocks.com
SIC: 2599 7641 Factory furniture & fixtures; furniture upholstery repair

(G-6204)
BARACOA DIPS
435 Ionia Ave Sw (49503-5161)
PHONE..................616 643-3204
EMP: 3
SQ FT: 1,000
SALES (est): 91.3K Privately Held
SIC: 2022 Mfg Cheese

(G-6205)
BATTJES BORING INC
3999 3 Mile Rd Ne (49525-9627)
PHONE..................616 363-1969
Douglas Battjes, *President*
EMP: 4
SALES (est): 306.1K Privately Held
SIC: 1081 Test boring, metal mining

(G-6206)
BATTS GROUP LTD (PA)
3855 Sparks Dr Se Ste 222 (49546-2427)
PHONE..................616 956-3053
John H Batts, *President*
EMP: 3
SQ FT: 1,400
SALES (est): 1.5MM Privately Held
SIC: 3089 6282 6211 Clothes hangers, plastic; investment advice; security brokers & dealers

(G-6207)
BAUER PRODUCTS INC
702 Evergreen St Se (49507-1890)
PHONE..................616 245-4540
Jon Bacon, *President*
J Norman, *Vice Pres*
Bruce Bacon, *Treasurer*
▲ EMP: 25 EST: 1957
SQ FT: 10,000
SALES (est): 4.5MM Privately Held
WEB: www.bauerproducts.com
SIC: 3429 Metal fasteners

(G-6208)
BELL PACKAGING CORP
2000 Beverly Ave Sw (49519-1719)
PHONE..................616 452-2111
Walter Reinhardt, *General Mgr*
EMP: 75
SALES (est): 5.5MM Privately Held
SIC: 3554 Box making machines, paper

(G-6209)
BELLA SPOSA BRIDAL & PROM
4972 Plainfield Ave Ne (49525-1019)
PHONE..................616 364-0777
Dwin Dykema, *Owner*
EMP: 4
SQ FT: 4,000
SALES: 350K Privately Held
WEB: www.bridaldiscounts.com
SIC: 7219 5621 5699 3144 Seamstress; bridal shops; designers, apparel; formal wear; dress shoes, women's; retail agent, laundry & drycleaning

(G-6210)
BENMILL LLC
Also Called: Kent Design & Manufacturing
3522 Lousma Dr Se (49548-2259)
PHONE..................616 243-7555
Chuck Bennett, *Principal*
Mike Miller, *VP Opers*
David Faulkner, *Sales Staff*
Larry Miller,
▲ EMP: 35
SQ FT: 79,500
SALES (est): 6.9MM Privately Held
WEB: www.kentdesign.com
SIC: 3496 Grilles & grillework, woven wire; woven wire products

(G-6211)
BENNETT STEEL LLC
1239 Randolph Ave Sw (49507-1517)
PHONE..................616 401-5271
Steven J Entingh, *Principal*
EMP: 13 EST: 2010
SALES (est): 2.4MM Privately Held
SIC: 3441 Fabricated structural metal

(G-6212)
BENTELER AUTOMOTIVE CORP
Also Called: Tubular Products Division
3721 Hagen Dr Se (49548-2331)
PHONE..................616 245-4607
Steve Bates, *Plant Mgr*
EMP: 510
SALES (corp-wide): 9.2B Privately Held
SIC: 3714 3317 Exhaust systems & parts, motor vehicle; steel pipe & tubes
HQ: Benteler Automotive Corporation
2650 N Opdyke Rd Ste B
Auburn Hills MI 48326
248 364-7190

(G-6213)
BEST METAL PRODUCTS CO INC
3570 Raleigh Dr Se (49512-2064)
PHONE..................616 942-7141
David Faasse, *CEO*
Augustine Iacopelli, *Vice Pres*
Noel Dreyer, *Maint Spvr*
Rachel Wright, *Production*
Kurt Skov, *Engineer*
▲ EMP: 115 EST: 1950
SQ FT: 30,000
SALES (est): 21MM Privately Held
WEB: www.best-hydraulic-cylinders.com
SIC: 3599 3593 Machine shop, jobbing & repair; fluid power cylinders & actuators

(G-6214)
BETZ INDUSTRIES INC
Also Called: Betz Castings
2121 Bristol Ave Nw (49504-1403)
PHONE..................616 453-4429
Karl Betz Sr, *Principal*
Mark Kraak, *Safety Mgr*
Robin Boire, *Purchasing*
William Tellefsen, *Technical Mgr*
Catherine Jenkins, *Research*
▲ EMP: 90
SQ FT: 500,000
SALES (est): 31MM Privately Held
WEB: www.betzindustries.com
SIC: 3321 Ductile iron castings; gray iron castings

(G-6215)
BEVERAGE SOLUTION TECHNOLGIES
955 Ken O Sha Ind Pk Dr S (49508-8246)
PHONE..................616 252-1700
EMP: 3
SALES (est): 68.6K Privately Held
SIC: 2085 Mfg Distilled/Blended Liquor

(G-6216)
BEYOND EMBROIDERY
2013 E Wyndham Hill Dr Ne # 102 (49505-7105)
PHONE..................616 726-7000
Steve Mieras, *Owner*
EMP: 3
SALES (est): 198.4K Privately Held
WEB: www.beyondembroidery.com
SIC: 2759 Screen printing

Grand Rapids - Kent County (G-6217) **GEOGRAPHIC SECTION**

(G-6217)
BG DEFENSE CO LLC
2291 Oak Industrial Dr Ne (49505-6015)
PHONE.................................616 710-0609
Brandon Gerke,
EMP: 10
SALES (est): 422.6K **Privately Held**
SIC: 3812 Defense systems & equipment

(G-6218)
BICO MICHIGAN INC (HQ)
Also Called: Bico Steel Service Centers
99 Steele St Nw (49534-8737)
PHONE.................................616 453-2400
Michael A Ensminger, *President*
▲ **EMP:** 30
SQ FT: 33,000
SALES (est): 37.1MM
SALES (corp-wide): 66.1MM **Privately Held**
SIC: 5051 3444 3325 Steel; sheet metalwork; steel foundries
PA: Bico Buyer, Inc
3100 Gilchrist Rd
Mogadore OH 44260
330 794-1716

(G-6219)
BIG DOME HOLDINGS INC
3044 Wilson Dr Nw (49534-7564)
PHONE.................................616 735-6228
Nat Rich, *President*
Brian Morrissey, *Vice Pres*
Jim Napora, *Site Mgr*
Dwight Wenta, *QC Mgr*
Abner Musonda, *IT/INT Sup*
▲ **EMP:** 55
SQ FT: 25,000
SALES (est): 14.1MM **Privately Held**
WEB: www.kenona.com
SIC: 3543 Industrial patterns

(G-6220)
BIG RAPIDS PRINTING
2801 Oak Industrial Dr Ne (49505-6046)
PHONE.................................231 796-8588
EMP: 6
SALES (est): 250K **Privately Held**
SIC: 2759 5943 Commercial Printing Ret Stationery

(G-6221)
BIG RAYS EXPRESS LUBE 28TH ST
2241 Alpine Ave Nw (49544-1952)
PHONE.................................616 447-9710
Hassan Baydoun, *Branch Mgr*
EMP: 3
SALES (corp-wide): 544.8K **Privately Held**
SIC: 2992 Lubricating oils
PA: Big Ray's Express Lube 28th Street Inc
1850 28th St Se Ofc 600
Grand Rapids MI 49508
616 241-6660

(G-6222)
BIMBO BAKERIES USA INC
210 28th St Se (49548-1106)
PHONE.................................616 252-2709
EMP: 400 **Privately Held**
SIC: 2051 2053 2099 2052 Bakery: wholesale or wholesale/retail combined; bread, all types (white, wheat, rye, etc): fresh or frozen; buns, bread type: fresh or frozen; frozen bakery products, except bread; food preparations; cookies & crackers
HQ: Bimbo Bakeries Usa, Inc
255 Business Center Dr # 200
Horsham PA 19044
215 347-5500

(G-6223)
BIOLYTE LABORATORIES LLC
Also Called: Biolyte Labs
310 Northern Dr Nw (49534-3700)
PHONE.................................616 350-9055
Lisa Ampulski, *QC Mgr*
Daniel Kaline, *Mng Member*
Joni Kaline, *Officer*
EMP: 4
SALES: 75K **Privately Held**
SIC: 2834 Pharmaceutical preparations

(G-6224)
BISSELL BETTER LIFE LLC
Also Called: Better Life Cleaning Products
2345 Walker Ave Nw (49544-2597)
PHONE.................................800 237-7691
James S Nicholson, *CFO*
EMP: 5
SALES (est): 229.7K
SALES (corp-wide): 919.8MM **Privately Held**
SIC: 2842 3589 3635 Specialty cleaning, polishes & sanitation goods; vacuum cleaners & sweepers, electric: industrial; household vacuum cleaners
HQ: Bissell Inc.
2345 Walker Ave Nw
Grand Rapids MI 49544
616 453-4451

(G-6225)
BISSELL HOMECARE INC (DH)
2345 Walker Ave Nw (49544-2597)
P.O. Box 3606 (49501-3606)
PHONE.................................616 453-4451
Mark J Bissell, *President*
◆ **EMP:** 208
SQ FT: 600,000
SALES (est): 194.7MM
SALES (corp-wide): 919.8MM **Privately Held**
SIC: 3635 Household vacuum cleaners
HQ: Bissell Inc.
2345 Walker Ave Nw
Grand Rapids MI 49544
616 453-4451

(G-6226)
BIVINS GRAPHICS
808 Carpenter Ave Nw (49504-3723)
PHONE.................................616 453-2211
Fred Bivins, *Owner*
EMP: 4 **Privately Held**
WEB: www.vinecroft.com
SIC: 2759 2396 Commercial printing; automotive & apparel trimmings
PA: Bivins Graphics
1614 Vinecroft St Nw
Grand Rapids MI 49544

(G-6227)
BIVINS GRAPHICS (PA)
Also Called: Vinecroft Studios
1614 Vinecroft St Nw (49544-1462)
PHONE.................................616 453-2211
Frederick Bivins, *Owner*
EMP: 7
SALES (est): 439.5K **Privately Held**
WEB: www.vinecroft.com
SIC: 7336 2759 2396 Graphic arts & related design; screen printing; automotive & apparel trimmings

(G-6228)
BLACK & DECKER (US) INC
3040 28th St Se (49512-1627)
PHONE.................................410 716-3900
EMP: 4
SALES (corp-wide): 13.9B **Publicly Held**
WEB: www.dewalt.com
SIC: 3546 Power-driven handtools
HQ: Black & Decker (U.S.) Inc.
1000 Stanley Dr
New Britain CT 06053
860 225-5111

(G-6229)
BLACKMER
Also Called: Psg Dover
1809 Century Ave Sw (49503-8017)
PHONE.................................616 241-1611
Carmine Bosco, *President*
Scott Jackson, *Manager*
▲ **EMP:** 81 **EST:** 2013
SALES (est): 17.5MM **Privately Held**
SIC: 3479 3533 Painting, coating & hot dipping; oil & gas field machinery

(G-6230)
BLACKMER DOVER RESOURCES INC
2662 Prairie St Sw (49519-2461)
PHONE.................................616 475-9285
Carmine Bosco, *President*
EMP: 6
SALES (est): 745.9K **Privately Held**
SIC: 3556 Pasta machinery

(G-6231)
BLISS & VINEGAR LLC
888 Forest Hill Ave Se (49546-2326)
PHONE.................................616 970-0732
Mark McNamara, *Principal*
EMP: 3 **EST:** 2014
SALES (est): 212.2K **Privately Held**
SIC: 2099 Vinegar

(G-6232)
BLOOM INDUSTRIES LLC (PA)
2218 Ashcreek Ct Nw (49534-2716)
PHONE.................................616 453-2946
Kristen R Inbody, *Principal*
EMP: 3
SALES (est): 680.6K **Privately Held**
SIC: 3999 Manufacturing industries

(G-6233)
BLUEWATER TECH GROUP INC
4245 44th St Se Ste 1 (49512-4053)
PHONE.................................616 656-9380
Gordon Vibbert, *Project Mgr*
Penny Crawford, *Purch Mgr*
Jeff Imhoff, *Accounts Exec*
Mack Truax, *Manager*
Mark Wilson, *Creative Dir*
EMP: 11
SALES (corp-wide): 35.9MM **Privately Held**
SIC: 3651 5064 7622 7359 Household audio & video equipment; electrical appliances, television & radio; radio & television repair; equipment rental & leasing
PA: Bluewater Technologies Group, Inc.
24050 Northwestern Hwy
Southfield MI 48075
248 356-4399

(G-6234)
BODYCOTE THERMAL PROC INC
3700 Eastern Ave Se (49508-2413)
PHONE.................................616 245-0465
Paula Ahonen, *Office Mgr*
Dean Smith, *Branch Mgr*
EMP: 55
SALES (corp-wide): 935.8MM **Privately Held**
SIC: 3398 Metal heat treating
HQ: Bodycote Thermal Processing, Inc.
12700 Park Central Dr # 700
Dallas TX 75251
214 904-2420

(G-6235)
BRECK GRAPHICS INCORPORATED (PA)
Also Called: Allegra Print & Imaging
3983 Linden Ave Se (49548-3431)
PHONE.................................616 248-4110
Ron Vetter, *CEO*
Eric Vetter, *President*
Beverly Vetter, *Corp Secy*
Lori Heimburger, *Project Mgr*
Jennifer Vetter, *Project Mgr*
EMP: 20
SQ FT: 17,000
SALES (est): 2.6MM **Privately Held**
SIC: 2752 2796 2791 2789 Commercial printing, offset; platemaking services; typesetting; bookbinding & related work

(G-6236)
BRIGHTFORMAT INC
5300 Corporate Grove Dr S (49512-5514)
PHONE.................................616 247-1161
Peter Houlihan, *President*
Staci Weaver, *Project Mgr*
Karen Wentworth, *Controller*
Linda Pearman, *Sr Project Mgr*
Eric Stone, *Data Proc Staff*
EMP: 20
SALES (est): 3.2MM **Privately Held**
SIC: 2759 7331 Commercial printing; mailing service

(G-6237)
BRUN LABORATORIES INC
1120 Monroe Ave Nw # 180 (49503-1075)
P.O. Box 2663 (49501-2663)
PHONE.................................616 456-1114
B Terrance Reagan, *President*
Norma Reagan, *Corp Secy*
EMP: 4
SQ FT: 4,000
SALES (est): 300K **Privately Held**
WEB: www.brunlabs.com
SIC: 2844 Toilet preparations

(G-6238)
BUCHER HYDRAULICS INC (DH)
1363 Michigan St Ne (49503-2003)
PHONE.................................616 458-1306
Dan Vaughan, *President*
Purav Patel, *Plant Mgr*
Keith Callaghan, *Materials Mgr*
John Bekker, *Engineer*
Greg Bergman, *Engineer*
▲ **EMP:** 140
SQ FT: 100,000
SALES (est): 49.1MM
SALES (corp-wide): 3B **Privately Held**
WEB: www.dynalift.com
SIC: 3594 3492 Pumps, hydraulic power transfer; fluid power valves & hose fittings
HQ: Bucher Hydraulics Ag
Industriestrasse 15
Neuheim ZG 6345
417 570-333

(G-6239)
BUITER TOOL & DIE INC
8187 Division Ave S (49548-7233)
PHONE.................................616 455-7410
John Buiter, *President*
Petronella Buiter, *Corp Secy*
Edward Buiter, *Vice Pres*
Steve Star, *Prgrmr*
EMP: 25 **EST:** 1962
SQ FT: 18,600
SALES: 2.5MM **Privately Held**
SIC: 3544 7692 Special dies & tools; welding repair

(G-6240)
BULL HN INFO SYSTEMS INC
2620 Horizon Dr Se D1 (49546-7520)
PHONE.................................616 942-7126
Paul Miller, *Branch Mgr*
EMP: 15
SALES (corp-wide): 166.6MM **Privately Held**
SIC: 3571 3577 7378 7373 Mainframe computers; computer peripheral equipment; computer & data processing equipment repair/maintenance; computer peripheral equipment repair & maintenance; systems integration services
HQ: Bull Hn Information Systems Inc.
285 Billerica Rd Ste 200
Chelmsford MA 01824
978 294-6000

(G-6241)
BULMAN PRODUCTS INC
1650 Mcreynolds Ave Nw (49504-2091)
PHONE.................................616 363-4416
Ann Kirkwood Hall, *President*
Rita Kirkwood, *Vice Pres*
John R Kirkwood, *Treasurer*
Cary Anderson, *Info Tech Dir*
EMP: 31
SQ FT: 26,000
SALES (est): 6.8MM **Privately Held**
WEB: www.bulmanproducts.com
SIC: 3499 Metal household articles

(G-6242)
BURGE INCORPORATED
Also Called: Burge Chemical Products
2751 Westbrook Dr Nw (49504-2348)
PHONE.................................616 791-2214
Terry L Wisner, *President*
Craig Wisner, *Vice Pres*
EMP: 6 **EST:** 1935
SQ FT: 18,000
SALES: 400K **Privately Held**
SIC: 2842 Cleaning or polishing preparations

(G-6243)
BURKE E PORTER MACHINERY CO (HQ)
Also Called: Burke Porter Machinery Co
730 Plymouth Ave Ne (49505-6034)
PHONE.................................616 234-1200
David Deboer, *CEO*
Jim Lehman, *Vice Pres*
◆ **EMP:** 200
SQ FT: 105,000

▲ = Import ▼=Export
◆ =Import/Export

GEOGRAPHIC SECTION — Grand Rapids - Kent County (G-6268)

SALES (est): 43.4MM **Privately Held**
WEB: www.bepco.com
SIC: **3823** 3559 3826 3825 Industrial instrmnts msrmnt display/control process variable; automotive maintenance equipment; analytical instruments; instruments to measure electricity; metalworking machinery

(G-6244)
BURKK INC
4455 Airwest Dr Se (49512-3939)
PHONE..................................616 365-0354
Brett Burkhardt, *President*
EMP: 8
SALES (est): 847.8K **Privately Held**
SIC: **3398** Metal heat treating

(G-6245)
BURNSIDE ACQUISITION LLC (PA)
1060 Kenosha Indus Dr Se (49508)
PHONE..................................616 243-2800
Matt Andreychuk, *Opers Mgr*
John Boll, *Mng Member*
Kevin Williams, *Executive*
Brian Burnside,
EMP: 2
SQ FT: 1,000
SALES (est): 11.3MM **Privately Held**
WEB: www.burnside-mfg.com
SIC: **3469** Stamping metal for the trade

(G-6246)
BUSCH INDUSTRIES INC
900 East Paris Ave Se # 304 (49546-3676)
PHONE..................................616 957-3737
Fax: 616 957-9951
EMP: 5
SQ FT: 1,500
SALES (est): 688.3K **Privately Held**
SIC: **8742** 3441 Management Consulting Services

(G-6247)
BUTTERBALL FARMS INC
1435 Buchanan Ave Sw (49507-1699)
PHONE..................................616 243-0105
Mark Peters, *CEO*
David Riemersma, *President*
Elinor Fultz, *QC Mgr*
Casey Brewer, *Engineer*
Ray Saturnio, *Human Res Mgr*
EMP: 135
SQ FT: 125,000
SALES (est): 49.3MM **Privately Held**
WEB: www.butterballfarms.com
SIC: **2099** 5143 Butter, renovated & processed; butter

(G-6248)
C D TOOL AND GAGE
3223 3 Mile Rd Nw (49534-1223)
PHONE 616 682-1111
EMP: 5
SALES (est): 443.5K **Privately Held**
SIC: **3599** Machine shop, jobbing & repair

(G-6249)
C G WITVOET & SONS COMPANY
356 Crown St Sw (49548-4279)
PHONE..................................616 534-6677
Brian Witvoet, *President*
EMP: 25
SALES (est): 4.7MM **Privately Held**
WEB: www.cgwitvoet.com
SIC: **3993** Signs & advertising specialties

(G-6250)
CAD CAM SERVICES INC
4017 Brockton Dr Se (49512-4084)
PHONE..................................616 554-5222
Michael Haverkamp, *President*
EMP: 10
SQ FT: 20,000
SALES (est): 1.6MM **Privately Held**
WEB: www.cadcamservices.com
SIC: **3544** Special dies & tools

(G-6251)
CAFFEINATED PRESS INC
3167 Kalamazoo Ave Se # 104 (49508-1475)
PHONE..................................888 809-1686
Jason Gillikin, *CEO*
Jennifer Brown, *Principal*
Amy Jo Johnson, *Principal*
John Winkelman, *Vice Chairman*
Brittany Wilson, *Treasurer*
EMP: 5
SALES (est): 268.4K **Privately Held**
SIC: **2741** Miscellaneous publishing

(G-6252)
CAMEO COUNTERTOPS INC
3550 3 Mile Rd Nw (49534-1230)
PHONE..................................616 458-8745
Sandy Garrett, *Sales Staff*
Tim Sorokin, *Manager*
EMP: 21 **Privately Held**
SIC: **2541** Counter & sink tops
PA: Cameo Countertops, Inc.
1610 Kieswetter Rd
Holland OH 43528

(G-6253)
CANAL STREET BREWING CO LLC
Also Called: Founders Ale House
235 Grandville Ave Sw (49503-4037)
PHONE..................................616 776-1195
Mike Stevens,
Dave Engbers,
David Engbers,
Jim Engbros,
John Green,
▲ EMP: 90 EST: 1996
SQ FT: 11,000
SALES (est): 37.8MM **Privately Held**
WEB: www.foundersbrewing.com
SIC: **2082** Beer (alcoholic beverage)

(G-6254)
CANNON MACHINE INC
1641 Davis Ave Nw (49504-2001)
PHONE..................................616 363-4014
Brian Meester, *President*
Ray Shalle Roberts, *Manager*
EMP: 9
SALES (est): 1.3MM **Privately Held**
WEB: www.cannonmachine.com
SIC: **3599** Machine shop, jobbing & repair

(G-6255)
CARAUSTAR CSTM PACKG GROUP INC
Grand Rapids Plant
1957 Beverly Ave Sw (49519-1720)
PHONE..................................616 247-0330
Russell Skeel, *Purch Mgr*
Don Aardema, *Engineer*
Dale Hoard, *Accountant*
Paul Curtis, *Branch Mgr*
Larry Howard, *Maintence Staff*
EMP: 23
SALES (corp-wide): 3.8B **Publicly Held**
SIC: **2653** 2657 Boxes, corrugated: made from purchased materials; folding paperboard boxes
HQ: Caraustar Custom Packaging Group, Inc.
5000 Austell Powder Sprin
Austell GA 30106
770 948-3101

(G-6256)
CARTER PRODUCTS COMPANY INC
2871 Northridge Dr Nw (49544-9109)
PHONE..................................616 647-3380
Peter Perez, *President*
Carroll Perez, *Corp Secy*
Terry Camp, *Vice Pres*
Kelli Tenbrock, *CFO*
▲ EMP: 15 EST: 1929
SQ FT: 16,000
SALES (est): 3.8MM **Privately Held**
WEB: www.carterproducts.com
SIC: **3553** 3549 Woodworking machinery; metalworking machinery

(G-6257)
CARTERS INC
Also Called: Carter's Children's Store
3390 Alpine Ave Nw (49544-1672)
PHONE..................................616 647-9452
EMP: 9

SALES (corp-wide): 3.4B **Publicly Held**
SIC: **5641** 5137 2369 Children's wear; children's goods; girls' & children's outerwear
PA: Carter's, Inc.
3438 Peachtree Rd Ne # 18
Atlanta GA 30326
678 791-1000

(G-6258)
CASCADE DIE CASTING GROUP INC (DH)
7441 Division Ave S A1 (49548-7979)
PHONE..................................616 281-1774
Theodore C Hohman, *Ch of Bd*
Patrick J Greene, *Vice Pres*
Rodney Manns, *QC Mgr*
Luis Castor, *Engineer*
Mark Preston, *Project Engr*
▲ EMP: 9
SQ FT: 2,700
SALES (est): 92.2MM
SALES (corp-wide): 83.8MM **Privately Held**
WEB: www.cascade-cdc.com
SIC: **3364** 3363 Zinc & zinc-base alloy die-castings; aluminum die-castings
HQ: T C H Industries Incorporated
7441 Div Ave S Ste A1
Grand Rapids MI 49548
616 942-0505

(G-6259)
CASCADE DIE CASTING GROUP INC
Also Called: Cascade Die Casting/Mid-State
7750 Division Ave S (49548-7226)
PHONE..................................616 455-4010
Dick Evans, *Branch Mgr*
EMP: 45
SALES (corp-wide): 83.8MM **Privately Held**
WEB: www.cascade-cdc.com
SIC: **3369** 3364 White metal castings (lead, tin, antimony), except die; nonferrous die-castings except aluminum
HQ: Cascade Die Casting Group Inc
7441 Division Ave S A1
Grand Rapids MI 49548
616 281-1774

(G-6260)
CASCADE ENGINEERING INC (PA)
Also Called: CASCADE CART SOLUTIONS
3400 Innovation Ct Se (49512-2085)
P.O. Box 888405 (49588-8405)
PHONE..................................616 975-4800
Christina Keller, *President*
Jim Gingrich, *General Mgr*
Dianna Stephens, *General Mgr*
Frederick P Keller, *Chairman*
Kenyatta Brame, *Exec VP*
◆ EMP: 850
SQ FT: 300,000
SALES (est): 577.9MM **Privately Held**
WEB: www.cascadeng.com
SIC: **3089** Injection molding of plastics

(G-6261)
CASCADE ENGINEERING INC
5050 33rd St Se (49512-2068)
PHONE..................................616 975-4800
Joe Maier, *Branch Mgr*
EMP: 150
SALES (corp-wide): 577.9MM **Privately Held**
SIC: **3089** Injection molding of plastics
PA: Cascade Engineering, Inc.
3400 Innovation Ct Se
Grand Rapids MI 49512
616 975-4800

(G-6262)
CASCADE ENGINEERING INC
Also Called: West Plant
5055 36th St Se (49512-2007)
PHONE..................................616 975-4923
Frederick Keller, *Chairman*
Jeff Totten, *Chief Engr*
James Kilduff, *Engineer*
EMP: 169
SALES (corp-wide): 577.9MM **Privately Held**
WEB: www.cascadeng.com
SIC: **3089** Injection molding of plastics

PA: Cascade Engineering, Inc.
3400 Innovation Ct Se
Grand Rapids MI 49512
616 975-4800

(G-6263)
CASCADE PAPER CONVERTERS LLC
4935 Starr St Se (49546-6350)
PHONE..................................616 974-9165
Tom Natale, *General Mgr*
Lori Natale,
Jodey Barnes,
John Falkenhagen,
EMP: 18
SQ FT: 40,000
SALES (est): 4.7MM **Privately Held**
WEB: www.cascadeconverters.com
SIC: **2655** 2298 2631 Tubes, fiber or paper: made from purchased material; binder & baler twine; packaging board

(G-6264)
CASCADE PRINTING AND GRAPHICS
Also Called: Budget Print Center
6504 28th St Se Ste A (49546-6929)
PHONE..................................616 222-2937
Brian Ebbers, *President*
Diane Ebbers, *Vice Pres*
EMP: 4
SALES (est): 558.5K **Privately Held**
WEB: www.cascadeprint.com
SIC: **2752** Commercial printing, offset

(G-6265)
CASE-FREE INC
Also Called: Coye's Canvas & Awnings
240 32nd St Se (49548-2221)
PHONE..................................616 245-3136
David Smith, *President*
EMP: 8
SALES: 450K **Privately Held**
WEB: www.awningsnow.com
SIC: **2394** 3089 3444 Awnings, fabric: made from purchased materials; canvas awnings & canopies; awnings, fiberglass & plastic combination; awnings & canopies

(G-6266)
CASTLETON VILLAGE CENTER INC
Also Called: Hightech Signs
3580 Rgr B Chaffee Mem Dr (49548-2328)
PHONE..................................616 247-8100
Mike Abramowski, *Vice Pres*
EMP: 4 **Privately Held**
WEB: www.hightech-signs.com
SIC: **3993** Signs, not made in custom sign painting shops
PA: Castleton Village Center Inc
6321 Huguenard Rd Ste A
Fort Wayne IN 46818

(G-6267)
CENTRAL INDUSTRIAL CORPORATION
Also Called: Central Industrial Packaging
2916 Walkent Dr Nw (49544-1483)
PHONE..................................616 784-9612
Lawrence Larsen, *President*
EMP: 9
SALES (est): 466.8K **Privately Held**
SIC: **3492** Hose & tube fittings & assemblies, hydraulic/pneumatic

(G-6268)
CHALLENGE MFG COMPANY
3200 Fruit Ridge Ave Nw (49544-9707)
PHONE..................................616 735-6500
Len Rinke, *Manager*
EMP: 150
SALES (corp-wide): 763MM **Privately Held**
SIC: **3465** 3469 Automotive stampings; metal stampings
PA: Challenge Mfg. Company, Llc
3200 Fruit Ridge Ave Nw
Walker MI 49544
616 735-6500

Grand Rapids - Kent County (G-6269) — GEOGRAPHIC SECTION

(G-6269)
CHAMES LLC
Also Called: Five Star Window Coatings
163 Ann St Ne Ste 1 (49505-6261)
PHONE..................................616 363-0000
Randall K Hutson, *Mng Member*
Melinda Hutson,
EMP: 8
SQ FT: 2,000
SALES (est): 1MM **Privately Held**
SIC: 1751 2899 Window & door (prefabricated) installation; household tints or dyes

(G-6270)
CHAMPION WINDOW & PATIO ROOM
4717 Broadmoor Ave Se J (49512-9330)
PHONE..................................616 554-1600
Jamey Dulin, *Principal*
EMP: 25
SALES (est): 2.1MM **Privately Held**
SIC: 2431 Window frames, wood

(G-6271)
CHARLES GROUP INC (PA)
7441 Div Ave S Ste A1 (49548)
PHONE..................................336 882-0186
Theodore C Hohman, *President*
Patrick Greene, *Vice Pres*
EMP: 275
SALES (est): 83.8MM **Privately Held**
SIC: 3364 3363 Zinc & zinc-base alloy die-castings; aluminum die-castings

(G-6272)
CHARTER INDS EXTRUSIONS INC (PA)
3900 S Greenbrooke Dr Se (49512-5326)
PHONE..................................616 245-3388
Pete Eardley, *President*
Chuck Eardley, *Vice Pres*
Christina Burke, *Marketing Staff*
▲ **EMP:** 8
SALES (est): 1.4MM **Privately Held**
WEB: www.charterindustries.com
SIC: 2491 Structural lumber & timber, treated wood

(G-6273)
CHASE PLASTIC SERVICES INC
1115 Cadillac Dr Se (49506-6503)
PHONE..................................616 246-7190
EMP: 4 **Privately Held**
SIC: 2821 Mfg Plastic Materials/Resins
PA: Chase Plastic Services, Inc.
6467 Waldon Center Dr # 200
Clarkston MI 48346

(G-6274)
CHILDRENS BIBLE HOUR INC (PA)
Also Called: Keys For Kids Ministries
2060 43rd St Se (49508-5099)
PHONE..................................616 647-4500
Davin Malin, *Business Mgr*
Dave Carpenter, *Accounts Mgr*
Greg Yoder, *Exec Dir*
Jennifer Potter, *Director*
EMP: 15
SQ FT: 12,000
SALES: 1.1MM **Privately Held**
WEB: www.childrensbiblehour.com
SIC: 7922 8699 2731 Radio producers; charitable organization; book publishing

(G-6275)
CHRISTIAN SCHOOLS INTL
3350 East Paris Ave Se (49512-2907)
PHONE..................................616 957-1070
John Wolters, *CFO*
Tom Quist, *Accountant*
Rachael Heyboer, *Manager*
Don Woo, *Regional*
EMP: 37 **EST:** 1920
SQ FT: 25,000
SALES: 2.2MM **Privately Held**
WEB: www.csionline.org
SIC: 8742 2731 Management consulting services; books: publishing & printing

(G-6276)
CHRISTY VAULT COMPANY INC
3669 Bridgehampton Dr Ne (49546-1444)
P.O. Box 717, Parkton MD (21120-0717)
PHONE..................................415 994-1378
EMP: 3
SALES (est): 221.8K **Privately Held**
SIC: 3272 Burial vaults, concrete or precast terrazzo

(G-6277)
CLASSIC DIE INC
610 Plymouth Ave Ne (49505-6040)
PHONE..................................616 454-3760
Daniel J Parmeter Sr, *President*
Todd Verwys, *President*
Joyce Parmeter, *Corp Secy*
Andy Bourn, *Project Mgr*
Mike Wright, *Engineer*
▲ **EMP:** 21
SQ FT: 12,000
SALES (est): 4.3MM **Privately Held**
SIC: 3089 3544 Injection molding of plastics; special dies, tools, jigs & fixtures

(G-6278)
CLEAN ROOMS INTERNATIONAL INC
4939 Starr St Se (49546-6350)
PHONE..................................616 452-8700
Timothy D Werkema, *President*
Nelson G Werkema, *President*
Bret Asper, *COO*
Keith Weber, *Vice Pres*
Melissa Joslin, *Administration*
EMP: 30
SQ FT: 36,000
SALES: 11.4MM **Privately Held**
WEB: www.cleanroomsint.com
SIC: 3564 Ventilating fans: industrial or commercial

(G-6279)
CLEAR ADVANTAGE MECHANICAL
Also Called: Honeywell Authorized Dealer
1620 Acacia Dr Nw (49504-2302)
PHONE..................................616 520-5884
Matthew Vanheulen, *Principal*
EMP: 3
SALES (est): 253.6K **Privately Held**
SIC: 3585 Air conditioning condensers & condensing units

(G-6280)
CLEAR CUT WATER JET MACHINING
4515 Patterson Ave Se (49512-5304)
PHONE..................................616 534-9119
Kirk Vetter, *Principal*
EMP: 5
SALES (est): 457.3K **Privately Held**
SIC: 3541 Machine tools, metal cutting type

(G-6281)
CLIPPER BELT LACER COMPANY
1995 Oak Industrial Dr Ne (49505-6071)
PHONE..................................616 459-3196
Rick White, *President*
John Meulenberg, *Manager*
John Collier, *Administration*
▲ **EMP:** 84
SQ FT: 90,000
SALES: 12MM
SALES (corp-wide): 131.6MM **Privately Held**
WEB: www.flexco.com
SIC: 3496 3599 Miscellaneous fabricated wire products; custom machinery
PA: Flexible Steel Lacing Company Inc
2525 Wisconsin Ave
Downers Grove IL 60515
800 323-3444

(G-6282)
CND PRODUCTS LLC
1642 Broadway Ave Nw 3n (49504-2046)
PHONE..................................616 361-1000
Jeffrey D Tyner,
EMP: 5
SQ FT: 1,000
SALES (est): 500K **Privately Held**
WEB: www.cndproducts.com
SIC: 3841 Surgical & medical instruments

(G-6283)
CNS INC
1621 Leonard St Ne Ofc 11 (49505-5658)
PHONE..................................616 242-7704
Jay Brady, *Manager*
EMP: 5
SALES (corp-wide): 39.5B **Privately Held**
SIC: 2834 Pharmaceutical preparations
HQ: Cns, Inc.
1000 Gsk Dr
Coraopolis PA

(G-6284)
COATINGS PLUS INC
675 Chestnut St Sw (49503-4938)
PHONE..................................616 451-2427
Jeff Stegmeier, *President*
Bob Rabe, *Vice Pres*
EMP: 25
SQ FT: 40,000
SALES (est): 3.1MM **Privately Held**
SIC: 3479 Coating of metals & formed products

(G-6285)
COCA-COLA REFRESHMENTS USA INC
1440 Butterworth St Sw (49504-6094)
PHONE..................................616 458-4536
Marty Piet, *Branch Mgr*
Matt Barribou, *Manager*
Jim Clark, *Manager*
EMP: 100
SALES (corp-wide): 31.8B **Publicly Held**
WEB: www.cokecce.com
SIC: 2086 Bottled & canned soft drinks
HQ: Coca-Cola Refreshments Usa, Inc.
2500 Windy Ridge Pkwy Se
Atlanta GA 30339
770 989-3000

(G-6286)
COFFMAN ELECTRICAL EQP CO
Also Called: Steadypower
3300 Jefferson Ave Se (49548-2242)
PHONE..................................616 452-8708
Richard E Coffman, *President*
Marcia Coffman, *Corp Secy*
Paul Coffman, *Vice Pres*
Lillian Grimminck, *Vice Pres*
Steve Coffman, *Marketing Staff*
EMP: 20
SQ FT: 27,000
SALES: 5.3MM **Privately Held**
SIC: 5063 3524 Generators; lighting fixtures; snowblowers & throwers, residential

(G-6287)
COIT AVENUE GRAVEL CO INC
4772 Coit Ave Ne (49525-1198)
PHONE..................................616 363-7777
Greg Jaaueowski, *President*
EMP: 30 **EST:** 1948
SQ FT: 6,000
SALES (est): 4.4MM **Privately Held**
SIC: 3273 Ready-mixed concrete

(G-6288)
COLES QUALITY FOODS INC (PA)
38 Commerce Ave Sw # 400 (49503-4144)
PHONE..................................231 722-1651
Wesley S Devon Jr, *CEO*
Cynthia A Havard, *COO*
Monte Nis, *Plant Mgr*
Kathy Cain, *Purch Mgr*
Jane Kendall, *Accountant*
EMP: 200
SQ FT: 86,000
SALES: 65MM **Privately Held**
WEB: www.coles.com
SIC: 2051 Bakery: wholesale or wholesale/retail combined; bread, all types (white, wheat, rye, etc): fresh or frozen

(G-6289)
COLOR HOUSE GRAPHICS INC
3505 Eastern Ave Se (49508-2408)
PHONE..................................616 241-1916
Ken Postema, *President*
Steve Landheer, *Corp Secy*
Britni Rickson, *Project Mgr*
Robert Tissot, *Project Mgr*
Dan Roest, *Purch Agent*
▲ **EMP:** 45
SQ FT: 27,000
SALES (est): 7.4MM **Privately Held**
WEB: www.colorhousegraphics.com
SIC: 2752 Commercial printing, offset

(G-6290)
COLORHUB LLC
4950 Kraft Ave Se (49512-9708)
PHONE..................................616 333-4411
Hal G Ostrow,
EMP: 12
SALES (est): 2.4MM **Privately Held**
SIC: 2752 Commercial printing, lithographic

(G-6291)
COMPATICO INC
5005 Kraft Ave Se Ste A (49512-9707)
PHONE..................................616 940-1772
John REA, *President*
Richard Posthumus, *President*
William Boer, *Chairman*
Carrie Boer, *Corp Secy*
Patrick Mullen, *Shareholder*
◆ **EMP:** 45
SQ FT: 45,000
SALES (est): 8.7MM **Privately Held**
WEB: www.compatico.com
SIC: 2541 Wood partitions & fixtures

(G-6292)
COMPETITIVE EDGE DESIGNS INC
4506 R B Chaffee Mem Dr S (49548)
PHONE..................................616 257-0565
James Houda, *President*
EMP: 5
SQ FT: 3,500
SALES (est): 442.8K **Privately Held**
WEB: www.comp-edge.com
SIC: 8711 3599 Mechanical engineering; designing: ship, boat, machine & product; machine shop, jobbing & repair

(G-6293)
COMPLETE SOURCE INC
4455 44th St Se (49512-4010)
PHONE..................................616 285-9110
Paul Schweitze, *President*
Sandy Smiley, *VP Sales*
Robert Carpenter, *Sales Staff*
Loren Boebel, *Sales Associate*
Nicki Witek, *Consultant*
EMP: 7 **EST:** 1989
SALES (est): 1.3MM **Privately Held**
WEB: www.completesourceinc.com
SIC: 2759 7319 Screen printing; display advertising service

(G-6294)
COMPONENT ENGRG SOLUTIONS LLC
1740 Chicago Dr Sw (49519-1207)
PHONE..................................616 514-1343
John Lallo, *President*
EMP: 14
SQ FT: 15,000
SALES (est): 3.3MM **Privately Held**
WEB: www.tpprobes.com
SIC: 3545 Gauges (machine tool accessories)

(G-6295)
COMPOSITION UNLIMITED INC
1375 Monroe Ave Nw (49505-4621)
PHONE..................................616 451-2222
Barbara Turner, *President*
Barb Turner, *President*
Dick Irwin, *Vice Pres*
Ben Butler, *Shareholder*
Dave Snyder, *Admin Sec*
EMP: 3
SQ FT: 1,000
SALES (est): 295.2K **Privately Held**
SIC: 2791 Typesetting

(G-6296)
COMPRESSOR TECHNOLOGIES INC
Also Called: CTI
4420 40th St Se (49512-4035)
PHONE..................................616 949-7000
Tom Russell, *President*
EMP: 15

GEOGRAPHIC SECTION
Grand Rapids - Kent County (G-6322)

SQ FT: 25,000
SALES (est): 5MM Privately Held
SIC: 5084 3564 7699 5075 Compressors, except air conditioning; blowers & fans; compressor repair; dehumidifiers, except portable

(G-6297)
COMPUCARE
Also Called: Boone, Eugene
3247 Brooklyn Ave Se (49508-2439)
PHONE..................................616 245-5371
Eugene Boone, *Owner*
EMP: 3
SALES (est): 221.7K Privately Held
SIC: 7372 7371 Prepackaged software; computer software systems analysis & design, custom

(G-6298)
CONCEPT TOOLING SYSTEMS INC
555 Plymouth Ave Ne (49505-6029)
PHONE..................................616 301-6906
Mark Eberlein, *President*
EMP: 34
SALES (est): 3.2MM Privately Held
SIC: 3544 Special dies, tools, jigs & fixtures

(G-6299)
CONICAL CUTTING TOOLS INC
Also Called: Conical Tool Company
3890 Buchanan Ave Sw (49548-3111)
PHONE..................................616 531-8500
Robert M Shindors, *President*
Michael Deklein, *Opers Staff*
EMP: 30 EST: 1944
SQ FT: 10,000
SALES (est): 8.5MM Privately Held
WEB: www.conicaltool.com
SIC: 3545 End mills

(G-6300)
CONLEY COMPOSITES LLC
Also Called: An Andronaco Industries Co
4855 Broadmoor Ave Se (49512-5360)
PHONE..................................918 299-5051
Ronald V Andronaco, *CEO*
Colin Cruttenden, *Plant Mgr*
Richard Smith, *Opers Mgr*
David Chaney, *Production*
Scott Price, *Purch Mgr*
▲ EMP: 45
SALES (est): 19MM
SALES (corp-wide): 147.8MM Privately Held
WEB: www.conleyfrp.com
SIC: 3084 3089 3491 2891 Plastics pipe; fittings for pipe, plastic; industrial valves; adhesives, plastic; epoxy adhesives; valves & pipe fittings
PA: Andronaco, Inc.
4855 Broadmoor Ave Se
Kentwood MI 49512
616 554-4600

(G-6301)
CONSOLDTED RSOURCE IMAGING LLC
2943 S Wilson Ct Nw (49534-7567)
PHONE..................................616 735-2080
Nathan Crawford, *Owner*
John Schroeder, *Electrical Engi*
EMP: 31
SALES (est): 5.2MM Privately Held
SIC: 8731 7629 8999 3812 Electronic research; electronic equipment repair; scientific consulting; infrared object detection equipment; electrical or electronic engineering

(G-6302)
CONSOLIDATED METAL PDTS INC
3831 Clay Ave Sw (49548-3012)
PHONE..................................616 538-1000
Gary Becker, *President*
John Becker, *Treasurer*
David Becker, *Admin Sec*
EMP: 5
SQ FT: 4,800
SALES (est): 810.6K Privately Held
WEB: www.cmp-incorp.com
SIC: 3469 3599 7692 3452 Stamping metal for the trade; machine shop, jobbing & repair; welding repair; bolts, nuts, rivets & washers; sheet metalwork

(G-6303)
CONTECH (US) INC
Also Called: Pherotech
314 Straight Ave Sw (49504-6439)
PHONE..................................616 459-4139
Mark Grambart, *President*
◆ EMP: 50
SALES (est): 7.9MM Privately Held
SIC: 3524 Lawn & garden equipment

(G-6304)
CONTRACT FLAVORS INC
Also Called: CFC
3855 Linden Ave Se (49548-3429)
PHONE..................................616 454-5950
Frederick High, *President*
EMP: 19
SQ FT: 2,000
SALES (est): 2.6MM Privately Held
SIC: 2087 Syrups, drink

(G-6305)
CONTRACT SOURCE & ASSEMBLY INC
Also Called: C S A
5230 33rd St Se (49512-2070)
PHONE..................................616 897-2185
Chris Cooper, *President*
▲ EMP: 40
SQ FT: 30,000
SALES (est): 3.6MM Privately Held
SIC: 2522 Office furniture, except wood

(G-6306)
CONTRACTORS STEEL COMPANY
2768 Dormax St Sw (49519-2406)
PHONE..................................616 531-4000
Keith D Ford, *Opers-Prdtn-Mfg*
EMP: 44
SALES (corp-wide): 357MM Privately Held
WEB: www.contractorssteel.com
SIC: 5051 3542 Steel; machine tools, metal forming type
HQ: Contractors Steel Company
36555 Amrhein Rd
Livonia MI 48150
734 464-4000

(G-6307)
CONTROLLED PLATING TECH INC
1100 Godfrey Ave Sw (49503-5008)
PHONE..................................616 243-6622
Steve Slot, *President*
Douglas Slot, *Manager*
Glenn Schuemann, *Supervisor*
EMP: 36
SQ FT: 30,000
SALES (est): 4.6MM Privately Held
WEB: www.controlledplating.com
SIC: 3471 Electroplating of metals or formed products

(G-6308)
CONWAY PRODUCTS CORPORATION
Also Called: Emerald Spa
4150 East Paris Ave Se # 1 (49512-3995)
PHONE..................................616 698-2601
Paul Slagh, *President*
Duncan McColl, *Opers Staff*
Tracy Kempkers, *Accountant*
Thomas Kneeshaw, *Executive*
John Kennedy, *Shareholder*
◆ EMP: 25
SQ FT: 84,000
SALES (est): 5.1MM Privately Held
WEB: www.emeraldspa.com
SIC: 3999 3088 3949 Hot tubs; plastics plumbing fixtures; sporting & athletic goods

(G-6309)
CONWAY-CLEVELAND CORP (PA)
2320 Oak Industrial Dr Ne (49505-6090)
PHONE..................................616 458-0056
Daniel Conway, *President*
Linda Conway, *Vice Pres*
▲ EMP: 5
SQ FT: 7,000
SALES: 750K Privately Held
WEB: www.conwaycleveland.com
SIC: 3829 2851 3553 3546 Measuring & controlling devices; wood fillers or sealers; woodworking machinery; power-driven handtools; gum & wood chemicals

(G-6310)
CORIUM INTERNATIONAL INC
4558 50th St Se (49512-5401)
PHONE..................................616 656-4563
Bobby Singh, *Vice Pres*
Mike Sayfie, *Mfg Dir*
Jennifer Loniewski, *Opers Staff*
Kathy Buist, *Mfg Staff*
Garrett Collins, *Mfg Staff*
EMP: 30
SALES (corp-wide): 31.8MM Privately Held
WEB: www.coriumintl.com
SIC: 2834 Adrenal pharmaceutical preparations
HQ: Corium, Inc.
235 Constitution Dr
Menlo Park CA 94025

(G-6311)
CORLETT-TURNER CO
Also Called: G. A. Richards - Corlett Turner
1060 Kn O Sha Indus Dr Se (49508)
PHONE..................................616 772-9082
EMP: 4
SALES (est): 695.1K Privately Held
SIC: 3444 Sheet metalwork

(G-6312)
COROTECH ACQUISITION CO
Also Called: Corotech Masonry
1222 Burton St Se (49507-3302)
PHONE..................................616 456-5557
R Jeffrey Dean, *President*
James Polonczyk, *Principal*
Jeff Dills, *Vice Pres*
EMP: 10
SQ FT: 10,500
SALES (est): 1.7MM Privately Held
WEB: www.corotech.com
SIC: 1791 1799 8711 3443 Storage tanks, metal: erection; coating of metal structures at construction site; engineering services; fabricated plate work (boiler shop); unsupported plastics film & sheet

(G-6313)
CORVAC COMPOSITES LLC
4450 36th St Se (49512-1917)
PHONE..................................812 256-2287
Christine Black, *Manager*
EMP: 40
SALES (corp-wide): 171MM Privately Held
SIC: 3559 Automotive related machinery
HQ: Corvac Composites, Llc
104 84th St Sw
Byron Center MI 49315

(G-6314)
CORVAC COMPOSITES LLC
4450 36th St Se (49512-1917)
PHONE..................................616 281-2430
James Sitzell, *Mng Member*
EMP: 250
SALES (corp-wide): 171MM Privately Held
SIC: 3559 Automotive related machinery
HQ: Corvac Composites, Llc
104 84th St Sw
Byron Center MI 49315

(G-6315)
CREATIVE STEEL RULE DIES INC
4157 Stafford Ave Sw (49548-3053)
PHONE..................................630 307-8880
Larry T Corriere, *President*
Sandra Corriere, *Admin Sec*
EMP: 15
SALES (est): 1MM Privately Held
SIC: 3544 Dies, steel rule

(G-6316)
CREEK DIESEL SERVICES INC
Also Called: Van Eck Diesel Services
3748 Water Leaf Ct Ne (49525-8604)
PHONE..................................800 974-4600
Tracey Garrett, *Manager*
EMP: 12 EST: 1990
SQ FT: 8,250
SALES (est): 1.5MM Privately Held
WEB: www.vaneckdiesel.com
SIC: 7538 3519 7699 Engine repair; general truck repair; internal combustion engines; marine engine repair

(G-6317)
CROP MARKS PRINTING
128 Coldbrook St Ne (49503-1010)
PHONE..................................616 356-5555
Russ Colter, *Owner*
EMP: 5
SALES (est): 372.3K Privately Held
SIC: 2752 Commercial printing, offset

(G-6318)
CROSS PATHS CORP
955 Ken O Sha Ind Park Dr (49508-8246)
PHONE..................................616 248-5371
Clifford Cross, *President*
Steve Siekman, *Treasurer*
EMP: 7
SQ FT: 3,000
SALES: 605K Privately Held
WEB: www.crosspathscorp.com
SIC: 3545 3599 Gauges (machine tool accessories); machine shop, jobbing & repair

(G-6319)
CROWN EQUIPMENT CORPORATION
Also Called: Crown Lift Trucks
4131 Roger Chaffee Mem Se (49548)
PHONE..................................616 530-3000
Fax: 616 530-7061
EMP: 46
SALES (corp-wide): 3.1B Privately Held
SIC: 3537 Mfg Industrial Trucks/Tractors
PA: Crown Equipment Corporation
44 S Washington St
New Bremen OH 45869
419 629-2311

(G-6320)
CSN MANUFACTURING INC
1750 Elizabeth Ave Nw (49504-2060)
PHONE..................................616 364-0027
Fax: 616 364-0082
EMP: 35
SQ FT: 25,000
SALES (est): 5.1MM Privately Held
SIC: 2821 Mfg Plastic Materials/Resins

(G-6321)
CUMMINS INC
3715 Clay Ave Sw (49548-3010)
PHONE..................................616 281-2211
Dan Zammitt, *General Mgr*
Greg Cryderman, *Manager*
EMP: 45
SALES (corp-wide): 23.7B Publicly Held
WEB: www.bridgewaypower.com
SIC: 5063 3519 Generators; internal combustion engines
PA: Cummins Inc.
500 Jackson St
Columbus IN 47201
812 377-5000

(G-6322)
CUP ACQUISITION LLC (PA)
Also Called: Custom Profile
2535 Waldorf Ct Nw (49544-1469)
PHONE..................................616 735-4410
Richard Sweers, *Materials Mgr*
Mike Rocheleau, *Purchasing*
Jim Lynema, *Project Engr*
Dave Shullenberger, *Sales Engr*
Bob Rhoades, *Sales Staff*
EMP: 135
SALES (est): 5.1MM Privately Held
SIC: 3089 Injection molding of plastics

Grand Rapids - Kent County (G-6323)

(G-6323)
CUSTOM COUNTER TOP COMPANY
4444 Division Ave S (49548-4360)
PHONE..................616 534-5894
Dorothy Kaechele, *Owner*
EMP: 3
SQ FT: 2,400
SALES (est): 274.9K **Privately Held**
SIC: 2541 Table or counter tops, plastic laminated

(G-6324)
CUSTOM GEARS INC
3761 Linden Ave Se Ste B (49548-3459)
PHONE..................616 243-2723
Ronald C Deyoung, *President*
EMP: 6
SALES (est): 1MM **Privately Held**
WEB: www.customgears.com
SIC: 3566 Gears, power transmission, except automotive

(G-6325)
CUSTOM POWDER COATING LLC
1601 Madison Ave Se Ste 1 (49507-2566)
PHONE..................616 454-9730
Lynda Vanos,
EMP: 5
SALES (est): 726.9K **Privately Held**
SIC: 3399 3479 Silver powder; metal coating & allied service

(G-6326)
CUSTOM PRINTERS INC
Also Called: Pageworks
2801 Oak Industrial Dr Ne (49505-6046)
PHONE..................616 454-9224
Daniel M Goris, *President*
Rob Driscoll, *President*
Debra Goris, *Vice Pres*
Debbie Goris, *CFO*
Karen Eggerding, *Sales Staff*
EMP: 60
SQ FT: 35,000
SALES: 8MM **Privately Held**
WEB: www.customprinters.com
SIC: 2752 2789 2759 Commercial printing, offset; bookbinding & related work; commercial printing

(G-6327)
D & B HEAT TRANSFER PDTS INC
8031 Division Ave S Ste C (49548-7205)
PHONE..................616 827-0028
Dale Deboer, *President*
Brian Amante, *Vice Pres*
Mark De Groot, *Manager*
EMP: 10
SQ FT: 18,000
SALES (est): 3.2MM **Privately Held**
SIC: 5013 3585 Radiators; evaporative condensers, heat transfer equipment

(G-6328)
D & D BUILDING INC
Also Called: Advantage Millwork
3959 Linden Ave Se (49548-3431)
PHONE..................616 248-7908
Jim Keuning, *Branch Mgr*
EMP: 10
SALES (corp-wide): 36.7MM **Privately Held**
SIC: 5031 2431 Millwork; millwork
PA: D & D Building, Inc.
3264 Union Ave Se
Wyoming MI 49548
616 243-5633

(G-6329)
D & D BUSINESS MACHINES INC
Also Called: Neopost Mailing Equipment
3545 Brandau Dr Ne (49525-2881)
PHONE..................616 364-8446
Ron Weidenfeller, *President*
EMP: 6
SALES (est): 882.8K **Privately Held**
SIC: 2893 Duplicating ink

(G-6330)
D & D PRINTING CO
342 Market Ave Sw Unit 1 (49503-4000)
PHONE..................616 454-7710

Mike Bardwell, *President*
Scott McCardy, *Vice Pres*
Larry Bardwell, *Treasurer*
Richard McCarty, *Admin Sec*
EMP: 27
SQ FT: 20,000
SALES (est): 5.1MM **Privately Held**
WEB: www.ddprinting.net
SIC: 2752 Commercial printing, offset

(G-6331)
D A C INDUSTRIES INC
600 11th St Nw (49504-4458)
PHONE..................616 235-0140
Dan W Hickey, *President*
EMP: 5
SQ FT: 400
SALES (est): 784.3K **Privately Held**
WEB: www.dacindustries.com
SIC: 3429 Door opening & closing devices, except electrical

(G-6332)
DAGENHAM MILLWORKS LLC
4525 Airwest Dr Se (49512-3951)
PHONE..................616 698-8883
Doug Deeder, *President*
EMP: 4
SALES (est): 350K **Privately Held**
SIC: 2431 Millwork

(G-6333)
DAIRY QUEEN
956 Fulton St W (49504-6261)
PHONE..................616 235-0102
Alex McKowski, *Owner*
EMP: 13
SALES (est): 333K **Privately Held**
SIC: 5812 2024 Ice cream stands or dairy bars; ice cream & frozen desserts

(G-6334)
DAMAR MACHINERY CO
3389 3 Mile Rd Nw (49534-1221)
PHONE..................616 453-4655
David Crysler, *President*
Douglas Crysler, *Vice Pres*
Becky Crysler, *Admin Sec*
EMP: 15
SQ FT: 20,000
SALES (est): 3MM **Privately Held**
WEB: www.damarmachinery.com
SIC: 3599 Machine shop, jobbing & repair

(G-6335)
DANLY IEM
4300 40th St Se (49512-4101)
PHONE..................800 243-2659
James Skalitzky, *Purch Mgr*
Harvey Van Huizen, *VP Sales*
John Petrocelly, *Mktg Dir*
Danly IEM, *Manager*
EMP: 5
SALES (est): 557.5K **Privately Held**
SIC: 3544 Die sets for metal stamping (presses)

(G-6336)
DATUM INDUSTRIES LLC
4740 44th St Se (49512-4017)
PHONE..................616 977-1995
Scott Leasure,
▲ EMP: 66
SQ FT: 50,000
SALES (est): 13.4MM **Privately Held**
WEB: www.datumind.com
SIC: 3544 Special dies & tools

(G-6337)
DAWN FOOD PRODUCTS INC
2885 Clydon Ave Sw (49519-2401)
P.O. Box 14391, Louisville KY (40214)
PHONE..................800 654-4843
Jerry Hoogterp, *Manager*
EMP: 150
SALES (corp-wide): 1.6B **Privately Held**
WEB: www.dawnfoods.com
SIC: 2045 Doughs & batters; from purchased flour
HQ: Dawn Food Products, Inc.
3333 Sargent Rd
Jackson MI 49201

(G-6338)
DC BYERS CO/GRAND RAPIDS INC (PA)
Also Called: Byers, D C Company
5946 Clay Ave Sw (49548-5768)
PHONE..................616 538-7300
Bernard L Bouma, *CEO*
Douglas Lectka, *Exec VP*
John Stevenson Jr, *VP Sales*
EMP: 15
SQ FT: 10,000
SALES (est): 3.4MM **Privately Held**
WEB: www.dcbyers.com
SIC: 1799 3471 Caulking (construction); plating & polishing

(G-6339)
DE VRU PRINTING CO
1446 Eastern Ave Se (49507-2054)
PHONE..................616 452-5451
Carl Huisman, *Owner*
EMP: 4 EST: 1969
SQ FT: 6,500
SALES (est): 374.2K **Privately Held**
SIC: 2752 2759 2791 2789 Commercial printing, offset; letterpress printing; typesetting; bookbinding & related work

(G-6340)
DECADE PRODUCTS LLC (PA)
Also Called: Dolav
3400 Innovation Ct Se (49512-2085)
PHONE..................616 975-4965
Frederick Keller, *CEO*
Raphael Harris, *President*
Matt Kramer, *Opers Staff*
Michael Sweers, *President*
Mike Begin, *Sales Staff*
◆ EMP: 10
SALES (est): 3.3MM **Privately Held**
WEB: www.decadeproducts.com
SIC: 3089 Plastic containers, except foam

(G-6341)
DECC COMPANY INC
Also Called: Cascade Rental Centers
1266 Wallen Ave Sw (49507-1586)
PHONE..................616 245-0431
Fred Mellema, *President*
Curt Jacob, *Controller*
Shannon Vallarino, *Human Resources*
▲ EMP: 50 EST: 1964
SQ FT: 100,000
SALES (est): 7MM **Privately Held**
WEB: www.decc.com
SIC: 3479 Coating of metals & formed products

(G-6342)
DEDINAS & FRANZAK ENTPS INC
Also Called: Cheeze Kurls
2915 Walkent Dr Nw (49544-1400)
PHONE..................616 784-6095
Tim De Dinas, *President*
Robert Franzak Jr, *Vice Pres*
Laura Franzak, *Controller*
▲ EMP: 80
SQ FT: 100,000
SALES (est): 17.8MM **Privately Held**
SIC: 2099 2096 Food preparations; potato chips & similar snacks

(G-6343)
DERK PIETER CO INC
Also Called: Sir Speedy
4513 Broadmoor Ave Se A (49512-5313)
PHONE..................616 554-7777
Rudy Dykhuis, *President*
EMP: 4
SQ FT: 2,000
SALES (est): 721.5K **Privately Held**
SIC: 2752 7338 2791 2789 Commercial printing, lithographic; secretarial & court reporting; typesetting; bookbinding & related work

(G-6344)
DESIGN CONVERTING INC
3470 Raleigh Dr Se (49512-2042)
PHONE..................616 942-7780
Randy Stout, *President*
Arthur Brand, *Vice Pres*
EMP: 17
SQ FT: 23,000

SALES (est): 4.1MM **Privately Held**
WEB: www.designconverting.com
SIC: 2675 3714 Paperboard die-cutting; motor vehicle body components & frame

(G-6345)
DESIGN DESIGN INC
Also Called: As
19 La Grave Ave Se (49503-4225)
P.O. Box 2266 (49501-2266)
PHONE..................866 935-2648
Donald J Kallil, *President*
Gregory Devries, *Vice Pres*
Jennifer Kallil, *Vice Pres*
Lauren Kallil, *Project Mgr*
Kelly Garcia, *Purch Agent*
◆ EMP: 160
SQ FT: 5,700
SALES (est): 29.6MM **Privately Held**
WEB: www.designdesign.us
SIC: 2771 Greeting cards

(G-6346)
DESIGN TECH LLC
Also Called: Designtech
2192 Trillium Ln Nw (49534-9597)
PHONE..................616 459-2885
Jerry Snyder, *Partner*
Kay Snyder, *Partner*
Brad Akerberg, *Director*
EMP: 4
SQ FT: 2,500
SALES (est): 309.5K **Privately Held**
SIC: 2396 2395 Screen printing on fabric articles; embroidery & art needlework

(G-6347)
DEWITT PACKAGING CORPORATION
5080 Kraft Ave Se (49512-9707)
PHONE..................616 698-0210
Steven Dewitt, *President*
Gordon Jack Dewitt, *Vice Pres*
Jill Dewitt, *Treasurer*
Dorothy Dewitt, *Admin Sec*
EMP: 48
SQ FT: 35,000
SALES (est): 10.2MM **Privately Held**
WEB: www.dewittpackaging.com
SIC: 2653 Boxes, corrugated: made from purchased materials

(G-6348)
DI-ANODIC FINISHING CORP
736 Ottawa Ave Nw 38 (49503-1428)
PHONE..................616 454-0470
A James Wanczuk, *President*
EMP: 23
SQ FT: 7,500
SALES (est): 2MM **Privately Held**
SIC: 3471 Anodizing (plating) of metals or formed products

(G-6349)
DIE-MATIC LLC
4309 Aldrich Ave Sw (49509-4031)
PHONE..................616 531-0060
Chad Folkema, *President*
Julie Sjaarda, *Administration*
EMP: 35
SALES (est): 6.2MM **Privately Held**
SIC: 3542 Sheet metalworking machines

(G-6350)
DIE-NAMIC TOOL CORP
4541 Patterson Ave Se (49512-5304)
PHONE..................616 954-7882
Rogelio A Ramirez, *President*
EMP: 6
SQ FT: 6,000
SALES (est): 999.5K **Privately Held**
SIC: 3544 Special dies & tools

(G-6351)
DIE-TECH AND ENGINEERING INC
4620 Herman Ave Sw (49509-5140)
PHONE..................616 530-9030
William H Berry III, *President*
Sandra Berry, *Corp Secy*
Thomas Gray, *Vice Pres*
EMP: 40
SQ FT: 25,000
SALES (est): 12.6MM **Privately Held**
SIC: 3544 Special dies & tools

▲ = Import ▼ = Export
◆ = Import/Export

GEOGRAPHIC SECTION   Grand Rapids - Kent County (G-6379)

(G-6352)
DIMENSION GRAPHICS INC
800 Burton St Se (49507-3320)
PHONE..................................616 245-1447
Ken Blessing, *President*
Donna Blessing, *Treasurer*
EMP: 8
SQ FT: 8,200
SALES (est): 897.6K **Privately Held**
SIC: 3993 Signs, not made in custom sign painting shops

(G-6353)
DIRECT AIM MEDIA LLC
1778 Grand Ct Ne (49525-7040)
PHONE..................................800 817-7101
Robert Raff, *Mng Member*
EMP: 20 EST: 2015
SALES (est): 77.4K **Privately Held**
SIC: 7319 2741 Advertising;

(G-6354)
DISCOUNT PALLETS
4580 Airwest Dr Se (49512-3950)
PHONE..................................616 453-5455
Randy Vanderveen, *President*
EMP: 5
SQ FT: 7,500
SALES (est): 596.8K **Privately Held**
SIC: 2448 Pallets, wood

(G-6355)
DISCOVERY HOUSE PUBLISHERS
Also Called: MIDWEST MEDIA MANAGEMENT DIV
3000 Kraft Ave Se (49512-2024)
P.O. Box 2222 (49555-0001)
PHONE..................................616 942-9218
Martin Dehaan, *President*
Dave Branon, *Editor*
Robert K De Vries, *Vice Pres*
Max E Smith, *CFO*
Anne Bauman, *Marketing Staff*
▲ EMP: 25
SQ FT: 65,000
SALES: 6.1MM
SALES (corp-wide): 43.8MM **Privately Held**
WEB: www.rbc.net
SIC: 2741 Miscellaneous publishing
PA: Rbc Ministries
    3000 Kraft Ave Se
    Grand Rapids MI 49512
    616 942-6770

(G-6356)
DISPLAY PACK INC
1600 Monroe Ave Nw (49505-4659)
PHONE..................................616 451-3061
Roger Hansen, *Principal*
EMP: 500
SQ FT: 40,000
SALES (corp-wide): 132.3MM **Privately Held**
WEB: www.displaypack.com
SIC: 3089 Plastic processing
PA: Display Pack, Inc.
    650 West St
    Cedar Springs MI 49319
    616 451-3061

(G-6357)
DOMART LLC
3923 28th St Se (49512-1805)
PHONE..................................616 285-9177
Martin Doorn, *Owner*
EMP: 3
SALES (est): 221.9K **Privately Held**
SIC: 4783 2759 7331 7389 Packing goods for shipping; commercial printing; mailing service; packaging & labeling services

(G-6358)
DOOR SEC SOLUTIONS OF MICH
6757 Cascade Rd Se 304 (49546-6849)
PHONE..................................616 301-1991
Jim Grondin, *President*
EMP: 10
SQ FT: 958
SALES (est): 980K **Privately Held**
SIC: 3429 Door locks, bolts & checks

(G-6359)
DOUBLE OTIS INC
Also Called: DOUBLEO O SUPPLY & CRAFTSMEN
1415 Division Ave S (49507-1601)
PHONE..................................616 878-3998
Michael F Otis, *President*
Linda N Otis, *Corp Secy*
William Riley, *Vice Pres*
Tom Ralya, *Sales Mgr*
Neil Krumrei, *Manager*
EMP: 35
SQ FT: 40,000
SALES: 8MM **Privately Held**
WEB: www.doubleoincorporated.com
SIC: 5031 2431 1793 Doors & windows; windows & window parts & trim, wood; windows, wood; glass & glazing work

(G-6360)
DOWN INC
635 Evergreen St Se (49507-1891)
PHONE..................................616 241-3922
Terry Tucker, *President*
▲ EMP: 30
SQ FT: 8,700
SALES: 3.5MM
SALES (corp-wide): 22.9MM **Privately Held**
WEB: www.down.com
SIC: 2392 Comforters & quilts: made from purchased materials; pillows, bed: made from purchased materials
HQ: Eurasia Feather, Inc.
    635 Evergreen St Se
    Grand Rapids MI 49507
    616 245-5496

(G-6361)
DREWS MANUFACTURING CO
5753 Division Ave S (49548-5726)
PHONE..................................616 534-3482
Larry Drew, *President*
EMP: 3
SQ FT: 22,000
SALES: 750K **Privately Held**
WEB: www.drewsmanufacturing.com
SIC: 3451 Screw machine products

(G-6362)
DTE ENERGY CO
444 Wealthy St Sw (49503-4023)
PHONE..................................616 632-2663
EMP: 14
SALES (est): 2.4MM **Privately Held**
SIC: 1311 Natural gas production

(G-6363)
DYNA PLATE INC
344 Mart St Sw (49548-1015)
PHONE..................................616 452-6763
Craig Hill, *President*
Richard Hill, *Vice Pres*
EMP: 22 EST: 1979
SQ FT: 40,000
SALES (est): 2.5MM **Privately Held**
WEB: www.dynaplate.com
SIC: 3471 Electroplating of metals or formed products

(G-6364)
EAGILE INCORPORATED
1880 Turner Ave Nw Ste A (49504)
PHONE..................................616 243-1200
Gary Burns, *CEO*
Peter Phaneuf, *President*
Matthew Wiersum, *Materials Mgr*
Jon Ryskamp, *Production*
Mark Dulemba, *Engineer*
▼ EMP: 15
SQ FT: 40,000
SALES (est): 1.4MM **Privately Held**
SIC: 3825 2754 Radio frequency measuring equipment; labels: gravure printing

(G-6365)
EAGLE INDUS GROUP FEDERAL LLC
555 Plymouth Ave Ne (49505-6029)
PHONE..................................616 863-8623
Chad Boersma,
EMP: 6
SALES (est): 473.8K **Privately Held**
SIC: 3544 Special dies & tools

(G-6366)
EARTHBOUND INC
1116 Plnfeld Ave Ne Ste 2 (49503)
PHONE..................................616 774-0096
Nyleene Dodgson, *President*
Karen Jones, *Manager*
EMP: 4
SALES: 300K **Privately Held**
SIC: 2759 2395 Screen printing; embroidery & art needlework

(G-6367)
EAST MUSKEGON ROOFG SHTMTL CO
Also Called: Certified Sheet Metal
2458 Waldorf Ct Nw (49544-1472)
PHONE..................................616 791-6900
Andrew Kanaar, *Branch Mgr*
EMP: 10
SALES (est): 1.1MM
SALES (corp-wide): 16.4MM **Privately Held**
SIC: 1761 3444 Sheet metalwork; sheet metalwork
PA: East Muskegon Roofing & Sheet Metal Co Inc
    1665 Holton Rd
    Muskegon MI 49445
    231 744-2461

(G-6368)
EATON AEROSPACE LLC
3675 Patterson Ave Se (49512-4022)
PHONE..................................616 949-1090
David Rosin, *General Mgr*
Brian Woloszyk, *Project Dir*
Matthew Lytle, *Materials Mgr*
Denise Mann, *Mfg Staff*
Neil Richards, *Buyer*
EMP: 300 **Privately Held**
WEB: www.eaton.com
SIC: 3625 3714 3594 3559 Motor controls & accessories; motor starters & controllers, electric; actuators, industrial; motor vehicle engines & parts; motor vehicle transmissions, drive assemblies & parts; motor vehicle steering systems & parts; pumps, hydraulic power transfer; motors: hydraulic, fluid power or air; semiconductor manufacturing machinery; personal computers (microcomputers)
HQ: Eaton Aerospace Llc
    1000 Eaton Blvd
    Cleveland OH 44122
    216 523-5000

(G-6369)
ECOPRINT SERVICES LLC
549 Ottawa Ave Nw Ste 103 (49503-1474)
PHONE..................................616 254-8019
Paul Bott,
EMP: 6
SALES (est): 728.7K **Privately Held**
WEB: www.ecoprint.com
SIC: 2759 Commercial printing

(G-6370)
EISELE CONNECTORS INC
99 Monroe Ave Nw Ste 200 (49503-2639)
PHONE..................................616 726-7714
Thomas Maier, *CEO*
Beate Sauerer, *Admin Asst*
EMP: 3
SALES (est): 170.5K **Privately Held**
SIC: 3479 Metal coating & allied service

(G-6371)
EL MILAGRO OF MICHIGAN
1846 Clyde Park Ave Sw (49509-1502)
PHONE..................................616 452-6625
Rafael Lopez, *Principal*
Jesse Lopez, *Mng Member*
Minerva Duran, *Mng Member*
Melissa Rincones, *Manager*
EMP: 8
SALES (est): 769.8K **Privately Held**
SIC: 2099 Tortillas, fresh or refrigerated

(G-6372)
EL VOCERO HISPANO INC
2818 Vineland Ave Se (49508-1453)
P.O. Box 7287 (49510-7287)
PHONE..................................616 246-6023
Andres Abreu, *President*
Amy Ramos, *Manager*
EMP: 10
SQ FT: 2,000
SALES (est): 861.2K **Privately Held**
WEB: www.elvocerohispano.com
SIC: 2711 Newspapers: publishing only, not printed on site

(G-6373)
ELECTRO CHEMICAL FINISHING CO
379 44th St Sw (49548-4122)
PHONE..................................616 531-1250
Tom Beckwith, *Branch Mgr*
EMP: 50
SALES (corp-wide): 21.4MM **Privately Held**
WEB: www.ecfinc.com
SIC: 3471 Electroplating of metals or formed products
PA: Electro Chemical Finishing Co.
    2610 Remico St Sw
    Wyoming MI 49519
    616 531-0670

(G-6374)
ELEMENT 80 ENGRAVING LLC
519 Macomb Ave Nw (49534-3570)
PHONE..................................616 318-7407
Alfred Hartl, *Principal*
EMP: 3
SALES (est): 183.1K **Privately Held**
SIC: 2819 Elements

(G-6375)
ELEVATED TECHNOLOGIES INC
15 Ionia Ave Sw Ste 310 (49503-4185)
PHONE..................................616 288-9817
Nathan McFabden, *President*
EMP: 12
SQ FT: 2,500
SALES (est): 2.2MM **Privately Held**
WEB: www.esigr.com
SIC: 1796 7699 1541 1791 Elevator installation & conversion; elevators: inspection, service & repair; industrial buildings & warehouses; structural steel erection; sheet metalwork; stair elevators, motor powered

(G-6376)
EMERALD GRAPHICS INC
4949 W Greenbrooke Dr Se (49512-5400)
PHONE..................................616 871-3020
Ann Kennedy, *President*
Mark Kennedy, *President*
EMP: 6
SALES (est): 670K **Privately Held**
SIC: 2759 Screen printing

(G-6377)
EMPIRICAL BIOSCIENCE INC
2007 Eastcastle Dr Se (49508-8773)
PHONE..................................877 479-9949
Craig Pippel, *Principal*
Elisabeth Reus, *Accountant*
Beth Lowe, *Manager*
EMP: 5
SALES (est): 765.8K **Privately Held**
SIC: 2819 Chemicals, reagent grade: refined from technical grade

(G-6378)
ENERTEMP INC
3961 Eastern Ave Se (49508-2416)
PHONE..................................616 243-2752
Clair D Norder, *President*
Joel T Teft, *Vice Pres*
Phil Vandenheuvel, *Engineer*
Michael Schellenboom, *Sales Engr*
Diane Braun, *Office Mgr*
EMP: 23
SQ FT: 5,000
SALES (est): 5.4MM **Privately Held**
WEB: www.enertemp.com
SIC: 3822 Auto controls regulating residntl & coml environmt & applncs

(G-6379)
ENGINEERED PRFMCE COATINGS INC
4881 Kendrick St Se (49512-9602)
PHONE..................................616 988-7927
Matthew Wolfe, *General Mgr*
EMP: 3
SQ FT: 7,500

Grand Rapids - Kent County (G-6380)   GEOGRAPHIC SECTION

SALES: 3MM **Privately Held**
SIC: 3479 Coating of metals & formed products
HQ: Engineered Performance Coatings Ltd
Lanesborough House The Laurels,
Heol Y Rhosog
Cardiff S GLAM CF3 2
292 166-0155

(G-6380)
ENGINEERED TOOLING SYSTEMS INC
Also Called: Tsg Tooling Systems Group.com
2780 Courier Dr Nw (49534-1247)
PHONE..................................616 647-5063
Jim Grotenrath, *President*
Kurtis Van Vels, *Vice Pres*
Drew Boresma, *Admin Sec*
▲ **EMP:** 12
SQ FT: 16,000
SALES (est): 4.3MM **Privately Held**
SIC: 3544 Special dies & tools
HQ: Advanced Tooling Systems, Inc.
1166 7 Mile Rd Nw
Comstock Park MI 49321
616 784-7513

(G-6381)
ENGRAVE & GRAPHIC INC
Also Called: Engrave & Graphic Inc Fax
1605 Eastern Ave Se (49507-2027)
PHONE..................................616 245-8082
Michael Trenshaw, *President*
Kay Trenshaw, *Treasurer*
EMP: 3
SQ FT: 5,200
SALES: 175K **Privately Held**
SIC: 3479 7336 Engraving jewelry silverware, or metal; silk screen design

(G-6382)
EOVATIONS LLC
2801 E Beltline Ave Ne (49525-9680)
PHONE..................................616 361-7136
Patrick Lockwood, *Owner*
EMP: 5
SALES (est): 334.6K **Privately Held**
SIC: 2421 Sawmills & planing mills, general

(G-6383)
ERWIN QUARDER INC
5101 Kraft Ave Se Ste B (49512-9737)
PHONE..................................616 575-1600
Martin Quarder, *President*
Jim Oberstadt, *Controller*
Scott Brown, *Sales Engr*
▲ **EMP:** 95 **EST:** 1998
SQ FT: 80,000
SALES: 34.3MM
SALES (corp-wide): 131.8MM **Privately Held**
SIC: 3089 3544 3714 7692 Injection molding of plastics; automotive parts, plastic; special dies, tools, jigs & fixtures; motor vehicle parts & accessories; welding repair
HQ: Erwin Quarder Systemtechnik Gmbh
Fritz-Souchon-Str. 2
Espelkamp 32339
577 291-140

(G-6384)
ESCO COMPANY LLC
2330 East Paris Ave Se (49546-6131)
PHONE..................................231 726-3106
Cal Collins, *CEO*
Robert Anderson, *President*
Eric Blackburn, *Senior VP*
Kevin Thomas, *Senior VP*
Ray Verlinich, *Senior VP*
▲ **EMP:** 60 **EST:** 2007
SALES (est): 17.2MM **Privately Held**
WEB: www.escocompany.com
SIC: 2865 Cyclic crudes & intermediates
HQ: Mitsui Chemicals America, Inc.
800 Westchester Ave N607
Rye Brook NY 10573
914 253-0777

(G-6385)
ESCO GROUP INC (PA)
2887 3 Mile Rd Nw (49534-1319)
PHONE..................................616 453-5458
Richard Hungerford Jr, *CEO*
EMP: 10

SALES (est): 10.3MM **Privately Held**
SIC: 3599 3541 Air intake filters, internal combustion engine, except auto; drilling & boring machines

(G-6386)
ESSILOR LABORATORIES AMER INC
Also Called: Optical Supply
1526 Plainfield Ave Ne (49505-4923)
PHONE..................................616 361-6000
John Dehommel, *General Mgr*
Bill Reese, *General Mgr*
Deborah Hutchison, *Sales Executive*
EMP: 200
SALES (corp-wide): 1.4MM **Privately Held**
WEB: www.crizal.com
SIC: 3851 3229 2522 2511 Contact lenses; pressed & blown glass; office furniture, except wood; wood household furniture
HQ: Essilor Laboratories Of America, Inc.
13515 N Stemmons Fwy
Dallas TX 75234
972 241-4141

(G-6387)
ETO MAGNETIC CORP (DH)
5925 Patterson Ave Se (49512-9618)
PHONE..................................616 957-2570
Stefan Jacob, *CEO*
Michael Ignaczak, *President*
Steve Lankfer, *COO*
Greg Peters, *Vice Pres*
Eric Schaefer, *Engineer*
▲ **EMP:** 74
SQ FT: 70,000
SALES: 25MM
SALES (corp-wide): 267.9K **Privately Held**
WEB: www.etomagnetic.com
SIC: 3679 3625 3647 Solenoids for electronic applications; solenoid switches (industrial controls); automotive lighting fixtures
HQ: Eto Magnetic Gmbh
Hardtring 8
Stockach 78333
777 180-90

(G-6388)
EVANS TEMPCON DELAWARE LLC
3260 Eagle Park Dr Ne Ne100 (49525-4569)
PHONE..................................616 361-2681
Mark L Smith, *President*
Rodney Roderick, *CFO*
EMP: 8
SALES (est): 364.1K
SALES (corp-wide): 52.4MM **Privately Held**
SIC: 3585 Air conditioning, motor vehicle
HQ: Proair Holdings Corporation
6630 E State Highway 114
Haslet TX 76052
817 636-2308

(G-6389)
EVANS TOOL & ENGINEERING INC
4287 3 Mile Rd Nw (49534-1144)
PHONE..................................616 791-6333
Michael Evans, *CEO*
Jacquelin Evans, *Vice Pres*
EMP: 12
SQ FT: 12,000
SALES (est): 1.2MM **Privately Held**
WEB: www.evanstool.com
SIC: 3545 Cutting tools for machine tools; diamond cutting tools for turning, boring, burnishing, etc.

(G-6390)
EVEN-CUT ABRASIVE COMPANY
3890 Buchanan Ave Sw (49548-3111)
PHONE..................................216 881-9595
Arthur Ellison, *President*
▲ **EMP:** 70
SQ FT: 65,000
SALES: 9.7MM **Privately Held**
WEB: www.evencut.com
SIC: 3291 Abrasive products

(G-6391)
EXCELLENCE MANUFACTURING INC
629 Ionia Ave Sw (49503-5148)
PHONE..................................616 456-9928
John P Carrier, *President*
David Collins, *Vice Pres*
David Savage, *Vice Pres*
Jim Sumners, *Vice Pres*
EMP: 100
SQ FT: 40,000
SALES (est): 11.9MM **Privately Held**
SIC: 3714 Motor vehicle parts & accessories

(G-6392)
EXPECTANCY LEARNING LLC
3152 Peregrine Dr Ne # 110 (49525-9723)
PHONE..................................866 829-9533
Jeremy Erard,
EMP: 7
SQ FT: 3,000
SALES (est): 168K **Privately Held**
SIC: 7372 Educational computer software

(G-6393)
EXPERT COATING COMPANY INC
2855 Marlin Ct Nw (49534-1293)
PHONE..................................616 453-8261
Erik Klimek, *President*
Walter Klimek, *Vice Pres*
Mennow Klimek, *Treasurer*
Patricia Lesinski, *Admin Sec*
EMP: 10 **EST:** 1940
SQ FT: 15,000
SALES (est): 1.1MM **Privately Held**
WEB: www.expertcoating.net
SIC: 3471 3479 Plating of metals or formed products; coating of metals with plastic or resins

(G-6394)
EXTREME SCREEN PRINTS
3723 Burlingame Ave Sw (49509-3701)
PHONE..................................616 889-8305
Daniel Lund, *Owner*
EMP: 4
SALES (est): 440.5K **Privately Held**
SIC: 2752 Commercial printing, lithographic

(G-6395)
EXTRUDE HONE LLC
Thermoburr Michigan West
2882 Northridge Dr Nw (49544-9109)
PHONE..................................616 647-9050
EMP: 10
SALES (corp-wide): 174.2MM **Privately Held**
SIC: 3541 Mfg Machine Tools-Cutting
HQ: Extrude Hone Llc
235 Industry Blvd
Irwin PA 15642
724 863-5900

(G-6396)
EXTRUSIONS DIVISION INC (PA)
201 Cottage Grove St Se (49507-1701)
PHONE..................................616 247-3611
James Azzar, *President*
Linda Azzar, *Admin Sec*
EMP: 5
SALES (est): 598.8K **Privately Held**
SIC: 3089 Extruded finished plastic products

(G-6397)
FAITH ALIVE CHRISTN RESOURCES (PA)
1700 28th St Se (49508-1414)
PHONE..................................800 333-8300
Paul Faber, *Editor*
Mike Dykema, *Finance Mgr*
Gary Mulder, *Exec Dir*
▲ **EMP:** 35
SQ FT: 22,000
SALES (est): 2.7MM **Privately Held**
SIC: 2721 2731 5049 Periodicals: publishing only; books: publishing & printing; pamphlets: publishing & printing; religious supplies

(G-6398)
FARNESE NORTH AMERICA INC
4095 Embassy Dr Se (49546-2456)
PHONE..................................616 844-8651
Jon Taylor, *Director*
EMP: 2 **EST:** 2014
SQ FT: 2,500
SALES: 1.5MM **Privately Held**
SIC: 3281 Cut stone & stone products

(G-6399)
FASTCO INDUSTRIES INC (PA)
2685 Mullins Ct Nw (49534-1219)
P.O. Box 141427 (49514-1427)
PHONE..................................616 453-5428
Arvin L Tap, *Ch of Bd*
Bruce Tap, *President*
Ken Chesterman, *COO*
Scott Smith, *Vice Pres*
Aaron Headrick, *Purch Agent*
▲ **EMP:** 66
SQ FT: 46,000
SALES (est): 20.3MM **Privately Held**
WEB: www.fastcoind.com
SIC: 3452 Bolts, nuts, rivets & washers

(G-6400)
FASTCO INDUSTRIES INC
2700 Courier Dr Nw (49534-1247)
PHONE..................................616 389-1390
Emily Bradfield, *Manager*
EMP: 60
SALES (corp-wide): 19.8MM **Privately Held**
SIC: 3452 Bolts, nuts, rivets & washers
PA: Fastco Industries, Inc.
2685 Mullins Ct Nw
Grand Rapids MI 49534
616 453-5428

(G-6401)
FASTCO INDUSTRIES INC
2759 Mullins Ave (49534)
PHONE..................................616 453-5428
Jane Fuller, *Branch Mgr*
EMP: 7
SALES (corp-wide): 20.3MM **Privately Held**
SIC: 3452 Bolts, nuts, rivets & washers
PA: Fastco Industries, Inc.
2685 Mullins Ct Nw
Grand Rapids MI 49534
616 453-5428

(G-6402)
FATHOM DRONES INC
401 Hall St Sw Ste 213 (49503-4997)
PHONE..................................586 216-7047
Matthew Gira, *CEO*
EMP: 4
SQ FT: 100
SALES (est): 175.8K **Privately Held**
SIC: 3429 Marine hardware

(G-6403)
FD LAKE COMPANY
3313 Lousma Dr Se (49548-2278)
PHONE..................................616 241-5639
Caryl Carlsen, *CEO*
Michael W Posey, *President*
Sue Elyn Johnson, *Controller*
Dennis Humphrey, *Sales Staff*
▲ **EMP:** 14
SQ FT: 12,000
SALES (est): 3.2MM **Privately Held**
WEB: www.fdlake.com
SIC: 1796 3731 Machine moving & rigging; marine rigging

(G-6404)
FEDEX OFFICE & PRINT SVCS INC
Also Called: Fedex Office Print & Ship Ctr
233 Fulton St W (49503-2668)
PHONE..................................616 336-1900
Richard Schmiedicke, *District Mgr*
EMP: 20
SALES (corp-wide): 69.6B **Publicly Held**
WEB: www.kinkos.com
SIC: 7334 2791 2789 2672 Photocopying & duplicating services; typesetting; bookbinding & related work; coated & laminated paper

GEOGRAPHIC SECTION

Grand Rapids - Kent County (G-6431)

HQ: Fedex Office And Print Services, Inc.
7900 Legacy Dr
Plano TX 75024
800 463-3339

(G-6405)
FEDEX OFFICE & PRINT SVCS INC
3614 28th St Se (49512-1606)
PHONE.................................616 957-7888
EMP: 29
SALES (corp-wide): 69.6B **Publicly Held**
WEB: www.kinkos.com
SIC: 7334 5943 2791 Photocopying & duplicating services; stationery stores; typesetting
HQ: Fedex Office And Print Services, Inc.
7900 Legacy Dr
Plano TX 75024
800 463-3339

(G-6406)
FIREBOY-XINTEX INC (HQ)
Also Called: Aetna Engineering
O-379 Lake Michigan Dr Nw (49534-3355)
PHONE.................................616 735-9380
Larry Akins, *CEO*
Tim Shively, *President*
Ron Wiersum, *Controller*
▲ **EMP:** 19
SQ FT: 30,000
SALES (est): 5.1MM
SALES (corp-wide): 200MM **Privately Held**
WEB: www.fireboy-xintex.com
SIC: 3531 Marine related equipment
PA: W. S. Darley & Co.
325 Spring Lake Dr
Itasca IL 60143
630 735-3500

(G-6407)
FIREHOUSE WOODWORKS LLC
1945 Kalamazoo Ave Se (49507-2832)
PHONE.................................616 285-2300
Troy Yarbrough,
EMP: 5 **EST:** 2015
SQ FT: 1,200
SALES (est): 291.2K **Privately Held**
SIC: 2599 Factory furniture & fixtures

(G-6408)
FIRSTRONIC LLC
1655 Michigan St Ne (49503-2015)
PHONE.................................616 456-9220
John Sammut, *President*
Steve Fraser, *Vice Pres*
Wally Johnson, *Vice Pres*
Carlos Melendez, *Buyer*
Nancy Quero, *Buyer*
▲ **EMP:** 500
SALES (est): 158.6MM **Privately Held**
SIC: 3559 Electronic component making machinery
HQ: Lacroix Group
8 Impasse Du Bourrelier
Saint-Herblain 44800
972 916-607

(G-6409)
FIXALL ELECTRIC MOTOR SERVICE
737 Butterworth St Sw (49504-6394)
PHONE.................................616 454-6863
Chuck Baar, *President*
EMP: 7 **EST:** 1950
SQ FT: 2,500
SALES (est): 1.8MM **Privately Held**
WEB: www.fixallelectric.com
SIC: 7694 Electric motor repair

(G-6410)
FLAME SPRAY TECHNOLOGIES INC
4881 Kendrick St Se (49512-9602)
PHONE.................................616 988-2622
Terry Wilmert, *President*
Marco Prosperini, *Vice Pres*
EMP: 3
SQ FT: 1,100
SALES (est): 557.5K **Privately Held**
WEB: www.flamespraytechnologies.com
SIC: 3563 Spraying outfits: metals, paints & chemicals (compressor)

(G-6411)
FLEX-N-GATE CORPORATION
3075 Breton Rd Se (49512-1747)
PHONE.................................616 222-3296
Donald Griffin, *Project Mgr*
Jim Goolsby, *Branch Mgr*
EMP: 450
SALES (corp-wide): 3.3B **Privately Held**
WEB: www.meridianautosystems.com
SIC: 3714 Bumpers & bumperettes, motor vehicle
PA: Flex-N-Gate Llc
1306 E University Ave
Urbana IL 61802
217 384-6600

(G-6412)
FLEXFAB LLC
5333 33rd St Se (49512-2022)
PHONE.................................269 945-3533
Brian Bowman, *Mfg Staff*
Matthew Decamp, *Branch Mgr*
EMP: 25
SALES (corp-wide): 115MM **Privately Held**
SIC: 3052 Rubber & plastics hose & beltings
HQ: Flexfab, Llc
1699 W M 43 Hwy
Hastings MI 49058
269 945-2433

(G-6413)
FLEXIBLE STEEL LACING COMPANY
Also Called: Flexco
1995 Oak Industrial Dr Ne (49505-6009)
PHONE.................................616 459-3196
Doug Saunders, *Opers Mgr*
Noel Cormier, *Engineer*
Michelle Young, *Engineer*
Derek Wright, *Senior Engr*
Nancy Ayres, *Branch Mgr*
EMP: 100
SALES (corp-wide): 131.6MM **Privately Held**
SIC: 3429 Metal fasteners
PA: Flexible Steel Lacing Company Inc
2525 Wisconsin Ave
Downers Grove IL 60515
800 323-3444

(G-6414)
FLOORCOVERING ENGINEERS LLC
2489 Maplevalley Dr Se (49512-3801)
PHONE.................................616 299-1007
John Quillan,
EMP: 1
SALES: 5MM **Privately Held**
SIC: 5023 3996 Carpets; hard surface floor coverings

(G-6415)
FOREMOST GRAPHICS LLC
Also Called: Dana Trading
2921 Wilson Dr Nw (49534-7565)
PHONE.................................616 453-4747
Brian Vanderhooning, *VP Mfg*
Mike Butterfield, *Purch Mgr*
Larry Schutt, *CFO*
Donna Perschbacher, *Controller*
Sarah Devries, *Human Res Mgr*
EMP: 70
SQ FT: 80,000
SALES (est): 10MM **Privately Held**
WEB: www.foremostdirect.com
SIC: 2752 2791 2789 Lithographing on metal; typesetting; bookbinding & related work

(G-6416)
FORMAX MANUFACTURING CORP
168 Wealthy St Sw (49503-4019)
PHONE.................................616 456-5458
Andrew Johnston, *President*
Gordon Johnston, *VP Mfg*
EMP: 25 **EST:** 1938
SQ FT: 50,000
SALES (est): 3.6MM **Privately Held**
WEB: www.formaxmfg.com
SIC: 3291 2842 Buffing or polishing wheels, abrasive or nonabrasive; abrasive buffs, bricks, cloth, paper, stones, etc.; sticks, abrasive; specialty cleaning, polishes & sanitation goods

(G-6417)
FORWARD METAL CRAFT INC
329 Summer Ave Nw (49504-5316)
PHONE.................................616 459-6051
Ward Schenck, *President*
Scot Schenck, *President*
EMP: 10
SQ FT: 40,000
SALES (est): 1.8MM **Privately Held**
WEB: www.forwardmetalcraft.com
SIC: 3465 3469 Automotive stampings; furniture components, porcelain enameled

(G-6418)
FRANKLIN PRESS INC
2426 28th St Sw (49519-2188)
PHONE.................................616 538-5320
Vic Helder, *President*
Dan De Ruischer, *Sales Staff*
EMP: 11
SQ FT: 5,500
SALES (est): 1.5MM **Privately Held**
WEB: www.franklinpressinc.com
SIC: 2752 Commercial printing, lithographic

(G-6419)
FRONTLINES PUBLISHING
Also Called: Pregnancy Resource Center
72 Ransom Ave Ne Ofc (49503-3217)
PHONE.................................616 887-6256
EMP: 21
SALES (est): 1.1MM **Privately Held**
SIC: 2741 Misc Publishing

(G-6420)
FROST INC (PA)
2900 Northridge Dr Nw (49544-9119)
PHONE.................................616 785-9030
Charles C Frost, *President*
Fred Sytsema, *Vice Pres*
EMP: 2
SQ FT: 79,000
SALES (est): 18.8MM **Privately Held**
WEB: www.frostindustries.com
SIC: 3535 3536 Overhead conveyor systems; trolley conveyors; hoists, cranes & monorails; hand hoists

(G-6421)
FROST INCORPORATED (HQ)
Also Called: CMS
2900 Northridge Dr Nw (49544-9119)
PHONE.................................616 453-7781
Chad Frost, *President*
John Yahmpun, *Vice Pres*
◆ **EMP:** 50 **EST:** 1915
SQ FT: 79,000
SALES (est): 20.4MM **Privately Held**
WEB: www.frostinc.com
SIC: 3535 3562 3537 3536 Overhead conveyor systems; trolley conveyors; ball & roller bearings; industrial trucks & tractors; hand hoists
PA: Frost Inc.
2900 Northridge Dr Nw
Grand Rapids MI 49544
616 785-9030

(G-6422)
FROST LINKS (PA)
2900 Northridge Dr Nw (49544-9119)
PHONE.................................616 785-9030
Paula Miller, *President*
▲ **EMP:** 7
SALES (est): 2.9MM **Privately Held**
SIC: 3535 Conveyors & conveying equipment

(G-6423)
FUCHS LUBRICANTS CO
3535 R B Chaffee Mem Dr (49548)
PHONE.................................708 333-8900
Mike Messer, *Manager*
EMP: 5

SALES (corp-wide): 2.9B **Privately Held**
WEB: www.fuchs.com
SIC: 2992 Lubricating oils & greases
HQ: Fuchs Lubricants Co.
17050 Lathrop Ave
Harvey IL 60426
708 333-8901

(G-6424)
FUN PROMOTION LLC
Also Called: Fun Promotion Services
2225 Lake Michigan Dr Nw (49504-5964)
P.O. Box 1383 (49501-1383)
PHONE.................................616 453-4245
Brent Walk,
EMP: 3
SALES: 120K **Privately Held**
WEB: www.funpromotions.com
SIC: 5199 3914 Advertising specialties; trophies

(G-6425)
FURNITURE CITY GLASS CORP
1012 Ken O Sha Ind Park (49508-8216)
PHONE.................................616 784-5500
Michael Greengard, *President*
EMP: 22
SQ FT: 40,000
SALES (est): 2.5MM **Privately Held**
SIC: 3211 3231 Building glass, flat; products of purchased glass

(G-6426)
G & W MACHINE CO
2107 Merlin St Ne (49525-2855)
PHONE.................................616 363-4435
Steven Wojciakowski, *Partner*
Thomas Wojciakowski, *Partner*
EMP: 4 **EST:** 1979
SQ FT: 6,000
SALES (est): 457.3K **Privately Held**
SIC: 3541 Machine tools, metal cutting type

(G-6427)
G A RICHARDS COMPANY (PA)
1060 Ken O Sha Ind (49508)
PHONE.................................616 243-2800
John Boll, *President*
Scott Uzarski, *Prdtn Mgr*
Paul Meeter, *Buyer*
Jay Pearson, *Purchasing*
Brooke Schreur, *Purchasing*
▲ **EMP:** 70
SQ FT: 75,000
SALES (est): 17.1MM **Privately Held**
SIC: 3444 Sheet metalwork

(G-6428)
G DEFENSE COMPANY B
823 Ottawa Ave Nw (49503-1429)
PHONE.................................616 202-4500
EMP: 3 **EST:** 2017
SALES (est): 160K **Privately Held**
SIC: 3812 Defense systems & equipment

(G-6429)
GABRIEL NORTH AMERICA INC
560 5th St Nw Ste 210 (49504-5296)
PHONE.................................616 202-5770
Claus Toftegaard, *Director*
EMP: 4
SALES (est): 250K **Privately Held**
SIC: 2299 Upholstery filling, textile

(G-6430)
GATEWAY ENGINEERING INC
6534 Clay Ave Sw (49548-7832)
PHONE.................................616 284-1425
Dan Owen, *President*
EMP: 50
SQ FT: 4,000
SALES: 1MM **Privately Held**
SIC: 3568 Power transmission equipment

(G-6431)
GE AVIATION SYSTEMS LLC
3290 Patterson Ave Se (49512-1934)
PHONE.................................616 224-6480
EMP: 25
SALES (corp-wide): 122B **Publicly Held**
SIC: 3812 Mfg Search/Navigation Equipment

Grand Rapids - Kent County (G-6432)

GEOGRAPHIC SECTION

HQ: Ge Aviation Systems Llc
1 Neumann Way
Cincinnati OH 45215
937 898-9600

(G-6432)
GE HEALTHCARE INC
Also Called: Nico Med Amersham
4380 Brockton Dr Se Ste 3 (49512-4108)
PHONE..................616 554-5717
Mary Presontaine, *Manager*
EMP: 20
SALES (corp-wide): 121.6B **Publicly Held**
SIC: 2834 5122 Pharmaceutical preparations; drugs, proprietaries & sundries
HQ: Ge Healthcare Inc.
100 Results Way
Marlborough MA 01752
800 526-3593

(G-6433)
GEM PLASTICS INC
2533 Thornwood St Sw (49519-2148)
PHONE..................616 538-5966
Michael Deyman, *President*
EMP: 6
SQ FT: 15,000
SALES (est): 1.1MM **Privately Held**
WEB: www.gemplastics.com
SIC: 3089 Injection molding of plastics

(G-6434)
GEMINI CORPORATION
Also Called: Gemini Publications
401 Hall St Sw Ste 331a (49503-6501)
PHONE..................616 459-4545
John Zwarensteyn, *CEO*
Chris Ehrlich, *Editor*
Karla Jeltema, *Editor*
Jenn Maksimowski, *Sales Mgr*
Jennifer Maksimowski, *Sales Mgr*
EMP: 46
SALES (est): 5.1MM **Privately Held**
WEB: www.grmag.com
SIC: 2721 2711 2741 Magazines: publishing only, not printed on site; newspapers: publishing only, not printed on site; miscellaneous publishing

(G-6435)
GENERAL DIE & ENGINEERING INC (PA)
6500 Clay Ave Sw (49548-7832)
PHONE..................616 698-6961
Leon McCudden, *CEO*
Charles Kukulis, *President*
Doug Kukulis, *COO*
John Rose, *Vice Pres*
Justin Ackley, *Engineer*
EMP: 46
SQ FT: 68,000
SALES (est): 7.4MM **Privately Held**
WEB: www.gendie.com
SIC: 3544 Special dies & tools

(G-6436)
GENESIS SEATING INC
Also Called: Genesis Seating 0519
3445 East Paris Ave Se (49512-2960)
PHONE..................616 954-1040
EMP: 5
SALES (corp-wide): 4.2B **Publicly Held**
SIC: 5021 2511 2426 Office & public building furniture; wood household furniture; hardwood dimension & flooring mills
HQ: Genesis Seating, Inc.
3445 East Paris Ave Se
Grand Rapids MI 49512

(G-6437)
GENESIS SEATING INC (HQ)
Also Called: Genesis Seating 0519
3445 East Paris Ave Se (49512-2960)
PHONE..................616 954-1040
Kevin Kuske, *CEO*
Jeff Agar, *Vice Pres*
Christopher Barnes, *Engineer*
Rick Williams, *Director*
◆ **EMP:** 9
SQ FT: 129,000

SALES (est): 23.2MM
SALES (corp-wide): 4.2B **Publicly Held**
WEB: www.genesis-seating.com
SIC: 5021 2521 2511 2426 Office & public building furniture; wood office furniture; wood household furniture; hardwood dimension & flooring mills
PA: Leggett & Platt, Incorporated
1 Leggett Rd
Carthage MO 64836
417 358-8131

(G-6438)
GILL CORPORATION (HQ)
Also Called: GRS&s
706 Bond Ave Nw (49503-1434)
PHONE..................616 453-4491
James J Zawacki, *President*
Tom Deemter, *Engineer*
Paul Von Eitzen, *Engineer*
Ted Hohman, *Treasurer*
▲ **EMP:** 280
SQ FT: 120,000
SALES (est): 122.1MM
SALES (corp-wide): 376.6MM **Privately Held**
WEB: www.grs-s.com
SIC: 3469 3312 3495 3493 Metal stampings; tool & die steel; wire springs; steel springs, except wire; miscellaneous fabricated wire products; automotive stampings
PA: Gill Holding Company, Inc.
5271 Plainfield Ave Ne
Grand Rapids MI 49525
616 559-2700

(G-6439)
GILL CORPORATION
Stumpp Schuele Somappa Spring
706 Bond Ave Nw (49503-1434)
PHONE..................616 453-4491
EMP: 165
SALES (corp-wide): 376.6MM **Privately Held**
WEB: www.grs-s.com
SIC: 3496 3312 3495 3493 Miscellaneous fabricated wire products; blast furnaces & steel mills; wire springs; steel springs, except wire
HQ: Gill Corporation
706 Bond Ave Nw
Grand Rapids MI 49503
616 453-4491

(G-6440)
GILL HOLDING COMPANY INC (PA)
5271 Plainfield Ave Ne (49525-1046)
PHONE..................616 559-2700
Richard Perreault, *CEO*
J Timothy Gargaro, *CFO*
EMP: 31 **EST:** 2011
SALES (est): 376.6MM **Privately Held**
SIC: 3465 3544 Automotive stampings; special dies & tools

(G-6441)
GILL INDUSTRIES INC (HQ)
Also Called: Gill Manufacturing Co.
5271 Plainfield Ave Ne (49525-1046)
PHONE..................616 559-2700
Rita Williams, *CEO*
Joe Gill, *Vice Pres*
Charles Scholfield, *Vice Pres*
Bob Sutter, *Vice Pres*
Rita Woodruff, *Vice Pres*
◆ **EMP:** 112 **EST:** 1964
SQ FT: 150,000
SALES (est): 253.3MM
SALES (corp-wide): 376.6MM **Privately Held**
WEB: www.gill-industries.com
SIC: 3465 3544 Automotive stampings; special dies & tools
PA: Gill Holding Company, Inc.
5271 Plainfield Ave Ne
Grand Rapids MI 49525
616 559-2700

(G-6442)
GILL INDUSTRIES INC
Also Called: Gill Manufacturing
5271 Plainfield Ave Nw (49525)
PHONE..................616 559-2700
John Woodruff, *Branch Mgr*

EMP: 150
SALES (corp-wide): 376.6MM **Privately Held**
WEB: www.gill-industries.com
SIC: 3423 Hand & edge tools
HQ: Gill Industries, Inc.
5271 Plainfield Ave Ne
Grand Rapids MI 49525
616 559-2700

(G-6443)
GINSAN LIQUIDATING COMPANY LLC
Also Called: Trusco
3611 3 Mile Rd Nw (49534-1251)
PHONE..................616 791-8100
Sigrid Valk-Feeney, *President*
Marlene Redner, *Credit Staff*
Garrick Greathouse, *Marketing Staff*
Dan Kamsickas, *Technical Staff*
◆ **EMP:** 95
SQ FT: 45,000
SALES (est): 19.4MM **Privately Held**
WEB: www.ginsan.com
SIC: 3589 2899 Car washing machinery; water treating compounds

(G-6444)
GM COMPONENTS HOLDINGS LLC
Gmch Grand Rapids
2100 Burlingame Ave Sw (49509-1753)
PHONE..................616 246-2000
Fred Brown, *Branch Mgr*
Ed Di Enno, *Executive*
EMP: 50 **EST:** 1940
SIC: 3519 3714 3594 3492 Internal combustion engines; fuel systems & parts, motor vehicle; hydraulic fluid power pumps for auto steering mechanism; fluid power pumps & motors; fluid power valves & hose fittings
HQ: Gm Components Holdings, Llc
300 Renaissance Ctr
Detroit MI 48243

(G-6445)
GO BEYOND HEALTHY LLC
2290 Christine Ct Se (49546-6468)
PHONE..................407 255-0314
Scott Graves, *Mng Member*
EMP: 3
SALES (est): 171.8K **Privately Held**
SIC: 2076 7922 5149 Coconut oil; beauty contest production; juices

(G-6446)
GONZALEZ JR PALLETS LLC
1601 Madison St Sw (49507)
PHONE..................616 885-0201
Valentin Gonzalez,
EMP: 7
SQ FT: 16,000
SALES: 350K **Privately Held**
SIC: 2448 Pallets, wood

(G-6447)
GONZALEZ UNIVERSAL PALLETS LLC
955 Godfrey Ave Sw (49503-5003)
PHONE..................616 243-5524
Alfonso Gonzalez Ortiz,
EMP: 8
SALES (est): 1.3MM **Privately Held**
SIC: 2448 Pallets, wood & wood with metal

(G-6448)
GOODALE ENTERPRISES LLC (PA)
21 Fennessey St Sw (49534-5896)
PHONE..................616 453-7690
Patrick Goodale, *Mng Member*
EMP: 7
SALES (est): 2.1MM **Privately Held**
SIC: 1311 Crude petroleum production

(G-6449)
GR BAKING COMPANY
Also Called: Sunrise Bread Co
900 Division Ave S (49507-1563)
PHONE..................616 245-3446
Daniel P Herman, *President*
EMP: 12

SALES: 500K **Privately Held**
SIC: 2051 Bread, all types (white, wheat, rye, etc): fresh or frozen

(G-6450)
GRAND NORTHERN PRODUCTS
400 Mart St Sw (49548-1015)
PHONE..................800 968-1811
William Currie, *Principal*
EMP: 3
SALES (est): 244K **Privately Held**
SIC: 3471 5085 Finishing, metals or formed products; abrasives

(G-6451)
GRAND RAPIDS BEDDING CO (PA)
Also Called: Spring Air Mattress Company
630 Myrtle St Nw (49504-3129)
PHONE..................616 459-8234
Kenneth R Clapp, *President*
▲ **EMP:** 30 **EST:** 1889
SQ FT: 65,000
SALES (est): 4.5MM **Privately Held**
SIC: 2515 Mattresses, innerspring or box spring

(G-6452)
GRAND RAPIDS CARVERS INC
4465 Roger B Chaffee Se (49548-7522)
PHONE..................616 538-0022
Kevin J Slagter, *President*
Robert Buehler, *Vice Pres*
Rhonda Slagter, *Treasurer*
Tammy Buehler, *Executive*
EMP: 32 **EST:** 1940
SQ FT: 42,000
SALES: 3MM **Privately Held**
WEB: www.grcarvers.com
SIC: 2431 2426 3543 2531 Millwork; furniture dimension stock, hardwood; frames for upholstered furniture, wood; industrial patterns; public building & related furniture; wood office furniture; wood household furniture

(G-6453)
GRAND RAPIDS ELC MTR SVC LLC
1057 Cottage Grove St Se (49507-2003)
PHONE..................616 243-8866
Trent Bremer,
EMP: 8
SALES (est): 101.3K **Privately Held**
SIC: 7694 Electric motor repair

(G-6454)
GRAND RAPIDS GRAVEL COMPANY (PA)
Also Called: Port City Redi-Mix
2700 28th St Sw (49519-2110)
P.O. Box 9160 (49509-0160)
PHONE..................616 538-9000
Andrew Dykema, *President*
James Dykema, *Admin Sec*
EMP: 10 **EST:** 1920
SQ FT: 10,000
SALES (est): 26.5MM **Privately Held**
WEB: www.grgravel.com
SIC: 3273 1422 8741 1442 Ready-mixed concrete; calcareous tufa, crushed & broken-quarrying; management services; construction sand & gravel

(G-6455)
GRAND RAPIDS LABEL COMPANY
2351 Oak Industrial Dr Ne (49505-6017)
PHONE..................616 459-8134
William M Muir, *President*
Elizabeth J Crosby, *Vice Pres*
John Crosby, *Vice Pres*
Scott Dobrowolski, *Mfg Dir*
Brian Sparks, *Purch Mgr*
EMP: 72 **EST:** 1884
SQ FT: 103,000
SALES (est): 18.9MM **Privately Held**
WEB: www.grlabel.com
SIC: 2759 7389 Flexographic printing; packaging & labeling services

(G-6456)
GRAND RAPIDS LEGAL NEWS
1430 Monroe Ave Nw # 140 (49505-4678)
PHONE..................616 454-9293

GEOGRAPHIC SECTION

Grand Rapids - Kent County (G-6483)

Ben Piseo, *Principal*
EMP: 6 **EST:** 2011
SALES (est): 329K **Privately Held**
SIC: 2711 Newspapers, publishing & printing

(G-6457)
GRAND RAPIDS LETTER SERVICE
315 Fuller Ave Ne (49503-3630)
PHONE..............................616 459-4711
EMP: 4
SQ FT: 3,500
SALES (est): 300K **Privately Held**
SIC: 2752 2759 Offset Printing Shop

(G-6458)
GRAND RAPIDS MACHINE REPAIR
3710 Linden Ave Se (49548-3428)
PHONE..............................616 248-4760
Ron Brow Jr, *President*
EMP: 40
SALES (est): 3MM **Privately Held**
SIC: 3599 Machine shop, jobbing & repair

(G-6459)
GRAND RAPIDS MACHINE REPR INC
4000 Eastern Ave Se (49508-3402)
PHONE..............................616 245-9102
Ronald Brow Sr, *President*
Ron Walker, *Plant Mgr*
EMP: 34
SQ FT: 15,000
SALES (est): 5.5MM **Privately Held**
WEB: www.grmr.com
SIC: 7699 3812 Aircraft & heavy equipment repair services; aircraft flight instruments

(G-6460)
GRAND RAPIDS METALTEK INC
2860 Marlin Ct Nw (49534-1217)
PHONE..............................616 791-2373
Paul Bultinck, *President*
Karla Cook, *Vice Pres*
Kris Hurley, *Project Mgr*
Aaron Scott, *Project Mgr*
Trena Bresky, *Treasurer*
EMP: 49
SQ FT: 23,000
SALES (est): 5MM **Privately Held**
WEB: www.grmetaltek.com
SIC: 7692 3599 7389 3545 Welding repair; machine shop, jobbing & repair; grinding, precision: commercial or industrial; precision tools, machinists'

(G-6461)
GRAND RAPIDS PRESS INC
3102 Walker Ridge Dr Nw (49544-9125)
PHONE..............................616 459-1400
Sheri Compton, *Principal*
Ryan Knizner, *Sales Staff*
Sally Loftis, *Executive Asst*
EMP: 17 **EST:** 2008
SALES (est): 1.7MM **Privately Held**
SIC: 2711 Newspapers

(G-6462)
GRAND RAPIDS PRINTING INK CO (PA)
4920 Starr St Se (49546-6351)
PHONE..............................616 241-5681
John Toigo, *President*
Joe Toigo, *Treasurer*
▲ **EMP:** 13
SQ FT: 17,000
SALES (est): 2.5MM **Privately Held**
WEB: www.graphicarts.org
SIC: 2893 5085 Printing ink; ink, printers'

(G-6463)
GRAND RAPIDS SALSA
1301 Benjamin Ave Se (49506-3228)
PHONE..............................616 780-1801
Tom Carrick, *Principal*
EMP: 3
SALES (est): 104.3K **Privately Held**
SIC: 2099 Dips, except cheese & sour cream based

(G-6464)
GRAND RAPIDS STRIPPING CO
1933 Will Ave Nw (49504-2035)
P.O. Box 3730 (49501-3730)
PHONE..............................616 361-0794
Michael Murphy, *President*
Phyllis Murphy, *Corp Secy*
EMP: 5
SQ FT: 8,000
SALES (est): 380K **Privately Held**
WEB: www.grandrapidsfertility.com
SIC: 3471 Cleaning & descaling metal products

(G-6465)
GRAND RAPIDS TECHNOLOGIES INC
3133 Madison Ave Se Ste B (49548-1277)
PHONE..............................616 245-7700
Gregory R Toman, *President*
EMP: 8
SQ FT: 5,000
SALES (est): 1.3MM **Privately Held**
WEB: www.grtavionics.com
SIC: 3728 Aircraft parts & equipment

(G-6466)
GRAND RAPIDS TIMES INC
2016 Eastern Ave Se (49507-3235)
P.O. Box 7258 (49510-7258)
PHONE..............................616 245-8737
Patricia Pulliam, *President*
Sallie Calloway, *Director*
EMP: 11
SALES (est): 677.6K **Privately Held**
SIC: 2711 Commercial printing & newspaper publishing combined; newspapers, publishing & printing

(G-6467)
GRAND RIVER ASEPTIC MFG INC (PA)
Also Called: Gram
140 Front Ave Sw Ste 3 (49504-6426)
PHONE..............................616 464-5072
Jerry Arthur, *CEO*
Gregory Gonzales, *President*
Jason Steele, *Business Mgr*
Matthew Vangessel, *QC Mgr*
Nick Bykerk, *Finance*
EMP: 11 **EST:** 2010
SALES (est): 7.2MM **Privately Held**
WEB: www.grandriveraseptimfg.com
SIC: 5047 2834 Medical equipment & supplies; solutions, pharmaceutical

(G-6468)
GRAND RIVER INTERIORS INC
Also Called: Echo Etching
974 Front Ave Nw Ste 2 (49504-4456)
PHONE..............................616 454-2800
David Wiest, *CEO*
Charles Luepnitz, *President*
John Hogenson, *VP Mktg*
EMP: 20
SQ FT: 30,000
SALES (est): 2.5MM **Privately Held**
WEB: www.grandriverinteriors.com
SIC: 1752 5023 3231 Carpet laying; linoleum installation; ceramic floor tile installation; floor coverings; decorated glassware: chipped, engraved, etched, etc.

(G-6469)
GRAND RPIDS WILBERT BURIAL VLT
2500 3 Mile Rd Nw (49534-1314)
PHONE..............................616 453-9429
William F Sturrus, *President*
Dave Sturrus, *General Mgr*
David Sturrus, *Vice Pres*
Todd Sturrus, *Treasurer*
Cheryl Kampfschulte, *Admin Asst*
EMP: 25 **EST:** 1936
SQ FT: 12,000
SALES (est): 3.7MM **Privately Held**
SIC: 3272 Burial vaults, concrete or precast terrazzo; septic tanks, concrete; manhole covers or frames, concrete; covers, catch basin: concrete

(G-6470)
GRAND RUSTIC PALLET CO
1105 Aberdeen St Ne (49505-3820)
PHONE..............................231 329-5035
Josh O'Donnell, *Principal*
EMP: 4
SALES (est): 225.4K **Privately Held**
SIC: 2448 Pallets, wood & wood with metal

(G-6471)
GRAND VALLEY WOOD PRODUCTS INC
Also Called: Sunstone Granite & Marble Co
3113 Hillcroft Ave Sw (49548-1036)
PHONE..............................616 475-5890
Terry Idema, *President*
Shawn Hager, *Vice Pres*
Geoff Allen, *Project Mgr*
EMP: 50
SQ FT: 34,000
SALES (est): 7.8MM **Privately Held**
SIC: 2431 2542 2541 3442 Millwork; counters or counter display cases: except wood; cabinets, except refrigerated: show, display, etc.: wood; display fixtures, wood; table or counter tops, plastic laminated; metal doors, sash & trim; wood office furniture

(G-6472)
GRANITEONECOM INC
639 Hoyt St Se (49507-3213)
P.O. Box 5050, Pine Ridge SD (57770-5050)
PHONE..............................616 452-8372
EMP: 4 **EST:** 2003
SALES: 100K **Privately Held**
SIC: 1423 Crushed/Broken Granite

(G-6473)
GRAPHIC ARTS SERVICE & SUP INC (PA)
Also Called: Speciality Grinding Co.
3933 S Greenbrooke Dr Se (49512-5382)
PHONE..............................616 698-9300
Brian Tubergen, *President*
▲ **EMP:** 10
SQ FT: 5,000
SALES (est): 4.5MM **Privately Held**
WEB: www.gasupply.com
SIC: 5084 3554 7699 Printing trades machinery, equipment & supplies; cutting machines, paper; knife, saw & tool sharpening & repair

(G-6474)
GRAPHIC IMPRESSIONS INC
Also Called: Matrix Printing & Mailing
6621 Division Ave S (49548-7805)
PHONE..............................616 455-0303
Matthew Van Dore, *President*
EMP: 5
SQ FT: 2,200
SALES: 400K **Privately Held**
SIC: 2759 2789 2752 Commercial printing; bookbinding & related work; commercial printing, lithographic

(G-6475)
GRAPHIC SPECIALTIES INC (PA)
Also Called: G S I
2350 Brton Indus Pk Dr Se (49508-1548)
PHONE..............................616 247-0060
Dale Hutchins, *President*
Mathew Hutchins, *Vice Pres*
Tj Moran, *Sales Dir*
EMP: 40
SQ FT: 6,000
SALES (est): 27.4MM **Privately Held**
WEB: www.gs-sg.com
SIC: 3497 2675 2759 2796 Metal foil & leaf; die-cut paper & board; embossing on paper; platemaking services; bookbinding & related work

(G-6476)
GRAPHICS EMBOSSED IMAGES INC
1975 Waldorf St Nw Ste A (49544-1404)
PHONE..............................616 791-0404
Ron Feenstra, *President*
Meredyth Hasenjaeger, *Vice Pres*
Michele Matthews, *Vice Pres*
EMP: 9

SALES: 800K **Privately Held**
WEB: www.graphicsembossedimages.com
SIC: 2759 Embossing on paper

(G-6477)
GREAT LAKES BINDERY INC
3741 Linden Ave Se (49548-3427)
PHONE..............................616 245-5264
Stephen W Landheer, *President*
Dan Dafoe, *Vice Pres*
Brian Willemstyn, *Plant Mgr*
Sharon Kershner, *Controller*
EMP: 18
SQ FT: 5,000
SALES: 2MM **Privately Held**
WEB: www.greatlakesbindery.com
SIC: 2789 Binding only: books, pamphlets, magazines, etc.

(G-6478)
GREAT LAKES GRILLING CO
2685 Northridge Dr Nw C (49544-9111)
PHONE..............................616 791-8600
Randy Barnard, *President*
EMP: 10
SALES (est): 1.1MM **Privately Held**
WEB: www.greatlakesgrilling.com
SIC: 3496 Grilles & grillework, woven wire

(G-6479)
GREAT LAKES HYDRA CORPORATION
Also Called: Glm Products
4170 36th St Se (49512-2903)
PHONE..............................616 949-8844
Arthur Apkarian, *President*
Larry Laham, *Vice Pres*
David Plants, *Vice Pres*
EMP: 11
SQ FT: 18,000
SALES (est): 3.8MM **Privately Held**
WEB: www.glhydraulics.com
SIC: 3566 7699 5084 3594 Speed changers, drives & gears; hydraulic equipment repair; hydraulic systems equipment & supplies; fluid power pumps & motors; valves & pipe fittings

(G-6480)
GREAT LAKES-TRIAD PLASTIC (PA)
Also Called: Glt Packaging
3939 36th St Se (49512-2917)
PHONE..............................616 241-6441
Brian Burns, *President*
Kevin Burns, *Corp Secy*
Steven White, *CFO*
EMP: 85 **EST:** 1974
SQ FT: 83,000
SALES (est): 20.5MM
SALES (corp-wide): 11.4MM **Privately Held**
WEB: www.gltpkg.com
SIC: 2653 Boxes, corrugated: made from purchased materials

(G-6481)
GREAT LKES FSTIDA HOLDINGS INC
Also Called: Festida Foods
219 Canton St Sw Ste A (49507-1098)
PHONE..............................616 241-0400
Joseph Riley, *CEO*
Don Reynolds, *CFO*
▲ **EMP:** 15
SQ FT: 150,000
SALES: 35MM **Privately Held**
WEB: www.festidafoods.com
SIC: 2096 Potato chips & similar snacks

(G-6482)
GREYSTONE IMAGING LLC
5510 33rd St Se Ste 1 (49512-2060)
PHONE..............................616 742-3810
Frederick Nagle Jr, *Bd of Directors*
EMP: 4
SALES (est): 289.4K **Privately Held**
SIC: 2759 Commercial printing

(G-6483)
GRW TECHNOLOGIES INC
4460 44th St Se Ste B (49512-4096)
PHONE..............................616 575-8119
Walter Soehner, *President*
Joechim Hollimius, *Vice Pres*

Grand Rapids - Kent County (G-6484)
GEOGRAPHIC SECTION

Jana Borrink, *Production*
Rosemarie Soehner, *Admin Sec*
▲ **EMP:** 160 **EST:** 2008
SQ FT: 24,000
SALES (est): 29MM
SALES (corp-wide): 177.9K **Privately Held**
WEB: www.grwtechnologies.com
SIC: 3544 3089 Special dies, tools, jigs & fixtures; injection molding of plastics
PA: Sohnergroup Gmbh
　Daimlerstr. 13
　Schwaigern
　713 822-0

(G-6484)
GUERREROS PALLETS
1601 Madison Ave Se (49507-2566)
PHONE 616 808-4721
Jennifer Hinojosa, *Principal*
EMP: 4 **EST:** 2012
SALES (est): 231.8K **Privately Held**
SIC: 2448 Pallets, wood & wood with metal

(G-6485)
GUILFORD OF MAINE MARKETING CO
5300 Corporate Grove Dr S (49512-5512)
PHONE 616 554-2250
Brian Demoura, *President*
Renee Mascolo, *Accounts Exec*
EMP: 75 **EST:** 1996
SALES (est): 5MM
SALES (corp-wide): 300K **Privately Held**
WEB: www.guilfordofmaine.com
SIC: 2299 Upholstery filling, textile
HQ: Duvaltex (Us), Inc.
　9 Oak St
　Guilford ME 04443
　207 873-3331

(G-6486)
GUNDRY MEDIA INC
Also Called: Throbak Electronics
800 Monroe Ave Nw Ste 220 (49503-1450)
PHONE 616 734-8977
Jonathan Gundry, *President*
EMP: 3
SALES (est): 105.6K **Privately Held**
SIC: 5736 3931 Musical instrument stores; guitars & parts, electric & nonelectric

(G-6487)
H & R INDUSTRIES INC (PA)
3020 Stafford Ave Sw (49548-1098)
PHONE 616 247-1165
Janet L Herr, *President*
Christine Page, *Vice Pres*
David A Herr, *Admin Sec*
EMP: 14
SQ FT: 6,000
SALES (est): 4.7MM **Privately Held**
WEB: www.hr-industries.com
SIC: 5084 3699 3561 Cleaning equipment, high pressure, sand or steam; pumps & pumping equipment; cleaning equipment, ultrasonic, except medical & dental; pumps & pumping equipment

(G-6488)
H S DIE & ENGINEERING INC (PA)
O-215 Lake Michigan Dr Nw (49534-3397)
PHONE 616 453-5451
Marcia Steele, *CEO*
Dale Hermiller, *General Mgr*
Jeff Hearn, *COO*
Jeff Travis, *Purchasing*
Dave Brothers, *Engineer*
▼ **EMP:** 179
SQ FT: 90,000
SALES (est): 69.1MM **Privately Held**
WEB: www.hsdie.com
SIC: 3544 Special dies & tools

(G-6489)
HANDICAP SIGN INC
1142 Wealthy St Se (49506-1543)
PHONE 616 454-9416
Charles J Tasma, *President*
Kim Tasma, *Treasurer*
EMP: 8 **EST:** 1956
SQ FT: 5,500

SALES (est): 791.5K **Privately Held**
WEB: www.handicapsigns.com
SIC: 7389 3993 Sign painting & lettering shop; signs & advertising specialties

(G-6490)
HANDORN INC
Also Called: Custom Counters By Handorn
636 Crofton St Se (49507-1819)
PHONE 616 241-6181
Seth Erlandson, *President*
EMP: 20
SQ FT: 20,000
SALES (est): 3.3MM **Privately Held**
SIC: 2434 Wood kitchen cabinets

(G-6491)
HANGER INC
5005 Cascade Rd Se Ste C (49546-8411)
PHONE 616 949-0075
EMP: 14
SALES (corp-wide): 1B **Publicly Held**
SIC: 3842 Surgical appliances & supplies
PA: Hanger, Inc.
　10910 Domain Dr Ste 300
　Austin TX 78758
　512 777-3800

(G-6492)
HANGER INC
230 Michigan St Ne Ste 200 (49503-2502)
PHONE 616 458-8080
EMP: 27
SALES (corp-wide): 1B **Publicly Held**
SIC: 3842 Surgical appliances & supplies
PA: Hanger, Inc.
　10910 Domain Dr Ste 300
　Austin TX 78758
　512 777-3800

(G-6493)
HANGER INC
5005 Cascade Rd Se Ste C (49546-8411)
PHONE 616 940-0878
Thomas Kirk PHD, *CEO*
EMP: 99
SALES (corp-wide): 1B **Publicly Held**
SIC: 3842 Prosthetic appliances
PA: Hanger, Inc.
　10910 Domain Dr Ste 300
　Austin TX 78758
　512 777-3800

(G-6494)
HANSEN MACHINE & TOOL CORP
457 Clover Ct Nw (49504-5204)
PHONE 616 361-2842
Bill Hansen, *President*
EMP: 3
SALES (est): 437.2K **Privately Held**
SIC: 3423 Hand & edge tools

(G-6495)
HART & COOLEY INC (DH)
5030 Corp Exch Blvd Se (49512)
P.O. Box 2930, Milwaukee WI (53201-2930)
PHONE 616 656-8200
Michael Winn, *President*
Mary De Vree, *Credit Mgr*
▲ **EMP:** 130
SALES (est): 667.2MM **Privately Held**
SIC: 3446 3822 Registers (air), metal; auto controls regulating residntl & coml environmt & applncs
HQ: Air Distribution Technologies, Inc.
　605 Shiloh Rd
　Plano TX 75074
　972 943-6100

(G-6496)
HARVEST ENERGY INC
2820 Division Ave S (49548-1127)
PHONE 269 838-4595
Thomas O'Hara, *President*
EMP: 18 **EST:** 2008
SALES (est): 4.5MM **Privately Held**
SIC: 3823 Industrial process measurement equipment

(G-6497)
HAVILAND ENTERPRISES INC (PA)
421 Ann St Nw (49504-2019)
PHONE 616 361-6691
H Richard Garner, *Principal*
Arthur F Harre, *Vice Pres*
Michael J Marmo, *Vice Pres*
Rich Held, *Research*
Rob Pawson, *Regl Sales Mgr*
▲ **EMP:** 145
SQ FT: 850,000
SALES (est): 173.2MM **Privately Held**
SIC: 2899 Chemical preparations

(G-6498)
HAVILAND PRODUCTS COMPANY (HQ)
421 Ann St Nw (49504-2075)
PHONE 616 361-6691
E Bernard Haviland, *President*
Brian Schoen, *Opers Mgr*
John Klocko, *Production*
Jerry Schoen, *CFO*
Thomas Simmons, *CFO*
◆ **EMP:** 150
SQ FT: 150,000
SALES (est): 120MM
SALES (corp-wide): 173.2MM **Privately Held**
WEB: www.haviland.org
SIC: 2819 Industrial inorganic chemicals
PA: Haviland Enterprises, Inc.
　421 Ann St Nw
　Grand Rapids MI 49504
　616 361-6691

(G-6499)
HAVILAND PRODUCTS COMPANY
521 Ann St Nw (49504)
PHONE 800 456-1134
E Bernard Haviland, *President*
EMP: 8
SALES (corp-wide): 173.2MM **Privately Held**
SIC: 2819 Industrial inorganic chemicals
HQ: Haviland Products Company
　421 Ann St Nw
　Grand Rapids MI 49504
　616 361-6691

(G-6500)
HB FULLER COMPANY
Hbf Grand Rapids
2727 Kinney Ave Nw (49534-1198)
PHONE 616 453-8271
Monte Hadlock, *Opers-Prdtn-Mfg*
EMP: 31
SALES (corp-wide): 3B **Publicly Held**
WEB: www.hbfuller.com
SIC: 2891 2851 Adhesives; sealants; lacquers, varnishes, enamels & other coatings
PA: H.B. Fuller Company
　1200 Willow Lake Blvd
　Saint Paul MN 55110
　651 236-5900

(G-6501)
HEB DEVELOPMENT LLC (PA)
1946 Turner Ave Nw (49504-2034)
PHONE 616 363-3825
Bill Mast, *Managing Prtnr*
Heath Baxter, *Managing Prtnr*
Bruce G Visser, *Managing Prtnr*
Eric Todd Visser, *Managing Prtnr*
EMP: 4
SALES (est): 3.1MM **Privately Held**
SIC: 3251 Structural brick & blocks

(G-6502)
HEKMAN FURNITURE COMPANY
Also Called: Alexis Manufacturing Div
3188 Wilson Dr Nw (49534-7564)
PHONE 616 735-3905
Dan Ahlem, *Branch Mgr*
EMP: 58
SALES (corp-wide): 99.1MM **Privately Held**
WEB: www.hekman.com
SIC: 2521 Wood office furniture

HQ: Hekman Furniture Company
　860 E Main Ave
　Zeeland MI 49464
　616 748-2660

(G-6503)
HEL INC
Also Called: Hastings Equipment
450 Market Ave Sw (49503-4943)
PHONE 616 774-9032
Richard Van Dam, *President*
Randall Van Dam, *Treasurer*
John Van Dam, *Admin Sec*
EMP: 15
SQ FT: 43,000
SALES (est): 2.6MM **Privately Held**
SIC: 7699 7692 7629 Industrial machinery & equipment repair; welding repair; electrical repair shops

(G-6504)
HELLO LIFE INC (PA)
Also Called: Vetionx
4635 40th St Se (49512-4038)
PHONE 616 808-3290
Albert Duoibes, *CEO*
Curtis Hagberg, *Principal*
Fekadu Tonna, *Principal*
Nancy Falkowski, *Opers Mgr*
▲ **EMP:** 15 **EST:** 2010
SQ FT: 2,800
SALES (est): 4.1MM **Privately Held**
SIC: 5499 2834 Dietetic foods; pharmaceutical preparations; cough medicines

(G-6505)
HELLO LIFE INC
Vetionx
4460 44th St Se Ste C600 (49512-4150)
PHONE 616 808-3290
Albert Duoibes, *CEO*
EMP: 18
SALES (corp-wide): 4.1MM **Privately Held**
SIC: 2834 5499 8731 Pharmaceutical preparations; health & dietetic food stores; medical research, commercial
PA: Hello Life, Inc.
　4635 40th St Se
　Grand Rapids MI 49512
　616 808-3290

(G-6506)
HERALD NEWSPAPERS COMPANY INC
Grand Rapids Paper, The
3102 Walker Ridge Dr Nw (49544-9125)
P.O. Box 2168 (49501-2168)
PHONE 616 222-5400
Nancy Clay, *Manager*
Rick Sullivan, *Exec Dir*
Steve Wells, *Maintence Staff*
EMP: 100
SALES (corp-wide): 5.5B **Privately Held**
WEB: www.post-standard.com
SIC: 2711 Newspapers, publishing & printing
HQ: The Herald Newspapers Company Inc
　220 S Warren St
　Syracuse NY 13202
　315 470-0011

(G-6507)
HERALD NEWSPAPERS COMPANY INC
Also Called: Ann Arbor News
3102 Walker Ridge Dr Nw (49544-9125)
PHONE 734 834-6376
Laurel Champion, *Exec Dir*
EMP: 100
SALES (corp-wide): 5.5B **Privately Held**
WEB: www.post-standard.com
SIC: 2711 Newspapers
HQ: The Herald Newspapers Company Inc
　220 S Warren St
　Syracuse NY 13202
　315 470-0011

(G-6508)
HERALD PUBLISHING COMPANY LLC
Also Called: Mlive Media Group
169 Monroe Ave Nw (49503-6213)
PHONE 616 222-5400
Dan Gaydou, *President*

GEOGRAPHIC SECTION

Grand Rapids - Kent County (G-6535)

Sara Scott, *Editor*
Matthew Brzezinski, *Accounts Mgr*
John Markham, *Accounts Mgr*
Holly Schonert, *Accounts Mgr*
EMP: 8
SALES (corp-wide): 5.5B **Privately Held**
SIC: 2711 Newspapers, publishing & printing
HQ: The Herald Publishing Company Llc
3102 Walker Ridge Dr Nw
Walker MI 49544
616 222-5400

(G-6509)
HERMAN MILLER INC
2915 Stonewood St Nw (49504-8003)
PHONE..................616 453-5995
Ross Vanderklok, *Branch Mgr*
EMP: 3
SALES (corp-wide): 2.5B **Publicly Held**
SIC: 3429 Furniture hardware
PA: Herman Miller, Inc.
855 E Main Ave
Zeeland MI 49464
616 654-3000

(G-6510)
HIGH GRADE MATERIALS COMPANY
10561 Linden Dr Nw (49534-9647)
PHONE..................616 677-1271
Curt Hanson, *Manager*
EMP: 10
SALES (corp-wide): 28.3MM **Privately Held**
SIC: 3273 Ready-mixed concrete
PA: High Grade Materials Company
9266 Snows Lake Rd
Greenville MI 48838
616 754-5545

(G-6511)
HILCO FIXTURE FINDERS LLC
Also Called: Supermarket Liquidation
1345 Monroe Ave Nw # 321 (49505-4671)
PHONE..................616 453-1300
Scott Hoek, *CEO*
▼ **EMP:** 40
SALES (est): 9.3MM **Privately Held**
SIC: 2541 Store fixtures, wood
HQ: Hilco Merchant Resources, Llc
5 Revere Dr Ste 206
Northbrook IL 60062

(G-6512)
HILCO INDUSTRIAL PLASTICS LLC
4999 36th St Se (49512-2005)
PHONE..................616 323-1330
EMP: 3
SALES (corp-wide): 23.7MM **Privately Held**
SIC: 3089 Molding primary plastic
PA: Hilco Industrial Plastics, Llc
4172 Danvers Ct Se
Grand Rapids MI 49512
616 957-1081

(G-6513)
HILL BROTHERS
Also Called: Hill Bros Orchards
6159 Peach Ridge Ave Nw (49544-9110)
PHONE..................616 784-2767
Walter Hill, *Partner*
David Hill, *Partner*
Arlene Hill, *Principal*
EMP: 5
SALES (est): 339.2K **Privately Held**
SIC: 0175 2099 2086 Apple orchard; cider, nonalcoholic; bottled & canned soft drinks

(G-6514)
HILL MACHINERY CO
4585 Danvers Dr Se (49512-4040)
PHONE..................616 940-2800
Donald V Bos Jr, *President*
Shane O'Neill, *Vice Pres*
Vickie Totten, *Purch Agent*
Jerry Falicki, *Engineer*
Jeff Senn, *Controller*
EMP: 60 **EST:** 1897
SQ FT: 45,000
SALES: 21.9MM **Privately Held**
WEB: www.hillmachinery.com
SIC: 3544 3494 Special dies & tools; jigs & fixtures; valves & pipe fittings

(G-6515)
HOMAG MACHINERY NORTH AMER INC
4577 Patterson Ave Se (49512-5308)
PHONE..................616 254-8181
Frank Wegener, *President*
Jens Fahlbusch, *Corp Comm Staff*
▲ **EMP:** 19
SQ FT: 32,000
SALES (est): 4.4MM
SALES (corp-wide): 4.4B **Privately Held**
SIC: 3553 Woodworking machinery
PA: Durr Ag
Carl-Benz-Str. 34
Bietigheim-Bissingen 74321
714 278-0

(G-6516)
HORMEL FOODS CORPORATION
801 Broadway Ave Nw (49504-4462)
PHONE..................616 454-0418
EMP: 118
SALES (corp-wide): 9.5B **Publicly Held**
SIC: 2011 Meat packing plants
PA: Hormel Foods Corporation
1 Hormel Pl
Austin MN 55912
507 437-5611

(G-6517)
HOWE US INC
401 Hall St Sw Ste 230 (49503-4988)
PHONE..................616 419-2226
Michael Jacobsen, *President*
EMP: 52
SALES (est): 445.8K
SALES (corp-wide): 14.2MM **Privately Held**
SIC: 2521 Wood office furniture
PA: Howe A/S
Filosofgangen 18
Odense 5000
634 164-00

(G-6518)
HUDSONVILLE PRODUCTS LLC
1735 Elizabeth Ave Nw (49504-2003)
P.O. Box 140501 (49514-0501)
PHONE..................616 836-1904
Ben Douzman, *Mng Member*
EMP: 6 **EST:** 2017
SALES (est): 436.1K **Privately Held**
SIC: 2541 5046 Store & office display cases & fixtures; store fixtures & display equipment

(G-6519)
HUTCHINSON ANTIVIBRATION (DH)
Also Called: Hutchinson Automotive
460 Fuller Ave Ne (49503-1912)
PHONE..................616 459-4541
Madan Achuri, *CEO*
Monica Draper, *Buyer*
Tammi Doolittle, *Accountant*
▲ **EMP:** 350 **EST:** 1986
SALES: 250MM
SALES (corp-wide): 8.4B **Publicly Held**
SIC: 3069 3061 Molded rubber products; mechanical rubber goods
HQ: Hutchinson Corporation
460 Fuller Ave Ne
Grand Rapids MI 49503
616 459-4541

(G-6520)
HUTCHINSON CORPORATION (DH)
460 Fuller Ave Ne (49503-1912)
P.O. Box 1886 (49501-1886)
PHONE..................616 459-4541
Yves Rene Manot, *Ch of Bd*
Gerard Gehin, *President*
Tim Burbank, *Purchasing*
Franck Larmande, *VP Engrg*
Toan Nguyen, *Draft/Design*
◆ **EMP:** 5
SQ FT: 305,868
SALES (est): 1B
SALES (corp-wide): 8.4B **Publicly Held**
SIC: 3069 3011 Molded rubber products; mittens, rubber; tires, cushion or solid rubber
HQ: Hutchinson
2 Rue Balzac
Paris 8e Arrondissement 75008
140 748-300

(G-6521)
HZ INDUSTRIES INC
706 Bond Ave Nw (49503-1434)
PHONE..................616 453-4491
EMP: 350
SQ FT: 120,000
SALES: 50MM **Privately Held**
SIC: 3469 3495 Machine parts, stamped or pressed metal; wire springs

(G-6522)
I C S CORPORATION AMERICA INC
Also Called: Ics Filtration Products
4675 Talon Ct Se (49512-5408)
PHONE..................616 554-9300
Sherwin D Doorn, *President*
Norman Hoekman, *Treasurer*
EMP: 11
SQ FT: 14,500
SALES (est): 1.9MM **Privately Held**
SIC: 2819 Nonmetallic compounds

(G-6523)
I D MEDICAL SYSTEMS INC
3954 44th St Se (49512-3942)
PHONE..................616 698-0535
Robert O'Connor, *President*
EMP: 4
SQ FT: 3,500
SALES (est): 480.1K **Privately Held**
SIC: 3844 0742 X-ray apparatus & tubes; veterinary services, specialties

(G-6524)
ICON INDUSTRIES INC
1522 Madison Ave Se (49507-1715)
PHONE..................616 241-1877
Thomas D Jacques, *President*
Robert J Zieger, *Vice Pres*
EMP: 6
SQ FT: 80,000
SALES (est): 3.4MM **Privately Held**
WEB: www.miconind.com
SIC: 5084 7389 3089 Industrial machinery & equipment; design, commercial & industrial; plastic processing

(G-6525)
IDEAL PRINTING COMPANY (PA)
2801 Oak Industrial Dr Ne (49505-6046)
PHONE..................616 454-9224
Howard Goris, *Ch of Bd*
Dan Goris, *President*
Marian Goris, *Treasurer*
Debbie Goris, *Admin Sec*
EMP: 20
SQ FT: 8,000
SALES (est): 2.6MM **Privately Held**
WEB: www.idealprinting.net
SIC: 2752 Lithographing on metal; commercial printing, offset

(G-6526)
IGA ABRASIVES LLC
3011 Hillcroft Ave Sw (49548-1099)
PHONE..................616 243-5566
SL Munson,
▼ **EMP:** 35
SQ FT: 35,000
SALES (est): 3.9MM **Privately Held**
SIC: 3291 Abrasive products

(G-6527)
IHS INC
2851 Charlevoix Ave Ne # 314 (49546-7092)
PHONE..................616 464-4224
EMP: 4 **Privately Held**
SIC: 3537 Mfg Industrial Trucks/Tractors
HQ: Ihs Inc.
15 Inverness Way E
Englewood CO 80112
303 790-0600

(G-6528)
IMPERIAL CLINICAL RES SVCS INC
Also Called: Imperial Graphics
3100 Walkent Dr Nw (49544-1402)
PHONE..................616 784-0100
Matthew Bissell, *President*
Steven Balk, *Vice Pres*
▼ **EMP:** 150 **EST:** 1965
SQ FT: 100,000
SALES (est): 29.3MM **Privately Held**
WEB: www.imperialcrs.com
SIC: 2761 5112 2759 2732 Manifold business forms; stationery & office supplies; commercial printing; book printing; medical research

(G-6529)
IMPERIAL LASER INC
11473 1st Ave Nw (49534-3364)
PHONE..................616 735-9315
Mark Meade, *President*
EMP: 5
SQ FT: 5,000
SALES (est): 499.2K **Privately Held**
SIC: 3699 Laser systems & equipment

(G-6530)
IMPERIAL METAL PRODUCTS CO
835 Hall St Sw (49503-4820)
PHONE..................616 452-1700
Jeff Dean, *President*
Ken Preston, *Vice Pres*
Tim Looman, *Manager*
EMP: 45 **EST:** 1993
SQ FT: 49,000
SALES (est): 10.2MM **Privately Held**
WEB: www.imperialmetalproducts.com
SIC: 3599 Machine shop, jobbing & repair

(G-6531)
INDELCO PLASTICS CORPORATION
3322 Lousma Dr Se (49548-2200)
PHONE..................616 452-7077
EMP: 3
SALES (est): 90K **Privately Held**
SIC: 2821 Molding compounds, plastics

(G-6532)
INDEPENDENT DIE CUTTING INC
1265 Godfrey Ave Sw (49503-5009)
PHONE..................616 452-3197
EMP: 10
SQ FT: 25,000
SALES (est): 1.9MM **Privately Held**
SIC: 2672 Die Cut Pressure Sensitive Tapes Mylar Foam Ect

(G-6533)
INDUSTRIAL SERVICE TECH INC
Also Called: International Sports Timing
3286 Kentland Ct Se (49548-2310)
PHONE..................616 288-3352
Richard Farnsworth, *President*
Jennifer Farnsworth, *Corp Secy*
EMP: 11
SQ FT: 4,800
SALES: 1.8MM **Privately Held**
WEB: www.istime.com
SIC: 7629 3569 8711 5734 Electronic equipment repair; robots, assembly line: industrial & commercial; engineering services; computer software & accessories

(G-6534)
INFOR (US) INC
Also Called: Ssa Global
3040 Charlevoix Dr Se # 200 (49546-7065)
PHONE..................616 258-3311
John Harding, *Administration*
EMP: 225
SALES (corp-wide): 3.1B **Privately Held**
SIC: 7372 Application computer software
HQ: Infor (Us), Inc.
13560 Morris Rd Ste 4100
Alpharetta GA 30004
678 319-8000

(G-6535)
INFOTECH IMAGING INC
1843 Oak Industrial Dr Ne (49505-6007)
PHONE..................616 458-8686

Grand Rapids - Kent County (G-6536)

George Hood, *President*
EMP: 12
SQ FT: 32,000
SALES (est): 2.2MM **Privately Held**
WEB: www.infotechimaging.com
SIC: 7372 Business oriented computer software

(G-6536)
INNER BOX LOADING SYSTEMS INC
Also Called: Load All
3058 Eastern Ave Se (49508-1321)
PHONE..................................616 241-4330
Paul Verwys, *President*
Russell Liscomb, *Vice Pres*
Scott Teunissen, *Vice Pres*
Jeff Bender, *CFO*
EMP: 3
SQ FT: 4,500
SALES (est): 219.6K **Privately Held**
WEB: www.loadall.com
SIC: 3448 Ramps: prefabricated metal

(G-6537)
INNOVATIVE CLEANING EQP INC
Also Called: Foam-It
3833 Soundtech Ct Se (49512-4116)
PHONE..................................616 656-9225
Dan Jacques, *President*
Ann Jacques, *Corp Secy*
◆ **EMP:** 25
SQ FT: 20,000
SALES (est): 4.8MM **Privately Held**
WEB: www.foamit.com
SIC: 3559 Chemical machinery & equipment

(G-6538)
INNOVATIVE IRON INC
3370 Jefferson Ave Se (49548-2242)
PHONE..................................616 248-4250
John Versluys, *President*
Thomas Hoffman, *Vice Pres*
EMP: 6
SQ FT: 9,000
SALES (est): 1.2MM **Privately Held**
SIC: 3441 Fabricated structural metal

(G-6539)
INTAGLIO LLC
Also Called: Dialogue
3106 3 Mile Rd Nw (49534-1326)
PHONE..................................616 243-3300
Rich Tomlinson, *Design Engr*
Bill Streb, *Accounts Exec*
Bill Dawson, *Sales Engr*
Kirk Grimshaw, *Mng Member*
Chris Van Zoest, *Manager*
EMP: 12
SALES (est): 2.4MM **Privately Held**
SIC: 3651 7622 4899 Household audio equipment; radio repair & installation; data communication services

(G-6540)
INTERNAL GRINDING ABRASIVES
3011 Hillcroft Ave Sw (49548-1099)
PHONE..................................616 243-5566
Susan Smith, *President*
Donald Kranenberg Sr, *President*
John Hoekstra, *Treasurer*
EMP: 35 **EST:** 1958
SQ FT: 25,000
SALES: 1.2MM **Privately Held**
SIC: 3291 3541 Grinding balls, ceramic; hones; coated abrasive products; machine tools, metal cutting type

(G-6541)
INTERNATIONAL MET SYSTEMS INC
Also Called: Intermet Systems
4767 Broadmoor Ave Se # 7 (49512-9397)
PHONE..................................616 971-1005
Frederick Clowney, *President*
Joseph Parini, *Chairman*
Joe Barnes, *Vice Pres*
Justin Meulenberg, *Marketing Staff*
▲ **EMP:** 15
SQ FT: 5,000

SALES: 3MM **Privately Held**
WEB: www.intermetsystems.com
SIC: 3829 Meteorologic tracking systems; meteorological instruments

(G-6542)
INTERNATIONAL WOOD INDS INC
2801 E Beltline Ave Ne (49525-9680)
PHONE..................................800 598-9663
Patrick M Webster, *Principal*
EMP: 3 **EST:** 2008
SALES (est): 143.1K **Privately Held**
SIC: 3999 Manufacturing industries

(G-6543)
INTRALOX LLC
1430 Monroe Ave Nw # 180 (49505-4678)
PHONE..................................616 259-7471
Jeff Batchelder, *President*
EMP: 8
SALES (corp-wide): 396.9MM **Privately Held**
SIC: 3535 Conveyors & conveying equipment
HQ: Intralox, L.L.C.
301 Plantation Rd
Harahan LA 70123
504 733-6739

(G-6544)
IONXHEALTH INC
Also Called: Vetionx
4635 40th St Se (49512-4038)
PHONE..................................616 808-3290
EMP: 40 **EST:** 2007
SALES: 1MM **Privately Held**
SIC: 0752 2834 5499 Animal Services Mfg Pharmaceutical Preparations Ret Misc Foods

(G-6545)
IRWIN SEATING HOLDING COMPANY (PA)
3251 Fruit Ridge Ave Nw (49544-9748)
P.O. Box 2429 (49501-2429)
PHONE..................................616 574-7400
Earle S Irwin, *President*
Dale I Tanis, *Senior VP*
Ryan Kent, *Project Mgr*
Ronnie Groves, *Purch Mgr*
Jon Cotton, *Engineer*
◆ **EMP:** 400
SQ FT: 400,000
SALES (est): 81.9MM **Privately Held**
SIC: 7641 2531 Furniture repair & maintenance; furniture refinishing; antique furniture repair & restoration; school furniture

(G-6546)
J HANSEN-BALK STL TREATING CO
1230 Monroe Ave Nw (49505-4620)
PHONE..................................616 458-1414
James Balk II, *President*
Steve Balk, *Bookkeeper*
Eleazar Lopez, *Info Tech Mgr*
Shirley Balk, *Admin Sec*
EMP: 35
SQ FT: 60,000
SALES (est): 8.2MM **Privately Held**
WEB: www.hansenbalk.com
SIC: 3398 Metal heat treating

(G-6547)
J KALTZ & CO
3987 Brockton Dr Se Ste C (49512-4070)
PHONE..................................616 942-6070
Sue Bothwell, *Manager*
EMP: 7
SALES (corp-wide): 4.7MM **Privately Held**
SIC: 5251 3083 Hardware; laminated plastics plate & sheet
PA: J. Kaltz & Co.
730 E 9 Mile Rd
Ferndale MI 48220
248 541-8800

(G-6548)
J MARK SYSTEMS INC
3696 Northridge Dr Nw # 10 (49544-9002)
PHONE..................................616 784-6005
Mark Zeilbeck, *President*
Todd McNulty, *General Mgr*

EMP: 7
SQ FT: 6,400
SALES (est): 1.2MM **Privately Held**
WEB: www.jmarksystems.com
SIC: 3589 Water treatment equipment, industrial

(G-6549)
J W HOLDINGS INC
Also Called: U S Engineering
2530 Thornwood St Sw B (49519-2178)
PHONE..................................616 530-9889
Dennis Madden, *President*
EMP: 40
SQ FT: 33,000
SALES (est): 12.7MM **Privately Held**
WEB: www.usengineeringcorp.com
SIC: 3548 3549 3541 Resistance welders, electric; assembly machines, including robotic; machine tools, metal cutting type

(G-6550)
JACKSON MANUFACTURING & DISTRG
470 Market Ave Sw Unit 34 (49503-4994)
P.O. Box 3774 (49501-3774)
PHONE..................................616 451-3030
EMP: 3
SQ FT: 2,500
SALES (est): 97K **Privately Held**
SIC: 2392 5023 Mfg Household Furnishings Whol Homefurnishings

(G-6551)
JAMES E SULLIVAN & ASSOCIATES
Also Called: Carpet Crafters
4617 Sundial Dr Ne (49525-9492)
PHONE..................................616 453-0345
James E Sullivan, *Owner*
EMP: 4
SALES: 2.4MM **Privately Held**
SIC: 5023 2273 Carpets; carpets, textile fiber

(G-6552)
JANELLE PETERSON
Also Called: Pages In Time
5274 Plainfield Ave Ne (49525-1047)
PHONE..................................616 447-9070
Fax: 616 457-8425
EMP: 7 **EST:** 1997
SQ FT: 2,300
SALES (est): 310K **Privately Held**
SIC: 2782 Mfg Blankbooks/Binders

(G-6553)
JAPHIL INC
Also Called: Postema Sign Co
7475 Division Ave S (49548-7137)
PHONE..................................616 455-0260
Sandy Postema, *President*
Mark Postema, *Office Mgr*
Brenda Frazee,
EMP: 9
SQ FT: 4,900
SALES: 1.5MM **Privately Held**
WEB: www.postemasign.com
SIC: 3993 Electric signs

(G-6554)
JASPER WELLER LLC (HQ)
Also Called: Weller Truck Parts
1500 Gezon Pkwy Sw (49509-9585)
PHONE..................................616 724-2000
Terry Stranz, *President*
Stephen Donahue, *Regional Mgr*
Bill Lewis, *Regional Mgr*
Amy Hurley, *Business Mgr*
Paul Weller, *COO*
▲ **EMP:** 200
SALES: 244MM
SALES (corp-wide): 521.6MM **Privately Held**
SIC: 3714 Transmissions, motor vehicle
PA: Jasper Engine Exchange, Inc.
815 Wernsing Rd
Jasper IN 47546
812 482-1041

(G-6555)
JBL ENTERPRISES
Also Called: Abl Enterprises
3535 Wentworth Dr Sw (49519-3161)
PHONE..................................616 530-8647

Jeffrey R Godfrey, *Owner*
EMP: 5
SALES (est): 327.2K **Privately Held**
WEB: www.jbl-enterprises.com
SIC: 3479 2396 5199 Engraving jewelry silverware, or metal; screen printing on fabric articles; badges

(G-6556)
JEAN SMITH DESIGNS
2704 Boston St Se (49506-4718)
PHONE..................................616 942-9212
Jean Smith, *Owner*
EMP: 20
SALES (est): 871.4K **Privately Held**
WEB: www.jeansmithdesigns.com
SIC: 2395 2396 Embroidery & art needlework; automotive & apparel trimmings

(G-6557)
JEDCO INC (PA)
1615 Broadway Ave Nw (49504-2026)
PHONE..................................616 459-5161
Daniel Szymanski, *Ch of Bd*
Larry Sharp, *Partner*
John Boeschenstein, *Vice Pres*
Traci Grose, *Vice Pres*
Robert Nyquist, *Vice Pres*
EMP: 150
SQ FT: 75,000
SALES (est): 40.1MM **Privately Held**
WEB: www.jedinc.com
SIC: 3728 Aircraft parts & equipment

(G-6558)
JELD-WEN INC
Jeld-Wen Doors
4200 Roger B Chaffee Se (49548-3446)
PHONE..................................616 531-5440
Jeff Koger, *Manager*
EMP: 80 **Publicly Held**
WEB: www.jeld-wen.com
SIC: 2431 Doors, wood
HQ: Jeld-Wen, Inc.
2645 Silver Crescent Dr
Charlotte NC 28273
800 535-3936

(G-6559)
JETCO PACKAGING SOLUTIONS LLC
Also Called: Jetco Federal Supply
525 Ottawa Ave Nw Lev (49503-1403)
PHONE..................................616 588-2492
Susan Tellier, *President*
Jon Tellier, *Vice Pres*
EMP: 4
SALES (est): 958.8K **Privately Held**
SIC: 2671 2653 Packaging paper & plastics film, coated & laminated; boxes, corrugated: made from purchased materials

(G-6560)
JEWELERS WORKSHOP
1624 Leonard St Nw (49504-3950)
P.O. Box 141271 (49514-1271)
PHONE..................................616 791-6500
Ronald A Patton, *President*
Linda J Eatten, *Vice Pres*
EMP: 3
SALES (est): 520.2K **Privately Held**
SIC: 5944 3911 7631 Jewelry, precious stones & precious metals; jewelry, precious metal; jewelry repair services

(G-6561)
JOAN ARNOUDSE
2499 Omega Dr Ne (49525-6710)
PHONE..................................616 364-9075
Joan Arnoudse, *Owner*
EMP: 5 **EST:** 2001
SALES (est): 325.2K **Privately Held**
SIC: 2211 Laundry fabrics, cotton

(G-6562)
JOHN H DEKKER & SONS INC
Also Called: Dekker Bookbinding
2941 Clydon Ave Sw (49519-2403)
PHONE..................................616 257-4120
John M Dekker Jr, *President*
Chris Dekker, *Vice Pres*
Corbin Dekker, *Vice Pres*
Noel Hentschel, *Plant Mgr*
Mark Huber, *Production*
▼ **EMP:** 60 **EST:** 1928
SQ FT: 95,000

GEOGRAPHIC SECTION

Grand Rapids - Kent County (G-6590)

SALES (est): 8MM **Privately Held**
WEB: www.dekkerbook.com
SIC: 2789 Binding only: books, pamphlets, magazines, etc.

(G-6563)
JOHNSON CONTROLS INC
3312 Lousma Dr Se (49548-2252)
PHONE 866 252-3677
EMP: 6 **Privately Held**
SIC: 2531 Seats, automobile
HQ: Johnson Controls, Inc.
   5757 N Green Bay Ave
   Milwaukee WI 53209
   414 524-1200

(G-6564)
JONATHAN STEVENS MATTRESS CO (PA)
Also Called: Acme Bedding Company
3800 Division Ave S (49548-3275)
PHONE 616 243-4342
Ronald Zagel, *President*
John Huff, *Vice Pres*
EMP: 3 **EST:** 1945
SQ FT: 10,000
SALES (est): 4.9MM **Privately Held**
SIC: 5712 2515 Bedding & bedsprings; mattresses, innerspring or box spring

(G-6565)
K C M INC
1010 Chicago Dr Sw (49509-1108)
PHONE 616 245-8599
Bruno Unzens, *President*
EMP: 12
SQ FT: 6,000
SALES (est): 1.7MM **Privately Held**
WEB: www.kcm.com
SIC: 2841 Soap & other detergents

(G-6566)
K-BUR ENTERPRISES INC
Also Called: Sign-A-Rama
5120 Plainfield Ave Ne (49525-2084)
PHONE 616 447-7446
Brian Burmanai, *President*
Kevin Curtiss, *Vice Pres*
EMP: 4
SQ FT: 960
SALES (est): 381.6K **Privately Held**
SIC: 3993 Signs & advertising specialties

(G-6567)
K12 INC
678 Front Ave Nw (49504-5325)
PHONE 616 309-1600
EMP: 227
SALES (corp-wide): 1B **Publicly Held**
SIC: 3999 Education aids, devices & supplies
PA: K12 Inc.
   2300 Corporate Park Dr
   Herndon VA 20171
   703 483-7000

(G-6568)
KALAMAZOO PACKAGING SYSTEMS
900 47th St Sw Ste I (49509-5142)
P.O. Box 88141 (49518-0141)
PHONE 616 534-2600
Charles Rencurrel, *President*
Penny Rencurrel, *Corp Secy*
EMP: 5
SQ FT: 6,000
SALES (est): 1MM **Privately Held**
WEB: www.kalpack.com
SIC: 3565 Packaging machinery

(G-6569)
KAMPS INC (PA)
Also Called: Kamps Wood Resources
2900 Peach Ridge Ave Nw (49534-1333)
PHONE 616 453-9676
Bernard Kamps, *President*
Ken Haines, *CFO*
George Ophoff, *Sales Staff*
Daniel Williams, *Sales Staff*
John Carpenter, *Manager*
EMP: 60
SQ FT: 19,600
SALES (est): 157.4MM **Privately Held**
WEB: www.kampspallets.com
SIC: 2448 2499 Pallets, wood; mulch, wood & bark

(G-6570)
KAWASAKI PRCISION MCHY USA INC
3838 Broadmoor Ave Se (49512-3927)
PHONE 616 975-3100
Noriaki Kanekiyo, *President*
Jack Konishi, *President*
Takashi Miki, *Engineer*
Joseph Klooster, *Finance*
Ryan Lucarelli, *Sales Mgr*
▲ **EMP:** 32
SALES (est): 7.7MM **Privately Held**
SIC: 3594 Fluid power pumps & motors
PA: Kawasaki Heavy Industries, Ltd.
   1-1-3, Higashikawasakicho, Chuo-Ku
   Kobe HYO 650-0

(G-6571)
KEANE SAUNDERS & ASSOCIATES
6350 Cascade Pointe Dr Se (49546-8711)
PHONE 616 954-7088
John Keane, *Owner*
EMP: 4
SALES (est): 404.9K **Privately Held**
SIC: 3569 General industrial machinery

(G-6572)
KELLOGGS CORPORATION
5300 Patterson Ave Se (49512-5663)
PHONE 616 219-6100
EMP: 10
SALES (est): 3.7MM
SALES (corp-wide): 13.5B **Publicly Held**
SIC: 2041 Flour & other grain mill products
PA: Kellogg Company
   1 Kellogg Sq
   Battle Creek MI 49017
   269 961-2000

(G-6573)
KENNEDY ACQUISITION INC (PA)
Also Called: Emerald Graphics
4949 W Greenbrooke Dr Se (49512-5400)
PHONE 616 871-3020
John Kennedy, *President*
Nicole Taylor, *Opers Staff*
Paul Slagh, *Treasurer*
Stu Cheney, *Admin Sec*
EMP: 3
SALES (est): 13.9MM **Privately Held**
SIC: 2759 Screen printing

(G-6574)
KENONA INDUSTRIES LLC
3044 Wilson Dr Nw (49534-7564)
PHONE 616 735-6228
Bryan Morrissey, *President*
Chris Afendoulis, *CFO*
EMP: 140
SALES (est): 50MM **Privately Held**
SIC: 3714 Motor vehicle parts & accessories

(G-6575)
KENT COMMUNICATIONS INC
Also Called: Kci Printsource
3901 East Paris Ave Se (49512-3906)
PHONE 616 957-2120
Joe Wujkowski, *CEO*
Brian Quist, *President*
Eric Liggett, *General Mgr*
Jean Stuckey, *Accountant*
Miriam Franken, *Accounts Mgr*
EMP: 62
SQ FT: 32,000
SALES (est): 13.4MM **Privately Held**
WEB: www.kcidata.com
SIC: 7331 2752 2789 7336 Mailing list compilers; mailing service; commercial printing, lithographic; bookbinding & related work; commercial art & graphic design

(G-6576)
KENT DOOR & SPECIALTY INC
Also Called: Kent Door Supply
2535 28th St Sw (49519-2105)
PHONE 616 534-9691
David Hees, *President*
David Homrich, *Vice Pres*
EMP: 25
SQ FT: 85,000
SALES (est): 8.6MM **Privately Held**
WEB: www.kentdoor.com
SIC: 5031 2431 Doors; millwork

(G-6577)
KENT MANUFACTURING COMPANY
2200 Oak Industrial Dr Ne (49505-6016)
PHONE 616 454-9495
Kenneth Muraski, *President*
Robert Glowacki, *Partner*
Tom Muraski, *Exec VP*
Michael Muraski, *Vice Pres*
Thomas Muraski, *Vice Pres*
EMP: 60 **EST:** 1940
SQ FT: 45,000
SALES (est): 29.2MM **Privately Held**
WEB: www.kent-mfg.com
SIC: 2672 3053 3069 2891 Tape, pressure sensitive: made from purchased materials; adhesive papers, labels or tapes: from purchased material; gaskets & sealing devices; gasket materials; medical & laboratory rubber sundries & related products; tape, pressure sensitive: rubber; foam rubber; adhesives; plastics foam products; laminated plastics plate & sheet

(G-6578)
KENT WELDING INC
1915 Sterling Ave Nw (49504-2023)
PHONE 616 363-4414
Mathew Delano, *President*
EMP: 4
SQ FT: 5,200
SALES (est): 500K **Privately Held**
SIC: 7692 Welding repair

(G-6579)
KENTWOOD MANUFACTURING CO
103 76th St Sw Ste C (49548-7254)
PHONE 616 698-6370
James Fennema Jr, *CEO*
Dawn Fennema, *Admin Sec*
▲ **EMP:** 25 **EST:** 1954
SALES (est): 4.1MM **Privately Held**
WEB: www.kentwoodmfg.com
SIC: 2426 2511 3231 Hardwood dimension & flooring mills; wood household furniture; products of purchased glass

(G-6580)
KENTWOOD POWDER COAT INC
3900 Swank Dr Se (49512-3961)
PHONE 616 698-8181
Leonard Vining, *President*
EMP: 36
SALES (est): 4.2MM **Privately Held**
WEB: www.kentwoodpowder.com
SIC: 3479 Coating of metals & formed products; painting, coating & hot dipping

(G-6581)
KERKSTRA MECHANICAL LLC
4345 44th St Se Ste C (49512-4089)
PHONE 616 532-6100
Terry Kerkstra,
EMP: 7 **EST:** 2007
SALES (est): 781.1K **Privately Held**
SIC: 3714 Water pump, motor vehicle

(G-6582)
KERRY FOODS
4444 52nd St Se (49512-9674)
P.O. Box 8846, Kentwood (49518-8846)
PHONE 616 871-9940
Rhonda Gonzalez, *Principal*
EMP: 6
SALES (est): 642.9K **Privately Held**
SIC: 2099 Food preparations

(G-6583)
KINDEL FURNITURE COMPANY LLC (PA)
Also Called: Karges Furniture Co
4047 Eastern Ave Se (49508-3401)
PHONE 616 243-3676
Robert Burch, *CEO*
James Fisher, *President*
Dennis Patterson, *Vice Pres*
Amy Wolbert, *Vice Pres*
Carol Oren, *Accountant*
▲ **EMP:** 160
SQ FT: 150,000
SALES (est): 36.3MM **Privately Held**
WEB: www.kindelfurniture.com
SIC: 2511 7641 Dining room furniture: wood; tables, household: wood; chairs, household, except upholstered: wood; re-upholstery & furniture repair

(G-6584)
KINGS SELF DEFENSE LLC
6769 Bent Grass Dr Se (49508-7873)
PHONE 910 890-4322
Jared Reyes, *Principal*
EMP: 3
SALES (est): 199.2K **Privately Held**
SIC: 3812 Defense systems & equipment

(G-6585)
KNAPE & VOGT MANUFACTURING CO (DH)
2700 Oak Industrial Dr Ne (49505-6081)
PHONE 616 459-3311
Peter Martin, *President*
Jon P Elordi, *Vice Pres*
Gordon Kirsch, *Vice Pres*
Andy Marzolf, *Vice Pres*
Gary Ottenjan, *Vice Pres*
◆ **EMP:** 582 **EST:** 1898
SQ FT: 444,000
SALES (est): 189.9MM
SALES (corp-wide): 1.4B **Privately Held**
WEB: www.knapeandvogt.com
SIC: 2541 3429 2542 Wood partitions & fixtures; shelving, office & store, wood; display fixtures, wood; furniture builders' & other household hardware; shelving, office & store: except wood

(G-6586)
KNICKERBOCKER
417 Bridge St Nw (49504-5305)
PHONE 616 345-5642
EMP: 4
SALES (est): 302.5K **Privately Held**
SIC: 2082 Malt beverages

(G-6587)
KNOLL INC
Also Called: Knoll Group
4300 36th St Se (49512-2993)
PHONE 616 949-1050
Leslie Rakestraw, *Buyer*
David Overholt, *Branch Mgr*
Rick Vledder, *Software Dev*
David Haigler, *Director*
EMP: 250 **Publicly Held**
WEB: www.knoll.com
SIC: 2521 2541 Wood office furniture; wood partitions & fixtures
PA: Knoll, Inc.
   1235 Water St
   East Greenville PA 18041

(G-6588)
KOEZE COMPANY (PA)
Also Called: Koeze Direct
2555 Burlingame Ave Sw (49509-2237)
P.O. Box 9470 (49509-0470)
PHONE 616 724-2601
Jeffrey Koeze, *Ch of Bd*
William E Malpass, *Corp Secy*
John Feenstra, *Purch Mgr*
Mark Minkus, *Controller*
Martin Andree, *Marketing Mgr*
◆ **EMP:** 33 **EST:** 1910
SQ FT: 92,000
SALES (est): 10.7MM **Privately Held**
WEB: www.koeze.com
SIC: 5441 2068 2095 Candy; salted & roasted nuts & seeds; roasted coffee

(G-6589)
KRAFT HEINZ
3950 Sparks Dr Se (49546-6146)
PHONE 616 940-2260
EMP: 3
SALES (est): 72.7K **Privately Held**
SIC: 2022 Processed cheese

(G-6590)
KRAFT HEINZ FOODS COMPANY
Also Called: Kraft Foods
3950 Sparks Dr Se (49546-6146)
PHONE 616 447-0481
EMP: 450

Grand Rapids - Kent County (G-6591)   GEOGRAPHIC SECTION

SALES (corp-wide): 26.2B **Publicly Held**
SIC: 2033 Canned fruits & specialties
HQ: Kraft Heinz Foods Company
   1 Ppg Pl Fl 34
   Pittsburgh PA 15222
   412 456-5700

(G-6591)
KRIEGER CRAFTSMEN INC
2758 3 Mile Rd Nw (49534-1318)
PHONE.................................616 735-9200
Tim Krieger, *President*
EMP: 32
SQ FT: 5,000
SALES (est): 7.1MM **Privately Held**
WEB: www.kriegercraftsmen.com
SIC: 3544 Industrial molds

(G-6592)
KVA ENGINEERING INC
1248 Plymouth Ave Ne (49505-5641)
PHONE.................................616 745-7483
Kenneth Vranish, *Principal*
EMP: 5
SALES (est): 444.1K **Privately Held**
SIC: 3812 Search & navigation equipment

(G-6593)
L3 AVIATION PRODUCTS INC (DH)
Also Called: L3 Commnctons Avionics Systems
5353 52nd St Se (49512-9702)
PHONE.................................616 949-6600
Christopher E Kubasik, *CEO*
Jay Lafoy, *President*
EMP: 300
SQ FT: 110,000
SALES (est): 154.1MM
SALES (corp-wide): 6.8B **Publicly Held**
SIC: 3812 Aircraft flight instruments; gyroscopes; automatic pilots, aircraft; radar systems & equipment
HQ: L3 Technologies, Inc.
   600 3rd Ave Fl 34
   New York NY 10016
   212 697-1111

(G-6594)
LACH DIAMOND
4350 Airwest Dr Se Ofc A (49512-3969)
PHONE.................................616 698-0101
Horst Lach, *President*
Sue Wilder, *Finance Spvr*
Amber Clisso, *Sales Staff*
Lonn Beaver, *Manager*
Jon Cade, *Admin Sec*
EMP: 26
SQ FT: 12,000
SALES (est): 4.2MM **Privately Held**
WEB: www.lach-diamond.com
SIC: 3423 7699 Hand & edge tools; knife, saw & tool sharpening & repair

(G-6595)
LACKS ENTERPRISES INC
4221 Airlane Dr Se (49512-3960)
PHONE.................................616 949-6570
Richard Lacks Jr, *President*
Jim Morrissey, *Opers Staff*
Michael Pokrywka, *Purch Mgr*
Heather Vandyke, *Purch Agent*
Scott Palmatier, *Manager*
EMP: 65
SALES (corp-wide): 715.6MM **Privately Held**
SIC: 3089 Molding primary plastic
PA: Lacks Enterprises, Inc.
   5460 Cascade Rd Se
   Grand Rapids MI 49546
   616 949-6570

(G-6596)
LACKS ENTERPRISES INC
4365 52nd St Se (49512-9673)
PHONE.................................616 656-2910
Richard Lacks Jr, *President*
EMP: 100
SALES (corp-wide): 715.6MM **Privately Held**
SIC: 3089 Molding primary plastic
PA: Lacks Enterprises, Inc.
   5460 Cascade Rd Se
   Grand Rapids MI 49546
   616 949-6570

(G-6597)
LACKS ENTERPRISES INC
Also Called: Plastic Plate Plt 2
4251 Brockton Ct Se (49512-4049)
PHONE.................................616 698-2030
Bob Sweeney, *Manager*
Mary Taylor, *Exec Dir*
EMP: 100
SALES (corp-wide): 715.6MM **Privately Held**
SIC: 3089 3471 Molding primary plastic; plating & polishing
PA: Lacks Enterprises, Inc.
   5460 Cascade Rd Se
   Grand Rapids MI 49546
   616 949-6570

(G-6598)
LACKS ENTERPRISES INC (PA)
5460 Cascade Rd Se (49546-6406)
PHONE.................................616 949-6570
Richard Lacks Jr, *President*
Bob Bieri, *General Mgr*
Jeff Lacross, *General Mgr*
John Lacks, *Principal*
Chris Walker, *Principal*
EMP: 60
SQ FT: 19,000
SALES (est): 715.6MM **Privately Held**
SIC: 3089 Molding primary plastic

(G-6599)
LACKS EXTERIOR SYSTEMS LLC
Also Called: Lacks Enterprises
4245 52nd St Se (49512-9570)
PHONE.................................616 554-3419
Michael Snider, *Purchasing*
Tom Lewis, *Manager*
Jon Smith, *Director*
EMP: 200
SALES (corp-wide): 715.6MM **Privately Held**
WEB: www.lacksenterprises.com
SIC: 3479 Etching & engraving
HQ: Lacks Exterior Systems, Llc
   5460 Cascade Rd Se
   Grand Rapids MI 49546
   616 949-6570

(G-6600)
LACKS EXTERIOR SYSTEMS LLC (HQ)
Also Called: Lacks Trim Systems
5460 Cascade Rd Se (49546-6406)
PHONE.................................616 949-6570
Beb Bieri, *General Mgr*
Kurt Lacks, *Vice Pres*
Jason McFarlane, *Engineer*
Patrick Knight, *Plant Engr*
Dane Fortney, *Sales Staff*
◆ **EMP:** 1000
SALES (est): 367.8MM
SALES (corp-wide): 715.6MM **Privately Held**
WEB: www.lacksenterprises.com
SIC: 3089 Plastic hardware & building products
PA: Lacks Enterprises, Inc.
   5460 Cascade Rd Se
   Grand Rapids MI 49546
   616 949-6570

(G-6601)
LACKS EXTERIOR SYSTEMS LLC
5010 52nd St Se (49512)
PHONE.................................616 949-6570
Joe Strouse, *Director*
EMP: 25
SALES (corp-wide): 715.6MM **Privately Held**
SIC: 3089 Plastic hardware & building products
HQ: Lacks Exterior Systems, Llc
   5460 Cascade Rd Se
   Grand Rapids MI 49546
   616 949-6570

(G-6602)
LACKS EXTERIOR SYSTEMS LLC
5711 Kraft Ave Se (49512)
PHONE.................................616 949-6570
Dan Centille, *Branch Mgr*
EMP: 180
SALES (corp-wide): 715.6MM **Privately Held**
SIC: 3089 Automotive parts, plastic
HQ: Lacks Exterior Systems, Llc
   5460 Cascade Rd Se
   Grand Rapids MI 49546
   616 949-6570

(G-6603)
LACKS EXTERIOR SYSTEMS LLC
5801 Kraft Ave Se (49512-9683)
PHONE.................................616 949-6570
Joel Goward, *Branch Mgr*
EMP: 125
SALES (corp-wide): 715.6MM **Privately Held**
SIC: 3089 Automotive parts, plastic
HQ: Lacks Exterior Systems, Llc
   5460 Cascade Rd Se
   Grand Rapids MI 49546
   616 949-6570

(G-6604)
LACKS EXTERIOR SYSTEMS LLC
4315 52nd St Se (49512)
PHONE.................................616 949-6570
Jason Fogelsonger, *Branch Mgr*
EMP: 225
SALES (corp-wide): 715.6MM **Privately Held**
SIC: 3089 Automotive parts, plastic
HQ: Lacks Exterior Systems, Llc
   5460 Cascade Rd Se
   Grand Rapids MI 49546
   616 949-6570

(G-6605)
LACKS EXTERIOR SYSTEMS LLC
3703 Patterson Sw (49512)
PHONE.................................616 949-6570
Jeff Reest, *Manager*
EMP: 300
SALES (corp-wide): 715.6MM **Privately Held**
SIC: 2396 Automotive & apparel trimmings
HQ: Lacks Exterior Systems, Llc
   5460 Cascade Rd Se
   Grand Rapids MI 49546
   616 949-6570

(G-6606)
LACKS INDUSTRIES INC
Kentwood Division
4260 Airwest Dr Se (49512-3948)
PHONE.................................616 698-6890
Joe Sullivan, *Manager*
EMP: 150
SALES (corp-wide): 715.6MM **Privately Held**
SIC: 3089 3714 3429 Molding primary plastic; motor vehicle parts & accessories; manufactured hardware (general)
HQ: Lacks Industries, Inc.
   5460 Cascade Rd Se
   Grand Rapids MI 49546
   616 949-6570

(G-6607)
LACKS INDUSTRIES INC
4375 52nd St Se (49512-9673)
PHONE.................................616 698-3600
Joe Sullivan, *Manager*
EMP: 200
SALES (corp-wide): 715.6MM **Privately Held**
SIC: 3089 Plastic processing
HQ: Lacks Industries, Inc.
   5460 Cascade Rd Se
   Grand Rapids MI 49546
   616 949-6570

(G-6608)
LACKS INDUSTRIES INC
Also Called: Lacks Trim Systems
4090 Barden Dr (49512)
PHONE.................................616 698-6854
Steve Morrissey, *Plant Mgr*
Bill Mull, *Manager*
EMP: 75
SALES (corp-wide): 715.6MM **Privately Held**
SIC: 3089 Molding primary plastic
HQ: Lacks Industries, Inc.
   5460 Cascade Rd Se
   Grand Rapids MI 49546
   616 949-6570

(G-6609)
LACKS INDUSTRIES INC
4260 Airlane Dr Se (49512-3959)
PHONE.................................616 698-9852
Jim Morsey, *Manager*
EMP: 250
SALES (corp-wide): 715.6MM **Privately Held**
SIC: 2396 3471 Automotive trimmings, fabric; plating & polishing
HQ: Lacks Industries, Inc.
   5460 Cascade Rd Se
   Grand Rapids MI 49546
   616 949-6570

(G-6610)
LACKS INDUSTRIES INC
Also Called: Lacks Wheel Trim Systems
3505 Kraft Ave Se (49512-2033)
PHONE.................................616 554-7134
Timothy Laven, *QA Dir*
Mitch Brummel, *Research*
Kevin Chinavare, *Engineer*
Lary O'Tool, *Branch Mgr*
Jennifer Etchison, *Manager*
EMP: 100
SALES (corp-wide): 715.6MM **Privately Held**
SIC: 3089 Plastic containers, except foam
HQ: Lacks Industries, Inc.
   5460 Cascade Rd Se
   Grand Rapids MI 49546
   616 949-6570

(G-6611)
LACKS INDUSTRIES INC
Also Called: Airwest Engineering
4275 Airwest Dr Se (49512-3949)
PHONE.................................616 698-2776
Doug Reams, *Principal*
Peggy Russell, *Vice Pres*
Kimberly Zoerman, *QA Dir*
Peter Bottorff, *Engineer*
Scott Hoogerhyde, *Engineer*
EMP: 75
SALES (corp-wide): 715.6MM **Privately Held**
SIC: 3089 Molding primary plastic
HQ: Lacks Industries, Inc.
   5460 Cascade Rd Se
   Grand Rapids MI 49546
   616 949-6570

(G-6612)
LACKS INDUSTRIES INC
4365 52nd St Se (49512-9673)
PHONE.................................616 656-2910
Chris Ober, *Manager*
EMP: 100
SALES (corp-wide): 715.6MM **Privately Held**
SIC: 3089 3714 Plastic hardware & building products; motor vehicle parts & accessories
HQ: Lacks Industries, Inc.
   5460 Cascade Rd Se
   Grand Rapids MI 49546
   616 949-6570

(G-6613)
LACKS WHEEL TRIM SYSTEMS LLC (PA)
5460 Cascade Rd Se (49546-6406)
PHONE.................................616 949-6570
Mike Clover, *CFO*
Chet Anisko, *Finance*
Dane Fortney, *Sales Staff*
EMP: 50 **EST:** 1998
SQ FT: 40,000
SALES (est): 7.2MM **Privately Held**
SIC: 3089 Injection molding of plastics

(G-6614)
LAKELAND FINISHING CORPORATION
5400 36th St Se (49512-2016)
PHONE.................................616 949-8001
Thomas A Smith, *President*

GEOGRAPHIC SECTION

Grand Rapids - Kent County (G-6640)

Kabrina Alcorn, *QC Mgr*
Traci Clark, *Project Engr*
John Behrend, *Accounts Mgr*
EMP: 60
SQ FT: 85,000
SALES (est): 18.4MM
SALES (corp-wide): 6.5MM **Privately Held**
SIC: 3714 Motor vehicle parts & accessories
PA: Monroe Group Holdings, Llc
4490 44th St Se
Grand Rapids MI 49512
616 942-9820

(G-6615)
LAKELAND PALLETS INC (PA)
3801 Kraft Ave Se (49512-2039)
PHONE..................616 949-9515
Dan Bodbyl, *President*
Joel Bodbyl, *General Mgr*
EMP: 34
SALES (est): 5.6MM **Privately Held**
SIC: 2448 Pallets, wood; pallets, wood & wood with metal

(G-6616)
LAMININ MEDICAL PRODUCTS INC
3760 East Paris Ave Se (49512-3903)
PHONE..................616 871-3390
Jon Rudolph, *President*
Don Armbrester, *Exec VP*
▲ **EMP:** 20 **EST:** 2011
SALES (est): 5.1MM **Privately Held**
SIC: 2672 Adhesive backed films, foams & foils

(G-6617)
LAND & HOMES INC
1701 Porter St Sw Ste 6 (49519-1771)
PHONE..................616 534-5792
Paul Land, *President*
Roger Lucas, *Vice Pres*
Daniel Hibma, *Treasurer*
Dan Himba, *Treasurer*
EMP: 4
SALES (est): 430.6K **Privately Held**
SIC: 2721 Periodicals

(G-6618)
LASER ACCESS INC
3691 Northridge Dr Nw # 10 (49544-9007)
PHONE..................616 459-5496
Daniel Szymanski, *President*
Glenn Jarrell, *Controller*
Ted Terhune, *Manager*
Kay Ostrowski, *Technology*
EMP: 120
SALES (est): 20.2MM
SALES (corp-wide): 40.1MM **Privately Held**
WEB: www.laseraccess.com
SIC: 3699 7692 Laser welding, drilling & cutting equipment; welding repair
PA: Jedco, Inc.
1615 Broadway Ave Nw
Grand Rapids MI 49504
616 459-5161

(G-6619)
LASERCUTTING SERVICES INC
Also Called: Michigan Lasercut
4101 40th St Se Ste 7 (49512-4124)
PHONE..................616 975-2000
Steve Schroder, *President*
Les Wong, *Chairman*
Brian Curtis, *Vice Pres*
Tony Klima, *Sales Staff*
Michele Schilling, *Administration*
EMP: 19
SQ FT: 12,500
SALES (est): 3.3MM **Privately Held**
WEB: www.michiganlasercut.com
SIC: 3544 Dies, steel rule

(G-6620)
LASERS RESOURCE INC
4775 40th St Se (49512-4076)
PHONE..................616 554-5555
Thomas Senecal, *President*
Amy West, *Controller*
Joe Greene, *Accounts Mgr*
Adrian Lopez, *Sales Staff*
Debra Senecal, *Admin Sec*
EMP: 20

SQ FT: 12,000
SALES (est): 4.8MM **Privately Held**
WEB: www.lasersresource.com
SIC: 3861 7378 Toners, prepared photographic (not made in chemical plants); computer peripheral equipment repair & maintenance

(G-6621)
LASERS UNLIMITED INC
4600 36th St Se (49512-1920)
PHONE..................616 977-2668
Alan Bush, *President*
Dale Parker, *Sales Staff*
EMP: 16
SQ FT: 41,000
SALES (est): 3.7MM **Privately Held**
SIC: 3441 Fabricated structural metal

(G-6622)
LATIN AMERICAN INDUSTRIES LLC
3120 Kn O Sha Indus Ct Se (49508)
PHONE..................616 301-1878
Olivia Benitez, *Mng Member*
EMP: 7
SALES (est): 1.3MM **Privately Held**
SIC: 3089 3544 Molding primary plastic; special dies, tools, jigs & fixtures

(G-6623)
LEATHERCRAFTS BY BEAR
751 Brownwood Ave Nw (49504-3645)
PHONE..................616 453-8308
John Downer, *Owner*
Maureen Downer, *Co-Owner*
EMP: 4
SALES: 68K **Privately Held**
SIC: 3199 Leather garments

(G-6624)
LEEDY MANUFACTURING CO LLC
210 Hall St Sw (49507-1034)
PHONE..................616 245-0517
Gary King, *Opers Mgr*
Roy Hagle, *QC Dir*
Steve Traynor, *VP Finance*
Harold Leedy Jr,
Donald Freehafer,
▲ **EMP:** 70 **EST:** 1947
SQ FT: 75,000
SALES (est): 22.9MM **Privately Held**
WEB: www.leedymfg.com
SIC: 3714 3531 3568 3536 Gears, motor vehicle; transmissions, motor vehicle; winches; sprockets (power transmission equipment); pulleys, power transmission; hoists, cranes & monorails

(G-6625)
LEGACY METAL FABRICATING LLC
21 N Park St Nw (49544-6932)
PHONE..................616 258-8406
Ryan McComb, *Vice Pres*
Kim McComb,
EMP: 20
SQ FT: 12,000
SALES (est): 5.1MM **Privately Held**
SIC: 3444 Sheet metalwork

(G-6626)
LELAND INTERNATIONAL INC (PA)
5695 Eagle Dr Se (49512-2057)
PHONE..................616 975-9260
Timothy Korzon, *President*
Brenda Amato, *Sls & Mktg Exec*
Shanna Korzon, *Manager*
▲ **EMP:** 33
SALES (est): 7.2MM **Privately Held**
WEB: www.lelandinternational.com
SIC: 2512 Wood upholstered chairs & couches

(G-6627)
LIGHT SPEED USA LLC
Also Called: Phenosynthesis LLC
1971 E Beltlin Ave Ne 106-130 (49525-7045)
PHONE..................616 308-0054
Anthony Cairo, *Managing Dir*
EMP: 895

SALES (est): 5MM **Privately Held**
SIC: 3229 8999 8748 Reflectors for lighting equipment, pressed or blown glass; scientific consulting; systems analysis & engineering consulting services

(G-6628)
LILY PRODUCTS MICHIGAN INC
2070 Calvin Ave Se (49507-3373)
PHONE..................616 245-9193
Steven Popma, *CEO*
Jason Popma, *President*
Ryan Murray, *Vice Pres*
EMP: 6 **EST:** 1968
SQ FT: 18,000
SALES (est): 1MM **Privately Held**
WEB: www.lilyproducts.com
SIC: 2819 Industrial inorganic chemicals

(G-6629)
LIVESPACE LLC
Also Called: Audiospace
4995 Starr St Se (49546-6350)
PHONE..................616 929-0191
Jason McCleon, *CFO*
Todd Ernst, *Sales Staff*
Richards Bacans, *Mng Member*
EMP: 15
SQ FT: 16,000
SALES (est): 3MM **Privately Held**
SIC: 3663 7941 Studio equipment, radio & television broadcasting; stadium event operator services

(G-6630)
LONG ROAD DISTILLERS LLC
537 Leonard St Nw (49504-4263)
PHONE..................616 356-1770
Kyle Van Strien, *Owner*
EMP: 7 **EST:** 2014
SALES (est): 631.1K **Privately Held**
SIC: 2085 Distillers' dried grains & solubles & alcohol

(G-6631)
LOUIS PADNOS IRON AND METAL CO
601 Lettellier St Sw (49504-6435)
PHONE..................616 459-4208
Shelley Padnos, *Branch Mgr*
EMP: 36
SALES (corp-wide): 520.8MM **Privately Held**
SIC: 5093 3341 3231 2611 Ferrous metal scrap & waste; secondary nonferrous metals; products of purchased glass; pulp mills
PA: Louis Padnos Iron And Metal Company
185 W 8th St
Holland MI 49423
616 396-6521

(G-6632)
LOUIS PADNOS IRON AND METAL CO
Also Called: Burton Street Recycling
719 Burton St Sw (49503-8005)
PHONE..................616 452-6037
Bill Varberg, *Manager*
EMP: 8
SALES (corp-wide): 520.8MM **Privately Held**
SIC: 4953 3341 Recycling, waste materials; secondary nonferrous metals
PA: Louis Padnos Iron And Metal Company
185 W 8th St
Holland MI 49423
616 396-6521

(G-6633)
LOWERY CORPORATION (PA)
Also Called: Applied Imaging
5555 Glnwood Hlls Pkwy Se (49512-2091)
PHONE..................616 554-5200
John Lowery, *President*
John Konyonbelt, *Vice Pres*
Allen Husted, *Prdtn Mgr*
Rob Henderson, *Production*
Patrick Okuley, *Production*
EMP: 150
SQ FT: 13,000
SALES (est): 109.1MM **Privately Held**
WEB: www.imagingnow.com
SIC: 5044 7379 2759 Copying equipment; ; commercial printing

(G-6634)
LUB-TECH INC
Also Called: Lt Global
470 Market Ave Sw Unit 13 (49503-4981)
PHONE..................616 299-3540
▲ **EMP:** 4
SALES (est): 342.1K **Privately Held**
SIC: 2992 5085 Mfg Lubricating Oils/Greases & Filters

(G-6635)
LUDWICKS FROZEN DONUTS INC
Also Called: Ludwick's Sour Cream Donuts
3217 3 Mile Rd Nw (49534-1223)
PHONE..................616 453-6880
Tom Ludwick, *President*
EMP: 19 **EST:** 1957
SQ FT: 11,000
SALES: 1.1MM **Privately Held**
SIC: 2053 2052 Doughnuts, frozen; cookies & crackers

(G-6636)
LUMENFLOW CORP
3685 Hagen Dr Se (49548-2340)
P.O. Box 216, Caledonia (49316-0216)
PHONE..................269 795-9007
Paul Bourget, *President*
Brian Zatzke, *Corp Secy*
Harold Brunt, *Vice Pres*
Brian Post, *Vice Pres*
EMP: 6
SALES (est): 1.1MM **Privately Held**
WEB: www.lumenflow.com
SIC: 3827 Optical instruments & lenses

(G-6637)
LUMICHRON INC
2215 29th St Se Ste B4 (49508-1580)
PHONE..................616 245-8888
Ian Macartney, *President*
Karen Macartney, *Vice Pres*
▼ **EMP:** 4
SQ FT: 3,500
SALES (est): 370K **Privately Held**
WEB: www.lumichron.com
SIC: 3873 Clocks, except timeclocks

(G-6638)
M & E MANUFACTURING INC
530 32nd St Se (49548-2304)
P.O. Box 897 (49518-0897)
PHONE..................616 241-5509
Russ Visner, *President*
Roger Potgeter, *Principal*
Dale Vokerding, *Principal*
EMP: 8
SQ FT: 13,000
SALES (est): 830K **Privately Held**
SIC: 3321 Sewer pipe, cast iron; soil pipe & fittings: cast iron; water pipe, cast iron

(G-6639)
MACALI INC
Also Called: Sovereign Machine
1615 Monroe Ave Nw Ste 2 (49505-4677)
PHONE..................616 447-1202
Mark Vanderwal, *President*
EMP: 3
SQ FT: 1,100
SALES (est): 250K **Privately Held**
SIC: 7699 3553 Industrial machinery & equipment repair; woodworking machinery

(G-6640)
MAGNA MIRRORS AMERICA INC (DH)
Also Called: Magna Engineered Glass
5085 Kraft Ave Se (49512-9707)
PHONE..................616 786-5120
James L Brodie, *CEO*
Niall R Lynam, *Senior VP*
Aaron McCarthy, *Vice Pres*
Darrell Commans, *Engineer*
◆ **EMP:** 20 **EST:** 1905

Grand Rapids - Kent County (G-6641)   GEOGRAPHIC SECTION

SALES (est): 1.7B
SALES (corp-wide): 40.8B **Privately Held**
WEB: www.donnelly.com
SIC: 3231 3647 3827 Mirrors, truck & automobile: made from purchased glass; windshields, glass: made from purchased glass; dome lights, automotive; automotive lighting fixtures; optical instruments & lenses

(G-6641)
MALL CITY CONTAINERS INC
88 54th St Sw Unit 105 (49548-5683)
PHONE..................................616 249-3657
Gary Coster, *Manager*
EMP: 6
SALES (est): 600.9K
SALES (corp-wide): 10.1MM **Privately Held**
WEB: www.mallcitycontainers.com
SIC: 2653 Boxes, corrugated: made from purchased materials
PA: Mall City Containers, Inc.
2710 N Pitcher St
Kalamazoo MI 49004
269 381-2706

(G-6642)
MAR-MED INC
Also Called: Mar-Med Co.
333 Fuller Ave Ne (49503-3630)
PHONE..................................616 454-3000
Joseph Marogil, *President*
Joel Marogil, *Treasurer*
Jerry Marogil, *Admin Sec*
▲ **EMP:** 3
SALES: 500K **Privately Held**
SIC: 3841 Surgical & medical instruments

(G-6643)
MARK MAKER COMPANY INC (PA)
4157 Stafford Ave Sw (49548-3053)
PHONE..................................616 538-6980
Robert Pettijohn, *President*
Charles Bobeldyk, *Vice Pres*
Ronna Schultz, *Vice Pres*
Steven Stout, *Vice Pres*
Troy Brouwer, *Opers Mgr*
EMP: 38
SQ FT: 15,000
SALES (est): 6.4MM **Privately Held**
WEB: www.mark-makerco.com
SIC: 3953 3544 2796 Printing dies, rubber or plastic, for marking machines; dies & die holders for metal cutting, forming, die casting; platemaking services

(G-6644)
MARKIT PRODUCTS
2430 Turner Ave Nw Ste D (49544-2005)
PHONE..................................616 458-7881
Heather Grimes, *Owner*
EMP: 4
SALES (est): 160K **Privately Held**
SIC: 2395 Embroidery products, except schiffli machine

(G-6645)
MARSHALL RYERSON CO
7440 Lime Hollow Dr Se (49546-7437)
PHONE..................................616 299-1751
Marshall Ryerson, *President*
EMP: 10
SALES (est): 720K **Privately Held**
SIC: 8742 3826 2851 2952 Marketing consulting services; instruments measuring thermal properties; polyurethane coatings; roofing felts, cements or coatings; waterproofing compounds; insulation, thermal

(G-6646)
MARTIN AND HATTIE RASCHE INC
Also Called: Valley City Plating Company
3353 Eastern Ave Se (49508-2404)
PHONE..................................616 245-1223
Jon Rasche, *President*
Carol Rasche, *Vice Pres*
Jeff Rasche, *Vice Pres*
David Lammers, *Purchasing*
Jack Zimmerman, *Treasurer*
EMP: 65 **EST:** 1988
SQ FT: 75,000
SALES (est): 8.4MM **Privately Held**
WEB: www.brassplater.com
SIC: 3471 2514 Buffing for the trade; polishing, metals or formed products; plating of metals or formed products; metal household furniture

(G-6647)
MARTON TOOL & DIE CO INC
610 Plymouth Ave Ne (49505-6040)
PHONE..................................616 361-7337
Dan Parmeter, *President*
EMP: 8
SALES (est): 927.9K **Privately Held**
WEB: www.classicdie.com
SIC: 3544 Special dies & tools

(G-6648)
MASTER FINISH CO
2020 Nelson Ave Se # 103 (49507-3300)
PHONE..................................877 590-5819
Dale Mulder, *President*
Aaron Mulder, *Vice Pres*
Douglas Roetman, *Vice Pres*
John Haley, *Maint Spvr*
Matt Lomasney, *Engineer*
EMP: 150 **EST:** 1959
SQ FT: 56,000
SALES (est): 13.5MM **Privately Held**
WEB: www.masterfinishco.com
SIC: 3471 Plating of metals or formed products; polishing, metals or formed products

(G-6649)
MATRIX MANUFACTURING INC
862 47th St Sw Ste B2 (49509-5141)
PHONE..................................616 532-6000
Jeffrey J Rodgers, *President*
▲ **EMP:** 6
SALES (est): 1.1MM **Privately Held**
SIC: 3089 Injection molding of plastics

(G-6650)
MATTSON TOOL & DIE CORP
4174 5 Mile Rd Ne (49525-9570)
PHONE..................................616 447-9012
EMP: 5 **EST:** 2013
SALES (est): 375.8K **Privately Held**
SIC: 3544 Mfg Dies/Tools/Jigs/Fixtures

(G-6651)
MBWWPRODUCTS INC
825 Buchanan Ave Sw (49507-1004)
P.O. Box 501, Cannonsburg, (49317-0501)
PHONE..................................616 464-1650
Michael D Petersen, *President*
EMP: 12
SALES (est): 1MM **Privately Held**
SIC: 2499 Dishes, wood; carved & turned wood; decorative wood & woodwork; furniture inlays (veneers)

(G-6652)
MCCARTHY GROUP INCORPORATED (PA)
5505 52nd St Se (49512-9700)
PHONE..................................616 977-2900
John McCarthy, *President*
Derrick McCarthy, *Vice Pres*
Theressa Henderson, *Finance*
◆ **EMP:** 5
SQ FT: 2,000
SALES (est): 1MM **Privately Held**
SIC: 2399 2843 4226 Automotive covers, except seat & tire covers; textile processing assistants; textile warehousing

(G-6653)
MCCLURE METALS GROUP INC
6161 28th St Se Ste 5 (49546-6931)
PHONE..................................616 957-5955
Steve McClure, *President*
▲ **EMP:** 4
SALES: 500K **Privately Held**
WEB: www.mcclmetals.com
SIC: 3315 Steel wire & related products

(G-6654)
MCCOY CRAFTSMAN LLC
1642 Broadway Ave Nw (49504-2046)
PHONE..................................616 634-7455
Jeffrey Bystry,
EMP: 12
SALES (est): 428.7K **Privately Held**
SIC: 2431 Millwork

(G-6655)
MDM ENTERPRISES INC
Also Called: Enamelite Industries
3829 Roger B Chaffee Mem (49548-3437)
PHONE..................................616 452-1591
Roger Rollman, *President*
EMP: 19 **EST:** 1967
SQ FT: 20,000
SALES (est): 2.5MM
SALES (corp-wide): 16MM **Privately Held**
WEB: www.enamelite-ind.com
SIC: 3479 Coating of metals with plastic or resins
PA: Model Die & Mold, Inc.
3859 Roger B Chaffee Se
Grand Rapids MI
616 243-6996

(G-6656)
MEDBIO INC (PA)
5346 36th St Se (49512-2014)
PHONE..................................616 245-0214
Christopher Williams, *President*
Ronald A Williams, *Chairman*
Rajesh Kothari, *Corp Secy*
Sean Callaghan, *Vice Pres*
Steve Morgan, *QC Mgr*
▲ **EMP:** 76
SQ FT: 65,000
SALES (est): 18.5MM **Privately Held**
WEB: www.medbioinc.com
SIC: 3089 Injection molding of plastics

(G-6657)
MEDISURGE LLC
Also Called: Surge Cardiovascular
333 Bridge St Nw Ste 1125 (49504-5367)
PHONE..................................888 307-1144
Robert Taylor, *Mng Member*
EMP: 10
SALES (est): 377.1K **Privately Held**
SIC: 3841 Surgical & medical instruments

(G-6658)
MEDTRONIC INC
620 Watson St Sw (49504-6340)
PHONE..................................616 643-5200
Fax: 616 643-1017
EMP: 8 **Publicly Held**
SIC: 3841 3845 3842 Mfg Surgical/Medical Instruments Mfg Electromedical Equipment Mfg Surgical Appliances/Supplies
HQ: Medtronic, Inc.
710 Medtronic Pkwy
Minneapolis MN 55432
763 514-4000

(G-6659)
MEDTRONIC INC
520 Watson St Sw (49504-6450)
PHONE..................................616 643-5200
Gary Bernauer, *Manager*
EMP: 11 **Privately Held**
WEB: www.medtronic.com
SIC: 3841 Surgical & medical instruments
HQ: Medtronic, Inc.
710 Medtronic Pkwy
Minneapolis MN 55432
763 514-4000

(G-6660)
METAL COMPONENTS LLC (PA)
Also Called: M C
3281 Roger B (49548)
PHONE..................................616 252-1900
Craig Balow, *General Mgr*
▲ **EMP:** 80
SQ FT: 85,000
SALES (est): 19.4MM **Privately Held**
WEB: www.metalcomponentsinc.com
SIC: 2522 3444 Office furniture, except wood; metal housings, enclosures, casings & other containers

(G-6661)
METAL COMPONENTS EMPLOYMENT
3281 Rog B Chaffee Mem Dr (49548)
PHONE..................................616 252-1900
Todd Schreiber,
EMP: 86
SALES: 950K **Privately Held**
SIC: 3444 Sheet metalwork

(G-6662)
METRO ENGRG OF GRND RAPIDS
845 Ottawa Ave Nw (49503-1429)
PHONE..................................616 458-2823
John Taylor, *President*
EMP: 11
SQ FT: 24,000
SALES (est): 1.4MM **Privately Held**
WEB: www.metroengineering.com
SIC: 3999 Models, general, except toy

(G-6663)
METRO GRAPHIC ARTS INC
900 40th St Se (49508-2401)
PHONE..................................616 245-2271
David Gaebel, *President*
William B Clifford, *Vice Pres*
Diane Gaebel, *Treasurer*
Linda Clifford, *Admin Sec*
EMP: 19
SQ FT: 15,000
SALES: 850K **Privately Held**
SIC: 2741 5999 5199 Maps: publishing & printing; maps & charts; maps & charts

(G-6664)
METZGAR CONVEYOR CO
5801 Clay Ave Sw Ste A (49548-3033)
PHONE..................................616 784-0930
Patricia Metzgar, *Ch of Bd*
D Robert Metzgar, *President*
Dave Stevens, *Purch Mgr*
Jon Goeman, *Manager*
EMP: 40
SALES (est): 8.8MM **Privately Held**
WEB: www.metzgarconveyors.com
SIC: 3535 5084 3537 Conveyors & conveying equipment; industrial machinery & equipment; industrial trucks & tractors

(G-6665)
MEXAMERICA FOODS LLC
219 Canton St Sw Ste A (49507-1098)
PHONE..................................814 781-1447
Raymond Gunn, *CEO*
▲ **EMP:** 47
SQ FT: 25,000
SALES (est): 13.9MM **Privately Held**
SIC: 2099 2096 5812 Tortillas, fresh or refrigerated; ready-to-eat meals, salads & sandwiches; potato chips & similar snacks; eating places

(G-6666)
MICHCOR CONTAINER INC
1151 Sheldon Ave Se (49507-1135)
PHONE..................................616 452-7089
John Pettengill, *President*
Charity Dawson, *CFO*
Luann Shepardson, *Controller*
EMP: 27
SQ FT: 40,000
SALES (est): 6.3MM **Privately Held**
WEB: www.michcor.com
SIC: 2653 Boxes, corrugated: made from purchased materials

(G-6667)
MICHIGAN AGRICULTURAL FUEL
2411 Santigo Ave Se (49546-6740)
PHONE..................................419 490-6599
Anthony Senagore, *CEO*
EMP: 3
SALES (est): 192.1K **Privately Held**
SIC: 2869 Industrial organic chemicals

(G-6668)
MICHIGAN BINGO BUGLE
2604 Pohens Ave Nw (49544-1857)
PHONE..................................616 784-9344
Sandra Webber, *Owner*
EMP: 3
SALES: 96K **Privately Held**
SIC: 2711 Newspapers, publishing & printing

(G-6669)
MICHIGAN COATING PRODUCTS INC
3761 Eastern Ave Se (49508-2412)
PHONE..................................616 456-8800
Tom Lilley, *President*
Dawn Wustman, *Executive Asst*

▲ = Import ▼ = Export
◆ = Import/Export

Grand Rapids - Kent County (G-6696)

EMP: 9
SQ FT: 15,000
SALES (est): 1.6MM Privately Held
SIC: 2851 Paints & paint additives

(G-6670)
MICHIGAN ENVELOPE INC
6650 Clay Ave Sw (49548-7833)
PHONE..................616 554-3404
Lloyd H De Vries, *President*
Phyllis De Vries, *Vice Pres*
EMP: 7
SQ FT: 12,000
SALES (est): 1.7MM Privately Held
SIC: 2677 Envelopes

(G-6671)
MICHIGAN FOAM PRODUCTS INC
1820 Chicago Dr Sw (49519-1209)
PHONE..................616 452-9611
Jack Goodale, *President*
Brian Anderson, *General Mgr*
Scot Van Airsdale, *Sales Engr*
▲ EMP: 15
SQ FT: 450,000
SALES (est): 3.2MM Privately Held
WEB: www.michiganfoam.com
SIC: 3086 5199 Insulation or cushioning material, foamed plastic; packaging & shipping materials, foamed plastic; plastics foam

(G-6672)
MICHIGAN GENERAL GRINDING LLC
328 Winter Ave Nw (49504-5348)
PHONE..................616 454-5089
Dan Huver,
EMP: 6
SQ FT: 14,000
SALES (est): 843.2K Privately Held
WEB: www.michigangeneralgrinding.com
SIC: 3599 Grinding castings for the trade

(G-6673)
MICHIGAN LIGHTNING PROTECTION
2401 O Brien Rd Sw (49534-7009)
PHONE..................616 453-1174
Terrence K Portfleet, *President*
EMP: 5
SALES (est): 718.9K Privately Held
WEB: www.michiganlightning.com
SIC: 3648 Lighting equipment

(G-6674)
MICHIGAN PATTERN WORKS INC
872 Grandville Ave Sw (49503-5152)
PHONE..................616 245-9259
Randy Toppel, *President*
Gary Rauser, *Treasurer*
Mary Kay Toppel, *Office Mgr*
EMP: 20 EST: 1945
SQ FT: 10,500
SALES (est): 3.3MM Privately Held
SIC: 3543 Industrial patterns

(G-6675)
MICHIGAN PAVING AND MTLS CO
1100 Market Ave Sw (49503-4837)
PHONE..................616 459-9545
Dave Wilson, *Branch Mgr*
Asphalt Sealcoating, *Products*
EMP: 40
SALES (corp-wide): 30.6B Privately Held
SIC: 2951 Asphalt paving mixtures & blocks
HQ: Michigan Paving And Materials Company
2575 S Haggerty Rd # 100
Canton MI 48188
734 397-2050

(G-6676)
MICHIGAN TURKEY PRODUCERS
1100 Hall St Sw (49503-4861)
PHONE..................616 245-2221
Brian Boerigter, *Branch Mgr*
EMP: 17

SALES (est): 2.6MM
SALES (corp-wide): 113.3MM Privately Held
WEB: www.miturkey.com
SIC: 2015 Turkey processing & slaughtering
PA: Michigan Turkey Producers Cooperative, Inc.
2140 Chicago Dr Sw
Wyoming MI 49519
616 245-2221

(G-6677)
MICHIGAN WHEEL OPERATIONS LLC (DH)
Also Called: Michigan Wheel Marine
1501 Buchanan Ave Sw (49507-1697)
PHONE..................616 452-6941
Kenneth Creech, *CFO*
Susan Gray, *Cust Mgr*
Stan Heide, *Mng Member*
Nicholas Graham, *Supervisor*
◆ EMP: 41
SQ FT: 157,480
SALES (est): 13.9MM Privately Held
SIC: 3366 3429 3599 Propellers, ship: cast brass; manufactured hardware (general); ties, form: metal

(G-6678)
MICHIGAN WIRE EDM SERVICES
1246 Scribner Ave Nw (49504-3230)
PHONE..................616 742-0940
Khoa Tran, *President*
EMP: 9
SALES (est): 1MM Privately Held
SIC: 3599 Machine shop, jobbing & repair

(G-6679)
MICO INDUSTRIES INC (PA)
2929 32nd St Se Ste 8 (49512-1784)
PHONE..................616 245-6426
Terence Sammon, *CEO*
Henry Visser, *President*
M Christina De La Garza, *Vice Pres*
Chris Nott, *VP Finance*
EMP: 100
SQ FT: 50,000
SALES (est): 26.8MM Privately Held
WEB: www.micoindustries.com
SIC: 3469 7692 3711 Stamping metal for the trade; automotive welding; automobile assembly, including specialty automobiles

(G-6680)
MICO INDUSTRIES INC
2725 Prairie St Sw (49519-2458)
PHONE..................616 245-6426
Bryan Henderson, *Purchasing*
Terence Sammon, *Manager*
EMP: 10
SALES (corp-wide): 26.8MM Privately Held
WEB: www.micoindustries.com
SIC: 3469 Stamping metal for the trade
PA: Mico Industries, Inc.
2929 32nd St Se Ste 8
Grand Rapids MI 49512
616 245-6426

(G-6681)
MICO INDUSTRIES INC
219 Canton St Sw Ste B (49507-1098)
PHONE..................616 514-1143
EMP: 50
SALES (corp-wide): 32.7MM Privately Held
SIC: 3469 Metal Stampings, Nec, Nsk
PA: Mico Industries, Inc.
2929 32nd St Se
Grand Rapids MI 49512
616 245-6426

(G-6682)
MICRON MFG COMPANY
1722 Kloet St Nw (49504-1421)
P.O. Box 141667 (49514-1667)
PHONE..................616 453-5486
Michael Preston, *President*
Jaqueline Preston, *Treasurer*
EMP: 45 EST: 1952
SQ FT: 30,000
SALES (est): 6MM Privately Held
WEB: www.micronmfg.net
SIC: 3599 Machine shop, jobbing & repair

(G-6683)
MID MICHIGAN PIPE INC
977 Ada Place Dr Se Ste A (49546-8412)
P.O. Box 123, Mount Pleasant (48804-0123)
PHONE..................989 772-5664
Doug Darnell, *President*
Donald Campbell, *Vice Pres*
EMP: 7
SQ FT: 6,000
SALES (est): 994.5K Privately Held
WEB: www.mid-michiganpipe.com
SIC: 1623 5051 3544 3441 Pipeline construction; pipe & tubing, steel; special dies & tools; fabricated structural metal; excavation work; snowplowing

(G-6684)
MIDDLETON PRINTING INC
Also Called: Campaign-Stickers.com
200 32nd St Se Ste A (49548-2269)
PHONE..................616 247-8742
Steven Middleton, *President*
EMP: 7 EST: 1956
SQ FT: 14,000
SALES (est): 980.6K Privately Held
WEB: www.tlwsolutions.com
SIC: 2759 2679 Flexographic printing; letterpress printing; tags & labels, paper

(G-6685)
MIDWEST PLATING COMPANY INC
613 North Ave Ne (49503-1695)
PHONE..................616 451-2007
Brian L Wortman, *President*
Beth McCullough, *Corp Secy*
Doug Wortman, *Vice Pres*
Garry Wortman, *VP Opers*
Thomas Wortman, *VP Prdtn*
EMP: 25 EST: 1945
SQ FT: 35,000
SALES (est): 2.8MM Privately Held
WEB: www.midwestplating.com
SIC: 3471 Plating of metals or formed products

(G-6686)
MIDWEST SAFETY PRODUCTS INC
4929 East Paris Ave Se (49512-5351)
PHONE..................616 554-5155
Banah Miller, *President*
Kurt Solomon, *Vice Pres*
Matthew Motta, *Purch Mgr*
Alli Beggs, *Buyer*
Theresa Wheeler, *Purchasing*
EMP: 25
SQ FT: 40,000
SALES (est): 9.7MM Privately Held
WEB: www.midwestsafety.com
SIC: 5099 3993 Safety equipment & supplies; signs & advertising specialties

(G-6687)
MIDWEST SEATING SOLUTIONS INC
2234 Burning Tree Dr Se (49546-5513)
P.O. Box 6159 (49516-6159)
PHONE..................616 222-0636
Jon Reed, *Principal*
EMP: 10
SALES (est): 1MM Privately Held
SIC: 2531 Stadium seating

(G-6688)
MIEN COMPANY INC
2547 3 Mile Rd Nw Ste F (49534-1358)
PHONE..................616 818-1970
Johan Bergsma, *President*
Jacob Vanderlaan, *Principal*
Jason Deweerd, *Vice Pres*
Donna Rice, *Sales Staff*
Lacey Steward, *Sales Staff*
▲ EMP: 13
SALES (est): 2MM Privately Held
SIC: 2511 Wood household furniture

(G-6689)
MII DISPOSITION INC
4717 Talon Ct Se (49512-5408)
PHONE..................616 554-9696
Joseph Baldwin, *President*
Angie Kulesza, *General Mgr*
Eric Hadesh, *Sls & Mktg Exec*

EMP: 20 EST: 1964
SQ FT: 20,000
SALES (est): 3.8MM Privately Held
WEB: www.michiganinstruments.com
SIC: 3845 3842 Electromedical equipment; surgical appliances & supplies

(G-6690)
MILL STEEL CO (PA)
Also Called: Mill Steel Company
2905 Lucerne Dr Se # 100 (49546-7160)
PHONE..................616 949-6700
David Samrick, *Ch of Bd*
Pam Heglund, *President*
Joe Poot, *Senior VP*
George Crone, *Plant Supt*
Melvin Weldon, *Plant Supt*
EMP: 60
SALES (est): 270.8MM Privately Held
WEB: www.millsteel.com
SIC: 5051 3312 Ferrous metals; blast furnaces & steel mills

(G-6691)
MITTEN BREWING COMPANY LLC
527 Leonard St Nw (49504-4278)
PHONE..................616 608-5612
James Yarbrough, *Principal*
EMP: 9 EST: 2012
SALES (est): 931.1K Privately Held
SIC: 2082 Malt beverages

(G-6692)
MIX STREET
1328 Burton St Se (49507-3304)
PHONE..................616 241-6550
Hai Doan, *Administration*
EMP: 5 EST: 2007
SALES (est): 382.1K Privately Held
SIC: 3273 Ready-mixed concrete

(G-6693)
MOBILE OFFICE VEHICLE INC
Also Called: Go Office.com
4053 Brockton Dr Se Ste A (49512-4071)
PHONE..................616 971-0080
Charles E Lippert, *President*
◆ EMP: 4
SQ FT: 10,000
SALES (est): 57.5K Privately Held
WEB: www.gooffice.com
SIC: 2522 Office furniture, except wood

(G-6694)
MOD SIGNS INC
Also Called: Postema Signs & Graphics
7475 Division Ave S (49548-7137)
PHONE..................616 455-0260
Olga Dubois, *President*
EMP: 11
SALES (est): 347.5K Privately Held
SIC: 3993 Signs & advertising specialties

(G-6695)
MOELLER MFG COMPANY LLC
Also Called: Moeller Manufacturing Co
3757 Broadmoor Ave Se (49512-3908)
PHONE..................616 285-5012
Kevin Atkinson, *President*
EMP: 3
SALES (corp-wide): 255.7MM Privately Held
SIC: 3724 Turbines, aircraft type
HQ: Moeller Mfg. Company, Llc
30100 Beck Rd
Wixom MI 48393
248 960-3999

(G-6696)
MOL BELTING SYSTEMS INC
Also Called: Mol Belting Company
2532 Waldorf Ct Nw (49544-1478)
P.O. Box 141095 (49514-1095)
PHONE..................616 453-2484
Edward Mol, *President*
David Hathaway, *Vice Pres*
Dan Mol, *Vice Pres*
Tim Jousma, *Engineer*
Jim Anderson, *Sales Staff*
▲ EMP: 75
SQ FT: 52,000

Grand Rapids - Kent County (G-6697) — GEOGRAPHIC SECTION

SALES (est): 15.8MM **Privately Held**
WEB: www.molindustries.com
SIC: 3052 3535 3446 Rubber belting; conveyors & conveying equipment; architectural metalwork

(G-6697)
MOLD TOOLING SYSTEMS INC
2972 Wilson Dr Nw (49534-7564)
PHONE 616 735-6653
Daniel Jay Vanenk, *President*
Drew Boersma, *Vice Pres*
EMP: 10
SQ FT: 16,300
SALES (est): 1.3MM **Privately Held**
SIC: 3544 Special dies & tools

(G-6698)
MOLLERS NORTH AMERICA INC
5215 52nd St Se (49512-9702)
P.O. Box 888820 (49588-8820)
PHONE 616 942-6504
Thomas Wagner, *Exec VP*
Tom Wagner, *Exec VP*
Peter Engelhardt, *Admin Sec*
▲ **EMP:** 65 **EST:** 1978
SQ FT: 100,000
SALES: 25MM
SALES (corp-wide): 355.8K **Privately Held**
WEB: www.mollersna.com
SIC: 3537 7389 Palletizers & depalletizers; packaging & labeling services
PA: Birkenfeld Holding Gmbh
 Sudhoferweg 93
 Beckum
 252 188-0

(G-6699)
MONARCH METAL MFG INC
3303 Union Ave Se (49548-2311)
PHONE 616 247-0412
Gordon Sironen, *President*
Jane Sironen, *Vice Pres*
EMP: 6
SQ FT: 5,500
SALES: 600K **Privately Held**
SIC: 3444 Sheet metalwork

(G-6700)
MONDRELLA PROCESS SYSTEMS LLC
2049 Innwood Dr Se (49508-5078)
PHONE 616 281-9836
Michael J Mondrella, *Administration*
EMP: 4
SALES (est): 411.2K **Privately Held**
SIC: 3535 Conveyors & conveying equipment

(G-6701)
MONOCO INC
351 Ney Ave Sw (49503-4043)
P.O. Box 3226 (49501-3226)
PHONE 616 459-9800
Scott Hanisch, *President*
EMP: 4 **EST:** 1961
SQ FT: 10,000
SALES (est): 650K **Privately Held**
WEB: www.monoco.com
SIC: 3644 Insulators & insulation materials, electrical

(G-6702)
MONROE LLC
4490 44th St Se Ste A (49512-4064)
PHONE 616 942-9820
Norm Day, *Opers Mgr*
Chris Blanker,
EMP: 285
SALES (est): 59.5MM **Privately Held**
SIC: 3089 3542 3544 Molding primary plastic; machine tools, metal forming type; special dies, tools, jigs & fixtures

(G-6703)
MONROE INC
4490 44th St Se Ste A (49512-4064)
PHONE 616 284-3358
EMP: 7
SALES (est): 951.1K **Privately Held**
SIC: 3089 Injection molding of plastics

(G-6704)
MOONLIGHT GRAPHICS INC
3144 Broadmoor Ave Se (49512-1845)
PHONE 616 243-3166
Paul J Block, *President*
EMP: 6
SQ FT: 3,500
SALES (est): 590K **Privately Held**
WEB: www.moonlight-graphics.com
SIC: 2759 Commercial printing

(G-6705)
MOONPEACE
615 Parkwood St Ne (49503-3413)
PHONE 616 456-1128
Greg Stuart, *Owner*
EMP: 3
SALES (est): 173.5K **Privately Held**
SIC: 2759 Calendars: printing

(G-6706)
MOORECO INC
Also Called: Vanerum Stelter
549 Ionia Ave Sw (49503-5138)
PHONE 616 451-7800
EMP: 25 **Privately Held**
SIC: 2521 2522 5021 Manufactures Wood Office Furniture Office Furniture-Nonwood Wholesales Furniture
HQ: Mooreco, Inc.
 2885 Lorraine Ave
 Temple TX 76501

(G-6707)
MOSS AUDIO CORPORATION
Also Called: Moss Telecommunications Svcs
561 Century Ave Sw (49503-4903)
PHONE 616 451-9933
Jerry Schaefer, *CEO*
Gerard J Schaefer, *President*
Jeff Schaefer, *Opers Mgr*
Chris Lipka, *CFO*
Dave Taylor, *Sales Engr*
EMP: 65 **EST:** 1977
SQ FT: 16,000
SALES: 15MM **Privately Held**
WEB: www.mosstele.com
SIC: 3651 Speaker systems

(G-6708)
MPD WELDING - GRAND RAPIDS INC
Also Called: Fire-Kote
1903 Clyde Park Ave Sw (49509-1592)
P.O. Box 9341 (49509-0341)
PHONE 616 248-9353
David Sinquefield, *President*
Ryan A Stambaugh, *Corp Secy*
EMP: 29
SQ FT: 30,000
SALES (est): 2.2MM **Privately Held**
WEB: www.firekote.com
SIC: 7692 3398 Welding repair; metal heat treating

(G-6709)
MULTI TECH PRECISION INC
3403 Lousma Dr Se (49548-2265)
PHONE 616 514-1415
Steve Steketee, *President*
EMP: 5
SQ FT: 15,000
SALES (est): 590.2K **Privately Held**
SIC: 3599 Machine shop, jobbing & repair

(G-6710)
N-K MANUFACTURING TECH LLC (PA)
1134 Freeman Ave Sw (49503-4816)
PHONE 616 248-3200
Austin Sikes, *Warehouse Mgr*
Rachel Miles, *Purchasing*
Saumil Joshi, *Project Engr*
Bonnie Kettner, *Controller*
Armen Kassouni, *Sales Executive*
▲ **EMP:** 38
SQ FT: 75,000
SALES (est): 14.2MM **Privately Held**
WEB: www.nkmfgtech.com
SIC: 3089 Injection molding of plastics

(G-6711)
N-K SEALING TECHNOLOGIES LLC (PA)
Also Called: Caldwell Gasket Company
1134 Freeman Ave Sw (49503-4816)
PHONE 616 248-3200
Bonnie Kettner, *Comptroller*
Haig Kassouni,
Armen Kassouni,
EMP: 6
SQ FT: 15,000
SALES (est): 939.8K **Privately Held**
SIC: 3053 Gaskets & sealing devices

(G-6712)
NATURES SELECT INC (PA)
833 Kenmoor Ave Se Ste D (49546-2390)
PHONE 616 956-1105
Peter Assaly, *President*
EMP: 4
SQ FT: 120
SALES (est): 332K **Privately Held**
SIC: 2099 Food preparations

(G-6713)
NELSONITE CHEMICAL PRODUCTS
2320 Oak Industrial Dr Ne (49505-6018)
PHONE 616 456-7098
Daniel Conway, *President*
Linda Conway, *Vice Pres*
EMP: 4
SQ FT: 8,000
SALES (est): 515.4K
SALES (corp-wide): 750K **Privately Held**
WEB: www.conwaycleveland.com
SIC: 2819 2899 Chemicals, high purity: refined from technical grade; chemical preparations
PA: Conway-Cleveland Corp
 2320 Oak Industrial Dr Ne
 Grand Rapids MI 49505
 616 458-0056

(G-6714)
NEPTUNE CHEMICAL PUMP COMPANY (HQ)
Also Called: Neptune Mixer
1809 Century Ave Sw (49503-8017)
PHONE 215 699-8700
Michael Dowse, *CEO*
Sivasankaran Somasundaram, *President*
William Barton, *Corp Secy*
John Allen, *Vice Pres*
▲ **EMP:** 128
SALES (est): 32.6MM
SALES (corp-wide): 6.9B **Publicly Held**
WEB: www.neptune1.com
SIC: 3561 3586 Industrial pumps & parts; measuring & dispensing pumps
PA: Dover Corporation
 3005 Highland Pkwy # 200
 Downers Grove IL 60515
 630 541-1540

(G-6715)
NEW 9 INC
Also Called: G W I Engineering Division
1411 Michigan St Ne (49503-2005)
PHONE 616 459-8274
Peter Cordes, *President*
Mark Blanding, *Vice Pres*
Christopher Cordes, *Vice Pres*
Jerry Coeling, *Chief Engr*
Bruce Gilbert, *Engineer*
EMP: 50 **EST:** 1955
SQ FT: 47,000
SALES (est): 8MM **Privately Held**
WEB: www.gwiengineering.com
SIC: 3569 Firefighting apparatus & related equipment

(G-6716)
NEW HOLLAND BREWERY
427 Bridge St Nw (49504-5305)
PHONE 616 202-7200
EMP: 6
SALES (est): 582.6K **Privately Held**
SIC: 2082 Malt beverages

(G-6717)
NOBLE POLYMERS LLC
4855 37th St Se (49512-4068)
P.O. Box 888405 (49588-8405)
PHONE 616 975-4800
Frederick P Keller,
EMP: 17 **EST:** 1997
SALES: 3MM
SALES (corp-wide): 577.9MM **Privately Held**
WEB: www.noblepolymers.com
SIC: 3089 Automotive parts, plastic
PA: Cascade Engineering, Inc.
 3400 Innovation Ct Se
 Grand Rapids MI 49512
 616 975-4800

(G-6718)
NORTEK INC
2547 3 Mile Rd Nw Ste A (49534-1358)
PHONE 616 719-5588
EMP: 3
SALES (corp-wide): 11B **Privately Held**
SIC: 3585 Refrigeration & heating equipment
HQ: Nortek, Inc.
 8000 Phoenix Pkwy
 O Fallon MO 63368
 636 561-7300

(G-6719)
NORTH AMERICA FUEL SYSTEMS R
4232 Brockton Dr Se (49512-4048)
PHONE 616 541-1100
Russ Anthony, *Facilities Mgr*
Stephen Rose, *IT/INT Sup*
Jeff Lecklich,
Jeff Latkiewitz,
EMP: 140
SQ FT: 52,000
SALES (est): 32.4MM
SALES (corp-wide): 191.6B **Privately Held**
WEB: www.detroitdiesel.com
SIC: 3561 Pumps & pumping equipment
HQ: Detroit Diesel Corporation
 13400 W Outer Dr
 Detroit MI 48239
 313 592-5000

(G-6720)
NORTHWEST METAL PRODUCTS INC
Also Called: Transet
2055 Walker Ct Nw (49544-1411)
PHONE 616 453-0556
Mark Scholten, *President*
EMP: 10 **EST:** 1980
SQ FT: 12,500
SALES (est): 1.5MM **Privately Held**
WEB: www.northwestmetalproducts.com
SIC: 3429 Furniture hardware

(G-6721)
NORTHWEST POLISHING & BUFFING
3738 Walker Ave Nw (49544-9705)
PHONE 616 899-2682
Michelle Klein, *President*
EMP: 3 **EST:** 1976
SALES (est): 169.3K **Privately Held**
SIC: 3471 Cleaning, polishing & finishing; buffing for the trade

(G-6722)
NOTIONS MARKETING
1500 Buchanan Ave Sw (49507-1613)
PHONE 616 243-8424
Steve Pietentol, *President*
Tom Nakfoor, *VP Opers*
Chad Bush, *Opers Mgr*
Dean Lantinga, *Facilities Mgr*
Melissa Saganski, *Buyer*
EMP: 500
SALES (est): 56.3K **Privately Held**
SIC: 2284 Hand knitting thread

(G-6723)
NOVARES US LLC
Also Called: Key Plastics
5375 Intl Pkwy Se (49512)
PHONE 616 554-3555
Andrew James, *Manager*
John Choponis, *Maintence Staff*
EMP: 350

GEOGRAPHIC SECTION

Grand Rapids - Kent County (G-6749)

SALES (corp-wide): 102.8MM **Privately Held**
WEB: www.keyplastics.com
SIC: 3089 3714 3085 Injection molded finished plastic products; motor vehicle parts & accessories; plastics bottles
HQ: Novares Us Llc
19575 Victor Pkwy Ste 400
Livonia MI 48152
248 449-6100

(G-6724)
NU TEK SALES
3366 Kraft Ave Se Ste A (49512-3148)
PHONE 616 258-0631
Doug Watkoski, *Owner*
EMP: 10
SALES (est): 1.1MM **Privately Held**
SIC: 3672 Circuit boards, television & radio printed

(G-6725)
NUWAVE TECHNOLOGY PARTNERS LLC
4079 Park East Ct Se A (49546-8815)
PHONE 616 942-7520
Richard Paalman, *Executive*
EMP: 11 **Privately Held**
SIC: 3661 7371 Telephone & telegraph apparatus; custom computer programming services
PA: Nuwave Technology Partners, Llc
5268 Azo Dr
Kalamazoo MI 49048

(G-6726)
OBRIEN HARRIS WOODWORKS LLC
1125 41st St Se Ste A (49507)
PHONE 616 248-0779
Stephen Chausow, *Mng Member*
EMP: 25
SQ FT: 33,000
SALES (est): 688K **Privately Held**
SIC: 2434 Wood kitchen cabinets

(G-6727)
OCUSANO INC
600 Union Ave Se 1 (49503-5428)
PHONE 734 730-5407
EMP: 3
SALES (est): 214.6K **Privately Held**
SIC: 2834 Mfg Pharmaceutical Preparations

(G-6728)
OLIVER PRODUCTS COMPANY (HQ)
Also Called: Oliver Healthcare Packaging
445 6th St Nw (49504-5298)
PHONE 616 456-7711
Mike Benevento, *President*
Julian Benavides, *Regional Mgr*
Temple Phipps, *Business Mgr*
John Sullivan, *Business Mgr*
Phil Kaufman, *Plant Mgr*
EMP: 89
SALES (est): 292.5MM
SALES (corp-wide): 2.9B **Privately Held**
SIC: 5084 5199 3053 Processing & packaging equipment; packaging materials; packing materials
PA: Berwind Corporation
3000 Ctr Sq W 1500 Mkt St 1500 W
Philadelphia PA 19102
215 563-2800

(G-6729)
OMEGA INDUSTRIES MICHIGAN LLC
3744 Linden Ave Se (49548-3428)
P.O. Box 818, Rockford (49341-0818)
PHONE 616 460-0500
Lori Maher, *Mng Member*
Jeff Twyman,
EMP: 5
SALES: 800K **Privately Held**
SIC: 5085 3559 5075 Filters, industrial; metal finishing equipment for plating, etc.; air filters

(G-6730)
ONE BEER AT A TIME LLC
Also Called: Brewery Vivant
925 Cherry St Se Ste 1-2 (49506-1403)
PHONE 616 719-1604
Brooks Twist, *Opers Staff*
Jason Spaulding, *Mng Member*
EMP: 45
SQ FT: 9,000
SALES (est): 2MM **Privately Held**
SIC: 5921 2082 Beer (packaged); brewers' grain

(G-6731)
ONION CROCK OF MICHIGAN INC
1221 Mcreynolds Ave Nw (49504-3116)
PHONE 616 458-2922
Eugene Lacroix, *President*
EMP: 4
SALES (est): 250K **Privately Held**
SIC: 2032 2099 Soups & broths: canned, jarred, etc.; sauces: gravy, dressing & dip mixes

(G-6732)
OPERATOR SPECIALTY COMPANY INC
Also Called: Osco
2547 3 Mile Rd Nw (49534-1358)
PHONE 616 675-5050
William Hildebrand, *President*
▲ **EMP:** 54 **EST:** 1975
SQ FT: 25,000
SALES (est): 13.2MM
SALES (corp-wide): 11B **Privately Held**
WEB: www.operatorspecialty.com
SIC: 3699 Door opening & closing devices, electrical
HQ: Nortek Security & Control Llc
5919 Sea Otter Pl Ste 100
Carlsbad CA 92010
760 438-7000

(G-6733)
ORANGEBOX US INC
4595 Broadmoor Ave Se # 120 (49512-5300)
PHONE 616 988-8624
Remo Vernaschi, *Principal*
Kayleigh Bower, *Admin Asst*
EMP: 3
SALES (est): 376.7K
SALES (corp-wide): 3.4B **Publicly Held**
SIC: 2599 Boards: planning, display, notice
HQ: Orangebox Group Limited
Parc Nantgarw
Cardiff S GLAM CF15
144 381-6604

(G-6734)
ORTHOPAEDIC ASSOCIATES MICH (PA)
Also Called: Orthopaedic Associates Mich
4665 44th St Se Ste A190 (49512-4135)
PHONE 616 459-7101
Patrick Reid, *CEO*
Joseph Brown, *Principal*
Kenneth Easton, *Principal*
Paul Schutt, *Principal*
Christa Ebmeyer, *Materials Mgr*
EMP: 80
SQ FT: 19,000
SALES (est): 15.4MM **Privately Held**
WEB: www.injurypros.net
SIC: 8011 3842 Orthopedic physician; surgeon; surgical appliances & supplies

(G-6735)
OTTAWA TOOL & MACHINE LLC
2188 Leonard St Nw (49534-9514)
PHONE 616 677-1743
Charles Chambers,
EMP: 4
SALES: 15K **Privately Held**
SIC: 3499 Fabricated metal products

(G-6736)
OUTFRONT MEDIA LLC
Also Called: Outdoor Systems Advertising
1355 Century Ave Sw (49503-8008)
PHONE 616 452-3171
Kelly Duff, *Human Res Dir*
Jeff Campbell, *Accounts Exec*
David Smreker, *Accounts Exec*
Lueida Grady, *Executive*
EMP: 18
SALES (corp-wide): 1.6B **Publicly Held**
SIC: 7312 3993 Outdoor advertising services; signs & advertising specialties
HQ: Outfront Media Llc
405 Lexington Ave Fl 14
New York NY 10174
212 297-6400

(G-6737)
PAC-CNC INC
4045 Remembrance Rd Nw (49534-1109)
PHONE 616 288-3389
Roger Hoogewind, *President*
Randy Hoogewind, *Business Mgr*
EMP: 34
SQ FT: 15,000
SALES: 5.1MM **Privately Held**
WEB: www.paccnc.com
SIC: 3469 Stamping metal for the trade

(G-6738)
PACIFIC EPOXY POLYMERS INC
3450 Charlevoix Dr Se (49546-7054)
PHONE 616 949-1634
Charles E Bennett, *President*
Micky Burnham, *General Mgr*
Gholi Darehshori, *Shareholder*
EMP: 28
SQ FT: 45,000
SALES (est): 3.4MM **Privately Held**
SIC: 2821 2851 Epoxy resins; paints & allied products

(G-6739)
PADNOS LEITELT INC
Also Called: Leitelt Iron Works
2301 Turner Ave Nw (49544-2002)
PHONE 616 363-3817
Douglas Kesler, *Principal*
Francis Abrahams, *Vice Pres*
Joe Brechting, *Vice Pres*
Eda Lynn Sandstorm, *Manager*
EMP: 15 **EST:** 1862
SQ FT: 90,000
SALES (est): 1.9MM
SALES (corp-wide): 520.8MM **Privately Held**
WEB: www.leitelt.com
SIC: 7699 3599 5051 Industrial machinery & equipment repair; machine shop, jobbing & repair; steel
PA: Louis Padnos Iron And Metal Company
185 W 8th St
Holland MI 49423
616 396-6521

(G-6740)
PALADIN IND INC
4990 W Greenbrooke Dr Se (49512-5400)
PHONE 616 698-7495
Larry E Bell, *CEO*
Craig C Bell, *President*
Thad Bell, *Vice Pres*
Barbara Bell, *Admin Mgr*
Barbara R Bell, *Admin Sec*
EMP: 30
SQ FT: 54,000
SALES (est): 6.4MM **Privately Held**
WEB: www.paladinind.com
SIC: 2599 2521 Factory furniture & fixtures; wood office furniture

(G-6741)
PARAGON DIE & ENGINEERING CO (PA)
Also Called: Paragon D&E
5225 33rd St Se (49512-2071)
PHONE 616 949-2220
Dave Muir, *CEO*
Jon Hamming, *General Mgr*
Chad Burger, *Project Mgr*
Michael Stephens, *QC Mgr*
Ryan James, *Engineer*
▲ **EMP:** 154 **EST:** 1954
SQ FT: 180,000
SALES (est): 32.3MM **Privately Held**
WEB: www.paragondie.com
SIC: 3544 Special dies & tools

(G-6742)
PARKER ENGINEERING AND MFG CO
11 N Park St Nw (49544-6932)
PHONE 616 784-6500
Douglas Parker, *President*
Linda Parker, *Vice Pres*
EMP: 7
SQ FT: 40,000
SALES (est): 600K **Privately Held**
WEB: www.slugbuster.com
SIC: 3699 Electronic training devices

(G-6743)
PARKER TOOLING & DESIGN INC
Also Called: Vacuum Farm Tools
2563 3 Mile Rd Nw (49534-1313)
PHONE 616 791-1080
John Ervine, *President*
EMP: 15
SQ FT: 10,000
SALES (est): 2.1MM **Privately Held**
WEB: www.parkertooling.net
SIC: 7692 3544 3543 Welding repair; special dies, tools, jigs & fixtures; industrial patterns

(G-6744)
PATRIOT SOLUTIONS LLC
525 Ottawa Ave Nw Lvl (49503-1403)
PHONE 616 240-8164
Chad Boersma, *President*
Jon Tellier, *Vice Pres*
EMP: 4
SALES (est): 622.7K **Privately Held**
SIC: 2653 Boxes, corrugated: made from purchased materials

(G-6745)
PAZZEL INC
100 Stevens St Sw (49507-1526)
PHONE 616 291-0257
Aaron Vandergalien, *President*
Joshua Conran, *Admin Sec*
EMP: 9
SQ FT: 7,000
SALES (est): 850K **Privately Held**
SIC: 2434 2521 2517 Wood kitchen cabinets; cabinets, office: wood; wood television & radio cabinets

(G-6746)
PEISELER LLC
601 Crosby St Nw (49504-3104)
PHONE 616 235-8460
Ronald Kwiatkowski, *General Mgr*
▲ **EMP:** 5
SALES (est): 681.6K **Privately Held**
WEB: www.peiseler.com
SIC: 3541 Machine tools, metal cutting type

(G-6747)
PEPSI-COLA METRO BTLG CO INC
3700 Kraft Ave Se (49512-0704)
PHONE 616 285-8200
Will Warren, *Manager*
EMP: 100
SALES (corp-wide): 64.6B **Publicly Held**
WEB: www.joy-of-cola.com
SIC: 2086 4225 5149 Carbonated soft drinks, bottled & canned; general warehousing; groceries & related products
HQ: Pepsi-Cola Metropolitan Bottling Company, Inc.
1111 Westchester Ave
White Plains NY 10604
914 767-6000

(G-6748)
PERFECTED GRAVE VAULT CO
2500 3 Mile Rd Nw (49534-1314)
PHONE 616 243-3375
Kenneth Kornoelje Jr, *President*
EMP: 7 **EST:** 1921
SQ FT: 15,000
SALES (est): 1.1MM **Privately Held**
SIC: 3559 3272 Parking facility equipment & supplies; grave markers, concrete

(G-6749)
PERFORMANCE SYSTEMATIX INC (PA)
5569 33rd St Se (49512-2061)
PHONE 616 949-9090
Karlis Vizulis, *CEO*
Glenn Dunn, *President*
Metra Krautmanis, *Vice Pres*

Grand Rapids - Kent County (G-6750) GEOGRAPHIC SECTION

Wayne Bolle, *Supervisor*
◆ **EMP:** 60
SQ FT: 64,000
SALES: 20MM **Privately Held**
WEB: www.psix.com
SIC: 3089 3841 Plastic containers, except foam; plastic hardware & building products; surgical & medical instruments

(G-6750)
PERFORMNCE DCUTTING FINSHG LLC
955 Godfrey Ave Sw (49503-5003)
PHONE..................................616 245-3636
Wayne Vanderlaan, *Administration*
EMP: 4
SALES (est): 353.4K **Privately Held**
SIC: 3423 Cutting dies, except metal cutting

(G-6751)
PERRIGO PRINTING INC
125 Ottawa Ave Nw Ste 160 (49503-2898)
PHONE..................................616 454-6761
P Richard Perrigo, *President*
Nicolas Ford, *Director*
EMP: 4
SQ FT: 985
SALES (est): 500K **Privately Held**
SIC: 2752 Commercial printing, offset

(G-6752)
PET SUPPLIES PLUS
6159 Kalamazoo Ave Se (49508-7805)
PHONE..................................616 554-3600
Steve Adams, *Owner*
Mike Klothe, *Owner*
EMP: 16
SALES (est): 772.6K **Privately Held**
SIC: 5999 3999 Pets & pet supplies; pet supplies

(G-6753)
PHASE III GRAPHICS INC (PA)
255 Colrain St Sw Ste 1 (49548-1057)
PHONE..................................616 949-9290
Jeffrey Veine, *President*
Janet Veine, *Vice Pres*
EMP: 6
SALES (est): 622.1K **Privately Held**
WEB: www.phase3graphics.com
SIC: 2752 2791 2789 Commercial printing, offset; typesetting; bookbinding & related work

(G-6754)
PHIL ELENBAAS MILLWORK INC (PA)
3000 Wilson Dr Nw (49534-7564)
PHONE..................................616 791-1616
Ben Elenbaas, *President*
EMP: 28
SQ FT: 10,000
SALES (est): 3.1MM **Privately Held**
WEB: www.elenbaasmillwork.com
SIC: 2431 5211 Moldings, wood: unfinished & prefinished; millwork & lumber

(G-6755)
PIONEER MOLDED PRODUCTS INC
5505 52nd St Se (49512-9700)
PHONE..................................616 977-4172
John McCarthy, *Ch of Bd*
Derrick McCarthy, *President*
▲ **EMP:** 45
SALES (est): 12.7MM **Privately Held**
SIC: 3089 Injection molding of plastics

(G-6756)
PLASTIC MOLD TECHNOLOGY INC
Also Called: Woldering Plastic Mold Tech
3870 Model Ct Se (49512-3938)
PHONE..................................616 698-9810
Gary Proos, *Owner*
EMP: 4
SALES (corp-wide): 14.2MM **Privately Held**
WEB: www.plasticmold.com
SIC: 3089 3544 Injection molding of plastics; special dies, tools, jigs & fixtures

PA: Plastic Mold Technology, Inc.
4201 Broadmoor Ave Se
Kentwood MI 49512
616 698-9810

(G-6757)
PLASTIC PLATE LLC (HQ)
3500 Raleigh Dr Se (49512-2064)
PHONE..................................616 455-5240
Richard Lacks Jr, *President*
Anthony Riley, *Engineer*
Brian Cavanaugh, *Executive*
EMP: 50
SQ FT: 35,000
SALES (est): 24.9MM
SALES (corp-wide): 715.6MM **Privately Held**
SIC: 3714 Motor vehicle parts & accessories
PA: Lacks Enterprises, Inc.
5460 Cascade Rd Se
Grand Rapids MI 49546
616 949-6570

(G-6758)
PLASTIC-PLATE INC
5460 Cascade Rd Se (49546-6406)
PHONE..................................616 698-2030
Richard Lacks, *Principal*
Jeff Chiu, *Business Mgr*
Tom Hawkins, *Engineer*
Dennis Lang, *Maintence Staff*
EMP: 18
SALES (est): 3.8MM **Privately Held**
SIC: 3544 Forms (molds), for foundry & plastics working machinery

(G-6759)
POSITECH INC
4134 36th St Se (49512-2903)
P.O. Box 888250 (49588-8250)
PHONE..................................616 949-4024
Charles W Boelkins, *President*
EMP: 6
SQ FT: 8,000
SALES (est): 2MM **Privately Held**
SIC: 3569 Lubrication machinery, automatic

(G-6760)
PRATT INDUSTRIES INC
Also Called: Corrugating Division
2000 Beverly Ave Sw (49519-1719)
PHONE..................................616 452-2111
Jamie Waltermire, *General Mgr*
Lisa Tschoerner-Pete, *Controller*
Stuart Baskin, *Sales Staff*
EMP: 120
SALES (corp-wide): 2.5B **Privately Held**
SIC: 2653 Corrugated & solid fiber boxes
PA: Pratt Industries, Inc.
1800 Sarasot Bus Pkwy Ne C
Conyers GA 30013
770 918-5678

(G-6761)
PRAXAIR INC
1000 Scribner Ave Nw (49504-4212)
PHONE..................................231 796-3266
John Soller, *Branch Mgr*
EMP: 20 **Privately Held**
SIC: 2813 Industrial gases
HQ: Praxair, Inc.
10 Riverview Dr
Danbury CT 06810
203 837-2000

(G-6762)
PRAXAIR DISTRIBUTION INC
1000 Scribner Ave Nw (49504-4212)
PHONE..................................616 451-3055
Tom Chambers, *Branch Mgr*
EMP: 20 **Privately Held**
SIC: 2813 5084 5999 Carbon dioxide; dry ice, carbon dioxide (solid); oxygen, compressed or liquefied; welding machinery & equipment; welding supplies
HQ: Praxair Distribution, Inc.
10 Riverview Dr
Danbury CT 06810
203 837-2000

(G-6763)
PRECISE CNC ROUTING INC
2605 Thornwood St Sw A (49519-2179)
PHONE..................................616 538-8608

Richard Lemson, *President*
Laura Lemson, *Corp Secy*
EMP: 20
SQ FT: 66,000
SALES (est): 4.9MM **Privately Held**
SIC: 3545 Precision tools, machinists'

(G-6764)
PRECISION AEROSPACE CORP
5300 Corporate Grv (49512-5514)
PHONE..................................616 243-8112
William R Hoyer, *President*
Roger Heyboer, *Vice Pres*
Michael Banachowski, *Project Engr*
Stacey Schichtel, *Technician*
EMP: 158 **EST:** 1966
SQ FT: 80,000
SALES (est): 44.1MM
SALES (corp-wide): 56.9MM **Privately Held**
WEB: www.precision-aerospace.com
SIC: 3599 Machine shop, jobbing & repair
PA: Tribus Aerospace Llc
10 S Wacker Dr Ste 3300
Chicago IL 60606
312 876-7267

(G-6765)
PRECISION FINISHING CO INC
1010 Chicago Dr Sw (49509-1199)
PHONE..................................616 245-2255
Bruno Unzens, *President*
EMP: 25 **EST:** 1967
SQ FT: 10,000
SALES (est): 3MM **Privately Held**
WEB: www.precisionfinishing.com
SIC: 3471 Finishing, metals or formed products

(G-6766)
PRECISION WIRE EDM SERVICE
3180 3 Mile Rd Nw (49534-1326)
PHONE..................................616 453-4360
Frank Kruzel, *President*
EMP: 12
SQ FT: 12,000
SALES (est): 1.9MM **Privately Held**
SIC: 3599 Machine shop, jobbing & repair

(G-6767)
PREGIS LLC
Also Called: Pregis Film
1100 Hynes Ave Sw Ste B (49507-1084)
PHONE..................................616 520-1550
Travis Stick, *Manager*
EMP: 12
SALES (corp-wide): 4.7B **Privately Held**
SIC: 3086 Packaging & shipping materials, foamed plastic
HQ: Pregis Llc
1650 Lake Cook Rd Ste 400
Deerfield IL 60015
847 597-2200

(G-6768)
PREMIER FINISHING INC
3180 Fruit Ridge Ave Nw (49544-9707)
PHONE..................................616 785-3070
Andy Ribbens, *President*
Carin Ribbens, *Vice Pres*
Josh Ribbens, *Exec Dir*
EMP: 20
SQ FT: 22,000
SALES (est): 1.9MM **Privately Held**
WEB: www.premierfinishing.com
SIC: 3471 Plating & polishing

(G-6769)
PREMIER SOFTWARE INC
Also Called: Premier Software Systems
3501 Lake Dr Se Ste 140 (49546-4339)
PHONE..................................616 940-8601
Robert Baerens, *President*
EMP: 3
SALES (est): 241K **Privately Held**
SIC: 7372 Prepackaged software

(G-6770)
PRESSURE RELEASES CORPORATION (PA)
Also Called: Status Transportation
2035 Porter St Sw (49519-2271)
PHONE..................................616 531-8116
Len Collins, *President*
Daniel R Collins, *Senior VP*
Priscilla Elaine Myers, *VP Mktg*

EMP: 10
SALES (est): 1.4MM **Privately Held**
SIC: 4212 2721 Delivery service, vehicular; periodicals: publishing only

(G-6771)
PRESTIGE PRINTING INC
4437 Eastern Ave Se Ste 1 (49508-7530)
PHONE..................................616 532-5133
Fax: 616 532-1128
EMP: 6
SALES (est): 300K **Privately Held**
SIC: 2752 Lithographic Commercial Printing Service

(G-6772)
PRESTO PRINT INC
3409 Plainfield Ave Ne (49525-2716)
PHONE..................................616 364-7132
Carroll Cook, *President*
Pam Olsen, *Vice Pres*
Pamela K Olson, *Vice Pres*
EMP: 10
SQ FT: 2,000
SALES (est): 1.6MM **Privately Held**
WEB: www.prestoprintinc.com
SIC: 2752 Commercial printing, offset

(G-6773)
PREUSSER JEWELERS
125 Ottawa Ave Nw Ste 195 (49503-2840)
PHONE..................................616 458-1425
David H Kammeraad, *President*
Sharon Straight, *Accountant*
EMP: 8
SQ FT: 2,300
SALES (est): 1.1MM **Privately Held**
WEB: www.preusserjewelers.com
SIC: 5944 7631 3961 Jewelry, precious stones & precious metals; watches; silverware; watch repair; jewelry repair services; costume jewelry

(G-6774)
PRIDGEON & CLAY INC (PA)
50 Cottage Grove St Sw (49507-1685)
PHONE..................................616 241-5675
Robert Edwin Clay, *Ch of Bd*
Lou Kocsondy, *President*
Donald C Clay, *Principal*
Rick Martin, *Vice Pres*
Bill McKibben, *Vice Pres*
▲ **EMP:** 575
SQ FT: 285,000
SALES (est): 180.7MM **Privately Held**
WEB: www.pridgeonandclay.com
SIC: 3714 3465 Motor vehicle parts & accessories; automotive stampings

(G-6775)
PRIME PRODUCTS INC
2755 Remico St Sw (49519-2494)
PHONE..................................616 531-8970
James Mc Kenzie, *President*
Chrissie Jacobs, *QC Mgr*
Jj McKenzie, *VP Sales*
Amanda Miner, *Cust Mgr*
EMP: 40
SQ FT: 17,000
SALES (est): 6.9MM **Privately Held**
WEB: www.primeproductsinc.com
SIC: 3728 Aircraft parts & equipment

(G-6776)
PRINTING CONSOLIDATION CO LLC (PA)
190 Monroe Ave Nw Ste 600 (49503-2628)
PHONE..................................616 233-3161
Aaron Day, *CEO*
John Ruther, *CFO*
EMP: 3
SALES (est): 5.6MM **Privately Held**
SIC: 2759 Commercial printing

(G-6777)
PRINTING PRODUCTIONS INK
3852 44th St Se (49512-3944)
PHONE..................................616 871-9292
Shawn Wylie, *President*
Sandy Frazier,
EMP: 5
SQ FT: 1,900
SALES: 125K **Privately Held**
SIC: 2752 Commercial printing, offset

Grand Rapids - Kent County (G-6805)

(G-6778)
PRISTINE GLASS COMPANY
647 Ottawa Ave Nw (49503-1426)
PHONE..................................616 454-2092
Thomas Blackburn, *President*
John Vanderweele, *Vice Pres*
L Craig Davis, *Admin Sec*
EMP: 7 **EST:** 1979
SQ FT: 3,000
SALES: 400K **Privately Held**
SIC: 7699 3231 China & glass repair; ornamental glass: cut, engraved or otherwise decorated

(G-6779)
PRO SEALANTS
3683 Maplebrook Dr Nw (49534-2709)
PHONE..................................616 318-6067
Jason Hendricks, *President*
EMP: 3
SALES (est): 196.3K **Privately Held**
SIC: 2891 Sealants

(G-6780)
PRO STAMP PLUS LLC
1988 Alpine Ave Nw (49504-2808)
PHONE..................................616 447-2988
Shawn Tilstra, *General Mgr*
Sally Moyers, *QC Mgr*
Clark Schuiteman,
EMP: 8
SALES (est): 1.2MM **Privately Held**
SIC: 3469 Metal stampings

(G-6781)
PRO-FINISH POWDER COATING INC
1000 Kn O Sha Indus Dr Se (49508)
PHONE..................................616 245-7550
Jeff Hutchinson, *Principal*
EMP: 30
SQ FT: 17,000
SALES (est): 3.1MM **Privately Held**
WEB: www.pro-finish.net
SIC: 3479 Coating of metals & formed products

(G-6782)
PROFESSIONAL FABRICATING INC
Also Called: Professional Fabricating & Mfg
902 47th St Sw Ste A (49509-5143)
PHONE..................................616 531-1240
John Moran, *President*
Mandy Walston, *Purch Agent*
Mark Postiech, *CFO*
EMP: 35
SQ FT: 20,000
SALES (est): 8.5MM **Privately Held**
WEB: www.profabgr.com
SIC: 3444 Sheet metal specialties, not stamped

(G-6783)
PROFESSIONAL METAL FINISHERS
2474 Turner Ave Nw Ste 4 (49544-2060)
PHONE..................................616 365-2620
Bepsy Boss, *President*
EMP: 15
SQ FT: 10,000
SALES (est): 2MM **Privately Held**
SIC: 3471 Anodizing (plating) of metals or formed products; electroplating of metals or formed products

(G-6784)
PROFICIENT MACHINING INC
3455 3 Mile Rd Nw (49534-1227)
PHONE..................................616 453-9496
Lawrence Rozendaal, *President*
Kristie Rozenbaal, *Vice Pres*
Lawrence R Rozendaal, *Purch Mgr*
EMP: 12
SALES (est): 2.5MM **Privately Held**
SIC: 3599 Machine shop, jobbing & repair

(G-6785)
PROFILE INDUSTRIAL PACKG CORP
Also Called: Profile Films
1976 Avastar Pkwy Nw (49544-1936)
PHONE..................................616 245-7260
Steve Ehmann, *President*
Jennifer B Coffman, *Vice Pres*
Brian Hoeksema, *Vice Pres*
Jesse Flegel, *Maintence Staff*
EMP: 150
SQ FT: 100,000
SALES (est): 70.5MM **Privately Held**
WEB: www.profilefilms.com
SIC: 3081 Polyethylene film

(G-6786)
PROGRESSIVE SURFACE INC (PA)
4695 Danvers Dr Se (49512-4077)
PHONE..................................616 957-0871
Lewis Van Kuiken, *President*
Gerald Molitor, *Vice Pres*
James Whalen, *Vice Pres*
Jill Machuta, *Accountant*
▼ **EMP:** 52 **EST:** 1967
SQ FT: 80,500
SALES (est): 17MM **Privately Held**
WEB: www.ptihome.com
SIC: 3569 7699 Blast cleaning equipment, dustless; industrial machinery & equipment repair

(G-6787)
PROGRESSIVE SURFACE INC
4671 Danvers Dr Se (49512-4018)
PHONE..................................616 957-0871
Lewis Van Kuiken, *President*
EMP: 21
SALES (corp-wide): 17MM **Privately Held**
SIC: 3569 7699 Blast cleaning equipment, dustless; industrial machinery & equipment repair
PA: Progressive Surface, Inc.
   4695 Danvers Dr Se
   Grand Rapids MI 49512
   616 957-0871

(G-6788)
PROJECT DIE AND MOLD INC
228 Wesley St Se (49548-1258)
PHONE..................................616 862-8689
Scott Garber, *President*
EMP: 6
SALES (est): 739.4K **Privately Held**
SIC: 3544 Industrial molds

(G-6789)
PRONG HORN
Also Called: Pronghorn Imprinting Co
6757 Cascade Rd Se # 164 (49546-6849)
PHONE..................................616 456-1903
David Horn, *Owner*
David Prong, *Co-Owner*
EMP: 7
SALES (est): 270K **Privately Held**
SIC: 2261 Screen printing of cotton broadwoven fabrics

(G-6790)
PROOF & UNION LLC
605 Greenwood Ave Se (49506-2912)
PHONE..................................312 919-0191
Brian May,
Eric Teodoro Franco,
Alden Hoksbergen,
EMP: 3
SALES (est): 91.3K **Privately Held**
SIC: 2085 Cordials & premixed alcoholic cocktails; cocktails, alcoholic

(G-6791)
PROOS MANUFACTURING INC
Also Called: Office Furniture Accessories
2140 Oak Industrial Dr Ne (49505-6014)
PHONE..................................616 454-5622
Amy Proos, *CEO*
Amy Engelsman, *Principal*
Larry Engelsman, *Vice Pres*
EMP: 62 **EST:** 1919
SQ FT: 66,000
SALES (est): 23.1MM **Privately Held**
SIC: 3469 3949 Stamping metal for the trade; fishing equipment

(G-6792)
PROSPECTORS LLC
Also Called: Prospectors Cold Brew Coffee
5035 W Greenbrooke Dr Se # 2 (49512-5491)
PHONE..................................616 634-8260
David Wentworth, *Principal*
EMP: 3
SALES (est): 342.1K **Privately Held**
SIC: 5046 7389 2095 Coffee brewing equipment & supplies; coffee service; freeze-dried coffee

(G-6793)
PROTO-CAM INC
1009 Ottawa Ave Nw (49503-1407)
PHONE..................................616 454-9810
William Tingley, *President*
Daniel Bradley, *Vice Pres*
EMP: 10
SQ FT: 10,000
SALES: 1MM **Privately Held**
WEB: www.bendtooling.com
SIC: 3599 Machine shop, jobbing & repair

(G-6794)
PRS MANUFACTURING INC
3745 Dykstra Dr Nw (49544-9745)
PHONE..................................616 784-4409
Dennis Kowalczyk, *President*
Chad Kowalczyk, *Vice Pres*
EMP: 7 **EST:** 1961
SQ FT: 8,200
SALES: 850K **Privately Held**
SIC: 3499 3471 Fire- or burglary-resistive products; plating & polishing

(G-6795)
PUMP HOUSE
2090 Celebration Dr Ne # 120 (49525-9200)
PHONE..................................616 647-5481
Karen Avrey, *Owner*
EMP: 4
SALES (est): 203.6K **Privately Held**
SIC: 2024 Ice cream & frozen desserts

(G-6796)
PUMP SOLUTIONS GROUP
Blackmer Pump
1809 Century Ave Sw (49503-8017)
PHONE..................................616 241-1611
Rick Foster, *Engineer*
Clark Naroleski, *Branch Mgr*
Jeff Taft, *Info Tech Mgr*
Dennis Gort, *Technology*
Sydney Aiello, *IT/INT Sup*
EMP: 260
SALES (corp-wide): 6.9B **Publicly Held**
WEB: www.blackmer.com
SIC: 3594 3561 Motors: hydraulic, fluid power or air; pumps & pumping equipment
HQ: Dover Energy, Inc.
   1815 S Meyers Rd
   Oakbrook Terrace IL 60181
   630 487-2240

(G-6797)
PUMP SOLUTIONS GROUP
Also Called: Blackmer System One
1809 Century Ave Sw (49503-8017)
PHONE..................................616 241-1611
Clark Naroleski, *Manager*
EMP: 20
SALES (corp-wide): 6.9B **Publicly Held**
SIC: 3561 Pump jacks & other pumping equipment
HQ: Dover Energy, Inc.
   1815 S Meyers Rd
   Oakbrook Terrace IL 60181
   630 487-2240

(G-6798)
PWV STUDIOS LTD
1650 Broadway Ave Nw (49504-2027)
PHONE..................................616 361-5659
Carol Vsoske, *President*
Paul Vsoske, *Vice Pres*
EMP: 15
SALES (est): 2.3MM
SALES (corp-wide): 74.7MM **Privately Held**
WEB: www.pwvstudios.com
SIC: 2273 Carpets & rugs
PA: Scott Group Custom Carpets, Llc
   3232 Kraft Ave Se Ste A
   Grand Rapids MI 49512
   616 954-3200

(G-6799)
QUALITY METAL FABRICATING
1324 Burke Ave Ne (49505-5543)
PHONE..................................616 901-5510
Ernest Altman, *Principal*
EMP: 4
SALES (est): 425K **Privately Held**
SIC: 3499 Fabricated metal products

(G-6800)
QUALITY MODEL & PATTERN CO
2663 Elmridge Dr Nw (49534-1329)
PHONE..................................616 791-1156
Ed Doyle, *President*
Kristin Adams, *Business Mgr*
Mary Tuttle, *Corp Secy*
Donald Tuttle, *Vice Pres*
EMP: 28
SQ FT: 10,000
SALES (est): 5MM **Privately Held**
SIC: 3543 3544 3354 Foundry patternmaking; special dies, tools, jigs & fixtures; aluminum extruded products

(G-6801)
QUALITY PRINTING & GRAPHICS
Also Called: Abby's Printing
3109 Broadmoor Ave Se (49512-1877)
PHONE..................................616 949-3400
Maher Karadsheh, *President*
EMP: 5
SQ FT: 3,200
SALES: 400K **Privately Held**
WEB: www.abbysprinting.com
SIC: 2752 Commercial printing, offset

(G-6802)
QUICK PRINTING COMPANY INC
2642 Division Ave S (49507-3467)
PHONE..................................616 241-0506
Lori Weyers, *President*
Mark Weyers, *Vice Pres*
EMP: 4
SQ FT: 3,000
SALES (est): 302.5K **Privately Held**
WEB: www.qpco.com
SIC: 2752 2791 Commercial printing, offset; typesetting

(G-6803)
R L ADAMS PLASTICS INC
5955 Crossroads Commerce (49519-9572)
PHONE..................................616 261-4400
Craig Adams, *CEO*
Cathy Taylor, *CFO*
Curt Vandyke, *Director*
David Gardner, *Maintence Staff*
EMP: 100
SALES (est): 28.9MM **Privately Held**
WEB: www.adamsplasticsinc.com
SIC: 3089 Trays, plastic; extruded finished plastic products

(G-6804)
R T LONDON COMPANY (PA)
Also Called: Rt London
1642 Broadway Ave Nw # 1 (49504-2046)
PHONE..................................616 364-4800
Richard Postma, *President*
Steve Eldserveld, *COO*
Dale Haley, *VP Opers*
Linda Iagnemma, *Regl Sales Mgr*
▲ **EMP:** 100
SQ FT: 275,000
SALES: 18MM **Privately Held**
WEB: www.rtlondon.com
SIC: 2531 2521 Public building & related furniture; wood office furniture

(G-6805)
RADLEY CORPORATION
Also Called: Radley Corp of Grand Rapids
4595 Broadmoor Ave Se # 115 (49512-5300)
PHONE..................................616 554-9060
David Barks, *Vice Pres*
Dave Ley, *Branch Mgr*
Paula Simpson, *Consultant*
Bobbie Jarvi, *Director*
EMP: 20
SALES (est): 1.7MM
SALES (corp-wide): 8.5MM **Privately Held**
WEB: www.radley.com
SIC: 7371 5045 7372 Computer software development; computers, peripherals & software; prepackaged software

Grand Rapids - Kent County (G-6806)

PA: Radley Corporation
23077 Greenfield Rd # 440
Southfield MI 48075
248 559-6858

(G-6806)
RAENELL PRESS LLC
3637 Clyde Park Ave Sw # 6 (49509-4095)
PHONE..................................616 534-8890
Daniel Britten, *Partner*
Gerald R Britten, *Partner*
Jack Britten, *Partner*
Kevin Britten, *Partner*
Gerald Britten, *Mng Member*
EMP: 5
SQ FT: 1,000
SALES (est): 460K **Privately Held**
SIC: 2752 2759 Commercial printing, offset; letterpress printing

(G-6807)
RAM DIE CORP
Also Called: Rdc
2980 3 Mile Rd Nw (49534-1322)
PHONE..................................616 647-2855
Matt Alcumbrack, *President*
Chad Boersma, *Principal*
Rich Alflen, *Vice Pres*
Rodney Beggs, *Plant Mgr*
Jon Demeester, *Program Mgr*
EMP: 11
SALES (est): 1.7MM **Privately Held**
WEB: www.ramdiecorp.com
SIC: 7389 3312 Design services; tool & die steel

(G-6808)
RANIR LLC (PA)
4701 East Paris Ave Se (49512-5353)
P.O. Box 8877 (49518-8877)
PHONE..................................616 698-8880
Rich Sororta, *President*
Mark McCumby, *Senior VP*
Julie Nass, *Vice Pres*
Andre Lebaron, *CFO*
Steve Weinberger, *CFO*
▲ **EMP:** 420
SQ FT: 150,000
SALES (est): 122MM **Privately Held**
WEB: www.ranir.com
SIC: 3843 3991 Dental equipment & supplies; toothbrushes, except electric

(G-6809)
RANIR GLOBAL HOLDINGS LLC
4701 East Paris Ave Se (49512-5353)
P.O. Box 8877 (49518-8877)
PHONE..................................616 698-8880
Rich Sorota, *President*
EMP: 650 **EST:** 2008
SALES (est): 969.6K **Privately Held**
SIC: 3843 Dental equipment & supplies
PA: Perrigo Company Public Limited Company
Treasury Building
Dublin 2

(G-6810)
RAPID EDM SERVICE INC
3051 Hillcroft Ave Sw (49548-1034)
PHONE..................................616 243-5781
Pat Roys, *President*
EMP: 3
SALES (est): 210.8K **Privately Held**
SIC: 3599 Electrical discharge machining (EDM)

(G-6811)
RAPID-PACKAGING CORPORATION
5151 52nd St Se (49512-9718)
PHONE..................................616 949-0950
James R Spees, *Ch of Bd*
Russell H Spees II, *President*
Jerry Shepard, *Vice Pres*
Jim Spees, *Plant Mgr*
Dean Carstensen, *Director*
EMP: 35 **EST:** 1961
SQ FT: 60,000
SALES (est): 8.1MM **Privately Held**
WEB: www.rapid-packagingcorp.com
SIC: 2657 Folding paperboard boxes

(G-6812)
RBC MINISTRIES (PA)
Also Called: Midwest Media Management Div
3000 Kraft Ave Se (49512-2092)
P.O. Box 2222 (49555-0001)
PHONE..................................616 942-6770
Katy Pent, *President*
Max Smith, *President*
Karlene Schmid, *Partner*
Anne Cetas, *Editor*
John Crupper, *Editor*
▲ **EMP:** 155
SQ FT: 110,000
SALES: 43.8MM **Privately Held**
WEB: www.rbc.net
SIC: 7922 2731 Radio producers; pamphlets: publishing & printing

(G-6813)
REARDEN DEVELOPMENT CORP
5960 Tahoe Dr Se Ste 103 (49546-7124)
PHONE..................................616 464-4434
Michael Neuhaus, *President*
EMP: 5
SALES (est): 323.5K **Privately Held**
WEB: www.reardendevelopment.com
SIC: 7372 Prepackaged software

(G-6814)
RECON TECHNOLOGIES LLC
1522 Madison Ave Se (49507-1715)
PHONE..................................616 241-1877
Thomas Jacques,
EMP: 4
SALES (est): 543.1K **Privately Held**
SIC: 3523 Dairy equipment (farm)

(G-6815)
RECYCLING CONCEPTS W MICH INC
5015 52nd St Se (49512-9731)
PHONE..................................616 942-8888
John Dewitt, *President*
Tim White, *Vice Pres*
EMP: 55
SQ FT: 90,133
SALES (est): 32.2MM **Privately Held**
SIC: 5162 2611 5085 5093 Plastics materials & basic shapes; pulp manufactured from waste or recycled paper; glass bottles; metal scrap & waste materials

(G-6816)
RED STAMP INC
3800 Patterson Ave Se (49512-4027)
PHONE..................................616 878-7771
Timothy Vetter, *President*
Jack Spaans, *Opers Mgr*
Barbara Frost, *Accounting Mgr*
Scott Dutton, *Regl Sales Mgr*
Matthew Cobble, *Sales Staff*
EMP: 35
SQ FT: 4,700
SALES (est): 12MM **Privately Held**
WEB: www.redstamp.com
SIC: 3565 Packing & wrapping machinery

(G-6817)
REFLECTIVE ART INC
4030 Eastern Ave Se (49508-3402)
PHONE..................................616 452-0712
Thomas Hoover, *President*
Eugene Murray, *Prdtn Mgr*
Henry Art, *Controller*
Eric Anderson, *Sales Executive*
Shene Smith, *Director*
▲ **EMP:** 21
SQ FT: 55,000
SALES (est): 2.1MM **Privately Held**
WEB: www.reflectiveartinc.com
SIC: 2741 Miscellaneous publishing

(G-6818)
RELIANCE FINISHING CO
1236 Judd Ave Sw (49509-1094)
PHONE..................................616 241-4436
Michael Mosey, *CEO*
Mary Mosey, *Vice Pres*
Kraig Meuser, *Opers Staff*
EMP: 75
SQ FT: 40,000
SALES (est): 9.1MM **Privately Held**
WEB: www.relfn.com
SIC: 3479 Aluminum coating of metal products; coating of metals & formed products

(G-6819)
RELIANCE SPRAY MASK CO INC
2825 Northridge Dr Nw (49544-9109)
PHONE..................................616 784-3664
Timothy Blanch, *President*
Richard Blanch, *Vice Pres*
Terri Lynn Blanch, *Admin Sec*
EMP: 11
SQ FT: 7,200
SALES (est): 500K **Privately Held**
WEB: www.fatiguesarmynavy.com
SIC: 5013 3544 Body repair or paint shop supplies, automotive; special dies, tools, jigs & fixtures

(G-6820)
REVUE HOLDING COMPANY
Also Called: Revue Magazine
2422 Burton St Se (49546-4809)
PHONE..................................616 608-6170
Brian Edwards, *Principal*
EMP: 8
SQ FT: 1,500
SALES (est): 400K **Privately Held**
WEB: www.revuewm.com
SIC: 2721 Magazines: publishing only, not printed on site

(G-6821)
REYNOLDS BUS SOLUTIONS LLC
3610 Sandy Lane Ct Se (49546-9221)
PHONE..................................616 293-6449
William G Reynolds,
EMP: 3 **EST:** 2007
SALES (est): 53.2K **Privately Held**
SIC: 2759 Promotional printing

(G-6822)
RHINO LININGS OF GRAND RAPIDS
1520 Rupert St Ne (49525-2817)
PHONE..................................616 361-9786
Steve French, *General Mgr*
EMP: 7
SALES (est): 443K **Privately Held**
SIC: 2842 Automobile polish

(G-6823)
RICHARDS QUALITY BEDDING CO
3443 Manderley Dr Ne (49525-2033)
PHONE..................................616 363-0070
EMP: 30
SQ FT: 75,000
SALES (est): 2.8MM **Privately Held**
SIC: 2515 5712 Mfg Mattresses/Bedsprings Ret Furniture

(G-6824)
RICHWOOD INDUSTRIES INC (PA)
2700 Buchanan Ave Sw (49548-1040)
PHONE..................................616 243-2700
Rick Start, *President*
Lisa V Schelven, *Exec VP*
Jim Bennor, *Manager*
▲ **EMP:** 45
SQ FT: 110,000
SALES (est): 10.8MM **Privately Held**
WEB: www.richwoodind.com
SIC: 2499 5021 2426 Handles, poles, dowels & stakes: wood; furniture; hardwood dimension & flooring mills

(G-6825)
RIDGEVIEW INDUSTRIES INC
2727 3 Mile Rd Nw (49534-1317)
PHONE..................................616 453-8636
Gil Rushlau, *Manager*
Kurt Christensen, *Planning*
EMP: 275
SALES (corp-wide): 107MM **Privately Held**
SIC: 3469 Metal stampings
PA: Ridgeview Industries, Inc.
3093 Northridge Dr Nw
Grand Rapids MI 49544
616 453-8636

(G-6826)
RIDGEVIEW INDUSTRIES INC (PA)
3093 Northridge Dr Nw (49544-9132)
PHONE..................................616 453-8636
David Nykamp, *President*
Ron Vanderlaan, *Plant Mgr*
Linda Lafountain, *Production*
Cindy West, *Buyer*
Troy Hendges, *Technical Mgr*
▲ **EMP:** 200
SQ FT: 200,000
SALES (est): 107MM **Privately Held**
WEB: www.ridgeview-ind.com
SIC: 3469 7692 Metal stampings; welding repair

(G-6827)
RIVER CITY STUDIOS LTD
1935 Monroe Ave Nw (49505-6242)
PHONE..................................616 456-1404
Dan Trierweiler, *President*
Joe McCargar, *Manager*
Roy Wallace, *Instructor*
EMP: 6
SALES (est): 748.6K **Privately Held**
WEB: www.rivercitystudios.com
SIC: 3652 Master records or tapes, preparation of

(G-6828)
RIVERSIDE PRTG OF GRND RAPIDS
1375 Monroe Ave Nw (49505-4621)
PHONE..................................616 458-8011
Gregg Cobb, *President*
Rich Van Ess, *Vice Pres*
Ken Van Ess, *Treasurer*
Matt Cobb, *Admin Sec*
EMP: 5 **EST:** 1976
SQ FT: 8,000
SALES: 950K **Privately Held**
SIC: 2752 Commercial printing, offset

(G-6829)
RIVERSIDE TOOL CORP
Also Called: Carbide Specialties
88 54th St Sw Unit 106 (49548-5683)
PHONE..................................616 241-1424
Thomas Roth, *President*
EMP: 21 **Privately Held**
SIC: 3541 Lathes, metal cutting & polishing
HQ: Riverside Tool Corp.
3504 Henke St
Elkhart IN 46514
574 522-6798

(G-6830)
ROBB MACHINE TOOL CO
4301 Clyde Park Ave Sw (49509-4036)
PHONE..................................616 532-6642
Phillip Parsh, *President*
EMP: 5
SQ FT: 5,000
SALES: 800K **Privately Held**
SIC: 3544 Special dies, tools, jigs & fixtures

(G-6831)
ROBERT J LIDZAN
Also Called: Mr TS Screenprinting
2147 Airway St Ne (49525-1546)
PHONE..................................616 361-6446
Bob Lidzan, *Owner*
EMP: 3
SALES: 72K **Privately Held**
WEB: www.mrtsscreenprinting.com
SIC: 2759 Screen printing

(G-6832)
ROCK RIVER FABRICATIONS INC
7670 Caterpillar Ct Sw (49548-7203)
PHONE..................................616 281-5769
Chris Kowalski, *Principal*
John Herweyer, *Safety Mgr*
EMP: 30
SQ FT: 75,000
SALES (est): 3.7MM **Privately Held**
SIC: 3498 3317 Tube fabricating (contract bending & shaping); steel pipe & tubes

Grand Rapids - Kent County (G-6860)

(G-6833)
ROCKY MOUNTAIN RV
7145 Division Ave S (49548-7131)
PHONE.................................435 713-4242
Thomas J Selvius, *Administration*
EMP: 3
SALES (est): 229.7K **Privately Held**
SIC: 3799 Recreational vehicles

(G-6834)
RODENHOUSE INC
974 Front Ave Nw Ste 4 (49504-4456)
P.O. Box 141184 (49514-1184)
PHONE.................................616 454-3100
Robert H Rodenhouse, *President*
EMP: 4
SQ FT: 4,000
SALES (est): 555.3K **Privately Held**
WEB: www.rodenhouse-inc.com
SIC: 3965 Fasteners

(G-6835)
ROLLIE WILLIAMS PAINT SPOT
2570 Walker Ave Nw (49544-1303)
PHONE.................................616 791-6100
Michael Perry, *Office Mgr*
Calvin Kerwalker, *Branch Mgr*
Nick Ramsay, *Technical Staff*
EMP: 7
SALES (corp-wide): 23.7MM **Privately Held**
WEB: www.rwps.com
SIC: 2851 Paints & allied products
PA: Rollie Williams Paint Spot Inc
  1179 Kent St
  Elkhart IN 46514
  574 264-3174

(G-6836)
ROLLSTOCK INC
3680 44th St Se Ste 100a (49512-3966)
PHONE.................................616 803-5370
James D Azzar, *President*
EMP: 3
SALES (est): 203.2K **Privately Held**
SIC: 3565 Packaging machinery

(G-6837)
ROSE ENGRAVING COMPANY
1971 E Beltline Ave Ne # 240
  (49525-7059)
PHONE.................................616 243-3108
Harry Westers, *President*
EMP: 5
SALES (est): 652.5K **Privately Held**
SIC: 2796 3469 Steel line engraving for the printing trade; metal stampings

(G-6838)
ROSE TECHNOLOGIES COMPANY
Also Called: Rose Medical
1440 Front Ave Nw (49504-3221)
PHONE.................................616 233-3000
Todd Grimm, *President*
Eric Vroegop, *Vice Pres*
Carson Tobias, *Engineer*
Brian Wilterink, *Engineer*
Chris Zandstra, *Project Engr*
EMP: 24
SQ FT: 35,000
SALES (est): 6MM **Privately Held**
WEB: www.rose-technologies.com
SIC: 3841 Surgical & medical instruments

(G-6839)
ROSKAM BAKING COMPANY (PA)
Also Called: Starr Puff Factory
4880 Corp Exch Blvd Se (49512)
P.O. Box 202 (49501-0202)
PHONE.................................616 574-5757
Robert Roskam, *President*
Devin McCarthy, *Production*
Jessica Lamp, *Buyer*
Rachael Ashiwer, *Purchasing*
CFS C Lehtinen, *Research*
◆ **EMP:** 200 **EST:** 1918
SALES (est): 470.9MM **Privately Held**
SIC: 2051 2043 7389 Bread, cake & related products; cereal breakfast foods; packaging & labeling services

(G-6840)
ROSKAM BAKING COMPANY
Also Called: M1 Plant
3225 32nd St Se (49512-1870)
PHONE.................................616 574-5757
EMP: 67
SALES (corp-wide): 470.9MM **Privately Held**
SIC: 2051 Bread, cake & related products
PA: Roskam Baking Company
  4880 Corp Exch Blvd Se
  Grand Rapids MI 49512
  616 574-5757

(G-6841)
ROSKAM BAKING COMPANY
Also Called: M2 Plant
3035 32nd St Se (49512-1753)
PHONE.................................616 574-5757
EMP: 144
SALES (corp-wide): 470.9MM **Privately Held**
SIC: 2051 Bread, cake & related products
PA: Roskam Baking Company
  4880 Corp Exch Blvd Se
  Grand Rapids MI 49512
  616 574-5757

(G-6842)
ROSKAM BAKING COMPANY
Also Called: Doughnut World
4855 52nd St Se (49512-9701)
PHONE.................................616 554-9160
Pete Roessler, *QC Dir*
Bob Roskam, *Branch Mgr*
Chris Outman, *Manager*
EMP: 157
SALES (corp-wide): 470.9MM **Privately Held**
SIC: 2051 Bakery: wholesale or wholesale/retail combined
PA: Roskam Baking Company
  4880 Corp Exch Blvd Se
  Grand Rapids MI 49512
  616 574-5757

(G-6843)
ROSKAM BAKING COMPANY
Also Called: S1 Plant
5353 Broadmoor Ave Se (49512-9601)
PHONE.................................616 574-5757
Corey Ball, *Branch Mgr*
Rob Ralph, *Manager*
Rich Perna, *IT/INT Sup*
Alexandria Otis, *Administration*
EMP: 354
SALES (corp-wide): 470.9MM **Privately Held**
SIC: 2051 Bread, cake & related products
PA: Roskam Baking Company
  4880 Corp Exch Blvd Se
  Grand Rapids MI 49512
  616 574-5757

(G-6844)
ROTHBURY FARMS INC
3061 Shaffer Ave Se (49512-1709)
P.O. Box 202 (49501-0202)
PHONE.................................616 574-5757
Robert O Roskam, *President*
EMP: 1000
SALES (est): 128.9MM **Privately Held**
WEB: www.rothburyfarms.com
SIC: 5149 2051 2043 Bakery products; bread, cake & related products; cereal breakfast foods

(G-6845)
ROUTE ONE
7290 Division Ave S (49548-7237)
PHONE.................................616 455-4883
Bruce Schler, *Owner*
EMP: 4
SALES (est): 231.8K **Privately Held**
WEB: www.routeone.net
SIC: 3993 Signs & advertising specialties

(G-6846)
ROWSTER COFFEE INC
100 Stevens St Sw (49507-1526)
PHONE.................................616 780-7777
Kurt Stauffer, *President*
EMP: 20
SALES (est): 671.8K **Privately Held**
SIC: 2095 Coffee roasting (except by wholesale grocers)

(G-6847)
ROYCE ROLLS RINGER COMPANY
16 Riverview Ter Ne (49505-6245)
P.O. Box 1831 (49501-1831)
PHONE.................................616 361-9266
Charles Royce Jr, *CEO*
Matthew L Royce, *President*
Angie Tant, *Sales Dir*
Bill Swartz, *Manager*
Dan Hesse, *Info Tech Mgr*
EMP: 20 **EST:** 1925
SQ FT: 32,000
SALES (est): 4MM **Privately Held**
WEB: www.roycerolls.net
SIC: 3589 Mop wringers; janitors' carts

(G-6848)
S & S TOOL INC
1310 Taylor Ave N (49505-4941)
PHONE.................................616 458-3219
Scott Slenker, *President*
EMP: 5
SQ FT: 3,600
SALES (est): 400K **Privately Held**
SIC: 3599 Machine shop, jobbing & repair

(G-6849)
S F GILMORE INC
321 Terminal St Sw (49548-1018)
PHONE.................................616 475-5100
Scott F Gilmore, *President*
Brandon Fowler, *Manager*
Robert Clark, *Information Mgr*
Amanda Powell,
▲ **EMP:** 120
SQ FT: 50,000
SALES (est): 22.1MM **Privately Held**
WEB: www.gilmorefurnitureinc.com
SIC: 2521 Wood office furniture

(G-6850)
SAGE DIRECT INC
3400 Raleigh Dr Se (49512-2042)
PHONE.................................616 940-8311
Gary Sage, *President*
Ann Marie Priddy, *General Mgr*
Pamela Sage, *Vice Pres*
EMP: 17
SQ FT: 12,000
SALES (est): 2.7MM **Privately Held**
WEB: www.sagedirect.com
SIC: 8742 7374 2759 Marketing consulting services; data processing service; laser printing

(G-6851)
SAVORY FOODS INC
900 Hynes Ave Sw Ofc (49507-1091)
P.O. Box 2583 (49501-2583)
PHONE.................................616 241-2583
Dan Abraham, *President*
Gerald Abraham, *Principal*
Kathy Abraham, *Vice Pres*
Dien Le, *Vice Pres*
Jan Krings, *Human Res Mgr*
▲ **EMP:** 55 **EST:** 1971
SQ FT: 54,000
SALES (est): 15.3MM **Privately Held**
WEB: www.savoryfoods.com
SIC: 2051 2099 2053 2052 Bakery: wholesale or wholesale/retail combined; food preparations; frozen bakery products, except bread; cookies & crackers

(G-6852)
SAW TUBERGEN SERVICE INC
Also Called: Tubergen Cutting Tools
5252 Division Ave S (49548-5606)
PHONE.................................616 534-0701
Andrew Tubergen, *President*
EMP: 6 **EST:** 1907
SQ FT: 2,500
SALES (est): 1MM **Privately Held**
SIC: 3425 7699 Saw blades, chain type; knife, saw & tool sharpening & repair

(G-6853)
SCHNITZELSTEIN BAKING CO
1305 Fulton St E (49503-3851)
PHONE.................................616 988-2316
Brian De Bries, *Principal*
EMP: 4
SALES (est): 231.8K **Privately Held**
SIC: 2051 Bread, all types (white, wheat, rye, etc): fresh or frozen

(G-6854)
SCOTT GROUP CUSTOM CARPETS LLC (PA)
Also Called: Scott Group Studio
3232 Kraft Ave Se Ste A (49512-2040)
PHONE.................................616 954-3200
Mike Ruggeri, *President*
Rachel Janowitz, *Regional Mgr*
John Hart, *Exec VP*
Tim Hill, *Vice Pres*
Rich Ruggeri, *Vice Pres*
▲ **EMP:** 195 **EST:** 1969
SQ FT: 140,000
SALES (est): 74.7MM **Privately Held**
WEB: www.scott-group.com
SIC: 2273 Carpets, textile fiber

(G-6855)
SCREEN IDEAS INC
3257 Union Ave Se (49548-2311)
PHONE.................................616 458-5119
Mark Schumaker, *President*
Susan Schumaker, *Treasurer*
EMP: 4
SQ FT: 10,000
SALES (est): 683.8K **Privately Held**
WEB: www.screenideas.net
SIC: 5199 5099 2759 Advertising specialties; signs, except electric; screen printing

(G-6856)
SCREEN PRINT DEPARTMENT
1181 Taylor Ave N (49503-1000)
PHONE.................................616 235-2200
Carl Perrin, *President*
Doug Hindley, *Sales Staff*
Mary Perrin, *Officer*
EMP: 21
SALES (est): 3.4MM **Privately Held**
WEB: www.screenprintdept.com
SIC: 2759 Screen printing

(G-6857)
SELKIRK CORPORATION (DH)
5030 Corp Exch Blvd Se (49512)
PHONE.................................616 656-8200
Brooks F Sherman,
▲ **EMP:** 50
SALES (est): 160.3MM **Privately Held**
WEB: www.selkirkusa.com
SIC: 3444 Metal ventilating equipment
HQ: Johnson Controls, Inc.
  5757 N Green Bay Ave
  Milwaukee WI 53209
  414 524-1200

(G-6858)
SETCO INC
314 Straight Ave Sw (49504-6439)
PHONE.................................616 459-6311
Jeff Clark, *President*
Geraldine Vander Werff, *Admin Sec*
EMP: 5 **EST:** 1973
SQ FT: 1,400
SALES: 500K **Privately Held**
SIC: 2499 2449 Garment hangers, wood; wood containers

(G-6859)
SHELTER CARPET SPECIALTIES
2025 Calvin Ave Se (49507-3305)
PHONE.................................616 475-4944
EMP: 4
SALES (est): 319.3K **Privately Held**
SIC: 2273 Carpets & rugs

(G-6860)
SHERIDAN PUBG GRND RAPIDS INC
5100 33rd St Se (49512-2062)
PHONE.................................616 957-5100
Chris Kurtzman, *President*
Ben Matalamaki, *CFO*
EMP: 100
SALES (est): 2.2MM
SALES (corp-wide): 536.1MM **Privately Held**
SIC: 2732 Book printing
PA: Cjk Group, Inc.
  3323 Oak St
  Brainerd MN 56401
  218 829-2877

Grand Rapids - Kent County (G-6861)

GEOGRAPHIC SECTION

(G-6861)
SIEMENS INDUSTRY INC
4147 Eastern Ave Se (49508-3405)
PHONE.....................616 913-7700
Dave Zaleski, *Branch Mgr*
EMP: 150
SALES (corp-wide): 95B **Privately Held**
WEB: www.sea.siemens.com
SIC: 3535 8711 1796 5084 Conveyors & conveying equipment; engineering services; machinery installation; conveyor systems
HQ: Siemens Industry, Inc.
1000 Deerfield Pkwy
Buffalo Grove IL 60089
847 215-1000

(G-6862)
SIGNCOMP LLC
Also Called: Signtech
3032 Walker Ridge Dr Nw (49544-9129)
PHONE.....................616 784-0405
Peter Lamberts, *CEO*
Jeremy Breihof, *Regl Sales Mgr*
◆ **EMP:** 37
SQ FT: 50,000
SALES (est): 13.3MM **Privately Held**
WEB: www.signcomp.com
SIC: 3354 Aluminum extruded products

(G-6863)
SIGNMAKERS LTD
7290 Division Ave S Ste A (49548-7237)
PHONE.....................616 455-4220
Eric Sheler, *President*
Michelle Sheler, *Vice Pres*
EMP: 4
SQ FT: 3,600
SALES (est): 557.9K **Privately Held**
SIC: 3993 Neon signs

(G-6864)
SIGNWORKS OF MICHIGAN INC (PA)
4612 44th St Se (49512-4015)
PHONE.....................616 954-2554
Ann Frass, *President*
EMP: 7
SALES (est): 813.8K **Privately Held**
WEB: www.signworksofmi.com
SIC: 3993 Signs, not made in custom sign painting shops

(G-6865)
SIMCO AUTOMOTIVE TRIM INC
Also Called: Ufp Technologies
3831 Patterson Ave Se (49512-4026)
PHONE.....................616 608-9818
R Jeffrey Bailly, *President*
Ronald J Lataille, *Treasurer*
Daniel Hart, *Technology*
Laurie Vanderkodde, *Technician*
▲ **EMP:** 20 **EST:** 1961
SQ FT: 70,000
SALES (est): 4.1MM
SALES (corp-wide): 190.4MM **Publicly Held**
WEB: www.ufpt.com
SIC: 3086 Plastics foam products
PA: Ufp Technologies, Inc.
100 Hale St
Newburyport MA 01950
978 352-2200

(G-6866)
SIMMONS & COURTRIGHT PLASTIC
Also Called: S & C Plastic Coating
2701a West River Dr Nw (49544-2013)
PHONE.....................616 365-0045
Gary Courtright, *CFO*
Sam Simmons, *Mng Member*
EMP: 7
SQ FT: 25,000
SALES: 500K **Privately Held**
WEB: www.scplasticcoating.com
SIC: 3479 Coating of metals with plastic or resins

(G-6867)
SK ENTERPRISES INC
Also Called: Pets Supplys Plus
3593 Alpine Ave Nw (49544-1635)
PHONE.....................616 785-1070
Jan Gandy, *Manager*
EMP: 16
SALES (est): 996.7K **Privately Held**
SIC: 3999 3569 Pet supplies; general industrial machinery

(G-6868)
SMARTCOAST LLC
3200 Broadmoor Ave Se (49512-2865)
PHONE.....................231 571-2020
Greg Vandenbosch,
EMP: 5 **EST:** 2013
SALES (est): 650K **Privately Held**
SIC: 3549 Assembly machines, including robotic

(G-6869)
SMARTSTART MEDICAL LLC
4334 Brockton Dr Se Ste E (49512-4117)
PHONE.....................616 227-4560
Matthew Lapham,
Ryan Erickson,
EMP: 3
SALES (est): 315.9K **Privately Held**
SIC: 2671 Packaging paper & plastics film, coated & laminated

(G-6870)
SOLARBOS
2685 Northridge Dr Nw A (49544-9111)
PHONE.....................616 588-7270
EMP: 7
SALES (corp-wide): 1B **Publicly Held**
SIC: 3613 Switchgear & switchboard apparatus
HQ: Solarbos
310 Stealth Ct
Livermore CA 94551

(G-6871)
SOUNDTECH INC
3880 Soundtech Ct Se (49512-4115)
PHONE.....................616 575-0866
Amy Sparks, *President*
Cardell Taylor, *Engineer*
Pam Stebbins, *Finance Dir*
Nancy Ellis, *Shareholder*
Kimberly Zetter, *Shareholder*
▼ **EMP:** 100
SQ FT: 150,000
SALES (est): 52.7MM **Privately Held**
WEB: www.soundtechinc.com
SIC: 3446 Partitions & supports/studs, including accoustical systems

(G-6872)
SOURCEONE IMAGING LLC
Also Called: Vizcom Media
3223 Kraft Ave Se (49512-2063)
PHONE.....................616 452-2001
Tim Benton,
Scott Benton,
EMP: 7
SALES (est): 1.3MM **Privately Held**
SIC: 2752 Commercial printing, offset

(G-6873)
SOUTHERN LITHOPLATE INC
4150 Danvers Ct Se (49512-4041)
PHONE.....................616 957-2650
EMP: 54
SALES (corp-wide): 47.8MM **Privately Held**
SIC: 2796 Lithographic plates, positives or negatives
PA: Southern Lithoplate Inc.
105 Jeffrey Way
Youngsville NC 27596
919 556-9400

(G-6874)
SOUTHWESTERN FOAM TECH INC (HQ)
1700 Alpine Ave Nw (49504-2810)
PHONE.....................616 726-1677
Richard W Amann, *President*
EMP: 20
SALES (est): 2.4MM
SALES (corp-wide): 214.9MM **Privately Held**
SIC: 3086 Plastics foam products
PA: Grand Rapids Foam Technologies, Inc.
2788 Remico St Sw
Wyoming MI 49519
616 726-1677

(G-6875)
SPARKS BELTING COMPANY INC (HQ)
3800 Stahl Dr Se (49546-6148)
PHONE.....................616 949-2750
Bruce Dieleman, *VP Sales*
▲ **EMP:** 78
SALES (est): 33.5MM
SALES (corp-wide): 550.2MM **Privately Held**
SIC: 3535 3052 Conveyors & conveying equipment; rubber belting
PA: Jsj Corporation
700 Robbins Rd
Grand Haven MI 49417
616 842-6350

(G-6876)
SPARTA SHEET METAL INC
2200 Bristol Ave Nw (49544-1406)
PHONE.....................616 784-9035
Melvin Stoepker, *President*
Michele Kelly, *Business Mgr*
Linda Stoepker, *Vice Pres*
Terry Hiler, *Foreman/Supr*
EMP: 15 **EST:** 1956
SALES (est): 3.2MM **Privately Held**
SIC: 3444 1799 Sheet metalwork; welding on site

(G-6877)
SPARTAN CENTRAL KITCHEN
463 44th St Se (49548-4327)
PHONE.....................616 878-8940
Gary Sputfky, *Manager*
EMP: 6
SALES (est): 772.5K **Privately Held**
SIC: 2099 Food preparations

(G-6878)
SPEC INTERNATIONAL INC
739 Cottage Grove St Se (49507-1815)
PHONE.....................616 248-9116
Kim McComb, *Manager*
EMP: 50 **Privately Held**
WEB: www.specinternational.com
SIC: 2392 Sheets, fabric: made from purchased materials
PA: Spec International, Inc.
1530 Eastern Ave Se
Grand Rapids MI 49507

(G-6879)
SPEC INTERNATIONAL INC (PA)
1530 Eastern Ave Se (49507-2028)
PHONE.....................616 248-3022
J Marcus Stephenson, *President*
Orlando Stephenson III, *Corp Secy*
EMP: 10
SQ FT: 24,000
SALES (est): 10.7MM **Privately Held**
WEB: www.specinternational.com
SIC: 3999 2514 Coin-operated amusement machines; slot machines; metal household furniture

(G-6880)
SPECIALTY TOOL & MOLD INC
4542 Roger B Chaffee Mem (49548-7522)
PHONE.....................616 531-3870
Erik Rogenbuck, *President*
EMP: 7
SQ FT: 5,500
SALES (est): 1MM **Privately Held**
WEB: www.spectoolinc.com
SIC: 3544 Special dies & tools

(G-6881)
SPECIALTY TOOLING SYSTEMS INC
Also Called: STS
4315 3 Mile Rd Nw (49534-1136)
PHONE.....................616 784-2353
Dave Ruthven, *President*
Drew Boersma, *Treasurer*
EMP: 36
SALES (est): 525K **Privately Held**
SIC: 3599 Machine shop, jobbing & repair
PA: Tooling Systems Group Inc.
555 Plymouth Ave Ne
Grand Rapids MI 49505

(G-6882)
SPECIALTY TUBE LLC
Also Called: Beverlin Manufacturing
3515 Raleigh Dr Se (49512-2041)
PHONE.....................616 949-5990
Richard Watson, *President*
Paul Cole, *Vice Pres*
Michael Watson, *Vice Pres*
Zachary Slott, *Engineer*
John Watson,
EMP: 30
SQ FT: 50,000
SALES (est): 6.1MM **Privately Held**
WEB: www.beverlin.com
SIC: 3469 Metal stampings

(G-6883)
SPECTRUM CUBIC INC (PA)
13 Mcconnell St Sw (49503-5126)
PHONE.....................616 459-8751
Jay Bassett, *CEO*
Kevin Bassett, *President*
Keith Bassett, *Vice Pres*
Gina Tniick, *CFO*
▲ **EMP:** 75
SQ FT: 122,000
SALES (est): 9.9MM **Privately Held**
SIC: 3714 Motor vehicle parts & accessories

(G-6884)
SPECTRUM INDUSTRIES INC (PA)
Also Called: Spectrum Cubic
700 Wealthy St Sw (49504-6440)
PHONE.....................616 451-0784
I Jay Bassett, *President*
Keith Bassett, *Vice Pres*
Robert Wilder, *Vice Pres*
Steve Creasap, *VP Sales*
Carla F Leuck, *Marketing Mgr*
▲ **EMP:** 69
SQ FT: 122,000
SALES: 16.9MM **Privately Held**
SIC: 3479 3471 Enameling, including porcelain, of metal products; plating & polishing

(G-6885)
SPINDEL CORP SPECIALIZED
Also Called: Spindel Electronics
4517 Broadmoor Ave Se (49512-5339)
PHONE.....................616 554-2200
Boris Polic, *President*
Otto M Muller, *Vice Pres*
EMP: 10
SALES (est): 1.1MM **Privately Held**
WEB: www.spindelcorp.com
SIC: 3566 Speed changers, drives & gears

(G-6886)
SPINNAKER FORMS SYSTEMS CORP
6812 Old 28th St Se Ste L (49546-6933)
PHONE.....................616 956-7677
EMP: 4 **EST:** 1983
SQ FT: 400
SALES: 300K **Privately Held**
SIC: 5112 2752 5199 Whol Business Forms

(G-6887)
STATE HEAT TREATING COMPANY
520 32nd St Se (49548-2304)
PHONE.....................616 243-0178
Susan Boll, *President*
Paul Meengs, *Vice Pres*
EMP: 20 **EST:** 1946
SQ FT: 50,000
SALES (est): 4.3MM **Privately Held**
WEB: www.stateheattreating.com
SIC: 3398 Tempering of metal

(G-6888)
STEEL SUPPLY & ENGINEERING CO (PA)
Also Called: SS&e Metalcraft
2020 Newark Ave Se (49507-3356)
PHONE.....................616 452-3281
R Jeffrey Dean, *President*
Steve J Entingh, *Vice Pres*
Roy P Lorenz, *Vice Pres*
Jim Schueler, *Vice Pres*
Jeff Dills, *Manager*

GEOGRAPHIC SECTION **Grand Rapids - Kent County (G-6912)**

EMP: 45 **EST:** 1996
SQ FT: 76,000
SALES (est): 14.4MM **Privately Held**
WEB: www.steelsupplyengineering.com
SIC: 1791 3441 Structural steel erection; fabricated structural metal

(G-6889)
STEELCASE INC (PA)
901 44th St Se (49508-7594)
P.O. Box 1967 (49501-1967)
PHONE..................616 247-2710
Robert C Pew III, *Ch of Bd*
James P Keane, *President*
Ulrich H E Gwinner, *President*
Vanessa Derks, *Business Mgr*
Guillaume M Alvarez, *Senior VP*
◆ **EMP:** 583 **EST:** 1912
SALES: 3.4B **Publicly Held**
WEB: www.steelcase.com
SIC: 2522 2521 3648 8748 Office furniture, except wood; chairs, office: padded or plain, except wood; desks, office: except wood; cabinets, office: except wood; wood office furniture; chairs, office: padded, upholstered or plain: wood; desks, office: wood; cabinets, office: wood; lighting equipment; business consulting

(G-6890)
STEELCASE INC
1120 S 36th (49508)
P.O. Box 1967 (49501-1967)
PHONE..................616 247-2710
Steve Sanders, *General Mgr*
EMP: 100
SQ FT: 1,379,792
SALES (corp-wide): 3.4B **Publicly Held**
WEB: www.steelcase.com
SIC: 2522 Office furniture, except wood
PA: Steelcase Inc.
  901 44th St Se
  Grand Rapids MI 49508
  616 247-2710

(G-6891)
STEELTECH LTD (PA)
1251 Phillips Ave Sw (49507-1589)
PHONE..................616 243-7920
Gary L Salerno, *President*
Jeff Dyk, *Accountant*
Bob Otvos, *Sales Mgr*
Kevin Bozym, *Sales Staff*
Jordan Jensen, *Sales Staff*
▲ **EMP:** 70
SQ FT: 40,000
SALES (est): 19.1MM **Privately Held**
WEB: www.steeltechltd.com
SIC: 3325 3321 Alloy steel castings, except investment; gray iron castings

(G-6892)
STEPHENS PIPE & STEEL LLC
Also Called: Stephens Fence Supply
3400 Roger B Chaffee Mem (49548-2326)
PHONE..................616 248-3433
Terry Powell, *Manager*
EMP: 30 **Privately Held**
WEB: www.stephenspipeandsteel.com
SIC: 5051 3315 3523 Pipe & tubing, steel; steel wire & related products; farm machinery & equipment
HQ: Stephens Pipe & Steel, Llc
  2224 E Highway 619
  Russell Springs KY 42642
  270 866-3331

(G-6893)
STONEY CREEK COLLECTION INC
Also Called: Marilyn's Needlework
4336 Plnfeld Ave Ne Ste H (49525)
PHONE..................616 363-4858
Marilynn Vredevelt, *President*
Sally Smith, *Corp Secy*
EMP: 22
SQ FT: 35,000
SALES (est): 2.7MM **Privately Held**
WEB: www.stoneycreek.com
SIC: 2731 5949 2721 Books: publishing only; sewing, needlework & piece goods; periodicals

(G-6894)
STOVALL WELL DRILLING CO
Also Called: Stovall Drilling
2132 4 Mile Rd Ne (49525-2449)
PHONE..................616 364-4144
Howard Stovall, *President*
Doris A Stovall, *Corp Secy*
EMP: 8
SALES (est): 504.8K **Privately Held**
SIC: 1389 1381 Oil & gas wells: building, repairing & dismantling; drilling oil & gas wells

(G-6895)
STUMP SCHLELE SOMAPPA SPRNG
Also Called: SSS Spring & Wire
5161 Woodfield Ct Ne (49525-1027)
PHONE..................616 361-2791
Derek Saynor, *Sales Mgr*
Ravi Machani, *Mng Member*
Pauline Saynor, *Executive*
▲ **EMP:** 22
SQ FT: 30,000
SALES: 3MM **Privately Held**
SIC: 3495 Wire springs

(G-6896)
STUMPP SCHUELE SOMAPPA USA INC
5161 Woodfield Ct Ne (49525-1027)
PHONE..................616 361-2791
Derek Saynor,
EMP: 12 **EST:** 2007
SALES (est): 1.1MM **Privately Held**
SIC: 3495 Wire springs

(G-6897)
SUMMIT TRAINING SOURCE INC (PA)
4170 Embassy Dr Se (49546-2417)
P.O. Box 809298, Chicago IL (60680-9298)
PHONE..................800 842-0466
Bill Clendenen, *CEO*
Valerie R Overheul, *President*
Dave Myers, *CFO*
EMP: 45
SQ FT: 15,000
SALES (est): 2.8MM **Privately Held**
WEB: www.safetyontheweb.com
SIC: 8331 2741 3652 Skill training center; miscellaneous publishing; pre-recorded records & tapes

(G-6898)
SUNHILL AMERICA LLC (PA)
Also Called: American Trading International
5300 Broadmoor Ave Se B (49512-9654)
PHONE..................616 249-3600
Raymond Wiedenfeller, *Mng Member*
▲ **EMP:** 5
SALES (est): 719.3K **Privately Held**
SIC: 3562 Ball & roller bearings

(G-6899)
SUNMED LLC (HQ)
2710 Northridge Dr Nw A (49544-9112)
PHONE..................616 259-8400
Jenny Chen, *Buyer*
Jared Potgeter, *Engineer*
Richard Cao, *Project Engr*
Kristi Neeley, *Human Res Mgr*
Emily Walters, *Mktg Coord*
▲ **EMP:** 58 **EST:** 2008
SQ FT: 30,000
SALES (est): 44.8MM **Privately Held**
SIC: 3841 Surgical & medical instruments
PA: Sunmed Holdings, Llc
  2710 Northridge Dr Nw
  Grand Rapids MI 49544
  616 259-8400

(G-6900)
SUNMED HOLDINGS LLC (PA)
2710 Northridge Dr Nw (49544-9112)
PHONE..................616 259-8400
John Sommerdyke, *Mng Member*
EMP: 12 **EST:** 2013
SALES (est): 44.8MM **Privately Held**
SIC: 3841 6719 Surgical & medical instruments; investment holding companies, except banks

(G-6901)
SUNSHINE SYSTEMS INC
3700 Buchanan Ave Sw B (49548-3100)
PHONE..................616 363-9272
Curtis Clemens, *President*
EMP: 3
SALES (est): 436.8K **Privately Held**
WEB: www.sunshinesystemsinc.com
SIC: 3645 1799 Garden, patio, walkway & yard lighting fixtures: electric; desk lamps; mobile home site setup & tie down; awning installation

(G-6902)
SUPERIOR DISTRIBUTION SVCS LLC
4001 3 Mile Rd Nw (49534-1132)
P.O. Box 1768 (49501-1768)
PHONE..................616 453-6358
James Leonard, *Mng Member*
EMP: 3
SALES (est): 605.8K
SALES (corp-wide): 493.4MM **Privately Held**
SIC: 3537 4212 Trucks: freight, baggage, etc.: industrial, except mining; local trucking, without storage
HQ: S. Abraham & Sons, Inc.
  4001 3 Mile Rd Nw
  Grand Rapids MI 49534
  616 453-6358

(G-6903)
SUPERIOR FIXTURE & TOOLING LLC
425 36th St Se (49548-2313)
PHONE..................616 828-1566
Mark Mastbergen, *CEO*
EMP: 7
SALES (est): 1MM **Privately Held**
SIC: 2599 Factory furniture & fixtures

(G-6904)
SUPERIOR STEEL COMPONENTS INC (PA)
180 Monroe Ave Nw Ste 2r (49503-2626)
P.O. Box 68, Marne (49435-0068)
PHONE..................616 866-4759
Eric Greenfield, *President*
Titus R Hager, *Chairman*
Dennis Van Wyk, *Treasurer*
EMP: 80
SQ FT: 16,000
SALES (est): 10.5MM **Privately Held**
WEB: www.lgst.com
SIC: 3443 Truss plates, metal

(G-6905)
SUPERTRAMP CUSTOM TRAMPOLINE
5161 Woodfield Ct Ne # 1 (49525-1027)
PHONE..................616 634-2010
Paul Hagan, *Owner*
EMP: 17
SQ FT: 400
SALES (est): 330K **Privately Held**
SIC: 3949 Trampolines & equipment

(G-6906)
SUSPA INCORPORATED (DH)
3970 R B Chaffee Mem Dr (49548)
PHONE..................616 241-4200
Steve Garvelink, *President*
Jim Doyle, *General Mgr*
Penny Drougal, *General Mgr*
Jonathan Bruin, *Engineer*
Jim Zanden, *Engineer*
▲ **EMP:** 109 **EST:** 1974
SQ FT: 165,000
SALES (est): 27.8MM
SALES (corp-wide): 494K **Privately Held**
WEB: www.suspa-inc.com
SIC: 3593 Fluid power cylinders & actuators
HQ: Suspa Gmbh
  Muhlweg 33
  Altdorf B. Nurnberg 90518
  918 793-00

(G-6907)
SWAROVSKI NORTH AMERICA LTD
3175 28th St Se (49512-1663)
PHONE..................616 977-5008
EMP: 4
SALES (corp-wide): 4.7B **Privately Held**
SIC: 3961 Costume jewelry
HQ: Swarovski North America Limited
  1 Kenney Rd
  Cranston RI 02920
  401 463-6400

(G-6908)
SWIFT PRINTING CO
Also Called: Swift Printing and Comm
404 Bridge St Nw (49504-5379)
PHONE..................616 459-4263
Walter D Gutowski, *CEO*
Walter Gutowski Jr, *Treasurer*
Kathy Schramski, *Corp Comm Staff*
Steve Hale, *Graphic Designe*
EMP: 10 **EST:** 1955
SQ FT: 6,000
SALES (est): 1.7MM **Privately Held**
WEB: www.swiftprinting.com
SIC: 2759 2752 Screen printing; commercial printing, lithographic

(G-6909)
SWOBODA INC
4108 52nd St Se (49512-9636)
PHONE..................616 554-6161
Thomas Hecksel, *CEO*
Michael Follmann Ceo, *Principal*
Erina Hanka, *Principal*
Christoph Hirt, *Principal*
Samir Gandhi, *COO*
▲ **EMP:** 120
SQ FT: 60,000
SALES (est): 26.1MM
SALES (corp-wide): 226.5K **Privately Held**
WEB: www.swobodaus.com
SIC: 3714 Motor vehicle engines & parts
HQ: Swoboda Wiggensbach Kg
  Max-Swoboda-Str. 1
  Wiggensbach 87487
  837 091-00

(G-6910)
SYNOD OF GREAT LAKES
4500 60th St Se (49512-9685)
PHONE..................616 698-7071
Bill Verhulst, *Treasurer*
Dave Schutt, *Director*
West Graneerg-Michaelson, *Director*
EMP: 112
SQ FT: 5,000
SALES (est): 3.5MM **Privately Held**
WEB: www.cranhillranch.com
SIC: 8661 2741 8741 Reformed Church; newsletter publishing; management services

(G-6911)
SYSTEM 2/90 INC
Also Called: 2/90 Sign Systems
5350 Corprte Grv Dr Se (49512-5500)
P.O. Box 888289 (49588-8289)
PHONE..................616 656-4310
Albert J Perry, *President*
Michael A Benedict, *Vice Pres*
Michael Herweyer, *Vice Pres*
Kathleen Kluck, *Vice Pres*
Waldy Carey, *Technical Staff*
▼ **EMP:** 95
SQ FT: 88,000
SALES (est): 16.8MM **Privately Held**
WEB: www.290signs.com
SIC: 3993 Electric signs

(G-6912)
T C H INDUSTRIES INCORPORATED (HQ)
7441 Div Ave S Ste A1 (49548)
PHONE..................616 942-0505
Theodore C Hohman, *President*
Patrick J Greene, *Vice Pres*
EMP: 9
SALES (est): 92.2MM
SALES (corp-wide): 83.8MM **Privately Held**
SIC: 3364 3363 Zinc & zinc-base alloy die-castings; aluminum die-castings
PA: Charles Group, Inc.
  7441 Div Ave S Ste A1
  Grand Rapids MI 49548
  336 882-0186

Grand Rapids - Kent County (G-6913) — GEOGRAPHIC SECTION

(G-6913)
TABLETTING INC
4201 Danvers Ct Se (49512-4041)
PHONE..................................616 957-0281
Bryan Koster, *President*
Dale Koster, *Vice Pres*
EMP: 7
SQ FT: 5,000
SALES (est): 1.1MM **Privately Held**
SIC: 2834 Tablets, pharmaceutical

(G-6914)
TABS WALL SYSTEMS LLC
4515 Airwest Dr Se (49512-3951)
PHONE..................................616 554-5400
Ron Losse, *Manager*
EMP: 3 **EST:** 2010
SALES (est): 374.9K **Privately Held**
SIC: 3251 Brick clay: common face, glazed, vitrified or hollow

(G-6915)
TATUM BINDERY COMPANY
Also Called: Tatum Bookbinding
666 Wealthy St Se (49503-5447)
PHONE..................................616 458-8991
James H McMullen, *Owner*
James B McMullen, *Co-Owner*
EMP: 3 **EST:** 1904
SQ FT: 5,000
SALES (est): 244.5K **Privately Held**
SIC: 2789 2752 Binding only: books, pamphlets, magazines, etc.; commercial printing, lithographic

(G-6916)
TAYLOR FREEZER MICHIGAN INC
2111 Walker Ct Nw (49544-1411)
PHONE..................................616 453-0531
Rick Senica, *Vice Pres*
EMP: 16
SALES (corp-wide): 16.6MM **Privately Held**
WEB: www.taylor-michigan.com
SIC: 3556 5046 5078 Ice cream manufacturing machinery; commercial equipment; ice cream cabinets
PA: Taylor Freezer Of Michigan, Inc.
13341 Stark Rd
Livonia MI
800 292-0031

(G-6917)
TAYLOR TOOLING GROUP LLC
4303 3 Mile Rd Nw (49534-1136)
PHONE..................................616 805-3917
James Taylor, *Mng Member*
Thomas Taylor,
EMP: 20
SQ FT: 18,000
SALES: 1.6MM **Privately Held**
SIC: 3312 Tool & die steel

(G-6918)
TECH FORMS METAL LTD
2437 Coit Ave Ne (49505-4017)
PHONE..................................616 956-0430
Timothy G Gleason, *President*
▲ **EMP:** 7
SALES (est): 650.3K **Privately Held**
SIC: 3353 Aluminum sheet & strip

(G-6919)
TEKTON INC
Also Called: Michigan Industrial Tools
3707 R B Chaffee Memrl Dr (49548)
PHONE..................................616 243-2443
Attallah Amash, *President*
Marie Amash, *Vice Pres*
Greg Hawkins, *Opers Mgr*
Brent McBride, *Prdtn Mgr*
Jordan Flickinger, *QC Mgr*
◆ **EMP:** 90
SQ FT: 140,000
SALES (est): 14.6MM **Privately Held**
WEB: www.mit-tool.com
SIC: 3423 5072 Hand & edge tools; hand tools

(G-6920)
TEN X PLASTICS LLC
610 Maryland Ave Ne Ste A (49505-6052)
PHONE..................................616 813-3037
Robert Velte,
EMP: 7
SALES (est): 813.5K **Privately Held**
SIC: 3089 Injection molding of plastics

(G-6921)
TENIBAC-GRAPHION INC
2925 Northridge Dr Nw (49544-9120)
PHONE..................................616 647-3333
Tony Pettigrew, *Branch Mgr*
EMP: 11
SALES (corp-wide): 791.5MM **Publicly Held**
WEB: www.tenibac.com
SIC: 3469 Patterns on metal
HQ: Tenibac-Graphion, Inc.
35155 Automation Dr
Clinton Township MI 48035
586 792-0150

(G-6922)
TER MOLEN & HART INC
3056 Eastern Ave Se Ste C (49508-8250)
PHONE..................................616 458-4832
Steve Van Zytveld, *President*
EMP: 8
SQ FT: 3,000
SALES (est): 1MM **Privately Held**
WEB: www.termolenhart.com
SIC: 3449 Bars, concrete reinforcing: fabricated steel

(G-6923)
TERRYBERRY COMPANY LLC (PA)
Also Called: Stange Company
2033 Oak Industrial Dr Ne (49505-6011)
P.O. Box 502 (49501-0502)
PHONE..................................616 458-1391
Tad Evans, *Plant Mgr*
Mike Byam,
David Beemer,
◆ **EMP:** 131 **EST:** 1918
SQ FT: 30,000
SALES: 42.2MM **Privately Held**
WEB: www.talisman-jewelry.com
SIC: 3911 Rings, finger: precious metal

(G-6924)
TESA TAPE INC
2945 Walkent Ct Nw (49544-1481)
PHONE..................................616 785-6970
Fabiana Espino, *Finance*
Tom Dupont, *Branch Mgr*
EMP: 9
SALES (corp-wide): 11.8B **Privately Held**
WEB: www.tesatape.com
SIC: 2672 3842 3644 2671 Tape, pressure sensitive: made from purchased materials; surgical appliances & supplies; noncurrent-carrying wiring services; packaging paper & plastics film, coated & laminated
HQ: Tesa Tape, Inc.
5825 Carnegie Blvd
Charlotte NC 28209
704 554-0707

(G-6925)
TG MANUFACTURING LLC
Aim Industries
146 Monroe Center St Nw # 710 (49503-2816)
PHONE..................................616 842-1503
Jeanne Duthler, *Principal*
EMP: 30
SALES (est): 8.4MM **Privately Held**
SIC: 3469 Stamping metal for the trade
PA: Tg Manufacturing, Llc
8197 Clyde Park Ave Sw
Byron Center MI 49315

(G-6926)
THIERICA INC (HQ)
Also Called: Thierica Display Products
900 Clancy Ave Ne (49503-1599)
PHONE..................................616 458-1538
Forrest Frank, *CEO*
James Stein, *President*
Paul Doyle, *General Mgr*
Sandra Frank, *Vice Pres*
Jeff Jenkins, *Prdtn Mgr*
▲ **EMP:** 85 **EST:** 1946
SQ FT: 57,000
SALES (est): 27.5MM **Privately Held**
WEB: www.thiincorporated.com
SIC: 3812 3479 3829 Aircraft flight instruments; coating of metals & formed products; measuring & controlling devices

(G-6927)
THIERICA CONTROLS INC
Also Called: Automatrics
4400 Donkers Ct Se (49512-4054)
PHONE..................................616 956-5500
Forrest Frank, *President*
Kazim Aya, *General Mgr*
Keith Rollenhagen, *Electrical Engi*
Richard Nagy, *Sales Staff*
John Crousse, *Info Tech Mgr*
EMP: 17
SALES: 2.6MM **Privately Held**
WEB: www.automatrics.com
SIC: 3613 Control panels, electric
PA: Thi Incorporated
900 Clancy Ave Ne
Grand Rapids MI 49503

(G-6928)
THIERICA EQUIPMENT CORPORATION
Also Called: Thi Equipment
3147 N Wilson Ct Nw (49534-7566)
PHONE..................................616 453-6570
Forrest Frank, *CEO*
James Stein, *President*
Gregorio Garza, *General Mgr*
Sandra Frank, *Vice Pres*
Dan Van, *Purchasing*
▼ **EMP:** 45
SQ FT: 57,000
SALES (est): 13.4MM **Privately Held**
WEB: www.thiincorporated.com
SIC: 3599 3991 3842 3563 Machine & other job shop work; brooms & brushes; surgical appliances & supplies; air & gas compressors; sheet metalwork
PA: Thi Incorporated
900 Clancy Ave Ne
Grand Rapids MI 49503

(G-6929)
THIRD WAVE COMPUTING
2176 Wealthy St Se 2 (49506-3041)
PHONE..................................616 855-5501
John Bajema, *Partner*
Dave Anderson, *Vice Pres*
EMP: 3 **EST:** 1995
SALES: 240K **Privately Held**
WEB: www.3rdwavecomputing.com
SIC: 7372 Prepackaged software

(G-6930)
THYSSENKRUPP ELEVATOR CORP
5169 Northland Dr Ne (49525-1015)
PHONE..................................616 942-4710
Scott Barron, *Manager*
EMP: 12
SALES (corp-wide): 39.8B **Privately Held**
WEB: www.tyssenkrupp.com
SIC: 3534 1796 Elevators & moving stairways; installing building equipment
HQ: Thyssenkrupp Elevator Corporation
11605 Haynes Bridge Rd # 650
Alpharetta GA 30009
678 319-3240

(G-6931)
TICKETS PLUS INC (PA)
Also Called: Star Tickets Plus
620 Century Ave Sw # 300 (49503-4977)
PHONE..................................616 222-4000
Henry Mast, *Ch of Bd*
Jack Krasula, *President*
Robert Struyk, *President*
Larry D Fredericks, *Treasurer*
Kevin Einfeld, *Director*
EMP: 35
SQ FT: 1,500
SALES (est): 4.2MM **Privately Held**
WEB: www.ticketsplus.net
SIC: 2759 7999 Tickets: printing; ticket sales office for sporting events, contract

(G-6932)
TON-TEX CORPORATION
4245 44th St Se Ste 1 (49512-4053)
PHONE..................................616 957-3200
Michael Hough, *Sales Mgr*
Robert Beaman, *Branch Mgr*
EMP: 7
SALES (est): 639.2K
SALES (corp-wide): 5.9MM **Privately Held**
SIC: 3568 Power transmission equipment
PA: Ton-Tex Corporation
4029 E Grv Unit 7
Greenville MI 48838
616 957-3200

(G-6933)
TOOLING SYSTEMS GROUP INC (PA)
Also Called: Tooling Systems Enterprises
555 Plymouth Ave Ne (49505-6029)
P.O. Box 152053 (49515-2053)
PHONE..................................616 863-8623
Julie Boersma, *CEO*
Drew Boersma, *President*
Kyle Twardy, *Project Engr*
▲ **EMP:** 12
SALES (est): 11.7MM **Privately Held**
SIC: 3544 Special dies, tools, jigs & fixtures

(G-6934)
TOWER AUTOMOTIVE OPERATIONS I
4695 44th St Se Ste B175 (49512-4140)
PHONE..................................616 802-1600
Orrie Jones, *Manager*
EMP: 52
SALES (corp-wide): 2.2B **Privately Held**
SIC: 3465 Automotive stampings
HQ: Tower Automotive Operations Usa I, Llc
17672 N Laurel Park Dr 400e
Livonia MI 48152

(G-6935)
TOWER INTERNATIONAL INC
4695 44th St Se Ste B175 (49512-4140)
PHONE..................................616 802-1600
Nanette Dudek, *Vice Pres*
Phil Parker, *Analyst*
EMP: 4
SALES (corp-wide): 2.2B **Privately Held**
SIC: 3441 Fabricated structural metal
HQ: Tower International, Inc.
17672 N Laurel Park Dr
Livonia MI 48152

(G-6936)
TREAT OF DAY LLC
Also Called: Totd
2540 Ridgemoor Dr Se (49512-1635)
PHONE..................................616 706-1717
Bakeer Muhammad,
Clifton Jura,
EMP: 15
SALES (est): 528.5K **Privately Held**
SIC: 2095 Coffee roasting (except by wholesale grocers)

(G-6937)
TRIDENT LIGHTING LLC
2929 32nd St Se (49512-1771)
PHONE..................................616 957-9500
Anthony Shaw, *CEO*
Carol Levy,
▲ **EMP:** 195 **EST:** 1895
SQ FT: 330,000
SALES (est): 19.1MM **Privately Held**
SIC: 3647 3714 3641 Automotive lighting fixtures; motor vehicle parts & accessories; electric lamps

(G-6938)
TRUE TEKNIT INC
5300 Corprte Grv Dr Se De (49512-5514)
PHONE..................................616 656-5111
Alain Dueal, *CEO*
EMP: 25
SQ FT: 40,000
SALES: 3.5MM **Privately Held**
SIC: 2281 Knitting yarn, spun

(G-6939)
TRUE TOOL CNC REGRINDING & MFG
14110 Ironwood Dr Nw (49534-1034)
PHONE..................................616 677-1751
Tom Balzeski, *President*
Lisa Belzeski, *Admin Sec*

GEOGRAPHIC SECTION   **Grand Rapids - Kent County (G-6965)**

EMP: 4
SQ FT: 3,000
SALES (est): 467.2K **Privately Held**
SIC: 3599 Grinding castings for the trade

(G-6940)
TUFF AUTOMATION INC
2751 Courier Dr Nw (49534-1247)
PHONE..................................616 735-3939
Monte R Tuffs, *President*
Scott V Buren, *Info Tech Dir*
▲ EMP: 25
SQ FT: 12,000
SALES (est): 5.1MM **Privately Held**
WEB: www.tuffautomation.com
SIC: 3599 Custom machinery

(G-6941)
TURNKEY FABRICATION LLC
1530 Eastern Ave Se (49507-2028)
PHONE..................................616 248-9116
EMP: 6
SALES (est): 488.4K **Privately Held**
SIC: 1761 3444 Sheet metalwork; sheet metalwork

(G-6942)
TVB INC
544 Richmond St Nw (49504-2007)
P.O. Box 651, Howard City (49329-0651)
PHONE..................................616 456-9629
Tom Van Blooys, *President*
EMP: 12
SQ FT: 16,000
SALES (est): 1.4MM **Privately Held**
WEB: www.tvb-inc.com
SIC: 2522 5712 Office furniture, except wood; furniture stores

(G-6943)
TWINLAB HOLDINGS INC
3133 Orchard Vista Dr Se (49546-7033)
PHONE..................................800 645-5626
Jerry Seidl, *Vice Pres*
David Vick, *Vice Pres*
Hoa Khong, *Production*
Niki Simoneaux, *Marketing Staff*
Joseph Sopracasa, *Director*
EMP: 4
SALES (corp-wide): 98.1MM **Privately Held**
SIC: 2099 Tea blending
PA: Twinlab Holdings, Inc.
 4800 T Rex Ave
 Boca Raton FL 33431
 800 645-5626

(G-6944)
UEI INC
Also Called: U E I
2771 West River Dr Nw (49544-2013)
PHONE..................................616 361-6093
Greg Usher, *President*
Sean Eshraghi, *Purchasing*
Jeanine Usher, *Treasurer*
EMP: 30
SQ FT: 16,000
SALES (est): 6.2MM **Privately Held**
SIC: 3469 3544 Metal stampings; special dies & tools

(G-6945)
UFP ATLANTIC LLC
2801 E Beltline Ave Ne (49525-9680)
PHONE..................................616 364-6161
Michael Cole, *Principal*
EMP: 9
SALES (est): 1.3MM
SALES (corp-wide): 4.4B **Publicly Held**
SIC: 2421 5031 1796 Sawmills & planing mills, general; lumber, plywood & millwork; installing building equipment
PA: Universal Forest Products, Inc.
 2801 E Beltline Ave Ne
 Grand Rapids MI 49525
 616 364-6161

(G-6946)
UFP EASTERN DIVISION INC (HQ)
Also Called: Universal Forest Products
2801 E Beltline Ave Ne (49525-9680)
PHONE..................................616 364-6161
C Scott Greene, *President*
Elaine Garrett, *Sales Staff*
◆ EMP: 31

SALES (est): 5.9MM
SALES (corp-wide): 4.4B **Publicly Held**
WEB: www.ufpi.com
SIC: 2421 Sawmills & planing mills, general
PA: Universal Forest Products, Inc.
 2801 E Beltline Ave Ne
 Grand Rapids MI 49525
 616 364-6161

(G-6947)
UFP GRAND RAPIDS LLC
825 Buchanan Ave Sw (49507-1004)
PHONE..................................616 464-1650
EMP: 16
SALES (est): 2.3MM
SALES (corp-wide): 4.4B **Publicly Held**
SIC: 2421 Building & structural materials, wood; lumber: rough, sawed or planed
PA: Universal Forest Products, Inc.
 2801 E Beltline Ave Ne
 Grand Rapids MI 49525
 616 364-6161

(G-6948)
UFP TECHNOLOGIES INC
Also Called: United Foam Products
3831 Patterson Ave Se (49512-4026)
PHONE..................................616 949-8100
R Jeffrey Bailly, *Branch Mgr*
EMP: 100
SALES (corp-wide): 190.4MM **Publicly Held**
SIC: 3086 3714 3296 2821 Plastics foam products; motor vehicle parts & accessories; mineral wool; plastics materials & resins; packaging paper & plastics film, coated & laminated
PA: Ufp Technologies, Inc.
 100 Hale St
 Newburyport MA 01950
 978 352-2200

(G-6949)
UFP WEST CENTRAL LLC
2801 E Beltline Ave Ne (49525-9680)
PHONE..................................616 364-6161
David Tutas,
EMP: 3
SALES (est): 256.4K **Privately Held**
SIC: 2421 5031 1796 Sawmills & planing mills, general; lumber, plywood & millwork; installing building equipment

(G-6950)
UNIBAND USA LLC
2555 Oak Industrial Dr Ne C (49505-6056)
PHONE..................................616 676-6011
Milco Marchetti, *Mng Member*
Shae Husted, *Assistant*
▲ EMP: 18
SALES (est): 3.1MM **Privately Held**
SIC: 7374 3535 Data processing service; belt conveyor systems, general industrial use

(G-6951)
UNIST INC (PA)
4134 36th St Se (49512-2903)
PHONE..................................616 949-0853
Wally Boelkins, *CEO*
Charles Boelkins, *President*
Tim Walker, *Vice Pres*
Timothy Bangma, *Design Engr*
Kevin Varnes, *Design Engr*
EMP: 25
SALES (est): 5.2MM **Privately Held**
WEB: www.unist.com
SIC: 3523 5172 3563 3494 Sprayers & spraying machines, agricultural; lubricating oils & greases; air & gas compressors; valves & pipe fittings; manufactured hardware (general)

(G-6952)
UNITED FOAM A UFP TECH BRND
3831 Patterson Ave Se (49512-4026)
PHONE..................................616 949-8100
R J Bailly, *CEO*
Larry W Barrows, *Vice Pres*
Michael Dale, *Vice Pres*
Daniel C Croteau, *Sales/Mktg Dir*
Jack Pigott, *VP Sales*
◆ EMP: 100
SQ FT: 265,000

SALES (est): 27.4MM
SALES (corp-wide): 190.4MM **Publicly Held**
WEB: www.steplaw.com
SIC: 3086 3714 5013 2821 Plastics foam products; motor vehicle parts & accessories; motor vehicle supplies & new parts; plastics materials & resins; computers, peripherals & software
PA: Ufp Technologies, Inc.
 100 Hale St
 Newburyport MA 01950
 978 352-2200

(G-6953)
UNIVERSAL CONSUMER PDTS INC (HQ)
Also Called: U C P
2801 E Beltline Ave Ne (49525-9680)
PHONE..................................616 364-6161
Bob Coleman, *Exec VP*
Eric S Maxey, *Vice Pres*
▲ EMP: 3
SALES (est): 12.5MM
SALES (corp-wide): 4.4B **Publicly Held**
SIC: 2821 Molding compounds, plastics
PA: Universal Forest Products, Inc.
 2801 E Beltline Ave Ne
 Grand Rapids MI 49525
 616 364-6161

(G-6954)
UNIVERSAL FOREST PRODUCTS INC (PA)
2801 E Beltline Ave Ne (49525-9680)
PHONE..................................616 364-6161
Matthew J Missad, *CEO*
William G Currie, *Ch of Bd*
Patrick Benton, *President*
Allen Peters, *President*
Allen T Peters, *President*
▼ EMP: 120 **EST:** 1955
SALES: 4.4B **Publicly Held**
WEB: www.ufpinc.com
SIC: 2421 1796 Building & structural materials, wood; lumber: rough, sawed or planed; installing building equipment

(G-6955)
UNIVERSAL SIGN INC
5001 Falcon View Ave Se (49512-5405)
PHONE..................................616 554-9999
Michael Penkevich, *President*
Mark Koster, *Foreman/Supr*
EMP: 20
SQ FT: 24,000
SALES: 3.9MM **Privately Held**
SIC: 3993 Electric signs

(G-6956)
VACLOVERS INC
3611 3 Mile Rd Nw (49534-1231)
PHONE..................................616 246-1700
Dewey I Doyle III, *President*
Joseph P Doyle, *Corp Secy*
EMP: 48
SQ FT: 25,000
SALES (est): 5.4MM **Privately Held**
WEB: www.industrialvacuumsystems.com
SIC: 3589 Vacuum cleaners & sweepers, electric; industrial

(G-6957)
VAN DAM IRON WORKS INC
1813 Chicago Dr Sw (49519-1250)
PHONE..................................616 452-8627
James Stickland, *President*
Jack Goodale, *Owner*
Neal Stickland, *Vice Pres*
Dana Berkeley, *Project Mgr*
Dave Wiedlund, *Purch Agent*
EMP: 32
SQ FT: 42,000
SALES: 5.5MM **Privately Held**
WEB: www.vdiw.net
SIC: 3441 Fabricated structural metal

(G-6958)
VAN ZEE ACQUISITIONS INC
Also Called: Superior Furniture Company
4047 Eastern Ave Se (49508-3401)
PHONE..................................616 855-7000
Sue Ann Burns, *Ch of Bd*
William J Lee II, *President*
▲ EMP: 22 **EST:** 1936
SQ FT: 65,000

SALES (est): 2.3MM **Privately Held**
WEB: www.superiorfurnitureco.com
SIC: 2511 Wood household furniture

(G-6959)
VAN ZEE CORPORATION
Also Called: Taylor Company, The
4047 Eastern Ave Se (49508-3401)
PHONE..................................616 245-9000
John Van Zee, *President*
Clarence Medema, *Shareholder*
EMP: 85
SQ FT: 90,000
SALES (est): 795.4K **Privately Held**
SIC: 2541 Wood partitions & fixtures

(G-6960)
VANDER MILL LLC (PA)
505 Ball Ave Ne (49503-2011)
PHONE..................................616 259-8828
Amanda Vander Heide, *Mng Member*
Paul Vander Heide, *Mng Member*
Stuart Vander Heide, *Mng Member*
EMP: 65
SQ FT: 55,000
SALES (est): 7.6MM **Privately Held**
SIC: 2084 Wines

(G-6961)
VANS PATTERN CORP
11 Sweet St Nw (49505-4633)
P.O. Box 1971 (49501-1971)
PHONE..................................616 364-9483
Daniel E Vandermolen, *CEO*
EMP: 25 **EST:** 1960
SQ FT: 40,000
SALES (est): 4.2MM **Privately Held**
SIC: 3543 Industrial patterns

(G-6962)
VECTOR DISTRIBUTION LLC
1642 Broadway Ave Nw (49504-2046)
PHONE..................................616 361-2021
Scott Soltys, *Prdtn Mgr*
Valerie Harkema, *Purchasing*
Marleigh Plachecki, *Human Resources*
Cory Bowser, *Manager*
Derek Foltz, *Manager*
▲ EMP: 6
SALES (est): 987.5K **Privately Held**
SIC: 2759 Screen printing

(G-6963)
VELOCITY WORLDWIDE INC
Also Called: Velocity USA
2280 29th St Se (49508-1560)
PHONE..................................616 243-3400
Tom Black, *President*
Linda Black, *Vice Pres*
Dave Deyoung, *Manager*
Theresa Steinbeck, *Info Tech Dir*
▲ EMP: 17
SALES (est): 2.4MM **Privately Held**
WEB: www.velocityusa.com
SIC: 3751 Bicycles & related parts

(G-6964)
VENOM MOTORSPORTS INC
5174 Plainfield Ave Ne (49525-1083)
PHONE..................................616 635-2519
Flikkema John Jr, *Administration*
EMP: 3
SALES (est): 180K **Privately Held**
SIC: 2836 Venoms

(G-6965)
VENTRA GRAND RAPIDS 5 LLC
3075 Breton Rd Se (49512-1747)
PHONE..................................616 222-3296
Jim Zsebok, *Treasurer*
Laura Kenndy, *Controller*
Shahid R Khan,
EMP: 300
SALES (est): 95.1MM
SALES (corp-wide): 3.3B **Privately Held**
SIC: 3465 Body parts, automobile: stamped metal
PA: Flex-N-Gate Llc
 1306 E University Ave
 Urbana IL 61802
 217 384-6600

Grand Rapids - Kent County (G-6966)   **GEOGRAPHIC SECTION**

(G-6966)
VERMEULEN & ASSOCIATES INC
4665 Cascade Rd Se # 140 (49546-3766)
PHONE...................................616 291-1255
Doug Vermeulen, *CEO*
Arnie Morren, *Corp Secy*
EMP: 3
SALES: 640K **Privately Held**
SIC: 1442 Construction sand & gravel

(G-6967)
VERSATILITY INC
Also Called: Union First Promotions
2610 Berwyck Rd Se (49506-4816)
PHONE...................................616 957-5555
Stephen Zain, *President*
Joe Wilson, *General Mgr*
EMP: 5
SALES (est): 566.4K **Privately Held**
WEB: www.versatilityinc.com
SIC: 3993 Advertising novelties

(G-6968)
VERSTRAETE CONVEYABILITY INC
Also Called: Conveyability, Inc.
2889 Northridge Dr Nw (49544-9109)
PHONE...................................800 798-0410
Pete Verstraete, *President*
EMP: 24
SQ FT: 24,000
SALES (est): 10.3MM **Privately Held**
WEB: www.conveyability.com
SIC: 3535 Conveyors & conveying equipment

(G-6969)
VI-CHEM CORP
55 Cottage Grove St Sw (49507-1646)
PHONE...................................616 247-8501
Leonard Slott, *President*
Michael Murphy, *Prdtn Mgr*
Derek Fountaine, *Research*
Mike Lourim, *CFO*
Stas Lopushansky, *Controller*
▲ **EMP:** 30
SQ FT: 120,000
SALES (est): 39.7MM
SALES (corp-wide): 206MM **Privately Held**
WEB: www.vichem.com
SIC: 2821 Polyvinyl chloride resins (PVC); elastomers, nonvulcanizable (plastics)
PA: Americhem, Inc.
    2000 Americhem Way
    Cuyahoga Falls OH 44221
    330 929-4213

(G-6970)
VIABLE INC
Also Called: Cleo
44 Grandville Ave Sw (49503-4083)
PHONE...................................616 774-2022
Scott Sikkema, *President*
EMP: 8
SALES (est): 358.8K **Privately Held**
SIC: 2521 Wood office furniture

(G-6971)
VIANT MEDICAL INC
620 Watson St Sw (49504-6340)
PHONE...................................616 643-5200
Dan Croteau, *Branch Mgr*
EMP: 96
SALES (corp-wide): 368.7MM **Privately Held**
SIC: 3841 Surgical & medical instruments
HQ: Viant Medical, Inc.
    6 Century Ln
    South Plainfield NJ 07080
    908 561-0717

(G-6972)
VIERSON BOILER & REPAIR CO
3700 Patterson Ave Se (49512-4097)
PHONE...................................616 949-0500
Neil Vierson III, *President*
Lydia Vierson, *Treasurer*
Christopher Castillo, *Manager*
EMP: 10
SQ FT: 8,000
SALES (est): 2MM **Privately Held**
WEB: www.viersonboiler.com
SIC: 1711 1796 3443 Boiler maintenance contractor; installing building equipment; boiler & boiler shop work; process vessels, industrial: metal plate

(G-6973)
VINTAGE VIEWS PRESS
959 Ogden Ave Se (49506-3560)
PHONE...................................616 475-7662
Thomas Wilson, *Principal*
EMP: 3
SALES (est): 137.3K **Privately Held**
SIC: 2711 Newspapers

(G-6974)
VOGT INDUSTRIES INC
4530 Roger B Chaffee Se (49548-7522)
PHONE...................................616 531-4830
James Vogt, *President*
Marcia Vogt, *Corp Secy*
EMP: 6
SQ FT: 25,000
SALES: 280K **Privately Held**
SIC: 3446 3429 Acoustical suspension systems, metal; manufactured hardware (general)

(G-6975)
W SOULE & CO
Also Called: W Soule & Company
4925 Kendrick St Se (49512-9602)
PHONE...................................616 975-6272
Jeff Voss, *Manager*
EMP: 20
SALES (corp-wide): 81.3MM **Privately Held**
WEB: www.wsoule.com
SIC: 3444 3498 Sheet metal specialties, not stamped; fabricated pipe & fittings
PA: W. Soule & Co.
    7125 S Sprinkle Rd
    Portage MI 49002
    269 324-7001

(G-6976)
WADDELL ELECTRIC COMPANY
4279 3 Mile Rd Nw (49534-1144)
PHONE...................................616 791-4860
Warren French, *President*
EMP: 6
SQ FT: 2,400
SALES (est): 791.3K **Privately Held**
SIC: 1731 7694 General electrical contractor; electric motor repair

(G-6977)
WALKER TOOL & DIE INC
2411 Walker Ave Nw (49544-1377)
PHONE...................................616 453-5471
David N Hendricks, *CEO*
Todd Finley, *President*
Jeff Umlor, *Plant Mgr*
Robert Huisken, *Project Mgr*
Dick Pierce, *Facilities Mgr*
◆ **EMP:** 95 **EST:** 1959
SQ FT: 100,000
SALES: 20MM **Privately Held**
WEB: www.walkertool.com
SIC: 3544 Special dies, tools, jigs & fixtures

(G-6978)
WALTHER TROWAL LLC
4540 East Paris Ave Se F (49512-5444)
PHONE...................................616 455-8940
Konrad Stadler, *President*
Ken Raby, *Vice Pres*
Gregg Ottaway, *Manager*
◆ **EMP:** 12 **EST:** 2016
SQ FT: 11,000
SALES: 7.9MM
SALES (corp-wide): 31.6MM **Privately Held**
SIC: 3694 5084 3449 Engine electrical equipment; machine tools & metalworking machinery; miscellaneous metalwork
PA: Walther Trowal Gmbh & Co. Kg
    Rheinische Str. 35-37
    Haan 42781
    212 957-10

(G-6979)
WALTHER TROWAL GMBH & CO KG
4540 East Paris Ave Se (49512-5444)
PHONE...................................616 871-0031
▲ **EMP:** 5
SALES (est): 608.1K **Privately Held**
SIC: 3714 Motor vehicle parts & accessories

(G-6980)
WEALTHY STREET CORPORATION
Also Called: Spectrum Industries
700 Wealthy St Sw (49504-6440)
PHONE...................................616 451-0784
I Jay Bassett, *President*
Keith Bassett, *Vice Pres*
Kevin Bassett, *Vice Pres*
EMP: 140
SQ FT: 144,000
SALES (est): 18.5MM **Privately Held**
WEB: www.wealthystreetbakery.com
SIC: 3479 Coating of metals & formed products

(G-6981)
WEAVER INSTRUCTIONAL SYSTEMS
6161 28th St Se Ste 9 (49546-6931)
PHONE...................................616 942-2891
Harry Weaver, *President*
EMP: 5
SALES (est): 456K **Privately Held**
SIC: 7372 5049 5046 5087 Application computer software; school supplies; teaching machines, electronic; service establishment equipment

(G-6982)
WEBER MACHINE (USA) INC
4717 Broadmoor Ave Se B (49512-9330)
PHONE...................................207 947-4990
Peter Witt, *President*
◆ **EMP:** 8
SALES (est): 2.7MM **Privately Held**
WEB: www.webermt.com
SIC: 3531 Soil compactors: vibratory

(G-6983)
WEISS TECHNIK NORTH AMER INC (DH)
Also Called: Envirotronics
3881 N Greenbrooke Dr Se (49512-5328)
PHONE...................................616 554-5020
Robert Levert, *CEO*
Daryl Penfold, *President*
Cheryl Martin, *Buyer*
Gregg Gilles, *Research*
Brenda Gordon, *Engineer*
▲ **EMP:** 100
SQ FT: 50,000
SALES: 45.2MM
SALES (corp-wide): 1.2B **Privately Held**
SIC: 8734 3569 Testing laboratories; testing chambers for altitude, temperature, ordnance, power
HQ: Weiss Umwelttechnik Gmbh
    Greizer Str. 41-49
    Reiskirchen 35447
    640 884-0

(G-6984)
WERKEMA MACHINE COMPANY INC
7300 Division Ave S (49548-7136)
PHONE...................................616 455-7650
Thomas Werkema, *President*
Kathleen Werkema, *Corp Secy*
Mike Mehler, *Project Engr*
Grant Allison, *Design Engr*
EMP: 11 **EST:** 1970
SQ FT: 10,000
SALES (est): 1MM **Privately Held**
WEB: www.werkemamachine.com
SIC: 3599 Machine shop, jobbing & repair

(G-6985)
WEST MICH PRCSION MCHINING INC
2500 Waldorf Ct Nw (49544-1416)
PHONE...................................616 791-1970
Phil Allen, *CEO*
EMP: 17
SALES (est): 3MM **Privately Held**
SIC: 3599 Machine shop, jobbing & repair

(G-6986)
WEST MICHIGAN COATING LLC
3150 Fruit Ridge Ave Nw (49544-9707)
PHONE...................................616 647-9509
David H Nykamp,
EMP: 23
SQ FT: 50,000
SALES (est): 2.5MM **Privately Held**
SIC: 3479 Coating of metals & formed products

(G-6987)
WEST MICHIGAN TAG & LABEL INC
Also Called: Wmtl
5300 Broadmoor Ave Se F (49512-9654)
PHONE...................................616 235-0120
Richard Rice, *President*
Joe Robach, *Sales Staff*
Lou Robach, *Sales Staff*
EMP: 20
SQ FT: 13,000
SALES (est): 3.2MM **Privately Held**
SIC: 2752 5199 Commercial printing, offset; tags, lithographed; packaging materials

(G-6988)
WEST MICHIGAN TECHNICAL SUPPLY
11331 3rd Ave Nw (49534-3582)
PHONE...................................616 735-0991
Timothy P Irwin, *President*
▲ **EMP:** 3
SALES (est): 476.4K **Privately Held**
SIC: 3613 Distribution cutouts

(G-6989)
WEST THOMAS PARTNERS LLC
Also Called: The Gluten Free Bar, The
4053 Brockton Dr Se Ste A (49512-4071)
PHONE...................................616 430-7585
Anastasia Pennington, *Plant Mgr*
Amanda Dorda, *Business Anlyst*
Ben Wahl,
Marshall Rader,
▼ **EMP:** 40
SALES: 7.8MM **Privately Held**
SIC: 2051 Bakery: wholesale or wholesale/retail combined

(G-6990)
WH MANUFACTURING INC
2606 Thornwood St Sw (49519-2151)
PHONE...................................616 534-7560
Debbie Williams, *President*
Mary Bolt, *Office Mgr*
EMP: 25
SQ FT: 4,500
SALES (est): 1.2MM **Privately Held**
SIC: 3679 5063 Harness assemblies for electronic use: wire or cable; electronic wire & cable

(G-6991)
WIKOFF COLOR CORPORATION
3410 Jefferson Ave Se (49548-2244)
PHONE...................................616 245-3930
Gary Hildebrand, *Branch Mgr*
Dave Rose, *Manager*
EMP: 20
SALES (corp-wide): 145.1MM **Privately Held**
WEB: www.wikoff.com
SIC: 2893 Printing ink
PA: Wikoff Color Corporation
    1886 Merritt Rd
    Fort Mill SC 29715
    803 548-2210

(G-6992)
WIL-KAST INC
8025 Division Ave S (49548-7231)
PHONE...................................616 281-2850
Tom Wilkerson, *Principal*
Scott Fisher, *QC Mgr*
Steve Homrich, *Engineer*
Mike Wilkerson, *Manager*
EMP: 45
SQ FT: 42,000

GEOGRAPHIC SECTION

Grandville - Kent County (G-7018)

SALES (est): 11.1MM **Privately Held**
WEB: www.wilkast.com
SIC: 3369 Zinc & zinc-base alloy castings, except die-castings

(G-6993)
WILEY & CO
4186 Plainfield Ave Ne (49525-1610)
PHONE.................................616 361-7110
John Connell, *President*
Elizabeth Connell, *Admin Sec*
EMP: 3
SALES (est): 248.5K **Privately Held**
SIC: 3069 5087 5947 Balloons, advertising & toy: rubber; carnival & amusement park equipment; gift, novelty & souvenir shop

(G-6994)
WILLIAM B EERDMANS PUBG CO
4035 Park East Ct Se (49546-8818)
PHONE.................................616 459-4591
Anita Eerdmans, *President*
David Bratt, *Editor*
James Ernest, *Vice Pres*
Klaas Wolterstorff, *Vice Pres*
Michele Reynolds, *Credit Mgr*
▲ EMP: 42 EST: 1911
SQ FT: 80,000
SALES: 7MM **Privately Held**
WEB: www.eerdmans.com
SIC: 2731 2732 Books: publishing only; textbooks: publishing only, not printed on site; pamphlets: publishing only, not printed on site; books: printing & binding; textbooks: printing & binding, not publishing; pamphlets: printing & binding, not published on site

(G-6995)
WIZ WHEELZ INC
Also Called: Terratrike
4460 40th St Se (49512-4035)
PHONE.................................616 455-5988
Jack Wiswell, *CEO*
Wayne Oom, *CFO*
Jeff Yonker, *Marketing Staff*
▲ EMP: 12
SQ FT: 8,000
SALES (est): 2MM **Privately Held**
WEB: www.wizwheelz.com
SIC: 3751 5941 Bicycles & related parts; sporting goods & bicycle shops

(G-6996)
WOLVERINE COIL SPRING COMPANY
818 Front Ave Nw (49504-4495)
PHONE.................................616 459-3504
Jay Dunwell, *President*
Jerry Walker, *Plant Mgr*
Donna Crowl, *Opers Mgr*
Mike Konyndyk, *Engineer*
Douglas Miron, *CFO*
EMP: 70 EST: 1946
SQ FT: 45,000
SALES (est): 14.1MM **Privately Held**
WEB: www.wolverinecoilspring.com
SIC: 3495 Wire springs

(G-6997)
WOLVERINE CRANE & SERVICE INC (PA)
2557 Thornwood St Sw (49519-2148)
PHONE.................................616 538-4870
Rich Kelps, *President*
▲ EMP: 45
SQ FT: 60,000
SALES (est): 14MM **Privately Held**
WEB: www.wolverinecrane.com
SIC: 3536 7699 Cranes, overhead traveling; industrial equipment services

(G-6998)
WOLVERINE GAS AND OIL CORP (PA)
1 Riverfront Plz # 55 (49503)
PHONE.................................616 458-1150
Sidney J Jansma Jr, *President*
David Rozendal, *Business Mgr*
Gary Bleeker, *Vice Pres*
Sidney Jansma Jr III, *Vice Pres*
Richard Moritz, *Vice Pres*
EMP: 35

SALES (est): 6.8MM **Privately Held**
WEB: www.wolvgas.com
SIC: 1382 Oil & gas exploration services

(G-6999)
WOLVERINE PRINTING COMPANY LLC
Also Called: Spectrum Graphics
315 Grandville Ave Sw (49503-4098)
PHONE.................................616 451-2075
Ray Boisvenue, *VP Human Res*
Mike Fauble, *Sales Staff*
Kurt Burmeister, *Marketing Staff*
Virginia Fish, *Mng Member*
Deb Redmond, *Consultant*
EMP: 32 EST: 1963
SQ FT: 36,000
SALES (est): 5.1MM **Privately Held**
WEB: www.wolverineprinting.com
SIC: 2791 2789 2752 Typesetting; bookbinding & related work; commercial printing, offset

(G-7000)
WOLVERINE SPECIAL TOOL INC
1857 Waldorf St Nw (49544-1433)
PHONE.................................616 791-1027
Guy Chilton, *President*
Paul Tenbrock, *Corp Secy*
EMP: 20
SQ FT: 5,500
SALES: 1.2MM **Privately Held**
WEB: www.wsti.biz
SIC: 3545 7389 5084 Cutting tools for machine tools; grinding, precision: commercial or industrial; machine tools & metalworking machinery

(G-7001)
WOMENS LIFESTYLE INC
3500 3 Mile Rd Nw A (49534-1230)
PHONE.................................616 458-2121
Victoria Upton, *President*
EMP: 3
SALES: 400K **Privately Held**
WEB: www.womenslifestylemagazine.com
SIC: 2721 Magazines: publishing & printing

(G-7002)
WONDERLAND GRAPHICS INC
4030 Eastern Ave Se (49508-3402)
PHONE.................................616 452-0712
Mark Hoover, *President*
Diane Krugh, *Corp Secy*
Tom Hooper, *Manager*
Shene Smith, *Director*
Marge Crischer, *Admin Sec*
EMP: 16
SQ FT: 17,000
SALES (est): 1.2MM **Privately Held**
WEB: www.reflective-art.com
SIC: 3299 Art goods: plaster of paris, papier mache & scagliola

(G-7003)
WOODWAYS INDUSTRIES LLC (PA)
Also Called: Woodways Custom Built
4265 28th St Se Ste A (49512-5670)
PHONE.................................616 956-3070
Samuel Martonosi, *Engineer*
Suzanne Rudnitzki,
Volker Rudnitzki,
EMP: 30
SQ FT: 22,000
SALES (est): 8.5MM **Privately Held**
SIC: 2434 2511 1751 Wood kitchen cabinets; wood household furniture; carpentry work

(G-7004)
WORTHEN INDUSTRIES INC
Also Called: Worthen Coated Fabrics
1125 41st St Se (49508)
PHONE.................................616 742-8990
EMP: 25
SALES (corp-wide): 66.2MM **Privately Held**
SIC: 2891 2295 Adhesives; coated fabrics, not rubberized
HQ: Worthen Industries, Inc.
3 E Spit Brook Rd
Nashua NH 03060
603 888-5443

(G-7005)
WYKE DIE & ENGINEERING INC
4334 Brockton Dr Se Ste I (49512-4117)
PHONE.................................616 871-1175
Robert Wykoski, *President*
EMP: 8
SQ FT: 3,000
SALES (est): 790K **Privately Held**
SIC: 3544 Special dies & tools

(G-7006)
X-RITE INCORPORATED (HQ)
Also Called: X-Rite Company, The
4300 44th St Se (49512-4009)
PHONE.................................616 803-2100
Thomas J Vacchiano Jr, *CEO*
Ondrej Kruk, *President*
Jan-Paul V Maaren, *President*
Iris Mangelschots, *President*
Terri Bartlett, *Business Mgr*
▲ EMP: 186 EST: 1958
SALES (est): 50MM
SALES (corp-wide): 19.8B **Publicly Held**
WEB: www.xrite.com
SIC: 3827 3823 3826 3613 Optical instruments & lenses; industrial instrmnts msrmnt display/control process variable; analytical instruments; switchgear & switchboard apparatus; densitometers
PA: Danaher Corporation
2200 Penn Ave Nw Ste 800w
Washington DC 20037
202 828-0850

(G-7007)
YARD & HOME LLC
2801 E Beltline Ave Nw (49525)
PHONE.................................844 927-3466
EMP: 3
SALES (est): 444K
SALES (corp-wide): 4.4B **Publicly Held**
SIC: 2421 1796 Building & structural materials, wood; lumber: rough, sawed or planed; installing building equipment
PA: Universal Forest Products, Inc.
2801 E Beltline Ave Ne
Grand Rapids MI 49525
616 364-6161

(G-7008)
YELLO DUMPSTER
1505 Steele Ave Sw (49507-1522)
PHONE.................................616 915-0506
EMP: 4
SALES (est): 157.5K **Privately Held**
SIC: 3443 Dumpsters, garbage

(G-7009)
YONKER WELDING SERVICE INC
3975 Linden Ave Se (49548-3431)
PHONE.................................616 534-2774
Edward Yonker Sr, *President*
Rynard Yonker, *Admin Sec*
EMP: 3
SQ FT: 3,000
SALES (est): 230K **Privately Held**
SIC: 1799 7692 Welding on site; welding repair

(G-7010)
YOUR SHOWER DOOR
2958 28th St Se (49512-1625)
PHONE.................................616 940-0900
David Knoynbyk, *General Mgr*
EMP: 7 EST: 2013
SALES (est): 678.9K **Privately Held**
SIC: 3088 Shower stalls, fiberglass & plastic

(G-7011)
ZAYNA LLC
Also Called: Harnel Company
1600 Marshall Ave Se Side (49507-2069)
PHONE.................................616 452-4522
James Tuffs, *President*
EMP: 5
SQ FT: 30,000
SALES (est): 765.4K **Privately Held**
WEB: www.harnelcase.com
SIC: 3089 3412 Plastic containers, except foam; metal barrels, drums & pails

(G-7012)
ZINGER SHEET METAL INC
4005 Roger B Chaffee Mem (49548-3441)
PHONE.................................616 532-3121
Nelson Capestany, *President*
Sandra Capestany, *Admin Sec*
EMP: 18 EST: 1954
SQ FT: 10,200
SALES: 1.2MM **Privately Held**
WEB: www.zingersheetmetal.com
SIC: 3444 Sheet metal specialties, not stamped

(G-7013)
ZONDERVAN CORPORATION LLC (DH)
Also Called: Zondervan Publishing House
3900 Sparks Dr Se (49546-6146)
PHONE.................................616 698-6900
Rich Tatum, *Publisher*
Dirk Buursma, *Editor*
Stephanie S Smith, *Editor*
Phil Herich, *Buyer*
Chris Warners, *Financial Analy*
▲ EMP: 315
SQ FT: 306,000
SALES (est): 53.1MM
SALES (corp-wide): 10B **Publicly Held**
SIC: 2731 Books: publishing only; textbooks: publishing only, not printed on site
HQ: Harpercollins Publishers L.L.C.
195 Broadway
New York NY 10007
212 207-7000

(G-7014)
ZOOMER DISPLAY LLC
522 Stocking Ave Nw (49504-5504)
PHONE.................................616 734-0300
Jackson Martin, *President*
EMP: 5
SQ FT: 40,000
SALES (est): 495.2K **Privately Held**
SIC: 2741 2653 7389 Miscellaneous publishing; display items, solid fiber: made from purchased materials; packaging & labeling services

Grandville
Kent County

(G-7015)
A KOPPEL COLOR IMAGE COMPANY
Also Called: Koppel A Color Image
4025 Chicago Dr Sw (49418-1201)
PHONE.................................616 534-3600
John Koppel, *Partner*
Kim Koppel, *Partner*
EMP: 6
SALES (est): 976.2K **Privately Held**
WEB: www.koppelprint.com
SIC: 2752 2791 2789 Commercial printing, lithographic; typesetting; bookbinding & related work

(G-7016)
ACTION DIE & TOOL INC
4621 Spartan Indus Dr Sw (49418-2511)
PHONE.................................616 538-2326
Tim Vandeclock, *President*
EMP: 8
SQ FT: 3,500
SALES (est): 1.3MM **Privately Held**
SIC: 3544 Special dies & tools

(G-7017)
ADVANCED CNC MACHINING LLC
3086 Dixie Ave Sw Ste E (49418-1196)
PHONE.................................616 226-6706
James Kozak,
EMP: 9
SQ FT: 4,000
SALES: 800K **Privately Held**
SIC: 3599 Machine shop, jobbing & repair

(G-7018)
AEC SYSTEMS USA INC
3665 Iris Dr Sw (49418-1886)
P.O. Box 10 (49468-0010)
PHONE.................................616 257-9502

Grandville - Kent County (G-7019)

GEOGRAPHIC SECTION

Darrel Wilcox, CEO
EMP: 25
SALES: 950K **Privately Held**
SIC: 3582 Commercial laundry equipment

(G-7019)
ALTER CYCLES LTD
2910 Quarter Ct Sw (49418)
PHONE..................313 737-1196
John Walton, CEO
EMP: 7
SALES (corp-wide): 1MM **Privately Held**
SIC: 3751 Bicycles & related parts
PA: Alter Cycles, Ltd.
    2910 Porter Ct Sw
    Grandville MI 49418
    313 737-1196

(G-7020)
ALUMINUM TEXTURES INC
2925 Remico St Sw Ste A (49418-2722)
PHONE..................616 538-3144
G T Boylan, President
Tom Dykstra, Vice Pres
Charles Bellgraph, VP Opers
EMP: 40
SQ FT: 25,000
SALES (est): 5MM **Privately Held**
SIC: 3089 3469 3442 3354 Plastic processing; metal stampings; metal doors, sash & trim; aluminum extruded products

(G-7021)
BAY HOME MEDICAL AND REHAB INC (PA)
5752 Stonebridge Dr Sw (49418-3239)
PHONE..................231 933-1200
Timothy Keller, President
Karen Keller, Treasurer
EMP: 23
SQ FT: 4,500
SALES (est): 3.1MM **Privately Held**
WEB: www.bayhomemedical.com
SIC: 5999 5047 3999 Medical apparatus & supplies; hospital equipment & furniture; wheelchair lifts

(G-7022)
BELWITH PRODUCTS LLC
3100 Broadway Ave Sw (49418-1581)
PHONE..................616 247-4000
Andy Sidor, President
EMP: 10
SQ FT: 340,000 **Privately Held**
SIC: 3469 3429 3452 3366 Metal stampings; furniture hardware; bolts, nuts, rivets & washers; copper foundries
PA: Belwith Products, Llc
    3100 Broadway Ave Sw
    Grandville MI 49418

(G-7023)
BLACK & DECKER (US) INC
Also Called: Dewalt Industrial Tool
2982 28th St Sw (49418-2703)
PHONE..................616 261-0425
Dale Smith, Manager
EMP: 5
SALES (corp-wide): 13.9B **Publicly Held**
WEB: www.dewalt.com
SIC: 3546 Power-driven handtools
HQ: Black & Decker (U.S.) Inc.
    1000 Stanley Dr
    New Britain CT 06053
    860 225-5111

(G-7024)
BMC BIL-MAC CORPORATION
Also Called: BMC Bil-Mac Company
2995 44th St Sw (49418-2565)
PHONE..................616 538-1930
Mike Bowen, President
Nicholas Bowen, Vice Pres
Alexander Calverley, Engineer
Ellen Olson, Office Mgr
Brian King, Supervisor
EMP: 77
SQ FT: 65,000
SALES (est): 15.4MM **Privately Held**
WEB: www.bmcbil-mac.com
SIC: 3451 Screw machine products

(G-7025)
BUSINESS CONNECT L3C
3888 16th Ave Sw (49418-9607)
PHONE..................616 443-8070
Lou Haveman,
Jeffrey Haveman,
Jereme Lambert,
EMP: 5 **EST:** 2014
SALES: 450K **Privately Held**
SIC: 3589 7389 Water purification equipment, household type;

(G-7026)
CLASSIC DESIGNS CSTM AREA RUGS
4370 Chicago Dr Sw # 220 (49418-1694)
PHONE..................616 530-0740
Chad Scholten, President
EMP: 3
SQ FT: 2,500
SALES (est): 390.9K **Privately Held**
WEB: www.classicdesignsrugs.com
SIC: 2273 Rugs, hand & machine made

(G-7027)
DEPPE MOLD & TOOLING INC
2814 Franklin Ave Sw (49418-1262)
PHONE..................616 530-1331
Jeff Deppe, President
Sheryl Deppe, Admin Sec
EMP: 23
SQ FT: 4,000
SALES (est): 1.4MM **Privately Held**
SIC: 3544 Industrial molds

(G-7028)
DIGITAL TOOL & DIE INC
2606 Sanford Ave Sw (49418-1069)
PHONE..................616 532-8020
Michael Gill, President
Dennis Gill, Vice Pres
Nancy Allen, Manager
▲ **EMP:** 47
SQ FT: 20,000
SALES (est): 10.1MM **Privately Held**
WEB: www.digitaltool-die.com
SIC: 3544 Special dies, tools, jigs & fixtures

(G-7029)
EJS ENGRAVING
4450 Blackfoot Dr Sw (49418-2274)
PHONE..................616 534-8104
Susan Streeter, Partner
Kathy Olsen, Partner
Edward Streeter, Partner
EMP: 3
SALES: 170K **Privately Held**
SIC: 3089 3479 Engraving of plastic; etching & engraving

(G-7030)
ELECTRIC MOTOR SERVICE CTR INC
3565 Viaduct St Sw (49418-1057)
PHONE..................616 532-6007
Michael Dertien, President
Adam Dertien, Vice Pres
Samuel Dertien, Treasurer
EMP: 3
SQ FT: 3,000
SALES (est): 395K **Privately Held**
SIC: 7694 Electric motor repair

(G-7031)
ELECTRO CHEMICAL FINISHING CO
2973 Dormax St Sw (49418-1165)
PHONE..................616 531-0670
Alex Duck, Principal
Tony Cockrill, Engineer
▲ **EMP:** 13
SALES (est): 1.3MM **Privately Held**
SIC: 3471 Electroplating of metals or formed products

(G-7032)
ELECTRO CHEMICAL FINISHING CO
2949 Remico St Sw (49418-1188)
PHONE..................616 249-7092
Judy Lee, Manager
EMP: 5
SALES (corp-wide): 21.4MM **Privately Held**
WEB: www.ecfinc.com
SIC: 3471 Plating & polishing
PA: Electro Chemical Finishing Co.
    2610 Remico St Sw
    Wyoming MI 49519
    616 531-0670

(G-7033)
ENTERPRISE TOOL & DIE LLC
4270 White St Sw (49418-1254)
PHONE..................616 538-0920
Doug Groom, CEO
Leslie Larsen, President
Dan Hipp, Project Mgr
Eric Smith, Project Mgr
Rob Groom, Foreman/Supr
EMP: 55 **EST:** 1961
SQ FT: 45,000
SALES (est): 10MM **Privately Held**
WEB: www.enterprisedie.com
SIC: 3544 Special dies & tools

(G-7034)
EXTREME SCREENPRINTS
3030 Sangra Ave Sw (49418-2723)
PHONE..................616 889-8305
EMP: 3
SALES (est): 88.6K **Privately Held**
SIC: 2759 Publication printing

(G-7035)
EXTREME WIRE EDM SERVICE INC
3636 Busch Dr Sw (49418-1340)
PHONE..................616 249-3901
Carl Berndt, President
Brian Berndt, Vice Pres
EMP: 8
SALES (est): 375K **Privately Held**
SIC: 3544 Special dies & tools

(G-7036)
FAMILY SAFETY PRODUCTS INC
2879 Remico St Sw (49418-1139)
PHONE..................616 530-6540
Jim Workman, Chairman
EMP: 9
SALES (est): 1.1MM **Privately Held**
SIC: 3829 Gas detectors

(G-7037)
GIVE-EM A BRAKE SAFETY LLC
2610 Sanford Ave Sw (49418-1069)
PHONE..................616 531-8705
Jamie Lemke, General Mgr
Brad Peterman, Foreman/Supr
Chris Heyboer, Branch Mgr
Jeff Macdermaid, Branch Mgr
Dan Babcock, Mng Member
EMP: 20
SQ FT: 10,000
SALES (est): 6.2MM **Privately Held**
WEB: www.gebsafety.com
SIC: 3499 3669 Barricades, metal; traffic signals, electric

(G-7038)
GRAND RAPIDS GRAVEL COMPANY
3706 Busch (49418)
P.O. Box 9160, Grand Rapids (49509-0160)
PHONE..................616 538-9000
Brad Rahn, Branch Mgr
Mary Joe, Administration
EMP: 3
SALES (corp-wide): 26.5MM **Privately Held**
WEB: www.grgravel.com
SIC: 3273 Ready-mixed concrete
PA: Grand Rapids Gravel Company
    2700 28th St Sw
    Grand Rapids MI 49519
    616 538-9000

(G-7039)
GRANDVILLE INDUSTRIES INC
4270 White St Sw (49418-1254)
P.O. Box 439 (49468-0439)
PHONE..................616 538-0920
Robert C Johnson, CEO
Russell Wiersma, President
John Szot, Treasurer
EMP: 70
SQ FT: 45,000
SALES (est): 5.7MM **Privately Held**
SIC: 3544 Special dies & tools; dies, plastics forming

(G-7040)
GRANDVILLE PRINTING CO
4719 Ivanrest Ave Sw (49418-9141)
P.O. Box 247 (49468-0247)
PHONE..................616 534-8647
Jeffrey C Brewer, Ch of Bd
Patrick J Brewer, President
Rickard A Durham, Vice Pres
Curtis J Cooke, CFO
▼ **EMP:** 222
SQ FT: 157,000
SALES (est): 79.1MM **Privately Held**
WEB: www.gpco.com
SIC: 2752 Commercial printing, offset

(G-7041)
GRANDVILLE TRACTOR SVCS LLC
3408 Busch Dr Sw Ste E (49418-3422)
PHONE..................616 530-2030
EMP: 17
SALES (est): 1.9MM **Privately Held**
SIC: 3524 Mfg Lawn/Garden Equipment

(G-7042)
H & L ADVANTAGE INC
3500 Busch Dr Sw (49418-1321)
PHONE..................616 532-1012
Brad Alkema, President
Lawrence Hobbie, Vice Pres
▲ **EMP:** 50 **EST:** 1974
SQ FT: 36,000
SALES (est): 12.1MM **Privately Held**
WEB: www.hladvantage.com
SIC: 3429 5162 Furniture hardware; plastics materials & basic shapes

(G-7043)
HADLEY PRODUCTS CORPORATION (HQ)
Also Called: B & R Manufacturing Division
2851 Prairie St Sw Ste A (49418-2179)
PHONE..................616 530-1717
James Humphrey, CEO
John W Humphrey, Ch of Bd
Robert Dubsky, President
Raoul Stasse, Business Mgr
James Green, Vice Pres
◆ **EMP:** 138
SQ FT: 117,000
SALES (est): 38.5MM
SALES (corp-wide): 171MM **Privately Held**
WEB: www.hadley-products.com
SIC: 3714 Motor vehicle parts & accessories
PA: Humphrey Companies Llc
    2851 Prairie St Sw
    Grandville MI 49418
    616 530-1717

(G-7044)
HARBOR FOAM INC
2950 Pririe St Sw Ste 300 (49418)
PHONE..................616 855-8150
Laura Kuperus, President
Ryan Dyke, Sales Staff
▲ **EMP:** 8
SALES (est): 1.7MM **Privately Held**
WEB: www.harborfoaminc.com
SIC: 3086 Insulation or cushioning material, foamed plastic

(G-7045)
HARLO CORPORATION (PA)
4210 Ferry St Sw (49418-1573)
P.O. Box 129 (49468-0129)
PHONE..................616 538-0550
Mary Helen Crooks, CEO
Craig Crooks, Chairman
Richard G Crooks, Vice Pres
Benjamin Usher, Design Engr
Jim Johnson, Controller
EMP: 107 **EST:** 1938
SQ FT: 84,000
SALES (est): 40.4MM **Privately Held**
WEB: www.harlo.com
SIC: 3537 3613 Lift trucks, industrial: fork, platform, straddle, etc.; control panels, electric

GEOGRAPHIC SECTION
Grandville - Kent County (G-7072)

(G-7046)
HARLO CORPORATION
Also Called: Control Panel Div
4210 Ferry St Sw (49418-1573)
P.O. Box 129 (49468-0129)
PHONE..................................616 538-0550
Mike Birkmeier, *Branch Mgr*
EMP: 45
SALES (corp-wide): 40.4MM **Privately Held**
WEB: www.harlo.com
SIC: 3537 3613 Lift trucks, industrial: fork, platform, straddle, etc.; switchgear & switchboard apparatus
PA: Harlo Corporation
4210 Ferry St Sw
Grandville MI 49418
616 538-0550

(G-7047)
HARLO PRODUCTS CORPORATION (HQ)
4210 Ferry St Sw (49418-1545)
P.O. Box 129 (49468-0129)
PHONE..................................616 538-0550
Mary Helen Crooks, *CEO*
Craig Crooks, *Chairman*
Richard G Crooks, *Exec VP*
▲ **EMP:** 30 **EST:** 1958
SQ FT: 63,000
SALES (est): 10.4MM
SALES (corp-wide): 40.4MM **Privately Held**
SIC: 3537 Forklift trucks
PA: Harlo Corporation
4210 Ferry St Sw
Grandville MI 49418
616 538-0550

(G-7048)
HUMPHREY COMPANIES LLC (PA)
2851 Prairie St Sw (49418-2179)
PHONE..................................616 530-1717
James A Humphrey, *CEO*
John W Humphrey, *Chairman*
James D Green, *CFO*
Scott Finkhouse, *Manager*
EMP: 195
SALES (est): 176.8MM
SALES (corp-wide): 171MM **Privately Held**
SIC: 3537 3714 3089 5023 Industrial trucks & tractors; motor vehicle parts & accessories; molding primary plastic; home furnishings; plastics sheets & rods

(G-7049)
I MACHINE LLC
2606 Sanford Ave Sw (49418-1069)
PHONE..................................616 532-8020
Michael Gill, *Manager*
Dennis Gill,
EMP: 3
SALES (est): 246.3K **Privately Held**
SIC: 3549 Wiredrawing & fabricating machinery & equipment, ex. die

(G-7050)
I2 INTERNATIONAL DEV LLC
2905 Wilson Ave Sw # 200 (49418-1295)
PHONE..................................616 534-8100
David Byker, *CEO*
Bill Stewart, *President*
Abdul Swalhah, *Vice Pres*
EMP: 12 **EST:** 2015
SQ FT: 3,000
SALES (est): 332.3K **Privately Held**
SIC: 3211 5039 Construction glass; glass construction materials

(G-7051)
IFCA INTERNATIONAL INC (PA)
3520 Fairlanes Ave Sw (49418-1536)
P.O. Box 810 (49468-0810)
PHONE..................................616 531-1840
Royce Sprague, *President*
Les Lofquist, *Exec Dir*
Rick Jeske, *Bd of Directors*
Thomas Margie, *Admin Asst*
EMP: 8
SQ FT: 6,000
SALES (est): 1.1MM **Privately Held**
WEB: www.ifca.org
SIC: 2741 8661 Miscellaneous publishing; religious organizations

(G-7052)
INDUSTRIAL INNOVATIONS INC
Also Called: Spray Right
2936 Dormax St Sw (49418-1166)
PHONE..................................616 249-1525
Troy W Turnbull, *President*
John W Hayes, *Vice Pres*
EMP: 10 **EST:** 1980
SQ FT: 10,000
SALES (est): 2.4MM **Privately Held**
WEB: www.industrialinnovations.com
SIC: 3542 3469 Die casting machines; metal stampings

(G-7053)
JIREH METAL PRODUCTS INC
3635 Nardin St Sw (49418-1066)
PHONE..................................616 531-7581
Michael Davenport, *President*
Andy Otteman, *Director*
EMP: 100
SQ FT: 114,000
SALES (est): 19.2MM **Privately Held**
WEB: www.jirehmetal.com
SIC: 3469 Stamping metal for the trade

(G-7054)
KERKSTRA PRECAST INC
Also Called: Spancrete Great Lakes
3373 Busch Dr Sw (49418-1341)
PHONE..................................616 457-4920
Greg Kerkstra, *CEO*
Derek Hunderman, *President*
Steve Haskill, *Vice Pres*
Susan Rollins, *Safety Dir*
Andy Eustice, *Project Mgr*
▲ **EMP:** 150
SALES (est): 44.6MM **Privately Held**
SIC: 3432 3272 Plumbing fixture fittings & trim; septic tanks, concrete

(G-7055)
LEGACY PRECISION MOLDS INC
4668 Spartan Indus Dr Sw (49418-2512)
PHONE..................................616 532-6536
Tom Van Ree, *Owner*
EMP: 7
SQ FT: 4,000
SALES (est): 1.1MM **Privately Held**
SIC: 3544 Forms (molds), for foundry & plastics working machinery

(G-7056)
LEJ INVESTMENTS LLC
Also Called: Nanoplas
2950 Pririe St Sw Ste 900 (49418)
PHONE..................................616 452-3707
John B Hoff,
EMP: 3
SALES (est): 328.9K **Privately Held**
SIC: 2821 Molding compounds, plastics

(G-7057)
MICHIGAN LEGAL PUBLISHING LTD
2885 Sanford Ave Sw (49418-1342)
PHONE..................................877 525-1990
Jeff Steinport, *Principal*
EMP: 3
SALES (est): 66.5K **Privately Held**
SIC: 2741 Miscellaneous publishing

(G-7058)
MIDWEST VIBRO INC
Also Called: H & M Vibro
3715 28th St Sw (49418-1314)
P.O. Box 245 (49468-0245)
PHONE..................................616 532-7670
Edwin Haverkamp, *President*
Douglas Haverkamp, *Vice Pres*
Nancy Haverkamp, *Admin Sec*
EMP: 5
SQ FT: 10,500
SALES (est): 1.2MM **Privately Held**
WEB: www.hmvibro.com
SIC: 3531 7359 7699 Vibrators for concrete construction; equipment rental & leasing; professional instrument repair services

(G-7059)
MULL-IT-OVER PRODUCTS INC
4275 White St Sw (49418-1253)
PHONE..................................616 843-6470
Bruce Brugess, *Principal*
EMP: 3
SALES (est): 400K **Privately Held**
SIC: 3531 Construction machinery

(G-7060)
MULTIAX INTERNATIONAL INC
3000 Remico St Sw (49418-1189)
PHONE..................................616 534-4530
Eduard Dauthier, *Managing Dir*
Darin De Clark, *Principal*
EMP: 5
SALES (est): 884.3K **Privately Held**
SIC: 8741 3661 Management services; modems

(G-7061)
MUSICAL SNEAKERS INCORPORATED (PA)
2885 Snford Ave Sw 3533 (49418)
P.O. Box 310, New York NY (10029-0241)
PHONE..................................888 410-7050
EMP: 16
SALES (est): 2.8MM **Privately Held**
SIC: 3021 Mfg Rubber/Plastic Footwear

(G-7062)
PACKAGING CORPORATION AMERICA
Also Called: PCA Grandville
3251 Chicago Dr Sw (49418-1003)
PHONE..................................616 530-5700
Mary Newmarch, *Principal*
Holly Koschtial, *Human Res Dir*
Bob Park, *Branch Mgr*
Robert Yoder, *Supervisor*
EMP: 125
SALES (corp-wide): 7B **Publicly Held**
WEB: www.pactiv.com
SIC: 2653 Boxes, corrugated: made from purchased materials; boxes, solid fiber: made from purchased materials
PA: Packaging Corporation Of America
1 N Field Ct
Lake Forest IL 60045
847 482-3000

(G-7063)
PEERLESS STEEL COMPANY
3280 Century Center St Sw (49418-3101)
PHONE..................................616 530-6695
Gary W Bradley, *Manager*
James Kandt, *Technology*
EMP: 28
SALES (est): 4.4MM
SALES (corp-wide): 81.9MM **Privately Held**
WEB: www.peerlesssteel.com
SIC: 5051 3322 3316 3312 Steel; malleable iron foundries; cold finishing of steel shapes; blast furnaces & steel mills
PA: Peerless Steel Company
2450 Austin Dr
Troy MI 48083
248 528-3200

(G-7064)
PLASMA BIOLIFE SERVICES L P
6331 Kenowa Ave Sw (49418-9414)
PHONE..................................616 667-0264
EMP: 4
SALES (corp-wide): 15.1B **Privately Held**
SIC: 2834 3841 2835 3842 Pharmaceutical preparations; intravenous solutions; solutions, pharmaceutical; surgical & medical instruments; catheters; medical instruments & equipment, blood & bone work; surgical instruments & apparatus; blood derivative diagnostic agents; surgical appliances & supplies
HQ: Biolife Plasma Services L.P.
1200 Lakeside Dr
Bannockburn IL

(G-7065)
PRAISE SIGN COMPANY
3404 Busch Dr Sw Ste F (49418-1000)
PHONE..................................616 439-0315
John Vanocker, *Owner*
EMP: 9
SALES (est): 55.7K **Privately Held**
SIC: 3993 1731 Signs & advertising specialties; general electrical contractor

(G-7066)
PRECISION LABEL INC
4181 Spartan Indus Dr Sw (49418-2553)
PHONE..................................616 534-9935
David Greiner, *President*
Tom Pikaart, *General Mgr*
EMP: 7 **EST:** 1994
SQ FT: 5,000
SALES (est): 832.1K **Privately Held**
SIC: 2759 Labels & seals: printing

(G-7067)
PROGRESS CHEMICAL INC
3015 Dormax St Sw (49418-1167)
P.O. Box 275 (49468-0275)
PHONE..................................616 534-6103
Eric H Stacey, *President*
Dan J Stacey, *Vice Pres*
Gregory H Stacey, *Vice Pres*
Michael C Stacey, *VP Mfg*
Brian Stacey, *Natl Sales Mgr*
▼ **EMP:** 5 **EST:** 1946
SQ FT: 14,000
SALES (est): 2.4MM **Privately Held**
WEB: www.progresschemical.com
SIC: 2842 Cleaning or polishing preparations; metal polish

(G-7068)
QUALITY EQP INSTALLATIONS
3404 Busch Dr Sw Ste A (49418-1000)
PHONE..................................616 249-3649
William Stick, *President*
EMP: 7 **EST:** 2000
SALES (est): 610K **Privately Held**
SIC: 3599 Custom machinery

(G-7069)
RAND WORLDWIDE SUBSIDIARY INC
4445 Wilson Ave Sw Ste 4 (49418-2351)
PHONE..................................616 261-8183
EMP: 4
SALES (corp-wide): 81MM **Publicly Held**
SIC: 3131 Mfg Footwear Cut Stock
HQ: Rand Worldwide Subsidiary, Inc.
11201 Dlfeld Blvd Ste 112
Owings Mills MD 21117
877 726-3243

(G-7070)
SCOTTS SIGNS
3386 Olivet St Sw (49418-1088)
P.O. Box 827 (49468-0827)
PHONE..................................616 532-2034
Scott Bouma, *Owner*
EMP: 4
SQ FT: 3,750
SALES (est): 402.6K **Privately Held**
SIC: 7389 3993 Sign painting & lettering shop; signs & advertising specialties

(G-7071)
SIGNET MACHINE INC
3119 Chicago Dr Sw (49418-1117)
PHONE..................................616 261-2939
Michael Tubergen, *President*
EMP: 3
SALES (est): 500K **Privately Held**
WEB: www.signetmachine.com
SIC: 3549 3599 5072 Metalworking machinery; machine shop, jobbing & repair; nozzles

(G-7072)
STANDALE LUMBER AND SUPPLY CO
2971 Franklin Ave Sw (49418-1266)
PHONE..................................616 530-8200
Tom Powers, *Manager*
EMP: 55
SALES (corp-wide): 46.1MM **Privately Held**
WEB: www.standalelumber.com
SIC: 5713 2431 5211 Floor covering stores; carpets; millwork; lumber products
PA: Standale Lumber And Supply Company
4100 Lake Michigan Dr Nw
Grand Rapids MI 49534
616 453-8207

Grandville - Kent County (G-7073)

GEOGRAPHIC SECTION

(G-7073)
TAPESTRY INC
3700 Rivertown Pkwy Sw # 1184
(49418-3085)
PHONE..................616 538-5802
Mike Krueger, *Branch Mgr*
EMP: 13
SALES (corp-wide): 6B **Publicly Held**
WEB: www.coach.com
SIC: 3199 5699 Embossed leather goods; customized clothing & apparel
PA: Tapestry, Inc.
10 Hudson Yards
New York NY 10001
212 594-1850

(G-7074)
THERM TECHNOLOGY CORP
2879 Remico St Sw (49418-1139)
PHONE..................616 530-6540
Jim Workman, *Ch of Bd*
▲ **EMP:** 8
SQ FT: 25,000
SALES (est): 1MM **Privately Held**
WEB: www.fuelcellss.com
SIC: 3634 Heaters, space electric

(G-7075)
VAN DYKEN MECHANICAL INC
4275 Spartan Indus Dr Sw (49418-2503)
PHONE..................616 224-7030
Arnold Van Dyken, *Ch of Bd*
Randal Van Dyken, *President*
John Herdegen, *Business Mgr*
Joe Vandenberg, *Exec VP*
Bill Barrett, *Vice Pres*
EMP: 85 **EST:** 1949
SQ FT: 6,000
SALES (est): 17.2MM **Privately Held**
WEB: www.vdminc.com
SIC: 1711 8711 3499 Warm air heating & air conditioning contractor; mechanical contractor; engineering services; fire- or burglary-resistive products

(G-7076)
WOOD-CUTTERS TOOLING INC
4685 Spartan Indus Dr Sw (49418-2511)
PHONE..................616 257-7930
Charlie Bosscher, *President*
EMP: 6
SQ FT: 4,400
SALES (est): 841.5K **Privately Held**
SIC: 3545 7699 Cutting tools for machine tools; knife, saw & tool sharpening & repair

Grant
Newaygo County

(G-7077)
ALLIED MACHINE INC
11171 Spruce Ave (49327-9342)
PHONE..................231 834-0050
Kenneth Cronk, *President*
David Thompson, *Vice Pres*
David Lutz, *Manager*
EMP: 27
SQ FT: 19,600
SALES: 3MM **Privately Held**
SIC: 3599 7692 3444 Machine shop, jobbing & repair; welding repair; sheet metalwork

(G-7078)
AMERICAN PALLET COMPANY LLC
11421 S Peach Ave (49327-8759)
PHONE..................231 834-5056
Henry Dehaan,
EMP: 3
SALES (est): 119.9K **Privately Held**
SIC: 2448 Wood pallets & skids

(G-7079)
CHIVIS SPORTSMAN CASES
1192 E 112th St (49327-7423)
PHONE..................231 834-1162
Gary Chivis, *President*
EMP: 5
SALES (est): 203.6K **Privately Held**
SIC: 2499 Wood products

(G-7080)
KEITH FALAN
14097 S Mason Dr (49327-9645)
PHONE..................231 834-7358
Keith Falan, *Principal*
EMP: 3
SALES (est): 180.3K **Privately Held**
SIC: 2411 Logging

(G-7081)
QUALITY FINISHING SYSTEMS
333 W 136th St (49327-9646)
P.O. Box 372 (49327-0372)
PHONE..................231 834-9131
Loren Courson, *President*
Brent Courson, *Accountant*
EMP: 18
SALES: 2MM **Privately Held**
SIC: 3441 3444 Fabricated structural metal; sheet metalwork

(G-7082)
RIDGE CIDER
351 W 136th St (49327-8456)
PHONE..................231 674-2040
Matt Delong, *Owner*
EMP: 6 **EST:** 2015
SALES (est): 434K **Privately Held**
SIC: 2099 Cider, nonalcoholic

Grass Lake
Jackson County

(G-7083)
AGGREGATE INDUSTRIES - MWR INC
4950 Loveland Rd (49240-9106)
PHONE..................734 475-2531
Todd Yetzke, *Foreman/Supr*
Randy Allen, *Manager*
EMP: 6
SALES (corp-wide): 27.6B **Privately Held**
SIC: 3273 Ready-mixed concrete
HQ: Aggregate Industries - Mwr, Inc.
2815 Dodd Rd
Eagan MN 55121
651 683-0600

(G-7084)
AGGREGATE INDUSTRIES CENTL REG
4950 Loveland Rd (49240-9106)
PHONE..................734 475-2531
David Allen, *Plant Mgr*
EMP: 3
SALES (est): 163.1K **Privately Held**
SIC: 3273 Ready-mixed concrete

(G-7085)
AMERICAN TOOLING CENTER INC (PA)
4111 Mount Hope Rd (49240-9513)
PHONE..................517 522-8411
John J Basso, *President*
Linda Garrisi, *Vice Pres*
Julie Bristow, *Purch Mgr*
Julie Howard, *Purch Mgr*
Sonia Basso, *Treasurer*
▲ **EMP:** 78
SQ FT: 65,000
SALES (est): 30.3MM **Privately Held**
WEB: www.americantoolingcenter.com
SIC: 3544 Special dies & tools

(G-7086)
COY LABORATORY PRODUCTS INC
14500 Coy Dr (49240-9207)
PHONE..................734 433-9296
Richard A Coy, *President*
Brian Coy, *President*
Carol Ann Coy, *Corp Secy*
Kevin Coy, *Corp Secy*
Ashley Coy, *Director*
▼ **EMP:** 22 **EST:** 1969
SQ FT: 20,000
SALES: 5.4MM **Privately Held**
WEB: www.coylab.com
SIC: 3821 Laboratory apparatus & furniture

(G-7087)
DOERKEN CORPORATION
11200 Cedar Knoll Dr (49240-9622)
P.O. Box 429 (49240-0429)
PHONE..................517 522-4600
Frederick A Schultz, *President*
▲ **EMP:** 4
SQ FT: 24,000
SALES (est): 2MM
SALES (corp-wide): 347.5MM **Privately Held**
WEB: www.doerkenusa.com
SIC: 2899 Corrosion preventive lubricant
PA: Ewald DOrken Ag
Wetterstr. 58
Herdecke 58313
233 063-0

(G-7088)
GRASS LAKE COMMUNITY PHARMACY
Also Called: Indispensable Health
116 E Michigan Ave (49240-9680)
PHONE..................517 522-4100
Todd Raehtz, *President*
EMP: 7
SALES (est): 465.6K **Privately Held**
SIC: 2834 8742 Druggists' preparations (pharmaceuticals); hospital & health services consultant

(G-7089)
LOVEN SPOONFUL
119 E Main St (49240)
PHONE..................517 522-3953
Shelly Hart, *Owner*
EMP: 5
SALES (est): 270K **Privately Held**
SIC: 2024 Ice cream & frozen desserts

(G-7090)
P L SCHMITT CRBIDE TOOLING LLC
8865 Seymour Rd (49240-9565)
PHONE..................313 706-5756
Paul Schmitt,
EMP: 5
SALES (est): 564.2K **Privately Held**
SIC: 3545 End mills

(G-7091)
PDF MFG INC
11000 Cedar Knoll Dr (49240-9811)
P.O. Box 186 (49240-0186)
PHONE..................517 522-8431
Lee Declaire, *President*
Glen A Primrose, *Treasurer*
Bruce Fielder, *Shareholder*
EMP: 5
SQ FT: 5,500
SALES (est): 774.9K **Privately Held**
SIC: 3599 3312 3544 Electrical discharge machining (EDM); tool & die steel; special dies, tools, jigs & fixtures

(G-7092)
PL SCHMITT CRBIDE TOLING LLC
133 Drake St (49240-8302)
PHONE..................517 522-6891
Paul Schmitt, *Mng Member*
EMP: 8 **EST:** 2014
SALES (est): 1.6MM **Privately Held**
SIC: 3545 Cutting tools for machine tools

(G-7093)
SOLID MANUFACTURING INC
125 W Michigan Ave (49240-9188)
P.O. Box 280 (49240-0280)
PHONE..................517 522-5895
George T Husak II, *CEO*
George Husak Jr, *President*
Connie Husak, *Vice Pres*
George Husak Sr, *Vice Pres*
EMP: 20
SQ FT: 15,000
SALES (est): 4.3MM **Privately Held**
WEB: www.solidmfg.com
SIC: 3599 Machine shop, jobbing & repair

(G-7094)
STR COMPANY
6442 Wooster Rd (49240-9505)
PHONE..................517 206-6058
Susann K Moore, *Owner*
EMP: 4
SALES (est): 190K **Privately Held**
SIC: 2679 Paperboard products, converted

(G-7095)
TENNECO AUTOMOTIVE OPER CO INC
3901 Willis Rd (49240-9791)
P.O. Box 157 (49240-0157)
PHONE..................517 522-5520
Joe Czarnecki, *Opers-Prdtn-Mfg*
James Pettit, *Engineer*
Rich Harms, *Program Mgr*
Jason Timmerman, *Program Mgr*
Sampangiappa Sankarbabu, *Manager*
EMP: 245
SQ FT: 50,000
SALES (corp-wide): 11.7B **Publicly Held**
WEB: www.tenneco-automotive.com
SIC: 3714 Motor vehicle parts & accessories
HQ: Tenneco Automotive Operating Company, Inc.
500 N Field Dr
Lake Forest IL 60045
847 482-5000

Grawn
Grand Traverse County

(G-7096)
ALTUS BRANDS LLC (PA)
6893 Sullivan Rd (49637-9542)
PHONE..................231 421-3810
Shannon Plamondon, *Office Mgr*
Brian Breneman, *Mng Member*
◆ **EMP:** 12
SALES (est): 2.8MM **Privately Held**
SIC: 3999 Advertising display products

(G-7097)
APPLE FENCE CO
1893 Pine Tree (49637-9776)
PHONE..................231 276-9888
Gary Sheffer, *President*
Scott Sheffer, *Corp Secy*
EMP: 15 **EST:** 1982
SQ FT: 2,560
SALES (est): 3.3MM **Privately Held**
WEB: www.applefence.com
SIC: 5211 2499 1799 Fencing; fencing, wood; drapery track installation

(G-7098)
GREAT LAKES WELLHEAD INC (PA)
4243 S M 37 (49637-9745)
PHONE..................231 943-9100
Bruce Rosema, *President*
Lisa Hernandez, *Branch Mgr*
Bruce Lautner, *Senior Mgr*
Kyle Fitzpatrick, *Nurse*
EMP: 3
SQ FT: 4,000
SALES (est): 4MM **Privately Held**
SIC: 7353 5082 1389 Oil equipment rental services; oil field equipment; oil & gas wells; building, repairing & dismantling

(G-7099)
MATERNE NORTH AMERICA CORP
Also Called: Gogosqueez
6331 Us Highway 31 (49637-9620)
P.O. Box 268 (49637-0268)
PHONE..................231 346-6600
Michel Larroche, *CEO*
EMP: 20
SALES (corp-wide): 7.4MM **Privately Held**
SIC: 2033 Apple sauce: packaged in cans, jars, etc.
HQ: Materne North America, Corp.
20 W 22nd St Fl 12
New York NY 10010
212 675-7881

(G-7100)
RIETH-RILEY CNSTR CO INC
4435 S M 37 (49637-9745)
PHONE..................231 263-2100
Jeff Saylor, *Manager*

GEOGRAPHIC SECTION

EMP: 10
SQ FT: 864
SALES (corp-wide): 205.9MM **Privately Held**
WEB: www.reithriley.com
SIC: **1611** 2951 Surfacing & paving; asphalt paving mixtures & blocks
PA: Rieth-Riley Construction Co., Inc.
3626 Elkhart Rd
Goshen IN 46526
574 875-5183

Grayling
Crawford County

(G-7101)
A J D FOREST PDTS LTD PARTNR
4440 W 4 Mile Rd (49738-9779)
P.O. Box 629 (49738-0629)
PHONE.................................989 348-5412
David J Stephenson, *Partner*
A D F 1 Corp, *Partner*
Fred Fisher, *Partner*
Albert L Quaal, *Partner*
EMP: 55
SQ FT: 54,000
SALES (est): 2.6MM
SALES (corp-wide): 6.8B **Publicly Held**
WEB: www.ajdforestproducts.com
SIC: **2421** Lumber: rough, sawed or planed
PA: Cms Energy Corporation
1 Energy Plaza Dr
Jackson MI 49201
517 788-0550

(G-7102)
AIR WAY AUTOMATION INC
2268 Industrial Dr (49738-7849)
P.O. Box 563 (49738-0563)
PHONE.................................989 348-1802
Robert G Toms, *President*
David Starkey, *Corp Secy*
John Ammond, *Vice Pres*
Tim Coggins, *Engineer*
Don Schlehuber, *Engineer*
◆ EMP: 44
SQ FT: 51,700
SALES: 13.4MM **Privately Held**
WEB: www.airwayautomation.com
SIC: **3599** Machine shop, jobbing & repair

(G-7103)
ARAUCO NORTH AMERICA INC
5851 Arauco Rd (49738-9707)
PHONE.................................800 261-4896
EMP: 200 **Privately Held**
SIC: **2493** Flakeboard
HQ: Arauco North America, Inc
400 Perimeter Center Ter
Atlanta GA 30346

(G-7104)
CRAWFORD COUNTY AVALANCHE
108 E Michigan Ave (49738-1741)
P.O. Box 490 (49738-0490)
PHONE.................................989 348-6811
Ann Marie Milliman, *President*
EMP: 5
SALES (est): 343.5K **Privately Held**
SIC: **2711** Job printing & newspaper publishing combined

(G-7105)
CSI EMERGENCY APPARATUS LLC
2332 Dupont St (49738-7836)
PHONE.................................989 348-2877
Chuck Quiney, *Mng Member*
Mark Brown,
Scott Patchin,
EMP: 16
SQ FT: 16,000
SALES (est): 3.4MM **Privately Held**
WEB: www.csiea.com
SIC: **3713** Truck bodies (motor vehicles)

(G-7106)
FRED KELLY PICKS LLC
4333 W N Down River Rd (49738-7891)
P.O. Box 532 (49738-0532)
PHONE.................................989 348-2938
Fred Kelly, *Mng Member*
Helen Kelly,
EMP: 6 EST: 1976
SQ FT: 3,200
SALES: 250K **Privately Held**
SIC: **3931** Guitars & parts, electric & non-electric

(G-7107)
GEORGIA-PACIFIC LLC
4113 W 4 Mile Rd (49738-9779)
PHONE.................................989 348-7275
Steve Randall, *Manager*
EMP: 35
SALES (corp-wide): 40.6B **Privately Held**
WEB: www.gp.com
SIC: **3087** 2869 2821 Custom compound purchased resins; industrial organic chemicals; plastics materials & resins
HQ: Georgia-Pacific Llc
133 Peachtree St Nw
Atlanta GA 30303
404 652-4000

(G-7108)
IMM INC
758 Isenhauer Rd (49738-8638)
P.O. Box 747 (49738-0747)
PHONE.................................989 344-7662
Elizabeth Doering, *President*
Mark Saxton, *Vice Pres*
EMP: 40
SQ FT: 45,000
SALES (est): 1.5MM **Privately Held**
SIC: **3441** 1791 Fabricated structural metal; structural steel erection

(G-7109)
JACK MILLIKIN INC
4680 W N Down River Rd (49738-7892)
PHONE.................................989 348-8411
JC M Millikin, *Corp Secy*
Brian Pratt, *Vice Pres*
EMP: 9 EST: 1941
SQ FT: 12,400
SALES (est): 860K **Privately Held**
SIC: **1794** 1442 5039 Excavation work; common sand mining; gravel mining; septic tanks

(G-7110)
LC MATERIALS
3881 W 4 Mile Rd (49738-8079)
PHONE.................................989 344-0235
Dave Gildey, *President*
EMP: 6
SALES (corp-wide): 8MM **Privately Held**
SIC: **3273** Ready-mixed concrete
PA: Lc Materials
805 W 13th St
Cadillac MI 49601
231 825-2473

(G-7111)
MAY-DAY WINDOW MANUFACTURING
403 N Wilcox Bridge Rd (49738-8613)
PHONE.................................989 348-2809
Mark Swiercz, *President*
David Swiercz, *Vice Pres*
EMP: 4
SQ FT: 12,000
SALES (est): 260K **Privately Held**
SIC: **3089** Windows, plastic

(G-7112)
MICHIGAN WOOD PELLET LLC
2211 Industrial Dr (49738-7849)
PHONE.................................989 348-4100
Susan L Hees, *Principal*
Mike Hees,
EMP: 10
SALES (est): 1.4MM **Privately Held**
SIC: **3532** Pellet mills (mining machinery)

(G-7113)
MONARCH MILLWORK INC (PA)
2211 Industrial Dr (49738-7849)
PHONE.................................989 348-8292
Michael D Hees, *President*
EMP: 8
SQ FT: 20,000
SALES (est): 2MM **Privately Held**
SIC: **2431** Doors, wood

(G-7114)
NORTHERN WOODCRAFTERS
4562 W N Down River Rd (49738-7892)
PHONE.................................989 348-2553
Scott Page, *Owner*
EMP: 6
SQ FT: 16,000
SALES (est): 2.7MM **Privately Held**
SIC: **3553** Furniture makers' machinery, woodworking

(G-7115)
PADDLE HARD DISTRIBUTING LLC
118 E Michigan Ave (49738-1741)
PHONE.................................513 309-1192
Dave Vargo,
EMP: 5 EST: 2016
SQ FT: 3,000
SALES (est): 169.2K **Privately Held**
SIC: **2082** Beer (alcoholic beverage)

(G-7116)
SYLVESTERS (PA)
Also Called: Cheers Embroidery
5610 W M 72 Hwy (49738-1226)
PHONE.................................989 348-9097
Larry Raymond, *Owner*
EMP: 3
SQ FT: 3,800
SALES (est): 502.5K **Privately Held**
WEB: www.sylvesters.net
SIC: **2396** 2395 5999 2759 Screen printing on fabric articles; embroidery & art needlework; trophies & plaques; screen printing; signs & advertising specialties

(G-7117)
T WARREN SAWMILL
6187 Warren Trl (49738-8013)
PHONE.................................989 619-0840
Tony G Warren, *Principal*
EMP: 3
SALES (est): 233.1K **Privately Held**
SIC: **2421** Sawmills & planing mills, general

(G-7118)
WEYERHAEUSER COMPANY
4111 W 4 Mile Rd (49738-9702)
PHONE.................................989 348-2881
Rina Bethany, *Plant Mgr*
Phil Dennett, *Opers-Prdtn-Mfg*
Bonnie Doremire, *Finance Mgr*
EMP: 200
SALES (corp-wide): 7.4B **Publicly Held**
SIC: **2421** 2493 Lumber: rough, sawed or planed; reconstituted wood products
PA: Weyerhaeuser Company
220 Occidental Ave S
Seattle WA 98104
206 539-3000

(G-7119)
YAMAHA LOGGING
2682 Sandy Trl (49738-9434)
P.O. Box 90 (49738-0090)
PHONE.................................989 657-1706
EMP: 3
SALES (est): 127.4K **Privately Held**
SIC: **2411** Logging

Greenbush
Alcona County

(G-7120)
HAVERCROFT TOOL & DIE INC
5002 Main St (48738-9698)
PHONE.................................989 724-5913
Timothy Havercroft, *CEO*
EMP: 5
SALES (est): 484K **Privately Held**
SIC: **3544** Special dies & tools

(G-7121)
W & S DEVELOPMENT INC
4957 Main St (48738-9696)
PHONE.................................989 724-5463
Thomas L Stojsik, *President*
EMP: 18
SQ FT: 12,000
SALES (est): 3.1MM **Privately Held**
WEB: www.wsdredge.com
SIC: **3531** Dredging machinery

Greenville
Montcalm County

(G-7122)
AGGRESSIVE TOOLING INC
608 Industrial Park Dr (48838-9792)
PHONE.................................616 754-1404
Richard Jones, *President*
Jon Heaton, *Vice Pres*
Pam Moore, *Manager*
Dan Slezak, *Manager*
Arden Bremmer, *Technology*
EMP: 43
SQ FT: 16,000
SALES (est): 8.3MM **Privately Held**
WEB: www.aggressivetooling.com
SIC: **3544** 7692 Special dies & tools; welding repair

(G-7123)
BLACKSMITH SHOP LLC
809 Callaghan St (48838-7146)
PHONE.................................616 754-4719
Loie Byville, *Office Mgr*
William Byville,
EMP: 5
SQ FT: 10,000
SALES: 500K **Privately Held**
SIC: **3446** Architectural metalwork

(G-7124)
CITY OF GREENVILLE
Also Called: Silent Observer
415 S Lafayette St (48838-2353)
PHONE.................................616 754-0100
Bruce Schnepp, *Director*
EMP: 27 **Privately Held**
SIC: **2711** Newspapers
PA: City Of Greenville
411 S Lafayette St
Greenville MI 48838
616 754-5644

(G-7125)
CLARION TECHNOLOGIES INC
501 S Cedar St (48838-2003)
PHONE.................................616 754-1199
Fred Gradisher, *Manager*
EMP: 225
SALES (corp-wide): 63.6MM **Privately Held**
WEB: www.clariontechnologies.com
SIC: **3089** Molding primary plastic
PA: Clarion Technologies, Inc.
170 College Ave Ste 300
Holland MI 49423
616 698-7277

(G-7126)
D-M-E USA INC
Also Called: Master Unit Die Products, Inc.
1117 E Fairplains St (48838-2808)
PHONE.................................616 754-4601
Dennis Smith, *CEO*
Ken Jasina, *General Mgr*
Mary Wall, *Principal*
◆ EMP: 48 EST: 1958
SALES (est): 23.3K
SALES (corp-wide): 1.2B **Privately Held**
SIC: **3544** 3443 Forms (molds), for foundry & plastics working machinery; fabricated plate work (boiler shop)
HQ: Dme Company Llc
29111 Stephenson Hwy
Madison Heights MI 48071

(G-7127)
DICASTAL NORTH AMERICA INC
1 Dicastal Dr (48838-9594)
PHONE.................................616 303-0306
Bernard Polzin, *President*
Mike James, *Engineer*
Scott Petzold, *Human Res Dir*
EMP: 268
SQ FT: 623,749
SALES (est): 1.2MM **Privately Held**
SIC: **3714** Wheels, motor vehicle

Greenville - Montcalm County (G-7128)

HQ: Citic Dicastal Co., Ltd.
No.185, Longhai Avenue, Economic
And Technological Development Z
Qinhuangdao 06601
335 535-8751

(G-7128)
DLT INDUSTRIES INC
1760 Callaghan St (48838-7109)
PHONE..................616 754-2762
Dave Tamblyn, *President*
▲ **EMP:** 3
SQ FT: 6,000
SALES (est): 505.9K **Privately Held**
WEB: www.dltindustries.com
SIC: 3544 Special dies & tools

(G-7129)
EAGLE GROUP II LTD
8384 Peck Rd (48838-9715)
PHONE..................616 754-7777
Roy Ferguson Jr, *President*
Roy J Ferguson III, *President*
Roy J Ferguson Sr, *President*
Hal Soucie, *Vice Pres*
Al Magaluk, *Project Mgr*
EMP: 25
SQ FT: 16,000
SALES (est): 6.8MM **Privately Held**
WEB: www.eaglegroupltd.com
SIC: 3523 Farm machinery & equipment

(G-7130)
FABX INDUSTRIES INC
Also Called: Aquest Machining & Assembly
715 Callaghan St (48838-7157)
PHONE..................616 225-1724
Gopikrishna Ganta, *President*
EMP: 21
SALES (est): 694.8K **Privately Held**
SIC: 3599 Machine shop, jobbing & repair

(G-7131)
FEDERAL-MOGUL POWERTRAIN LLC
409 E Cass St (48838-1903)
PHONE..................616 754-1272
EMP: 8
SALES (corp-wide): 11.7B **Publicly Held**
SIC: 3559 Degreasing machines, automotive & industrial
HQ: Federal-Mogul Powertrain Llc
27300 W 11 Mile Rd
Southfield MI 48034

(G-7132)
FEDERAL-MOGUL POWERTRAIN LLC
510 E Grove St (48838-1881)
PHONE..................616 754-5681
Damien Vezol, *Branch Mgr*
EMP: 350
SALES (corp-wide): 11.7B **Publicly Held**
SIC: 3714 3568 Bearings, motor vehicle; power transmission equipment
HQ: Federal-Mogul Powertrain Llc
27300 W 11 Mile Rd
Southfield MI 48034

(G-7133)
GREENVILLE CABINET DISTRI
425 E Fairplains St (48838-2469)
PHONE..................616 225-2424
Byron Reynolds, *Owner*
EMP: 8
SALES (est): 510K **Privately Held**
SIC: 2434 Wood kitchen cabinets

(G-7134)
GREENVILLE ENGINEERED & TOOLED
Also Called: Great Products
12525 Sassafras Rd Ne (48838-9018)
PHONE..................616 292-0701
Derek Cushman, *President*
EMP: 3
SALES (est): 2MM **Privately Held**
SIC: 3499 Aerosol valves, metal

(G-7135)
GREENVILLE TOOL & DIE CO
Also Called: Z. Real Estate Company
1215 S Lafayette St (48838-9386)
P.O. Box 310 (48838-0310)
PHONE..................616 754-5693
Dale Hartway, *CEO*
Larry Caverley, *President*
Ted Bush, *Exec VP*
Rob Rahn, *Design Engr*
Gregg Peters, *Controller*
▲ **EMP:** 140
SQ FT: 109,000
SALES (est): 24.6MM **Privately Held**
WEB: www.gtd.com
SIC: 3544 Special dies & tools

(G-7136)
GREENVILLE TRCK WLDG SUPS LLC (PA)
Also Called: Greenville Truck and Welding
201 W Greenville West Dr (48838-1162)
P.O. Box 933 (48838-0933)
PHONE..................616 754-6120
Jeffrey Loding, *President*
Peter Gibson, *Vice Pres*
Pete Gibson, *Sales Staff*
Brenda Ladermann, *Office Mgr*
EMP: 12
SALES (est): 2.9MM **Privately Held**
SIC: 5999 2813 Welding supplies; acetylene

(G-7137)
GREENVILLE VENTR PARTNERS LLC
6501 Fitzner Rd (48838-9783)
PHONE..................616 303-2400
Michael Doyle, *President*
EMP: 30
SALES (est): 942.1K **Privately Held**
SIC: 2022 2026 2023 2021 Cheese, natural & processed; fluid milk; condensed milk; evaporated whey; powdered milk; creamery butter
PA: Foremost Farms Usa Cooperative
E10889 Penny Ln
Baraboo WI 53913

(G-7138)
HIGH GRADE MATERIALS COMPANY (PA)
9266 Snows Lake Rd (48838-8753)
PHONE..................616 754-5545
James Sturrus, *President*
Dave Cole, *Controller*
Patty Sturrus, *Human Res Mgr*
Sharon Schultz, *Technology*
Roger Roberts, *Master*
EMP: 27
SQ FT: 34,000
SALES (est): 28.3MM **Privately Held**
SIC: 3273 3272 1442 Ready-mixed concrete; concrete products; construction sand & gravel

(G-7139)
HUNTINGTON FOAM LLC
1323 Moore St (48838-8767)
PHONE..................661 225-9951
Sidney Montes, *Branch Mgr*
Robert Staffo, *Manager*
John Thompson, *Manager*
EMP: 40 **Privately Held**
SIC: 3086 Plastics foam products
PA: Huntington Foam, Llc
125 Caliber Ridge Dr # 200
Greer SC 29651

(G-7140)
JORGENSENS INC
Also Called: Jorgensen's Supermarket
1325 W Washington St (48838-2191)
PHONE..................989 831-8338
Mark Deihl, *Manager*
EMP: 30
SALES (corp-wide): 6.3MM **Privately Held**
WEB: www.jorgensens.com
SIC: 5411 5912 5812 2051 Grocery stores; drug stores & proprietary stores; eating places; bread, cake & related products
PA: Jorgensen's Inc
215 N State St
Stanton MI 48888
989 831-8345

(G-7141)
K&W TOOL AND MACHINE INC
1216 Shearer Rd Ste A (48838-9102)
PHONE..................616 754-7540
Joseph H Kohn, *President*
Laura Kohn, *Human Resources*
EMP: 19
SQ FT: 105,000
SALES (est): 2.2MM **Privately Held**
SIC: 3599 7389 Custom machinery; metal cutting services

(G-7142)
KENT FOUNDRY COMPANY
1413 Callaghan St (48838-8127)
P.O. Box 187 (48838-0187)
PHONE..................616 754-1100
Gerald A Poorman, *President*
Jim Perski, *General Mgr*
Jo Ann Poorman, *Corp Secy*
Richard Dykhouse, *QC Mgr*
Kathy Porter, *Sales Staff*
EMP: 46
SQ FT: 33,000
SALES (est): 13MM **Privately Held**
WEB: www.kentfoundry.com
SIC: 3321 Ductile iron castings; gray iron castings

(G-7143)
KNAPP PRINTING SERVICES INC
Also Called: Arrow Swift Prtg & Copy Ctr
6540 S Greenville Rd (48838-1021)
PHONE..................616 754-9159
Mike Knapp, *President*
EMP: 7
SQ FT: 2,500
SALES (est): 1.1MM **Privately Held**
SIC: 2752 Commercial printing, offset

(G-7144)
LINDE GAS LLC
510 E Grove St (48838-1878)
PHONE..................616 754-7575
Wolfgang Reitzle, *CEO*
EMP: 3
SALES (est): 160.7K **Privately Held**
SIC: 2813 Nitrogen

(G-7145)
MASTER PRECISION PRODUCTS INC
Also Called: Master Precision Molds
1212 E Fairplains St (48838-2809)
P.O. Box 70 (48838-0070)
PHONE..................616 754-5483
Stephen D Drake Jr, *President*
Gary Bowen, *Plant Mgr*
Rick Gunderson, *Engineer*
Marcus Hansen, *Engineer*
Ray Sova, *Program Mgr*
◆ **EMP:** 30
SQ FT: 30,000
SALES (est): 5.8MM **Privately Held**
WEB: www.masterprecision.com
SIC: 3544 Forms (molds), for foundry & plastics working machinery

(G-7146)
MERSEN USA GREENVILLE-MI CORP
712 Industrial Park Dr (48838-9792)
P.O. Box 637 (48838-0637)
PHONE..................616 754-5671
Todd N Taylor, *President*
Doug Adams, *General Mgr*
Shane Dennis, *Accounts Mgr*
▲ **EMP:** 115
SQ FT: 110,000
SALES (est): 24.5MM
SALES (corp-wide): 2MM **Privately Held**
WEB: www.graphite-eng.com
SIC: 3624 Carbon & graphite products
HQ: Mersen Usa Ptt Corp.
400 Myrtle Ave
Boonton NJ 07005
973 334-0700

(G-7147)
NORTHLAND CORPORATION
Also Called: Marvel Industries
1260 E Van Deinse St (48838-1400)
P.O. Box 400 (48838-0400)
PHONE..................616 754-5601
William Harris, *Plant Mgr*
Robert Ailes, *Purch Agent*
Richard Burns, *Purch Agent*
Richard Detrick, *Engineer*
Erskine Ratchford, *Engineer*
EMP: 100
SALES (corp-wide): 2.7B **Publicly Held**
WEB: www.northlandka.net
SIC: 3444 Sheet metalwork
HQ: Northland Corporation
1260 E Van Deinse St
Greenville MI 48838
616 754-5601

(G-7148)
NORTHLAND CORPORATION (DH)
Also Called: Northland Refrigeration
1260 E Van Deinse St (48838-1400)
PHONE..................616 754-5601
William McGrath, *CEO*
Bradley S Stauffer, *Senior VP*
◆ **EMP:** 141 **EST:** 1892
SQ FT: 175,000
SALES (est): 28.7MM
SALES (corp-wide): 2.7B **Publicly Held**
WEB: www.northlandnka.net
SIC: 3632 3444 Freezers, home & farm; sheet metalwork

(G-7149)
P C S COMPANIES INC
Also Called: Powder Coating Services
1251 Callaghan St (48838-8178)
PHONE..................616 754-2229
Patrick J Emerson, *President*
Jim Bullinger, *Vice Pres*
EMP: 7
SQ FT: 10,000
SALES (est): 605.2K **Privately Held**
SIC: 1721 1521 3479 Industrial painting; single-family housing construction; coating of metals & formed products

(G-7150)
QUAD/GRAPHICS INC
1321 E Van Deinse St (48838-7192)
P.O. Box 220 (48838-0220)
PHONE..................616 754-3672
Keith Fleming, *President*
Cathy De Leon, *Sales Executive*
Joe Corcoran, *Manager*
EMP: 200
SALES (corp-wide): 4.1B **Publicly Held**
WEB: www.vertisinc.com
SIC: 2752 Commercial printing, offset
PA: Quad/Graphics Inc.
N61w23044 Harrys Way
Sussex WI 53089
414 566-6000

(G-7151)
S & H TROPHY & SPORTS
1224 Blackburn St (48838-1519)
PHONE..................616 754-0005
James Hinton, *Owner*
EMP: 3
SALES (est): 253K **Privately Held**
SIC: 5941 5999 2395 2396 Sporting goods & bicycle shops; trophies & plaques; embroidery products, except schiffli machine; screen printing on fabric articles

(G-7152)
SCREENWORKS CSTM SCRN PRINTG &
9470 Sw Greenville Rd (48838-9487)
PHONE..................616 754-7762
Dave Kluzak, *Owner*
Nancy Kluzak, *Co-Owner*
EMP: 3
SALES: 67K **Privately Held**
SIC: 2759 Screen printing

(G-7153)
SIMMONS GRAVEL CO
5123 Youngman Rd (48838-9205)
PHONE..................616 754-7073
John Simmons, *Owner*
EMP: 3 **EST:** 1971
SALES: 65K **Privately Held**
SIC: 1442 3272 Gravel mining; septic tanks, concrete

GEOGRAPHIC SECTION

(G-7154)
STAFFORD MEDIA INC (PA)
Also Called: Newsweb
109 N Lafayette St (48838-1853)
P.O. Box 340 (48838-0340)
PHONE.................................616 754-9301
Chris Loiselle, *CEO*
Robert Stafford, *President*
Richard Ellafrits, *CPA*
Ruth Pate, *Human Res Mgr*
John Moy, *VP Sales*
EMP: 40
SQ FT: 10,000
SALES (est): 20.6MM **Privately Held**
WEB: www.greenvillenews.net
SIC: 2791 2711 2752 2741 Typesetting; commercial printing & newspaper publishing combined; commercial printing, lithographic; miscellaneous publishing

(G-7155)
STAFFORD MEDIA INC
1005 E Fairplains St (48838-2806)
PHONE.................................616 754-1178
John Moy, *Manager*
Peter Meade, *Executive*
EMP: 71
SALES (corp-wide): 20.6MM **Privately Held**
SIC: 2791 Typesetting
PA: Stafford Media, Inc.
  109 N Lafayette St
  Greenville MI 48838
  616 754-9301

(G-7156)
SYNTHETIC LUBRICANTS INC
1411 Callaghan St (48838-8127)
PHONE.................................616 754-1050
Anthony Draper, *President*
Tony Draper, *Research*
EMP: 5 **EST:** 1973
SQ FT: 7,500
SALES: 1MM **Privately Held**
WEB: www.synlube-mi.com
SIC: 3471 Cleaning & descaling metal products

(G-7157)
TAW PLASTICS LLC (PA)
1118 S Edgewood St (48838-2522)
PHONE.................................616 302-0954
Timothy A Weaver, *Mng Member*
EMP: 2
SALES: 1.4MM **Privately Held**
SIC: 3089 Molding primary plastic; injection molding of plastics

(G-7158)
TON-TEX CORPORATION (PA)
4029 E Grv Unit 7 (48838)
P.O. Box 397 (48838-0397)
PHONE.................................616 957-3200
Robert H Beaman, *Ch of Bd*
Robert L Fox, *President*
EMP: 37 **EST:** 1926
SQ FT: 32,500
SALES (est): 5.9MM **Privately Held**
SIC: 3568 3535 3052 2296 Power transmission equipment; conveyors & conveying equipment; rubber & plastics hose & beltings; tire cord & fabrics; conveyor belts

(G-7159)
TRAFFIC DISPLAYS LLC
9363 S Grow Rd (48838-9741)
PHONE.................................616 225-8865
Jason Johnson,
EMP: 6
SALES (est): 781.4K **Privately Held**
WEB: www.trafficdisplays.com
SIC: 3993 Signs, not made in custom sign painting shops

(G-7160)
WELLS HELICOPTER SERVICE INC
Also Called: S & W Marine System
10860 11 Mile Rd Ne (48838-9334)
PHONE.................................616 874-6255
Robert Wells, *President*
Patricia Wells, *Vice Pres*
EMP: 3 **EST:** 1971
SQ FT: 2,420
SALES (est): 212.3K **Privately Held**
SIC: 0721 4581 3599 Crop spraying services; aircraft cleaning & janitorial service; custom machinery

(G-7161)
WMC LLC
Also Called: West Michigan Compounding
1300 Moore St (48838-8768)
PHONE.................................616 560-4142
Ashley Everin, *Vice Pres*
Scott Barnard,
▲ **EMP:** 20
SALES (est): 7.5MM **Privately Held**
SIC: 2821 Plastics materials & resins

(G-7162)
WOODS GRAPHICS
Also Called: Wood Graphics Signs
9180 Wabasis Ave Ne (48838-9331)
PHONE.................................616 691-8025
John Frueh, *Owner*
EMP: 10 **EST:** 1994
SALES (est): 393.9K **Privately Held**
SIC: 3993 Signs & advertising specialties

Greenwood
St. Clair County

(G-7163)
WITCO INC
6401 Bricker Rd (48006-2521)
PHONE.................................810 387-4231
Georgina Witt, *CEO*
Kevin Witt, *President*
David E Witt, *Vice Pres*
Hyens Mark, *Engineer*
Shane Koch, *Sales Mgr*
EMP: 52
SQ FT: 45,000
SALES (est): 11.8MM **Privately Held**
WEB: www.witcoinc.com
SIC: 3545 Precision tools, machinists'

Gregory
Livingston County

(G-7164)
BOOS PRODUCTS INC
Also Called: Michigan Gear & Engineering
20416 Kaiser Rd (48137-9713)
PHONE.................................734 498-2207
Bill Jewell, *President*
Darwin Snider, *Vice Pres*
Tim Boos, *Admin Sec*
EMP: 15
SQ FT: 14,500
SALES: 1.9MM **Privately Held**
WEB: www.michigangear.com
SIC: 3599 3462 Machine shop, jobbing & repair; gears, forged steel

(G-7165)
P & M INDUSTRIES INC
5901 Weller Rd (48137-9523)
P.O. Box 141 (48137-0141)
PHONE.................................517 223-1000
Glen V Pantke, *President*
Susan C Pantke, *Vice Pres*
EMP: 10
SQ FT: 6,000
SALES (est): 1.1MM **Privately Held**
WEB: www.pm-industries.com
SIC: 3599 Machine shop, jobbing & repair

(G-7166)
TOOLCRAFT MACHINE CO INC
5390 Weller Rd (48137-9524)
PHONE.................................517 223-9265
Robert Fanto, *President*
Caroline Fanto, *Corp Secy*
Joseph Fanto, *Vice Pres*
EMP: 3
SALES (est): 468.7K **Privately Held**
SIC: 3498 Tube fabricating (contract bending & shaping); pipe sections fabricated from purchased pipe

Grosse Ile
Wayne County

(G-7167)
ASSOCIATED PRINT & GRAPHICS
9617 Island Dr (48138-1464)
PHONE.................................734 676-8896
Charlotte Williams, *Owner*
EMP: 6
SALES (est): 298.1K **Privately Held**
SIC: 2752 Commercial printing, lithographic

(G-7168)
CUSTARD CORNER INC
2972 W Jefferson Ave (48138)
PHONE.................................734 771-4396
Nicole Gall, *President*
EMP: 7
SALES (est): 324.2K **Privately Held**
SIC: 2024 Ice cream & frozen desserts

(G-7169)
DAILY CONTRACTS LLC
7779 Grays Dr (48138-1505)
PHONE.................................734 676-0903
Dan Daily, *Principal*
EMP: 3
SALES (est): 170.9K **Privately Held**
SIC: 2711 Newspapers, publishing & printing

(G-7170)
DIVERSIFIED TOOL & ENGINEERING
10340 Ruthmere Ave (48138-2133)
PHONE.................................734 692-1260
Patrick Manick, *President*
Kyle Beck, *Vice Pres*
EMP: 10
SQ FT: 6,000
SALES (est): 770K **Privately Held**
SIC: 3544 3599 Special dies & tools; jigs & fixtures; machine shop, jobbing & repair

(G-7171)
DOUGLAS WEST COMPANY INC
Also Called: Sharewell
9177 Groh Rd Bldg 43 (48138-1950)
PHONE.................................734 676-8882
Douglas Bodrie, *President*
EMP: 7
SALES (est): 380K **Privately Held**
SIC: 3444 Sheet metal specialties, not stamped

(G-7172)
EIKLAE PRODUCTS
10286 Boucher Rd (48138-2002)
PHONE.................................734 671-0752
Clayton Brundage, *Owner*
Clayton Grundage, *Owner*
EMP: 4 **EST:** 1987
SALES (est): 131.2K **Privately Held**
SIC: 2741 Business service newsletters: publishing & printing

(G-7173)
FUEL SOURCE LLC
29112 E River Rd (48138-1941)
PHONE.................................313 506-0448
Klaus P Uhse, *Administration*
EMP: 4
SALES (est): 443.4K **Privately Held**
SIC: 2992 Re-refining lubricating oils & greases

(G-7174)
NORTHERN PACKAGING MI INC
27665 Elba Dr (48138-1905)
PHONE.................................734 692-4700
Scott Wright, *President*
EMP: 17
SQ FT: 20,000
SALES (est): 1.4MM **Privately Held**
SIC: 2449 Rectangular boxes & crates, wood

(G-7175)
PFIZER INC
18141 Meridian Rd (48138-1088)
PHONE.................................734 679-7368
John Poslajko, *Branch Mgr*
EMP: 3
SALES (corp-wide): 53.6B **Publicly Held**
SIC: 2834 Pharmaceutical preparations
PA: Pfizer Inc.
  235 E 42nd St
  New York NY 10017
  212 733-2323

(G-7176)
SOLAR CONTROL SYSTEMS
8463 Thorntree Dr (48138-1587)
PHONE.................................734 671-6899
Thomas Llewelyn, *Owner*
EMP: 5 **EST:** 1977
SALES (est): 278.7K **Privately Held**
WEB: www.solarcontrolsystems.com
SIC: 3433 Solar heaters & collectors

(G-7177)
SYDELINE CORPORATION
9155 Groh Rd (48138-1950)
P.O. Box 229 (48138-0229)
PHONE.................................734 675-9330
Barbara Bennett, *President*
Mary J Conflitti, *President*
EMP: 8 **EST:** 1975
SQ FT: 6,000
SALES (est): 776.9K **Privately Held**
SIC: 3231 Industrial glassware: made from purchased glass

Grosse Pointe
Wayne County

(G-7178)
DEWEYS LUMBERVILLE INC
757 Notre Dame St (48230-1239)
PHONE.................................313 885-0960
Joseph A Dewey Jr, *President*
EMP: 5 **EST:** 1939
SQ FT: 12,500
SALES: 1MM **Privately Held**
SIC: 5211 2511 Lumber & other building materials; unassembled or unfinished furniture, household: wood

(G-7179)
GOURMET HOLDINGS LLC
Also Called: Teta Foods
37519 Harper Ave (48230)
PHONE.................................313 432-2121
Tarek Abouljoud, *Mng Member*
EMP: 3 **EST:** 2010
SALES: 250K **Privately Held**
SIC: 2035 Pickles, sauces & salad dressings

(G-7180)
GRAYTON INTEGRATED PUBG LLC
886 Washington Rd (48230-1291)
PHONE.................................313 881-1734
Sue Cavallaro,
Peter Haapaniemi,
Sheila Young Tomkowiak,
EMP: 3
SALES: 367K **Privately Held**
WEB: www.graytonpub.com
SIC: 2741 Miscellaneous publishing

(G-7181)
PAGE LITHO INC
7 Wellington Pl (48230-1919)
PHONE.................................313 885-8555
Joy Pecherski, *President*
Denise Pecherski, *Vice Pres*
Jeff Pecherski, *Vice Pres*
Timothy Clement, *CFO*
EMP: 30
SQ FT: 60,000
SALES (est): 3MM **Privately Held**
SIC: 2789 2752 Binding only: books, pamphlets, magazines, etc.; commercial printing, lithographic

(G-7182)
POLYHEDRON LLC
Also Called: Libstack
203 Lakeland St (48230-1922)
PHONE..................................313 318-4807
David Kircos, *Principal*
EMP: 3
SALES (est): 166K **Privately Held**
SIC: 7372 Prepackaged software

(G-7183)
SEQUOIA MOLDING
820 Lakeland St (48230-1273)
PHONE..................................586 463-4400
EMP: 3 EST: 2009
SALES (est): 226.4K **Privately Held**
SIC: 3089 Molding primary plastic

(G-7184)
STUNT3 MULTIMEDIA LLC
829 Rivard Blvd (48230-1256)
PHONE..................................313 417-0909
Brian G Kruger, *Principal*
EMP: 5
SALES: 950K **Privately Held**
SIC: 7372 Prepackaged software

Grosse Pointe Farms
Wayne County

(G-7185)
J HOUSE LLC
71 Lake Shore Rd (48236-3765)
PHONE..................................313 220-4449
Jennifer Dunbar,
EMP: 6
SALES (est): 349K **Privately Held**
SIC: 2033 Vegetable juices: fresh

(G-7186)
MEDIA SWING LLC
14 Radnor Cir (48236-3813)
PHONE..................................313 885-2525
David Paschke, *CEO*
EMP: 3
SALES (est): 900K **Privately Held**
SIC: 8999 8742 7389 1799 Communication services; marketing consulting services; ; sign installation & maintenance; signs, not made in custom sign painting shops

(G-7187)
SCHROTH ENTERPRISES INC (PA)
95 Tonnacour Pl (48236-3032)
PHONE..................................586 759-4240
James L Schroth, *President*
Robert A Connelly, *Vice Pres*
Dean Barr, *QC Mgr*
EMP: 21
SALES (est): 3.4MM **Privately Held**
SIC: 3398 3496 3069 3479 Metal heat treating; woven wire products; molded rubber products; hard rubber & molded rubber products; painting of metal products

(G-7188)
SHOCK-TEK LLC
21 Kercheval Ave Ste 225 (48236-3651)
PHONE..................................313 886-0530
Arthur Porter, *Principal*
Valk Estate, *Mng Member*
A Spitzer Glvoe,
EMP: 5
SQ FT: 3,000
SALES (est): 517.2K **Privately Held**
WEB: www.shocktek.com
SIC: 3842 Bandages & dressings

Grosse Pointe Park
Wayne County

(G-7189)
ALTERNATIVE FUEL TECH LLC
1350 Buckingham Rd (48230-1140)
PHONE..................................313 417-9212
EMP: 4
SALES (est): 362.3K **Privately Held**
SIC: 8731 3714 Commercial Physical Research Mfg Motor Vehicle Parts/Accessories

(G-7190)
ANTEEBO PUBLISHERS INC
Also Called: Grosse Pointe News
16980 Kercheval Pl (48230-1554)
PHONE..................................313 882-6900
Robert G Edgar, *President*
Robert G Liggett Jr, *Publisher*
Jody McVeigh, *Editor*
Terry Minnis, *Vice Pres*
Sara Birmingham, *Accounts Exec*
EMP: 50
SQ FT: 4,000
SALES (est): 2.8MM **Privately Held**
WEB: www.grossepointenews.com
SIC: 2711 2791 Newspapers: publishing only, not printed on site; typesetting

(G-7191)
ATWATER IN PARK
1175 Lakepointe St (48230-1319)
PHONE..................................313 344-5104
Brady Hunt, *President*
EMP: 5 EST: 2014
SALES (est): 358.5K **Privately Held**
SIC: 2082 Beer (alcoholic beverage)

(G-7192)
COLD STONE CREAMERY
16823 Kercheval Ave (48230-1532)
PHONE..................................313 886-4020
EMP: 3
SALES (est): 279.1K **Privately Held**
SIC: 2024 5143 5812 Ice cream & frozen desserts; ice cream & ices; ice cream stands or dairy bars

(G-7193)
FRASER TOOL & GAUGE LLC
1352 Harvard Rd (48230-1134)
PHONE..................................313 882-9192
David Lawrence, *Managing Dir*
Geoff Lawrence, *Sales Staff*
Ralph Lawrence, *Mng Member*
▲ EMP: 5
SALES: 4MM **Privately Held**
SIC: 3545 Gauges (machine tool accessories)

(G-7194)
GREEN ZEBRA FOODS INCORPORATED
620 Middlesex Rd (48230-1740)
PHONE..................................248 291-7339
Katherine Berschback, *Principal*
EMP: 3
SALES (est): 165.8K **Privately Held**
SIC: 2099 Food preparations

(G-7195)
POINTE PRINTING INC
1103 Balfour St (48230-1326)
PHONE..................................313 821-0030
James M Odell, *President*
James A Odell, *Owner*
EMP: 9 EST: 1949
SQ FT: 4,200
SALES (est): 610K **Privately Held**
SIC: 2752 2759 Commercial printing, offset; letterpress printing

(G-7196)
ST JOHN
1056 Yorkshire Rd (48230-1450)
PHONE..................................313 499-4065
Frank Bever, *Principal*
EMP: 3
SALES (est): 195K **Privately Held**
SIC: 2339 Sportswear, women's

(G-7197)
UNIVERSAL PRODUCT MKTG LLC
854 Edgemont Park (48230-1855)
PHONE..................................248 585-9959
Jose Reyes, *President*
▲ EMP: 9
SALES: 2.3MM **Privately Held**
SIC: 2676 Sanitary paper products

Grosse Pointe Shores
Wayne County

(G-7198)
DYNAMIC SUPPLY SOLUTIONS INC
56 Sunningdale Dr (48236-1664)
PHONE..................................248 987-2205
Debbie Mifsud, *Vice Pres*
Bill Bolton, *Vice Pres*
Will Bolton, *Vice Pres*
EMP: 5
SALES (est): 836.3K **Privately Held**
SIC: 3679 Antennas, receiving

(G-7199)
HARPER DERMATOLOGY PC
21 Stillmeadow Ln (48236-1117)
PHONE..................................586 776-7546
Usha Sood, *President*
EMP: 4
SALES (est): 588.3K **Privately Held**
SIC: 8011 2834 Dermatologist; dermatologicals

(G-7200)
M-SEAL PRODUCTS CO LLC
55 Fairford Rd (48236-2617)
PHONE..................................313 884-6147
Paul Van Der Hoeven, *Principal*
EMP: 4 EST: 2008
SALES (est): 384.4K **Privately Held**
SIC: 3053 Gaskets, packing & sealing devices

Grosse Pointe Woods
Wayne County

(G-7201)
CIRCUITS OF SOUND
840 Shoreham Rd (48236-2446)
PHONE..................................313 886-5599
Edward Bartos, *Principal*
EMP: 3
SALES (est): 253.8K **Privately Held**
SIC: 3679 Electronic circuits

(G-7202)
CONTINENTAL BLDG SVS OF CINCI
Also Called: Blue Flash Supply Co
580 Cook Rd (48236-2708)
PHONE..................................313 336-8543
Richard E Beck, *President*
Dave Divozzo, *Vice Pres*
Anna Beck, *Admin Sec*
EMP: 10
SQ FT: 3,600
SALES: 500K **Privately Held**
SIC: 7349 2841 Building maintenance, except repairs; soap & other detergents

(G-7203)
GEORGE KOUEITER JEWELERS
19815 Mack Ave (48236-2505)
PHONE..................................313 882-1110
Marie Koueiter, *Owner*
John Brennan, *Sales Staff*
EMP: 3
SQ FT: 1,400
SALES (est): 292.9K **Privately Held**
WEB: www.koueiterjewelers.com
SIC: 5944 3911 Jewelry, precious stones & precious metals; jewelry, precious metal

(G-7204)
JOSEFS FRENCH PASTRY SHOP CO
21150 Mack Ave (48236-1044)
PHONE..................................313 881-5710
Joseph Bogosian, *President*
Eileen Bogosian, *Vice Pres*
Rebecca Brown, *Admin Sec*
EMP: 30
SQ FT: 2,600
SALES (est): 1.2MM **Privately Held**
SIC: 5461 2051 Pastries; bread, cake & related products

(G-7205)
JOSEPH A DIMAGGIO
Also Called: Dimaggio Jseph A Mstr Gldsmith
19876 Mack Ave (48236-2363)
PHONE..................................313 881-5353
Joseph A Dimaggio, *Owner*
EMP: 4
SALES (est): 450.3K **Privately Held**
SIC: 7353 3911 Cranes & aerial lift equipment, rental or leasing; jewelry, precious metal

(G-7206)
LITTLE BLUE BOOK INC
Also Called: Ble Book Publishing
19803 Mack Ave (48236-2505)
PHONE..................................313 469-0052
Kim Towar, *President*
Brandy Towar, *Vice Pres*
EMP: 11 EST: 1948
SQ FT: 3,000
SALES (est): 1.4MM **Privately Held**
WEB: www.littlebluebook.net
SIC: 2741 Telephone & other directory publishing

(G-7207)
MICHIGAN FUELS
20700 Mack Ave (48236-1436)
PHONE..................................313 886-7110
Atto Assi, *Manager*
EMP: 3
SALES (est): 177.5K **Privately Held**
SIC: 2869 Fuels

(G-7208)
PRINT XPRESS
20373 Mack Ave (48236-1610)
PHONE..................................313 886-6850
Tony Alfonsi, *Partner*
Terrie Mc Lauchlan, *Partner*
EMP: 7
SQ FT: 2,800
SALES (est): 1.1MM **Privately Held**
WEB: www.printxpress.com
SIC: 2752 Commercial printing, offset

(G-7209)
SPECTRA LINK
21885 River Rd (48236-1139)
PHONE..................................313 417-3723
Mike Moore, *Principal*
EMP: 3
SALES (est): 219.9K **Privately Held**
SIC: 3661 Telephone & telegraph apparatus

(G-7210)
TEMPERANCE FUEL STOP INC
2110 Anita Ave (48236-1430)
PHONE..................................734 206-2676
EMP: 3 EST: 2013
SALES (est): 245.7K **Privately Held**
SIC: 2869 Fuels

Gulliver
Schoolcraft County

(G-7211)
CARMEUSE LIME & STONE INC
15 W County Rd 432 (49840)
PHONE..................................906 283-3456
James Weber, *Opers Mgr*
Dana Neadow, *Buyer*
Gary Kaiser, *Maintence Staff*
EMP: 80
SALES (corp-wide): 177.9K **Privately Held**
SIC: 1422 Limestones, ground
HQ: Carmeuse Lime & Stone, Inc.
11 Stanwix St Fl 21
Pittsburgh PA 15222
412 995-5500

(G-7212)
R & I REPAIR SHOP
1129n N Gulliver Rd (49840-9041)
PHONE..................................906 283-6000
Mark Swaim, *Owner*
EMP: 3
SALES (est): 198.3K **Privately Held**
SIC: 3599 Machine shop, jobbing & repair

GEOGRAPHIC SECTION

(G-7213)
SPENCER FOREST PRODUCTS
1110n Townline Rd (49840-9106)
PHONE................................906 341-6791
James Spencer, *Owner*
Barbara Spencer, *Principal*
EMP: 6
SALES (est): 625.2K **Privately Held**
SIC: 2411 Logging camps & contractors

(G-7214)
TUTTLE FOREST PRODUCTS
1964 W Hwy Us 2 (49840)
PHONE................................906 283-3871
Betty Tuttle, *Owner*
EMP: 4
SALES (est): 373.4K **Privately Held**
WEB: www.tuttlescedaryard.com
SIC: 2411 Logging camps & contractors; pulpwood contractors engaged in cutting; wooden logs

Gwinn
Marquette County

(G-7215)
ARGONICS INC (PA)
520 9th St (49841-3110)
PHONE................................906 226-9747
Robert Flood, *President*
Douglas Maves, *Engineer*
Bob Ucoli, *Finance*
Joe Roell, *Sales Staff*
Bob Welker, *Sales Staff*
▼ **EMP:** 90
SQ FT: 10,040
SALES (est): 22MM **Privately Held**
WEB: www.argonics.com
SIC: 2821 Elastomers, nonvulcanizable (plastics)

(G-7216)
AVERY COLOR STUDIOS INC
511 Avenue D (49841-3307)
PHONE................................906 346-3908
Wells Chapin, *President*
Amy Chapin, *Vice Pres*
EMP: 4
SALES (est): 518.6K **Privately Held**
WEB: www.atlanticwreckdivers.com
SIC: 2752 2741 Commercial printing, offset; miscellaneous publishing

(G-7217)
CANUSA INC
Also Called: Canusa Wood Products
502 2nd St (49841-3301)
PHONE................................906 446-3327
Francis Fournier, *President*
Sherry Fournier, *Vice Pres*
EMP: 8
SALES: 300K **Privately Held**
SIC: 2431 Planing mill, millwork

(G-7218)
CCO HOLDINGS LLC
105 W State Highway M35 (49841-9179)
PHONE................................906 346-1000
EMP: 3
SALES (corp-wide): 43.6B **Publicly Held**
SIC: 5064 4841 3663 3651 Electrical appliances, television & radio; cable & other pay television services; radio & TV communications equipment; household audio & video equipment
HQ: Cco Holdings, Llc
400 Atlantic St
Stamford CT 06901
203 905-7801

(G-7219)
GERALD FROBERG
Also Called: Froberg's Clothing Store
25 E Stephenson Ave (49841-9148)
P.O. Box 351 (49841-0351)
PHONE................................906 346-3311
Gerald Froberg, *Owner*
EMP: 3
SQ FT: 2,880
SALES (est): 198K **Privately Held**
SIC: 5651 5136 2326 Family clothing stores; caps, men's & boys'; hats, men's & boys'; hosiery, men's & boys'; gloves, men's & boys'; men's & boys' work clothing

(G-7220)
NATIONAL CARBON TECH LLC
513 4th St (49841-3304)
PHONE................................651 330-4063
EMP: 25
SALES (corp-wide): 1.8MM **Privately Held**
SIC: 3624 Carbon specialties for electrical use
PA: National Carbon Technologies, Llc
3510 Hopkins Pl N
Saint Paul MN 55128
651 330-4063

(G-7221)
NORTHWOODS WREATHING COMPANY
143 E Johnson Lake Rd (49841-9045)
PHONE................................906 202-2888
Amy L Kuivanen, *Owner*
EMP: 3
SALES (est): 122.2K **Privately Held**
SIC: 3999 Wreaths, artificial

(G-7222)
POTLATCHDELTIC CORPORATION
Also Called: Own Lumber Mill
650 Avenue A (49841-3300)
PHONE................................906 346-3215
Ron Salisbury, *Branch Mgr*
EMP: 170
SALES (corp-wide): 974.5MM **Publicly Held**
WEB: www.potlatchcorp.com
SIC: 2421 2426 Lumber: rough, sawed or planed; sawdust, shavings & wood chips; hardwood dimension & flooring mills
PA: Potlatchdeltic Corporation
601 W 1st Ave Ste 1600
Spokane WA 99201
509 835-1500

(G-7223)
SUPERIOR EXTRUSION INC
Also Called: SEI
118 Avenue G (49841-3107)
PHONE................................906 346-7308
Daniel Amberg, *President*
Dean Borlace, *CFO*
Dean Borlace, *Controller*
Janet Yager, *Personnel Exec*
Dan Richards, *VP Sales*
◆ **EMP:** 170
SQ FT: 103,000
SALES (est): 79.7MM **Privately Held**
WEB: www.superiorextrusion.com
SIC: 3354 Aluminum extruded products

Hale
Iosco County

(G-7224)
CONTAINER SPECIALTIES INC
Darton Archery Div
3540 Darton Rd (48739-8500)
P.O. Box 68 (48739-0068)
PHONE................................989 728-4231
Rex Darlington, *Branch Mgr*
EMP: 25
SALES (corp-wide): 2.2MM **Privately Held**
SIC: 3949 5941 Bows, archery; arrows, archery; skateboards; archery supplies
PA: Container Specialties, Inc
G3261 Flushing Rd
Flint MI

Hamburg
Livingston County

(G-7225)
FLEXIBLE METAL INC
7495 E M 36 (48139)
PHONE................................810 231-1300
Joseph Baxter, *Manager*
EMP: 75
SALES (corp-wide): 96.5MM **Privately Held**
SIC: 3498 Fabricated pipe & fittings
HQ: Flexible Metal, Inc.
1685 Brandywine Ave
Chula Vista CA 91911
678 280-0127

(G-7226)
NATIONAL CONTROL SYSTEMS INC
10737 Hamburg Rd (48139-1216)
P.O. Box 266 (48139-0266)
PHONE................................810 231-2901
Thomas Treiber, *Ch of Bd*
Robert Socia, *President*
Mike Arpi, *Vice Pres*
Patrick Jeski, *Admin Sec*
EMP: 7
SQ FT: 5,000
SALES (est): 1MM **Privately Held**
WEB: www.ncsmail.com
SIC: 3625 Relays & industrial controls

(G-7227)
PICKO FERRUM FABRICATING LLC
10800 Featherly Dr (48139-1212)
PHONE................................810 626-7086
Mike Jecks, *President*
EMP: 6 **EST:** 2017
SALES (est): 950.7K **Privately Held**
SIC: 3498 Tube fabricating (contract bending & shaping)

Hamilton
Allegan County

(G-7228)
ADVANCE CNC MACHINE INC
3051 Lincoln Rd (49419-9527)
P.O. Box 272 (49419-0272)
PHONE................................269 751-7005
Lyle Lugten, *President*
Douglas Boals, *Vice Pres*
EMP: 7
SQ FT: 5,500
SALES (est): 832.8K **Privately Held**
SIC: 3599 Machine shop, jobbing & repair

(G-7229)
ALLEGAN METAL FABRICATORS INC
3280 Lincoln Rd (49419-9531)
P.O. Box 251 (49419-0251)
PHONE................................269 751-7130
Eric Nyhof, *President*
Henry M Nyhof, *Admin Sec*
EMP: 6
SQ FT: 25,200
SALES (est): 1.2MM **Privately Held**
SIC: 7692 3441 Welding repair; fabricated structural metal

(G-7230)
AMERIVET ENGINEERING LLC
3146 53rd St (49419-9626)
PHONE................................269 751-9092
Scott Russell,
EMP: 4
SALES (est): 190.2K **Privately Held**
SIC: 8711 3559 Consulting engineer; automotive related machinery

(G-7231)
DARLING INGREDIENTS INC
5900 Old Allegan Rd (49419-9314)
PHONE................................269 751-0560
Terry Pfannestill, *Principal*
EMP: 37
SALES (corp-wide): 3.3B **Publicly Held**
WEB: www.krugerinc.com
SIC: 2077 2076 2048 2013 Animal & marine fats & oils; vegetable oil mills; prepared feeds; sausages & other prepared meats; commodity brokers, contracts
PA: Darling Ingredients Inc.
5601 N Macarthur Blvd
Irving TX 75038
972 717-0300

(G-7232)
HAMILTON BLOCK & READY MIX CO
4510 132nd Ave (49419-9530)
P.O. Box 7 (49419-0007)
PHONE................................269 751-5129
Curt Pieper, *President*
Paul Haverdink, *Vice Pres*
Dorothy Motman, *Treasurer*
Margaret Scharf, *Admin Sec*
EMP: 17
SQ FT: 2,500
SALES (est): 2.3MM **Privately Held**
WEB: www.hamiltonbr.com
SIC: 3273 Ready-mixed concrete

(G-7233)
HAMILTON INDUSTRIAL PRODUCTS
4555 134th Ave (49419-8579)
P.O. Box 157 (49419-0157)
PHONE................................269 751-5153
Reinhold Petry, *President*
Eva Petry, *Vice Pres*
Eva J Petry, *Admin Sec*
EMP: 50
SQ FT: 56,000
SALES (est): 6MM **Privately Held**
SIC: 3599 7629 3542 Machine shop, jobbing & repair; custom machinery; electrical repair shops; machine tools, metal forming type

(G-7234)
HAMILTON STEEL FABRICATIONS
3290 Lincoln Rd (49419-9531)
PHONE................................269 751-8757
Rudy Lampen, *President*
Blake Lampen, *Opers Mgr*
EMP: 7
SQ FT: 18,000
SALES (est): 1MM **Privately Held**
WEB: www.hamiltonsteelfab.com
SIC: 3441 Fabricated structural metal

(G-7235)
LENWAY MACHINE COMPANY INC
Also Called: Len-Way Machine & Tool
3165 60th St (49419-9657)
PHONE................................269 751-5183
Jeanette Sluis, *President*
EMP: 9
SQ FT: 4,000
SALES (est): 800K **Privately Held**
WEB: www.lenwaymachine.com
SIC: 3599 3544 Machine shop, jobbing & repair; special dies, tools, jigs & fixtures

(G-7236)
LITE LOAD SERVICES LLC
3866 40th St (49419-9737)
PHONE................................269 751-6037
Jeff Garvelink, *Mng Member*
EMP: 10
SALES (est): 707K **Privately Held**
SIC: 1771 2951 Blacktop (asphalt) work; asphalt paving mixtures & blocks

(G-7237)
POST HARDWOODS INC
3544 38th St (49419-9500)
PHONE................................269 751-2221
Robert Post, *President*
August Jay Post, *Vice Pres*
EMP: 11
SQ FT: 10,000
SALES (est): 1.2MM **Privately Held**
SIC: 2421 Lumber: rough, sawed or planed; furniture dimension stock, softwood

(G-7238)
PROTOTYPES PLUS INC
3537 Lincoln Rd (49419-9601)
PHONE......................................269 751-7141
James H Lemson, *President*
EMP: 5
SALES (est): 945.9K **Privately Held**
WEB: www.proto-plus.com
SIC: 3714 Motor vehicle parts & accessories

(G-7239)
R & D CNC MACHINING INC
3506 Lincoln Rd (49419-9601)
P.O. Box 218 (49419-0218)
PHONE......................................269 751-4171
Rienhold Petry, *Owner*
EMP: 16
SALES (est): 2.2MM **Privately Held**
SIC: 3599 Machine shop, jobbing & repair

(G-7240)
T-PRINT USA
3410 136th Ave (49419-9543)
PHONE......................................269 751-4603
Chris Malley, *Executive Asst*
EMP: 3
SALES (est): 255K **Privately Held**
SIC: 2752 Commercial printing, offset

(G-7241)
TRESTLE PLASTIC SERVICES LLC
3393 Lincoln Rd (49419-8588)
P.O. Box 142 (49419-0142)
PHONE......................................616 262-5484
Rick Evstile, *Mng Member*
EMP: 4
SQ FT: 6,000
SALES: 47K **Privately Held**
SIC: 3089 Injection molding of plastics

(G-7242)
WEBER BROS & WHITE METAL WORKS
4715 136th Ave (49419-9722)
P.O. Box 187 (49419-0187)
PHONE......................................269 751-5193
Stuart W White, *President*
Sara S Van Doornik, *Vice Pres*
Betty White, *Treasurer*
Harold Kirke White Jr, *Shareholder*
EMP: 4
SQ FT: 15,000
SALES: 300K **Privately Held**
WEB: www.weberbros-white.com
SIC: 3469 Spinning metal for the trade

Hamtramck
Wayne County

(G-7243)
18TH STREET DELI INC
8800 Conant St (48211-1401)
PHONE......................................313 921-7710
David Salerno, *President*
EMP: 5
SALES (est): 908.7K **Privately Held**
WEB: www.18thstreetdeli.com
SIC: 2099 5141 Food preparations; groceries, general line

(G-7244)
MELIX SERVICES INC
2359 Livernois Rd Ste 300 (48212)
PHONE......................................248 387-9303
Melis Lejlic, *President*
EMP: 7
SALES: 200K **Privately Held**
SIC: 1389 6531 Construction, repair & dismantling services; real estate leasing & rentals

(G-7245)
RAPID CNC SOLUTIONS
9605 Buffalo St (48212-3322)
PHONE......................................586 850-6385
Ryan Glowacki, *Co-Owner*
EMP: 3
SQ FT: 1,000
SALES (est): 122.5K **Privately Held**
SIC: 3541 Numerically controlled metal cutting machine tools

(G-7246)
SEVEN MILE AND GRND RIVER FUEL
Also Called: BP
5099 Fredro St (48212-2838)
PHONE......................................313 535-3000
EMP: 5
SALES (est): 401.1K **Privately Held**
SIC: 2869 Fuels

Hancock
Houghton County

(G-7247)
A & S INDUSTRIAL LLC
19273 Kiiskila Rd (49930-9668)
PHONE......................................906 482-8007
Larry Anderson, *Principal*
EMP: 4
SALES (est): 215.5K **Privately Held**
SIC: 3441 Fabricated structural metal

(G-7248)
BOOK CONCERN PRINTERS
129 E Franklin St (49930-1807)
P.O. Box 330 (49930-0330)
PHONE......................................906 482-1250
Jack Eberhard, *President*
▲ EMP: 7
SQ FT: 5,800
SALES (est): 957K **Privately Held**
SIC: 2752 7336 Commercial printing, offset; graphic arts & related design

(G-7249)
BRENT BASTIAN LOGGING LLC
54215 Salo Rd (49930-9651)
PHONE......................................906 482-6378
Brent Bastian, *Principal*
EMP: 6
SALES (est): 517.1K **Privately Held**
SIC: 2411 Logging

(G-7250)
CELEBRATIONS
Also Called: Celebrations Bridal & Formal
110 E Quincy St (49930-2138)
PHONE......................................906 482-4946
Diane Eshbach, *Owner*
EMP: 4
SQ FT: 2,000
SALES: 165K **Privately Held**
WEB: www.celebrationsbridal.net
SIC: 5621 7221 7299 5699 Bridal shops; photographic studios, portrait; tuxedo rental; formal wear; shoes, orthopedic; invitation & stationery printing & engraving

(G-7251)
HANCOCK BOTTLING CO INC
Also Called: Coca-Cola
1800 Birch St (49930-1067)
PHONE......................................906 482-3701
Robert L Scholie Jr, *President*
Gary Scholie, *Vice Pres*
EMP: 14
SALES: 3.8MM **Privately Held**
SIC: 2086 Bottled & canned soft drinks

(G-7252)
INFRARED TELEMETRICS INC
Also Called: Ir Telemetrics
1780 Birch St (49930-1072)
P.O. Box 70, Houghton (49931-0070)
PHONE......................................906 482-0012
Glen L Barna, *President*
Paul La Vigne, *Vice Pres*
Carl L Anderson, *Treasurer*
EMP: 12
SQ FT: 5,000
SALES (est): 1.2MM **Privately Held**
WEB: www.irtelemetrics.com
SIC: 3829 3825 3823 8711 Measuring & controlling devices; instruments to measure electricity; industrial instrmnts msrmnt display/control process variable; professional engineer

(G-7253)
JOHN V GEDDA JR
Also Called: Gedda's Electrical Repair
715 Pine St (49930-1613)
PHONE......................................906 482-5037
John V Gedda Jr, *Owner*
EMP: 3
SQ FT: 4,500
SALES: 100K **Privately Held**
SIC: 7694 1731 Rewinding services; general electrical contractor

(G-7254)
NORTH POST INC
Also Called: Northwoods Trading Post
120 Quincy St (49930-1856)
PHONE......................................906 482-5210
Richard Freeman, *President*
Carol Freeman, *Corp Secy*
EMP: 7 EST: 1957
SQ FT: 6,500
SALES (est): 725.6K **Privately Held**
SIC: 3949 Fishing equipment; hunting equipment

(G-7255)
PLASTIC FLOW LLC
540 Depot St (49930-2031)
PHONE......................................906 483-0691
Mahesh Gupta, *President*
EMP: 3
SALES (est): 265.8K **Privately Held**
SIC: 2821 Plastics materials & resins

(G-7256)
RIPLEY PRODUCTS COMPANY INC
21194 Royce Rd (49930-2427)
PHONE......................................906 482-1380
Lawrence Julio, *President*
Elizabeth Ann Julio, *Corp Secy*
EMP: 3 EST: 1956
SQ FT: 3,000
SALES (est): 210K **Privately Held**
SIC: 7692 Welding repair

(G-7257)
SUPERIOR MARINE PRODUCTS LLC
Also Called: Pronav Marine
20134 Gagnon Cir (49930-2276)
PHONE......................................906 370-9908
Neil Anderson,
EMP: 3
SALES (est): 121.5K **Privately Held**
SIC: 3949 Fishing equipment

(G-7258)
VANDCO INCORPORATED
Also Called: Vollwerth & Co
200 Hancock St (49930-2004)
P.O. Box 239 (49930-0239)
PHONE......................................906 482-1550
Adam M Manderfield, *President*
James Schaaf, *Vice Pres*
Jim Schaaf, *Vice Pres*
Adam Manderfield, *Prdtn Mgr*
Robert Ruelle, *Manager*
EMP: 35 EST: 1915
SQ FT: 20,000
SALES: 3.9MM **Privately Held**
WEB: www.vollwerth.com
SIC: 2013 5141 Sausages from purchased meat; smoked meats from purchased meat; groceries, general line

(G-7259)
WOODSIDE LOGGING LLC
23763 Woodside Ln (49930-9334)
PHONE......................................906 482-0150
Alayne Kangas, *Office Mgr*
Shane Kangas, *Administration*
EMP: 3 EST: 2015
SALES (est): 147.9K **Privately Held**
SIC: 2411 Timber, cut at logging camp

Hanover
Jackson County

(G-7260)
GREAT LAKE FOAM TECHNOLOGIES
104 W Main St (49241-9811)
PHONE......................................517 563-8030
William Maccready, *President*
EMP: 13
SQ FT: 9,000
SALES (est): 1.3MM **Privately Held**
SIC: 3069 Foam rubber

(G-7261)
LEVY MACHINING LLC
11901 Strait Rd (49241-9781)
PHONE......................................517 563-2013
Ryan Levy,
Michael Levy,
Sherilene Levy,
EMP: 5
SALES: 250K **Privately Held**
SIC: 3599 Machine shop, jobbing & repair

(G-7262)
TRI-STATE TECHNICAL SERVICES
9659 Grover Rd (49241-9776)
PHONE......................................517 563-8743
Wendy Valentine,
Ross Valentine,
EMP: 4
SALES (est): 609.7K **Privately Held**
WEB: www.usetsts.com
SIC: 3552 Embroidery machines

Harbor Beach
Huron County

(G-7263)
AG MANUFACTURING INC
319 Industrial Dr (48441-1014)
PHONE......................................989 479-9590
Victor Edozien, *CEO*
Kevin Schwanz, *COO*
Diane Hartman, *Engineer*
Mike Onianwah, *CFO*
Gail McConnachie, *Manager*
▲ EMP: 30
SQ FT: 55,000
SALES (est): 9.3MM **Privately Held**
WEB: www.agmanufacturing.com
SIC: 3315 Steel wire & related products

(G-7264)
CLASSY THREADZ
310 State St (48441-1207)
PHONE......................................989 479-9595
Cindy Simen, *Owner*
EMP: 4
SALES (est): 174.8K **Privately Held**
SIC: 2395 Embroidery products, except schiffli machine

(G-7265)
DOW AGROSCIENCES LLC
305 N Huron Ave (48441-1120)
PHONE......................................989 479-3245
Paul Vammer, *Manager*
EMP: 5
SALES (corp-wide): 30.6B **Publicly Held**
SIC: 2879 Agricultural chemicals
HQ: Dow Agrosciences Llc
9330 Zionsville Rd
Indianapolis IN 46268
317 337-3000

(G-7266)
HARBOR BEACH TIMES
123 N 1st St (48441-1102)
PHONE......................................989 479-3605
Fax: 989 479-9697
EMP: 4
SALES (est): 177.2K **Privately Held**
SIC: 2711 Newspapers-Publishing/Printing

GEOGRAPHIC SECTION

Harbor Springs - Emmet County

(G-7267)
HARBOR TOOL AND MACHINE
225 Hunter Industrial Dr (48441-9346)
PHONE...................................989 479-6708
Bob Glaza, *Partner*
Lucille Glaza, *Corp Secy*
Dennis Glaza, *Vice Pres*
Gary Glaza, *Manager*
EMP: 10
SALES (est): 1.4MM **Privately Held**
SIC: 3599 Machine shop, jobbing & repair

(G-7268)
JUPITER MANUFACTURING
8661 Sand Beach Rd (48441-9435)
PHONE...................................989 551-0519
Thomas Booms, *Manager*
EMP: 3
SALES (est): 269.9K **Privately Held**
SIC: 3999 Manufacturing industries

(G-7269)
LEADER TOOL COMPANY - HB INC
630 N Huron Ave (48441-1007)
P.O. Box 66 (48441-0066)
PHONE...................................989 479-3281
Bryan Gunn, *President*
Allen D Gunn, *President*
Joan Gunn, *Vice Pres*
EMP: 60
SQ FT: 30,000
SALES (est): 8.1MM **Privately Held**
SIC: 3544 3452 Special dies & tools; bolts, nuts, rivets & washers

(G-7270)
SENSIENT FLAVORS LLC
79 State St (48441-1255)
PHONE...................................989 479-3211
EMP: 8 EST: 2008
SALES (est): 121.5K **Privately Held**
SIC: 2087 2099 Flavoring extracts & syrups; yeast

(G-7271)
SENSIENT TECHNOLOGIES CORP
79 State St (48441-1255)
PHONE...................................989 479-3211
Jim Tenbusch, *Branch Mgr*
EMP: 62
SALES (corp-wide): 1.3B **Publicly Held**
WEB: www.sensient-tech.com
SIC: 2099 2087 Yeast; seasonings & spices; chili pepper or powder; seasonings: dry mixes; beverage bases
PA: Sensient Technologies Corporation
 777 E Wisconsin Ave # 1100
 Milwaukee WI 53202
 414 271-6755

Harbor Springs
Emmet County

(G-7272)
AMERICAN GATOR TOOL COMPANY
1225 W Conway Rd Unit C (49740-9604)
PHONE...................................231 347-3222
Donald Berg, *President*
Carol Berg, *Vice Pres*
EMP: 5
SQ FT: 6,000
SALES (est): 270K **Privately Held**
SIC: 3541 3545 5084 Tapping machines; machine tool attachments & accessories; metalworking tools (such as drills, taps, dies, files); tapping attachments

(G-7273)
AMERICAN LAP COMPANY
220 Franklin Park (49740-9614)
P.O. Box 106 (49740-0106)
PHONE...................................231 526-7121
Arthur J Hackman Jr, *CEO*
Alan T Hackman, *President*
Mary Alice Hackman, *Corp Secy*
EMP: 5
SQ FT: 5,000
SALES (est): 665.5K **Privately Held**
WEB: www.americanlap.com
SIC: 3545 Cutting tools for machine tools

(G-7274)
BEAR CUB HOLDINGS INC
8761 M 119 (49740)
P.O. Box 291 (49740-0291)
PHONE...................................231 242-1152
Mike Walda, *President*
Emylee Walda, *Vice Pres*
EMP: 4
SALES (est): 13.8K **Privately Held**
SIC: 2891 Sealing compounds for pipe threads or joints

(G-7275)
BOYER GLASSWORKS INC
207 State St (49740-1528)
P.O. Box 733 (49740-0733)
PHONE...................................231 526-6359
Harry Boyer, *President*
EMP: 4
SALES (est): 344.2K **Privately Held**
SIC: 3231 Art glass: made from purchased glass

(G-7276)
CEEFLOW INC
5334 S Lake Shore Dr (49740-9199)
PHONE...................................231 526-5579
Peter A Cummings, *President*
David Cummings, *Admin Sec*
EMP: 4
SQ FT: 5,000
SALES (est): 850K **Privately Held**
SIC: 3444 Skylights, sheet metal

(G-7277)
CENTRAL INDUSTRIAL MFG INC
Also Called: Walls Holding Company
1211 W Conway Rd (49740-9683)
PHONE...................................231 347-5920
Erika Walls, *President*
EMP: 11
SQ FT: 5,700
SALES (est): 1.9MM **Privately Held**
SIC: 3544 Special dies & tools

(G-7278)
CONTRACTORS SHEET METAL INC
974 W Conway Rd Ste 15 (49740-9488)
PHONE...................................231 348-0753
Scott Cavell, *President*
EMP: 3
SALES (est): 261.7K **Privately Held**
SIC: 3444 Sheet metalwork

(G-7279)
CORNILLIE CONCRETE
710 W Conway Rd (49740-9585)
PHONE...................................231 439-9200
Rick Deneweth, *Owner*
EMP: 20 EST: 1997
SALES (est): 218.3K **Privately Held**
SIC: 3273 Ready-mixed concrete

(G-7280)
CREATIVE MILLWORK CORPORATION
385 Franklin Park (49740-9628)
PHONE...................................231 526-0201
John David Lewis, *Owner*
Jim Hawkins, *Foreman/Supr*
EMP: 6
SQ FT: 2,500
SALES (est): 619.1K **Privately Held**
WEB: www.creativemillworks.com
SIC: 2431 Interior & ornamental woodwork & trim

(G-7281)
DECKA DIGITAL LLC
1227 W Conway Rd (49740-9683)
PHONE...................................231 347-1253
Doug Potts, *President*
Cathy Kalahar, *Vice Pres*
Kathy Potts,
EMP: 3 EST: 2012
SALES (est): 50K **Privately Held**
SIC: 2752 Commercial printing, offset

(G-7282)
DENNIS OBRYAN OD
8422 M 119 (49740-9595)
PHONE...................................231 348-1255
Dennis Obryan, *Owner*
EMP: 3
SALES (est): 180K **Privately Held**
SIC: 3851 Eyeglasses, lenses & frames

(G-7283)
HARBOR SPRNG VNYRDS WINERY LLC
Also Called: Tunnel Vision Brewery
5699 S Lake Shore Dr (49740-9784)
PHONE...................................231 242-4062
James Palmer,
James Spencer IV,
Sharon Spencer,
EMP: 6
SQ FT: 2,000
SALES (est): 185.1K **Privately Held**
SIC: 2084 Wines

(G-7284)
HYDRONIX LTD
Also Called: Hydronix Americas
692 W Conway Rd 24 (49740-9489)
PHONE...................................231 439-5000
Lindsay Fall, *Asst Office Mgr*
EMP: 3 **Privately Held**
SIC: 3822 Hydronic pressure or temperature controls
PA: Hydronix Limited
 Unit 7 The Riverside Business Centre
 Walnut Tree Close
 Guildford

(G-7285)
JERVIS B WEBB COMPANY
8212 M 119 (49740-9070)
PHONE...................................231 347-3931
Tammy Brendly, *Purch Agent*
Dennis Tippett, *Manager*
EMP: 160 **Privately Held**
WEB: www.jervisbwebb.com
SIC: 3535 Conveyors & conveying equipment
HQ: Jervis B. Webb Company
 30100 Cabot Dr
 Novi MI 48377
 248 553-1000

(G-7286)
LARIBITS KEATON PUBL GROUP
8959 Sturgeon Bay Dr (49740-9746)
PHONE...................................231 537-3330
Larry Ribits, *Principal*
EMP: 3
SALES (est): 182K **Privately Held**
SIC: 2721 Periodicals

(G-7287)
LITTLE TRAVERSE DISPOSAL LLC
1128 Mcbride Park Dr (49740-9508)
PHONE...................................231 487-0780
Arvin Warner, *Owner*
EMP: 5
SALES (est): 790.4K **Privately Held**
SIC: 3089 Garbage containers, plastic

(G-7288)
LUCKY PRESS LLC
4929 Turfway Trl (49740-9273)
PHONE...................................614 309-0048
Janice Phelps, *Principal*
EMP: 3
SALES (est): 134.3K **Privately Held**
SIC: 2741 Miscellaneous publishing

(G-7289)
MOELLER AEROSPACE TECH INC
8725 Moeller Dr (49740-9583)
PHONE...................................231 347-9575
David Davidson, *Opers Staff*
Jeff Beaubien, *Manager*
EMP: 225
SQ FT: 19,000
SALES (est): 42.1MM **Privately Held**
SIC: 3724 Aircraft engines & engine parts

(G-7290)
NORTH COUNTRY PUBLISHING CORP
Also Called: Harbor Light Newspaper
211 E 3rd St (49740-1534)
P.O. Box 4545 (49740-4545)
PHONE...................................231 526-2191
Kevin Oneill, *Publisher*
Ruth Oneill, *Treasurer*
EMP: 4
SQ FT: 2,500
SALES (est): 525.9K **Privately Held**
WEB: www.harborlightnews.com
SIC: 2759 Newspapers: printing; invitations: printing

(G-7291)
PHIL ELENBAAS MILLWORK INC
341 Franklin Park (49740-9628)
PHONE...................................231 526-8399
Yli Rabeiro, *Branch Mgr*
EMP: 3
SALES (est): 255.1K
SALES (corp-wide): 3.1MM **Privately Held**
SIC: 2431 Millwork
PA: Phil Elenbaas Millwork, Inc.
 3000 Wilson Dr Nw
 Grand Rapids MI 49534
 616 791-1616

(G-7292)
RED IRON STRL CONSULTING CORP
170 Royalview Rd (49740-8727)
PHONE...................................810 364-5100
Kenneth O Shaw, *President*
Mark Lietke, *Vice Pres*
Kevin Shaw, *Vice Pres*
Dave Dziubinski, *Data Proc Dir*
Karen Shaw, *Admin Sec*
EMP: 2
SALES (est): 2.4MM **Privately Held**
SIC: 3441 7389 Fabricated structural metal;

(G-7293)
SEALEX INC
8850 Moeller Dr (49740-9461)
PHONE...................................231 348-5020
Robert Hagen, *President*
Peter R Hagen, *Chairman*
Matthias Hagan, *Vice Pres*
EMP: 7
SQ FT: 10,000
SALES (est): 1.1MM **Privately Held**
WEB: www.sealexinc.com
SIC: 2891 Adhesives & sealants

(G-7294)
SMART SWATTER LLC
3229 Valleyview Trl (49740-9325)
P.O. Box 96, Alanson (49706-0096)
PHONE...................................989 763-2626
Rod McDonald, *Mng Member*
EMP: 4
SALES: 25K **Privately Held**
SIC: 3999 Flyswatters

(G-7295)
TIMBERTECH INC
8796 Moeller Dr (49740-9583)
P.O. Box 546 (49740-0546)
PHONE...................................231 348-2750
John F Phillips, *President*
Deborah Baker, *Sales Mgr*
Angie Olson, *Graphic Designe*
EMP: 24
SQ FT: 13,500
SALES (est): 3.4MM **Privately Held**
SIC: 2752 2761 2759 2671 Business forms, lithographed; manifold business forms; commercial printing; packaging paper & plastics film, coated & laminated; automotive & apparel trimmings

(G-7296)
TRAVERSE BAY CANVAS INC
787 W Conway Rd (49740-9585)
PHONE...................................231 347-3001
Carol E Kleinert, *President*
Carol Kleinert, *President*
EMP: 8
SQ FT: 6,000

Harbor Springs - Emmet County (G-7297)

SALES (est): 572.4K **Privately Held**
WEB: www.traversebaycanvas.com
SIC: **2394** Awnings, fabric: made from purchased materials

(G-7297)
VENTILATION + PLUS EQP INC
670 W Conway Rd 1 (49740-9489)
P.O. Box 811 (49740-0811)
PHONE 231 487-1156
Gary Teffens, *President*
EMP: 4
SALES (est): 658.8K **Privately Held**
SIC: **3444** Metal ventilating equipment

(G-7298)
WOODPECKER INDUSTRIES LLC
375 Franklin Park 2 (49740-9628)
PHONE 231 347-0970
Alan Dika,
EMP: 3
SALES: 470K **Privately Held**
WEB: www.wpind.com
SIC: **3544** Special dies, tools, jigs & fixtures

Harper Woods
Wayne County

(G-7299)
AVIDASPORTS LLC
20844 Harper Ave (48225-1172)
PHONE 313 447-5670
Bruce Burton, *Principal*
EMP: 3
SALES (est): 289.8K **Privately Held**
SIC: **2329** Bathing suits & swimwear: men's & boys'

(G-7300)
BULLION TOOL TECHNOLOGY LLC
20044 E 8 Mile Rd (48225-1101)
PHONE 313 881-1404
James Bordeau, *Engineer*
Ronda Boscarino,
EMP: 3
SALES: 950K **Privately Held**
SIC: **3545** Cutting tools for machine tools

(G-7301)
HARVILLE ASSOCIATES INC
Also Called: Detroit Brew Factory
19666 Old Homestead Dr (48225-2003)
PHONE 313 839-5712
Sandra Harville, *President*
EMP: 3
SALES: 250K **Privately Held**
SIC: **2082** Malt beverages

(G-7302)
MASLIN CORPORATION (PA)
Also Called: Sir Speedy
20304 Harper Ave (48225-1701)
PHONE 586 777-7500
Thomas J Coughlin, *President*
Catherine Coughlin, *Corp Secy*
EMP: 4
SALES (est): 750.7K **Privately Held**
SIC: **2752** Commercial printing, lithographic

(G-7303)
REFINERY CORPORATION AMERICA
20008 Kelly Rd (48225-1919)
P.O. Box 361420, Grosse Pointe (48236-5420)
PHONE 877 881-0336
Ashia Paul, *President*
EMP: 6
SQ FT: 4,000
SALES (est): 264.4K **Privately Held**
SIC: **1311** Gas & hydrocarbon liquefication from coal

(G-7304)
SBR LLC
Also Called: Steve's Back Room
19872 Kelly Rd (48225-1918)
P.O. Box 180611, Utica (48318-0611)
PHONE 313 350-8799
Stephen Kalil, *Mng Member*
EMP: 25 EST: 2009
SALES (est): 2.6MM **Privately Held**
SIC: **2032** 5499 5812 Italian foods: packaged in cans, jars, etc.; Spanish foods: packaged in cans, jars, etc.; gourmet food stores; eating places

(G-7305)
SHANNONS INNOVATIVE CREAT LLC
20410 Lochmoor St (48225-1750)
PHONE 313 282-2724
Shannon Ridley,
EMP: 3 EST: 2013
SALES (est): 214.4K **Privately Held**
SIC: **2759** Commercial printing

(G-7306)
SWEETHEART BAKERY OF MICHIGAN
Also Called: Michelle's Restaurant
19200 Kelly Rd (48225-1902)
P.O. Box 88, Roseville (48066-0088)
PHONE 586 795-1660
Michael Gralewski, *President*
Amelia Gralewski, *Vice Pres*
EMP: 100
SQ FT: 13,000
SALES (est): 2.5MM **Privately Held**
SIC: **5812** 5461 2051 Family restaurants; bakeries; bread, cake & related products

Harrison
Clare County

(G-7307)
AMERICAN HYDRO-WORKS ENGRG LLC
6817 Swallow Dr (48625-9097)
PHONE 906 282-8890
Suzanne Posluszny,
Larry Posluszny,
EMP: 3
SALES (est): 140K **Privately Held**
SIC: **3544** Special dies, tools, jigs & fixtures

(G-7308)
BADGER PIPE & PILING LLC
2090 E Mannsiding Rd (48625-9567)
PHONE 989 965-0126
Lee Fritzinger,
EMP: 3
SALES (est): 89.5K **Privately Held**
SIC: **1389** Building oil & gas well foundations on site

(G-7309)
BECKMAN PRODUCTION SVCS INC
4400 N Clare Ave (48625-8521)
PHONE 989 539-7126
Chuck Pardue, *General Mgr*
Chuck Taylor, *Branch Mgr*
EMP: 25
SALES (corp-wide): 827.1MM **Publicly Held**
WEB: www.dartenergy.com
SIC: **1389** 1382 Oil field services; oil & gas exploration services
HQ: Beckman Production Services, Inc.
3786 Beebe Rd
Kalkaska MI 49646
231 258-9524

(G-7310)
CLARE COUNTY CLEAVER INC
183 W Main St (48625)
P.O. Box 436 (48625-0436)
PHONE 989 539-7496
Glen Bucholz, *President*
Martin Bucholz, *Vice Pres*
Mable Bucholz, *Treasurer*
EMP: 8

SALES (est): 599.5K **Privately Held**
SIC: **2711** Newspapers, publishing & printing; job printing & newspaper publishing combined

(G-7311)
FEDERAL BROACH & MCH CO LLC
1961 Sullivan Dr (48625-9455)
PHONE 989 539-7420
Daniel Bickersteth, *COO*
Dan Dennis, *Vice Pres*
Joe Witer, *Vice Pres*
Kami Knop, *Production*
Christian Carmack, *Engineer*
▲ EMP: 116
SQ FT: 82,000
SALES (est): 28.8MM **Privately Held**
WEB: www.federalbroach.com
SIC: **3541** 3545 Broaching machines; broaches (machine tool accessories)
HQ: Mitsubishi Heavy Industries America, Inc.
20 Greenway Plz
Houston TX 77046
346 308-8800

(G-7312)
GAMBLES REDI-MIX INC
1415 N Clare Ave (48625-8218)
P.O. Box 692 (48625-0692)
PHONE 989 539-6460
Walter W Gamble, *President*
Cathy Gamble, *Vice Pres*
EMP: 12
SQ FT: 2,400
SALES (est): 1.5MM **Privately Held**
SIC: **3273** 3272 Ready-mixed concrete; concrete products

(G-7313)
JAMES L MILLER
Also Called: Runnin Gears
2500 Major Mountain Rd (48625-8211)
PHONE 989 539-5540
James L Miller, *Owner*
EMP: 4
SQ FT: 10,000
SALES (est): 515.9K **Privately Held**
SIC: **2411** 5082 Logging; logging & forestry machinery & equipment

(G-7314)
LONG LAKE FOREST PRODUCTS
2330 E Haskell Lake Rd (48625-8512)
PHONE 989 239-6527
Harvey J Hose Jr, *Managing Prtnr*
Julie Wymer, *Partner*
Larry Wymer, *Partner*
EMP: 3
SALES: 300K **Privately Held**
SIC: **5099** 2611 2411 Timber products, rough; pulpwood; pulp mills; logging

(G-7315)
MARINE AUTOMATED DOC SYSTEM
2900 Doc Dr (48625-7329)
PHONE 989 539-9010
Greg Heintz, *President*
Tom Dewey, *Vice Pres*
EMP: 12
SALES (est): 1.5MM **Privately Held**
WEB: www.madsdirect.com
SIC: **3448** Docks: prefabricated metal

(G-7316)
SABERTOOTH ENTERPRISES LLC
Also Called: Billsby Lumber Company
2725 Larch Rd (48625-9211)
P.O. Box 530 (48625-0530)
PHONE 989 539-9842
Ray Billsby, *President*
Pamela Brown, *Principal*
Doris Billsby, *Vice Pres*
Joel Woodruff,
EMP: 16
SQ FT: 6,240
SALES (est): 3MM **Privately Held**
SIC: **2421** Sawmills & planing mills, general

Harrison Township
Macomb County

(G-7317)
A & C ELECTRIC COMPANY
Also Called: A & C Electric Motor Sls & Svc
41225 Irwin Dr (48045-1330)
PHONE 586 773-2746
Jewell Arker, *President*
Daniel Arker, *Vice Pres*
Nancy Fountain, *Treasurer*
Lisa Jacobson, *Admin Sec*
EMP: 21
SQ FT: 15,000
SALES (est): 5MM **Privately Held**
SIC: **7694** 5063 Electric motor repair; motors, electric

(G-7318)
ALLIANCE TOOL
41239 Irwin Dr (48045-1330)
PHONE 586 465-3960
Cynthia Thompson, *Owner*
EMP: 5
SQ FT: 5,000
SALES (est): 500K **Privately Held**
WEB: www.alliancetool.net
SIC: **3541** Machine tools, metal cutting type

(G-7319)
AMP INNOVATIVE TECH LLC
42050 Executive Dr (48045-1311)
PHONE 586 465-2700
EMP: 25
SALES (est): 2.7MM **Privately Held**
SIC: **3089** Mfg Plastic Products

(G-7320)
AQUARIUS RECREATIONAL PRODUCTS
41201 Production Dr (48045-1353)
PHONE 586 469-4600
Josephine Adas, *President*
EMP: 4
SQ FT: 4,000
SALES (est): 100K **Privately Held**
SIC: **3499** 3446 Ladders, portable: metal; furniture parts, metal; railings, prefabricated metal

(G-7321)
ARISTO-COTE INC (PA)
Also Called: Aristo Industries
24951 Henry B Joy Blvd (48045-1115)
PHONE 586 336-9421
Matt Murray, *President*
Pat Abel, *Plant Mgr*
EMP: 30
SQ FT: 42,515
SALES: 30.8MM **Privately Held**
WEB: www.aristo-cote.com
SIC: **3479** Coating of metals & formed products; coating of metals with plastic or resins; coating of metals with silicon; coating or wrapping steel pipe

(G-7322)
ARTHUR R SOMMERS
Also Called: Sommers Marine
41700 Conger Bay Dr (48045-1432)
PHONE 586 469-1280
Arthur R Sommers, *Owner*
EMP: 6 EST: 1955
SALES (est): 507.7K **Privately Held**
SIC: **7699** 3568 3566 Marine engine repair; power transmission equipment; speed changers, drives & gears

(G-7323)
BEACON MARINE SALES & SERVICE
36400 Jefferson Ave (48045-2904)
PHONE 586 465-2539
Edward Keller, *President*
EMP: 3
SALES (est): 370.4K **Privately Held**
SIC: **3732** Boat building & repairing

GEOGRAPHIC SECTION — Harrison Township - Macomb County (G-7353)

(G-7324)
BREITEN BOX & PACKAGING CO INC
42828 Executive Dr (48045-1317)
P.O. Box 576, Mount Clemens (48046-0576)
PHONE 586 469-0800
Tom Szajna, *President*
Kim Szajna, *Vice Pres*
EMP: 7
SQ FT: 10,900
SALES (est): 600K **Privately Held**
SIC: 2448 5031 Wood pallets & skids; lumber: rough, dressed & finished

(G-7325)
C F PLASTIC FABRICATING INC
41590 Production Dr (48045-1357)
PHONE 586 954-1296
Charles Fowler, *President*
Dennis Fowler, *Vice Pres*
Margaret Fowler, *Admin Sec*
EMP: 7 EST: 1976
SQ FT: 4,500
SALES (est): 1MM **Privately Held**
SIC: 2542 Fixtures: display, office or store: except wood

(G-7326)
CAMBRO PRODUCTS INC
41135 Irwin Dr (48045-1329)
PHONE 586 468-8847
Kevin Cameron, *President*
Cheryl Cameron, *Treasurer*
EMP: 25
SQ FT: 31,000
SALES (est): 3.8MM **Privately Held**
WEB: www.cambroproducts.com
SIC: 3714 Motor vehicle brake systems & parts

(G-7327)
CRANE 1 SERVICES INC
Also Called: Mt. Clemens Crane
42827 Irwin Dr (48045-1342)
PHONE 586 468-0909
Matthew Milton, *President*
Lisa Miketich, *CFO*
Charles Albright, *Manager*
Bill Janssen, *Manager*
EMP: 25
SALES (corp-wide): 47MM **Privately Held**
SIC: 7699 5084 3536 Industrial machinery & equipment repair; cranes, industrial; hoists, cranes & monorails
PA: Crane 1 Services, Inc.
1027 Byers Rd
Miamisburg OH 45342
937 704-9900

(G-7328)
D M C INTERNATIONAL INC
42470 Executive Dr (48045-1313)
PHONE 586 465-1112
William Schneider, *Vice Pres*
▲ EMP: 6
SQ FT: 8,200
SALES (est): 966.4K **Privately Held**
WEB: www.dmcinter.com
SIC: 3599 Machine shop, jobbing & repair

(G-7329)
DOCKSIDE CANVAS CO INC
29939 S River Rd (48045-3031)
PHONE 586 463-1231
John P Bowen, *President*
EMP: 17
SQ FT: 7,500
SALES (est): 1.8MM **Privately Held**
SIC: 2394 Awnings, fabric: made from purchased materials; convertible tops, canvas or boat: from purchased materials

(G-7330)
FERRO INDUSTRIES INC
35200 Union Lake Rd (48045-6100)
P.O. Box 86, Mount Clemens (48046-0086)
PHONE 586 792-6001
Joseph V Clemente, *President*
Marilyn Clemente, *Vice Pres*
Dean Clemente, *Marketing Mgr*
Becky Durlock, *Manager*
EMP: 45 EST: 1962
SQ FT: 30,000
SALES (est): 5.8MM **Privately Held**
SIC: 3291 3089 Abrasive products; injection molding of plastics

(G-7331)
FOX MFG CO
32535 S River Rd (48045-5703)
PHONE 586 468-1421
Richard Fox, *President*
Steven Fox, *President*
Eunice Fox, *Treasurer*
Anne Fox, *Admin Sec*
EMP: 25 EST: 1933
SQ FT: 12,000
SALES (est): 4.8MM **Privately Held**
WEB: www.foxmanufacturing.com
SIC: 3451 Screw machine products

(G-7332)
HENRY PLAMBECK
Also Called: American Dowel & Fastener
40962 Production Dr (48045-1352)
PHONE 586 463-3410
Henry Plambeck, *Owner*
EMP: 6
SALES (est): 1MM **Privately Held**
SIC: 3452 Dowel pins, metal

(G-7333)
J E ENTERPRISES
Also Called: River Bend Driving Range
38154 Willowmere St (48045-5327)
PHONE 586 463-5129
EMP: 5
SALES: 210K **Privately Held**
SIC: 3599 Machine Shop

(G-7334)
JENE HOLLY DESIGNS INC
39876 Shoreline Dr (48045-1638)
PHONE 586 954-0255
Christine Ewald, *President*
Leslie Ewald, *Vice Pres*
EMP: 6
SALES: 50K **Privately Held**
WEB: www.hollyjenedesigns.com
SIC: 2395 7389 5231 Embroidery products, except schiffli machine; advertising, promotional & trade show services; glass

(G-7335)
KENT SAIL CO INC
35942 Jefferson Ave (48045-3252)
PHONE 586 791-2580
Kent T Schwandt, *President*
Susan Heins, *Vice Pres*
Timothy Schwandt, *Vice Pres*
EMP: 3 EST: 1969
SALES (est): 349.3K **Privately Held**
SIC: 2394 Sails: made from purchased materials; liners & covers, fabric: made from purchased materials

(G-7336)
KRING PIZZA INC
35415 Jefferson Ave (48045-3240)
PHONE 586 792-0049
John Kring, *President*
EMP: 8
SALES (est): 588.2K **Privately Held**
SIC: 2099 2038 5812 Spices, including grinding; frozen specialties; pizza restaurants

(G-7337)
LASER CUTTING CO
42300 Executive Dr (48045-1312)
PHONE 586 468-5300
Cheryl A Scullion, *President*
Melissa Pizzo, *Vice Pres*
Melissa R Scullion, *Vice Pres*
John Hopf, *Plant Mgr*
Justin Craft, *Engineer*
EMP: 27 EST: 1967
SQ FT: 37,432
SALES (est): 5.7MM **Privately Held**
WEB: www.lasercuttinginc.com
SIC: 3599 3469 3465 Machine shop, jobbing & repair; metal stampings; automotive stampings

(G-7338)
LIBERTYS HIGH PRFMCE PDTS INC
41775 Production Dr (48045-1370)
PHONE 586 469-1140
Craig Liberty, *President*
Jennifer Plutschuck, *Principal*
Casey Patterson, *Vice Pres*
▼ EMP: 12
SQ FT: 8,800
SALES (est): 2.3MM **Privately Held**
SIC: 3714 Gears, motor vehicle

(G-7339)
MASTERLINE DESIGN & MFG
41580 Production Dr (48045-1357)
PHONE 586 463-5888
Kathleen Pomaville, *President*
Dennis Pomaville, *Vice Pres*
EMP: 28
SQ FT: 7,000
SALES (est): 5.3MM **Privately Held**
SIC: 3568 Shafts, flexible

(G-7340)
MILLERS CUSTOM BOAT TOP INC
41700 Conger Bay Dr (48045-1432)
PHONE 586 468-5533
Dennis Miller, *President*
Cheryl Miller, *Vice Pres*
EMP: 6
SQ FT: 3,000
SALES (est): 513.4K **Privately Held**
SIC: 2394 Liners & covers, fabric: made from purchased materials

(G-7341)
NORTHERN INDUSTRIAL MFG CORP
41000 Executive Dr (48045-1303)
PHONE 586 468-2790
Harvey Hohlfeldt, *CEO*
Dale Hohlfelot, *President*
Howard Powell, *Vice Pres*
Jeff Hohlfeldt, *Sales Staff*
Kaye Hohlfeldt, *Webmaster*
EMP: 25
SALES (est): 5.3MM **Privately Held**
WEB: www.northernindmfg.com
SIC: 3465 3469 3452 Automotive stampings; metal stampings; bolts, nuts, rivets & washers

(G-7342)
OERLIKON BLZERS CATING USA INC
42728 Executive Dr (48045-1316)
PHONE 586 465-0412
Fax: 586 465-1968
EMP: 50
SALES (corp-wide): 3.3B **Privately Held**
SIC: 3479 Coating/Engraving Service
HQ: Oerlikon Balzers Coating Usa Inc.
1475 E Wdfield Rd Ste 201
Schaumburg IL 60173
847 619-5541

(G-7343)
POWER INDUSTRIES CORP
42279 Irwin Dr (48045-1339)
PHONE 586 783-3818
Karen Lee Johnston, *President*
Glenn Johnston, *Vice Pres*
EMP: 6
SQ FT: 5,400
SALES (est): 400K **Privately Held**
SIC: 3462 3443 3441 Machinery forgings, ferrous; fabricated plate work (boiler shop); fabricated structural metal

(G-7344)
POWER MARINE LLC
38303 Mast St (48045-2751)
PHONE 586 344-1192
Gerald Knotts, *Principal*
EMP: 4
SALES (est): 349K **Privately Held**
SIC: 3443 Boilers: industrial, power, or marine

(G-7345)
R AND T SPORTING CLAYS INC
37853 Elmlane (48045-2713)
P.O. Box 46701, Mount Clemens (48046-6701)
PHONE 586 215-9861
Tom Shather, *President*
Rick Stover, *Vice Pres*
EMP: 4
SALES (est): 240.8K **Privately Held**
SIC: 3949 Hunting equipment

(G-7346)
RA PRCSION GRNDING MTLWRKS INC
40801 Irwin Dr (48045-1326)
PHONE 586 783-7776
Roger Belanger, *President*
Linda Belanger, *Vice Pres*
EMP: 18 EST: 2015
SALES: 1.4MM **Privately Held**
SIC: 3541 Grinding machines, metalworking

(G-7347)
ROUSSIN M & UBELHOR R INC
Also Called: Shores Tool and Mfg
41903 Irwin Dr (48045-1336)
PHONE 586 783-6015
Mark Roussin, *President*
EMP: 4
SQ FT: 2,500
SALES: 300K **Privately Held**
SIC: 3541 Machine tools, metal cutting: exotic (explosive, etc.)

(G-7348)
SELFRIDGE PLATING INC
Also Called: Selfridge Technologies
42081 Irwin Dr (48045-1337)
PHONE 586 469-3141
Howard Staudaker, *CEO*
Craig Studaker, *President*
Elyce Rausch, *Vice Pres*
Wanda Staudaker, *Treasurer*
EMP: 55 EST: 1970
SQ FT: 34,000
SALES (est): 8MM **Privately Held**
WEB: www.selfridgeplating.com
SIC: 3471 Plating of metals or formed products

(G-7349)
SIGN FABRICATORS INC
37675 Lakeville St (48045-2882)
PHONE 586 468-7360
Timothy White, *Principal*
EMP: 3
SALES (est): 215.5K **Privately Held**
SIC: 3993 Signs & advertising specialties

(G-7350)
SR INJECTION MOLDING INC
41565 Production Dr (48045-1358)
PHONE 586 260-2360
Scott Rheeder, *President*
EMP: 5
SALES (est): 235.3K **Privately Held**
SIC: 3089 Injection molding of plastics

(G-7351)
STERLING PROD MACHINING LLC
42522 Executive Dr (48045-1314)
PHONE 586 493-0633
Stevo Sljivic, *Mng Member*
Donna Sljivic,
EMP: 4
SQ FT: 13,000
SALES: 500K **Privately Held**
SIC: 3599 Machine shop, jobbing & repair

(G-7352)
TAZZ BROACH AND MACHINE INC
41565 Production Dr (48045-1358)
PHONE 586 296-7755
Fax: 586 294-5850
EMP: 9
SQ FT: 2,800
SALES (est): 730K **Privately Held**
SIC: 3545 7389 Mfg Broaches & Precision Grinding Service

(G-7353)
TEMP RITE STEEL TREATING INC
42386 Executive Dr (48045-1312)
PHONE 586 469-3071
Delphine Decook, *President*
David De Cook, *Vice Pres*
Paul De Cook, *Vice Pres*
Doreen Dulics, *Treasurer*
Aimee Alvarez, *Manager*

EMP: 20
SQ FT: 20,000
SALES (est): 4.1MM **Privately Held**
SIC: 3398 Shot peening (treating steel to reduce fatigue); brazing (hardening) of metal

(G-7354)
TRI MATICS MFG INC
25500 Henry B Joy Blvd (48045-1322)
PHONE..................................586 469-3150
Robert Saunders, *President*
EMP: 7
SQ FT: 4,000
SALES (est): 350K **Privately Held**
SIC: 3599 Machine shop, jobbing & repair

(G-7355)
WILSON-GARNER COMPANY
40935 Production Dr (48045-1351)
P.O. Box 1167, Mount Clemens (48046-1167)
PHONE..................................586 466-5880
Timothy Pinchback, *President*
Joe Pinchback, *General Mgr*
Tyrus Pinchback, *Chairman*
Keith Pinchback, *Vice Pres*
Robert Lemons, *Plant Mgr*
EMP: 20
SQ FT: 26,000
SALES: 1MM **Privately Held**
WEB: www.placebolt.com
SIC: 3452 Bolts, metal

(G-7356)
WOLVERINE BROACH CO INC (PA)
41200 Executive Dr (48045-1305)
PHONE..................................586 468-4445
Bernard Aude, *President*
EMP: 24
SQ FT: 11,600
SALES: 5.6MM **Privately Held**
SIC: 3545 Broaches (machine tool accessories)

(G-7357)
WOLVERINE PRODUCTION & ENGRG
41160 Executive Dr (48045-1304)
PHONE..................................586 468-2890
Bernard Aude Jr, *President*
John R Ferguson, *Plant Mgr*
EMP: 18
SQ FT: 15,000
SALES (est): 2.2MM **Privately Held**
SIC: 3545 Machine tool accessories

(G-7358)
YANFENG US AUTOMOTIVE
Also Called: Yanfeng Automotive Interiors
42150 Executive Dr (48045-1376)
PHONE..................................586 354-2101
Jennifer Johnson, *Exec Dir*
Marilyn Brooks, *Admin Asst*
EMP: 10
SALES (corp-wide): 55MM **Privately Held**
SIC: 2531 Seats, automobile
HQ: Yanfeng Us Automotive Interior Systems I Llc
41935 W 12 Mile Rd
Novi MI 48377
248 319-7333

(G-7359)
YANFENG USA AUTOMOTIVE TRIM SY (DH)
42150 Executive Dr (48045-1376)
PHONE..................................586 354-2101
Johannes Roters, *CEO*
David Wang, *President*
Thomas Truax, *Engineer*
Michael Kleinheksel, *CFO*
▲ **EMP:** 52
SQ FT: 1,000
SALES (est): 81MM
SALES (corp-wide): 55MM **Privately Held**
SIC: 2396 Automotive & apparel trimmings
HQ: Yanfeng Global Automotive Interior Systems Co., Ltd.
No.399, Liuzhou Road, Xuhui District
Shanghai 20023
213 338-1000

Harrison Twp
Macomb County

(G-7360)
SARNS INDUSTRIES INC
Also Called: Sarns Machine
41451 Irwin Dr (48045-1331)
PHONE..................................586 463-5829
Jerry Flowers, *President*
EMP: 15
SQ FT: 13,000
SALES (est): 1.8MM **Privately Held**
WEB: www.sarnsindustries.com
SIC: 7699 3559 Hydraulic equipment repair; automotive related machinery

Harrisville
Alcona County

(G-7361)
ALCONA COUNTY REVIEW
111 N Lake St (48740-9696)
P.O. Box 548 (48740-0548)
PHONE..................................989 724-6384
Cheryl L Peterson, *Owner*
John Boufford, *Co-Owner*
EMP: 4
SQ FT: 2,250
SALES (est): 475.1K **Privately Held**
WEB: www.alconareview.com
SIC: 2711 Newspapers: publishing only, not printed on site

(G-7362)
ALCONA TOOL & MACHINE INC (PA)
3040 E Carbide Dr (48740-9610)
P.O. Box 340, Lincoln (48742-0340)
PHONE..................................989 736-8151
Monty L Kruttlin, *President*
Joe James, *Corp Secy*
EMP: 48
SQ FT: 12,000
SALES (est): 7.3MM **Privately Held**
WEB: www.alconatool.com
SIC: 3544 3599 Special dies & tools; machine shop, jobbing & repair

(G-7363)
ESR
2225 E Tait Rd (48740-9532)
PHONE..................................989 619-7160
Craig Stoley, *President*
Jeff Evjen, *Manager*
EMP: 4
SALES (est): 373.3K **Privately Held**
SIC: 3541 Machine tools, metal cutting type

(G-7364)
LINCOLN TOOL CO INC
3140 E M 72 (48740-9714)
PHONE..................................989 736-8711
Kenneth G Manning, *President*
Florence V Manning, *Corp Secy*
EMP: 4
SQ FT: 5,000
SALES (est): 505.2K **Privately Held**
WEB: www.lincolntoolco.com
SIC: 3544 7699 Special dies, tools, jigs & fixtures; industrial tool grinding

(G-7365)
MANUS TOOL INC
510 S 3rd St (48740-9319)
P.O. Box 248 (48740-0248)
PHONE..................................989 724-7171
Keith Nedo, *President*
Guy Holm, *Vice Pres*
EMP: 25
SQ FT: 5,000
SALES (est): 2.3MM **Privately Held**
SIC: 3599 Machine shop, jobbing & repair

(G-7366)
SUNRISE TOOL PRODUCTS INC
604 S 3rd St (48740-9320)
P.O. Box 373 (48740-0373)
PHONE..................................989 724-6688
Kevin Johnson, *President*
Michelle Johnson, *Principal*
Jaymie Sutton, *Principal*
Timothy Sutton, *Vice Pres*
EMP: 14
SQ FT: 6,200
SALES (est): 1.1MM **Privately Held**
SIC: 3541 Machine tools, metal cutting type

(G-7367)
WEISER METAL PRODUCTS INC
3040 E Carbide Dr (48740-9610)
P.O. Box 370, Lincoln (48742-0370)
PHONE..................................989 736-6055
Terry Lenard, *President*
Joe James, *Corp Secy*
Keith Karuttlin, *Vice Pres*
EMP: 8
SQ FT: 7,000
SALES (est): 1MM **Privately Held**
WEB: www.weisermetal.com
SIC: 2819 Carbides

Harsens Island
St. Clair County

(G-7368)
BEARDSLEE INVESTMENTS INC
2256 N Channel Dr (48028-9790)
PHONE..................................810 748-9951
Richard Engle, *CEO*
John Falkiewicz, *President*
Steven Popkie, *Vice Pres*
EMP: 15
SQ FT: 26,000
SALES (est): 2.6MM **Privately Held**
SIC: 3731 3732 Shipbuilding & repairing; yachts, building & repairing

(G-7369)
HOLLOWAY EQUIPMENT CO INC
4856 Middle Channel Dr (48028-9667)
PHONE..................................810 748-9577
Paul J Hollowaty, *President*
Shirley A Hollowaty, *Admin Sec*
EMP: 15
SQ FT: 26,000
SALES (est): 1.6MM **Privately Held**
WEB: www.hollowayequipment.com
SIC: 3599 Custom machinery

Hart
Oceana County

(G-7370)
DALE ROUTLEY LOGGING
1870 N 100th Ave (49420-8826)
PHONE..................................231 861-2596
Dale R Routley, *Principal*
EMP: 3
SALES (est): 258K **Privately Held**
SIC: 2411 Logging

(G-7371)
GHSP INC
Also Called: Ghsp Hart Plant
1500 Industrial Park Dr (49420-8148)
PHONE..................................231 873-3300
Dave Christmas, *Engineer*
Mark Gaultney, *Engineer*
Jerry Scott, *Branch Mgr*
Noah Witte, *Technician*
EMP: 16
SALES (corp-wide): 550.2MM **Privately Held**
SIC: 3089 3714 Injection molded finished plastic products; motor vehicle parts & accessories
HQ: Ghsp, Inc.
1250 S Beechtree St
Grand Haven MI 49417
616 842-5500

(G-7372)
GRAY & COMPANY (HQ)
3325 W Polk Rd (49420-8149)
PHONE..................................231 873-5628
James G Reynolds, *Ch of Bd*
Joshua E Reynolds, *Exec VP*
Ray Hacker, *Purch Agent*
Clyde Hendrick, *Manager*
Ronald Greenman, *Admin Sec*
◆ **EMP:** 150
SQ FT: 5,000
SALES (est): 72.4MM
SALES (corp-wide): 1.2B **Publicly Held**
WEB: www.cherryman.com
SIC: 2033 Maraschino cherries: packaged in cans, jars, etc.
PA: Seneca Foods Corporation
3736 S Main St
Marion NY 14505
315 926-8100

(G-7373)
HART FREEZE PACK LLC
Also Called: Michigan Freeze Pack
835 S Griswold St (49420-9756)
P.O. Box 30 (49420-0030)
PHONE..................................231 873-2175
Mary Riddell, *Manager*
Al Karnemaat,
Scott Greiner,
Ralph Oomen,
Richard Oomen,
EMP: 10
SQ FT: 100,000
SALES (est): 2.4MM **Privately Held**
WEB: www.michiganfreezepack.com
SIC: 2037 Fruits, quick frozen & cold pack (frozen); vegetables, quick frozen & cold pack, excl. potato products

(G-7374)
INDIAN SUMMER COOPERATIVE INC
409 Wood St (49420-1351)
P.O. Box 31 (49420-0031)
PHONE..................................231 873-7504
Denny Spear, *Plant Mgr*
Roger Warrmuskerkem, *Manager*
EMP: 20
SALES (corp-wide): 89.1MM **Privately Held**
SIC: 3556 2099 Dehydrating equipment, food processing; food preparations
PA: Indian Summer Cooperative Inc
3958 W Chauvez Rd Ste 1
Ludington MI 49431
231 845-6248

(G-7375)
KARDUX WELDING & FABRICATING
Also Called: Blast-All Sandblasting
1827 E Minke Rd (49420-8637)
P.O. Box 859 (49420-0859)
PHONE..................................231 873-4648
Todd Kardux, *Owner*
EMP: 3
SQ FT: 3,000
SALES (est): 100K **Privately Held**
SIC: 7692 1799 Welding repair; sandblasting of building exteriors

(G-7376)
MAKKEDAH MT PROC & BULK FD STR
1813 N 136th Ave (49420-8809)
PHONE..................................231 873-2113
Ronald Marks, *President*
EMP: 5
SALES (est): 34.4K **Privately Held**
SIC: 2011 Meat packing plants

(G-7377)
NORTHLAND CASTINGS CORPORATION (PA)
4130 W Tyler Rd (49420-8213)
P.O. Box 472 (49420-0472)
PHONE..................................231 873-4974
John L Orzechowski, *President*
Kirk Dow, *Owner*
Charmaine Orzechowski, *Vice Pres*
EMP: 15 **EST:** 1974
SQ FT: 15,000
SALES (est): 2.4MM **Privately Held**
WEB: www.northlandcastings.com
SIC: 3321 Gray iron castings

GEOGRAPHIC SECTION

(G-7378)
OCEANAS HERALD-JOURNAL INC
Also Called: Freeway
123 S State St (49420-1124)
P.O. Box 190 (49420-0190)
PHONE..................................231 873-5602
James Young, *President*
Mary Sanford, *Editor*
Lance Corey, *Branch Mgr*
Margaret Clune, *Executive*
EMP: 16
SQ FT: 3,000
SALES (est): 1.1MM **Privately Held**
WEB: www.oceanaheraldjournal.com
SIC: 2711 2741 Job printing & newspaper publishing combined; shopping news: publishing only, not printed on site

(G-7379)
RAN-MARK CO
2978 E Hazel Rd (49420-8807)
PHONE..................................231 873-5103
Randy Fedo, *Owner*
EMP: 10
SQ FT: 3,200
SALES: 450K **Privately Held**
SIC: 3544 0161 Special dies, tools, jigs & fixtures; asparagus farm

(G-7380)
TURCHETTI SPAGHETTI CO LLC
1535 Industrial Park Dr (49420-8377)
PHONE..................................616 706-4766
Rick Turchetti,
Kathy Turchetti,
Reed Turchetti,
EMP: 3
SALES (est): 91.3K **Privately Held**
SIC: 2032 Italian foods: packaged in cans, jars, etc.

Hartford
Van Buren County

(G-7381)
AMHAWK LLC (PA)
200 Dunbar St (49057-8748)
PHONE..................................269 468-4177
Deb A Ashley, *Plant Supt*
Regi Kurien, *Mng Member*
EMP: 23
SQ FT: 800,000
SALES (est): 6.9MM **Privately Held**
WEB: www.amhawk.com
SIC: 3443 3444 3441 Fabricated plate work (boiler shop); sheet metalwork; fabricated structural metal

(G-7382)
BURNETTE FOODS INC
87171 County Road 687 (49057-8602)
PHONE..................................269 621-3181
William Sherman Jr, *Plant Mgr*
Ted Sherman, *Opers Mgr*
Pete Inman, *Production*
John Wyatt, *Engineer*
John H Wyatt, *Sales/Mktg Mgr*
EMP: 55
SALES (corp-wide): 92.7MM **Privately Held**
WEB: www.burnettefoods.com
SIC: 2033 Fruits: packaged in cans, jars, etc.; vegetable juices: packaged in cans, jars, etc.; fruit juices: packaged in cans, jars, etc.
PA: Burnette Foods, Inc.
 701 S Us Highway 31
 Elk Rapids MI 49629
 231 264-8116

(G-7383)
DOVER METALS INC
117 Paras Hill Dr (49057-1164)
PHONE..................................269 849-1411
Deborah Bedwell, *President*
Nick Anders, *Vice Pres*
▲ **EMP:** 8
SQ FT: 4,000
SALES (est): 1MM **Privately Held**
WEB: www.dovermetals.com
SIC: 3999 Advertising display products

(G-7384)
KEELER-GLASGOW COMPANY INC
80444 County Road 687 (49057-8606)
P.O. Box 158 (49057-0158)
PHONE..................................269 621-2415
Ernest Glasgow, *President*
EMP: 20
SQ FT: 15,000
SALES (est): 3.6MM **Privately Held**
SIC: 3448 3231 1542 Greenhouses: prefabricated metal; products of purchased glass; nonresidential construction

(G-7385)
MANN METAL FINISHING INC
200 Prospect St (49057-1057)
PHONE..................................269 621-6359
Jewell D Mann Sr, *President*
Greg Collins, *Vice Pres*
Tammy Collins, *Vice Pres*
Shirley Mann, *Admin Sec*
EMP: 70
SQ FT: 100,000
SALES (est): 7.8MM **Privately Held**
WEB: www.mannmetal.com
SIC: 3471 5051 Polishing, metals or formed products; buffing for the trade; finishing, metals or formed products; metals service centers & offices

(G-7386)
PRO SLOT LTD
12 W Main St (49057-1005)
PHONE..................................616 897-6000
Daniel De Bella, *President*
Sherly De Bella, *Corp Secy*
Dan Debella, *Manager*
▲ **EMP:** 6
SQ FT: 5,000
SALES: 490K **Privately Held**
WEB: www.proslot.com
SIC: 3621 3089 3451 Motors, electric; injection molding of plastics; screw machine products

(G-7387)
SINCLAIR GRAPHICS LLC
315 N Center St (49057-1199)
PHONE..................................269 621-3651
Scott C Sinclair, *Partner*
Peter R Sinclair, *Partner*
EMP: 4 EST: 1950
SALES (est): 501.5K **Privately Held**
SIC: 2752 Promotional printing, lithographic

Hartland
Livingston County

(G-7388)
C & V SERVICES INC
2755 Ore Valley Dr (48353-2809)
PHONE..................................810 632-9677
Constantine Vorias, *President*
EMP: 3
SALES (est): 290K **Privately Held**
SIC: 3663 Satellites, communications

(G-7389)
DENALI INCORPORATED
11600 Maxfield Blvd (48353-3425)
PHONE..................................517 574-0047
Ryan James Kincaid, *Branch Mgr*
EMP: 3 **Privately Held**
SIC: 3089 Air mattresses, plastic
PA: Denali Incorporated
 7134 S Yale Ave Ste 560
 Tulsa OK 74136

(G-7390)
HECK INDUSTRIES INCORPORATED
1498 Old Us 23 Hwy (48353)
P.O. Box 425 (48353-0425)
PHONE..................................810 632-5400
Philip H Heck, *President*
Deborah Heck, *Treasurer*
▲ **EMP:** 18 EST: 1970
SQ FT: 10,000
SALES (est): 6MM **Privately Held**
SIC: 5084 3546 Industrial machinery & equipment; power-driven handtools

(G-7391)
HERFF JONES LLC
3556 Avon St (48353-7706)
PHONE..................................810 632-6500
John Risser, *Manager*
EMP: 4
SALES (corp-wide): 1.1B **Privately Held**
WEB: www.herffjones.com
SIC: 3911 Rings, finger: precious metal
HQ: Herff Jones, Llc
 4501 W 62nd St
 Indianapolis IN 46268
 800 419-5462

(G-7392)
INTERNATIONAL MCH TL SVCS LLC
4028 Hartland Rd (48353-1004)
PHONE..................................734 667-2233
Carol Passmore,
Dave Passmore,
EMP: 8
SALES (est): 521.3K **Privately Held**
SIC: 3599 Machine shop, jobbing & repair

(G-7393)
J W MANCHESTER COMPANY INC
3552 Hartland Rd Ste 201 (48353)
P.O. Box 159 (48353-0159)
PHONE..................................810 632-5409
John W Manchester, *Ch of Bd*
Doug Steele, *President*
Grant Weidman, *Accounts Mgr*
Susane Nurnberger, *Admin Sec*
EMP: 7
SQ FT: 1,400
SALES (est): 1.6MM **Privately Held**
WEB: www.manchesterbag.com
SIC: 5199 2671 Packaging materials; packaging paper & plastics film, coated & laminated

(G-7394)
TNT MARBLE AND STONE INC
1240 Bogie Lake Rd (48353)
PHONE..................................248 887-8237
Robert Taylor, *President*
EMP: 5
SALES (est): 565.5K **Privately Held**
SIC: 3281 1411 Table tops, marble; granite, cut & shaped; dimension stone

(G-7395)
VILLAGE & COUNTRY WATER TRTMNT (PA)
2875 N Old Us Highway 23 (48353)
P.O. Box 448 (48353-0448)
PHONE..................................810 632-7880
Richard Abel, *President*
John Beauchamp, *President*
EMP: 12 EST: 1974
SALES (est): 2.7MM **Privately Held**
SIC: 5999 7389 4971 3432 Water purification equipment; water softener service; water distribution or supply systems for irrigation; plastic plumbing fixture fittings, assembly

Haslett
Ingham County

(G-7396)
BAKER INC
Also Called: Baker Drive Train
9804 Old M 78 (48840-9310)
PHONE..................................517 339-3835
Lisa D Baker, *President*
Bert Baker, *Vice Pres*
EMP: 20
SQ FT: 8,000
SALES (est): 4.6MM **Privately Held**
WEB: www.bakerdrivetrain.com
SIC: 3568 Drive chains, bicycle or motorcycle

(G-7397)
MERIDIAN ENERGY CORPORATION
6009 Marsh Rd (48840-8988)
PHONE..................................517 339-8444
Richard B Patterson, *President*
Michelle Rich, *Info Tech Mgr*
James R Patterson, *Admin Sec*
EMP: 14
SQ FT: 3,000
SALES (est): 2.3MM **Privately Held**
WEB: www.meridianlandgroup.com
SIC: 1382 6541 Oil & gas exploration services; title abstract offices

(G-7398)
PROFESSIONAL METAL WORKS INC
8109 Old M 78 (48840-9307)
PHONE..................................517 351-7411
Fred Boling, *President*
Jerry McKenna, *Vice Pres*
EMP: 30
SQ FT: 12,000
SALES (est): 10.8MM **Privately Held**
WEB: www.prometalworks.com
SIC: 3444 Sheet metalwork

(G-7399)
SLIDING SYSTEMS INC
8080 E Old M (48840)
PHONE..................................517 339-1455
Duane A Swenson, *Administration*
EMP: 20
SALES (corp-wide): 4.1MM **Privately Held**
WEB: www.slidingsystems.com
SIC: 3714 Motor vehicle body components & frame
PA: Sliding Systems, Inc.
 12300 W Center St Ste 200
 Milwaukee WI 53222
 414 258-0500

(G-7400)
SULZER MIXPAC USA INC (DH)
Also Called: Cox North America, Inc.
8181 Coleman Rd (48840-9338)
PHONE..................................517 339-3330
Victoria Ringler, *COO*
EMP: 12
SQ FT: 5,000
SALES (est): 3.2MM
SALES (corp-wide): 3.3B **Privately Held**
WEB: www.cox-applicators.com
SIC: 3423 Caulking tools, hand
HQ: Sulzer Mixpac (Uk) Ltd
 1-2 Tealgate
 Hungerford BERKS RG17
 148 864-7800

Hastings
Barry County

(G-7401)
AWEBA TOOL & DIE CORP
1004 E State St (49058-9166)
PHONE..................................478 296-2002
Karsten Dittrich, *CEO*
Matthias Gerber, *COO*
Robyn Thomas, *Executive Asst*
▲ **EMP:** 15
SALES: 500K
SALES (corp-wide): 6.9B **Privately Held**
SIC: 3312 Tool & die steel & alloys
HQ: Aweba Werkzeugbau Gmbh Aue
 Damaschkestr. 7
 Aue 08280
 377 127-30

(G-7402)
BROADMOOR MOTOR SALES INC
1420 S Hanover St (49058-2545)
PHONE..................................269 320-6304
Henry Koning, *Branch Mgr*
EMP: 6
SALES (est): 325.9K
SALES (corp-wide): 2.1MM **Privately Held**
SIC: 7514 3993 Rent-a-car service; signs & advertising specialties
PA: Broadmoor Motor Sales Inc
 6890 Broadmoor Ave Se
 Caledonia MI 49316
 616 698-9595

Hastings - Barry County (G-7403)

(G-7403)
CNB INTERNATIONAL INC
Also Called: Niagara Machine
1004 S East St (49058)
PHONE..................................269 948-3300
Pete Straube, *CEO*
Charles Bahr, *CEO*
Richard J Laski, *President*
Michael Ponsetto, *Design Engr*
Michael Cygan, *CFO*
EMP: 100 **EST:** 1879
SQ FT: 400,000
SALES (est): 19.2MM **Privately Held**
SIC: 3542 Bending machines

(G-7404)
CO-DEE STAMPING INC
1657 Star School Rd (49058-9351)
PHONE..................................269 948-8631
Robert Redman, *President*
Clint Neal, *Vice Pres*
EMP: 8
SQ FT: 10,000
SALES: 1MM **Privately Held**
WEB: www.codeestamping.com
SIC: 3469 Stamping metal for the trade

(G-7405)
D T R SIGN CO LLC
6315 Thornapple Valley Dr (49058-8287)
PHONE..................................616 889-8927
Ted Reidsma, *Principal*
EMP: 3
SALES (est): 247.5K **Privately Held**
SIC: 3993 Signs & advertising specialties

(G-7406)
DIAMOND PRESS SOLUTIONS LLC
1611 S Hanover St (49058-2604)
PHONE..................................269 945-1997
Steve Diamond, *President*
EMP: 5
SQ FT: 1,200
SALES (est): 597.9K **Privately Held**
SIC: 3469 Metal stampings

(G-7407)
DIMOND MACHINERY COMPANY INC
922 N M 37 Hwy (49058-8266)
PHONE..................................269 945-5908
Russell Dimond, *President*
EMP: 27 **EST:** 1964
SQ FT: 15,680
SALES: 1.4MM **Privately Held**
WEB: www.affordablemachinery.com
SIC: 3541 3542 5084 5082 Machine tools, metal cutting type; mechanical (pneumatic or hydraulic) metal forming machines; industrial machinery & equipment; construction & mining machinery

(G-7408)
ELECTRIC MOTOR SERVICE
1569 S M 37 Hwy (49058-8321)
PHONE..................................269 945-5113
Rick James, *Owner*
EMP: 3
SQ FT: 2,000
SALES: 280K **Privately Held**
SIC: 7694 5063 5999 Electric motor repair; rewinding stators; motors, electric; motors, electric

(G-7409)
FLEXFAB HORIZONS INTL INC (PA)
Also Called: Fhi Family of Companies
102 Cook Rd (49058-9629)
PHONE..................................269 945-4700
Matt Decamp, *CEO*
Douglas A Decamp, *Ch of Bd*
Marty Walsh, *Vice Pres*
Rita Brasseur, *Engineer*
Scott Larsen, *Engineer*
▲ **EMP:** 50 **EST:** 1961
SQ FT: 52,000
SALES: 115MM **Privately Held**
WEB: www.flexfab.com
SIC: 3599 3052 3053 2822 Flexible metal hose, tubing & bellows; rubber & plastics hose & beltings; gaskets, packing & sealing devices; synthetic rubber

(G-7410)
FLEXFAB LLC (HQ)
Also Called: Flexfab De Mexico
1699 W M 43 Hwy (49058-9285)
PHONE..................................269 945-2433
Satish Sharma, *Vice Pres*
Jeff Weiden, *Vice Pres*
Tim Larsen, *VP Opers*
Jason Stevenson, *Maint Spvr*
Dave Anderson, *Purch Mgr*
▲ **EMP:** 8
SQ FT: 120,000
SALES (est): 93.8MM
SALES (corp-wide): 115MM **Privately Held**
SIC: 3052 2822 Rubber & plastics hose & beltings; synthetic rubber
PA: Flexfab Horizons International, Inc.
102 Cook Rd
Hastings MI 49058
269 945-4700

(G-7411)
GIBBYS TRANSPORT LLC
719 E Woodlawn Ave (49058-8455)
PHONE..................................269 838-2794
Timmy Allen Rosenberg, *Mng Member*
EMP: 4
SQ FT: 1,742,400
SALES: 260K **Privately Held**
SIC: 3792 Travel trailers & campers

(G-7412)
HASTINGS FIBER GLASS PDTS INC
1301 W Green St (49058-1718)
P.O. Box 218 (49058-0218)
PHONE..................................269 945-9541
Larry Baum, *CEO*
Earl L Mc Mullin, *Ch of Bd*
David Baum, *President*
Earlene Baum, *Corp Secy*
Mark Schmidt, *Engineer*
◆ **EMP:** 93 **EST:** 1959
SQ FT: 52,500
SALES (est): 26.4MM **Privately Held**
WEB: www.hfgp.com
SIC: 3423 Hand & edge tools

(G-7413)
HASTINGS MANUFACTURING COMPANY
325 N Hanover St (49058-1598)
PHONE..................................269 945-2491
Robert M Kollar, *CEO*
Ken Holbrook, *CEO*
Jeffrey P Guenther, *Vice Pres*
Richard L Zwiernikowski, *CFO*
▲ **EMP:** 99 **EST:** 2013
SALES (est): 22.4MM **Privately Held**
SIC: 3592 Carburetors, pistons, rings, valves

(G-7414)
HURLESS MACHINE SHOP INC
2450 Lower Lake Rd (49058-8406)
PHONE..................................269 945-9362
Mark Hurless, *President*
Danise Regan, *Treasurer*
EMP: 9
SQ FT: 6,000
SALES: 450K **Privately Held**
SIC: 3599 Machine shop, jobbing & repair

(G-7415)
I M F INC
437 E Walnut St (49058-1963)
PHONE..................................269 948-2345
George Littlejohn, *President*
EMP: 3
SQ FT: 10,000
SALES: 260K **Privately Held**
WEB: www.fimanagement.com
SIC: 3599 5084 3544 Machine shop, jobbing & repair; industrial machinery & equipment; special dies, tools, jigs & fixtures

(G-7416)
J-AD GRAPHICS INC (PA)
Also Called: Reminder, The
1351 N M 43 Hwy (49058-8499)
P.O. Box 188 (49058-0188)
PHONE..................................800 870-7085
John Jacobs, *President*
Brett Bremer, *Editor*
Shelly Sulser, *Editor*
Fred Jacobs, *Vice Pres*
Jennie Yonker, *Sales Mgr*
EMP: 85
SQ FT: 100,000
SALES (est): 15.3MM **Privately Held**
WEB: www.j-adgraphics.com
SIC: 2741 2711 2752 2791 Guides: publishing & printing; newspapers, publishing & printing; commercial printing, offset; typesetting; bookbinding & related work; commercial printing

(G-7417)
JMJ INC
1029 Enterprise Dr (49058-7804)
PHONE..................................269 948-2828
Mick Suter, *President*
▼ **EMP:** 22
SALES (est): 3.8MM **Privately Held**
WEB: www.jmjinc.net
SIC: 2542 Partitions & fixtures, except wood

(G-7418)
K & E TACKLE INC
2530 Barber Rd (49058-9416)
PHONE..................................269 945-4496
James Sprague, *President*
Jennifer Sprague, *Corp Secy*
Kenneth Sprague, *Director*
EMP: 11
SQ FT: 4,560
SALES (est): 1.6MM **Privately Held**
WEB: www.stopperlures.com
SIC: 3949 Bait, artificial: fishing; fishing tackle, general

(G-7419)
KASTEN MACHINERY INC
1611 S Hanover St Ste 107 (49058-2604)
PHONE..................................269 945-1999
Steve Diamond, *President*
Carmen Solano, *Vice Pres*
▼ **EMP:** 4
SALES (est): 310.6K **Privately Held**
WEB: www.kastenmachinery.com
SIC: 3542 Presses: forming, stamping, punching, sizing (machine tools)

(G-7420)
MENSCH MANUFACTURING LLC
2333 S M 37 Hwy (49058-9370)
P.O. Box 418 (49058-0418)
PHONE..................................269 945-5300
Donald Mensch, *President*
Nathan Wilkins, *Electrical Engi*
Sarah Mensch, *Manager*
EMP: 3
SALES (est): 464.3K **Privately Held**
SIC: 3523 Farm machinery & equipment

(G-7421)
MENSCH MFG MAR DIV INC
Also Called: Rubber Round-Up
2499 S M 37 Hwy (49058-9369)
P.O. Box 418 (49058-0418)
PHONE..................................269 945-5300
Donald L Mensch, *President*
EMP: 25
SQ FT: 16,000
SALES (est): 8.5MM **Privately Held**
WEB: www.menschmfg.com
SIC: 3523 Farm machinery & equipment

(G-7422)
NEWTON WELL SERVICE INC
550 E Cloverdale Rd (49058-9331)
PHONE..................................269 945-5084
EMP: 3
SALES (est): 371.1K **Privately Held**
SIC: 1381 Oil/Gas Well Drilling

(G-7423)
PROGRESSIVE GRAPHICS
115 S Jefferson St (49058-1825)
PHONE..................................269 945-9249
Doug Acker, *Owner*
EMP: 5
SQ FT: 1,200
SALES (est): 768.2K **Privately Held**
SIC: 2759 Screen printing

(G-7424)
QUALITY ALUM ACQUISITION LLC (PA)
429 S Michigan Ave (49058-2250)
PHONE..................................800 550-1667
Mike Clark, *General Mgr*
Bob Clark, *Plant Mgr*
David Schillim, *Buyer*
Robert Clark, *Treasurer*
Blaze Tomich, *Finance Mgr*
EMP: 100
SQ FT: 30,000
SALES: 41MM **Privately Held**
WEB: www.qualityaluminum.com
SIC: 3444 3354 Siding, sheet metal; aluminum extruded products

(G-7425)
SABRE MANUFACTURING
2324 S M 37 Hwy (49058-9370)
PHONE..................................269 945-4120
Steve Reaser, *President*
Larry Monroe, *General Mgr*
EMP: 8
SALES: 300K **Privately Held**
SIC: 3312 Tool & die steel

(G-7426)
SANINOCENCIO LOGGING
2900 Roush Rd (49058-8817)
PHONE..................................269 945-3567
James R Dull, *Principal*
EMP: 3 **EST:** 2011
SALES (est): 164.8K **Privately Held**
SIC: 2411 Logging

(G-7427)
SOARING CONCEPTS AEROSPACE LLC
3001 W Airport Rd (49058-9774)
PHONE..................................574 286-9670
Galen Geigley, *Mng Member*
EMP: 16
SALES: 3.2MM **Privately Held**
SIC: 3721 3541 Aircraft; numerically controlled metal cutting machine tools

(G-7428)
VIKING CORPORATION (DH)
210 Industrial Park Dr (49058-9631)
PHONE..................................269 945-9501
Thomas G Deegan, *President*
Paul Coble, *General Mgr*
Karl Barton, *Business Mgr*
Doug Bensinger, *Vice Pres*
Gary W Buckley, *Vice Pres*
◆ **EMP:** 270 **EST:** 1897
SQ FT: 180,000
SALES (est): 235.7MM **Privately Held**
WEB: www.vikingcorp.com
SIC: 3499 Fire- or burglary-resistive products

(G-7429)
VIKING FABRICATION SVCS LLC (DH)
210 Industrial Park Dr (49058-9706)
PHONE..................................269 945-9501
Mike Dosma, *President*
Tom Deegan, *Vice Pres*
Jennifer McKeever, *Analyst*
▲ **EMP:** 400
SALES (est): 83MM **Privately Held**
SIC: 3499 Fire- or burglary-resistive products
HQ: Minimax Viking Gmbh
Industriestr. 10/
Bad Oldesloe 23843
453 180-30

Hawks
Presque Isle County

(G-7430)
PRELLS SAW MILL INC
Also Called: Prell's Sawmill
8571 F-21 Hwy (49743-8723)
P.O. Box 121 (49743-0121)
PHONE..................................989 734-2939
Joseph A Kuznizki, *President*
Linda K Kuznizki, *Admin Sec*
EMP: 25

SQ FT: 400
SALES (est): 1.3MM **Privately Held**
SIC: 2421 5211 Sawmills & planing mills, general; custom sawmill; kiln drying of lumber; lumber products

(G-7431)
RECOLLECTIONS CO
7956 F-21 Hwy (49743-8716)
PHONE..................989 734-0566
Steven Koenig, *Partner*
EMP: 20
SALES (est): 1.9MM **Privately Held**
SIC: 2335 5621 Dresses, paper: cut & sewn; women's clothing stores

Hazel Park
Oakland County

(G-7432)
ADVANCED ASSEMBLY PRODUCTS INC (PA)
Also Called: A A P
1300 E 9 Mile Rd (48030-1959)
PHONE..................248 543-2427
Chain Sandhu, *President*
Jay Sandhu, *CFO*
Ravinder Sandhu, *Director*
▲ **EMP:** 6 **EST:** 1963
SQ FT: 20,000
SALES (est): 15.4MM **Privately Held**
SIC: 3714 Motor vehicle parts & accessories

(G-7433)
ALMAR INDUSTRIES INC
21005 Dequindre Rd (48030-2610)
PHONE..................248 541-5617
Margaret Bogaert, *President*
EMP: 3
SQ FT: 2,000
SALES: 190K **Privately Held**
WEB: www.almarinductionheating.com
SIC: 3398 Metal heat treating

(G-7434)
AMCOL CORPORATION
Also Called: American Charcoal
21435 Dequindre Rd (48030-2350)
PHONE..................248 414-5700
James Dyla, *President*
Patty Craig, *Production*
Chris Dyla, *Sales Staff*
Michelle Vaughn, *Sales Staff*
Richard Howe, *Manager*
◆ **EMP:** 25
SQ FT: 27,000
SALES (est): 8.4MM **Privately Held**
WEB: www.amcolcorp.com
SIC: 2992 3569 Oils & greases, blending & compounding; lubricating equipment

(G-7435)
BRONCO PRINTING COMPANY
21841 Dequindre Rd (48030-2103)
PHONE..................248 544-1120
Walter Ziemniak, *President*
Mary Ann Toporek, *Vice Pres*
Sharon Zelmanski, *Treasurer*
EMP: 6 **EST:** 1947
SQ FT: 2,200
SALES: 500K **Privately Held**
SIC: 2752 3993 2791 2789 Commercial printing, offset; signs & advertising specialties; typesetting; bookbinding & related work; commercial printing

(G-7436)
CHIODINI & SONS PRINTING
21721 Dequindre Rd (48030-2102)
PHONE..................248 548-0064
John Chiodini, *Partner*
Richard Chiodini, *Partner*
EMP: 3
SQ FT: 1,800
SALES: 150K **Privately Held**
SIC: 2752 Commercial printing, offset

(G-7437)
EXLTERRA INC
618 E 10 Mile Rd (48030-1259)
PHONE..................248 268-2336
Frank Muller, *CEO*

Denis Gobet, *Vice Pres*
Nathan Rose, *Manager*
EMP: 4 **EST:** 2016
SALES (est): 209.1K **Privately Held**
SIC: 3541 Drilling machine tools (metal cutting)

(G-7438)
FOX ALUMINUM PRODUCTS INC
Also Called: Weldore Manufacturing
1355 E Woodward Hts Blvd (48030-1628)
PHONE..................248 399-4288
James Fox, *President*
Judith Fox, *Treasurer*
▲ **EMP:** 20
SQ FT: 42,000
SALES (est): 3.3MM **Privately Held**
WEB: www.foxweldoor.com
SIC: 3442 5211 Storm doors or windows, metal; windows, storm: wood or metal; doors, storm: wood or metal

(G-7439)
J & L PRODUCTS INC
Also Called: J & L Plating & Sand Blasting
21733 Dequindre Rd (48030-2195)
PHONE..................248 544-8500
Lynn Persyn, *President*
Timothy Jurban, *Vice Pres*
Nancy Jurban, *Treasurer*
EMP: 6 **EST:** 1957
SQ FT: 15,000
SALES: 750K **Privately Held**
SIC: 3471 Sand blasting of metal parts; plating of metals or formed products

(G-7440)
KC JONES PLATING CO
Jones, K C Plating Division
321 W 10 Mile Rd (48030-1184)
PHONE..................248 399-8500
Al Kay, *Purch Dir*
Marty Hartrick, *Branch Mgr*
EMP: 40
SQ FT: 25,000
SALES (corp-wide): 21.4MM **Privately Held**
WEB: www.kcjplating.com
SIC: 3471 Electroplating of metals or formed products
PA: K.C. Jones Plating Co.
2845 E 10 Mile Rd
Warren MI 48091
586 755-4900

(G-7441)
LG ELECTRONICS VEHICLE COMPONE (DH)
1400 E 10 Mile Rd Ste 100 (48030-1278)
PHONE..................248 268-5851
Kenneth Cheng, *President*
EMP: 140
SALES: 2.6B **Privately Held**
SIC: 3694 Automotive electrical equipment
HQ: Lg Electronics U.S.A., Inc.
1000 Sylvan Ave
Englewood Cliffs NJ 07632
201 816-2000

(G-7442)
M C M FIXTURE COMPANY INC
Also Called: M C M Stainless Fabricating
21306 John R Rd (48030-2211)
PHONE..................248 547-9280
Gary Brown, *President*
Seymour Brown, *Shareholder*
EMP: 25 **EST:** 1953
SQ FT: 20,000
SALES (est): 3.9MM **Privately Held**
WEB: www.mcmstainless.com
SIC: 3444 2514 2511 Restaurant sheet metalwork; metal household furniture; wood household furniture

(G-7443)
METRA INC
24211 John R Rd (48030-1110)
PHONE..................248 543-3500
Mary Sappington, *President*
Henry Stafij, *Vice Pres*
Kenneth Lamparski, *Admin Sec*
EMP: 4 **EST:** 1979
SQ FT: 3,000
SALES: 500K **Privately Held**
SIC: 2721 Magazines: publishing & printing

(G-7444)
MICHIGAN PLATING LLC
21733 Dequindre Rd (48030-2102)
PHONE..................248 544-3500
Patrick Smith,
EMP: 6
SALES (est): 414.8K **Privately Held**
SIC: 3471 Plating of metals or formed products; electroplating of metals or formed products

(G-7445)
MICHIGAN SPLINE GAGE CO INC
1626 E 9 Mile Rd (48030-1937)
P.O. Box 69 (48030-0069)
PHONE..................248 544-7303
Bernard Hagen, *President*
Cathy Bongilrno, *Admin Sec*
EMP: 18 **EST:** 1950
SQ FT: 10,000
SALES (est): 4.5MM **Privately Held**
WEB: www.michiganspline.com
SIC: 3829 Measuring & controlling devices

(G-7446)
MICRO GRIND CO INC
Also Called: Micro Gind
1648 E 9 Mile Rd (48030-1937)
PHONE..................248 398-9770
Daniel Fiantaco, *President*
Barbara Fiantaco, *Vice Pres*
EMP: 4 **EST:** 1981
SQ FT: 2,500
SALES: 200K **Privately Held**
SIC: 3599 Machine shop, jobbing & repair

(G-7447)
NEW MONITOR
23082 Reynolds Ave (48030-1441)
PHONE..................248 439-1863
EMP: 3
SALES (est): 114K **Privately Held**
SIC: 2711 Newspapers, publishing & printing

(G-7448)
NINJA TEES N MORE
505 W 9 Mile Rd Ste B (48030-1714)
PHONE..................248 541-2547
Shawn Loiko, *Partner*
Mike Wilamowski, *Partner*
EMP: 5
SALES (est): 156.9K **Privately Held**
SIC: 2759 Screen printing

(G-7449)
P & G TECHNOLOGIES INC
938 E 10 Mile Rd (48030-1220)
PHONE..................248 399-3135
Gary Bowden, *President*
Adam Bowden, *Vice Pres*
Colleen Osemlak, *Office Mgr*
EMP: 8
SQ FT: 6,700
SALES (est): 907.5K **Privately Held**
SIC: 3599 Machine shop, jobbing & repair

(G-7450)
PACORA RIVER DEFENSE LLC
21323 John R Rd (48030-2210)
PHONE..................248 546-1142
Ronald J Eisbrenner,
EMP: 3
SALES (est): 206.8K **Privately Held**
SIC: 3593 Fluid power cylinders & actuators

(G-7451)
R E D INDUSTRIES INC
1671 E 9 Mile Rd (48030-1957)
PHONE..................248 542-2211
Lila Elmhirst, *President*
EMP: 15
SQ FT: 10,000
SALES (est): 2.6MM **Privately Held**
SIC: 3469 Stamping metal for the trade

(G-7452)
RAZE-IT PRINTING
24221 John R Rd (48030-1110)
PHONE..................248 543-3813
Barbara Schmitz, *Principal*
EMP: 4

SALES (est): 330.8K **Privately Held**
SIC: 2752 Commercial printing, offset

(G-7453)
ROCON LLC
1755 E 9 Mile Rd (48030-1939)
P.O. Box 249 (48030-0249)
PHONE..................248 542-9635
Lars Rosaen, *Principal*
Erik Rosaen,
EMP: 7
SALES (est): 611.5K
SALES (corp-wide): 11.5MM **Privately Held**
SIC: 3491 5084 Water works valves; industrial machinery & equipment
PA: Universal Flow Monitors, Inc.
1755 E 9 Mile Rd
Hazel Park MI 48030
248 542-9635

(G-7454)
SCOTT IRON WORKS INC
24529 John R Rd (48030-1141)
PHONE..................248 548-2822
John H Petit, *President*
Virginia Petit, *Corp Secy*
Robert Petit, *Vice Pres*
Laura Van Almen, *Sales Staff*
Arthur Petit, *Shareholder*
EMP: 10 **EST:** 1960
SQ FT: 30,000
SALES (est): 1.4MM **Privately Held**
SIC: 3446 3442 Gates, ornamental metal; railings, bannisters, guards, etc.: made from metal pipe; storm doors or windows, metal

(G-7455)
SHELLBACK MANUFACTURING CO
1320 E Elza Ave (48030-2354)
PHONE..................248 544-4600
William Nielsen, *President*
EMP: 9 **EST:** 1934
SQ FT: 1,664
SALES (est): 1.8MM **Privately Held**
SIC: 3561 Pumps, domestic: water or sump

(G-7456)
STEADFAST LAB
21928 John R Rd (48030-2021)
PHONE..................248 242-2291
EMP: 4 **EST:** 2018
SALES (est): 363.7K **Privately Held**
SIC: 3999

(G-7457)
UNIVERSAL FLOW MONITORS INC (PA)
Also Called: Ufm
1755 E 9 Mile Rd (48030-1939)
P.O. Box 249 (48030-0249)
PHONE..................248 542-9635
Lars O Rosaen, *President*
Erik Rosaen, *Principal*
EMP: 45
SQ FT: 42,000
SALES (est): 11.5MM **Privately Held**
WEB: www.flowmeters.com
SIC: 3823 Flow instruments, industrial process type

(G-7458)
WALLACE PUBLISHING LLC
1127 E Pearl Ave (48030-1922)
P.O. Box 162 (48030-0162)
PHONE..................248 416-7259
EMP: 28 **EST:** 2010
SALES (est): 1.7MM **Privately Held**
SIC: 2741 Misc Publishing

Hemlock
Saginaw County

(G-7459)
ANDERSONS INC
485 S Hemlock Rd (48626-8784)
PHONE..................989 642-5291
EMP: 6

Hemlock - Saginaw County (G-7460)

SALES (corp-wide): 3B **Publicly Held**
SIC: **5153** 0723 5191 2874 Grains; crop preparation services for market; farm supplies; phosphatic fertilizers; rental of railroad cars
PA: The Andersons Inc
1947 Briarfield Blvd
Maumee OH 43537
419 893-5050

(G-7460)
CORNERSTONE FABG & CNSTR INC (PA)
667 Watson Rd (48626-9795)
PHONE..................989 642-5241
Robert Bishop, *President*
Tony Mansfield, *Opers Mgr*
Heather Frederick, *Manager*
EMP: 29
SQ FT: 3,600
SALES (est): 10.4MM **Privately Held**
WEB: www.cornerstonefab.com
SIC: **3535** 3441 Conveyors & conveying equipment; fabricated structural metal

(G-7461)
DOUGLAS KING INDUSTRIES INC
Also Called: Dki
16425 Northern Pintail Dr (48626-8787)
P.O. Box 6575, Saginaw (48608-6575)
PHONE..................989 642-2865
Douglas W King, *President*
Deborah King, *Vice Pres*
Gerry Mueller, *Vice Pres*
Gene Slachta, *Vice Pres*
EMP: 42
SALES (est): 3.8MM **Privately Held**
WEB: www.dki-inc.com
SIC: **3599** 3441 3544 3444 Machine shop, jobbing & repair; fabricated structural metal; special dies, tools, jigs & fixtures; sheet metalwork; nonferrous foundries; steel investment foundries

(G-7462)
DOW SILICONES CORPORATION
Also Called: Healthcare Inds Mtls Site
1635 N Gleaner Rd (48626)
P.O. Box 20 (48626-0020)
PHONE..................800 248-2481
Doug Kempf, *Engineer*
Jim Cross, *Branch Mgr*
EMP: 150
SALES (corp-wide): 61B **Publicly Held**
WEB: www.dowcorning.com
SIC: **2869** Industrial organic chemicals
HQ: Dow Silicones Corporation
2200 W Salzburg Rd
Auburn MI 48611
989 496-4000

(G-7463)
HEMLOCK SMCNDCTOR OPRTIONS LLC
12334 Geddes Rd (48626-9409)
P.O. Box 80 (48626-0080)
PHONE..................989 642-5201
Richard Doorndos, *President*
Brooke Beebe, *Vice Pres*
Mark Loboda, *Vice Pres*
Andy Ault, *VP Mfg*
William Wittke, *Engineer*
▲ EMP: 400 EST: 1959
SALES (est): 228.8MM
SALES (corp-wide): 61B **Publicly Held**
WEB: www.hscpoly.com
SIC: **3674** Semiconductors & related devices
HQ: Dow Silicones Corporation
2200 W Salzburg Rd
Auburn MI 48611
989 496-4000

(G-7464)
URS ENERGY & CONSTRUCTION INC
12334 Geddes Rd (48626-9409)
PHONE..................989 642-4190
EMP: 235
SALES (corp-wide): 10.9B **Publicly Held**
SIC: **1622** 1629 1081 4953 Bridge/Tunnel Cnstn Heavy Construction Metal Mining Services Refuse Systems

HQ: Urs Energy & Construction, Inc.
7800 E Union Ave Ste 100
Denver CO 90067
303 843-2000

Henderson
Shiawassee County

(G-7465)
AJ LOGGING
8203 N M 52 (48841-9714)
PHONE..................989 725-9610
Alan Sjoberg, *Owner*
EMP: 13 EST: 1990
SALES (est): 893.1K **Privately Held**
SIC: **2411** Logging camps & contractors

Hermansville
Menominee County

(G-7466)
STEWART MANUFACTURING LLC
N16415 Earle Dr (49847)
P.O. Box 219 (49847-0219)
PHONE..................906 498-7600
Harry Bergquist, *Engineer*
Gregory Stewart,
▲ EMP: 85
SQ FT: 77,000
SALES (est): 19.2MM **Privately Held**
WEB: www.stewart-mfg.com
SIC: **3999** Barber & beauty shop equipment

(G-7467)
SUPERIOR WELDING & MFG INC
5704 Old Us 2 Rd 43 (49847)
P.O. Box 145 (49847-0145)
PHONE..................906 498-7616
Kelly Plunger, *President*
Steve Geyser, *Engineer*
Nick Arduin, *Treasurer*
Rick Arduin, *Admin Sec*
◆ EMP: 45
SALES (est): 5.6MM **Privately Held**
SIC: **7692** Welding repair

(G-7468)
WENDRICKS TRUSS INC (PA)
W5728 Old Us 2 Road No 43 (49847-9553)
P.O. Box 160 (49847-0160)
PHONE..................906 498-7709
Kelly Plunger, *President*
Melissa Gatien, *Safety Mgr*
Robin Newlin, *Manager*
Steve Kluskens, *Officer*
EMP: 40 EST: 1975
SQ FT: 40,000
SALES (est): 7.3MM **Privately Held**
WEB: www.wendrickstruss.com
SIC: **2439** Trusses, wooden roof

(G-7469)
WHITENS KILN & LUMBER INC
125801 Coney Rd (49847)
P.O. Box 154 (49847-0154)
PHONE..................906 498-2116
Russell Jay Whitens, *President*
Roger A Whitens, *Vice Pres*
EMP: 10
SQ FT: 31,596
SALES (est): 1.5MM **Privately Held**
SIC: **2421** 2426 Lumber: rough, sawed or planed; kiln drying of lumber; hardwood dimension & flooring mills

Herron
Alpena County

(G-7470)
SSRM MACHINE SHOP INC
4346 S Herron Rd (49744-9759)
PHONE..................989 379-4075
Steven Armstrong, *President*
Shirley Armstrong, *Vice Pres*
EMP: 8 EST: 1978

SQ FT: 15,780
SALES (est): 1MM **Privately Held**
SIC: **3544** Jigs & fixtures

Hersey
Osceola County

(G-7471)
CARGILL INCORPORATED
1395 135th Ave (49639-8746)
PHONE..................810 989-7242
Rob Plosz, *Branch Mgr*
EMP: 80
SALES (corp-wide): 114.7B **Privately Held**
WEB: www.imcglobal.com
SIC: **1474** Potash, soda & borate minerals
PA: Cargill, Incorporated
15407 Mcginty Rd W
Wayzata MN 55391
952 742-7575

(G-7472)
ENERTECH CORPORATION
210 S Division St (49639-5117)
P.O. Box 183 (49639-0183)
PHONE..................231 832-5587
Pamela J Hall, *President*
EMP: 10
SQ FT: 18,000
SALES (est): 1.7MM **Privately Held**
WEB: www.enertechcorp.com
SIC: **3679** Harness assemblies for electronic use: wire or cable

(G-7473)
LAIDCO SALES INC
4753 175th Ave (49639-8790)
PHONE..................231 832-1327
Patrick Laidlaw, *President*
Bill Bondy, *Vice Pres*
EMP: 5
SQ FT: 2,000
SALES (est): 4.5MM **Privately Held**
SIC: **3229** Glass lighting equipment parts

(G-7474)
MOSIAC POTASH HERSEY LLC
1395 135th Ave (49639-8746)
PHONE..................231 832-3755
EMP: 8
SALES (est): 168.8K **Privately Held**
SIC: **1474** Potash/Soda/Borate Mining

(G-7475)
RIDGEWOOD STOVES LLC
1293 170th Ave (49639-8451)
PHONE..................989 488-3397
EMP: 6
SALES (est): 399.4K **Privately Held**
SIC: **2421** Outdoor wood structural products

(G-7476)
VINYL CRAFT WINDOW LLC
14654 Hersey Rd (49639-8518)
PHONE..................231 832-8905
Lewis Hostetler, *President*
EMP: 10
SALES (est): 1.1MM **Privately Held**
SIC: **3089** Window frames & sash, plastic

Hesperia
Oceana County

(G-7477)
CHARLES WILLIAM CARR SR
Also Called: Carr Logging
6379 S Maple Island Rd (49421-8936)
PHONE..................231 854-3643
Charles William Carr Sr, *Principal*
EMP: 3
SALES (est): 163.7K **Privately Held**
SIC: **2411** Logging camps & contractors

(G-7478)
LOWRY JOANELLEN
Also Called: Cj's Smoked Spc Dom Game Proc
7833 Lincoln St (49421)
PHONE..................231 873-2323

Joanellen Lowry, *Owner*
EMP: 6
SALES: 100K **Privately Held**
SIC: **3556** Meat processing machinery

(G-7479)
NORTHERN LABEL INC
265 S Division St (49421-9601)
PHONE..................231 854-6301
William P Walch, *President*
Sandy Kilborne, *Corp Secy*
Desmer Walch, *Vice Pres*
EMP: 7
SQ FT: 11,100
SALES: 510.8K **Privately Held**
WEB: www.northernlabel.com
SIC: **2759** Labels & seals: printing

(G-7480)
WHITE RIVER SUGAR BUSH
2840 E Garfield Rd (49421-8531)
PHONE..................231 861-4860
Earl Girard, *Partner*
Marilyn Girard, *Partner*
EMP: 3
SALES (est): 189.9K **Privately Held**
SIC: **2099** 2064 Maple syrup; candy & other confectionery products

Hessel
Mackinac County

(G-7481)
MAPLES SAWMILL INC
2736 Chard Rd (49745-9115)
P.O. Box 185 (49745-0185)
PHONE..................906 484-3926
Luke Jaroche, *President*
Lynelle Jaroche, *Admin Sec*
EMP: 27
SQ FT: 9,500
SALES (est): 2MM **Privately Held**
WEB: www.maplessawmill.com
SIC: **2421** Lumber: rough, sawed or planed

Higgins Lake
Roscommon County

(G-7482)
CLASSIC LOG HOMES INCORPORATED
Also Called: Richard L Martin Construction
7340 Hillcrest Rd (48627)
P.O. Box 125 (48627-0125)
PHONE..................989 821-6118
Richard Martin, *President*
EMP: 10
SALES: 1.4MM **Privately Held**
WEB: www.richardlmartinconstruction.com
SIC: **2452** Log cabins, prefabricated, wood

Highland
Oakland County

(G-7483)
A B C PRINTING INC
2983 E Highland Rd (48356-2811)
PHONE..................248 887-0010
Tim Camble, *President*
Tim Campbell, *Accounts Mgr*
Harmony Patterson, *Marketing Staff*
EMP: 4
SQ FT: 800
SALES (est): 573.4K **Privately Held**
SIC: **2752** 2759 Commercial printing, offset; letterpress printing

(G-7484)
ADVANCE CONCRETE PRODUCTS CO
975 N Milford Rd (48357-4551)
P.O. Box 549 (48357-0549)
PHONE..................248 887-4173
Ronald P Kirchner, *President*
Richard Kirschner, *Exec VP*
Greg Pollard, *Vice Pres*
EMP: 30 EST: 1966
SQ FT: 32,000

GEOGRAPHIC SECTION

SALES (est): 5.9MM **Privately Held**
SIC: 3272 5211 Concrete products, precast; masonry materials & supplies

(G-7485)
ADVANCED TECHNOLOGY AND DESIGN
1458 Energy Way (48357-3803)
PHONE................................248 889-5658
Robert Board, *Vice Pres*
EMP: 3
SQ FT: 4,000
SALES: 150K **Privately Held**
SIC: 3543 Industrial patterns

(G-7486)
ARTISTS PALLET
203 S Milford Rd (48357-4646)
PHONE................................248 889-2440
Karen Beardsley, *Manager*
EMP: 4
SALES (est): 341.5K **Privately Held**
SIC: 2448 Pallets, wood & wood with metal

(G-7487)
CARDINAL HEALTH INC
2675 S Milford Rd Ste B (48357-4986)
PHONE................................248 685-9655
Greg Agoston, *Branch Mgr*
EMP: 240
SALES (corp-wide): 145.5B **Publicly Held**
SIC: 3841 Surgical & medical instruments
PA: Cardinal Health, Inc.
  7000 Cardinal Pl
  Dublin OH 43017
  614 757-5000

(G-7488)
COMMERCIAL FABRICATING & ENGRG (PA)
1395 Energy Way (48357-3801)
P.O. Box 503 (48357-0503)
PHONE................................248 887-1595
James W Shoner, *President*
Dennis R Baker, *Vice Pres*
EMP: 10
SQ FT: 25,000
SALES (est): 5.3MM **Privately Held**
SIC: 3444 Metal housings, enclosures, casings & other containers; sheet metal specialties, not stamped

(G-7489)
COMPLETE METALCRAFT LLC
184 W Wardlow Rd (48357-3841)
PHONE................................248 990-0850
Jason Swider, *Mng Member*
EMP: 5
SALES (est): 256.2K **Privately Held**
SIC: 3469 Metal stampings

(G-7490)
CONSIDINE SALES & MARKETING
611 S Milford Rd (48357-4846)
P.O. Box 1208 (48357-1208)
PHONE................................248 889-7887
James Considine Jr, *President*
James W Considine III, *Vice Pres*
EMP: 8
SALES (est): 847.6K **Privately Held**
WEB: www.considinesales.com
SIC: 8742 3559 5531 Sales (including sales management) consultant; automotive maintenance equipment; automotive parts

(G-7491)
D T M 1 INC
1450 N Milford Rd Ste 101 (48357-4505)
PHONE................................248 889-9210
Michael Denton, *President*
Drew Sweetman, *Vice Pres*
▲ **EMP:** 33
SQ FT: 20,000
SALES (est): 9.1MM **Privately Held**
SIC: 3465 2821 3089 Body parts, automobile: stamped metal; thermoplastic materials; injection molding of plastics

(G-7492)
EXPERT AIR CLEANER MAINT
359 Meribah (48356-1028)
PHONE................................248 889-3760
EMP: 3 **EST:** 1997
SALES (est): 140K **Privately Held**
SIC: 3564 Mfg Blowers/Fans

(G-7493)
HERITAGE GLASS INC
672 N Milford Rd Ste 140 (48357-4572)
PHONE................................248 887-1010
Tony Bugis, *President*
EMP: 3
SALES (est): 262.8K **Privately Held**
SIC: 3231 Products of purchased glass

(G-7494)
HIGHLAND SUPPLY INC
294 W Wardlow Rd (48357-3843)
P.O. Box 1041 (48357-1041)
PHONE................................248 714-8355
Mike Maher, *Owner*
EMP: 17
SQ FT: 6,000
SALES (est): 3.2MM **Privately Held**
SIC: 2631 Container, packaging & boxboard

(G-7495)
INNOVATIVE AIR MANAGEMENT LLC
1255 S Milford Rd (48357-4860)
PHONE................................586 201-3513
Jerry Douglas,
▲ **EMP:** 3
SQ FT: 1,200
SALES: 2.5MM **Privately Held**
SIC: 3677 Filtration devices, electronic; air filters; filters, general line: industrial; alcoholic beverage making equipment & supplies

(G-7496)
MAC MATERIAL ACQUISITION CO
1197 Craven Dr (48356-1130)
PHONE................................248 685-8393
Lynn McDunnough, *President*
Kevin McDunnough, *Vice Pres*
EMP: 5
SALES (est): 488.2K **Privately Held**
SIC: 2821 5149 7699 5084 Molding compounds, plastics; soft drinks; industrial machinery & equipment repair; industrial machinery & equipment

(G-7497)
MAGNETIC PRODUCTS INC
Also Called: Mpi
683 Town Center Dr (48356-2965)
P.O. Box 529 (48357-0529)
PHONE................................248 887-5600
Keith Rhodes, *President*
Matthew Wiggins, *Opers Mgr*
Tim Anderson, *Engineer*
Adam Blanchard, *Engineer*
Tom Perry, *Engineer*
▲ **EMP:** 60
SQ FT: 40,000
SALES (est): 17.5MM **Privately Held**
WEB: www.mpimagnet.com
SIC: 3535 5085 3559 3444 Conveyors & conveying equipment; industrial supplies; separation equipment, magnetic; sheet metalwork; fabricated plate work (boiler shop)

(G-7498)
NEPTECH INC
2000 E Highland Rd (48356-3058)
PHONE................................810 225-2222
Michael P Seacord Sr, *President*
EMP: 20
SQ FT: 20,000
SALES: 4MM **Privately Held**
WEB: www.neptechinc.com
SIC: 3491 3634 3829 3826 Process control regulator valves; blankets, electric; thermocouples; coulometric analyzers, except industrial process type

(G-7499)
PARKWAY TOOL DIE
4576 Bretton Ln (48356-1036)
PHONE................................248 889-3490
Margaret Sue Kruger, *Principal*
EMP: 3
SALES (est): 295.1K **Privately Held**
SIC: 3544 Special dies & tools

(G-7500)
SURGITECH SURGICAL SVCS INC
1477 Schooner Cv (48356-2259)
PHONE................................248 593-0797
Garret Smith, *President*
EMP: 20
SQ FT: 1,300
SALES: 3.2MM **Privately Held**
WEB: www.surgitechonline.com
SIC: 3841 Surgical & medical instruments

(G-7501)
UNITED FABRICATING COMPANY
160 N Saint John Rd (48357-4648)
P.O. Box 8 (48357-0008)
PHONE................................248 887-7289
Gordon Langlois, *President*
Jeffrey Langlois, *Vice Pres*
EMP: 6 **EST:** 1959
SQ FT: 8,000
SALES (est): 366K **Privately Held**
SIC: 3441 Fabricated structural metal

Highland Park
Wayne County

(G-7502)
COCA-COLA BOTTLING CO
12225 Oakland Pkwy (48203-3500)
PHONE................................313 868-2167
Kathy Cole, *Manager*
EMP: 4
SALES (est): 83K **Privately Held**
SIC: 2086 Bottled & canned soft drinks

(G-7503)
FAURECIA AUTO SEATING LLC
13000 Oakland Park Blvd (48203)
PHONE................................248 563-9241
Dan Hodgins, *Branch Mgr*
EMP: 390
SALES (corp-wide): 38.2MM **Privately Held**
SIC: 2531 Seats, automobile
HQ: Faurecia Automotive Seating, Llc
  2800 High Meadow Cir
  Auburn Hills MI 48326
  248 288-1000

(G-7504)
FAURECIA AUTO SEATING LLC
12900 Oakland Park Blvd (48203)
PHONE................................248 563-9241
Dan Hodgins, *Branch Mgr*
EMP: 174
SALES (corp-wide): 38.2MM **Privately Held**
SIC: 2531 Seats, automobile
HQ: Faurecia Automotive Seating, Llc
  2800 High Meadow Cir
  Auburn Hills MI 48326
  248 288-1000

(G-7505)
FTE AUTOMOTIVE USA INC
12700 Oakland Park Blvd (48203)
PHONE................................248 209-8239
Uwe Krueger, *President*
Robert A Stead, *Treasurer*
◆ **EMP:** 188
SALES: 46.2MM
SALES (corp-wide): 12.5MM **Privately Held**
SIC: 3714 Motor vehicle transmissions, drive assemblies & parts
HQ: Fte Automotive Gmbh
  Andreas-Humann-Str. 2
  Ebern 96106
  953 181-0

(G-7506)
GREAT LAKES WINE & SPIRITS LLC (PA)
Also Called: J. Lewis Cooper Co.
373 Victor St (48203-3117)
PHONE................................313 278-5400
Lew Cooper III, *CEO*
Syd Ross, *CEO*
J Lewis Cooper Jr, *Ch of Bd*
Matthew Goetz, *Division Mgr*
Mark Sabatini, *Division Mgr*
▲ **EMP:** 185
SQ FT: 40,000
SALES (est): 381.5MM **Privately Held**
WEB: www.jlewiscooper.com
SIC: 5182 2084 Wine; wine coolers, alcoholic; liquor; wines, brandy & brandy spirits

(G-7507)
SHERWOOD PROTOTYPE INC
124 Victor St (48203-3130)
PHONE................................313 883-3880
Peter Paxton, *President*
EMP: 12
SALES: 1.5MM **Privately Held**
WEB: www.sherwoodprototype.com
SIC: 3599 Machine shop, jobbing & repair

Hillman
Montmorency County

(G-7508)
CHEBOYGAN CEMENT PRODUCTS INC
Also Called: Gilners Concrete
800 E Progress St (49746-8942)
PHONE................................989 742-4107
Rick Hopp, *Finance Mgr*
Eugene Jameson, *Manager*
Paul Nowosad, *Manager*
EMP: 4
SALES (corp-wide): 8.6MM **Privately Held**
SIC: 3272 3273 Concrete products; ready-mixed concrete
PA: Cheboygan Cement Products Inc
  702 Lafayette Ave
  Cheboygan MI 49721
  231 627-5631

(G-7509)
PATCHWOOD PRODUCTS INC (PA)
14797 State St (49746-8034)
PHONE................................989 742-2605
Jim Paczkowski, *President*
EMP: 5 **EST:** 2014
SALES (est): 1.8MM **Privately Held**
SIC: 2448 Pallets, wood

(G-7510)
WAYNE WIRE CLOTH PRODUCTS INC
Hillman Division
221 Garfield St (49746-9206)
PHONE................................989 742-4591
Alice Thompson, *Plant Mgr*
Karen Piper, *Purch Mgr*
Steve Waugh, *Branch Mgr*
EMP: 150
SALES (corp-wide): 64MM **Privately Held**
WEB: www.waynewire.com
SIC: 3569 3564 3496 3494 Filters; blowers & fans; miscellaneous fabricated wire products; valves & pipe fittings
PA: Wayne Wire Cloth Products Inc
  200 E Dresden St
  Kalkaska MI 49646
  231 258-9187

(G-7511)
WIDELL INDUSTRIES INC
24601 Veterans Mem Hwy (49746-8671)
PHONE................................989 742-4528
Chuck Lisowe, *Manager*
EMP: 25
SQ FT: 11,000
SALES (est): 2.7MM
SALES (corp-wide): 14.5MM **Privately Held**
WEB: www.widell.com
SIC: 3545 3544 5251 Taps, machine tool; special dies & tools; tools
PA: Widell Industries, Inc.
  6622 Industrial Ave
  Port Richey FL 34668
  800 237-5963

Hillsdale
Hillsdale County

(G-7512)
ABRASIVE MATERIALS LLC
90 W Fayette St (49242-1013)
PHONE..................................517 437-4796
Clay Miller, *General Mgr*
Christi Olmstead, *Info Tech Mgr*
Mike Trotta,
▲ **EMP:** 7
SALES (est): 896.2K **Privately Held**
WEB: www.abrasivematerials.com
SIC: 3291 Abrasive products

(G-7513)
ACME MILLS COMPANY
Also Called: Fairway Products Division
301 Arch Ave (49242-1080)
PHONE..................................517 437-8940
Steven Firavich, *Manager*
EMP: 125
SALES (corp-wide): 83.5MM **Privately Held**
WEB: www.greatlakesfilters.com
SIC: 5131 3429 2674 2394 Textile converters; manufactured hardware (general); bags: uncoated paper & multiwall; canvas & related products; textile bags; men's & boys' work clothing
PA: Acme Mills Company
33 Bloomfield Hills Pkwy
Bloomfield Hills MI 48304
248 203-2000

(G-7514)
ACME MILLS COMPANY
Great Lakes Filter
301 Arch Ave (49242-1080)
PHONE..................................517 437-8940
Brian Balliet, *Manager*
EMP: 20
SALES (corp-wide): 83.5MM **Privately Held**
WEB: www.greatlakesfilters.com
SIC: 3569 Filters
PA: Acme Mills Company
33 Bloomfield Hills Pkwy
Bloomfield Hills MI 48304
248 203-2000

(G-7515)
ACT TEST PANELS LLC
273 Industrial Dr (49242-1078)
PHONE..................................517 439-1485
Frank Lutze, *CEO*
Burt Johns, *Prdtn Mgr*
Craig Armstrong, *Maint Spvr*
Mike Janes, *QC Mgr*
Rob Lancaster, *QC Mgr*
▲ **EMP:** 33
SQ FT: 74,000
SALES (est): 7.5MM **Privately Held**
SIC: 3479 Painting of metal products

(G-7516)
AUTORACK TECHNOLOGIES INC
20 Superior St (49242-1735)
P.O. Box 672 (49242-0672)
PHONE..................................517 437-4800
Scott Bowerman, *President*
EMP: 20
SQ FT: 21,000
SALES (est): 2MM **Privately Held**
SIC: 7692 Welding repair

(G-7517)
BECKER & SCRIVENS CON PDTS INC
3340 Beck Rd (49242-9406)
PHONE..................................517 437-4250
Gordon Scrivens, *President*
Aaron Scrivens, *Treasurer*
EMP: 24 **EST:** 1940
SQ FT: 3,000
SALES (est): 1.8MM **Privately Held**
SIC: 3273 3272 Ready-mixed concrete; septic tanks, concrete

(G-7518)
BOB EVANS FARMS INC
200 N Wolcott St (49242-1762)
P.O. Box 226 (49242-0226)
PHONE..................................517 437-3349
Tery Camp, *Manager*
EMP: 100
SQ FT: 18,000 **Publicly Held**
WEB: www.bobevans.com
SIC: 2011 Sausages from meat slaughtered on site
HQ: Bob Evans Farms, Inc.
8200 Walton Pkwy
New Albany OH 43054
614 491-2225

(G-7519)
BUNDY CORPORATION
200 Arch Ave (49242-1079)
PHONE..................................517 439-1132
Tom Neill, *Principal*
EMP: 4
SALES (est): 281.8K **Privately Held**
SIC: 3498 Fabricated pipe & fittings

(G-7520)
CAMBRIA TOOL AND MACHINE INC
121 Mechanic Rd (49242-5025)
P.O. Box 248 (49242-0248)
PHONE..................................517 437-3500
Troy Balser, *President*
Andrea Daniels, *Admin Sec*
EMP: 10 **EST:** 1953
SQ FT: 14,250
SALES (est): 1.6MM **Privately Held**
WEB: www.cambriatool.com
SIC: 3544 3599 3714 Special dies & tools; jigs & fixtures; custom machinery; drive shafts, motor vehicle

(G-7521)
CARDINAL GROUP INDUSTRIES CORP
266 Industrial Dr (49242-1077)
PHONE..................................517 437-6000
Tracy McCullough, *President*
EMP: 50
SQ FT: 10,000
SALES: 5MM **Privately Held**
SIC: 7389 8742 3451 Brokers' services; management consulting services; screw machine products

(G-7522)
DAYCO PRODUCTS LLC
215 Industrial Dr (49242-1076)
PHONE..................................517 439-0689
John Traylor, *Vice Pres*
David Kelly, *Vice Pres*
Sam Trego, *Vice Pres*
Del Melloch, *Purchasing*
William Oteney, *Purchasing*
EMP: 30
SQ FT: 15,000
SALES (corp-wide): 178.8MM **Privately Held**
SIC: 3559 3714 Automotive related machinery; motor vehicle parts & accessories
HQ: Dayco Products, Llc
1650 Research Dr Ste 200
Troy MI 48083

(G-7523)
DOW CHEMICAL COMPANY
195 Uran St (49242)
PHONE..................................517 439-4400
Tim Dill, *Manager*
EMP: 175
SALES (corp-wide): 61B **Publicly Held**
WEB: www.dow.com
SIC: 5085 2899 2891 Industrial supplies; chemical preparations; adhesives & sealants
HQ: The Dow Chemical Company
2211 H H Dow Way
Midland MI 48642
989 636-1000

(G-7524)
FOUST ELECTRO MOLD INC
277 Industrial Dr (49242-1078)
PHONE..................................517 439-1062
Alan Foust, *President*
Jeffrey Foust, *Agent*
EMP: 9
SQ FT: 7,500
SALES: 400K **Privately Held**
SIC: 3544 Forms (molds), for foundry & plastics working machinery; industrial molds

(G-7525)
FRANK CONDON INC
Also Called: Hillsdale Terminal
250 Industrial Dr (49242-1075)
PHONE..................................517 849-2505
Frank Condon, *President*
Jim Condon, *Vice Pres*
John Condon, *Vice Pres*
Tom Condon, *Treasurer*
Bill Johnson, *Sales Staff*
▲ **EMP:** 40
SQ FT: 35,000
SALES (est): 11.7MM **Privately Held**
SIC: 3643 Connectors & terminals for electrical devices

(G-7526)
GENERAL AUTOMATIC MCH PDTS CO
Also Called: Gampco
266 Industrial Dr (49242-1077)
PHONE..................................517 437-6000
Tracy McCullough, *President*
Ralph Schafer, *Chairman*
Scott Schafer, *Treasurer*
EMP: 50 **EST:** 1944
SQ FT: 79,287
SALES (est): 8.8MM **Privately Held**
SIC: 3495 Mechanical springs, precision

(G-7527)
HILLSDALE PALLET LLC
1242 E Montgomery Rd (49242-8504)
PHONE..................................517 254-4777
Shannon Miller,
EMP: 8
SALES (est): 944.5K **Privately Held**
SIC: 2448 Pallets, wood & wood with metal

(G-7528)
LITEX INC
400 Arch Ave (49242-1081)
PHONE..................................517 439-9361
Mary Playford, *Branch Mgr*
EMP: 35
SALES (corp-wide): 9.1MM **Privately Held**
WEB: www.litex.com
SIC: 3442 Metal doors
PA: Litex, Inc.
2774 Product Dr
Rochester Hills MI 48309
248 852-0661

(G-7529)
MAR-VO MINERAL COMPANY INC
115 E Bacon St (49242-1655)
P.O. Box 86, Osseo (49266-0086)
PHONE..................................517 523-2669
David Wheeler, *President*
Jana Wheeler, *Vice Pres*
EMP: 4
SALES: 750K **Privately Held**
SIC: 2048 Mineral feed supplements

(G-7530)
METALLIST INC
200 Development Dr (49242-5013)
PHONE..................................517 437-4476
Michael J Vaillancourt, *President*
Linda Hartley, *Controller*
EMP: 6 **EST:** 1960
SQ FT: 20,000
SALES (est): 1MM **Privately Held**
WEB: www.metallistinc.com
SIC: 3444 Sheet metal specialties, not stamped

(G-7531)
MICRO PLASTICS MFG & SLS
2944 Lakeview Ct (49242-9327)
PHONE..................................517 320-2488
Steve Ward, *President*
Kathie A Ward, *Vice Pres*
EMP: 3
SQ FT: 2,000
SALES (est): 257.7K **Privately Held**
WEB: www.microplasticshillsdale.com
SIC: 3089 Injection molding of plastics

(G-7532)
MORRIS COMMUNICATIONS CO LLC
Also Called: Hillsdale Daily News
33 Mccollum St (49242-1688)
P.O. Box 287 (49242-0287)
PHONE..................................517 437-3253
Jim Pruitt, *Manager*
EMP: 45
SQ FT: 5,000 **Privately Held**
WEB: www.morris.com
SIC: 2711 Newspapers, publishing & printing
HQ: Morris Communications Company Llc
725 Broad St
Augusta GA 30901
706 724-0851

(G-7533)
PARAGON METALS LLC (PA)
Also Called: New Venture Foundry
3010 Mechanic Rd (49242-1095)
PHONE..................................517 639-4629
Michael Smith, *CEO*
David Smith, *Vice Pres*
Tom Nichols, *Director*
▲ **EMP:** 7
SQ FT: 10,000
SALES (est): 25.3MM **Privately Held**
WEB: www.paragonmetals.com
SIC: 3321 3322 3324 3369 Gray & ductile iron foundries; malleable iron foundries; steel investment foundries; nonferrous foundries; steel foundries; aluminum die-castings

(G-7534)
PRECISION GAGE INC
256 Industrial Dr (49242-1077)
P.O. Box 277 (49242-0277)
PHONE..................................517 439-1690
John Spratt, *President*
Eric Lewis, *Vice Pres*
Kenette Spratt, *Treasurer*
EMP: 56
SQ FT: 56,000
SALES (est): 11.4MM **Privately Held**
SIC: 3714 3599 3545 3544 Motor vehicle body components & frame; machine shop, jobbing & repair; machine tool accessories; special dies, tools, jigs & fixtures; strain gages, solid state; prosthetic appliances

(G-7535)
QUALITE INC
Also Called: Qualite Sports Lighting
215 W Mechanic St (49242-5042)
P.O. Box 765 (49242-0765)
PHONE..................................517 439-4316
Dwight C Shaneour Jr, *Ch of Bd*
Russ McCoy, *President*
Georgia Clark, *Corp Secy*
Nic Page, *Vice Pres*
Ashley Huscio, *Manager*
▲ **EMP:** 20
SQ FT: 20,000
SALES (est): 5.8MM
SALES (corp-wide): 68.1MM **Privately Held**
WEB: www.shanegroup.com
SIC: 3648 Area & sports luminaries
HQ: The Shane Group Llc
215 W Mechanic St
Hillsdale MI 49242
517 439-4316

(G-7536)
QUALITY INDUSTRIES INC
215 W Mechanic St (49242-5042)
P.O. Box 765 (49242-0765)
PHONE..................................517 439-1591
Robert Kuchowicz, *CEO*
Keith Addleman,
Gary Van Deusen, *Vice Pres*
EMP: 40
SQ FT: 85,000
SALES: 2.1MM
SALES (corp-wide): 68.1MM **Privately Held**
WEB: www.shanegroup.com
SIC: 3949 Playground equipment

GEOGRAPHIC SECTION

HQ: The Shane Group Llc
215 W Mechanic St
Hillsdale MI 49242
517 439-4316

(G-7537)
RON WATKINS
Also Called: H & R Enterprises
4080 State Rd (49242-9753)
PHONE..................517 439-5451
Ron Watkins, *Owner*
EMP: 5
SQ FT: 2,000
SALES: 260K **Privately Held**
SIC: 3751 Motorcycle accessories

(G-7538)
RUMLER BROTHERS INC
Also Called: Arrow Swift Printing
72 W Carleton Rd (49242-1202)
PHONE..................517 437-2990
Jerry Rumler, *President*
Doug Adams, *Graphic Designe*
EMP: 5
SQ FT: 1,800
SALES (est): 805.8K **Privately Held**
SIC: 2752 7334 Commercial printing, offset; photocopying & duplicating services

(G-7539)
SCRANTON MACHINE INC
266 Industrial Dr (49242-1077)
PHONE..................517 437-6000
Scott Schafer, *CEO*
Ralph Schafer, *President*
EMP: 17
SQ FT: 80,000
SALES (est): 980K **Privately Held**
SIC: 3599 Machine shop, jobbing & repair

(G-7540)
SEMMLER ELECTRIC LLC
2500 Mechanic Rd (49242-1098)
PHONE..................517 869-2211
Douglas Scmmler, *Mng Member*
EMP: 3
SALES: 200K **Privately Held**
SIC: 3699 Appliance cords for household electrical equipment

(G-7541)
SHANE GROUP LLC (HQ)
215 W Mechanic St (49242-5042)
P.O. Box 765 (49242-0765)
PHONE..................517 439-4316
Eric Boorom, *President*
Alan Dimmers, *Corp Secy*
Dwight Shaneour Jr, *Exec VP*
Marci Bates, *Human Res Dir*
▲ **EMP:** 3 **EST:** 1974
SQ FT: 20,000
SALES (est): 66.7MM
SALES (corp-wide): 68.1MM **Privately Held**
WEB: www.shanegroup.com
SIC: 5074 3949 3429 Plumbing fittings & supplies; playground equipment; animal traps, iron or steel
PA: Worth Investment Group, Llc
3634 Mccain Rd Ste 8
Jackson MI 49203
517 750-9900

(G-7542)
SWISS INDUSTRIES INC
305 Arch Ave (49242-1080)
PHONE..................517 437-3682
Robert P Krick, *President*
Irene Krick, *Corp Secy*
William E Krick, *Vice Pres*
EMP: 8 **EST:** 1957
SQ FT: 8,000
SALES (est): 450K **Privately Held**
WEB: www.swissindustries.com
SIC: 3451 Screw machine products

(G-7543)
TI GROUP AUTO SYSTEMS LLC
200 Arch Ave (49242-1079)
PHONE..................517 437-7462
Tom Neill, *Mng Member*
Earl Medlen, *Manager*
Paula Miller, *Director*
EMP: 60
SALES (corp-wide): 3.9B **Privately Held**
WEB: www.tiautomotive.com
SIC: 3462 3052 3714 3312 Automotive forgings, ferrous: crankshaft, engine, axle, etc.; rubber hose; motor vehicle parts & accessories; blast furnaces & steel mills
HQ: Ti Group Automotive Systems, Llc
2020 Taylor Rd
Auburn Hills MI 48326
248 296-8000

Holland
Ottawa County

(G-7544)
A & B PACKING EQUIPMENT INC
414 E 40th St (49423-5383)
PHONE..................616 294-3539
Michael Williamson, *CEO*
EMP: 4
SALES (corp-wide): 26.2MM **Privately Held**
SIC: 3565 Packaging machinery
PA: A & B Packing Equipment, Inc.
732 W Saint Joseph St
Lawrence MI 49064
269 539-4700

(G-7545)
ABCOR INDUSTRIES LLC
4690 128th Ave (49424-8028)
PHONE..................616 994-9577
Ed Kleinjan, *Prdtn Mgr*
Jason Fynewever, *QC Mgr*
Maddison Edwards, *Cust Mgr*
Josh Foreman, *Cust Mgr*
Jay T Weis, *Mng Member*
EMP: 16
SQ FT: 67,000
SALES (est): 4.5MM **Privately Held**
SIC: 2493 Reconstituted wood products

(G-7546)
ABCOR PARTNERS LLC
4690 128th Ave (49424-8028)
PHONE..................616 994-9577
Jt Weis, *CEO*
EMP: 24
SALES (est): 2.9MM **Privately Held**
SIC: 2411 Wooden logs

(G-7547)
ACCURATE ENGINEERING & MFG LLC
13569 New Holland St (49424-8467)
PHONE..................616 738-1261
Larry Koyers, *Principal*
EMP: 12
SALES (est): 1.8MM **Privately Held**
SIC: 3444 Sheet metalwork

(G-7548)
ACME PALLET INC
13450 New Holland St (49424-9407)
P.O. Box 1438 (49422-1438)
PHONE..................616 738-6452
Asher L Tourison, *President*
James Vandervoord, *Corp Secy*
Dan Lampe, *Vice Pres*
Mark Machiele, *Pediatrics*
EMP: 32
SQ FT: 90,000
SALES (est): 5.9MM **Privately Held**
WEB: www.acmepallet.com
SIC: 2448 Pallets, wood

(G-7549)
ADIENT US LLC
205 Douglas Ave (49424-6569)
PHONE..................616 394-8510
Bob Cook, *Manager*
Ramesh Akkala, *Manager*
Michael Chabot, *Director*
EMP: 150 **Privately Held**
SIC: 3714 Motor vehicle parts & accessories
HQ: Adient Us Llc
49200 Halyard Dr
Plymouth MI 48170
734 254-5000

(G-7550)
ADRIANS SCREEN PRINT
Also Called: Adrian's T-Shirt Printery
3735 Hollywood St (49424-1134)
PHONE..................734 994-1367
Adrian J Cleypool, *Owner*
EMP: 4
SQ FT: 2,100
SALES: 350K **Privately Held**
WEB: www.adrianstshirts.com
SIC: 2759 Screen printing

(G-7551)
AGRITEK INDUSTRIES INC
4211 Hallacy Dr (49424-8723)
PHONE..................616 786-9200
Larry Kooiker, *President*
Sid Widmayer, *Prdtn Mgr*
Nick Joung, *Purchasing*
Ken Kreuze, *Engineer*
Romie Anderson, *VP Finance*
▲ **EMP:** 100
SQ FT: 70,000
SALES (est): 26.2MM **Privately Held**
WEB: www.agritek.com
SIC: 3523 3714 2522 Farm machinery & equipment; motor vehicle parts & accessories; office furniture, except wood

(G-7552)
AHS LLC (DH)
Also Called: Heaven Saunas
25 W 8th St Ste 200 (49423-3173)
PHONE..................888 355-3050
Colleen Raymond, *Bookkeeper*
Richard M Mouw, *Mng Member*
EMP: 10
SQ FT: 600
SALES: 2.3MM
SALES (corp-wide): 1.2MM **Privately Held**
WEB: www.almostheaven.com
SIC: 5999 2452 Sauna equipment & supplies; sauna rooms, prefabricated, wood
HQ: Harvia Us Inc.
25 W 8th St Ste 200
Holland MI 49423
888 355-3050

(G-7553)
AIR FORCE INC
933 Butternut Dr (49424-1513)
PHONE..................616 399-8511
Piero Policicchio DDS, *President*
▲ **EMP:** 3 **EST:** 1995
SALES (est): 306.9K **Privately Held**
WEB: www.dentalairforce.com
SIC: 3843 Dental equipment & supplies

(G-7554)
ALL METAL DESIGNS INC
Also Called: A M D
13131 Reflections Dr (49424-7262)
PHONE..................616 392-3696
Russell Fincher, *President*
Mike Kragt, *Vice Pres*
EMP: 8
SQ FT: 12,000
SALES (est): 1.2MM **Privately Held**
WEB: www.allmetal.com
SIC: 3599 Custom machinery; machine shop, jobbing & repair

(G-7555)
ALSENTIS LLC
1261 S Waverly Rd (49423-9332)
PHONE..................616 395-8254
David Caldwell, *President*
EMP: 6
SALES (est): 1MM **Privately Held**
SIC: 3674 Light sensitive devices

(G-7556)
AMERICAN BOTTLING COMPANY
545 E 32nd St (49423-5411)
PHONE..................616 396-1281
Drake Eckert, *Branch Mgr*
EMP: 70 **Publicly Held**
WEB: www.cs-americas.com
SIC: 2086 Soft drinks: packaged in cans, bottles, etc.
HQ: The American Bottling Company
5301 Legacy Dr
Plano TX 75024

(G-7557)
AMERICAN BOTTLING COMPANY
Also Called: 7 Up Holland
900 Brooks Ave Ste 1 (49423-5337)
PHONE..................616 392-2124
Ellen Jolley, *Office Mgr*
Ken Gerrits, *Manager*
EMP: 40 **Publicly Held**
WEB: www.cs-americas.com
SIC: 2086 Soft drinks: packaged in cans, bottles, etc.
HQ: The American Bottling Company
5301 Legacy Dr
Plano TX 75024

(G-7558)
AMERICAN CLASSIC HOMES INC
Also Called: Select Building Supplies
13352 Van Buren St (49424-9248)
PHONE..................616 594-5900
Scott Christopher, *CEO*
EMP: 8
SQ FT: 2,500
SALES: 2MM **Privately Held**
SIC: 2421 Sawmills & planing mills, general

(G-7559)
AMNEON ACQUISITIONS LLC
Also Called: Jdti
199 E 17th St (49423-4385)
PHONE..................616 895-6640
Reggie Vanden Bosch, *President*
EMP: 35
SQ FT: 49,000
SALES (est): 5.9MM **Privately Held**
WEB: www.amneon.com
SIC: 2522 Office furniture, except wood

(G-7560)
AQUA FINE INC
Also Called: Aqua Water System of Holland
1120 Washington Ave Ste A (49423-5399)
PHONE..................616 392-7843
Steven Eurich, *President*
Randy Wabeke, *Director*
EMP: 3
SALES (est): 290K **Privately Held**
SIC: 5074 2086 7389 Water purification equipment; mineral water, carbonated: packaged in cans, bottles, etc.; water softener service

(G-7561)
AUTOFORM DEVELOPMENT INC
Also Called: Pro Body
257 E 32nd St Ste 2 (49423-5413)
PHONE..................616 392-4909
Steve Dreyer, *President*
Anette Goozman, *Manager*
EMP: 10
SQ FT: 6,000
SALES (est): 650K **Privately Held**
WEB: www.autoformgroup.com
SIC: 7532 3714 3711 Top & body repair & paint shops; motor vehicle parts & accessories; motor vehicles & car bodies

(G-7562)
AUTOMATION SPECIALISTS INC
12555 Superior Ct (49424-8287)
PHONE..................616 738-8288
Mitch Weener, *President*
Rick Berens, *Engineer*
Jeff Padding, *Manager*
EMP: 15
SQ FT: 20,000
SALES (est): 3.3MM **Privately Held**
SIC: 3549 Metalworking machinery

(G-7563)
AXIS MACHINE & TOOL INC
7217 W Olive Rd (49424-9415)
PHONE..................616 738-2196
Timothy Ebels, *President*
EMP: 5
SQ FT: 5,000
SALES (est): 758.8K **Privately Held**
WEB: www.axismachine.com
SIC: 3544 Special dies & tools

Holland - Ottawa County (G-7564)

(G-7564)
B & W WOODWORK INC
11362 James St (49424-8627)
PHONE..................616 772-4577
Bruce Kruithoff, *President*
EMP: 8
SQ FT: 17,000
SALES: 1MM **Privately Held**
SIC: 2431 2599 5211 Doors, wood; door trim, wood; cabinets, factory; millwork & lumber

(G-7565)
BEECHBED MIX
120 James St (49424-1824)
PHONE..................616 263-7422
Charles German, *Principal*
EMP: 5
SALES (est): 516.1K **Privately Held**
SIC: 3273 Ready-mixed concrete

(G-7566)
BEI INTERNATIONAL LLC
10753 Macatawa Dr (49424-9572)
PHONE..................616 204-8274
Richard McKibben, *Vice Pres*
▼ **EMP:** 26 **EST:** 1959
SQ FT: 28,000
SALES (est): 4.7MM **Privately Held**
WEB: www.bei-inc.com
SIC: 3523 Harvesters, fruit, vegetable, tobacco, etc.; sprayers & spraying machines, agricultural; planting, haying, harvesting & processing machinery

(G-7567)
BENTELER ALUMINIUM SYSTEMS
533 Ottawa Ave (49423-5903)
P.O. Box 77246, Detroit (48277-0246)
PHONE..................616 396-6591
EMP: 9
SALES (corp-wide): 9.2B **Privately Held**
SIC: 3714 Motor vehicle parts & accessories
HQ: Benteler Aluminium Systems Michigan Inc.
533 Ottawa Ave
Holland MI 49423

(G-7568)
BENTELER ALUMINIUM SYSTEMS (HQ)
533 Ottawa Ave (49423-5903)
PHONE..................616 396-6591
Dirk Feidler, *Plant Mgr*
Elena Sgroia, *Finance Mgr*
▲ **EMP:** 50
SQ FT: 450,000
SALES (est): 27.4MM
SALES (corp-wide): 9.2B **Privately Held**
SIC: 3341 3354 Secondary nonferrous metals; aluminum extruded products
PA: Benteler International Aktiengesellschaft
SchillerstraBe 25
Salzburg 5020
662 228-30

(G-7569)
BIG DUTCHMAN INC (HQ)
Also Called: Cyclone International
3900 John F Donnelly Dr (49424-7277)
P.O. Box 1017 (49422-1017)
PHONE..................616 392-5981
Clovis Rayzel, *President*
Andrew King, *Regional Mgr*
Jeff Adams, *Vice Pres*
Chris Jozwiak, *Vice Pres*
Steve Langley, *Vice Pres*
◆ **EMP:** 85 **EST:** 1975
SQ FT: 94,000
SALES: 17.6MM
SALES (corp-wide): 1.1B **Privately Held**
WEB: www.bigdutchman.com
SIC: 3523 Poultry brooders, feeders & waterers
PA: Big Dutchman Aktiengesellschaft
Auf Der Lage 2
Vechta 49377
444 780-10

(G-7570)
BILLCO ACQUISITION LLC
Also Called: Billco Products
1373 Lincoln Ave (49423-9389)
PHONE..................616 928-0637
Tom Sligh, *President*
▲ **EMP:** 25
SQ FT: 45,000
SALES (est): 3.9MM **Privately Held**
SIC: 2599 Restaurant furniture, wood or metal; hotel furniture

(G-7571)
BLUJAY SOLUTIONS CO
915 E 32nd St Ste B (49423-9123)
PHONE..................616 738-6400
Douglas Braun, *CEO*
Timothy Hinson, *COO*
Troy Grabel, *Marketing Staff*
Gabe Judson, *Manager*
EMP: 4
SALES (est): 1.1MM **Privately Held**
SIC: 4731 7372 Freight transportation arrangement; business oriented computer software

(G-7572)
BOARS HEAD PROVISIONS CO INC
284 Roost Ave (49424-2032)
PHONE..................941 955-0994
Van Ayvazain, *President*
EMP: 270
SALES (est): 42.2MM
SALES (corp-wide): 221.8MM **Privately Held**
SIC: 5147 2013 2011 Meats & meat products; luncheon meat from purchased meat; meat packing plants
PA: Boar's Head Provisions Co., Inc.
1819 Main St Ste 800
Sarasota FL 34236
941 955-0994

(G-7573)
BODYCOTE THERMAL PROC INC
3270 John F Donnelly Dr (49424-8222)
PHONE..................616 399-6880
Jodi Underhill, *Office Mgr*
Harrison Tiemann, *Manager*
EMP: 95
SALES (corp-wide): 935.8MM **Privately Held**
SIC: 3398 Metal heat treating
HQ: Bodycote Thermal Processing, Inc.
12700 Park Central Dr # 700
Dallas TX 75251
214 904-2420

(G-7574)
BRACY & ASSOCIATES LTD
965 N Baywood Dr (49424-2585)
PHONE..................616 298-8120
Arnold Bracey, *Partner*
EMP: 5
SALES (est): 343.2K **Privately Held**
WEB: www.bracyassociates.com
SIC: 2531 Altars & pulpits

(G-7575)
BRADFORD COMPANY (PA)
Also Called: Bradford Packaging
13500 Quincy St (49424-9460)
P.O. Box 1199 (49422-1199)
PHONE..................616 399-3000
Judson A Bradford, *Ch of Bd*
Thomas R Bradford, *President*
Jud Bradford, *Vice Pres*
Chuck Slager, *Vice Pres*
Mike Bale, *Prdtn Mgr*
▲ **EMP:** 160 **EST:** 1924
SQ FT: 184,000
SALES (est): 77.1MM **Privately Held**
WEB: www.bradfordcompany.com
SIC: 2653 3535 2675 Partitions, solid fiber: made from purchased materials; unit handling conveying systems; die-cut paper & board

(G-7576)
BRAWN MIXER INC
12838 Stainless Dr (49424-8218)
PHONE..................616 399-5600
Jerry Fleishman, *President*

Dan Keller, *General Mgr*
George McIntosh, *Vice Pres*
Andrea Paul, *Engineer*
Steve Canaley, *Sales Mgr*
EMP: 17
SQ FT: 21,000
SALES (est): 5MM **Privately Held**
WEB: www.brawnmixer.com
SIC: 3531 5084 Mixers: ore, plaster, slag, sand, mortar, etc.; industrial machinery & equipment

(G-7577)
BREWER SAND & GRAVEL INC
877 Chicago Dr (49423-3005)
PHONE..................616 393-8990
James Brewer, *President*
Dan Brewer, *Vice Pres*
Jerry Brewer, *Vice Pres*
Joan Brewer, *Admin Sec*
EMP: 6
SQ FT: 2,400
SALES (est): 1.4MM **Privately Held**
SIC: 1442 Construction sand & gravel

(G-7578)
BREWERS CITY DOCK INC
24 Pine Ave (49423-2838)
PHONE..................616 396-6563
Phillip Brewer, *President*
Ronald Lucas, *Vice Pres*
EMP: 25
SQ FT: 28,000
SALES (est): 4.1MM **Privately Held**
SIC: 3273 5032 Ready-mixed concrete; sand, construction

(G-7579)
BRON MACHINE INC
821 Productions Pl (49423-9168)
PHONE..................616 392-5320
Ron Grenadier, *President*
EMP: 13
SQ FT: 8,500
SALES (est): 1.5MM **Privately Held**
WEB: www.bronmachine.com
SIC: 3599 Machine shop, jobbing & repair

(G-7580)
BUFFOLI NORTH AMERICA CORP
4508 128th Ave (49424-9257)
PHONE..................616 610-4362
William Damian, *Principal*
EMP: 3 **EST:** 2018
SALES (est): 400.2K **Privately Held**
SIC: 3599 Industrial machinery

(G-7581)
BUHLERPRINCE INC (DH)
670 Windcrest Dr (49423-5410)
PHONE..................616 394-8248
Mark Los, *President*
Bob Aylsworth, *Opers Mgr*
▲ **EMP:** 128
SQ FT: 700,000
SALES (est): 34.8MM
SALES (corp-wide): 3.3B **Privately Held**
WEB: www.idraprince.com
SIC: 3542 Die casting machines
HQ: Buhler Ag
Gupfenstrasse 5
Uzwil SG 9240
719 551-111

(G-7582)
BUSSCHER SEPTIC TANK SERVICE
Also Called: Busscher Septic Tank Company
11305 E Lakewood Blvd (49424-9605)
PHONE..................616 392-9653
Verne J Lubbers, *President*
Virginia Lubbers, *Vice Pres*
EMP: 9
SALES (est): 1.4MM **Privately Held**
WEB: www.busscherssseptic.com
SIC: 3272 7699 Septic tanks, concrete; burial vaults, concrete or precast terrazzo; septic tank cleaning service

(G-7583)
C T L ENTERPRISES INC
Also Called: Signs Now
832 Productions Pl (49423-9168)
PHONE..................616 392-1159
Leslie Louisell, *President*

Timothy Louisell, *President*
Mitchell Kroll, *Engineer*
Michelle Robillard, *Accounting Dir*
Vern Bosch, *Finance Mgr*
EMP: 12
SQ FT: 9,600
SALES (est): 1.7MM **Privately Held**
WEB: www.signsnowhollandinc.com
SIC: 3993 Signs & advertising specialties

(G-7584)
CANVAS INNOVATIONS LLC
11276 E Lakewood Blvd (49424-8601)
PHONE..................616 393-4400
Christopher Ritsema, *Principal*
EMP: 8 **EST:** 2010
SALES (est): 986.8K **Privately Held**
SIC: 2211 Canvas

(G-7585)
CARRY-ALL PRODUCTS INC
Also Called: Mobile Installations
4498 128th Ave (49424-9257)
PHONE..................616 399-8080
Chuck Rademacher, *President*
Kenneth Rademacher, *Vice Pres*
Bruce Williams, *Manager*
EMP: 12
SQ FT: 7,500
SALES: 1MM **Privately Held**
SIC: 2211 3552 Canvas; silk screens for textile industry

(G-7586)
CASEQ TECHNOLOGIES INC
657 Commerce Ct Ste 40 (49424-2941)
PHONE..................734 730-5407
Stanley Samuel, *President*
EMP: 3 **EST:** 2015
SQ FT: 2,000
SALES (est): 234.8K **Privately Held**
SIC: 2813 Carbon dioxide

(G-7587)
CHALLENGE MFG COMPANY
1401 Washington Ave (49423-8747)
PHONE..................616 396-2079
Christine Chappell, *Purchasing*
Link Rinke, *Branch Mgr*
EMP: 700
SALES (corp-wide): 763MM **Privately Held**
SIC: 3465 3469 Automotive stampings; metal stampings
PA: Challenge Mfg. Company, Llc
3200 Fruit Ridge Ave Nw
Walker MI 49544
616 735-6500

(G-7588)
CHARLES BOWMAN & COMPANY
3328 John F Donnelly Dr (49424-9294)
PHONE..................616 786-4000
John Ripley, *CEO*
Cara Larsen, *Vice Pres*
Brett Helgeson, *VP Opers*
Anthony Evans, *VP Sls/Mktg*
George Tilton, *Director*
◆ **EMP:** 19
SQ FT: 20,000
SALES (est): 9.7MM **Privately Held**
WEB: www.charlesbowman.com
SIC: 2834 Druggists' preparations (pharmaceuticals)

(G-7589)
CHRISTENSEN FIBERGLASS LLC
126 Aniline Ave N (49424-6407)
PHONE..................616 738-1219
Bill Christensen, *Mng Member*
EMP: 20
SALES (est): 3.7MM **Privately Held**
WEB: www.christensenfiberglasstooling.com
SIC: 3544 Industrial molds

(G-7590)
CHROMATIC GRAPHICS INC
654 E Lakewood Blvd (49424-2025)
PHONE..................616 393-0034
Glen Windemuller, *President*
Judy Windemuller, *Corp Secy*
Steve Windemuller, *Vice Pres*
EMP: 8

GEOGRAPHIC SECTION

Holland - Ottawa County (G-7619)

SQ FT: 6,000
SALES (est): 825.9K **Privately Held**
SIC: 2396 2397 Screen printing on fabric articles; schiffli machine embroideries

(G-7591)
CIRCUS PROCESSION LLC
622 Graafschap Rd (49423-4549)
PHONE..................................616 834-8048
EMP: 4
SALES (est): 218.3K **Privately Held**
SIC: 2084 Wines

(G-7592)
CLARION TECHNOLOGIES INC (PA)
170 College Ave Ste 300 (49423-2982)
PHONE..................................616 698-7277
Steven W Olmstead, *CEO*
John Brownlow, *President*
Mark Alexander, *General Mgr*
Craig A Wierda, *Chairman*
Paul Byrne, *Safety Dir*
▲ EMP: 110
SQ FT: 130,000
SALES (est): 63.6MM **Privately Held**
WEB: www.clariontechnologies.com
SIC: 3089 Injection molding of plastics

(G-7593)
COASTAL CONTAINER CORPORATION
Also Called: Coastal Energy
1201 Indl Ave (49423)
PHONE..................................616 355-9800
Brent E Patterson, *President*
Bill Baumgartner, *Vice Pres*
Tamara Jalving, *Vice Pres*
EMP: 75
SQ FT: 235,000
SALES (est): 21.2MM **Privately Held**
WEB: www.coastalfc.com
SIC: 2653 Corrugated & solid fiber boxes

(G-7594)
CODE BLUE CORPORATION
259 Hedcor St Ste 1 (49423-9314)
PHONE..................................616 392-8296
Kenneth Genzink, *Ch of Bd*
Doug Vanderveen, *Technical Staff*
▲ EMP: 36
SQ FT: 35,000
SALES (est): 9.9MM **Privately Held**
WEB: www.codeblue.com
SIC: 3669 5065 3661 Emergency alarms; security control equipment & systems; telephone & telegraph apparatus

(G-7595)
COMPAC SPECIALTIES INC
13444 Barry St (49424-8495)
PHONE..................................616 786-9100
Donald Schutt, *Ch of Bd*
Mike Schutt, *President*
Rick Schutt, *Vice Pres*
Elaine Zwagerman, *Office Mgr*
EMP: 10
SALES (est): 1.4MM **Privately Held**
SIC: 3559 Recycling machinery

(G-7596)
COMPOSITE BUILDERS LLC
430 W 18th St (49423-3904)
PHONE..................................616 377-7767
Danielle Macinnes,
Brian Macinnes,
EMP: 4
SALES (est): 400.3K **Privately Held**
SIC: 3624 Carbon & graphite products

(G-7597)
CONAGRA FOODS
147 E 6th St (49423-2911)
PHONE..................................616 392-2359
Daryl Horton, *President*
EMP: 3
SALES (est): 189.3K **Privately Held**
SIC: 2099 Food preparations

(G-7598)
CONSUMERS CONCRETE CORPORATION
4312 M 40 (49423)
PHONE..................................616 392-6190
Bill Kirby, *Manager*
EMP: 7
SALES (corp-wide): 102.9MM **Privately Held**
WEB: www.consumersconcrete.com
SIC: 3273 Ready-mixed concrete
PA: Consumers Concrete Corporation
    3508 S Sprinkle Rd
    Kalamazoo MI 49001
    269 342-0136

(G-7599)
CRAFTWOOD INDUSTRIES INC
2530 Kamar Dr (49424-8964)
P.O. Box 2068 (49422-2068)
PHONE..................................616 796-1209
Terry W Beckering, *President*
Roger Steensma, *Treasurer*
Kathy Prominski, *Admin Sec*
EMP: 35
SQ FT: 32,750
SALES (est): 5.1MM **Privately Held**
WEB: www.craftwoodindustries.com
SIC: 2522 2531 2426 2511 Office furniture, except wood; public building & related furniture; hardwood dimension & flooring mills; wood household furniture; wood office furniture

(G-7600)
CREATIVE PRODUCTS INTL
Also Called: CPI Creative Products
A-4699 61st St Unit H (49423)
PHONE..................................616 335-3333
Dave Maurer, *President*
Maritza Voorhurst, *Business Mgr*
▲ EMP: 12
SALES (est): 773.5K **Privately Held**
SIC: 7699 5087 3589 Cleaning services; carpet & rug cleaning equipment & supplies, commercial; vacuum cleaning systems; commercial cleaning equipment; janitors' carts

(G-7601)
CUSTOM SOCKETS INC
1896 Russel Ct (49423-8749)
PHONE..................................616 355-1971
Chris Lance, *President*
EMP: 5 EST: 1997
SQ FT: 3,000
SALES (est): 800K **Privately Held**
SIC: 3423 Hand & edge tools

(G-7602)
CUTTING EDGE TECHNOLOGIES INC
13305 New Holland St B (49424-7442)
PHONE..................................616 738-0800
Jim Dirette, *Vice Pres*
Pete Kornoelje, *Vice Pres*
Craig Kane, *Treasurer*
EMP: 12 EST: 2001
SQ FT: 14,000
SALES (est): 1.2MM **Privately Held**
SIC: 3544 Special dies, tools, jigs & fixtures

(G-7603)
D B INTERNATIONAL LLC
650 Riley St Ste C (49424-1592)
PHONE..................................616 796-0679
Khamtanh Sayavong, *Mng Member*
EMP: 5
SALES (est): 389.9K **Privately Held**
SIC: 3089 Plastics products

(G-7604)
D SIGN LLC
Also Called: D-Sign
511 Chicago Dr (49423-2939)
PHONE..................................616 392-3841
Joy Smith, *MIS Dir*
Douglas Smith,
EMP: 5
SQ FT: 2,000
SALES (est): 423.5K **Privately Held**
SIC: 3993 Neon signs

(G-7605)
DANIEL PRUITOFF
Also Called: Holland Automotive Machine
271 E 26th St (49423-5445)
PHONE..................................616 392-1371
Daniel Pruitoff, *Owner*
EMP: 5
SQ FT: 3,000
SALES: 600K **Privately Held**
SIC: 7538 7539 3599 Engine rebuilding: automotive; machine shop, automotive; crankshafts & camshafts, machining

(G-7606)
DEES LOGGING
1907 W 32nd St (49423-4364)
PHONE..................................616 796-8050
EMP: 3 EST: 2010
SALES (est): 140K **Privately Held**
SIC: 2411 Logging

(G-7607)
DEMATIC
11818 James St (49424-7789)
PHONE..................................616 395-8671
EMP: 5
SALES (corp-wide): 9.1B **Privately Held**
SIC: 3535 7371 3537 Conveyors & conveying equipment; custom computer programming services; industrial trucks & tractors
HQ: Dematic Corp.
    3550 Lenox Rd Ne
    Atlanta GA 30326
    877 725-7500

(G-7608)
DIVERSIFIED PDTS & SVCS LLC
500 E 8th St (49423-3770)
P.O. Box 2081 (49422-2081)
PHONE..................................616 836-6600
EMP: 8 EST: 2014
SALES (est): 480K **Privately Held**
SIC: 2421 2441 2448 2449 Sawmill/Planing Mill Mfg Wood Boxes/Shooks Mfg Wood Pallets/Skids Mfg Wood Containers

(G-7609)
DIVERSIFIED WELDING & FABG
12813 Riley St (49424-9201)
PHONE..................................616 738-0400
Calvin Lawson, *President*
Karen Lawson, *Vice Pres*
EMP: 5
SQ FT: 5,000
SALES (est): 613.2K **Privately Held**
SIC: 7692 Welding repair

(G-7610)
DONUTVILLE
676 Michigan Ave Ste 1 (49423-4912)
PHONE..................................616 396-1160
Thomas Lee, *Manager*
EMP: 3
SALES (est): 111.7K **Privately Held**
SIC: 5461 2051 Doughnuts; doughnuts, except frozen

(G-7611)
DR PEPPER SNAPPLE GROUP
777 Brooks Ave (49423-5340)
PHONE..................................616 393-5800
Stephanie Vantil, *Recruiter*
EMP: 4 EST: 2018
SALES (est): 208.9K **Privately Held**
SIC: 2086 Bottled & canned soft drinks

(G-7612)
DRI-DESIGN INC
12480 Superior Ct Ste 1 (49424-7241)
P.O. Box 1286 (49422-1286)
PHONE..................................616 355-2970
Bradley J Zeeff, *President*
Dale Bauer, *Project Mgr*
Jim Haas, *Project Mgr*
Leif Haugen, *Project Mgr*
Michael Hemmeke, *Project Mgr*
EMP: 22 EST: 1996
SQ FT: 20,000
SALES (est): 8.9MM **Privately Held**
WEB: www.dri-design.com
SIC: 3444 Siding, sheet metal
HQ: Kingspan Insulated Panels Inc.
    726 Summerhill Dr
    Deland FL 32724
    386 626-6789

(G-7613)
DYNAMIC CORPORATION (PA)
Also Called: Dynamic Metrology Services
2565 Van Ommen Dr (49424-8208)
PHONE..................................616 399-9391
Hugh F Broersma, *President*
Ray Atwood, *Vice Pres*
Steve Connelly, *Vice Pres*
Cheryl Moulder, *Assistant*
EMP: 70
SQ FT: 10,000
SALES (est): 8.4MM **Privately Held**
WEB: www.ah.dynamicinc.com
SIC: 8711 8744 8734 3544 Consulting engineer; facilities support services; product certification, safety or performance; calibration & certification; special dies, tools, jigs & fixtures; metal stampings; screw machine products

(G-7614)
DYNAMIC STAFFING SOLUTIONS (PA)
2565 Van Ommen Dr (49424-8208)
PHONE..................................616 399-5220
Hugh Broersma, *President*
Steve Connelly, *Vice Pres*
EMP: 15
SQ FT: 14,000
SALES (est): 1.3MM **Privately Held**
WEB: www.sag.dynamicinc.com
SIC: 2869 Laboratory chemicals, organic

(G-7615)
E M I CONSTRUCTION PRODUCTS
526 E 64th St (49423-8717)
PHONE..................................616 392-7207
Edward Shidler, *President*
Marlene Shidler, *Corp Secy*
▼ EMP: 55
SALES (est): 8.4MM **Privately Held**
SIC: 5082 5211 3531 3496 Masonry equipment & supplies; masonry materials & supplies; construction machinery; miscellaneous fabricated wire products; hand & edge tools

(G-7616)
EBW ELECTRONICS INC
Also Called: Ebwe
13110 Ransom St (49424-8715)
PHONE..................................616 786-0575
Leo Le Blanc, *CEO*
James Cory Steeby, *President*
Craig Maghielse, *Vice Pres*
Phil De Vries, *Engineer*
Luanne Verner, *Systems Staff*
▲ EMP: 40
SQ FT: 12,000
SALES (est): 18.1MM **Privately Held**
WEB: www.ebw-electronics.com
SIC: 3679 3612 8731 Electronic circuits; transformers, except electric; electronic research

(G-7617)
ECO - COMPOSITES LLC
Also Called: Ccd Holdings
845 Allen Dr (49423-4501)
PHONE..................................616 395-8902
Carey J Boote,
EMP: 5
SALES (est): 609K **Privately Held**
SIC: 3089 Molding primary plastic

(G-7618)
EDMAR MANUFACTURING INC
Also Called: EMI Construction Products
526 E 64th St (49423-8717)
PHONE..................................616 392-7218
Dave Shidler, *President*
Edward Shidler, *President*
David Shidler, *General Mgr*
David Van Hekken, *Vice Pres*
Jerry Higgins, *Mfg Dir*
▲ EMP: 52
SALES (est): 21.8MM **Privately Held**
WEB: www.edmarmfg.com
SIC: 3469 3544 Metal stampings; special dies, tools, jigs & fixtures

(G-7619)
EGEMIN AUTOMATION INC
Also Called: Egemin Group, Inc.
11818 James St (49424-7789)
PHONE..................................616 393-0101
Jan Vercammen, *CEO*
Robert Moskin, *Vice Pres*
Craig Hoeve, *Purchasing*
Seth Cooper, *Engineer*
Marc Guns, *Ch Credit Ofcr*
▲ EMP: 180

Holland - Ottawa County (G-7620) GEOGRAPHIC SECTION

SQ FT: 58,000
SALES (est): 46MM
SALES (corp-wide): 9.1B **Privately Held**
WEB: www.egeminusa.com
SIC: 3535 7371 3537 Conveyors & conveying equipment; custom computer programming services; industrial trucks & tractors
PA: Kion Group Ag
Thea-Rasche-Str. 8
Frankfurt Am Main 60549
692 011-00

(G-7620)
ELDEAN YACHT BASIN LTD (PA)
Also Called: Yach Basin Marina
1862 Ottawa Beach Rd (49424-2444)
PHONE..................................616 786-2205
Herbert Eldean, *President*
Tom Denherder, *Treasurer*
EMP: 25
SALES (est): 2MM **Privately Held**
SIC: 4493 3732 Marinas; boat building & repairing

(G-7621)
ELITE ACTIVE WEAR INC
701 Washington Ave (49423-6935)
PHONE..................................616 396-1229
Tim Elhart, *President*
Michelle Elhart, *Treasurer*
EMP: 5
SQ FT: 2,500
SALES (est): 564.3K **Privately Held**
WEB: www.eliteactivewear.com
SIC: 2396 Screen printing on fabric articles

(G-7622)
EMI CONSTRUCTION PRODUCTS
455 E 64th St (49423-8732)
PHONE..................................800 603-9965
Dan Cressey, *Sales Staff*
▼ EMP: 8
SALES (est): 771.9K **Privately Held**
SIC: 3444 Concrete forms, sheet metal

(G-7623)
ENSIGN EQUIPMENT INC
12523 Superior Ct (49424-8287)
PHONE..................................616 738-9000
David Pulver, *President*
Al Grollem, *Vice Pres*
EMP: 8
SALES (est): 2.2MM
SALES (corp-wide): 31.8MM **Privately Held**
WEB: www.ensignequipment.com
SIC: 3535 Bulk handling conveyor systems
PA: Excalibur Group L.L.C.
1160 Amboy Ave
Perth Amboy NJ 08861
732 442-8425

(G-7624)
ENVISION MACHINE AND MFG LLC
Also Called: Envision Machine & Mfg
741 Waverly Ct (49423-9387)
PHONE..................................616 953-8580
Tim Vander Toorn, *President*
Josh Vander Toorn, *Vice Pres*
Eric Jones, *Sales Engr*
EMP: 8
SQ FT: 9,000
SALES: 1MM **Privately Held**
SIC: 7692 Welding repair

(G-7625)
ESS TEC INC
3347 128th Ave (49424-9263)
PHONE..................................616 394-0230
Larry W Essenburg, *President*
Constance S Essenburg, *Corp Secy*
Jim Davis, *Vice Pres*
Travis Chambers, *Materials Mgr*
Jose Gomez, *QC Mgr*
EMP: 89
SQ FT: 20,000
SALES (est): 9MM **Privately Held**
WEB: www.ess-tec.com
SIC: 3089 3559 Injection molded finished plastic products; plastics working machinery

(G-7626)
EURO-LOCKS INC
124 James St (49424-1824)
PHONE..................................616 994-0490
▲ EMP: 12
SQ FT: 3,400
SALES (est): 2.1MM
SALES (corp-wide): 105.2MM **Privately Held**
SIC: 3429 Locks or lock sets
PA: Lowe And Fletcher Limited
Moorcroft Drive
Wednesbury W MIDLANDS WS10
121 505-0400

(G-7627)
EVEREST EXPEDITION LLC
Also Called: Worden Company, The
199 E 17th St (49423-4385)
PHONE..................................616 392-1848
Steve Deloof, *President*
Stephanie White, *Human Res Mgr*
Tom Gerber, *Director*
James Hendrickson, *Executive*
EMP: 99 EST: 2013
SQ FT: 25,000
SALES (est): 13.1MM **Privately Held**
SIC: 2531 Library furniture

(G-7628)
EVIA LEARNING INC
720 E 8th St Ste 4 (49423-3079)
PHONE..................................616 393-8803
Lee Sorester, *President*
EMP: 7
SALES (est): 588.4K **Privately Held**
SIC: 2731 Books: publishing & printing

(G-7629)
EVOQUA WATER TECHNOLOGIES LLC
2155 112th Ave (49424-9609)
PHONE..................................616 772-9011
Ken Hollidge, *Branch Mgr*
EMP: 100
SALES (corp-wide): 1.3B **Publicly Held**
SIC: 3589 Water treatment equipment, industrial
HQ: Evoqua Water Technologies Llc
210 6th Ave Ste 3300
Pittsburgh PA 15222
724 772-0044

(G-7630)
FIBERGLASS CONCEPTS WEST MICH
257 E 32nd St Ste 2 (49423-5413)
PHONE..................................616 392-4909
Steven Dreiyer, *President*
EMP: 3
SALES (est): 200K **Privately Held**
SIC: 3296 Fiberglass insulation

(G-7631)
FILLMORE BEEF COMPANY INC
5812 142nd Ave (49423-9338)
P.O. Box 1316 (49422-1316)
PHONE..................................616 396-6693
Larry Slank, *President*
Marika Slenk, *Vice Pres*
EMP: 3 EST: 1963
SQ FT: 25,000
SALES (est): 412.6K **Privately Held**
SIC: 2011 Meat packing plants

(G-7632)
FLEXPOST INC
2236 112th Ave Ste 80 (49424-8502)
PHONE..................................616 928-0829
Thomas Stanley, *CEO*
John Kandra, *President*
EMP: 8
SALES (est): 557.4K **Privately Held**
SIC: 3315 Fence gates posts & fittings: steel

(G-7633)
FOCUS MARKETING
2495 112th Ave Ste 8 (49424-9657)
PHONE..................................616 355-4362
EMP: 20
SALES (est): 1.6MM **Privately Held**
SIC: 2759 Commercial Printing

(G-7634)
FOREFRONT CONTROL SYSTEMS LLC
4314 136th Ave Ste 200 (49424-7467)
PHONE..................................616 796-3495
Garryl Roon, *Owner*
Susan Roon, *Administration*
EMP: 5
SALES (est): 869.2K **Privately Held**
SIC: 3823 Controllers for process variables, all types

(G-7635)
FORMED SOLUTIONS INC
1900 Lamar Ct (49423-8750)
PHONE..................................616 395-5455
Lyle Schut, *President*
CAM Streidl, *Vice Pres*
◆ EMP: 15
SQ FT: 37,500
SALES (est): 2.8MM **Privately Held**
WEB: www.formedsolutions.com
SIC: 3089 Thermoformed finished plastic products; injection molding of plastics

(G-7636)
FORTRESS STBLZTION SYSTEMS LLC
184 W 64th St (49423-9302)
PHONE..................................616 355-1421
Edward Wheatley,
EMP: 8
SQ FT: 25,000
SALES (est): 1.3MM **Privately Held**
WEB: www.fortressstabilization.com
SIC: 3624 Fibers, carbon & graphite

(G-7637)
FSI LABEL COMPANY
Also Called: Argo Systems
6227 136th Ave (49424-8289)
P.O. Box 36480, Grosse Pointe (48236-0480)
PHONE..................................586 776-4110
Emily Kopko, *President*
Christopher Roman, *Vice Pres*
Matt Kopko, *Representative*
EMP: 20
SQ FT: 30,000
SALES (est): 3.5MM **Privately Held**
WEB: www.fsilabel.com
SIC: 2759 5112 Labels & seals: printing; office filing supplies; file folders

(G-7638)
FURNITURE PARTNERS LLC
199 E 17th St (49423-4385)
PHONE..................................616 355-3051
James Weaver, *President*
Kenneth Filippini, *Principal*
EMP: 99 EST: 2015
SQ FT: 135,000
SALES (est): 3.7MM **Privately Held**
SIC: 2531 Public building & related furniture

(G-7639)
G P REEVES INC
4551 Holland Ave (49424-9200)
PHONE..................................616 399-8893
Gordon P Reeves, *President*
Shirley Reeves, *Vice Pres*
Brad Alvesteffer, *Engineer*
Larry Jackson, *Sales Mgr*
Ken Walker, *Sales Engr*
EMP: 25
SQ FT: 27,000
SALES (est): 2.8MM **Privately Held**
WEB: www.gpreeves.com
SIC: 3569 Lubrication equipment, industrial

(G-7640)
GENERAL PROCESSING SYSTEMS INC
Also Called: Product Saver
12838 Stainless Dr (49424-8218)
PHONE..................................630 554-7804
EMP: 10 EST: 1966
SQ FT: 10,000
SALES (est): 897.1K **Privately Held**
SIC: 3599 5084 Mfg Industrial Machinery Whol Industrial Equipment

(G-7641)
GENERAL TECHNOLOGY INC
4521 48th St (49423-9515)
PHONE..................................269 751-7516
Gregory Laarman, *President*
Betty Laarman, *Admin Sec*
EMP: 15
SQ FT: 600
SALES: 750K **Privately Held**
SIC: 3599 Machine shop, jobbing & repair

(G-7642)
GENERATION PRESS INC
Also Called: Schreur Printing
10861 Paw Paw Dr (49424-8991)
PHONE..................................616 392-4405
Tim Schreur, *President*
Mary Jane Schreur, *Vice Pres*
EMP: 9 EST: 1945
SALES: 500K **Privately Held**
WEB: www.schreurprinting.com
SIC: 2752 7331 Commercial printing, offset; mailing service

(G-7643)
GENESIS INNOVATION GROUP LLC
13827 Port Sheldon St (49424-9413)
PHONE..................................616 294-1026
Robert Ball, *Mng Member*
Jeff Ondrla,
Don Running,
EMP: 3 EST: 2016
SALES (est): 290.1K **Privately Held**
SIC: 3841 Diagnostic apparatus, medical

(G-7644)
GLW FINISHING
741 Waverly Ct (49423-9387)
P.O. Box 1738 (49422-1738)
PHONE..................................616 395-0112
EMP: 25
SQ FT: 33,000
SALES (est): 2.3MM **Privately Held**
SIC: 3479 Coating/Engraving Service

(G-7645)
GNS HOLLAND INC
Also Called: Gns America Co.
13341 Quincy St (49424-9460)
PHONE..................................616 796-0433
Sukje Lee, *President*
Morey Wagenmaker, *Business Mgr*
Chris Delange, *Engineer*
Dan Gilbert, *Engineer*
Rod Sluis, *Engineer*
▲ EMP: 2
SQ FT: 100,000
SALES: 45MM
SALES (corp-wide): 83.5MM **Privately Held**
SIC: 3469 Perforated metal, stamped
PA: Gns North America, Inc.
13341 Quincy St
Holland MI 49424
616 796-0433

(G-7646)
GNS NORTH AMERICA INC (PA)
13341 Quincy St (49424-9460)
PHONE..................................616 796-0433
Moon Gyu-Kong, *President*
Todd Dale, *COO*
EMP: 6 EST: 2009
SQ FT: 1,750
SALES (est): 83.5MM **Privately Held**
SIC: 6719 3465 Investment holding companies, except banks; body parts, automobile: stamped metal

(G-7647)
GRAHAM PACKAGING COMPANY LP
926 S Waverly Rd (49423-9306)
P.O. Box 1198 (49422-1198)
PHONE..................................616 355-0479
Todd James, *General Mgr*
Heather Merritt, *Admin Mgr*
EMP: 35
SALES (corp-wide): 14.1MM **Privately Held**
WEB: www.grahampackaging.com
SIC: 3089 3085 Plastic containers, except foam; plastics bottles

GEOGRAPHIC SECTION

Holland - Ottawa County (G-7672)

HQ: Graham Packaging Company, L.P.
700 Indian Springs Dr # 100
Lancaster PA 17601
717 849-8500

(G-7648)
GRAND RAPIDS GRAVEL COMPANY
Kalkman Redi-Mix Division
13180 Quincy St (49424-9474)
P.O. Box 9160, Wyoming (49509-0160)
PHONE..................................616 538-9000
Randy Venhuizen, *Office Mgr*
EMP: 23
SQ FT: 10,000
SALES (corp-wide): 26.5MM **Privately Held**
WEB: www.grgravel.com
SIC: 3273 8611 Ready-mixed concrete; business associations
PA: Grand Rapids Gravel Company
2700 28th St Sw
Grand Rapids MI 49519
616 538-9000

(G-7649)
GRAND RIVER GRANITE INC
13688 Port Sheldon St (49424-9244)
PHONE..................................616 399-9324
Sorin Stef, *President*
David Miller, *Vice Pres*
Jack Miller, *Admin Sec*
EMP: 4
SQ FT: 2,000
SALES (est): 331.9K **Privately Held**
WEB: www.grandrivergranite.com
SIC: 3281 Granite, cut & shaped

(G-7650)
GRAPHIX SIGNS & EMBROIDERY
Also Called: Mle
11223 E Lakewood Blvd (49424-8601)
PHONE..................................616 396-0009
Marcia Essenburg, *Partner*
Beth Essenburg, *Partner*
EMP: 8
SQ FT: 5,200
SALES (est): 743.5K **Privately Held**
SIC: 3993 7299 Signs & advertising specialties; stitching, custom

(G-7651)
GREAT LAKE WOODS INC
3303 John F Donnelly Dr (49424-9207)
P.O. Box 1738 (49422-1738)
PHONE..................................616 399-3300
Keith Malmstadt, *Principal*
Guillermo Sanchez, *Supervisor*
▼ EMP: 150
SQ FT: 103,000
SALES (est): 30.9MM **Privately Held**
WEB: www.greatlakewoods.com
SIC: 2851 2431 Vinyl coatings, strippable; moldings, wood: unfinished & prefinished

(G-7652)
GREAT LAKES CASTINGS LLC
12970 Ransom St (49424-9277)
PHONE..................................616 399-9710
Tim Stefanick, *Manager*
EMP: 50 **Privately Held**
WEB: www.glccadv.com
SIC: 3321 Gray iron castings
HQ: Great Lakes Castings Llc
800 N Washington Ave
Ludington MI 49431
231 843-2501

(G-7653)
GREAT LAKES NCW LLC
386 Bay Park Dr Ste 10 (49424-2083)
PHONE..................................616 355-2626
Steve Guillory, *President*
EMP: 5
SALES (est): 323.8K **Privately Held**
SIC: 3589 Car washing machinery

(G-7654)
GREEN PLASTICS LLC
13370 Barry St Ste A (49424-7451)
PHONE..................................616 295-2718
Dan English, *Mng Member*
Holly Bouwens,
Nick English,
EMP: 20

SALES (est): 2.3MM **Privately Held**
SIC: 3089 Injection molding of plastics

(G-7655)
GT SOLUTIONS LLC
Also Called: Matech Lighting Systems
31 E 8th St Ste 310 (49423-3541)
PHONE..................................616 259-0700
Jeffery Teroller, *Mng Member*
Julie Mesman, *Admin Asst*
EMP: 4
SALES: 1.5MM **Privately Held**
SIC: 8748 3648 3646 Business consulting; lighting equipment; commercial indusl & institutional electric lighting fixtures

(G-7656)
H E MORSE CO
Also Called: Morse-Hemco
455 Douglas Ave (49424-2772)
PHONE..................................616 396-4604
Christopher A Wysong, *President*
Laurence Wysong, *Chairman*
Michael Hop, *Vice Pres*
Renee Wilson, *Human Res Mgr*
Nancy Wennersten, *Admin Sec*
EMP: 60
SQ FT: 36,000
SALES (est): 11.7MM **Privately Held**
WEB: www.hemcogages.com
SIC: 3545 Gauges (machine tool accessories)

(G-7657)
HARBOR STEEL AND SUPPLY CORP
2385 112th Ave (49424-9553)
PHONE..................................616 786-0002
Brian Bovia, *Branch Mgr*
EMP: 14
SALES (corp-wide): 95.2MM **Privately Held**
WEB: www.harborsteel.com
SIC: 5051 3498 3446 Steel; tube fabricating (contract bending & shaping); open flooring & grating for construction
HQ: Harbor Steel And Supply Corporation
1115 E Broadway Ave
Norton Shores MI 49444
231 739-7152

(G-7658)
HARVEY BOCK CO
141 Central Ave Ste 120 (49423-2861)
PHONE..................................616 566-1372
Harvey Bock, *Owner*
EMP: 3 EST: 2015
SALES (est): 103.7K **Privately Held**
SIC: 2711 Newspapers

(G-7659)
HAWORTH INC (HQ)
1 Haworth Ctr (49423-8820)
PHONE..................................616 393-3000
Franco Bianchi, *President*
Matthew Haworth, *Chairman*
Jos Amaral, *Vice Pres*
Todd James, *Vice Pres*
Mark Lobb, *Vice Pres*
◆ EMP: 3200 EST: 1959
SQ FT: 1,550,000
SALES (est): 1.8B **Privately Held**
WEB: www.haworth-furn.com
SIC: 2522 2521 Office furniture, except wood; wood office furniture
PA: Haworth International, Ltd.
1 Haworth Ctr
Holland MI 49423
616 393-3000

(G-7660)
HAWORTH INTERNATIONAL LTD (PA)
1 Haworth Ctr (49423-8820)
PHONE..................................616 393-3000
Matthew Haworth, *Ch of Bd*
Frankco Bianchi, *President*
Steve Heyer, *Design Engr*
Eric Meyers, *Sales Staff*
Nicole Decou, *Manager*
◆ EMP: 3000 EST: 1948
SQ FT: 1,500,000
SALES (est): 1.8B **Privately Held**
WEB: www.haworth.com
SIC: 2522 2521 Office furniture, except wood; wood office furniture

(G-7661)
HEMP GLOBAL PRODUCTS INC
503 Essenburg Dr (49424-1623)
PHONE..................................616 617-6476
Israel Quintanilla, *President*
Bryce Taylor, *Treasurer*
EMP: 4
SQ FT: 3,000
SALES: 250K **Privately Held**
SIC: 2329 5199 2339 5136 Athletic (warmup, sweat & jogging) suits: men's & boys'; general merchandise, non-durable; women's & misses' outerwear; men's & boys' clothing; women's & children's clothing

(G-7662)
HERMAN MILLER INC
10201 Adams St (49424)
PHONE..................................616 654-7456
Greg Wrona, *General Mgr*
Dave Emenheiser, *Director*
EMP: 24
SALES (corp-wide): 2.5B **Publicly Held**
WEB: www.hermanmiller.com
SIC: 2521 Wood office furniture
PA: Herman Miller, Inc.
855 E Main Ave
Zeeland MI 49464
616 654-3000

(G-7663)
HERMAN MILLER INC
10001 Adams St (49424)
PHONE..................................616 654-8078
EMP: 24
SALES (corp-wide): 2.5B **Publicly Held**
SIC: 2521 Wood office furniture
PA: Herman Miller, Inc.
855 E Main Ave
Zeeland MI 49464
616 654-3000

(G-7664)
HGC WESTSHORE LLC
Also Called: Westshore Design
3440 Windquest Dr (49424-8069)
PHONE..................................616 796-1218
Gary Van Dyke,
EMP: 61
SALES (est): 6.1MM **Privately Held**
SIC: 3672 Printed circuit boards

(G-7665)
HIGH Q LIGHTING INC
11439 E Lakewood Blvd (49424-9663)
P.O. Box 2817 (49422-2817)
PHONE..................................616 396-3591
Michael A Goheen, *President*
Michael Serr, *Vice Pres*
Carlyle Serr, *Treasurer*
EMP: 35
SQ FT: 20,000
SALES (est): 5.8MM **Privately Held**
WEB: www.hql.net
SIC: 3646 3648 3641 Fluorescent lighting fixtures, commercial; lighting equipment; electric lamps

(G-7666)
HIGH-TECH INDS OF HOLLAND
3269 John F Donnelly Dr (49424-8223)
PHONE..................................616 399-5430
David Tenbrink, *President*
EMP: 33
SQ FT: 20,000
SALES: 3.2MM **Privately Held**
WEB: www.hightechindustries.com
SIC: 3369 Castings, except die-castings, precision

(G-7667)
HOLLAND ALLOYS INC
534 Chicago Dr (49423-2940)
P.O. Box 2459 (49422-2459)
PHONE..................................616 396-6444
Richard O Hagen, *President*
Carolyn Hagen, *Vice Pres*
Bonnie De Kleine, *Admin Sec*
EMP: 37
SQ FT: 1,000

SALES (est): 470.4K
SALES (corp-wide): 4.7MM **Privately Held**
WEB: www.hollandpattern.com
SIC: 3369 3366 3365 3325 Castings, except die-castings, precision; copper foundries; aluminum foundries; steel foundries; malleable iron foundries; gray & ductile iron foundries
PA: Holland Pattern Co
534 Chicago Dr
Holland MI 49423
616 396-6348

(G-7668)
HOLLAND BAR STOOL COMPANY
Also Called: Holland Honey Cake Co.
12839 Corporate Circle Pl (49424-7267)
PHONE..................................616 399-5530
Larry Bensink, *President*
Ling Bensink, *Vice Pres*
Daniel Vriesman, *Graphic Designe*
▲ EMP: 17
SQ FT: 60,000
SALES (est): 3.7MM **Privately Held**
WEB: www.hollandbarstool.com
SIC: 2599 Bar, restaurant & cafeteria furniture

(G-7669)
HOLLAND BOWL MILL
120 James St (49424-1824)
P.O. Box 2102 (49422-2102)
PHONE..................................616 396-6513
Donna B Phillips, *Partner*
Dave Gier, *Partner*
EMP: 40
SQ FT: 18,000
SALES (est): 4.2MM **Privately Held**
WEB: www.hollandbowlmill.com
SIC: 2499 Bowls, wood

(G-7670)
HOLLAND COMMUNITY HOSP AUX INC
Also Called: Behavioral Health
854 Wshington Ave Ste 330 (49423)
PHONE..................................616 355-3926
Steve Sorenson, *Branch Mgr*
Adam Duncan, *Manager*
Nathan Silva, *Software Engr*
Mark Laman, *Director*
Bobga Fomunung, *Psychiatry*
EMP: 20
SALES (corp-wide): 258.6MM **Privately Held**
SIC: 3821 8734 8071 Clinical laboratory instruments, except medical & dental; testing laboratories; medical laboratories
PA: Holland Community Hospital Auxiliary, Inc.
602 Michigan Ave
Holland MI 49423
616 748-9346

(G-7671)
HOLLAND ELECTRIC MOTOR CO
11598 E Lakewood Blvd B (49424-7932)
PHONE..................................616 392-1115
James Achterhof, *President*
Paul Achterhof, *Vice Pres*
Philip Holtrop, *Treasurer*
Mike Vanderwall, *Manager*
Delwyn Mokma, *Asst Sec*
EMP: 5
SQ FT: 3,300
SALES (est): 1.1MM **Privately Held**
WEB: www.hollandelectricmotor.com
SIC: 7694 5063 Electric motor repair; generators

(G-7672)
HOLLAND HOUSE CANDLES INC (PA)
16656 Riley St (49424-5811)
PHONE..................................800 238-8467
Valerie Nichols, *President*
William Nichols, *Treasurer*
EMP: 14 EST: 1974
SALES (est): 1.2MM **Privately Held**
WEB: www.hollandhousecandles.com
SIC: 3999 5999 Candles; candle shops

Holland - Ottawa County (G-7673) — GEOGRAPHIC SECTION

(G-7673)
HOLLAND PALLET REPAIR INC
13370 Barry St Ste A (49424-7451)
PHONE.................................616 875-8642
John Breslin, *President*
Dave Mason, *Treasurer*
EMP: 45
SQ FT: 7,000
SALES (est): 7.6MM **Privately Held**
SIC: 2448 Wood pallets & skids

(G-7674)
HOLLAND PANEL PRODUCTS INC
615 E 40th St (49423-5314)
PHONE.................................616 392-1826
Eric Smith, *President*
Kristine Elders, *HR Admin*
EMP: 26
SALES (est): 6.2MM
SALES (corp-wide): 95.4MM **Privately Held**
WEB: www.panel.com
SIC: 2493 Wallboard, except gypsum
PA: Panel Processing, Inc.
  120 N Industrial Hwy
  Alpena MI 49707
  800 433-7142

(G-7675)
HOLLAND PATTERN CO (PA)
534 Chicago Dr (49423-2999)
P.O. Box 2459 (49422-2459)
PHONE.................................616 396-6348
Richard O Hagen, *President*
Carolyn Hagen, *Vice Pres*
David Tackett, *Facilities Mgr*
Randy Schutt, *Engineer*
Alice Reinhardt, *Marketing Staff*
EMP: 37
SQ FT: 6,000
SALES (est): 4.7MM **Privately Held**
SIC: 3543 3369 Industrial patterns; castings, except die-castings, precision

(G-7676)
HOLLAND PRINTING CENTER INC (PA)
Also Called: Allegra Print & Imaging
4314 136th Ave Ste 100 (49424-7467)
PHONE.................................616 786-3101
Richard Schwander, *President*
Jeff Schwander, *Vice Pres*
EMP: 16
SQ FT: 10,000
SALES (est): 1MM **Privately Held**
SIC: 2752 Commercial printing, offset

(G-7677)
HOLLAND SCREEN PRINT INC
4665 44th St (49423-9031)
PHONE.................................616 396-7630
Steve Dickerson, *President*
Tom Dickerson, *General Mgr*
Amy Dickerson, *Vice Pres*
EMP: 7
SQ FT: 20,000
SALES (est): 400K **Privately Held**
SIC: 2759 Screen printing

(G-7678)
HOLLAND STITCHCRAFT INC
13163 Reflections Dr (49424-7262)
PHONE.................................616 399-3868
Tami Jo Beltman, *Owner*
Ernest Overkamp, *Principal*
Brian Beltman, *Vice Pres*
EMP: 12 **EST:** 1982
SQ FT: 12,000
SALES (est): 1.8MM **Privately Held**
SIC: 2521 2599 Wood office furniture; bar, restaurant & cafeteria furniture

(G-7679)
HOLLAND TOOL & DIE LLC
4472 48th St (49423-9597)
PHONE.................................269 751-5862
Douglas W Bolman,
EMP: 3
SQ FT: 1,200
SALES (est): 372.1K **Privately Held**
SIC: 3544 Special dies & tools

(G-7680)
HOLLAND TRANSPLANTER CO INC
510 E 16th St (49423-3702)
P.O. Box 1527 (49422-1527)
PHONE.................................616 392-3579
Howard Poll, *President*
Ken Poll, *VP Sales*
EMP: 20 **EST:** 1927
SQ FT: 100,000
SALES: 1.5MM **Privately Held**
WEB: www.transplanter.com
SIC: 3523 Transplanters

(G-7681)
HOUSEPARTY
6 Bellwood Dr (49423-5226)
PHONE.................................616 422-1226
Charles Murillo, *CEO*
EMP: 3
SALES: 50K **Privately Held**
SIC: 3944 7389 7299 Games, toys & children's vehicles; artists' agents & brokers; ; home improvement & renovation contractor agency

(G-7682)
HTI ASSOCIATES LLC
Also Called: High-Tech Industries
3269 John F Donnelly Dr (49424-8223)
PHONE.................................616 399-5430
Jodi Wszolek, *Comptroller*
Leonor De Ochoteco, *Human Res Mgr*
David Tenbrink, *Mng Member*
EMP: 30 **EST:** 1983
SALES (est): 4.5MM **Privately Held**
SIC: 3469 5084 Machine parts, stamped or pressed metal; industrial machine parts

(G-7683)
HTTM LLC
300 E 48th St (49423-5301)
PHONE.................................616 820-2500
Patrick A Thompson, *Mng Member*
EMP: 11
SALES (est): 1.3MM
SALES (corp-wide): 50.8MM **Privately Held**
SIC: 3691 Storage batteries
PA: Trans-Matic Mfg Co Incorporated
  300 E 48th St
  Holland MI 49423
  616 820-2500

(G-7684)
HUDSONVLLE CRMRY ICE CREAM LLC
345 E 48th St Ste 200 (49423-5301)
PHONE.................................616 546-4005
Dan Dejonge, *Facilities Mgr*
Kevin Phillips, *CFO*
Rhonda Dittman, *Human Resources*
Steve Ulrey, *Sales Mgr*
CJ Ellens, *Mktg Dir*
EMP: 28 **EST:** 1895
SQ FT: 65,000
SALES (est): 8.9MM **Privately Held**
SIC: 2024 Ice cream, bulk

(G-7685)
I S TWO
262 E 26th St (49423-5457)
PHONE.................................616 396-5634
Rick Obbink, *Owner*
EMP: 8
SALES (est): 935.1K **Privately Held**
SIC: 2434 Wood kitchen cabinets

(G-7686)
ICON SHELTERS INC
Also Called: Icon Shelter Systems
1455 Lincoln Ave (49423-9389)
PHONE.................................616 396-0919
Davi Dayton, *President*
Bob Jaskulski, *Principal*
Richard Lubbers, *Vice Pres*
Tim Postma, *Vice Pres*
Ellen Fisher, *VP Mfg*
EMP: 24
SQ FT: 18,000
SALES (est): 9.4MM **Privately Held**
WEB: www.iconshelters.com
SIC: 3448 Buildings, portable: prefabricated metal

(G-7687)
IMAGEN ORTHOPEDICS LLC
13827 Port Sheldon St (49424-9413)
PHONE.................................616 294-1026
Don Running, *CEO*
EMP: 3 **EST:** 2016
SALES (est): 126.6K **Privately Held**
SIC: 3841 7371 Surgical & medical instruments; computer software development

(G-7688)
IMPACT FAB INC
3440 John F Donnelly Dr (49424-9294)
PHONE.................................616 399-9970
Dave Haan, *President*
EMP: 10
SALES (est): 1.8MM **Privately Held**
WEB: www.impactfab.com
SIC: 3599 Machine shop, jobbing & repair

(G-7689)
IMPRES ENGINEERING SVCS LLC
147 Douglas Ave (49424-6584)
P.O. Box 8518 (49422-8518)
PHONE.................................616 283-4112
Ross Hoek, *Mng Member*
EMP: 8
SQ FT: 14,000
SALES (est): 1.5MM **Privately Held**
WEB: www.rosshoek.com
SIC: 3549 Metalworking machinery

(G-7690)
INTERIOR SPC OF HOLLAND
262 E 26th St (49423-5457)
PHONE.................................616 396-5634
Arthur Wormet, *President*
EMP: 25
SQ FT: 14,000
SALES (est): 3.1MM **Privately Held**
SIC: 5211 2434 Cabinets, kitchen; wood kitchen cabinets

(G-7691)
INTERNATIONAL MATERIAL CO
Also Called: Imcs
510 E 40th St (49423-5313)
PHONE.................................616 355-2800
Rodney Webb, *President*
David Geschwendt, *Vice Pres*
EMP: 12
SQ FT: 30,000
SALES (est): 3.9MM **Privately Held**
SIC: 3535 Conveyors & conveying equipment

(G-7692)
IXL MACHINE SHOP INC
117 W 7th St (49423-2823)
P.O. Box 1979 (49422-1979)
PHONE.................................616 392-9803
Stuart B Padnos, *President*
EMP: 60
SQ FT: 10,000
SALES (est): 3.6MM
SALES (corp-wide): 520.8MM **Privately Held**
WEB: www.ixlmachine.com
SIC: 3599 Machine shop, jobbing & repair
PA: Louis Padnos Iron And Metal Company
  185 W 8th St
  Holland MI 49423
  616 396-6521

(G-7693)
JAMESWAY TOOL AND DIE INC
401 120th Ave (49424-2119)
PHONE.................................616 396-3731
James Rozeboom, *President*
Mark Rozeboom, *Corp Secy*
David Rozeboom, *Vice Pres*
EMP: 32
SQ FT: 17,400
SALES (est): 5.6MM **Privately Held**
SIC: 3544 Dies & die holders for metal cutting, forming, die casting; industrial molds

(G-7694)
JMS OF HOLLAND INC
1010 Productions Ct (49423-9122)
PHONE.................................616 796-2727
Harold Jordan, *President*
Leon Jordan, *Vice Pres*
Travis Stevens, *QC Mgr*

Rodney Culver, *Treasurer*
Jason Raak, *Sales Mgr*
▼ **EMP:** 100
SQ FT: 64,000
SALES: 21.1MM **Privately Held**
SIC: 3469 Stamping metal for the trade

(G-7695)
JOHN A VAN DEN BOSCH CO (PA)
Also Called: V D B
4511 Holland Ave (49424-9200)
P.O. Box 1786 (49422-1786)
PHONE.................................616 848-2000
David V Den Bosch, *CEO*
Jim D Bosch, *Vice Pres*
Michael V Bosch, *Accounting Mgr*
Abby Siebern, *Sales Dir*
Brock Hyder, *Accounts Mgr*
EMP: 27 **EST:** 1932
SQ FT: 118,000
SALES (est): 8.9MM **Privately Held**
WEB: www.vbosch.com
SIC: 2048 Livestock feeds

(G-7696)
JOHNSON CONTROLS INC
921 E 32nd St (49423-9246)
PHONE.................................616 283-5578
David Sniegowski, *Branch Mgr*
John Tomcala, *Director*
EMP: 93 **Privately Held**
SIC: 2531 Seats, automobile
HQ: Johnson Controls, Inc.
  5757 N Green Bay Ave
  Milwaukee WI 53209
  414 524-1200

(G-7697)
JOHNSON CONTROLS INC
1 Prince Ctr (49423-5486)
PHONE.................................616 392-5151
Bob Bieri, *Manager*
EMP: 300 **Privately Held**
SIC: 3714 Motor vehicle parts & accessories
HQ: Johnson Controls, Inc.
  5757 N Green Bay Ave
  Milwaukee WI 53209
  414 524-1200

(G-7698)
JR AUTOMATION TECH LLC (HQ)
Also Called: Jr Automation
13365 Tyler St (49424-9421)
PHONE.................................616 399-2168
Mike Dubose, *Ch of Bd*
Bryan Jones, *Co-CEO*
Barry Kohn, *CFO*
Sean Ryan, *Asst Controller*
Clay Darrow, *Technician*
▲ **EMP:** 250
SQ FT: 120,000
SALES: 200MM
SALES (corp-wide): 230.4MM **Privately Held**
SIC: 3549 Assembly machines, including robotic
PA: Jr Technology Group, Llc
  13365 Tyler St
  Holland MI 49424
  616 399-2168

(G-7699)
JR AUTOMATION TECH LLC
4433 Holland Ave (49424-8279)
PHONE.................................616 399-2168
Sarah Renee Jaromin, *President*
EMP: 4
SQ FT: 45,000
SALES (corp-wide): 230.4MM **Privately Held**
SIC: 3549 Assembly machines, including robotic
HQ: J.R. Automation Technologies, Llc
  13365 Tyler St
  Holland MI 49424
  616 399-2168

(G-7700)
JR AUTOMATION TECH LLC
4412 136th Ave (49424-9452)
PHONE.................................616 399-2168
EMP: 3
SQ FT: 10,000

GEOGRAPHIC SECTION

Holland - Ottawa County (G-7729)

SALES (corp-wide): 230.4MM **Privately Held**
SIC: 3549 Assembly machines, including robotic
HQ: J.R. Automation Technologies, Llc
13365 Tyler St
Holland MI 49424
616 399-2168

(G-7701)
JR AUTOMATION TECH LLC
100 Aniline Ave N (49424-6681)
PHONE..................................616 399-2168
EMP: 3
SALES (corp-wide): 230.4MM **Privately Held**
SIC: 3549 Assembly machines, including robotic
HQ: J.R. Automation Technologies, Llc
13365 Tyler St
Holland MI 49424
616 399-2168

(G-7702)
JR TECHNOLOGY GROUP LLC (PA)
Also Called: Jr Automation Technologies
13365 Tyler St (49424-9421)
PHONE..................................616 399-2168
Mike Dubose, *Ch of Bd*
Bryan Jones, *Co-CEO*
Barry Kohn, *CFO*
Jim Kramer, *VP Sales*
EMP: 250
SALES (est): 230.4MM **Privately Held**
SIC: 3549 Assembly machines, including robotic

(G-7703)
JRT ENTERPRISES LLC
Also Called: Sparkeology
199 E 17th St (49423-4385)
PHONE..................................877 318-7661
Robin H Lane, *Vice Pres*
Tavan Hendrick,
Robin Lane,
Jamie Stuursma,
EMP: 3
SALES (est): 240K **Privately Held**
SIC: 2531 7389 Public building & related furniture;

(G-7704)
K M S COMPANY
5072 Lakeshore Dr (49424-1068)
P.O. Box 34, Ferrysburg (49409-0034)
PHONE..................................616 994-7000
Kirk M Schutter, *President*
EMP: 4
SALES (est): 106.4K **Privately Held**
SIC: 3546 Guns, pneumatic: chip removal

(G-7705)
KAM PLASTICS CORP (PA)
611 Ottawa Ave (49423-4068)
PHONE..................................616 355-5900
Peter Prouty, *President*
Barbara Dawson, *Vice Pres*
Dan Rietveld, *Vice Pres*
Ray Cederholm, *Engineer*
Farah Miller, *Engineer*
▲ EMP: 75
SQ FT: 70,000
SALES: 10MM **Privately Held**
WEB: www.kamplastics.com
SIC: 3089 Injection molding of plastics

(G-7706)
KAMEX MOLDED PRODUCTS LLC
611 Ottawa Ave (49423-4068)
PHONE..................................616 355-5900
Pete Prouty, *President*
EMP: 3 EST: 2007
SALES (est): 265.9K **Privately Held**
SIC: 3089 Injection molded finished plastic products

(G-7707)
KARR SPRING COMPANY
Also Called: Omni Die & Engineering
966 Brooks Ave (49423-5371)
PHONE..................................616 394-1277
Henry Vugteveen, *President*
Henry Vugteveen, *President*
Doug Vugteveen, *Production*

Gregg Insley, *Sales Mgr*
EMP: 22 EST: 1928
SQ FT: 12,000
SALES (est): 4.9MM **Privately Held**
WEB: www.omnidie.com
SIC: 3545 Machine tool accessories

(G-7708)
KEGLOVE LLC
6403 Sand Castle Vw (49423-8527)
P.O. Box 396, Saugatuck (49453-0396)
PHONE..................................616 610-7289
Mark Young,
Bridget Young,
EMP: 25 EST: 2007
SALES (est): 2.4MM **Privately Held**
WEB: www.keglove.com
SIC: 5084 5078 5046 3429 Brewery products manufacturing machinery, commercial; beverage coolers; commercial cooking & food service equipment; ice chests or coolers, portable, except foam plastic

(G-7709)
KENOWA INDUSTRIES INC (PA)
11405 E Lakewood Blvd (49424-9663)
PHONE..................................616 392-7080
Ed Amaya, *President*
Douglas Devries, *Principal*
Michael Devries, *Principal*
EMP: 40
SQ FT: 38,000
SALES (est): 5.9MM **Privately Held**
WEB: www.kenowa.com
SIC: 3449 7692 Miscellaneous metalwork; welding repair

(G-7710)
KENRIE INC
500 E 8th St Ste 1100 (49423-4751)
PHONE..................................616 494-3200
Kenneth Vennesland, *President*
EMP: 11
SALES (est): 2.3MM **Privately Held**
WEB: www.kenrie.com
SIC: 3545 5084 Precision tools, machinists'; industrial machine parts

(G-7711)
KESKA LLC
87 Chriscraft Ln (49424-6680)
PHONE..................................616 283-7056
Steven Hoek, *President*
EMP: 4
SQ FT: 1,000
SALES (est): 180K **Privately Held**
SIC: 3672 Printed circuit boards

(G-7712)
KOETJE WOOD PRODUCTS INC
11743 Greenway Dr (49424-8654)
PHONE..................................616 393-9191
Terry Koetje, *President*
Jeff Bussler, *Treasurer*
EMP: 4
SQ FT: 6,000
SALES: 700K **Privately Held**
SIC: 2499 Decorative wood & woodwork

(G-7713)
KRAFT HEINZ FOODS COMPANY
431 W 16th St (49423-3445)
PHONE..................................616 396-6557
Jerry Shoup, *Manager*
EMP: 300
SALES (corp-wide): 26.2B **Publicly Held**
SIC: 2032 2099 2033 Canned specialties; vinegar; canned fruits & specialties
HQ: Kraft Heinz Foods Company
1 Ppg Pl Fl 34
Pittsburgh PA 15222
412 456-5700

(G-7714)
KYLER INDUSTRIES INC
192 E 48th St (49423-9307)
PHONE..................................616 392-1042
Thomas J Bratt, *President*
EMP: 5
SALES (est): 807.2K **Privately Held**
SIC: 2591 Blinds vertical; mini blinds

(G-7715)
L & W INC
Also Called: L & W Engineering Co
808 E 32nd St (49423-9128)
PHONE..................................616 394-9665
Jim Swanston, *Branch Mgr*
EMP: 250
SALES (corp-wide): 2.2B **Privately Held**
SIC: 3465 3443 Automotive stampings; bins, prefabricated metal plate
HQ: L & W, Inc.
17757 Woodland Dr
New Boston MI 48164
734 397-6300

(G-7716)
L PERRIGO COMPANY
13295 Reflections Dr (49424-8220)
PHONE..................................616 738-0150
David Gibbons, *Ch of Bd*
Todd Geerlings, *Opers Mgr*
Matthew Laduke, *Research*
John Anderson, *Engineer*
Zachary Wilkinson, *Engineer*
EMP: 365 **Privately Held**
SIC: 2834 Vitamin, nutrient & hematinic preparations for human use
HQ: L Perrigo Company
515 Eastern Ave
Allegan MI 49010
269 673-8451

(G-7717)
LAKE MICHIGAN WIRE LLC
4211 Hallacy Dr (49424-8723)
PHONE..................................616 786-9200
Eric Anderson, *Mng Member*
EMP: 15
SALES: 2.8MM **Privately Held**
SIC: 3312 Wire products, steel or iron

(G-7718)
LAKESIDE PROPERTY SERVICES
14250 Ottawa Creek Ln (49424-8534)
PHONE..................................863 455-9038
Andrew Fikoski, *President*
EMP: 5
SALES (est): 111.6K **Privately Held**
SIC: 0782 3953 4959 Mowing services, lawn; stencils, painting & marking; road, airport & parking lot maintenance services

(G-7719)
LANDSCAPE STONE SUPPLY INC
5960 136th Ave (49424-9477)
PHONE..................................616 953-2028
EMP: 3
SALES (est): 109.5K **Privately Held**
SIC: 3281 Cut stone & stone products

(G-7720)
LAS BRAZAS TORTILLAS
3416 Crystal Valley Ct (49424-8517)
PHONE..................................616 886-0737
Isaias Sanchez, *Partner*
Juligta Rodriguez, *Partner*
EMP: 7
SQ FT: 3,500
SALES: 475K **Privately Held**
SIC: 2099 Tortillas, fresh or refrigerated

(G-7721)
LEON INTERIORS INC (DH)
Also Called: Leon Automotive Interiors
88 E 48th St (49423-9307)
PHONE..................................616 422-7479
Shannon White, *CEO*
Roger Nelson, *Business Mgr*
Beth Haseley, *Opers Staff*
Dave Scheidmantel, *VP Sales*
Jim Gorant, *Accounts Mgr*
▲ EMP: 370
SALES (est): 156.8MM
SALES (corp-wide): 573.9MM **Privately Held**
SIC: 3089 3714 3086 Molding primary plastic; motor vehicle parts & accessories; plastics foam products
HQ: Motus Llc
88 E 48th St
Holland MI 49423
616 422-7557

(G-7722)
LG CHEM MICHIGAN INC (HQ)
Also Called: Lgcmi
1 Lg Way (49423-8574)
PHONE..................................616 494-7100
Prabhakar Patil, *CEO*
Nick Kassanos, *President*
◆ EMP: 138
SQ FT: 618,000
SALES: 197.3MM **Privately Held**
WEB: www.compactpower.com
SIC: 3691 Storage batteries

(G-7723)
LIBERTY AUTOMOTIVE TECH LLC
4554 128th Ave (49424-9257)
PHONE..................................269 487-8114
Scott Irwin,
EMP: 5
SALES (est): 150.7K **Privately Held**
SIC: 3999 Manufacturing industries

(G-7724)
LIBERTY PLASTICS INC
13170 Ransom St (49424-8715)
PHONE..................................616 994-7033
Richard Lynema, *President*
Matt Lynema, *Prdtn Mgr*
Bryce Tenckinck, *QC Mgr*
EMP: 7 EST: 2000
SQ FT: 2,500
SALES: 2MM **Privately Held**
SIC: 3089 Injection molding of plastics

(G-7725)
LIGHTNING MACHINE HOLLAND LLC
128 Manufacturers Dr (49424-1893)
PHONE..................................616 786-9280
Rich Tanis,
EMP: 10
SQ FT: 8,600
SALES (est): 1.7MM **Privately Held**
WEB: www.lightningmachine.com
SIC: 3545 3599 Boring machine attachments (machine tool accessories); precision measuring tools; machine shop, jobbing & repair

(G-7726)
LITTLE MAN WINERY LLC
1666 Pinta Dr (49424-6215)
PHONE..................................616 292-3983
Deborah Murdoch, *Principal*
EMP: 3
SALES (est): 123.4K **Privately Held**
SIC: 2084 Wines

(G-7727)
LOTUS CORPORATION
100 Aniline Ave N Ste 180 (49424-6682)
PHONE..................................616 494-0112
Anthony Ho, *President*
Anh Ho, *Exec VP*
EMP: 7
SQ FT: 14,000
SALES: 710K **Privately Held**
WEB: www.lotuscorporation.com
SIC: 3544 Special dies, tools, jigs & fixtures

(G-7728)
M2 SCIENTIFICS LLC
400 136th Ave Ste 100a (49424-2903)
PHONE..................................616 379-9080
EMP: 7
SALES (est): 529.9K **Privately Held**
SIC: 3821 3231 3596 7389 Centrifuges, laboratory; balances, laboratory; clinical laboratory instruments, except medical & dental; laboratory glassware; scales & balances, except laboratory;

(G-7729)
MAAS ENTERPRISES MICHIGAN LLC
Also Called: Top Notch Tree Service
7938 112th Ave (49424-9498)
PHONE..................................616 875-8099
Paul Maas, *Principal*
EMP: 4
SALES (est): 24.6K **Privately Held**
SIC: 2064 Candy & other confectionery products

Holland - Ottawa County (G-7730)

(G-7730)
MAC BAITS
669 Douglas Ave (49424-2783)
PHONE..................................616 392-2553
Jerry Doornewerd, *Owner*
EMP: 3
SALES (est): 200.1K **Privately Held**
SIC: 2048 Fish food

(G-7731)
MACHINE GUARD & COVER CO
6187 136th Ave (49424-8290)
PHONE..................................616 392-8188
William Labarge Jr, *President*
W Labarge Jr, *Vice Pres*
Becky Haveman, *Human Res Mgr*
EMP: 6
SALES: 750K **Privately Held**
WEB: www.machineguard.com
SIC: 3432 Plastic plumbing fixture fittings, assembly

(G-7732)
MAGNA
3401 128th Ave (49424-9263)
PHONE..................................616 786-7403
Michael Baur, *Manager*
EMP: 6
SALES (est): 111.6K **Privately Held**
SIC: 3231 3442 Products of purchased glass; metal doors, sash & trim

(G-7733)
MAGNA INTERNATIONAL AMER INC
Magna Closures Engineered GL
3501 John F Donnelly Dr (49424-9284)
PHONE..................................616 786-7000
EMP: 8
SALES (corp-wide): 40.8B **Privately Held**
SIC: 3211 Laminated glass
HQ: Magna International Of America, Inc.
750 Tower Dr 7000
Troy MI 48098

(G-7734)
MAGNA MIRRORS AMERICA INC
Also Called: Donnelly
49 W 3rd St (49423-2813)
PHONE..................................616 786-7000
Erika Cates, *Production*
Brenda Kyle, *Production*
Paul Whaley, *Engineer*
Becky Jones, *Human Res Dir*
John Fenech, *Sales Staff*
EMP: 5
SALES (corp-wide): 40.8B **Privately Held**
SIC: 3231 3647 3827 Mirrors, truck & automobile: made from purchased glass; dome lights, automotive; optical instruments & lenses
HQ: Magna Mirrors Of America, Inc.
5085 Kraft Ave Se
Grand Rapids MI 49512
616 786-5120

(G-7735)
MAGNA MIRRORS AMERICA INC
40th Street Divison
414 E 40th St (49423-5383)
PHONE..................................616 786-7300
John Roberts, *General Mgr*
EMP: 100
SALES (corp-wide): 40.8B **Privately Held**
SIC: 3231 3647 3827 Mirrors, truck & automobile: made from purchased glass; windshields, glass: made from purchased glass; dome lights, automotive; automotive lighting fixtures; optical instruments & lenses
HQ: Magna Mirrors Of America, Inc.
5085 Kraft Ave Se
Grand Rapids MI 49512
616 786-5120

(G-7736)
MAGNA MIRRORS AMERICA INC
Also Called: Jfd North
3601 John F Donnelly Dr (49424-9338)
PHONE..................................616 738-0115
Jim Brodie, *Branch Mgr*
EMP: 400

SALES (corp-wide): 40.8B **Privately Held**
WEB: www.donnelly.com
SIC: 3231 Mirrored glass
HQ: Magna Mirrors Of America, Inc.
5085 Kraft Ave Se
Grand Rapids MI 49512
616 786-5120

(G-7737)
MAGNA MIRRORS AMERICA INC
3401 128th Ave (49424-9263)
PHONE..................................616 786-7000
Michael Baur, *Branch Mgr*
EMP: 116
SQ FT: 25,000
SALES (corp-wide): 40.8B **Privately Held**
WEB: www.donnelly.com
SIC: 5013 3231 Automotive servicing equipment; mirrors, truck & automobile: made from purchased glass
HQ: Magna Mirrors Of America, Inc.
5085 Kraft Ave Se
Grand Rapids MI 49512
616 786-5120

(G-7738)
MAGNA MIRRORS AMERICA INC
Also Called: Magna Sealing & Glass Systems
3501 John F Donnelly Dr (49424-9284)
PHONE..................................616 786-7772
Jong Kang, *Engineer*
Edward Scott, *Engineer*
Stacey Burroughs, *Branch Mgr*
EMP: 800
SALES (corp-wide): 40.8B **Privately Held**
WEB: www.donnelly.com
SIC: 3231 Mirrors, truck & automobile: made from purchased glass
HQ: Magna Mirrors Of America, Inc.
5085 Kraft Ave Se
Grand Rapids MI 49512
616 786-5120

(G-7739)
MARCUS AUTOMOTIVE LLC
257 W Lakewood Blvd # 20 (49424-1973)
PHONE..................................616 494-6400
Konrad Marcus, *CEO*
Jonathan Marcus, *President*
EMP: 5 **EST:** 2008
SQ FT: 1,500
SALES: 250K **Privately Held**
SIC: 3465 Moldings or trim, automobile: stamped metal

(G-7740)
MASLO FABRICATION LLC
155 Manufacturers Dr (49424-1894)
PHONE..................................616 298-7700
Jim England, *Mng Member*
EMP: 4
SALES: 330K **Privately Held**
SIC: 3441 4492 Fabricated structural metal; towing & tugboat service

(G-7741)
MB FLUID SERVICES LLC
11372 E Lakewood Blvd (49424-9605)
PHONE..................................616 392-7036
Mike Boes,
EMP: 10
SALES (est): 495.7K **Privately Held**
SIC: 2992 Lubricating oils & greases

(G-7742)
MECHANICAL TRANSPLANTER CO LLC
1150 Central Ave (49423-5230)
PHONE..................................616 396-8738
Steve Van Loo, *Mng Member*
Dan Timmer,
▲ **EMP:** 20 **EST:** 1953
SQ FT: 58,000
SALES: 4.7MM **Privately Held**
WEB: www.mechanicaltransplanter.com
SIC: 3523 Transplanters

(G-7743)
METAL FLOW CORPORATION
11694 James St (49424-8963)
PHONE..................................616 392-7976
Leslie Brown, *Ch of Bd*
Robert K Knittel, *President*

Kelly Springer, *COO*
Chuck Caesar, *Exec VP*
Chad Hindley, *Engineer*
▲ **EMP:** 230
SQ FT: 150,000
SALES: 70MM **Privately Held**
WEB: www.metalflow.com
SIC: 3469 Stamping metal for the trade

(G-7744)
METAL STANDARD CORP
286 Hedcor St (49423-9364)
PHONE..................................616 396-6356
Mike Wiersema, *CEO*
Brian Scalabrino, *Finance Dir*
Beth Lundquist, *HR Admin*
Lou Haller, *Maintence Staff*
▲ **EMP:** 90
SQ FT: 36,000
SALES (est): 18.3MM **Privately Held**
WEB: www.metalstd.com
SIC: 3499 Aerosol valves, metal

(G-7745)
METALUTION TOOL DIE
60 W 64th St (49423-9356)
PHONE..................................616 355-9700
Mike Finsky, *Principal*
EMP: 11 **EST:** 2010
SALES (est): 1.5MM **Privately Held**
SIC: 3599 Machine shop, jobbing & repair

(G-7746)
MHR INC
Also Called: Mix Head Repair
78 Veterans Dr (49423-7813)
PHONE..................................616 394-0191
Doug Breuker, *President*
Larry Dyke, *General Mgr*
Patricia Breuker, *Admin Sec*
EMP: 10
SQ FT: 6,400
SALES: 1.5MM **Privately Held**
WEB: www.mhr-inc.com
SIC: 7699 3569 5084 Industrial machinery & equipment repair; pumps & pumping equipment repair; assembly machines, non-metalworking; industrial machinery & equipment

(G-7747)
MICHIGAN WOOD FUELS LLC
1125 Industrial Ave (49423-5318)
PHONE..................................616 355-4955
Benjamin Rose, *CEO*
James Ackerson, *Plant Mgr*
Kevin Dumont, *Plant Mgr*
Randall Grinwis, *Safety Mgr*
Dalemarie James, *Administration*
EMP: 16
SALES (est): 2.5MM
SALES (corp-wide): 1.3MM **Privately Held**
SIC: 2499 Mulch or sawdust products, wood
PA: Northern Biomass Fuels Llc
341 W Belden Ave
Chicago IL 60614
773 697-7186

(G-7748)
MORRIS COMMUNICATIONS CO LLC
Also Called: Holland Sentinel
54 W 8th St (49423-3104)
PHONE..................................616 546-4200
Mike Hengel, *Manager*
EMP: 100 **Privately Held**
WEB: www.morris.com
SIC: 2721 2752 2711 Periodicals; commercial printing, lithographic; newspapers
HQ: Morris Communications Company Llc
725 Broad St
Augusta GA 30901
706 724-0851

(G-7749)
MOTUS HOLDINGS LLC (DH)
88 E 48th St (49423-9307)
PHONE..................................616 422-7557
Shannon White, *Mng Member*
EMP: 761

SALES (corp-wide): 573.9MM **Privately Held**
SIC: 6719 3465 Investment holding companies, except banks; body parts, automobile: stamped metal
HQ: Motus Us Holding B.V.
Prof. J.H. Bavinckiaan 2
Amstelveen
205 214-777

(G-7750)
MOTUS LLC (DH)
Also Called: Motus Integrated Technologies
88 E 48th St (49423-9307)
PHONE..................................616 422-7557
Garn Evans, *Vice Pres*
Stacy Spondike, *Vice Pres*
Doug Redder, *Plant Mgr*
Marco Gonzalez, *Opers Mgr*
Jennifer Wagner, *Purchasing*
▲ **EMP:** 180 **EST:** 2013
SALES (est): 165.5MM
SALES (corp-wide): 573.9MM **Privately Held**
SIC: 3465 Body parts, automobile: stamped metal
HQ: Motus Holdings Llc
88 E 48th St
Holland MI 49423
616 422-7557

(G-7751)
MULTI PACKAGING SOLUTIONS INC
13 W 4th St (49423-2815)
PHONE..................................616 355-6024
Gary Kremers, *Principal*
Jack Frost, *Site Mgr*
EMP: 20
SALES (corp-wide): 16.2B **Publicly Held**
SIC: 2759 Commercial printing
HQ: Multi Packaging Solutions, Inc.
885 3rd Ave Fl 28
New York NY 10022

(G-7752)
NATIONAL BULK EQUIPMENT INC (PA)
12838 Stainless Dr (49424-8218)
PHONE..................................616 399-2220
Joe Reed, *CEO*
Todd Reed, *President*
Dic K Dykema, *Vice Pres*
Ellen Kaines, *Vice Pres*
Will Bryan, *Project Mgr*
◆ **EMP:** 110 **EST:** 1976
SQ FT: 65,000
SALES: 11MM **Privately Held**
SIC: 3599 5084 Custom machinery; industrial machinery & equipment

(G-7753)
NELSON STEEL PRODUCTS INC
410 E 48th St (49423-8535)
PHONE..................................616 396-1515
Wallace Ryzenga Jr, *President*
Ross Ryzenga, *Plant Mgr*
Mark Simmons, *Opers Mgr*
Bob Hulst, *Purch Mgr*
Mark Ryzenga, *Manager*
EMP: 55 **EST:** 1963
SQ FT: 57,000
SALES (est): 11.5MM **Privately Held**
WEB: www.nelsonsteelproducts.com
SIC: 3444 7692 3469 3443 Sheet metalwork; welding repair; stamping metal for the trade; fabricated plate work (boiler shop)

(G-7754)
NEW 11 INC
Also Called: Power Manufacturing
1886 Russel Ct (49423-8749)
PHONE..................................616 494-9370
Todd Mulder, *Owner*
EMP: 25
SQ FT: 40,000
SALES (est): 5.1MM **Privately Held**
SIC: 3469 3317 Stamping metal for the trade; steel pipe & tubes

(G-7755)
NEW CNC ROUTERCOM INC
510 E 40th St (49423-5313)
PHONE..................................616 994-8844
Doug Huizenga, *Principal*

GEOGRAPHIC SECTION

Holland - Ottawa County (G-7785)

◆ EMP: 4
SALES (est): 420.2K **Privately Held**
SIC: 3569 Assembly machines, non-metalworking

(G-7756)
NEW HOLLAND BREWERY
690 Commerce Ct (49424-2913)
PHONE..................................616 298-7727
EMP: 15 EST: 2016
SALES (est): 2.3MM **Privately Held**
SIC: 2082 Malt beverages

(G-7757)
NEW HOLLAND BREWING CO LLC
684 Commerce Ct (49424-2913)
PHONE..................................616 355-2941
Shawna Cantu, *General Mgr*
Eli Harper, *General Mgr*
Mike Boysen, *Opers Staff*
Brad Kamphuis, *Opers Staff*
Patricia McGovern, *Buyer*
▲ EMP: 200
SALES (est): 46.8MM **Privately Held**
WEB: www.newhollandbrew.com
SIC: 2082 5813 5812 Beer (alcoholic beverage); drinking places; eating places

(G-7758)
NEW PRODUCT DEVELOPMENT LLC
785 Mary Ave (49424-1615)
PHONE..................................616 399-6253
Jack Hartman, *Owner*
EMP: 5
SALES (est): 314.6K **Privately Held**
SIC: 3089 Flower pots, plastic

(G-7759)
NORTEK AIR SOLUTIONS LLC
Also Called: Mammoth
4433 Holland Ave (49424-8279)
PHONE..................................616 738-7148
EMP: 60
SALES (corp-wide): 1B **Privately Held**
SIC: 3585 3567 3564 3561 Mfg Refrig/Heat Equip Indstl Furnace/Ovens Blowers/Fans Pumps/Pumping Equip
HQ: Nortek Air Solutions, Llc
4001 Valley Indus Blvd S
Shakopee MN 63368
952 358-6600

(G-7760)
NUVAR INC
895 E 40th St (49423-5397)
PHONE..................................616 394-5779
Mark Kuyper, *President*
Jerry Vande Wege, *Treasurer*
Jason Birky, *Human Res Mgr*
Ken Doss, *Admin Sec*
▲ EMP: 30
SQ FT: 40,000
SALES (est): 5.3MM **Privately Held**
WEB: www.nuvar.com
SIC: 2511 Wood household furniture

(G-7761)
NUWOOD COMPONENTS
759 E 48th St (49423-8562)
PHONE..................................616 395-1905
Bob Genovese, *Principal*
EMP: 3
SALES (est): 330.5K **Privately Held**
SIC: 2499 1751 Decorative wood & woodwork; carpentry work

(G-7762)
OCEANS SANDS SCUBA
780 Columbia Ave (49423-7047)
PHONE..................................616 396-0068
Charles Larsen, *Owner*
EMP: 3
SQ FT: 4,000
SALES (est): 150K **Privately Held**
WEB: www.oceanssandsscuba.com
SIC: 5941 3544 1629 Skin diving, scuba equipment & supplies; industrial molds; marine construction

(G-7763)
OMT VEYHL
4430 136th Ave Ste 3 (49424-8499)
PHONE..................................616 738-6688
David Guy, *Vice Pres*
Jim Roy, *Project Mgr*
Jordan Sloan, *Production*
Brian Kooshian, *Purch Agent*
Joel Knierim, *Engineer*
▲ EMP: 5
SALES (est): 785.4K **Privately Held**
SIC: 3499 Furniture parts, metal

(G-7764)
OMT-VEYHL USA CORPORATION
11511 James St (49424-8962)
PHONE..................................616 738-6688
Lars Reuter, *President*
Steve Ozaistowicz, *Production*
David Fouchea, *Purch Agent*
Dan Lerz, *Engineer*
Bruce Weiderman, *Controller*
▲ EMP: 35 EST: 2005
SALES (est): 10.5MM
SALES (corp-wide): 826.1K **Privately Held**
SIC: 2521 Wood office furniture
PA: Omt-Veyhl America Gmbh
Hertzstr. 1-3
Hoya 27318
425 181-60

(G-7765)
PANDA KING EXPRESS
520 Butternut Dr Ste 30 (49424-1587)
PHONE..................................616 796-3286
Yong Lin, *Principal*
EMP: 4
SALES (est): 213K **Privately Held**
SIC: 2741 Miscellaneous publishing

(G-7766)
PAR MOLDS INC
850 Maple Ave (49423-7199)
PHONE..................................616 396-5249
Alvin J Dozeman, *Ch of Bd*
Ken Dozeman, *President*
Roger Langworthy, *President*
Kendall M Dozeman, *Vice Pres*
EMP: 14
SQ FT: 10,500
SALES (est): 1.8MM **Privately Held**
SIC: 3544 Industrial molds; special dies & tools

(G-7767)
PARKWAY ELC COMMUNICATIONS LLC (PA)
Also Called: Westshore Testing
11952 James St Ste A (49424-9618)
PHONE..................................616 392-2788
Doug Mitchell, *COO*
Joshua Emmons, *Warehouse Mgr*
EMP: 78 EST: 1945
SQ FT: 20,000
SALES (est): 30MM **Privately Held**
WEB: www.parkwayelectric.com
SIC: 1731 3679 General electrical contractor; voice controls

(G-7768)
PEERLESS WASTE SOLUTIONS LLC
510 E 40th St (49423-5313)
PHONE..................................616 355-2800
Donald Pellegrini, *President*
David Geschwendt,
EDP PWS LLC,
Rodney Webb,
EMP: 7
SQ FT: 30,000
SALES (est): 3MM **Privately Held**
SIC: 3821 Sterilizers

(G-7769)
PERMALOC CORPORATION
Also Called: Permaloc Aluminum Edging
13505 Barry St (49424-9411)
PHONE..................................616 399-9600
Dan Zwier, *President*
Sally Zwier, *Vice Pres*
▼ EMP: 13
SQ FT: 14,000
SALES (est): 3.1MM **Privately Held**
WEB: www.permaloc.com
SIC: 3469 3353 Stamping metal for the trade; aluminum sheet, plate & foil

(G-7770)
PERRIGO COMPANY
3896 58th St (49423-9348)
PHONE..................................616 396-0941
EMP: 8 **Privately Held**
SIC: 2834 Pharmaceutical preparations
HQ: Perrigo Company
515 Eastern Ave
Allegan MI 49010
269 673-8451

(G-7771)
PETRA ELECTRONIC MFG INC
3440 Windquest Dr (49424-8069)
PHONE..................................616 877-1991
Jack Doornbos, *President*
Jamie Vanderhaar, *Accounting Mgr*
Mike Stebbins, *Sales Mgr*
EMP: 18
SALES (est): 3.6MM **Privately Held**
WEB: www.petraelec.com
SIC: 3672 Printed circuit boards

(G-7772)
PMS PRODUCTS INC
Also Called: Boeshield
76 Veterans Dr Ste 110 (49423-7823)
PHONE..................................616 355-6615
Peter M Schwarz, *President*
EMP: 3
SQ FT: 2,700
SALES (est): 280K **Privately Held**
WEB: www.boeshield.com
SIC: 2992 8748 Lubricating oils; business consulting

(G-7773)
PORTER CORP
Also Called: Poligon
4240 136th Ave (49424-8442)
PHONE..................................616 399-1963
Gary Vandyke, *President*
Mark Anderson, *Administration*
EMP: 92 EST: 1964
SQ FT: 112,000
SALES (est): 38.4MM **Privately Held**
WEB: www.poligon.com
SIC: 3448 Panels for prefabricated metal buildings; prefabricated metal buildings

(G-7774)
PRE-CUT PATTERNS INC
76 Veterans Dr Ste 130 (49423-7823)
PHONE..................................616 392-4415
Lori Corbat-Appeldoo, *President*
EMP: 5
SALES (est): 290.4K **Privately Held**
WEB: www.pre-cut.com
SIC: 3543 Industrial patterns

(G-7775)
PRIME WOOD PRODUCTS INC (PA)
Also Called: De Antigua
308 N River Ave (49424-2146)
PHONE..................................616 399-4700
Herman Raad, *President*
EMP: 9
SQ FT: 7,500
SALES (est): 871.9K **Privately Held**
WEB: www.primewoodproducts.com
SIC: 2431 5023 2511 2434 Interior & ornamental woodwork & trim; mirrors & pictures, framed & unframed; wood household furniture; wood kitchen cabinets

(G-7776)
PRINT HAUS
295 120th Ave Ste 10 (49424-2192)
PHONE..................................616 786-4030
William Maclean, *President*
EMP: 5
SALES (est): 705.1K **Privately Held**
WEB: www.printhaus.com
SIC: 2752 Commercial printing, offset

(G-7777)
PRINTERY INC
79 Clover St (49423-2941)
PHONE..................................616 396-4655
Robert Hydenberk, *President*
EMP: 35
SALES (est): 4.3MM
SALES (corp-wide): 16.2B **Publicly Held**
SIC: 2752 2791 2789 2759 Commercial printing, offset; typesetting; bookbinding & related work; commercial printing
HQ: Mps Holdco, Inc.
5800 W Grand River Ave
Lansing MI 48906

(G-7778)
PURPLE COW CREAMERY
234 Charles St (49424-2088)
PHONE..................................616 494-1933
EMP: 6 EST: 2013
SALES (est): 512.1K **Privately Held**
SIC: 2021 Creamery butter

(G-7779)
QUALITY MACHINE & AUTOMATION
184 Manufacturers Dr (49424-1893)
PHONE..................................616 399-4415
Scott Steggerda, *President*
EMP: 16
SQ FT: 12,000
SALES (est): 3.5MM **Privately Held**
WEB: www.qmautomation.com
SIC: 3599 Machine shop, jobbing & repair

(G-7780)
QUICK - BURN LLC
14518 Edmeer Dr (49424-6316)
PHONE..................................616 402-4874
Richard Campbell,
EMP: 3
SALES: 10K **Privately Held**
SIC: 3499 Fabricated metal products

(G-7781)
QUINCY STREET INC
13350 Quincy St (49424-9460)
PHONE..................................616 399-3330
Douglas M Miller, *CEO*
Philip A Holtrop, *CFO*
EMP: 165
SQ FT: 100,000
SALES (est): 26.5MM **Privately Held**
SIC: 2013 Prepared pork products from purchased pork
HQ: Indiana Packers Corporation
Hwy 421 S & Cr 100 N
Delphi IN 46923
765 564-3680

(G-7782)
R & R TOOL INC
192 E 48th St (49423-9307)
PHONE..................................616 394-4200
Derksen Ramsey, *Administration*
EMP: 3
SALES (est): 311.5K **Privately Held**
SIC: 3599 Machine shop, jobbing & repair

(G-7783)
R B MACHINE
5904 142nd Ave Lot 93 (49423-9394)
PHONE..................................616 928-8690
Ronald Weighmink, *Owner*
EMP: 3
SQ FT: 8,000
SALES (est): 160K **Privately Held**
SIC: 3599 3441 3559 Machine shop, jobbing & repair; fabricated structural metal; automotive related machinery

(G-7784)
R S L TOOL LLC
13417 New Hlland St Ste 2 (49424)
PHONE..................................616 786-2880
Robert Jacobs, *Mng Member*
Lauralee L Jacobs,
EMP: 5 EST: 1998
SQ FT: 1,800
SALES: 300K **Privately Held**
SIC: 3544 Special dies & tools

(G-7785)
RARE BIRD HOLDINGS LLC
849 Allen Dr (49423-4501)
PHONE..................................616 335-9463
Leon Devisser, *Principal*
EMP: 3
SALES (est): 73.3K **Privately Held**
SIC: 2082 Malt beverages

Holland - Ottawa County (G-7786) — GEOGRAPHIC SECTION

(G-7786)
REKMAKKER MILLWORK INC
6035 145th Ave (49423-8905)
PHONE..................616 546-3680
Randy Spykerman, *Principal*
EMP: 4
SALES (est): 533.1K **Privately Held**
SIC: 2431 Millwork

(G-7787)
REPCOLITE PAINTS INC (PA)
Also Called: Repcolite Decorating Center
473 W 17th St (49423-3495)
PHONE..................616 396-5213
Daniel Altena, *President*
David Altena, *Vice Pres*
Karen Michner, *Human Res Mgr*
Dave Helmholdt, *Cust Mgr*
EMP: 65 **EST:** 1948
SQ FT: 22,000
SALES (est): 12.4MM **Privately Held**
WEB: www.repcolite.com
SIC: 2851 5231 Paints & paint additives; paint; paint brushes, rollers, sprayers & other supplies

(G-7788)
RJ CORP
Also Called: Red Wing Bags
2127 112th Ave (49424-9626)
P.O. Box 2877 (49422-2877)
PHONE..................616 396-0552
Randy Lamer, *President*
Lisa Lamer, *Vice Pres*
▲ **EMP:** 14
SQ FT: 5,000
SALES: 850K **Privately Held**
WEB: www.rjcorporation.com
SIC: 2396 Printing & embossing on plastics fabric articles

(G-7789)
RJ OPERATING COMPANY
217 E 24th St Ste 102 (49423-4973)
PHONE..................616 392-7101
Robert L Sligh, *President*
David A Crouch,
John C Kennedy,
William P Peterson,
▲ **EMP:** 10
SQ FT: 7,500
SALES (est): 1.5MM **Privately Held**
SIC: 2521 2522 Desks, office: wood; cabinets, office: wood; filing cabinets (boxes), office: wood; bookcases, office: wood; office furniture, except wood

(G-7790)
ROD CHOMPER INC
4249 58th St (49423-9315)
PHONE..................616 392-9677
Wayne A Bouwman, *President*
Harold Tanis, *Sales Mgr*
▼ **EMP:** 11
SQ FT: 2,800
SALES (est): 1.9MM **Privately Held**
WEB: www.rodchomper.com
SIC: 3549 3547 3541 3496 Metalworking machinery; rolling mill machinery; machine tools, metal cutting type; miscellaneous fabricated wire products; blast furnaces & steel mills

(G-7791)
RUSSELLS TECHNICAL PDTS INC
1883 Russel Ct (49423-8749)
PHONE..................616 392-3161
Gary Molenaar, *President*
Bill Bench, *Vice Pres*
William J Bench, *Vice Pres*
Ray Resseguie, *Plant Mgr*
Dave Jolly, *Engineer*
EMP: 45
SQ FT: 31,000
SALES (est): 12.8MM **Privately Held**
WEB: www.russells-tech.com
SIC: 3829 Measuring & controlling devices

(G-7792)
RUTHERFORD & ASSOCIATES INC
1009 Productions Ct (49423-9122)
PHONE..................616 392-5000
Mike Rutherford, *President*
Sebastien Charroud, *Vice Pres*
Brian Rutherford, *Vice Pres*
Fred Dobrowitsky, *Opers Staff*
Paul Rutherford, *Treasurer*
EMP: 25
SALES (est): 5.6MM **Privately Held**
WEB: www.eostar.com
SIC: 3695 5734 5961 7372 Computer software tape & disks: blank, rigid & floppy; software, business & non-game; software, computer games; computer software, mail order; prepackaged software

(G-7793)
S 2 YACHTS INC (PA)
Also Called: Tiara Yachts
725 E 40th St (49423-5392)
PHONE..................616 392-7163
Leon R Slikkers, *Ch of Bd*
Robert L Slikkers, *President*
David A Slikkers, *COO*
Dave Dejonge, *CFO*
Tom Van, *Info Tech Mgr*
▼ **EMP:** 600 **EST:** 1974
SQ FT: 450,000
SALES: 4.7MM **Privately Held**
WEB: www.s2yachts.com
SIC: 3732 Boats, fiberglass: building & repairing; motorboats, inboard or outboard: building & repairing

(G-7794)
SAF-HOLLAND INC
467 Ottawa Ave (49423-3983)
PHONE..................616 396-6501
Lance Gage, *Engineer*
Kevin Kent, *Human Res Mgr*
Judy Champ, *HR Admin*
Richard Muzzy, *Branch Mgr*
Brian Veldhof, *Admin Asst*
EMP: 10
SALES (corp-wide): 177.9M **Privately Held**
SIC: 3714 3713 Motor vehicle parts & accessories; truck & bus bodies
HQ: Saf-Holland, Inc.
   1950 Industrial Blvd
   Muskegon MI 49442
   231 773-3271

(G-7795)
SAF-HOLLAND INC
430 W 18th St (49423-3904)
PHONE..................616 396-6501
Richard Muzzy, *CEO*
Samuel Martin, *Branch Mgr*
Bill Kindt, *Executive*
EMP: 145
SALES (corp-wide): 177.9M **Privately Held**
SIC: 3714 3715 Motor vehicle parts & accessories; trailer bodies
HQ: Saf-Holland, Inc.
   1950 Industrial Blvd
   Muskegon MI 49442
   231 773-3271

(G-7796)
SANDCASTLE FOR KIDS INC
Also Called: Sand Castle For Kids, The
2 E 8th St (49423-3502)
PHONE..................616 396-5955
Ellie Bremer, *President*
W Michael Bremer, *Vice Pres*
EMP: 10
SQ FT: 2,000
SALES (est): 873.5K **Privately Held**
SIC: 5945 5947 5641 3612 Toys & games; gift shop; children's wear; toy transformers

(G-7797)
SEASONED HOME LLC
43 E 8th St Ste 100 (49423-3530)
PHONE..................616 392-8350
Jodeea Lacombe, *CEO*
Cristina Bensinger, *Co-Owner*
EMP: 7
SALES (est): 970.8K **Privately Held**
SIC: 3469 Household cooking & kitchen utensils, metal

(G-7798)
SEBRIGHT MACHINING INC
613 Commerce Ct (49424-2924)
PHONE..................616 399-0445
Gerald E Sebright, *President*
Carolyn E Sebright, *Corp Secy*
EMP: 11
SQ FT: 6,000
SALES (est): 1.6MM **Privately Held**
SIC: 3599 Custom machinery; machine shop, jobbing & repair

(G-7799)
SEKISUI POLYMR INNOVATIONS LLC
1305 Lincoln Ave (49423-9381)
PHONE..................616 392-9004
Ronn Cort, *President*
EMP: 100 **Privately Held**
SIC: 2821 Plastics materials & resins
HQ: Sekisui Polymer Innovations, Llc
   6685 Lowe St
   Bloomsburg PA 17815
   570 387-6997

(G-7800)
SHORELINE CONTAINER INC (PA)
Also Called: Shoreline Container and Packg
4450 136th Ave (49424-9452)
P.O. Box 1993 (49422-1993)
PHONE..................616 399-2088
Bruce Patterson, *President*
Bob Zuker, *VP Opers*
Jeff Mooney, *Prdtn Mgr*
Rick Vandyke, *Purch Mgr*
Rob Forrest, *Engineer*
EMP: 163 **EST:** 1963
SQ FT: 203,000
SALES (est): 62MM **Privately Held**
WEB: www.shorelinecontainer.com
SIC: 2653 2671 Boxes, corrugated: made from purchased materials; partitions, corrugated: made from purchased materials; packaging paper & plastics film, coated & laminated

(G-7801)
SHORELINE CREATIONS LTD (PA)
Also Called: Group Tour Magazines
2465 112th Ave (49424-9657)
PHONE..................616 393-2077
Carl Wassink, *President*
Ruth Wassink, *Exec VP*
EMP: 23
SQ FT: 7,500
SALES (est): 4.5MM **Privately Held**
WEB: www.grouptour.com
SIC: 2721 2741 Magazines: publishing only, not printed on site; guides: publishing only, not printed on site

(G-7802)
SHORELINE MANUFACTURING LLC
155 Manufacturers Dr (49424-1894)
PHONE..................616 834-1503
EMP: 3 **EST:** 2014
SALES (est): 255.1K **Privately Held**
SIC: 3999 Manufacturing industries

(G-7803)
SHOULDER INNOVATIONS INC
13827 Port Sheldon St (49424-9413)
PHONE..................616 294-1029
Matthew Ahearn, *President*
Matt Ahearn, *COO*
Jeff Ondrla, *Exec VP*
EMP: 4
SALES (est): 240.3K **Privately Held**
SIC: 3841 Surgical & medical instruments

(G-7804)
SIGVARIS INC
13055 Riley St Ste 30 (49424-7240)
PHONE..................616 741-4281
Dan Karadsheh, *Manager*
EMP: 25
SALES (corp-wide): 202.8MM **Privately Held**
SIC: 3842 Surgical appliances & supplies
HQ: Sigvaris Inc
   1119 Highway 74 S
   Peachtree City GA 30269
   770 631-1778

(G-7805)
SILENT OBSERVER
89 W 8th St (49423-3103)
PHONE..................616 392-4443
EMP: 3
SALES (est): 108.9K **Privately Held**
SIC: 2711 Newspapers-Publishing/Printing

(G-7806)
SLOAN TRANSPORTATION PDTS INC
534 E 48th St (49423-9502)
PHONE..................616 395-5600
Thomas Bronz, *President*
▲ **EMP:** 70
SQ FT: 105,000
SALES (est): 18.5MM **Privately Held**
WEB: www.bldproducts.com
SIC: 3625 3561 3491 3714 Relays & industrial controls; pumps & pumping equipment; industrial valves; fuel systems & parts, motor vehicle

(G-7807)
SMALL SCALE DEFENSE
2779 132nd Ave (49424-9205)
P.O. Box 64, Michigamme (49861-0064)
PHONE..................616 238-2671
Thomas Springer, *Principal*
EMP: 3
SALES (est): 153.8K **Privately Held**
SIC: 3812 Defense systems & equipment

(G-7808)
SMW TOOLING INC
Also Called: S M W
11781 Greenway Dr (49424-8654)
PHONE..................616 355-9822
Steve Zeerip, *President*
Elizabeth Zeerip, *Treasurer*
EMP: 10
SQ FT: 12,000
SALES (est): 1.7MM **Privately Held**
SIC: 3541 Milling machines

(G-7809)
SOLAR STREET LIGHTS USA LLC
169 Manufacturers Dr # 1 (49424-1904)
PHONE..................616 399-6166
Craig Brumels,
◆ **EMP:** 6
SALES (est): 1.1MM **Privately Held**
SIC: 3829 Solarimeters

(G-7810)
SOLID LOGIC LLC
Also Called: Smooth Logics
3455 John F Donnelly Dr (49424-9207)
PHONE..................616 738-8922
Rj Boersema, *Software Engr*
Benjamin Fogg,
EMP: 13 **EST:** 2010
SALES (est): 240.4K **Privately Held**
SIC: 7372 Business oriented computer software

(G-7811)
SPINDANCE INC
150 E 8th St (49423-3504)
PHONE..................616 355-7000
Kevin Virta, *President*
Eric Smith, *Vice Pres*
Tom Miller, *Vice Pres*
Keith Pustover, *VP Opers*
Brendan Rabb, *Engineer*
EMP: 9 **EST:** 2000
SALES (est): 126.5K **Privately Held**
SIC: 5045 7372 Computer software; application computer software

(G-7812)
SPINE ALIGN INC
Also Called: Holland Bedding
741 Chicago Dr (49423-3003)
P.O. Box 2723 (49422-2723)
PHONE..................616 395-5407
Thomas Buis, *President*
EMP: 3
SQ FT: 12,000

▲ = Import ▼ = Export ◆ = Import/Export

GEOGRAPHIC SECTION
Holland - Ottawa County (G-7836)

SALES (est): 375.1K **Privately Held**
WEB: www.airplanekit.com
SIC: 2515 Mattresses & foundations

(G-7813)
STARBUCK MACHINING INC
13413 New Holland St (49424-9407)
PHONE..................................616 399-9720
Richard Starbuck, *President*
Amy Starbuck, *Purch Mgr*
Susan Starbuck, *Office Mgr*
EMP: 14
SQ FT: 12,000
SALES (est): 2.8MM **Privately Held**
WEB: www.starbuckmachining.com
SIC: 3599 Ties, form: metal; machine shop, jobbing & repair

(G-7814)
STEKETEE-VAN HUIS INC
Also Called: MPS Holland
13 W 4th St (49423-2886)
PHONE..................................616 392-2326
Marc Shore, *CEO*
Theodore Etheridge, *President*
Dennis Kaltman, *President*
Gary Kremers, *COO*
William Ockerland, *CFO*
EMP: 140
SQ FT: 69,000
SALES (est): 27.2MM
SALES (corp-wide): 16.2B **Publicly Held**
WEB: www.svhgroup.com
SIC: 2657 2752 Folding paperboard boxes; commercial printing, offset
HQ: Mps Holdco, Inc.
    5800 W Grand River Ave
    Lansing MI 48906

(G-7815)
STM MFG INC (PA)
Also Called: S T M
494 E 64th St (49423-9324)
PHONE..................................616 392-4656
Roger Blauwkamp, *President*
Jacquelyn Blauwkamp, *Corp Secy*
Brent Vorac, *COO*
Kevin Dannenberg, *Vice Pres*
Jeff Lampen, *Project Mgr*
EMP: 60 **EST:** 1977
SQ FT: 22,000
SALES (est): 14.8MM **Privately Held**
WEB: www.stmtooling.com
SIC: 3544 Special dies & tools

(G-7816)
STOW COMPANY (PA)
130 Central Ave Ste 400 (49423-2852)
PHONE..................................616 399-3311
Frank Newman, *President*
Elisabeth Devos, *Chairman*
Richard Devos, *Chairman*
Scott Sliva, *Vice Pres*
Barry Williams, *Opers Staff*
▲ EMP: 200 **EST:** 1984
SQ FT: 186,000
SALES (est): 39.9MM **Privately Held**
WEB: www.windquestco.com
SIC: 2511 Wood household furniture

(G-7817)
STRIK-WSTFEN-DYNARAD FRNC CORP (DH)
Also Called: Striko Dynarad
301 Hoover Blvd Ste 200 (49423-3776)
PHONE..................................616 355-2327
Martin Reeves, *Opers Staff*
David Kozman, *Sales Staff*
▲ EMP: 6
SQ FT: 25,000
SALES (est): 4MM **Privately Held**
SIC: 3567 8742 Metal melting furnaces, industrial: electric; automation & robotics consultant
HQ: Strikowestofen Gmbh
    Hohe Str. 14
    Gummersbach 51643
    226 170-910

(G-7818)
STUS WELDING & FABRICATION
4249 58th St (49423-9315)
PHONE..................................616 392-8459
Wayne Bouwman, *President*
Phyllis Bouwman, *President*
EMP: 8

SQ FT: 18,750
SALES: 1MM **Privately Held**
SIC: 7692 3599 3446 3469 Welding repair; machine shop, jobbing & repair; balconies, metal; metal stampings; sheet metalwork

(G-7819)
SUBASSEMBLY PLUS INC
11359 James St (49424-8627)
PHONE..................................616 395-2075
Rick Zuverink, *President*
David Beckman, *Corp Secy*
EMP: 45
SALES (est): 7.6MM **Privately Held**
WEB: www.subassemblyplus.com
SIC: 2531 Assembly hall furniture

(G-7820)
SUN RAY SIGN GROUP INC
376 Roost Ave (49424-2032)
PHONE..................................616 392-2824
Harvey Streur, *President*
Scott Tardiff, *Vice Pres*
EMP: 4 **EST:** 1973
SQ FT: 6,000
SALES (est): 275K **Privately Held**
WEB: www.itworld.com
SIC: 3993 7389 Electric signs; sign painting & lettering shop

(G-7821)
SUPERIOR CUTTING SERVICE INC
4740 136th Ave (49424-8413)
PHONE..................................616 796-0114
Fax: 616 399-9631
EMP: 14
SQ FT: 12,000
SALES (est): 3MM **Privately Held**
SIC: 3599 Mfg Industrial Machinery

(G-7822)
SURE-LOC ALUMINUM EDGING INC
Also Called: Sure -Loc Edging-Wolverine Tls
310 E 64th St (49423-8731)
PHONE..................................616 392-3209
Roger Blauwkamp, *Principal*
Kevin Dannenberg, *Vice Pres*
Tammy Stegink, *Purch Mgr*
◆ EMP: 7
SALES (est): 1.6MM
SALES (corp-wide): 14.8MM **Privately Held**
WEB: www.surelocedging.com
SIC: 3524 0781 3423 Edgers, lawn; landscape planning services; shovels, spades (hand tools)
PA: Stm Mfg., Inc.
    494 E 64th St
    Holland MI 49423
    616 392-4656

(G-7823)
TANIS TECHNOLOGIES LLC
645 Commerce Ct Ste 10 (49424-2934)
PHONE..................................616 796-2712
Richard Tanis,
Jamie Tanis,
EMP: 6
SQ FT: 10,000
SALES (est): 1MM **Privately Held**
SIC: 3564 Air purification equipment; filters, air: furnaces, air conditioning equipment, etc.

(G-7824)
TECHNO-COAT INC
861 E 40th St (49423-5397)
PHONE..................................616 396-6446
Ike Vande Wege, *President*
Lois Ramaker, *Vice Pres*
Michael Wiersema, *Vice Pres*
Scott Eisen, *Engineer*
Norma V Wege, *Financial Exec*
EMP: 135
SQ FT: 90,000
SALES (est): 21.7MM **Privately Held**
WEB: www.technocoat.com
SIC: 3479 Coating of metals & formed products

(G-7825)
TED VOSS & SONS INC
Also Called: Voss T & Sons Septic Tanks
995 Lincoln Ave (49425-5326)
PHONE..................................616 396-8344
David A Voss, *President*
Ronald J Voss, *Vice Pres*
EMP: 4 **EST:** 1948
SQ FT: 1,200
SALES (est): 579K **Privately Held**
SIC: 3272 1794 Septic tanks, concrete; excavation & grading, building construction

(G-7826)
TENNANT COMMERCIAL
12875 Ransom St (49424-9273)
PHONE..................................616 994-4000
Debby Davis, *Principal*
▼ EMP: 270 **EST:** 2009
SQ FT: 250,000
SALES (est): 50.5MM
SALES (corp-wide): 1.1B **Publicly Held**
WEB: www.tennantco.com
SIC: 3589 2842 Commercial cleaning equipment; specialty cleaning, polishes & sanitation goods
PA: Tennant Company
    701 Lilac Dr N
    Minneapolis MN 55422
    763 540-1200

(G-7827)
TENNANT COMPANY
12875 Ransom St (49424-9273)
PHONE..................................616 994-4000
Steve Westveld, *General Mgr*
Dave Horn, *Engineer*
Chris Smith, *Engineer*
Lynn Klug, *Accounts Mgr*
Tim Gardner, *Manager*
EMP: 8
SALES (corp-wide): 1.1B **Publicly Held**
SIC: 3589 Commercial cleaning equipment
PA: Tennant Company
    701 Lilac Dr N
    Minneapolis MN 55422
    763 540-1200

(G-7828)
TERRYS PRECAST PRODUCTS INC
4248 58th St (49423-9315)
PHONE..................................616 396-7042
Terry Bouwman, *President*
Chad Bouwman, *Vice Pres*
Ryan Bouwman, *Admin Sec*
EMP: 3
SQ FT: 17,500
SALES: 350K **Privately Held**
WEB: www.terrys-precast.com
SIC: 3272 Concrete products, precast

(G-7829)
THERMOTRON INDUSTRIES INC
875 Brooks Ave (49423-5338)
PHONE..................................616 928-9044
EMP: 35
SALES (corp-wide): 146.4MM **Privately Held**
SIC: 3599 Machine & other job shop work
HQ: Thermotron Industries, Inc.
    291 Kollen Park Dr
    Holland MI 49423

(G-7830)
THERMOTRON INDUSTRIES INC (HQ)
291 Kollen Park Dr (49423-3487)
PHONE..................................616 392-1491
Ron Lampen, *President*
Brian Nahey, *Principal*
Alan Hall, *Regional Mgr*
Lynn Ternan, *Vice Pres*
Gary Keelean, *Facilities Mgr*
▼ EMP: 340
SALES (est): 93.6MM
SALES (corp-wide): 146.4MM **Privately Held**
WEB: www.thermotron.com
SIC: 3829 Measuring & controlling devices
PA: Venturedyne, Ltd.
    600 College Ave
    Pewaukee WI 53072
    262 691-9900

(G-7831)
TOTAL INNOVATIVE MFG LLC
13395 Tyler St (49424-9421)
PHONE..................................616 399-9903
Kenneth Assink, *Owner*
EMP: 26
SQ FT: 48,000
SALES: 3.5MM **Privately Held**
SIC: 2522 Panel systems & partitions, office: except wood

(G-7832)
TPK AMERICA LLC
Also Called: TOUCH REVOLUTION
215 Central Ave Ste 200 (49423-3237)
PHONE..................................616 786-5300
Gene Halfy, *Mng Member*
▲ EMP: 12 **EST:** 2010
SQ FT: 1,600
SALES: 65MM **Privately Held**
SIC: 3669 Visual communication systems
HQ: Tpk U.S.A., Llc
    999 Baker Way Ste 120
    San Mateo CA 94404

(G-7833)
TRAMEC SLOAN LLC (HQ)
Also Called: Sloan Transportation Products
534 E 48th St (49423-9502)
PHONE..................................616 395-5600
Thomas Bronz, *President*
▲ EMP: 70
SALES (est): 24.8MM
SALES (corp-wide): 110MM **Privately Held**
SIC: 3714 3625 3561 Motor vehicle parts & accessories; relays & industrial controls; pumps & pumping equipment
PA: Tramec, L.L.C.
    30 Davis St
    Iola KS 66749
    620 365-6977

(G-7834)
TRANS-MATIC MFG CO INC (PA)
300 E 48th St (49423-5391)
PHONE..................................616 820-2500
Patrick A Thompson, *CEO*
Patrick J Thompson, *President*
Mary Wiley, *Production*
Dan Dekker, *Senior Buyer*
Dennis Wynalda, *Engineer*
▲ EMP: 225
SQ FT: 150,000
SALES (est): 50.8MM **Privately Held**
WEB: www.transmatic.com
SIC: 3465 3469 Automotive stampings; stamping metal for the trade

(G-7835)
TRANS-MATIC MFG CO INC
Transmatic Mfg
471 E 40th St (49423-5344)
PHONE..................................616 820-2541
Mark Parker, *Manager*
EMP: 3
SALES (corp-wide): 50.8MM **Privately Held**
SIC: 3469 Metal stampings
PA: Trans-Matic Mfg Co Incorporated
    300 E 48th St
    Holland MI 49423
    616 820-2500

(G-7836)
TRENDWAY CORPORATION (HQ)
13467 Quincy St (49424-9484)
P.O. Box 9016 (49422-9016)
PHONE..................................616 399-3900
John Fellowes, *President*
Ashley Bundy, *Mfg Staff*
Bryant Ruch, *Manager*
Jim Ford, *Director*
Sara Lee, *Analyst*
◆ EMP: 310 **EST:** 1968
SQ FT: 650,000

Holland - Ottawa County (G-7837)

SALES (est): 57.4MM
SALES (corp-wide): 582MM **Privately Held**
WEB: www.trendway.com
SIC: **2522** 2521 Panel systems & partitions, office: except wood; desks, office: except wood; filing boxes, cabinets & cases: except wood; cabinets, office: except wood; panel systems & partitions (free-standing), office: wood; desks, office: wood; filing cabinets (boxes), office: wood; cabinets, office: wood
PA: Fellowes, Inc.
  1789 Norwood Ave
  Itasca IL 60143
  630 893-1600

(G-7837)
TRENDWAY SVCS ORGANIZATION LLC
Also Called: Catapult Business Services
13467 Quincy St (49424-9460)
PHONE..................................616 994-5327
Eva Meekhof, *CEO*
Benjamin Lampen, *Controller*
EMP: 4
SALES (est): 155.8K **Privately Held**
SIC: **2522** Office furniture, except wood

(G-7838)
TRI TECH TOOLING INC
11615 Greenway Dr (49424-7701)
P.O. Box 1137 (49422-1137)
PHONE..................................616 396-6000
Michael Bouma, *President*
Chris Schaefer, *Vice Pres*
Harwyn Berens, *Treasurer*
▲ EMP: 10
SALES (est): 1.2MM **Privately Held**
WEB: www.tritechtooling.com
SIC: **3544** Special dies & tools

(G-7839)
TRIANGLE PRODUCT DISTRIBUTORS
5750 Lakeshore Dr (49424-1021)
PHONE..................................970 609-9001
Charles Hozer, *CEO*
Charles L Hozer II, *President*
◆ EMP: 17 EST: 1975
SQ FT: 4,800
SALES (est): 2.5MM **Privately Held**
SIC: **3577** 5074 5045 Computer peripheral equipment; heating equipment & panels, solar; computer software

(G-7840)
TRIC TOOL LTD
3760 John F Donnelly Dr (49424-7278)
PHONE..................................616 395-1530
Thomas Jackson, *President*
James Carden, *Vice Pres*
Jim Carden, *Vice Pres*
Brian Vandragt, *Project Engr*
EMP: 28
SQ FT: 20,000
SALES (est): 5.8MM **Privately Held**
WEB: www.trictool.com
SIC: **3544** 3599 Special dies & tools; machine shop, jobbing & repair

(G-7841)
TRIGON STEEL COMPONENTS INC
1448 Lincoln Ave (49423-9389)
PHONE..................................616 834-0506
Isaac Koert, *President*
Cortney Sluiter, *Vice Pres*
Corey Bakker, *Prdtn Mgr*
Alec Bobko, *Manager*
EMP: 4
SQ FT: 8,200
SALES (est): 684.5K **Privately Held**
SIC: **3448** Prefabricated metal components

(G-7842)
UNITED MANUFACTURING INC
Also Called: Umi
4150 Sunnyside Dr (49424-8716)
PHONE..................................616 738-8888
Randall Bezile, *President*
Mark Chase, *Vice Pres*
Keith Fox, *Vice Pres*
Bob Hanson, *Vice Pres*
EMP: 35
SQ FT: 30,000
SALES (est): 6.3MM **Privately Held**
WEB: www.unitedmfginc.com
SIC: **3469** Metal stampings

(G-7843)
VARATECH INC
1141 Ambertrace Ln Apt 8 (49424-5335)
PHONE..................................616 393-6408
Robert Gardner Jr, *President*
Gary Crispin, *CFO*
Hwei-Min Lu, *CTO*
EMP: 10
SALES: 850K **Privately Held**
WEB: www.varatech.com
SIC: **8711** 7373 7372 Consulting engineer; systems software development services; prepackaged software

(G-7844)
VELDHEER TULIP GARDEN INC
Also Called: De Klomp Wden Shoe Delft Fctry
12755 Quincy St (49424-8285)
PHONE..................................616 399-1900
Vernon Veldheer, *CEO*
James Veldheer, *President*
▲ EMP: 70
SALES (est): 3.6MM **Privately Held**
WEB: www.veldheer.com
SIC: **0181** 3269 2499 5191 Bulbs, growing of; flowers: grown under cover (e.g. greenhouse production); art & ornamental ware, pottery; shoe & boot products, wood; flower & field bulbs; flowers, fresh; men's footwear, except athletic

(G-7845)
VENNTIS TECHNOLOGIES LLC
1261 S Waverly Rd (49423-9332)
PHONE..................................616 395-8254
Erich Roehl, *Partner*
Robert Bos, *Engineer*
David Caldwell,
Katherine Boeve, *Administration*
EMP: 16
SALES (est): 2.5MM **Privately Held**
SIC: **3679** 8711 Electronic circuits; consulting engineer

(G-7846)
VENTUREDYNE LTD
Thermotron Industries
291 Kollen Park Dr (49423-3460)
PHONE..................................616 392-1491
Leon Kragt, *Engineer*
Daniel O'Keefe, *Branch Mgr*
Mark Lamers, *Info Tech Mgr*
EMP: 37
SALES (corp-wide): 146.4MM **Privately Held**
WEB: www.venturedyne.com
SIC: **3569** 3826 Testing chambers for altitude, temperature, ordnance, power; environmental testing equipment
PA: Venturedyne, Ltd.
  600 College Ave
  Pewaukee WI 53072
  262 691-9900

(G-7847)
VENTUREDYNE LTD
Thermotron Industries
836 Brooks Ave (49423-5339)
PHONE..................................616 392-6550
Dan O'Keefe, *Manager*
John Harbison, *Analyst*
EMP: 500
SALES (corp-wide): 146.4MM **Privately Held**
SIC: **3826** Environmental testing equipment
PA: Venturedyne, Ltd.
  600 College Ave
  Pewaukee WI 53072
  262 691-9900

(G-7848)
VISION DESIGNS INC
774 Columbia Ave (49423-7047)
PHONE..................................616 994-7054
Karen Bruursema, *President*
EMP: 3
SQ FT: 1,200
SALES (est): 198.1K **Privately Held**
SIC: **7336** 2759 Commercial art & graphic design; screen printing

(G-7849)
VIVATAR INC
935 E 40th St (49423-5384)
PHONE..................................616 928-0750
Brian Schelstraete, *CEO*
John Mugridge, *CFO*
EMP: 26
SALES (est): 6.4MM **Privately Held**
SIC: **3089** Injection molding of plastics

(G-7850)
VOLTA POWER SYSTEMS LLC
12550 Superior Ct 40 (49424-8287)
PHONE..................................616 226-4224
Jack Johnson, *COO*
Todd Ritter,
Randy Vanklompenburg,
EMP: 3 EST: 2014
SALES (est): 187.5K **Privately Held**
SIC: **3825** 8748 Integrating electricity meters; energy conservation consultant

(G-7851)
W-LOK CORPORATION
861 Productions Pl (49423-9168)
PHONE..................................616 355-4015
Rudell Broekhuis, *President*
Waterson Chen, *Vice Pres*
Nana Wang, *Treasurer*
Landon McDonald, *Maintence Staff*
EMP: 4 EST: 1998
SALES (est): 145.2K **Privately Held**
SIC: **3429** Keys, locks & related hardware

(G-7852)
WALTERS SEED CO LLC
Also Called: Promogarden.com
65 Veterans Dr (49423-7813)
PHONE..................................616 355-7333
Kenneth Slager, *Partner*
Kate Abrahams, *Sales Staff*
Sandra Slager,
EMP: 10
SALES: 999.9K **Privately Held**
WEB: www.walters-seed.com
SIC: **5261** 2679 Nursery stock, seeds & bulbs; paper products, converted

(G-7853)
WELCHDRY INC
4270 Sunnyside Dr (49424-8653)
PHONE..................................616 399-2711
Dave Vander Heide, *President*
Sean Schaap, *Vice Pres*
◆ EMP: 16
SQ FT: 60,000
SALES (est): 2.3MM **Privately Held**
WEB: www.welchlaboratories.com
SIC: **2834** Powders, pharmaceutical

(G-7854)
WEST MICHIGAN ALPACAS
15747 Greenly St (49424-5947)
PHONE..................................616 990-0556
Rhonda Faber, *Principal*
EMP: 3
SALES (est): 186.4K **Privately Held**
SIC: **2231** Alpacas, mohair: woven

(G-7855)
WEST MICHIGAN CANVAS COMPANY
Also Called: West Mich Awning
11041 Paw Paw Dr (49424-8992)
PHONE..................................616 355-7855
Karen De Jonge, *President*
Jay Win, *President*
EMP: 9
SALES (est): 1MM **Privately Held**
SIC: **2221** Manmade & synthetic broadwoven fabrics; vinal broadwoven fabrics

(G-7856)
WEST MICHIGAN SPLINE INC
156 Manufacturers Dr (49424-1893)
PHONE..................................616 399-4078
Gary R Hill, *President*
Greg Hill, *Engineer*
Marie Hill, *Treasurer*
▲ EMP: 12
SQ FT: 11,750
SALES (est): 1.3MM **Privately Held**
WEB: www.westmichiganspline.com
SIC: **3542** Spline rolling machines

(G-7857)
WESTERN MICHIGAN PLASTICS
5745 143rd Ave (49423-8746)
PHONE..................................616 394-9269
Gregory Cook, *President*
Tom O'Neal, *Vice Pres*
▲ EMP: 12
SALES (est): 2.2MM **Privately Held**
SIC: **3089** Injection molding of plastics

(G-7858)
WESTERN PEGASUS INC (PA)
728 E 8th St Ste 3 (49423-3080)
PHONE..................................616 393-9580
Heather Wincel, *President*
James Mc Gurk, *Owner*
Karen Johnson, *Accountant*
Katie Hoye, *Executive Asst*
EMP: 6
SQ FT: 2,000
SALES (est): 7.1MM **Privately Held**
WEB: www.westpeg.com
SIC: **3545** Gauges (machine tool accessories)

(G-7859)
WINDOW DESIGNS INC (PA)
Also Called: Great Lakes Draperies
753 Lincoln Ave (49423-5482)
PHONE..................................616 396-5295
Dorothy Willemstyn, *President*
Chet Willemstyn Sr, *Corp Secy*
Chet Willemstyn Jr, *Vice Pres*
EMP: 10
SQ FT: 7,000
SALES (est): 1.4MM **Privately Held**
SIC: **5714** 7389 2211 2221 Draperies; design services; draperies & drapery fabrics, cotton; draperies & drapery fabrics, manmade fiber & silk

(G-7860)
WOODEN RUNABOUT CO
4261 58th St (49423-9315)
PHONE..................................616 396-7248
Mike Teusink, *Owner*
EMP: 5
SALES (est): 385.4K **Privately Held**
SIC: **3732** Boat building & repairing

(G-7861)
WORDEN GROUP LLC
199 E 17th St (49423-4385)
PHONE..................................616 392-1848
James Weaver, *President*
Kenneth Filippini, *Principal*
EMP: 99 EST: 2012
SQ FT: 25,000
SALES (est): 9MM **Privately Held**
SIC: **2531** Library furniture

(G-7862)
WORLD CLASS PROTOTYPES INC
400 Center St (49423-3717)
PHONE..................................616 355-0200
James Leonard, *President*
Susan Leonard, *Vice Pres*
Gary Leonard, *Teacher*
EMP: 10
SQ FT: 2,000
SALES (est): 1MM **Privately Held**
WEB: www.worldclassprototypes.com
SIC: **3089** Injection molding of plastics

(G-7863)
YANFENG US AUTOMOTIVE
Also Called: Holland Pmsc
1776 Airport Park Ct (49423-9370)
PHONE..................................616 392-5151
Michael Devine, *Plant Mgr*
EMP: 30
SALES (corp-wide): 55MM **Privately Held**
SIC: **3714** Motor vehicle parts & accessories
HQ: Yanfeng Us Automotive Interior Systems I Llc
  41935 W 12 Mile Rd
  Novi MI 48377
  248 319-7333

GEOGRAPHIC SECTION

Holly - Oakland County (G-7889)

(G-7864)
YANFENG US AUTOMOTIVE
915 E 32nd St (49423-9120)
PHONE..................................616 392-5151
Jeffrey Stout, *Engineer*
Dan White, *Branch Mgr*
EMP: 94
SALES (corp-wide): 55MM **Privately Held**
SIC: 3714 5531 Motor vehicle parts & accessories; automotive parts
HQ: Yanfeng Us Automotive Interior Systems I Llc
41935 W 12 Mile Rd
Novi MI 48377
248 319-7333

(G-7865)
YANFENG US AUTOMOTIVE
Also Called: Yanfeng Auto Intr Systems
701 S Waverly Rd (49423-9121)
PHONE..................................616 394-1199
Chris Prestridge, *Controller*
Joseph Derrico, *Manager*
Michael Silverman, *Manager*
Scott Postma, *Director*
Michael Reider, *Maintence Staff*
EMP: 31
SALES (corp-wide): 55MM **Privately Held**
SIC: 2531 Seats, automobile
HQ: Yanfeng Us Automotive Interior Systems I Llc
41935 W 12 Mile Rd
Novi MI 48377
248 319-7333

(G-7866)
YANFENG US AUTOMOTIVE
Yanfeng Virtual City
915 32nd St Tech Ctr (49423)
PHONE..................................616 394-1523
Court Manns, *Branch Mgr*
EMP: 4
SALES (corp-wide): 55MM **Privately Held**
SIC: 8741 2531 Management services; seats, automobile
HQ: Yanfeng Us Automotive Interior Systems I Llc
41935 W 12 Mile Rd
Novi MI 48377
248 319-7333

(G-7867)
YOST VISES LLC
388 W 24th St (49423-4037)
PHONE..................................616 396-2063
Fred J Nelis Jr, *President*
Kevin Nelis, *Vice Pres*
Ryan Nelis, *Sales Staff*
Patrick Nelis, *Admin Sec*
▲ **EMP:** 7
SQ FT: 31,000
SALES (est): 1.1MM **Privately Held**
SIC: 3545 Vises, machine (machine tool accessories)

Holly
Oakland County

(G-7868)
ACUMENT GLOBAL TECH INC
Also Called: Ring Screw
4160 Baldwin Rd (48442-9328)
PHONE..................................810 953-4575
Mike Tracy, *General Mgr*
Pamela Chavez, *Mfg Staff*
Mike Abbott, *Engineer*
Lori Johnson, *Corp Comm Staff*
Michelle Kelly, *Manager*
EMP: 175
SALES (corp-wide): 30.9MM **Privately Held**
SIC: 3452 Bolts, nuts, rivets & washers
HQ: Acument Global Technologies, Inc.
6125 18 Mile Rd
Sterling Heights MI 48314
586 254-3900

(G-7869)
AFCO MANUFACTURING CORP
428 Cogshall St (48442-1756)
P.O. Box 230 (48442-0230)
PHONE..................................248 634-4415
Dawn Holbrook, *President*
EMP: 16
SQ FT: 35,000
SALES (est): 5.5MM **Privately Held**
SIC: 3441 Building components, structural steel

(G-7870)
BARLOWS GOURMET PRODUCTS INC
1815 Parker Rd (48442-8539)
PHONE..................................248 245-0393
Stephanie M Barlow, *President*
Dale J B Barlow, *Vice Pres*
Dale Barlow, *Vice Pres*
EMP: 3
SALES: 100K **Privately Held**
SIC: 2035 7389 Seasonings, meat sauces (except tomato & dry);

(G-7871)
BARS PRODUCTS INC (PA)
Also Called: Insealator
10386 N Holly Rd (48442-9302)
P.O. Box 187 (48442-0187)
PHONE..................................248 634-8278
Robert Mermuys, *President*
Michael Mermuys, *Vice Pres*
Clayton Parks, *Vice Pres*
Malinda Strickert, *Sales Staff*
Chad Geiersbach, *Manager*
▲ **EMP:** 35
SQ FT: 45,000
SALES (est): 5.4MM **Privately Held**
WEB: www.barsproducts.com
SIC: 2899 2891 Chemical preparations; sealants

(G-7872)
COVENTRY INDUSTRIES LLC
313 E Sherman St (48442-1656)
PHONE..................................248 761-8462
Michael Coventry, *Principal*
EMP: 5
SALES (est): 440.9K **Privately Held**
SIC: 3999 Barber & beauty shop equipment

(G-7873)
DAVID NICKELS
6455 Lahring Rd (48442-9602)
PHONE..................................248 634-5420
David Nickels, *Principal*
EMP: 4 **EST:** 2009
SALES (est): 406.8K **Privately Held**
SIC: 3356 Nickel

(G-7874)
DELTA TUBE & FABRICATING CORP (PA)
4149 Grange Hall Rd (48442-1113)
PHONE..................................248 634-8267
Howard W Campbell Jr, *President*
Betty Campbell, *Corp Secy*
Todd Campbell, *Vice Pres*
EMP: 20 **EST:** 1973
SQ FT: 12,000
SALES (est): 28.4MM **Privately Held**
SIC: 3496 3743 3317 Miscellaneous fabricated wire products; railroad car rebuilding; steel pipe & tubes

(G-7875)
DELTA TUBE & FABRICATING CORP
Also Called: Delta Rail Division
4149 Grange Hall Rd (48442-1113)
PHONE..................................248 634-8267
Howard Campbell, *Owner*
Richard Clark, *Manager*
EMP: 150
SALES (corp-wide): 28.4MM **Privately Held**
SIC: 3547 3537 3444 3412 Pipe & tube mills; industrial trucks & tractors; sheet metalwork; metal barrels, drums & pails; metal cans; railroad & subway construction
PA: Delta Tube & Fabricating Corporation
4149 Grange Hall Rd
Holly MI 48442
248 634-8267

(G-7876)
DIEHLS ORCHARD & CIDER MILL
1479 Ranch Rd (48442-8668)
PHONE..................................248 634-8981
John W Diehl, *President*
Sue Burton, *Principal*
Mike Diehl, *Vice Pres*
EMP: 3
SQ FT: 12,000
SALES (est): 224.4K **Privately Held**
WEB: www.diehlsorchard.com
SIC: 0175 2086 Apple orchard; bottled & canned soft drinks

(G-7877)
DUMPSTER EXPRESS LLC
11177 Horton Rd (48442-9472)
PHONE..................................855 599-7255
EMP: 3
SALES (est): 166.8K **Privately Held**
SIC: 3443 Dumpsters, garbage

(G-7878)
FALCON MOTORSPORTS INC
Also Called: A P Engineering
255 Elm St (48442-1404)
PHONE..................................248 328-2222
Carl D Lemke, *President*
Jeffery Lemke, *Vice Pres*
Kathleen Lemke, *Treasurer*
EMP: 7
SQ FT: 2,200
SALES (est): 1.1MM **Privately Held**
SIC: 3541 7699 3545 Machine tools, metal cutting type; marine propeller repair; machine tool accessories

(G-7879)
GARCIA COMPANY
10255 Fish Lake Rd (48442-8626)
PHONE..................................248 459-0952
John Garcia, *President*
EMP: 5
SALES (est): 440K **Privately Held**
SIC: 2441 Cases, wood

(G-7880)
GENOAK MATERIALS INC (PA)
14300 Shields Rd (48442-9731)
P.O. Box 182 (48442-0182)
PHONE..................................248 634-8276
Bernhard Rumbold, *President*
Hugh Carr, *Corp Secy*
Scott Mc Kay, *Vice Pres*
EMP: 106
SALES: 16.8MM **Privately Held**
SIC: 1442 4212 1611 1623 Gravel mining; local trucking, without storage; highway & street paving contractor; water, sewer & utility lines

(G-7881)
GIBRALTAR NATIONAL CORPORATION
Also Called: Quikrete Gibraltar National
14311 Cmi Dr (48442-9752)
PHONE..................................248 634-8257
Paul Robbins, *Manager*
EMP: 15
SQ FT: 8,000 **Privately Held**
SIC: 3272 Concrete products
HQ: Gibraltar National Corporation
8951 Schaefer Hwy
Detroit MI 48228
313 491-3500

(G-7882)
GRAND BLANC PROCESSING LLC
10151 Gainey Rd (48442-9313)
PHONE..................................810 694-6000
Matt Takahashi, *President*
Takashi Ono, *Financial Exec*
Jeff Newbill, *Technology*
Erica Crabb, *Executive*
Greg Edwards, *Maintence Staff*
▲ **EMP:** 58
SALES (est): 14.3MM **Privately Held**
WEB: www.shinsho.com
SIC: 3398 Metal heat treating
HQ: The Shinsho American Corporation
26200 Town Center Dr # 220
Novi MI 48375
248 675-0058

(G-7883)
HPC HOLDINGS INC (PA)
111 Rosette St (48442-1304)
P.O. Box 158 (48442-0158)
PHONE..................................248 634-9361
David Bubnar, *President*
Nancy Bubnar, *Corp Secy*
Paul J Bubnar III, *Vice Pres*
EMP: 25 **EST:** 1969
SQ FT: 20,000
SALES (est): 5.1MM **Privately Held**
SIC: 3471 Electroplating of metals or formed products

(G-7884)
LANGS INC
5469 Jacobs Dr (48442-9566)
PHONE..................................248 634-6048
Scott Lang, *President*
EMP: 8
SQ FT: 1,000
SALES (est): 910K **Privately Held**
SIC: 2026 5143 Fermented & cultured milk products; cheese

(G-7885)
MAGNA E-CAR USA LLC (HQ)
10410 N Holly Rd (48442-9332)
PHONE..................................248 606-0600
Burge Young, *Vice Pres*
Roy Taylor, *Engineer*
Roger Barcia, *Project Engr*
Ted Robertson,
EMP: 190
SALES (est): 757.7K
SALES (corp-wide): 40.8B **Privately Held**
SIC: 3621 Motors & generators
PA: Magna International Inc
337 Magna Dr
Aurora ON L4G 7
905 726-2462

(G-7886)
MAGNA E-CAR USA LLC
10410 N Holly Rd (48442-9332)
PHONE..................................248 606-0600
EMP: 3
SALES (corp-wide): 40.8B **Privately Held**
SIC: 3621 Motors & generators
HQ: Magna E-Car Usa Llc
10410 N Holly Rd
Holly MI 48442

(G-7887)
MAGNA ELECTRONICS TECH INC (DH)
10410 N Holly Rd (48442-9332)
PHONE..................................810 606-0145
David Turnbull, *President*
Kenneth Wagner, *Treasurer*
Jayson Wolkove, *Admin Sec*
▲ **EMP:** 21
SALES (est): 3MM
SALES (corp-wide): 40.8B **Privately Held**
SIC: 3714 Motor vehicle parts & accessories

(G-7888)
METROPOULOS AMPLIFICATION INC
10460 N Holly Rd (48442-9319)
PHONE..................................810 614-3905
George Metropoulos, *Administration*
EMP: 7
SALES (est): 1MM **Privately Held**
SIC: 3699 Electrical equipment & supplies

(G-7889)
NORTHERN OAK BREWERY INC
806 N Saginaw St (48442-1347)
PHONE..................................248 634-7515
Ed Krupa, *President*
Andrew Stark, *Vice Pres*
EMP: 11
SALES: 400K **Privately Held**
SIC: 5813 2082 Bars & lounges; beer (alcoholic beverage)

Holly - Oakland County (G-7890) — GEOGRAPHIC SECTION

(G-7890)
PATRICIA HUELLMANTEL PUBG
2323 Academy Rd (48442-8353)
PHONE..................248 634-9894
David Huellmantel, *Principal*
EMP: 3
SALES (est): 123.3K **Privately Held**
SIC: 3999 Education aids, devices & supplies

(G-7891)
QUALITY WAY PRODUCTS LLC
407 Hadley St (48442-1637)
PHONE..................248 634-2401
Brian D Mann Jr,
EMP: 10
SALES: 3.5MM **Privately Held**
SIC: 3272 Columns, concrete

(G-7892)
QUANTUM VENTURES LLC
Also Called: Uantum Lifecare
18055 Fish Lake Rd (48442-8624)
PHONE..................248 325-8380
Pamelia M Jobes, *Principal*
EMP: 5
SALES (est): 505.4K **Privately Held**
SIC: 3572 Computer storage devices

(G-7893)
RANKIN BIOMEDICAL CORPORATION
14515 Mackey Rd (48442-9738)
PHONE..................248 625-4104
Robert Rankin, *Principal*
Brent Rankin, *Vice Pres*
Amy Wright, *Finance Mgr*
▼ **EMP:** 10
SQ FT: 10,400
SALES: 1.8MM **Privately Held**
WEB: www.rankinbiomed.com
SIC: 5047 5049 3821 Medical equipment & supplies; laboratory equipment, except medical or dental; microtomes

(G-7894)
RING SCREW LLC
Holly Operations At Baldwin
4146 Baldwin Rd (48442-9328)
PHONE..................810 695-0800
EMP: 90
SQ FT: 32,000 **Privately Held**
SIC: 3452 Mfg Bolts/Screws/Rivets
HQ: Ring Screw Llc
6125 18 Mile Rd
Sterling Heights MI 48314
586 997-5600

(G-7895)
RUSH AIR INC
Also Called: Rush Technologies
200 Quality Way (48442-9480)
PHONE..................810 694-5763
Kelly Rushmore, *President*
Diane L Rushmore, *Admin Sec*
EMP: 12
SQ FT: 36,000
SALES (est): 1.5MM **Privately Held**
SIC: 3585 Air conditioning equipment, complete

(G-7896)
S T A INC
4150 Grange Hall Rd (48442-1112)
PHONE..................248 328-5000
Charles E Phyle, *Chairman*
Dan Ross, *Design Engr*
Rich Stoolmaker, *Design Engr*
Pat Brendle, *Sales Staff*
EMP: 33
SQ FT: 25,000
SALES (est): 6.2MM **Privately Held**
WEB: www.astmi.com
SIC: 3571 7378 Electronic computers; computer maintenance & repair

(G-7897)
SOUTH FLINT GRAVEL INC
Also Called: Aldridge Trucking
6090 Belford Rd (48442-9443)
PHONE..................810 232-8971
Robert Aldridge, *Owner*
EMP: 6
SALES (est): 468.3K **Privately Held**
SIC: 1442 Gravel mining

(G-7898)
STRUCTURAL PLASTICS INC
3401 Chief (48442-9333)
PHONE..................810 953-9400
Stephen Aho, *President*
Mike Giampetroni, *Sales Mgr*
Matt Bennett, *Manager*
Bree Cady, *Manager*
Jordan Cheek, *Manager*
EMP: 20
SQ FT: 4,000
SALES (est): 4.6MM **Privately Held**
WEB: www.spcindustrial.com
SIC: 2542 Partitions & fixtures, except wood

(G-7899)
TMI CLIMATE SOLUTIONS INC (DH)
200 Quality Way (48442-9400)
PHONE..................810 603-3300
Jim Huff, *CEO*
James Huff, *COO*
George Bishop, *Project Mgr*
Keione Hargrow, *Engineer*
George Gary, *Electrical Engi*
EMP: 133
SQ FT: 160,000
SALES (est): 55.2MM
SALES (corp-wide): 225.3B **Publicly Held**
WEB: www.tminc.net
SIC: 3585 Refrigeration & heating equipment
HQ: Mitek Industries, Inc.
16023 Swinly Rdg
Chesterfield MO 63017
314 434-1200

(G-7900)
TRI-CITY AGGREGATES INC
14300 Shields Rd (48442-9731)
P.O. Box 182 (48442-0182)
PHONE..................248 634-8276
Bernhard C Rumbold, *President*
Hugh Carr, *Corp Secy*
Scott Mc Kay, *Vice Pres*
Michael Krakowski, *Project Mgr*
EMP: 35
SQ FT: 5,000
SALES (est): 8.5MM **Privately Held**
SIC: 1442 4212 2951 Sand mining; gravel & pebble mining; local trucking, without storage; asphalt paving mixtures & blocks
PA: Genoak Materials Inc
14300 Shields Rd
Holly MI 48442

(G-7901)
VINYL TECH WINDOW SYSTEMS INC
405 Cogshall St (48442-1736)
PHONE..................248 634-8900
Paul Baker, *President*
EMP: 18
SQ FT: 6,500
SALES (est): 6.7MM **Privately Held**
SIC: 3089 Windows, plastic

(G-7902)
WOLVERINE MACHINE PRODUCTS CO
319 Cogshall St (48442-1761)
P.O. Box 209 (48442-0209)
PHONE..................248 634-9952
Brian K Hickman, *CEO*
Kenneth H Walker, *President*
Blaine Walker, *Vice Pres*
Bruce H Walker, *Vice Pres*
Kenneth H Walker, *Sales Mgr*
EMP: 22
SQ FT: 1,200
SALES (est): 2.4MM **Privately Held**
SIC: 3568 3541 3451 Power transmission equipment; machine tools, metal cutting type; screw machine products

(G-7903)
YANKEE SCREW PRODUCTS COMPANY
212 Elm St (48442-1403)
PHONE..................248 634-3011
Michael Yankee, *Ch of Bd*
EMP: 14 **EST:** 1944
SQ FT: 40,000
SALES (est): 2.2MM **Privately Held**
SIC: 3451 Screw machine products

Holt
Ingham County

(G-7904)
BACH ORNAMENTAL & STRL STL INC
4140 Keller Rd (48842-1254)
PHONE..................517 694-4311
EMP: 4
SALES: 1.4MM **Privately Held**
SIC: 3449 7692 Mfg Misc Structural Metalwork Welding Repair

(G-7905)
CAPITAL STEEL & BUILDERS SUP
3897 Holt Rd (48842-9774)
P.O. Box 279 (48842-0279)
PHONE..................517 694-0451
William A Buyak, *President*
EMP: 13
SQ FT: 13,000
SALES (est): 2.8MM **Privately Held**
SIC: 3441 5051 5211 Fabricated structural metal; steel; lumber & other building materials

(G-7906)
D & M SILKSCREENING
4202 Charlar Dr Ste 3 (48842-6808)
PHONE..................517 694-4199
Michael Denison, *Owner*
Lynn Denison, *Principal*
EMP: 6
SALES: 200K **Privately Held**
SIC: 2759 2395 Screen printing; embroidery products, except schiffli machine

(G-7907)
DAKKOTA INTEGRATED SYSTEMS LLC
4147 Keller Rd (48842-1253)
PHONE..................517 694-6500
Peter Goguen, *Manager*
EMP: 20
SALES (corp-wide): 242.2MM **Privately Held**
SIC: 3711 3714 Automobile assembly, including specialty automobiles; motor vehicle parts & accessories
PA: Dakkota Integrated Systems, Llc
123 Brighton Lake Rd # 202
Brighton MI 48116
517 694-6500

(G-7908)
DAKKOTA LIGHTING TECH LLC (HQ)
4147 Keller Rd (48842-1253)
PHONE..................517 993-7700
Andra Rush, *Chairman*
Mark Licovitch, *Vice Pres*
Gary Caldwell,
Michael McCarthy,
Linda McMahan,
EMP: 24
SQ FT: 150,000
SALES (est): 1.9MM
SALES (corp-wide): 242.2MM **Privately Held**
SIC: 3648 Lighting equipment
PA: Dakkota Integrated Systems, Llc
123 Brighton Lake Rd # 202
Brighton MI 48116
517 694-6500

(G-7909)
DART CONTAINER MICHIGAN LLC
2148 Depot St (48842-1816)
PHONE..................517 694-9455
Larry McCaffrey, *Plant Mgr*
Randy Robinson, *Project Engr*
EMP: 40 **Privately Held**
WEB: www.dartcontainer.com
SIC: 3086 2656 Cups & plates, foamed plastic; paper cups, plates, dishes & utensils
HQ: Dart Container Of Michigan Llc
500 Hogsback Rd
Mason MI 48854
800 248-5960

(G-7910)
DELHI LEASING INC (PA)
Also Called: Albert Sand & Gravel
1185 N Eifert Rd (48842-9698)
PHONE..................517 694-8578
Larry Albert, *President*
Alan Albert, *Corp Secy*
Steven Albert, *Vice Pres*
EMP: 3 **EST:** 1967
SALES (est): 435.8K **Privately Held**
SIC: 1442 7353 7513 Construction sand mining; gravel mining; heavy construction equipment rental; truck leasing, without drivers

(G-7911)
ENERGY ACQUISITION CORP
2385 Delhi Commerce Dr # 5 (48842-2192)
PHONE..................517 339-0249
Naomi Weitzman, *Admin Sec*
EMP: 10
SQ FT: 800
SALES (est): 897.3K **Privately Held**
SIC: 1381 Directional drilling oil & gas wells

(G-7912)
HOLT PRODUCTS COMPANY
4200 Legion Dr (48842)
P.O. Box 98, Mason, (48854-0098)
PHONE..................517 699-2111
Thomas L Hunt, *Ch of Bd*
Todd E Hunt, *Corp Secy*
Phyllis Ann Hunt, *Shareholder*
EMP: 55
SQ FT: 10,000
SALES (est): 9.7MM **Privately Held**
SIC: 3451 Screw machine products

(G-7913)
INDUSTRIAL MARKING PRODUCTS
1415 Grovenburg Rd (48842-8613)
P.O. Box 314 (48842-0314)
PHONE..................517 699-2160
Gale Wilson, *President*
Larry Osborn, *Vice Pres*
EMP: 6
SQ FT: 2,500
SALES (est): 930.3K **Privately Held**
SIC: 3312 Plate, steel

(G-7914)
INNOVATIVE PACKG SOLUTIONS LLC
2075 Dean Ave Ste 2 (48842-1314)
PHONE..................517 213-3169
EMP: 4
SALES (est): 249.1K **Privately Held**
SIC: 3089 7389 Mfg Plastic Products Business Services At Non-Commercial Site

(G-7915)
MANTISSA INDUSTRIES INC
2362 Jarco Dr (48842-1210)
PHONE..................517 694-2260
Jeffrey Holoweiko, *President*
Sam Holoweiko, *Sales Staff*
EMP: 5
SQ FT: 7,000
SALES (est): 1.5MM **Privately Held**
WEB: www.mantissainds.com
SIC: 3089 3543 Injection molding of plastics; industrial patterns

(G-7916)
MOLDED PLASTIC INDUSTRIES INC
Also Called: Mpi
2382 Jarco Dr (48842-1210)
P.O. Box 70 (48842-0070)
PHONE..................517 694-7434
Frank Phillips Jr, *President*
Steven A Carlson, *CFO*
Scott Parker, *Shareholder*
EMP: 37
SQ FT: 55,000

GEOGRAPHIC SECTION

Homer - Calhoun County (G-7943)

SALES: 5MM **Privately Held**
WEB: www.moldedplastic.com
SIC: 3089 Injection molding of plastics

(G-7917)
MOLDED PLASTICS & TOOLING
2200 Depot St (48842-1818)
PHONE.................................517 268-0849
Frank Phillips, *Owner*
EMP: 4
SALES (est): 204.1K **Privately Held**
SIC: 3089 Injection molding of plastics

(G-7918)
OCCASIONS (PA)
3575 Scholar Ln (48842-9423)
PHONE.................................517 694-6437
Mary Bower, *Owner*
EMP: 5
SALES (est): 761.5K **Privately Held**
SIC: 2754 Stationery & invitation printing, gravure

(G-7919)
ORCHID ORTHPD SLTONS ORGAN INC
Also Called: Orchid Connecticut
1489 Cedar St (48842-1875)
PHONE.................................203 877-3341
Michael E Miller, *President*
Walter Kopec, *Plant Mgr*
Derrick Phillips, *Engineer*
Ted Bloomfield, *Director*
Jorge Ramos, *Admin Sec*
EMP: 69
SALES: 13.1MM
SALES (corp-wide): 319MM **Privately Held**
SIC: 3841 Bone plates & screws
PA: Tulip Us Holdings, Inc.
   1489 Cedar St
   Holt MI 48842
   517 694-2300

(G-7920)
ORCHID ORTHPD SOLUTIONS LLC (HQ)
Also Called: Orchid Lansing
1489 Cedar St (48842-1875)
PHONE.................................517 694-2300
Michael E Miller, *President*
Clay Clayton, *General Mgr*
Jeff Wippel, *General Mgr*
Nick Belloli, *Business Mgr*
Mark Burba, *Exec VP*
EMP: 215
SQ FT: 65,000
SALES (est): 55.5MM
SALES (corp-wide): 319MM **Privately Held**
WEB: www.orchid-orthopedics.com
SIC: 3841 Surgical & medical instruments
PA: Tulip Us Holdings, Inc.
   1489 Cedar St
   Holt MI 48842
   517 694-2300

(G-7921)
PAGEANT HOMES INC
Also Called: Lumbertown
4000 Holt Rd (48842-1844)
P.O. Box 39 (48842-0039)
PHONE.................................517 694-0431
Kenneth Hope, *President*
Louis Legg Jr, *Treasurer*
Bruce Korstange, *Admin Sec*
EMP: 9 EST: 1957
SQ FT: 11,500
SALES (est): 1.1MM **Privately Held**
WEB: www.pageanthomes.com
SIC: 2452 2541 Prefabricated buildings, wood; wood partitions & fixtures

(G-7922)
PRINTING CENTRE INC
Also Called: Paper Image Printing Centres
1900 Cedar St (48842-1806)
PHONE.................................517 694-2400
Cindy Heister, *President*
EMP: 10
SQ FT: 2,000
SALES (est): 1.7MM **Privately Held**
WEB: www.paperimage.com
SIC: 2752 2791 7334 Commercial printing, offset; typesetting; photocopying & duplicating services

(G-7923)
RODCO LTD
2118 Cedar St (48842-1458)
P.O. Box 198, Mason (48854-0198)
PHONE.................................517 244-0200
Richard O Deibler, *President*
EMP: 3
SALES: 500K **Privately Held**
WEB: www.rodco-ltd.com
SIC: 3999 2844 5099 5122 Novelties, bric-a-brac & hobby kits; candles; perfumes & colognes; novelties, durable; cosmetics, perfumes & hair products

(G-7924)
S F R PRECISION TURNING INC
2200 Depot St (48842-1818)
PHONE.................................517 709-3367
Harvey Wright, *President*
Kevin Jurus, *Vice Pres*
Allen Dase, *Treasurer*
EMP: 5
SQ FT: 2,000
SALES (est): 638K **Privately Held**
SIC: 3312 3544 Tubes, steel & iron; special dies, tools, jigs & fixtures

(G-7925)
SANITATION STRATEGIES LLC
1798 Holloway Dr Ste A (48842-7726)
PHONE.................................517 268-3303
Sherman McDonald, *President*
EMP: 11
SQ FT: 2,000
SALES (est): 2.2MM **Privately Held**
WEB: www.sanitationstrategies.com
SIC: 2841 Soap & other detergents

(G-7926)
SCITEX LLC
Also Called: Trick Titanium
2046 Depot St Bldg B (48842-1814)
PHONE.................................517 694-7449
Michael Miller, *President*
EMP: 7
SALES (est): 1MM **Privately Held**
SIC: 3356 Titanium

(G-7927)
SCITEX LLC
Also Called: Trick Titanium
3982 Holt Rd (48842-9701)
P.O. Box 428 (48842-0428)
PHONE.................................517 694-7449
John Gulliver, *Controller*
Mike Miller,
EMP: 20
SALES: 2.8MM **Privately Held**
SIC: 3356 Titanium

(G-7928)
SET LIQUIDATION INC (PA)
Also Called: Stealth Medical Technologies
1489 Cedar St (48842-1875)
PHONE.................................517 694-2300
Michael E Miller, *Ch of Bd*
Lawrence Peek, *President*
Mary Callaghan, *Corp Secy*
▲ EMP: 70
SQ FT: 12,800
SALES (est): 5.7MM **Privately Held**
WEB: www.stealth-medical.com
SIC: 3842 3494 8711 Implants, surgical; valves & pipe fittings; engineering services

(G-7929)
SHAYLESLIE CORPORATION
Also Called: Gaffey & Associates
2385 Delhi Commerce Dr # 1 (48842-2192)
P.O. Box 137 (48842-0137)
PHONE.................................517 694-4115
David J Gaffey, *President*
Shay Leslie Gaffey, *Vice Pres*
EMP: 4
SQ FT: 10,000
SALES (est): 549.5K **Privately Held**
WEB: www.gaffeyassociates.com
SIC: 5112 5199 2752 Business forms; office supplies; data processing supplies; advertising specialties; commercial printing, offset

(G-7930)
THUNDER BAY PRESS INC
2325 Jarco Dr (48842-1209)
P.O. Box 637 (48842-0637)
PHONE.................................517 694-3205
Vicky L Eaves, *President*
Samuel Speigel, *Admin Sec*
▲ EMP: 25
SQ FT: 30,000
SALES (est): 1.5MM
SALES (corp-wide): 123.2MM **Privately Held**
WEB: www.partnersbook.com
SIC: 2731 Book clubs: publishing only, not printed on site
PA: Partners Book Distributing, Inc.
   2325 Jarco Dr
   Holt MI 48842
   517 694-3205

(G-7931)
TULIP US HOLDINGS INC (PA)
Also Called: Orchid Orthopedic Solutions
1489 Cedar St (48842-1875)
PHONE.................................517 694-2300
Jerome Jurkiewicz, *CEO*
Barry Torrey, *Materials Mgr*
Tracy Tindell, *Buyer*
John Mathews, *Engineer*
Mark Owen, *Engineer*
EMP: 40 EST: 2011
SALES: 319MM **Privately Held**
SIC: 3842 Orthopedic appliances

Holton
Muskegon County

(G-7932)
H & M PALLET LLC
9148 S 200th Ave (49425-9601)
PHONE.................................231 821-8800
Melvin Miller, *Mng Member*
Jerry Miller,
EMP: 10
SQ FT: 18,000
SALES: 3MM **Privately Held**
SIC: 2448 Pallets, wood & wood with metal

(G-7933)
JOSEPH MILLER
Also Called: Summit Truss
7781 Brickyard Rd (49425-9516)
PHONE.................................231 821-2430
Joseph Miller, *Principal*
EMP: 3
SQ FT: 7,700
SALES: 1.3MM **Privately Held**
SIC: 2439 Trusses, wooden roof

(G-7934)
MILLERS CANVAS SHOP
6531 Meinert Rd (49425-9543)
PHONE.................................231 821-0771
Andy Miller, *Owner*
EMP: 3
SQ FT: 2,500
SALES: 100K **Privately Held**
SIC: 2394 Canvas covers & drop cloths

(G-7935)
VOGEL ENGINEERING INC
6688 Maple Island Rd (49425-7547)
PHONE.................................231 821-2125
Wayne Vogel, *President*
David Vogel, *Vice Pres*
Karen Vogel, *Treasurer*
EMP: 9
SQ FT: 35,000
SALES (est): 2MM **Privately Held**
SIC: 3561 Pumps & pumping equipment

Homer
Calhoun County

(G-7936)
AMSTED RAIL COMPANY INC
124 W Platt St (49245-1033)
PHONE.................................517 568-4161
EMP: 6
SALES (est): 459.7K **Privately Held**
SIC: 3743 Railroad equipment

(G-7937)
BREMBO NORTH AMERICA INC
5851 30 Mile Rd (49245-9524)
PHONE.................................517 568-4398
Katrina Marsh, *Principal*
Ted Finch, *Engineer*
Johnny Wilson, *Engineer*
Jim Burge, *Electrical Engi*
Melissa Radzi, *Manager*
EMP: 20 **Privately Held**
SIC: 3714 Motor vehicle brake systems & parts
HQ: Brembo North America, Inc.
   47765 Halyard Dr
   Plymouth MI 48170

(G-7938)
BREMBO NORTH AMERICA INC
29991 E M 60 (49245-9753)
PHONE.................................517 568-3301
EMP: 25
SQ FT: 250,000 **Privately Held**
WEB: www.ibraco.com
SIC: 3599 Machine shop, jobbing & repair
HQ: Brembo North America, Inc.
   47765 Halyard Dr
   Plymouth MI 48170

(G-7939)
BREMBO NORTH AMERICA HOMER INC
29991 E M 60 (49245-9753)
PHONE.................................517 568-4398
Dan Sandeburg, *CEO*
EMP: 50
SALES (est): 7.1MM **Privately Held**
SIC: 3599 Machine shop, jobbing & repair
HQ: Brembo North America, Inc.
   47765 Halyard Dr
   Plymouth MI 48170

(G-7940)
CALHOUN FOUNDRY COMPANY INC
506 S Clay St (49245-1359)
P.O. Box 218 (49245-0218)
PHONE.................................517 568-4415
George J Petredean, *Ch of Bd*
Micheal Hamaker, *President*
Melodie Avery, *Engineer*
Mike Hamaker, *Engineer*
Suzanne Nelson, *Treasurer*
EMP: 62 EST: 1943
SQ FT: 70,000
SALES (est): 12.9MM **Privately Held**
WEB: www.calhounfoundry.com
SIC: 3321 Gray iron castings

(G-7941)
D J S SYSTEMS INC
801 S Hillsdale St (49245-9701)
P.O. Box 70 (49245-0070)
PHONE.................................517 568-4444
Dave Swope, *President*
▲ EMP: 40
SQ FT: 20,000
SALES (est): 8.5MM **Privately Held**
WEB: www.djssystems.com
SIC: 3565 Packaging machinery

(G-7942)
F M T PRODUCTS INC
140 W Main St (49245-1046)
PHONE.................................517 568-3373
Thomas Grant, *President*
▲ EMP: 9
SQ FT: 10,000
SALES (est): 1.2MM **Privately Held**
SIC: 5013 3647 Automotive supplies & parts; motor vehicle lighting equipment

(G-7943)
HANKS WELDING SERVICE INC
2379 29 Mile Rd (49245-9516)
PHONE.................................517 568-3804
Jerry Renfroe, *President*
June Refroe, *Vice Pres*
Ruth Renfroe, *Vice Pres*
EMP: 3
SALES (est): 159.5K **Privately Held**
SIC: 7692 Welding repair

(G-7944)
HOMER INDEX
122 E Main St (49245-1137)
P.O. Box 236 (49245-0236)
PHONE....................517 568-4646
Michael Warner, *Partner*
Sharon Warner, *Partner*
EMP: 4
SALES: 130K **Privately Held**
SIC: 2711 Newspapers, publishing & printing

(G-7945)
MCCONNELL & SCULLY INC (PA)
146 W Main St (49245-1046)
PHONE....................517 568-4104
Ron Mc Connell, *President*
Elaine M Seitz, *Corp Secy*
Tom Mc Nicholas, *Vice Pres*
EMP: 40 **EST:** 1966
SQ FT: 11,000
SALES (est): 7.5MM **Privately Held**
SIC: 1389 Oil field services

(G-7946)
MCS INDUSTRIES INC
Also Called: Steel Products
124 W Platt St (49245-1033)
P.O. Box 217 (49245-0217)
PHONE....................517 568-4161
Chris Miller, *President*
EMP: 22
SQ FT: 8,000
SALES (est): 3.5MM **Privately Held**
WEB: www.steelproducts-mcs.com
SIC: 3441 Fabricated structural metal

(G-7947)
NAGEL MEAT PROCESSING
3265 22 Mile Rd (49245-9647)
PHONE....................517 568-5035
Joseph Nagel, *Owner*
EMP: 12
SALES (est): 1MM **Privately Held**
SIC: 2011 7299 Meat packing plants; butcher service, processing only

(G-7948)
RSB NORTH AMERICA LLC (DH)
24425 W M 60 (49245-9651)
P.O. Box 68 (49245-0068)
PHONE....................517 568-4171
Mike Koerner, *Principal*
Mathura Singh, *Vice Pres*
EMP: 4
SALES (est): 576K **Privately Held**
SIC: 3599 Machine shop, jobbing & repair
HQ: Rsb Transmissions Na, Inc.
24425 W M 60
Homer MI 49245
517 568-4171

(G-7949)
RSB TRANSMISSIONS NA INC (DH)
24425 W M 60 (49245-9651)
P.O. Box 68 (49245-0068)
PHONE....................517 568-4171
Paul Metzbar, *General Mgr*
Paul Metzgar, *General Mgr*
Nishit Behera, *Managing Dir*
Pradipta Swain, *Dept Chairman*
Mike Good, *Mfg Mgr*
▲ **EMP:** 19
SQ FT: 75,000
SALES (est): 20.7MM **Privately Held**
WEB: www.millerbrosmfg.com
SIC: 3599 Machine shop, jobbing & repair

(G-7950)
TEKKRA SYSTEMS INC
300 S Elm St (49245-1337)
PHONE....................517 568-4121
Nels E Vorm, *President*
EMP: 26
SQ FT: 20,000
SALES (est): 5.5MM **Privately Held**
WEB: www.tekkrasystems.com
SIC: 3565 Packaging machinery

(G-7951)
TROJAN HEAT TREAT INC
Also Called: Trojan Heat Treat Company
809 S Byron St (49245-9761)
P.O. Box 97 (49245-0097)
PHONE....................517 568-4403
Ronald Di Salvio, *President*
Jeff Jones, *Plant Engr*
John Dibble, *Manager*
EMP: 50
SQ FT: 46,000
SALES: 2.5MM
SALES (corp-wide): 22.7MM **Privately Held**
WEB: www.trojanheattreat.com
SIC: 3398 Metal heat treating
PA: Heat Treating Services Corporation Of America
217 Central Ave
Pontiac MI 48341
248 858-2230

Honor
Benzie County

(G-7952)
FIELD CRAFTS INC (PA)
Also Called: Bookwear
9930 Honor Hwy (49640-9534)
PHONE....................231 325-1122
John Gyr, *President*
EMP: 20
SQ FT: 9,400
SALES (est): 2.3MM **Privately Held**
WEB: www.fieldcrafts.com
SIC: 2396 2759 Screen printing on fabric articles; commercial printing

(G-7953)
RAK WELDING
7739 Valley Rd (49640-9732)
PHONE....................231 651-0732
Roger Kerby, *Principal*
EMP: 8
SALES (est): 88.7K **Privately Held**
SIC: 7692 Welding repair

Hope
Midland County

(G-7954)
INTERNATIONAL ENGRG & MFG INC
Also Called: IEM
6054 N Meridian Rd (48628-9786)
P.O. Box 316, Edenville (48620-0316)
PHONE....................989 689-4911
Robert Musselman, *President*
Serena Gardener, *Human Res Dir*
Serena Gardiner, *Assistant*
▲ **EMP:** 96 **EST:** 1968
SQ FT: 27,640
SALES (est): 21.7MM **Privately Held**
WEB: www.wiem.com
SIC: 3429 Manufactured hardware (general)

(G-7955)
L & M MFG INC
6016 N Meridian Rd (48628-9786)
PHONE....................989 689-4010
Mark Wilkins, *President*
EMP: 4
SQ FT: 6,800
SALES (est): 549.6K **Privately Held**
SIC: 3536 Boat lifts

(G-7956)
ROSES SUSIES FEATHER
7191 Middle Rd (48628-9307)
PHONE....................989 689-6570
Mark Stewart, *Owner*
EMP: 4
SALES (est): 157.5K **Privately Held**
SIC: 3999 Flowers, artificial & preserved

(G-7957)
TRI-CITY REPAIR COMPANY
6700 Middle Rd (48628-9306)
PHONE....................989 835-4784
Melvin R Vanmeter, *President*
Chris R Vanmeter, *Vice Pres*
Beverly J Riggie, *Treasurer*
Betty L Vanmeter, *Admin Sec*
EMP: 5
SQ FT: 2,400
SALES (est): 275K **Privately Held**
SIC: 7699 3599 Industrial machinery & equipment repair; machine shop, jobbing & repair

(G-7958)
YACKS DRY DOCK
6227 N Meridian Rd (48628-9740)
PHONE....................989 689-6749
EMP: 4 **EST:** 2010
SALES (est): 210K **Privately Held**
SIC: 3421 Mfg Cutlery

Hopkins
Allegan County

(G-7959)
MILLER SAND & GRAVEL COMPANY
1466 120th Ave (49328-9626)
PHONE....................269 672-5601
Tom E Miller, *President*
Marvin Miller, *Vice Pres*
Helena Miller, *Treasurer*
Mary Carlson, *Admin Sec*
EMP: 8
SQ FT: 2,500
SALES (est): 520K **Privately Held**
SIC: 1442 3273 4212 Common sand mining; gravel mining; ready-mixed concrete; dump truck haulage

(G-7960)
SEBRIGHT PRODUCTS INC (PA)
127 N Water St (49328-5116)
P.O. Box 296 (49328-0296)
PHONE....................269 793-7183
David Sebright, *Ch of Bd*
Brent Sebright, *President*
Stuart Sebright, *General Mgr*
Lee Murray, *Vice Pres*
Janet Wozniak, *Purch Mgr*
EMP: 20
SQ FT: 5,100
SALES (est): 18.3MM **Privately Held**
SIC: 3589 5084 Garbage disposers & compactors, commercial; industrial machinery & equipment

(G-7961)
SHRED-PAC INC
Also Called: Sp Industries
2982 22nd St (49328-9783)
PHONE....................269 793-7978
Dennis Pool, *President*
Roger Arndt, *Exec VP*
Elise Dones, *Treasurer*
EMP: 37 **EST:** 1980
SQ FT: 45,000
SALES (est): 8.4MM **Privately Held**
WEB: www.sp-industries.com
SIC: 3589 3531 Garbage disposers & compactors, commercial; construction machinery

(G-7962)
SMITH LOGGING LLC
2717 134th Ave (49328-9528)
PHONE....................616 558-0729
Dudley Smith, *Principal*
EMP: 3
SALES (est): 107.3K **Privately Held**
SIC: 2411 Logging camps & contractors

Horton
Jackson County

(G-7963)
CHOCOLATE VAULT LLC
8475 Chicago Rd (49246-9684)
PHONE....................517 688-3388
James McCann,
Barbara McCann,
Robert McCann,
EMP: 7
SALES (est): 410K **Privately Held**
WEB: www.chocolatevault.com
SIC: 2026 5441 2064 Milk, chocolate; candy; candy bars, including chocolate covered bars; chocolate candy, except solid chocolate

(G-7964)
HUTSONS MACHINE & TOOL INC
408 Maitland Dr (49246-9758)
PHONE....................517 688-3674
John T Hutson Jr, *President*
Kathryn Hutson, *Vice Pres*
EMP: 3
SALES (est): 300K **Privately Held**
SIC: 3599 Machine shop, jobbing & repair

(G-7965)
LOMAR MACHINE & TOOL CO
5931 Coats Rd (49246-9405)
PHONE....................517 563-8136
Ronald Geisman, *Manager*
Ronald E Geisman, *Manager*
EMP: 34
SALES (corp-wide): 26.6MM **Privately Held**
SIC: 3599 Machine shop, jobbing & repair
PA: Lomar Machine & Tool Co.
135 Main St
Horton MI 49246
517 563-8136

(G-7966)
LOMAR MACHINE & TOOL CO (PA)
135 Main St (49246-9540)
P.O. Box 128 (49246-0128)
PHONE....................517 563-8136
James L Geisman, *CEO*
Ronald E Geisman, *President*
Kelly Kohn, *Business Mgr*
Charles Murphy, *Vice Pres*
Jason Dorian, *Project Mgr*
EMP: 21
SQ FT: 630,000
SALES (est): 26.6MM **Privately Held**
SIC: 3549 3544 Assembly machines, including robotic; special dies & tools; jigs & fixtures

(G-7967)
LOMAR MACHINE & TOOL CO
7595 Moscow Rd (49246-9301)
PHONE....................517 563-8136
EMP: 3
SALES (est): 188.9K **Privately Held**
SIC: 3599 Machine shop, jobbing & repair

(G-7968)
LOMAR MACHINE & TOOL CO
Also Called: Low Mar
7595 Moscow Rd (49246-9301)
PHONE....................517 563-8800
Ron Geisman, *President*
EMP: 36
SALES (corp-wide): 26.6MM **Privately Held**
SIC: 3599 Machine shop, jobbing & repair
PA: Lomar Machine & Tool Co.
135 Main St
Horton MI 49246
517 563-8136

(G-7969)
MEDICAL ENGINEERING & DEV
4910 Dancer Rd (49246-9016)
PHONE....................517 563-2352
Bruce Harshe, *President*
Sharon Harshe, *Vice Pres*
EMP: 4
SQ FT: 200
SALES (est): 301.6K **Privately Held**
WEB: www.med-engrg.com
SIC: 8731 3841 Commercial physical research; surgical & medical instruments

(G-7970)
RACK & PINION INC
7595 Moscow Rd (49246-9301)
P.O. Box 128 (49246-0128)
PHONE....................517 563-8872
James L Geisman, *President*
Ron E Geisman, *Vice Pres*
Chuck Murphy, *Treasurer*
EMP: 7

SQ FT: 11,000
SALES (est): 644.3K **Privately Held**
WEB: www.rack-and-pinion.com
SIC: 3714 3462 Motor vehicle body components & frame; iron & steel forgings

Houghton
Houghton County

(G-7971)
ANDERSON LOGGING INC
50433 Canal Rd (49931-9793)
PHONE..................................906 482-7505
Dawn Anderson, *Principal*
EMP: 3
SALES (est): 343.4K **Privately Held**
SIC: 2411 Logging camps & contractors

(G-7972)
CONSISTACOM INC
47420 State Highway M26 # 27 (49931-2819)
P.O. Box 293 (49931-0293)
PHONE..................................906 482-7653
Steven C Fitzgerald, *President*
EMP: 6
SALES (est): 570K **Privately Held**
WEB: www.telecominstitute.com
SIC: 7372 Business oriented computer software

(G-7973)
KEWEENAW BREWING COMPANY LLC (PA)
408 Shelden Ave (49931-2138)
PHONE..................................906 482-5596
David Lawrence, *General Mgr*
Richard J Gray,
Paul Boissevain,
▲ EMP: 14
SALES (est): 2.6MM **Privately Held**
SIC: 2082 Beer (alcoholic beverage)

(G-7974)
LAWRENCE J JULIO LLC
Also Called: Lawrence Co
47212 Main St (49931-9753)
P.O. Box 604 (49931-0604)
PHONE..................................906 483-4781
Lawrence Julio,
EMP: 5
SALES: 80K **Privately Held**
SIC: 3531 Construction machinery

(G-7975)
LITEBRAKE TECH LLC
406 2nd St Houghton (49931)
PHONE..................................906 523-2007
Scott Huang, *Mng Member*
Xiaodi Huang, *Manager*
Nannon Huang,
EMP: 5
SALES (est): 277.7K **Privately Held**
SIC: 3714 Motor vehicle brake systems & parts

(G-7976)
LITSENBERGER PRINT SHOP
Also Called: Print Shop, The
224 Shelden Ave (49931-2134)
PHONE..................................906 482-3903
Thomas A Litsenberger, *Owner*
Bobbie Jean Litsenberger, *Co-Owner*
Brendan Graphic, *Director*
Bobbi Jean Litsenberger, *Graphic Designe*
EMP: 8 EST: 1976
SQ FT: 3,000
SALES (est): 933.1K **Privately Held**
WEB: www.theprintshophoughton.com
SIC: 2752 2791 2789 2672 Commercial printing, offset; typesetting; bookbinding & related work; coated & laminated paper

(G-7977)
LYMPHOGEN INC
1914 Middle Pointe Ln (49931-2746)
PHONE..................................906 281-7372
Jeremy Goldman, *Director*
EMP: 3
SALES (est): 238.5K **Privately Held**
SIC: 2834 Pharmaceutical preparations

(G-7978)
NANO INNOVATIONS LLC
22151 Ridge Rd (49931-9010)
PHONE..................................906 231-2101
Yoke Khin Yap,
John Diebel,
EMP: 4
SALES (est): 255.7K **Privately Held**
SIC: 3299 Ceramic fiber

(G-7979)
NUTTING NEWSPAPERS INC
Also Called: Daily Mining Gazette
206 Shelden Ave (49931-2134)
P.O. Box 368 (49931-0368)
PHONE..................................906 482-1500
Cathy O Connell, *Human Res Dir*
Michael Scott, *Manager*
Craig Peterson, *Manager*
Jennifer Robinson, *Manager*
Josh Vissers, *Assoc Editor*
EMP: 40 **Privately Held**
WEB: www.salemnews.net
SIC: 2711 2752 7313 Newspapers: publishing only, not printed on site; commercial printing, lithographic; newspaper advertising representative
PA: The Nutting Newspapers Inc
1500 Main St
Wheeling WV 26003

(G-7980)
PEPSI COLA BOTLING CO HOUGHTON
Also Called: Pepsico
309 E Sharon Ave (49931-1908)
PHONE..................................906 482-0161
William Harvey, *Owner*
Jim Holmquest, *General Mgr*
EMP: 14
SALES (est): 2.6MM **Privately Held**
SIC: 2086 Carbonated soft drinks, bottled & canned

(G-7981)
QUINCY WOODWRIGHTS LLC (PA)
408 E Montezuma Ave (49931-2115)
PHONE..................................808 397-0818
Jonathan D Julien,
EMP: 5 EST: 2013
SQ FT: 26,000
SALES (est): 522K **Privately Held**
SIC: 2435 Veneer stock, hardwood

(G-7982)
SCOTT JOHNSON FOREST PDTS CO
43850 Superior Rd (49931-9770)
PHONE..................................906 482-3978
Scott Johnson, *President*
EMP: 7
SALES (est): 563K **Privately Held**
SIC: 2411 Logging camps & contractors

(G-7983)
SOMERO ENTERPRISES INC (PA)
46980 State Hwy M 26 26 M (49931)
P.O. Box 309 (49931-0309)
PHONE..................................906 482-7252
Jack Cooney, *President*
Nicole Blake, *Principal*
Mike Miemela, *CFO*
◆ EMP: 93
SALES (est): 34.7MM **Privately Held**
WEB: www.somero.com
SIC: 3559 Concrete products machinery

(G-7984)
SUPERIOR BLOCK COMPANY INC
100 Isle Royale St (49931)
P.O. Box 6 (49931-0006)
PHONE..................................906 482-2731
Daniel P Lorenzetti, *President*
Joan Lorenzetti, *Corp Secy*
EMP: 15 EST: 1946
SQ FT: 12,000
SALES (est): 2.1MM **Privately Held**
SIC: 3271 Blocks, concrete or cinder: standard

(G-7985)
SUPERIOR GRAPHICS STUDIOS LTD
19923 W Sharon Ave (49931-2515)
PHONE..................................906 482-7891
Gary Gutshall, *Owner*
Diane Gutshall, *Vice Pres*
EMP: 3 EST: 1998
SALES (est): 185K **Privately Held**
WEB: www.superiorgraphicsmi.com
SIC: 2752 3993 Commercial printing, lithographic; signs & advertising specialties

(G-7986)
THOMAS J MOYLE JR INCORPORATED (PA)
Also Called: Moyle Lumber
46702 Hwy M 26 (49931)
P.O. Box 414 (49931-0414)
PHONE..................................906 482-3000
Tom Moyle, *CEO*
Andy Moyle, *President*
Kimberly Moyle, *Corp Secy*
EMP: 20
SQ FT: 3,200
SALES (est): 6.8MM **Privately Held**
SIC: 1542 1521 3531 5211 Commercial & office building, new construction; new construction, single-family houses; concrete plants; lumber products; gravel

Houghton Lake
Roscommon County

(G-7987)
BOS FIELD MACHINING INC
Also Called: Beano's On Site Machining
1750 Maywood Rd (48629-9238)
P.O. Box 383 (48629-0383)
PHONE..................................517 204-1688
Beano Sterns, *CEO*
Trish Stearns, *Office Mgr*
EMP: 6
SALES (est): 550K **Privately Held**
WEB: www.bosmachining.com
SIC: 3599 Machine shop, jobbing & repair

(G-7988)
CHAMPION FORTUNE CORPORATION
387 S Harrison Rd (48629-8613)
P.O. Box 849 (48629-0849)
PHONE..................................989 422-6130
Gregg Hetzinger, *President*
EMP: 17
SQ FT: 30,000
SALES (est): 2.8MM **Privately Held**
SIC: 3599 Machine shop, jobbing & repair

(G-7989)
CLIFFS SAND & GRAVEL INC
1128 Federal Ave (48629-8945)
PHONE..................................989 422-3463
Clifton Halliday, *President*
EMP: 6 EST: 1973
SALES (est): 412.7K **Privately Held**
SIC: 1442 Construction sand mining; gravel mining

(G-7990)
HALLIDAY SAND & GRAVEL INC
1128 Federal Ave (48629-8945)
PHONE..................................989 422-3463
Clifton Halliday, *President*
Edah Halliday, *Corp Secy*
EMP: 40 EST: 1963
SALES (est): 5.5MM **Privately Held**
SIC: 1442 Construction sand mining; gravel mining

(G-7991)
HAMP
126 Winding Dr (48629-9153)
PHONE..................................989 366-5341
Eric M Hamp, *Principal*
EMP: 3 EST: 2010
SALES (est): 125.8K **Privately Held**
SIC: 2711 Newspapers, publishing & printing

(G-7992)
HL OUTDOORS
308 Huron St (48629-9756)
P.O. Box 1013 (48629-1013)
PHONE..................................989 422-3264
Steven L Johnston, *Owner*
EMP: 4
SALES (est): 250.3K **Privately Held**
SIC: 5091 3949 Fishing tackle; fishing tackle, general

(G-7993)
HOUGHTON LAKE RESORTER INC
4049 W Houghton Lake Dr (48629-9208)
P.O. Box 248 (48629-0248)
PHONE..................................989 366-5341
Thoams W Hamp, *President*
Thomas W Hamp, *President*
Eric Hamp, *Editor*
Patricia Hamp, *Corp Secy*
Robert J Hamp Jr, *Vice Pres*
EMP: 20
SQ FT: 5,000
SALES (est): 1.5MM **Privately Held**
WEB: www.houghtonlakeresorter.com
SIC: 2711 2752 2759 Newspapers: publishing only, not printed on site; commercial printing, offset; letterpress printing

(G-7994)
KUZIMSKI ENTERPRISES INC
Also Called: North Central Machine
9100 Knapp Rd (48629-8800)
PHONE..................................989 422-5377
Kurt Kuzimski, *Principal*
EMP: 8
SALES (est): 150.6K **Privately Held**
SIC: 3599 Machine shop, jobbing & repair

(G-7995)
LC MATERIALS
9142 Knapp Rd (48629-8847)
PHONE..................................989 422-4202
Steve Diss, *Branch Mgr*
EMP: 8
SALES (corp-wide): 8MM **Privately Held**
SIC: 3273 Ready-mixed concrete
PA: Lc Materials
805 W 13th St
Cadillac MI 49601
231 825-2473

(G-7996)
RONALD BRADLEY
224 Welch Rd (48629-9631)
PHONE..................................989 422-5609
Ronald Bradley, *Principal*
EMP: 3
SALES (est): 170K **Privately Held**
SIC: 2611 Pulp mills

(G-7997)
SPICERS BOAT CY OF HOUGHTON LK
4165 W Houghton Lake Dr (48629-8277)
PHONE..................................989 366-8384
Phillip Spicer, *President*
Shaw Stanley, *Sales Staff*
EMP: 50 EST: 1959
SQ FT: 16,500
SALES (est): 11.8MM **Privately Held**
WEB: www.spicersboatcity.com
SIC: 5551 5599 4493 3732 Motor boat dealers; marine supplies; snowmobiles; boat yards, storage & incidental repair; boat building & repairing

(G-7998)
STAR BUYERS GUIDE
4772 W Houghton Lake Dr (48629-8221)
PHONE..................................989 366-8341
EMP: 4 EST: 2011
SALES (est): 150K **Privately Held**
SIC: 2741 Misc Publishing

(G-7999)
SUPERIOR AUTO GLASS OF MICH
7006 W Houghton Lake Dr (48629-9715)
PHONE..................................989 366-9691
Allyn C Packman, *President*
Albert J Taylor, *Vice Pres*
EMP: 5

Howard City - Montcalm County (G-8000) — GEOGRAPHIC SECTION

SALES (est): 546.9K **Privately Held**
SIC: 7536 3211 Automotive glass replacement shops; tempered glass

Howard City
Montcalm County

(G-8000)
CUSTOM DESIGN COMPONENTS INC
19569 W Edgar Rd (49329-9207)
PHONE.................................231 937-6166
Robert Deurloo, *President*
Robert E Deurloo, *President*
Bob Deurloo, *Financial Exec*
EMP: 19
SQ FT: 3,024
SALES (est): 2MM **Privately Held**
SIC: 3599 Machine shop, jobbing & repair

(G-8001)
HUSH PUPPIES RETAIL LLC
214 Washburn St (49329-9012)
PHONE.................................231 937-1004
Steve Johnston, *Director*
EMP: 50
SALES (corp-wide): 2.2B **Publicly Held**
WEB: www.wwwinc.com
SIC: 3143 5139 Men's footwear, except athletic; footwear
HQ: Hush Puppies Retail, Llc
   9341 Courtland Dr Ne
   Rockford MI 49351
   616 866-5500

(G-8002)
INFLATABLE MARINE PRODUCTS INC
Also Called: Sea Wolf
9485 N Reed Rd Ste C (49329-8621)
PHONE.................................616 723-8140
Robert Johnson, *President*
David Johnson, *President*
EMP: 5
SALES (est): 290K **Privately Held**
SIC: 3089 5551 Plastic boats & other marine equipment; inflatable boats

(G-8003)
LINDY PRESS INC
9794 Locust Ave (49329-9641)
PHONE.................................231 937-6169
Deborah Sturgeon, *President*
EMP: 4
SQ FT: 3,000
SALES: 270K **Privately Held**
WEB: www.lindypressgr.com
SIC: 2752 Commercial printing, offset

(G-8004)
NORTHERN CABLE & AUTOMTN LLC (PA)
Also Called: Flex Cable
5822 Henkel Rd (49329-8668)
PHONE.................................231 937-8000
Erwin Kroulik, *Chief Engr*
Randy Nettle, *Sales Engr*
Tonia Bennett, *Sales Staff*
Stuart Borman, *Mng Member*
Chris McCall, *Maintence Staff*
EMP: 50
SQ FT: 50,000
SALES (est): 18.1MM **Privately Held**
WEB: www.flexcable.com
SIC: 3496 Miscellaneous fabricated wire products

(G-8005)
PRECISE MACHINING INC
17279 Almy Rd (49329-9588)
PHONE.................................231 937-7957
Carol Deurloo, *CEO*
John Deurloo, *President*
EMP: 5
SALES: 92K **Privately Held**
SIC: 3599 Machine shop, jobbing & repair

(G-8006)
RIVERSIDE PLASTIC CO
138 Washburn St (49329-9008)
PHONE.................................231 937-7333
Chuck Freeman, *President*
Wesely Freeman, *Shareholder*
EMP: 20 **EST:** 1989
SQ FT: 20,000
SALES (est): 3.1MM **Privately Held**
WEB: www.riversideplastics.com
SIC: 3089 Extruded finished plastic products

(G-8007)
UNIVERSAL MAGNETICS INC
5555 N Amy School Rd (49329-9722)
PHONE.................................231 937-5555
George H Ravell, *President*
Dorothy Ravell, *Corp Secy*
EMP: 7
SQ FT: 4,400
SALES (est): 1MM **Privately Held**
WEB: www.univmag.com
SIC: 3559 3812 3499 Separation equipment, magnetic; electronic field detection apparatus (aeronautical); magnets, permanent: metallic

Howell
Livingston County

(G-8008)
A S R C INC
4285 Westhill Dr (48843-9492)
PHONE.................................517 545-7430
Richard M Keough, *President*
Jennifer Keough, *Corp Secy*
John Keough, *Vice Pres*
EMP: 3
SQ FT: 1,500
SALES: 1MM **Privately Held**
WEB: www.asrc.net
SIC: 3554 Folding machines, paper

(G-8009)
AA GEAR LLC
Also Called: Ann Arbor Gear
1045 Durant Dr (48843-9536)
PHONE.................................517 552-3100
Pete Lazik, *Principal*
Marty Jablonowski, *Engineer*
Randy Turner, *Admin Sec*
EMP: 18
SQ FT: 112,000
SALES (est): 4.1MM **Privately Held**
SIC: 3714 Gears, motor vehicle

(G-8010)
ALBRIGHT PRECISION INC
4921 W Grand River Ave (48855-8713)
PHONE.................................517 545-7642
Mark Albright, *President*
EMP: 3
SQ FT: 2,500
SALES (est): 345.7K **Privately Held**
SIC: 3599 Machine shop, jobbing & repair

(G-8011)
ALPHA TECHNOLOGY CORPORATION
Also Called: Altec
1450 Mcpherson Park Dr (48843-1936)
P.O. Box 168 (48844-0168)
PHONE.................................517 546-9700
Stephen Sweda, *President*
Shigeki Nagano, *President*
Mark Goodman, *General Mgr*
Akio Kobayashi, *Vice Pres*
▲ **EMP:** 21
SQ FT: 6,000
SALES: 70MM **Privately Held**
WEB: www.altec-us.com
SIC: 3714 5013 3429 Motor vehicle parts & accessories; automotive supplies & parts; keys, locks & related hardware
PA: Alpha Corporation
   1-6-8, Fukuura, Kanazawa-Ku
   Yokohama KNG 236-0

(G-8012)
ALUDYNE NORTH AMERICA INC
2280 W Grand River Ave (48843-8515)
PHONE.................................248 728-8642
Larry Dunn, *Engineer*
Michael Hayden, *Supervisor*
EMP: 120
SALES (corp-wide): 1.3B **Privately Held**
SIC: 3714 Motor vehicle parts & accessories
HQ: Aludyne North America Inc.
   300 Galleria Ofcntr Ste 5
   Southfield MI 48034
   248 728-8642

(G-8013)
AMERICAN CONCRETE PRODUCTS INC
4944 Mason Rd (48843-9697)
PHONE.................................517 546-2810
Toll Free:..888 -
Brad Jonckheere, *President*
Alicia Jonckheere, *Corp Secy*
EMP: 6
SQ FT: 1,000
SALES (est): 1.1MM **Privately Held**
WEB: www.americanconprod.com
SIC: 3273 Ready-mixed concrete

(G-8014)
ANDERSEN OAKLEAF INC
4330 Jewell Rd (48843-9503)
PHONE.................................517 546-1805
Les Andersen, *President*
Elaine Andersen, *Corp Secy*
Harold Andersen, *Vice Pres*
EMP: 3
SALES: 40K **Privately Held**
SIC: 3523 Farm machinery & equipment

(G-8015)
ANTOLIN INTERIORS USA INC
Antolin Howell
3705 W Grand River Ave (48855-8792)
PHONE.................................517 548-0052
Matt Edwards, *General Mgr*
Todd Van Bynen, *Executive*
Michael North, *Administration*
EMP: 718
SALES (corp-wide): 33.3MM **Privately Held**
WEB: www.atreum.com
SIC: 3714 3429 Motor vehicle parts & accessories; manufactured hardware (general)
HQ: Antolin Interiors Usa, Inc.
   1700 Atlantic Blvd
   Auburn Hills MI 48326
   248 373-1749

(G-8016)
ARROWMAT LLC
6540 Munsell Rd (48843-9638)
PHONE.................................800 920-6035
Kim Acker, *President*
EMP: 3
SQ FT: 800
SALES: 120K **Privately Held**
SIC: 3949 Targets, archery & rifle shooting

(G-8017)
BOTTLING GROUP INC
755 Mcpherson Park Dr (48843-1933)
PHONE.................................517 545-2624
EMP: 5 **EST:** 2017
SALES (est): 344.7K **Privately Held**
SIC: 2086 Bottled & canned soft drinks

(G-8018)
C & D GAGE INC
8736 Glen Haven Dr (48843-8116)
PHONE.................................517 548-7049
Dennis J Colegrove, *President*
Harold D Kaupp, *Vice Pres*
EMP: 5
SQ FT: 1,600
SALES (est): 486.5K **Privately Held**
SIC: 3543 Industrial patterns

(G-8019)
CARCOUSTICS USA INC
1400 Durant Dr (48843-8572)
PHONE.................................517 548-6700
Alexander Elsing, *Business Mgr*
Burkhard Graske, *Opers Mgr*
Gary Leonard, *Purchasing*
Dorie Phillips, *Human Res Mgr*
Mario Contreras, *Sales Dir*
▲ **EMP:** 100
SQ FT: 25,000
SALES: 32.2MM
SALES (est): 355.8K **Privately Held**
WEB: www.carcoustics.com
SIC: 3086 Padding, foamed plastic
HQ: Carcoustics International Gmbh
   Neuenkamp 8
   Leverkusen 51381
   217 190-00

(G-8020)
CENTECH INC
1325 Grand Oaks Dr (48843-8579)
PHONE.................................517 546-9185
Keith E Burrison, *President*
EMP: 12
SQ FT: 4,240
SALES: 1.5MM **Privately Held**
SIC: 3599 Custom machinery

(G-8021)
CHEM-TREND HOLDING INC
1445 Mcpherson Park Dr (48843-3999)
PHONE.................................517 545-7980
Devanir Moraes, *Principal*
Wangbin Zhang, *Sales Mgr*
Amy Bartrum, *Sales Staff*
Lori Davis, *Sales Staff*
Patricia Villeneuve, *Technical Staff*
◆ **EMP:** 7 **EST:** 2001
SALES (est): 1.4MM
SALES (corp-wide): 11B **Privately Held**
SIC: 2899 Chemical preparations
PA: Freudenberg & Co. Kg
   Hohnerweg 2-4
   Weinheim 69469
   620 180-0

(G-8022)
CHEM-TREND LIMITED PARTNERSHIP (HQ)
1445 Mcpherson Park Dr (48843-3999)
P.O. Box 860 (48844-0860)
PHONE.................................517 546-4520
Devanir Moraes, *Partner*
Dan Hays, *Area Mgr*
Mark Marshall, *COO*
Carl Poslusdny, *Exec VP*
Subramanian Hariharan, *Vice Pres*
◆ **EMP:** 150
SQ FT: 70,000
SALES (est): 80.9MM
SALES (corp-wide): 11B **Privately Held**
WEB: www.chemtrend.com
SIC: 2899 2869 Chemical preparations; hydraulic fluids, synthetic base
PA: Freudenberg & Co. Kg
   Hohnerweg 2-4
   Weinheim 69469
   620 180-0

(G-8023)
CHEM-TREND LIMITED PARTNERSHIP
3205 E Grand River Ave (48843-8552)
PHONE.................................517 546-4520
Mitchell H Berger, *Principal*
EMP: 16
SALES (corp-wide): 11B **Privately Held**
WEB: www.chemtrend.com
SIC: 2899 Chemical preparations
HQ: Chem-Trend Limited Partnership
   1445 Mcpherson Park Dr
   Howell MI 48843
   517 546-4520

(G-8024)
CHROME WHEEL EXCHANGE LLC
4337 E Grand River Ave (48843-6583)
PHONE.................................810 360-0298
Mike Byler, *Mng Member*
EMP: 3
SALES: 740K **Privately Held**
SIC: 3312 Wheels

(G-8025)
CRASH TOOL INC
1225 Fendt Dr (48843-7594)
PHONE.................................517 552-0250
Joseph M Goers, *President*
EMP: 11
SQ FT: 10,800
SALES (est): 1.5MM **Privately Held**
SIC: 3544 Special dies & tools; jigs & fixtures

GEOGRAPHIC SECTION

Howell - Livingston County (G-8055)

(G-8026)
CRB CRANE SERVICES INC (PA)
1194 Austin Ct (48843-9556)
PHONE...................517 552-5699
Craig Bendidict, *President*
Patrica Benedict, *Shareholder*
EMP: 21
SQ FT: 24,000
SALES (est): 5.9MM **Privately Held**
SIC: 3536 Hoists, cranes & monorails

(G-8027)
CRW PLASTICS USA INC
5775 Brighton Pines Ct (48843-6403)
PHONE...................517 545-0900
Derian Campos, *President*
▲ **EMP:** 200
SQ FT: 6,000
SALES (est): 57MM **Privately Held**
SIC: 3089 Automotive parts, plastic
PA: Crw Plasticos Usa Business, Inc.
2036 Ewall St
Mount Pleasant SC 29464

(G-8028)
DESIGNTEC SERVICES INC
3050 Centennial Ct (48843-8837)
PHONE...................734 216-6051
Allen Stawick, *President*
Melanie Tshirhart, *Bookkeeper*
EMP: 3 **EST:** 1994
SALES: 200K **Privately Held**
SIC: 4212 2521 Furniture moving, local: without storage; wood office furniture

(G-8029)
DEWITTS RADIATOR LLC
1275 Grand Oaks Dr (48843-8578)
P.O. Box 288 (48844-0288)
PHONE...................517 548-0600
Jeff Scales, *President*
EMP: 12
SQ FT: 3,000
SALES (est): 2.3MM **Privately Held**
SIC: 3519 Radiators, stationary engine

(G-8030)
DIAMOND CHROME PLATING INC
604 S Michigan Ave (48843-2605)
P.O. Box 557 (48844-0557)
PHONE...................517 546-0150
John L Raymond, *President*
April Smith, *VP Human Res*
EMP: 60 **EST:** 1953
SQ FT: 30,000
SALES: 4MM
SALES (corp-wide): 6.7MM **Privately Held**
WEB: www.diamondchromeplating.com
SIC: 3471 Electroplating of metals or formed products
PA: Superior Technology Corp.
Lacey Pl
Southport CT 06890
203 255-1501

(G-8031)
DMI AUTOMOTIVE INC
1200 Durant Dr (48843-9539)
PHONE...................517 548-1414
Dieter Schormann, *President*
EMP: 18
SQ FT: 14,000
SALES (est): 2MM **Privately Held**
WEB: www.dmiautomotive.com
SIC: 3471 Chromium plating of metals or formed products

(G-8032)
DONALYN ENTERPRISES INC
Also Called: First Impression Prtg Howell
907 Fowler St (48843-2320)
PHONE...................517 546-9798
Donald Cortez, *President*
Sandie Cortez, *Vice Pres*
EMP: 15
SQ FT: 6,000
SALES (est): 2.6MM **Privately Held**
WEB: www.fipdirect.com
SIC: 2752 4783 Commercial printing, offset; packing goods for shipping

(G-8033)
DONTECH SOLUTIONS LLC
4755 Treasure Lake Dr (48843-9473)
P.O. Box 5021, Dearborn (48128-0021)
PHONE...................248 789-3086
Edward Parpart,
EMP: 27
SALES (est): 2.2MM **Privately Held**
SIC: 3714 Automotive wiring harness sets

(G-8034)
DOWN HOME INC (PA)
Also Called: Down & Associates
110 W Grand River Ave (48843-2237)
PHONE...................517 545-5955
William Down, *President*
EMP: 5 **EST:** 1983
SALES (est): 685.3K **Privately Held**
SIC: 3499 Novelties & giftware, including trophies

(G-8035)
DRATHS CORPORATION
236 Crystal Ct (48843-6141)
PHONE...................517 349-0668
Willard D Brown, *President*
EMP: 32
SQ FT: 12,500
SALES: 600K **Privately Held**
SIC: 2869 Industrial organic chemicals

(G-8036)
DUSEVOIR ACQUISITIONS LLC
Also Called: Dusevoir Metal Products
1609 White Blossom Ln (48843-8215)
PHONE...................313 562-5550
Fax: 313 562-7731
EMP: 16
SALES (est): 1.8MM
SALES (corp-wide): 1.8MM **Privately Held**
SIC: 3599 Supplier Of Production Prototype And Experimental Manufactured Metal Components
PA: Double Eagle Defense, Llc
25205 Trowbridge St
Dearborn MI 48124
313 562-5550

(G-8037)
ELECTRIC APPARATUS COMPANY
409 Roosevelt St Ste 100 (48843-1860)
P.O. Box 227 (48844-0227)
PHONE...................248 682-7992
Carmen Biller, *President*
Jim Bloomfield, *Purchasing*
EMP: 40 **EST:** 1915
SQ FT: 100,000
SALES (est): 8.2MM **Privately Held**
SIC: 3621 Motors, electric

(G-8038)
ELEMENT SERVICES LLC
3650 Norton Rd (48843-8909)
PHONE...................517 672-1005
Steven Tinskey, *Principal*
EMP: 4
SALES (est): 301.5K **Privately Held**
SIC: 2819 Elements

(G-8039)
EXPERT CLEANING SOLUTIONS INC
Also Called: Ecs Production
2440 W Highland Rd (48843-8623)
PHONE...................517 545-9095
EMP: 7 **EST:** 1998
SALES (est): 500K **Privately Held**
SIC: 2841 Mfg Soap/Other Detergents

(G-8040)
FALCON STAMPING INC
1125 Grand Oaks Dr (48843-8511)
PHONE...................517 540-6197
Mark Mobley, *President*
Cheryl Swaim, *Corp Secy*
▼ **EMP:** 9
SALES: 2.1MM **Privately Held**
WEB: www.falconstamping.com
SIC: 3469 Stamping metal for the trade

(G-8041)
FIORE CONSTRUCTION
936 Pingree Rd (48843-7695)
PHONE...................517 404-0000
Melissa Sambiagio, *Owner*
EMP: 8
SALES: 500K **Privately Held**
SIC: 1389 Construction, repair & dismantling services

(G-8042)
FRAGRANCE OUTLET INC
1475 N Burkhart Rd E115 (48855-8288)
PHONE...................517 552-9545
EMP: 5
SALES (corp-wide): 42.4MM **Privately Held**
SIC: 2844 Mfg Toilet Preparations
PA: The Fragrance Outlet Inc
11920 Miramar Pkwy
Miramar FL 33025
305 654-8015

(G-8043)
GANNETT CO INC
Also Called: Brighton Argus, The
323 E Grand River Ave (48843-2322)
PHONE...................517 548-2000
Buddy Moorehouse, *Director*
EMP: 15
SALES (corp-wide): 2.9B **Publicly Held**
SIC: 2711 Newspapers
PA: Gannett Co., Inc.
7950 Jones Branch Dr
Mc Lean VA 22102
703 854-6000

(G-8044)
GLOBAL STRAPPING LLC
Also Called: Kubinec Strapping Solutions
895 Grand Oaks Dr (48843-8512)
P.O. Box 1943, Brighton (48116-5743)
PHONE...................517 545-4900
Christopher Pagett, *Owner*
▲ **EMP:** 7
SQ FT: 10,000
SALES (est): 1.5MM **Privately Held**
WEB: www.kubinecstrapping.com
SIC: 2241 Tie tapes, woven or braided

(G-8045)
GREEN SHEET
323 E Grand River Ave (48843-2322)
PHONE...................517 548-2570
EMP: 3
SALES (est): 117.8K **Privately Held**
SIC: 2711 Newspapers-Publishing/Printing

(G-8046)
GUESS INC
Also Called: Guess Factory Store 185
1475 N Burkhart Rd B100 (48855-7325)
PHONE...................517 546-2933
Brandi Pendle, *Manager*
EMP: 13
SALES (corp-wide): 2.6B **Publicly Held**
WEB: www.guess.com
SIC: 5611 5621 2325 2339 Clothing, sportswear, men's & boys'; women's sportswear; men's & boys' jeans & dungarees; women's & misses' outerwear
PA: Guess, Inc.
1444 S Alameda St
Los Angeles CA 90021
213 765-3100

(G-8047)
HATCH STAMPING COMPANY LLC
1051 Austin Ct (48843-5515)
PHONE...................517 540-1021
Scott Holloway, *Branch Mgr*
EMP: 105
SALES (corp-wide): 863.9MM **Privately Held**
WEB: www.hatchstamping.com
SIC: 3465 3544 3469 Body parts, automobile: stamped metal; special dies & tools; metal stampings
HQ: Hatch Stamping Company Llc
635 E Industrial Dr
Chelsea MI 48118
734 475-8628

(G-8048)
HIGHLAND ENGINEERING INC
Also Called: HEI
1153 Grand Oaks Dr (48843-8511)
PHONE...................517 548-4372
Ralph S Beebe, *President*
Stephanie Rife, *Vice Pres*
Jacob Schumacher, *Project Mgr*
Raymond A Beebe Jr, *CFO*
▼ **EMP:** 45
SQ FT: 50,000
SALES: 7.9MM **Privately Held**
WEB: www.high-eng.com
SIC: 3535 3599 3441 3469 Conveyors & conveying equipment; machine shop, jobbing & repair; fabricated structural metal; stamping metal for the trade; special dies, tools, jigs & fixtures; fabricated plate work (boiler shop)

(G-8049)
HILLJACK INDUSTRIES LLC
3146 New Holland Dr (48843-6906)
P.O. Box 406 (48844-0406)
PHONE...................517 552-3874
Alison Tiihonen, *Principal*
EMP: 3
SALES (est): 165K **Privately Held**
SIC: 3999 Manufacturing industries

(G-8050)
HOLE INDUSTRIES INCORPORATED
600 Chukker Cv (48843-8685)
PHONE...................517 548-4229
Scott Hole, *President*
EMP: 7
SQ FT: 3,500
SALES (est): 750K **Privately Held**
WEB: www.holeindustries.com
SIC: 3568 3825 Power transmission equipment; instruments to measure electricity

(G-8051)
HORIZON BROS PAINTING CORP
1053 Kendra Ln (48843-8434)
PHONE...................810 632-3362
Dino Djolaj, *President*
EMP: 8
SQ FT: 3,000
SALES (est): 1.6MM **Privately Held**
SIC: 1721 3589 Commercial painting; sandblasting equipment

(G-8052)
HOWELL TOOL SERVICE INC
5818 Sterling Dr (48843-8861)
PHONE...................517 548-1114
EMP: 15
SQ FT: 19,000
SALES (est): 1MM **Privately Held**
SIC: 3291 3545 Mfg Abrasive Products Mfg Machine Tool Accessories

(G-8053)
HOWELLS MAINSTREET WINERY
201 W Grand River Ave (48843-2238)
PHONE...................517 545-9463
Sandy Vyletel, *Owner*
EMP: 6
SALES (est): 576.9K **Privately Held**
SIC: 5921 2084 Wine; wines

(G-8054)
JAM-LIVE LLC
2677 Brewer Rd (48855-8758)
PHONE...................517 282-5410
Marjorie McKenzie, *General Mgr*
Lee R McKenzie,
EMP: 3
SALES (est): 120.3K **Privately Held**
SIC: 7372 Educational computer software

(G-8055)
JESS ENTERPRISES LLC
Also Called: Lectra Tool Company
5776 E Grand River Ave (48843-9106)
PHONE...................517 546-5818
Joseph Patrell,
EMP: 9
SQ FT: 4,000

Howell - Livingston County (G-8056)

GEOGRAPHIC SECTION

SALES (est): 1.6MM **Privately Held**
WEB: www.lectratool.com
SIC: 3599 Machine shop, jobbing & repair

(G-8056)
JJ JINKLEHEIMER & CO INC
2705 E Grand River Ave # 1 (48843-6634)
P.O. Box 446 (48844-0446)
PHONE 517 546-4345
Art Coloma, *President*
EMP: 17
SQ FT: 5,000
SALES: 2.5MM **Privately Held**
WEB: www.jjink.com
SIC: 2395 7389 Embroidery products, except schiffli machine; advertising, promotional & trade show services

(G-8057)
KOPPERT BIOLOGICAL SYSTEMS
1502 N Old Us 23 (48843-9036)
PHONE 734 641-3763
Paul Koppert, *President*
Rene Ruiter, *General Mgr*
Tom Stall, *Prdtn Mgr*
Ryan Hill, *Department Mgr*
Brad Kaniski, *Planning*
▲ **EMP:** 50
SQ FT: 22,000
SALES (est): 13.5MM
SALES (corp-wide): 183.7K **Privately Held**
WEB: www.koppert.com
SIC: 2836 Biological products, except diagnostic
HQ: Koppert B.V.
    Veilingweg 14
    Berkel En Rodenrijs 2651
    105 140-444

(G-8058)
LIVINGSTON MACHINE INC
7445 Schrepfer Rd (48855-9392)
PHONE 517 546-4253
James Philburn, *President*
Linda Philburn, *Vice Pres*
EMP: 20
SQ FT: 16,000
SALES: 2MM **Privately Held**
SIC: 3599 Machine shop, jobbing & repair

(G-8059)
M S MACHINING SYSTEMS INC (PA)
5833 Fisher Rd (48855-8228)
PHONE 517 546-1170
Leo Voglrieder, *President*
Greg Cook, *Purchasing*
EMP: 15
SQ FT: 20,000
SALES (est): 3.1MM **Privately Held**
WEB: www.msmsi.com
SIC: 3541 Numerically controlled metal cutting machine tools

(G-8060)
MASONITE INTERNATIONAL CORP
Also Called: A & F Wood Products
5665 Sterling Dr (48843-9555)
PHONE 517 545-5811
EMP: 19
SALES (corp-wide): 2.1B **Publicly Held**
SIC: 2431 Doors, wood
PA: Masonite International Corporation
    201 N Franklin St Ste 300
    Tampa FL 33602
    800 895-2723

(G-8061)
MERCHANTS METALS INC
830 Grand Oaks Dr (48843-8512)
PHONE 810 227-3036
Andrew Combs, *Credit Mgr*
Alexander Baturlin, *Financial Analy*
Christopher Desm, *Manager*
EMP: 20
SALES (corp-wide): 2.9B **Privately Held**
SIC: 3496 Fencing, made from purchased wire
HQ: Merchants Metals Llc
    211 Perimeter Center Pkwy
    Atlanta GA 30346
    770 741-0306

(G-8062)
MERITOR SPECIALTY PRODUCTS LLC
Also Called: Aa Gear & Manufacturing
1045 Durant Dr (48843-9536)
PHONE 517 545-5800
EMP: 94 **Publicly Held**
SIC: 3714 Transmission housings or parts, motor vehicle; gears, motor vehicle
HQ: Meritor Specialty Products Llc
    151 Lawrence Dr
    Livermore CA 94551
    248 435-1000

(G-8063)
MICA CRAFTERS INC
1400 Old Pinckney Rd (48843-8870)
PHONE 517 548-2924
Terrance Newman, *President*
Pat Newman, *Corp Secy*
EMP: 20
SALES (est): 2.3MM **Privately Held**
SIC: 2541 1799 Counter & sink tops; counter top installation

(G-8064)
MICCUS INC
Also Called: Blubridge
3336 Lakewood Shores Dr (48843-7858)
PHONE 616 604-4449
Jeremy S Kovacs, *President*
Karin Rautiola, *Corp Secy*
▲ **EMP:** 10
SQ FT: 4,000
SALES (est): 341K **Privately Held**
SIC: 3313 Electrometallurgical products

(G-8065)
MICHIGAN ROD PRODUCTS INC (PA)
1326 Grand Oaks Dr (48843-8579)
PHONE 517 552-9812
Edward Lumm, *President*
Jerry Bendert, *Principal*
John Allen, *Vice Pres*
Timothy F Brown, *Vice Pres*
Dave Niec, *Vice Pres*
◆ **EMP:** 90
SQ FT: 128,000
SALES (est): 20.4MM **Privately Held**
WEB: www.michrod.com
SIC: 3496 3469 3452 3312 Miscellaneous fabricated wire products; metal stampings; bolts, nuts, rivets & washers; blast furnaces & steel mills

(G-8066)
MICHIGAN TOOL & GAUGE INC
1010 Packard Dr (48843-7338)
PHONE 517 548-4604
Wesley Brown, *President*
Glenda Brown, *Vice Pres*
Jason Stiles, *Sales Staff*
EMP: 25
SQ FT: 13,000
SALES: 3MM **Privately Held**
WEB: www.michigantool.com
SIC: 3544 Special dies & tools; jigs & fixtures

(G-8067)
MOTOR CITY WRAPS LLC
3510 Brophy Rd (48855-9744)
PHONE 734 812-4580
Nicholas J Zuk, *Administration*
Nicholas Zuk,
EMP: 3 **EST:** 2013
SALES (est): 154.5K **Privately Held**
SIC: 3993 Signs & advertising specialties

(G-8068)
NESCO TOOL & FIXTURE LLC
530 Fowler St (48843-2367)
PHONE 517 618-7052
Bryan Norris,
EMP: 3
SALES: 600K **Privately Held**
SIC: 3544 Special dies & tools

(G-8069)
NORTH GROUP INC
Also Called: Tenmec
2790 W Grand River Ave # 100 (48843-8424)
PHONE 517 540-0038

Ken Hartwig, *President*
EMP: 7
SALES (est): 280K **Privately Held**
SIC: 2851 Paints & allied products

(G-8070)
NORTHSTAR WHOLESALE
5818 Sterling Dr (48843-8861)
P.O. Box 2273, Brighton (48116-6073)
PHONE 517 545-2379
Dennis Norwood, *President*
▲ **EMP:** 5
SALES (est): 480.3K **Privately Held**
SIC: 3585 Heating & air conditioning combination units

(G-8071)
NOVARES US LLC
1301 Mcpherson Park Dr (48843-1935)
PHONE 517 546-1900
Joe McKinley, *General Mgr*
Joe Bourassa, *Plant Mgr*
EMP: 245
SQ FT: 26,000
SALES (corp-wide): 102.8MM **Privately Held**
WEB: www.keyplastics.com
SIC: 3089 Injection molded finished plastic products; coloring & finishing of plastic products
HQ: Novares Us Llc
    19575 Victor Pkwy Ste 400
    Livonia MI 48152
    248 449-6100

(G-8072)
NUGENTEC OILFIELD CHEM LLC
1105 Grand Oaks Dr (48843-8511)
PHONE 517 518-2712
Kelley Behrendt, *Principal*
EMP: 3
SALES (est): 191.2K **Privately Held**
SIC: 2819 Industrial inorganic chemicals

(G-8073)
NYATEX CHEMICAL COMPANY
2112 Industrial Dr (48843-2406)
P.O. Box 124 (48844-0124)
PHONE 517 546-4046
William H Hulbert, *President*
Shannon Orlowski, *Vice Pres*
EMP: 10
SQ FT: 12,000
SALES (est): 2MM **Privately Held**
SIC: 2891 Adhesives

(G-8074)
ORVIS MACHINE TOOL INC
5253 Clyde Rd (48855-6705)
PHONE 517 548-7638
Everett Orvis, *President*
EMP: 3
SALES: 500K **Privately Held**
SIC: 3599 Machine shop, jobbing & repair

(G-8075)
OVIDON MANUFACTURING LLC
1200 Grand Oaks Dr (48843-8578)
P.O. Box 189002, Utica (48318-9002)
PHONE 517 548-4005
Daniel Koppenhoefer, *Safety Mgr*
Charlene Evans, *Purchasing*
Rick Doyen, *Engineer*
Tom Lawrence, *Sales Engr*
Dave Marshall, *Sales Staff*
EMP: 56
SQ FT: 52,000
SALES (est): 13.1MM **Privately Held**
SIC: 3544 3469 Extrusion dies; metal stampings

(G-8076)
PATRICK CARBIDE DIE LLC
840 Victory Dr Ste 200 (48843-6633)
PHONE 517 546-5646
Mark Cook, *Mng Member*
EMP: 6
SQ FT: 4,000
SALES: 850K **Privately Held**
SIC: 3544 Special dies, tools, jigs & fixtures

(G-8077)
PEPSI BOTTLING GROUP
Also Called: Pepsico
404 Mason Rd (48843-3928)
PHONE 517 546-2777
Kelvin Greene, *Plant Mgr*
EMP: 12
SALES (est): 2.6MM **Privately Held**
SIC: 2086 Carbonated soft drinks, bottled & canned

(G-8078)
PEPSI-COLA METRO BTLG CO INC
725 Mcpherson St (48843-1472)
PHONE 517 546-2777
Chuck Frame, *Branch Mgr*
EMP: 100
SALES (corp-wide): 64.6B **Publicly Held**
WEB: www.joy-of-cola.com
SIC: 2086 Carbonated soft drinks, bottled & canned
HQ: Pepsi-Cola Metropolitan Bottling Company, Inc.
    1111 Westchester Ave
    White Plains NY 10604
    914 767-6000

(G-8079)
PEPSI-NEW BERN-HOWELL-151
755 Mcpherson Park Dr (48843-1933)
PHONE 517 546-7542
Andre El-Khoury, *Principal*
EMP: 5
SALES (est): 514.5K **Privately Held**
SIC: 2086 Carbonated soft drinks, bottled & canned

(G-8080)
PERFORMANCE INDUCTION
1475 Four Seasons Dr (48843-6117)
PHONE 734 658-1676
Cary M Chouinard,
EMP: 3
SQ FT: 5,000
SALES (est): 260K **Privately Held**
SIC: 3677 Inductors, electronic

(G-8081)
PRECISE FINISHING SYSTEMS INC
1650 N Burkhart Rd (48855-9690)
PHONE 517 552-9200
Michael McLean, *President*
Cary Lyons, *Principal*
Frank A Taube III, *Principal*
Michelle Loiselle, *Purch Agent*
McGregor Neville, *Treasurer*
EMP: 25
SQ FT: 23,000
SALES (est): 6.1MM **Privately Held**
WEB: www.preciseusa.com
SIC: 3823 3443 Temperature measurement instruments, industrial; industrial vessels, tanks & containers

(G-8082)
PRECISION STAMPING CO INC
1244 Grand Oaks Dr (48843-8578)
PHONE 517 546-5656
John P Parke Jr, *President*
John P Parke Sr, *Chairman*
EMP: 50 **EST:** 1946
SQ FT: 50,000
SALES (est): 10.6MM **Privately Held**
WEB: www.precisionstamping.com
SIC: 3465 3469 Body parts, automobile; stamped metal; appliance parts, porcelain enameled

(G-8083)
PREFERRED AVIONICS INSTRS LLC
3679 Bowen Rd (48855-7755)
PHONE 800 521-5130
Randy Weller, *Business Mgr*
Charles Olivier, *Manager*
Christopher Turner,
Wendy Loruss, *Admin Asst*
EMP: 11
SALES (est): 1.3MM **Privately Held**
SIC: 3812 Aircraft/aerospace flight instruments & guidance systems

GEOGRAPHIC SECTION

Howell - Livingston County (G-8114)

(G-8084)
R & D SCREW PRODUCTS INC
810 Fowler St (48843-2319)
PHONE.................................517 546-2380
Norman C Dymond, *President*
Bob Dymond, *Vice Pres*
Robert J Dymond, *Vice Pres*
Clint Adkins, *Plant Mgr*
Holly Matvchuk, *Office Mgr*
EMP: 42
SQ FT: 10,000
SALES (est): 7.7MM **Privately Held**
WEB: www.rdscrew.com
SIC: 3451 Screw machine products

(G-8085)
R AND J DUMPSTERS LLC
5886 Lange Rd (48843-9611)
PHONE.................................248 863-8579
Robert Ellwart, *Principal*
EMP: 4 **EST:** 2017
SALES (est): 268K **Privately Held**
SIC: 3443 Dumpsters, garbage

(G-8086)
R CONCEPTS INCORPORATED
10083 Bergin Rd (48843-7049)
PHONE.................................810 632-4857
Ray Sinke, *President*
Chad Sinke, *Vice Pres*
EMP: 7
SALES (est): 1.1MM **Privately Held**
SIC: 3569 3823 5084 Robots, assembly line; industrial & commercial; industrial instrmnts msrmnt display/control process variable; industrial machinery & equipment

(G-8087)
RADIOLGICAL FABRICATION DESIGN
Also Called: Rf Design
10187 Bergin Rd (48843-7048)
PHONE.................................810 632-6000
Paul Price, *President*
EMP: 5
SQ FT: 3,000
SALES: 500K **Privately Held**
WEB: www.rfdesign.com
SIC: 3842 5047 3356 Radiation shielding aprons, gloves, sheeting, etc.; X-ray film & supplies; nonferrous rolling & drawing

(G-8088)
RC DIRECTIONAL BORING INC
3402 Cedar Lake Rd (48843-5434)
P.O. Box 706 (48844-0706)
PHONE.................................517 545-4887
Cale Gillett, *President*
Ron Musial, *Vice Pres*
Becky Bowers, *Office Mgr*
EMP: 19
SALES: 3.2MM **Privately Held**
SIC: 1381 1711 3542 Directional drilling oil & gas wells; mechanical contractor; robots for metal forming: pressing, extruding, etc.

(G-8089)
RED LASER INC
5684 E Highland Rd (48843-9735)
PHONE.................................517 540-1300
Teresa Deacon, *Principal*
EMP: 8
SALES (est): 1.6MM **Privately Held**
SIC: 3441 Fabricated structural metal

(G-8090)
RETRO-A-GO-GO LLC
214 S Michigan Ave (48843-2215)
PHONE.................................734 476-0300
Kirsten Pagacz, *Principal*
▲ **EMP:** 3
SALES (est): 247.2K **Privately Held**
SIC: 2389 7389 Apparel & accessories; apparel designers, commercial

(G-8091)
REULAND ELECTRIC CO
4500 E Grand River Ave (48843-7567)
PHONE.................................517 546-4400
Bobby Moody, *Branch Mgr*
EMP: 60
SALES (corp-wide): 42.4MM **Privately Held**
WEB: www.reuland.com
SIC: 3621 Motors, electric
PA: Reuland Electric Co.
17969 Railroad St
City Of Industry CA 91748
626 964-6411

(G-8092)
REX MATERIALS INC (PA)
1600 Brewer Rd (48855-8760)
PHONE.................................517 223-3787
David D Rex, *President*
Abe Forbeck, *Engineer*
Lindsey Gregory, *Admin Sec*
EMP: 20
SALES (est): 17.6MM **Privately Held**
SIC: 3599 5033 3297 Oil filters, internal combustion engine, except automotive; insulation materials; nonclay refractories

(G-8093)
ROOTO CORPORATION
3505 W Grand River Ave (48855-9610)
PHONE.................................517 546-8330
Joon S Moon, *President*
EMP: 10
SQ FT: 5,000
SALES (est): 1.1MM **Privately Held**
WEB: www.rootocorp.com
SIC: 2842 2899 Drain pipe solvents or cleaners; concrete curing & hardening compounds

(G-8094)
RUSTOP TECHNOLOGIES LLC (PA)
4831 W Grand River Ave (48855-8713)
PHONE.................................517 223-5098
Ciara Looney, *Controller*
Robert Daymon,
John C Cook,
▼ **EMP:** 7
SQ FT: 20,000
SALES: 875K **Privately Held**
WEB: www.rustoptech.com
SIC: 2899 Anti-glare material

(G-8095)
S & G ERECTION COMPANY
2055 N Lima Center Dr (48843)
PHONE.................................517 546-9240
Tom Good, *President*
EMP: 11
SQ FT: 5,000
SALES (est): 870K **Privately Held**
SIC: 3441 Fabricated structural metal

(G-8096)
SHELLYS PINS N NEEDLES
484 Brighton Rd (48843-9427)
PHONE.................................517 861-7110
EMP: 3
SALES (est): 174K **Privately Held**
SIC: 3452 Mfg Bolts/Screws/Rivets

(G-8097)
SIGN WORKS INC
5380 E Grand River Ave (48843-9101)
PHONE.................................517 546-3620
Daniel Haberl, *President*
Robert Haberl, *Corp Secy*
Andy Haberl, *Vice Pres*
EMP: 6
SQ FT: 3,000
SALES (est): 705.2K **Privately Held**
SIC: 3993 Electric signs; neon signs

(G-8098)
SKS INDUSTRIES INC (PA)
Also Called: Armor Protective Packaging
1551 N Burkhart Rd (48855-9603)
P.O. Box 828 (48844-0828)
PHONE.................................517 546-1117
John Holden, *CEO*
Robin McConnell, *President*
David Yancho, *Vice Pres*
Jeff Goodsall, *Opers Mgr*
Steve Evans, *Mfg Staff*
▼ **EMP:** 10
SQ FT: 16,000
SALES: 15.5MM **Privately Held**
SIC: 2899 2679 Corrosion preventive lubricant; paper products, converted

(G-8099)
SMART LABEL SOLUTIONS LLC
2287 Grand Commerce Dr (48855-7320)
PHONE.................................800 996-7343
Cheryl Pearson, *Manager*
Jeff Hudson,
Kaye Pearson,
EMP: 6
SQ FT: 2,400
SALES (est): 1.7MM **Privately Held**
SIC: 3825 7373 Radio frequency measuring equipment; systems integration services

(G-8100)
SMULLEN FIRE APP SALES & SVCS
3680 W Grand River Ave (48855-7605)
P.O. Box 530 (48844-0530)
PHONE.................................517 546-8898
Jim Smullen, *General Mgr*
Estelle Kirby, *Principal*
James Smullen,
EMP: 6
SALES (est): 40K **Privately Held**
SIC: 3569 General industrial machinery

(G-8101)
SPIRAL INDUSTRIES INC
1572 N Old Hwy Us23 (48843)
PHONE.................................810 632-6300
Harry Linfield, *CEO*
Don Schellenberg, *Sales Staff*
EMP: 50 **EST:** 1969
SQ FT: 50,000
SALES (est): 11.2MM **Privately Held**
WEB: www.spiralindustries.com
SIC: 3492 3498 3429 Hose & tube fittings & assemblies, hydraulic/pneumatic; fabricated pipe & fittings; manufactured hardware (general)

(G-8102)
SPIRIT OF LIVINGSTON INC
3280 W Grand River Ave (48855-9605)
PHONE.................................517 545-8831
Carol Maczik, *President*
Daniel Maczik, *Vice Pres*
EMP: 4
SALES (est): 356.7K **Privately Held**
SIC: 2395 Embroidery products, except schiffli machine

(G-8103)
STEEL SKINZ LLC
Also Called: Steel Skinz Graphics
4836 Pinckney Rd (48843-7807)
PHONE.................................517 545-9955
EMP: 6
SALES (est): 521K **Privately Held**
SIC: 7312 7336 3993 Outdoor Advertising Svcs Coml Art/Graphic Design Mfg Signs/Ad Specialties

(G-8104)
SYD ENTERPRISES
Also Called: We're Rolling Pretzel Company
3850 E Grand River Ave (48843-8593)
PHONE.................................517 719-2740
Bob Dedarmo, *Owner*
Stacey Degarmo, *Co-Owner*
EMP: 7
SALES (est): 345.5K **Privately Held**
SIC: 2052 Pretzels

(G-8105)
TECHNCAL AUDIO VIDEO SOLUTIONS
5695 Whispering Oaks Dr (48855-9791)
PHONE.................................810 899-5546
EMP: 4 **EST:** 2010
SALES (est): 190K **Privately Held**
SIC: 3669 Mfg Communications Equipment

(G-8106)
TESMA INSTRUMENTS LLC
8770 Giovanni Ct (48855-6300)
P.O. Box 274, Hartland (48353-0274)
PHONE.................................517 940-1362
Kaitlin Mattes, *Principal*
EMP: 3
SALES (est): 104.8K **Privately Held**
SIC: 3841 Medical instruments & equipment, blood & bone work

(G-8107)
THAI SUMMIT AMERICA CORP (HQ)
1480 Mcpherson Park Dr (48843-1936)
PHONE.................................517 548-4900
Brian Miller, *Opers Staff*
Pete Leventis, *Production*
Timothy Bratton, *Engineer*
Jim Darkangelo, *Engineer*
Koji Kaneko, *Engineer*
◆ **EMP:** 100
SQ FT: 1,000,000
SALES (est): 188.6MM **Privately Held**
SIC: 3469 Metal stampings

(G-8108)
THOMPSON JOHN
Also Called: Thompson Glass Co
5345 Crooked Lake Rd (48843-8806)
PHONE.................................810 225-8780
John Thompson, *Owner*
EMP: 6
SALES (est): 280K **Privately Held**
SIC: 3229 1793 Glass fiber products; glass & glazing work

(G-8109)
THOMSON PLASTICS INC
3970 Parsons Rd (48855-9617)
PHONE.................................517 545-5026
Rick Kibbey, *Principal*
EMP: 92 **Privately Held**
SIC: 3949 3089 Sporting & athletic goods; plastic containers, except foam; injection molding of plastics
PA: Thomson Plastics, Inc.
130 Quality Dr
Thomson GA 30824

(G-8110)
THREE 60 CORPORATION
741 Victory Dr (48843-7591)
PHONE.................................517 545-3600
Bruce P Barton Jr, *President*
▲ **EMP:** 16
SQ FT: 12,200
SALES (est): 3.1MM **Privately Held**
WEB: www.three60corp.com
SIC: 3089 Molding primary plastic

(G-8111)
TITAN SPRINKLER LLC
1987 Sundance Rdg (48843-7999)
PHONE.................................517 540-1851
Timothy Kandow, *Mng Member*
EMP: 4
SALES (est): 442.2K **Privately Held**
WEB: www.titansprinkler.com
SIC: 3432 Lawn hose nozzles & sprinklers

(G-8112)
TK HOLDINGS INC
1199 Austin Ct (48843-9556)
PHONE.................................517 545-9535
EMP: 195
SALES (corp-wide): 8B **Privately Held**
SIC: 2399 Seat belts, automobile & aircraft; seat covers, automobile
HQ: Tk Holdings Inc.
4611 Wiseman Blvd
San Antonio TX 78251
210 509-0762

(G-8113)
TOMTEK HVAC INC
Also Called: Honeywell Authorized Dealer
627 Dearborn St (48843-2348)
PHONE.................................517 546-0357
Tom Fortney, *President*
EMP: 6
SALES (est): 324.5K **Privately Held**
SIC: 1711 3567 Warm air heating & air conditioning contractor; industrial furnaces & ovens

(G-8114)
TRI-MATIC SCREW PRODUCTS CO
5684 E Highland Rd (48843-9735)
PHONE.................................517 548-6414
Robert M Race Jr, *President*
Joseph F Race, *Vice Pres*
EMP: 20
SQ FT: 6,000

Howell - Livingston County (G-8115)

SALES (est): 3.9MM **Privately Held**
WEB: www.trimatic.net
SIC: **3451** Screw machine products

(G-8115)
TRIBAR MANUFACTURING LLC (HQ)
2211 Grand Commerce Dr (48855-7320)
PHONE.................................248 516-1600
Robert L Bretz, *General Mgr*
Frank Gray, *Opers Staff*
John Dragonov, *Purch Mgr*
Ivy Fox, *Purchasing*
Lou Lafrate, *Engineer*
EMP: 350
SQ FT: 65,000
SALES (est): 55.2MM
SALES (corp-wide): 55.3MM **Privately Held**
WEB: www.tribarmfg.com
SIC: **3089** Injection molded finished plastic products
PA: Tribar Technologies, Inc.
   48668 Alpha Dr
   Wixom MI 48393
   248 516-1600

(G-8116)
TURBO-SPRAY MIDWEST INC (PA)
1172 Fendt Dr Ste 3 (48843-7590)
PHONE.................................517 548-9096
James E Hynds, *President*
Jodie Lambert, *Vice Pres*
Kim Borgert, *Design Engr*
Ficaro Martin, *VP Sales*
EMP: 17
SQ FT: 10,000
SALES: 6.3MM **Privately Held**
WEB: www.turbospray.com
SIC: **3599** Custom machinery

(G-8117)
ULTIMATE SOFTWARE GROUP INC
809 E Grand River Ave A (48843-2500)
PHONE.................................517 540-9718
Scott Sheare, *Branch Mgr*
EMP: 44
SALES (corp-wide): 1.1B **Privately Held**
SIC: **7372** Business oriented computer software
PA: The Ultimate Software Group Inc
   2000 Ultimate Way
   Weston FL 33326
   954 331-7000

(G-8118)
UNIFIED INDUSTRIES INC (HQ)
Also Called: Plastic Tool Company American
1033 Sutton St (48843-1714)
PHONE.................................517 546-3220
Mark D Morelli, *President*
William Cuellar, *Sales Staff*
Alan S Korman, *Admin Sec*
▲ EMP: 13
SQ FT: 34,700
SALES (est): 5.3MM
SALES (corp-wide): 876.2MM **Publicly Held**
WEB: www.unified-ind.com
SIC: **3498** **3536** Fabricated pipe & fittings; cranes, overhead traveling
PA: Columbus Mckinnon Corporation
   205 Crosspoint Pkwy
   Getzville NY 14068
   716 689-5400

(G-8119)
UNIVERSAL COMPONENTS LLC
510 S Hughes Rd (48843-9180)
PHONE.................................517 861-7064
Mary M Novak, *President*
EMP: 3
SQ FT: 3,000
SALES: 50K **Privately Held**
SIC: **3965** **3011** Fasteners; tires & inner tubes

(G-8120)
UPCYCLE POLYMERS LLC
1145 Sutton St (48843-1715)
PHONE.................................248 446-8750
Dan Root,
EMP: 3

SQ FT: 24,000
SALES: 2MM **Privately Held**
SIC: **2611** **5093** Pulp mills, chemical & semichemical processing; plastics scrap

(G-8121)
VIC BOND SALES INC
2225 W Grand River Ave (48843-8515)
PHONE.................................517 548-0107
Gary Swick, *Principal*
EMP: 7
SALES (est): 386.3K
SALES (corp-wide): 28.8MM **Privately Held**
SIC: **5251** **5084** **5075** **3432** Pumps & pumping equipment; pumps & pumping equipment; warm air heating equipment & supplies; plumbing fixture fittings & trim
PA: Vic Bond Sales, Inc.
   1240 E Coldwater Rd
   Flint MI 48505
   810 787-5321

(G-8122)
WOW FACTOR TABLES AND EVENTS
4337 E Grand River Ave (48843-6583)
PHONE.................................248 550-5922
Cincarla Goddard, *Owner*
EMP: 4
SQ FT: 500
SALES (est): 165.9K **Privately Held**
SIC: **2051** Bakery, for home service delivery

(G-8123)
ZENITH GLOBAL LLC
1100 Sutton St (48843-1716)
PHONE.................................517 546-7402
Suman Tetarbe,
EMP: 6
SALES (est): 1.3MM
SALES (corp-wide): 2.5B **Privately Held**
SIC: **3081** Unsupported plastics film & sheet
HQ: Pmc, Inc.
   12243 Branford St
   Sun Valley CA 91352
   818 896-1101

(G-8124)
ZENWOLF TECHNOLOGIES GROUP
815 E Grand River Ave (48843-2431)
PHONE.................................517 618-2000
Kirk Lanam, *President*
EMP: 26
SQ FT: 2,880
SALES: 1.8MM **Privately Held**
SIC: **7311** **4813** **2741** Advertising consultant; ;

Hubbard Lake
Alpena County

(G-8125)
FAIR & SQUARE PALLET & LBR CO
5700 Ratz Rd (49747-9547)
PHONE.................................989 727-3949
Robin Wilke, *Partner*
Randolph Wilke, *Partner*
Richard Wilke, *Partner*
Rory Wilke, *Partner*
Rudolph Wilke, *Partner*
EMP: 4
SALES: 260K **Privately Held**
SIC: **2448** Wood pallets & skids

Hubbell
Houghton County

(G-8126)
KOPPERS PERFORMANCE CHEM INC
Also Called: Peninsula Copper Industries
52430 Duncan Ave (49934-9777)
PHONE.................................906 296-8271
Kevin Codere, *Branch Mgr*
EMP: 38

SALES (corp-wide): 1.7B **Publicly Held**
SIC: **2819** **4213** Copper compounds or salts, inorganic; trucking, except local
HQ: Koppers Performance Chemicals Inc.
   1016 Everee Inn Rd
   Griffin GA 30224
   770 228-8434

Hudson
Lenawee County

(G-8127)
ARC METAL STAMPING LLC
Also Called: Kecy Metal Technologies
4111 Munson Hwy (49247-9551)
PHONE.................................517 448-8954
EMP: 90 **EST:** 2014
SALES (est): 4.6MM **Privately Held**
SIC: **3465** Automotive stampings

(G-8128)
ARC-KECY LLC
4111 Munson Hwy (49247-9551)
PHONE.................................517 448-8954
Raymond Cox, *Principal*
EMP: 90
SALES (est): 7.5MM **Privately Held**
SIC: **3465** Automotive stampings

(G-8129)
HERALD BI-COUNTY INC
115 S Church St (49247-1301)
PHONE.................................517 448-2201
John W Monohan, *President*
Geri Monohan, *Vice Pres*
Karen Downing, *Treasurer*
EMP: 6
SALES (est): 588.2K **Privately Held**
SIC: **2741** **2752** Shopping news: publishing only, not printed on site; commercial printing, lithographic

(G-8130)
HI-LEX CONTROLS INCORPORATED
15780 Steger Indus Dr (49247-9574)
PHONE.................................517 448-2752
Bill Spencer, *Vice Pres*
Takuju Murayama, *Manager*
EMP: 165 **Privately Held**
SIC: **3714** **3625** Motor vehicle parts & accessories; relays & industrial controls
HQ: Hi-Lex Controls Incorporated
   152 Simpson Dr
   Litchfield MI 49252
   517 542-2955

(G-8131)
HORNET MANUFACTURING INC
14587 Day Rd (49247-9268)
PHONE.................................517 448-8203
Matt Shallsky, *CEO*
William Tsompanidis, *Opers Staff*
Christi Shallsky, *Admin Sec*
EMP: 7
SQ FT: 23,000
SALES (est): 1.6MM **Privately Held**
SIC: **3443** Fabricated plate work (boiler shop)

(G-8132)
HUDSON POST GAZETTE
113 S Market St (49247-1317)
P.O. Box 70 (49247-0070)
PHONE.................................517 448-2611
Edward Potter, *Owner*
EMP: 4 **EST:** 1858
SQ FT: 2,000
SALES: 120K **Privately Held**
SIC: **2711** Newspapers: publishing only, not printed on site

(G-8133)
KECY CORPORATION
4111 Munson Hwy (49247-9551)
PHONE.................................517 448-8954
Ray Cox, *President*
Dave Zerbey, *Vice Pres*
▲ EMP: 38
SALES (est): 7.8MM **Privately Held**
SIC: **3469** Metal stampings

(G-8134)
KECY PRODUCTS INC
4111 Munson Hwy (49247-9551)
P.O. Box 150 (49247-0150)
PHONE.................................517 448-8954
Jack Donaldson, *President*
Minoru Kitsuda, *Vice Pres*
▲ EMP: 60
SQ FT: 26,000
SALES (est): 10.5MM **Privately Held**
WEB: www.kecyproducts.com
SIC: **3465** **5084** **3469** Body parts, automobile: stamped metal; industrial machinery & equipment; metal stampings

(G-8135)
MALABAR MANUFACTURING INC
4255 Munson Hwy (49247-9551)
P.O. Box 128 (49247-0128)
PHONE.................................517 448-2155
Bart Malarney, *President*
John W Malarney, *Principal*
EMP: 15
SQ FT: 13,000
SALES (est): 1.8MM **Privately Held**
SIC: **3451** Screw machine products

(G-8136)
MALMAC TOOL AND FIXTURE INC
4255 Munson Hwy (49247-9551)
P.O. Box 128 (49247-0128)
PHONE.................................517 448-8244
John W Malarney, *President*
Dale Mc Faul, *Vice Pres*
EMP: 5
SQ FT: 3,500
SALES (est): 300K **Privately Held**
SIC: **3545** **3544** Tools & accessories for machine tools; special dies, tools, jigs & fixtures

(G-8137)
NORTHSHORE PONTOON
3985 Munson Hwy (49247-9800)
PHONE.................................517 547-8877
Doug Haskell, *Owner*
EMP: 5
SALES (est): 283.3K **Privately Held**
SIC: **3732** **5551** Boats, fiberglass: building & repairing; motor boat dealers

(G-8138)
PASCHAL BURIAL VAULT SVC LLC
Also Called: Paschal Burial Vaults
431 School St (49247-1427)
PHONE.................................517 448-8868
Lee Paschal, *Mng Member*
EMP: 5
SALES: 500K **Privately Held**
WEB: www.paschalburialvaultllc.com
SIC: **3272** Burial vaults, concrete or precast terrazzo

(G-8139)
PRO SHOP THE/P S GRAPHICS
309 W Main St (49247-1051)
P.O. Box 27 (49247-0027)
PHONE.................................517 448-8490
Dave Sheeley, *Owner*
Janet Sheely, *Owner*
EMP: 8 **EST:** 1979
SQ FT: 2,500
SALES (est): 125K **Privately Held**
SIC: **2261** **5941** **5999** **2759** Screen printing of cotton broadwoven fabrics; sporting goods & bicycle shops; trophies & plaques; screen printing

(G-8140)
PURITY FOODS INC
417 S Meridian Rd (49247-9709)
PHONE.................................517 448-7440
Jaclyn Bowen, *Principal*
◆ EMP: 11 **EST:** 1979
SQ FT: 3,000
SALES (est): 5.4MM
SALES (corp-wide): 3B **Publicly Held**
WEB: www.purityfoods.com
SIC: **5153** **5191** **5149** **2041** Grains; corn; soybeans; seeds: field, garden & flower; pasta & rice; flour & other grain mill products

PA: The Andersons Inc
1947 Briarfield Blvd
Maumee OH 43537
419 893-5050

(G-8141)
RIMA MANUFACTURING COMPANY (PA)
3850 Munson Hwy (49247-9804)
PHONE 517 448-8921
Edward J Engle Jr, *President*
Laura Tomasello, *Exec VP*
Dolores Randolph, *Human Resources*
Rich Willett, *Manager*
Jim Prestidge, *Supervisor*
EMP: 100 **EST:** 1955
SQ FT: 50,000
SALES (est): 20.8MM **Privately Held**
WEB: www.rimamfg.com
SIC: 3451 3599 Screw machine products; machine shop, jobbing & repair

(G-8142)
SOLUTIONS FOR INDUSTRY INC
13240 Egypt Rd (49247-9237)
PHONE 517 448-8608
Kevin V Kuhn, *President*
Jane Stewart, *Vice Pres*
EMP: 6
SALES (est): 975K **Privately Held**
WEB: www.solutionsforindustryinc.com
SIC: 3625 7539 8711 Control equipment, electric; electrical services; machine tool design

Hudsonville
Ottawa County

(G-8143)
ADVANTAGE SIGN SUPPLY INC (PA)
Also Called: Advantage Sign Grphic Slutions
4182 Royal Ct (49426-7957)
P.O. Box 888684, Grand Rapids (49588-8684)
PHONE 877 237-4464
Gary Van Dyke, *CEO*
Steve Kloosterman, *President*
Dan Irrer, *Vice Pres*
Katy Vandewaa, *Marketing Mgr*
Katy Kloosterman, *Admin Sec*
▲ **EMP:** 50
SQ FT: 50,000
SALES: 55MM **Privately Held**
WEB: www.advantagesignsupply.com
SIC: 3993 Signs & advertising specialties

(G-8144)
ALTRON AUTOMATION INC
3523 Highland Dr (49426-1916)
PHONE 616 669-7711
Ronald G McNees, *President*
Arnold Lacombe, *Vice Pres*
Patrick Cooper, *CFO*
EMP: 60
SQ FT: 60,000
SALES (est): 25.6MM **Privately Held**
WEB: www.altronautomation.com
SIC: 3535 Unit handling conveying systems

(G-8145)
ALTRONICS ENERGY LLC
3523 Highland Dr (49426-1916)
PHONE 616 662-7401
Ronald McNees,
EMP: 10
SALES (est): 833.4K **Privately Held**
SIC: 3674 3511 Solar cells; hydraulic turbines

(G-8146)
APTIV SERVICES US LLC
4254 Oak Meadow Dr (49426-8656)
PHONE 248 813-2000
James Kikkert, *Engineer*
EMP: 6
SALES (corp-wide): 16.6B **Privately Held**
SIC: 3714 Motor vehicle parts & accessories
HQ: Aptiv Services Us, Llc
5725 Innovation Dr
Troy MI 48098

(G-8147)
BAKER FASTENING SYSTEMS INC
5030 40th Ave (49426-9481)
PHONE 616 669-7400
Rick Sousley, *President*
▲ **EMP:** 7
SALES (est): 1.2MM **Privately Held**
SIC: 3965 Fasteners

(G-8148)
BLOEM LLC (PA)
Also Called: Bloem Living
3301 Hudson Trail Dr (49426-7401)
P.O. Box 583 (49426-0583)
PHONE 616 622-6344
Brian Rudy, *CFO*
Ryan Mast,
Ramel Steede, *Maintence Staff*
Sarah Ryan,
Kevin Wilson,
EMP: 10
SALES (est): 4.5MM **Privately Held**
SIC: 3089 Planters, plastic

(G-8149)
BLUE PONY LLC
Also Called: Joleado
3479 8th Ave (49426-9639)
PHONE 616 291-5554
Michael Emaus,
EMP: 8
SQ FT: 5,000
SALES (est): 325.2K **Privately Held**
SIC: 7372 8748 8742 Business oriented computer software; communications consulting; marketing consulting services; financial consultant

(G-8150)
CHRISTMAS SPORTS ENTERPRISE
7490 Taylor St (49426-9525)
PHONE 616 895-6238
Morris Klinger, *CEO*
EMP: 3
SALES (est): 172.8K **Privately Held**
SIC: 3799 Recreational vehicles

(G-8151)
CREME CURLS BAKERY INC
5292 Lawndale Ave (49426-1213)
P.O. Box 276 (49426-0276)
PHONE 616 669-6230
Gary A Bierling, *President*
Paul H Bierling, *Vice Pres*
EMP: 120 **EST:** 1966
SQ FT: 66,000
SALES (est): 10.8MM **Privately Held**
WEB: www.cremecurls.com
SIC: 2051 Bakery: wholesale or wholesale/retail combined

(G-8152)
CUSTOM MACHINING BY FARLEY
2792 24th Ave (49426-9603)
PHONE 616 896-8469
Robert Van Farowe, *President*
Marene Van Farowe, *Vice Pres*
EMP: 4
SQ FT: 2,400
SALES (est): 549.6K **Privately Held**
SIC: 3599 Machine shop, jobbing & repair

(G-8153)
CUSTOM TOOL & DIE SERVICE INC
5090 40th Ave Ste A (49426-9595)
PHONE 616 662-1068
Jacob Broekema, *President*
Beverly Broekema, *Treasurer*
EMP: 8 **EST:** 1976
SQ FT: 10,000
SALES (est): 770K **Privately Held**
SIC: 3544 Special dies & tools

(G-8154)
D&JS PLASTICS LLC
2322 Edson Dr (49426-7789)
PHONE 616 745-5798
Doug Reams,
Jon Price,
Justin Price,
Colin Reams,
Tom Reams,
EMP: 5 **EST:** 2006
SALES (est): 425.6K **Privately Held**
SIC: 3089 2673 Battery cases, plastic or plastic combination; garment bags (plastic film): made from purchased materials

(G-8155)
EMERGENCY TECHNOLOGY INC
Also Called: Sound-Off Signal
3900 Central Pkwy (49426-7884)
P.O. Box 206 (49426-0206)
PHONE 616 896-7100
Mark Litke, *President*
George Boerigter, *Chairman*
Marni Epstein, *Vice Pres*
Greg Leatherman, *Prdtn Mgr*
Scott Huyser, *Mfg Staff*
▲ **EMP:** 100
SQ FT: 40,000
SALES (est): 46.9MM **Privately Held**
WEB: www.soundoffsignal.com
SIC: 3648 3625 3699 3647 Lighting equipment; control circuit devices, magnet & solid state; electric sound equipment; motor vehicle lighting equipment; emergency alarms

(G-8156)
ESPEC CORP
4141 Central Pkwy (49426-7828)
PHONE 616 896-6100
EMP: 28
SALES (est): 6.5MM **Privately Held**
WEB: www.espec.com
SIC: 3826 Environmental testing equipment

(G-8157)
GRAPHICS UNLIMITED INC
2340 Chicago Dr (49426-2404)
PHONE 616 662-0455
Tim Ritsema, *President*
EMP: 4
SALES (est): 350K **Privately Held**
SIC: 2893 Printing ink

(G-8158)
GUARNERI HOUSE LLC
5645 Balsam Dr Ste 800 (49426-1156)
PHONE 616 451-4960
Linda Reiley,
Aaron Reiley,
EMP: 4
SQ FT: 7,500
SALES (est): 450K **Privately Held**
SIC: 3931 7359 Strings, musical instrument; musical instrument rental services

(G-8159)
HARBOR MASTER LTD
3127 Highland Blvd (49426-7934)
PHONE 616 669-3170
Tim Contreras, *President*
EMP: 10
SQ FT: 24,000
SALES (est): 1.5MM **Privately Held**
WEB: www.harbor-master.com
SIC: 3536 Boat lifts

(G-8160)
INNOVTIVE DSPLAY SOLUTIONS LLC
Also Called: IDS
4256 Corp Exch Dr Ste A (49426)
PHONE 616 896-6080
Brian Newenhouse,
EMP: 10 **EST:** 2007
SALES (est): 2MM **Privately Held**
SIC: 2431 2499 Doors & door parts & trim, wood; laundry products, wood

(G-8161)
KENT QUALITY FOODS INC
3426 Quincy St (49426-7835)
PHONE 616 459-4595
Charles M Soet, *President*
Karl Soet, *Vice Pres*
Jim Zubkus, *Vice Pres*
Steve Airo, *Human Res Dir*
Chris Vandervelde, *Info Tech Dir*
EMP: 145
SALES (est): 51.1MM **Privately Held**
WEB: www.kentqualityfoods.com
SIC: 2011 2013 Meat packing plants; sausages & other prepared meats

(G-8162)
LOL TELCOM INC
Also Called: G-Town Techs
6897 Springfield Ave (49426-9340)
P.O. Box 161 (49426-0161)
PHONE 616 888-6171
Jeffery Webb, *President*
EMP: 300
SQ FT: 20,000
SALES: 3MM **Privately Held**
SIC: 5999 3661 8742 Telephone & communication equipment; fiber optics communications equipment; business consultant

(G-8163)
M&D DUMPSTERS LLC
6117 Polk St (49426-8501)
P.O. Box 676, Jenison (49429-0676)
PHONE 616 299-0234
Mike Oosterhouse, *Principal*
EMP: 5
SALES (est): 542.9K **Privately Held**
SIC: 3443 Dumpsters, garbage

(G-8164)
MARKED TOOL INC
2934 Highland Blvd (49426-9455)
PHONE 616 669-3201
Mark W Overway, *President*
Sally Rae Overway, *Corp Secy*
EMP: 8
SQ FT: 7,000
SALES (est): 1.3MM **Privately Held**
WEB: www.markedtool.com
SIC: 3599 Machine shop, jobbing & repair

(G-8165)
MCCLURE TABLES INC
4939 Big Bass Dr (49426-8608)
PHONE 616 662-5974
Todd McClure, *CEO*
EMP: 7
SALES (corp-wide): 1.2MM **Privately Held**
SIC: 3949 Shuffleboards & shuffleboard equipment
PA: Mcclure Tables Inc.
6661 Roger Dr Ste C
Jenison MI 49428
616 662-5974

(G-8166)
MESSENGER PRINTING & COPY SVC
5300 Plaza Ave (49426-1491)
P.O. Box 302 (49426-0302)
PHONE 616 669-5620
Martin De Young, *President*
Kenneth Jipping, *Vice Pres*
EMP: 5
SQ FT: 1,500
SALES (est): 363K **Privately Held**
SIC: 2752 Commercial printing, offset

(G-8167)
MFP AUTOMATION ENGINEERING INC
4404 Central Pkwy (49426-7831)
PHONE 616 538-5700
Roger Betten, *CEO*
Roger L Betten Jr, *President*
Kari Kars, *General Mgr*
Brad Kirk, *COO*
Joe Tidd, *Warehouse Mgr*
EMP: 68
SQ FT: 47,500
SALES: 33.1MM **Privately Held**
WEB: www.mifp.com
SIC: 5084 3594 Hydraulic systems equipment & supplies; pneumatic tools & equipment; power plant machinery; fluid power pumps & motors

(G-8168)
MICHIGAN CELERY PROMOTION COOP
5009 40th Ave (49426-9481)
P.O. Box 306 (49426-0306)
PHONE 616 669-1250

Hudsonville - Ottawa County (G-8169)

Gary Wruble, *General Mgr*
Duane Frens, *General Mgr*
EMP: 25
SALES (est): 9.6MM **Privately Held**
WEB: www.michigancelery.com
SIC: 5148 2099 Vegetables; food preparations

(G-8169)
MICHIGAN VEAL INC
3007 Van Buren St (49426-1524)
P.O. Box 155 (49426-0155)
PHONE.................................616 669-6688
Ed Deyoung, *President*
Ed De Young, *President*
Lisa De Young, *Admin Sec*
EMP: 12 **EST:** 1920
SQ FT: 30,000
SALES: 15MM **Privately Held**
SIC: 2011 Lamb products from lamb slaughtered on site; boxed beef from meat slaughtered on site; veal from meat slaughtered on site

(G-8170)
MIGHTY CO
Also Called: Mighty In The Midwest
50 Louis St Nw 520 (49426)
PHONE.................................616 822-1013
Clifton Wegner, *President*
Danni Shultz, *Project Mgr*
Stephanie Malburg, *Opers Mgr*
EMP: 24
SALES: 1.6MM **Privately Held**
SIC: 7372 Prepackaged software

(G-8171)
MMM MEAT LLC
Also Called: Tolman's Wholesale Meats
4598 Buttermilk Dr (49426-1953)
PHONE.................................616 669-6140
Brandon Bassett, *CEO*
EMP: 17
SALES (est): 586.7K **Privately Held**
SIC: 2011 Meat packing plants

(G-8172)
MYPAC INC
1570 36th Ave (49426-7612)
PHONE.................................616 896-9359
Edward Myaard, *President*
Ed Myard, *President*
Jack Myaard, *Vice Pres*
EMP: 2
SQ FT: 12,000
SALES (est): 1.2MM **Privately Held**
WEB: www.mypac.myers.edu
SIC: 2011 Meat packing plants

(G-8173)
ON GREEN LOGOS
2430 Chicago Dr (49426-2406)
PHONE.................................616 669-1928
David Thompson, *Principal*
EMP: 3
SALES (est): 333.2K **Privately Held**
SIC: 2395 Embroidery & art needlework

(G-8174)
PROCESS PARTNERS INC
3770 Chicago Dr (49426-1637)
PHONE.................................616 875-2156
James Breslin, *President*
Sheila Breslin, *CFO*
EMP: 8
SALES: 1.8MM **Privately Held**
WEB: www.processpartners.com
SIC: 8711 3556 Engineering services; food products machinery

(G-8175)
RAPIDTEK LLC
Also Called: Rapid-Veyor
3825 Central Pkwy Ste A (49426-7844)
PHONE.................................616 662-0954
H Alan Denning, *President*
Quinn Denning, *Mng Member*
Alan Denning,
▼ **EMP:** 8
SQ FT: 11,000
SALES (est): 1.1MM **Privately Held**
WEB: www.rapidautomated.com
SIC: 3799 5084 Towing bars & systems; industrial machinery & equipment

(G-8176)
ROYAL PLASTICS LLC
3765 Quincy St (49426-8836)
PHONE.................................616 669-3393
Paul Vanderlaan, *President*
EMP: 3
SALES (est): 234.3K **Privately Held**
SIC: 3089 Injection molding of plastics

(G-8177)
ROYAL TECHNOLOGIES CORPORATION
3133 Highland Blvd (49426-7495)
PHONE.................................616 667-4102
Doyle Gerrig, *Branch Mgr*
EMP: 150
SALES (est): 14.5MM
SALES (corp-wide): 228.8MM **Privately Held**
WEB: www.royal-plastics.com
SIC: 3089 Injection molding of plastics
PA: Royal Technologies Corporation
3765 Quincy St
Hudsonville MI 49426
616 669-3393

(G-8178)
ROYAL TECHNOLOGIES CORPORATION (PA)
Also Called: Hi-Tech Plastics
3765 Quincy St (49426-8408)
PHONE.................................616 669-3393
James H Vanderkolk, *President*
Perry Franco, *Vice Pres*
Tom Kennedy, *Vice Pres*
Richard C Klamer, *Vice Pres*
Kirk Lambers, *Vice Pres*
◆ **EMP:** 700
SQ FT: 82,000
SALES (est): 228.8MM **Privately Held**
WEB: www.royal-plastics.com
SIC: 3089 Injection molded finished plastic products

(G-8179)
ROYAL TECHNOLOGIES CORPORATION
3712 Quincy St (49426-8408)
PHONE.................................616 667-4102
Jim Scott, *Manager*
EMP: 150
SALES (corp-wide): 228.8MM **Privately Held**
WEB: www.royal-plastics.com
SIC: 3089 Injection molded finished plastic products
PA: Royal Technologies Corporation
3765 Quincy St
Hudsonville MI 49426
616 669-3393

(G-8180)
ROYAL TECHNOLOGIES CORPORATION
2905 Corporate Grove Dr (49426-8020)
PHONE.................................616 669-3393
Ed Bos, *Manager*
EMP: 150
SALES (est): 16MM
SALES (corp-wide): 228.8MM **Privately Held**
WEB: www.royal-plastics.com
SIC: 3089 Injection molding of plastics
PA: Royal Technologies Corporation
3765 Quincy St
Hudsonville MI 49426
616 669-3393

(G-8181)
RT BALDWIN ENTERPRISES INC
Also Called: R.T. Baldwin Hardwood Floors
4322 Cent Pkwy Ste A (49426)
PHONE.................................616 669-1626
Lance Baldwin, *President*
EMP: 8
SALES: 700K **Privately Held**
SIC: 2426 Flooring, hardwood

(G-8182)
SHEFIT INC
5340 Plaza Ave Ste B (49426-1446)
P.O. Box 396 (49426-0396)
PHONE.................................616 209-7003
Robert Moylan, *President*
Rachel Tuttleman, *Opers Staff*
Rachelle Tuttleman, *Controller*
Sara Moylan, *Shareholder*
EMP: 10
SQ FT: 3,000
SALES (est): 200K **Privately Held**
SIC: 2342 Brassieres

(G-8183)
TOLMANS PROCESSING
Also Called: Tolman Meat Processing
7405 Port Sheldon St (49426-9513)
PHONE.................................616 875-8598
Jerry Nyenbrink, *Owner*
EMP: 3
SALES (est): 56.2K **Privately Held**
SIC: 7299 2011 Butcher service, processing only; computer photography or portrait; pillow rental service; cured meats from meat slaughtered on site; dried meats from meat slaughtered on site; sausages from meat slaughtered on site

(G-8184)
TOPCRAFT METAL PRODUCTS INC
Also Called: T M P
5112 40th Ave (49426-8433)
PHONE.................................616 669-1790
Kelly Weener, *President*
Yalonda Bonds, *Principal*
Ronda Burwell, *Principal*
Joseph Heller, *Principal*
Brian Sherwood, *Principal*
▲ **EMP:** 45 **EST:** 1971
SQ FT: 24,500
SALES (est): 9.5MM **Privately Held**
WEB: www.topcraftmetal.com
SIC: 3451 Screw machine products

(G-8185)
WB PALLETS INC
4440 Chicago Dr (49426-9483)
PHONE.................................616 669-3000
Warren Busscher, *President*
Diane Joy Busscher, *Vice Pres*
EMP: 24
SQ FT: 32,000
SALES: 4.3MM **Privately Held**
SIC: 2448 Pallets, wood

(G-8186)
WEST MICHIGAN CABINET SUPPLY
Also Called: Wmcs
4366 Central Pkwy (49426-7830)
PHONE.................................616 896-6990
Steve Sterk, *President*
Roland Hoezee, *Vice Pres*
EMP: 10
SQ FT: 5,000
SALES (est): 1MM **Privately Held**
WEB: www.wmcabinetdoors.com
SIC: 2434 Wood kitchen cabinets

(G-8187)
WHATS SCOOP
3667 Baldwin St (49426-9767)
PHONE.................................616 662-6423
Chandler Bullheis, *Owner*
EMP: 3 **EST:** 2008
SALES (est): 237.4K **Privately Held**
SIC: 2024 Ice cream, bulk

Huntington Woods
Oakland County

(G-8188)
HI TECH GEAR INC
26020 Allor Ave (48070-1402)
PHONE.................................248 548-8649
Carol Ann Marvick, *Corp Secy*
Dennis Durant, *Vice Pres*
EMP: 3
SALES (est): 240K **Privately Held**
SIC: 3462 Gears, forged steel

(G-8189)
LORNE HANLEY
Also Called: Custom Workroom
10085 Lincoln Dr (48070-1507)
PHONE.................................248 547-9865
Lorne Hanley, *Owner*
EMP: 6
SALES (est): 368.2K **Privately Held**
SIC: 2391 2591 Curtains & draperies; drapery hardware & blinds & shades

(G-8190)
MINOWITZ MANUFACTURING CO (PA)
26311 Woodward Ave (48070-1331)
PHONE.................................586 779-5940
David Pereira, *President*
Paul Pereira, *Chairman*
Eleanor Pereira, *Treasurer*
James Sopala, *Office Mgr*
▲ **EMP:** 25 **EST:** 1966
SQ FT: 38,000
SALES (est): 9.6MM **Privately Held**
WEB: www.minowitz.com
SIC: 3069 3714 3519 3694 Hard rubber & molded rubber products; drive shafts, motor vehicle; fuel pumps, motor vehicle; gas tanks, motor vehicle; parts & accessories, internal combustion engines; engine electrical equipment; generators, automotive & aircraft; motors & generators; carburetors, pistons, rings, valves

(G-8191)
POLYMERICA LIMITED COMPANY (PA)
Also Called: Global Enterprises
26909 Woodward Ave (48070-1365)
PHONE.................................248 542-2000
William Kunz, *Managing Prtnr*
Manuel Gueterrez, *Partner*
Chris Cormier, *Partner*
Patricia Kladzyk, *Partner*
Marilyn Kunz, *Partner*
▲ **EMP:** 225
SQ FT: 2,400
SALES (est): 86MM **Privately Held**
WEB: www.globalent.org
SIC: 3089 Extruded finished plastic products

(G-8192)
TWIN BEGINNINGS LLC (PA)
13308 Lasalle Blvd (48070-1029)
PHONE.................................248 542-6250
Karla A Scanlan,
Karen Kuhn,
EMP: 3
SALES (est): 240K **Privately Held**
SIC: 3556 Dairy & milk machinery

Ida
Monroe County

(G-8193)
CCO HOLDINGS LLC
3245 Lewis Ave (48140-9708)
PHONE.................................734 868-5044
EMP: 3
SALES (corp-wide): 43.6B **Publicly Held**
SIC: 5064 4841 3663 3651 Electrical appliances, television & radio; cable & other pay television services; radio & TV communications equipment; household audio & video equipment
HQ: Cco Holdings, Llc
400 Atlantic St
Stamford CT 06901
203 905-7801

(G-8194)
TRUE ANLYTICS MFG SLUTIONS LLC
5400 Douglas Rd (48140-9512)
PHONE.................................517 902-9700
David Morley, *Principal*
EMP: 4 **EST:** 2016
SALES (est): 119K **Privately Held**
SIC: 7372 7389 Application computer software;

Imlay City
Lapeer County

(G-8195)
ALL SIZE PALLETS
4005 N Van Dyke Rd (48444-8902)
PHONE...................................810 721-1999
Carman Daly, *Owner*
EMP: 27
SALES (est): 2.3MM **Privately Held**
WEB: www.allsizepallets.com
SIC: 2448 Pallets, wood

(G-8196)
ANAND NVH NORTH AMERICA INC
2083 Reek Rd (48444-9203)
PHONE...................................810 724-2400
Mark R Selleke, *President*
Kraig L Selleke, *Vice Pres*
▲ **EMP**: 244
SQ FT: 105,057
SALES (est): 41.1MM **Privately Held**
WEB: www.rubberenterprises.com
SIC: 3069 3714 3061 3052 Molded rubber products; motor vehicle parts & accessories; mechanical rubber goods; rubber & plastics hose & beltings; metal stampings

(G-8197)
CHAMPION BUS INC
331 Graham Rd (48444-9738)
P.O. Box 158 (48444-0158)
PHONE...................................810 724-1753
John Resnik, *President*
▲ **EMP**: 300
SQ FT: 172,000
SALES (est): 60.8MM **Publicly Held**
WEB: www.championbus.com
SIC: 3711 Motor vehicles & car bodies
PA: Rev Group, Inc.
111 E Kilbourn Ave # 2600
Milwaukee WI 53202

(G-8198)
DIETECH TOOL & MFG INC
385 Industrial Dr (48444-1337)
PHONE...................................810 724-0505
Arthur Adam, *Ch of Bd*
Gary Adam, *President*
Ronald Adam, *Vice Pres*
Norman Adam, *Treasurer*
Steve Dyer, *Manager*
EMP: 94
SQ FT: 30,000
SALES (est): 18MM **Privately Held**
WEB: www.dietechtool.com
SIC: 3469 Stamping metal for the trade

(G-8199)
G & L MFG INC
2 Mountain Dr (48444-8819)
PHONE...................................810 724-4101
Pete Lutz, *President*
EMP: 6
SALES (est): 23.2K **Privately Held**
SIC: 3999 Manufacturing industries

(G-8200)
GENERAL COACH AMERICA INC (HQ)
275 Graham Rd (48444-9738)
PHONE...................................810 724-6474
John Resnik, *President*
Theresa Smith, *Vice Pres*
Dominic Romeo, *Treasurer*
T Michael Pangburn, *Admin Sec*
EMP: 9
SALES (est): 19.4MM **Publicly Held**
SIC: 3711 Buses, all types, assembly of

(G-8201)
GRAPENTIN SPECIALTIES INC
Also Called: Xstream Tackle
5599 Bowers Rd (48444-8919)
PHONE...................................810 724-0636
Diane L Grapentin, *President*
Laura Vradelis, *Managing Dir*
Jeffrey Grapentin, *Vice Pres*
EMP: 4
SQ FT: 4,000
SALES: 350K **Privately Held**
SIC: 5091 5941 3949 Fishing tackle; hunting equipment & supplies; camping equipment & supplies; fishing equipment; camping equipment; fishing tackle, general

(G-8202)
HYPONEX CORPORATION
Scotts- Hyponex
332 Graham Rd (48444-9600)
PHONE...................................810 724-2875
Nick Prusakiewicz, *Plant Mgr*
Mary Davis, *Manager*
Jill Rowe, *Manager*
Ron Kampo, *Maintence Staff*
EMP: 50
SALES (corp-wide): 2.6B **Publicly Held**
SIC: 2873 2875 Plant foods, mixed: from plants making nitrog. fertilizers; fertilizers, mixing only
HQ: Hyponex Corporation
14111 Scottslawn Rd
Marysville OH 43040
937 644-0011

(G-8203)
IMLAY CITY CONCRETE INC (PA)
Also Called: Homer Concrete Products
205 S Cedar St (48444-1389)
PHONE...................................810 724-3905
James Homer, *President*
Jeremy Homer, *Vice Pres*
EMP: 13
SQ FT: 30,000
SALES (est): 2.7MM **Privately Held**
SIC: 3273 3272 Ready-mixed concrete; septic tanks, concrete

(G-8204)
IMLAY CITY MOLDED PDTS CORP
593 S Cedar St (48444-1333)
PHONE...................................810 721-9100
Charles Tesnow, *President*
Corey Drayer, *Principal*
Coleen Felstow, *Corp Secy*
Mary Theresa Justice, *Vice Pres*
Bonita Liebler, *Vice Pres*
EMP: 25
SQ FT: 30,000
SALES (est): 4MM **Privately Held**
WEB: www.imlaycitymolded.com
SIC: 3089 Injection molded finished plastic products; injection molding of plastics

(G-8205)
JEFF SCHALLER TRANSPORT INC
2835 N Van Dyke Rd (48444-8985)
PHONE...................................810 724-7640
Jeffrey Schaller, *President*
Wendy Schaller, *Vice Pres*
EMP: 5
SALES (est): 680.6K **Privately Held**
SIC: 3711 Motor vehicles & car bodies

(G-8206)
KING HUGHES FASTENERS INC
Also Called: King-Hughes Fasteners
550 W 4th St (48444-1066)
P.O. Box 98 (48444-0098)
PHONE...................................810 721-0300
John King, *President*
▲ **EMP**: 20
SQ FT: 24,000
SALES (est): 4.1MM **Privately Held**
WEB: www.kinghughes.com
SIC: 3496 Wire fasteners

(G-8207)
LUMBERJACK SHACK INC
7230 Webster Rd (48444-9655)
PHONE...................................810 724-7230
Dave Zgnilec, *President*
EMP: 8
SQ FT: 1,200
SALES (est): 1.2MM **Privately Held**
WEB: www.lumberjackshack.com
SIC: 5261 5571 7538 3546 Lawn & garden supplies; all-terrain vehicles; recreational vehicle repairs; saws & sawing equipment

(G-8208)
MIG MOLDING LLC
611 Industrial Park Dr (48444-1351)
PHONE...................................810 724-7400
Jim Schoonover,
Brad Johnson,
Weizhong Mu,
EMP: 4
SQ FT: 70,000
SALES (est): 567.8K **Privately Held**
SIC: 3449 Custom roll formed products

(G-8209)
PAGE ONE INC
Also Called: Tri City Times
594 N Almont Ave (48444-1000)
P.O. Box 278 (48444-0278)
PHONE...................................810 724-0254
Dolores Heim, *President*
EMP: 30
SALES (est): 2MM **Privately Held**
SIC: 2711 Newspapers: publishing only, not printed on site

(G-8210)
PINNACLE FOODS GROUP LLC
415 S Blacks Corners Rd (48444-9761)
PHONE...................................810 724-6144
Sarah Ehrenfeucht, *Asst Controller*
Jan Knight, *Marketing Staff*
Donnie Miller, *Manager*
Lynn Holiday, *Manager*
Zhifan Xu, *Manager*
EMP: 300
SALES (corp-wide): 9.5B **Publicly Held**
WEB: www.aurorafoods.com
SIC: 2038 Frozen specialties
HQ: Pinnacle Foods Group Llc
399 Jefferson Rd
Parsippany NJ 07054

(G-8211)
PRINT SHOP 4U LLC
Also Called: Print Shop, The
110 N Almont Ave (48444-1003)
PHONE...................................810 721-7500
Rebecca Homer,
EMP: 3 **EST**: 2018
SALES (est): 97.5K **Privately Held**
SIC: 2759 Publication printing

(G-8212)
TOYO SEAT USA CORPORATION (HQ)
2155 S Almont Ave (48444-9732)
PHONE...................................606 849-3009
Seizo Yamaguchi, *President*
Brian Fike, *Purchasing*
David Bruce, *Engineer*
Drew Meier, *Engineer*
Joe Metzger, *Engineer*
▲ **EMP**: 200
SQ FT: 125,000
SALES (est): 73.5MM **Privately Held**
SIC: 2531 8742 3714 3429 Seats, automobile; management consulting services; motor vehicle parts & accessories; manufactured hardware (general); automotive supplies & parts

(G-8213)
VALTEC LLC
565 S Cedar St (48444-1333)
PHONE...................................810 724-5048
Larry J Winget Jr, *President*
Nick Demiro, *Partner*
Colleen Buckhanon, *QC Mgr*
Shellie Simons, *Human Resources*
Tim Howell,
EMP: 120
SALES (est): 36.8MM **Privately Held**
SIC: 3089 Injection molding of plastics

(G-8214)
VINTECH INDUSTRIES INC (PA)
Also Called: M & S Extrusions
611 Industrial Park Dr (48444-1351)
PHONE...................................810 724-7400
Jim Schoonover, *President*
Frank Mu, *Vice Pres*
Anna Warner, *Accounts Mgr*
▲ **EMP**: 160
SQ FT: 72,500
SALES: 11MM **Privately Held**
WEB: www.vintechplastics.com
SIC: 3089 Extruded finished plastic products

(G-8215)
VINTECH MEXICO HOLDINGS LLC (PA)
611 Industrial Park Dr (48444-1351)
PHONE...................................810 387-3224
Jason Powell,
EMP: 3 **EST**: 2014
SALES (est): 528.7K **Privately Held**
SIC: 3089 3469 Toilets, portable chemical; plastic; metal stampings

(G-8216)
WILLENBORG ASSOCIATES INC
Also Called: Leblond Lathe Service
620 Industrial Park Dr (48444-1349)
PHONE...................................810 724-5678
Michael Willenborg, *President*
▲ **EMP**: 12
SALES (est): 2.2MM **Privately Held**
SIC: 3599 Machine shop, jobbing & repair

Indian River
Cheboygan County

(G-8217)
G B WOLFGRAM AND SONS INC
Also Called: Indian River Custom Log Homes
6083 River St (49749-5129)
PHONE...................................231 238-4638
Gerald Wolfgram, *President*
Bob Davis, *Vice Pres*
Faye Wolfgram, *Admin Sec*
EMP: 10
SQ FT: 1,000
SALES: 1MM **Privately Held**
WEB: www.indianriverloghomes.com
SIC: 2452 1521 Log cabins, prefabricated, wood; single-family housing construction

(G-8218)
G L NELSON INC
Also Called: Today Publications
290 Patrick Dr (49749-9174)
PHONE...................................630 682-5958
Sharon Nelson, *President*
Gerald L Nelson, *President*
Sharon R Nelson, *Corp Secy*
EMP: 4
SALES: 350K **Privately Held**
SIC: 2741 2721 Shopping news: publishing & printing; periodicals

(G-8219)
LINK MANUFACTURING INC
Also Called: Link Industries
2208 S Straits Hwy (49749-9792)
PHONE...................................231 238-8741
Jeffrey Veryer, *Manager*
EMP: 25 **Privately Held**
SIC: 3545 Drills (machine tool accessories)
HQ: Link Manufacturing, Inc.
43855 Plymouth Oaks Blvd
Plymouth MI 48170
734 453-0800

(G-8220)
MICHIGAN PURE ICE CO LLC
126 N Straits Hwy (49749-9147)
PHONE...................................231 420-9896
Crystal Schley, *CEO*
EMP: 5
SQ FT: 6,000
SALES: 70K **Privately Held**
SIC: 2097 Ice cubes

(G-8221)
MILAN SUPPLY COMPANY
6031 S Straits Hwy (49749-9469)
PHONE...................................231 238-9200
Wyatt Hart, *Sales Staff*
John Kukulka, *Manager*
EMP: 3
SALES (corp-wide): 1.3B **Publicly Held**
WEB: www.milansupply.com
SIC: 3533 Water well drilling equipment

Indian River - Cheboygan County (G-8222)

HQ: Milan Supply Company
7125 E Pickard Rd
Mount Pleasant MI 48858
989 773-5933

(G-8222)
SCREEN GRAPHICS CO INC
5859 S Straits Hwy (49749-8430)
PHONE...............................231 238-4499
Wes Allen, *President*
Maxwell Allen, *President*
Leigh Allen, *Vice Pres*
Wesley Allen, *Vice Pres*
EMP: 5
SQ FT: 16,500
SALES (est): 1.6MM **Privately Held**
SIC: 2759 Screen printing

(G-8223)
STRAITSLAND RESORTER
3636 S Straits Hwy (49749-5136)
P.O. Box 579 (49749-0579)
PHONE...............................231 238-7362
L Scott Swanson, *Partner*
Kathy Swanson, *Partner*
EMP: 3
SALES (est): 235.6K **Privately Held**
WEB: www.resorter.com
SIC: 2711 Newspapers: publishing only, not printed on site

Ingalls
Menominee County

(G-8224)
LAPOINTE CEDAR PRODUCTS INC
N7247 17.75 Ln (49848-9215)
PHONE...............................906 753-4072
Joseph Lapointe, *President*
EMP: 15
SALES: 761K **Privately Held**
SIC: 2511 Lawn furniture: wood

Inkster
Wayne County

(G-8225)
BIRLON GROUP LLC
Also Called: Birlon Sacs
3801 Inkster Rd Ste 2 (48141-3069)
PHONE...............................313 551-5341
Gina Allen,
EMP: 7
SALES (est): 65.4K **Privately Held**
SIC: 3161 2393 3172 3199 Clothing & apparel carrying cases; canvas bags; leather money holders; equestrian related leather articles; fur apparel; leather goods, except luggage & shoes

(G-8226)
COPPERTEC INC
Also Called: Nu-Core
2424 Beech Daly Rd (48141-2449)
PHONE...............................313 278-0139
Ted Fells, *CEO*
Bob Grove, *President*
Deanna Hohn, *Principal*
◆ **EMP:** 50
SQ FT: 12,000
SALES (est): 7.9MM **Privately Held**
WEB: www.nu-core.com
SIC: 7692 3643 3357 Welding repair; current-carrying wiring devices; nonferrous wiredrawing & insulating

(G-8227)
FLOSS AUTOMOTIVE GROUP
1742 Lexington Pkwy (48141-1571)
PHONE...............................734 773-2524
Mark Robinson, *Owner*
EMP: 3 **EST:** 2011
SALES (est): 51.6K **Privately Held**
SIC: 7538 5521 7542 3743 General automotive repair shops; used car dealers; washing & polishing, automotive; freight cars & equipment

(G-8228)
INKSTER FUEL & FOOD INC
1021 Inkster Rd (48141-1825)
PHONE...............................313 565-8230
Paula Abdul, *Owner*
EMP: 5
SALES (est): 521.2K **Privately Held**
SIC: 2869 Fuels

(G-8229)
LARRYS TARPAULIN SHOP LLC
3452 Beech Daly Rd (48141-2625)
PHONE...............................313 563-2292
Larry C Smith,
EMP: 4
SQ FT: 3,260
SALES (est): 255.4K **Privately Held**
SIC: 2394 Tarpaulins, fabric: made from purchased materials

(G-8230)
OIL EXCHANGE 6 INC
140 Middlebelt Rd (48141-1171)
PHONE...............................734 641-4310
EMP: 5
SALES (est): 370K **Privately Held**
SIC: 1389 Oil/Gas Field Services

(G-8231)
PLASTEEL CORPORATION
26970 Princeton St (48141-2314)
P.O. Box 555 (48141-0555)
PHONE...............................313 562-5400
William E Ohlsson, *President*
Jane Ohlsson, *Vice Pres*
Bill Ohlsson, *VP Mktg*
Wendy Langlois, *Admin Sec*
▲ **EMP:** 15
SQ FT: 14,500
SALES (est): 2.8MM **Privately Held**
WEB: www.antennatoppers.com
SIC: 3086 2821 Insulation or cushioning material, foamed plastic; plastics materials & resins

(G-8232)
PRECISION MTL HDLG EQP LLC (HQ)
26700 Princeton St (48141-2310)
PHONE...............................313 789-8101
Edward Walker, *CEO*
Leona Burja, *President*
EMP: 100
SQ FT: 90,000
SALES (est): 3.3MM
SALES (corp-wide): 20.3MM **Privately Held**
SIC: 3441 Fabricated structural metal
PA: W International, Llc
31720 Stephenson Hwy
Madison Heights MI
248 577-0364

(G-8233)
PROTO-CAST INC
2699 John Daly St (48141-3704)
PHONE...............................313 565-5400
William H Covington, *President*
Don E Clapham, *Vice Pres*
EMP: 20
SQ FT: 31,000
SALES (est): 4.3MM **Privately Held**
WEB: www.protocast.com
SIC: 3364 3543 3369 Zinc & zinc-base alloy die-castings; industrial patterns; nonferrous foundries

(G-8234)
QUICK DRAW TARPAULIN SYSTEMS
26125 Trowbridge St (48141-2408)
PHONE...............................313 561-0554
EMP: 13 **Privately Held**
SIC: 2394 Tarpaulins, fabric: made from purchased materials
PA: Quick Draw Tarpaulin Systems Inc
10200 Ford Rd
Dearborn MI 48126

(G-8235)
W W J FORM TOOL COMPANY INC
26122 Michigan Ave (48141-2462)
PHONE...............................313 565-0015
Arthur Tykoski Jr, *President*

Jennifer Tykoski, *Treasurer*
Suzanne Baughman, *Manager*
EMP: 6 **EST:** 1959
SQ FT: 1,600
SALES: 250K **Privately Held**
SIC: 3541 Machine tools, metal cutting: exotic (explosive, etc.)

Interlochen
Grand Traverse County

(G-8236)
BIG JON SPORTS INC
11455 Us Highway 31 (49643-9355)
PHONE...............................231 275-1010
Jerry Carlson, *President*
John Pampu, *Director*
EMP: 3
SALES (est): 385K **Privately Held**
SIC: 2048 Fish food

(G-8237)
BRITTEN WOODWORKS INC
1954 Betsie River Rd (49643-9690)
PHONE...............................231 275-5457
Paul Britten, *President*
Michael Bean, *Vice Pres*
EMP: 32
SALES: 4MM **Privately Held**
SIC: 2431 Interior & ornamental woodwork & trim

(G-8238)
CANVAS CO INC
5962 Penn Lock Colony Rd (49643-9478)
PHONE...............................231 276-3083
Michael McWilliams, *Principal*
EMP: 3
SALES (est): 300.2K **Privately Held**
SIC: 2211 Canvas

(G-8239)
DEERINGS JERKY CO LLC
2015 Sandy Dr (49643-9388)
PHONE...............................231 590-5687
Paul M Deering, *Mng Member*
EMP: 5 **EST:** 2013
SALES (est): 153.8K **Privately Held**
SIC: 2013 Snack sticks, including jerky: from purchased meat

(G-8240)
FISH ON SPORTS INC
11838 Us Highway 31 (49643-9365)
PHONE...............................231 342-5231
EMP: 5
SALES (est): 433.1K **Privately Held**
SIC: 3949 Fishing equipment; rods & rod parts, fishing

(G-8241)
GRAND TRAVERSE MECH CONTG LLC
1500 Melody Ln (49643-9711)
P.O. Box 1168, Traverse City (49685-1168)
PHONE...............................231 943-7400
William Riley, *Sls & Mktg Exec*
EMP: 3
SALES: 197K **Privately Held**
SIC: 1711 3585 Heating & air conditioning contractors; refrigeration & heating equipment

(G-8242)
GRAND TRAVERSE WOMAN MAG
Interlochen State Park (49643)
P.O. Box 22 (49643-0022)
PHONE...............................231 276-5105
Kerry Winkler, *Principal*
Jason Hubbard, *Assistant VP*
Kristal Nolf, *Technology*
Bill Sears, *Teacher*
EMP: 5 **EST:** 2004
SALES (est): 311.1K **Privately Held**
SIC: 2721 Magazines: publishing only, not printed on site

(G-8243)
INTERLOCHEN BOAT SHOP INC
11512 Us Highway 31 (49643-9739)
PHONE...............................231 275-7112
Scott Worden, *President*

EMP: 3
SALES: 350K **Privately Held**
SIC: 5551 3536 3599 Marine supplies & equipment; boat lifts; machine shop, jobbing & repair

(G-8244)
OMNI UNITED (USA) INC (HQ)
5350 Birch Point Dr (49643-9579)
P.O. Box 158 (49643-0158)
PHONE...............................231 943-9804
Gajendra Sareen, *CEO*
Scott Rhodes, *Vice Pres*
Phillip D Caris, *Exec Dir*
Sagra Maceira De Rosen,
EMP: 8
SQ FT: 55,000
SALES: 200MM
SALES (corp-wide): 4.4MM **Privately Held**
SIC: 3011 Tires & inner tubes
PA: Omni United (S) Pte. Ltd.
1 Raffles Place
Singapore 04861
642 315-86

(G-8245)
SAWMILL BILL LUMBER INC
18657 Us Highway 31 (49643-9394)
PHONE...............................231 275-3000
William Reitz, *Owner*
Denise Reitz, *Vice Pres*
EMP: 5
SQ FT: 22,000
SALES (est): 595.2K **Privately Held**
WEB: www.sawmillbill.com
SIC: 2431 Millwork

(G-8246)
WILLOW MFG INC
11455 Us Highway 31 (49643-9355)
PHONE...............................231 275-1026
Jerry A Carlson, *President*
EMP: 5
SALES (est): 729.4K **Privately Held**
SIC: 3999 Barber & beauty shop equipment

Ionia
Ionia County

(G-8247)
CUSTOM COMPONENTS CORPORATION
1111 E Main St Ionia (48846)
PHONE...............................616 523-1111
Ryan Pawloski, *CEO*
David Leonard, *President*
Jenna Hurless, *Principal*
Tammy Pawloski, *Principal*
Collin Pawloski, *Engineer*
EMP: 15
SQ FT: 96,000
SALES (est): 3.4MM **Privately Held**
SIC: 2599 2521 2522 5047 Hotel furniture; wood office furniture; office furniture, except wood; hospital furniture; table or counter tops, plastic laminated

(G-8248)
MATCOR AUTOMOTIVE MICHIGAN INC
401 S Steele St (48846-9401)
P.O. Box 503 (48846-0503)
PHONE...............................616 527-4050
Art Artuso, *President*
Gilliano Tiberini, *Vice Pres*
Anca Matache, *Engineer*
Tracy McClintock, *Manager*
EMP: 120
SALES (est): 29.2MM **Privately Held**
SIC: 3465 5013 Body parts, automobile: stamped metal; automotive stampings

(G-8249)
MIDWEST INTERNATIONAL DIST LLC
433 Union St (48846-1206)
PHONE...............................616 901-4621
Alan Kasper,
EMP: 3

GEOGRAPHIC SECTION

Iron Mountain - Dickinson County (G-8277)

SALES (corp-wide): 952K **Privately Held**
SIC: **3694** Distributors, motor vehicle engine
PA: Midwest International Distribution Llc
7550 Bluewater Hwy
Saranac MI 48881
616 841-1265

(G-8250)
ORION MANUFACTURING INC
480 Apple Tree Dr (48846-8512)
PHONE................................616 527-5994
Joseph D Stewart, *President*
Tony Sorsen, *Plant Mgr*
EMP: 16
SQ FT: 25,000
SALES (est): 3.2MM **Privately Held**
WEB: www.orionmfg.net
SIC: **3465** 3429 Automotive stampings; manufactured hardware (general); furniture builders' & other household hardware

(G-8251)
REURINK SALES & SERVICE LLC
Also Called: Reurink Roofing and Siding Sls
1243 W Lincoln Ave (48846-8551)
PHONE................................616 522-9100
Todd Reurink, *Mng Member*
EMP: 7 EST: 2007
SALES (est): 925.6K **Privately Held**
SIC: **3444** Metal roofing & roof drainage equipment

(G-8252)
VENTRA IONIA MAIN LLC
1790 E Bluewater Hwy (48846-9774)
PHONE................................616 597-3220
John Atkinson, *Branch Mgr*
EMP: 50
SALES (corp-wide): 3.3B **Privately Held**
SIC: **3469** 3089 5198 Metal stampings; molding primary plastic; paints
HQ: Ventra Ionia Main, Llc
14 Beardsley St
Ionia MI 48846

(G-8253)
VENTRA IONIA MAIN LLC (HQ)
14 Beardsley St (48846-9789)
PHONE................................616 597-3220
Scott Wieber, *Engineer*
Michael Helsel, *Human Res Mgr*
Shahid R Khan, *Mng Member*
Michael Prebble, *Program Mgr*
John Atkinson,
▲ EMP: 135
SALES (est): 126.5MM
SALES (corp-wide): 3.3B **Privately Held**
SIC: **3469** 3089 5198 Metal stampings; molding primary plastic; paints
PA: Flex-N-Gate Llc
1306 E University Ave
Urbana IL 61802
217 384-6600

(G-8254)
VOLCOR FINISHING INC
510 Apple Tree Dr (48846-8512)
PHONE................................616 527-5555
David Doug, *Ch of Bd*
John Fisher, *President*
Jim Erickson, *Maintence Staff*
EMP: 23
SQ FT: 25,000
SALES (est): 5MM **Privately Held**
WEB: www.volcor.com
SIC: **3479** Rust proofing (hot dipping) of metals & formed products

Ira
St. Clair County

(G-8255)
EST TOOLS AMERICA INC
10138 Radiance Dr (48023-1424)
PHONE................................810 824-3323
Kenneth Nemec, *Administration*
EMP: 5
SALES (est): 443.3K **Privately Held**
SIC: **3545** Machine tool accessories

(G-8256)
G & G DIE AND ENGINEERING INC
6091 Corporate Dr (48023-1423)
PHONE................................586 716-8099
William Gilley, *President*
▲ EMP: 20
SQ FT: 10,000
SALES (est): 3.1MM **Privately Held**
SIC: **3544** Dies & die holders for metal cutting, forming, die casting

(G-8257)
HTC SALES CORPORATION
Also Called: Htc Products
6560 Bethuy Rd (48023-1810)
PHONE................................800 624-2027
Charles Russell, *President*
▲ EMP: 30
SQ FT: 38,000
SALES (est): 3MM **Privately Held**
WEB: www.htcproductsinc.com
SIC: **3545** 5084 Machine tool accessories; industrial machinery & equipment

(G-8258)
IIG-DSS TECHNOLOGIES LLC
6100 Bethuy Rd (48023-1120)
PHONE................................586 725-5300
Francis G Leo, *Mng Member*
Doug Dawson,
Sekou Shorter,
Greg Yezback,
▲ EMP: 48
SQ FT: 68,000
SALES (est): 4.6MM **Privately Held**
SIC: **3089** Injection molded finished plastic products; injection molding of plastics

(G-8259)
KEHRIG STEEL INC
9279 Marine City Hwy (48023-1222)
PHONE................................586 716-9700
Robert Kehrig, *President*
EMP: 4
SQ FT: 8,000
SALES (est): 1.2MM **Privately Held**
SIC: **3441** Fabricated structural metal

(G-8260)
MATERIAL HANDLING TECH INC
9023 Marine City Hwy B (48023-1225)
PHONE................................586 725-5546
David Vavro, *President*
Don Robert Vavro, *Vice Pres*
▲ EMP: 70
SQ FT: 66,000
SALES (est): 17MM **Privately Held**
SIC: **3444** 7692 5084 Hoppers, sheet metal; welding repair; materials handling machinery

(G-8261)
MOD INTERIORS INC
9301 Marine City Hwy (48023-1223)
PHONE................................586 725-8227
Donald Megie, *President*
Matthew Gaglio, *Vice Pres*
Kennita Megie, *Controller*
EMP: 27
SQ FT: 20,000
SALES (est): 12.7MM **Privately Held**
WEB: www.modinteriorsinc.com
SIC: **2431** 1751 Millwork; cabinet building & installation

(G-8262)
MODERN PRINTING SERVICES INC
8850 Dixie Hwy (48023-2489)
PHONE................................586 792-9700
Steve Podlaskowski, *Shareholder*
EMP: 3
SALES (est): 351.3K **Privately Held**
SIC: **2752** Commercial printing, lithographic

(G-8263)
MODIFIED TECHNOLOGIES INC
6500 Bethuy Rd (48023-1810)
PHONE................................586 725-0448
Charles Russell, *President*
Jim Boelstler, *General Mgr*
Colleen Kowalski, *Manager*
Donna Russell, *Admin Sec*
EMP: 52
SQ FT: 44,000
SALES (est): 7.5MM **Privately Held**
WEB: www.modifiedtech.com
SIC: **3544** Special dies, tools, jigs & fixtures

(G-8264)
MURLEYS MARINE
8174 Dixie Hwy (48023-2513)
PHONE................................586 725-7446
Michael Murley, *Owner*
EMP: 4
SQ FT: 3,600
SALES (est): 200K **Privately Held**
SIC: **3732** 7699 Motorized boat, building & repairing; marine engine repair

(G-8265)
P D Q PRESS INC
7752 Dixie Hwy (48023-2728)
PHONE................................586 725-1888
Thomas Gratopp, *President*
Willard Gratopp, *Vice Pres*
William Gratopp, *Treasurer*
EMP: 5
SALES (est): 486.2K **Privately Held**
SIC: **2759** 2791 7331 7384 Ready prints; typesetting, computer controlled; direct mail advertising services; film developing & printing

(G-8266)
P T M CORPORATION (PA)
Also Called: Quasar Prototype and Tool Co.
6560 Bethuy Rd (48023-1810)
PHONE................................586 725-2211
Charles T Russell, *President*
Rick Burchett, *General Mgr*
Donna Russell, *Vice Pres*
Steve Kuhr, *Opers Staff*
Tammy Redman, *Production*
EMP: 96 EST: 1965
SQ FT: 121,500
SALES (est): 19MM **Privately Held**
WEB: www.ptmcorporation.com
SIC: **3714** 3545 Motor vehicle parts & accessories; tools & accessories for machine tools

(G-8267)
R E GALLAHER CORP
9601 Marine City Hwy (48023-1116)
PHONE................................586 725-3333
James A Gallaher III, *President*
James A Gallaher IV, *Vice Pres*
EMP: 21
SQ FT: 20,000
SALES: 783K **Privately Held**
SIC: **3541** Screw machines, automatic

(G-8268)
RIVERHILL PUBLICATIONS & PRTG
8850 Dixie Hwy (48023-2489)
PHONE................................586 468-6011
Louis Cattaneo, *Vice Pres*
EMP: 10 EST: 1971
SQ FT: 6,000
SALES (est): 1.1MM **Privately Held**
WEB: www.riverhillpartners.com
SIC: **2759** Commercial printing

(G-8269)
SATTLER INC
6024 Corporate Dr (48023-1422)
PHONE................................586 725-1140
Paul Sattler, *President*
Robert Stattler Jr, *Vice Pres*
EMP: 10
SALES (est): 1.7MM **Privately Held**
WEB: www.sattler.com
SIC: **3599** Machine shop, jobbing & repair

(G-8270)
SEJASMI INDUSTRIES INC
Also Called: Bosch
6100 Bethuy Rd (48023-1120)
PHONE................................586 725-5300
Samir Patel, *President*
D S Patel, *Vice Pres*
▲ EMP: 125
SALES (est): 24.2MM **Privately Held**
SIC: **3052** Automobile hose, plastic

(G-8271)
SKILL-CRAFT COMPANY INC
10125 Radiance Dr (48023-1424)
PHONE................................586 716-4300
James E Thurman, *President*
Donald P Thurman, *Vice Pres*
Dave Thurman, *Engineer*
Matt Thurman, *Engineer*
Lisa Vici, *Manager*
EMP: 10 EST: 1952
SQ FT: 7,000
SALES (est): 1.5MM **Privately Held**
SIC: **3545** Chucks: drill, lathe or magnetic (machine tool accessories); collets (machine tool accessories)

(G-8272)
STANDBY POWER USA LLC
7770 Bouvier Blvd (48023-2708)
PHONE................................586 716-9610
Robert Martin,
EMP: 3
SQ FT: 2,000
SALES: 1.2MM **Privately Held**
SIC: **3621** Generators & sets, electric

(G-8273)
SUPREME INDUSTRIES LLC
6015 Corporate Dr (48023-1423)
PHONE................................586 725-2500
Rick Winarski,
EMP: 5
SALES (est): 578.1K **Privately Held**
WEB: www.supremeindustries.com
SIC: **3089** Injection molding of plastics

Iron Mountain
Dickinson County

(G-8274)
ALL-LIFT SYSTEMS INC
1400 Cedar Ave (49801-4729)
PHONE................................906 779-1620
Mickey Meiers, *Manager*
EMP: 11
SALES (corp-wide): 15MM **Privately Held**
WEB: www.all-liftsystems.com
SIC: **3531** Construction machinery
PA: All-Lift Systems, Inc.
2146 W Pershing St
Appleton WI 54914
920 738-0800

(G-8275)
AUTO CLINIC
411 Carpenter Ave (49801-3330)
P.O. Box 2491, Kingsford (49802-2491)
PHONE................................906 774-5780
Mitch Leinen, *Owner*
EMP: 3
SALES (est): 141.6K **Privately Held**
SIC: **5013** 7539 3691 5063 Body repair or paint shop supplies, automotive; electrical services; storage batteries; batteries

(G-8276)
BERTOLDI OIL SERVICE INC
N2395 Cemetary Ln (49801)
P.O. Box 646 (49801-0646)
PHONE................................906 774-1707
James Bertoldi, *President*
John Bertoldi, *Vice Pres*
George Bertoldi, *Treasurer*
EMP: 9
SQ FT: 10,000
SALES (est): 1.2MM **Privately Held**
SIC: **2911** Petroleum refining

(G-8277)
BINKS COCA-COLA BOTTLING CO
617 Industrial Dr (49801-1423)
PHONE................................906 774-3202
Todd Charpier, *Manager*
EMP: 17
SALES (corp-wide): 7.4MM **Privately Held**
SIC: **2086** Bottled & canned soft drinks
PA: Bink's Coca-Cola Bottling Co
3001 Danforth Rd
Escanaba MI 49829
906 786-4144

Iron Mountain - Dickinson County (G-8278)

(G-8278)
BK MATTSON ENTERPRISES INC
Also Called: Bk Enterprises
410 S Stephenson Ave (49801-3455)
P.O. Box 248 (49801-0248)
PHONE..................................906 774-0097
Brenda Mattson, *President*
EMP: 3
SQ FT: 1,000
SALES (est): 324.8K **Privately Held**
WEB: www.bkengravesit.com
SIC: 2759 5947 7389 5999 Engraving; gift shop; engraving service; rubber stamps; engraving jewelry silverware, or metal

(G-8279)
CCO HOLDINGS LLC
104 N Stephenson Ave (49801-2934)
PHONE..................................906 239-3763
EMP: 3
SALES (corp-wide): 43.6B **Publicly Held**
SIC: 5064 4841 3663 3651 Electrical appliances, television & radio; cable & other pay television services; radio & TV communications equipment; household audio & video equipment
HQ: Cco Holdings, Llc
400 Atlantic St
Stamford CT 06901
203 905-7801

(G-8280)
CHAMPION CHARTER SLS & SVC INC
180 Traders Mine Rd (49801-1447)
P.O. Box 490 (49801-0490)
PHONE..................................906 779-2300
Gary Benjamin, *Ch of Bd*
Thomas Jacko, *President*
Jim Rose, *Safety Dir*
Daniel Wentarmini, *Treasurer*
John Roberts, *Sales Mgr*
EMP: 7
SALES: 11.8MM **Privately Held**
SIC: 3491 3543 Industrial valves; industrial patterns

(G-8281)
CUMMINS INC
1901 N Stephenson Ave (49801-1483)
P.O. Box 5070, De Pere WI (54115-5070)
PHONE..................................906 774-2424
Dan Carlson, *Branch Mgr*
EMP: 218
SALES (corp-wide): 23.7B **Publicly Held**
WEB: www.cummins.com
SIC: 3714 Fuel systems & parts, motor vehicle
PA: Cummins Inc.
500 Jackson St
Columbus IN 47201
812 377-5000

(G-8282)
CUSTOMER METAL FABRICATION INC (PA)
W8762 Lakeview Dr (49801-9320)
P.O. Box 669 (49801-0669)
PHONE..................................906 774-3216
Richard Sparapani, *President*
Lori Machus, *Corp Secy*
David Ethington, *Vice Pres*
Thomas Wickman, *Vice Pres*
EMP: 50
SQ FT: 16,000
SALES (est): 5.4MM **Privately Held**
WEB: www.customermetal.com
SIC: 3599 7692 3444 Machine shop, jobbing & repair; welding repair; sheet metalwork

(G-8283)
FAIRCHILDS DAUGHTERS & SON LLC
Also Called: FDS Engineering
617 N Stephenson Ave (49801-2200)
PHONE..................................906 239-6061
Jesse Fairchild, *President*
EMP: 3 **EST:** 2014
SQ FT: 1,000
SALES (est): 182.8K **Privately Held**
SIC: 8711 7389 3613 Electrical or electronic engineering; drafting service, except temporary help; time switches, electrical switchgear apparatus

(G-8284)
H U R ENTERPRISES INC
Also Called: Lighthouse, The
717 W Hughitt St (49801-2743)
PHONE..................................906 774-0833
Harry U Rahoi, *President*
Mary Rahoi, *Corp Secy*
EMP: 3
SQ FT: 3,200
SALES: 490K **Privately Held**
SIC: 3645 Residential lighting fixtures

(G-8285)
INTERSTATE POWER SYSTEMS INC
Also Called: Interstate Powersystems
600 Industrial Park Dr (49801)
PHONE..................................952 854-2044
Terry Edmonds, *Branch Mgr*
EMP: 16
SALES (corp-wide): 228MM **Privately Held**
SIC: 3714 5084 Motor vehicle parts & accessories; industrial machinery & equipment
HQ: Interstate Power Systems, Inc.
2901 E 78th St
Minneapolis MN 55425
952 854-2044

(G-8286)
JERED LLC
821 East Blvd (49802-4435)
P.O. Box 1074 (49801-8074)
PHONE..................................906 776-1800
Mike Gerard, *Branch Mgr*
EMP: 4
SALES (corp-wide): 267.6MM **Privately Held**
WEB: www.jered.com
SIC: 3625 3536 Marine & navy auxiliary controls; hoists, cranes & monorails
HQ: Jered Llc
3000 Sidney Lanier Dr
Brunswick GA 31525
912 262-2000

(G-8287)
LA ROZINAS INC
921 Eagle Dr (49802-1228)
PHONE..................................906 779-2181
Dennis Strand, *President*
Janis Strand, *Corp Secy*
EMP: 3
SQ FT: 3,000
SALES: 470K **Privately Held**
SIC: 2098 2033 Noodles (e.g. egg, plain & water), dry; tomato sauce: packaged in cans, jars, etc.

(G-8288)
LAYDON ENTERPRISES INC (PA)
Also Called: Eagle Tool
101 Woodward Ave (49802-4736)
P.O. Box 459 (49801-0459)
PHONE..................................906 774-4633
John G Laydon, *President*
Dan Wender, *Vice Pres*
EMP: 43
SQ FT: 15,000
SALES (est): 8.9MM **Privately Held**
SIC: 3545 3398 3599 3541 Broaches (machine tool accessories); metal heat treating; machine shop, jobbing & repair; machine tools, metal cutting type

(G-8289)
LAYDON TECHNOLOGY INC
1005 Pinewood Ct (49801-4464)
PHONE..................................906 774-5780
James Laydon, *President*
EMP: 3
SALES (est): 147K **Privately Held**
WEB: www.laydon.com
SIC: 7372 Prepackaged software

(G-8290)
MILLER PRODUCTS & SUPPLY CO
1801 N Stephenson Ave (49801-1407)
PHONE..................................906 774-1243
Robert Fayas, *President*
Ryan Fayas, *Supervisor*
EMP: 10
SQ FT: 6,000
SALES (est): 3.1MM **Privately Held**
SIC: 5032 3271 Concrete & cinder block; concrete block & brick

(G-8291)
NELSON PAINT COMPANY MICH INC
1 Nelson Dr (49802-4561)
P.O. Box 2040 (49802-2040)
PHONE..................................906 774-5566
EMP: 8
SALES (est): 667.2K **Privately Held**
SIC: 2851 5231 Mfg Paints/Allied Products Ret Paint/Glass/Wallpaper

(G-8292)
NELSON TECHNOLOGIES INC
1 Nelson Dr (49802-4561)
P.O. Box 2040 (49802-2040)
PHONE..................................906 774-5566
Barbara Louys, *President*
Richard Louys, *President*
Karen Cox, *Vice Pres*
Brian Tollefson, *Controller*
EMP: 60
SALES (est): 10MM **Privately Held**
WEB: www.nelsontechinc.com
SIC: 3949 Sporting & athletic goods

(G-8293)
NORTHERN PRODUCTS OF WISCONSIN
W8969 Frei Dr (49801-9449)
PHONE..................................715 589-4417
David Lavarnway, *President*
EMP: 8
SALES (est): 540K **Privately Held**
SIC: 2421 Sawmills & planing mills, general

(G-8294)
NORTHSIDE NOODLE
609 Vulcan St (49801-2351)
PHONE..................................906 779-2181
Michael P Celello, *Administration*
EMP: 8
SALES (est): 595K **Privately Held**
SIC: 2098 Noodles (e.g. egg, plain & water), dry

(G-8295)
NOW OGDEN NEWS PUBG OF MICH
Also Called: Advertiser, The
421 S Stephenson Ave (49801-3454)
P.O. Box 786 (49801-0786)
PHONE..................................906 774-3708
EMP: 10 **EST:** 1975
SQ FT: 3,000
SALES (est): 735.3K **Privately Held**
SIC: 2711 Newspapers, publishing & printing

(G-8296)
OGDEN NEWSPAPERS INC
Also Called: Daily News, The
215 E Ludington St (49801-2917)
PHONE..................................906 774-2772
Corky Deroeck, *Principal*
EMP: 12 **Privately Held**
SIC: 2711 Newspapers: publishing only, not printed on site
HQ: The Ogden Newspapers Inc
1500 Main St
Wheeling WV 26003
304 233-0100

(G-8297)
ORBIT TECHNOLOGY INC
100 W Brown St (49801-2802)
P.O. Box 1043 (49801-8043)
PHONE..................................906 776-7248
Gary Marsden, *President*
Gary Unrein, *Vice Pres*
Amanda Harvath, *Office Mgr*
EMP: 7
SALES (est): 679.1K **Privately Held**
WEB: www.orbittec.com
SIC: 7372 5044 Prepackaged software; copying equipment

(G-8298)
RICE JUICE COMPANY INC
873 Evergreen Ct (49802-1107)
PHONE..................................906 774-1733
Larry Rice, *President*
EMP: 7 **EST:** 1950
SQ FT: 13,050
SALES (est): 756.3K **Privately Held**
SIC: 2033 5149 Fruit juices: packaged in cans, jars, etc.; juices; soft drinks

(G-8299)
SCHNEIDER IRON & METAL INC
Also Called: East Kingsford Iron & Metal Co
100 E Superior St (49801)
PHONE..................................906 774-0644
Ronald Schneider, *Owner*
EMP: 14
SQ FT: 1,800
SALES (est): 1.3MM
SALES (corp-wide): 6.3MM **Privately Held**
SIC: 5093 3444 3341 Ferrous metal scrap & waste; culverts, sheet metal; secondary nonferrous metals
PA: Schneider Iron & Metal Inc
1929 Elmer St
Niagara WI 54151
906 774-0644

(G-8300)
SHIRT TAILS INC
408 S Stephenson Ave (49801-3469)
PHONE..................................906 774-3370
John Benzie, *President*
EMP: 3
SQ FT: 1,800
SALES (est): 319.9K **Privately Held**
WEB: www.shirttails.com
SIC: 2759 5699 Screen printing; customized clothing & apparel

(G-8301)
SMITH CASTINGS INC
Ford Plant (49802)
PHONE..................................906 774-4956
Eric Frantz, *President*
Rick Sadler, *Facilities Mgr*
April Rugg, *Administration*
EMP: 24
SQ FT: 35,000
SALES (est): 4.7MM **Privately Held**
WEB: www.smithcastings.com
SIC: 3321 3366 3369 3325 Gray iron castings; castings (except die); nonferrous foundries; steel foundries; malleable iron foundries

(G-8302)
SUPERIOR EQUIPMENT & SUPPLY CO
1515 S Stephenson Ave (49801-3633)
P.O. Box 339 (49801-0339)
PHONE..................................906 774-1789
David Johnson, *President*
Mary Johnson, *Corp Secy*
EMP: 5
SQ FT: 2,200
SALES (est): 1.2MM **Privately Held**
SIC: 5084 3537 5082 Industrial machinery & equipment; lift trucks, industrial: fork, platform, straddle, etc.; mining machinery & equipment, except petroleum

(G-8303)
TIMBER PDTS MICH LTD PARTNR (PA)
104 E B St (49801-3468)
P.O. Box 378, Munising (49862-0378)
PHONE..................................906 779-2000
Joseph Gonyea, *Partner*
EMP: 2
SALES (est): 23.6MM **Privately Held**
WEB: www.teamtp.com
SIC: 2435 2426 Veneer stock, hardwood; lumber, hardwood dimension

GEOGRAPHIC SECTION

Ironwood - Gogebic County (G-8330)

(G-8304)
TORO COMPANY
Also Called: Boss Snowplow
2007-2010 Boss Way (49801)
PHONE.................................888 492-6841
Dave Brule, *Branch Mgr*
EMP: 300
SALES (corp-wide): 2.6B **Publicly Held**
SIC: 3531 Snow plow attachments
PA: The Toro Company
  8111 Lyndale Ave S
  Bloomington MN 55420
  952 888-8801

(G-8305)
WENDER LOGGING INC
W7487 Upper Pine Creek Dr (49801-9616)
PHONE.................................906 779-1483
Gary Wender, *President*
EMP: 3
SALES (est): 320.9K **Privately Held**
SIC: 2411 Logging camps & contractors

(G-8306)
Z & R ELECTRIC SERVICE INC
619 Industrial Park Dr (49801)
P.O. Box 740, Schofield WI (54476-0740)
PHONE.................................906 774-0468
Ricki Bieti, *President*
EMP: 11
SQ FT: 20,000
SALES: 2.2MM **Privately Held**
SIC: 5063 7694 5999 3599 Motors, electric; electric motor repair; electronic parts & equipment; machine shop, jobbing & repair; motors & generators

Iron River
Iron County

(G-8307)
ALEXA FOREST PRODUCTS
137 Dirkman Rd (49935)
PHONE.................................906 265-2347
David Alexa, *Owner*
EMP: 6
SALES (est): 519.3K **Privately Held**
SIC: 2411 Logging camps & contractors

(G-8308)
DINA MIA KITCHENS INC
751 N 4th Ave (49935-1394)
PHONE.................................906 265-9082
Peter Saving, *President*
Linda Saving, *Corp Secy*
EMP: 18 EST: 1961
SQ FT: 5,000
SALES (est): 541.4K **Privately Held**
WEB: www.dinamiakitchens.com
SIC: 2038 2098 2035 2013 Pizza, frozen; spaghetti & meatballs, frozen; macaroni & spaghetti; pickles, sauces & salad dressings; sausages & other prepared meats
PA: Linda Mia Inc
  751 N 4th Ave
  Iron River MI 49935

(G-8309)
GAASTRA WELDING & SUPPLY INC
Also Called: Gaastra John's
928 Selden Rd (49935-8943)
P.O. Box 498 (49935-0498)
PHONE.................................906 265-4288
John Lundahl, *CEO*
EMP: 3
SQ FT: 6,400
SALES (est): 250K **Privately Held**
SIC: 3599 7692 Machine shop, jobbing & repair; welding repair

(G-8310)
IRON RIVER MFG CO INC
Also Called: Lester Detterbeck Enterprises
3390 Us Highway 2 (49935-8578)
PHONE.................................906 265-5121
John Detterbeck, *President*
EMP: 40
SQ FT: 20,000
SALES (est): 3.5MM
SALES (corp-wide): 8.2MM **Privately Held**
WEB: www.lesterdetterbeck.com
SIC: 3541 5084 Machine tools, metal cutting type; industrial machinery & equipment
PA: Lester Detterbeck Enterprises, Ltd.
  3390 Us Highway 2
  Iron River MI 49935
  906 265-5121

(G-8311)
JAMES SPICER INC
Also Called: Spicer's
1571 W Adams St (49935-1266)
PHONE.................................906 265-2385
Tony Spicer, *President*
EMP: 6
SALES (est): 704.7K **Privately Held**
SIC: 4212 2411 Local trucking, without storage; logging camps & contractors

(G-8312)
JKL HARDWOODS INC
1101 Homer Rd (49935-9692)
P.O. Box 428 (49935-0428)
PHONE.................................906 265-9130
John Ricker, *President*
EMP: 12
SQ FT: 100
SALES: 2MM **Privately Held**
SIC: 2491 Structural lumber & timber, treated wood

(G-8313)
LAKE SHORE SYSTEMS INC
1520 W Adams St (49935-1265)
P.O. Box 467 (49935-0467)
PHONE.................................906 265-5414
Dan Bruso, *Exec VP*
Jerry Schallock, *Human Res Mgr*
EMP: 99
SALES (corp-wide): 77MM **Privately Held**
SIC: 3534 3731 3532 Elevators & moving stairways; shipbuilding & repairing; mining machinery
PA: Lake Shore Systems, Inc.
  2141 Woodward Ave
  Kingsford MI 49802
  906 774-1500

(G-8314)
LESTER DETTERBECK ENTPS LTD (PA)
3390 Us Highway 2 (49935-8578)
PHONE.................................906 265-5121
John Detterbeck, *President*
EMP: 25
SALES (est): 8.2MM **Privately Held**
WEB: www.lesterdetterbeck.com
SIC: 3541 3545 3544 3451 Machine tools, metal cutting: exotic (explosive, etc.); machine tool accessories; special dies, tools, jigs & fixtures; screw machine products

(G-8315)
LOW IMPACT LOGGING INC
3172 Us Highway 2 (49935-8568)
PHONE.................................906 250-5117
Ted R Benson, *Principal*
EMP: 6 EST: 2007
SALES (est): 645.7K **Privately Held**
SIC: 2411 Logging

(G-8316)
MOTTES MATERIALS INC
4084 Us Highway 2 (49935-7972)
P.O. Box 112 (49935-0112)
PHONE.................................906 265-9955
Eugene Mottes, *President*
EMP: 28 EST: 1977
SQ FT: 5,000
SALES (est): 1.6MM **Privately Held**
WEB: www.mottesmaterials.com
SIC: 1442 3273 Sand mining; gravel mining; ready-mixed concrete

(G-8317)
NICOLET SIGN & DESIGN
Also Called: Nicolet Sign & Construction
612 W Adams St (49935-1322)
PHONE.................................906 265-5220
Kris Hughes, *Owner*
EMP: 3
SALES (est): 119.7K **Privately Held**
SIC: 3993 Signs & advertising specialties

(G-8318)
NORTHLAND PUBLISHERS INC
Also Called: Reporter & Shoppers Guide
801 W Adams St (49935-1218)
P.O. Box 311 (49935-0311)
PHONE.................................906 265-9927
Eugene A Halker, *President*
EMP: 14 EST: 1968
SALES (est): 559.9K **Privately Held**
WEB: www.ironcountyreporter.com
SIC: 2711 5943 Newspapers, publishing & printing; office forms & supplies

(G-8319)
PIWARSKI BROTHERS LOGGING INC
941 Gibbs City Rd (49935-9632)
PHONE.................................906 265-2914
Larry Piwarski, *President*
Leonard Piwarski, *Partner*
Dell Piwarski, *Vice Pres*
EMP: 5
SALES (est): 607.3K **Privately Held**
SIC: 2411 Logging camps & contractors

(G-8320)
SHAMCO INC
4128 Us Highway 2 (49935-7976)
P.O. Box 436 (49935-0436)
PHONE.................................906 265-5065
Jerry Shamion, *President*
Todd Shamion, *Vice Pres*
Chris Shamion, *Treasurer*
Eric Shamion, *Treasurer*
Scott Shamion, *Treasurer*
EMP: 4
SALES (est): 810K **Privately Held**
SIC: 2411 Logging camps & contractors

(G-8321)
SHAMION BROTHERS
4128 Us Highway 2 (49935-7976)
P.O. Box 454 (49935-0454)
PHONE.................................906 265-5065
Jerry Shamion, *Partner*
Richard Shamion, *Partner*
Ronald Shamion, *Partner*
EMP: 20
SQ FT: 9,000
SALES (est): 1.9MM **Privately Held**
SIC: 2411 Logging camps & contractors

Irons
Lake County

(G-8322)
ROTHIG FOREST PRODUCTS INC
3600 N M 37 (49644)
P.O. Box 340, Luther (49656-0340)
PHONE.................................231 266-8292
Ross Rothig, *President*
Robert Morgan, *Vice Pres*
Julie Morgan, *Admin Sec*
EMP: 25
SALES: 4MM **Privately Held**
SIC: 5031 0851 2411 Lumber: rough, dressed & finished; forest management services; logging

Ironwood
Gogebic County

(G-8323)
BURTON INDUSTRIES INC
1260 Wall St (49938-1763)
P.O. Box 279, Goodrich (48438-0279)
PHONE.................................906 932-5970
Clark E Johnson, *President*
Mike De Vries, *CPA*
▲ EMP: 50 EST: 1966
SQ FT: 50,000
SALES (est): 14.3MM **Privately Held**
SIC: 3549 3559 Assembly machines, including robotic; automotive maintenance equipment

(G-8324)
BURTON INDUSTRIES INC
1260 Wall St (49938-1763)
PHONE.................................906 932-5970
Gary Burett, *Manager*
EMP: 40
SALES (corp-wide): 27.6MM **Privately Held**
WEB: www.burtonindustries.com
SIC: 3672 Printed circuit boards
PA: Burton Industries, Inc.
  9821 Cedar Falls Rd
  Hazelhurst WI 54531
  906 932-5970

(G-8325)
CCO HOLDINGS LLC
121 E Aurora St (49938-2109)
PHONE.................................906 285-6497
EMP: 4
SALES (corp-wide): 43.6B **Publicly Held**
SIC: 5064 4841 3663 3651 Electrical appliances, television & radio; cable & other pay television services; radio & TV communications equipment; household audio & video equipment
HQ: Cco Holdings, Llc
  400 Atlantic St
  Stamford CT 06901
  203 905-7801

(G-8326)
CRAMBLITS WELDING LLC
Also Called: Fine Art Metalwork
1215 Wall St (49938-1764)
PHONE.................................906 932-1908
Ron Tankka, *Mng Member*
Julann Cramblit,
EMP: 5
SQ FT: 19,200
SALES: 486K **Privately Held**
SIC: 7692 1799 5999 Welding repair; ornamental metal work; welding supplies

(G-8327)
EVERSON TOOL & MACHINE LTD
620 Easy St (49938-1766)
P.O. Box 466 (49938-0466)
PHONE.................................906 932-3440
Michael Key, *Principal*
EMP: 15
SQ FT: 12,000
SALES (est): 1.1MM **Privately Held**
WEB: www.precisionmold.biz
SIC: 3544 Industrial molds

(G-8328)
FABRIC PATCH LTD
100 W Mcleod Ave (49938-2526)
PHONE.................................906 932-5260
Joanne Kuula, *President*
EMP: 4
SQ FT: 1,000
SALES (est): 372.2K **Privately Held**
SIC: 3496 5722 Fabrics, woven wire; sewing machines

(G-8329)
GLOBE INDUSTRIES INCORPORATED
Also Called: Globe Sand & Gravel
121 Mill St (49938-3025)
PHONE.................................906 932-3540
Mark Ruppe, *President*
EMP: 15
SALES (est): 2.2MM **Privately Held**
SIC: 3531 Bituminous, cement & concrete related products & equipment

(G-8330)
IRONWOOD PLASTICS INC (PA)
1235 Wall St (49938-1764)
PHONE.................................906 932-5025
Gordon K Stephens, *President*
Rick Faustich, *President*
Mark K Stephens, *President*
Robert L Stephens, *Vice Pres*
Scott D Stephens, *Vice Pres*
▲ EMP: 210
SQ FT: 54,000
SALES (est): 59.6MM **Privately Held**
SIC: 3089 Injection molded finished plastic products

Ironwood - Gogebic County (G-8331)

(G-8331)
IRONWOOD READY MIX & TRUCKING
500 Bonnie Rd (49938-3405)
P.O. Box 100, Iron Belt WI (54536-0100)
PHONE.................................906 932-4531
Nancy Luppino, *President*
Paul Luppino, *Corp Secy*
EMP: 6
SQ FT: 4,000
SALES (est): 780.5K **Privately Held**
SIC: 3273 1442 Ready-mixed concrete; construction sand mining; gravel mining

(G-8332)
JACQUART FABRIC PRODUCTS INC
1238 Wall St (49938-1763)
PHONE.................................906 932-1339
Robert J Jacquart, *President*
Bob Jacquart, *President*
Dennis McRae, *Purch Mgr*
Becky Maki, *Engineer*
Leann Tregembo, *Controller*
▲ **EMP:** 141 **EST:** 1956
SQ FT: 63,600
SALES (est): 18.7MM **Privately Held**
WEB: www.jacquarts.com
SIC: 2394 2392 7389 3842 Awnings, fabric: made from purchased materials; pillows, bed: made from purchased materials; sewing contractor; surgical appliances & supplies; furniture upholstery repair

(G-8333)
KAUFMAN CUSTOM SHEET M
400 W Aurora St (49938-2537)
PHONE.................................906 932-2130
Otto Gebhardt Jr,
EMP: 5
SQ FT: 6,000
SALES: 60K **Privately Held**
SIC: 3531 1761 Snow plow attachments; sheet metalwork

(G-8334)
LEE J CUMMINGS
N11689 Lake Rd (49938-9575)
PHONE.................................906 932-3298
Lee Cummings, *Principal*
EMP: 3
SALES (est): 193.4K **Privately Held**
SIC: 2411 Logging

(G-8335)
MENDOTA MANTELS LLC
E6638 Maple Creek Rd (49938)
PHONE.................................651 271-7544
Tom Schoeller, *Manager*
EMP: 4
SALES (est): 330.1K **Privately Held**
SIC: 2431 Mantels, wood

(G-8336)
OTTAWA FOREST PRODUCTS INC
1243 Wall St (49938-1764)
P.O. Box 99 (49938-0099)
PHONE.................................906 932-9701
Charles Baxter, *President*
Aaron Somero, *General Mgr*
James Sweet, *VP Mfg*
Val Mower, *VP Sales*
EMP: 40
SALES (est): 7.5MM **Privately Held**
SIC: 2421 2426 2448 Lumber: rough, sawed or planed; hardwood dimension & flooring mills; wood pallets & skids

(G-8337)
PEARSON DEAN EXCAVATING & LOG
E3233 Lake Rd (49938-9743)
PHONE.................................906 932-3513
Dean N Pearson, *Administration*
EMP: 3
SALES (est): 286.7K **Privately Held**
SIC: 2411 Logging camps & contractors

(G-8338)
PRECISION TOOL & MOLD LLC
620 Easy St (49938-1766)
P.O. Box 466 (49938-0466)
PHONE.................................906 932-3440
Michael Key, *President*
Mark Maccani, *Production*
EMP: 15
SQ FT: 12,000
SALES (est): 2.1MM **Privately Held**
SIC: 3544 Industrial molds

(G-8339)
RUPPE MANUFACTURING COMPANY (PA)
Also Called: Ironwood Testing & Design Div
100 Mill St (49938)
PHONE.................................906 932-3540
Mark Ruppe, *President*
EMP: 20
SQ FT: 30,000
SALES (est): 3.6MM **Privately Held**
SIC: 1442 3273 1794 3271 Construction sand mining; gravel mining; ready-mixed concrete; excavation & grading, building construction; blocks, concrete or cinder: standard

(G-8340)
SAWDUST BIN INC
629 W Cloverland Dr Ste 5 (49938-1006)
PHONE.................................906 932-5518
Jeff Wesenberg, *President*
EMP: 11
SQ FT: 3,000
SALES: 1.4MM **Privately Held**
WEB: www.sawdustbin.com
SIC: 2434 2511 Wood kitchen cabinets; wood stands & chests, except bedside stands; tables, household: wood

(G-8341)
WOODTECH BUILDERS INC
219 E Frederick St (49938-2013)
PHONE.................................906 932-8055
Rick Tippett, *President*
EMP: 13
SALES (est): 1.5MM **Privately Held**
WEB: www.woodtechbuilders.com
SIC: 1521 2452 New construction, single-family houses; single-family home remodeling, additions & repairs; prefabricated wood buildings

Ishpeming
Marquette County

(G-8342)
A LINDBERG & SONS INC (PA)
599 Washington St (49849-1239)
P.O. Box 308 (49849-0308)
PHONE.................................906 485-5705
Roger Crimmins, *President*
David J Crimmins, *Vice Pres*
Shirley Crimmins, *Treasurer*
Jerry Sicotte, *Admin Sec*
EMP: 50 **EST:** 1920
SQ FT: 3,600
SALES (est): 16.9MM **Privately Held**
WEB: www.lindberginc.com
SIC: 1442 1611 1794 1623 Gravel mining; highway & street construction; excavation work; water main construction; sewer line construction

(G-8343)
CLEVELAND-CLIFFS INC
Cleveland Cliffs Michigan Oper
101 Tilden Mine Rd (49849)
P.O. Box 2000 (49849-0901)
PHONE.................................906 475-3547
Joe Carrabba, *Branch Mgr*
Patricia Persico, *Director*
John T Baldwin, *Bd of Directors*
Robert P Fisher, *Bd of Directors*
Joseph Rutkowski, *Bd of Directors*
EMP: 700
SALES (corp-wide): 2.3B **Publicly Held**
SIC: 1011 Iron ores
PA: Cleveland-Cliffs Inc.
  200 Public Sq Ste 3300
  Cleveland OH 44114
  216 694-5700

(G-8344)
DYNO NOBEL INC
Also Called: Dyno Nobel Midwest
9045 County Road 476 (49849-8996)
P.O. Box 8 (49849-0008)
PHONE.................................906 486-4473
Mike Dayton, *Branch Mgr*
EMP: 15 **Privately Held**
SIC: 2892 Explosives
HQ: Dyno Nobel Inc.
  2795 E Cottonwood Pkwy # 500
  Salt Lake City UT 84121
  801 364-4800

(G-8345)
GLOBE PRINTING & SPECIALTIES
200 W Division St (49849-2301)
P.O. Box 378 (49849-0378)
PHONE.................................906 485-1033
Curt Gronvall, *President*
Stacey Willey, *Treasurer*
EMP: 10 **EST:** 1953
SQ FT: 3,325
SALES (est): 1.4MM **Privately Held**
SIC: 2752 2759 Commercial printing, offset; screen printing

(G-8346)
HOLLI FOREST PRODUCTS
900 Cooper Lake Rd (49849-3350)
P.O. Box 117 (49849-0117)
PHONE.................................906 486-9352
David Holli, *President*
EMP: 25
SALES (est): 3.1MM **Privately Held**
SIC: 2411 Logging

(G-8347)
ISHPEMING CONCRETE CORPORATION
400 Stone St (49849-2349)
PHONE.................................906 485-5851
Patrick Moyle, *President*
EMP: 5
SQ FT: 300
SALES (est): 697.2K **Privately Held**
SIC: 3273 Ready-mixed concrete

(G-8348)
LAKE BROTHERS FOREST PRODUCTS
3039 County Road 496 (49849-9432)
PHONE.................................906 485-5639
Robert Lake, *President*
Randolf Lake, *Vice Pres*
EMP: 3
SALES (est): 235.8K **Privately Held**
SIC: 2411 Logging camps & contractors

(G-8349)
MARK HONKALA LOGGING INC
18261 County Road Cd (49849-9379)
PHONE.................................906 485-1570
Mark Honkala, *Principal*
EMP: 3
SALES (est): 315K **Privately Held**
SIC: 2411 Logging camps & contractors

(G-8350)
NORTHERN TIRE INC
1880 Us Highway 41 W (49849-3168)
PHONE.................................906 486-4463
Lee T Woods, *President*
Elizabeth A Woods, *Vice Pres*
EMP: 10 **EST:** 1961
SQ FT: 17,600
SALES (est): 4.5MM **Privately Held**
SIC: 5014 3069 7534 Tires & tubes; rubber automotive products; tire retreading & repair shops

(G-8351)
OASIS FUEL CORPORATION
417 E Hematite Dr (49849-1846)
PHONE.................................906 486-4126
Ali Safieddine, *Principal*
EMP: 6
SALES (est): 662.1K **Privately Held**
SIC: 2869 Fuels

(G-8352)
PEPIN-IRECO INC
9045 County Road 476 (49849-8996)
P.O. Box 8 (49849-0008)
PHONE.................................906 486-4473
Joseph A Pepin, *President*
Kathleen Pepin, *Admin Sec*
EMP: 21
SALES (est): 2.9MM **Privately Held**
SIC: 5169 2892 Explosives; explosives

(G-8353)
RUSSO BROS INC
1710 Us Highway 41 W (49849-3197)
PHONE.................................906 485-5250
John Korhonen, *President*
Jean Korhonen, *Admin Sec*
EMP: 34
SALES (est): 3.6MM **Privately Held**
WEB: www.mamarusso.com
SIC: 2099 5421 5921 Emulsifiers, food; meat markets, including freezer provisioners; beer (packaged); wine

(G-8354)
TILDEN MINING COMPANY LC
Also Called: Tilden Mine
2 Miles S Of Ishpeming (49849)
P.O. Box 2000 (49849-0901)
PHONE.................................906 475-3400
David B Brake, *Manager*
EMP: 700
SALES (corp-wide): 2.3B **Publicly Held**
SIC: 1011 Iron ores
HQ: Tilden Mining Company L.C.
  200 Public Sq Ste 3300
  Cleveland OH 44114
  216 694-5700

Ithaca
Gratiot County

(G-8355)
A B PUBLISHING INC
Also Called: Angela's Book Shelf
3039 S Bagley Rd (48847-9570)
P.O. Box 83, North Star (48862-0083)
PHONE.................................989 875-4985
Mike Foster, *President*
Katya Foster, *Admin Sec*
▲ **EMP:** 5
SQ FT: 16,000
SALES (est): 1.9MM **Privately Held**
WEB: www.abpub.com
SIC: 5192 2731 Books; books: publishing only

(G-8356)
AIRCRAFT PRECISION PDTS INC
185 Industrial Pkwy (48847-9476)
P.O. Box 340 (48847-0340)
PHONE.................................989 875-4186
William Henderson III, *President*
Gary Henderson, *Corp Secy*
Gary King, *Manager*
EMP: 60
SQ FT: 58,000
SALES: 11MM **Privately Held**
WEB: www.aircraftprecision.net
SIC: 3592 3728 3053 3492 Carburetors, pistons, rings, valves; aircraft parts & equipment; gaskets, packing & sealing devices; fluid power valves & hose fittings; aircraft engines & engine parts

(G-8357)
CAU ACQUISITION COMPANY LLC (PA)
Also Called: Cartridges Are US
100 Raycraft Dr (48847-1762)
PHONE.................................989 875-8133
Daniel Ruhl,
James Cerkleski,
William Saracco,
▲ **EMP:** 52 **EST:** 1997
SALES (est): 21.9MM **Privately Held**
WEB: www.cartridgesareus.com
SIC: 3955 2899 Print cartridges for laser & other computer printers; chemical preparations

GEOGRAPHIC SECTION

(G-8358)
CONNELL LIMITED PARTNERSHIP
Danly Die Set
255 Industrial Pkwy (48847-9476)
PHONE...................................989 875-5135
Jeffrey Hood, *Exec VP*
Vahid Tabatavai, *VP Opers*
Kelly Robbennolt, *Safety Mgr*
Colleen Simon, *Mktg Coord*
Rich Overla, *Manager*
EMP: 70
SQ FT: 60,000
SALES (corp-wide): 500MM Privately Held
WEB: www.connell-lp.com
SIC: 3544 3363 Die sets for metal stamping (presses); aluminum die-castings
PA: Connell Limited Partnership
 1 International Pl Fl 31
 Boston MA 02110
 617 737-2700

(G-8359)
E & S GRAPHICS INC
300 Industrial Pkwy (48847-9489)
P.O. Box 98 (48847-0098)
PHONE...................................989 875-2828
Scott Gray, *President*
Nick Houghton, *Managing Prtnr*
Douglas Sias, *Vice Pres*
John Gille, *Info Tech Dir*
EMP: 9
SQ FT: 5,000
SALES (est): 1.5MM Privately Held
WEB: www.esgraphics.com
SIC: 2752 2759 Commercial printing, offset; letterpress printing

(G-8360)
HUTCHINSON AROSPC & INDUST INC
1300 S County Farm Rd (48847-9480)
P.O. Box 160 (48847-0160)
PHONE...................................989 875-2052
Chuck Daniels, *Branch Mgr*
EMP: 17
SALES (corp-wide): 8.4B Publicly Held
WEB: www.barrycontrols.com
SIC: 3462 Automotive forgings, ferrous: crankshaft, engine, axle, etc.
HQ: Hutchinson Aerospace & Industry, Inc.
 82 South St
 Hopkinton MA 01748
 508 417-7000

(G-8361)
ITHACA MANUFACTURING CORP
1210 Avenue A (48847-8400)
P.O. Box 78 (48847-0078)
PHONE...................................989 875-4949
Scott Merchant, *President*
Jason Ebright, *Corp Secy*
Benjamin Cooley, *Vice Pres*
EMP: 7
SALES: 556K Privately Held
SIC: 7692 Welding repair

(G-8362)
M & E PLASTICS LLC
205 Industrial Pkwy (48847-9476)
PHONE...................................989 875-4191
John Kungz,
EMP: 10
SALES (est): 393.6K Privately Held
SIC: 3089 Injection molding of plastics

(G-8363)
MACDONALD PUBLICATIONS INC
Also Called: Gratiot County Herald
123 N Main St (48847-1131)
P.O. Box 10 (48847-0010)
PHONE...................................989 875-4151
Patricia Macdonald, *President*
Thomas Macdonald, *Vice Pres*
Greg Nelson, *Relations*
EMP: 12
SQ FT: 4,200
SALES (est): 847.1K Privately Held
SIC: 2711 2741 2752 Newspapers, publishing & printing; shopping news: publishing & printing; commercial printing, offset

(G-8364)
MID-STATE PRINTING INC
145 Industrial Pkwy (48847-9476)
P.O. Box 277 (48847-0277)
PHONE...................................989 875-4163
Tom McDonald, *Principal*
John Belles, *Vice Pres*
EMP: 15
SQ FT: 9,000
SALES (est): 2MM Privately Held
WEB: www.gcherald.com
SIC: 2752 2791 2789 2759 Newspapers, lithographed only; typesetting; bookbinding & related work; commercial printing

(G-8365)
MISUMI INVESTMENT USA CORP
255 Industrial Pkwy (48847-9476)
PHONE...................................989 875-5400
Steve Zerio, *Branch Mgr*
EMP: 18 Privately Held
SIC: 3544 Die sets for metal stamping (presses)
HQ: Misumi Investment Usa Corporation
 500 Progress Rd
 Dayton OH 45449
 937 859-5111

(G-8366)
MOBILE PROSTHETICS
1326 E Center St Ste 200 (48847-1619)
PHONE...................................989 875-7000
EMP: 3
SALES (est): 120K Privately Held
SIC: 3842 Mfg Surgical Appliances/Supplies

(G-8367)
STAGE STOP
Also Called: Columbus Tree The
5348 Us 127 S (48847)
PHONE...................................989 838-4039
Beverly Nelson, *President*
Ronald Nelson, *Owner*
EMP: 8
SQ FT: 9,000
SALES (est): 350K Privately Held
WEB: www.thestagestop.com
SIC: 3312 Forgings, iron & steel

Jackson
Jackson County

(G-8368)
127 BREWING
3090 Shirley Dr (49201-7010)
PHONE...................................517 258-1346
Jeff Tolonen, *Owner*
EMP: 3 **EST:** 2016
SALES (est): 75.4K Privately Held
SIC: 2082 Malt beverages

(G-8369)
A J TOOL CO
3525 Scheele Dr Ste A (49202-1284)
PHONE...................................517 787-5755
EMP: 12
SALES (est): 1.1MM Privately Held
SIC: 3544 Mfg Dies/Tools/Jigs/Fixtures

(G-8370)
A&LB CUSTOM FRAMING LLC
Also Called: I've Been Framed
866 N Wisner St (49202-3141)
PHONE...................................517 783-3810
Aimee Bozinoff,
EMP: 3
SALES (est): 84.1K Privately Held
SIC: 5719 2499 Pictures, wall; picture frame molding, finished

(G-8371)
ACCUBILT AUTOMATED SYSTEMS LLC
2365 Research Dr (49203-6407)
P.O. Box 844 (49204-0844)
PHONE...................................517 787-9353
Rob Rooney, *President*
John Cross, *Treasurer*
EMP: 22
SQ FT: 24,000
SALES (est): 5.1MM Privately Held
WEB: www.accubilt.com
SIC: 3544 3541 Special dies, tools, jigs & fixtures; machine tool replacement & repair parts, metal cutting types

(G-8372)
ADVANCE PACKAGING CORPORATION
2400 E High St (49203-6418)
PHONE...................................616 949-6610
Dave Knickerbocker, *Manager*
EMP: 65
SALES (corp-wide): 147MM Privately Held
WEB: www.advancepkg.com
SIC: 2653 Boxes, corrugated: made from purchased materials
PA: Advance Packaging Corporation
 4459 40th St Se
 Grand Rapids MI 49512
 616 949-6610

(G-8373)
ADVANCE TURNING AND MFG INC (PA)
4005 Morrill Rd (49201-7013)
PHONE...................................517 783-2713
John Macchia Jr, *CEO*
John Rappleye, *President*
John Macchia Sr, *Chairman*
Scott Halstead, *Vice Pres*
Scott Lawson, *Vice Pres*
EMP: 101
SQ FT: 38,000
SALES (est): 24.9MM Privately Held
WEB: www.advanceturning.com
SIC: 3769 3599 3451 3728 Guided missile & space vehicle parts & auxiliary equipment; machine shop, jobbing & repair; machine & other job shop work; screw machine products; aircraft power transmission equipment; aircraft engines & engine parts

(G-8374)
ADVANCE TURNING AND MFG INC
Also Called: McDivitt Road Facility
4901 James Mcdevitt St (49201-8958)
PHONE...................................517 750-3580
Scott Halstead, *Vice Pres*
Nicole Burks, *Accountant*
EMP: 40
SQ FT: 22,500
SALES (corp-wide): 24.9MM Privately Held
WEB: www.advanceturning.com
SIC: 3599 Machine shop, jobbing & repair
PA: Advance Turning And Manufacturing, Inc.
 4005 Morrill Rd
 Jackson MI 49201
 517 783-2713

(G-8375)
AERTECH MACHINING & MFG INC
2020 Micor Dr (49203-3448)
PHONE...................................517 782-4644
Michael D Macchia, *CEO*
Todd Cochrane, *President*
Adam Bauerly, *QC Mgr*
Jenny Griffis, *CFO*
Gina Macchia, *Manager*
EMP: 30
SQ FT: 10,000
SALES (est): 6.6MM Privately Held
SIC: 3599 3812 Machine shop, jobbing & repair; search & navigation equipment

(G-8376)
AFX INDUSTRIES LLC
4111 County Farm Rd (49201-4100)
PHONE...................................517 768-8993
D Sommerville, *Vice Pres*
EMP: 4
SALES (corp-wide): 440.5MM Privately Held
SIC: 3111 Cutting of leather
HQ: Afx Industries, L.L.C.
 1411 3rd St Ste G
 Port Huron MI 48060
 810 966-4650

(G-8377)
AIR-HYDRAULICS INC
545 Hupp Ave (49203-1929)
P.O. Box 831 (49204-0831)
PHONE...................................517 787-9444
Joseph R Miller, *President*
David C Miller, *Vice Pres*
Joseph Leo Miller, *Vice Pres*
Philip G Miller, *Vice Pres*
Howard C Patch, *Admin Sec*
EMP: 18 **EST:** 1945
SQ FT: 13,000
SALES: 1.2MM Privately Held
WEB: www.airhydraulics.com
SIC: 3542 3559 3544 3537 Presses: hydraulic & pneumatic, mechanical & manual; automotive related machinery; plastics working machinery; punches, forming & stamping; tables, lift: hydraulic

(G-8378)
AIRMETAL CORPORATION
1309 Bagley Ave (49203-3303)
PHONE...................................517 784-6000
Bruce Rogers, *President*
Steve Marcinkiewicz, *Vice Pres*
EMP: 10
SQ FT: 8,800
SALES: 1.1MM Privately Held
WEB: www.airmetalcorp.com
SIC: 3599 3544 Machine shop, jobbing & repair; special dies & tools

(G-8379)
AIRWAY WELDING INC
2415 E High St (49203-3421)
PHONE...................................517 789-6125
Douglas R Rogers, *President*
Rick L Rogers, *Treasurer*
EMP: 11 **EST:** 1962
SQ FT: 23,500
SALES: 2.1MM Privately Held
SIC: 7692 Welding repair

(G-8380)
ALLIED CHUCKER AND ENGRG CO (PA)
Also Called: Acecd
3529 Scheele Dr (49202-1296)
PHONE...................................517 787-1370
Melvin Schalhamer, *Ch of Bd*
William P Schomer, *President*
Morris Thorrez, *Corp Secy*
Patrick McCann, *Vice Pres*
Albert Thorrez, *Vice Pres*
EMP: 140
SQ FT: 15,000
SALES (est): 69.1MM Privately Held
SIC: 3599 Machine shop, jobbing & repair

(G-8381)
ALLIED CHUCKER AND ENGRG CO
3525 Scheele Dr (49202-1284)
PHONE...................................517 787-1370
Frank Zielinski, *Branch Mgr*
EMP: 150
SALES (corp-wide): 69.1MM Privately Held
SIC: 3599 Machine shop, jobbing & repair
PA: Allied Chucker And Engineering Company
 3529 Scheele Dr
 Jackson MI 49202
 517 787-1370

(G-8382)
ALRO RIVERSIDE LLC
Also Called: Riverside Grinding Co
829 Belden Rd (49203-2189)
PHONE...................................517 782-8322
E G Miller, *Principal*
Kevin McCann, *Opers Mgr*
Phill Miller,
Kathy Brady,
EMP: 6
SQ FT: 10,000
SALES (est): 531.5K Privately Held
SIC: 3599 3443 Grinding castings for the trade; fabricated plate work (boiler shop)

Jackson - Jackson County (G-8383)

(G-8383)
AMERICAN TOOLING CENTER INC
11505 Elm St (49202)
PHONE.....................517 522-8411
John J Basso, *President*
EMP: 6
SALES (corp-wide): 30.3MM **Privately Held**
SIC: 3544 Special dies & tools
PA: American Tooling Center, Inc.
 4111 Mount Hope Rd
 Grass Lake MI 49240
 517 522-8411

(G-8384)
ANDERTON MACHINING LLC
2400 Enterprise St 1 (49203-6425)
PHONE.....................517 905-5155
Richard A Walawender,
EMP: 5
SALES (est): 880.2K
SALES (corp-wide): 780.2K **Privately Held**
SIC: 3089 Automotive parts, plastic
PA: Anderton Industries, Inc.
 3001 W Big Beaver Rd # 310
 Troy MI 48084
 248 430-6650

(G-8385)
AUTOMOTIVE SERVICE CO
603 E Washington Ave (49203-6110)
P.O. Box 129 (49204-0129)
PHONE.....................517 784-6131
Toll Free:..................................888 -
Duane R Zwick Jr, *President*
Charlie Zwick, *Vice Pres*
Craig D Zwick, *Vice Pres*
Mike Caldwell, *Manager*
EMP: 10
SQ FT: 32,000
SALES (est): 1MM **Privately Held**
WEB: www.automotiveserviceco.com
SIC: 3715 3713 5531 5013 Truck trailers; truck bodies (motor vehicles); truck equipment & parts; trailer hitches, automotive; truck parts & accessories; trailer parts & accessories

(G-8386)
B & R GEAR COMPANY INC
2102 River St (49202-1719)
PHONE.....................517 787-8381
Michael Null, *President*
EMP: 11 **EST:** 1959
SQ FT: 8,000
SALES (est): 1.1MM **Privately Held**
SIC: 3599 Machine shop, jobbing & repair

(G-8387)
BAILEY SAND & GRAVEL CO
6505 W Michigan Ave (49201-8997)
PHONE.....................517 750-4889
Jerald Bailey, *President*
Jeffery Bailey, *Vice Pres*
James Bailey, *Treasurer*
EMP: 18
SQ FT: 8,000
SALES (est): 3.2MM **Privately Held**
SIC: 1442 Sand mining; gravel & pebble mining

(G-8388)
BAXTER MACHINE & TOOL CO
103 N Horton St (49202-3719)
P.O. Box 530 (49204-0530)
PHONE.....................517 782-2808
Larry G Baxter, *President*
Sandra K Baxter, *Vice Pres*
Sam Genix, *Prdtn Mgr*
Michael Baxter, *Engineer*
Scott McCarty, *Engineer*
EMP: 35
SQ FT: 25,000
SALES (est): 6.4MM **Privately Held**
WEB: www.baxtermachine.com
SIC: 3544 3599 3545 Special dies & tools; industrial molds; machine shop, jobbing & repair; machine tool accessories

(G-8389)
BIG STEEL RACK LLC
2427 Research Dr (49203-6409)
P.O. Box 4010 (49204-4010)
PHONE.....................517 740-5428
Paul Brockie, *Natl Sales Mgr*
Ronald W Johncox,
Ronnie Johncox,
EMP: 3
SQ FT: 50,000
SALES (est): 306.1K **Privately Held**
SIC: 3443 Containers, shipping (bombs, etc.): metal plate

(G-8390)
BIOMEDICAL DESIGNS
306 W Washington Ave # 105 (49201-2141)
PHONE.....................517 784-6617
Joe Hunter, *President*
EMP: 3
SALES (est): 297.6K **Privately Held**
SIC: 3842 Surgical appliances & supplies

(G-8391)
BISBEE INFRARED SERVICES INC
569 Wildwood Ave Unit 2 (49201-1048)
P.O. Box 51 (49204-0051)
PHONE.....................517 787-4620
Penny Wilson-Chrzan, *President*
EMP: 9
SQ FT: 400
SALES (est): 1.1MM **Privately Held**
SIC: 3823 Industrial instrmnts msrmnt display/control process variable

(G-8392)
BOBBYS MOBILE SERVICE LLC
1188 Herbert J Ave (49202-1928)
PHONE.....................517 206-6026
Roberty Holmes, *Principal*
EMP: 6 **EST:** 2012
SALES (est): 684.4K **Privately Held**
SIC: 3715 Bus trailers, tractor type

(G-8393)
BOONES WELDING & FABRICATING
1309 Westlane St (49203-5024)
PHONE.....................517 782-7461
Stephen A Boone, *President*
Deborah H Boone, *Corp Secy*
EMP: 7
SALES (est): 1.1MM **Privately Held**
SIC: 3441 Fabricated structural metal

(G-8394)
BOYERS TOOL AND DIE INC
1729 W Ganson St (49202-4030)
PHONE.....................517 782-7869
R Tucker Boyers, *President*
Robert D Boyers, *Treasurer*
EMP: 8
SQ FT: 6,000
SALES (est): 1.1MM **Privately Held**
WEB: www.boyers-tool.com
SIC: 3544 Special dies & tools

(G-8395)
BRIGGS MOLD & DIE INC
414 N Jackson St 97-12 (49201-1249)
PHONE.....................517 784-6908
Howard Briggs, *President*
EMP: 4 **EST:** 1997
SALES (est): 403.3K **Privately Held**
SIC: 3544 Special dies & tools

(G-8396)
C & H STAMPING INC
205 Obrien Rd (49201-8919)
PHONE.....................517 750-3600
David T Parshall, *President*
John Parshall, *President*
Lynne Parshall, *Vice Pres*
EMP: 30
SQ FT: 36,000
SALES (est): 5.3MM **Privately Held**
SIC: 3465 3544 Automotive stampings; special dies & tools

(G-8397)
C & K BOX COMPANY INC
423 Barrett Ave (49202-3901)
P.O. Box 1817 (49204-1817)
PHONE.....................517 784-1779
Robert C Stevens, *CEO*
Mark Stevens, *President*
Amy Stevens, *Corp Secy*
EMP: 20 **EST:** 1960
SQ FT: 35,000
SALES (est): 3.5MM **Privately Held**
SIC: 2448 2441 2449 Pallets, wood; boxes, wood; wood containers

(G-8398)
C C WELDING
429 Hill St (49202-2203)
PHONE.....................517 783-2305
Charles Heines Sr, *Partner*
EMP: 3
SALES (est): 229.2K **Privately Held**
SIC: 7692 Welding repair

(G-8399)
C THORREZ INDUSTRIES INC (PA)
4909 W Michigan Ave (49201-7909)
PHONE.....................517 750-3160
Albert F Thorrez, *Ch of Bd*
Camiel E Thorrez, *President*
Henry C Thorrez, *Vice Pres*
Michael Thorrez, *Vice Pres*
Morris C Thorrez, *Admin Sec*
▲ **EMP:** 52 **EST:** 1968
SQ FT: 48,000
SALES (est): 21.8MM **Privately Held**
SIC: 3451 Screw machine products

(G-8400)
CAMSHAFT ACQUISITION INC
Also Called: Camshaft Machine Company
717 Woodworth Rd (49202-1636)
PHONE.....................517 787-2040
Jeremy Lumbrezer, *President*
EMP: 41 **EST:** 2014
SALES (est): 4.6MM **Privately Held**
SIC: 3714 Camshafts, motor vehicle

(G-8401)
CAMSHAFT MACHINE COMPANY LLC (PA)
717 Woodworth Rd (49202-1636)
PHONE.....................517 787-2040
Rodney Delong, *COO*
Chris Easterday, *Buyer*
Jacqueline Fagan, *QC Mgr*
Wendy Tyslenko, *Controller*
Wendy Willis, *Human Res Mgr*
EMP: 45
SALES (est): 9.2MM **Privately Held**
WEB: www.camshaftmachine.com
SIC: 3714 Camshafts, motor vehicle

(G-8402)
CARB-A-TRON TOOL CO
4615 S Jackson Rd (49203-8382)
PHONE.....................517 782-2249
John Trammell, *President*
Joan Fayette, *Vice Pres*
EMP: 9
SQ FT: 7,800
SALES (est): 1MM **Privately Held**
WEB: www.carb-a-tron.com
SIC: 3541 3556 Machine tools, metal cutting: exotic (explosive, etc.); cutting, chopping, grinding, mixing & similar machinery

(G-8403)
CASALBI COMPANY INC
Also Called: Globe Tumbling Barrel Eqp
540 Wayne St (49202-4099)
PHONE.....................517 782-0345
Steven J Sparks, *President*
William Bregg, *Treasurer*
EMP: 11
SQ FT: 10,000
SALES (est): 500K **Privately Held**
SIC: 3541 Deburring machines

(G-8404)
CDGJL INC (PA)
Also Called: Comfort-Aire
1900 Wellworth (49203-6428)
PHONE.....................517 787-2100
Donald Peck, *Ch of Bd*
Lou Rasmussen, *Vice Pres*
David Duane, *CFO*
Tracy Volz, *Credit Mgr*
Leon Cogswell, *Sales Staff*
◆ **EMP:** 45 **EST:** 1933
SQ FT: 175,000
SALES (est): 12MM **Privately Held**
WEB: www.heatcontroller.com
SIC: 3585 3634 3564 Air conditioning equipment, complete; humidifiers, electric: household; dehumidifiers, electric: room; air purification equipment

(G-8405)
CERTAINTEED CORPORATION
Wolverine Vinyl Siding
701 E Washington Ave (49203-6132)
PHONE.....................517 787-8898
Sheldon Thorpe, *Branch Mgr*
EMP: 400
SQ FT: 550,000
SALES (corp-wide): 215.9MM **Privately Held**
WEB: www.certainteed.net
SIC: 3089 3444 Siding, plastic; sheet metalwork
HQ: Certainteed Llc
 20 Moores Rd
 Malvern PA 19355
 610 893-5000

(G-8406)
CERTAINTEED CORPORATION
803 Belden Rd (49203-1908)
PHONE.....................517 787-1737
Dave Beck, *Manager*
EMP: 48
SALES (corp-wide): 215.9MM **Privately Held**
WEB: www.certainteed.net
SIC: 8731 3444 Commercial research laboratory; sheet metalwork
HQ: Certainteed Llc
 20 Moores Rd
 Malvern PA 19355
 610 893-5000

(G-8407)
CHATEAU ARONAUTIQUE WINERY LLC
101 Chief Dr (49201-8154)
PHONE.....................517 569-2132
Lorenzo Lizarralde,
EMP: 5
SALES (est): 411.9K **Privately Held**
SIC: 2084 Wines

(G-8408)
CHEMETALL US INC
Also Called: Chemetall Americas
1100 Technology Dr (49201-2256)
PHONE.....................517 787-4846
EMP: 18
SALES (corp-wide): 71.7B **Privately Held**
SIC: 2842 2899 2851 Bleaches, household: dry or liquid; chemical preparations; paints & allied products
HQ: Chemetall U.S., Inc.
 675 Central Ave
 New Providence NJ 07974
 908 464-6900

(G-8409)
CHRISTOPHER S CAMPION
Also Called: Connected Prfmce Cmpt Cnslting
258 Ackerson Lake Dr (49201-8755)
PHONE.....................517 414-6796
EMP: 3 **EST:** 2015
SALES (est): 145.2K **Privately Held**
SIC: 3571 5734 7371 7373 Mfg Electronic Computers Ret Computers/Software Computer Programming Svc Computer Systems Design Business Consulting Svcs

(G-8410)
CLASSIC CABINETS INTERIORS LLC
807 S Brown St (49203-1430)
PHONE.....................517 817-5650
Besty Writer, *Manager*
EMP: 3
SALES (corp-wide): 2.5MM **Privately Held**
SIC: 2434 Wood kitchen cabinets
PA: Classic Cabinets And Interiors, Llc
 118 W Chicago Blvd
 Tecumseh MI 49286
 517 423-2600

GEOGRAPHIC SECTION
Jackson - Jackson County (G-8434)

(G-8411)
CLASSIC METAL FINISHING INC
Also Called: Precision Metal Finishing
2500 W Argyle St (49202-1969)
PHONE..................................517 990-0011
Scott A Brockie, *President*
Bradely E Nall, *Vice Pres*
Sam Absher, *Engineer*
Jason Braden, *Technician*
EMP: 29
SALES (est): 5.8MM **Privately Held**
SIC: 3599 3471 Machine shop, jobbing & repair; anodizing (plating) of metals or formed products

(G-8412)
CLASSIC TURNING INC (PA)
Also Called: Cnc
3000 E South St (49201-8741)
PHONE..................................517 764-1335
Alex Webster, *President*
Philip J Curtis, *Owner*
EMP: 55
SQ FT: 65,000
SALES (est): 23.1MM **Privately Held**
WEB: www.classicturning.com
SIC: 3599 Amusement park equipment; machine shop, jobbing & repair

(G-8413)
CMS ENTERPRISES COMPANY (HQ)
1 Energy Plaza Dr (49201-2357)
PHONE..................................517 788-0550
Thomas W Elward, *President*
M Clifford Lawrenso, *Vice Pres*
William H Stephens, *Vice Pres*
Joseph P Tomasik, *Vice Pres*
Joe Eckert, *Opers Mgr*
▼ **EMP:** 145
SALES (est): 79MM
SALES (corp-wide): 6.8B **Publicly Held**
SIC: 4911 1382 Generation, electric power; geophysical exploration, oil & gas field
PA: Cms Energy Corporation
1 Energy Plaza Dr
Jackson MI 49201
517 788-0550

(G-8414)
CODO MACHINE & TOOL INC
1418 Lewis St (49203-3326)
PHONE..................................517 789-5113
David C Brautigam, *President*
Dorothy L Brautigam, *Corp Secy*
Corey O Brautigam, *Vice Pres*
EMP: 4
SQ FT: 3,000
SALES (est): 260K **Privately Held**
SIC: 3599 Machine shop, jobbing & repair

(G-8415)
COLONIAL CHEMICAL CORP
720 E Mansion St (49203-4400)
P.O. Box 459, Canal Fulton OH (44614-0459)
PHONE..................................517 789-8161
Wayne F Aben, *President*
Pat Thibert, *Vice Pres*
▲ **EMP:** 4
SQ FT: 8,500
SALES (est): 440.2K **Privately Held**
SIC: 2842 Cleaning or polishing preparations

(G-8416)
COMMONWEALTH ASSOCIATES INC (PA)
2700 W Argyle St (49202-1975)
P.O. Box 1124 (49204-1124)
PHONE..................................517 788-3000
Richard N Collins, *President*
Stephen Arnold, *Senior VP*
Samuel R Barnes, *Vice Pres*
Linda Gray, *Vice Pres*
Allen Vasaris, *Vice Pres*
EMP: 170
SQ FT: 49,000
SALES: 37MM **Privately Held**
WEB: www.cai-engr.com
SIC: 8711 3822 Consulting engineer; auto controls regulating residntl & coml environmt & applncs

(G-8417)
COMTRONICS
4909 W Michigan Ave (49201-7909)
PHONE..................................517 750-3160
EMP: 3
SALES (est): 120.5K **Privately Held**
SIC: 3451 Screw machine products

(G-8418)
CONCENT GRINDING INC (HQ)
2620 Saradan Dr (49202-1214)
P.O. Box 1188 (49204-1188)
PHONE..................................517 787-8172
Mark S Melling, *President*
Thomas C Evanson, *Corp Secy*
▲ **EMP:** 1
SALES (est): 8.7MM
SALES (corp-wide): 265MM **Privately Held**
SIC: 3714 Motor vehicle parts & accessories
PA: Melling Tool Co.
2620 Saradan Dr
Jackson MI 49202
517 787-8172

(G-8419)
CONSUMERS CONCRETE CORPORATION
3342 Page Ave (49203-2259)
PHONE..................................517 784-9108
Roger Butterfield, *Manager*
EMP: 10
SALES (corp-wide): 102.9MM **Privately Held**
WEB: www.consumersconcrete.com
SIC: 1771 3273 3272 Concrete work; ready-mixed concrete; concrete products
PA: Consumers Concrete Corporation
3508 S Sprinkle Rd
Kalamazoo MI 49001
269 342-0136

(G-8420)
CONTOUR TOOL AND MACHINE INC
2393 Research Dr (49203-6407)
PHONE..................................517 787-6806
Richard Johnson, *President*
EMP: 7 **EST:** 1978
SQ FT: 12,800
SALES (est): 875K **Privately Held**
WEB: www.contourtoolinc.com
SIC: 3545 3599 Tools & accessories for machine tools; machine shop, jobbing & repair

(G-8421)
CONTROLLED TURNING INC
1607 S Gorham St (49203-3412)
P.O. Box 1364 (49204-1364)
PHONE..................................517 782-0517
Jerome Broughman, *President*
Carol Broughman, *Vice Pres*
EMP: 9
SQ FT: 10,000
SALES (est): 1.4MM **Privately Held**
SIC: 3599 Machine shop, jobbing & repair

(G-8422)
COX BROTHERS MACHINING INC
2300 E Ganson St (49202-3770)
PHONE..................................517 796-4662
Russell E Cox, *Owner*
Teri Cox, *Corp Secy*
Clinton Cox, *QC Mgr*
EMP: 20 **EST:** 1995
SQ FT: 2,400
SALES (est): 2.7MM **Privately Held**
WEB: www.coxbro.com
SIC: 3441 3479 Fabricated structural metal; coating of metals & formed products

(G-8423)
CRANKSHAFT MACHINE COMPANY (HQ)
Also Called: Lindberg Fluid Power Division
314 N Jackson St (49201-1246)
P.O. Box 1127 (49204-1127)
PHONE..................................517 787-3791
Craig Little, *President*
EMP: 35 **EST:** 1916
SQ FT: 50,000
SALES: 8MM
SALES (corp-wide): 312.9MM **Privately Held**
WEB: www.crankshaft.net
SIC: 3593 3541 Fluid power cylinders, hydraulic or pneumatic; crankshaft regrinding machines; grinding machines, metalworking; broaching machines
PA: Avis Industrial Corporation
1909 S Main St
Upland IN 46989
765 998-8100

(G-8424)
CREATIVE GRAPHICS INC
430 N Mechanic St (49201-1307)
PHONE..................................517 784-0391
Gary Bailey, *President*
Nancy Vandworth, *Admin Sec*
EMP: 7 **EST:** 1978
SQ FT: 7,500
SALES (est): 903.8K **Privately Held**
SIC: 2732 Books: printing only

(G-8425)
CROWN INDUSTRIAL SERVICES INC
Also Called: Miwi
2080 Brooklyn Rd (49203-4744)
P.O. Box 970197, Ypsilanti (48197-0026)
PHONE..................................517 905-5300
Steven Bullock, *Branch Mgr*
EMP: 40
SALES (corp-wide): 17.4MM **Privately Held**
SIC: 3471 Cleaning, polishing & finishing
PA: Crown Industrial Services Inc
2480 Airport Dr
Ypsilanti MI 48198
734 483-7270

(G-8426)
D W MACHINE INC
2501 Precision St (49202-3925)
PHONE..................................517 787-9929
Fax: 517 787-2151
EMP: 10
SQ FT: 8,500
SALES: 450K **Privately Held**
SIC: 3544 3541 Tool & Die Shop & Mfg Turrets

(G-8427)
DAWN EQUIPMENT COMPANY INC
Also Called: Dawn Food Products
2021 Micor Dr (49203-3473)
PHONE..................................517 789-4500
Carrie Barber Jones, *President*
Paul Caske, *Vice Pres*
Gretchen Tello, *Safety Mgr*
Mike Bowers, *Production*
Joe Benn, *Buyer*
EMP: 120
SALES (est): 114MM
SALES (corp-wide): 1.6B **Privately Held**
SIC: 5046 3556 Bakery equipment & supplies; bakery machinery
PA: Dawn Foods, Inc.
3333 Sargent Rd
Jackson MI 49201
517 789-4400

(G-8428)
DAWN FOOD PRODUCTS INC
Also Called: Brothers Baking
3333 Sargent Rd (49201-8847)
PHONE..................................517 789-4400
Tom Wegner, *Manager*
EMP: 107
SALES (corp-wide): 1.6B **Privately Held**
WEB: www.dawnfoods.com
SIC: 2045 Doughnut mixes, prepared: from purchased flour
HQ: Dawn Food Products, Inc.
3333 Sargent Rd
Jackson MI 49201

(G-8429)
DAWN FOOD PRODUCTS INC (HQ)
3333 Sargent Rd (49201-8847)
PHONE..................................517 789-4400
Carrie L Barber, *CEO*
Miles E Jones, *Ch of Bd*
Ronald L Jones, *Ch of Bd*
Phil Batty, *President*
Carey Dassatti, *President*
◆ **EMP:** 200
SQ FT: 95,000
SALES (est): 760.3MM
SALES (corp-wide): 1.6B **Privately Held**
WEB: www.dawnfoods.com
SIC: 2045 5046 3556 Doughnut mixes, prepared: from purchased flour; cake mixes, prepared: from purchased flour; bakery equipment & supplies; bakery machinery
PA: Dawn Foods, Inc.
3333 Sargent Rd
Jackson MI 49201
517 789-4400

(G-8430)
DAWN FOODS INC (PA)
3333 Sargent Rd (49201-8847)
PHONE..................................517 789-4400
Carrie Jones-Barber, *CEO*
Serhat Unsal, *CEO*
Maria Figueras, *General Mgr*
Don Schwartzman, *General Mgr*
Jim Whalen, *General Mgr*
◆ **EMP:** 200 **EST:** 1925
SALES (est): 1.6B **Privately Held**
SIC: 2053 2045 3556 5046 Cakes, bakery: frozen; pastries (danish): frozen; doughnut mixes, prepared: from purchased flour; bakery machinery; bakery equipment & supplies; investment holding companies, except banks

(G-8431)
DAWN FOODS INTERNATIONAL CORP
3333 Sargent Rd (49201-8847)
PHONE..................................517 789-4400
Ronald L Jones, *President*
Miles Jones, *COO*
Jerry Baglien, *CFO*
Patrick Willemsen, *Manager*
Marvel Jones, *Admin Sec*
EMP: 220
SALES (est): 19.7MM
SALES (corp-wide): 1.6B **Privately Held**
SIC: 2045 Prepared flour mixes & doughs
PA: Dawn Foods, Inc.
3333 Sargent Rd
Jackson MI 49201
517 789-4400

(G-8432)
DEXTER STAMPING COMPANY LLC
1013 Thorrez Rd (49201-8903)
PHONE..................................517 750-3414
Tracey Swarthout, *Vice Pres*
Tom Knox, *Purchasing*
John Berkemeier, *Engineer*
Ken Lowry, *Engineer*
Denise Moeckel, *Controller*
▲ **EMP:** 52
SQ FT: 100,000
SALES (est): 11.2MM **Privately Held**
WEB: www.dsc-1.com
SIC: 3465 Body parts, automobile: stamped metal

(G-8433)
DIE-NAMIC TOOL & DESIGN LLC
147 Hobart St (49202-2497)
PHONE..................................517 787-4900
Robert Whiting,
Chad Whiting,
EMP: 13
SQ FT: 7,000
SALES (est): 1.1MM **Privately Held**
SIC: 3544 Special dies & tools

(G-8434)
DIVERSIFIED ENGRG & PLAS LLC
1801 Wildwood Ave (49202-4044)
PHONE..................................517 789-8118
Anita-Mara Quillen, *President*
EMP: 80
SALES (est): 21MM **Privately Held**
SIC: 3089 Injection molding of plastics

Jackson - Jackson County (G-8435)

(G-8435)
DOROTHY DAWSON FOOD PRODUCTS
251 W Euclid Ave (49203-4101)
P.O. Box 312 (49204-0312)
PHONE..................517 788-9830
Pj Dawson, *President*
Brett Crosthwaite, *CFO*
William Kuhl, *Treasurer*
Becky Haltom, *Executive Asst*
EMP: 32 **EST:** 1954
SQ FT: 10,000
SALES (est): 9.2MM **Privately Held**
SIC: 2099 2045 2051 2041 Food preparations; prepared flour mixes & doughs; bakery products, partially cooked (except frozen); flour & other grain mill products

(G-8436)
EAGLE BUCKETS INC
703 S Cooper St (49203-1886)
PHONE..................517 787-0385
EMP: 3
SQ FT: 60,000
SALES (est): 300.5K
SALES (corp-wide): 2.6MM **Privately Held**
SIC: 3531 3535 3412 Mfg Construction Machinery Conveyors/Equipment & Metal Barrels/Pails
PA: John Crowley, Inc.
703 S Cooper St
Jackson MI
517 782-0491

(G-8437)
EAGLE POWDER COATING
2218 E High St Ste C (49203-3553)
PHONE..................517 784-2556
Matthew Olinyk, *Owner*
EMP: 30
SQ FT: 65,000
SALES (est): 3.3MM **Privately Held**
WEB: www.epcpowder.com
SIC: 3479 Coating of metals & formed products

(G-8438)
EATON AEROSPACE LLC
300 S East Ave (49203-1973)
PHONE..................517 787-8121
Nicholas Goerke, *President*
EMP: 12 **Privately Held**
SIC: 3721 Aircraft
HQ: Eaton Aerospace Llc
1000 Eaton Blvd
Cleveland OH 44122
216 523-5000

(G-8439)
EATON CORPORATION
Jackson Plant
2425 W Michigan Ave (49202-3964)
PHONE..................517 787-7220
Lisa Baarns, *Buyer*
Andrew Kellogg, *Buyer*
Tameko Watts, *Buyer*
Randy Pepper, *Purchasing*
Clay Carroll, *QC Mgr*
EMP: 200
SQ FT: 116,624 **Privately Held**
WEB: www.eaton.com
SIC: 3594 3593 3494 Fluid power pumps & motors; fluid power cylinders & actuators; valves & pipe fittings
HQ: Eaton Corporation
1000 Eaton Blvd
Cleveland OH 44122
440 523-5000

(G-8440)
EATON-AEROQUIP LLC
Also Called: Aerospace Group
300 S East Ave (49203-1973)
PHONE..................949 452-9575
Scott Thompson, *General Mgr*
Terri Vernon Cleary, *Contract Law*
EMP: 350 **Privately Held**
WEB: www.eaton.com
SIC: 3492 3728 3594 3494 Fluid power valves for aircraft; aircraft parts & equipment; fluid power pumps & motors; valves & pipe fittings; manufactured hardware (general); rubber & plastics hose & beltings
HQ: Eaton Aeroquip Llc
1000 Eaton Blvd
Cleveland OH 44122
216 523-5000

(G-8441)
EDWARDS MACHINING INC
Also Called: Edwards Machine & Tool Co
2335 Research Dr (49203-6407)
PHONE..................517 782-2568
Scott Penrod, *President*
Kevin Immonen, *Manager*
EMP: 22 **EST:** 2002
SALES (est): 5.9MM **Privately Held**
WEB: www.edwardsmachining.com
SIC: 3544 Special dies, tools, jigs & fixtures

(G-8442)
EILER BROTHERS INC
2201 Brooklyn Rd (49203-4797)
PHONE..................517 784-0970
Jeffrey Stout, *President*
Jeanetta Stout, *Corp Secy*
EMP: 12 **EST:** 1968
SQ FT: 15,000
SALES (est): 2.3MM **Privately Held**
SIC: 3599 Machine shop, jobbing & repair

(G-8443)
ELCO ENTERPRISES INC
Also Called: Wire Wizard Welding Products
5750 Marathon Dr Ste B (49201-7711)
PHONE..................517 782-8040
Edward Cooper, *President*
▲ **EMP:** 20
SQ FT: 23,000
SALES (est): 7.5MM **Privately Held**
WEB: www.wire-wizard.com
SIC: 3315 Wire & fabricated wire products

(G-8444)
ELM PLATING
533 Hupp Ave (49203-1929)
PHONE..................517 795-1574
EMP: 3
SALES (est): 153.3K **Privately Held**
SIC: 3471 Plating & polishing

(G-8445)
F & H MANUFACTURING CO INC
149 W Porter St (49202-2319)
PHONE..................517 783-2311
Scott Kellenberger, *President*
EMP: 35
SQ FT: 20,000
SALES (est): 7.4MM **Privately Held**
SIC: 3451 Screw machine products

(G-8446)
F & S TOOL & GAUGE CO INC
1027 E South St (49203-4404)
PHONE..................517 787-2661
Andrew Essenmacher, *President*
Andy Essenmacher, *Engineer*
EMP: 8 **EST:** 1956
SQ FT: 3,000
SALES (est): 1MM **Privately Held**
WEB: www.fstool.com
SIC: 3545 Machine tool attachments & accessories; gauges (machine tool accessories)

(G-8447)
FAB-ALLOY COMPANY
1163 E Morrell St (49203-1986)
P.O. Box 1429 (49204-1429)
PHONE..................517 787-4313
Philip H Clark, *President*
Kathleen M Levy, *Treasurer*
Dorothea Clark, *Admin Sec*
EMP: 9
SQ FT: 20,000
SALES (est): 1.5MM **Privately Held**
WEB: www.fab-alloy.com
SIC: 3499 3444 3443 Fire- or burglary-resistive products; sheet metalwork; fabricated plate work (boiler shop)

(G-8448)
FABRICATION SERVICES INC
Also Called: FSI
1505 E High St (49203-3317)
PHONE..................517 796-1975
John Day, *President*
Rob Wood, *Vice Pres*
EMP: 7
SQ FT: 12,000
SALES: 650K **Privately Held**
SIC: 3443 Industrial vessels, tanks & containers

(G-8449)
FITNESS FINDERS INC
1007 Hurst Rd (49201-8905)
PHONE..................517 750-1500
Richard Fairbanks, *COO*
EMP: 20
SALES: 950K **Privately Held**
SIC: 5961 3089 Catalog sales; novelties, plastic

(G-8450)
FORSONS INC
Also Called: Insty-Prints
139 S Mechanic St (49201-2325)
PHONE..................517 787-4562
Carolyn Matteson, *President*
EMP: 8 **EST:** 1969
SQ FT: 1,400
SALES (est): 1.1MM **Privately Held**
SIC: 2752 2791 2789 8743 Commercial printing, lithographic; typesetting; bookbinding & related work; sales promotion; advertising, promotional & trade show services; presorted mail service; business service newsletters: publishing & printing

(G-8451)
FOURWAY MACHINERY SALES CO
3215 Gregory Rd (49202-2613)
PHONE..................517 782-9371
Lynn Hinkley Sr, *President*
Mark Vancalo, *Owner*
Mark Vancalbergh, *Vice Pres*
Tim Cole, *Plant Supt*
EMP: 13
SQ FT: 52,000
SALES (est): 3.2MM **Privately Held**
WEB: www.fourway.com
SIC: 5084 3541 Machine tools & accessories; machine tools, metal cutting type

(G-8452)
FRY KRISP FOOD PRODUCTS INC
Also Called: Fry Krisp Company, The
3514 Wayland Dr (49202-1234)
PHONE..................517 784-8531
Richard G Neuenfeldt, *President*
Richard J Neuenfeldt, *President*
Steve Hartz, *Vice Pres*
EMP: 12
SQ FT: 8,000
SALES: 3MM **Privately Held**
WEB: www.frykrisp.com
SIC: 2045 Prepared flour mixes & doughs

(G-8453)
FULGHAM MACHINE & TOOL COMPANY
Also Called: Brokenbolt
2347 W High St (49203-2737)
PHONE..................517 937-8316
Charles Fulgham, *President*
Lana Fulgham, *Corp Secy*
EMP: 3
SQ FT: 9,900
SALES (est): 200K **Privately Held**
SIC: 3544 3545 Special dies & tools; drills (machine tool accessories)

(G-8454)
FULL SPECTRUM SOLUTIONS INC (PA)
2021 Wellworth (49203-3451)
P.O. Box 1087 (49204-1087)
PHONE..................517 783-3800
Michael Nevins, *President*
Natasha Spink, *Purchasing*
▲ **EMP:** 39
SQ FT: 72,000
SALES (est): 7.7MM **Privately Held**
WEB: www.paralite.com
SIC: 3645 5063 Residential lighting fixtures; lighting fixtures

(G-8455)
GERDAU MACSTEEL INC
Macsteel Division
3100 Brooklyn Rd (49203-4809)
P.O. Box 1101 (49204-0411)
PHONE..................517 764-3920
John Fisher, *Vice Pres*
EMP: 350 **Privately Held**
WEB: www.macsteel.com
SIC: 3312 3316 Bars & bar shapes, steel, cold-finished: own hot-rolled; cold finishing of steel shapes
HQ: Gerdau Macsteel, Inc.
5591 Morrill Rd
Jackson MI 49201

(G-8456)
GERDAU MACSTEEL INC (DH)
Also Called: Nitro Steel
5591 Morrill Rd (49201-7084)
PHONE..................517 782-0415
Mark Marcucci, *President*
Michael Parham, *Production*
Adam Esterline, *Buyer*
Renu Krishnan, *Engineer*
Nicholas Nelson, *Engineer*
◆ **EMP:** 50
SQ FT: 20,000
SALES (est): 338.5MM **Privately Held**
WEB: www.macsteel.com
SIC: 3316 3312 Cold finishing of steel shapes; bars & bar shapes, steel, cold-finished: own hot-rolled

(G-8457)
GIBBS PRECAST CO INC
2412 Lansing Ave (49202-1645)
PHONE..................517 768-9100
Bill Gibbs, *President*
Donald Gibbs, *Vice Pres*
Sherry Gibbs, *Treasurer*
EMP: 3
SALES (est): 262.9K **Privately Held**
SIC: 3272 Precast terrazo or concrete products

(G-8458)
GLOBAL MFG & ASSEMBLY CORP
1801 Wildwood Ave (49202-4044)
P.O. Box 983 (49204-0983)
PHONE..................517 789-8116
Armida Pearse, *CEO*
Travis Pearse Jr, *President*
EMP: 331 **EST:** 2001
SALES (est): 24.3MM **Privately Held**
SIC: 3089 Plastic containers, except foam

(G-8459)
GREAT LAKES INDUSTRY INC
Also Called: G I
1927 Wildwood Ave (49202-4061)
PHONE..................517 784-3153
Lawrence Schultz, *President*
Michael D Dwyer, *Vice Pres*
Jim Dettloff, *Purchasing*
Michael Edwards, *QC Mgr*
Bob Haughey, *Engineer*
▲ **EMP:** 45
SQ FT: 52,000
SALES (est): 11.7MM **Privately Held**
WEB: www.greatlakesind.com
SIC: 3568 3462 Clutches, except vehicular; couplings, shaft: rigid, flexible, universal joint, etc.; sprockets (power transmission equipment); iron & steel forgings

(G-8460)
GREAT LAKES METAL FINSHG LLC
3000 E South St (49201-8741)
PHONE..................517 764-1335
Philip J Curtis,
EMP: 24 **EST:** 2012
SALES (est): 1.7MM
SALES (corp-wide): 23.1MM **Privately Held**
SIC: 3471 Coloring & finishing of aluminum or formed products
PA: Classic Turning, Inc.
3000 E South St
Jackson MI 49201
517 764-1335

(G-8461)
H & M WELDING AND FABRICATING
3600 Page Ave (49203-2322)
PHONE.....................517 764-3630
Richard Miller, *President*
EMP: 5 EST: 1969
SQ FT: 14,000
SALES: 700K **Privately Held**
SIC: 7692 3444 3443 3441 Welding repair; sheet metalwork; fabricated plate work (boiler shop); fabricated structural metal

(G-8462)
HANDLEY INDUSTRIES INC
2101 Brooklyn Rd (49203-4792)
PHONE.....................517 787-8821
Robert E Handley, *President*
Rick Harbaugh, *Plant Mgr*
Howard Patch, *Treasurer*
Barbara D Huggett, *Admin Sec*
▲ EMP: 10 EST: 1925
SQ FT: 55,000
SALES: 2.3MM **Privately Held**
WEB: www.handleyind.com
SIC: 3089 Boxes, plastic

(G-8463)
HAYES-ALBION CORPORATION
1999 Wildwood Ave (49202)
PHONE.....................517 629-2141
Chad Baase, *President*
EMP: 12
SQ FT: 7,000
SALES (est): 1.6MM **Privately Held**
SIC: 3714 3471 3711 2396 Motor vehicle parts & accessories; cleaning, polishing & finishing; motor vehicles & car bodies; automotive trimmings, fabric

(G-8464)
HERALD NEWSPAPERS COMPANY INC
Also Called: Jackson Citizen Patriot
1750 S Cooper St (49203-4417)
PHONE.....................517 787-2300
Sandy Petykiewicz, *Director*
EMP: 198
SALES (corp-wide): 5.5B **Privately Held**
WEB: www.post-standard.com
SIC: 2711 Newspapers, publishing & printing
HQ: The Herald Newspapers Company Inc
220 S Warren St
Syracuse NY 13202
315 470-0011

(G-8465)
HI-TECH FLEXIBLE PRODUCTS INC
2000 Townley St (49203-4414)
PHONE.....................517 783-5911
Ron Phillips, *President*
Stephanie Cronkright, *Office Admin*
EMP: 11
SQ FT: 8,000
SALES (est): 1.9MM **Privately Held**
WEB: www.hi-techflex.com
SIC: 3069 Molded rubber products

(G-8466)
HOLIDAY DISTRIBUTING CO
Also Called: Addison Awning Co
3990 Francis St (49203-5434)
PHONE.....................517 782-7146
Anthony J Krupa Jr, *President*
Gary L Krupa, *President*
Bill Vinson, *Sales Mgr*
Ashley Tackett, *Admin Asst*
EMP: 40 EST: 1955
SQ FT: 26,000
SALES (est): 8.7MM **Privately Held**
WEB: www.krupas.com
SIC: 5551 2394 Marine supplies; awnings, fabric: made from purchased materials

(G-8467)
HYDRAULIC SYSTEMS INC
1505 E High St (49203-3317)
PHONE.....................517 787-7818
John Day, *President*
EMP: 20 EST: 1983
SQ FT: 20,000
SALES (est): 2.5MM **Privately Held**
WEB: www.hydraulicsystems.net
SIC: 3594 3569 Pumps, hydraulic power transfer; motors: hydraulic, fluid power or air; filter elements, fluid, hydraulic line

(G-8468)
HYTROL MANUFACTURING INC
4005 Morrill Rd (49201-7013)
PHONE.....................734 261-8030
Fred R Waldecker, *CEO*
Scott Lawson, *President*
Steve Leger, *Vice Pres*
EMP: 40
SQ FT: 15,000
SALES (est): 6.7MM **Privately Held**
WEB: www.hytrolmfg.com
SIC: 3728 3764 3812 Aircraft parts & equipment; engines & engine parts, guided missile; search & navigation equipment

(G-8469)
IMAGECRAFT
100 Robinson Rd (49203-1053)
PHONE.....................517 750-0077
John F Dawson, *Owner*
EMP: 5 EST: 1977
SALES: 260K **Privately Held**
SIC: 5999 3479 Trophies & plaques; engraving jewelry silverware, or metal

(G-8470)
INDUSTRIAL STEEL TREATING CO
Also Called: Ist
613 Carroll Ave (49202-3169)
P.O. Box 98 (49204-0098)
PHONE.....................517 787-6312
Timothy Levy, *President*
Mark Egan, *Project Mgr*
Jim Matthews, *Facilities Mgr*
James Wildenhaus, *Purch Mgr*
Doug Scott, *Human Res Mgr*
EMP: 85
SQ FT: 175,000
SALES (est): 22.1MM **Privately Held**
WEB: www.indstl.com
SIC: 3398 Metal heat treating

(G-8471)
INTERN METALS AND ENERGY (PA)
Also Called: Imet
522 Hupp Ave (49203-1974)
PHONE.....................248 765-7747
Julius J Rim, *President*
Elena Rim, *Vice Pres*
EMP: 6
SQ FT: 200,000
SALES: 1MM **Privately Held**
SIC: 7549 4226 3341 Emissions testing without repairs, automotive; special warehousing & storage; secondary nonferrous metals

(G-8472)
INTERNATIONAL SMART TAN NETWRK
Also Called: Tanning Trends
3101 Page Ave (49203-2254)
P.O. Box 1630 (49204-1630)
PHONE.....................517 841-4920
Dale Parrott, *President*
EMP: 20
SQ FT: 6,000
SALES (est): 2MM **Privately Held**
WEB: www.smarttanohio.com
SIC: 2721 Magazines: publishing only, not printed on site

(G-8473)
J & J INDUSTRIES INC
260 W Euclid Ave (49203-4161)
PHONE.....................517 784-3586
Jim Maes, *President*
Regina Maes, *Manager*
EMP: 6 EST: 1997
SALES: 400K **Privately Held**
SIC: 3714 3451 Oil pump, motor vehicle; screw machine products

(G-8474)
JACKSON ARCHITCTURAL MTL FABRI
1421 S Cooper St (49203-4410)
PHONE.....................517 782-8884
Mike Mason, *Principal*
EMP: 7 EST: 2012
SALES (est): 1.1MM **Privately Held**
SIC: 3444 Sheet metalwork

(G-8475)
JACKSON CANVAS COMPANY
2100 Brooklyn Rd (49203-4746)
PHONE.....................517 768-8459
Thedore Mac Cready, *President*
David Herman, *Vice Pres*
John Rappleye, *Treasurer*
EMP: 26 EST: 1943
SQ FT: 9,000
SALES (est): 5.5MM **Privately Held**
WEB: www.jackson-canvas.com
SIC: 2394 Awnings, fabric: made from purchased materials

(G-8476)
JACKSON GRINDING CO INC
1300 Bagley Ave (49203-3304)
P.O. Box 964 (49204-0964)
PHONE.....................517 782-8080
Michael Alexander, *President*
Thomas Evanson, *Corp Secy*
EMP: 10
SQ FT: 9,000
SALES (est): 1.7MM **Privately Held**
WEB: www.jacksongrinding.com
SIC: 3599 Machine shop, jobbing & repair

(G-8477)
JACKSON INDUSTRIAL COATING SVC
3600 Scheele Dr Ste A (49202-1283)
PHONE.....................517 782-8169
Richard Friedlund, *President*
Ron Markowski, *Treasurer*
EMP: 6
SQ FT: 31,000
SALES (est): 675.2K **Privately Held**
SIC: 3479 Coating of metals & formed products

(G-8478)
JACKSON OVEN SUPPLY INC
3507 Wayland Dr (49202-1233)
PHONE.....................517 784-9660
Dennis Cones, *CEO*
Jean Cones, *Controller*
EMP: 10
SALES: 2MM **Privately Held**
WEB: www.jacksonoven.com
SIC: 3567 Industrial furnaces & ovens

(G-8479)
JACKSON PRECISION INDS INC
1900 Cooper St (49202-1710)
PHONE.....................517 782-8103
John Ziemba, *President*
Patricia Ziemba, *Vice Pres*
Steven Ziemba, *Admin Sec*
EMP: 48
SQ FT: 75,000
SALES (est): 14.4MM **Privately Held**
WEB: www.fine-blanking.com
SIC: 3469 Stamping metal for the trade

(G-8480)
JACKSON PRINTING COMPANY INC
3136 Francis St Ste 69 (49203-5047)
PHONE.....................517 783-2705
Douglas Hoyt, *President*
Randy Hoyt, *Vice Pres*
Charles H Aymond, *Director*
Kevin Hoyt, *Director*
Edward L Hoyt, *Shareholder*
EMP: 18 EST: 1940
SQ FT: 15,000
SALES (est): 1.9MM **Privately Held**
WEB: www.jacksonprinting.com
SIC: 2752 Commercial printing, offset

(G-8481)
JACKSON TUMBLE FINISH CORP
1801 Mitchell St (49203-3393)
P.O. Box 4007 (49204-4007)
PHONE.....................517 787-0368
Denise Losey, *President*
EMP: 47
SQ FT: 40,000
SALES: 6MM **Privately Held**
WEB: www.jacksontumble.com
SIC: 3471 Polishing, metals or formed products; buffing for the trade

(G-8482)
JANSEN INDUSTRIES INC
2400 Enterprise St (49203-6425)
PHONE.....................517 788-6800
James P Jansen, *President*
Thomas Jansen, *Vice Pres*
EMP: 100
SQ FT: 440,000
SALES (est): 19.1MM **Privately Held**
WEB: www.productionengineering.net
SIC: 3599 Machine shop, jobbing & repair

(G-8483)
JFP ACQUISITION LLC
Also Called: Jackson Flexible Products
7765 Clinton Rd (49201-9418)
PHONE.....................517 787-8877
Tim Dickerson, *CEO*
Ken Trupke, *CEO*
Lacey Fausneaucht, *COO*
Chris Rose, *Prdtn Mgr*
Cody Shepherd, *QC Mgr*
EMP: 25 EST: 1969
SQ FT: 35,000
SALES: 3.9MM
SALES (corp-wide): 1.1MM **Privately Held**
WEB: www.jacksonflex.com
SIC: 3069 Molded rubber products
PA: Tillerman Jfp, Llc
10451 W Garbow Rd
Middleville MI 49333
616 443-8346

(G-8484)
JOHNSON SIGN COMPANY INC
2240 Lansing Ave (49202-1641)
PHONE.....................517 784-3720
James Jay Johnson, *President*
Jim Johnson, *Vice Pres*
Will Johnson, *Opers Staff*
Greg Keeler, *Production*
Brion Martin, *Human Resources*
EMP: 16
SQ FT: 12,000
SALES (est): 3.3MM **Privately Held**
WEB: www.johnsonsign.com
SIC: 3993 Signs, not made in custom sign painting shops; electric signs

(G-8485)
JSP INTERNATIONAL LLC
4335 County Farm Rd (49201-9078)
PHONE.....................517 748-5200
Rob Doerr, *Branch Mgr*
EMP: 100 **Privately Held**
SIC: 2821 Polypropylene resins
HQ: Jsp International Llc
1285 Drummers Ln Ste 301
Wayne PA 19087
610 651-8600

(G-8486)
JTC INC
Also Called: Jackson Typesetting Company
1820 W Ganson St (49202-4033)
PHONE.....................517 784-0576
Jay Foust, *President*
Dan Fals, *Vice Pres*
EMP: 20
SQ FT: 20,000
SALES (est): 1.6MM **Privately Held**
SIC: 2791 Typesetting

(G-8487)
K&A MACHINE AND TOOL INC
4821 W Michigan Ave (49201-8902)
P.O. Box 1173 (49204-1173)
PHONE.....................517 750-9244
Karl P Fridd, *President*
Constance M Fridd, *Vice Pres*
Melissa Heydenburg, *Manager*

Jackson - Jackson County (G-8488)

EMP: 68
SQ FT: 19,000
SALES: 10MM **Privately Held**
WEB: www.kamachine.com
SIC: **3599** Machine shop, jobbing & repair

(G-8488)
KELLOGG CRANKSHAFT CO
3524 Wayland Dr (49202-1294)
PHONE..................517 788-9200
Allen E Spiess Jr, *President*
E Leroy Kincaid, *Production*
Allen E Spiess Sr, *Treasurer*
EMP: 89 EST: 1956
SQ FT: 100,000
SALES (est): 15.9MM **Privately Held**
WEB: www.kelloggcrankshaft.com
SIC: **3714** Crankshaft assemblies, motor vehicle

(G-8489)
KMAK INC
Also Called: American Speedy Printing
1232 S West Ave (49203-2959)
PHONE..................517 784-8800
Amy Lienhard, *President*
Jim Yekle, *Manager*
EMP: 4
SQ FT: 2,200
SALES (est): 459.5K **Privately Held**
WEB: www.americanspeedyprintingjackson.com
SIC: **2752** 7334 Commercial printing, offset; photocopying & duplicating services

(G-8490)
KRT PRECISION TOOL & MFG CO
1300 Mitchell St (49203-3341)
PHONE..................517 783-5715
Tim Hawkins, *President*
Kevin Hawkins, *Admin Sec*
EMP: 5 EST: 1955
SQ FT: 7,200
SALES (est): 652.6K **Privately Held**
SIC: **3599** 3544 Machine shop, jobbing & repair; special dies & tools

(G-8491)
L & L MACHINE & TOOL INC
415 Condad Ave (49202-3911)
PHONE..................517 784-5575
Larry Hager, *President*
EMP: 6
SQ FT: 8,500
SALES (est): 440K **Privately Held**
WEB: www.lnltool.com
SIC: **3544** 3398 Special dies & tools; metal heat treating

(G-8492)
L3HARRIS TECHNOLOGIES INC
3516 Wayland Dr (49202-1234)
PHONE..................517 780-0695
Sally Huyghebart, *Branch Mgr*
EMP: 3
SALES (corp-wide): 6.8B **Publicly Held**
SIC: **3812** Search & navigation equipment
PA: L3harris Technologies, Inc.
1025 W Nasa Blvd
Melbourne FL 32919
321 727-9100

(G-8493)
LABOR AIDING SYSTEMS CORP
3101 Hart Rd (49201-8746)
PHONE..................517 768-7478
Joseph Simon, *CEO*
EMP: 28 EST: 2013
SALES (est): 5.2MM **Privately Held**
SIC: **3544** Special dies, tools, jigs & fixtures

(G-8494)
LAMPCO INDUSTRIES INC
1635 Losey Ave (49203-3439)
PHONE..................517 783-3414
Phil Lewan, *President*
Diana Beveridge, *Corp Secy*
EMP: 4
SQ FT: 2,800
SALES (est): 737.1K **Privately Held**
SIC: **3569** 3589 Filters; metalworking machinery; metalworking tools (such as drills, taps, dies, files)

(G-8495)
LAMPCO MANUFACTURING COMPANY
1635 Losey Ave (49203-3439)
PHONE..................517 784-4393
Michael Lewandowski, *President*
Philip Lewandowski, *Vice Pres*
Evelyn Lewandowski, *Treasurer*
Linda Lewandowski, *Admin Sec*
EMP: 3
SALES: 150K **Privately Held**
SIC: **3479** Coating of metals & formed products

(G-8496)
LE WARREN INC
1600 S Jackson St (49203-4295)
PHONE..................517 784-8701
Leo E Warren, *President*
Jeff Warren, *Sales Staff*
EMP: 16 EST: 1941
SQ FT: 22,500
SALES (est): 1.3MM **Privately Held**
WEB: www.lewarren.com
SIC: **3599** Machine shop, jobbing & repair

(G-8497)
LEMATIC INC
2410 W Main St (49203-1099)
P.O. Box 787 (49204-0787)
PHONE..................517 787-3301
Dale J Le Crone, *CEO*
John Hamilton, *President*
Tammy Sanford, *CFO*
◆ EMP: 60
SQ FT: 35,000
SALES (est): 21.3MM **Privately Held**
WEB: www.lematic.com
SIC: **3556** Bakery machinery

(G-8498)
LEONARD MACHINE & TOOLING INC
508 Condad Ave (49202-3913)
PHONE..................517 782-8140
James L Boobyer, *President*
Jerry L Boobyer, *Vice Pres*
Laura Riker, *Admin Sec*
EMP: 8
SQ FT: 10,000
SALES (est): 1.2MM **Privately Held**
SIC: **3599** Machine shop, jobbing & repair

(G-8499)
LIBRA INDUSTRIES INC MICHIGAN (PA)
Also Called: Work Apparel Division
1435 N Blackstone St (49202-2227)
P.O. Box 1105 (49204-1105)
PHONE..................517 787-5675
Beth Yoxheimer, *President*
Sheila Archer, *Division Mgr*
Todd Parshall, *Sales Mgr*
John Matthews, *Accounts Mgr*
Marty Job, *Sales Staff*
EMP: 4
SQ FT: 70,000
SALES (est): 75.7MM **Privately Held**
WEB: www.librami.com
SIC: **5084** 3559 1741 Recycling machinery & equipment; recycling machinery; tuckpointing or restoration

(G-8500)
LRH & ASSOCIATES INC
Also Called: Karl Lyn Systems
111 Randolph St (49203-4259)
P.O. Box 6172 (49204-6172)
PHONE..................517 784-1055
Lynwood Harr, *President*
John Harr, *Vice Pres*
Karen Harr, *Admin Sec*
EMP: 3
SQ FT: 12,000
SALES: 1MM **Privately Held**
SIC: **3535** 8741 8742 Pneumatic tube conveyor systems; construction management; construction project management consultant

(G-8501)
M & M AUTOMATIC PRODUCTS INC
420 Ingham St (49201-1251)
PHONE..................517 782-0577
Joseph Miller, *President*
Mary Lynn Miller, *Admin Sec*
EMP: 10
SQ FT: 10,000
SALES: 714.3K **Privately Held**
SALES (corp-wide): 13.2MM **Privately Held**
WEB: www.trinityholding.com
SIC: **3599** Machine shop, jobbing & repair
PA: Trinity Holding, Inc.
420 Ingham St
Jackson MI 49201
517 787-3100

(G-8502)
M AND G LAMINATED PRODUCTS
507 W Michigan Ave (49201-2033)
PHONE..................517 784-4974
Chet Malone, *CEO*
Dale Gazlay, *President*
EMP: 7
SQ FT: 10,000
SALES (est): 698.4K **Privately Held**
SIC: **2599** 5031 2541 2434 Cabinets, factory; kitchen cabinets; wood partitions & fixtures; wood kitchen cabinets

(G-8503)
M P JACKSON LLC
1824 River St (49202-1755)
PHONE..................517 782-0391
Rich Regole, *President*
James C Allison, *Vice Pres*
R Mark Baker, *CFO*
EMP: 21
SQ FT: 55,000
SALES (est): 2.2MM **Privately Held**
WEB: www.mechprod.com
SIC: **3625** 3613 Control circuit devices, magnet & solid state; power circuit breakers

(G-8504)
MAES TOOL & DIE CO INC
1074 Toro Dr (49201-8946)
PHONE..................517 750-3131
Joseph Maes, *President*
Jerome Maes, *Vice Pres*
EMP: 15
SQ FT: 25,500
SALES (est): 1.3MM **Privately Held**
SIC: **3544** 3823 3545 3541 Special dies & tools; industrial instrmnts msrmnt display/control process variable; machine tool accessories; machine tools, metal cutting type

(G-8505)
MAG-TEC CASTING CORPORATION
2411 Research Dr (49203-6409)
PHONE..................517 789-8505
Allen F Schroeder, *President*
James R Malloch, *Vice Pres*
Bill Wilson, *Vice Pres*
▲ EMP: 20
SQ FT: 27,500
SALES (est): 5.2MM **Privately Held**
WEB: www.mag-teccasting.com
SIC: **3364** 3363 Magnesium & magnesium-base alloy die-castings; aluminum die-castings

(G-8506)
MAIN & COMPANY
2700 Cooper St (49201-9555)
PHONE..................517 789-7183
Gerald Brown, *President*
Frank Main, *Chairman*
Howard Patch, *Admin Sec*
EMP: 17 EST: 1956
SQ FT: 12,592
SALES: 5.6MM **Privately Held**
WEB: www.maincompany.com
SIC: **3599** Machine shop, jobbing & repair

(G-8507)
MAKE IT YOURS
6982 Surrey Ln (49201-2443)
PHONE..................517 990-6799
Peggy Hill, *Owner*
EMP: 6
SALES (est): 280K **Privately Held**
SIC: **3269** Art & ornamental ware, pottery

(G-8508)
MALACHI PRINTING LLC
444 E Prospect St (49204-4439)
PHONE..................517 395-4813
Derek Fankhauser, *Owner*
EMP: 4
SALES (est): 175K **Privately Held**
SIC: **2759** Screen printing

(G-8509)
MARATHON WELD GROUP LLC
5750 Marathon Dr (49201-7711)
PHONE..................517 782-8040
Michelle Cooper, *COO*
Edward Cooper,
EMP: 30
SALES (est): 4.2MM **Privately Held**
SIC: **5084** 3315 Welding machinery & equipment; wire & fabricated wire products

(G-8510)
MATTHEWS PLATING INC
405 N Mechanic St (49201-1306)
PHONE..................517 784-3535
Norman Niceswander, *General Mgr*
Brandon Niceswander, *Vice Pres*
EMP: 21
SALES (est): 3MM **Privately Held**
SIC: **3471** Finishing, metals or formed products

(G-8511)
MAX MANUFACTURING
205 Watts Rd (49203-2324)
PHONE..................517 990-9180
O Donnell Docks, *Owner*
Todd Hardcastle, *General Mgr*
EMP: 15
SALES (est): 500.3K **Privately Held**
SIC: **3732** Boat building & repairing

(G-8512)
MELLING INDUSTRIES INC
2620 Saradan Dr (49202-1214)
P.O. Box 1188 (49204-1188)
PHONE..................517 787-8172
Mark Melling, *President*
Scot Gazlay, *General Mgr*
Dan McDonell, *General Mgr*
Kevin Oleary, *General Mgr*
Karyn Clow, *Business Mgr*
EMP: 50
SQ FT: 27,000
SALES (est): 10.3MM
SALES (corp-wide): 265MM **Privately Held**
SIC: **3599** Machine shop, jobbing & repair
PA: Melling Tool Co.
2620 Saradan Dr
Jackson MI 49202
517 787-8172

(G-8513)
MELLING MANUFACTURING INC
4901 James Mcdevitt St (49201-8958)
PHONE..................517 750-3580
Mark Melling, *President*
Thomas C Evanson, *Corp Secy*
David K Horthrop, *Vice Pres*
EMP: 42
SALES (est): 3.4MM
SALES (corp-wide): 265MM **Privately Held**
SIC: **3599** 3841 3728 Machine shop, jobbing & repair; surgical & medical instruments; aircraft parts & equipment
PA: Melling Tool Co.
2620 Saradan Dr
Jackson MI 49202
517 787-8172

(G-8514)
MELLING TOOL CO (PA)
Also Called: Melling Automotive Products
2620 Saradan Dr (49202-1258)
P.O. Box 1188 (49204-1188)
PHONE..................517 787-8172
Mark Melling, *President*
Brian Shaughnessy, *General Mgr*
John Shellberg, *Purch Mgr*
Michelle Kinch, *QC Mgr*
Cale Risinger, *Technical Mgr*
◆ EMP: 320 EST: 1956
SQ FT: 275,000

GEOGRAPHIC SECTION
Jackson - Jackson County (G-8541)

SALES (est): 265MM **Privately Held**
SIC: **3451** 3714 3625 3568 Screw machine products; oil pump, motor vehicle; relays & industrial controls; power transmission equipment; pumps & pumping equipment; valves & pipe fittings

(G-8515)
MERRIMAN PRODUCTS INC
1302 W Ganson St (49202-4298)
PHONE..................................517 787-1825
Jacque J Lake, *President*
Robert Kingsbury, *Vice Pres*
James Peters, *Vice Pres*
Janet E Putman, *Admin Sec*
EMP: 4 EST: 1951
SQ FT: 2,000
SALES (est): 510.2K **Privately Held**
WEB: www.merrimanproducts.com
SIC: **3544** Jigs & fixtures

(G-8516)
METALFORM LLC
2223 Rives Eaton Rd (49201-8222)
PHONE..................................517 569-3313
Clifford Hanchett, *Owner*
EMP: 5
SQ FT: 12,000
SALES (est): 603.2K **Privately Held**
SIC: **3544** Special dies, tools, jigs & fixtures

(G-8517)
METRO DUCT INC
485 E South St (49203-4440)
PHONE..................................517 783-2646
Joanne Applegate, *President*
EMP: 30
SQ FT: 45,000
SALES (est): 2.6MM **Privately Held**
SIC: **3444** Sheet metalwork

(G-8518)
MICHIGAN ALUMINUM EXTRUSION
Also Called: Michigan Extruded Aluminum
205 Watts Rd (49203-2324)
P.O. Box 1109 (49204-1109)
PHONE..................................517 764-5400
Jeffrey L Jacobs, *President*
Nancy J Jacobs, *Vice Pres*
EMP: 75
SQ FT: 160,000
SALES (est): 19.4MM **Privately Held**
WEB: www.extrude.net
SIC: **3354** Aluminum extruded products

(G-8519)
MICHIGAN BRLLE TRNSCRBING FUND
3500 N Elm Ave (49201-8887)
PHONE..................................517 780-5096
Cindy Omstead, *President*
EMP: 3
SALES: 736.5K **Privately Held**
SIC: **2732** Books: printing only

(G-8520)
MICHIGAN PAVING AND MTLS CO
1600 N Elm Ave (49202-1745)
P.O. Box 1134 (49204-1134)
PHONE..................................517 787-4200
Mike Jackson, *Division Mgr*
John Peters, *General Mgr*
EMP: 60
SALES (corp-wide): 30.6B **Privately Held**
SIC: **7549** 2952 2951 Road service, automotive; asphalt felts & coatings; asphalt paving mixtures & blocks
HQ: Michigan Paving And Materials Company
2575 S Haggerty Rd # 100
Canton MI 48188
734 397-2050

(G-8521)
MICHNER PLATING COMPANY
Also Called: Metal Treat
1690 Shoemaker Dr (49203-2779)
PHONE..................................517 789-6627
Walter J Michner, *President*
James Michner II, *Vice Pres*
Jason Michner, *Vice Pres*
Camillia Cavanaugh, *Treasurer*
Suzanne Hamilton, *Admin Sec*
EMP: 98 EST: 1941
SQ FT: 200,000
SALES (est): 8.2MM **Privately Held**
SIC: **3471** Plating of metals or formed products; chromium plating of metals or formed products

(G-8522)
MICROMATIC SCREW PRODUCTS INC
825 Carroll Ave (49202-3142)
PHONE..................................517 787-3666
Harold A Burke, *President*
Carolyn Burke, *General Mgr*
EMP: 18
SQ FT: 8,000
SALES (est): 3.1MM **Privately Held**
WEB: www.microspi.com
SIC: **3451** Screw machine products

(G-8523)
MICROTECH GAGING LLC
4801 W Michigan Ave (49201-8902)
PHONE..................................517 750-2169
Bob Ekin, *Owner*
Tom Jackson, *Principal*
Eve Warren, *Manager*
EMP: 3
SALES (est): 285.6K **Privately Held**
SIC: **3599** Machine shop, jobbing & repair

(G-8524)
MICROTECH MACHINE COMPANY
4801 W Michigan Ave (49201-8902)
PHONE..................................517 750-4422
Robert C Ekin, *President*
Kathleen L Ekin, *Vice Pres*
EMP: 7
SQ FT: 9,500
SALES (est): 772K **Privately Held**
SIC: **3599** Machine shop, jobbing & repair

(G-8525)
MIDBROOK INC (PA)
2621 E Kimmel Rd (49201-8724)
PHONE..................................800 966-9274
Milton F Lutz II, *Ch of Bd*
Joanne Houghton, *President*
Ernest Houghton, *Vice Pres*
Rick Bennet, *Foreman/Supr*
Brian Rockwell, *Foreman/Supr*
◆ EMP: 100 EST: 1976
SQ FT: 200,000
SALES (est): 19MM **Privately Held**
WEB: www.midbrook.com
SIC: **3559** 3444 Degreasing machines, automotive & industrial; sheet metalwork

(G-8526)
MIDBROOK MEDICAL DIST INC
Also Called: Copperforhealthcare
2080 Brooklyn Rd (49203-4744)
PHONE..................................517 787-3481
Milton F Lutz II, *Director*
EMP: 7
SALES (est): 113.7K
SALES (corp-wide): 19MM **Privately Held**
SIC: **3351** 5047 Tubing, copper & copper alloy; medical equipment & supplies
PA: Midbrook, Inc.
2621 E Kimmel Rd
Jackson MI 49201
800 966-9274

(G-8527)
MIDWAY STRL PIPE & SUP INC (PA)
Also Called: Lannis Fence Systems
1611 Clara St (49203-3471)
P.O. Box 742 (49204-0742)
PHONE..................................517 787-1350
Robin Brannan, *President*
Alan Brannan, *COO*
Douglas Murray, *CFO*
EMP: 8
SQ FT: 6,000
SALES (est): 7MM **Privately Held**
WEB: www.midwaystructural.com
SIC: **3317** 5039 5051 Steel pipe & tubes; wire fence, gates & accessories; pipe & tubing, steel

(G-8528)
MILLER INDUSTRIAL PRODUCTS INC
801 Water St (49203-1963)
PHONE..................................517 783-2756
William R Miller, *President*
Bernie F Miller, *Exec VP*
EMP: 30
SQ FT: 150,000
SALES (est): 7.3MM **Privately Held**
WEB: www.jacksonmi.com
SIC: **3429** 3714 Motor vehicle hardware; motor vehicle parts & accessories

(G-8529)
MILLER TOOL & DIE CO
Also Called: Miller Machine & Technologies
829 Belden Rd (49203-1994)
PHONE..................................517 782-0347
Philip G Miller, *President*
Emmanuel G Miller, *Chairman*
Steven B Anspaugh, *Vice Pres*
Patrick G Miller, *Vice Pres*
Scott Anderson, *Project Mgr*
▼ EMP: 43
SQ FT: 60,000
SALES (est): 13.3MM **Privately Held**
WEB: www.millertd.com
SIC: **3542** 3541 3544 3545 Machine tools, metal forming type; machine tools, metal cutting type; special dies, tools, jigs & fixtures; machine tool accessories

(G-8530)
MILLERS SHOE PARLOR INC
103 W Michigan Ave (49201-1368)
PHONE..................................517 783-1258
James E Shotwell Jr, *President*
James E Shotwell Sr, *Vice Pres*
Letha Shotwell, *Admin Sec*
EMP: 5 EST: 1912
SQ FT: 4,200
SALES: 305K **Privately Held**
SIC: **5661** 3143 3144 Men's shoes; women's shoes; children's shoes; shoes, orthopedic; orthopedic shoes, men's; orthopedic shoes, women's

(G-8531)
MILSCO LLC
Milsco Michigan Seat
2313 Brooklyn Rd (49203-4776)
PHONE..................................517 787-3650
EMP: 300
SALES (corp-wide): 612.9MM **Publicly Held**
WEB: www.jasoninc.com
SIC: **3069** 2531 3537 3524 Foam rubber; vehicle furniture; industrial trucks & tractors; lawn & garden equipment
HQ: Milsco, Llc
1301 W Canal St
Milwaukee WI 53233
414 354-0500

(G-8532)
MKI PRODUCTS
1410 W Ganson St Ste 9 (49202-4060)
PHONE..................................517 748-5075
Debra Masqudlier, *Owner*
EMP: 3 EST: 2016
SALES: 300K **Privately Held**
SIC: **3564** Blowers & fans

(G-8533)
MLIVE COM
214 S Jackson St (49201-2267)
PHONE..................................517 768-4984
Scott Hagen, *Principal*
EMP: 3
SALES (est): 101.8K **Privately Held**
SIC: **2711** Newspapers, publishing & printing

(G-8534)
MMP MOLDED MAGNESIUM PDTS LLC
2336 E High St (49203-3422)
PHONE..................................517 789-8505
Bill Wilson, *General Mgr*
Zach Lankton, *Opers Mgr*
Gavin McGraw, *Controller*
EMP: 8
SALES: 2MM **Privately Held**
SIC: **3575** 5251 3949 Computer terminals, monitors & components; tools; sporting & athletic goods

(G-8535)
MODERN BUILDERS SUPPLY INC
Also Called: Mbs
2401 Brooklyn Rd (49203-4803)
PHONE..................................517 787-3633
Larry Leggett, *President*
EMP: 7
SALES (corp-wide): 347.7MM **Privately Held**
WEB: www.polaristechnologies.com
SIC: **5072** 3089 Builders' hardware; windows, plastic; doors, folding: plastic or plastic coated fabric
PA: Modern Builders Supply, Inc.
3500 Phillips Ave
Toledo OH 43608
419 241-3961

(G-8536)
MODERN MACHINE TOOL CO
2005 Losey Ave (49203-3499)
PHONE..................................517 788-9120
Steven G Walker, *President*
Gregory Walker, *Vice Pres*
Drennan Darin, *Engineer*
EMP: 16 EST: 1916
SQ FT: 42,000
SALES (est): 4.6MM **Privately Held**
WEB: www.modernmachinetool.com
SIC: **3541** Cutoff machines (metalworking machinery)

(G-8537)
MP HOLLYWOOD LLC
Also Called: Mechanical Products Co
1824 River St (49202-1755)
PHONE..................................517 782-0391
Rich Regole, *COO*
James C Allison,
Larry Bajorek,
▲ EMP: 19
SQ FT: 20,000
SALES (est): 1.9MM **Privately Held**
SIC: **3613** Power circuit breakers

(G-8538)
MULTIMATIC MICHIGAN LLC
2400 Enterprise St (49203-6425)
PHONE..................................517 962-7190
Peter Czapka, *President*
EMP: 25
SQ FT: 100,000
SALES (est): 1.3MM
SALES (corp-wide): 6.2MM **Privately Held**
SIC: **3465** Automotive stampings
PA: Multimatic Holdings Inc
8688 Woodbine Ave Suite 200
Markham ON L3R 8
905 470-9149

(G-8539)
MVP SPORTS STORE
5000 Ann Arbor Rd (49201-8801)
PHONE..................................517 764-5165
Raymond Hines, *President*
Ray Hines, *Owner*
Mark Buckland, *Vice Pres*
Kelley Hines, *Treasurer*
EMP: 4
SALES (est): 405.9K **Privately Held**
SIC: **2396** 5137 Screen printing on fabric articles; uniforms, women's & children's

(G-8540)
MYRTLE INDUSTRIES INC
1810 E High St Ste 2 (49203-6433)
PHONE..................................517 784-8579
James Jenks, *President*
Russell Lyke, *Vice Pres*
▲ EMP: 10
SQ FT: 5,000
SALES (est): 810K **Privately Held**
SIC: **3429** Clamps & couplings, hose

(G-8541)
NATIONWIDE COMMUNICATIONS LLC
5263 Thames Ct (49201-8347)
PHONE..................................517 990-1223

Jackson - Jackson County (G-8542)

EMP: 4
SALES (est): 390K **Privately Held**
SIC: 3669 Mfg Communications Equipment

(G-8542)
NELSON COMPANY
654 Hupp Ave (49203-1930)
PHONE..................................517 788-6117
Amber Harrell, *Manager*
EMP: 7
SALES (corp-wide): 23.1MM **Privately Held**
WEB: www.smartrax.net
SIC: 2448 Pallets, wood
PA: The Nelson Company
4517 North Point Blvd
Baltimore MD 21219
410 477-3000

(G-8543)
NORTHWEST MARKET
7051 Standish Rd (49201-9417)
PHONE..................................517 787-5005
Jack Milligan, *Owner*
EMP: 5
SQ FT: 2,000
SALES (est): 305.8K **Privately Held**
WEB: www.northwestmarket.com
SIC: 5421 5921 2011 Meat markets, including freezer provisioners; beer (packaged); wine; meat packing plants

(G-8544)
NORTHWEST TOOL & MACHINE INC
1014 Hurst Rd (49201-8905)
P.O. Box 201 (49204-0201)
PHONE..................................517 750-1332
Kent A Pickett, *President*
Kent Pickett Jr, *Vice Pres*
Jennifer Dysert, *Admin Sec*
EMP: 25
SQ FT: 20,000
SALES: 2.5MM **Privately Held**
WEB: www.machiningexperts.com
SIC: 3544 3599 3549 5047 Special dies & tools; machine shop, jobbing & repair; metalworking machinery; medical & hospital equipment

(G-8545)
ORBITFORM GROUP LLC
1600 Executive Dr (49203-3469)
PHONE..................................800 957-4838
Michael J Shirkey, *President*
Phil Sponsler, *President*
EMP: 68
SQ FT: 107,000
SALES: 17.7MM
SALES (corp-wide): 27.2MM **Privately Held**
WEB: www.orbitform.com
SIC: 3542 Riveting machines
PA: Smsg, L.L.C.
1600 Executive Dr
Jackson MI 49203
517 787-9447

(G-8546)
OVERKILL RESEARCH & DEV LABS
2010 Micor Dr (49203-3448)
PHONE..................................517 768-8155
Martin D Sears, *President*
Mike Vogel, *Vice Pres*
EMP: 8
SQ FT: 15,000
SALES: 100K **Privately Held**
WEB: www.overkillarchery.net
SIC: 3949 Archery equipment, general

(G-8547)
PATRICK EXPLORATION COMPANY
301 W Michigan Ave (49201-2120)
PHONE..................................517 787-6633
Mark Patrick, *Manager*
EMP: 3
SALES (est): 174.1K **Privately Held**
SIC: 1382 Oil & gas exploration services
PA: Patrick Exploration Company
415 W Wall St Ste 1705
Midland TX

(G-8548)
PC SOLUTIONS
Also Called: PC Solutions of Michigan
1200 S West Ave (49203-2959)
PHONE..................................517 787-9934
Allen Huber, *Owner*
EMP: 12
SALES (est): 1.5MM **Privately Held**
SIC: 7372 Prepackaged software

(G-8549)
PENTAR STAMPING INC
1821 Wildwood Ave (49202-4044)
P.O. Box 1449 (49204-1449)
PHONE..................................517 782-0700
Joe Tippins, *Partner*
Robert Moore, *Partner*
Dale Moretz, *Partner*
Todd Ostrander, *Mfg Dir*
Harley Burch, *Engineer*
EMP: 30 **EST:** 1998
SQ FT: 14,369
SALES (est): 5.2MM **Privately Held**
WEB: www.pentarstamping.com
SIC: 3469 Machine parts, stamped or pressed metal

(G-8550)
PERFECTION BAKERIES INC
Also Called: Jackson 043
1001 Hurst Rd (49201-8905)
PHONE..................................517 750-1818
Bob Resor, *Branch Mgr*
EMP: 37
SALES (corp-wide): 535.8MM **Privately Held**
WEB: www.perfectionpastries.com
SIC: 2051 Bread, cake & related products
PA: Perfection Bakeries, Inc.
350 Pearl St
Fort Wayne IN 46802
260 424-8245

(G-8551)
PETTY MACHINE & TOOL INC
4035 Morrill Rd (49201-7013)
PHONE..................................517 782-9355
Bobby Petty, *President*
Sandra Petty, *Vice Pres*
Sandy Petty, *Vice Pres*
Laura Garver, *Purch Mgr*
John Walker, *Buyer*
EMP: 32
SQ FT: 13,000
SALES (est): 5.9MM **Privately Held**
WEB: www.pettymachine.com
SIC: 3541 Machine tools, metal cutting type

(G-8552)
PIONEER FOUNDRY COMPANY INC (PA)
606 Water St (49203-1980)
P.O. Box 1425 (49204-1425)
PHONE..................................517 782-9469
James A Lefere, *CEO*
Bob Lefere, *President*
Ted Lefere, *Vice Pres*
Howard Patch, *Admin Sec*
EMP: 13 **EST:** 1905
SQ FT: 60,000
SALES (est): 1.7MM **Privately Held**
SIC: 3321 Gray iron castings

(G-8553)
PLASTGAGE CSTM FABRICATION LLC
250 W Monroe St (49202-2252)
PHONE..................................517 817-0719
Lisa Minor, *Office Mgr*
Dennis Minor,
EMP: 4
SALES (est): 478.6K **Privately Held**
SIC: 3496 Miscellaneous fabricated wire products

(G-8554)
PLATING SYSTEMS AND TECH INC
Also Called: PS & T
317 N Mechanic St (49201-1305)
PHONE..................................517 783-4776
Thomas Rochester, *President*
David Rochester, *Vice Pres*
Stacy Richardson, *Manager*
Rita Nau, *Officer*
▲ **EMP:** 7
SQ FT: 15,000
SALES (est): 1.6MM **Privately Held**
SIC: 2899 Plating compounds

(G-8555)
PPG INDUSTRIES INC
Also Called: PPG 9356
167 W North St (49202-3362)
PHONE..................................517 784-6138
Craig Tingley, *Branch Mgr*
EMP: 24
SALES (corp-wide): 15.3B **Publicly Held**
WEB: www.ppg.com
SIC: 2851 Paints & allied products
PA: Ppg Industries, Inc.
1 Ppg Pl
Pittsburgh PA 15272
412 434-3131

(G-8556)
PRESCOTT PRODUCTS INC (HQ)
2620 Saradan Dr (49202-1214)
PHONE..................................517 787-8172
Harry S Melling, *President*
Thomas C Evanson, *Corp Secy*
David Horthrop, *Vice Pres*
William Marx, *Vice Pres*
EMP: 2
SQ FT: 43,000
SALES (est): 1.6MM
SALES (corp-wide): 265MM **Privately Held**
WEB: www.prescottproducts.com
SIC: 3451 Screw machine products
PA: Melling Tool Co.
2620 Saradan Dr
Jackson MI 49202
517 787-8172

(G-8557)
PRIME CUTS OF JACKSON LLC
1821 Horton Rd (49203-5130)
PHONE..................................517 768-8090
Walt McGaskey,
EMP: 20 **EST:** 2007
SALES (est): 2.2MM **Privately Held**
SIC: 2011 Meat by-products from meat slaughtered on site

(G-8558)
PSP OFFICE SOLUTIONS LLC
Also Called: Printer Source Plus
1737 Spring Arbor Rd # 219 (49203-2701)
PHONE..................................517 817-0680
Joseph Sharpe, *Principal*
EMP: 12
SALES (est): 616.2K **Privately Held**
SIC: 2752 Commercial printing, lithographic

(G-8559)
PT&T PRECISE MACHINING LLC
Also Called: PT&t Properties
325 Watts Rd (49203-2326)
PHONE..................................517 748-9325
Phillip Vincent, *Mng Member*
Ted Kenell, *Mng Member*
EMP: 8
SQ FT: 8,500
SALES: 850K **Privately Held**
WEB: www.pttprecise.com
SIC: 3599 Machine shop, jobbing & repair

(G-8560)
R J MICHAELS INC
515 S West Ave (49203-1639)
P.O. Box 1467 (49204-1467)
PHONE..................................517 783-2637
Bonnie Gretzner, *Editor*
EMP: 12
SQ FT: 2,000
SALES (est): 1.6MM **Privately Held**
WEB: www.rjmichaels.com
SIC: 7311 2721 Advertising consultant; periodicals

(G-8561)
RAY PRINTING COMPANY INC
201 Brookley Ave (49202-2399)
PHONE..................................517 787-4130
Gary Emerson, *President*
Gary Lewis, *Vice Pres*
EMP: 16
SQ FT: 7,000
SALES (est): 2.6MM **Privately Held**
SIC: 2752 7331 2759 Commercial printing, offset; direct mail advertising services; letterpress printing

(G-8562)
REFRIGERATION SALES INC
1810 E High St Ste 2 (49203-6433)
PHONE..................................517 784-8579
Russell Lyke, *President*
Vern R Lyke, *Vice Pres*
▲ **EMP:** 9
SQ FT: 2,000
SALES (est): 1.7MM **Privately Held**
WEB: www.refsales.com
SIC: 3429 Manufactured hardware (general)

(G-8563)
RIVMAX MANUFACTURING INC
2218 E High St Ste C (49203-3553)
PHONE..................................517 784-2556
Matthew Olinyk, *President*
EMP: 10
SALES (est): 832.8K **Privately Held**
WEB: www.rivmaxinc.com
SIC: 2514 Cabinets, radio & television: metal

(G-8564)
ROE PUBLISHING DEPARTMENT
2535 Grey Tower Rd (49201-9120)
P.O. Box 309, Grass Lake (49240-0309)
PHONE..................................517 522-3598
Nathaniel Pop, *Owner*
EMP: 6 **EST:** 2000
SALES (est): 197.5K **Privately Held**
SIC: 2741 Miscellaneous publishing

(G-8565)
ROYAL CABINET INC
Also Called: Kitchen Supply Co
3900 Francis St (49203-5434)
P.O. Box 177 (49204-0177)
PHONE..................................517 787-2940
Richard W Ehnis, *President*
Beverly A Ehnis, *Vice Pres*
EMP: 15
SQ FT: 18,000
SALES: 860K **Privately Held**
WEB: www.kitchensupplyco.com
SIC: 2541 Cabinets, except refrigerated: show, display, etc.: wood; table or counter tops, plastic laminated

(G-8566)
RSM & ASSOCIATES CO
Also Called: RSM Auto Co.
4107 W Michigan Ave (49202-1830)
PHONE..................................517 750-9330
Robert Martens, *CEO*
▲ **EMP:** 18
SALES (est): 2.4MM **Privately Held**
SIC: 3799 5511 Midget autos, power driven; automobiles, new & used

(G-8567)
RTD MANUFACTURING INC
1150 S Elm Ave (49203-3306)
PHONE..................................517 783-1550
Bryant Ramsey, *President*
Donna Ramsey, *Corp Secy*
BJ Ramsey, *Vice Pres*
Dave Smith, *Executive*
EMP: 22
SQ FT: 120,000
SALES (est): 3.7MM **Privately Held**
WEB: www.rtdtool.com
SIC: 3599 7389 Machine shop, jobbing & repair; design, commercial & industrial

(G-8568)
S R P INC
1927 Wildwood Ave (49202-4046)
PHONE..................................517 784-3153
Lawrence H Schultz, *President*
Douglas H Dold, *Admin Sec*
EMP: 65 **EST:** 1979
SQ FT: 52,000
SALES (est): 4.5MM **Privately Held**
SIC: 3568 Clutches, except vehicular; couplings, shaft: rigid, flexible, universal joint, etc.; sprockets (power transmission equipment)

GEOGRAPHIC SECTION
Jackson - Jackson County (G-8596)

(G-8569)
SALCO ENGINEERING AND MFG INC
2030 Micor Dr (49203-3448)
PHONE.................................517 789-9010
James Flack, *President*
Walter J Michner, *Corp Secy*
Rick Harbaugh, *Plant Mgr*
EMP: 17 EST: 1962
SQ FT: 60,000
SALES (est): 3.9MM **Privately Held**
SIC: 3496 Miscellaneous fabricated wire products

(G-8570)
SCHUTTE MSA LLC
4055 Morrill Rd (49201-7013)
PHONE.................................517 782-3600
C James Trunk, *Mng Member*
▲ EMP: 13
SQ FT: 15,000
SALES: 7MM **Privately Held**
WEB: www.schuttemsa.com
SIC: 5084 3541 Machine tools & accessories; machine tools, metal cutting type

(G-8571)
SCOTT MACHINE INC
4025 Morrill Rd (49201-7013)
P.O. Box 468 (49204-0468)
PHONE.................................517 787-6616
Tom Dobbin, *President*
Edward R Scott, *Chairman*
Charles Donall, *Exec VP*
Michael Embury, *Vice Pres*
Chris Ganpon, *Vice Pres*
EMP: 50 EST: 1946
SQ FT: 27,000
SALES (est): 9.9MM **Privately Held**
WEB: www.scottmachineinc.com
SIC: 3728 3494 3492 Aircraft parts & equipment; valves & pipe fittings; fluid power valves & hose fittings

(G-8572)
SHAFER REDI-MIX INC
5405 E Michigan Ave (49201-8406)
PHONE.................................517 764-0517
Jerry Shafer, *Principal*
EMP: 55
SQ FT: 5,000
SALES (corp-wide): 22.1MM **Privately Held**
SIC: 3273 Ready-mixed concrete
PA: Shafer Redi-Mix, Inc.
29150 C Dr N
Albion MI 49224
517 629-4800

(G-8573)
SLED SHED ENTERPRISES LLC
1150 S Elm Ave (49203-3306)
PHONE.................................517 783-5136
Bryant Ramsey, *Mng Member*
EMP: 6
SQ FT: 25,000
SALES (est): 490.7K **Privately Held**
WEB: www.sledshed234.net
SIC: 3799 Recreational vehicles

(G-8574)
SMSG LLC (PA)
Also Called: Orbitform Group
1600 Executive Dr (49203-3469)
PHONE.................................517 787-9447
Mark Shirkey, *CFO*
Mike Shirkey,
EMP: 2
SALES (est): 27.2MM **Privately Held**
WEB: www.orbitform.com
SIC: 3452 Rivets, metal

(G-8575)
SPENCER ZDANOWITZ INC
Also Called: Great Lakes Metal Finshg Inc
120 S Dwight St (49203-2083)
PHONE.................................517 841-9380
John Spencer, *CEO*
Dennis L Zdanowitz, *COO*
EMP: 4
SQ FT: 14,000
SALES (est): 577.5K
SALES (corp-wide): 23.1MM **Privately Held**
SIC: 3471 Coloring & finishing of aluminum or formed products

PA: Classic Turning, Inc.
3000 E South St
Jackson MI 49201
517 764-1335

(G-8576)
SPIRIT STEEL CO INC
212 W Monroe St (49202-2252)
PHONE.................................517 750-4885
Howard K Martin, *President*
Elizabeth A Martin, *Corp Secy*
William A Martin, *Vice Pres*
EMP: 3
SQ FT: 3,500
SALES: 200K **Privately Held**
SIC: 3441 Building components, structural steel

(G-8577)
STEINKE-FENTON FABRICATORS
1355 Page Ave (49203-2158)
PHONE.................................517 782-8174
Robert D Chatfield, *President*
Todd Chatfield, *Vice Pres*
EMP: 15
SQ FT: 18,000
SALES (est): 2.9MM **Privately Held**
SIC: 3444 Sheet metal specialties, not stamped

(G-8578)
STERLING SPRING LLC
2001 Wellworth (49203-3451)
PHONE.................................517 782-2479
Pat Grant, *Branch Mgr*
EMP: 25
SALES (corp-wide): 23.2MM **Privately Held**
SIC: 3495 Wire springs
PA: Sterling Spring, L.L.C.
5432 W 54th St
Chicago IL 60638
773 582-6464

(G-8579)
SUPERIOR SURFACE PROTECTION CO
Also Called: Ahh Publishing
3728 Luella St (49201-8632)
P.O. Box 4285 (49204-4285)
PHONE.................................517 206-1541
David Asaro, *President*
EMP: 3
SALES (est): 450K **Privately Held**
WEB: www.ahapublishing.com
SIC: 3086 Packaging & shipping materials, foamed plastic

(G-8580)
T&M USA INC
4115 County Farm Rd (49201-4100)
PHONE.................................517 789-9420
Toshiya Matsui, *Principal*
◆ EMP: 15
SQ FT: 6,680
SALES (est): 1.2MM **Privately Held**
WEB: www.tmusa.com
SIC: 2499 Decorative wood & woodwork

(G-8581)
TAC INDUSTRIAL GROUP LLC
1164 Lexington Blvd (49201-9856)
P.O. Box 761, Grass Lake (49240-0761)
PHONE.................................517 917-8976
Michael Kulka,
EMP: 3
SALES (est): 109.4K **Privately Held**
SIC: 3599 5084 Crankshafts & camshafts, machining; industrial machinery & equipment

(G-8582)
TAC MANUFACTURING INC (DH)
4111 County Farm Rd (49201-9065)
PHONE.................................517 789-7000
Hiro Ysui, *President*
Kiyoshi Sasaki, *President*
Y Hirai, *Vice Pres*
Salarrium Jones, *Production*
Corey Prior, *Buyer*
▲ EMP: 290
SQ FT: 110,000
SALES (est): 108.1MM **Privately Held**
SIC: 3714 3625 Motor vehicle engines & parts; relays & industrial controls

HQ: Tram, Inc.
47200 Port St
Plymouth MI 48170
734 254-8500

(G-8583)
TALKIN TACKLE LLC
205 S Sandstone Rd (49201-8925)
PHONE.................................517 474-6241
Ronald Kerver, *President*
Ralph McGonegal, *Managing Prtnr*
Kay Kerver, *Vice Pres*
Laurie Miller, *Admin Sec*
EMP: 4
SALES (est): 266.7K **Privately Held**
SIC: 3812 7389 Sonar systems & equipment;

(G-8584)
TECH TOOLING SPECIALTIES INC
1708 Cooper St (49202)
PHONE.................................517 782-8898
Robert Woodard, *President*
EMP: 13
SQ FT: 12,000
SALES (est): 2.2MM **Privately Held**
SIC: 3544 3541 3599 3542 Special dies & tools; machine tools, metal cutting type; machine shop, jobbing & repair; machine tools, metal forming type

(G-8585)
TECHNIQUE INC
1500 Technology Dr (49201-2700)
P.O. Box 4010 (49204-4010)
PHONE.................................517 789-8988
Ronnie Johncox, *President*
Steve Hines, *Manager*
EMP: 75
SQ FT: 126,000
SALES (est): 15.4MM **Privately Held**
WEB: www.tirps.com
SIC: 3469 3465 7692 3751 Metal stampings; automotive stampings; automotive welding; frames, motorcycle & bicycle; exhaust systems (mufflers, tail pipes, etc.); exhaust systems & parts, motor vehicle

(G-8586)
TENNECO AUTOMOTIVE OPER CO INC
2701 N Dettman Rd (49201-8883)
PHONE.................................517 522-5525
Bill Dreyer, *Principal*
Anthony Bartotti, *Engineer*
EMP: 60
SALES (corp-wide): 11.7B **Publicly Held**
WEB: www.tenneco-automotive.com
SIC: 3714 Motor vehicle parts & accessories
HQ: Tenneco Automotive Operating Company, Inc.
500 N Field Dr
Lake Forest IL 60045
847 482-5000

(G-8587)
TERRY TOOL & DIE CO
1080 Toro Dr (49201-8946)
PHONE.................................517 750-1771
Janet Schrader, *President*
Ryan Schrader, *Vice Pres*
Ron Markowski, *Treasurer*
John Dobben, *Admin Sec*
EMP: 10
SQ FT: 18,000
SALES (est): 1.3MM **Privately Held**
SIC: 3451 3544 Screw machine products; special dies, tools, jigs & fixtures

(G-8588)
THOMAN TOOL INC
313 Oak St (49201-1425)
PHONE.................................517 768-0114
Bud Thoman, *President*
EMP: 4 EST: 1958
SQ FT: 5,000
SALES: 250K **Privately Held**
SIC: 3599 Machine shop, jobbing & repair

(G-8589)
THOMAS FRANKINI
Also Called: Westlund Mfg
1415 S Cooper St (49203-4410)
PHONE.................................517 783-2400

Thomas Frankini, *Owner*
EMP: 3
SALES (est): 181.7K **Privately Held**
WEB: www.westlundmfg.com
SIC: 3471 Plating of metals or formed products

(G-8590)
TMS INTERNATIONAL LLC
3100 Brooklyn Rd (49203-4809)
PHONE.................................517 764-5123
Dustyn Greenhelgh, *Owner*
EMP: 5 **Privately Held**
SIC: 3312 Blast furnaces & steel mills
HQ: Tms International, Llc
2835 E Carson St Fl 3
Glassport PA 15203
412 678-6141

(G-8591)
TREGETS TOOL & ENGINEERING CO
1021 Airport Rd (49202-1850)
PHONE.................................517 782-0044
Steven Dygert, *President*
George Dygert, *Treasurer*
Dorothy Dygert, *Admin Sec*
EMP: 8
SQ FT: 15,680
SALES: 500K **Privately Held**
SIC: 3544 Special dies & tools

(G-8592)
TRICO INCORPORATED
7401 Foxworth Ct (49201-8486)
PHONE.................................517 764-1780
Harold Jones, *President*
Shelley Jones, *Vice Pres*
EMP: 7 EST: 1943
SALES (est): 1.2MM **Privately Held**
WEB: www.trico.com
SIC: 2796 Gravure printing plates or cylinders, preparation of

(G-8593)
TRINITY HOLDING INC (PA)
420 Ingham St (49201-1251)
PHONE.................................517 787-3100
Joseph R Miller, *President*
Phyllis L Miller, *Chairman*
Mary Lynn Miller, *Corp Secy*
EMP: 17
SQ FT: 40,000
SALES: 13.2MM **Privately Held**
WEB: www.trinityholding.com
SIC: 5084 4214 6531 3451 Industrial machinery & equipment; local trucking with storage; real estate agents & managers; screw machine products

(G-8594)
TRUFORM MACHINE INC
2510 Precision St (49202-3967)
PHONE.................................517 782-8523
Frank Phillips, *CEO*
Jeff Risk, *President*
EMP: 35
SQ FT: 12,000
SALES (est): 6.3MM **Privately Held**
WEB: www.truformmachine.com
SIC: 3599 3841 3812 3769 Machine shop, jobbing & repair; surgical & medical instruments; search & navigation equipment; guided missile & space vehicle parts & auxiliary equipment; fluid power pumps & motors

(G-8595)
TRULIFE
2010 E High St (49203-3416)
PHONE.................................800 492-1088
Noel Murphy, *President*
EMP: 30
SALES (est): 2.5MM **Privately Held**
WEB: www.trulife.com
SIC: 3842 Prosthetic appliances

(G-8596)
TRULIFE INC (DH)
Also Called: Discount Vitamin Store
2010 E High St (49203-3416)
PHONE.................................517 787-1600
Noel J Murphy, *CEO*
Alan Cooke, *CEO*
Laurie Bouchard, *Human Res Mgr*
Shelly Vaughn, *Executive*

Jackson - Jackson County (G-8597)

▲ **EMP:** 50
SQ FT: 75,000
SALES (est): 65.7MM **Privately Held**
SIC: 3842 8011 Belts: surgical, sanitary & corrective; braces, orthopedic; supports: abdominal, ankle, arch, kneecap, etc.; offices & clinics of medical doctors

(G-8597)
UNIFIED TOOL AND DIE INC
2010 Micor Dr (49203-3448)
PHONE...................517 768-8070
Michael Vogel, *President*
Marty Sears, *Treasurer*
EMP: 7
SQ FT: 2,700
SALES: 600K **Privately Held**
SIC: 3544 Special dies & tools

(G-8598)
UNION BUILT PC INC
Also Called: Midwest Regional Office
4202 Ann Arbor Rd (49202-2810)
PHONE...................248 910-3955
Brandon Weber, *Branch Mgr*
EMP: 3
SALES (corp-wide): 908.9K **Privately Held**
WEB: www.unionbuiltpc.com
SIC: 3575 7371 1731 Computer terminals; computer software development; computerized controls installation
PA: Union Built Pc Inc.
716 Bradley Rd Unit A
Ocean City MD 21842
410 250-5300

(G-8599)
UNITED METAL TECHNOLOGY INC
144 W Monroe St (49202-2398)
PHONE...................517 787-7940
Dennis G Rulewicz, *President*
Stephen J Rulewicz, *Vice Pres*
EMP: 15 **EST:** 1981
SQ FT: 18,500
SALES (est): 3MM **Privately Held**
WEB: www.unitedmetaltech.com
SIC: 3714 3533 Motor vehicle parts & accessories; oil field machinery & equipment

(G-8600)
VERITAS VINEYARD LLC (PA)
Also Called: Grand River Brewery.
117 W Louis Glick Hwy (49201-1327)
PHONE...................517 962-2427
John Burtka,
Denise E Burtka,
EMP: 25 **EST:** 2002
SQ FT: 12,500
SALES: 2MM **Privately Held**
SIC: 2084 8741 5921 Wines; restaurant management; wine & beer

(G-8601)
VOGEL TOOLING & MACHINE LLC
2010 Micor Dr (49203-3448)
PHONE...................517 414-7635
Michael Vogel,
EMP: 3 **EST:** 2011
SQ FT: 20,000
SALES (est): 187.8K **Privately Held**
SIC: 3544 Die sets for metal stamping (presses); welding positioners (jigs); jigs & fixtures; punches, forming & stamping

(G-8602)
W2 INC
Also Called: Gilbert's Chocolates
233 N Jackson St (49201-1203)
PHONE...................517 764-3141
William R Blakemore, *President*
EMP: 7
SQ FT: 1,500
SALES (est): 611.6K **Privately Held**
SIC: 5441 5145 2064 Candy; candy; candy & other confectionery products

(G-8603)
WALLER MACHINE CO INC
433 Condad Ave (49202-3911)
PHONE...................517 789-7707
Carl Waller, *President*
John Waller, *Vice Pres*
EMP: 3
SQ FT: 2,500
SALES (est): 358.4K **Privately Held**
WEB: www.wallermachine.com
SIC: 3728 Aircraft assemblies, subassemblies & parts

(G-8604)
WALTONS SAWMILL
1004 Hamilton St (49202-3332)
PHONE...................517 841-5241
Eric Walton, *Owner*
EMP: 3
SALES (est): 254.8K **Privately Held**
SIC: 2421 Sawmills & planing mills, general

(G-8605)
WAY BAKERY (HQ)
2100 Enterprise St (49203-6412)
PHONE...................517 787-6720
John F Popp, *President*
Jay E Miller, *Vice Pres*
EMP: 230 **EST:** 1884
SQ FT: 62,000
SALES (est): 56.9MM
SALES (corp-wide): 535.8MM **Privately Held**
SIC: 2051 Buns, bread type: fresh or frozen
PA: Perfection Bakeries, Inc.
350 Pearl St
Fort Wayne IN 46802
260 424-8245

(G-8606)
WEATHERPROOF INC
385 Watts Rd (49203-2333)
PHONE...................517 764-1330
Terri Jo, *President*
Carol Goldsmith, *President*
Lisa Haynes, *Vice Pres*
Terri Nichols, *Vice Pres*
EMP: 34
SQ FT: 15,000
SALES (est): 6.8MM **Privately Held**
WEB: www.weatherproof.net
SIC: 2821 3442 3211 2431 Vinyl resins; storm doors or windows, metal; insulating glass, sealed units; awnings, blinds & shutters, wood

(G-8607)
WILLBEE CONCRETE PRODUCTS CO
2323 Brooklyn Rd (49203-4751)
PHONE...................517 782-8246
EMP: 14 **EST:** 1922
SQ FT: 15,000
SALES (est): 2MM **Privately Held**
SIC: 3272 7261 5087 Mfg Concrete Products Funeral Service/Crematory Whol Service Establishment Equipment

(G-8608)
WILLBEE TRANSIT-MIX CO INC
2323 Brooklyn Rd (49203-4749)
P.O. Box 427 (49204-0427)
PHONE...................517 782-9493
Andrew Willbee, *President*
Gregory Sherwood, *Vice Pres*
EMP: 25
SQ FT: 1,200
SALES (est): 4.7MM **Privately Held**
SIC: 3273 5032 Ready-mixed concrete; brick, stone & related material

(G-8609)
WILLIAMS WELDING AND REPAIR
2445 Brooklyn Rd (49203-4803)
PHONE...................517 783-3977
Gary Williams, *President*
Elizabeth Williams, *Corp Secy*
EMP: 3
SQ FT: 4,000
SALES (est): 365.2K **Privately Held**
SIC: 7692 Welding repair

(G-8610)
WOLVERINE TRAILERS INC (PA)
116 Frost St (49202-2371)
P.O. Box 1829 (49204-1829)
PHONE...................517 782-4950
Lyle Johnson, *CEO*
EMP: 4
SQ FT: 5,000
SALES: 5MM **Privately Held**
SIC: 3715 Truck trailers

(G-8611)
WOLVERINE TRAILERS INC
1500 Chanter Rd (49201-9563)
P.O. Box 1829 (49204-1829)
PHONE...................517 782-4950
Lyle Johnson, *Branch Mgr*
EMP: 8
SALES (corp-wide): 5MM **Privately Held**
SIC: 3715 Truck trailers
PA: Wolverine Trailers, Inc.
116 Frost St
Jackson MI 49202
517 782-4950

(G-8612)
WOLVERINE TRAILERS INC
1500 Chanter Rd (49201-9563)
P.O. Box 1829 (49204-1829)
PHONE...................517 782-4950
EMP: 17
SALES (corp-wide): 5MM **Privately Held**
SIC: 3713 Utility truck bodies
PA: Wolverine Trailers, Inc.
116 Frost St
Jackson MI 49202
517 782-4950

(G-8613)
WOODIE MANUFACTURING INC
1400 Wildwood Ave (49202-4027)
PHONE...................517 782-7663
John Flannery, *President*
EMP: 8
SQ FT: 3,000
SALES: 600K **Privately Held**
SIC: 3599 Machine shop, jobbing & repair

(G-8614)
YOXHEIMER TILE CO
919 E South St (49203-4404)
PHONE...................517 788-7542
Scott Yoxheimer, *President*
EMP: 14
SQ FT: 1,260
SALES (est): 1.5MM **Privately Held**
WEB: www.yoxheimertile.com
SIC: 1743 3253 5032 Tile installation, ceramic; floor tile, ceramic; granite building stone

(G-8615)
ZIMMER MARBLE CO INC
1812 River St (49202-1755)
PHONE...................517 787-1500
Joseph A Campau, *President*
Philip F Campau, *Vice Pres*
EMP: 14
SQ FT: 54,000
SALES (est): 2.2MM **Privately Held**
SIC: 3281 3088 Marble, building: cut & shaped; plastics plumbing fixtures

Jenison
Ottawa County

(G-8616)
ADVANTAGE INDUSTRIES INC
2196 Port Sheldon St (49428-9315)
PHONE...................616 669-2400
Kirk Klynstra, *President*
William Bos, *President*
Morris Kolff, *Vice Pres*
Doug Dornbos, *Treasurer*
Bob Forward, *Admin Sec*
EMP: 40
SQ FT: 20,000
SALES (est): 9MM **Privately Held**
WEB: www.advind.com
SIC: 3543 3544 7373 1731 Industrial patterns; industrial molds; jigs: inspection, gauging & checking; computer-aided design (CAD) systems service; electrical work

(G-8617)
APPAREL SALES INC
2712 Edward St Ste A (49428-8187)
PHONE...................616 842-5650
Jon Johnson, *President*
Robert Dykstra, *Vice Pres*
▲ **EMP:** 5
SQ FT: 28,000
SALES (est): 1.2MM **Privately Held**
WEB: www.apparelsalesonline.com
SIC: 5136 2759 2395 Sportswear, men's & boys'; screen printing; embroidery & art needlework

(G-8618)
AUTOMATED MACHINE SYSTEMS INC
6651 Pine Ridge Ct Sw (49428-9254)
PHONE...................616 662-1309
Kris Chayer, *President*
Kevin Grinwis, *Vice Pres*
Kevin Rowe, *Project Mgr*
Anne Wiersum, *Office Mgr*
Micah Farraher, *Technical Staff*
EMP: 23
SQ FT: 5,000
SALES (est): 7.2MM **Privately Held**
SIC: 3537 Palletizers & depalletizers

(G-8619)
BOLHOUSE LLC
2704 Edward St (49428-8187)
PHONE...................616 209-7543
Scott Bolhouse, *Mng Member*
Kyle Dykstria, *Manager*
EMP: 3 **EST:** 2010
SQ FT: 200
SALES (est): 456.5K **Privately Held**
SIC: 3585 Refrigeration & heating equipment; air conditioning equipment, complete; heating equipment, complete

(G-8620)
CELLULOSE MTL SOLUTIONS LLC
Also Called: CMS
2472 Port Sheldon St (49428-9342)
PHONE...................616 669-2990
Matt Henderson, *Vice Pres*
Mark Henderson, *Mng Member*
EMP: 7
SALES (est): 297.6K **Privately Held**
WEB: www.cmsgreen.com
SIC: 2392 Blankets: made from purchased materials

(G-8621)
COMPOSITE SIGN PRODUCTS INC
Also Called: Aerotech Caps
2148 Center Industrial Ct (49428-8347)
PHONE...................616 252-9110
Brian Kronemeyer, *President*
▼ **EMP:** 3 **EST:** 2011
SALES (est): 350K **Privately Held**
SIC: 3799 Automobile trailer chassis

(G-8622)
CONCRETE LIFTERS INC
7520 Main St Ste 6 (49428)
PHONE...................616 669-0400
Gerald Miedema, *Principal*
EMP: 5
SALES (est): 274.2K **Privately Held**
SIC: 1389 1771 Mud service, oil field drilling; concrete work

(G-8623)
DEWENT REDI-MIX LLC
1601 Chicago Dr (49428-9740)
PHONE...................616 457-2100
Cheryl Zwagerman, *Principal*
EMP: 3
SALES (est): 169.9K **Privately Held**
SIC: 3273 Ready-mixed concrete

(G-8624)
ELENBAAS HARDWOOD INCORPORATED (PA)
2363 Port Sheldon Ct (49428-8220)
P.O. Box 8 (49429-0008)
PHONE...................616 669-3085
Dave Elenbaas, *President*
EMP: 4 **EST:** 1950
SQ FT: 30,000
SALES (est): 1.7MM **Privately Held**
SIC: 2431 Moldings, wood: unfinished & prefinished

GEOGRAPHIC SECTION

Jonesville - Hillsdale County (G-8653)

(G-8625)
EMBROIDERY HOUSE INC
2688 Edward St (49428-8187)
PHONE..................................616 669-6400
Kurt Vander Loon, *President*
Derek Stark, *Sales Staff*
EMP: 7
SQ FT: 5,200
SALES (est): 679K **Privately Held**
WEB: www.embroideryhouseinc.com
SIC: 2395 2396 5199 2752 Embroidery products, except schiffli machine; emblems, embroidered; screen printing on fabric articles; advertising specialties; business form & card printing, lithographic

(G-8626)
FABRI-TECH INC (PA)
Also Called: Anterior Quest
6719 Pine Ridge Ct Sw (49428-9253)
PHONE..................................616 662-0150
Dennis Jonker, *President*
David Brandsen, *Vice Pres*
Daniel Holtrop, *Vice Pres*
Curt Van Koevering, *Technical Staff*
Scott Bowron, *Admin Sec*
▲ EMP: 30
SQ FT: 22,000
SALES (est): 5.4MM **Privately Held**
SIC: 3552 5949 Embroidery machines; sewing, needlework & piece goods

(G-8627)
GLUCO INC
794 Chicago Dr (49428-9195)
PHONE..................................616 457-1212
Morry Pysarchik, *President*
George Lemmon, *Corp Secy*
John F Northway, *Vice Pres*
▲ EMP: 3 EST: 1964
SQ FT: 21,000
SALES (est): 57.8K **Privately Held**
WEB: www.gluco.com
SIC: 3559 5084 Plastics working machinery; industrial machinery & equipment

(G-8628)
H&H AUTOMATION CONTROLS
7633 Bluebird Dr (49428-7954)
PHONE..................................616 457-5994
Hung Pham, *Electrical Engi*
Pham Hung, *Administration*
EMP: 3
SALES (est): 286.7K **Privately Held**
SIC: 3625 Relays & industrial controls

(G-8629)
HUIZENGA GRAVEL COMPANY INC
1861 Filmore St (49428)
PHONE..................................616 457-1030
Bruce Huizenga, *President*
EMP: 3
SALES (corp-wide): 4.5MM **Privately Held**
SIC: 1442 Gravel mining
PA: Huizenga Gravel Company, Inc.
   10075 Gordon St
   Zeeland MI 49464
   616 772-6241

(G-8630)
INNOVATIVE MACHINES INC
1811 Chicago Dr (49428-9740)
PHONE..................................616 669-1649
Arlen Van Os, *President*
Don Ogle, *Vice Pres*
Lois Ogle, *Opers Staff*
Todd Schwartzkopf, *Engineer*
▲ EMP: 8
SQ FT: 90,000
SALES (est): 967.3K **Privately Held**
WEB: www.innovativemachines.com
SIC: 3555 Printing trades machinery

(G-8631)
KDI TECHNOLOGIES INC
Also Called: Dienetics
2206 Pine Ridge Dr Sw (49428-9229)
PHONE..................................616 667-1600
Bruce Krouskop, *CEO*
EMP: 60 EST: 1955
SQ FT: 54,000
SALES (est): 10.9MM **Privately Held**
WEB: www.dienetics.com
SIC: 3544 Special dies & tools

(G-8632)
LARKHITE DEVELOPMENT SYSTEM
1501 Port Sheldon St (49428-9320)
P.O. Box 989 (49429-0989)
PHONE..................................616 457-6722
David Maier, *President*
EMP: 7
SALES (est): 651.5K **Privately Held**
SIC: 2451 Mobile homes

(G-8633)
MCCLURE TABLES INC (PA)
6661 Roger Dr Ste C (49428-9248)
PHONE..................................616 662-5974
Todd McClure, *CEO*
Judy McClure, *President*
EMP: 1
SQ FT: 5,000
SALES (est): 1.2MM **Privately Held**
SIC: 3949 Shuffleboards & shuffleboard equipment

(G-8634)
NEXT LEVEL MANUFACTURING LLC
6778 18th Ave (49428-8385)
PHONE..................................269 397-1220
David Warner, *President*
Tim Creamer, *Opers Mgr*
EMP: 30
SALES (est): 4MM **Privately Held**
SIC: 3999 Atomizers, toiletry

(G-8635)
NU-WOOL CO INC
Also Called: Business Software Services
2472 Port Sheldon St (49428-9342)
PHONE..................................800 748-0128
Mark Henderson, *President*
Jack Golden, *Area Mgr*
Matt Henderson, *Vice Pres*
Valerie Henderson, *Vice Pres*
Mercy Schaab, *Controller*
▲ EMP: 68 EST: 1949
SQ FT: 90,000
SALES (est): 12.1MM **Privately Held**
WEB: www.nuwool.com
SIC: 2499 2493 Mulch, wood & bark; insulation board, cellular fiber

(G-8636)
PERFORMANCE ENGRG RACG ENGS
2176 Center Industrial Ct (49428-8347)
PHONE..................................616 669-5800
Kathleen Huizinga, *President*
EMP: 6
SQ FT: 8,100
SALES (est): 950.4K **Privately Held**
WEB: www.pereng.com
SIC: 3714 Motor vehicle engines & parts

(G-8637)
PREFERRED MACHINE LLC
6673 Pine Ridge Ct Sw C (49428-9278)
PHONE..................................616 272-6334
Nathan Holstege, *Mng Member*
Corey Westra, *Manager*
EMP: 30 EST: 2009
SALES (est): 5MM **Privately Held**
SIC: 3599 Machine shop, jobbing & repair

(G-8638)
PROTXS INC (PA)
7974 Parkside Ct (49428-9100)
PHONE..................................989 255-3836
Nathan Blury, *President*
Dr Michael Halliday, *Founder*
▼ EMP: 217
SQ FT: 4,556
SALES (est): 3.2MM **Privately Held**
SIC: 3571 Electronic computers

(G-8639)
QUILTING BY CHERYL
8092 Emberly Dr (49428-9167)
PHONE..................................616 669-5636
Cheryl Klein, *Owner*
EMP: 3
SALES: 100K **Privately Held**
SIC: 2395 Quilting, for the trade

(G-8640)
R & R HARWOOD INC
Also Called: Hardwoods Prtg & Advg Servic
2688 Edward St (49428-8187)
PHONE..................................616 669-6400
Morton Harwood Sr, *President*
Morton Harwood Jr, *President*
Mabel Harwood, *Principal*
Randy Harwood, *Vice Pres*
EMP: 5 EST: 1939
SQ FT: 2,000
SALES: 1MM **Privately Held**
SIC: 2741 2752 2759 2789 Miscellaneous publishing; commercial printing, lithographic; commercial printing; bookbinding & related work; signs & advertising specialties; advertising specialties

(G-8641)
RANDALL TOOL & MFG LLC
Also Called: Randall Tool & Manufacturing
2514 Port Sheldon St # 3 (49428-7311)
PHONE..................................616 669-1260
Aaron Timmer, *Owner*
Aaron T Timmer, *Manager*
EMP: 3 EST: 1972
SQ FT: 4,000
SALES (est): 370K **Privately Held**
SIC: 3599 Machine shop, jobbing & repair

(G-8642)
SCHRIER PLASTICS CORP
2019 Pine Ridge Dr Sw (49428-9228)
PHONE..................................616 669-7174
Jeffrey Schrier, *President*
Pamela Schrier, *Corp Secy*
EMP: 20
SQ FT: 15,000
SALES (est): 1.5MM **Privately Held**
WEB: www.schrierplastics.com
SIC: 3089 Plastic hardware & building products; plastic processing

(G-8643)
SERVISCREEN INC
1765 Chicago Dr (49428-9740)
PHONE..................................616 669-1640
Allen Van Os, *CEO*
Lowell Vanos, *Exec VP*
Allen Os, *Vice Pres*
Arlen Van Os, *Vice Pres*
Lowell Van Os, *Vice Pres*
EMP: 100
SQ FT: 53,645
SALES (est): 23.6MM **Privately Held**
WEB: www.serviscreen.com
SIC: 2759 3479 Screen printing; painting, coating & hot dipping; painting of metal products

(G-8644)
TANNEWITZ INC
Also Called: Ramco
794 Chicago Dr (49428-9195)
PHONE..................................616 457-5999
Morry Pysarchik, *President*
Debbie Prew, *General Mgr*
David Oltouse, *Vice Pres*
Celeste Schade, *Controller*
▲ EMP: 24
SQ FT: 21,000
SALES (est): 7.5MM **Privately Held**
SIC: 3549 3553 Metalworking machinery; woodworking machinery

(G-8645)
TRUSSWAY
8450 Winona Dr (49428-9540)
P.O. Box 27, Sparta (49345-0027)
PHONE..................................713 691-6900
Ron Wiersum, *Principal*
EMP: 4 EST: 2010
SALES (est): 250.3K **Privately Held**
SIC: 2439 Trusses, wooden roof

(G-8646)
USA SIGN FRAME & STAKE INC
2150 Center Industrial Ct (49428-8347)
PHONE..................................616 662-9100
Gary Moshluk, *President*
Brian Kronemeyer, *President*
EMP: 5
SQ FT: 8,000
SALES: 850K **Privately Held**
SIC: 3993 Signs, not made in custom sign painting shops

(G-8647)
VANEX MOLD INC
2240 Pine Ridge Dr Sw (49428-9229)
PHONE..................................616 662-4100
Tom Vanek, *President*
Ken Vanek, *Vice Pres*
EMP: 4
SQ FT: 9,000
SALES (est): 680.3K **Privately Held**
WEB: www.vanextooling.com
SIC: 3544 Industrial molds

(G-8648)
VIBRATION RESEARCH CORPORATION
1294 Chicago Dr (49428-9308)
PHONE..................................616 669-3028
John Van Baren, *President*
EMP: 20
SQ FT: 8,000
SALES (est): 5.5MM **Privately Held**
WEB: www.vibrationresearch.com
SIC: 3829 Measuring & controlling devices

Johannesburg
Otsego County

(G-8649)
EASTPORT GROUP INC
9301 M 32 E (49751-9548)
P.O. Box 277 (49751-0277)
PHONE..................................989 732-0030
William C Myler Jr, *President*
Thomas J Myler, *Vice Pres*
EMP: 15
SALES (est): 1.2MM **Privately Held**
WEB: www.eastportgroup.com
SIC: 1389 Gas field services; oil field services

(G-8650)
RCS SERVICES COMPANY LLC
10850 Hetherton Rd (49751-8730)
P.O. Box 38 (49751-0038)
PHONE..................................989 732-7999
Robert Jones, *Mng Member*
Connie Madej, *Administration*
EMP: 12
SALES (est): 1.1MM **Privately Held**
SIC: 1389 Oil field services

Jones
Cass County

(G-8651)
DANIEL OLSON
Also Called: Maple Row Sugarhouse
12646 Born St (49061-9735)
PHONE..................................269 816-1838
Daniel Olson, *Owner*
EMP: 3
SALES (est): 135.1K **Privately Held**
SIC: 2099 Maple syrup

(G-8652)
ODONNELLS DOCKS
12097 M 60 (49061-8768)
P.O. Box 1 (49061-0001)
PHONE..................................269 244-1446
Shawn Odonnell, *Principal*
EMP: 4
SALES (est): 512.2K **Privately Held**
WEB: www.odonnellsdocks.com
SIC: 3536 4491 Boat lifts; docks, incl. buildings & facilities: operation & maintenance

Jonesville
Hillsdale County

(G-8653)
BAY ALPHI MANUFACTURING INC
576 Beck St (49250-9472)
P.O. Box 9229, Green Bay WI (54308-9229)
PHONE..................................517 849-9945

Jonesville - Hillsdale County (G-8654)

Daniel A Schmidt, *CEO*
Ronn Kleinschmidt, *CFO*
Eric Maystead, *Manager*
Gloria J Schmidt, *Director*
EMP: 50
SALES (est): 1.8MM **Privately Held**
SIC: 3714 Mufflers (exhaust), motor vehicle
PA: Aws/Gb Corporation
2929 Walker Dr
Green Bay WI 54311

(G-8654)
EXPRESS CNC & FABRICATION LLC
3041 North Adams Rd (49250-9200)
PHONE.................................517 937-8760
Tommy Schuette, *Vice Pres*
EMP: 7
SQ FT: 145,000
SALES (est): 653.3K **Privately Held**
SIC: 3599 Machine shop, jobbing & repair

(G-8655)
GONZALEZ GROUP JONESVILLE LLC
3980 Beck Rd (49250-8400)
P.O. Box 360, Litchfield (49252-0360)
PHONE.................................517 849-9908
EMP: 50
SALES (corp-wide): 8.4MM **Privately Held**
SIC: 3498 Fabricated Pipe And Fittings
PA: Gonzalez Group, Llc
935 Anderson Rd
Litchfield MI 49252
517 542-2928

(G-8656)
INTERDYNE INC
530 Industrial Pkwy (49250-9006)
P.O. Box 165 (49250-0165)
PHONE.................................517 849-2281
Antonin Slovacek, *President*
Matt Slovacek, *Admin Sec*
EMP: 25
SQ FT: 62,500
SALES (est): 4.3MM **Privately Held**
WEB: www.interdyneinc.com
SIC: 3069 Molded rubber products

(G-8657)
JAG INDUSTRIAL SERVICES INC
225 E Chicago St (49250-1002)
PHONE.................................678 592-6860
Douglas Charles Huff, *CEO*
Helena Jagielski, *General Mgr*
Joshua Huff Christopher, *Admin Sec*
EMP: 3
SALES (est): 392.6K **Privately Held**
SIC: 3731 Shipbuilding & repairing

(G-8658)
JT MANUFACTURING INC
Also Called: Jonesville Tool and Mfg
540 Industrial Pkwy (49250-9004)
P.O. Box 4364, Jackson (49204-4364)
PHONE.................................517 849-2923
Neil Caulkins, *President*
Cary Addleman, *Vice Pres*
Jim Parker, *Vice Pres*
Dan Waterstraut, *QC Mgr*
Cary Addleman, *Engineer*
EMP: 48
SQ FT: 32,500
SALES (est): 12MM **Privately Held**
WEB: www.jonesvilletool.com
SIC: 3599 3545 Machine shop, jobbing & repair; precision tools, machinists'

(G-8659)
K & K TANNERY LLC
561 Industrial Pkwy (49250-9004)
PHONE.................................517 849-9720
Gary Kies, *Owner*
EMP: 4
SALES (est): 304.8K **Privately Held**
WEB: www.kandktannery.com
SIC: 3111 Hides: tanning, currying & finishing

(G-8660)
MACK ANDREW & SON BRUSH CO
216 E Chicago St (49250-1003)
P.O. Box 157 (49250-0157)
PHONE.................................517 849-9272
Jon M Fast, *President*
Betty J Fast, *Vice Pres*
Jonathan C Fast, *Vice Pres*
EMP: 9 EST: 1891
SQ FT: 1,500
SALES (est): 1.2MM **Privately Held**
WEB: www.mackbrush.com
SIC: 5231 3991 Paint brushes, rollers, sprayers & other supplies; paint brushes

(G-8661)
MARTINREA INDUSTRIES INC
Mj US
260 Gaige St (49250-9431)
PHONE.................................517 849-2195
Pete Bertolini, *General Mgr*
Tom Schneider, *Safety Mgr*
John Perrin, *Purch Mgr*
EMP: 14
SALES (corp-wide): 2.7B **Privately Held**
SIC: 3714 Motor vehicle parts & accessories
HQ: Martinrea Industries, Inc.
10501 Mi State Road 52
Manchester MI 48158
734 428-2400

(G-8662)
MARTINREA JONESVILLE LLC (HQ)
260 Gaige St (49250-9431)
PHONE.................................517 849-2195
Nick Orlando, *CEO*
Sheryl Miller, *Buyer*
Andre Larosa,
▲ **EMP:** 89
SQ FT: 500,000
SALES (est): 145.6MM
SALES (corp-wide): 2.7B **Privately Held**
SIC: 3465 Body parts, automobile: stamped metal
PA: Martinrea International Inc
3210 Langstaff Rd
Vaughan ON
416 749-0314

(G-8663)
MEGA SCREEN CORP
549 Industrial Pkwy (49250-9004)
P.O. Box 152 (49250-0152)
PHONE.................................517 849-7057
Mark L Domack, *President*
Stacy Domack, *Treasurer*
EMP: 6
SQ FT: 9,000
SALES (est): 703.4K **Privately Held**
WEB: www.epicgames.com
SIC: 2759 3089 3549 Screen printing; plastic processing; injection molding of plastics; metalworking machinery

(G-8664)
NORTH EAST FABRICATION CO INC
Also Called: Nefco
113 Deal Pkwy (49250-9351)
P.O. Box 231 (49250-0231)
PHONE.................................517 849-8090
Steve Harding, *President*
EMP: 12
SQ FT: 5,000
SALES (est): 1.9MM **Privately Held**
SIC: 3499 5999 Welding tips, heat resistant: metal; welding supplies

(G-8665)
NYLONCRAFT OF MICHIGAN INC
1640 E Chicago Rd (49250-9110)
P.O. Box 35 (49250-0035)
PHONE.................................517 849-9911
James Krzyzewski, *President*
Glenn Scolnik, *Chairman*
Roland Erb, *Vice Pres*
Terry Rensberger, *Vice Pres*
Tom Smith, *Plant Mgr*
▲ **EMP:** 260
SQ FT: 145,000
SALES (est): 69.9MM
SALES (corp-wide): 333.7MM **Privately Held**
WEB: www.nyloncraft.com
SIC: 3089 Injection molding of plastics
HQ: Nyloncraft, Inc.
616 W Mckinley Ave
Mishawaka IN 46545
574 256-1521

(G-8666)
PELHAMS CONSTRUCTION LLC
10800 Concord Rd (49250-9635)
PHONE.................................517 549-8276
Terry R Pelham, *Mng Member*
EMP: 4
SALES (est): 500K **Privately Held**
SIC: 1389 Gas field services

(G-8667)
QUICKMITT INC
2400 E Chicago Rd (49250-9749)
PHONE.................................517 849-2141
Scott D Smith, *President*
EMP: 4
SALES (est): 302K **Privately Held**
WEB: www.quickmitt.com
SIC: 2298 Slings, rope; cordage: abaca, sisal, henequen, hemp, jute or other fiber

(G-8668)
RITZ-CRAFT CORP PA INC
Also Called: Ritz Craft Corp of Michigan
118 Deal Pkwy (49250-9351)
PHONE.................................517 849-7425
Paul Lindley, *General Mgr*
Brook R Bindus, *Principal*
EMP: 40
SALES (corp-wide): 82.5MM **Privately Held**
WEB: www.ritz-craft.com
SIC: 5211 2452 Modular homes; modular homes, prefabricated, wood
PA: Ritz-Craft Corporation Of Pennsylvania, Inc.
15 Industrial Park Rd
Mifflinburg PA 17844
570 966-1053

(G-8669)
TECHNIPLAS LLC
1640 E Chicago Rd (49250-9110)
PHONE.................................517 849-9911
EMP: 260
SALES (corp-wide): 303.3MM **Privately Held**
SIC: 3089 Plastic processing
PA: Techniplas, Llc
N44w33341 Wtrtwn Plnk Rd
Nashotah WI 53058
262 369-5555

Kalamazoo
Kalamazoo County

(G-8670)
A & D LIGHTING
3711 New Farm St (49048-8640)
PHONE.................................269 327-1126
Andrew Kragt, *Owner*
EMP: 3
SALES (est): 270.1K **Privately Held**
SIC: 3645 Residential lighting fixtures

(G-8671)
A 1 PRINTING AND COPY CENTER
129 E Michigan Ave 131 (49007-3907)
PHONE.................................269 381-0093
Sandra Gilman, *President*
Steven Gilman, *Corp Secy*
Gerald Gilman, *Vice Pres*
EMP: 3
SQ FT: 4,000
SALES (est): 344.9K **Privately Held**
WEB: www.a1printing.com
SIC: 2752 2791 7334 Commercial printing, offset; typesetting; photocopying & duplicating services

(G-8672)
A D JOHNSON ENGRAVING CO INC
2129 Portage St (49001-6145)
PHONE.................................269 385-0044
Donovan J Kindle, *President*
EMP: 12
SQ FT: 2,000
SALES (est): 250K **Privately Held**
WEB: www.adjohnson.com
SIC: 7389 3446 3993 3544 Engraving service; architectural metalwork; signs & advertising specialties; special dies, tools, jigs & fixtures; platemaking services

(G-8673)
AGGREGATE INDUSTRIES - MWR INC
822 Schuster Ave (49001-3203)
P.O. Box 19760 (49019-0760)
PHONE.................................269 321-3800
Tom Jansen, *Manager*
EMP: 50
SALES (corp-wide): 27.6B **Privately Held**
SIC: 3273 Ready-mixed concrete
HQ: Aggregate Industries - Mwr, Inc.
2815 Dodd Rd
Eagan MN 55121
651 683-0600

(G-8674)
AGRESTAL HYGIENICS LLC
10463 W H Ave (49009-8506)
PHONE.................................800 410-9053
Marc Deforest,
▲ **EMP:** 3
SALES (est): 164K **Privately Held**
SIC: 2844 Cosmetic preparations

(G-8675)
ALLNEX USA INC
2715 Miller Rd (49001-4138)
PHONE.................................269 385-1205
William Doukas, *Opers Mgr*
Carl Walker, *Engineer*
Dan Kersting, *Manager*
EMP: 99
SALES (corp-wide): 177.9K **Privately Held**
SIC: 2821 Acrylic resins
HQ: Allnex Usa Inc.
9005 Westside Pkwy
Alpharetta GA
800 433-2873

(G-8676)
ALLYNN CORP
7868 Douglas Ave (49009-6327)
PHONE.................................269 383-1199
Larry Loviska, *President*
Kevin Marcy, *Vice Pres*
EMP: 9
SQ FT: 3,000
SALES (est): 1.2MM **Privately Held**
WEB: www.allynncorp.com
SIC: 3599 7692 Machine shop, jobbing & repair; welding repair

(G-8677)
ALTERNATIVE SYSTEMS INC
5519 E Cork St Ste A (49048-8634)
PHONE.................................269 384-2008
Daniel J Olinger, *President*
Troy Butler, *Vice Pres*
Linda Olinger, *Admin Sec*
EMP: 10
SQ FT: 10,000
SALES (est): 1.7MM **Privately Held**
WEB: www.alternativesysteminc.com
SIC: 3089 Plates, plastic

(G-8678)
ALUMINUM FINISHING COMPANY
615 W Ransom St (49007-3311)
PHONE.................................269 382-4010
Jahan Assadi, *Principal*
EMP: 4
SQ FT: 10,000
SALES (est): 300K **Privately Held**
SIC: 3471 Anodizing (plating) of metals or formed products

GEOGRAPHIC SECTION
Kalamazoo - Kalamazoo County (G-8706)

(G-8679)
APPLE BLOSSOM WINERY LLC
Also Called: Texas Corners Brewing Company
6970 Texas Dr (49009-9795)
PHONE 269 668-3724
Denise Schultz, *Principal*
EMP: 12 **EST:** 2012
SQ FT: 200
SALES: 300K **Privately Held**
SIC: 2082 2083 Malt liquors; malt

(G-8680)
APPLIED COATINGS SOLUTIONS LLC
1830 Reed Ave (49001-4049)
PHONE 269 341-9757
Gary Yost,
EMP: 5
SALES (est): 597.9K
SALES (corp-wide): 14.2MM **Privately Held**
WEB: www.unifabcorporation.com
SIC: 3479 Coating of metals & formed products
PA: Weber Specialties Company
15230 Us Highway 131 S
Schoolcraft MI 49087
269 679-5160

(G-8681)
AQUEOUS ORBITAL SYSTEMS LLC
301 N 26th St (49048-4830)
PHONE 269 501-7461
James D Sutton, *Principal*
EMP: 7 **EST:** 2017
SALES (est): 278.3K **Privately Held**
SIC: 3714 Motor vehicle transmissions, drive assemblies & parts

(G-8682)
ARCHITECTURAL GLASS & MTLS INC (PA)
604 S 8th St (49009-8041)
P.O. Box 19067 (49019-0067)
PHONE 269 375-6165
Bob Fujawa, *President*
Robin Wendland, *Corp Secy*
EMP: 15
SQ FT: 20,000
SALES (est): 6.3MM **Privately Held**
SIC: 1751 3442 Window & door (prefabricated) installation; window & door frames

(G-8683)
ARGYLE SOCKS LLC
3800 Winding Way (49004-3738)
PHONE 269 615-0097
Craig Pennings, *Principal*
EMP: 3
SALES (est): 229.9K **Privately Held**
SIC: 2252 Socks

(G-8684)
ARTIGY PRINTING
5285 E Fg Ave (49004-9638)
PHONE 269 373-6591
Roger Jackson, *Owner*
Sean Campbell, *Manager*
Kevin Muraszewski, *Manager*
EMP: 5
SQ FT: 1,750
SALES (est): 566.7K **Privately Held**
WEB: www.artigy.com
SIC: 2752 Commercial printing, offset

(G-8685)
ARVCO CONTAINER CORPORATION (PA)
Also Called: Arvco Speciality Packaging
845 Gibson St (49001-2573)
PHONE 269 381-0900
Joann Arvanigian, *CEO*
Greg Arvanigian, *President*
Bob Ford, *Vice Pres*
John Vrbensky, *Vice Pres*
Jack Secord, *VP Mfg*
▲ **EMP:** 25 **EST:** 1971
SQ FT: 170,000
SALES (est): 58.8MM **Privately Held**
WEB: www.arvco.com
SIC: 2653 Boxes, corrugated: made from purchased materials; sheets, corrugated: made from purchased materials

(G-8686)
ARVCO CONTAINER CORPORATION
Also Called: Arvan Specialty Products
845 Gibson St (49001-2573)
PHONE 269 381-0900
Greg Arvanigian, *Branch Mgr*
EMP: 200
SALES (corp-wide): 58.8MM **Privately Held**
WEB: www.arvco.com
SIC: 2653 Boxes, corrugated: made from purchased materials; sheets, corrugated: made from purchased materials
PA: Arvco Container Corporation
845 Gibson St
Kalamazoo MI 49001
269 381-0900

(G-8687)
ARVCO CONTAINER CORPORATION
351 Rochester Ave (49007-4932)
PHONE 269 381-0900
Greg Arvanigian, *Branch Mgr*
EMP: 30
SALES (corp-wide): 58.8MM **Privately Held**
WEB: www.arvco.com
SIC: 2653 Boxes, corrugated: made from purchased materials; sheets, corrugated: made from purchased materials
PA: Arvco Container Corporation
845 Gibson St
Kalamazoo MI 49001
269 381-0900

(G-8688)
AUREOGEN INC
Also Called: Aureogen Biosciences
4717 Campus Dr Ste 2300 (49008-5620)
PHONE 269 353-3805
Ake Elhemmer, *CEO*
Jerry Slighten, *COO*
EMP: 8
SQ FT: 4,000
SALES: 1MM **Privately Held**
WEB: www.aureogen.com
SIC: 2833 Antibiotics

(G-8689)
AXONIA MEDICAL INC
4321 Roxbury Ln (49008-3314)
PHONE 269 615-6632
Harry C Ledebur Jr, *CEO*
EMP: 5
SALES (est): 538K **Privately Held**
SIC: 2836 Biological products, except diagnostic

(G-8690)
AZON USA INC (PA)
643 W Crosstown Pkwy (49008-1910)
PHONE 269 385-5942
James M Dunstan, *Ch of Bd*
David Mills, *President*
Ruth L Dunstan, *Exec VP*
Matt Deittrick, *Vice Pres*
Patrick Muessig, *Vice Pres*
▲ **EMP:** 18
SQ FT: 18,000
SALES: 40MM **Privately Held**
WEB: www.azoninet.com
SIC: 3087 3599 Custom compound purchased resins; custom machinery

(G-8691)
AZON USA INC
2204 Ravine Rd (49004-3506)
PHONE 269 385-5942
David Mills, *Branch Mgr*
EMP: 27
SALES (corp-wide): 13.6MM **Privately Held**
WEB: www.azoninet.com
SIC: 3087 3599 Custom compound purchased resins; custom machinery
PA: Azon Usa, Inc.
643 W Crosstown Pkwy
Kalamazoo MI 49008
269 385-5942

(G-8692)
B L HARROUN AND SON INC (PA)
1018 Staples Ave (49007-2319)
PHONE 269 345-8657
Willard S Harroun, *President*
Craig Harroun, *Vice Pres*
Todd Harroun, *Treasurer*
Carole Holmes, *Admin Sec*
EMP: 20 **EST:** 1939
SQ FT: 40,000
SALES (est): 6.6MM **Privately Held**
WEB: www.blharroun.com
SIC: 3498 1711 8741 Fabricated pipe & fittings; fire sprinkler system installation; management services

(G-8693)
BECKAN INDUSTRIES INC
2700 N Pitcher St (49004-3490)
PHONE 269 381-6984
Graham Ouding, *President*
EMP: 27 **EST:** 1978
SALES (est): 4.9MM **Privately Held**
SIC: 3599 Machine shop, jobbing & repair

(G-8694)
BECKTOLD ENTERPRISES INC
Also Called: Michigan Power Cleaning
2101 Palmer Ave (49001-4129)
PHONE 269 349-3656
Bryon Becktold, *President*
▲ **EMP:** 5
SQ FT: 3,500
SALES: 800K **Privately Held**
WEB: www.michiganpowercleaning.com
SIC: 3561 5084 Industrial pumps & parts; industrial machinery & equipment

(G-8695)
BELLS BREWERY INC
355 E Kalamazoo Ave (49007-3807)
PHONE 269 382-1402
Jason Reicherts, *Branch Mgr*
EMP: 18
SALES (corp-wide): 19MM **Privately Held**
SIC: 2082 Beer (alcoholic beverage)
PA: Bell's Brewery, Inc.
8690 Krum Ave
Galesburg MI 49053
269 382-2338

(G-8696)
BENSON DISTRIBUTION INC
5792 Stoney Brook Rd (49009-7705)
PHONE 269 344-5529
Chris Benson, *President*
EMP: 4
SALES (est): 336.2K **Privately Held**
SIC: 2711 Newspapers

(G-8697)
BIO KLEEN PRODUCTS INC
810 Lake St (49001-3045)
PHONE 269 567-9400
Tim Kowalski, *President*
Tracy Hall, *Natl Sales Mgr*
▼ **EMP:** 9
SQ FT: 15,000
SALES (est): 825K **Privately Held**
WEB: www.biokleen.com
SIC: 2842 5087 Specialty cleaning preparations; service establishment equipment

(G-8698)
BKM FUELS LLC
5566 Gull Rd (49048-1017)
PHONE 269 342-9576
Robert Willmarth, *Principal*
EMP: 4
SALES (est): 428.6K **Privately Held**
SIC: 2869 Fuels

(G-8699)
BOLD FUSION FABG & CUSTOMS LLC
5383 E Cd Ave (49004-8625)
PHONE 269 345-0681
Joseph Beilby, *Owner*
EMP: 3
SALES (est): 195.1K **Privately Held**
SIC: 3842 Welders' hoods

(G-8700)
BORROUGHS CORPORATION (PA)
3002 N Burdick St (49004-3458)
PHONE 800 748-0227
Tim Tyler, *President*
Zac Sweetland, *Vice Pres*
Greg Worsnop, *VP Opers*
Ted Lyle IV, *Director*
Wanda Myrick, *Director*
◆ **EMP:** 100
SQ FT: 465,000
SALES (est): 51.5MM **Privately Held**
SIC: 2542 Partitions & fixtures, except wood

(G-8701)
BRITISH CNVRTNG SLTNS NRTH AME
259 E Michigan Ave # 305 (49007-3949)
PHONE 281 764-6651
▲ **EMP:** 24 **EST:** 2013
SQ FT: 300
SALES (est): 2.3MM
SALES (corp-wide): 16.9MM **Privately Held**
SIC: 3565 Mfg Packaging Machinery
HQ: British Converting Solutions Limited
Townsend Industrial Estate
Dunstable BEDS LU5 5
152 537-9359

(G-8702)
BUDDY TDA INC
Also Called: T D A
383 E D Ave Ste B (49009-6307)
PHONE 269 349-8105
David A Elliott, *President*
Crystal Lobretto, *Office Mgr*
EMP: 3
SQ FT: 14,000
SALES (est): 447.1K **Privately Held**
WEB: www.tdabuddy.com
SIC: 3545 Tools & accessories for machine tools

(G-8703)
CALCOMCO INC (PA)
5544 S Red Pine Cir (49009-4087)
PHONE 313 885-9228
Edwin Frederickson, *President*
EMP: 7
SALES (est): 12.5MM **Privately Held**
SIC: 2711 Newspapers

(G-8704)
CCO HOLDINGS LLC
2103 Parkview Ave (49008-3925)
PHONE 269 216-6680
EMP: 3
SALES (corp-wide): 43.6B **Publicly Held**
SIC: 5064 4841 3663 3651 Electrical appliances, television & radio; cable & other pay television services; radio & TV communications equipment; household audio & video equipment
HQ: Cco Holdings, Llc
400 Atlantic St
Stamford CT 06901
203 905-7801

(G-8705)
CHALQ LLC
5200 Croyden Ave (49009-3320)
PHONE 269 330-1514
Andy Peninger,
EMP: 3 **EST:** 2014
SALES (est): 90.9K **Privately Held**
SIC: 7372 Application computer software

(G-8706)
CLAUSING INDUSTRIAL INC
Also Called: Clausing Industrial Svc Ctr
3963 Emerald Dr (49001-7923)
PHONE 269 345-7155
Greg Chidister, *Branch Mgr*
EMP: 32
SALES (corp-wide): 29.9MM **Privately Held**
WEB: www.clausing-industrial.com
SIC: 5084 3541 3546 Machine tools & accessories; drill presses; saws & sawing machines; power-driven handtools

Kalamazoo - Kalamazoo County (G-8707) — GEOGRAPHIC SECTION

PA: Clausing Industrial, Inc.
3963 Emerald Dr
Kalamazoo MI 49001
269 345-7155

(G-8707)
CLAUSING INDUSTRIAL INC (PA)
Also Called: Pratt Burnerd America
3963 Emerald Dr (49001-7923)
PHONE..................................269 345-7155
Donald J Haselton, *CEO*
Paul Peters, *District Mgr*
B J Lillibridge, *Vice Pres*
Kevin F Mungovan, *Vice Pres*
Dennis W Pepper, *Vice Pres*
▲ **EMP:** 57
SQ FT: 150,000
SALES (est): 29.9MM **Privately Held**
WEB: www.clausing-industrial.com
SIC: 5084 3541 3546 Machine tools & accessories; drill presses; saws & sawing machines; power-driven handtools

(G-8708)
CLM VIBETECH INC
Also Called: Custom Lining and Molding
7025 E K Ave (49048-6047)
PHONE..................................269 344-3878
William Money, *President*
EMP: 16
SQ FT: 46,000
SALES (est): 3MM **Privately Held**
WEB: www.clmvibetech.com
SIC: 3541 Deburring machines

(G-8709)
COMMERCIAL INDUS A SLTIONS LLC
6830 E Michigan Ave (49048-9532)
PHONE..................................269 373-8797
EMP: 4 **EST:** 2006
SALES (est): 340K **Privately Held**
SIC: 3444 Mfg Sheet Metalwork

(G-8710)
COMMUNITY ACCESS CENTER
359 S Kalamazoo Mall # 300 (49007-4845)
PHONE..................................269 343-2211
Jerry Brown, *Chairman*
Harry Haach, *Exec Dir*
EMP: 15
SQ FT: 5,600
SALES: 674.3K **Privately Held**
SIC: 4841 3663 Cable & other pay television services; studio equipment, radio & television broadcasting

(G-8711)
COMPLETE METAL FINISHING INC
4301 Manchester Rd Ste A (49001-0833)
PHONE..................................269 343-0500
Ken Matheis, *President*
Partrick Greene, *Vice Pres*
EMP: 10
SALES (est): 1.2MM **Privately Held**
SIC: 3471 Finishing, metals or formed products

(G-8712)
COMSTOCK CREAMERY LLC
6086 E Michigan Ave (49048-6017)
PHONE..................................269 929-7693
Serih Smelker, *Mng Member*
EMP: 4
SQ FT: 3,200
SALES (est): 116.1K **Privately Held**
SIC: 2024 2064 Ice cream & frozen desserts; candy bars, including chocolate covered bars

(G-8713)
CONSORT CORPORATION (PA)
Also Called: Consort Display Group
2129 Portage St (49001-6145)
PHONE..................................269 388-4532
Roger M Lepley, *President*
Steven Hanson, *Mfg Staff*
Judy Little, *Cust Mgr*
Kathleen Barkley, *Sales Staff*
Corey Rolfe, *Sales Staff*
EMP: 24
SQ FT: 13,500
SALES (est): 3.9MM **Privately Held**
WEB: www.consort.com
SIC: 2399 3429 3993 2599 Banners, made from fabric; metal fasteners; signs & advertising specialties; factory furniture & fixtures

(G-8714)
CONSUMERS CONCRETE CORP
3809 E Michigan Ave (49048-2417)
P.O. Box 2229 (49003-2229)
PHONE..................................269 384-0977
Tom W Thomas, *President*
Stephen A Thomas, *Vice Pres*
Randy Parsons, *Purch Mgr*
Gregory Thomas, *Treasurer*
Patrick Cook, *Technical Staff*
EMP: 40
SQ FT: 4,000
SALES (est): 4.3MM
SALES (corp-wide): 102.9MM **Privately Held**
WEB: www.consumersconcrete.com
SIC: 3271 3273 Blocks, concrete or cinder: standard; ready-mixed concrete
PA: Consumers Concrete Corporation
3508 S Sprinkle Rd
Kalamazoo MI 49001
269 342-0136

(G-8715)
CONSUMERS CONCRETE CORPORATION (PA)
Also Called: Consumers Sand & Gravel Co
3508 S Sprinkle Rd (49001-0813)
P.O. Box 2229 (49003-2229)
PHONE..................................269 342-0136
Stephen A Thomas, *President*
Steve Thomas, *President*
Josh Wooden, *General Mgr*
Tom W Thomas, *Chairman*
Holly Statler, *Vice Pres*
EMP: 21
SQ FT: 12,000
SALES (est): 102.9MM **Privately Held**
WEB: www.consumersconcrete.com
SIC: 3273 3271 5032 Ready-mixed concrete; blocks, concrete or cinder: standard; gravel; sand, construction

(G-8716)
CONSUMERS CONCRETE CORPORATION
700 Nazareth Rd (49048-1100)
P.O. Box 2229 (49003-2229)
PHONE..................................269 342-5983
Ken Baker, *Manager*
EMP: 15
SALES (corp-wide): 102.9MM **Privately Held**
WEB: www.consumersconcrete.com
SIC: 3273 Ready-mixed concrete
PA: Consumers Concrete Corporation
3508 S Sprinkle Rd
Kalamazoo MI 49001
269 342-0136

(G-8717)
COOPER FOUNDRY INC
8216 Douglas Ave (49009-5255)
PHONE..................................269 343-2808
David Hollerbach, *President*
EMP: 11
SQ FT: 18,000
SALES (est): 1.8MM **Privately Held**
WEB: www.cooperfoundry.com
SIC: 3364 3363 Brass & bronze die-castings; aluminum die-castings

(G-8718)
CORNERS LIMITED (PA)
Also Called: Esto Connectors
628 S 8th St (49009-8041)
PHONE..................................269 353-8311
James J Pestoor, *President*
Grace Pestoor, *Vice Pres*
EMP: 8 **EST:** 1981
SALES (est): 1MM **Privately Held**
WEB: www.cornerslimited.com
SIC: 3496 Cages, wire; shelving, made from purchased wire

(G-8719)
CORPORATE COLORS INC
3638 Miller Rd Ste A (49001-4656)
PHONE..................................269 323-2000
Allen Harris, *President*
EMP: 3
SQ FT: 1,800
SALES: 300K **Privately Held**
SIC: 2759 7299 Screen printing; stitching services

(G-8720)
COXLINE INC
Also Called: Wellsaw
2829 N Burdick St (49004-3457)
PHONE..................................269 345-1132
Robert Boyle, *President*
Mary Gucma, *Principal*
Delores Boyle, *Corp Secy*
Daniel Truskowski, *Vice Pres*
EMP: 20
SALES (est): 5MM **Privately Held**
WEB: www.wellsaw.com
SIC: 3553 3444 3546 Bandsaws, woodworking; metal housings, enclosures, casings & other containers; saws & sawing equipment

(G-8721)
CUMMINS LABEL COMPANY
2230 Glendenning Rd (49001-4115)
PHONE..................................269 345-3386
Phil Nagle, *President*
Debbie Hamming, *Corp Secy*
EMP: 21
SQ FT: 26,000
SALES (est): 3.1MM **Privately Held**
WEB: www.cumminslabel.com
SIC: 2759 2671 2672 Flexographic printing; packaging paper & plastics film, coated & laminated; coated & laminated paper

(G-8722)
CYTEC INDUSTRIES INC
3115 Miller Rd (49001-4103)
PHONE..................................269 349-6677
Ed Elsinore, *Branch Mgr*
EMP: 115
SALES (corp-wide): 12.8MM **Privately Held**
SIC: 2899 2821 2824 2672 Chemical preparations; plastics materials & resins; acrylic fibers; adhesive backed films, foams & foils; industrial inorganic chemicals; aerospace castings, aluminum
HQ: Cytec Industries Inc.
4500 Mcginnis Ferry Rd
Alpharetta GA 30005

(G-8723)
DAVIS STEEL RULE DIE
2222 Glendenning Rd 9b (49001-4159)
PHONE..................................269 492-9908
Mike Davis, *Owner*
EMP: 5
SALES (est): 474.4K **Privately Held**
WEB: www.davissteelruledie.com
SIC: 3544 Special dies & tools

(G-8724)
DEKOFF & SONS INC
Also Called: D & D Printing
2531 Azo Dr (49048-9540)
PHONE..................................269 344-5816
John Dekoff, *President*
John De Koff, *President*
EMP: 5
SQ FT: 4,000
SALES (est): 813.1K **Privately Held**
WEB: www.danddprinting.com
SIC: 2752 2759 2791 Commercial printing, offset; letterpress printing; typesetting

(G-8725)
DIAGNOSTIC SYSTEMS ASSOCIATION
6190 Technology Ave (49009-8179)
P.O. Box 467, Oshtemo (49077-0467)
PHONE..................................269 544-9000
Robert Mitchell, *President*
EMP: 10
SQ FT: 10,000
SALES (est): 1.2MM **Privately Held**
SIC: 7549 3825 Emissions testing without repairs, automotive; engine electrical test equipment

(G-8726)
DIAMOND GRAPHICS INC
2328 Lake St (49048-3270)
PHONE..................................269 345-1164
Fax: 269 345-3026
EMP: 6 **EST:** 1975
SQ FT: 4,230
SALES (est): 540K **Privately Held**
SIC: 2796 Mfg Engraved Printing Plates

(G-8727)
DIGITAL IMPACT DESIGN INC
Also Called: Fastsigns
403 Balch St (49001-2769)
PHONE..................................269 337-4200
Steve Trottier, *President*
Matt Trottier, *General Mgr*
Dee Trottier, *Corp Secy*
EMP: 5 **EST:** 1998
SQ FT: 2,400
SALES: 320K **Privately Held**
SIC: 3993 Signs & advertising specialties

(G-8728)
DIMPLEX THERMAL SOLUTIONS INC (HQ)
2625 Emerald Dr (49001-4542)
PHONE..................................269 349-6800
William Bohr, *President*
Kristin Anderson, *Vice Pres*
Keith Roberts, *Vice Pres*
Howard Barnes, *Buyer*
Todd Arndt, *Engineer*
▲ **EMP:** 183
SALES (est): 37.5MM
SALES (corp-wide): 4.1MM **Privately Held**
WEB: www.koolant.com
SIC: 3585 Refrigeration & heating equipment
PA: Glen Dimplex Unlimited Company
Old Airport Road
Dublin
185 234-00

(G-8729)
DMS ELECTRIC APPARATUS SERVICE
630 Gibson St (49007-4921)
P.O. Box 50644 (49005-0644)
PHONE..................................269 349-7000
Tim Fielding, *CEO*
EMP: 32 **EST:** 1950
SQ FT: 35,000
SALES (est): 9.4MM **Privately Held**
WEB: www.teamdms.net
SIC: 5063 7694 3599 3621 Motors, electric; electric motor repair; machine shop, jobbing & repair; motors & generators

(G-8730)
DN-LAWRENCE INDUSTRIES INC
423 Walbridge St (49007-3625)
P.O. Box 141, Plainwell (49080-0141)
PHONE..................................269 552-4999
Ruth Lovelace Murphy, *President*
Michael Lovelace, *Treasurer*
EMP: 13 **EST:** 1964
SQ FT: 12,000
SALES (est): 1.1MM **Privately Held**
SIC: 3471 Plating of metals or formed products; polishing, metals or formed products

(G-8731)
DOMER INDUSTRIES LLC
Also Called: Agio Imaging
3434 S Burdick St (49001-4836)
PHONE..................................269 226-4000
Robert Lihosit, *President*
Jonathan Rykse, *Vice Pres*
Marc Androsky, *Accounts Exec*
Kip Dice, *Accounts Exec*
Ryan Herder, *Accounts Exec*
EMP: 14
SQ FT: 11,000
SALES (est): 2.5MM **Privately Held**
WEB: www.agioimaging.com
SIC: 2759 7336 Screen printing; commercial art & graphic design

(G-8732)
DUNKLEY INTERNATIONAL INC
1910 Lake St (49001-3274)
PHONE..................................269 343-5583

GEOGRAPHIC SECTION

Kalamazoo - Kalamazoo County (G-8757)

Richard L Bogard, *President*
Nick Hatzinikolis, *General Mgr*
EMP: 115
SQ FT: 36,400
SALES (est): 19.3MM
SALES (corp-wide): 133MM **Privately Held**
WEB: www.dunkleyinternational.com
SIC: 3556 3535 Juice extractors, fruit & vegetable: commercial type; conveyors & conveying equipment
PA: Cherry Central Cooperative, Inc.
1771 N Us 31 S
Traverse City MI 49685
231 946-1860

(G-8733)
ELENBAAS HARDWOOD INCORPORATED
3751 Alvan Rd (49001-4652)
PHONE.................................269 343-7791
Craig Dobbs, *Manager*
EMP: 5
SALES (corp-wide): 1.7MM **Privately Held**
SIC: 2431 Moldings, wood: unfinished & prefinished
PA: Elenbaas Hardwood, Incorporated
2363 Port Sheldon Ct
Jenison MI 49428
616 669-3085

(G-8734)
ELITE TOOLING LLC
Also Called: Elite Tooling Aerospace
3816 Miller Rd (49001-4637)
PHONE.................................269 383-9714
Shane Smith,
EMP: 6
SALES: 1.2MM **Privately Held**
SIC: 3541 3812 Machine tools, metal cutting type; acceleration indicators & systems components, aerospace

(G-8735)
ELKAY INDUSTRIES INC
Also Called: Elkay Fastening Systems
1804 Reed Ave (49001-4049)
PHONE.................................269 381-4266
Shirley A Knapp, *President*
Roger Knapp, *Vice Pres*
EMP: 14
SQ FT: 50,000
SALES (est): 2.4MM **Privately Held**
SIC: 5072 3965 Miscellaneous fasteners; rivets; washers (hardware); screws; fasteners

(G-8736)
EMERGENCY VEHICLE PRODUCTS
2975 Interstate Pkwy (49048-9600)
PHONE.................................269 342-0973
Craig McDonald, *President*
EMP: 3
SALES (est): 361.5K **Privately Held**
SIC: 3714 Motor vehicle parts & accessories

(G-8737)
ENCORE PUBLISHING GROUP INC
Also Called: Encore Magazine
350 S Kalamazoo Mall # 214 (49007-4820)
PHONE.................................269 383-4433
Richard Briscoe, *President*
EMP: 3
SALES (est): 287.6K **Privately Held**
WEB: www.encorekalamazoo.com
SIC: 2741 Miscellaneous publishing

(G-8738)
ENERGY SUPPLIERS LLC
Also Called: Michigan Biofuels
2813 W Main St (49006-2901)
PHONE.................................269 342-9482
Mark Meulendyk,
EMP: 10
SQ FT: 5,000
SALES: 1.6MM **Privately Held**
SIC: 3559 Refinery, chemical processing & similar machinery

(G-8739)
ENVIRODYNE TECHNOLOGIES INC (HQ)
Also Called: Kalamazoo Fabricating
7574 E Michigan Ave (49048-9531)
P.O. Box 2121 (49003-2121)
PHONE.................................269 342-1918
Tim Hanna, *President*
Jarrod Herington, *Mfg Spvr*
▲ **EMP:** 28
SQ FT: 30,000
SALES: 8MM
SALES (corp-wide): 40.9MM **Privately Held**
WEB: www.kalfab.com
SIC: 3444 Sheet metalwork
PA: Kalamazoo Manufacturing Corporation Global
5944 E N Ave
Kalamazoo MI 49048
269 382-8200

(G-8740)
FABRI-KAL CORPORATION
4141 Manchester Rd (49001-1893)
PHONE.................................269 385-5050
Rick Collins, *Principal*
Craig Bashore, *Vice Pres*
Tom Bush, *Vice Pres*
David Schaller, *Engineer*
Laura Cochran, *Credit Staff*
EMP: 20
SALES (corp-wide): 372.3MM **Privately Held**
SIC: 3089 Thermoformed finished plastic products
HQ: Fabri-Kal Corporation
600 Plastics Pl
Kalamazoo MI 49001
269 385-5050

(G-8741)
FABRICATED FLEX & HOSE SUP INC
2037 Palmer Ave (49001-4162)
PHONE.................................269 342-2221
Craig Williams, *President*
Dennis Munson, *Corp Secy*
Dina Hershberger, *Administration*
EMP: 7
SQ FT: 4,000
SALES (est): 1.4MM **Privately Held**
WEB: www.fabflexhose.com
SIC: 3052 Rubber & plastics hose & beltings

(G-8742)
FERNAND CORPORATION
Also Called: Comfoot Shoes
326 W Kalamazoo Ave # 105 (49007-3388)
PHONE.................................231 882-9622
Steven Fernand, *President*
EMP: 4
SALES (est): 405.2K **Privately Held**
WEB: www.fernandfootwear.com
SIC: 3021 Shoes, rubber or plastic molded to fabric

(G-8743)
FIBERS OF KALAMAZOO INC
436 W Willard St Ste A (49007-3369)
P.O. Box 51028 (49005-1028)
PHONE.................................269 344-3122
Robert Boyle, *CEO*
William Boyle, *President*
Buddy Peterson, *President*
Colin Raymond, *Chairman*
Mike Horton, *Vice Pres*
EMP: 40 EST: 1981
SQ FT: 92,680
SALES (est): 10.4MM **Privately Held**
WEB: www.fibersofkzoo.com
SIC: 2679 5113 Paper products, converted; industrial & personal service paper

(G-8744)
FLARE FITTINGS INCORPORATED
2980 Interstate Pkwy (49048-9600)
PHONE.................................269 344-7600
Bernard F Havlock, *President*
Mary Ann Havlock, *Treasurer*
▲ **EMP:** 33
SQ FT: 18,000
SALES (est): 7.2MM **Privately Held**
WEB: www.flarefittings.com
SIC: 3364 5941 Brass & bronze die-castings; sporting goods & bicycle shops

(G-8745)
FLINT GROUP US LLC
Also Called: Flint Ink North America Div
2309 N Burdick St (49007-1876)
PHONE.................................269 381-1955
John Croskey, *Principal*
EMP: 20
SALES (corp-wide): 177.9K **Privately Held**
WEB: www.flintink.com
SIC: 2893 Printing ink
HQ: Flint Group Us Llc
17177 N Laurel Park Dr # 300
Livonia MI 48152
734 781-4600

(G-8746)
FLOWSERVE US INC
2100 Factory St (49001-4161)
PHONE.................................269 381-2650
Tyler Harden, *District Mgr*
Cory Griffin, *Project Mgr*
Tom Pawlak, *Project Mgr*
Ron Klatt, *Facilities Mgr*
Lance Rome, *Mfg Spvr*
EMP: 250
SALES (corp-wide): 3.8B **Publicly Held**
SIC: 3053 Gaskets, packing & sealing devices
HQ: Flowserve Us Inc.
5215 N Oconnor Blvd Ste Connor
Irving TX 75039
972 443-6500

(G-8747)
FORREST COMPANY
7877 N 12th St (49009-9084)
PHONE.................................269 384-6120
Jann Forrest, *President*
EMP: 7
SQ FT: 4,500
SALES: 600K **Privately Held**
SIC: 3544 Special dies & tools

(G-8748)
GENCO ALLIANCE LLC
630 Gibson St (49007-4921)
PHONE.................................269 216-5500
Douglas Gipson, *CEO*
Timothy Fielding, *COO*
▲ **EMP:** 33
SQ FT: 60,000
SALES (est): 2.4MM **Privately Held**
SIC: 5063 3621 3441 7629 Electrical apparatus & equipment; motors & generators; fabricated structural metal; electrical repair shops

(G-8749)
GENERAL MILLS INC
6805 Beatrice Dr (49009-9559)
PHONE.................................763 764-7600
Steve Pearcowski, *Branch Mgr*
EMP: 100
SALES (corp-wide): 16.8B **Publicly Held**
WEB: www.generalmills.com
SIC: 2043 Cereal breakfast foods
PA: General Mills, Inc.
1 General Mills Blvd
Minneapolis MN 55426
763 764-7600

(G-8750)
GENERAL MILLS INC
3800 Midlink Dr (49048-8802)
PHONE.................................269 337-0288
Edith Tuddel, *Manager*
EMP: 5
SALES (corp-wide): 16.8B **Publicly Held**
WEB: www.generalmills.com
SIC: 5143 2041 4225 Yogurt; flour mixes; general warehousing & storage
PA: General Mills, Inc.
1 General Mills Blvd
Minneapolis MN 55426
763 764-7600

(G-8751)
GENX CORPORATION
2911 Emerald Dr (49001-4530)
PHONE.................................269 341-4242
Russ Ureel, *President*
EMP: 4
SALES (est): 392.3K **Privately Held**
SIC: 3827 Optical comparators

(G-8752)
GETECHA INC
2914 Business One Dr (49048-8719)
PHONE.................................269 373-8896
Chris Koffend, *President*
▲ **EMP:** 6
SQ FT: 18,000
SALES: 1.7MM
SALES (corp-wide): 9.5MM **Privately Held**
WEB: www.getechaus.com
SIC: 3589 Shredders, industrial & commercial
PA: Getecha Gmbh
Am Gemeindegraben 13
Aschaffenburg 63741
602 184-000

(G-8753)
GLASSMASTER CONTROLS CO INC
831 Cobb Ave (49007-2444)
PHONE.................................269 382-2010
Steven Trewhella, *President*
Wayne Nicolen, *General Mgr*
Andrew Cook, *IT/INT Sup*
Melinda Vanmeter, *Executive*
▲ **EMP:** 45
SQ FT: 90,000
SALES (est): 11.4MM **Privately Held**
WEB: www.glassmaster.com
SIC: 3496 3812 3714 3672 Miscellaneous fabricated wire products; search & navigation equipment; motor vehicle parts & accessories; printed circuit boards; relays & industrial controls; nonferrous wire-drawing & insulating

(G-8754)
GRAPHIC PACKAGING INTL LLC
1500 N Pitcher St (49007-2539)
PHONE.................................269 383-5000
Andy Black, *Opers Mgr*
Sue Dehollander, *Buyer*
Diana Sackrider, *Buyer*
Rusty Miller, *VP Engrg*
Manny Garza, *Project Engr*
EMP: 100 **Publicly Held**
SIC: 2631 Paperboard mills
HQ: Graphic Packaging International, Llc
1500 Riveredge Pkwy # 100
Atlanta GA 30328

(G-8755)
GRAPHIC PACKAGING INTL LLC
1421 N Pitcher St (49007-2579)
PHONE.................................269 343-6104
Rob Bradsher, *Plant Mgr*
Gary Ingersoll, *Maint Spvr*
Brian Gwin, *Sales Staff*
Gary Leeman, *Branch Mgr*
EMP: 409 **Publicly Held**
SIC: 2631 Paperboard mills
HQ: Graphic Packaging International, Llc
1500 Riveredge Pkwy # 100
Atlanta GA 30328

(G-8756)
GRAPHICS & PRINTING CO INC
5356 N Riverview Dr (49004-1543)
PHONE.................................269 381-1482
Gayle Bullard, *President*
Larry Bullard, *Admin Sec*
EMP: 6
SQ FT: 3,000
SALES (est): 569.7K **Privately Held**
SIC: 2752 Commercial printing, offset

(G-8757)
GREEN BAY PACKAGING INC
Kalamazoo Container Division
5350 E N Ave (49048-9776)
P.O. Box 3007 (49003-3007)
PHONE.................................269 552-1000
Dean Murphy, *General Mgr*
Loren Smith, *Human Res Mgr*
EMP: 140

Kalamazoo - Kalamazoo County (G-8758)   GEOGRAPHIC SECTION

SALES (corp-wide): 1.2B **Privately Held**
WEB: www.gbp.com
SIC: 2653 3412 Boxes, corrugated: made from purchased materials; metal barrels, drums & pails
PA: Green Bay Packaging Inc.
1700 N Webster Ave
Green Bay WI 54302
920 433-5111

(G-8758)
GREEN LINK INC
5519 E Cork St Ste A (49048-8634)
PHONE......................................269 216-9229
Phillip Georgeau, *CEO*
EMP: 10
SALES (est): 545.3K **Privately Held**
SIC: 2952 Roofing materials

(G-8759)
HAMMOND MACHINERY INC
1600 Douglas Ave (49007-1630)
PHONE......................................269 345-7151
Robert E Hammond, *President*
EMP: 78
SQ FT: 145,000
SALES (est): 14.9MM
SALES (corp-wide): 29.8MM **Privately Held**
SIC: 3541 3564 3291 Deburring machines; grinding machines, metalworking; buffing & polishing machines; robots for drilling, cutting, grinding, polishing, etc.; dust or fume collecting equipment, industrial; abrasive products
PA: The Kalamazoo Company
1600 Douglas Ave
Kalamazoo MI 49007
269 345-7151

(G-8760)
HAPMAN
6002 E N Ave (49048-9775)
PHONE......................................269 343-1675
Ned Thompson, *Owner*
EMP: 14 **EST:** 2014
SALES (est): 2.7MM **Privately Held**
SIC: 3535 Conveyors & conveying equipment

(G-8761)
HARRISON PACKING CO INC (PA)
3420 Stadium Pkwy (49009-6767)
PHONE......................................269 381-3837
Rush Harrison, *President*
Bradley Harrison, *Admin Sec*
EMP: 15
SQ FT: 40,000
SALES (est): 2.1MM **Privately Held**
WEB: www.harrisonpacking.com
SIC: 2035 Pickles, vinegar; vegetables, pickled

(G-8762)
HECO INC
Also Called: Hatfield Electric Industrial
3509 S Burdick St (49001-4835)
PHONE......................................269 381-7200
Terrell Lee Hatfield, *Ch of Bd*
Mark S Hatfield, *President*
Joyce Hatfield, *Principal*
Kathy Bishop, *Vice Pres*
Brad S Hatfield, *Vice Pres*
EMP: 55 **EST:** 1959
SQ FT: 80,000
SALES (est): 49.8MM **Privately Held**
SIC: 5063 7694 3699 3677 Motors, electric; armature rewinding shops; electric motor repair; electrical equipment & supplies; electronic coils, transformers & other inductors; motors & generators; scales & balances, except laboratory

(G-8763)
HELIOS SOLAR LLC
248 W Michigan Ave (49007-3735)
PHONE......................................269 343-5581
Connor Field, *CEO*
Samuel Field, *CFO*
EMP: 4 **EST:** 2009
SALES: 1MM **Privately Held**
SIC: 8711 3674 Engineering services; solar cells

(G-8764)
HERALD NEWSPAPERS COMPANY INC
Also Called: Kalamazoo Gazette
6825 Beatrice Dr Ste C (49009-7263)
PHONE......................................269 345-3511
Jim Stephanak, *Manager*
EMP: 241
SALES (corp-wide): 5.5B **Privately Held**
WEB: www.post-standard.com
SIC: 2711 Newspapers, publishing & printing
HQ: The Herald Newspapers Company Inc
220 S Warren St
Syracuse NY 13202
315 470-0011

(G-8765)
HERALD NEWSPAPERS COMPANY INC
423 S Burdick St (49007-5217)
PHONE......................................269 373-7100
Michael Castranova, *Branch Mgr*
EMP: 20
SALES (corp-wide): 5.5B **Privately Held**
WEB: www.post-standard.com
SIC: 2711 Newspapers: publishing only, not printed on site
HQ: The Herald Newspapers Company Inc
220 S Warren St
Syracuse NY 13202
315 470-0011

(G-8766)
HERALD NEWSPAPERS COMPANY INC
Also Called: Kalamazoo Gazette
401 S Burdick St (49007-6215)
PHONE......................................269 388-8501
EMP: 100
SALES (corp-wide): 2B **Privately Held**
SIC: 2711 Newspapers-Publishing/Printing
HQ: The Herald Newspapers Company Inc
1 Clinton Sq
Syracuse NY 13202
315 470-0011

(G-8767)
HERCULES LLC
5325 Autumn Glen St (49009-8184)
P.O. Box 118 (49004-0118)
PHONE......................................269 388-8676
John Prevost, *Branch Mgr*
EMP: 75
SALES (corp-wide): 3.7B **Publicly Held**
WEB: www.herc.com
SIC: 2869 2899 Chemical warfare gases: phosgene, mustard gas, tear gas; chemical preparations
HQ: Hercules Llc
500 Hercules Rd
Wilmington DE 19808
302 594-5000

(G-8768)
HERITAGE GUITAR INC
225 Parsons St Ste 286 (49007-3593)
PHONE......................................269 385-5721
J P Moats, *President*
Daniel Struve, *Opers Mgr*
Bill Paige, *Treasurer*
James Deurloo, *Shareholder*
Marvin Lamb, *Shareholder*
EMP: 17
SQ FT: 22,000
SALES (est): 2.2MM **Privately Held**
SIC: 3931 5736 Fretted instruments & parts; guitars & parts, electric & nonelectric; mandolins & parts; banjos & parts; musical instrument stores

(G-8769)
HIGH GRADE MATERIALS COMPANY
2700 E Cork St (49001-4648)
PHONE......................................269 349-8222
Wyatt Brown, *Executive*
EMP: 15
SALES (corp-wide): 28.3MM **Privately Held**
SIC: 3273 Ready-mixed concrete
PA: High Grade Materials Company
9266 Snows Lake Rd
Greenville MI 48885
616 754-5545

(G-8770)
HUMPHREY PRODUCTS COMPANY (PA)
5070 E N Ave (49048-9785)
P.O. Box 2008 (49003-2008)
PHONE......................................269 381-5500
Robert P Humphrey, *Ch of Bd*
David A Maurer, *President*
Scott Ludwig, *Facilities Mgr*
Torok Joeseph, *Buyer*
Deron Kaczorowski, *Technical Mgr*
▲ EMP: 225 **EST:** 1901
SQ FT: 150,000
SALES: 34MM **Privately Held**
WEB: www.humphrey-products.com
SIC: 3492 Control valves, fluid power: hydraulic & pneumatic

(G-8771)
HYCORR LLC
3654 Midlink Dr (49048-8806)
PHONE......................................269 381-6349
Robert Shafer, *President*
Lance Head, *Director*
EMP: 16 **EST:** 2012
SALES (est): 3MM **Privately Held**
SIC: 3554 7336 Paper mill machinery: plating, slitting, waxing, etc.; graphic arts & related design

(G-8772)
HYDRO EXTRUSION NORTH AMER LLC
Sapa Kalamazoo
5575 N Riverview Dr (49004-1547)
PHONE......................................269 349-6626
Samone Harper, *Safety Mgr*
Sat Adufumill, *Manager*
EMP: 300
SALES (corp-wide): 18.9B **Privately Held**
WEB: www.hydroaluminumna.com
SIC: 3354 3444 Aluminum extruded products; sheet metalwork
HQ: Hydro Extrusion North America, Llc
6250 N River Rd
Rosemont IL 60018
877 710-7272

(G-8773)
INTERKAL LLC (DH)
5981 E Cork St (49048-9638)
P.O. Box 2107 (49003-2107)
PHONE......................................269 349-1521
Dave Petersen, *Plant Mgr*
Bob Mihelich, *Materials Mgr*
Brian Ellis, *Traffic Mgr*
Ken Sipes, *Parts Mgr*
Curt Finch, *Purch Agent*
◆ EMP: 102 **EST:** 1958
SQ FT: 190,000
SALES (est): 20.5MM **Privately Held**
WEB: www.interkal.com
SIC: 2531 Stadium seating
HQ: Kotocorp (Usa), Inc.
5981 E Cork St
Kalamazoo MI 49048
269 349-1521

(G-8774)
INTERSRCE RECOVERY SYSTEMS INC (PA)
1470 S 8th St (49009-9327)
PHONE......................................269 375-5100
William D Nemedi, *President*
Robert J Nemedi, *Treasurer*
EMP: 25
SALES (est): 2.4MM **Privately Held**
WEB: www.inter-source.com
SIC: 3569 3535 Lubricating equipment; unit handling conveying systems

(G-8775)
INVITATIONS BY DESIGN
223 S Kalamazoo Mall (49007-4812)
PHONE......................................269 342-8551
Patrica Hirsch, *Mng Member*
EMP: 4
SALES (est): 229.9K **Privately Held**
SIC: 2759 Invitation & stationery printing & engraving

(G-8776)
J STERLING INDUSTRIES LLC
6825 Beatrice Dr Ste A (49009-7263)
PHONE......................................269 492-6922

David Van Slingerland, *CEO*
Libni Cano, *QC Mgr*
Tara Vandestreek, *Accounts Mgr*
EMP: 15
SQ FT: 30,000
SALES (est): 3.6MM **Privately Held**
SIC: 3841 Medical instruments & equipment, blood & bone work

(G-8777)
JBT BOTTLING LLC
8322 Waterwood Dr (49048-4832)
PHONE......................................269 377-4905
Nelson H Tansey, *President*
EMP: 3
SALES (est): 136.2K **Privately Held**
SIC: 2086 Bottled & canned soft drinks

(G-8778)
JIRGENS MODERN TOOL CORP
3536 Gembrit Cir (49001-4616)
PHONE......................................269 381-5588
Maija Jirgens, *President*
EMP: 10
SQ FT: 10,000
SALES (est): 1.3MM **Privately Held**
WEB: www.jirgensmoderntoolcorp.com
SIC: 3544 Special dies & tools

(G-8779)
JK MACHINING INC
5955 W D Ave (49009-9012)
PHONE......................................269 344-0870
Henry Kalkman, *President*
EMP: 16
SQ FT: 6,125
SALES: 2.5MM **Privately Held**
WEB: www.jkmachining.com
SIC: 3089 Injection molding of plastics

(G-8780)
JOHN L HINKLE HOLDING CO INC
1206 E Crosstown Pkwy (49001-2563)
P.O. Box 2153 (49003-2153)
PHONE......................................269 344-3640
John Hinkle, *President*
◆ EMP: 20 **EST:** 1941
SQ FT: 10,000
SALES (est): 3.3MM **Privately Held**
WEB: www.nationalflavors.com
SIC: 2087 Extracts, flavoring

(G-8781)
JOHNSON CONTROLS INC
7684 N Sprinkle Rd (49004)
PHONE......................................269 323-0988
Scott Dixon, *Branch Mgr*
EMP: 22 **Privately Held**
SIC: 2531 Seats, automobile
HQ: Johnson Controls, Inc.
5757 N Green Bay Ave
Milwaukee WI 53209
414 524-1200

(G-8782)
JUNKLESS FOODS INC
5782 Hyde Park Ave (49009-4128)
PHONE......................................616 560-7895
Laurence Beyer, *CEO*
EMP: 3
SALES (est): 227.3K **Privately Held**
SIC: 2064 Breakfast bars

(G-8783)
KAISER ALUMINUM CORPORATION
5205 Midlink Dr (49048-9648)
PHONE......................................269 488-0957
Charles Eyster, *Buyer*
Kathy Ankney, *Human Resources*
EMP: 18
SALES (corp-wide): 1.5B **Publicly Held**
SIC: 3354 Aluminum extruded products
PA: Kaiser Aluminum Corporation
27422 Portola Pkwy # 350
Foothill Ranch CA 92610
949 614-1740

(G-8784)
KAISER ALUMINUM FAB PDTS LLC
5205 Kaiser Dr (49048-8804)
PHONE......................................269 250-8400
EMP: 51

GEOGRAPHIC SECTION

Kalamazoo - Kalamazoo County (G-8811)

SALES (corp-wide): 1.5B **Publicly Held**
SIC: 3334 3353 3354 Primary aluminum; aluminum sheet, plate & foil; aluminum rod & bar
HQ: Kaiser Aluminum Fabricated Products, Llc
27422 Portola Pkwy # 200
Foothill Ranch CA 92610

(G-8785)
KALAMAZOO CANDLE COMPANY
5111 E Ml Ave Ste A15 (49048-8581)
PHONE..................................269 532-9816
Adam McFarlin,
EMP: 10
SALES (est): 283.1K **Privately Held**
SIC: 3999 Candles

(G-8786)
KALAMAZOO COMPANY (PA)
Also Called: Hammound Roto-Finish
1600 Douglas Ave (49007-1630)
PHONE..................................269 345-7151
Robert E Hammond, *President*
Brenda Long, *General Mgr*
EMP: 50
SQ FT: 115,000
SALES (est): 29.8MM **Privately Held**
WEB: www.hammondmach.com
SIC: 3541 5085 3291 Deburring machines; grinding machines, metalworking; buffing & polishing machines; robots for drilling, cutting, grinding, polishing, etc.; abrasives; abrasive products

(G-8787)
KALAMAZOO DENTAL SUPPLY
710 Gibson St (49007-4923)
PHONE..................................269 345-0260
Gary Gray, *Owner*
EMP: 3
SQ FT: 17,000
SALES (est): 1MM **Privately Held**
SIC: 5047 3843 Dental equipment & supplies; dental equipment; dental chairs; dental laboratory equipment

(G-8788)
KALAMAZOO ELECTRIC MOTOR INC
414 Mills St (49001-2529)
PHONE..................................269 345-7802
Kristen Salvesen, *President*
Rick Curtis, *Manager*
EMP: 5
SQ FT: 5,880
SALES (est): 550K **Privately Held**
SIC: 5999 5251 7694 5063 Motors, electric; hardware; tools, hand; electric motor repair; motors, electric

(G-8789)
KALAMAZOO HOLDINGS INC (PA)
Also Called: Kalazack
3713 W Main St (49006-2842)
P.O. Box 50511 (49005-0511)
PHONE..................................269 349-9711
George Todd, *President*
Paul Todd, *Chairman*
Gary Hainrihar, *Vice Pres*
Donn Baird, *Treasurer*
◆ **EMP:** 4
SQ FT: 85,000
SALES (est): 82.2MM **Privately Held**
SIC: 2099 Spices, including grinding

(G-8790)
KALAMAZOO MECHANICAL INC
Also Called: Honeywell Authorized Dealer
5507 E Cork St (49048-9668)
PHONE..................................269 343-5351
Irving Cornish, *President*
Carson Cornish, *Vice Pres*
EMP: 19
SQ FT: 6,500
SALES: 7.5MM **Privately Held**
SIC: 1761 1711 3444 Sheet metalwork; warm air heating & air conditioning contractor; sheet metalwork

(G-8791)
KALAMAZOO METAL FINISHERS INC
2019 Glendenning Rd (49001-4112)
P.O. Box 2650 (49003-2650)
PHONE..................................269 382-1611
Lisa Halliday, *CEO*
Richard Halliday, *President*
EMP: 15
SQ FT: 22,000
SALES (est): 2.6MM **Privately Held**
SIC: 3471 Electroplating of metals or formed products

(G-8792)
KALAMAZOO MFG CORP GLOBL (PA)
Also Called: Prab
5944 E N Ave (49048-9776)
P.O. Box 2121 (49003-2121)
PHONE..................................269 382-8200
Edward Thompson, *President*
Robert W Klinge, *CFO*
EMP: 128
SALES (est): 40.9MM **Privately Held**
SIC: 3535 5084 Conveyors & conveying equipment; industrial machinery & equipment

(G-8793)
KALAMAZOO ORTHOTICS & DBTC
Also Called: Corey's Bootery
1016 E Cork St (49001-4823)
PHONE..................................269 349-2247
James F Bloomfield III, *President*
Craig Corey, *Executive*
EMP: 10
SQ FT: 1,200
SALES (est): 1MM **Privately Held**
SIC: 3143 5139 5661 Orthopedic shoes, men's; shoes; custom & orthopedic shoes

(G-8794)
KALAMAZOO PHOTO COMP SVCS
Also Called: Kpc Graphics
701 Commerce Ln (49004-1128)
P.O. Box 614, Richland (49083-0614)
PHONE..................................269 345-3706
Judy Appelgren, *President*
EMP: 30
SQ FT: 6,600
SALES (est): 2.4MM **Privately Held**
SIC: 2791 7336 2796 Typesetting; graphic arts & related design; platemaking services

(G-8795)
KALAMAZOO PLASTICS COMPANY
3723 Songbird Ln (49008-3358)
PHONE..................................269 381-0010
Ted Hartridge, *CEO*
Mellisa Hartridge, *President*
EMP: 20
SALES (est): 1.6MM **Privately Held**
WEB: www.kalamazooplastics.com
SIC: 3086 Packaging & shipping materials, foamed plastic

(G-8796)
KALAMAZOO PROMISE
125 W Exchange Pl (49007-4709)
PHONE..................................269 337-0037
Janice Brown, *Exec Dir*
Von Washington, *Exec Dir*
EMP: 1
SALES (est): 10.5MM **Privately Held**
SIC: 3999 Education aids, devices & supplies

(G-8797)
KALAMAZOO REGALIA INC
728 W Michigan Ave (49007-4538)
PHONE..................................269 344-4299
James Bellinger, *President*
Terry Squires, *Manager*
EMP: 12
SQ FT: 10,000
SALES (est): 550K **Privately Held**
WEB: www.kalamazooregalia.com
SIC: 2389 2396 Regalia; automotive & apparel trimmings

(G-8798)
KALAMAZOO SPORTSWEAR INC
728 W Michigan Ave (49007-4538)
PHONE..................................269 344-4242
Jim Bellinger, *President*
EMP: 18
SQ FT: 10,000
SALES: 970K **Privately Held**
WEB: www.kazoosports.com
SIC: 2396 Screen printing on fabric articles

(G-8799)
KALSEC INC (HQ)
3713 W Main St (49006-2842)
P.O. Box 50511 (49005-0511)
PHONE..................................269 349-9711
Scott M Nykaza, *President*
James Justice, *Trustee*
Roger Nahas, *Vice Pres*
Paul Moxon, *Mfg Staff*
Craig Cameron, *Production*
◆ **EMP:** 257 **EST:** 1958
SQ FT: 80,000
SALES (est): 83.4MM
SALES (corp-wide): 82.2MM **Privately Held**
WEB: www.kalsec.com
SIC: 2099 2087 Spices, including grinding; flavoring extracts & syrups
PA: Kalamazoo Holdings Inc
3713 W Main St
Kalamazoo MI 49006
269 349-9711

(G-8800)
KAMPS INC
1122 E Crosstown Pkwy (49001-2512)
PHONE..................................269 342-8113
Daniel De Verries, *Principal*
EMP: 20
SALES (corp-wide): 157.4MM **Privately Held**
WEB: www.kampspallets.com
SIC: 2448 Pallets, wood
PA: Kamps, Inc.
2900 Peach Ridge Ave Nw
Grand Rapids MI 49534
616 453-9676

(G-8801)
KEYSTONE MANUFACTURING LLC
6387 Technology Ave Ste B (49009-8193)
PHONE..................................269 343-4108
Len Stoehr, *Project Engr*
Jim Medsker,
▲ **EMP:** 16
SALES (est): 3.6MM **Privately Held**
SIC: 3841 Surgical & medical instruments

(G-8802)
KOTOCORP (USA) INC (HQ)
5981 E Cork St (49048-9609)
PHONE..................................269 349-1521
Mike Amemiya, *Chairman*
◆ **EMP:** 1 **EST:** 1997
SALES (est): 20.5MM **Privately Held**
WEB: www.interkal.com
SIC: 2531 Stadium seating

(G-8803)
KRAFTBRAU BREWERY INC
402 E Kalamazoo Ave (49007-3810)
PHONE..................................269 384-0288
James Quinn, *President*
EMP: 6
SALES (est): 250.5K **Privately Held**
SIC: 2082 Malt beverages

(G-8804)
LAKE MICHIGAN MAILERS INC (PA)
Also Called: Marana Group
3777 Sky King Blvd (49009-6953)
P.O. Box 19157 (49019-0157)
PHONE..................................269 383-9333
Robert J Rhoa, *CEO*
Karen Rhoa, *Ch of Bd*
David Rhoa, *President*
Marti Veld, *Plant Mgr*
EMP: 55
SQ FT: 23,800

SALES (est): 9.2MM **Privately Held**
WEB: www.barcodemail.com
SIC: 7331 4783 2752 7336 Mailing service; packing goods for shipping; commercial printing, lithographic; promotional printing, lithographic; commercial art & graphic design

(G-8805)
LAPINE METAL PRODUCTS INC
5232 Azo Ct (49048-8560)
P.O. Box 3156 (49003-3156)
PHONE..................................269 388-5900
Craig Lapine, *President*
Nathaniel P Burkett, *Vice Pres*
EMP: 15
SQ FT: 40,000
SALES: 1.9MM **Privately Held**
WEB: www.lapinemetalproducts.com
SIC: 3498 Coils, pipe: fabricated from purchased pipe

(G-8806)
LAWTON RIDGE WINERY LLC
8456 Stadium Dr (49009-9481)
PHONE..................................269 372-9463
Haltom Crick, *Owner*
Haltom Cricks, *Owner*
EMP: 4
SALES (est): 267.6K **Privately Held**
SIC: 2084 Wines

(G-8807)
LEADERS INC
Also Called: Leaders RPM
8500 W Main St (49009-9231)
PHONE..................................269 372-1072
Dale R Resh, *President*
Brent D Resh, *General Mgr*
Matthew R Resh, *Principal*
Nathan E Resh, *Principal*
Ethel Resh, *Corp Secy*
EMP: 4
SQ FT: 19,000
SALES (est): 1MM **Privately Held**
WEB: www.leadersmarine.com
SIC: 3433 5599 5551 Stoves, wood & coal burning; snowmobiles; outboard motors

(G-8808)
LEE-COBB COMPANY
415 W Maple St (49001-3642)
PHONE..................................269 553-0873
Willie Cobb, *Partner*
Sang Ae Lee-Cobb, *Partner*
▲ **EMP:** 4
SQ FT: 7,000
SALES (est): 374.5K **Privately Held**
SIC: 2386 Coats & jackets, leather & sheep-lined; hats & caps, leather; garments, leather; pants, leather

(G-8809)
LIBERTY CIRCUITS CORPORATION
630 E Walnut St Ste 1 (49007-4944)
PHONE..................................269 226-8743
Karl Person, *President*
Roger Person, *Vice Pres*
EMP: 5
SALES (est): 365K **Privately Held**
SIC: 7389 3679 Design services; electronic circuits

(G-8810)
LMM GROUP INC
443 E D Ave (49009-6312)
PHONE..................................269 276-9909
Michael Laughlin, *Principal*
EMP: 7 **EST:** 1999
SQ FT: 10,000
SALES (est): 385.8K **Privately Held**
SIC: 3599 Machine shop, jobbing & repair

(G-8811)
LUITEN GREENHOUSE TECH
1316 Howland Ave (49001-5112)
P.O. Box 3213 (49003-3213)
PHONE..................................269 381-4020
Arie Luiten, *Owner*
▲ **EMP:** 3
SALES (est): 468.7K **Privately Held**
WEB: www.luitenshading.com
SIC: 3448 0782 Greenhouses: prefabricated metal; lawn & garden services

Kalamazoo - Kalamazoo County (G-8812)   GEOGRAPHIC SECTION

(G-8812)
M & A MACHINING INC
1523 N Burdick St (49007-2597)
PHONE..................................269 342-0026
Alexander Pinto, *President*
EMP: 18
SQ FT: 7,000
SALES (est): 1.8MM **Privately Held**
SIC: 3599 Machine shop, jobbing & repair

(G-8813)
M B B M INC
Also Called: M & B Associates
6967 E Mn Ave (49048-9612)
PHONE..................................269 344-6361
William Maskill, *President*
Kenneth Buelow, *Vice Pres*
EMP: 5
SALES (est): 351.9K **Privately Held**
SIC: 5941 3949 Team sports equipment; sporting & athletic goods

(G-8814)
MACKENZIES BAKERY (PA)
527 Harrison St (49007-3662)
PHONE..................................269 343-8440
John R Mac Kenzie, *Owner*
Barb Schiebergen, *Executive*
EMP: 40
SQ FT: 5,000
SALES (est): 4.2MM **Privately Held**
WEB: www.mackenziesbakery.com
SIC: 5461 2051 Bread; bread, cake & related products

(G-8815)
MAINE PLASTICS INCORPORATED
3939 Emerald Dr (49001-7923)
PHONE..................................269 679-3988
Robert Render, *President*
EMP: 50
SALES (corp-wide): 47.4MM **Privately Held**
WEB: www.maineplastics.com
SIC: 3089 Plastic processing
PA: Maine Plastics, Incorporated
 1817 Kenosha Rd
 Zion IL 60099
 847 379-9100

(G-8816)
MALL CITY ALUMINUM INC
850 E Crosstown Pkwy (49001-2506)
PHONE..................................269 349-5088
Robert Grosser, *President*
Maxine Grosser, *Vice Pres*
EMP: 7
SQ FT: 15,000
SALES (est): 1.2MM **Privately Held**
SIC: 3365 Aluminum & aluminum-based alloy castings

(G-8817)
MALL CITY CONTAINERS INC (PA)
2710 N Pitcher St (49004-3490)
P.O. Box 69 (49004-0069)
PHONE..................................269 381-2706
Cleo Boersma, *Vice Pres*
Dave Johnston, *Accounts Mgr*
Steve Huyser, *Info Tech Dir*
EMP: 49
SQ FT: 120,000
SALES (est): 10.1MM **Privately Held**
WEB: www.mallcitycontainers.com
SIC: 2653 Boxes, corrugated: made from purchased materials; pads, corrugated: made from purchased materials; display items, corrugated: made from purchased materials; hampers, corrugated: made from purchased materials

(G-8818)
MANN + HUMMEL USA INC
3411 Ctr Park Plz (49048)
PHONE..................................248 857-8501
Michael Ternes, *Vice Pres*
EMP: 30
SALES (corp-wide): 4.5B **Privately Held**
SIC: 3089 3714 Injection molding of plastics; motor vehicle parts & accessories
HQ: Mann + Hummel Usa, Inc.
 6400 S Sprinkle Rd
 Portage MI 49002
 269 329-3900

(G-8819)
MC NALLY ELEVATOR COMPANY (PA)
223 W Ransom St (49007-3635)
PHONE..................................269 381-1860
Joseph Mc Nally, *President*
Mary C Mc Nally, *Corp Secy*
EMP: 18
SQ FT: 10,000
SALES (est): 3MM **Privately Held**
SIC: 1796 7699 3534 Elevator installation & conversion; elevators: inspection, service & repair; elevators & equipment

(G-8820)
MEGEE PRINTING INC
Also Called: Megee Print Document Solutions
509 Mills St (49001-2530)
PHONE..................................269 344-3226
Roger Megee, *President*
EMP: 12
SQ FT: 15,000
SALES: 1MM **Privately Held**
WEB: www.megeeonline.com
SIC: 2752 7334 Commercial printing, offset; photocopying & duplicating services

(G-8821)
MEINTS GLASS BLOWING
436 N Park St Ste 119 (49007-3376)
PHONE..................................269 349-1958
Frank Meintz, *Owner*
EMP: 3
SQ FT: 2,000
SALES: 54K **Privately Held**
SIC: 3229 Glassware, art or decorative

(G-8822)
METABOLIC SOLUTIONS DEV CO LLC
161 E Michigan Ave Fl 4 (49007-3926)
PHONE..................................269 343-6732
EMP: 14
SALES (est): 2.6MM **Privately Held**
SIC: 2833 8731 Mfg Medicinal/Botanical Products Commercial Physical Research

(G-8823)
MICHIGAN BIODIESEL LLC
2813 W Main St (49006-2901)
PHONE..................................269 427-0804
John Oakley,
EMP: 8
SALES (est): 651.7K **Privately Held**
SIC: 2079 Soybean oil, refined: not made in soybean oil mills

(G-8824)
MICRO MACHINE COMPANY LLC
Also Called: M2 Micro Machine
2429 N Burdick St (49007-1875)
PHONE..................................269 388-2440
Clive Scott, *CEO*
Lisa Terry, *Purch Agent*
EMP: 68
SQ FT: 25,000
SALES (est): 12.8MM **Privately Held**
WEB: www.micromachineco.com
SIC: 3599 Machine shop, jobbing & repair

(G-8825)
MICRO PRECISION MOLDS INC
3915 Ravine Rd (49006-1452)
PHONE..................................269 344-2044
William Longjohn, *President*
Tom Berglund Jr, *President*
Jack Buck, *Vice Pres*
EMP: 80
SQ FT: 7,000
SALES (est): 6.6MM **Privately Held**
SIC: 3544 Industrial molds

(G-8826)
MIDW INC
Also Called: Midwest Electric Motor
2734 Miller Rd (49001-4167)
PHONE..................................269 343-7090
Steve Olmsted, *President*
EMP: 7
SQ FT: 6,000
SALES (est): 1.2MM **Privately Held**
SIC: 7694 5063 Electric motor repair; motors, electric

(G-8827)
MIDWEST CUSTOM EMBROIDERY CO
621 E North St (49007-3536)
PHONE..................................269 381-7660
Marshall Pallett, *President*
David Davies, *Treasurer*
EMP: 8
SQ FT: 2,400
SALES (est): 768.5K **Privately Held**
WEB: www.midwest-embroidery.com
SIC: 2395 Embroidery products, except schiffli machine

(G-8828)
MILLER ENERGY INC
277 S Rose St Ste 3300 (49007-4722)
P.O. Box 632, Traverse City (49685-0632)
PHONE..................................269 352-5960
C John Miller, *CEO*
Michael J Miller, *President*
EMP: 15
SALES (est): 2.5MM **Privately Held**
WEB: www.millerenergy.com
SIC: 1382 Oil & gas exploration services

(G-8829)
MITTEN FRUIT COMPANY LLC
Also Called: Mitten Fruit Company, The
3680 Stadium Pkwy (49009-9743)
PHONE..................................269 585-8541
Daniel C Hinkle,
EMP: 4 EST: 2014
SALES (est): 116.1K **Privately Held**
SIC: 2033 Fruit juices: fresh

(G-8830)
MODERN NEON SIGN CO INC
1219 E Vine St (49001-3197)
PHONE..................................269 349-8636
Oliver Laclair, *President*
Oliver La Clair, *President*
Mary Ann La Clair, *Vice Pres*
Pamela De Young, *Admin Sec*
EMP: 12
SQ FT: 10,000
SALES (est): 1.1MM **Privately Held**
WEB: www.modernmansion.com
SIC: 1799 3993 Sign installation & maintenance; neon signs

(G-8831)
MOPHIE LLC
Also Called: Mstation
6244 Technology Ave (49009-8113)
PHONE..................................269 743-1340
Daniel Huang, *CEO*
▲ EMP: 99
SALES (est): 17.6MM **Publicly Held**
SIC: 3692 4812 8999 Primary batteries, dry & wet; cellular telephone services; communication services
HQ: Mophie Inc.
 15495 Sand Canyon Ave # 4
 Irvine CA 92618
 888 866-7443

(G-8832)
MRC INDUSTRIES INC (PA)
2538 S 26th St (49048-9610)
PHONE..................................269 343-0747
Christine Zeigler, *CEO*
Christine Ziegler, *CEO*
Margaret Miller, *Admin Asst*
EMP: 85 EST: 1950
SQ FT: 21,000
SALES (est): 4MM **Privately Held**
WEB: www.mrcindustries.org
SIC: 8331 2653 2631 Vocational rehabilitation agency; corrugated & solid fiber boxes; paperboard mills

(G-8833)
NATIONAL FLAVORS LLC
3680 Stadium Park Way (49009)
PHONE..................................800 525-2431
Dan Hinkle, *President*
▼ EMP: 26
SALES (est): 6.3MM **Privately Held**
SIC: 2869 Perfumes, flavorings & food additives

(G-8834)
NATIONAL PRODUCT CO
1206 E Crosstown Pkwy (49001-2563)
P.O. Box 2153 (49003-2153)
PHONE..................................269 344-3640
John Polzin, *Principal*
EMP: 7
SALES (est): 715.2K **Privately Held**
SIC: 2087 Flavoring extracts & syrups

(G-8835)
NEW ISSUES POETRY AND PROSE
Also Called: New Issues Press
1903 W Michigan Ave (49008-5463)
PHONE..................................269 387-8185
Kimberly Kolbe, *Managing Dir*
William Olsen, *Director*
EMP: 6
SALES (est): 100K **Privately Held**
SIC: 2731 Book publishing

(G-8836)
NUCON SCHOKBETON
3102 E Cork St (49001-4606)
PHONE..................................269 381-1550
Dennis Declerk, *President*
EMP: 110
SALES (est): 9.8MM **Privately Held**
WEB: www.stressconindustries.com
SIC: 3272 Concrete products, precast
PA: Stress Con Industries, Inc.
 1321 Industrial Pkwy N # 500
 Brunswick OH 44212

(G-8837)
NUWAVE TECHNOLOGY PARTNERS LLC (PA)
Also Called: Nuwave Medical Solutions
5268 Azo Dr (49048-9541)
PHONE..................................269 342-4400
Bill Knapp, *Vice Pres*
Doug Carroll, *Engineer*
David Alkema, *Network Engineer*
Kevin Chall, *Network Engineer*
Richard Paalman,
EMP: 12
SALES (est): 8.3MM **Privately Held**
SIC: 3661 7371 Telephone & telegraph apparatus; custom computer programming services

(G-8838)
O I K INDUSTRIES INC
7882 Douglas Ave (49009-6327)
P.O. Box 67 (49004-0067)
PHONE..................................269 382-1210
Dennis J Scheffers, *President*
David Scheffers, *Vice Pres*
Tim Scheffers, *Vice Pres*
EMP: 20
SQ FT: 22,600
SALES (est): 4.3MM **Privately Held**
WEB: www.oikindustries.com
SIC: 3446 Architectural metalwork

(G-8839)
OLDCASTLE MATERIALS INC
Also Called: Globe Construction
2300 Glendenning Rd (49001-4115)
P.O. Box 2857 (49003-2857)
PHONE..................................269 343-4659
Rusty Stafford, *Branch Mgr*
EMP: 50
SQ FT: 7,500
SALES (corp-wide): 30.6B **Privately Held**
WEB: www.oldcastlematerials.com
SIC: 1611 2951 General contractor, highway & street construction; asphalt paving mixtures & blocks
HQ: Oldcastle Materials, Inc.
 900 Ashwood Pkwy Ste 700
 Atlanta GA 30338

(G-8840)
PANOPLATE LITHOGRAPHICS INC
101 N Riverview Dr (49004-1397)
PHONE..................................269 343-4644
Bob Cox, *President*
EMP: 5 EST: 1976
SQ FT: 7,800

GEOGRAPHIC SECTION

Kalamazoo - Kalamazoo County (G-8866)

SALES (est): 340K **Privately Held**
WEB: www.panoplate.com
SIC: 2796 3952 Lithographic plates, positives or negatives; lead pencils & art goods

(G-8841)
PARAMONT MACHINE CO LLC
2810 N Burdick St (49004-3637)
PHONE..................330 339-3489
EMP: 7 **EST:** 2015
SALES (est): 881.1K **Privately Held**
SIC: 3599 Machine shop, jobbing & repair

(G-8842)
PARKER HSD
2220 Palmer Ave (49001-4122)
PHONE..................269 384-3915
Kyle Oberlee, *Principal*
Nicole Obriecht, *Engineer*
David Vanvels, *Engineer*
Darryl Watkins, *Engineer*
Chad Vliek, *Program Mgr*
EMP: 11
SALES (est): 1.7MM **Privately Held**
SIC: 3594 Fluid power pumps & motors

(G-8843)
PARKER-HANNIFIN CORPORATION
Hydraulic Systems Division
2220 Palmer Ave (49001-4122)
PHONE..................269 384-3459
Richard Soderquist, *Facilities Mgr*
Keith Jensen, *Senior Buyer*
Sarah Wegrzyn, *Purchasing*
Rod Carnes, *Engineer*
Chris Dykstra, *Engineer*
EMP: 450
SALES (corp-wide): 14.3B **Publicly Held**
WEB: www.parker.com
SIC: 3728 3812 3769 3625 Aircraft parts & equipment; search & navigation equipment; guided missile & space vehicle parts & auxiliary equipment; relays & industrial controls; fluid power pumps & motors; fluid power cylinders & actuators
PA: Parker-Hannifin Corporation
    6035 Parkland Blvd
    Cleveland OH 44124
    216 896-3000

(G-8844)
PARKER-HANNIFIN CORPORATION
Parker Abex
2220 Palmer Ave (49001-4122)
PHONE..................269 384-3400
Bill Cartmill, *Manager*
EMP: 650
SALES (corp-wide): 14.3B **Publicly Held**
WEB: www.parker.com
SIC: 3594 Fluid power pumps
PA: Parker-Hannifin Corporation
    6035 Parkland Blvd
    Cleveland OH 44124
    216 896-3000

(G-8845)
PAW ENTERPRISES LLC
Also Called: P.A.w Hardwood Flooring & Sups
3308 Covington Rd Ste 1 (49001-1801)
PHONE..................269 329-1865
Edward R Westfall III, *Principal*
EMP: 15
SALES (est): 3.1MM **Privately Held**
SIC: 2426 Flooring, hardwood

(G-8846)
PEPSI-COLA METRO BTLG CO INC
2725 E Kilgore Rd (49001-0840)
PHONE..................269 226-6400
Jacob Peterson, *Warehouse Mgr*
John Hoffman, *Manager*
Dave Vander, *Manager*
EMP: 53
SALES (corp-wide): 64.6B **Publicly Held**
WEB: www.joy-of-cola.com
SIC: 2086 Carbonated soft drinks, bottled & canned
HQ: Pepsi-Cola Metropolitan Bottling Company, Inc.
    1111 Westchester Ave
    White Plains NY 10604
    914 767-6000

(G-8847)
PERFECTION BAKERIES INC
Also Called: Perfection Bakery
807 Palmer Ave (49001-3880)
PHONE..................269 343-1217
Chad Kubasiak, *Manager*
EMP: 80
SALES (corp-wide): 535.8MM **Privately Held**
WEB: www.perfectionpastries.com
SIC: 2051 Bakery: wholesale or wholesale/retail combined
PA: Perfection Bakeries, Inc.
    350 Pearl St
    Fort Wayne IN 46802
    260 424-8245

(G-8848)
PFIZER INC
7171 Portage Rd (49001-0100)
PHONE..................269 833-5143
Gregory Brandt, *Engineer*
Jim Taylor, *Engineer*
Sandy Cobine, *Branch Mgr*
Jaime Lozada, *Director*
EMP: 146
SALES (corp-wide): 53.6B **Publicly Held**
WEB: www.pfizer.com
SIC: 2834 Pharmaceutical preparations
PA: Pfizer Inc.
    235 E 42nd St
    New York NY 10017
    212 733-2323

(G-8849)
PHARMACIA & UPJOHN COMPANY LLC
7000 Portage Rd (49001-0199)
PHONE..................908 901-8000
Philip Carra, *Branch Mgr*
EMP: 54
SALES (corp-wide): 53.6B **Publicly Held**
SIC: 8743 2834 2833 Public relations & publicity; pharmaceutical preparations; organic medicinal chemicals: bulk, uncompounded
HQ: Pharmacia & Upjohn Company Llc
    100 Rte 206 N
    Peapack NJ 07977
    908 901-8000

(G-8850)
PICWOOD USA LLC
Also Called: Picwood USA
2002 Charles Ave (49048-2072)
P.O. Box 50762 (49005-0762)
PHONE..................844 802-1599
Thomas Dockham, *President*
EMP: 4
SALES (est): 76.2K **Privately Held**
SIC: 2511 Chairs, bentwood

(G-8851)
PIERSON FINE ART
Also Called: Spirit of Apparel, The
3415 Meadowcroft Ave (49004-3131)
PHONE..................269 385-4974
Le Shon Pierson, *Owner*
EMP: 5
SALES: 180K **Privately Held**
SIC: 8412 2395 Art gallery; embroidery & art needlework

(G-8852)
PINTO PRODUCTS INC
2525 Miller Rd (49001-4141)
PHONE..................269 383-0015
Matthew Pinto, *CEO*
David Pinto, *President*
Cathy Pinto, *Technology*
EMP: 7
SQ FT: 24,000
SALES (est): 1.1MM **Privately Held**
WEB: www.pintoproducts.com
SIC: 3829 Aircraft & motor vehicle measurement equipment; gauging instruments, thickness ultrasonic

(G-8853)
PIPE FABRICATORS INC
1018 Staples Ave (49007-2319)
PHONE..................269 345-8657
Willard Harroun, *President*
Craig Harroun, *Vice Pres*
EMP: 54 **EST:** 1940
SQ FT: 6,000
SALES (est): 5.6MM
SALES (corp-wide): 6.6MM **Privately Held**
WEB: www.blharroun.com
SIC: 3498 7692 Fabricated pipe & fittings; welding repair
PA: B L Harroun And Son, Inc.
    1018 Staples Ave
    Kalamazoo MI 49007
    269 345-8657

(G-8854)
PRAB INC (HQ)
Also Called: Prab and Hapman
5944 E N Ave (49048-9776)
P.O. Box 2121 (49003-2121)
PHONE..................269 382-8200
Edward Thompson, *Ch of Bd*
David B Fisher, *President*
Robert W Klinge, *CFO*
Patrick Burgio, *Manager*
Alec Ingram, *Manager*
▲ **EMP:** 116 **EST:** 1961
SQ FT: 72,000
SALES: 32MM
SALES (corp-wide): 40.9MM **Privately Held**
WEB: www.prab.com
SIC: 3535 5084 Conveyors & conveying equipment; industrial machinery & equipment
PA: Kalamazoo Manufacturing Corporation Global
    5944 E N Ave
    Kalamazoo MI 49048
    269 382-8200

(G-8855)
PRAB INC
Hapman Conveyors
5944 E N Ave (49048-9776)
P.O. Box 2121 (49003-2121)
PHONE..................269 343-1675
Greg Patterson, *Vice Pres*
EMP: 81
SALES (corp-wide): 40.9MM **Privately Held**
WEB: www.prab.com
SIC: 3535 Conveyors & conveying equipment
HQ: Prab, Inc.
    5944 E N Ave
    Kalamazoo MI 49048
    269 382-8200

(G-8856)
PRAXAIR INC
1119 E Walnut St (49001-2447)
PHONE..................269 276-0442
Ken Blocker, *Branch Mgr*
EMP: 20 **Privately Held**
SIC: 2813 Industrial gases
HQ: Praxair, Inc.
    10 Riverview Dr
    Danbury CT 06810
    203 837-2000

(G-8857)
PRECISION DIAL CO
7240 W Kl Av (49009-7993)
PHONE..................269 375-5601
Myrna Babushka, *President*
Myrna Babushka, *President*
Robert Babushka, *Vice Pres*
EMP: 8
SQ FT: 3,600
SALES: 590K **Privately Held**
WEB: www.precisiondial.com
SIC: 2759 Screen printing

(G-8858)
PRECISION HEAT TREATING CO
660 Gull Rd (49007-3565)
P.O. Box 50326 (49005-0326)
PHONE..................269 382-4660
Mary Jeanne Juzwiak, *President*
Donald Juzwiak, *Vice Pres*
EMP: 25

SQ FT: 16,000
SALES (est): 4MM **Privately Held**
SIC: 3398 Metal heat treating

(G-8859)
PRECISION METALS PLUS INC
7574 E Mich Ave Kalamazoo (49048)
P.O. Box 678, Richland (49083-0678)
PHONE..................269 342-6330
Jeremy Brooks, *President*
EMP: 8
SQ FT: 9,000
SALES (est): 1MM **Privately Held**
SIC: 3441 Fabricated structural metal

(G-8860)
PRECISION POLYMER MFG INC
3915 Ravine Rd (49006-1452)
PHONE..................269 344-2044
William Longjohn, *President*
Tom Berglund, *Vice Pres*
Jack Buck, *Vice Pres*
▲ **EMP:** 40
SALES (est): 7.6MM **Privately Held**
WEB: www.ppmanufacturing.com
SIC: 3089 3429 7692 3229 Injection molding of plastics; aircraft hardware; welding repair; pressed & blown glass

(G-8861)
PREMIERE TOOL & DIE CAST
6146 W Main St Ste C (49009-4047)
PHONE..................269 782-3030
EMP: 4
SALES (est): 177.3K **Privately Held**
SIC: 3369 Nonferrous foundries

(G-8862)
PRINTMILL INC
4001 Portage St (49001-4912)
PHONE..................269 382-0428
William Schley, *President*
Steve Chapman, *President*
EMP: 6
SQ FT: 1,100
SALES (est): 689.5K **Privately Held**
WEB: www.printmill.com
SIC: 2752 Commercial printing, offset

(G-8863)
PURE PULP PRODUCTS INC
600 Plastics Pl (49001-4882)
PHONE..................269 385-5050
Richard H Young, *President*
Michael Roader, *Chairman*
Tyler Sheerer, *Admin Sec*
EMP: 20
SQ FT: 60,000
SALES (est): 3.9MM
SALES (corp-wide): 372.3MM **Privately Held**
SIC: 2621 Wrapping & packaging papers
PA: Two Mitts, Inc.
    600 Plastics Pl
    Kalamazoo MI 49001
    800 888-5054

(G-8864)
QUALITY CASTINGS CO
903 Hotop Ave (49048-1737)
PHONE..................269 349-7449
Jim A Wendel, *Owner*
EMP: 3
SALES: 130K **Privately Held**
SIC: 3363 Aluminum die-castings

(G-8865)
QUALITY CYLINDER SERVICE
106 W Mosel Ave (49004-3470)
PHONE..................269 345-0699
William Bilyk, *Owner*
EMP: 4
SQ FT: 4,000
SALES (est): 250K **Privately Held**
SIC: 3593 Fluid power cylinders, hydraulic or pneumatic

(G-8866)
QUALITY PRECAST INC
7800 Adobe (49009-5002)
PHONE..................269 342-0539
Jeff Schierbeek, *President*
Dan Schierbeek, *Vice Pres*
EMP: 20

Kalamazoo - Kalamazoo County (G-8867)   GEOGRAPHIC SECTION

SALES (est): 2.3MM **Privately Held**
SIC: **3272** Precast.terrazo or concrete products

(G-8867)
R H & COMPANY INC
Also Called: Spirit Shoppe
4510 W Kl Ave (49006-5725)
PHONE..............................269 345-7814
Richard Scheffers, *President*
Heather Scheffers, *Treasurer*
EMP: 10
SQ FT: 3,000
SALES (est): 850K **Privately Held**
SIC: **5699** 5947 5136 2396 Sports apparel; gift shop; sportswear, men's & boys'; screen printing on fabric articles; embroidering of advertising on shirts, etc.

(G-8868)
R H CROSS ENTERPRISES INC
731 Porter St (49007-3577)
PHONE..............................269 488-4009
Ronald H Cross, *CEO*
Jackie Edwards, *Vice Pres*
EMP: 4
SALES (est): 527.5K **Privately Held**
SIC: **3841** Surgical & medical instruments

(G-8869)
REALBIO TECHNOLOGY INC
8390 Canary Dr (49009-0803)
PHONE..............................269 544-1088
Paul Neeb, *CEO*
EMP: 4
SALES: 250K **Privately Held**
SIC: **3089** Injection molding of plastics

(G-8870)
RICHARD-ALLAN SCIENTIFIC CO (DH)
Also Called: Thermo Fischer Scientific
4481 Campus Dr (49008-2590)
PHONE..............................269 544-5600
Mark Casper, *CEO*
◆ EMP: 23
SQ FT: 120,000
SALES (est): 24.9MM
SALES (corp-wide): 24.3B **Publicly Held**
WEB: www.rallansci.com
SIC: **3826** Analytical instruments
HQ: Fisher Scientific International Llc
81 Wyman St
Waltham MA 02451
781 622-1000

(G-8871)
RIEDEL USA INC
2315 Cambridge Dr (49001-4536)
PHONE..............................734 595-9820
Sean O Driscoll, *Ch of Bd*
Bernhard Wieck, *Vice Pres*
Wolftang Todt, *Director*
▲ EMP: 4
SALES: 5MM
SALES (corp-wide): 4.1MM **Privately Held**
WEB: www.riedel-usa.com
SIC: **3585** Refrigeration & heating equipment
PA: Glen Dimplex Unlimited Company
Old Airport Road
Dublin
185 234-00

(G-8872)
RITSEMA PRCISION MACHINING INC
3221 Redmond Ave (49001-4828)
PHONE..............................269 344-8882
Joel Ritsema, *President*
Kris Ritsema, *Treasurer*
Fred Ritsema, *Shareholder*
EMP: 4
SQ FT: 12,000
SALES (est): 800K **Privately Held**
SIC: **3599** Machine shop, jobbing & repair

(G-8873)
RIVER RUN PRESS INC
Also Called: Economy Printing
600 Shoppers Ln (49004-1195)
PHONE..............................269 349-7603
Alfred Higdon, *President*
Josh Hannapel, *Opers Mgr*
John Arnsman, *Purchasing*
Jennifer Higdon, *Treasurer*
Ed Ramage, *Accounts Mgr*
EMP: 32 EST: 1979
SQ FT: 9,600
SALES (est): 5.4MM **Privately Held**
WEB: www.riverrunpress.com
SIC: **2752** 2791 2789 2759 Commercial printing, offset; typesetting; bookbinding & related work; commercial printing

(G-8874)
ROOT SPRING SCRAPER CO
527 W North St (49007-2494)
PHONE..............................269 382-2025
Frederick Root Jr, *President*
William Root, *Corp Secy*
Rodney Root, *Vice Pres*
Suzanna King, *Accountant*
Tim Rayman, *Manager*
▼ EMP: 45 EST: 1891
SQ FT: 57,000
SALES: 2.6MM **Privately Held**
WEB: www.rootsnowplows.com
SIC: **3531** 3524 Snow plow attachments; scrapers (construction machinery); lawn & garden equipment

(G-8875)
ROTO-FINISH COMPANY INC
Also Called: Hammond Machinery
1600 Douglas Ave (49007-1630)
PHONE..............................269 327-7071
Robert E Hammond, *Ch of Bd*
Michael Carl, *Corp Secy*
John Davidson, *Sales Mgr*
◆ EMP: 20
SQ FT: 115,000
SALES: 3.9MM
SALES (corp-wide): 29.8MM **Privately Held**
WEB: www.hammondmach.com
SIC: **3541** 5085 3291 Machine tools, metal cutting type; abrasives; abrasive products
PA: The Kalamazoo Company
1600 Douglas Ave
Kalamazoo MI 49007
269 345-7151

(G-8876)
RUSSELL FARMS INC
5616 N Riverview Dr (49004-1548)
PHONE..............................269 349-6120
Gail Russell, *President*
Rickard Russell, *Vice Pres*
EMP: 4
SALES: 150K **Privately Held**
SIC: **3111** 2499 Hides: tanning, currying & finishing; food handling & processing products, wood

(G-8877)
RWL SIGN CO LLC
Also Called: R Wl Sign Co
6185 W Kl Ave (49009-8060)
PHONE..............................269 372-3629
Jason Hadley, *Project Mgr*
Jason Headley, *Project Mgr*
Robert Leet, *Mng Member*
EMP: 7
SALES: 1.5MM **Privately Held**
WEB: www.rwlsign.com
SIC: **3993** Electric signs

(G-8878)
RX OPTICAL LABORATORIES INC (PA)
1825 S Park St (49001-2762)
PHONE..............................269 342-5958
Edward J Fletcher, *CEO*
Stephan J Jepson, *President*
George Jepson, *Vice Pres*
Steve Yonke, *CFO*
Joni Lapointe, *Controller*
EMP: 55
SQ FT: 12,000
SALES (est): 43.3MM **Privately Held**
WEB: www.rxoptical.com
SIC: **5995** 5048 3851 Opticians; ophthalmic goods; ophthalmic goods

(G-8879)
RX OPTICAL LABORATORIES INC
5349 W Main St Ofc (49009-1007)
PHONE..............................269 349-7627
Stacey Parsons, *Manager*
EMP: 4
SALES (corp-wide): 43.3MM **Privately Held**
WEB: www.rxoptical.com
SIC: **5995** 3851 Opticians; ophthalmic goods
PA: Rx Optical Laboratories, Inc
1825 S Park St
Kalamazoo MI 49001
269 342-5958

(G-8880)
S & C INDUSTRIES INC
Also Called: Oakes Carton Company
5575 Collingwood Ave (49004-1598)
PHONE..............................269 381-6022
James L Oakes, *President*
EMP: 19 EST: 1949
SQ FT: 30,000
SALES (est): 3.9MM **Privately Held**
SIC: **2657** Folding paperboard boxes

(G-8881)
SALES DRIVEN LTD LIABILITY CO
Also Called: Raybend
2723 Kersten Ct (49048-9301)
PHONE..............................269 254-8497
Joseph Mauro, *President*
Dagne Clark, *Controller*
◆ EMP: 30
SQ FT: 22,500
SALES (est): 6MM **Privately Held**
SIC: **3561** Pumps & pumping equipment

(G-8882)
SALES PAGE TECHNOLOGIES INC
227 N Rose St (49007-3935)
PHONE..............................269 567-7401
EMP: 5 EST: 2014
SALES (est): 193.8K **Privately Held**
SIC: **7372** Prepackaged software

(G-8883)
SALESPAGE TECHNOLOGIES LLC (PA)
600 E Michigan Ave # 103 (49007-4906)
P.O. Box 2707 (49003-2707)
PHONE..............................269 567-7400
Melissa Jobe, *President*
Beek Scott Vande, *Vice Pres*
Warren Fitzpatrick, *Technical Mgr*
Rick Bailey, *Engineer*
Amy Avis, *Controller*
EMP: 65
SQ FT: 11,500
SALES (est): 3.5MM **Privately Held**
WEB: www.salespage.com
SIC: **7372** Business oriented computer software

(G-8884)
SCHAWK INC (PA)
2325 N Burdick St (49007-1876)
PHONE..............................269 381-3820
Mike Bartusch, *President*
EMP: 9
SALES (est): 1.7MM **Privately Held**
SIC: **2796** Platemaking services

(G-8885)
SCOTT ROBERTS
Also Called: Sign Depot
3711 Gembrit Cir (49001-4617)
P.O. Box 367, Mattawan (49071-0367)
PHONE..............................269 668-5355
Scott Roberts, *Owner*
EMP: 3
SQ FT: 14,000
SALES: 500K **Privately Held**
WEB: www.scottroberts.com
SIC: **3993** Neon signs

(G-8886)
SHIELDS & SHIELDS ENTERPRISES
Also Called: Sign Shop, The
4302 S Westnedge Ave (49008-3227)
PHONE..............................269 345-7744
William Shields, *President*
Susan Shields, *President*
EMP: 4

SALES (est): 487.7K **Privately Held**
SIC: **3993** 5999 Signs & advertising specialties; banners

(G-8887)
SIGMA MACHINE INC
3358 Center Park Pl (49048-8646)
PHONE..............................269 345-6316
Jim Van Weelden, *President*
Jim L Van Weelden, *Corp Secy*
EMP: 100
SQ FT: 100,000
SALES (est): 13.5MM **Privately Held**
SIC: **3451** Screw machine products

(G-8888)
SIGN ART INC (PA)
5757 E Cork St (49048-9668)
PHONE..............................269 381-3012
Michael P Williams, *President*
EMP: 48
SQ FT: 47,550
SALES (est): 9MM **Privately Held**
SIC: **3993** Electric signs

(G-8889)
SIGN CENTER OF KALAMAZOO INC
711 Portage St (49001-2566)
PHONE..............................269 381-6869
Robert M Cook, *President*
EMP: 6
SQ FT: 2,500
SALES (est): 852.3K **Privately Held**
SIC: **3993** 7336 Signs & advertising specialties; commercial art & graphic design

(G-8890)
SIGN CITY INC
7178 Stadium Dr (49009-9423)
PHONE..............................269 375-1385
Steve Ellis, *President*
EMP: 7
SQ FT: 6,000
SALES: 500K **Privately Held**
WEB: www.signcity.com
SIC: **3993** Signs & advertising specialties

(G-8891)
SIGN IMPRESSIONS INC
3929 Ravine Rd (49006-1452)
PHONE..............................269 382-5152
Paul Havenaar, *President*
Kim Havenaar, *Vice Pres*
EMP: 5
SQ FT: 5,280
SALES: 375K **Privately Held**
WEB: www.signimpressionsinc.com
SIC: **7336** 3993 7389 Silk screen design; signs & advertising specialties; lettering service

(G-8892)
SIGN ON INC
Also Called: Sign Center
711 Portage St (49001-2566)
PHONE..............................269 381-6869
Ryan Talcott, *Principal*
EMP: 8
SALES (est): 263.4K **Privately Held**
SIC: **3993** Signs & advertising specialties

(G-8893)
SOUTHWEST MICH INNOVATION CTR
4717 Campus Dr Ste 100 (49008-5602)
PHONE..............................269 353-1823
Robert H Dewit, *President*
Molly Watson, *Corp Comm Staff*
Doug Morton, *Manager*
Richard West, *Manager*
EMP: 4
SALES: 2.9MM **Privately Held**
SIC: **3821** Incubators, laboratory

(G-8894)
SOUTHWEST MICHIGAN LIVING
1346 Floral Dr (49008-2810)
PHONE..............................269 344-7438
Kaye Collins, *Mng Member*
Karan Valantine,
EMP: 3
SALES: 60K **Privately Held**
SIC: **2721** Magazines: publishing only, not printed on site

▲ = Import ▼=Export
◆ =Import/Export

GEOGRAPHIC SECTION

Kalamazoo - Kalamazoo County (G-8923)

(G-8895)
SPARK GAMES LLC
5243 Torrey Pines Dr (49009-3840)
PHONE.....................269 303-7201
Parag Gupta,
Arun Pandey,
EMP: 3
SALES (est): 368.2K **Privately Held**
SIC: 3944 Bingo boards (games)

(G-8896)
SPARTAN PAPERBOARD COMPANY INC
8062 Stadium Dr (49009-9424)
P.O. Box 505, Oshtemo (49077-0505)
PHONE.....................269 381-0192
Jeff Cavanaugh, *President*
◆ **EMP:** 11 **EST:** 1978
SQ FT: 40,000
SALES (est): 3.6MM **Privately Held**
WEB: www.spartanpaper.com
SIC: 2631 Paperboard mills

(G-8897)
SPECILTY ADHESIVES COATING INC
3334 N Pitcher St (49004-3494)
PHONE.....................269 345-3801
Mark Cox, *General Mgr*
EMP: 11
SALES (corp-wide): 49.5MM **Privately Held**
WEB: www.specialtyadhesivesinc.com
SIC: 2891 Adhesives
PA: Specialty Adhesives & Coating, Inc.
   3791 Air Park St
   Memphis TN 38118
   800 728-9171

(G-8898)
SPLASH IN TIME LLC
Also Called: Cse Print
2015 Lake St (49001-3220)
PHONE.....................269 775-1204
Scott Roosenberg,
Charles Roosenberg,
EMP: 4
SALES (est): 97.9K **Privately Held**
SIC: 2711 Commercial printing & newspaper publishing combined

(G-8899)
STRESS CON INDUSTRIES INC
3102 E Cork St (49001-4606)
PHONE.....................269 381-1550
EMP: 336 **Privately Held**
SIC: 3272 Precast terrazo or concrete products
PA: Stress Con Industries, Inc.
   1321 Industrial Pkwy N # 500
   Brunswick OH 44212

(G-8900)
STURAK BROTHERS INC
2450 S Sprinkle Rd (49001-4624)
PHONE.....................269 345-2929
EMP: 8
SALES (est): 677.7K **Privately Held**
SIC: 1382 Oil/Gas Exploration Services

(G-8901)
SUMMIT POLYMERS INC
5858 E N Ave (49048-9776)
PHONE.....................269 324-9330
Daniel Brown, *Manager*
EMP: 275
SALES (corp-wide): 444.7MM **Privately Held**
SIC: 3089 Injection molding of plastics
PA: Summit Polymers, Inc.
   6715 S Sprinkle Rd
   Portage MI 49002
   269 324-9330

(G-8902)
SUNSET ENTERPRISES INC (PA)
Also Called: The Signwriter
633 W Michigan Ave (49007-3715)
PHONE.....................269 373-6440
Mark W Wrench, *President*
Melissa J Wrench, *Vice Pres*
Amy Livingston, *Electrical Engi*
EMP: 11
SALES (est): 1.7MM **Privately Held**
SIC: 3993 Signs & advertising specialties

(G-8903)
SUPERIOR EQUIPMENT LLC
7008 E N Ave (49048-9784)
PHONE.....................269 388-2871
Robert E Hammond II, *Principal*
Michelle Hammond,
EMP: 4
SALES (est): 800K **Privately Held**
WEB: www.superiorequip.net
SIC: 3991 Street sweeping brooms, hand or machine

(G-8904)
SUPERIOR IMAGING SERVICES INC
4001 Portage St (49001-4912)
PHONE.....................269 382-0428
Paul Verschoof, *President*
Derek McElvain, *Business Mgr*
EMP: 7
SQ FT: 3,360
SALES (est): 600K **Privately Held**
WEB: www.superiorimagingservices.com
SIC: 2752 Commercial printing, offset

(G-8905)
SUPERIOR TYPESETTING SERVICE
Also Called: Superior Imaging
4001 Portage St (49001-4912)
PHONE.....................269 382-0428
Paul Verschoof, *President*
Derek McElvain, *Vice Pres*
EMP: 8
SALES (est): 787.1K **Privately Held**
SIC: 2752 Commercial printing, offset

(G-8906)
SWEET MANUFACTURING INC
3421 S Burdick St (49001-4835)
PHONE.....................269 344-2086
Randall J Sweet, *President*
Joe Mathu, *Supervisor*
Joann Roberts, *Admin Asst*
EMP: 29
SQ FT: 20,000
SALES (est): 7.3MM **Privately Held**
SIC: 3714 Motor vehicle steering systems & parts

(G-8907)
T - SHIRT PRINTING PLUS INC
8608 W Main St Ste B (49009-8232)
PHONE.....................269 383-3666
Gary Peshl, *President*
Kathryn Peshl, *Vice Pres*
EMP: 15
SALES (est): 1.5MM **Privately Held**
SIC: 2396 2395 Screen printing on fabric articles; embroidery & art needlework

(G-8908)
TEAM PHARMA
2022 Fulford St (49001-2085)
PHONE.....................269 344-8326
Daniel Torres, *Principal*
John Lee, *Research*
EMP: 5
SALES (est): 310K **Privately Held**
SIC: 2834 Pharmaceutical preparations

(G-8909)
TECLAB INC (PA)
Also Called: Kalamazoo Technical Furniture
6450 Valley Industrial Dr (49009-9591)
PHONE.....................269 372-6000
Darren Draves, *President*
Ken Kasparek, *General Mgr*
Gil Vanderlip, *Vice Pres*
EMP: 50 **EST:** 1982
SQ FT: 32,500
SALES (est): 11.1MM **Privately Held**
WEB: www.teclab.com
SIC: 3821 Laboratory furniture

(G-8910)
THE SPOTT
550 E Cork St (49001-4873)
PHONE.....................269 459-6462
EMP: 5
SALES (est): 462.8K **Privately Held**
SIC: 3999 5812 ; eating places

(G-8911)
THERMO FISHER SCIENTIFIC INC
Also Called: Epredia
4481 Campus Dr (49008-2590)
PHONE.....................269 544-5600
Bill Yates, *Opers Mgr*
Kevin Verhulst, *Buyer*
Jennifer Freeland, *Research*
Peter Kilner, *Marketing Mgr*
Jerry Frendburgh, *Manager*
EMP: 307
SALES (corp-wide): 24.3B **Publicly Held**
WEB: www.thermo.com
SIC: 3826 Analytical instruments
PA: Thermo Fisher Scientific Inc.
   168 3rd Ave
   Waltham MA 02451
   781 622-1000

(G-8912)
THERMO SHANDON INC
4481 Campus Dr (49008-2590)
PHONE.....................269 544-7500
Kurt Kimbler, *President*
EMP: 3
SALES (est): 237.1K **Privately Held**
SIC: 3826 Analytical instruments

(G-8913)
TIRE WHOLESALERS COMPANY
3883 Emerald Dr (49001-7919)
PHONE.....................269 349-9401
Joe Krol, *Manager*
EMP: 94
SALES (corp-wide): 75MM **Privately Held**
WEB: www.twitire.com
SIC: 3011 5531 Tires & inner tubes; automotive tires
PA: Tire Wholesalers Company
   1783 E 14 Mile Rd
   Troy MI 48083
   248 589-9910

(G-8914)
TOTAL PLASTICS RESOURCES LLC (HQ)
Also Called: Total Plastics International
2810 N Burdick St Ste A (49004-3637)
PHONE.....................269 344-0009
Thomas Garrett, *President*
Rick Crisp, *Director*
▲ **EMP:** 75
SQ FT: 12,500
SALES: 135MM
SALES (corp-wide): 863.9MM **Privately Held**
WEB: www.totalplastics.com
SIC: 5162 3083 Plastics sheets & rods; laminated plastics plate & sheet
PA: Prophet Equity Lp
   1460 Main St Ste 200
   Southlake TX 76092
   817 898-1500

(G-8915)
TWO MITTS INC (PA)
600 Plastics Pl (49001-4882)
PHONE.....................800 888-5054
Michael Roeder, *President*
Gary Galia, *CFO*
John Kittredge, *Chief Mktg Ofcr*
Todd Carlson, *Officer*
EMP: 1 **EST:** 2014
SQ FT: 25,000
SALES (est): 372.3MM **Privately Held**
SIC: 3089 Thermoformed finished plastic products

(G-8916)
ULTRA FORMS PLUS INC
301 Peekstock Rd (49001-4844)
P.O. Box 2528 (49003-2528)
PHONE.....................269 337-6000
Kim Kugler, *President*
Ken Heegeman, *Vice Pres*
EMP: 14
SALES (est): 2MM **Privately Held**
WEB: www.ultraformsplus.com
SIC: 2761 Computer forms, manifold or continuous

(G-8917)
VANDER ROEST HOMES FINE WDWKG
2419 N 3rd St (49009-8518)
PHONE.....................269 353-3175
Dan V Roest, *Principal*
EMP: 4 **EST:** 2011
SALES (est): 490.7K **Privately Held**
SIC: 2431 Millwork

(G-8918)
VERSANT MEDICAL PHYSICS
116 S Riverview Dr (49004-1328)
PHONE.....................888 316-3644
Marcie Ramsay, *Managing Dir*
Nadeem Khan, *Director*
Sandra Konerth, *Director*
Eric Ramsay, *Director*
EMP: 20
SALES (est): 1.8MM **Privately Held**
SIC: 8099 8748 2835 0742 Medical services organization; safety training service; radioactive diagnostic substances; animal hospital services, pets & other animal specialties

(G-8919)
VISIONS CAR & TRUCK ACC
8250 Douglas Ave (49009-5255)
PHONE.....................269 342-2962
Mark Cottingham, *Owner*
EMP: 4
SALES (est): 319.6K **Privately Held**
SIC: 3714 Motor vehicle parts & accessories

(G-8920)
W SOULE & CO
Also Called: Sheet Metal Division
5175 King Hwy (49048-5910)
P.O. Box 2169 (49003-2169)
PHONE.....................269 344-0139
Jeremy Lagalo, *Accounting Mgr*
Susie Young, *Branch Mgr*
Brian Snyder, *Manager*
Howard Dembs, *CIO*
Ken Schneider, *Info Tech Mgr*
EMP: 150
SALES (corp-wide): 81.3MM **Privately Held**
WEB: www.wsoule.com
SIC: 1711 3444 3535 3443 Mechanical contractor; sheet metalwork; conveyors & conveying equipment; fabricated plate work (boiler shop)
PA: W. Soule & Co.
   7125 S Sprinkle Rd
   Portage MI 49002
   269 324-7001

(G-8921)
WABER TOOL & ENGINEERING CO
Also Called: Zip Cut
1335 Ravine Rd (49004-3501)
PHONE.....................269 342-0765
Heidi Waber, *President*
Vicky Roy, *Human Res Dir*
EMP: 20
SQ FT: 25,000
SALES (est): 3.1MM **Privately Held**
WEB: www.zipcut.com
SIC: 3541 3599 3829 3546 Machine tools, metal cutting type; machine shop, jobbing & repair; measuring & controlling devices; power-driven handtools; special dies, tools, jigs & fixtures

(G-8922)
WEST COLONY GRAPHIC INC
Also Called: West Colony Printing
2519 Summerdale Ave (49004-1922)
PHONE.....................269 375-6625
Richard Reynolds, *President*
Michael Kemple, *Vice Pres*
EMP: 5
SQ FT: 1,900
SALES (est): 370K **Privately Held**
WEB: www.westcolony.com
SIC: 2752 Commercial printing, offset

(G-8923)
WEST MICH OFF INTERIORS INC
3308 S Westnedge Ave (49008-4925)
PHONE.....................269 344-0768

Chuck Scheap, *Principal*
EMP: 6
SALES (corp-wide): 11MM **Privately Held**
WEB: www.wmoi.com
SIC: 2521 2522 4225 5712 Panel systems & partitions (free-standing), office: wood; panel systems & partitions, office: except wood; general warehousing & storage; furniture stores; furniture
PA: West Michigan Office Interiors, Inc.
300 E 40th St
Holland MI 49423
616 396-7303

(G-8924)
WICWAS PRESS
1620 Miller Rd (49001-4514)
PHONE.................................269 344-8027
Lawrence Connor, *Principal*
EMP: 4
SALES (est): 331.9K **Privately Held**
SIC: 2741 Miscellaneous publishing

(G-8925)
WILD FLAVORS INC
Also Called: A.M. Todd
1717 Douglas Ave (49007-1600)
PHONE.................................269 216-2603
EMP: 50
SALES (corp-wide): 64.3B **Publicly Held**
SIC: 2087 2869 Extracts, flavoring; flavors or flavoring materials, synthetic; perfume materials, synthetic
HQ: Wild Flavors, Inc.
1261 Pacific Ave
Erlanger KY 41018

(G-8926)
WONDER MAKERS ENVIRONMENTAL
2117 Lane Blvd (49001-4102)
P.O. Box 50209 (49005-0209)
PHONE.................................269 382-4154
Michael Pinto, *CEO*
Dave Batts, *Director*
EMP: 15
SQ FT: 10,000
SALES (est): 1.7MM **Privately Held**
WEB: www.wondermakers.com
SIC: 8742 3589 3463 Industrial hygiene consultant; asbestos removal equipment; aluminum forgings

(G-8927)
WOOD SMITHS INC
1180 S 8th St (49009-9327)
PHONE.................................269 372-6432
Kenneth C Smith, *President*
Robert Angle, *Principal*
▲ **EMP:** 16
SQ FT: 11,500
SALES: 2.5MM **Privately Held**
SIC: 2431 5211 7699 Millwork; doors, wood or metal, except storm; door & window repair

(G-8928)
WORLD OF CD-ROM
Also Called: World of Cd-Rom, The
4026 S Westnedge Ave D (49008-4135)
PHONE.................................269 382-3766
John Turcott, *Owner*
Mike Clapp, *Manager*
Joe Taylor, *Manager*
EMP: 10
SALES (est): 570K **Privately Held**
WEB: www.worldofcd-rom.com
SIC: 5734 7372 Computer & software stores; prepackaged software

(G-8929)
ZOETIS LLC
2605 E Kilgore Rd (49001-5505)
PHONE.................................888 963-8471
Mark Markillie, *Technician*
EMP: 21
SALES (corp-wide): 5.8B **Publicly Held**
SIC: 2834 Pharmaceutical preparations
HQ: Zoetis Llc
10 Sylvan Way Ste 105
Parsippany NJ 07054
973 822-7000

Kaleva
Manistee County

(G-8930)
BOWLING ENTERPRISES INC
Also Called: Bowling Hydroseeding
9091 Chief Rd (49645-9731)
P.O. Box 457, Bear Lake (49614-0457)
PHONE.................................231 864-2653
Floyd Bowling, *President*
Patti Bowling, *Admin Sec*
EMP: 4
SALES (est): 340K **Privately Held**
WEB: www.bowlinghydroseeding.com
SIC: 3449 0721 Bars, concrete reinforcing: fabricated steel; crop seeding services

(G-8931)
CREAM CUP DAIRY
7377 Feldhak Rd (49645-9653)
PHONE.................................231 889-4158
David Miller,
EMP: 4 **EST:** 2008
SALES: 110K **Privately Held**
SIC: 0241 2026 Dairy farms; milk processing (pasteurizing, homogenizing, bottling)

(G-8932)
FISCHER TANKS LLC
13884 Rengo Ave (49645)
PHONE.................................231 362-8265
Dustin Haw,
EMP: 60
SQ FT: 85,000
SALES (est): 9.1MM
SALES (corp-wide): 41.3MM **Privately Held**
SIC: 3443 7699 Fuel tanks (oil, gas, etc.): metal plate; tank repair
PA: Granby Industries Limited Partnership
98 Rue Des Industries
Cowansville QC J2K 0
450 378-2334

(G-8933)
FRUIT HAVEN NURSERY INC
Also Called: Calvin Lutz Farm
8576 Chief Rd (49645-9607)
PHONE.................................231 889-9973
Calvin Lutz II, *President*
Mark Coe, *Principal*
Mike Feliczak, *Principal*
Calvin Lutz III, *Principal*
Ralph Smith, *Principal*
EMP: 8
SALES (est): 1.7MM **Privately Held**
WEB: www.fruithavennursery.com
SIC: 0161 3999 0782 Corn farm, sweet; asparagus farm; Christmas trees, artificial; landscape contractors

(G-8934)
NORTHERN CHAIN SPECIALTIES
7329 Chief Rd (49645-9712)
PHONE.................................231 889-3151
James Kelly, *President*
Barry Crawford, *Vice Pres*
EMP: 12
SQ FT: 20,000
SALES (est): 2.2MM **Privately Held**
WEB: www.northernchain.com
SIC: 3441 Fabricated structural metal

Kalkaska
Kalkaska County

(G-8935)
1ST CHOICE TRCKG & RENTL INC
1256 Thomas Rd (49646)
P.O. Box 970 (49646-0970)
PHONE.................................231 258-0417
Roger Wilkinson, *President*
Brenda Goosman, *Shareholder*
James Vowels, *Shareholder*
Lyle Vowels, *Shareholder*
Joe Waterman, *Admin Sec*
EMP: 9
SALES: 200K **Privately Held**
SIC: 1389 Haulage, oil field

(G-8936)
ARROW DRILLING SERVICES LLC
4030 Columbus Dr Ne (49646-8484)
PHONE.................................231 258-4596
Stephen J Harrigan,
George Molski,
EMP: 30
SALES (est): 2.4MM **Privately Held**
SIC: 1381 Drilling oil & gas wells

(G-8937)
BARBRON CORPORATION
200 E Dresden St (49646-8589)
PHONE.................................586 716-3530
EMP: 30
SQ FT: 8,500
SALES (est): 2.4MM **Privately Held**
SIC: 3569 3497 3496 3494 Mfg General Indstl Mach Mfg Metal Foil/Leaf Mfg Misc Fab Wire Prdts Mfg Valves/Pipe Fittings

(G-8938)
BEAVER LOG HOMES INC
850 S Cedar St (49646-8031)
P.O. Box 3 (49646-0003)
PHONE.................................231 258-5020
Richard Beaver, *President*
EMP: 10
SQ FT: 864
SALES (est): 1.3MM **Privately Held**
WEB: www.beaverloghomes.net
SIC: 2452 Log cabins, prefabricated, wood

(G-8939)
BECKMAN PRODUCTION SVCS INC (HQ)
Also Called: Indril
3786 Beebe Rd (49646-8014)
P.O. Box 670 (49646-0670)
PHONE.................................231 258-9524
Tom Cyculla, *CEO*
Ed Sarin, *Safety Mgr*
Mark Bishop, *CFO*
Tom Cybulla, *Manager*
EMP: 67 **EST:** 1970
SALES (est): 165.8MM
SALES (corp-wide): 827.1MM **Publicly Held**
SIC: 1389 Oil field services
PA: Nine Energy Service, Inc.
2001 Kirby Dr Ste 200
Houston TX 77019
281 730-5100

(G-8940)
D & W FLOW TESTING INC (PA)
1770 M 72 Se (49646-9717)
P.O. Box 448 (49646-0448)
PHONE.................................231 258-4926
Derrell W Eldridge, *President*
Wanda Eldridge, *Admin Sec*
EMP: 3
SQ FT: 2,000
SALES: 400K **Privately Held**
SIC: 1389 5084 Oil field services; petroleum industry machinery

(G-8941)
D J AND G ENTERPRISE INC
Also Called: Patton Welding
402 E Dresden St (49646-9701)
PHONE.................................231 258-9925
Don Patton, *President*
Jenny Patton, *Corp Secy*
EMP: 6
SQ FT: 6,000
SALES: 400K **Privately Held**
SIC: 3548 Welding wire, bare & coated

(G-8942)
EXODUS PRESSURE CONTROL
110 W Park Dr (49646-9702)
P.O. Box 2053 (49646-2053)
PHONE.................................231 258-8001
Jeff Bergman, *Partner*
Troy Fisher, *Partner*
EMP: 6
SALES (est): 736.3K **Privately Held**
SIC: 1389 Construction, repair & dismantling services

(G-8943)
GREAT LAKES CONTAINMENT INC
731 S Cedar St (49646-9460)
P.O. Box 51 (49646-0051)
PHONE.................................231 258-8800
Larry Anderson, *President*
Randy Kinney, *President*
EMP: 10
SQ FT: 10,000
SALES (est): 840K **Privately Held**
WEB: www.greatlakescontainment.com
SIC: 3081 Unsupported plastics film & sheet

(G-8944)
ILLINOIS TOOL WORKS INC
ITW Coding Products
111 W Park Dr (49646-9702)
PHONE.................................231 258-5521
Mark Thelen, *Exec Dir*
EMP: 80
SQ FT: 14,000
SALES (corp-wide): 14.7B **Publicly Held**
SIC: 3497 Metal foil & leaf
PA: Illinois Tool Works Inc.
155 Harlem Ave
Glenview IL 60025
847 724-7500

(G-8945)
JK MANUFACTURING CO
520 E Dresden St (49646-9701)
PHONE.................................231 258-2638
Jody L Keener, *President*
EMP: 11
SALES (est): 220.6K **Privately Held**
SIC: 3999 Barber & beauty shop equipment

(G-8946)
KALKASKA SCREW PRODUCTS INC
775 Rabourn Rd Ne (49646-8959)
PHONE.................................231 258-2560
Tedd H Stewart, *President*
Steve Hartzell, *Purch Agent*
Tim Eagleton, *QC Mgr*
Ric Helmreich, *Engineer*
EMP: 24
SQ FT: 30,000
SALES (est): 6.9MM **Privately Held**
WEB: www.kalkaskascrew.com
SIC: 3451 Screw machine products

(G-8947)
KEY ENERGY SERVICES INC
4030 Columbus Dr Ne (49646-8484)
PHONE.................................231 258-9637
Duke Upaul, *Manager*
EMP: 50
SALES (corp-wide): 521.7MM **Publicly Held**
WEB: www.keyenergy.com
SIC: 1381 Drilling oil & gas wells
PA: Key Energy Services, Inc.
1301 Mckinney St Ste 1800
Houston TX 77010
713 651-4300

(G-8948)
LC MATERIALS
Also Called: L C Redi Mix
500 M 72 (49646)
PHONE.................................231 258-8633
Calvin Hutchinson, *Manager*
EMP: 10
SALES (corp-wide): 8MM **Privately Held**
SIC: 3273 Ready-mixed concrete
PA: Lc Materials
805 W 13th St
Cadillac MI 49601
231 825-2473

(G-8949)
MARSH INDUSTRIAL SERVICES INC
Also Called: Marsh Welding
135 E Mile Rd (49646-9485)
P.O. Box 1107 (49646-1107)
PHONE.................................231 258-4870
Donald R Marsh, *President*
Debra Marsh, *Corp Secy*
EMP: 15
SQ FT: 12,000

GEOGRAPHIC SECTION

SALES (est): 2.8MM **Privately Held**
SIC: **3443** 1799 7692 3713 Fabricated plate work (boiler shop); welding on site; welding repair; truck & bus bodies; industrial trucks & tractors; sheet metalwork

(G-8950)
MERIT ENERGY COMPANY LLC
1510 E Thomas Rd (49646)
PHONE.....................................231 258-6401
Randy Sanders, *Branch Mgr*
EMP: 20
SALES (corp-wide): 3.9B **Privately Held**
SIC: **1311** Crude petroleum production; natural gas production
PA: Merit Energy Company, Llc
13737 Noel Rd Ste 1200
Dallas TX 75240
972 701-8377

(G-8951)
MICHAEL NIEDERPRUEM
Also Called: Print Shop, The
880 Lake Dr Ne (49646-9642)
PHONE.....................................231 935-0241
Michael Niederpruem, *Owner*
EMP: 4
SQ FT: 1,100
SALES (est): 180K **Privately Held**
SIC: **2759** Commercial printing

(G-8952)
MICHIGAN AGGR SAND/GRAVEL HAUL
765 Rabourn Rd Ne (49646-8959)
PHONE.....................................231 258-8237
Frank Peters, *President*
Olive Peters, *Vice Pres*
Timothy Peters, *Treasurer*
EMP: 10 **EST:** 1973
SQ FT: 3,000
SALES (est): 1.7MM **Privately Held**
WEB: www.michiganagg.com
SIC: **1442** Construction sand & gravel

(G-8953)
MIDWEST TOOL AND CUTLERY CO
Also Called: Forge Div Midwest Tl & Cutly
222 Seeley Rd Ne (49646-9483)
PHONE.....................................231 258-2341
Gordon German, *Plant Mgr*
Scott Musser, *Branch Mgr*
EMP: 15
SALES (corp-wide): 16.2MM **Privately Held**
WEB: www.midwestsnips.com
SIC: **3421** 3542 Scissors, shears, clippers, snips & similar tools; forging machinery & hammers
PA: Midwest Tool And Cutlery Company
1210 Progress St
Sturgis MI 49091
269 651-2476

(G-8954)
MIKES STEAMER SERVICE INC
355 Columbus Dr Ne (49646-8029)
P.O. Box 1260 (49646-1260)
PHONE.....................................231 258-8500
Michael Beehler, *President*
EMP: 45
SQ FT: 3,000
SALES (est): 4.5MM **Privately Held**
WEB: www.mikessteamer.com
SIC: **1389** Oil field services

(G-8955)
NORTHERN A 1 SERVICES INC
Also Called: Pollution Control Services
3947 Us Highway 131 Ne (49646-8428)
P.O. Box 1030 (49646-1030)
PHONE.....................................231 258-9961
Gregg Orr, *President*
Mike Ascione, *President*
EMP: 20
SALES (est): 2.1MM **Privately Held**
SIC: **1389** Servicing oil & gas wells

(G-8956)
NORTHERN DESIGN SERVICES INC
424 E Dresden St (49646-9701)
PHONE.....................................231 258-9900
Dan Minder, *President*

Leo Dutton, *Treasurer*
EMP: 20
SQ FT: 14,000
SALES (est): 2MM **Privately Held**
SIC: **7692** Welding repair

(G-8957)
PATTON WELDING INC
Also Called: Michigan Modular Service
402 E Dresden St (49646-9701)
PHONE.....................................231 258-9925
Donald Patton, *President*
Barney Hunter, *Manager*
EMP: 18
SALES: 300K **Privately Held**
SIC: **3498** Fabricated pipe & fittings

(G-8958)
SHETLER FAMILY DAIRY LLC
5436 Tyler Rd Se (49646-7923)
PHONE.....................................231 258-8216
George Shetler,
EMP: 10
SALES (est): 1.4MM **Privately Held**
SIC: **2024** 2026 Ice cream & ice milk; fluid milk

(G-8959)
SUPERIOR INSPECTION SVC
1864 Prough Rd Sw (49646-7809)
P.O. Box 1509 (49646-1509)
PHONE.....................................231 258-9400
EMP: 7
SALES (est): 539.2K **Privately Held**
SIC: **1389** Construction, repair & dismantling services

(G-8960)
TARGET OIL TOOLS LLC
3540 Us Highway 131 Ne (49646-8430)
P.O. Box 621 (49646-0621)
PHONE.....................................231 258-4960
Brent Bell, *Mng Member*
Brent W Bell,
EMP: 3
SALES (est): 571.9K **Privately Held**
SIC: **1389** Oil field services

(G-8961)
TEAM SERVICES LLC
1587 Enterprise Dr (49646-8255)
P.O. Box 1104 (49646-1104)
PHONE.....................................231 258-9130
Steve Kwapis, *CEO*
EMP: 36
SALES (est): 7.6MM **Privately Held**
SIC: **1389** Servicing oil & gas wells

(G-8962)
TEAM SPOOLING SERVICES LLC
Also Called: Team Acquistions
209 E Park Dr (49646-9785)
P.O. Box 1104 (49646-1104)
PHONE.....................................231 258-9130
Tim Tinker,
EMP: 4 **EST:** 2001
SALES (est): 403.9K **Privately Held**
SIC: **1389** Servicing oil & gas wells

(G-8963)
THIN LINE PUMP
208 Court St (49646-8209)
P.O. Box 292 (49646-0292)
PHONE.....................................231 258-2692
Charles Tartriedge, *Owner*
EMP: 6
SQ FT: 2,000
SALES (est): 150K **Privately Held**
SIC: **3561** Industrial pumps & parts

(G-8964)
TODDS WELDING SERVICE INC
Also Called: T W S Wldg & Cstm Fabrication
8604 Us 131 N (49646)
P.O. Box 1113 (49646-1113)
PHONE.....................................231 587-9969
Todd Chwastek, *President*
Renee Chwastek, *Vice Pres*
EMP: 16
SQ FT: 13,000
SALES (est): 3.4MM **Privately Held**
SIC: **7692** Welding repair

(G-8965)
TREND SERVICES COMPANY
311 Maple St (49646-5101)
P.O. Box 458 (49646-0458)
PHONE.....................................231 258-9951
Michael E Babcock, *President*
Charles Witt, *Accountant*
David Babcock, *Technician*
Steve Dipzinski, *Technician*
Josh Hicks, *Technician*
EMP: 7
SQ FT: 8,500
SALES (est): 4MM **Privately Held**
WEB: www.trendservices.net
SIC: **1389** Construction, repair & dismantling services; measurement of well flow rates, oil & gas

(G-8966)
WAYNE WIRE A BAG CMPONENTS INC
200 E Dresden St (49646-8589)
PHONE.....................................231 258-9187
Michael G Brown, *President*
▲ **EMP:** 45
SALES: 20MM
SALES (corp-wide): 64MM **Privately Held**
WEB: www.waynewire.com
SIC: **3496** Miscellaneous fabricated wire products
PA: Wayne Wire Cloth Products Inc
200 E Dresden St
Kalkaska MI 49646
231 258-9187

(G-8967)
WAYNE WIRE CLOTH PRODUCTS INC (PA)
Also Called: Wayne Wire Airbag Components
200 E Dresden St (49646-8589)
PHONE.....................................231 258-9187
Michael G Brown, *President*
David Brown, *President*
Steve Brown, *President*
M G Brown, *Chairman*
Dave Allison, *Plant Mgr*
EMP: 100 **EST:** 1943
SQ FT: 175,000
SALES (est): 64MM **Privately Held**
WEB: www.waynewire.com
SIC: **3496** Miscellaneous fabricated wire products

(G-8968)
WOODLAND CREEK FURNITURE INC (PA)
Also Called: Arhouzz
546 M 72 E (49646-9417)
P.O. Box 2048 (49646-2048)
PHONE.....................................231 518-4084
Rob Evina, *President*
Wendy Watson, *Manager*
▲ **EMP:** 30
SALES (est): 5.2MM **Privately Held**
SIC: **2511** 5712 Wood household furniture; custom made furniture, except cabinets

Kawkawlin
Bay County

(G-8969)
ACME SEPTIC TANK CO
2888 S Huron Rd (48631-9107)
P.O. Box 336 (48631-0336)
PHONE.....................................989 684-3852
Brian Marsh, *President*
Audrey Marsh, *Vice Pres*
EMP: 12 **EST:** 1950
SALES (est): 1.8MM **Privately Held**
SIC: **3272** 1711 1389 Septic tanks, concrete; septic system construction; servicing oil & gas wells

(G-8970)
BAILER AND DE SHAW
204 S Old Kawkawlin Rd (48631-2507)
PHONE.....................................989 684-3610
Douglas I Bailer, *Partner*
Herman J De Shaw, *Partner*
EMP: 7 **EST:** 1962
SQ FT: 240

SALES (est): 725.5K **Privately Held**
SIC: **1311** Crude petroleum production

(G-8971)
GLENN KNOCHEL
Also Called: Maple Lane Ag-Bag
2152 E Beaver Rd (48631-9422)
PHONE.....................................989 684-7869
Glenn Knochel, *Owner*
EMP: 4
SALES (est): 481.6K **Privately Held**
SIC: **3523** 5999 Crop storage bins; farm equipment & supplies

(G-8972)
HOLSINGER MANUFACTURING CORP
2922 S Huron Rd (48631-9177)
P.O. Box 645 (48631-0645)
PHONE.....................................989 684-3101
Joe Martuch, *President*
Harley Owen Holsinger, *President*
EMP: 12
SQ FT: 26,000
SALES: 632.1K **Privately Held**
WEB: www.holsingermfg.com
SIC: **2541** 2599 Store fixtures, wood; bar fixtures, wood; office fixtures, wood; bar, restaurant & cafeteria furniture

(G-8973)
HUGO BROTHERS PALLET MFG
2474 River Rd (48631-9409)
PHONE.....................................989 684-5564
Daniel Hugo, *President*
William Hugo, *Corp Secy*
EMP: 8
SQ FT: 6,720
SALES (est): 710K **Privately Held**
SIC: **2448** Pallets, wood

(G-8974)
KAWKAWLIN MANUFACTURING CO
Also Called: Kawkawlin Church Furniture
300 Spring St (48631)
P.O. Box 368 (48631-0368)
PHONE.....................................989 684-5470
Frank King Jr, *President*
EMP: 8
SALES (corp-wide): 871.9K **Privately Held**
SIC: **2531** Public building & related furniture
PA: Kawkawlin Manufacturing Co Inc
2707 Highbrook Dr
Midland MI 48642
989 684-5470

(G-8975)
SAGINAW BAY PLASTICS INC
2768 S Huron Rd (48631-9176)
P.O. Box 507 (48631-0507)
PHONE.....................................989 686-7860
David Burke, *President*
Graham Greene, *QC Mgr*
Connie Scott, *Admin Asst*
▲ **EMP:** 65
SQ FT: 30,000
SALES (est): 11.8MM **Privately Held**
WEB: www.saginawbayplastics.com
SIC: **3089** Injection molding of plastics

(G-8976)
WOODLAND INDUSTRIES
112 S Huron Rd (48631-9127)
P.O. Box 504 (48631-0504)
PHONE.....................................989 686-6176
Michael Ferguson, *Owner*
EMP: 5
SQ FT: 4,000
SALES (est): 417.5K **Privately Held**
SIC: **3715** 5599 Truck trailers; utility trailers

(G-8977)
X L T ENGINEERING INC
2595 S Huron Rd (48631-9170)
P.O. Box 126 (48631-0126)
PHONE.....................................989 684-4344
Mike Staszak, *President*
Stacie Staszak, *Vice Pres*
EMP: 18
SALES: 1.5MM **Privately Held**
SIC: **3599** 3544 Machine shop, jobbing & repair; special dies, tools, jigs & fixtures

Keego Harbor
Oakland County

(G-8978)
B & B ELECTRICAL INC
2804 Orchard Lake Rd # 203 (48320-1449)
PHONE..................................248 391-3800
Richard Linnell, *President*
Margaret M Linnell, *Vice Pres*
EMP: 3
SALES (est): 500.1K **Privately Held**
WEB: www.bbelec.com
SIC: 3429 Manufactured hardware (general)

(G-8979)
HYDROSCIENCES LLC
3477 Orchard Lake Rd (48320-1315)
PHONE..................................248 890-8116
EMP: 3
SALES (est): 290K **Privately Held**
SIC: 2869 Developer Of Chemical Technology

(G-8980)
I JAMS LLC
1497 Beachland Blvd (48320-1002)
PHONE..................................248 756-1380
EMP: 3
SALES (est): 144K **Privately Held**
SIC: 2033 Jams, jellies & preserves: packaged in cans, jars, etc.

(G-8981)
POWERSPORTS DALES LLC
2142 Beechmont St (48320-1171)
PHONE..................................248 682-4200
Dale Wilte, *President*
Dale Wiltse, *Mng Member*
EMP: 4
SALES (est): 271.6K **Privately Held**
SIC: 3732 Jet skis

(G-8982)
WINDWORD PRESS
3109 Portman St (48320-1208)
PHONE..................................248 681-7905
Stanley H Finsilver, *President*
Sheri Finsilver, *Corp Secy*
Barry Rudner, *Vice Pres*
EMP: 3
SALES (est): 138.8K **Privately Held**
WEB: www.windwardreports.com
SIC: 2731 Book publishing

Kendall
Van Buren County

(G-8983)
CZUK STUDIO
26922 County Road 388 (49062-5100)
P.O. Box 67 (49062-0067)
PHONE..................................269 628-2568
Peter Czuk, *Owner*
EMP: 3
SALES: 140K **Privately Held**
WEB: www.czukstudio.com
SIC: 2499 3873 2511 2441 Engraved wood products; watches, clocks, watchcases & parts; wood household furniture; nailed wood boxes & shook

Kenockee
St. Clair County

(G-8984)
BOBS WELDING & FABRICATING
Also Called: B W and F Excavating
5375 Kilgore Rd (48006-3229)
PHONE..................................810 324-2592
Robert Goolsby, *Owner*
EMP: 10
SALES (est): 683.8K **Privately Held**
SIC: 7692 Welding repair

(G-8985)
MCPHAILS PALLETS INC
9871 Bryce Rd (48006-3725)
PHONE..................................810 384-6458
Ronald McPhail, *President*
Tim McPhail, *Vice Pres*
EMP: 10
SQ FT: 5,000
SALES: 900K **Privately Held**
SIC: 2448 2421 Pallets, wood; wood chips, produced at mill

Kent City
Kent County

(G-8986)
2255SRV LLV
2825 17 Mile Rd Ste A (49330-8921)
PHONE..................................616 678-4900
Dale Flanery,
EMP: 29
SALES (est): 5.8MM **Privately Held**
SIC: 3089 Injection molded finished plastic products; injection molding of plastics

(G-8987)
BARBER CREEK SAND & GRAVEL
15666 Barber Creek Ave (49330-9734)
P.O. Box 185 (49330-0185)
PHONE..................................616 675-7619
Daniel C Groenke, *President*
EMP: 11 **EST:** 1976
SQ FT: 3,840
SALES (est): 2.7MM **Privately Held**
SIC: 1442 Gravel mining

(G-8988)
C & T FABRICATION LLC
90 Spring St (49330-9303)
P.O. Box 310 (49330-0310)
PHONE..................................616 678-5133
Dan Boyd, *Partner*
▲ **EMP:** 6
SALES (est): 504.1K **Privately Held**
SIC: 1761 3444 Sheet metalwork; sheet metalwork

(G-8989)
COUNTY LINE PALLET
Also Called: Fisk Wood Products
2031 22 Mile Rd (49330-9450)
PHONE..................................231 834-8416
EMP: 8
SALES (est): 490K **Privately Held**
SIC: 2448 Mfg Wood Pallets/Skids

(G-8990)
G & C CARPORTS
1324 17 Mile Rd (49330-9058)
PHONE..................................616 678-4308
Narcizo Gutierrez, *Owner*
EMP: 12
SALES (est): 2MM **Privately Held**
WEB: www.customcarports.net
SIC: 3448 Carports: prefabricated metal

(G-8991)
GT PLASTICS & EQUIPMENT LLC
13425 Peach Ridge Ave (49330-9155)
P.O. Box 158 (49330-0158)
PHONE..................................616 678-7445
Grady Ogle,
EMP: 12
SQ FT: 10,000
SALES (est): 1.8MM **Privately Held**
SIC: 3089 5084 Blow molded finished plastic products; plastic products machinery

(G-8992)
KALINIAK DESIGN LLC
13984 Eagle Ridge Dr (49330-9086)
PHONE..................................616 675-3850
Andrew Kaliniak, *President*
Edie Kaliniak, *Opers Mgr*
EMP: 7
SQ FT: 8,000
SALES: 500K **Privately Held**
SIC: 2511 2434 Wood household furniture; wood kitchen cabinets

(G-8993)
KENT CITY PLASTICS LLC
90 Spring St Ste B (49330-9305)
PHONE..................................616 678-4900
Michael Tatman, *Mng Member*
Joseph Pohlen,
EMP: 15
SALES (est): 2.6MM **Privately Held**
SIC: 3089 Plastic containers, except foam; injection molding of plastics

(G-8994)
SMITH DUMPSTERS
13546 Kenowa Ave (49330-9502)
PHONE..................................616 675-9399
Ronald R Smith, *Principal*
EMP: 3
SALES (est): 150.8K **Privately Held**
SIC: 3443 Dumpsters, garbage

Kenton
Ontonagon County

(G-8995)
EAST BRANCH FOREST PRODUCTS
5160 E Hwy 28 (49967)
PHONE..................................906 852-3315
EMP: 5
SALES (est): 334.9K **Privately Held**
SIC: 2411 Logging

(G-8996)
INTEGRITY FOREST PRODUCTS LLC
844 Hwy M28 (49967)
PHONE..................................513 871-8988
James Stoehr III, *President*
Patrick Folz, *CFO*
EMP: 7
SALES (est): 285.1K **Privately Held**
SIC: 2421 Sawmills & planing mills, general

Kentwood
Kent County

(G-8997)
ABACO PARTNERS LLC
Also Called: Surefil
4560 Danvers Dr Se (49512-4039)
PHONE..................................616 532-1700
Andrea Hecker, *Project Mgr*
Chuck Blaauw, *Purch Mgr*
Tim Kauffman, *Controller*
Luisa Shumpert, *Marketing Staff*
William Currie, *Mng Member*
▲ **EMP:** 110
SQ FT: 5,000
SALES (est): 41.6MM **Privately Held**
SIC: 2844 2834 2082 Mouthwashes; druggists' preparations (pharmaceuticals); malt beverages

(G-8998)
ANDRONACO INC (PA)
4855 Broadmoor Ave Se (49512-5360)
PHONE..................................616 554-4600
Ronald V Andronaco, *CEO*
Adam Hanson, *Engineer*
Scott Palmitier, *CFO*
Bob Varela, *Sales Dir*
Colleen Reeves, *Sales Staff*
EMP: 4
SALES (est): 147.8MM **Privately Held**
SIC: 3052 Air line or air brake hose, rubber or rubberized fabric

(G-8999)
ARCANUM ALLOYS INC
4460 44th St Se Ste F (49512-4096)
PHONE..................................312 810-4479
Daniel Bullard, *CEO*
Ravi Oswal, *Vice Pres*
Joseph McDermott, *VP Mfg*
David Keifer, *VP Sales*
Jared Warrick, *Director*
EMP: 7 **EST:** 2011
SALES (est): 1.5MM **Privately Held**
SIC: 3325 Alloy steel castings, except investment

(G-9000)
AUTOCAM CORPORATION (HQ)
Also Called: Autocam Prcsion Cmpnents Group
4180 40th St Se (49512-4122)
P.O. Box 42404, Indianapolis IN (46242-0404)
PHONE..................................616 698-0707
John R Buchan, *COO*
Frank Zacsek, *Engineer*
Warren A Veltman, *CFO*
Ernest Barnett, *Maintence Staff*
▲ **EMP:** 325
SQ FT: 190,000
SALES (est): 335.5MM
SALES (corp-wide): 770.6MM **Publicly Held**
SIC: 3572 3841 5084 3714 Computer disk & drum drives & components; surgical & medical instruments; fuel injection systems; motor vehicle brake systems & parts
PA: Nn, Inc.
6210 Ardrey Kell Rd
Charlotte NC 28277
980 264-4300

(G-9001)
AUTOCAM CORPORATION
4070 East Paris Ave Se (49512-3963)
PHONE..................................616 698-0707
John Swistak, *Engineer*
John C Kennedy, *Branch Mgr*
Mike Chambers, *Technology*
EMP: 113
SALES (corp-wide): 770.6MM **Publicly Held**
SIC: 3714 Motor vehicle parts & accessories
HQ: Autocam Corporation
4180 40th St Se
Kentwood MI 49512
616 698-0707

(G-9002)
AUTOCAM MED DVC HOLDINGS LLC (PA)
4152 East Paris Ave Se (49512-3911)
PHONE..................................616 541-8080
John C Kennedy, *President*
Warren A Veltman, *Officer*
EMP: 2
SQ FT: 190,000
SALES (est): 35.5MM **Privately Held**
SIC: 3841 3842 Surgical & medical instruments; implants, surgical

(G-9003)
BIOCORRECT ORTHOTICS LAB
5147 East Paris Ave Se # 21 (49512-5457)
PHONE..................................616 356-5030
Stacy Parent, *Mng Member*
EMP: 3
SALES (est): 353.4K **Privately Held**
SIC: 3842 Orthopedic appliances

(G-9004)
CORVAC COMPOSITES LLC
4450 36th St Se (49512-1917)
PHONE..................................616 281-4059
Christine Black, *Controller*
EMP: 200
SALES (corp-wide): 171MM **Privately Held**
SIC: 3714 Motor vehicle parts & accessories
HQ: Corvac Composites, Llc
104 84th St Sw
Byron Center MI 49315

(G-9005)
ETHYLENE LLC
4855 Broadmoor Ave Se (49512-5360)
PHONE..................................616 554-3464
Ron V Andronaco,
Michael R Sheridan,
▲ **EMP:** 26 **EST:** 1950
SQ FT: 64,000

GEOGRAPHIC SECTION — Kentwood - Kent County (G-9030)

SALES (est): 6.4MM
SALES (corp-wide): 147.8MM **Privately Held**
SIC: 3084 3089 3441 Plastics pipe; fittings for pipe, plastic; fabricated structural metal
PA: Andronaco, Inc.
4855 Broadmoor Ave Se
Kentwood MI 49512
616 554-4600

(G-9006)
FLOWCOR LLC (PA)
4855 Broadmoor Ave Se (49512-5360)
PHONE 616 554-1100
Ronald V Andronaco, *Mng Member*
EMP: 5
SALES (est): 1.1MM **Privately Held**
SIC: 3592 Valves

(G-9007)
FRESHWATER DGTAL MDIA PRTNRS
4585 40th St Se (49512-4036)
PHONE 616 446-1771
Jonathan Dodge, *Exec VP*
Mathew Downey, *Mng Member*
EMP: 13
SALES (est): 931.9K **Privately Held**
SIC: 3993 7812 7336 Signs & advertising specialties; video production; graphic arts & related design

(G-9008)
HAERTER STAMPING LLC
3840 Model Ct Se (49512-3938)
PHONE 616 871-9400
Martin Haerter, *Managing Dir*
Greg May, *Engineer*
Wolfgang Haerter,
◆ EMP: 60
SQ FT: 80,385
SALES (est): 21.3MM **Privately Held**
WEB: www.haerter.com
SIC: 3469 Ornamental metal stampings

(G-9009)
HEARTHSIDE FOOD SOLUTIONS LLC
Also Called: H4 Plant
4185 44th St Se (49512-4004)
PHONE 616 871-6240
EMP: 223 **Privately Held**
SIC: 2043 2048 Cereal breakfast foods; prepared feeds
PA: Hearthside Food Solutions, Llc
3500 Lacey Rd Ste 300
Downers Grove IL 60515

(G-9010)
HEARTHSIDE FOOD SOLUTIONS LLC
Also Called: H1 Plant
3061 Shaffer Ave Se (49512-1709)
PHONE 616 574-2000
Perry Kogelschatz, *Manager*
EMP: 395 **Privately Held**
SIC: 2043 Cereal breakfast foods
PA: Hearthside Food Solutions, Llc
3500 Lacey Rd Ste 300
Downers Grove IL 60515

(G-9011)
HILLS-MCCANNA LLC
4855 Broadmoor Ave Se (49512-5360)
PHONE 616 554-9308
Paul Tenbrook, *CFO*
Ronald Andronaco, *Mng Member*
Rick Vinning, *Info Tech Mgr*
▲ EMP: 90 EST: 2008
SALES (est): 13.3MM
SALES (corp-wide): 147.8MM **Privately Held**
SIC: 3491 Industrial valves
PA: Andronaco, Inc.
4855 Broadmoor Ave Se
Kentwood MI 49512
616 554-4600

(G-9012)
ID ENGNRING ATMTED SYSTEMS INC
3650 44th St Se (49512-3916)
P.O. Box 888861 (49588-8861)
PHONE 616 656-0182
Dana Sutterfield, *CEO*
Keith Pagel, *President*
Kraig Vruggink, *Vice Pres*
Leonard Kogut, *Manager*
EMP: 19
SQ FT: 21,470
SALES (est): 5.8MM **Privately Held**
WEB: www.idengineering.com
SIC: 3599 Custom machinery

(G-9013)
KENTWOOD FUEL INC
1980 44th St Se (49508-5049)
PHONE 616 455-2387
EMP: 4 EST: 2015
SALES (est): 181.6K **Privately Held**
SIC: 2869 Mfg Industrial Organic Chemicals

(G-9014)
KHALSA METAL PRODUCTS INC
3142 Broadmoor Ave Se (49512-1845)
PHONE 616 791-4794
Manjinder Singh, *President*
Manpreet Singh, *Opers Mgr*
Menganber Singh, *Manager*
EMP: 6
SALES (est): 500K **Privately Held**
SIC: 3545 Precision tools, machinists'

(G-9015)
LACKS EXTERIOR SYSTEMS LLC
4655 Patterson Ave Se (49512-5337)
PHONE 616 554-7805
Brian Benedict, *Branch Mgr*
EMP: 17
SALES (corp-wide): 715.6MM **Privately Held**
SIC: 3089 Plastic hardware & building products
HQ: Lacks Exterior Systems, Llc
5460 Cascade Rd Se
Grand Rapids MI 49546
616 949-6570

(G-9016)
LACKS EXTERIOR SYSTEMS LLC
Also Called: Lacks Trim Systems
3703 Patterson Ave Se (49512-4024)
PHONE 616 554-7180
Richard Lacks,
EMP: 20
SALES (corp-wide): 715.6MM **Privately Held**
SIC: 3465 Body parts, automobile: stamped metal
HQ: Lacks Exterior Systems, Llc
5460 Cascade Rd Se
Grand Rapids MI 49546
616 949-6570

(G-9017)
LACKS INDUSTRIES INC
Also Called: Lacks Wheel Trim Systems
4655 Patterson Ave Se D (49512-5337)
PHONE 616 554-7135
Bill Mull, *Branch Mgr*
EMP: 50
SALES (corp-wide): 715.6MM **Privately Held**
SIC: 3089 Plastic processing; molding primary plastic
HQ: Lacks Industries, Inc.
5460 Cascade Rd Se
Grand Rapids MI 49546
616 949-6570

(G-9018)
MAGNA EXTRORS INTRORS AMER INC
5085 Kraft Ave Se (49512-9707)
PHONE 616 786-7000
Fulker Rudnitzki, *Manager*
EMP: 5
SALES (corp-wide): 40.8B **Privately Held**
WEB: www.magnaint.com
SIC: 3479 Coating of metals & formed products
HQ: Magna Exteriors Of America, Inc.
750 Tower Dr
Troy MI 48098
248 631-1100

(G-9019)
MAGNA MIRRORS AMERICA INC
Also Called: Engineering Center
5085 Kraft Ave Se (49512-9707)
PHONE 616 786-7000
David O'Connell, *Branch Mgr*
EMP: 20
SALES (corp-wide): 40.8B **Privately Held**
WEB: www.donnelly.com
SIC: 3231 Mirrors, truck & automobile: made from purchased glass
HQ: Magna Mirrors Of America, Inc.
5085 Kraft Ave Se
Grand Rapids MI 49512
616 786-5120

(G-9020)
MICRON HOLDINGS INC
4436 Broadmoor Ave Se (49512-5305)
PHONE 616 698-0707
John C Kennedy, *President*
John R Buchan, *COO*
Eduardo Renner De Castilho, *COO*
John F X Daly, *Vice Pres*
Jack Daly, *Vice Pres*
EMP: 2612
SQ FT: 190,000
SALES (est): 144.3MM **Privately Held**
SIC: 3714 Motor vehicle parts & accessories

(G-9021)
NIL-COR LLC
4855 Broadmoor Ave Se (49512-5360)
PHONE 616 554-3100
Ronald Andronaco, *CEO*
Lisa Miller, *Purch Agent*
Joe Beaumont, *Engineer*
Scott Palmitier, *CFO*
Kaila Hicks, *Executive Asst*
▲ EMP: 200
SALES (est): 17MM
SALES (corp-wide): 147.8MM **Privately Held**
SIC: 3491 Industrial valves
PA: Andronaco, Inc.
4855 Broadmoor Ave Se
Kentwood MI 49512
616 554-4600

(G-9022)
PLASTIC MOLD TECHNOLOGY INC (PA)
4201 Broadmoor Ave Se (49512-3934)
PHONE 616 698-9810
Gary K Proos, *President*
Dave Filling, *Principal*
Gary S Proos - Plant, *Manager*
▲ EMP: 51 EST: 1958
SQ FT: 33,000
SALES (est): 14.2MM **Privately Held**
WEB: www.plasticmold.com
SIC: 3089 Injection molding of plastics

(G-9023)
PLASTIC PLATE LLC
5675 Kraft Ave Se (49512-9624)
PHONE 616 698-3678
Jeff Cowdrey, *Manager*
EMP: 150
SALES (corp-wide): 715.6MM **Privately Held**
SIC: 3714 Motor vehicle parts & accessories
HQ: Plastic Plate, Llc
3500 Raleigh Dr Se
Grand Rapids MI 49512
616 455-5240

(G-9024)
PLASTIC PLATE LLC
3505 Kraft Ave Se (49512-2033)
PHONE 616 949-6570
John Crosby, *Maintence Staff*
EMP: 100
SALES (corp-wide): 715.6MM **Privately Held**
SIC: 3714 Motor vehicle parts & accessories
HQ: Plastic Plate, Llc
3500 Raleigh Dr Se
Grand Rapids MI 49512
616 455-5240

(G-9025)
POLYVALVE LLC
Also Called: An Andronaco Industries Co
4855 Broadmoor Ave Se (49512-5360)
PHONE 616 656-2264
Ronald V Andronaco, *President*
▲ EMP: 1
SALES (est): 2.5MM
SALES (corp-wide): 147.8MM **Privately Held**
SIC: 3592 Valves
PA: Andronaco, Inc.
4855 Broadmoor Ave Se
Kentwood MI 49512
616 554-4600

(G-9026)
PUREFLEX INC
4855 Broadmoor Ave Se (49512-5360)
PHONE 616 554-1100
Ronald V Andronaco, *CEO*
Dave Knoop, *Purchasing*
Scott Palmitier, *CFO*
Mike Sczepanski, *Cust Svc Dir*
Mike Szepanski, *Sales Executive*
▲ EMP: 200
SQ FT: 200,000
SALES (est): 46.5MM
SALES (corp-wide): 147.8MM **Privately Held**
WEB: www.pureflex.com
SIC: 3052 Rubber hose
PA: Andronaco, Inc.
4855 Broadmoor Ave Se
Kentwood MI 49512
616 554-4600

(G-9027)
R J REYNOLDS TOBACCO COMPANY
3156 Breton Rd Se (49512-1750)
PHONE 616 949-3740
Mike Kakabeeke, *Branch Mgr*
EMP: 8
SALES (corp-wide): 31.4B **Privately Held**
WEB: www.carolinagroup.com
SIC: 5194 2111 Tobacco & tobacco products; cigarettes
HQ: R. J. Reynolds Tobacco Company
401 N Main St
Winston Salem NC 27101
336 741-5000

(G-9028)
RAMPARTS LLC
4855 Broadmoor Ave Se (49512-5360)
PHONE 616 656-2250
Ronald V Andronaco, *CEO*
Dan Urquhart, *Engineer*
Scott Palmitier, *CFO*
EMP: 200
SALES (est): 42.9MM
SALES (corp-wide): 147.8MM **Privately Held**
SIC: 3561 Pumps & pumping equipment
PA: Andronaco, Inc.
4855 Broadmoor Ave Se
Kentwood MI 49512
616 554-4600

(G-9029)
RLS INTERVENTIONAL INC
Also Called: Inrad
4375 Donkers Ct Se (49512-4054)
PHONE 616 301-7800
Steve Field, *CEO*
Susan Field, *Vice Pres*
EMP: 10
SQ FT: 2,500
SALES (est): 1.7MM **Privately Held**
WEB: www.inrad-inc.com
SIC: 3841 Biopsy instruments & equipment

(G-9030)
ROBERT BOSCH FUEL SYSTEMS LLC
4700 S Broadmoor Ste 100 (49512)
PHONE 616 554-6500
Dave Winfree, *Senior Engr*
Charlie Syrcuse, *Mng Member*
EMP: 200 EST: 2003

SALES (est): 113.9K
SALES (corp-wide): 294.8MM **Privately Held**
SIC: 3714 Fuel systems & parts, motor vehicle
HQ: Robert Bosch Llc
2800 S 25th Ave
Broadview IL 60155
248 876-1000

(G-9031)
SASSY 14 LLC (DH)
3729 Patterson Ave Se (49512-4024)
P.O. Box 888654 (49588-8654)
PHONE.................................616 243-0767
Tom Bratton, *CEO*
Cel Minster, *COO*
Tammy Symonds, *VP Finance*
EMP: 39 **EST:** 2014
SALES (est): 19.7MM
SALES (corp-wide): 300K **Privately Held**
SIC: 3944 5945 Games, toys & children's vehicles; hobby, toy & game shops; children's toys & games, except dolls
HQ: Holding Angelcare Inc, Le
201 Boul De L'industrie Bureau 104
Candiac QC J5R 6
514 761-0511

(G-9032)
SC CUSTOM DISPLAY INC
Also Called: Studiocraft
3010 Shaffer Ave Se Ste 1 (49512-1773)
PHONE.................................616 940-0563
EMP: 8
SQ FT: 9,000
SALES (est): 610K **Privately Held**
SIC: 2542 Mfg Partitions/Fixtures-Nonwood

(G-9033)
THERMOFORMS INC
4374 Donkers Ct Se (49512-4054)
PHONE.................................616 974-0055
Timmothy Zych, *President*
Pat Murphy, *Plant Mgr*
Belinda Dehaven, *Opers Staff*
EMP: 19
SQ FT: 27,000
SALES: 2.6MM **Privately Held**
WEB: www.thermoformsinc.com
SIC: 3089 Injection molded finished plastic products

(G-9034)
TMC FURNITURE INC (PA)
4525 Airwest Dr Se (49512-3951)
PHONE.................................734 622-0080
Blake Ratcliffe, *President*
EMP: 30
SQ FT: 25,000
SALES (est): 3.3MM **Privately Held**
WEB: www.tmcfurniture.com
SIC: 2531 School furniture; library furniture

(G-9035)
YANFENG US AUTOMOTIVE
5050 Kendrick St Se (49512-9205)
PHONE.................................616 975-4000
Jennifer Wendt, *Branch Mgr*
EMP: 150
SALES (corp-wide): 55MM **Privately Held**
SIC: 3799 Off-road automobiles, except recreational vehicles
HQ: Yanfeng Us Automotive Interior Systems Ii Llc
5757 N Green Bay Ave
Milwaukee WI 53209
205 477-4225

(G-9036)
ZOE HEALTH
5715 Christie Ave Se (49508-6236)
PHONE.................................616 485-1909
Sharon Chase, *Owner*
EMP: 4
SALES: 800K **Privately Held**
SIC: 3999 Manufacturing industries

Kewadin
Antrim County

(G-9037)
COYNE MACHINE & TOOL LLC
13275 Winters Rd (49648-9139)
PHONE.................................231 944-8755
Ruth Coyne,
Ron Coyne Jr,
Ronald Coyne Sr,
EMP: 3
SQ FT: 2,000
SALES (est): 462.6K **Privately Held**
SIC: 3545 7699 Machine tool accessories; knife, saw & tool sharpening & repair

(G-9038)
GEOMEMBRANE SERVICES INC
6516 Birch Lake Rd (49648-9081)
P.O. Box 312 (49648-0312)
PHONE.................................231 264-9030
James Lundy, *President*
EMP: 12
SALES (est): 2.6MM **Privately Held**
SIC: 3443 Liners/lining

(G-9039)
GREAT LAKES PACKING CO
6556 Quarterline Rd (49648-8907)
PHONE.................................231 264-5561
Jon Beliqutte, *President*
Norman Veliquette, *President*
Dean Veliquette, *Vice Pres*
Jon T Veliquette, *Admin Sec*
▼ **EMP:** 20
SQ FT: 30,000
SALES (est): 3.5MM **Privately Held**
SIC: 0723 2033 Fruit (fresh) packing services; canned fruits & specialties

(G-9040)
SMOOTHIES
11937 Stone Circle Dr (49648-8003)
PHONE.................................231 498-2374
Jeffrey C Urbanavage, *Owner*
EMP: 3 **EST:** 2014
SALES (est): 143.8K **Privately Held**
SIC: 2037 Frozen fruits & vegetables

Keweenaw Bay
Baraga County

(G-9041)
SUPERIOR TOOL & FABG LLC
13529 Old 41 Rd (49908-9022)
PHONE.................................906 353-7588
EMP: 8 **EST:** 2010
SQ FT: 6,000
SALES: 500K **Privately Held**
SIC: 3593 Mfg Fluid Power Cylinders

Kimball
St. Clair County

(G-9042)
AUTO QUIP INC
70 Airport Dr (48074-4404)
PHONE.................................810 364-3366
Paul Sossi, *President*
Annemarie Sossi, *Vice Pres*
EMP: 10
SQ FT: 11,100
SALES: 1MM **Privately Held**
WEB: www.autoquipinc.com
SIC: 3291 Abrasive products

(G-9043)
F C SIMPSON LIME CO
1293 Wadhams Rd (48074-3112)
PHONE.................................810 367-3510
R Kurt Simpson, *President*
EMP: 5 **EST:** 1959
SALES (est): 483.1K **Privately Held**
SIC: 0711 2874 4212 Lime spreading services; soil chemical treatment services; calcium meta-phosphate; animal & farm product transportation services

(G-9044)
HAMMARS CONTRACTING LLC
Also Called: Hammar's Welding
1177 Wadhams Rd (48074-3111)
PHONE.................................810 367-3037
Timothy Hammar, *Owner*
Robert Hammar, *Owner*
EMP: 14
SQ FT: 2,500
SALES (est): 1.8MM **Privately Held**
SIC: 7699 3443 Industrial equipment services; dumpsters, garbage

(G-9045)
MPP CORP
Also Called: Massobrio Precision Products
82 Airport Dr (48074-4404)
P.O. Box 275, Marysville (48040-0275)
PHONE.................................810 364-2939
Carlo Massobrio, *President*
Aurelio Massobrio, *Vice Pres*
Frank Nothelle, *Manager*
▲ **EMP:** 28
SQ FT: 13,800
SALES (est): 5.6MM **Privately Held**
WEB: www.mppcorp.net
SIC: 3544 Forms (molds), for foundry & plastics working machinery

(G-9046)
PEPSI BOTTLING GROUP
Also Called: Pepsico
2111 Wadhams Rd (48074-1914)
PHONE.................................810 966-8060
Brian Connelly, *Principal*
EMP: 7
SALES (est): 615.3K **Privately Held**
SIC: 2086 Soft drinks: packaged in cans, bottles, etc.

(G-9047)
PEPSI-COLA METRO BTLG CO INC
2111 Wadhams Rd (48074-1914)
PHONE.................................810 987-2181
Brian Connelly, *Manager*
EMP: 25
SALES (corp-wide): 64.6B **Publicly Held**
WEB: www.joy-of-cola.com
SIC: 4225 2086 General warehousing & storage; carbonated beverages, nonalcoholic: bottled & canned
HQ: Pepsi-Cola Metropolitan Bottling Company, Inc.
1111 Westchester Ave
White Plains NY 10604
914 767-6000

(G-9048)
PREFERRED INDUSTRIES INC
11 Ash Dr (48074-4401)
PHONE.................................810 364-4090
Charles Kott, *President*
Alex Morton, *General Mgr*
Katie Lezin, *Technology*
▲ **EMP:** 30
SQ FT: 20,000
SALES (est): 7.1MM **Privately Held**
SIC: 3544 5051 Special dies & tools; metals service centers & offices

(G-9049)
WIRETECH WIRE EDM SERVICE INC
2243 Wadhams Rd Ste A (48074-1931)
PHONE.................................810 966-9912
Roy Cole, *President*
EMP: 3
SQ FT: 2,750
SALES (est): 406K **Privately Held**
SIC: 3599 Electrical discharge machining (EDM)

Kincheloe
Chippewa County

(G-9050)
E U P WOODS SHAVINGS
16816 S Hugginin St (49788-1900)
PHONE.................................906 495-1141
Mickey Hoffman, *Principal*
EMP: 3

SALES (est): 270.6K **Privately Held**
SIC: 2421 Sawdust, shavings & wood chips

(G-9051)
FLORIDA COCA-COLA BOTTLING CO
4760 W Curtis St (49788-1584)
PHONE.................................906 495-2261
Julane Underhill, *Manager*
EMP: 15
SALES (corp-wide): 31.8B **Publicly Held**
WEB: www.ge.cokecce.com
SIC: 2086 Bottled & canned soft drinks
HQ: Florida Coca-Cola Bottling Company
521 Lake Kathy Dr
Brandon FL 33510
813 569-2600

(G-9052)
KINROSS FAB & MACHINE INC
17422 S Dolan St (49788-1615)
PHONE.................................906 495-1900
Charles Esson, *President*
Paul Odom, *Info Tech Mgr*
EMP: 22
SALES: 500K **Privately Held**
SIC: 7692 Welding repair

(G-9053)
SUPERIOR FABRICATION CO LLC
17499 S Dolan St Bldg 434 (49788-1615)
PHONE.................................906 495-5634
Jay Miller, *Vice Pres*
Angela Fuller, *Accountant*
Joseph Dobrowolski, *Mng Member*
Larry Fitzpatrick, *Manager*
David Hill, *Manager*
▲ **EMP:** 100
SQ FT: 130,000
SALES (est): 32.1MM **Privately Held**
WEB: www.supfab.com
SIC: 3812 3531 Defense systems & equipment; construction machinery

Kingsford
Dickinson County

(G-9054)
BAUMAN ENGRAVING & SIGNS INC
808 John Mcneil Dr (49802-4446)
PHONE.................................906 774-9460
Dean C Bauman, *CEO*
EMP: 4
SQ FT: 1,692
SALES (est): 431.5K **Privately Held**
WEB: www.baumanengraving.com
SIC: 3993 Signs & advertising specialties

(G-9055)
C J GRAPHICS INC
121 S Carpenter Ave (49802-4520)
PHONE.................................906 774-8636
Nicole Lutz, *President*
EMP: 9
SQ FT: 4,600
SALES (est): 840K **Privately Held**
WEB: www.cjgraphics.com
SIC: 2752 Commercial printing, offset

(G-9056)
COUNTRY SCHOOLHOUSE KINGSFORD
600 East Blvd (49802-4508)
PHONE.................................906 828-1971
EMP: 3 **EST:** 2016
SALES (est): 90K **Privately Held**
SIC: 2861 Charcoal, except activated

(G-9057)
DICKINSON HOMES INC (PA)
1500 W Breitung Ave (49802-5127)
P.O. Box 2245, Iron Mountain (49802-2245)
PHONE.................................906 774-5800
Albert Santoni, *President*
Paul Santoni, *Vice Pres*
Steve Kindness, *Project Mgr*
Peter Demboski, *Engineer*
Anthony Santoni, *Engineer*

GEOGRAPHIC SECTION

EMP: 40
SQ FT: 80,000
SALES (est): 9.5MM **Privately Held**
WEB: www.dickinsonhomes.com
SIC: **2452** Modular homes, prefabricated, wood

(G-9058)
GREDE LLC
Iron Mountain Foundry
801 S Carpenter Ave (49802-5511)
PHONE..................906 774-7250
Randy Priem, *VP Opers*
EMP: 500
SALES (corp-wide): 7.2B **Publicly Held**
WEB: www.grede.com
SIC: **3321** 3322 Gray iron castings; malleable iron foundries
HQ: Grede Llc
  20750 Civic Center Dr # 100
  Southfield MI 48076

(G-9059)
HARVEY PATTERN WORKS INC
410 North Blvd (49802-4414)
P.O. Box 2024 (49802-2024)
PHONE..................906 774-4285
Jeff Harvey, *President*
EMP: 10
SQ FT: 8,000
SALES (est): 1.3MM **Privately Held**
SIC: **3543** Foundry patternmaking

(G-9060)
KINGSFORD BROACH & TOOL INC
2200 Maule Dr (49802-5101)
P.O. Box 2277 (49802-2277)
PHONE..................906 774-4917
Dominic Shultz, *President*
Jack Raney, *Vice Pres*
Keith Baldwin, *Prdtn Mgr*
Angela Anderson, *IT/INT Sup*
EMP: 42
SQ FT: 22,000
SALES: 5.3MM **Privately Held**
WEB: www.kingsfordbroach.com
SIC: **3545** 7389 Broaches (machine tool accessories);

(G-9061)
LAKE SHORE SYSTEMS INC (PA)
2141 Woodward Ave (49802-4206)
PHONE..................906 774-1500
Jessica Frost, *CEO*
Bart Lamers, *CFO*
Kelly Gaucher, *Controller*
Kevin Lindholm, *Program Mgr*
▲ EMP: 78
SQ FT: 20,000
SALES (est): 77MM **Privately Held**
SIC: **3537** 3532 3731 Industrial trucks & tractors; mining machinery; shipbuilding & repairing

(G-9062)
LODAL INC
620 N Hooper St (49802-5400)
PHONE..................906 779-1700
Bernard Leger, *President*
John R Giuliani, *Corp Secy*
◆ EMP: 70 EST: 1946
SQ FT: 360,000
SALES (est): 16.7MM **Privately Held**
WEB: www.lodal.com
SIC: **3713** Truck bodies (motor vehicles)

(G-9063)
NELSON PAINT CO OF MICH INC (PA)
Also Called: Nelson Technologies
1 Nelson Dr (49802-4561)
P.O. Box 2040 (49802-2040)
PHONE..................906 774-5566
Richard Louys, *President*
Karen Cox, *Vice Pres*
EMP: 3
SQ FT: 20,000
SALES (est): 1.3MM **Privately Held**
WEB: www.nelsonpaint.com
SIC: **2851** 5941 3953 Paints, waterproof; sporting goods & bicycle shops; marking devices

(G-9064)
NELSON PAINT COMPANY ALA INC (PA)
1 Nelson Dr (49802-4561)
P.O. Box 2040 (49802-2040)
PHONE..................906 774-5566
Barbara N Louys, *President*
Richard Louys, *Vice Pres*
John Hannon, *Plant Mgr*
Marsha Geib, *Manager*
Karen Cox, *Admin Sec*
EMP: 3
SQ FT: 33,000
SALES (est): 1MM **Privately Held**
WEB: www.nelson-paint.com
SIC: **2851** Paints & paint additives

(G-9065)
NORTHWOODS MANUFACTURING INC
850 East Blvd (49802-4436)
P.O. Box 2294 (49802-2294)
PHONE..................906 779-2370
Jon Pipp, *President*
Joe Schutte, *Plant Mgr*
Jason Paupore, *Human Resources*
Greg Linsmeyer, *Executive*
▲ EMP: 70
SQ FT: 100,000
SALES (est): 22MM **Privately Held**
WEB: www.northwoodsmanufacturing.com
SIC: **3444** 3441 3548 5211 Culverts, flumes & pipes; fabricated structural metal for ships; welding & cutting apparatus & accessories; insulation material, building; barber & beauty shop equipment; fire- or burglary-resistive products

(G-9066)
SM SMITH CO
1105 Westwood Ave (49802-6601)
PHONE..................906 774-8258
Steve M Smith, *President*
Sharon L Ray, *Vice Pres*
▲ EMP: 3
SQ FT: 2,500
SALES: 200K **Privately Held**
WEB: www.smsmithco.com
SIC: **2311** Firemen's uniforms: made from purchased materials

(G-9067)
STANDARD ELECTRIC COMPANY
701 Valsam St (49802)
PHONE..................906 774-4455
Mary Brooks, *Branch Mgr*
EMP: 20
SALES (corp-wide): 210.4MM **Privately Held**
SIC: **5063** 3825 Electrical supplies; electrical fittings & construction materials; electrical construction materials; frequency meters: electrical, mechanical & electronic
PA: Standard Electric Company
  2650 Trautner Dr
  Saginaw MI 48604
  989 497-2100

(G-9068)
WILBERT BURIAL VAULT WORKS
609 S Carpenter Ave (49802-5521)
P.O. Box 688, Iron Mountain (49801-0688)
PHONE..................906 786-0261
Alvin Grabowski, *President*
Keith Grabowski, *Vice Pres*
EMP: 8 EST: 1938
SQ FT: 11,520
SALES: 390K **Privately Held**
SIC: **3272** 7261 Burial vaults, concrete or precast terrazzo; septic tanks, concrete; crematory

Kingsley
Grand Traverse County

(G-9069)
5 STAR DRCTIONAL DRLG SVCS IND
8553 Blackman Rd (49649-9671)
P.O. Box 194 (49649-0194)
PHONE..................231 263-2050
Trevor Yetter, *President*
Mike Newman, *Vice Pres*
EMP: 4
SQ FT: 10,000
SALES: 475K **Privately Held**
SIC: **1381** Directional drilling oil & gas wells

(G-9070)
BACH SERVICES & MFG CO LLC
2777 Lynx Ln (49649-9528)
PHONE..................231 263-2777
Robin Bach,
Rick Bach,
EMP: 35
SALES (est): 4.7MM **Privately Held**
SIC: **1389** Construction, repair & dismantling services

(G-9071)
EM A GIVE BREAK SAFETY
6502 M 37 (49649-9773)
PHONE..................231 263-6625
Jeff Mac Dermaid, *Manager*
EMP: 11
SALES (est): 509.7K **Privately Held**
SIC: **8742** 3669 Quality assurance consultant; pedestrian traffic control equipment

(G-9072)
MICHAEL CHRIS STORMS
Also Called: Fire-Pit Pellets
1401 W Center Rd (49649-9734)
PHONE..................231 263-7516
Michael Chris Storms, *Owner*
Joy Storms, *Co-Owner*
EMP: 5
SALES (est): 469.5K **Privately Held**
WEB: www.cherrypitstore.com
SIC: **2448** Wood pallets & skids

Kingston
Tuscola County

(G-9073)
MIDYNACO LLC
Also Called: MI Dynaco
3719 Ross St (48741-9775)
PHONE..................989 550-8552
Dale Manor,
Dave Gibson,
EMP: 4 EST: 2004
SALES (est): 331K
SALES (corp-wide): 1MM **Privately Held**
SIC: **3442** Metal doors, sash & trim
PA: Memtech, Inc.
  9033 General Dr
  Plymouth MI 48170
  734 455-8550

La Salle
Monroe County

(G-9074)
REED YACHT SALES LLC (PA)
11840 Toledo Beach Rd (48145-9767)
PHONE..................419 304-4405
Cheryl Bogedain,
EMP: 6
SALES (est): 4.5MM **Privately Held**
SIC: **3732** Yachts, building & repairing

Lachine
Alpena County

(G-9075)
NORTHERN MICH CHRSTN CUNSELING
5010 Beaushaw Rd (49753-8705)
PHONE..................989 278-2590
EMP: 3 EST: 2016
SALES (est): 100K **Privately Held**
SIC: **2435** Hardwood veneer & plywood

(G-9076)
NORTHERN MICHIG
Also Called: Northern Promotions
12595 Long Rapids Rd (49753-9630)
PHONE..................989 340-1272
Kevan R Rogers,
EMP: 10
SQ FT: 1,500
SALES: 1MM **Privately Held**
SIC: **3861** 7336 Printing frames, photographic; commercial art & illustration

(G-9077)
PATCHWOOD PRODUCTS INC
105 Stagecoach Dr (49753-9610)
PHONE..................989 742-2605
Patricia Paczkowski, *Branch Mgr*
James Paczkowski, *Admin Sec*
EMP: 10
SQ FT: 50,000
SALES (corp-wide): 1.8MM **Privately Held**
SIC: **2448** Pallets, wood
PA: Patchwood Products, Inc.
  14797 State St
  Hillman MI 49746
  989 742-2605

(G-9078)
ROBERT CRAWFORD & SON LOGGING
15490 Green Farm Rd (49753-9359)
PHONE..................989 379-2712
Robert Crawford, *CEO*
EMP: 4
SALES (est): 452.9K **Privately Held**
SIC: **2411** Logging camps & contractors

(G-9079)
VIA-TECH CORP
11715 M 32 W (49753-9659)
P.O. Box 233, Alpena (49707-0233)
PHONE..................989 358-7028
Gregory C Winter, *President*
Deborah J Winter, *Corp Secy*
EMP: 11
SQ FT: 11,000
SALES (est): 2.7MM **Privately Held**
SIC: **3535** Conveyors & conveying equipment

Laingsburg
Shiawassee County

(G-9080)
LAINGSBURG SCREW INC
9805 Round Lake Rd (48848-9404)
PHONE..................517 651-2757
Brian Grable, *President*
Leslie Graham, *Treasurer*
EMP: 6
SQ FT: 2,400
SALES (est): 663.7K **Privately Held**
SIC: **3544** Special dies, tools, jigs & fixtures

(G-9081)
TOASTMASTERS INTERNATIONAL
6687 Westview Dr (48848-9489)
PHONE..................517 651-6507
Johnson Baugh, *Treasurer*
EMP: 34

SALES (corp-wide): 31.3MM **Privately Held**
WEB: www.d70toastmasters.org
SIC: 8299 2721 Educational service, non-degree granting: continuing educ.; magazines: publishing only, not printed on site
PA: Toastmasters International
9127 S Jamaica St Ste 400
Englewood CO 80112
949 858-8255

Lake
Clare County

(G-9082)
GDS ENTERPRISES
6500 N Brinton Rd (48632-9769)
PHONE 989 644-3115
Gilbert Schrock, *Owner*
EMP: 3
SALES (est): 190K **Privately Held**
SIC: 3594 3533 7699 Fluid power pumps & motors; drilling tools for gas, oil or water wells; hydraulic equipment repair

Lake Ann
Benzie County

(G-9083)
ALL DEALER INVENTORY LLC
8148 Maple City Hwy (49650-9620)
P.O. Box 32054, Tucson AZ (85751-2054)
PHONE 231 342-9823
Kimberly Deatrick, *Principal*
EMP: 3 EST: 2009
SALES (est): 117.5K **Privately Held**
SIC: 7319 7313 2721 Distribution of advertising material or sample services; electronic media advertising representatives; printed media advertising representatives; magazines: publishing only, not printed on site

(G-9084)
ANN LAKE HARDWOOD INC
17437 Almira Rd (49650-9600)
PHONE 231 275-6406
Mark E Gabrick, *President*
Michael Brigham, *Treasurer*
EMP: 8
SQ FT: 8,000
SALES (est): 750K **Privately Held**
WEB: www.lakeannhardwoods.com
SIC: 2421 Lumber: rough, sawed or planed

Lake City
Missaukee County

(G-9085)
BOHNING COMPANY LTD (PA)
7361 N 7 Mile Rd (49651-9293)
PHONE 231 229-4247
Larry Griffith, *President*
Dale E Voice, *Vice Pres*
Tara Carlson, *Buyer*
Keith Allan, *Engineer*
Bob Potter, *Design Engr*
◆ EMP: 38
SQ FT: 31,400
SALES (est): 4.6MM **Privately Held**
WEB: www.bohning.com
SIC: 3949 2899 Archery equipment, general; golf equipment; chemical preparations

(G-9086)
BOHNING COMPANY LTD
7650 N 7 Mile Rd (49651)
PHONE 231 229-4247
Larry R Griffith, *President*
EMP: 20
SQ FT: 13,000
SALES (corp-wide): 4.6MM **Privately Held**
WEB: www.bohning.com
SIC: 3949 Archery equipment, general; golf equipment

PA: Bohning Company Ltd.
7361 N 7 Mile Rd
Lake City MI 49651
231 229-4247

(G-9087)
GAGE NUMERICAL INC
Also Called: Inspection Control Company
900 S 7 Mile Rd (49651-8537)
PHONE 231 328-4426
Glen F Corwin, *President*
Phyllis L Corwin, *Vice Pres*
EMP: 5
SQ FT: 5,168
SALES: 350K **Privately Held**
WEB: www.thermogauge.com
SIC: 3545 8734 Gauge blocks; calibration & certification

(G-9088)
HOLLOWAY FUR DRESSING
3590 W Sanborn Rd (49651-8408)
PHONE 231 258-5200
EMP: 3
SALES (est): 128.8K **Privately Held**
SIC: 3999 5632 Fur Dressing & Processing Service & Ret Fur Coats Hats & Mittens

(G-9089)
JOHN A BIEWER LUMBER COMPANY
1560 W Houghton Lake Rd (49651-9672)
PHONE 231 839-7646
Lawrence Markey Jr, *President*
Jason Otto, *Plant Mgr*
EMP: 8
SALES (est): 1.1MM
SALES (corp-wide): 53.8MM **Privately Held**
SIC: 2421 Sawmills & planing mills, general
PA: John A. Biewer Lumber Company
812 S Riverside Ave
Saint Clair MI 48079
810 329-4789

(G-9090)
LC MANUFACTURING LLC (PA)
Also Called: Lake City Forge
4150 N Wolcott Rd (49651-9126)
PHONE 231 839-7102
Peter Baenen, *CEO*
Doug Crosby, *Purch Agent*
Scott Smith,
EMP: 170 EST: 1975
SQ FT: 5,200
SALES (est): 51.1MM **Privately Held**
WEB: www.lcmanufacturingllc.com
SIC: 3462 3544 Automotive forgings, ferrous: crankshaft, engine, axle, etc.; special dies & tools

(G-9091)
LC MATERIALS
1317 E Sanborn Rd (49651)
PHONE 231 839-4319
Kenneth Gilde, *Manager*
EMP: 25
SALES (corp-wide): 8MM **Privately Held**
SIC: 1442 Common sand mining; gravel mining
PA: Lc Materials
805 W 13th St
Cadillac MI 49601
231 825-2473

(G-9092)
MARK BEEM
Also Called: Beem Fence
861 N Green Rd (49651-9230)
P.O. Box 685 (49651-0685)
PHONE 231 510-8122
Mark Beem, *Owner*
EMP: 6
SALES (est): 292.6K **Privately Held**
SIC: 1799 2499 7389 Fence construction; fencing, docks & other outdoor wood structural products;

(G-9093)
MID MICHIGAN LOGGING
9620 N Nelson Rd (49651-9742)
PHONE 231 229-4501
Terry Frever, *Partner*
Larry Niebrzydowski, *Partner*

EMP: 12
SALES: 2.8MM **Privately Held**
SIC: 2411 Logging camps & contractors; wood chips, produced in the field

(G-9094)
MISSAUKEE MOLDED RUBBER INC
6400 W Blue Rd (49651-8948)
PHONE 231 839-5309
Jay W Price, *President*
Kathy Price, *Treasurer*
EMP: 13
SQ FT: 3,456
SALES: 1.5MM **Privately Held**
WEB: www.mmri-crc.com
SIC: 3069 Molded rubber products

(G-9095)
PARKS SAWMILL PRODUCTS
9775 N Vander Meulen Rd (49651-9279)
PHONE 231 229-4551
Raymond Park, *Principal*
EMP: 3 EST: 2010
SALES (est): 178.1K **Privately Held**
SIC: 2421 Sawmills & planing mills, general

(G-9096)
RIVERSIDE DEFENSE TRAINING LLC
5360 S Dickerson Rd (49651-8662)
PHONE 231 825-2895
Richard A Bradley, *Principal*
EMP: 3
SALES (est): 186.2K **Privately Held**
SIC: 3812 Defense systems & equipment

(G-9097)
VAN DUINEN FOREST PRODUCTS
4680 E Houghton Lake Rd (49651-9546)
PHONE 231 328-4507
Carmen Van Duinen, *President*
Charles Van Duinen, *Principal*
Ave Van Duinen, *Treasurer*
EMP: 12
SALES: 1.3MM **Privately Held**
SIC: 2411 Logging

Lake Leelanau
Leelanau County

(G-9098)
45 NORTH VINEYARD & WINERY
8580 E Horn Rd (49653-9645)
PHONE 231 271-1188
Alanna Grossnickle, *General Mgr*
Steve Grossnickle, *Co-Owner*
Lori Grossnickle, *Co-Owner*
Brian Grossnickle, *Manager*
▲ EMP: 15
SALES (est): 568.8K **Privately Held**
SIC: 2084 Wines

(G-9099)
AURORA CELLARS 2015 LLC
7788 E Horn Rd (49653-9640)
PHONE 231 994-3188
Joanna Simpson,
Samuel Simpson,
EMP: 10 EST: 2015
SALES (est): 367.6K **Privately Held**
SIC: 2084 Wine cellars, bonded: engaged in blending wines

(G-9100)
BAA BAA ZUZU
1006 S Sawmill Rd (49653-8706)
PHONE 231 256-7176
Sue Burns, *President*
Kevin Burns, *Vice Pres*
EMP: 3
SALES (est): 350K **Privately Held**
WEB: www.baabaazuzu.com
SIC: 2339 Women's & misses' athletic clothing & sportswear

(G-9101)
BLUSTONE PARTNERS LLC
Also Called: Blustone Vineyards
780 N Sylt Rd (49653)
P.O. Box 292 (49653-0292)
PHONE 231 256-0146
Tom Knighton, *Mng Member*
EMP: 12
SALES (est): 267.6K **Privately Held**
SIC: 2084 Wines

(G-9102)
E S I INDUSTRIES
10 S Highland Dr (49653-9413)
PHONE 231 256-9345
Larry Hudson, *President*
Stanley Hudson, *Vice Pres*
Jerry Dykema, *Treasurer*
EMP: 15
SQ FT: 10,000
SALES (est): 1.1MM **Privately Held**
WEB: www.esiindustries.com
SIC: 3291 Paper, abrasive: garnet, emery, aluminum oxide coated

(G-9103)
FONTAINE CHATEAU
2290 S French Rd (49653-9558)
PHONE 231 256-0000
Dan Matthias, *Owner*
EMP: 5
SALES (est): 192.3K **Privately Held**
SIC: 2084 5921 5182 Wines; wine; wine

(G-9104)
LEELANAU ENTERPRISE INC
7200 E Duck Lake Rd (49653-9779)
PHONE 231 256-9827
Alan C Campbell, *President*
Pat Varley, *Graphic Designe*
EMP: 12
SALES (est): 846.8K **Privately Held**
WEB: www.leelanaunews.com
SIC: 2711 Newspapers: publishing only, not printed on site

(G-9105)
PDM COMPANY
Also Called: PDM Lumber Co
2563 S Sandy Ridge Rd (49653-9720)
PHONE 231 946-4444
Robert G Kelly, *Principal*
Robert Kelly, *President*
Pamela Kelly, *Treasurer*
EMP: 10
SQ FT: 15,000
SALES (est): 1.2MM **Privately Held**
SIC: 2421 5031 Kiln drying of lumber; lumber: rough, dressed & finished

(G-9106)
PLAMONDON OIL CO INC
525 W Main St (49653-9499)
P.O. Box 139 (49653-0139)
PHONE 231 256-9261
Michele Gipun, *Principal*
EMP: 4
SALES (est): 521.9K **Privately Held**
SIC: 3569 Gas producers, generators & other gas related equipment

Lake Linden
Houghton County

(G-9107)
CW CHAMPION WELDING ALLOYS LLC
52705 State Highway M26 (49945-1343)
P.O. Box 10 (49945-0010)
PHONE 906 296-9633
Charlie Kiilunen, *Principal*
EMP: 3
SALES (est): 252.9K **Privately Held**
SIC: 7692 Welding repair

(G-9108)
LAWRENCE BEAUDOIN LOGGING
52972 Sawmill Rd (49945-9752)
PHONE 906 296-0549
Lawrence Beaudoin, *Principal*
EMP: 3

GEOGRAPHIC SECTION
Lake Orion - Oakland County (G-9136)

SALES (est): 211.9K **Privately Held**
SIC: 2411 Logging camps & contractors

(G-9109)
PENINSULA PRODUCTS INC
54385 Cemetery Rd (49945-1278)
PHONE 906 296-9801
Larry R Joosten, *President*
Marcia M Joosten, *Corp Secy*
EMP: 4
SQ FT: 2,500
SALES: 200K **Privately Held**
SIC: 3272 Burial vaults, concrete or precast terrazzo; septic tanks, concrete

Lake Odessa
Ionia County

(G-9110)
A & L WOODS
5670 Brown Rd (48849-9609)
PHONE 616 374-7820
EMP: 3
SALES (est): 359.7K **Privately Held**
SIC: 2431 Mfg Millwork

(G-9111)
AUTOMATED PROCESS EQUIPMENT (PA)
Also Called: Apec
1201 4th Ave (48849-1301)
PHONE 616 374-1000
Kendall Wilcox, *CEO*
Garrett Billmire, *Vice Pres*
Terry Stemler, *Vice Pres*
▼ **EMP:** 40
SQ FT: 60,000
SALES (est): 6.8MM **Privately Held**
WEB: www.apecusa.com
SIC: 3556 Food products machinery

(G-9112)
CARBON GREEN BIOENERGY LLC
7795 Saddlebag Lake Rd (48849-9319)
PHONE 616 374-4000
Mitchell Miller, *CEO*
Maggie Benham, *Principal*
Jason Jerke, *CFO*
Jim Murphy,
EMP: 45
SALES (est): 8.2MM **Privately Held**
SIC: 2869 5169 Ethyl alcohol, ethanol; alcohols

(G-9113)
COBB ROBERT 3 RACHEL
2237 W Musgrove Hwy (48849-8521)
PHONE 616 374-7420
Robert Cobb, *Principal*
EMP: 3 **EST:** 2007
SALES (est): 279K **Privately Held**
SIC: 2992 Lubricating oils

(G-9114)
FRANKLIN METAL TRADING CORP
Also Called: Champion Alloys
609 Tupper Lake St (48849-1062)
PHONE 616 374-7171
William Boorstein, *President*
Laurie Martin, *Controller*
EMP: 28
SQ FT: 150,000
SALES (est): 7.4MM **Privately Held**
WEB: www.franklincompanies.com
SIC: 5093 3341 Ferrous metal scrap & waste; secondary nonferrous metals

(G-9115)
GREAT LAKES SAND & GRAVEL LLC
7940 Woodland Rd (48849-9300)
PHONE 616 374-3169
Bob Dejong, *Owner*
EMP: 5
SALES (est): 542.8K **Privately Held**
SIC: 3273 Ready-mixed concrete

(G-9116)
LAKE ODESSA MEAT PROCESSING
1423 Clark St (48849-9404)
PHONE 616 374-8392
Burt Bowen, *Owner*
Don Bowen, *Finance Other*
EMP: 3
SALES (est): 113.1K **Privately Held**
SIC: 2011 7299 Meat packing plants; butcher service, processing only

(G-9117)
MICHIGAN AG SERVICES INC (PA)
Also Called: Michigan Glass Lined Storage
3587 W Tupper Lake Rd (48849-9804)
P.O. Box 573 (48849-0573)
PHONE 616 374-8803
Martinus Koorn, *President*
Larry Ackerson, *General Mgr*
Laverne Lettinga, *Vice Pres*
▲ **EMP:** 18
SQ FT: 10,000
SALES (est): 2.1MM **Privately Held**
WEB: www.michiganag.com
SIC: 3523 1542 Farm machinery & equipment; silo construction, agricultural

(G-9118)
MICHIGAN DUTCH BARNS INC
9811 Thompson Rd (48849-9713)
PHONE 616 693-2754
Steve Swartz, *President*
April Swartz, *Treasurer*
EMP: 15
SQ FT: 960
SALES (est): 2.2MM **Privately Held**
WEB: www.michigandutchbarns.com
SIC: 2452 Prefabricated buildings, wood

(G-9119)
SMITH WELDING AND REPAIR LLC
7430 Velte Rd (48849-9483)
PHONE 616 374-1445
Ed Smith, *Owner*
EMP: 3
SALES (est): 282.6K **Privately Held**
SIC: 7692 Welding repair

(G-9120)
TWIN CITY FOODS INC
801 Lincoln St (48849-1399)
PHONE 616 374-4002
Ken Stensen, *Div Sub Head*
Sherry Tischer, *Human Res Dir*
EMP: 115
SQ FT: 120,000
SALES (corp-wide): 204.7MM **Privately Held**
WEB: www.twincityfoods.com
SIC: 2037 2038 2033 2099 Vegetables, quick frozen & cold pack, excl. potato products; frozen specialties; canned fruits & specialties; food preparations
PA: Twin City Foods, Inc.
10130 269th Pl Nw
Stanwood WA 98292
206 515-2400

Lake Orion
Oakland County

(G-9121)
51 NORTH BREWING
51 N Broadway St (48362-3101)
PHONE 248 690-7367
Mary Gindhart, *Principal*
EMP: 6 **EST:** 2011
SALES (est): 509.3K **Privately Held**
SIC: 2082 Malt beverages

(G-9122)
ACCRA TOOL INC
1218 Cottonwood Dr (48360-1464)
PHONE 248 680-9936
Donald Mancier, *President*
Joycelyn Mancier, *Vice Pres*
EMP: 4
SALES (est): 438.9K **Privately Held**
WEB: www.accratool.com
SIC: 3541 Machine tool replacement & repair parts, metal cutting types

(G-9123)
ACME MANUFACTURING COMPANY
101 Premier Dr (48359-1882)
PHONE 248 393-7300
Clark Merriman, *Director*
EMP: 10
SALES (corp-wide): 15.4MM **Privately Held**
SIC: 3541 Machine tools, metal cutting type
PA: Acme Manufacturing Company
4240 N Atlantic Blvd
Auburn Hills MI 48326
248 393-7300

(G-9124)
AIMRITE LLC
Also Called: Aim-Rite Hauling
941 Hinford Ave (48362-2647)
PHONE 248 693-8925
David Bressman, *Owner*
EMP: 4 **EST:** 1998
SALES (est): 390K **Privately Held**
SIC: 3537 Trucks: freight, baggage, etc.: industrial, except mining

(G-9125)
AMERICAN BATTERY SOLUTIONS INC
3768 S Lapeer Rd (48359-1324)
PHONE 248 462-6364
Subhash Dhar, *CEO*
EMP: 38
SALES (est): 1.3MM **Privately Held**
SIC: 3999 Manufacturing industries

(G-9126)
BMS GREAT LAKES LLC
4577 S Lapeer Rd Ste G (48359-2413)
PHONE 248 390-1598
David Hodgson, *Principal*
EMP: 4
SALES (est): 186.5K **Privately Held**
SIC: 3842 Abdominal supporters, braces & trusses

(G-9127)
C & C MACHINE TOOL INC
1584 Oneida Trl (48362-1242)
PHONE 248 693-3347
Richard W Cole, *President*
Clayton E Cobb, *Corp Secy*
EMP: 5
SQ FT: 10,800
SALES: 600K **Privately Held**
WEB: www.ccmachinetool.com
SIC: 3599 Machine shop, jobbing & repair

(G-9128)
COBRA TORCHES INC
Also Called: Detroit Torch Company
180 Engelwood Dr Ste J (48359-2417)
P.O. Box 169, Clarkston (48347-0169)
PHONE 248 499-8122
Mark Scholl, *President*
Mary Cycholl, *Vice Pres*
EMP: 5
SALES (est): 933.5K **Privately Held**
WEB: www.cobratorches.com
SIC: 7692 Welding repair

(G-9129)
COLE CARBIDE INDUSTRIES INC (PA)
4930 S Lapeer Rd (48359-2412)
PHONE 248 276-1278
John M Cole, *President*
Amy Kranker, *Exec VP*
Scott Kelley, *VP Mfg*
James McNally, *Manager*
Nancy Schroth, *Admin Sec*
EMP: 17 **EST:** 1936
SQ FT: 11,000
SALES (est): 14.3MM **Privately Held**
SIC: 3545 Cutting tools for machine tools

(G-9130)
COLE TOOLING SYSTEMS INC
Also Called: Millstar
4930 S Lapeer Rd (48359-2412)
PHONE 586 573-9450
Donald Gleklen, *Principal*
EMP: 19
SALES (est): 2.9MM
SALES (corp-wide): 14.3MM **Privately Held**
SIC: 3544 Special dies, tools, jigs & fixtures
PA: Cole Carbide Industries, Inc.
4930 S Lapeer Rd
Lake Orion MI 48359
248 276-1278

(G-9131)
COMPLETE AUTO-MATION INC
Also Called: Bbi Group
1776d W Clarkston Rd (48362-2267)
P.O. Box 65 (48361-0065)
PHONE 248 693-0500
Kenneth J Matheis Sr, *President*
John H Matheis, *Vice Pres*
Kenneth J Matheis Jr, *Vice Pres*
Ian Chornoby, *Project Mgr*
Jason Farhat, *Project Mgr*
EMP: 100
SQ FT: 49,000
SALES (est): 28.3MM **Privately Held**
SIC: 3823 Industrial flow & liquid measuring instruments

(G-9132)
COMPLETE FILTRATION INC
Also Called: Complete Companies
1776d W Clarkston Rd (48362-2267)
P.O. Box 65 (48361-0065)
PHONE 248 693-0500
Kenneth J Matheis Sr, *President*
John H Matheis, *Vice Pres*
Kenneth J Matheis Jr, *Vice Pres*
Ian Chornoby, *Project Mgr*
Karin Tinus, *Safety Mgr*
▲ **EMP:** 16
SQ FT: 20,000
SALES (est): 6.2MM **Privately Held**
SIC: 3564 3567 Filters, air: furnaces, air conditioning equipment, etc.; air purification equipment; industrial furnaces & ovens

(G-9133)
CUSTOM THREADS AND SPORTS LLC
260 Engelwood Dr Ste A (48359-2443)
PHONE 248 391-0088
Mark McCord,
Linda McCord,
EMP: 5
SALES: 852.7K **Privately Held**
WEB: www.customthreadsandsports.com
SIC: 2759 Commercial printing

(G-9134)
DATACOVER INC
1070 W Silverbell Rd (48359-1327)
PHONE 248 391-2163
EMP: 13
SALES: 500K **Privately Held**
SIC: 3089 Mfg Plastic Hardware

(G-9135)
DAVES DIAMOND INC
416 S Broadway St (48362-2742)
PHONE 248 693-2482
David Schurman, *President*
Cynthia Schurman, *Vice Pres*
EMP: 11 **EST:** 1976
SQ FT: 3,000
SALES (est): 1.2MM **Privately Held**
SIC: 5944 3911 Jewelry, precious stones & precious metals; jewelry apparel

(G-9136)
GENENTECH INC
362 Kirksway Ln (48362-2279)
PHONE 650 225-1000
Nancy Vitale, *Principal*
EMP: 3
SALES (corp-wide): 57.2B **Privately Held**
SIC: 2834 Pharmaceutical preparations

Lake Orion - Oakland County (G-9137)

GEOGRAPHIC SECTION

HQ: Genentech, Inc.
1 Dna Way
South San Francisco CA 94080
650 225-1000

(G-9137)
GM ORION ASSEMBLY
4555 Giddings Rd (48359-1713)
PHONE..................................248 377-5260
Gary Malkus, *Manager*
EMP: 3 **EST:** 2016
SALES (est): 326.9K **Privately Held**
SIC: 3711 Motor vehicles & car bodies

(G-9138)
HILITE INDUSTRIES INC
250 Kay Industrial Dr (48359-2402)
PHONE..................................248 475-4580
Marvin Koler, *Manager*
Michael Flory, *Technician*
EMP: 5
SALES (corp-wide): 43.3B **Privately Held**
SIC: 3495 3469 Clock springs, precision; metal stampings
HQ: Hilite Industries Inc
1671 S Broadway St
Carrollton TX 75006
972 242-2116

(G-9139)
INFINITY CONTROLS & ENGRG INC
3039 Cedar Key Dr (48360-1515)
PHONE..................................248 397-8267
EMP: 8
SALES: 2MM **Privately Held**
SIC: 3625 8711 Mfg Relays/Industrial Controls Engineering Services

(G-9140)
INFONORM INC
4820 Joslyn Rd (48359-2232)
PHONE..................................248 276-9027
Stefan Kubli, *President*
Amy B Kubli, *Managing Prtnr*
Robert Rudorf, *Sales Staff*
EMP: 4
SQ FT: 750
SALES: 750K **Privately Held**
SIC: 5099 3993 Signs, except electric; signs & advertising specialties

(G-9141)
KAY SCREEN PRINTING INC (DH)
Also Called: Kay Automotive Graphics
57 Kay Industrial Dr (48359-1832)
PHONE..................................248 377-4999
Joseph Kowalczyk, *President*
Al Bonnell, *Vice Pres*
William Farnen, *Vice Pres*
Terry Young, *Project Mgr*
Cindy Williamson, *QC Mgr*
▲ **EMP:** 171
SQ FT: 130,000
SALES (est): 66.4MM
SALES (corp-wide): 661.1MM **Privately Held**
WEB: www.kayautomotive.com
SIC: 2752 2396 Commercial printing, offset; automotive & apparel trimmings
HQ: Orafol International, Inc.
1100 Oracal Pkwy
Black Creek GA 31308
912 851-5000

(G-9142)
KPMF USA INC
67 Kay Industrial Dr (48359)
PHONE..................................248 377-4999
Joseph Kowalczyk, *President*
EMP: 10
SALES (est): 573.9K
SALES (corp-wide): 661.1MM **Privately Held**
SIC: 2759 Screen printing
HQ: Kay Screen Printing, Inc.
57 Kay Industrial Dr
Lake Orion MI 48359
248 377-4999

(G-9143)
LABORTRIO ELTTROFISICO USA INC
Also Called: Le USA Walker Scientific
40 Engelwood Dr Ste H (48359-2419)
PHONE..................................248 340-7040
Brian Palakow, *President*
Brian R Palakow, *Vice Pres*
Roger Fei, *Sales Mgr*
Luca Zanon, *Sales Mgr*
Jacob Hohner, *Sales Staff*
EMP: 5
SALES (est): 1.3MM **Privately Held**
SIC: 3823 3829 Industrial instrmnts msrmnt display/control process variable; pressure measurement instruments, industrial; measuring & controlling devices

(G-9144)
LAKE ORION CONCRETE ORNA PDTS
62 W Scripps Rd (48360-2116)
PHONE..................................248 693-8683
EMP: 4
SQ FT: 2,000
SALES (est): 37.6K **Privately Held**
SIC: 3272 5261 Mfg Concrete Products Ret Nursery/Garden Supplies

(G-9145)
LASER CRAFT LLC
151 Premier Dr (48359-1882)
PHONE..................................248 340-8922
Richard Ortisis,
Tom Griffin,
Terry Grsyb,
Richard Ortisi,
EMP: 13
SQ FT: 20,000
SALES (est): 1.5MM **Privately Held**
SIC: 3441 Fabricated structural metal

(G-9146)
LIGHTNING TECHNOLOGIES LLC
315 W Silverbell Rd (48359-1752)
PHONE..................................248 977-5566
Jeffrey Owen, *CEO*
EMP: 17
SALES (corp-wide): 11.5MM **Privately Held**
SIC: 2448 Wood pallets & skids
PA: Lightning Technologies, Llc
2171 Xcelsior Dr
Oxford MI 48371
248 572-6700

(G-9147)
MANUFACTURING & INDUS TECH INC
Also Called: Mit
525 Goldengate St Ste 100 (48362-3413)
PHONE..................................248 814-8544
Joyce Folts, *President*
Robert Folts, *Vice Pres*
EMP: 50
SALES (est): 3MM **Privately Held**
WEB: www.mfgind.com
SIC: 7363 8733 3721 3724 Temporary help service; industrial help service; non-commercial biological research organization; aircraft; aircraft engines & engine parts; aircraft parts & equipment; engineering services

(G-9148)
MAR COR PURIFICATION INC
180 Engelwood Dr Ste D (48359-2417)
PHONE..................................248 373-7844
Gary Youness, *Branch Mgr*
EMP: 10
SALES (corp-wide): 918.1MM **Publicly Held**
WEB: www.marcorservices.com
SIC: 3589 Water treatment equipment, industrial
HQ: Mar Cor Purification, Inc.
4450 Township Line Rd
Skippack PA 19474
800 633-3080

(G-9149)
MINT STEEL FORGE INC
162 Northpointe Dr (48359-1863)
PHONE..................................248 276-9000
Terry Kohler, *President*
Allen Gohl, *President*
Jane Boyer, *Vice Pres*
▲ **EMP:** 15
SQ FT: 27,500
SALES (est): 3.3MM **Privately Held**
WEB: www.minttool.com
SIC: 3714 Motor vehicle parts & accessories

(G-9150)
MORRISON & BARNETT ANESTH
830 Hemingway Rd (48362-2635)
PHONE..................................248 814-0609
Steve Barneth, *Partner*
Russell Morrison, *Partner*
EMP: 3
SALES (est): 275.5K **Privately Held**
SIC: 3841 Anesthesia apparatus

(G-9151)
NORMA MICHIGAN INC
Torca Products
325 W Silverbell Rd (48359-1764)
PHONE..................................248 373-4300
Norma Alamar, *Branch Mgr*
EMP: 10
SALES (corp-wide): 1.2B **Privately Held**
SIC: 3714 3429 3713 Motor vehicle parts & accessories; manufactured hardware (general); clamps, metal; truck & bus bodies
HQ: Norma Michigan, Inc.
2430 E Walton Blvd
Auburn Hills MI 48326
248 373-4300

(G-9152)
OAKLAND STAMPING LLC
4555 Giddings Rd (48359-1713)
PHONE..................................248 340-2520
EMP: 4 **Privately Held**
SIC: 3469 Stamping metal for the trade
HQ: Oakland Stamping, Llc
1200 Woodland St
Detroit MI 48211

(G-9153)
ODYSSEY INDUSTRIES LLC
3020 Indianwood Rd (48362-1113)
PHONE..................................248 814-8800
Paul Walsh, *President*
Mike Cavender, *General Mgr*
Kurt Nanney, *Vice Pres*
Dawn Steele, *Purch Mgr*
Tim Andrews, *Data Proc Spvr*
EMP: 219
SQ FT: 210,000
SALES (est): 42.6MM
SALES (corp-wide): 386.8MM **Privately Held**
WEB: www.odysseytooling.com
SIC: 3728 Aircraft parts & equipment
HQ: Ascent Aerospace, Llc
16445 23 Mile Rd
Macomb MI 48042
586 726-0500

(G-9154)
OERLIKON BLZERS CATING USA INC
199 Kay Industrial Dr (48359-1833)
PHONE..................................248 409-5900
EMP: 35
SALES (corp-wide): 2.6B **Privately Held**
SIC: 3479 Coating of metals & formed products
HQ: Oerlikon Balzers Coating Usa Inc.
1700 E Golf Rd Ste 200
Schaumburg IL 60173
847 619-5541

(G-9155)
PLATT MOUNTS - USA INC
100 Engelwood Dr Ste D (48359-2411)
PHONE..................................586 202-2920
Wilfred Platt, *President*
EMP: 4
SALES: 1MM **Privately Held**
WEB: www.plattmounts.com
SIC: 3599 Industrial machinery

(G-9156)
ROMA TOOL INC
50 Northpointe Dr (48359-1846)
PHONE..................................248 218-1889
Mark Bowery, *Principal*
Joe Pavlik, *Vice Pres*
EMP: 17
SALES (est): 3.6MM **Privately Held**
SIC: 3549 Assembly machines, including robotic

(G-9157)
RS DEFENSE TACTICS
31 Beebe St (48362-3021)
PHONE..................................248 693-2337
EMP: 3
SALES (est): 145.3K **Privately Held**
SIC: 3812 Defense systems & equipment

(G-9158)
SA INDUSTRIES 2 INC (PA)
1081 Indianwood Rd (48362-1327)
P.O. Box 5 (48361-0005)
PHONE..................................248 693-9100
Bonnie Schulz, *Principal*
EMP: 9
SALES (est): 1.8MM **Privately Held**
SIC: 3452 Screws, metal

(G-9159)
SEEO INC
3740 S Lapeer Rd (48359-1324)
PHONE..................................510 782-7336
Hal Zarem, *President*
Hany Eitouni, *Vice Pres*
▲ **EMP:** 17
SALES: 4.5MM
SALES (corp-wide): 294.8MM **Privately Held**
SIC: 3691 Storage batteries
HQ: Robert Bosch Llc
2800 S 25th Ave
Broadview IL 60155
248 876-1000

(G-9160)
SHELL OIL COMPANY
378 S Broadway St (48362-2741)
PHONE..................................248 693-0036
EMP: 3
SALES (corp-wide): 388.3B **Privately Held**
SIC: 1311 Crude petroleum & natural gas
HQ: Shell Oil Company
150 N Dairy Ashford Rd A
Houston TX 77079
713 241-6161

(G-9161)
SHERMAN PUBLICATIONS INC
Also Called: Lake Orion Review, The
30 N Broadway St (48362-3100)
PHONE..................................248 693-8331
James Sherman, *President*
EMP: 4
SALES (est): 279K
SALES (corp-wide): 5.5MM **Privately Held**
WEB: www.oxfordleader.com
SIC: 2711 Newspapers: publishing only, not printed on site
PA: Sherman Publications Inc
666 S Lapeer Rd
Oxford MI 48371
248 628-4801

(G-9162)
SODECIA AUTO DETROIT CORP
Also Called: Sodecia North America
325 W Silverbell Rd (48359-1764)
PHONE..................................586 759-2200
Rick Sutter, *Branch Mgr*
EMP: 163 **Privately Held**
SIC: 3465 Automotive stampings
HQ: Sodecia Auto Detroit Corp.
969 Chicago Rd
Troy MI 48083
586 759-2200

(G-9163)
SONIMA CORP
325 W Silverbell Rd # 250 (48359-1764)
PHONE..................................302 450-6452
EMP: 9

GEOGRAPHIC SECTION

Lanse - Baraga County (G-9190)

SALES (est): 429.9K
SALES (corp-wide): 31.5MM **Privately Held**
SIC: 3674 Modules, solid state
PA: Sonima Gmbh
Ruhweg 17
Gollheim 67307
635 199-9970

(G-9164)
SU-DAN COMPANY (PA)
Also Called: Sudan
190 Northpointe Dr (48359-1863)
P.O. Box 81700, Rochester (48308-1700)
PHONE..................................248 651-6035
Dennis J Keat, *President*
David Salkowski, *President*
Cindy Keat, *Chairman*
Douglas Braun, *Vice Pres*
▲ **EMP:** 60 **EST:** 1966
SQ FT: 32,000
SALES (est): 26.5MM **Privately Held**
WEB: www.su-dan.com
SIC: 3465 3469 Body parts, automobile: stamped metal; appliance parts, porcelain enameled

(G-9165)
SU-DAN PLASTICS INC (PA)
190 Northpointe Dr (48359-1863)
P.O. Box 81700, Rochester (48308-1700)
PHONE..................................248 651-6035
Richard G Dryden, *Ch of Bd*
Dennis J Keat, *President*
EMP: 19 **EST:** 1977
SQ FT: 2,500
SALES (est): 24.6MM **Privately Held**
SIC: 3714 Motor vehicle parts & accessories

(G-9166)
TOTAL REPAIR EXPRESS MI LLC
118 Indianwood Rd Ste C (48362-4013)
PHONE..................................248 690-9410
Kirt Bennett,
EMP: 15
SALES (est): 397K **Privately Held**
SIC: 3999 Manufacturing industries

(G-9167)
TRU-SYZYGY INC
1151 Sunset Hills Dr (48360-1412)
PHONE..................................248 622-7211
Donald Dietz, *Principal*
EMP: 6
SALES (est): 181.3K **Privately Held**
SIC: 7371 7372 7373 7374 Computer software systems analysis & design, custom; business oriented computer software; systems software development services; computer processing services; computer related consulting services

(G-9168)
US FARATHANE HOLDINGS CORP
325 W Silverbell Rd # 220 (48359-1764)
PHONE..................................248 754-7000
John Lojewski, *Manager*
EMP: 15
SALES (corp-wide): 876MM **Privately Held**
SIC: 3089 Injection molding of plastics
PA: U.S. Farathane Holdings Corp.
11650 Park Ct
Shelby Township MI 48315
586 726-1200

(G-9169)
WEBER SAND AND GRAVEL INC (PA)
1401 E Silverbell Rd (48360-2342)
PHONE..................................248 373-0900
Everett Jack Weber, *President*
Geraldine Weber, *Corp Secy*
EMP: 10 **EST:** 1950
SALES (est): 2.6MM **Privately Held**
SIC: 1442 Gravel mining

(G-9170)
WESTERN ENGINEERED PRODUCTS
540 N Lapeer Rd Ste 390 (48362-1582)
PHONE..................................248 371-9259
Donald F Stephanic, *President*
EMP: 7
SQ FT: 7,000
SALES: 2MM **Privately Held**
WEB: www.westernep.com
SIC: 3398 3469 3471 Annealing of metal; metal stampings; plating of metals or formed products

Lakeview
Montcalm County

(G-9171)
COUNTRY SIDE SAWMILL
7682 N Greenville Rd (48850-9575)
PHONE..................................989 352-7198
Eli Schrock, *Administration*
EMP: 3
SALES (est): 275.2K **Privately Held**
SIC: 2421 Sawmills & planing mills, general

(G-9172)
FARM COUNTRY CHEESE HOUSE
7263 Kendalville Rd (48850)
PHONE..................................989 352-7779
Jim Nunley, *Owner*
Julie Nunley, *Owner*
EMP: 10
SQ FT: 4,000
SALES (est): 756.5K **Privately Held**
SIC: 2022 Natural cheese

(G-9173)
GRIFCO INC
Also Called: Lakeview Sand & Gravel
10451 Orchard Ln (48850-9142)
P.O. Box 93 (48850-0093)
PHONE..................................989 352-7965
Kevin Griffith, *President*
EMP: 1
SQ FT: 1,800
SALES: 1MM **Privately Held**
SIC: 1442 Construction sand & gravel

(G-9174)
INTREPID PLASTICS MFG INC
7675 Howard Cy Edmore Rd (48850-9116)
PHONE..................................616 901-5718
Bonnie Knopf, *President*
EMP: 15
SQ FT: 6,000
SALES (est): 1.3MM **Privately Held**
WEB: www.intrepidplastics.com
SIC: 3089 Injection molding of plastics

(G-9175)
MARKHAM PEAT CORP
9475 Jefferson Rd (48850-9616)
PHONE..................................800 851-7230
Lee Clemence, *President*
Penny Clemence, *Corp Secy*
EMP: 13
SQ FT: 7,500
SALES (est): 1.5MM **Privately Held**
WEB: www.gummerpeat.com
SIC: 1499 2048 2875 Peat mining; bird food, prepared; fertilizers, mixing only

(G-9176)
STEEPLECHASE TOOL & DIE INC
9307 Howard Cy Edmore Rd (48850-9470)
PHONE..................................989 352-5544
Michael Baird, *President*
Mike Garvey, *Plant Mgr*
Joe Ritter, *Purchasing*
Tim Johnson, *Manager*
EMP: 40
SQ FT: 29,000
SALES (est): 9.3MM **Privately Held**
WEB: www.steeplechasetool.com
SIC: 3544 Special dies & tools

Lakeville
Oakland County

(G-9177)
BERGAMOT INC
110 Lena Hill Dr (48367-4213)
PHONE..................................586 372-7109
Marin M Klink, *Principal*
EMP: 4
SALES (est): 266.7K **Privately Held**
SIC: 3499 Magnets, permanent: metallic

(G-9178)
KBA DEFENSE
409 Race St (48367-6613)
PHONE..................................586 552-9268
Joseph Bigger, *Principal*
EMP: 3 **EST:** 2017
SALES (est): 160.4K **Privately Held**
SIC: 3812 Defense systems & equipment

(G-9179)
NATIONAL CRANE & HOIST SERVICE
1630 Noble Rd (48367-1658)
P.O. Box 88, Troy (48099-0088)
PHONE..................................248 789-4535
Jack Myers, *President*
Deette Myers, *Admin Sec*
EMP: 5
SALES: 500K **Privately Held**
SIC: 3625 Crane & hoist controls, including metal mill

(G-9180)
THOR TOOL AND MACHINE LLC
401 E Elmwood (48367-1807)
P.O. Box 786, Leonard (48367-0786)
PHONE..................................248 628-3185
Andrew A Koski,
Axel R Koski,
EMP: 5 **EST:** 1996
SQ FT: 18,800
SALES (est): 268.2K **Privately Held**
SIC: 3599 Machine shop, jobbing & repair

Lambertville
Monroe County

(G-9181)
CREATIVE PROMOTIONS
3325 W Temperance Rd (48144-9706)
PHONE..................................734 854-2292
Robert A Lindecker, *Owner*
EMP: 3
SQ FT: 800
SALES: 525K **Privately Held**
WEB: www.creativepromotions.net
SIC: 3993 5199 2395 2262 Signs & advertising specialties; advertising specialties; embroidery & art needlework; screen printing: manmade fiber & silk broadwoven fabrics

(G-9182)
CUSTER TOOL & MFG LLC
7714 Secor Rd (48144-8672)
PHONE..................................734 854-5943
Lewis Custer,
EMP: 4
SALES (est): 609.1K **Privately Held**
SIC: 3544 Special dies, tools, jigs & fixtures

(G-9183)
INNOVATIVE CARGO SYSTEMS LLC
Also Called: Wheelchair Carrier
7325 Douglas Rd (48144-9491)
PHONE..................................734 568-6084
David Makulinski, *General Mgr*
Mike Siler,
EMP: 7 **EST:** 1978
SQ FT: 100,000
SALES (est): 1.2MM **Privately Held**
WEB: www.wheelchaircarrier.com
SIC: 3842 Wheelchairs

(G-9184)
QUEST - IV INCORPORATED
7116 Summerfield Rd (48144-9415)
PHONE..................................734 847-5487
Donald McCullough Jr, *President*
Randy Mc Cullough, *Vice Pres*
F Bart Fannin, *Treasurer*
EMP: 15
SQ FT: 2,700
SALES (est): 1.1MM **Privately Held**
WEB: www.questiv.com
SIC: 7372 Business oriented computer software

(G-9185)
STEVENSON BUILDING AND SUP CO
8197 Secor Rd (48144-8673)
PHONE..................................734 856-3931
Arthur G Stevenson, *President*
Dave Stevenson, *Vice Pres*
EMP: 8 **EST:** 1953
SQ FT: 1,200
SALES (est): 1.6MM **Privately Held**
SIC: 3273 5211 Ready-mixed concrete; masonry materials & supplies

(G-9186)
TEMPERANCE PRINTING
Also Called: Bedford Press
3363 Hemmingway Ln (48144-9653)
PHONE..................................419 290-6846
Karen Daggett, *Owner*
EMP: 5
SQ FT: 1,500
SALES: 290K **Privately Held**
SIC: 2752 7331 Commercial printing, offset; direct mail advertising services

(G-9187)
VX-LLC
8336 Monroe Rd Rm 201 (48144-9340)
P.O. Box 828, Holland OH (43528-0828)
PHONE..................................734 854-8700
EMP: 9
SALES (est): 1.1MM **Privately Held**
SIC: 3321 3351 Rolling mill rolls, cast iron; copper rolling & drawing; brass rolling & drawing

Lanse
Baraga County

(G-9188)
C D C LOGGING
17311 Kent St (49946-8096)
PHONE..................................906 524-6369
Charles D Cavanaugh, *Owner*
EMP: 6
SALES (est): 435.1K **Privately Held**
SIC: 2411 Logging camps & contractors

(G-9189)
CERTAINTEED GYPSUM INC
Also Called: Bpb/Celotex
200 S Main St (49946-1036)
PHONE..................................906 524-6101
Chet Van Aken, *Plant Mgr*
Chet Igan, *Manager*
EMP: 120
SALES (corp-wide): 215.9MM **Privately Held**
WEB: www.bpb-na.com
SIC: 3296 Acoustical board & tile, mineral wool
HQ: Certainteed Gypsum, Inc.
20 Moores Rd
Malvern PA 19355

(G-9190)
COLLINS BROTHERS SAWMILL INC
17579 Watters St (49946)
P.O. Box 265 (49946-0265)
PHONE..................................906 524-5511
Tom Collins, *President*
Dave Collins, *Corp Secy*
Judy Collins, *Administration*
EMP: 15
SALES (est): 1.9MM **Privately Held**
SIC: 2421 Sawmills & planing mills, general

Lanse - Baraga County

(G-9191)
ERICKSON LUMBER & TRUE VALUE
17752 Us Hwy 41 (49946)
P.O. Box 145 (49946-0145)
PHONE..................906 524-6295
Robert Erickson, *President*
Ann Leclaire, *Corp Secy*
Donna Baxter, *Vice Pres*
Cindy Erickson, *Shareholder*
Jim Erickson, *Shareholder*
EMP: 8 EST: 1992
SALES (est): 5.1MM **Privately Held**
SIC: 5251 5211 2426 Hardware; lumber & other building materials; hardwood dimension & flooring mills

(G-9192)
HERMAN HILLBILLIES FARM LLC
Also Called: Herman Hills Sugar Bush
18194 Lahti Rd (49946-8047)
PHONE..................906 201-0760
James Ballor,
Anita Taisto,
EMP: 6
SQ FT: 1,200
SALES (est): 300.1K **Privately Held**
SIC: 2099 Maple syrup

(G-9193)
JESSE JAMES LOGGING
16938 Dynamite Hill Rd (49946-8085)
P.O. Box 55 (49946-0055)
PHONE..................906 395-6819
James Lahti, *Principal*
EMP: 3
SALES (est): 232.4K **Privately Held**
SIC: 2411 Logging

(G-9194)
JOHN VUK & SON INC
Vuk Rd (49946)
PHONE..................906 524-6074
John A Vuk Jr, *President*
John Vuk Sr, *Corp Secy*
EMP: 4
SALES: 300K **Privately Held**
SIC: 2411 Logging

(G-9195)
JOHNSON & BERRY MFG INC
15442 Roth Rd (49946-9005)
PHONE..................906 524-6433
William Johnson, *President*
Cory Frisk, *Corp Secy*
EMP: 7
SQ FT: 2,500
SALES (est): 985.9K **Privately Held**
SIC: 3599 Machine shop, jobbing & repair

(G-9196)
KETOLA LOGGING
16369 Bayshore Rd (49946-8303)
PHONE..................906 524-6479
Reino Ketola, *Owner*
EMP: 3
SALES (est): 226.8K **Privately Held**
SIC: 2411 Logging camps & contractors

(G-9197)
KK LOGGING
16234 Skanee Rd (49946-9017)
PHONE..................906 524-6047
Ken Ketola, *Principal*
EMP: 3
SALES (est): 243K **Privately Held**
SIC: 2411 Logging camps & contractors

(G-9198)
L D J INC
Also Called: L'Anse Sentinel
202 N Main St (49946-1118)
P.O. Box 7 (49946-0007)
PHONE..................906 524-6194
Edward Danner, *President*
EMP: 10
SQ FT: 5,500
SALES (est): 531.9K **Privately Held**
WEB: www.lansesentinel.com
SIC: 2711 5943 2752 Newspapers, publishing & printing; office forms & supplies; commercial printing, offset

(G-9199)
PATRICK NEWLAND LOGGING LTD
14738 Pequaming Rd (49946-8335)
PHONE..................906 524-2255
Patrick Newland, *President*
EMP: 6
SALES: 210K **Privately Held**
SIC: 2411 Logging camps & contractors

(G-9200)
R H HUHTALA AGGREGATES INC
18154 Us Highway 41 (49946-8005)
PHONE..................906 524-7758
Roland H Huhtala, *Owner*
EMP: 4
SQ FT: 2,940
SALES (est): 298.1K **Privately Held**
SIC: 1442 1611 Construction sand mining; gravel mining; general contractor, highway & street construction

Lansing
Clinton County

(G-9201)
ADAMS OUTDOOR ADVG LTD PARTNR
3801 Capitol City Blvd (48906-2109)
PHONE..................517 321-2121
Jacquelen Timm, *Sales Mgr*
John Hamilton, *Accounts Exec*
Jeannine Dodson, *Manager*
EMP: 50
SALES (corp-wide): 50.5MM **Privately Held**
WEB: www.adamsoutdoor.com
SIC: 7312 3993 Billboard advertising; signs & advertising specialties
PA: Adams Outdoor Advertising Limited Partnership
500 Colonial Center Pkwy
Roswell GA 30076
770 333-0399

(G-9202)
AMERICAN TOOLING CENTER INC
705 E Oakland Ave (48906-5314)
PHONE..................517 522-8411
John J Basso, *President*
EMP: 6
SALES (corp-wide): 30.3MM **Privately Held**
SIC: 3544 Special dies & tools
PA: American Tooling Center, Inc.
4111 Mount Hope Rd
Grass Lake MI 49240
517 522-8411

(G-9203)
ARCOSA SHORING PRODUCTS INC
Pro-Tech Equipment
4837 W Grand River Ave (48906-9122)
PHONE..................800 292-1225
Ron Wey, *Branch Mgr*
EMP: 11
SALES (corp-wide): 1.4B **Publicly Held**
SIC: 7353 3531 Heavy construction equipment rental; construction machinery
HQ: Arcosa Shoring Products, Inc.
8530 M 60
Union City MI 49094
517 741-4300

(G-9204)
ARDO GRANITE LLC
Also Called: Blue Granite & Marble
919 Filley St Ste B (48906-2968)
PHONE..................517 253-7139
Aldmar Ferreira, *Mng Member*
EMP: 10
SALES: 1.1MM **Privately Held**
SIC: 3281 Curbing, granite or stone; marble, building; cut & shaped

(G-9205)
BANNASCH WELDING INC
Also Called: Grills To Go At Bannasch Wldg
807 Lake Lansing Rd Ste 1 (48906-4292)
PHONE..................517 482-2916
William Bannasch, *President*
Sandy Bannasch, *Vice Pres*
EMP: 11
SQ FT: 14,000
SALES (est): 1.3MM **Privately Held**
WEB: www.bannaschwelding.com
SIC: 7692 Welding repair

(G-9206)
BONWRX LTD
924 Terminal Rd (48906-3063)
PHONE..................517 481-2924
Erengul Rose Carmicheal, *Administration*
EMP: 3
SALES (est): 206.4K **Privately Held**
SIC: 3841 Surgical & medical instruments

(G-9207)
CAPITAL CITY BLUE PRINT INC
Also Called: Capital City Reprographics
1110 Center St (48906-5297)
PHONE..................517 482-5431
Mark Odeen, *President*
EMP: 8
SQ FT: 11,000
SALES (est): 610K **Privately Held**
WEB: www.capitalcityblueprint.com
SIC: 7334 2752 Blueprinting service; commercial printing, lithographic

(G-9208)
CENTRAL MICHIGAN ENGRAVERS
412 W Gier St (48906-2945)
P.O. Box 15006 (48901-5006)
PHONE..................517 485-5865
Fred Root, *President*
EMP: 9 EST: 1960
SQ FT: 4,800
SALES (est): 1.7MM **Privately Held**
SIC: 3579 Paper handling machines

(G-9209)
CHALLENGE MFG COMPANY
6375 W Grand River Ave (48906)
PHONE..................616 735-6500
Douglas Bradley, *Vice Pres*
EMP: 5
SQ FT: 1,000
SALES (corp-wide): 763MM **Privately Held**
SIC: 3449 Miscellaneous metalwork
PA: Challenge Mfg. Company, Llc
3200 Fruit Ridge Ave Nw
Grand Rapids MI 49544
616 735-6500

(G-9210)
COMMUNITY MENTAL HEALTH
Also Called: Tri-County Diversified Inds
3200 Remy Dr (48906-2759)
PHONE..................517 323-9558
Susan Spears, *Director*
EMP: 100
SQ FT: 11,000
SALES (corp-wide): 123.8MM **Privately Held**
WEB: www.ceicmh.org
SIC: 8621 2759 Health association; promotional printing
PA: Community Mental Health Authority Of Clinton, Eaton & Ingham Counties
812 E Jolly Rd
Lansing MI 48910
517 346-8000

(G-9211)
CUSTOM EMBROIDERY PLUS LLC
420 E Saginaw St Ste 112 (48906-5255)
PHONE..................517 316-9902
Kirk Gartside, *Branch Mgr*
EMP: 3
SALES (est): 328.7K
SALES (corp-wide): 675K **Privately Held**
SIC: 2752 Commercial printing, lithographic

PA: Custom Embroidery Plus Llc
304 N Lansing St
Saint Johns MI 48879
989 227-9432

(G-9212)
CUSTOM QUILTS
14667 S Lowell Rd (48906-9326)
PHONE..................517 626-6399
Susan Myers, *Partner*
Cindy Hogan, *Partner*
EMP: 3
SALES: 20K **Privately Held**
SIC: 2392 Comforters & quilts: made from purchased materials

(G-9213)
DAKKOTA INTEGRATED SYSTEMS LLC
16130 Grove Rd (48906)
PHONE..................517 321-3064
James Horwarth,
EMP: 75
SALES (corp-wide): 242.2MM **Privately Held**
SIC: 3711 Automobile assembly, including specialty automobiles
PA: Dakkota Integrated Systems, Llc
123 Brighton Lake Rd # 202
Brighton MI 48116
517 694-6500

(G-9214)
DELTA PACKAGING INTERNATIONAL
3463 Millwood Rd (48906-2492)
PHONE..................517 321-6548
Mario S Diaz, *President*
Dolores J Diaz, *Corp Secy*
▲ EMP: 6
SQ FT: 12,000
SALES: 750K **Privately Held**
SIC: 2448 2449 Pallets, wood; containers, plywood & veneer wood

(G-9215)
DELTA SPORTS SERVICE & EMB
1611 N Grand River Ave (48906-3995)
PHONE..................517 482-6565
Tom Schaberg, *President*
Gerald Schaberg, *Treasurer*
EMP: 8
SQ FT: 5,500
SALES (est): 1.1MM **Privately Held**
SIC: 5136 5091 2759 2395 Sportswear, men's & boys'; sporting & recreation goods; screen printing; embroidery products, except schiffli machine

(G-9216)
DEMMER CORPORATION
Also Called: Demmer - Porter St.
728 Porter St (48906)
PHONE..................517 703-3116
Ron Patrick, *Manager*
EMP: 100
SALES (corp-wide): 136.7MM **Privately Held**
WEB: www.demmercorp.com
SIC: 3795 3599 Tanks & tank components; machine & other job shop work
HQ: Demmer Corporation
4520 N Grand River Ave
Lansing MI 48906
517 321-3600

(G-9217)
DEMMER CORPORATION (HQ)
4520 N Grand River Ave (48906-2615)
PHONE..................517 321-3600
John E Demmer, *Ch of Bd*
William A Demmer, *President*
Paul Pakkala, *Plant Mgr*
Heather Shawa De Cook, *CFO*
Duane A Wagner, *CPA*
▲ EMP: 160
SALES (est): 114.8MM
SALES (corp-wide): 136.7MM **Privately Held**
WEB: www.demmercorp.com
SIC: 3795 3812 3544 3465 Tanks & tank components; acceleration indicators & systems components, aerospace; special dies, tools, jigs & fixtures; automotive stampings; fabricated structural metal

GEOGRAPHIC SECTION
Lansing - Clinton County (G-9242)

PA: Loc Performance Products, Inc.
13505 N Haggerty Rd
Plymouth MI 48170
734 453-2300

(G-9218)
DEMMER CORPORATION
705 E Oakland Ave (48906-5314)
PHONE.................................517 703-3163
Matt Heppler, *Principal*
EMP: 65
SALES (corp-wide): 136.7MM **Privately Held**
WEB: www.demmercorp.com
SIC: 3795 3599 Tanks & tank components; machine & other job shop work
HQ: Demmer Corporation
4520 N Grand River Ave
Lansing MI 48906
517 321-3600

(G-9219)
DEMMER CORPORATION
720 Porter St (48906)
PHONE.................................517 703-3131
Jerry Frazier, *Branch Mgr*
EMP: 100
SALES (corp-wide): 136.7MM **Privately Held**
WEB: www.demmercorp.com
SIC: 3795 3599 Tanks & tank components; machine & other job shop work
HQ: Demmer Corporation
4520 N Grand River Ave
Lansing MI 48906
517 321-3600

(G-9220)
DEMMER CORPORATION
16325 Felton Rd (48906-9144)
PHONE.................................517 323-4504
Matt Heppler, *General Mgr*
EMP: 63
SALES (corp-wide): 136.7MM **Privately Held**
WEB: www.demmercorp.com
SIC: 3795 3711 Tanks & tank components; military motor vehicle assembly
HQ: Demmer Corporation
4520 N Grand River Ave
Lansing MI 48906
517 321-3600

(G-9221)
DEMMER INVESTMENTS INC (PA)
4520 N Grand River Ave (48906-2615)
PHONE.................................517 321-3600
Stan Sjober, *CEO*
Heather Shawa Decook, *Treasurer*
Edward Demmer, *Shareholder*
Marguerite Demmer, *Shareholder*
William Demmer, *Shareholder*
EMP: 6
SALES (est): 12MM **Privately Held**
SIC: 3549 3469 3829 Wiredrawing & fabricating machinery & equipment, ex. die; metal stampings; testing equipment: abrasion, shearing strength, etc.

(G-9222)
DENTAL ART LABORATORIES INC
1721 N Grand River Ave # 1 (48906-3982)
PHONE.................................517 485-2200
Tom Daulton, *CEO*
Richard Blundy, *President*
Bryan Medler, *Vice Pres*
EMP: 88 **EST:** 1950
SALES (est): 5.7MM
SALES (corp-wide): 151.4MM **Privately Held**
WEB: www.dentalartlab.com
SIC: 8072 8021 3843 Artificial teeth production; crown & bridge production; offices & clinics of dentists; dental equipment & supplies
HQ: National Dentex, Llc
11601 Kew Gardens Ave # 200
Palm Beach Gardens FL 33410
561 537-8300

(G-9223)
ELITE ELECTRO COATERS INC
16261 Grove Rd (48906-9330)
PHONE.................................517 886-1020
Mike Mushong, *President*
Carole Mushong, *President*
EMP: 3
SQ FT: 7,000
SALES: 200K **Privately Held**
SIC: 3699 1721 Electrostatic particle accelerators; painting & paper hanging

(G-9224)
EMERGENT BIODEF OPER LNSNG LLC
3500 N Martin Luther King (48906-2933)
PHONE.................................517 327-1500
Fuad El-Hibri, *Ch of Bd*
Robert Myers, *Exec VP*
Mark Alley, *Vice Pres*
Tom Waytes, *Vice Pres*
Jessica Harding, *Project Mgr*
EMP: 300
SALES (est): 110.2MM
SALES (corp-wide): 782.4MM **Publicly Held**
WEB: www.emergentbiosolutions.com
SIC: 2836 2834 Vaccines; pharmaceutical preparations
PA: Emergent Biosolutions Inc.
400 Professional Dr # 400
Gaithersburg MD 20879
240 631-3200

(G-9225)
ENGINEERING GRAPHICS INC
16333 S Us Highway 27 (48906-1563)
PHONE.................................517 485-5828
Mark Lamond, *President*
Robert Lamond, *President*
Vivian Lamond, *Corp Secy*
EMP: 6
SQ FT: 8,200
SALES (est): 483.3K **Privately Held**
WEB: www.e-graphicsinc.com
SIC: 7335 3999 Commercial photography; novelties, bric-a-brac & hobby kits

(G-9226)
ENPROTECH INDUSTRIAL TECH LLC
Enprotech Mechanical Svcs
16740 16800 Indus Pkwy (48906)
PHONE.................................517 372-0950
Pedro Garcia, *President*
Glenn Fountain, *Engineer*
John Morton, *Engineer*
Laura Fackelman, *Human Res Mgr*
Rick Crosslin, *Regl Sales Mgr*
EMP: 122 **Privately Held**
WEB: www.enpromech.com
SIC: 3542 Machine tools, metal forming type
HQ: Enprotech Industrial Technologies, Llc
4259 E 49th St
Cleveland OH 44125
216 883-3220

(G-9227)
FAIRFAX PRINTS LTD
Also Called: Frazeli Prints
4918 Delta River Dr (48906-9013)
PHONE.................................517 321-5590
Gary E Fairfax, *Owner*
EMP: 4
SALES (est): 469.6K **Privately Held**
WEB: www.fairfaxprints.com
SIC: 5199 5999 2752 Posters; posters; posters, lithographed

(G-9228)
FAITH PUBLISHING SERVICE
1500 E Saginaw St Ofc C (48906-5517)
PHONE.................................517 853-7600
Carl Mengeling, *Principal*
Elizabeth Solsburg, *Director*
EMP: 30
SALES (est): 6.1MM **Privately Held**
SIC: 2721 Magazines: publishing & printing

(G-9229)
FLIGHT MANAGEMENT CORPORATION
16637 Corporate Avi Dr (48906-9188)
PHONE.................................517 327-0400
Rajan Sheth, *Principal*
EMP: 3
SALES (est): 289.9K **Privately Held**
SIC: 3812 Aircraft flight instruments

(G-9230)
FORESIGHT GROUP INC (PA)
2822 N Martin Luther (48906)
PHONE.................................517 485-5700
William K Christofferson, *President*
Scott McPherson, *Vice Pres*
Scott Mossbarger, *Opers Mgr*
Jill Dimmitt, *Accounts Exec*
Britton Goetz, *Accounts Exec*
EMP: 36
SQ FT: 24,000
SALES: 6.4MM **Privately Held**
WEB: www.foresightgr.com
SIC: 2759 5199 Screen printing; advertising specialties

(G-9231)
FRANCHINO MOLD & ENGRG CO
5867 W Grand River Ave (48906-9117)
PHONE.................................517 321-5609
Robert Franchino, *President*
Mike Hetherington, *Vice Pres*
Todd Phillips, *Vice Pres*
John Dyer, *Buyer*
John Kingsley, *QC Mgr*
EMP: 82 **EST:** 1955
SQ FT: 36,000
SALES (est): 20.8MM **Privately Held**
WEB: www.franchino.com
SIC: 3544 Industrial molds

(G-9232)
FRIEDLAND INDUSTRIES INC
Also Called: FI
405 E Maple St (48906-5237)
P.O. Box 14180 (48901-4180)
PHONE.................................517 482-3000
Lawrence A Bass, *President*
Randolph Rifkin, *Treasurer*
EMP: 40
SQ FT: 6,000
SALES (est): 14.1MM **Privately Held**
WEB: www.friedlandindustries.com
SIC: 5093 4953 3341 2611 Ferrous metal scrap & waste; nonferrous metals scrap; waste paper; recycling, waste materials; secondary nonferrous metals; pulp mills

(G-9233)
H A ECKHART & ASSOCIATES INC
16185 National Pkwy (48906-9114)
PHONE.................................517 321-7700
Andrew Storm, *CEO*
Daniel Burseth, *Vice Pres*
Kevin Marr, *Opers Mgr*
Robert A Breard, *Treasurer*
Michael Weber, *Controller*
EMP: 40
SQ FT: 50,000
SALES: 26MM
SALES (corp-wide): 3.6MM **Privately Held**
WEB: www.eckhartusa.com
SIC: 3559 Automotive related machinery
HQ: Eckhart Holdings, Inc.
16185 National Pkwy
Lansing MI 48906
517 321-7700

(G-9234)
HEART TRUSS & ENGINEERING CORP
1830 N Grand River Ave (48906-3905)
PHONE.................................517 372-0850
Curtis Schaberg, *President*
Joe Butcher, *Vice Pres*
EMP: 100 **EST:** 1963
SQ FT: 20,000
SALES (est): 22.7MM **Privately Held**
WEB: www.hearttruss.net
SIC: 2439 Trusses, wooden roof

(G-9235)
HIGH GRADE MATERIALS COMPANY
1800 Turner St (48906-4049)
PHONE.................................517 374-1029
Andy Gibbs, *Branch Mgr*
EMP: 15
SALES (corp-wide): 28.3MM **Privately Held**
WEB: www.highgradematerials.com
SIC: 3273 Ready-mixed concrete

PA: High Grade Materials Company
9266 Snows Lake Rd
Greenville MI 48838
616 754-5545

(G-9236)
INNOVATIVE ENGINEERING MICH
712 Terminal Rd (48906-3059)
PHONE.................................517 977-0460
Ryan Cutler, *President*
EMP: 5
SQ FT: 8,000
SALES: 497.8K **Privately Held**
SIC: 2851 5199 3559 3089 Polyurethane coatings; rubber, crude; plastics working machinery; molding primary plastic

(G-9237)
INTER STATE FOODS INC (PA)
Also Called: Paramount Coffee Co.
5133 W Grand River Ave (48906-9117)
P.O. Box 13068 (48901-3068)
PHONE.................................517 372-5500
Fax: 517 372-2870
EMP: 10 **EST:** 1935
SQ FT: 40,000
SALES (est): 5MM **Privately Held**
SIC: 2095 Mfg Roasted Coffee

(G-9238)
JDS SMALL MACHINE REPAIR
1515 Biltmore Blvd (48906-2802)
PHONE.................................517 323-7236
Jeffrey Deline, *Owner*
EMP: 3
SALES (est): 156.3K **Privately Held**
SIC: 3599 Machine shop, jobbing & repair

(G-9239)
KANSMACKERS MANUFACTURING CO
Also Called: Source Vending
312 W Willow St (48906-4740)
PHONE.................................248 249-6666
Nick Yono, *President*
EMP: 15
SQ FT: 5,000
SALES (est): 2.5MM **Privately Held**
WEB: www.kansmacker.com
SIC: 3559 Recycling machinery

(G-9240)
LANSING ICE AND FUEL COMPANY (PA)
911 Center St (48906-5298)
P.O. Box 20097 (48901-0697)
PHONE.................................517 372-3850
Ron Bewersborss, *President*
Ronald Beversdorff, *President*
Floyd Conklin, *Corp Secy*
Robert J Reutter, *Vice Pres*
EMP: 16 **EST:** 1906
SQ FT: 20,000
SALES (est): 17.8MM **Privately Held**
SIC: 5983 5172 2097 Fuel oil dealers; fuel oil; manufactured ice

(G-9241)
LANSING PLATING COMPANY
1303 Case St (48906-4599)
PHONE.................................517 485-6915
Dean Vohwinkle, *President*
Lynn Vohwinkle, *Vice Pres*
EMP: 6
SQ FT: 15,500
SALES: 1.2MM **Privately Held**
SIC: 3471 Plating of metals or formed products

(G-9242)
LOC PERFORMANCE PRODUCTS INC
1600 N Larch St (48906-4168)
PHONE.................................734 453-2300
Teena L Kowalski, *Finance*
Timothy Horner, *Branch Mgr*
EMP: 160
SALES (corp-wide): 136.7MM **Privately Held**
SIC: 3541 Machine tools, metal cutting type

Lansing - Clinton County (G-9243)

PA: Loc Performance Products, Inc.
13505 N Haggerty Rd
Plymouth MI 48170
734 453-2300

(G-9243)
MADAR METAL FABRICATING LLC
3310 Ranger Rd (48906-2725)
PHONE......................517 267-9610
Greg Madar,
EMP: 12
SALES (est): 1.7MM **Privately Held**
SIC: 3441 Fabricated structural metal

(G-9244)
MARKERBOARD PEOPLE INC
1611 N Grand River Ave # 1 (48906-3995)
P.O. Box 80560 (48908-0560)
PHONE......................517 372-1666
Harold Spaeth, *President*
Dean Hibler, *General Mgr*
Josh Struble, *Office Mgr*
Chris Zimmerman, *Info Tech Mgr*
▲ **EMP:** 26
SQ FT: 35,000
SALES (est): 3.9MM **Privately Held**
WEB: www.dryerase.com
SIC: 3952 Boards, drawing, artists'

(G-9245)
MICHALSKI ENTERPRISES INC
Also Called: Tool Craft
16733 Industrial Pkwy (48906-9136)
PHONE......................517 703-0777
Michael Michalski, *President*
William Michalski, *Vice Pres*
EMP: 22 **EST:** 1966
SQ FT: 6,000
SALES (est): 4.5MM **Privately Held**
SIC: 3544 2542 3543 Jigs & fixtures; office & store showcases & display fixtures; industrial patterns

(G-9246)
MPS HOLDCO INC (DH)
Also Called: MPS Holdings
5800 W Grand River Ave (48906-9111)
PHONE......................517 886-2526
Marc Shore, *CEO*
Dennis Kalpman, *President*
Tim Schultz, *Senior VP*
Sandra Marshall, *Opers Staff*
Christine Barto, *Purch Mgr*
EMP: 151
SALES (est): 330.9MM
SALES (corp-wide): 16.2B **Publicly Held**
SIC: 2759 Advertising literature: printing

(G-9247)
MPS HRL LLC
Also Called: John Henry
5800 W Grand River Ave (48906-9111)
PHONE......................800 748-0517
EMP: 14
SALES (est): 2.2MM
SALES (corp-wide): 16.2B **Publicly Held**
SIC: 2759 Commercial printing
HQ: Multi Packaging Solutions, Inc.
885 3rd Ave Fl 28
New York NY 10022

(G-9248)
MPS LANSING INC (DH)
5800 W Grand River Ave (48906-9111)
PHONE......................517 323-9000
Marc Shore, *CEO*
Dennis Kaltman, *President*
Michael Klein, *Opers Staff*
Greg Bomers, *Treasurer*
Becky Bush, *Natl Sales Mgr*
◆ **EMP:** 800 **EST:** 1946
SQ FT: 350,000
SALES (est): 250.7MM
SALES (corp-wide): 16.2B **Publicly Held**
WEB: www.thejohnhenrycompany.com
SIC: 2759 2731 2761 3089 Commercial printing; screen printing; letterpress printing; tags: printing; books: publishing & printing; continuous forms, office & business; identification cards, plastic; packaging paper & plastics film, coated & laminated

(G-9249)
MPS/IH LLC
5800 W Grand River Ave (48906-9111)
PHONE......................517 323-9001
Dennis Kaltman, *Manager*
EMP: 4
SALES (est): 248.8K **Privately Held**
SIC: 2752 Commercial printing, offset

(G-9250)
MULTI PACKG SOLUTIONS INTL LTD
5800 W Grand River Ave (48906-9111)
PHONE......................517 323-9000
EMP: 640
SALES (corp-wide): 14.8B **Publicly Held**
SIC: 2759 Business forms: printing; letterpress printing; tags: printing
HQ: Multi Packaging Solutions International Limited
885 3rd Ave Fl 28
New York NY 10022
646 885-0005

(G-9251)
PALMER ENGINEERING INC
3525 Capitol City Blvd (48906-2101)
P.O. Box 12030 (48901-2030)
PHONE......................517 321-3600
William Demmer, *President*
Tim McKenna, *Executive*
EMP: 25 **EST:** 1947
SQ FT: 15,000
SALES (est): 3.8MM **Privately Held**
SIC: 3469 Stamping metal for the trade

(G-9252)
PECKHAM VOCATIONAL INDS INC (PA)
3510 Capitol City Blvd (48906-2102)
PHONE......................517 316-4000
Mitchell Tomlinson, *CEO*
Karen Jury, *President*
Stuart Muladore, *President*
Curt Munson, *President*
Melanie Grafft, *Business Mgr*
EMP: 1000
SQ FT: 190,000
SALES: 196.1MM **Privately Held**
SIC: 8331 2396 2311 2331 Vocational rehabilitation agency; automotive trimmings, fabric; men's & boys' suits & coats; women's & misses' blouses & shirts; women's & misses' outerwear; men's & boys' work clothing

(G-9253)
PECKHAM VOCATIONAL INDS INC
2511 N Martin Lthr King J (48906-3865)
PHONE......................517 316-4478
Wayne Parsons, *Principal*
EMP: 175
SALES (corp-wide): 196.1MM **Privately Held**
SIC: 8331 2396 2311 2331 Vocational rehabilitation agency; automotive trimmings, fabric; men's & boys' suits & coats; women's & misses' blouses & shirts; motor vehicle parts & accessories
PA: Peckham Vocational Industries, Inc.
3510 Capitol City Blvd
Lansing MI 48906
517 316-4000

(G-9254)
PEPSI-COLA METRO BTLG CO INC
4900 W Grand River Ave (48906-9128)
PHONE......................517 321-0231
Paul Hermann, *Manager*
Scott Conant, *Manager*
EMP: 100
SALES (corp-wide): 64.6B **Publicly Held**
WEB: www.joy-of-cola.com
SIC: 2086 Carbonated soft drinks, bottled & canned
HQ: Pepsi-Cola Metropolitan Bottling Company, Inc.
1111 Westchester Ave
White Plains NY 10604
914 767-6000

(G-9255)
PIERCE ENGINEERS INC
5122 N Grand River Ave # 1 (48906-5810)
PHONE......................517 321-5051
John W Pierce, *President*
Jim Nordhof, *Manager*
EMP: 4
SALES: 375K **Privately Held**
WEB: www.pierceengineeringltd.com
SIC: 3484 Guns (firearms) or gun parts, 30 mm. & below

(G-9256)
PINE NEEDLE PEOPLE LLC
Also Called: Alien Resources
934 Clark St Ste 4 (48906-5425)
PHONE......................517 242-4752
Kevin Karpinski, *CEO*
EMP: 3
SALES (est): 200.7K **Privately Held**
SIC: 3559 Robots, molding & forming plastics

(G-9257)
PIZZA CRUST COMPANY INC
728 E Cesar E Chavez Ave (48906-5340)
PHONE......................517 482-3368
Keith A Guyer, *President*
Eloy Guyer, *Treasurer*
EMP: 10
SQ FT: 1,500
SALES (est): 1MM **Privately Held**
SIC: 2045 Pizza doughs, prepared: from purchased flour; bread & bread type roll mixes: from purchased flour

(G-9258)
PLANNING & ZONING CENTER INC
Also Called: Planning & Zoning News
715 N Cedar St Ste 2 (48906-5275)
PHONE......................517 886-0555
Mark A Wyckoff, *President*
Carolyn Freebury, *Vice Pres*
Leslie Hoover, *Treasurer*
Cheryl Petchell, *Office Mgr*
EMP: 4
SALES (est): 448K **Privately Held**
WEB: www.pzcenter.com
SIC: 2721 Magazines: publishing & printing

(G-9259)
PLAS-LABS INCORPORATED
401 E North St Ste 1 (48906-4434)
PHONE......................517 372-7178
David L Regan, *President*
▲ **EMP:** 20 **EST:** 1967
SQ FT: 9,000
SALES (est): 5MM **Privately Held**
WEB: www.plas-labs.com
SIC: 3821 Laboratory equipment: fume hoods, distillation racks, etc.

(G-9260)
PRO-SOIL SITE SERVICES INC
3323 N East St (48906-2037)
P.O. Box 12217 (48901-2217)
PHONE......................517 267-8767
Nicole Tews, *President*
Darren Tews, *Vice Pres*
EMP: 5
SALES (est): 776.8K **Privately Held**
SIC: 3315 1799 5039 Fence gates posts & fittings: steel; construction site cleanup; fence construction; post-disaster renovations; wire fence, gates & accessories

(G-9261)
PRODUCT RESOURCE COMPANY
2220 Raymond Dr (48906-3918)
PHONE......................517 484-8400
Chris Spalding, *President*
Jack Spalding, *Project Mgr*
EMP: 3
SALES: 430K **Privately Held**
SIC: 5122 3999 Toilet articles; fire extinguishers, portable

(G-9262)
PURITY CYLINDER GASES INC
1035 Mak Tech Dr Ste A (48906-5618)
PHONE......................517 321-9555
Don Grifwald, *Branch Mgr*
EMP: 9
SALES (corp-wide): 111.1MM **Privately Held**
WEB: www.puritygas.com
SIC: 5169 3548 5084 Gases, compressed & liquefied; welding apparatus; welding machinery & equipment
HQ: Purity Cylinder Gases, Inc.
2580 28th St Sw
Wyoming MI 49519
616 532-2375

(G-9263)
SPARTAN METAL FAB LLC
4905 N Grand River Ave (48906-2541)
PHONE......................517 322-9050
Greg Simmer, *Mng Member*
EMP: 4
SALES (est): 300K **Privately Held**
SIC: 3446 1799 5051 3441 Stairs, staircases, stair treads: prefabricated metal; fence construction; steel; fabricated structural metal

(G-9264)
SPARTAN PRINTING INC
15551 S Us Highway 27 (48906-1409)
PHONE......................517 372-6910
Steve Root, *President*
James Fournier, *Accounts Exec*
▲ **EMP:** 38 **EST:** 1960
SQ FT: 10,000
SALES (est): 6.7MM **Privately Held**
WEB: www.spartanprintinginc.com
SIC: 2752 2791 2789 Commercial printing, offset; typesetting; bookbinding & related work

(G-9265)
SPIETH ANDERSON USA LC
Also Called: SA Sport
3327 Ranger Rd (48906-2726)
PHONE......................817 536-3366
EMP: 12
SQ FT: 22,000
SALES (est): 1.8MM
SALES (corp-wide): 4.1MM **Privately Held**
SIC: 3949 Mfg Sporting/Athletic Goods
PA: Spieth-Anderson International Inc
135 Forestview Rd
Oro-Medonte ON L3V 0
705 325-2274

(G-9266)
SPIRIT INDUSTRIES INC
2900 7th Ave (48906-3347)
PHONE......................517 371-7840
James Parker Jr, *President*
EMP: 6
SQ FT: 9,000
SALES: 1.7MM **Privately Held**
SIC: 3559 3089 3599 3469 Plastics working machinery; blow molded finished plastic products; machine shop, jobbing & repair; metal stampings

(G-9267)
STAMP-RITE INCORPORATED
Also Called: Stamprite Supersine
2822 N M Luther King Jr (48906)
PHONE......................517 487-5071
Wendell W Parsons, *President*
Scott W Parsons, *Exec VP*
Pam Frei, *Admin Sec*
EMP: 29 **EST:** 1955
SQ FT: 16,000
SALES (est): 4.1MM **Privately Held**
WEB: www.stamprite.com
SIC: 3993 3953 2752 2759 Signs, not made in custom sign painting shops; embossing seals & hand stamps; commercial printing, offset; labels & seals: printing; platemaking services; packaging paper & plastics film, coated & laminated

(G-9268)
STATEWIDE PRINTING LLC
16230 S Lowell Rd (48906-9324)
P.O. Box 81166 (48908-1166)
PHONE......................517 485-4466
Steve Goble, *President*
EMP: 6
SQ FT: 2,800

GEOGRAPHIC SECTION

Lansing - Eaton County (G-9294)

SALES (est): 750K **Privately Held**
WEB: www.advancedimagingusa.com
SIC: **2759** 2791 Commercial printing; typesetting

(G-9269)
TENNECO AUTOMOTIVE OPER CO INC
4722 Grand Riv (48906)
PHONE.....................734 243-8000
Marthy Partin, *Branch Mgr*
EMP: 50
SALES (corp-wide): 11.7B **Publicly Held**
SIC: **3714** 3699 Shock absorbers, motor vehicle; electrical equipment & supplies
HQ: Tenneco Automotive Operating Company, Inc.
500 N Field Dr
Lake Forest IL 60045
847 482-5000

(G-9270)
TOP SHOP INC
2526 N Grand River Ave (48906-3915)
PHONE.....................517 323-9085
Vic Toune, *President*
Joseph Sutton, *Vice Pres*
Sam Eyde, *Admin Sec*
EMP: 5
SQ FT: 7,000
SALES (est): 607.1K **Privately Held**
SIC: **2542** Counters or counter display cases: except wood

(G-9271)
VAN-ROB INC
Also Called: Van Rob Lansing
16325 Felton Rd (48906-9144)
PHONE.....................517 657-2450
Steven Meyer, *Plant Mgr*
EMP: 135
SALES (corp-wide): 1.8B **Privately Held**
SIC: **3465** 5013 Automotive stampings; automotive supplies & parts
HQ: Kirchhoff Automotive Canada Inc
25 Mural St
Richmond ON L4B 1
905 727-8585

Lansing
Eaton County

(G-9272)
AIR LIFT COMPANY (PA)
Also Called: Suspension Solutions
2727 Snow Rd (48917-9595)
P.O. Box 80167 (48908-0167)
PHONE.....................517 322-2144
Thomas J Waier, *President*
Kevin Mehigh, *President*
Dorothy Scripsma, *Vice Pres*
Adam Koch, *Plant Mgr*
Kelly Parker, *Engineer*
◆ EMP: 50 EST: 1947
SQ FT: 30,000
SALES (est): 9.2MM **Privately Held**
WEB: www.airliftcompany.com
SIC: **3714** Motor vehicle parts & accessories

(G-9273)
ALLIANCE INTERIORS LLC
4521 W Mount Hope Hwy (48917-9501)
PHONE.....................517 322-0711
Steve Phillips, *CEO*
John Lychos, *Principal*
Gary Stanis, *CFO*
John Pendleton,
Wayne Robbison,
▲ EMP: 54
SQ FT: 200,000
SALES (est): 20.8MM **Privately Held**
WEB: www.dtigroup.biz/allianceinteriors.htm
SIC: **3446** Partitions & supports/studs, including accoustical systems
PA: Detroit Technologies, Inc.
32500 Telg Rd Ste 207
Bingham Farms MI 48025

(G-9274)
ALLOY MACHINING LLC
437 N Rosemary St (48917-4915)
PHONE.....................517 204-3306
EMP: 4 EST: 2011
SALES (est): 200.1K **Privately Held**
SIC: **3369** Nonferrous foundries

(G-9275)
ALPINE SIGN AND PRTG SUP INC
Also Called: Michigan Sign Supplies
3105 Sanders Rd (48917-9512)
P.O. Box 504, Portland (48875-0504)
PHONE.....................517 487-1400
Robert Heindel, *President*
EMP: 12
SQ FT: 6,000
SALES: 2.5MM **Privately Held**
SIC: **3555** Printing trades machinery

(G-9276)
ANDROID INDUSTRIES LLC
8175 Millett Hwy (48917-8512)
PHONE.....................517 322-0141
▲ EMP: 3
SALES (est): 280K **Privately Held**
SIC: **3999** Barber & beauty shop equipment

(G-9277)
ANDROID INDUSTRIES-DELTA TOWNS
Also Called: Ai-Delta Township
2051 S Canal Rd (48917-8598)
PHONE.....................517 322-0657
Jerry Elson,
▲ EMP: 170
SALES (est): 22.2MM
SALES (corp-wide): 559.5MM **Privately Held**
SIC: **3714** Motor vehicle parts & accessories
PA: Android Industries, L.L.C.
2155 Executive Hills Dr
Auburn Hills MI 48326
248 454-0500

(G-9278)
ART CRAFT DISPLAY INC (PA)
500 Business Centre Dr (48917-3796)
PHONE.....................517 485-2221
Barry Freed, *President*
David Beeman, *General Mgr*
Steve Carr, *General Mgr*
Doug Goin, *General Mgr*
Jeanette Kapusto, *Corp Secy*
EMP: 100 EST: 1958
SQ FT: 20,000
SALES (est): 15MM **Privately Held**
WEB: www.artcraftdisplay.com
SIC: **7389** 2759 Convention & show services; commercial printing

(G-9279)
BRIDGEWATER INTERIORS LLC
Also Called: Johnson Controls
2369 S Canal Rd (48917-8589)
PHONE.....................517 322-4800
Lillie Rucker, *President*
EMP: 12 **Privately Held**
SIC: **2531** Seats, automobile
HQ: Bridgewater Interiors, L.L.C.
4617 W Fort St
Detroit MI 48209
313 842-3300

(G-9280)
CAPITOL TOOL GRINDING CO
437 N Rosemary St (48917-4915)
PHONE.....................517 321-8230
Jack L Yeakey, *President*
Betty L Yeakey, *Corp Secy*
Daniel J Yeakey, *Vice Pres*
EMP: 3
SALES: 115K **Privately Held**
SIC: **7699** 3545 Knife, saw & tool sharpening & repair; machine tool accessories

(G-9281)
CHAIN-SYS CORPORATION (PA)
8530 Ember Glen Pass (48917-8844)
PHONE.....................517 627-1173
Sundaramurugan Rathinam, *President*
Frank Malangone, *Technical Mgr*
EMP: 11
SQ FT: 6,000
SALES (est): 3.4MM **Privately Held**
SIC: **7379** 7371 7372 Computer related consulting services; computer software systems analysis & design, custom; prepackaged software

(G-9282)
CLASSIC SEA SCAPES
7232 Glen Terra Dr (48917-7819)
P.O. Box 80303 (48908-0303)
PHONE.....................517 323-7775
EMP: 3 EST: 1996
SALES: 190K **Privately Held**
SIC: **3999** Manufactures And Wholesale Artificial Flower Arrangements For Aquariam Decoration

(G-9283)
COCA-COLA REFRESHMENTS USA INC
3300 S Creyts Rd (48917-8508)
PHONE.....................517 322-2349
John F Brock, *CEO*
EMP: 250
SALES (corp-wide): 31.8B **Publicly Held**
WEB: www.cokecce.com
SIC: **2086** 2087 5149 Bottled & canned soft drinks; syrups, drink; concentrates, drink; groceries & related products
HQ: Coca-Cola Refreshments Usa, Inc.
2500 Windy Ridge Pkwy Se
Atlanta GA 30339
770 989-3000

(G-9284)
CON-VEL INC
7020 Old River Trl (48917-9746)
PHONE.....................864 281-2228
Raymond L Kaser, *President*
Frederick W Standfest III, *Admin Sec*
EMP: 3
SQ FT: 24,000
SALES (est): 331.7K **Privately Held**
SIC: **3568** 3714 Joints & couplings; motor vehicle parts & accessories

(G-9285)
CORE TECHNOLOGY CORPORATION
5859 W Saginaw Hwy 217 (48917-2460)
PHONE.....................517 627-1521
David Hadsall, *President*
EMP: 16
SQ FT: 7,000
SALES (est): 1.5MM
SALES (corp-wide): 1.4MM **Privately Held**
WEB: www.ctc-core.com
SIC: **7372** 7371 Business oriented computer software; custom computer programming services
PA: Harris Systems Usa, Inc

Jersey City NJ
613 226-5511

(G-9286)
DEE CRAMER INC
2623 W Saint Joseph St (48917-3877)
PHONE.....................517 485-5519
Marshael Nations, *Branch Mgr*
EMP: 30
SALES (corp-wide): 36MM **Privately Held**
WEB: www.deecramer.com
SIC: **1711** 3444 Ventilation & duct work contractor; mechanical contractor; warm air heating & air conditioning contractor; sheet metalwork
PA: Dee Cramer, Inc.
4221 Baldwin Rd
Holly MI 48442
810 579-5000

(G-9287)
DEMMER CORPORATION
Also Called: Delta Stamping Div
2904 Snow Rd (48917-9545)
PHONE.....................517 321-3600
Tim McKenna, *Branch Mgr*
EMP: 45
SQ FT: 55,000
SALES (corp-wide): 136.7MM **Privately Held**
WEB: www.demmercorp.com
SIC: **3795** 3599 Tanks & tank components; machine & other job shop work
HQ: Demmer Corporation
4520 N Grand River Ave
Lansing MI 48906
517 321-3600

(G-9288)
DOUGLAS STEEL FABRICATING CORP
1312 S Waverly Rd (48917-4259)
P.O. Box 27277 (48909-7277)
PHONE.....................517 322-2050
James D Buzzie, *President*
Charles Dunn, *Plant Supt*
Dan Harris, *Project Mgr*
Michael Mortenson, *Purch Agent*
Chris Lowe, *Purchasing*
EMP: 58 EST: 1952
SQ FT: 50,000
SALES: 17MM **Privately Held**
WEB: www.douglassteel.com
SIC: **1791** 8711 3441 Iron work, structural; sanitary engineers; fabricated structural metal for ships

(G-9289)
FLAVORED GROUP LLC
437 Lentz Ct (48917-3702)
PHONE.....................517 775-4371
Juan Hernandez, *Partner*
Eric Fuentes, *Administration*
EMP: 3
SALES (est): 237.1K **Privately Held**
SIC: **2759** 7389 Screen printing; apparel designers, commercial

(G-9290)
GENERAL MOTORS LLC
4400 W Mount Hope Hwy (48917-9501)
PHONE.....................517 885-6669
Barb Pohlman, *Manager*
EMP: 700 **Publicly Held**
SIC: **5511** 3714 Automobiles, new & used; motor vehicle parts & accessories
HQ: General Motors Llc
300 Renaissance Ctr L1
Detroit MI 48243

(G-9291)
GENERAL MOTORS LLC
8175 Millett Hwy (48917-8512)
PHONE.....................517 721-2000
Kevin Slocum, *Fire Chief*
Pat Donohue, *Branch Mgr*
EMP: 230 **Publicly Held**
SIC: **3465** Automotive stampings
HQ: General Motors Llc
300 Renaissance Ctr L1
Detroit MI 48243

(G-9292)
HOLDER CORPORATION
2538 W Main St (48917-4341)
PHONE.....................517 484-5453
Kenneth Holz, *President*
Melissa Holz, *Corp Secy*
EMP: 7
SQ FT: 7,000
SALES: 500K **Privately Held**
SIC: **3599** Machine shop, jobbing & repair

(G-9293)
HP INC
7335 Westshire Dr Ste 101 (48917-9703)
PHONE.....................650 857-1501
Earl Smith, *Manager*
EMP: 6
SALES (corp-wide): 58.4B **Publicly Held**
SIC: **3571** Personal computers (microcomputers)
PA: Hp, Inc.
1501 Page Mill Rd
Palo Alto CA 94304
650 857-1501

(G-9294)
ICON SIGN & DESIGN INC
3308 W Saint Joseph St (48917-3706)
PHONE.....................517 372-1104
David Finley, *President*
Elaine Slawski, *Vice Pres*
EMP: 7

SQ FT: 3,000
SALES (est): 784.7K **Privately Held**
SIC: 3993 Electric signs

(G-9295)
IDV SOLUTIONS LLC (HQ)
6000 W St Joe Hwy Ste 100 (48917-4873)
PHONE.................................517 853-3755
Travis Conti, *Manager*
Rick Peterson, *Manager*
John McPherson, *Info Tech Mgr*
Yusuke Hasegawa, *Software Dev*
Peter Tirrell, *Software Dev*
EMP: 35
SALES (est): 5.6MM
SALES (corp-wide): 147MM **Publicly Held**
WEB: www.idvsolutions.com
SIC: 7372 Business oriented computer software
PA: Everbridge, Inc.
25 Corporate Dr Ste 400
Burlington MA 01803
818 230-9700

(G-9296)
IM A BEER HOUND
602 N Grace St (48917-4912)
PHONE.................................517 331-0528
Chuck Brown, *Owner*
EMP: 3
SALES (est): 147.7K **Privately Held**
SIC: 2082 Beer (alcoholic beverage)

(G-9297)
INCO DEVELOPMENT CORPORATION
Also Called: Inco Graphics
1628 Alan Ln (48917-1247)
PHONE.................................517 323-8448
Richard J Abood, *President*
Robert Blowers, *Vice Pres*
Timothy W Brown, *Vice Pres*
Adam H Hunt, *Vice Pres*
Jennifer L Abood, *Treasurer*
EMP: 90 EST: 1963
SQ FT: 41,750
SALES (est): 10MM **Privately Held**
WEB: www.incographics.net
SIC: 2752 Commercial printing, offset; promotional printing, lithographic; periodicals, lithographed

(G-9298)
INDUSTRIAL PATTERN OF LANSING
5901 W Willow Hwy (48917-1228)
PHONE.................................517 482-9835
W Herbert Sturdevant, *Ch of Bd*
Dennis J Schmidt, *President*
EMP: 3 EST: 1956
SALES (est): 219.6K **Privately Held**
WEB: www.ind-patt.com
SIC: 3999 3089 Models, except toy; thermoformed finished plastic products

(G-9299)
INSTY-PRINTS WEST INC
3121 W Saginaw St Ste A (48917-5301)
PHONE.................................517 321-7091
Robert Porter, *President*
EMP: 3
SALES: 400K **Privately Held**
SIC: 2752 7334 Commercial printing, lithographic; photocopying & duplicating services

(G-9300)
JOB SHOP INK INC
2321 W Main St (48917-4338)
PHONE.................................517 372-3900
Scott McCulloch, *President*
Scott Mc Kenna, *Vice Pres*
EMP: 5 EST: 1999
SALES: 400K **Privately Held**
SIC: 2752 2759 Commercial printing, lithographic; commercial printing

(G-9301)
K&H SUPPLY OF LANSING INC (PA)
3503 W Saint Joseph St (48917-3692)
PHONE.................................517 482-7600
Dave Tebben, *President*
EMP: 7

SALES (est): 870.8K **Privately Held**
SIC: 3531 Concrete grouting equipment

(G-9302)
KAMPS INC
4201 S Creyts Rd (48917-9583)
PHONE.................................517 322-2500
Eric Lee, *Warehouse Mgr*
Tony Sokoloski, *Manager*
EMP: 54
SALES (corp-wide): 157.4MM **Privately Held**
WEB: www.kampspallets.com
SIC: 2448 Pallets, wood
PA: Kamps, Inc.
2900 Peach Ridge Ave Nw
Grand Rapids MI 49534
616 453-9676

(G-9303)
KAREMOR INC
Also Called: Auntie Anne's
5242 W Saginaw Hwy (48917)
PHONE.................................517 323-3042
Karen Mory, *President*
EMP: 9 **Privately Held**
SIC: 5461 2052 Pretzels; pretzels
PA: Karemor Inc
5778 Whisperwood Dr
Haslett MI 48840

(G-9304)
KENOWA INDUSTRIES INC
2924 Sanders Rd (48917-8570)
PHONE.................................517 322-0311
Gerry Hawkins, *Manager*
EMP: 4
SALES (corp-wide): 5.9MM **Privately Held**
WEB: www.kenowa.com
SIC: 3449 3441 Miscellaneous metalwork; fabricated structural metal
PA: Kenowa Industries, Inc.
11405 E Lakewood Blvd
Holland MI 49424
616 392-7080

(G-9305)
LANSING ATHLETICS
5572 W Saginaw Hwy (48917-1919)
PHONE.................................517 327-8828
Alfonso Salas, *Owner*
EMP: 5
SQ FT: 1,000
SALES (est): 366.7K **Privately Held**
SIC: 5699 5941 2759 2395 Sports apparel; team sports equipment; screen printing; embroidery products, except schiffli machine

(G-9306)
LANSING LABOR NEWS INC
210 Clare St Ste A (48917-3889)
PHONE.................................517 484-7408
Nancy Sears, *Principal*
Mike Bestero, *Treasurer*
Harold Foster, *Director*
EMP: 4
SQ FT: 2,200
SALES: 179.6K **Privately Held**
SIC: 2711 Newspapers: publishing only, not printed on site

(G-9307)
LANSING PALLET
4201 S Creyts Rd (48917-9583)
PHONE.................................517 322-2500
Bill Viveen, *Principal*
EMP: 4 EST: 2009
SALES (est): 302.9K **Privately Held**
SIC: 2448 Pallets, wood

(G-9308)
LEIF DISTRIBUTION LLC
Also Called: Leif Led
7704 Lanac St (48917-9572)
PHONE.................................517 481-2122
Toby Leifker, *Mng Member*
▲ EMP: 25
SQ FT: 40,000

SALES (est): 440.9K **Privately Held**
SIC: 3648 3646 Street lighting fixtures; outdoor lighting equipment; commercial indusl & institutional electric lighting fixtures; ornamental lighting fixtures, commercial; fluorescent lighting fixtures, commercial

(G-9309)
LOUIS PADNOS IRON AND METAL CO
1900 W Willow St (48917-1838)
PHONE.................................517 372-6600
Todd Pastoor, *Branch Mgr*
EMP: 30
SALES (corp-wide): 520.8MM **Privately Held**
SIC: 5093 3341 4953 Metal scrap & waste materials; ferrous metal scrap & waste; nonferrous metals scrap; secondary nonferrous metals; recycling, waste materials
PA: Louis Padnos Iron And Metal Company
185 W 8th St
Holland MI 49423
616 396-6521

(G-9310)
MELANGE COMPUTER SERVICES INC
808 Century Blvd Ste 100 (48917-8243)
PHONE.................................517 321-8434
Rick White, *President*
Ronald Austin, *Vice Pres*
Rick Bean, *Vice Pres*
Harrold Rappold, *Vice Pres*
EMP: 34
SQ FT: 11,536
SALES (est): 2.5MM
SALES (corp-wide): 4.4MM **Privately Held**
WEB: www.melange-inc.com
SIC: 7371 7374 7372 Computer software development; data processing service; prepackaged software
PA: Planet Bingo Llc
75190 Gerald Ford Dr
Palm Desert CA 92211
760 773-0197

(G-9311)
MILLBROOK PRESS WORKS
Also Called: Gladstone Printing
517 S Waverly Rd (48917-3617)
PHONE.................................517 323-2111
Travis Millbrook, *Owner*
EMP: 4 EST: 1979
SQ FT: 3,000
SALES (est): 380.5K **Privately Held**
WEB: www.gladstoneprinting.com
SIC: 2752 Commercial printing, offset

(G-9312)
MILLIMAN COMMUNICATIONS INC (PA)
4601 W Saginaw Hwy Apt 2 (48917-2756)
PHONE.................................517 327-8407
Dirk Milliman, *President*
Teresa Fitzwater, *Vice Pres*
Ann Marie Milliman, *Treasurer*
EMP: 4 EST: 1992
SQ FT: 1,000 **Privately Held**
SIC: 2711 Newspapers, publishing & printing

(G-9313)
MONROE SP INC
437 Lentz Ct (48917-3702)
PHONE.................................517 374-6544
Steve Monroe, *President*
EMP: 9
SALES: 420K **Privately Held**
WEB: www.monroescreenprinting.com
SIC: 2759 Screen printing

(G-9314)
NORPLAS INDUSTRIES INC
Also Called: Dexsys
5589 W Mount Hope Hwy (48917-9559)
PHONE.................................517 999-1400
Eric Jorgensen, *Controller*
Chris Wood, *Manager*
EMP: 60

SALES (corp-wide): 40.8B **Privately Held**
SIC: 3714 Bumpers & bumperettes, motor vehicle
HQ: Norplas Industries Inc.
7825 Caple Blvd
Northwood OH 43619
419 662-3317

(G-9315)
NUWAVE TECHNOLOGY PARTNERS LLC
6709 Centurion Dr Ste 200 (48917-8293)
PHONE.................................517 322-2200
Richard Paalman, *Branch Mgr*
EMP: 12 **Privately Held**
SIC: 3661 Telephone & telegraph apparatus
PA: Nuwave Technology Partners, Llc
5268 Azo Dr
Kalamazoo MI 49048

(G-9316)
OAKWOOD SPORTS INC (PA)
1025 Clark Rd (48917-2129)
PHONE.................................517 321-6852
Greg Bria, *President*
Willard Boast, *Vice Pres*
EMP: 8
SQ FT: 8,500
SALES (est): 609.7K **Privately Held**
WEB: www.oakwoodsports.com
SIC: 2499 Decorative wood & woodwork

(G-9317)
PAXTON PRODUCTS INC
Also Called: Paxton Countertops
1340 S Waverly Rd (48917-5206)
P.O. Box 174, Grand Ledge (48837-0174)
PHONE.................................517 627-3688
Stephen Paxton, *President*
Rachel Paxton Schroeder, *Principal*
David Paxton, *Vice Pres*
Jane Paxton, *Admin Sec*
EMP: 22
SQ FT: 10,000
SALES (est): 2.7MM **Privately Held**
SIC: 2541 Counter & sink tops

(G-9318)
PIRA TESTING LLC
Also Called: Pira International
6539 Westland Way Ste 24 (48917-9581)
PHONE.................................517 574-4297
Michael Dannemiller, *Manager*
Barbara Rojas, *Director*
Michael Kuebler,
EMP: 15
SALES (est): 2MM **Privately Held**
SIC: 2869 Industrial organic chemicals

(G-9319)
PURINA MILLS LLC
5620 Millett Hwy (48917-8556)
PHONE.................................517 322-0200
Lawrence Moorman, *Manager*
EMP: 50
SALES (corp-wide): 6.8B **Privately Held**
WEB: www.purina-mills.com
SIC: 2048 5191 5149 Prepared feeds; animal feeds; groceries & related products
HQ: Purina Mills, Llc
555 Maryvle Univ Dr 200
Saint Louis MO 63141

(G-9320)
ROBERTS SINTO CORPORATION (DH)
Also Called: Shalco Systems
3001 W Main St (48917-4352)
P.O. Box 39, Grand Ledge (48837-0039)
PHONE.................................517 371-2460
Richard Stewart, *CEO*
Michael Halsband, *Exec VP*
Wendell Kauffman, *Vice Pres*
Bill Traeger, *Vice Pres*
Anthony Price, *Project Mgr*
▲ EMP: 120
SQ FT: 25,000
SALES: 32MM **Privately Held**
WEB: www.robertssinto.com
SIC: 3559 3535 5084 Foundry machinery & equipment; conveyors & conveying equipment; machine tools & metalworking machinery

GEOGRAPHIC SECTION

Lansing - Ingham County (G-9345)

HQ: Sinto America, Inc.
3001 W Main St
Lansing MI 48917
517 371-2460

(G-9321)
RYDER INTEGRATED LOGISTICS INC
2901 S Canal Rd (48917-8594)
PHONE.................517 492-4446
Greg Reinke, *Manager*
Bill Sheerin, *Manager*
EMP: 956
SQ FT: 2,760,000
SALES (corp-wide): 8.4B **Publicly Held**
SIC: 4225 3714 General warehousing & storage; motor vehicle parts & accessories
PA: Ryder Integrated Logistics, Inc.
11690 Nw 105th St
Medley FL 33178
305 500-3726

(G-9322)
SHAPESHIFT LLC
4500 Empire Way Ste 11 (48917-9580)
PHONE.................517 910-3078
Robert Gilreath,
EMP: 3 **EST:** 2018
SALES: 350K **Privately Held**
SIC: 2821 Plastics materials & resins

(G-9323)
SINTO AMERICA INC (HQ)
3001 W Main St (48917-4352)
P.O. Box 40760 (48901-7960)
PHONE.................517 371-2460
James A Donlan, *Ch of Bd*
▲ **EMP:** 25
SQ FT: 25,000
SALES: 45MM **Privately Held**
SIC: 3559 3535 5084 3823 Foundry machinery & equipment; conveyors & conveying equipment; industrial machinery & equipment; industrial instrmnts msrmnt display/control process variable

(G-9324)
SUGAR BERRY
5451 W Saginaw Hwy (48917-1982)
PHONE.................517 321-0177
Sarah Pham, *Owner*
EMP: 5
SALES (est): 298.8K **Privately Held**
SIC: 2026 Yogurt

(G-9325)
TEE TO GREEN PRINT & PROMO PRO
3030 Sanders Rd Ste 1 (48917-8552)
PHONE.................517 322-3088
Bruce Chapman, *President*
EMP: 6
SALES (est): 510K **Privately Held**
WEB: www.t2gprintpromo.com
SIC: 2752 Commercial printing, lithographic

(G-9326)
TOP SHELF BARBER SUPPLIES LLC (PA)
5400 Pierson Hwy W (48917-9513)
PHONE.................586 453-6809
Trevor Burch, *Vice Pres*
Anna Mrdeza, *Vice Pres*
Ned Milana, *VP Sales*
Jake Wilk, *Chief Mktg Ofcr*
Douglas Mrdeza, *Mng Member*
◆ **EMP:** 6
SALES (est): 7.6MM **Privately Held**
SIC: 3999 Barber & beauty shop equipment

(G-9327)
TOPDUCK PRODUCTS LLC
2902 Sanders Rd (48917-8570)
PHONE.................517 322-3202
Donald Kettles, *President*
EMP: 10
SQ FT: 7,000
SALES (est): 1.3MM **Privately Held**
WEB: www.topduckproducts.com
SIC: 2899 Corrosion preventive lubricant

(G-9328)
UFP LANSING LLC
Also Called: Universal Forest Products
2509 Snow Rd (48917-9506)
PHONE.................517 322-0025
EMP: 5
SALES (est): 506K
SALES (corp-wide): 3.9B **Publicly Held**
SIC: 2491 2499 Wood Preserving Mfg Wood Products
PA: Universal Forest Products, Inc.
2801 E Beltline Ave Ne
Grand Rapids MI 49525
616 364-6161

(G-9329)
XYZ MCHINE TL FABRICATIONS INC
2127 W Willow St (48917-1862)
PHONE.................517 482-3668
John Wieber, *President*
EMP: 8
SQ FT: 6,000
SALES (est): 1.4MM **Privately Held**
SIC: 3842 Surgical appliances & supplies

Lansing
Ingham County

(G-9330)
2 BROTHERS HOLDINGS LLC
Also Called: Tommark Lansing
1115 S Penn Ave Ste B (48912-1658)
PHONE.................517 487-3900
Michael Olds, *Manager*
EMP: 6
SALES (corp-wide): 10.9MM **Privately Held**
WEB: www.tommark.com
SIC: 3829 3494 5075 Measuring & controlling devices; valves & pipe fittings; warm air heating & air conditioning
PA: 2 Brothers Holdings, Llc
7653 Blue Gentian Ct
Dexter MI 48130
517 782-0557

(G-9331)
917 CHITTOCK STREET LLC
Also Called: A Dependable Property MGT
114 Bank St (48910-9159)
PHONE.................866 945-0269
Neil Wright, *Mng Member*
Janell S Wright,
EMP: 10
SQ FT: 2,200
SALES: 500K **Privately Held**
SIC: 8741 6531 1389 Business management; real estate agents & managers; construction, repair & dismantling services

(G-9332)
ACUMEDIA MANUFACTURERS INC
620 Lesher Pl (48912-1509)
PHONE.................517 372-9200
Deb Cook, *Admin Sec*
EMP: 30
SQ FT: 40,000
SALES (est): 207.8K
SALES (corp-wide): 414.1MM **Publicly Held**
SIC: 2656 Sanitary food containers
PA: Neogen Corporation
620 Lesher Pl
Lansing MI 48912
517 372-9200

(G-9333)
ADVANCED C & T MANUFACTURERS
Also Called: Aadvanced Truck Caps Mfrs
3315 S Cedar St (48910-3435)
PHONE.................517 882-2444
Bill Loveall, *CEO*
EMP: 4
SALES (est): 180K **Privately Held**
SIC: 3713 Truck bodies & parts

(G-9334)
ALDINGER INC
1669 E Jolly Rd (48910-7142)
PHONE.................517 394-2424
Alan Godfrey, *CEO*
Alan D Godfrey, *CEO*
Douglas Bushard, *President*
Shelby Waters, *Vice Pres*
Jim Lohman, *Sales Staff*
EMP: 30
SQ FT: 23,000
SALES (est): 4.3MM **Privately Held**
WEB: www.aldingerinc.com
SIC: 7331 2791 2759 2752 Mailing service; typesetting; commercial printing; commercial printing, lithographic

(G-9335)
ALRO STEEL CORPORATION
1800 W Willow St (48915-1430)
PHONE.................517 371-9600
Dave Forquer, *Manager*
EMP: 40
SALES (corp-wide): 2.2B **Privately Held**
WEB: www.alro.com
SIC: 5051 3316 Steel; cold finishing of steel shapes
PA: Alro Steel Corporation
3100 E High St
Jackson MI 49203
517 787-5500

(G-9336)
AMBASSADOR STEEL CORPORATION
Also Called: Harris Rebar
1501 E Jolly Rd (48910-7133)
PHONE.................517 455-7216
William Wear, *Principal*
Kevin Nunn, *Project Mgr*
Jeff Weingarten, *Sales/Mktg Mgr*
Melissa Vannortrick, *Administration*
EMP: 23
SALES (corp-wide): 25B **Publicly Held**
WEB: www.ambassadorsteel.com
SIC: 3449 3496 3443 3441 Miscellaneous metalwork; miscellaneous fabricated wire products; fabricated plate work (boiler shop); fabricated structural metal
HQ: Ambassador Steel Corporation
1340 S Grandstaff Dr
Auburn IN 46706
260 925-5440

(G-9337)
APPAREL PRINTERS LIMITED
Also Called: Apparel Printers, The
3505 S Cedar St Ste A (48912-4607)
PHONE.................517 882-5700
Sheila M Boucher, *President*
Bob Benge, *Vice Pres*
EMP: 3
SQ FT: 1,500
SALES: 200K **Privately Held**
WEB: www.apparelprinters.com
SIC: 2759 Screen printing

(G-9338)
APPLAUSE INC
Also Called: On-The-Spot-engraving
2519 S Cedar St (48910-3137)
PHONE.................517 485-9880
John Williams, *President*
Betty Williams, *Vice Pres*
Bethany Bigelow, *Opers Mgr*
EMP: 4
SQ FT: 2,600
SALES (est): 445.3K **Privately Held**
WEB: www.applauseinc.com
SIC: 7389 2396 Engraving service; automotive & apparel trimmings

(G-9339)
APPLICTION SPCLIST KOMPANY INC
Also Called: Application Specialists Co
316 Moores River Dr (48910-1434)
PHONE.................517 676-6633
Dave Paul, *CEO*
Michael Maddocx, *President*
Michael Brown, *Vice Pres*
Thomas Wendling, *Project Engr*
Erik Jacobsen, *Sales Staff*
EMP: 12
SALES (est): 3.7MM **Privately Held**
WEB: www.justask.net
SIC: 7371 3577 Computer software writing services; printers & plotters

(G-9340)
ARCTIC GLACIER TEXAS INC
5635 Commerce St Ste B (48911-5347)
PHONE.................517 999-3500
Jim Forsburg, *Regional Mgr*
EMP: 7
SALES (corp-wide): 2.4B **Publicly Held**
SIC: 2097 Block ice
HQ: Arctic Glacier Texas Inc.
130 E 42nd St
Lubbock TX

(G-9341)
ASAP PRINTING INC
1110 Keystone Ave (48911-4032)
PHONE.................517 882-3500
Edward Guile, *Branch Mgr*
EMP: 7
SALES (est): 789.2K **Privately Held**
SIC: 2752 Commercial printing, offset
PA: Asap Printing, Inc.
2323 Jolly Rd
Okemos MI 48864

(G-9342)
ATMOSPHERE ANNEALING LLC (HQ)
209 W Mount Hope Ave # 2 (48910-9084)
PHONE.................517 485-5090
Steve Wyatt, *Mng Member*
EMP: 75 **EST:** 2010
SQ FT: 13,400
SALES: 40MM
SALES (corp-wide): 81.9MM **Privately Held**
SIC: 3398 Annealing of metal
PA: Premier Thermal Solutions, Llc
209 W Mount Hope Ave # 2
Lansing MI 48910
517 485-5090

(G-9343)
ATMOSPHERE ANNEALING LLC
1801 Bassett St (48915-1597)
PHONE.................517 482-1374
Lew Fortune, *Manager*
EMP: 40
SALES (corp-wide): 81.9MM **Privately Held**
SIC: 3398 Annealing of metal
HQ: Atmosphere Annealing, Llc
209 W Mount Hope Ave # 2
Lansing MI 48910
517 485-5090

(G-9344)
AURORA SPCLTY CHEMISTRIES CORP
1520 Lake Lansing Rd (48912-3707)
P.O. Box 227, Lowell (49331-0227)
PHONE.................517 372-9121
Harry J Moyle, *President*
Timothy Pinter, *Vice Pres*
Bradley Moyle, *Technical Staff*
▲ **EMP:** 30
SQ FT: 15,000
SALES (est): 11.7MM **Privately Held**
WEB: www.auroraspchm.com
SIC: 2899 8731 Water treating compounds; commercial physical research

(G-9345)
BAKE N CAKES LP
3003 E Kalamazoo St (48912-4614)
PHONE.................517 337-2253
Jeffrey Johnson, *Partner*
Deborah Johnson, *General Ptnr*
Wilford Johnson, *Ltd Ptnr*
EMP: 6
SQ FT: 2,020
SALES (est): 583.7K **Privately Held**
WEB: www.bakencakes.com
SIC: 2048 5461 Dry pet food (except dog & cat); bakeries

Lansing - Ingham County (G-9346) — GEOGRAPHIC SECTION

(G-9346)
BARNES GROUP INC
Barnes Aerospace Lansing Div
5300 Aurelius Rd (48911-4116)
P.O. Box 30112, College Station TX (77842-3112)
PHONE.................517 393-5110
Patti Gibson, *Production*
Dylan Caddy, *Engineer*
Rob Stanley, *Engineer*
Stuart Kale, *Branch Mgr*
Sevie Jean, *Manager*
EMP: 1434
SALES (corp-wide): 1.5B **Publicly Held**
WEB: www.barnesgroupinc.com
SIC: 3724 Aircraft engines & engine parts
PA: Barnes Group Inc.
  123 Main St
  Bristol CT 06010
  860 583-7070

(G-9347)
BARONS INC
Also Called: Baron's Window Coverings
325 S Washington Sq (48933-2114)
PHONE.................517 484-1366
Donald Baron, *President*
Donald E Baron, *President*
Neil Baron, *Vice Pres*
EMP: 20
SQ FT: 10,800
SALES (est): 1.9MM **Privately Held**
WEB: www.baronsblinds.com
SIC: 2391 5714 Curtains, window: made from purchased materials; curtains

(G-9348)
BOOTH NEWSPAPER
108 S Washington Sq Ste 1 (48933-1726)
PHONE.................517 487-8888
Meegan Holland, *Manager*
EMP: 3
SALES (est): 174.9K **Privately Held**
SIC: 2711 Newspapers

(G-9349)
BRADFORD PRINTING INC
1020 E Jolly Rd (48910-7123)
PHONE.................517 887-0044
Barry L Bradford, *President*
Pamela A Bradford, *Treasurer*
EMP: 7
SQ FT: 4,000
SALES (est): 1.8MM **Privately Held**
SIC: 2759 Screen printing

(G-9350)
BRD PRINTING INC
912 W Saint Joseph St (48915-1687)
PHONE.................517 372-0268
Donald W Hough, *President*
Julie Brown, *Production*
David Campbell, *Accounts Mgr*
Lonnie Campbell, *Manager*
Mark Wells, *Manager*
EMP: 37 EST: 1977
SQ FT: 22,000
SALES (est): 7.5MM **Privately Held**
WEB: www.brdprinting.com
SIC: 2752 2789 Commercial printing, offset; bookbinding & related work

(G-9351)
BRETTS PRINTING SERVICE
2435 S Rundle Ave 39 (48910-2746)
PHONE.................517 482-2256
Pauline Brethauder, *Owner*
EMP: 5
SQ FT: 2,500
SALES (est): 80K **Privately Held**
SIC: 2752 Commercial printing, offset

(G-9352)
BRUCE INC
Also Called: Insty-Prints
209 S Washington Sq (48933-1807)
PHONE.................517 371-5205
Michael S Bruce, *President*
Annette Bruce, *Treasurer*
EMP: 5
SQ FT: 4,000
SALES (est): 895K **Privately Held**
SIC: 2752 2791 2789 7331 Commercial printing, lithographic; typesetting; bookbinding & related work; mailing service; poster advertising, outdoor

(G-9353)
CAMERON TOOL CORPORATION
1800 Bassett St (48915-1598)
PHONE.................517 487-3671
Tracy Selden, *President*
Kathy Bracey, *Exec VP*
Travis Adrion, *Project Mgr*
Carey Oberlin, *Human Res Mgr*
Keith Krupsky, *Info Tech Mgr*
▲ EMP: 60
SQ FT: 72,000
SALES (est): 18.6MM **Privately Held**
WEB: www.camerontool.com
SIC: 3544 3469 Special dies & tools; jigs & fixtures; metal stampings

(G-9354)
CAMPBELL INC PRESS REPAIR
925 River St (48912-1027)
PHONE.................517 371-1034
Peter Campbell, *President*
▲ EMP: 20
SQ FT: 35,000
SALES (est): 3.5MM **Privately Held**
WEB: www.campbellpress.com
SIC: 7692 5084 Welding repair; industrial machinery & equipment

(G-9355)
CAPITAL IMAGING INC
2521 E Michigan Ave (48912-4010)
PHONE.................517 482-2292
Granville Noles, *Principal*
Nia Noles, *Principal*
EMP: 15
SQ FT: 7,000
SALES (est): 2.7MM **Privately Held**
WEB: www.capital-imaging.com
SIC: 2752 2754 7334 Commercial printing, offset; commercial printing, gravure; blueprinting service

(G-9356)
CENTRAL MICH KNWRTH LNSING LLC
2556 Alamo Dr (48911-6351)
PHONE.................517 394-7000
Jesse CP Berger, *President*
EMP: 4
SALES (est): 329.3K **Privately Held**
SIC: 3713 4492 Truck bodies & parts; towing & tugboat service

(G-9357)
COMMERCIAL BLUEPRINT INC
3125 Pinetree Rd Ste 3b (48911-4231)
PHONE.................517 372-8360
Douglas Schmidt, *President*
Pete Dumond, *Vice Pres*
Stephanie Schmidt, *Treasurer*
Maureen Devota, *Incorporator*
Heidi Dumond, *Admin Sec*
EMP: 25
SQ FT: 14,000
SALES (est): 5.9MM **Privately Held**
WEB: www.commblue.com
SIC: 5049 7334 2759 Drafting supplies; blueprinting service; commercial printing

(G-9358)
CUSHION LRRY TRPHIES ENGRV LLC
300 N Clippert St Ste 14 (48912-4637)
PHONE.................517 332-1667
Leann Cushion-Groves,
EMP: 4
SALES (est): 280K **Privately Held**
SIC: 5999 3479 Trophies & plaques; name plates: engraved, etched, etc.

(G-9359)
DATAMATIC PROCESSING INC (PA)
5545 Enterprise Dr (48911-4131)
PHONE.................517 882-4401
Wesley Benzing, *President*
Alan Ross, *Vice Pres*
Weston Benzing, *CFO*
Marsha Benzing, *Admin Sec*
EMP: 25 EST: 1974
SQ FT: 20,000
SALES (est): 3.8MM **Privately Held**
WEB: www.datamatic.net
SIC: 7372 5045 7374 Business oriented computer software; computers, peripherals & software; data processing service

(G-9360)
DILLION RENEE ENTITIES
600 Baker St (48910-1708)
PHONE.................989 443-0654
Eddie Wells,
EMP: 5
SALES (est): 341.9K **Privately Held**
SIC: 6794 2741 Performance rights, publishing & licensing; miscellaneous publishing

(G-9361)
DIOCESE OF LANSING
Also Called: Liturgical Commission
1500 W Saginaw St Ste 2 (48915-1380)
PHONE.................517 484-4449
Mary Jo Gilliland, *Manager*
EMP: 11
SALES (corp-wide): 52.7MM **Privately Held**
WEB: www.stgerard.org
SIC: 8661 5942 2721 2731 Catholic Church; books, religious; periodicals: publishing & printing; books: publishing & printing; miscellaneous publishing
PA: Diocese Of Lansing
  228 N Walnut St
  Lansing MI 48933
  517 342-2440

(G-9362)
DOUGLAS E FULK
Also Called: Douglas Sign Company
1800 S Cedar St (48910-9102)
PHONE.................517 482-2090
Douglas E Fulk, *Owner*
EMP: 3 EST: 1968
SQ FT: 3,000
SALES (est): 392.2K **Privately Held**
SIC: 7312 3993 Billboard advertising; signs & advertising specialties

(G-9363)
EDWARDS INDUSTRIAL SALES INC
5646 Commerce St Ste D (48911-5335)
PHONE.................517 887-6100
David Salisbury, *Branch Mgr*
EMP: 4
SALES (corp-wide): 14.4MM **Privately Held**
SIC: 3621 5085 5063 Electric motor & generator parts; bearings; motors, electric
PA: Edwards Industrial Sales, Inc.
  424 Mills St
  Kalamazoo MI 49001
  269 349-7737

(G-9364)
ELMET NORTH AMERICA INC
4103 Grand Oak Dr B102 (48911-7404)
P.O. Box 459, Dimondale (48821-0459)
PHONE.................517 664-9011
Helmut Gaderer, *Principal*
EMP: 10 EST: 2012
SALES (est): 979.3K **Privately Held**
SIC: 3089 Injection molded finished plastic products

(G-9365)
ELSIE PUBLISHING INSTITUTE (PA)
500 W Ionia St (48933-1013)
P.O. Box 811, East Lansing (48826-0811)
PHONE.................517 371-5257
Penny Gardner, *President*
Denise Gruben, *Vice Pres*
Katie Watkins, *Manager*
EMP: 18
SALES (est): 518K **Privately Held**
SIC: 2721 7389 Magazines: publishing only, not printed on site;

(G-9366)
ENPROTECH INDUSTRIAL TECH LLC
2200 Olds Ave (48915-1054)
PHONE.................517 319-5306
Eric Pratt, *Managing Dir*
John Burgett, *Project Engr*
Scott Race, *Controller*
Nancy E Wilson, *Manager*
EMP: 23 **Privately Held**
SIC: 3542 Machine tools, metal forming type
HQ: Enprotech Industrial Technologies, Llc
  4259 E 49th St
  Cleveland OH 44125
  216 883-3220

(G-9367)
ETCHED GLASS WORKS & A BLDG CO
300 Hill St (48912-1333)
PHONE.................517 819-4343
Mark Kruger, *Owner*
EMP: 3
SALES (est): 255.7K **Privately Held**
SIC: 3231 Decorated glassware: chipped, engraved, etched, etc.

(G-9368)
FLORHEAT COMPANY
3130 Sovereign Dr (48911-4241)
PHONE.................517 272-4441
Charlie Karupa, *President*
Gary Smith, *Sales Mgr*
EMP: 7
SALES (est): 660K **Privately Held**
SIC: 3567 Radiant heating systems, industrial process

(G-9369)
FLUID CHILLERS INC
Also Called: Coolant Chillers
2730 Alpha Access St (48910-3686)
PHONE.................517 484-9190
Timothy Ayres, *President*
Tom Ayres, *Mfg Mgr*
Amy Vanburen, *Human Resources*
Brittany Kushion, *Assistant*
▲ EMP: 46
SALES (est): 13.4MM **Privately Held**
SIC: 3585 Parts for heating, cooling & refrigerating equipment

(G-9370)
GADGET FACTORY LLC
5157 Aurelius Rd (48911-4115)
PHONE.................517 449-1444
Mike Mosholder,
EMP: 6
SALES (est): 502.9K **Privately Held**
SIC: 3648 Lighting equipment

(G-9371)
GANNETT CO INC
Also Called: Lansing State Journal
300 S Wash Sq Ste 300 # 300 (48933-2102)
PHONE.................517 377-1000
Richard A Ramhoff, *President*
EMP: 77
SALES (corp-wide): 2.9B **Publicly Held**
WEB: www.gannett.com
SIC: 2711 2752 Newspapers; commercial printing, lithographic
PA: Gannett Co., Inc.
  7950 Jones Branch Dr
  Mc Lean VA 22102
  703 854-6000

(G-9372)
GENERAL MOTORS LLC
920 Townsend St (48933-2344)
PHONE.................517 242-2158
Mark Coucke, *Engineer*
Una Tan, *Mktg Dir*
Charles Geller, *Branch Mgr*
Nathan Malkus, *Analyst*
Mark Binge, *Maintence Staff*
EMP: 3 **Publicly Held**
SIC: 3441 Fabricated structural metal
HQ: General Motors Llc
  300 Renaissance Ctr L1
  Detroit MI 48243

(G-9373)
GERDAU MACSTEEL ATMOSPHERE ANN (DH)
209 W Mount Hope Ave # 1 (48910-9084)
PHONE.................517 782-0415
James McWilliams, *CFO*
Roger Webster, *Manager*
▲ EMP: 16 EST: 1978

GEOGRAPHIC SECTION
Lansing - Ingham County (G-9401)

SQ FT: 100,000
SALES (est): 14.2MM Privately Held
WEB: www.aaimac.com
SIC: 3398 Annealing of metal
HQ: Gerdau Ameristeel Us Inc.
  4221 W Boy Scout Blvd # 600
  Tampa FL 33607
  813 286-8383

(G-9374)
GERDAU MACSTEEL ATMOSPHERE ANN
1801 Bassett St (48915-1567)
PHONE.................517 482-1374
Jay Murthy, *Branch Mgr*
EMP: 40 Privately Held
WEB: www.aaimac.com
SIC: 3398 Metal heat treating
HQ: Gerdau Macsteel Atmosphere Annealing
  209 W Mount Hope Ave # 1
  Lansing MI 48910
  517 782-0415

(G-9375)
GONGWER NEWS SERVICE INC
101 S Wash Sq Ste 540 (48933-1733)
PHONE.................517 482-3500
Larry Lee, *Vice Pres*
EMP: 5
SQ FT: 800
SALES (corp-wide): 1.6MM Privately Held
WEB: www.gongwer.com
SIC: 2721 Magazines: publishing only, not printed on site
PA: Gongwer News Service Inc
  17 S High St Ste 630
  Columbus OH 43215
  614 221-1992

(G-9376)
GREATER LANSING BUS MONTHLY
221 W Saginaw St (48933-1254)
PHONE.................517 203-0123
J Chris Holman, *President*
EMP: 5
SALES (est): 496.4K Privately Held
WEB: www.ameriental.com
SIC: 2721 Magazines: publishing & printing

(G-9377)
GREATER LANSING ORTHOTIC CLINI
200 N Homer St Ste A (48912-4741)
PHONE.................517 337-0856
Joseph Springer, *President*
EMP: 6
SQ FT: 6,000
SALES (est): 617.7K Privately Held
WEB: www.springerprosthetics.com
SIC: 3842 5999 Braces, orthopedic; orthopedic & prosthesis applications

(G-9378)
GREENMARK BIOMEDICAL INC
3815 Tech Blvd Ste 1055 (48910)
PHONE.................517 336-4665
Steven Bloembergen, *Principal*
Joerg Lahann, *Director*
Kenneth Pienta, *Director*
Frank Van Luttikhuizen, *Director*
EMP: 5
SALES (est): 305.8K Privately Held
SIC: 2834 2835 Pharmaceutical preparations; in vitro & in vivo diagnostic substances

(G-9379)
GROWGENERATION MICHIGAN CORP (HQ)
Also Called: Superior Growers Supply
5711 Enterprise Dr (48911-4106)
PHONE.................248 473-0450
Michael Salaman, *President*
EMP: 2
SQ FT: 16,000
SALES: 4MM
SALES (corp-wide): 29MM Publicly Held
WEB: www.sgs-hydroponic.com
SIC: 5261 3423 Garden supplies & tools; garden & farm tools, including shovels

PA: Growgeneration Corp.
  1000 W Mississippi Ave
  Denver CO 80223
  800 935-8420

(G-9380)
HACKS KEY SHOP INC
1109 River St (48912-1031)
PHONE.................517 485-9488
Diana Engman, *President*
EMP: 11
SALES: 500K Privately Held
WEB: www.hackskeyshop.com
SIC: 3442 7699 7382 Metal doors; lock & key services; security systems services

(G-9381)
HANGER PRSTHETCS & ORTHO INC
Also Called: Institute Adv of Prosthetics
4424 S Pennsylvania Ave (48910-7625)
PHONE.................517 394-5850
Jerry Vilmanot, *VP Mktg*
Jerry Vilminot, *Director*
EMP: 10
SALES (corp-wide): 1B Publicly Held
SIC: 3842 5999 Prosthetic appliances; orthopedic & prosthesis applications
HQ: Hanger Prosthetics & Orthotics, Inc.
  10910 Domain Dr Ste 300
  Austin TX 78758
  512 777-3800

(G-9382)
HOTWATER WORKS INC (PA)
Also Called: Hot Tubs
2116 E Michigan Ave (48912-3026)
PHONE.................517 364-8827
James McFarland, *President*
▲ EMP: 4
SQ FT: 10,000
SALES (est): 1MM Privately Held
WEB: www.hotwaterworks.com
SIC: 5999 3431 Swimming pools, above ground; bathtubs: enameled iron, cast iron or pressed metal

(G-9383)
HYDRODYNAMICS INTERNATIONAL
5711 Enterprise Dr (48911-4106)
PHONE.................517 887-2007
Jeffrey A Gibson, *President*
▲ EMP: 6 EST: 1998
SALES (est): 1.4MM Privately Held
WEB: www.superiorgrowers.com
SIC: 2875 Fertilizers, mixing only

(G-9384)
IHICORE LLC
1305 S Cedar St (48910-1520)
PHONE.................800 960-0448
Agujiofomgala Maduka,
EMP: 3
SALES (est): 121.7K Privately Held
SIC: 3199 Leather goods

(G-9385)
INFOGUYS INC
Also Called: Mirs News
910 W Ottawa St (48915-1742)
PHONE.................517 482-2125
John T Reurink, *President*
Michelle Reurink, *Treasurer*
Mary Lou Reurink, *Admin Sec*
EMP: 6
SQ FT: 15,000
SALES: 480K Privately Held
WEB: www.mirsnews.com
SIC: 2711 2721 Newspapers; periodicals

(G-9386)
LAKE LANSING ASC PARTNERS LLC
1707 Lake Lansing Rd (48912-3742)
PHONE.................517 708-3333
Tom Mathews, *CEO*
Dan Hunt,
EMP: 15
SALES (est): 1.5MM
SALES (corp-wide): 18.3B Publicly Held
WEB: www.lansingsurgery.com
SIC: 3841 Surgical & medical instruments

PA: Tenet Healthcare Corporation
  1445 Ross Ave Ste 1400
  Dallas TX 75202
  469 893-2200

(G-9387)
LANGENBERG MACHINE PRODUCTS
1234 S Holmes St (48912-1928)
PHONE.................517 485-9450
Sigurd C Langenberg, *President*
EMP: 5
SQ FT: 3,000
SALES: 400K Privately Held
SIC: 3599 Machine shop, jobbing & repair

(G-9388)
LANSING FORGE INC (HQ)
5232 Aurelius Rd (48911-4114)
PHONE.................517 882-2056
Dennis M Mosholder, *President*
Matt Partin, *General Mgr*
EMP: 11 EST: 1957
SQ FT: 16,000
SALES (est): 1.7MM Privately Held
SIC: 3462 Iron & steel forgings
PA: Lansing Holding Company Inc
  5232 Aurelius Rd
  Lansing MI 48911
  517 882-2056

(G-9389)
LANSING FUEL VENTURES INC
601 W Saginaw St (48933-8023)
PHONE.................517 371-1198
EMP: 5
SALES (est): 310.9K Privately Held
SIC: 2869 Fuels

(G-9390)
LANSING HOLDING COMPANY INC (PA)
5232 Aurelius Rd (48911-4114)
PHONE.................517 882-2056
Dennis M Mosholder, *President*
Mike Mosholder, *Vice Pres*
EMP: 2
SQ FT: 16,000
SALES (est): 1.7MM Privately Held
SIC: 3462 Iron & steel forgings

(G-9391)
LECTRONIX INC (PA)
5858 Enterprise Dr (48911-4107)
PHONE.................517 492-1900
Allan Dale, *President*
Tom Bayerl, *Senior VP*
Frederick Roth, *Senior VP*
Rick Roth, *Senior VP*
Frank Pellitta, *Vice Pres*
EMP: 53
SQ FT: 80,000
SALES (est): 10.4MM Privately Held
WEB: www.lectronix.biz
SIC: 8711 3679 Electrical or electronic engineering; electronic circuits

(G-9392)
LIGHTNING LITHO INC
Also Called: Allegra Print Imaging-Lansing
5731 Enterprise Dr (48911-4106)
PHONE.................517 394-2995
Brad Naghtin, *President*
Shirley Naghtin, *Vice Pres*
EMP: 10 EST: 1973
SQ FT: 4,000
SALES (est): 1.9MM Privately Held
SIC: 2752 7334 Commercial printing, offset; photocopying & duplicating services

(G-9393)
LYONDELLBASELL INDUSTRIES INC
Also Called: Equistar Chemicals, LP
3610 Forest Rd Ste A (48910-3716)
PHONE.................517 336-4800
EMP: 14
SALES (corp-wide): 39.1B Privately Held
SIC: 2821 Polymethyl methacrylate resins (plexiglass)
HQ: Lyondellbasell Industries, Inc.
  1221 Mckinney St Ste 300
  Houston TX 77010

(G-9394)
MAGNA POWERTRAIN AMERICA INC
3140 Spanish Oak Dr (48911-4291)
PHONE.................517 316-1013
Jennifer Cantarella, *Manager*
David Anderson, *Prgrmr*
EMP: 4
SALES (corp-wide): 40.8B Privately Held
SIC: 3714 Motor vehicle parts & accessories
HQ: Magna Powertrain Of America, Inc.
  1870 Technology Dr
  Troy MI 48083

(G-9395)
MBCD INC
1520 E Malcolm X St (48912-2425)
PHONE.................517 484-4426
Dale Martin, *President*
EMP: 20 EST: 1940
SQ FT: 9,000
SALES (est): 2.4MM Privately Held
SIC: 3271 3296 3272 1442 Brick, concrete; mineral wool; concrete products; construction sand & gravel

(G-9396)
MERRITT PRESS INC
6534 Aurelius Rd (48911-7103)
P.O. Box 27578 (48909-0578)
PHONE.................517 394-0118
Scott Merritt, *President*
EMP: 12
SQ FT: 7,300
SALES (est): 2.1MM Privately Held
SIC: 2752 Commercial printing, offset

(G-9397)
MICHIGAN BANKER MAGAZINE
1430 E Michigan Ave (48912-2112)
P.O. Box 12236 (48901-2236)
PHONE.................517 484-0775
Miles Pilgrim, *President*
EMP: 3
SQ FT: 2,000
SALES: 383K Privately Held
SIC: 2721 8743 Periodicals: publishing & printing; public relations services

(G-9398)
MICHIGAN FORGE COMPANY LLC
2807 S Martin L Kng Jr Bl (48910-2653)
PHONE.................815 758-6400
Don Jones, *President*
EMP: 50
SALES (est): 3.8MM Privately Held
SIC: 3462 Iron & steel forgings

(G-9399)
MICHIGAN OIL AND GAS ASSN
124 W Allegan St Ste 1610 (48933-1750)
PHONE.................517 487-0480
Frank L Mortl, *President*
Daniel Wyohe, *Chairman*
Jennifer Clark, *Opers Staff*
Jim Stark, *Director*
EMP: 6 EST: 1934
SQ FT: 1,400
SALES: 786.4K Privately Held
WEB: www.michiganoilandgasassociation.org
SIC: 8611 2721 Trade associations; magazines: publishing only, not printed on site

(G-9400)
MICHIGRAIN DISTILLERY
523 E Shiawassee St (48912-1213)
PHONE.................517 580-8624
EMP: 3
SALES (est): 162K Privately Held
SIC: 2085 Distilled & blended liquors

(G-9401)
MIKE DEGROW
327 Seymour Ave (48933-1114)
PHONE.................734 353-4752
EMP: 3
SALES (est): 191.7K Privately Held
SIC: 3643 Mfg Conductive Wiring Devices

Lansing - Ingham County (G-9402) GEOGRAPHIC SECTION

(G-9402)
MOONLIGHT TIFFANIES LLC
1216 N Foster Ave (48912-3309)
PHONE..................517 372-2795
Robert F Hollis, *Owner*
EMP: 7
SALES (est): 380K **Privately Held**
SIC: 5023 2499 Lamps: floor, boudoir, desk; novelties, wood fiber

(G-9403)
MPT LANSING LLC
Also Called: Magna Powertrain Lansing
3140 Spanish Oak Dr Ste A (48911-4291)
PHONE..................517 316-1013
Heather Bickford, *Materials Mgr*
Rick Rinard,
◆ EMP: 140
SALES (est): 150.1MM
SALES (corp-wide): 40.8B **Privately Held**
SIC: 3714 Motor vehicle engines & parts
HQ: Magna Powertrain Usa, Inc.
1870 Technology Dr
Troy MI 48083
248 680-4900

(G-9404)
NANORETE INC
3815 Tech Blvd Ste 1050 (48910)
PHONE..................517 336-4680
Linda Chamberlain, *CEO*
EMP: 9
SALES (est): 975.6K **Privately Held**
SIC: 3825 2835 Instruments to measure electricity; in vitro diagnostics

(G-9405)
NEOGEN CORPORATION (PA)
620 Lesher Pl (48912-1509)
PHONE..................517 372-9200
James L Herbert, *Ch of Bd*
John E Adent, *President*
David Seidl, *General Mgr*
Joseph A Corbett, *Vice Pres*
Robert S Donofrio, *Vice Pres*
▲ EMP: 277
SQ FT: 300,000
SALES: 414.1MM **Publicly Held**
SIC: 3841 2836 2835 Veterinarians' instruments & apparatus; veterinary biological products; veterinary diagnostic substances

(G-9406)
NEWARK MORNING LEDGER CO
217 N Sycamore St (48933-1033)
PHONE..................517 487-8888
Meegan Holland, *Branch Mgr*
Medra Burdette, *Manager*
EMP: 20
SALES (corp-wide): 217.5MM **Privately Held**
SIC: 7383 7313 2711 News reporting services for newspapers & periodicals; newspaper advertising representative; newspapers
PA: Newark Morning Ledger Co.
1 Gateway Ctr Ste 1100
Newark NJ 07102
973 392-4141

(G-9407)
OMC ARCHTRIM
810 E Mount Hope Ave (48910-3260)
PHONE..................517 482-9411
Jack Olsen, *Principal*
EMP: 45
SALES (est): 3.5MM **Privately Held**
SIC: 3398 Metal heat treating

(G-9408)
OMNILINK COMMUNICATIONS CORP
3101 Technology Blvd (48910-8546)
PHONE..................517 336-1800
Franklin Tarquini, *President*
Henry H Graham, *CFO*
Robert Lindmann, *Officer*
EMP: 40
SQ FT: 13,000
SALES: 863K **Privately Held**
SIC: 3661 Telephone & telegraph apparatus

(G-9409)
PEANUT SHOP INC
117 S Washington Sq Ste 1 (48933-1789)
PHONE..................517 374-0008
Tamara Melser, *President*
Glenda Osterhouse, *Treasurer*
EMP: 5
SQ FT: 1,000
SALES: 348K **Privately Held**
WEB: www.thepeanutshop.com
SIC: 3556 Roasting machinery: coffee, peanut, etc.; confectionery machinery

(G-9410)
PEPSI-COLA METRO BTLG CO INC
3101 Grand Oak Dr (48911-4224)
PHONE..................517 272-2800
Matt Hilton, *Branch Mgr*
Cheryl Hinkle, *Manager*
EMP: 90
SALES (corp-wide): 64.6B **Publicly Held**
WEB: www.joy-of-cola.com
SIC: 2096 7623 7629 Potato chips & other potato-based snacks; refrigeration service & repair; electrical repair shops
HQ: Pepsi-Cola Metropolitan Bottling Company, Inc.
1111 Westchester Ave
White Plains NY 10604
914 767-6000

(G-9411)
PHILLIPS BROS SCREW PDTS CO
2909 S Martin Luther King (48910-2655)
PHONE..................517 882-0279
Donald Phillips, *Owner*
EMP: 5 EST: 1944
SQ FT: 7,000
SALES (est): 125K **Privately Held**
SIC: 3451 Screw machine products

(G-9412)
PPG INDUSTRIES INC
5633 Lamone Dr Ste B (48911-4047)
PHONE..................517 394-9093
Jay Hamilton, *Manager*
EMP: 22
SALES (corp-wide): 15.3B **Publicly Held**
SIC: 2851 Paints & paint additives
PA: Ppg Industries, Inc.
1 Ppg Pl
Pittsburgh PA 15272
412 434-3131

(G-9413)
PRATT & WHITNEY AUTOAIR INC
Also Called: Auto-Air Composites
5640 Enterprise Dr (48911-4103)
PHONE..................517 393-4040
Toll Free:..................888 -
Bennett Croswell, *President*
John McDonald, *Materials Mgr*
William Puetz, *Buyer*
Wright Lauren, *Purchasing*
Heather Barber, *Engineer*
▲ EMP: 258 EST: 1956
SQ FT: 225,000
SALES (est): 66.3MM
SALES (corp-wide): 66.5B **Publicly Held**
WEB: www.utc.com
SIC: 3724 3544 Aircraft engines & engine parts; special dies, tools, jigs & fixtures
PA: United Technologies Corporation
10 Farm Springs Rd
Farmington CT 06032
860 728-7000

(G-9414)
PRECISION POWER INC
630 Park Pl (48912-1164)
PHONE..................517 371-4274
Rexford G Curtiss, *President*
EMP: 3
SQ FT: 9,000
SALES (est): 414.8K **Privately Held**
WEB: www.precision-pwr.com
SIC: 3694 3621 Automotive electrical equipment; alternators, automotive; starters, for motors

(G-9415)
QUALITY AWNING SHOPS INC
4512 S Martin Luther King (48910-5297)
PHONE..................517 882-2491
Don Brand, *President*
Judith A Brand, *Corp Secy*
EMP: 6 EST: 1911
SQ FT: 12,800
SALES (est): 424.5K **Privately Held**
SIC: 2394 7641 Awnings, fabric: made from purchased materials; cloth, drop (fabric): made from purchased materials; reupholstery

(G-9416)
QUALITY DAIRY COMPANY
Also Called: Qdc Plastics
111 W Mount Hope Ave 3a (48910-9080)
PHONE..................517 319-4302
Stan Martin, *Owner*
EMP: 80
SALES (corp-wide): 106.8MM **Privately Held**
WEB: www.qdcplastics.com
SIC: 2821 Plastics materials & resins
PA: Quality Dairy Company
111 W Mount Hope Ave 3a
Lansing MI 48910
517 319-4100

(G-9417)
QUALITY DAIRY COMPANY
1400 S Washington Ave (48910-1655)
PHONE..................517 367-2400
Kenneth Martin, *Manager*
Tony Gauna, *Manager*
EMP: 30
SQ FT: 2,000
SALES (corp-wide): 106.8MM **Privately Held**
WEB: www.qdcplastics.com
SIC: 2026 2024 Milk processing (pasteurizing, homogenizing, bottling); ice cream & frozen desserts
PA: Quality Dairy Company
111 W Mount Hope Ave 3a
Lansing MI 48910
517 319-4100

(G-9418)
RIVERFRONT CYCLE INC
507 E Shiawassee St (48912-1213)
PHONE..................517 482-8585
David Hanson, *President*
EMP: 5
SQ FT: 3,500
SALES: 600K **Privately Held**
WEB: www.riverfrontcycle.com
SIC: 5941 7699 3949 7999 Bicycle & bicycle parts; exercise equipment; recreational sporting equipment repair services; bicycle repair shop; exercise equipment; bicycle rental; motorcycles

(G-9419)
ROMA BAKERY & IMPORTED FOODS
Also Called: Roma Bakery Deli & Fine Foods
1928 Vassar Dr (48912-5118)
PHONE..................517 485-9466
Philomania Castriciano, *Owner*
EMP: 20 EST: 1969
SALES (est): 2.5MM **Privately Held**
SIC: 2052 5461 5921 5411 Cookies & crackers; bread; beer (packaged); grocery stores, independent; bread, cake & related products

(G-9420)
S & S DIE CO
2727 Lyons Ave (48910-3338)
PHONE..................517 272-1100
David H Soltow, *President*
Diana G Hurst, *Vice Pres*
EMP: 24
SQ FT: 7,000
SALES (est): 4.5MM **Privately Held**
WEB: www.ssdie.com
SIC: 3544 Special dies & tools

(G-9421)
SCHINDLER ELEVATOR CORPORATION
3135 Pinetree Rd Ste 2b (48911-4242)
PHONE..................517 272-1234
Pete Long, *Manager*
EMP: 10
SALES (corp-wide): 10.9B **Privately Held**
WEB: www.us.schindler.com
SIC: 1796 5084 3534 Elevator installation & conversion; elevators; dumbwaiters
HQ: Schindler Elevator Corporation
20 Whippany Rd
Morristown NJ 07960
973 397-6500

(G-9422)
SCHNEIDER SHEET METAL SUP INC
6836 Aurelius Rd (48911-7112)
PHONE..................517 694-7661
William Schneider Jr, *President*
Kimberly Schneider, *Vice Pres*
EMP: 6
SQ FT: 19,000
SALES (est): 1MM **Privately Held**
SIC: 3444 Ducts, sheet metal

(G-9423)
SEELYE GROUP LTD
Also Called: Fresh Tracks
912 E Michigan Ave (48912-1418)
PHONE..................517 267-2001
Aaron Pouch, *Division Mgr*
Tim Spaulding, *Vice Pres*
EMP: 5
SALES (corp-wide): 3.2MM **Privately Held**
WEB: www.seelyegroupltd.com
SIC: 1752 2273 7349 Carpet laying; carpets & rugs; cleaning service, industrial or commercial
PA: Seelye Group, Ltd.
1411 Lake Lansing Rd
Lansing MI 48912
517 267-2007

(G-9424)
SLICK SHIRTS SCREEN PRINTING
805 Vine St (48912-1525)
PHONE..................517 371-3600
Brian Kavanagh, *President*
Victor Mendenhal, *Corp Secy*
EMP: 11
SQ FT: 12,000
SALES: 800K **Privately Held**
WEB: www.slickshirts.com
SIC: 2261 2759 2395 Screen printing of cotton broadwoven fabrics; commercial printing; embroidery products, except schiffli machine

(G-9425)
SOULFULL EARTH HERBALS
1131 S Washington Ave (48910-1648)
PHONE..................517 316-0547
EMP: 4
SALES (est): 328.7K **Privately Held**
SIC: 2844 Toilet preparations

(G-9426)
SPRINGER PRSTHTIC ORTHTIC SVCS (PA)
200 N Homer St (48912-4741)
PHONE..................517 337-0300
Joe Springer, *President*
Patricia Springer, *Vice Pres*
EMP: 11
SQ FT: 6,000
SALES (est): 1.7MM **Privately Held**
SIC: 3842 5999 Prosthetic appliances; artificial limbs

(G-9427)
SWAT ENVIRONMENTAL INC (PA)
2607 Eaton Rapids Rd (48911-6310)
PHONE..................517 322-2999
Jamey Gelina, *Principal*
EMP: 50
SALES (est): 10.1MM **Privately Held**
SIC: 7342 8744 5084 3822 Disinfecting & pest control services; ; pollution control equipment, air (environmental); hardware for environmental regulators

GEOGRAPHIC SECTION

Lapeer - Lapeer County (G-9455)

(G-9428)
SWAY MAGAZINE PUBLISHING
3612 W Miller Rd (48911-4446)
PHONE 517 394-4295
EMP: 3 **EST:** 2005
SALES (est): 240K **Privately Held**
SIC: 2721 Periodicals-Publishing/Printing

(G-9429)
SYMMETRY MEDICAL INC
5212 Aurelius Rd (48911-4114)
PHONE 517 887-3424
Misti Brayton, *Human Res Mgr*
Jason Tabor, *Info Tech Mgr*
EMP: 14
SALES (corp-wide): 697.6MM **Privately Held**
SIC: 3841 Surgical & medical instruments
HQ: Symmetry Medical Inc.
3724 N State Road 15
Warsaw IN 46582

(G-9430)
TECHNOLOGY MGT & BUDGT DEPT
Also Called: Office Services Division
7461 Crowner Dr (48913-0001)
P.O. Box 30026 (48909-7526)
PHONE 517 322-1897
Kristi Thompson, *Director*
EMP: 100 **Privately Held**
SIC: 2791 9311 2789 2752 Typesetting; ; bookbinding & related work; commercial printing, lithographic; coated & laminated paper
HQ: Management & Budget Department Of Technology
320 S Walnut St
Lansing MI 48933

(G-9431)
TECOMET INC
5212 Aurelius Rd (48911-4114)
PHONE 517 882-4311
Jennifer Dalling, *Human Res Mgr*
Clint Newman, *Program Mgr*
John Helmoth, *Manager*
EMP: 290
SALES (corp-wide): 697.6MM **Privately Held**
SIC: 3841 Surgical & medical instruments
PA: Tecomet Inc.
115 Eames St
Wilmington MA 01887
978 642-2400

(G-9432)
TENNECO CLEAN AIR US INC (HQ)
18765 Seaway Dr (48911)
PHONE 734 384-7867
EMP: 3
SALES (est): 261.2K
SALES (corp-wide): 11.7B **Publicly Held**
SIC: 3714 Motor vehicle engines & parts
PA: Tenneco Inc.
500 N Field Dr
Lake Forest IL 60045
847 482-5000

(G-9433)
W S TOWNSEND COMPANY
Also Called: Michigan Kitchen Distributors
5320 S Pennsylvania Ave (48911-4006)
PHONE 517 393-7300
Chuck Sayers, *Purchasing*
Melissa Monaghan, *Sales Staff*
Mark Voss, *Manager*
Jerry Doorlag, *Manager*
Mark Dixon, *Consultant*
EMP: 8
SALES (corp-wide): 24.4MM **Privately Held**
WEB: www.thekitchenshops.com
SIC: 2434 5211 1799 1521 Wood kitchen cabinets; millwork & lumber; kitchen & bathroom remodeling; single-family home remodeling, additions & repairs
PA: W. S. Townsend Company
106 E Oliver Dr
Marshall MI 49068
269 781-5131

(G-9434)
WOODWORKS & DESIGN COMPANY
109 E South St (48910-1622)
PHONE 517 482-6665
Thaddeus S Vance, *President*
EMP: 11
SQ FT: 6,000
SALES (est): 1.1MM **Privately Held**
SIC: 1521 1751 2431 General remodeling, single-family houses; carpentry work; millwork

(G-9435)
WRIGHT & FILIPPIS INC
1438 E Michigan Ave # 100 (48912-2160)
PHONE 517 484-2624
Beth Burke, *Manager*
EMP: 11
SALES (corp-wide): 51.4MM **Privately Held**
WEB: www.firsttoserve.com
SIC: 3842 5999 5047 3999 Surgical appliances & supplies; orthopedic & prosthesis applications; hospital equipment & furniture; wheelchair lifts
PA: Wright & Filippis, Inc.
2845 Crooks Rd
Rochester Hills MI 48309
248 829-8292

(G-9436)
XG SCIENCES INC
2100 S Washington Ave (48910-0824)
PHONE 517 316-2038
Scott Murray, *Vice Pres*
EMP: 11 **Privately Held**
SIC: 2821 Plastics materials & resins
PA: Xg Sciences, Inc.
3101 Grand Oak Dr
Lansing MI 48911

(G-9437)
XG SCIENCES INC (PA)
3101 Grand Oak Dr (48911-4224)
PHONE 517 703-1110
Philip Rose, *CEO*
Scott Murray, *Vice Pres*
Robert Privette, *Vice Pres*
Liya Wang, *Vice Pres*
John Colwell, *Mfg Staff*
▼ **EMP:** 9
SQ FT: 7,000
SALES (est): 8.4MM **Privately Held**
WEB: www.xgsciences.com
SIC: 2819 8731 Industrial inorganic chemicals; commercial physical research

(G-9438)
YORK ELECTRIC INC
1905 S Washington Ave (48910-9152)
PHONE 517 487-6400
EMP: 20
SALES (corp-wide): 16.4MM **Privately Held**
SIC: 3261 7694 Bathroom accessories/fittings, vitreous china or earthenware; electric motor repair
PA: York Electric, Inc.
611 Andre St
Bay City MI 48706
989 684-7460

Lapeer
Lapeer County

(G-9439)
21ST CENTURY NEWSPAPERS INC
1521 Imlay City Rd (48446-3175)
P.O. Box 220 (48446-0220)
PHONE 810 664-0811
Frank Shepherd, *Partner*
EMP: 100
SALES (corp-wide): 697.5MM **Privately Held**
WEB: www.macombdaily.com
SIC: 2711 Newspapers, publishing & printing
HQ: 21st Century Newspapers, Inc.
19176 Hall Rd Ste 200
Clinton Township MI 48038
586 469-4510

(G-9440)
ALBAR INDUSTRIES INC
780 Whitney Dr (48446-2570)
PHONE 810 667-0150
Edward A May, *President*
Lawrence May, *Vice Pres*
Ed Brown, *Maint Mgr*
David Smith, *Materials Mgr*
Sandy Griffin, *Production*
EMP: 300 **EST:** 1966
SQ FT: 103,000
SALES (est): 99.7MM **Privately Held**
WEB: www.albar.com
SIC: 3089 Coloring & finishing of plastic products

(G-9441)
B & M SONICS AND MACHINE LLC
4301 N Lapeer Rd (48446-8616)
PHONE 810 793-1236
Bill J Gomes Sr, *Owner*
EMP: 3
SALES (est): 328.4K **Privately Held**
SIC: 3699 Generators, ultrasonic

(G-9442)
B M INDUSTRIES INC
130 Harsen Rd (48446-2752)
PHONE 810 658-0052
EMP: 4
SALES (est): 230.1K **Privately Held**
SIC: 3451 Mfg Screw Machine Products

(G-9443)
BLUE WATER PRINTING CO INC
655 Mccormick Dr Ste B (48446-3925)
P.O. Box 241 (48446-0241)
PHONE 810 664-0643
Gene Becker, *President*
EMP: 7 **EST:** 1974
SQ FT: 6,500
SALES (est): 620K **Privately Held**
SIC: 2752 2759 Commercial printing, offset; commercial printing

(G-9444)
BRADFORD TOOL & DIE COMPANY
1130 Clark Rd (48446-3019)
PHONE 810 664-8653
EMP: 6 **EST:** 1966
SQ FT: 22,000
SALES (est): 895.1K **Privately Held**
SIC: 3544 Mfg Dies/Tools/Jigs/Fixtures

(G-9445)
BULLS-EYE WIRE & CABLE INC
1498 N Saginaw St Ste 4 (48446-1594)
P.O. Box 556, Lake Orion (48361-0556)
PHONE 810 245-8600
Kevin C Morrison, *President*
EMP: 7
SQ FT: 2,500
SALES: 1.5MM **Privately Held**
SIC: 3357 Nonferrous wiredrawing & insulating

(G-9446)
BYRNES MANUFACTURING CO LLC
870 Whitney Dr (48446-2565)
P.O. Box 40 (48446-0040)
PHONE 810 664-3686
Ryan Byrnes, *Principal*
Bruce Byrnes,
EMP: 4
SALES (est): 416.8K **Privately Held**
SIC: 3544 Dies, plastics forming

(G-9447)
BYRNES TOOL CO INC
870 Whitney Dr (48446-2565)
P.O. Box 40 (48446-0040)
PHONE 810 664-3686
Bruce Byrnes, *President*
Robert Byrnes Jr, *Corp Secy*
EMP: 7
SQ FT: 10,000
SALES (est): 200K **Privately Held**
SIC: 3544 Industrial molds

(G-9448)
C P I INC
1449 Bowers Rd (48446-3124)
PHONE 810 664-8686
Gerald Jasper, *President*
EMP: 4 **EST:** 1955
SQ FT: 5,100
SALES (est): 716K **Privately Held**
SIC: 3312 Tool & die steel

(G-9449)
CANCO INC
Also Called: Gregory's Canvass
1404 Imlay City Rd (48446-3114)
PHONE 810 664-3520
Stephen C Gregory, *President*
EMP: 3
SQ FT: 7,000
SALES (est): 355.3K **Privately Held**
SIC: 2298 2394 Slings, rope; canvas & related products

(G-9450)
CAPNESITY INC
1778 Imlay City Rd (48446-3206)
PHONE 317 401-6766
Jeffrey Gibson, *President*
EMP: 4
SALES (est): 149.2K **Privately Held**
SIC: 3841 Surgical & medical instruments

(G-9451)
CONTOUR MOLD CORPORATION
1830 N Lapeer Rd (48446-7771)
PHONE 810 245-4070
EMP: 3
SALES (est): 17.1K **Privately Held**
SIC: 3544 Industrial molds

(G-9452)
CRAIGS SIGNS
1498 N Saginaw St Ste 2 (48446-1594)
PHONE 810 667-7446
Craig Turner, *Owner*
EMP: 5
SALES (est): 417.3K **Privately Held**
SIC: 3993 Signs, not made in custom sign painting shops

(G-9453)
CYPRESS COMPUTER SYSTEMS INC
Also Called: Robot Space, The
1778 Imlay City Rd (48446-3206)
PHONE 810 245-2300
Paul Ahern, *President*
Anthony J Diodato, *Vice Pres*
▲ **EMP:** 11
SQ FT: 10,000
SALES (est): 1.5MM **Privately Held**
WEB: www.cypressworld.com
SIC: 7373 7371 3571 3699 Computer integrated systems design; computer software systems analysis & design, custom; electronic computers; security devices; security control equipment & systems; security devices, locks

(G-9454)
D T FOWLER MFG CO INC (PA)
101 N Mapleleaf Rd (48446-8003)
P.O. Box 70 (48446-0070)
PHONE 810 245-9336
Christina Fowler-White, *President*
EMP: 6 **EST:** 1950
SQ FT: 200,000
SALES (est): 8.8MM **Privately Held**
SIC: 2448 2653 Pallets, wood; corrugated & solid fiber boxes

(G-9455)
DADS PANELS INC
Also Called: Tool Organisations Service
2142 Imlay City Rd (48446-3260)
P.O. Box 1342 (48446-5342)
PHONE 810 245-1871
Charles English, *President*
Matthew English, *Opers Mgr*
Tom Fitzgerald, *Manager*
EMP: 5 **EST:** 1990

Lapeer - Lapeer County (G-9456) — GEOGRAPHIC SECTION

SALES: 270K **Privately Held**
WEB: www.toolorg.com
SIC: **2541** 2542 2431 Store & office display cases & fixtures; partitions & fixtures, except wood; millwork

(G-9456)
DALES LLC
348 Cty Center St (48446)
 PHONE.................................734 444-4620
Dale Tusek,
EMP: 4
SALES (est): 274.5K **Privately Held**
SIC: **2411** Fuel wood harvesting

(G-9457)
DURAKON INDUSTRIES INC (DH)
2101 N Lapeer Rd (48446-8799)
 PHONE.................................608 742-5301
Duane Braskamp, *CFO*
▲ EMP: 4
SALES: 57MM
SALES (corp-wide): 61.4MM **Privately Held**
WEB: www.durakon.com
SIC: **3714** 3713 3081 Motor vehicle parts & accessories; truck & bus bodies; unsupported plastics film & sheet

(G-9458)
ENERGY STEEL & SUPPLY CO
3123 John Conley Dr (48446-2987)
 PHONE.................................810 538-4990
James Lines, *CEO*
Joseph Aliasso, *General Mgr*
Bob Paton, *Vice Pres*
Robert J Paton, *Vice Pres*
Marcus Alexander, *Project Mgr*
▼ EMP: 55 EST: 1982
SQ FT: 60,000
SALES (est): 17.5MM
SALES (corp-wide): 91.8MM **Publicly Held**
WEB: www.energysteel.com
SIC: **3317** 5051 Steel pipe & tubes; pipe & tubing, steel
PA: The Graham Corporation
 20 Florence Ave
 Batavia NY 14020
 585 343-2216

(G-9459)
ESE LLC
3344 John Conley Dr (48446-4301)
 PHONE.................................810 538-1000
Steve Brusie, *Design Engr*
Derek Lehr, *Design Engr*
Kyle Smith, *Design Engr*
Eric Smith,
Aaron Oberle,
▲ EMP: 4
SQ FT: 10,500
SALES (est): 668.8K **Privately Held**
SIC: **3714** Instrument board assemblies, motor vehicle

(G-9460)
EVOLUTION TOOL INC
587 Mccormick Dr (48446-2575)
 PHONE.................................810 664-5500
EMP: 7
SALES (est): 696.8K **Privately Held**
SIC: **3544** Special dies & tools

(G-9461)
FABULOUS OPERATING PDTS LLC
401 Mccormick Dr (48446-2555)
 PHONE.................................810 245-5759
Lorin A Milks,
Steven D Hoffman,
Lorin Milks,
EMP: 8 EST: 2013
SALES (est): 1MM **Privately Held**
SIC: **3714** Motor vehicle parts & accessories

(G-9462)
GESTAMP ALABAMA LLC
100 E Fair St (48446-1502)
 PHONE.................................810 245-3100
Stephanie McComas, *Purch Mgr*
Joan Hall, *Buyer*
Danny Taylor, *Engineer*
Justin Lavender, *Finance Mgr*
Kessler James, *Credit Mgr*
EMP: 200
SALES (corp-wide): 120.9MM **Privately Held**
SIC: **3465** Body parts, automobile: stamped metal
HQ: Gestamp Alabama, Llc
 7000 Jefferson Metro Pkwy
 Mc Calla AL 35111
 205 497-6400

(G-9463)
GRH INC
Also Called: Good-Rich Honey
3409 W Sutton Rd (48446-9645)
 PHONE.................................888 344-6639
Jeff Melton, *President*
EMP: 3
SQ FT: 1,600
SALES (est): 331.3K **Privately Held**
WEB: www.goodrichhoney.com
SIC: **3999** Honeycomb foundations (beekeepers' supplies)

(G-9464)
HYDRAULIC TUBES & FITTINGS LLC
434 Mccormick Dr (48446-2518)
P.O. Box 219 (48446-0219)
 PHONE.................................810 660-8088
David Berney, *Mng Member*
EMP: 49
SQ FT: 95,000
SALES (est): 12MM **Privately Held**
SIC: **3312** Pipes, iron & steel

(G-9465)
JAMS MEDIA LLC
1521 Imlay City Rd (48446-3175)
P.O. Box 220 (48446-0220)
 PHONE.................................810 664-0811
Wes Smith, *President*
Angie Lang, *Executive*
EMP: 8
SALES (est): 622.5K **Privately Held**
SIC: **2711** Newspapers

(G-9466)
LAPEER FUEL VENTURES INC
252 S Main St (48446-2425)
 PHONE.................................810 664-8770
Jennifer Schank, *Principal*
EMP: 5
SALES (est): 826.1K **Privately Held**
SIC: **1389** Oil field services

(G-9467)
LAPEER INDUSTRIES INC (PA)
400 Mccormick Dr (48446-2572)
P.O. Box 69 (48446-0069)
 PHONE.................................810 664-1816
Bryan Deblois, *President*
Daniel C Schreiber, *Chairman*
Chris Erickson, *Vice Pres*
Chelsea Lang, *Buyer*
Matt Phelps, *Program Mgr*
▲ EMP: 182
SQ FT: 400,000
SALES (est): 22.5MM **Privately Held**
WEB: www.lapeerind.com
SIC: **3728** 3544 Military aircraft equipment & armament; turrets & turret drives, aircraft; turret test fixtures, aircraft; special dies & tools

(G-9468)
LAPEER PLATING & PLASTICS INC
395 Demille Rd (48446-3055)
P.O. Box 898 (48446-0898)
 PHONE.................................810 667-4240
Larry Gatt, *CEO*
Dan Brown, *QC Mgr*
EMP: 225
SALES (est): 77.9MM **Privately Held**
SIC: **2431** 3089 Moldings & baseboards, ornamental & trim; injection molded finished plastic products

(G-9469)
LESLEY ELIZABETH INC
449 Mccormick Dr (48446-2555)
 PHONE.................................810 667-4706
Lesley Mc Cowen, *President*
EMP: 7 **Privately Held**
SIC: **2099** Food preparations
PA: Lesley Elizabeth Inc.
 877 Whitney Dr
 Lapeer MI 48446

(G-9470)
LESLEY ELIZABETH INC (PA)
877 Whitney Dr (48446-2565)
 PHONE.................................810 667-0706
Lesley McCowen, *President*
Sally Burrell, *COO*
Catherine Moore, *Shareholder*
▲ EMP: 15
SQ FT: 8,200
SALES (est): 2.7MM **Privately Held**
SIC: **2099** Seasonings & spices

(G-9471)
LLC STAHL CROSS
110 N Saginaw St (48446-4600)
 PHONE.................................810 688-2505
John Stahl, *Mng Member*
EMP: 4 EST: 2010
SALES (est): 357.9K **Privately Held**
SIC: **3911** Jewelry apparel

(G-9472)
LUMBER & TRUSS INC
162 S Saginaw St (48446-2602)
P.O. Box 729 (48446-0729)
 PHONE.................................810 664-7290
Joseph O'Henley, *President*
Kim Brown, *Treasurer*
Thomas Butterfield, *Admin Sec*
▲ EMP: 22
SALES (est): 3.2MM **Privately Held**
SIC: **1531** 5211 5031 2439 Operative builders; lumber products; lumber, plywood & millwork; trusses, wooden roof; agricultural building contractors

(G-9473)
MANUFCTRING PARTNERS GROUP LLC
1639 Horton Lake Rd (48446-7504)
 PHONE.................................517 749-4050
James Krozek, *Principal*
EMP: 7
SALES (est): 94.4K **Privately Held**
SIC: **3999** Manufacturing industries

(G-9474)
MASCO CORPORATION OF INDIANA
211 Mccormick Dr (48446-2571)
 PHONE.................................810 664-8501
Rob Lyman, *Supervisor*
EMP: 85
SALES (corp-wide): 8.3B **Publicly Held**
SIC: **3088** Tubs (bath, shower & laundry), plastic
HQ: Masco Corporation Of Indiana
 55 E 111th St
 Indianapolis IN 46280
 317 848-1812

(G-9475)
MOLD MASTERS CO
1455 Imlay City Rd (48446-3142)
 PHONE.................................810 245-4100
Hugo Leonardi, *CEO*
Angela Swiatkowski, *Corp Secy*
Glenn Haines, *Maintence Staff*
Tony Visnaw, *Maintence Staff*
▲ EMP: 150 EST: 1973
SQ FT: 250,000
SALES (est): 38.4MM **Privately Held**
SIC: **3089** Injection molding of plastics

(G-9476)
MOTION MACHINE COMPANY
524 Mccormick Dr (48446-2518)
 PHONE.................................810 664-9901
Danny L Walters, *President*
David Clemens, *Vice Pres*
Brian Walters, *Engineer*
Thomas Niazy, *Treasurer*
EMP: 13
SQ FT: 14,200
SALES (est): 2.8MM **Privately Held**
WEB: www.motionmach.com
SIC: **3599** 3549 3535 Machine shop, jobbing & repair; metalworking machinery; unit handling conveying systems

(G-9477)
NOLANS OUTDOOR POWER INC
Also Called: Nolan's Farm Equipment
3120 N Lapeer Rd (48446-8766)
 PHONE.................................810 664-3798
Michael Nolan, *President*
Joe Nolan, *Vice Pres*
EMP: 8
SQ FT: 12,500
SALES (est): 970K **Privately Held**
SIC: **3524** Lawn & garden equipment

(G-9478)
OGILVIE MANUFACTURING COMPANY
2445 Henry Rd (48446-9037)
 PHONE.................................810 793-6598
Bruce Ogilvie, *President*
Lyle Ogilvie, *Treasurer*
EMP: 4 EST: 1962
SALES: 250K **Privately Held**
SIC: **3634** Heating units, for electric appliances

(G-9479)
P & P MANUFACTURING CO INC
260 Mccormick Dr (48446-2518)
 PHONE.................................810 667-2712
Jon M Kirsch, *President*
Jacqueline Linklater, *Controller*
EMP: 30 EST: 1962
SQ FT: 15,000
SALES (est): 1.7MM **Privately Held**
WEB: www.patcoairtools.com
SIC: **3545** Tools & accessories for machine tools

(G-9480)
PENTIER GROUP INC
587 S Court St Ste 300 (48446-2579)
P.O. Box 350 (48446-0350)
 PHONE.................................810 664-7997
Tony Anderson, *President*
George Adams, *Vice Pres*
EMP: 19
SQ FT: 16,400
SALES (est): 4.4MM **Privately Held**
WEB: www.pentier.com
SIC: **3599** Custom machinery

(G-9481)
POLLUMS NATURAL RESOURCES
732 S Elba Rd (48446-2775)
 PHONE.................................810 245-7268
Harry Pollum, *Principal*
EMP: 3
SALES (est): 262K **Privately Held**
SIC: **2421** Sawmills & planing mills, general

(G-9482)
PROFESSIONAL SFTWR ASSOC INC
Also Called: Psa
2517 Imlay City Rd (48446-3215)
 PHONE.................................727 724-0000
John Hertrich, *President*
Chris Hertrich, *CFO*
EMP: 3
SQ FT: 2,200
SALES (est): 500K **Privately Held**
WEB: www.psa-software.com
SIC: **7371** 7372 Computer software development & applications; prepackaged software

(G-9483)
PTL ENGINEERING INC
3333 John Conley Dr # 2 (48446-4308)
 PHONE.................................810 664-2310
Brian Trombley, *President*
EMP: 13
SALES (est): 3.1MM **Privately Held**
WEB: www.ptlengineering.com
SIC: **3442** Screen & storm doors & windows

(G-9484)
QUEST INDUSTRIES INC
3309 John Conley Dr (48446-4301)
 PHONE.................................810 245-4535
Dennis Hoover, *Owner*
Sonya Lee Hoover, *Vice Pres*
Scott Carey, *Program Mgr*

GEOGRAPHIC SECTION

Michael Cook, *Program Mgr*
John Neubecker, *Program Mgr*
EMP: 50
SQ FT: 42,000
SALES (est): 10.3MM **Privately Held**
SIC: 3599 Machine shop, jobbing & repair

(G-9485)
REO FAB LLC (PA)
1567 Imlay City Rd Ste A (48446-3196)
PHONE..................................810 969-4667
Robert E Fischer,
Tamara Fischer,
EMP: 3
SQ FT: 5,000
SALES: 749K **Privately Held**
SIC: 3441 Fabricated structural metal

(G-9486)
SHAWS ENTERPRISES INC
Also Called: SE Tools
415 Howard St (48446-2556)
PHONE..................................810 664-2981
Greg Shaw, *President*
Steven Shaw, *Vice Pres*
▲ **EMP:** 20 **EST:** 1930
SQ FT: 25,000
SALES (est): 4.3MM **Privately Held**
WEB: www.setools.com
SIC: 3423 Hand & edge tools

(G-9487)
SOURIS ENTERPRISES INC
Also Called: Lapeer Manufacturing Company
2045 N Lapeer Rd (48446-8628)
P.O. Box 370 (48446-0370)
PHONE..................................810 664-2964
Bernice L Souris, *President*
Nicholas Souris, *Vice Pres*
Kimberley Souris, *Admin Sec*
EMP: 10 **EST:** 1986
SQ FT: 13,000
SALES (est): 2.1MM **Privately Held**
WEB: www.knu-vise.com
SIC: 3429 Clamps, metal

(G-9488)
STADIUM BLEACHERS LLC
3597 Lippincott Rd (48446-9638)
PHONE..................................810 245-6258
EMP: 5
SALES (est): 360K **Privately Held**
SIC: 2531 Mfg Public Building Furniture

(G-9489)
URGENT DESIGN AND MFG INC
Also Called: 3 Dimensional Services
2547 Product Dr (48446)
PHONE..................................810 245-1300
Douglas Peterson, *President*
Michael Brabandt, *General Mgr*
Alan Peterson, *Vice Pres*
Andy Testerman, *Engineer*
David Turner, *Engineer*
EMP: 43 **EST:** 1999
SQ FT: 50,000
SALES (est): 12.4MM **Privately Held**
WEB: www.urgent-design.com
SIC: 3599 Machine shop, jobbing & repair

(G-9490)
VIDON PLASTICS INC
3171 John Conley Dr (48446-2987)
P.O. Box 56 (48446-0056)
PHONE..................................810 667-0634
Donald Dube, *President*
Matthew Dube, *Business Mgr*
Dave Barth, *Controller*
▼ **EMP:** 75
SQ FT: 75,000
SALES (est): 15.1MM **Privately Held**
WEB: www.vidonplastics.com
SIC: 3089 3084 3083 Extruded finished plastic products; plastics pipe; laminated plastics plate & sheet

(G-9491)
VILLAGE PRINTING & SUPPLY INC
349 Mccormick Dr (48446-2574)
PHONE..................................810 664-2270
Joseph Morey, *President*
Kara Lambourn, *Manager*
Ardith Westendorf, *Admin Sec*
EMP: 6
SQ FT: 2,500
SALES (est): 1.1MM **Privately Held**
SIC: 2752 2759 5084 Commercial printing, offset; invitation & stationery printing & engraving; printing trades machinery, equipment & supplies

(G-9492)
WOLVERINE TOOL CO
2045 N Lapeer Rd (48446-8628)
PHONE..................................810 664-2964
George Grenzke, *Ch of Bd*
Richard Grenzke, *President*
Norman F Grenzke Jr, *Vice Pres*
EMP: 14
SQ FT: 9,600
SALES (est): 1.3MM **Privately Held**
WEB: www.wolverinetool.com
SIC: 3544 3545 3599 Special dies & tools; jigs & fixtures; tools & accessories for machine tools; gauges (machine tool accessories); machine shop, jobbing & repair

(G-9493)
ZAREASON INC
333 N Washington St (48446-1949)
PHONE..................................510 868-5000
Cathy Malmrose, *CEO*
Earl Malmrose, *Chief Engr*
▲ **EMP:** 15
SALES (est): 2.3MM **Privately Held**
WEB: www.zareason.com
SIC: 3571 Electronic computers

(G-9494)
ZF CHASSIS COMPONENTS LLC (DH)
3300 John Conley Dr (48446-4301)
PHONE..................................810 245-2000
Kurt Mueller, *Vice Pres*
Bruce Wrenbeck, *Vice Pres*
Craig Meyer, *Engineer*
Chase Skipinski, *Design Engr*
Franz Kleiner, *CFO*
◆ **EMP:** 215
SALES (est): 216.3MM
SALES (corp-wide): 216.2K **Privately Held**
WEB: www.zf-group.com
SIC: 3714 Steering mechanisms, motor vehicle; tie rods, motor vehicle; ball joints, motor vehicle; motor vehicle steering systems & parts
HQ: Zf Friedrichshafen Ag
Lowentaler Str. 20
Friedrichshafen 88046
754 177-0

(G-9495)
ZF CHASSIS COMPONENTS LLC
930 S Saginaw St (48446-4601)
PHONE..................................810 245-2000
Bradley Schmuck, *Branch Mgr*
EMP: 260
SALES (corp-wide): 216.2K **Privately Held**
SIC: 3714 Steering mechanisms, motor vehicle
HQ: Zf Chassis Components, Llc
3300 John Conley Dr
Lapeer MI 48446
810 245-2000

(G-9496)
ZF LEMFORDER CORP
3300 John Conley Dr (48446-4301)
PHONE..................................810 245-7136
Larry Miner, *General Mgr*
Jeanette Johnstone, *Engineer*
Jason Link, *Engineer*
Kurt Brown, *Controller*
Adam Arntz, *Manager*
EMP: 13
SALES (est): 1.8MM **Privately Held**
SIC: 3714 Motor vehicle parts & accessories

Lathrup Village
Oakland County

(G-9497)
AFFORDABLE MOBILE DEVICES LLC
28211 Southfield Rd # 760092 (48076-7047)
PHONE..................................313 433-9242
Abraham Harris, *Director*
EMP: 3
SALES: 30K **Privately Held**
SIC: 3625 Switches, electronic applications

(G-9498)
AUTO PALLETS-BOXES INC (PA)
28000 Southfield Rd Fl 2 (48076-2864)
PHONE..................................248 559-7744
Mitchell B Foster, *President*
Chuck Foster, *Vice Pres*
James B Foster, *Vice Pres*
Greg V Dorn, *Finance*
Mitchell Foster, *CTO*
EMP: 15 **EST:** 1963
SQ FT: 7,000
SALES (est): 5.7MM **Privately Held**
WEB: www.apallets.com
SIC: 2448 2441 Pallets, wood; boxes, wood

(G-9499)
FEDEX OFFICE & PRINT SVCS INC
27661 Southfield Rd (48076-7902)
PHONE..................................248 443-2679
EMP: 26
SALES (corp-wide): 69.6B **Publicly Held**
WEB: www.kinkos.com
SIC: 7334 2789 Photocopying & duplicating services; bookbinding & related work
HQ: Fedex Office And Print Services, Inc.
7900 Legacy Dr
Plano TX 75024
800 463-3339

(G-9500)
IDEA MIA LLC
18513 San Quentin Dr (48076-7809)
PHONE..................................248 891-8939
Marco Cucco, *Principal*
Angie Cucco, *Vice Pres*
▲ **EMP:** 7
SALES (est): 877K **Privately Held**
SIC: 2673 Bags: plastic, laminated & coated

(G-9501)
SUPERSINE COMPANY
27634 Rackham Dr (48076-3303)
PHONE..................................313 892-6200
EMP: 20 **EST:** 1950
SQ FT: 12,500
SALES (est): 1.5MM **Privately Held**
SIC: 3993 Mfg Signs & Sign Parts

Laurium
Houghton County

(G-9502)
A & S ENTERPRISES LLC
175 Woodland Ave (49913-2049)
PHONE..................................906 482-9007
Alan D Anderson, *Mng Member*
EMP: 3
SALES: 320K **Privately Held**
SIC: 3499 Fire- or burglary-resistive products

(G-9503)
DESIGNOTYPE PRINTERS INC
22950 Airpark Blvd (49913-9241)
PHONE..................................906 482-2424
Brian Helminen, *President*
EMP: 4
SALES (est): 508.8K **Privately Held**
WEB: www.designotype.com
SIC: 2752 Commercial printing, offset

Lawrence
Van Buren County

(G-9504)
A & B PACKING EQUIPMENT INC (PA)
732 W Saint Joseph St (49064-9338)
PHONE..................................269 539-4700
Michael Williamson, *CEO*
Terry Draper, *COO*
Teresa Jamieson, *Human Res Mgr*
Luis Dominguez, *Accounts Mgr*
Robin Jayetileke, *Sales Staff*
▲ **EMP:** 126
SALES (est): 26.2MM **Privately Held**
WEB: www.a-bpack.net
SIC: 3523 Farm machinery & equipment

(G-9505)
LANPHEAR TOOL WORKS INC
Also Called: L T W
311 S Paw Paw St (49064-9686)
P.O. Box 680 (49064-0680)
PHONE..................................269 674-8877
John Lanphear, *President*
Mindy R Lanphear, *Vice Pres*
EMP: 12
SQ FT: 20,000
SALES (est): 1.2MM **Privately Held**
SIC: 3599 Machine shop, jobbing & repair

(G-9506)
QUALITY ASSURED PLASTICS INC
1200 Crandall Pkwy (49064-8778)
PHONE..................................269 674-3888
Annette Crandall, *President*
Eugene Crandall, *Vice Pres*
Barbara Daniel, *Treasurer*
Steve Barr, *Sales Staff*
Wendy K Sundberg, *Admin Sec*
EMP: 40
SQ FT: 28,000
SALES (est): 9.3MM **Privately Held**
WEB: www.qapinc.com
SIC: 3089 Injection molding of plastics

(G-9507)
RHINO PRODUCTS INC
Also Called: Bowditch
57100 48th Ave (49064-9013)
PHONE..................................269 674-8309
James A Mc Gowan, *President*
Susie Mc Gowan, *Admin Sec*
EMP: 15
SALES: 325K **Privately Held**
WEB: www.rhinoproducts.com
SIC: 3161 2241 Cases, carrying; narrow fabric mills; strapping webs

(G-9508)
SILL FARMS & MARKET INC
50241 Red Arrow Hwy (49064-8781)
PHONE..................................269 674-3755
Bob Ross, *President*
Jean M Sill, *Vice Pres*
Lois Ross, *Treasurer*
EMP: 25 **EST:** 1950
SQ FT: 25,000
SALES (est): 3.7MM **Privately Held**
SIC: 2037 Fruits, quick frozen & cold pack (frozen)

(G-9509)
USA QUALITY METAL FINSHG LLC
67131 56th St (49064-8757)
PHONE..................................269 427-9000
Dave Millword,
EMP: 15 **EST:** 2007
SALES (est): 1.4MM **Privately Held**
SIC: 3471 Finishing, metals or formed products

Lawton
Van Buren County

(G-9510)
AMJS INCORPORATED
Also Called: Byers Manufacturing
828 S Main St (49065-8743)
P.O. Box 386 (49065-0386)
Fax: 269 624-7322
EMP: 6
SALES (est): 923.3K **Privately Held**
SIC: 3444 Sheet Metalwork, Nsk

(G-9511)
DAVES CONCRETE PRODUCTS INC
79811 M 40 (49065-9355)
PHONE.................................269 624-4100
David Flory, *President*
Todd Docekal, *Vice Pres*
Susan Lockhart, *Manager*
EMP: 19
SALES (est): 2.9MM **Privately Held**
SIC: 3272 3273 Septic tanks, concrete; silos, prefabricated concrete; ready-mixed concrete

(G-9512)
KTS ENTERPRISES
Also Called: Ken's Tarp & Canvas Shop
121 W 2nd St (49065-9799)
PHONE.................................269 624-3435
Thomas Osborne, *Owner*
EMP: 3
SQ FT: 2,800
SALES: 100K **Privately Held**
SIC: 2394 5551 Shades, canvas: made from purchased materials; marine supplies

(G-9513)
PACKERS CANNING CO INC
Also Called: Honee Bear Canning Co
72100 M 40 (49065-8444)
P.O. Box 907 (49065-0907)
PHONE.................................269 624-4681
Robert R Packer, *President*
Steven C Packer, *Vice Pres*
Jim Farley, *Sales Staff*
Glen Rogers, *Manager*
Gail Coombs, *Supervisor*
◆ **EMP:** 55 **EST:** 1943
SQ FT: 200,000
SALES (est): 17.9MM **Privately Held**
WEB: www.honeebear.com
SIC: 2033 Fruits: packaged in cans, jars, etc.; vegetables: packaged in cans, jars, etc.; fruit juices: packaged in cans, jars, etc.; fruit pie mixes & fillings: packaged in cans, jars, etc.

(G-9514)
PERFORMANCE CNC INC
75289 M 40 (49065-8458)
P.O. Box 849 (49065-0849)
PHONE.................................269 624-3206
Kyle Yoder, *President*
EMP: 3
SQ FT: 3,200
SALES (est): 461.3K **Privately Held**
SIC: 3599 Machine shop, jobbing & repair

(G-9515)
STEARNS & STAFFORD INC
33081 County Road 358 (49065-9254)
P.O. Box 308 (49065-0308)
PHONE.................................269 624-4541
Tom Dietz, *President*
Rita Pfister, *Corp Secy*
EMP: 14 **EST:** 1923
SQ FT: 15,000
SALES: 1MM **Privately Held**
SIC: 3562 Roller bearings & parts

(G-9516)
WELCH FOODS INC A COOPERATIVE
Also Called: Lawton Plant
400 Walker St (49065-9711)
PHONE.................................269 624-4141
Hank Grosel, *Branch Mgr*
Randy Holmes, *Manager*
EMP: 85
SALES (corp-wide): 608.4MM **Privately Held**
WEB: www.welchs.com
SIC: 2033 2037 Fruit juices: packaged in cans, jars, etc.; preserves, including imitation: in cans, jars, etc.; frozen fruits & vegetables
HQ: Welch Foods Inc, A Cooperative
575 Virginia Rd
Concord MA 01742
978 371-1000

(G-9517)
WEST MICHIGAN AERIAL LLC
62422 M 40 (49065-7497)
P.O. Box 738, Mattawan (49071-0738)
PHONE.................................269 998-4455
Domonic Tykoski, *Mng Member*
EMP: 26
SALES (est): 5.3MM **Privately Held**
SIC: 3531 Aerial work platforms: hydraulic/elec. truck/carrier mounted

Lennon
Genesee County

(G-9518)
MET-PRO TECHNOLOGIES LLC
1172 S M 13 (48449-9301)
P.O. Box 459, Owosso (48867)
PHONE.................................989 725-8184
Fax: 989 725-8188
EMP: 68
SQ FT: 34,166
SALES (corp-wide): 417MM **Publicly Held**
SIC: 3564 Mfg Blowers/Fans
HQ: Met-Pro Technologies Llc
460 E Swedesford Rd # 2030
Wayne PA 19087
215 717-7909

(G-9519)
STEINER TRACTOR PARTS INC
1660 S M 13 (48449-9325)
P.O. Box 449 (48449-0449)
PHONE.................................810 621-3000
Daniel P Steiner, *President*
Leslie Steiner, *Corp Secy*
Jenny Bradshaw, *Vice Pres*
Andrew Wilberding, *Adv Mgr*
Michael Mackenzie, *Manager*
▲ **EMP:** 43 **EST:** 1960
SALES (est): 10.3MM **Privately Held**
WEB: www.steinertractor.com
SIC: 3523 5083 Farm machinery & equipment; agricultural machinery & equipment

Lenox
Macomb County

(G-9520)
ALBERS CABINET COMPANY
65151 Gratiot Ave (48050-2010)
PHONE.................................586 727-9090
George Alber, *Partner*
James Alber, *Partner*
▼ **EMP:** 9
SQ FT: 10,000
SALES (est): 1.2MM **Privately Held**
WEB: www.albersfireplaces.com
SIC: 2434 Wood kitchen cabinets

(G-9521)
LENOX CEMENT PRODUCTS INC
65601 Gratiot Ave (48050-2012)
PHONE.................................586 727-1488
Alvin Harms, *President*
Margaret Harms, *Vice Pres*
EMP: 3
SALES (est): 287.9K **Privately Held**
SIC: 3272 1711 5231 1793 Septic tanks, concrete; septic system construction; glass; glass & glazing work

(G-9522)
LENOX INC
Also Called: Lenox Septic Tanks
65601 Gratiot Ave (48050-2012)
PHONE.................................586 727-1488
Alvin J Harms, *President*
Lori Harms, *Treasurer*
Clarence E Harms, *Admin Sec*
EMP: 5
SQ FT: 100
SALES: 1MM **Privately Held**
SIC: 3272 Septic tanks, concrete; burial vaults, concrete or precast terrazzo

(G-9523)
PRODUCTION & PROTOTYPE SVC LLC
35820 31 Mile Rd (48050-1457)
PHONE.................................586 924-7479
Michael Pionk, *Principal*
EMP: 3
SALES: 200K **Privately Held**
SIC: 3999 Manufacturing industries

(G-9524)
RICHMOND MILLWORK INC
66375 S Forest Ave (48050-1918)
P.O. Box 338, Richmond (48062-0338)
PHONE.................................586 727-6747
Mark Huss, *President*
Jim Vannuck, *Vice Pres*
Kenneth Huss, *Treasurer*
EMP: 13
SQ FT: 10,000
SALES (est): 1.7MM **Privately Held**
SIC: 2431 Millwork

(G-9525)
SELECT FIRE LLC
32037 29 Mile Rd (48050-2414)
PHONE.................................586 924-1974
Phillip Camarda,
▲ **EMP:** 3
SALES: 500K **Privately Held**
SIC: 3669 Fire alarm apparatus, electric

Leonard
Oakland County

(G-9526)
AREA EXTERIORS
4075 Forest St (48367-1911)
PHONE.................................248 544-0706
Richard Stiltner,
EMP: 4
SALES (est): 417.6K **Privately Held**
SIC: 2431 Garage doors, overhead: wood

(G-9527)
COOPER-STANDARD AUTOMOTIVE INC
180 E Elmwood (48367-1801)
P.O. Box 680 (48367-0680)
PHONE.................................248 628-4899
Tom Capua, *Branch Mgr*
EMP: 100
SALES (corp-wide): 3.6B **Publicly Held**
WEB: www.cooperstandard.com
SIC: 3443 Heat exchangers, condensers & components
HQ: Cooper-Standard Automotive Inc.
39550 Orchard Hill Pl
Novi MI 48375
248 596-5900

(G-9528)
STEENSON ENTERPRISES
4444 Forest St (48367-1932)
PHONE.................................248 628-0036
Curt Steenson, *Partner*
Deborah Steenson, *Partner*
EMP: 5
SQ FT: 2,000
SALES (est): 484K **Privately Held**
SIC: 3544 Industrial molds

Leroy
Osceola County

(G-9529)
ADVANCED FIBERMOLDING INC
23095 14 Mile Rd (49655-8552)
PHONE.................................231 768-5177
Dennis Webster, *President*
Norma Jean Webster, *Corp Secy*
EMP: 40
SQ FT: 24,000
SALES (est): 11.5MM **Privately Held**
WEB: www.advancedfibermold.com
SIC: 3089 Plastic containers, except foam

(G-9530)
D J MCQUESTION & SONS INC
17708 18 Mile Rd (49655-8219)
PHONE.................................231 768-4403
Robert McQuestion, *President*
Julie Gugle, *Human Res Mgr*
Craig Todd, *Benefits Mgr*
Brandy Prosch,
EMP: 10
SQ FT: 3,000
SALES (est): 41.9MM **Privately Held**
SIC: 3295 1794 1611 Pulverized earth; excavation work; highway & street construction

(G-9531)
DYERS SAWMILL INC
17688 15 Mile Rd (49655-7501)
P.O. Box 20 (49655-0020)
PHONE.................................231 768-4438
Ross Rothig, *President*
EMP: 28
SQ FT: 12,500
SALES (est): 3.8MM **Privately Held**
SIC: 2421 2435 2426 Lumber: rough, sawed or planed; hardwood veneer & plywood; hardwood dimension & flooring mills

(G-9532)
EB ENTERPRISES LLC
17747 Leroy Rd (49655-7104)
PHONE.................................231 768-5072
Bertha Miller,
Ervin Miller,
EMP: 3
SALES (est): 32.2K **Privately Held**
SIC: 2511 7389 Wood lawn & garden furniture;

(G-9533)
LEROY TOOL & DIE INC
17951 180th Ave (49655-8427)
PHONE.................................231 768-4336
Terry Wanstead, *President*
Judy Wanstead, *Corp Secy*
▲ **EMP:** 70
SQ FT: 8,000
SALES (est): 9.9MM **Privately Held**
WEB: www.leroytool.com
SIC: 3544 Forms (molds), for foundry & plastics working machinery

(G-9534)
NORTHERN PRECISION PDTS INC
4790 Mackinaw Trl (49655-9320)
P.O. Box 202 (49655-0202)
PHONE.................................231 768-4435
Mary Nagengast, *CEO*
Bernard Nagengast, *Vice Pres*
Doug Thompson, *Sales Mgr*
EMP: 40
SQ FT: 23,000
SALES (est): 7.2MM **Privately Held**
WEB: www.northernprecisionproducts.com
SIC: 3451 Screw machine products

(G-9535)
PIONEER BROACH MIDWEST INC
13957 Pioneer Ave (49655-9402)
PHONE.................................231 768-5800
Gary Izor, *President*
EMP: 10
SQ FT: 35,000
SALES: 1.4MM
SALES (corp-wide): 9.2MM **Privately Held**
WEB: www.pioneerbroach.com
SIC: 3545 3541 Machine tool accessories; machine tools, metal cutting type
PA: Pioneer Broach Company
6434 Telegraph Rd
Commerce CA 90040
323 728-1263

GEOGRAPHIC SECTION

(G-9536)
PIONEER MICHIGAN BROACH CO
13957 Pioneer Ave (49655-9402)
PHONE.................................231 768-5800
Michael Ochs, *President*
Jerry Ezor, *Principal*
EMP: 15
SALES (est): 823.8K **Privately Held**
SIC: 3545 7699 Broaches (machine tool accessories); knife, saw & tool sharpening & repair

(G-9537)
RICHTER SAWMILL
20408 18 Mile Rd (49655-8370)
PHONE.................................231 829-3071
Warren Richter, *Owner*
EMP: 4
SALES (est): 318.6K **Privately Held**
SIC: 2421 Sawmills & planing mills, general

(G-9538)
SUPERIOR AUTOMOTIVE EQP INC
18153 150th Ave (49655-8210)
PHONE.................................231 829-9902
Michael Bell, *President*
▲ **EMP:** 4
SALES (est): 732.6K **Privately Held**
SIC: 3559 Automotive maintenance equipment

(G-9539)
UNOCO EXPLORATION CO
23382 17 Mile Rd (49655-8564)
PHONE.................................231 829-3235
Robert Feeley, *Owner*
EMP: 3
SALES (est): 300.7K **Privately Held**
SIC: 1382 1389 Oil & gas exploration services; oil & gas field services

Leslie
Ingham County

(G-9540)
AERO INSPECTION & TOOL LLC
856 Ewers Rd (49251-9524)
PHONE.................................517 525-7373
Nona Roe, *Principal*
EMP: 3
SALES (est): 296.2K **Privately Held**
SIC: 3721 Aircraft

(G-9541)
GORDON HACKWORTH LOGGING
3751 Meridian Rd (49251-9567)
PHONE.................................517 589-9218
Gordan Hackworth, *Owner*
EMP: 3
SALES (est): 164.8K **Privately Held**
SIC: 2411 Logging camps & contractors

(G-9542)
JD NORMAN INDUSTRIES INC
815 Rice St (49251-2500)
PHONE.................................517 589-8241
Beth Bryer, *Production*
Rich Foster, *Engineer*
Tom Mackinder, *Branch Mgr*
EMP: 90
SALES (corp-wide): 269MM **Privately Held**
SIC: 3568 Power transmission equipment
PA: Jd Norman Industries, Inc.
787 W Belden Ave
Addison IL 60101
630 458-3700

(G-9543)
JEFFREY L HACKWORTH
1162 W Fitchburg Rd (49251-9747)
PHONE.................................517 589-5884
Jeffrey Hackworth, *Principal*
EMP: 3
SALES (est): 234.7K **Privately Held**
SIC: 2411 Logging camps & contractors

(G-9544)
LOGAN DIESEL INCORPORATED
4567 Churchill Rd (49251-9732)
PHONE.................................517 589-8811
James L Logan, *President*
Sally Logan, *Admin Sec*
EMP: 5
SQ FT: 3,200
SALES: 500K **Privately Held**
SIC: 3519 3523 Diesel engine rebuilding; fertilizing, spraying, dusting & irrigation machinery

(G-9545)
MODERN FUR DRESSING LLC
801 Rice St (49251-2500)
P.O. Box 93 (49251-0093)
PHONE.................................517 589-5575
Roger G Smith,
EMP: 9
SQ FT: 2,000
SALES: 187K **Privately Held**
WEB: www.modernfurdressing.com
SIC: 3999 3111 Furs, dressed: bleached, curried, scraped, tanned or dyed; leather tanning & finishing

Levering
Emmet County

(G-9546)
SNIDER CONSTRUCTION INC
6711 E Levering Rd (49755-9589)
P.O. Box 95 (49755-0095)
PHONE.................................231 537-4851
Thomas Snider, *President*
Lois Snider, *Treasurer*
EMP: 3
SALES (est): 243.9K **Privately Held**
SIC: 1711 1442 1771 Septic system construction; gravel mining; concrete work

Lewiston
Montmorency County

(G-9547)
AMI INDUSTRIES INC (PA)
Also Called: Aggressive Mfg Innovations
5093 N Red Oak Rd (49756-8548)
P.O. Box 269 (49756-0269)
PHONE.................................989 786-3755
Jeff Evans, *President*
Vic Kellar, *Production*
Bill Scheid, *Engineer*
Carla Gordon, *Plant Engr*
Mick Lamagna, *Finance Mgr*
▲ **EMP:** 80
SQ FT: 30,000
SALES (est): 35.6MM **Privately Held**
WEB: www.ami-lewiston.com
SIC: 3559 Automotive related machinery

(G-9548)
FIELD TECH SERVICES INC
3860 County Road 491 (49756-9210)
PHONE.................................989 786-7046
Anthony Lucas, *President*
Mary Lucas, *Treasurer*
EMP: 7 **EST:** 2001
SALES (est): 1.2MM **Privately Held**
SIC: 1389 Oil field services

(G-9549)
GREAT LAKES COMPRESSION INC
3690 County Road 491 (49756-9310)
P.O. Box 945 (49756-0945)
PHONE.................................989 786-3788
Ron Bingham, *President*
Keith Koronak, *President*
EMP: 33
SALES (est): 1.6MM
SALES (corp-wide): 65.4MM **Publicly Held**
WEB: www.ngsgi.com
SIC: 1389 Oil field services

PA: Natural Gas Services Group, Inc.
508 W Wall St Ste 550
Midland TX 79701
432 262-2700

(G-9550)
HB CARBIDE COMPANY
4210 Doyle (49756-9083)
PHONE.................................989 786-4223
Norman B Lawton, *President*
Bradley L Lawton, *Vice Pres*
Richard Mc Leod, *Vice Pres*
Boyd E Moilanen, *Vice Pres*
Martin Woodhouse, *Vice Pres*
EMP: 100
SQ FT: 50,000
SALES (est): 24.9MM
SALES (corp-wide): 224.7MM **Privately Held**
WEB: www.hbcarbide.com
SIC: 3544 Special dies, tools, jigs & fixtures
PA: Star Cutter Co.
23461 Industrial Park Dr
Farmington Hills MI 48335
248 474-8200

(G-9551)
LEWISTON CONCRETE INC
6234 County Road 612 (49756-9287)
P.O. Box 448 (49756-0448)
PHONE.................................989 786-3722
Mike Van Coillie, *President*
Robert J Van Coillie, *Principal*
John Van Coillie, *Vice Pres*
EMP: 3 **EST:** 1971
SQ FT: 2,000
SALES (est): 388.9K **Privately Held**
SIC: 3273 Ready-mixed concrete

(G-9552)
LEWISTON SAND & GRAVEL INC
5122 County Road 612 (49756-7853)
P.O. Box 162 (49756-0162)
PHONE.................................989 786-2742
Tom May, *President*
EMP: 6 **EST:** 1959
SQ FT: 5,600
SALES (est): 890.7K **Privately Held**
SIC: 1794 3281 5999 5211 Excavation work; stone, quarrying & processing of own stone products; rock & stone specimens; sand & gravel

(G-9553)
N G S G I NATURAL GAS SER
3690 County Road 491 (49756-9310)
PHONE.................................989 786-3788
EMP: 3
SALES (est): 406.1K **Privately Held**
SIC: 3533 Oil & gas field machinery

(G-9554)
NORTHWEST HARDWOODS INC
3293 County Road 491 (49756-9227)
P.O. Box 599 (49756-0599)
PHONE.................................989 786-6100
Michael Avery, *Branch Mgr*
EMP: 36 **Privately Held**
SIC: 2421 Sawmills & planing mills, general
HQ: Northwest Hardwoods, Inc.
1313 Broadway Ste 300
Tacoma WA 98402

(G-9555)
STAR CUTTER CO
4210 Doyle (49756-9083)
PHONE.................................248 474-8200
Jeff Michael, *Chief Engr*
Lillian Kilgo, *Representative*
EMP: 5
SALES (corp-wide): 224.7MM **Privately Held**
SIC: 3541 Machine tools, metal cutting type
PA: Star Cutter Co.
23461 Industrial Park Dr
Farmington Hills MI 48335
248 474-8200

Lexington
Sanilac County

(G-9556)
CHARLES PHIPPS AND SONS LTD
6951 Lakeshore Rd (48450-9002)
PHONE.................................810 359-7141
Charles S Phipps Sr, *President*
Charles S Phipps Jr, *Vice Pres*
Stephan C Phipps, *Treasurer*
Andrew C Phipps, *Admin Sec*
EMP: 11
SQ FT: 3,200
SALES: 2MM **Privately Held**
SIC: 2511 Wood household furniture

(G-9557)
GIELOW PICKLES INC (PA)
5260 Main St (48450-9393)
PHONE.................................810 359-7680
Douglas R Gielow, *President*
Craig Gielow, *Vice Pres*
Marc Gielow, *Plant Mgr*
Lisa Disser, *Human Res Mgr*
Ken Karaba, *Natl Sales Mgr*
◆ **EMP:** 165
SQ FT: 30,000
SALES: 61.7MM **Privately Held**
WEB: www.gielowpickles.com
SIC: 2035 Cucumbers, pickles & pickle salting

(G-9558)
HURON INC (DH)
Also Called: Tube Assembly Manufacturing Co
6554 Lakeshore Rd (48450-9763)
PHONE.................................810 359-5344
Jerry Solar, *President*
Sally Bucholtz, *Engineer*
Ryan Jagoda, *Engineer*
Rick Cook, *CFO*
John Bowns, *Sales Mgr*
▲ **EMP:** 31
SQ FT: 122,000
SALES (est): 43.9MM
SALES (corp-wide): 22.3MM **Privately Held**
WEB: www.huroninc.com
SIC: 3498 3451 Fabricated pipe & fittings; screw machine products
HQ: Hdt Automotive Solutions Llc
38701 7 Mile Rd
Livonia MI 48152
810 359-5344

(G-9559)
PATTON TOOL AND DIE INC
Also Called: Mill Creek Industries
7185 Baker Rd (48450-9750)
P.O. Box 142 (48450-0142)
PHONE.................................810 359-5336
Dennis E Patton, *President*
David R Patton, *Vice Pres*
Sharon Patton, *Treasurer*
EMP: 10 **EST:** 1978
SQ FT: 7,200
SALES (est): 1.6MM **Privately Held**
WEB: www.cros-lex-chamber.com
SIC: 3089 3544 3469 Injection molding of plastics; injection molded finished plastic products; jigs & fixtures; metal stampings

(G-9560)
SUNRAISE INC
6547 Lakeshore Rd (48450-9761)
P.O. Box 9 (48450-0009)
PHONE.................................810 359-7301
Lindsey Rankin, *President*
Gary Rankin, *Admin Sec*
▲ **EMP:** 14
SQ FT: 18,000
SALES (est): 3.1MM **Privately Held**
WEB: www.sunraise.com
SIC: 3555 Printing presses

Lincoln
Alcona County

(G-9561)
ALCONA TOOL & MACHINE INC
325 N Lake St (48742)
PHONE..................989 736-8151
Mark Feldhiser, *General Mgr*
EMP: 4
SQ FT: 10,000
SALES (corp-wide): 7.3MM **Privately Held**
WEB: www.alconatool.com
SIC: 3544 Special dies & tools
PA: Alcona Tool & Machine, Inc.
3040 E Carbide Dr
Harrisville MI 48740
989 736-8151

(G-9562)
GREAT NORTHERN LUMBER MICH LLC
507 W Traverse Bay Rd (48742-9313)
PHONE..................989 736-6192
Joel Blohm, *Mng Member*
EMP: 27
SALES (est): 2.7MM **Privately Held**
SIC: 2421 2448 Custom sawmill; pallets, wood

(G-9563)
HILLMAN EXTRUSION TOOL INC
425 W Traverse Bay Rd (48742-9318)
P.O. Box 340 (48742-0340)
PHONE..................989 736-8010
Ted James, *President*
Joseph James, *Corp Secy*
Keith Kruttlin, *Vice Pres*
EMP: 3 EST: 1982
SQ FT: 6,600
SALES (est): 445.8K
SALES (corp-wide): 7.3MM **Privately Held**
WEB: www.alconatool.com
SIC: 3544 Special dies & tools
PA: Alcona Tool & Machine, Inc.
3040 E Carbide Dr
Harrisville MI 48740
989 736-8151

(G-9564)
HURON QUALITY MFG INC
481 State St (48742-9338)
P.O. Box 400 (48742-0400)
PHONE..................989 736-8121
Joseph James, *Treasurer*
Joseph P James, *Administration*
EMP: 8 EST: 2016
SALES (est): 356.4K **Privately Held**
SIC: 3599 Machine shop, jobbing & repair

(G-9565)
LINCOLN INDUSTRIES (PA)
202 S Second St (48742)
P.O. Box 388 (48742-0388)
PHONE..................989 736-6421
Gary H Becker, *President*
EMP: 2
SQ FT: 15,000
SALES (est): 1.1MM **Privately Held**
SIC: 3089 3479 Injection molding of plastics; identification cards, plastic; painting of metal products

(G-9566)
LINCOLN PRECISION CARBIDE INC
600 S 2nd St (48742)
P.O. Box 129 (48742-0129)
PHONE..................989 736-8113
Howard Stone, *President*
Kirk Sherwood, *Vice Pres*
Richard Weichel, *Vice Pres*
Steve Weichel, *Vice Pres*
EMP: 35
SQ FT: 12,000
SALES (est): 7.6MM **Privately Held**
WEB: www.lincolnprecision.com
SIC: 3541 3545 Machine tools, metal cutting type; machine tool accessories

(G-9567)
MODERN DIVERSIFIED PRODUCTS
202 S Second St (48742)
PHONE..................989 736-3430
Gary Becker, *President*
EMP: 5
SALES (est): 445.8K **Privately Held**
SIC: 3559 Automotive related machinery

(G-9568)
NORTHERN INDUSTRIAL WOOD INC
507 State St (48742-9313)
PHONE..................989 736-6192
Steve Rhone, *President*
EMP: 28
SALES: 3.6MM **Privately Held**
SIC: 2421 Lumber: rough, sawed or planed

(G-9569)
NORTHERN PRECISION INC
601 S Lake St (48742-9466)
P.O. Box 189 (48742-0189)
PHONE..................989 736-6322
Ralph E Diemond, *President*
Rita Kay Diemond, *Corp Secy*
EMP: 22
SQ FT: 4,800
SALES (est): 3.5MM **Privately Held**
SIC: 3544 3545 Special dies & tools; machine tool accessories

(G-9570)
QUALITY MANUFACTURING
481 W Traverse Bay Rd (48742-9338)
PHONE..................989 736-8121
Ronald Jilbert, *Partner*
Patricia Jilbert, *Partner*
EMP: 3
SQ FT: 3,500
SALES (est): 333.7K **Privately Held**
SIC: 3498 3496 Tube fabricating (contract bending & shaping); miscellaneous fabricated wire products

(G-9571)
WEISER METAL PRODUCTS INC
3431 E M 72 (48742)
P.O. Box 370 (48742-0370)
PHONE..................989 736-8151
Terry Lenard, *President*
Joe James, *Corp Secy*
Keith Kruttlin, *Vice Pres*
Ava Budreau, *Admin Sec*
EMP: 5
SALES (est): 485.3K **Privately Held**
SIC: 3493 Cold formed springs

Lincoln Park
Wayne County

(G-9572)
AMERICAN GRINDING MACHINING CO
1415 Dix Hwy (48146-1496)
PHONE..................313 388-0440
Wilbur C Thomas, *President*
William Northrup, *General Mgr*
EMP: 15 EST: 1955
SQ FT: 10,000
SALES (est): 1.3MM **Privately Held**
SIC: 3599 Grinding castings for the trade

(G-9573)
BASF CORPORATION
1512 John A Papalas Dr (48146-4708)
PHONE..................313 382-4250
John J Garrigan, *Manager*
EMP: 3
SALES (corp-wide): 71.7B **Privately Held**
WEB: www.basf.com
SIC: 2869 Industrial organic chemicals
HQ: Basf Corporation
100 Park Ave
Florham Park NJ 07932
973 245-6000

(G-9574)
BEST IMPRESSIONS
1412 Dix Hwy (48146-1402)
P.O. Box 615 (48146-0615)
PHONE..................313 389-1202
Fred Brown, *CEO*
EMP: 5
SALES (est): 272.1K **Privately Held**
SIC: 2759 Commercial printing

(G-9575)
CALDER BROS DAIRY INC
1020 Southfield Rd (48146-2604)
PHONE..................313 381-8858
William Calder, *President*
John Calder, *Vice Pres*
EMP: 30
SQ FT: 1,600
SALES (est): 996K **Privately Held**
SIC: 5812 5963 2026 Ice cream stands or dairy bars; milk delivery; fluid milk

(G-9576)
EVER-FLEX INC
1490 John A Papalas Dr (48146-1460)
PHONE..................313 389-2060
Merel Epstein, *President*
EMP: 30
SQ FT: 13,000
SALES (est): 4.5MM **Privately Held**
WEB: www.ever-flex.com
SIC: 3842 Surgical appliances & supplies

(G-9577)
FK FUEL INC
Also Called: Lincoln Park Fuel
1312 Fort St (48146-1815)
PHONE..................313 383-6005
John Kizy, *Principal*
EMP: 4
SQ FT: 2,000
SALES (est): 340K **Privately Held**
SIC: 2869 Fuels

(G-9578)
GARY PRINTING COMPANY INC
3330 Fort St (48146-3627)
P.O. Box 1006 (48146-1006)
PHONE..................313 383-3222
Russell Mathena, *President*
EMP: 3 EST: 1955
SQ FT: 3,000
SALES (est): 330.3K **Privately Held**
SIC: 2752 2759 Commercial printing, offset; letterpress printing

(G-9579)
GRAPHIC GEAR INC
Also Called: Accents Custom Printwear Plus
3018 Fort St (48146-2428)
PHONE..................734 283-3864
Julie Mascia, *President*
Vito Mascia, *Treasurer*
EMP: 7
SQ FT: 3,000
SALES (est): 281.8K **Privately Held**
WEB: www.accentscustomprintwear.com
SIC: 2339 2329 Uniforms, athletic: women's, misses' & juniors'; men's & boys' athletic uniforms

(G-9580)
LAS TORTUGAS PALLET CO
1583 Austin Ave (48146-2101)
PHONE..................313 283-3279
Carlos Ruiz, *Principal*
EMP: 3
SALES (est): 119.9K **Privately Held**
SIC: 2448 Wood pallets & skids

(G-9581)
LIBERTY BELL POWDR COATING LLC
Also Called: Liberty Powder Coating
1468 John A Papalas Dr (48146-1460)
PHONE..................586 557-6328
Timothy Garavaglia, *Mng Member*
EMP: 4 EST: 2012
SQ FT: 3,000
SALES: 300K **Privately Held**
SIC: 3479 Coating of metals & formed products

(G-9582)
OLIVO LLC
1609 Applewood Ave (48146-2130)
PHONE..................313 573-7202
Yeisson Olivio, *Principal*
Zulmarie Baez-Polanco, *Principal*
Luis M Verdejo Esperanza, *Vice Pres*
EMP: 3
SALES (est): 169.1K **Privately Held**
SIC: 5411 5499 2674 3484 Grocery stores; water: distilled mineral or spring; shopping bags: made from purchased materials; pistols or pistol parts, 30 mm. & below; food storage & trash bags (plastic)

(G-9583)
PIERINO FROZEN FOODS INC
1695 Southfield Rd (48146-2275)
PHONE..................313 928-0950
Gianni Guglielmetti, *President*
Maria Karizat, *Treasurer*
Silvana Villarreal, *Admin Sec*
▲ EMP: 44
SQ FT: 25,000
SALES (est): 12.1MM **Privately Held**
WEB: www.pierinofrozenfoods.com
SIC: 2038 2099 2098 Frozen specialties; packaged combination products: pasta, rice & potato; macaroni & spaghetti

(G-9584)
R P T CINCINNATI INC
1636 John A Papalas Dr (48146-1462)
PHONE..................313 382-5880
Tom Stefani, *President*
▲ EMP: 9 EST: 2001
SQ FT: 7,500
SALES: 2.5MM **Privately Held**
WEB: www.cincinnatirpt.com
SIC: 3541 Machine tool replacement & repair parts, metal cutting types

(G-9585)
SHAFTMASTERS
1668 John A Papalas Dr (48146-1462)
PHONE..................313 383-6347
Robert A Eppich, *President*
EMP: 4
SALES (est): 496.8K **Privately Held**
SIC: 3714 Drive shafts, motor vehicle

(G-9586)
TREND MILLWORK LLC
1300 John A Papalas Dr (48146-1356)
PHONE..................313 383-6300
David Muzzatti, *CEO*
Brian Zuccaro, *COO*
Luke Bonanni, *Vice Pres*
Matt Parent, *Plant Mgr*
Paul Urbano, *CFO*
EMP: 20
SQ FT: 15,000
SALES (est): 4.1MM **Privately Held**
WEB: www.trendmillwork.com
SIC: 2431 Millwork

(G-9587)
VENTURE LABELS USA INC
855 Southfield Rd (48146-2601)
PHONE..................313 928-2545
Alex Stevanov, *President*
Gary Stevanov, *General Mgr*
Angela Lamarre, *Vice Pres*
Jelica Stevanov, *Treasurer*
EMP: 3
SQ FT: 6,000
SALES (est): 300.8K **Privately Held**
WEB: www.venturelabels.com
SIC: 2679 Labels, paper: made from purchased material

(G-9588)
WILLIAM PENN SYSTEMS INC
Also Called: Harvest Tax Services
3510 Helen Ave (48146-3462)
PHONE..................313 383-8299
Petrina Arapakis, *President*
Bill Cantrell, *Partner*
Robert L Phillips, *Vice Pres*
Robert Phillips, *Vice Pres*
EMP: 3 EST: 1996
SALES (est): 314.7K **Privately Held**
SIC: 3571 Electronic computers

GEOGRAPHIC SECTION

(G-9589)
WRIGHT & FILIPPIS INC
Also Called: Fordson Health Care
4050 Fort St (48146-4123)
PHONE.................................313 386-3330
Steve Filippis, *Manager*
EMP: 20
SALES (corp-wide): 51.4MM **Privately Held**
WEB: www.firsttoserve.com
SIC: 5999 3842 3841 Medical apparatus & supplies; surgical appliances & supplies; surgical & medical instruments
PA: Wright & Filippis, Inc.
2845 Crooks Rd
Rochester Hills MI 48309
248 829-8292

Linden
Genesee County

(G-9590)
FARNELL CONTRACTING INC
3355 Lahring Rd (48451-9434)
PHONE.................................810 714-3421
Doug Farnell, *President*
Sheila Morley, *Project Mgr*
Sally Spencer, *Project Mgr*
Kathleen M Farnell, *Treasurer*
Kathy Farnell, *Treasurer*
EMP: 14
SALES (est): 2.7MM **Privately Held**
SIC: 2521 Cabinets, office: wood

(G-9591)
GREEN BRIDGE TECH INTL INC (PA)
15091 Poberezny Ct (48451-9161)
PHONE.................................810 410-8177
Mike Roth, *CEO*
Len Baxter, *President*
EMP: 8
SQ FT: 2,000
SALES (est): 1.9MM **Privately Held**
WEB: www.hissusa.com
SIC: 3812 Search & navigation equipment

(G-9592)
HI-TRAC INDUSTRIES INC
5161 Harp Dr (48451-9060)
PHONE.................................810 625-7193
Joseph W Hood, *Vice Pres*
EMP: 4
SQ FT: 15,000
SALES (est): 260K **Privately Held**
SIC: 3842 Crutches & walkers; canes, orthopedic

(G-9593)
MCINTYRE SOFTWATER SERVICE
Also Called: Sunshine Water Conditioner
1014 N Bridge St (48451-8821)
PHONE.................................810 735-5778
James Mc Intyre, *President*
EMP: 23 **EST:** 1960
SQ FT: 11,000
SALES (est): 3.1MM **Privately Held**
WEB: www.mcintyrewater.com
SIC: 3589 7389 5499 Water filters & softeners, household type; water softener service; water: distilled mineral or spring

(G-9594)
MID AMERICA COMMODITIES LLC
7420 Majestic Woods Dr (48451-8836)
PHONE.................................810 936-0108
Katarzyna Chapple,
Brad Chapple,
▲ **EMP:** 5
SQ FT: 2,000
SALES (est): 650K **Privately Held**
SIC: 2038 Dinners, frozen & packaged

(G-9595)
ROKAN CORP
5929 Deerfield Indus Dr (48451-8303)
PHONE.................................810 735-9170
Rod Kannisto, *President*
EMP: 5
SQ FT: 10,000
SALES (est): 736K **Privately Held**
WEB: www.rokanreels.com
SIC: 2655 Reels (fiber), textile: made from purchased material

(G-9596)
SOFTAIRE DIFFUSERS INC
4198 Neal Ct (48451-8463)
PHONE.................................810 730-1668
Gary Hodges, *President*
Garry Hodges, *Manager*
EMP: 4
SALES (est): 330K **Privately Held**
WEB: www.softairediffusers.com
SIC: 3822 1711 Air flow controllers, air conditioning & refrigeration; plumbing, heating, air-conditioning contractors

(G-9597)
STRAATSMA ASSOCIATES INC
110 S Bridge St (48451-7706)
P.O. Box 312 (48451-0312)
PHONE.................................810 735-6957
Michael T Murray, *President*
EMP: 3
SALES (est): 495.6K **Privately Held**
WEB: www.straatsmainc.com
SIC: 3535 Conveyors & conveying equipment

Linwood
Bay County

(G-9598)
LINWOOD BAKERY
Also Called: Judy's Famous Pies
11 S Huron Rd (48634-9489)
PHONE.................................989 697-4430
Judy Davis, *Partner*
EMP: 4
SALES (est): 296.2K **Privately Held**
SIC: 2051 Pies, bakery: except frozen

(G-9599)
WILLIAMS CHEESE CO
Also Called: Amish Country Cheese
998 N Huron Rd (48634-9219)
P.O. Box 249 (48634-0249)
PHONE.................................989 697-4492
Michael Williams, *CEO*
EMP: 50 **EST:** 1944
SQ FT: 16,000
SALES (est): 21.6MM **Privately Held**
WEB: www.pinconning.com
SIC: 5143 2022 Cheese; cheese, natural & processed

Litchfield
Hillsdale County

(G-9600)
BASIS MACHINING LLC
8998 Anderson Rd (49252)
P.O. Box 43 (49252-0043)
PHONE.................................517 542-3818
Jason Stych,
EMP: 3
SQ FT: 3,000
SALES: 181K **Privately Held**
SIC: 3599 3549 Machine shop, jobbing & repair; wiredrawing & fabricating machinery & equipment, ex. die

(G-9601)
FINISHING TOUCH INC
Also Called: F T I
191 Simpson Dr (49252-9601)
PHONE.................................517 542-3581
Thomas A Van Auken, *President*
Darlene D Van Auken, *Vice Pres*
Treva McNair, *Purchasing*
EMP: 23
SQ FT: 24,000
SALES (est): 2.4MM **Privately Held**
WEB: www.ftipaint.com
SIC: 1721 3471 Industrial painting; finishing, metals or formed products

(G-9602)
HARVARD CLOTHING COMPANY
411 Marshall St (49252-9703)
P.O. Box 330 (49252-0330)
PHONE.................................517 542-2986
Richard Barker Jr, *President*
EMP: 18 **EST:** 1926
SQ FT: 24,000
SALES (est): 2.1MM **Privately Held**
WEB: www.harvardclothing.com
SIC: 2329 2339 Men's & boys' sportswear & athletic clothing; jackets (suede, leatherette, etc.), sport: men's & boys'; women's & misses' outerwear; jackets, untailored: women's, misses' & juniors'; jogging & warmup suits: women's, misses' & juniors'

(G-9603)
HI-LEX AMERICA INCORPORATED
152 Simpson Dr (49252-9601)
PHONE.................................517 542-2955
Katsuaki Tokuhrio, *Branch Mgr*
EMP: 7 **Privately Held**
WEB: www.hci.hi-lex.com
SIC: 3496 Miscellaneous fabricated wire products
HQ: Hi-Lex America, Incorporated
5200 Wayne Rd
Battle Creek MI 49037
269 968-0781

(G-9604)
HI-LEX CONTROLS INCORPORATED (DH)
152 Simpson Dr (49252-9601)
PHONE.................................517 542-2955
Tom Strickland, *President*
Tomoharu Otane, *COO*
Randy Seegert, *Maintenance Dir*
Gavin Carr, *Mfg Spvr*
Steve Bowen, *Purch Mgr*
▲ **EMP:** 12
SQ FT: 160,000
SALES (est): 49.2MM **Privately Held**
SIC: 3714 Motor vehicle electrical equipment
HQ: Tsk Of America, Inc.
152 Simpson Dr
Litchfield MI 49252
517 542-2955

(G-9605)
JEMS OF LITCHFIELD INC
174 Simpson Dr (49252-9601)
P.O. Box 449 (49252-0449)
PHONE.................................517 542-5367
Phil Reneau, *President*
Doud Hawkins, *Principal*
David Palmer, *Treasurer*
EMP: 18
SQ FT: 31,000
SALES (est): 7.6MM **Privately Held**
WEB: www.jemsoflitchfield.com
SIC: 3599 3498 3315 3544 Machine & other job shop work; tube fabricating (contract bending & shaping); steel wire & related products; forms (molds), for foundry & plastics working machinery

(G-9606)
JOHAN VAN DE WEERD CO INC
Also Called: Jvdw
916 Anderson Rd (49252-9776)
PHONE.................................517 542-3817
Johan Van De Weerd, *CEO*
Philip Wilson, *President*
EMP: 9
SALES (est): 1.4MM **Privately Held**
WEB: www.jvdw.com
SIC: 3545 Boring machine attachments (machine tool accessories)

(G-9607)
METALDYNE PWRTRAIN CMPNNTS INC
Also Called: Litchfield Mfg Facility
917 Anderson Rd (49252-9776)
PHONE.................................517 542-5555
Tom Lehman, *Manager*
EMP: 210
SALES (corp-wide): 7.2B **Publicly Held**
SIC: 3519 3714 Parts & accessories, internal combustion engines; motor vehicle parts & accessories
HQ: Metaldyne Powertrain Components, Inc.
1 Dauch Dr
Detroit MI 48211
313 758-2000

(G-9608)
METALDYNE PWRTRAIN CMPNNTS INC
Also Called: Litchfield Mfg Facility
917 Anderson Rd (49252-9776)
P.O. Box 177 (49252-0177)
PHONE.................................517 542-5555
EMP: 16
SALES (corp-wide): 7.2B **Publicly Held**
SIC: 3714 Motor vehicle parts & accessories
HQ: Metaldyne Powertrain Components, Inc.
1 Dauch Dr
Detroit MI 48211
313 758-2000

(G-9609)
MICHIGAN REBUILD & AUTOMTN INC
Also Called: M R A
7460 Herring Rd (49252)
PHONE.................................517 542-6000
Timothy Galloway, *President*
▼ **EMP:** 16
SQ FT: 17,500
SALES (est): 4.6MM **Privately Held**
WEB: www.mraweb.com
SIC: 3599 7699 Custom machinery; industrial machinery & equipment repair

(G-9610)
NEWCO INDUSTRIES LLC
Also Called: Nex Solutions
900 Anderson Rd (49252-9776)
P.O. Box 177 (49252-0177)
PHONE.................................517 542-0105
Rodney W Norris,
EMP: 45
SALES (est): 18.9MM **Privately Held**
SIC: 3441 Fabricated structural metal

(G-9611)
TENNECO AUTOMOTIVE OPER CO INC
929 Anderson Rd (49252-9776)
PHONE.................................517 542-5511
Bob Weyer, *Accounting Mgr*
Doud Minix, *Manager*
EMP: 204
SQ FT: 132,000
SALES (corp-wide): 11.7B **Publicly Held**
WEB: www.tenneco-automotive.com
SIC: 3714 Mufflers (exhaust), motor vehicle
HQ: Tenneco Automotive Operating Company, Inc.
500 N Field Dr
Lake Forest IL 60045
847 482-5000

(G-9612)
TSK OF AMERICA INC (HQ)
Also Called: Hi-Lex
152 Simpson Dr (49252-9601)
PHONE.................................517 542-2955
Brad Semp, *Partner*
Cindy Cummings, *Buyer*
John Steingass, *Engineer*
Brian Wild, *Engineer*
John Wyllie, *Engineer*
EMP: 13
SALES (est): 201.5MM **Privately Held**
SIC: 3357 Automotive wire & cable, except ignition sets: nonferrous

(G-9613)
WELLS EQUIPMENT SALES INC
534 Homer Rd (49252)
P.O. Box 208 (49252-0208)
PHONE.................................517 542-2376
Steven A Wells, *President*
Clifton F Wells, *Vice Pres*
Frances E Wells, *Treasurer*
Karen K Wells, *Admin Sec*

Livonia - Wayne County (G-9614)

EMP: 19 **EST:** 1952
SQ FT: 16,000
SALES: 13MM **Privately Held**
SIC: 5999 3524 5511 Farm equipment & supplies; lawn & garden tractors & equipment; trucks, tractors & trailers: new & used

Livonia
Wayne County

(G-9614)
+VANTAGE CORPORATION
12651 Newburgh Rd (48150-1001)
PHONE.................................734 432-5055
Timothy M White, *President*
◆ **EMP:** 43
SQ FT: 20,000
SALES: 13.5MM **Privately Held**
SIC: 3569 Assembly machines, non-metalworking

(G-9615)
3715-11TH STREET CORP
Also Called: Alpha Group of Companies, The
32711 Glendale St (48150-1611)
PHONE.................................734 523-1000
Nicholas Strumbos, *President*
Chuck Dardas, *COO*
EMP: 9
SALES (est): 941.8K **Privately Held**
SIC: 3465 Automotive stampings

(G-9616)
4-M INDUSTRIES INCORPORATED
33855 Capitol St (48150-1566)
PHONE.................................734 762-7200
Allen Marsh, *Manager*
EMP: 15
SALES (corp-wide): 15.2MM **Privately Held**
SIC: 3599 Machine shop, jobbing & repair
PA: 4-M Industries, Incorporated
35300 Glendale St
Livonia MI 48150
734 762-7200

(G-9617)
4-M INDUSTRIES INCORPORATED (PA)
35300 Glendale St (48150-1243)
PHONE.................................734 762-7200
Allen Marsh, *President*
Christopher Marsh, *Vice Pres*
Steven Marsh, *Vice Pres*
Roger Wyatt, *Plant Mgr*
Kim Delaforce, *Buyer*
EMP: 68
SQ FT: 38,000
SALES (est): 15.2MM **Privately Held**
WEB: www.4mindustries.com
SIC: 3599 Machine shop, jobbing & repair

(G-9618)
A & R PACKING CO INC
34165 Autry St (48150-1333)
PHONE.................................734 422-2060
Larry Kornacki, *President*
Ken Schwarz, *Vice Pres*
EMP: 40
SQ FT: 50,000
SALES (est): 7MM **Privately Held**
SIC: 2013 2011 Smoked meats from purchased meat; cured meats from meat slaughtered on site

(G-9619)
A B M TOOL & DIE INC
38281 Schoolcraft Rd D (48150-5000)
PHONE.................................734 432-6060
EMP: 5
SQ FT: 3,000
SALES: 1.5MM **Privately Held**
SIC: 3544 Mfg Dies/Tools/Jigs/Fixtures

(G-9620)
A&G CORPORATE HOLDINGS LLC
Also Called: Trigon Metal Products
12725 Inkster Rd (48150-2216)
PHONE.................................734 513-3488
Stephen Gordon, *President*
EMP: 8 **EST:** 2016
SQ FT: 22,000
SALES (est): 777K **Privately Held**
SIC: 3499 Machine bases, metal

(G-9621)
A123 SYSTEMS LLC
28200 Plymouth Rd (48150-2398)
PHONE.................................734 466-6521
Mujeeb Ijaz, *Principal*
EMP: 222
SALES (corp-wide): 2.9B **Privately Held**
WEB: www.a123systems.com
SIC: 3691 Batteries, rechargeable
HQ: A123 Systems Llc
27101 Cabaret Dr
Novi MI 48377
248 412-9249

(G-9622)
AA ANDERSON & CO INC
35569 Industrial Rd (48150-1233)
PHONE.................................734 432-9800
Dan Ely, *Branch Mgr*
EMP: 7
SALES (corp-wide): 29.4MM **Privately Held**
SIC: 3561 5063 5084 Pumps & pumping equipment; electrical apparatus & equipment; pumps & pumping equipment
PA: A.A. Anderson & Co., Inc.
21365 Gateway Ct
Brookfield WI 53045
262 784-3340

(G-9623)
AACTUS INC
12671 Richfield Ct (48150-1062)
PHONE.................................734 425-1212
John Haapala, *President*
Rayleen Morgan, *Bookkeeper*
EMP: 9
SQ FT: 8,000
SALES (est): 4.2MM **Privately Held**
SIC: 5085 5072 5113 5198 Industrial supplies; staples; pressure sensitive tape; closures, paper & disposable plastic; paints, varnishes & supplies; personal safety equipment; container, packaging & boxboard

(G-9624)
ABC ACQUISITION COMPANY LLC
Also Called: Aetna Bearing Company
31778 Enterprise Dr (48150-1960)
PHONE.................................734 335-4083
Kal Beibas, *Mng Member*
Joe Galvin, *Technical Staff*
James Trauscht,
▲ **EMP:** 50
SALES (est): 9.6MM **Privately Held**
SIC: 3562 Ball bearings & parts

(G-9625)
ACCESS HEATING & COOLING INC
39001 Ann Arbor Trl (48150-4545)
P.O. Box 510681 (48151-6681)
PHONE.................................734 464-0566
Kathen Hans, *President*
Edsel D Sloan Jr, *Treasurer*
Kathleen Sloan, *Admin Sec*
EMP: 1
SALES: 11MM **Privately Held**
SIC: 1711 3444 Mechanical contractor; warm air heating & air conditioning contractor; sheet metalwork

(G-9626)
ACCURATE MACHINED SERVICE INC
Also Called: Accurate Machine Service
30948 Industrial Rd (48150-2024)
PHONE.................................734 421-4660
Frank J Kowal, *President*
Andrew Kowal, *Vice Pres*
EMP: 6
SQ FT: 20,000
SALES (est): 530K **Privately Held**
SIC: 3541 Grinding machines, metalworking

(G-9627)
ACORN INDUSTRIES INC (PA)
Also Called: Contamination Control
11844 Brookfield St (48150-1701)
PHONE.................................734 261-2940
Philip Austin, *President*
Philip R Austin, *President*
Edward Schiller, *General Mgr*
Philip J Austin, *Vice Pres*
Gynell Rock, *Engineer*
EMP: 60
SQ FT: 25,000
SALES (est): 9.3MM **Privately Held**
WEB: www.acornind.com
SIC: 8742 3471 Industrial hygiene consultant; training & development consultant; plating & polishing

(G-9628)
ADVANCED ELASTOMERS CORP
34481 Industrial Rd (48150-1307)
PHONE.................................734 458-4194
Chris Campbell, *President*
James Pruitt, *Vice Pres*
EMP: 8
SQ FT: 5,000
SALES: 1.5MM **Privately Held**
SIC: 2821 Plastics materials & resins

(G-9629)
ADVANTAGE LASER INC
35684 Veronica St (48150-1204)
PHONE.................................734 367-9936
Michael Lubig, *President*
Brenda Brock, *Treasurer*
EMP: 4
SQ FT: 13,600
SALES (est): 540K **Privately Held**
WEB: www.advantage-laser.com
SIC: 3444 Sheet metalwork

(G-9630)
AERO SYSTEMS
13475 Wayne Rd (48150-1245)
PHONE.................................253 269-3000
Jennifer Whales, *Chairman*
EMP: 12
SALES (est): 685.9K **Privately Held**
SIC: 3669 Emergency alarms

(G-9631)
AEROFFICIENT LLC
12001 Farmington Rd (48150-1725)
PHONE.................................847 784-8100
James A Reiman, *CEO*
Herbert Golding, *President*
EMP: 3
SALES (est): 233.7K **Privately Held**
SIC: 3713 Truck bodies & parts

(G-9632)
AIR FILTER & EQUIPMENT INC
Also Called: Exfil
37007 Industrial Rd (48150-1146)
PHONE.................................734 261-1860
Fred Marshall, *Branch Mgr*
EMP: 5
SALES (corp-wide): 5.9MM **Privately Held**
WEB: www.airfilterequipment.com
SIC: 3564 Filters, air: furnaces, air conditioning equipment, etc.
PA: Air Filter & Equipment, Inc
4110 S 9th St
Kalamazoo MI 49009
269 544-2444

(G-9633)
AIRFLOW SCIENCES EQUIPMENT LLC
12190 Hubbard St (48150-1737)
PHONE.................................734 525-0300
Andrew Banka, *Vice Pres*
Robert Mudry,
EMP: 29
SALES (est): 2.3MM **Privately Held**
SIC: 3823 Flow instruments, industrial process type

(G-9634)
ALL AMERICAN EMBROIDERY INC
Also Called: All American Essentials
31600 Plymouth Rd (48150-1930)
PHONE.................................734 421-9292
Sandeep Narang, *President*
EMP: 10
SALES: 3.6MM **Privately Held**
SIC: 3953 3993 3552 Screens, textile printing; signs & advertising specialties; embroidery machines

(G-9635)
ALLIE BROTHERS INC
Also Called: Allie Brothers Men's Wear
20295 Middlebelt Rd (48152-2001)
PHONE.................................248 477-4434
Hassen J Allie, *President*
Robert Allie, *CFO*
EMP: 14 **EST:** 1971
SQ FT: 7,500
SALES: 2.7MM **Privately Held**
WEB: www.alliebrothers.com
SIC: 5699 5611 2311 Uniforms; men's & boys' clothing stores; suits, men's; clothing accessories: men's & boys'; men's & boys' uniforms

(G-9636)
ALPHA COATINGS INC
Also Called: Alpha Group
32711 Glendale St (48150-1611)
PHONE.................................734 523-9000
Nicholas Strumbos, *President*
EMP: 22
SALES (est): 3.1MM **Privately Held**
WEB: www.alphausa.com
SIC: 3479 Coating of metals & formed products

(G-9637)
ALPHA STEEL TREATING INC
32969 Glendale St (48150-1613)
PHONE.................................734 523-1035
George Strumbos, *Ch of Bd*
Nicholas Strumbos, *President*
Stanley Martinez, *Exec VP*
Catherine Strumbos, *Vice Pres*
EMP: 45
SQ FT: 80,000
SALES (est): 4MM **Privately Held**
SIC: 3398 Metal heat treating

(G-9638)
ALTA EQUIPMENT HOLDINGS INC (PA)
13211 Merriman Rd (48150-1826)
PHONE.................................248 449-6700
Steven Greenawalt, *CEO*
Rob Chiles, *President*
Jeremy Cionca, *President*
Derek Vantichelt, *President*
Latrice Levy, *General Mgr*
EMP: 26
SALES (est): 110.6MM **Privately Held**
SIC: 3537 5084 Industrial trucks & tractors; lift trucks & parts

(G-9639)
ALTON BORING CO INC
Also Called: Cowens & Sons
30950 Industrial Rd Ste A (48150-2059)
PHONE.................................734 522-9595
Alton Cowen, *President*
EMP: 3
SQ FT: 2,900
SALES: 300K **Privately Held**
SIC: 3599 Machine shop, jobbing & repair

(G-9640)
AM TECH SERVICES LLC
29647 Oakley St (48154-3758)
PHONE.................................734 762-7209
EMP: 3
SALES (est): 123.2K **Privately Held**
SIC: 2891 Adhesives & sealants

(G-9641)
AMANDA MANUFACTURING LLC
Also Called: Msd Stamping
34450 Industrial Rd (48150-1308)
PHONE.................................740 385-9380
Dewey Johnson, *Plant Mgr*
Robert Grufchow, *Mng Member*

▲ = Import ▼ = Export
◆ = Import/Export

GEOGRAPHIC SECTION — Livonia - Wayne County (G-9665)

EMP: 50
SQ FT: 35,000
SALES (est): 14MM
SALES (corp-wide): 100MM **Privately Held**
SIC: 3452 Bolts, nuts, rivets & washers
PA: Deshler Group, Inc.
    34450 Industrial Rd
    Livonia MI 48150
    734 525-9100

(G-9642) AMERI-PRINT INC
Also Called: Saturn Printing & Mailing
35175 Plymouth Rd (48150-1422)
PHONE 734 427-2887
Duane Macdonald, *CEO*
Graham Currie, *Principal*
Melanie Leeson, *Controller*
EMP: 25
SQ FT: 9,000
SALES (est): 4.2MM **Privately Held**
WEB: www.saturnprinting.com
SIC: 2752 Commercial printing, offset

(G-9643) AMERICAN HOUSEHOLD INC
Also Called: Sunbeam
33067 Industrial Rd (48150-1619)
P.O. Box 860, Freeport IL (61032-0860)
PHONE 601 296-5000
EMP: 4
SALES (corp-wide): 8.6B **Publicly Held**
WEB: www.sunbeam.com
SIC: 3631 Barbecues, grills & braziers (outdoor cooking)
HQ: American Household, Inc.
    2381 Nw Executive Ctr Dr
    Boca Raton FL 33431
    561 912-4100

(G-9644) AMERICAN RING MANUFACTURING
Also Called: Artco Mfg
35955 Veronica St (48150-1207)
PHONE 734 402-0426
Gary Howell, *President*
Robert H Morissey, *Principal*
Jack Morrissey, *Vice Pres*
EMP: 15
SQ FT: 15,000
SALES (est): 2.6MM **Privately Held**
WEB: www.americanringmfg.com
SIC: 3493 Steel springs, except wire

(G-9645) AMERICAN ROLL SHUTTER AWNG CO
Also Called: Maygrove Awning Co.
12700 Merriman Rd (48150-1818)
PHONE 734 422-7110
Michael Falahee, *President*
▲ **EMP:** 45
SQ FT: 17,000
SALES (est): 5.2MM **Privately Held**
SIC: 2394 3444 3442 5714 Awnings, fabric: made from purchased materials; awnings, sheet metal; metal doors, sash & trim; drapery & upholstery stores

(G-9646) AMI LIVONIA LLC
36930 Industrial Rd (48150-1135)
PHONE 734 428-3132
Vincent Henderson, *CEO*
EMP: 75
SQ FT: 100,000
SALES: 7MM
SALES (corp-wide): 25.2MM **Privately Held**
SIC: 3465 Automotive stampings
PA: Gallant Steel, Inc.
    17951 W Austin Rd
    Manchester MI

(G-9647) AMTRADE SYSTEMS INC
12885 Wayne Rd (48150-1244)
PHONE 734 522-9500
Joe Glaser, *President*
◆ **EMP:** 5
SQ FT: 10,000
SALES (est): 1.7MM **Privately Held**
WEB: www.amtrade-systems.com
SIC: 5063 1796 7692 Generators; installing building equipment; welding repair

(G-9648) ANDERSEN CORPORATION
37720 Amrhein Rd (48150-1012)
PHONE 734 237-1052
Rob Mannooch, *Branch Mgr*
EMP: 600
SALES (corp-wide): 2.8B **Privately Held**
SIC: 2431 Windows, wood; doors, wood
PA: Andersen Corporation
    100 4th Ave N
    Bayport MN 55003
    651 264-5150

(G-9649) ANTONIOS LEATHER EXPERTS
12409 Stark Rd (48150-1552)
PHONE 734 762-5000
Lea Antonios, *Principal*
EMP: 7
SALES (est): 540.5K **Privately Held**
SIC: 2819 Tanning agents, synthetic inorganic

(G-9650) AP IMPRESSIONS INC (PA)
Also Called: Personal Tuch By AP Imprssions
17360 N Laurel Park Dr (48152-3916)
PHONE 734 464-8009
Paul Ahn, *President*
EMP: 5
SQ FT: 700
SALES: 120K **Privately Held**
WEB: www.kpcmd.org
SIC: 2759 5199 2791 2752 Screen printing; general merchandise, non-durable; typesetting; commercial printing, lithographic; automotive & apparel trimmings; pleating & stitching

(G-9651) APPLIED PROCESS INC (HQ)
Also Called: AP Southridge
12202 Newburgh Rd (48150-1046)
PHONE 734 464-8000
Harold Karp, *CEO*
Steve Metz, *Vice Pres*
John Wagner, *Vice Pres*
Jerry Hayward, *Plant Mgr*
Bob Prusky, *Plant Mgr*
▲ **EMP:** 39
SQ FT: 49,900
SALES (est): 5.5MM **Privately Held**
WEB: www.appliedprocess.com
SIC: 3398 Metal heat treating

(G-9652) ARGENT LIMITED
11966 Brookfield St (48150-1736)
PHONE 734 427-5533
EMP: 7 **EST:** 1977
SQ FT: 15,000
SALES (est): 1.3MM **Privately Held**
SIC: 2992 Mfg Lubricating Oils/Greases

(G-9653) ASAO LLC
Also Called: American Shortening and Oil Co
34115 Industrial Rd (48150-1305)
PHONE 734 522-6333
Anthony Gavol, *President*
William W Brown, *President*
Vivian Brown, *Corp Secy*
Ron Manni, *Buyer*
Hugo Coronado, *QC Mgr*
EMP: 10 **EST:** 1936
SALES (est): 1.4MM **Privately Held**
SIC: 2079 2077 5145 Shortening & other solid edible fats; animal & marine fats & oils; confectionery

(G-9654) ASSA ABLOY ENTRANCE SYSTEMS US
38291 Schoolcraft Rd # 103 (48150-5042)
PHONE 734 462-2348
Shaun Pransch, *General Mgr*
EMP: 20
SALES (corp-wide): 9.3B **Privately Held**
SIC: 3699 1796 Door opening & closing devices, electrical; installing building equipment
HQ: Assa Abloy Entrance Systems Us Inc.
    1900 Airport Rd
    Monroe NC 28110
    704 290-5520

(G-9655) ATEQ CORPORATION (HQ)
Also Called: Ateq Leak Detecting Service
35980 Industrial Rd (48150-1274)
PHONE 734 838-3100
Guy Dewailly, *President*
Carl Hardt, *Sales Engr*
Shaun Hadley, *Sales Staff*
Zak McGraw, *Sales Staff*
Heidi Franklin, *Marketing Mgr*
▲ **EMP:** 15
SQ FT: 5,200
SALES (est): 7MM
SALES (corp-wide): 38.1MM **Privately Held**
WEB: www.atequsa.com
SIC: 3829 Measuring & controlling devices
PA: Ateq
    Zone Industrielle Des Dames
    Les Clayes-Sous-Bois 78340
    130 801-020

(G-9656) ATEQ TPMS TOOLS LC
35990 Industrial Rd (48150)
PHONE 734 838-3104
Guy Dewailly, *President*
EMP: 15
SALES: 7MM
SALES (corp-wide): 38.1MM **Privately Held**
SIC: 3823 Pressure measurement instruments, industrial
HQ: Ateq Corporation
    35980 Industrial Rd
    Livonia MI 48150
    734 838-3100

(G-9657) ATS ASSEMBLY AND TEST INC
Assembly Technology & Test
12841 Stark Rd (48150-1525)
PHONE 734 266-4713
David Osborne, *Project Mgr*
Greg Munn, *Opers Mgr*
Cheryl Hulbert, *Senior Buyer*
Paul Chamberlain, *Engineer*
Amanda Harshbarger, *Engineer*
EMP: 60
SQ FT: 90,000
SALES (corp-wide): 947.9MM **Privately Held**
WEB: www.assembly-testww.com
SIC: 8711 3549 3829 3536 Designing: ship, boat, machine & product; metalworking machinery; measuring & controlling devices; hoists, cranes & monorails
HQ: Ats Assembly And Test, Inc.
    1 Ats Dr
    Wixom MI 48393
    937 222-3030

(G-9658) B/E AEROSPACE INC
34073 Schoolcraft Rd (48150-1313)
PHONE 734 425-6200
Amin J Khoury, *Ch of Bd*
EMP: 4
SALES (corp-wide): 66.5B **Publicly Held**
SIC: 2531 3728 3647 Seats, aircraft; aircraft parts & equipment; aircraft lighting fixtures
HQ: B/E Aerospace, Inc.
    1400 Corporate Center Way
    Wellington FL 33414
    561 791-5000

(G-9659) BACKOS ENGINEERING CO
17310 Farmington Rd (48152-3158)
PHONE 734 513-0020
Sanford Backos, *President*
EMP: 4
SQ FT: 1,600
SALES (est): 300K **Privately Held**
SIC: 3561 8711 Pumps & pumping equipment; mechanical engineering

(G-9660) BASF CORPORATION
B A S F Colors & Colorants
13000 Levan Rd (48150-1228)
PHONE 734 591-5560
Bill Depopompolo, *Branch Mgr*
EMP: 68
SQ FT: 20,000
SALES (corp-wide): 71.7B **Privately Held**
WEB: www.basf.com
SIC: 2869 2899 2821 Industrial organic chemicals; chemical preparations; plastics materials & resins
HQ: Basf Corporation
    100 Park Ave
    Florham Park NJ 07932
    973 245-6000

(G-9661) BCS AUTOMOTIVE INTERFACE SOLUT
12000 Tech Center Dr (48150-2121)
PHONE 734 855-3297
EMP: 6 **Privately Held**
SIC: 3714 Motor vehicle parts & accessories
HQ: Bcs Automotive Interface Solutions Us, Llc
    5676 Industrial Park Rd
    Winona MN 55987
    507 494-2813

(G-9662) BEAVER AEROSPACE & DEFENSE INC (HQ)
11850 Mayfield St (48150-1708)
PHONE 734 853-5003
Frederick Gagne, *President*
Stephane Arsenault, *Principal*
Gilles Labbe, *Vice Pres*
William Michalski, *Vice Pres*
Matt Seng, *Production*
◆ **EMP:** 92 **EST:** 1952
SQ FT: 82,200
SALES: 30MM
SALES (corp-wide): 365.8MM **Privately Held**
WEB: www.beaver-online.com
SIC: 3452 3593 3812 3728 Screws, metal; fluid power cylinders & actuators; acceleration indicators & systems components, aerospace; gears, aircraft power transmission; aircraft maintenance & repair services
PA: Heroux-Devtek Inc
    1111 Rue Saint-Charles O Bureau 600
    Longueuil QC J4K 5
    450 679-3330

(G-9663) BECK & BOYS CUSTOM APPAREL
33650 5 Mile Rd (48154-2866)
PHONE 734 458-4015
Kitty Beck, *President*
EMP: 5
SALES (est): 392K **Privately Held**
SIC: 2395 Embroidery products, except schiffli machine

(G-9664) BELL AND HOWELL LLC
Also Called: Sensible Technologies
12794 Currie Ct (48150-1109)
PHONE 734 421-1727
EMP: 4
SALES (corp-wide): 1.4B **Privately Held**
SIC: 7372 Prepackaged Software Services
HQ: Bell And Howell, Llc
    3791 S Alston Ave
    Durham NC 27713

(G-9665) BIMBO BAKERIES USA INC
13280 Newburgh Rd (48150-1006)
PHONE 734 953-5741
Peter Bimbo, *Branch Mgr*
EMP: 18 **Privately Held**
SIC: 2051 Bakery: wholesale or wholesale/retail combined
HQ: Bimbo Bakeries Usa, Inc
    255 Business Center Dr # 200
    Horsham PA 19044
    215 347-5500

Livonia - Wayne County (G-9666)

(G-9666)
BODYCOTE THERMAL PROC INC
31888 Glendale St (48150-1827)
PHONE................................734 427-6814
Kenneth Smith, *General Mgr*
EMP: 10
SALES (corp-wide): 935.8MM **Privately Held**
SIC: 3398 Metal heat treating
HQ: Bodycote Thermal Processing, Inc.
12700 Park Central Dr # 700
Dallas TX 75251
214 904-2420

(G-9667)
BODYCOTE THERMAL PROC INC
31888 Glendale St (48150-1827)
PHONE................................734 427-6814
Biji George, *Manager*
EMP: 10
SALES (corp-wide): 935.8MM **Privately Held**
SIC: 3398 Metal heat treating
HQ: Bodycote Thermal Processing, Inc.
12700 Park Central Dr # 700
Dallas TX 75251
214 904-2420

(G-9668)
BORGWARNER POWDERED METALS INC (HQ)
32059 Schoolcraft Rd (48150-1833)
PHONE................................734 261-5322
Timothy M Manganello, *CEO*
Art Barrows, *Vice Pres*
David Sommers, *Electrical Engi*
Dave Hall, *VP Human Res*
EMP: 37
SQ FT: 65,000
SALES (est): 21.6MM
SALES (corp-wide): 10.5B **Publicly Held**
SIC: 3714 3568 3463 3462 Motor vehicle transmissions, drive assemblies & parts; power transmission equipment; nonferrous forgings; iron & steel forgings
PA: Borgwarner Inc.
3850 Hamlin Rd
Auburn Hills MI 48326
248 754-9200

(G-9669)
BOWER TOOL & MANUFACTURING INC
27481 Schoolcraft Rd (48150-2201)
PHONE................................734 522-0444
Lois Bower, *President*
Robbie Bower, *Corp Secy*
William Bower, *Vice Pres*
EMP: 4
SQ FT: 4,000
SALES (est): 754.3K **Privately Held**
SIC: 3545 Gauges (machine tool accessories)

(G-9670)
BRENNER ORTHTIC PRSTHETIC LABS
Also Called: Michigan Institute For Elect
32975 8 Mile Rd (48152-1337)
PHONE................................248 615-0600
Carl D Brenner, *President*
Teressa M Brenner, *Admin Sec*
EMP: 3 **EST:** 1944
SALES: 22.1K **Privately Held**
SIC: 5999 3842 Orthopedic & prosthesis applications; braces, orthopedic

(G-9671)
BUCKINGHAM TOOL CORP
11915 Market St (48150-1163)
PHONE................................734 591-2333
Matt Dixon, *President*
Robin Dixon, *Treasurer*
EMP: 15 **EST:** 1941
SQ FT: 10,000
SALES (est): 2.2MM **Privately Held**
WEB: www.buckinghamtool.com
SIC: 3544 Special dies & tools

(G-9672)
C E S INDUSTRIES INC
12751 Inkster Rd (48150-2216)
PHONE................................734 425-0522
Charles E Strong, *President*
Frances Strong, *Vice Pres*
EMP: 35 **EST:** 1965
SQ FT: 6,000
SALES (est): 3.7MM **Privately Held**
SIC: 3599 Machine shop, jobbing & repair

(G-9673)
CAN-AM ENGINEERED PRODUCTS
30850 Industrial Rd (48150-2022)
PHONE................................734 427-2020
Michael H Bunnell, *President*
Carol Secco, *Bookkeeper*
EMP: 3
SQ FT: 10,000
SALES (est): 559.7K **Privately Held**
WEB: www.canamengineered.com
SIC: 3563 5013 Spraying outfits: metals, paints & chemicals (compressor); automotive supplies & parts

(G-9674)
CAPARO VEHICLE COMPONENTS INC (PA)
Also Called: Grand River Fabricating
13060 Merriman Rd (48150-1816)
PHONE................................734 513-2859
Colin Scott, *President*
Don Piper, *CFO*
Mike Dustmann, *Admin Sec*
▼ **EMP:** 64 **EST:** 1973
SQ FT: 202,000
SALES (est): 21.6MM **Privately Held**
WEB: www.polynorm.com
SIC: 3465 Body parts, automobile: stamped metal

(G-9675)
CARBOLINE COMPANY
32820 Capitol St (48150-1706)
PHONE................................734 525-2824
Richard Preston, *Branch Mgr*
EMP: 20
SALES (corp-wide): 5.5B **Publicly Held**
SIC: 2851 Lacquers, varnishes, enamels & other coatings
HQ: Carboline Company
2150 Schuetz Rd Fl 1
Saint Louis MO 63146
314 644-1000

(G-9676)
CARBON TOOL & MANUFACTURING
12735 Inkster Rd (48150-2216)
PHONE................................734 422-0380
Daniel Kochanek, *President*
EMP: 11
SQ FT: 6,000
SALES: 1MM **Privately Held**
WEB: www.carbon-tool.com
SIC: 3599 Machine shop, jobbing & repair

(G-9677)
CARLSON TECHNOLOGY INC
Also Called: Pitstop Engineering
30945 8 Mile Rd (48152-1605)
PHONE................................248 476-0013
Dennis Carlson, *President*
EMP: 4
SQ FT: 1,000
SALES (est): 340.8K **Privately Held**
WEB: www.carlsontechnology.com
SIC: 8731 3842 Medical research, commercial; respiratory protection equipment, personal

(G-9678)
CDP DIAMOND PRODUCTS INC
Also Called: Construction Diamond Products
11919 Globe St (48150-1133)
P.O. Box 51727 (48151-5727)
PHONE................................734 591-1041
James Dillon, *Vice Pres*
Jim Dillon, *Vice Pres*
Craig Campbell, *Sales Staff*
EMP: 22
SQ FT: 14,020
SALES (est): 4.4MM **Privately Held**
WEB: www.cdpdiamond.com
SIC: 3545 3291 Machine tool accessories; abrasive products

(G-9679)
CELANO PRECISION MFG INC
30016 Richland St (48150-3051)
P.O. Box 51448 (48151-5448)
PHONE................................734 748-1744
Peter Celano, *President*
Cindy Celano, *Vice Pres*
EMP: 4
SALES (est): 96.6K **Privately Held**
SIC: 3599 Machine shop, jobbing & repair

(G-9680)
CENTRAL ADMXTURE PHRM SVCS INC
Also Called: C A P S
37497 Schoolcraft Rd (48150-1007)
PHONE................................734 953-6760
Margaret Byrd, *Warehouse Mgr*
Glenn Pangrazzi, *Manager*
EMP: 25
SALES (corp-wide): 2.6MM **Privately Held**
WEB: www.capspharmacy.com
SIC: 2834 5122 Pharmaceutical preparations; pharmaceuticals
HQ: Central Admixture Pharmacy Services, Inc.
2525 Mcgaw Ave
Irvine CA 92614

(G-9681)
CENTURY INSTRUMENT COMPANY
11865 Mayfield St (48150-1707)
PHONE................................734 427-0340
Azeir O Sigurdsson, *President*
Roger Bingham, *Principal*
Franklin Nau, *Principal*
Azeir Sigurdsson, *CIO*
Nancy Bowers, *Admin Sec*
▲ **EMP:** 33 **EST:** 1950
SQ FT: 19,000
SALES (est): 6.5MM **Privately Held**
WEB: www.centuryinstrument.com
SIC: 3491 3822 Pressure valves & regulators, industrial; temperature controls, automatic

(G-9682)
CENTURY TRUSS
17199 N Laurel Park Dr # 402 (48152-7905)
PHONE................................248 486-4000
Ronald Bergeron, *Principal*
EMP: 3
SALES (est): 378.6K **Privately Held**
SIC: 2439 Trusses, wooden roof

(G-9683)
CJG LLC
Also Called: Golden Refrigerant
31800 Industrial Rd (48150-1820)
PHONE................................734 793-1400
Carl Grolle, *Mng Member*
EMP: 19
SQ FT: 101,000
SALES (est): 5.8MM **Privately Held**
WEB: www.goldenrefrigerant.com
SIC: 2869 1799 Freon; antenna installation

(G-9684)
CLASSIC CONTAINER CORPORATION
32432 Capitol St (48150-1703)
PHONE................................734 853-3000
Craig Beaudoin, *General Mgr*
EMP: 50
SQ FT: 75,000
SALES (est): 5.8MM
SALES (corp-wide): 2.5B **Privately Held**
WEB: www.prattindustries.com
SIC: 3086 2653 2675 2671 Packaging & shipping materials, foamed plastic; corrugated & solid fiber boxes; die-cut paper & board; packaging paper & plastics film, coated & laminated; paperboard mills; wood containers
PA: Pratt Industries, Inc.
1800 Sarasot Bus Pkwy Ne C
Conyers GA 30013
770 918-5678

(G-9685)
COGSDILL TOOL PRODUCTS INC
Also Called: E-Z Burr Tool
11757 Globe St (48150-1133)
PHONE................................734 744-4500
EMP: 9
SALES (corp-wide): 10.8MM **Privately Held**
SIC: 3545 Cutting tools for machine tools
PA: Cogsdill Tool Products, Inc.
1001 Guion Dr
Lugoff SC 29078
803 438-4000

(G-9686)
COMPLETE SERVICES LLC
32401 8 Mile Rd (48152-1301)
PHONE................................248 470-8247
Johnny R Thompson, *Administration*
EMP: 10
SALES (est): 381.8K **Privately Held**
SIC: 8742 8331 2731 2741 Management consulting services; job training & vocational rehabilitation services; book publishing; miscellaneous publishing; language school

(G-9687)
CONTOUR MACHINING INC
11837 Brookfield St (48150-1701)
PHONE................................734 525-4877
Frank Schlampp, *President*
EMP: 10
SQ FT: 4,000
SALES (est): 1.2MM **Privately Held**
SIC: 3599 Machine shop, jobbing & repair

(G-9688)
COOPER-STANDARD AUTOMOTIVE INC
11820 Globe St (48150-1171)
P.O. Box 8034, Novi (48376-8034)
PHONE................................734 542-6300
Karl Deline, *Manager*
EMP: 93
SALES (corp-wide): 3.6B **Publicly Held**
WEB: www.cooperstandard.com
SIC: 3714 Motor vehicle parts & accessories
HQ: Cooper-Standard Automotive Inc.
39550 Orchard Hill Pl
Novi MI 48375
248 596-5900

(G-9689)
CORELED SYSTEMS LLC
31478 Industrial Rd # 400 (48150-1839)
PHONE................................734 516-2060
Stephen Godwin, *Design Engr*
Derek Mallory,
EMP: 4
SALES (est): 321.5K **Privately Held**
SIC: 3648 Lighting equipment

(G-9690)
CORRUGATED PRATT
32432 Capitol St (48150-1703)
PHONE................................734 853-3030
Brian McPheely, *CEO*
EMP: 4 **EST:** 2010
SALES (est): 344.1K **Privately Held**
SIC: 2653 Corrugated & solid fiber boxes

(G-9691)
COUNTRY FRESH LLC
Also Called: Embest
31770 Enterprise Dr (48150-1960)
PHONE................................734 261-7980
Bruce Evans, *Manager*
EMP: 250 **Publicly Held**
SIC: 2026 Fluid milk
HQ: Country Fresh, Llc
2711 N Haskell Ave # 3400
Dallas TX 75204
616 243-0173

GEOGRAPHIC SECTION — Livonia - Wayne County (G-9720)

(G-9692)
CREATIVE AUTOMATION SOLUTIONS
34552 Dover Ave (48150-3659)
PHONE..................313 790-4848
Ahmad Khreis, *Owner*
EMP: 6
SALES: 155K **Privately Held**
SIC: 3711 Automobile assembly, including specialty automobiles

(G-9693)
CROWNE GROUP LLC
17199 N Laurel Park Dr # 322 (48152-2679)
PHONE..................734 855-4512
EMP: 4
SALES: 391.7K **Privately Held**
SIC: 3714 Motor vehicle parts & accessories

(G-9694)
CURBELL PLASTICS INC
28455 Schoolcraft Rd # 5 (48152-2238)
PHONE..................734 513-0531
Dave Barney, *Purch Agent*
Tim Cassani, *Manager*
EMP: 8
SALES (corp-wide): 216.5MM **Privately Held**
WEB: www.curbellplastics.com
SIC: 5162 3669 3842 Plastics products; plastics sheets & rods; plastics materials; plastics film; intercommunication systems, electric; surgical appliances & supplies
HQ: Curbell Plastics, Inc.
7 Cobham Dr
Orchard Park NY 14127

(G-9695)
CUSTOM METAL PRODUCTS CORP
12283 Levan Rd (48150-1499)
PHONE..................734 591-2500
James C Veale, *President*
Charles W Veale, *Vice Pres*
EMP: 7 EST: 1945
SQ FT: 10,000
SALES (est): 1MM **Privately Held**
SIC: 3444 Sheet metal specialties, not stamped

(G-9696)
CUTEX INC
12496 Globe St (48150-1144)
PHONE..................734 953-8908
Boguslaw Gierek, *President*
EMP: 6
SQ FT: 5,600
SALES (est): 926.7K **Privately Held**
SIC: 3541 Machine tools, metal cutting type

(G-9697)
D MAC INDUSTRIES INC
31492 Glendale St (48150-1834)
PHONE..................734 536-7754
Dennis Macdonald, *President*
EMP: 10
SALES (est): 1.2MM **Privately Held**
SIC: 3463 Automotive forgings, nonferrous

(G-9698)
DAVID H BOSLEY & ASSOCIATES
Also Called: Insty-Prints
16329 Middlebelt Rd (48154-3360)
PHONE..................734 261-8390
David H Bosley, *President*
Beverly Bosley, *Admin Sec*
EMP: 3
SQ FT: 1,800
SALES (est): 460.4K **Privately Held**
SIC: 2752 2789 Commercial printing, lithographic; bookbinding & related work

(G-9699)
DAVISON-RITE PRODUCTS CO
12921 Stark Rd (48150-1525)
PHONE..................734 513-0505
Arthur G Krol, *President*
George German, *Plant Mgr*
Art Krol, *Finance*
EMP: 34 EST: 1947
SQ FT: 23,000
SALES (est): 5.2MM **Privately Held**
WEB: www.davison-rite.com
SIC: 3451 3545 3541 Screw machine products; machine tool accessories; machine tools, metal cutting type

(G-9700)
DB COMMUNICATIONS INC
32922 Brookside Cir (48152-1419)
PHONE..................800 692-8200
David Bartnick, *President*
EMP: 11
SQ FT: 2,500
SALES: 2MM **Privately Held**
SIC: 3661 Headsets, telephone

(G-9701)
DEARBORN LITHOGRAPH INC
12380 Globe St (48150-1181)
PHONE..................734 464-4242
Russell Masura, *President*
Judith Masura, *Vice Pres*
EMP: 21
SQ FT: 17,250
SALES (est): 4.6MM **Privately Held**
WEB: www.dearbornlithograph.com
SIC: 2752 2796 Commercial printing, offset; platemaking services

(G-9702)
DEBURRING COMPANY
12690 Newburgh Rd (48150-1002)
PHONE..................734 542-9800
Robert E Van Schoick Jr, *President*
EMP: 12
SQ FT: 13,000
SALES (est): 1.3MM **Privately Held**
WEB: www.deburringcompany.com
SIC: 3471 Cleaning & descaling metal products

(G-9703)
DELTA 6 LLC
Also Called: Delta Six
20341 Parker St (48150-1363)
PHONE..................248 778-6414
Nabil Nouman, *Principal*
EMP: 4 EST: 2014
SALES (est): 254K **Privately Held**
SIC: 3949 7389 Camping equipment & supplies; shooting equipment & supplies, general; target shooting equipment;

(G-9704)
DELTA GEAR INC
36251 Schoolcraft Rd (48150-1216)
PHONE..................734 525-8000
Robert Sakuta, *President*
Ken McConnell, *Mfg Mgr*
Michael Pierz, *Chief Engr*
Thomas Acker, *Marketing Staff*
▲ EMP: 37
SQ FT: 20,000
SALES (est): 8.7MM **Privately Held**
WEB: www.delrecorp.com
SIC: 3599 Machine shop, jobbing & repair

(G-9705)
DELTA RESEARCH CORPORATION
32971 Capitol St (48150-1705)
PHONE..................734 261-6400
Robert Sakuta, *President*
Bob Sakuta, *President*
Tony Werschky, *Partner*
Don McHugh, *Vice Pres*
Scott Sakuta, *Manager*
▲ EMP: 50 EST: 1952
SQ FT: 43,000
SALES (est): 12.2MM **Privately Held**
WEB: www.delrecorp.com
SIC: 3714 Motor vehicle parts & accessories

(G-9706)
DESHLER GROUP INC (PA)
34450 Industrial Rd (48150-1308)
PHONE..................734 525-9100
Robert Gruschow, *President*
Mark Brodie, *Vice Pres*
Wilbur Darst, *Vice Pres*
Damian Fernandez, *Vice Pres*
Gerald A Gentile, *Vice Pres*
EMP: 150 EST: 1968
SQ FT: 100,000
SALES (est): 100MM **Privately Held**
WEB: www.deshlergroup.com
SIC: 3496 3599 Miscellaneous fabricated wire products; custom machinery

(G-9707)
DESIGN USA INC
36117 Schoolcraft Rd (48150-1216)
PHONE..................734 233-8677
John Mulgrew, *Principal*
Bradley Springer, *Office Mgr*
EMP: 3
SALES (est): 396.4K
SALES (corp-wide): 893.1K **Privately Held**
SIC: 3714 Motor vehicle parts & accessories
PA: Des Group (Pty) Ltd
26 - 32 Palmgate Cres Southgate Business Park
Amanzimtoti KN 4126
319 143-120

(G-9708)
DETROIT QULTY BRUSH MFG CO INC
Also Called: Dqb Industries
32165 Schoolcraft Rd (48150-1833)
PHONE..................734 525-5660
Donald Weinbaum, *President*
Wim Demees, *Safety Mgr*
Kathy Hamill, *Buyer*
Bev Martin, *Controller*
Diane Deckard, *Accounting Dir*
▲ EMP: 81 EST: 1919
SQ FT: 100,000
SALES (est): 13.4MM **Privately Held**
WEB: www.dqb.com
SIC: 3991 Brushes, household or industrial; push brooms

(G-9709)
DEWSBURY MANUFACTURING COMPANY
12502 Globe St (48150-1144)
P.O. Box 627, Trenton (48183-0627)
PHONE..................734 839-6376
Richard Wykle, *Manager*
EMP: 3
SALES (est): 196K **Privately Held**
SIC: 3999 Manufacturing industries

(G-9710)
DIAMOND AUTOMATION LTD
32235 Industrial Rd (48150-1836)
PHONE..................734 838-7138
Jeffrey Bucher, *President*
Andrew Sieczka, *Vice Pres*
◆ EMP: 4
SQ FT: 62,000
SALES: 400K **Privately Held**
WEB: www.diamondautomation.com
SIC: 3549 3535 Assembly machines, including robotic; conveyors & conveying equipment

(G-9711)
DIECRAFTERS INC
27487 Schoolcraft Rd (48150-2201)
PHONE..................734 425-8000
Richard C Johnson, *President*
Bruce Martin, *Corp Secy*
Mark A Gdowski, *Vice Pres*
EMP: 3
SQ FT: 2,000
SALES (est): 250K **Privately Held**
SIC: 3544 Dies, steel rule

(G-9712)
DIGITAL DIE SOLUTIONS INC
13281 Merriman Rd (48150-1815)
PHONE..................734 542-2222
Frank Barkman, *Director*
EMP: 12
SALES: 700K **Privately Held**
SIC: 3542 Die casting & extruding machines

(G-9713)
DIPSOL OF AMERICA INC
Also Called: Dipsol Chemicals
34005 Schoolcraft Rd (48150-1313)
PHONE..................734 367-0530
Cara Mahlawi, *President*
Adam Walsh, *Engineer*
Jason Boyce, *Technical Staff*
Jamie Flesch, *Technical Staff*
Steven Kokotovich, *Technician*
▲ EMP: 26
SQ FT: 26,000
SALES (est): 7.1MM **Privately Held**
WEB: www.dipsolamerica.com
SIC: 3559 8711 Metal finishing equipment for plating, etc.; pollution control engineering
HQ: Dipsol Chemicals Co., Ltd.
2-7-12, Yaesu
Chuo-Ku TKY 104-0

(G-9714)
DON DUFF REBUILDING
31130 Industrial Rd (48150-2034)
PHONE..................734 522-7700
▲ EMP: 5
SQ FT: 8,000
SALES (est): 665K **Privately Held**
SIC: 3694 Mfg Engine Electrical Equipment

(G-9715)
DPM MANUFACTURING LLC
35451 Schoolcraft Rd (48150-1222)
PHONE..................248 349-6375
▲ EMP: 15
SALES (est): 2.8MM **Privately Held**
SIC: 3544 3452 3451 Mfg Dies/Tools/Jigs/Fixtures Mfg Bolts/Screws/Rivets Mfg Screw Machine Products

(G-9716)
DYNAMIC SOFTWARE GROUP LLC
33006 7 Mile Rd (48152-1358)
PHONE..................734 716-0925
Joseph M Gomez,
EMP: 10
SALES (est): 311.8K **Privately Held**
SIC: 3571 Electronic computers

(G-9717)
E & R BINDERY SERVICE INC
Also Called: Ink On Paper Printing
37477 Schoolcraft Rd (48150-1007)
PHONE..................734 464-7954
Howard V Bolitho, *President*
Daniel Flavian, *Corp Secy*
Raymond Connell, *Vice Pres*
EMP: 5
SQ FT: 2,700
SALES: 300K **Privately Held**
SIC: 2789 Trade binding services

(G-9718)
E D P TECHNICAL SERVICES INC
36704 Commerce St (48150-1164)
PHONE..................734 591-9176
Richard Bezerko, *President*
Dedra Egler, *Purchasing*
Margaret M Bezerko, *Admin Sec*
EMP: 3
SALES (est): 237.1K **Privately Held**
SIC: 2741 8711 8734 Technical manual & paper publishing; engineering services; automobile proving & testing ground

(G-9719)
EATON STEEL CORPORATION
Also Called: Hercules Drawn Steel Div
38901 Amrhein Rd (48150-1042)
PHONE..................248 398-3434
Mark Goodman, *Branch Mgr*
EMP: 70
SALES (corp-wide): 215MM **Privately Held**
SIC: 5051 3312 Structural shapes, iron or steel; bars & bar shapes, steel, cold-finished: own hot-rolled
PA: Eaton Steel Corporation
10221 Capital St
Oak Park MI 48237
248 398-3434

(G-9720)
ECLIPSE PRINT EMPORIUM INC
32753 8 Mile Rd (48152-1302)
PHONE..................248 477-8337
Domingo Nieto, *President*
EMP: 4

Livonia - Wayne County (G-9721)   GEOGRAPHIC SECTION

SALES (est): 422.1K **Privately Held**
WEB: www.eclipsedetroit.com
SIC: 2759 5199 Screen printing; advertising specialties

(G-9721)
ECOGRANITE LLC
20495 Melvin St (48152-1832)
PHONE 248 820-9196
David Popp,
EMP: 3 EST: 2011
SALES (est): 188.5K **Privately Held**
SIC: 3281 Granite, cut & shaped

(G-9722)
EIS INC
Also Called: Egeler Industrial Services
31478 Industrial Rd # 100 (48150-1839)
PHONE 734 266-6500
Timothy A Westerdale, *President*
P Vernon Links, *Vice Pres*
Zona Faye Davis, *Treasurer*
EMP: 15
SQ FT: 10,000
SALES (est): 1.7MM **Privately Held**
SIC: 1381 Drilling oil & gas wells

(G-9723)
ELECTRODYNAMICS INC
31091 Schoolcraft Rd (48150-2029)
PHONE 734 422-5420
Andy Low, *President*
Chris Tucker, *Technician*
▲ EMP: 5
SQ FT: 1,700
SALES (est): 804.2K **Privately Held**
WEB: www.electrodynam.com
SIC: 3694 7389 3825 Battery charging generators, automobile & aircraft; design, commercial & industrial; battery testers, electrical

(G-9724)
ELECTRONIC DESIGN & PACKG CO
Also Called: EDP Company
36704 Commerce St (48150-1164)
PHONE 734 591-9176
Richard Bezerko, *President*
Margaret M Bezerko, *Vice Pres*
Chris Henning, *Technician*
EMP: 18
SQ FT: 19,000
SALES (est): 3.7MM **Privately Held**
WEB: www.edpcompany.com
SIC: 3812 3699 Detection apparatus: electronic/magnetic field, light/heat; electrical equipment & supplies

(G-9725)
ELRING KLINGER SEALING SYSTEMS
35955 Veronica St (48150-1207)
PHONE 734 542-1522
Henry Horbestel, *Principal*
EMP: 3
SALES (est): 143.2K **Privately Held**
SIC: 3465 Automotive stampings

(G-9726)
ELSIE INC
Also Called: Blind Xpress
12752 Stark Rd Ste 1 (48150-1594)
PHONE 734 421-8844
Lawrence Carollo, *President*
EMP: 14
SQ FT: 23,000
SALES (est): 3.8MM **Privately Held**
SIC: 5023 2591 Venetian blinds; vertical blinds; venetian blinds; blinds vertical; mini blinds

(G-9727)
ENTERPRISE SERVICES LLC
12200 Middlebelt Rd (48150-2454)
PHONE 734 523-6525
Melanie Relitz, *Manager*
EMP: 17
SALES (corp-wide): 11.5B **Publicly Held**
WEB: www.eds.com
SIC: 7374 7371 6321 6159 Data processing service; custom computer programming services; accident & health insurance; machinery & equipment finance leasing; prepackaged software

HQ: Perspecta Enterprise Solutions Llc
13600 Eds Dr A3s
Herndon VA 20171
703 245-9675

(G-9728)
ENVIRONMENTAL PRODUCTS CORP
30421 8 Mile Rd (48152-1701)
PHONE 248 471-4770
Gool Santchurn, *Branch Mgr*
Bob Jones, *Manager*
EMP: 5
SALES (corp-wide): 745.2K **Privately Held**
SIC: 3559 Recycling machinery
HQ: Environmental Products Corporation
99 Great Hill Rd
Naugatuck CT 06770
203 720-4059

(G-9729)
EPI PRINTERS INC
13305 Wayne Rd (48150-1245)
PHONE 734 261-9400
Patrick Kolodziejczak, *Vice Pres*
John Zagada, *Plant Mgr*
Pat Kolodziejczak, *Manager*
Dale Umphrey, *Manager*
EMP: 80
SQ FT: 30,000
SALES (corp-wide): 198.2MM **Privately Held**
WEB: www.epiinc.com
SIC: 2752 3993 2759 2732 Advertising posters, lithographed; periodicals, lithographed; signs & advertising specialties; commercial printing; book printing
PA: Epi Printers, Inc.
5404 Wayne Rd
Battle Creek MI 49037
800 562-9733

(G-9730)
ERA TOOL & ENGINEERING CO
35551 Schoolcraft Rd (48150-1249)
PHONE 810 227-3509
Douglas E Thorwall, *President*
Daniel E Thorwall, *Treasurer*
EMP: 10
SQ FT: 18,000
SALES (est): 1.1MM **Privately Held**
WEB: www.eratool.com
SIC: 3544 Special dies & tools; jigs & fixtures

(G-9731)
EXCEL GRAPHICS
31647 8 Mile Rd (48152-4217)
PHONE 248 442-9390
Ruth Dober, *Owner*
EMP: 4
SQ FT: 2,400
SALES: 250K **Privately Held**
SIC: 2752 Commercial printing, offset; publication printing, lithographic

(G-9732)
F & G TOOL COMPANY
11863 Brookfield St (48150-1701)
PHONE 734 261-0022
Finn Gammerath, *President*
Rick Henegar, *Admin Sec*
EMP: 9
SQ FT: 6,000
SALES: 1MM **Privately Held**
SIC: 3599 Machine shop, jobbing & repair

(G-9733)
FABULOUS PRINTING INC
15076 Middlebelt Rd (48154-4033)
PHONE 734 422-5555
Kevin Solomon, *President*
EMP: 5
SALES (est): 1.2MM **Privately Held**
SIC: 2759 Commercial printing

(G-9734)
FAIRFIELD INVESTMENT CO
Also Called: Lazer Images
32738 Barkley St (48154-3517)
PHONE 734 427-4141
David D Berger, *President*
▲ EMP: 4
SQ FT: 1,900

SALES (est): 511.5K **Privately Held**
WEB: www.lazerimages.com
SIC: 3993 Letters for signs, metal

(G-9735)
FARMINGTON CABINET COMPANY
30795 8 Mile Rd (48152-1601)
PHONE 248 476-2666
Fax: 248 476-6438
EMP: 17
SQ FT: 11,500
SALES (est): 1.7MM **Privately Held**
SIC: 2434 5712 Mfg & Ret Of Wood Kitchen Cabinets

(G-9736)
FL TOOL HOLDERS LLC
36010 Industrial Rd (48150-1200)
PHONE 734 591-0134
Edward Vella, *President*
EMP: 20 EST: 1965
SQ FT: 15,500
SALES (est): 4.3MM
SALES (corp-wide): 988.5K **Privately Held**
WEB: www.fltoolholders.com
SIC: 3545 Tool holders
HQ: Marposs Corporation
3300 Cross Creek Pkwy
Auburn Hills MI 48326
248 370-0404

(G-9737)
FLINT GROUP NORTH AMERICA LLC
17177 N Laurel Park Dr # 300 (48152-2693)
PHONE 734 781-4600
William B Miller, *CEO*
Gerardo Orta, *General Mgr*
Greg Rodulfo, *General Mgr*
Mike Buystedt, *Vice Pres*
Michael Kellen, *Vice Pres*
◆ EMP: 125
SALES (est): 2.1B
SALES (corp-wide): 177.9K **Privately Held**
WEB: www.flintink.com
SIC: 2893 Printing ink
HQ: Flint Group Us Llc
17177 N Laurel Park Dr # 300
Livonia MI 48152
734 781-4600

(G-9738)
FLINT GROUP PACKAGING INKS
17177 N Laurel Park Dr # 300 (48152-2693)
PHONE 513 619-2085
Pierre-Marie De Leener, *Chairman*
EMP: 6
SALES (est): 196.5K
SALES (corp-wide): 1.3MM **Privately Held**
SIC: 2396 Printing & embossing on plastics fabric articles
PA: Flint Group Packaging Inks North America Holdings Llc
17177 N Laurel Park Dr # 300
Livonia MI 48152
734 781-4600

(G-9739)
FLINT GROUP PACKAGING INKS (PA)
17177 N Laurel Park Dr # 300 (48152-2693)
PHONE 734 781-4600
Peter M Schreck,
EMP: 0
SALES (est): 1.3MM **Privately Held**
SIC: 6719 2396 Investment holding companies, except banks; printing & embossing on plastics fabric articles

(G-9740)
FLINT GROUP US LLC (DH)
Also Called: Cdr Pigments & Dispersions
17177 N Laurel Park Dr # 300 (48152-2693)
PHONE 734 781-4600
Michelle Domas, *Vice Pres*
Jeff Almaraz, *Accounts Mgr*
Dave Cofer, *Manager*

Corina Freier, *Manager*
Marie Luetmer, *Manager*
◆ EMP: 300 EST: 1920
SALES (est): 2.4B
SALES (corp-wide): 177.9K **Privately Held**
WEB: www.flintink.com
SIC: 2865 2893 Color pigments, organic; printing ink
HQ: Flint Group Germany Gmbh
Sieglestr. 25
Stuttgart 70469
711 981-60

(G-9741)
FLINT GROUP US LLC
Also Called: Flint Group Print Media N Amer
17177 N Laurel Park Dr # 300 (48152-2693)
PHONE 734 781-4600
EMP: 1400
SALES (corp-wide): 177.9K **Privately Held**
SIC: 2759 3069 5169 Flexographic printing; printers' rolls & blankets: rubber or rubberized fabric; chemicals & allied products
HQ: Flint Group Us Llc
17177 N Laurel Park Dr # 300
Livonia MI 48152
734 781-4600

(G-9742)
FLO-TEC INC
13033 Fairlane St (48150-1325)
PHONE 734 455-7655
Timothy Yarnell, *President*
Dawn Bratcher, *Purch Mgr*
Wes Yarnell, *Marketing Staff*
EMP: 65 EST: 1983
SALES (est): 9MM **Privately Held**
SIC: 2399 Hammocks, fabric: made from purchased materials

(G-9743)
FORD MOTOR COMPANY
36200 Plymouth Rd (48150-1498)
PHONE 734 377-4954
Madhu Deme, *Engineer*
David Hinman, *Engineer*
Mark Panetta, *Engineer*
Stephen Patrone, *Engineer*
Mike Schmitz, *Engineer*
EMP: 3209
SQ FT: 3,300,000
SALES (corp-wide): 160.3B **Publicly Held**
WEB: www.ford.com
SIC: 5511 3714 Automobiles, new & used; motor vehicle parts & accessories
PA: Ford Motor Company
1 American Rd
Dearborn MI 48126
313 322-3000

(G-9744)
FORD MOTOR COMPANY
11871 Middlebelt Rd (48150-2310)
PHONE 734 523-3000
Js Volpi, *Engineer*
David McTague, *Branch Mgr*
EMP: 1516
SALES (corp-wide): 160.3B **Publicly Held**
WEB: www.ford.com
SIC: 5511 3713 3714 6153 Automobiles, new & used; truck & bus bodies; motor vehicle parts & accessories; financing of dealers by motor vehicle manufacturers organ.; financing: automobiles, furniture, etc., not a deposit bank; passenger car leasing
PA: Ford Motor Company
1 American Rd
Dearborn MI 48126
313 322-3000

(G-9745)
FUSION STRATEGIES LLC
15658 Brookfield St (48154-3006)
PHONE 734 776-1734
Sean Jahn, *Principal*
EMP: 3
SALES (est): 83.9K **Privately Held**
SIC: 3999 Manufacturing industries

▲ = Import ▼ =Export
◆ =Import/Export

GEOGRAPHIC SECTION
Livonia - Wayne County (G-9773)

(G-9746)
G M PARIS BAKERY INC
28418 Joy Rd (48150-4133)
PHONE..................734 425-2060
Daniel Domzalski, *President*
Michael Domzalski, *Vice Pres*
EMP: 23 **EST:** 1956
SQ FT: 3,200
SALES (est): 855.8K **Privately Held**
SIC: 5461 2051 Cakes; bread, cake & related products

(G-9747)
GAGS AND GAMES INC (DH)
Also Called: Man Store, The
35901 Veronica St (48150-1207)
PHONE..................734 591-1717
John Mc Intire, *Co-President*
Christopher Bearss, *Co-President*
▲ **EMP:** 35
SQ FT: 34,400
SALES (est): 56.1MM
SALES (corp-wide): 2.4B **Publicly Held**
SIC: 2389 5947 Costumes; party favors
HQ: Party City Holdings Inc.
80 Grasslands Rd
Elmsford NY 10523
973 453-8600

(G-9748)
GALLAGHER FIRE EQUIPMENT CO
30895 8 Mile Rd (48152-1600)
PHONE..................248 477-1540
Alan Ross, *President*
Roger Bebow, *Human Res Dir*
EMP: 36
SQ FT: 5,000
SALES: 1.8MM **Privately Held**
WEB: www.fire-equipment.com
SIC: 7389 5999 7382 1711 Fire extinguisher servicing; fire protection service other than forestry or public; fire extinguishers; safety supplies & equipment; fire alarm maintenance & monitoring; fire sprinkler system installation; sprinkler systems, fire: automatic

(G-9749)
GARCO GASKETS INC
11865 Globe St (48150-1133)
PHONE..................734 728-4912
Garabet S Arslanian, *President*
▲ **EMP:** 5
SQ FT: 4,000
SALES (est): 1MM **Privately Held**
SIC: 3053 Gaskets, all materials

(G-9750)
GEMPHIRE THERAPEUTICS INC
17199 N Laurel Park Dr # 401 (48152-7905)
PHONE..................734 245-1700
Charles L Bisgaier, *Ch of Bd*
Steven Gullans, *President*
Seth Reno, *Ch Credit Ofcr*
EMP: 18 **EST:** 2008
SQ FT: 5,300
SALES (est): 2.7MM **Privately Held**
SIC: 2834 Pharmaceutical preparations

(G-9751)
GEOLEAN USA LLC
11998 Merriman Rd (48150-1919)
PHONE..................313 859-9780
Luman Temby, *President*
EMP: 15 **EST:** 2016
SALES (est): 440.3K **Privately Held**
SIC: 8742 3599 Management consulting services; custom machinery

(G-9752)
GIV LLC
Also Called: Sofpoint
38705 7 Mile Rd Ste 405 (48152-3990)
PHONE..................248 467-6852
Mark R Slotta,
Chad Slotta,
Sandra Slotta,
EMP: 3 **EST:** 1999
SALES (est): 330K **Privately Held**
WEB: www.sofpoint.com
SIC: 3069 Molded rubber products

(G-9753)
GLOBAL STRGC SUP SOLUTIONS LLC
Also Called: Gs3
34450 Industrial Rd (48150-1308)
PHONE..................734 525-9100
Robert Gruschow, *General Mgr*
Lisa Lunsford, *Mng Member*
◆ **EMP:** 100
SQ FT: 140,000
SALES (est): 6.4MM **Privately Held**
SIC: 8711 3559 3441 3542 Engineering services; automotive related machinery; fabricated structural metal; machine tools, metal forming type

(G-9754)
GORDON METAL PRODUCTS INC
31373 Industrial Rd (48150-2035)
PHONE..................586 445-0960
Gary Wyner, *President*
EMP: 18
SQ FT: 43,000
SALES (est): 2.5MM **Privately Held**
SIC: 3469 Stamping metal for the trade

(G-9755)
GRAKON LLC
Also Called: Grakon Michigan
19500 Victor Pkwy Ste 325 (48152-1084)
PHONE..................734 462-1201
EMP: 5
SALES (corp-wide): 80.7MM **Privately Held**
SIC: 3714 Motor vehicle electrical equipment
PA: Grakon, Llc
1911 S 218th St
Des Moines WA 98198
206 824-6000

(G-9756)
GRANITE CITY INC
31693 8 Mile Rd (48152-4217)
PHONE..................248 478-0033
Jon Williams, *Principal*
EMP: 2
SALES (est): 1.7MM **Privately Held**
SIC: 3281 5032 Curbing, granite or stone; granite, cut & shaped; granite building stone

(G-9757)
GRANITE PLANET LLC
30411 Schoolcraft Rd (48150-2008)
PHONE..................734 522-0190
Calbe Hartmann, *Mng Member*
EMP: 5
SALES (est): 683.3K **Privately Held**
SIC: 2541 Counter & sink tops

(G-9758)
GRAPHICOLOR SYSTEMS INC
Also Called: Graphicolor Exhibits
12788 Currie Ct (48150-1109)
PHONE..................248 347-0271
Anita Mitzel, *President*
Don Mitzel, *Treasurer*
EMP: 7
SQ FT: 8,000
SALES (est): 1.1MM **Privately Held**
WEB: www.graphicolor.com
SIC: 7389 2759 Promoters of shows & exhibitions; promotional printing

(G-9759)
GREAT LAKES FISH DECOY COLLECT
35824 W Chicago St (48150-2522)
PHONE..................734 427-7768
Dick Walters, *President*
Frank R Baron, *Corp Secy*
EMP: 3
SALES (est): 160K **Privately Held**
WEB: www.glfda.org
SIC: 8641 3949 Social club, membership; sporting & athletic goods

(G-9760)
GREAT LAKES LABORATORIES INC
27537 Schoolcraft Rd (48150-2217)
PHONE..................734 525-8300
J Edward Schwartz, *President*
L Stanford Evans, *Admin Sec*
EMP: 3 **EST:** 1971
SQ FT: 6,800
SALES (est): 630K **Privately Held**
WEB: www.greatlakeslaboratories.com
SIC: 2842 5169 Cleaning or polishing preparations; chemicals & allied products

(G-9761)
GUARDIAN MANUFACTURING CORP
12193 Levan Rd (48150-1403)
PHONE..................734 591-1454
Melvin Stevens, *President*
Sheryl Kudla, *Vice Pres*
Keith M Stevens, *Vice Pres*
Keith Stevens, *Vice Pres*
Don Connelly, *Engineer*
EMP: 35
SQ FT: 18,800
SALES: 8MM **Privately Held**
WEB: www.guardman.com
SIC: 3545 Machine tool accessories

(G-9762)
GUIDED PER BUS & PROF SVCS LLC
17361 Deering St (48152-3703)
PHONE..................248 567-2121
Gilbert Williams Jr, *Principal*
EMP: 3
SALES (est): 81.4K **Privately Held**
SIC: 1389 Hot shot service

(G-9763)
HAL INTERNATIONAL INC
Also Called: Dynapath Systems Inc.
34155 Industrial Rd (48150-1305)
PHONE..................248 488-0440
Jacob Pien, *President*
Michael Radiwon, *Purchasing*
Nick Pitsillos, *CFO*
▲ **EMP:** 7
SQ FT: 8,000
SALES (est): 1.6MM **Privately Held**
SIC: 3541 Machine tools, metal cutting type

(G-9764)
HAMILTON ENGINEERING INC
Also Called: Agritemp
34000 Autry St (48150-1333)
PHONE..................734 419-0200
Jeffrey E Deal, *CEO*
Tyler Segur, *Regional Mgr*
Diana Deal, *Vice Pres*
Shawn Edmonds, *Engineer*
Paul Lenhard, *Marketing Mgr*
▲ **EMP:** 35
SQ FT: 76,000
SALES (est): 15MM **Privately Held**
WEB: www.hamiltonengineering.com
SIC: 3433 5074 Burners, furnaces, boilers & stokers; boilers, hot water heating

(G-9765)
HANGER INC
32975 8 Mile Rd (48152-1337)
PHONE..................248 615-0601
EMP: 23
SALES (corp-wide): 1B **Publicly Held**
SIC: 3842 Surgical appliances & supplies
PA: Hanger, Inc.
10910 Domain Dr Ste 300
Austin TX 78758
512 777-3800

(G-9766)
HANLO GAUGES & ENGINEERING CO
34403 Glendale St (48150-1301)
PHONE..................734 422-4224
Barbara A Williams, *CEO*
Rick Williams, *President*
Mike Williams, *Corp Secy*
EMP: 7
SQ FT: 9,820
SALES: 1.5MM **Privately Held**
WEB: www.hanlogages.com
SIC: 3545 Gauges (machine tool accessories)

(G-9767)
HDT AUTOMOTIVE SOLUTIONS LLC (HQ)
38701 7 Mile Rd (48152-1091)
PHONE..................810 359-5344
Patrick Paige, *President*
Rick Cook, *President*
EMP: 8 **EST:** 2017
SALES (est): 43.9MM
SALES (corp-wide): 22.3MM **Privately Held**
SIC: 3714 Motor vehicle parts & accessories
PA: Ardian Holding
20 Place Vendome
Paris 1er Arrondissement 75001
141 719-200

(G-9768)
HENSLEY PRECISION CARBIDE INC
8825 Nevada St (48150-3845)
PHONE..................734 727-0810
Derona Geiger, *President*
Sharon Raymond, *Corp Secy*
Victoria Lever, *Office Mgr*
EMP: 10 **EST:** 1957
SQ FT: 16,260
SALES (est): 1.4MM **Privately Held**
WEB: www.hensleyprecisioncarbide.com
SIC: 3599 Machine shop, jobbing & repair; grinding castings for the trade

(G-9769)
HIDEN ANALYTICAL INC
37699 Schoolcraft Rd (48150-5031)
PHONE..................734 542-6666
Mark Buckley, *President*
EMP: 3
SALES (corp-wide): 20.8MM **Privately Held**
WEB: www.hideninc.com
SIC: 3826 Analytical instruments
HQ: Hiden Analytical, Inc
75 Hancock Rd Ste H
Peterborough NH 03458
603 924-5008

(G-9770)
HIGH TECH INSULATORS INC
34483 Glendale St (48150-1301)
PHONE..................734 525-9030
James D Allen, *President*
EMP: 20
SALES (est): 1.9MM **Privately Held**
SIC: 3086 Insulation or cushioning material, foamed plastic

(G-9771)
HIROSE ELECTRIC USA INC
37727 Prof Ctr Dr 100c (48154)
PHONE..................734 542-9963
Nick Shukuya, *Manager*
EMP: 55
SALES (est): 4.8MM **Privately Held**
SIC: 3699 Electron beam metal cutting, forming or welding machines

(G-9772)
HOLBROOK RACING ENGINES
31831 Schoolcraft Rd (48150-1825)
PHONE..................734 762-4315
Chris Holbrook, *General Mgr*
Donald M Soenen,
EMP: 10
SQ FT: 9,000
SALES: 800K **Privately Held**
WEB: www.holbrookracingengines.com
SIC: 3711 3519 Motor vehicles & car bodies; internal combustion engines

(G-9773)
HOLO-SOURCE CORPORATION
12280 Hubbard St (48150-1737)
PHONE..................734 427-1530
Deryl C Lacey, *President*
Robert H Levy, *Vice Pres*
▲ **EMP:** 4
SQ FT: 5,000
SALES: 1.6MM **Privately Held**
WEB: www.holo-source.com
SIC: 2671 Packaging paper & plastics film, coated & laminated

Livonia - Wayne County (G-9774)

(G-9774)
HOUGHTON INTERNATIONAL INC
17177 N Laurel Park Dr # 212 (48152-2693)
PHONE...............................248 641-3231
EMP: 16
SALES (corp-wide): 867.5MM Publicly Held
WEB: www.houghtonfluidcare.com
SIC: 2899 Chemical preparations
HQ: Houghton International Inc.
945 Madison Ave
Norristown PA 19403
888 459-9844

(G-9775)
HUEBNER E W & SON MFG CO INC
12871 Farmington Rd (48150-1607)
PHONE...............................734 427-2600
Max Riehl, President
EMP: 6 EST: 1952
SQ FT: 5,000
SALES (est): 690K Privately Held
SIC: 3548 Electrodes, electric welding

(G-9776)
HUGHES ELECTRONICS PDTS CORP (PA)
34467 Industrial Rd (48150-1305)
PHONE...............................734 427-8310
Richard L Smith Jr, President
Christopher Thomas, Vice Pres
Pauline Smith, Treasurer
EMP: 21 EST: 1982
SQ FT: 7,000
SALES (est): 4.6MM Privately Held
WEB: www.hugheselectronics.com
SIC: 3672 Circuit boards, television & radio printed

(G-9777)
I D ENTERPRISES LLC
Also Called: Idadee Enterprises
32788 5 Mile Rd Ste 2 (48154-6002)
PHONE...............................734 513-0800
Michael W Frasier,
EMP: 5
SALES (est): 854K Privately Held
WEB: www.id-enterprises.com
SIC: 2752 Offset & photolithographic printing

(G-9778)
IDEAL FABRICATORS INC
30579 Schoolcraft Rd (48150-2008)
PHONE...............................734 422-5320
John P Fisher, President
Mark Logan, Vice Pres
EMP: 35
SQ FT: 22,000
SALES (est): 9.8MM Privately Held
WEB: www.idealfab.com
SIC: 3443 Tanks, standard or custom fabricated: metal plate

(G-9779)
ILLINOIS TOOL WORKS INC
Also Called: TRW Engineered Fas Components
12200 Tech Center Dr (48150-2177)
PHONE...............................734 855-3709
Tammy Bass, Branch Mgr
EMP: 25
SALES (corp-wide): 14.7B Publicly Held
SIC: 3469 Metal stampings
PA: Illinois Tool Works Inc.
155 Harlem Ave
Glenview IL 60025
847 724-7500

(G-9780)
IMMUNO CONCEPTS NA LTD
17199 N Laurel Park Dr # 320 (48152-7904)
PHONE...............................734 464-0701
EMP: 40
SALES (est): 4.1MM Privately Held
SIC: 2836 Mfg Biological Products

(G-9781)
IMS/CHINATOOL JV LLC (PA)
Also Called: CT Automotive
17199 N Laurel Park Dr # 412 (48152-7905)
PHONE...............................734 466-5151
Robert Schaffer,
▲ EMP: 9
SALES (est): 5.9MM Privately Held
SIC: 3559 3089 Automotive related machinery; automotive parts, plastic

(G-9782)
INFINEON TECH AMERICAS CORP
19401 Victor Pkwy (48152-1001)
PHONE...............................734 464-0891
Shawn Slusser, VP Sales
Surekha Hunjan, Sales Staff
EMP: 75
SALES (corp-wide): 8.7B Privately Held
WEB: www.infineon-ncs.com
SIC: 3674 Semiconductors & related devices
HQ: Infineon Technologies Americas Corp.
101 N Pacific Coast Hwy
El Segundo CA 90245
310 726-8000

(G-9783)
INGERSOLL-RAND COMPANY
13551 Merriman Rd (48150-1815)
PHONE...............................734 525-6030
Scott Martin, Sales/Mktg Mgr
Ian McCloud, Manager
EMP: 20 Privately Held
WEB: www.ingersoll-rand.com
SIC: 3561 Pumps & pumping equipment
HQ: Ingersoll-Rand Company
800 Beaty St Ste B
Davidson NC 28036
704 655-4000

(G-9784)
INTERNTONAL SPECIALTY TUBE LLC
Also Called: Ist
17199 N Laurl Prk Dr # 322 (48152-2679)
PHONE...............................313 923-2000
Donna Schultz, Plant Mgr
Jim Darmer, QC Mgr
Thomas Payne, Engineer
Mike Roeder, Controller
Latara Larsosa, Accountant
EMP: 108
SQ FT: 150,000
SALES: 60.2MM
SALES (corp-wide): 830.8MM Privately Held
WEB: www.istube.com
SIC: 3317 Tubes, wrought: welded or lock joint
PA: Crowne Group, Llc
127 Public Sq Ste 5110
Cleveland OH 44114
216 589-0198

(G-9785)
INVENTRON INC
30927 Schoolcraft Rd (48150-2038)
PHONE...............................248 473-9250
Arthur Merkl, Branch Mgr
EMP: 8
SALES (corp-wide): 1.7MM Privately Held
SIC: 3829 Ultrasonic testing equipment
PA: Inventron Inc
5642 Drake Hollow Dr E
West Bloomfield MI
734 513-7700

(G-9786)
IPS ASSEMBLY CORP
12077 Merriman Rd (48150-1912)
PHONE...............................734 391-0080
Ishvar Sutariya, President
Perry Sutariya, Vice Pres
EMP: 16
SQ FT: 6,000
SALES: 2.2MM Privately Held
SIC: 3672 Circuit boards, television & radio printed

(G-9787)
J & J UNITED INDUSTRIES LLC
Also Called: United Fabrications
39111 6 Mile Rd (48152-3926)
P.O. Box 1104, New Boston (48164-1104)
PHONE...............................734 443-3737
EMP: 6
SALES: 14.3K Privately Held
SIC: 7389 3441 Business Services Structural Metal Fabrication

(G-9788)
J & S LIVONIA INC
Also Called: Jaimes Industries
12658 Richfield Ct (48150-1062)
PHONE...............................734 793-9000
Ghassan Yonan, President
EMP: 8
SALES (est): 1.5MM Privately Held
SIC: 3441 Building components, structural steel

(G-9789)
J C GIBBONS MFG INC
35055 Glendale St (48150-1230)
PHONE...............................734 266-5544
Jerry Gibbons, President
Jeff Gibbons, Vice Pres
Jeffery Gibbons, VP Opers
Dan Gibbons, QC Mgr
EMP: 20 EST: 1959
SQ FT: 22,000
SALES (est): 4.2MM Privately Held
SIC: 3451 Screw machine products

(G-9790)
J DRUMMOND SERVICE INC
31758 Enterprise Dr (48150-1960)
PHONE...............................248 624-0190
James Drummond, President
David Nowakowski, Vice Pres
EMP: 3
SALES: 400K Privately Held
SIC: 3714 Hydraulic fluid power pumps for auto steering mechanism

(G-9791)
JACOBSEN INDUSTRIES INC
12173 Market St (48150-1166)
PHONE...............................734 591-6111
Lee S Jacobsen, President
▲ EMP: 80 EST: 1946
SQ FT: 20,000
SALES (est): 11.7MM Privately Held
WEB: www.jacobsenindustries.com
SIC: 2675 3544 3053 Die-cut paper & board; dies, steel rule; gaskets, packing & sealing devices

(G-9792)
JADE PHARMACEUTICALS ENTP LLC
32229 Schoolcraft Rd (48150-4302)
PHONE...............................248 716-8333
Sam Alawieh, Mng Member
Abraham Alaouie,
EMP: 4
SQ FT: 15,600
SALES (est): 156.7K Privately Held
SIC: 2834 Pharmaceutical preparations

(G-9793)
JOES TRAILER MANUFACTURING
13374 Farmington Rd Ste A (48150-4206)
P.O. Box 51908 (48151-5908)
PHONE...............................734 261-0050
Douglas J Vandenberg, President
Marilynne G Vandenberg, Corp Secy
EMP: 5
SQ FT: 18,000
SALES (est): 84.5K Privately Held
WEB: www.greatlakestrailers.com
SIC: 3715 5531 Truck trailers; truck equipment & parts

(G-9794)
KELLER TOOL LTD (PA)
Also Called: O. Keller Tool Engineering Co.
12701 Inkster Rd (48150-2216)
PHONE...............................734 425-4500
Barry W La Chance, CEO
Brian Van Norman, President
EMP: 55
SQ FT: 30,000
SALES (est): 5.8MM Privately Held
SIC: 3544 3545 3537 Jigs & fixtures; gauges (machine tool accessories); pallets, metal

(G-9795)
KELLEY BROTHERS LC
Also Called: Honeywell Authorized Dealer
37100 Amrhein Rd (48150-1107)
PHONE...............................734 462-6266
Pat Kelley,
EMP: 18
SALES (est): 4.8MM Privately Held
SIC: 3585 Heating & air conditioning combination units

(G-9796)
KERRY J MCNEELY
Also Called: Kerry's Pallets
15810 Harrison St (48154-3410)
PHONE...............................734 776-1928
Kerry J McNeely, Principal
EMP: 4
SALES (est): 264K Privately Held
SIC: 2448 Pallets, wood & wood with metal

(G-9797)
KITTY CONDO LLC
17197 N Laurel Park Dr # 402 (48152-7910)
PHONE...............................419 690-9063
Michael L Stewart,
Jack L Berry,
Harry Shallop,
Harvy Solway,
EMP: 20
SQ FT: 20,000
SALES: 600K Privately Held
SIC: 3999 Pet supplies

(G-9798)
KKT INC
Also Called: Lockwood Manufacturing Company
31251 Industrial Rd (48150-2035)
PHONE...............................734 425-5330
David Lamson, President
▼ EMP: 40
SQ FT: 60,000
SALES (est): 12.8MM Privately Held
WEB: www.lockwoodusa.com
SIC: 3334 Primary aluminum

(G-9799)
KOPACZ INDUSTRIAL PAINTING
12225 Merriman Rd (48150-1912)
PHONE...............................734 427-6740
Edward F Kopacz Jr, President
EMP: 3
SQ FT: 5,000
SALES: 430K Privately Held
SIC: 3479 Painting of metal products

(G-9800)
KORE GROUP INC
Also Called: Fastsigns
37148 6 Mile Rd (48152-2730)
PHONE...............................248 449-6500
Kevin Miller, Manager
EMP: 4 Privately Held
WEB: www.koreinc.com
SIC: 3993 Signs & advertising specialties
PA: Kore Group Inc.
3500 Washtenaw Ave
Ann Arbor MI 48104

(G-9801)
KRUPP INDUSTRIES LLC
Also Called: Universal Sprial Air
37050 Plymouth Rd (48150-1132)
PHONE...............................734 261-0410
David C Krupp,
EMP: 100
SALES (corp-wide): 17.1MM Privately Held
SIC: 3444 Ducts, sheet metal
PA: Krupp Industries Llc
2735 West River Dr Nw
Walker MI 49544
616 475-5905

▲ = Import ▼=Export
◆ =Import/Export

GEOGRAPHIC SECTION

Livonia - Wayne County (G-9827)

(G-9802)
KURTIS MFG & DISTRG CORP (PA)
Also Called: Kurtis Kitchen & Bath Centers
12500 Merriman Rd (48150-1928)
PHONE.................................734 522-7600
Howard Kuretzky, *Principal*
Steve Edelman, *Vice Pres*
Wayne Weintraub, *Vice Pres*
Dave Curtis, *Director*
EMP: 50
SQ FT: 83,000
SALES (est): 31.6MM **Privately Held**
WEB: www.kurtiskitchen.com
SIC: 5021 5211 5031 5712 Household furniture; counter tops; kitchen cabinets; cabinet work, custom; wood kitchen cabinets; wood partitions & fixtures

(G-9803)
L I S MANUFACTURING INC
15223 Farmington Rd Ste 8 (48154-5411)
PHONE.................................734 525-3070
Michael G Jeffery, *President*
EMP: 10
SQ FT: 700
SALES (est): 1.3MM **Privately Held**
SIC: 2841 Soap & other detergents

(G-9804)
LAM INDUSTRIES
12985 Wayne Rd (48150-1269)
PHONE.................................734 266-1404
Larry Lam, *President*
EMP: 5
SALES (est): 456.9K **Privately Held**
SIC: 3599 Machine shop, jobbing & repair

(G-9805)
LEAPERS INC (PA)
32700 Capitol St (48150-1742)
PHONE.................................734 542-1500
Tina Ding, *President*
David Ding, *Vice Pres*
Nick Lee, *Project Engr*
Hongda Shen, *Cust Mgr*
Tom Zhu, *Sales Staff*
◆ **EMP:** 45
SQ FT: 150,000
SALES (est): 41.8MM **Privately Held**
WEB: www.leapers.com
SIC: 5091 3827 Sporting & recreation goods; gun sights, optical

(G-9806)
LETTERING INC OF MICHIGAN
13324 Farmington Rd (48150-4203)
PHONE.................................248 223-9700
Karin Krumpelbeck, *President*
Russell Mull, *General Mgr*
Russel Hall, *Manager*
John Krumpelbeck, *Admin Sec*
EMP: 10
SQ FT: 25,000
SALES: 900K
SALES (corp-wide): 2MM **Privately Held**
WEB: www.letteringinc.com
SIC: 3993 Signs & advertising specialties
PA: Lettering Inc Of New York
  255 Mill Rd
  Stamford CT 06903
  203 329-7759

(G-9807)
LINAMAR HOLDING NEVADA INC (HQ)
Also Called: McLaren Engineering
32233 8 Mile Rd (48152-1361)
PHONE.................................248 477-6240
Linda Hasenfratz, *CEO*
Jim Jarrell, *President*
Mike Vandieren, *Vice Pres*
Mitch Holland, *Engineer*
Dale Schneider, *CFO*
EMP: 10
SQ FT: 77,622
SALES (est): 55.8MM
SALES (corp-wide): 5.7B **Privately Held**
SIC: 3545 Precision measuring tools
PA: Linamar Corporation
  287 Speedvale Ave W
  Guelph ON N1H 1
  519 836-7550

(G-9808)
LINCOLN SERVICE LLC (PA)
11862 Brookfield St (48150-1701)
PHONE.................................734 793-0083
Mark Lippincott,
EMP: 7
SALES (est): 2.1MM **Privately Held**
WEB: www.lincolnservicecenter.com
SIC: 5063 7694 Motors, electric; motor repair services

(G-9809)
LINEAR MOLD & ENGINEERING LLC
34435 Glendale St (48150-1301)
PHONE.................................734 744-4548
John Tenbusch, *Branch Mgr*
EMP: 46
SALES (corp-wide): 26MM **Privately Held**
SIC: 3462 Iron & steel forgings
PA: Linear Mold & Engineering, Llc
  12163 Globe St
  Livonia MI 48150
  734 422-6060

(G-9810)
LINEAR MOLD & ENGINEERING LLC (PA)
Also Called: Linear AMS
12163 Globe St (48150-1142)
PHONE.................................734 422-6060
John Tenbusch, *CEO*
Lou Young, *President*
Garrett Remines, *Mfg Staff*
Brian Ackerman, *Purch Mgr*
Jim Koing, *Controller*
▲ **EMP:** 15
SQ FT: 13,000
SALES (est): 26MM **Privately Held**
SIC: 3462 Automotive & internal combustion engine forgings

(G-9811)
LINK MECHANICAL SOLUTIONS LLC
11970 Mayfield St (48150-1710)
PHONE.................................734 744-5616
Sean Koneff, *President*
Dave Lively, *Engineer*
EMP: 12 **EST:** 2010
SALES (est): 2.5MM **Privately Held**
SIC: 3599 Custom machinery

(G-9812)
LISI AUTOMOTIVE HI VOL INC
11813 Hubbard St (48150-1732)
PHONE.................................734 266-6958
Randy Hinz, *Vice Pres*
EMP: 10
SALES (corp-wide): 177.9K **Privately Held**
SIC: 5084 3399 Fuel injection systems; metal fasteners
HQ: Lisi Automotive Hi Vol Inc.
  12955 Inkster Rd
  Livonia MI 48150
  734 266-6900

(G-9813)
LISI AUTOMOTIVE HI VOL INC (DH)
12955 Inkster Rd (48150-2212)
PHONE.................................734 266-6900
Christian Darville, *President*
Randy Hinz, *Vice Pres*
Tim Waters, *Engineer*
EMP: 130
SQ FT: 60,000
SALES (est): 12.7MM
SALES (corp-wide): 177.9K **Privately Held**
WEB: www.trimascorp.com
SIC: 3462 Iron & steel forgings
HQ: Lisi Automotive
  2 Rue Juvenal Viellard
  Grandvillars 90600
  384 586-300

(G-9814)
LIVONIA AUTOMATIC INCORPORATED
12650 Newburgh Rd (48150-1002)
PHONE.................................734 591-0321
Gerald L Crespi, *President*
Robert J Crespi, *Vice Pres*
EMP: 5
SQ FT: 5,000
SALES (est): 649.5K **Privately Held**
SIC: 3451 Screw machine products

(G-9815)
LIVONIA OBSERVER
8928 Virginia St (48150-3643)
PHONE.................................734 525-4657
Norene Hanchett, *Principal*
EMP: 3 **EST:** 2010
SALES (est): 124.8K **Privately Held**
SIC: 2711 Newspapers, publishing & printing

(G-9816)
LIVONIA TROPHY & SCREEN PRTG
38065 Ann Arbor Rd (48150-3499)
PHONE.................................734 464-9191
Scott Wilson, *President*
EMP: 7
SQ FT: 2,400
SALES (est): 851.2K **Privately Held**
SIC: 5999 2759 Trophies & plaques; screen printing

(G-9817)
LLOYD WATERS & ASSOCIATES (PA)
33180 Industrial Rd Ste A (48150-4200)
PHONE.................................734 525-2777
Robert T Waters, *President*
W Lloyd Waters, *Treasurer*
Kim Ross, *Manager*
EMP: 5 **EST:** 1957
SQ FT: 2,400
SALES (est): 1.4MM **Privately Held**
WEB: www.lloydwaters.com
SIC: 7389 7336 2752 Printing broker; graphic arts & related design; commercial printing, offset

(G-9818)
LOONEY BAKER OF LIVONIA INC
13931 Farmington Rd (48154-5403)
PHONE.................................734 425-8569
John N Strauch, *President*
EMP: 20
SQ FT: 2,500
SALES (est): 680K **Privately Held**
SIC: 5461 2051 Cookies; doughnuts; bread, cake & related products

(G-9819)
LOVE MACHINERY INC
36232 Lawrence Dr (48150-2506)
PHONE.................................734 427-0824
William J Love, *President*
Francis Love, *Corp Secy*
EMP: 5
SQ FT: 4,500
SALES (est): 499.8K **Privately Held**
SIC: 3541 Machine tools, metal cutting type

(G-9820)
M & J GRAPHICS ENTERPRISES INC
Also Called: Reprographics One
36060 Industrial Rd (48150-1200)
PHONE.................................734 542-8800
Marianne Lewis, *CEO*
Joseph Kapp, *President*
EMP: 20
SQ FT: 22,000
SALES (est): 2.4MM **Privately Held**
WEB: www.reprographicsone.com
SIC: 2759 5734 Commercial printing; printers & plotters: computers

(G-9821)
MANUFACTURERS / MCH BLDRS SVCS
Also Called: Mmbs
13035 Wayne Rd (48150-1268)
PHONE.................................734 748-3706
Chanya Neal, *President*
Glen Neal, *Principal*
Patrick Bomia, *Admin Sec*
EMP: 4
SQ FT: 10,400
SALES (est): 1.3MM **Privately Held**
WEB: www.mmbscorp.com
SIC: 3549 Metalworking machinery

(G-9822)
MANUFACTURING ASSOCIATES INC
39201 Amrhein Rd (48150-5018)
PHONE.................................248 421-4943
Mark Ashworth, *President*
EMP: 6
SQ FT: 10,000
SALES (est): 460K **Privately Held**
SIC: 3541 Milling machines; lathes; numerically controlled metal cutting machine tools

(G-9823)
MARIE MINNIE BAKERS INC
Also Called: Awrey Bakeries
12301 Farmington Rd (48150-1747)
PHONE.................................734 522-1100
Ronald Beebe, *Ch of Bd*
Diane Lynch, *Vice Pres*
EMP: 120
SALES (est): 50.2MM **Privately Held**
SIC: 2053 2051 Frozen bakery products, except bread; bread, cake & related products

(G-9824)
MARYGROVE AWNINGS
12700 Merriman Rd (48150-1818)
PHONE.................................734 422-7110
EMP: 11
SALES (est): 1.1MM **Privately Held**
SIC: 3993 Signs & advertising specialties

(G-9825)
MASCO BUILDING PRODUCTS CORP (HQ)
17450 College Pkwy (48152-2300)
PHONE.................................313 274-7400
Allan Barry, *President*
Yvette Vanriper, *Counsel*
Eugene Gargaro, *Vice Pres*
Lebo Larry, *Vice Pres*
Cathy Hensley, *Credit Staff*
EMP: 8
SALES (est): 1.8B
SALES (corp-wide): 8.3B **Publicly Held**
SIC: 3429 3639 3644 Door locks, bolts & checks; major kitchen appliances, except refrigerators & stoves; outlet boxes (electric wiring devices)
PA: Masco Corporation
  17450 College Pkwy
  Livonia MI 48152
  313 274-7400

(G-9826)
MASCO CORPORATION (PA)
17450 College Pkwy (48152-2300)
PHONE.................................313 274-7400
J Michael Losh, *Ch of Bd*
Keith J Allman, *President*
Joseph B Gross, *President*
Jai Shah, *President*
Amit Bhargava, *Vice Pres*
◆ **EMP:** 559 **EST:** 1929
SALES: 8.3B **Publicly Held**
WEB: www.masco.com
SIC: 3432 3088 3429 1742 Faucets & spigots, metal & plastic; plumbers' brass goods: drain cocks, faucets, spigots, etc.; plastic plumbing fixture fittings, assembly; plastics plumbing fixtures; tubs (bath, shower & laundry), plastic; bathroom fixtures, plastic; hot tubs, plastic or fiberglass; builders' hardware; locks or lock sets; acoustical & insulation work; vanities, bathroom: wood

(G-9827)
MASCO SERVICES INC
17450 College Pkwy (48152-2300)
PHONE.................................313 274-7400
Eugene A Gargaro Jr, *Principal*
EMP: 6
SALES (est): 448.9K
SALES (corp-wide): 8.3B **Publicly Held**
WEB: www.masco.com
SIC: 2434 Wood kitchen cabinets

Livonia - Wayne County (G-9828)

PA: Masco Corporation
17450 College Pkwy
Livonia MI 48152
313 274-7400

(G-9828)
MASTER AUTOMATIC MCH CO INC
12271 Globe St (48150-1142)
PHONE.................................734 414-0500
John D Evasic, *Ch of Bd*
EMP: 50
SALES (corp-wide): 30.2MM **Privately Held**
SIC: 3559 Automotive related machinery
PA: Master Automatic Machine Company, Inc.
40485 Schoolcraft Rd
Plymouth MI 48170
734 414-0500

(G-9829)
MAZZELLA LIFTING TECH INC
12671 Richfield Ct (48150-1062)
PHONE.................................734 953-7300
EMP: 6 **Privately Held**
SIC: 3496 Manufactures Hoisting And Lifting Devices
HQ: Mazzella Lifting Technologies, Inc.
21000 Aerospace Pkwy
Cleveland OH 44142
440 239-7000

(G-9830)
MCCLATCHY NEWSPAPERS INC
31572 Industrial Rd # 400 (48150-1837)
PHONE.................................734 525-2224
Nancy Pierce, *Branch Mgr*
EMP: 95
SALES (corp-wide): 807.2MM **Publicly Held**
WEB: www.sacbee.com
SIC: 2711 Newspapers, publishing & printing
HQ: Mcclatchy Newspapers, Inc.
2100 Q St
Sacramento CA 95816
916 321-1855

(G-9831)
MCDONALD ENTERPRISES INC
36650 Plymouth Rd (48150-1129)
PHONE.................................734 464-4664
Richard Larance, *President*
EMP: 10
SQ FT: 11,000
SALES: 1.5MM **Privately Held**
SIC: 3599 Machine shop, jobbing & repair

(G-9832)
MCGEAN-ROHCO INC
38521 Schoolcraft Rd (48150-1031)
PHONE.................................216 441-4900
Jim Rector, *Manager*
Lisa Allman, *Executive*
EMP: 20
SALES (corp-wide): 62.8MM **Privately Held**
WEB: www.mcgean.com
SIC: 2899 2819 3471 2842 Chemical preparations; industrial inorganic chemicals; plating & polishing; specialty cleaning, polishes & sanitation goods
PA: Mcgean-Rohco, Inc.
2910 Harvard Ave
Newburgh Heights OH 44105
216 441-4900

(G-9833)
MCKESSON CORPORATION
Also Called: McEsson Drug Company
38220 Plymouth Rd (48150-1050)
PHONE.................................734 953-2523
Craig Vanderburg, *Manager*
Garima Pandey, *Manager*
Lori Baronet, *IT/INT Sup*
Hamsa Konanur, *Director*
EMP: 99
SALES (corp-wide): 214.3B **Publicly Held**
WEB: www.imckesson.com
SIC: 5122 2834 Pharmaceuticals; pharmaceutical preparations

PA: Mckesson Corporation
6555 State Highway 161
Irving TX 75039
972 446-4800

(G-9834)
MCKESSON PHARMACY SYSTEMS LLC (HQ)
30881 Schoolcraft Rd (48150-2010)
PHONE.................................800 521-1758
Emilie Ray, *President*
Brian Grobbel, *President*
EMP: 554
SALES (est): 39.5MM
SALES (corp-wide): 214.3B **Publicly Held**
WEB: www.imckesson.com
SIC: 7372 5122 Prepackaged software; pharmaceuticals
PA: Mckesson Corporation
6555 State Highway 161
Irving TX 75039
972 446-4800

(G-9835)
MEASURING TOOL SERVICES
8984 Russell St (48150-3535)
PHONE.................................734 261-1107
Brian K Pope, *CEO*
Jani Pope, *General Mgr*
EMP: 3
SALES: 150K **Privately Held**
SIC: 3545 7699 Precision measuring tools; professional instrument repair services

(G-9836)
MECAPLAST USA LLC
19575 Victor Pkwy Ste 400 (48152-7026)
PHONE.................................248 594-8082
David Brassell, *Mng Member*
▲ **EMP:** 5
SQ FT: 4,000
SALES: 500K
SALES (corp-wide): 102.8MM **Privately Held**
SIC: 3089 Injection molding of plastics
HQ: Novares Group
361 Avenue Du General De Gaulle
Clamart 92140
155 955-560

(G-9837)
MELODY FARMS LLC
31770 Enterprise Dr (48150-1960)
PHONE.................................734 261-7980
Jerry Shannon,
EMP: 40
SQ FT: 15,000
SALES (est): 3.3MM **Privately Held**
SIC: 2026 Fluid milk

(G-9838)
MERITOR SPECIALTY PRODUCTS LLC
Also Called: Fabco Holdings Inc.
12623 Newburgh Rd (48150-1001)
PHONE.................................248 435-1000
Gerard L Giudici, *President*
EMP: 4 **EST:** 2011
SALES (est): 255.4K **Publicly Held**
SIC: 3714 Motor vehicle parts & accessories
PA: Meritor, Inc.
2135 W Maple Rd
Troy MI 48084

(G-9839)
METALCRAFT IMPRESSION DIE CO
Also Called: Metal Craft Impression Die
11914 Brookfield St (48150-1736)
PHONE.................................734 513-8058
Bryan Stenman, *President*
EMP: 6
SQ FT: 5,000
SALES (est): 1MM **Privately Held**
SIC: 3544 Special dies & tools

(G-9840)
METRO MEDICAL EQP MFG INC
38415 Schoolcraft Rd (48150-1031)
PHONE.................................734 522-8400
Paul Mocur, *President*
Sylvia Mocur, *Treasurer*

EMP: 65
SQ FT: 10,000
SALES (est): 8.7MM **Privately Held**
SIC: 7352 5999 3842 Medical equipment rental; hospital equipment & supplies; prosthetic appliances

(G-9841)
METTES PRINTERY INC
27454 Plymouth Rd (48150-2317)
PHONE.................................734 261-6262
Bruce C Mette, *President*
Toni Mette, *Corp Secy*
EMP: 7
SQ FT: 4,000
SALES (est): 670K **Privately Held**
WEB: www.mettesprinting.com
SIC: 2752 Commercial printing, offset

(G-9842)
MICHIGAN OVERHEAD DOOR
Also Called: Raynor Overhead Door
11615 Inkster Rd (48150-2343)
PHONE.................................734 425-0295
Donald R Funk, *President*
Ralph Moore, *Vice Pres*
Nancy Moore, *Treasurer*
Isabelle Funk, *Admin Sec*
EMP: 13
SQ FT: 7,500
SALES: 900K **Privately Held**
WEB: www.raynordetroit.com
SIC: 2431 Garage doors, overhead: wood

(G-9843)
MID-WEST SCREW PRODUCTS CO
Also Called: Unco Automotive Products
11975 Globe St (48150-1133)
PHONE.................................734 591-1800
Kevin Johnson, *President*
Christina Rowland, *Controller*
EMP: 12 **EST:** 1953
SQ FT: 11,000
SALES: 2MM **Privately Held**
SIC: 3451 Screw machine products

(G-9844)
MIDWEST STAINLESS FABRICATING
32433 8 Mile Rd (48152-1301)
PHONE.................................248 476-4502
James Day, *President*
Mark Hall, *Vice Pres*
Tammi Milewski, *Controller*
EMP: 8
SQ FT: 7,500
SALES: 900K **Privately Held**
SIC: 3589 Commercial cooking & food-warming equipment

(G-9845)
MILLENNIUM SCREW MACHINE INC
13311 Stark Rd (48150-1548)
PHONE.................................734 525-5235
Frederick D Mercaldo, *President*
John Baughman, *Vice Pres*
Jerome Genders, *Vice Pres*
Virginia Mercaldo, *Admin Sec*
EMP: 5
SQ FT: 11,000
SALES: 320K **Privately Held**
SIC: 3541 Machine tools, metal cutting type

(G-9846)
MJ CREATIVE PRINTING LLC
19566 Hardy St (48152-1587)
PHONE.................................248 891-1117
Marianne Groth, *Principal*
EMP: 8
SALES (est): 1MM **Privately Held**
SIC: 2752 Commercial printing, lithographic

(G-9847)
MOHECO PRODUCTS COMPANY
34410 Rosati Ave (48150-1429)
PHONE.................................734 855-4194
Gerald Herrmann, *President*
EMP: 5
SQ FT: 16,000

SALES: 600K **Privately Held**
WEB: www.moheco.com
SIC: 3356 3429 Nonferrous rolling & drawing; furniture hardware

(G-9848)
MORSTAR INC
12868 Farmington Rd (48150-1603)
PHONE.................................248 605-3291
Qiumin Su, *President*
William Guo, *Vice Pres*
EMP: 18 **EST:** 2009
SALES: 1MM **Privately Held**
SIC: 3699 3315 Grids, electric; wire & fabricated wire products

(G-9849)
MOTOR CITY QUICK LUBE ONE INC
11900 Middlebelt Rd Ste A (48150-2300)
PHONE.................................734 367-6457
Emad Bazzi, *Principal*
EMP: 5
SALES (est): 670K **Privately Held**
SIC: 2911 Oils, fuel; oils, lubricating; fuel additives

(G-9850)
MOTOR TOOL MANUFACTURING CO
14710 Flamingo St (48154-3610)
PHONE.................................734 425-3300
Jack D Kastelic, *President*
Julius Konosky, *Vice Pres*
EMP: 4 **EST:** 1937
SQ FT: 5,600
SALES (est): 506.6K **Privately Held**
WEB: www.americangator.com
SIC: 3545 Cutting tools for machine tools

(G-9851)
MOTUS LLC
13975 Farmington Rd (48154-5454)
PHONE.................................734 266-3237
Kevin Connors, *Sales Mgr*
EMP: 8
SALES (corp-wide): 573.9MM **Privately Held**
SIC: 3089 Injection molding of plastics
HQ: Motus Llc
88 E 48th St
Holland MI 49423
616 422-7557

(G-9852)
MP-TEC INC
32920 Capitol St (48150-1743)
PHONE.................................734 367-1284
Toshiro Yamagata, *Principal*
EMP: 21 **EST:** 2007
SALES (est): 2.9MM **Privately Held**
SIC: 2295 Resin or plastic coated fabrics

(G-9853)
MR PEEL INC
33975 Autry St (48150-1323)
PHONE.................................734 266-2022
El Roma, *Owner*
EMP: 5
SALES (est): 317.7K **Privately Held**
WEB: www.mrpeel.com
SIC: 2064 Fruit & fruit peel confections

(G-9854)
MTU AMERICA INCORPORATED
30946 Industrial Rd (48150-2054)
PHONE.................................734 261-0309
EMP: 5
SALES (corp-wide): 20.2B **Privately Held**
SIC: 3519 Diesel engine rebuilding
HQ: Mtu America Inc.
39525 Mackenzie Dr
Novi MI 48377
248 560-8000

(G-9855)
N A ACTUAPLAST INC
31690 Glendale St (48150-1827)
PHONE.................................734 744-4010
Ronan Perennou, *CEO*
Virginie Tymen, *Admin Mgr*
▲ **EMP:** 10

GEOGRAPHIC SECTION

Livonia - Wayne County (G-9879)

SALES (est): 1.1MM
SALES (corp-wide): 6.6MM **Privately Held**
SIC: 3089 Blow molded finished plastic products
PA: Actuaplast Group
Lieu Dit La Grande Halte
La Foret-Fouesnant 29940
298 569-462

(G-9856)
NAGLE PAVING COMPANY
36780 Amrhein Rd (48150-1104)
PHONE....................734 591-1484
Steve Santi, *Branch Mgr*
EMP: 129
SALES (corp-wide): 47.7MM **Privately Held**
WEB: www.naglepaving.com
SIC: 1771 2951 Blacktop (asphalt) work; asphalt paving mixtures & blocks
PA: Nagle Paving Company
39525 W 13 Mile Rd # 300
Novi MI 48377
248 553-0600

(G-9857)
NANKIN WELDING CO INC
12620 Fairlane St (48150-1300)
PHONE....................734 458-3980
Richard F Colwell, *President*
EMP: 3 EST: 1980
SQ FT: 10,000
SALES: 500K **Privately Held**
SIC: 3444 3544 Sheet metalwork; forms (molds), for foundry & plastics working machinery

(G-9858)
NANOMAG LLC
13753 Otterson Ct (48150-1220)
PHONE....................734 261-2800
Stephen Lebeau, *Partner*
EMP: 7
SALES: 500K **Privately Held**
SIC: 3356 Magnesium

(G-9859)
NASSAU CANDY MIDWEST L L C
35521 Industrial Rd (48150-1233)
PHONE....................734 464-2787
Dam Squilliets, *General Mgr*
EMP: 79
SALES (est): 5.3MM
SALES (corp-wide): 212MM **Privately Held**
WEB: www.nassaucandy.com
SIC: 2064 Candy & other confectionery products
HQ: Nassau Candy Distributors, Inc.
530 W John St
Hicksville NY 11801
516 433-7100

(G-9860)
NATIONAL INSTRUMENTS CORP
20255 Victor Pkwy Ste 195 (48152-7021)
PHONE....................734 464-2310
EMP: 338
SALES (corp-wide): 1.2B **Publicly Held**
SIC: 7372 Provides Prepackaged Computer Software
PA: National Instruments Corporation
11500 N Mopac Expy
Austin TX 78759
512 338-9119

(G-9861)
NATIONAL TOOL & DIE WELDING
13340 Merriman Rd (48150-1830)
PHONE....................734 522-0072
Stephan Skrobot, *President*
Jeff Skrobot, *Vice Pres*
EMP: 10
SQ FT: 13,000
SALES (est): 1.1MM **Privately Held**
SIC: 7692 Welding repair

(G-9862)
NCI MFG INC
12665 Richfield Ct (48150-1062)
PHONE....................248 380-4151
Koji Iwata, *Branch Mgr*
EMP: 10

SALES (est): 850.7K **Privately Held**
SIC: 5531 3053 1711 Automotive parts; gaskets, packing & sealing devices; plumbing, heating, air-conditioning contractors
PA: Nci Mfg, Inc.
209 Lnnie E Crawford Blvd
Scottsboro AL 35769

(G-9863)
NORTHAMERICAN REPRODUCTION
34943 6 Mile Rd (48152-2991)
PHONE....................734 421-6800
Taras A Filas, *President*
Cheryl Evenson, *General Mgr*
EMP: 15
SQ FT: 3,000
SALES (est): 1.7MM **Privately Held**
SIC: 2752 Commercial printing, offset

(G-9864)
NORTHROP GRMMN SPCE & MSSN SYS
12025 Tech Center Dr (48150-2122)
PHONE....................734 266-2600
EMP: 900 **Publicly Held**
SIC: 3714 Mfg Vehicle Brakes Systems & Parts
HQ: Northrop Grumman Space & Mission Systems Corp.
6377 San Ignacio Ave
San Jose CA 95119
703 280-2900

(G-9865)
NOVARES CORPORATION US INC (DH)
19575 Victor Pkwy Ste 400 (48152-7026)
PHONE....................248 449-6100
Terry Gohl, *CEO*
Scott Wawrzyniak, *Vice Pres*
EMP: 3
SALES (est): 1.1B
SALES (corp-wide): 102.8MM **Privately Held**
SIC: 3089 7389 Automotive parts, plastic; design services
HQ: Novares Group
361 Avenue Du General De Gaulle
Clamart 92140
155 955-560

(G-9866)
NOVARES US LLC (DH)
Also Called: Novares Group
19575 Victor Pkwy Ste 400 (48152-7026)
PHONE....................248 449-6100
Dean Proney, *President*
Fernando Duarte, *Vice Pres*
Kimberlie Cole, *Materials Mgr*
David McLaughlin-Smit, *Mfg Spvr*
George Awad, *Engineer*
▲ EMP: 64
SQ FT: 24,500
SALES (est): 1.1B
SALES (corp-wide): 102.8MM **Privately Held**
WEB: www.keyplastics.com
SIC: 3089 Automotive parts, plastic
HQ: Novares Corporation Us Inc.
19575 Victor Pkwy Ste 400
Livonia MI 48152
248 449-6100

(G-9867)
NU CON CORPORATION
34100 Industrial Rd (48150-1335)
PHONE....................734 525-0770
David Stormont, *President*
David L Bernhardt, *Exec VP*
M Robert Barnes, *Treasurer*
Allen Stevens, *Shareholder*
EMP: 32
SQ FT: 5,000
SALES: 4.2MM **Privately Held**
WEB: www.nuconcorp.com
SIC: 3511 3728 3724 3714 Turbines & turbine generator sets; aircraft parts & equipment; aircraft engines & engine parts; motor vehicle parts & accessories

(G-9868)
NUKO PRECISION LLC
35455 Schoolcraft Rd (48150-1222)
PHONE....................734 464-6856
Rani G Thuluri, *Mng Member*
Ram Thuluri,
▲ EMP: 17
SQ FT: 17,000
SALES (est): 1MM **Privately Held**
SIC: 3451 Screw machine products

(G-9869)
NYX INC
Also Called: Nyx Plymouth
38700 Plymouth Rd (48150-1055)
PHONE....................734 464-0800
Dan Taylor, *Manager*
EMP: 300
SALES (corp-wide): 607.1MM **Privately Held**
WEB: www.nyxinc.com
SIC: 3559 3643 3537 Automotive related machinery; current-carrying wiring devices; industrial trucks & tractors
PA: Nyx, Llc
36111 Schoolcraft Rd
Livonia MI 48150
734 462-2385

(G-9870)
NYX INC
Also Called: Nyx Livonia Plant II
28350 Plymouth Rd (48150-2790)
PHONE....................734 261-7535
Dan Taylor, *Branch Mgr*
EMP: 300
SALES (corp-wide): 607.1MM **Privately Held**
SIC: 3714 3089 3565 2671 Motor vehicle parts & accessories; injection molding of plastics; packaging machinery; packaging paper & plastics film, coated & laminated
PA: Nyx, Llc
36111 Schoolcraft Rd
Livonia MI 48150
734 462-2385

(G-9871)
NYX LLC (PA)
Also Called: Nyx Technologies
36111 Schoolcraft Rd (48150-1216)
PHONE....................734 462-2385
Lev Lilov, *Vice Pres*
Pawan Dhaliwal, *Project Engr*
Jeannine Laible, *Human Res Dir*
Todd McCaig, *Manager*
Napinder Singh, *Manager*
▲ EMP: 225
SQ FT: 45,000
SALES (est): 607.1MM **Privately Held**
WEB: www.nyxinc.com
SIC: 3089 3714 3565 2671 Injection molding of plastics; motor vehicle parts & accessories; packaging machinery; packaging paper & plastics film, coated & laminated

(G-9872)
NYX LLC
30111 Schoolcraft Rd (48150-2006)
PHONE....................734 421-3850
Chain S Sandhu, *CEO*
EMP: 120
SALES (corp-wide): 607.1MM **Privately Held**
WEB: www.nyxinc.com
SIC: 3089 Injection molding of plastics
PA: Nyx, Llc
36111 Schoolcraft Rd
Livonia MI 48150
734 462-2385

(G-9873)
O KELLER TOOL ENGRG CO LLC
12701 Inkster Rd (48150-2216)
P.O. Box 510327 (48151-6327)
PHONE....................734 425-4500
Barry W La Chance, *CEO*
Brian Van Norman, *President*
Daniel Grayson, *COO*
Phillip Williams, *Purch Mgr*
Stephanie London, *Office Mgr*
EMP: 49
SQ FT: 30,000

SALES: 9.3MM
SALES (corp-wide): 5.8MM **Privately Held**
SIC: 3545 3544 3537 Gauges (machine tool accessories); jigs & fixtures; pallets, metal
PA: Keller Tool Ltd
12701 Inkster Rd
Livonia MI 48150
734 425-4500

(G-9874)
ODYSSEY ELECTRONICS INC
12886 Fairlane St (48150-1327)
PHONE....................734 421-8340
Ernest V Flamont, *President*
Mark Estes, *Vice Pres*
Traci Cauchi, *QC Mgr*
Laura Henning, *QC Mgr*
Jason Cassar, *Supervisor*
▲ EMP: 70
SQ FT: 18,420
SALES (est): 31.4MM **Privately Held**
WEB: www.odyssey-oei.com
SIC: 3672 5065 Printed circuit boards; electronic parts & equipment

(G-9875)
ONE-WAY TOOL & DIE INC
32845 8 Mile Rd (48152-1337)
PHONE....................248 477-2964
Adam Bowser, *President*
EMP: 5 EST: 1978
SQ FT: 1,800
SALES: 400K **Privately Held**
WEB: www.oneway.ca
SIC: 3544 Special dies, tools, jigs & fixtures

(G-9876)
ONEGENE AMERICA INC
38777 6 Mile Rd (48152-2694)
PHONE....................734 855-4460
Daewook Kim, *CEO*
▲ EMP: 3
SALES (est): 490K **Privately Held**
SIC: 3679 Electronic loads & power supplies

(G-9877)
OVERSEAS AUTO PARTS INC
32400 Plymouth Rd (48150-1712)
PHONE....................734 427-4840
John Demrovsky, *President*
Andrew Demrovsky, *President*
Helen Demrovsky, *Treasurer*
Sam Demrovsky, *Admin Sec*
Samuel Demrovsky, *Admin Sec*
EMP: 24
SQ FT: 20,000
SALES: 3MM **Privately Held**
SIC: 5013 3694 Motor vehicle supplies & new parts; automotive electrical equipment

(G-9878)
OXBOW MACHINE PRODUCTS INC (PA)
12743 Merriman Rd (48150-1800)
PHONE....................734 422-7730
John R Tiano, *CEO*
Robert C Tiano, *President*
Michael J Tiano, *Vice Pres*
EMP: 30
SQ FT: 27,800
SALES (est): 12.1MM **Privately Held**
WEB: www.oxbow-machine.com
SIC: 3544 Special dies, tools, jigs & fixtures

(G-9879)
P M Z TECHNOLOGY INC
Also Called: Video Service Center
33302 7 Mile Rd (48152-1369)
PHONE....................248 471-0447
Paul Zsenyuk, *President*
Steve Zsenyuk, *Treasurer*
Mariann Zsenyuk, *Admin Sec*
EMP: 4
SQ FT: 1,200
SALES: 300K **Privately Held**
SIC: 3672 Printed circuit boards

Livonia - Wayne County (G-9880) GEOGRAPHIC SECTION

(G-9880)
PA PRODUCTS INC
Also Called: P A Products
33709 Schoolcraft Rd (48150-1505)
PHONE.................................734 421-1060
Tim Pilzner, *President*
Timothy Pilzner, *President*
Ellen Pilzner, *Corp Secy*
▲ **EMP:** 7
SQ FT: 13,500
SALES (est): 1.2MM **Privately Held**
SIC: 3496 5072 5046 Screening, woven wire: made from purchased wire; cutlery; restaurant equipment & supplies

(G-9881)
PACKAGING CORPORATION AMERICA
Also Called: PCA
28330 Plymouth Rd (48150-2790)
PHONE.................................734 266-1877
EMP: 7
SALES (corp-wide): 7B **Publicly Held**
SIC: 2653 Boxes, corrugated: made from purchased materials
PA: Packaging Corporation Of America
   1 N Field Ct
   Lake Forest IL 60045
   847 482-3000

(G-9882)
PALLET MASTERS
16352 Farmington Rd (48154-2945)
PHONE.................................313 995-1131
Fax: 313 995-1131
EMP: 3
SALES (est): 119.9K **Privately Held**
SIC: 2448 Mfg Wood Pallets/Skids

(G-9883)
PANEL PRO LLC
16809 Ryan Rd (48154-6232)
PHONE.................................734 427-1691
Thomas Lee, *Principal*
EMP: 4
SALES (est): 345.7K **Privately Held**
SIC: 3643 Electric switches

(G-9884)
PARKWAY DRAPERY & UPHL CO INC
Also Called: Parkway Contract Group
12784 Currie Ct (48150-1109)
PHONE.................................734 779-1300
Robert Zaguroli, *President*
EMP: 9
SQ FT: 4,000
SALES: 1.6MM **Privately Held**
SIC: 2591 2391 7641 5023 Window blinds; blinds vertical; draperies, plastic & textile: from purchased materials; re-upholstery; carpets; drapery material, woven; millwork

(G-9885)
PEPPERIDGE FARM INCORPORATED
Also Called: Pepperidge Farm Thrift Store
29115 8 Mile Rd (48152-2009)
PHONE.................................734 953-6729
Pamela Baker, *Manager*
EMP: 6
SALES (corp-wide): 8.1B **Publicly Held**
WEB: www.pepperidgefarm.com
SIC: 5461 2052 2099 2053 Bakeries; cookies; bread crumbs, not made in bakeries; frozen bakery products, except bread
HQ: Pepperidge Farm, Incorporated
   595 Westport Ave
   Norwalk CT 06851
   203 846-7000

(G-9886)
PERFIT CORPORATION
Also Called: Michigan Engine Pro
13090 Fairlane St (48150-1326)
PHONE.................................734 524-9208
Nathan Brown, *Branch Mgr*
EMP: 3
SALES (corp-wide): 4.8MM **Privately Held**
SIC: 3519 Parts & accessories, internal combustion engines
PA: The Perfit Corporation
   728 Division Ave S
   Grand Rapids MI 49503
   616 247-4634

(G-9887)
PERFORMNCE ASSMBLY SLTIONS LLC
28190 Plymouth Rd (48150-2398)
PHONE.................................734 466-6380
Facundo Bravo, *President*
John Torvinen, *Vice Pres*
Victoria Borg, *Planning*
▲ **EMP:** 24
SQ FT: 29,000
SALES (est): 10.5MM **Privately Held**
SIC: 3714 Motor vehicle parts & accessories

(G-9888)
PHOENIX IMAGING INC (PA)
Also Called: Phoenix Imaging Machine Vision
29865 6 Mile Rd (48152-3673)
PHONE.................................248 476-4200
Gerald Budd, *President*
Jean Cox, *Vice Pres*
Lauren Krawec, *Treasurer*
John A Cook, *Admin Sec*
▼ **EMP:** 3
SQ FT: 3,400
SALES (est): 1MM **Privately Held**
WEB: www.phoeniximaging.com
SIC: 3827 3648 Optical test & inspection equipment; lighting equipment

(G-9889)
PLASTOMER CORPORATION
37819 Schoolcraft Rd (48150-1096)
PHONE.................................734 464-0700
Walter Baughman III, *President*
David Baughman, *Exec VP*
Roger Baughman, *Treasurer*
Donald Show, *Controller*
▲ **EMP:** 200 **EST:** 1954
SQ FT: 175,000
SALES (est): 30MM **Privately Held**
WEB: www.plastomer.com
SIC: 3053 Gaskets, all materials

(G-9890)
PLYMOUTH COMPUTER &
Also Called: Pcnphone.com
27840 Plymouth Rd (48150-2325)
PHONE.................................734 744-9563
Malek Abunab,
EMP: 3 **EST:** 2014
SQ FT: 3,000
SALES (est): 98K **Privately Held**
SIC: 7622 3672 3663 3571 Household antenna installation & service; printed circuit boards; mobile communication equipment; personal computers (microcomputers)

(G-9891)
POWER-BRITE OF MICHIGAN INC
12053 Levan Rd (48150-1449)
PHONE.................................734 591-7911
Spence P Babcock, *President*
Dorothy Babcock, *Corp Secy*
T Fred Moseley, *Vice Pres*
EMP: 13 **EST:** 1978
SQ FT: 10,000
SALES (est): 2MM **Privately Held**
SIC: 3589 Car washing machinery

(G-9892)
POWERTHRU INC
11825 Mayfield St (48150-1707)
PHONE.................................734 583-5004
EMP: 8 **EST:** 2012
SALES (est): 710K
SALES (corp-wide): 37.9MM **Privately Held**
SIC: 3621 Mfg Motors/Generators
PA: Phillips Service Industries, Inc.
   11878 Hubbard St
   Livonia MI 48170
   734 853-5000

(G-9893)
POWERTHRU INC
11825 Mayfield St (48150-1707)
P.O. Box 3313 (48151-3313)
PHONE.................................734 853-5004
William S Phillips, *CEO*
Lawrence E Perlin, *CFO*
EMP: 11
SALES (est): 1.7MM
SALES (corp-wide): 365.8MM **Privately Held**
SIC: 3621 Motors & generators
HQ: Beaver Aerospace & Defense, Inc.
   11850 Mayfield St
   Livonia MI 48150
   734 853-5003

(G-9894)
PPG COATING SERVICES
Also Called: Crown Group Livonia Plant, The
31774 Enterprise Dr (48150-1960)
PHONE.................................734 421-7300
Ed Dickinson, *Business Mgr*
Jason Garcia, *Engineer*
Chris Behnam, *Accounting Dir*
Stacy Chmelko, *Benefits Mgr*
Eric Vermillion, *Branch Mgr*
EMP: 75
SALES (corp-wide): 15.3B **Publicly Held**
SIC: 3479 2851 Coating of metals & formed products; paints & allied products
HQ: Ppg Coating Services
   5875 New King Ct
   Troy MI 48098
   586 575-9800

(G-9895)
PRATT INDUSTRIES INC
32432 Capitol St (48150-1703)
PHONE.................................734 853-3000
Craig Beaudoin, *General Mgr*
Terry Teller, *Info Tech Dir*
Hanna Beaudoin, *Executive*
Sharon Curry, *Executive*
EMP: 5
SALES (corp-wide): 2.5B **Privately Held**
SIC: 2653 Corrugated & solid fiber boxes
PA: Pratt Industries, Inc.
   1800 Sarasot Bus Pkwy Ne C
   Conyers GA 30013
   770 918-5678

(G-9896)
PRECIOUS FURS LLC
35912 Joy Rd (48150-3591)
PHONE.................................734 262-6262
Nicole Ortiz-Rich, *Principal*
EMP: 3
SALES (est): 221.8K **Privately Held**
SIC: 3999 Furs

(G-9897)
PREMIER PANEL COMPANY
12300 Merriman Rd (48150-1917)
PHONE.................................734 427-1700
Tim Oliver, *President*
Jeff Crampton, *President*
Melvin Guthery, *Principal*
William Gutherie, *Admin Sec*
EMP: 20
SQ FT: 16,000
SALES: 375K **Privately Held**
SIC: 2452 Prefabricated wood buildings

(G-9898)
PRIDE SOURCE CORPORATION
Also Called: Between The Lines
20222 Farmington Rd (48152-1412)
PHONE.................................734 293-7200
Susan Horowitz, *Publisher*
Janet R Stevenson, *CFO*
EMP: 15
SALES (est): 1.8MM **Privately Held**
WEB: www.pridesource.com
SIC: 2721 Periodicals

(G-9899)
PSI REPAIR SERVICES INC (HQ)
Also Called: PSI Semicon Services
11900 Mayfield St (48150-1785)
P.O. Box 3313 (48151-3313)
PHONE.................................734 853-5000
Scott Phillips, *CEO*
William S Phllps, *President*
Kelly Ryan, *General Mgr*
William T Phillips, *Chairman*
Bob Phillips, *Vice Pres*
EMP: 200
SQ FT: 5,800
SALES: 30MM
SALES (corp-wide): 67.8MM **Privately Held**
WEB: www.psirepair-online.com
SIC: 7699 7694 7629 Pumps & pumping equipment; valve repair, industrial; electric motor repair; circuit board repair
PA: Phillips Service Industries, Inc.
   14492 N Sheldon Rd # 300
   Plymouth MI 48170
   734 853-5000

(G-9900)
QUALITY METALCRAFT INC (HQ)
28101 Schoolcraft Rd (48150-2239)
PHONE.................................734 261-6700
Kurt Saldana, *CEO*
Ken Lerg, *COO*
Ej Long, *Engineer*
Scott Bain, *CFO*
▲ **EMP:** 149
SALES (est): 107.2MM
SALES (corp-wide): 10.2MM **Privately Held**
WEB: www.qualitymetalcraft.com
SIC: 3544 3465 3469 3444 Special dies & tools; automotive stampings; body parts, automobile: stamped metal; metal stampings; sheet metalwork
PA: Watermill-Qmc Holdings, Corp.
   750 Marrett Rd Ste 401
   Lexington MA 02421
   781 398-9460

(G-9901)
QUANTUM CHEMICAL LLC
Also Called: Chemsol
12944 Farmington Rd (48150-4201)
PHONE.................................734 429-0033
Robert Skandalaris, *President*
EMP: 9
SQ FT: 8,000
SALES: 2.1MM **Privately Held**
SIC: 2851 5085 5169 Paints & paint additives; undercoatings, paint; polyurethane coatings; abrasives & adhesives; adhesives & sealants; industrial chemicals

(G-9902)
QUANTUM INNOVATIONS LLC
33680 5 Mile Rd (48154-2866)
PHONE.................................734 576-2000
EMP: 3 **EST:** 2011
SALES (est): 295.1K **Privately Held**
SIC: 3572 Mfg Computer Storage Devices

(G-9903)
R & B INDUSTRIES INC
12055 Globe St (48150-1142)
PHONE.................................734 462-9478
Mark Schloff, *President*
Facundo Bravo, *Principal*
▼ **EMP:** 35
SQ FT: 40,000
SALES (est): 4.4MM **Privately Held**
SIC: 3599 3545 Machine shop, jobbing & repair; machine tool accessories

(G-9904)
R CUSHMAN & ASSOCIATES INC
Also Called: Fabco Automotive
12623 Newburgh Rd (48150-1001)
PHONE.................................248 477-9900
Richard Cushman, *President*
Sarah Smith, *Human Resources*
JB Derderian, *Director*
▲ **EMP:** 35 **EST:** 1966
SQ FT: 60,000
SALES (est): 10.2MM **Publicly Held**
WEB: www.rcushman.com
SIC: 3714 8711 Transmissions, motor vehicle; industrial engineers
HQ: Meritor Specialty Products Llc
   151 Lawrence Dr
   Livermore CA 94551
   248 435-1000

(G-9905)
R L SCHMITT COMPANY INC
34506 Glendale St (48150-1304)
PHONE.................................734 525-9310
Paul L Schmitt, *President*
Bruce J Schmitt, *Vice Pres*
EMP: 24 **EST:** 1947

GEOGRAPHIC SECTION
Livonia - Wayne County (G-9936)

SQ FT: 12,000
SALES (est): 4MM **Privately Held**
WEB: www.rlschmitt.com
SIC: **3545** 2819 Cutting tools for machine tools; industrial inorganic chemicals

(G-9906)
RED TIE GROUP INC
11898 Belden Ct (48150-1465)
PHONE.................................734 458-2011
Matt Stoney, *Branch Mgr*
EMP: 12
SALES (corp-wide): 145.1MM **Privately Held**
WEB: www.bsink.com
SIC: **2893** Printing ink
HQ: Red Tie Group, Inc.
3650 E 93rd St
Cleveland OH 44105
216 271-2300

(G-9907)
REEMCO INCORPORATED
11801 Belden Ct (48150-1460)
PHONE.................................734 522-8988
Hanna M Ackall, *President*
Richard C Schultz, *Partner*
EMP: 6
SQ FT: 10,000
SALES (est): 1MM **Privately Held**
WEB: www.reemco.com
SIC: **3599** Machine shop, jobbing & repair

(G-9908)
REGGIE MCKENZIE INDUS MTLS
34401 Schoolcraft Rd (48150-1332)
P.O. Box 1186, Jackson (49204-1186)
PHONE.................................734 261-0844
Reggie McKenzie, *President*
EMP: 7
SALES (est): 1MM **Privately Held**
SIC: **3541** Saws, power (metalworking machinery)

(G-9909)
RICK WYKLE LLC
Also Called: Dewsbury Manufactruing Company
12502 Globe St (48150-1144)
P.O. Box 627, Trenton (48183-0627)
PHONE.................................734 839-6376
Rick Wykle, *Owner*
EMP: 5
SQ FT: 5,400
SALES (est): 200K **Privately Held**
SIC: **5065** 3444 3625 Electronic parts & equipment; metal housings, enclosures, casings & other containers; relays & industrial controls

(G-9910)
RK BORING INC
35425 Schoolcraft Rd (48150-1222)
PHONE.................................734 542-7920
Kevin Stevens, *President*
EMP: 7
SQ FT: 3,300
SALES (est): 982.3K **Privately Held**
SIC: **3544** Special dies & tools

(G-9911)
ROUSH ENTERPRISES INC
12447 Levan Rd (48150-1405)
PHONE.................................734 779-7006
EMP: 787 **Privately Held**
SIC: **3714** Motor vehicle parts & accessories
PA: Roush Enterprises, Inc.
34300 W 9 Mile Rd
Farmington MI 48335

(G-9912)
ROUSH INDUSTRIES INC
36580 Commerce St (48150-1121)
PHONE.................................734 779-7016
Jeff Johnston, *Vice Pres*
EMP: 25 **Privately Held**
SIC: **8711** 3714 8734 7948 Engineering services; motor vehicle parts & accessories; testing laboratories; racing, including track operation
HQ: Roush Industries, Inc.
12447 Levan Rd
Livonia MI 48150
734 779-7006

(G-9913)
ROUSH INDUSTRIES INC
11874 Market St (48150-1123)
PHONE.................................734 779-7013
Tom Topper, *Branch Mgr*
EMP: 45 **Privately Held**
SIC: **8711** 3714 8734 Engineering services; motor vehicle engines & parts; motor vehicle transmissions, drive assemblies & parts; automobile proving & testing ground
HQ: Roush Industries, Inc.
12447 Levan Rd
Livonia MI 48150
734 779-7006

(G-9914)
ROUSH INDUSTRIES INC
12447 Levan Rd Bldg 6 (48150-1405)
PHONE.................................734 779-7000
Doug Smith, *Branch Mgr*
EMP: 125 **Privately Held**
SIC: **3599** Machine & other job shop work
HQ: Roush Industries, Inc.
12447 Levan Rd
Livonia MI 48150
734 779-7006

(G-9915)
ROUSH MANUFACTURING INC (HQ)
12447 Levan Rd (48150-1405)
PHONE.................................734 779-7006
Evan Lyall, *CEO*
Jeff Johnston, *Exec VP*
Dean Massab, *Exec VP*
Steve Sciatto, *Vice Pres*
▲ EMP: 130
SALES (est): 33.4MM **Privately Held**
SIC: **3714** 8711 Motor vehicle parts & accessories; engineering services

(G-9916)
S & C TOOL & MANUFACTURING
30954 Industrial Rd Ste A (48150-2061)
PHONE.................................313 378-1003
John L Spiteri, *President*
Sandra K Spiteri, *Admin Sec*
EMP: 4
SQ FT: 2,000
SALES (est): 535.2K **Privately Held**
SIC: **3599** Machine shop, jobbing & repair

(G-9917)
S & L TOOL INC
11833 Brookfield St (48150-1701)
PHONE.................................734 464-4200
Stephen Lindsay, *President*
Betty Burns, *Office Mgr*
EMP: 7
SALES (est): 940.1K **Privately Held**
SIC: **3541** 3542 Machine tools, metal cutting type; rebuilt machine tools, metal forming types

(G-9918)
S P JIG GRINDING
32465 Schoolcraft Rd (48150-4300)
PHONE.................................734 525-6335
Larry Saganski, *Owner*
EMP: 3 EST: 1974
SQ FT: 1,000
SALES (est): 750K **Privately Held**
SIC: **3599** Grinding castings for the trade

(G-9919)
SALES & ENGINEERING INC
32920 Industrial Rd (48150-1617)
PHONE.................................734 525-9030
James D Allen, *President*
Cynthia Allen, *Vice Pres*
EMP: 50 EST: 1971
SQ FT: 31,000
SALES (est): 10.6MM **Privately Held**
WEB: www.sales-eng.com
SIC: **3465** 3498 3441 Body parts, automobile: stamped metal; tube fabricating (contract bending & shaping); fabricated structural metal

(G-9920)
SAMPLING BAG TECHNOLOGIES LLC
27491 Schoolcraft Rd (48150-2201)
PHONE.................................734 525-8600
George Smith, *General Mgr*
Arthur Coleman, *Mng Member*
EMP: 6
SALES (est): 250K **Privately Held**
WEB: www.samplingbagtech.com
SIC: **3634** Blankets, electric

(G-9921)
SB INVESTMENTS LLC
Also Called: Reinhart Industries
12055 Globe St (48150-1142)
PHONE.................................734 462-9478
Wally Bishop, *Plant Mgr*
Mark J Schloff, *Mng Member*
EMP: 22
SQ FT: 28,000
SALES: 15MM **Privately Held**
SIC: **3549** 3545 Marking machines, metalworking; arbors (machine tool accessories)

(G-9922)
SCHEELS CONCRETE INC
33146 Grennada St (48154-4171)
PHONE.................................734 782-1464
EMP: 8 EST: 1919
SQ FT: 20,000
SALES (est): 1MM **Privately Held**
SIC: **3273** Mfg Ready-Mixed Concrete

(G-9923)
SCRAPPY CHIC
33523 8 Mile Rd Ste C1 (48152-4104)
PHONE.................................248 426-9020
Chris Nicholson, *Executive Asst*
EMP: 4
SALES (est): 395.1K **Privately Held**
SIC: **2782** Scrapbooks

(G-9924)
SECURITY COUNTERMEASURES TECH
37637 5 Mile Rd (48154-1543)
PHONE.................................248 237-6263
William Tisaby, *Principal*
EMP: 4
SALES (est): 444.3K **Privately Held**
SIC: **3131** Counters

(G-9925)
SENSCOMP INC
36704 Commerce St (48150-1164)
PHONE.................................734 953-4783
Richard Berzerko, *President*
EMP: 25
SALES (est): 3MM **Privately Held**
WEB: www.senscomp.com
SIC: **3812** Search & navigation equipment

(G-9926)
SIEMENS PRODUCT LIFE MGMT SFTW
38695 7 Mile Rd Ste 300 (48152-7097)
PHONE.................................734 953-2700
Lovquist George, *Branch Mgr*
Mary Charnley, *Manager*
William Prete, *Technical Staff*
EMP: 100
SALES (corp-wide): 95B **Privately Held**
SIC: **7372** Business oriented computer software
HQ: Siemens Industry Software Inc.
5800 Granite Pkwy Ste 600
Plano TX 75024
972 987-3000

(G-9927)
SIGMA DIAGNOSTICS INC
Also Called: Immunospec
14155 Farmington Rd Ste D (48154-5422)
PHONE.................................734 744-4846
Mojeeb Shahbain, *Principal*
▲ EMP: 6
SALES (est): 638K **Privately Held**
SIC: **2835** In vitro & in vivo diagnostic substances

(G-9928)
SIGMA INTERNATIONAL INC (PA)
36800 Plymouth Rd (48150-1136)
PHONE.................................248 230-9681
Christopher J Naidoo, *CEO*
◆ EMP: 20
SQ FT: 8,150
SALES (est): 10.8MM **Privately Held**
WEB: www.sigmaintl.com
SIC: **2396** 2821 3471 Fabric printing & stamping; plastics materials & resins; electroplating & plating

(G-9929)
SIGMA LUMINOUS LLC
36800 Plymouth Rd (48150-1136)
PHONE.................................800 482-1327
Christopher Naidoo, *President*
Waseem Ksebati, *Business Anlyst*
▲ EMP: 6
SQ FT: 10,000
SALES: 2MM **Privately Held**
SIC: **3674** Light emitting diodes

(G-9930)
SIGN & ART INC
12321 Stark Rd Ste 2 (48150-5506)
PHONE.................................734 522-0520
Timothy Foley, *President*
Colleen Foley, *Vice Pres*
EMP: 5
SALES (est): 404.3K **Privately Held**
WEB: www.signatureart.com
SIC: **3993** Signs & advertising specialties

(G-9931)
SIGN STUFF INC
13604 Merriman Rd (48150-1814)
PHONE.................................734 458-1055
William J Buyers IV, *President*
Danny Desjardin, *Manager*
EMP: 5
SQ FT: 3,100
SALES (est): 791K **Privately Held**
WEB: www.signstuff.com
SIC: **3993** Signs & advertising specialties

(G-9932)
SL WHEELS INC
Also Called: Speedline
38701 7 Mile Rd Ste 155 (48152-3970)
PHONE.................................734 744-8500
Michele Mazzucconi, *President*
▲ EMP: 5
SALES (est): 838.2K
SALES (corp-wide): 25.8MM **Privately Held**
SIC: **3312** Wheels
HQ: Speedline Srl
Via Salgari 6
Santa Maria Di Sala VE 30036
041 572-9832

(G-9933)
SLOTTING INGRAM & MACHINE
32175 Industrial Rd (48150-1836)
PHONE.................................248 478-2430
David Ingram, *President*
EMP: 10
SQ FT: 6,300
SALES: 750K **Privately Held**
SIC: **3599** Machine shop, jobbing & repair; custom machinery

(G-9934)
SNOW TECHNOLOGIES INCORPORATED
13015 Fairlane St (48150-1325)
PHONE.................................734 425-3600
Earl Mott, *President*
EMP: 3
SALES (est): 722K **Privately Held**
WEB: www.snow-tech.com
SIC: **3585** Heating equipment, complete

(G-9935)
SOL-I-COR INDUSTRIES
Also Called: Corian By Solicor Industries
30795 8 Mile Rd (48152-1601)
PHONE.................................248 476-0670
Gary Bohr, *Owner*
EMP: 18
SALES (est): 1MM **Privately Held**
SIC: **3441** Fabricated structural metal

(G-9936)
SOUTHWIN LTD
11800 Sears St (48150-2107)
PHONE.................................734 525-9000
Fred Greco, *General Mgr*
EMP: 20 EST: 2011
SALES (est): 2.8MM **Privately Held**
SIC: **2842** Window cleaning preparations

Livonia - Wayne County (G-9937) GEOGRAPHIC SECTION

(G-9937)
SPARE DIE INC
30948 Industrial Rd (48150-2024)
PHONE..................................734 522-2508
Ron Clymer, *President*
EMP: 4
SALES (est): 292.8K **Privately Held**
SIC: 3544 Special dies & tools

(G-9938)
SPECTRUM AUTOMATION COMPANY
34447 Schoolcraft Rd (48150-1316)
PHONE..................................734 522-2160
Richard D Zimmerman, *President*
Thomas Zimmerman, *Corp Secy*
EMP: 25
SQ FT: 26,000
SALES (est): 6.6MM **Privately Held**
WEB: www.spectrumautomation.com
SIC: 3535 Unit handling conveying systems

(G-9939)
SPEEDWAY ORDERING SYSTEMS INC
Also Called: Robicon
27601 Schoolcraft Rd C (48150-2242)
PHONE..................................734 420-0482
Theos Strates, *President*
Strates Theos, *President*
Christine Theos, *Admin Sec*
EMP: 3 **EST:** 1961
SQ FT: 1,500
SALES (est): 180K **Privately Held**
SIC: 3571 5044 Computers, digital, analog or hybrid; cash registers

(G-9940)
SPX CORPORATION
13324 Farmington Rd (48150-4203)
PHONE..................................313 768-2103
Rich Huber, *Principal*
EMP: 97
SALES (corp-wide): 1.5B **Publicly Held**
WEB: www.spx.com
SIC: 3443 Cooling towers, metal plate
PA: Spx Corporation
13320a Balntyn Corp Pl
Charlotte NC 28277
980 474-3700

(G-9941)
STANDARD DIE INTERNATIONAL INC (PA)
12980 Wayne Rd (48150-1259)
PHONE..................................800 838-5464
Douglas C Menzies, *President*
Tim Plymale, *COO*
Alan R Menzies, *Vice Pres*
Jill Krol, *Project Mgr*
Gregory Gagner, *Purchasing*
EMP: 50
SQ FT: 30,000
SALES (est): 12.4MM **Privately Held**
WEB: www.standarddie.com
SIC: 3544 3469 Special dies & tools; stamping metal for the trade

(G-9942)
STANDFAST INDUSTRIES INC
13570 Wayne Rd (48150-1270)
PHONE..................................248 380-3223
Brian D O'Connor, *President*
Gary T Riddell, *Corp Secy*
Laurette Walsh, *Vice Pres*
EMP: 28
SQ FT: 27,500
SALES (est): 5.6MM **Privately Held**
WEB: www.standfastnitrogencylinders.com
SIC: 3561 Cylinders, pump

(G-9943)
STANFORD DENTAL PLLC
34441 8 Mile Rd Ste 114 (48152-4013)
PHONE..................................248 476-4500
Mark A Stanford, *Principal*
EMP: 8
SALES (est): 905.3K **Privately Held**
SIC: 3843 Enamels, dentists'

(G-9944)
STAR DESIGN METRO DETROIT LLC
32401 8 Mile Rd Ste 1-1 (48152-1301)
PHONE..................................734 740-0189
Ali Ayesh,
EMP: 41
SQ FT: 1,000
SALES (est): 262.9K **Privately Held**
SIC: 7336 7819 2741 3993 Commercial art & graphic design; developing & printing of commercial motion picture film; posters: publishing & printing; electric signs

(G-9945)
STEELCRAFT TOOL CO INC
12930 Wayne Rd (48150-1272)
PHONE..................................734 522-7130
James P Glaser, *President*
Nancy G Marr, *Vice Pres*
EMP: 32 **EST:** 1943
SQ FT: 13,000
SALES (est): 4MM **Privately Held**
WEB: www.steelcrafttool.com
SIC: 3545 3423 Cutting tools for machine tools; hand & edge tools

(G-9946)
STORCH PRODUCTS COMPANY INC
Also Called: Storch Magnetics
11827 Globe St (48150-1188)
PHONE..................................734 591-2200
Marjorie A Storch, *President*
Thomas Papora, *Vice Pres*
Todd Papora, *Vice Pres*
Robert Mount, *Engineer*
Dawn Sparagowski, *Clerk*
▲ **EMP:** 17
SQ FT: 25,500
SALES (est): 4.2MM **Privately Held**
WEB: www.storchmagnetics.com
SIC: 3695 3535 Magnetic & optical recording media; conveyors & conveying equipment

(G-9947)
SUGRU INC
38120 Amrhein Rd (48150-5016)
PHONE..................................877 990-9888
EMP: 3
SALES (est): 126.9K **Privately Held**
SIC: 2891 Glue
PA: Formformform Ltd
Unit 2 47-49 Tudor Road
London E9 7S

(G-9948)
SUPERIOR INFORMATION TECH LLC
Also Called: Anantics
38701 7 Mile Rd Ste 285 (48152-4123)
PHONE..................................734 666-9963
Anurag Kulshrestha,
EMP: 10
SQ FT: 2,500
SALES: 1MM **Privately Held**
SIC: 7371 7372 7373 7389 Custom computer programming services; application computer software; utility computer software; systems engineering, computer related; turnkey vendors, computer systems; photogrammatic mapping

(G-9949)
SWIRLBERRY
17382 Haggerty Rd (48152-2608)
PHONE..................................734 779-0830
EMP: 4 **EST:** 2010
SALES (est): 248.8K **Privately Held**
SIC: 2024 Mfg Ice Cream/Frozen Desert

(G-9950)
SYNCON INC
31001 Schoolcraft Rd (48150-2029)
P.O. Box 23042, Dearborn (48123-2867)
PHONE..................................313 914-4481
Ryan Klacking, *President*
Chris Klacking, *Vice Pres*
Renee Ferguson, *Treasurer*
Lee Swallow, *Director*
EMP: 48
SALES (est): 3.9MM **Privately Held**
SIC: 3531 Surfacers, concrete grinding

(G-9951)
SYSTEM CONTROLS INC
35245 Schoolcraft Rd (48150-1209)
PHONE..................................734 427-0440
Donald Rende, *President*
EMP: 30 **EST:** 2003
SALES (est): 6.6MM **Privately Held**
SIC: 3822 Appliance regulators

(G-9952)
T F G GAGE COMPONENTS
11901 Brookfield St (48150-1736)
P.O. Box 3334 (48151-3334)
PHONE..................................734 427-2274
Frank C Murtland III, *Partner*
Gregory H Murtland, *Partner*
Terri Murtland, *Partner*
EMP: 3
SQ FT: 9,000
SALES (est): 463.2K **Privately Held**
WEB: www.transcom.mil
SIC: 5084 3452 Industrial machinery & equipment; bolts, nuts, rivets & washers

(G-9953)
TARA INDUSTRIES INC (PA)
30105 8 Mile Rd (48152-1811)
PHONE..................................248 477-6520
Ravi K Tandon, *CEO*
Adam Tandon, *President*
Selma Cimsit, *Treasurer*
EMP: 10
SQ FT: 8,800
SALES (est): 1.7MM **Privately Held**
SIC: 3444 3612 3613 Metal housings, enclosures, casings & other containers; lighting transformers, fluorescent; switchboards & parts, power

(G-9954)
TECHNI CAM AND MANUFACTURING
30633 Schoolcraft Rd A (48150-2008)
PHONE..................................734 261-6477
Chris Meadows, *President*
Greg Meadows, *Vice Pres*
EMP: 10
SQ FT: 10,000
SALES (est): 1MM **Privately Held**
WEB: www.technicam.com
SIC: 3545 3599 7538 Cams (machine tool accessories); machine shop, jobbing & repair; general automotive repair shops

(G-9955)
TESTRON INCORPORATED
34153 Industrial Rd (48150-1305)
PHONE..................................734 513-6820
Brian E Dombrowsky, *President*
EMP: 16
SQ FT: 8,500
SALES (est): 300K **Privately Held**
SIC: 3829 3825 3823 3643 Physical property testing equipment; instruments to measure electricity; industrial instrmnts msrmnt display/control process variable; current-carrying wiring devices

(G-9956)
THERMAL SOLUTIONS MFG (PA)
35255 Glendale St (48150-1254)
PHONE..................................734 655-7145
EMP: 3
SALES (est): 2MM **Privately Held**
SIC: 3714 Motor vehicle parts & accessories

(G-9957)
TOOLING & EQUIPMENT INTL CORP
12550 Tech Center Dr (48150-2192)
PHONE..................................734 522-1422
Oliver Johnson, *President*
Robert Showalter, *Sales Staff*
EMP: 120
SQ FT: 80,000
SALES (est): 35.8MM **Privately Held**
WEB: www.teintl.net
SIC: 3365 Aluminum & aluminum-based alloy castings; aerospace castings, aluminum; machinery castings, aluminum

(G-9958)
TOWER ACQUISITION CO II LLC
17672 N Laurel Park Dr (48152-3984)
PHONE..................................248 675-6000
EMP: 4
SALES (est): 243K
SALES (corp-wide): 2.2B **Privately Held**
SIC: 3465 Body parts, automobile: stamped metal
HQ: Tower International, Inc.
17672 N Laurel Park Dr
Livonia MI 48152

(G-9959)
TOWER AUTMTVE OPRTNS USA III (DH)
17672 N Laurel Park Dr (48152-3984)
PHONE..................................248 675-6000
Mark Malcolm, *President*
EMP: 5
SALES (est): 1.6MM
SALES (corp-wide): 2.2B **Privately Held**
SIC: 3465 Automotive stampings

(G-9960)
TOWER AUTO HOLDINGS I LLC
17672 N Laurel Park Dr 400e (48152-3984)
PHONE..................................248 675-6000
Mark Malcolm, *President*
Seth Gardner, *President*
Jeffrey Lomasky, *Treasurer*
▲ **EMP:** 6
SALES (est): 1.4MM
SALES (corp-wide): 2.2B **Privately Held**
SIC: 3465 Automotive stampings
HQ: Tower International, Inc.
17672 N Laurel Park Dr
Livonia MI 48152

(G-9961)
TOWER AUTO HOLDINGS II A LLC
17672 N Laurel Park Dr 400e (48152-3984)
PHONE..................................248 675-6000
Mark Malcolm, *Principal*
Seth Gardner, *Principal*
Jeffrey L Lomasky, *Principal*
EMP: 3
SALES (est): 206.9K
SALES (corp-wide): 2.2B **Privately Held**
SIC: 3465 Automotive stampings
HQ: Tower International, Inc.
17672 N Laurel Park Dr
Livonia MI 48152

(G-9962)
TOWER AUTO HOLDINGS II B LLC
17672 N Laurel Park Dr (48152-3984)
PHONE..................................248 675-6000
Jim Gouin, *CEO*
EMP: 4
SALES (est): 248.4K
SALES (corp-wide): 2.2B **Privately Held**
SIC: 3465 Automotive stampings
HQ: Tower International, Inc.
17672 N Laurel Park Dr
Livonia MI 48152

(G-9963)
TOWER AUTO HOLDINGS USA LLC (DH)
Also Called: Tower International
17672 N Laurel Park Dr 400e (48152-3984)
PHONE..................................248 675-6000
Ken Kundrick, *President*
Mark Malcolm, *Bd of Directors*
Seth Gardner,
James Gouin,
Jeffrey L Lomasky,
▲ **EMP:** 19
SALES (est): 963.4MM
SALES (corp-wide): 2.2B **Privately Held**
SIC: 3465 Automotive stampings

(G-9964)
TOWER AUTOMOTIVE OPERATIONS (DH)
17672 N Laurel Park Dr 400e (48152-3984)
PHONE..................................248 675-6000

GEOGRAPHIC SECTION

Livonia - Wayne County (G-9989)

Dev B Kapadia, *President*
Seth Gardner, *Vice Pres*
Jeffrey L Lomasky, *Treasurer*
Christopher Pyzik, *Administration*
▲ **EMP:** 100
SALES (est): 893.5MM
SALES (corp-wide): 2.2B **Privately Held**
SIC: 3465 Automotive stampings

(G-9965)
TOWER AUTOMOTIVE OPERATIONS (DH)
17672 N Laurel Park Dr 400e (48152-3984)
PHONE..................248 675-6000
Mark Malcolm, *President*
Seth Gardner, *Vice Pres*
Pilar Alvarez, *Materials Mgr*
John Tockstein, *Senior Buyer*
Studstill Daryl, *Buyer*
▲ **EMP:** 3
SALES (est): 82.8MM
SALES (corp-wide): 2.2B **Privately Held**
SIC: 3465 Automotive stampings

(G-9966)
TOWER DEFENSE & AEROSPACE LLC
Also Called: W Industries
17672 N Laurel Park Dr (48152-3984)
PHONE..................248 675-6000
Michael Rajkovic, *Mng Member*
Ron Lecronier,
▲ **EMP:** 250
SALES (est): 34.5MM
SALES (corp-wide): 2.2B **Privately Held**
SIC: 3465 3365 3443 Automotive stampings; aerospace castings, aluminum; metal parts
HQ: Tower International, Inc.
   17672 N Laurel Park Dr
   Livonia MI 48152

(G-9967)
TOWER INTERNATIONAL INC (HQ)
17672 N Laurel Park Dr (48152-3984)
PHONE..................248 675-6000
George Thanopoulos, *President*
▲ **EMP:** 300
SQ FT: 76,000
SALES: 1.5B
SALES (corp-wide): 2.2B **Privately Held**
SIC: 3465 Body parts, automobile: stamped metal
PA: Autokiniton Us Holdings, Inc.
   485 Lexington Ave Fl 31
   New York NY 10017
   212 338-5100

(G-9968)
TRADE BINDERY SERVICE INC
35400 Plymouth Rd (48150-1425)
PHONE..................734 425-7500
Steven Pair, *President*
EMP: 7
SQ FT: 10,500
SALES (est): 959.4K **Privately Held**
SIC: 2789 Bookbinding & repairing: trade, edition, library, etc.

(G-9969)
TRANE US INC
33725 Schoolcraft Rd (48150-1505)
PHONE..................734 367-0700
David Westbrook, *Branch Mgr*
EMP: 7 **Privately Held**
SIC: 3585 Refrigeration & heating equipment
HQ: Trane U.S. Inc.
   3600 Pammel Creek Rd
   La Crosse WI 54601
   608 787-2000

(G-9970)
TRANE US INC
37001 Industrial Rd (48150-1146)
PHONE..................734 452-2000
Mark Wagner, *Branch Mgr*
EMP: 100 **Privately Held**
SIC: 3585 Refrigeration & heating equipment

HQ: Trane U.S. Inc.
   3600 Pammel Creek Rd
   La Crosse WI 54601
   608 787-2000

(G-9971)
TRIGON METAL PRODUCTS INC
12725 Inkster Rd (48150-2216)
PHONE..................734 513-3488
John F Stankey, *President*
Johanna E Stankey, *Corp Secy*
Traci Krohn, *Purchasing*
EMP: 8 **EST:** 1974
SQ FT: 22,000
SALES (est): 1.3MM **Privately Held**
WEB: www.corrosionsource.com
SIC: 3444 Sheet metal specialties, not stamped; metal housings, enclosures, casings & other containers

(G-9972)
TRU-LINE SCREW PRODUCTS INC (PA)
Also Called: Tru-Line Metal Products Co
15223 Farmington Rd Ste 5 (48154-5411)
P.O. Box 510323 (48151-6323)
PHONE..................734 261-8780
Thomas E Gresham, *President*
Gary H Burton, *Vice Pres*
EMP: 30 **EST:** 1950
SQ FT: 6,600
SALES (est): 5.2MM **Privately Held**
WEB: www.trulinemetal.com
SIC: 3451 Screw machine products

(G-9973)
TRU-LINE SCREW PRODUCTS INC
Also Called: Tru-Line Metal Products
30649 Schoolcraft Rd (48150-2008)
PHONE..................734 261-8780
Tom Gresham, *President*
EMP: 20
SALES (corp-wide): 5.2MM **Privately Held**
WEB: www.trulinemetal.com
SIC: 3451 Screw machine products
PA: Tru-Line Screw Products Incorporated
   15223 Farmington Rd Ste 5
   Livonia MI 48154
   734 261-8780

(G-9974)
TRW AUTO HOLDINGS INC (DH)
12001 Tech Center Dr (48150-2122)
PHONE..................734 855-2600
John Plant, *Principal*
Clive Trickey, *Project Mgr*
Thomas Rossman, *Manager*
Felicia Wirgau, *Manager*
Shannon Armstrong, *Supervisor*
EMP: 1
SALES (est): 2.4MM
SALES (corp-wide): 216.2K **Privately Held**
SIC: 3714 Motor vehicle parts & accessories
HQ: Zf Friedrichshafen Ag
   Lowentaler Str. 20
   Friedrichshafen 88046
   754 177-0

(G-9975)
TRW AUTOMOTIVE JV LLC (DH)
12001 Tech Center Dr (48150-2122)
PHONE..................734 855-2787
John Plant,
EMP: 7
SALES (est): 173.6K
SALES (corp-wide): 216.2K **Privately Held**
SIC: 3714 Connecting rods, motor vehicle engine
HQ: Zf Trw Automotive Holdings Corp.
   12001 Tech Center Dr
   Livonia MI 48150
   734 855-2600

(G-9976)
TRW EAST INC
12001 Tech Center Dr (48150-2122)
PHONE..................734 855-2600
EMP: 4

SALES (est): 242.2K
SALES (corp-wide): 216.2K **Privately Held**
SIC: 3714 Motor vehicle parts & accessories
HQ: Zf Trw Automotive Holdings Corp.
   12001 Tech Center Dr
   Livonia MI 48150
   734 855-2600

(G-9977)
TRW ODYSSEY MEXICO LLC
12001 Tech Center Dr (48150-2122)
PHONE..................734 855-2600
Tom Wells, *President*
EMP: 4
SALES (est): 309.6K
SALES (corp-wide): 216.2K **Privately Held**
SIC: 3714 Motor vehicle parts & accessories
HQ: Zf Trw Automotive Holdings Corp.
   12001 Tech Center Dr
   Livonia MI 48150
   734 855-2600

(G-9978)
TURBINE TOOL & GAGE INC
11901 Brookfield St (48150-1736)
P.O. Box 3334 (48151-3334)
PHONE..................734 427-2270
Audrey Murtland, *President*
Gregory Murtland, *Vice Pres*
Gregory H Murtland, *Treasurer*
Bruce Rossler, *Supervisor*
EMP: 17 **EST:** 1966
SQ FT: 9,000
SALES (est): 3MM **Privately Held**
WEB: www.turbinetoolandgage.com
SIC: 3545 3544 3823 Gauges (machine tool accessories); jigs & fixtures; draft gauges, industrial process type

(G-9979)
U S FABRICATION & DESIGN LLC
32890 Capitol St (48150-1706)
PHONE..................248 919-2910
Mark Perry,
Robert Provow,
EMP: 12
SQ FT: 25,000
SALES (est): 4.1MM **Privately Held**
SIC: 3441 Fabricated structural metal

(G-9980)
UIS INDUSTRIES LLC
39111 6 Mile Rd (48152-3926)
PHONE..................734 443-3737
John Pierce,
EMP: 4
SALES (est): 132.5K **Privately Held**
SIC: 3999 Manufacturing industries

(G-9981)
UNITED STATE PHRM GROUP
39209 6 Mile Rd (48152-2688)
PHONE..................734 462-3685
Tracy Frey, *Manager*
EMP: 3
SALES (est): 187.8K **Privately Held**
SIC: 2834 Pharmaceutical preparations

(G-9982)
UPPER LEVEL GRAPHICS INC
13193 Wayne Rd (48150-1266)
P.O. Box 5345, Plymouth (48170-5345)
PHONE..................734 525-7111
Betty Rojek, *CEO*
Matthew Rojek, *President*
EMP: 3
SQ FT: 1,000
SALES (est): 398.7K **Privately Held**
WEB: www.ulgraphics.com
SIC: 3993 Signs & advertising specialties

(G-9983)
US GREEN ENERGY SOLUTIONS LLC
9532 Harrison St (48150-3130)
PHONE..................810 955-2992
Patrick Smith,
Cassandra Smith,
Edgar Smith,
Peiyi Yao,
EMP: 5

SALES (est): 216K **Privately Held**
SIC: 3612 7389 Transformers, except electric;

(G-9984)
UV PARTNERS INC (PA)
Also Called: Uv Angel
38099 Schoolcraft Rd # 165 (48150-1029)
PHONE..................616 204-5416
Douglas Sharp, *VP Finance*
EMP: 8
SALES (est): 946.3K **Privately Held**
SIC: 3845 5731 Electromedical equipment; consumer electronic equipment

(G-9985)
VALASSIS COMMUNICATIONS INC (DH)
19975 Victor Pkwy (48152-7001)
PHONE..................734 591-3000
Cali Tran, *President*
Alan F Schultz, *Chairman*
Ronald L Goolsby, *COO*
James D Parkinson, *Exec VP*
Todd L Wiseley, *Exec VP*
▲ **EMP:** 148
SALES (est): 800.4MM **Privately Held**
WEB: www.valassis.com
SIC: 7319 7331 7372 Distribution of advertising material or sample services; direct mail advertising services; business oriented computer software
HQ: Harland Clarke Holdings Corp.
   15955 La Cantera Pkwy
   San Antonio TX 78256
   210 697-8888

(G-9986)
VALASSIS COMMUNICATIONS INC
38905 6 Mile Rd (48150-3933)
PHONE..................734 432-8000
Ruth Libbey, *Branch Mgr*
EMP: 180 **Privately Held**
WEB: www.valassis.com
SIC: 7319 7331 7372 Distribution of advertising material or sample services; direct mail advertising services; business oriented computer software
HQ: Valassis Communications, Inc.
   19975 Victor Pkwy
   Livonia MI 48152
   734 591-3000

(G-9987)
VALASSIS INTERNATIONAL INC (DH)
19975 Victor Pkwy (48152-7001)
PHONE..................734 591-3000
Rob Mason, *President*
Todd Wiseley, *Exec VP*
Blaine Gerber, *Vice Pres*
Brandon Garoutte, *Sales Staff*
Darren Ryder, *Sales Staff*
EMP: 350
SQ FT: 85,000
SALES (est): 288.7MM **Privately Held**
SIC: 8743 3993 2759 2752 Promotion service; sales promotion; signs & advertising specialties; commercial printing; commercial printing, lithographic
HQ: Valassis Communications, Inc.
   19975 Victor Pkwy
   Livonia MI 48152
   734 591-3000

(G-9988)
VENUS CONTROLS INC
30105 8 Mile Rd (48152-1811)
PHONE..................248 477-0448
Ravi Tandon, *President*
Kristin Tandon, *Corp Secy*
Adam Tandon, *Vice Pres*
EMP: 15
SQ FT: 8,800
SALES (est): 3MM **Privately Held**
SIC: 3625 Relays & industrial controls

(G-9989)
VERBIO NORTH AMERICA CORP (PA)
17199 N Laurel Park Dr # 409 (48152-7911)
PHONE..................866 306-4777
Claus Sauter, *Director*

Livonia - Wayne County (G-9990)

EMP: 3
SALES (est): 612.5K **Privately Held**
SIC: 1389 Cementing oil & gas well casings

(G-9990)
VISOTEK INC
11700 Belden Ct (48150-1428)
PHONE.................................734 427-4800
Sheila Jensen, *President*
Elmer Wang, *Electrical Engi*
EMP: 10
SQ FT: 15,000
SALES (est): 2.2MM
SALES (corp-wide): 19.9MM **Privately Held**
WEB: www.visotekinc.com
SIC: 3699 3827 Laser welding, drilling & cutting equipment; optical instruments & apparatus
PA: Laser Mechanisms, Inc.
25325 Regency Dr
Novi MI 48375
248 474-9480

(G-9991)
VOILA PRINT INC
37000 Industrial Rd (48150-1135)
PHONE.................................866 942-1677
Fatima Ahmed, *President*
EMP: 3
SALES: 1MM
SALES (corp-wide): 1.6MM **Privately Held**
SIC: 2752 Commercial printing, lithographic
PA: Instant Printing And Graphics, Inc.
31373 Industrial Rd
Livonia MI

(G-9992)
VSR TECHNOLOGIES INC
12270 Belden Ct (48150-1459)
PHONE.................................734 425-7172
John Vella, *President*
John A Vella, *Vice Pres*
EMP: 10
SQ FT: 6,000
SALES: 6.5MM **Privately Held**
WEB: www.vsrtech.com
SIC: 3825 Test equipment for electronic & electric measurement

(G-9993)
VTEC GRAPHICS INC (PA)
12487 Globe St (48150-1134)
PHONE.................................734 953-9729
Steven Smith, *President*
Mark Mazur, *Vice Pres*
Eric Westberg, *Prdtn Mgr*
Jon Tkacz, *Art Dir*
EMP: 8
SQ FT: 7,500
SALES (est): 1.3MM **Privately Held**
WEB: www.vtecprint.com
SIC: 2752 7336 Offset & photolithographic printing; graphic arts & related design

(G-9994)
WAL FUEL SYSTEMS (USA) INC
39111 6 Mile Rd Ste 167 (48152-3926)
PHONE.................................248 579-4147
Tao MA, *President*
EMP: 5
SQ FT: 1,000
SALES (est): 1.3MM
SALES (corp-wide): 24.1MM **Privately Held**
SIC: 3569 Filters
PA: Wal Fuel Systems (Hefei) Co., Ltd
No.59, Fozhang Rd., Eco-Tech Development Zone
Hefei 23060
551 638-4710

(G-9995)
WALLIN BROTHERS INC
35270 Glendale St Ste 1 (48150-1264)
PHONE.................................734 525-7750
Ernest Johnson, *President*
Marlene Johnson, *Vice Pres*
EMP: 6 **EST:** 1946
SQ FT: 13,000
SALES: 1MM **Privately Held**
SIC: 3544 3469 Special dies & tools; metal stampings

(G-9996)
WAMU FUEL LLC
17151 Middlebelt Rd (48152-3609)
PHONE.................................313 386-8700
Wassef Zahr, *Principal*
EMP: 4
SALES (est): 378K **Privately Held**
SIC: 2869 Fuels

(G-9997)
WARN INDUSTRIES INC
37002 Industrial Rd (48150-1135)
PHONE.................................734 953-9870
Sean Blasch, *Director*
EMP: 4
SALES (corp-wide): 11.8B **Publicly Held**
SIC: 3714 Motor vehicle parts & accessories
HQ: Warn Industries, Inc.
12900 Se Capps Rd
Clackamas OR 97015
503 722-1200

(G-9998)
WARREN SCREW WORKS INC
Also Called: Warren Autometric Fasteners
13360 Wayne Rd (48150-1246)
PHONE.................................734 525-2920
Andrew Wojcik, *General Mgr*
EMP: 5
SQ FT: 10,000
SALES (est): 672.3K **Privately Held**
SIC: 3452 5072 Dowel pins, metal; miscellaneous fasteners; bolts; nuts (hardware)

(G-9999)
WASHERS INCORPORATED (PA)
Also Called: Alphausa
33375 Glendale St (48150-1615)
PHONE.................................734 523-1000
George Strumbos, *Ch of Bd*
Nicholas Strumbos, *President*
Douglas Johnson, *Controller*
Veronica Cruz, *Human Resources*
EMP: 129
SQ FT: 100,000
SALES (est): 32.9MM **Privately Held**
WEB: www.alphastamping.com
SIC: 3452 3465 Washers, metal; automotive stampings

(G-10000)
WASHERS INCORPORATED
32711 Glendale St (48150-1611)
PHONE.................................734 523-1000
Nicholas Strumbos, *President*
EMP: 4
SALES (corp-wide): 32.9MM **Privately Held**
SIC: 3452 3465 Washers, metal; automotive stampings
PA: Washers, Incorporated
33375 Glendale St
Livonia MI 48150
734 523-1000

(G-10001)
WAYNE-CRAFT INC
Also Called: Wayne Craft
13525 Wayne Rd (48150-1245)
PHONE.................................734 421-8800
Steven McFall, *President*
Steven Mc Fall, *President*
Kathleen Mc Fall, *Controller*
EMP: 18
SQ FT: 35,000
SALES (est): 4.9MM **Privately Held**
WEB: www.waynecraft.com
SIC: 5039 2431 3334 5051 Awnings; awnings, wood; primary aluminum; aluminum bars, rods, ingots, sheets, pipes, plates, etc.

(G-10002)
WEBASTO ROOF SYSTEMS INC
Also Called: Websto Stamping
36930 Industrial Rd (48150-1135)
PHONE.................................734 452-2600
Robert Eames, *Mfg Mgr*
Steve Skornicka, *Opers Staff*
Marius Mihalceanu, *Mfg Staff*
Kristin Blitz, *Buyer*
Martin Goschnick, *Buyer*
EMP: 225
SALES (corp-wide): 411.9K **Privately Held**
WEB: www.webasto.com
SIC: 3714 3469 Sun roofs, motor vehicle; metal stampings
HQ: Webasto Roof Systems Inc.
1757 Northfield Dr
Rochester Hills MI 48309
248 997-5100

(G-10003)
WELDCRAFT INC
11881 Belden Ct (48150-1460)
PHONE.................................734 779-1303
Chris Novack, *President*
EMP: 5
SQ FT: 3,000
SALES (est): 200K **Privately Held**
WEB: www.weldcraftwheels.com
SIC: 7692 Welding repair

(G-10004)
WELK-KO FABRICATORS INC (PA)
11885 Mayfield St (48150-1707)
PHONE.................................734 425-6840
Ronald S Karaisz II, *President*
Timothy P Karaisz, *Vice Pres*
EMP: 10 **EST:** 1967
SALES (est): 3.7MM **Privately Held**
WEB: www.kar-ent.com
SIC: 3444 3699 Sheet metal specialties, not stamped; electrical equipment & supplies

(G-10005)
WELLINGTON FRAGRANCE
33306 Glendale St (48150-1616)
PHONE.................................734 261-5531
William Waack, *Principal*
▲ **EMP:** 4
SALES (est): 469K **Privately Held**
SIC: 2844 Perfumes & colognes

(G-10006)
WELZ TOOL MCH & BORING CO INC
11952 Hubbard St (48150-1733)
PHONE.................................734 425-3920
Zef Vuljevic, *President*
EMP: 25
SQ FT: 20,000
SALES (est): 6MM **Privately Held**
SIC: 3599 Machine shop, jobbing & repair

(G-10007)
WEST/WIN LTD
11800 Sears St (48150-2107)
PHONE.................................734 525-9000
William Dubose, *President*
Blaine Dubose, *Vice Pres*
EMP: 5
SALES (est): 843.8K **Privately Held**
SIC: 3714 Windshield wiper systems, motor vehicle

(G-10008)
WESTCO METALCRAFT INC
31846 Glendale St (48150-1827)
PHONE.................................734 425-0900
Penny Johnson, *President*
Matt Johnson, *Vice Pres*
George Sharpe, *Vice Pres*
Patricia Westergaard, *Treasurer*
Harry Keolian, *Admin Sec*
EMP: 10
SQ FT: 11,000
SALES (est): 1.3MM **Privately Held**
WEB: www.westcometalcraft.com
SIC: 3444 Sheet metal specialties, not stamped

(G-10009)
WILLIAMS DIVERSIFIED INC
13170 Merriman Rd (48150-1816)
PHONE.................................734 421-6100
George Hieronymus, *President*
EMP: 42 **EST:** 1962
SQ FT: 19,000
SALES (est): 4.5MM **Privately Held**
WEB: www.williamsfinishing.com
SIC: 3471 3999 Plating of metals or formed products; custom pulverizing & grinding of plastic materials

(G-10010)
WILLIAMS FINISHING INC
13170 Merriman Rd (48150-1816)
PHONE.................................734 421-6100
George Williams, *Owner*
EMP: 6
SALES (est): 193.1K **Privately Held**
SIC: 3471 Plating of metals or formed products

(G-10011)
WIRED TECHNOLOGIES LLC
31099 Schoolcraft Rd (48150)
PHONE.................................313 800-1611
Muhannad Saleh, *Mng Member*
EMP: 7
SALES: 500K **Privately Held**
SIC: 3625 Control circuit relays, industrial

(G-10012)
WORKFORCE SOFTWARE LLC (PA)
38705 7 Mile Rd Ste 300 (48152-3979)
PHONE.................................734 542-4100
Mike Morini, *CEO*
David Farquhar, *COO*
Ron Lev, *Vice Pres*
Matthew Yacoub, *Vice Pres*
Molly Gapp, *Project Dir*
EMP: 160
SQ FT: 10,500
SALES (est): 84.7MM **Privately Held**
WEB: www.workforcesoftware.com
SIC: 7372 7371 Business oriented computer software; custom computer programming services

(G-10013)
ZF ACTIVE SAFETY & ELEC US LLC
12025 Tech Center Dr (48150-2122)
PHONE.................................586 843-2100
Eric Weiss, *Manager*
John Leidy, *Director*
EMP: 627
SALES (corp-wide): 216.2K **Privately Held**
WEB: www.trw.mediaroom.com
SIC: 3714 Motor vehicle parts & accessories
HQ: Zf Active Safety & Electronics Us Llc
12001 Tech Center Dr
Livonia MI 48150
734 855-2600

(G-10014)
ZF ACTIVE SAFETY & ELEC US LLC (DH)
Also Called: Active and Passive Safety
12001 Tech Center Dr (48150-2122)
PHONE.................................734 855-2600
John C Plant, *CEO*
Joseph S Cantie, *Exec VP*
Steven Lunn, *Exec VP*
Carsten Maziul, *Project Mgr*
Galo Leon, *Opers Mgr*
◆ **EMP:** 200
SALES (est): 2.6MM
SALES (corp-wide): 216.2K **Privately Held**
WEB: www.trw.mediaroom.com
SIC: 3679 3469 3089 Electronic switches; metal stampings; plastic processing
HQ: Zf Trw Automotive Holdings Corp.
12001 Tech Center Dr
Livonia MI 48150
734 855-2600

(G-10015)
ZF ACTIVE SAFETY US INC (DH)
Also Called: TRW Automotive Inc.
12001 Tech Center Dr (48150-2122)
PHONE.................................734 855-2542
John C Plant, *President*
Steven Lunn, *Exec VP*
Mark Stewart, *Exec VP*
Aly A Badawy, *Vice Pres*
Joseph Cantie, *Vice Pres*
▲ **EMP:** 500

SALES (est): 33.2MM
SALES (corp-wide): 216.2K **Privately Held**
SIC: 3714 Connecting rods, motor vehicle engine; steering mechanisms, motor vehicle; brake drums, motor vehicle; hydraulic fluid power pumps for auto steering mechanism
HQ: Zf Trw Automotive Holdings Corp.
12001 Tech Center Dr
Livonia MI 48150
734 855-2600

(G-10016)
ZF ACTIVE SAFETY US INC (DH)
12001 Tech Center Dr (48150-2122)
P.O. Box 51970 (48151-5970)
PHONE..................................734 812-6979
Edward Carpenter, *CEO*
◆ **EMP:** 14
SALES (est): 201K
SALES (corp-wide): 216.2K **Privately Held**
SIC: 3714 Motor vehicle engines & parts
HQ: Zf Trw Automotive Holdings Corp.
12001 Tech Center Dr
Livonia MI 48150
734 855-2600

(G-10017)
ZF ACTIVE SAFETY US INC
12200 Tech Center Dr (48150-2177)
PHONE..................................734 855-2470
Mike Wong, *Manager*
EMP: 40
SALES (corp-wide): 216.2K **Privately Held**
SIC: 3714 Connecting rods, motor vehicle engine
HQ: Zf Active Safety Us Inc.
12001 Tech Center Dr
Livonia MI 48150
734 812-6979

(G-10018)
ZF PASSIVE SAFETY
12075 Tech Center Dr (48150-6103)
P.O. Box 51970 (48151-5970)
PHONE..................................734 855-3631
EMP: 3
SALES (corp-wide): 216.2K **Privately Held**
SIC: 3469 Metal stampings
HQ: Zf Active Safety & Electronics Us Llc
12001 Tech Center Dr
Livonia MI 48150
734 855-2600

(G-10019)
ZF PASSIVE SAFETY US INC (DH)
12001 Tech Center Dr (48150-2122)
PHONE..................................734 855-2600
Wolf-Henning Scheider, *CEO*
John Harju, *Exec VP*
Dr Peter Holdmann, *Exec VP*
Peter Lake, *Exec VP*
Christophe Marnat, *CFO*
▲ **EMP:** 10
SALES (est): 810.4K
SALES (corp-wide): 216.2K **Privately Held**
SIC: 3714 Motor vehicle parts & accessories
HQ: Zf Trw Automotive Holdings Corp.
12001 Tech Center Dr
Livonia MI 48150
734 855-2600

(G-10020)
ZF STRING ACTIVE SAFETY US INC (DH)
12001 Tech Center Dr (48150-2122)
PHONE..................................734 855-2600
John C Plant, *President*
John Plant, *President*
Joseph Cantie, *CFO*
Mark Oswald, *Director*
▲ **EMP:** 5
SALES (est): 3MM
SALES (corp-wide): 216.2K **Privately Held**
SIC: 3714 Motor vehicle parts & accessories

HQ: Zf Trw Automotive Holdings Corp.
12001 Tech Center Dr
Livonia MI 48150
734 855-2600

(G-10021)
ZF TRW AUTO HOLDINGS CORP (DH)
12001 Tech Center Dr (48150-2122)
PHONE..................................734 855-2600
Franz Kleiner, *CEO*
John Plant, *Co-CEO*
Peter Holdmann, *Exec VP*
Peter J Lake, *Exec VP*
Neil E Marchuk, *Exec VP*
◆ **EMP:** 800
SALES: 39.3MM
SALES (corp-wide): 216.2K **Privately Held**
SIC: 3714 3711 Motor vehicle parts & accessories; motor vehicles & car bodies; chassis, motor vehicle
HQ: Zf North America, Inc.
15811 Centennial Dr 48
Northville MI 48168
734 416-6200

Lowell
Kent County

(G-10022)
ADVANCED METAL FABRICATORS
12958 Christopher Dr (49331-9420)
PHONE..................................616 570-4847
Michael Perdok, *Principal*
EMP: 7
SALES (est): 1MM **Privately Held**
SIC: 3499 Fabricated metal products

(G-10023)
ATTWOOD CORPORATION (HQ)
1016 N Monroe St (49331-1197)
PHONE..................................616 897-9241
James B Fox, *President*
Randy Gray, *Vice Pres*
Thomas Powell, *Vice Pres*
Peter D Zimmer, *Vice Pres*
Jordan Sinclair, *Opers Staff*
◆ **EMP:** 150 **EST:** 1905
SQ FT: 432,000
SALES (est): 41.5MM
SALES (corp-wide): 5.1B **Publicly Held**
WEB: www.attwoodmarine.com
SIC: 3429 Marine hardware
PA: Brunswick Corporation
26125 N Riverwoods Blvd # 500
Mettawa IL 60045
847 735-4700

(G-10024)
BLOUGH INC
9885 Centerline Rd (49331-9224)
PHONE..................................616 897-8407
Arthur Blough, *President*
Phyllis Huver, *Personnel*
EMP: 90
SQ FT: 50,000
SALES (est): 9.5MM **Privately Held**
SIC: 3471 Finishing, metals or formed products

(G-10025)
BUYERS GUIDE
Also Called: Lowell Litho
105 N Broadway St (49331-1085)
P.O. Box 128 (49331-0128)
PHONE..................................616 897-9261
Roger Brown, *Owner*
Terese Brown, *Co-Owner*
EMP: 15
SQ FT: 1,500
SALES (est): 904.2K **Privately Held**
SIC: 2741 2711 Shopping news: publishing only, not printed on site; newspapers

(G-10026)
CINDYS SUDS LLC
12415 Downes St Ne (49331-9762)
PHONE..................................616 485-1983
EMP: 3

SALES (est): 177.2K **Privately Held**
SIC: 2841 5122 5999 Soap: granulated, liquid, cake, flaked or chip; toilet soap; toiletries, cosmetics & perfumes

(G-10027)
ENVISION ENGINEERING LLC
12650 Envision Dr Se (49331-1902)
PHONE..................................616 897-0599
Michael Vanderwilp, *Engineer*
Scott Roerig,
Mike Vanderwilt,
▲ **EMP:** 5
SALES (est): 1.4MM **Privately Held**
WEB: www.envisioneng.com
SIC: 3444 5049 Sheet metalwork; scientific & engineering equipment & supplies

(G-10028)
FLOR TEC INC
4475 Causeway Dr Ne (49331-9412)
PHONE..................................616 897-3122
Freeman L Billock, *President*
EMP: 7
SALES (est): 400K **Privately Held**
SIC: 3996 1542 Hard surface floor coverings; commercial & office buildings, renovation & repair

(G-10029)
FOREVER FLOORING AND MORE LLC
10880 Woodbushe Dr Se (49331-9625)
PHONE..................................517 745-6194
Earl Gordon, *Mng Member*
Theresa Valdez, *Mng Member*
EMP: 3
SALES (est): 237.5K **Privately Held**
SIC: 2273 7389 Carpets & rugs;

(G-10030)
HAPPY BUMS
201 Montcalm Ave Se (49331-9101)
PHONE..................................616 987-3159
Cheryl Pratt, *Owner*
EMP: 3
SALES (est): 160K **Privately Held**
SIC: 2676 Infant & baby paper products

(G-10031)
INDUSTRIAL SERVICES GROUP
683 Lincoln Lake Ave Se (49331-9416)
PHONE..................................269 945-5291
David Kensington, *Principal*
EMP: 30
SALES (est): 3.9MM **Privately Held**
SIC: 3999 Manufacturing industries

(G-10032)
J & T MACHINING INC
681 Lincoln Lake Ave Se (49331-9416)
PHONE..................................616 897-6744
John Thomas, *President*
Pat Thomas, *Vice Pres*
Patrick Thomas, *Vice Pres*
Robert Thomas, *Vice Pres*
EMP: 8
SQ FT: 4,800
SALES (est): 1MM **Privately Held**
WEB: www.jtmach.com
SIC: 3599 Machine shop, jobbing & repair

(G-10033)
KING MILLING COMPANY
115 S Broadway St (49331-1666)
PHONE..................................616 897-9264
Brian Doyle, *President*
James M Doyle, *Senior VP*
Stephen Doyle, *Vice Pres*
Julie Cantrell, *Officer*
Michael V Harren, *Admin Sec*
◆ **EMP:** 55 **EST:** 1890
SALES: 76.4MM **Privately Held**
WEB: www.kingflour.com
SIC: 2041 Wheat flour

(G-10034)
LITEHOUSE INC
1400 Foreman St (49331-1076)
P.O. Box 287 (49331-0287)
PHONE..................................616 897-5911
Susan Sherne, *Manager*
Joe Hansen, *Manager*
EMP: 140

SALES (corp-wide): 316.2MM **Privately Held**
WEB: www.litehousefoods.com
SIC: 2035 2099 2022 Dressings, salad: raw & cooked (except dry mixes); food preparations; cheese, natural & processed
PA: Litehouse, Inc.
100 Litehouse Dr
Sandpoint ID 83864
208 920-2000

(G-10035)
LYONNAIS INC
3760 Snow Ave Se (49331-8921)
PHONE..................................616 868-6625
EMP: 1
SALES: 1MM **Privately Held**
SIC: 3531 Mfg Construction Machinery

(G-10036)
MAGNESIUM ALUM MACHINING LLC
533 Godfrey St (49331-1002)
PHONE..................................616 309-1202
Rick Manos, *Mng Member*
EMP: 45
SQ FT: 55,000
SALES (est): 4.2MM
SALES (corp-wide): 20.8MM **Privately Held**
SIC: 3599 Machine shop, jobbing & repair
HQ: Magnesium Aluminum Michigan Corporation
3559 Kraft Ave Se
Grand Rapids MI

(G-10037)
METRIC MANUFACTURING CO INC
1001 Foreman St (49331-1094)
P.O. Box 226 (49331-0226)
PHONE..................................616 897-5959
Charles S Thomas, *President*
Pat Gilbert, *Vice Pres*
Greg Thomas, *Vice Pres*
Jim Allerding, *Engineer*
Bruce Kraft, *Exec Dir*
EMP: 115 **EST:** 1978
SQ FT: 55,000
SALES: 12.5MM **Privately Held**
WEB: www.metricmfg.com
SIC: 3599 Machine shop, jobbing & repair

(G-10038)
NATHAN SLAGTER
Also Called: Inventors Industries
730 Lincoln Lake Ave Se (49331-9421)
PHONE..................................616 648-7423
Nathan Slagter, *Owner*
EMP: 3
SALES (est): 61.8K **Privately Held**
SIC: 3999 Manufacturing industries

(G-10039)
OPTEC INC
199 Smith St (49331-1399)
PHONE..................................616 897-9351
Jeff Dickerman, *President*
Tina Dickerman, *Treasurer*
EMP: 10
SQ FT: 3,700
SALES (est): 1.7MM **Privately Held**
WEB: www.optecinc.com
SIC: 3827 Optical instruments & lenses

(G-10040)
ORGANICORP INC
11455 36th St Se (49331-9555)
PHONE..................................616 540-0295
Mark McKitrick, *Principal*
EMP: 3
SALES (est): 171.6K **Privately Held**
SIC: 2869 Fuels

(G-10041)
PURFORMS INC
615 Chatham St Ste 1 (49331-1387)
PHONE..................................616 897-3000
Richard A Raimer, *President*
Lori Raimer, *Human Res Mgr*
Richard Raimer, *Manager*
▼ **EMP:** 36
SQ FT: 66,000

Lowell - Kent County (G-10042)

SALES: 3.5MM **Privately Held**
WEB: www.purforms.com
SIC: 3089 Injection molding of plastics

(G-10042)
ROOT-LOWELL MANUFACTURING CO
Also Called: Rl Flo-Master
1000 Foreman St (49331-1074)
PHONE...................................616 897-9211
Tony Asselta, *President*
David Longfield, *Business Mgr*
Lisa Lahr, *Purch Agent*
Tony Christie, *QC Mgr*
Stephanie Ackley, *Sales Staff*
◆ EMP: 100
SQ FT: 100,000
SALES (est): 34.8MM **Privately Held**
WEB: www.rlflomaster.com
SIC: 3523 Sprayers & spraying machines, agricultural

(G-10043)
SWEET MELLISAS CUPCAKES
4413 Causeway Dr Ne (49331-9412)
PHONE...................................616 889-3998
Mellisa Verstrate, *Principal*
EMP: 4 EST: 2012
SALES (est): 218.9K **Privately Held**
SIC: 2051 Bread, cake & related products

(G-10044)
SWIVL - EZE MARINE
1016 N Monroe St (49331-1167)
PHONE...................................616 897-9241
Brunswick Corporation, *Partner*
Perry Kirkland, *Principal*
▲ EMP: 45
SALES (est): 6.2MM
SALES (corp-wide): 5.1B **Publicly Held**
WEB: www.swivleze.com
SIC: 3732 Boat building & repairing
PA: Brunswick Corporation
    26125 N Riverwoods Blvd # 500
    Mettawa IL 60045
    847 735-4700

(G-10045)
WHITES BRIDGE TOOLING INC
1395 Bowes Rd (49331-8882)
P.O. Box 8 (49331-0008)
PHONE...................................616 897-4151
Peter Odland, *President*
William Dulyea, *Vice Pres*
EMP: 25
SQ FT: 8,400
SALES (est): 5.4MM **Privately Held**
WEB: www.wbtooling.com
SIC: 3569 7692 3535 Assembly machines, non-metalworking; welding repair; conveyors & conveying equipment

(G-10046)
WHITES INDUSTRIAL SERVICE
5010 Abraham Dr Ne (49331-9733)
PHONE...................................616 291-3706
Michael White, *President*
EMP: 5
SALES: 600K **Privately Held**
SIC: 1752 3479 Floor laying & floor work; painting, coating & hot dipping

---
Ludington
Mason County

(G-10047)
ABRAHAMSON MARINE INC
820 1st St (49431-2400)
PHONE...................................231 843-2142
Steven Abrahamson, *President*
EMP: 3
SALES (est): 381.3K **Privately Held**
SIC: 3732 Boat building & repairing

(G-10048)
AMERICAN CLASSICS CORP
3750 W Hansen Rd (49431-8604)
P.O. Box 310 (49431-0310)
PHONE...................................231 843-0523
David Gwiazdowski, *Principal*
EMP: 6
SALES (est): 568K **Privately Held**
SIC: 2099 Food preparations

(G-10049)
ANDREW J REISTERER D D S PLLC
902 E Ludington Ave (49431-2438)
PHONE...................................231 845-8989
John Piopelle, *Principal*
EMP: 4
SALES (est): 428.2K **Privately Held**
SIC: 3843 Enamels, dentists'

(G-10050)
BRILL COMPANY INC
715 S James St (49431-2362)
PHONE...................................231 843-2430
David Field, *President*
Ken Gibbs, *Vice Pres*
Bill Shaub, *Vice Pres*
Bill Sniegowski, *Purch Mgr*
Cindy Swan, *Manager*
▲ EMP: 40
SQ FT: 84,000
SALES (est): 7.8MM **Privately Held**
WEB: www.brillcompany.com
SIC: 2531 2599 Public building & related furniture; restaurant furniture, wood or metal

(G-10051)
CAL-CHLOR CORP
5379 W 6th St (49431-9322)
P.O. Box 622 (49431-0622)
PHONE...................................231 843-1147
Wayne Wagner, *Manager*
EMP: 30
SALES (corp-wide): 156.4MM **Privately Held**
SIC: 4783 2819 Packing goods for shipping; industrial inorganic chemicals
PA: Cal-Chlor Corp.
    627 Jefferson St
    Lafayette LA 70501
    337 264-1449

(G-10052)
CHANGE PARTS INCORPORATED
185 S Jebavy Dr (49431-2460)
PHONE...................................231 845-5107
Ronald Sarto, *CEO*
Gregory Simsa, *CFO*
Lorne Sparks, *Regl Sales Mgr*
Denise Hoge, *Manager*
EMP: 40
SQ FT: 40,000
SALES: 4.5MM **Privately Held**
WEB: www.changeparts.com
SIC: 3569 3565 3535 Assembly machines, non-metalworking; packaging machinery; conveyors & conveying equipment

(G-10053)
CHANGEOVER INTEGRATION LLC
787 S Pere Marquette Hwy (49431-2662)
PHONE...................................231 845-5320
Dan Sarto, *President*
Tom Latala, *Sales Engr*
Lorena Buchholz, *Office Mgr*
EMP: 17 EST: 2007
SALES (est): 2.3MM **Privately Held**
SIC: 3471 3479 3541 Anodizing (plating) of metals or formed products; etching & engraving; buffing & polishing machines

(G-10054)
CONE DRIVE OPERATIONS INC
Also Called: Cone Drive Textron
5115 Progress Dr (49431-9205)
PHONE...................................231 843-3393
John Cummins, *Plant Mgr*
John Hammonds, *Branch Mgr*
EMP: 30
SALES (corp-wide): 3.5B **Publicly Held**
WEB: www.conedrive.com
SIC: 3566 Reduction gears & gear units for turbines, except automotive
HQ: Cone Drive Operations Inc.
    240 E Twelfth St
    Traverse City MI 49684
    231 946-8410

(G-10055)
DEBBINK AND SONS INC
1010 Conrad Industrial Dr (49431-2677)
P.O. Box 868 (49431-0868)
PHONE...................................231 845-6421
Craig Debbink, *President*
EMP: 5
SALES: 2MM **Privately Held**
SIC: 2521 2512 1521 Cabinets, office: wood; upholstered household furniture; single-family housing construction

(G-10056)
DOW CHEMICAL COMPANY
1600 S Madison St (49431-2597)
PHONE...................................231 845-4285
John Hockstra, *Branch Mgr*
EMP: 75
SALES (corp-wide): 61B **Publicly Held**
WEB: www.dow.com
SIC: 2821 Thermoplastic materials
HQ: The Dow Chemical Company
    2211 H H Dow Way
    Midland MI 48642
    989 636-1000

(G-10057)
DREAMWEAVER LURE COMPANY INC
5712 Brookwood Pl (49431-1972)
PHONE...................................231 843-3652
Roger Bogner, *Principal*
Shane Rupoyianes, *Vice Pres*
▲ EMP: 10 EST: 1995
SQ FT: 7,000
SALES (est): 771.6K **Privately Held**
SIC: 3949 Fishing equipment

(G-10058)
DUNA USA INC
5900 6th St (49431-2646)
PHONE...................................231 425-4300
Alex Skinner, *President*
Kelly Haas, *Sales Staff*
EMP: 7
SALES (corp-wide): 26.9K **Privately Held**
SIC: 3086 Plastics foam products
HQ: Duna Usa Inc.
    4210 Fm 1405 Rd
    Baytown TX 77523
    281 383-3862

(G-10059)
FLORACRAFT CORPORATION (PA)
Also Called: Floracraft Cares
1 Longfellow Pl (49431-1591)
P.O. Box 400 (49431-0400)
PHONE...................................231 845-5127
James V Scatena, *CEO*
Russell Lee Schoenherr, *Ch of Bd*
Victor Burwell, *Exec VP*
Conny Bax, *Vice Pres*
Bill Hellwarth, *Vice Pres*
◆ EMP: 125
SQ FT: 350,000
SALES: 50MM **Privately Held**
WEB: www.floracraft.com
SIC: 3086 2211 Plastics foam products; chenilles, tufted textile

(G-10060)
GOLD COAST ICE MAKERS LLC
Also Called: Gold Coast Icemakers
3785 W Us Highway 10 (49431-9601)
PHONE...................................231 845-2745
Rose Lennox, *President*
EMP: 5
SALES: 220K **Privately Held**
SIC: 2097 Manufactured ice

(G-10061)
GREAT LAKES CASTINGS LLC (HQ)
800 N Washington Ave (49431-1500)
PHONE...................................231 843-2501
Robert Killips, *President*
David Scott, *Maint Spvr*
Ben Meyer, *Purch Agent*
Thomas Aument, *Engineer*
Carol Henke, *VP Finance*
EMP: 160 EST: 1945
SQ FT: 150,000
SALES (est): 36.3MM **Privately Held**
WEB: www.glccadv.com
SIC: 3321 Gray & ductile iron foundries

(G-10062)
HARSCO CORPORATION
Also Called: Harsco Rail
200 S Jackson Rd (49431-2483)
PHONE...................................231 843-3431
Rodger Nash, *Manager*
EMP: 60
SALES (corp-wide): 1.7B **Publicly Held**
WEB: www.harsco.com
SIC: 3531 3743 3536 3678 Construction machinery; railroad equipment; hoists, cranes & monorails; electronic connectors
PA: Harsco Corporation
    350 Poplar Church Rd
    Camp Hill PA 17011
    717 763-7064

(G-10063)
HARSCO CORPORATION
Harsco Track Technologies
200 S Jackson Rd (49431-2483)
PHONE...................................231 843-3431
EMP: 13
SALES (corp-wide): 1.7B **Publicly Held**
WEB: www.harsco.com
SIC: 3531 Construction machinery
PA: Harsco Corporation
    350 Poplar Church Rd
    Camp Hill PA 17011
    717 763-7064

(G-10064)
HAWORTH INC
Also Called: Ludington Components
5170 Progress Dr (49431-9205)
PHONE...................................231 845-0607
Michael Fedrigo, *Principal*
EMP: 52
SALES (corp-wide): 1.8B **Privately Held**
WEB: www.haworth-furn.com
SIC: 2522 3646 Office furniture, except wood; commercial indusl & institutional electric lighting fixtures
HQ: Haworth, Inc.
    1 Haworth Ctr
    Holland MI 49423
    616 393-3000

(G-10065)
HOBE INC
Also Called: Ludington Concrete Products
605 S Pere Marquette Hwy (49431-2660)
P.O. Box 714 (49431-0714)
PHONE...................................231 845-5196
Sandra Holcombe, *President*
Tim Martin, *Sales Mgr*
EMP: 4
SALES: 2.2MM **Privately Held**
SIC: 3271 Blocks, concrete or cinder: standard

(G-10066)
HOUSE OF FLAVORS INC (HQ)
110 N William St (49431-2092)
PHONE...................................231 845-7369
Whit Gallagher, *President*
Pat Calder, *COO*
Sarah R Holmes, *Controller*
Sarah Holmes, *Controller*
Terry Carr, *Maintence Staff*
▼ EMP: 150
SQ FT: 17,000
SALES: 105.2MM **Privately Held**
WEB: www.houseofflavors.com
SIC: 2024 Ice cream, packaged: molded, on sticks, etc.
PA: Protein Holdings Inc.
    10 Moulton St Ste 5
    Portland ME 04101
    207 771-0965

(G-10067)
INDIAN SUMMER COOPERATIVE INC (PA)
3958 W Chauvez Rd Ste 1 (49431-8200)
PHONE...................................231 845-6248
Roy D Hackert, *President*
Doyle Fenner, *Opers Mgr*
Scott Quillan, *Purch Agent*
Steven Hull, *Treasurer*
Ted Lasley, *Controller*
◆ EMP: 250 EST: 1973

▲ = Import ▼=Export
◆ =Import/Export

GEOGRAPHIC SECTION

SQ FT: 15,000
SALES (est): 89.1MM **Privately Held**
SIC: **2033** 0723 4213 2035 Apple sauce: packaged in cans, jars, etc.; fruit juices: packaged in cans, jars, etc.; fruits: packaged in cans, jars, etc.; fruit (fresh) packing services; trucking, except local; contract haulers; pickles, sauces & salad dressings

(G-10068)
JACKSON PANDROL INC
200 S Jackson Rd (49431-2409)
PHONE...................................231 843-3431
Bruce Bradshaw, *Vice Pres*
Roy J Orrow, *CFO*
EMP: 300
SQ FT: 150,000
SALES (est): 10.9MM
SALES (corp-wide): 2.6MM **Privately Held**
SIC: **4789** 3531 Railroad maintenance & repair services; railroad related equipment; tampers, powered
HQ: Pandrol International Limited
    Osprey House, 63 Station Road
    Addlestone
    193 283-4500

(G-10069)
LUDINGTON DAILY NEWS INC
Also Called: Shoreline Media
202 N Rath Ave (49431-1663)
P.O. Box 340 (49431-0340)
PHONE...................................231 845-5181
David R Jackson, *President*
Ray McGrew, *President*
Linda Farley, *Sales Staff*
Jeffrey Evans, *Asst Sec*
EMP: 52 EST: 1933
SQ FT: 20,000
SALES: 3.2MM **Privately Held**
WEB: www.ludingtondailynews.com
SIC: **2711** 2741 Commercial printing & newspaper publishing combined; directories, telephone: publishing & printing; shopping news: publishing & printing

(G-10070)
M & M ASSOCIATES (PA)
Also Called: Sassafras Tees
4010 S Pere Marquette Hwy (49431-9729)
PHONE...................................231 845-7034
David Mack, *Owner*
EMP: 3
SQ FT: 1,800
SALES (est): 400K **Privately Held**
SIC: **2396** Screen printing on fabric articles

(G-10071)
MERDEL GAME MANUFACTURING CO
Also Called: Carrom Company
218 E Dowland St (49431-2309)
P.O. Box 649 (49431-0649)
PHONE...................................231 845-1263
Norman Rosen, *President*
▲ EMP: 7 EST: 1961
SQ FT: 70,000
SALES (est): 1.6MM **Privately Held**
WEB: www.carrom.com
SIC: **3944** 2511 Games, toys & children's vehicles; wood household furniture
PA: The Lightning Group Inc
    722 N Market St
    Duncannon PA 17020
    717 834-3031

(G-10072)
MET INC
640 S Pere Marquette Hwy (49431-2661)
PHONE...................................231 845-1737
Dennis G Eggert, *President*
John Babbin, *Principal*
Mark Todd, *Shareholder*
EMP: 8
SQ FT: 18,000
SALES (est): 799.3K **Privately Held**
SIC: **2421** Furniture dimension stock, softwood; kiln drying of lumber

(G-10073)
METALWORKS INC (PA)
Also Called: Great Openings
902 4th St (49431-2693)
PHONE...................................231 845-5136
G William Paine, *Ch of Bd*
Thomas W Paine, *President*
Karlan Young, *Buyer*
David Gowen, *Engineer*
Bob Hayes, *Project Engr*
EMP: 243 EST: 1969
SQ FT: 125,000
SALES (est): 52.6MM **Privately Held**
WEB: www.metalwrks.com
SIC: **3499** 3444 Furniture parts, metal; sheet metalwork

(G-10074)
NORTHWOOD SIGNS INC
5111 W Us Highway 10 # 4 (49431-8686)
PHONE...................................231 843-3956
Dianna Bondeson, *President*
Linwood Bondeson, *Vice Pres*
EMP: 8
SQ FT: 9,500
SALES (est): 350K **Privately Held**
SIC: **3993** Signs, not made in custom sign painting shops

(G-10075)
OCCIDENTAL CHEMICAL CORP
1600 S Madison St (49431-2568)
PHONE...................................231 845-4411
Bill Berrett, *Branch Mgr*
EMP: 20
SALES (corp-wide): 18.9B **Publicly Held**
SIC: **2812** Chlorine, compressed or liquefied
HQ: Occidental Chemical Corporation
    14555 Dallas Pkwy Ste 400
    Dallas TX 75254
    972 404-3800

(G-10076)
ODEN MACHINERY INC
185 S Jebavy Dr (49431-2460)
PHONE...................................716 874-3000
Gregory E Simsa, *Manager*
EMP: 4
SALES (est): 278.9K
SALES (corp-wide): 4.5MM **Privately Held**
SIC: **3823** Thermometers, filled system: industrial process type
PA: Oden Machinery, Inc.
    600 Ensminger Rd
    Tonawanda NY 14150
    716 874-3000

(G-10077)
OMIMEX ENERGY INC
4854 W Angling Rd (49431)
PHONE...................................231 845-7358
Ken Prior, *Manager*
EMP: 11
SALES (corp-wide): 38.2MM **Privately Held**
WEB: www.omimexgroup.com
SIC: **1311** Crude petroleum production; natural gas production
HQ: Omimex Energy, Inc.
    7950 John T White Rd
    Fort Worth TX 76120

(G-10078)
SIGNA GROUP INC
Also Called: Whitehall Industries
5175 W 6th St (49431-9322)
PHONE...................................231 845-5101
EMP: 338
SALES (corp-wide): 25.7MM **Privately Held**
SIC: **3441** Building components, structural steel
PA: Signa Group, Inc.
    540 W Frontage Rd # 2105
    Northfield IL 60093
    847 386-7639

(G-10079)
SSW HOLDING COMPANY LLC
902 N Rowe St Ste 200 (49431-1495)
PHONE...................................231 780-0230
Jim Marrison, *Branch Mgr*
EMP: 7
SALES (corp-wide): 470.1MM **Privately Held**
SIC: **3496** Miscellaneous fabricated wire products
PA: Ssw Holding Company, Llc
    3501 Tulsa St
    Fort Smith AR 72903
    479 646-1651

(G-10080)
STRAITS STEEL AND WIRE COMPANY (HQ)
902 N Rowe St Ste 100 (49431-1495)
P.O. Box 589 (49431-0589)
PHONE...................................231 843-3416
Paul Kara, *President*
Sam J Flocks, *CFO*
◆ EMP: 85
SQ FT: 95,000
SALES (est): 7.6MM
SALES (corp-wide): 470.1MM **Privately Held**
SIC: **3479** 3496 4212 3315 Painting, coating & hot dipping; miscellaneous fabricated wire products; shelving, made from purchased wire; local trucking, without storage; steel wire & related products
PA: Ssw Holding Company, Llc
    3501 Tulsa St
    Fort Smith AR 72903
    479 646-1651

(G-10081)
SURFACE EXPRESSIONS LLC
904 1st St (49431-2435)
PHONE...................................231 843-8282
Tim Husted,
EMP: 6
SALES (est): 518.5K **Privately Held**
WEB: www.surfaceexpressions.com
SIC: **1799** 2434 Kitchen & bathroom remodeling; wood kitchen cabinets

(G-10082)
THERADAPT PRODUCTS INC
922 N Washington Ave (49431-1543)
PHONE...................................231 480-4008
Julia McNally, *CEO*
Eric W McNally, *President*
EMP: 5
SQ FT: 10,000
SALES: 500K **Privately Held**
WEB: www.theradapt.com
SIC: **5047** 2511 Therapy equipment; wood household furniture

(G-10083)
TYES INC
Also Called: Safety Decals
5236 W 1st St (49431-9349)
PHONE...................................888 219-6301
Nicholas Tykoski, *CEO*
EMP: 10
SQ FT: 8,400
SALES: 900K **Privately Held**
SIC: **3993** Signs & advertising specialties

(G-10084)
UACJ AUTO WHITEHALL INDS INC
801 S Madison St (49431-2529)
PHONE...................................231 845-5101
Bobbi Areklet, *Engineer*
Drew Pehrson, *Manager*
Kim Haner, *Manager*
EMP: 200 **Privately Held**
SIC: **3354** Aluminum extruded products
HQ: Uacj Automotive Whitehall Industries, Inc.
    5175 W 6th St
    Ludington MI 49431
    231 845-5101

(G-10085)
UACJ AUTOMOTIVE WHITEHALL INDS
4960 Progress Dr (49431-9231)
PHONE...................................231 845-5101
Teruo Kawashima, *President*
EMP: 137
SALES (est): 4.7MM **Privately Held**
SIC: **3441** Fabricated structural metal

(G-10086)
VANDERVEST ELECTRIC MTR & FABG
5635 W Dewey Rd (49431-9599)
PHONE...................................231 843-6196
Brian Vandervest, *Owner*
EMP: 4
SQ FT: 4,800
SALES (est): 275K **Privately Held**
SIC: **3621** Motors, electric

(G-10087)
WEST MICHIGAN WIRE CO
Also Called: Kaines West Michigan Co
211 E Dowland St (49431-2308)
P.O. Box 603 (49431-0603)
PHONE...................................231 845-1281
Les Kaines, *CEO*
John L Kaines, *President*
Jim Karner, *Production*
John Applegarth, *Purch Dir*
Mike Felty, *Engineer*
▲ EMP: 85
SQ FT: 48,000
SALES: 10MM **Privately Held**
WEB: www.kwmco.com
SIC: **3496** 3315 Miscellaneous fabricated wire products; steel wire & related products

(G-10088)
WESTERN LAND SERVICES INC (PA)
1100 Conrad Industrial Dr (49431-2679)
PHONE...................................231 843-8878
John K Wilson, *President*
Todd Stowe, *Vice Pres*
Jim Aksamit, *Project Mgr*
Ravi Sharma, *Project Mgr*
Dan Stevenson, *Project Mgr*
EMP: 75
SQ FT: 21,000
SALES: 70.7MM **Privately Held**
WEB: www.westernls.com
SIC: **1382** Oil & gas exploration services

(G-10089)
WORTEN COPY CENTER INC
Also Called: Kwik Print Plus
601 N Washington Ave (49431-1503)
PHONE...................................231 845-7030
Timothy A Alley, *President*
Tim Alley, *Vice Pres*
Debra H Alley, *Treasurer*
Aaron Alley, *Manager*
EMP: 6
SQ FT: 1,600
SALES (est): 843.4K **Privately Held**
WEB: www.kwikprintplus.com
SIC: **2752** 2791 Commercial printing, offset; typesetting

Lum
Lapeer County

(G-10090)
LUMCO MANUFACTURING COMPANY
2027 Mitchell Lake Rd (48412-9243)
PHONE...................................810 724-0582
Patrick J Gleason, *President*
John T Gleason, *Vice Pres*
Margaret Gleason, *Treasurer*
EMP: 10 EST: 1968
SQ FT: 30,000
SALES (est): 2.4MM **Privately Held**
WEB: www.lumco.com
SIC: **3545** Machine tool accessories

Lupton
Ogemaw County

(G-10091)
BRINDLEY LUMBER & PALLET CO
Also Called: Brindley Pallets
1971 State Rd (48635-9762)
PHONE...................................989 345-3497
James Brindley, *President*
Richard Brindley, *Vice Pres*
EMP: 8
SQ FT: 15,000
SALES: 500K **Privately Held**
SIC: **2448** Pallets, wood

Lupton - Ogemaw County (G-10092) — GEOGRAPHIC SECTION

(G-10092)
MARK A NELSON
332 Oneil Rd (48635-9759)
PHONE...................989 305-5769
Mark A Nelson, *Principal*
EMP: 3
SALES (est): 246.2K **Privately Held**
SIC: 2411 Logging

Luther
Lake County

(G-10093)
JEFFERY LUCAS
10975 E Old M 63 (49656-9384)
PHONE...................231 797-5152
Jeffrey Lucas, *Principal*
EMP: 3
SALES (est): 243.9K **Privately Held**
SIC: 2411 Logging camps & contractors

Lyons
Ionia County

(G-10094)
MID MICHIGAN WOOD SPECIALITES
1370 Divine Hwy (48851-8718)
PHONE...................989 855-3667
James Smith, *Owner*
EMP: 10 **EST:** 2014
SALES (est): 786.9K **Privately Held**
SIC: 2434 Wood kitchen cabinets

(G-10095)
PREMIUM MACHINE & TOOL INC
207 Water St (48851-5105)
P.O. Box 286 (48851-0286)
PHONE...................989 855-3326
Mark L Schneider, *President*
EMP: 11
SQ FT: 10,000
SALES: 500K **Privately Held**
SIC: 2514 2522 Metal household furniture; office furniture, except wood

Macatawa
Ottawa County

(G-10096)
ELDEAN COMPANY
Also Called: Eldean Shipyard & Yacht Sales
2223 S Shore Dr (49434-9800)
P.O. Box 6 (49434-0006)
PHONE...................616 335-5843
Herbert Eldean, *President*
Matt Eldean, *Manager*
EMP: 35
SQ FT: 180,000
SALES (est): 4.8MM **Privately Held**
WEB: www.eldean.com
SIC: 4493 3732 Boat yards, storage & incidental repair; boat building & repairing

Mackinac Island
Mackinac County

(G-10097)
ORIGINAL MURDICKS FUDGE CO (PA)
Also Called: Murdick's Fudge Kitchen
7363 Main St (49757)
P.O. Box 481 (49757-0481)
PHONE...................906 847-3530
Robert J Benser, *President*
EMP: 30 **EST:** 1955
SQ FT: 1,250
SALES (est): 2.4MM **Privately Held**
SIC: 5441 2064 5812 2066 Candy; fudge (candy); ice cream stands or dairy bars; chocolate & cocoa products

Mackinaw City
Cheboygan County

(G-10098)
BIERE DE MAC BREW WORKS LLC
14277 N Mackinaw Hwy (49701-8622)
P.O. Box 208 (49701-0208)
PHONE...................616 862-8018
George Ranville, *President*
EMP: 3 **EST:** 2015
SQ FT: 3,281
SALES (est): 137.2K **Privately Held**
SIC: 2082 Malt beverages

(G-10099)
MARSHALLS TRAIL INC
Also Called: Marshall's Fudge
308 E Central Ave (49701-9801)
P.O. Box 639 (49701-0639)
PHONE...................231 436-5082
Joseph D Scheerens, *President*
Mary J Scheerens, *Corp Secy*
Bruce T Thrasher, *Vice Pres*
Michael J Thrasher, *Vice Pres*
EMP: 12
SQ FT: 5,000
SALES (est): 862.5K **Privately Held**
WEB: www.marshallsfudge.com
SIC: 5441 5812 5947 2099 Confectionery produced for direct sale on the premises; delicatessen (eating places); gift shop; food preparations; chocolate & cocoa products; candy & other confectionery products

(G-10100)
NICHOLASS BLACK RIVER VINEYAR
156 S Huron Ave (49701)
PHONE...................231 436-5770
Nick J Koklanaris, *Branch Mgr*
EMP: 3
SALES (est): 102.8K
SALES (corp-wide): 318.1K **Privately Held**
SIC: 2084 Wines
PA: Nicholas's Black River Vineyards & Winery Inc
6209 N Black River Rd
Cheboygan MI 49721
231 625-9060

(G-10101)
SIGN OF THE LOON GIFTS INC
311 W Central Ave (49701-9701)
P.O. Box 309 (49701-0309)
PHONE...................231 436-5155
Jeffrey Alexander, *President*
Ethyl Alexander, *Vice Pres*
EMP: 4
SALES (est): 266.7K **Privately Held**
SIC: 5947 2261 Gift shop; screen printing of cotton broadwoven fabrics

Macomb
Macomb County

(G-10102)
ADMORE INC
Also Called: Colorworx
24707 Wood Ct (48042-5378)
PHONE...................586 949-8200
Keith Walters, *CEO*
Paul Brancaleone, *Prdtn Mgr*
Amy Joseph, *Human Res Mgr*
Brian Doppke, *Sales Staff*
Michelle McCanham, *Technician*
EMP: 52 **EST:** 1947
SQ FT: 57,500
SALES (est): 23.8MM
SALES (corp-wide): 400.7MM **Publicly Held**
WEB: www.admoreonline.com
SIC: 2752 Commercial printing, offset
PA: Ennis, Inc.
2441 Presidential Pkwy
Midlothian TX 76065
972 775-9801

(G-10103)
ADVANCED SYSTEMS & CONTRLS INC
15773 Leone Dr (48042-4006)
PHONE...................586 992-9684
Andrew Zundel, *President*
Kevin P Pray, *Vice Pres*
EMP: 34
SQ FT: 7,100
SALES (est): 8MM **Privately Held**
WEB: www.advancedsyst.com
SIC: 3829 3825 Aircraft & motor vehicle measurement equipment; instruments to measure electricity

(G-10104)
AEROSPACE NYLOK CORPORATION (PA)
15260 Hallmark Ct (48042-4007)
PHONE...................586 786-0100
Max F Dorflinger, *President*
James J Walsh, *Treasurer*
Jerry D Mac Leith, *Admin Sec*
Sharon Easton, *Asst Sec*
▲ **EMP:** 3
SALES (est): 599K **Privately Held**
SIC: 3452 Bolts, nuts, rivets & washers

(G-10105)
ALL AMERICAN CONTAINER CORP
24600 Wood Ct (48042-5919)
PHONE...................586 949-0000
Harold B Berquist, *CEO*
Dale E Cartwright, *President*
Amber Lapinta, *General Mgr*
Amanda Garon, *Sales Staff*
EMP: 15
SQ FT: 54,000
SALES (est): 5.2MM **Privately Held**
SIC: 5113 2448 Corrugated & solid fiber boxes; pallets, wood

(G-10106)
ALLIANCE INDUSTRIES INC
51820 Regency Center Dr (48042-4133)
PHONE...................248 656-3473
Todd Sangster, *President*
Thomas A Fournier, *Admin Sec*
EMP: 30
SQ FT: 11,000
SALES (est): 5.8MM **Privately Held**
SIC: 3544 Industrial molds

(G-10107)
ANDRETTA & ASSOCIATES INC
Also Called: Midwest International Wines
48945 Austrian Pine Dr (48044-6126)
PHONE...................586 557-6226
Sandro Andretta, *President*
▲ **EMP:** 10
SALES: 1MM **Privately Held**
SIC: 2084 Wines

(G-10108)
ASCENT AEROSPACE LLC (HQ)
16445 23 Mile Rd (48042-4005)
PHONE...................586 726-0500
Michael Mahfet, *CEO*
Daniel Nowicki, *CFO*
Sean Roberts, *Finance Dir*
Alan Shagena, *Manager*
Ron Mack, *Director*
EMP: 950
SQ FT: 200,000
SALES: 250MM
SALES (corp-wide): 386.8MM **Privately Held**
SIC: 3544 8711 3541 Industrial molds; aviation &/or aeronautical engineering; machine tools, metal cutting type
PA: Ascent Aerospace Holdings Llc
16445 23 Mile Rd
Macomb MI 48042
212 916-8142

(G-10109)
ASCENT AEROSPACE HOLDINGS LLC (PA)
Also Called: Aip Aerospace
16445 23 Mile Rd (48042-4005)
PHONE...................212 916-8142
Michael Mahfet, *CEO*
Jonathon Levine, *CFO*
Sean Roberts, *Finance Dir*
Dino Cusomano, *Director*
EMP: 4 **EST:** 2012
SQ FT: 20,000
SALES (est): 386.8MM **Privately Held**
SIC: 6799 3721 Investors; aircraft

(G-10110)
ASCENT INTEGRATED PLATFORMS
Also Called: Aip Aerospace
16445 23 Mile Rd (48042-4005)
PHONE...................586 726-0500
Ray Kauffman, *Mng Member*
EMP: 14
SALES (est): 2.5MM **Privately Held**
SIC: 3369 Nonferrous foundries

(G-10111)
BAKER INDUSTRIES INC (HQ)
16936 Enterprise Dr (48044-1006)
PHONE...................586 286-4900
Kevin M Baker, *President*
▲ **EMP:** 116
SQ FT: 220,000
SALES (est): 86.5MM
SALES (corp-wide): 3B **Publicly Held**
WEB: www.bakermachining.com
SIC: 3544 Forms (molds), for foundry & plastics working machinery
PA: Lincoln Electric Holdings, Inc.
22801 Saint Clair Ave
Cleveland OH 44117
216 481-8100

(G-10112)
BLUE WATER BORING LLC
46522 Erb Dr (48042-5915)
PHONE...................586 421-2100
Sandra Vezina, *Mng Member*
Michele Vezina,
EMP: 4
SQ FT: 4,000
SALES (est): 293.8K **Privately Held**
SIC: 3599 Machine shop, jobbing & repair

(G-10113)
C&C DOORS INC
51805 Milano Dr (48042-4052)
PHONE...................586 232-4538
Joe Cusumano, *President*
Salvatore Cusumano, *Vice Pres*
EMP: 3
SQ FT: 500
SALES (est): 194.1K **Privately Held**
SIC: 2434 Wood kitchen cabinets

(G-10114)
CARROLL TOOL AND DIE CO
46650 Erb Dr (48042-5348)
PHONE...................586 949-7670
Thomas J Plotzke, *President*
Tony Plotzke, *Vice Pres*
Catherine Plotzke, *Admin Sec*
EMP: 40
SQ FT: 20,000
SALES (est): 6.3MM **Privately Held**
WEB: www.carrolltool.com
SIC: 3544 Special dies & tools

(G-10115)
CENTURY PLASTICS LLC
51102 Quadrate Dr (48042)
PHONE...................586 697-5752
Bob Stafford, *Manager*
EMP: 5
SALES (corp-wide): 118.8MM **Privately Held**
SIC: 3089 Injection molding of plastics
HQ: Century Plastics, Llc
15030 23 Mile Rd
Shelby Township MI 48315
586 566-3900

(G-10116)
DETROIT CYCLE PUB LLC
16089 Diamante Dr (48044-1183)
PHONE...................231 286-5257
Nicholas Blaszczyk, *Principal*
EMP: 4
SALES (est): 75.4K **Privately Held**
SIC: 2082 Malt beverages

GEOGRAPHIC SECTION
Macomb - Macomb County (G-10144)

(G-10117)
DETROIT TECHNOLOGIES INC
Also Called: Dti Plastic Products
51258 Quadrate Dr (48042-4055)
PHONE...................248 647-0400
Gary Stanus, *Manager*
EMP: 12 **Privately Held**
SIC: 3714 Motor vehicle parts & accessories
PA: Detroit Technologies, Inc.
32500 Telg Rd Ste 207
Bingham Farms MI 48025

(G-10118)
DSE INDUSTRIES LLC
51315 Regency Center Dr (48042-4131)
PHONE...................313 530-6668
Ron Scott, *Managing Dir*
Ronald Scott, *CFO*
EMP: 5
SQ FT: 15,000
SALES (est): 387.3K **Privately Held**
SIC: 3672 8711 7389 3714 Printed circuit boards; engineering services; ; motor vehicle parts & accessories; injection molding of plastics

(G-10119)
ELITE MACHINING
46516 Erb Dr (48042-5915)
PHONE...................586 598-9008
Jeff R Hayes, *Owner*
Carol Hayes, *Co-Owner*
EMP: 3
SALES: 140K **Privately Held**
SIC: 3599 Machine shop, jobbing & repair

(G-10120)
ESIRPAL INC
55549 Danube Ave (48042-2362)
PHONE...................586 337-7848
Vincent Laprise, *President*
EMP: 7
SALES (est): 848.3K **Privately Held**
WEB: www.hotwaterlobster.com
SIC: 3825 3569 Semiconductor test equipment; assembly machines, non-metalworking

(G-10121)
FABTRONIC INC
51685 Industrial Dr (48042-4027)
PHONE...................586 786-6114
Howard G Baisch, *President*
Jeremy Baisch, *Vice Pres*
Victoria Baisch, *Vice Pres*
EMP: 50
SQ FT: 16,000
SALES: 6.6MM **Privately Held**
WEB: www.fabtronic.com
SIC: 3312 Tool & die steel & alloys

(G-10122)
FIVE STAR INDUSTRIES INC
51550 Hayes Rd (48042-4008)
PHONE...................586 786-0500
Shirley Tomayko, *President*
Randal Tomayko, *Vice Pres*
EMP: 25
SQ FT: 21,225
SALES (est): 5.3MM **Privately Held**
SIC: 3545 3544 3541 Comparators (machinists' precision tools); special dies, tools, jigs & fixtures; machine tools, metal cutting type

(G-10123)
FUN LEARNING COMPANY LLC
21341 Fairfield Dr (48044-2966)
PHONE...................269 362-0651
Cathy Joyce, *Mng Member*
EMP: 14
SALES (est): 927.7K **Privately Held**
SIC: 3999 Education aids, devices & supplies

(G-10124)
G T GUNDRILLING INC
51195 Regency Center Dr (48042-4130)
PHONE...................586 992-3301
Richard Thibault, *President*
EMP: 6
SQ FT: 10,500
SALES (est): 550K **Privately Held**
SIC: 3429 Manufactured hardware (general)

(G-10125)
GENERAL DYNAMICS CORPORATION
55518 Belle Ln (48042-2366)
PHONE...................586 825-8228
EMP: 44
SALES (corp-wide): 36.1B **Publicly Held**
SIC: 3731 Submarines, building & repairing
PA: General Dynamics Corporation
11011 Sunset Hills Rd
Reston VA 20190
703 876-3000

(G-10126)
GLITTERBUG USA
47587 Goldridge Ln (48044-2419)
PHONE...................586 247-7569
J Young, *Principal*
EMP: 3
SALES (est): 167.8K **Privately Held**
SIC: 3911 Jewelry apparel

(G-10127)
GLOBAL TOOLING SYSTEMS LLC
16445 23 Mile Rd (48042-4005)
PHONE...................586 726-0500
Paul Walsh, *President*
Jamie Franz, *QC Mgr*
Tracy Grabman, *QC Mgr*
Eugene Darlak, *Engineer*
Dan Nowicki, *CFO*
▼ **EMP**: 50
SQ FT: 215,000
SALES: 65MM
SALES (corp-wide): 386.8MM **Privately Held**
WEB: www.global-tooling-systems.com
SIC: 3545 3569 Cutting tools for machine tools; gas producers, generators & other gas related equipment
HQ: Ascent Aerospace, Llc
16445 23 Mile Rd
Macomb MI 48042
586 726-0500

(G-10128)
HARRYS STEERING GEAR REPAIR
52197 Sawmill Creek Dr (48042-5698)
PHONE...................586 677-5580
Harry Nowak, *President*
Josephine Nowak, *Corp Secy*
EMP: 7
SALES: 420K **Privately Held**
SIC: 7538 3714 General automotive repair shops; motor vehicle parts & accessories

(G-10129)
HICKS PLASTICS COMPANY INC
51308 Industrial Dr (48042-4025)
PHONE...................586 786-5640
Tim Hicks, *President*
Gail P Hicks, *Exec VP*
John Jagoda, *Plant Mgr*
Jeff Ward, *Plant Mgr*
Saul Perez, *Purch Mgr*
EMP: 100
SQ FT: 70,000
SALES (est): 49.3MM **Privately Held**
SIC: 3089 Injection molding of plastics
PA: Sea Link International Irb Inc.
13151 66th St
Largo FL 33773

(G-10130)
HYDRA-TECH INC
1483 Quadrate Dr Ste C (48042)
PHONE...................586 232-4479
Eugene Nelson, *President*
Jo Ann Nelson, *Admin Sec*
EMP: 8
SQ FT: 6,000
SALES (est): 2.9MM **Privately Held**
WEB: www.hydra-tech.net
SIC: 3561 5084 Industrial pumps & parts; hydraulic systems equipment & supplies

(G-10131)
INOVATECH AUTOMATION INC
16105 Leone Dr (48042-4063)
PHONE...................586 210-9010
Mark Rathbone, *Principal*
EMP: 15
SALES (est): 3.3MM **Privately Held**
SIC: 3569 Liquid automation machinery & equipment

(G-10132)
ITALIAN TRIBUNE
21852 23 Mile Rd (48042-4422)
PHONE...................586 783-3260
Marilyn Borner, *Principal*
EMP: 5
SALES (est): 207.4K **Privately Held**
SIC: 2711 Commercial printing & newspaper publishing combined; newspapers, publishing & printing

(G-10133)
JOINT PRODUCTION TECH INC (PA)
Also Called: Jpt
15381 Hallmark Ct (48042-4016)
PHONE...................586 786-0080
Robert B Peuterbaugh, *President*
David A Gifford, *Vice Pres*
Ronald Peuterbaugh, *Plant Mgr*
Roy Morris, *Engineer*
John Wirtanen, *Sales Engr*
EMP: 26
SQ FT: 24,000
SALES (est): 2.5MM **Privately Held**
WEB: www.jointproduction.com
SIC: 3545 Cutting tools for machine tools

(G-10134)
KID BY KID INC
54249 Myrica Dr (48042-2224)
P.O. Box 511, Warren (48090-0511)
PHONE...................586 781-2345
Michelle Pylar, *President*
Daniel Cooper, *Vice Pres*
Laurie Cooper, *Vice Pres*
Christina Parker, *Vice Pres*
Jeffery Parker, *Vice Pres*
EMP: 6
SALES: 50K **Privately Held**
WEB: www.kidbykid.com
SIC: 3944 Games, toys & children's vehicles

(G-10135)
KIMBERLY-CLARK CORPORATION
21346 Summerfield Dr (48044-2967)
PHONE...................586 949-1649
EMP: 202
SALES (corp-wide): 18.4B **Publicly Held**
SIC: 2621 2676 Sanitary tissue paper; infant & baby paper products
PA: Kimberly-Clark Corporation
351 Phelps Dr
Irving TX 75038
972 281-1200

(G-10136)
L & M TOOL CO INC
51261 Milano Dr (48042-4049)
PHONE...................586 677-4700
Mary Jane West, *President*
Donald West, *Vice Pres*
EMP: 10 **EST**: 1964
SQ FT: 42,000
SALES (est): 1.2MM **Privately Held**
SIC: 3599 3545 3544 Machine shop, jobbing & repair; machine tool accessories; special dies, tools, jigs & fixtures

(G-10137)
LUMASMART TECHNOLOGY INTL INC
Also Called: Lst Lighting
15379 Claire Ct (48042-4024)
PHONE...................586 232-4125
Dennis Dobosz, *President*
Chris Lee, *Business Mgr*
Peter Mues, *Materials Mgr*
Johnny Achkar, *Engineer*
Joseph Niksa, *Electrical Engi*
▲ **EMP**: 117
SALES (est): 32.5K **Privately Held**
SIC: 3648 Lighting equipment

(G-10138)
MAJESTIC INDUSTRIES INC
15378 Hallmark Ct (48042-4017)
PHONE...................586 786-9100
James Butler, *President*
Svetlana Rozhik, *Vice Pres*
Eric Sherman, *Vice Pres*
Alan Janiszewski, *Treasurer*
▲ **EMP**: 77
SQ FT: 65,000
SALES (est): 16.2MM **Privately Held**
WEB: www.majesticindustries.com
SIC: 3544 Special dies & tools; jigs & fixtures
HQ: Tooling Technology Holdings, Llc
100 Enterprise Dr
Fort Loramie OH 45845
937 295-3672

(G-10139)
MARK SIKORSKI MD
16800 24 Mile Rd (48042-2990)
PHONE...................586 786-1800
Mark Sikorski, *Principal*
EMP: 3
SALES (est): 141.2K **Privately Held**
SIC: 2711 Newspapers, publishing & printing

(G-10140)
MATERIAL DIFFERENCE TECH LLC
51195 Regency Center Dr (48042-4130)
PHONE...................888 818-1283
Lori Cerqua, *Accountant*
Matt Fields, *Sales Staff*
Jacob Love, *Manager*
Adam Armstrong, *Technical Staff*
EMP: 10
SALES (corp-wide): 19.3MM **Privately Held**
SIC: 5162 3087 Plastics materials & basic shapes; custom compound purchased resins
PA: Material Difference Technologies Llc
1501 Sarasota Center Blvd
Sarasota FL 34240
888 818-1283

(G-10141)
METALBUILT TACTICAL LLC
51820 Regency Center Dr (48042-4133)
PHONE...................586 786-9106
EMP: 3 **EST**: 2009
SQ FT: 24,000
SALES (est): 210K **Privately Held**
SIC: 3499 Mfg Fabricated Metal Prod

(G-10142)
MICHIGAN PROD MACHINING INC (PA)
Also Called: Mpm
16700 23 Mile Rd (48044-1100)
PHONE...................586 228-9700
Mary Jane West, *Corp Secy*
Kevin West, *Vice Pres*
Leroy Seiber, *QC Mgr*
James Newport, *Engineer*
Dan Myers, *CFO*
▲ **EMP**: 113 **EST**: 1973
SQ FT: 108,000
SALES (est): 81MM **Privately Held**
WEB: www.michpro.com
SIC: 3599 Machine shop, jobbing & repair

(G-10143)
MICHIGAN TOOL & ENGINEERING
16963 Crystal Dr (48042-2913)
PHONE...................586 786-0540
Joseph T Ciborowski, *President*
EMP: 3
SQ FT: 6,000
SALES: 140K **Privately Held**
SIC: 3544 Special dies & tools

(G-10144)
MISC PRODUCTS
16730 Enterprise Dr (48044-1006)
PHONE...................586 263-3300
William Corbit, *President*
Bill Younggren, *Vice Pres*
Dan Jasman, *QC Mgr*
Cathy First, *Manager*
▼ **EMP**: 63 **EST**: 1970
SQ FT: 28,080

(PA)=Parent Co (HQ)=Headquarters (DH)=Div Headquarters
✪ = New Business established in last 2 years

Macomb - Macomb County (G-10145)

SALES (est): 10MM Privately Held
WEB: www.misc1.com
SIC: 3714 Motor vehicle parts & accessories

(G-10145)
MLS SIGNS INC
50617 Plaza Dr (48042-4634)
PHONE....................586 948-0200
Bill Siewert, *President*
Amber Linhart, *Agent*
EMP: 10
SALES (est): 1.4MM Privately Held
WEB: www.mlssigns.com
SIC: 3993 Signs, not made in custom sign painting shops

(G-10146)
MPI PLASTICS
51315 Regency Center Dr (48042-4131)
PHONE....................201 502-1534
EMP: 3
SALES (est): 155.7K Privately Held
SIC: 3089 Injection molding of plastics

(G-10147)
MULTI-FORM PLASTICS INC
51315 Regency Center Dr (48042-4131)
PHONE....................586 786-4229
Jenny Travis, *President*
Lorenzo Borbolla, *Vice Pres*
EMP: 10
SQ FT: 8,275
SALES (est): 1.5MM Privately Held
SIC: 3089 Injection molding of plastics

(G-10148)
NETWAVE
20539 Country Side Dr (48044-3589)
PHONE....................586 263-4469
Randy Hyduk, *President*
April Hyduk, *Technology*
EMP: 12
SALES (est): 1.3MM Privately Held
SIC: 3825 Network analyzers

(G-10149)
NYLOK LLC (PA)
15260 Hallmark Ct (48042-4007)
PHONE....................586 786-0100
Greg Rawlings, *General Mgr*
Gus Anagnostopoulos, *Vice Pres*
David Deanda, *Mfg Mgr*
Bill Geatches, *Maint Spvr*
Jeremy Bugay, *QC Mgr*
EMP: 3
SALES (est): 18MM Privately Held
SIC: 3399 Metal fasteners

(G-10150)
OPEN AIR LIFESTYLES LLC
16009 Leone Dr Bldg A (48042-4063)
PHONE....................586 716-2233
Erin Haddad, *President*
▲ EMP: 12
SALES (est): 2MM Privately Held
SIC: 2421 Outdoor wood structural products

(G-10151)
P2R METAL FABRICATION INC
49620 Hayes Rd (48044-1509)
PHONE....................888 727-5587
Patrick McAleer, *President*
Ryan Novak, *Treasurer*
Jessica Guseila, *Admin Sec*
EMP: 6
SALES (est): 279.4K Privately Held
SIC: 3599 3799 3711 3721 Machine & other job shop work; trailers & trailer equipment; military motor vehicle assembly; aircraft; engineering services

(G-10152)
PANAGON SYSTEMS INC
51375 Regency Center Dr (48042-4131)
PHONE....................586 786-3920
Karl Toth, *President*
Ken Gladfelter, *General Mgr*
Matt Orr, *Purch Agent*
Don Brown, *Sales Staff*
Kelly Suess, *Sales Staff*
▲ EMP: 20
SQ FT: 16,000
SALES (est): 2.5MM Privately Held
WEB: www.panagonsystems.com
SIC: 3714 Hydraulic fluid power pumps for auto steering mechanism

(G-10153)
PPG INDUSTRIES INC
54197 Myrica Dr (48042-2223)
PHONE....................248 640-4174
Keith Larson, *Principal*
EMP: 23
SALES (corp-wide): 15.3B Publicly Held
SIC: 2851 Paints & allied products
PA: Ppg Industries, Inc.
    1 Ppg Pl
    Pittsburgh PA 15272
    412 434-3131

(G-10154)
PRAET TOOL & ENGINEERING INC
51214 Industrial Dr (48042-4025)
PHONE....................586 677-3800
Alan Praet, *President*
Dennis Praet, *Vice Pres*
EMP: 29
SQ FT: 30,000
SALES (est): 5.2MM Privately Held
WEB: www.praettool.com
SIC: 3544 3599 8711 Special dies & tools; machine shop, jobbing & repair; engineering services

(G-10155)
PRAXAIR DISTRIBUTION INC
46025 Gratiot St (48042)
PHONE....................586 598-9020
Harold Wilson, *Manager*
EMP: 18 Privately Held
WEB: www.parxair.com
SIC: 3499 5084 Welding tips, heat resistant: metal; industrial machinery & equipment
HQ: Praxair Distribution, Inc.
    10 Riverview Dr
    Danbury CT 06810
    203 837-2000

(G-10156)
PREMIER FIREPLACE CO LLC
46566 Erb Dr (48042-5916)
PHONE....................586 949-4315
EMP: 3
SALES (est): 210K Privately Held
SIC: 5719 1799 3272 Ret Misc Homefurnishings Trade Contractor Mfg Concrete Products

(G-10157)
PRISM PRINTING
51168 Milano Dr (48042-4018)
PHONE....................586 786-1250
Rick Medwith, *Owner*
EMP: 6 EST: 1990
SALES (est): 399.7K Privately Held
SIC: 2752 Commercial printing, lithographic

(G-10158)
PROBOTIC SERVICES LLC
17920 Country Club Dr (48042-1166)
PHONE....................586 524-9589
Lindsay Richcardson,
EMP: 3
SALES (est): 150K Privately Held
SIC: 3429 Manufactured hardware (general)

(G-10159)
PTI ENGINEERED PLASTICS INC
50900 Corporate Dr (48044-1008)
PHONE....................586 263-5100
Mark Rathbone, *CEO*
Kurt Nerva, *President*
Larry Terryn, *Plant Mgr*
Chris Behring, *Opers Mgr*
Diana Matthews, *Materials Mgr*
▲ EMP: 300
SQ FT: 150,000
SALES (est): 78.5MM Privately Held
WEB: www.teampti.com
SIC: 3089 3544 Injection molded finished plastic products; forms (molds), for foundry & plastics working machinery

(G-10160)
QUARTECH CORPORATION
15923 Angelo Dr (48042-4050)
PHONE....................586 781-0373
Perry Muckenthaler, *President*
Keevin Bigelow, *Treasurer*
EMP: 3
SQ FT: 3,600
SALES (est): 320K Privately Held
WEB: www.quartechcorp.com
SIC: 3577 Tape print units, computer

(G-10161)
SIMCO AUTOMOTIVE TRIM
51362 Quadrate Dr (48042-4055)
PHONE....................800 372-3172
Jeffrey Bailly, *CEO*
EMP: 60
SQ FT: 32,000
SALES (est): 3.8MM
SALES (corp-wide): 190.4MM Publicly Held
WEB: www.uspt.com
SIC: 2211 Seat cover cloth, automobile: cotton
PA: Ufp Technologies, Inc.
    100 Hale St
    Newburyport MA 01950
    978 352-2200

(G-10162)
STEEL-GUARD COMPANY LLC
51407 Milano Dr (48042-4044)
PHONE....................586 232-3909
Evis Kola,
EMP: 3
SALES (est): 104K Privately Held
SIC: 3444 Machine guards, sheet metal

(G-10163)
STERLING DIE & ENGINEERING INC
15767 Claire Ct (48042-4024)
PHONE....................586 677-0707
Chet Wisniewski, *President*
Donna Wisniewski, *President*
EMP: 35
SALES (est): 10MM Privately Held
SIC: 3465 3496 3544 3469 Automotive stampings; miscellaneous fabricated wire products; special dies, tools, jigs & fixtures; metal stampings; manufactured hardware (general)

(G-10164)
SURFACE ENCOUNTERS LLC
16280 23 Mile Rd (48044-1004)
PHONE....................586 566-7557
Chuck Russo, *CEO*
Sandy Aluia, *Principal*
▲ EMP: 60
SALES (est): 9.3MM Privately Held
SIC: 1411 5032 1741 Granite, dimension-quarrying; granite building stone; marble masonry, exterior construction

(G-10165)
SWISS PRECISION MACHINING INC
54370 Oconee Dr (48042-6123)
PHONE....................586 677-7558
Roger Kappeli, *President*
Linda Kappeli, *Vice Pres*
Rolf Kappeli, *Treasurer*
Evelyn Kappeli, *Admin Sec*
EMP: 15 EST: 1959
SQ FT: 7,850
SALES (est): 1.1MM Privately Held
WEB: www.spmswiss.com
SIC: 3599 3812 Machine shop, jobbing & repair; search & navigation equipment

(G-10166)
TEC INTERNATIONAL II
Also Called: Matrix Metalcraft
15721 Leone Dr (48042-4006)
PHONE....................586 469-9611
Nicholas A Salvatore, *Partner*
Michael Buscaino, *Sales Staff*
Mike Dilisio, *Manager*
EMP: 25
SALES (corp-wide): 5MM Privately Held
SIC: 3444 Sheet metalwork
PA: Tec International Ii, A Michigan Limited Partnership, Llp
    68 S Squirrel Rd
    Auburn Hills MI 48326
    248 724-1800

(G-10167)
TECH ELECTRIC CO LLC
16177 Leone Dr (48042-4063)
PHONE....................586 697-5095
James Gallo, *Principal*
EMP: 4
SALES (est): 505.9K Privately Held
SIC: 3699 1731 Electrical equipment & supplies; electrical work

(G-10168)
TITANIUM BUILDING CO INC
53355 Fairchild Rd (48042-3334)
PHONE....................586 634-8580
Denise Kakos, *Principal*
EMP: 4
SALES (est): 455.7K Privately Held
SIC: 3356 Titanium

(G-10169)
TOOLING TECHNOLOGY LLC (PA)
Also Called: Tooling Tech Group
51223 Quadrate Dr (48042)
P.O. Box 319, Fort Loramie OH (45845-0319)
PHONE....................937 381-9211
Anthony Seger, *CEO*
Gary Peppelman, *President*
Keith Hummel, *Controller*
Todd Wodzinski, *Ch Credit Ofcr*
Aaron Barhorst, *Sales Staff*
EMP: 80
SQ FT: 42,000
SALES (est): 48.7MM Privately Held
SIC: 3544 3363 3365 3322 Industrial molds; aluminum die-castings; aluminum foundries; malleable iron foundries

(G-10170)
TRIUMPH GEAR SYSTEMS - MACOMB
15375 23 Mile Rd (48042-4000)
PHONE....................586 781-2800
Dan Hennen, *President*
Bill Tucker, *QC Mgr*
Tj Belmont, *Engineer*
Carey Hock, *Engineer*
Dennis Blitz, *CFO*
◆ EMP: 198 EST: 1977
SQ FT: 85,000
SALES (est): 63.8MM Publicly Held
WEB: www.triumphgrp.com
SIC: 3728 3599 3462 3444 Gears, aircraft power transmission; machine shop, jobbing & repair; iron & steel forgings; sheet metalwork; gray & ductile iron foundries
PA: Triumph Group, Inc.
    899 Cassatt Rd Ste 210
    Berwyn PA 19312

(G-10171)
UNITED MACHINING INC
51362 Quadrate Dr (48042-4055)
PHONE....................586 323-4300
Lou Sabel, *General Mgr*
EMP: 5
SALES (corp-wide): 526.8MM Privately Held
SIC: 3714 Motor vehicle parts & accessories
HQ: United Machining Inc.
    6300 18 1/2 Mile Rd
    Sterling Heights MI 48314
    586 323-4300

(G-10172)
VAIVE WOOD PRODUCTS CO
24935 21 Mile Rd (48042-5114)
PHONE....................586 949-4900
Richard Vaive, *President*
Allan R Scroggs, *Vice Pres*
Constance Vaive, *Admin Sec*
EMP: 50
SQ FT: 16,800
SALES (est): 6.5MM Privately Held
SIC: 2448 2441 Pallets, wood & metal combination; shipping cases, wood: nailed or lock corner

GEOGRAPHIC SECTION
Madison Heights - Oakland County (G-10200)

(G-10173)
VISION GLOBAL INDUSTRIES
16041 Leone Dr (48042-4063)
P.O. Box 471, Armada (48005-0471)
PHONE..................248 390-5805
Deborah Paterra, *President*
Mike Locke, *Vice Pres*
EMP: 4
SALES (est): 233.3K **Privately Held**
SIC: 8711 3544 3999 Professional engineer; industrial molds; atomizers, toiletry

(G-10174)
VOLOS TUBE FORM INC
50395 Corporate Dr (48044-1007)
PHONE..................586 416-3600
Stanley Volos, *President*
EMP: 20
SQ FT: 42,600
SALES: 4.9MM **Privately Held**
WEB: www.volostubeform.com
SIC: 3498 3569 Tube fabricating (contract bending & shaping); assembly machines, non-metalworking

Madison Heights
Oakland County

(G-10175)
A C STEEL RULE DIES INC
324 E Mandoline Ave (48071-4738)
PHONE..................248 588-5600
Randy Genord, *President*
EMP: 9 EST: 1964
SQ FT: 5,600
SALES (est): 1.5MM **Privately Held**
WEB: www.acsteelrule.com
SIC: 3544 3555 Dies, steel rule; printing trades machinery

(G-10176)
A-OK GRINDING CO
32466 Townley St (48071-4760)
PHONE..................248 589-3070
Wayne A Koskinen, *President*
Kristine Koskinen, *Admin Sec*
EMP: 4 EST: 1968
SQ FT: 2,000
SALES (est): 478.2K **Privately Held**
SIC: 3599 Grinding castings for the trade

(G-10177)
AACTRON INC
29306 Stephenson Hwy (48071-2317)
PHONE..................248 543-6740
Erik M Kafarski, *President*
Mitchell I Kafarski, *Chairman*
Roman J Kafarski, *Vice Pres*
Ron Wroblewski, *Plant Mgr*
Lisa Bushon, *QC Mgr*
EMP: 22 EST: 1965
SQ FT: 25,000
SALES: 1.2MM **Privately Held**
WEB: www.aactron.com
SIC: 3479 Coating of metals & formed products

(G-10178)
ABI INTERNATIONAL
Also Called: Inland Craft Products
32052 Edward Ave (48071-1420)
PHONE..................248 583-7150
EMP: 3
SALES (est): 305.1K **Privately Held**
SIC: 3531 Grinders, stone: portable

(G-10179)
ABRASIVE DIAMOND TOOL COMPANY (PA)
Also Called: Adtco
30231 Stephenson Hwy (48071-1661)
P.O. Box 71278 (48071-0278)
PHONE..................248 588-4800
Ellen Lucas, *Ch of Bd*
Thomas M Lucas, *President*
Dave Plosky, *Vice Pres*
EMP: 25 EST: 1935
SQ FT: 15,000
SALES: 2MM **Privately Held**
SIC: 3545 3599 3291 Dressers, abrasive wheel: diamond point or other; diamond cutting tools for turning, boring, burnishing, etc.; machine shop, jobbing & repair; abrasive products

(G-10180)
ACRYLIC SPECIALTIES
32336 Edward Ave (48071-1432)
PHONE..................248 588-4390
Kathy Jerue, *President*
EMP: 6
SALES (est): 794K **Privately Held**
SIC: 3089 Injection molding of plastics

(G-10181)
ADAM ELECTRONICS INCORPORATED
32020 Edward Ave (48071-1420)
PHONE..................248 583-2000
Dan Kayganich, *CEO*
EMP: 20
SALES (est): 5.8MM **Privately Held**
SIC: 3629 7389 Electronic generation equipment; design services

(G-10182)
ADVANCED PRINTWEAR INC
31171 Stephenson Hwy (48071-1639)
PHONE..................248 585-4412
Dale Wrubel, *President*
EMP: 8
SQ FT: 8,800
SALES (est): 765.8K **Privately Held**
SIC: 2395 2261 Embroidery & art needlework; screen printing of cotton broadwoven fabrics

(G-10183)
AERO FILTER INC
Also Called: Air Filter Sales & Service
1604 E Avis Dr (48071-1501)
PHONE..................248 837-4100
Gerald V Festian, *President*
Pam Festian, *Treasurer*
David Polens, *Sales Mgr*
Bob Buckley, *Sales Staff*
Jeff Easton, *Manager*
EMP: 28 EST: 1978
SQ FT: 30,905
SALES (est): 8.9MM **Privately Held**
WEB: www.aerofilter.com
SIC: 3564 5075 Filters, air: furnaces, air conditioning equipment, etc.; air filters

(G-10184)
AJAX SPRING AND MFG CO
700 Ajax Dr (48071-2488)
PHONE..................248 588-5700
Werner Boelstler, *President*
Nicole Boelstler, *Vice Pres*
▲ EMP: 15 EST: 1952
SQ FT: 20,000
SALES (est): 2.5MM **Privately Held**
SIC: 3469 3496 3493 3465 Stamping metal for the trade; miscellaneous fabricated wire products; steel springs, except wire; automotive stampings; bolts, nuts, rivets & washers

(G-10185)
AJAX TOCCO MAGNETHERMIC CORP
30100 Stephenson Hwy (48071-1630)
PHONE..................248 589-2524
Kieth Anderson, *Principal*
Chris Pedder, *Technical Staff*
EMP: 50
SALES (corp-wide): 1.6B **Publicly Held**
WEB: www.ajaxtocco.com
SIC: 3567 3612 7699 Metal melting furnaces, industrial: electric; electric furnace transformers; industrial machinery & equipment repair
HQ: Ajax Tocco Magnethermic Corporation
1745 Overland Ave Ne
Warren OH 44483
330 372-8511

(G-10186)
AJAX TOCCO MAGNETHERMIC CORP
32350 Howard Ave (48071-1429)
PHONE..................248 585-1140
Jeff Lao, *Purch Agent*
Keith Anderson, *Branch Mgr*
EMP: 15
SALES (corp-wide): 1.6B **Publicly Held**
WEB: www.ajaxtocco.com
SIC: 3567 3612 7699 Metal melting furnaces, industrial: electric; electric furnace transformers; industrial machinery & equipment repair
HQ: Ajax Tocco Magnethermic Corporation
1745 Overland Ave Ne
Warren OH 44483
330 372-8511

(G-10187)
ALL PACKAGING SOLUTIONS INC
Also Called: Allpacks
29380 John R Rd (48071-5404)
PHONE..................248 880-1548
Robert Morales, *President*
Joe Silorey, *Warehouse Mgr*
EMP: 7
SALES: 2.5MM **Privately Held**
SIC: 2653 Corrugated & solid fiber boxes

(G-10188)
ALLIED BINDERY LLC
32501 Dequindre Rd (48071-1520)
PHONE..................248 588-5990
Jarrad Barrick, *Purch Mgr*
Edward Doyle, *Human Res Mgr*
Chris Cook,
EMP: 45
SQ FT: 48,000
SALES (est): 5.3MM **Privately Held**
WEB: www.alliedbindery.com
SIC: 2789 7389 Binding only: books, pamphlets, magazines, etc.; mailing & messenger services

(G-10189)
AMERICAN SCREW PRODUCTS INC
29866 John R Rd (48071-5408)
PHONE..................248 543-0991
Sekhar Chinasigari, *President*
EMP: 5
SQ FT: 5,100
SALES (est): 511.1K **Privately Held**
SIC: 3451 Screw machine products

(G-10190)
AMERICAN THERMOGRAPHERS INC
291 E 12 Mile Rd (48071-2557)
PHONE..................248 398-3810
Kerry J Welborn, *Owner*
EMP: 20
SQ FT: 2,300
SALES: 750K **Privately Held**
SIC: 2759 Thermography

(G-10191)
ANCHOR DANLY INC
95 E 10 Mile Rd (48071-4202)
PHONE..................519 966-4431
Terry Cutshay, *Manager*
EMP: 8
SALES (corp-wide): 7.5MM **Privately Held**
SIC: 3544 Special dies, tools, jigs & fixtures
HQ: Anchor Danly Inc
2590 Ouellette Ave
Windsor ON N8X 1
519 966-4431

(G-10192)
ANDERSON BRAZING CO INC
1544 E 11 Mile Rd (48071-3810)
PHONE..................248 399-5155
Robert Stewart, *President*
EMP: 4 EST: 1943
SQ FT: 3,000
SALES (est): 386.6K **Privately Held**
SIC: 7692 Brazing

(G-10193)
APMS INCORPORATED
Also Called: Associated Print & Marketing
31211 Stvnson Hwy Ste 100 (48071)
PHONE..................248 268-1477
Thomas David Elle, *President*
Cameron Elle, *Vice Pres*
Heather Elle, *Treasurer*
EMP: 5
SALES: 1.5MM **Privately Held**
SIC: 2752 Commercial printing, lithographic

(G-10194)
AQUA TOOL LLC
32360 Edward Ave Ste 100 (48071-1445)
PHONE..................248 307-1984
Keith Reiber, *General Mgr*
Stephen Kamp,
Gary Reiber,
EMP: 20
SQ FT: 9,875
SALES (est): 3.2MM **Privately Held**
WEB: www.aquatool.com
SIC: 3599 Machine shop, jobbing & repair

(G-10195)
ARGON TOOL INC
Also Called: Argon & Tool Manufacturing Co
32309 Milton Ave (48071-5601)
PHONE..................248 583-1605
Ted Wright, *General Mgr*
▲ EMP: 12
SQ FT: 25,000
SALES (est): 1.9MM **Privately Held**
WEB: www.steelstamps.com
SIC: 3953 Marking devices

(G-10196)
ARTECH PRINTING INC
26346 John R Rd (48071-3610)
PHONE..................248 545-0088
Thomas Brien, *Director*
Kathryn Kauer, *Graphic Designe*
EMP: 7
SQ FT: 2,200
SALES (est): 948.2K **Privately Held**
SIC: 2752 Commercial printing, offset

(G-10197)
ASTRO-NETICS INC
1780 E 14 Mile Rd (48071-1543)
PHONE..................248 585-4890
James Boston, *President*
William R Roberts, *Vice Pres*
Richard J Janes, *Treasurer*
Lawrence D Heitsch, *Admin Sec*
EMP: 90
SQ FT: 35,000
SALES (est): 12.6MM **Privately Held**
SIC: 3543 Industrial patterns

(G-10198)
ATLAS GEAR COMPANY
32801 Edward Ave (48071-1450)
PHONE..................248 583-2964
Robert A Bouren, *President*
Robert Bouren, *VP Opers*
Debbie Preston, *Office Mgr*
John Mock, *Manager*
Mary Bouren, *Clerk*
▲ EMP: 14 EST: 1946
SQ FT: 15,000
SALES (est): 3.6MM **Privately Held**
WEB: www.atlasg.com
SIC: 3566 3714 Gears, power transmission, except automotive; gears, motor vehicle

(G-10199)
AUTHORITY CUSTOMWEAR LTD
Also Called: Skyline Screen Printing & EMB
32046 Edward Ave (48071-1420)
PHONE..................248 588-8075
Steven Khalil, *President*
David Khalil, *Corp Secy*
EMP: 20
SQ FT: 18,000
SALES (est): 1.8MM **Privately Held**
SIC: 7389 7336 2396 2395 Embroidering of advertising on shirts, etc.; silk screen design; automotive & apparel trimmings; pleating & stitching

(G-10200)
BAND-AYD SYSTEMS INTL INC
355 E Whitcomb Ave (48071-4754)
PHONE..................586 294-8851
Susan De Benedetti, *President*
Brenda Vanderheyden, *Vice Pres*
EMP: 10
SQ FT: 20,000

Madison Heights - Oakland County (G-10201)

SALES (est): 960.5K **Privately Held**
WEB: www.band-ayd.com
SIC: **7389** 3699 1731 7359 Advertising, promotional & trade show services; convention & show services; trade show arrangement; electric sound equipment; lighting contractor; sound equipment specialization; sound & lighting equipment rental; audio-visual equipment & supply rental; party supplies rental services

(G-10201)
BARNES INDUSTRIES INC
1161 E 11 Mile Rd (48071-3801)
P.O. Box 71543 (48071-0543)
PHONE..................................248 541-2333
Glen R Barnes, *President*
Eric Miller, *Sales Engr*
Robert Blanton, *Marketing Staff*
EMP: 50
SQ FT: 62,500
SALES (est): 12.3MM **Privately Held**
WEB: www.barnesballscrew.com
SIC: **3568** Power transmission equipment

(G-10202)
BARON ACQUISITION LLC (PA)
Also Called: Baron Industries
999 E Mandoline Ave (48071-1436)
PHONE..................................248 585-0444
Jaime Hartom, *QC Mgr*
EMP: 3
SALES (est): 1.3MM **Privately Held**
SIC: **3479** Etching & engraving

(G-10203)
BEHCO INC
1666 E Lincoln Ave (48071-4141)
PHONE..................................586 755-0200
Stephen J Ellis, *President*
EMP: 19
SQ FT: 12,000
SALES (est): 12.3MM **Privately Held**
WEB: www.behco.com
SIC: **5084** 3593 Hydraulic systems equipment & supplies; pneumatic tools & equipment; fluid power cylinders, hydraulic or pneumatic

(G-10204)
BESPRO PATTERN INC
31301 Mally Dr (48071-1629)
PHONE..................................586 268-6970
John J Basso, *President*
Sonjia A Basso, *Vice Pres*
EMP: 15
SQ FT: 15,000
SALES (est): 2.4MM **Privately Held**
WEB: www.bespropattern.com
SIC: **3543** 3553 3086 Industrial patterns; pattern makers' machinery, woodworking; plastics foam products

(G-10205)
BORITE MANUFACTURING CORP
31711 Sherman Ave (48071-1428)
PHONE..................................248 588-7260
Andrew Lankin, *President*
Sheila Emmons, *Manager*
EMP: 8 EST: 1960
SQ FT: 8,100
SALES (est): 888K **Privately Held**
SIC: **3545** Boring machine attachments (machine tool accessories); headstocks, lathe (machine tool accessories)

(G-10206)
BRASCO INTERNATIONAL INC
32400 Industrial Dr (48071-1527)
PHONE..................................313 393-0393
William Noecker, *President*
Douglas N Pew, *COO*
Vanessa Bagwell, *Project Mgr*
Vanessa Toce, *Project Mgr*
Brett House, *Design Engr*
◆ EMP: 60
SQ FT: 57,000
SALES (est): 21.7MM **Privately Held**
WEB: www.brasco.com
SIC: **3448** Buildings, portable: prefabricated metal

(G-10207)
BROWE INC
30870 Stephenson Hwy C (48071-1614)
PHONE..................................248 877-3800
Brian K Browe, *President*
EMP: 5
SALES (est): 1.1MM **Privately Held**
SIC: **3827** Optical instruments & lenses

(G-10208)
CENTRAL GEAR INC
Also Called: Machining Specialties
540 Ajax Dr (48071-2494)
PHONE..................................800 589-1602
Herschel Breazeale, *President*
Richard Moores, *Vice Pres*
Lorraine Breazeale, *Admin Sec*
EMP: 18
SALES (est): 2.7MM **Privately Held**
WEB: www.centralgear.com
SIC: **3599** Machine shop, jobbing & repair

(G-10209)
CHEMICAL PROCESS INDS LLC
25428 John R Rd (48071-4012)
PHONE..................................248 547-5200
Bruce Kafarski, *President*
EMP: 10
SALES (est): 989K **Privately Held**
SIC: **3471** Plating of metals or formed products

(G-10210)
CLEARY DEVELOPMENTS INC (PA)
Also Called: Belmont Equipment Company
32055 Edward Ave (48071-1419)
P.O. Box 71013 (48071-0013)
PHONE..................................248 588-7011
Lawrence J Ianitelli, *Ch of Bd*
Robert J Ianitelli, *President*
Tony Tyll, *General Mgr*
Julie Carr, *Warehouse Mgr*
Natalie Pettibone, *Purch Mgr*
▲ EMP: 45
SQ FT: 22,000
SALES: 45MM **Privately Held**
WEB: www.belmont4edm.com
SIC: **5084** 5085 3599 3541 Machine tools & accessories; industrial supplies; electrical discharge machining (EDM); machine tools, metal cutting type

(G-10211)
CLEARY DEVELOPMENTS INC
Primeway Tool & Engrg Co Div
32033 Edward Ave (48071-1419)
PHONE..................................248 588-6614
Larry Ianitelli, *President*
Don Ligrow, *Manager*
EMP: 25
SALES (corp-wide): 45MM **Privately Held**
SIC: **3599** 3544 Machine shop, jobbing & repair; special dies, tools, jigs & fixtures
PA: Cleary Developments Incorporated
  32055 Edward Ave
  Madison Heights MI 48071
  248 588-7011

(G-10212)
CNI ENTERPRISES INC (DH)
Also Called: Futuris Automotive
1451 E Lincoln Ave (48071-4136)
PHONE..................................248 586-3300
Merv Dunn, *CEO*
Ray Bomya, *COO*
William K Peterson, *CFO*
Paul Williams, *Sales Staff*
▲ EMP: 1
SQ FT: 5,000
SALES (est): 240.9MM **Privately Held**
SIC: **2396** Automotive trimmings, fabric
HQ: Futuris Automotive (Us) Inc.
  14925 W 11 Mile Rd
  Oak Park MI 48237
  248 439-7800

(G-10213)
CNI-OWOSSO LLC
Also Called: Futuris Automotive
1451 E Lincoln Ave (48071-4136)
PHONE..................................248 586-3300
Merv Dunn, *CEO*
Bill Peterson, *CFO*
▲ EMP: 1
SQ FT: 35,000
SALES (est): 7.1MM **Privately Held**
SIC: **2396** Automotive trimmings, fabric
HQ: Cni Enterprises, Inc.
  1451 E Lincoln Ave
  Madison Heights MI 48071
  248 586-3300

(G-10214)
COBRA ENTERPRISES INC
32303 Howard Ave (48071-1427)
PHONE..................................248 588-2669
Eric Myers, *President*
Derek Myers, *Vice Pres*
EMP: 10
SQ FT: 7,000
SALES (est): 940K **Privately Held**
SIC: **3599** Machine shop, jobbing & repair

(G-10215)
COBRA PATTERNS & MODELS INC
Also Called: Cobra Enterprises
32303 Howard Ave (48071-1427)
PHONE..................................248 588-2669
Eric Myers, *President*
Derek Myers, *Admin Sec*
EMP: 50
SQ FT: 7,000
SALES (est): 7.2MM **Privately Held**
SIC: **3543** 3364 Industrial patterns; non-ferrous die-castings except aluminum

(G-10216)
COLOR COAT PLATING COMPANY
355 W Girard Ave (48071-1841)
PHONE..................................248 744-0445
Jeffery Swanson, *President*
EMP: 12 EST: 1999
SQ FT: 6,500
SALES (est): 1.7MM **Privately Held**
SIC: **3471** Plating of metals or formed products

(G-10217)
COMMERCIAL STEEL TREATING CORP (PA)
31440 Stephenson Hwy (48071-1693)
P.O. Box 908, Troy (48099-0908)
PHONE..................................248 588-3300
Ralph Hoensheid, *Principal*
Jack Howard, *Treasurer*
Duane Drobnich, *Commercial*
▲ EMP: 82
SQ FT: 140,000
SALES (est): 27.3MM **Privately Held**
WEB: www.commercialsteel.com
SIC: **3479** 3398 Coating of metals & formed products; tempering of metal

(G-10218)
COMPUTER COMPOSITION CORP
1401 W Girard Ave (48071-4400)
PHONE..................................248 545-4330
Peter Fulton, *President*
Allan Germic, *Vice Pres*
EMP: 13
SQ FT: 10,000
SALES (est): 1.7MM **Privately Held**
WEB: www.computercomposition.com
SIC: **2791** 2741 Typesetting, computer controlled; directories: publishing only, not printed on site

(G-10219)
COMPUTERIZED SEC SYSTEMS INC (DH)
Also Called: Saflok
31750 Sherman Ave (48071-1423)
PHONE..................................248 837-3700
Riet Cadonau, *CEO*
Frank Belflower, *President*
▲ EMP: 135
SQ FT: 29,000
SALES (est): 30.5MM
SALES (corp-wide): 2.8B **Privately Held**
WEB: www.saflok.com
SIC: **3699** Door opening & closing devices, electrical
HQ: Kaba Ilco Corp.
  400 Jeffreys Rd
  Rocky Mount NC 27804
  252 446-3321

(G-10220)
COPILOT PRINTING
285 E 12 Mile Rd (48071-2557)
PHONE..................................248 398-5301
Ryan Malerman, *Owner*
EMP: 4
SALES (est): 434.1K **Privately Held**
SIC: **2752** Commercial printing, offset

(G-10221)
COWS LOCOMOTIVE MFG CO (PA)
32052 Edward Ave (48071-1420)
PHONE..................................248 583-7150
Richard K Wiand, *CEO*
Donald Hirst, *President*
Sharon Meadows, *Vice Pres*
Linda Redman, *Vice Pres*
▲ EMP: 20
SQ FT: 20,000
SALES (est): 1.7MM **Privately Held**
WEB: www.inlandcraft.com
SIC: **3423** 3545 3532 2899 Hand & edge tools; machine tool accessories; mining machinery; chemical preparations

(G-10222)
CREATIVE CONTROLS INC
Also Called: Creative Controls Handicapped
32217 Stephenson Hwy (48071-5519)
PHONE..................................248 577-9800
Thomas R Stowers, *President*
▲ EMP: 15
SQ FT: 6,500
SALES (est): 193.4K **Privately Held**
WEB: www.creativecontrolsinc.com
SIC: **3714** Motor vehicle parts & accessories

(G-10223)
CTA ACOUSTICS INC (PA)
25211 Dequindre Rd (48071-4211)
PHONE..................................248 544-2580
James J Pike, *Ch of Bd*
Thomas Brown, *President*
Barry Gaines, *Vice Pres*
Amy Hopkins, *Purchasing*
Barry Hickey, *Info Tech Dir*
▲ EMP: 50
SQ FT: 400,000
SALES (est): 201.1MM **Privately Held**
WEB: www.ctaacoustics.com
SIC: **3714** Motor vehicle body components & frame

(G-10224)
CURTIS METAL FINISHING CO
31440 Stephenson Hwy (48071-1621)
PHONE..................................248 588-3300
Scott Hoensheid, *President*
EMP: 4 EST: 2017
SALES (est): 358.5K **Privately Held**
SIC: **3398** Metal heat treating

(G-10225)
CUSTOM VALVE CONCEPTS INC
Also Called: W.A. Kates Company, The
31651 Research Park Dr (48071-4626)
PHONE..................................248 597-8999
John D Taube, *President*
◆ EMP: 25 EST: 1946
SQ FT: 13,000
SALES (est): 6.9MM **Privately Held**
WEB: www.wakates.com
SIC: **3823** 5084 Flow instruments, industrial process type; industrial machinery & equipment

(G-10226)
DAIRY FREEZZZ TOO LLC
621 E 11 Mile Rd (48071-3703)
PHONE..................................248 629-6666
Susan Cox,
EMP: 7
SALES (est): 211.9K **Privately Held**
SIC: **2024** Ice cream & frozen desserts

(G-10227)
DALE CORPORATION
28091 Dequindre Rd # 301 (48071-3047)
PHONE..................................248 542-2400
Dale Z Jablonski, *President*
Vespa Anthony, *Project Mgr*
EMP: 20 EST: 1969

GEOGRAPHIC SECTION
Madison Heights - Oakland County (G-10253)

SALES (est): 2.3MM **Privately Held**
SIC: 8743 2721 Public relations & publicity; periodicals: publishing only; magazines: publishing only, not printed on site

(G-10228)
DATA MAIL SERVICES INC
Also Called: Intelligent Document Solutions
747 E Whitcomb Ave (48071-1409)
PHONE.................................248 588-2415
William P Hayden, *President*
EMP: 50
SQ FT: 26,000
SALES (est): 16.6MM
SALES (corp-wide): 64.6MM **Privately Held**
WEB: www.datamailservices.com
SIC: 2759 7331 Commercial printing; mailing service
HQ: Intelligent Document Solutions, Inc.
747 E Whitcomb Ave
Madison Heights MI 48071

(G-10229)
DESIGN FABRICATIONS INC
Also Called: D Fab
1100 E Mandoline Ave A (48071-1426)
PHONE.................................248 597-0988
Gregory Geralds, *President*
Bruce Dych, *Chairman*
Tony Camilletti, *Vice Pres*
James Donohue, *Project Mgr*
Laura Higgins, *Project Mgr*
▲ **EMP:** 100 **EST:** 1973
SQ FT: 100,000
SALES (est): 14.7MM **Privately Held**
WEB: www.dfidesign.com
SIC: 7389 2541 3993 Design, commercial & industrial; wood partitions & fixtures; signs & advertising specialties

(G-10230)
DETROIT WIRE ROPE SPLCING CORP
31623 Stephenson Hwy (48071-1646)
PHONE.................................248 585-1063
Charles W Richards, *President*
Kent Richards, *Vice Pres*
EMP: 12
SQ FT: 12,000
SALES (est): 1.8MM **Privately Held**
SIC: 5084 3496 Materials handling machinery; cable, uninsulated wire: made from purchased wire; slings, lifting: made from purchased wire

(G-10231)
DIVERSIFIED E D M INC
1019 E 10 Mile Rd (48071-4226)
PHONE.................................248 547-2320
Billie Huffman, *President*
Larry Huffman, *Vice Pres*
EMP: 5
SQ FT: 1,200
SALES (est): 471.2K **Privately Held**
SIC: 3599 Electrical discharge machining (EDM)

(G-10232)
DIVERSIFIED TOOLING GROUP INC
31240 Stephenson Hwy (48071-1620)
PHONE.................................248 837-5828
Jay Warner, *Vice Pres*
James Curtin, *Mfg Mgr*
John Visger, *Chief Engr*
Brooks McLaughlin, *Engineer*
Gary Gizinski, *Treasurer*
EMP: 14 **EST:** 2002
SALES (est): 2MM **Privately Held**
SIC: 3443 Liners, industrial: metal plate

(G-10233)
DME COMPANY LLC (DH)
29111 Stephenson Hwy (48071-2383)
PHONE.................................248 398-6000
Robert Salhaney, *President*
Fred Schroeder, *Engineer*
Lisa Close, *Financial Analy*
Nykita Berry, *Sales Staff*
Donna Craner, *Sales Staff*
▲ **EMP:** 274
SALES (est): 83.7MM
SALES (corp-wide): 1.2B **Privately Held**
SIC: 3544 3545 Industrial molds; precision measuring tools

(G-10234)
DOUGLAS STAMPING COMPANY
25531 Dequindre Rd (48071-4236)
PHONE.................................248 542-3940
Nick Maylen, *President*
Matthew Maylen, *Vice Pres*
David Maylen III, *Admin Sec*
EMP: 9 **EST:** 1947
SQ FT: 6,900
SALES (est): 1.6MM **Privately Held**
WEB: www.dougstampco.com
SIC: 3465 3469 Automotive stampings; stamping metal for the trade

(G-10235)
DUNHAMS ATHLEISURE CORPORATION
32101 John R Rd (48071-4722)
PHONE.................................248 658-1382
Jeremy Miller, *Branch Mgr*
EMP: 16
SALES (corp-wide): 380MM **Privately Held**
SIC: 5941 5699 5091 3949 Specialty sport supplies; sports apparel; sporting & recreation goods; sporting & athletic goods
HQ: Dunham's Athleisure Corporation
5607 New King Dr Ste 125
Troy MI 48098
248 530-6700

(G-10236)
DURA THREAD GAGE INC
971 E 10 Mile Rd (48071-4288)
PHONE.................................248 545-2890
Mary Oliveto, *President*
John Oliveto, *Vice Pres*
Sam Oliveto, *Admin Sec*
EMP: 10 **EST:** 1963
SQ FT: 7,400
SALES (est): 1.2MM **Privately Held**
SIC: 3544 3823 3545 Special dies, tools, jigs & fixtures; industrial instrmnts msrmnt display/control process variable; gauges (machine tool accessories)

(G-10237)
EAST - LIND HEAT TREAT INC
32045 Dequindre Rd (48071-1521)
PHONE.................................248 585-1415
Robert L Easterbrook Sr, *President*
Sue Cardillo, *Controller*
EMP: 31
SQ FT: 27,149
SALES (est): 4.2MM **Privately Held**
WEB: www.eastlind.com
SIC: 3398 Metal heat treating

(G-10238)
ECOLO-TECH INC
1743 E 10 Mile Rd (48071-4229)
PHONE.................................248 541-1100
Roy Costello, *President*
Roy E Costello, *President*
Thomas Costello, *Vice Pres*
EMP: 12
SQ FT: 4,500
SALES (est): 1.8MM **Privately Held**
SIC: 3444 Ducts, sheet metal

(G-10239)
ECOSTRAT USA INC
201 W 13 Mile Rd (48071-1870)
PHONE.................................416 968-8884
Jordan Solomon, *CEO*
EMP: 3
SALES (est): 122.2K **Privately Held**
SIC: 2421 Sawmills & planing mills, general

(G-10240)
EFD INDUCTION INC
Also Called: E F D
31511 Dequindre Rd (48071-1537)
PHONE.................................248 658-0700
Tom Crocker, *President*
Johan Larsen, *Vice Pres*
▲ **EMP:** 17
SQ FT: 16,000
SALES (est): 3.1MM
SALES (corp-wide): 578.5MM **Privately Held**
WEB: www.efd-induction.com
SIC: 3567 Industrial furnaces & ovens
HQ: Efd Induction As
Bolevegen 10
Skien 3724
355 060-00

(G-10241)
EGT PRINTING SOLUTIONS LLC
32031 Townley St (48071-1320)
PHONE.................................248 583-2500
Mike Gillette, *President*
Michael Gonte, *Vice Pres*
Drew Johnson, *VP Sales*
Todd Gillick, *Sales Staff*
Sean McInerney, *Sales Staff*
▲ **EMP:** 104 **EST:** 1975
SQ FT: 75,000
SALES (est): 22.7MM
SALES (corp-wide): 6.8B **Publicly Held**
WEB: www.egtgo.com
SIC: 2752 Commercial printing, offset
HQ: Consolidated Graphics, Inc.
5858 Westheimer Rd # 200
Houston TX 77057
713 787-0977

(G-10242)
ELECTRO-PLATING SERVICE INC
945 E 10 Mile Rd (48071-4290)
PHONE.................................248 541-0035
EMP: 15
SQ FT: 11,500
SALES (est): 1.6MM **Privately Held**
SIC: 3471 Plating / Polishing Service

(G-10243)
ELECTROCOM MIDWEST SALES INC (PA)
32500 Concord Dr Ste 298 (48071-1100)
PHONE.................................248 449-2643
Steve Blank, *President*
Brian Blank, *Treasurer*
EMP: 6
SQ FT: 1,300
SALES: 800K **Privately Held**
WEB: www.electrocommidwest.com
SIC: 3643 Current-carrying wiring devices

(G-10244)
ELEVEN MILE TRCK FRME & AX
Also Called: Eleven Mile Truck Collision Co
1750 E 11 Mile Rd (48071-3814)
PHONE.................................248 399-7536
Milan S Krstich, *President*
Ken Krstich, *General Mgr*
Lois Krstich, *Vice Pres*
Rick Krstich, *Admin Sec*
EMP: 55
SQ FT: 32,000
SALES (est): 7MM **Privately Held**
WEB: www.11miletruck.com
SIC: 7538 7532 3713 General truck repair; collision shops, automotive; truck & bus bodies

(G-10245)
EMERALD CONSULTING GROUP LLC
31650 Stephenson Hwy (48071-1642)
PHONE.................................248 720-0573
Joe Ankley, *Vice Pres*
Eric Jones, *QC Mgr*
Jim Schorsch, *Plant Engr*
Randy Hopkins, *Sales Mgr*
Greg Bondie, *Accounts Mgr*
▲ **EMP:** 35
SALES (est): 19.8MM
SALES (corp-wide): 100MM **Privately Held**
SIC: 3398 Annealing of metal
PA: Shannon Precision Fastener, Llc
31600 Stephenson Hwy
Madison Heights MI 48071
248 589-9670

(G-10246)
ENDLESS POSSIBILITIES INC
672 Ajax Dr (48071-2414)
PHONE.................................248 262-7443
Joyce Murphy, *Owner*
▲ **EMP:** 7
SALES (est): 544.3K **Privately Held**
SIC: 3999 Education aids, devices & supplies

(G-10247)
ENERGY PRODUCTS INC (PA)
1551 E Lincoln Ave # 101 (48071-4159)
PHONE.................................248 545-7700
Kurt H Smith, *CEO*
▲ **EMP:** 60
SQ FT: 100,000
SALES: 60MM **Privately Held**
WEB: www.energyprod.com
SIC: 7699 7539 5063 3625 Battery service & repair; automotive repair shops; storage batteries, industrial; relays & industrial controls; industrial machinery & equipment

(G-10248)
ENGINEERED HEAT TREAT INC
31271 Stephenson Hwy (48071-1682)
PHONE.................................248 588-5141
Phillip D Pilibosian, *Chairman*
Keith Pilibosian, *Vice Pres*
Greg Crampton, *Opers Mgr*
Ronald Pilibosian, *Treasurer*
Greg Pilibosian, *Manager*
◆ **EMP:** 35 **EST:** 1959
SQ FT: 47,000
SALES (est): 8.5MM **Privately Held**
WEB: www.ehtinc.com
SIC: 3398 Metal heat treating

(G-10249)
EQUIP CONSUMABLE GROUP
32035 Edward Ave (48071-1419)
PHONE.................................248 588-9981
Sandra Kerwin, *Principal*
EMP: 3 **EST:** 2015
SALES (est): 95K **Privately Held**
SIC: 3599 Industrial machinery

(G-10250)
EUREKA WELDING ALLOYS INC
2000 E Avis Dr (48071-1551)
PHONE.................................248 588-0001
Ralph Lameti, *Chairman*
David Vinson, *Regional Mgr*
John Kerchkof, *Vice Pres*
Kathleen Nataline, *Human Res Mgr*
Kathy Nataline, *Manager*
◆ **EMP:** 38
SQ FT: 58,000
SALES (est): 9.4MM **Privately Held**
WEB: www.eurekaweldingalloys.com
SIC: 3548 3356 5084 5085 Electrodes, electric welding; welding rods; welding machinery & equipment; welding supplies

(G-10251)
F J MANUFACTURING CO
32329 Milton Ave (48071-5601)
PHONE.................................248 583-4777
Gary Parlove, *President*
Marion Brown, *Purchasing*
EMP: 14 **EST:** 1957
SQ FT: 11,700
SALES (est): 1.4MM **Privately Held**
SIC: 3599 Machine shop, jobbing & repair

(G-10252)
FEG GAGE INC
Also Called: Feg Gage & Engineering
32329 Milton Ave (48071-5601)
PHONE.................................248 616-3631
Daniel Ellis, *President*
EMP: 12 **EST:** 1978
SQ FT: 10,000
SALES (est): 1.6MM **Privately Held**
SIC: 3544 8731 Jigs & fixtures; commercial physical research

(G-10253)
FICOSA NORTH AMERICA CORP (HQ)
30870 Stephenson Hwy (48071-1614)
PHONE.................................248 307-2230
Javier Pujol, *President*
Fred Zicard, *Exec VP*
Pawel Pernal, *QC Mgr*
Jordi Aubert, *Engineer*
Jose Espinosa, *Engineer*
▲ **EMP:** 30
SQ FT: 16,750
SALES (est): 564.4MM
SALES (corp-wide): 68.5MM **Privately Held**
SIC: 3711 Motor vehicles & car bodies

Madison Heights - Oakland County (G-10254)

PA: Ficosa International, Sa
Calle Gran Via Carles Iii, 98 - 5o
Planta
Barcelona 08028
933 391-814

(G-10254)
FIRST OPTOMETRY LAB
195 Ajax Dr (48071-2425)
PHONE..................................248 546-1300
EMP: 9 **EST:** 1997
SALES (est): 850K **Privately Held**
SQ FT: 1,600
SIC: 3827 Mfg Optical Instruments/Lenses

(G-10255)
GAGE PATTERN & MODEL INC
32070 Townley St (48071-1304)
PHONE..................................248 361-6609
Werner Schulte, *President*
Eric Schulte, *Corp Secy*
Ilse Schulte, *Vice Pres*
Lori Vuljaj, *CFO*
EMP: 50
SQ FT: 12,000
SALES (est): 7.5MM **Privately Held**
WEB: www.gpminc.com
SIC: 3543 3544 3714 Industrial patterns; jigs & fixtures; motor vehicle parts & accessories

(G-10256)
GALCO INDUSTRIAL ELEC INC
1001 Lincoln St (48071)
PHONE..................................248 542-9090
Michael Conwell, *Exec VP*
Cory Hall, *Materials Mgr*
Amber Adams, *Purch Agent*
Doug Bauman, *Sales Staff*
Tina Sheck, *Sales Staff*
EMP: 9
SALES (corp-wide): 3B **Privately Held**
WEB: www.galco.com
SIC: 5065 7629 3625 Electronic parts; rectifiers, electronic; capacitors, electronic; electronic equipment repair; relays & industrial controls
HQ: Galco Industrial Electronics, Inc.
26010 Pinehurst Dr
Madison Heights MI 48071
248 542-9090

(G-10257)
GHI ELECTRONICS LLC
501 E Whitcomb Ave (48071-1408)
PHONE..................................248 397-8856
Ghassan Issa, *Principal*
Michael Bagnaschi, *Prdtn Mgr*
Gary Beaver, *Opers Staff*
◆ **EMP:** 12
SQ FT: 18,000
SALES (est): 1MM **Privately Held**
SIC: 5999 3672 5065 Electronic parts & equipment; printed circuit boards; electronic parts

(G-10258)
GRAPHIC ENTERPRISES INC
1200 E Avis Dr (48071-1507)
PHONE..................................248 616-4900
EMP: 85
SALES (est): 4.6MM **Privately Held**
SIC: 7336 2752 7335 2796 Coml Art/Graphic Design Lithographic Coml Print Commercial Photography Platemaking Services Commercial Printing

(G-10259)
GRAPHITE PRODUCTS CORP
1797 E 10 Mile Rd (48071-4229)
PHONE..................................248 548-7800
Gilbert Liske, *President*
▲ **EMP:** 7 **EST:** 1965
SQ FT: 9,000
SALES (est): 680K **Privately Held**
WEB: www.graphiteproductscorp.com
SIC: 3599 Machine shop, jobbing & repair

(G-10260)
GREAT LAKES EMBROIDERY
1191 E 10 Mile Rd (48071-4207)
PHONE..................................248 543-5164
Robin Tasker, *Owner*
EMP: 3
SQ FT: 1,600
SALES (est): 180K **Privately Held**
SIC: 2396 Printing & embossing on plastics fabric articles

(G-10261)
GREAT LAKES FOOD CENTER LLC
32102 Howard Ave (48071-1451)
PHONE..................................248 397-8166
Ronnie Ayar,
◆ **EMP:** 21
SQ FT: 310,000
SALES: 4MM **Privately Held**
SIC: 2035 Seasonings & sauces, except tomato & dry

(G-10262)
GREAT LAKES LASER SERVICES
147 E 10 Mile Rd (48071-4203)
P.O. Box 868, Royal Oak (48068-0868)
PHONE..................................248 584-1828
Carl R Hildebrand, *CEO*
Carl J Hildebrand, *President*
Bath Buccarielli, *Vice Pres*
Gary Johns, *Manager*
EMP: 6
SQ FT: 1,600
SALES (est): 687.6K **Privately Held**
WEB: www.greatlakeslaser.com
SIC: 3599 3548 Machine shop, jobbing & repair; resistance welders, electric

(G-10263)
H & L TOOL COMPANY INC
32701 Dequindre Rd (48071-1595)
PHONE..................................248 585-7474
Michael Bourg, *President*
Tony Langlois, *Plant Mgr*
Tim Whiting, *Plant Mgr*
Paul Snider, *Opers Mgr*
Dennis Chestnut, *Engineer*
EMP: 100
SQ FT: 95,000
SALES (est): 21.4MM
SALES (corp-wide): 37.1MM **Publicly Held**
WEB: www.chicagorivetsw.com
SIC: 3451 3452 3316 Screw machine products; rivets, metal; bolts, metal; cold finishing of steel shapes
PA: Chicago Rivet & Machine Co.
901 Frontenac Rd
Naperville IL 60563
630 357-8500

(G-10264)
HENKEL LOCTITE CORPORATION
32100 Stephenson Hwy (48071-5514)
PHONE..................................787 264-7534
Jeffrey C Piccolomini, *CEO*
Bob Miller, *Business Mgr*
Susan Wahl, *Purch Mgr*
John Zimmerman, *Research*
Mike Hogan, *Engineer*
EMP: 3
SALES (corp-wide): 22.7B **Privately Held**
SIC: 2891 Adhesives
HQ: Henkel Loctite Corporation
1 Henkel Way
Rocky Hill CT 06067
860 571-5100

(G-10265)
HENKEL SURFACE TECHNOLOGIES
31200 Stephenson Hwy (48071-1620)
PHONE..................................248 307-0240
Fax: 248 589-4806
▲ **EMP:** 6
SALES (est): 1.4MM **Privately Held**
SIC: 2842 Mfg Polish/Sanitation Goods

(G-10266)
HENKEL US OPERATIONS CORP
Also Called: Henkel Surface Technologies
32100 Stephenson Hwy (48071-5514)
P.O. Box 27950, Scottsdale AZ (85255-0149)
PHONE..................................248 588-1082
Mark Zahradnik, *General Mgr*
Patrick Apsey, *Business Mgr*
Scott Baldwin, *Business Mgr*
Greg Barrier, *Business Mgr*
John Dudiak, *Business Mgr*
EMP: 300
SQ FT: 250,000
SALES (corp-wide): 22.7B **Privately Held**
SIC: 2899 2869 2819 3823 Corrosion preventive lubricant; industrial organic chemicals; industrial inorganic chemicals; industrial process control instruments
HQ: Henkel Us Operations Corporation
1 Henkel Way
Rocky Hill CT 06067
860 571-5100

(G-10267)
HIGHLAND MANUFACTURING INC
339 E Whitcomb Ave (48071-4754)
PHONE..................................248 585-8040
Hilarion Bibicoff, *President*
Hilarion Larry Bibicoff, *President*
Hilarion Bibicoff VI, *Vice Pres*
EMP: 18
SQ FT: 11,600
SALES (est): 3.3MM **Privately Held**
SIC: 3599 3714 Machine shop, jobbing & repair; oil pump, motor vehicle

(G-10268)
HOT WHEELS CITY INC (PA)
32451 Dequindre Rd (48071-1596)
PHONE..................................248 589-8800
Nazhat Abouna, *President*
Amber Rompz, *Admin Sec*
▲ **EMP:** 21
SQ FT: 6,288
SALES (est): 11.3MM **Privately Held**
SIC: 5531 3011 3312 5013 Automotive tires; tire & inner tube materials & related products; wheels; wheels, motor vehicle

(G-10269)
HOWARD FINISHING LLC (PA)
Also Called: Hf
32565 Dequindre Rd (48071-1520)
PHONE..................................248 588-9050
James E Grimes, *President*
William Aikens,
EMP: 120
SQ FT: 150,000
SALES (est): 26.1MM **Privately Held**
WEB: www.howardfinishing.com
SIC: 3449 Miscellaneous metalwork

(G-10270)
HQT INC
324 E Mandoline Ave (48071-4738)
PHONE..................................248 589-7960
Joanne Hicks, *President*
Greg Bailey, *Manager*
EMP: 3
SQ FT: 6,000
SALES (est): 330K **Privately Held**
SIC: 3544 Special dies & tools

(G-10271)
HR TECHNOLOGIES INC
32500 N Avis Dr (48071-1558)
PHONE..................................248 284-1170
Tushar Patel, *President*
▲ **EMP:** 144
SQ FT: 111,000
SALES (est): 35.1MM **Privately Held**
WEB: www.hrtechinc.com
SIC: 2273 Mats & matting

(G-10272)
I E & E INDUSTRIES INC (PA)
111 E 10 Mile Rd (48071-4203)
PHONE..................................248 544-8181
Ron Webber, *President*
Judy Miles, *Vice Pres*
EMP: 19 **EST:** 1957
SQ FT: 10,000
SALES (est): 1.3MM **Privately Held**
WEB: www.ie-e.com
SIC: 3544 Jigs & fixtures

(G-10273)
IDENTIFY INC
25163 Dequindre Rd (48071-4240)
PHONE..................................313 802-2015
Robert Suszynski, *President*
John Rademaker, *Business Mgr*
Gerald Alfred, *Vice Pres*
Thomas Mezza, *Treasurer*
Mike Simmons, *Manager*
EMP: 17
SALES (est): 2.8MM **Privately Held**
SIC: 3699 Security devices

(G-10274)
INFUSYSTEM HOLDINGS INC (PA)
31700 Research Park Dr (48071-4627)
PHONE..................................248 291-1210
Richard Diiorio, *President*
Scott Shuda, *Chairman*
Carrie Lachance, *COO*
Michael McReynolds, *Exec VP*
Sean W Schembri, *Exec VP*
EMP: 89
SALES: 67.1MM **Publicly Held**
SIC: 3841 Surgical & medical instruments

(G-10275)
INGERSOLL-RAND COMPANY
29555 Stephenson Hwy (48071-2332)
PHONE..................................248 398-6200
Lisa O'Dell, *Manager*
EMP: 30 **Privately Held**
WEB: www.ingersoll-rand.com
SIC: 3432 Plumbing fixture fittings & trim
HQ: Ingersoll-Rand Company
800 Beaty St Ste B
Davidson NC 28036
704 655-4000

(G-10276)
INLAND DIAMOND PRODUCTS CO
32051 Howard Ave (48071-1473)
PHONE..................................248 585-1762
Ronald K Wiand, *President*
Dennis Raffaelli, *COO*
Mike Boon, *Engineer*
Irene Shotkin, *CFO*
Bruce Kesselring, *Sales Mgr*
▲ **EMP:** 50
SQ FT: 20,000
SALES (est): 8.3MM **Privately Held**
WEB: www.inlanddiamond.com
SIC: 3291 3851 Wheels, abrasive; ophthalmic goods

(G-10277)
INTERNATIONAL NOODLE CO INC
32811 Groveland St (48071-1330)
PHONE..................................248 583-2479
Bob Ip, *President*
EMP: 8
SQ FT: 700
SALES (est): 1.1MM **Privately Held**
SIC: 2099 Food preparations

(G-10278)
IONBOND LLC (DH)
1823 E Whitcomb Ave (48071-1413)
PHONE..................................248 398-9100
Joe Haggerty, *CEO*
Debbie Degraaf, *General Mgr*
Kyle Puska, *Plant Mgr*
Joe Rogers, *Plant Mgr*
Jerry Fabbri, *Prdtn Mgr*
▲ **EMP:** 60
SQ FT: 36,767
SALES (est): 109.4MM **Privately Held**
WEB: www.ionbond.com
SIC: 3398 3479 Metal heat treating; bonderizing of metal or metal products
HQ: Ihi Ionbond Ag
Industriestrasse 9
Dulliken SO 4657
622 878-686

(G-10279)
J E WOOD CO
395 W Girard Ave (48071-1841)
PHONE..................................248 585-5711
James E Wood, *Ch of Bd*
Brian Fish, *President*
John Kistela, *Vice Pres*
EMP: 15 **EST:** 1958
SQ FT: 10,000
SALES (est): 1.3MM **Privately Held**
WEB: www.jewood.com
SIC: 3545 Cutting tools for machine tools

▲ = Import ▼ = Export
◆ = Import/Export

GEOGRAPHIC SECTION
Madison Heights - Oakland County (G-10305)

(G-10280)
J H P INC (PA)
Also Called: Royal Design
32401 Stephenson Hwy (48071-5521)
PHONE..................248 588-0110
Rodney D Paulick, *Ch of Bd*
Patrick Eveland, *President*
EMP: 2
SQ FT: 16,000
SALES (est): 11.4MM **Privately Held**
WEB: www.royaldesign.com
SIC: **3559** 7372 2542 Automotive related machinery; operating systems computer software; racks, merchandise display or storage: except wood

(G-10281)
J J PATTERN & CASTINGS INC (PA)
1780 E 11 Mile Rd (48071-3816)
PHONE..................248 543-7119
Martin Steudle, *President*
Eric Steudle, *Vice Pres*
Bob Kress, *Sales Staff*
EMP: 7
SQ FT: 7,000
SALES (est): 1MM **Privately Held**
SIC: **3543** 5051 Industrial patterns; castings, rough: iron or steel

(G-10282)
JAMES STEEL & TUBE COMPANY (HQ)
29774 Stephenson Hwy (48071-2340)
PHONE..................248 547-4200
Jim Petkus, *President*
EMP: 20
SQ FT: 106,000
SALES (est): 3.7MM
SALES (corp-wide): 312.9MM **Privately Held**
WEB: www.jamessteel.com
SIC: **3317** Tubes, wrought: welded or lock joint
PA: Avis Industrial Corporation
1909 S Main St
Upland IN 46989
765 998-8100

(G-10283)
JD PLATING COMPANY INC (PA)
25428 John R Rd (48071-4098)
PHONE..................248 547-5200
George E Wines, *Ch of Bd*
▲ EMP: 30 EST: 1947
SQ FT: 15,000
SALES (est): 2.2MM **Privately Held**
SIC: **3471** 3479 Electroplating of metals or formed products; coating of metals & formed products

(G-10284)
JO-AD INDUSTRIES INC
31465 Stephenson Hwy (48071-1683)
PHONE..................248 588-4810
Patrick Wagner, *President*
David Gilbert, *Vice Pres*
Jim Davis, *Safety Mgr*
Amy Kaip, *Executive*
EMP: 35 EST: 1957
SQ FT: 50,000
SALES (est): 6.8MM **Privately Held**
WEB: www.jo-ad.com
SIC: **3544** Special dies & tools; forms (molds), for foundry & plastics working machinery; jigs & fixtures

(G-10285)
JSP INTERNATIONAL LLC
1443 E 12 Mile Rd (48071-2653)
PHONE..................248 397-3200
Nurul Huda, *Engineer*
Kevin J Brophy, *Director*
EMP: 15 **Privately Held**
SIC: **3081** Polyethylene film; polypropylene film & sheet
HQ: Jsp International Llc
1285 Drummers Ln Ste 301
Wayne PA 19087
610 651-8600

(G-10286)
JUST WING IT INC
Also Called: Savers Wholesale Printing
31681 Dequindre Rd (48071-1522)
PHONE..................248 549-9338
Doreen Wing, *Principal*
EMP: 6
SALES (est): 381K **Privately Held**
SIC: **2759** Commercial printing

(G-10287)
KA-WOOD GEAR & MACHINE CO
32500 Industrial Dr (48071-5003)
PHONE..................248 585-8870
Joseph J Kloka III, *President*
Don Carlson, *Vice Pres*
Marge Kloka, *Vice Pres*
Tanya Carlson, *Treasurer*
EMP: 29
SALES (est): 8.6MM **Privately Held**
WEB: www.kawoodgear.com
SIC: **3469** 7389 Machine parts, stamped or pressed metal;

(G-10288)
KAR NUT PRODUCTS COMPANY LLC
Also Called: Kar's Nuts
1200 E 14 Mile Rd Ste A (48071-1421)
PHONE..................248 588-1903
Victor Mehren, *CEO*
Nick Nicolay, *Chairman*
William P Elam, *Vice Pres*
Dan Bailey, *Opers Dir*
Eric Martin, *Production*
EMP: 140
SQ FT: 131,000
SALES (est): 131.4MM
SALES (corp-wide): 178.7MM **Privately Held**
WEB: www.karsnuts.com
SIC: **5145** 2068 Nuts, salted or roasted; nuts: dried, dehydrated, salted or roasted
PA: Knpc Holdco, Llc
1200 E 14 Mile Rd
Madison Heights MI 48071
248 588-1903

(G-10289)
KASPER MACHINE CO (HQ)
29275 Stephenson Hwy (48071-2379)
PHONE..................248 547-3150
Raffeale Ghilardi, *President*
Jim Danek, *Project Mgr*
Vincent Skaarud, *Mfg Staff*
Tracey Skaarud, *Purchasing*
Elizabeth Smith, *Office Mgr*
▲ EMP: 14
SQ FT: 46,000
SALES (est): 2.3MM
SALES (corp-wide): 356.3MM **Privately Held**
WEB: www.kaspermachine.com
SIC: **3541** 3545 Boring mills; vertical turning & boring machines (metalworking); machine tool attachments & accessories
PA: Samson Ag
Weismullerstr. 3
Frankfurt Am Main 60314
694 009-0

(G-10290)
KERR SCREW PRODUCTS CO INC
32069 Milton Ave (48071-1407)
PHONE..................248 589-2200
Frank B Kerr, *President*
Patricia Kerr, *Corp Secy*
W Rex Keller, *Vice Pres*
Debbie Keller, *Sales Mgr*
EMP: 9 EST: 1959
SQ FT: 12,000
SALES (est): 1.3MM **Privately Held**
WEB: www.kerrscrew.com
SIC: **3451** Screw machine products

(G-10291)
KNICKERBOCKER BAKING INC
26040 Pinehurst Dr (48071-4139)
PHONE..................248 541-2110
Steven Corinatis, *President*
Daniel Rubino, *Vice Pres*
Patricia Corinatis, *Treasurer*
EMP: 20
SQ FT: 7,000
SALES (est): 1.7MM **Privately Held**
SIC: **2051** Bread, all types (white, wheat, rye, etc): fresh or frozen; rolls, bread type: fresh or frozen; bagels, fresh or frozen

(G-10292)
KNPC HOLDCO LLC (PA)
1200 E 14 Mile Rd (48071-1421)
PHONE..................248 588-1903
Ernest L Nicolay III, *President*
Karen Marton, *Human Res Mgr*
EMP: 4
SALES (est): 178.7MM **Privately Held**
SIC: **2068** 6719 Nuts: dried, dehydrated, salted or roasted; investment holding companies, except banks

(G-10293)
KOINS CORP
25169 Dequindre Rd (48071-4240)
PHONE..................248 548-3038
Gran Lobeck, *Vice Pres*
▲ EMP: 3
SALES (est): 430.1K **Privately Held**
SIC: **3559** Foundry machinery & equipment

(G-10294)
KREFT INJECTION TECHNOLOGY LLC
799 E Mandoline Ave (48071-1437)
PHONE..................248 589-9202
John Marshall,
EMP: 3
SQ FT: 19,016
SALES: 60K **Privately Held**
SIC: **3089** Injection molded finished plastic products

(G-10295)
KS LIQUIDATING LLC
Also Called: Korstone
32031 Howard Ave (48071-1430)
PHONE..................248 577-8220
James Agley, *Principal*
Timothy Price,
EMP: 25
SQ FT: 18,000
SALES (est): 2.3MM **Privately Held**
SIC: **2541** Counter & sink tops

(G-10296)
LANCE INDUSTRIES LLC
1260 Kempar Ave (48071-1424)
PHONE..................248 549-1968
Matt Floore, *Treasurer*
Michelle Pfaendtner, *Sales Staff*
John Witt, *Mng Member*
EMP: 5
SQ FT: 5,000
SALES (est): 590K **Privately Held**
WEB: www.lancetools.com
SIC: **3545** Sockets (machine tool accessories)

(G-10297)
LAND ENTERPRISES INC
26641 Townley St (48071-3619)
P.O. Box 71730 (48071-0730)
PHONE..................248 398-7276
Shelley Vasseur, *President*
EMP: 8
SALES (est): 683.2K **Privately Held**
SIC: **3446** Open flooring & grating for construction

(G-10298)
LASERTEC INC
Also Called: Intelligent Document Solutions
747 E Whitcomb Ave (48071-1409)
PHONE..................586 274-4500
Wendy Lokken, *President*
Wendy Schulte, *President*
Ben Danielak, *Production*
William Hayden, *Admin Sec*
EMP: 35
SQ FT: 28,950
SALES (est): 5.4MM
SALES (corp-wide): 64.6MM **Privately Held**
WEB: www.lasertecinc.com
SIC: **2759** 2791 Laser printing; typesetting
HQ: Intelligent Document Solutions, Inc.
747 E Whitcomb Ave
Madison Heights MI 48071

(G-10299)
LINKED LIVE INC
30550 Brush St (48071-1876)
PHONE..................248 345-5993
Gheorghe Herdean, *CEO*
EMP: 9
SALES (est): 244K **Privately Held**
SIC: **7372** Prepackaged software

(G-10300)
LUBO USA INC
32250 Howard Ave (48071-1452)
PHONE..................810 244-5826
Young Seok Kim, *CEO*
Yeoung Weon Kim, *Corp Secy*
Ilyeob Choi, *Director*
Haejong Lim, *Director*
▲ EMP: 5
SQ FT: 15,000
SALES (est): 927K **Privately Held**
WEB: www.luboinc.com
SIC: **3364** Brass & bronze die-castings

(G-10301)
MAPLE PRESS LLC
31211 Stephenson Hwy # 100 (48071-1637)
PHONE..................248 733-9669
James Alexander,
EMP: 12
SQ FT: 12,000
SALES (est): 1.4MM **Privately Held**
SIC: **2741** Miscellaneous publishing

(G-10302)
MARTIN FLUID POWER COMPANY (PA)
Also Called: Enhanced MSC
900 E Whitcomb Ave (48071-5612)
PHONE..................248 585-8170
Wayne Michael King, *CEO*
Ryan King, *President*
Michael Geddes, *Purch Mgr*
Bridget Gelle, *Purch Agent*
James McLauchlan, *Research*
▲ EMP: 100
SQ FT: 10,000
SALES (est): 55.9MM **Privately Held**
WEB: www.mfpseals.com
SIC: **5085** 3053 Seals, industrial; gaskets & sealing devices

(G-10303)
MAZZELLA LIFTING TECH INC
31623 Stephenson Hwy (48071-1646)
PHONE..................248 585-1063
Mark Shubel, *Vice Pres*
EMP: 9 **Privately Held**
SIC: **3496** Miscellaneous fabricated wire products
HQ: Mazzella Lifting Technologies, Inc.
21000 Aerospace Pkwy
Cleveland OH 44142
440 239-7000

(G-10304)
MICHIGAN AUTO BENDING CORP
Also Called: Mabco
1700 E 14 Mile Rd (48071-1543)
PHONE..................248 528-1150
Louis St Laurent, *President*
Robert Shaw, *Principal*
EMP: 30
SQ FT: 20,000
SALES (est): 5.5MM **Privately Held**
SIC: **3544** 7538 Special dies & tools; general automotive repair shops

(G-10305)
MICHIGAN DIVERSFD HOLDINGS INC
Also Called: Sutherland Felt Co
700 E Whitcomb Ave (48071-1416)
PHONE..................248 280-0450
Thomas Shoan, *CEO*
Sue Toth, *General Mgr*
Michele Shoan, *Corp Secy*
Matt Callies, *Sales Engr*
EMP: 13 EST: 1902
SQ FT: 10,000
SALES (est): 5.3MM **Privately Held**
WEB: www.slfco.com
SIC: **5199** 3111 Felt; die-cutting of leather

Madison Heights - Oakland County (G-10306)

(G-10306)
MIDWEST CABINET COUNTERS
650 E Mandoline Ave (48071-1455)
PHONE.....................248 586-4260
Jeff Valenti, *Principal*
EMP: 6
SALES (est): 919.4K **Privately Held**
SIC: 3131 Counters

(G-10307)
MILTON CHILI COMPANY INC
511 E Whitcomb Ave (48071-1408)
PHONE.....................248 585-0300
Chris Shafkalis, *President*
EMP: 3 **EST:** 1967
SQ FT: 3,600
SALES: 275K **Privately Held**
SIC: 2099 Food preparations

(G-10308)
MNP CORPORATION
Also Called: MNP Corporation Division 2
1524 E 14 Mile Rd (48071-1542)
PHONE.....................248 585-5010
Bob Lewell, *Manager*
EMP: 50
SALES (corp-wide): 232.6MM **Privately Held**
WEB: www.mnp.com
SIC: 3452 3714 Bolts, nuts, rivets & washers; motor vehicle parts & accessories
PA: Mnp Corporation
  44225 Utica Rd
  Utica MI 48317
  586 254-1320

(G-10309)
MOLD-MSTERS INJCTIONEERING LLC
29111 Stephenson Hwy (48071-2330)
PHONE.....................905 877-0185
John Watt, *Project Mgr*
Chris Loftus, *Project Engr*
David Adey, *Sales Mgr*
Doug Hugo, *Manager*
Adam Domurat, *Manager*
EMP: 19
SALES (est): 3.8MM **Privately Held**
SIC: 3089 Molding primary plastic

(G-10310)
MRI CONSULTANTS LLC
30785 Stephenson Hwy (48071-1618)
P.O. Box 517, Roseville (48066-0517)
PHONE.....................248 619-9771
Ram Gunabalan, *Med Doctor*
EMP: 3
SQ FT: 2,000
SALES: 415K **Privately Held**
SIC: 3829 Medical diagnostic systems, nuclear

(G-10311)
MSI MACHINE TOOL PARTS INC
1619 Donna Ave (48071-2063)
PHONE.....................248 589-0515
John Wallace, *President*
EMP: 10
SALES (est): 550K **Privately Held**
SIC: 3599 Machine shop, jobbing & repair

(G-10312)
MSX INTERNATIONAL INC
30031 Stephenson Hwy (48071-1605)
PHONE.....................248 585-6654
Dennis Groesbeck, *Manager*
EMP: 60
SALES (corp-wide): 15.3B **Privately Held**
WEB: www.msxi.com
SIC: 7363 3544 Help supply services; special dies, tools, jigs & fixtures
HQ: Msx International, Inc.
  500 Woodward Ave Ste 2150
  Detroit MI 48226
  248 829-6300

(G-10313)
MUNIDEALS LLC
Also Called: Munideals.com
29401 Stephenson Hwy (48071-2331)
PHONE.....................248 945-0991
Janis A Valenti,
Jay F Higgins,
EMP: 3
SALES (est): 266.9K
SALES (corp-wide): 2MM **Privately Held**
SIC: 2759 Commercial printing
PA: Computing Source Litigation Support Services, Llc
  29401 Stephenson Hwy
  Madison Heights MI 48071
  248 213-1500

(G-10314)
NATIONAL MILLWORK INC
32350 Howard Ave (48071-1429)
PHONE.....................248 307-1299
Dennis T Figiel, *President*
Michael K Figiel, *Treasurer*
EMP: 16
SQ FT: 13,000
SALES: 1.1MM **Privately Held**
SIC: 2541 Store & office display cases & fixtures; store fixtures, wood

(G-10315)
NAVISTAR DEFENSE LLC
1675 E Whitcomb Ave (48071-1411)
PHONE.....................248 680-7505
Michael Lyons, *Manager*
Rosana Stein, *Director*
EMP: 8
SALES (corp-wide): 10.2B **Publicly Held**
SIC: 3812 Defense systems & equipment
HQ: Navistar Defense Llc
  10400 W North Ave
  Melrose Park IL 60160
  708 617-4500

(G-10316)
OCTAPHARMA PLASMA INC
401 E 13 Mile Rd (48071-2176)
PHONE.....................248 597-0314
Rachel Isbelle, *Manager*
EMP: 5
SALES (corp-wide): 2B **Privately Held**
SIC: 2836 Plasmas
HQ: Octapharma Plasma, Inc.
  10644 Westlake Dr
  Charlotte NC 28273
  704 654-4600

(G-10317)
ONEIRIC SYSTEMS INC (PA)
31711 Sherman Ave (48071-1428)
PHONE.....................248 554-3090
Everett Hall, *President*
Jennifer Brown, *Opers Mgr*
EMP: 5
SALES (est): 945K **Privately Held**
SIC: 3559 Degreasing machines, automotive & industrial

(G-10318)
OSTRANDER COMPANY INC
Also Called: John Ostrander Company
1200 W 12 Mile Rd (48071-4439)
PHONE.....................248 646-6680
John Ostrander, *President*
Robin Denby, *Office Mgr*
EMP: 2
SALES: 3MM **Privately Held**
SIC: 3585 Refrigeration & heating equipment

(G-10319)
P X TOOL CO
Also Called: Peerless Tooling Components
32354 Edward Ave (48071-1432)
PHONE.....................248 585-9330
Edmund M Nowak, *President*
Dawn Wagner, *Manager*
EMP: 6
SQ FT: 6,000
SALES (est): 788K **Privately Held**
WEB: www.pxtool.com
SIC: 3544 Jigs & fixtures

(G-10320)
P3 PRODUCT SOLUTIONS INC ◆
1225 Spartan St (48071-3829)
PHONE.....................248 703-7724
Colin Goldsmith, *President*
EMP: 18 **EST:** 2019
SALES (est): 720.2K
SALES (corp-wide): 428.7MM **Privately Held**
SIC: 3714 Motor vehicle electrical equipment
HQ: P3-North America, Inc.
  25650 W 11 Mile Rd # 300
  Southfield MI 48034

(G-10321)
PARRY PRECISION INC
845 E Mandoline Ave (48071-1472)
PHONE.....................248 585-1234
Donald Payne, *President*
Leon Parry, *President*
Mike Parry, *President*
EMP: 15
SQ FT: 8,000
SALES (est): 2.2MM **Privately Held**
SIC: 3544 Jigs & fixtures

(G-10322)
PENKA TOOL CORPORATION
Also Called: Penka Cutter Grinding
1717 E 10 Mile Rd (48071-4229)
PHONE.....................248 543-3940
Paul Marinello, *President*
Sharon Marinello, *Vice Pres*
EMP: 8
SQ FT: 4,500
SALES (est): 880K **Privately Held**
SIC: 3542 Machine tools, metal forming type

(G-10323)
PETERSON AMERICAN CORPORATION
Peterson Spring Div
32601 Industrial Dr (48071-1517)
PHONE.....................248 616-3380
Elizabeth Klotz, *Superintendent*
Brian Rambo, *Manager*
Tim Campbell, *Technician*
EMP: 45
SQ FT: 26,489
SALES (corp-wide): 290.5MM **Privately Held**
WEB: www.pspring.com
SIC: 3495 3493 Mechanical springs, precision; steel springs, except wire
PA: Peterson American Corporation
  21200 Telegraph Rd
  Southfield MI 48033
  248 799-5400

(G-10324)
PETERSON AMERICAN CORPORATION
679 E Mandoline Ave (48071-1442)
PHONE.....................248 799-5400
Travis Bell, *General Mgr*
EMP: 3
SALES (corp-wide): 290.5MM **Privately Held**
SIC: 3495 Wire springs
PA: Peterson American Corporation
  21200 Telegraph Rd
  Southfield MI 48033
  248 799-5400

(G-10325)
PEZCO INDUSTRIES INC
380 E Mandoline Ave (48071-4738)
PHONE.....................248 589-1140
Thomas J Pesamoska, *President*
Barbara J Pesamoska, *Vice Pres*
EMP: 6
SQ FT: 2,800
SALES (est): 450K **Privately Held**
SIC: 3599 Machine shop, jobbing & repair

(G-10326)
PILLAR INDUCTION
30100 Stephenson Hwy (48071-1630)
PHONE.....................586 254-8470
Mike Felvey, *President*
EMP: 8
SALES (est): 873.6K
SALES (corp-wide): 1.6B **Publicly Held**
SIC: 3567 Induction heating equipment
HQ: Ajax Tocco Magnethermic Corporation
  1745 Overland Ave Ne
  Warren OH 44483
  330 372-8511

(G-10327)
PIONEER MACHINE AND TECH INC
1167 E 10 Mile Rd (48071-4207)
P.O. Box 184, Hazel Park (48030-0184)
PHONE.....................248 546-4451
Jeffrey Harris, *President*
Steven Harrris, *Vice Pres*
Chanel Harris, *Treasurer*
EMP: 9
SQ FT: 5,500
SALES (est): 1.4MM **Privately Held**
SIC: 3599 3441 Machine shop, jobbing & repair; fabricated structural metal

(G-10328)
PITNEY BOWES INC
30200 Stephenson Hwy (48071-1612)
PHONE.....................248 591-2800
Bryan Bonnici, *Branch Mgr*
EMP: 10
SALES (corp-wide): 3.5B **Publicly Held**
SIC: 3579 7359 Postage meters; business machine & electronic equipment rental services
PA: Pitney Bowes Inc.
  3001 Summer St Ste 3
  Stamford CT 06905
  203 356-5000

(G-10329)
PLASON SCRAPING CO INC
32825 Dequindre Rd (48071-1519)
PHONE.....................248 588-7280
James Sultana, *President*
Mark Hickerson, *Vice Pres*
Tim Hickerson, *Vice Pres*
EMP: 9 **EST:** 1959
SQ FT: 3,500
SALES (est): 1.4MM **Privately Held**
SIC: 3541 7699 Machine tools, metal cutting type; industrial machinery & equipment repair

(G-10330)
PLATING SPECIALTIES INC (PA)
1625 E 10 Mile Rd (48071-4219)
PHONE.....................248 547-8660
Thomas Baker, *President*
EMP: 14
SQ FT: 15,000
SALES (est): 1.3MM **Privately Held**
WEB: www.platingspecialties.com
SIC: 3471 Plating of metals or formed products

(G-10331)
POLY TECH INDUSTRIES INC
395 W Lincoln Ave Ste B (48071-3967)
PHONE.....................248 589-9950
Douglas Dick, *President*
Jeremy Dick, *Prgrmr*
EMP: 8
SALES (est): 440K **Privately Held**
SIC: 2791 Typesetting, computer controlled

(G-10332)
POPCORN PRESS INC
32400 Edward Ave Ste A (48071-1447)
PHONE.....................248 588-4444
Al Glasby, *President*
EMP: 23
SQ FT: 8,000
SALES (est): 4.3MM **Privately Held**
WEB: www.popcornpress.net
SIC: 2752 Commercial printing, offset

(G-10333)
POWERTRAIN INTEGRATION LLC (PA)
Also Called: Power Solutions International
32505 Industrial Dr (48071-5004)
PHONE.....................248 577-0010
Robert Pachla,
Ron Meganck,
▲ **EMP:** 12
SQ FT: 47,000
SALES (est): 4.9MM **Privately Held**
SIC: 3568 3519 Power transmission equipment; gasoline engines

GEOGRAPHIC SECTION

Madison Heights - Oakland County (G-10358)

(G-10334)
PREFERRED TOOL & MACHINE LTD
595 E 10 Mile Rd (48071-4204)
PHONE.................................248 399-6919
Scott T Stewart, *President*
EMP: 4
SQ FT: 4,000
SALES (est): 350K **Privately Held**
SIC: 3599 Machine shop, jobbing & repair

(G-10335)
PRESTIGE ADVANCED INC
30031 Stephenson Hwy (48071-1605)
PHONE.................................586 868-4000
William G Fritts, *President*
Dennis Groesbeck, *Vice Pres*
EMP: 54
SQ FT: 5,400
SALES (est): 9MM **Privately Held**
SIC: 3465 Automotive stampings

(G-10336)
PRESTIGE ENGRG RSRCES TECH INC
Also Called: Prestige Advance
30031 Stephenson Hwy (48071-1605)
PHONE.................................586 573-3070
Dennis Groesbeck, *Controller*
Dennis M Groesbeck, *Administration*
EMP: 50
SALES (est): 1.9MM
SALES (corp-wide): 13.9MM **Privately Held**
SIC: 3599 3714 Amusement park equipment; motor vehicle engines & parts
PA: Prestige Engineering Resources & Technologies Inc.
24700 Capital Blvd
Clinton Township MI 48036
586 573-3070

(G-10337)
PRIMARY TOOL & CUTTER GRINDING
32388 Edward Ave (48071-1432)
PHONE.................................248 588-1530
Paul Borthwick, *President*
Joe Paupert, *Vice Pres*
Gary Dassatt, *Treasurer*
EMP: 12
SQ FT: 7,200
SALES (est): 1.8MM **Privately Held**
WEB: www.primarytool.com
SIC: 3545 Cutting tools for machine tools

(G-10338)
PRINCIPAL DIAMOND WORKS
32750 Townley St (48071-1333)
PHONE.................................248 589-1111
Ron Mikolajczyk, *Owner*
EMP: 3
SQ FT: 4,000
SALES: 200K **Privately Held**
SIC: 3545 Diamond cutting tools for turning, boring, burnishing, etc.

(G-10339)
PRINT MASTERS INC
Also Called: Print Masters Printing Co
26039 Dequindre Rd (48071-3820)
PHONE.................................248 548-7100
James Gerds, *President*
Laura Carlin, *Vice Pres*
Judie Rumps, *Mng Member*
EMP: 13
SQ FT: 6,000
SALES (est): 2.2MM **Privately Held**
SIC: 2752 7336 7331 2791 Commercial printing, offset; commercial art & graphic design; direct mail advertising services; typesetting

(G-10340)
PYRO SERVICE COMPANY
25812 John R Rd (48071-4020)
PHONE.................................248 547-2552
Gerry Hambright, *President*
▲ **EMP:** 5
SQ FT: 6,000
SALES: 350K **Privately Held**
SIC: 3823 3822 Pyrometers, industrial process type; thermocouples, vacuum; glass

(G-10341)
QC TECH LLC
Also Called: Qcr Tech
1605 E Avis Dr (48071-1514)
PHONE.................................248 597-3984
Mike Withee, *Controller*
William Young,
Eva Young,
EMP: 55
SQ FT: 17,000
SALES: 8MM **Privately Held**
WEB: www.qcrtech.com
SIC: 3544 Industrial molds

(G-10342)
QMI GROUP INC
Also Called: Q M I
1645 E Avis Dr (48071-1514)
PHONE.................................248 589-0505
Barbara A Shereda, *President*
James J Shereda Sr, *Vice Pres*
Mary Schumacher, *Sales Staff*
Patrick Smith, *Manager*
Joann Streebing, *Manager*
EMP: 25 **EST:** 1975
SQ FT: 15,000
SALES (est): 5.3MM **Privately Held**
WEB: www.qmigroupinc.com
SIC: 3555 5999 3993 3471 Printing trades machinery; trophies & plaques; signs & advertising specialties; plating & polishing; automotive & apparel trimmings

(G-10343)
QUALITY STAINLESS MFG CO
1150 E 11 Mile Rd (48071-3802)
PHONE.................................248 546-4141
Diana Rudzewicz, *President*
Dan Jankowski, *Vice Pres*
EMP: 10
SQ FT: 8,500
SALES (est): 1.1MM **Privately Held**
WEB: www.qualitystainlessmfg.com
SIC: 3444 1711 Restaurant sheet metalwork; mechanical contractor

(G-10344)
ROTARY MULTIFORMS INC
Also Called: R M I
1340 E 11 Mile Rd (48071-3806)
P.O. Box 641009, Detroit (48264-1009)
PHONE.................................586 558-7960
William R Condon, *President*
Jeff Flynn, *Administration*
Rachel Seng, *Graphic Designe*
Kim Causley, *Representative*
Ron Malinowski, *Representative*
EMP: 9
SALES: 3.5MM **Privately Held**
WEB: www.rmi-printing.com
SIC: 2761 Continuous forms, office & business; strip forms (manifold business forms)

(G-10345)
ROYAL ARC INC
520 Sheffield Dr (48071-2206)
PHONE.................................586 758-0718
Joseph P Lonero, *President*
Joseph Lonero, *Owner*
Nancy Lonero, *Admin Sec*
EMP: 5 **EST:** 1955
SQ FT: 5,600
SALES (est): 500.2K **Privately Held**
SIC: 3544 Special dies, tools, jigs & fixtures

(G-10346)
ROYAL DESIGN & MANUFACTURING
32401 Stephenson Hwy (48071-1093)
PHONE.................................248 588-0110
Rodney D Paulick, *Chairman*
Patrick J Eveland, *Vice Pres*
▼ **EMP:** 65 **EST:** 1951
SQ FT: 16,000
SALES (est): 11.4MM **Privately Held**
WEB: www.royaltoolmanagement.com
SIC: 3559 2542 3824 3545 Automotive related machinery; racks, merchandise display or storage; except wood; fluid meters & counting devices; machine tool accessories; metal cans

PA: J H P Inc
32401 Stephenson Hwy
Madison Heights MI 48071
248 588-0110

(G-10347)
S & L MACHINE PRODUCTS INC
30250 Stephenson Hwy (48071-1612)
PHONE.................................248 543-6633
John Backer, *President*
EMP: 15
SQ FT: 15,000
SALES (est): 3MM **Privately Held**
SIC: 3599 Machine shop, jobbing & repair

(G-10348)
SANTANNA TOOL & DESIGN LLC
Also Called: Bulldog Factory Service
25880 Commerce Dr (48071-4151)
PHONE.................................248 541-3500
Gary Newton, *Opers Staff*
Kathy Celani, *Office Mgr*
Jamilce Newton, *Mng Member*
Tracy Hutchinson, *Administration*
Joseph Newton,
EMP: 70
SQ FT: 50,000
SALES: 30MM **Privately Held**
WEB: www.bulldogfactory.com
SIC: 3535 3548 Conveyors & conveying equipment; welding apparatus

(G-10349)
SCOTT & ITOH MACHINE COMPANY
31690 Stephenson Hwy (48071-1642)
PHONE.................................248 585-5385
Jeffrey Scott, *President*
Rebecca Scott, *CFO*
EMP: 21
SQ FT: 36,000
SALES (est): 4.2MM
SALES (corp-wide): 22.5MM **Privately Held**
WEB: www.scott-itoh.com
SIC: 3599 Machine shop, jobbing & repair
PA: Allan Tool & Machine Co., Inc.
1822 E Maple Rd
Troy MI 48083
248 585-2910

(G-10350)
SHANNON PRECISION FASTENER LLC
Also Called: Shannon Distribution Center
800 E 14 Mile Rd (48071-1425)
PHONE.................................248 658-3015
Jerry Iwanski, *Branch Mgr*
Kyle Marchetti, *Supervisor*
EMP: 50
SALES (corp-wide): 100MM **Privately Held**
SIC: 3542 3452 Machine tools, metal forming type; bolts, nuts, rivets & washers
PA: Shannon Precision Fastener, Llc
31600 Stephenson Hwy
Madison Heights MI 48071
248 589-9670

(G-10351)
SHANNON PRECISION FASTENER LLC (PA)
Also Called: Shannon Distribution Center
31600 Stephenson Hwy (48071-1642)
PHONE.................................248 589-9670
Glenn Purvin, *Vice Pres*
Robb Thompson, *Vice Pres*
Chris Collins, *Project Mgr*
John Varani, *Maint Spvr*
Phil Menzies, *Research*
▲ **EMP:** 95
SQ FT: 83,000
SALES: 100MM **Privately Held**
WEB: www.shannonpf.com
SIC: 3452 Bolts, nuts, rivets & washers

(G-10352)
SIKA AUTO EATON RAPIDS INC (DH)
Also Called: Sika Advanced Resins US
30800 Stephenson Hwy (48071-1614)
PHONE.................................248 588-2270
Marty Poljan, *President*
Melissa Stutz, *Division Mgr*

Jayne Thomas, *Controller*
▲ **EMP:** 10 **EST:** 1979
SALES (est): 16.2MM
SALES (corp-wide): 7.1B **Privately Held**
SIC: 7389 3999 2821 Building scale models; models, except toy; elastomers, non-vulcanizable (plastics)
HQ: Sika Corporation
201 Polito Ave
Lyndhurst NJ 07071
201 933-8800

(G-10353)
SIKA CORPORATION
Also Called: Sika Industry
30800 Stephenson Hwy (48071-1614)
PHONE.................................248 577-0020
Thomas Labelle, *Managing Dir*
Kevin Bohannon, *District Mgr*
David Yeskey, *Maint Spvr*
Michelle Climie, *Research*
Zach Barnhart, *Engineer*
EMP: 100
SALES (corp-wide): 7.1B **Privately Held**
WEB: www.sikacorp.com
SIC: 3721 8742 8731 2899 Aircraft; management consulting services; commercial physical research; chemical preparations; adhesives & sealants
HQ: Sika Corporation
201 Polito Ave
Lyndhurst NJ 07071
201 933-8800

(G-10354)
SIMIRON INC
Also Called: Epoxi-Pro
32700 Industrial Dr (48071-5005)
PHONE.................................248 585-7500
Simon Palushi, *President*
▲ **EMP:** 30
SQ FT: 45,000
SALES (est): 13.8MM **Privately Held**
WEB: www.epoxi-pro.com
SIC: 2851 Epoxy coatings

(G-10355)
SOURCE ONE DIST SVCS INC
900 Tech Row (48071-4624)
PHONE.................................248 399-5060
Joseph Gurak Sr, *President*
Joseph Gurak Jr, *Vice Pres*
Michelle August, *Manager*
Chris Gurak, *Manager*
EMP: 10
SQ FT: 19,800
SALES: 1.9MM **Privately Held**
WEB: www.sourceone-dist.com
SIC: 2759 7331 Laser printing; mailing service

(G-10356)
SPECIAL DRILL AND REAMER CORP
408 E 14 Mile Rd (48071-1458)
P.O. Box 71105 (48071-0105)
PHONE.................................248 588-5333
Michael Obloy, *President*
Phyllis Hudeck, *Vice Pres*
EMP: 18
SQ FT: 26,000
SALES (est): 2.5MM **Privately Held**
SIC: 3545 Drilling machine attachments & accessories; reamers, machine tool

(G-10357)
SPECIAL FABRICATORS INC
31649 Stephenson Hwy (48071-1684)
PHONE.................................248 588-6717
Richard Tieman, *President*
EMP: 7
SQ FT: 10,000
SALES (est): 638.6K **Privately Held**
SIC: 3441 Fabricated structural metal

(G-10358)
SPECTRUM NEON CO
1280 Kempar Ave (48071-1424)
PHONE.................................248 246-1142
EMP: 3
SALES (est): 135.6K **Privately Held**
SIC: 2813 Neon

(PA)=Parent Co (HQ)=Headquarters (DH)=Div Headquarters
❂ – New Business established in last 2 years

Madison Heights - Oakland County (G-10359)

(G-10359)
STANDARD COATING INC
32565 Dequindre Rd (48071-1520)
PHONE....................................248 297-6650
Michael Mitchell, *President*
Jeff Mertz, *Exec Dir*
EMP: 75
SALES (est): 7.9MM **Privately Held**
SIC: 3449 Miscellaneous metalwork

(G-10360)
STANHOPE TOOL INC
Also Called: J E Wood Comp
395 W Girard Ave (48071-1896)
PHONE....................................248 585-5711
Brian Fish, *President*
James Dayf, *Vice Pres*
EMP: 13 **EST:** 1962
SQ FT: 5,000
SALES (est): 2.4MM **Privately Held**
WEB: www.stanhopetool.com
SIC: 3545 3541 3599 3544 Gauges (machine tool accessories); precision measuring tools; machine tools, metal cutting type; machine & other job shop work; special dies, tools, jigs & fixtures

(G-10361)
STAR TEXTILE INC
1000 Tech Row (48071-4679)
PHONE....................................888 527-5700
Noha Mikhail, *Owner*
▲ **EMP:** 50
SALES (est): 6.6MM **Privately Held**
SIC: 2392 2259 Blankets, comforters & beddings; curtains & bedding, knit

(G-10362)
STEC USA INC (PA)
31900 Sherman Ave (48071-5605)
PHONE....................................248 307-1440
Shuo Wang, *President*
EMP: 10 **EST:** 2014
SQ FT: 30,500
SALES (est): 1.7MM **Privately Held**
SIC: 3559 Automotive maintenance equipment

(G-10363)
SULFO-TECHNOLOGIES LLC
32300 Howard Ave (48071-1429)
PHONE....................................248 307-9150
Larry Gladchun,
Samuel Greenewalt,
Richard Kaspers,
▲ **EMP:** 8
SQ FT: 3,600
SALES: 1.2MM **Privately Held**
WEB: www.sulfotech.com
SIC: 2821 Plasticizer/additive based plastic materials

(G-10364)
SUPERIOR CAM INC
31240 Stephenson Hwy (48071-1620)
PHONE....................................248 588-1100
John J Basso, *President*
Donn Helfer, *Plant Supt*
John Basso, *Engineer*
Sonia Basso, *Treasurer*
Gus Ruprecht, *Program Mgr*
EMP: 100
SQ FT: 67,000
SALES (est): 25.4MM **Privately Held**
WEB: www.superiorcam.com
SIC: 3465 Body parts, automobile: stamped metal; fenders, automobile: stamped or pressed metal

(G-10365)
SUPPLEMENT GROUP INC
32787 Stephenson Hwy (48071-5527)
PHONE....................................248 588-2055
EMP: 15
SQ FT: 11,500
SALES (est): 3.5MM **Privately Held**
SIC: 2834 Mfg Pharmaceutical Preparations

(G-10366)
TC MOULDING
31811 Sherman Ave (48071-5606)
PHONE....................................248 588-2333
Ed Bax, *Principal*
EMP: 3
SALES (est): 281K **Privately Held**
SIC: 5023 2499 Frames & framing, picture & mirror; picture frame molding, finished

(G-10367)
TEXTRON INC
25225 Dequindre Rd (48071-4211)
PHONE....................................248 545-2035
EMP: 4
SALES (corp-wide): 14.2B **Publicly Held**
SIC: 3721 Mfg Aviation Aircrafts
PA: Textron Inc.
40 Westminster St
Providence RI 02903
401 421-2800

(G-10368)
TOTAL BUSINESS SYSTEMS INC (PA)
Also Called: Deluxe Data Printers
30800 Montpelier Dr (48071-5108)
PHONE....................................248 307-1076
Robert G Finnerty, *President*
Tom Lustig, *Plant Supt*
Justus J Austin Jr, *Treasurer*
EMP: 18
SQ FT: 9,000
SALES (est): 15.5MM **Privately Held**
WEB: www.tbsddp.com
SIC: 2761 2752 Manifold business forms; business forms, lithographed

(G-10369)
TRIAD MANUFACTURING CO INC
32020 Edward Ave (48071-1420)
P.O. Box 71591 (48071-0591)
PHONE....................................248 583-9636
Hartmut Rothacker, *President*
EMP: 12
SQ FT: 12,000
SALES (est): 1.5MM **Privately Held**
SIC: 3599 Machine shop, jobbing & repair

(G-10370)
TRIG TOOL INC
1143 E 10 Mile Rd (48071-4207)
PHONE....................................248 543-2550
Andrey Duzyt, *President*
Andrey Duzyj, *Corp Secy*
EMP: 6
SQ FT: 3,750
SALES (est): 700K **Privately Held**
SIC: 3545 Machine tool accessories

(G-10371)
TRYNEX INTERNATIONAL LLC
531 Ajax Dr (48071-2429)
PHONE....................................248 586-3500
James Janik, *CEO*
Andy Miller, *Mfg Staff*
Donna Owiesny, *Accountant*
Larry Ursell, *Office Mgr*
▲ **EMP:** 15
SQ FT: 14,500
SALES (est): 5.5MM **Publicly Held**
SIC: 3711 5082 Snow plows (motor vehicles), assembly of; blades for graders, scrapers, dozers & snow plows
PA: Douglas Dynamics, Inc.
7777 N 73rd St
Milwaukee WI 53223

(G-10372)
UNCLE RONS WOODWORKING
611 W Girard Ave (48071-5104)
PHONE....................................248 585-7837
Ronald Gilbert, *Principal*
EMP: 3
SALES (est): 233.6K **Privately Held**
SIC: 2431 Millwork

(G-10373)
UNIVERSAL FABRICATORS INC
25855 Commerce Dr (48071-4152)
PHONE....................................248 399-7565
Anthony F Usakoski Jr, *President*
Bonnie S Usakoski, *Treasurer*
Marylu Guida, *Manager*
EMP: 30
SQ FT: 4,500
SALES (est): 4.5MM **Privately Held**
WEB: www.universalfabricators.com
SIC: 3444 Sheet metalwork

(G-10374)
UNIVERSAL TRIM INC
Also Called: Mari Leather Works, Inc.
1451 E Lincoln Ave (48071-4136)
PHONE....................................248 586-3300
Merv Dunn, *CEO*
Steven Deyouv, *Finance*
▲ **EMP:** 25 **EST:** 1982
SALES (est): 383.2K **Privately Held**
SIC: 2396 Automotive trimmings, fabric
HQ: Cni Enterprises, Inc.
1451 E Lincoln Ave
Madison Heights MI 48071
248 586-3300

(G-10375)
USI INC
Also Called: Ultimate Systems
31302 Stephenson Hwy A (48071-1634)
PHONE....................................248 583-9337
Sheryl Chinn, *President*
Robert Reck, *CFO*
EMP: 10
SALES (est): 1.6MM **Privately Held**
WEB: www.ultsystems.com
SIC: 3594 Motors: hydraulic, fluid power or air

(G-10376)
VIGEL NORTH AMERICA INC (DH)
32375 Howard Ave (48071-1433)
PHONE....................................734 947-9900
Ron Scariol, *President*
EMP: 8
SALES (est): 1.1MM
SALES (corp-wide): 92.9K **Privately Held**
SIC: 3545 Machine tool accessories
HQ: Vigel Spa
Via Mappano 15/A
Borgaro Torinese TO 10071
011 470-4104

(G-10377)
VIKING TECHNOLOGIES INC
25169 Dequindre Rd (48071-4240)
PHONE....................................586 914-0819
Leif Goran Lowback, *President*
Ann Lowback, *Vice Pres*
Ida Lowback, *Admin Sec*
▼ **EMP:** 7 **EST:** 2009
SQ FT: 4,200
SALES (est): 494.9K **Privately Held**
SIC: 3674 5065 Memories, solid state; modems, computer

(G-10378)
VISUAL PRECISION INC
111 E 10 Mile Rd (48071-4203)
PHONE....................................248 546-7984
Ron Webber, *President*
Judy Miles, *Administration*
EMP: 5
SQ FT: 5,000
SALES (est): 600K **Privately Held**
WEB: www.vpcharts.com
SIC: 3827 Optical comparators

(G-10379)
WALL CO INCORPORATED (PA)
101 W Girard Ave (48071-1880)
PHONE....................................248 585-6400
William P Clark Jr, *President*
Joseph A Drobot Jr, *Corp Secy*
Joseph M Maria, *Vice Pres*
Mike Edwards, *CFO*
Bob Heminger, *MIS Dir*
◆ **EMP:** 30
SQ FT: 15,000
SALES (est): 71.7MM **Privately Held**
SIC: 3399 3398 Powder, metal; brazing (hardening) of metal

(G-10380)
WALL COLMONOY CORPORATION (HQ)
101 W Girard Ave (48071-1880)
PHONE....................................248 585-6400
William P Clark, *President*
Robert Heminger, *Vice Pres*
Ed Mohrbach, *Treasurer*
Justin Madrid, *Prdtn Mgr*
Christopher Corrick, *Buyer*
◆ **EMP:** 20 **EST:** 1953
SQ FT: 9,000
SALES (est): 64.5MM
SALES (corp-wide): 71.7MM **Privately Held**
WEB: www.wallcolmonoy.com
SIC: 2891 Adhesives & sealants
PA: Wall Co., Incorporated
101 W Girard Ave
Madison Heights MI 48071
248 585-6400

(G-10381)
WHITLOCK BUSINESS SYSTEMS INC
275 E 12 Mile Rd (48071-2557)
PHONE....................................248 548-1040
Curtis Bledsoe, *Vice Pres*
Kenneth Noonan, *Treasurer*
Brian Bledsoe, *Accounts Mgr*
EMP: 30
SQ FT: 16,000
SALES (est): 14.3MM **Privately Held**
WEB: www.wbsusa.com
SIC: 5112 2761 Business forms; manifold business forms

(G-10382)
WHITLOCK DISTRIBUTION SVCS LLC
275 E 12 Mile Rd (48071-2557)
PHONE....................................248 548-1040
Kenneth Noonan, *Mng Member*
EMP: 60
SQ FT: 5,000
SALES (est): 228.7K **Privately Held**
SIC: 2759 Commercial printing

(G-10383)
WOLVERINE HYDRAULICS & MFG CO
25329 John R Rd (48071-4009)
PHONE....................................248 543-5261
James F Mc Faul, *President*
Michelle Schulmeister, *Treasurer*
EMP: 5
SQ FT: 5,000
SALES (est): 460K **Privately Held**
SIC: 3548 Welding & cutting apparatus & accessories

Mancelona
Antrim County

(G-10384)
A S RIVARD AND SON WELL DRLG
2085 Twin Lake Rd Ne (49659-8203)
PHONE....................................231 331-4508
Tony Rivard, *President*
Sandra Rivard, *Vice Pres*
EMP: 4
SALES (est): 432.3K **Privately Held**
SIC: 3317 Well casing, wrought: welded, lock joint or heavy riveted

(G-10385)
ADVANCE TOOL CO
407 Rose St (49659-8305)
P.O. Box 588 (49659-0588)
PHONE....................................231 587-5286
William R McGillivray, *Owner*
EMP: 12
SALES (est): 778K **Privately Held**
SIC: 3544 Special dies, tools, jigs & fixtures

(G-10386)
ANTRIM MACHINE PRODUCTS INC
9142 Johnson Rd (49659-7964)
P.O. Box 379 (49659-0379)
PHONE....................................231 587-9114
Gerald Witowski, *President*
Jacob Kelly, *Plant Mgr*
Noel Zocharski, *Office Mgr*
EMP: 25
SALES (est): 1.5MM **Privately Held**
WEB: www.antrimmachine.com
SIC: 3599 3812 Machine shop, jobbing & repair; defense systems & equipment; acceleration indicators & systems components, aerospace

▲ = Import ▼ = Export
◆ = Import/Export

GEOGRAPHIC SECTION

Manistee - Manistee County (G-10413)

(G-10387)
BUCK-N-HAM MACHINES INC (HQ)
413 Dale Ave (49659-9328)
PHONE.....................231 587-5322
Virginia Lapointe, *President*
Henry La Pointe, *Corp Secy*
Shannon Hampton, *Vice Pres*
Bnhmachines Lapointe, *Engineer*
Charles Lapointe, *Sales Mgr*
EMP: 5
SQ FT: 7,500
SALES (est): 523.9K **Privately Held**
WEB: www.bnhmachines.com
SIC: 3599 Machine shop, jobbing & repair

(G-10388)
BURT MOEKE & SON HARDWOODS
2509 Valley Rd (49659-9344)
P.O. Box 500 (49659-0500)
PHONE.....................231 587-5388
Fax: 231 587-0550
EMP: 50
SQ FT: 7,000
SALES (est): 5.6MM **Privately Held**
SIC: 2421 2426 Sawmill/Planing Mill Hardwood Dimension/Floor Mill

(G-10389)
EL PASO LLC
8616 Anr Storage Rd Ne (49659-8205)
PHONE.....................231 587-0704
Bill Brown, *Manager*
EMP: 4 **Publicly Held**
WEB: www.elpaso.com
SIC: 1389 Gas field services
HQ: El Paso Llc
1001 Louisiana St
Houston TX 77002
713 420-2600

(G-10390)
FAHL FOREST PRODUCTS INC
2509 Valley Rd (49659-9344)
P.O. Box 500 (49659-0500)
PHONE.....................231 258-9734
Sam Fahl, *Owner*
John Penfold, *Buyer*
EMP: 56
SALES (est): 670.2K **Privately Held**
SIC: 2411 Logging camps & contractors

(G-10391)
FLANNERY MACHINE & TOOL INC
8420 S Us Highway 131 (49659)
PHONE.....................231 587-5076
Kenneth W Flannery, *President*
Darryl A Antcliff, *Purch Mgr*
Ken Flannery, *Sales Executive*
Lance Sedwick, *Manager*
Allison Trudell, *Manager*
EMP: 30
SQ FT: 9,600
SALES (est): 6.8MM **Privately Held**
SIC: 3544 Special dies & tools

(G-10392)
HAK INC (PA)
413 Dale Ave (49659-9328)
PHONE.....................231 587-5322
Henry J Lapointe, *President*
EMP: 6
SQ FT: 4,700
SALES (est): 714.2K **Privately Held**
SIC: 3549 Metalworking machinery

(G-10393)
LANZEN FABRICATING NORTH INC
611 N East Limits St (49659-7600)
PHONE.....................231 587-8200
Terry K Lanzen, *President*
Kelly McPhaile, *General Mgr*
EMP: 32
SQ FT: 64,000
SALES (est): 5.5MM **Privately Held**
SIC: 3599 Machine shop, jobbing & repair

(G-10394)
MEEDERS DIM & LBR PDTS CO
7810 S M 88 Hwy (49659-8753)
PHONE.....................231 587-8611
Tim Meeder, *CEO*
Shannon Meeder, *President*
D Mitchell Meeder, *Vice Pres*
EMP: 6 **EST:** 1963
SQ FT: 10,000
SALES (est): 340K **Privately Held**
SIC: 2426 2511 Furniture dimension stock, hardwood; wood household furniture

(G-10395)
MEEDERS LUMBER CO
7810 S M 88 Hwy (49659-8753)
PHONE.....................231 587-8611
Shannon Meeder, *CEO*
EMP: 8 **EST:** 1947
SQ FT: 12,400
SALES (est): 610K **Privately Held**
SIC: 2421 Lumber: rough, sawed or planed; kiln drying of lumber

(G-10396)
MERRITT RACEWAY LLC
7300 N Maple Valley Rd Ne (49659-7940)
PHONE.....................231 590-4431
Ricky Ancel, *Principal*
EMP: 3
SALES (est): 259.8K **Privately Held**
SIC: 3644 Raceways

(G-10397)
MODERNE SLATE INC
8333 County Road 571 Ne (49659-9501)
PHONE.....................231 584-3499
Sylvia Leonard, *President*
EMP: 4
SALES (est): 359.4K **Privately Held**
SIC: 3281 Slate products

(G-10398)
REDTAIL SOFTWARE
1414 Plum Valley Rd Ne (49659-9589)
PHONE.....................231 587-0720
Robert Baldwin, *Principal*
EMP: 5 **EST:** 2008
SALES (est): 359.2K **Privately Held**
SIC: 7372 Prepackaged software

(G-10399)
STEEL TANK & FABRICATING CO
9517 Lake St (49659-7968)
PHONE.....................231 587-8412
Charles Harding, *Manager*
EMP: 50
SALES (corp-wide): 14.1MM **Privately Held**
SIC: 3443 Fabricated plate work (boiler shop)
PA: Steel Tank & Fabricating Co.
4701 White Lake Rd
Clarkston MI 48346
248 625-8700

(G-10400)
UP NORTH PUBLICATIONS INC
Also Called: Antrim County News
112 E State St (49659-8017)
P.O. Box 647 (49659-0647)
PHONE.....................231 587-8471
Fax: 231 587-9617
EMP: 3
SALES (corp-wide): 1.5MM **Privately Held**
SIC: 2711 Newspapers-Publishing/Printing
PA: Up North Publications Inc
415 Cass St Ste 1d
Traverse City MI
231 258-4600

Manchester
Washtenaw County

(G-10401)
AMCOR RIGID PACKAGING USA LLC
10521 S M 52 (48158-9474)
PHONE.....................734 336-3812
Kim Chiarito, *Manager*
EMP: 118 **Privately Held**
SIC: 3089 Plastic containers, except foam
HQ: Amcor Rigid Packaging Usa, Llc
40600 Ann Arbor Rd E # 201
Plymouth MI 48170

(G-10402)
AMERICAN ENGNRED CMPONENTS INC (PA)
Also Called: His Stamping Division
17951 W Austin Rd (48158-8668)
P.O. Box 338 (48158-0338)
PHONE.....................734 428-8301
John Morrison, *Ch of Bd*
Frederick W Schoen, *President*
William F McGregor, *VP Mfg*
Charles L Dardas, *CFO*
EMP: 139
SQ FT: 108,000
SALES (est): 32.9MM **Privately Held**
SIC: 3469 Metal stampings

(G-10403)
CEI COMPOSITE MATERIALS LLC
Also Called: Cei
800 E Duncan St (48158-9425)
PHONE.....................734 212-3006
Jeff Henry, *COO*
Jason Sherrill, *COO*
Garrett Harris, *Project Mgr*
Rob Napper, *Project Mgr*
Nick Sodt, *Project Mgr*
EMP: 20
SQ FT: 16,000
SALES (est): 5.2MM **Privately Held**
SIC: 3446 Architectural metalwork

(G-10404)
CONTINENTAL STRCTRL PLSTC MCH
Also Called: CSP Stamping
17951 W Austin Rd (48158-8668)
PHONE.....................734 428-8301
Steve Rooney, *CEO*
▲ **EMP:** 85
SQ FT: 89,000
SALES (est): 25MM **Privately Held**
SIC: 3469 Metal stampings
HQ: Csp Holding Corp.
255 Rex Blvd
Auburn Hills MI 48326
248 237-7800

(G-10405)
ENKON LLC
Also Called: Broadway
10521 Mi State Road 52 (48158-9474)
PHONE.....................937 890-5678
Kelly Ferguson, *President*
Debra L Doyle,
EMP: 14
SALES (est): 3MM
SALES (corp-wide): 36.5MM **Privately Held**
SIC: 3089 3544 3599 8711 Injection molding of plastics; molding plastic; dies, plastics forming; machine & other job shop work; machine tool design; steel wool
PA: The Eco-Groupe Inc
6161 Ventnor Ave
Dayton OH 45414
937 898-2603

(G-10406)
FASTENER ADVANCE PDT CO LTD
750 Hogan Rd (48158-9590)
PHONE.....................734 428-8070
Jang-Chon Wang, *President*
John Langer, *General Mgr*
▲ **EMP:** 15
SQ FT: 20,000
SALES (est): 2.5MM **Privately Held**
SIC: 3452 Bolts, nuts, rivets & washers

(G-10407)
MAC ENTERPRISES INC (PA)
11940 Hieber Rd (48158-9438)
PHONE.....................313 846-4567
Sylvia McCaffery, *President*
Lila D McCaffery, *President*
Mary Ann Nye, *General Mgr*
Paula S McCaffery, *Corp Secy*
▲ **EMP:** 15 **EST:** 1951
SALES (est): 2.9MM **Privately Held**
SIC: 3944 5092 3952 Craft & hobby kits & sets; arts & crafts equipment & supplies; lead pencils & art goods

(G-10408)
MARTINREA INDUSTRIES INC (HQ)
10501 Mi State Road 52 (48158-9432)
PHONE.....................734 428-2400
Morris Rowlett, *CEO*
Robert Wildeboer, *Ch of Bd*
Fred Jaekel, *President*
Brad Graves, *General Mgr*
Chris Oginski, *General Mgr*
▲ **EMP:** 25
SALES (est): 454.1MM
SALES (corp-wide): 2.7B **Privately Held**
WEB: www.reedcitytool.com
SIC: 3714 3317 3089 3544 Motor vehicle parts & accessories; steel pipe & tubes; plastic containers, except foam; special dies, tools, jigs & fixtures
PA: Martinrea International Inc
3210 Langstaff Rd
Vaughan ON
416 749-0314

(G-10409)
OBERTRON ELECTRONIC MFG INC
10098 Mi State Road 52 (48158-9743)
PHONE.....................734 428-0722
Bradley Oberleiter, *President*
▲ **EMP:** 10
SQ FT: 10,000
SALES (est): 1.8MM **Privately Held**
SIC: 3672 Printed circuit boards

(G-10410)
PINNACLE ENGINEERING CO INC
10250 Mi State Road 52 (48158-9757)
PHONE.....................734 428-7039
Murray Smith, *President*
Gertrude Smith, *Corp Secy*
Gary Smith, *Vice Pres*
EMP: 17 **EST:** 1969
SQ FT: 14,400
SALES (est): 2.5MM **Privately Held**
SIC: 3544 3541 7692 Special dies & tools; industrial molds; machine tools, metal cutting type; welding repair

(G-10411)
POST PRODUCTION SOLUTIONS LLC
110 Division St Ste 1 (48158-8803)
PHONE.....................734 428-7000
Pete Berger, *General Mgr*
Richard Berger, *Mng Member*
EMP: 10
SALES (est): 1.6MM **Privately Held**
SIC: 3599 Machine shop, jobbing & repair

(G-10412)
TIDY MRO ENTERPRISES LLC
520 Wolverine St (48158-9567)
PHONE.....................734 649-1122
Daniel Alber, *Principal*
EMP: 3 **EST:** 2016
SALES (est): 292.8K **Privately Held**
SIC: 3724 Aircraft engines & engine parts

Manistee
Manistee County

(G-10413)
A & A MARINE & MFG INC
270 3rd St (49660-1736)
P.O. Box 244 (49660-0244)
PHONE.....................231 723-8308
Michael R Kamaloski, *President*
Nan Kamnlaosdki, *President*
David Kamaloski, *Office Mgr*
EMP: 3
SQ FT: 6,000
SALES (est): 596.3K **Privately Held**
WEB: www.classicboating.com
SIC: 5088 3429 Marine supplies; marine hardware

Manistee - Manistee County (G-10414)

(G-10414)
AMOR SIGN STUDIOS INC
Also Called: Amor Imagepro
443 Water St (49660-1550)
P.O. Box 433 (49660-0433)
PHONE.................................231 723-8361
Thomas E Amor, *President*
Thomas H Amor, *Vice Pres*
EMP: 17
SQ FT: 9,000
SALES (est): 2.7MM **Privately Held**
WEB: www.amorsign.com
SIC: 7359 7389 3993 Sign rental; lettering & sign painting services; electric signs

(G-10415)
AMPTECH INC (HQ)
201 Glocheski Dr (49660-2640)
PHONE.................................231 464-5492
Lee R Wyatt, *President*
Dave Rogers, *Engineer*
Paul Zajac, *Design Engr*
Kim Graczyk, *Manager*
▲ **EMP:** 1
SQ FT: 53,000
SALES (est): 14.3MM **Privately Held**
WEB: www.amptechinc.com
SIC: 3679 Electronic circuits

(G-10416)
BLACK RIVER OIL CORP
65 Maple St (49660-1555)
PHONE.................................231 723-6502
EMP: 3 **EST:** 1981
SALES (est): 319.2K **Privately Held**
SIC: 1311 Crude petroleum production; natural gas production

(G-10417)
BOS MANUFACTURING LLC (PA)
100 Glocheski Dr (49660-2600)
PHONE.................................231 398-3328
David Boothe, *President*
Tonya Guinan, *Accounting Mgr*
Brian Boothe,
Tim Stone,
◆ **EMP:** 4
SQ FT: 45,000
SALES (est): 3MM **Privately Held**
SIC: 3535 Conveyors & conveying equipment

(G-10418)
CONINE PUBLISHING INC (DH)
75 Maple St (49660-1554)
P.O. Box 317 (49660-0317)
PHONE.................................231 723-3592
John A Batdorff, *President*
EMP: 30
SQ FT: 8,000
SALES (est): 7.5MM
SALES (corp-wide): 8.3B **Privately Held**
WEB: www.pioneergroup.net
SIC: 2711 2741 Commercial printing & newspaper publishing combined; miscellaneous publishing
HQ: Pgi Holdings, Inc.
115 N Michigan Ave
Big Rapids MI 49307
231 796-4831

(G-10419)
DYNAMIC DEVELOPMENT INC
314 W Parkdale Ave (49660-1132)
P.O. Box 336 (49660-0336)
PHONE.................................231 723-8318
Gerald Hamilton, *President*
Joseph A Pienta, *Vice Pres*
EMP: 5
SQ FT: 2,000
SALES (est): 584.1K **Privately Held**
SIC: 1382 Oil & gas exploration services

(G-10420)
ENVIRODINE INC
Also Called: Green Screen
317 Washington St (49660-1259)
P.O. Box 451 (49660-0451)
PHONE.................................231 723-5905
Denis Meikle, *President*
EMP: 3
SALES (est): 339.6K **Privately Held**
WEB: www.greenscreen1.com
SIC: 2879 Insecticides & pesticides

(G-10421)
FAB-LITE INC
330 Washington St (49660-1260)
P.O. Box 353 (49660-0353)
PHONE.................................231 398-8280
Stephen Paine, *President*
Scott Lakari, *VP Opers*
Brian Maxey, *Prdtn Mgr*
Tina Kelley, *Mfg Mgr*
Pete Anderson, *Manager*
EMP: 95
SQ FT: 40,000
SALES (est): 12.2MM **Privately Held**
WEB: www.fablite.com
SIC: 3441 Fabricated structural metal

(G-10422)
FORBES SANITATION & EXCAVATION
1878 E Parkdale Ave (49660-9359)
PHONE.................................231 723-2311
Don Forbes, *President*
EMP: 10
SALES (est): 1.6MM **Privately Held**
SIC: 1711 1794 3272 7699 Septic system construction; excavation & grading, building construction; septic tanks, concrete; septic tank cleaning service; water, sewer & utility lines

(G-10423)
GENTZ FOREST ROBERT PRODUCTS (PA)
9644 Guenthardt Rd (49660-9362)
PHONE.................................231 398-9194
Robert Gentz, *President*
David Gentz, *Vice Pres*
Duane Gentz, *Vice Pres*
Paula Gentz, *Vice Pres*
EMP: 18
SALES (est): 2.6MM **Privately Held**
SIC: 2411 Saw logs; pulpwood contractors engaged in cutting; wood chips, produced in the field

(G-10424)
IMAGEPRO INC
443 Water St (49660-1550)
P.O. Box 433 (49660-0433)
PHONE.................................231 723-7906
Tom Amor Jr, *President*
EMP: 3 **EST:** 2001
SALES (est): 652.1K **Privately Held**
WEB: www.imageproled.com
SIC: 5065 3993 Electronic parts & equipment; signs & advertising specialties

(G-10425)
JACKPINE PRESS INCORPORATED (PA)
Also Called: Jackpine Business Center
76 Filer St (49660-2717)
PHONE.................................231 723-8344
Jeff Trucks, *President*
Lee Trucks, *Vice Pres*
Sally Koon, *Admin Sec*
EMP: 15
SQ FT: 12,000
SALES (est): 3.1MM **Privately Held**
WEB: www.jackpine.com
SIC: 5943 5999 2752 Office forms & supplies; business machines & equipment; commercial printing, offset

(G-10426)
LIQUID DUSTLAYER INC
3320 Grant Hwy (49660)
PHONE.................................231 723-3750
Richard C Rademaker, *President*
Tina Rademaker, *Admin Sec*
EMP: 6 **EST:** 1941
SQ FT: 10,000
SALES (est): 530K **Privately Held**
WEB: www.liquiddustlayer.com
SIC: 2819 Calcium chloride & hypochlorite

(G-10427)
MANISTEE NEWS ADVOCATE
75 Maple St (49660-1554)
PHONE.................................231 723-3592
EMP: 16 **EST:** 2007
SALES (est): 675.7K **Privately Held**
SIC: 2741 Misc Publishing

(G-10428)
MANISTEE WLDG & PIPING SVC INC (PA)
325 Oakgrove St (49660-1121)
P.O. Box 68 (49660-0068)
PHONE.................................231 723-2551
George Edmondson, *President*
Reta Racine, *Corp Secy*
EMP: 7 **EST:** 1952
SQ FT: 3,500
SALES: 1.6MM **Privately Held**
SIC: 1541 7692 3498 3441 Renovation, remodeling & repairs: industrial buildings; welding repair; fabricated pipe & fittings; fabricated structural metal; blast furnaces & steel mills

(G-10429)
MARTIN MRETTA MAGNESIA SPC LLC
1800 E Lake Rd (49660-9394)
P.O. Box 398 (49660-0398)
PHONE.................................231 723-2577
Jim Reithel, *Branch Mgr*
EMP: 30 **Publicly Held**
SIC: 3297 Cement, magnesia
HQ: Martin Marietta Magnesia Specialties, Llc
755 Lime Rd
Woodville OH 43469
419 849-4223

(G-10430)
MI FROZEN FOOD LLC
Also Called: Michigan Farm To Freezer
33 Lake St (49660-1437)
P.O. Box 7069, Detroit (48207-0069)
PHONE.................................231 357-4334
Brandon Seng, *Mng Member*
EMP: 7
SQ FT: 100
SALES (est): 600K **Privately Held**
SIC: 2037 Frozen fruits & vegetables

(G-10431)
MORTON SALT INC
180 6th St (49660-3000)
PHONE.................................231 398-0758
Jacob Bialik, *Facilities Mgr*
Michael Ganger, *QC Mgr*
Candace Owens, *Human Res Mgr*
Phil Carlton, *Branch Mgr*
Robert Kinney, *Maintence Staff*
EMP: 12
SALES (corp-wide): 4.6B **Privately Held**
SIC: 1479 Salt & sulfur mining
HQ: Morton Salt, Inc.
444 W Lake Ste 3000
Chicago IL 60606

(G-10432)
NATURAL ATTRACTION
25 Cross St (49660-1431)
PHONE.................................231 398-0787
John Mundschau, *Owner*
EMP: 3
SALES: 125K **Privately Held**
SIC: 2339 Women's & misses' athletic clothing & sportswear

(G-10433)
NORON COMPOSITE TECHNOLOGIES
650 W Hoague Rd (49660-9503)
PHONE.................................231 723-9277
Ronny Melchert, *President*
EMP: 20
SQ FT: 36,000
SALES (est): 4.2MM **Privately Held**
WEB: www.noroncomposites.com
SIC: 3083 Plastic finished products, laminated

(G-10434)
PERFECT SIGNS
338 4th St (49660-2932)
PHONE.................................231 233-3721
Bruce Schaub, *Owner*
Jeneva Schaub, *Co-Owner*
EMP: 7
SALES (est): 222.1K **Privately Held**
SIC: 3993 Signs & advertising specialties

(G-10435)
PGI HOLDINGS INC
Also Called: Manistee News-Advocate
75 Maple St (49660-1554)
P.O. Box 317 (49660-0317)
PHONE.................................231 723-3592
Jack Batdorff, *President*
EMP: 30
SQ FT: 9,000
SALES (corp-wide): 8.3B **Privately Held**
WEB: www.bigrapidsnews.com
SIC: 2711 Newspapers: publishing only, not printed on site
HQ: Pgi Holdings, Inc.
115 N Michigan Ave
Big Rapids MI 49307
231 796-4831

(G-10436)
PIONEER PRESS
Also Called: Pioneer Group, The
75 Maple St (49660-1554)
PHONE.................................231 723-3592
Jack Batdorff, *Branch Mgr*
EMP: 20
SALES (corp-wide): 4.8MM **Privately Held**
SIC: 2759 7311 Commercial printing; advertising agencies
PA: Pioneer Press
22405 18 Mile Rd
Big Rapids MI 49307
231 796-8072

(G-10437)
SPORTS INK SCREEN PRTG EMB LLC
316 W Parkdale Ave (49660-1132)
PHONE.................................231 723-5696
Sharon Monnot, *Owner*
EMP: 4
SALES (est): 280.5K **Privately Held**
SIC: 2752 5699 Commercial printing, lithographic; designers, apparel

---

Manistique
Schoolcraft County

(G-10438)
ADVISOR INC
311 Oak St (49854-1409)
P.O. Box 99 (49854-0099)
PHONE.................................906 341-2424
John J Ozanich, *President*
EMP: 6 **EST:** 1948
SALES: 4.5MM **Privately Held**
WEB: www.advisor.com
SIC: 2721 Periodicals

(G-10439)
BOSANIC LWRNCE SONS TMBER PDTS
1840n W Kendall Rd (49854-9159)
PHONE.................................906 341-5609
Lawrence Bosanic, *Owner*
Greg Bosanic, *Manager*
Greggguy Bosanic, *Manager*
Steave Bosanic, *Manager*
EMP: 8
SALES: 600K **Privately Held**
SIC: 2411 Logging camps & contractors

(G-10440)
FOUR SEASONS PUBLISHING INC
Also Called: Manistique Pioneer Tribune
212 Walnut St (49854-1445)
PHONE.................................906 341-5200
Richard Demers, *Principal*
EMP: 7 **EST:** 1998
SALES (est): 618K **Privately Held**
SIC: 2711 Newspapers, publishing & printing

(G-10441)
JOE BOSANIC FOREST PRODUCTS
1808 Nw Kendall Rd (49854)
PHONE.................................906 341-2037
Joseph Bosanic, *Owner*
EMP: 7

SALES (est): 454.4K **Privately Held**
SIC: 2411 Skidding logs

(G-10442)
JOSEPH LAKOSKY LOGGING
Also Called: Excavation
10502w Government Rd (49854-9383)
PHONE..................................906 573-2783
Joseph Lakosky, *Owner*
EMP: 7
SALES (est): 350K **Privately Held**
SIC: 2411 Logging camps & contractors; veneer logs

(G-10443)
MANISTIQUE RENTALS INC
415 Chippewa Ave (49854-1350)
PHONE..................................906 341-6955
Elizabeth Slining, *Corp Secy*
George James Slining Jr, *Vice Pres*
David Slining, *Foreman/Supr*
Debbie Musgrave, *Persnl Mgr*
EMP: 5
SQ FT: 18,000
SALES: 1MM **Privately Held**
SIC: 3273 4953 Ready-mixed concrete; refuse collection & disposal services

(G-10444)
NORTHFORK READI MIX INC
5665w Us Highway 2 (49854-9211)
PHONE..................................906 341-3445
Brian Skok, *President*
EMP: 6
SALES (est): 669.9K **Privately Held**
SIC: 3273 Ready-mixed concrete

(G-10445)
ONLINE ENGINEERING INC
400 N Cedar St (49854-1250)
PHONE..................................906 341-0090
James Gardener, *President*
Marilyn Gardener, *Vice Pres*
EMP: 19
SQ FT: 11,000
SALES: 2.3MM **Privately Held**
WEB: www.online-engineering.com
SIC: 3823 3559 Industrial instrmnts msrmnt display/control process variable; screening equipment, electric

(G-10446)
U P FABRICATING CO INC
Manistique Machine
342 Elm St (49854-1247)
PHONE..................................906 341-2868
Mike Kumpula, *Engineer*
Mike Mahoney, *Engineer*
Scott Carey, *Manager*
EMP: 5
SALES (corp-wide): 6.3MM **Privately Held**
SIC: 3599 Machine shop, jobbing & repair
PA: U. P. Fabricating Co. Inc.
120 Us Highway 41 E Ste A
Negaunee MI 49866
906 475-4400

(G-10447)
UP COIN & CULTIVATION LLC (PA)
321 Deer St (49854-1145)
PHONE..................................906 341-4769
Jason J Gregurash,
EMP: 3
SALES: 400K **Privately Held**
SIC: 3524 Lawn & garden equipment

Manitou Beach
Lenawee County

(G-10448)
HARDY-REED TOOL & DIE CO INC
Also Called: Kbd Properties
16269 Manitou Beach Rd (49253-9649)
PHONE..................................517 547-7107
Scott Strodtman, *President*
Debbie Isenhower, *Office Mgr*
Debra Isenhower, *Office Mgr*
EMP: 13
SQ FT: 13,800

SALES: 830K **Privately Held**
SIC: 3544 3599 3545 Die sets for metal stamping (presses); custom machinery; tools & accessories for machine tools

(G-10449)
STRIKER TOOLS LLC
210 Park St (49253-9123)
P.O. Box 206 (49253-0206)
PHONE..................................248 990-7767
Kelly Nielsen, *CEO*
Margaret Cunningham, *President*
Jami Miller, *CFO*
EMP: 6
SALES (est): 547.9K **Privately Held**
SIC: 3546 7389 Hammers, portable: electric or pneumatic, chipping, etc.;

Manton
Wexford County

(G-10450)
ALLEN WHITEHOUSE
Also Called: Whitehouse Logging & Hardwood
1270 E 16 1/2 Rd (49663-9721)
PHONE..................................231 824-3000
Allen Whitehouse, *Owner*
EMP: 6
SALES (est): 412.1K **Privately Held**
SIC: 2411 Logging camps & contractors

(G-10451)
BUNDY LOGGING
Also Called: Bundy, Bundy
4114 E 16 Rd (49663-8592)
PHONE..................................231 824-6054
Bruce Bundy, *President*
EMP: 5
SALES (est): 478K **Privately Held**
SIC: 2411 Pulpwood contractors engaged in cutting

(G-10452)
DANNY K BUNDY
2630 E 16 1/2 Rd (49663-9719)
PHONE..................................231 590-6924
Danny K Bundy, *Principal*
EMP: 3 **EST:** 2010
SALES (est): 204.4K **Privately Held**
SIC: 2411 Logging camps & contractors

(G-10453)
DJL LOGGING INC
5905 N Brown Rd (49663-9090)
PHONE..................................231 590-2012
Dustin Lutke, *Principal*
EMP: 3
SALES (est): 270.7K **Privately Held**
SIC: 2411 Logging

(G-10454)
HELSELS TREE SERVICE INC
320 Rose St (49663-9472)
PHONE..................................231 879-3666
Eric Helsel, *President*
EMP: 3
SALES (est): 25K **Privately Held**
SIC: 0783 3999 1629 Ornamental shrub & tree services; custom pulverizing & grinding of plastic materials; land clearing contractor

(G-10455)
HILLSIDE PALLETS
4093 N 35 Rd (49663-9688)
PHONE..................................231 824-3761
Tobias C Hochstetler, *Owner*
EMP: 3
SALES: 300K **Privately Held**
SIC: 2448 Pallets, wood & wood with metal

(G-10456)
JASON LUTKE
Also Called: Lutke Forest Products
615 Rw Harris Dr (49663)
PHONE..................................231 824-6655
Jason Lutke, *Owner*
EMP: 50
SALES (est): 5.7MM **Privately Held**
SIC: 2411 Logging camps & contractors

(G-10457)
R & B GRINDING SERVICE INC
641 R W Harris Dr (49663-9785)
PHONE..................................231 824-6798
Ray Fisher, *President*
Donald Fisher, *Vice Pres*
EMP: 5
SQ FT: 3,000
SALES: 100K **Privately Held**
SIC: 3599 Grinding castings for the trade

(G-10458)
UPNORTH DESIGN & REPAIR INC
10811 E 20 Rd (49663-9441)
PHONE..................................231 824-6025
Allan Van Dyke, *President*
Rebecca Vandyke, *Vice Pres*
EMP: 3
SALES: 110K **Privately Held**
SIC: 3441 Fabricated structural metal

(G-10459)
WILDCAT BUILDINGS INC
656 Rw Hrris Indus Prk Dr (49663)
PHONE..................................231 824-6406
Janet M Triplett, *President*
Tim Loving, *Vice Pres*
Lisa Kimbel, *Admin Sec*
EMP: 15
SQ FT: 4,000
SALES (est): 3.6MM **Privately Held**
WEB: www.wildcatbuildings.com
SIC: 3448 Buildings, portable: prefabricated metal

Maple City
Leelanau County

(G-10460)
BINSFELD ENGINEERING INC
4571 Mcfarlane Rd (49664-9673)
PHONE..................................231 334-4383
Stephen B Tarsa, *CEO*
Michael W Binsfeld, *President*
Dan Daigger, *Mfg Staff*
Bob Holden, *Sales Executive*
EMP: 12
SQ FT: 4,000
SALES: 2.5MM **Privately Held**
WEB: www.binsfeld.com
SIC: 3823 8711 Industrial process measurement equipment; consulting engineer

(G-10461)
KASSON SAND & GRAVEL CO INC
10282 S Pierce Rd (49664-9742)
PHONE..................................231 228-5455
Robert W Noonan, *President*
EMP: 14
SQ FT: 2,800
SALES (est): 4MM **Privately Held**
WEB: www.kassonsandandgravel.com
SIC: 1442 Construction sand mining; gravel mining

(G-10462)
LEELANAU REDI-MIX INC
Also Called: Leelanau Redi-Mix & Gravel
12488 S Newman Rd (49664-9734)
PHONE..................................231 228-5005
Marilyn Flaska, *President*
Charles Flaska, *Chairman*
Elizabeth Warnes, *Treasurer*
Jerry Flaska, *Manager*
EMP: 43 **EST:** 1950
SQ FT: 4,000
SALES (est): 7.3MM **Privately Held**
WEB: www.fisherscottages.com
SIC: 3273 3272 1771 Ready-mixed concrete; tanks, concrete; flooring contractor

(G-10463)
MAPLE VALLEY PALLET CO
9285 S Nash Rd (49664-9746)
P.O. Box 134 (49664-0134)
PHONE..................................231 228-6641
Everett Lautner, *Partner*
Janice Lautner, *Partner*
EMP: 11
SQ FT: 13,800

SALES (est): 640K **Privately Held**
SIC: 2448 Pallets, wood

Marcellus
Cass County

(G-10464)
FAB MASTERS COMPANY INC
51787 M 40 (49067-8718)
P.O. Box 278 (49067-0278)
PHONE..................................269 646-5315
Ronald L Troxell, *President*
Gail Klein, *Corp Secy*
Brian Phillips, *Prdtn Mgr*
Kim Fox, *Manager*
EMP: 100
SQ FT: 59,000
SALES (est): 17MM **Privately Held**
WEB: www.fabmasters.net
SIC: 3441 Fabricated structural metal

(G-10465)
FAITH PLASTICS LLC
239 E Main St (49067-5103)
P.O. Box 217 (49067-0217)
PHONE..................................269 646-2294
Joe Occhipiniti, *President*
Laura Occhipinti, *Vice Pres*
EMP: 30
SQ FT: 14,000
SALES: 2.4MM
SALES (corp-wide): 50.4MM **Privately Held**
SIC: 3089 Injection molding of plastics
PA: Gdc, Inc.
815 Logan St
Goshen IN 46528
574 533-3128

(G-10466)
MOORMANN PRINTING INC (PA)
Also Called: Marcellus News
149 W Main St (49067-5104)
P.O. Box 277 (49067-0277)
PHONE..................................269 646-2101
Ramona Moormann, *President*
David Moormann, *Vice Pres*
EMP: 3 **EST:** 1946
SQ FT: 8,500
SALES (est): 660.5K **Privately Held**
WEB: www.marcellusnews.com
SIC: 2711 2752 Newspapers, publishing & printing; commercial printing, lithographic

(G-10467)
POWCO INC
56165 Moorlag Rd (49067-9525)
PHONE..................................269 646-5385
L Judson Brown, *President*
EMP: 10
SQ FT: 30,000
SALES (est): 495K **Privately Held**
WEB: www.powco.com
SIC: 3479 Coating of metals & formed products

(G-10468)
SPEED CINCH INC
22724 96th Ave (49067-9700)
P.O. Box 739 (49067-0739)
PHONE..................................269 646-2016
James R Bainbridge, *President*
Cindy Peague, *General Mgr*
▼**EMP:** 4
SQ FT: 4,000
SALES: 500K **Privately Held**
SIC: 3089 Injection molding of plastics

(G-10469)
TRI-STAR MOLDING INC
51540 M 40 (49067-7717)
PHONE..................................269 646-0062
Nick Dekoning, *Co-Owner*
David McMorrow, *Co-Owner*
Tim Dekoning, *Purchasing*
Julie Dekoning, *Manager*
EMP: 46
SQ FT: 33,000
SALES (est): 16.2MM **Privately Held**
WEB: www.tristarmolding.com
SIC: 3089 Injection molding of plastics

Marine City - St. Clair County (G-10470)

GEOGRAPHIC SECTION

Marine City
St. Clair County

(G-10470)
B ERICKSON MANUFACTURING LTD
6317 King Rd (48039-1428)
P.O. Box 934, New Baltimore (48047-0934)
PHONE..................810 765-1144
Brent Erickson, *President*
Constance Erickson, *Corp Secy*
▲ **EMP:** 10
SQ FT: 100
SALES (est): 2MM **Privately Held**
SIC: 2241 Strapping webs

(G-10471)
BUTLER PLASTICS COMPANY
766 Degurse Ave (48039-1526)
P.O. Box 100 (48039-0100)
PHONE..................810 765-8811
Kelly Drummond, *President*
Kevin Drummond, *Vice Pres*
Kristy Domerese, *Engineer*
▼ **EMP:** 29
SQ FT: 15,000
SALES (est): 4.8MM **Privately Held**
SIC: 3089 Injection molding of plastics

(G-10472)
CUSTOM METAL WORKS INC
316 S Belle River Ave # 11 (48039-3562)
PHONE..................810 420-0390
Robert B Peterson, *President*
EMP: 4
SQ FT: 10,000
SALES: 600K **Privately Held**
SIC: 3444 Booths, spray: prefabricated sheet metal; sheet metal specialties, not stamped

(G-10473)
FISHER-BAKER CORPORATION
420 S Water St (48039-1690)
P.O. Box 248 (48039-0248)
PHONE..................810 765-3548
Virginia Ladensack, *President*
Robert J Baker, *Vice Pres*
▲ **EMP:** 6
SALES (est): 1.2MM **Privately Held**
WEB: www.fisherbaker.com
SIC: 5084 3647 Industrial machinery & equipment; automotive lighting fixtures

(G-10474)
INTELLICHEM LLC
887 Chartier (48039-2324)
PHONE..................810 765-4075
Jamey Westrick, *Purch Agent*
Mike Westrick, *
EMP: 10
SALES: 400K **Privately Held**
SIC: 3569 Lubrication equipment, industrial

(G-10475)
ISLAND MACHINE AND ENGRG LLC
847 Degurse Ave (48039-1532)
P.O. Box 247 (48039-0247)
PHONE..................810 765-8228
Tony Skudrna, *Mng Member*
EMP: 8
SQ FT: 5,000
SALES (est): 998.2K **Privately Held**
SIC: 8711 7699 3599 Engineering services; industrial equipment services; machine shop, jobbing & repair

(G-10476)
KLINGLER CONSULTING & MFG
Also Called: Rockford Carving Co
837 Degurse Ave (48039-1532)
PHONE..................810 765-3700
Robert Klingler, *President*
Sara Klinger, *Admin Sec*
▲ **EMP:** 12
SQ FT: 50,000
SALES (est): 910K **Privately Held**
SIC: 3931 Saxophones & parts; trumpets & parts; banjos & parts; guitars & parts, electric & nonelectric

(G-10477)
MECHANICAL FABRICATORS INC
770 Degurse Ave (48039-1526)
PHONE..................810 765-8853
Jeff Colman, *President*
Carl Colman, *Vice Pres*
EMP: 15 **EST:** 1961
SQ FT: 10,000
SALES (est): 1.1MM **Privately Held**
SIC: 3441 Building components, structural steel

(G-10478)
MIDWEST FBRGLAS FBRICATORS INC
1796 S Parker St (48039-2337)
PHONE..................810 765-7445
Anthony Simon, *President*
Anne Costello, *Vice Pres*
EMP: 10
SQ FT: 30,000
SALES (est): 1.5MM **Privately Held**
SIC: 3053 3296 Gaskets, packing & sealing devices; fiberglass insulation

(G-10479)
PARKSIDE PRINTING INC
611 Broadway St (48039-1612)
P.O. Box 32 (48039-0032)
PHONE..................810 765-4500
Donna Paulus, *President*
James Paulus, *Treasurer*
EMP: 3
SALES (est): 150K **Privately Held**
SIC: 2752 2759 7338 2791 Commercial printing, offset; invitation & stationery printing & engraving; secretarial & court reporting; typesetting; bookbinding & related work

(G-10480)
PRO RELEASE INC
420 S Water St 275 (48039-1690)
PHONE..................810 512-4120
Gary J Todd, *President*
▲ **EMP:** 5
SQ FT: 8,000
SALES (est): 422.5K **Privately Held**
WEB: www.prorelease.com
SIC: 3949 Archery equipment, general; bows, archery

(G-10481)
RIVERSIDE SPLINE & GEAR INC
1390 S Parker St (48039-2334)
P.O. Box 340 (48039-0340)
PHONE..................810 765-8302
Wayne Forest, *President*
Aaron Forest, *Vice Pres*
Valerie Forest, *Vice Pres*
Jeff Krause, *Mfg Mgr*
Matthew J McBride, *CFO*
EMP: 35 **EST:** 1964
SQ FT: 20,700
SALES (est): 7MM **Privately Held**
WEB: www.splineandgear.com
SIC: 3462 3568 3541 3545 Gear & chain forgings; power transmission equipment; machine tools, metal cutting type; machine tool accessories; paints & allied products

(G-10482)
SEAWAY PLASTICS CORPORATION
814 Degurse Ave (48039-1528)
PHONE..................810 765-8864
EMP: 35
SQ FT: 17,200
SALES (est): 323.9K **Privately Held**
SIC: 3089 Mfg Plastic Products

(G-10483)
SELECTIVE INDUSTRIES INC
6100 King Rd (48039-1401)
PHONE..................810 765-4666
John Osterman, *CEO*
Michael Osterman, *President*
Brian Burns, *General Mgr*
Nick Black, *Project Mgr*
EMP: 85
SQ FT: 24,000
SALES (est): 13.7MM **Privately Held**
WEB: www.selectiveinc.com
SIC: 3469 Metal stampings

(G-10484)
THEUT PRODUCTS INC
1910 S Parker St (48039-2339)
PHONE..................810 765-9321
David Theut, *Branch Mgr*
EMP: 12
SALES (corp-wide): 15.4MM **Privately Held**
WEB: www.theutproducts.com
SIC: 3273 Ready-mixed concrete
PA: Theut Products, Inc.
73408 Van Dyke Rd
Bruce Twp MI 48065
586 752-4541

(G-10485)
USMATS INC
Also Called: Woodcraft Industries
6347 King Rd (48039-1428)
P.O. Box 455, Algonac (48001-0455)
PHONE..................810 765-4545
Dale Nevison, *President*
Anna Nevison, *Treasurer*
EMP: 8
SQ FT: 10,000
SALES (est): 1MM **Privately Held**
WEB: www.usmats.com
SIC: 2273 Carpets & rugs

(G-10486)
V J INDUSTRIES INC
827 Degurse Ave (48039-1532)
PHONE..................810 364-6470
EMP: 12
SALES (est): 1.6MM **Privately Held**
SIC: 7539 3545 Automotive Repair Mfg Machine Tool Accessories

(G-10487)
WM KLOEFFLER INDUSTRIES INC
Also Called: Kloeffler, Wm Industries
6033 King Rd (48039-1403)
PHONE..................810 765-4068
William H Kloeffler Jr, *President*
Gail Kloeffler, *Admin Sec*
EMP: 25
SQ FT: 18,000
SALES (est): 1.6MM **Privately Held**
SIC: 7692 3441 2599 3444 Welding repair; fabricated structural metal; stools, factory; sheet metalwork

(G-10488)
WORSWICK MOLD & TOOL INC
6232 King Rd (48039-1400)
P.O. Box 308 (48039-0308)
PHONE..................810 765-1700
Stanley Worswick, *President*
Sharon Worswick, *Vice Pres*
Annette Pelaccio, *Prdtn Mgr*
Dawn Prowse, *Treasurer*
EMP: 10
SQ FT: 22,000
SALES (est): 1.7MM **Privately Held**
SIC: 3089 3544 Injection molded finished plastic products; special dies & tools

Marion
Osceola County

(G-10489)
ALBERTS MACHINE TOOL INC
16971 10th Ave (49665-8272)
PHONE..................231 743-2457
Steve Alberts, *President*
Terri Alberts, *Vice Pres*
EMP: 3
SQ FT: 1,000
SALES: 100K **Privately Held**
SIC: 3545 3569 Gauges (machine tool accessories); liquid automation machinery & equipment

(G-10490)
LOCK AND LOAD CORP
3390 16 Mile Rd (49665-8414)
PHONE..................800 975-9658
EMP: 4

SALES (est): 330K **Privately Held**
SIC: 2448 3537 3499 Mfg Wood Pallets/Skids Mfg Industrial Trucks/Tractors Mfg Misc Fabricated Metal Products

(G-10491)
MARION PALLET
7414 20 Mile Rd (49665-8440)
PHONE..................231 743-6124
Daniel Beachy, *Principal*
EMP: 4
SALES (est): 407.3K **Privately Held**
SIC: 2448 Pallets, wood & wood with metal

(G-10492)
NIVERS SAND GRAVEL
19937 M 115 (49665-8078)
PHONE..................231 743-6126
Don Nivers, *Owner*
EMP: 14
SALES (est): 546K **Privately Held**
SIC: 1442 Construction sand & gravel

(G-10493)
POLLINGTON MACHINE TOOL INC
Also Called: Buck Pole Archery Deerranch
20669 30th Ave (49665-8305)
PHONE..................231 743-2003
Claude S Pollington, *President*
Ross Richards, *Treasurer*
Penny Miller, *Admin Sec*
▲ **EMP:** 30
SQ FT: 20,000
SALES: 6.9MM **Privately Held**
WEB: www.buckpole.com
SIC: 3599 3544 Custom machinery; special dies, tools, jigs & fixtures

Marlette
Sanilac County

(G-10494)
BARTLETT MANUFACTURING CO LLC
Also Called: Bartlett Arborist Sup & Mfrs
7876 S Van Dyke Rd Ste 10 (48453-9156)
PHONE..................989 635-8900
John Nelson, *President*
EMP: 6 **EST:** 1912
SQ FT: 20,000
SALES (est): 1.2MM **Privately Held**
WEB: www.bartlettman.com
SIC: 3423 Hand & edge tools

(G-10495)
DGP INC
3260 Fenner St (48453-1229)
P.O. Box 155 (48453-0155)
PHONE..................989 635-7531
Steve Quade, *President*
Chris Clark Jr, *Vice Pres*
Christopher G Clark, *Marketing Staff*
EMP: 40
SQ FT: 26,000
SALES (est): 6.6MM **Privately Held**
SIC: 3296 4131 Fiberglass insulation; intercity & rural bus transportation

(G-10496)
EXPERNCED PRCSION MCHINING INC
2720 Lamotte St (48453-1034)
PHONE..................989 635-2299
Keith P Mexico, *President*
Glenn Mexico, *Vice Pres*
Jim Mexico, *Vice Pres*
Betty Mexico, *Treasurer*
EMP: 6
SALES: 356.4K **Privately Held**
SIC: 3714 3724 3599 Motor vehicle parts & accessories; aircraft engines & engine parts; machine shop, jobbing & repair

(G-10497)
GRUPO ANTOLIN MICHIGAN INC (DH)
6300 Euclid St (48453-1424)
PHONE..................989 635-5055
Jesus Pascual Santos, *CEO*
Maria Victoria Hidalgo Castao, *CFO*
Jason Kodat, *Supervisor*

GEOGRAPHIC SECTION

Marquette - Marquette County (G-10527)

▲ EMP: 160
SQ FT: 180,000
SALES (est): 45.4MM
SALES (corp-wide): 33.3MM **Privately Held**
SIC: 3714 Motor vehicle body components & frame
HQ: Grupo Antolin North America, Inc.
1700 Atlantic Blvd
Auburn Hills MI 48326
248 373-1749

(G-10498)
LUPA R A AND SONS REPAIR
3580 Willis Rd (48453-9323)
PHONE..................................810 346-3579
Roger A Lupa, *Owner*
EMP: 6
SQ FT: 2,100
SALES (est): 1.5MM **Privately Held**
SIC: 3715 7539 7538 Truck trailers; trailer repair; general truck repair

(G-10499)
M & B WELDING INC
6411 Euclid St (48453-1402)
PHONE..................................989 635-8017
Matthew Blatt, *President*
EMP: 6
SQ FT: 10,000
SALES: 380K **Privately Held**
SIC: 7692 Welding repair

(G-10500)
MARINE INDUSTRIES INC
2900 Boyne Rd (48453-9773)
P.O. Box 368 (48453-0368)
PHONE..................................989 635-3644
Lowell Driver, *President*
EMP: 20
SQ FT: 34,000
SALES (est): 3.8MM **Privately Held**
SIC: 3429 Marine hardware

(G-10501)
MEN OF STEEL INC
2920 Municipal Dr (48453-1378)
P.O. Box 308 (48453-0308)
PHONE..................................989 635-4866
Brian Vanderpool, *President*
Brian K Vanderpool, *President*
Lori A Vanderpool, *Treasurer*
EMP: 14 EST: 1996
SQ FT: 4,800
SALES (est): 2.2MM **Privately Held**
WEB: www.menofsteel.com
SIC: 1791 3441 Structural steel erection; fabricated structural metal

(G-10502)
SANILAC STEEL INC
2487 S Van Dyke Rd (48453-9781)
P.O. Box 185 (48453-0185)
PHONE..................................989 635-2992
James O'Morrow, *President*
David Christensen, *Vice Pres*
James O'Morrow Jr, *Vice Pres*
EMP: 15
SQ FT: 6,300
SALES: 2.8MM **Privately Held**
WEB: www.sanilacsteel.com
SIC: 3441 Fabricated structural metal

Marne
Ottawa County

(G-10503)
2 E FABRICATING
1202 Comstock St (49435-8750)
PHONE..................................616 498-7036
EMP: 3
SALES (est): 291.2K **Privately Held**
SIC: 3599 Machine shop, jobbing & repair

(G-10504)
AXIS ENTERPRISES INC
15300 8th Ave (49435-9610)
PHONE..................................616 677-5281
Jon Dewys, *President*
C T Martin, *Vice Pres*
EMP: 100

SALES (est): 7.6MM **Privately Held**
SIC: 3965 Eyelets, metal: clothing, fabrics, boots or shoes

(G-10505)
BORGIA DIE & ENGINEERING INC
14750 Raymer Cir (49435)
P.O. Box 65 (49435-0065)
PHONE..................................616 677-3595
Frank Borgia Jr, *President*
Frank Borgia Sr, *Vice Pres*
James Marckini, *Admin Sec*
EMP: 15
SQ FT: 7,000
SALES: 400K **Privately Held**
SIC: 3544 Special dies & tools

(G-10506)
D MARSH COMPANY INC
3186 Leonard St (49435-9657)
P.O. Box 261, Thiensville WI (53092-0261)
PHONE..................................616 677-5276
Don Marsh, *President*
EMP: 3
SALES: 800K **Privately Held**
SIC: 3559 Automotive maintenance equipment

(G-10507)
DEWYS MANUFACTURING INC
Also Called: American Grow Rack
15300 8th Ave (49435-9600)
PHONE..................................616 677-5281
Jon Dewys, *CEO*
C T Martin, *President*
Mark Schoenborn, *COO*
Jake Blink, *Accountant*
▲ EMP: 180
SQ FT: 90,000
SALES (est): 41.2MM **Privately Held**
WEB: www.dewysmfg.com
SIC: 3444 Sheet metalwork

(G-10508)
HATFIELD ENTERPRISES
15627 24th Ave (49435-8767)
PHONE..................................616 677-5215
Dennis Hatfield, *Owner*
EMP: 3
SALES (est): 197K **Privately Held**
SIC: 2048 Fish food

(G-10509)
KAILING MACHINE SHOP
14464 16th Ave (49435-9700)
PHONE..................................616 677-3629
Thomas Kailing, *Partner*
EMP: 3
SALES (est): 227.2K **Privately Held**
SIC: 3549 Metalworking machinery

(G-10510)
PARADIGM CONVEYOR LLC
15342 24th Ave (49435-8766)
P.O. Box 21 (49435-0021)
PHONE..................................,616 520-1926
Ken Alkema, *Engineer*
Kenneth Alkema, *Mng Member*
EMP: 5
SALES: 450K **Privately Held**
SIC: 3535 Conveyors & conveying equipment

(G-10511)
PARAMOUNT TOOL AND DIE INC
1245 Comstock St (49435-8750)
P.O. Box 120 (49435-0120)
PHONE..................................616 677-0000
Robert Burnett, *President*
Todd Van Loon, *Vice Pres*
Cindee Nowicki, *Office Mgr*
EMP: 14
SQ FT: 20,000
SALES (est): 2.6MM **Privately Held**
WEB: www.paratool.com
SIC: 3544 Industrial molds; special dies & tools

(G-10512)
R ANDREWS PALLET CO INC
1035 Comstock St (49435-9603)
PHONE..................................616 677-3270
EMP: 10 EST: 1987
SQ FT: 12,000

SALES: 1.2MM **Privately Held**
SIC: 2448 5031 Mfg Wood Pallets/Skids Whol Lumber/Plywood/Millwork

(G-10513)
SOLAIRE MEDICAL STORAGE LLC
1239 Comstock St (49435-8750)
PHONE..................................888 435-2256
Benjamin Barber, *Principal*
Christopher Barber, *Principal*
Daniel Schroeder, *Vice Pres*
EMP: 60 EST: 2011
SALES (est): 235K **Privately Held**
SIC: 2426 5047 Turnings, furniture: wood; medical equipment & supplies

(G-10514)
UNDER PRESSURE PWR WASHERS LLC
885 Meyer Ln (49435-8637)
PHONE..................................616 292-4289
Les Williamson, *Owner*
EMP: 5 EST: 2009
SALES (est): 391.1K **Privately Held**
SIC: 3452 Washers

(G-10515)
VAN RON STEEL SERVICES LLC
1100 Comstock St (49435-8753)
PHONE..................................616 813-6907
Mark Vanportfliet,
EMP: 10
SALES (est): 1.5MM **Privately Held**
SIC: 3315 Steel wire & related products

(G-10516)
WOOD-N-STUFF INC
12151 Linden Dr (49435-9684)
PHONE..................................616 677-0177
Robert Lupton, *President*
EMP: 3
SALES (est): 287.5K **Privately Held**
SIC: 2493 Reconstituted wood products

Marquette
Marquette County

(G-10517)
AMERICAN BLDRS CONTRS SUP INC
Also Called: ABC Supply 693
908 W Baraga Ave (49855-4029)
PHONE..................................906 226-9665
Brian Russell, *Branch Mgr*
EMP: 8
SALES (corp-wide): 457.2MM **Privately Held**
WEB: www.norandex.com
SIC: 2431 5031 Windows & window parts & trim, wood; lumber, plywood & millwork
HQ: American Builders & Contractors Supply Co., Inc.
1 Abc Pkwy
Beloit WI 53511
608 362-7777

(G-10518)
ASSRA
Also Called: Single Shot Rifle Journal
625 Pine St (49855-3723)
PHONE..................................906 225-1828
John Merz, *President*
Dale McGee, *Vice Pres*
Richard Eeesley, *Treasurer*
Charles Persons, *Director*
Laurie Gapko, *Admin Sec*
EMP: 10
SALES (est): 470.1K **Privately Held**
SIC: 3949 Targets, archery & rifle shooting

(G-10519)
BINGHAM BOAT WORKS LTD
58 Middle Island Point Rd (49855-9726)
PHONE..................................906 225-0050
Joe Bingham, *President*
EMP: 5
SALES (est): 350K **Privately Held**
SIC: 3732 7699 Boat building & repairing; boat repair

(G-10520)
BLACKROCKS BREWERY LLC
950 W Washington St (49855-4019)
PHONE..................................906 273-1333
EMP: 6 **Privately Held**
SIC: 2082 5813 Beer (alcoholic beverage); bars & lounges
PA: Blackrocks Brewery, Llc
424 N 3rd St
Marquette MI 49855

(G-10521)
BLACKROCKS BREWERY LLC (PA)
424 N 3rd St (49855-3555)
PHONE..................................906 273-1333
David Manson,
EMP: 6
SQ FT: 2,000
SALES: 875K **Privately Held**
SIC: 5813 2082 Bars & lounges; beer (alcoholic beverage)

(G-10522)
CHICAGO BLOW PIPE COMPANY
405 Lakewood Ln (49855-9510)
PHONE..................................773 533-6100
EMP: 16 EST: 1919
SQ FT: 30,000
SALES (est): 3.9MM **Privately Held**
SIC: 3444 3714 3564 3443 Mfg Sheet Metalwork Mfg Motor Vehicle Parts Mfg Blowers/Fans Mfg Fabricated Plate Wrk Structural Metal Fabrctn

(G-10523)
CLAIR SAWYER
Also Called: Marquette Machining & Fabg
1225 W Washington St (49855-3111)
PHONE..................................906 228-8242
Clair Sawyer, *Owner*
EMP: 7
SQ FT: 5,000
SALES (est): 640.4K **Privately Held**
SIC: 3599 7692 3441 Machine shop, jobbing & repair; welding repair; fabricated structural metal

(G-10524)
COMPANY B GRAPHIC DESIGN INC
1200 Wright St Ste 4 (49855-1837)
PHONE..................................906 228-5887
Gretta Berg, *President*
EMP: 3
SALES (est): 170K **Privately Held**
SIC: 3993 Signs & advertising specialties

(G-10525)
COMPUDYNE INC
925 W Washington St # 104 (49855-4061)
PHONE..................................906 360-9081
Thomas F Vidovic, *Branch Mgr*
EMP: 14
SALES (corp-wide): 7.8MM **Privately Held**
SIC: 3571 Personal computers (microcomputers)
PA: Compudyne, Inc.
1524 E 37th St
Hibbing MN 55746
218 263-3624

(G-10526)
DONCKERS CANDIES & GIFTS
137 W Washington St (49855-4319)
PHONE..................................906 226-6110
Tom Vear, *Owner*
Fred Donckers, *Owner*
EMP: 3
SALES (est): 222.1K **Privately Held**
SIC: 5441 5947 2064 Candy; gift shop; candy & other confectionery products

(G-10527)
DUQUAINE INCORPORATED
Also Called: Honeywell Authorized Dealer
1744 Presque Isle Ave (49855-2197)
PHONE..................................906 228-7290
Mark Duquaine, *President*
Karen Duquaine, *Admin Sec*
EMP: 9
SQ FT: 5,800

Marquette - Marquette County (G-10528)

GEOGRAPHIC SECTION

SALES (est): 1.7MM **Privately Held**
SIC: **1711** 3469 Refrigeration contractor; warm air heating & air conditioning contractor; kitchen fixtures & equipment: metal, except cast aluminum

(G-10528)
EASTSIDE SPOT INC
129 E Hewitt Ave (49855-3707)
PHONE..................906 226-9431
Rich Pascoe, *President*
EMP: 6
SALES (est): 488.6K **Privately Held**
SIC: **2082** Beer (alcoholic beverage)

(G-10529)
EMBROIDERY WEARHOUSE
2112 Us Highway 41 W # 3 (49855-2480)
PHONE..................906 228-5818
Barbara Oneiol, *Owner*
EMP: 4
SALES (est): 214.7K **Privately Held**
SIC: **2395** Embroidery products, except schiffli machine; embroidery & art needlework

(G-10530)
ETNA DISTRIBUTORS LLC
1922 Enterprise St (49855-1819)
PHONE..................906 273-2331
Perry Wooden, *Branch Mgr*
EMP: 3
SALES (corp-wide): 184.2MM **Privately Held**
SIC: **5251** 5074 3432 Pumps & pumping equipment; plumbing fittings & supplies; plumbing fixture fittings & trim
PA: Etna Distributors, Llc
4901 Clay Ave Sw
Grand Rapids MI 49548
616 245-4373

(G-10531)
F & A ENTERPRISES OF MICHIGAN
Also Called: Fred's Rubber Stamp Shop
519 N Lakeshore Blvd (49855-3819)
PHONE..................906 228-3222
Frederick M Warren, *President*
Audrey Warren, *Vice Pres*
EMP: 4 EST: 1977
SQ FT: 2,500
SALES (est): 480.1K **Privately Held**
SIC: **3953** 2759 7389 2796 Marking devices; commercial printing; laminating service; platemaking services

(G-10532)
FRACO
200 Cherry Creek Rd (49855-8909)
PHONE..................906 249-1476
Peter W Frazier, *President*
Lincoln B Frazier Jr, *Vice Pres*
Peggy A Frazier, *Treasurer*
Mike Cousineau, *Sales Executive*
Terry Bengry, *Executive*
EMP: 10
SQ FT: 40,000
SALES (est): 1.1MM **Privately Held**
WEB: www.fracoinc.com
SIC: **3271** 3273 Blocks, concrete or cinder: standard; ready-mixed concrete

(G-10533)
FRONTIER RNWABLE RESOURCES LLC (PA)
210 N Front St Ste 1 (49855-4200)
PHONE..................906 228-7960
William J Brady, *CEO*
Stephen Hicks, *CFO*
Karen D Anderson, *Admin Mgr*
Bruce Jamerson,
EMP: 5
SALES (est): 479K **Privately Held**
SIC: **2869** Fuels

(G-10534)
HEIDTMAN LOGGING INC
748 County Road 550 (49855)
PHONE..................906 249-3914
John L Heidtman, *President*
John B Heidtman, *Director*
Gary A Heidtman, *Admin Sec*
EMP: 7
SALES (est): 800K **Privately Held**
SIC: **2411** Logging camps & contractors

(G-10535)
J M LONGYEAR HEIRS INC (PA)
210 N Front St Ste 1 (49855-4200)
PHONE..................906 228-7960
Ralph M Roberts,
Rusell Bennett,
Charlotte Burton,
Catherine Springer,
EMP: 5
SQ FT: 18,000
SALES (est): 1.7MM **Privately Held**
SIC: **6519** 1499 Real property lessors; precious stones mining

(G-10536)
JANDRON II
605 Couty Rd Hq (49855)
PHONE..................906 225-9600
Neil Jandron, *Owner*
Kathie Jandron, *Co-Owner*
EMP: 9
SALES (est): 726.6K **Privately Held**
SIC: **3479** Engraving jewelry silverware, or metal

(G-10537)
JG DISTRIBUTING INC
120 Morgan Meadows Rd (49855-8683)
PHONE..................906 225-0882
John Manchester, *CEO*
EMP: 5
SALES (est): 574.6K **Privately Held**
SIC: **3531** Snow plow attachments

(G-10538)
LAKE SUPERIOR PRESS INC
802 S Lake St (49855-5224)
P.O. Box 308 (49855-0308)
PHONE..................906 228-7450
Thomas E Dubow, *President*
EMP: 10
SQ FT: 5,000
SALES (est): 1.5MM **Privately Held**
SIC: **2752** Commercial printing, offset

(G-10539)
LANDERS DRAFTING INC
Also Called: Sign Solutions
105 Garfield Ave (49855-4013)
PHONE..................906 228-8690
Dan Landers, *President*
Matt Landers, *Executive*
EMP: 5 EST: 1936
SQ FT: 2,000
SALES (est): 945.2K **Privately Held**
WEB: www.cooksign.com
SIC: **7389** 3993 Sign painting & lettering shop; electric signs

(G-10540)
LEVI OHMAN MICAH
Also Called: Marquette Maple Company
320 W College Ave Apt 1 (49855-3055)
PHONE..................612 251-1293
Micah Ohman, *Owner*
EMP: 3 EST: 2014
SALES (est): 76.6K **Privately Held**
SIC: **2099** Maple syrup

(G-10541)
MACKINAW POWER LLC
102 W Washington St # 222 (49855-4368)
PHONE..................906 264-5025
Ricahrd Vander Veen III,
EMP: 3
SALES (est): 311.4K **Privately Held**
SIC: **3621** Windmills, electric generating

(G-10542)
MAQUET MONTHLY
810 N 3rd St (49855-3502)
PHONE..................906 226-6500
Patricia Ryan Oday, *President*
EMP: 5
SALES (est): 252.3K **Privately Held**
WEB: www.mmnow.com
SIC: **7313** 2711 Newspaper advertising representative; newspapers

(G-10543)
MARQUETTE DISTILLERY
844 W Bluff St (49855-4122)
PHONE..................906 869-4933
Chris Gale, *Principal*
EMP: 3

SALES (est): 83K **Privately Held**
SIC: **2082** Malt beverages

(G-10544)
MARQUETTE FENCE COMPANY INC
1446 State Highway M28 E (49855-9562)
PHONE..................906 249-8000
Robert L Northrup, *President*
EMP: 5
SQ FT: 4,000
SALES: 1.5MM **Privately Held**
SIC: **1799** 3446 Fence construction; fences, gates, posts & flagpoles

(G-10545)
MARQUETTE MEATS IN CITY LLC
3060 Us Highway 41 W (49855-2293)
PHONE..................906 226-8333
Susan Korton, *Mng Member*
Dan Meadows, *Mng Member*
EMP: 3 EST: 2008
SQ FT: 2,000
SALES: 400K **Privately Held**
SIC: **5421** 2013 Meat markets, including freezer provisioners; snack sticks, including jerky: from purchased meat

(G-10546)
MINING JRNL BSNESS OFFC-DTRIAL
249 W Washington St (49855-4387)
P.O. Box 430 (49855-0430)
PHONE..................906 228-2500
Fax: 906 228-2617
EMP: 20
SALES (est): 1.4MM **Privately Held**
SIC: **2711** Newspapers-Publishing/Printing

(G-10547)
NORTH WIND STUDENT NEWSPAPER
2310 University Ctr (49855)
PHONE..................906 227-2545
Christine Mosier, *Chief*
EMP: 35
SALES (est): 984K **Privately Held**
WEB: www.thenorthwind.org
SIC: **2711** Newspapers, publishing & printing

(G-10548)
OGDEN NEWSPAPERS INC
Also Called: Mining Journal
249 W Washington St (49855-4321)
PHONE..................906 228-2500
Tom Grady, *Warehouse Mgr*
Emily Xu, *Accounting Mgr*
Larry Doyle, *Adv Dir*
Jim Reevs, *Branch Mgr*
Jason Briggs, *Branch Mgr*
EMP: 98 **Privately Held**
WEB: www.miningjournal.net
SIC: **2711** Commercial printing & newspaper publishing combined; newspapers: publishing only, not printed on site
HQ: The Ogden Newspapers Inc
1500 Main St
Wheeling WV 26003
304 233-0100

(G-10549)
OGDEN NEWSPAPERS VIRGINIA LLC
Also Called: Action Shopper
249 W Washington St (49855-4321)
P.O. Box 610 (49855-0610)
PHONE..................906 228-8920
Richard Havican, *Manager*
EMP: 9 **Privately Held**
SIC: **2711** Newspapers, publishing & printing
HQ: Ogden Newspapers Of Virginia, Llc
1500 Main St
Wheeling WV 26003
304 233-0100

(G-10550)
ORE DOCK BREWING COMPANY LLC
14 Spring St (49855)
PHONE..................906 228-8888
Weston Pernsteiner,

EMP: 9
SALES (est): 882.1K **Privately Held**
SIC: **2082** Brewers' grain

(G-10551)
PARK MOLDED SPECIALTIES INC
150 Huron Woods Dr (49855-9699)
PHONE..................906 225-0385
Thomas Chiodini, *President*
Thomas A Chiodini, *President*
Stephen P Chiodini, *Corp Secy*
Michael Chiodini, *Vice Pres*
EMP: 7 EST: 1948
SQ FT: 14,000
SALES: 900K **Privately Held**
SIC: **3089** Injection molding of plastics

(G-10552)
PIONEER SURGICAL TECH INC (HQ)
Also Called: Rti Surgical
375 River Park Cir (49855-1781)
PHONE..................906 226-9909
Jeffery W Millin, *President*
M Shane Ray, *General Mgr*
Fred J Taccolini, *Principal*
Eric Baldwin, *COO*
Jim St John, *Vice Pres*
EMP: 170
SQ FT: 28,000
SALES (est): 40.4MM
SALES (corp-wide): 280.8MM **Publicly Held**
SIC: **3841** Surgical & medical instruments
PA: Rti Surgical, Inc.
11621 Research Cir
Alachua FL 32615
386 418-8888

(G-10553)
PLASMA BIOLIFE SERVICES L P
175 Hawley St (49855-1788)
PHONE..................906 226-9080
Marcia Hodges, *Manager*
Trudy Vlahos, *Manager*
EMP: 40
SALES (corp-wide): 15.1B **Privately Held**
SIC: **2835** Blood derivative diagnostic agents
HQ: Biolife Plasma Services L.P.
1200 Lakeside Dr
Bannockburn IL

(G-10554)
PRIDE PRINTING INC
2847 Us Highway 41 W (49855-2252)
PHONE..................906 228-8182
Richard Wester, *President*
EMP: 6
SQ FT: 3,200
SALES: 425K **Privately Held**
WEB: www.prideprintingonline.com
SIC: **2752** 5199 Commercial printing, offset; advertising specialties

(G-10555)
QUICKTROPHY LLC
446 E Crescent St (49855-3621)
PHONE..................906 228-2604
Terrence Dehring, *Mng Member*
Janet Wells, *Manager*
▼ EMP: 15
SQ FT: 14,000
SALES: 1.7MM **Privately Held**
WEB: www.quicktrophy.com
SIC: **3914** 3993 5999 Trophies; signs & advertising specialties; trophies & plaques

(G-10556)
SCREENED IMAGE GRAPHIC DESIGN
Also Called: Hayes, Lorrie
149 W Washington St (49855-4319)
PHONE..................906 226-6112
Lorrie Hayes, *Owner*
EMP: 3
SALES: 110K **Privately Held**
WEB: www.thescreenedimage.com
SIC: **2759** Screen printing

(G-10557)
SIGNS UNLIMITED
1401 S Front St (49855-5142)
PHONE..................906 226-7446

Doug Sladek, *Owner*
Greg Steltenpohl, *Manager*
EMP: 3
SALES (est): 221.8K **Privately Held**
SIC: 3993 Signs, not made in custom sign painting shops

(G-10558)
SUPERIOR ELC MTR SLS & SVC INC
Also Called: Superior Elc Mtr Sls & Svc
1740 Presque Isle Ave (49855-2196)
PHONE..................................906 226-9051
Franklin Michael Smith, *President*
Kevin Nylund, *Sales Mgr*
EMP: 7
SQ FT: 4,940
SALES (est): 1.6MM **Privately Held**
WEB: www.superiorelectriccompany.com
SIC: 7694 5063 Electric motor repair; rewinding stators; motors, electric

(G-10559)
SUPERIOR HOCKEY LLC (PA)
401 E Fair Ave (49855-2951)
PHONE..................................906 225-9008
EMP: 7
SALES (est): 1MM **Privately Held**
SIC: 3949 Hockey equipment & supplies, general

(G-10560)
UP CATHOLIC NEWSPAPER
347 Rock St (49855-4725)
P.O. Box 1000 (49855-1000)
PHONE..................................906 226-8821
Fax: 906 226-6941
EMP: 5 EST: 1946
SALES (est): 170K **Privately Held**
SIC: 2711 Newspapers-Publishing/Printing

(G-10561)
WATTSSON & WATTSSON JEWELERS
Also Called: Dockside Imports
118 W Washington St # 100 (49855-4353)
PHONE..................................906 228-5775
Ron Wattsson, *CEO*
Linda Wilson, *Vice Pres*
EMP: 12
SQ FT: 18,000
SALES (est): 1MM **Privately Held**
SIC: 5944 3911 7631 Jewelry, precious stones & precious metals; jewelry apparel; jewelry repair services

Marshall
Calhoun County

(G-10562)
AUTOCAM CORPORATION
1511 George Brown Dr (49068-9596)
PHONE..................................269 789-4000
Brian Simon, *Plant Mgr*
Jeff Goodman, *Manager*
EMP: 78
SALES (corp-wide): 770.6MM **Publicly Held**
SIC: 3714 Motor vehicle engines & parts
HQ: Autocam Corporation
  4180 40th St Se
  Kentwood MI 49512
  616 698-0707

(G-10563)
BORGWARNER THERMAL SYSTEMS INC (HQ)
Also Called: Borgwarner Automotive
1507 S Kalamazoo Ave (49068-8310)
PHONE..................................269 781-1228
James R Verrier, *CEO*
Timothy M Manganello, *Chairman*
Robin J Adams, *Exec VP*
Jamal M Farhat, *Vice Pres*
Anthony D Hensel, *Vice Pres*
▲ **EMP:** 105
SALES (est): 196.7MM
SALES (corp-wide): 10.5B **Publicly Held**
SIC: 3714 Motor vehicle parts & accessories

PA: Borgwarner Inc.
  3850 Hamlin Rd
  Auburn Hills MI 48326
  248 754-9200

(G-10564)
CHELSEA MILLING COMPANY
C & S Carton Division
310 W Oliver Dr (49068-9506)
P.O. Box 70 (49068-0070)
PHONE..................................269 781-2823
Donald Stephan, *Manager*
EMP: 16
SALES (corp-wide): 86.6MM **Privately Held**
WEB: www.jiffymix.com
SIC: 2652 5113 Boxes, newsboard, metal edged: made from purchased materials; bags, paper & disposable plastic
PA: Chelsea Milling Company
  201 W North St
  Chelsea MI 48118
  734 475-1361

(G-10565)
CRYSTAL FLASH INC
1021 E Michigan Ave (49068-9301)
PHONE..................................269 781-8221
Rick Gillette, *Manager*
EMP: 7 **Privately Held**
SIC: 1381 Drilling oil & gas wells
PA: Crystal Flash, Inc.
  1754 Alpine Ave Nw
  Grand Rapids MI 49504

(G-10566)
EATON CORPORATION
19218 B Dr S (49068-8600)
PHONE..................................269 781-0200
Jeff Romig, *Vice Pres*
Stacey Drumm, *Buyer*
Timothy Waxler, *Buyer*
David Berlinger, *QC Mgr*
Randy Graves, *Chief Engr*
EMP: 300 **Privately Held**
WEB: www.eaton.com
SIC: 3724 8734 Research & development on aircraft engines & parts; testing laboratories
HQ: Eaton Corporation
  1000 Eaton Blvd
  Cleveland OH 44122
  440 523-5000

(G-10567)
FABRILASER MFG LLC
1308 S Kalamazoo Ave (49068-1971)
PHONE..................................269 789-9490
Joey Morales, *Manager*
Gregory Harris,
EMP: 20
SALES (est): 4MM **Privately Held**
SIC: 3699 3443 3444 5084 Laser systems & equipment; metal parts; forming machine work, sheet metal; welding machinery & equipment; metal cutting services

(G-10568)
FUG INC
315 Woolley Dr (49068-9500)
P.O. Box 305, Tekonsha (49092-0305)
PHONE..................................269 781-8036
Donald Kujawa, *President*
EMP: 8
SALES (est): 790K **Privately Held**
SIC: 3993 2759 Signs & advertising specialties; screen printing

(G-10569)
GREAT LAKES METAL WORKS
819 Industrial Rd (49068-1744)
PHONE..................................269 789-2342
Myron Katz, *President*
William Howard, *Vice Pres*
EMP: 5
SALES (est): 562.7K **Privately Held**
SIC: 3441 Fabricated structural metal

(G-10570)
GRONDIN PRINTING AND AWARDS
Also Called: Grondin & Associates
13492 W Michigan Ave (49068-8505)
P.O. Box 754 (49068-0754)
PHONE..................................269 781-5447

Everett F Grondin, *Owner*
EMP: 3
SALES (est): 164.1K **Privately Held**
SIC: 2752 Commercial printing, offset

(G-10571)
HARVEY RICHARD JOHN
Also Called: Oak Frost Kennel
19611 16 Mile Rd (49068-9467)
PHONE..................................269 781-5801
Richard J Harvey, *Owner*
EMP: 3
SALES (est): 174.6K **Privately Held**
SIC: 2047 0752 Dog food; boarding services, kennels

(G-10572)
J & L MANUFACTURING CO INC (PA)
1507 George Brown Dr (49068-9596)
P.O. Box 189 (49068-0189)
PHONE..................................269 789-1507
Jim Dominique, *President*
▲ **EMP:** 35
SQ FT: 1,000
SALES: 5MM **Privately Held**
WEB: www.jlmanufacturing.com
SIC: 3498 Tube fabricating (contract bending & shaping)

(G-10573)
J-AD GRAPHICS INC
Community Ad-Visor
514 S Kalamazoo Ave (49068-1719)
P.O. Box 111 (49068-0111)
PHONE..................................269 945-9554
John Jacobs, *President*
EMP: 8
SQ FT: 1,000
SALES (corp-wide): 15.3MM **Privately Held**
WEB: www.j-adgraphics.com
SIC: 2741 2711 Guides: publishing & printing; commercial printing & newspaper publishing combined
PA: J-Ad Graphics, Inc.
  1351 N M 43 Hwy
  Hastings MI 49058
  800 870-7085

(G-10574)
MANUFACTURED HOMES INC
Also Called: Permabilt Homes
330 S Kalamazoo Ave (49068-1715)
P.O. Box 269 (49068-0269)
PHONE..................................269 781-2887
John Monk, *President*
Thomas Legg, *Corp Secy*
Bob Hayes, *Vice Pres*
EMP: 35 EST: 1952
SALES (est): 3.2MM **Privately Held**
WEB: www.manufacturedhomes.com
SIC: 2452 Prefabricated buildings, wood

(G-10575)
MARSHALL BLDG COMPONENTS CORP
1605 Brooks Dr (49068-9587)
P.O. Box 724 (49068-0724)
PHONE..................................269 781-4236
Leigh Iobe, *President*
EMP: 12
SQ FT: 13,000
SALES (est): 2MM **Privately Held**
WEB: www.marbc.com
SIC: 2439 Trusses, except roof: laminated lumber; trusses, wooden roof

(G-10576)
MARSHALL EXCELSIOR CO
1508 George Brown Dr (49068-9596)
PHONE..................................269 789-6700
EMP: 3
SALES (corp-wide): 1.4B **Privately Held**
SIC: 3433 Heating equipment, except electric
HQ: Marshall Excelsior Co.
  1506 George Brown Dr
  Marshall MI 49068
  269 789-6700

(G-10577)
MARSHALL EXCELSIOR CO (HQ)
1506 George Brown Dr (49068-9596)
PHONE..................................269 789-6700
Jeff Begg, *President*
Allen Begg, *Admin Sec*
◆ **EMP:** 50
SQ FT: 25,000
SALES (est): 8.5MM
SALES (corp-wide): 1.4B **Privately Held**
SIC: 3433 3599 3498 3494 Heating equipment, except electric; machine shop, jobbing & repair; fabricated pipe & fittings; valves & pipe fittings; gaskets, packing & sealing devices
PA: Harbour Group Ltd.
  7733 Forsyth Blvd Fl 23
  Saint Louis MO 63105
  314 727-5550

(G-10578)
MARSHALL GAS CONTROLS INC
450 Leggitt Rd (49068-9555)
PHONE..................................269 781-3901
Don C Leggitt Sr, *Ch of Bd*
Don C Leggitt Jr, *President*
Jean T Clearman, *Corp Secy*
Dorothy Mc Redmond, *Asst Treas*
Donald J Brewer, *Asst Sec*
EMP: 5
SQ FT: 75,000
SALES (est): 419.3K
SALES (corp-wide): 53.6MM **Privately Held**
WEB: www.marshallgascontrols.com
SIC: 3491 Automatic regulating & control valves
PA: S. H. Leggitt Company
  1000 Civic Center Loop
  San Marcos TX 78666
  956 504-6440

(G-10579)
MARSHALL METAL PRODUCTS INC
1006 E Michigan Ave (49068-9301)
PHONE..................................269 781-3924
Dan Stulberg, *President*
Ron Holcomb, *Manager*
EMP: 6
SQ FT: 14,000
SALES: 800K **Privately Held**
WEB: www.marshallmetalproducts.com
SIC: 3469 Stamping metal for the trade

(G-10580)
MARSHALL WELDING & FABRICATION
817 Industrial Rd (49068-1744)
PHONE..................................269 781-4010
Nick Heemsoth, *Owner*
EMP: 3
SALES (est): 293.1K **Privately Held**
SIC: 7692 1799 Welding repair; welding on site

(G-10581)
MAVERICK MACHINE TOOL
101 E Oliver Dr (49068-9505)
P.O. Box 647 (49068-0647)
PHONE..................................269 789-1617
Wanda Martin, *Partner*
Jim Dominique, *Partner*
Neil Martin, *Partner*
EMP: 20
SQ FT: 12,000
SALES (est): 2.6MM **Privately Held**
SIC: 3599 Machine shop, jobbing & repair

(G-10582)
MCELROY METAL MILL INC
311 Oliver Dr (49068-9574)
P.O. Box 527 (49068-0527)
PHONE..................................269 781-8313
Mark Brotherton, *Branch Mgr*
EMP: 40
SALES (corp-wide): 373.4MM **Privately Held**
WEB: www.mcelroymetal.com
SIC: 3448 3444 2952 Prefabricated metal buildings; sheet metalwork; asphalt felts & coatings

Marshall - Calhoun County (G-10583)

PA: Mcelroy Metal Mill, Inc.
1500 Hamilton Rd
Bossier City LA 71111
318 747-8000

(G-10583)
MICHIGAN RIFLE AND PISTOL ASSN
Also Called: Mrpa
215 N Linden St (49068-1402)
P.O. Box 71 (49068-0071)
PHONE..................................269 781-1223
Leo I Cebula, *President*
EMP: 3
SALES: 39K **Privately Held**
WEB: www.michrpa.com
SIC: 8699 3482 Amateur sports promotion; pellets & BB's, pistol & air rifle ammunition

(G-10584)
MOR-DALL ENTERPRISES INC
Also Called: Darkhorse Brewing Company, The
511 S Kalamazoo Ave (49068-1718)
PHONE..................................269 558-4915
Erin Moore, *President*
Jim Anderson, *Shareholder*
▲ **EMP:** 6
SQ FT: 2,100
SALES (est): 1MM **Privately Held**
SIC: 2082 Beer (alcoholic beverage)

(G-10585)
PROGRESSIVE DYNAMICS INC
507 Industrial Rd (49068-1750)
PHONE..................................269 781-4241
Ralph McGee, *President*
Delores Schoenborn, *General Mgr*
Tom Phlipo, *Exec VP*
Mike Walters, *Vice Pres*
Randy Rial, *VP Opers*
▲ **EMP:** 90 **EST:** 1964
SQ FT: 157,000
SALES: 19MM **Privately Held**
WEB: www.progressivedyn.com
SIC: 3679 3647 3841 Static power supply converters for electronic applications; vehicular lighting equipment; surgical & medical instruments

(G-10586)
QUALITY ENGRAVING SERVICE
221 W Michigan Ave (49068-1523)
PHONE..................................269 781-4822
James Stadtfeld, *President*
Thomas Brownell, *Owner*
Paula Gwin, *Corp Secy*
EMP: 5
SALES (est): 385.7K **Privately Held**
SIC: 2759 5999 Engraving; trophies & plaques

(G-10587)
QUALTEK INC
1611 Brooks Dr (49068-9587)
P.O. Box 224 (49068-0224)
PHONE..................................269 781-2835
Margaret Milhoan, *President*
Michael Hayes, *Treasurer*
Fred L Hayes, *Admin Sec*
EMP: 7 **EST:** 1966
SQ FT: 8,500
SALES (est): 470K **Privately Held**
SIC: 3451 Screw machine products

(G-10588)
SH LEGGITT COMPANY
Also Called: Marshall Brass Co
450 Leggitt Rd (49068-9555)
PHONE..................................269 781-3901
Don C Leggitt Sr, *Branch Mgr*
EMP: 170
SALES (corp-wide): 53.6MM **Privately Held**
WEB: www.shleggitt.com
SIC: 3451 3714 3612 3494 Screw machine products; motor vehicle parts & accessories; transformers, except electric; valves & pipe fittings; industrial valves; plumbing fixture fittings & trim
PA: S. H. Leggitt Company
1000 Civic Center Loop
San Marcos TX 78666
956 504-6440

(G-10589)
SPRAY METAL MOLD TECHNOLOGY
200 Woolley Dr (49068-9588)
PHONE..................................269 781-7151
Mark Warner, *President*
EMP: 5
SQ FT: 2,000
SALES (est): 647.7K **Privately Held**
WEB: www.metal-molds.com
SIC: 3544 Industrial molds

(G-10590)
TENNECO AUTOMOTIVE OPER CO INC
904 Industrial Rd (49068-1741)
PHONE..................................269 781-1350
Randy Rial, *Manager*
EMP: 204
SALES (corp-wide): 11.7B **Publicly Held**
WEB: www.tenneco-automotive.com
SIC: 3714 Mufflers (exhaust), motor vehicle
HQ: Tenneco Automotive Operating Company, Inc.
500 N Field Dr
Lake Forest IL 60045
847 482-5000

(G-10591)
TRIBAL MANUFACTURING INC (PA)
450 Leggitt Rd (49068-9555)
PHONE..................................269 781-3901
Joseph N Ismert, *CEO*
Skip Nelson, *Plant Mgr*
Abby Roberts, *Purch Agent*
Tim Rowley, *Engineer*
Dominic Ismert, *CFO*
▲ **EMP:** 43
SALES (est): 12.7MM **Privately Held**
SIC: 3494 3451 3599 Valves & pipe fittings; screw machine products; machine shop, jobbing & repair

(G-10592)
W L HAMILTON & CO
325 Cherry St (49068-1489)
P.O. Box 766 (49068-0766)
PHONE..................................269 781-6941
Jeffery A Begg, *President*
▲ **EMP:** 10 **EST:** 1961
SALES (est): 2MM **Privately Held**
WEB: www.wlhamiltonco.com
SIC: 3494 Sprinkler systems, field

(G-10593)
W S TOWNSEND COMPANY (PA)
Also Called: Michigan Kitchen Distributors
106 E Oliver Dr (49068-9505)
PHONE..................................269 781-5131
Jack W Townsend, *CEO*
Steve Townsend, *President*
Gregory L Nyenhuis, *Corp Secy*
Jacquelynn Tucker, *CFO*
Mike Ostafin, *Manager*
EMP: 120
SQ FT: 54,000
SALES (est): 24.4MM **Privately Held**
WEB: www.thekitchenshops.com
SIC: 1799 5031 1751 2434 Closet organizers, installation & design; millwork; carpentry work; wood kitchen cabinets; wood partitions & fixtures

Martin
Allegan County

(G-10594)
ASH INDUSTRIES INC
362 116th Ave (49070-8702)
P.O. Box 147 (49070-0147)
PHONE..................................269 672-9630
Gordon Ash, *President*
Margaret Smith, *Principal*
Mary Jo Ash, *Corp Secy*
EMP: 12
SALES (est): 1.9MM **Privately Held**
SIC: 3519 Parts & accessories, internal combustion engines

(G-10595)
CAM FAB
643 112th Ave (49070-9752)
PHONE..................................269 685-1000
George A Campbell, *Owner*
EMP: 3
SQ FT: 18,000
SALES (est): 180K **Privately Held**
SIC: 3443 3441 Fabricated plate work (boiler shop); fabricated structural metal

(G-10596)
MPF ACQUISITIONS INC
Also Called: Marshall Plastic Film
904 E Allegan St (49070-9797)
P.O. Box 125 (49070-0125)
PHONE..................................269 672-5511
John Roggow, *President*
Ann Jameson, *CFO*
Heidi Hildebrand, *Human Res Mgr*
▲ **EMP:** 49
SQ FT: 40,000
SALES (est): 16.6MM
SALES (corp-wide): 339.4MM **Privately Held**
WEB: www.marshallplastic.com
SIC: 3081 Plastic film & sheet
PA: Transcendia, Inc.
9201 Belmont Ave
Franklin Park IL 60131
847 678-1800

(G-10597)
SEYMOUR DEHAAN
Also Called: Independent Water Service
1613 10th St (49070-8710)
P.O. Box 207 (49070-0207)
PHONE..................................269 672-7377
Seymore Dehaan, *Owner*
EMP: 3
SQ FT: 2,000
SALES (est): 244.4K **Privately Held**
SIC: 3589 5149 Water treatment equipment, industrial; water, distilled

Marysville
St. Clair County

(G-10598)
AMERICAN METAL RESTORATION
Also Called: Wilkie Brothers
1765 Michigan Ave Ste 2 (48040-2046)
P.O. Box 219 (48040-0219)
PHONE..................................810 364-4820
Robert B Wilkie, *President*
Paul Naz, *Vice Pres*
Donald Wilkie, *Vice Pres*
◆ **EMP:** 6
SQ FT: 3,000
SALES: 1MM **Privately Held**
SIC: 7349 3471 Cleaning service, industrial or commercial; plating & polishing

(G-10599)
BLUE WATER MANUFACTURING INC
1765 Michigan Ave (48040-2046)
P.O. Box 219 (48040-0219)
PHONE..................................810 364-6170
Paul Naz, *President*
▲ **EMP:** 11
SQ FT: 20,000
SALES (est): 5.1MM **Privately Held**
WEB: www.bluewatermanufacturing.com
SIC: 3535 Conveyors & conveying equipment

(G-10600)
CAMPBELL & SHAW STEEL INC
1705 Michigan Ave (48040-1805)
PHONE..................................810 364-5100
Karen Lietke, *President*
Mark Lietke, *Vice Pres*
Jake Paull, *Project Mgr*
Karen Shaw, *Admin Sec*
EMP: 14 **EST:** 2011
SALES (est): 5.2MM **Privately Held**
WEB: www.campbellshawsteel.com
SIC: 5051 1791 3441 3449 Steel; structural steel erection; fabricated structural metal; miscellaneous metalwork; fire- or burglary-resistive products

(G-10601)
CONFORMANCE COATINGS PROTOTYPE
2321 Busha Hwy (48040-1946)
PHONE..................................810 364-4333
Allan Fahner, *President*
Bruce Douglass, *Corp Secy*
Robert Marchione, *Vice Pres*
EMP: 37
SQ FT: 12,700
SALES (est): 1.2MM **Privately Held**
SIC: 3479 Painting, coating & hot dipping

(G-10602)
DARRELL R HANSON
579 Michigan Ave (48040-1111)
PHONE..................................810 364-7892
Darrell Hanson, *President*
EMP: 3
SALES (est): 292.5K **Privately Held**
SIC: 3599 Industrial machinery

(G-10603)
HEARTLAND STEEL PRODUCTS LLC
Also Called: Spacerak
2420 Wills St (48040-1978)
PHONE..................................810 364-7421
Pat Peplowski, *CEO*
Wesley Boyne, *Mfg Mgr*
Darryl Strongheart, *Mfg Mgr*
Rich Eastman, *Engineer*
Dan Wendell, *Design Engr*
EMP: 50
SALES (est): 12.9MM **Privately Held**
SIC: 3291 Abrasive metal & steel products

(G-10604)
INTERTAPE POLYMER CORP
317 Kendall St (48040-1911)
PHONE..................................810 364-9000
Thomas Wendt, *Principal*
Brian Ciesielski, *Engineer*
Kim Peens, *Manager*
Kristi Humphrey, *Graphic Designe*
EMP: 120
SALES (corp-wide): 1B **Privately Held**
WEB: www.unitedtape.com
SIC: 2672 Tape, pressure sensitive: made from purchased materials; adhesive backed films, foams & foils
HQ: Intertape Polymer Corp.
100 Paramount Dr Ste 300
Sarasota FL 34232
888 898-7834

(G-10605)
JONES & HOLLANDS INC
Also Called: Jones Equipment Rental
1777 Busha Hwy (48040-1815)
PHONE..................................810 364-6400
Derek Fleury, *Manager*
EMP: 5 **Privately Held**
SIC: 7353 3546 7359 5083 Heavy construction equipment rental; saws & sawing equipment; equipment rental & leasing; farm & garden machinery
PA: Jones & Hollands, Inc.
4600 24th Ave
Fort Gratiot MI 48059

(G-10606)
MARYSVILLE HYDROCARBONS LLC (DH)
2510 Busha Hwy (48040-1904)
PHONE..................................586 445-2300
Rai Bhargava, *President*
EMP: 35
SQ FT: 3,000
SALES (est): 4.3MM
SALES (corp-wide): 9.8B **Publicly Held**
WEB: www.dartenergy.com
SIC: 2911 Fractionation products of crude petroleum, hydrocarbons

(G-10607)
METER USA LLC
1765 Michigan Ave (48040-2046)
PHONE..................................810 388-9373
▲ **EMP:** 15
SALES (est): 1MM **Privately Held**
SIC: 3499 Mfg Misc Fabricated Metal Products

GEOGRAPHIC SECTION

Mason - Ingham County (G-10631)

(G-10608)
MUELLER IMPACTS COMPANY INC
2409 Wills St (48040-1979)
PHONE.................................810 364-3700
James H Rourke, *President*
▼ **EMP:** 125
SQ FT: 140,000
SALES (est): 26.1MM
SALES (corp-wide): 2.5B **Publicly Held**
WEB: www.muellerbrass.com
SIC: 3469 3354 3463 Metal stampings; aluminum extruded products; nonferrous forgings
HQ: Mueller Brass Co.
8285 Tournament Dr # 150
Memphis TN 38125
901 753-3200

(G-10609)
ONTARIO DIE COMPANY AMERICA (HQ)
1755 Busha Hwy (48040-1815)
PHONE.................................810 987-5060
Gary Levene, *President*
▲ **EMP:** 60 **EST:** 1974
SALES (est): 14.6MM
SALES (corp-wide): 1.6MM **Privately Held**
WEB: www.ontariodie.com
SIC: 3544 3423 Special dies & tools; knives, agricultural or industrial
PA: Ontario Die International Inc
235 Gage Ave
Kitchener ON N2M 2
519 745-1002

(G-10610)
PAUMAC TUBING LLC (PA)
315 Cuttle Rd (48040-1804)
PHONE.................................810 985-9400
Kevin Bronson, *Purchasing*
Kelly Russell, *Purchasing*
Sue Miller, *Human Res Mgr*
Norman McDonald, *Mng Member*
Alexandra Houston, *Administration*
EMP: 90
SQ FT: 65
SALES (est): 17.7MM **Privately Held**
SIC: 3498 Tube fabricating (contract bending & shaping)

(G-10611)
PREGIS LLC
2700 Wills St (48040-2459)
PHONE.................................810 320-3005
EMP: 67
SALES (corp-wide): 4.7B **Privately Held**
SIC: 3086 Plastics foam products
HQ: Pregis Llc
1650 Lake Cook Rd Ste 400
Deerfield IL 60015
847 597-2200

(G-10612)
PUNCH TECH
2701 Busha Hwy (48040-1905)
PHONE.................................810 364-4811
EMP: 33
SQ FT: 14,400
SALES (est): 2.1MM **Privately Held**
SIC: 3541 3965 3544 Mfg Machine Tools-Cutting Mfg Fasteners/Buttons/Pins Mfg Dies/Tools/Jigs/Fixtures

(G-10613)
SCHEFENALKER VISION SYSTEMS
1855 Busha Hwy (48040-1892)
PHONE.................................810 388-2511
Ronald Egan, *Principal*
EMP: 3 **EST:** 2008
SALES (est): 323.1K **Privately Held**
SIC: 3231 Products of purchased glass

(G-10614)
SIGNAL MEDICAL CORPORATION (PA)
400 Pyramid Dr Ste 2 (48040-2463)
PHONE.................................810 364-7070
Drleo Whiteside, *President*
Leo Whiteside, *President*
EMP: 11
SALES: 1.7MM **Privately Held**
WEB: www.signalmd.com
SIC: 3842 5999 Surgical appliances & supplies; medical apparatus & supplies

(G-10615)
SMR ATMTIVE MRROR INTL USA INC (DH)
1855 Busha Hwy (48040-1892)
PHONE.................................810 364-4141
Char Zawadzinski, *President*
▲ **EMP:** 402
SALES (est): 337.2MM
SALES (corp-wide): 1B **Privately Held**
SIC: 3231 Products of purchased glass
HQ: Smr Automotive Technology Holdings Usa Partners Llp
1855 Busha Hwy
Marysville MI 48040
810 364-4141

(G-10616)
SMR AUTOMOTIVE SYSTEMS USA INC (DH)
Also Called: Samvardhana Mtherson Reflectec
1855 Busha Hwy (48040-1892)
PHONE.................................810 364-4141
Char Zawadzinski, *President*
SAI Tatineni, *Vice Pres*
Anthony D'Andrea, *Project Mgr*
Jacqueline Johnson, *Buyer*
Paul Bouverette, *QA Dir*
▲ **EMP:** 1000
SQ FT: 175,000
SALES (est): 332.1MM
SALES (corp-wide): 1B **Privately Held**
WEB: www.schefenacker.com
SIC: 3231 Mirrors, truck & automobile: made from purchased glass
HQ: Smr Automotive Mirror International Usa Inc.
1855 Busha Hwy
Marysville MI 48040
810 364-4141

(G-10617)
SMR AUTOMOTIVE TECHNOLOGY (DH)
1855 Busha Hwy (48040-1892)
PHONE.................................810 364-4141
Char Zawadzinski,
▲ **EMP:** 12 **EST:** 2000
SALES (est): 337.7MM
SALES (corp-wide): 1B **Privately Held**
SIC: 3231 Products of purchased glass
HQ: Smr Automotive Mirror Parts And Holdings Uk Limited
Portchester 2
Fareham HANTS
239 221-0022

(G-10618)
SOUTH PARK WELDING SUPS LLC (PA)
50 Gratiot Blvd (48040-1199)
PHONE.................................810 364-6521
Judy Darczy,
Lou Darczy,
EMP: 13
SQ FT: 3,500
SALES (est): 4.2MM **Privately Held**
SIC: 2813 5084 Industrial gases; welding machinery & equipment

(G-10619)
ST CLAIR PACKAGING INC
Also Called: St. Clair Paper & Supply
2121 Busha Hwy (48040-1943)
PHONE.................................810 364-4230
David Miotke, *CEO*
Todd Lawson, *President*
Dan Toler, *Plant Mgr*
Mark St Pierre, *Opers Mgr*
Jennifer Page, *Controller*
▲ **EMP:** 35 **EST:** 1980
SQ FT: 100,000
SALES (est): 8.8MM **Privately Held**
WEB: www.stclairpackaging.com
SIC: 5113 2653 Corrugated & solid fiber boxes; paper & products, wrapping or coarse; boxes, corrugated: made from purchased materials; boxes, solid fiber: made from purchased materials

(G-10620)
TARPON INDUSTRIES INC
2420 Wills St (48040-1978)
PHONE.................................810 364-7421
James W Bradshaw, *Ch of Bd*
Patrick J Hook, *President*
Patrick G Peplowski, *Exec VP*
Joseph T Lendo, *CFO*
Debbie Boyne, *Manager*
EMP: 154
SQ FT: 200,000
SALES (est): 17.5MM **Privately Held**
WEB: www.tarponind.com
SIC: 3317 2542 Tubes, wrought: welded or lock joint; racks, merchandise display or storage: except wood

(G-10621)
THEUT PRODUCTS INC
1444 Gratiot Blvd (48040-1179)
PHONE.................................810 364-7132
Jim Roberts, *Sales/Mktg Mgr*
EMP: 15
SALES (corp-wide): 15.4MM **Privately Held**
WEB: www.theutproducts.com
SIC: 3251 Brick & structural clay tile
PA: Theut Products, Inc.
73408 Van Dyke Rd
Bruce Twp MI 48065
586 752-4541

(G-10622)
THORPE PRINTING SERVICES INC
Also Called: Studio 626
604 Busha Hwy (48040-1310)
PHONE.................................810 364-6222
Lance Thorpe, *President*
Stacie Thorpe, *Exec VP*
Darin Magneson, *Graphic Designe*
EMP: 7
SQ FT: 6,550
SALES (est): 951.6K **Privately Held**
WEB: www.thorpeprinting.com
SIC: 2752 2399 7336 2791 Commercial printing, offset; banners, pennants & flags; graphic arts & related design; typesetting, computer controlled; bookbinding & related work; commercial printing

(G-10623)
TI GROUP AUTO SYSTEMS LLC
Also Called: Fluid Systems Division
184 Gratiot Blvd (48040-1147)
PHONE.................................810 364-3277
Dawn Hayes, *Materials Mgr*
Silke Smith, *Personnel*
Jim Springer, *Branch Mgr*
EMP: 120
SQ FT: 30,000
SALES (corp-wide): 3.9B **Privately Held**
WEB: www.tiautomotive.com
SIC: 3714 3089 Motor vehicle parts & accessories; plastic processing
HQ: Ti Group Automotive Systems, Llc
2020 Taylor Rd
Auburn Hills MI 48326
248 296-8000

(G-10624)
TROLLEY REBUILDERS INC
1765 Michigan Ave (48040-2046)
P.O. Box 219 (48040-0219)
PHONE.................................810 364-4820
Don Wilkie, *Owner*
EMP: 3
SALES (est): 335.8K **Privately Held**
SIC: 1542 3599 Commercial & office building contractors; industrial machinery

(G-10625)
VAN KEHRBERG VERN
Also Called: Copy Cat Sign & Print
914 Gratiot Blvd Ste 3 (48040-1141)
PHONE.................................810 364-1066
Vern Van Kehrberg, *Owner*
EMP: 4
SQ FT: 8,500
SALES (est): 165K **Privately Held**
SIC: 2759 3993 Commercial printing; signs, not made in custom sign painting shops

(G-10626)
WILKIE BROS CONVEYORS INC
1765 Michigan Ave Ste 2 (48040-2046)
P.O. Box 219 (48040-0219)
PHONE.................................810 364-4820
Donald Wilkie, *President*
Robert B Wilkie, *President*
▼ **EMP:** 50
SQ FT: 120,000
SALES (est): 14.2MM **Privately Held**
SIC: 3535 3568 3566 3462 Overhead conveyor systems; power transmission equipment; speed changers, drives & gears; iron & steel forgings

(G-10627)
ZF AXLE DRIVES MARYSVILLE LLC
Also Called: Division P
2900 Busha Hwy (48040-2439)
PHONE.................................810 989-8702
Jeff Beach, *Safety Mgr*
Christie Handlon, *Production*
Carrie Smith, *Engineer*
David White, *Sales Mgr*
Eric Vaneenoo, *Manager*
▲ **EMP:** 340
SALES (est): 73.1MM
SALES (corp-wide): 216.2K **Privately Held**
SIC: 3714 Motor vehicle parts & accessories
HQ: Zf North America, Inc.
15811 Centennial Dr 48
Northville MI 48168
734 416-6200

Mason
Ingham County

(G-10628)
A R C WELDING & REPAIR
5261 Bunker Rd (48854-9732)
PHONE.................................517 628-2475
Andrew Hudson, *Partner*
Douglas Hudson, *Partner*
EMP: 6
SALES (est): 319.1K **Privately Held**
SIC: 7692 Welding repair

(G-10629)
CONCENTRIC LABS INC
715 Hall Blvd (48854-1705)
P.O. Box 164 (48854-0164)
PHONE.................................517 969-3038
Joshua Woodland, *President*
EMP: 3
SALES (est): 162.1K **Privately Held**
SIC: 3625 Electric controls & control accessories, industrial

(G-10630)
CONTECH ENGNERED SOLUTIONS LLC
661 Jerico Dr (48854-9384)
PHONE.................................517 676-3000
Paul Depuy, *Manager*
EMP: 5 **Privately Held**
SIC: 3443 Fabricated plate work (boiler shop)
HQ: Contech Engineered Solutions Llc
9025 Centre Pointe Dr # 400
West Chester OH 45069
513 645-7000

(G-10631)
DART CONTAINER CORP GEORGIA (PA)
500 Hogsback Rd (48854-9547)
PHONE.................................517 676-3800
Robert C Dart, *President*
Leslie White, *COO*
Randy Lamie, *Engineer*
Kevin Fox, *Treasurer*
Christine Sheetz, *Sales Staff*
◆ **EMP:** 300 **EST:** 1983
SQ FT: 50,000
SALES (est): 146.4MM **Privately Held**
SIC: 3089 Cups, plastic, except foam

Mason - Ingham County (G-10632) — GEOGRAPHIC SECTION

(G-10632)
DART CONTAINER CORP KENTUCKY (PA)
Also Called: Dart Polymers
500 Hogsback Rd (48854-9547)
PHONE................517 676-3800
Robert C Dart, *CEO*
Mike Kerekes, *Engineer*
Collin Nelson, *Engineer*
Kevin Fox, *Treasurer*
Yadira Bernal, *Human Res Mgr*
◆ EMP: 277
SALES (est): 105.1MM **Privately Held**
SIC: 2821 3086 Plastics materials & resins; cups & plates, foamed plastic

(G-10633)
DART CONTAINER CORPORATION (PA)
500 Hogsback Rd (48854-9547)
PHONE................800 248-5960
Robert C Dart, *President*
Stanley Gilhool, *Counsel*
Charles Blevins, *Vice Pres*
Teri Hull, *Vice Pres*
James D Lammers, *Vice Pres*
◆ EMP: 780
SALES (est): 2.4B **Privately Held**
SIC: 3086 Plastics foam products

(G-10634)
DART CONTAINER MICHIGAN LLC (HQ)
500 Hogsback Rd (48854-9547)
PHONE................800 248-5960
Robert C Dart, *CEO*
William A Dart, *Vice Pres*
Timothy Hickey, *Vice Pres*
Rose Short, *Purchasing*
Richard Hall, *Research*
▲ EMP: 50
SQ FT: 50,000
SALES (est): 285MM **Privately Held**
WEB: www.dartcontainer.com
SIC: 3086 2656 Cups & plates, foamed plastic; paper cups, plates, dishes & utensils

(G-10635)
DART CONTAINER MICHIGAN LLC
432 Hogsback Rd (48854-9548)
PHONE................517 676-3803
Steven Hills, *Engineer*
Peter Matysiak, *Engineer*
Diane Mauk, *Engineer*
Matt Turner, *Project Engr*
Jim Kuerbitz, *Manager*
EMP: 215 **Privately Held**
SIC: 3086 Cups & plates, foamed plastic
HQ: Dart Container Of Michigan Llc
500 Hogsback Rd
Mason MI 48854
800 248-5960

(G-10636)
DIGITAL SUCCESS NETWORK
Also Called: D S N Satellites
205 S Cedar St (48854-1432)
P.O. Box 265 (48854-0265)
PHONE................517 244-0771
Bruce Ware, *President*
Amber Wyman, *Manager*
EMP: 20
SQ FT: 5,200
SALES (est): 2.9MM **Privately Held**
WEB: www.dsndish.com
SIC: 4841 2741 Satellite master antenna systems services (SMATV);

(G-10637)
ESL SUPPLIES LLC
600 N College Rd (48854-9544)
PHONE................517 525-7877
Rebecca Schwartz,
EMP: 3
SALES (est): 172.5K **Privately Held**
SIC: 3999 5961 5999 8748 Education aids, devices & supplies; educational supplies & equipment, mail order; education aids, devices & supplies; educational consultant

(G-10638)
FIRST DUE FIRE SUPPLY COMPANY
207 E Kipp Rd (48854-8201)
PHONE................517 969-3065
Daniel Hamel, *President*
EMP: 7
SALES (est): 1.1MM **Privately Held**
SIC: 3569 Firefighting apparatus & related equipment

(G-10639)
FW SHORING COMPANY (PA)
Also Called: Efficiency Shoring and Supply
685 Hull Rd (48854-9271)
PHONE................517 676-8800
Kenneth Forsberg, *President*
Rod Austin, *Vice Pres*
Gary Bushong, *Vice Pres*
Michael West, *Admin Sec*
EMP: 100 EST: 1971
SQ FT: 79,000
SALES (est): 24.8MM **Privately Held**
WEB: www.efficiencyproduction.com
SIC: 3531 Construction machinery

(G-10640)
GENESIS INTERNATIONAL LLC
Also Called: Genesis Casket Company
200 E Kipp Rd (48854-9291)
PHONE................317 777-6700
Wm Anthony Colson, *CEO*
Judy Rossom, *Mng Member*
Denny Knigga,
Adrian Lee,
Billingsley Scott,
◆ EMP: 25
SALES (est): 4.7MM **Privately Held**
SIC: 3995 Burial caskets

(G-10641)
GESTAMP MASON LLC
200 E Kipp Rd (48854-9291)
PHONE................517 244-8800
Jeffrey Wilson, *CEO*
John Craig, *President*
Mary Dunivon, *Buyer*
Miguel Ferrandez, *Research*
James Barry, *CFO*
◆ EMP: 489
SQ FT: 230,000
SALES (est): 172.9MM
SALES (corp-wide): 120.9MM **Privately Held**
SIC: 3398 5013 3714 3711 Metal heat treating; motor vehicle supplies & new parts; motor vehicle parts & accessories; motor vehicles & car bodies; automotive stampings
HQ: Gestamp North America, Inc.
2701 Troy Center Dr # 150
Troy MI 48084
248 743-3400

(G-10642)
H & H WELDING & REPAIR LLC
700 Acme Dr (48854)
P.O. Box 371 (48854-0371)
PHONE................517 676-1800
Dale Good, *Manager*
Scott Summerville,
Kris Cook,
EMP: 54
SQ FT: 27,000
SALES (est): 6.7MM **Privately Held**
SIC: 7692 Welding repair

(G-10643)
KENT NUTRITION GROUP INC
725 Hull Rd (48854-9272)
PHONE................517 676-9544
Joe Frushour, *Manager*
EMP: 12
SALES (corp-wide): 449.1MM **Privately Held**
WEB: www.kentfeeds.com
SIC: 2048 Livestock feeds; poultry feeds
HQ: Kent Nutrition Group, Inc.
1600 Oregon St
Muscatine IA 52761
866 647-1212

(G-10644)
LEAR CORPORATION
Also Called: GM Division Plant
454 North St (48854-1588)
PHONE................248 447-1500
Tom Stark, *Controller*
Bret Badertscher, *Manager*
EMP: 600
SALES (corp-wide): 21.1B **Publicly Held**
WEB: www.lear.com
SIC: 2396 2531 Automotive & apparel trimmings; public building & related furniture
PA: Lear Corporation
21557 Telegraph Rd
Southfield MI 48033
248 447-1500

(G-10645)
MASON FORGE & DIE INC
Also Called: Mason Specialty Forge
841 Hull Rd (48854-9273)
P.O. Box 321 (48854-0321)
PHONE................517 676-2992
EMP: 10
SQ FT: 17,500
SALES (est): 1.3MM **Privately Held**
SIC: 3714 3462 Mfg Steering Components And Steel Forgings

(G-10646)
MICHIGAN PACKAGING COMPANY (DH)
Also Called: Southeastern Packaging
700 Eden Rd (48854-9277)
PHONE................517 676-8700
Geoffrey A Jollay, *CEO*
Donna Mills, *Vice Pres*
Chris Zimmerman, *Prdtn Mgr*
Jody Stewart, *Purchasing*
John Klein, *Chief Mktg Ofcr*
▲ EMP: 100
SQ FT: 210,000
SALES (est): 25MM
SALES (corp-wide): 3.8B **Publicly Held**
SIC: 2653 Sheets, corrugated: made from purchased materials
HQ: Corrchoice, Inc.
777 3rd St Nw
Massillon OH 44647
330 833-5705

(G-10647)
MICHIGAN WOODWORK
1234 Christian Way (48854-9817)
PHONE................517 204-4394
Matthew Gustafson, *Owner*
EMP: 3 EST: 2013
SALES (est): 474.7K **Privately Held**
SIC: 2431 Millwork

(G-10648)
MONSANTO COMPANY
1440 Okemos Rd (48854-9314)
PHONE................517 676-2479
Erwin Felton, *Manager*
EMP: 3
SALES (corp-wide): 45.3B **Privately Held**
WEB: www.monsanto.com
SIC: 2879 Agricultural chemicals
HQ: Monsanto Company
800 N Lindbergh Blvd
Saint Louis MO 63167
314 694-1000

(G-10649)
NITREX INC (DH)
822 Kim Dr (48854-9366)
P.O. Box 155 (48854-0155)
PHONE................517 676-6370
Chris Morawski, *President*
Jerry Snow, *Maintence Staff*
▲ EMP: 25
SQ FT: 20,000
SALES (est): 12.8MM
SALES (corp-wide): 419.3K **Privately Held**
WEB: www.nitrexmetaltech.com
SIC: 3398 3714 Metal heat treating; motor vehicle parts & accessories
HQ: Nitrex Metal Inc
3474 Boul Poirier
Saint-Laurent QC H4R 2
514 335-7191

(G-10650)
OMIMEX ENERGY INC
3505 W Barnes Rd (48854-8720)
P.O. Box 258 (48854-0258)
PHONE................517 628-2820
Kem Pryor, *Manager*
EMP: 6
SALES (corp-wide): 38.2MM **Privately Held**
WEB: www.omimexgroup.com
SIC: 1311 Crude petroleum & natural gas production
HQ: Omimex Energy, Inc.
7950 John T White Rd
Fort Worth TX 76120

(G-10651)
PARKER-HANNIFIN CORPORATION
Also Called: Hose Products Division
1355 N Cedar Rd (48854-9586)
PHONE................517 694-0491
Bryan Wilton, *Engineer*
Lonnie Gallup, *Branch Mgr*
Jared Balistreri, *Manager*
EMP: 105
SALES (corp-wide): 14.3B **Publicly Held**
WEB: www.parker.com
SIC: 3494 Pipe fittings
PA: Parker-Hannifin Corporation
6035 Parkland Blvd
Cleveland OH 44124
216 896-3000

(G-10652)
RALYAS AUTO BODY INCORPORATED
1250 N Cedar Rd (48854-9530)
PHONE................517 694-6512
Tim Ralya, *Owner*
EMP: 3 EST: 2007
SALES (est): 326.5K **Privately Held**
SIC: 3711 3713 7532 Automobile bodies, passenger car, not including engine, etc.; truck & bus bodies; exterior repair services

(G-10653)
S G PUBLICATIONS INC (PA)
Also Called: The Shopping Guide
140 E Ash St (48854-2603)
PHONE................517 676-5100
George Raymund, *President*
George Raymund, *President*
John Raymund, *Treasurer*
EMP: 15
SQ FT: 1,800
SALES (est): 2.8MM **Privately Held**
WEB: www.theshoppingguide.com
SIC: 2741 Shopping news: publishing & printing

(G-10654)
SCHUNK OIL FIELD SERVICE INC
4161 Legion Dr (48854-2547)
P.O. Box 382 (48854-0382)
PHONE................517 676-8900
Jeff Schunk, *President*
EMP: 6
SQ FT: 200
SALES: 500K **Privately Held**
SIC: 1389 Oil field services

(G-10655)
SCIC LLC (PA)
500 Hogsback Rd (48854-8523)
PHONE................800 248-5960
Robert C Dart, *CEO*
Ronald Whaley, *Principal*
Mike Lonsway, *Exec VP*
Abu Husain, *Software Dev*
▼ EMP: 32
SALES (est): 965.8MM **Privately Held**
SIC: 3089 2656 Cups, plastic, except foam; paper cups, plates, dishes & utensils

(G-10656)
SF HOLDINGS GROUP INC (DH)
Also Called: Solo Cup
500 Hogsback Rd (48854-8523)
PHONE................800 248-5960
Robert C Dart, *CEO*
Linda Ridgley, *Vice Pres*

GEOGRAPHIC SECTION

Carrie Anderson, *Human Res Dir*
◆ **EMP:** 59
SALES (est): 112.5MM
SALES (corp-wide): 965.8MM **Privately Held**
SIC: 2656 Plates, paper: made from purchased material; food containers (liquid tight), including milk cartons
HQ: Solo Cup Company Llc
500 Hogsback Rd
Mason MI 48854
800 248-5960

(G-10657)
SOLO CUP COMPANY LLC (HQ)
500 Hogsback Rd (48854-8523)
PHONE....................800 248-5960
Robert C Dart, *CEO*
Jan Stern Reed, *Vice Pres*
Mike Northington, *Warehouse Mgr*
Sheree Wills, *Production*
Breck Armstrong, *Engineer*
▲ **EMP:** 150
SQ FT: 133,218
SALES (est): 965.8MM **Privately Held**
SIC: 3089 2656 Cups, plastic, except foam; straws, drinking: made from purchased material
PA: Scic Llc
500 Hogsback Rd
Mason MI 48854
800 248-5960

(G-10658)
SOLO CUP OPERATING CORPORATION (DH)
500 Hogsback Rd (48854-8523)
PHONE....................800 248-5960
Robert C Dart, *President*
John Mc Gregor, *Director*
F Purdum, *Admin Asst*
▼ **EMP:** 60
SALES (est): 31MM
SALES (corp-wide): 996.7MM **Privately Held**
WEB: www.sweetheart.com
SIC: 3089 2656 Plastic kitchenware, tableware & houseware; cups, plastic, except foam; plates, plastic; plastic containers, except foam; paper cups, plates, dishes & utensils; cups, paper: made from purchased material; plates, paper: made from purchased material; straws, drinking: made from purchased material
HQ: Sf Holdings Group, Inc.
500 Hogsback Rd
Mason MI 48854
800 248-5960

(G-10659)
SPECIAL PROJECTS ENGINEERING
2072 Tomlinson Rd (48854-9203)
P.O. Box 413 (48854-0413)
PHONE....................517 676-8525
Edward Goodman, *President*
Sarah J Goodman, *Vice Pres*
▲ **EMP:** 8
SQ FT: 7,000
SALES: 600K **Privately Held**
SIC: 3086 Plastics foam products

(G-10660)
SPORTS STOP
Also Called: Sports Stop Sportswear
124 W Ash St (48854-1648)
PHONE....................517 676-2199
Rick L Washburn, *Owner*
EMP: 5
SQ FT: 1,800
SALES (est): 425K **Privately Held**
SIC: 5699 2396 2395 Sports apparel; screen printing on fabric articles; emblems, embroidered

Mass City
Ontonagon County

(G-10661)
DEHAAN FOREST PRODUCTS INC
25367 Mud Creek Rd (49948-9530)
PHONE....................906 883-3417
Richard Dehaan, *President*
Martin Dehaan, *Vice Pres*
Sharon Dehaan, *Treasurer*
EMP: 10
SALES: 3.5MM **Privately Held**
SIC: 2411 0191 Logging; general farms, primarily crop

Mattawan
Van Buren County

(G-10662)
BASF CONSTRUCTION CHEM LLC
23930 Concord Ave (49071-9566)
PHONE....................269 668-3371
Larry Labelle, *Manager*
EMP: 34
SALES (corp-wide): 71.7B **Privately Held**
WEB: www.chemrex.com
SIC: 2899 2851 Concrete curing & hardening compounds; paints & allied products
HQ: Basf Construction Chemicals, Llc
889 Valley Park Dr
Shakopee MN 55379
952 496-6000

(G-10663)
CODY KRESTA VINEYARD & WINERY
45727 27th St (49071-9736)
PHONE....................269 668-3800
Cody Kresta, *Executive*
EMP: 4
SALES (est): 361K **Privately Held**
SIC: 2084 Wines

(G-10664)
FACTORY PRODUCTS INC
26375 60th Ave (49071-9513)
P.O. Box 159 (49071-0159)
PHONE....................269 668-3329
Karina Kerby, *President*
Mildred L Kerby, *President*
EMP: 3 **EST:** 1958
SQ FT: 8,000
SALES (est): 326.8K **Privately Held**
SIC: 3052 3089 Rubber belting; transmission belting, rubber; plastic hose; plastic processing

(G-10665)
MALLORY POLE BUILDINGS INC
24359 Red Arrow Hwy Ste A (49071-7758)
PHONE....................269 668-2627
Stephen A Mallory, *President*
Angie Mallory, *Vice Pres*
EMP: 15
SQ FT: 7,800
SALES (est): 1.2MM **Privately Held**
SIC: 2452 Prefabricated wood buildings

(G-10666)
MOL-SON INC
Also Called: Western Diversified
53196 N Main St (49071-8305)
PHONE....................269 668-3377
Ronald A Molitor, *President*
Carl Shinabargar, *Engineer*
Bill Oesterle, *Plant Engr*
Shawn Hansen, *Design Engr*
Susan Fritzer, *CFO*
EMP: 100
SQ FT: 12,000
SALES (est): 43.1MM **Privately Held**
WEB: www.mol-son.com
SIC: 3544 Special dies & tools

(G-10667)
PRODUCTION TOOLING INC
23650 French Rd (49071-9331)
P.O. Box 399 (49071-0399)
PHONE....................269 668-6789
Thomas Henry, *President*
Karen Henry, *Corp Secy*
EMP: 9
SQ FT: 5,000
SALES (est): 1.3MM **Privately Held**
SIC: 3599 Machine shop, jobbing & repair

(G-10668)
PUSHARD WELDING LLC
25222 Red Arrow Hwy (49071-9767)
PHONE....................269 760-9611
Chris Pushard,
EMP: 6
SALES (est): 120.3K **Privately Held**
SIC: 7692 Welding repair

(G-10669)
SHEPHERD CASTER CORP
22186 Woodhenge Dr (49071-9720)
PHONE....................269 668-4800
EMP: 3 **EST:** 2014
SALES (est): 129.6K **Privately Held**
SIC: 3562 Casters

(G-10670)
TRI-MATION INDUSTRIES INC
53160 N Main St Plant 12 (49071)
P.O. Box 249 (49071-0249)
PHONE....................269 668-4333
Blaine Borkowski, *President*
EMP: 17
SALES (est): 5.4MM **Privately Held**
WEB: www.tri-mation.com
SIC: 3549 Metalworking machinery

(G-10671)
WESTERN DIVERSIFIED PLAS LLC (PA)
53150 N Main St (49071-8305)
PHONE....................269 668-3393
Dave Ward, *Production*
Richard Schau, *Engineer*
Pam Monroe, *Cust Mgr*
Dirk Dragt, *Marketing Staff*
Kirk Boeskool, *Program Mgr*
EMP: 1
SALES (est): 3.1MM **Privately Held**
SIC: 3089 Injection molding of plastics

Maybee
Monroe County

(G-10672)
SECURITYSNARES INC
10683 Bitz Rd (48159-9703)
PHONE....................734 308-5106
Jonathan Cunningham, *Co-Owner*
EMP: 3
SALES (est): 71.1K **Privately Held**
SIC: 7372 Application computer software

(G-10673)
STONECO INC
6837 Scofield Rd (48159-9706)
PHONE....................734 587-7125
Mark Parron, *Manager*
EMP: 20
SALES (corp-wide): 30.6B **Privately Held**
WEB: www.stoneco.net
SIC: 1611 1422 General contractor, highway & street construction; crushed & broken limestone
HQ: Stoneco, Inc.
1700 Fostoria Ave Ste 200
Findlay OH 45840
419 422-8854

(G-10674)
STUFF A PAL
14401 Cone Rd (48159-9741)
PHONE....................734 646-3775
Anne Herlocher, *Principal*
EMP: 3
SALES (est): 321.9K **Privately Held**
SIC: 3523 Clippers, for animal use: hand or electric

Mayville
Tuscola County

(G-10675)
MOUNT OF OLIVE OIL COMPANY
1821 Ambrose Rd (48744-9755)
PHONE....................989 928-9030
Dustin Riness, *Principal*
EMP: 3 **EST:** 2018
SALES (est): 91.3K **Privately Held**
SIC: 2079 Olive oil

(G-10676)
WILKINSON CHEMICAL CORPORATION
8290 Lapeer Rd (48744-9305)
PHONE....................989 843-6163
Irene Wilkinson, *President*
EMP: 15 **EST:** 1948
SQ FT: 5,400
SALES (est): 2.3MM **Privately Held**
SIC: 2819 Calcium chloride & hypochlorite; magnesium compounds or salts, inorganic

Mc Bain
Missaukee County

(G-10677)
BD CLASSIC SEWING
1890 E Stoney Corners Rd (49657-9515)
PHONE....................231 825-2628
Betty Randall, *Partner*
Deanna Lucas, *Partner*
EMP: 5 **EST:** 1992
SALES: 36.5K **Privately Held**
SIC: 2395 Embroidery products, except schiffli machine

(G-10678)
BIEWER FOREST MANAGEMENT LLC
6400 W Gerwoude Dr (49657-9113)
PHONE....................231 825-2855
Wes Windover, *Info Tech Mgr*
Timothy Biewer,
EMP: 5
SALES (est): 531K **Privately Held**
SIC: 2421 Specialty sawmill products

(G-10679)
BIEWER SAWMILL INC
6251 W Gerwoude Dr (49657-9105)
P.O. Box 497, Saint Clair (48079-0497)
PHONE....................231 825-2855
Richard N Biewer, *President*
Brian B Biewer, *Vice Pres*
Shawn Johnston, *Plant Mgr*
Steve Koryba, *Human Res Dir*
Leo Colantuono, *Sales Mgr*
EMP: 30
SQ FT: 2,500
SALES (est): 4.8MM
SALES (corp-wide): 120.2MM **Privately Held**
WEB: www.biewerlumber.com
SIC: 2491 2429 Structural lumber & timber, treated wood; barrels & barrel parts
PA: Biewer Lumber, Inc.
812 S Riverside Ave
Saint Clair MI 48079
810 326-3930

(G-10680)
BRINKS FAMILY CREAMERY LLC
3560 E Mulder Rd (49657)
PHONE....................231 826-0099
Ron Brinks, *Principal*
Barb Brinks, *Principal*
Kathy Lucas, *Principal*
Kenda Rivera, *Principal*
EMP: 5
SALES: 60K **Privately Held**
SIC: 2021 Creamery butter

(G-10681)
HYDROLAKE INC (HQ)
6151 W Gerwoude Dr (49657-9110)
PHONE....................231 825-2233
Franklin C Wheatlake, *President*
Roland L Lyons, *Vice Pres*
EMP: 2
SALES (est): 2.3MM **Privately Held**
SIC: 2499 Poles, wood

Mc Bain - Missaukee County (G-10682)

(G-10682)
JOHN A BIEWER LUMBER COMPANY
Also Called: Biewer Sawmill
6251 W Gerwoude Dr (49657-9105)
PHONE.................................231 825-2855
Rich Reinemann, *Manager*
EMP: 95
SALES (corp-wide): 53.8MM **Privately Held**
SIC: 2491 2426 2421 Structural lumber & timber, treated wood; hardwood dimension & flooring mills; sawmills & planing mills, general
PA: John A. Biewer Lumber Company
812 S Riverside Ave
Saint Clair MI 48079
810 329-4789

(G-10683)
QUALITY PALLETS LLC
9773 S Burkett Rd (49657-9788)
PHONE.................................231 825-8361
Kenneth Otto, *Mng Member*
EMP: 15
SQ FT: 30,000
SALES: 3.1MM **Privately Held**
SIC: 2448 Pallets, wood

(G-10684)
ROGER BAZUIN & SONS INC
8750 W Stoney Corners Rd (49657-9414)
PHONE.................................231 825-2889
Roger Bazuin, *President*
Mae Bazuin, *Corp Secy*
Jerry Bazuin, *Vice Pres*
Robert Bazuin, *Director*
EMP: 27
SQ FT: 20,000
SALES: 1.5MM **Privately Held**
SIC: 2411 Logging camps & contractors

Mc Millan
Luce County

(G-10685)
GRACE CONTRACTING SERVICES LLC
25688 County Road 98 (49853-9360)
PHONE.................................906 630-4680
Raymond Plesscher,
EMP: 4
SALES (est): 200K **Privately Held**
SIC: 1781 1791 1799 1389 Water well drilling; precast concrete structural framing or panels, placing of; erection & dismantling of forms for poured concrete; grading oil & gas well foundations; demolition, buildings & other structures;

Mears
Oceana County

(G-10686)
CHASSIS SHOP PRFMCE PDTS INC
1931 N 24th Ave (49436-9687)
PHONE.................................231 873-3640
Stuart Spears, *President*
EMP: 7
SQ FT: 10,000
SALES (est): 1.1MM **Privately Held**
WEB: www.chassisshop.com
SIC: 3799 Recreational vehicles

Mecosta
Mecosta County

(G-10687)
CHROUCH COMMUNICATIONS INC
Also Called: CCI
6644 9 Mile Rd (49332-9703)
PHONE.................................231 972-0339
Kevin Courtnay, *Manager*
EMP: 4

SALES (corp-wide): 1.9MM **Privately Held**
WEB: www.chrouch.com
SIC: 3679 5731 Headphones, radio; electronic circuits; radios, receiver type; radios, two-way, citizens' band, weather, short-wave, etc.
PA: Chrouch Communications, Inc.
7860 Morrison Lake Rd
Saranac MI 48881
616 642-3881

(G-10688)
LUTCO INC
8800 Midstate Dr (49332-9538)
P.O. Box 107 (49332-0107)
PHONE.................................231 972-5566
Janet L Luttman, *Administration*
EMP: 8 EST: 2009
SALES (est): 846.1K **Privately Held**
SIC: 3546 3544 Power-driven handtools; special dies, tools, jigs & fixtures

(G-10689)
MANNIX RE HOLDINGS LLC
8965 Midstate Dr (49332)
PHONE.................................231 972-0088
Mike Alvey,
EMP: 5
SALES (est): 835.8K **Privately Held**
SIC: 3325 Steel foundries

(G-10690)
MAXS CONCRETE INC
15323 75th Ave (49332-9609)
PHONE.................................231 972-7558
Max Goltz, *President*
Mike Goltz, *Vice Pres*
Marjorie Story, *Treasurer*
Brian Bakos, *Admin Sec*
EMP: 9
SALES: 1MM **Privately Held**
SIC: 3273 3272 Ready-mixed concrete; septic tanks, concrete

Melvin
Sanilac County

(G-10691)
MARK GRIESSEL
7068 Jordan Rd (48454-9750)
PHONE.................................810 378-6060
Mark Griessel, *Principal*
EMP: 4
SALES (est): 321.7K **Privately Held**
SIC: 3679 Rheostats, for electronic end products

Melvindale
Wayne County

(G-10692)
ACCULIFT INC
17516 Dix Rd (48122-1316)
PHONE.................................313 382-5121
William Szekesy, *President*
EMP: 4
SALES (est): 340K **Privately Held**
SIC: 3625 Actuators, industrial

(G-10693)
COMPRESSOR INDUSTRIES LLC
17162 Francis St (48122-2316)
PHONE.................................313 389-2800
Paul Linares,
EMP: 14
SALES (est): 1.9MM **Privately Held**
SIC: 3585 Compressors for refrigeration & air conditioning equipment

(G-10694)
CORE ELECTRIC COMPANY INC
Also Called: Michigan Pump
25125 Outer Dr (48122-1955)
PHONE.................................313 382-7140
John L Goodman, *President*
Jeanne Tritt, *Persnl Mgr*
Leona Goodman, *Admin Sec*
EMP: 15
SQ FT: 40,000

SALES (est): 4.4MM **Privately Held**
WEB: www.coreelectric.net
SIC: 7694 7699 5063 3451 Electric motor repair; coil winding service; pumps & pumping equipment repair; motors, electric; screw machine products

(G-10695)
DARLING INGREDIENTS INC
3350 Greenfield Rd (48122-1280)
P.O. Box 3185 (48122-0185)
PHONE.................................313 928-7400
Helen Donahoe, *Office Mgr*
Don Muchow, *Manager*
Mike Selke, *Manager*
Al Steiger, *Manager*
EMP: 79
SALES (corp-wide): 3.3B **Publicly Held**
WEB: www.darlingii.com
SIC: 2077 2076 2048 2833 Grease rendering, inedible; tallow rendering, inedible; bone meal, except as animal feed; meat meal & tankage, except as animal feed; vegetable oil mills; prepared feeds; animal oils, medicinal grade: refined or concentrated
PA: Darling Ingredients Inc.
5601 N Macarthur Blvd
Irving TX 75038
972 717-0300

(G-10696)
DRYE CUSTOM PALLETS INC
19400 Allen Rd (48122-2204)
PHONE.................................313 381-2681
Michael A Kostrzewa, *President*
Eric Anderson, *Vice Pres*
David Radcliffe, *Vice Pres*
EMP: 55
SQ FT: 33,000
SALES (est): 5.4MM **Privately Held**
SIC: 2448 Pallets, wood

(G-10697)
EBONEX CORPORATION (PA)
Also Called: Keystone Universal
18400 Rialto St (48122-1946)
P.O. Box 3247 (48122-0247)
PHONE.................................313 388-0063
Michelle Toennids, *President*
Michael F Szczepanik, *President*
Shelly Toenniges, *Manager*
▲ **EMP:** 11
SQ FT: 30,000
SALES (est): 2.4MM **Privately Held**
WEB: www.cosmicblack.com
SIC: 2816 5169 Bone black; chemicals & allied products

(G-10698)
FLYING COLORS IMPRINTING INC
19500 Allen Rd (48122-1622)
PHONE.................................734 641-1300
Mark Dabiero, *President*
Carla Dabiero, *Sales Dir*
EMP: 16
SALES (est): 2.2MM **Privately Held**
SIC: 2759 Imprinting

(G-10699)
HEMINGWAY SCREW PRODUCTS INC
17840 Dix Rd (48122-1320)
PHONE.................................313 383-7300
Randy Stojanovich, *President*
EMP: 4
SQ FT: 9,500
SALES (est): 330K **Privately Held**
SIC: 3451 3599 Screw machine products; machine shop, jobbing & repair

(G-10700)
IDEAL GAS INC
2750 Oakwood Blvd (48122-1359)
PHONE.................................734 365-7192
Ferrel D Moore, *President*
Shannon Zokoe, *Manager*
EMP: 3
SALES (est): 405.3K **Privately Held**
SIC: 3825 Standards & calibrating equipment, laboratory

(G-10701)
J I B PROPERTIES LLC
17100 Francis St (48122-2316)
P.O. Box 3245 (48122-0245)
PHONE.................................313 382-3234
Fax: 313 382-5530
EMP: 8
SQ FT: 37,500
SALES (est): 530K **Privately Held**
SIC: 7699 1796 3599 Repairs Rebuilds Services & Installs Steel Processing Equipment

(G-10702)
MONARCH ELECTRIC SERVICE CO
Also Called: Monarch Electric Apparatus Svc
18800 Meginnity St (48122-1931)
PHONE.................................313 388-7800
Dennis Boik, *Branch Mgr*
EMP: 30
SALES (corp-wide): 855.2MM **Privately Held**
WEB: www.monarch-electric.com
SIC: 7699 5063 7694 3621 Industrial machinery & equipment repair; electrical apparatus & equipment; armature rewinding shops; motors & generators
HQ: Monarch Electric Service Company
5325 W 130th St
Cleveland OH 44130
216 433-7800

(G-10703)
MOTOR CONTROL INCORPORATED
17100 Francis St (48122-2316)
PHONE.................................313 389-4000
Corbett R Crider Sr, *President*
EMP: 5
SALES (est): 440K **Privately Held**
SIC: 3625 5063 Control equipment, electric; motors, electric

(G-10704)
ONODI TOOL & ENGINEERING CO
19150 Meginnity St (48122-1934)
PHONE.................................313 386-6682
John Onodi, *President*
Sandy Onodi, *Vice Pres*
▲ **EMP:** 40 EST: 1974
SQ FT: 100,000
SALES: 11.3MM **Privately Held**
WEB: www.onoditool.com
SIC: 3711 3365 3369 3324 Military motor vehicle assembly; aerospace castings, aluminum; aerospace castings, nonferrous: except aluminum; aerospace investment castings, ferrous

(G-10705)
PIPING COMPONENTS INC
Also Called: PCI
4205 Oakwood Blvd (48122-1409)
PHONE.................................313 382-6400
Neil R Matthews, *President*
Chris Joyce Powell, *CFO*
EMP: 6
SQ FT: 10,000
SALES (est): 2.3MM **Privately Held**
WEB: www.pipingcomponents.com
SIC: 5051 8711 3823 Pipe & tubing, steel; consulting engineer; flow instruments, industrial process type

(G-10706)
QUALITY MODELS INTL INC
17516 Dix Rd (48122-1316)
PHONE.................................519 727-4255
William Szekesy, *President*
Judy Szekesy, *Vice Pres*
▲ **EMP:** 6
SALES (est): 802K **Privately Held**
SIC: 3089 Injection molding of plastics

(G-10707)
STANDARD PLAQUE INCORPORATED
17271 Francis St (48122-1338)
PHONE.................................313 383-7233
Nick Tarcia, *President*
Robert S Tarcia, *Vice Pres*
EMP: 10
SQ FT: 6,000

GEOGRAPHIC SECTION

Menominee - Menominee County (G-10733)

SALES: 800K **Privately Held**
WEB: www.standardplaque.com
SIC: **3089** Plastic hardware & building products

(G-10708)
VISIONARY VITAMIN CO
3205 Mckitrick St (48122-1112)
PHONE.................................734 788-5934
Marino Apollinari, *President*
EMP: 4
SALES (est): 156.7K **Privately Held**
SIC: **2833** Vitamins, natural or synthetic: bulk, uncompounded

Memphis
St. Clair County

(G-10709)
G5 OUTDOORS LLC (PA)
34775 Potter St (48041-4613)
PHONE.................................866 456-8836
Matt Grace, *Engineer*
Brian Anderson, *Accounts Mgr*
Joel Harris, *Marketing Mgr*
Tim Checkeroski, *Marketing Staff*
Louis Grace,
▲ EMP: 4
SALES (est): 647.3K **Privately Held**
SIC: **3949** Archery equipment, general

(G-10710)
GRACE ENGINEERING CORP
34775 Potter St (48041-4613)
P.O. Box 202 (48041-0202)
PHONE.................................810 392-2181
Matt Grace, *Principal*
▲ EMP: 90
SQ FT: 65,000
SALES (est): 19.2MM **Privately Held**
WEB: www.graceeng.com
SIC: **3451 3841** Screw machine products; surgical & medical instruments

Mendon
St. Joseph County

(G-10711)
AFFINITY CUSTOM MOLDING INC
21198 M 60 (49072-8757)
P.O. Box 9 (49072-0009)
PHONE.................................269 496-8423
David Cook, *President*
Todd Cook, *Corp Secy*
Jim Batten, *Trustee*
Kathy Brueck, *Manager*
▲ EMP: 43
SQ FT: 40,000
SALES (est): 9.3MM **Privately Held**
WEB: www.affinitycustommolding.com
SIC: **3089 3544** Injection molding of plastics; forms (molds), for foundry & plastics working machinery; industrial molds

(G-10712)
CIRCLE C MOLD & PLASTICS GROUP
55664 Parkville Rd (49072-9748)
PHONE.................................269 496-5515
F Earl Carr Jr, *President*
Frederick Earl Carr Jr, *President*
Linda Carr, *Vice Pres*
EMP: 10
SQ FT: 15,000
SALES: 650K **Privately Held**
SIC: **3544** Industrial molds

(G-10713)
HILLSIDE CREATIONS LLC
58267 Walterspaugh Rd (49072-9500)
PHONE.................................269 496-7041
Ed Kauffman,
Melvin Bondtrager,
EMP: 3
SALES (est): 137.5K **Privately Held**
SIC: **2499** Decorative wood & woodwork

(G-10714)
JONATHAN SHOWALTER
Also Called: Bee Line Apiaries & Woodenware
20960 M 60 (49072-8724)
PHONE.................................269 496-7001
Jonathan Showalter, *Owner*
EMP: 4
SALES (est): 349.3K **Privately Held**
SIC: **0279 2499** Apiary (bee & honey farm); beekeeping supplies, wood

(G-10715)
LEAR CORPORATION
236 Clark St (49072-9794)
PHONE.................................269 496-2215
Ken Way, *Branch Mgr*
EMP: 271
SALES (corp-wide): 21.1B **Publicly Held**
WEB: www.lear.com
SIC: **2531 3714** Seats, automobile; motor vehicle electrical equipment; instrument board assemblies, motor vehicle; automotive wiring harness sets; motor vehicle body components & frame
PA: Lear Corporation
 21557 Telegraph Rd
 Southfield MI 48033
 248 447-1500

(G-10716)
MANCHESTER INDUSTRIES INC VA
26920 M 60 (49072-9654)
PHONE.................................269 496-2715
Ranse McKinney, *Branch Mgr*
EMP: 40 **Publicly Held**
SIC: **2679** Paperboard products, converted
HQ: Manchester Industries Inc. Of Virginia
 200 Orleans St
 Richmond VA 23231
 804 226-4250

(G-10717)
PENTAGON MOLD CO
21015 M 60 (49072-8739)
PHONE.................................269 496-7072
Jay Crabtree, *President*
Todd Batten, *Vice Pres*
EMP: 4
SQ FT: 4,600
SALES: 300K **Privately Held**
SIC: **3544** Industrial molds

(G-10718)
SANDERSON INSULATION
840 Avery Dr (49072-9667)
PHONE.................................269 496-7660
Marvin J Sanderson, *Owner*
Gloria Sanderson, *Principal*
EMP: 5
SALES: 360K **Privately Held**
SIC: **3357 1761** Nonferrous wiredrawing & insulating; siding contractor; roofing contractor

(G-10719)
TH PLASTICS INC (PA)
106 E Main St (49072-9650)
P.O. Box 188 (49072-0188)
PHONE.................................269 496-8495
Patrick J Haas, *CEO*
Chris Haas, *President*
Michael McCaw, *Vice Pres*
Elizabeth Mitchell, *Vice Pres*
Scott Mitchell, *Vice Pres*
▲ EMP: 340
SQ FT: 210,000
SALES (est): 142MM **Privately Held**
WEB: www.thplastics.com
SIC: **3089** Injection molded finished plastic products; injection molding of plastics

(G-10720)
TH PLASTICS INC
Also Called: Plant 2
106 E Main St (49072-9650)
P.O. Box 188 (49072-0188)
PHONE.................................269 496-8495
Scott Mitchell, *Manager*
EMP: 100
SALES (corp-wide): 142MM **Privately Held**
WEB: www.thplastics.com
SIC: **3089 3714** Plastic containers, except foam; motor vehicle parts & accessories

PA: Th Plastics, Inc.
 106 E Main St
 Mendon MI 49072
 269 496-8495

Menominee
Menominee County

(G-10721)
ADVANCED BLNDING SOLUTIONS LLC
Also Called: ABS
949 1st St (49858-3265)
P.O. Box 37, Wallace (49893-0037)
PHONE.................................906 914-4180
Joe Gardon, *Project Mgr*
Janet Kolaszewski, *Purch Agent*
Keith Coroneos, *Engineer*
Andrew Eland, *Engineer*
Brent A Berquist, *Sales Dir*
▲ EMP: 17
SQ FT: 12,000
SALES (est): 4.3MM **Privately Held**
SIC: **3634 7629** Blenders, electric; electrical household appliance repair

(G-10722)
ANCHOR COUPLING INC (HQ)
5520 13th St (49858-1014)
PHONE.................................906 863-2672
Bonnie Fetch, *President*
Dave Bozeman, *Principal*
Rick Brown, *Vice Pres*
John Pressler, *Vice Pres*
Dan V Avond, *Maint Spvr*
◆ EMP: 225
SQ FT: 88,000
SALES (est): 95.1MM
SALES (corp-wide): 54.7B **Publicly Held**
WEB: www.anchorcoupling.com
SIC: **3429** Clamps & couplings, hose
PA: Caterpillar Inc.
 510 Lake Cook Rd Ste 100
 Deerfield IL 60015
 224 551-4000

(G-10723)
ANDERSON MANUFACTURING CO INC (PA)
Also Called: Ultimate Bed
5300 13th St (49858-1044)
PHONE.................................906 863-8223
Robert F Anderson, *President*
Eric Anderson, *Vice Pres*
Deb Carley, *Treasurer*
Lois A Anderson, *Admin Sec*
EMP: 12
SQ FT: 50,000
SALES (est): 1.9MM **Privately Held**
WEB: www.ultimatebed.com
SIC: **2511** Dressers, household: wood

(G-10724)
AQUILA RESOURCES INC (PA)
414 10th Ave Ste 1 (49858-3066)
PHONE.................................906 352-4024
Thomas Quigley, *Principal*
Dan Blondeau, *Manager*
EMP: 8 EST: 2011
SALES (est): 1.8MM **Privately Held**
SIC: **6211 1481** Oil & gas lease brokers; nonmetallic mineral services

(G-10725)
BEAVER CREEK WOOD PRODUCTS LLC
993 26th St (49858-2212)
P.O. Box 456, Marinette WI (54143-0456)
PHONE.................................920 680-9663
David Koertge, *Mng Member*
EMP: 25 EST: 2006
SALES (est): 2.5MM **Privately Held**
SIC: **2499** Mulch, wood & bark

(G-10726)
BOBURKA CUSTOM MOLD
805 6th St (49858-3109)
P.O. Box 651 (49858-0651)
PHONE.................................906 864-9930
Mike Boburka, *Mng Member*
EMP: 10
SALES (est): 1.1MM **Privately Held**
SIC: **3599** Machine shop, jobbing & repair

(G-10727)
CMB MFG LLC
630 7th St (49858-3159)
PHONE.................................920 915-2079
EMP: 3
SALES (est): 173.7K **Privately Held**
SIC: **3999** Manufacturing industries

(G-10728)
COLEMAN MACHINE INC (PA)
Also Called: Coleman Racing Products
N1597 Us Highway 41 (49858-9692)
PHONE.................................906 863-1113
Gene Coleman, *President*
Donna Coleman, *Vice Pres*
▲ EMP: 30 EST: 1965
SQ FT: 10,000
SALES (est): 4MM **Privately Held**
WEB: www.colemanracing.com
SIC: **3599 3549** Machine shop, jobbing & repair; metalworking machinery

(G-10729)
COMPONENT SOLUTIONS LLC
2219 10th Ave (49858-2301)
P.O. Box 1074, Marinette WI (54143-6074)
PHONE.................................906 863-2682
Kari Jo Bunting, *Owner*
EMP: 45
SALES (est): 19MM **Privately Held**
SIC: **5031 2426** Lumber, plywood & millwork; lumber, hardwood dimension

(G-10730)
DUFF BRUSH LLC
630 7th St (49858-3159)
PHONE.................................906 863-3319
Matthew Duffrin,
EMP: 6
SALES (est): 566.9K **Privately Held**
SIC: **3991** Brooms & brushes

(G-10731)
ENSTROM HELICOPTER CORPORATION
2209 22nd St (49858-3515)
PHONE.................................906 863-1200
Matthew Francour, *CEO*
Gong WEI, *Ch of Bd*
Guo Huaqiang, *Principal*
Lori Okrasinski, *Purch Mgr*
Stephanie Bergstrom, *Treasurer*
◆ EMP: 220 EST: 1959
SQ FT: 88,000
SALES (est): 45MM
SALES (corp-wide): 45.8MM **Privately Held**
WEB: www.enstromhelicopter.com
SIC: **3721** Helicopters
PA: Chongqing General Aviation Industry Group Co., Ltd.
 No.19,Yinlong Rd.,Longxing Town,Yubei District
 Chongqing 40113
 238 872-8555

(G-10732)
EVEN WEIGHT BRUSH LLC
603 6th St (49858-3163)
P.O. Box 34 (49858-0034)
PHONE.................................906 863-3319
EMP: 4
SALES (est): 300K **Privately Held**
SIC: **3991** Mfg Brooms/Brushes

(G-10733)
FIBREK INC
Also Called: Resolute Forest Products
701 4th Ave (49858-3353)
P.O. Box 277 (49858-0277)
PHONE.................................906 864-9125
Robert Garland, *President*
Michael Klumb, *Engineer*
Sue Keer, *Controller*
Dana Peterson, *Accountant*
Todd Enderby, *Manager*
EMP: 214
SALES (est): 41.2MM
SALES (corp-wide): 3.7B **Privately Held**
SIC: **2611** Pulp mills
PA: Resolute Forest Products Inc
 111 Boul Robert-Bourassa Bureau 5000
 Montreal QC H3C 2
 514 875-2160

Menominee - Menominee County (G-10734)

(G-10734)
FIBREK RECYCLING US INC
Also Called: Great Lakes Pulp & Fibre
701 4th Ave (49858-3353)
P.O. Box 277 (49858-0277)
PHONE..................................906 863-8137
Richard Garneau, *President*
Alain Boivin, *Vice Pres*
Peter Staiger, *Treasurer*
Jacques Vachon, *Admin Sec*
◆ **EMP:** 108
SQ FT: 5,000
SALES: 37.2MM
SALES (corp-wide): 3.7B **Privately Held**
SIC: 2611 Pulp mills, chemical & semi-chemical processing
PA: Resolute Forest Products Inc
111 Boul Robert-Bourassa Bureau 5000
Montreal QC H3C 2
514 875-2160

(G-10735)
FIBREK US INC
701 4th Ave (49858-3353)
PHONE..................................906 864-9125
Richard Garneau, *President*
EMP: 5
SALES (est): 1MM
SALES (corp-wide): 3.7B **Privately Held**
SIC: 2611 Pulp mills
PA: Resolute Forest Products Inc
111 Boul Robert-Bourassa Bureau 5000
Montreal QC H3C 2
514 875-2160

(G-10736)
FLANDERS INDUSTRIES INC
Also Called: Lloyd Flanders Industries
3010 10th St (49858-1704)
P.O. Box 550 (49858-0550)
PHONE..................................906 863-4491
Dudley K Flanders, *President*
Jeffrey H Starks, *Corp Secy*
Eugene B Davenport, *Exec VP*
Lou Rosebrock, *Senior VP*
Norman Rosebrock, *Senior VP*
◆ **EMP:** 110 **EST:** 1929
SALES: 1.2MM **Privately Held**
SIC: 2519 2514 Wicker furniture: padded or plain; metal lawn & garden furniture; lawn furniture: metal

(G-10737)
GARDEN BAY WINERY LLC
817 48th Ave (49858-1234)
PHONE..................................906 361-6136
EMP: 4
SALES (est): 170K **Privately Held**
SIC: 2084 Mfg Wines/Brandy/Spirits

(G-10738)
GIBOUTS SASH & DOOR
2208 10th Ave (49858-2302)
PHONE..................................906 863-2224
Jacob Menacher, *Partner*
Daniel J Menacher, *Partner*
Gerald Menacher, *Partner*
EMP: 3
SQ FT: 5,250
SALES: 140K **Privately Held**
SIC: 2431 Doors, wood

(G-10739)
IRON CITY ENTERPRISES INC
N2404 Us Highway 41 (49858-9675)
PHONE..................................906 863-2630
Thomas J Nemetz, *President*
Marilyn J Nemetz, *Corp Secy*
Robert Nemetz, *Vice Pres*
EMP: 3
SQ FT: 2,100
SALES (est): 626.8K **Privately Held**
SIC: 3272 Septic tanks, concrete

(G-10740)
JP SKIDMORE LLC
W5634 Evergreen Road No 3 (49858-9604)
PHONE..................................906 424-4127
EMP: 9
SALES (est): 2MM **Privately Held**
SIC: 3531 Forestry related equipment

(G-10741)
L E JONES COMPANY
1200 34th Ave (49858-1695)
PHONE..................................906 863-1043
David Doll, *CEO*
Peter Vennema, *Ch of Bd*
Douglas Dooley, *Vice Pres*
Dan Bancroft, *Director*
▲ **EMP:** 390
SQ FT: 110,000
SALES (est): 77.5MM **Privately Held**
WEB: www.lejones.com
SIC: 3592 3545 Valves, engine; machine tool accessories

(G-10742)
LUMBER JACK HARDWOODS INC (PA)
N2509 O1 Dr (49858-9674)
P.O. Box 397 (49858-0397)
PHONE..................................906 863-7090
John Fleetwood, *President*
Candace Fleetwood, *Corp Secy*
Nathan Fleetwood, *Vice Pres*
EMP: 15 **EST:** 1976
SALES (est): 5.5MM **Privately Held**
WEB: www.sturgeonmillwork.com
SIC: 2426 2421 Hardwood dimension & flooring mills; kiln drying of lumber

(G-10743)
MARSHALL MIDDLEBY HOLDING LLC
Also Called: Nu-Vu Food Service Systems
5600 13th St (49858-1029)
PHONE..................................906 863-4401
◆ **EMP:** 10
SALES (est): 978.8K
SALES (corp-wide): 2.7B **Publicly Held**
SIC: 3556 Food products machinery
PA: The Middleby Corporation
1400 Toastmaster Dr
Elgin IL 60120
847 741-3300

(G-10744)
MARTIN SAW & TOOL INC (PA)
1212 19th Ave (49858-2718)
PHONE..................................906 863-6812
William W Martin, *President*
Jeffrey Martin, *Vice Pres*
Randy Martin, *Vice Pres*
Phyllis Martin, *Treasurer*
EMP: 7
SQ FT: 21,260
SALES: 500K **Privately Held**
SIC: 3599 3425 Machine shop, jobbing & repair; saw blades & handsaws

(G-10745)
MENOMINEE ACQUISITION CORP
Also Called: Clearwater Paper - Menominee
144 1st St (49858-3302)
PHONE..................................906 863-5595
Russell Taylor, *President*
Tom Moore, *Vice Pres*
Dianne Scheu, *CFO*
Hugo Vivero, *VP Sales*
▼ **EMP:** 125
SALES (est): 27.7MM
SALES (corp-wide): 139.6MM **Privately Held**
WEB: www.menomineepaper.com
SIC: 2621 Paper mills
HQ: Dunn Paper, Inc.
218 Riverview St
Port Huron MI 48060
810 984-5521

(G-10746)
MENOMINEE CITY OF MICHIGAN
Also Called: Waste Water Treatment
1301 5th Ave (49858)
P.O. Box 453 (49858-0453)
PHONE..................................906 863-3050
Mike Thorsen, *Manager*
EMP: 4 **Privately Held**
WEB: www.cityofmenominee.org
SIC: 3589 Water treatment equipment, industrial
PA: Menominee City Of Michigan
2511 10th St
Menominee MI 49858
906 863-2656

(G-10747)
MENOMINEE SAW AND SUPPLY CO (PA)
Also Called: Menominee Carbide Cutting Tls
900 16th St (49858-2600)
P.O. Box 515 (49858-0515)
PHONE..................................906 863-2609
Felix Ben Mroz, *President*
Marilyn K Mroz, *Treasurer*
▼ **EMP:** 27
SQ FT: 11,000
SALES (est): 3.7MM **Privately Held**
WEB: www.menomineesaw.com
SIC: 7699 5084 3546 3541 Knife, saw & tool sharpening & repair; sawmill machinery & equipment; power-driven handtools; machine tools, metal cutting type; saw blades & handsaws

(G-10748)
MENOMINEE SAW AND SUPPLY CO
2134 13th St (49858-2104)
PHONE..................................906 863-8998
Terry Champeau, *Manager*
EMP: 4
SALES (corp-wide): 3.7MM **Privately Held**
WEB: www.menomineesaw.com
SIC: 7692 Welding repair
PA: Saw Menominee And Supply Company
900 16th St
Menominee MI 49858
906 863-2609

(G-10749)
MENOMINEE RVER LBR DMNSIONS LLC
2219 10th Ave (49858-2301)
P.O. Box 1074, Marinette WI (54143-6074)
PHONE..................................906 863-2682
Kari Bunting, *President*
Dave Geier, *Vice Pres*
▲ **EMP:** 40
SQ FT: 60,000
SALES (est): 5MM **Privately Held**
WEB: www.mrlandd.com
SIC: 5211 2426 Planing mill products & lumber; dimension, hardwood

(G-10750)
MIDDLEBY CORPORATION
Nu-Vu Food Service Systems
5600 13th St (49858-1029)
PHONE..................................906 863-4401
Gary Hahn, *Branch Mgr*
EMP: 103
SALES (corp-wide): 2.7B **Publicly Held**
WEB: www.middleby.com
SIC: 3556 Ovens, bakery
PA: The Middleby Corporation
1400 Toastmaster Dr
Elgin IL 60120
847 741-3300

(G-10751)
MINERALS PROCESSING CORP
414 10th Ave (49858-3066)
PHONE..................................906 352-4024
EMP: 4 **EST:** 2013
SALES (est): 267.3K **Privately Held**
SIC: 1081 Metal mining exploration & development services

(G-10752)
N PACK SHIP CENTER
1045 10th St (49858-3025)
PHONE..................................906 863-4095
April Davis, *Owner*
EMP: 5
SALES (est): 498.5K **Privately Held**
SIC: 3086 4731 Packaging & shipping materials, foamed plastic; agents, shipping

(G-10753)
NORTHERN COATINGS & CHEM CO
705 6th Ave (49858-3115)
PHONE..................................906 863-2641
Larry Melgary, *President*
Susan Ellie, *Vice Pres*
Mark Lavalley, *Vice Pres*
Doyle Yoder, *Project Mgr*
Chad Christensen, *Production*
▼ **EMP:** 37 **EST:** 1971
SQ FT: 100,000
SALES: 7MM **Privately Held**
WEB: www.northern-coatings.com
SIC: 2851 2899 2869 Paints & paint additives; chemical preparations; industrial organic chemicals

(G-10754)
NORTHERN FAB & MACHINE LLC
5601 13th St (49858-1045)
PHONE..................................906 863-8506
Daniel Drifka,
EMP: 12
SALES (est): 2MM **Privately Held**
SIC: 3599 3443 Hose, flexible metallic; weldments

(G-10755)
PLUTCHAK FAB
Also Called: Krane
N1715 Us Highway 41 (49858-9607)
PHONE..................................906 864-4650
Tim Plutchak,
EMP: 8
SQ FT: 20,000
SALES (est): 3.3MM **Privately Held**
SIC: 5084 3441 Cranes, industrial; fabricated structural metal

(G-10756)
R W FERNSTRUM & COMPANY
1716 11th Ave (49858-2500)
P.O. Box 97 (49858-0097)
PHONE..................................906 863-5553
Paul W Fernstrum, *President*
Dale Gusick, *Export Mgr*
Jean Granum, *CFO*
Todd Fernstrum, *Treasurer*
▲ **EMP:** 35
SQ FT: 34,300
SALES (est): 8.5MM **Privately Held**
WEB: www.fernstrum.com
SIC: 3443 3429 Fabricated plate work (boiler shop); manufactured hardware (general)

(G-10757)
STRIDER SOFTWARE INC
1605 7th St (49858-2815)
P.O. Box 513, Marinette WI (54143-0513)
PHONE..................................906 863-7798
Kenneth Stillman, *President*
EMP: 6
SALES (est): 473.8K **Privately Held**
WEB: www.typestyler.com
SIC: 7372 Application computer software

(G-10758)
SUPERIOR ATTACHMENT INC
N3522 Us Highway 41 (49858-9653)
PHONE..................................906 864-1708
Rich Linsmeier, *Principal*
EMP: 4
SALES (est): 559.1K **Privately Held**
SIC: 3523 Farm machinery & equipment

(G-10759)
UNIQUE NAMECRAFT INC
N297 River Dr (49858-9428)
PHONE..................................906 863-3644
Richard Boye, *President*
Tom Brockman, *Partner*
Nelvin Reman, *Partner*
EMP: 3
SALES (est): 154.9K **Privately Held**
SIC: 2499 Decorative wood & woodwork

Merrill
Saginaw County

(G-10760)
MERRILL TECHNOLOGIES GROUP INC
Also Called: Merrill Tool & Machine
21659 Gratiot Rd (48637-8717)
PHONE..................................989 643-7981
Robert Yackel, *CEO*
Robin Schmaltz, *Business Mgr*
EMP: 123
SALES (corp-wide): 60MM **Privately Held**
SIC: 3599 Machine shop, jobbing & repair

▲ = Import ▼ = Export
◆ = Import/Export

GEOGRAPHIC SECTION

Michigan Center - Jackson County (G-10786)

PA: Merrill Technologies Group, Inc.
400 Florence St
Saginaw MI 48602
989 791-6676

(G-10761)
SILER PRECISION MACHINE INC
136 E Saginaw St (48637-2528)
P.O. Box 37 (48637-0037)
PHONE..................989 643-7793
Steven J Siler, *President*
George Siler, *Treasurer*
EMP: 4
SQ FT: 14,000
SALES (est): 698.5K **Privately Held**
SIC: 3599 Machine shop, jobbing & repair

(G-10762)
SUPERIOR VAULT CO
345 E Mahoney (48637-9337)
P.O. Box 118 (48637-0118)
PHONE..................989 643-4200
John Hutchinson, *Owner*
EMP: 4 EST: 2001
SALES (est): 348.5K **Privately Held**
SIC: 3272 5087 Burial vaults, concrete or precast terrazzo; concrete burial vaults & boxes

Merritt
Missaukee County

(G-10763)
HOWEY TREE BALER CORPORATION
6069 E Gaukel Rd (49667-9738)
PHONE..................231 328-4321
Stephen Howey Jr, *President*
Darleana Howey, *Corp Secy*
Gary Howey, *Vice Pres*
Greg Howey, *Vice Pres*
Stephen Howey Sr, *Vice Pres*
EMP: 5
SQ FT: 8,000
SALES (est): 866.6K **Privately Held**
SIC: 3523 Balers, farm: hay, straw, cotton, etc.; elevators, farm

(G-10764)
LONEYS WELDING & EXCVTG INC
6735 E Houghton Lake Rd (49667-9743)
PHONE..................231 328-4408
Michael Loney, *President*
Lesia Loney, *Admin Sec*
EMP: 5
SALES (est): 1.1MM **Privately Held**
SIC: 1382 7692 Oil & gas exploration services; welding repair

(G-10765)
TRONOX INCORPORATED
4176 N Dorr Rd (49667-9774)
PHONE..................231 328-4986
Steve Walker, *Branch Mgr*
EMP: 5
SALES (corp-wide): 1.7B **Privately Held**
WEB: www.tieandtimber.com
SIC: 1311 1321 Crude petroleum & natural gas; natural gas liquids
HQ: Tronox Incorporated
1 Stamford Plz
Stamford CT 06901
203 705-3800

Mesick
Wexford County

(G-10766)
BECKMAN PRODUCTION SVCS INC
23862 13 Mile Rd (49668-9604)
PHONE..................231 885-1665
Ron Sedlacek, *Area Mgr*
EMP: 6
SALES (corp-wide): 827.1MM **Publicly Held**
SIC: 1389 Oil field services

HQ: Beckman Production Services, Inc.
3786 Beebe Rd
Kalkaska MI 49646
231 258-9524

(G-10767)
BLUEWATER TECH GROUP INC
6305 W 115 (49668)
PHONE..................231 885-2600
Mack Truax, *Branch Mgr*
EMP: 6
SALES (corp-wide): 35.9MM **Privately Held**
SIC: 3651 5064 7622 7359 Household audio & video equipment; electrical appliances, television & radio; radio & television repair; equipment rental & leasing
PA: Bluewater Technologies Group, Inc.
24050 Northwestern Hwy
Southfield MI 48075
248 356-4399

(G-10768)
CASSELMAN LOGGING
23400 13 Mile Rd (49668-9604)
PHONE..................231 885-1040
James A Casselman, *Partner*
Patty Casselman, *Partner*
EMP: 6
SALES (est): 290K **Privately Held**
SIC: 2411 2421 Pulpwood contractors engaged in cutting; sawmills & planing mills, general

(G-10769)
DART ENERGY CORPORATION
23862 13 Mile Rd (49668-9604)
PHONE..................231 885-1665
Danny Cagel, *Branch Mgr*
EMP: 14 **Privately Held**
WEB: www.dartenergy.com
SIC: 1311 1382 Crude petroleum production; natural gas production; oil & gas exploration services

(G-10770)
HOUSLER SAWMILL INC
222 E 16 Rd (49668-9726)
PHONE..................231 824-6353
Leslie Housler, *President*
Wayl D Housler, *Vice Pres*
EMP: 15
SALES (est): 2.4MM **Privately Held**
SIC: 2421 Sawmills & planing mills, general

(G-10771)
MESICK MOLD CO
4901 Industrial Dr (49668-9525)
PHONE..................231 885-1304
Chancey Spencer, *President*
Dave Spencer, *General Mgr*
David Spencer, *Vice Pres*
Jon Slabaugh, *Engineer*
Mark Giberson, *Design Engr*
EMP: 25
SQ FT: 6,000
SALES: 4.5MM **Privately Held**
WEB: www.mesickmold.com
SIC: 3544 Forms (molds), for foundry & plastics working machinery; industrial molds

Metamora
Lapeer County

(G-10772)
AURORA CAD CAM INC
Also Called: Cad CAM
1643 E Brocker Rd (48455-9789)
PHONE..................810 678-2128
Ron Jovanovitz, *President*
EMP: 10
SALES (est): 1.7MM **Privately Held**
SIC: 3543 Industrial patterns

(G-10773)
CENTERPOINT TUNGSTEN LLC
4427 Snook Rd (48455-9736)
PHONE..................810 797-5196
Ronald G Kline, *Owner*
EMP: 3

SALES (est): 304.9K **Privately Held**
SIC: 3532 Grinders, stone: stationary

(G-10774)
CROSS COUNTRY OILFLD SVCS INC
4833 Linda Ln (48455-8935)
PHONE..................337 366-3840
Sherri Dupuis, *President*
EMP: 4
SALES (est): 174.9K **Privately Held**
SIC: 1389 Oil field services

(G-10775)
GRAPHITE MACHINING INC
4141 S Oak St (48455-9240)
PHONE..................810 678-2227
Tim Bears, *Manager*
EMP: 10
SALES (corp-wide): 17.8MM **Privately Held**
WEB: www.graphitemachinginc.com
SIC: 3599 3624 3295 Machine shop, jobbing & repair; carbon & graphite products; graphite, natural: ground, pulverized, refined or blended
PA: Graphite Machining, Inc.
240 N Main St
Topton PA 19562
610 682-0080

(G-10776)
INDOCOMP SYSTEMS INC
3383 S Lapeer Rd (48455-8968)
PHONE..................810 678-3990
Mike Keerl, *President*
Brian Daye, *President*
Thomas Floyd, *Vice Pres*
Thomas Foley, *CFO*
EMP: 15
SALES (est): 2MM **Privately Held**
WEB: www.indocomp.com
SIC: 3571 7373 Electronic computers; systems integration services

(G-10777)
JOHN R SAND & GRAVEL CO INC
1717 E Dryden Rd (48455)
PHONE..................810 678-3715
Edward R Evatz Jr, *President*
EMP: 4
SALES (est): 645.5K **Privately Held**
SIC: 1442 Common sand mining; gravel mining

(G-10778)
L & J ENTERPRISES INC
Also Called: Lady Jane Gourmet Seed Co.
3181 Wynns Mill Ct (48455-8956)
PHONE..................586 995-4153
Laura Noble, *President*
Joe Noble, *Vice Pres*
EMP: 4
SALES (est): 307.9K **Privately Held**
SIC: 2099 Food preparations

(G-10779)
OXFORD BIOMEDICAL RESEARCH INC (PA)
4600 Gardner Rd (48455-9108)
P.O. Box 522, Oxford (48371-0522)
PHONE..................248 852-8815
Denis M Callewaert, *President*
Karen Callewaert, *Treasurer*
EMP: 2
SQ FT: 4,000
SALES (est): 2.6MM **Privately Held**
WEB: www.oxfordlabs.com
SIC: 5122 8731 2836 Biologicals & allied products; biological research; biological products, except diagnostic

(G-10780)
SHADOWOOD TECHNOLOGY INC
4221 Meadow Pond Ln (48455-9751)
P.O. Box 284, Hadley (48440-0284)
PHONE..................810 358-2569
Todd Hemingway, *President*
Wendy K Hemingway, *CFO*
EMP: 8
SQ FT: 10,000

SALES (est): 795.1K **Privately Held**
SIC: 3519 Diesel, semi-diesel or duel-fuel engines, including marine; diesel engine rebuilding; engines, diesel & semi-diesel or dual-fuel; governors, pump, for diesel engines

(G-10781)
SUPERIOR DESIGN & MFG
4180 Pleasant St (48455-9403)
P.O. Box 204 (48455-0204)
PHONE..................810 678-3950
Patrick Clouse, *President*
David Denise, *Treasurer*
Dave Denise, *Manager*
EMP: 10
SQ FT: 4,500
SALES (est): 1.2MM **Privately Held**
SIC: 3545 3569 3599 Machine tool accessories; assembly machines, non-metalworking; machine shop, jobbing & repair

(G-10782)
TEC-3 PROTOTYPES INC
4321 Blood Rd (48455-9243)
PHONE..................810 678-8909
EMP: 20
SQ FT: 9,200
SALES (est): 2.7MM **Privately Held**
SIC: 3465 3496 3495 3444 Mfg Automotive Stampings Mfg Misc Fab Wire Prdts Mfg Wire Springs Mfg Sheet Metalwork Mfg Hardware

Michigan Center
Jackson County

(G-10783)
ADCO GLOBAL INC
Also Called: Adco Products
4401 Page Ave (49254-1037)
PHONE..................517 764-0334
Jim Turner, *Principal*
Connie Kearns, *Chief Mktg Ofcr*
EMP: 300
SALES (corp-wide): 3B **Publicly Held**
WEB: www.adcoglobal.com
SIC: 2891 Adhesives
HQ: Adco Global, Inc.
100 Tri State Intl # 135
Lincolnshire IL 60069
847 282-3485

(G-10784)
ADCO PRODUCTS LLC
Also Called: Adco Products, Inc.
4401 Page Ave (49254-1037)
P.O. Box 457 (49254-0457)
PHONE..................517 841-7238
John Knox, *CEO*
Glenn Frommer, *President*
Tim Oneill, *General Mgr*
Dan Dixon, *Safety Mgr*
Eric Weidner, *Project Engr*
EMP: 220
SQ FT: 200,000
SALES (est): 58.9K
SALES (corp-wide): 3B **Publicly Held**
WEB: www.adcocorp.com
SIC: 2891 Adhesives & sealants
HQ: Adco Global, Inc.
100 Tri State Intl # 135
Lincolnshire IL 60069
847 282-3485

(G-10785)
CENTER MACHINE & TOOL LLC
150 Factory Rd (49254-1010)
PHONE..................517 748-2500
Craig Ahrens,
EMP: 7
SQ FT: 8,000
SALES (est): 1MM **Privately Held**
SIC: 3599 Machine shop, jobbing & repair

(G-10786)
ETERNABOND INC
4401 Page Ave (49254-1037)
PHONE..................847 540-0600
Christopher Margarites, *President*
Gail Margarites, *Vice Pres*
▲ EMP: 7
SQ FT: 5,000

Michigan Center - Jackson County (G-10787)

SALES (est): 4.7MM **Privately Held**
WEB: www.eternabond.com
SIC: 2891 Adhesives

(G-10787)
MILLENNIUM ADHESIVE PRODUCTS (PA)
4401 Page Ave (49254-1037)
PHONE 800 248-4010
EMP: 8
SALES (est): 1.2MM **Privately Held**
SIC: 2891 Adhesives

(G-10788)
MONARCH PRINT SOLUTIONS LLC
4000 Page Ave Ste E (49254-1028)
P.O. Box 807 (49254-0807)
PHONE 517 522-8457
EMP: 4
SALES (est): 598.5K **Privately Held**
SIC: 2752 Commercial printing, offset

(G-10789)
PRECISION GUIDES LLC
151 Factory Rd (49254-1009)
PHONE 517 536-7234
Lee Cole,
Kurt Cole,
Scott Cole,
EMP: 5 EST: 2011
SQ FT: 2,500
SALES: 400K **Privately Held**
SIC: 3541 Machine tools, metal cutting type

(G-10790)
ROYAL ADHESIVES & SEALANTS LLC
4401 Page Ave (49254-1037)
PHONE 517 764-0334
EMP: 65
SALES (corp-wide): 3B **Publicly Held**
SIC: 2891 Sealants
HQ: Royal Adhesives And Sealants Llc
2001 W Washington St
South Bend IN 46628
574 246-5000

(G-10791)
SYNCHRONOUS MANUFACTURING INC
4050 Page Ave (49254-1030)
PHONE 517 764-6930
Michael Thorrez, *President*
Albert A Thorrez, *Treasurer*
▲ EMP: 50
SALES (est): 8.3MM **Privately Held**
WEB: www.thorrez.com
SIC: 3499 3625 3714 Fire- or burglary-resistive products; relays & industrial controls; motor vehicle parts & accessories

(G-10792)
UNISORB INC (HQ)
Also Called: Unisorb Installation Tech
4117 Felters Rd Ste A (49254-1076)
P.O. Box 1000, Jackson (49204-1000)
PHONE 517 764-6060
Michael A Considine, *Ch of Bd*
Peter M Moore, *President*
John Richter, *Vice Pres*
Wayne H Whittaker, *Vice Pres*
▲ EMP: 40
SQ FT: 64,000
SALES (est): 5.4MM **Privately Held**
WEB: www.unisorb.com
SIC: 3499 Machine bases, metal
PA: Considine Financial Corporation
101 N Indian Hill Blvd C1-206
Claremont CA 91711
626 793-1000

Middleton
Gratiot County

(G-10793)
MEYERS JOHN
Also Called: Johnny Meyers Trucking
5752 Cleveland Rd (48856)
PHONE 989 236-5400
John Meyers, *Owner*
EMP: 4
SQ FT: 30,000
SALES (est): 252.5K **Privately Held**
SIC: 3711 Truck & tractor truck assembly

(G-10794)
MID MCHGAN FEED INGRDIENTS LLC
4585 S Garfield Rd (48856)
PHONE 989 236-5014
Kris D Duflo,
EMP: 5
SALES (est): 958.4K **Privately Held**
SIC: 2048 Prepared feeds

(G-10795)
SHADY NOOK FARMS (PA)
Also Called: M.R. Village Pizzeria
129 S Newton St (48856)
PHONE 989 236-7240
Richard Schaffer, *President*
Don Schaffer, *Vice Pres*
EMP: 4
SALES (est): 853.3K **Privately Held**
SIC: 2099 4225 Pizza, refrigerated: except frozen; miniwarehouse, warehousing

Middleville
Barry County

(G-10796)
ACCURATE MACHINE & TL USA LTD
987 Grand Rapids St (49333-9498)
PHONE 269 205-2610
Steve Zawacki, *Manager*
EMP: 13
SALES (corp-wide): 14.4MM **Privately Held**
SIC: 3599 Machine shop, jobbing & repair
PA: Accurate Machine & Tool Limited
1844 Wilson Ave
North York ON M9M 1
416 742-8301

(G-10797)
ALLIANCE SHEET METAL INC
6262 N Moe Rd (49333-8749)
PHONE 269 795-2954
Tim Flohe, *President*
EMP: 13
SQ FT: 44,000
SALES (est): 1.6MM **Privately Held**
WEB: www.alliancesheetmetal.com
SIC: 3444 Sheet metalwork

(G-10798)
BAIRDS MACHINE SHOP
8300 W Garbow Rd (49333-9454)
PHONE 269 795-9524
Eric Baird, *Owner*
EMP: 3
SALES (est): 150K **Privately Held**
SIC: 3599 7692 Machine shop, jobbing & repair; welding repair

(G-10799)
BRADFORD-WHITE CORPORATION
200 Lafayette St (49333-7048)
PHONE 269 795-3364
Nicholas J Giuffre, *CEO*
Eric Lannes, *Senior VP*
Bruce Hill, *VP Engrg*
EMP: 900
SQ FT: 300,000
SALES (corp-wide): 222.6MM **Privately Held**
WEB: www.bradfordwhite.com
SIC: 3639 Hot water heaters, household
PA: Bradford White Corporation
725 Talamore Dr
Ambler PA 19002
215 641-9400

(G-10800)
COMMERCIAL WORKS
200 Lafayette St (49333-9492)
PHONE 269 795-2060
Bradford-White Corporation, *Partner*
Eugene West, *Opers Mgr*
EMP: 110
SQ FT: 70,000
SALES (est): 8.5MM **Privately Held**
SIC: 3433 Heating equipment, except electric

(G-10801)
CORNERSTONE FURNITURE INC
915 Grand Rapids St (49333-9498)
P.O. Box 276 (49333-0276)
PHONE 269 795-3379
Quentin Mulder, *President*
EMP: 4
SQ FT: 8,000
SALES (est): 516.4K **Privately Held**
WEB: www.cornerstonefurniture.com
SIC: 2521 Desks, office: wood

(G-10802)
FORZZA CORPORATION
915 Grand Rapids St (49333-9498)
PHONE 616 884-6121
EMP: 16
SALES (corp-wide): 1.9MM **Privately Held**
SIC: 3585 Parts for heating, cooling & refrigerating equipment
PA: Forzza Corporation
222 N Lake St
Madison OH 44057
440 998-6300

(G-10803)
GREAT LAKES JIG & FIXTURE
11610 Bowens Mill Rd (49333-9758)
PHONE 269 795-4349
Scott Palazzolo, *Owner*
Steve Palazzolo, *General Mgr*
EMP: 7
SQ FT: 2,200
SALES (est): 1MM **Privately Held**
SIC: 3544 Special dies, tools, jigs & fixtures

(G-10804)
H & L MANUFACTURING CO
900 E Mn St (49333)
PHONE 269 795-5000
Steve Sawdy, *CEO*
Roger Van Dyke, *Manager*
Tanya Sawdy, *Admin Sec*
EMP: 130 EST: 1964
SQ FT: 28,000
SALES (est): 32.7MM **Privately Held**
SIC: 3714 3694 Motor vehicle parts & accessories; engine electrical equipment

(G-10805)
MIDDLEVILLE TOOL & DIE CO INC
1900 Patterson Rd (49333-8410)
PHONE 269 795-3646
Gary Middleton, *CEO*
Ross Martin, *President*
Mike Cornell, *VP Mfg*
Tim Hayman, *Materials Mgr*
Rick Cain, *QC Mgr*
EMP: 70 EST: 1966
SQ FT: 53,000
SALES (est): 25.8MM **Privately Held**
WEB: www.mtd-inc.com
SIC: 3469 3544 3465 Stamping metal for the trade; special dies & tools; automotive stampings

(G-10806)
REURINK ROOF MAINT & COATING
12795 Jackson Rd (49333-8596)
PHONE 269 795-2337
Richard H Reurink, *President*
James Reurink, *Treasurer*
Mary Reurink, *Admin Sec*
EMP: 4
SALES (est): 400K **Privately Held**
SIC: 1761 2952 Roofing contractor; roofing felts, cements or coatings

(G-10807)
SOUTH KENT GRAVEL INC
3700 Patterson Rd (49333-9150)
PHONE 269 795-3500
Bob Thompson, *President*
EMP: 23
SQ FT: 30,000
SALES (est): 1.3MM
SALES (corp-wide): 30.6B **Privately Held**
SIC: 1442 Construction sand & gravel
HQ: Michigan Paving And Materials Company
2575 S Haggerty Rd # 100
Canton MI 48188
734 397-2050

(G-10808)
SOUTHWESTERN HARDWOODS LLC
4450 Village Edge Dr (49333-9195)
PHONE 269 795-0004
EMP: 3 EST: 2008
SALES (est): 211.5K **Privately Held**
SIC: 2421 Sawmills & planing mills, general

(G-10809)
STICKMANN BAECKEREI
11332 W M 179 Hwy (49333-8429)
PHONE 269 205-2444
Rebecca Denney, *Principal*
EMP: 3
SALES (est): 198.8K **Privately Held**
SIC: 2095 Roasted coffee

(G-10810)
TILLERMAN JFP LLC (PA)
10451 W Garbow Rd (49333-8557)
PHONE 616 443-8346
Remos Lenio, *Mng Member*
EMP: 25
SALES (est): 1.1MM **Privately Held**
SIC: 3069 Molded rubber products

(G-10811)
U S BAIRD CORPORATION
J M Systems Div
8121 108th St Se (49333-9302)
PHONE 616 826-5013
John Mitteer, *General Mgr*
EMP: 10
SALES (corp-wide): 4.2MM **Privately Held**
WEB: www.usbaird.com
SIC: 3542 Spinning, spline rolling & winding machines
PA: The U S Baird Corporation
1700 Stratford Ave
Stratford CT
203 375-3361

Midland
Midland County

(G-10812)
AGRIGENETICS INC
2030 Dow Ctr (48674-1500)
PHONE 317 337-3000
Robert M Isackson, *Principal*
EMP: 8
SALES (est): 1.8MM
SALES (corp-wide): 61B **Publicly Held**
SIC: 2873 Fertilizers: natural (organic), except compost
HQ: The Dow Chemical Company
2211 H H Dow Way
Midland MI 48642
989 636-1000

(G-10813)
ALLOY CONSTRUCTION SERVICE INC (PA)
3500 Contractors Dr (48642-6962)
PHONE 989 486-6960
Ronnie J Neumann, *President*
Michael Laundra, *Vice Pres*
EMP: 25 EST: 1981
SQ FT: 13,000
SALES (est): 5.7MM **Privately Held**
SIC: 3441 Fabricated structural metal

(G-10814)
AMPM INC
7403 W Wackerly St (48642-7435)
P.O. Box 1887 (48641-1887)
PHONE 989 837-8800
Mark Bush, *President*
William Trethaway, *Chairman*
Hugo Cruz, *Site Mgr*
Enrique Hernandez, *Site Mgr*
Eldon Price, *Site Mgr*
EMP: 13
SQ FT: 6,400

SALES: 1.5MM **Privately Held**
SIC: 7311 3577 8732 Advertising consultant; graphic displays, except graphic terminals; market analysis or research

(G-10815)
ANIMAL MEDICAL CTR OF LAPEER
4925 Jefferson Ave (48640-2905)
PHONE.................................989 631-3350
Daniel White, *Branch Mgr*
EMP: 10
SALES (est): 1.4MM **Privately Held**
SIC: 3841 0742 Surgical & medical instruments; veterinarian, animal specialties
PA: Animal Medical Center Of Lapeer Inc
490 Oak St
Lapeer MI 48446

(G-10816)
APTARGROUP INC
Also Called: LMS
2202 Ridgewood Dr (48642-5841)
PHONE.................................989 631-8030
James Manning, *President*
Andrew Smith, *General Mgr*
Greg Cole, *Engineer*
Chad Smith, *Engineer*
Tyler Witt, *Engineer*
EMP: 105 **Publicly Held**
SIC: 3069 4225 2822 Molded rubber products; general warehousing; synthetic rubber
PA: Aptargroup, Inc.
265 Exchange Dr Ste 100
Crystal Lake IL 60014

(G-10817)
BLUE CUBE HOLDING LLC (DH)
2030 Dow Ctr (48674-1500)
PHONE.................................989 636-1000
Thomas Macphee, *President*
Duncan Stuart, *Vice Pres*
Ignacio Molina, *Treasurer*
Daniel Dub, *Admin Sec*
EMP: 20 EST: 2013
SALES (est): 2.8MM
SALES (corp-wide): 6.9B **Publicly Held**
SIC: 2819 Industrial inorganic chemicals
HQ: Blue Cube Spinco Inc.
190 Carondelet Plz # 1530
Saint Louis MO 63105
314 480-1400

(G-10818)
BOSTONTEC INC (PA)
2700 James Savage Rd (48642-6529)
P.O. Box 2044 (48641-2044)
PHONE.................................989 496-9510
Richard Vander Velle, *President*
Dave Clark, *Exec VP*
David L Clark, *Exec VP*
Mike Chapman, *Design Engr*
Bob Doucette, *Natl Sales Mgr*
▼ EMP: 10
SQ FT: 180,000
SALES (est): 1.5MM **Privately Held**
WEB: www.bostontec.com
SIC: 2522 Office furniture, except wood

(G-10819)
BUCKEYS CONTRACTING & SERVICE
707 Jefferson Ave (48640-5391)
PHONE.................................989 835-9512
Richard Buckey, *President*
Janet K Buckey, *Vice Pres*
EMP: 7
SQ FT: 4,800
SALES (est): 1.4MM **Privately Held**
SIC: 1542 7692 Nonresidential construction; welding repair

(G-10820)
BURCH TANK & TRUCK INC
Also Called: Burch Truck and Trailer Parts
4200 James Savage Rd (48642-6522)
PHONE.................................989 495-0342
Tony Near, *Business Mgr*
EMP: 5 **Privately Held**
SIC: 3795 5088 Tanks & tank components; tanks & tank components
PA: Burch Tank & Truck, Inc.
2253 Enterprise Dr
Mount Pleasant MI 48858

(G-10821)
CABOT CORPORATION
3603 S Saginaw Rd (48640-7612)
PHONE.................................989 495-2113
Jean Cronin, *Administration*
EMP: 25
SALES (corp-wide): 3.2B **Publicly Held**
WEB: www.cabot-corp.com
SIC: 2819 2899 1446 Silica compounds; chemical preparations; industrial sand
PA: Cabot Corporation
2 Seaport Ln Ste 1300
Boston MA 02210
617 345-0100

(G-10822)
CASE SYSTEMS INC
2700 James Savage Rd (48642-6529)
P.O. Box 2044 (48641-2044)
PHONE.................................989 496-9510
Robert W Bowden, *Ch of Bd*
Richard W Vanderweele, *President*
David L Clark, *General Mgr*
Kelly Wehner, *Vice Pres*
Amy Tomchick, *Buyer*
EMP: 190
SQ FT: 160,000
SALES (est): 33.5MM **Privately Held**
WEB: www.casesystems.com
SIC: 2521 3821 2434 Cabinets, office: wood; filing cabinets (boxes), office: wood; laboratory apparatus & furniture; wood kitchen cabinets

(G-10823)
CENTEN AG LLC (DH)
Also Called: Centen AG Inc
2030 Dow Ctr (48674-1500)
PHONE.................................989 636-1000
Mark A Bachman, *President*
EMP: 3
SALES (est): 401.6K
SALES (corp-wide): 61B **Publicly Held**
SIC: 2879 Agricultural chemicals
HQ: The Dow Chemical Company
2211 H H Dow Way
Midland MI 48642
989 636-1000

(G-10824)
CIRCLE K SERVICE CORPORATION
4300 James Savage Rd (48642-6523)
PHONE.................................989 496-0511
Rodney Kloha, *President*
EMP: 20
SQ FT: 15,000
SALES (est): 3.8MM **Privately Held**
WEB: www.circlekservice.com
SIC: 7538 3537 General truck repair; industrial trucks & tractors

(G-10825)
COBBLESTONE PRESS
4516 Washington St (48642-3583)
PHONE.................................989 832-0166
Harvey Hirsch, *Owner*
EMP: 5
SALES (est): 191.4K **Privately Held**
SIC: 2741 Miscellaneous publishing

(G-10826)
COMPUCOM COMPUTERS INC
28 Ashman Cir (48640-4530)
PHONE.................................989 837-1895
Randy Chisums, *Owner*
Henry Dufour, *Manager*
EMP: 3 **Privately Held**
WEB: www.compucomcomputers.com
SIC: 3674 7378 Computer logic modules; computer maintenance & repair
PA: Compucom Computers, Inc
3453 Court St
Saginaw MI

(G-10827)
CQ SIMPLE LLC
5103 Eastman Ave Ste 125 (48640-6724)
PHONE.................................989 492-7068
Elaine Blodgett, *Sales Staff*
Dave Root,
EMP: 7
SALES (est): 283.1K **Privately Held**
SIC: 7372 Business oriented computer software

(G-10828)
DAILY BILL
610 W Saint Andrews Rd (48640-3354)
PHONE.................................989 631-2068
Bill Daily, *Principal*
EMP: 5
SALES (est): 258.2K **Privately Held**
SIC: 2711 Newspapers, publishing & printing

(G-10829)
DDP SPECIALTY ELECTNC (DH)
2200 W Salzburg Rd (48686-0001)
PHONE.................................989 496-4400
Mark A Bachman, *President*
EMP: 1
SQ FT: 9,000
SALES (est): 1.3MM
SALES (corp-wide): 61B **Publicly Held**
SIC: 2869 Silicones
HQ: Dow Silicones Corporation
2200 W Salzburg Rd
Auburn MI 48611
989 496-4000

(G-10830)
DENDRITECH INC
3110 Schuette Rd (48642-6944)
PHONE.................................989 496-1152
S Emery Scheibert, *President*
Sebastian Scheibert, *General Mgr*
Joe Rousseau, *Lab Dir*
EMP: 6
SQ FT: 6,540
SALES (est): 1.2MM **Privately Held**
WEB: www.dendritech.com
SIC: 2822 Ethylene-propylene rubbers, EPDM polymers

(G-10831)
DENDRITIC NANOTECHNOLOGIES INC
1515 Commerce Dr Ste C (48642-8531)
PHONE.................................989 774-3096
Robert Berry, *CEO*
EMP: 9
SALES (est): 490K **Privately Held**
WEB: www.dnanotech.com
SIC: 3089 Plastic processing

(G-10832)
DIAZEM CORP
1406 E Pine St (48642-5323)
PHONE.................................989 832-3612
EMP: 8
SQ FT: 25,000
SALES (est): 847.1K **Privately Held**
SIC: 2819 Manufactures Chemicals

(G-10833)
DOW AGROSCIENCES LLC
433 Bldg (48674-0001)
P.O. Box 2009 (48641-2009)
PHONE.................................989 636-4400
David Duepre, *Branch Mgr*
EMP: 35
SALES (corp-wide): 30.6B **Publicly Held**
SIC: 2879 Trace elements (agricultural chemicals)
HQ: Dow Agrosciences Llc
9330 Zionsville Rd
Indianapolis IN 46268
317 337-3000

(G-10834)
DOW CHEMICAL COMPANY (HQ)
2211 H H Dow Way (48642-4815)
PHONE.................................989 636-1000
James R Fitterling, *CEO*
Howard Ungerleider, *President*
Tony Reed, *Business Mgr*
Darryl Frickey, *Counsel*
Johanna Soderstrom, *Senior VP*
◆ EMP: 277 EST: 1897
SALES: 60.2B
SALES (corp-wide): 61B **Publicly Held**
WEB: www.dow.com
SIC: 2821 3081 3086 2812 Thermoplastic materials; thermosetting materials; plasticizer/additive based plastic materials; molding compounds, plastics; plastic film & sheet; plastics foam products; insulation or cushioning material, foamed plastic; alkalies & chlorine; fungicides, herbicides; insecticides, agricultural or household; pesticides, agricultural or household
PA: Dow Inc.
2211 H H Dow Way
Midland MI 48642
989 636-1000

(G-10835)
DOW CHEMICAL COMPANY
2511 S Saginaw Rd (48640-5688)
PHONE.................................989 636-1000
Kelly Warner, *Engineer*
Pamela Elkins, *Finance*
Deb Plaver, *Branch Mgr*
EMP: 75
SALES (corp-wide): 61B **Publicly Held**
SIC: 2821 Thermoplastic materials
HQ: The Dow Chemical Company
2211 H H Dow Way
Midland MI 48642
989 636-1000

(G-10836)
DOW CHEMICAL COMPANY
1801 Larkin Center Dr (48642-8605)
PHONE.................................989 636-4406
Bobbi Sauer, *Principal*
EMP: 150
SALES (corp-wide): 61B **Publicly Held**
WEB: www.dow.com
SIC: 3081 3086 2879 0181 Plastic film & sheet; plastics foam products; fungicides, herbicides; insecticides, agricultural or household; pesticides, agricultural or household; bulbs & seeds; pharmaceutical preparations; laxatives; cough medicines; cold remedies
HQ: The Dow Chemical Company
2211 H H Dow Way
Midland MI 48642
989 636-1000

(G-10837)
DOW CHEMICAL COMPANY
3800 S Saginaw Rd Gate17 (48640)
PHONE.................................989 708-6737
EMP: 3
SALES (corp-wide): 61B **Publicly Held**
SIC: 2821 Thermoplastic materials; thermosetting materials; plasticizer/additive based plastic materials; molding compounds, plastics
HQ: The Dow Chemical Company
2211 H H Dow Way
Midland MI 48642
989 636-1000

(G-10838)
DOW CHEMICAL COMPANY
2511 E Patrick Rd (48642)
PHONE.................................989 636-1000
EMP: 4
SALES (corp-wide): 61B **Publicly Held**
SIC: 2821 Thermoplastic materials
HQ: The Dow Chemical Company
2211 H H Dow Way
Midland MI 48642
989 636-1000

(G-10839)
DOW CHEMICAL COMPANY
2030 Dow Ctr 263 (48674-1500)
PHONE.................................989 636-8587
EMP: 3
SALES (corp-wide): 61B **Publicly Held**
SIC: 2821 Plastics materials & resins
HQ: The Dow Chemical Company
2211 H H Dow Way
Midland MI 48642
989 636-1000

(G-10840)
DOW CHEMICAL COMPANY
S Saginaw Bldg 304 (48667-0001)
PHONE.................................989 636-1000

Midland - Midland County (G-10841)

EMP: 4
SALES (corp-wide): 61B **Publicly Held**
SIC: 2821 3081 Plastics materials & resins; tile, unsupported plastic
HQ: The Dow Chemical Company
2211 H H Dow Way
Midland MI 48642
989 636-1000

(G-10841)
DOW CHEMICAL COMPANY
2007 Austin St (48642-6180)
P.O. Box 2186 (48641)
PHONE....................989 496-2246
Joe Plant, *Manager*
EMP: 180
SALES (corp-wide): 61B **Publicly Held**
WEB: www.dow.com
SIC: 2869 Industrial organic chemicals
HQ: The Dow Chemical Company
2211 H H Dow Way
Midland MI 48642
989 636-1000

(G-10842)
DOW CHEMICAL COMPANY
100 Larkin Ctr (48674-0001)
PHONE....................989 636-2636
Jennifer Butcher, *Branch Mgr*
EMP: 106
SALES (corp-wide): 61B **Publicly Held**
WEB: www.dow.com
SIC: 2869 Industrial organic chemicals
HQ: The Dow Chemical Company
2211 H H Dow Way
Midland MI 48642
989 636-1000

(G-10843)
DOW CHEMICAL COMPANY
2050 Abbott Rd (48674-0001)
PHONE....................989 636-5430
Chelsea Sandborn, *Research*
Catherine M Baase, *Manager*
David Asiala, *Director*
EMP: 68
SALES (corp-wide): 61B **Publicly Held**
WEB: www.dow.com
SIC: 3086 Plastics foam products
HQ: The Dow Chemical Company
2211 H H Dow Way
Midland MI 48642
989 636-1000

(G-10844)
DOW CHEMICAL COMPANY
2040 Dow Ctr (48674-1500)
P.O. Box 6004 (48641-6004)
PHONE....................989 832-1000
William Davis, *Manager*
EMP: 150
SALES (corp-wide): 61B **Publicly Held**
WEB: www.dow.com
SIC: 2821 5169 Thermoplastic materials; chemicals & allied products
HQ: The Dow Chemical Company
2211 H H Dow Way
Midland MI 48642
989 636-1000

(G-10845)
DOW CHEMICAL COMPANY
1320 Waldo Ave Ste 300 (48642-5868)
PHONE....................989 636-0540
Anne Mitchell, *Branch Mgr*
EMP: 75
SALES (corp-wide): 61B **Publicly Held**
WEB: www.dow.com
SIC: 2821 3081 3086 2879 Plastics materials & resins; unsupported plastics film & sheet; plastics foam products; agricultural chemicals; ornamental nursery products
HQ: The Dow Chemical Company
2211 H H Dow Way
Midland MI 48642
989 636-1000

(G-10846)
DOW CHEMICAL COMPANY
Gpc Building (48667-0001)
P.O. Box 2047 (48641-2047)
PHONE....................989 638-6441
Ann Mitchell, *Admin Sec*
EMP: 20
SALES (corp-wide): 61B **Publicly Held**
WEB: www.dow.com
SIC: 2869 Industrial organic chemicals
HQ: The Dow Chemical Company
2211 H H Dow Way
Midland MI 48642
989 636-1000

(G-10847)
DOW CHEMICAL COMPANY
Bldg 1710 (48674-0001)
PHONE....................989 636-6351
Paul Vammer, *Manager*
EMP: 100
SALES (corp-wide): 61B **Publicly Held**
WEB: www.dow.com
SIC: 2821 Thermoplastic materials
HQ: The Dow Chemical Company
2211 H H Dow Way
Midland MI 48642
989 636-1000

(G-10848)
DOW CHEMICAL COMPANY
3700 James Savage Rd (48642-6517)
P.O. Box 2560 (48641-2560)
PHONE....................989 636-5409
EMP: 75
SALES (corp-wide): 61B **Publicly Held**
SIC: 2821 3081 3086 2812 Thermoplastic materials; thermosetting materials; plasticizer/additive based plastic materials; molding compounds, plastics; plastic film & sheet; plastics foam products; insulation or cushioning material, foamed plastic; alkalies & chlorine; fungicides, herbicides; insecticides, agricultural or household; pesticides, agricultural or household
HQ: The Dow Chemical Company
2211 H H Dow Way
Midland MI 48642
989 636-1000

(G-10849)
DOW CORNING CORPORATION
1404 Peppermill Cir (48642-3066)
PHONE....................989 839-2808
Jim Fitterling, *CEO*
Howard Ungerleider, *CFO*
Michael Altes, *Manager*
EMP: 3
SALES (est): 147.1K **Privately Held**
SIC: 2869 2822 Silicones; silicone rubbers

(G-10850)
DOW CREDIT CORPORATION
2030 Dow Ctr Unit E228 (48674-1500)
PHONE....................989 636-8949
EMP: 3
SALES (est): 299.1K
SALES (corp-wide): 48.7B **Publicly Held**
SIC: 2899 Mfg Chemical Preparations
PA: The Dow Chemical Company
2030 Dow Ctr
Midland MI 48642
989 636-1000

(G-10851)
DOW INC (PA)
2211 H H Dow Way (48642-4815)
PHONE....................989 636-1000
James R Fitterling, *CEO*
EMP: 8
SALES (est): 61B **Publicly Held**
SIC: 2821 3081 3086 Thermoplastic materials; thermosetting materials; plasticizer/additive based plastic materials; molding compounds, plastics; plastic film & sheet; plastics foam products; insulation or cushioning material, foamed plastic

(G-10852)
DOW INTERNATIONAL HOLDINGS CO (DH)
2030 Dow Ctr (48674-1500)
PHONE....................989 636-1000
Andrew N Liveris, *Ch of Bd*
EMP: 4
SALES (est): 21.9MM
SALES (corp-wide): 61B **Publicly Held**
SIC: 2821 Thermoplastic materials
HQ: The Dow Chemical Company
2211 H H Dow Way
Midland MI 48642
989 636-1000

(G-10853)
DOW SILICONES CORPORATION
Also Called: Solar Solutions
3901 S Saginaw Rd (48640-5670)
PHONE....................989 496-4400
Mike Syrylo, *Mfg Staff*
James Beck, *Research*
Brett Burkhart, *Engineer*
Peter Moore, *Sales Dir*
Jere Marciniak, *Branch Mgr*
EMP: 125
SALES (corp-wide): 61B **Publicly Held**
WEB: www.dowcorning.com
SIC: 2869 Industrial organic chemicals
HQ: Dow Silicones Corporation
2200 W Salzburg Rd
Auburn MI 48611
989 496-4000

(G-10854)
DOW SILICONES CORPORATION
2651 Salzburg St (48640-8595)
PHONE....................989 496-4000
EMP: 133
SALES (corp-wide): 61B **Publicly Held**
SIC: 2869 Silicones
HQ: Dow Silicones Corporation
2200 W Salzburg Rd
Auburn MI 48611
989 496-4000

(G-10855)
DOW SILICONES CORPORATION
2651 Salzburg St (48640-8595)
P.O. Box 0998 (48640)
PHONE....................989 496-4137
EMP: 100
SALES (corp-wide): 61B **Publicly Held**
SIC: 2821 2869 Silicone resins; silicones
HQ: Dow Silicones Corporation
2200 W Salzburg Rd
Auburn MI 48611
989 496-4000

(G-10856)
DUNKIN DONUTS & BASKIN-ROBBINS
5000 Foxcroft Dr (48642-3299)
PHONE....................989 835-8412
Gale Letcher, *Owner*
EMP: 20
SALES (est): 680K **Privately Held**
SIC: 5461 2051 5812 Doughnuts, except frozen; ice cream, soft drink & soda fountain stands

(G-10857)
EAGLEBURGMANN INDUSTRIES LP
1821 Austin St (48642-6955)
PHONE....................989 486-1571
Pat McCann, *Manager*
EMP: 7
SALES (corp-wide): 11B **Privately Held**
SIC: 3999 Atomizers, toiletry
HQ: Eagleburgmann Industries Lp
10035 Brookriver Dr
Houston TX 77040
713 939-9515

(G-10858)
ECO BIO PLASTICS MIDLAND INC
4037 S Saginaw Rd (48640-8501)
PHONE....................989 496-1934
Jim Plonka, *CEO*
Takamichi Matsushita, *Chairman*
Fukuji Saotome, *COO*
Kenichi Toguchi, *COO*
Adrian Merrington, *Chief Engr*
▲ **EMP:** 10 **EST:** 2011
SQ FT: 38,000
SALES (est): 1.7MM **Privately Held**
SIC: 3087 Custom compound purchased resins
PA: Eco Research Institute Ltd.
16-29, Nampeidaicho
Shibuya-Ku TKY 150-0

(G-10859)
ELECTRO PANEL INC
4501 Forestview Dr (48642-6610)
PHONE....................989 832-2110
John Lefler, *President*
Richard Lefler, *Vice Pres*
EMP: 5
SQ FT: 10,000
SALES: 1MM **Privately Held**
SIC: 3679 Harness assemblies for electronic use: wire or cable

(G-10860)
ELEMENT SALON AND DAY SPA
3917 E Patrick Rd (48642-6501)
PHONE....................989 708-6006
Michael Jones, *Principal*
EMP: 5
SALES (est): 620.9K **Privately Held**
SIC: 2819 Elements

(G-10861)
FISHER SAND AND GRAVEL COMPANY
Also Called: Allied Concrete Products
921 Jefferson Ave (48640-5318)
P.O. Box 1703 (48641-1703)
PHONE....................989 835-7187
James O Fisher, *President*
Ralph Fisher Jr, *Corp Secy*
John Fischer, *Vice Pres*
EMP: 25
SQ FT: 2,000
SALES (est): 4.9MM **Privately Held**
SIC: 3273 5032 5211 Ready-mixed concrete; concrete & cinder block; concrete & cinder block

(G-10862)
FLOWSERVE US INC
2420 Schuette Rd (48642-5974)
PHONE....................989 496-3897
Brad Harrelson, *Manager*
EMP: 5
SALES (corp-wide): 3.8B **Publicly Held**
SIC: 3561 Pumps & pumping equipment
HQ: Flowserve Us Inc.
5215 N Oconnor Blvd Ste Connor
Irving TX 75039
972 443-6500

(G-10863)
FULCRUM COMPOSITES INC
110 E Main St Apt 301 (48640-5105)
PHONE....................989 636-1025
Chris Edwards, *President*
▲ **EMP:** 4
SALES (est): 548.2K **Privately Held**
WEB: www.fulcrumcomposites.com
SIC: 2221 Fiberglass fabrics

(G-10864)
GANTEC INC
777 E Isabella Rd (48640-8333)
PHONE....................989 631-9300
Richard Olson, *President*
Lanny Robins, *Principal*
Joe Affholter, *Chairman*
Joseph Afflholter, *Chairman*
EMP: 7
SALES (est): 700K **Privately Held**
WEB: www.gantec.com
SIC: 2879 2873 Pesticides, agricultural or household; fertilizers: natural (organic), except compost

(G-10865)
GCI WATER SOLUTIONS LLC
5202 Dale St (48642-3289)
PHONE....................312 928-9992
Michael Schuette, *Principal*
EMP: 6
SALES (est): 292.1K **Privately Held**
SIC: 3589 Water treatment equipment, industrial

(G-10866)
GLAXOSMITHKLINE LLC
2518 Abbott Rd Apt V11 (48642-5010)
PHONE....................989 280-1225
EMP: 26
SALES (corp-wide): 39.5B **Privately Held**
SIC: 2834 Pharmaceutical preparations

HQ: Glaxosmithkline Llc
5 Crescent Dr
Philadelphia PA 19112
215 751-4000

(G-10867)
HARRIS SHEET METAL CO
3313 S Saginaw Rd (48640-5697)
PHONE..................................989 496-3080
Mark E Harris, *President*
Mark Harris, *President*
Scott Cergnul, *Vice Pres*
EMP: 12
SQ FT: 9,600
SALES (est): 1.6MM **Privately Held**
SIC: 3444 1761 Ducts, sheet metal; sheet metal specialties, not stamped; sheet metalwork

(G-10868)
HEALTH ENHANCEMENT SYSTEMS INC (PA)
800 Cambridge St Ste 101 (48642-7600)
P.O. Box 1035 (48641-1035)
PHONE..................................989 839-0852
Dean Witherspoon, *President*
Kaitlyn Baase, *Accounts Mgr*
Lisa Cochran, *Manager*
Kristen Fernandes, *Manager*
John Stanfield, *Info Tech Dir*
EMP: 12
SQ FT: 3,000
SALES (est): 1.2MM **Privately Held**
WEB: www.hesonline.com
SIC: 2741 Miscellaneous publishing

(G-10869)
HEATHER N HOLLY
228 E Main St (48640-5114)
PHONE..................................989 832-6460
Pamela Gallagher, *Owner*
EMP: 3
SALES (est): 268.2K **Privately Held**
SIC: 2066 Chocolate bars, solid

(G-10870)
INGERSOLL CM SYSTEMS LLC
3505 Centennial Dr (48642-6940)
PHONE..................................989 495-5000
Chuck Rozewski, *Materials Mgr*
Brian Kennedy, *Opers Staff*
Gary Maday, *Buyer*
Rebel Bates, *Purchasing*
Mark St Pierre, *Engineer*
▲ **EMP:** 57
SALES (est): 13.1MM **Privately Held**
SIC: 3541 Machine tools, metal cutting type

(G-10871)
INTERACT WEBSITES INC
Also Called: Interactrv
3526 E Curtis Rd (48642-8432)
P.O. Box 2291 (48641-2291)
PHONE..................................800 515-9672
Kevin Wallenbeck, *President*
Ron Cheney, *Vice Pres*
Nicolette Matt, *Marketing Staff*
Alex Schimp, *Prgrmr*
EMP: 17
SALES (est): 1.6MM **Privately Held**
SIC: 7372 Prepackaged software

(G-10872)
INTERKAL LLC
2701 Highbrook Dr (48642-3923)
PHONE..................................989 486-1788
Kurt Hemmer, *President*
EMP: 5 **Privately Held**
SIC: 2531 Public building & related furniture
HQ: Interkal, Llc
5981 E Cork St
Kalamazoo MI 49048
269 349-1521

(G-10873)
INTERNATIONAL BUS MCHS CORP
Also Called: IBM
2125 Ridgeview Dr (48642-5836)
PHONE..................................989 832-6000
EMP: 25
SALES (corp-wide): 79.1B **Publicly Held**
SIC: 3571 Mfg Electronic Computers

PA: International Business Machines Corporation
1 New Orchard Rd Ste 1 # 1
Armonk NY 10504
914 499-1900

(G-10874)
JAMES G GALLAGHER
Also Called: JDG Service
5609 Summerset Dr (48640-2930)
PHONE..................................989 832-3458
James D Gallagher, *Owner*
EMP: 3
SALES (est): 260K **Privately Held**
SIC: 3822 Temperature controls, automatic

(G-10875)
JLM ELEC
1854 Smith Ct (48640-8946)
PHONE..................................989 486-3788
Michael Gravis, *Principal*
EMP: 3
SALES (est): 243.8K **Privately Held**
SIC: 3621 Generators & sets, electric

(G-10876)
JOHN CRANE INC
3300 Centennial Dr (48642-5958)
PHONE..................................989 496-9292
Jerry Smith, *Manager*
EMP: 10
SALES (corp-wide): 4.2B **Privately Held**
WEB: www.johncrane.com
SIC: 3053 Oil seals, rubber; packing: steam engines, pipe joints, air compressors, etc.
HQ: John Crane Inc.
227 W Monroe St Ste 1800
Chicago IL 60606
312 605-7800

(G-10877)
JONES RAY WELL SERVICING INC
172 N 11 Mile Rd (48640-9118)
PHONE..................................989 832-8071
Jeanne Yost, *President*
David Yost, *Vice Pres*
EMP: 20
SALES (est): 910.5K **Privately Held**
SIC: 1389 Servicing oil & gas wells

(G-10878)
JUMPIN JOHNNYS INC
1309 W Reardon St Apt 2 (48640-4817)
PHONE..................................989 832-0160
John Klein, *President*
Michael Kangas, *Chairman*
EMP: 5
SQ FT: 3,000
SALES (est): 320K **Privately Held**
WEB: www.jumpinjohnnys.com
SIC: 2086 Bottled & canned soft drinks

(G-10879)
KAWKAWLIN MANUFACTURING CO (PA)
Also Called: Kawkawlin Church Furn Mfg Co
2707 Highbrook Dr (48642-3923)
PHONE..................................989 684-5470
Frank King Jr, *President*
Janelle Adamczyk, *Admin Sec*
EMP: 6 **EST:** 1940
SALES (est): 871.9K **Privately Held**
SIC: 2531 Pews, church; church furniture; benches for public buildings

(G-10880)
KINETIC WAVE POWER LLC
2861 N Tupelo Dr (48640-8829)
PHONE..................................989 839-9757
Joseph Blackmore,
EMP: 5
SALES (est): 418.1K **Privately Held**
SIC: 3511 Turbines & turbine generator sets

(G-10881)
LAMONS
807 Pershing St (48640-5611)
PHONE..................................989 488-4580
Terry Allen, *Manager*
EMP: 4
SALES (est): 375K **Privately Held**
SIC: 3053 Gaskets, all materials

(G-10882)
LIVING WORD INTERNATIONAL INC
Also Called: Mark Barclay Ministries
2010 N Stark Rd (48640-9439)
PHONE..................................989 832-7547
Mark Barclay, *President*
Josh Barclay, *Vice Pres*
Jonathan Dolan, *Info Tech Mgr*
Bethany Bedtelyon, *Director*
William Bailey, *Admin Sec*
EMP: 26
SQ FT: 18,000
SALES (est): 2.7MM **Privately Held**
WEB: www.mbmmail.com
SIC: 8661 2731 2721 Covenant & Evangelical Church; book publishing; periodicals

(G-10883)
MCKAY PRESS INC
7600 W Wackerly St (48642-7405)
P.O. Box 2749 (48641-2749)
PHONE..................................989 631-2360
Corey Christiansen, *President*
Jim Nigro, *Vice Pres*
Jim McFarlane, *Opers Staff*
Bob Smith, *Controller*
Todd Fisher, *Accounts Exec*
EMP: 135 **EST:** 1994
SQ FT: 93,000
SALES (est): 18.7MM
SALES (corp-wide): 6.8B **Publicly Held**
WEB: www.mckaypress.com
SIC: 2759 Commercial printing
PA: R. R. Donnelley & Sons Company
35 W Wacker Dr
Chicago IL 60601
312 326-8000

(G-10884)
MHR INVESTMENTS INC
Also Called: Mc Creadie Sales
601 S Saginaw Rd (48640-4610)
PHONE..................................989 832-5395
Richard McCreadie, *President*
Richard Mc Creadie, *President*
EMP: 14
SQ FT: 5,500
SALES (est): 1.2MM **Privately Held**
WEB: www.mccreadiesales.com
SIC: 5699 5812 3993 Shirts, custom made; T-shirts, custom printed; fast-food restaurant, independent; signs & advertising specialties

(G-10885)
MICHIGAN GYPSUM CO
6105 Jefferson Ave (48640-2935)
PHONE..................................989 792-8734
Francesanna Sargent, *President*
Thomas Webber, *Vice Pres*
EMP: 19 **EST:** 1953
SQ FT: 18,000
SALES (est): 1.7MM **Privately Held**
WEB: www.michigangypsum.com
SIC: 1499 Gypsum mining

(G-10886)
MID MICHIGAN REPAIR SERVICE
680 S Poseyville Rd (48640-8911)
PHONE..................................989 835-6014
Ruhl R Hoover, *President*
EMP: 8
SQ FT: 3,200
SALES (est): 712.3K **Privately Held**
SIC: 7699 5084 7692 3548 Welding equipment repair; welding machinery & equipment; welding repair; welding apparatus

(G-10887)
MIDLAND BREWING CO LLC
Also Called: Brewing Company
5011 N Saginaw Rd (48642)
PHONE..................................989 631-3041
EMP: 7 **EST:** 2010
SALES (est): 220K **Privately Held**
SIC: 5813 2082 Drinking Place Mfg Malt Beverages

(G-10888)
MIDLAND CMPNDING CNSULTING INC
3802 James Savage Rd (48642-6518)
PHONE..................................989 495-9367
Thayer Brown, *President*
EMP: 7
SQ FT: 24,000
SALES (est): 2MM **Privately Held**
WEB: www.midlandcompounding.com
SIC: 2899 2611 Insulating compounds; pulp mills, mechanical & recycling processing

(G-10889)
MIDLAND IRON WORKS INC
57 W Chippewa River Rd (48640-9039)
PHONE..................................989 832-3041
Stephen D Dent, *President*
Dixie Dent, *Admin Sec*
EMP: 10
SQ FT: 1,600
SALES (est): 1.8MM **Privately Held**
SIC: 3321 Gray iron castings; ductile iron castings

(G-10890)
MIDLAND MOLD & MACHINING INC
1406 E Pine St Ste 5 (48640-5323)
PHONE..................................989 832-9534
Lynwood K Barnard, *President*
Bernard Lindon, *Corp Secy*
Kris Hepinstall, *Vice Pres*
EMP: 3
SQ FT: 1,200
SALES (est): 150K **Privately Held**
SIC: 3544 Forms (molds), for foundry & plastics working machinery

(G-10891)
MIDLAND PUBLISHING COMPANY
Also Called: Midland Daily News
124 S Mcdonald St (48640-5161)
PHONE..................................989 835-7171
Jenny Anderson, *President*
Cathy Bott, *General Mgr*
Pam Shauger, *Advt Staff*
Carol Vansluyters, *Manager*
Victoria Ritter, *Clerk*
EMP: 105 **EST:** 1858
SQ FT: 27,000
SALES (est): 5.5MM
SALES (corp-wide): 8.3B **Privately Held**
WEB: www.ourmidland.com
SIC: 2711 2752 Newspapers: publishing only, not printed on site; commercial printing, lithographic
PA: The Hearst Corporation
300 W 57th St Fl 42
New York NY 10019
212 649-2000

(G-10892)
MITCHART INC
2611 Schuette Rd Ste A (48642-6965)
PHONE..................................989 835-3964
Krista Mc Donald, *Principal*
Jamie M McDonald, *COO*
Krista McDonald, *Sales Dir*
EMP: 6
SALES (est): 845.6K **Privately Held**
SIC: 3993 Signs & advertising specialties

(G-10893)
MMGG INC (PA)
120 Waldo Ave (48642-5965)
PHONE..................................616 405-3807
Mark Groulx, *President*
Gretchen Groulx, *Corp Secy*
Mike Groulx, *Vice Pres*
EMP: 3
SQ FT: 5,000
SALES (est): 5.1MM **Privately Held**
SIC: 3531 Construction machinery

(G-10894)
MMGG INC
Also Called: Falcon Rme
120 Waldo Ave (48642-5965)
PHONE..................................989 495-9332
Mike Groulx, *Vice Pres*
EMP: 30
SQ FT: 23,000

Midland - Midland County (G-10895)

SALES (corp-wide): 5.1MM **Privately Held**
SIC: 3531 Construction machinery
PA: Mmgg, Inc.
120 Waldo Ave
Midland MI 48642
616 405-3807

(G-10895)
MODERN METALCRAFT INC
2033 Roxbury Ct (48642-8002)
PHONE.................................989 835-3716
John Mc Peak, *President*
Tamara Schuman, *Controller*
EMP: 16
SQ FT: 29,000
SALES (est): 2.4MM **Privately Held**
WEB: www.modernmetalcraft.com
SIC: 3444 3599 Sheet metal specialties, not stamped; machine shop, jobbing & repair

(G-10896)
N F P INC
Also Called: Wysong
7550 Eastman Ave (48642-7809)
PHONE.................................989 631-0009
Jill Barton, *Principal*
EMP: 5
SALES (est): 366.1K
SALES (corp-wide): 1.3MM **Privately Held**
SIC: 8721 5499 2834 2099 Billing & bookkeeping service; health & dietetic food stores; pharmaceutical preparations; food preparations; prepared feeds
PA: N F P Inc
N5475 Crossman Rd
Lake Mills WI 53551
920 648-3003

(G-10897)
NUVOSUN INC
2040 Abbott Rd (48674-1000)
PHONE.................................408 514-6200
Kirk Thompson, *President*
Bruce Hachtmann, *Vice Pres*
Tom Valeri, *Vice Pres*
Art Wall, *Vice Pres*
▲ EMP: 62
SQ FT: 102,000
SALES (est): 12.8MM
SALES (corp-wide): 61B **Publicly Held**
SIC: 3674 Photovoltaic devices, solid state
HQ: The Dow Chemical Company
2211 H H Dow Way
Midland MI 48642
989 636-1000

(G-10898)
OAKLAND ORTHOPEDIC APPLS INC
422 W Wackerly St (48640-4701)
PHONE.................................989 839-9241
Kelly Hetherington, *Manager*
EMP: 3
SQ FT: 1,200
SALES (corp-wide): 6.8MM **Privately Held**
SIC: 5999 3842 Orthopedic & prosthesis applications; orthopedic appliances
PA: Oakland Orthopedic Appliances, Inc.
515 Mulholland St
Bay City MI 48708
989 893-7544

(G-10899)
OIL CITY VENTURE INC
Also Called: G & H Producers
172 N 11 Mile Rd (48640-9118)
PHONE.................................989 832-8071
David Yost, *President*
Jeanne Yost, *Vice Pres*
EMP: 4
SALES (est): 255K **Privately Held**
SIC: 1311 Crude petroleum & natural gas

(G-10900)
ORACLE AMERICA INC
2200 Salzburg St (48640-8531)
PHONE.................................989 495-0465
EMP: 46
SALES (corp-wide): 39.5B **Publicly Held**
SIC: 7372 Prepackaged software

HQ: Oracle America, Inc.
500 Oracle Pkwy
Redwood City CA 94065
650 506-7000

(G-10901)
OWENS BUILDING CO INC
Also Called: Owens Cabinet & Trim
1928 N Stark Rd (48642-9438)
PHONE.................................989 835-1293
EMP: 25
SQ FT: 21,000
SALES: 2.5MM **Privately Held**
SIC: 2431 2541 5211 1799 Millwork; wood partitions & fixtures; cabinets, kitchen; counter top installation; cabinet & finish carpentry; vanities, bathroom: wood

(G-10902)
PAROUSIA PLASTICS INC
2412 Judith Ct (48642-4751)
PHONE.................................989 832-4054
Robert Yore, *President*
EMP: 3
SALES (est): 170.2K **Privately Held**
SIC: 3089 Injection molding of plastics

(G-10903)
PRECISION TORQUE CONTROL INC
220 Arrow Cv (48642-6950)
PHONE.................................989 495-9330
Michael Scott, *President*
Mike Degraw, *Manager*
Angela Licht, *Admin Mgr*
▲ EMP: 10
SALES (est): 1.5MM **Privately Held**
WEB: www.precisiontork.com
SIC: 3714 3568 Clutches, motor vehicle; power transmission equipment

(G-10904)
QG LLC
Also Called: Worldcolor Midland
1700 James Savage Rd (48642-5812)
PHONE.................................989 496-3333
Jim Houvener, *Branch Mgr*
EMP: 326
SALES (corp-wide): 4.1B **Publicly Held**
SIC: 2752 Commercial printing, offset
HQ: Qg, Llc
N61w23044 Harrys Way
Sussex WI 53089

(G-10905)
QRP INC (PA)
Also Called: Quick and Reliable Printing
94 Ashman Cir (48640-4627)
PHONE.................................989 496-2955
Robert A Anderson, *President*
Nancy Anderson, *Vice Pres*
Jim Haring, *Sales Executive*
EMP: 7
SQ FT: 3,600
SALES (est): 6.3MM **Privately Held**
WEB: www.qrp-printing.com
SIC: 2752 5999 2796 2791 Commercial printing, offset; banners, flags, decals & posters; platemaking services; typesetting; bookbinding & related work; coated & laminated paper

(G-10906)
QRP INC
Also Called: Quick Reliable Printing
3000 James Savage Rd (48642-6533)
PHONE.................................989 496-2955
Bob Anderson, *President*
Ken Trethaway, *Accounts Exec*
Jenny Schaefer, *Department Mgr*
Amy Anderson, *Manager*
Hal Grunwell, *MIS Mgr*
EMP: 40
SALES (corp-wide): 6.3MM **Privately Held**
WEB: www.qrp-printing.com
SIC: 2752 2791 2789 2759 Commercial printing, offset; typesetting; bookbinding & related work; commercial printing
PA: Qrp, Inc.
94 Ashman Cir
Midland MI 48640
989 496-2955

(G-10907)
QUAD/GRAPHICS INC
1700 James Savage Rd (48642-5812)
PHONE.................................989 698-5598
Rachelle Ebach, *Principal*
Jessica Solano, *Purch Mgr*
Jennie Lippie, *Controller*
Kevin Dumond, *Admin Asst*
EMP: 13
SALES (corp-wide): 4.1B **Publicly Held**
SIC: 2752 Commercial printing, offset
PA: Quad/Graphics Inc.
N61w23044 Harrys Way
Sussex WI 53089
414 566-6000

(G-10908)
RIDER TYPE & DESIGN
3600 E Mary Jane Dr (48642-9758)
PHONE.................................989 839-0015
Robert Rider, *President*
EMP: 4
SALES: 400K **Privately Held**
SIC: 2791 2752 Typesetting; commercial printing, lithographic

(G-10909)
ROHM HAAS DNMARK INVSTMNTS LLC
2030 Dow Ctr (48674-1500)
PHONE.................................989 636-1463
EMP: 7 EST: 2015
SALES (est): 148.8K
SALES (corp-wide): 61B **Publicly Held**
SIC: 2821 Plastics materials & resins
HQ: The Dow Chemical Company
2211 H H Dow Way
Midland MI 48642
989 636-1000

(G-10910)
S AND P DRCTNAL BORING SVC LLC
Also Called: L L C
801 W Meadowbrook Dr (48640-6023)
PHONE.................................989 832-7716
Patrick Zilfki,
▲ EMP: 4
SALES (est): 307.7K **Privately Held**
SIC: 1381 Directional drilling oil & gas wells

(G-10911)
SAGINAW VALLEY INST MTLS INC
4800 James Savage Rd (48642-6528)
PHONE.................................989 496-2307
Rebecca Cox, *President*
Theodore Selby, *President*
Jean Selby, *Treasurer*
EMP: 4
SALES (est): 327.5K **Privately Held**
SIC: 1389 8734 Oil field services; testing laboratories

(G-10912)
SARGENT SAND CO
6105 Jefferson Ave (48640-2935)
PHONE.................................989 792-8734
Francesanna Sargent, *President*
Doug Horacek, *Office Mgr*
EMP: 3 EST: 1923
SALES (est): 1.5MM **Privately Held**
SIC: 1446 Foundry sand mining

(G-10913)
SEADRIFT PIPELINE CORP
2030 Dow Ctr (48674-1500)
PHONE.................................989 636-6636
K C Weyer, *Principal*
EMP: 10
SALES (est): 1.2MM **Privately Held**
SIC: 3317 Seamless pipes & tubes

(G-10914)
SECURECOM INC
3079 E Commercial Dr (48642-7840)
P.O. Box 1309 (48641-1309)
PHONE.................................989 837-4005
Kevin L Wray, *Principal*
EMP: 3
SALES (est): 234.5K **Privately Held**
SIC: 3699 Security control equipment & systems

(G-10915)
SERENUS JOHNSON PORTABLES LLC
1928 N Stark Rd (48642-9438)
PHONE.................................989 839-2324
Brian Johnson, *President*
EMP: 15
SALES: 1,000K **Privately Held**
SIC: 3448 Prefabricated metal buildings

(G-10916)
SIGNATURE WALL SOLUTIONS INC
Also Called: Swiftwall Solutions
1928 N Stark Rd (48642-9438)
P.O. Box 1601 (48641-1601)
PHONE.................................616 366-4242
Joe Afiala, *CEO*
Rick Brouwer, *Co-Founder*
Eli Rytlewsky, *Director*
EMP: 5
SQ FT: 30,000
SALES: 1MM **Privately Held**
SIC: 3499 1791 Barricades, metal; exterior wall system installation

(G-10917)
SNOW MACHINES INCORPORATED (PA)
Also Called: SMI Evaporative Systems
1512 Rockwell Dr (48642-9318)
PHONE.................................989 631-6091
Joseph M Vanderkelen, *President*
Matt Leinberger, *Design Engr*
Steve Fellman, *Sales Mgr*
Wes Cashwell, *Sales Staff*
Nic Horgan, *Manager*
▲ EMP: 24
SQ FT: 9,000
SALES (est): 5.3MM **Privately Held**
WEB: www.snowmakers.com
SIC: 3585 3821 Snowmaking machinery; evaporation apparatus, laboratory type

(G-10918)
SOURCE POINT PRESS
3603 Orchard Dr (48640-2676)
PHONE.................................269 501-3690
Travis Macintire, *Administration*
EMP: 3
SALES (est): 45.4K **Privately Held**
SIC: 2741 Miscellaneous publishing

(G-10919)
SPECIALTY PRODUCTS US LLC (DH)
2211 H H Dow Way (48642-4815)
PHONE.................................989 636-4341
Mark A Bachman, *President*
EMP: 7
SALES (est): 1.1MM
SALES (corp-wide): 61B **Publicly Held**
SIC: 2821 2869 Plastics materials & resins; industrial organic chemicals
HQ: The Dow Chemical Company
2211 H H Dow Way
Midland MI 48642
989 636-1000

(G-10920)
SPORTS JUNCTION
6823 Eastman Ave Ste 11 (48642-7896)
PHONE.................................989 835-9696
David Bedford, *Partner*
EMP: 3
SALES (corp-wide): 872.7K **Privately Held**
SIC: 5699 5941 2759 2395 Sports apparel; sporting goods & bicycle shops; screen printing; embroidery products, except schiffli machine
PA: Sports Junction
5605 State St
Saginaw MI 48603
989 791-5900

(G-10921)
TRINSEO
3700 James Savage Rd (48642-6517)
PHONE.................................989 636-5409
EMP: 5
SALES (est): 890.7K **Privately Held**
SIC: 2821 Plastics materials & resins

GEOGRAPHIC SECTION
Milan - Monroe County (G-10949)

(G-10922)
TRINSEO LLC
409 Ashman St Ste 1 (48640-5057)
PHONE..................................888 789-7661
Jeff Denton, *Manager*
EMP: 40 **Publicly Held**
SIC: 3089 3069 Air mattresses, plastic; latex, foamed
HQ: Trinseo Llc
1000 Chesterbrook Blvd # 300
Berwyn PA 19312

(G-10923)
W & W TOOL AND DIE INC
1508 E Grove St (48640-5299)
PHONE..................................989 835-5522
Dennis Duford, *President*
Kenneth Friedle, *Corp Secy*
EMP: 9 **EST:** 1946
SQ FT: 4,100
SALES (est): 1.1MM **Privately Held**
SIC: 3544 Forms (molds), for foundry & plastics working machinery

(G-10924)
WYSONG CORPORATION
7550 Eastman Ave (48642-7809)
PHONE..................................989 631-0009
Randy L Wysong, *Owner*
Joyce Morton, *Sales Mgr*
Lucas Wysong, *Marketing Mgr*
About Wysong, *Director*
EMP: 5
SALES (est): 804.7K **Privately Held**
SIC: 2048 Feeds, specialty: mice, guinea pig, etc.

(G-10925)
WYSONG MEDICAL CORPORATION
7550 Eastman Ave (48642-7809)
PHONE..................................989 631-0009
Randy L Wysong, *President*
EMP: 20 **EST:** 1976
SQ FT: 16,050
SALES (est): 3.2MM **Privately Held**
WEB: www.wysong.net
SIC: 2048 2047 2099 3841 Feeds, specialty: mice, guinea pig, etc.; feed concentrates; feed supplements; dog food; cat food; food preparations; surgical & medical instruments

(G-10926)
XAERUS PERFORMANCE FLUIDS LLC
2825 Schuette Rd (48642-6945)
PHONE..................................989 631-7871
EMP: 4
SALES (est): 551.4K **Privately Held**
SIC: 2899 Corrosion preventive lubricant
PA: Xaerus Performance Fluids, L.L.C.
1605 Ashman St
Midland MI 48640

(G-10927)
XAERUS PERFORMANCE FLUIDS LLC (PA)
Also Called: Xaerus Performance Fluids Intl
1605 Ashman St (48640-5451)
PHONE..................................989 631-7871
Dan Tolfa, *President*
John A Carras, *CFO*
EMP: 27
SALES (est): 10.5MM **Privately Held**
SIC: 2992 Lubricating oils

(G-10928)
XALT ENERGY LLC (DH)
2700 S Saginaw Rd (48640-6845)
PHONE..................................989 486-8501
Jeff Michalski, *President*
Martin Klein, *Vice Pres*
Joseph Tenbusch, *Program Mgr*
▲ **EMP:** 15
SQ FT: 17,500
SALES (est): 25.7MM
SALES (corp-wide): 11B **Privately Held**
SIC: 3691 Storage batteries
HQ: Tobul Accumulator Incorporated
61 Innovation Dr
Bamberg SC 29003
803 245-2400

(G-10929)
XALT ENERGY LLC
2700 S Saginaw Rd (48640-6845)
PHONE..................................816 525-1153
EMP: 5
SALES (corp-wide): 29.9MM **Privately Held**
SIC: 3629 Mfg Electrical Industrial Apparatus
HQ: Xalt Energy, Llc
2700 S Saginaw Rd
Midland MI 48640

(G-10930)
XALT ENERGY MI LLC
2700 S Saginaw Rd (48640-6845)
PHONE..................................989 486-8501
Subhash Dhar, *CEO*
Richard Cundiff, *Vice Chairman*
Matt Hanson, *CFO*
◆ **EMP:** 60
SALES (est): 20MM
SALES (corp-wide): 11B **Privately Held**
SIC: 3691 Storage batteries
HQ: Xalt Energy, Llc
2700 S Saginaw Rd
Midland MI 48640

Milan
Monroe County

(G-10931)
ADAMS JERROLL ORGAN BUILDER
226 E Main St Ste 228 (48160-1506)
PHONE..................................734 439-7203
Jerroll H Adams, *Owner*
EMP: 3
SALES (est): 200K **Privately Held**
SIC: 3931 7699 Pipes, organ; organ tuning & repair

(G-10932)
AMEX MFG & DISTRG CO INC
640 Ash St (48160-1074)
PHONE..................................734 439-8560
Phil Varnhagen, *Manager*
EMP: 5
SALES (est): 490K **Privately Held**
WEB: www.amexmfg.com
SIC: 3541 Screw machines, automatic

(G-10933)
CHEMINCON INC
Also Called: Bimac
345 E Main St (48160-1556)
PHONE..................................734 439-2478
Bernhard C Rumhold, *President*
Sally Cooper, *Corp Secy*
EMP: 3
SQ FT: 21,000
SALES (est): 371.2K **Privately Held**
SIC: 3297 8711 Cement refractories, nonclay; industrial engineers

(G-10934)
CHEMTOOL INCORPORATED
415 Squires Dr (48160-1253)
PHONE..................................734 439-7010
Fax: 734 439-7509
EMP: 7
SALES (corp-wide): 210.8B **Publicly Held**
SIC: 2992 3412 Mfg Lubricating Oils/Greases Mfg Metal Barrels/Pails
HQ: Chemtool Incorporated
801 W Rockton Rd
Rockton IL 61072
815 957-4140

(G-10935)
CLARK PERFORATING COMPANY INC
15875 Allen Rd (48160-9278)
P.O. Box 179 (48160-0179)
PHONE..................................734 439-1170
Sally Clark Freeman, *President*
Ken Clark, *Vice Pres*
EMP: 11 **EST:** 1993
SQ FT: 20,000
SALES (est): 2.2MM **Privately Held**
SIC: 3469 Perforated metal, stamped

(G-10936)
DIAMOND SETTERS INC
13 W Main St (48160-1213)
P.O. Box 28 (48160-0028)
PHONE..................................734 439-8655
Joseph Wilkenson, *President*
EMP: 3
SALES (est): 251.1K **Privately Held**
WEB: www.the-diamond-setters.com
SIC: 3911 7631 Jewel settings & mountings, precious metal; jewelry repair services

(G-10937)
FINCH SAND & GRAVEL LLC
10980 N Platt Rd (48160-9619)
P.O. Box 269 (48160-0269)
PHONE..................................734 439-1044
EMP: 6
SALES (est): 360K **Privately Held**
SIC: 1442 Construction Sand/Gravel

(G-10938)
GEORGIA-PACIFIC LLC
951 County St (48160-9785)
PHONE..................................734 439-2441
Dennis Guenther, *Manager*
EMP: 100
SQ FT: 200,000
SALES (corp-wide): 40.6B **Privately Held**
WEB: www.gp.com
SIC: 2653 3412 Corrugated & solid fiber boxes; metal barrels, drums & pails
HQ: Georgia-Pacific Llc
133 Peachtree St Nw
Atlanta GA 30303
404 652-4000

(G-10939)
GOTTS TRANSIT MIX INC
605 S Platt Rd (48160-9304)
P.O. Box 240 (48160-0240)
PHONE..................................734 439-1528
Tom Gotts, *President*
Gary Brown, *Vice Pres*
Paul Raetzel, *Dispersing Agnt*
EMP: 23
SQ FT: 5,000
SALES (est): 4.6MM **Privately Held**
SIC: 5032 3273 Concrete mixtures; ready-mixed concrete

(G-10940)
HARRISON PARTNERS INV GROUP
33 E Main St (48160-1475)
PHONE..................................419 708-8154
Edward Harrison III, *Principal*
Edward R Harrison III, *Principal*
EMP: 3
SALES (est): 166.4K **Privately Held**
SIC: 1541 5084 3523 4731 Food products manufacturing or packing plant construction; food product manufacturing machinery; windmills for pumping water, agricultural; freight transportation arrangement

(G-10941)
INNOVATIVE FLUIDS LLC
415 Squires Dr (48160-1253)
PHONE..................................734 241-5699
Barbara Hober, *Office Mgr*
Steven Peters, *Mng Member*
EMP: 16
SQ FT: 19,000
SALES (est): 4.8MM **Privately Held**
SIC: 2842 Cleaning or polishing preparations

(G-10942)
JAYTEC LLC
620 S Platt Rd (48160-9305)
PHONE..................................734 713-4500
Josh Forquer, *Manager*
EMP: 10
SALES (corp-wide): 2.2B **Privately Held**
SIC: 3465 Automotive stampings
HQ: Jaytec, Llc
17757 Woodland Dr
New Boston MI 48164
517 451-8272

(G-10943)
LIBERTY RESEARCH CO INC
291 Squires Dr (48160-1253)
PHONE..................................734 508-6237
Derrick Perkins, *Branch Mgr*
EMP: 5
SALES (corp-wide): 2.2MM **Privately Held**
SIC: 3451 Screw machine products
PA: Liberty Research Co, Inc.
7 Nadeau Dr
Rochester NH 03867
603 332-2730

(G-10944)
LIBERTY TURNED COMPONENTS LLC (PA)
Also Called: Ltc
291 Squires Dr (48160-1253)
P.O. Box 160 (48160-0160)
PHONE..................................734 508-6237
Derrick Perkins, *CEO*
Michele Perkins, *President*
EMP: 18
SQ FT: 5,400
SALES (est): 5.4MM **Privately Held**
SIC: 3451 Screw machine products

(G-10945)
LILLIAN FUEL INC
1200 Dexter St (48160-1100)
PHONE..................................734 439-8505
EMP: 4 **EST:** 2011
SALES (est): 360.6K **Privately Held**
SIC: 2869 Mfg Industrial Organic Chemicals

(G-10946)
MILAN BURIAL VAULT INC
Also Called: Milan Vault
10475 N Ann Arbor Rd (48160-9275)
PHONE..................................734 439-1538
Daniel C Wagner, *President*
Linda J Wagner, *Corp Secy*
Sam Wagner, *Vice Pres*
EMP: 13 **EST:** 1941
SQ FT: 10,000
SALES: 2MM **Privately Held**
WEB: www.milanvault.com
SIC: 3272 Burial vaults, concrete or precast terrazzo; septic tanks, concrete; concrete products, precast

(G-10947)
MILAN CAST METAL CORPORATION
13905 N Sanford Rd (48160-8809)
PHONE..................................734 439-0510
Donald Kondor, *President*
Steve Coburn, *General Mgr*
David Kondor, *Vice Pres*
Jason Arnold, *Manager*
Shelly Coburn, *Admin Sec*
EMP: 26 **EST:** 1946
SQ FT: 32,000
SALES (est): 5MM **Privately Held**
WEB: www.milancastmetal.com
SIC: 3365 Aluminum & aluminum-based alloy castings

(G-10948)
MILAN METAL SYSTEMS LLC
555 S Platt Rd (48160-9303)
PHONE..................................734 439-1546
Jeff Carter,
▲ **EMP:** 145
SQ FT: 15,000
SALES (est): 34.7MM
SALES (corp-wide): 4.1B **Privately Held**
SIC: 3465 Body parts, automobile: stamped metal
HQ: Global Automotive Systems, Llc
1780 Pond Run
Auburn Hills MI 48326
248 299-7500

(G-10949)
MILAN SCREW PRODUCTS INC
291 Squires Dr (48160-1253)
P.O. Box 180 (48160-0180)
PHONE..................................734 439-2431
Charles Tellas, *President*
Lorena Tellas, *Vice Pres*
EMP: 30
SQ FT: 37,000

Milan - Monroe County (G-10950)

SALES (est): 4.4MM **Privately Held**
SIC: 3451 3568 3429 Screw machine products; power transmission equipment; manufactured hardware (general)

(G-10950)
PRECISION DEVICES INC
606 County St (48160-9606)
P.O. Box 220 (48160-0220)
PHONE..................734 439-2462
Thomas L Preston, *President*
Joseph M Kormos, *Corp Secy*
EMP: 49 EST: 1971
SQ FT: 31,550
SALES (est): 10.6MM **Privately Held**
WEB: www.predev.com
SIC: 3829 3545 Physical property testing equipment; precision tools, machinists'

(G-10951)
STEVEN J DEVLIN
268 S Platt St (48160-1246)
PHONE..................734 439-1325
Steven J Devlin, *Principal*
EMP: 4
SALES (est): 203.3K **Privately Held**
SIC: 3724 Research & development on aircraft engines & parts

Milford
Oakland County

(G-10952)
4D BUILDING INC
Also Called: McDonald Modular Solutions
54500 Pontiac Trl (48381-4345)
PHONE..................248 799-7384
William Duffield, *President*
Colleen Rocha, *Sales Staff*
EMP: 18
SQ FT: 11,000
SALES (est): 3.6MM **Privately Held**
SIC: 2452 7359 Prefabricated wood buildings; equipment rental & leasing; shipping container leasing

(G-10953)
A & F ENTERPRISES INC
Also Called: Armstrong Graphics
1203 N Milford Rd (48381-1033)
PHONE..................248 714-6529
Dave Armstrong, *President*
EMP: 10
SALES (est): 950K **Privately Held**
SIC: 2721 Magazines: publishing only, not printed on site

(G-10954)
AMERICAN AWARDS & ENGRV LLC
1240 S Garner Rd (48380-4118)
PHONE..................810 229-5911
Susan Bates, *President*
Wendy Staniszeski, *President*
EMP: 3
SALES (est): 294K **Privately Held**
SIC: 3914 7389 5999 Trophies, plated (all metals); engraving service; trophies & plaques

(G-10955)
BISCAYNE AND ASSOCIATES INC
2515 Charms Rd (48381-3001)
PHONE..................248 304-0600
Keven Smith, *President*
Nigel Adkins, *Info Tech Mgr*
Arlene Santiago, *Info Tech Mgr*
Michelle Klaudt, *Prgrmr*
EMP: 24
SALES (est): 4.3MM **Privately Held**
WEB: www.mortgagebuilder.com
SIC: 7372 Prepackaged software

(G-10956)
BREESPORT HOLDINGS INC
Also Called: Cft Company
1235 Holden Ave (48381-3137)
PHONE..................248 685-9500
Robert E Dalton, *President*
James Heller, *Corp Secy*
Peter K Rosenkrands, *Vice Pres*
Christine Updike, *Human Res Mgr*

Arthur King, *CTO*
▼ EMP: 120 EST: 1946
SQ FT: 52,000
SALES (est): 23.5MM **Privately Held**
WEB: www.abheller.com
SIC: 3599 3545 Machine shop, jobbing & repair; cutting tools for machine tools

(G-10957)
BURNERS INC
4901 Mccarthy Dr (48381-3947)
P.O. Box 735 (48381-0735)
PHONE..................248 676-9141
W Michael Bockelman, *President*
Robert Bockelman, *Vice Pres*
Scott Bockelman, *Vice Pres*
Pamela Osinski, *Vice Pres*
▲ EMP: 9
SQ FT: 12,000
SALES (est): 1MM **Privately Held**
WEB: www.burnersinc.com
SIC: 3433 3625 Gas burners, industrial; control equipment, electric

(G-10958)
CLASSIC DESIGN CONCEPTS LLC
53194 Pontiac Trl (48381-4331)
PHONE..................248 504-5202
George Huisman, *Branch Mgr*
Lori Huisman,
▼ EMP: 11
SQ FT: 10,000
SALES (est): 2.1MM **Privately Held**
WEB: www.classicdesignconcepts.com
SIC: 3714 Exhaust systems & parts, motor vehicle; motor vehicle body components & frame
HQ: Tecstar, Lp
  3033 Excelsior Blvd # 300
  Minneapolis MN

(G-10959)
DAG R&D
1677 Melody Ln (48380-2145)
PHONE..................248 444-0575
Eric McBride, *Owner*
EMP: 5
SALES (est): 186.3K **Privately Held**
SIC: 3499 Fabricated metal products

(G-10960)
DENLIN INDUSTRIES INC
371 Mill Pond Ln (48381-1035)
PHONE..................586 303-5209
David C Peck, *President*
EMP: 5
SALES (est): 687.8K **Privately Held**
SIC: 3444 Sheet metalwork

(G-10961)
DIMITRI MANSOUR
Also Called: Blue Grill Foods
426 N Main St (48381-1958)
PHONE..................248 684-4545
Dimitri Mansour, *Owner*
EMP: 5
SQ FT: 1,100
SALES (est): 163.9K **Privately Held**
SIC: 2035 Pickles, sauces & salad dressings

(G-10962)
EIDEMLLER PRCSION MCHINING INC
4998 Mccarthy Dr (48381-3945)
PHONE..................248 669-2660
Martin Eidemiller, *President*
Renee Lagrow, *Purch Agent*
Jennifer Dominick, *Personnel*
EMP: 20
SALES (est): 4.3MM **Privately Held**
SIC: 3599 Machine shop, jobbing & repair

(G-10963)
ELECTRONIC APPS SPECLSTS INC
Also Called: E A S I
1250 Holden Ave (48381-3134)
PHONE..................248 491-4988
Michael Dechape, *President*
Jeffrey Dechape, *Vice Pres*
◆ EMP: 3
SQ FT: 2,200

SALES (est): 340.7K **Privately Held**
SIC: 3825 3829 3823 Test equipment for electronic & electrical circuits; physical property testing equipment; industrial instrmnts msrmnt display/control process variable

(G-10964)
GAILS CARPET CARE REPAIR
3110 Beach Lake Dr E (48380-2865)
PHONE..................248 684-8789
Gail Veiloeux, *Owner*
EMP: 3
SALES (est): 122.8K **Privately Held**
SIC: 2392 Linings, carpet: textile, except felt

(G-10965)
GREAT LAKES POST LLC
12466 Scenic View Ct (48380-2861)
PHONE..................248 941-1349
Stefan Kogler,
Jennifer Kogler,
EMP: 5
SALES (est): 117.9K **Privately Held**
SIC: 2711 Newspapers, publishing & printing

(G-10966)
INDUSTRIAL FABG SYSTEMS INC
4965 Technical Dr (48381-3952)
PHONE..................248 685-7373
Michael P Quin Jr, *President*
Cheryl M Quin, *Vice Pres*
EMP: 20
SQ FT: 11,000
SALES (est): 4.4MM **Privately Held**
SIC: 3443 Industrial vessels, tanks & containers; metal parts

(G-10967)
KLEIN BROS FENCE & STAKES LLC
2400 E Buno Rd (48381-3658)
PHONE..................248 684-6919
David Klein Jr, *Mng Member*
EMP: 5 EST: 1957
SQ FT: 1,800
SALES (est): 800K **Privately Held**
SIC: 2499 Surveyors' stakes, wood

(G-10968)
LANDIS PRECISION INC (PA)
937 S Main St (48381-2369)
PHONE..................248 685-8032
Lawrence P Donnellon, *President*
Lawrence Donnellon Sr, *President*
EMP: 3
SALES (est): 350K **Privately Held**
SIC: 3829 5084 Physical property testing equipment; machinists' precision measuring tools

(G-10969)
MICHIGAN SCIENTIFIC CORP (PA)
321 E Huron St (48381-2352)
PHONE..................248 685-3939
Hugh W Larsen, *President*
Michael Castiglione, *Vice Pres*
Andrew Cook, *Vice Pres*
Richard Wurst, *Vice Pres*
Jason Cichon, *Project Engr*
◆ EMP: 40 EST: 1960
SALES (est): 16.7MM **Privately Held**
WEB: www.michsci.com
SIC: 3829 8711 Testing equipment: abrasion, shearing strength, etc.; engineering services

(G-10970)
MILFORD JEWELERS INC
441 N Main St (48381-1960)
PHONE..................248 676-0721
Pamar Chopjin, *Principal*
EMP: 4
SQ FT: 4,286
SALES (est): 373.7K **Privately Held**
WEB: www.milfordjewelers.com
SIC: 5944 3911 Jewelry, precious stones & precious metals; jewelry, precious metal

(G-10971)
MILFORD REDI-MIX COMPANY
800 Concrete Dr (48381-1511)
PHONE..................248 684-1465
Keith Shorr, *President*
Charles Shorr, *Vice Pres*
EMP: 20
SQ FT: 5,000
SALES (est): 6.3MM **Privately Held**
WEB: www.milfordredimix.com
SIC: 3273 5032 Ready-mixed concrete; concrete building products

(G-10972)
MILLWORK DESIGN GROUP LLC
1280 Holden Ave Ste 127 (48381-3171)
PHONE..................248 472-2178
Gerald A Rauschenberger,
EMP: 5 EST: 1984
SQ FT: 3,000
SALES (est): 4.8MM **Privately Held**
SIC: 2434 5211 Wood kitchen cabinets; cabinets, kitchen

(G-10973)
MYCO INDUSTRIES INC
510 Highland Ave 332 (48381-1516)
PHONE..................248 685-2496
John Choate, *President*
Carol Choate, *Vice Pres*
Carol Briston-Choate, *Mng Member*
EMP: 3
SQ FT: 2,500
SALES (est): 500K **Privately Held**
WEB: www.mycoindustries.net
SIC: 3841 Ophthalmic instruments & apparatus

(G-10974)
NANO MATERIALS & PROCESSES INC
659 Heritage Dr (48381-2739)
PHONE..................248 529-3873
Andrey Factor, *Vice Pres*
Marshall Weingarden, *Administration*
EMP: 4
SALES (est): 796K **Privately Held**
SIC: 5169 2911 3479 2821 Oil additives; fuel additives; metal coating & allied service; painting, coating & hot dipping; epoxy resins; plasticizer/additive based plastic materials; custom compound purchased resins

(G-10975)
NATURAL AGGREGATES CORPORATION (PA)
3362 Muir Rd (48380-2947)
P.O. Box 2183, Brighton (48116-5983)
PHONE..................248 685-1502
Daniel N Pevos, *President*
Harold Lipsitz, *Vice Pres*
EMP: 13 EST: 1964
SQ FT: 800
SALES (est): 2.3MM **Privately Held**
SIC: 1442 Construction sand mining; gravel mining

(G-10976)
NEW WAY AIR SOLUTION COMPANY (PA)
4030 Sleeth Rd (48380)
PHONE..................248 676-9418
J Kenneth Simmons, *President*
EMP: 4
SQ FT: 5,000
SALES (est): 480K **Privately Held**
SIC: 3564 1711 Purification & dust collection equipment; plumbing, heating, air-conditioning contractors

(G-10977)
NOIR LASER COMPANY LLC
Also Called: Laser Shield
4975 Technical Dr (48381-3952)
P.O. Box 159, South Lyon (48178-0159)
PHONE..................800 521-9746
Mark Gleichert, *Mng Member*
Mike Smiglewski, *Manager*
Luanne Johnsen, *Technology*
A Brooks Gleicher,
Marc Gleichert,
EMP: 25 EST: 1996
SQ FT: 4,000

SALES (est): 4.2MM **Privately Held**
WEB: www.noirlaser.com
SIC: 3851 Protectors, eye

(G-10978)
NOIR MEDICAL TECHNOLOGIES LLC (PA)
Also Called: Noir Manufacturing Co
4975 Technical Dr (48381-3952)
PHONE.................................734 769-5565
Arthur B Gleichert,
David Bothner,
Marc Gleicher,
Linda Gleichert,
Anna Smiglewski,
EMP: 27
SALES: 5MM **Privately Held**
WEB: www.noir-medical.com
SIC: 3851 Glasses, sun or glare

(G-10979)
PICPATCH LLC
2488 Pearson Rd (48380-4322)
P.O. Box 779 (48381-0779)
PHONE.................................248 670-2681
David Mamo, *Mng Member*
▼ EMP: 5
SQ FT: 2,000
SALES: 100K **Privately Held**
SIC: 3699 Security devices

(G-10980)
PRECISION MACHINING
4998 Mccarthy Dr (48381-3945)
PHONE.................................248 669-2660
Martin Eidelmiller, *President*
EMP: 50
SQ FT: 22,000
SALES (est): 4.3MM **Privately Held**
SIC: 3599 Machine shop, jobbing & repair
HQ: Elopak-Americas, Inc.
46962 Liberty Dr
Wixom MI 48393
248 486-4600

(G-10981)
QUALITY STEEL PRODUCTS INC
4978 Technical Dr (48381-3950)
PHONE.................................248 684-0555
Joesph Schwegman, *President*
Paul Dolan, *Exec VP*
Marion Purdy, *Admin Sec*
EMP: 45
SQ FT: 60,000
SALES (est): 10.8MM **Privately Held**
SIC: 3462 3714 3568 Automotive forgings, ferrous: crankshaft, engine, axle, etc.; chains, forged steel; motor vehicle parts & accessories; power transmission equipment

(G-10982)
RADIUS LLC
4922 Technical Dr (48381-3950)
PHONE.................................248 685-0773
Steve Kozerski,
Bill Romero,
EMP: 4
SALES (est): 529.4K **Privately Held**
WEB: www.radius-eng.com
SIC: 3625 Actuators, industrial

(G-10983)
RPD MANUFACTURING LLC
3171 Rolling Green Ct (48380-4472)
PHONE.................................248 760-4796
EMP: 3 EST: 2012
SALES (est): 179.7K **Privately Held**
SIC: 3999 Manufacturing industries

(G-10984)
SCHAEFFLER GROUP USA INC
4574 Windswept Dr (48380-2776)
PHONE.................................810 360-0294
EMP: 347
SALES (corp-wide): 68.1B **Privately Held**
SIC: 3562 Roller bearings & parts
HQ: Schaeffler Group Usa Inc.
308 Springhill Farm Rd
Fort Mill SC 29715
803 548-8500

(G-10985)
SILVER SLATE LLC
4964 Technical Dr (48381-3950)
PHONE.................................248 486-3989
Ray Merlo, *Mng Member*
Pamela Merlo,
EMP: 20
SALES (est): 2.1MM **Privately Held**
SIC: 1221 Bituminous coal & lignite-surface mining

(G-10986)
SOUTH HILL SAND AND GRAVEL
4303 S Hill Rd (48381-3807)
PHONE.................................248 685-7020
Tom Powell, *Manager*
EMP: 5 **Privately Held**
SIC: 1442 Gravel mining
PA: South Hill Sand And Gravel, Inc
5877 Livernois Rd Ste 103
Troy MI 48098

(G-10987)
STERLING PERFORMANCE INC
54420 Pontiac Trl (48381-4344)
PHONE.................................248 685-7811
Michael J D'Anniballe, *President*
Jeff Burrill, *Vice Pres*
▲ EMP: 25
SQ FT: 8,000
SALES: 3.5MM **Privately Held**
SIC: 3714 3732 Motor vehicle engines & parts; motorboats, inboard or outboard: building & repairing

(G-10988)
TECHNOLOGY & MANUFACTURING INC
3190 Pine Cone Ct (48381-3398)
PHONE.................................248 755-1444
Paul Diaz, *CEO*
▲ EMP: 7
SALES (est): 721.3K **Privately Held**
SIC: 3559 Automotive related machinery

(G-10989)
TRIAD PROCESS EQUIPMENT INC
4922 Technical Dr (48381-3950)
PHONE.................................248 685-9938
Steve Kozerski, *President*
William Romero, *Vice Pres*
▲ EMP: 9
SQ FT: 1,000
SALES (est): 1.2MM **Privately Held**
WEB: www.triadprocess.com
SIC: 3491 5085 Industrial valves; industrial supplies

(G-10990)
VERTEX STEEL INC
2175 Fyke Dr (48381-3687)
PHONE.................................248 684-4177
Mike Dimet, *President*
Ralph Wood, *Plant Mgr*
Jim Cortopassi, *Project Mgr*
Sandy Richardson, *Manager*
EMP: 30
SQ FT: 14,000
SALES (est): 9.1MM **Privately Held**
WEB: www.vertexsteel.com
SIC: 3442 Sash, door or window: metal

Millersburg
Presque Isle County

(G-10991)
CEDAR LOG LBR MILLERSBURG INC
6019 Millersburg Rd (49759-8726)
PHONE.................................989 733-2676
Tyler Tollini, *President*
Rita Tollini, *Vice Pres*
EMP: 10
SALES (est): 1.6MM **Privately Held**
SIC: 5211 5031 2431 Lumber products; lumber, plywood & millwork; woodwork, interior & ornamental

(G-10992)
PNEUMATIC INNOVATIONS LLC
5369 Main St (49759-9435)
P.O. Box 111 (49759-0111)
PHONE.................................989 734-3435
Dennis Trestain, *Partner*
Jane Trestain, *Partner*
EMP: 3
SALES (est): 750K **Privately Held**
SIC: 5084 3914 Conveyor systems; trays, stainless steel

Millington
Tuscola County

(G-10993)
ADS US INC (PA)
Also Called: Advanced Decorative Systems
4705 Industrial Dr (48746-9300)
PHONE.................................989 871-4550
James Conaty, *CEO*
John Allard, *President*
Terry Aymer, *President*
Csaba Bedo, *Managing Dir*
Carrie Joseph, *COO*
▲ EMP: 124
SQ FT: 52,000
SALES: 19MM **Privately Held**
WEB: www.kaumagraph.com
SIC: 3714 3429 Motor vehicle parts & accessories; manufactured hardware (general)

(G-10994)
DYNA SALES & SERVICE LLC
Also Called: Dynas Products
8440 State Rd (48746-9445)
PHONE.................................231 734-4433
Nathan Miller,
Louie Weaver, *Products*
Omer Miller,
Stephen Miller,
EMP: 9
SALES: 5.4MM **Privately Held**
SIC: 3599 Machine shop, jobbing & repair

(G-10995)
E & S SHEET METAL
9450 Belsay Rd (48746-9587)
PHONE.................................989 871-2067
Eugene Root, *Owner*
EMP: 3
SQ FT: 216
SALES (est): 276.7K **Privately Held**
SIC: 3444 Sheet metalwork

(G-10996)
HOME STYLE CO
Also Called: Up To Date Painting
8400 Caine Rd (48746-9132)
PHONE.................................989 871-3654
Donna J Dipzinski, *Owner*
EMP: 5
SALES: 120K **Privately Held**
SIC: 7389 1721 2499 Interior designer; painting & paper hanging; handles, wood

(G-10997)
LOUDON STEEL INC
8208 Ellis Rd (48746-9402)
P.O. Box 312 (48746-0312)
PHONE.................................989 871-9353
Gregg Loudon, *President*
EMP: 80
SQ FT: 26,000
SALES (est): 25.5MM **Privately Held**
SIC: 3441 3535 3537 3496 Fabricated structural metal; conveyors & conveying equipment; industrial trucks & tractors; miscellaneous fabricated wire products; partitions & fixtures, except wood

(G-10998)
STEMCO PRODUCTS INC
4641 Industrial Dr (48746-9300)
PHONE.................................888 854-6474
EMP: 3
SALES (corp-wide): 1.5B **Publicly Held**
SIC: 3714 3465 Brake drums, motor vehicle; hub caps, automobile: stamped metal

HQ: Stemco Products, Inc.
300 Industrial Dr
Longview TX 75602
734 416-8911

(G-10999)
WOOD BURN LLC
8106 Vassar Rd (48746-9479)
PHONE.................................810 614-4204
Joseph Payne, *Mng Member*
EMP: 4
SALES (est): 270K **Privately Held**
SIC: 3433 Burners, furnaces, boilers & stokers

Minden City
Sanilac County

(G-11000)
MINDEN CITY HERALD
Also Called: Engel Printing Company
1524 Main St (48456-9404)
P.O. Box 38 (48456-0038)
PHONE.................................989 864-3630
Paul Engel, *Partner*
Janice Ann Engel, *Partner*
EMP: 3 EST: 1945
SQ FT: 1,000
SALES (est): 266.2K **Privately Held**
SIC: 2752 2711 Commercial printing, lithographic; newspapers: publishing only, not printed on site

(G-11001)
SURFACE MAUSOLEUM COMPANY INC
1799 Main St (48456-9301)
P.O. Box 27 (48456-0027)
PHONE.................................989 864-3460
Phillip G Moses, *President*
Jane Moses, *Corp Secy*
EMP: 6 EST: 1932
SQ FT: 8,800
SALES (est): 730.9K **Privately Held**
SIC: 3272 Burial vaults, concrete or precast terrazzo; septic tanks, concrete

Mio
Oscoda County

(G-11002)
GILCHRIST PREMIUM LUMBER PDTS (PA)
Also Called: Woodhaven Log & Lumber
1284 Mapes Rd (48647-9516)
P.O. Box 964 (48647-0964)
PHONE.................................989 826-8300
Richard Bills, *President*
Anita Bills, *Vice Pres*
EMP: 12
SQ FT: 240
SALES: 2.5MM **Privately Held**
SIC: 2421 Lumber: rough, sawed or planed; siding (dressed lumber)

(G-11003)
GYMS SAWMILL
931 W Kittle Rd (48647-9713)
PHONE.................................989 826-8299
Michael Gingerich, *Partner*
Nate Hochstetler, *Partner*
Titus Lambright, *Partner*
Ivan Miller, *Partner*
EMP: 4
SALES: 800K **Privately Held**
SIC: 2421 Sawmills & planing mills, general

(G-11004)
METALFAB MANUFACTURING INC
378 Booth Rd (48647-9771)
PHONE.................................989 826-2301
Joel Yoder, *President*
Jim Weaver, *Plant Mgr*
Jerry Anderson, *Sales Mgr*
Michelle Yoder, *Admin Sec*
Trevor Blamer, *Maintence Staff*
EMP: 20

Mio - Oscoda County (G-11005)

SALES: 4MM **Privately Held**
SIC: 3441 Fabricated structural metal

(G-11005)
METALFAB TOOL & MACHINE INC
Also Called: Metal Fab Tool & Machine
55 W Kittle Rd (48647-9704)
PHONE..................989 826-6044
Thomas Holzwarth, *President*
Elizabeth Holzwarth, *Manager*
EMP: 6
SQ FT: 4,320
SALES: 674.8K **Privately Held**
SIC: 3544 Special dies & tools; jigs & fixtures

(G-11006)
MORSE CONCRETE & EXCAVATING
106 S Vine St (48647-9459)
P.O. Box 518 (48647-0518)
PHONE..................989 826-3975
Dennis Morse, *President*
Audrey Reghi, *General Mgr*
EMP: 10
SQ FT: 1,200
SALES (est): 1MM **Privately Held**
SIC: 3273 1794 1711 1795 Ready-mixed concrete; excavation work; septic system construction; demolition, buildings & other structures

(G-11007)
NORTHWOOD LUMBER
937 W Kittle Rd (48647-9713)
PHONE..................989 826-1751
Neil Bontrager, *Partner*
Leon Hershberger, *Partner*
Nathan Ponpreger, *Partner*
EMP: 5 EST: 2001
SALES (est): 1MM **Privately Held**
SIC: 2421 Sawmills & planing mills, general

(G-11008)
R & N LUMBER
1388 Caldwell Rd (48647-8738)
PHONE..................989 848-5553
John Miller, *Managing Prtnr*
Samuel Beachy, *Partner*
David Yoder, *Partner*
EMP: 6
SALES (est): 649.6K **Privately Held**
SIC: 2421 Lumber: rough, sawed or planed

(G-11009)
SPECIALTY TUBE SOLUTIONS
Also Called: STS
339 E Miller Rd (48647-9660)
PHONE..................989 848-0880
Cortney L Sears, *Administration*
EMP: 6 EST: 2014
SALES (est): 771.1K **Privately Held**
SIC: 3317 Pipes, wrought: welded, lock joint or heavy riveted

Moline
Allegan County

(G-11010)
GLD HOLDINGS INC
4560 Division (49335)
P.O. Box 337 (49335-0337)
PHONE..................616 877-4288
Gary L De Young, *President*
Matt McCauley, *Vice Pres*
EMP: 13
SQ FT: 15,000
SALES (est): 3.2MM **Privately Held**
SIC: 5511 3443 7699 Trucks, tractors & trailers: new & used; tanks, lined: metal plate; tank repair

(G-11011)
JONES MFG & SUP CO INC
1177 Electric Ave (49335)
P.O. Box 343 (49335-0343)
PHONE..................616 877-4442
Gary Jones, *President*
Jason Kelly, *Vice Pres*
Jim Cyrak, *Foreman/Supr*
Jill Kelly, *Treasurer*
EMP: 20 EST: 1974
SQ FT: 25,000
SALES (est): 4.1MM **Privately Held**
WEB: www.jonesmanufacturing.com
SIC: 3444 Sheet metal specialties, not stamped

Monroe
Monroe County

(G-11012)
ACTUATOR SERVICES LLC
Also Called: Actuator Specialties
1620 Rose St (48162-5699)
PHONE..................734 242-5456
Mallory Setzler, *CEO*
Wendy Wright, *Treasurer*
EMP: 5
SQ FT: 11,000
SALES (est): 778.1K **Privately Held**
WEB: www.actuatorspecialties.com
SIC: 3999 Education aids, devices & supplies

(G-11013)
ADVANCED HEAT TREAT CORP
1625 Rose St (48162-5607)
PHONE..................734 243-0063
Gary Sharp, *President*
Matt Cunningham, *Maintence Staff*
EMP: 20
SALES (corp-wide): 12.5MM **Privately Held**
WEB: www.ahtweb.com
SIC: 3398 Metal heat treating
PA: Advanced Heat Treat Corp.
 2825 Midport Blvd
 Waterloo IA 50703
 319 232-5221

(G-11014)
AJ AIRCRAFT
2410 N Monroe St (48162-4216)
PHONE..................734 244-4015
EMP: 3
SALES (est): 220.7K **Privately Held**
SIC: 3728 Aircraft parts & equipment

(G-11015)
BACKYARD PRODUCTS LLC (PA)
Also Called: Handy Home
1000 Ternes Dr (48162-5224)
PHONE..................734 242-6900
Chuck Halasi, *Maint Spvr*
Brennan Deitsch, *Marketing Mgr*
Jeremiah Walters, *IT/INT Sup*
Leonard Baker, *Director*
Thomas Van Der Meulen,
▲ EMP: 6
SQ FT: 250,000
SALES (est): 244.4MM **Privately Held**
SIC: 2452 Prefabricated wood buildings; play pens, children's: wood

(G-11016)
BACKYARD SERVICES LLC
1000 Ternes Dr (48162-5224)
PHONE..................734 242-6900
Daniel R Dalach, *CFO*
Duane Daniels, *Controller*
Thomas Van Der Meulen,
EMP: 220
SALES (est): 8.6MM **Privately Held**
SIC: 2511 Storage chests, household: wood; children's wood furniture
PA: Backyard Products, Llc
 1000 Ternes Dr
 Monroe MI 48162

(G-11017)
BAGNALL ENTERPRISES INC
Also Called: American Speedy Printing
1110 N Telegraph Rd Ste 8 (48162-3340)
PHONE..................734 457-0500
Debra A Bagnall, *President*
EMP: 7
SALES: 350K **Privately Held**
SIC: 2752 Commercial printing, offset

(G-11018)
BALL HARD MUSIC GROUP LLC (PA)
330 E Elm Ave (48162-2655)
PHONE..................734 636-0038
Quentine Turnage, *President*
Berlon Watson, *Vice Pres*
EMP: 4
SALES: 40K **Privately Held**
SIC: 7389 7929 2741 Music recording producer; ; entertainment service; miscellaneous publishing

(G-11019)
BAR PROCESSING CORPORATION
550 Ternes Dr (48162-5000)
PHONE..................734 243-8937
Jack Starkey, *Sales Staff*
John Wilson, *Manager*
EMP: 60
SALES (corp-wide): 39.9MM **Privately Held**
SIC: 3471 Finishing, metals or formed products; polishing, metals or formed products
HQ: Bar Processing Corporation
 26601 W Huron River Dr
 Flat Rock MI 48134
 734 782-4454

(G-11020)
BAY CORRUGATED CONTAINER INC
1655 W 7th St (48161-1688)
P.O. Box 667 (48161-0667)
PHONE..................734 243-5400
Connie Reuther, *CEO*
John Reuther, *President*
Phillip Dress, *Vice Pres*
James Goiins, *Vice Pres*
James Goins, *Vice Pres*
▲ EMP: 215
SQ FT: 400,000
SALES (est): 66MM **Privately Held**
WEB: www.baycorr.com
SIC: 2653 Boxes, corrugated: made from purchased materials

(G-11021)
BEKTROM FOODS INC
15610 S Telegraph Rd (48161-4067)
PHONE..................734 241-3796
Tom Barbela, *Branch Mgr*
EMP: 12
SALES (corp-wide): 12.5MM **Privately Held**
SIC: 2045 Prepared flour mixes & doughs
PA: Bektrom Foods, Inc.
 6800 Jericho Tpke 207w
 Syosset NY 11791
 516 802-3800

(G-11022)
BEKTROM FOODS INC
1010 Detroit Ave (48162-2543)
PHONE..................734 241-3711
EMP: 5
SALES (corp-wide): 12.5MM **Privately Held**
SIC: 2099 Spices, including grinding
PA: Bektrom Foods, Inc.
 6800 Jericho Tpke 207w
 Syosset NY 11791
 516 802-3800

(G-11023)
BENESH CORPORATION (PA)
1910 N Telegraph Rd (48162-8900)
P.O. Box 906 (48161-0906)
PHONE..................734 244-4143
Peter Benesh, *President*
Edward Benesh, *Manager*
Kathryn Benesh, *Admin Sec*
EMP: 20 EST: 1943
SQ FT: 18,000
SALES: 1.7MM **Privately Held**
SIC: 3465 3535 3829 3845 Body parts, automobile: stamped metal; conveyors & conveying equipment; measuring & controlling devices; electromedical equipment; instruments to measure electricity; switchgear & switchboard apparatus

(G-11024)
CCO HOLDINGS LLC
2101 Mall Rd (48162-8863)
PHONE..................734 244-8028
EMP: 3
SALES (corp-wide): 43.6B **Publicly Held**
SIC: 5064 4841 3663 3651 Electrical appliances, television & radio; cable & other pay television services; radio & TV communications equipment; household audio & video equipment
HQ: Cco Holdings, Llc
 400 Atlantic St
 Stamford CT 06901
 203 905-7801

(G-11025)
COMPLETE PACKAGING INC
633 Detroit Ave (48162-2587)
P.O. Box 735 (48161-0735)
PHONE..................734 241-2794
Robert Maul, *President*
Jeff Ball, *Plant Mgr*
Sue Brey, *Controller*
Gregg Reau, *Mktg Dir*
EMP: 50
SQ FT: 60,000
SALES (est): 13MM **Privately Held**
WEB: www.completepkg.com
SIC: 2441 2653 2657 2448 Boxes, wood; corrugated & solid fiber boxes; folding paperboard boxes; wood pallets & skids

(G-11026)
D S C SERVICES INC (PA)
1510 E 1st St (48161-1915)
PHONE..................734 241-9500
Mark Berryman, *Principal*
Tammy Aldrich, *Marketing Mgr*
EMP: 6
SALES (est): 57.5MM **Privately Held**
SIC: 3433 Stokers, mechanical: domestic or industrial

(G-11027)
DD PARKER ENTERPRISES INC
Also Called: Monroe Mold
1402 W 7th St (48161-1681)
PHONE..................734 241-6898
James Ghesquire, *President*
John Kwiechen, *President*
EMP: 28
SQ FT: 4,000
SALES (est): 3.2MM **Privately Held**
WEB: www.monroemold.com
SIC: 3599 3544 Machine shop, jobbing & repair; special dies, tools, jigs & fixtures

(G-11028)
DETROIT STOKER COMPANY
1510 E 1st St (48161-1915)
PHONE..................734 241-9500
Gary K Ludwig, *CEO*
Rich Clasby, *Business Mgr*
Michael Dimonte, *Vice Pres*
John Murray, *Vice Pres*
Tom Rosen, *Plant Mgr*
▲ EMP: 225 EST: 1898
SQ FT: 300,000
SALES (est): 57.5MM **Privately Held**
WEB: www.detroitstoker.com
SIC: 3433 Stokers, mechanical: domestic or industrial
PA: D S C Services Inc
 1510 E 1st St
 Monroe MI 48161

(G-11029)
ECHO ENGRG & PROD SUPS INC
Also Called: Ammex Plastics
725 Ternes Dr (48162-5005)
PHONE..................734 241-9622
David Ayala, *General Mgr*
Chris Wells, *Maintence Staff*
EMP: 54
SALES (corp-wide): 14.9MM **Privately Held**
SIC: 3089 Plastic processing
PA: Echo Engineering & Production Supplies Inc.
 7150 Winton Dr Ste 300
 Indianapolis IN 46268
 317 876-8848

GEOGRAPHIC SECTION
Monroe - Monroe County (G-11055)

(G-11030)
EVENING NEWS
20 W 1st St (48161-2333)
PHONE..................................734 242-1100
Lonnie Peppler-Moyer, *Principal*
EMP: 6
SALES (est): 331.5K **Privately Held**
SIC: 2711 Newspapers

(G-11031)
FINISHERS UNLIMITED MONROE INC
757 S Telegraph Rd (48161-1674)
PHONE..................................734 243-3502
Eric Kuehnlein, *President*
Jim Mackin, *Vice Pres*
Jackie Nocella, *Sales Associate*
EMP: 20
SQ FT: 15,000
SALES (est): 2.6MM **Privately Held**
SIC: 3479 Painting of metal products

(G-11032)
GENESIS MANUFACTURING ENTPS
348 Ruff Dr (48162-3525)
PHONE..................................734 243-5302
EMP: 3
SQ FT: 8,000
SALES (est): 200.6K **Privately Held**
SIC: 3086 Mfg Foam Packaging Products

(G-11033)
GERDAU MACSTEEL INC
Also Called: Gerdau Special Steel N Amer
3000 E Front St (48161-1973)
P.O. Box 1200 (48161-6200)
PHONE..................................734 243-2446
Darrel Moore, *Branch Mgr*
EMP: 536 **Privately Held**
SIC: 3312 Bars & bar shapes, steel, hot-rolled
HQ: Gerdau Macsteel, Inc.
  5591 Morrill Rd
  Jackson MI 49201

(G-11034)
GERDAU MACSTEEL INC
Also Called: Macsteel Monroe
3000 E Front St (48161-1973)
P.O. Box 1200 (48161-6200)
PHONE..................................734 243-2446
Otto Alvarado, *Safety Mgr*
Marcus Tremper, *Production*
Fred Clark, *Engineer*
Wendy Craig, *Engineer*
Christopher Paull, *Engineer*
EMP: 380
SQ FT: 552 **Privately Held**
WEB: www.quanex.com
SIC: 3312 3316 Bars & bar shapes, steel, cold-finished: own hot-rolled; cold finishing of steel shapes
HQ: Gerdau Macsteel, Inc.
  5591 Morrill Rd
  Jackson MI 49201

(G-11035)
GERKEN MATERIALS INC
15205 S Telegraph Rd (48161)
PHONE..................................734 243-1851
Rob Jankowski, *Manager*
EMP: 3
SALES (corp-wide): 80.7MM **Privately Held**
SIC: 3531 Asphalt plant, including gravel-mix type
PA: Gerken Materials, Inc.
  9072 County Road 424
  Napoleon OH 43545
  419 533-2421

(G-11036)
GLOBAL DIGITAL PRINTING
20 W 1st St (48161-2333)
PHONE..................................734 244-5010
EMP: 3
SALES (est): 101.5K **Privately Held**
SIC: 2752 Commercial printing, lithographic

(G-11037)
GREAT LAKES TOWERS LLC
Also Called: Ventower Industries
111 Borchert Park Dr (48161-1986)
P.O. Box 589 (48161-0589)
PHONE..................................734 682-4000
Gregory Adanin,
Christy Follbaum, *Administration*
Scott Viciana,
▲ **EMP:** 180
SQ FT: 115,000
SALES (est): 31.6MM **Privately Held**
SIC: 3441 Fabricated structural metal

(G-11038)
HANWHA ADVANCED MTLS AMER LLC
Also Called: Hanwha L&C Alabama
1530 E Front St (48161-2456)
PHONE..................................810 629-2496
Larry Rood, *Branch Mgr*
EMP: 23 **Privately Held**
SIC: 3714 Motor vehicle parts & accessories
HQ: Hanwha Advanced Materials America Llc
  4400 N Park Dr
  Opelika AL 36801
  334 741-7725

(G-11039)
HILGRAEVE INC
115 E Elm Ave (48162-2650)
P.O. Box 941 (48161-0941)
PHONE..................................734 243-0576
Patty Thompson, *President*
Robert Everett,
John Hile,
EMP: 5
SALES (est): 690.6K **Privately Held**
WEB: www.hilgraeve.com
SIC: 7372 Prepackaged software

(G-11040)
HYDROCHEM LLC
Also Called: Hydrochempsc
987 W Hurd Rd (48162-9401)
PHONE..................................313 841-5800
Rodney Baugher, *Safety Dir*
Steve McMahan, *Opers Mgr*
Tim Gaudet, *Human Res Dir*
Gary Noto, *Branch Mgr*
EMP: 200
SALES (corp-wide): 607.5MM **Privately Held**
SIC: 3589 Vacuum cleaners & sweepers, electric: industrial
HQ: Hydrochem Llc
  900 Georgia Ave
  Deer Park TX 77536
  713 393-5600

(G-11041)
INDEPENDENT DAIRY INC (PA)
126 N Telegraph Rd (48162-3299)
PHONE..................................734 241-6016
Michael Cheney, *President*
Jeffery Hutchinson, *Treasurer*
EMP: 20
SQ FT: 18,000
SALES (est): 3.8MM **Privately Held**
SIC: 2024 5143 5411 Ice cream, bulk; ice cream, packaged: molded, on sticks, etc.; milk & cream, fluid; ice cream & ices; convenience stores, chain

(G-11042)
INTER-PACK CORPORATION (PA)
399 Detroit Ave (48162-2538)
P.O. Box 691 (48162-0691)
PHONE..................................734 242-7755
J Benjiman Watson, *President*
Douglas Southworth, *Shareholder*
EMP: 25 **EST:** 1967
SQ FT: 80,000
SALES: 2MM **Privately Held**
WEB: www.lakelandindustries.com
SIC: 2653 3086 7389 Boxes, corrugated: made from purchased materials; plastics foam products; packaging & labeling services

(G-11043)
JERRYS PALLETS
232 E Hurd Rd (48162-9213)
PHONE..................................734 242-1577
EMP: 4 **EST:** 2009
SALES (est): 190K **Privately Held**
SIC: 2448 Mfg Wood Pallets/Skids

(G-11044)
JR KANDLER & SONS
13657 Laplaisance Rd (48161-4753)
PHONE..................................734 241-0270
John Kandler, *Owner*
EMP: 3
SALES (est): 236.2K **Privately Held**
SIC: 3441 Fabricated structural metal

(G-11045)
KUHLMAN CORPORATION
Also Called: Kuhlman Concrete
15370 S Dixie Hwy (48161-3773)
PHONE..................................734 241-8692
Stan Radabaugh, *Manager*
EMP: 7
SALES (est): 819.1K
SALES (corp-wide): 53.5MM **Privately Held**
WEB: www.kuhlman-corp.com
SIC: 3273 Ready-mixed concrete
PA: Kuhlman Corporation
  1845 Indian Wood Cir
  Maumee OH 43537
  419 897-6000

(G-11046)
L & C HANWHA
1530 E Front St (48161-2456)
PHONE..................................734 457-5600
EMP: 7
SALES (est): 1.3MM **Privately Held**
SIC: 3714 Motor vehicle parts & accessories

(G-11047)
LA-Z-BOY CASEGOODS INC (HQ)
Also Called: La-Z-Boy Greensboro, Inc.
1 Lazboy Dr (48162-5138)
PHONE..................................734 242-1444
Kurt L Darrow, *CEO*
Steven M Kincaid, *Principal*
Louis M Riccio, *Vice Pres*
James P Klarr, *Admin Sec*
▲ **EMP:** 20
SALES (est): 9.4MM
SALES (corp-wide): 1.7B **Publicly Held**
WEB: www.hammary.com
SIC: 2511 5714 Wood household furniture; upholstery materials
PA: La-Z-Boy Incorporated
  1 Lazboy Dr
  Monroe MI 48162
  734 242-1444

(G-11048)
LA-Z-BOY GLOBAL LIMITED
1 Lazboy Dr (48162-5138)
PHONE..................................734 241-2438
Kurt Droow, *Principal*
EMP: 3
SALES (est): 192.2K
SALES (corp-wide): 1.7B **Publicly Held**
SIC: 2512 Chairs: upholstered on wood frames
PA: La-Z-Boy Incorporated
  1 Lazboy Dr
  Monroe MI 48162
  734 242-1444

(G-11049)
LA-Z-BOY INCORPORATED (PA)
1 Lazboy Dr (48162-5138)
PHONE..................................734 242-1444
Kurt L Darrow, *Ch of Bd*
Dave Bergman, *General Mgr*
Daren Davison, *General Mgr*
Richard Hawkes, *General Mgr*
Thomas Mox, *General Mgr*
◆ **EMP:** 550 **EST:** 1927
SALES: 1.7B **Publicly Held**
WEB: www.lazyboy.com
SIC: 2512 2511 5712 Chairs: upholstered on wood frames; couches, sofas & davenports: upholstered on wood frames; recliners: upholstered on wood frames; rockers: upholstered on wood frames; wood household furniture; furniture stores

(G-11050)
LAMOUR PRINTING CO
123 E Front St (48161-2198)
PHONE..................................734 241-6006
Robert Lamour, *Partner*
John Lamour, *Partner*
Brian Lamour, *Manager*
EMP: 4
SQ FT: 2,000
SALES: 250K **Privately Held**
SIC: 2759 2752 Letterpress printing; commercial printing, offset

(G-11051)
LZB MANUFACTURING INC (HQ)
Also Called: La-Z-Boy
1 Lazboy Dr (48162-5138)
PHONE..................................734 242-1444
Mark S Bacon Sr, *President*
R Rand Tucker, *Vice Pres*
Louis M Riccio, *CFO*
Greg A Brinks, *Treasurer*
James P Klarr, *Admin Sec*
▲ **EMP:** 5
SALES (est): 167.2MM
SALES (corp-wide): 1.7B **Publicly Held**
SIC: 2512 Upholstered household furniture
PA: La-Z-Boy Incorporated
  1 Lazboy Dr
  Monroe MI 48162
  734 242-1444

(G-11052)
MIDWAY PRODUCTS GROUP INC (PA)
1 Lyman E Hoyt Dr (48161)
P.O. Box 737 (48161-0737)
PHONE..................................734 241-7242
James E Hoyt, *President*
Lloyd A Miller, *Vice Pres*
Scott Morton, *Project Mgr*
Craig Anschuetz, *Engineer*
Brian Behm, *Engineer*
▲ **EMP:** 120
SALES (est): 186.8MM **Privately Held**
SIC: 3465 Automotive stampings

(G-11053)
MOBILE MIX
15519 Westwood Dr (48161-4053)
PHONE..................................734 497-3256
Samantha Needham, *Principal*
EMP: 3
SALES (est): 170.4K **Privately Held**
SIC: 3273 Ready-mixed concrete

(G-11054)
MONROE ENVIRONMENTAL CORP
810 W Front St (48161-1627)
PHONE..................................734 242-2420
Gary Pashaian, *President*
Debbie Machnak, *Project Mgr*
Rob Cardella, *Opers Mgr*
Joseph Dragich, *Purch Mgr*
Larry Deranek, *Engineer*
◆ **EMP:** 44
SQ FT: 40,000
SALES (est): 14.8MM **Privately Held**
WEB: www.monroeenvironmental.com
SIC: 3589 Water treatment equipment, industrial

(G-11055)
MONROE EVENING NEWS
7460 White Horse Cir (48161-5009)
PHONE..................................734 242-1100
Larry D Gray, *Principal*
Tyler Eagle, *Editor*
Barbara Krolak, *Editor*
Barb McMullen, *Purchasing*
Vicki Price, *Sales Staff*
EMP: 8
SALES (est): 450.2K **Privately Held**
SIC: 2711 Newspapers

Monroe - Monroe County (G-11056) — GEOGRAPHIC SECTION

(G-11056)
MONROE MOLD LLC
1402 W 7th St (48161-1681)
PHONE 734 241-6898
Jim Ghesquire, *President*
Mark Gardner, *Vice Pres*
Perry Schwemmin, *Engineer*
EMP: 3
SALES (est): 2.2MM **Privately Held**
SIC: 3089 Molding primary plastic; injection molding of plastics

(G-11057)
MONROE PUBLISHING COMPANY (HQ)
20 W 1st St (48161-2333)
P.O. Box 1176 (48161-6176)
PHONE 734 242-1100
Lonnie L Peppler-Moyer, *President*
Jay Hollon, *Corp Secy*
Kristi Prater, *Advt Staff*
Kendra Wall, *Advt Staff*
Jamie West, *Advt Staff*
EMP: 69
SQ FT: 25,000
SALES (est): 13.4MM
SALES (corp-wide): 1.5B **Privately Held**
WEB: www.monroenews.com
SIC: 2759 2711 Commercial printing; newspapers, publishing & printing
PA: New Media Investment Group Inc.
1345 Avenue Of The Americ
New York NY 10105
212 479-3160

(G-11058)
MONROE SUCCESS VLC
1000 S Monroe St (48161-3901)
PHONE 734 682-3720
EMP: 3
SALES (est): 103.3K **Privately Held**
SIC: 2711 Newspapers

(G-11059)
NATIONAL GALVANIZING LP
1500 Telb St (48162-2572)
PHONE 734 243-1882
Mike Robinson, *Principal*
Becky Riley, *Human Res Mgr*
EMP: 1000
SQ FT: 15,000
SALES (est): 174.4MM **Privately Held**
WEB: www.nationalgalvanizing.com
SIC: 3312 3316 3471 3341 Sheet or strip, steel, hot-rolled; strip steel, cold-rolled: from purchased hot-rolled; plating & polishing; secondary nonferrous metals; metals service centers & offices

(G-11060)
PAUL C DOERR
Also Called: Kraus & Co
407 E Front St (48161-2048)
PHONE 734 242-2058
Paul C Doerr, *Owner*
EMP: 4 **EST:** 1947
SQ FT: 6,500
SALES (est): 320K **Privately Held**
SIC: 2752 2791 2789 Advertising posters, lithographed; typesetting; bookbinding & related work

(G-11061)
PHYSICIANS TECHNOLOGY LLC
Also Called: Willow
23 E Front St Ste 200 (48161-2210)
PHONE 734 241-5060
David Sutton, *CEO*
EMP: 12
SALES (est): 1.5MM **Privately Held**
SIC: 3845 Laser systems & equipment, medical

(G-11062)
PIONEER METAL FINISHING LLC
525 Ternes Dr (48162-5001)
PHONE 734 384-9000
Ann Shealer, *Branch Mgr*
EMP: 150
SALES (corp-wide): 93MM **Privately Held**
WEB: www.pioneermetal.com
SIC: 3398 3471 Metal heat treating; plating & polishing
PA: Pioneer Metal Finishing, Llc
480 Pilgrim Way Ste 1400
Green Bay WI 54304
877 721-1100

(G-11063)
PRO-POWERSPORTS
7779 Townway Dr (48161-4725)
PHONE 734 457-0829
Chris Danish, *Partner*
EMP: 5
SALES (est): 507.8K **Privately Held**
WEB: www.sledauction.com
SIC: 3799 Snowmobiles

(G-11064)
PULLMAN COMPANY (DH)
1 International Dr (48161-9345)
PHONE 734 243-8000
Thomas E Evans, *President*
James Gray, *President*
▲ **EMP:** 19
SQ FT: 185,000
SALES (est): 132MM
SALES (corp-wide): 11.7B **Publicly Held**
SIC: 3714 3715 3061 Motor vehicle parts & accessories; trailer bodies; automotive rubber goods (mechanical)
HQ: Tenneco Automotive Operating Company, Inc.
500 N Field Dr
Lake Forest IL 60045
847 482-5000

(G-11065)
SIGNMEUPCOM INC
1285 N Telegraph Rd (48162-3368)
PHONE 312 343-1263
Todd Bellino, *Principal*
EMP: 3
SALES (est): 126.6K **Privately Held**
SIC: 7372 Prepackaged software

(G-11066)
SOURCE CAPITAL BACKYARD LLC
1000 Ternes Dr (48162-5224)
PHONE 734 242-6900
Thomas Van Der Meulen, *Mng Member*
EMP: 2
SQ FT: 250,000
SALES: 85MM **Privately Held**
SIC: 2511 2452 Play pens, children's: wood; prefabricated wood buildings

(G-11067)
SPARTAN STEEL COATING LLC
3300 Wolverine (48162-9393)
PHONE 734 289-5400
Brian Skolnik, *Officer*
Neil Bruss,
Dave Brandau,
EMP: 62
SQ FT: 293,000
SALES (est): 7.6MM
SALES (corp-wide): 3.7B **Publicly Held**
SIC: 3479 Galvanizing of iron, steel or end-formed products
PA: Worthington Industries, Inc.
200 W Wlson Bridge Rd
Worthington OH 43085
614 438-3210

(G-11068)
SPILLSON LTD
878 Regents Park Dr (48161-9762)
PHONE 734 384-0284
John Spillson, *President*
George Spillson, *Corp Secy*
Sophia Spillson, *Vice Pres*
EMP: 4
SQ FT: 4,000
SALES: 250K **Privately Held**
WEB: www.spillsonsricepudding.com
SIC: 2011 Canned meats (except baby food), meat slaughtered on site

(G-11069)
SPIRATEX COMPANY
Also Called: SPIRATEX COMPANY THE
1916 Frenchtown Ctr Dr (48162-9375)
PHONE 734 289-4800
Gary Markel, *Vice Pres*
EMP: 60
SALES (corp-wide): 25MM **Privately Held**
WEB: www.spiratex.com
SIC: 3089 3083 3082 Injection molding of plastics; laminated plastics plate & sheet; unsupported plastics profile shapes
PA: The Spiratex Company
6333 Cogswell St
Romulus MI 48174
734 722-0100

(G-11070)
STONECO OF MICHIGAN INC (PA)
15203 S Telegraph Rd (48161-4072)
PHONE 734 241-8966
Dennis Rickard, *President*
EMP: 31
SALES (est): 25.1MM **Privately Held**
SIC: 3531 Construction machinery

(G-11071)
SWANSON ORTHTIC PRSTHETICS CTR
Also Called: Novacare Prosthetics Orthotics
1174 W Front St (48162-2465)
PHONE 734 241-4397
David S Chernow, *President*
Vern Swanson, *Principal*
EMP: 4 **Privately Held**
SIC: 3842 Limbs, artificial
HQ: Swanson Orthotic & Prosthetics Center Inc
855 Springdale Dr Ste 200
Exton PA 19341

(G-11072)
TENNECO AUTOMOTIVE OPER CO INC
13910 Lake Dr (48161-3845)
PHONE 734 243-8039
Thorne Decarlo, *Manager*
EMP: 4
SALES (corp-wide): 11.7B **Publicly Held**
WEB: www.tenneco-automotive.com
SIC: 3714 Motor vehicle engines & parts
HQ: Tenneco Automotive Operating Company, Inc.
500 N Field Dr
Lake Forest IL 60045
847 482-5000

(G-11073)
TENNECO AUTOMOTIVE OPER CO INC
1 International Dr (48161-9386)
PHONE 734 243-4615
Nicholas Dennis, *Manager*
EMP: 15
SALES (corp-wide): 11.7B **Publicly Held**
WEB: www.tenneco-automotive.com
SIC: 3714 Motor vehicle parts & accessories
HQ: Tenneco Automotive Operating Company, Inc.
500 N Field Dr
Lake Forest IL 60045
847 482-5000

(G-11074)
TENNECO AUTOMOTIVE OPER CO INC
1 International Dr (48161-9386)
PHONE 734 243-8000
Joe Pomaranski, *Manager*
EMP: 288
SALES (corp-wide): 11.7B **Publicly Held**
SIC: 3714 Shock absorbers, motor vehicle
HQ: Tenneco Automotive Operating Company, Inc.
500 N Field Dr
Lake Forest IL 60045
847 482-5000

(G-11075)
THOMAS L SNAREY & ASSOC INC (PA)
Also Called: Premier Industries
513 N Dixie Hwy (48162-2563)
PHONE 734 241-8474
Thomas L Snarey, *President*
James Cameron, *Vice Pres*
Lee Wilder, *Sales Engr*
Kathleen Vadun, *Admin Sec*
▲ **EMP:** 13
SQ FT: 40,000
SALES (est): 7.3MM **Privately Held**
WEB: www.premierindustries.com
SIC: 3599 Machine shop, jobbing & repair

(G-11076)
TITE NEON CAT
3175 Comboni Way (48162-9214)
PHONE 734 755-7349
EMP: 3
SALES (est): 123.2K **Privately Held**
SIC: 2813 Neon

(G-11077)
TMS INTERNATIONAL LLC
3000 E Front St (48161-1973)
PHONE 734 241-3007
EMP: 3 **Privately Held**
SIC: 3312 Blast furnaces & steel mills
HQ: Tms International, Llc
2835 E Carson St Fl 3
Glassport PA 15203
412 678-6141

(G-11078)
TMS INTERNATIONAL LLC
3000 E Front St (48161-1973)
P.O. Box 843 (48161-0843)
PHONE 734 241-3007
EMP: 18
SQ FT: 672 **Privately Held**
SIC: 3295 Minerals, Ground Or Treated, Nsk

(G-11079)
TOMAN INDUSTRIES INC
1652 E Hurd Rd (48162-9314)
PHONE 734 289-1393
Jeffrey S Toman, *President*
EMP: 2
SALES: 1.2MM **Privately Held**
SIC: 3549 Assembly machines, including robotic

(G-11080)
TWB COMPANY LLC (HQ)
1600 Nadeau Rd (48162-9317)
PHONE 734 289-6400
Ivan Meltzer, *President*
Ryan Kane, *Principal*
Thomas Mulherin, *Engineer*
Wayne Huisman, *Project Engr*
Jeff Keaton, *Human Resources*
▲ **EMP:** 220
SQ FT: 178,000
SALES (est): 190.9MM
SALES (corp-wide): 3.7B **Publicly Held**
WEB: www.twbcompany.com
SIC: 3465 Automotive stampings
PA: Worthington Industries, Inc.
200 W Wlson Bridge Rd
Worthington OH 43085
614 438-3210

(G-11081)
TWB OF INDIANA INC
1600 Nadeau Rd (48162-9317)
PHONE 734 289-6400
Tom Fant, *President*
Manfred Nagel, *Exec VP*
Mike Lowrey, *Vice Pres*
Ivan Meltzer, *Vice Pres*
EMP: 30 **EST:** 2001
SQ FT: 127,800
SALES (est): 3MM **Privately Held**
SIC: 3429 Motor vehicle hardware

(G-11082)
VAN DAELES INC
Also Called: Al's Cabinet Shop
8830 Ida Maybee Rd (48162-9112)
PHONE 734 587-7165
Leonard Van Daele, *President*
Shirley Van Daele, *Corp Secy*

GEOGRAPHIC SECTION

Jerry Van Daele, *Vice Pres*
EMP: 9
SQ FT: 7,824
SALES: 876.7K **Privately Held**
SIC: 2434 5712 Wood kitchen cabinets; cabinet work, custom

(G-11083)
WASHINGTON STREET PRINTERS LLC
17 Washington St (48161-2234)
PHONE.................................734 240-5541
EMP: 3
SALES (est): 224.3K **Privately Held**
SIC: 2752 Commercial printing, offset

(G-11084)
WEST BROTHERS LLC
815 Scarlet Oak Dr (48162-3481)
PHONE.................................734 457-0083
Charles West, *Mng Member*
Julie West, *Mng Member*
EMP: 4
SALES: 100K **Privately Held**
SIC: 2099 Sauces: gravy, dressing & dip mixes

(G-11085)
WOWZA ME LLC
122 W Noble Ave (48162-2743)
PHONE.................................734 636-4460
Derek Young, *CEO*
Dawn Young,
EMP: 3
SALES (est): 104.1K **Privately Held**
SIC: 7372 7389 Prepackaged software;

(G-11086)
YANFENG US AUTOMOTIVE
Also Called: Johnson Controls
1833 Frenchtown Ctr Dr (48162-9375)
PHONE.................................734 289-4841
EMP: 96
SALES (corp-wide): 55MM **Privately Held**
SIC: 2531 Public building & related furniture
HQ: Yanfeng Us Automotive Interior Systems Ii Llc
5757 N Green Bay Ave
Milwaukee WI 53209
205 477-4225

(G-11087)
YANFENG US AUTOMOTIVE
1833 Frenchtown Ctr Dr (48162-9375)
PHONE.................................734 289-4841
Brad Meyers, *Branch Mgr*
EMP: 150
SALES (corp-wide): 55MM **Privately Held**
SIC: 3089 Plastic containers, except foam
HQ: Yanfeng Us Automotive Interior Systems I Llc
41935 W 12 Mile Rd
Novi MI 48377
248 319-7333

(G-11088)
ZHONGDING SALING PARTS USA INC (HQ)
Also Called: Allied Baltic Rubber
400 Detroit Ave (48162-2783)
PHONE.................................734 241-8870
Steve Seketa, *CEO*
Dennis Cruz, *Manager*
▲ **EMP**: 4
SQ FT: 80,000
SALES: 200MM
SALES (corp-wide): 1.7B **Privately Held**
WEB: www.allied-baltic.com
SIC: 3069 Molded rubber products; rubber automotive products
PA: Anhui Zhongding Sealing Parts Co., Ltd.
Zhongding Industrial Park, Economic & Technological Development
Ningguo 24230
563 418-9703

Montague
Muskegon County

(G-11089)
CLAYBANKS KIDS LLC
7473 W Skeels Rd (49437-9139)
PHONE.................................231 893-4071
Annie Rupert,
Stephanie Mallery,
EMP: 3
SALES (est): 191.4K **Privately Held**
SIC: 3944 Games, toys & children's vehicles

(G-11090)
DYER CORPORATION
Also Called: Pin-Key Manufacturing Co
6200 W Old Channel Trl (49437-9305)
PHONE.................................231 894-4282
Robert A Dyer, *CEO*
John E Dyer, *President*
EMP: 5
SQ FT: 942
SALES (est): 738.2K **Privately Held**
SIC: 3452 Pins; dowel pins, metal; machine keys

(G-11091)
INTERNATIONAL MASTER PDTS CORP (PA)
Also Called: Master Tag
9751 Us Hhwy 31 (49437)
PHONE.................................231 894-5651
Richard K Hughes Jr, *President*
Michelle Turner, *Project Mgr*
Tina Forbes, *Production*
William Tripp, *Purch Mgr*
Juan Loera, *QC Mgr*
EMP: 125 **EST**: 1951
SQ FT: 38,000
SALES (est): 38.9MM **Privately Held**
WEB: www.mastertag.com
SIC: 2752 2759 2671 Tags, lithographed; commercial printing; packaging paper & plastics film, coated & laminated

(G-11092)
INTERNATIONAL MASTER PDTS CORP
Also Called: Mastertag
9751 Us Highway 31 (49437-9555)
PHONE.................................800 253-0439
Richard K Hughes, *Branch Mgr*
EMP: 8
SALES (corp-wide): 20.9MM **Privately Held**
SIC: 2752 Commercial printing, lithographic
PA: International Master Products Corporation
9751 Us Highway 31
Montague MI 49437
231 894-5651

(G-11093)
LEADING EDGE FABRICATING INC
5315 Industrial Park Rd (49437-1529)
PHONE.................................231 893-2605
Patricia Vanderwest, *President*
EMP: 3
SQ FT: 2,500
SALES (est): 585.1K **Privately Held**
SIC: 3599 Machine shop, jobbing & repair

(G-11094)
LUKER ENTERPRISES INC
Also Called: Luker Custom Canvas
4530 Dowling St (49437-1201)
PHONE.................................231 894-9702
Diane Luker, *President*
EMP: 7
SALES (est): 601.3K **Privately Held**
SIC: 2394 Sails: made from purchased materials

(G-11095)
MONTAGUE METAL PRODUCTS INC
4101 Fruitvale Rd (49437-9531)
PHONE.................................231 893-0547
Mary Morris, *President*
Mark Morris, *Vice Pres*
John Morris, *Treasurer*
Tyler Morris, *Admin Sec*
EMP: 25
SQ FT: 14,000
SALES: 1.7MM **Privately Held**
WEB: www.montaguemetalproducts.com
SIC: 3363 Aluminum die-castings

(G-11096)
PAPPYS PAD LLC
8812 Ferry St (49437-1293)
PHONE.................................231 894-0888
Mark Peets, *Mng Member*
EMP: 4
SALES (est): 176.1K **Privately Held**
SIC: 3993 Signs & advertising specialties

(G-11097)
SHELLCAST INC
5230 Industrial Park Rd (49437-1528)
PHONE.................................231 893-8245
Robert F Johnson, *President*
Robert J Johnson, *Purch Mgr*
Scott Miller, *QC Mgr*
EMP: 22 **EST**: 1961
SQ FT: 35,000
SALES (est): 4.8MM **Privately Held**
WEB: www.shellcastinc.com
SIC: 3369 Castings, except die-castings, precision

(G-11098)
SPECTRUM ILLUMINATION CO INC
5114 Industrial Park Rd (49437-1526)
PHONE.................................231 894-4590
Naomi Muyskens, *President*
Valerie Muyskens, *Admin Sec*
EMP: 5
SQ FT: 2,400
SALES (est): 864.9K **Privately Held**
SIC: 3648 Lighting equipment

(G-11099)
WHITE RIVER
7386 Post Rd (49437-9706)
PHONE.................................231 894-9216
Mike Cockerill, *Principal*
Deborah Harris, *Treasurer*
Joanne Lehman, *Admin Sec*
EMP: 5
SALES (est): 470.8K **Privately Held**
SIC: 3674 Hall effect devices

Montgomery
Branch County

(G-11100)
WATSON SALES
7821 Topinabee Dr (49255-9015)
PHONE.................................517 296-4275
David Watson, *Owner*
EMP: 3
SALES (est): 301.9K **Privately Held**
SIC: 2679 2671 7389 Tags & labels, paper; paper coated or laminated for packaging; packaging & labeling services

Montrose
Genesee County

(G-11101)
BASF CORPORATION
10406 Farrand Rd (48457-9733)
PHONE.................................810 639-0492
Kurt Bock, *Branch Mgr*
EMP: 100
SALES (corp-wide): 71.7B **Privately Held**
SIC: 2869 Industrial organic chemicals
HQ: Basf Corporation
100 Park Ave
Florham Park NJ 07932
973 245-6000

(G-11102)
GOODYEAR HORSESHOE SUPPLY INC
Also Called: Goodyear Supply
9372 Seymour Rd (48457-9122)
PHONE.................................810 639-2591
Therese Ketchum, *President*
EMP: 3
SALES (est): 354.5K **Privately Held**
SIC: 3462 Horseshoes

(G-11103)
M-57 AGGREGATE COMPANY
170 W State St (48457-9807)
PHONE.................................810 639-7516
Shane Powell, *Vice Pres*
EMP: 7 **EST**: 2009
SALES (est): 383.6K **Privately Held**
SIC: 1442 7389 Construction sand & gravel;

(G-11104)
MARSHALLS CROSSING
12050 Trident Blvd (48457-8902)
PHONE.................................810 639-4740
Wendy Brotherton, *Manager*
EMP: 8
SALES (est): 560.2K **Privately Held**
WEB: www.marshallscrossing.com
SIC: 2452 6552 6531 Modular homes, prefabricated, wood; subdividers & developers; real estate agents & managers

(G-11105)
MONTROSE TRAILERS INC
180 Ruth St (48457-9450)
PHONE.................................810 639-7431
Gary Palinsky, *President*
Barbara Palinsky, *Corp Secy*
EMP: 8 **EST**: 1971
SQ FT: 8,800
SALES: 800K **Privately Held**
WEB: www.montrosetrailers.com
SIC: 3799 3792 3715 3537 Trailers & trailer equipment; travel trailers & campers; truck trailers; industrial trucks & tractors; mobile homes

(G-11106)
TRU-COAT INC
10428 Seymour Rd (48457-9015)
PHONE.................................810 785-3331
Ronald Loafman, *President*
Phil Wood, *General Mgr*
EMP: 5
SQ FT: 8,000
SALES (est): 635.2K **Privately Held**
SIC: 3471 Plating of metals or formed products

Moran
Mackinac County

(G-11107)
GUSTAFSON SMOKED FISH
Also Called: T & J Uphl Sp & Marathon Svc
W4467 Us 2 (49760-9819)
PHONE.................................906 292-5424
Thomas Gustafson, *Owner*
EMP: 4
SQ FT: 2,500
SALES (est): 295.3K **Privately Held**
SIC: 2091 7641 5541 Fish, smoked; reupholstery; filling stations, gasoline

(G-11108)
SAND PRODUCTS CORPORATION
W5021 Us Hwy 2 (49760)
PHONE.................................906 292-5432
Robert C Cook, *Manager*
EMP: 5
SALES (corp-wide): 359.7MM **Privately Held**
SIC: 1446 Foundry sand mining
PA: Sand Products Corporation
13495 92nd St Se
Alto MI 49302
231 722-6691

Morenci
Lenawee County

(G-11109)
GENERAL BROACH COMPANY (HQ)
307 Salisbury St (49256-1043)
PHONE..................................517 458-7555
Robert Roseliep, *President*
Larry Stover, *General Mgr*
Doyle Collar, *General Mgr*
Chris McCaskey, *Mfg Staff*
Diane Jackson, *Purchasing*
▲ **EMP**: 46
SQ FT: 62,640
SALES (est): 13MM
SALES (corp-wide): 565.7MM **Privately Held**
SIC: 3545 3541 Broaches (machine tool accessories); broaching machines
PA: Utica Enterprises, Inc.
5750 New King Dr Ste 200
Troy MI 48098
586 726-4300

(G-11110)
GENERAL BROACH COMPANY
555 W Main St Ste C (49256-1481)
PHONE..................................517 458-7555
Larry Stover, *Branch Mgr*
EMP: 20
SALES (corp-wide): 565.7MM **Privately Held**
SIC: 3545 Broaches (machine tool accessories)
HQ: General Broach Company
307 Salisbury St
Morenci MI 49256

(G-11111)
GREEN MANUFACTURING INC
9650 Packard Rd (49256-9557)
PHONE..................................517 458-1500
Kevin Green, *President*
Brian Holly, *COO*
EMP: 9
SQ FT: 2,500
SALES (est): 4.7MM **Privately Held**
WEB: www.greenteeth.com
SIC: 3545 Tools & accessories for machine tools

(G-11112)
LENAWEE TOOL & AUTOMATION INC
235 Salisbury St (49256-1020)
PHONE..................................517 458-7222
Michael Dwyer, *President*
EMP: 6 **EST**: 1970
SQ FT: 14,000
SALES: 800K **Privately Held**
SIC: 3535 Conveyors & conveying equipment

(G-11113)
MORENCI OBSERVER (PA)
Also Called: State Line Observer, The
120 North St (49256-1446)
PHONE..................................517 458-6811
David G Green, *Owner*
Steve Amick, *Author*
EMP: 3
SQ FT: 1,600
SALES (est): 280.3K **Privately Held**
SIC: 2711 Newspapers: publishing only, not printed on site

(G-11114)
ROTH FABRICATING INC
9600 Skyline Dr (49256-9709)
PHONE..................................517 458-7541
Simone Haas, *President*
Jeanie Sarnac, *Vice Pres*
Shane Sarnac, *Admin Sec*
EMP: 25
SQ FT: 22,000
SALES (est): 5.7MM **Privately Held**
WEB: www.rothfabricating.com
SIC: 3444 Sheet metalwork

(G-11115)
TILLER TOOL AND DIE INC
Also Called: Versacut Industries
555 W Main St (49256-1480)
PHONE..................................517 458-6602
Gerald T Tiller, *President*
Cyndi Tiller, *Vice Pres*
Gerald Tiller, *VP Sls/Mktg*
EMP: 15
SQ FT: 68,000
SALES: 1.3MM **Privately Held**
WEB: www.versacutind.com
SIC: 3544 Special dies & tools

(G-11116)
TRIPLE K FARMS INC
Also Called: Grain and Cattle Farm
13648 Wabash Rd (49256-9724)
PHONE..................................517 458-9741
Steven Kutzley, *President*
Terry Kutzley, *Vice Pres*
EMP: 4 **EST**: 1996
SQ FT: 10,000
SALES (est): 978.6K **Privately Held**
SIC: 0211 0119 3523 Beef cattle feedlots; bean (dry field & seed) farm; irrigation equipment, self-propelled

Morley
Mecosta County

(G-11117)
PEACOCKS ECO LOG & SAWMILL LLC
14823 4 Mile Rd (49336-9509)
PHONE..................................231 250-3462
Travis Peacock, *Principal*
EMP: 3
SALES (est): 195.5K **Privately Held**
SIC: 2411 Logging camps & contractors

(G-11118)
SUMMIT TOOLING & MFG INC
451 N Cass St (49336-9575)
PHONE..................................231 856-7037
EMP: 6
SQ FT: 15,000
SALES (est): 330K **Privately Held**
SIC: 3423 Mfg Hand & Edge Tools

Morrice
Shiawassee County

(G-11119)
FLETCHER PRINTING
9517 S Morrice Rd (48857-9784)
PHONE..................................517 625-7030
David Fletcher, *Owner*
EMP: 3
SQ FT: 1,152
SALES: 220K **Privately Held**
SIC: 2759 2752 Letterpress printing; commercial printing, offset

(G-11120)
MATHIE ENERGY SUPPLY CO INC
7840 Gale Rd (48857-9771)
P.O. Box 334, Perry (48872-0334)
PHONE..................................517 625-3646
Michael Mathie, *President*
Melissa Mathie, *Admin Sec*
EMP: 2
SALES: 1MM **Privately Held**
SIC: 2048 Feeds from meat & from meat & vegetable meals

(G-11121)
MEAL AND MORE INCORPORATED
130 W 3rd Ave (48857-2547)
P.O. Box 376 (48857-0376)
PHONE..................................517 625-3186
Elizabeth Andrus, *President*
Timothy Kline, *Software Engr*
Jack Mc Eowen, *Admin Sec*
EMP: 26
SQ FT: 2,400
SALES (est): 4.4MM **Privately Held**
SIC: 2048 Livestock feeds

Mount Clemens
Macomb County

(G-11122)
A B C ROLL CO
301 Church St (48043-2180)
PHONE..................................586 465-9125
Stan Florka, *President*
EMP: 5 **EST**: 1959
SQ FT: 10,000
SALES (est): 876.8K **Privately Held**
WEB: www.a1roll.com
SIC: 3312 Bars & bar shapes, steel, cold-finished: own hot-rolled

(G-11123)
ARTS CRAFTS HARDWARE
169 Smith St (48043-2345)
PHONE..................................586 231-5344
EMP: 10
SALES (est): 1MM **Privately Held**
SIC: 3861 Mfg Photographic Equipment/Supplies

(G-11124)
AUTO-TECH PLASTICS INC
Also Called: Pt Woody
164 Grand Ave (48043-5415)
PHONE..................................586 783-0103
Ronald Schuman, *President*
Beverly Schuman, *Principal*
EMP: 4
SALES (est): 643.3K **Privately Held**
WEB: www.flexchrome.com
SIC: 3714 Motor vehicle parts & accessories

(G-11125)
BETTER-BILT CABINET CO
99 Cass Ave (48043-2382)
PHONE..................................586 469-0080
Aldo Valitutti, *President*
Angeline Valitutti, *Vice Pres*
Lisa Valitutti, *Vice Pres*
EMP: 5 **EST**: 1974
SQ FT: 4,000
SALES (est): 764.5K **Privately Held**
SIC: 2434 2439 Wood kitchen cabinets; structural wood members

(G-11126)
CAN YOU HANDLEBAR LLC
239 Church St (48043-2184)
PHONE..................................248 821-2171
Doug Geiger, *Mng Member*
EMP: 10 **EST**: 2016
SALES (est): 208.4K **Privately Held**
SIC: 2844 Toilet preparations

(G-11127)
CONCORD TOOL AND MFG INC
118 N Groesbeck Hwy Ste E (48043-5453)
PHONE..................................586 465-6537
Ronald Dichtel, *Ch of Bd*
Mark Dichtel, *President*
David Bozek, *Vice Pres*
Justin Babcock, *Purch Mgr*
Kim Barone, *Purch Agent*
▲ **EMP**: 165
SQ FT: 100,000
SALES (est): 35.5MM **Privately Held**
WEB: www.concordtool.com
SIC: 3465 3544 Body parts, automobile: stamped metal; die sets for metal stamping (presses)

(G-11128)
D-MARK INC
130 N Groesbeck Hwy (48043-1529)
PHONE..................................586 949-3610
James W Kasmark Jr, *President*
James Reinke, *Human Res Mgr*
EMP: 30
SQ FT: 19,000
SALES: 5.3MM **Privately Held**
WEB: www.dmarkinc.com
SIC: 3564 Filters, air: furnaces, air conditioning equipment, etc.

(G-11129)
DETROIT CUSTOM SERVICES INC (PA)
Also Called: Vertical Vics
150 N Groesbeck Hwy (48043-1529)
PHONE..................................586 465-3631
Mitch Bazinski, *President*
Rebecca Bazinski, *Vice Pres*
EMP: 35
SQ FT: 20,000
SALES (est): 2.3MM **Privately Held**
SIC: 2391 2591 5714 5719 Draperies, plastic & textile: from purchased materials; window blinds; draperies; vertical blinds; drapery track installation; window treatment installation

(G-11130)
FCA US LLC
151 Lafayette St (48043-1557)
PHONE..................................586 468-2891
Michael Lyell, *General Mgr*
EMP: 195
SALES (corp-wide): 126.4B **Privately Held**
SIC: 3711 Motor vehicles & car bodies
HQ: Fca Us Llc
1000 Chrysler Dr
Auburn Hills MI 48326

(G-11131)
FOURNIER ENTERPRISES INC
17 N Rose St Ste A (48043-5462)
PHONE..................................586 323-9160
Ronald J Fournier, *President*
Nicole Fournier, *Vice Pres*
EMP: 5
SQ FT: 2,500
SALES (est): 737.3K **Privately Held**
WEB: www.fournierenterprises.com
SIC: 3499 Furniture parts, metal

(G-11132)
HELICAL LAP & MANUFACTURING CO (HQ)
121 Madison Ave (48043-1624)
PHONE..................................586 307-8322
Stephen Griffin, *President*
Ken Werner, *Vice Pres*
Mark Gray, *Treasurer*
Donna Lebeda, *Asst Treas*
EMP: 13 **EST**: 1958
SQ FT: 9,200
SALES (est): 1.8MM
SALES (corp-wide): 39.6MM **Privately Held**
WEB: www.helicallap.com
SIC: 3541 Lapping machines
PA: Engis Corporation
105 W Hintz Rd
Wheeling IL 60090
847 808-9400

(G-11133)
HYDRA-LOCK CORPORATION
25000 Joy Blvd (48043-6021)
PHONE..................................586 783-5007
Eugene R Andre Sr, *President*
William M Andre, *Corp Secy*
Eugene R Andre Jr, *Vice Pres*
EMP: 40
SQ FT: 18,000
SALES (est): 7.4MM **Privately Held**
WEB: www.hydralock.com
SIC: 3545 Arbors (machine tool accessories); chucks: drill, lathe or magnetic (machine tool accessories); gauges (machine tool accessories)

(G-11134)
INDEPENDENT NEWSPAPERS INC (DH)
Also Called: The Daily Tribune
100 Macomb Daily Dr (48043-5802)
PHONE..................................586 469-4510
Ronald J Wood, *President*
Jerry Bammel, *Vice Pres*
▲ **EMP**: 125
SALES (est): 23.7MM
SALES (corp-wide): 697.5MM **Privately Held**
SIC: 2711 Newspapers, publishing & printing

GEOGRAPHIC SECTION

Mount Morris - Genesee County (G-11161)

HQ: 21st Century Newspapers, Inc.
19176 Hall Rd Ste 200
Clinton Township MI 48038
586 469-4510

(G-11135)
J B CUTTING INC
Also Called: MCO
171 Grand Ave (48043-5413)
PHONE 586 468-4765
Joann Filthaut, *President*
William Filthaut, *Vice Pres*
EMP: 9
SQ FT: 16,000
SALES (est): 1.4MM **Privately Held**
WEB: www.jbcutting.com
SIC: 2511 Wood household furniture

(G-11136)
JEX MANUFACTURING INC
41 Eldredge St (48043-5410)
PHONE 586 463-4274
Jex Harrison, *President*
EMP: 4
SQ FT: 1,800
SALES (est): 379K **Privately Held**
SIC: 3599 Machine shop, jobbing & repair

(G-11137)
JOURNAL REGISTER COMPANY
Also Called: Macomb Daily
100 Macomb Daily Dr (48043-5802)
PHONE 586 790-1600
Ted Eagan, *Director*
EMP: 63
SALES (corp-wide): 697.5MM **Privately Held**
SIC: 2711 Newspapers, publishing & printing
PA: Journal Register Company
5 Hanover Sq Fl 25
New York NY 10004

(G-11138)
KROPP WOODWORKING INC
154 S Rose St (48043-2176)
PHONE 586 463-2300
Paul Kropp, *President*
EMP: 19 **EST:** 2010
SALES (est): 3.2MM **Privately Held**
SIC: 2431 Millwork

(G-11139)
LIQUID DRIVE CORPORATION
Also Called: Easco-Sparcatron
18 1st St (48043-2523)
P.O. Box 207, Holly (48442-0207)
PHONE 248 634-5382
Robert G Nelson, *President*
Gary Brown, *Vice Pres*
EMP: 20 **EST:** 1945
SQ FT: 28,000
SALES (est): 3.4MM **Privately Held**
WEB: www.liquiddrive.com
SIC: 3541 3568 8299 Electron-discharge metal cutting machine tools; couplings, shaft: rigid, flexible, universal joint, etc.; vehicle driving school

(G-11140)
MALL TOOLING & ENGINEERING
150 Grand Ave (48043-5415)
PHONE 586 463-6520
Gregory P Theokas, *President*
EMP: 12
SQ FT: 12,000
SALES (est): 1.6MM
SALES (corp-wide): 2.4MM **Privately Held**
WEB: www.oepushrods.com
SIC: 3714 Motor vehicle engines & parts
PA: Oe Push Rods Inc
150 Grand Ave
Mount Clemens MI 48043
586 463-6520

(G-11141)
MCCOMB COUNTY LEGAL NEWS
148 S Main St Ste 100 (48043-7900)
PHONE 586 463-4300
Melanie Deeds, *Manager*
EMP: 3
SALES (est): 165.5K **Privately Held**
WEB: www.macomblegalnews.com
SIC: 2711 Newspapers

(G-11142)
MILJOCO CORP (PA)
200 Elizabeth St (48043-1643)
PHONE 586 777-4280
Howard O Trerice, *President*
Heath M Trerice, *Vice Pres*
▲ **EMP:** 62
SQ FT: 45,000
SALES (est): 13.5MM **Privately Held**
WEB: www.miljoco.com
SIC: 3829 Measuring & controlling devices

(G-11143)
PARKER PATTERN INC
195 Malow St (48043-2114)
PHONE 586 466-5900
Jerry Parker, *President*
Fred Parker, *Vice Pres*
EMP: 10
SQ FT: 9,600
SALES (est): 400K **Privately Held**
SIC: 3543 Industrial patterns

(G-11144)
PETSCHKE MANUFACTURING COMPANY
187 Hubbard St (48043-5420)
PHONE 586 463-0841
James Petschke, *President*
Steven Petschke, *Corp Secy*
Ann Petschke, *Vice Pres*
Steve Petschke, *Sales Mgr*
EMP: 14 **EST:** 1943
SQ FT: 13,000
SALES (est): 1.9MM **Privately Held**
SIC: 3496 3354 3451 Miscellaneous fabricated wire products; aluminum rod & bar; aluminum pipe & tube; screw machine products

(G-11145)
POWDER COTE II INC (PA)
50 N Rose St (48043-5405)
P.O. Box 368 (48046-0368)
PHONE 586 463-7040
Eric Trott, *CEO*
Charlie J Trott, *Vice Pres*
Michael Coon, *Manager*
▲ **EMP:** 185 **EST:** 1980
SQ FT: 43,000
SALES (est): 26.2MM **Privately Held**
WEB: www.powdercoteii.com
SIC: 3479 Coating of metals & formed products

(G-11146)
POWDER COTE II INC
60 N Rose St (48043-5405)
P.O. Box 368 (48046-0368)
PHONE 586 463-7040
Michael Coon, *Manager*
EMP: 4
SALES (est): 300.1K
SALES (corp-wide): 26.2MM **Privately Held**
SIC: 3479 Coating of metals & formed products
PA: Powder Cote Ii, Inc.
50 N Rose St
Mount Clemens MI 48043
586 463-7040

(G-11147)
RB CONSTRUCTION COMPANY (PA)
249 Cass Ave (48043-2118)
PHONE 586 264-9478
Russell C Beaver, *President*
John Stapleton, *Vice Pres*
EMP: 21
SQ FT: 2,000
SALES: 26MM **Privately Held**
SIC: 1542 3448 Commercial & office building, new construction; commercial & office buildings, renovation & repair; prefabricated metal buildings

(G-11148)
REBECCA EIBEN
Also Called: R&R Tool & Gage
191 Grand Ave (48043-5413)
PHONE 586 231-0548
Rebecca Eiben, *Owner*
Ronald Eiben, *Principal*
Rebekah Eiben, *Office Mgr*
EMP: 5
SQ FT: 3,500
SALES (est): 700K **Privately Held**
SIC: 3599 Machine shop, jobbing & repair

(G-11149)
SECURE DOOR LLC
75 Lafayette St (48043-1613)
PHONE 586 792-2402
Scott Mayes, *Mng Member*
EMP: 13 **EST:** 2009
SALES (est): 3MM **Privately Held**
SIC: 3442 Shutters, door or window: metal

(G-11150)
SHARADANS LEATHER GOODS INC
237 N River Rd R19 (48043-1920)
PHONE 586 468-0666
EMP: 3
SALES (est): 600K **Privately Held**
SIC: 3199 Mfg Leather Goods Mfg Leather Goods

(G-11151)
T M SMITH TOOL INTL CORP (PA)
360 Hubbard St (48043-5403)
P.O. Box 1065 (48046-1065)
PHONE 586 468-1465
D F Smith, *Ch of Bd*
Gerald R Norton, *President*
David F Smith II, *Vice Pres*
Jeff McKown, *Safety Dir*
James Sanders, *CFO*
EMP: 30 **EST:** 1952
SQ FT: 22,000
SALES (est): 6.3MM **Privately Held**
WEB: www.tmsmith.com
SIC: 3545 Tool holders

(G-11152)
TRU TECH SYSTEMS LLC (HQ)
24550 N River Rd (48043-1910)
P.O. Box 46965 (48046-6965)
PHONE 586 469-2700
Steve Smarsh, *President*
Shari Michels, *Vice Pres*
Tom Lebel, *Manager*
EMP: 60
SQ FT: 25,000
SALES (est): 18.3MM **Privately Held**
WEB: www.trutechsystems.com
SIC: 7389 3541 Grinding, precision: commercial or industrial; grinding, polishing, buffing, lapping & honing machines

(G-11153)
WEBER SECURITY GROUP INC
Also Called: East Side Locksmith
95 S Rose St Ste A (48043-2187)
PHONE 586 582-0000
William D Weber Jr, *President*
EMP: 6
SQ FT: 10,000
SALES: 1.2MM **Privately Held**
WEB: www.webersecurity.com
SIC: 3429 3699 Locks or lock sets; security control equipment & systems

(G-11154)
WICKEDGLOW INDUSTRIES INC
Also Called: Body Faders
248 Nrthbound Gratiot Ave (48043-5749)
PHONE 586 776-4132
Loretta Monley, *President*
Karl Clayton, *Vice Pres*
EMP: 8
SQ FT: 2,000
SALES (est): 795.1K **Privately Held**
WEB: www.bodyfaders.com
SIC: 3641 2253 Glow lamp bulbs; T-shirts & tops, knit

Mount Morris
Genesee County

(G-11155)
A GAME APPAREL
4330 W Mount Morris Rd # 1 (48458-9380)
PHONE 810 564-2600
Don Damonth, *Partner*
EMP: 12
SALES (est): 1MM **Privately Held**
WEB: www.agameapparel.com
SIC: 2396 Screen printing on fabric articles

(G-11156)
ADNIC PRODUCTS CO
6261 N Saginaw St (48458-2454)
PHONE 810 789-0321
Anne D Nickola, *President*
Vicki Haley, *Vice Pres*
R Diane Bayeh, *Admin Sec*
EMP: 4
SQ FT: 2,400
SALES (est): 325.9K **Privately Held**
WEB: www.adnicproducts.com
SIC: 3644 Electric outlet, switch & fuse boxes

(G-11157)
AMERICAN BOTTLING COMPANY
Also Called: 7-Up Flint
7300 Enterprise Pkwy (48458-9356)
PHONE 810 564-1432
Ron Blair, *General Mgr*
Brian Blossom, *Info Tech Mgr*
EMP: 70 **Publicly Held**
SIC: 2086 Soft drinks: packaged in cans, bottles, etc.
HQ: The American Bottling Company
5301 Legacy Dr
Plano TX 75024

(G-11158)
BEST BUY BONES INC
7426 N Dort Hwy (48458-2232)
P.O. Box 39 (48458-0039)
PHONE 810 631-6971
Delbert McCord, *President*
Deldert McCord, *President*
EMP: 6
SALES (est): 777.7K **Privately Held**
SIC: 3999 Pet supplies

(G-11159)
C W A MANUFACTURING CO INC
7406 N Dort Hwy (48458-2232)
P.O. Box 10 (48458-0010)
PHONE 810 686-3030
Fax: 810 686-2410
EMP: 40 **EST:** 1951
SQ FT: 23,000
SALES (est): 2.5MM **Privately Held**
SIC: 7389 3714 Commercial Packaging & Labeling & Small Automotive Component Assembly

(G-11160)
DANIEL WARD
Also Called: Colorized Prints
7352 N Tort Hi W Y Ste 2 (48458)
PHONE 810 965-6535
Daniel Ward, *Owner*
EMP: 4
SALES: 84K **Privately Held**
SIC: 2752 7334 Business form & card printing, lithographic; blueprinting service

(G-11161)
HAMMOND PUBLISHING COMPANY
G7166 N Saginaw St (48458)
PHONE 810 686-8879
Leo F Flynn, *President*
Ann Flynn, *Treasurer*
EMP: 4
SQ FT: 6,000
SALES (est): 447.7K **Privately Held**
SIC: 2741 2493 5192 Miscellaneous publishing; reconstituted wood products; books, periodicals & newspapers

Mount Morris - Genesee County (G-11162)

(G-11162)
HOMETOWN AMERICA LLC
2197 E Mount Morris Rd (48458-8709)
PHONE................810 686-7020
Matt Whorton, *Administration*
EMP: 6
SALES (corp-wide): 36.7MM **Privately Held**
WEB: www.hometownamerica.com
SIC: 2451 Mobile homes, personal or private use
PA: Hometown America, L.L.C.
150 N Wacker Dr Ste 2800
Chicago IL 60606
312 604-7500

(G-11163)
KINDER COMPANY INC
Also Called: Rockwell Team Sports
7070 N Saginaw Rd (48458-2141)
PHONE................810 240-3065
Daren Kinder, *President*
EMP: 6
SALES (est): 330K **Privately Held**
SIC: 2329 Vests (suede, leatherette, etc.), sport: men's & boys'

(G-11164)
LOPER CORPORATION
6031 N Clio Rd (48458-8220)
PHONE................810 620-0202
Karl Loper, *President*
EMP: 3
SQ FT: 5,000
SALES (est): 160K **Privately Held**
SIC: 3089 2671 Plastic processing; packaging paper & plastics film, coated & laminated

(G-11165)
MICHIGAN CHURCH SUPPLY CO INC (PA)
7166 N Saginaw Rd (48458-2165)
P.O. Box 279 (48458-0279)
PHONE................810 686-8877
Leo F Flynn, *President*
Leann Cooper, *Corp Secy*
Ann C Lynn, *Vice Pres*
Michael Malik, *Analyst*
EMP: 17
SQ FT: 28,000
SALES (est): 4.1MM **Privately Held**
WEB: www.michiganchurchsupply.com
SIC: 5049 3089 Religious supplies; injection molded finished plastic products

(G-11166)
MICHIGAN MACHINING INC
3322 E Mount Morris Rd (48458-8958)
PHONE................810 686-6655
Charles M Wood, *President*
EMP: 6
SALES (est): 816K **Privately Held**
WEB: www.michiganmachining.com
SIC: 3599 Machine shop, jobbing & repair

(G-11167)
ZODIAC ENTERPRISES LLC
1000 Church St Ste 1 (48458-2084)
PHONE................810 640-7146
Charles Harburn, *Manager*
EMP: 6
SALES (est): 702.5K **Privately Held**
SIC: 2759 Screen printing

Mount Pleasant
Isabella County

(G-11168)
AIR BRAKE SYSTEMS INC
4356 E Valley Rd (48858-8621)
P.O. Box 270 (48804-0270)
PHONE................989 775-8880
William E Washington, *CEO*
EMP: 4
SQ FT: 3,200
SALES (est): 340K **Privately Held**
WEB: www.absbrakes.com
SIC: 3592 Valves

(G-11169)
AMERICAN MITSUBA CORPORATION
2945 Three Leaves Dr (48858-4596)
PHONE................989 773-0377
Mike Goin, *Manager*
EMP: 235 **Privately Held**
SIC: 3621 Motors, electric
HQ: American Mitsuba Corporation
2945 Three Leaves Dr
Mount Pleasant MI 48858
989 779-4962

(G-11170)
AMERICAN MITSUBA CORPORATION (HQ)
2945 Three Leaves Dr (48858-4596)
PHONE................989 779-4962
Masayoshi Shirato, *President*
Mishel Ashtary, *Senior VP*
David Stevens, *Senior VP*
Hideaki Fujii, *Vice Pres*
Takashi Ichinokawa, *Vice Pres*
◆ **EMP:** 365
SALES: 606.5MM **Privately Held**
SIC: 3714 Motor vehicle parts & accessories

(G-11171)
ASPIRE PHARMACY
121 E Broadway St D (48858-2312)
PHONE................989 773-7849
James Horton, *General Mgr*
EMP: 5
SALES (est): 439.6K **Privately Held**
SIC: 2834 Pharmaceutical preparations

(G-11172)
B & H CEMENTING SERVICES INC
5580 Venture Way (48858-1149)
PHONE................989 773-5975
Steve Bagard, *President*
EMP: 5
SQ FT: 2,000
SALES (est): 310.1K **Privately Held**
SIC: 1389 Oil field services

(G-11173)
B & H TRACTOR & TRUCK INC
5580 Venture Way (48858-1149)
PHONE................989 773-5975
Steven Bagard, *President*
Ricky Huggard, *Vice Pres*
Tim Burggraf, *Manager*
Jeana Falfetta, *Admin Sec*
EMP: 9 EST: 1998
SQ FT: 5,000
SALES (est): 500K **Privately Held**
SIC: 1389 Haulage, oil field

(G-11174)
BAKER HGHES OLFLD OPRTIONS LLC
Also Called: Baker Oil Tools
1950 Commercial Dr (48858-8913)
P.O. Box 508 (48804-0508)
PHONE................989 772-1600
EMP: 9
SALES (corp-wide): 122B **Publicly Held**
SIC: 1389 Sales And Gas Services
HQ: Baker Hughes Oilfield Operations Llc
17021 Aldine Westfield Rd
Houston TX 77073
713 879-1000

(G-11175)
BAKER HGHES OLFLD OPRTIONS LLC
Also Called: Baker Atlas
2222 Enterprise Dr (48858-2335)
PHONE................989 773-7992
Jason Warrens, *Manager*
Steve Pressley, *Manager*
EMP: 14
SALES (corp-wide): 22.8B **Privately Held**
WEB: www.bakeratlas.com
SIC: 1389 1382 Oil field services; well logging; seismograph surveys
HQ: Baker Hughes Oilfield Operations Llc
17021 Aldine Westfield Rd
Houston TX 77073
713 879-1000

(G-11176)
BAKER HUGHES A GE COMPANY LLC
Also Called: Baker Hughes Incorporat...
2222 Enterprise Dr (48858-2335)
PHONE................989 506-2167
Deborah Payne, *Branch Mgr*
EMP: 4
SALES (corp-wide): 22.8B **Privately Held**
SIC: 1389 Construction, repair & dismantling services
PA: Baker Hughes, A Ge Company Llc
17021 Aldine Westfield Rd
Houston TX 77073
713 439-8600

(G-11177)
BEAR PACKAGING AND SUPPLY
4265 Corporate Dr (48858-1083)
PHONE................989 772-2268
Scott Schafer, *Manager*
EMP: 6 EST: 1967
SQ FT: 10,000
SALES: 1.5MM **Privately Held**
WEB: www.bearclawbags.net
SIC: 2673 5199 Plastic bags: made from purchased materials; packaging materials

(G-11178)
BIGARD & HUGGARD DRILLING INC
5580 Venture Way (48858-1149)
PHONE................989 775-6608
Steven Bigard, *President*
Ricky Huggard, *Vice Pres*
EMP: 85
SQ FT: 4,000
SALES (est): 17.9MM **Privately Held**
SIC: 1381 Directional drilling oil & gas wells

(G-11179)
BILLS CUSTOM FAB INC
1836 Gover Pkwy (48858-8166)
PHONE................989 772-5817
William T Quakenbush, *President*
Michelle Quakenbush, *Vice Pres*
Eric Quakenbush, *Manager*
EMP: 15
SQ FT: 5,200
SALES: 1.2MM **Privately Held**
SIC: 3443 5051 Fabricated plate work (boiler shop); steel

(G-11180)
BIOLIFE PLASMA SERVICES LP
4279 E Blue Grass Rd (48858-8096)
PHONE................989 773-1500
Gary Ciegenselder, *Principal*
EMP: 9
SALES (corp-wide): 15.1B **Privately Held**
SIC: 2836 Plasmas
HQ: Biolife Plasma Services L.P.
1200 Lakeside Dr
Bannockburn IL

(G-11181)
BURCH TANK & TRUCK INC (PA)
Also Called: Burch Truck and Trailer Parts
2253 Enterprise Dr (48858-2347)
PHONE................989 772-6266
Jeffrey Harrison, *President*
Craig Haley, *Opers Mgr*
Jason Harrison, *Engineer*
Al Lamphere, *Manager*
EMP: 75
SQ FT: 3,000
SALES (est): 6MM **Privately Held**
SIC: 3795 5088 Tanks & tank components; tanks & tank components

(G-11182)
C & C ENTERPRISES INC
1106 Packard Rd (48858-5324)
PHONE................989 772-5095
Charles Caszatt, *President*
Christopher Holsworth, *Corp Secy*
Levi Woodbury, *Sales Staff*
Chris Holsworth, *Marketing Staff*
EMP: 5
SQ FT: 1,600
SALES (est): 2.1MM **Privately Held**
SIC: 5084 2396 Safety equipment; screen printing on fabric articles

(G-11183)
CENTRAL ASPHALT INC
900 S Bradley St (48858-3046)
P.O. Box 389 (48804-0389)
PHONE................989 772-0720
Vance Johnson, *President*
James O Fisher, *Corp Secy*
Arthur J Fisher, *Vice Pres*
Aaron White, *Vice Pres*
Jeff Hyde, *Controller*
EMP: 12
SQ FT: 4,000
SALES (est): 2.4MM **Privately Held**
WEB: www.centralasphalt.com
SIC: 1611 2951 1771 Resurfacing contractor; asphalt paving mixtures & blocks; concrete work

(G-11184)
CENTRAL MICH CMENTING SVCS LLC
1961 Commercial Dr (48858-8913)
PHONE................989 775-0940
Mike Ball, *Opers Mgr*
John Keathley,
Michael Machuta,
EMP: 6
SALES (est): 837K **Privately Held**
SIC: 1389 Cementing oil & gas well casings

(G-11185)
CENTRAL MICHIGAN RAPID PRINT
1206 N Fancher Ave (48858-4608)
PHONE................989 772-3110
Dolores M Venable, *President*
Robert M Venable, *Vice Pres*
Debra Venable, *Admin Sec*
EMP: 3
SQ FT: 1,600
SALES (est): 376.5K **Privately Held**
SIC: 2752 Commercial printing, offset

(G-11186)
CENTRAL MICHIGAN UNIVERSITY
Also Called: Student Publications
436 Moore Hall (48859-0001)
PHONE................989 774-3493
Neil Hott, *Director*
EMP: 6
SALES (corp-wide): 314.3MM **Privately Held**
WEB: www.cm-life.com
SIC: 2711 Newspapers, publishing & printing
PA: Central Michigan University
1200 S Franklin St
Mount Pleasant MI 48859
989 774-4000

(G-11187)
CENTRAL MICHIGAN UNIVERSITY
Also Called: Cmu University Press
160 Combined Svcs Bldg (48859-0001)
PHONE................989 774-3216
John Jackson, *Info Tech Mgr*
Rhonda Kohler, *Director*
EMP: 15
SALES (corp-wide): 314.3MM **Privately Held**
WEB: www.cm-life.com
SIC: 2731 8221 Book publishing; university
PA: Central Michigan University
1200 S Franklin St
Mount Pleasant MI 48859
989 774-4000

(G-11188)
CIRCULAR MOTION LLC
4265 Corporate Dr (48858-1083)
PHONE................989 779-9040
Kevin Kennedy,
▲ **EMP:** 3
SALES (est): 241.5K **Privately Held**
WEB: www.circularmotion.com
SIC: 2257 Dyeing & finishing circular knit fabrics

GEOGRAPHIC SECTION

Mount Pleasant - Isabella County (G-11218)

(G-11189)
CMU
802 Industrial Dr (48858-4646)
PHONE..................................989 774-7143
Yoon Auh, *Principal*
EMP: 17 **EST:** 2008
SALES (est): 1.2MM **Privately Held**
SIC: 2711 Newspapers

(G-11190)
COIL DRILLING TECHNOLOGIES INC
2362 Northway Dr (48858-1289)
PHONE..................................989 773-6504
Pat Jarman, *President*
EMP: 8
SQ FT: 85,000
SALES (est): 1MM **Privately Held**
SIC: 1389 Oil field services

(G-11191)
DAYCO PRODUCTS LLC
1799 Gover Pkwy (48858-8140)
PHONE..................................989 775-0689
Lisa Dewyse, *Buyer*
Mike Byrne, *Branch Mgr*
EMP: 117
SALES (corp-wide): 178.8MM **Privately Held**
SIC: 3559 3714 Automotive related machinery; motor vehicle parts & accessories
HQ: Dayco Products, Llc
1650 Research Dr Ste 200
Troy MI 48083

(G-11192)
DELFIELD COMPANY LLC
980 S Isabella Rd (48858-9200)
PHONE..................................989 773-7981
Graham Tillotson, *Exec VP*
Jay Rivers, *Controller*
Robert Howes, *Credit Mgr*
Denise Maeder, *Sales Staff*
▲ **EMP:** 875
SQ FT: 345,000
SALES (est): 228.8MM
SALES (corp-wide): 1.5B **Publicly Held**
SIC: 3589 Commercial cooking & food-warming equipment
PA: Welbilt, Inc.
2227 Welbilt Blvd
Trinity FL 34655
727 375-7010

(G-11193)
FOLTZ SCREEN PRINTING
2094 S Isabella Rd (48858-2016)
PHONE..................................989 772-3947
Joe Foltz, *Owner*
EMP: 5
SQ FT: 5,500
SALES: 350K **Privately Held**
SIC: 2752 Commercial printing, lithographic

(G-11194)
GEOSTAR CORPORATION (PA)
2480 W Campus Dr Ste C (48858-5416)
PHONE..................................989 773-7050
Tom Robinson, *President*
Tony Ferguson, *Exec VP*
John Parrott, *Exec VP*
EMP: 20
SQ FT: 10,000
SALES (est): 18.9MM **Privately Held**
SIC: 1382 Oil & gas exploration services

(G-11195)
GRAPH-ADS PRINTING INC
711 W Pickard St Ste I (48858-1587)
P.O. Box 447 (48804-0447)
PHONE..................................989 779-6000
Al Frattura, *President*
EMP: 130
SQ FT: 20,000
SALES (est): 5.9MM
SALES (corp-wide): 697.5MM **Privately Held**
SIC: 2752 Newspapers, lithographed only
HQ: Morning Star Publishing Company
311 E Superior St Ste A
Alma MI 48801
989 779-6000

(G-11196)
HUBSCHER & SON INC (PA)
1101 N Franklin Ave (48858-4617)
P.O. Box 411 (48804-0411)
PHONE..................................989 773-5369
Paul Hubscher, *President*
G Charles Hubscher, *Vice Pres*
EMP: 1
SQ FT: 1,000
SALES (est): 2.6MM **Privately Held**
SIC: 1442 Gravel mining

(G-11197)
INTEGRTED DATABASE SYSTEMS INC
2625 Denison Dr A (48858-5596)
PHONE..................................989 546-4512
Lance Ferden, *President*
Lisa Ferden, *Vice Pres*
Siva Yerramsetty, *Engineer*
Julie Wallace, *Marketing Staff*
EMP: 12
SALES (est): 1.2MM **Privately Held**
SIC: 7372 Application computer software

(G-11198)
INTERMODAL TECHNOLOGIES INC
915 S Deer Run (48858-7400)
P.O. Box 270 (48804-0270)
PHONE..................................989 775-3799
EMP: 3 **EST:** 2002
SQ FT: 3,200
SALES (est): 220K **Privately Held**
SIC: 3715 Sales And Manufacturing Of Semi Trailers And Thrust Inhibitors

(G-11199)
J & W MACHINE INC
Also Called: J & W Machine & Tool
315 E Pickard St (48858-1553)
P.O. Box 315 (48804-0315)
PHONE..................................989 773-9951
Vernon L Powis Jr, *President*
Dan Sheahan, *President*
EMP: 5
SALES (est): 885.8K **Privately Held**
SIC: 3541 Drilling machine tools (metal cutting); screw & thread machines

(G-11200)
JO WELL SERVICE AND TSTG INC
Also Called: J O Well Service
6825 Lea Pick Dr (48858-8911)
PHONE..................................989 772-4221
Kirk Miller, *President*
Greg Elser, *Vice Pres*
Tim Auker, *Treasurer*
EMP: 4
SQ FT: 2,500
SALES: 500K **Privately Held**
SIC: 1389 Servicing oil & gas wells; oil field services

(G-11201)
KONWINSKI KABNETS INC
1900 Gover Pkwy (48858-8137)
PHONE..................................989 773-2906
Jerel Konwinski, *President*
EMP: 5
SALES (est): 430K **Privately Held**
SIC: 2521 Cabinets, office: wood

(G-11202)
LEASE MANAGEMENT INC (PA)
503 Industrial Dr (48858-4639)
P.O. Box 290 (48804-0290)
PHONE..................................989 773-5948
John R Harkins, *President*
Rudolph J Kler, *Treasurer*
EMP: 8
SQ FT: 4,080
SALES (est): 5.5MM **Privately Held**
SIC: 1389 1311 Servicing oil & gas wells; crude petroleum production; natural gas production

(G-11203)
MANESS PETROLEUM CORP
1425 S Mission Rd (48858-4665)
P.O. Box 313 (48804-0313)
PHONE..................................989 773-5475
David Maness, *President*
Lora Beatty, *Office Mgr*
EMP: 6
SQ FT: 1,500
SALES: 1.5MM **Privately Held**
WEB: www.manesspetr.com
SIC: 1382 8711 Oil & gas exploration services; consulting engineer

(G-11204)
MICHAEL ENGINEERING LTD
Also Called: Rook Metering Equipment
5625 Venture Way (48858-1152)
PHONE..................................989 772-4073
Ralph M Prewett, *CEO*
Eric V Prewett, *Vice Pres*
Eric Prewett, *Vice Pres*
Chuck Murrey, *Plant Mgr*
Deb Bongard, *Train & Dev Mgr*
EMP: 20
SQ FT: 20,000
SALES (est): 4.9MM **Privately Held**
WEB: www.michaelengineering.com
SIC: 3829 Measuring & controlling devices

(G-11205)
MICHIGAN WIRELINE SERVICE
4854 E River Rd (48858)
P.O. Box 782 (48804-0782)
PHONE..................................989 772-5075
Dennis McConahy, *President*
Ed Crain, *President*
Brian Sharrar, *Corp Secy*
EMP: 12
SQ FT: 4,500
SALES: 2MM **Privately Held**
SIC: 1389 Oil field services

(G-11206)
MICHIWEST ENERGY INC
1425 S Mission Rd Ste 2 (48858-4665)
PHONE..................................989 772-2107
William J Strickler, *President*
EMP: 5
SQ FT: 600
SALES (est): 540K **Privately Held**
WEB: www.stricklerresources.com
SIC: 1381 Drilling oil & gas wells

(G-11207)
MID STATE OIL TOOLS INC (PA)
1934 Commercial Dr (48858-8913)
PHONE..................................989 773-4114
John Keathley, *President*
Michael Machuta, *Vice Pres*
Brian Tafts, *Controller*
EMP: 40
SQ FT: 9,000
SALES (est): 8.5MM **Privately Held**
WEB: www.midstateoiltools.com
SIC: 1389 Oil field services

(G-11208)
MID-MICHIGAN INDUSTRIES INC (PA)
Also Called: Mmi of Central Michigan
2426 Parkway Dr (48858-4723)
PHONE..................................989 773-6918
Alan J Schilling, *President*
Jeremy Murphy, *General Mgr*
Doug Ouellette, *Chairman*
Jori Coster, *Human Res Dir*
W Sidney, *Supervisor*
EMP: 70
SQ FT: 22,000
SALES: 5.9MM **Privately Held**
WEB: www.mmionline.com
SIC: 8331 3471 2396 Vocational training agency; plating & polishing; automotive & apparel trimmings

(G-11209)
MONTCALM AGGREGATES INC
2201 Commerce St Ste 4 (48858-9060)
PHONE..................................989 772-7038
Jim Zalud, *President*
Deanne Travis, *Manager*
EMP: 4
SALES (est): 764K **Privately Held**
SIC: 3295 Perlite, aggregate or expanded

(G-11210)
MOUNT PLEASANT BREWING COMPANY
506 W Broadway St (48858-2441)
PHONE..................................989 400-4666
Robert Trines, *Principal*
EMP: 5
SALES (est): 367.5K **Privately Held**
SIC: 2082 Beer (alcoholic beverage)

(G-11211)
MOUNTAIN TOWN STN BREW PUB LLC
Also Called: Mountain Town Stn Brewing Co &
506 W Broadway St (48858-2441)
PHONE..................................989 775-2337
Jim Holton, *President*
EMP: 135
SQ FT: 8,700
SALES (est): 2.1MM **Privately Held**
WEB: www.mountaintown.com
SIC: 5812 2082 Steak restaurant; beer (alcoholic beverage)

(G-11212)
MTW PERFORMANCE & FAB
706 W Pickard St (48858-9854)
PHONE..................................989 317-3301
Kevin Curtiss, *Principal*
EMP: 3
SALES (est): 392.8K **Privately Held**
SIC: 3441 Fabricated structural metal

(G-11213)
MVM7 LLC
210 W Pickard St (48858-1560)
PHONE..................................989 317-3901
Michael Otterbine, *Mng Member*
EMP: 35
SQ FT: 5,100
SALES: 5MM **Privately Held**
SIC: 3792 Travel trailers & campers

(G-11214)
NANOSYNTHONS LLC
1200 N Fancher Ave (48858-4608)
PHONE..................................989 317-3737
Donald Tomalia, *CEO*
Janet E Tomalia, *CFO*
EMP: 7
SALES (est): 803.8K **Privately Held**
SIC: 2899 Chemical preparations

(G-11215)
OILPATCH MACHINE TOOL INC
Also Called: Oil Patch Machine & Tool
6773 E Pickard Rd (48858-8907)
PHONE..................................989 772-0637
Mark Arends, *President*
Deborah Klunzinger, *Controller*
EMP: 9
SQ FT: 6,000
SALES: 290K **Privately Held**
SIC: 7539 7692 3498 Machine shop, automotive; welding repair; fabricated pipe & fittings

(G-11216)
ON THE MARK INC
801 Industrial Dr (48858-4645)
PHONE..................................989 317-8033
Alexander Hollenbeck, *President*
Martha Hollenbeck, *Treasurer*
EMP: 8
SQ FT: 35,000
SALES (est): 250K **Privately Held**
SIC: 3549 3482 Metalworking machinery; small arms ammunition

(G-11217)
PINNACLE CABINET COMPANY INC
1121 N Fancher Ave (48858-4605)
PHONE..................................989 772-3866
Eric McDonald, *President*
Eric Mc Donald, *President*
Joe Mc Donald, *Corp Secy*
Fred Mc Donald, *Vice Pres*
Deb Mc Donald, *VP Finance*
EMP: 20
SALES: 2MM **Privately Held**
SIC: 2599 2542 2434 Cabinets, factory; partitions & fixtures, except wood; wood kitchen cabinets

(G-11218)
PIONEER OIL TOOLS INC
5179 W Weidman Rd (48858)
P.O. Box 131 (48804-0131)
PHONE..................................989 644-6999
Glenn Smith, *President*

Mount Pleasant - Isabella County (G-11219)

EMP: 7
SQ FT: 6,000
SALES (est): 296K **Privately Held**
SIC: 1389 Oil & gas wells: building, repairing & dismantling; oil field services

(G-11219)
PLEASANT GRAPHICS INC
6835 Lea Pick Dr (48858-8911)
PHONE..................989 773-7777
Douglas Neff, *President*
Hans Schwarzkopf, *Consultant*
▲ EMP: 12
SQ FT: 7,000
SALES (est): 1.7MM **Privately Held**
WEB: www.pleasantgraphics.com
SIC: 2752 Commercial printing, offset

(G-11220)
PREMIER CASING CREWS INC
5580 Venture Way (48858-1149)
PHONE..................989 775-7436
Steve Bigard, *President*
Ricky Huagard, *Vice Pres*
EMP: 7 EST: 1997
SALES: 360K **Privately Held**
SIC: 1389 Construction, repair & dismantling services; oil field services

(G-11221)
PRINT TECH PRINTING PLACE INC
1610 W Lyons St (48858-3038)
PHONE..................989 772-6109
Denise Anderson, *President*
Loren Anderson, *Treasurer*
EMP: 3
SQ FT: 4,000
SALES: 325K **Privately Held**
SIC: 2752 7334 2759 Commercial printing, offset; photocopying & duplicating services; commercial printing

(G-11222)
QUALITY DOOR & MORE INC
1102 Packard Rd Ste B (48858-5326)
PHONE..................989 317-8314
Ryan W Tebo, *Administration*
EMP: 9
SALES: 2.5MM **Privately Held**
SIC: 5211 3699 Doors, wood or metal, except storm; door opening & closing devices, electrical

(G-11223)
REFRIGERATION RESEARCH INC
Also Called: Oak Division
2174 Commerce St (48858-9060)
PHONE..................989 773-7540
Mike Cummings, *Principal*
EMP: 7
SALES (corp-wide): 11.6MM **Privately Held**
WEB: www.refresearch.com
SIC: 3585 Refrigeration equipment, complete
PA: Refrigeration Research, Inc.
525 N 5th St
Brighton MI 48116
810 227-1151

(G-11224)
RELATIVE PATH LLC
4775 Commons Dr Unit Gg09 (48858-4447)
PHONE..................217 840-6376
Michael Wayman, *Principal*
EMP: 3
SALES (est): 121.3K **Privately Held**
SIC: 7372 Prepackaged software

(G-11225)
RISE MACHINE COMPANY INC
905 N Kinney Ave (48858-1700)
P.O. Box 321 (48804-0321)
PHONE..................989 772-2151
Kenneth Rise, *President*
Donald J Rise Sr, *President*
EMP: 7 EST: 1965
SQ FT: 6,480
SALES: 300K **Privately Held**
SIC: 3599 7692 Machine shop, jobbing & repair; welding repair

(G-11226)
SHUTTERS CHANDELIERS LLC
600 S Mission St Ste B (48858-2790)
PHONE..................989 773-0929
Elizabeth Walters, *Principal*
EMP: 3
SALES (est): 159.6K **Privately Held**
SIC: 3442 Shutters, door or window: metal

(G-11227)
SMITH & SONS MEAT PROC INC
5080 E Broadway Rd (48858-8413)
PHONE..................989 772-6048
Russell Smith, *President*
EMP: 8 EST: 1936
SQ FT: 10,000
SALES: 1MM **Privately Held**
SIC: 2011 5421 Meat packing plants; meat & fish markets; meat markets, including freezer provisioners

(G-11228)
SMITH - SONS ME
5080 E Broadway Rd (48858-8413)
PHONE..................989 772-6048
Ken Rau, *Principal*
EMP: 3
SALES (est): 206.6K **Privately Held**
SIC: 2011 Meat packing plants

(G-11229)
SOLAR EZ INC
5340 E Jordan Rd (48858-9220)
PHONE..................989 773-3347
EMP: 15
SALES (est): 666K **Privately Held**
SIC: 1799 3433 Trade Contractor Mfg Heating Equipment-Nonelectric

(G-11230)
STEEL-FAB WILSON & MACHINE
1219 N Mission St (48858-1050)
PHONE..................989 773-6046
David L Wilson, *President*
Tim Wilson, *Vice Pres*
EMP: 6
SQ FT: 4,000
SALES (est): 1MM **Privately Held**
SIC: 3599 Custom machinery: machine shop, jobbing & repair

(G-11231)
STEELHEAD INDUSTRIES LLC
121 E Broadway St (48858-2312)
PHONE..................989 506-7416
Tim Sponseller,
Greg McCarthy,
EMP: 14 EST: 2015
SQ FT: 50,000
SALES: 2MM **Privately Held**
SIC: 3537 Engine stands & racks, metal

(G-11232)
T L V INC
Also Called: Tumbl Trak
5747 W Isabella Rd (48858-9302)
P.O. Box 289 (48804-0289)
PHONE..................989 773-4362
Doug Davis, *President*
Douglas Davis, *President*
Stacy Finnerty, *Vice Pres*
Darlene Keely, *Accountant*
Monica Betker, *Marketing Staff*
▲ EMP: 11
SQ FT: 3,600
SALES (est): 1.9MM **Privately Held**
WEB: www.tumbltrak.com
SIC: 3949 5091 Gymnasium equipment; gymnasium equipment

(G-11233)
TOLAS OIL GAS EXPLORATION CO
Also Called: Tolas Brothers
306 E Broadway St Ste 1 (48858-2659)
P.O. Box 308 (48804-0308)
PHONE..................989 772-2599
Peter J Tolas, *President*
James Tolas, *Treasurer*
George Tolas, *Admin Sec*
EMP: 3 EST: 1980
SQ FT: 4,000
SALES (est): 400K **Privately Held**
SIC: 1311 Crude petroleum production; natural gas production

(G-11234)
TOTAL LEE SPORTS INC
1575 Airway Dr (48858-8922)
P.O. Box 47 (48804-0047)
PHONE..................989 772-6121
Robert Lee, *President*
Karen Lee, *Corp Secy*
Mary Ann Lee, *Vice Pres*
EMP: 4
SQ FT: 2,000
SALES (est): 580.1K **Privately Held**
SIC: 2759 5091 5941 Letterpress & screen printing; sporting & recreation goods; sporting goods & bicycle shops

(G-11235)
WEBER BROS SAWMILL INC
2862 N Winn Rd (48858-9736)
PHONE..................989 644-2206
Ed Weber, *President*
John Weber, *President*
Ben Weber, *Corp Secy*
EMP: 27 EST: 1956
SQ FT: 15,500
SALES (est): 3.7MM **Privately Held**
SIC: 2421 2426 Lumber: rough, sawed or planed; hardwood dimension & flooring mills

(G-11236)
YOUR CUSTOM IMAGE
2021 E River Rd (48858-8047)
P.O. Box 478, Edmore (48829-0478)
PHONE..................989 621-2250
Nick Houghton, *Owner*
EMP: 4
SALES: 200K **Privately Held**
SIC: 2711 Newspapers

Muir
Ionia County

(G-11237)
CCO HOLDINGS LLC
156 Superior St (48860-8705)
PHONE..................989 853-2008
EMP: 3
SALES (corp-wide): 43.6B **Publicly Held**
SIC: 5064 4841 3663 3651 Electrical appliances, television & radio; cable & other pay television services; radio & TV communications equipment; household audio & video equipment
HQ: Cco Holdings, Llc
400 Atlantic St
Stamford CT 06901
203 905-7801

Mulliken
Eaton County

(G-11238)
ALR PRODUCTS INC
Also Called: Polly Products
12 Charlotte St (48861-9701)
PHONE..................517 649-2243
Steve Ault, *CEO*
EMP: 25
SALES: 250K **Privately Held**
SIC: 2531 Public building & related furniture

(G-11239)
KELLOGG COMPANY
235 Potter St (48861-9663)
PHONE..................269 961-9387
Leslie Lauderbaugh, *Principal*
EMP: 385
SALES (corp-wide): 13.5B **Publicly Held**
SIC: 2043 Cereal breakfast foods
PA: Kellogg Company
1 Kellogg Sq
Battle Creek MI 49017
269 961-2000

(G-11240)
RECYCLETECH PRODUCTS INC
12 Charlotte St (48861-9701)
PHONE..................517 649-2243
Tom Vanderhenst, *President*
EMP: 35
SALES (est): 2.7MM **Privately Held**
WEB: www.recycletechproducts.com
SIC: 2531 5941 Picnic tables or benches, park; playground equipment

Munger
Bay County

(G-11241)
COMPUTERS EDGE
230 W Brown Rd (48747-9304)
PHONE..................989 659-3179
William Wazny, *Owner*
William F Wazny, *Owner*
EMP: 3
SALES (est): 250K **Privately Held**
SIC: 5045 3577 Computers & accessories, personal & home entertainment; computer peripheral equipment; computer peripheral equipment

(G-11242)
IKES WELDING SHOP AND MFG
50 N Finn Rd (48747-9780)
PHONE..................989 892-2783
Jefferdon Behmlander, *Partner*
Randy Bowman, *Principal*
Roger Bowman, *Principal*
EMP: 6
SALES (est): 570K **Privately Held**
SIC: 3523 Potato diggers, harvesters & planters; grading, cleaning, sorting machines, fruit, grain, vegetable

Munising
Alger County

(G-11243)
HARMONY PRODUCTS
118 E Superior St (49862-1122)
P.O. Box 96 (49862-0096)
PHONE..................906 387-5411
Nancy Webster, *Owner*
EMP: 3
SALES (est): 254.1K **Privately Held**
SIC: 2873 Nitrogenous fertilizers

(G-11244)
HIAWATHA LOG HOMES INC
M-28 East (49862)
PHONE..................877 275-9090
Paul Essinger, *President*
Rick Rhoades, *General Mgr*
EMP: 24
SQ FT: 10,000
SALES (est): 3MM **Privately Held**
WEB: www.hiawatha.com
SIC: 2452 2411 Log cabins, prefabricated, wood; wooden logs

(G-11245)
MANNISTO FOREST PRODUCTS INC
E7720 Knuttila Rd (49862-8984)
PHONE..................906 387-3836
David L Mannisto, *CEO*
EMP: 3
SALES (est): 250K **Privately Held**
SIC: 2411 Logging

(G-11246)
NEENAH PAPER INC
501 E Munising Ave (49862-1490)
PHONE..................906 387-2700
Chris Simard, *Mfg Staff*
Patrick McDonald, *Project Engr*
Jim Pytyck, *Manager*
Vicky Lindquist, *Maintence Staff*
EMP: 340
SALES (corp-wide): 1B **Publicly Held**
WEB: www.neenah.com
SIC: 2621 Paper mills
PA: Neenah, Inc.
3460 Preston Ridge Rd # 150
Alpharetta GA 30005
678 566-6500

GEOGRAPHIC SECTION

Muskegon - Muskegon County (G-11272)

(G-11247)
PETERSON PUBLISHING INC
Also Called: Algen County Shopper
132 E Superior St (49862-1122)
PHONE..................................906 387-3282
Willie J Peterson, *President*
EMP: 8 **EST:** 1945
SQ FT: 8,600
SALES (est): 592.9K **Privately Held**
SIC: 2711 5943 Job printing & newspaper publishing combined; office forms & supplies

(G-11248)
PONTOON RENTALS
Also Called: Seaberg Pontoon Rentals
1330 Commercial St (49862-1358)
PHONE..................................906 387-2685
Sharon Seaberg, *Principal*
EMP: 4
SALES (est): 412.4K **Privately Held**
SIC: 3728 7999 Pontoons, aircraft; pleasure boat rental

(G-11249)
S & S FOREST PRODUCTS
905 W Munising Ave (49862-1321)
PHONE..................................906 892-8268
Earl Steinhoff, *President*
Milo Steinhoff, *Partner*
EMP: 5
SALES (est): 370K **Privately Held**
SIC: 2411 Logging

(G-11250)
TIMBER PRODUCTS CO LTD PARTNR
Also Called: Michigan Hrdwood Vneer Lbr Div
Hwy M 28 E (49862)
P.O. Box 378 (49862-0378)
PHONE..................................906 452-6221
David Gonyea, *Vice Pres*
Millard Larsen, *Manager*
EMP: 250
SALES (corp-wide): 340.8MM **Privately Held**
WEB: www.sor.teamtp.com
SIC: 2421 2435 Sawmills & planing mills, general; hardwood veneer & plywood
PA: Timber Products Co. Limited Partnership
  305 S 4th St
  Springfield OR 97477
  541 747-4577

(G-11251)
TIMBERLAND FORESTRY
E6971 Wildwood Rd (49862-8836)
PHONE..................................906 387-4350
Tom Nolta, *Owner*
EMP: 12
SALES (est): 1.3MM **Privately Held**
SIC: 3531 Forestry related equipment

Munith
Jackson County

(G-11252)
CENTERLESS REBUILDERS INC
9053 Plum Orchard Rd (49259-9805)
PHONE..................................517 596-3233
Bill Stagier, *Manager*
EMP: 11
SALES (corp-wide): 7.6MM **Privately Held**
WEB: www.centerless.net
SIC: 3599 Machine shop, jobbing & repair
PA: Centerless Rebuilders, Inc.
  57877 Main St
  New Haven MI 48048
  586 749-6529

(G-11253)
PERSONAL & HOME DEFENSE LLC
8795 Portage Lake Rd (49259-9604)
PHONE..................................517 596-3027
EMP: 3
SALES (est): 160.4K **Privately Held**
SIC: 3812 Defense systems & equipment

(G-11254)
R T C ENVIRO FAB INC
9043 M 106 (49259)
P.O. Box 99, Pleasant Lake (49272-0099)
PHONE..................................517 596-2987
Virginia Bubp, *President*
Ronald Bubp, *General Mgr*
EMP: 15
SQ FT: 12,000
SALES (est): 2.6MM **Privately Held**
SIC: 3443 3441 Tanks, lined: metal plate; fabricated structural metal

Muskegon
Muskegon County

(G-11255)
A & B WELDING & FABRICATING
Also Called: A&B Welding
2532 S Getty St (49444-1797)
PHONE..................................231 733-2661
Thomas Baker, *President*
Ted Baker, *Vice Pres*
Timothy Baker, *Vice Pres*
Gary Baker, *Treasurer*
Sandra Zahart, *Admin Sec*
EMP: 6
SQ FT: 12,000
SALES: 2MM **Privately Held**
SIC: 3449 7692 3444 3443 Custom roll formed products; welding repair; sheet metalwork; fabricated plate work (boiler shop)

(G-11256)
A & D RUN OFF INC
Also Called: Wells Index Division
701 W Clay Ave (49440-1064)
PHONE..................................231 759-0950
Rick Robison, *President*
EMP: 6
SQ FT: 16,000
SALES (est): 650K **Privately Held**
WEB: www.wellsindex.com
SIC: 3541 3545 Electrochemical milling machines; milling machine attachments (machine tool accessories)

(G-11257)
A B ELECTRICAL INC
2246 Olthoff St (49444-2644)
PHONE..................................231 737-9200
West Leiter, *Owner*
EMP: 35
SALES (est): 1.8MM **Privately Held**
SIC: 3679 Harness assemblies for electronic use: wire or cable

(G-11258)
AB ELECTRICAL WIRES INC
2240 Glade St (49444-1316)
P.O. Box 1873 (49443-1873)
PHONE..................................231 737-9200
Wes Leiter, *President*
EMP: 33
SQ FT: 15,000
SALES (est): 4.1MM **Privately Held**
SIC: 3496 3613 3625 3679 Miscellaneous fabricated wire products; control panels, electric; crane & hoist controls, including metal mill; harness assemblies for electronic use: wire or cable

(G-11259)
ACCESS WORKS INC
Also Called: Fleet Engineers
1800 E Keating Ave (49442-6121)
PHONE..................................231 777-2537
Wesley K Eklund, *President*
Louis E Eklund, *Treasurer*
EMP: 9
SQ FT: 240,000
SALES (est): 736.3K **Privately Held**
SIC: 3714 Motor vehicle parts & accessories

(G-11260)
ADAC PLASTICS INC
2653 Olthoff St (49444-2680)
PHONE..................................231 777-2645
Stacey Henkel, *Exec Dir*
EMP: 167
SALES (corp-wide): 263.6MM **Privately Held**
SIC: 3089 Injection molding of plastics
PA: Adac Plastics, Inc.
  5920 Tahoe Dr Se
  Grand Rapids MI 49546
  616 957-0311

(G-11261)
ADAC PLASTICS INC
2050 Port City Blvd (49442-6134)
PHONE..................................616 957-0520
Dennis Comstock, *Engineer*
Stacey Henkel, *Branch Mgr*
Eric McDonald, *Technology*
EMP: 250
SALES (corp-wide): 263.6MM **Privately Held**
SIC: 3089 3714 Injection molding of plastics; motor vehicle parts & accessories
PA: Adac Plastics, Inc.
  5920 Tahoe Dr Se
  Grand Rapids MI 49546
  616 957-0311

(G-11262)
ADAC PLASTICS INC
Also Called: Adac Automotive
1801 E Keating Ave (49442-6120)
PHONE..................................616 957-0311
Jeff Taylor, *Mfg Staff*
Jon Wildern, *Project Engr*
Brad Wingett, *Branch Mgr*
Rick Vandekopple, *Exec Dir*
EMP: 500
SALES (corp-wide): 263.6MM **Privately Held**
SIC: 3089 3714 Injection molding of plastics; motor vehicle parts & accessories
PA: Adac Plastics, Inc.
  5920 Tahoe Dr Se
  Grand Rapids MI 49546
  616 957-0311

(G-11263)
AERO FOIL INTERNATIONAL INC
Also Called: Afi
1920 Port City Blvd (49442-6132)
PHONE..................................231 773-0200
Stephen Kutches, *President*
Trevor McClung, *Engineer*
▼ **EMP:** 50
SQ FT: 30,000
SALES: 2MM **Privately Held**
WEB: www.afiusa.net
SIC: 3544 Special dies & tools

(G-11264)
AGGREGTES EXCVTG LOGISTICS LLC
Also Called: Franklin AEL
951 E Barney Ave Ste B (49444-1708)
PHONE..................................231 737-4949
Jaime Franklin,
EMP: 3
SALES (est): 671.7K **Privately Held**
SIC: 1442 Construction sand & gravel

(G-11265)
ALLOY RESOURCES LLC
Also Called: Alloy Resources Corp.
1985 E Laketon Ave (49442-6127)
PHONE..................................231 777-3941
Bruce J Essex Jr, *President*
EMP: 50
SALES: 19.5MM
SALES (corp-wide): 101.3MM **Privately Held**
SIC: 3312 Tool & die steel & alloys
HQ: Port City Group, Inc.
  1985 E Laketon Ave
  Muskegon MI 49442
  231 777-3941

(G-11266)
AMERICAN ATHLETIC
418 W Hackley Ave (49444-1032)
P.O. Box 1881 (49443-1881)
PHONE..................................231 798-7300
Timothy Ehilietart, *Partner*
John McDonald, *Partner*
Mark Scott, *Partner*
Marianne White, *Admin Asst*
EMP: 12
SALES (est): 1.7MM **Privately Held**
SIC: 2531 Bleacher seating, portable

(G-11267)
AMERICAN CHEM SOLUTIONS LLC
2406 Roberts St (49444-1843)
PHONE..................................231 655-5840
Todd Zahn,
EMP: 14 **EST:** 2018
SALES (est): 1.5MM **Privately Held**
SIC: 2899 Chemical preparations

(G-11268)
AMERICAN PORCELAIN ENAMEL CO
1709 Ruddiman Dr (49445-3041)
PHONE..................................231 744-3013
Robert Long Jr, *President*
Harry E Long, *Treasurer*
Donna Buit, *Manager*
EMP: 27
SQ FT: 36,000
SALES: 5MM **Privately Held**
SIC: 3479 Enameling, including porcelain, of metal products

(G-11269)
AMERIFORM ACQUISITION CO LLC
Also Called: Hemisphere Design Works
700 Terrace Point Dr # 200 (49440-1166)
PHONE..................................231 733-2725
Dan Harris, *General Mgr*
Gary Rose, *Plant Engr*
Thomas Harris, *Mng Member*
Daniel Harris,
David Harris,
◆ **EMP:** 300
SQ FT: 500,000
SALES (est): 52.7MM **Privately Held**
WEB: www.klindustries.com
SIC: 3732 7359 Non-motorized boat, building & repairing; portable toilet rental

(G-11270)
ANDERSON GLOBAL INC
500 W Sherman Blvd (49444-1315)
PHONE..................................231 733-2164
John R Mc Intyre, *President*
John McIntyre, *President*
Troy Leroux, *Opers Mgr*
Joe Merrill, *Engineer*
Rex Pease, *Engineer*
▲ **EMP:** 135 **EST:** 1982
SQ FT: 45,000
SALES (est): 38.3MM **Privately Held**
WEB: www.andersonglobal.com
SIC: 3543 Foundry patternmaking

(G-11271)
APPARELMASTER-MUSKEGON INC
Also Called: Blue Ribbon Linen and Mat Svcs
341 E Apple Ave (49442-3465)
P.O. Box 5337 (49445-0337)
PHONE..................................231 728-5406
Eric Anderson, *President*
Donald Harakas, *Vice Pres*
Lori Anderson, *Treasurer*
Nancy Anderson, *Admin Sec*
EMP: 22
SQ FT: 11,000
SALES: 1.5MM **Privately Held**
SIC: 2273 7213 Mats & matting; uniform supply

(G-11272)
ASPHALT PAVING INC
1000 E Sherman Blvd (49444-1808)
P.O. Box 4190 (49444-0190)
PHONE..................................231 733-1409
Joseph Burns, *President*
Nelson Van Leeuwen, *Principal*
Gary Verplank, *Principal*
L J Verplank, *Principal*
Ken Johnson, *Vice Pres*
EMP: 18
SQ FT: 1,000
SALES (est): 3.2MM **Privately Held**
SIC: 1611 3272 Surfacing & paving; resurfacing contractor; paving materials, prefabricated concrete

Muskegon - Muskegon County (G-11273)

(G-11273)
AZKO MANUFACTURING INC
560 E Broadway Ave (49444-2261)
PHONE.................................231 733-0888
Adam Ziganthaler, *President*
Ross Ziganthaler, *Vice Pres*
EMP: 6
SALES: 180K **Privately Held**
SIC: 3543 Foundry patternmaking

(G-11274)
AZKO PATTERN MFG INC
560 E Broadway Ave (49444-2261)
PHONE.................................231 733-0888
A Ross Ziegenthaler, *Principal*
EMP: 8 **EST:** 2009
SALES (est): 890.2K **Privately Held**
SIC: 3543 Industrial patterns

(G-11275)
BASF
1740 Whitehall Rd (49445-1354)
PHONE.................................231 719-3019
EMP: 4
SALES (est): 472.3K **Privately Held**
SIC: 2899 Chemical preparations

(G-11276)
BAUER SHEET METAL & FABG INC (PA)
1550 Evanston Ave (49442-5327)
PHONE.................................231 773-3244
Michael Bauer, *President*
Mike Heath, *Project Mgr*
Ron Sejat, *Opers Mgr*
Jeff Nason, *Sales Staff*
EMP: 35 **EST:** 1933
SQ FT: 17,000
SALES (est): 8.8MM **Privately Held**
WEB: www.bauersheetmetal.com
SIC: 1761 3441 3444 Sheet metalwork; fabricated structural metal; sheet metalwork

(G-11277)
BAYER CROPSCIENCE LP
Also Called: Muskegon Formulation Plant
1740 Whitehall Rd (49445-1354)
PHONE.................................231 744-4711
James Dowd, *Plant Mgr*
Richard Pospisil, *Warehouse Mgr*
Steve Smythe, *Branch Mgr*
David Sova, *Manager*
Debra Deyoung, *Technician*
EMP: 80
SQ FT: 4,500
SALES (corp-wide): 71.7B **Privately Held**
SIC: 2879 Agricultural chemicals
HQ: Bayer Cropscience Lp
  2 Tw Alexander Dr
  Durham NC 27709
  919 549-2000

(G-11278)
BBP INVESTMENT HOLDINGS LLC (PA)
Also Called: Brunswick Bowling Products
525 W Laketon Ave (49441-2601)
PHONE.................................231 725-4966
Corey Dykstra, *Mng Member*
Cheyney Rushing, *Info Tech Mgr*
Mark Kolbe, *Analyst*
EMP: 18 **EST:** 2015
SQ FT: 430,000
SALES (est): 91.2MM **Privately Held**
SIC: 3949 6719 Bowling equipment & supplies; investment holding companies, except banks

(G-11279)
BERT HAZEKAMP & SON INC
Also Called: Hazekamps Wholesale Meat Co
3933 S Brooks Rd (49444-9721)
PHONE.................................231 773-8302
David Hazekamp, *President*
Mike Hazekamp, *Vice Pres*
Julie Hazekamp, *Admin Sec*
EMP: 110 **EST:** 1905
SQ FT: 85,000
SALES (est): 21.8MM **Privately Held**
SIC: 2013 2011 Sausages & other prepared meats; meat packing plants

(G-11280)
BMC/INDUSTRIAL EDUCTL SVCS INC
Also Called: BMC Laboratory Casework
2831 Maffett St (49444-2153)
P.O. Box 4089 (49444-0089)
PHONE.................................231 733-1206
Joel Gauthier, *President*
EMP: 30 **EST:** 1970
SQ FT: 40,000
SALES (est): 5.7MM **Privately Held**
WEB: www.bmclab.com
SIC: 5047 3444 3821 Hospital equipment & supplies; medical laboratory equipment; sheet metalwork; laboratory equipment: fume hoods, distillation racks, etc.

(G-11281)
BOARS BELLY
333 W Western Ave (49440-1266)
PHONE.................................231 722-2627
EMP: 4
SALES (est): 471K **Privately Held**
SIC: 2599 Bar, restaurant & cafeteria furniture

(G-11282)
BOLD COMPANIES INC
Also Called: Bold Furniture
2291 Olthoff St (49444-2643)
PHONE.................................231 773-8026
David Folkert, *CEO*
Todd Folkert, *President*
Kylene Smith, *CFO*
Nick Milanowski, *Manager*
EMP: 88
SQ FT: 75,000
SALES (est): 18.3MM **Privately Held**
WEB: www.boldfurniture.com
SIC: 2521 Wood office furniture

(G-11283)
BORGMAN TOOL & ENGINEERING LLC
2912 Hamilton Rd (49445-8318)
PHONE.................................231 733-4133
John Borgim,
EMP: 5
SALES (est): 734.1K **Privately Held**
SIC: 3544 Special dies, tools, jigs & fixtures

(G-11284)
BOYD MANUFACTURING LLC
1838 Ruddiman Dr (49445-3146)
PHONE.................................734 649-9765
William Boyd, *Info Tech Mgr*
EMP: 5
SALES (est): 737.7K **Privately Held**
WEB: www.boyd-engineering.com
SIC: 3672 3699 3821 5049 Printed circuit boards; laser systems & equipment; physics laboratory apparatus; laboratory equipment, except medical or dental; consulting engineer; electrical or electronic engineering

(G-11285)
BRUNSWICK BOWLING PRODUCTS LLC (HQ)
525 W Laketon Ave (49441-2601)
P.O. Box 329 (49443-0329)
PHONE.................................231 725-3300
Corey J Dykstra, *CEO*
Austin Rothbard, *President*
Kelly Meloche, *Buyer*
Jerry Taylor, *Design Engr*
Corey Dykstra, *CFO*
◆ **EMP:** 500
SQ FT: 160,000
SALES (est): 101.7MM
SALES (corp-wide): 91.2MM **Privately Held**
WEB: www.bowlbrunswick.com
SIC: 3949 Bowling equipment & supplies
PA: Bbp Investment Holdings, Llc
  525 W Laketon Ave
  Muskegon MI 49441
  231 725-4966

(G-11286)
BULLSEYE POWER
2134 Northwoods Ave (49442-6850)
PHONE.................................231 788-5209
John Workman, *Partner*
Mark Fazakerley, *Partner*
David M Hall, *Partner*
Charles D Portera, *Partner*
Bill Devine, *Manager*
▲ **EMP:** 9
SALES (est): 1.2MM **Privately Held**
WEB: www.bullseyepower.com
SIC: 3714 Motor vehicle parts & accessories

(G-11287)
BUYERS GUIDE
1781 5th St Ste 1 (49441-2600)
PHONE.................................231 722-3784
Dale Bush, *Owner*
Barb Bary, *Manager*
EMP: 16
SQ FT: 8,000
SALES (est): 1.3MM **Privately Held**
SIC: 2741 Shopping news: publishing only, not printed on site

(G-11288)
C W MARSH COMPANY (PA)
1385 Hudson St (49441-1814)
P.O. Box 598 (49443-0598)
PHONE.................................231 722-3781
David Utzinger, *President*
James Bradbury, *Chairman*
Elizabeth Bradbury, *Vice Pres*
EMP: 22
SQ FT: 16,000
SALES: 2.6MM **Privately Held**
WEB: www.cwmarsh.com
SIC: 3199 3172 3053 Leather belting & strapping; personal leather goods; gaskets, packing & sealing devices

(G-11289)
CAMCAR PLASTICS INC
1732 Glade St (49441-2313)
PHONE.................................231 726-5000
Courtney Gust III, *President*
Teresa Gust, *Vice Pres*
EMP: 14
SQ FT: 18,000
SALES: 1.9MM **Privately Held**
WEB: www.ccplasticparts.com
SIC: 3089 Injection molding of plastics

(G-11290)
CAMERON INTERNATIONAL CORP
Also Called: Cameron/Schlumberger
2076 Northwoods Ave (49442-6849)
PHONE.................................231 788-7020
Becky Jones, *Human Res Mgr*
Phillip Vaughan, *Branch Mgr*
EMP: 49 **Publicly Held**
SIC: 3533 Oil field machinery & equipment
HQ: Cameron International Corporation
  4646 W Sam Houston Pkwy N
  Houston TX 77041

(G-11291)
CCO HOLDINGS LLC
1595 Lakeshore Dr (49441-1636)
PHONE.................................231 720-0688
EMP: 3
SALES (corp-wide): 43.6B **Publicly Held**
SIC: 5064 4841 3663 3651 Electrical appliances, television & radio; cable & other pay television services; radio & TV communications equipment; household audio & video equipment
HQ: Cco Holdings, Llc
  400 Atlantic St
  Stamford CT 06901
  203 905-7801

(G-11292)
CEL PLASTICS INC
Also Called: Port City Custom Plastics
1985 E Laketon Ave (49442-6127)
PHONE.................................231 777-3941
Mark Pickett, *President*
Bruce Essex, *Vice Pres*
John Essex, *Vice Pres*
EMP: 10
SQ FT: 10,000
SALES: 4.5MM
SALES (corp-wide): 101.3MM **Privately Held**
SIC: 3089 Injection molded finished plastic products
HQ: Pace Industries, Llc
  481 S Shiloh Dr
  Fayetteville AR 72704
  479 443-1455

(G-11293)
CENTURY FOUNDRY INC
339 W Hovey Ave (49444-1306)
P.O. Box 4438 (49444-0438)
PHONE.................................231 733-1572
Scott Le Roux, *President*
Laura Ellis, *Human Res Dir*
Cindy Snyder, *Human Res Mgr*
EMP: 50
SQ FT: 45,000
SALES (est): 13.2MM **Privately Held**
WEB: www.centuryfoundry.com
SIC: 3365 Machinery castings, aluminum

(G-11294)
CLASS A TOOL & MACHINE LLC
770 S Maple Island Rd (49442-9480)
PHONE.................................231 788-3822
Ron Pavlich, *President*
EMP: 5
SQ FT: 7,500
SALES (est): 450K **Privately Held**
WEB: www.classatool.com
SIC: 3544 Industrial molds

(G-11295)
COLES QUALITY FOODS INC
1188 Lakeshore Dr (49441-1613)
PHONE.................................231 722-1651
Wesley S Devon, *CEO*
EMP: 22
SALES (corp-wide): 65MM **Privately Held**
WEB: www.coles.com
SIC: 5149 2051 2038 Specialty food items; bread, cake & related products; frozen specialties
PA: Cole's Quality Foods, Inc.
  38 Commerce Ave Sw # 400
  Grand Rapids MI 49503
  231 722-1651

(G-11296)
COLUMBUS MCKINNON CORPORATION
Also Called: Budgit Hoists
414 W Broadway Ave (49444)
PHONE.................................800 955-5541
Pam Goven, *Branch Mgr*
EMP: 5
SALES (corp-wide): 876.2MM **Publicly Held**
WEB: www.cmworks.com
SIC: 3496 3535 3537 Chain, welded; conveyor belts; conveyors & conveying equipment; tables, lift: hydraulic
PA: Columbus Mckinnon Corporation
  205 Crosspoint Pkwy
  Getzville NY 14068
  716 689-5400

(G-11297)
COMBAT ADVANCED PROPULSION LLC
76 S Getty St (49442-1242)
PHONE.................................231 724-2100
Micheal Saunders, *Mng Member*
▲ **EMP:** 3
SALES (est): 446.5K **Privately Held**
SIC: 3519 Internal combustion engines

(G-11298)
COMPACT ENGINEERING CORP
4512 Iris Ct (49442-1768)
PHONE.................................231 788-5470
Larry Terwilliger, *President*
Rick Van Heukelom, *Vice Pres*
EMP: 12
SALES (est): 1.1MM **Privately Held**
WEB: www.compactstoragesystems.com
SIC: 3448 2542 2522 Prefabricated metal buildings; partitions & fixtures, except wood; office furniture, except wood

(G-11299)
COMPETITIVE EDGE WOOD SPC INC
711 E Savidge Spring Mi 4 (49441)
PHONE.................................616 842-1063
EMP: 60

GEOGRAPHIC SECTION

Muskegon - Muskegon County (G-11328)

SQ FT: 20,000
SALES (est): 5.5MM **Privately Held**
SIC: **2541** Wood Partitions And Fixtures

(G-11300)
CONSUMERS CONCRETE CORPORATION
4450 Evanston Ave (49442-6525)
PHONE..................231 777-3981
Dick Woodward, *Accounts Mgr*
Mike Gerose, *Exec Dir*
EMP: 15
SALES (corp-wide): 102.9MM **Privately Held**
WEB: www.consumersconcrete.com
SIC: **3273** 3271 5032 Ready-mixed concrete; blocks, concrete or cinder: standard; gravel; sand, construction
PA: Consumers Concrete Corporation
3508 S Sprinkle Rd
Kalamazoo MI 49001
269 342-0136

(G-11301)
COUNTY OF MUSKEGON
Also Called: Drain Commissioner
141 E Apple Ave (49442-3404)
PHONE..................231 724-6219
David Fisher, *Commissioner*
EMP: 3
SQ FT: 1,344 **Privately Held**
WEB: www.visit-muskegon.org
SIC: **1629** 2842 Drainage system construction; drain pipe solvents or cleaners
PA: County Of Muskegon
990 Terrace St
Muskegon MI 49442
231 724-6520

(G-11302)
COUNTY OF MUSKEGON
Also Called: Muskegon Pioneer County Park
1563 Scenic Dr (49445-9612)
PHONE..................231 744-3580
Jim Wood, *Superintendent*
EMP: 18 **Privately Held**
WEB: www.visit-muskegon.org
SIC: **3792** Camping trailers & chassis
PA: County Of Muskegon
990 Terrace St
Muskegon MI 49442
231 724-6520

(G-11303)
CUSTOM SERVICE PRINTERS INC
916 E Keating Ave (49442-5953)
PHONE..................231 726-3297
Stephen Kamp, *President*
Gregory Kamp, *Vice Pres*
Joseph Rupar, *Vice Pres*
EMP: 12 EST: 1960
SQ FT: 17,500
SALES: 2.2MM **Privately Held**
WEB: www.csp-inc.com
SIC: **2752** Commercial printing, offset

(G-11304)
D & J MFG & MACHINING
507 W Hovey Ave (49444-1361)
PHONE..................231 830-9522
Joann Perley, *Owner*
EMP: 5
SALES (est): 485.4K **Privately Held**
SIC: **3599** Machine shop, jobbing & repair

(G-11305)
DENTAL IMPRESSIONS
1915 Holton Rd (49445-1533)
PHONE..................231 719-0033
S Dadd, *Principal*
EMP: 4
SALES (est): 614.8K **Privately Held**
SIC: **3843** Enamels, dentists'

(G-11306)
DOBB PRINTING INC
2431 Harvey St (49442-6104)
PHONE..................231 722-1060
Michael L Dobb, *Owner*
Joe Dobb, *Vice Pres*
Kristi Monette, *Office Mgr*
EMP: 21
SQ FT: 22,000
SALES (est): 3.9MM **Privately Held**
SIC: **2752** 2789 2759 Commercial printing, offset; letters, circular or form: lithographed; bookbinding & related work; commercial printing

(G-11307)
DSC LABORATORIES INC
1979 Latimer Dr (49442-6229)
PHONE..................800 492-5988
Edward Kling, *President*
▲ EMP: 40 EST: 1969
SALES (est): 14.6MM **Privately Held**
WEB: www.dsclab.com
SIC: **2842** 2834 2841 Cleaning or polishing preparations; automobile polish; pharmaceutical preparations; soap & other detergents

(G-11308)
DYNAMIC FINISHING LLC
823 W Western Ave Ste B (49441-1795)
PHONE..................231 727-8811
Steven Sanson,
EMP: 3 **Privately Held**
SIC: **3471** Plating of metals or formed products
PA: Dynamic Finishing Llc
69 S 2nd Ave
Fruitport MI 49415

(G-11309)
EAGLE ALUMINUM CAST PDTS INC
664 W Clay Ave (49440-1035)
PHONE..................231 788-4884
Mark Fazakerley, *President*
EMP: 8
SALES (corp-wide): 4.3MM **Privately Held**
SIC: **3365** Aluminum & aluminum-based alloy castings
PA: Eagle Aluminum Cast Products Inc
2134 Northwoods Ave
Muskegon MI 49442
231 788-4884

(G-11310)
EAGLE PRECISION CAST PARTS INC
5112 Evanston Ave (49442-4852)
PHONE..................231 788-3318
Mark Fazakerley, *President*
John Workman, *Vice Pres*
Dean Buikema, *Accountant*
Rob Kriger, *Technician*
EMP: 42
SQ FT: 37,500
SALES: 6.5MM **Privately Held**
WEB: www.eaglegroupmanufacturers.com
SIC: **3324** Steel investment foundries

(G-11311)
EAGLE T M C TECHNOLOGIES
Also Called: Eagle Cnc Technology
2357 Whitehall Rd (49445-1043)
PHONE..................231 766-3914
Mark Fazakerley, *President*
John Workman, *Vice Pres*
Dena Buikema,
EMP: 15
SQ FT: 12,000
SALES (est): 1.1MM **Privately Held**
SIC: **3599** Machine shop, jobbing & repair

(G-11312)
EARLE PRESS INC
Also Called: Earle Press Printing
2140 Latimer Dr (49442-6234)
P.O. Box 327 (49443-0327)
PHONE..................231 773-2111
Jerry M Grevel, *President*
Wes Pearcy, *Exec VP*
Whitney Eckert, *CFO*
Amy Grevel, *Manager*
EMP: 32 EST: 1920
SQ FT: 24,000
SALES (est): 4.7MM **Privately Held**
WEB: www.earlepress.com
SIC: **2752** 5112 2791 2789 Commercial printing, offset; business forms; typesetting; bookbinding & related work; manifold business forms; commercial printing

(G-11313)
EAST MUSKEGON ROOFG SHTMTL CO (PA)
Also Called: CERTIFIED SHEET METAL
1665 Holton Rd (49445-1450)
PHONE..................231 744-2461
Gregory R Kanaar, *President*
Joseph Kastl, *General Mgr*
Jesse Adkins, *Superintendent*
Matthew N Bradley, *Project Mgr*
Matthew D Brink, *Project Mgr*
EMP: 85
SALES: 16.4MM **Privately Held**
SIC: **1761** 3444 Sheet metalwork; roofing contractor; sheet metalwork

(G-11314)
EAST RIVER MACHINE & TOOL INC
1701 Wierengo Dr (49442-6257)
PHONE..................231 767-1701
Dan Wemsumius, *President*
Les Furst, *Vice Pres*
Tim Huizenga, *Vice Pres*
EMP: 9
SQ FT: 4,900
SALES: 700K **Privately Held**
SIC: **3544** Special dies & tools

(G-11315)
ECO BRUSHES AND FIBERS
Also Called: Eco Brushes and Fibers S.A.s
2658 Heights Ravenna Rd (49444-3430)
P.O. Box 193 (49443-0193)
PHONE..................231 683-9202
Virginia Tawney, *Owner*
EMP: 4 EST: 2014
SALES (est): 164.9K **Privately Held**
SIC: **3991** 7389 Street sweeping brooms, hand or machine;

(G-11316)
EMC WELDING & FABRICATION INC
4966 Evanston Ave (49442-4828)
PHONE..................231 788-4172
Jerry Locke, *Mng Member*
EMP: 8
SQ FT: 5,700
SALES (est): 1.3MM **Privately Held**
SIC: **3441** Fabricated structural metal

(G-11317)
EMERGENCY SERVICES LLC
Also Called: Great Lakes Coach
1660 Dodson Dr (49442-6604)
PHONE..................231 727-7400
Robert George, *Principal*
Dean Hull,
EMP: 4
SALES (est): 1.3MM **Privately Held**
SIC: **7538** 3714 General automotive repair shops; motor vehicle transmissions, drive assemblies & parts

(G-11318)
EXCELL MACHINE & TOOL CO LLC
1084 E Hackley Ave (49444-1887)
PHONE..................231 728-1210
Joe Wood, *Mng Member*
EMP: 8
SQ FT: 1,500
SALES: 800K **Privately Held**
SIC: **3544** Special dies & tools; jigs & fixtures

(G-11319)
FABJUNKY LLC
1908 Euro Dr (49444-4567)
PHONE..................323 572-4988
Tiffannie Porter, *Mng Member*
EMP: 3
SALES (est): 113.3K **Privately Held**
SIC: **2389** 5961 Apparel & accessories;

(G-11320)
FAIRWAY OPTICAL INC
4490 W Giles Rd (49445-9690)
PHONE..................231 744-6168
Gerald Prince, *President*
EMP: 4
SALES: 300K **Privately Held**
SIC: **3851** 5049 Lenses, ophthalmic; optical goods

(G-11321)
FEB INC
Also Called: Muskegon Awning & Fabrication
2333 Henry St (49441-3019)
PHONE..................231 759-0911
David Bayne, *President*
EMP: 12 EST: 2005
SALES (est): 1.1MM **Privately Held**
SIC: **2394** Awnings, fabric: made from purchased materials

(G-11322)
FINEEYE COLOR SOLUTIONS INC
1218 Tall Tree Ln (49445-1265)
PHONE..................616 988-6119
Stephen A Macdonald, *CEO*
Peder W Nelson, *President*
Dawn Nelson, *Sales Staff*
Michael Dicosola, *Admin Sec*
▲ EMP: 4
SQ FT: 2,500
SALES (est): 1.2MM **Privately Held**
WEB: Www.chromaticity.com
SIC: **2679** Paper products, converted

(G-11323)
FIVE PEAKS TECHNOLOGY LLC
700 Terrace Point Dr # 200 (49440-1166)
PHONE..................231 830-8099
Reg Adams, *Mng Member*
Dave Harris, *Admin Sec*
◆ EMP: 26
SALES (est): 3.4MM **Privately Held**
SIC: **3089** Toilets, portable chemical: plastic

(G-11324)
FLEET ENGINEERS INC (PA)
1800 E Keating Ave (49442-6189)
PHONE..................231 777-2537
Wesley Eklund, *President*
Kevin Allman, *Business Mgr*
Ray Steinhauer, *Purch Agent*
Jennifer Schucker, *Buyer*
Bruce Medema, *QC Mgr*
▲ EMP: 122 EST: 1963
SQ FT: 240,000
SALES (est): 18.6MM **Privately Held**
WEB: www.fleetengineers.com
SIC: **3714** Motor vehicle parts & accessories

(G-11325)
FOMCORE LLC
1360 E Laketon Ave (49442-6026)
PHONE..................231 366-4791
Jeffery Zack,
Jeremy Leffring,
EMP: 80 EST: 2016
SALES (est): 11.9MM **Privately Held**
SIC: **3086** Plastics foam products

(G-11326)
FORMING TECHNOLOGIES LLC
1885 E Laketon Ave (49442-6123)
P.O. Box 2246, Brighton (48116-6046)
PHONE..................231 777-7030
David M Hembree, *Mng Member*
Dean W Miller,
Bryan B Ward,
EMP: 60
SQ FT: 25,000
SALES (est): 10.7MM **Privately Held**
WEB: www.formingtechnologies.com
SIC: **3089** Thermoformed finished plastic products

(G-11327)
FREEDOM TOOL & MFG CO
Also Called: Tool and Die
1741 S Wolf Lake Rd (49442-4879)
PHONE..................231 788-2898
Carl Barber, *President*
Cynthia Barber, *Admin Sec*
EMP: 7
SQ FT: 4,800
SALES: 700K **Privately Held**
SIC: **3544** Special dies & tools

(G-11328)
FROSTY COVE
2133 Lakeshore Dr (49441-1413)
PHONE..................231 343-6643
Marcia Dula, *Principal*

Muskegon - Muskegon County (G-11329)

EMP: 5 EST: 2010
SALES (est): 285.4K **Privately Held**
SIC: 2024 Ice cream, bulk

(G-11329)
GEERPRES INC
1780 Harvey St (49442-5396)
P.O. Box 658 (49443-0658)
PHONE..................................231 773-3211
Scott E Ribbe, *President*
Sam Waites, *Vice Pres*
Bryan Depree, *CFO*
Bryan De Pree, *Manager*
▲ EMP: 20
SQ FT: 85,000
SALES (est): 5.2MM **Privately Held**
WEB: www.geerpres.com
SIC: 3444 3589 3412 Sheet metalwork; commercial cleaning equipment; mop wringers; janitors' carts; metal barrels, drums & pails

(G-11330)
GLASSICART DECORATIVE GLWR
3128 7th St (49444-2834)
PHONE..................................231 739-5956
Michael Stapleton, *Owner*
EMP: 5
SALES (est): 263.6K **Privately Held**
SIC: 3229 Art, decorative & novelty glassware

(G-11331)
GMI COMPOSITES INC
1355 W Sherman Blvd (49441-3538)
PHONE..................................231 755-1611
Bob Brady, *President*
Charles Brady, *Principal*
Louis Simoncini, *Principal*
Jerry Dykstra, *Corp Secy*
▲ EMP: 62 EST: 1920
SALES (est): 21.6MM **Privately Held**
WEB: www.gmicomposites.com
SIC: 3089 Molding primary plastic

(G-11332)
GRAND RAPIDS GRAVEL COMPANY
Also Called: Port City Redi-Mix Co
1780 S Sheridan Dr (49442-4404)
P.O. Box 9160, Wyoming (49509-0160)
PHONE..................................231 777-2777
Tom Williams, *Manager*
EMP: 20
SALES (corp-wide): 26.5MM **Privately Held**
WEB: www.grgravel.com
SIC: 3273 Ready-mixed concrete
PA: Grand Rapids Gravel Company
2700 28th St Sw
Grand Rapids MI 49519
616 538-9000

(G-11333)
GRAPHICS HOUSE PUBLISHING
Also Called: Graphics House Printing
2632 Peck St (49444-2028)
PHONE..................................231 739-4004
Daniel Mc Kinnon, *President*
EMP: 20
SALES (est): 3.6MM **Privately Held**
SIC: 2752 Commercial printing, offset

(G-11334)
GRAPHICS HSE SPT PRMOTIONS INC (PA)
Also Called: Gh Imaging
444 Irwin Ave (49442-5009)
PHONE..................................231 739-4004
Brent McKinnon, *President*
Dan McKinnon, *CFO*
Steve Bolthouse, *Sales Staff*
Greg Petrongelli, *Sales Staff*
EMP: 43
SALES (est): 9.1MM **Privately Held**
WEB: www.graphicshouse.net
SIC: 2711 2721 2741 Newspapers; magazines: publishing only, not printed on site; miscellaneous publishing

(G-11335)
GRAPHICS HSE SPT PRMOTIONS INC
United Sign Co.
444 Irwin Ave (49442-5009)
PHONE..................................231 733-1877
Brent McKinnon, *President*
EMP: 20
SALES (corp-wide): 9.1MM **Privately Held**
SIC: 3993 Signs & advertising specialties
PA: Graphics House Sports Promotions, Inc.
444 Irwin Ave
Muskegon MI 49442
231 739-4004

(G-11336)
GRAPHICS UNLIMITED INC
2304 Olthoff St (49444-2646)
PHONE..................................231 773-2696
Wayne Kamp, *President*
EMP: 5
SQ FT: 4,000
SALES (est): 695.3K **Privately Held**
WEB: www.trafficgraffix.com
SIC: 2791 2752 5699 7336 Typesetting; commercial printing, lithographic; T-shirts, custom printed; graphic arts & related design

(G-11337)
GREAT LAKES DIE CAST CORP (PA)
701 W Laketon Ave (49441-2925)
PHONE..................................231 726-4002
Con J Nolan, *President*
Bob Johnson, *President*
▲ EMP: 62 EST: 2002
SQ FT: 105,000
SALES (est): 31.6MM **Privately Held**
WEB: www.gldiecast.com
SIC: 3363 3089 Aluminum die-castings; injection molded finished plastic products

(G-11338)
GREAT LAKES FINISHING INC
510 W Hackley Ave (49444-1046)
PHONE..................................231 733-9566
Diana Bench, *CEO*
Bruce Vollmer, *Plant Mgr*
EMP: 13
SALES (est): 1.7MM **Privately Held**
SIC: 3471 Electroplating of metals or formed products

(G-11339)
GREAT LAKES NURSERY SOILS INC
680 S Maple Island Rd (49442-9407)
PHONE..................................231 788-3123
Fax: 231 788-2770
EMP: 10
SALES (est): 1.6MM **Privately Held**
SIC: 2875 Mfg Fertilizers-Mix Only

(G-11340)
GRIFFON INC
820 S Broton Rd (49442-9488)
P.O. Box 1403 (49443-1403)
PHONE..................................231 788-4630
Craig A Zimmer, *President*
Lorraine Zimmer, *Vice Pres*
▼ EMP: 15
SQ FT: 10,000
SALES (est): 2.1MM **Privately Held**
WEB: www.griffoncompanies.com
SIC: 3993 Signs, not made in custom sign painting shops; letters for signs, metal

(G-11341)
GROSS VENTURES INC
Also Called: Iroquois Hoods
2176 E Laketon Ave (49442-6224)
PHONE..................................231 767-1301
Mike Gross, *President*
EMP: 5 EST: 1964
SQ FT: 20,000
SALES (est): 940.6K **Privately Held**
WEB: www.iroquoishoods.com
SIC: 3821 Laboratory equipment: fume hoods, distillation racks, etc.

(G-11342)
HACKLEY HEALTH VENTURES INC (DH)
Also Called: Hackley Hearing Center
1675 Leahy St Ste 101 (49442-5538)
PHONE..................................231 728-5720
Richard Witham, *Ch of Bd*
Robert Hovey, *Vice Ch Bd*
Michael T Baker, *President*
David Gingras, *Corp Secy*
EMP: 5
SQ FT: 1,000
SALES: 575K
SALES (corp-wide): 18.3B **Privately Held**
SIC: 8741 5912 3842 8011 Hospital management; nursing & personal care facility management; drug stores; prosthetic appliances; health maintenance organization; rehabilitation center, outpatient treatment; occupational therapist
HQ: Mercy Health Partners
1675 Leahy St Ste 101
Muskegon MI 49442
231 728-4032

(G-11343)
HARBORFRONT INTERIORS INC
2300 Black Creek Rd (49444-2672)
PHONE..................................231 777-3838
David Rikkers, *President*
James Duncan, *President*
Ruth Duncan, *Treasurer*
Anette Buchholz, *Manager*
Dave Carpenter, *Manager*
EMP: 13
SQ FT: 12,000
SALES (est): 2.4MM **Privately Held**
WEB: www.harborfront.com
SIC: 8711 2599 Designing: ship, boat, machine & product; restaurant furniture, wood or metal

(G-11344)
HERALD NEWSPAPERS COMPANY INC
Also Called: Muskegon Chronicle
379 W Western Ave Ste 100 (49440-1265)
PHONE..................................231 722-3161
Gary Ostrom, *Principal*
EMP: 100
SALES (corp-wide): 5.5B **Privately Held**
WEB: www.post-standard.com
SIC: 2711 Newspapers, publishing & printing
HQ: The Herald Newspapers Company Inc
220 S Warren St
Syracuse NY 13202
315 470-0011

(G-11345)
HY LIFT JOHNSON INC
1185 E Keating Ave (49442-6018)
PHONE..................................231 722-1100
David Pop, *General Mgr*
Dave Popp, *General Mgr*
▲ EMP: 3
SALES (est): 344.6K **Privately Held**
SIC: 3462 Automotive & internal combustion engine forgings

(G-11346)
IED INC
1938 Sanford St (49441-2517)
PHONE..................................231 728-9154
L Scott McNeill, *President*
EMP: 6
SQ FT: 14,000
SALES (est): 1MM **Privately Held**
SIC: 3559 5084 Metal finishing equipment for plating, etc.; metal refining machinery & equipment

(G-11347)
INDUSTRIAL TOOLING TECH INC
3253 Whitehall Rd (49445-1061)
PHONE..................................231 766-2155
Jim Sweet, *Principal*
▲ EMP: 13 EST: 1970
SALES (est): 1.3MM **Privately Held**
WEB: www.ittgage.com
SIC: 3544 Special dies & tools

(G-11348)
INNOVATIVE SHEET METALS
1681 S Wolf Lake Rd (49442-4839)
PHONE..................................231 788-5751
Andrew Stevens, *Principal*
EMP: 4
SALES (est): 644K **Privately Held**
SIC: 3444 Sheet metalwork

(G-11349)
INTEGRATED CONVEYOR LTD
301 W Laketon Ave (49441-2629)
PHONE..................................231 747-6430
Dick Perri, *President*
Joe Garzolonie, *Manager*
EMP: 4
SALES (est): 550K **Privately Held**
SIC: 3535 5084 Conveyors & conveying equipment; industrial machinery & equipment

(G-11350)
ITT GAGE INC
3253 Whitehall Rd (49445-1061)
PHONE..................................231 766-2155
EMP: 5
SALES (est): 733K **Privately Held**
SIC: 3544 Special dies & tools

(G-11351)
J & J MACHINE LTD
3011 S Milliron Rd (49444-3689)
PHONE..................................231 773-4100
Joseph Hammerle, *President*
John Hammerle, *Vice Pres*
EMP: 10
SQ FT: 3,300
SALES: 660K **Privately Held**
WEB: www.jjmachine99.com
SIC: 3599 Machine shop, jobbing & repair; machine & other job shop work

(G-11352)
JBS SHEET METAL INC
2226 S Getty St (49444-1208)
PHONE..................................231 777-2802
Steven Six, *President*
Bryan Six, *Vice Pres*
EMP: 4
SALES (est): 480.1K **Privately Held**
SIC: 3444 Ducts, sheet metal

(G-11353)
JET FUEL
Also Called: Muskegon Gas and Fuel
2177 S Mill Iron Rd (49442-6445)
PHONE..................................231 767-9566
M Athar, *Manager*
EMP: 9 EST: 2010
SALES (est): 1.1MM **Privately Held**
SIC: 2911 Jet fuels

(G-11354)
JOHNSON TECHNOLOGY INC (DH)
Also Called: GE Aviation Muskegon
2034 Latimer Dr (49442-6232)
PHONE..................................231 777-2685
Kevin Prindable, *President*
Robert McFalls, *Engineer*
Stephanie Niezurawski, *Engineer*
Bill Miller, *Project Engr*
Rhonda Boyd, *Director*
▲ EMP: 345
SQ FT: 101,000
SALES (est): 224.2MM
SALES (corp-wide): 121.6B **Publicly Held**
SIC: 3724 Turbines, aircraft type
HQ: Ge Aircraft Engines Holdings, Inc.
1 Neumann Way
Cincinnati OH 45215
888 999-5103

(G-11355)
JOLMAN & JOLMAN ENTERPRISES
1384 Linden Dr (49445-2524)
PHONE..................................231 744-4500
Daniel Jolman, *Owner*
EMP: 6 EST: 2008
SALES: 50K **Privately Held**
SIC: 0782 3531 4971 Lawn care services; snow plow attachments; irrigation systems

GEOGRAPHIC SECTION

Muskegon - Muskegon County (G-11381)

(G-11356)
JONES ELECTRIC COMPANY
1965 Sanford St (49441-2516)
P.O. Box 785 (49443-0785)
PHONE..................................231 726-5001
Rodney Dobb, *President*
EMP: 12
SQ FT: 9,000
SALES (est): 1.8MM **Privately Held**
SIC: 7694 7629 Electric motor repair; electrical repair shops

(G-11357)
KAUTEX INC
CWC Textron
1085 W Sherman Blvd (49441-3500)
PHONE..................................231 739-2704
Jim Heethuis, *Branch Mgr*
EMP: 275
SALES (corp-wide): 13.9B **Publicly Held**
WEB: www.textronautotrim.com
SIC: 3714 Camshafts, motor vehicle
HQ: Kautex Inc.
 750 Stephenson Hwy # 200
 Troy MI 48083
 248 616-5100

(G-11358)
KRAUSE WELDING INC
4350 Evanston Ave (49442-6523)
PHONE..................................231 773-4443
Brian Krause, *CEO*
Berl W Krause, *President*
David K Krause, *Vice Pres*
Cheryl K Krause, *Treasurer*
EMP: 10
SQ FT: 8,000
SALES (est): 1.1MM **Privately Held**
SIC: 7692 Automotive welding

(G-11359)
L & L PATTERN INC
2401 Park St (49444-1393)
PHONE..................................231 733-2646
Robert C Oosting, *President*
William K Oosting, *Corp Secy*
EMP: 8
SQ FT: 4,000
SALES (est): 500K **Privately Held**
SIC: 3543 3599 3366 Industrial patterns; machine & other job shop work; castings (except die)

(G-11360)
L & P LLC
Also Called: Fun Foods
2376 Dels Dr (49444-2676)
PHONE..................................231 733-1415
Lisa Kordecki,
Patti Derouin,
EMP: 14
SQ FT: 3,800
SALES (est): 541.7K **Privately Held**
SIC: 5199 2099 General merchandise, non-durable; ready-to-eat meals, salads & sandwiches; pizza, refrigerated: except frozen

(G-11361)
L3 TECHNOLOGIES INC
Also Called: L-3 Combat Propulsion Systems
76 S Getty St (49442-1242)
PHONE..................................231 724-2151
Michael Soimar, *President*
EMP: 999
SALES (corp-wide): 6.8B **Publicly Held**
SIC: 3663 Radio & TV communications equipment
HQ: L3 Technologies, Inc.
 600 3rd Ave Fl 34
 New York NY 10016
 212 697-1111

(G-11362)
LAFARGE NORTH AMERICA INC
1047 7th St (49441-1604)
PHONE..................................231 726-3291
William Conwill, *Manager*
David Matuzeski, *Manager*
EMP: 5
SALES (corp-wide): 27.6B **Privately Held**
WEB: www.lafargenorthamerica.com
SIC: 3273 Ready-mixed concrete
HQ: Lafarge North America Inc.
 8700 W Bryn Mawr Ave
 Chicago IL 60631
 773 372-1000

(G-11363)
LAKESIDE CANVAS & UPHOLSTERY
3200 Lakeshore Dr (49441-1292)
PHONE..................................231 755-2514
Joe Vanlente, *President*
Elizabeth Vanlente, *Vice Pres*
EMP: 4
SALES: 170K **Privately Held**
SIC: 7532 2394 Top & body repair & paint shops; canvas & related products

(G-11364)
LAKESIDE SPRING PRODUCTS INC
2615 Temple St (49444-1937)
PHONE..................................616 847-2706
Samuel Lowry, *President*
EMP: 3
SALES: 2MM **Privately Held**
SIC: 3495 Wire springs

(G-11365)
LEE INDUSTRIES INC
1800 E Keating Ave (49442-6121)
PHONE..................................231 777-2537
Wesley K Eklund, *President*
Bob Durso, *Engineer*
Mike McAlister, *Manager*
Robert Eklund, *Admin Sec*
EMP: 21
SQ FT: 10,000
SALES (est): 2.3MM **Privately Held**
SIC: 3714 3471 2789 1031 Trailer hitches, motor vehicle; plating & polishing; bookbinding & related work; lead & zinc ores

(G-11366)
LORENZ PROPELLERS & ENGRG CO
600 W Southern Ave (49441-2300)
PHONE..................................231 728-3245
Eldon Lorenz, *Ch of Bd*
Jack Lorenz, *President*
EMP: 8
SQ FT: 60,000
SALES (est): 800.7K **Privately Held**
SIC: 3599 Propellers, ship & boat: machined

(G-11367)
LORIN INDUSTRIES INC (PA)
Also Called: Coil Anodizing
1960 Roberts St (49442-6087)
PHONE..................................231 722-1631
Park Kersman, *CEO*
Robert L Kersman, *Ch of Bd*
L Philip Kelly, *Corp Secy*
John Montague, *Vice Pres*
Clinton Rollins, *Purch Mgr*
◆ **EMP:** 90 EST: 1943
SQ FT: 300,000
SALES (est): 35.8MM **Privately Held**
WEB: www.lorin.com
SIC: 3471 Anodizing (plating) of metals or formed products

(G-11368)
LOUIS PADNOS IRON AND METAL CO
259 Ottawa St (49441-1008)
PHONE..................................231 722-6081
EMP: 16
SALES (corp-wide): 520.8MM **Privately Held**
SIC: 4491 3599 5093 Waterfront terminal operation; machine shop, jobbing & repair; metal scrap & waste materials
PA: Louis Padnos Iron And Metal Company
 185 W 8th St
 Holland MI 49423
 616 396-6521

(G-11369)
LUMBERTOWN PORTABLE SAWMILL
1650 Madison St (49442-5945)
PHONE..................................231 206-4600
EMP: 3 EST: 2011

SALES (est): 289.1K **Privately Held**
SIC: 3559 Kilns

(G-11370)
M & N MACHINE LLC
755 Access Hwy (49442-1236)
PHONE..................................231 722-7085
Kenneth Anderson, *Mng Member*
EMP: 3
SQ FT: 70,000
SALES: 600K **Privately Held**
SIC: 3451 Screw machine products

(G-11371)
M 37 CONCRETE PRODUCTS INC (PA)
Also Called: High Grade Concrete Pdts Co
767 E Sherman Blvd (49442-2254)
PHONE..................................231 733-8247
Thomas J Sturrus, *President*
EMP: 50
SQ FT: 5,000
SALES (est): 6.9MM **Privately Held**
SIC: 3273 Ready-mixed concrete

(G-11372)
MAHLE INDUSTRIES INCORPORATED
2020 Sanford St (49444-1000)
PHONE..................................231 722-1300
Sue Rynberg, *General Mgr*
Joe Hamelink, *Chief Engr*
Thomas Dunning, *Engineer*
Steve Joneson, *Engineer*
Eric Passow, *Engineer*
EMP: 120
SALES (corp-wide): 504.6K **Privately Held**
WEB: www.glacier-vandervell.com
SIC: 3714 Bearings, motor vehicle
HQ: Mahle Industries, Incorporated
 23030 Mahle Dr
 Farmington Hills MI 48335
 248 305-8200

(G-11373)
MERCY HEALTH PARTNERS (DH)
1675 Leahy St Ste 101 (49442-5538)
PHONE..................................231 728-4032
Richard C Lague, *Ch of Bd*
Gordon A Mudler, *President*
David Gingras, *Vice Pres*
H Richard Morgenstern, *Treasurer*
Mandy McCarl, *Executive Asst*
EMP: 85
SQ FT: 100,000
SALES: 666MM
SALES (corp-wide): 18.3B **Privately Held**
SIC: 8741 6512 3812 Hospital management; nursing & personal care facility management; nonresidential building operators; compasses & accessories
HQ: Trinity Health-Michigan
 20555 Victor Pkwy
 Livonia MI 48152
 810 985-1500

(G-11374)
MERCY HEALTH PARTNERS
Also Called: Orthotics and Prosthetics
1560 E Sherman Blvd # 145 (49444-1850)
PHONE..................................231 672-4886
Gary Allore, *CFO*
Megan Hudson, *Consultant*
EMP: 9
SALES (corp-wide): 18.3B **Privately Held**
SIC: 3842 Surgical appliances & supplies
HQ: Mercy Health Partners
 1675 Leahy St Ste 101
 Muskegon MI 49442
 231 728-4032

(G-11375)
METAL ARC INC
3792 E Ellis Rd (49444-8764)
PHONE..................................231 865-3111
Ray Gerdes, *President*
Denise Karel, *Office Mgr*
Shannon Conaty, *Manager*
Gregory Gerdes, *Admin Sec*
▲ **EMP:** 28
SQ FT: 47,000

###
SALES (est): 6.2MM **Privately Held**
WEB: www.metalarc.com
SIC: 3599 3821 2522 Machine & other job shop work; laboratory furniture; office furniture, except wood

(G-11376)
METAL FINISHING TECHNOLOGY
2652 Hoyt St (49444-2142)
PHONE..................................231 733-9736
David Bernd, *President*
EMP: 5
SALES (est): 458.7K **Privately Held**
SIC: 3479 3471 Coating of metals & formed products; plating & polishing

(G-11377)
METAL-LINE CORP
Also Called: Versatile Manufacturing
2708 9th St (49441-1945)
PHONE..................................231 723-7041
Joe Balaskovitz, *President*
Brian Fauble, *Principal*
Dan Balaskovitz, *Corp Secy*
Jennifer Larsen, *Office Mgr*
EMP: 25
SQ FT: 21,000
SALES (est): 4MM **Privately Held**
WEB: www.metallinecorp.com
SIC: 3599 7694 7692 3541 Machine shop, jobbing & repair; rewinding services; electric motor repair; welding repair; machine tools, metal cutting type; boring mills

(G-11378)
MICHIGAN INDUS MET PDTS INC
1674 S Getty St (49442-5857)
PHONE..................................616 786-3922
Maryann Griffin, *President*
John J Griffin, *General Mgr*
EMP: 30
SALES (est): 5.3MM **Privately Held**
SIC: 3441 1542 Fabricated structural metal; nonresidential construction

(G-11379)
MICHIGAN SPRING & STAMPING LLC (HQ)
2700 Wickham Dr (49441-3532)
PHONE..................................231 755-1691
Bir Singh, *President*
Dan Wallington, *President*
Jeff Stewart, *Business Mgr*
Paul Vanderlaan, *VP Opers*
Dick Carter, *Engineer*
▲ **EMP:** 110
SALES (est): 27.7MM
SALES (corp-wide): 204.2MM **Privately Held**
SIC: 3495 Mechanical springs, precision
PA: Hines Corporation
 1218 E Pontaluna Rd Ste B
 Norton Shores MI 49456
 231 799-6240

(G-11380)
MID-WEST SPRING & STAMPING INC
1935 E Laketon Ave (49442-6125)
PHONE..................................231 777-2707
Jeff Kamp, *General Mgr*
Chuck Mann, *Manager*
EMP: 42
SQ FT: 50,000
SALES (corp-wide): 17.6MM **Privately Held**
WEB: www.mwspring.com
SIC: 3495 3496 3493 Wire springs; miscellaneous fabricated wire products; steel springs, except wire
HQ: Spring Mid-West And Stamping Inc
 1404 N Joliet Rd Ste C
 Romeoville IL 60446
 630 739-3800

(G-11381)
MIDWEST PRODUCT SPC INC
2190 Aurora Dr (49442-6295)
PHONE..................................231 767-9942
Michael Snyder, *President*
Michone E Snyder, *Vice Pres*
▲ **EMP:** 6

(PA)=Parent Co (HQ)=Headquarters (DH)=Div Headquarters
✪ = New Business established in last 2 years

Muskegon - Muskegon County (G-11382)

SALES (est): 759.4K **Privately Held**
SIC: 3297 Nonclay refractories

(G-11382)
MOBILE HAULAWAY LLC
4365 Evanston Ave (49442-6522)
PHONE.................................616 402-7878
Jerry McDowell, *Branch Mgr*
EMP: 3
SALES (corp-wide): 993.1K **Privately Held**
SIC: 3713 Dump truck bodies
PA: Mobile Haulaway Llc
1972 Miner Ave
Muskegon MI 49441
616 402-4589

(G-11383)
MODERN AGE PATTERN MFG INC
7265 Hall Rd (49442-9408)
PHONE.................................231 788-1222
EMP: 8
SQ FT: 9,004
SALES: 800K **Privately Held**
SIC: 3543 Industrial patterns

(G-11384)
MONARCH WELDING & ENGRG INC
519 W Hackley Ave (49444-1045)
PHONE.................................231 733-7222
Johan Bartels, *Branch Mgr*
EMP: 14
SALES (corp-wide): 13.7MM **Privately Held**
SIC: 1711 7692 3444 Mechanical contractor; boiler & furnace contractors; welding repair; sheet metalwork
PA: Monarch Welding & Engineering, Inc.
23635 Mound Rd
Warren MI 48091
586 754-5400

(G-11385)
MONROES CUSTOM CAMPERS INC
Also Called: Monroe Truck and Auto ACC
2915 E Apple Ave (49442-4503)
PHONE.................................231 773-0005
Nicholas Monroe, *President*
Michael Monroe, *Vice Pres*
EMP: 8
SQ FT: 20,000
SALES (est): 1.3MM **Privately Held**
WEB: www.monroecustom.com
SIC: 3792 5531 Campers, for mounting on trucks; pickup covers, canopies or caps; automotive & home supply stores

(G-11386)
MR AXLE
6336 E Apple Ave (49442-4974)
PHONE.................................231 788-4624
Mike Crowell, *Owner*
EMP: 11
SQ FT: 2,800
SALES (est): 1.3MM **Privately Held**
SIC: 3714 5531 5015 Axles, motor vehicle; automotive parts; automotive parts & supplies, used

(G-11387)
MUSKEGON AWNING & MFG CO
2333 Henry St (49441-3097)
PHONE.................................231 759-0911
David Bayne, *President*
Ruth Luker, *Corp Secy*
Gordon Moen, *Vice Pres*
Jeffrey Lindell, *Sales Staff*
EMP: 25 EST: 1898
SQ FT: 14,196
SALES (est): 3.2MM **Privately Held**
WEB: www.muskegonawning.com
SIC: 2394 3444 2591 Awnings, fabric: made from purchased materials; canvas covers & drop cloths; sheet metalwork; drapery hardware & blinds & shades

(G-11388)
MUSKEGON CASTINGS LLC
1985 E Laketon Ave (49442-6127)
PHONE.................................231 777-3941
John Essex, *CEO*
Mark Pickett, *President*
Dale Keyser, *CFO*
▲ EMP: 127
SQ FT: 36,500
SALES (est): 1MM
SALES (corp-wide): 101.3MM **Privately Held**
SIC: 3363 Aluminum die-castings
HQ: Port City Group, Inc.
1985 E Laketon Ave
Muskegon MI 49442
231 777-3941

(G-11389)
MUSKEGON INDUSTRIAL FINISHNG
2000 Sanford St (49444-1000)
PHONE.................................231 733-7663
EMP: 5
SALES (est): 436.3K **Privately Held**
SIC: 3471 Plating/Polishing Service

(G-11390)
MUSKEGON MONUMENT & STONE CO
Also Called: Designs In Stones
1396 Pine St (49442-3599)
PHONE.................................231 722-2730
James Bauer, *President*
EMP: 5 EST: 1901
SQ FT: 5,000
SALES: 300K **Privately Held**
SIC: 3281 5999 1743 Monuments, cut stone (not finishing or lettering only); stone, quarrying & processing of own stone products; monuments, finished to custom order; monuments & tombstones; terrazzo, tile, marble, mosaic work

(G-11391)
MUSKEGON TOOLS LLC
5142 Evanston Ave (49442-4852)
PHONE.................................231 788-4633
Mark Fazakerley,
Mike Coffey,
Wayne Jarvis,
John Workman,
EMP: 4
SALES: 250K **Privately Held**
SIC: 3423 Wrenches, hand tools

(G-11392)
OKTOBER LLC
1657 S Getty St Ste 17 (49442-5872)
PHONE.................................231 750-1998
Joshua Van Den Heuvel, *Mng Member*
Dennis Grumm,
Clint Leatrea,
▼ EMP: 9
SQ FT: 3,500
SALES: 1MM **Privately Held**
SIC: 3411 Aluminum cans

(G-11393)
ORION MACHINE INC
392 Irwin Ave (49442-5008)
PHONE.................................231 728-1229
George R Zukiewicz, *President*
EMP: 5
SQ FT: 10,800
SALES (est): 614.6K **Privately Held**
SIC: 3599 Machine shop, jobbing & repair

(G-11394)
PACE INDUSTRIES LLC
Also Called: Port City Die Cast
2121 Latimer Dr (49442-6233)
PHONE.................................231 777-3941
Mark Pickett, *President*
EMP: 57
SALES (corp-wide): 101.3MM **Privately Held**
SIC: 3363 Aluminum die-castings
HQ: Pace Industries, Llc
481 S Shiloh Dr
Fayetteville AR 72704
479 443-1455

(G-11395)
PACE INDUSTRIES LLC
Also Called: Port City Custom Plastics
1868 Port City Blvd (49442-6130)
PHONE.................................231 773-4491
EMP: 48
SALES (corp-wide): 101.3MM **Privately Held**
SIC: 3363 Aluminum die-castings
HQ: Pace Industries, Llc
481 S Shiloh Dr
Fayetteville AR 72704
479 443-1455

(G-11396)
PACE INDUSTRIES LLC
Port City Group
1985 E Laketon Ave (49442-6127)
PHONE.................................231 777-3941
John Essex, *Branch Mgr*
EMP: 530
SALES (corp-wide): 101.3MM **Privately Held**
SIC: 3542 3089 Die casting & extruding machines; casting of plastic
HQ: Pace Industries, Llc
481 S Shiloh Dr
Fayetteville AR 72704
479 443-1455

(G-11397)
PACE INDUSTRIES LLC
Also Called: Port City Metal Products
2350 Black Creek Rd (49444)
PHONE.................................231 777-5615
Mark Pickett, *President*
EMP: 10
SALES (corp-wide): 101.3MM **Privately Held**
SIC: 3544 Special dies, tools, jigs & fixtures
HQ: Pace Industries, Llc
481 S Shiloh Dr
Fayetteville AR 72704
479 443-1455

(G-11398)
PACIFIC STAMEX CLG SYSTEMS INC
2259 S Sheridan Dr (49442-6252)
PHONE.................................231 773-1330
Larry W Hines, *CEO*
Dave Nelson, *President*
Bob Friedman, *General Mgr*
Kip Kauffman, *Engineer*
Chelsea Houseman, *Marketing Mgr*
▲ EMP: 26 EST: 1953
SQ FT: 36,000
SALES: 7.3MM
SALES (corp-wide): 204.2MM **Privately Held**
WEB: www.pacificfloorcare.com
SIC: 3589 Floor washing & polishing machines, commercial
PA: Hines Corporation
1218 E Pontaluna Rd Ste B
Norton Shores MI 49456
231 799-6240

(G-11399)
PARK STREET MACHINE INC
2201 Park St (49444-1324)
PHONE.................................231 739-9165
Joel Kowalski, *President*
EMP: 25
SQ FT: 50,000
SALES: 2MM **Privately Held**
SIC: 3599 3544 Custom machinery; special dies, tools, jigs & fixtures

(G-11400)
PORT CITY GROUP INC (DH)
1985 E Laketon Ave (49442-6127)
PHONE.................................231 777-3941
B John Essex Jr, *President*
Mark Pickett, *COO*
Jim Hurley, *CFO*
Steve Lawrence, *Manager*
Paul Toppen, *Supervisor*
EMP: 15 EST: 2012
SQ FT: 520,000
SALES: 194.1MM
SALES (corp-wide): 101.3MM **Privately Held**
SIC: 3089 3542 Casting of plastic; die casting & extruding machines
HQ: Pace Industries, Llc
481 S Shiloh Dr
Fayetteville AR 72704
479 443-1455

(G-11401)
PORT CITY INDUSTRIAL FINISHING
1867 Huizenga St (49442-5900)
PHONE.................................231 726-4288
Eric G Fri, *President*
EMP: 75
SQ FT: 40,000
SALES (est): 7.9MM **Privately Held**
SIC: 3471 Finishing, metals or formed products

(G-11402)
PORT CITY PAINTS MFG INC
Also Called: Benjamin Moore Authorized Ret
1250 9th St (49440-1092)
PHONE.................................231 726-5911
Jerry Klinger, *President*
Roy Spencer, *Admin Sec*
EMP: 6
SQ FT: 20,000
SALES (est): 530.3K **Privately Held**
SIC: 5231 2851 Paint; paints: oil or alkyd vehicle or water thinned; varnishes

(G-11403)
PORT CY ARCHTCTRAL SIGNAGE LLC
2350 S Getty St (49444-1702)
PHONE.................................231 739-3463
Tim Mills, *Mng Member*
Murdock Mills,
▲ EMP: 6
SALES (est): 918K **Privately Held**
SIC: 3993 Signs, not made in custom sign painting shops

(G-11404)
PORTER STEEL & WELDING COMPANY
831 E Hovey Ave (49444-1794)
PHONE.................................231 733-4495
Robert L Smith, *President*
EMP: 10
SQ FT: 20,000
SALES (est): 1.4MM **Privately Held**
WEB: www.psw.net
SIC: 3449 7692 Custom roll formed products; welding repair

(G-11405)
PRAXAIR INC
363 Ottawa St (49442-1032)
PHONE.................................231 722-3773
EMP: 21 **Privately Held**
SIC: 2813 Industrial gases
HQ: Praxair, Inc.
10 Riverview Dr
Danbury CT 06810
203 837-2000

(G-11406)
PRECISION TOOL COMPANY INC
2839 Henry St (49441-4011)
PHONE.................................231 733-0811
David A Reck, *President*
Franklin Zadonick, *Vice Pres*
EMP: 25 EST: 1942
SQ FT: 12,200
SALES (est): 1.8MM **Privately Held**
SIC: 3545 3544 Cutting tools for machine tools; jigs: inspection, gauging & checking

(G-11407)
PRODUCTION FABRICATORS INC
Also Called: Profab
1608 Creston St (49442-6012)
PHONE.................................231 777-3822
Patrick Bauer, *President*
Michael Bauer, *Corp Secy*
Jordan Hoofman, *Plant Mgr*
Mark Vanappel, *Purchasing*
Ben Hoofman, *Accounts Mgr*
▲ EMP: 30
SQ FT: 30,000
SALES (est): 10.3MM **Privately Held**
WEB: www.profablaser.com
SIC: 3496 3542 3469 3444 Miscellaneous fabricated wire products; machine tools, metal forming type; metal stampings; sheet metalwork; fabricated plate work (boiler shop); fabricated structural metal

GEOGRAPHIC SECTION
Muskegon - Muskegon County (G-11436)

(G-11408)
PULPWOOD & FORESTRY PRODUCTS
131 S Maple Island Rd (49442-9412)
PHONE.................................231 788-3088
Melvin V Whitten Jr, *President*
Ola E Torenga, *Corp Secy*
EMP: 10
SQ FT: 4,200
SALES (est): 1.3MM **Privately Held**
SIC: 2421 Wood chips, produced at mill

(G-11409)
QUALITY PALLET INC
Also Called: Peregrine Wood Products
7220 Hall Rd (49442-9408)
PHONE.................................231 788-5161
Corky Williams, *President*
EMP: 4
SALES (est): 877.1K **Privately Held**
SIC: 2448 Pallets, wood

(G-11410)
QUALITY TOOL & STAMPING CO INC
Also Called: Qts
541 E Sherman Blvd (49444-2277)
PHONE.................................231 733-2538
Edward Kuznar, *President*
Ed Kuznar, *President*
Dan Kuznar, *Vice Pres*
Mike Kuznar, *Plant Mgr*
Kurt Kastelic, *Engineer*
▲ **EMP:** 112 **EST:** 1957
SQ FT: 80,000
SALES: 35MM **Privately Held**
WEB: www.qtstamping.com
SIC: 3469 Stamping metal for the trade

(G-11411)
QWIK TOOL & MFG INC
480 W Hume Ave (49444-1386)
PHONE.................................231 739-8849
EMP: 4
SALES (est): 350K **Privately Held**
SIC: 3544 Manufactures Special Dies Tools Die Sets Jigs Fixtures Or Molds

(G-11412)
R J WOODWORKING INC
3108 Whitehall Rd (49445-1060)
PHONE.................................231 766-2511
Robert J Carter Jr, *President*
Kay L Carter, *Corp Secy*
Tonya Hayes, *Admin Asst*
EMP: 15
SQ FT: 32,000
SALES: 950K **Privately Held**
WEB: www.rjwoodworking.com
SIC: 2521 Wood office desks & tables

(G-11413)
RE-SOURCE INDUSTRIES INC
1485 S Getty St (49442-5103)
PHONE.................................231 728-1155
Paul Kuyt, *President*
Kim Fleming, *General Mgr*
Patrick Conran, *Project Mgr*
Randi Kuyt, *Treasurer*
EMP: 38
SQ FT: 27,000
SALES (est): 6.4MM **Privately Held**
WEB: www.re-sourceindustries.com
SIC: 3599 Machine shop, jobbing & repair

(G-11414)
REAL STEEL MANUFACTURING LLC
304 W Delano Ave (49444-1003)
PHONE.................................231 457-4673
Rick Terpstra, *Owner*
EMP: 3
SALES (est): 54.2K **Privately Held**
SIC: 3999 Manufacturing industries

(G-11415)
ROE LLC
Also Called: Women Lifestyle Northshore
1446 Randolph Ave (49441-3133)
PHONE.................................231 755-5043
Jenni Naffie, *President*
EMP: 5
SALES (est): 468.7K **Privately Held**
SIC: 2721 Magazines: publishing only, not printed on site

(G-11416)
ROGER D RAPOPORT
Also Called: Rdr Books
1487 Glen Ave (49441-3101)
P.O. Box 1231 (49443-1231)
PHONE.................................231 755-6665
Roger Rapoport, *Owner*
EMP: 4
SALES (est): 170.4K **Privately Held**
WEB: www.rdrbooks.com
SIC: 2731 Book publishing

(G-11417)
SAF-HOLLAND INC (DH)
Also Called: Saf-Holland USA
1950 Industrial Blvd (49442-6114)
P.O. Box 425 (49443-0425)
PHONE.................................231 773-3271
Steffen Schewerda, *President*
Ken Hauman, *Vice Pres*
Cheral Stiegmann, *Vice Pres*
John Wieringa, *Vice Pres*
Erich Gering, *Mfg Staff*
◆ **EMP:** 261
SQ FT: 18,000
SALES: 81MM
SALES (corp-wide): 177.9K **Privately Held**
WEB: www.aerway.com
SIC: 3715 3568 3537 3452 Truck trailers; power transmission equipment; industrial trucks & tractors; bolts, nuts, rivets & washers; trailer hitches, motor vehicle
HQ: Saf-Holland Gmbh
Hauptstr. 26
Bessenbach 63856
609 530-10

(G-11418)
SAND PRODUCTS WISCONSIN LLC
560 Mart St (49440-1044)
PHONE.................................231 722-6691
Chuck Cainstraight, *Principal*
EMP: 3 **EST:** 2012
SALES (est): 233.7K **Privately Held**
SIC: 1442 Sand mining

(G-11419)
SCHERDEL SALES & TECH INC (DH)
3440 E Laketon Ave (49442-6438)
PHONE.................................231 777-7774
Sander Schoos, *CEO*
Rolf Shumacher, *President*
Janina Schmieder, *Opers Mgr*
Margaret Alexander, *CFO*
▲ **EMP:** 61
SQ FT: 22,500
SALES (est): 14.9MM
SALES (corp-wide): 3MM **Privately Held**
SIC: 3495 Wire springs
HQ: Scherdel Gmbh
Scherdelstr. 2
Marktredwitz 95615
923 160-30

(G-11420)
SECURITY STEELCRAFT CORP
2636 Sanford St (49444-2007)
P.O. Box 118 (49443-0118)
PHONE.................................231 733-1101
Stanley L Horness, *President*
Beth Hudson, *Admin Sec*
EMP: 20 **EST:** 1954
SQ FT: 73,000
SALES (est): 1.5MM **Privately Held**
SIC: 3821 3444 Laboratory furniture; laboratory equipment: fume hoods, distillation racks, etc.; sheet metalwork; sheet metal specialties, not stamped; cowls or scoops, air (ship ventilators): sheet metal

(G-11421)
SHAPE DYNAMICS INTL INC
500 W Sherman Blvd (49444-1315)
PHONE.................................231 733-2164
John Mc Intyre, *CEO*
EMP: 3
SALES (est): 269.7K **Privately Held**
SIC: 3545 3542 Cutting tools for machine tools; machine tools, metal forming type

(G-11422)
SHOE SHOP
Also Called: West Michigan Pedorthics
3324 Glade St (49444-2708)
PHONE.................................231 739-2174
John Yarrington, *Owner*
EMP: 4
SQ FT: 8,000
SALES (est): 381.6K **Privately Held**
WEB: www.shoe-shop.com
SIC: 3143 Orthopedic shoes, men's

(G-11423)
SHORELINE MTAL FABRICATORS INC
1880 Park St (49441-2638)
PHONE.................................231 722-4443
Gary Bird, *President*
Sandy Bird, *Office Mgr*
EMP: 30
SQ FT: 9,000
SALES (est): 6.2MM **Privately Held**
SIC: 3441 Fabricated structural metal

(G-11424)
SHORELINE RECYCLING & SUPPLY
259 Ottawa St (49442-1008)
PHONE.................................231 722-6081
Jeffrey Padnos, *President*
John Jones, *Vice Pres*
EMP: 32
SALES (est): 3.3MM **Privately Held**
SIC: 5093 3341 3312 Metal scrap & waste materials; secondary nonferrous metals; blast furnaces & steel mills

(G-11425)
SIGN CABINETS INC
2000 9th St (49444-1081)
PHONE.................................231 725-7187
Georg Michael Abraham, *President*
Mike Abraham, *President*
Patrick Abraham, *Office Mgr*
EMP: 4
SQ FT: 10,000
SALES (est): 746.7K **Privately Held**
WEB: www.signcabinetsinc.com
SIC: 3354 Shapes, extruded aluminum

(G-11426)
SIGNCRAFTERS INC
2325 Black Creek Rd (49444-2673)
PHONE.................................231 773-3343
Steven Carlson, *President*
Vicki Carlson, *Vice Pres*
EMP: 4
SQ FT: 5,400
SALES: 500K **Privately Held**
SIC: 3993 Signs, not made in custom sign painting shops

(G-11427)
SOLUS INNOVATIONS LLC
4275 Ford Rd (49445-9619)
PHONE.................................231 744-9832
Becky Bennett,
David Bennett,
EMP: 3
SALES (est): 209.2K **Privately Held**
SIC: 3842 Prosthetic appliances

(G-11428)
SPEC ABRASIVES AND FINISHING
Also Called: Spec Abrasive
543 W Southern Ave (49441-2323)
PHONE.................................231 722-1926
Larry Anderson, *President*
EMP: 14
SQ FT: 9,500
SALES (est): 1.9MM **Privately Held**
SIC: 3471 Sand blasting of metal parts; finishing, metals or formed products

(G-11429)
SPX CORPORATION
700 Terrace Point Dr (49440-1158)
PHONE.................................704 752-4400
Curtis T Atkisson Jr, *Branch Mgr*
EMP: 8
SALES (corp-wide): 1.5B **Publicly Held**
SIC: 3999 Barber & beauty shop equipment
PA: Spx Corporation
13320a Balntyn Corp Pl
Charlotte NC 28277
980 474-3700

(G-11430)
STAR 10 INC
575 W Hume Ave Ste 1 (49444-1375)
PHONE.................................231 830-8070
EMP: 3
SALES (est): 431.1K **Privately Held**
SIC: 2851 Mfg Paints/Allied Products

(G-11431)
SUN CHEMICAL CORPORATION
5025 Evanston Ave (49442-4899)
PHONE.................................513 681-5950
Thom Bolen, *President*
Steve Ferski, *Principal*
Phyllis Wright, *Purchasing*
Don Houston, *Manager*
▲ **EMP:** 17
SALES (est): 1.4MM **Privately Held**
SIC: 5999 2851 2865 Toiletries, cosmetics & perfumes; polyurethane coatings; dyes & pigments

(G-11432)
SUN CHEMICAL CORPORATION
Pigments Division
4835 Evanston Ave (49442-4825)
PHONE.................................231 788-2371
Thom Bolen, *Vice Pres*
Greg Stackey, *Branch Mgr*
John Dewind, *Manager*
EMP: 200 **Privately Held**
WEB: www.sunchemical.com
SIC: 2816 2865 Inorganic pigments; cyclic crudes & intermediates
HQ: Sun Chemical Corporation
35 Waterview Blvd Ste 100
Parsippany NJ 07054
973 404-6000

(G-11433)
SUPERIOR MONUMENTS CO (PA)
354 Ottawa St (49442-1033)
PHONE.................................231 728-2211
David Sietsema, *President*
Cristine Kramer, *CFO*
Nancy Sietsema, *Treasurer*
EMP: 8
SALES (est): 782.1K **Privately Held**
WEB: www.superiormonument.com
SIC: 5999 3272 3281 Monuments, finished to custom order; monuments & tombstones; monuments & grave markers, except terrazo; cut stone & stone products

(G-11434)
T Q MACHINING INC
450 W Hackley Ave (49444-1032)
PHONE.................................231 726-5914
John Dyer Sr, *President*
Jack Smith, *Vice Pres*
Jason Dyer, *Mfg Staff*
EMP: 20
SQ FT: 48,000
SALES (est): 4.5MM **Privately Held**
SIC: 3724 Aircraft engines & engine parts

(G-11435)
TERRELL MANUFACTURING SVCS INC
7245 Hall Rd (49442-9408)
PHONE.................................231 788-2000
Terry Williams, *CEO*
EMP: 16
SQ FT: 8,000
SALES (est): 1.7MM **Privately Held**
SIC: 3569 8711 Liquid automation machinery & equipment; machine tool design; industrial engineers

(G-11436)
TFI INC
Also Called: Thompson Fabrication Inds
2620 Park St (49444-1936)
PHONE.................................231 728-2310
Mark Thompson, *President*
Ed Vugteveen, *Sales Staff*
EMP: 23
SQ FT: 31,000

Muskegon - Muskegon County (G-11437)   GEOGRAPHIC SECTION

SALES: 2.8MM Privately Held
WEB: www.thompsonfab.net
SIC: 3441 Fabricated structural metal

(G-11437)
TIGER NEUROSCIENCE LLC
200 Viridian Dr (49440-1141)
PHONE..................................872 903-1904
Steve Adams, *Mng Member*
EMP: 6
SALES (est): 260.6K Privately Held
SIC: 3841 Surgical & medical instruments

(G-11438)
TISCHCO SIGNS
Also Called: Tischco Signs & Service
2107 Henry St Ste 1 (49441-3087)
PHONE..................................231 755-5529
Matthew Tisch, *President*
EMP: 5
SALES (est): 517.3K Privately Held
WEB: www.tischcosigns.com
SIC: 3993 Signs & advertising specialties

(G-11439)
TOTAL QUALITY MACHINING INC
2620 Park St (49444-1936)
PHONE..................................231 767-1825
Paul Reid, *President*
EMP: 13
SALES (est): 1.8MM
SALES (corp-wide): 1.3B Privately Held
WEB: www.tqmachining.com
SIC: 3599 Machine shop, jobbing & repair
HQ: Essentra Components Company
    3123 Station Rd
    Erie PA 16510
    231 777-3951

(G-11440)
TRI-STATE ALUMINUM LLC (HQ)
1060 E Keating Ave (49442-5962)
PHONE..................................231 722-7825
Randy Clark, *President*
EMP: 10
SQ FT: 12,800
SALES (est): 1.6MM
SALES (corp-wide): 3MM Privately Held
WEB: www.tsacc.com
SIC: 3363 Aluminum die-castings
PA: Tri-State Cast Technologies Co, Inc
    926 N Lake St
    Boyne City MI 49712
    231 582-0452

(G-11441)
TRINITY EQUIPMENT CO
3918 Holton Rd (49445-8535)
PHONE..................................231 719-1813
Keith Massey, *President*
Jennie Kriger, *Marketing Mgr*
▲ EMP: 5
SALES: 1.5MM Privately Held
SIC: 3743 Railroad equipment

(G-11442)
TRIPLE C GEOTHERMAL INC
487 W Forest Ave (49441-2463)
PHONE..................................517 282-7249
Joel Soelberg, *President*
EMP: 5
SALES (est): 176K Privately Held
SIC: 3089 Injection molded finished plastic products; injection molding of plastics; automotive parts, plastic; handles, brush or tool: plastic

(G-11443)
TRUSS TECHNOLOGIES INC
Also Called: West Michigan Truss Company
404 S Maple Island Rd (49442-9407)
PHONE..................................231 788-6330
Dan Bekkering, *Manager*
EMP: 50 Privately Held
WEB: www.trusstechnologies.com
SIC: 2439 Trusses, wooden roof
PA: Truss Technologies, Inc.
    4141 16 Mile Rd Ne
    Cedar Springs MI 49319

(G-11444)
VAN KAM INC
Also Called: Vankam Trailer Sales & Mfg
1316 Whitehall Rd (49445-2432)
PHONE..................................231 744-2658

Leona Vanderberg, *President*
Michael Vanderberg, *Vice Pres*
EMP: 10
SQ FT: 7,000
SALES (est): 1.5MM Privately Held
WEB: www.vankam.com
SIC: 3792 Campers, for mounting on trucks; pickup covers, canopies or caps; trailer coaches, automobile

(G-11445)
VANS CAR WASH INC
1600 Whitehall Rd (49445-1352)
PHONE..................................231 744-4831
Mike Vanderstelt, *Manager*
EMP: 10
SALES (corp-wide): 9.4MM Privately Held
SIC: 3589 Car washing machinery
PA: Van's Car Wash Inc
    1230 W Sherman Blvd
    Muskegon MI 49441
    231 759-7777

(G-11446)
VERSATILE FABRICATION CO INC
2708 9th St (49444-1945)
PHONE..................................231 739-7115
Joe Balaskovitz, *President*
Gwen Henning, *Controller*
Ron Balaskovitz, *Sales Staff*
EMP: 44
SQ FT: 12,000
SALES (est): 13MM Privately Held
WEB: www.versatilefab.com
SIC: 3537 3444 3441 Industrial trucks & tractors; sheet metalwork; fabricated structural metal

(G-11447)
WESTECH CORP
2357 Whitehall Rd (49445-1043)
P.O. Box 5210 (49445-0210)
PHONE..................................231 766-3914
William Seyferth, *President*
Holly Wiles, *Prdtn Mgr*
Larry Herzhaft, *QC Mgr*
Pat Galla, *Manager*
Andera Cuthbertson, *Executive*
EMP: 30
SQ FT: 36,000
SALES (est): 4.2MM Privately Held
WEB: www.westechcorp.com
SIC: 3599 3545 Machine shop, jobbing & repair; machine tool accessories

(G-11448)
WESTPACK INC
1204 W Western Ave Ste 3 (49441-1674)
PHONE..................................231 725-9200
Dale Deveau, *President*
Carsten Birk, *Accounts Mgr*
Jesper Jensen, *Accounts Mgr*
Jeanne Rasmussen, *Sales Staff*
EMP: 7
SQ FT: 11,000
SALES (est): 1.2MM Privately Held
WEB: www.westpack.com
SIC: 3086 Packaging & shipping materials, foamed plastic

(G-11449)
WILBERT BURIAL VAULT COMPANY (PA)
Also Called: West Michigan Crematory Svc
1510 S Getty St (49442-5164)
PHONE..................................231 773-6631
John King, *President*
William King, *Corp Secy*
Virginia King, *Vice Pres*
EMP: 1 EST: 1949
SQ FT: 8,500
SALES (est): 1MM Privately Held
SIC: 3272 5087 7261 Burial vaults, concrete or precast terrazzo; caskets; crematory

(G-11450)
WILBERT BURIAL VAULT COMPANY
1546 S Getty St (49442-5164)
PHONE..................................231 773-6631
John King, *Manager*
EMP: 6

SALES (corp-wide): 1MM Privately Held
SIC: 3272 Burial vaults, concrete or precast terrazzo
PA: Wilbert Burial Vault Company Inc
    1510 S Getty St
    Muskegon MI 49442
    231 773-6631

(G-11451)
WILBUR PRODUCTS INC
950 W Broadway Ave (49441-3522)
PHONE..................................231 755-3805
Scott Wilbur, *President*
Scott Hewitt, *Marketing Mgr*
Kevin Keck, *Manager*
EMP: 10
SQ FT: 1,500
SALES (corp-wide): 4.9MM Privately Held
WEB: www.tech-lineproducts.com
SIC: 5091 2842 2992 2891 Sharpeners, sporting goods; cleaning or polishing preparations; lubricating oils & greases; adhesives & sealants; chemical preparations
PA: Wilbur Products, Inc.
    18570 Trimble Ct
    Spring Lake MI 49456
    616 850-9868

(G-11452)
WILDE SIGNS
Also Called: Wilde Group
771 Access Hwy (49442-1236)
PHONE..................................231 727-1200
Jim Wilde, *Owner*
EMP: 10
SALES (est): 1.8MM Privately Held
SIC: 3993 Signs & advertising specialties

(G-11453)
WINDTRONICS INC
380 W Western Ave Ste 301 (49440-1169)
PHONE..................................231 332-1200
EMP: 3 EST: 2013
SALES (est): 160K Privately Held
SIC: 3511 Mfg Turbines/Generator Sets

(G-11454)
WM TUBE & WIRE FORMING INC
2724 9th St (49444-1945)
P.O. Box 4589 (49444-0589)
PHONE..................................231 830-9393
Eugene Pease, *President*
Charles Colligan, *Vice Pres*
Chuck E Colligan, *Vice Pres*
Steven Colligan, *Vice Pres*
EMP: 19
SQ FT: 25,000
SALES (est): 6.9MM Privately Held
SIC: 3315 3312 Wire, ferrous/iron; pipes & tubes

(G-11455)
WORKMAN PRINTING INC
Also Called: Advanced Printing & Graphics
1261 Holton Rd (49445-2517)
PHONE..................................231 744-5500
Brian Balski, *President*
EMP: 8
SALES (est): 1.2MM Privately Held
SIC: 2752 Commercial printing, offset

(G-11456)
Z & A NEWS
1239 W Giles Rd (49445-1267)
PHONE..................................231 747-6232
EMP: 4
SALES (est): 175.5K Privately Held
SIC: 2711 Newspapers, publishing & printing

Mussey
St. Clair County

(G-11457)
KEIHIN MICHIGAN MFG LLC
14898 Koehn Rd (48014-4310)
PHONE..................................317 462-3015
Yasufhi Takahashi, *CEO*
Dave Thomas, *Vice Pres*
Thom Bennett,

Shigeru Iwaki,
▲ EMP: 160
SALES (est): 26.5MM Privately Held
WEB: www.kipt-inc.com
SIC: 3714 Motor vehicle parts & accessories
HQ: Keihin North America, Inc.
    2701 Enterprise Dr
    Anderson IN 46013
    765 298-6030

Nashville
Barry County

(G-11458)
JUSTIN CARRIAGE WORKS LLC
7615 S M 66 Hwy (49073-9425)
P.O. Box 336 (49073-0336)
PHONE..................................517 852-9743
Roxie Andler, *Owner*
▼ EMP: 3
SALES: 300K Privately Held
SIC: 0752 3799 Breeding services, horses: racing & non-racing; carriages, horse drawn

(G-11459)
LEEP LOGGING INC
8445 Guy Rd (49073-8512)
PHONE..................................517 852-1540
Thomas Leep, *Principal*
EMP: 6
SALES (est): 441.3K Privately Held
SIC: 2411 Logging

(G-11460)
MAPLE VALLEY CONCRETE PRODUCTS
725 Durkee St (49073-9570)
P.O. Box 357 (49073-0357)
PHONE..................................517 852-1900
Ronald Ohler, *President*
Cornelia Ohler, *Corp Secy*
EMP: 3 EST: 1978
SQ FT: 5,000
SALES (est): 341.2K Privately Held
SIC: 3271 5211 5074 5031 Concrete block & brick; sand & gravel; cement; plumbing & hydronic heating supplies; millwork; construction sand & gravel

(G-11461)
MIKE HUGHES
Also Called: Meh Logging Co
6054 Marshall Rd (49073-9537)
PHONE..................................269 377-3578
Mike Hughes, *Owner*
EMP: 3
SALES (est): 123.4K Privately Held
SIC: 2411 Logging camps & contractors

(G-11462)
MOO-VILLE INC
Also Called: Moo-Ville Creamery
5875 S M 66 Hwy (49073-9431)
PHONE..................................517 852-9003
Douglas J Westendorp, *President*
Louisa Westendorp, *Vice Pres*
EMP: 20
SQ FT: 10,000
SALES (est): 3.1MM Privately Held
SIC: 2024 2021 5451 Ice cream & frozen desserts; creamery butter; ice cream (packaged)

(G-11463)
OHLER MACHINE
725 Durkee St (49073-9570)
P.O. Box 357 (49073-0357)
PHONE..................................517 852-1900
Ronald Ohler, *Owner*
EMP: 3
SALES (est): 114K Privately Held
SIC: 3599 Machine shop, jobbing & repair

National City
Iosco County

(G-11464)
NEW NGC INC
Also Called: Gold Bond
2375 S National City Rd (48748-9623)
PHONE..................989 756-2741
Rick Penn, *Branch Mgr*
EMP: 25
SALES (corp-wide): 723.5MM **Privately Held**
WEB: www.natgyp.com
SIC: 3275 Gypsum products
HQ: New Ngc, Inc.
 2001 Rexford Rd
 Charlotte NC 28211

Naubinway
Mackinac County

(G-11465)
D A U P CORP
Also Called: Makinaw Fudge Co
Us 2 (49762)
PHONE..................906 477-1148
Joel Schultz, *President*
EMP: 3
SALES (est): 143.8K **Privately Held**
SIC: 2064 Candy & other confectionery products

Negaunee
Marquette County

(G-11466)
5 PYN INC
Also Called: Signs Now
363 Us Highway 41 E Ste 1 (49866-9698)
PHONE..................906 228-2828
Mark B Pynnonen, *President*
EMP: 7 **EST:** 1998
SQ FT: 4,000
SALES: 250K **Privately Held**
SIC: 3993 7336 Signs & advertising specialties; commercial art & graphic design

(G-11467)
ASSOCIATED CONSTRUCTORS LLC
Also Called: Associated Redi Mix and Block
14 Industrial Park Dr (49866-9627)
P.O. Box 970, Marquette (49855-0970)
PHONE..................906 226-6505
Peter O'Dovero, *Mng Member*
Jim O'Dovero,
EMP: 80
SALES (est): 22.9MM **Privately Held**
SIC: 3273 Ready-mixed concrete

(G-11468)
CAIN BROTHERS LOGGING INC
1001 County Road 510 (49866-9746)
PHONE..................906 345-9252
Kim Cain, *President*
EMP: 4
SALES (est): 369.6K **Privately Held**
SIC: 2411 Logging camps & contractors

(G-11469)
CUMMINS NPOWER LLC
75 Us Hwy 41 N (49866)
PHONE..................906 475-8800
Tim Kleikamp, *Branch Mgr*
EMP: 35
SALES (corp-wide): 23.7B **Publicly Held**
SIC: 5084 5063 3519 Engines & parts, diesel; generators; internal combustion engines
HQ: Cummins Npower Llc
 1600 Buerkle Rd
 White Bear Lake MN 55110
 800 642-0085

(G-11470)
GREAT LAKES WOOD PRODUCTS
434 Us Highway 41 E (49866-9626)
PHONE..................906 228-3737
James Thompson, *Owner*
EMP: 4 **EST:** 1985
SQ FT: 7,200
SALES (est): 419K **Privately Held**
SIC: 5251 2511 2431 Tools, power; wood lawn & garden furniture; millwork

(G-11471)
JOHNSON GLASS CLEANING INC
5 Pond Rd (49866-9608)
PHONE..................906 361-0361
Randall Johnson, *President*
EMP: 3
SALES (est): 195K **Privately Held**
SIC: 3211 Building glass, flat; window glass, clear & colored

(G-11472)
OAK NORTH MANUFACTURING INC
114 Us Highway 41 E (49866-9682)
PHONE..................906 475-7992
Thomas Mahaney, *President*
Brock Micklew, *Vice Pres*
EMP: 12
SQ FT: 10,000
SALES (est): 1MM **Privately Held**
SIC: 2434 2431 Wood kitchen cabinets; millwork

(G-11473)
PELLOW PRINTING CO
318 Iron St (49866-1893)
PHONE..................906 475-9431
Wayne Gerberding, *Owner*
EMP: 3
SQ FT: 1,000
SALES (est): 272.3K **Privately Held**
SIC: 2759 2752 Letterpress printing; lithographing on metal

(G-11474)
REFRESHMENT PRODUCT SVCS INC
201 Summit St Bldg 53 (49866-9581)
PHONE..................906 475-7003
EMP: 4
SALES (corp-wide): 31.8B **Publicly Held**
SIC: 2086 2087 Soft drinks: packaged in cans, bottles, etc.; concentrates, drink
HQ: Refreshment Product Services, Inc.
 1 Coca Cola Plz Nw
 Atlanta GA 30313
 404 676-2121

(G-11475)
ROBBINS INC
844 Highway M 28 (49866)
PHONE..................513 619-5936
Dave Fulton, *CEO*
EMP: 9
SALES (corp-wide): 71.2MM **Privately Held**
SIC: 2426 Flooring, hardwood
PA: Robbins, Inc.
 4777 Eastern Ave
 Cincinnati OH 45226
 513 871-8988

(G-11476)
RUDY GOUPILLE & SONS INC
Also Called: Redi-Crete
118 Midway Dr (49866-9680)
PHONE..................906 475-9816
Adele Goupille, *President*
EMP: 8
SALES (est): 1.2MM **Privately Held**
SIC: 3272 3273 1794 4212 Septic tanks, concrete; ready-mixed concrete; excavation work; local trucking, without storage

(G-11477)
STEPHEN HAAS
Also Called: Haas Food Services
96 Croix St Apt 6 (49866-1157)
PHONE..................906 475-4826
Stephen Haas, *Principal*
EMP: 6
SALES (est): 282K **Privately Held**
SIC: 2099 Box lunches, for sale off premises

(G-11478)
U P FABRICATING CO INC (PA)
Also Called: Manistique Machine
120 Us Highway 41 E Ste A (49866-9703)
PHONE..................906 475-4400
Richard W Kauppila, *President*
EMP: 30
SQ FT: 28,000
SALES (est): 6.3MM **Privately Held**
SIC: 3531 3532 3441 Construction machinery; mining machinery; fabricated structural metal

New Baltimore
Macomb County

(G-11479)
AMF DEFENSE
51528 Industrial Dr (48047-4148)
PHONE..................586 684-3365
Gloria Rentz, *Principal*
EMP: 3 **EST:** 2017
SALES (est): 156.9K **Privately Held**
SIC: 3812 Defense systems & equipment

(G-11480)
ANCHOR BAY POWDER COAT LLC
51469 Birch St (48047-1587)
PHONE..................586 725-3255
Robert Thomas, *Principal*
EMP: 13
SALES (est): 1.3MM **Privately Held**
SIC: 3479 Coating of metals & formed products

(G-11481)
BAYSHORE KITCHEN AND BATH INC
51180 Washington St (48047-2159)
PHONE..................586 725-8800
Jerold O Ettel, *Owner*
EMP: 4
SALES (est): 413.8K **Privately Held**
SIC: 2434 Wood kitchen cabinets

(G-11482)
CALIBER METALS INC
36870 Green St (48047-1605)
PHONE..................586 465-7650
William M Harber Sr, *President*
Andrew Ligda, *Corp Secy*
Ned Cavallaro, *Vice Pres*
EMP: 20
SQ FT: 96,000
SALES (est): 5.1MM **Privately Held**
WEB: www.calibermetals.com
SIC: 5033 3442 Roofing & siding materials; metal doors, sash & trim

(G-11483)
DLH ROLLFORM LLC
51751 County Line Rd (48047-1147)
PHONE..................586 231-0507
Ken Hesse, *Owner*
Rick Humby, *Owner*
EMP: 4
SALES (est): 603.5K **Privately Held**
SIC: 3449 Custom roll formed products

(G-11484)
EXPAN INC (PA)
51513 Industrial Dr (48047-4149)
P.O. Box 267 (48047-0267)
PHONE..................586 725-0405
William Mc Cormick, *President*
◆ **EMP:** 49
SQ FT: 26,000
SALES (est): 2.9MM **Privately Held**
WEB: www.expaninc.com
SIC: 3469 3339 Perforated metal, stamped; primary nonferrous metals

(G-11485)
I & G TOOL CO INC
51528 Industrial Dr (48047-4148)
PHONE..................586 777-7690
Sigfried Charow, *President*
Peter Charow, *Vice Pres*
Gloria Rentz, *Manager*
EMP: 22 **EST:** 1984
SQ FT: 14,000
SALES (est): 3.5MM **Privately Held**
SIC: 3545 3544 Cutting tools for machine tools; special dies, tools, jigs & fixtures

(G-11486)
INDUCTION ENGINEERING INC
51517 Industrial Dr (48047-4149)
PHONE..................586 716-4700
Jack Muller, *President*
EMP: 15
SQ FT: 25,000
SALES (est): 1.4MM **Privately Held**
WEB: www.inductionengineering.com
SIC: 3398 3677 3621 Metal heat treating; electronic coils, transformers & other inductors; motors & generators

(G-11487)
KBE PRECISION PRODUCTS LLC
Also Called: Kbe Hoist
51537 Industrial Dr (48047-4149)
PHONE..................586 725-4200
Jay Baumgarten,
Chuck Baumgarten,
Karen Baumgarten,
EMP: 8
SQ FT: 1,400
SALES (est): 1.3MM **Privately Held**
SIC: 3541 Machine tools, metal cutting type

(G-11488)
MAGNUM INDUCTION INC
51517 Industrial Dr (48047-4149)
PHONE..................586 716-4700
Jack Muller, *President*
John Muller, *Vice Pres*
EMP: 22
SQ FT: 5,000
SALES (est): 3MM **Privately Held**
WEB: www.magnuminduction.com
SIC: 3398 Metal heat treating

(G-11489)
NASS CORPORATION
Also Called: Nass Controls
51509 Birch St (48047-1588)
PHONE..................586 725-6610
Randy Bennett, *President*
K Kirchheim, *Principal*
C Ullrich, *Principal*
Cindy Secondino, *Human Resources*
▲ **EMP:** 10
SQ FT: 12,000
SALES (est): 1.6MM **Privately Held**
WEB: www.nasscontrols.com
SIC: 3679 5085 Solenoids for electronic applications; valves & fittings

(G-11490)
R & DS MANUFACTURING LLC
51690 Birch St (48047-1585)
PHONE..................586 716-9900
Daniel Q Pfaendtner,
EMP: 4
SALES (est): 97.4K **Privately Held**
SIC: 3444 Sheet metalwork

(G-11491)
S & G PROTOTYPE INC
51540 Industrial Dr (48047-4148)
P.O. Box 129 (48047-0129)
PHONE..................586 716-3600
Scott Grove, *President*
Deanna Grove, *Vice Pres*
EMP: 15
SQ FT: 15,000
SALES (est): 1.6MM **Privately Held**
SIC: 3465 Automotive stampings

(G-11492)
SER INC
51529 Birch St (48047-1588)
P.O. Box 26 (48047-0026)
PHONE..................586 725-0192
William J McCormick, *President*
Charles McCormick, *COO*
▲ **EMP:** 45 **EST:** 1966
SQ FT: 29,000

New Baltimore - Macomb County (G-11493) — GEOGRAPHIC SECTION

SALES (est): 8.6MM Privately Held
WEB: www.rseincorporated.com
SIC: 3564 Filters, air: furnaces, air conditioning equipment, etc.

(G-11493)
SNOEKS AUTOMOTIVE N AMER INC
35035 Cricklewood Blvd (48047-1535)
PHONE.................586 716-9588
Johan Veenstra, *Principal*
EMP: 4 EST: 2016
SALES (est): 115.8K Privately Held
SIC: 2399 Automotive covers, except seat & tire covers

(G-11494)
TRANSNAV HOLDINGS INC (PA)
35105 Cricklewood Blvd (48047-1530)
PHONE.................586 716-5600
Gerrit A Vreeken, *Partner*
Adrian Gerardo, *Opers Mgr*
Ted Light, *Engineer*
Percy Vreeken, *Treasurer*
Ilja Vreeken, *Admin Sec*
EMP: 200
SQ FT: 152,000
SALES (est): 75.6MM Privately Held
SIC: 3089 3111 Injection molding of plastics; leather processing

(G-11495)
TRANSNAV TECHNOLOGIES INC (HQ)
35105 Cricklewood Blvd (48047-1530)
PHONE.................888 249-9955
Gerrit A Vreeken, *President*
Percy P Vreeken, *Treasurer*
Aaron Prout, *Program Mgr*
Natalie Szymberski, *Technology*
Ilja J Vreeken, *Admin Sec*
▲ EMP: 200
SQ FT: 152,000
SALES (est): 46.7MM Privately Held
SIC: 3089 Injection molded finished plastic products

New Boston
Wayne County

(G-11496)
AJF INC
37015 Pennsylvania Rd (48164-9372)
P.O. Box 697 (48164-0697)
PHONE.................734 753-4410
Michael O'Leary, *President*
Michael O'Lear, *Vice Pres*
James McGuire, *Sales Executive*
Jeremy Richardson, *Administration*
▲ EMP: 29
SALES (est): 4.6MM Privately Held
SIC: 3297 5051 Graphite refractories: carbon bond or ceramic bond; foundry products

(G-11497)
BONSAL AMERICAN INC
Also Called: Bonsan American
36506 Sibley Rd (48164-9290)
PHONE.................734 753-4413
Roger Thomas, *Manager*
EMP: 15
SALES (corp-wide): 30.6B Privately Held
WEB: www.bonsalamerican.com
SIC: 3272 3273 Building materials, except block or brick: concrete; ready-mixed concrete
HQ: Bonsal American, Inc.
    625 Griffith Rd Ste 100
    Charlotte NC 28217
    704 525-1621

(G-11498)
BROSE NEW BOSTON INC (DH)
23400 Bell Rd (48164-9183)
PHONE.................248 339-4021
Jurgen Otto, *CEO*
Jan Kowal, *President*
Volker Herdin, *Corp Secy*
Marco Braeutigam, *QC Mgr*
Joseph Larussa, *Engineer*
◆ EMP: 113

SALES (est): 55.6MM
SALES (corp-wide): 1.2B Privately Held
SIC: 3694 Automotive electrical equipment
HQ: Brose North America, Inc.
    3933 Automation Ave
    Auburn Hills MI 48326
    248 339-4000

(G-11499)
CHAMPION FOODS LLC
23900 Bell Rd (48164-9226)
PHONE.................734 753-3663
David W Kowal, *President*
Evan Litvak, *Vice Pres*
Max Stark, *Information Mgr*
EMP: 300
SALES (est): 26.5MM Privately Held
SIC: 2099 Pizza, refrigerated: except frozen
PA: Ilitch Holdings, Inc.
    2211 Woodward Ave
    Detroit MI 48201

(G-11500)
JAYTEC LLC (DH)
17757 Woodland Dr (48164-9265)
PHONE.................517 451-8272
Wayne Jones, *Mng Member*
▲ EMP: 10
SALES (est): 25.3MM
SALES (corp-wide): 2.2B Privately Held
WEB: www.jaytec.net
SIC: 3465 Automotive stampings
HQ: L & W, Inc.
    17757 Woodland Dr
    New Boston MI 48164
    734 397-6300

(G-11501)
KURRENT WELDING INC
18488 Wahrman Rd (48164-9509)
PHONE.................734 753-9197
Jeff Komisar, *President*
EMP: 4
SQ FT: 2,800
SALES (est): 494.6K Privately Held
SIC: 7692 3443 Welding repair; fabricated plate work (boiler shop)

(G-11502)
L & W INC (HQ)
Also Called: L & W Engineering
17757 Woodland Dr (48164-9265)
PHONE.................734 397-6300
Scott L Jones, *President*
Brian Matney, *General Mgr*
Kurt Spencer, *General Mgr*
Steven Schafer, *COO*
Bob Koss, *Treasurer*
▲ EMP: 100
SQ FT: 30,670
SALES (est): 630.9MM
SALES (corp-wide): 2.2B Privately Held
SIC: 3465 3469 3441 3429 Automotive stampings; stamping metal for the trade; fabricated structural metal; manufactured hardware (general)
PA: Autokiniton Us Holdings, Inc.
    485 Lexington Ave Fl 31
    New York NY 10017
    212 338-5100

(G-11503)
LC MANUFACTURING LLC
Also Called: New Boston Forge
36485 S Huron Rd (48164-9275)
PHONE.................734 753-3990
Floyd Simmons, *Branch Mgr*
EMP: 50
SALES (corp-wide): 51.1MM Privately Held
WEB: www.lcmanufacturingllc.com
SIC: 3462 Iron & steel forgings
PA: Lc Manufacturing, Llc
    4150 N Wolcott Rd
    Lake City MI 49651
    231 839-7102

(G-11504)
NEW BOSTON CANDLE COMPANY
21941 Merriman Rd (48164-9458)
PHONE.................734 782-5809
Ellen Rees, *President*
Ron Rees, *Admin Sec*
EMP: 13

SQ FT: 2,500
SALES: 500K Privately Held
WEB: www.newbostoncandle.com
SIC: 3999 5947 Candles; gift, novelty & souvenir shop

(G-11505)
NEW BOSTON RTM INC
19155 Shook Rd (48164-9288)
P.O. Box 188 (48164-0188)
PHONE.................734 753-9956
Michael Angerer, *President*
EMP: 23
SQ FT: 18,000
SALES (est): 4.5MM Privately Held
SIC: 2821 Plastics materials & resins

(G-11506)
OAKLAND STAMPING LLC
17757 Woodland Dr (48164-9265)
PHONE.................313 867-3700
EMP: 3
SQ FT: 500 Privately Held
SIC: 3465 Automotive stampings
HQ: Oakland Stamping, Llc
    1200 Woodland St
    Detroit MI 48211

(G-11507)
OS HOLDINGS LLC (PA)
17757 Woodland Dr (48164-9265)
PHONE.................734 397-6300
Scott Jones, *Mng Member*
EMP: 7
SALES (est): 49.3MM Privately Held
SIC: 3469 Metal stampings

(G-11508)
PLASTIC OMINIUM AUTO INERGY
Also Called: Huron Township Plant
36000 Bruelle Ave (48164-8957)
PHONE.................734 753-1350
John Dunn, *Vice Pres*
EMP: 350
SQ FT: 300,000
SALES (corp-wide): 10.4MM Privately Held
SIC: 3714 Fuel systems & parts, motor vehicle
HQ: Plastic Omnium Auto Inergy (Usa) Llc
    2710 Bellingham Dr
    Troy MI 48083
    248 743-5700

(G-11509)
QUALITY PIPE PRODUCTS INC
17275 Huron River Dr (48164-8955)
P.O. Box 667 (48164-0667)
PHONE.................734 606-5100
Roger Melton, *CEO*
Steve Abrams, *Vice Pres*
Sylvia Melton, *Treasurer*
George Rennie, *Treasurer*
Katherine Klages, *Controller*
◆ EMP: 50
SQ FT: 31,000
SALES (est): 23.4MM Privately Held
WEB: www.qualitypipeproducts.com
SIC: 3494 3498 3541 5085 Valves & pipe fittings; pipe sections fabricated from purchased pipe; pipe cutting & threading machines; industrial supplies

(G-11510)
RAVEN CARBIDE DIE LLC
17901 Wdlnd Dr Ste 1100 (48164)
PHONE.................313 228-8776
EMP: 6 EST: 2014
SALES (est): 413.9K Privately Held
SIC: 2819 Carbides

(G-11511)
SOUTHTEC LLC
17757 Woodland Dr (48164-9265)
PHONE.................734 397-6300
EMP: 4
SALES (corp-wide): 2.2B Privately Held
SIC: 3469 Automobile license tags, stamped metal
HQ: Southtec, Llc
    17757 Woodland Dr
    New Boston MI 48164
    734 397-6300

(G-11512)
SOUTHTEC LLC (DH)
17757 Woodland Dr (48164-9265)
PHONE.................734 397-6300
Wayne Jones, *CEO*
Scott Jones, *President*
Bob Koss, *Vice Pres*
▲ EMP: 250 EST: 2001
SALES (est): 22.6MM
SALES (corp-wide): 2.2B Privately Held
WEB: www.southtec.com
SIC: 3469 Automobile license tags, stamped metal; perforated metal, stamped; ash trays, stamped metal
HQ: L & W, Inc.
    17757 Woodland Dr
    New Boston MI 48164
    734 397-6300

(G-11513)
THREADWORKS LTD INC
29907 N Park Ct (48164-7818)
PHONE.................517 548-9745
David Wendlandt, *President*
EMP: 3
SALES (est): 279.1K Privately Held
SIC: 2759 2395 Letterpress & screen printing; screen printing; embroidery & art needlework

New Buffalo
Berrien County

(G-11514)
FUSION DESIGN GROUP LTD
30 N Brton St New Bffalo (49117)
P.O. Box 498 (49117-0498)
PHONE.................269 469-8226
Tim S Rogers, *President*
EMP: 4
SALES: 156K Privately Held
WEB: www.fusiondg.com
SIC: 7336 4813 2741 7311 Commercial art & graphic design; ; ; advertising agencies; marketing consulting services

(G-11515)
GHOST ISLAND BREWERY
17656 Us Highway 12 (49117-9714)
P.O. Box 822 (49117-0822)
PHONE.................219 242-4800
Sima Robert Louis, *Owner*
EMP: 3 EST: 2017
SALES (est): 68.6K Privately Held
SIC: 2082 Malt beverages

(G-11516)
NEW BUFFALO CONCRETE PRODUCTS
Also Called: Ozinga Ready Mix
825 S Whittaker St (49117-1771)
PHONE.................269 469-2515
Richard Wittenberg, *Partner*
Robert Wittenberg, *Partner*
Brent Van Dyk, *Manager*
EMP: 350
SQ FT: 8,100
SALES (est): 22.8MM Privately Held
SIC: 3273 3271 Ready-mixed concrete; blocks, concrete or cinder: standard

(G-11517)
NEW BUFFALO TIMES
430 S Whittaker St (49117-1764)
P.O. Box 369 (49117-0369)
PHONE.................269 469-1100
Dee Dee Duhn, *Owner*
EMP: 6
SALES (est): 347.6K Privately Held
SIC: 2711 Newspapers: publishing only, not printed on site

(G-11518)
VINYL EXPRESS
19654 Ash Ct (49117-9280)
P.O. Box 159 (49117-0159)
PHONE.................269 469-5165
Janet Freier, *President*
EMP: 3
SALES (est): 196.7K Privately Held
SIC: 3993 Electric signs

▲ = Import ▼ = Export
◆ = Import/Export

New ERA
Oceana County

(G-11519)
BURNETTE FOODS INC
4856 1st St (49446-9677)
PHONE..................................231 861-2151
Joel Smith, *Plant Mgr*
Jeremy Hartwick, *Opers Mgr*
Abe Farias, *Warehouse Mgr*
John Pelizzari, *Branch Mgr*
EMP: 222
SALES (corp-wide): 92.7MM **Privately Held**
SIC: 2033 Canned fruits & specialties
PA: Burnette Foods, Inc.
 701 S Us Highway 31
 Elk Rapids MI 49629
 231 264-8116

(G-11520)
COUNTRY DAIRY INC (PA)
3476 S 80th Ave (49446-9776)
PHONE..................................231 861-4636
Wendell Van Gunst, *President*
Robert S Eekhoff, *Vice Pres*
Robert Eekhoff, *Vice Pres*
Paul D Arkema, *Treasurer*
Amy Vangunst, *Human Res Mgr*
EMP: 58 **EST:** 1964
SQ FT: 600
SALES (est): 8.8MM **Privately Held**
WEB: www.countrydairy.com
SIC: 0241 2026 Dairy farms; fluid milk

(G-11521)
NEW ERA CANNING COMPANY
4856 1st St (49446-9608)
P.O. Box 68 (49446-0068)
PHONE..................................231 861-2151
Rick Ray, *President*
EMP: 250
SQ FT: 200,000
SALES (est): 36.3MM **Privately Held**
WEB: www.neweracanning.com
SIC: 2033 Fruits: packaged in cans, jars, etc.

New Haven
Macomb County

(G-11522)
CARGILL AMERICAS INC
31029 Comcast Dr Ste 100 (48048-2784)
PHONE..................................810 989-7689
EMP: 98 **EST:** 2015
SALES (est): 7.4MM **Privately Held**
SIC: 2015 Poultry slaughtering & processing

(G-11523)
CENTERLESS REBUILDERS INC (PA)
Also Called: C R I
57877 Main St (48048-2664)
P.O. Box 480549 (48048-0549)
PHONE..................................586 749-6529
Gerald A Filipek, *President*
▲ **EMP:** 35
SQ FT: 42,000
SALES (est): 7.6MM **Privately Held**
WEB: www.centerless.net
SIC: 3542 Rebuilt machine tools, metal forming types

(G-11524)
JMA TOOL COMPANY INC
Also Called: Jma Manufacturing
58233 Gratiot Ave (48048-2777)
PHONE..................................586 270-6706
Christine Arciniaga, *President*
John Anguish, *Vice Pres*
EMP: 22
SALES (est): 3.6MM **Privately Held**
SIC: 3089 Injection molded finished plastic products; injection molding of plastics

(G-11525)
MOTE INDUSTRIES INC
57446 River Oaks Dr (48048-3301)
PHONE..................................248 613-3413
James Mote, *CEO*
EMP: 15
SALES (est): 752.6K **Privately Held**
WEB: www.mote-inc.com
SIC: 3999 Manufacturing industries

(G-11526)
STURDY GRINDING MACHINING INC
58600 Rosell Rd (48048-2649)
PHONE..................................586 463-8880
Ray Blake, *President*
Donna Blake, *Admin Sec*
EMP: 18
SQ FT: 13,600
SALES (est): 3MM **Privately Held**
WEB: www.sturdygrinding.com
SIC: 3599 Machine shop, jobbing & repair

(G-11527)
SUPERB MACHINE REPAIR INC (PA)
59180 Havenridge Rd (48048-1908)
P.O. Box 480579 (48048-0579)
PHONE..................................586 749-8800
Robert Vanthomme, *President*
James Leonard, *Vice Pres*
EMP: 15
SQ FT: 20,000
SALES (est): 3.3MM **Privately Held**
SIC: 3599 Air intake filters, internal combustion engine, except auto

(G-11528)
TI AUTOMOTIVE LLC
30600 Commerce Blvd (48048)
PHONE..................................586 948-6036
Debra Geier, *Purch Agent*
Jim Harrison, *Engineer*
EMP: 14
SALES (corp-wide): 3.9B **Privately Held**
SIC: 3317 Steel pipe & tubes
HQ: Ti Automotive, L.L.C.
 2020 Taylor Rd
 Auburn Hills MI 48326
 248 494-5000

(G-11529)
TRIANGLE GRINDING COMPANY INC
57877 Main St (48048-2664)
P.O. Box 480549 (48048-0549)
PHONE..................................586 749-6540
Mark Plantrich, *CEO*
Paul Duffy, *Vice Pres*
EMP: 22 **EST:** 1955
SQ FT: 6,400
SALES (est): 2.6MM **Privately Held**
WEB: www.trianglegrinding.com
SIC: 3599 Machine shop, jobbing & repair; grinding castings for the trade

New Hudson
Oakland County

(G-11530)
ALTA CONSTRUCTION EQP LLC
56195 Pontiac Trl (48165-9702)
PHONE..................................248 356-5200
Steve Greenawalt, *Mng Member*
Theodore M Schafer,
EMP: 52
SALES (est): 13.1MM **Privately Held**
SIC: 3531 Construction machinery
PA: Alta Equipment Holdings, Inc.
 13211 Merriman Rd
 Livonia MI 48150

(G-11531)
BIELOMATIK INC
55397 Lyon Industrial Dr (48165-8545)
PHONE..................................248 446-9910
Ulrik Frodermann, *President*
▲ **EMP:** 28
SQ FT: 20,000
SALES (est): 7.9MM
SALES (corp-wide): 1.1MM **Privately Held**
WEB: www.bielomatik.com
SIC: 3548 Welding & cutting apparatus & accessories
HQ: Bielomatik Leuze Gmbh + Co. Kg
 Daimlerstr 6-10
 Neuffen 72639
 702 512-0

(G-11532)
BIELOMATIK USA INC
55397 Lyon Industrial Dr (48165-8545)
PHONE..................................248 446-9910
Porten Warnatsch, *President*
EMP: 50 **EST:** 2003
SALES (est): 2.1MM
SALES (corp-wide): 1.1MM **Privately Held**
SIC: 3541 Machine tools, metal cutting type
HQ: Bielomatik Leuze Gmbh + Co. Kg
 Daimlerstr 6-10
 Neuffen 72639
 702 512-0

(G-11533)
BVA INC
Also Called: BVA OILS
29222 Trident Indus Blvd (48165-8559)
P.O. Box 930301, Wixom (48393-0301)
PHONE..................................248 348-4920
David J Vincent, *President*
◆ **EMP:** 21
SQ FT: 25,000
SALES (est): 21.8MM **Privately Held**
WEB: www.bvaoils.com
SIC: 5172 2911 Lubricating oils & greases; oils, lubricating

(G-11534)
CONTINENTAL ALUMINUM LLC
29201 Milford Rd (48165-9741)
PHONE..................................248 437-1001
Edward O Merz, *Manager*
EMP: 50
SQ FT: 130,000
SALES (est): 19.2MM **Privately Held**
SIC: 3341 Aluminum smelting & refining (secondary)
PA: Lefton Metal Enterprises Corporation
 111 West Port Plz Ste 700
 Saint Louis MO 63146
 314 434-3500

(G-11535)
CUMMINS BRIDGEWAY GROVE CY LLC
21810 Clessie Ct (48165-8573)
PHONE..................................614 604-6000
Dan Ogg, *Principal*
EMP: 3
SALES (est): 1.1MM
SALES (corp-wide): 23.7B **Publicly Held**
WEB: www.bridgewaypower.com
SIC: 5084 3519 Engines & parts, diesel; internal combustion engines
PA: Cummins Inc.
 500 Jackson St
 Columbus IN 47201
 812 377-5000

(G-11536)
CUMMINS INC
54250 Grand River Ave (48165-9561)
PHONE..................................248 573-1900
Dave Dunbrach, *Manager*
EMP: 30
SALES (corp-wide): 23.7B **Publicly Held**
WEB: www.bridgewaypower.com
SIC: 5084 3519 Engines & parts, diesel; internal combustion engines
PA: Cummins Inc.
 500 Jackson St
 Columbus IN 47201
 812 377-5000

(G-11537)
DEMARIA BUILDING COMPANY INC
Taft Steel Div
53655 Grand River Ave (48165-8523)
PHONE..................................248 486-2598
Rick Flynn, *Controller*
Larry Lesniak, *Manager*
EMP: 8
SALES (corp-wide): 19.2MM **Privately Held**
SIC: 3441 Fabricated structural metal
PA: Demaria Building Company, Inc.
 45500 Grand River Ave
 Novi MI 48374
 248 348-8710

(G-11538)
DRAUGHT HORSE GROUP LLC
57721 Grand River Ave (48165-8542)
PHONE..................................231 631-5218
Brad Tiernan, *Principal*
EMP: 7
SALES (est): 752.5K **Privately Held**
SIC: 2082 Malt beverages

(G-11539)
EMTRON CORPORATION INC
Also Called: Emtron Gauge
57401 Travis Rd (48165-9753)
PHONE..................................248 347-3333
John G Kelly, *President*
EMP: 17 **EST:** 1974
SQ FT: 5,000
SALES (est): 2.5MM **Privately Held**
SIC: 3545 Gauges (machine tool accessories); tools & accessories for machine tools

(G-11540)
ENVIRONMENTAL RESOURCES
56901 Grand River Ave (48165-8540)
P.O. Box 235 (48165-0235)
PHONE..................................248 446-9639
John Evans, *Principal*
EMP: 3
SALES (est): 303.5K **Privately Held**
SIC: 3589 Water filters & softeners, household type

(G-11541)
GLOBAL AUTOPACK LLC
30428 Milford Rd Ste 2000 (48165-8583)
PHONE..................................248 390-2434
EMP: 3 **EST:** 2004
SALES (est): 250K **Privately Held**
SIC: 3086 Mfg Automotive Foam/Packaging

(G-11542)
HARRELLS LLC
53410 Grand River Ave (48165-8521)
PHONE..................................248 446-8070
EMP: 6
SALES (corp-wide): 113.6MM **Privately Held**
SIC: 3524 Mfg Lawn/Garden Equipment
HQ: Harrell's, Llc
 5105 New Tampa Hwy
 Lakeland FL 33815

(G-11543)
HENROB CORPORATION (DH)
30000 S Hill Rd (48165-9828)
PHONE..................................248 493-3800
Keith Jones, *CEO*
Robert Le Fevre, *Opers Mgr*
Philip J Whitehead, *CFO*
Holly Watkins, *Admin Asst*
◆ **EMP:** 80
SQ FT: 60,000
SALES (est): 25.7MM
SALES (corp-wide): 10.5B **Privately Held**
WEB: www.henrob.com
SIC: 3452 5085 5084 Bolts, nuts, rivets & washers; fasteners, industrial: nuts, bolts, screws, etc.; machine tools & accessories
HQ: Atlas Copco North America Llc
 6 Century Dr Ste 310
 Parsippany NJ 07054
 973 397-3400

(G-11544)
HILLTOP MANUFACTURING CO INC
56849 Rice St (48165-8530)
P.O. Box E (48165-0334)
PHONE..................................248 437-2530
Patrick Allen, *President*
John Allen, *Corp Secy*
EMP: 3
SQ FT: 7,000

New Hudson - Oakland County (G-11545)

SALES (est): 382K **Privately Held**
SIC: 3548 3465 3469 Welding & cutting apparatus & accessories; automotive stampings; metal stampings

(G-11545)
IDEAL HEATED KNIVES INC
57007 Pontiac Trl (48165-9748)
P.O. Box 187 (48165-0187)
PHONE...................................248 437-1510
John T Sukenik, *President*
Margie Andrews, *Bookkeeper*
EMP: 4 **EST:** 1966
SQ FT: 1,000
SALES (est): 620.4K **Privately Held**
SIC: 3545 Cutting tools for machine tools

(G-11546)
K & S PROPERTY INC (PA)
Also Called: Cummins Bridgeway
21810 Clessie Ct (48165-8573)
PHONE...................................248 573-1600
Gregory Boll, *President*
Cheryl Chapman, *Engineer*
Bhakti Rane, *Engineer*
Ken Clark, *CFO*
Kenneth Clark, *CFO*
EMP: 630
SQ FT: 14,500
SALES: 110MM **Privately Held**
SIC: 5084 3519 Engines & parts, diesel; internal combustion engines

(G-11547)
MACDERMID INCORPORATED
Also Called: Allied Kelite
29111 Milford Rd (48165-9741)
PHONE...................................248 437-8161
David Crotty, *Research*
Tony Cangelosi, *Research*
EMP: 23
SALES (corp-wide): 1.9B **Publicly Held**
WEB: www.macdermid.com
SIC: 2899 Chemical preparations
HQ: Macdermid, Incorporated
245 Freight St
Waterbury CT 06702
203 575-5700

(G-11548)
MAGNA INTERNATIONAL INC
Also Called: Cosma Body Assembly Michigan
54725 Grand River Ave (48165-8526)
PHONE...................................248 617-3200
Mike Zimmerman, *General Mgr*
Dale Greer, *Opers Staff*
Ken Reid, *Purch Mgr*
Jason Durfee, *Research*
Dan Davis, *Engineer*
EMP: 14
SALES (corp-wide): 40.8B **Privately Held**
SIC: 3714 Motor vehicle parts & accessories
PA: Magna International Inc
337 Magna Dr
Aurora ON L4G 7
905 726-2462

(G-11549)
NETWORKS ENTERPRISES INC
57450 Travis Rd (48165-9753)
P.O. Box 930063, Wixom (48393-0063)
PHONE...................................248 446-8590
Douglas J Ross, *President*
Kenneth J Ross, *Vice Pres*
EMP: 5
SALES (est): 809.3K **Privately Held**
WEB: www.cargonets.com
SIC: 2298 Cargo nets

(G-11550)
NORTECH LLC
30163 Research Dr (48165-8548)
PHONE...................................248 446-7575
Michael Walker, *President*
Richard Cameron, *Principal*
Tracy Schichl, *Office Mgr*
Robert Boroniek,
EMP: 25
SALES (est): 6MM **Privately Held**
WEB: www.nortechllc.com
SIC: 3499 Automobile seat frames, metal

(G-11551)
PERFORMANCE SPRINGS INC
57575 Travis Rd (48165-9753)
PHONE...................................248 486-3372
Steve Bown, *President*
Dave Boyer, *Plant Mgr*
Lawrence Luchi, *Treasurer*
EMP: 19
SQ FT: 14,000
SALES (est): 3.7MM **Privately Held**
SIC: 3714 Motor vehicle engines & parts

(G-11552)
REFRIGERANT SERVICES LLC
54000 Grand River Ave (48165-8514)
PHONE...................................248 586-6988
Scotty Stanley,
EMP: 4
SQ FT: 8,000
SALES (est): 197K **Privately Held**
SIC: 3822 Auto controls regulating residntl & coml environmt & applncs

(G-11553)
RICHARD TOOL & DIE CORPORATION
29700 Wk Smith Dr (48165-9488)
PHONE...................................248 486-0900
Richard A Heidrich, *President*
Steven S Rowe, *Exec VP*
Robert Heidrich, *Vice Pres*
▲ **EMP:** 80 **EST:** 1966
SALES (est): 15.1MM **Privately Held**
WEB: www.rtdcorp.com
SIC: 3544 Special dies & tools

(G-11554)
ROY A HUTCHINS COMPANY
57455 Travis Rd (48165-9351)
P.O. Box 340 (48165-1340)
PHONE...................................248 437-3470
Harold Thomas, *CEO*
Lincoln Thomas, *President*
Gail Merwin, *Corp Secy*
EMP: 4
SQ FT: 9,000
SALES (est): 665.5K **Privately Held**
SIC: 5084 3452 3541 Industrial machinery & equipment; bolts, nuts, rivets & washers; drilling & boring machines

(G-11555)
SLOAN VALVE COMPANY
Sloan Flushmate
30075 Research Dr (48165-8548)
PHONE...................................248 446-5300
Chuck Eden, *COO*
Jim Galidio, *Purchasing*
Jerry Sobolewski, *Engineer*
Paul Deboo, *Chief Mktg Ofcr*
Joseph Bosman, *Branch Mgr*
EMP: 85
SALES (corp-wide): 199.1MM **Privately Held**
WEB: www.sloanvalve.com
SIC: 3494 3443 3431 Valves & pipe fittings; fabricated plate work (boiler shop); metal sanitary ware
PA: Sloan Valve Company
10500 Seymour Ave
Franklin Park IL 60131
847 671-4300

(G-11556)
SUPERIOR MACHINING INC
55378 Lyon Industrial Dr (48165-8544)
PHONE...................................248 446-9451
Dennis Roggers, *President*
EMP: 12
SQ FT: 14,000
SALES (est): 975K **Privately Held**
WEB: www.superiormachining.com
SIC: 3465 Automotive stampings

(G-11557)
TAIT GRINDING SERVICE INC
57401 Travis Rd (48165-9353)
P.O. Box 158 (48165-0158)
PHONE...................................248 437-5100
Richard H Tait, *President*
EMP: 5
SQ FT: 4,000
SALES (est): 613K **Privately Held**
WEB: www.taitcc.com
SIC: 3599 Grinding castings for the trade

(G-11558)
TEC INDUSTRIES INC
Also Called: Maple Industries
55309 Lyon Industrial Dr (48165-8545)
PHONE...................................248 446-9560
Patricia Kuschell, *President*
EMP: 7 **EST:** 1973
SQ FT: 5,000
SALES (est): 1.2MM **Privately Held**
SIC: 3545 Tool holders

(G-11559)
WELK-KO FABRICATORS INC
53655 Grand River Ave (48165-8523)
PHONE...................................248 486-2598
EMP: 6
SALES (corp-wide): 3.7MM **Privately Held**
SIC: 3312 3449 Blast furnaces & steel mills; bars, concrete reinforcing: fabricated steel
PA: Welk-Ko Fabricators, Inc.
11885 Mayfield St
Livonia MI 48150
734 425-6840

New Troy
Berrien County

(G-11560)
TERRY HANOVER
Also Called: Center of The World Woodshop
4102 Hanover Rd (49119)
P.O. Box 105 (49119-0105)
PHONE...................................269 426-4199
Terry Hanover, *Owner*
EMP: 3
SQ FT: 2,250
SALES (est): 214.2K **Privately Held**
SIC: 2511 1751 1521 Wood household furniture; cabinet & finish carpentry; general remodeling, single-family houses

(G-11561)
TRU DIE CAST CORPORATION
13066 California Rd (49119-5112)
P.O. Box 366 (49119-0366)
PHONE...................................269 426-3361
Bruno Lehmann, *President*
▲ **EMP:** 20
SQ FT: 60,000
SALES: 3.8MM **Privately Held**
WEB: www.trudiecast.com
SIC: 3364 3363 Zinc & zinc-base alloy die-castings; aluminum die-castings

(G-11562)
VICKERS ENGINEERING INC
3604 Glendora Rd (49119-5108)
P.O. Box 346 (49119-0346)
PHONE...................................269 426-8545
Matthew S Tyler, *President*
Scott Gourlay, *Vice Pres*
Jeffrey Vickers, *Vice Pres*
David York, *Vice Pres*
Matthew Sorenson, *Engineer*
EMP: 120
SQ FT: 120,000
SALES (est): 34.3MM **Privately Held**
WEB: www.vickerseng.com
SIC: 3599 Machine shop, jobbing & repair; custom machinery; machine & other job shop work

Newaygo
Newaygo County

(G-11563)
ARMSTRONG DISPLAY CONCEPTS
480 S Park St (49337-8940)
P.O. Box 668 (49337-0668)
PHONE...................................231 652-1675
Ronald Armstrong, *President*
Laura Lyons, *Business Mgr*
Pamala Stevens, *Business Mgr*
Scott Faulkner, *CFO*
Michelle Wood, *Department Mgr*
EMP: 13
SQ FT: 6,000
SALES (est): 2MM **Privately Held**
WEB: www.armstrongdisplay.com
SIC: 2653 3993 2394 Display items, solid fiber: made from purchased materials; signs & advertising specialties; canvas & related products

(G-11564)
BUCHER HYDRAULICS INC
201 Cooperative Center Dr (49337-8957)
PHONE...................................231 652-2773
Kimberly Gillespie, *Purchasing*
Jainil Chikani, *Engineer*
Andrew Trombley, *Design Engr*
Dan Vaughan, *Branch Mgr*
EMP: 25
SALES (corp-wide): 3B **Privately Held**
WEB: www.dynalift.com
SIC: 3594 3593 3592 3537 Pumps, hydraulic power transfer; fluid power cylinders, hydraulic or pneumatic; valves; industrial trucks & tractors; valves & pipe fittings; fluid power valves & hose fittings
HQ: Bucher Hydraulics, Inc.
1363 Michigan St Ne
Grand Rapids MI 49503
616 458-1306

(G-11565)
COLONIAL SIGN CO
Also Called: Colonial Neon Sign Co
1170 230th Ave (49337-9412)
PHONE...................................616 534-1400
Richard Ryman, *Owner*
EMP: 3
SQ FT: 3,000
SALES: 375K **Privately Held**
SIC: 3993 7389 Neon signs; sign painting & lettering shop

(G-11566)
CREEKSIDE LUMBER
3810 W 72nd St (49337-9784)
PHONE...................................231 924-1934
Irvin Beachy, *Owner*
EMP: 4
SALES (est): 443.6K **Privately Held**
SIC: 2421 Sawmills & planing mills, general

(G-11567)
DONNELLY CORP
700 Park St (49337-8956)
PHONE...................................231 652-8425
Roger Donga, *Principal*
▲ **EMP:** 14
SALES (est): 3.1MM **Privately Held**
SIC: 3714 Motor vehicle parts & accessories

(G-11568)
G-M WOOD PRODUCTS INC (PA)
Also Called: G-M Graphics
531 S Clay St (49337-8521)
P.O. Box 266 (49337-0266)
PHONE...................................231 652-2201
Mark Micho, *President*
Kevin Karrip, *Vice Pres*
J Kevin Kirrip, *Vice Pres*
Craig Witzman, *Production*
Jane Lang, *Purch Agent*
◆ **EMP:** 80
SQ FT: 150,000
SALES (est): 32.4MM **Privately Held**
SIC: 2431 5199 Windows & window parts & trim, wood; art goods & supplies

(G-11569)
GRAPHICUS SIGNS & DESIGNS
477 S Park St (49337-8940)
PHONE...................................231 652-9160
Sergio Bassetto, *Owner*
Sandra Bassetto, *Co-Owner*
EMP: 5
SALES (est): 358.3K **Privately Held**
SIC: 3993 Signs & advertising specialties

(G-11570)
JERKIES JERKY FACTORY
48 W State Rd (49337-8127)
PHONE...................................231 652-8008
Carrrie Sekach, *Owner*
EMP: 4 **EST:** 2010

▲ = Import ▼ = Export
◆ = Import/Export

SALES (est): 367.7K **Privately Held**
SIC: 3421 Table & food cutlery, including butchers'

(G-11571)
KARR UNLIMITED INC
515 S Division St (49337-8858)
P.O. Box 471, Grant (49327-0471)
PHONE..................................231 652-9045
Karen S Berndt, *President*
Robert Berndt, *Corp Secy*
EMP: 7 **EST:** 1997
SQ FT: 5,250
SALES: 400K **Privately Held**
SIC: 3544 Special dies & tools

(G-11572)
LEGACY TOOL LLC
9023 S Baldwin Ave (49337-9674)
PHONE..................................231 335-8983
Dean A Shue,
EMP: 5
SALES (est): 482.6K **Privately Held**
SIC: 3545 Machine tool accessories

(G-11573)
MAGNA MIRRORS AMERICA INC
Also Called: Magna Mirrors Newaygo Division
579 S Park St (49337-8994)
PHONE..................................616 942-0163
EMP: 177
SALES (corp-wide): 40.8B **Privately Held**
SIC: 3231 3647 3827 Mirrors, truck & automobile: made from purchased glass; dome lights, automotive; optical instruments & lenses
HQ: Magna Mirrors Of America, Inc.
5085 Kraft Ave Se
Grand Rapids MI 49512
616 786-5120

(G-11574)
MAGNA MIRRORS AMERICA INC
700 Park St (49337-8956)
P.O. Box 618 (49337-0618)
PHONE..................................231 652-4450
Brian Chadwell, *General Mgr*
Carl Commons, *General Mgr*
Brian Doom, *Materials Mgr*
Scott Goldman, *Maint Spvr*
Christine Shand, *Production*
EMP: 350
SALES (corp-wide): 40.8B **Privately Held**
WEB: www.donnelly.com
SIC: 3231 3699 3429 Mirrors, truck & automobile: made from purchased glass; door opening & closing devices, electrical; door opening & closing devices, except electrical
HQ: Magna Mirrors Of America, Inc.
5085 Kraft Ave Se
Grand Rapids MI 49512
616 786-5120

(G-11575)
MICHAEL ANDERSON
Also Called: Anderson Screen Printing
4933 E Croton Dr (49337-9012)
PHONE..................................231 652-5717
Michael Anderson, *Owner*
EMP: 4
SALES (est): 277.5K **Privately Held**
SIC: 2759 5999 2396 Screen printing; trophies & plaques; automotive & apparel trimmings

(G-11576)
RIVERSIDE INTERNET SERVICES (PA)
Also Called: Riverside Computer
45 W Gene Furgason Ln (49337-7116)
PHONE..................................231 652-2562
Dan Boutell, *Owner*
EMP: 3
SALES (est): 261.8K **Privately Held**
WEB: www.riverview.net
SIC: 7372 Prepackaged software

(G-11577)
RON ROWE (PA)
Also Called: Copy Shop of Newaygo
8140 S Mason Dr (49337-8802)
PHONE..................................231 652-2642

Ron Rowe, *Owner*
EMP: 3
SQ FT: 1,000
SALES (est): 666.9K **Privately Held**
SIC: 2752 2789 2672 Commercial printing, offset; photo-offset printing; bookbinding & related work; coated & laminated paper

(G-11578)
TECH-SOURCE INTERNATIONAL INC
1000 Park St (49337-8916)
PHONE..................................231 652-9100
Michael N Wilson, *President*
David Hummel, *Corp Secy*
EMP: 30
SQ FT: 17,000
SALES: 2.5MM **Privately Held**
WEB: www.tech-source-intl.com
SIC: 3699 Electrical equipment & supplies

Newberry
Luce County

(G-11579)
EAST END SPORTS AWARDS INC
Also Called: 4 Mile Graphics
13367 State Highway M123 (49868-7624)
PHONE..................................906 293-8895
Dewey Lyke Jr, *President*
Shawn Lyke, *Vice Pres*
EMP: 3
SQ FT: 4,160
SALES (est): 160K **Privately Held**
SIC: 3499 7336 2396 Trophies, metal, except silver; silk screen design; graphic arts & related design; fabric printing & stamping

(G-11580)
MCNAMARA & MCNAMARA
Also Called: Clarence McNamara Logging
13123 State Highway M123 (49868-7625)
PHONE..................................906 293-5281
Clarence E McNamara Jr, *Owner*
EMP: 10 **EST:** 1969
SQ FT: 3,360
SALES: 2.5MM **Privately Held**
SIC: 2411 4212 Logging camps & contractors; timber trucking, local

(G-11581)
NEUMANN ENTERPRISES INC
1011 Newberry Ave (49868-1510)
PHONE..................................906 293-8122
Joyce Neumann, *President*
EMP: 6
SQ FT: 1,200
SALES (est): 243.3K **Privately Held**
SIC: 2711 5992 Newspapers; florists

(G-11582)
NEWBERRY BOTTLING CO INC (PA)
Also Called: Pepsicola
80 N Newberry Ave (49868)
P.O. Box 76 (49868-0076)
PHONE..................................906 293-5189
Jacob Maki, *President*
EMP: 5 **EST:** 1938
SQ FT: 30,000
SALES: 5MM **Privately Held**
SIC: 2086 Carbonated soft drinks, bottled & canned

(G-11583)
NEWBERRY NEWS INC
316 Newberry Ave (49868-1105)
P.O. Box 46 (49868-0046)
PHONE..................................906 293-8401
Bill Diem, *President*
Jackie Applin, *Admin Sec*
EMP: 6 **EST:** 1886
SALES (est): 464.2K **Privately Held**
SIC: 2711 2752 Newspapers: publishing only, not printed on site; commercial printing, offset

(G-11584)
NEWBERRY REDI-MIX INC (PA)
307 E Victory Way (49868)
P.O. Box 404 (49868-0404)
PHONE..................................906 293-5178
William J Burton, *President*
Sandra L Burton, *Admin Sec*
EMP: 8
SQ FT: 3,000
SALES (est): 1.4MM **Privately Held**
SIC: 3273 5211 3272 Ready-mixed concrete; brick; cement; septic tanks, concrete

(G-11585)
NEWBERRY WOOD ENTERPRISES INC
7300 N County Road 403 (49868-7871)
PHONE..................................906 293-3131
Dave Dismuke, *Manager*
EMP: 15
SALES (corp-wide): 1.8MM **Privately Held**
SIC: 2499 Fencing, wood
PA: Newberry Wood Enterprises Inc
12223 Prospect Rd
Strongsville OH 44149
440 238-6127

(G-11586)
NORTHERN WINGS REPAIR INC (PA)
6679 County Road 392 (49868-8170)
P.O. Box 1070, Brookfield WI (53008-1070)
PHONE..................................906 477-6176
David Goudreau, *President*
Christopher Burger, *Opers Mgr*
Dan Hackman, *Opers Staff*
Drew Zitnik, *Sales Staff*
◆ **EMP:** 25
SQ FT: 13,000
SALES: 12MM **Privately Held**
WEB: www.nwrepair.com
SIC: 4581 3728 Aircraft maintenance & repair services; aircraft parts & equipment

Newport
Monroe County

(G-11587)
CENTERLINE INDUS FABRICATION
7397 Mentel Rd (48166-9365)
PHONE..................................313 977-9056
Gerlad Irvine, *Principal*
EMP: 3
SALES (est): 471K **Privately Held**
SIC: 3441 Fabricated structural metal

(G-11588)
J&D INDUSTRIES LLC
4611 Pointe Aux Peaux (48166-9519)
PHONE..................................734 430-6582
Denise Lockard, *Principal*
EMP: 3
SALES (est): 138.6K **Privately Held**
SIC: 3999 Manufacturing industries

(G-11589)
LEVIATHAN DEFENSE GROUP
7720 N Dixie Hwy (48166-9133)
PHONE..................................419 575-7792
James Jacob, *Principal*
EMP: 3
SALES (est): 310.7K **Privately Held**
SIC: 3812 Defense systems & equipment

(G-11590)
ROCKWOOD QUARRY LLC
7500 Reaume Rd (48166-9709)
PHONE..................................734 783-7400
Bill Begley, *General Mgr*
EMP: 8
SALES (est): 530.5K
SALES (corp-wide): 14.4MM **Privately Held**
SIC: 3281 Stone, quarrying & processing of own stone products
PA: Rockwood Quarry, Llc
5699 Ready Rd
South Rockwood MI 48179
734 783-7415

(G-11591)
STONECO OF MICHIGAN INC
7250 Reaume Rd (48166-9709)
PHONE..................................734 236-6538
Dean Vanderveld, *Manager*
EMP: 7 **Privately Held**
SIC: 3531 Construction machinery
PA: Stoneco Of Michigan Inc
15203 S Telegraph Rd
Monroe MI 48161

Niles
Berrien County

(G-11592)
AACOA EXTRUSIONS INC
2005 Mayflower Rd (49120-8625)
PHONE..................................269 697-6063
Dan Formsma, *President*
Barry Bundesman, *Project Engr*
Michael Mann, *Finance Mgr*
Jeff Teeple, *VP Sales*
Carl Holderbaum, *Manager*
EMP: 220
SQ FT: 91,000
SALES (est): 90.2MM **Privately Held**
WEB: www.aacoa.com
SIC: 3354 Aluminum extruded products
HQ: Aacoa, Inc.
2551 County Road 10 W
Elkhart IN 46514
574 262-4685

(G-11593)
ACCESS MANUFACTURING TECHN
1530 W River Rd (49120-8953)
PHONE..................................224 610-0171
Tom Rissmann, *Principal*
▲ **EMP:** 12
SALES (est): 1.1MM **Privately Held**
SIC: 3999 Manufacturing industries

(G-11594)
AMERICAN AGGREGATE INC
2041 M 140 (49120-1131)
PHONE..................................269 683-6160
Betty Smith, *President*
EMP: 8
SALES (est): 1.5MM **Privately Held**
SIC: 1429 1442 5032 Sandstone, crushed & broken-quarrying; gravel mining; sand, construction; gravel

(G-11595)
ASTAR INC
71135 Fir Rd (49120-5960)
PHONE..................................574 234-2137
Sidney Moore Jr, *President*
Dorothy Moore, *Corp Secy*
EMP: 40 **EST:** 1980
SQ FT: 40,000
SALES (est): 8MM **Privately Held**
WEB: www.astar.com
SIC: 3089 3544 Injection molding of plastics; forms (molds), for foundry & plastics working machinery

(G-11596)
BAUER SOFT WATER CO
1760 Mayflower Rd (49120-8753)
P.O. Box 72 (49120-0072)
PHONE..................................269 695-7900
Matthew Bauer, *President*
EMP: 6
SQ FT: 10,000
SALES (est): 892.1K **Privately Held**
WEB: www.bauerwater.com
SIC: 3589 7389 Water filters & softeners, household type; water softener service

(G-11597)
BLOCKMATIC INC
Also Called: Blockmatic Company
2519 S 17th St (49120-4597)
PHONE..................................269 683-1655
Jeffery A Cichos, *President*
Sigmund P Cichos, *Vice Pres*
EMP: 7
SQ FT: 5,000
SALES: 1.3MM **Privately Held**
SIC: 3559 Concrete products machinery

Niles - Berrien County (G-11598)

(G-11598)
C & S MACHINE PRODUCTS INC (PA)
2929 Saratore Dr (49120-8703)
PHONE...................269 695-6859
Joseph J Saratore, *President*
Dominick Saratore, *President*
Rachel Saratore, *Corp Secy*
Denice Hartline, *Vice Pres*
Andrea Adams, *Purchasing*
EMP: 41
SQ FT: 18,000
SALES: 11.4MM **Privately Held**
WEB: www.candsmachine.com
SIC: 3599 Machine shop, jobbing & repair

(G-11599)
CNC PRODUCTS LLC
2126 S 11th St (49120-4096)
PHONE...................269 684-5500
Fritz Knauf, *President*
EMP: 20 **EST:** 1987
SQ FT: 41,000
SALES (est): 4.2MM **Privately Held**
WEB: www.cncproducts-llc.com
SIC: 3444 Sheet metal specialties, not stamped; metal housings, enclosures, casings & other containers

(G-11600)
COLORFUL STITCHES
225 E Main St (49120-2303)
PHONE...................269 683-6442
Elsie Lancaster, *Owner*
EMP: 3
SALES (est): 218.8K **Privately Held**
SIC: 2395 Embroidery products, except schiffli machine; embroidery & art needlework

(G-11601)
CONSUMERS CONCRETE CORPORATION
1523 Lake St (49120-1235)
PHONE...................269 684-8760
Matt Tober, *Manager*
EMP: 9
SALES (corp-wide): 102.9MM **Privately Held**
WEB: www.consumersconcrete.com
SIC: 3273 Ready-mixed concrete
PA: Consumers Concrete Corporation
3508 S Sprinkle Rd
Kalamazoo MI 49001
269 342-0136

(G-11602)
CRAFT PRESS PRINTING INC
312 Bell Rd (49120-4063)
PHONE...................269 683-9694
James Dahlgren, *President*
Gina Dahlgren, *Vice Pres*
EMP: 5
SQ FT: 2,800
SALES: 229.4K **Privately Held**
SIC: 2752 3552 Commercial printing, offset; business form & card printing, lithographic; business forms, lithographic; silk screens for textile industry

(G-11603)
CROSS ALUMINUM PRODUCTS INC
1770 Mayflower Rd (49120-8753)
PHONE...................269 697-8340
Patrick J Leets, *President*
Michael Leets, *Vice Pres*
Jackie Leets, *Treasurer*
Jacob Leets, *Admin Sec*
▲ **EMP:** 15 **EST:** 1977
SQ FT: 38,180
SALES: 2.7MM **Privately Held**
WEB: www.crossaluminum.com
SIC: 3442 Metal doors; casements, aluminum; window & door frames

(G-11604)
CUSTOM MARINE CARPET
Also Called: CMC
423 N 9th St (49120-2531)
PHONE...................269 684-1922
John Peterson, *Owner*
▼ **EMP:** 6
SQ FT: 25,000
SALES: 750K **Privately Held**
WEB: www.snapincarpet.com
SIC: 2273 Carpets & rugs

(G-11605)
CUT-TECH
1951 Industrial Dr (49120-1228)
PHONE...................269 687-9005
William Glossinger, *President*
Henry Kruger, *Vice Pres*
EMP: 3
SQ FT: 10,000
SALES: 250K **Privately Held**
SIC: 2865 3599 Dyes & pigments; machine shop, jobbing & repair

(G-11606)
DAUGHTRY NWSPAPERS INVESTMENTS
Also Called: Dowagiac Daily News
217 N 4th St (49120-2301)
PHONE...................269 683-2100
L P Daughtry, *President*
Les P Daughtry, *President*
Daniel G Dean, *Vice Pres*
Wade J Parker, *Treasurer*
EMP: 13
SQ FT: 6,000
SALES (est): 706.8K **Privately Held**
SIC: 2711 5994 Newspapers: publishing only, not printed on site; news dealers & newsstands

(G-11607)
DEHRING MOLD E-D-M
1450 Jerome St (49120-3462)
PHONE...................269 683-5970
Dennis Dehring, *Owner*
EMP: 7 **EST:** 1976
SQ FT: 16,000
SALES (est): 642.8K **Privately Held**
SIC: 3544 Industrial molds

(G-11608)
DELTA MACHINING INC
2361 Reum Rd (49120-5037)
PHONE...................269 683-7775
Wannis Parris, *CEO*
Doug Liggett, *Engineer*
Michael Smith, *CFO*
William R Robison, *Treasurer*
Pam Laporte, *Controller*
▲ **EMP:** 70
SQ FT: 100,000
SALES: 9.9MM **Privately Held**
WEB: www.deltamach.com
SIC: 3599 3494 Machine shop, jobbing & repair; valves & pipe fittings

(G-11609)
DSS VALVE PRODUCTS INC
Also Called: Valves D S S
1760 Mayflower Rd (49120-8753)
PHONE...................269 409-6080
Trenton Runyon, *President*
David Bergeron, *COO*
James Pellegrini, *Vice Pres*
Jim Pellegrini, *Vice Pres*
Jennifer Foulks, *Controller*
EMP: 14
SQ FT: 2,500
SALES (est): 2.3MM **Privately Held**
SIC: 3491 Industrial valves

(G-11610)
DW-NATIONAL STANDARD-NILES LLC
1631 Lake St (49120-1270)
PHONE...................269 683-8100
Tim Francis,
Brent Steffen,
▲ **EMP:** 135
SALES (est): 48.6MM **Privately Held**
SIC: 3315 Wire & fabricated wire products
HQ: National-Standard, Llc
1631 Lake St
Niles MI 49120
269 683-9902

(G-11611)
FONTIJNE GROTNES INC
30257 Redfield St (49120-5958)
PHONE...................269 262-4700
Mike Walker, *CEO*
Mark Varda, *Engineer*
▲ **EMP:** 40
SALES: 10MM **Privately Held**
WEB: www.fontijnegrotnes.com
SIC: 3714 3549 3543 3545 Wheel rims, motor vehicle; metalworking machinery; rolling mill machinery; machine tool accessories; machine tools, metal forming type

(G-11612)
FRENCH PAPER COMPANY
100 French St (49120-2854)
P.O. Box 398 (49120-0398)
PHONE...................269 683-1100
Jerry French, *CEO*
Shane Fenske, *VP Mfg*
◆ **EMP:** 85 **EST:** 1871
SQ FT: 3,362
SALES (est): 32.8MM
SALES (corp-wide): 75.7MM **Privately Held**
SIC: 2621 Book paper; text paper; offset paper; specialty papers
PA: Finch Paper Holdings Llc
1 Glen St
Glens Falls NY 12801
800 833-9983

(G-11613)
GAMCO INC
3001 S 11th St (49120-4753)
P.O. Box 272 (49120-0272)
PHONE...................269 683-4280
Gary E Smith, *President*
Martha Smith, *Vice Pres*
▲ **EMP:** 10
SALES (est): 1.5MM **Privately Held**
WEB: www.gamcoinc.com
SIC: 2392 Household furnishings

(G-11614)
GARDEN CITY PRODUCTS INC
833 Carberry Rd (49120-5012)
P.O. Box 967 (49120-0967)
PHONE...................269 684-6264
Larry Reichanadter, *President*
Larry Rechanadter, *President*
Lydia Reichanadter, *Vice Pres*
EMP: 15
SQ FT: 6,500
SALES (est): 1.9MM **Privately Held**
SIC: 3599 7389 7692 3544 Machine shop, jobbing & repair; engraving service; welding repair; special dies, tools, jigs & fixtures

(G-11615)
GREAT LAKES PRECISION MACHINE
Also Called: Great Lakes Metal Fabricating
1760 Foundation Dr (49120-8987)
PHONE...................269 695-4580
Keith Fulbright, *President*
EMP: 11
SQ FT: 11,000
SALES (est): 1.8MM **Privately Held**
SIC: 3599 Machine shop, jobbing & repair; machine & other job shop work

(G-11616)
HOOSIER TANK AND MANUFACTURING
2190 Industrial Dr (49120-1233)
PHONE...................269 683-2550
EMP: 3
SALES (est): 175.7K **Privately Held**
SIC: 3999 Manufacturing industries

(G-11617)
INDUSTRIAL MACHINE TECH LLC
32736 Bertrand St (49120-7656)
PHONE...................269 683-4689
Trent Vaughn, *Mng Member*
EMP: 5
SALES: 400K **Privately Held**
SIC: 3599 Machine shop, jobbing & repair

(G-11618)
INERTIA CYCLEWORKS
211 E Main St (49120-2303)
PHONE...................269 684-2000
EMP: 3
SALES (est): 220.1K **Privately Held**
SIC: 3625 Relays & industrial controls

(G-11619)
INNOVATION MACHINING CORP
1461 S 3rd St (49120-4024)
PHONE...................269 683-3343
Charles Lord, *President*
EMP: 12
SQ FT: 9,000
SALES (est): 831.7K **Privately Held**
SIC: 3599 Machine shop, jobbing & repair

(G-11620)
INNOVATIVE PDTS UNLIMITED INC
2120 Industrial Dr (49120-1233)
PHONE...................269 684-5050
Fritz Heerdt, *President*
William Becker, *Vice Pres*
Melissa Asmus, *Purch Agent*
▲ **EMP:** 35
SQ FT: 10,000
SALES (est): 5.8MM **Privately Held**
WEB: www.ipu.com
SIC: 2599 2519 Hospital beds; fiberglass & plastic furniture

(G-11621)
INTRA BUSINESS LLC
70600 Batchelor Dr (49120-7624)
PHONE...................269 262-0863
John Kampars, *Mng Member*
EMP: 5
SALES (est): 445.7K **Privately Held**
SIC: 5112 7389 2893 Office supplies; ; printing ink

(G-11622)
JOY PRODUCTS INC
1930 S 3rd St (49120-4004)
PHONE...................269 683-1662
Michael Stewart, *President*
EMP: 4
SQ FT: 8,000
SALES (est): 420K **Privately Held**
SIC: 3086 Ice chests or coolers (portable), foamed plastic

(G-11623)
LEADER PUBLICATIONS LLC (PA)
Also Called: Niles Daily Star
217 N 4th St (49120-2301)
P.O. Box 391 (49120-0391)
PHONE...................269 683-2100
Scott Novak, *Editor*
Rhonda Rauen, *Accounting Mgr*
Phil Langer, *Marketing Staff*
Lisa Oxender, *Marketing Staff*
Cindy Klingerman, *Manager*
EMP: 75
SQ FT: 8,000
SALES (est): 4.4MM **Privately Held**
WEB: www.leaderpub.com
SIC: 2711 2752 2741 Newspapers, publishing & printing; commercial printing, lithographic; miscellaneous publishing

(G-11624)
MASSEE PRODUCTS LTD
2612 N 5th St (49120-1174)
PHONE...................269 684-8255
Jesse Townsend, *President*
Margaret Townsend, *Corp Secy*
EMP: 5
SQ FT: 11,000
SALES (est): 400K **Privately Held**
SIC: 3069 Foam rubber

(G-11625)
MEGAPRO MARKETING USA INC
2710 S 3rd St (49120-4406)
PHONE...................866 522-3652
Hermann Fruhm, *President*
EMP: 10
SQ FT: 21,000
SALES: 6MM **Privately Held**
SIC: 3423 Hand & edge tools

(G-11626)
MICHIANA AGGREGATE INC
3265 W Us Highway 12 (49120-8761)
PHONE...................269 695-7669
John S Yerington II, *President*
EMP: 9
SQ FT: 600

▲ = Import ▼ = Export
◆ = Import/Export

GEOGRAPHIC SECTION

North Adams - Hillsdale County (G-11654)

SALES (est): 707.4K **Privately Held**
SIC: 1442 Sand mining; gravel mining

(G-11627)
MODINEER CO (PA)
2190 Industrial Dr (49120-1233)
P.O. Box 640 (49120-0640)
PHONE.................................269 683-2550
Jonathon Stough, *General Mgr*
Michael J Dreher, *Chairman*
Gary Dreher, *Vice Pres*
Dave Graham, *Opers Mgr*
Michael Busby, *Production*
◆ EMP: 130 EST: 1940
SQ FT: 96,000
SALES (est): 138.8MM **Privately Held**
WEB: www.modineer.com
SIC: 3469 3599 3544 Stamping metal for the trade; machine shop, jobbing & repair; special dies & tools

(G-11628)
MODINEER CO
1501 S 3rd St (49120-4026)
PHONE.................................269 684-3138
Allan Hoffman, *Branch Mgr*
EMP: 140
SALES (corp-wide): 138.8MM **Privately Held**
WEB: www.modineer.com
SIC: 3469 3599 3544 Stamping metal for the trade; machine shop, jobbing & repair; special dies & tools
PA: Modineer Co.
2190 Industrial Dr
Niles MI 49120
269 683-2550

(G-11629)
N & K FULBRIGHT LLC
Also Called: Great Lakes X-Cel
1760 Foundation Dr (49120-8987)
PHONE.................................269 695-4580
Keith Fultright,
EMP: 30
SALES (est): 6.1MM **Privately Held**
SIC: 3449 Bars, concrete reinforcing: fabricated steel

(G-11630)
NATIONAL-STANDARD LLC (HQ)
1631 Lake St (49120-1270)
PHONE.................................269 683-9902
Eric Lupa, *Purch Mgr*
Jim Hillebrandt,
Wendy Miller, *Technician*
▲ EMP: 242 EST: 2008
SQ FT: 456,000
SALES (est): 84.2MM **Privately Held**
WEB: www.nationalstandard.com
SIC: 3315 3496 Wire & fabricated wire products; wire, ferrous/iron; wire products, ferrous/iron: made in wiredrawing plants; miscellaneous fabricated wire products; wire cloth & woven wire products

(G-11631)
NCP COATINGS INC (PA)
225 Fort St (49120-3429)
P.O. Box 307 (49120-0307)
PHONE.................................269 683-3377
Neil Hannewyk, *President*
Cornelius M Hannewyk III, *President*
Jennifer Moore, *General Mgr*
M Sherman Drew Jr, *Vice Pres*
Sherman Drew, *Vice Pres*
EMP: 95
SQ FT: 6,300
SALES (est): 17.9MM **Privately Held**
WEB: www.ncpcoatings.com
SIC: 2851 Paints & paint additives

(G-11632)
NILES ALUMINUM PRODUCTS INC
1434 S 9th St (49120-4208)
P.O. Box 607 (49120-0607)
PHONE.................................269 683-1191
Donald Ort, *President*
Vicki Ort, *Corp Secy*
Ginger Andres, *Manager*
Christina Lee, *Manager*
EMP: 12
SQ FT: 23,000
SALES (est): 2MM **Privately Held**
SIC: 3446 Architectural metalwork

(G-11633)
NILES MACHINE & TOOL COMPANY
2124 S 11th St (49120-4061)
PHONE.................................269 684-2594
Richard Robbins, *Owner*
EMP: 5
SQ FT: 6,000
SALES (est): 1.2MM **Privately Held**
SIC: 3599 Machine shop, jobbing & repair

(G-11634)
NILES PRECISION COMPANY
1308 Fort St (49120-3898)
P.O. Box 548 (49120-0548)
PHONE.................................269 683-0585
Jay C Skalla, *President*
Eric C Vinnedge, *Vice Pres*
Kalie Wieger, *Technology*
John Dykema, *Admin Sec*
EMP: 168 EST: 1950
SQ FT: 60,000
SALES (est): 33.9MM **Privately Held**
WEB: www.nilesprecision.com
SIC: 3724 3728 3812 Aircraft engines & engine parts; aircraft parts & equipment; search & navigation equipment

(G-11635)
PADDLETEK LLC
1990 S 11th St Ste 3 (49120-4072)
PHONE.................................269 340-5967
Curtis Smith, *Owner*
Janeth Vance, *Office Mgr*
EMP: 14
SALES (est): 1MM **Privately Held**
SIC: 2499 Oars & paddles, wood

(G-11636)
PARAGON TEMPERED GLASS LLC (PA)
1830 Terminal Rd (49120-1246)
PHONE.................................269 684-5060
Terry Orourke, *President*
EMP: 26
SALES (est): 9MM **Privately Held**
SIC: 3231 Products of purchased glass

(G-11637)
PATRIOT TOOL & DIE INC
2116 Progressive Dr (49120-1285)
PHONE.................................269 687-9024
Paul Mooney, *President*
George Forray, *Vice Pres*
EMP: 5
SQ FT: 1,200
SALES (est): 510.2K **Privately Held**
SIC: 3544 Special dies & tools

(G-11638)
PERFORMANCE MACHINING INC
Also Called: On Sight Armory
919 Michigan St (49120-3330)
PHONE.................................269 683-4370
Susan Millin, *President*
EMP: 9
SALES (est): 1MM **Privately Held**
SIC: 3599 Machine shop, jobbing & repair

(G-11639)
PHILLIP ANDERSON
Also Called: Cut Above Wood Designs
2536 Detroit Rd (49120-9447)
P.O. Box 455 (49120-0455)
PHONE.................................269 687-7166
Phillip Anderson, *Owner*
EMP: 3 EST: 1997
SALES (est): 389.3K **Privately Held**
SIC: 5712 2521 Cabinet work, custom; cabinets, office: wood

(G-11640)
PILKINGTON NORTH AMERICA INC
Also Called: Pilkington Glass - Niles
2121 W Chicago Rd Ste E (49120-8647)
PHONE.................................269 687-2100
Peter Carpenter, *Plant Mgr*
Eric Quinn, *Safety Mgr*
Doug Wait, *Branch Mgr*
EMP: 302 **Privately Held**
WEB: www.low-eglass.com
SIC: 3211 Construction glass
HQ: Pilkington North America, Inc.
811 Madison Ave Fl 3
Toledo OH 43604
419 247-3731

(G-11641)
R & M MANUFACTURING COMPANY
2424 N 5th St (49120-1193)
PHONE.................................269 683-9550
Timothy Mead, *President*
Roger Larson, *Director*
Diana Mead, *Admin Sec*
EMP: 18 EST: 1948
SQ FT: 10,000
SALES (est): 2.5MM **Privately Held**
WEB: www.rmmco.com
SIC: 3599 Machine shop, jobbing & repair

(G-11642)
REED FUEL LLC
1445 S 3rd St (49120-4024)
PHONE.................................574 520-3101
Reed Ryan, *Administration*
EMP: 3
SALES (est): 202.8K **Privately Held**
SIC: 2869 Fuels

(G-11643)
REVWIRES LLC
1631 Lake St (49120-1270)
PHONE.................................269 683-8100
Brent Steffen,
EMP: 8
SALES (est): 1MM **Privately Held**
WEB: www.revwires.com
SIC: 3399 Brads: aluminum, brass or other nonferrous metal or wire

(G-11644)
RTI PRODUCTS LLC
1451 Lake St (49120-1235)
PHONE.................................269 684-9960
Ronald G Witchie, *Mng Member*
Linda L Witchie,
▲ EMP: 18
SQ FT: 30,000
SALES (est): 2.9MM **Privately Held**
WEB: www.rti-products.com
SIC: 3661 Telephone & telegraph apparatus

(G-11645)
SHIVELY CORP
Also Called: West River Machine
2604 S 11th St (49120-4418)
PHONE.................................269 683-9503
Don Shively, *President*
Betty Shively, *Vice Pres*
EMP: 10
SALES (est): 897K **Privately Held**
SIC: 3599 Machine shop, jobbing & repair

(G-11646)
SOUTHAST BERRIEN CNTY LANDFILL
1540 Mayflower Rd (49120-8729)
PHONE.................................269 695-2500
Carla Cole, *Ch of Bd*
Barry Miller, *Opers Mgr*
EMP: 19
SQ FT: 454,400
SALES (est): 5.1MM **Privately Held**
SIC: 4953 2611 4212 Sanitary landfill operation; pulp manufactured from waste or recycled paper; garbage collection & transport, no disposal

(G-11647)
SPARTAN TOOL LLC (DH)
1618 Terminal Rd (49120-1298)
PHONE.................................815 539-7411
Kevin Walsh, *President*
Brian Binns, *Engineer*
Ross Wilson, *Engineer*
Kevin Dineen, *Project Engr*
Kyle Marscola, *Controller*
▲ EMP: 25
SALES (est): 26.1MM
SALES (corp-wide): 1.2B **Privately Held**
WEB: www.spartantool.com
SIC: 3589 Sewer cleaning equipment, power
HQ: Pettibone L.L.C.
27501 Bella Vista Pkwy
Warrenville IL 60555
630 353-5000

(G-11648)
SPECIALTY PDTS & POLYMERS INC
2100 Progressive Dr (49120-1285)
PHONE.................................269 684-5931
Rick Rey, *President*
Enriqueto C Rey, *Admin Sec*
Kristen Fellows, *Technician*
▲ EMP: 25
SQ FT: 30,000
SALES (est): 5.7MM **Privately Held**
SIC: 3069 Custom compounding of rubber materials

(G-11649)
TOEFCO ENGINEERING INC
Also Called: Toefco Engnred Coating Systems
1220 N 14th St (49120-1897)
PHONE.................................269 683-0188
Artie McElwee, *CEO*
Arthur McElwee III, *President*
Patricia McElwee, *Exec VP*
Scott Kucela, *Controller*
Craig Ponsler, *Accounts Mgr*
EMP: 35 EST: 1955
SQ FT: 47,000
SALES (est): 5.9MM **Privately Held**
WEB: www.toefco.com
SIC: 3479 Coating of metals & formed products

(G-11650)
TRU BLU INDUSTRIES LLC
1920 Industrial Dr (49120-1229)
PHONE.................................269 684-4989
David Kalling, *Manager*
EMP: 90
SALES (est): 10.9MM **Privately Held**
SIC: 2679 Paperboard products, converted

(G-11651)
WHITE ENGINEERING INC
Also Called: White Tool & Engineering
3000 E Geyer Rd (49120-9066)
PHONE.................................269 695-0825
Rolf Krueger, *President*
Hildegarde Krueger, *Corp Secy*
Kurt Krueger, *Vice Pres*
EMP: 4
SQ FT: 4,000
SALES (est): 580.8K **Privately Held**
SIC: 3544 Special dies & tools

(G-11652)
YERINGTON BROTHERS INC
3265 W Us Highway 12 (49120-8761)
PHONE.................................269 695-7669
John Yerington, *President*
John S Yerington II, *Treasurer*
Denise Skala, *Admin Sec*
EMP: 8
SQ FT: 500
SALES (est): 550K **Privately Held**
SIC: 3532 4212 Mining machinery; dump truck haulage

(G-11653)
ZELLCO PRECISION INC
1710 E Main St (49120-3832)
PHONE.................................269 684-1720
Eric Zellmer, *President*
Ingrid Zellmer, *Treasurer*
EMP: 5
SQ FT: 5,000
SALES (est): 741.9K **Privately Held**
SIC: 3599 Machine shop, jobbing & repair

North Adams
Hillsdale County

(G-11654)
F & F MOLD INC
5931 Knowles Rd (49262-9708)
PHONE.................................517 287-5866
EMP: 7
SQ FT: 7,500

North Adams - Hillsdale County (G-11655)

GEOGRAPHIC SECTION

SALES: 1.2MM **Privately Held**
SIC: 3544 Mfg Dies/Tools/Jigs/Fixtures

(G-11655)
J AND K PALLET
10990 N Adams Rd (49262-9760)
PHONE 517 648-5974
EMP: 3
SALES (est): 143.1K **Privately Held**
SIC: 2448 Pallets, wood & wood with metal

(G-11656)
MARTINREA METAL INDUSTRIES INC
4800 Knowles Rd (49262)
PHONE 517 849-2195
Carl Brewer, *Principal*
EMP: 75
SALES (corp-wide): 2.7B **Privately Held**
SIC: 3559 Automotive related machinery
HQ: Martinrea Metal Industries, Inc.
2100 N Opdyke Rd
Auburn Hills MI 48326
248 392-9700

North Branch
Lapeer County

(G-11657)
CCO HOLDINGS LLC
3989 Huron St (48461-6122)
PHONE 810 270-1002
EMP: 3
SALES (corp-wide): 43.6B **Publicly Held**
SIC: 5064 4841 3663 3651 Electrical appliances, television & radio; cable & other pay television services; radio & TV communications equipment; household audio & video equipment
HQ: Cco Holdings, Llc
400 Atlantic St
Stamford CT 06901
203 905-7801

(G-11658)
CUSTOM MOLD TOOL AND DIE CORP
6779 Lincoln St (48461-7700)
P.O. Box 3571 (48461-0571)
PHONE 810 688-3711
Norm Morey, *President*
EMP: 8
SQ FT: 6,060
SALES (est): 306.1K **Privately Held**
SIC: 3312 Tool & die steel

(G-11659)
DAVID JENKS
5955 Chapman Rd (48461-9532)
PHONE 810 793-7340
David Jenks, *Principal*
EMP: 3
SALES (est): 230.5K **Privately Held**
SIC: 2411 Logging camps & contractors

(G-11660)
JOHNSON WALKER & ASSOC LLC
Also Called: Imperial Plastics Mfg
4337 Mill St (48461-8727)
PHONE 810 688-1600
Charles Snooks, *CFO*
Craig S Johnson, *Mng Member*
Tom Walker, *Mng Member*
EMP: 8
SALES (est): 1.4MM **Privately Held**
SIC: 3089 Extruded finished plastic products

(G-11661)
KEIZER-MORRIS INTL INC
Also Called: Km International
6561 Bernie Kohler Dr (48461-8886)
PHONE 810 688-1234
Bryan Burke, *CEO*
Clifford Cameron, *President*
Cliff Cameron, *General Mgr*
Greg Welke, *Manager*
EMP: 32
SQ FT: 37,500
SALES (est): 10.3MM **Privately Held**
WEB: www.kminfrared.com
SIC: 3531 Construction machinery

(G-11662)
KK WELDING SERVICES INC
3903 Five Lakes Rd (48461-8400)
PHONE 810 664-5564
Kirt Lawicki, *President*
EMP: 5
SALES (est): 403.9K **Privately Held**
SIC: 7692 Welding repair

(G-11663)
MK CHAMBERS COMPANY (PA)
2251 Johnson Mill Rd (48461-9744)
PHONE 810 688-3750
Gerald Chambers, *President*
Robert Chambers, *Senior VP*
Merle K Chambers, *Vice Pres*
Sharon Chase, *Vice Pres*
Paul Rogers, *Plant Mgr*
▲ EMP: 50 EST: 1957
SQ FT: 70,000
SALES (est): 17.1MM **Privately Held**
WEB: www.mkchambers.com
SIC: 3451 Screw machine products

(G-11664)
PRECISION MACHINING COMPANY
6637 Bernie Kohler Dr (48461-6112)
PHONE 810 688-8674
Mark Grimem, *President*
EMP: 24 EST: 1986
SQ FT: 10,500
SALES (est): 4.3MM **Privately Held**
WEB: www.precision-machiningco.com
SIC: 3599 Machine shop, jobbing & repair

(G-11665)
PRODUCTION THREADED PARTS CO
Also Called: Orr Lumber
6829 Lincoln St (48461-8440)
P.O. Box 320 (48461-0320)
PHONE 810 688-3186
Ralph Deshetsky, *President*
Wilfred Deshetsky, *Vice Pres*
Tracey Delong, *Admin Sec*
Marjorie Deshetsky, *Asst Sec*
EMP: 18 EST: 1955
SQ FT: 28,000
SALES (est): 3.5MM **Privately Held**
WEB: www.orrlumber.com
SIC: 3541 Machine tools, metal cutting type

(G-11666)
VANCO STEEL INC
6573 Bernie Kohler Dr (48461-8886)
P.O. Box 178 (48461-0178)
PHONE 810 688-4333
John Vanecek, *President*
Nick Vanecek, *Vice Pres*
EMP: 14
SALES (est): 2.1MM **Privately Held**
SIC: 3441 Fabricated structural metal

North Star
Gratiot County

(G-11667)
SMITH CONCRETE PRODUCTS
3282 S Crapo Rd (48862)
PHONE 989 875-4687
Robert Smith, *Owner*
EMP: 4
SALES (est): 359.5K **Privately Held**
SIC: 3272 Burial vaults, concrete or precast terrazzo

North Street
St. Clair County

(G-11668)
PROFILE GEAR INC
4777 Brott Rd (48049-2317)
PHONE 810 324-2731
Edmond P Cloutier II, *President*
Carol Cloutier, *Vice Pres*
▲ EMP: 7 EST: 1977
SQ FT: 10,000
SALES: 800K **Privately Held**
SIC: 3599 Machine shop, jobbing & repair

(G-11669)
TYLER CROCKETT MARINE ENGINES
Also Called: Crockett, Tyler Marine Engines
4600 Brott Rd (48049-2907)
PHONE 810 324-2720
Tyler Crockett, *Owner*
EMP: 3
SALES: 130K **Privately Held**
WEB: www.crockettmarineengines.com
SIC: 3599 Machine shop, jobbing & repair

Northport
Leelanau County

(G-11670)
MASTER CRAFT EXTRUSION TLS INC
771 N Mill St (49670-9701)
PHONE 231 386-5149
Donald Allington, *President*
Diane Allington, *CFO*
Juli Waldrup, *Office Mgr*
EMP: 11
SQ FT: 10,000
SALES: 1.3MM **Privately Held**
SIC: 3544 Special dies & tools

(G-11671)
SHERWOOD MANUFACTURING CORP
922 N Mill St (49670-9779)
P.O. Box 366 (49670-0366)
PHONE 231 386-5132
Gerald R Woods, *President*
Raymond Keith Woods, *Vice Pres*
Linda E Woods, *Treasurer*
EMP: 20
SQ FT: 20,000
SALES (est): 3.7MM **Privately Held**
SIC: 3441 7692 Fabricated structural metal; welding repair

(G-11672)
SPARTAN FLAG COMPANY INC
323 S Shabwasung St (49670)
PHONE 231 386-5150
Cheryl Seipke, *President*
Milton Seipke, *Vice Pres*
EMP: 15 EST: 1950
SQ FT: 3,400
SALES (est): 1.6MM **Privately Held**
SIC: 2399 Flags, fabric; pennants

(G-11673)
THOMAS AND MILLIKEN MLLWK INC (PA)
931 N Mill St (49670-9779)
P.O. Box 265 (49670-0265)
PHONE 231 386-7236
Andrew Thomas, *President*
Todd Huck, *Plant Mgr*
Kent Strawderman, *Sales Staff*
Gloria Thomas, *Admin Sec*
EMP: 18
SQ FT: 13,000
SALES (est): 3.7MM **Privately Held**
WEB: www.tmmill.com
SIC: 2431 1751 Millwork; cabinet building & installation

Northville
Wayne County

(G-11674)
5 WATER SOCKS LLC
17679 Stonebrook Dr (48168-4328)
PHONE 248 735-1730
EMP: 3 EST: 2013
SALES (est): 138.6K **Privately Held**
SIC: 2252 Mfg Hosiery

(G-11675)
A A ANCHOR BOLT INC
7390 Salem Rd (48168-9404)
PHONE 248 349-6565
Robert P Horton, *President*
Robert M Horton, *Vice Pres*
Kellie Duffy, *Manager*
EMP: 15
SQ FT: 15,000
SALES (est): 3.5MM **Privately Held**
WEB: www.aaanchorbolt.com
SIC: 3545 3452 Threading tools (machine tool accessories); bolts, metal

(G-11676)
AISIN HOLDINGS AMERICA INC
15300 Centennial Dr (48168-8687)
PHONE 734 453-5551
Jun Mukai, *Branch Mgr*
EMP: 5 **Privately Held**
SIC: 2395 2499 Emblems, embroidered; seats, toilet
HQ: Aisin Holdings Of America, Inc.
1665 E 4th Street Rd
Seymour IN 47274
812 524-8144

(G-11677)
AISIN TECHNICAL CTR AMER INC
15300 Centennial Dr (48168-8687)
PHONE 734 453-5551
Yoshiaki Kato, *President*
Takashi Araki, *Treasurer*
♦ EMP: 71
SALES (est): 16.3MM **Privately Held**
SIC: 3559 Automotive related machinery
PA: Aisin Seiki Co., Ltd.
2-1, Asahimachi
Kariya AIC 448-0

(G-11678)
BELANGER INC
1001 Doheny Dr (48167-1957)
PHONE 248 349-7010
EMP: 3
SALES (corp-wide): 6.9B **Publicly Held**
SIC: 3291 Abrasive products
HQ: Belanger, Inc.
9393 Prnceton Glendale Rd
West Chester OH 45011
517 870-3206

(G-11679)
BELANGER ABRASIVES INC
Also Called: Belanger Industrial Products
19414 Gerald St (48167-2517)
PHONE 248 735-8900
Lee Belanger, *President*
Richard Belanger, *Vice Pres*
▲ EMP: 70
SQ FT: 26,000
SALES (est): 8.2MM
SALES (corp-wide): 612.9MM **Publicly Held**
WEB: www.belangerabrasives.com
SIC: 3291 Abrasive wheels & grindstones, not artificial
HQ: Schaffner Manufacturing Co Inc
21 Herron Ave
Pittsburgh PA 15202
412 761-9902

(G-11680)
BOHLEY INDUSTRIES
9595 5 Mile Rd (48168-9403)
PHONE 734 455-3430
Virgil Bohley, *Principal*
EMP: 3
SALES (est): 330K **Privately Held**
SIC: 5051 2431 1799 Steel; staircases, stairs & railings; special trade contractors

(G-11681)
BROWNDOG CREAMERY LLC
118 E Main St (48167-1620)
PHONE 248 361-3759
Paul Gabriel, *Principal*
EMP: 3
SALES (est): 191K **Privately Held**
SIC: 2021 Creamery butter

(G-11682)
CAMBRIDGE FOODS LLC
Also Called: Elizabeth Jeans Pie Kits
47765 Bellagio Dr (48167-9803)
PHONE 248 348-3800
Elizabeth Guidobono, *Mng Member*
Mark Guidobono,
Mark F Guidobono,
EMP: 3 EST: 2008

GEOGRAPHIC SECTION

SALES (est): 244K **Privately Held**
SIC: 2051 7389 Cakes, pies & pastries;

(G-11683)
COMPETITIVE CMPT INFO TECH INC
Also Called: Land and Sea Group
100 Maincentre Ste 1 (48167-1579)
PHONE..................................732 829-9699
Vijey R Seri, *CEO*
Srilaz MI, *President*
EMP: 25 EST: 1997
SALES: 3MM **Privately Held**
SIC: 7371 7372 7379 Computer software development; prepackaged software; computer related consulting services

(G-11684)
CORR PACK IN
9833 5 Mile Rd (48168-9403)
PHONE..................................248 348-4188
Larry Gutowsky, *President*
EMP: 7
SQ FT: 20,000
SALES: 1.5MM **Privately Held**
SIC: 2653 Boxes, corrugated: made from purchased materials

(G-11685)
CURVY LLC (PA)
2959 Charing Cross (48167-8679)
PHONE..................................917 960-3774
Marketa Simot, *CEO*
Srinizas Nunna,
EMP: 3
SALES: 60K **Privately Held**
SIC: 2741 7389 ;

(G-11686)
CW MANUFACTURING LLC
Also Called: Cw Bearing
15200 Technology Dr (48168-2849)
PHONE..................................734 781-4000
John Lirong Hu,
EMP: 27 EST: 2015
SALES (est): 1.2MM **Privately Held**
SIC: 3562 Ball & roller bearings

(G-11687)
DEARBORN COLLISION SERVICE INC
39407 Jasmine Cir (48167-3901)
PHONE..................................734 455-3299
John Krueger, *President*
EMP: 7
SQ FT: 10,000
SALES (est): 710K **Privately Held**
WEB: www.dearborncollision.com
SIC: 3824 Fluid meters & counting devices

(G-11688)
DEUWAVE LLC
200 S Wing St (48167-1854)
PHONE..................................888 238-9283
Alvar Sushma, *Administration*
Sushma Alvar,
EMP: 4
SALES (est): 247.3K **Privately Held**
SIC: 3841 Diagnostic apparatus, medical

(G-11689)
EDENS TECHNOLOGIES LLC
Also Called: Optishot Golf
115 N Center St Ste 202 (48167-1469)
PHONE..................................517 304-1324
▲ EMP: 10
SQ FT: 1,000
SALES (est): 991.5K **Privately Held**
SIC: 3949 Mfg Sporting/Athletic Goods

(G-11690)
ENTRON COMPUTER SYSTEMS INC
44554 Chedworth Ct (48167-8934)
PHONE..................................248 349-8898
Tim Evans, *President*
Harry Rodgers, *Marketing Staff*
EMP: 5
SALES: 231.3K **Privately Held**
WEB: www.entron.net
SIC: 3571 Electronic computers

(G-11691)
FLORANCE TURNING COMPANY INC
44862 Aspen Ridge Dr (48168-4435)
PHONE..................................248 347-0068
Frank L Florance, *President*
Linda Florance, *Admin Sec*
EMP: 4
SQ FT: 1,800
SALES (est): 280K **Privately Held**
SIC: 3544 Special dies, tools, jigs & fixtures

(G-11692)
FONTS ABOUT INC
143 Cadycentre 130 (48167-1119)
PHONE..................................248 767-7504
Aubrie Ann Glennon, *President*
EMP: 5
SALES: 50K **Privately Held**
SIC: 7336 2759 Graphic arts & related design; promotional printing

(G-11693)
GAS RECOVERY SYSTEMS LLC
10611 5 Mile Rd (48168-9402)
PHONE..................................248 305-7774
Jay Walkinhood, *Manager*
EMP: 14
SALES (corp-wide): 198.8MM **Privately Held**
SIC: 1389 Removal of condensate gasoline from field (gathering) lines
HQ: Gas Recovery Systems, Llc
1 N Lexington Ave Ste 620
White Plains NY 10601
914 421-4903

(G-11694)
GENTHERM INCORPORATED (PA)
21680 Haggerty Rd Ste 101 (48167-8994)
PHONE..................................248 504-0500
Oscar B Marx III, *Ch of Bd*
Phillip Eyler, *President*
Klaus Wilhelm, *General Mgr*
Yijing H Brentano, *Senior VP*
James Paloyan, *Senior VP*
▲ EMP: 263
SQ FT: 82,000
SALES: 1B **Publicly Held**
WEB: www.amerigon.com
SIC: 3714 Motor vehicle electrical equipment

(G-11695)
GREAT LAKES INFOTRONICS INC (PA)
22300 Haggerty Rd 100 (48167-8987)
PHONE..................................248 476-2500
James Rheinhart, *Ch of Bd*
Christopher Ciapala, *President*
Alan Witts, *Corp Secy*
Vicki Rytel, *Opers Staff*
Vicki Beasley, *Accounting Mgr*
EMP: 25
SQ FT: 19,800
SALES (est): 7.8MM **Privately Held**
WEB: www.infotronics.com
SIC: 5065 7371 7372 Electronic parts & equipment; custom computer programming services; prepackaged software

(G-11696)
GUERNSEY DAIRY STORES INC
Also Called: Guernsey Farms Dairy
21300 Novi Rd (48167-9701)
PHONE..................................248 349-1466
Martin McGuire, *President*
Gregory McGuire, *Vice Pres*
Matthew McGuire, *Vice Pres*
Rita Rice, *CFO*
Stacey Sharp, *Accountant*
EMP: 170
SQ FT: 28,000
SALES: 12MM **Privately Held**
SIC: 2024 5812 5451 Ice cream & frozen desserts; ice cream, soft drink & soda fountain stands; dairy products stores

(G-11697)
HELLA CORPORATE CENTER USA INC (DH)
Also Called: Hella North America, Inc.
15951 Technology Dr (48168-2849)
PHONE..................................586 232-4788
Joseph V Borruso, *CEO*
Steve Lietaert, *President*
Tony Grado, *Project Mgr*
Mike Dolan, *Engineer*
Antonio Wells, *Engineer*
◆ EMP: 40 EST: 1978
SALES (est): 178.2MM
SALES (corp-wide): 7.8B **Privately Held**
SIC: 3625 5013 5088 3822 Industrial electrical relays & switches; automotive supplies & parts; marine supplies; auto controls regulating residntl & coml environmt & applncs; refrigeration & heating equipment; manufactured hardware (general)
HQ: Hella Holding International Gmbh
Rixbecker Str. 75
Lippstadt
294 138-0

(G-11698)
HPI PRODUCTS INC
Also Called: Allpro Vector Group
640 Griswold St Ste 200 (48167-1691)
PHONE..................................248 773-7460
William E Garvey, *Owner*
EMP: 5
SQ FT: 600
SALES (corp-wide): 10.5MM **Privately Held**
SIC: 2879 5191 Insecticides & pesticides; pesticides
PA: Hpi Products, Inc.
222 Sylvanie St
Saint Joseph MO 64501
816 233-1237

(G-11699)
HULET BODY CO INC
19700 Meadowbrook Rd (48167-9556)
PHONE..................................313 931-6000
Tom Letvin, *CEO*
Dee Letvin, *Vice Pres*
EMP: 20
SQ FT: 15,000
SALES (est): 3.7MM **Privately Held**
WEB: www.huletbody.com
SIC: 3713 3715 7532 7538 Truck bodies (motor vehicles); trailer bodies; body shop, trucks; general automotive repair shops

(G-11700)
INNOVATIVE MACHINE TECHNOLOGY
Also Called: IMT
7591 Chubb Rd (48168-9616)
PHONE..................................248 348-1630
Bret Smith, *President*
Corine Smith, *Corp Secy*
EMP: 12
SQ FT: 6,400
SALES (est): 1.9MM **Privately Held**
SIC: 3599 Machine shop, jobbing & repair

(G-11701)
INTERNATIONAL FENESTRATION (PA)
Also Called: Ifc
917 Pond Island Ct (48167-1089)
PHONE..................................248 735-6880
Valerie Mc Keegan, *Treasurer*
John McKeegan,
EMP: 12
SALES (est): 311K **Privately Held**
WEB: www.ifctechonline.com
SIC: 3365 3553 Aluminum & aluminum-based alloy castings; woodworking machinery

(G-11702)
JAY INDUSTRIES INC
7455 Fox Hill Ln (48168-9544)
PHONE..................................313 240-7535
Theodore Maged, *President*
EMP: 6
SALES: 1MM **Privately Held**
WEB: www.jayindustries.com
SIC: 3441 Fabricated structural metal

(G-11703)
JOGUE INC
Also Called: Northville Laboratories
100 Rural Hill St (48167-1538)
PHONE..................................248 349-1501
Andrew Huber, *CFO*
EMP: 14
SALES (corp-wide): 12.2MM **Privately Held**
SIC: 2087 2844 2099 Flavoring extracts & syrups; perfumes & colognes; food preparations
PA: Jogue, Inc.
14731 Helm Ct
Plymouth MI 48170
734 207-0100

(G-11704)
KEMAI (USA) CHEMICAL CO LTD
48948 Freestone Dr (48168-8005)
PHONE..................................248 924-2225
Lizhi LI, *General Mgr*
John Zhang, *Sales Mgr*
▲ EMP: 5
SQ FT: 2,700
SALES: 41MM **Privately Held**
SIC: 2869 Laboratory chemicals, organic

(G-11705)
LYDALL PERFORMANCE MTLS US INC
22260 Haggerty Rd Ste 200 (48167-8969)
PHONE..................................248 596-2800
Louis Dannibale, *Manager*
EMP: 5
SALES (corp-wide): 785.9MM **Publicly Held**
WEB: www.sealinfo.com
SIC: 2631 Paperboard mills
HQ: Lydall Performance Materials (Us), Inc.
216 Wohlsen Way
Lancaster PA 17603

(G-11706)
LYDALL SEALING SOLUTIONS INC
22260 Haggerty Rd Ste 200 (48167-8969)
PHONE..................................248 596-2800
Franklin Fox, *President*
EMP: 100
SALES (corp-wide): 785.9MM **Publicly Held**
WEB: www.bfsealingproducts.com
SIC: 3053 5013 Gaskets, packing & sealing devices; motor vehicle supplies & new parts
HQ: Lydall Sealing Solutions, Inc.
410 S 1st Ave
Marshalltown IA 50158

(G-11707)
LYNX DX INC
120 W Main St Ste 300 (48167-1584)
PHONE..................................734 274-3144
Yashar Niknafs, *Principal*
Arul Chinnaiyan, *Principal*
Jeff Tosoian, *Principal*
EMP: 3
SALES (est): 123.2K **Privately Held**
SIC: 2835 In vitro & in vivo diagnostic substances

(G-11708)
MACH II ENTERPRISES INC
Also Called: Mach II Tax Service
200 S Main St Ste A (48167-2680)
PHONE..................................248 347-8822
EMP: 7
SALES (est): 503.6K **Privately Held**
SIC: 2395 7291 Embroidery & Income Tax Service

(G-11709)
MEIDEN AMERICA INC (HQ)
15800 Centennial Dr (48168-9629)
PHONE..................................734 459-1781
Ko Yamamoto, *President*
Junzo Inamura, *Principal*
Hidefumi Miura, *Principal*
Tetsuya Nishiguchi, *Engineer*
▲ EMP: 17
SQ FT: 78,000

Northville - Wayne County (G-11710) — GEOGRAPHIC SECTION

SALES (est): 3.4MM **Privately Held**
SIC: 3825 3612 Engine electrical test equipment; distribution transformers, electric

(G-11710)
MITSUBISHI ELC AUTO AMER INC
15603 Centennial Dr (48168-8690)
PHONE.................734 453-2617
Mike Delano, *President*
Harold Fernandez, *Credit Staff*
Mark Yantek, *Sales Staff*
Kurt Burkett, *Manager*
James Cass, *Manager*
EMP: 80 **Privately Held**
SIC: 3651 Amplifiers: radio, public address or musical instrument
HQ: Mitsubishi Electric Automotive America, Inc.
4773 Bethany Rd
Mason OH 45040
513 573-6614

(G-11711)
MITSUBISHI ELECTRIC US INC
15603 Centennial Dr (48168-8690)
PHONE.................734 453-6200
Pokiyoshi Shima, *President*
Nyna Springer, *Opers Staff*
Susan Parzych, *Engineer*
Kurt Burkett, *Manager*
Mohammad Horani, *Manager*
EMP: 100 **Privately Held**
WEB: www.diamond-vision.com
SIC: 5045 1796 5065 3534 Computer peripheral equipment; elevator installation & conversion; electronic parts & equipment; escalators, passenger & freight
HQ: Mitsubishi Electric Us, Inc.
5900 Katella Ave Ste C
Cypress CA 90630
714 220-2500

(G-11712)
MOSER RACING INC
43641 Serenity Dr (48167-8930)
PHONE.................248 348-6502
Robert Moser, *Owner*
EMP: 12
SALES (est): 939.3K **Privately Held**
WEB: www.moserracing.net
SIC: 3711 Automobile assembly, including specialty automobiles

(G-11713)
MYCO ENTERPRISES INC (PA)
200 S Wing St (48167-1854)
P.O. Box 113 (48167-0113)
PHONE.................248 348-3806
Frank Firek Jr, *President*
Frank Firek Sr, *Owner*
◆ **EMP:** 7
SQ FT: 3,500
SALES (est): 861.4K **Privately Held**
SIC: 3498 Pipe sections fabricated from purchased pipe; tube fabricating (contract bending & shaping)

(G-11714)
NORMAC INCORPORATED
720 Baseline Rd (48167-1266)
P.O. Box 245 (48167-0245)
PHONE.................248 349-2644
Chuck McDonald, *Research*
Emmanuel Gauzer, *Product Mgr*
EMP: 18
SQ FT: 7,000
SALES (corp-wide): 7.1MM **Privately Held**
WEB: www.normac.com
SIC: 3541 Machine tool replacement & repair parts, metal cutting types
PA: Normac Incorporated
93 Industrial Dr
Hendersonville NC 28739
828 209-9000

(G-11715)
NORTHVILLE CIDER MILL INC
714 Baseline Rd (48167-1266)
PHONE.................248 349-3181
Diane Jones, *President*
Cheryl Nelson, *Vice Pres*
Robert Nelson, *Treasurer*
Melvin Jones, *Admin Sec*
EMP: 50
SQ FT: 3,200
SALES: 250K **Privately Held**
WEB: www.northvillecider.com
SIC: 5431 5499 5921 2086 Fruit stands or markets; beverage stores; wine; bottled & canned soft drinks; wines, brandy & brandy spirits; canned fruits & specialties

(G-11716)
NORTHVILLE LABORATORIES INC
Also Called: Flavors & Fragrances
100 Rural Hill St (48167-1538)
P.O. Box 190 (48167-0190)
PHONE.................248 349-1500
Patrick Kilpatrick, *President*
EMP: 15 **EST:** 1929
SQ FT: 48,000
SALES (est): 914.4K **Privately Held**
SIC: 2087 Extracts, flavoring

(G-11717)
NORTHVILLE STITCHING POST
Also Called: Mark II Enterprises
200 S Main St Ste A (48167-2680)
PHONE.................248 347-7622
Nancy Lewis, *Partner*
Bruce Mach, *Partner*
EMP: 5
SQ FT: 1,900
SALES (est): 360K **Privately Held**
SIC: 2395 Embroidery products, except schiffli machine

(G-11718)
NORTHVILLE WINERY
630 Baseline Rd (48167-1265)
PHONE.................248 320-6507
Nelson Carina, *Administration*
EMP: 16
SALES (est): 1.7MM **Privately Held**
SIC: 2084 Wines

(G-11719)
ONCOFUSION THERAPEUTICS INC
120 W Main St Ste 300 (48167-1584)
PHONE.................248 361-3341
Arul M Chinnaiyan, *Principal*
Kenneth Pienta, *Principal*
Shaomeng Wang, *Principal*
EMP: 6
SALES (est): 239.1K **Privately Held**
SIC: 3845 Electrotherapeutic apparatus

(G-11720)
OX ENGINEERED PRODUCTS LLC (PA)
22260 Haggerty Rd Ste 365 (48167-8970)
PHONE.................248 289-9950
Dave Ulmer, *CEO*
Cris Fauline, *COO*
Jeff Wolf, *CFO*
James Lanham, *Sales Staff*
Charlie Devine, *Representative*
EMP: 12 **EST:** 2012
SALES (est): 1.4MM **Privately Held**
SIC: 2493 Wall tile, fiberboard

(G-11721)
REJOICE INTERNATIONAL CORP
21800 Haggerty Rd Ste 203 (48167-8981)
PHONE.................855 345-5575
Rowyda H Mackie, *Principal*
EMP: 7
SALES (est): 1MM **Privately Held**
SIC: 2844 Toilet preparations

(G-11722)
SALEM TOOL COMPANY
7811 Salem Rd (48168-9423)
PHONE.................248 349-2632
Leonard Bourgoin, *President*
EMP: 4
SQ FT: 2,400
SALES: 395K **Privately Held**
SIC: 3599 Machine shop, jobbing & repair

(G-11723)
SANDBOX SOLUTIONS INC
1001 Doheny Dr (48167-1957)
P.O. Box 5470 (48167-5470)
PHONE.................248 349-7010
L G Belanger, *CEO*
M J Belanger, *President*
Barry Turner, *Vice Pres*
Robert Wentworth, *Vice Pres*
Sue Harteg, *Buyer*
▲ **EMP:** 212
SQ FT: 80,000
SALES (est): 45.6MM **Privately Held**
WEB: www.belangerinc.com
SIC: 3589 3291 1542 6719 Commercial cooking & foodwarming equipment; abrasive products; nonresidential construction; investment holding companies, except banks

(G-11724)
SCHAFFNER MANUFACTURING CO
19414 Gerald St (48167-2517)
PHONE.................248 735-8900
Lee Belanger, *President*
EMP: 6
SALES (est): 263.8K **Privately Held**
SIC: 3291 2842 Wheels, abrasive; specialty cleaning, polishes & sanitation goods

(G-11725)
SENSATA TECHNOLOGIES INC
235 E Main St Ste 102a (48167-1546)
PHONE.................805 523-2000
EMP: 3
SALES (corp-wide): 3.5B **Privately Held**
SIC: 3679 Transducers, electrical
HQ: Sensata Technologies, Inc.
529 Pleasant St
Attleboro MA 02703
508 236-3800

(G-11726)
SKYWORKS LLC
Also Called: Artificial Sky
15461 Bay Hill Dr (48168-9643)
PHONE.................972 284-9093
Mark Jenzen, *Mng Member*
EMP: 10
SALES: 2MM **Privately Held**
SIC: 3646 Ceiling systems, luminous

(G-11727)
SPIDERS SOFTWARE SOLUTIONS LLC
Also Called: Corporate
49831 Parkside Dr (48167-6822)
PHONE.................248 305-3225
Jagadish Boddapati, *CEO*
Gita Boddapati, *President*
EMP: 20
SALES (est): 2.1MM **Privately Held**
SIC: 7379 7372 Computer related consulting services; prepackaged software

(G-11728)
TENNECO AUTOMOTIVE OPER CO
15701 Technology Dr (48168)
PHONE.................248 849-1258
Roger Wood, *CEO*
Lynnette Vollink, *Human Resources*
EMP: 300
SALES: 50MM
SALES (corp-wide): 11.7B **Publicly Held**
SIC: 3714 Motor vehicle wheels & parts
PA: Tenneco Inc.
500 N Field Dr
Lake Forest IL 60045
847 482-5000

(G-11729)
TOM NICKELS
22000 Garfield Rd (48167-9731)
PHONE.................248 348-7974
Tom Nickels, *Principal*
EMP: 3
SALES (est): 184.7K **Privately Held**
SIC: 3356 Nickel

(G-11730)
TRELLBORG SLING SLTIONS US INC
15701 Centennial Dr (48168-8691)
PHONE.................734 354-1250
EMP: 7
SALES (corp-wide): 3.7B **Privately Held**
SIC: 3089 Plastic processing

HQ: Trelleborg Sealing Solutions Us, Inc.
2531 Bremer Rd
Fort Wayne IN 46803
260 749-9631

(G-11731)
TRELLEBORG AUTOMOTIVE USA INC
15701 Centennial Dr (48168-8691)
PHONE.................734 254-9140
Robert Peacock, *Vice Pres*
Steven Molesworth, *Engineer*
Jenna Maisonville, *Project Engr*
Erich Merrill, *Project Engr*
Tristan Roeda, *Project Engr*
EMP: 30
SALES (corp-wide): 2.4B **Privately Held**
SIC: 3061 Mechanical rubber goods
HQ: Vibracoustic Usa, Inc.
400 Aylworth Ave
South Haven MI 49090
269 637-2116

(G-11732)
TS ENTERPRISE ASSOCIATES INC
Also Called: Advanced Technologies Cons
110 W Main St (48167-1521)
P.O. Box 905 (48167-0905)
PHONE.................248 348-2963
Thomas S Close, *CEO*
Susan Close, *President*
Lisa Hunter, *Business Mgr*
Gregg Zydeck, *Vice Pres*
Bob Kelly, *Regl Sales Mgr*
▲ **EMP:** 14
SQ FT: 3,000
SALES (est): 4.5MM **Privately Held**
SIC: 3826 Analytical instruments

(G-11733)
UNDERSTATED CORRUGATED LLC
635 Horton St (48167-1209)
PHONE.................248 880-5767
Paul Roberts, *Principal*
EMP: 4
SALES (est): 18.4K **Privately Held**
SIC: 2653 Corrugated & solid fiber boxes

(G-11734)
WEBSTER COLD FORGE CO
47652 Pine Creek Ct (48168-8527)
PHONE.................313 554-4500
Robert Webster, *President*
Jack McGill, *Principal*
EMP: 18 **EST:** 1925
SQ FT: 100,000
SALES (est): 2MM **Privately Held**
WEB: www.webstercoldforge.com
SIC: 3462 3465 3469 Iron & steel forgings; automotive stampings; metal stampings

(G-11735)
ZF NORTH AMERICA INC (DH)
Also Called: Division Z
15811 Centennial Dr 48 (48168-9629)
PHONE.................734 416-6200
Franz Kleiner, *CEO*
Werner Engl, *General Mgr*
Holzner Joachim, *General Mgr*
Paul Olexa, *Vice Pres*
Karyn Taylor, *Project Mgr*
◆ **EMP:** 500 **EST:** 1979
SQ FT: 5,000
SALES (est): 21.5B
SALES (corp-wide): 216.2K **Privately Held**
SIC: 3714 5013 Motor vehicle parts & accessories; automotive supplies & parts
HQ: Zf Friedrichshafen Ag
Lowentaler Str. 20
Friedrichshafen 88046
754 177-0

(G-11736)
ZF NORTH AMERICA INC
15811 Centennial Dr (48168-9629)
PHONE.................734 416-6200
EMP: 3
SALES (corp-wide): 216.2K **Privately Held**
SIC: 3714 5013 Motor vehicle parts & accessories; automotive supplies & parts

▲ = Import ▼ = Export
◆ = Import/Export

Norton Shores - Muskegon County (G-11762)

HQ: Zf North America, Inc.
15811 Centennial Dr 48
Northville MI 48168
734 416-6200

Norton Shores
Muskegon County

(G-11737)
AEROVISION AIRCRAFT SVCS LLC
620 E Ellis Rd (49441-5672)
PHONE..................................231 799-9000
Jeffrey Barnes, *President*
Greg Van Boxel,
EMP: 42
SALES (est): 6.4MM
SALES (corp-wide): 11.8B **Publicly Held**
SIC: 3724 3728 Aircraft engines & engine parts; aircraft parts & equipment
PA: Lkq Corporation
500 W Madison St Ste 2800
Chicago IL 60661
312 621-1950

(G-11738)
AEROVISION INTERNATIONAL LLC
620 E Ellis Rd (49441-5672)
PHONE..................................231 799-9000
Dominick P Zarcone, *President*
EMP: 42
SQ FT: 12,000
SALES (est): 3.5MM
SALES (corp-wide): 11.8B **Publicly Held**
WEB: www.aerovi.com
SIC: 3724 3728 4581 Aircraft engines & engine parts; aircraft parts & equipment; aircraft maintenance & repair services
PA: Lkq Corporation
500 W Madison St Ste 2800
Chicago IL 60661
312 621-1950

(G-11739)
AIR MASTER SYSTEMS CORP
6480 Norton Center Dr (49441-6034)
PHONE..................................231 798-1111
Don Nelson, *CEO*
Rachelle Papp, *Project Mgr*
Jason Nelson, *Opers Mgr*
Adam Mastenbrook, *Facilities Mgr*
Luis Corrales, *Engineer*
EMP: 25
SQ FT: 60,000
SALES (est): 6.5MM **Privately Held**
WEB: www.airmastersystems.com
SIC: 3821 Laboratory equipment: fume hoods, distillation racks, etc.

(G-11740)
AVI INVENTORY SERVICES LLC (PA)
620 E Ellis Rd (49441-5672)
PHONE..................................231 799-9000
Rick Cramblet, *Exec VP*
Angela Baker, *Vice Pres*
Pete Gibson, *VP Business*
Sam Rice, *VP Sales*
Natalie Medema, *Sales Staff*
EMP: 26 **EST:** 2009
SALES (est): 5.4MM **Privately Held**
SIC: 3724 3728 Aircraft engines & engine parts; aircraft parts & equipment

(G-11741)
BRY MAC INC
Also Called: Dietech
865 E Porter Rd (49441-5972)
PHONE..................................231 799-2211
Brian McCarthy, *President*
Bob Tilden, *Engineer*
EMP: 16
SQ FT: 4,000
SALES: 1.4MM **Privately Held**
WEB: www.dietechinc.com
SIC: 3544 Special dies, tools, jigs & fixtures

(G-11742)
BUSH CONCRETE PRODUCTS INC
3584 Airline Rd (49444-3865)
PHONE..................................231 733-1904
Gerald McGrath, *President*
Teresa Wesley, *Office Mgr*
EMP: 12 **EST:** 1928
SQ FT: 15,000
SALES (est): 2.4MM **Privately Held**
WEB: www.bushconcreteproducts.com
SIC: 3272 Concrete products, precast; tanks, concrete; burial vaults, concrete or precast terrazzo

(G-11743)
CAKE FLOUR
1811 W Norton Ave (49441-4284)
PHONE..................................231 571-3054
Nicholas Sean Johnson, *Owner*
EMP: 4
SALES (est): 103.4K **Privately Held**
SIC: 2041 Cake flour

(G-11744)
CANNON-MUSKEGON CORPORATION
2875 Lincoln St (49441-3313)
P.O. Box 506, Muskegon (49443-0506)
PHONE..................................231 755-1681
Mark Dunagan, *Ch of Bd*
Douglas Orr, *President*
Alva Bettis, *Vice Pres*
Kenneth Harris, *Vice Pres*
Nick Huston, *Materials Mgr*
▲ **EMP:** 180 **EST:** 1952
SQ FT: 130,000
SALES (est): 89.3MM
SALES (corp-wide): 225.3B **Publicly Held**
WEB: www.c-mgroup.com
SIC: 3313 3341 3339 3312 Alloys, additive, except copper: not made in blast furnaces; secondary nonferrous metals; primary nonferrous metals; blast furnaces & steel mills
HQ: Sps Technologies, Llc
301 Highland Ave
Jenkintown PA 19046
215 572-3000

(G-11745)
CHALLENGE MACHINERY COMPANY (PA)
6125 Norton Center Dr (49441-6081)
PHONE..................................231 799-8484
Larry J Ritsema, *President*
Edgar Martin, *Chairman*
Lawrence D Schrader, *Treasurer*
Susan Hilliard, *Admin Sec*
▲ **EMP:** 45
SQ FT: 40,000
SALES (est): 9.4MM **Privately Held**
WEB: www.challengemachinery.com
SIC: 3554 Die cutting & stamping machinery, paper converting; cutting machines, paper; folding machines, paper

(G-11746)
CLASSIC STAMP & SIGNS
772 W Broadway Ave (49441-3518)
PHONE..................................231 737-0200
David A Peters, *Owner*
Brad Peters, *Manager*
EMP: 3
SALES (est): 332.4K **Privately Held**
WEB: www.classicstampandsign.com
SIC: 5099 3993 Rubber stamps; signs & advertising specialties

(G-11747)
DAMA TOOL & GAUGE COMPANY
Also Called: Unicor
6175 Norton Center Dr (49441-6081)
PHONE..................................616 842-9631
Cesar Castro, *President*
Mary Castro, *Vice Pres*
EMP: 13
SQ FT: 9,000
SALES (est): 1.2MM **Privately Held**
WEB: www.unicor.net
SIC: 1389 3566 Oil field services; drives, high speed industrial, except hydrostatic

(G-11748)
DYNAMIC CONVEYOR CORPORATION
Also Called: Dyna-Con
5980 Grand Haven Rd (49441-6012)
PHONE..................................231 798-0014
Curtis Chambers, *Chairman*
Tammy Jacobs, *Admin Mgr*
Jean Chambers, *Shareholder*
Kim Chambers, *Shareholder*
EMP: 20
SQ FT: 48,000
SALES (est): 5.8MM **Privately Held**
WEB: www.dynamicconveyor.com
SIC: 3535 Conveyors & conveying equipment

(G-11749)
EAGLE MACHINE TOOL CORPORATION
6060 Grand Haven Rd (49441-6014)
PHONE..................................231 798-8473
Theodore Fleis, *President*
Mary Lou Fleis, *Corp Secy*
EMP: 8
SQ FT: 5,000
SALES (est): 161K **Privately Held**
SIC: 3542 Machine tools, metal forming type

(G-11750)
EAGLE QUEST INTERNATIONAL LTD
Also Called: Eqi, Ltd.
5797 Harvey St Ste D (49444-6727)
PHONE..................................616 850-2630
Blake Phillips, *President*
◆ **EMP:** 11
SQ FT: 1,800
SALES (est): 2.6MM **Privately Held**
SIC: 3321 5084 Gray & ductile iron foundries; industrial machine parts

(G-11751)
EARTHTRONICS INC
800 E Ellis Rd Ste 574 (49441-5646)
PHONE..................................231 332-1188
Kevin Youngquist, *Exec VP*
Lesley Budde, *Sales Staff*
EMP: 22 **EST:** 2007
SALES (est): 5.4MM **Privately Held**
SIC: 3641 Electric light bulbs, complete

(G-11752)
EMERALD TOOL INC
6305 Norton Center Dr (49441-6031)
PHONE..................................231 799-9193
Tom Reidy, *President*
Travis Reidy, *Admin Sec*
EMP: 9
SQ FT: 14,000
SALES (est): 1.3MM **Privately Held**
SIC: 3599 Machine shop, jobbing & repair

(G-11753)
EQI LTD
5797 Harvey St (49444-7783)
PHONE..................................616 850-2630
Blake Phillips, *CEO*
EMP: 6
SALES (est): 541K **Privately Held**
SIC: 3321 Gray & ductile iron foundries

(G-11754)
ERMANCO
1300 E Mount Garfield Rd (49441-6097)
PHONE..................................231 798-4547
Steve Drelles, *Site Mgr*
CAM Oconnor, *Purch Mgr*
Tom Brower, *Engineer*
Pete Hansen, *Engineer*
Kevin Hardie, *Engineer*
EMP: 17 **EST:** 2009
SALES (est): 3.7MM **Privately Held**
SIC: 3535 Conveyors & conveying equipment

(G-11755)
FIRST PLACE MANUFACTURING LLC
6234 Norton Center Dr (49441-6030)
PHONE..................................231 798-1694
Erik Sportell, *Mng Member*
EMP: 4
SQ FT: 5,000
SALES: 1MM **Privately Held**
SIC: 3312 Tool & die steel

(G-11756)
FLAIRWOOD INDUSTRIES INC
6230 Norton Center Dr (49441-6030)
PHONE..................................231 798-8324
EMP: 30
SQ FT: 32,000
SALES (est): 5MM **Privately Held**
SIC: 2431 2541 3993 2521 Mfg Millwork Mfg Wood Partitions/Fixt Mfg Signs/Ad Specialties Mfg Wood Office Furn Mfg Wood Household Furn

(G-11757)
GE AVIATION MUSKEGON
6060 Norton Center Dr (49441-6087)
PHONE..................................231 777-2685
Joyce Carlyle Swartz, *Manager*
Timothy Adams, *Planning*
EMP: 11
SALES (corp-wide): 121.6B **Publicly Held**
SIC: 3724 Turbines, aircraft type
HQ: Johnson Technology, Inc.
2034 Latimer Dr
Muskegon MI 49442

(G-11758)
GREAT LAKES PRTG SOLUTIONS INC
5163 Robert Hunter Dr (49441-6547)
PHONE..................................231 799-6000
David Anderson, *President*
Paul Sikkenga, *Prdtn Mgr*
Ann Fraser, *Accountant*
Lacey Layman, *Sales Staff*
George Myler, *Sales Executive*
EMP: 16
SQ FT: 45,000
SALES (est): 2MM **Privately Held*
WEB: www.glpsi.com
SIC: 2752 Commercial printing, lithographic

(G-11759)
HARDING ENERGY INC
509 E Ellis Rd (49441-5629)
PHONE..................................231 798-7033
Stev Morgan, *President*
Ed Hanenburg, *Chairman*
▲ **EMP:** 32
SQ FT: 20,000
SALES (est): 6.7MM **Privately Held**
WEB: www.questbatteries.com
SIC: 3691 Storage batteries

(G-11760)
HESTIA INC
Also Called: American Panel
650 Airport Pl (49441-6550)
PHONE..................................231 747-8157
Jeffrey R Kreiser, *President*
Ann Kreiser, *Vice Pres*
EMP: 8
SQ FT: 22,000
SALES: 2MM **Privately Held**
SIC: 2298 Insulator pads, cordage

(G-11761)
ID SYSTEMS INC
Also Called: Inter Dyne Systems
676 E Ellis Rd (49441-5672)
PHONE..................................231 799-8760
Ann Moore, *President*
Jack Andree, *Vice Pres*
Jennifer Huizenga, *Opers Staff*
EMP: 15
SQ FT: 4,000
SALES (est): 3.6MM **Privately Held**
WEB: www.interdynesystems.com
SIC: 3821 Laboratory equipment: fume hoods, distillation racks, etc.

(G-11762)
INTELLIGENT MCH SOLUTIONS INC
Also Called: IMS
1269 E Mt Grfeld Rd Ste D (49441)
PHONE..................................616 607-9751
Aaron Russick, *President*
Gilbert McDonald, *Exec VP*
Van Brewer, *Engineer*
Domanic Viterna, *Master*
▲ **EMP:** 19

Norton Shores - Muskegon County (G-11763)

GEOGRAPHIC SECTION

SALES (est): 4.2MM **Privately Held**
SIC: 3599 Machine shop, jobbing & repair

(G-11763)
INTRICATE GRINDING MCH SPC INC
1081 S Gateway Blvd (49441-6074)
PHONE..................................231 798-2154
Brenda Amaya, *President*
EMP: 24
SQ FT: 16,000
SALES (est): 2.6MM **Privately Held**
WEB: www.intricategrinding.com
SIC: 3599 Machine shop, jobbing & repair

(G-11764)
J & M MACHINE PRODUCTS INC
1821 Manor Dr (49441-3498)
PHONE..................................231 755-1622
Joseph J Rahrig, *President*
Robert Lindstrom, *Vice Pres*
Pat Smith, *QC Mgr*
Chris Rahrig, *Treasurer*
John Douglass, *Sales Engr*
▲ EMP: 80 EST: 1980
SQ FT: 30,000
SALES (est): 18.8MM **Privately Held**
WEB: www.jmmachine.com
SIC: 3599 3365 3441 3325 Machine shop, jobbing & repair; aluminum foundries; fabricated structural metal; steel foundries; sheet metalwork

(G-11765)
J F MCCAUGHIN CO (DH)
2817 Mccracken St (49441-3420)
PHONE..................................231 759-7304
Pat Mc Caughin, *President*
▲ EMP: 29
SQ FT: 20,000
SALES (est): 3.3MM
SALES (corp-wide): 667.6MM **Privately Held**
WEB: www.argueso.com
SIC: 3999 Candles
HQ: Paramelt Usa, Inc.
2817 Mccracken St
Norton Shores MI 49441
231 759-7304

(G-11766)
KAYDON CORPORATION
Kaydon Bearings Division
2860 Mccracken St (49441-3495)
P.O. Box 688, Muskegon (49443-0688)
PHONE..................................231 755-3741
Jim Bandelin, *Opers Staff*
Cindy Wagner, *Buyer*
Juan Leal, *QC Mgr*
Leeann Thompson, *QC Mgr*
Branden Workman, *QC Mgr*
EMP: 160
SALES (corp-wide): 9.5B **Privately Held**
WEB: www.kaydon.com
SIC: 3562 5085 3568 8711 Ball & roller bearings; industrial supplies; bearings; power transmission equipment; engineering services
HQ: Kaydon Corporation
2723 S State St Ste 300
Ann Arbor MI 48104
734 747-7025

(G-11767)
KNOLL INC
2800 Estes St (49441-3407)
PHONE..................................231 755-2270
Richard Vales, *Vice Pres*
David Noel, *VP Mktg*
Sherry Zufelt, *Supervisor*
Martin Winicki, *Maintence Staff*
EMP: 45 **Publicly Held**
WEB: www.knoll.com
SIC: 2521 2522 Wood office furniture; office furniture, except wood; panel systems & partitions, office: except wood
PA: Knoll, Inc.
1235 Water St
East Greenville PA 18041

(G-11768)
KOPPEL TOOL & ENGINEERING LLC
1099 N Gateway Blvd (49441-6092)
PHONE..................................616 638-2611
Matthew C Koppel,
Alexander J Koppel,
EMP: 7
SQ FT: 17,000
SALES: 800K **Privately Held**
SIC: 3599 Machine shop, jobbing & repair

(G-11769)
LA COLOMBE TORREFACTION
1269 E Mount Garfield Rd (49441-5694)
PHONE..................................231 798-9853
Todd Carmichael, *CEO*
JP Iberti, *President*
EMP: 3
SALES (est): 165.5K **Privately Held**
SIC: 2095 Roasted coffee

(G-11770)
LAKETON TRUSS INC
1527 Scranton Dr (49441-5245)
PHONE..................................231 798-3467
Charles Morton, *Principal*
EMP: 3
SALES (est): 230.7K **Privately Held**
SIC: 2439 Structural wood members

(G-11771)
M ARGUESO & CO INC
Also Called: Paramelt
2817 Mccracken St (49441-3420)
PHONE..................................231 759-7304
David Pekala, *President*
Greg Schuetz, *Human Res Mgr*
◆ EMP: 144
SALES (est): 296.5K
SALES (corp-wide): 667.6MM **Privately Held**
SIC: 2891 Sealing wax
HQ: Paramelt B.V.
Costerstraat 18
Heerhugowaard 1704
725 750-600

(G-11772)
MAW VENTURES INC
6230 Norton Center Dr (49441-6030)
PHONE..................................231 798-8324
Wayne Baxter, *CEO*
Joel Pyper, *President*
EMP: 30
SQ FT: 50,000
SALES (est): 1MM **Privately Held**
SIC: 2431 2541 3993 Woodwork, interior & ornamental; showcases, except refrigerated: wood; signs & advertising specialties

(G-11773)
MICRGRAPHICS PRINTING INC (PA)
Also Called: Lee Printing & Graphics
2637 Emerson Blvd (49441-3503)
PHONE..................................231 739-6575
Richard Voss, *Principal*
Marcia Banninga, *Vice Pres*
EMP: 20
SALES (est): 1.4MM **Privately Held**
WEB: www.micrgraphics.com
SIC: 2752 2759 2791 2789 Commercial printing, offset; letterpress printing; typesetting; bookbinding & related work; manifold business forms

(G-11774)
MICRO-SYSTEMS INC
129 Woodslee Ct (49444-7796)
PHONE..................................616 481-1601
Pamela Ann Schumaker, *CEO*
Mark P Schumaker, *President*
EMP: 3
SQ FT: 1,500
SALES: 329.9K **Privately Held**
SIC: 7389 3824 Design, commercial & industrial; controls, revolution & timing instruments

(G-11775)
MONARCH POWDER COATING INC
5906 Grand Haven Rd (49441-6012)
PHONE..................................231 798-1422
Steven Johnson, *President*
EMP: 5
SQ FT: 5,000
SALES (est): 578.6K **Privately Held**
SIC: 3479 Coating of metals & formed products

(G-11776)
MUSKEGON BRAKE & DISTRG CO LLC (PA)
Also Called: Muskegon Brake & Parts
848 E Broadway Ave (49444-2328)
PHONE..................................231 733-0874
Rita Sikkenga, *Human Res Dir*
Robert Cutler,
EMP: 27
SALES (est): 15.6MM **Privately Held**
WEB: www.muskegonbrake.com
SIC: 5531 5013 3493 7539 Automotive tires; motor vehicle supplies & new parts; steel springs, except wire; automotive repair shops

(G-11777)
MUSKEGON HEIGHTS WATER FILTER
2323 Seminole Rd (49441-4230)
PHONE..................................231 780-3415
Bonnie McGlothin, *Mayor*
Darryl Van Dyke, *Director*
EMP: 8 EST: 1977
SALES (est): 1MM **Privately Held**
SIC: 3569 Filters

(G-11778)
NATIONAL AMBUCS INC
Also Called: Ambucs Muskegon Chapter
708 Mapleway Dr (49441-6500)
PHONE..................................231 798-4244
Kevin Dick, *President*
Robert Kendall, *Treasurer*
EMP: 35
SALES (est): 2.4MM **Privately Held**
SIC: 3944 7389 Tricycles;

(G-11779)
NAUTICRAFT CORPORATION
5980 Grand Haven Rd (49441-6012)
PHONE..................................231 798-8440
Curtis Chambers, *President*
EMP: 3
SQ FT: 48,000
SALES (est): 53.5K **Privately Held**
WEB: www.nauticraft.com
SIC: 3732 Boats, rigid: plastics

(G-11780)
NEWS ONE INC
Also Called: Mibiz
4080 Oak Hollow Ct (49441-4565)
PHONE..................................231 798-4669
William R Lowry, *President*
Renee Looman, *Marketing Staff*
EMP: 14
SALES (est): 1.6MM **Privately Held**
WEB: www.mibiz.com
SIC: 2711 Newspapers, publishing & printing

(G-11781)
NMP INC
Also Called: Nowak Machine Products
6170 Norton Center Dr (49441-6080)
PHONE..................................231 798-8851
Kenneth Nowak, *President*
Ken Nowak, *Engineer*
Russ Nyblade, *CFO*
Scott Waldo, *Controller*
Donielle Routt, *Human Resources*
EMP: 50
SQ FT: 60,000
SALES (est): 9.1MM **Privately Held**
WEB: www.nowakmp.com
SIC: 3599 Machine shop, jobbing & repair

(G-11782)
NON-FERROUS CAST ALLOYS INC
1146 N Gateway Blvd (49441-6083)
PHONE..................................231 799-0550
Dale Boersema, *President*
Ben Boersema, *Vice Pres*
Amy S Rademaker, *Opers Staff*
Chantalle Wagenmaker, *Project Engr*
Corey Swiftney, *Treasurer*
▼ EMP: 52
SQ FT: 61,000
SALES (est): 12.6MM **Privately Held**
WEB: www.nfca.com
SIC: 3366 3471 3369 3365 Brass foundry; bronze foundry; plating & polishing; nonferrous foundries; aluminum foundries

(G-11783)
NORTHERN MACHINE TOOL COMPANY
761 Alberta Ave (49441-3002)
PHONE..................................231 755-1603
Gerhard Olsen, *Ch of Bd*
Stephen Olsen, *President*
Steve Olsen, *General Mgr*
Brian Kieft, *Design Engr*
Dan Olsen, *Treasurer*
EMP: 40 EST: 1946
SQ FT: 32,000
SALES (est): 7.2MM **Privately Held**
WEB: www.nmtdie.com
SIC: 3544 Special dies & tools

(G-11784)
NU-PAK SOLUTIONS INC
2850 Lincoln St (49441-3314)
PHONE..................................231 755-1662
Herbert Bevelhymer, *President*
EMP: 10
SQ FT: 50,000
SALES (est): 1.6MM **Privately Held**
SIC: 3086 Packaging & shipping materials, foamed plastic

(G-11785)
NUGENT SAND COMPANY INC
2925 Lincoln St (49441-3393)
PHONE..................................231 755-1686
Robert Chandonnet, *Ch of Bd*
John A Nevedal, *Vice Pres*
David L Terpsma, *Treasurer*
EMP: 45 EST: 1912
SQ FT: 6,000
SALES (est): 12.8MM **Privately Held**
SIC: 1442 Construction sand & gravel

(G-11786)
PARAMELT USA INC (DH)
2817 Mccracken St (49441-3420)
P.O. Box 126, Muskegon (49443-0126)
PHONE..................................231 759-7304
David Pekala, *President*
Mark Ostrum, *Materials Mgr*
Adrienne Frasier, *Purch Agent*
Gordon Green, *Accounts Mgr*
Marcelo Anibarro, *Manager*
◆ EMP: 112 EST: 2009
SQ FT: 60,000
SALES (est): 32.3MM
SALES (corp-wide): 667.6MM **Privately Held**
SIC: 2891 Adhesives & sealants
HQ: Paramelt B.V.
Costerstraat 18
Heerhugowaard 1704
725 750-600

(G-11787)
PATTERSON PRECISION MFG INC
Also Called: Ace Tooling
1188 E Broadway Ave (49444-2356)
PHONE..................................231 733-1913
John Patterson, *President*
EMP: 16
SALES: 1.4MM **Privately Held**
SIC: 3599 Machine shop, jobbing & repair

(G-11788)
PEPSI-COLA METRO BTLG CO INC
4900 Paul Ct (49441-5566)
PHONE..................................231 798-1274
Dave Purple, *Manager*
EMP: 30
SALES (corp-wide): 64.6B **Publicly Held**
WEB: www.joy-of-cola.com
SIC: 2086 Soft drinks: packaged in cans, bottles, etc.
HQ: Pepsi-Cola Metropolitan Bottling Company, Inc.
1111 Westchester Ave
White Plains NY 10604
914 767-6000

GEOGRAPHIC SECTION

Norton Shores - Ottawa County (G-11813)

(G-11789)
R & D MACHINE AND TOOL INC
6059 Norton Center Dr (49441-6082)
PHONE.................................231 798-8500
Dan Wilson, *President*
Robert Smith III, *Exec VP*
EMP: 9
SQ FT: 6,000
SALES (est): 930K Privately Held
WEB: www.rdmachineandtool.com
SIC: 3599 3544 Custom machinery; special dies, tools, jigs & fixtures

(G-11790)
RIVERCITY ROLLFORM INC
1130 E Mount Garfield Rd (49441-6076)
PHONE.................................231 799-9550
Roy Johnson Jr, *President*
Theran Nordstrom, *Engineer*
Kris Rake, *Office Mgr*
EMP: 13
SQ FT: 20,000
SALES (est): 3MM Privately Held
WEB: www.rivercityrollform.com
SIC: 3544 Special dies & tools

(G-11791)
SAFECUTTERS INC
800 E Ellis Rd Ste 245 (49441-5646)
PHONE.................................866 865-7171
Sally J Fri, *President*
Tom Fri, *Principal*
Mandy Olsen, *Sales Staff*
▲ **EMP:** 3
SALES (est): 379.2K Privately Held
WEB: www.safecutters.com
SIC: 3423 Hand & edge tools

(G-11792)
SEABROOK PLASTICS INC
1869 Lindberg Dr (49441-3410)
PHONE.................................231 759-8820
Serge Cousins, *Ch of Bd*
Carol Cousins, *Admin Sec*
▲ **EMP:** 23
SQ FT: 24,000
SALES (est): 5.6MM Privately Held
WEB: www.seabrookplastics.com
SIC: 3089 Injection molding of plastics

(G-11793)
SILVER CREEK MANUFACTURING INC
696 Airport Pl (49441-6550)
PHONE.................................231 798-3003
Susan Bush, *President*
Andy Bush, *Vice Pres*
EMP: 10
SQ FT: 20,000
SALES (est): 2.7MM Privately Held
WEB: www.silvercreekmfg.com
SIC: 3469 Stamping metal for the trade

(G-11794)
SMART VISION LIGHTS LLC
5113 Robert Hunter Dr (49441-6547)
PHONE.................................231 722-1199
Dave Spalding, *President*
Matt Van Bogart, *Vice Pres*
Matt Pinter, *Design Engr*
EMP: 18
SALES (est): 3.9MM Privately Held
SIC: 1531 3646 ; commercial indusl & institutional electric lighting fixtures

(G-11795)
SNOOK INC
6430 Norton Center Dr (49441-6034)
PHONE.................................231 799-3333
Jack De Horn, *President*
EMP: 12
SQ FT: 1,000
SALES (est): 1.9MM Privately Held
WEB: www.snookinc.com
SIC: 3052 Hose, pneumatic: rubber or rubberized fabric

(G-11796)
SOILS AND STRUCTURES INC
6480 Grand Haven Rd (49441-6060)
PHONE.................................800 933-3959
David Hohmeyer, *President*
Joy Hohmeyer, *Human Res Dir*
Nancy Cook, *Personnel*
Eric Tourre, *Manager*
Stephen Hohmeyer, *Admin Sec*
EMP: 30
SQ FT: 4,000
SALES (est): 3.6MM Privately Held
WEB: www.soilsandstructures.com
SIC: 0711 8711 7389 3541 Soil testing services; engineering services; civil engineering; drafting service, except temporary help; drilling & boring machines

(G-11797)
SOURCE ONE DIGITAL LLC
1137 N Gateway Blvd (49441-6099)
PHONE.................................231 799-4040
Randy Crow, *CEO*
Abby Crow, *President*
Jane Savidge, *Vice Pres*
Amy Byrnes, *Sales Staff*
Kristen Strait, *Sales Staff*
EMP: 39
SQ FT: 25,000
SALES (est): 6.8MM Privately Held
WEB: www.sourceonedigital.com
SIC: 2759 Commercial printing

(G-11798)
STRUCTURAL CONCEPTS CORP (PA)
888 E Porter Rd (49441-5895)
PHONE.................................231 798-8888
James Doss, *Ch of Bd*
David P Geerts, *President*
Steve Meyers, *COO*
Jeff Schneider, *Senior VP*
Bob Matych, *Vice Pres*
◆ **EMP:** 293
SQ FT: 180,000
SALES (est): 87.1MM Privately Held
SIC: 2542 Cabinets: show, display or storage: except wood; counters or counter display cases: except wood

(G-11799)
TARGET MOLD CORPORATION
4088 Treeline Dr (49441-4500)
PHONE.................................231 798-3535
Charles Fishel, *Co-President*
EMP: 13
SALES (est): 2MM Privately Held
SIC: 3544 3545 Industrial molds; jigs & fixtures; gauges (machine tool accessories)

(G-11800)
TGW SYSTEMS INC (DH)
1300 E Mount Garfield Rd (49441-6097)
PHONE.................................231 798-4547
Mario Hernel, *CEO*
Shelley Steinhauer, *Editor*
Lynn Metzger, *Business Mgr*
Markus Sturm, *Vice Pres*
Leigh Baker, *Opers Mgr*
◆ **EMP:** 207
SALES (est): 50.4MM
SALES (corp-wide): 242.1K Privately Held
WEB: www.tgw-group.com
SIC: 3535 Conveyors & conveying equipment
HQ: Tgw Mechanics Gmbh
   CollmannstraBe 2
   Wels 4600
   724 248-60

(G-11801)
THERM-O-DISC INCORPORATED
851 E Porter Rd (49441-5972)
PHONE.................................231 799-4100
Marie Pierson, *Branch Mgr*
EMP: 451
SALES (corp-wide): 17.4B Publicly Held
SIC: 3823 Industrial instrmnts msrmnt display/control process variable
HQ: Therm-O-Disc, Incorporated
   1320 S Main St
   Mansfield OH 44907
   419 525-8500

(G-11802)
THERM-O-DISC MIDWEST INC
851 E Porter Rd (49441-5972)
PHONE.................................231 799-4100
Dave Stebnicki, *General Mgr*
Keith Kuipers, *General Mgr*
Gary Bergeron, *Engineer*
EMP: 18
SALES (est): 2.3MM Privately Held
SIC: 3823 Industrial instrmnts msrmnt display/control process variable

(G-11803)
TITAN TOOL & DIE INC
6435 Schamber Dr (49444-9752)
PHONE.................................231 799-8680
Fernando Vicente, *President*
EMP: 7
SALES (est): 1.2MM Privately Held
WEB: www.titantoolanddieinc.com
SIC: 3544 Special dies & tools

(G-11804)
WACKER NEUSON CORPORATION
1300 E Mount Garfield Rd (49441-6097)
PHONE.................................231 799-4500
EMP: 15
SALES (corp-wide): 1.8B Privately Held
SIC: 3531 Mfg Construction Mach
HQ: Wacker Neuson Corporation
   N92w15000 Anthony Ave
   Menomonee Falls WI 53051
   262 255-0500

(G-11805)
WEST MICHIGAN GRINDING SVC INC
Also Called: Wmgm
1188 E Broadway Ave (49444-2356)
P.O. Box 4471, Muskegon (49444-0471)
PHONE.................................231 739-4245
Donald A Martines, *President*
Damon Hoeltzel, *Manager*
EMP: 18 **EST:** 1962
SQ FT: 20,000
SALES (est): 3.1MM Privately Held
WEB: www.westmichigangrinding.com
SIC: 7699 7389 3599 Industrial tool grinding; grinding, precision: commercial or industrial; machine & other job shop work

Norton Shores
Ottawa County

(G-11806)
ACEMCO INCORPORATED
Also Called: Acemco Automotive
7297 Enterprise Dr (49456-9695)
PHONE.................................231 799-8612
Jeffrey Giangrande, *Ch of Bd*
Erik Rasmussen, *Exec VP*
Terry Luce, *Maint Spvr*
Glenn Schneider, *Purch Mgr*
Ken Wilson, *Purchasing*
▲ **EMP:** 200
SQ FT: 185,000
SALES (est): 53.1MM Privately Held
WEB: www.acemco.com
SIC: 3465 3469 Automotive stampings; stamping metal for the trade

(G-11807)
ADHESIVES AND PROCESSES TECH
Also Called: Aptec
1202 E Pontaluna Rd Ste B (49456-8610)
PHONE.................................231 737-4418
Mark Kemple, *President*
Jim White, *Vice Pres*
Craig Wiknader, *Manager*
EMP: 4
SALES (est): 548K Privately Held
SIC: 2891 Adhesives

(G-11808)
BENNETT COMMERCIAL PUMP CO
1218 E Pontaluna Rd Ste A (49456-9634)
PHONE.................................231 798-1310
Thomas A Thompson, *President*
EMP: 100
SALES (est): 10MM
SALES (corp-wide): 204.2MM Privately Held
SIC: 3586 Gasoline pumps, measuring or dispensing
PA: Hines Corporation
   1218 E Pontaluna Rd Ste B
   Norton Shores MI 49456
   231 799-6240

(G-11809)
BPC ACQUISITION COMPANY
Also Called: Bennett Pump Company
1218 E Pontaluna Rd (49456-9634)
PHONE.................................231 798-1310
Thomas A Thompson, *President*
James Collier, *Vice Pres*
Pedro Ruiz, *Vice Pres*
Bill Graybeal, *Regl Sales Mgr*
EMP: 70 **EST:** 1996
SQ FT: 68,000
SALES (est): 7.2MM
SALES (corp-wide): 204.2MM Privately Held
WEB: www.bennettpump.com
SIC: 8742 3586 Management consulting services; gasoline pumps, measuring or dispensing
PA: Hines Corporation
   1218 E Pontaluna Rd Ste B
   Norton Shores MI 49456
   231 799-6240

(G-11810)
BURNSIDE ACQUISITION LLC
6830 Grand Haven Rd (49456-9616)
PHONE.................................231 798-3394
Kevin Mesler, *Branch Mgr*
Nick Maes, *Manager*
EMP: 88 Privately Held
WEB: www.burnside-mfg.com
SIC: 3469 Stamping metal for the trade
PA: Burnside Acquisition, Llc
   1060 Kenosha Indus Dr Se
   Grand Rapids MI 49508

(G-11811)
BURNSIDE INDUSTRIES LLC
Also Called: G.A. Rchrds Indstrial Oprtions
6830 Grand Haven Rd (49456-9616)
PHONE.................................231 798-3394
Brian Burnside, *Mng Member*
Megan Martin, *Manager*
EMP: 70 **EST:** 1932
SQ FT: 66,000
SALES (est): 12.9MM
SALES (corp-wide): 17.1MM Privately Held
SIC: 3469 3496 Machine parts, stamped or pressed metal; miscellaneous fabricated wire products
PA: G. A. Richards Company
   1060 Ken O Sha Ind
   Grand Rapids MI 49508
   616 243-2800

(G-11812)
HINES CORPORATION (PA)
1218 E Pontaluna Rd Ste B (49456-9634)
PHONE.................................231 799-6240
Larry Hines, *President*
Dominic Maher, *Managing Dir*
Robert Trujillo, *Managing Dir*
Michele Buckley, *Vice Pres*
Michael Chiat, *Vice Pres*
◆ **EMP:** 12
SQ FT: 4,000
SALES (est): 204.2MM Privately Held
SIC: 3443 3823 3589 3531 Boilers: industrial, power, or marine; fluidic devices, circuits & systems for process control; floor washing & polishing machines, commercial; construction machinery; roofing equipment; conveyors & conveying equipment; general construction machinery & equipment

(G-11813)
POLYCEM LLC
1271 Judson Rd (49456-9681)
P.O. Box 349, Ferrysburg (49409-0349)
PHONE.................................231 799-1040
Milton Kuyers,
Davee Wiersma, *Maintence Staff*
EMP: 30
SALES (est): 6.1MM Privately Held
SIC: 3272 Concrete products

Norton Shores - Ottawa County

(G-11814)
PROGRESS MACHINE & TOOL INC
1155 Judson Rd (49456-9635)
PHONE..................................231 798-3410
Lance H Norris, *President*
Fred Ploughman, *General Mgr*
Brad Sprague, *General Mgr*
Inja Norris, *Vice Pres*
Angie Keasey, *Production*
EMP: 40
SQ FT: 20,000
SALES (est): 6.9MM **Privately Held**
WEB: www.progressmachine.biz
SIC: 3599 Machine shop, jobbing & repair

(G-11815)
SHAPE CORP
1218 E Pontaluna Rd Ste D (49456-9634)
PHONE..................................616 846-8700
Jeff Piper, *Exec VP*
Chris Prince, *Engineer*
Dan Vanderboon, *Engineer*
EMP: 6
SALES (corp-wide): 565.6MM **Privately Held**
SIC: 3449 Miscellaneous metalwork
PA: Shape Corp.
  1900 Hayes St
  Grand Haven MI 49417
  616 846-8700

Norway
Dickinson County

(G-11816)
CURRENT
605 Saginaw St (49870-1143)
PHONE..................................906 563-5212
Bob Wurzer, *Owner*
EMP: 5
SALES (est): 217.4K **Privately Held**
SIC: 2711 Newspapers, publishing & printing

(G-11817)
LOADMASTER CORPORATION
100 E 9th Ave (49870-1107)
P.O. Box 186 (49870-0186)
PHONE..................................906 563-9226
David Brisson, *President*
Terry Barnes, *Vice Pres*
Forrest Hayes, *Engineer*
Ethan Brisson, *Sales Associate*
Andrew Brisson, *Manager*
◆ **EMP:** 50 **EST:** 1932
SQ FT: 45,000
SALES (est): 16MM **Privately Held**
WEB: www.loadmaster.org
SIC: 3713 3559 Garbage, refuse truck bodies; recycling machinery

(G-11818)
NICKELS LOGGING
1108 Railroad Ave (49870-1432)
P.O. Box 213 (49870-0213)
PHONE..................................906 563-5880
Jeffrey Nickels, *Partner*
Robert Nickels, *Partner*
EMP: 5
SALES (est): 672K **Privately Held**
SIC: 2411 4212 Logging camps & contractors; lumber (log) trucking, local

(G-11819)
RENEWABLE WORLD ENERGIES LLC
1001 Stephenson St Ste C (49870-1173)
PHONE..................................906 828-0808
William Bill Harris, *President*
EMP: 10 **EST:** 2012
SALES (est): 1.6MM **Privately Held**
SIC: 3679 Electronic loads & power supplies

(G-11820)
STEINBRECHER STONE CORP (PA)
Also Called: Norway Granite Marble
N1443 Forest Dr (49870-2007)
P.O. Box 41 (49870-0041)
PHONE..................................906 563-5852
James Steinbrecher, *President*
Kay Steinbrecher, *Corp Secy*
EMP: 7
SQ FT: 3,800
SALES (est): 913.2K **Privately Held**
SIC: 3281 5099 5999 Monuments, cut stone (not finishing or lettering only); monuments & grave markers; monuments, finished to custom order

(G-11821)
VERSO CORPORATION
Us Hwy 2 (49870)
PHONE..................................906 779-3371
Thomas Dubose, *Engineer*
Mike Sussman, *Branch Mgr*
EMP: 400 **Publicly Held**
SIC: 2621 Paper mills
PA: Verso Corporation
  8540 Gander Creek Dr
  Miamisburg OH 45342

Novi
Oakland County

(G-11822)
A123 SYSTEMS LLC (HQ)
27101 Cabaret Dr (48377-3312)
PHONE..................................248 412-9249
Peter Cirino, *President*
Thomas Spiril, *General Mgr*
Jason Forcier, *Vice Pres*
Lisa Steedman, *Vice Pres*
Joe Palo, *Plant Mgr*
▼ **EMP:** 493 **EST:** 2001
SALES (est): 409.8MM
SALES (corp-wide): 2.9B **Privately Held**
SIC: 5063 3691 Batteries; storage batteries
PA: Wanxiang Group Corporation
  Xiaoshan Economic And Technological Development Zone
  Hangzhou 31121
  571 828-3299

(G-11823)
ACCURATE TECHNOLOGIES INC (PA)
Also Called: ATI
26999 Meadowbrook Rd (48377-3523)
PHONE..................................248 848-9200
Robert Kasprzyk, *President*
Hans Bornemann, *General Mgr*
Umesh Patel, *Business Mgr*
Ronald Drexler, *Vice Pres*
Bruce Porcaro, *Prdtn Mgr*
EMP: 65
SQ FT: 22,000
SALES (est): 12.3MM **Privately Held**
SIC: 3825 Test equipment for electronic & electric measurement

(G-11824)
AMARIS INTERNATIONAL LLC
23481 Haggerty Rd (48375-3727)
PHONE..................................248 427-0472
Rebekah Beal, *Mng Member*
Robert Lewis, *Mng Member*
EMP: 3
SALES: 1.5MM **Privately Held**
WEB: www.amarisinternational.com
SIC: 2679 Paper products, converted

(G-11825)
AMPHENOL CORPORATION
41180 Bridge St (48375-1300)
PHONE..................................256 417-4338
EMP: 3
SALES (corp-wide): 8.2B **Publicly Held**
SIC: 3678 Electronic connectors
PA: Amphenol Corporation
  358 Hall Ave
  Wallingford CT 06492
  203 265-8900

(G-11826)
ANCHOR LAMINA AMERICA INC (DH)
Also Called: Anchor Die Supply
39830 Grand River Ave B-2 (48375-2134)
PHONE..................................248 489-9122
Micahel Purchase, *President*
Michael Purchase, *President*
Scott Jones, *General Mgr*
Sawato Hayashi, *Chairman*
Bill Mills, *Vice Pres*
▲ **EMP:** 21
SQ FT: 7,800
SALES (est): 69.4MM **Privately Held**
WEB: www.anchorlamina.com
SIC: 3544 3546 3443 3366 Die sets for metal stamping (presses); drills, portable, except rock: electric or pneumatic; fabricated plate work (boiler shop); copper foundries; nonferrous rolling & drawing
HQ: Dayton Lamina Corporation
  500 Progress Rd
  Dayton OH 45449
  937 859-5111

(G-11827)
ANCHOR PRINTING COMPANY
Also Called: Anchor Flexible Packg & Label
22790 Heslip Dr (48375-4143)
PHONE..................................248 335-7440
Martin Weitz, *President*
Linda Weitz, *Corp Secy*
Andrew Weitz, *Vice Pres*
▲ **EMP:** 32
SQ FT: 15,000
SALES (est): 5.8MM **Privately Held**
WEB: www.anchorprinting.com
SIC: 2759 2752 Flexographic printing; commercial printing, offset

(G-11828)
ANDRITZ METALS INC
26800 Meadowbrook Rd (48377-3540)
PHONE..................................248 305-2969
Peter Winkler, *General Mgr*
EMP: 5
SALES (corp-wide): 6.9B **Privately Held**
SIC: 7692 5999 Welding repair; welding supplies
HQ: Andritz Metals Inc.
  500 Technology Dr
  Canonsburg PA 15317

(G-11829)
AR2 ENGINEERING LLC (PA)
Also Called: Screen Works
26600 Heyn Dr (48374-1821)
PHONE..................................248 735-9999
Amit Soman,
EMP: 28 **EST:** 2015
SALES (est): 7.4MM **Privately Held**
SIC: 7336 2759 3993 Commercial art & graphic design; screen printing; signs & advertising specialties

(G-11830)
ASCO LP
46280 Dylan Dr Ste 100 (48377-4910)
PHONE..................................248 596-3200
Joe Malloi, *Branch Mgr*
Dana Greenly, *Manager*
EMP: 125
SALES (corp-wide): 17.4B **Publicly Held**
WEB: www.numatics-frl.com
SIC: 3491 Valves, automatic control
HQ: Asco, L.P.
  160 Park Ave
  Florham Park NJ 07932
  800 972-2726

(G-11831)
ASMO DETROIT INC
39575 Lewis Dr Ste 800 (48377-2987)
PHONE..................................248 359-4440
Hiromi Okugawa, *President*
Yasunori Yamada, *President*
▲ **EMP:** 8
SALES (est): 1.3MM **Privately Held**
SIC: 3714 Motor vehicle parts & accessories
PA: Denso Corporation
  1-1, Showacho
  Kariya AIC 448-0

(G-11832)
ASSISTIVE TECHNOLOGY MICH INC
Also Called: Assistive Technology Cal
43000 W 9 Mile Rd Ste 113 (48375-4180)
PHONE..................................248 348-7161
Ghassan Souri, *President*
EMP: 4
SALES (est): 400K **Privately Held**
WEB: www.atofmich.com
SIC: 3842 5047 5999 Technical aids for the handicapped; technical aids for the handicapped; technical aids for the handicapped

(G-11833)
AUTODESK INC
26200 Town Center Dr # 300 (48375-1220)
PHONE..................................248 347-9650
Robert Kross, *Branch Mgr*
Steven Trudeau, *Manager*
Brad Ingram, *Sr Software Eng*
Jeffrey Sannes, *Executive*
EMP: 61
SALES (corp-wide): 2.5B **Publicly Held**
WEB: www.autodesk.com
SIC: 7372 7371 Prepackaged software; custom computer programming services
PA: Autodesk, Inc.
  111 Mcinnis Pkwy
  San Rafael CA 94903
  415 507-5000

(G-11834)
AUTOMATED CONTROL SYSTEMS INC
25168 Seeley Rd (48375-2044)
PHONE..................................248 476-9490
James B Mellas, *President*
Ryan Mellas, *Mfg Mgr*
David Skarzynski, *Materials Mgr*
Rob Simpson, *Sales Mgr*
Larry Walker, *Program Mgr*
EMP: 8
SQ FT: 8,000
SALES (est): 1.9MM **Privately Held**
SIC: 3625 Electric controls & control accessories, industrial

(G-11835)
AUTOMATIC VALVE CORP
Also Called: Automatic Valve Nuclear
22550 Heslip Dr (48375-4139)
PHONE..................................248 474-6761
Todd Hutchins, *CEO*
▲ **EMP:** 50 **EST:** 1945
SQ FT: 14,600
SALES (est): 9.6MM **Privately Held**
WEB: www.automaticvalve.com
SIC: 3492 3494 5085 3491 Fluid power valves & hose fittings; valves & pipe fittings; valves & fittings; industrial valves

(G-11836)
AUTONEUM NORTH AMERICA INC (HQ)
29293 Haggerty Rd (48375-5501)
PHONE..................................248 848-0100
Richard Derr, *President*
Jian Pan, *Principal*
Timothy Judy, *Vice Pres*
Robert Larney, *CFO*
John Lenga, *CFO*
▲ **EMP:** 100 **EST:** 1979
SQ FT: 50,000
SALES (est): 732.2MM
SALES (corp-wide): 2.3B **Privately Held**
WEB: www.rieter.com
SIC: 3714 Motor vehicle parts & accessories
PA: Autoneum Holding Ag
  Schlosstalstrasse 43
  Winterthur ZH
  522 448-282

(G-11837)
BAKELITE N SUMITOMO AMER INC (HQ)
Also Called: Sbhpp
46820 Magellan Dr Ste C (48377-2454)
PHONE..................................248 313-7000
Shintaro Ishiwata, *CEO*
EMP: 1
SALES (est): 95.2MM **Privately Held**
SIC: 2821 Molding compounds, plastics

(G-11838)
BLOSSOM BERRY
44325 W 12 Mile Rd H-172 (48377-2534)
PHONE..................................517 775-6978
Toan K Chau, *Principal*
EMP: 4

▲ = Import ▼ = Export
◆ = Import/Export

GEOGRAPHIC SECTION

Novi - Oakland County (G-11863)

SALES (est): 199.4K **Privately Held**
SIC: 2024 5143 Ice cream & frozen desserts; frozen dairy desserts; ice cream & ices

(G-11839)
BOROPHARM INC (PA)
39555 Orchard Hill Pl # 600 (48375-5374)
PHONE 248 348-5776
Todd Zahn, *President*
Andrew Cipa, *Business Mgr*
Paul Herrinton, *Vice Pres*
Alex Baker, *Engineer*
EMP: 3
SQ FT: 30,000
SALES: 12MM **Privately Held**
SIC: 2819 Boron compounds, not from mines

(G-11840)
BRASSCRAFT MANUFACTURING CO (HQ)
Also Called: Brass Craft Mfg Co
39600 Orchard Hill Pl (48375-5331)
PHONE 248 305-6000
Rick Mejia, *President*
Thomas Assante, *President*
Wade Henderson, *Senior VP*
Dawn Rowley, *Vice Pres*
Scott Kay, *CFO*
▲ **EMP:** 146 **EST:** 1946
SQ FT: 60,000
SALES (est): 217.2MM
SALES (corp-wide): 8.3B **Publicly Held**
WEB: www.brasscraft.com
SIC: 3432 Plumbers' brass goods: drain cocks, faucets, spigots, etc.
PA: Masco Corporation
17450 College Pkwy
Livonia MI 48152
313 274-7400

(G-11841)
BROOKS UTILITY PRODUCTS GROUP (PA)
Also Called: Brooks Meter Devices
43045 W 9 Mile Rd (48375-4116)
PHONE 248 477-0250
Susan Cook, *Principal*
Allen Pruehs, *Senior Engr*
◆ **EMP:** 31
SALES (est): 6.8MM **Privately Held**
SIC: 3643 3469 Sockets, electric; electronic enclosures, stamped or pressed metal

(G-11842)
CAMBRIC CORPORATION
41050 W 11 Mile Rd (48375-1902)
PHONE 801 415-7300
Timothy Hayes, *President*
Ronald Rainson, *President*
Florin Muntean, *Vice Pres*
Merilee Hunt, *Admin Sec*
EMP: 420
SQ FT: 10,000
SALES (est): 16.7MM
SALES (corp-wide): 9.7B **Privately Held**
WEB: www.cambric.com
SIC: 8711 3462 Engineering services; automotive & internal combustion engine forgings
HQ: Tata Technologies, Inc.
41050 W 11 Mile Rd
Novi MI 48375
248 426-1482

(G-11843)
CARCONE CO
43422 W Oaks Dr (48377-3300)
PHONE 248 348-2677
Susan Carcone, *Principal*
EMP: 3
SALES (est): 245.8K **Privately Held**
SIC: 3953 Marking devices

(G-11844)
CASCO PRODUCTS CORPORATION
25921 Meadowbrook Rd (48375-1853)
PHONE 248 957-0400
Susan Verellen, *Director*
EMP: 10
SALES (est): 199.4K **Privately Held**
WEB: www.cascoglobal.com
SIC: 3714 Motor vehicle parts & accessories
HQ: Casco Products Corporation
1000 Lafayette Blvd # 100
Bridgeport CT 06604

(G-11845)
CAV TOOL COMPANY
22605 Heslip Dr (48375-4142)
PHONE 248 349-7860
Michael Ciaverilla, *President*
EMP: 12
SQ FT: 4,500
SALES (est): 1.6MM **Privately Held**
WEB: www.cavtool.com
SIC: 3544 Special dies & tools

(G-11846)
CELERITY SYSTEMS N AMER INC
28175 Haggerty Rd (48377-2903)
PHONE 248 994-7696
Michael Hurst, *Vice Pres*
EMP: 7 **EST:** 2014
SALES (est): 343.4K **Privately Held**
SIC: 3621 Rotors, for motors

(G-11847)
CHANGER & DRESSER INC
40000 Grand River Ave # 106 (48375-2133)
PHONE 256 832-4392
Lois Garlock, *Administration*
EMP: 5 **Privately Held**
SIC: 3699 Welding machines & equipment, ultrasonic
HQ: Changer & Dresser, Inc.
1527 Itc Way
Anniston AL 36207
256 832-4392

(G-11848)
CITATION MICHIGAN LLC
27275 Haggerty Rd Ste 420 (48377-3636)
PHONE 248 522-4500
Doug Grimm, *CEO*
EMP: 21
SALES (est): 3.4MM **Privately Held**
SIC: 3321 Gray iron castings

(G-11849)
CLARK INSTRUMENT INC
46590 Ryan Ct (48377-1730)
PHONE 248 669-3100
Richard Antonick, *President*
EMP: 10
SQ FT: 4,000
SALES (est): 766.8K
SALES (corp-wide): 2.1MM **Privately Held**
WEB: www.clarkinstrument.com
SIC: 3829 Measuring & controlling devices
PA: Sun-Tec, Corp.
46590 Ryan Ct
Novi MI 48377
248 669-3100

(G-11850)
CLARKSON CONTROLS & EQP CO
Also Called: Maspac International
42572 Cherry Hill Rd (48375-2511)
PHONE 248 380-9915
Don Clarkson, *President*
Kenneth J Clarkson, *Vice Pres*
EMP: 6 **EST:** 1973
SQ FT: 2,000
SALES: 500K **Privately Held**
SIC: 3823 3564 Industrial instrmnts msrmnt display/control process variable; air cleaning systems

(G-11851)
COMAU LLC
Also Called: Autotech
43900 Grand River Ave (48375-1117)
PHONE 248 305-9662
Christopher Murdoch, *Division Mgr*
Lance Pierce, *Plant Mgr*
EMP: 105
SALES (corp-wide): 126.4B **Privately Held**
SIC: 3548 Resistance welders, electric

HQ: Comau Llc
21000 Telegraph Rd
Southfield MI 48033
248 353-8888

(G-11852)
CONDUCTIVE BOLTON SYSTEMS LLC
Also Called: New Bolton Conductive Systems
28001 Cabot Dr Ste 100 (48377-2958)
PHONE 248 669-7080
William M Lasky, *Ch of Bd*
William Bolton,
Martin Kochis,
Floyd Joseph Malecke,
EMP: 100
SALES (est): 13.9MM
SALES (corp-wide): 866.2MM **Publicly Held**
SIC: 3613 Control panels, electric
PA: Stoneridge, Inc.
39675 Mackenzie Dr # 400
Novi MI 48377
248 489-9300

(G-11853)
COOPER-STANDARD AUTO OH LLC
39550 Orchard Hill Pl (48375-5329)
PHONE 248 596-5900
Allen J Campbell,
EMP: 6
SALES (est): 680.4K
SALES (corp-wide): 3.6B **Publicly Held**
SIC: 4111 3714 Local & suburban transit; motor vehicle parts & accessories
PA: Cooper-Standard Holdings Inc.
39550 Orchard Hill Pl
Novi MI 48375
248 596-5900

(G-11854)
COOPER-STANDARD AUTOMOTIVE INC (HQ)
39550 Orchard Hill Pl (48375-5329)
PHONE 248 596-5900
Jeffrey S Edwards, *CEO*
Jeffrey Debest, *President*
D William Pumphrey Jr, *President*
Keith D Stephenson, *COO*
Christopher Couch, *Vice Pres*
▲ **EMP:** 275 **EST:** 1936
SALES (est): 3B
SALES (corp-wide): 3.6B **Publicly Held**
WEB: www.cooperstandard.com
SIC: 3714 Motor vehicle parts & accessories
PA: Cooper-Standard Holdings Inc.
39550 Orchard Hill Pl
Novi MI 48375
248 596-5900

(G-11855)
COOPER-STANDARD FHS LLC (DH)
39550 Orchard Hill Pl (48375-5329)
PHONE 248 596-5900
Jeffrey S Edwards, *CEO*
Allen J Campbell, *Vice Pres*
Juan Fernando De Miguel, *Vice Pres*
Timothy W Hefferon, *Vice Pres*
Barry V Lanken, *Vice Pres*
▲ **EMP:** 9
SALES (est): 898.5K
SALES (corp-wide): 3.6B **Publicly Held**
SIC: 3714 Motor vehicle parts & accessories
HQ: Cooper-Standard Automotive Inc.
39550 Orchard Hill Pl
Novi MI 48375
248 596-5900

(G-11856)
COOPER-STANDARD HOLDINGS INC (PA)
Also Called: Cooper Standard
39550 Orchard Hill Pl (48375-5329)
PHONE 248 596-5900
Jeffrey S Edwards, *CEO*
Patrick R Clark, *Senior VP*
Christopher E Couch, *Senior VP*
Susan P Kampe, *Senior VP*
Sharon S Wenzl, *Senior VP*
EMP: 5

SALES (est): 3.6B **Publicly Held**
SIC: 3714 Motor vehicle parts & accessories

(G-11857)
CREED DEVELOPMENT
22635 Venture Dr (48375-4182)
P.O. Box 270 (48376-0270)
PHONE 248 926-9811
EMP: 4
SALES (est): 198.3K **Privately Held**
SIC: 3089 Mfg Plastic Products

(G-11858)
CREFORM CORPORATION
29795 Hudson Dr (48377-1736)
PHONE 248 926-2555
Robert Lauzon, *Engineer*
Jason Verlee, *Engineer*
Matt Slack, *Sales Mgr*
Lilia White, *Cust Mgr*
Brandon Cross, *Sales Engr*
EMP: 18 **Privately Held**
WEB: www.creform.com
SIC: 3312 3449 3494 Pipes & tubes; joists, fabricated bar; pipe fittings
HQ: Creform Corporation
1628 Poplar Drive Ext
Greer SC 29651
864 877-7405

(G-11859)
CSA SERVICES INC
39550 Orchard Hill Pl (48375-5329)
PHONE 248 596-6184
Scott D Zaret, *Principal*
EMP: 6
SALES (est): 273.5K **Privately Held**
SIC: 4111 3714 Local & suburban transit; motor vehicle parts & accessories

(G-11860)
CSQUARED INNOVATIONS INC
45145 W 12 Mile Rd (48377-2517)
PHONE 734 998-8330
Steve Annear, *CEO*
Pravansu Mohanty, *President*
EMP: 10
SALES (est): 550K **Privately Held**
SIC: 8731 3479 Commercial physical research; coating electrodes

(G-11861)
DACO HAND CONTROLLERS INC
24404 Catherine Industria (48375-2456)
PHONE 248 982-3266
Roy Engel, *President*
◆ **EMP:** 10
SQ FT: 3,825
SALES: 2.5MM
SALES (corp-wide): 14.1MM **Privately Held**
SIC: 3577 Computer peripheral equipment
PA: Daco Scientific Limited
Unit 1, Vulcan House
Reading BERKS RG7 8
118 981-7311

(G-11862)
DAIFUKU NORTH AMERICA HOLDG CO (HQ)
30100 Cabot Dr (48377-4000)
PHONE 248 553-1000
Aki Nishimura, *President*
John Doychish, *Vice Pres*
Aleem Ali, *Project Mgr*
Andrew Goody, *Project Mgr*
Marvin Delaney, *Engineer*
EMP: 47
SALES (est): 501.5MM **Privately Held**
SIC: 3535 Conveyors & conveying equipment

(G-11863)
DELPHINUS MEDICAL TECHNOLOGIES
45525 Grand River Ave (48374-1308)
PHONE 248 522-9600
Mark Forchette, *CEO*
Francis X Dobscha, *Vice Pres*
Shawn O'Brien, *VP Finance*
EMP: 45
SALES (est): 9.7MM **Privately Held**
SIC: 3841 Surgical & medical instruments

Novi - Oakland County (G-11864)

(G-11864)
DETROIT DIAMETERS INC
45380 W Park Dr (48377-1369)
PHONE 248 669-2330
Craig Spitery, *President*
Scott Spitery, *Shareholder*
EMP: 9 **EST:** 1955
SQ FT: 4,800
SALES (est): 850K **Privately Held**
WEB: www.detdia.com
SIC: 3599 Machine shop, jobbing & repair

(G-11865)
DETROIT RECYCLED CONCRETE CO (PA)
39525 W 13 Mile Rd # 300 (48377-2361)
PHONE 248 553-0600
Michael Santi, *Principal*
James Oliver, *Principal*
EMP: 7
SALES (est): 1.1MM **Privately Held**
SIC: 3272 Dry mixture concrete

(G-11866)
DETROIT TESTING MACHINE CO
46590 Ryan Ct (48377-1730)
PHONE 248 669-3100
Richard Antonik, *President*
EMP: 4
SALES (est): 282.6K **Privately Held**
WEB: www.detroittestingmachine.com
SIC: 3829 Measuring & controlling devices

(G-11867)
DEXKO GLOBAL INC (DH)
Also Called: Dragon Acqstion Intrmdate Hldc
39555 Orchard Hill Pl (48375-5374)
PHONE 248 533-0029
Fred Bentley, *CEO*
Adam Dexter, *President*
Ed Meador, *COO*
Matt Griffith, *Vice Pres*
Jeff Richard, *CFO*
EMP: 5
SALES (est): 322.9MM
SALES (corp-wide): 324.9MM **Privately Held**
SIC: 3799 Trailers & trailer equipment
HQ: Dragon Acquisition Intermediate Holdco, Llc
39555 Orchard Hill Pl # 52
Novi MI 48375
248 692-4367

(G-11868)
DI-COAT CORPORATION
42900 W 9 Mile Rd (48375-4123)
PHONE 248 349-1211
Zigmund Grutza, *President*
Alan Davis, *Exec VP*
Jeffery Boudrie, *Opers Staff*
David Asselin, *Director*
EMP: 47
SQ FT: 14,000
SALES (est): 12.7MM **Privately Held**
WEB: www.dicoat.com
SIC: 3545 3841 3531 3291 Diamond cutting tools for turning, boring, burnishing, etc.; surgical & medical instruments; construction machinery; abrasive products

(G-11869)
DIKAR TOOL COMPANY INC
22635 Heslip Dr (48375-4142)
P.O. Box 916 (48376-0916)
PHONE 248 348-0010
Robert J Forsyth, *President*
Edward E Forsyth, *Vice Pres*
Joann Forsyth, *Admin Sec*
EMP: 12 **EST:** 1956
SQ FT: 10,000
SALES: 2MM **Privately Held**
SIC: 3541 Machine tools, metal cutting type

(G-11870)
DIVERSFIED TCHNCAL SYSTEMS INC
25881 Meadowbrook Rd (48375-1851)
PHONE 248 513-6050
Steve Moss, *President*
EMP: 44 **Privately Held**
SIC: 3679 Electronic circuits
PA: Diversified Technical Systems, Inc.
1720 Apollo Ct
Seal Beach CA 90740

(G-11871)
DRAGON ACQUISITION INTERMEDIAT (HQ)
39555 Orchard Hill Pl # 52 (48375-5374)
PHONE 248 692-4367
Fred Bentley, *CEO*
EMP: 3
SALES (est): 323MM
SALES (corp-wide): 324.9MM **Privately Held**
SIC: 3799 Trailers & trailer equipment
PA: Dragon Acquisition Parent, Inc.
39555 Orchard Hill Pl # 52
Novi MI 48375
248 692-4367

(G-11872)
DRAGON ACQUISITION PARENT INC (PA)
39555 Orchard Hill Pl # 52 (48375-5374)
PHONE 248 692-4367
Fred Bentley, *CEO*
EMP: 5
SQ FT: 1,300
SALES (est): 324.9MM **Privately Held**
SIC: 3799 Trailers & trailer equipment

(G-11873)
DURA SILL CORPORATION
22500 Heslip Dr (48375-4139)
PHONE 248 348-2490
Raymond B Morianti, *President*
EMP: 5
SALES: 560K **Privately Held**
SIC: 3281 Marble, building: cut & shaped

(G-11874)
DUREZ CORPORATION (DH)
46820 Magellan Dr Ste C (48377-2454)
PHONE 248 313-7000
John W Fisher, *CEO*
David L Faust, *Treasurer*
Kelly Lane, *Sales Staff*
Keiichiro Miyajima, *Admin Sec*
◆ **EMP:** 156
SALES (est): 79.1MM **Privately Held**
WEB: www.durez.com
SIC: 2865 2821 Phenol, alkylated & cumene; molding compounds, plastics

(G-11875)
E D M SPECIALTIES INC
26111 Lannys Rd (48375-1025)
P.O. Box 696 (48376-0696)
PHONE 248 344-4080
Douglas Higley, *President*
Erik Higley, *Treasurer*
EMP: 7
SQ FT: 3,948
SALES (est): 869.9K **Privately Held**
SIC: 3544 Special dies, tools, jigs & fixtures

(G-11876)
EBERSPAECHER NORTH AMERICA INC
43700 Gen Mar (48375-1667)
PHONE 248 778-5231
Bal Sharma, *Prgrmr*
EMP: 42
SALES (corp-wide): 5.2B **Privately Held**
SIC: 3714 Motor vehicle parts & accessories
HQ: Eberspaecher North America, Inc.
29101 Haggerty Rd
Novi MI 48377
248 994-7010

(G-11877)
EBERSPAECHER NORTH AMERICA INC (DH)
Also Called: Catem North America
29101 Haggerty Rd (48377-2913)
PHONE 248 994-7010
Ken Chisholm, *General Mgr*
Gunter Baumann, *Chairman*
Pete Laplante, *Regional Mgr*
Heinrich Baumann, *COO*
Klaus Beetz, *COO*
◆ **EMP:** 42

SALES (est): 229.7MM
SALES (corp-wide): 5.2B **Privately Held**
WEB: www.eberspacher.com
SIC: 3714 Exhaust systems & parts, motor vehicle
HQ: Eberspacher Climate Control Systems Gmbh & Co. Kg
176 South St
Eberspacherstr. 24
Esslingen Am Neckar 73730
711 939-00

(G-11878)
ECCO TOOL CO INC
42525 W 11 Mile Rd (48375-1701)
PHONE 248 349-0840
Floyd Peterson, *President*
EMP: 8
SQ FT: 8,000
SALES: 1.1MM **Privately Held**
WEB: www.eccotool.com
SIC: 3545 Cutting tools for machine tools

(G-11879)
ECOLAB INC
28550 Cabot Dr Ste 100 (48377-2988)
PHONE 248 697-0202
David Bourgeois, *Branch Mgr*
EMP: 34
SALES (corp-wide): 14.6B **Publicly Held**
WEB: www.ecolab.com
SIC: 2841 Soap & other detergents
PA: Ecolab Inc.
1 Ecolab Pl
Saint Paul MN 55102
800 232-6522

(G-11880)
EDW C LEVY CO
Cadillac Asphalt Paving
27575 Wixom Rd (48374-1127)
PHONE 248 349-8600
Ron Jones, *Manager*
EMP: 50
SALES (corp-wide): 368.1MM **Privately Held**
WEB: www.edwclevy.com
SIC: 1611 2951 Highway & street paving contractor; asphalt paving mixtures & blocks
PA: Edw. C. Levy Co.
9300 Dix
Dearborn MI 48120
313 429-2200

(G-11881)
EKSTROM INDUSTRIES INC
Also Called: Brooks Utility Products Group
43045 W 9 Mile Rd (48375-4116)
PHONE 248 477-0040
Jeff Hanft, *President*
▼ **EMP:** 82 **EST:** 1954
SQ FT: 38,200
SALES (est): 12.5MM
SALES (corp-wide): 444.9MM **Privately Held**
WEB: www.surgeprotectiondevices.com
SIC: 3643 3544 Current-carrying wiring devices; special dies & tools; jigs & fixtures
HQ: E.J. Brooks Company
409 Hoosier Dr
Angola IN 46703
800 348-4777

(G-11882)
ELMET LLC
40028 Grand River Ave # 400 (48375-2165)
PHONE 248 473-2924
Arthur Griebel,
EMP: 3
SQ FT: 2,500
SALES: 970K **Privately Held**
SIC: 3825 Analog-digital converters, electronic instrumentation type

(G-11883)
EMC CORPORATION
39555 Orchard Hill Pl # 138 (48375-5374)
PHONE 248 374-5009
Gary Van Buhler, *Manager*
EMP: 3

SALES (corp-wide): 90.6B **Publicly Held**
WEB: www.emc.com
SIC: 7372 5734 Business oriented computer software; computer & software stores
HQ: Emc Corporation
176 South St
Hopkinton MA 01748
508 435-1000

(G-11884)
ENERGY EXPLORATION
40411 Oakwood Dr (48375-4453)
PHONE 248 579-6531
Richard T Buttery, *Administration*
EMP: 3 **EST:** 2010
SALES (est): 215.5K **Privately Held**
SIC: 1382 Oil & gas exploration services

(G-11885)
ESPAR INC
43700 Gen Mar 3 (48375-1667)
PHONE 248 994-7010
Gokcen Tural, *Opers Mgr*
EMP: 9 **EST:** 2013
SALES (est): 352.2K
SALES (corp-wide): 5.2B **Privately Held**
SIC: 3585 Air conditioning, motor vehicle
HQ: Eberspacher Climate Control Systems Gmbh & Co. Kg
Eberspacherstr. 24
Esslingen Am Neckar 73730
711 939-00

(G-11886)
EZM LLC
39555 Orchard Hill Pl # 600 (48375-5374)
PHONE 248 438-6570
Tom V Esch,
Carine Woldanski,
EMP: 13
SALES: 1.5MM **Privately Held**
SIC: 3825 3829 Electrical energy measuring equipment; measuring & controlling devices

(G-11887)
FREMONT COMMUNITY DIGESTER LLC
23955 Novi Rd (48375-3244)
PHONE 248 735-6684
Anand Gangadharan,
EMP: 18
SALES: 950K **Privately Held**
SIC: 2813 4911 Industrial gases; electric services

(G-11888)
FROUDE INC
Also Called: Go Power Systems
41123 Jo Dr Ste A (48375-1920)
PHONE 248 579-4295
John G Harris, *CEO*
Andrew Sadlon, *President*
◆ **EMP:** 2
SQ FT: 1,800
SALES (est): 9.6MM **Privately Held**
WEB: www.froudehofmann.com
SIC: 3829 Dynamometer instruments
HQ: Wintergreen Management Limited
Unit 3 Ashted Lock
Birmingham W MIDLANDS

(G-11889)
FXI NOVI
28700 Cabot Dr (48377-2943)
PHONE 248 994-0630
EMP: 3
SALES (est): 169.3K **Privately Held**
SIC: 3086 Plastics foam products

(G-11890)
GENERAL FILTERS INC (PA)
Also Called: Gar-Ber
43800 Grand River Ave (48375-1115)
PHONE 248 476-5100
Carl R Redner, *President*
Robert P Redner, *Vice Pres*
Gary Danis, *Purch Agent*
Paige Freeland, *Marketing Mgr*
John A Redner, *Admin Sec*
▲ **EMP:** 50
SQ FT: 110,000

SALES (est): 14.5MM **Privately Held**
WEB: www.generalfilters.com
SIC: 3585 3564 Humidifying equipment, except portable; filters, air: furnaces, air conditioning equipment, etc.; air purification equipment

(G-11891)
GICMAC INDUSTRIAL INC
43155 Main St (48375-1777)
PHONE..................................248 308-2743
Marco Arie Canizo, *President*
EMP: 2
SALES (est): 4.9MM **Privately Held**
SIC: 3543 Industrial patterns

(G-11892)
GUHRING INC
Also Called: Guhring-Michigan
24975 Trans X Rd (48375-2435)
PHONE..................................262 784-6730
Henry Kenneweg, *Branch Mgr*
EMP: 20
SALES (corp-wide): 1.3B **Privately Held**
WEB: www.guhring.com
SIC: 3545 Cutting tools for machine tools
HQ: Guhring, Inc.
1445 Commerce Ave
Brookfield WI 53045
262 784-6730

(G-11893)
HANON SYSTEMS USA LLC (DH)
39600 Lewis Dr (48375-2953)
PHONE..................................248 907-8000
Bob Hickson, *President*
Robert Willing, *Managing Prtnr*
Kwangtaek Hong, *Vice Pres*
Jay Son, *Vice Pres*
Cherie Nuttall, *Purch Mgr*
EMP: 263 **EST:** 2012
SALES (est): 201.5MM **Privately Held**
SIC: 3714 3585 3699 Air conditioner parts, motor vehicle; radiators & radiator shells & cores, motor vehicle; heaters, motor vehicle; compressors for refrigeration & air conditioning equipment; heat emission operating apparatus

(G-11894)
HARADA INDUSTRY AMERICA INC (HQ)
22925 Venture Dr (48375-4181)
PHONE..................................248 374-2587
Toru Sasaki, *CEO*
Shoji Harada, *Ch of Bd*
Yoichi Hiyama, *President*
Sandy Hammett, *General Mgr*
Israel Cruzado, *Vice Pres*
▲ **EMP:** 75
SQ FT: 12,000
SALES (est): 20.3MM **Privately Held**
WEB: www.haradamail.com
SIC: 3663 Antennas, transmitting & communications

(G-11895)
HARBROOK TOOL INC
40391 Grand River Ave (48375-2123)
PHONE..................................248 477-8040
Kim Bergerson, *President*
William Bergerson, *Vice Pres*
EMP: 12
SQ FT: 6,000
SALES (est): 2MM **Privately Held**
WEB: www.harbrooktool.com
SIC: 3544 Special dies & tools

(G-11896)
HARMAN BECKER AUTO SYSTEMS INC (DH)
Also Called: Harman Consumer Group
30001 Cabot Dr (48377-2910)
P.O. Box 550, Farmington (48332-0550)
PHONE..................................248 785-2361
Klaus Blickle, *President*
Dinesh C Paliwal, *Principal*
Herbert K Parker, *Exec VP*
Paul Devries, *Engineer*
Jonathan Lane, *Director*
◆ **EMP:** 500
SQ FT: 182,000

SALES (est): 903.2MM **Privately Held**
SIC: 3812 3931 Navigational systems & instruments; autophones (organs with perforated music rolls)
HQ: Harman International Industries Incorporated
400 Atlantic St Ste 15
Stamford CT 06901
203 328-3500

(G-11897)
HARRYS MEME LLC
41679 Magnolia Ct (48377-4529)
PHONE..................................248 977-0168
Hai Gu,
EMP: 7 **EST:** 2017
SALES (est): 298.2K **Privately Held**
SIC: 2322 Men's & boys' underwear & nightwear

(G-11898)
HAYES LEMMERZ INTL-GA LLC
39500 Orchard Hill Pl (48375-5370)
PHONE..................................734 737-5000
Fred Bentley, *COO*
John A Salvette, *CFO*
▲ **EMP:** 200
SALES (est): 8.6MM **Privately Held**
SIC: 3312 3714 Wheels, locomotive & car: iron & steel; motor vehicle parts & accessories
HQ: Maxion Wheels U.S.A. Llc
39500 Orchard Hill Pl # 500
Novi MI 48375
734 737-5000

(G-11899)
HENGST OF NORTH AMERICA INC
29770 Hudson Dr (48377-1736)
PHONE..................................586 757-2995
Tim Hanelt, *Engineer*
Constantine Diehl, *Branch Mgr*
EMP: 4
SALES (corp-wide): 499.7MM **Privately Held**
SIC: 3714 Filters: oil, fuel & air, motor vehicle
HQ: Hengst Of North America, Inc.
29 Hengst Blvd
Camden SC 29020
803 432-5992

(G-11900)
HEPHAESTUS HOLDINGS LLC (DH)
39475 W 13 Mile Rd # 105 (48377-2359)
PHONE..................................248 479-2700
George Thanopolous, *CEO*
EMP: 1
SALES (est): 284.9MM
SALES (corp-wide): 7.2B **Publicly Held**
SIC: 3462 3463 Iron & steel forgings; nonferrous forgings
HQ: Forging Holdings, Llc
1 Dauch Dr
Detroit MI 48211
313 758-2000

(G-11901)
HIGH TOUCH HEALTHCARE LLC
29307 Douglas Dr (48377-2891)
PHONE..................................248 513-2425
Bhuvan Doneecudi, *Mng Member*
Ravi Kamepalli,
EMP: 4
SALES: 350K **Privately Held**
SIC: 7372 7389 Application computer software;

(G-11902)
HOWA USA HOLDINGS INC (HQ)
40220 Grand River Ave (48375-2116)
PHONE..................................248 715-4000
Katsuro Saito, *CEO*
Makoto ITOH, *General Mgr*
Mikio Ishihara, *Sales Staff*
EMP: 0
SALES (est): 18.1MM **Privately Held**
SIC: 6719 3552 Personal holding companies, except banks; textile machinery

(G-11903)
HUHNSEAL USA INC
41650 Gardenbrook Rd (48375-1321)
PHONE..................................248 347-0606

Fulvio Ginobri, *Principal*
EMP: 3
SALES (est): 123.6K **Privately Held**
SIC: 2891 Sealing compounds for pipe threads or joints

(G-11904)
HYDRO CHEM LABORATORIES INC
22859 Heslip Dr (48375-4146)
PHONE..................................248 348-1737
James V Boyd, *President*
Michael Trzos, *Vice Pres*
EMP: 4
SQ FT: 2,400
SALES (est): 709.3K **Privately Held**
WEB: www.hgcinc.com
SIC: 2899 Water treating compounds

(G-11905)
IMC DATAWORKS LLC
39555 Orchard Hill Pl # 225 (48375-5374)
PHONE..................................248 356-4311
Andrew Jesudowich, *Mng Member*
EMP: 8
SALES (est): 978.1K **Privately Held**
WEB: www.imcdataworks.com
SIC: 3823 Industrial process measurement equipment

(G-11906)
INTEGRATED SECURITY CORP
46755 Magellan Dr (48377-2453)
PHONE..................................248 624-0700
Morton Noveck, *President*
Tammy Wilson, *Clerk*
▼ **EMP:** 18
SALES (est): 3.9MM **Privately Held**
WEB: www.integratedsecuritycorp.com
SIC: 3699 3823 Security control equipment & systems; industrial instrmnts msrmnt display/control process variable

(G-11907)
IOCHPE HOLDINGS LLC (HQ)
39500 Orchard Hill Pl # 500 (48375-5370)
PHONE..................................734 737-5000
Dan Ioschpe, *CEO*
Steve Esau, *Vice Pres*
John Salvette, *Vice Pres*
Eric Moraw, *Treasurer*
Colleen Hanley, *Director*
EMP: 100
SQ FT: 20,000
SALES (est): 1.8B **Privately Held**
SIC: 3714 Motor vehicle parts & accessories

(G-11908)
IPG PHOTONICS CORPORATION
Also Called: Ipg Phtnics - Mdwest Oprations
46695 Magellan Dr (48377-2442)
PHONE..................................248 863-5001
William Carlson, *Engineer*
Mike Klos, *Manager*
EMP: 12
SALES (corp-wide): 1.4B **Publicly Held**
SIC: 3699 Laser systems & equipment
PA: Ipg Photonics Corporation
50 Old Webster Rd
Oxford MA 01540
508 373-1100

(G-11909)
ITT MOTION TECH AMER LLC
Also Called: ITT Koni America, LLC
46785 Magellan Dr (48377-2453)
PHONE..................................248 863-2161
Denise L Ramos, *CEO*
▲ **EMP:** 18
SALES (est): 2.6MM
SALES (corp-wide): 2.7B **Publicly Held**
SIC: 3751 3446 3625 Brakes, friction clutch & other: bicycle; acoustical suspension systems, metal; control equipment, electric
HQ: Itt Llc
1133 Westchester Ave N-100
White Plains NY 10604
914 641-2000

(G-11910)
J H BENNETT AND COMPANY INC (PA)
22975 Venture Dr (48375-4181)
PHONE..................................248 596-5100

Bill Vincent, *President*
David Cassel, *Exec VP*
Joey Selmants, *Sales Engr*
▲ **EMP:** 33
SQ FT: 32,000
SALES: 36.6MM **Privately Held**
WEB: www.jhbennett.com
SIC: 3594 5084 Fluid power pumps & motors; hydraulic systems equipment & supplies

(G-11911)
JD GROUP INC
26600 Heyn Dr (48374-1821)
PHONE..................................248 735-9999
Michael Grzych, *President*
Michael Tamm, *Vice Pres*
EMP: 42
SQ FT: 14,000
SALES (est): 5.9MM **Privately Held**
WEB: www.screenworksinc.net
SIC: 2759 3993 Screen printing; signs & advertising specialties

(G-11912)
JERVIS B WEBB COMPANY (HQ)
30100 Cabot Dr (48377-4000)
PHONE..................................248 553-1000
Dina Salehi, *CEO*
Timothy Hund, *President*
Deon Oley, *Engineer*
Alex Wuchte, *Engineer*
Takao Saruhashi, *CFO*
◆ **EMP:** 300 **EST:** 1919
SQ FT: 180,000
SALES (est): 271.3MM **Privately Held**
WEB: www.jervisbwebb.com
SIC: 3536 3462 3537 3613 Cranes & monorail systems; cranes, industrial plant; monorail systems; iron & steel forgings; chains, forged steel; stacking machines, automatic; tractors, used in plants, docks, terminals, etc.: industrial; control panels, electric; overhead conveyor systems

(G-11913)
KALTEC SCIENTIFIC INC
22425 Heslip Dr (48375-4138)
P.O. Box 762 (48376-0762)
PHONE..................................248 349-8100
Jon T Dean, *President*
▼ **EMP:** 4
SQ FT: 8,000
SALES: 650K **Privately Held**
WEB: www.kaltecsci.com
SIC: 3823 7699 Viscosimeters, industrial process type; scientific equipment repair service

(G-11914)
KERN INDUSTRIES INC
43000 W 10 Mile Rd Frnt (48375-5443)
PHONE..................................248 349-4866
Patrick Kern, *President*
Thomas Kern, *Corp Secy*
James Kern, *Vice Pres*
Michael Kern, *Vice Pres*
EMP: 20
SQ FT: 14,000
SALES: 1.2MM **Privately Held**
SIC: 3544 Special dies & tools

(G-11915)
KIDDE SAFETY
39550 W 13 Mile Rd # 101 (48377-2360)
PHONE..................................800 880-6788
EMP: 8
SALES (est): 614.9K **Privately Held**
SIC: 3999 Fire extinguishers, portable

(G-11916)
KISTLER INSTRUMENT CORPORATION (HQ)
30280 Hudson Dr (48377-4115)
PHONE..................................248 668-6900
Nick Wilks, *President*
William Zwolinski, *Vice Pres*
Aaron Schumacher, *Technical Mgr*
Eren Kiziltug, *Sales Dir*
Jin-SOO Kim, *Manager*
▲ **EMP:** 75
SQ FT: 33,000
SALES (est): 9.7MM
SALES (corp-wide): 478.9MM **Privately Held**
SIC: 3829 Measuring & controlling devices

Novi - Oakland County (G-11917)

PA: Kistler Holding Ag
Eulachstrasse 22
Winterthur ZH 8408
522 241-111

(G-11917)
KONECRANES INC
Also Called: Crane Pro Services
42970 W 10 Mile Rd (48375-5421)
PHONE..................248 380-2626
Margie Bryant, *Manager*
Rick Colombo, *Manager*
EMP: 20
SALES (corp-wide): 3.6B **Privately Held**
WEB: www.kciusa.com
SIC: 3536 Hoists, cranes & monorails
HQ: Konecranes, Inc.
4401 Gateway Blvd
Springfield OH 45502

(G-11918)
KONGSBERG AUTOMOTIVE INC (HQ)
27275 Haggerty Rd Ste 610 (48377-3635)
PHONE..................248 468-1300
Hans Peter Havdal, *CEO*
Joachim Magnusson, *Exec VP*
Jarle Nymoen, *Exec VP*
Anders Nystrm, *Exec VP*
Trond Stabekk, *Exec VP*
▲ EMP: 100
SALES (est): 249.5MM
SALES (corp-wide): 1.2B **Privately Held**
WEB: www.kongsbergautomotive.com
SIC: 3714 Heaters, motor vehicle
PA: Kongsberg Automotive Asa
Dyrmyrgata 48
Kongsberg 3611
327 705-00

(G-11919)
KONGSBERG HOLDING I INC (PA)
27275 Haggerty Rd Ste 610 (48377-3635)
PHONE..................248 468-1300
EMP: 4
SALES (est): 879.5K **Privately Held**
SIC: 3714 Motor vehicle parts & accessories

(G-11920)
KONGSBERG HOLDING III INC (HQ)
Also Called: Kongsberg Automotive
27275 Haggerty Rd Ste 610 (48377-3635)
PHONE..................248 468-1300
Raymond Boyma, *President*
EMP: 25
SALES (est): 178.3MM
SALES (corp-wide): 1.2B **Privately Held**
SIC: 3714 Motor vehicle parts & accessories
PA: Kongsberg Automotive Asa
Dyrmyrgata 48
Kongsberg 3611
327 705-00

(G-11921)
KONGSBERG INTR SYSTEMS I INC (DH)
27275 Haggerty Rd Ste 610 (48377-3635)
PHONE..................956 465-4541
Hans Peter Havdal, *CEO*
Raymond Bonya, *President*
Anders Mystron, *Exec VP*
Trond Stabekk, *Exec VP*
▲ EMP: 19
SQ FT: 137,000
SALES (est): 55.8MM
SALES (corp-wide): 1.2B **Privately Held**
SIC: 3714 Motor vehicle parts & accessories

(G-11922)
KUBICA CORP
Also Called: Prime Technologies
22575 Heslip Dr (48375-4140)
P.O. Box 812, Northville (48167-0812)
PHONE..................248 344-7750
Dennis Kubica, *CEO*
Katherine Hall, *Engineer*
Jennifer Kubica, *CFO*
Daniel Gorman, *Office Mgr*
Erik Aitken, *Software Dev*
EMP: 14

SQ FT: 15,800
SALES (est): 3.4MM **Privately Held**
WEB: www.kubicacorp.net
SIC: 8711 7371 3823 Consulting engineer; computer software development & applications; industrial process control instruments

(G-11923)
KYB AMERICAS CORPORATION
26800 Meadowbrook Rd # 115 (48377-3540)
PHONE..................248 374-0100
EMP: 4 **Privately Held**
SIC: 5012 3711 Automobile auction; motor vehicles & car bodies
HQ: Kyb Americas Corporation
2625 N Morton St
Franklin IN 46131
317 736-7774

(G-11924)
KYOEI ELECTRONICS AMERICA INC
39555 Orchard Hill Pl (48375-5374)
PHONE..................248 773-3690
Hiroyuki Komiya, *President*
EMP: 11
SALES (est): 381.2K **Privately Held**
SIC: 3931 String instruments & parts
PA: Kyoei Sangyo Co., Ltd.
2-20-4, Shoto
Shibuya-Ku TKY 150-0

(G-11925)
L N T INC
24300 Catherne Ind Dr # 405 (48375-2457)
PHONE..................248 347-6006
Richard Fink, *President*
EMP: 4
SALES (est): 438.6K **Privately Held**
SIC: 3915 Jewelers' castings

(G-11926)
LACKS EXTERIOR SYSTEMS LLC
39500 Mackenzie Dr # 500 (48377-1603)
PHONE..................248 351-0555
Christopher Thoreson, *Branch Mgr*
EMP: 15
SALES (corp-wide): 715.6MM **Privately Held**
SIC: 3089 Plastic hardware & building products
HQ: Lacks Exterior Systems, Llc
5460 Cascade Rd Se
Grand Rapids MI 49546
616 949-6570

(G-11927)
LACKS WHEEL TRIM SYSTEMS LLC
39500 Mackenzie Dr # 500 (48377-1603)
PHONE..................248 351-0555
Mark Montone, *Principal*
EMP: 15
SALES (corp-wide): 7.7MM **Privately Held**
SIC: 3089 Injection molding of plastics
PA: Lacks Wheel Trim Systems, Llc
5460 Cascade Rd Se
Grand Rapids MI 49546
616 949-6570

(G-11928)
LACY TOOL COMPANY INC
40375 Grand River Ave (48375-2123)
PHONE..................248 476-5250
Evan Lacy, *President*
Thelma Lacy, *Corp Secy*
EMP: 6
SQ FT: 12,500
SALES: 960K **Privately Held**
SIC: 3465 3469 Automotive stampings; metal stampings

(G-11929)
LASER MECHANISMS INC (PA)
25325 Regency Dr (48375-2159)
PHONE..................248 474-9480
William G Fredrick, *President*
Greg Stone, *Vice Pres*
Richard Lee, *Mfg Engineer*
John Brower, *Engineer*

Gerry Hermann, *Engineer*
EMP: 75
SQ FT: 25,000
SALES: 19.9MM **Privately Held**
WEB: www.lasermech-rps.com
SIC: 3699 Laser systems & equipment

(G-11930)
LUEBKE & VOGT CORPORATION
25889 Meadowbrook Rd (48375-1851)
PHONE..................248 449-3232
Paul Nikl, *President*
Karin Demuth, *Admin Asst*
◆ EMP: 4
SALES (est): 539.6K **Privately Held**
SIC: 3069 Molded rubber products

(G-11931)
M-TEK INC
29065 Cabot Dr 300 (48377-2951)
PHONE..................248 553-1581
EMP: 15
SALES (corp-wide): 1.8B **Privately Held**
SIC: 3714 Mfg Plastic Products
HQ: M-Tek, Inc.
1020 Volunteer Pkwy
Manchester TN 37129
931 728-4122

(G-11932)
MAGNA SEATING AMERICA INC (HQ)
Also Called: Intier Automotive Seating
30020 Cabot Dr (48377-2910)
PHONE..................248 567-4000
Joseph Pittel, *President*
Mike Bisson, *President*
John Oilar, *President*
Simon Kew, *General Mgr*
Glen Copeland, *Vice Pres*
▲ EMP: 450
SQ FT: 300,000
SALES (est): 640.9MM
SALES (corp-wide): 40.8B **Privately Held**
SIC: 3714 Motor vehicle parts & accessories
PA: Magna International Inc
337 Magna Dr
Aurora ON L4G 7
905 726-2462

(G-11933)
MAGNETECH CORPORATION
22809 Heslip Dr (48375-4146)
P.O. Box 931 (48376-0931)
PHONE..................248 426-8840
Victor Lu, *President*
Tina Yang, *Vice Pres*
▲ EMP: 3
SQ FT: 2,400
SALES: 840.4K **Privately Held**
SIC: 3625 8711 3679 3621 Brakes, electromagnetic; control equipment, electric; engineering services; electronic circuits; coils, for electric motors or generators; control panels, electric

(G-11934)
MARBELITE CORP
22500 Heslip Dr (48375-4139)
PHONE..................248 348-1900
Larry Morianti, *President*
Steve Sist, *Vice Pres*
EMP: 40
SQ FT: 16,000
SALES (est): 5.2MM **Privately Held**
WEB: www.marbelitecorp.com
SIC: 3281 3431 2434 Bathroom fixtures, cut stone; metal sanitary ware; wood kitchen cabinets

(G-11935)
MASTER JIG GRINDING & GAGE CO
43050 W 10 Mile Rd (48375-3206)
PHONE..................248 380-8515
Lyle F Vidergar, *President*
EMP: 5 EST: 1962
SQ FT: 5,000
SALES (est): 800.6K **Privately Held**
WEB: www.mjgg.com
SIC: 3545 3544 Gauges (machine tool accessories); jigs: inspection, gauging & checking

(G-11936)
MASTERY TECHNOLOGIES INC
41214 Bridge St (48375-1301)
PHONE..................248 888-8420
William M Marker, *President*
Jeff Holth, *Partner*
Kirk V Berry, *Vice Pres*
Kirk Berry, *Vice Pres*
Carl Allard, *Accounts Exec*
EMP: 11
SQ FT: 3,300
SALES (est): 1.7MM **Privately Held**
WEB: www.industrialbestpractices.com
SIC: 7372 Business oriented computer software

(G-11937)
MATHWORKS INC
39555 Orchard Hill Pl # 280 (48375-5538)
PHONE..................248 596-7920
Olgha Qaqish, *Principal*
Camil Jreige, *Engineer*
Mark McBroom, *Engineer*
Steven Conahan, *Software Engr*
Zhiquan He, *Software Engr*
EMP: 18
SALES (corp-wide): 1B **Privately Held**
SIC: 7372 Application computer software
PA: The Mathworks Inc
1 Apple Hill Dr Ste 2
Natick MA 01760
508 647-7000

(G-11938)
MAXION FUMAGALLI AUTO USA
39500 Orchard Hill Pl (48375-5370)
PHONE..................734 737-5000
EMP: 75
SALES (est): 5.4MM **Privately Held**
SIC: 3714 Mfg Motor Vehicle Parts/Accessories

(G-11939)
MAXION IMPORT LLC
39500 Orchard Hill Pl # 500 (48375-5370)
PHONE..................734 737-5000
John Salvette, *Vice Pres*
Steven Esau, *Vice Pres*
William Wardle, *Vice Pres*
Eric Moraw, *Treasurer*
▲ EMP: 10
SQ FT: 1,000
SALES (est): 2MM **Privately Held**
SIC: 3714 Motor vehicle parts & accessories
HQ: Iochpe Holdings Llc
39500 Orchard Hill Pl # 500
Novi MI 48375
734 737-5000

(G-11940)
MAXION WHEELS (DH)
Also Called: Hayes Lemmerz International
39500 Orchard Hill Pl # 500 (48375-5370)
PHONE..................734 737-5000
Pieter Klinkers, *CEO*
Kai Kronenberg, *President*
Don Polk, *President*
Steven Esau, *Vice Pres*
Giorgio Mariani, *Vice Pres*
◆ EMP: 100
SQ FT: 30,000
SALES (est): 1.8B **Privately Held**
WEB: www.hayes-lemmerz.com
SIC: 3714 Wheels, motor vehicle
HQ: Iochpe Holdings Llc
39500 Orchard Hill Pl # 500
Novi MI 48375
734 737-5000

(G-11941)
MAXION WHEELS AKRON LLC
39500 Orchard Hill Pl # 500 (48375-5370)
PHONE..................734 737-5000
Joslyn Lawson, *Branch Mgr*
EMP: 4 **Privately Held**
SIC: 3714 Motor vehicle parts & accessories
HQ: Maxion Wheels Akron Llc
428 Seiberling St
Akron OH 44306

(G-11942)
MAXION WHEELS USA LLC (DH)
39500 Orchard Hill Pl # 500 (48375-5370)
PHONE..................734 737-5000

GEOGRAPHIC SECTION
Novi - Oakland County (G-11968)

Pieter Klinkers, *CEO*
Steve Esau, *Vice Pres*
John Salvette, *Vice Pres*
Karl Rode, *VP Opers*
Kenny Angle, *Opers Mgr*
EMP: 100
SQ FT: 20,000
SALES (est): 809.1MM **Privately Held**
SIC: 3714 Wheels, motor vehicle
HQ: Maxion Wheels
   39500 Orchard Hill Pl # 500
   Novi MI 48375
   734 737-5000

(G-11943)
MEDTRONIC INC
41850 W 11 Mile Rd (48375-1819)
PHONE...............................248 349-6987
Greg Burrell, *Manager*
EMP: 7 **Privately Held**
WEB: www.medtronic.com
SIC: 3841 Surgical & medical instruments
HQ: Medtronic, Inc.
   710 Medtronic Pkwy
   Minneapolis MN 55432
   763 514-4000

(G-11944)
MEDTRONIC USA INC
39555 Orchard Hill Pl # 500 (48375-5374)
PHONE...............................248 449-5027
Greg Burrell, *Branch Mgr*
EMP: 4 **Privately Held**
WEB: www.medtronic.com
SIC: 3841 Surgical & medical instruments
HQ: Medtronic Usa, Inc.
   710 Medtronic Pkwy
   Minneapolis MN 55432
   763 514-4000

(G-11945)
METALSA STRUCTURAL PDTS INC (DH)
29545 Hudson Dr (48377-1733)
PHONE...............................248 669-3704
Polo Cedillo, *CEO*
Jose Jaime Salazar Reyes, *President*
David Altemar Sanchez Hernande, *Vice Pres*
Laura Johnson, *Treasurer*
Fernando Perez Valdes, *Admin Sec*
▲ **EMP:** 70
SALES (est): 581.9MM **Privately Held**
SIC: 3714 Motor vehicle parts & accessories

(G-11946)
MICHIGAN CUSTOM MACHINES INC
Also Called: McM
22750 Heslip Dr (48375-4143)
PHONE...............................248 347-7900
Michael Schena, *President*
Larry Palovich, *Purchasing*
Nissa Rademacher Wise, *Purchasing*
Steven Hobson, *Electrical Engi*
April Gazo Arthurs, *Office Mgr*
EMP: 35
SQ FT: 35,600
SALES: 16MM **Privately Held*
WEB: www.mcm1.com
SIC: 3599 Machine shop, jobbing & repair

(G-11947)
MICHIGAN MILK PRODUCERS ASSN (PA)
41310 Bridge St (48375-1302)
P.O. Box 8002 (48376-8002)
PHONE...............................248 474-6672
John Dilland, *CEO*
Kenneth Nobis, *President*
Bob Kran, *Vice Pres*
Kris Wardin, *Vice Pres*
Dave Davis, *Plant Mgr*
EMP: 40
SQ FT: 20,000
SALES (est): 854MM **Privately Held**
WEB: www.mimilk.com
SIC: 5143 2023 2021 8611 Milk & cream, fluid; dried milk; condensed milk; creamery butter; business associations; fluid milk

(G-11948)
MICHIGAN SPRING & STAMP
41850 W 11 Mile Rd # 105 (48375-1857)
PHONE...............................248 344-1459
Gerald Baker, *Principal*
Jessica Morse, *Human Res Mgr*
EMP: 4
SALES (est): 36.9K **Privately Held**
SIC: 3495 Wire springs

(G-11949)
MIDWEST SUPERIOR ABRASIVES
24517 Cavendish Ave E (48375-2361)
PHONE...............................248 202-0454
Gopal Malkani, *Owner*
▲ **EMP:** 3 **EST:** 2012
SALES (est): 147.9K **Privately Held**
SIC: 3291 Abrasive wheels & grindstones, not artificial

(G-11950)
MTU AMERICA INC (DH)
39525 Mackenzie Dr (48377-1602)
PHONE...............................248 560-8000
Thomas Koenig, *President*
David Brunette, *General Mgr*
Joe Lewis, *General Mgr*
Joanna Vardas, *General Mgr*
Mary Anne Lloyd, *Opers Mgr*
▲ **EMP:** 250 **EST:** 1978
SALES (est): 204.2MM
SALES (corp-wide): 20.2B **Privately Held**
WEB: www.mtu-online.com
SIC: 3519 Diesel, semi-diesel or duel-fuel engines, including marine
HQ: Mtu Friedrichshafen Gmbh
   Maybachplatz 1
   Friedrichshafen 88045
   754 190-0

(G-11951)
NAGLE PAVING COMPANY (PA)
39525 W 13 Mile Rd # 300 (48377-2361)
PHONE...............................248 553-0600
Michael Santi, *President*
Lawrence Brennan, *Vice Pres*
Robert Nagle, *Vice Pres*
James P Oliver, *Vice Pres*
James Oliver, *Vice Pres*
EMP: 11
SQ FT: 3,240
SALES (est): 47.7MM **Privately Held**
WEB: www.naglepaving.com
SIC: 1611 2951 Surfacing & paving; asphalt & asphaltic paving mixtures (not from refineries)

(G-11952)
NAKAGAWA SPECIAL STL AMER INC
42400 Grand River Ave # 102 (48375-2571)
PHONE...............................248 449-6050
Akihiko Saigo, *Principal*
EMP: 6
SALES (est): 535.8K **Privately Held**
SIC: 3291 Abrasive metal & steel products

(G-11953)
NITS SOLUTIONS INC
40850 Grand River Ave 100a (48375-5705)
PHONE...............................248 231-2267
Neetu Seth, *President*
Laura Socaciu, *Administration*
EMP: 15
SALES (est): 1.3MM **Privately Held**
SIC: 7371 7372 7374 8732 Computer software development; application computer software; calculating service (computer); survey service: marketing, location, etc.; telemarketing services

(G-11954)
NITTO INC
45880 Dylan Dr (48377-4905)
PHONE...............................248 449-2300
EMP: 5 **Privately Held**
SIC: 2241 Fabric tapes
HQ: Nitto, Inc.
   1990 Rutgers Blvd
   Lakewood NJ 08701
   732 901-7905

(G-11955)
NORTHWEST ORTHOTICS-PROSTHETIC
39830 Grand River Ave B1d (48375-2134)
PHONE...............................248 477-1443
Michael Henry,
EMP: 5
SQ FT: 2,600
SALES (est): 558.9K **Privately Held**
SIC: 3842 5999 Orthopedic appliances; prosthetic appliances; orthopedic & prosthesis applications

(G-11956)
NOVELIS CORPORATION
39550 W 13 Mile Rd # 150 (48377-2360)
PHONE...............................248 668-5111
EMP: 8
SALES (corp-wide): 6.3B **Privately Held**
SIC: 3353 Foil, aluminum
HQ: Novelis Corporation
   3560 Lenox Rd Ne Ste 2000
   Atlanta GA 30326
   404 760-4000

(G-11957)
NOVI CRUSHED CONCRETE LLC
46900 W 12 Mile Rd (48375-3217)
PHONE...............................248 305-6020
Howard K Copeland, *Principal*
EMP: 4 **EST:** 1999
SALES (est): 570.1K **Privately Held**
SIC: 3273 Ready-mixed concrete

(G-11958)
NOVI MANUFACTURING CO
Also Called: U-Haul
25555 Seeley Rd (48375-2053)
PHONE...............................248 476-4350
Henry P Kelly, *President*
EMP: 82 **EST:** 1963
SALES (est): 9.4MM
SALES (corp-wide): 3.7B **Publicly Held**
SIC: 3713 Truck & bus bodies
PA: Amerco
   5555 Kietzke Ln Ste 100
   Reno NV 89511
   775 688-6300

(G-11959)
NPR OF AMERICA INC
41650 Gardenbrook Rd # 180 (48375-1323)
PHONE...............................248 449-8955
▲ **EMP:** 19 **Privately Held**
SIC: 3089 Automotive parts, plastic
HQ: Npr Of America, Inc.
   7001 Village Dr Ste 240
   Buena Park CA 90621
   562 207-6882

(G-11960)
NSSC AMERICA INCORPORATED
42400 Grand River Ave # 102 (48375-2572)
PHONE...............................248 449-6050
Yoichiro Nakatawa, *President*
Shu Hashimoto, *Senior VP*
Shuhei Kawamura, *Vice Pres*
▲ **EMP:** 3
SQ FT: 1,000
SALES (est): 339.1K **Privately Held**
SIC: 3398 Metal heat treating
PA: Nakagawa Special Steel Inc.
   8-1, Akashicho
   Chuo-Ku TKY 104-0

(G-11961)
OAKLAND AUTOMATION LLC
25475 Trans X Rd (48375-2445)
PHONE...............................810 874-3061
Bryan Tolles,
Dan Bickersteth,
EMP: 10
SALES (est): 452.9K **Privately Held**
SIC: 3599 8711 Custom machinery; engineering services

(G-11962)
OBARA CORPORATION USA (HQ)
Also Called: Hercules Welding Products
26800 Meadowbrook Rd # 111 (48377-3540)
PHONE...............................586 755-1250
Sota Iwasaki, *President*
Dan Wellman, *Managing Dir*
Allen Tribbe, *Engineer*
Joseph Sanda, *Controller*
▲ **EMP:** 9
SALES (est): 11.6MM **Privately Held**
WEB: www.obarausa.com
SIC: 3548 Electrodes, electric welding

(G-11963)
OKUNO INTERNATIONAL CORP
40000 Grand River Ave # 103 (48375-2121)
PHONE...............................248 536-2727
Katuyoshi Okuno, *President*
Naoki Okuno, *Vice Pres*
Dayne Kono, *Admin Sec*
▲ **EMP:** 5
SALES (est): 80K **Privately Held**
SIC: 3563 Dusting outfits for metals, paints & chemicals

(G-11964)
OMRON AUTOMOTIVE ELECTRONICS
29185 Cabot Dr (48377-2936)
PHONE...............................248 893-0200
Eric Dezries, *President*
Jerry Bricker, *Vice Pres*
Deanna Velasco, *Manager*
EMP: 30
SQ FT: 9,000
SALES (est): 4.2MM **Privately Held**
WEB: www.omronauto.com
SIC: 3694 Automotive electrical equipment

(G-11965)
OMRON AUTOMOTIVE ELECTRONICS
29185 Cabot Dr (48377-2936)
PHONE...............................248 893-0200
EMP: 38
SALES (corp-wide): 7.1B **Publicly Held**
SIC: 3694 Mfg Engine Electrical Equipment
HQ: Omron Automotive Electronics, Inc.
   3709 Ohio Ave
   Saint Charles IL 60174
   630 443-6800

(G-11966)
OPTIMEMS TECHNOLOGY INC
43422 W Oaks Dr Ste 183 (48377-3300)
PHONE...............................248 660-0380
Z Joe Huang, *Administration*
EMP: 3 **EST:** 2013
SALES (est): 191.5K **Privately Held**
SIC: 3674 Semiconductors & related devices

(G-11967)
OROTEX CORPORATION
22475 Venture Dr (48375-4177)
PHONE...............................248 773-8630
Kenichi Miura, *President*
Ritsuko McCarthy, *Accountant*
▲ **EMP:** 150
SQ FT: 60,000
SALES: 25.7MM **Privately Held**
SIC: 3714 Motor vehicle parts & accessories
PA: Iida Industry Co.,Ltd.
   759, Ichichowari, Mukuicho
   Inazawa AIC 492-8

(G-11968)
OWENS CORNING SALES LLC
46500 Humboldt Dr (48377-2434)
PHONE...............................248 668-7500
Gary Nieman, *Vice Pres*
EMP: 40 **Publicly Held**
WEB: www.owenscorning.com
SIC: 3296 Mineral wool
HQ: Owens Corning Sales, Llc
   1 Owens Corning Pkwy
   Toledo OH 43659
   419 248-8000

Novi - Oakland County (G-11969)

(G-11969)
OXID CORPORATION
25325 Regency Dr (48375-2159)
PHONE.....................248 474-9817
William G Fredrick Jr, *President*
Ann Raske, *Technician*
EMP: 30
SALES: 8.4MM **Privately Held**
SIC: 3599 Machine shop, jobbing & repair

(G-11970)
PACIFIC ENGINEERING CORP
Also Called: PEC of America
39555 Orchard Hill Pl (48375-5374)
PHONE.....................248 359-7823
Hirohisa Ogawa, *Ch of Bd*
Takahisa Ogawa, *President*
Norio Io, *Exec VP*
EMP: 6
SALES (est): 487.3K **Privately Held**
SIC: 3465 8711 Body parts, automobile: stamped metal; engineering services

(G-11971)
PCB PIEZOTRONICS INC
4000 Grand River Blvd (48375)
PHONE.....................888 684-0014
Jeff Case, *Branch Mgr*
EMP: 10
SALES (corp-wide): 778MM **Publicly Held**
SIC: 3829 3679 Measuring & controlling devices; transducers, electrical
HQ: Pcb Piezotronics, Inc.
3425 Walden Ave
Depew NY 14043
716 684-0001

(G-11972)
PEC OF AMERICA CORPORATION (HQ)
39555 Orchard Hill Pl # 220 (48375-5374)
PHONE.....................248 675-3130
Takahisa Ogawa, *CEO*
Koichiro Mabuchi, *CFO*
▲ **EMP:** 15
SQ FT: 1,200
SALES (est): 50MM **Privately Held**
SIC: 3613 3469 Fuses, electric; machine parts, stamped or pressed metal

(G-11973)
PERMACEL CORPORATION
45880 Dylan Dr (48377-4905)
PHONE.....................248 347-2843
EMP: 3 **EST:** 2009
SALES (est): 230K **Privately Held**
SIC: 2241 Narrow Fabric Mill

(G-11974)
POLYWORKS USA TRAINING CENTER
41700 Gardenbrook Rd (48375-1324)
PHONE.....................216 226-1617
EMP: 5
SALES (est): 367K **Privately Held**
SIC: 7372 Prepackaged software

(G-11975)
POWER PROCESS ENGRG CO INC
24300 Catherne Ind Dr # 403 (48375-2457)
PHONE.....................248 473-8450
John Walsh, *President*
Donald J Fichter Jr, *Vice Pres*
EMP: 8
SQ FT: 5,000
SALES: 3MM **Privately Held**
SIC: 3494 Valves & pipe fittings

(G-11976)
POWERLASE PHOTONICS INC
26800 Meadowbrook Rd # 113 (48377-3540)
PHONE.....................248 305-2963
EMP: 3
SALES (est): 184.7K **Privately Held**
SIC: 3674 Semiconductors & related devices

(G-11977)
PPG INDUSTRIES INC
Also Called: PPG 5622
40400 Grand River Ave C (48375-2872)
PHONE.....................248 478-1300
Tony Bronvich, *Branch Mgr*
EMP: 24
SALES (corp-wide): 15.3B **Publicly Held**
WEB: www.ppg.com
SIC: 2851 Paints & allied products
PA: Ppg Industries, Inc.
1 Ppg Pl
Pittsburgh PA 15272
412 434-3131

(G-11978)
PRESTOLITE ELECTRIC LLC (DH)
30120 Hudson Dr (48377-4115)
PHONE.....................248 313-3807
Peter J Corrigan, *COO*
Penny Henry, *Purch Agent*
Kenneth C Cornelius, *CFO*
P Kim Packard, *Mng Member*
Roberto Buaron,
▲ **EMP:** 8
SALES (est): 182.4MM
SALES (corp-wide): 1.2B **Privately Held**
SIC: 3643 3824 3621 3625 Electric switches; electromechanical counters; motors, electric; electric controls & control accessories, industrial; motors, starting: automotive & aircraft

(G-11979)
PRESTOLITE ELECTRIC HOLDING
Also Called: Prestolite International Holdg
30120 Hudson Dr (48377-4115)
PHONE.....................248 313-3807
Michael Shen, *CEO*
Charles Lu, *Ch of Bd*
Tom Hogan, *President*
Kerry Zhang, *CFO*
Tony Wong, *Administration*
EMP: 2500
SQ FT: 25,000
SALES (est): 168.8MM
SALES (corp-wide): 1.2B **Privately Held**
SIC: 3621 3694 Motors, electric; motors, starting: automotive & aircraft; ignition apparatus, internal combustion engines; alternators, automotive
HQ: Prestolite Electric, Llc
30120 Hudson Dr
Novi MI 48377
248 313-3807

(G-11980)
PRESTOLITE ELECTRIC INC (DH)
30120 Hudson Dr (48377-4115)
PHONE.....................866 463-7078
Tony Wong, *President*
Denise Wilmot, *Buyer*
Dave Bernard, *Engineer*
Zoltan Takacs, *Engineer*
Mike Brown, *Regl Sales Mgr*
▲ **EMP:** 12
SQ FT: 50,000
SALES (est): 121MM
SALES (corp-wide): 1.2B **Privately Held**
SIC: 3621 3694 Starters, for motors; alternators, automotive

(G-11981)
PRINTASTIC LLC
46555 Humboldt Dr Ste 200 (48377-2455)
PHONE.....................248 761-5697
EMP: 11
SALES (est): 1.4MM **Privately Held**
SIC: 3993 Signs & advertising specialties

(G-11982)
PRINTING INDUSTRIES OF MICH
41300 Beacon Rd (48375-5202)
PHONE.....................248 946-5895
Nick Wagner, *President*
EMP: 5
SALES: 275K **Privately Held**
WEB: www.printwire.net
SIC: 2752 Commercial printing, offset

(G-11983)
PROGRAMMED PRODUCTS CORP
Also Called: Ppc Design
44311 Grand River Ave (48375-1128)
PHONE.....................248 348-7755
Charles Voydanoff, *President*
John E Zafarana, *Chairman*
▼ **EMP:** 70
SQ FT: 75,000
SALES (est): 7.7MM **Privately Held**
WEB: www.ppcretaildesign.com
SIC: 3993 2541 2435 Signs & advertising specialties; wood partitions & fixtures; hardwood veneer & plywood

(G-11984)
R H M RUBBER & MANUFACTURING
203 Bernstadt St (48377-1918)
PHONE.....................248 624-8277
Raymond Hoyer, *President*
Kim Cooley, *Partner*
Cathie Hall, *Office Mgr*
EMP: 4 **EST:** 1964
SQ FT: 7,500
SALES: 300K **Privately Held**
SIC: 3069 3061 3053 Molded rubber products; mechanical rubber goods; gaskets, packing & sealing devices

(G-11985)
REDEEM POWER SERVICES
43422 W Oaks Dr Ste 178 (48377-3300)
PHONE.....................248 679-5277
Anthony Johnson,
Blanca Johnson,
EMP: 5 **EST:** 2012
SQ FT: 900
SALES (est): 282.6K **Privately Held**
SIC: 3629 3691 Inverters, nonrotating: electrical; rectifiers (electrical apparatus); storage batteries; batteries, rechargeable

(G-11986)
REVERE PLASTICS SYSTEMS LLC (DH)
39555 Orchard Hill Pl # 362 (48375-5389)
PHONE.....................419 547-6918
Brian Kinnie, *Vice Pres*
Chad Smith, *Engineer*
Ryan Southwell, *Engineer*
Toni Tackett, *Engineer*
Kathy Elchert, *Credit Staff*
▲ **EMP:** 277
SALES: 165.6MM
SALES (corp-wide): 22.3MM **Privately Held**
SIC: 3089 Injection molding of plastics
HQ: Ardian
20 Place Vendome
Paris 1er Arrondissement
141 719-200

(G-11987)
ROBERT BOSCH LLC
Novi Research Park (48377)
PHONE.....................248 921-9054
Pres Lawhon, *Branch Mgr*
EMP: 50
SALES (corp-wide): 294.8MM **Privately Held**
SIC: 3714 3694 5013 5064 Motor vehicle parts & accessories; motors, starting: automotive & aircraft; automotive supplies & parts; radios, motor vehicle; packaging machinery; deburring machines
HQ: Robert Bosch Llc
2800 S 25th Ave
Broadview IL 60155
248 876-1000

(G-11988)
RSI GLOBAL SOURCING LLC
Also Called: Stable ARC
43630 Wendingo Ct (48375-5432)
PHONE.....................734 604-2448
Randy S Stevens, *President*
EMP: 12
SQ FT: 1,500
SALES: 1MM **Privately Held**
SIC: 3441 3541 3548 Fabricated structural metal; plasma process metal cutting machines; welding apparatus

(G-11989)
SAGE INTERNATIONAL INC (DH)
Also Called: Jayco Manufacturing
26600 Heyn Dr (48374-1821)
PHONE.....................972 623-2004
Amit Soman, *Mng Member*
Michael Rakiter,
EMP: 57
SALES: 15.1MM **Privately Held**
SIC: 3469 3431 3444 Stamping metal for the trade; plumbing fixtures: enameled iron cast iron or pressed metal; metal roofing & roof drainage equipment

(G-11990)
SCS EMBEDDED TECH LLC
Also Called: Signal Conditioning Solutions
41100 Bridge St (48375-1300)
PHONE.....................248 615-2244
Rachel Rathsburg, *General Mgr*
EMP: 9
SALES: 3MM **Privately Held**
SIC: 3577 5065 5085 Input/output equipment, computer; electronic parts & equipment; industrial supplies

(G-11991)
SEG AUTOMOTIVE NORTH AMER LLC (DH)
27275 Haggerty Rd Ste 420 (48377-3636)
PHONE.....................248 465-2602
Jonathan Husby, *CEO*
EMP: 15
SALES (est): 3.9MM
SALES (corp-wide): 3.7B **Privately Held**
SIC: 3542 3714 3694 Press brakes; air brakes, motor vehicle; alternators, automotive; battery charging alternators & generators
HQ: Seg Automotive Germany Gmbh
Lotterbergstr. 30
Stuttgart 70499
711 400-9800

(G-11992)
SENSOR MANUFACTURING COMPANY
40750 Grand River Ave (48375-2812)
P.O. Box 955 (48376-0955)
PHONE.....................248 474-7300
Robert L Byrum, *President*
Robert Byrum Jr, *Vice Pres*
Dawn Jones, *Vice Pres*
Richard S Hamlin, *Admin Sec*
EMP: 14 **EST:** 1977
SQ FT: 9,300
SALES (est): 1.8MM **Privately Held**
WEB: www.sensormfg.com
SIC: 3679 Loads, electronic

(G-11993)
SERVICE DIAMOND TOOL COMPANY
Also Called: Service Physical Testers Div
46590 Ryan Ct (48377-1730)
PHONE.....................248 669-3100
Richard Antonik, *President*
EMP: 9 **EST:** 1942
SQ FT: 10,000
SALES (est): 732.2K **Privately Held**
SIC: 3545 3829 Diamond cutting tools for turning, boring, burnishing, etc.; hardness testing equipment

(G-11994)
SETCO SALES COMPANY
41129 Jo Dr (48375-1920)
PHONE.....................248 888-8989
Dave Kirkpatrick, *Principal*
EMP: 11
SALES (corp-wide): 323.1MM **Privately Held**
SIC: 3545 7694 Machine tool accessories; armature rewinding shops
HQ: Setco Sales Company
5880 Hillside Ave
Cincinnati OH 45233
513 941-5110

(G-11995)
SHAPE CORP
39625 Lewis Dr Ste 700 (48377-2962)
PHONE.....................248 788-8444
Budd Brink, *Branch Mgr*
EMP: 133

GEOGRAPHIC SECTION

Novi - Oakland County (G-12019)

SALES (corp-wide): 565.6MM **Privately Held**
SIC: **3449** Miscellaneous metalwork
PA: Shape Corp.
1900 Hayes St
Grand Haven MI 49417
616 846-8700

(G-11996)
SHIKOKU CABLE NORTH AMER INC
28175 Haggerty Rd (48377-2903)
PHONE.................................248 488-8620
Eiji Hayakawa, *CEO*
EMP: 2
SALES: 3.2MM **Privately Held**
SIC: **3357** Coaxial cable, nonferrous

(G-11997)
SIGNAL GROUP LLC
Also Called: Solid Signal
22285 Roethel Dr (48375-4700)
PHONE.................................248 479-1517
Jerry Chapman, *President*
Allan McKenzie, *Warehouse Mgr*
Autumn Mady, *Purch Mgr*
Abdel Anbari, *Finance Mgr*
Ruthie Weiss, *Human Res Mgr*
▼ EMP: 50
SQ FT: 20,000
SALES (est): 14.2MM **Privately Held**
WEB: www.signalgroupllc.com
SIC: **3663** Space satellite communications equipment

(G-11998)
SIMERICS INC
39500 Orchard Hill Pl # 155 (48375-5540)
PHONE.................................248 513-3200
Deming Wang, *Branch Mgr*
EMP: 6
SALES (est): 310.4K
SALES (corp-wide): 1.1MM **Privately Held**
SIC: **7372** **7379** Application computer software; computer related consulting services
PA: Simerics, Inc.
1750 112th Ave Ne C250
Bellevue WA 98004
256 489-1480

(G-11999)
SLACO TOOL AND MANUFACTURING
46089 Grand River Ave (48374-1319)
PHONE.................................248 449-9911
Judith Anderson, *President*
Sheridan Anderson, *Vice Pres*
Kenneth Anderson, *Treasurer*
EMP: 6
SQ FT: 128,000
SALES (est): 725.6K **Privately Held**
SIC: **3599** Machine shop, jobbing & repair

(G-12000)
SOLEO HEALTH INC
26800 Meadowbrook Rd # 119 (48377-3540)
PHONE.................................248 513-8687
EMP: 9
SALES (corp-wide): 56.4MM **Privately Held**
SIC: **2834** **5912** Druggists' preparations (pharmaceuticals); drug stores & proprietary stores
HQ: Soleo Health Inc.
950 Calcon Hook Rd Ste 19
Sharon Hill PA 19079
888 244-2340

(G-12001)
SOUTEC DIV OF ANDRITZ BRICMONT
26800 Meadowbrook Rd # 113 (48377-3540)
PHONE.................................248 305-2955
Lance Wan, *Manager*
EMP: 5
SALES (est): 173.9K **Privately Held**
SIC: **7011** **7692** Hostels; welding repair

(G-12002)
SOUTHEASTERN EQUIPMENT CO INC
48545 Grand River Ave (48374-1245)
PHONE.................................248 349-9922
Mike Zelewski, *Manager*
EMP: 6
SALES (est): 440K **Privately Held**
SIC: **2426** Brush blocks, wood; turned & shaped

(G-12003)
STARTECH SOFTWARE SYSTEMS INC
Also Called: Fdi Group
39500 High Pointe Blvd # 400 (48375-5505)
PHONE.................................248 344-2266
Mark Churella, *President*
EMP: 6
SALES (est): 332K
SALES (corp-wide): 40MM **Privately Held**
SIC: **7372** Prepackaged software
PA: Financial Designs, Inc.
39500 High Pointe Blvd # 400
Novi MI 48375
248 348-8200

(G-12004)
STONERIDGE INC (PA)
39675 Mackenzie Dr # 400 (48377-1607)
PHONE.................................248 489-9300
Jonathan B Degaynor, *President*
Robert Willig, *President*
Robert R Krakowiak, *CFO*
Laurent Borne, *CTO*
Daniel M Kusiak, *Officer*
◆ EMP: 7
SQ FT: 37,713
SALES: 866.2MM **Publicly Held**
WEB: www.stoneridge.com
SIC: **3714** **3679** **3625** Motor vehicle electrical equipment; instrument board assemblies, motor vehicle; harness assemblies for electronic use: wire or cable; electronic switches; actuators, industrial

(G-12005)
STONERIDGE CONTROL DEVICES INC
39675 Mackenzie Dr # 400 (48377-1607)
PHONE.................................248 489-9300
Jonathan B Degaynor, *President*
Robert R Krakowiak, *Treasurer*
Kristy Eichar, *Human Res Mgr*
Paul Nicol, *Manager*
Thomas M Dono Jr, *Admin Sec*
EMP: 5
SALES (est): 1.4MM
SALES (corp-wide): 866.2MM **Publicly Held**
SIC: **3625** Industrial electrical relays & switches
PA: Stoneridge, Inc.
39675 Mackenzie Dr # 400
Novi MI 48377
248 489-9300

(G-12006)
STRYKER CORPORATION
27275 Haggerty Rd Ste 680 (48377-3634)
PHONE.................................248 374-6352
John Hebner, *Principal*
Chris Nadeau, *Sales Staff*
EMP: 4
SALES (corp-wide): 13.6B **Publicly Held**
SIC: **3841** Surgical & medical instruments
PA: Stryker Corporation
2825 Airview Blvd
Portage MI 49002
269 385-2600

(G-12007)
STUARTS OF NOVI
41390 W 10 Mile Rd (48375-3404)
PHONE.................................248 615-2955
Paul Gabriel, *Manager*
EMP: 6
SALES (est): 444.7K **Privately Held**
SIC: **2024** Yogurt desserts, frozen

(G-12008)
SUMITOMO CHEMICAL AMERICA INC
45525 Grand River Ave # 200 (48374-1308)
PHONE.................................248 284-4797
David Risetter, *Branch Mgr*
EMP: 5 **Privately Held**
WEB: www.sumichem.com
SIC: **3089** Plastic processing
HQ: Sumitomo Chemical America, Inc.
150 E 42nd St Rm 701
New York NY 10017
212 572-8200

(G-12009)
SUN-TEC CORP (PA)
46590 Ryan Ct (48377-1730)
PHONE.................................248 669-3100
Richard Antonik, *President*
Mark Antonik, *Vice Pres*
▲ EMP: 3 EST: 1995
SQ FT: 10,000
SALES (est): 2.1MM **Privately Held**
WEB: www.sunteccorp.com
SIC: **3829** **7699** Physical property testing equipment; professional instrument repair services

(G-12010)
SUPPLY LINE INTERNATIONAL LLC
42350 Grand River Ave (48375-1838)
PHONE.................................248 242-7140
Joshua Kaplan, *Mng Member*
EMP: 18
SQ FT: 11,000
SALES: 10MM **Privately Held**
SIC: **3714** Motor vehicle parts & accessories

(G-12011)
TA DELAWARE INC (PA)
Also Called: Tower International
17672 N Laure Park Dr Ste (48377)
PHONE.................................248 675-6000
Mark Malcom, *President*
Michael Rajkovic, *COO*
James Gouin, *Exec VP*
Ken Kundrick, *Vice Pres*
Dennis Pike, *Vice Pres*
EMP: 48
SALES (est): 13.6MM **Privately Held**
SIC: **3469** Metal stampings

(G-12012)
TEMPERFORM LLC
25425 Trans X Rd (48375-2445)
P.O. Box 767 (48376-0767)
PHONE.................................248 349-5230
Bruce Boettger, *CEO*
Dan Bickersteth, *Director*
▲ EMP: 50
SQ FT: 50,000
SALES: 14MM
SALES (corp-wide): 55.2MM **Privately Held**
WEB: www.temperform.com
SIC: **3325** Alloy steel castings, except investment
PA: Blackeagle Partners, Llc
6905 Telegraph Rd Ste 119
Bloomfield Hills MI 48301
313 647-5340

(G-12013)
TEXAS INSTRUMENTS INCORPORATED
39555 Orchard Hill Pl # 525 (48375-5395)
PHONE.................................248 305-5718
William Milus, *Engineer*
John Rice, *Engineer*
Bob Dodd, *Sales Mgr*
Darrell Kolomyski, *Manager*
EMP: 12
SALES (corp-wide): 15.7B **Publicly Held**
WEB: www.ti.com
SIC: **3674** Semiconductors & related devices
PA: Texas Instruments Incorporated
12500 Ti Blvd
Dallas TX 75243
214 479-3773

(G-12014)
THERMAL DESIGNS & MFG
41069 Vincenti Ct (48375-1923)
PHONE.................................248 476-2978
Harold J Gardynik, *President*
EMP: 20
SQ FT: 26,000
SALES (est): 209.3K
SALES (corp-wide): 20MM **Privately Held**
WEB: www.commercecontrols.com
SIC: **3567** Infrared ovens, industrial
PA: Commerce Controls, Inc.
41069 Vincenti Ct
Novi MI 48375
248 476-1442

(G-12015)
THIELENHAUS MICROFINISH CORP (DH)
42925 W 9 Mile Rd (48375-4115)
PHONE.................................248 349-9450
J Peter Thielenhaus, *President*
Manfred Sieringhaus, *Chairman*
Fred Becker, *Technology*
Aloys K Schwarz, *Admin Sec*
▲ EMP: 38
SQ FT: 27,000
SALES: 17.5MM
SALES (corp-wide): 562.9K **Privately Held**
WEB: www.thielenhaususa.com
SIC: **3541** **3829** **3549** **3545** Machine tools, metal cutting type; measuring & controlling devices; metalworking machinery; machine tool accessories
HQ: Thielenhaus Technologies Gmbh
Schwesterstr. 50
Wuppertal 42285
202 481-0

(G-12016)
THUNDERHEAD ENTERPRISES LLC
Also Called: Thunderhead Gaming
26916 Gornada St (48377-3714)
PHONE.................................248 210-1146
Paul Jones, *CEO*
EMP: 3 EST: 2014
SALES (est): 60.1K **Privately Held**
SIC: **7372** Publishers' computer software

(G-12017)
TIMKENSTEEL CORPORATION
Also Called: Timkensteel Detroit Off Novi
28125 Cabot Dr Ste 204 (48377-2985)
PHONE.................................248 994-4422
Tim Claybaugh, *Regional Mgr*
Timothy Haubenstricker, *Vice Pres*
EMP: 6
SALES (corp-wide): 1.6B **Publicly Held**
SIC: **3312** Blast furnaces & steel mills
PA: Timkensteel Corporation
1835 Dueber Ave Sw
Canton OH 44706
330 471-7000

(G-12018)
TOYOTA INDUSTRIES ELCTC SYS N
28700 Cabot Dr Ste 100 (48377-2948)
PHONE.................................248 489-7700
Sadanori Suzuki, *President*
EMP: 4 EST: 2013
SALES (est): 410.5K **Privately Held**
SIC: **3559** Electronic component making machinery
HQ: Toyota Industries North America, Inc.
3030 Barker Dr
Columbus IN 47201
812 341-3810

(G-12019)
TVA KANE INC (PA)
45380 W 10 Mile Rd # 100 (48377-3000)
PHONE.................................248 946-4670
James C McCaffrey, *Administration*
EMP: 7 EST: 2011
SALES (est): 438.7K **Privately Held**
SIC: **5944** **3911** Jewelry, precious stones & precious metals; jewelry, precious metal

Novi - Oakland County (G-12020)

(G-12020)
U S TOOL & CUTTER CO
42525 W 11 Mile Rd (48375-1701)
PHONE..................................248 553-7745
David P Price, *President*
B Karen Oliver, *President*
EMP: 15
SQ FT: 17,000
SALES: 1.8MM **Privately Held**
WEB: www.ustool.us
SIC: 3541 Machine tools, metal cutting type

(G-12021)
U-SHIN AMERICA INC
40000 Grand River Ave # 105 (48375-2121)
PHONE..................................248 449-3155
Satoru Tsukui, *COO*
Mark Frey, *Research*
▲ EMP: 4
SALES (est): 491.4K **Privately Held**
SIC: 3714 Motor vehicle parts & accessories

(G-12022)
UCHIYAMA MKTG & DEV AMER LLC
46805 Magellan Dr (48377-2444)
PHONE..................................248 859-3986
Masatomo Sueki, *CEO*
EMP: 15
SQ FT: 18,212
SALES (est): 2.5MM **Privately Held**
SIC: 3061 Automotive rubber goods (mechanical)
PA: Uchiyama Manufacturing Corp.
338, Enami, Naka-Ku
Okayama OKA 702-8

(G-12023)
UNIFILTER INC
Also Called: Unifilter Company
43800 Grand River Ave (48375-1115)
P.O. Box 8025 (48376-8025)
PHONE..................................248 476-5100
Robert R Redner, *President*
John Redner, *President*
Carl Redner, *Vice Pres*
Robert R Redner, *Vice Pres*
Robert P Redner, *Vice Pres*
EMP: 50
SQ FT: 60,000
SALES (est): 5.5MM **Privately Held**
SIC: 5013 3714 Filters, air & oil; motor vehicle parts & accessories

(G-12024)
VECTOR NORTH AMERICA INC
39500 Orchard Hill Pl (48375-5370)
PHONE..................................248 449-9290
Tony Mascolo, *CEO*
Jeff Rothenberg, *Business Mgr*
Yvette Michels, *Treasurer*
Michael Macdonald, *Accounts Mgr*
Mark Jensen, *Manager*
EMP: 80
SQ FT: 27,000
SALES (est): 15.3MM
SALES (corp-wide): 632.5K **Privately Held**
WEB: www.vector-cantech.com
SIC: 7372 7373 Prepackaged software; computer integrated systems design
HQ: Vector Informatik Gmbh
Ingersheimer Str. 24
Stuttgart 70499
711 806-700

(G-12025)
VENTURE TECHNOLOGY GROUPS INC (PA)
Also Called: Process Technology & Controls
24300 Catherine Industria (48375-2457)
PHONE..................................248 473-8450
Don Fichter Jr, *Vice Pres*
EMP: 15
SQ FT: 16,000
SALES (est): 21.4MM **Privately Held**
WEB: www.venturegroups.com
SIC: 5051 5085 3999 Pipe & tubing, steel; industrial supplies; atomizers, toiletry

(G-12026)
VERITAS USA CORPORATION
39555 Orchard Hill Pl # 600 (48375-5374)
PHONE..................................248 374-5019
EMP: 5
SALES (est): 321.7K
SALES (corp-wide): 740.6MM **Privately Held**
SIC: 3714 Fuel systems & parts, motor vehicle
HQ: Veritas Ag
Stettiner Str. 1-9
Gelnhausen 63571
605 182-10

(G-12027)
YANFENG US AUTOMOTIVE (DH)
41935 W 12 Mile Rd (48377-3135)
PHONE..................................248 319-7333
Johannes Roters, *CEO*
Wenguang Wu, *CEO*
James Bos, *Vice Pres*
Ryan Lawson, *Warehouse Mgr*
Joanne Flemming, *Buyer*
EMP: 277
SALES (est): 148.8MM
SALES (corp-wide): 55MM **Privately Held**
SIC: 2531 Seats, automobile
HQ: Yanfeng Hungary Automotive Interior Systems Korlatolt Felelossegu
Tarsasag
Juhar Utca 17.
Papa 8500
895 117-00

(G-12028)
YANFENG US AUTOMOTIVE
41935 W 12 Mile Rd (48377-3135)
PHONE..................................517 721-0179
Joe White, *Branch Mgr*
EMP: 12
SALES (corp-wide): 55MM **Privately Held**
SIC: 3089 Plastic processing
HQ: Yanfeng Us Automotive Interior Systems Ii Llc
5757 N Green Bay Ave
Milwaukee WI 53209
205 477-4225

(G-12029)
YEUNGS LOTUS EXPRESS
27500 Novi Rd (48377-3418)
PHONE..................................248 380-3820
Dawn Ship, *Principal*
EMP: 4
SALES (est): 191.3K **Privately Held**
SIC: 2741 Miscellaneous publishing

(G-12030)
YORKSHIRE EDM INC
44825 Exeter Ct (48375-2707)
PHONE..................................248 349-3017
Thomas G Fleming, *President*
Terrance Dunn, *Vice Pres*
EMP: 3
SQ FT: 3,500
SALES (est): 290K **Privately Held**
SIC: 3599 Machine shop, jobbing & repair

Nunica
Ottawa County

(G-12031)
ADVANCED RECOVERY TECH CORP
16684 130th Ave (49448-9445)
PHONE..................................231 788-2911
Dewie D Jordan, *President*
Nancy Jordan, *Vice Pres*
EMP: 11
SQ FT: 8,000
SALES (est): 3.3MM **Privately Held**
SIC: 3569 1796 7389 Filters; pollution control equipment installation; air pollution measuring service

(G-12032)
ALPHA TRAN ENGINEERING CO
12575 Cleveland St (49448-9617)
PHONE..................................616 837-7341
Allen Lemieux, *President*
Richard Pearce, *Vice Pres*
EMP: 32
SQ FT: 10,000
SALES: 2MM **Privately Held**
WEB: www.alpha-tran.com
SIC: 3613 Control panels, electric

(G-12033)
C-PLASTICS INC
12463 Cleveland St (49448-9617)
PHONE..................................616 837-7396
Chris Kostecki, *President*
Stan Kostecki, *Vice Pres*
Bob Wurn, *Engineer*
EMP: 40
SQ FT: 27,000
SALES (est): 7.4MM **Privately Held**
SIC: 3089 Injection molding of plastics; plastic processing

(G-12034)
CONVERTING SYSTEMS INC
Also Called: Take A Label
16900 Power Dr (49448-9465)
PHONE..................................616 698-1882
EMP: 3
SQ FT: 10,000
SALES (est): 284.9K **Privately Held**
SIC: 3565 2759 Manufactures Labelers Dispensers & Flexographic Printer

(G-12035)
DENNISON AUTOMATICS LLC
16962 Woodlane Ste B (49448-9327)
PHONE..................................616 837-7063
Norman Anderson,
EMP: 9
SQ FT: 7,000
SALES: 850K **Privately Held**
SIC: 3451 Screw machine products

(G-12036)
DOLTEK ENTERPRISES INC
Also Called: Wood Dowel & Dimension
11335 Apple Dr (49448-9346)
P.O. Box 158 (49448-0158)
PHONE..................................616 837-7828
Mark Schroeder, *President*
Jack Schroeder, *Engineer*
EMP: 25
SQ FT: 50,000
SALES (est): 4.6MM **Privately Held**
WEB: www.wooddowelanddimension.com
SIC: 2499 2431 2426 Dowels, wood; moldings, wood: unfinished & prefinished; furniture stock & parts, hardwood

(G-12037)
J & B METAL FABRICATORS LLC
16913 Power Dr (49448-9465)
PHONE..................................616 837-6764
Robert Vink,
EMP: 6
SQ FT: 6,400
SALES: 1MM **Privately Held**
SIC: 3441 Fabricated structural metal

(G-12038)
J&S TECHNOLOGIES INC
16952 Woodlane (49448-9644)
PHONE..................................616 837-7080
Leon Sluis, *President*
Debra Sluis, *Vice Pres*
EMP: 4 EST: 1998
SQ FT: 6,000
SALES: 700K **Privately Held**
SIC: 3599 Machine shop, jobbing & repair

(G-12039)
JRM INDUSTRIES INC
Also Called: Integrity Trailers
12409 Cleveland St (49448-9617)
PHONE..................................616 837-9758
John Missimer, *President*
EMP: 10 EST: 1978
SALES (est): 1MM **Privately Held**
SIC: 3799 Trailers & trailer equipment; boat trailers

(G-12040)
LIVEROOF LLC
14109 Cleveland St (49448-9739)
P.O. Box 533, Spring Lake (49456-0533)
PHONE..................................616 842-1392
David McKenzie,
EMP: 25
SALES (est): 3.5MM
SALES (corp-wide): 10.7MM **Privately Held**
SIC: 2952 8611 Asphalt felts & coatings; growers' associations
PA: Hortech, Inc.
14109 Cleveland St
Nunica MI 49448
616 842-1392

(G-12041)
PRECISION ENGRG & MFG INC
16913 Power Dr (49448-9465)
PHONE..................................616 837-6764
Arthur Gajewski, *President*
Marcy Gajewski, *Director*
EMP: 9
SALES (est): 1.3MM **Privately Held**
SIC: 3999 Barber & beauty shop equipment

(G-12042)
PRECISION MFG GROUP INC
16913 Power Dr (49448-9465)
PHONE..................................616 837-6764
Scott Tilma, *President*
EMP: 13
SALES (est): 766.1K **Privately Held**
SIC: 3999 Manufacturing industries

(G-12043)
RIDGEVIEW INDUSTRIES INC
16933 144th Ave (49448-9667)
PHONE..................................616 414-6500
Tom Robbins, *Branch Mgr*
EMP: 90
SALES (corp-wide): 106.9MM **Privately Held**
SIC: 3469 Metal stampings
PA: Ridgeview Industries, Inc.
3093 Northridge Dr Nw
Grand Rapids MI 49544
616 453-8636

(G-12044)
TAKE-A-LABEL INC
16900 Power Dr (49448-9465)
PHONE..................................616 698-1882
EMP: 11
SQ FT: 10,000
SALES (est): 2.2MM **Privately Held**
SIC: 3565 Mfg Label Equipment

(G-12045)
TURBINE CONVERSIONS LTD
18155 120th Ave (49448-9310)
P.O. Box 8 (49448-0008)
PHONE..................................616 837-9428
William Hatfield, *President*
Nancy Hatfield, *Treasurer*
Ann Grahek, *Manager*
EMP: 4
SQ FT: 1,500
SALES (est): 549.6K **Privately Held**
WEB: www.turbineconversions.com
SIC: 3724 Turbines, aircraft type

(G-12046)
VARNEYS FAB & WELD LLC
5967 Maple Island Rd (49448-9511)
PHONE..................................231 865-6856
Tina Varney, *Office Mgr*
Scott Varney, *Mng Member*
EMP: 5
SQ FT: 740
SALES: 250K **Privately Held**
SIC: 3441 1799 Fabricated structural metal; welding on site

Oak Park
Oakland County

(G-12047)
A & A WOODWORK STUDIO LLC
8575 Capital St (48237-2301)
PHONE..................................248 691-8380
Nichole Smith, *Managing Prtnr*
EMP: 6 EST: 2010
SALES (est): 800K **Privately Held**
SIC: 2517 Home entertainment unit cabinets, wood

GEOGRAPHIC SECTION

(G-12048)
APOLLO HEAT TREATING PROC LLC
10400 Capital St (48237-3132)
PHONE..................248 398-3434
Jeff Goodman, *Mng Member*
EMP: 20
SALES (est): 2.3MM **Privately Held**
SIC: 3398 Metal heat treating

(G-12049)
ATLAS CUT STONE COMPANY
12920 Northend Ave (48237-3404)
PHONE..................248 545-5100
Carol Potrykus, *CEO*
William A Potrykus, *President*
Thelma Potrykus, *Corp Secy*
EMP: 4 **EST:** 1934
SQ FT: 4,800
SALES: 500K **Privately Held**
SIC: 3272 5032 Steps, prefabricated concrete; door frames, concrete; window sills, cast stone; limestone

(G-12050)
AUCTION MASTERS
8700 Capital St (48237-2360)
PHONE..................586 576-7777
EMP: 3
SALES (est): 130.1K **Privately Held**
SIC: 7389 3585 7699 5046 Auctioneers, fee basis; soda fountain & beverage dispensing equipment & parts; cold drink dispensing equipment (not coin-operated); restaurant equipment repair; restaurant equipment & supplies; retail trade consultant

(G-12051)
AUTO METAL CRAFT INC
Also Called: Auto Chem Craft
12741 Capital St (48237-3175)
PHONE..................248 398-2240
Patrick N Woody, *Chairman*
Kevin Woody, *Exec VP*
Kent Woody, *Vice Pres*
Kenneth Robinson, *Admin Sec*
EMP: 45
SQ FT: 22,000
SALES (est): 8.9MM **Privately Held**
WEB: www.autometal.com
SIC: 3465 3544 Automotive stampings; jigs & fixtures

(G-12052)
BORDRIN MOTOR CORPORATION INC
14925 W 11 Mile Rd (48237-1013)
PHONE..................877 507-3267
EMP: 4
SALES (est): 106.1K **Privately Held**
SIC: 3711 Automobile bodies, passenger car, not including engine, etc.

(G-12053)
BRILAR LLC
13200 Northend Ave (48237-3213)
PHONE..................248 547-6439
Larry Yaffa, *Mng Member*
Brian Yaffa,
EMP: 100
SALES (est): 21.3MM **Privately Held**
SIC: 3523 Grounds mowing equipment

(G-12054)
CORNBELT BEEF CORPORATION
14150 Ludlow Pl (48237-1355)
PHONE..................313 237-0087
Samuel Flatt, *President*
EMP: 45 **EST:** 1978
SQ FT: 50,000
SALES (est): 6.1MM **Privately Held**
SIC: 5147 2011 Meats, fresh; meat packing plants

(G-12055)
CRESCENT MACHINING INC
8720 Northend Ave (48237-2363)
PHONE..................248 541-7010
Greg Summer, *Principal*
EMP: 8 **EST:** 2005
SALES (est): 1.2MM **Privately Held**
SIC: 3089 Automotive parts, plastic

(G-12056)
CRESCENT PATTERN COMPANY
8720 Northend Ave (48237-2363)
PHONE..................248 541-1052
Greg Sommer, *President*
Mark Hagedorn, *Purchasing*
Kim Mace, *Executive*
EMP: 12 **EST:** 1945
SQ FT: 3,200
SALES (est): 2.5MM **Privately Held**
WEB: www.crescentpattern.com
SIC: 3543 Industrial patterns

(G-12057)
CUSTOM VERTICALS UNLIMITED
14621 Ludlow St (48237-4112)
PHONE..................734 522-1615
Martin Vittes, *President*
Howard Vittes, *Vice Pres*
Brian Vittes, *Treasurer*
EMP: 8
SALES (est): 958.2K **Privately Held**
WEB: www.freewaymarketing.com
SIC: 2591 5023 Blinds vertical; venetian blinds

(G-12058)
DEPENDABLE GAGE & TOOL CO
15321 W 11 Mile Rd (48237-1076)
PHONE..................248 545-2100
Leigh P Smith Jr, *President*
Jeff Smith, *Vice Pres*
Wayne Slowik, *Engineer*
Peggy Galka, *Adv Dir*
EMP: 18
SQ FT: 7,200
SALES (est): 3.5MM **Privately Held**
WEB: www.dependablegage.net
SIC: 3545 Precision tools, machinists'; gauges (machine tool accessories)

(G-12059)
DESIGN METAL INC
10841 Capital St (48237-3147)
PHONE..................248 547-4170
Carmelo Dimaggio, *President*
Sherri Dimaggio, *Vice Pres*
EMP: 19 **EST:** 1982
SQ FT: 15,000
SALES (est): 4.1MM **Privately Held**
WEB: www.designmetalinc.com
SIC: 3444 3465 Sheet metal specialties, not stamped; automotive stampings

(G-12060)
DRAE LLC
24221 Scotia Rd (48237-1728)
PHONE..................313 923-7230
Deena Rae Amolsch,
Braedon William Barkley,
Kalia Arielle Barkley,
Kieana Aliya Barkley,
EMP: 3
SALES (est): 71K **Privately Held**
SIC: 7372 7336 Business oriented computer software; art design services

(G-12061)
DURANT AND SONS INC
21850 Wyoming Pl (48237-3112)
PHONE..................248 548-8646
EMP: 3 **EST:** 1991
SALES (est): 240K **Privately Held**
SIC: 3451 Mfg Tools

(G-12062)
DYNAMIC ENERGY TECH LLC
22181 Morton St (48237-2931)
PHONE..................248 212-5904
David Hochberg,
EMP: 6
SALES (est): 410K **Privately Held**
SIC: 3511 Turbines & turbine generator sets

(G-12063)
E-ZEE SET WOOD PRODUCTS INC
21650 Coolidge Hwy (48237-3109)
PHONE..................248 398-0090
Jeff Lorenz, *President*
Karen Lorenz, *Vice Pres*
▲ **EMP:** 9 **EST:** 1969
SQ FT: 13,625
SALES: 1.5MM **Privately Held**
SIC: 2431 3442 Doors, wood; louver doors, wood; louvers, shutters, jalousies & similar items

(G-12064)
EATON STEEL CORPORATION (PA)
Also Called: Eaton Steel Bar Company
10221 Capital St (48237-3103)
PHONE..................248 398-3434
Mark Goodman, *President*
Mark Candy, *Vice Pres*
Gary Goodman, *Vice Pres*
Prachi Vesikar, *Engineer*
Brent Rolfe, *Sales Staff*
▲ **EMP:** 60
SQ FT: 188,000
SALES (est): 215MM **Privately Held**
SIC: 5051 3312 Structural shapes, iron or steel; bars & bar shapes, steel, cold-finished: own hot-rolled

(G-12065)
EJ USA INC
Also Called: E J I W
13001 Northend Ave (48237-3408)
P.O. Box 439, East Jordan (49727-0439)
PHONE..................248 546-2004
Frank Tainna, *Sales/Mktg Mgr*
EMP: 21
SQ FT: 3,296 **Privately Held**
WEB: www.ejiw.com
SIC: 3321 Manhole covers, metal
HQ: Ej Usa, Inc.
 301 Spring St
 East Jordan MI 49727
 800 874-4100

(G-12066)
ENGINEERED RESOURCES INC
Also Called: Dale Prentice
26511 Harding St (48237-1002)
PHONE..................248 399-5500
Larry Prentice, *President*
Bill Hunter, *Manager*
EMP: 6
SQ FT: 3,500
SALES (est): 690K **Privately Held**
SIC: 3599 Custom machinery

(G-12067)
FERGUSON LANDSCAPING
22020 Westhampton St (48237-2770)
PHONE..................248 761-1005
Phillip Ferguson,
EMP: 3
SALES (est): 20K **Privately Held**
SIC: 2075 Soybean oil mills

(G-12068)
FOREWARD LOGISTICS LLC
25900 Grnfeld Rd Ste 326 (48237)
PHONE..................877 488-9724
Tresa Fore, *President*
EMP: 4
SALES (est): 300K **Privately Held**
SIC: 4731 2393 5094 Truck transportation brokers; canvas bags; clocks, watches & parts

(G-12069)
FUTURIS AUTOMOTIVE (US) INC (DH)
14925 W 11 Mile Rd (48237-1013)
PHONE..................248 439-7800
Merv Dunn, *CEO*
▲ **EMP:** 50
SALES (est): 320.3MM **Privately Held**
SIC: 2396 Automotive trimmings, fabric
HQ: Futuris Global Holdings, Llc
 14925 W 11 Mile Rd
 Oak Park MI 48237
 248 439-7800

(G-12070)
FUTURIS GLOBAL HOLDINGS LLC (HQ)
Also Called: Futuris Automotive
14925 W 11 Mile Rd (48237-1013)
PHONE..................248 439-7800
Merv Dunn, *CEO*
Claire Zeki, *Finance*
John Brydell, *Manager*
Stacy Glezman, *Manager*
EMP: 100
SQ FT: 90,000
SALES: 500MM **Privately Held**
SIC: 2396 Automotive trimmings, fabric

(G-12071)
GONZALEZ PROD SYSTEMS INC
13200 W 8 Mile Rd (48237-3243)
PHONE..................248 209-1836
EMP: 3
SALES (corp-wide): 57.7MM **Privately Held**
SIC: 3544 Special dies, tools, jigs & fixtures
PA: Gonzalez Production Systems, Inc.
 1670 Highwood E
 Pontiac MI 48340
 248 548-6010

(G-12072)
H O TRERICE CO INC
12950 W 8 Mile Rd (48237-3214)
PHONE..................248 399-8000
Richard Picut, *President*
Brian Traicoff, *Asst Controller*
Steve Bradley, *Sales Staff*
Ken Comito, *Sales Staff*
Eric Lennon, *Sales Staff*
▲ **EMP:** 50
SQ FT: 40,000
SALES (est): 13.1MM **Privately Held**
SIC: 3823 Temperature measurement instruments, industrial; pressure measurement instruments, industrial
PA: Picut Industries Inc.
 140 Mount Bethel Rd
 Warren NJ 07059

(G-12073)
HOPEFUL HARVEST FOODS INC
21800 Greenfield Rd (48237-2507)
PHONE..................248 967-1500
EMP: 4
SQ FT: 5,000
SALES (est): 173K **Privately Held**
SIC: 2033 2035 0723 Mfg Canned Fruits/Vegetables Mfg Pickles/Sauces/Dressing Crop Preparation For Market

(G-12074)
IMPRESSIVE CABINETS INC
Also Called: Impressive Design
8575 Capital St (48237-2301)
PHONE..................248 542-1185
Joseph Devita, *President*
EMP: 10
SQ FT: 1,800
SALES (est): 903.8K **Privately Held**
SIC: 2434 Wood kitchen cabinets

(G-12075)
INNOVATIVE TOOL AND DESIGN INC
10725 Capital St (48237-3143)
PHONE..................248 542-1831
Marvin Quezada, *CEO*
▲ **EMP:** 50
SQ FT: 35,000
SALES (est): 8.6MM **Privately Held**
SIC: 3469 Stamping metal for the trade

(G-12076)
KERR PUMP AND SUPPLY INC
12880 Cloverdale St (48237-3206)
P.O. Box 37160 (48237-0160)
PHONE..................248 543-3880
Thomas Gross, *President*
Daryl Reddick, *COO*
Deborah Gerard, *Vice Pres*
Robert Kalfs, *Vice Pres*
John P Watson, *Vice Pres*
EMP: 48 **EST:** 1905
SQ FT: 24,000
SALES: 20.6MM **Privately Held**
WEB: www.kerrpump.com
SIC: 5084 3443 3561 Water pumps (industrial); compressors, except air conditioning; heat exchangers, condensers & components; pumps & pumping equipment

(G-12077)
LADUKE CORPORATION
Also Called: Laduke Roofing
10311 Capital St (48237-3139)
PHONE..................................248 414-6600
Roger Laduke, *President*
Roger La Duke, *President*
Tom Vasilofski, *Superintendent*
Todd Sumners, *Project Mgr*
Kathleen Laduke, *CFO*
EMP: 40
SQ FT: 18,000
SALES (est): 5.6MM **Privately Held**
WEB: www.ladukeroofing.com
SIC: 1761 3441 Roofing contractor; sheet metalwork; fabricated structural metal

(G-12078)
LUANS WELDING LLC
14120 Balfour St (48237-4106)
PHONE..................................248 787-5735
Luan Nilaj, *Mng Member*
EMP: 3
SALES: 600K **Privately Held**
SIC: 7692 1721 Welding repair; industrial painting

(G-12079)
M BESHARA INC
10020 Capital St (48237-3104)
PHONE..................................248 542-9220
John Beshara, *President*
Marc Beshara, *Vice Pres*
EMP: 8 **EST:** 1968
SALES (est): 1.2MM **Privately Held**
SIC: 2752 7336 Commercial printing, offset; graphic arts & related design

(G-12080)
MAGIC TREATZ LLC
24245 Coolidge Hwy (48237-1656)
PHONE..................................248 989-9956
Ronda Adams,
EMP: 6
SALES: 50K **Privately Held**
SIC: 2051 Cakes, bakery: except frozen

(G-12081)
MARBLECAST OF MICHIGAN INC
Also Called: Marblecast Kitchens & Baths
14831 W 11 Mile Rd (48237-1012)
PHONE..................................248 398-0600
Walter Olejniczak, *President*
Janet Olejniczak, *Vice Pres*
EMP: 13 **EST:** 1997
SQ FT: 8,000
SALES (est): 1.8MM **Privately Held**
WEB: www.marblecastofmichigan.com
SIC: 3281 Bathroom fixtures, cut stone

(G-12082)
MATTRESS WHOLESALE
14510 W 8 Mile Rd (48237-3046)
PHONE..................................248 968-2200
Ree Garmo, *Owner*
EMP: 12
SALES (est): 660K **Privately Held**
SIC: 2515 5021 Mattresses & bedsprings; mattresses

(G-12083)
MEHRING BOOKS INC
25900 Greenfield Rd # 258 (48237-1297)
PHONE..................................248 967-2924
Helen Halyard, *President*
Heather Jowsey, *Administration*
EMP: 5
SALES (est): 448.2K **Privately Held**
SIC: 2731 Books: publishing only

(G-12084)
MERCURY DRUGS LLC
22150 Coolidge Hwy (48237-2813)
PHONE..................................248 545-3600
Emad Mahmoud, *Principal*
EMP: 7 **EST:** 2012
SALES (est): 950.5K **Privately Held**
SIC: 2834 Pharmaceutical preparations

(G-12085)
MICHIGAN DESSERT CORPORATION
Also Called: MIDAS FOODS INTERNATIONAL
10750 Capital St (48237-3134)
PHONE..................................248 544-4574
Richard Elias, *President*
Gary Freeman, *Vice Pres*
EMP: 35
SQ FT: 45,000
SALES: 13MM **Privately Held**
WEB: www.midasfoods.com
SIC: 2099 Desserts, ready-to-mix

(G-12086)
MURRAYS WORLDWIDE INC
21841 Wyoming St Ste 1 (48237-3126)
PHONE..................................248 691-9156
Arthur E Berlin, *President*
Jeffrey Berlin, *Vice Pres*
Jim Berlin, *VP Pub Rel*
Dan Medow, *Manager*
Gerald Berlin, *Admin Sec*
◆ **EMP:** 13
SQ FT: 15,000
SALES (est): 3.4MM **Privately Held**
WEB: www.murrayspomade.com
SIC: 2844 Hair preparations, including shampoos

(G-12087)
NATIONAL TIME AND SIGNAL CORP
21800 Wyoming St (48237-3117)
PHONE..................................248 291-5867
Angeline Nathan, *Manager*
EMP: 30
SALES (corp-wide): 5.2MM **Privately Held**
WEB: www.natsco.net
SIC: 3669 3873 Signaling apparatus, electric; fire alarm apparatus, electric; clocks, except timeclocks
PA: National Time And Signal Corporation
28045 Oakland Oaks Ct
Wixom MI 48393
248 380-6264

(G-12088)
NCOC INC
Also Called: National Chemical & Oil
21251 Meyers Rd (48237-3201)
PHONE..................................248 548-5950
Ernest N Stacey Jr, *President*
Jagdeep Singh, *Vice Pres*
▲ **EMP:** 27
SQ FT: 23,000
SALES (est): 8.2MM **Privately Held**
WEB: www.ncocinc.com
SIC: 2899 3356 2891 2851 Metal treating compounds; frit; nonferrous rolling & drawing; adhesives & sealants; paints & allied products; metal heat treating

(G-12089)
NEW VINTAGE USA LLC
21840 Wyoming Pl Ste 1 (48237-3138)
PHONE..................................248 259-4964
Jennifer Surel, *Vice Pres*
Mark Surel,
▲ **EMP:** 4
SALES (est): 535.9K **Privately Held**
SIC: 3824 Vehicle instruments

(G-12090)
PCI INDUSTRIES INC
Also Called: Quiet Concepts
21717 Republic Ave (48237-2365)
PHONE..................................248 542-2570
Michael Pomish, *President*
Martin Mellin, *Vice Pres*
Dawn Sketch, *Bookkeeper*
Nancy Pomish, *Human Res Dir*
Bob Pomish, *VP Sales*
EMP: 53
SQ FT: 12,000
SALES (est): 13.5MM **Privately Held**
WEB: www.pcionesource.com
SIC: 1751 1721 2591 1742 Carpentry work; painting & paper hanging; drapery hardware & blinds & shades; plastering, drywall & insulation; wood partitions & fixtures; floor laying & floor work

(G-12091)
PURE VIRTUAL STUDIOS LLC (PA)
24281 Ridgedale St (48237-4626)
PHONE..................................248 250-4070
Gabriel Kwakyi,
Greg Klein,
EMP: 3
SALES (est): 263K **Privately Held**
SIC: 7372 Application computer software

(G-12092)
REB RESEARCH & CONSULTING CO
Also Called: Mr Hydrogen
12851 Capital St (48237-3160)
PHONE..................................248 545-0155
Robert Buxbaum, *Owner*
EMP: 4 **Privately Held**
SIC: 3569 Filters
PA: Reb Research & Consulting Co
25451 Gardner St
Detroit MI 48237

(G-12093)
ROLSTON HOCKEY ACADEMY LLC
13950 Oak Park Blvd (48237-2077)
PHONE..................................248 450-5300
Brian Rolston, *Principal*
EMP: 5
SALES (est): 175.9K **Privately Held**
SIC: 3949 Hockey equipment & supplies, general

(G-12094)
ROYAL CONTAINER INC
21100 Hubbell St (48237-3024)
PHONE..................................248 967-0910
Justin Mooter, *President*
J Anthony Mooter, *Admin Sec*
EMP: 24
SQ FT: 50,000
SALES (est): 5.1MM **Privately Held**
SIC: 2653 Boxes, corrugated: made from purchased materials

(G-12095)
ROYAL CREST INC
14851 W 11 Mile Rd (48237-1012)
PHONE..................................248 399-2476
Andrea Jeross, *President*
EMP: 6
SQ FT: 7,500
SALES (est): 738.5K **Privately Held**
WEB: www.royalcrestblinds.com
SIC: 2591 Window shades; blinds vertical

(G-12096)
RYAN POLISHING CORPORATION
10709 Capital St (48237-3143)
PHONE..................................248 548-6832
Warren Wood, *President*
Nancy Wood, *Vice Pres*
Billie Worden, *Manager*
EMP: 15 **EST:** 1961
SQ FT: 15,000
SALES: 1.5MM **Privately Held**
SIC: 3471 3451 Buffing for the trade; polishing, metals or formed products; screw machine products

(G-12097)
SAFARI MEATS LLC
24570 Oneida Blvd (48237-1716)
PHONE..................................313 539-3367
Max Doggett,
EMP: 5
SALES (est): 139.9K **Privately Held**
SIC: 2011 Sausages from meat slaughtered on site

(G-12098)
SANGLO INTERNATIONAL INC
21600 Wyoming St (48237-3101)
PHONE..................................248 894-1900
Anil Sanne, *President*
EMP: 3
SALES: 100K **Privately Held**
SIC: 3272 Concrete products

(G-12099)
SOCKS GALORE WHOLESALE INC
10355 Capital St (48237-3139)
PHONE..................................248 545-7625
Jim Toma, *President*
Chris Toma, *Vice Pres*
EMP: 3
SQ FT: 8,000
SALES (est): 575.5K **Privately Held**
SIC: 2252 Socks

(G-12100)
STAR LITE INTERNATIONAL LLC
14131 Ludlow Pl (48237-1354)
P.O. Box 965, Southfield (48037-0965)
PHONE..................................248 546-4489
David Benjamin, *General Mgr*
Sani Zeevi, *Mng Member*
EMP: 4
SALES (est): 450K **Privately Held**
WEB: www.starlite-intl.com
SIC: 5085 5065 5064 3812 Industrial tools; electric tools; communication equipment; amateur radio communications equipment; electrical entertainment equipment; search & navigation equipment

(G-12101)
T & W TOOL & DIE CORPORATION
21770 Wyoming Pl (48237-3112)
P.O. Box 36667, Grosse Pointe (48236-0667)
PHONE..................................248 548-5400
Herbert W Trute, *President*
Gary Nowakowski, *Vice Pres*
Carol L Trute, *Treasurer*
EMP: 50
SQ FT: 48,000
SALES (est): 5.6MM **Privately Held**
SIC: 3544 Special dies & tools

(G-12102)
VGAGE LLC
13250 Northend Ave (48237-3213)
PHONE..................................248 589-7455
David Adaline, *Sales Engr*
John T Malane, *Mng Member*
EMP: 55
SQ FT: 19,000
SALES (est): 13.3MM **Privately Held**
WEB: www.vgage.com
SIC: 3829 Aircraft & motor vehicle measurement equipment

(G-12103)
VILADON CORPORATION
Also Called: Viladon Laboratories
10411 Capital St (48237-3122)
PHONE..................................248 548-0043
Eliezer Meisler, *President*
Astrid Meisler, *Vice Pres*
EMP: 8
SQ FT: 12,500
SALES: 800K **Privately Held**
SIC: 3999 2844 Pet supplies; hair preparations, including shampoos

(G-12104)
WALKER PRINTERY INC
13351 Cloverdale St (48237-3275)
PHONE..................................248 548-5100
Lawrence J Traison, *President*
Barbara Traison, *Vice Pres*
Steven Traison, *Vice Pres*
▲ **EMP:** 19 **EST:** 1924
SQ FT: 16,000
SALES: 1MM **Privately Held**
SIC: 2752 Business forms, lithographed

(G-12105)
WEATHERGARD WINDOW COMPANY INC
Also Called: Weathergard Window Factory
14350 W 8 Mile Rd (48237-3050)
PHONE..................................248 967-8822
Albert Ben-Ezra, *President*
Elsy Ben-Ezra, *Vice Pres*
Shlome Benezra, *Vice Pres*
EMP: 100
SQ FT: 47,638

GEOGRAPHIC SECTION

SALES (est): 19.2MM **Privately Held**
SIC: 3089 5031 5211 Windows, plastic; doors, folding: plastic or plastic coated fabric; doors & windows; windows; doors; door & window products; windows, storm: wood or metal; doors, wood or metal, except storm

Oakland
Oakland County

(G-12106)
GARETT TUNISON
1829 Orion Rd (48363-1832)
PHONE..................................248 330-9835
Garett Tunison, *Partner*
Ray Omphroy, *Partner*
Jay Schnieder, *Partner*
Kenneth Tunison, *Partner*
EMP: 4
SALES (est): 221.6K **Privately Held**
SIC: 7373 3089 Computer-aided manufacturing (CAM) systems service; thermoformed finished plastic products; extruded finished plastic products; novelties, plastic; automotive parts, plastic

(G-12107)
MOSSWORLD ENTERPRISES INC
3577 Orion Rd (48363-2926)
PHONE..................................248 828-7460
Christine Moss, *President*
Michael Moss, *CFO*
▲ **EMP:** 3
SALES (est): 395.1K **Privately Held**
WEB: www.snacktrap.com
SIC: 2369 Girls' & children's outerwear

(G-12108)
SIMPLIFIED CONTROL SOLUTIONS
500 E Buell Rd (48306-1110)
PHONE..................................248 652-1449
Mike Crussler, *Partner*
Bob Grant, *Partner*
Jeffrey Donovan, *General Ptnr*
EMP: 3
SALES (est): 274.1K **Privately Held**
WEB: www.simplifiedcontrol.com
SIC: 3535 Robotic conveyors

(G-12109)
TJB INDUSTRIES
3622 Sweet Bay Ct (48363-2659)
PHONE..................................248 690-9608
Thomas Boyda,
EMP: 3
SALES (est): 314.5K **Privately Held**
SIC: 3999 Manufacturing industries

Oakland Township
Oakland County

(G-12110)
ANWC LLC
Also Called: Northern Wire & Cable
4236 Calumet Dr (48306-1463)
PHONE..................................248 759-1164
Robert H Brzustewicz,
EMP: 3
SQ FT: 1,500
SALES (est): 188.8K **Privately Held**
SIC: 3357 Aluminum wire & cable

Oakley
Saginaw County

(G-12111)
PNEUMATIC TUBE PRODUCTS CO
17108 S Hemlock Rd (48649-8747)
PHONE..................................503 968-0200
Ken Moeller, *President*
EMP: 7

SALES (est): 1.4MM **Privately Held**
WEB: www.ptubes.com
SIC: 3535 Pneumatic tube conveyor systems

Okemos
Ingham County

(G-12112)
AMERICAN PROSTHETIC INSTITUTE
Also Called: Stokosa Prosthetic Clinic
2145 University Park Dr # 100 (48864-3982)
PHONE..................................517 349-3130
Jan Stokosa, *President*
EMP: 5
SQ FT: 3,100
SALES (est): 797.1K **Privately Held**
WEB: www.stokosa.com
SIC: 3842 5999 Limbs, artificial; orthopedic & prosthesis applications

(G-12113)
AMERICAN TANK FABRICATION LLC
2222 W Grand (48864)
PHONE..................................780 663-3552
Sheila Slesher,
Shane Lazaro,
Joseph Wigington,
EMP: 15
SALES (est): 641.3K **Privately Held**
SIC: 3443 Tanks, standard or custom fabricated: metal plate

(G-12114)
ASAP PRINTING INC (PA)
2323 Jolly Rd (48864-3541)
PHONE..................................517 882-3500
Edward Guile, *President*
Bill Davis, *President*
EMP: 22
SQ FT: 1,500
SALES (est): 2.1MM **Privately Held**
WEB: www.asapprinting.net
SIC: 2752 2791 2789 Commercial printing, offset; typesetting; bookbinding & related work

(G-12115)
AVIDHRT INC
2721 Sophiea Pkwy (48864-2855)
PHONE..................................517 214-9041
Chandana Weebadde, *President*
EMP: 5
SALES (est): 338.1K **Privately Held**
SIC: 3829 Medical diagnostic systems, nuclear

(G-12116)
BARYAMES TUX SHOP INC
2421 W Grand River Ave (48864-1448)
PHONE..................................517 349-6555
Katina Baryames, *Owner*
EMP: 6
SALES (corp-wide): 957.5K **Privately Held**
WEB: www.baryames.com
SIC: 7299 2311 Tuxedo rental; men's & boys' suits & coats
PA: Baryames Tux Shop Inc
  3023 W Saginaw St
  Lansing MI 48917
  517 349-6555

(G-12117)
BIOPLSTIC PLYMERS CMPSITES LLC
4275 Conifer Cir (48864-3259)
PHONE..................................517 349-2970
Ramani Narayan, *President*
EMP: 5
SQ FT: 43,000
SALES (est): 120K **Privately Held**
SIC: 2673 8733 Bags: plastic, laminated & coated; noncommercial research organizations

(G-12118)
DALTON ARMOND PUBLISHERS INC
2867 Jolly Rd (48864-3547)
PHONE..................................517 351-8520
Dalton D Ward, *President*
Irene B Arens, *Exec VP*
Phyllis A Ward, *Exec VP*
Carol Borsum, *Opers Dir*
Tina Hawkins, *Assistant*
EMP: 5
SALES (est): 582.2K **Privately Held**
WEB: www.armonddalton.com
SIC: 2731 Books: publishing only

(G-12119)
DIGILINK TECHNOLOGY INC
Also Called: DIGILIANT
5100 Marsh Rd Ste E3 (48864-1152)
PHONE..................................517 381-8888
Ying Liu, *President*
Victor Bettenhaussen, *Store Mgr*
EMP: 12
SQ FT: 3,000
SALES (est): 2MM **Privately Held**
WEB: www.digiliant.com
SIC: 3572 7378 5734 Computer storage devices; computer maintenance & repair; personal computers

(G-12120)
EDIA TECHNOLOGIES INC
1907 Penobscot Dr (48864-2755)
PHONE..................................517 349-0322
David A Wilutis, *Principal*
EMP: 3
SALES (est): 310.4K **Privately Held**
SIC: 2789 Bookbinding & related work

(G-12121)
EFFECTIVE SCHOOLS PRODUCTS
2199 Jolly Rd Ste 160 (48864-5983)
PHONE..................................517 349-8841
Ruth Lezotte PHD, *President*
EMP: 6
SQ FT: 2,500
SALES (est): 1.2MM **Privately Held**
WEB: www.effectiveschools.com
SIC: 8748 2721 8732 Educational consultant; periodicals; educational research

(G-12122)
ELM INTERNATIONAL INC (PA)
4360 Hagadorn Rd (48864-2413)
P.O. Box 1740, East Lansing (48826-1740)
PHONE..................................517 332-4900
Marc Santucci, *President*
Etsuko Barrows, *Treasurer*
Deborah Santucci, *Admin Sec*
▲ **EMP:** 6
SQ FT: 1,400
SALES (est): 700K **Privately Held**
WEB: www.elm-intl.com
SIC: 2741 8732 8742 Directories: publishing & printing; market analysis or research; marketing consulting services

(G-12123)
FEDEX OFFICE & PRINT SVCS INC
4950 Marsh Rd 17 (48864-1654)
PHONE..................................517 347-8656
Paul Decker, *Manager*
EMP: 16
SALES (corp-wide): 69.6B **Publicly Held**
WEB: www.kinkos.com
SIC: 7334 7338 2791 2789 Photocopying & duplicating services; secretarial & court reporting; typesetting; bookbinding & related work
HQ: Fedex Office And Print Services, Inc.
  7900 Legacy Dr
  Plano TX 75024
  800 463-3339

(G-12124)
FRUIT FRO YO
5100 Marsh Rd (48864-1195)
PHONE..................................517 580-3967
Mary Cao, *Principal*
EMP: 3
SALES (est): 182.2K **Privately Held**
SIC: 2026 Yogurt

(G-12125)
GOLF STORE
1492 W Grand River Ave (48864-2307)
PHONE..................................517 347-8733
EMP: 6 **EST:** 2007
SALES (est): 280K **Privately Held**
SIC: 3949 Mfg Sporting/Athletic Goods

(G-12126)
INSTRUMENTED SENSOR TECH INC
Also Called: I.S.T.
4704 Moore St (48864-1722)
PHONE..................................517 349-8487
Gregory Hoshal, *President*
Celia Hoshal, *Vice Pres*
EMP: 8
SQ FT: 8,000
SALES: 2MM **Privately Held**
WEB: www.isthq.com
SIC: 3829 3825 3812 3674 Measuring & controlling devices; instruments to measure electricity; search & navigation equipment; semiconductors & related devices; scientific instruments

(G-12127)
KEVIN WHEAT & ASSOC LTD
Also Called: Wheat Jewelers
4990 Marsh Rd (48864-1194)
PHONE..................................517 349-0101
Kevin Wheat, *President*
Rebecca Liebman, *Sales Associate*
Nancy Pennell, *Office Mgr*
Archie Willoughby, *Manager*
EMP: 8
SQ FT: 5,000
SALES (est): 1.3MM **Privately Held**
WEB: www.spartanspirit.com
SIC: 3915 5094 5944 7631 Jewelers' materials & lapidary work; jewelry & precious stones; jewelry stores; jewelry repair services

(G-12128)
KISSMAN CONSULTING LLC
Also Called: Kissco Publishing
2109 Hamilton Rd Ste 113 (48864-1700)
P.O. Box 744 (48805-0744)
PHONE..................................517 256-1077
Tim Kissman,
EMP: 4
SALES (est): 320K **Privately Held**
SIC: 7311 2721 Advertising agencies; magazines: publishing & printing

(G-12129)
LUXOTTICA OF AMERICA INC
Also Called: Lenscrafters
1982 W Grand River Ave # 815 (48864-1736)
PHONE..................................517 349-0784
Sue Lobsiger, *Branch Mgr*
EMP: 25
SALES (corp-wide): 1.4MM **Privately Held**
WEB: www.lenscrafters.com
SIC: 5995 3851 Eyeglasses, prescription; ophthalmic goods
HQ: Luxottica Of America Inc.
  4000 Luxottica Pl
  Mason OH 45040

(G-12130)
MERIDIAN SCREEN PRTG & DESIGN
Also Called: Meridian Screen Prtg & Design
3362 Hulett Rd (48864-4204)
PHONE..................................517 351-2525
Felly Taylor, *President*
EMP: 6
SQ FT: 5,000
SALES (est): 678.5K **Privately Held**
SIC: 2395 7336 2261 Embroidery & art needlework; graphic arts & related design; printing of cotton broadwoven fabrics

(G-12131)
MICHIGAN ACDEMY FMLY PHYSCIANS
2164 Commons Pkwy (48864-3986)
PHONE..................................517 347-0098
Karlene Ketola, *CEO*
Peter Scuccimarri, *President*

Okemos - Ingham County (G-12132)

Fred Van Alstine, *Vice Pres*
Dana Lawrence, *Corp Comm Staff*
Christin Nohner, *Director*
EMP: 5
SALES: 346.9K **Privately Held**
WEB: www.mafp.com
SIC: 8621 2741 Health association; miscellaneous publishing

(G-12132)
MINOR CREATIONS INCORPORATED
693 W Grand River Ave (48864-3110)
PHONE 517 347-2900
Julia Story, *President*
Steve Carpenter, *Vice Pres*
Sarah Hayslet, *Sales Staff*
Tom Shipping, *Manager*
Justin Carpenter, *Technology*
▲ **EMP:** 15
SQ FT: 10,000
SALES (est): 1.4MM **Privately Held**
WEB: www.minorcreations.com
SIC: 2341 Nightgowns & negligees: women's & children's; chemises, camisoles & teddies: women's & children's

(G-12133)
MUHLECK ENTERPRISES INC
Also Called: Allegra Print & Imaging
2863 Jolly Rd (48864-3547)
PHONE 517 333-0713
David Muhleck, *President*
EMP: 15
SQ FT: 4,600
SALES (est): 1.4MM **Privately Held**
WEB: www.allegra-okemos.com
SIC: 2752 7334 Commercial printing, offset; photocopying & duplicating services

(G-12134)
POLLACK GLASS CO
2360 Jolly Rd (48864-6927)
PHONE 517 349-6380
Shari Montgomery, *Owner*
EMP: 12
SALES (corp-wide): 957.1K **Privately Held**
SIC: 3211 5231 Flat glass; glass
PA: Pollack Glass, Co
930 E Michigan Ave
Lansing MI 48912
517 482-1663

(G-12135)
POWER CONTROL SYSTEMS INC
2861 Jolly Rd Ste C (48864-3668)
P.O. Box 679 (48805-0679)
PHONE 517 339-1442
James Darnell, *President*
EMP: 15
SALES (est): 2.2MM **Privately Held**
WEB: www.powercontrolsys.com
SIC: 3612 Voltage regulating transformers, electric power

(G-12136)
ROYAL ACCOUTREMENTS INC
Also Called: Royal Coffee Maker
172 W Sherwood Rd (48864-1235)
PHONE 517 347-7983
Maria Maes, *President*
▲ **EMP:** 4
SALES: 80K **Privately Held**
WEB: www.royalcoffeemaker.com
SIC: 5499 3589 Coffee; coffee brewing equipment

(G-12137)
SCITEX TRICK TITANIUM LLC
4251 Hulett Rd (48864-3252)
PHONE 517 349-3736
Michael Miller, *Principal*
EMP: 4 EST: 2008
SALES (est): 338.5K **Privately Held**
SIC: 3356 Titanium

(G-12138)
TECHNOVA CORPORATION
3927 Dobie Rd (48864-3705)
PHONE 517 485-1402
Parviz Soroushian, *President*
Farangis Jamzadeh, *Vice Pres*
Maggie Soro, *Admin Sec*
EMP: 11
SQ FT: 30,000
SALES (est): 1.4MM **Privately Held**
SIC: 2655 8732 8742 Cans, composite: foil-fiber & other: from purchased fiber; commercial nonphysical research; marketing consulting services

(G-12139)
UMAKANTH CONSULTANTS INC
Also Called: Symbiosis International
3581 Cabaret Trl (48864-4082)
PHONE 517 347-7500
Uma Umakanth, *President*
Govindarajan Murali, *Vice Pres*
Thangavelu Suseela, *Admin Sec*
EMP: 16
SQ FT: 1,100
SALES (est): 1.5MM **Privately Held**
SIC: 7372 Prepackaged software

(G-12140)
VANGUARD PUBLICATIONS INC
4440 Hagadorn Rd (48864-2414)
PHONE 517 336-1600
Judy Scheidt, *President*
EMP: 4
SALES: 900K
SALES (corp-wide): 19.9MM **Privately Held**
WEB: www.corporateboard.com
SIC: 2721 2741 Magazines: publishing & printing; shopping news: publishing only, not printed on site
PA: American Collegiate Marketing, Inc.
4440 Hagadorn Rd
Okemos MI 48864
517 336-1600

Olivet
Eaton County

(G-12141)
FABRICATIONS PLUS INC
7898 Marshall Rd (49076-8613)
PHONE 269 749-3050
Randy Linn, *President*
Pat Hitchcock, *President*
Greg Shaver, *Principal*
EMP: 4
SALES (est): 610.3K **Privately Held**
SIC: 3444 Sheet metalwork

(G-12142)
MASTERBILT PRODUCTS CORP
719 N Main St (49076-9458)
P.O. Box 518 (49076-0518)
PHONE 269 749-4841
David Craig Masters, *President*
EMP: 20 EST: 1955
SQ FT: 40,000
SALES (est): 3.8MM **Privately Held**
SIC: 3498 3728 Tube fabricating (contract bending & shaping); aircraft parts & equipment

(G-12143)
OLIVET MACHINE TOOL ENGRG CO
Also Called: Omteco
423 N Main St (49076-9616)
P.O. Box 337 (49076-0337)
PHONE 269 749-2671
Bob Judd, *President*
Kathleen Judd, *Corp Secy*
Mike Judd, *Vice Pres*
EMP: 11 EST: 1946
SQ FT: 5,000
SALES (est): 1.3MM **Privately Held**
WEB: www.omteco.com
SIC: 3544 7692 3545 Special dies & tools; jigs & fixtures; welding repair; machine tool accessories

Omer
Arenac County

(G-12144)
LUBERDA WOOD PRODUCTS INC
1188 E Huron Rd (48749-9639)
PHONE 989 876-4334
Albert Luberda, *President*
EMP: 8
SALES (est): 815.7K **Privately Held**
SIC: 2448 2449 Wood pallets & skids; wood containers

Onaway
Presque Isle County

(G-12145)
BRUNING FOREST PRODUCTS
Also Called: Big Ridge Forest Products
16854 5 Mile Hwy (49765-9390)
PHONE 989 733-2880
Michael Bruning, *Owner*
▲ **EMP:** 105
SQ FT: 400
SALES (est): 3.5MM **Privately Held**
SIC: 5193 2411 0811 Nursery stock; timber, cut at logging camp; Christmas tree farm

(G-12146)
DON SAWMILL INC
17131 Twin School Hwy (49765-8887)
PHONE 989 733-2780
EMP: 7 EST: 2010
SALES (est): 779.2K **Privately Held**
SIC: 2421 Sawmills & planing mills, general

(G-12147)
METAL QUEST INC
11739 M68-33 Hwy (49765-8720)
P.O. Box 732 (49765-0732)
PHONE 989 733-2011
Thomas Moran, *CEO*
Rebecca Nash, *CFO*
EMP: 71
SALES (est): 2.3MM **Privately Held**
SIC: 3443 Plate work for the nuclear industry

(G-12148)
MORAN IRON WORKS INC
11739 M68-33 Hwy (49765-8720)
P.O. Box 732 (49765-0732)
PHONE 989 733-2011
Thomas J Moran, *President*
Danielle Chapman, *Principal*
David Kronberg, *Principal*
Mike Mroz, *Principal*
Keri Sheer, *Principal*
EMP: 65
SQ FT: 50,000
SALES (est): 17.9MM **Privately Held**
WEB: www.moraniron.com
SIC: 3441 Fabricated structural metal

(G-12149)
NU-WAY STOVE INC
6566 Rainey Lake Rd (49765)
PHONE 989 733-8792
Wayne Berry, *President*
Gary Schroeder, *Corp Secy*
▲ **EMP:** 5
SQ FT: 4,800
SALES (est): 903.9K **Privately Held**
SIC: 5064 3433 Electrical appliances, major; stoves, wood & coal burning

(G-12150)
PRECISION FORESTRY
4285 S County Line Rd (49765-7504)
P.O. Box 741 (49765-0741)
PHONE 989 619-1016
Michael Sturgill, *Owner*
EMP: 7
SALES (est): 1.2MM **Privately Held**
SIC: 2411 Logging camps & contractors

Onekama
Manistee County

(G-12151)
PORTAGE WIRE SYSTEMS INC
4853 Joseph Rd (49675-9754)
P.O. Box 567 (49675-0567)
PHONE 231 889-4215
Jerome Showalter, *President*
Andrew Showalter, *Admin Sec*
EMP: 30
SQ FT: 30,000
SALES (est): 3.3MM **Privately Held**
SIC: 3694 3444 Harness wiring sets, internal combustion engines; sheet metalwork

Onsted
Lenawee County

(G-12152)
EDWARD E YATES
8573 M 50 (49265-9612)
PHONE 517 467-4961
Bill Sturgill, *Principal*
EMP: 3
SALES (est): 205.9K **Privately Held**
SIC: 3273 Ready-mixed concrete

(G-12153)
GLOBAL QUALITY INGREDIENTS INC
Also Called: Gqi
10464 Bryan Hwy (49265-9551)
PHONE 651 337-2028
Chris Nubern, *CEO*
▲ **EMP:** 6 EST: 2014
SALES (est): 357.7K
SALES (corp-wide): 24.6MM **Privately Held**
SIC: 2099 Food preparations
PA: Natural American Foods, Inc.
10464 Bryan Hwy
Onsted MI 49265
517 467-2065

(G-12154)
MIDCO 2 INC
11703 Pentecost Hwy (49265-9700)
PHONE 517 467-2222
Tom D Johnson, *President*
Charles Roumell, *Corp Secy*
EMP: 5
SQ FT: 3,000
SALES: 600K **Privately Held**
SIC: 3441 Building components, structural steel

(G-12155)
NATURAL AMERICAN FOODS INC (PA)
Also Called: Sweet Harvest Foods
10464 Bryan Hwy. (49265-9551)
PHONE 517 467-2065
Lance Chambers, *CEO*
Jack Irvin, *CFO*
Gloria McMichael, *Human Res Mgr*
Rolf Richter, *Director*
Bruce Schultz, *Maintence Staff*
▲ **EMP:** 45
SQ FT: 20,000
SALES (est): 24.6MM **Privately Held**
SIC: 2099 Honey, strained & bottled

(G-12156)
S & S PARTS LLC
11000 Woerner Rd (49265-9564)
PHONE 517 467-6511
Sharon Lynn Gibbs,
Scott Gibbs,
Jeff Updike,
▲ **EMP:** 2 EST: 2009
SALES (est): 1MM **Privately Held**
SIC: 5051 3743 Steel; industrial locomotives & parts

GEOGRAPHIC SECTION

(G-12157)
ZONYA HEALTH INTERNATIONAL
Also Called: Zhi Publishing
7134 Donegal Dr (49265-9586)
PHONE 517 467-6995
Zonya Foco, *President*
EMP: 4
SALES (est): 338.2K **Privately Held**
WEB: www.zonya.com
SIC: 2731 Textbooks: publishing & printing

Ontonagon
Ontonagon County

(G-12158)
JAMES POLLARD LOGGING
37294 Tikka Rd (49953-9364)
PHONE 906 884-6744
James Pollard, *Principal*
EMP: 3
SALES (est): 279.9K **Privately Held**
SIC: 2411 Logging camps & contractors

(G-12159)
JCR FABRICATION LLC
23642 W State Highway M64 (49953-9035)
PHONE 906 235-2683
Jason Pestka, *Principal*
Carl Brees,
Roy Holmstrom,
EMP: 4
SALES (est): 547.2K **Privately Held**
SIC: 3449 Miscellaneous metalwork

(G-12160)
K AND W LANDFILL INC
Also Called: Waste Management
11877 State Highway M38 (49953-9351)
PHONE 906 883-3504
Murry Meyers, *President*
Dave Kempainen, *District Mgr*
EMP: 16 **EST:** 1998
SALES (est): 5.4MM
SALES (corp-wide): 14.9B **Publicly Held**
SIC: 3443 4953 Dumpsters, garbage; sanitary landfill operation
PA: Waste Management, Inc.
1001 Fannin St Ste 4000
Houston TX 77002
713 512-6200

(G-12161)
KARTTUNEN LOGGING
29015 W State Highway M64 (49953-9078)
PHONE 906 884-4312
Todd A Karttunen, *Owner*
EMP: 4
SALES (est): 198.5K **Privately Held**
SIC: 2411 Logging camps & contractors

(G-12162)
KOSKIS LOG HOMES INC
Also Called: Koski Log Homes
35993 Us Highway 45 (49953-9423)
PHONE 906 884-4937
Jerry Koski, *President*
Linda Koski, *Admin Sec*
EMP: 6
SALES: 650K **Privately Held**
SIC: 1521 2452 New construction, single-family houses; log cabins, prefabricated, wood

(G-12163)
ONTONAGON HERALD CO INC
326 River St (49953-1612)
PHONE 906 884-2826
Maureen Guzek, *President*
EMP: 8 **EST:** 1881
SQ FT: 2,000
SALES: 340K **Privately Held**
WEB: www.ontonagonherald.com
SIC: 2711 5943 Job printing & newspaper publishing combined; office forms & supplies

Orchard Lake
Oakland County

(G-12164)
3D POLYMERS INC
4084 Commerce Rd (48324-2300)
PHONE 248 588-5562
James A Chota, *President*
EMP: 60
SQ FT: 15,000
SALES (est): 7.6MM **Privately Held**
WEB: www.3dpolymers.com
SIC: 3089 3714 3544 Injection molding of plastics; motor vehicle parts & accessories; special dies, tools, jigs & fixtures

(G-12165)
DECOR GROUP INTERNATIONAL INC
3748 Sunset Blvd (48324-2957)
PHONE 248 307-2430
Dennis Knoblock, *President*
Kelly Davis, *Managing Prtnr*
EMP: 12
SALES: 2.5MM **Privately Held**
WEB: www.decorgroup.com
SIC: 3993 Signs & advertising specialties

(G-12166)
ESYNTRK INDUSTRIES LLC
4250 Pine Ln (48323-1647)
PHONE 248 730-0640
Takisha Jane Harper, *Principal*
William Harper, *Principal*
EMP: 8
SALES (est): 235K **Privately Held**
SIC: 3999 Atomizers, toiletry

(G-12167)
MARLIN CORPORATION
5243 Latimer St (48324-1442)
PHONE 248 683-1536
Marlin Berg, *President*
▲ **EMP:** 3
SALES (est): 367.9K **Privately Held**
WEB: www.marlins-motorcycles.com
SIC: 3751 Motorcycles & related parts; motorcycle accessories

(G-12168)
PAICE TECHNOLOGIES LLC
5843 Bravo Ct (48324-2911)
PHONE 248 376-1115
Richard Ferguson,
EMP: 5
SALES: 100K **Privately Held**
SIC: 3519 Internal combustion engines

(G-12169)
RED CARPET CAPITAL INC
3514 Arrowvale Dr (48324-1506)
PHONE 248 952-8583
Mitchell Rivet, *President*
EMP: 5
SALES (est): 156.5K **Privately Held**
SIC: 7922 1521 1389 1542 Theatrical production services; single-family housing construction; construction, repair & dismantling services; commercial & office building contractors; post office construction

(G-12170)
SUN DAILY
4226 Cherry Hill Dr (48323-1606)
PHONE 248 842-2925
EMP: 3
SALES (est): 120.4K **Privately Held**
SIC: 2711 Newspapers, publishing & printing

(G-12171)
TECHNA SYSTEMS INC
6850 Torybrooke Cir (48323-2165)
PHONE 248 681-1717
Ron Stav, *President*
EMP: 3
SALES (est): 414.7K **Privately Held**
SIC: 3677 Electronic coils, transformers & other inductors

Orion
Oakland County

(G-12172)
ADCOLE CORPORATION
40 Engelwood Dr Ste G (48359-2419)
PHONE 508 485-9100
Darren Dawes, *Branch Mgr*
EMP: 3
SALES (corp-wide): 33.6MM **Privately Held**
SIC: 3829 Aircraft & motor vehicle measurement equipment
HQ: Adcole Corporation
669 Forest St
Marlborough MA 01752
508 485-9100

(G-12173)
ADVANCED RESEARCH COMPANY
4140 S Lapeer Rd (48359-1865)
P.O. Box 408, Lake Orion (48361-0408)
PHONE 248 475-4770
William Sharp, *President*
Kim Frank, *Director*
EMP: 10
SQ FT: 18,000
SALES (est): 3.2MM **Privately Held**
WEB: www.advresearch.com
SIC: 7389 3699 Design services; electrical equipment & supplies

(G-12174)
BAIRD INVESTMENTS LLC
Also Called: Jaan Technologies
4140 S Lapeer Rd (48359-1865)
PHONE 586 665-0154
Steven Baird, *Branch Mgr*
EMP: 3 **Privately Held**
SIC: 3569 Assembly machines, non-metalworking
PA: Baird Investments, Llc
43333 Westview Dr
Sterling Heights MI 48313

(G-12175)
BECKER ROBOTIC EQUIPMENT CORP
260 Engelwood Dr Ste E (48359-2443)
PHONE 470 249-7880
Johan Broekhuijsen, *CEO*
EMP: 4
SALES (corp-wide): 2.8MM **Privately Held**
SIC: 3569 Robots, assembly line: industrial & commercial
PA: Becker Robotic Equipment Corp.
6420 Atl Blvd Ste 220
Norcross GA 30071
470 585-6593

(G-12176)
COLE KING LLC
4930 S Lapeer Rd (48359-2412)
PHONE 248 276-1278
John Cole, *President*
EMP: 3
SALES (est): 240.6K **Privately Held**
SIC: 2819 Carbides

(G-12177)
CORBAN INDUSTRIES INC
4590 Joslyn Rd (48359-2229)
PHONE 248 393-2720
Roderic C McIntosh, *President*
EMP: 88
SQ FT: 52,400
SALES (est): 10.8MM **Privately Held**
SIC: 3469 3544 7692 3441 Stamping metal for the trade; special dies & tools; welding repair; fabricated structural metal

(G-12178)
CREATIVE TECHNIQUES INC
200 Northpointe Dr (48359-2400)
PHONE 248 373-3050
Joeseph Banfield, *President*
David Matthews, *Vice Pres*
Richard Parker, *Vice Pres*
Ben Hood, *Project Mgr*
Tim Volke, *Purch Mgr*
EMP: 90
SQ FT: 62,000
SALES (est): 34.3MM **Privately Held**
WEB: www.creativetechniques.com
SIC: 3544 3089 Special dies, tools, jigs & fixtures; injection molded finished plastic products

(G-12179)
DARING COMPANY
180 Engelwood Dr Ste B (48359-2417)
PHONE 248 340-0741
Judy Soutar, *Office Mgr*
Larry Soutar, *Administration*
EMP: 7
SALES (est): 1.2MM **Privately Held**
SIC: 2891 Adhesives

(G-12180)
GEDIA MICHIGAN INC
269 Kay Industrial Dr (48359-2403)
PHONE 248 392-9090
Karl G Neef, *President*
Paul Sprainitis, *CFO*
EMP: 42
SALES (est): 1.8MM
SALES (corp-wide): 436.1K **Privately Held**
SIC: 3465 Automotive stampings
HQ: Gedia Gebruder Dingerkus Gmbh
Rontgenstr. 2-4
Attendorn 57439
272 269-10

(G-12181)
GEN-OAK FABRICATORS INC
2501 Brown Rd (48359-1811)
PHONE 248 373-1515
James Wilcox, *President*
William A Presson, *Corp Secy*
EMP: 3 **EST:** 1966
SQ FT: 15,600
SALES (est): 840K **Privately Held**
SIC: 3441 Fabricated structural metal

(G-12182)
LOTIS TECHNOLOGIES INC
100 Engelwood Dr Ste F (48359-2411)
PHONE 248 340-6065
Paul Dunstan, *President*
EMP: 5
SALES (est): 250.7K **Privately Held**
SIC: 7389 2631 Packaging & labeling services; container, packaging & boxboard

(G-12183)
LYMTAL INTERNATIONAL INC (PA)
4150 S Lapeer Rd (48359-1865)
PHONE 248 373-8100
Francis M Lymburner, *President*
Magdy M Talaat, *Vice Pres*
▼ **EMP:** 25
SQ FT: 34,000
SALES: 16.4MM **Privately Held**
WEB: www.lymtal.com
SIC: 2851 2899 2891 Polyurethane coatings; chemical preparations; sealants

(G-12184)
M P D WELDING INC (PA)
Also Called: Mpd Welding Center
4200 S Lapeer Rd (48359-1866)
P.O. Box 99277, Troy (48099-9277)
PHONE 248 340-0330
Rollin Bondar, *CEO*
Richard Bondar, *President*
Sue Godlewski, *General Mgr*
Dennis Wilette, *General Mgr*
Jerry Lilly, *Purch Mgr*
EMP: 34
SQ FT: 14,000
SALES (est): 5.9MM **Privately Held**
WEB: www.mpdweldinginc.com
SIC: 3544 7692 7699 3398 Special dies, tools, jigs & fixtures; welding repair; industrial machinery & equipment repair; shot peening (treating steel to reduce fatigue)

(G-12185)
MARKETPLACE SIGNS
681 Brown Rd (48359-2261)
PHONE 248 393-1609
EMP: 3

SALES (est): 20K **Privately Held**
SIC: **3993** Mfg Signs/Advertising Specialties

(G-12186)
NATIVE GREEN LLC
180 Engelwood Dr Ste A (48359-2417)
PHONE..................................248 365-4200
John Gagliardi, *General Mgr*
Linda Gcarrillo, *Mng Member*
Sherri Trivette, *Info Tech Mgr*
EMP: 13
SQ FT: 5,000
SALES: 192K **Privately Held**
WEB: www.gonativegreen.com
SIC: **2842** Specialty cleaning preparations

(G-12187)
ORACLE CORPORATION
3216 Hickory Dr (48359-1163)
PHONE..................................248 393-2498
Janice Lamothe Pmp, *Project Mgr*
William Rutan, *Branch Mgr*
Joe Kyriakoza, *Director*
EMP: 302
SALES (corp-wide): 39.5B **Publicly Held**
SIC: **7372** Business oriented computer software
PA: Oracle Corporation
500 Oracle Pkwy
Redwood City CA 94065
650 506-7000

(G-12188)
PATCO AIR TOOL INC
100 Engelwood Dr Ste G (48359-2411)
PHONE..................................248 648-8830
Jon M Kirsch, *President*
Joseph C Linklater, *General Mgr*
Jacqueline Linklater, *CFO*
EMP: 5
SQ FT: 15,000
SALES (est): 1.4MM **Privately Held**
SIC: **5085** 3423 5072 Tools; hand & edge tools; hardware

(G-12189)
ROBERT BOSCH BTRY SYSTEMS LLC (HQ)
3740 S Lapeer Rd (48359-1324)
PHONE..................................248 620-5700
Matt Jonas, *President*
Paul Branoff, *Director*
Reinhardt Peper,
Stephen Allen,
Joseph S Crocenzi,
▲ EMP: 100
SQ FT: 72,000
SALES (est): 76.5MM
SALES (corp-wide): 294.8MM **Privately Held**
WEB: www.cobasys.com
SIC: **3691** 3692 Storage batteries; primary batteries, dry & wet
PA: R O B E R T B O S C H S T I F T U N G Gesellschaft Mit Beschrankter Haftung
Heidehofstr. 31
Stuttgart 70184
711 460-840

(G-12190)
SODECIA AUTO DETROIT CORP
Also Called: AZ Automotive
4555 Giddings Rd 1 (48359-1713)
PHONE..................................248 276-6647
Rick Sutter, *Manager*
EMP: 163 **Privately Held**
SIC: **3465** Body parts, automobile: stamped metal
HQ: Sodecia Automotive Detroit Corp.
969 Chicago Rd
Troy MI 48083
586 759-2200

(G-12191)
US FARATHANE HOLDINGS CORP
4872 S Lapeer Rd (48359-1877)
PHONE..................................248 754-7000
Mike Sermo, *Branch Mgr*
EMP: 100
SALES (corp-wide): 876MM **Privately Held**
WEB: www.usfarathane.com
SIC: **3089** Injection molding of plastics

PA: U.S. Farathane Holdings Corp.
11650 Park Ct
Shelby Township MI 48315
586 726-1200

(G-12192)
VISUAL COMPONENTS N AMER CORP
2633 S Lapeer Rd Ste G (48360-2810)
PHONE..................................855 823-3746
Rober Axtman, *President*
Graham Wloch, *Technical Mgr*
EMP: 4
SALES (est): 1.4MM
SALES (corp-wide): 10.5MM **Privately Held**
SIC: **7372** Prepackaged software
PA: Visual Components Oy
Vanrikinkuja 2
Espoo 02600
925 240-800

Ortonville
Oakland County

(G-12193)
ANGSTROM AUTOMOTIVE GROUP LLC
85 Myron St (48462-8824)
PHONE..................................248 627-2871
Jack Boldt, *Branch Mgr*
EMP: 50 **Privately Held**
SIC: **3498** 3714 Tube fabricating (contract bending & shaping); motor vehicle parts & accessories
PA: Angstrom Automotive Group, Llc
26980 Trolley Indus Dr
Taylor MI 48180

(G-12194)
BEST RATE DUMPSTER RENTAL INC
256 Marrin (48462)
PHONE..................................248 391-5956
Brian Cummings, *President*
EMP: 8 EST: 1998
SALES (est): 507.6K **Privately Held**
SIC: **3443** Dumpsters, garbage

(G-12195)
BOB FLEMING WELL DRILLING
445 N Ortonville Rd (48462-8531)
PHONE..................................248 627-3511
Bob Fleming, *Owner*
Tom Fleming, *Co-Owner*
EMP: 3
SALES (est): 279.9K **Privately Held**
WEB: www.fleming-welldrilling.com
SIC: **1381** 1781 Drilling oil & gas wells; water well drilling

(G-12196)
BOONE EXPRESS
3920 S Hadley Rd (48462-9139)
PHONE..................................248 583-7080
M Vince, *Principal*
EMP: 4
SALES (est): 279K **Privately Held**
SIC: **2741** Miscellaneous publishing

(G-12197)
CITY PRESS INC
30 Rissman Ln (48462-9004)
PHONE..................................800 867-2626
Jeff Bidoli, *Principal*
EMP: 4 EST: 1947
SALES (est): 181.8K **Privately Held**
SIC: **2741** Miscellaneous publishing

(G-12198)
CLARKSTON CARBIDE TOOL & MCH (PA)
1959 Viola Dr (48462-8886)
PHONE..................................248 625-3182
Anthony Palazzola, *President*
Barbara Palazzola, *Corp Secy*
EMP: 7 EST: 1976
SALES (est): 758.6K **Privately Held**
SIC: **3599** Machine shop, jobbing & repair

(G-12199)
ETHER LLC
4950 Hummer Lake Rd (48462-9793)
PHONE..................................248 795-8830
Cole Denzler, *Principal*
EMP: 4
SALES (est): 119.8K **Privately Held**
SIC: **2869** Ethers

(G-12200)
MRJ SIGN COMPANY LLC
256 Narrin St (48462-8718)
PHONE..................................248 521-2431
Mark Johnson, *Vice Pres*
Mark R Johnson, *Mng Member*
Susan J Johnson,
EMP: 6
SALES (est): 636.9K **Privately Held**
WEB: www.mrjsign.com
SIC: **3993** Signs & advertising specialties

(G-12201)
PALFAM INDUSTRIES INC
Also Called: Wit-O-Matic
1959 Viola Dr (48462-8886)
PHONE..................................248 922-0590
Anthony Palazzola Sr, *President*
EMP: 15
SALES (est): 2MM **Privately Held**
WEB: www.wit-o-matic.com
SIC: **3541** Grinding machines, metalworking

(G-12202)
SATELLITE TRACKING SYSTEMS
2160 S Ortonville Rd (48462-8548)
PHONE..................................248 627-3334
Don Cargo, *President*
Mary Ann Cargo, *Corp Secy*
EMP: 3
SQ FT: 2,700
SALES: 600K **Privately Held**
WEB: www.satellitetracking.com
SIC: **7622** 5731 8748 3663 Radio & television receiver installation; phonograph repair; video repair; antennas, satellite dish; television sets; communications consulting; television broadcasting & communications equipment

(G-12203)
SHERI BOSTON
Also Called: Global Silks Gifts N Crafts
1119 Briar Ridge Ln (48462-9760)
PHONE..................................248 627-9576
Sheri Boston, *Owner*
EMP: 4
SALES: 75K **Privately Held**
WEB: www.globalsilks.com
SIC: **3999** 7299 Artificial flower arrangements;

(G-12204)
SHERMAN PUBLICATIONS INC
Also Called: Citizen Newspaper, The
12 South St (48462-7717)
P.O. Box 595 (48462-0595)
PHONE..................................248 627-4332
Alison Heffmer, *Branch Mgr*
EMP: 6
SALES (est): 269.6K
SALES (corp-wide): 5.5MM **Privately Held**
WEB: www.oxfordleader.com
SIC: **2711** Newspapers: publishing only, not printed on site
PA: Sherman Publications Inc
666 S Lapeer Rd
Oxford MI 48371
248 628-4801

Oscoda
Iosco County

(G-12205)
A W B INDUSTRIES INC
Also Called: Aircraft Tool Supply
1000 Ausable Rd (48750-9518)
P.O. Box 370 (48750-0370)
PHONE..................................989 739-1447
Desmond Lynch, *CEO*
Frank Barber, *Shareholder*

◆ EMP: 21
SQ FT: 38,000
SALES: 2.5MM **Privately Held**
WEB: www.aircraft-tool.com
SIC: **3546** 3542 5251 5961 Power-driven handtools; machine tools, metal forming type; hardware; catalog & mail-order houses

(G-12206)
COOPER-STANDARD AUTOMOTIVE INC
4700 Industrial Row (48750-9597)
PHONE..................................989 739-1423
Mike Billiel, *Plant Mgr*
Richard Smigelski, *Materials Mgr*
Stacey Curley, *Purch Agent*
Steven Warner, *Engineer*
Evelyn Clark, *Director*
EMP: 75
SALES (corp-wide): 3.6B **Publicly Held**
WEB: www.cooperstandard.com
SIC: **3443** Heat exchangers, condensers & components
HQ: Cooper-Standard Automotive Inc.
39550 Orchard Hill Pl
Novi MI 48375
248 596-5900

(G-12207)
COZY CUP COFFEE COMPANY LLC
4083 Denise Ct (48750-1062)
P.O. Box 495 (48750-0495)
PHONE..................................989 984-7619
Brian Colorite, *Mng Member*
Lance Thompson,
EMP: 4
SALES: 19K **Privately Held**
SIC: **2095** Coffee roasting (except by wholesale grocers)

(G-12208)
E A WOOD INC (PA)
6718 Loud Dr (48750-9676)
PHONE..................................989 739-9118
EMP: 10
SALES (est): 973.1K **Privately Held**
SIC: **3273** Mfg Ready-Mixed Concrete

(G-12209)
ENVIRO-BRITE SOLUTIONS LLC
4150 Arrow St (48750-1561)
PHONE..................................989 387-2758
Dean Wiltse, *Mng Member*
EMP: 5
SALES: 500K
SALES (corp-wide): 1.3MM **Privately Held**
SIC: **2842** 5087 Cleaning or polishing preparations; cleaning & maintenance equipment & supplies
PA: Wiltse's Restaurant Systems Inc
5606 F 41
Oscoda MI 48750
989 739-2231

(G-12210)
GT PLASTICS INCORPORATED
4681 Industrial Row (48750-8823)
PHONE..................................989 739-7803
Gary Thibault, *President*
Kevin Beliveau, *Webmaster*
Paula Thibault, *Admin Sec*
EMP: 17
SQ FT: 37,000
SALES: 5.4MM **Privately Held**
SIC: **3089** Injection molding of plastics

(G-12211)
INSTACOAT PREMIUM PRODUCTS LLC (PA)
5920 N Huron Ave (48750-2259)
PHONE..................................586 770-1773
Michael Dewald, *Mng Member*
Anthony Miriani,
◆ EMP: 7
SALES (est): 934K **Privately Held**
SIC: **2851** Paints & allied products

▲ = Import ▼=Export
◆ =Import/Export

GEOGRAPHIC SECTION

(G-12212)
IOSCO NEWS PRESS PUBLISHING CO (HQ)
Also Called: Oscoda Press
311 S State St (48750-1636)
P.O. Box 663 (48750-0663)
PHONE................................989 739-2054
Larry Berratto, *President*
Wayne Hemstreet, *Executive*
EMP: 9 **EST:** 1940
SQ FT: 2,000
SALES (est): 1.3MM **Privately Held**
WEB: www.oscodapress.com
SIC: 2711 Commercial printing & newspaper publishing combined

(G-12213)
LAKESHORE CEMENT PRODUCTS
5251 N Us Highway 23 (48750-9560)
PHONE................................989 739-9341
Larry Gerhardt, *Owner*
EMP: 4
SALES: 380K **Privately Held**
SIC: 3272 5211 5032 Precast terrazo or concrete products; concrete products, precast; paving materials, prefabricated concrete; masonry materials & supplies; paving stones; brick, stone & related material

(G-12214)
MIGATRON PRECISION PRODUCTS (PA)
Also Called: Fine Manufacturing & Tool Co
4296 E River Rd (48750-1027)
P.O. Box 100 (48750-0100)
PHONE................................989 739-1439
Ronald Edwards, *Vice Pres*
EMP: 13
SQ FT: 6,000
SALES (est): 1.1MM **Privately Held**
SIC: 3541 Machine tools, metal cutting type

(G-12215)
NTF MANUFACTURING USA LLC
Also Called: Ntf Filter
4691 Industrial Row (48750-8823)
PHONE................................989 739-8560
Cathy Williams, *Marketing Staff*
EMP: 13
SALES (est): 2.1MM **Privately Held**
SIC: 3677 Filtration devices, electronic

(G-12216)
OSCODA PLASTICS INC (PA)
Also Called: Jrb Enterprises
5585 N Huron Ave (48750-1583)
P.O. Box 189 (48750-0189)
PHONE................................989 739-6900
Tom Saeli, *CEO*
John Burt, *Ch of Bd*
Shawn Sny, *Exec VP*
Jason Tunney, *Exec VP*
Cory Gerger, *CFO*
EMP: 39
SQ FT: 130,000
SALES (est): 11.7MM **Privately Held**
WEB: www.oscodaplastics.com
SIC: 2821 3089 Polyvinyl chloride resins (PVC); floor coverings, plastic

(G-12217)
P&L DEVELOPMENT & MFG LLC
Also Called: P&L Development and Mfg
4025 Arrow St (48750-2214)
PHONE................................989 739-5203
David Langley,
EMP: 75 **EST:** 2007
SALES (est): 13.2MM **Privately Held**
SIC: 3545 Machine tool accessories

(G-12218)
PHOENIX CMPOSITE SOLUTIONS LLC
5911 Mission St (48750-1544)
PHONE................................989 739-7108
John F Scanlon, *President*
Erick Martin, *Division Mgr*
Lucas Jaqua, *Plant Mgr*
Ian Spragg, *QC Mgr*
Scott Phillips, *Engineer*
▲ **EMP:** 150
SQ FT: 118,000
SALES (est): 32.6MM **Privately Held**
WEB: www.phoenix-mi.com
SIC: 3728 Aircraft assemblies, subassemblies & parts

(G-12219)
SAGE CONTROL ORDNANCE INC
3455 Kings Corner Rd (48750-9667)
PHONE................................989 739-2200
John Klein, *President*
Marvin Clark, *Export Mgr*
▲ **EMP:** 15
SALES (est): 2.2MM **Privately Held**
WEB: www.sageco.com
SIC: 3482 Small arms ammunition

(G-12220)
SAGE INTERNATIONAL LIMITED
3455 Kings Corner Rd (48750-9667)
PHONE................................989 739-7000
John M Klein, *President*
Marvin Clark, *General Mgr*
Randall Marx, *Engineer*
Kristina Millard,
EMP: 15
SQ FT: 20,000
SALES: 1MM **Privately Held**
SIC: 3484 Small arms

(G-12221)
TIMCO ENGINE CENTER INC
Also Called: Haeco Americas Engine Services
3921 Arrow St (48750-2212)
PHONE................................989 739-2194
Ron Eutack, *President*
EMP: 60
SALES (est): 4.9MM **Privately Held**
SIC: 7694 Motor repair services
HQ: Haeco Americas, Llc
623 Radar Rd
Greensboro NC 27410
336 668-4410

(G-12222)
TIP-TOP SCREW MFG INC
4183 Forest St (48750-2335)
P.O. Box 665 (48750-0665)
PHONE................................989 739-5157
Thomas Saeli, *CEO*
Tom Hollingsworth, *Exec VP*
Shawn Sny, *Exec VP*
Jason Tunney, *Exec VP*
Thomas Lawler, *Vice Pres*
EMP: 20 **EST:** 1999
SQ FT: 50,000
SALES (est): 6.2MM **Privately Held**
WEB: www.tip-topscrew.com
SIC: 3452 Bolts, nuts, rivets & washers

(G-12223)
TUBE FORMING AND MACHINE INC
4614 Industrial Row (48750-9545)
PHONE................................989 739-3323
Jerome Orefice, *President*
Barbara Orefice, *Admin Sec*
▼ **EMP:** 20
SQ FT: 10,000
SALES (est): 1.5MM **Privately Held**
WEB: www.tubeforming.com
SIC: 3498 3547 Tube fabricating (contract bending & shaping); rolling mill machinery

(G-12224)
WELLMANS SPORT CENTER
Also Called: Wellman's Bait and Tackle
910 S State St (48750-1684)
PHONE................................989 739-2869
Ross Wellman, *Owner*
EMP: 3
SQ FT: 2,000
SALES (est): 316.2K **Privately Held**
SIC: 3949 Sporting & athletic goods

(G-12225)
YATES FOREST PRODUCTS INC
7110 Woodlea Rd (48750-9722)
PHONE................................989 739-8412
James Yates III, *President*
Steven Christopher Yates, *Vice Pres*
Faye Yates, *Admin Sec*
EMP: 6
SALES (est): 693K **Privately Held**
SIC: 2411 Logging

Osseo
Hillsdale County

(G-12226)
L & R MACHINE INC
6671 Hudson Rd (49266-9531)
PHONE................................517 523-2978
Vern Lee, *President*
VA Linda Milligan, *Corp Secy*
Robert Milligan, *Vice Pres*
EMP: 15
SQ FT: 10,300
SALES: 940K **Privately Held**
SIC: 3498 Tube fabricating (contract bending & shaping)

(G-12227)
MORGANS WELDING
6520 Skuse Rd (49266-9819)
PHONE................................517 523-3666
Thomas Morgan, *Owner*
EMP: 3 **EST:** 1978
SALES (est): 82.2K **Privately Held**
SIC: 7692 Welding repair

(G-12228)
R C PLASTICS INC
4790 Hudson Rd (49266-9626)
PHONE................................517 523-2112
Lewis L Cox, *President*
Greg Cox, *Vice Pres*
Sharon Cox, *Admin Sec*
Terry Cox, *Asst Sec*
♦ **EMP:** 16 **EST:** 1966
SQ FT: 24,000
SALES (est): 3MM **Privately Held**
SIC: 3089 Injection molded finished plastic products; injection molding of plastics

(G-12229)
SPRINGDALE AUTOMATICS INC
7201 Hudson Rd (49266-9534)
PHONE................................517 523-2424
Ronald Ball, *President*
Jennifer M Ball, *Corp Secy*
Andrew Ball, *Vice Pres*
Michael Ball, *Vice Pres*
EMP: 9 **EST:** 1997
SALES (est): 1.4MM **Privately Held**
SIC: 3451 Screw machine products

Ossineke
Alpena County

(G-12230)
OSSINEKE INDUSTRIES INC
10401 Piper Rd (49766-9653)
P.O. Box 82 (49766-0082)
PHONE................................989 471-2197
Brad Lawton, *President*
Bradley L Lawton, *Exec VP*
Jeffery Lawton, *Vice Pres*
Richard Mc Leod, *Vice Pres*
Boyd E Moilanen, *Vice Pres*
♦ **EMP:** 20
SQ FT: 25,000
SALES: 6.9MM
SALES (corp-wide): 224.7MM **Privately Held**
WEB: www.star-su.com
SIC: 3545 Drills (machine tool accessories)
PA: Star Cutter Co.
23461 Industrial Park Dr
Farmington Hills MI 48335
248 474-8200

(G-12231)
PURE PRODUCTS INTERNATIONAL IN
11925 Us Highway 23 S (49766-9507)
PHONE................................989 471-1104
Terry Derouin, *Owner*
EMP: 9
SALES (est): 1MM **Privately Held**
SIC: 2421 Building & structural materials, wood

Otisville
Genesee County

(G-12232)
LARSEN SERVICE INC
11018 Clar Eve Dr (48463-9434)
PHONE................................810 374-6132
Shawn Larsen, *President*
Dawn Larsen, *Admin Sec*
EMP: 4
SALES (est): 410K **Privately Held**
WEB: www.larsenservicerenovation.com
SIC: 3443 Retorts, industrial: smelting, etc.

(G-12233)
MASON TACKLE COMPANY
11273 Center St (48463-9707)
P.O. Box 56 (48463-0056)
PHONE................................810 631-4571
Daniel Powell, *Ch of Bd*
Richard A Powell, *President*
Doris M Powell, *Corp Secy*
Jeffrey D Powell, *Vice Pres*
▲ **EMP:** 20
SQ FT: 30,000
SALES (est): 2.8MM **Privately Held**
WEB: www.masontackle.com
SIC: 2298 3089 3949 3496 Fishing lines, nets, seines: made in cordage or twine mills; injection molded finished plastic products; sporting & athletic goods; miscellaneous fabricated wire products

(G-12234)
PROGRESSIVE CABINETS INC
112 S State Rd (48463-7735)
P.O. Box 36 (48463-0036)
PHONE................................810 631-4611
Billy Lee Weaver, *President*
Terry S Weaver, *President*
EMP: 3
SQ FT: 2,000
SALES (est): 500K **Privately Held**
WEB: www.progressivecabinets.com
SIC: 2434 1751 Wood kitchen cabinets; cabinet building & installation

Otsego
Allegan County

(G-12235)
COMMUNITY SHOPPERS GUIDE INC
117 N Farmer St (49078-1147)
P.O. Box 168 (49078-0168)
PHONE................................269 694-9431
Ron Bennett, *President*
Marty Bennet, *Vice Pres*
Grant Bennett, *Vice Pres*
EMP: 8
SQ FT: 2,500
SALES (est): 655.7K **Privately Held**
SIC: 2711 Newspapers, publishing & printing

(G-12236)
COMPOSITE DEVELOPMENT CORPORAT
1669 Oak St (49078-9318)
PHONE................................269 694-4159
David Merkel, *Principal*
EMP: 3
SALES (est): 185.2K **Privately Held**
SIC: 3089 Extruded finished plastic products

(G-12237)
CRONEN SIGNS LLC
515 E Allegan St (49078-1303)
PHONE................................269 692-2159
Mike Cronen,
Angela Cronen,
EMP: 3
SALES (est): 219K **Privately Held**
SIC: 3993 Signs & advertising specialties

Otsego - Allegan County (G-12238)

(G-12238)
ELECTRA-TEC INC
567 W M 89 Hwy (49078)
P.O. Box 17 (49078-0017)
PHONE..................................269 694-6652
Robert J Pawlowski, *President*
▲ **EMP:** 9
SQ FT: 20,000
SALES (est): 1MM **Privately Held**
WEB: www.electratec.com
SIC: 5021 2522 Office furniture; office furniture, except wood

(G-12239)
F & S ENTERPRISES INC
Also Called: Flame Spray
1473 14th St (49078-9718)
P.O. Box 67, Martin (49070-0067)
PHONE..................................269 672-7145
Scott Warner, *President*
Louella Warner, *Vice Pres*
EMP: 4 **EST:** 1976
SQ FT: 5,000
SALES: 300K **Privately Held**
SIC: 3599 Machine shop, jobbing & repair

(G-12240)
GEORGE WASHBURN
Also Called: Washburn Woodwork & Cabinet
515 S Wilmott St (49078-1444)
PHONE..................................269 694-2930
George Washburn, *Owner*
EMP: 5
SQ FT: 5,000
SALES: 500K **Privately Held**
SIC: 2434 2517 2431 Wood kitchen cabinets; wood television & radio cabinets; millwork

(G-12241)
IMPERT INDUSTRIES INC
Also Called: Electro Tech
557 Lincoln Rd (49078-1080)
P.O. Box 17 (49078-0017)
PHONE..................................269 694-2727
Brian Hoeksema, *President*
EMP: 4
SQ FT: 18,000
SALES: 300K **Privately Held**
SIC: 2542 3821 3443 Cabinets: show, display or storage: except wood; laboratory furniture; fabricated plate work (boiler shop)

(G-12242)
JIFFY PRINT
381 W Allegan St Ste C (49078-1089)
PHONE..................................269 692-3128
Jack Lawrence, *Owner*
EMP: 7
SALES (est): 360K **Privately Held**
SIC: 2752 Commercial printing, offset

(G-12243)
LAUCK PIPE ORGAN CO
92 24th St (49078-9633)
PHONE..................................269 694-4500
EMP: 8 **EST:** 1975
SQ FT: 3,000
SALES (est): 495K **Privately Held**
SIC: 3931 Pipes, organ

(G-12244)
MC PHERSON PLASTICS INC
1347 E M 89 89 M (49078)
P.O. Box 58 (49078-0058)
PHONE..................................269 694-9487
Timothy J Mc Pherson, *President*
Bernard C Mc Pherson Jr, *Vice Pres*
Hazel Mc Pherson, *Treasurer*
Melinda Kling, *Admin Sec*
EMP: 75
SQ FT: 45,000
SALES (est): 12.8MM **Privately Held**
WEB: www.mcpherson-plastics.com
SIC: 3089 Injection molding of plastics

(G-12245)
MILL ASSIST SERVICES INC
141 N Farmer St (49078-1165)
PHONE..................................269 692-3211
Denis Gloede, *President*
Bill Land, *Human Res Mgr*
EMP: 15 **EST:** 1997
SQ FT: 20,300
SALES (est): 2.3MM **Privately Held**
WEB: www.millassist.com
SIC: 3547 Primary rolling mill equipment

(G-12246)
MITECH ELECTRONICS CORPORATION
Also Called: Safari Circuit
411 Washington St (49078-1299)
PHONE..................................269 694-9471
Lawrence R Cain, *Ch of Bd*
Fred Lake, *Admin Sec*
EMP: 154
SQ FT: 110,000
SALES (est): 11MM **Privately Held**
WEB: www.safaricircuits.com
SIC: 3679 Electronic circuits
PA: Safari Circuits, Inc.
411 Washington St
Otsego MI 49078

(G-12247)
OTSEGO PAPER INC
320 N Farmer St (49078-1150)
PHONE..................................269 692-6141
Al Coleman, *Engineer*
EMP: 21
SALES (est): 4.4MM
SALES (corp-wide): 8.2B **Privately Held**
WEB: www.gypsumsolutions.com
SIC: 2621 Paper mills
HQ: Usg Corporation
550 W Adams St
Chicago IL 60661
312 436-4000

(G-12248)
PARKER & ASSOCIATES
338 W Franklin St (49078-1212)
P.O. Box 419 (49078-0419)
PHONE..................................269 694-6709
Charles Parker, *Owner*
▲ **EMP:** 4
SALES (est): 187.9K **Privately Held**
SIC: 2741 Miscellaneous publishing

(G-12249)
PARKER-HANNIFIN CORPORATION
Fluid System Connectors Div
300 Parker Dr (49078-1431)
PHONE..................................269 694-9411
Anthony Vanlerberghe, *Division Mgr*
Robert Moore, *Plant Mgr*
Angela Blaha, *Buyer*
Russ Kalis, *Branch Mgr*
Michael Dollar, *Manager*
EMP: 287
SALES (corp-wide): 14.3B **Publicly Held**
WEB: www.parker.com
SIC: 3366 3494 3432 Bushings & bearings, brass (nonmachined); valves & pipe fittings; plumbing fixture fittings & trim
PA: Parker-Hannifin Corporation
6035 Parkland Blvd
Cleveland OH 44124
216 896-3000

(G-12250)
PARKER-HANNIFIN CORPORATION
Also Called: Hydraulic Pump Division
100 Parker Dr (49078-1400)
PHONE..................................269 692-6254
Richard Dusa, *Principal*
Brad Nilson, *Buyer*
Sarah Johnson, *Engineer*
David Knight, *Engineer*
Greg Steffen, *Engineer*
EMP: 193
SALES (corp-wide): 14.3B **Publicly Held**
WEB: www.parker.com
SIC: 3594 Fluid power pumps & motors
PA: Parker-Hannifin Corporation
6035 Parkland Blvd
Cleveland OH 44124
216 896-3000

(G-12251)
PARKER-HANNIFIN CORPORATION
Also Called: Schrader Bellows
601 S Wilmott St (49078-1505)
PHONE..................................330 253-5239
Richard Surwicz, *General Mgr*
EMP: 85
SALES (corp-wide): 14.3B **Publicly Held**
WEB: www.parker.com
SIC: 3593 3492 3569 3053 Fluid power cylinders, hydraulic or pneumatic; control valves, fluid power: hydraulic & pneumatic; filter elements, fluid, hydraulic line; gaskets & sealing devices; aircraft & motor vehicle measurement equipment
PA: Parker-Hannifin Corporation
6035 Parkland Blvd
Cleveland OH 44124
216 896-3000

(G-12252)
PELOTON INC
124 E Allegan St (49078-1102)
P.O. Box 202 (49078-0202)
PHONE..................................269 694-9702
Nathan Hunt, *President*
Brian Ernst, *Design Engr*
Travis Loofboro, *Manager*
Mari Hill, *Executive Asst*
EMP: 9
SQ FT: 4,200
SALES (est): 1.6MM **Privately Held**
WEB: www.pelotoninc.com
SIC: 8711 3559 3544 Engineering services; paint making machinery; special dies, tools, jigs & fixtures

(G-12253)
PRIME SOLUTION INC
610 S Platt St (49078-1441)
PHONE..................................269 694-6666
Joseph Dendel, *President*
Larry Hartman, *Engineer*
Lisa Lewman, *Controller*
Kyle Parliament, *Manager*
Michele Arthur, *Info Tech Mgr*
EMP: 13
SQ FT: 40,000
SALES (est): 3.5MM **Privately Held**
WEB: www.primesolution1st.com
SIC: 3589 Sewage & water treatment equipment

(G-12254)
RADAM MOTORS LLC
545 Washington St (49078-1243)
PHONE..................................269 365-4982
Andrew Hirzel, *Partner*
EMP: 3 **EST:** 2014
SQ FT: 25,000
SALES (est): 177.9K **Privately Held**
SIC: 3625 Starter, electric motor

(G-12255)
SAFARI CIRCUITS INC (PA)
411 Washington St (49078-1241)
PHONE..................................269 694-9471
Lawrence R Cain, *CEO*
Michael L Kintz Jr, *President*
Eric Bearss, *Maint Spvr*
Joshua Quellet, *Engineer*
Aaron Wilson, *Electrical Engi*
▲ **EMP:** 165
SALES (est): 35.6MM **Privately Held**
WEB: www.safaricircuits.com
SIC: 3679 3661 3625 7812 Antennas, receiving; electronic circuits; fiber optics communications equipment; switches, electronic applications; control equipment, electric; video tape production; audio-visual program production

(G-12256)
TENGAM ENGINEERING INC
545 Washington St (49078-1243)
PHONE..................................269 694-9466
William R Mc Pherson, *President*
Bernard Mc Pherson Jr, *Vice Pres*
Mark M Pherson, *Plant Mgr*
Hazel Mc Pherson, *Treasurer*
Melinda Kling, *Admin Sec*
▲ **EMP:** 30
SQ FT: 21,000
SALES (est): 6.5MM **Privately Held**
WEB: www.tengam.com
SIC: 3499 3825 3264 Magnets, permanent: metallic; test equipment for electronic & electrical circuits; porcelain electrical supplies

(G-12257)
UNITED STATES GYPSUM COMPANY
Also Called: Otsego Paper
320 N Farmer St (49078-1150)
PHONE..................................269 384-6335
Henry Krell, *Plant Mgr*
Todd Oldham, *Manager*
EMP: 125
SALES (corp-wide): 8.2B **Privately Held**
SIC: 3275 Gypsum products
HQ: United States Gypsum Company
550 W Adams St Ste 1300
Chicago IL 60661
312 606-4000

(G-12258)
VANMEER CORPORATION
Also Called: E & B Machine Co
1754 106th Ave (49078-9763)
PHONE..................................269 694-6090
Douglas Vandermeulen, *President*
Douglas Vander Meulen, *President*
John Vander Meulen, *Vice Pres*
EMP: 12 **EST:** 1954
SQ FT: 14,000
SALES: 1MM **Privately Held**
SIC: 3444 Sheet metal specialties, not stamped

Ottawa Lake
Monroe County

(G-12259)
BISCHOFF ENTERPRISES LLC
5732 St Anthony Rd (49267)
PHONE..................................734 856-8490
Scott Bischoff, *Manager*
EMP: 4
SALES (est): 332.9K **Privately Held**
SIC: 3599 Machine shop, jobbing & repair

(G-12260)
COBRA TRUCK & FABRICATION
6248 Sterns Rd (49267-9524)
PHONE..................................734 854-5663
Greg Gruber, *Owner*
EMP: 3
SQ FT: 2,500
SALES: 700K **Privately Held**
SIC: 7692 3548 Welding repair; arc welders, transformer-rectifier

(G-12261)
CUSTOM INTERIORS OF TOLEDO
Also Called: Custombilt of Toledo
7979 Whiteford Rd (49267-8600)
PHONE..................................419 865-3090
Michael Thornton, *President*
Ted Weemes, *Manager*
EMP: 5
SQ FT: 11,500
SALES (est): 186.9K **Privately Held**
SIC: 7641 2511 Furniture upholstery repair; wood household furniture

(G-12262)
F&B TECHNOLOGIES
Also Called: Erie Technologies
6875 Memorial Hwy (49267)
PHONE..................................734 856-2118
Mark Bauman, *President*
Patrick Flynn, *Vice Pres*
Kristopher Hoag, *Project Mgr*
JD Korepta, *Engineer*
Debbie Chandler, *Controller*
EMP: 16
SQ FT: 2,000
SALES (est): 4.3MM **Privately Held**
SIC: 3449 7699 3536 Miscellaneous metalwork; industrial equipment services; hoists, cranes & monorails

(G-12263)
GALLATIN TANK WORKS LLC
6872 Memorial Hwy (49267-5908)
PHONE..................................734 856-5107
Marjorie Bauman,
Mark Bauman,
▲ **EMP:** 3
SALES (est): 250K **Privately Held**
SIC: 3499 Bank chests, metal

GEOGRAPHIC SECTION

Owosso - Shiawassee County (G-12289)

(G-12264)
GEORGETOWN STEEL LLC
8000 Yankee Rd Ste 440 (49267-9583)
PHONE.....................734 568-6148
John Jones,
EMP: 3
SQ FT: 5,200
SALES: 600K Privately Held
SIC: **3312** 5051 3316 Sheet or strip, steel, cold-rolled: own hot-rolled; sheet or strip, steel, hot-rolled; iron & steel (ferrous) products; sheet, steel, cold-rolled: from purchased hot-rolled

(G-12265)
LINK MANUFACTURING INC
Also Called: Link Engineering Company
8000 Yankee Rd Ste 105 (49267-9571)
PHONE.....................734 387-1001
Joe Wells, *Branch Mgr*
EMP: 12 Privately Held
SIC: **3829** Physical property testing equipment; testing equipment: abrasion, shearing strength, etc.
HQ: Link Manufacturing, Inc.
   43855 Plymouth Oaks Blvd
   Plymouth MI 48170
   734 453-0800

(G-12266)
MIDWEST II INC
6194 Section Rd (49267-9526)
PHONE.....................734 856-5200
Olin White, *President*
EMP: 130
SALES (est): 25.5MM Privately Held
SIC: **3471** Finishing, metals or formed products

(G-12267)
MIDWEST PRODUCTS FINSHG CO INC
6194 Section Rd (49267-9526)
PHONE.....................734 856-5200
Mike Alcala, *President*
EMP: 200
SQ FT: 150,000
SALES (est): 19.9MM Privately Held
SIC: **3479** Painting of metal products

(G-12268)
PINNACLE TECHNOLOGY GROUP
7076 Schnipke Dr (49267-9637)
PHONE.....................734 568-6600
Richard Wasserman, *President*
Scott Savage, *Admin Sec*
EMP: 60
SQ FT: 6,500
SALES (est): 21.7MM Privately Held
SIC: **3841** 3561 Diagnostic apparatus, medical; physiotherapy equipment, electrical; hydrojet marine engine units

(G-12269)
PURE LIBERTY MANUFACTURING LLC
Also Called: Global Builder Supply
7075 Schnipke Dr (49267-9637)
P.O. Box 107 (49267-0107)
PHONE.....................734 224-0333
Tyler Decker,
▲ EMP: 6
SALES (est): 1.1MM Privately Held
SIC: **3431** Bathroom fixtures, including sinks

(G-12270)
YAKKERTECH LIMITED
Also Called: Eleetus
8000 Yankee Rd Ste 350 (49267-9580)
PHONE.....................734 568-6162
William Bales, *CEO*
EMP: 8
SQ FT: 3,000
SALES (est): 614.6K Privately Held
SIC: **3699** Flight simulators (training aids), electronic; automotive driving simulators (training aids), electronic

Ovid
Clinton County

(G-12271)
CLINTON MACHINE INC
1300 S Main St (48866-9724)
P.O. Box 617 (48866-0617)
PHONE.....................989 834-2235
Terry Loznak, *President*
George L Burkitt, *Corp Secy*
Tom Domagala, *Vice Pres*
Loren Hall, *Controller*
EMP: 50 EST: 1964
SQ FT: 50,000
SALES (est): 15.2MM Privately Held
SIC: **3535** Conveyors & conveying equipment

(G-12272)
HOMETOWN PUBLISHING INC
Also Called: Meridian Weekly, The
200 S Main St (48866-9608)
P.O. Box 11 (48866-0011)
PHONE.....................989 834-2264
Deborah Price, *President*
EMP: 5
SALES (est): 334.2K Privately Held
SIC: **2711** Newspapers

(G-12273)
MICHIGAN MILK PRODUCERS ASSN
431 W Williams St (48866-9697)
P.O. Box 47 (48866-0047)
PHONE.....................989 834-2221
Kevin Bodensteimer, *Manager*
EMP: 100
SALES (corp-wide): 854MM Privately Held
WEB: www.mimilk.com
SIC: **2026** 2023 2021 5143 Milk processing (pasteurizing, homogenizing, bottling); dry, condensed, evaporated dairy products; creamery butter; dairy products, except dried or canned
PA: Michigan Milk Producers Association
   41310 Bridge St
   Novi MI 48375
   248 474-6672

(G-12274)
RESEARCH TOOL CORPORATION
1401 S Main St (48866-9720)
P.O. Box 76 (48866-0076)
PHONE.....................989 834-2246
Francis J Todosciuk, *President*
Harry Todosciuk, *Vice Pres*
Sandra Fongers, *Admin Sec*
EMP: 35 EST: 1959
SQ FT: 19,000
SALES (est): 6.1MM Privately Held
WEB: www.researchtoolcorp.com
SIC: **3544** Special dies & tools

Owosso
Shiawassee County

(G-12275)
ADVANCED DRAINAGE SYSTEMS INC
770 S Chestnut St (48867-3314)
PHONE.....................989 723-5208
Heath Duggan, *Sales Staff*
Dan Must, *Branch Mgr*
EMP: 60
SALES (corp-wide): 1.3B Publicly Held
WEB: www.ads-pipe.com
SIC: **3084** 3523 3317 3083 Plastics pipe; farm machinery & equipment; steel pipe & tubes; laminated plastics plate & sheet
PA: Advanced Drainage Systems, Inc.
   4640 Trueman Blvd
   Hilliard OH 43026
   614 658-0050

(G-12276)
AGNEW GRPHICS SIGNS PROMOTIONS
1905 W M 21 A (48867-9317)
PHONE.....................989 723-4621
Mark Agnew, *Owner*
Debi Agnew, *Manager*
EMP: 4
SALES (est): 164.2K Privately Held
WEB: www.agnewgraphics.com
SIC: **3993** 7336 Signs, not made in custom sign painting shops; commercial art & graphic design

(G-12277)
ALLIANCE HNI LLC
525 S Gould St (48867-3241)
PHONE.....................989 729-2804
Andrew Heyek, *President*
Greg Hedecore, *Vice Pres*
Debbie Athertin, *Manager*
EMP: 80
SALES (est): 10.4MM Privately Held
SIC: **3826** Magnetic resonance imaging apparatus

(G-12278)
ALLIED MOTION TECHNOLOGIES INC
201 S Delaney Rd (48867-9100)
PHONE.....................989 725-5151
Rob Pumford, *President*
Ken Laymen, *Branch Mgr*
EMP: 200
SALES (corp-wide): 310.6MM Publicly Held
SIC: **3621** Motors, electric
PA: Allied Motion Technologies Inc.
   495 Commerce Dr Ste 3
   Amherst NY 14228
   716 242-8634

(G-12279)
AMERICAN SPEEDY PRINTING CTRS
111 S Washington St (48867-2921)
PHONE.....................989 723-5196
John G Bennett, *Owner*
EMP: 4
SALES (est): 200K Privately Held
SIC: **2752** Commercial printing, offset

(G-12280)
ARGUS PRESS COMPANY
201 E Exchange St (48867-3094)
PHONE.....................989 725-5136
Tom E Campbell, *President*
Richard E Campbell, *Vice Pres*
EMP: 68 EST: 1894
SQ FT: 10,000
SALES: 3.2MM Privately Held
SIC: **2711** 2791 2752 Newspapers: publishing only, not printed on site; typesetting; commercial printing, lithographic

(G-12281)
CARGILL INCORPORATED
1510 Hathaway St (48867-2107)
PHONE.....................608 868-5150
Greg Hammond, *Plant Mgr*
EMP: 13
SALES (corp-wide): 114.7B Privately Held
SIC: **2075** 2046 2048 2011 Soybean oil, cake or meal; corn oil, refined; corn oil, meal; gluten meal; high fructose corn syrup (HFCS); prepared feeds; meat packing plants; beef products from beef slaughtered on site; poultry slaughtering & processing; wheat
PA: Cargill, Incorporated
   15407 Mcginty Rd W
   Wayzata MN 55391
   952 742-7575

(G-12282)
CLARK ENGINEERING CO (PA)
1470 Mcmillan Rd (48867-9702)
P.O. Box 166 (48867-0166)
PHONE.....................989 723-7930
Paul West, *President*
Daniel Craig, *President*
Scott Hewitt, *CFO*
EMP: 40
SQ FT: 42,000
SALES: 5MM Privately Held
WEB: www.clarkengineering.net
SIC: **3496** Miscellaneous fabricated wire products

(G-12283)
CLASSROOM FARMING LTD
708 Fletcher St (48867-3412)
PHONE.....................810 247-8410
Robert Hooper, *Principal*
EMP: 3
SALES (est): 119.4K Privately Held
SIC: **0191** 2051 General farms, primarily crop; bakery: wholesale or wholesale/retail combined

(G-12284)
CONSTINE INC
Also Called: Woods & Fields Community
2625 W M 21 (48867-8117)
PHONE.....................989 723-6043
Mike Constine, *President*
Mark Constine, *Vice Pres*
Rodney Constine, *Treasurer*
EMP: 50
SALES (est): 6MM Privately Held
WEB: www.constine.com
SIC: **1521** 4214 1011 General remodeling, single-family houses; local trucking with storage; underground iron ore mining; iron ore beneficiating

(G-12285)
CREST MARINE LLC
2710 S M 52 (48867-9203)
P.O. Box 190 (48867-0190)
PHONE.....................989 725-5188
Patrick D May,
Joe Antonneau,
Patrick May,
EMP: 50
SALES (est): 19.9MM
SALES (corp-wide): 466.3MM Publicly Held
SIC: **3732** Pontoons, except aircraft & inflatable
PA: Mastercraft Boat Holdings, Inc.
   100 Cherokee Cove Dr
   Vonore TN 37885
   423 884-2221

(G-12286)
CSH INCORPORATED
2151 W M 21 Ste A (48867-8161)
PHONE.....................989 723-8985
Dan Turnwall, *President*
EMP: 12 EST: 2011
SALES (est): 1.8MM Privately Held
SIC: **3699** Electrical equipment & supplies

(G-12287)
DANEKS GOODTIME ICE CO INC
210 N Gould St (48867-3238)
PHONE.....................989 725-5920
Lora Danek, *President*
James Patrick Danek, *Vice Pres*
EMP: 7
SQ FT: 2,220
SALES (est): 410K Privately Held
SIC: **2097** Manufactured ice

(G-12288)
DEANS HOBBY STOP
116 N Washington St (48867-2830)
PHONE.....................989 720-2137
Dean Sills, *Owner*
EMP: 3
SALES (est): 110K Privately Held
WEB: www.deanshobbystop.com
SIC: **3999** 5945 Miniatures; models, toy & hobby

(G-12289)
DETROIT ABRASIVES COMPANY
1500 W Oliver St (48867-2138)
P.O. Box 504 (48867-0504)
PHONE.....................989 725-2405
Darell Wallace, *Manager*
EMP: 7
SALES (corp-wide): 953.2K Privately Held
SIC: **3291** Abrasive products
PA: Detroit Abrasives Company
   11910 Dexter Chelsea Rd
   Chelsea MI 48118
   734 475-1651

(PA)=Parent Co (HQ)=Headquarters (DH)=Div Headquarters
○ = New Business established in last 2 years

(G-12290)
EDWARDS SIGN & SCREEN PRINTING
1585 S M 52 (48867-8915)
P.O. Box 727 (48867-0727)
PHONE...................989 725-2988
Arlington C Edwards, *Ch of Bd*
Douglas Edwards, *President*
Sandra K Hall, *Corp Secy*
EMP: 8
SQ FT: 4,000
SALES (est): 875.6K **Privately Held**
SIC: 7336 2759 5199 Art design services; screen printing; advertising specialties

(G-12291)
FISHER REDI MIX CONCRETE
599 Oakwood Ave (48867)
P.O. Box 916 (48867-0916)
PHONE...................989 723-1622
James Coldiron, *Manager*
EMP: 15 **EST:** 2001
SALES (est): 1.1MM **Privately Held**
SIC: 3273 Ready-mixed concrete

(G-12292)
FUOSS GRAVEL COMPANY
Also Called: Fuoss Bros
777 Busha Rd (48867-8114)
PHONE...................989 725-2084
Michael L Fuoss, *President*
James Fuoss, *Vice Pres*
Ronald Fuoss, *Treasurer*
Jon Fuoss, *Admin Sec*
EMP: 10 **EST:** 1948
SQ FT: 3,200
SALES (est): 2MM **Privately Held**
SIC: 1442 Construction sand mining; gravel mining

(G-12293)
GEORGIA-PACIFIC LLC
465 S Delaney Rd (48867-9114)
P.O. Box 130 (48867-0130)
PHONE...................989 725-5191
John Keyes, *Maint Spvr*
William Smith, *Sales & Mktg St*
EMP: 130
SALES (corp-wide): 40.6B **Privately Held**
WEB: www.gp.com
SIC: 2653 3412 Boxes, corrugated: made from purchased materials; metal barrels, drums & pails
HQ: Georgia-Pacific Llc
133 Peachtree St Nw
Atlanta GA 30303
404 652-4000

(G-12294)
HANKERDS SPORTSWEAR BASIC TS
116 W Exchange St (48867-2816)
PHONE...................989 725-2979
John Hankerd, *Owner*
EMP: 4
SALES (est): 299.3K **Privately Held**
WEB: www.basicts.com
SIC: 2396 Screen printing on fabric articles

(G-12295)
HEARTH-N-HOME INC (PA)
Also Called: Heart-N-Home
6990 W M 21 (48867-9344)
P.O. Box 108, Perry (48872-0108)
PHONE...................517 625-5586
Randy L Whitbeck, *President*
EMP: 5
SQ FT: 14,000
SALES (est): 1MM **Privately Held**
WEB: www.hearthman.com
SIC: 5719 3429 Fireplace equipment & accessories; fireplace equipment, hardware: andirons, grates, screens

(G-12296)
INDEPNDENT ADVSOR NWSPPR GROUP
Also Called: Shiawassee County Independent
1907 W M 21 (48867-9317)
PHONE...................989 723-1118
Michael Flores, *President*
EMP: 25
SALES (est): 1.3MM **Privately Held**
SIC: 2711 Newspapers: publishing only, not printed on site

(G-12297)
JT FOODS INC
Also Called: D-Licious Foods
220 N Park St (48867-3042)
PHONE...................810 772-9035
Jeremy Feskorn, *President*
Jennifer Frame, *CFO*
Thomas Polec, *Marketing Staff*
EMP: 3
SQ FT: 640
SALES (est): 91.3K **Privately Held**
SIC: 2033 Canned fruits & specialties

(G-12298)
KELLY BROS INC
2615 W Garrison Rd (48867-9728)
PHONE...................989 723-4543
David S Kelly, *President*
Shawn Kelly, *Vice Pres*
Kathleen Kelly, *Admin Sec*
EMP: 3
SALES: 550K **Privately Held**
SIC: 2097 Manufactured ice

(G-12299)
MACHINE TOOL & GEAR INC
401 S Chestnut St (48867-3307)
PHONE...................989 723-5486
EMP: 7
SALES (corp-wide): 118.8MM **Privately Held**
SIC: 3599 Machine shop, jobbing & repair
HQ: Machine Tool & Gear, Inc.
1021 N Shiawassee St
Corunna MI 48817
989 743-3936

(G-12300)
MARRS DISCOUNT FURNITURE
1544 E M 21 (48867-9051)
PHONE...................989 720-5436
Richard L Marr, *Owner*
EMP: 5 **EST:** 1970
SQ FT: 14,000
SALES (est): 506.1K **Privately Held**
WEB: www.marrs.com
SIC: 5712 5722 5941 2515 Furniture stores; electric household appliances, major; specialty sport supplies; mattresses & foundations; mattresses, innerspring or box spring

(G-12301)
MAURELL PRODUCTS INC
Also Called: Crest Boats
2710 S M 52 (48867-9203)
P.O. Box 190 (48867-0190)
PHONE...................989 725-5188
Linda Tomczak, *President*
Patrick May, *COO*
▲ **EMP:** 180
SQ FT: 75,000
SALES (est): 24.8MM **Privately Held**
WEB: www.crestpontoonboats.com
SIC: 3732 Houseboats, building & repairing

(G-12302)
MCLAREN INC
Also Called: McLaren Plumbing Htg & Coolg
2170 W M 21 (48867-9312)
PHONE...................989 720-4328
Sam McLaren, *President*
Gregory C Marsh, *General Mgr*
EMP: 5
SQ FT: 22,000
SALES (est): 1.1MM **Privately Held**
SIC: 1711 5074 5251 3492 Plumbing contractors; boiler maintenance contractor; warm air heating & air conditioning contractor; plumbing & hydronic heating supplies; hardware; control valves, fluid power: hydraulic & pneumatic

(G-12303)
MELCO DCTG & FURN RESTORATION
Also Called: Melco Interior
526 N Dewey St (48867-2428)
PHONE...................989 723-3335
W Gregory Cobb, *Owner*
EMP: 3
SALES: 125K **Privately Held**
SIC: 2391 7641 Draperies, plastic & textile: from purchased materials; reupholstery

(G-12304)
MIDWEST BUS CORPORATION (PA)
1940 W Stewart St (48867-4090)
P.O. Box 787 (48867-0787)
PHONE...................989 723-5241
Daniel D Morrill, *President*
Julie Velasco, *Admin Sec*
▲ **EMP:** 75
SQ FT: 39,000
SALES (est): 12.5MM **Privately Held**
WEB: www.midwestbus.com
SIC: 7532 5013 3713 Top & body repair & paint shops; motor vehicle supplies & new parts; truck & bus bodies

(G-12305)
MOTOR PRODUCTS CORPORATION (HQ)
201 S Delaney Rd (48867-9136)
P.O. Box 127 (48867-0127)
PHONE...................989 725-5151
Fred Stanuszek, *President*
▲ **EMP:** 150
SQ FT: 86,942
SALES (est): 9.8MM
SALES (corp-wide): 310.6MM **Publicly Held**
WEB: www.motorproducts.net
SIC: 3621 Motors, electric
PA: Allied Motion Technologies Inc.
495 Commerce Dr Ste 3
Amherst NY 14228
716 242-8634

(G-12306)
MRM INDUSTRIES INC
1655 Industrial Dr (48867-8979)
PHONE...................989 723-7443
Michael Mahan, *President*
Deborah Mahan, *Admin Sec*
EMP: 30
SQ FT: 32,000
SALES (est): 1.4MM **Privately Held**
WEB: www.mrmindustries.com
SIC: 2821 Molding compounds, plastics

(G-12307)
OWOSSO AUTOMATION INC
1650 E South St 488 (48867-9134)
P.O. Box 488 (48867-0488)
PHONE...................989 725-8804
Ernie Rivers, *President*
EMP: 7
SQ FT: 10,000
SALES: 1MM **Privately Held**
WEB: www.owossoautomation.com
SIC: 3545 3548 Hopper feed devices; electric welding equipment

(G-12308)
OWOSSO COUNTRY CLUB PRO SHOP
4200 N Chipman Rd (48867-9444)
P.O. Box 276 (48867-0276)
PHONE...................989 723-1470
Steve Wakulsky, *Owner*
EMP: 4 **EST:** 1971
SQ FT: 400
SALES (est): 472.8K **Privately Held**
SIC: 3949 5941 Sporting & athletic goods; golf goods & equipment

(G-12309)
OWOSSO GRAPHIC ARTS INC
151 N Delaney Rd (48867-1380)
P.O. Box 276 (48867-0276)
PHONE...................989 725-7112
Craig Ellenberg, *President*
Kathy Wilson, *Exec VP*
Dottie Roy, *Office Mgr*
Joe Holden, *Technical Staff*
▲ **EMP:** 35 **EST:** 1965
SQ FT: 45,500
SALES (est): 7.6MM **Privately Held**
WEB: www.owossographic.com
SIC: 2796 3643 3544 2789 Photoengraving plates, linecuts or halftones; current-carrying wiring devices; special dies, tools, jigs & fixtures; bookbinding & related work

(G-12310)
OWOSSO READY MIX CO
441 Cleveland Ave (48867-1369)
P.O. Box 484 (48867-0484)
PHONE...................989 723-1295
L Robert Ardelean, *President*
Arlene Ardelean, *Corp Secy*
Penney Hammond, *Teacher*
EMP: 8
SQ FT: 16,000
SALES (est): 1.3MM **Privately Held**
SIC: 3273 Ready-mixed concrete

(G-12311)
POLYMER PRODUCTS GROUP INC
3670 N M 52 (48867-1050)
P.O. Box 1084 (48867-6984)
PHONE...................989 723-9510
Daniel Clayton, *President*
Troy Clayton, *Vice Pres*
Vickie Clayton, *Treasurer*
Danielle Clayton, *Admin Sec*
EMP: 7
SALES: 750K **Privately Held**
SIC: 3061 Mechanical rubber goods

(G-12312)
RUESS WINCHESTER INC
Also Called: Rwi Manufacturing
705 Mcmillan Rd (48867-9776)
P.O. Box 847 (48867-0847)
PHONE...................989 725-5809
Bret Russ, *President*
John Pardell, *Vice Pres*
Jesse Mroz, *Agent*
EMP: 11
SALES (est): 1.5MM **Privately Held**
WEB: www.rwimfg.com
SIC: 3441 Fabricated structural metal

(G-12313)
RUGGED LINER INC
200 Universal Dr (48867-3539)
PHONE...................989 725-8354
William Reminder, *President*
Kelly Kneifl, *COO*
Jim Bresingham, *CFO*
Andy Brandes, *Controller*
Sherry Witt, *Sales Staff*
◆ **EMP:** 25
SALES (est): 7.8MM
SALES (corp-wide): 255.3MM **Privately Held**
SIC: 3714 Motor vehicle parts & accessories
HQ: Tectum Holdings, Inc.
5400 Data Ct
Ann Arbor MI 48108
734 677-0444

(G-12314)
SA AUTOMOTIVE LTD LLC
751 S Delaney Rd (48867-9122)
PHONE...................989 723-0425
Mike Lewis, *Branch Mgr*
EMP: 18
SALES (est): 1MM **Privately Held**
SIC: 8611 3714 Manufacturers' institute; motor vehicle parts & accessories
PA: Sa Automotive, Ltd.
1307 Highview Dr
Webberville MI 48892

(G-12315)
SAKOR TECHNOLOGIES INC
1900 Krouse Rd (48867-9116)
PHONE...................989 720-2700
Randal Beattie, *President*
Brian Beattie, *COO*
Greg Sigerson, *Mktg Coord*
Lori Bartlett, *Office Mgr*
Kamen Guentchev, *Director*
EMP: 11
SQ FT: 12,700
SALES (est): 3.1MM **Privately Held**
WEB: www.sakor.com
SIC: 3577 Computer peripheral equipment

(G-12316)
SOBAKS PHARMACY INC (PA)
112 W Exchange St (48867-2816)
PHONE...................989 725-2785
EMP: 17
SQ FT: 11,000

GEOGRAPHIC SECTION

Oxford - Oakland County (G-12342)

SALES (est): 2MM **Privately Held**
SIC: **3845** 5999 5947 Mfg Electromedical Equip Ret Misc Merchandise

(G-12317)
SONOCO PRTECTIVE SOLUTIONS INC
123 N Chipman St (48867-2028)
P.O. Box 627, Dekalb IL (60115-0627)
PHONE..................................989 723-3720
Tim Joseph, *Sales Staff*
Joe Bender, *Branch Mgr*
EMP: 80
SALES (corp-wide): 5.3B **Publicly Held**
WEB: www.tuscarora.com
SIC: **3086** Packaging & shipping materials, foamed plastic
HQ: Sonoco Protective Solutions, Inc.
  1 N 2nd St
  Hartsville SC 29550
  843 383-7000

(G-12318)
SPORTS RESORTS INTERNATIONAL
200 Universal Dr (48867-3539)
PHONE..................................989 725-8354
Donald J Williamson, *CEO*
Gregory T Strzynski, *CFO*
EMP: 82
SQ FT: 240,000
SALES (est): 11MM **Privately Held**
SIC: **3714** 7948 Pickup truck bed liners; race track operation

(G-12319)
SUPERIOR THREADING INC
Also Called: Oster Pipe Threaders
1535 N Hickory Rd (48867-9492)
P.O. Box 160 (48867-0160)
PHONE..................................989 729-1160
Doug Kenyon, *Ch of Bd*
EMP: 14 **EST:** 1893
SQ FT: 10,000
SALES (est): 3.1MM **Privately Held**
SIC: **3552** Thread making machines, spinning machinery

(G-12320)
SVRC INDUSTRIES INC
Also Called: Shiawssee Rhbilitation Program
2009 Corunna Ave (48867-3952)
PHONE..................................989 723-8205
Ruth Jandik, *Branch Mgr*
EMP: 59
SALES (corp-wide): 10.2MM **Privately Held**
WEB: www.svrcindustries.com
SIC: **8331** 2671 Vocational rehabilitation agency; packaging paper & plastics film, coated & laminated
PA: Svrc Industries, Inc.
  203 S Washington Ave # 310
  Saginaw MI 48607
  989 280-3038

(G-12321)
TED SENK TOOLING INC
1117 E Henderson Rd (48867-9460)
PHONE..................................989 725-6067
Larry Senk, *President*
Terri Senk, *Vice Pres*
EMP: 7
SQ FT: 4,300
SALES (est): 1.2MM **Privately Held**
SIC: **3599** Machine shop, jobbing & repair

(G-12322)
TIAL PRODUCTS INC
Also Called: Tial Sport
450 S Shiawassee St (48867-2751)
PHONE..................................989 729-8553
Gregg Jones, *President*
Eric Schultz, *Vice Pres*
Theodore Krupp, *Purchasing*
Julie Jones, *Engineer*
Fred Toman, *Engineer*
EMP: 25
SQ FT: 13,000
SALES (est): 6.9MM **Privately Held**
WEB: www.tialsport.com
SIC: **3449** Miscellaneous metalwork

(G-12323)
TRAMM TECH INC
807 S Delaney Rd (48867-9122)
P.O. Box 848 (48867-0848)
PHONE..................................989 723-2944
Thomas Walser, *President*
Ruth Ann Carlton, *Vice Pres*
EMP: 7
SQ FT: 8,000
SALES (est): 500K **Privately Held**
SIC: **3599** Machine shop, jobbing & repair

(G-12324)
TRANSIT BUS REBUILDERS INC
Also Called: Owosso Fabrication and Design
500 Smith Ave (48867-3639)
PHONE..................................989 277-3645
Scott Sterling, *President*
EMP: 26
SQ FT: 8,000
SALES (est): 2MM **Privately Held**
SIC: **3713** Bus bodies (motor vehicles)

(G-12325)
TUSCARORA INC -VS
123 N Chipman St (48867-2028)
PHONE..................................989 729-2780
Rob Cole, *Owner*
EMP: 3
SALES (est): 247.8K **Privately Held**
SIC: **3083** Plastic finished products, laminated

(G-12326)
UNIVERSAL HDLG EQP OWOSSO LLC
Also Called: Universal Handling Eqpt
1650 Industrial Dr (48867-8979)
PHONE..................................989 720-1650
Lance Hodges, *Mng Member*
EMP: 29
SALES: 7.3MM **Privately Held**
SIC: **3312** Blast furnaces & steel mills

(G-12327)
VIRON INTERNATIONAL CORP (PA)
505 N Hintz Rd (48867-9603)
PHONE..................................254 773-9292
Gary J Gregoricka, *President*
Larry M Gregoricka, *Vice Pres*
Terry S Gregoricka, *Vice Pres*
Scott Barton, *Project Mgr*
Jerry C Gregoricka, *Treasurer*
◆ **EMP:** 75
SQ FT: 32,000
SALES (est): 17MM **Privately Held**
WEB: www.vironintl.com
SIC: **3564** Air purification equipment

(G-12328)
WE PRINT EVERYTHING INC
215 N Ball St (48867-2813)
P.O. Box 399, Jeffersonville IN (47131-0399)
PHONE..................................989 723-6499
Richard E Stewart II, *President*
EMP: 3
SQ FT: 4,000
SALES (est): 268.9K **Privately Held**
SIC: **2791** Typesetting

(G-12329)
WILLIAMSTON PRODUCTS INC
615 N Delany Rd (48867)
PHONE..................................989 723-0149
Mike Issac, *CFO*
EMP: 100 **Privately Held**
SIC: **3089** Automotive parts, plastic
PA: Williamston Products, Inc.
  845 Progress Ct
  Williamston MI 48895

(G-12330)
WILLOUGHBY PRESS
1407 Corunna Ave (48867-3853)
P.O. Box 306 (48867-0306)
PHONE..................................989 723-3360
Terry J Kemp, *Owner*
EMP: 4
SQ FT: 1,800
SALES: 379.6K **Privately Held**
SIC: **2752** Commercial printing, offset

(G-12331)
WOODARD—CM LLC
210 S Delaney Rd (48867-9100)
PHONE..................................989 725-4265
Louis Zelenka, *Plant Mgr*
Troy Delcamp, *Opers Staff*
Brian March, *Production*
Reed Stauffer, *Engineer*
Carol Gaskin, *Human Res Mgr*
EMP: 27
SALES (corp-wide): 123.5MM **Privately Held**
SIC: **2511** 2521 2531 2599 Wood household furniture; wood office furniture; public building & related furniture; factory furniture & fixtures
HQ: Woodard—Cm, Llc
  650 S Royal Ln Ste 100
  Coppell TX 75019
  972 393-3800

Oxford
Oakland County

(G-12332)
ACORN STAMPING INC
600 S Glaspie St (48371-5134)
PHONE..................................248 628-5216
Bobby T Cox, *President*
Sandra K Cox, *Vice Pres*
Sandy Cox, *Vice Pres*
Jennifer Thompson, *Office Mgr*
Jeremy R Cox, *Sharcholder*
▲ **EMP:** 18
SQ FT: 26,400
SALES: 4MM **Privately Held**
WEB: www.acornstamping.com
SIC: **3469** 3443 5251 Stamping metal for the trade; heat exchangers: coolers (after, inter), condensers, etc.; door locks & lock sets

(G-12333)
ADVANCED AUTO TRENDS INC (PA)
2230 Metamora Rd (48371-2347)
PHONE..................................248 628-6111
Sandra L Cornell, *President*
Richard Koshorek, *QC Mgr*
Sydney A Cornell Jr, *Treasurer*
Stephanie Underwood, *Human Res Dir*
Donovan Heathcock, *Program Mgr*
▲ **EMP:** 40
SQ FT: 22,000
SALES (est): 29.6MM **Privately Held**
WEB: www.advancedautotrends.com
SIC: **3089** 3465 3469 3714 Injection molded finished plastic products; automotive stampings; metal stampings; motor vehicle parts & accessories

(G-12334)
ADVANCED AUTO TRENDS INC
Also Called: Aati
3485 Metamora Rd (48371-1619)
PHONE..................................248 628-4850
Charmain Bauerschmidt, *VP Opers*
Peter Reddish, *Production*
Crystal Rundell, *Purchasing*
Jay Cornell, *Engineer*
Ron Wilson, *Branch Mgr*
EMP: 50
SALES (corp-wide): 29.6MM **Privately Held**
WEB: www.advancedautotrends.com
SIC: **3089** 3465 3714 3544 Injection molded finished plastic products; automotive stampings; motor vehicle parts & accessories; special dies, tools, jigs & fixtures
PA: Advanced Auto Trends, Inc.
  2230 Metamora Rd
  Oxford MI 48371
  248 628-6111

(G-12335)
AMERICAN AXLE OXFORD
2300 Xcelsior Dr Ste 230 (48371-2300)
PHONE..................................248 361-6044
Richard Taugh, *Owner*
EMP: 30
SALES (est): 3.9MM **Privately Held**
SIC: **3312** Forgings, iron & steel

(G-12336)
APERION INFORMATION TECH INC (PA)
144 S Washington St (48371-4975)
PHONE..................................248 969-9791
Mark Comins, *President*
Randy Fietsam, *Vice Pres*
Patricia Comins, *Treasurer*
Jon Zupancic, *Marketing Mgr*
Nancy Pocs, *Admin Sec*
EMP: 18
SQ FT: 2,500
SALES (est): 3.7MM **Privately Held**
WEB: www.aperion.com
SIC: **7379** 3572 Computer related consulting services; computer storage devices

(G-12337)
BARRON INDUSTRIES INC (PA)
Also Called: Barron Cast
215 Plexus Dr (48371-2367)
P.O. Box 138 (48371-0138)
PHONE..................................248 628-4300
Bruce Barron, *President*
Michelle Drolshagen, *Corp Secy*
Greg Barron, *Vice Pres*
Jeff Barron, *Vice Pres*
Terri Frankenstein, *Purch Mgr*
◆ **EMP:** 75 **EST:** 1967
SQ FT: 48,000
SALES (est): 26.2MM **Privately Held**
SIC: **3366** 3369 3324 Castings (except die): bronze; nonferrous foundries; aerospace investment castings, ferrous

(G-12338)
BARRON INDUSTRIES INC
215 Plexus Dr (48371-2367)
P.O. Box 138 (48371-0138)
PHONE..................................248 628-4300
Bruce Barron, *Manager*
EMP: 75
SALES (est): 5.7MM
SALES (corp-wide): 26.2MM **Privately Held**
SIC: **3324** Commercial investment castings, ferrous
PA: Barron Industries, Inc.
  215 Plexus Dr
  Oxford MI 48371
  248 628-4300

(G-12339)
BBG NORTH AMERICA LTD PARTNR
2371 Xcelsior Dr (48371-2301)
PHONE..................................248 572-6550
Christian Fritz, *Principal*
EMP: 10
SALES: 4MM **Privately Held**
SIC: **3312** Tool & die steel

(G-12340)
BEAVER STAIR COMPANY
549 E Lakeville Rd (48371-5147)
P.O. Box 555 (48371-0555)
PHONE..................................248 628-0441
Robert Carbone, *President*
EMP: 15
SQ FT: 5,500
SALES (est): 2MM **Privately Held**
WEB: www.beaverstair.com
SIC: **2431** Staircases & stairs, wood; stair railings, wood

(G-12341)
CASEMER TOOL & MACHINE INC
2765 Metamora Rd (48371-2357)
PHONE..................................248 628-4807
Amy Reed, *President*
Robert E Trottier, *Vice Pres*
Jeanne M Trottier, *Treasurer*
Joe Penzien, *Exec Dir*
Robert E Trottier Jr, *Admin Sec*
▼ **EMP:** 20
SQ FT: 24,500
SALES (est): 5MM **Privately Held**
WEB: www.casemer.com
SIC: **3599** Machine shop, jobbing & repair

(G-12342)
CLAS CARBIDE
957 S Glaspie St (48371-5141)
PHONE..................................248 236-8353

Oxford - Oakland County (G-12343)

Rob Olsen, *Partner*
Les Olson, *Partner*
Jim Repeke, *Partner*
EMP: 3 **EST**: 1997
SQ FT: 1,900
SALES: 360K **Privately Held**
WEB: www.clascarbide.com
SIC: 3541 Machine tools, metal cutting type

(G-12343)
CLASSIC WOODWORKS OF MICHIGAN
3275 Metamora Rd Ste A (48371-1646)
PHONE.................................248 628-3356
Douglas Clayton, *Owner*
Laura Clayton, *Owner*
EMP: 3
SALES (est): 400.1K **Privately Held**
SIC: 2431 Millwork

(G-12344)
DRY COOLERS INC
575 S Glaspie St (48371-5133)
PHONE.................................248 969-3400
Brian Russell, *President*
Douglas Kowalski, *COO*
Margy Russell, *Admin Sec*
◆ **EMP**: 38
SQ FT: 20,000
SALES (est): 10.2MM **Privately Held**
WEB: www.drycoolers.com
SIC: 3724 Cooling systems, aircraft engine

(G-12345)
ELTRO SERVICES INC
Also Called: Eltropuls-Usa
3570 Thomas Rd (48371-1438)
PHONE.................................248 628-9790
Dr Siegfried Stramke, *President*
Craig Sytsma, *Director*
Dr Uweh Huchel, *Admin Sec*
EMP: 3
SQ FT: 4,000
SALES (est): 468.3K
SALES (corp-wide): 15.3MM **Privately Held**
WEB: www.eltroservices.com
SIC: 3398 Metal heat treating
PA: Eltro Gesellschaft Fur Elektrotechnik Mit Beschrankter Haftung
Arnold-Sommerfeld-Ring 3
Baesweiler 52499
240 180-970

(G-12346)
GIBBS SPORTS AMPHIBIANS INC
465 S Glaspie St Ste E (48371-5175)
P.O. Box 414, Imlay City (48444-0414)
PHONE.................................248 572-6670
Noel Lane, *CEO*
Dean Harlow, *CEO*
Alan Gibbs, *CTO*
▲ **EMP**: 90
SQ FT: 38,000
SALES: 8.9MM **Privately Held**
SIC: 3711 Motor vehicles & car bodies
PA: Gibbs Technologies Limited
Avenue Road
Nuneaton
247 638-8828

(G-12347)
GLAXOSMITHKLINE LLC
875 Island Lake Dr (48371-3721)
PHONE.................................989 928-6535
EMP: 26
SALES (corp-wide): 39.5B **Privately Held**
SIC: 2834 Pharmaceutical preparations
HQ: Glaxosmithkline Llc
5 Crescent Dr
Philadelphia PA 19112
215 751-4000

(G-12348)
HAMPTON BLOCK CO
Also Called: Hampton Block & Supply
465 Tanview Dr (48371-4770)
PHONE.................................248 628-1333
Eugene E Hampton, *President*
Robert E Hampton, *Vice Pres*
EMP: 4
SQ FT: 1,500
SALES (est): 408.7K **Privately Held**
SIC: 3271 Blocks, concrete or cinder: standard

(G-12349)
HOFF ENGINEERING CO INC (PA)
475 S Glaspie St (48371-5131)
PHONE.................................248 969-8272
Edward M Doyle, *President*
Mike Doyle, *Vice Pres*
Daniel E Argue, *VP Opers*
Edward Doyle, *Manager*
EMP: 9 **EST**: 1958
SQ FT: 13,000
SALES: 5MM **Privately Held**
WEB: www.hoffengineering.com
SIC: 3569 3714 Filters, general line: industrial; filters: oil, fuel & air, motor vehicle

(G-12350)
ILLINOIS TOOL WORKS INC
2425 N Lapeer Rd (48371-2425)
PHONE.................................248 969-4248
EMP: 91
SALES (corp-wide): 14.3B **Publicly Held**
SIC: 3089 Mfg Plastic & Metal Components & Fasteners
PA: Illinois Tool Works Inc.
155 Harlem Ave
Glenview IL 60025
847 724-7500

(G-12351)
INDUSTRIAL MACHINE PDTS INC
Also Called: I M P
32 Louck St (48371-4637)
P.O. Box 186 (48371-0186)
PHONE.................................248 628-3621
Timothy S Twork, *President*
Robert Twork, *Vice Pres*
Deborah Lock, *Accountant*
Brian Batten, *Accounts Mgr*
EMP: 55 **EST**: 1974
SQ FT: 35,000
SALES (est): 12.3MM **Privately Held**
WEB: www.industrialmachineprod.com
SIC: 3469 Metal stampings

(G-12352)
INTEGRITY DESIGN & MFG LLC
3285 Metamora Rd Ste A (48371-1648)
PHONE.................................248 628-6927
EMP: 4
SQ FT: 4,000
SALES (est): 582K **Privately Held**
SIC: 3541 8711 Engineering Services Mfg Machine Tools-Cutting

(G-12353)
KHI COATING
275 S Glaspie St Ste B (48371-5190)
P.O. Box 19 (48371-0019)
PHONE.................................248 236-2100
Fred Strnes, *President*
Steve Sleicher, *Manager*
EMP: 8
SALES: 1MM **Privately Held**
SIC: 2992 2899 Lubricating oils; chemical preparations

(G-12354)
KOENIG SAND & GRAVEL LLC
1955 E Lakeville Rd (48371-5264)
PHONE.................................248 628-2711
Norman Fredericks, *CEO*
EMP: 3
SALES (est): 273.1K **Privately Held**
SIC: 1442 Construction sand & gravel

(G-12355)
LIGHTNING TECHNOLOGIES LLC (PA)
2171 Xcelsior Dr (48371-2363)
PHONE.................................248 572-6700
Jeffrey Owen, *CEO*
Lars Wrebo, *Chairman*
Roland Heiberger, *Vice Pres*
Todd Vanbynen, *CFO*
Rosie Borowski, *Manager*
EMP: 26
SQ FT: 225,000
SALES (est): 11.5MM **Privately Held**
SIC: 2448 Wood pallets & skids

(G-12356)
LUMIFICIENT CORPORATION
1795 N Lapeer Rd (48371-2415)
PHONE.................................763 424-3702
Carey Burkett, *President*
Stacie Braford, *Vice Pres*
◆ **EMP**: 14
SQ FT: 13,200
SALES (est): 2MM
SALES (corp-wide): 99.9MM **Publicly Held**
SIC: 3646 Commercial indusl & institutional electric lighting fixtures
PA: Revolution Lighting Technologies, Inc.
177 Broad St Fl 12
Stamford CT 06901
203 504-1111

(G-12357)
M ANTONIK
690 Golf Villa Dr (48371-3695)
PHONE.................................248 236-0333
Michael Antonik, *Principal*
EMP: 7 **EST**: 2007
SQ FT: 4,800
SALES (est): 720.4K **Privately Held**
SIC: 3829 Testing equipment: abrasion, shearing strength, etc.

(G-12358)
M D HUBBARD SPRING CO INC
595 S Lapeer Rd (48371-5035)
P.O. Box 425 (48371-0425)
PHONE.................................248 628-2528
Charles D Hubbard, *President*
N M Hubbard, *Vice Pres*
Victor Psotka, *Sales Mgr*
Craig Bryce, *Manager*
▼ **EMP**: 30
SQ FT: 25,000
SALES (est): 6.6MM **Privately Held**
WEB: www.hubbardspring.com
SIC: 3496 3493 3495 3469 Miscellaneous fabricated wire products; coiled flat springs; wire springs; metal stampings

(G-12359)
MASTER MFG INC
3287 Metamora Rd (48371-1615)
P.O. Box 573 (48371-0573)
PHONE.................................248 628-9400
Renee Organek, *President*
Julie Ann Weedon, *Vice Pres*
Pradeep Saxena, *Broker*
EMP: 22
SQ FT: 20,000
SALES (est): 3.9MM **Privately Held**
WEB: www.mastermanufacturing.com
SIC: 3599 7694 3714 Machine shop, jobbing & repair; armature rewinding shops; motor vehicle parts & accessories

(G-12360)
MEDICAL LASER RESOURCES LLC
Also Called: Medical Laser Group
610 Gallagher Ct (48371-4191)
PHONE.................................248 628-8120
Alison Bouck,
▲ **EMP**: 4 **EST**: 2007
SALES (est): 557.3K **Privately Held**
SIC: 3841 Surgical lasers

(G-12361)
MIKE VAUGHN CUSTOM SPORTS INC
550 S Glaspie St (48371-5132)
PHONE.................................248 969-8956
Michael Vaughn, *President*
Arlene Vaughn, *Vice Pres*
▲ **EMP**: 42
SQ FT: 29,000
SALES (est): 5.5MM **Privately Held**
WEB: www.vaughnhockey.com
SIC: 3949 Pads: football, basketball, soccer, lacrosse, etc.; gloves, sport & athletic: boxing, handball, etc.; protectors: baseball, basketball, hockey, etc.; hockey equipment & supplies, general

(G-12362)
MSP INDUSTRIES CORPORATION
Also Called: Oxford Manufacturing Facility
45 W Oakwood Rd (48371-1631)
PHONE.................................248 628-4150
Micheal North, *President*
Ronald Kramer, *Principal*
John Peterson, *Mfg Spvr*
▲ **EMP**: 250
SQ FT: 72,000
SALES: 102.5MM
SALES (corp-wide): 7.2B **Publicly Held**
SIC: 3462 Automotive forgings, ferrous: crankshaft, engine, axle, etc.
HQ: American Axle & Manufacturing, Inc.
1 Dauch Dr
Detroit MI 48211

(G-12363)
PHONE GUY LLC
570 Golf Villa Dr (48371-3694)
PHONE.................................248 361-0132
Ronald Norkiewicz,
EMP: 8
SALES: 500K **Privately Held**
SIC: 3661 Telephone & telegraph apparatus

(G-12364)
PROCRAFT CUSTOM BUILDER
901 Markwood Dr (48370-2931)
PHONE.................................586 323-1605
Paul S Gilgallon, *Owner*
EMP: 3
SQ FT: 3,800
SALES (est): 157.2K **Privately Held**
SIC: 3069 Hard rubber & molded rubber products

(G-12365)
PURITAN MAGNETICS INC
533 S Lapeer Rd Ste C (48371-6512)
PHONE.................................248 628-3808
Al Crawshaw, *President*
Elaine Cantu, *Corp Secy*
Jack Hagen, *Vice Pres*
EMP: 15
SALES (est): 3.6MM **Privately Held**
WEB: www.puritanmagnetics.com
SIC: 3559 5084 Separation equipment, magnetic; industrial machinery & equipment

(G-12366)
R L M INDUSTRIES INC
100 Hummer Lake Rd (48371-2304)
P.O. Box 505 (48371-0505)
PHONE.................................248 628-5103
Louis Verville, *President*
Tammy Halsey, *Vice Pres*
Rick Meachum, *VP Sales*
Jackie Lawson, *CTO*
▲ **EMP**: 90
SQ FT: 45,000
SALES: 9.6MM **Privately Held**
WEB: www.rlmcastings.com
SIC: 3324 Steel investment foundries

(G-12367)
RAVEN ENGINEERING INC
725 S Glaspie St (48371-5137)
PHONE.................................248 969-9450
Robert Corbin, *President*
Andy Abraham, *General Mgr*
Tamie Bluthardt, *Purchasing*
Bruce Schafer, *Technical Mgr*
Jeff Hanft, *Sales Staff*
▲ **EMP**: 20
SQ FT: 10,000
SALES (est): 4.7MM **Privately Held**
WEB: www.raven-eng.com
SIC: 3541 Drilling & boring machines

(G-12368)
RELIABLE SALES CO
660 Lakes Edge Dr (48371-5229)
PHONE.................................248 969-0943
Robert L Moncrieff, *President*
Daniel Moncrieff, *Vice Pres*
EMP: 8 **EST**: 1975
SQ FT: 1,200
SALES: 700K **Privately Held**
SIC: 5084 3542 Industrial machinery & equipment; rebuilt machine tools, metal forming types

GEOGRAPHIC SECTION

(G-12369)
ROCHESTER WELDING COMPANY INC
2793 Metamora Rd (48371-2357)
P.O. Box 715, Lake Orion (48361-0715)
PHONE..................................248 628-0801
Thomas G Sears, *President*
Diane M Sears, *Corp Secy*
Roe Myung, *COO*
Stephanie Marracco, *Vice Pres*
EMP: 20 **EST:** 1976
SQ FT: 22,500
SALES (est): 5.4MM **Privately Held**
SIC: 3444 Sheet metalwork

(G-12370)
ROYAL OAK INDUSTRIES INC
700 S Glaspie St (48371-5136)
PHONE..................................248 628-2830
Fax: 248 628-2929
EMP: 60
SALES (corp-wide): 197.6MM **Privately Held**
SIC: 3599 Trade Contractor
PA: Oak Royal Industries Inc
39533 Woodward Ave # 175
Bloomfield Hills MI 48304
248 340-9200

(G-12371)
SASHABAW BEAD CO
2730 S Sashabaw Rd (48371-5422)
PHONE..................................248 969-1353
Cynthia Phillips, *Principal*
EMP: 7
SALES (est): 430K **Privately Held**
SIC: 3999 Stringing beads

(G-12372)
SHERMAN PUBLICATIONS INC (PA)
Also Called: Oxford Leader
666 S Lapeer Rd (48371-5034)
P.O. Box 108 (48371-0108)
PHONE..................................248 628-4801
James A Sherman, *President*
Luan Offer, *Treasurer*
Susan Speed, *Admin Sec*
EMP: 50 **EST:** 1898
SQ FT: 9,000
SALES (est): 5.5MM **Privately Held**
WEB: www.oxfordleader.com
SIC: 2711 Newspapers: publishing only, not printed on site

(G-12373)
STANISCI DESIGN AND MFG INC
700 S Glaspie St (48371-5136)
PHONE..................................586 752-3368
William Stanisci, *Owner*
Theresa Stanisci, *Vice Pres*
Adam Moore, *Sales Staff*
EMP: 8
SALES (est): 1.2MM **Privately Held**
SIC: 2434 Wood kitchen cabinets

(G-12374)
SUPERIOR ABRASIVE PRODUCTS
Also Called: Electro Diamond Tools
85 S Glaspie St Ste A (48371-5158)
PHONE..................................248 969-4090
Dennis Smornell, *President*
EMP: 20
SALES (est): 1.9MM **Privately Held**
SIC: 3291 Abrasive products

(G-12375)
THERMO VAC INC
201 W Oakwood Rd (48371-1635)
PHONE..................................248 969-0300
Walter Peterman, *President*
Stephen Boergert, *General Mgr*
Greg Johnson, *General Mgr*
Kim Johnson, *Purch Agent*
Gregory Johnston, *Engineer*
EMP: 52
SQ FT: 55,000
SALES (est): 20.5MM **Privately Held**
WEB: www.thermovac.com
SIC: 3564 3532 Blowing fans: industrial or commercial; exhaust fans: industrial or commercial; air purification equipment; crushing, pulverizing & screening equipment

(G-12376)
TOOLTECH MACHINERY INC (PA)
625 S Glaspie St (48371-5135)
P.O. Box 543 (48371-0543)
PHONE..................................248 628-1813
Robert E Trottier, *President*
Steve Trottier, *Vice Pres*
Jeanne Trottier, *Treasurer*
Melanie Trottier, *Manager*
EMP: 8
SQ FT: 5,000
SALES (est): 2.1MM **Privately Held**
WEB: www.michigantrap.org
SIC: 3545 Tools & accessories for machine tools

(G-12377)
TRISON TOOL AND MACHINE INC
925 S Glaspie St (48371-5141)
PHONE..................................248 628-8770
Robert E Trottier, *President*
Theodore F Trottier, *Vice Pres*
Jeanne Trottier, *Treasurer*
Tamara Lyerla, *Admin Sec*
EMP: 9
SQ FT: 6,250
SALES (est): 1.6MM **Privately Held**
SIC: 3599 Machine shop, jobbing & repair

(G-12378)
TURN KEY AUTOMOTIVE LLC
Also Called: Turn Key/Redico
3200 Adventure Ln 32-64 (48371-1638)
PHONE..................................248 628-5556
Lynn Rinke, *President*
EMP: 25
SALES (est): 3.7MM **Privately Held**
SIC: 3711 8711 Automobile assembly, including specialty automobiles; engineering services

(G-12379)
TURN KEY HARNESS & WIRE LLC
465 S Glaspie St (48371-5175)
PHONE..................................248 236-9915
EMP: 7
SALES (est): 146.3K **Privately Held**
SIC: 3355 3679 Aluminum wire & cable; harness assemblies for electronic use: wire or cable

(G-12380)
ULTRA FAB & MACHINE INC
465 S Glaspie St Ste D (48371-5175)
P.O. Box 747 (48371-0747)
PHONE..................................248 628-7065
Matt Blades, *President*
EMP: 4
SALES (est): 631.8K **Privately Held**
SIC: 3599 Custom machinery

Palmer
Marquette County

(G-12381)
EMPIRE IRON MINING PARTNERSHIP
Empire Mine Rd (49871)
P.O. Box 38 (49871-0038)
PHONE..................................906 475-3600
David B Blake, *Branch Mgr*
EMP: 620
SALES (corp-wide): 84.4MM **Privately Held**
SIC: 1011 Iron ores
PA: Empire Iron Mining Partnership
1100 Superior Ave E Fl 15
Cleveland OH 44114
216 694-5700

Paradise
Chippewa County

(G-12382)
ENVIRO INDUSTRIES INC
11874 N Whitefish Pt Rd (49768-9604)
PHONE..................................906 492-3402
Brent Biehl, *President*
EMP: 8
SQ FT: 25,000
SALES (est): 854.9K **Privately Held**
SIC: 2499 Mulch or sawdust products, wood

Paris
Mecosta County

(G-12383)
CREATIVE LOOP
21241 Northland Dr (49338-9476)
PHONE..................................231 629-8228
Leif Duddles, *Principal*
EMP: 3
SALES (est): 150.7K **Privately Held**
SIC: 2395 Embroidery products, except schiffli machine

(G-12384)
DOYLE FOREST PRODUCTS INC
21364 Meceola Rd (49338-9509)
PHONE..................................231 832-5586
Joseph D Doyle, *President*
EMP: 30
SALES (est): 3.3MM **Privately Held**
SIC: 2411 Logging

(G-12385)
HOPE NETWORK WEST MICHIGAN
21685 Northland Dr (49338-9794)
PHONE..................................231 796-4801
Jill Moerland, *Branch Mgr*
EMP: 126
SALES (corp-wide): 124.7MM **Privately Held**
SIC: 3469 3714 3479 0182 Metal stampings; motor vehicle parts & accessories; enameling, including porcelain, of metal products; hydroponic crops grown under cover
HQ: Hope Network West Michigan
795 36th St Se
Grand Rapids MI 49548
616 248-5900

(G-12386)
JOHNSON SIGN MINT CNSLTING LLC
5555 E 13 Mile Rd (49338-9629)
PHONE..................................231 796-8880
Loni J Johnson,
EMP: 11
SALES (est): 1.8MM **Privately Held**
SIC: 3993 Signs & advertising specialties

Parma
Jackson County

(G-12387)
BP GAS/ JB FUEL
107 W Main St (49269-8904)
PHONE..................................517 531-3400
EMP: 4 **EST:** 2009
SALES (est): 338.5K **Privately Held**
SIC: 2869 Mfg Industrial Organic Chemicals

(G-12388)
CAMERONS OF JACKSON LLC
Also Called: Fuel of Parma
107 W Main St (49269-8904)
PHONE..................................517 531-3400
Debbie Burnham, *Principal*
EMP: 4
SALES (est): 290.9K **Privately Held**
SIC: 2869 Fuels

(G-12389)
COUNTY PRESS
123 W Main St (49269-8904)
P.O. Box 279 (49269-0279)
PHONE..................................517 531-4542
Erika Sponsler, *President*
EMP: 3
SALES (est): 186K **Privately Held**
SIC: 2711 Commercial printing & newspaper publishing combined

(G-12390)
KNICKERBOCKER R YR BRICKR BLK
8997 Mccain Rd (49269-9701)
PHONE..................................517 531-5369
Roger Knickerbocker, *Owner*
EMP: 3
SALES (est): 60K **Privately Held**
SIC: 3229 Blocks & bricks, glass

(G-12391)
MICHIGAN AUTO COMPRSR INC (HQ)
Also Called: Maci
2400 N Dearing Rd (49269-9415)
PHONE..................................517 796-3200
Yuji Ishizaki, *President*
Masayuki Kobayashi, *General Mgr*
Scott Otsubo, *Vice Pres*
Bruce Verburg, *Vice Pres*
Timothy Boertman, *Facilities Mgr*
◆ **EMP:** 277
SQ FT: 457,000
SALES (est): 146.4MM **Privately Held**
WEB: www.michauto.com
SIC: 3585 3714 3568 3563 Air conditioning, motor vehicle; motor vehicle parts & accessories; power transmission equipment; air & gas compressors

(G-12392)
PARMA MANUFACTURING CO INC
120 N Union St (49269-9201)
P.O. Box 258 (49269-0258)
PHONE..................................517 531-4111
Michael Furtwangler, *President*
Judy Furtwangler, *Corp Secy*
Duane Furtwangler, *Vice Pres*
EMP: 3 **EST:** 1977
SQ FT: 10,000
SALES (est): 650K **Privately Held**
SIC: 3553 Bandsaws, woodworking

(G-12393)
R M BREWER & SON INC
215 S Harrington Rd (49269-9706)
PHONE..................................517 531-3022
Doug Brewer, *President*
Shaun Brewer, *Vice Pres*
Helen L Brewer, *Admin Sec*
EMP: 6 **EST:** 1922
SQ FT: 2,400
SALES (est): 400K **Privately Held**
SIC: 1381 Drilling water intake wells

(G-12394)
SPRAY FOAM FABRICATION LLC
3627 Pickett Rd (49269-9611)
PHONE..................................517 745-7885
Ryan McCormick,
EMP: 3
SALES (est): 481.5K **Privately Held**
SIC: 3563 Spraying & dusting equipment

(G-12395)
TRIPLE E LLC
8535 E Michigan Ave (49269-9785)
PHONE..................................517 531-4481
William Dobbins,
EMP: 23
SQ FT: 10,000
SALES (est): 3.2MM **Privately Held**
SIC: 3599 Machine shop, jobbing & repair

Paw Paw
Van Buren County

(G-12396)
AMBIANCE LLC
Also Called: Sweet Street Motor Car
42839 W Red Arrow Hwy (49079-9733)
PHONE.................................269 657-6027
William McFadden, *President*
EMP: 3 **EST:** 1976
SQ FT: 3,000
SALES (est): 200K **Privately Held**
SIC: 3829 Aircraft & motor vehicle measurement equipment

(G-12397)
BELLE FEEDS
34026 M 40 (49079)
PHONE.................................269 628-1231
Steve Stassek, *Partner*
EMP: 4
SALES (est): 281.5K **Privately Held**
SIC: 2048 Prepared feeds

(G-12398)
BIG BEAR PRODUCTS INC
Also Called: Arrow Material & Handling
32053 E Red Arrow Hwy (49079-8610)
PHONE.................................269 657-3550
Matt Serbenski, *President*
John Bainbridge, *Vice Pres*
EMP: 3 **EST:** 1997
SALES (est): 544.1K **Privately Held**
WEB: www.bigbearproducts.com
SIC: 2531 Public building & related furniture

(G-12399)
COCA-COLA COMPANY
38279 W Red Arrow Hwy (49079-9384)
P.O. Box 229 (49079-0229)
PHONE.................................269 657-3171
Dirk Lunsford, *Manager*
EMP: 500
SALES (corp-wide): 31.8B **Publicly Held**
WEB: www.cocacola.com
SIC: 2086 Bottled & canned soft drinks
PA: The Coca-Cola Company
1 Coca Cola Plz Nw
Atlanta GA 30313
404 676-2121

(G-12400)
COCA-COLA REFRESHMENTS USA INC
38279 W Red Arrow Hwy (49079-9384)
PHONE.................................269 657-8538
Carol Jackson, *Branch Mgr*
EMP: 72
SALES (corp-wide): 31.8B **Publicly Held**
SIC: 2086 Bottled & canned soft drinks
HQ: Coca-Cola Refreshments Usa, Inc.
2500 Windy Ridge Pkwy Se
Atlanta GA 30339
770 989-3000

(G-12401)
DAS TECHNOLOGIES INC
138 Ampey Rd (49079-1815)
P.O. Box 186 (49079-0186)
PHONE.................................269 657-0541
Clifton Runkle, *President*
EMP: 6
SALES (est): 1.3MM **Privately Held**
SIC: 3559 Electronic component making machinery

(G-12402)
DFORTE INC
57440 County Road 671 (49079-9726)
PHONE.................................269 657-6996
Amelio Dacoba, *President*
EMP: 10
SQ FT: 5,000
SALES (est): 612.9K **Privately Held**
SIC: 2038 3841 2099 2035 Frozen specialties; surgical & medical instruments; food preparations; dressings, salad: raw & cooked (except dry mixes)

(G-12403)
DIE CAST PRESS MFG CO INC (PA)
56480 Kasper Dr (49079-1197)
PHONE.................................269 657-6060
Kasper Smidt III, *President*
Mari Lynn Orosz, *Accountant*
Ken Smith, *Sales Mgr*
EMP: 30
SQ FT: 12,000
SALES (est): 4.2MM **Privately Held**
WEB: www.diecastpress.com
SIC: 3542 3452 5084 3429 Die casting machines; presses: hydraulic & pneumatic, mechanical & manual; bolts, nuts, rivets & washers; machine tools & metalworking machinery; manufactured hardware (general); blast furnaces & steel mills

(G-12404)
GLCC CO
39149 W Red Arrow Hwy (49079-9389)
P.O. Box 329 (49079-0329)
PHONE.................................269 657-3167
Jonathan Davis, *President*
Samantha Alderman, *Sales Staff*
▼ **EMP:** 20
SQ FT: 35,000
SALES (est): 2.2MM **Privately Held**
SIC: 2087 Concentrates, drink

(G-12405)
HARLOFF MANUFACTURING CO LLC
828 Duo Tang Rd Unit A (49079-1811)
PHONE.................................269 655-1097
Jason Harloff, *Mng Member*
EMP: 5
SALES (est): 58.1K **Privately Held**
SIC: 3569 Filters

(G-12406)
KNOUSE FOODS COOPERATIVE INC
815 S Kalamazoo St (49079-9230)
PHONE.................................269 657-5524
Frederick Jeffers, *Manager*
EMP: 100
SQ FT: 111,000
SALES (corp-wide): 281.7MM **Privately Held**
SIC: 2033 2099 2035 Fruit juices: fresh; apple sauce: packaged in cans, jars, etc.; food preparations; pickles, sauces & salad dressings
PA: Knouse Foods Cooperative, Inc.
800 Pach Glen Idaville Rd
Peach Glen PA 17375
717 677-8181

(G-12407)
LUCKY GIRL BRWING - CROSS RADS
34016 M 43 (49079-8464)
PHONE.................................630 723-4285
Jeffrey Wescott, *Principal*
EMP: 3
SALES (est): 68.6K **Privately Held**
SIC: 2082 Malt beverages

(G-12408)
MANNING ENTERPRISES INC
45872 30th St (49079-8004)
PHONE.................................269 657-2346
Steve Manning, *President*
Sheri Manning, *Controller*
EMP: 25
SQ FT: 10,000
SALES (est): 5.5MM **Privately Held**
WEB: www.manningmetal.com
SIC: 3444 7692 Sheet metalwork; welding repair

(G-12409)
MEYER WOOD PRODUCTS
32180 E Red Arrow Hwy (49079-8610)
PHONE.................................269 657-3450
Roy D Meyer, *Owner*
EMP: 3
SALES (est): 216.6K **Privately Held**
SIC: 2511 2452 Wood lawn & garden furniture; lawn furniture: wood; prefabricated buildings, wood

(G-12410)
MINUTE MAID CO
38279 W Red Arrow Hwy (49079-9384)
PHONE.................................269 657-3171
Candi Ewert, *Principal*
EMP: 5
SALES (est): 293.1K **Privately Held**
SIC: 2086 Bottled & canned soft drinks

(G-12411)
PAW PAW EVERLAST LABEL COMPANY
47161 M 40 (49079-8558)
P.O. Box 93 (49079-0093)
PHONE.................................269 657-4921
Steven Starbuck, *Owner*
EMP: 7
SALES (est): 200K **Privately Held**
SIC: 3469 Metal stampings

(G-12412)
PAW PAW FUEL STOP
60902 M 51 (49079-9769)
PHONE.................................269 657-7357
Cheryl Muirhead, *Manager*
EMP: 5
SALES (est): 478.6K **Privately Held**
SIC: 2869 Fuels

(G-12413)
SPORTING IMAGE INC
Also Called: Looksharp Marketing
37174 W Red Arrow Hwy (49079-9311)
P.O. Box 24 (49079-0024)
PHONE.................................269 657-5646
John Tapper III, *President*
Kerry Tapper, *Principal*
Linda Tapper, *Vice Pres*
Amy Rice, *Director*
EMP: 15
SQ FT: 15,000
SALES (est): 1.5MM **Privately Held**
WEB: www.looksharponline.com
SIC: 2396 2395 3993 Screen printing on fabric articles; embroidery products, except schiffli machine; signs, not made in custom sign painting shops

(G-12414)
ST JULIAN WINE COMPANY INC (PA)
716 S Kalamazoo St (49079-1558)
P.O. Box 127 (49079-0127)
PHONE.................................269 657-5568
David Braganini, *President*
David R Braganini, *President*
David Miller, *Vice Pres*
William Zuiderveen, *Vice Pres*
Phyllis Braganini, *Treasurer*
EMP: 35
SQ FT: 104,000
SALES (est): 10.9MM **Privately Held**
SIC: 2033 2084 Fruit juices: packaged in cans, jars, etc.; wines

(G-12415)
US SALON SUPPLY LLC
760 S Kalamazoo St (49079-1558)
PHONE.................................616 365-5790
Stan Woodward, *Principal*
▲ **EMP:** 9
SQ FT: 31,500
SALES (est): 919.2K **Privately Held**
SIC: 3999 5087 5112 5961 Barber & beauty shop equipment; beauty salon & barber shop equipment & supplies; stationery & office supplies; office supplies; cosmetics & perfumes, mail order

(G-12416)
VINEYARD PRESS INC
Also Called: Paw Paw Flashes
32280 E Red Arrow Hwy (49079-8764)
P.O. Box 129 (49079-0129)
PHONE.................................269 657-5080
Steven Racette, *President*
EMP: 15 **EST:** 1957
SQ FT: 2,200
SALES (est): 1.5MM **Privately Held**
SIC: 2741 2711 Shopping news: publishing only, not printed on site; newspapers: publishing only, not printed on site

(G-12417)
WARNER VINEYARDS INC (PA)
706 S Kalamazoo St (49079-1558)
P.O. Box 269 (49079-0269)
PHONE.................................269 657-3165
Patrick K Warner, *President*
Jim Warner, *Principal*
Kimberly Babcock, *Manager*
EMP: 5
SQ FT: 15,000
SALES (est): 522.8K **Privately Held**
WEB: www.warnerwines.com
SIC: 2084 2086 Wines; iced tea & fruit drinks, bottled & canned

Peck
Sanilac County

(G-12418)
AMETEK INC
Also Called: Ametek Automtn & Process Tech
6380 Brockway Rd (48466-9506)
PHONE.................................248 435-7540
EMP: 10
SALES (corp-wide): 4.8B **Publicly Held**
SIC: 3621 Motors & generators
PA: Ametek, Inc.
1100 Cassatt Rd
Berwyn PA 19312
610 647-2121

(G-12419)
JOHNSTON MEAT PROCESSING
4470 Sandusky Rd (48466-9715)
PHONE.................................810 378-5455
Jim Dhooghe, *Owner*
EMP: 3
SALES (est): 140K **Privately Held**
SIC: 0751 2013 Slaughtering: custom livestock services; sausages & other prepared meats

(G-12420)
PATRIOT SENSORS & CONTRLS CORP
Also Called: Ametek Patriot Sensors
6380 Brockway Rd (48466-9506)
PHONE.................................810 378-5511
Mark Overstreet, *Branch Mgr*
EMP: 95
SQ FT: 30,000
SALES (corp-wide): 4.8B **Publicly Held**
WEB: www.patriotsensors.com
SIC: 3625 3823 3613 Electric controls & control accessories, industrial; switches, electronic applications; brakes, electromagnetic; controllers for process variables, all types; current-carrying wiring devices; switchgear & switchboard apparatus
HQ: Patriot Sensors & Controls Corporation
1080 N Crooks Rd
Clawson MI 48017

Pelkie
Houghton County

(G-12421)
CDN LOADING INC
13470 State Highway M38 (49958-9278)
PHONE.................................906 338-2630
EMP: 3
SALES (est): 204.9K **Privately Held**
SIC: 2411 Logging camps & contractors

(G-12422)
KOSTAMO LOGGING
10408 Kostamo Rd (49958-9650)
PHONE.................................906 353-6171
Calvin Kostamo, *Principal*
EMP: 3
SALES (est): 210.7K **Privately Held**
SIC: 2411 Logging camps & contractors

(G-12423)
TOM CLISCH LOGGING INC
Hwy 134700 (49958)
PHONE.................................906 338-2900
Tom Clisch, *Owner*
EMP: 3

GEOGRAPHIC SECTION

Petoskey - Emmet County (G-12449)

SALES (est): 336.1K **Privately Held**
SIC: 2411 Logging camps & contractors

(G-12424)
TURPEINEN BROS INC
12920 State Highway M38 (49958-9271)
PHONE..................................906 338-2870
Peter R Turpeinen, *President*
EMP: 18 EST: 1966
SALES: 1.3MM **Privately Held**
SIC: 2411 Wood chips, produced in the field

Pellston
Emmet County

(G-12425)
DONALD LLL SONS LOGGING
260 Townline Rd (49769-9024)
PHONE..................................231 420-3800
Harvey L Sidell, *Principal*
EMP: 3
SALES (est): 180.5K **Privately Held**
SIC: 2411 Logging

(G-12426)
VTE INC
Also Called: Stella-Maris
5437 Robinson Rd (49769-9398)
P.O. Box 790 (49769-0790)
PHONE..................................231 539-8000
Willem Roelof Van Tielen, *President*
Brian R Hart, *Senior VP*
Brian Hart, *Engineer*
Julie Gorney, *Sales Mgr*
Samantha Gorney, *Supervisor*
▲ EMP: 27
SQ FT: 37,000
SALES (est): 5.3MM **Privately Held**
WEB: www.vteworld.com
SIC: 3069 3694 Molded rubber products; battery cable wiring sets for internal combustion engines; automotive electrical equipment

(G-12427)
ZULSKI LUMBER INC
2465 Zulski Rd (49769-9320)
PHONE..................................231 539-8909
Frank Zulski, *President*
Mary Zulski, *Corp Secy*
EMP: 7
SALES (est): 1.1MM **Privately Held**
SIC: 2421 Custom sawmill

Pentwater
Oceana County

(G-12428)
ARCHER WIRE INTERNATIONAL CORP
Pentwater Wire Products
474 S Carroll St (49449-8772)
PHONE..................................231 869-6911
Carl Youngstrom, *Manager*
EMP: 100
SALES (corp-wide): 35.3MM **Privately Held**
SIC: 3496 3993 3537 Shelving, made from purchased wire; signs & advertising specialties; industrial trucks & tractors
PA: Archer Wire International Corp.
7300 S Narragansett Ave
Bedford Park IL 60638
708 563-1700

(G-12429)
DENALI SEED CO
6237 S Pere Marquette Hwy (49449-9306)
P.O. Box 111425, Anchorage AK (99511-1425)
PHONE..................................907 344-0347
Reginald Yaple, *Owner*
EMP: 3 EST: 1966
SQ FT: 788
SALES (est): 265.8K **Privately Held**
WEB: www.thoughtsthatgrow.com
SIC: 5191 7033 2771 Seeds: field, garden & flower; trailer park; greeting cards

(G-12430)
RANCH PRODUCTION LLC
3908 W Hogan Rd (49449-9451)
PHONE..................................231 869-2050
Lynette Adams, *Mng Member*
Jennifer Adams, *Admin Sec*
EMP: 12
SALES (est): 2.1MM **Privately Held**
SIC: 3533 Oil & gas field machinery

(G-12431)
RIVERBEND WOODWORING
1293 W Adams Rd (49449-9473)
PHONE..................................231 869-4965
Karen Williams, *Owner*
EMP: 6
SALES (est): 304K **Privately Held**
SIC: 2491 Wood preserving

Perrinton
Gratiot County

(G-12432)
SHOOKS ASPHALT PAVING CO INC (PA)
3588 W Cleveland Rd (48871-9686)
PHONE..................................989 236-7740
Gary C Shook Jr, *President*
Debra Shook, *Vice Pres*
EMP: 10
SALES (est): 1.2MM **Privately Held**
SIC: 1611 2951 Highway & street paving contractor; asphalt paving mixtures & blocks

Perry
Shiawassee County

(G-12433)
CJ CHEMICALS LLC
1410 Milton Rd (48872-8516)
PHONE..................................888 274-1044
Cathy Lee, *President*
Josh Lee, *CFO*
Eric Earl, *Regl Sales Mgr*
Patrick Bruske, *Accounts Exec*
EMP: 17 EST: 2010
SALES (est): 3.8MM **Privately Held**
SIC: 2869 Industrial organic chemicals

Petersburg
Monroe County

(G-12434)
AMERICAN WELDING INC
16057 Ida West Rd (49270-8400)
P.O. Box 7 (49270-0007)
PHONE..................................734 279-1625
James Dusa, *President*
Stacey Dusa, *Admin Sec*
EMP: 4 EST: 1994
SALES: 337.4K **Privately Held**
SIC: 7692 Welding repair

(G-12435)
DTE HANKIN INC
Also Called: Hankins & Assoc
399 E Center St (49270-9702)
P.O. Box 66 (49270-0066)
PHONE..................................734 279-1831
Geary Hankin, *President*
EMP: 14
SQ FT: 10,000
SALES (est): 580.3K **Privately Held**
SIC: 8711 3541 Industrial engineers; milling machines

(G-12436)
GREAT LAKES SERVICE & SUPPLIES
5520 School Rd (49270-9316)
PHONE..................................734 854-8542
Gary Guilliam, *President*
EMP: 3
SQ FT: 1,200
SALES: 500K **Privately Held**
SIC: 3589 Sewer cleaning equipment, power

(G-12437)
MILAN METAL WORX LLC
Also Called: All Wood Log Splitters
16779 Ida West Rd (49270-9563)
PHONE..................................734 369-7115
Robert J Barta,
Robert F Barta, *Administration*
EMP: 3
SALES (est): 205.1K **Privately Held**
SIC: 3531 3535 Log splitters; conveyors & conveying equipment

(G-12438)
SUPERIOR ROLL LLC
Also Called: Superior Roll & Turning
399 E Center St (49270-9702)
P.O. Box 5 (49270-0005)
PHONE..................................734 279-1831
Jeff Johnson,
EMP: 10
SALES (est): 1.6MM **Privately Held**
WEB: www.superiorroll.com
SIC: 3599 Machine shop, jobbing & repair

Petoskey
Emmet County

(G-12439)
ADEPT DEFENSE LLC
1307 Howard St (49770-3002)
PHONE..................................231 758-2792
Jason Hitchings, *Principal*
EMP: 3
SALES (est): 166.7K **Privately Held**
SIC: 3812 Defense systems & equipment

(G-12440)
AMERICAN SPOON FOODS INC (PA)
1668 Clarion Ave (49770-9263)
P.O. Box 566 (49770-0566)
PHONE..................................231 347-9030
Justin Rashid, *President*
Noah Marshall-Rashid, *Vice Pres*
Jessica Kruskie, *QC Mgr*
Neal Pasciak, *Controller*
Chris Dettmer, *Marketing Staff*
EMP: 45
SQ FT: 12,000
SALES (est): 8MM **Privately Held**
WEB: www.americanspoon.com
SIC: 2035 2034 2032 2033 Pickles, sauces & salad dressings; dehydrated fruits, vegetables, soups; canned specialties; preserves, including imitation: in cans, jars, etc.

(G-12441)
BEARCUB OUTFITTERS LLC
321 E Lake St Unit 1 (49770-2479)
PHONE..................................231 439-9500
Rebecca Philipp-Kranig, *Vice Pres*
Becky Phillip-King, *Mng Member*
Barbara J Shawn,
Lawrence Shawn,
EMP: 10
SQ FT: 2,400
SALES (est): 978.6K **Privately Held**
WEB: www.bearcuboutfitters.com
SIC: 5641 5941 5699 2211 Children's & infants' wear stores; camping & backpacking equipment; sports apparel; apparel & outerwear fabrics, cotton

(G-12442)
BIXBY LOGGING
5056 Maxwell Rd (49770-8842)
PHONE..................................231 348-9794
Kristie Bixby, *Principal*
EMP: 3
SALES (est): 209K **Privately Held**
SIC: 2411 Logging

(G-12443)
BOESE ASSOCIATES INC
Also Called: Penta Associates
2395 Williams Rd (49770-9227)
PHONE..................................231 347-3995
Eric Boese, *President*
EMP: 3
SQ FT: 6,000
SALES: 250K **Privately Held**
SIC: 2511 2521 Wood household furniture; wood office furniture

(G-12444)
CIRCUIT CONTROLS CORPORATION
2277 M 119 (49770-8916)
PHONE..................................231 347-0760
Tetsu Yamamoto, *President*
Thomas Mason, *Vice Pres*
Donald W Winn, *Vice Pres*
Sabura Aihara, *Treasurer*
▲ EMP: 200
SQ FT: 80,000
SALES (est): 28.9MM **Privately Held**
WEB: www.circuitcontrols.com
SIC: 3714 Motor vehicle parts & accessories
HQ: Yazaki International Corporation
6801 N Haggerty Rd 4707e
Canton MI 48187

(G-12445)
COCA-COLA REFRESHMENTS USA INC
1884 M 119 (49770-9341)
PHONE..................................231 347-3242
Charlie Raymond, *Manager*
EMP: 25
SALES (corp-wide): 31.8B **Publicly Held**
WEB: www.cokecce.com
SIC: 2086 5149 Bottled & canned soft drinks; soft drinks
HQ: Coca-Cola Refreshments Usa, Inc.
2500 Windy Ridge Pkwy Se
Atlanta GA 30339
770 989-3000

(G-12446)
COMPASS INTERIORS LLC
Also Called: Quiet Moose
2666 Charlevoix Rd (49770-9707)
PHONE..................................231 348-5353
Mark Jensen,
EMP: 4
SQ FT: 10,000
SALES (est): 342.1K **Privately Held**
SIC: 0782 0781 5712 2511 Landscape contractors; landscape planning services; furniture stores; wood household furniture

(G-12447)
CYGNUS INC
829 Charlevoix Ave (49770-2255)
P.O. Box 292 (49770-0292)
PHONE..................................231 347-5404
Robert Waugh, *President*
EMP: 22
SQ FT: 1,000
SALES: 1.5MM **Privately Held**
WEB: www.cygnusinc.net
SIC: 2521 Cabinets, office: wood

(G-12448)
E K HYDRAULICS INC
1458 Tracy Ln (49770-8572)
PHONE..................................800 632-7112
William P Kalchik, *President*
Sandra Kalchik, *Vice Pres*
EMP: 8
SQ FT: 10,000
SALES (est): 2MM **Privately Held**
WEB: www.ekhydraulics.com
SIC: 5084 7699 3443 3593 Hydraulic systems equipment & supplies; hydraulic equipment repair; cylinders, pressure: metal plate; fluid power cylinders & actuators; manufactured hardware (general)

(G-12449)
GOING OUT ON A LIMB
4588 Greenwood Rd (49770-9560)
PHONE..................................231 347-4631
EMP: 3 EST: 2009
SALES (est): 120K **Privately Held**
SIC: 3842 Mfg Surgical Appliances/Supplies

Petoskey - Emmet County (G-12450) — GEOGRAPHIC SECTION

(G-12450)
GREENWELL MACHINE SHOP INC
1048 Emmet St (49770-2930)
PHONE................................231 347-3346
Gary Greenwell, *President*
EMP: 7 EST: 1947
SQ FT: 9,000
SALES (est): 1.3MM **Privately Held**
SIC: 5051 3599 3446 Steel; machine shop, jobbing & repair; stairs, staircases, stair treads: prefabricated metal

(G-12451)
HARBOR SOFTWARE INTL INC
231 State St Ste 5 (49770-2785)
P.O. Box 831 (49770-0831)
PHONE................................231 347-8866
Paul Fifer, *President*
EMP: 5
SALES (est): 332K **Privately Held**
WEB: www.harborsoft.com
SIC: 7371 7372 Computer software development; prepackaged software

(G-12452)
KILWINS QULTY CONFECTIONS INC (PA)
Also Called: Kilwins Chocolate Kitchen
1050 Bay View Rd (49770-9006)
PHONE................................231 347-3800
Don McCarty, *President*
Becky Lagerquist, *Controller*
EMP: 3 EST: 1995
SALES (est): 126.5K **Privately Held**
SIC: 2066 Chocolate bars, solid; chocolate candy, solid

(G-12453)
LAKEVIEW MANUFACTURING
1480 Mcdougal Rd (49770-9524)
PHONE................................231 348-2596
Gilbert Sevener, *Owner*
EMP: 3
SQ FT: 3,500
SALES: 150K **Privately Held**
SIC: 2431 Millwork

(G-12454)
LANZEN-PETOSKEY LLC
126 Fulton St (49770-2932)
PHONE................................231 881-9602
Terry Lanzen, *President*
EMP: 21
SALES (est): 873.6K
SALES (corp-wide): 28.8MM **Privately Held**
SIC: 3444 Sheet metalwork
PA: Lanzen, Incorporated
100 Peyerk Ct
Bruce Twp MI 48065
586 771-7070

(G-12455)
MAGNETIC SYSTEMS INTERNATIONAL
3890 Charlevoix Rd (49770-8422)
PHONE................................231 582-9600
Michael Markiewicz, *Manager*
EMP: 4
SALES (est): 335.4K **Privately Held**
SIC: 3572 Magnetic storage devices, computer

(G-12456)
MANTHEI INC
3996 Charlevoix Rd (49770-8426)
PHONE................................231 347-4672
Tom Manthei, *President*
James Manthei, *Vice Pres*
Daniel Manthei, *Treasurer*
Jason Miller, *Sales Dir*
Ben Manthei, *Shareholder*
▲ EMP: 150 EST: 1945
SQ FT: 142,000
SALES (est): 27.2MM **Privately Held**
WEB: www.mantheiinc.com
SIC: 2435 Veneer stock, hardwood

(G-12457)
MANTHEI DEVELOPMENT CORP
Also Called: N D C Contracting
3996 Charlevoix Rd (49770-8426)
PHONE................................231 347-6282
Joe Sladek, *Manager*
EMP: 6
SALES (corp-wide): 2.9MM **Privately Held**
WEB: www.mantheidevelopment.com
SIC: 3273 Ready-mixed concrete
PA: Manthei Development Corporation
5481 Us Highway 31 S
Charlevoix MI 49720
231 547-6595

(G-12458)
MANTHEI VENEER MILL INC
5491 Manthei Rd (49770-9744)
PHONE................................231 347-4688
Tom Manthei, *President*
James Manthei, *President*
Mark Manthei, *Admin Sec*
EMP: 3 EST: 2000
SALES (est): 291.1K **Privately Held**
SIC: 2435 Hardwood veneer & plywood

(G-12459)
MITCHELL GRAPHICS INC (PA)
2363 Mitchell Park Dr (49770-9600)
PHONE................................231 347-4635
Gary Fedus, *President*
Richard Dietrick, *Vice Pres*
Jeff Streelman, *Vice Pres*
Faith Sando, *Project Mgr*
Walter Lightfoot, *Purch Mgr*
▲ EMP: 42
SQ FT: 31,000
SALES (est): 6.2MM **Privately Held**
WEB: www.mitchellgraphics.com
SIC: 2752 2791 2789 Commercial printing, offset; post cards, picture: lithographed; typesetting; bookbinding & related work

(G-12460)
NORTHERN MICH HARDWOODS INC
5151 Manthei Rd (49770-9744)
PHONE................................231 347-4575
Philip Manthei, *President*
Steve Maniaci, *Treasurer*
Carol Manthei, *Admin Sec*
EMP: 15
SQ FT: 6,000
SALES (est): 2.7MM **Privately Held**
WEB: www.nmhardwoods.com
SIC: 2421 3442 2435 2431 Lumber: rough, sawed or planed; metal doors, sash & trim; hardwood veneer & plywood; millwork; hardwood dimension & flooring mills

(G-12461)
NORTHERN MICH PAIN SPECIALIST
1890 Us Highway 131 (49770-8344)
PHONE................................231 487-4650
Gary L Fuchs, *Principal*
Marilea Rogers, *Marketing Staff*
EMP: 5
SALES (est): 1.1MM **Privately Held**
SIC: 2435 Hardwood veneer & plywood

(G-12462)
NORTHERN MICH RGIONAL HLTH SYS
416 Connable Ave (49770-2212)
PHONE................................231 487-4094
David M Zechman, *President*
EMP: 10
SALES: 6MM **Privately Held**
SIC: 2435 Hardwood veneer & plywood

(G-12463)
NORTHERN MICHIGAN REVIEW INC (PA)
Also Called: Petoskey News Review
319 State St (49770-2746)
P.O. Box 528 (49770-0528)
PHONE................................231 547-6558
Doug Caldwell, *President*
Paul Gunderson, *General Mgr*
EMP: 49
SQ FT: 18,000
SALES (est): 9.2MM **Privately Held**
SIC: 2711 Commercial printing & newspaper publishing combined

(G-12464)
NORTHERN MICHIGAN REVIEW INC
Also Called: Charlevoix Courier, The
319 State St (49770-2746)
P.O. Box 117, Charlevoix (49720-0117)
PHONE................................231 547-6558
Jason Ellenburg, *Vice Pres*
Ken Winter, *Vice Pres*
Robert Morris, *VP Bus Dvlpt*
Kim Taylor, *Sales Staff*
Jeff Johnson, *Marketing Staff*
EMP: 4
SALES (corp-wide): 9.2MM **Privately Held**
SIC: 2711 Newspapers: publishing only, not printed on site
PA: Northern Michigan Review, Inc.
319 State St
Petoskey MI 49770
231 547-6558

(G-12465)
NORTHWOODS HOT SPRNG SPAS INC
2050 M 119 (49770-8962)
PHONE................................231 347-1134
Charlie Philliben, *President*
Christopher Lewis, *General Mgr*
EMP: 7 EST: 2016
SALES (est): 498.3K **Privately Held**
SIC: 5999 2452 Spas & hot tubs; sauna rooms, prefabricated, wood

(G-12466)
NU-TECH NORTH INC
445 E Mitchell St Ste 6 (49770-2670)
P.O. Box 486 (49770-0486)
PHONE................................231 347-1992
Joe Mullin, *President*
EMP: 7 EST: 1995
SALES (est): 527.3K **Privately Held**
SIC: 2759 Commercial printing

(G-12467)
PAUL W REED DDS
Also Called: Paul W Reed DDS Ms
414 Petoskey St (49770-2618)
PHONE................................231 347-4145
Paul W Reed, *Owner*
EMP: 11
SALES (est): 908.6K **Privately Held**
SIC: 3842 8021 Braces, orthopedic; offices & clinics of dentists

(G-12468)
PERSONAL GRAPHICS
270 Creekside Dr (49770-7606)
PHONE................................231 347-6347
Debra Baker, *Owner*
Jacobe Mooar, *Co-Owner*
EMP: 4
SALES (est): 331.9K **Privately Held**
WEB: www.personalgraphicsinc.com
SIC: 2395 2752 2759 Embroidery products, except schiffli machine; commercial printing, lithographic; screen printing

(G-12469)
PETOSKEY PLASTICS INC (PA)
1 Petoskey St (49770-2480)
PHONE................................231 347-2602
Paul C Keiswetter, *President*
Jason Keiswetter, *Exec VP*
Doug Stepanian, *Vice Pres*
Tony Ayoub, *Production*
Paul Shepard, *Purch Mgr*
◆ EMP: 30
SQ FT: 11,000
SALES (est): 139MM **Privately Held**
SIC: 3081 Plastic film & sheet

(G-12470)
PETOSKEY PLASTICS INC
4226 Us Highway 31 S (49770-9723)
PHONE................................231 347-2602
Allan Hopkins, *Plant Mgr*
Zander Keiswetter, *Sales Staff*
Michelle Witthoeft, *Sales Staff*
Alan Hopkins, *Branch Mgr*
Tim Harness, *Maintence Staff*
EMP: 180
SALES (corp-wide): 139MM **Privately Held**
SIC: 3081 Plastic film & sheet
PA: Petoskey Plastics, Inc.
1 Petoskey St
Petoskey MI 49770
231 347-2602

(G-12471)
PRINT SHOP
324 Michigan St (49770-2663)
PHONE................................231 347-2000
Denise Berger, *Owner*
EMP: 7
SQ FT: 2,000
SALES (est): 693.3K **Privately Held**
SIC: 2752 Commercial printing, offset

(G-12472)
REVIEW DIRECTORIES INC
Also Called: Phone Guide
311 E Mitchell St (49770-2615)
PHONE................................231 347-8606
Doug Caldwell, *President*
Beth Simon, *Production*
Phyllis Johnson, *Advt Staff*
EMP: 14
SALES (est): 823.8K **Privately Held**
WEB: www.thephoneguide.com
SIC: 2741 Telephone & other directory publishing

(G-12473)
ROSENTHAL LOGGING
577 Blanchard Rd (49770-9638)
PHONE................................231 348-8168
Klaus Rosenthal, *Principal*
EMP: 3 EST: 2000
SALES (est): 162.6K **Privately Held**
SIC: 2411 Logging camps & contractors

(G-12474)
RUFF LIFE LLC
309 Howard St (49770-2413)
PHONE................................231 347-1214
EMP: 4
SALES (est): 187.3K **Privately Held**
SIC: 5999 3999 Pet supplies; pet supplies

(G-12475)
SIGN AND DESIGN
427 Creekside Dr (49770-7624)
PHONE................................231 348-9256
Robert Scudder, *Owner*
EMP: 6
SALES (est): 456.6K **Privately Held**
WEB: www.signanddesign.com
SIC: 3993 Signs, not made in custom sign painting shops

(G-12476)
SLUDGEHAMMER GROUP LTD
4772 Us Highway 131 (49770-9220)
PHONE................................231 348-5866
Arthur Jenks, *CEO*
Daniel E Wickham, *President*
Anthony Wiegman, *COO*
EMP: 5
SALES: 1.8MM **Privately Held**
SIC: 3589 Sewage & water treatment equipment

(G-12477)
TIMS UNDERBODY
1702 Standish Ave Ste 1 (49770-8899)
PHONE................................231 347-9146
Tim Slappy, *Owner*
EMP: 3 EST: 2002
SALES (est): 132.3K **Privately Held**
SIC: 1389 Construction, repair & dismantling services

Pewamo
Ionia County

(G-12478)
DEVEREAUX SAW MILL INC
2872 N Hubbardston Rd (48873-9721)
P.O. Box 67 (48873-0067)
PHONE................................989 593-2552
Bruce Devereaux, *President*
Beth Smith, *Pub Rel Mgr*
Ann Thelen, *Treasurer*
▼ EMP: 60 EST: 1965

GEOGRAPHIC SECTION

Pinconning - Bay County (G-12506)

SALES (est): 11.5MM **Privately Held**
WEB: www.devereauxsawmill.com
SIC: **2421** 2426 Lumber: rough, sawed or planed; lumber, hardwood dimension

(G-12479)
GOODRICH BROTHERS INC (PA)
11409 E Blwter Hwy Pewamo (48873)
P.O. Box 362 (48873-0362)
PHONE..................................989 593-2104
Jerald Goodrich, *President*
Alfred Goodrich III, *Corp Secy*
Anthony Goodrich, *Vice Pres*
EMP: 28
SQ FT: 60,000
SALES (est): 6.1MM **Privately Held**
SIC: **5211** 2431 Millwork & lumber; door & window products; millwork; moldings, wood: unfinished & prefinished

(G-12480)
WESTENDORFF TRANSIT MIX
Also Called: Westendorff Redi-Mix
3344 N Hubbardston Rd (48873-9614)
PHONE..................................989 593-2488
Roy Westendorff, *Owner*
EMP: 6
SALES (est): 390.6K **Privately Held**
SIC: **3273** Ready-mixed concrete

Pickford
Chippewa County

(G-12481)
BEACOM ENTERPRISES INC
Also Called: Beacom's Chipping & Logging
6671 E Rockview Rd (49774-9038)
PHONE..................................906 647-3831
William Beacom, *President*
Rhoda Beacom, *Corp Secy*
EMP: 9
SALES (est): 2.5MM **Privately Held**
SIC: **2411** Logging camps & contractors

(G-12482)
NORTH ARROW LOG HOMES INC
5943 N 3 Mile Rd (49774-9023)
P.O. Box 645, Cedarville (49719-0645)
PHONE..................................906 484-5524
Lyle Kelley, *President*
Theresa Kelly, *Vice Pres*
EMP: 6
SALES (est): 785.3K **Privately Held**
WEB: www.northarrowloghomes.com
SIC: **2452** 1521 Log cabins, prefabricated, wood; prefabricated single-family house erection

(G-12483)
ROBINSON FENCE CO INC
Also Called: Michalski Wilbert Vault Co
24254 S Clegg Rd (49774-9194)
PHONE..................................906 647-3301
Thomas L Michalski, *President*
Mary Jean Michalski, *Vice Pres*
EMP: 3
SALES (est): 266.3K **Privately Held**
SIC: **1799** 3496 Fence construction; fencing, made from purchased wire

---

Pierson
Montcalm County

(G-12484)
LUMBERJACK LOGGING LLC
4778 Whitefish Woods Dr (49339-9448)
PHONE..................................616 799-4657
Dustin Hiler, *Administration*
EMP: 3
SALES (est): 161.8K **Privately Held**
SIC: **2411** Logging camps & contractors

Pigeon
Huron County

(G-12485)
ACTIVE FEED COMPANY (PA)
Also Called: Farm Crest Foods
7564 Pigeon Rd (48755-9597)
P.O. Box 350 (48755-0350)
PHONE..................................989 453-2472
Joseph J Maust, *President*
Emma Maust, *Vice Pres*
▲ EMP: 54 EST: 1960
SQ FT: 12,000
SALES (est): 29.3MM **Privately Held**
WEB: www.activefeedco.com
SIC: **5191** 0252 2048 Feed; chicken eggs; prepared feeds

(G-12486)
AXIS MACHINING INC
7061 Hartley St (48755-5191)
P.O. Box 170 (48755-0170)
PHONE..................................989 453-3943
Leroy Wurst, *President*
Devere Sturm, *Vice Pres*
Mark Smith, *Purch Mgr*
EMP: 100
SQ FT: 20,000
SALES (est): 17.9MM **Privately Held**
WEB: www.axismachining.net
SIC: **3325** Alloy steel castings, except investment

(G-12487)
BERNE ENTERPRISES INC
7190 Berne Rd (48755-9784)
PHONE..................................989 453-3235
Keith Wurst, *President*
EMP: 16
SQ FT: 35,000
SALES (est): 4.1MM **Privately Held**
WEB: www.berneenterprises.com
SIC: **3325** 3321 3369 Alloy steel castings, except investment; ductile iron castings; gray iron castings; nonferrous foundries

(G-12488)
D B TOOL COMPANY INC
6443 Dunn Rd (48755-9733)
PHONE..................................989 453-2429
David Bouck, *President*
Sue Bouck, *Corp Secy*
EMP: 8
SALES (est): 600K **Privately Held**
SIC: **3569** Filters

(G-12489)
GRM CORPORATION (PA)
39 N Caseville Rd (48755-9704)
P.O. Box 689 (48755-0689)
PHONE..................................989 453-2322
Lee Steinman, *CEO*
Sherril L Steinman, *Chairman*
EMP: 68
SQ FT: 16,000
SALES (est): 8.3MM **Privately Held**
SIC: **2822** 2869 3089 Silicone rubbers; industrial organic chemicals; molding primary plastic

(G-12490)
GRM CORPORATION
7375 Crescent Beach Rd (48755-9602)
PHONE..................................989 453-2322
James Steinman, *Manager*
EMP: 5 **Privately Held**
SIC: **3053** Gaskets & sealing devices
PA: Grm Corporation
   39 N Caseville Rd
   Pigeon MI 48755

(G-12491)
HURON CASTING INC (PA)
Also Called: H C I
7050 Hartley St (48755-5190)
P.O. Box 679 (48755-0679)
PHONE..................................989 453-3933
Leroy Wurst, *President*
Devere Sturm, *Vice Pres*
Duane Koroleski, *Plant Supt*
Linda Beyer, *Purchasing*
Dave Beachy, *Engineer*
◆ EMP: 450
SQ FT: 350,000
SALES (est): 104.7MM **Privately Held**
WEB: www.huroncasting.com
SIC: **3325** 3369 Alloy steel castings, except investment; nonferrous foundries

(G-12492)
RICHMONDS STEEL INC
6767 Pigeon Rd (48755-9502)
P.O. Box 290 (48755-0290)
PHONE..................................989 453-7010
Nick Pavlichek, *President*
Chris Pavlichek, *Vice Pres*
EMP: 15
SQ FT: 22,000
SALES (est): 1.5MM **Privately Held**
SIC: **3441** Fabricated structural metal

(G-12493)
THUMB TRUCK AND TRAILER CO
Also Called: Daryls Use Truck Sales
8305 Geiger Rd (48755-9562)
PHONE..................................989 453-3133
Daryl Elenbaum, *President*
Debra Heilig, *Admin Sec*
EMP: 9
SQ FT: 3,300
SALES (est): 1.3MM **Privately Held**
WEB: www.thumbtruck.com
SIC: **3715** Trailer bodies; semitrailers for truck tractors

(G-12494)
VOLLMER READY-MIX INC (PA)
196 S Caseville Rd 204 (48755-9531)
PHONE..................................989 453-2262
David R Vollmer, *President*
Audrey Vollmer, *Treasurer*
Jenny Vollmer, *Manager*
EMP: 5 EST: 1958
SQ FT: 4,000
SALES (est): 660K **Privately Held**
SIC: **3273** Ready-mixed concrete

Pinckney
Livingston County

(G-12495)
AKAMAI TECHNOLOGIES INC
9394 Anne St (48169-8933)
PHONE..................................734 424-1142
Thorn Vogel, *Principal*
EMP: 3
SALES (corp-wide): 2.7B **Publicly Held**
SIC: **7372** Prepackaged software
PA: Akamai Technologies, Inc.
   150 Broadway Ste 100
   Cambridge MA 02142
   617 444-3000

(G-12496)
ECONO PRINT INC
10312 Dexter Pinckney Rd (48169-8918)
P.O. Box 823 (48169-0823)
PHONE..................................734 878-5806
Ted Stilber, *President*
EMP: 8
SQ FT: 1,500
SALES (est): 1.1MM **Privately Held**
WEB: www.econoprintusa.com
SIC: **2752** 7331 2791 2789 Commercial printing, offset; direct mail advertising services; typesetting; bookbinding & related work

(G-12497)
FAMETHIS INC
10829 Wynns Rd (48169-8830)
PHONE..................................734 645-9100
Dustin Crawford, *Principal*
EMP: 3
SALES (est): 98K **Privately Held**
SIC: **2711** Newspapers

(G-12498)
FROYO PINCKNEY LLC
3282 Swarthout Rd (48169-9253)
PHONE..................................248 310-4465
Scott Roller, *Principal*
EMP: 3 EST: 2018
SALES (est): 140.2K **Privately Held**
SIC: **2024** Yogurt desserts, frozen

(G-12499)
LEXATRONICS LLC
9768 Cedar Lake Rd (48169-8826)
PHONE..................................734 878-6237
John Lincsay PHD, *President*
EMP: 4
SALES (est): 315.7K **Privately Held**
SIC: **3674** Radiation sensors

(G-12500)
MIDWEST AQUATICS GROUP INC
Also Called: Portage Yacht Club
8930 Dexter Pinckney Rd (48169-9430)
PHONE..................................734 426-4155
Thomas F Ehman, *President*
Ruth Ehman, *Vice Pres*
EMP: 8
SQ FT: 13,000
SALES (est): 357.5K **Privately Held**
WEB: www.ms-pyc.com
SIC: **5551** 7997 5088 5812 Sailboats & equipment; sailboats, unpowered; marine supplies; boating club, membership; marine crafts & supplies; marine supplies; eating places; marinas; boat building & repairing

(G-12501)
MJL PUBLISHING LLC
2898 Masters Ct (48169-8570)
PHONE..................................734 268-6187
Matthews Laviola,
EMP: 3 EST: 2007
SALES (est): 203.8K **Privately Held**
SIC: **2741** Miscellaneous publishing

(G-12502)
PINCKNEY AUTOMATIC & MFG
6128 Cedar Lake Rd (48169-8807)
P.O. Box 98 (48169-0098)
PHONE..................................734 878-3430
Robert Dudenhoefer, *President*
Barbara J Dudenhoefer, *Corp Secy*
EMP: 9
SQ FT: 3,000
SALES (est): 733.8K **Privately Held**
SIC: **3451** 3492 3452 Screw machine products; fluid power valves & hose fittings; bolts, nuts, rivets & washers

(G-12503)
PTSPOWER LLC
Also Called: Power-Technology-Solutions
10000 Stnchfield Woods Rd (48169-9452)
PHONE..................................734 268-6076
Mike Orginski, *President*
EMP: 3
SALES: 200K **Privately Held**
SIC: **3823** Combustion control instruments

(G-12504)
STEP INTO SUCCESS INC
Also Called: Ellsworth, Belinda
9940 Sunrise Dr (48169-9423)
P.O. Box 712, Lakeland (48143-0712)
PHONE..................................734 426-1075
Belinda Ellsworth, *President*
EMP: 8
SALES: 717K **Privately Held**
WEB: www.stepintosuccess.com
SIC: **8299** 8999 2759 Educational services; lecturing services; magazines: printing

(G-12505)
VORTEK
440 S Dexter St (48169-9070)
PHONE..................................248 767-2992
EMP: 4
SALES (est): 423.3K **Privately Held**
SIC: **3714** Motor vehicle parts & accessories

Pinconning
Bay County

(G-12506)
BERTHIAUME SLAUGHTER HOUSE
719 Jane St (48650-9404)
PHONE..................................989 879-4921

Robert Berthiaume, *President*
Charlie Berthiaume, *General Mgr*
EMP: 6
SALES: 370K **Privately Held**
SIC: 2011 0751 Meat packing plants; slaughtering: custom livestock services

(G-12507)
CONAIR NORTH AMERICA
Also Called: Iteg
503 S Mercer St (48650-9309)
PHONE..................................814 437-6861
Chris Weinrich, *General Mgr*
Michael Bloom, *Research*
EMP: 50
SALES (est): 4.4MM **Privately Held**
SIC: 3569 General industrial machinery

(G-12508)
KAISER FOODS INC
Also Called: Kaiser Pickles
1474 W Cody Estey Rd (48650-7962)
PHONE..................................989 879-2087
Lynnea Matthews, *Branch Mgr*
EMP: 11
SALES (corp-wide): 26.1MM **Privately Held**
SIC: 2035 Pickles, vinegar
PA: Kaiser Foods, Inc.
500 York St
Cincinnati OH 45214
513 621-2053

(G-12509)
LLOYDS CABINET SHOP INC
1947 N Huron Rd (48650-9773)
PHONE..................................989 879-3015
Ken Selle, *President*
EMP: 15
SQ FT: 24,000
SALES (est): 2.2MM **Privately Held**
WEB: www.lloydscabinetshop.com
SIC: 2434 5211 Wood kitchen cabinets; cabinets, kitchen

(G-12510)
MR CHIPS INC (HQ)
2628 N Huron Rd (48650-9512)
PHONE..................................989 879-3555
Joseph F Janicke, *President*
Randy Hugo, *Vice Pres*
Jay Janicke, *Vice Pres*
Sharon Janicke, *Vice Pres*
▲ **EMP:** 7 **EST:** 1969
SALES (est): 1.9MM
SALES (corp-wide): 92.1MM **Privately Held**
WEB: www.bayviewfoods.com
SIC: 2035 Pickles, sauces & salad dressings
PA: Bay View Food Products Company
2606 N Huron Rd
Pinconning MI
989 879-3555

(G-12511)
PINCONNING JOURNAL
110 E 3rd St (48650-9314)
P.O. Box 626 (48650-0626)
PHONE..................................989 879-3811
Thomas N Johnson, *Owner*
Marcia Johnson, *Co-Owner*
EMP: 3
SALES (est): 121K **Privately Held**
SIC: 2711 Newspapers, publishing & printing

(G-12512)
PINCONNING METALS INC
1140 E Cody Estey Rd (48650-8485)
P.O. Box 36 (48650-0036)
PHONE..................................989 879-3144
Richard Yaros, *President*
Bonnie Yaros, *Corp Secy*
Gary Yaros, *Manager*
EMP: 6
SQ FT: 10,000
SALES (est): 878.4K **Privately Held**
SIC: 3469 3465 3089 Stamping metal for the trade; body parts, automobile: stamped metal; molding primary plastic

(G-12513)
TIMS CABINET INC
Also Called: Tim's Cabinet Shop
5309 S Huron Rd (48650-6409)
PHONE..................................989 846-9831
Tim Jasman, *President*
Deborah Jasman, *Vice Pres*
EMP: 7
SQ FT: 5,000
SALES: 400K **Privately Held**
SIC: 1751 2521 2434 Cabinet building & installation; wood office filing cabinets & bookcases; wood kitchen cabinets

(G-12514)
TUBULAR METAL SYSTEMS LLC (DH)
401 E 5th St (48650-9321)
PHONE..................................989 879-2611
Dan Mullins,
▲ **EMP:** 48
SQ FT: 225,000
SALES (est): 30.5MM
SALES (corp-wide): 4.1B **Privately Held**
SIC: 3465 Body parts, automobile: stamped metal
HQ: Global Automotive Systems, Llc
1780 Pond Run
Auburn Hills MI 48326
248 299-7500

Pittsford
Hillsdale County

(G-12515)
BERLIN HOLDINGS LLC
Also Called: Alumi Span
4445 S Pittsford Rd (49271-9864)
P.O. Box 205 (49271-0205)
PHONE..................................517 523-2444
Rex D Hoover, *Ch of Bd*
David Berlin, *Mng Member*
EMP: 8 **EST:** 1957
SQ FT: 3,000
SALES: 1MM **Privately Held**
WEB: www.alumi-span.com
SIC: 3448 3999 Docks: prefabricated metal; dock equipment & supplies, industrial

Plainwell
Allegan County

(G-12516)
ACRO-TECH MANUFACTURING INC
12229 M 89 (49080-9049)
PHONE..................................269 629-4300
Hans Nikolaas, *President*
Robert Tenhoor, *Vice Pres*
Jan Nikolaas, *Treasurer*
EMP: 13
SALES (est): 1.8MM **Privately Held**
SIC: 3599 Machine shop, jobbing & repair

(G-12517)
AGGREGATE INDUSTRIES - MWR INC
475 12th St (49080-1901)
PHONE..................................269 685-5937
EMP: 20
SALES (corp-wide): 27.6B **Privately Held**
SIC: 3273 Ready-mixed concrete
HQ: Aggregate Industries - Mwr, Inc.
2815 Dodd Rd
Eagan MN 55121
651 683-0600

(G-12518)
ANO-KAL COMPANY
734 Jersey St (49080-1668)
PHONE..................................269 685-5743
Richard Kinsey, *Owner*
EMP: 10 **EST:** 2004
SALES (est): 1.2MM **Privately Held**
SIC: 3471 Anodizing (plating) of metals or formed products

(G-12519)
CHIPPEWA DEVELOPMENT INC
Also Called: Empire Forest Products Company
960 Industrial Pkwy (49080-1402)
PHONE..................................269 685-2646
William L Adams, *President*
▼ **EMP:** 14
SQ FT: 8,000
SALES (est): 1.5MM **Privately Held**
SIC: 2431 Millwork

(G-12520)
CONSUMERS CONCRETE CORPORATION
465 12th St (49080-1901)
PHONE..................................800 643-4235
Jerry Deboer, *Opers Mgr*
Brad Deneau, *Opers-Prdtn-Mfg*
Tom Thomas, *Engineer*
Mike Weber, *Marketing Mgr*
EMP: 6
SALES (corp-wide): 102.9MM **Privately Held**
WEB: www.consumersconcrete.com
SIC: 3273 Ready-mixed concrete
PA: Consumers Concrete Corporation
3508 S Sprinkle Rd
Kalamazoo MI 49001
269 342-0136

(G-12521)
DARBY METAL TREATING INC
892 Wakefield (49080-1425)
PHONE..................................269 204-6504
Tom Darby, *President*
EMP: 14
SALES (est): 2.2MM **Privately Held**
SIC: 3398 Metal heat treating

(G-12522)
DEANS ICE CREAM INC
307 N Sherwood Ave (49080-1330)
PHONE..................................269 685-6641
Gery Bentley, *President*
Gerald Bentley, *President*
EMP: 12 **EST:** 1920
SALES: 610K **Privately Held**
SIC: 2024 5812 Ice cream, bulk; drive-in restaurant

(G-12523)
DEDICATED CONVERTING GROUP INC
155 10th St (49080-9746)
PHONE..................................269 685-8430
John D Skelton II, *Branch Mgr*
EMP: 18
SALES (corp-wide): 5MM **Privately Held**
SIC: 2679 Paper products, converted
PA: Dedicated Converting Group, Inc.
3504 Norwood Cir
Richardson TX 75082
972 496-2588

(G-12524)
E LEET WOODWORKING
10175 3 Mile Rd (49080-9020)
PHONE..................................269 664-5203
Patrick J Leet, *Owner*
EMP: 5 **EST:** 1986
SALES (est): 593.8K **Privately Held**
SIC: 2431 Millwork

(G-12525)
FUSION FLEXO LLC
156 10th St (49080-9746)
P.O. Box 356 (49080-0356)
PHONE..................................269 685-5827
Grayce Lancaster, *Vice Pres*
Steve Berry, *Accounts Mgr*
Kristen Anderson, *Mng Member*
EMP: 20
SALES (corp-wide): 2.8MM **Privately Held**
SIC: 2796 Photoengraving plates, linecuts or halftones
PA: Fusion Flexo, Llc
6330 Canterwood Dr
Richland MI 49083
269 685-5827

(G-12526)
JBS PACKERLAND INC
11 11th St (49080-9711)
P.O. Box 247 (49080-0247)
PHONE..................................269 685-6886
Charlie Gach, *President*
Bob Pennock, *Vice Pres*
EMP: 24 **Publicly Held**
SIC: 2011 Boxed beef from meat slaughtered on site
HQ: Jbs Packerland, Inc.
1330 Lime Kiln Rd
Green Bay WI 54311
920 468-4000

(G-12527)
JBS PLAINWELL INC
11 11th St (49080-9711)
P.O. Box 247 (49080-0247)
PHONE..................................269 685-6886
Richard Besta, *Ch of Bd*
Paul Murray Jr, *President*
Craig Liegel, *Corp Secy*
Byron Marsh, *Purch Agent*
Joe Posada, *Purch Agent*
EMP: 250
SQ FT: 250,000
SALES (est): 32.7MM **Publicly Held**
SIC: 2011 Boxed beef from meat slaughtered on site
HQ: Jbs Usa Food Company
1770 Promontory Cir
Greeley CO 80634
970 506-8000

(G-12528)
KALAMAZOO METAL MUNCHER INC
3428 E B Ave (49080-8908)
PHONE..................................269 492-0268
Albert Kimball, *President*
James Lofts, *Vice Pres*
John Gay, *Treasurer*
EMP: 5 **EST:** 2011
SQ FT: 2,000
SALES (est): 381.9K **Privately Held**
SIC: 3441 Fabricated structural metal

(G-12529)
MAGIERA HOLDINGS INC
Also Called: Hytech Spring and Machine Co
950 Lincoln Pkwy (49080-1438)
PHONE..................................269 685-1768
Andrew Magiera, *President*
Mike Bowman, *Vice Pres*
EMP: 95
SQ FT: 63,438
SALES (est): 14.6MM **Privately Held**
WEB: www.hytechspring.com
SIC: 3495 3599 Wire springs; machine shop, jobbing & repair

(G-12530)
MICHIGAN PALLET INC
957 Industrial Pkwy (49080-1401)
PHONE..................................269 685-8802
Brad Dykstra, *Sales Mgr*
Paul Kamps, *Manager*
EMP: 15
SALES (corp-wide): 2.8MM **Privately Held**
SIC: 2448 Pallets, wood
PA: Michigan Pallet, Inc.
1225 N Saginaw St
Saint Charles MI 48655
989 865-9915

(G-12531)
MOTAN INC
320 Acorn St (49080-1412)
PHONE..................................269 685-1050
Mark McKibbin, *President*
Mark McKibben, *CFO*
Don Deluca, *Controller*
Sara Bassett, *Accounting Mgr*
Sara Reinhart, *Accounting Mgr*
▲ **EMP:** 30 **EST:** 1981
SQ FT: 30,000
SALES (est): 3.7MM
SALES (corp-wide): 150.7MM **Privately Held**
WEB: www.motan-inc.com
SIC: 3535 Conveyors & conveying equipment

GEOGRAPHIC SECTION Plymouth - Wayne County (G-12560)

PA: Motan Holding Gmbh
Stromeyersdorfstr. 12
Konstanz 78467
756 276-0

(G-12532)
OPTO SOLUTIONS INC
140 E Bridge St (49080-1718)
PHONE..................................269 254-9716
Todd Reynolds, *President*
Ryan Fisher, *Vice Pres*
EMP: 5 EST: 2010
SALES (est): 566.4K **Privately Held**
SIC: 3571 Electronic computers

(G-12533)
PACKERLAND PACKING CO
11 11th St (49080-9711)
P.O. Box 247 (49080-0247)
PHONE..................................269 685-6886
Paul Murray Sr, *President*
EMP: 3
SALES (est): 380.2K **Privately Held**
SIC: 2011 Meat packing plants

(G-12534)
PAUL MARSHALL & SON LOG LLC
7120 Marsh Rd (49080-9285)
PHONE..................................269 998-4440
Annette Bailey, *Principal*
EMP: 3 EST: 2010
SALES (est): 310.7K **Privately Held**
SIC: 2411 Logging camps & contractors

(G-12535)
PERCEPTIVE CONTROLS INC
140 E Bridge St (49080-1718)
PHONE..................................269 685-3040
Todd Reynolds, *President*
Ryan Fisher, *Vice Pres*
EMP: 29
SALES (est): 7.1MM **Privately Held**
SIC: 3823 Industrial process measurement equipment

(G-12536)
PERCEPTIVE INDUSTRIES INC
951 Industrial Pkwy (49080-1401)
PHONE..................................269 204-6768
Charles Dearman, *President*
Dean Decker, *Vice Pres*
Craig Sanford, *Engineer*
Pamela England, *Office Mgr*
Brad Hanna, *Manager*
EMP: 32
SQ FT: 26,000
SALES: 8MM **Privately Held**
WEB: www.perceptivecontrols.com
SIC: 3567 Industrial furnaces & ovens

(G-12537)
PLAINWELL ICE CREAM CO
621 E Bridge St (49080-1804)
PHONE..................................269 685-8586
Arthur Gaylord, *President*
Judy Gaylord, *Vice Pres*
EMP: 14
SQ FT: 2,100
SALES (est): 1.7MM **Privately Held**
SIC: 2024 Ice cream & frozen desserts

(G-12538)
PLAS-TECH MOLD AND DESIGN INC
946 Industrial Pkwy (49080-1402)
PHONE..................................269 225-1223
David J Williamson, *President*
Scott A Anson, *Vice Pres*
▲ EMP: 6
SQ FT: 5,000
SALES (est): 723.7K **Privately Held**
WEB: www.plas-techmold.com
SIC: 3544 Industrial molds

(G-12539)
PLASTISNOW LLC
Also Called: Msnow
200 Prince St (49080-1230)
PHONE..................................414 397-1233
Lucas Schrab, *Mng Member*
Adam Schrab,
EMP: 4
SALES: 433K **Privately Held**
SIC: 3949 7999 Snow skis; ski instruction

(G-12540)
PREFERRED PLASTICS INC (PA)
800 E Bridge St (49080-1800)
PHONE..................................269 685-5873
Tracy J Tucker, *CEO*
Daniel Julien, *Plant Mgr*
Fred Castaneda, *Engineer*
Greg Mathis, *Plant Engr*
Brittani Kincaid, *Human Res Mgr*
EMP: 80
SQ FT: 160,000
SALES (est): 15.7MM **Privately Held**
WEB: www.preferredplastics.net
SIC: 3089 Automotive parts, plastic; plastic processing

(G-12541)
RIDGE & KRAMER MOTOR SUPPLY CO
1286 M 89 (49080-1915)
PHONE..................................269 685-5838
Thomas Boerman, *Manager*
EMP: 4
SALES (corp-wide): 9.5MM **Privately Held**
SIC: 3714 Motor vehicle engines & parts
PA: Ridge & Kramer Motor Supply Co
123 W Napier Ave
Benton Harbor MI 49022
269 926-7151

(G-12542)
RIZZO PACKAGING INC
930 Lincoln Pkwy (49080-1438)
P.O. Box 278 (49080-0278)
PHONE..................................269 685-5808
Paul Rizzo, *President*
Bart A Rizzo, *Vice Pres*
Karen Weimer, *Accountant*
Phil Broekhuizen, *CIO*
Robert Fooy, *Executive*
EMP: 45
SQ FT: 40,000
SALES (est): 9.2MM **Privately Held**
WEB: www.rizzopackaging.com
SIC: 2631 2675 2621 Paperboard mills; cutouts, cardboard, die-cut; from purchased materials; packaging paper

(G-12543)
ROB ENTERPRISES INC
156 10th St (49080-9746)
P.O. Box 356 (49080-0356)
PHONE..................................269 685-5827
Brian Anderson, *CEO*
J Lee Murphy, *Admin Sec*
EMP: 15 EST: 1974
SQ FT: 10,000
SALES (est): 2.1MM **Privately Held**
WEB: www.hughesengraving.com
SIC: 2796 Photoengraving plates, linecuts or halftones

(G-12544)
SCHULTZ SAND GRAVEL LLC
173 8th St (49080-9724)
PHONE..................................269 720-7225
Denny L Schultz, *Principal*
EMP: 3
SALES (est): 183.6K **Privately Held**
SIC: 1442 Construction sand & gravel

(G-12545)
TALICOR INC (PA)
901 Lincoln Pkwy (49080-1452)
PHONE..................................269 685-2345
Nicole Hancock, *President*
Cheryl Sidhu, *Corp Secy*
▲ EMP: 20 EST: 1971
SQ FT: 21,500
SALES (est): 3.3MM **Privately Held**
WEB: www.talicor.com
SIC: 3944 Board games, children's & adults'

(G-12546)
TMD MACHINING INC
751 Wakefield (49080-1499)
P.O. Box 342 (49080-0342)
PHONE..................................269 685-3091
Tom Darby, *President*
Michelle Heeres, *Purch Agent*
Mike Myers, *Engineer*
Cody Stringham, *Human Res Mgr*
Jan Vernon, *Office Mgr*
EMP: 47
SQ FT: 18,000
SALES (est): 13.9MM **Privately Held**
WEB: www.tmdmach.com
SIC: 3599 Machine shop, jobbing & repair

(G-12547)
TOKUSEN HYTECH INC
Also Called: Hytech Spring and Machine Co.
950 Lincoln Pkwy (49080-1438)
PHONE..................................269 685-1768
Hiromi Kanai, *Ch of Bd*
Richard Graff, *President*
Kimberly Arthur, *Corp Secy*
Michael Bowman, *Vice Pres*
Barbara Magiera, *Vice Pres*
EMP: 125
SALES (est): 28.5MM **Privately Held**
SIC: 3495 3843 5047 Wire springs; dental metal; medical laboratory equipment; instruments, surgical & medical

(G-12548)
TOKUSEN HYTECH INC
Also Called: Hytech Spring and Machine
950 Lincoln Pkwy (49080-1438)
PHONE..................................269 658-1768
EMP: 99
SQ FT: 107,000
SALES (est): 8.8MM **Privately Held**
SIC: 3495 Mfg Wire Springs

(G-12549)
TRAVIS CREEK TOOLING
923 Industrial Pkwy (49080-1401)
P.O. Box 116, Kalamazoo (49004-0116)
PHONE..................................269 685-2000
Ronnie Bickings, *Owner*
EMP: 7
SQ FT: 4,000
SALES (est): 1MM **Privately Held**
SIC: 3089 Injection molding of plastics

(G-12550)
UCB ADVERTISING
12047 Oakridge Rd (49080-9273)
PHONE..................................269 808-2411
Tim Miller, *Vice Pres*
EMP: 4
SALES (est): 174.5K **Privately Held**
SIC: 3993 Electric signs

(G-12551)
WAYNE NOVICK
Also Called: Astral Projections Stage Ltg
113 4th St (49080-9717)
P.O. Box 645, Comstock (49041-0645)
PHONE..................................269 685-9818
Wayne Novick, *Owner*
EMP: 3
SALES: 150K **Privately Held**
SIC: 3648 7389 Decorative area lighting fixtures;

Pleasant Lake
Jackson County

(G-12552)
LARRYS TAXIDERMY INC
Also Called: Larry's Taxidermy Studio
8640 N Meridian Rd (49272-9752)
PHONE..................................517 769-6104
Larry W Angus, *President*
EMP: 5
SALES: 70K **Privately Held**
SIC: 7699 3111 Taxidermists; tanneries, leather

(G-12553)
PEAK MANUFACTURING INC
11855 Bunkerhill Rd (49272-9798)
PHONE..................................517 769-6900
Christopher A Salow, *CEO*
EMP: 30
SALES (est): 5.4MM **Privately Held**
WEB: www.peakmfgpro.com
SIC: 1241 7539 Coal mining services; machine shop, automotive

(G-12554)
SELFIES 2 HELPEASE INC
Also Called: Echopix
11855 Bunkerhill Rd (49272-9798)
PHONE..................................517 769-6900
Christopher Salow, *Principal*
EMP: 3
SALES (est): 71.1K **Privately Held**
SIC: 7372 Application computer software

Pleasant Ridge
Oakland County

(G-12555)
HANON PRINTING COMPANY
34 Cambridge Blvd (48069-1103)
PHONE..................................248 541-9099
C Robert Hanon, *President*
EMP: 4 EST: 1977
SQ FT: 3,400
SALES (est): 325.3K **Privately Held**
SIC: 2752 Commercial printing, offset

(G-12556)
TMC GROUP INC
26 Elm Park Blvd (48069-1105)
PHONE..................................248 819-6063
Kimberley Hanke, *President*
EMP: 15 EST: 2010
SALES (est): 721.6K **Privately Held**
SIC: 8711 8733 8999 3679 Professional engineer; scientific research agency; technical writing; electronic circuits; storage batteries; oils & greases, blending & compounding

Plymouth
Wayne County

(G-12557)
A & D PLASTICS INC
1255 S Mill St (48170-4318)
PHONE..................................734 455-2255
Gerald A Jagacki, *President*
EMP: 20 EST: 1968
SQ FT: 20,000
SALES (est): 1.8MM **Privately Held**
WEB: www.adplastic.com
SIC: 3544 Forms (molds), for foundry & plastics working machinery; special dies & tools

(G-12558)
A2 ENERGY SYSTEMS
45209 Helm St (48170-6023)
PHONE..................................734 622-9800
Glenn Theisen,
EMP: 5
SALES (est): 598K **Privately Held**
SIC: 3499 Machine bases, metal

(G-12559)
AA ANDERSON & CO INC
Also Called: Anderson Process
41304 Concept Dr (48170-4253)
P.O. Box 324, Farmington Hills (48332-0324)
PHONE..................................248 476-7782
David Tatro, *Manager*
EMP: 39
SALES (corp-wide): 29.4MM **Privately Held**
SIC: 5084 3569 Industrial machinery & equipment; liquid automation machinery & equipment
PA: A.A. Anderson & Co., Inc.
21365 Gateway Ct
Brookfield WI 53045
262 784-3340

(G-12560)
ABSOPURE WATER COMPANY LLC
8835 General Dr (48170-4623)
P.O. Box 701220 (48170-0961)
PHONE..................................734 459-8000
Michael Nagle, *Vice Pres*
Dennis Simmer, *Manager*
EMP: 300

Plymouth - Wayne County (G-12561)

GEOGRAPHIC SECTION

SALES (corp-wide): 94.7MM **Privately Held**
WEB: www.absopure.com
SIC: **2086** Water, pasteurized: packaged in cans, bottles, etc.
PA: Absopure Water Company Llc
  8845 General Dr
  Plymouth MI 48170
  313 898-1200

(G-12561)
ACTION PRINTECH INC
41079 Concept Dr (48170-4252)
PHONE..................................734 207-6000
Chris Dunlap, *President*
Estelle Dunlap, *Vice Pres*
Linda Dunlap, *Treasurer*
EMP: 20
SQ FT: 17,000
SALES (est): 4.3MM **Privately Held**
SIC: **2752** 7336 Commercial printing, offset; graphic arts & related design

(G-12562)
ADEPT BROACHING CO
6253 Barbara Ln (48170-5000)
PHONE..................................734 427-9221
Raymond Monticelli, *President*
Linda Monticelli, *Vice Pres*
EMP: 5 EST: 1962
SQ FT: 8,000
SALES: 400K **Privately Held**
SIC: **3599** Machine shop, jobbing & repair

(G-12563)
ADIENT INC (DH)
49200 Halyard Dr (48170-2481)
PHONE..................................734 254-5000
Doug Del Grosso, *CEO*
Nirav Patel, *Counsel*
Byron Foster, *Exec VP*
Neil Marchuk, *Exec VP*
Bruce McDonald, *Exec VP*
EMP: 79
SALES (est): 638.7MM **Privately Held**
SIC: **2531** Seats, automobile

(G-12564)
ADIENT US LLC (DH)
49200 Halyard Dr (48170-2481)
PHONE..................................734 254-5000
Cathleen Ebacher, *President*
Jim Conklin, *Vice Pres*
James Huang, *Vice Pres*
Mike Muncie, *Vice Pres*
Beth Dillard, *Production*
◆ EMP: 1100 EST: 1964
SQ FT: 70,000
SALES (est): 1.3B **Privately Held**
SIC: **3714** Motor vehicle parts & accessories

(G-12565)
ADIENT US LLC
47700 Halyard Dr (48170-2477)
P.O. Box 8010 (48170-8010)
PHONE..................................734 414-9215
Falko Jaehner, *Engineer*
Jim Keys, *Branch Mgr*
EMP: 300 **Privately Held**
SIC: **3714** Motor vehicle parts & accessories
HQ: Adient Us Llc
  49200 Halyard Dr
  Plymouth MI 48170
  734 254-5000

(G-12566)
ADIENT US LLC
45000 Helm St (48170-6046)
PHONE..................................734 414-9215
EMP: 8 **Privately Held**
SIC: **3714** Motor vehicle parts & accessories
HQ: Adient Us Llc
  49200 Halyard Dr
  Plymouth MI 48170
  734 254-5000

(G-12567)
ADVANCED AVIONICS INC
Also Called: Laser Blast
6118 Gotfredson Rd (48170-5073)
PHONE..................................734 259-5300
Carla Ewald, *President*
Timothy Ewald, *Vice Pres*
Mike Ewald, *Bd of Directors*
EMP: 9
SQ FT: 2,300
SALES (est): 1.9MM **Privately Held**
WEB: www.laser-blast.com
SIC: **3699** Heat emission operating apparatus

(G-12568)
ALLIANCE FRANCHISE BRANDS LLC (PA)
Also Called: Kwik Kopy Printing Canada
47585 Galleon Dr (48170-2466)
PHONE..................................248 596-8600
Carl Gerhardt, *CEO*
Julie Ledford, *Business Mgr*
Joe Haddad, *Exec VP*
Mike Cline, *Vice Pres*
Tom Hutchinson, *Vice Pres*
EMP: 20
SALES (est): 44.2MM **Privately Held**
SIC: **2752** Commercial printing, offset

(G-12569)
AMCOR RIGID PACKAGING USA LLC (HQ)
Also Called: Amcor Rigid Plas - Manchester
40600 Ann Arbor Rd E # 201 (48170-4675)
PHONE..................................734 428-9741
Michael Schmitt, *President*
Greg Rosati, *Business Mgr*
Scott Chambery, *Vice Pres*
Jeff McGroryjr, *Engineer*
Garry Noonan, *CFO*
◆ EMP: 58
SALES (est): 197.1MM **Privately Held**
WEB: www.slpcamericas.com
SIC: **3089** Plastic containers, except foam

(G-12570)
AMERICAN FURUKAWA INC (DH)
Also Called: A F I
47677 Galleon Dr (48170-2466)
PHONE..................................734 254-0344
Kazuhisa Sakata, *CEO*
Dave Thomas, *Senior VP*
Toru Umemoto, *Vice Pres*
Hisako Araki-Das, *Sales Staff*
Jeff Gearhart, *Sales Staff*
▲ EMP: 42
SQ FT: 24,000
SALES (est): 22.7MM **Privately Held**
WEB: www.americanfurukawa.com
SIC: **3357** 3572 5013 5065 Fiber optic cable (insulated); computer disk & drum drives & components; automotive supplies & parts; electronic parts

(G-12571)
AN CORPORATE CENTER LLC
Also Called: American Speedy Printing
47585 Galleon Dr (48170-2466)
PHONE..................................248 669-1188
Magda Dudek, *Human Res Dir*
Laura Pierce-Marutz, *Mng Member*
Mario Grech,
Michael Marcantonio,
Robert Milroy,
EMP: 22 EST: 1971
SQ FT: 25,000
SALES (est): 6.3MM
SALES (corp-wide): 44.2MM **Privately Held**
SIC: **2752** 7334 2789 2759 Commercial printing, offset; photocopying & duplicating services; bookbinding & related work; commercial printing
PA: Alliance Franchise Brands Llc
  47585 Galleon Dr
  Plymouth MI 48170
  248 596-8600

(G-12572)
ARGENT INTERNATIONAL INC
Also Called: Argent Automotive Systems
41016 Concept Dr (48170-4252)
P.O. Box 701007 (48170-0957)
PHONE..................................734 582-9800
Fred Perenic, *President*
◆ EMP: 128 EST: 1978
SQ FT: 84,000
SALES (est): 56.9MM **Privately Held**
WEB: www.argent-automotive.com
SIC: **2891** Adhesives

(G-12573)
ARGENT TAPE & LABEL INC (PA)
41016 Concept Dr Ste A (48170-4252)
P.O. Box 701007 (48170-0957)
PHONE..................................734 582-9956
Lynn Perenic, *President*
EMP: 16
SQ FT: 20,000
SALES (est): 4.1MM **Privately Held**
WEB: www.argent-label.com
SIC: **2672** 3714 2671 Adhesive papers, labels or tapes: from purchased material; motor vehicle parts & accessories; packaging paper & plastics film, coated & laminated

(G-12574)
ARTCRAFT PRINTING CORPORATION
Also Called: Elegant Invitations
14919 Maplewood Ln (48170-2655)
PHONE..................................734 455-8893
John J Zunich, *President*
EMP: 4
SALES: 300K **Privately Held**
SIC: **2752** Commercial printing, offset

(G-12575)
ATLAS TUBE (PLYMOUTH) INC
13101 Eckles Rd (48170-4245)
PHONE..................................734 738-5600
Barry M Zekelman, *CEO*
Dave Seeger, *President*
David W Seeger, *President*
Andrew Klaus, *Vice Pres*
Michael P McNamara, *Vice Pres*
◆ EMP: 60
SQ FT: 27,000
SALES (est): 15.2MM **Privately Held**
WEB: www.atlastube.com
SIC: **3317** Steel pipe & tubes
HQ: Atlas Holding Inc.
  1855 E 122nd St
  Chicago IL 60633

(G-12576)
ATRA PLASTICS INC (PA)
43938 Plymouth Oaks Blvd (48170-2584)
PHONE..................................734 237-3393
WEI Wang, *President*
Robert Say, *Vice Pres*
Matthew Winger, *Purchasing*
Pat Runnels, *QC Mgr*
Meng Wang, *Controller*
EMP: 14
SALES (est): 2.3MM **Privately Held**
SIC: **3544** Dies, plastics forming

(G-12577)
AUTOSYSTEMS AMERICA INC
Also Called: Litetek
46600 Port St (48170-6030)
PHONE..................................734 582-2300
Jeff Stecher, *President*
Nicole Randolph, *Buyer*
Jennifer Mitton, *Controller*
Shawn Bentley, *Manager*
Bradley Young, *Technical Staff*
EMP: 300
SQ FT: 150,000
SALES (est): 14.6MM
SALES (corp-wide): 40.8B **Privately Held**
SIC: **3647** Automotive lighting fixtures
PA: Magna International Inc
  337 Magna Dr
  Aurora ON L4G 7
  905 726-2462

(G-12578)
AVL MICHIGAN HOLDING CORP (DH)
47519 Halyard Dr (48170-2438)
PHONE..................................734 414-9600
Don Manvel, *CEO*
Helmut O List, *CEO*
Franz Kinzer, *Managing Dir*
Andreas Loecker, *Business Mgr*
Marko Dekena, *Exec VP*
EMP: 46
SALES (est): 64.8MM
SALES (corp-wide): 242.1K **Privately Held**
SIC: **3823** Industrial instrmnts msrmnt display/control process variable
HQ: Avl List Gmbh
  Hans-List-Platz 1
  Graz 8020
  316 787-0

(G-12579)
AVL NORTH AMER CORP SVCS INC
47603 Halyard Dr (48170-2429)
PHONE..................................734 414-9600
Chester S Ricker, *Principal*
Jennifer Fulton, *Accounting Mgr*
Huw Morris, *Director*
EMP: 609
SALES (est): 17.6MM
SALES (corp-wide): 242.1K **Privately Held**
SIC: **3569** Liquid automation machinery & equipment
HQ: Avl List Gmbh
  Hans-List-Platz 1
  Graz 8020
  316 787-0

(G-12580)
AVL TEST SYSTEMS INC
47603 Halyard Dr (48170-2429)
PHONE..................................734 414-9600
Don Manvel, *CEO*
Gregory Hopton, *President*
Joseph Strelow, *Business Mgr*
Chet Ricker, *Vice Pres*
Yin Wen, *Project Mgr*
▲ EMP: 121 EST: 1962
SQ FT: 68,500
SALES (est): 38MM
SALES (corp-wide): 242.1K **Privately Held**
SIC: **3823** 3829 3564 Industrial instrmnts msrmnt display/control process variable; measuring & controlling devices; blowers & fans
HQ: Avl Michigan Holding Corporation
  47519 Halyard Dr
  Plymouth MI 48170

(G-12581)
AW TRANSMISSION ENGRG USA INC (HQ)
Also Called: Awtech USA
14920 Keel St (48170-6006)
PHONE..................................734 454-1710
Takao Tohyama, *President*
Don Gioia, *Vice Pres*
▲ EMP: 97
SQ FT: 27,000
SALES (est): 14.7MM **Privately Held**
WEB: www.awtec.com
SIC: **3714** Transmissions, motor vehicle

(G-12582)
BARNES GROUP INC
Also Called: Associated Spring- Nat Sls
15150 Cleat St (48170-6014)
PHONE..................................734 737-0958
EMP: 6
SALES (corp-wide): 1.5B **Publicly Held**
WEB: www.barnesgroupinc.com
SIC: **3495** 3469 Wire springs; metal stampings
PA: Barnes Group Inc.
  123 Main St
  Bristol CT 06010
  860 583-7070

(G-12583)
BARNES GROUP INC
Also Called: Associated Spring
44330 Plymouth Oaks Blvd (48170-2584)
PHONE..................................734 429-2022
Robert Bruno, *Division Mgr*
Evan Van Stralen, *Buyer*
Tim Haller, *Branch Mgr*
Craig Smith, *Maintence Staff*
EMP: 40
SALES (corp-wide): 1.5B **Publicly Held**
WEB: www.barnesgroupinc.com
SIC: **3495** 3469 Wire springs; metal stampings
PA: Barnes Group Inc.
  123 Main St
  Bristol CT 06010
  860 583-7070

GEOGRAPHIC SECTION

Plymouth - Wayne County (G-12610)

(G-12584)
BEET LLC
45207 Helm St (48170-6023)
PHONE..................................248 432-0052
David Wang, *Mng Member*
Lance Lehmann, *Director*
Edward Kim,
EMP: 10
SQ FT: 5,000
SALES (est): 1.3MM **Privately Held**
SIC: 7371 3823 3829 8748 Computer software systems analysis & design, custom; primary elements for process flow measurement; aircraft & motor vehicle measurement equipment; systems analysis & engineering consulting services

(G-12585)
BERGER LLC
44160 Plymouth Oaks Blvd (48170-2584)
PHONE..................................734 414-0402
Klaus Niemann,
▲ **EMP:** 9
SALES (est): 1.1MM **Privately Held**
SIC: 3541 Grinding machines, metalworking

(G-12586)
BEST BINDING LLC
41230 Joy Rd (48170-4697)
PHONE..................................734 459-7785
James Decker,
EMP: 6 **EST:** 2011
SALES (est): 370K **Privately Held**
SIC: 2732 Books: printing & binding

(G-12587)
BIOSAVITA INC
46701 Commerce Center Dr (48170-2475)
PHONE..................................734 233-3146
James Kuo, *CEO*
Savita Nikam, *Research*
David Bramhill, *Director*
EMP: 3
SALES (est): 287.5K **Privately Held**
SIC: 2836 Biological products, except diagnostic

(G-12588)
BLACKBOX VISUAL DESIGN INC
265 Ann St (48170-1215)
PHONE..................................734 459-1307
Chadwick R Curry, *President*
Sharon Curry, *Exec VP*
EMP: 3
SALES: 160K **Privately Held**
WEB: www.blackboxvisdesign.com
SIC: 7389 3669 Design services; visual communication systems

(G-12589)
BR SAFETY PRODUCTS INC
1255 S Mill St (48170-4318)
PHONE..................................734 582-4499
Robert Milkowski, *CEO*
William Williamson, *Principal*
EMP: 4
SALES (est): 228K **Privately Held**
SIC: 3316 5051 Bars, steel, cold finished, from purchased hot-rolled; bars, metal

(G-12590)
BREMBO NORTH AMERICA INC (DH)
Also Called: Brembo Racing
47765 Halyard Dr (48170-2429)
PHONE..................................734 416-1275
Daniel Sandberg, *President*
Chris Husted, *Opers Dir*
Heid Ben, *Materials Mgr*
Kevin Duda, *Purch Mgr*
Emily Demeritt, *Purch Agent*
◆ **EMP:** 60
SQ FT: 45,000
SALES (est): 226.1MM **Privately Held**
WEB: www.ibraco.com
SIC: 3714 5013 Motor vehicle parts & accessories; motor vehicle supplies & new parts; automotive supplies & parts; automotive supplies
HQ: Freni Brembo Spa
Via Brembo 25
Curno BG 24035
035 605-2090

(G-12591)
BRUGOLA OEB INDSTRIALE USA INC
45555 Port St (48170-6051)
PHONE..................................734 468-0009
Egidio Brugola, *President*
▲ **EMP:** 13
SQ FT: 109,000
SALES (est): 5.4MM **Privately Held**
SIC: 3714 Motor vehicle parts & accessories
HQ: Brugola O.E.B. Industriale Spa
Piazza Papa Giovanni Xxiii 36
Lissone 20851
039 244-41

(G-12592)
BULLETIN MOON
44315 Plymouth Oaks Blvd (48170-2585)
PHONE..................................734 453-9985
Ted Boloven, *Owner*
EMP: 9
SALES (est): 290K **Privately Held**
SIC: 2711 Newspapers, publishing & printing

(G-12593)
CARDIAC ASSIST HOLDINGS LLC
Also Called: Hbeat Medical
46701 Commerce Center Dr (48170-2475)
PHONE..................................781 727-1391
Kurt Dasse,
Allen Kantrowitz,
EMP: 4
SQ FT: 700
SALES (est): 149.2K **Privately Held**
SIC: 3841 Surgical & medical instruments

(G-12594)
CELLAR 849 WINERY
849 Penniman Ave Ste 101 (48170-3776)
PHONE..................................734 254-0275
John Robert Corsi, *Owner*
EMP: 3
SALES (est): 192.1K **Privately Held**
SIC: 2084 Wines

(G-12595)
CEQUENT UK LTD
Also Called: Horizon Global Americas
47912 Halyard Dr Ste 100 (48170-2796)
PHONE..................................734 656-3000
EMP: 5
SALES (corp-wide): 968.4K **Privately Held**
SIC: 3714 Motor vehicle engines & parts
HQ: Cequent Uk Limited
Drome Road
Deeside CH5 2

(G-12596)
CHANGAN US RES & DEV CTR INC
Also Called: Changan US R&D Center
47799 Halyard Dr Ste 77 (48170-3771)
PHONE..................................734 259-6440
Hong Su, *Vice Pres*
Zeljko Medenica, *Engineer*
Craig Sutton, *Manager*
Allen Szemak, *Manager*
David Weber, *Manager*
▲ **EMP:** 4
SALES (est): 1.1MM **Privately Held**
SIC: 3069 Rubber automotive products
HQ: Changan Connected Car Technology Co., Ltd.
No.260 ,E(Ast) Jianxin Road,Jiangbei District
Chongqing 40002
139 832-7698

(G-12597)
CHRYSAN INDUSTRIES INC (PA)
14707 Keel St (48170-6001)
PHONE..................................734 451-5411
Suk Kyu Koh, *President*
Carolyn Booms, *Opers Staff*
Shanthi Subbiah, *Controller*
◆ **EMP:** 23 **EST:** 1977
SQ FT: 25,000
SALES: 40.5MM **Privately Held**
WEB: www.chrysanindustries.com
SIC: 2992 2842 Lubricating oils & greases; specialty cleaning preparations

(G-12598)
CLEAN TECH INC (HQ)
41605 Ann Arbor Rd E (48170-4304)
PHONE..................................734 455-3600
William C Young, *President*
Casey Chirite, *Engineer*
Peterson Ken, *Engineer*
Michael Plotzke, *CFO*
Tom Busard, *Executive*
▲ **EMP:** 50
SQ FT: 90,000
SALES (est): 15.1MM
SALES (corp-wide): 1.3B **Privately Held**
WEB: www.plastipak.com
SIC: 3087 4953 Custom compound purchased resins; recycling, waste materials
PA: Plastipak Holdings, Inc.
41605 Ann Arbor Rd E
Plymouth MI 48170
734 455-3600

(G-12599)
COFFEE EXPRESS CO
47722 Clipper St (48170-2437)
PHONE..................................734 459-4900
Thomas S Isaia, *President*
Donna Galdi, *Sales Staff*
Genevieve Boss, *Manager*
Sue Jelso, *Manager*
Joyce Novak, *Manager*
EMP: 12
SQ FT: 8,000
SALES (est): 2.2MM **Privately Held**
WEB: www.coffeeexpressco.com
SIC: 2095 Roasted coffee

(G-12600)
CONCRETE TO GO
702 Ann St (48170-1261)
PHONE..................................734 455-3531
Dorothy Miller, *Principal*
EMP: 5
SALES (est): 269.1K **Privately Held**
SIC: 3273 Ready-mixed concrete

(G-12601)
CONSOLIDATED CLIPS CLAMPS INC
Also Called: Clips & Clamps Industries
15050 Keel St (48170-6006)
PHONE..................................734 455-0880
Michael A Aznavorian, *President*
Alexandria Dul Mily, *Vice Pres*
Kathleen Dul Aznavorian, *Treasurer*
Jeffrey Szarek, *Supervisor*
Kotie Meghadri, *Technology*
EMP: 60
SQ FT: 37,600
SALES (est): 11.5MM **Privately Held**
WEB: www.clipsclamps.com
SIC: 3469 3496 3429 Stamping metal for the trade; miscellaneous fabricated wire products; manufactured hardware (general)

(G-12602)
COOPER GENOMICS
705 S Main St (48170-2089)
PHONE..................................313 579-9650
EMP: 4
SALES (est): 374.6K **Privately Held**
SIC: 2835 Microbiology & virology diagnostic products

(G-12603)
CROWN EQUIPMENT CORPORATION
Also Called: Crown Lift Trucks
43896 Plymouth Oaks Blvd (48170-2598)
PHONE..................................734 414-0160
Don Steele, *Manager*
EMP: 67
SQ FT: 24,000
SALES (corp-wide): 3.4B **Privately Held**
SIC: 3537 Lift trucks, industrial: fork, platform, straddle, etc.
PA: Crown Equipment Corporation
44 S Washington St
New Bremen OH 45869
419 629-2311

(G-12604)
DADCO INC (PA)
Also Called: Power Components
43850 Plymouth Oaks Blvd (48170-2598)
PHONE..................................734 207-1100
Michael C Diebolt, *President*
Kimberly Wadowski, *Vice Pres*
Jason Locke, *Purchasing*
Len Thompson, *Sales Mgr*
Bill Gross, *Sales Staff*
◆ **EMP:** 100
SQ FT: 125,000
SALES (est): 32.5MM **Privately Held**
WEB: www.dadco.net
SIC: 3593 3492 5084 Fluid power cylinders & actuators; fluid power valves & hose fittings; industrial machinery & equipment

(G-12605)
DARE AUTO INC
Also Called: Fzb Technology
47548 Halyard Dr Ste B (48170-3796)
PHONE..................................734 228-6243
Jim Yang, *CEO*
Yi LI, *President*
EMP: 30
SQ FT: 28,500
SALES (est): 1.2MM **Privately Held**
SIC: 3625 3594 Motor starters & controllers, electric; fluid power pumps & motors

(G-12606)
DAY INTERNATIONAL GROUP INC (DH)
14909 N Beck Rd (48170-2411)
PHONE..................................734 781-4600
William C Ferguson, *Ch of Bd*
Dennis R Wolters, *President*
Dwaine R Brooks, *Vice Pres*
David B Freimuth, *Vice Pres*
Thomas J Koenig, *Vice Pres*
◆ **EMP:** 30
SQ FT: 13,800
SALES (est): 144MM
SALES (corp-wide): 177.9K **Privately Held**
SIC: 3069 Printers' rolls & blankets: rubber or rubberized fabric
HQ: Flint Group Us Llc
17177 N Laurel Park Dr # 300
Livonia MI 48152
734 781-4600

(G-12607)
DELTAIC WELDING INC
11803 Turkey Run (48170-3727)
PHONE..................................734 207-1080
Douglas Bates, *President*
EMP: 3
SALES: 350K **Privately Held**
SIC: 7692 Welding repair

(G-12608)
DENTON ATD INC
47460 Galleon Dr (48170-2467)
PHONE..................................734 451-7878
Dave Stein, *Branch Mgr*
EMP: 55
SALES (corp-wide): 6.1MM **Privately Held**
SIC: 3999 Mannequins
PA: Denton Atd, Inc.
900 Denton Dr
Huron OH 44839
567 265-5200

(G-12609)
DESIGNSHIRTSCOM INC
Also Called: Versatranz
14777 Keel St (48170-6001)
PHONE..................................734 414-7604
Francesco Viola, *President*
James Sheridan, *Vice Pres*
EMP: 6
SALES (est): 1MM **Privately Held**
WEB: www.versatranz.com
SIC: 2759 Screen printing

(G-12610)
DHAKE INDUSTRIES INC
15169 Northville Rd (48170-2548)
PHONE..................................734 420-0101
Bhimashankar G Dhake, *President*
Robbie Mukherjee, *Business Mgr*

Plymouth - Wayne County (G-12611)

GEOGRAPHIC SECTION

Sapna Dhake, *Vice Pres*
Priyanka Dhake, *Finance Mgr*
Arjun Dhake, *VP Mktg*
EMP: 24
SQ FT: 30,000
SALES (est): 6.3MM **Privately Held**
WEB: www.dhakeindustries.com
SIC: 2851 Paints & allied products

(G-12611)
DIAMOND TOOL MANUFACTURING INC
14540 Jib St (48170-6013)
P.O. Box 701484 (48170-0965)
PHONE....................734 416-1900
Michael McHugh, *President*
Samantha Krall, *Finance*
Philip Clemens, *Shareholder*
EMP: 32
SQ FT: 10,400
SALES: 2.7MM **Privately Held**
WEB: www.diamondtoolmfg.com
SIC: 3545 3471 3291 Diamond cutting tools for turning, boring, burnishing, etc.; plating & polishing; abrasive products

(G-12612)
DIJET INCORPORATED (HQ)
45807 Helm St (48170-6025)
PHONE....................734 454-9100
Keiichiro Izumi, *President*
Sandy Szybisty, *Admin Sec*
▲ **EMP:** 8
SQ FT: 18,000
SALES (est): 1MM **Privately Held**
WEB: www.dijetusa.com
SIC: 3545 5084 Cutting tools for machine tools; metalworking tools (such as drills, taps, dies, files)

(G-12613)
DNR INC
45759 Helm St (48170-6025)
PHONE....................734 722-4000
Guy Roberts, *Vice Pres*
EMP: 5
SALES (corp-wide): 1.2MM **Privately Held**
SIC: 3471 7349 Tumbling (cleaning & polishing) of machine parts; cleaning service, industrial or commercial
PA: D.N.R. Inc.
38475 Webb Dr
Westland MI 48185
734 722-4000

(G-12614)
DVS TECHNOLOGY AMERICA INC
44099 Plymouth Oaks Blvd (48170-6527)
PHONE....................734 656-2080
Ralf Georg Eitel, *CEO*
EMP: 5
SQ FT: 4,500
SALES (est): 505.6K **Privately Held**
SIC: 3541 Machine tools, metal cutting type

(G-12615)
E & E MANUFACTURING CO INC (PA)
300 400 Indus Drv Plymuth (48170)
PHONE....................734 451-7600
Wallace E Smith, *President*
Tammy Adkins, *Project Mgr*
Neil Hoekstra, *Opers Mgr*
Michael McComb, *Buyer*
Clifford Barbee, *Engineer*
▼ **EMP:** 270 **EST:** 1962
SQ FT: 250,000
SALES (est): 100.9MM **Privately Held**
WEB: www.eemfg.com
SIC: 3469 Metal stampings

(G-12616)
E & E MANUFACTURING CO INC
200 Industrial Dr (48170-1804)
PHONE....................734 451-7600
Larry Joy, *Engineer*
Marian Nistor, *Engineer*
E Manufacturing, *Branch Mgr*
Dan Liu, *Info Tech Dir*
EMP: 23

SALES (corp-wide): 100.9MM **Privately Held**
SIC: 3465 Automotive stampings
PA: E & E Manufacturing Company, Inc.
300 400 Indus Drv Plymuth
Plymouth MI 48170
734 451-7600

(G-12617)
EMERSON ELECTRIC CO
15024 Robinwood Dr (48170-2677)
PHONE....................734 420-0832
Christophe Somercik, *Branch Mgr*
Dana Greenly, *Manager*
EMP: 4
SALES (corp-wide): 17.4B **Publicly Held**
WEB: www.gotoemerson.com
SIC: 3823 Industrial instrmnts msrmnt display/control process variable
PA: Emerson Electric Co.
8000 West Florissant Ave
Saint Louis MO 63136
314 553-2000

(G-12618)
ERNEST INDS ACQUISITION LLC
Also Called: Ernest Industries Company
14601 Keel St (48170-6002)
PHONE....................734 459-8881
EMP: 8
SALES (corp-wide): 7.2MM **Privately Held**
SIC: 3469 Mfg Metal Stampings
PA: Ernest Industries Acquisition, Llc
39133 Webb Dr
Westland MI 48185
734 595-9500

(G-12619)
ESPEROVAX INC
46701 Commerce Center Dr (48170-2475)
PHONE....................248 667-1845
David O'Hagan PHD, *Principal*
Roger Newton, *Principal*
Savita Nikam, *Principal*
EMP: 3 **Privately Held**
SIC: 2836 Biological products, except diagnostic

(G-12620)
FEDERAL-MOGUL POWERTRAIN LLC
47001 Port St (48170-6063)
PHONE....................734 254-0100
Jim Zabriskie, *Vice Pres*
Keri Westbrook, *Director*
Anne Russell, *Admin Asst*
EMP: 203
SALES (corp-wide): 11.7B **Publicly Held**
SIC: 3714 Motor vehicle parts & accessories
HQ: Federal-Mogul Powertrain Llc
27300 W 11 Mile Rd
Southfield MI 48034

(G-12621)
FLINT CPS INKS NORTH AMER LLC (PA)
14909 N Beck Rd (48170-2411)
PHONE....................734 781-4600
William B Miller,
Anila Ruseti,
Peter M Schreck,
EMP: 5
SALES (est): 3.6MM **Privately Held**
SIC: 2865 2893 Color pigments, organic; printing ink

(G-12622)
FLINT INK RECEIVABLES CORP
14909 N Beck Rd (48170-2411)
PHONE....................734 781-4600
EMP: 4
SALES (est): 316.9K **Privately Held**
SIC: 2893 Printing ink

(G-12623)
FREUDENBERG N AMER LTD PARTNR (DH)
47774 W Anchor Ct (48170-2456)
PHONE....................734 354-5505
Leesa A Smith, *President*
Maryellen Strabone, *Director*
◆ **EMP:** 7

SALES (est): 1.6B
SALES (corp-wide): 11B **Privately Held**
SIC: 2821 3714 3053 3061 Plastics materials & resins; motor vehicle parts & accessories; gaskets, packing & sealing devices; mechanical rubber goods
HQ: Freudenberg Sealing Technologies Gmbh & Co. Kg
Hohnerweg 2-4
Weinheim 69469
620 180-6666

(G-12624)
FREUDENBERG-NOK GENERAL PARTNR (DH)
Also Called: Freudenberg-Nok Sealing Tech
47774 W Anchor Ct (48170-2456)
PHONE....................734 451-0020
Mohsen M Sohi, *CEO*
Brad Norton, *President*
John Rice, *President*
Martin Wentzler, *Chairman*
Dr Michael Heidingsfelder, *Senior VP*
▲ **EMP:** 200 **EST:** 1989
SQ FT: 80,000
SALES (est): 1.4B
SALES (corp-wide): 11B **Privately Held**
WEB: www.freudenberg-nok.com
SIC: 2821 3714 3053 3061 Plastics materials & resins; motor vehicle parts & accessories; gaskets, packing & sealing devices; mechanical rubber goods

(G-12625)
FREUDENBERG-NOK GENERAL PARTNR
47805 Galleon Dr (48170-2434)
PHONE....................734 451-0020
James Eubanks, *Vice Pres*
Claus M Hlenkamp, *Branch Mgr*
EMP: 110
SALES (corp-wide): 11B **Privately Held**
SIC: 3053 Gaskets, packing & sealing devices
HQ: Freudenberg-Nok General Partnership
47774 W Anchor Ct
Plymouth MI 48170
734 451-0020

(G-12626)
GATCO INCORPORATED
42330 Ann Arbor Rd E (48170-4303)
PHONE....................734 453-2295
Mark E Sulkowski, *President*
EMP: 15 **EST:** 1913
SALES (est): 3MM **Privately Held**
WEB: www.gatcobushing.com
SIC: 3549 Metalworking machinery

(G-12627)
GI MILLWORKS INC
14970 Cleat St (48170-6053)
PHONE....................734 451-1100
John Malcom, *President*
Thomas Rener, *Principal*
EMP: 15
SALES (est): 1.6MM **Privately Held**
SIC: 2431 Moldings, wood: unfinished & prefinished

(G-12628)
GLASSLINE INCORPORATED
199 W Ann Arbor Trl (48170-1639)
PHONE....................734 453-2728
Guy R Kenny, *President*
EMP: 16 **EST:** 1963
SALES (est): 3.4MM **Privately Held**
SIC: 2221 Fiberglass fabrics

(G-12629)
GLOBAL CNC INDUSTRIES LTD
15150 Cleat St (48170-6014)
PHONE....................734 464-1920
Helen Stassinos, *President*
Catherine Stassinos, *Vice Pres*
Lambros Stassinos, *Treasurer*
Christine Stassinos, *Admin Sec*
▲ **EMP:** 34
SQ FT: 23,000
SALES (est): 8MM **Privately Held**
WEB: www.globalcnc.com
SIC: 3545 5084 3366 Cutting tools for machine tools; industrial machinery & equipment; copper foundries

(G-12630)
GLOBE TECH LLC
Also Called: Globe Tech Manufactured Pdts
40300 Plymouth Rd (48170-4210)
PHONE....................734 656-2200
Brian Swanson, *General Mgr*
John Meng, *CFO*
Joe Cheff, *Info Tech Mgr*
Matt Menchinger, *Info Tech Mgr*
▲ **EMP:** 20
SALES (est): 5MM **Privately Held**
WEB: www.globe-tech.biz
SIC: 3469 3465 3544 3542 Metal stampings; automotive stampings; special dies, tools, jigs & fixtures; machine tools, metal forming type; machine tools, metal cutting type

(G-12631)
GRAPH-X SIGNS
45650 Mast St (48170-6007)
PHONE....................734 420-0906
Tom Lunsford, *Owner*
Kara Vanderveen, *Accounts Mgr*
Thomas Lunsford, *Manager*
Ron Winters, *Representative*
EMP: 5
SALES: 750K **Privately Held**
WEB: www.graphxsigns.com
SIC: 3993 Neon signs

(G-12632)
GREKO PRINT & IMAGING INC
260 Ann Arbor Rd W (48170-2222)
PHONE....................734 453-0341
Paul Degrazia, *President*
Mario Degrazia, *Advt Staff*
EMP: 14
SALES (est): 2.5MM **Privately Held**
SIC: 2752 Commercial printing, offset

(G-12633)
GRIP STUDIOS
743 Wing St Rear Bldg (48170-6450)
PHONE....................248 757-0796
Dale Ryans, *Principal*
EMP: 6
SALES: 995K **Privately Held**
SIC: 3931 Guitars & parts, electric & non-electric

(G-12634)
HAVIS INC
47099 Five Mile Rd (48170-3765)
PHONE....................734 414-0699
Joe Bernert, *CEO*
Steve Ferarro, *CFO*
▲ **EMP:** 24
SALES (est): 5.1MM **Privately Held**
SIC: 3714 Directional signals, motor vehicle

(G-12635)
HAYDEN - MCNEIL LLC
14903 Pilot Dr (48170-3674)
PHONE....................734 455-7900
Patrick R Olson, *CEO*
Jeff McCarthy, *President*
EMP: 30
SQ FT: 11,500
SALES (est): 5.2MM
SALES (corp-wide): 1.6B **Privately Held**
WEB: www.hmpublishing.com
SIC: 2731 Textbooks: publishing only, not printed on site
HQ: Macmillan Holdings, Llc
120 Broadway Fl 22
New York NY 10271

(G-12636)
HELLA LIGHTING CORPORATION (DH)
43811 Plymouth Oaks Blvd (48170-2539)
PHONE....................734 414-0900
Raymund Heinen, *President*
John Bulger, *Admin Sec*
▲ **EMP:** 40
SALES (est): 9.7MM
SALES (corp-wide): 7.8B **Privately Held**
SIC: 3625 Industrial electrical relays & switches
HQ: Hella Corporate Center Usa, Inc.
15951 Technology Dr
Northville MI 48168
586 232-4788

GEOGRAPHIC SECTION

Plymouth - Wayne County (G-12660)

(G-12637)
HELM INCORPORATED (HQ)
47911 Halyard Dr (48170-3751)
PHONE..................................734 468-3700
Justin Gusick, *CEO*
Lorne Dubrowsky, *CFO*
▲ **EMP:** 99
SQ FT: 155,000
SALES (est): 40.1MM
SALES (corp-wide): 57.4MM **Privately Held**
WEB: www.helm.com
SIC: 7389 5199 2741 Packaging & labeling services; advertising specialties; technical manual & paper publishing
PA: Helm Holding Company
  47911 Halyard Dr
  Detroit MI 48203
  800 445-4831

(G-12638)
HERITAGE
1405 Gold Smith (48170-1082)
PHONE..................................734 414-0343
Gary Cummins, *Mng Member*
John Dempfey,
EMP: 5
SALES (est): 200K **Privately Held**
SIC: 3999 Embroidery kits

(G-12639)
HIGGINS PRINTING SERVICES LLC
1058 S Main St (48170-2050)
PHONE..................................734 414-6203
Timothy Higgins,
EMP: 3
SALES (est): 390.4K **Privately Held**
WEB: www.intlminutepress.com
SIC: 2752 Commercial printing, offset

(G-12640)
HITEC SENSOR DEVELOPMENTS INC
47460 Galleon Dr (48170-2467)
PHONE..................................313 506-2460
Terry Theodore, *Principal*
EMP: 23 **Privately Held**
SIC: 3823 Industrial process measurement equipment
PA: Hitec Sensor Developments, Inc.
  10 Elizabeth Dr Ste 5
  Chelmsford MA 01824

(G-12641)
HONEYWELL INTERNATIONAL INC
47548 Halyard Dr (48170-3796)
PHONE..................................734 392-5501
EMP: 50
SALES (corp-wide): 41.8B **Publicly Held**
WEB: www.honeywell.com
SIC: 3724 Aircraft engines & engine parts
PA: Honeywell International Inc.
  300 S Tryon St
  Charlotte NC 28202
  973 455-2000

(G-12642)
HOOVER UNIVERSAL INC (HQ)
Also Called: Johnson Cntrls-Bttle Creek Vnt
49200 Halyard Dr (48170-2481)
PHONE..................................734 454-0994
Keith E Wandell, *President*
Jeffrey S Edwards, *Vice Pres*
William J Kohler, *Vice Pres*
John David Major, *Vice Pres*
Jerome D Okarma, *Vice Pres*
▲ **EMP:** 20
SALES (est): 631.6MM **Privately Held**
SIC: 2531 Seats, automobile

(G-12643)
HORIZON GLOBAL AMERICAS INC (HQ)
Also Called: Cequent Performance Group
47912 Halyard Dr Ste 100 (48170-2796)
PHONE..................................734 656-3000
John Aleva, *President*
Tom Aepelbacher, *Vice Pres*
Marcie Albright, *Vice Pres*
Paul Caruso, *Vice Pres*
Mike Finos, *Vice Pres*
◆ **EMP:** 200

SALES (est): 491.8MM
SALES (corp-wide): 849.9MM **Publicly Held**
SIC: 3799 3714 Trailer hitches; trailer hitches, motor vehicle
PA: Horizon Global Corporation
  2600 W Big Beaver Rd # 555
  Troy MI 48084
  248 593-8820

(G-12644)
HUMAN SYNERGISTICS INC
39819 Plymouth Rd (48170-4290)
PHONE..................................734 459-1030
Robert A Cooke, *Principal*
Thomas W Cross, *Chairman*
Cheryl Boglarsky, *Research*
Jessica Cooke, *Director*
Geri Keener, *Director*
EMP: 22
SQ FT: 9,000
SALES: 3.3MM **Privately Held**
WEB: www.hscanada.com
SIC: 2741 8742 Miscellaneous publishing; business consultant

(G-12645)
IAC PLYMOUTH LLC
47785 W Anchor Ct (48170-2456)
PHONE..................................734 207-7000
Michael Gibson, *Business Anlyst*
EMP: 25
SALES (est): 4.9MM **Privately Held**
WEB: www.iaaawards.com
SIC: 3089 Automotive parts, plastic
HQ: International Automotive Components Group North America, Inc.
  28333 Telegraph Rd
  Southfield MI 48034

(G-12646)
ILMOR ENGINEERING INC (PA)
Also Called: Ilmor High Performance Marine
43939 Plymouth Oaks Blvd (48170-2557)
PHONE..................................734 456-3600
Paul Ray, *President*
Julie Bernard, *Vice Pres*
Wayne Bennett, *Opers Mgr*
Darren Dowding, *Opers Mgr*
Matthew Magers, *Maint Spvr*
▲ **EMP:** 75
SQ FT: 45,000
SALES (est): 42.8MM **Privately Held**
WEB: www.ilmor.com
SIC: 3714 Motor vehicle engines & parts

(G-12647)
INSTRUMENT AND VALVE SERVICES
14789 Keel St (48170-6001)
PHONE..................................734 459-0375
EMP: 4
SALES (est): 300K **Privately Held**
SIC: 3491 Mfg Industrial Valves

(G-12648)
INTERNATIONAL AUTOMOTIVE COMPO
47785 W Anchor Ct (48170-2456)
PHONE..................................734 456-2800
EMP: 283 **Privately Held**
SIC: 3089 Automotive parts, plastic
HQ: International Automotive Components Group North America, Inc.
  28333 Telegraph Rd
  Southfield MI 48034

(G-12649)
INTERTEC SYSTEMS LLC (DH)
45000 Helm St Ste 200 (48170-6046)
PHONE..................................734 254-3268
Randy Dunn, *Plant Mgr*
Robert Depotter, *Mng Member*
Michael Wells, *Department Mgr*
▲ **EMP:** 70
SQ FT: 70,000
SALES (est): 66.4MM **Privately Held**
WEB: www.intertecsystems.com
SIC: 3714 Instrument board assemblies, motor vehicle
HQ: Adient Us Llc
  49200 Halyard Dr
  Plymouth MI 48170
  734 254-5000

(G-12650)
ISHINO GASKET NORTH AMER LLC
Also Called: Freudenberg-Nok
47690 E Anchor Ct (48170-2400)
PHONE..................................734 451-0020
David Mickow, *Accounts Mgr*
Steve Philippart, *Mng Member*
David Sakata,
▲ **EMP:** 4
SQ FT: 177,000
SALES (est): 613.2K
SALES (corp-wide): 11B **Privately Held**
WEB: www.freudenberg-nok.com
SIC: 3053 Gaskets & sealing devices
HQ: Freudenberg-Nok General Partnership
  47774 W Anchor Ct
  Plymouth MI 48170
  734 451-0020

(G-12651)
J L BECKER ACQUISITION LLC
Also Called: J. L. Becker Co.
41150 Joy Rd (48170-4634)
PHONE..................................734 656-2000
Thomas Gasbarre, *CEO*
Benjamin Gasbarre, *President*
Ben Gasbarre, *General Mgr*
EMP: 40 **EST:** 1973
SQ FT: 55,640
SALES (est): 10.2MM
SALES (corp-wide): 40MM **Privately Held**
WEB: www.jlbecker.com
SIC: 3567 Industrial furnaces & ovens
PA: Gasbarre Products, Inc.
  590 Division St
  Du Bois PA 15801
  814 371-3015

(G-12652)
JACK RIPPER & ASSOCIATES INC
14708 Keel St (48170-6028)
PHONE..................................734 453-7333
John L Ripper, *President*
John E Ripper, *President*
Daniel Ripper, *Vice Pres*
David L Ripper, *Vice Pres*
EMP: 8
SQ FT: 28,000
SALES (est): 1.1MM **Privately Held**
WEB: www.jackripper.com
SIC: 2399 Banners, made from fabric

(G-12653)
JIER NORTH AMERICA INC
14975 Cleat St (48170-6015)
PHONE..................................734 404-6683
Zhiqiang Hao, *President*
Andrew Blakely, *Vice Pres*
▲ **EMP:** 10
SQ FT: 10,000
SALES: 26.5MM
SALES (corp-wide): 301.8MM **Privately Held**
SIC: 3542 Machine tools, metal forming type
PA: Jier Machine-Tool Group Co., Ltd.
  No.2 Jichuang Erchang Road, Huaiyin District
  Jinan 25002
  531 879-6432

(G-12654)
JOGUE INC (PA)
Also Called: Northville Laboratories
14731 Helm Ct (48170-6096)
P.O. Box 190, Northville, (48167-0190)
PHONE..................................734 207-0100
Anil Sastry, *President*
Ryan Richards, *Vice Pres*
Dr Dattu Sastry, *Vice Pres*
Pushpa Sastry, *Vice Pres*
Liz Stoughton, *Export Mgr*
◆ **EMP:** 27
SQ FT: 48,000
SALES (est): 12.2MM **Privately Held**
WEB: www.jogue.com
SIC: 2087 2844 2099 Extracts, flavoring; perfumes & colognes; food preparations

(G-12655)
JOHNSON CONTROLS INC
49200 Halyard Dr (48170-2465)
PHONE..................................734 254-5000
Robert Schommer, *Principal*
EMP: 500 **Privately Held**
SIC: 3713 2531 Truck bodies & parts; public building & related furniture
HQ: Johnson Controls, Inc.
  5757 N Green Bay Ave
  Milwaukee WI 53209
  414 524-1200

(G-12656)
JOHNSON CONTROLS INC
49200 Halyard Dr (48170-2465)
PHONE..................................734 254-5000
EMP: 163 **Privately Held**
SIC: 3714 Motor vehicle parts & accessories
HQ: Johnson Controls, Inc.
  5757 N Green Bay Ave
  Milwaukee WI 53209
  414 524-1200

(G-12657)
JOHNSON CONTROLS INC
47700 Halyard Dr (48170-2477)
PHONE..................................734 254-7200
Jim Keys, *Principal*
EMP: 25 **Privately Held**
SIC: 3714 Motor vehicle parts & accessories
HQ: Johnson Controls, Inc.
  5757 N Green Bay Ave
  Milwaukee WI 53209
  414 524-1200

(G-12658)
JOHNSON ELECTRIC N AMER INC (DH)
47660 Halyard Dr (48170-2453)
PHONE..................................734 392-5300
Ivan Dominguez, *General Mgr*
Patrick Shui-Chung Wang, *Chairman*
Shelley Ritchey, *Mfg Spvr*
Penny Calvert, *Buyer*
Kevin Swisher, *Purchasing*
▲ **EMP:** 100 **EST:** 1976
SQ FT: 5,000
SALES (est): 1.3B **Privately Held**
SIC: 5063 3625 3674 8711 Motors, electric; solenoid switches (industrial controls); microcircuits, integrated (semiconductor); engineering services

(G-12659)
JTEKT AUTOMOTIVE N AMER INC
47771 Halyard Dr (48170-2479)
PHONE..................................734 454-1500
Yoshio Tsuji, *President*
Charles Brandt, *Vice Pres*
Steve Spagnuolo, *Engineer*
Yoshiyuki INA, *Senior Engr*
Viola Hoover, *Accountant*
EMP: 1000 **EST:** 1988
SALES (est): 151.7MM **Privately Held**
SIC: 3714 Motor vehicle parts & accessories
HQ: Jtekt North America Corporation
  7 Research Dr Ste A
  Greenville SC 29607
  440 835-1000

(G-12660)
JTEKT NORTH AMERICA CORP
Also Called: Bearing Division
47771 Halyard Dr (48170-2479)
PHONE..................................734 454-1500
Ben Simpson, *General Mgr*
Graham Fullerton, *Manager*
EMP: 50 **Privately Held**
SIC: 3562 5085 Ball & roller bearings; industrial supplies
HQ: Jtekt North America Corporation
  7 Research Dr Ste A
  Greenville SC 29607
  440 835-1000

Plymouth - Wayne County (G-12661) — GEOGRAPHIC SECTION

(G-12661)
K-TOOL CORPORATION MICHIGAN (PA)
Also Called: K-Tool International
45225 Five Mile Rd (48170)
PHONE.................................863 603-0777
Robert E Geisinger, *President*
Bill Driscoll, *Corp Secy*
Andy Dunham, *Sales Staff*
Doreen Morris, *Sales Staff*
Nancy L Kay, *Admin Sec*
▲ **EMP:** 60
SQ FT: 104,000
SALES (est): 79.4MM **Privately Held**
WEB: www.ktool.com
SIC: 5013 5072 3545 3544 Tools & equipment, automotive; hardware; machine tool accessories; special dies, tools, jigs & fixtures; machine tools, metal cutting type

(G-12662)
KARMANN MANUFACTURING LLC
14967 Pilot Dr (48170-3674)
PHONE.................................734 582-5900
Stephen Chesna, *CFO*
Stephen P Chesna,
Annette Matthae,
Volker Rodeck,
EMP: 34
SALES (est): 28.8K
SALES (corp-wide): 411.9K **Privately Held**
WEB: www.karmann.com
SIC: 3999 Barber & beauty shop equipment
HQ: Webasto Convertibles Usa Inc.
14988 Pilot Dr
Plymouth MI 48170

(G-12663)
KEMIN INDUSTRIES INC
Also Called: Algal Scientific
14925 Galleon Ct (48170-6536)
PHONE.................................248 869-3080
EMP: 12
SALES (corp-wide): 346.6MM **Privately Held**
SIC: 4952 2048 8099 Sewerage systems; feed supplements; nutrition services
PA: Kemin Industries, Inc.
1900 Scott Ave
Des Moines IA 50317
515 559-5100

(G-12664)
KEMKRAFT ENGINEERING INC
47650 Clipper St (48170-2469)
PHONE.................................734 414-6500
Edward J Kemski Jr, *President*
Vickie Kemski, *Admin Sec*
EMP: 12
SALES: 493.8K **Privately Held**
WEB: www.kemkraft.com
SIC: 3829 Physical property testing equipment

(G-12665)
KEMNITZ FINE CANDIES
Also Called: Kemnitz Fine Candies & Gifts
896 W Ann Arbor Trl (48170-1602)
PHONE.................................734 453-0480
Cynthia Smith, *Owner*
Merle Hamlin, *Purchasing*
EMP: 8
SQ FT: 1,200
SALES (est): 431.3K **Privately Held**
SIC: 5441 2066 Candy; chocolate & cocoa products

(G-12666)
KESSLER USA INC
44099 Plymouth Oaks Blvd # 104 (48170-6527)
PHONE.................................734 404-0152
Ralf Mielke, *Manager*
EMP: 10
SALES (est): 2.2MM
SALES (corp-wide): 174MM **Privately Held**
SIC: 3694 Motors, starting: automotive & aircraft
HQ: Franz Kessler Gmbh
Franz-Kessler-Str. 2
Bad Buchau 88422
758 280-90

(G-12667)
KEY PLASTICS LLC
44191 Plymouth Oaks Blvd (48170-6530)
PHONE.................................248 449-6100
EMP: 7
SALES (est): 400.6K **Privately Held**
SIC: 3083 5162 Plastic finished products, laminated; plastics materials & basic shapes

(G-12668)
KIMPRINT INC
Also Called: PROGRESSIVE PRINTING
14875 Galleon Ct (48170-6523)
PHONE.................................734 459-2960
Kimberly A Price, *President*
Bruce M Price, *Vice Pres*
Bruce Price, *Vice Pres*
Todd Conte, *Opers Mgr*
Ron Phillips, *Sls & Mktg Exec*
EMP: 27
SQ FT: 18,500
SALES: 3.8MM **Privately Held**
WEB: www.progressiveprint.com
SIC: 7331 2752 Mailing service; commercial printing, offset

(G-12669)
KINGDOM CARTRIDGE INC
11704 Morgan Ave (48170-4439)
PHONE.................................734 564-1590
Dave Kozler, *President*
EMP: 3 **EST:** 2011
SALES (est): 270K **Privately Held**
SIC: 3577 Printers, computer

(G-12670)
KYOCERA INTERNATIONAL INC
46723 Five Mile Rd (48170-2422)
PHONE.................................734 416-8500
EMP: 12 **Publicly Held**
SIC: 3679 Electronic crystals
HQ: Kyocera International, Inc.
8611 Balboa Ave
San Diego CA 92123
858 492-1456

(G-12671)
LARSON-JUHL US LLC
47584 Galleon Dr (48170-2467)
PHONE.................................734 416-3302
EMP: 4
SALES (corp-wide): 225.3B **Publicly Held**
SIC: 2499 Applicators, wood
HQ: Larson-Juhl Us Llc
3900 Steve Reynolds Blvd
Norcross GA 30093
770 279-5200

(G-12672)
LAW ENFORCEMENT DEVELOPMENT CO
Also Called: Ledco-Chargeguard
47801 W Anchor Ct (48170-6018)
PHONE.................................734 656-4100
Joe Bernert, *CEO*
Michael J Bernert, *President*
Michael Zani, *COO*
Steve Ferraro, *CFO*
Lori Layer, *Director*
▲ **EMP:** 55
SQ FT: 26,000
SALES (est): 10.9MM
SALES (corp-wide): 129.2MM **Privately Held**
SIC: 3577 Computer peripheral equipment
PA: Havis, Inc.
75 Jacksonville Rd
Warminster PA 18974
215 957-0720

(G-12673)
LINK MANUFACTURING INC (HQ)
Also Called: Link Engineering Company
43855 Plymouth Oaks Blvd (48170-2539)
PHONE.................................734 453-0800
Roy Link, *Ch of Bd*
Warren Brown, *Vice Pres*
Timothy Olex, *Vice Pres*
Derek Stoneburg, *CFO*
John Ligerakism, *Sales Mgr*
▲ **EMP:** 119 **EST:** 1953
SQ FT: 73,000
SALES (est): 69.7MM **Privately Held**
SIC: 3829 Physical property testing equipment; testing equipment: abrasion, shearing strength, etc.

(G-12674)
LOC PERFORMANCE PRODUCTS INC (PA)
13505 N Haggerty Rd (48170-4251)
PHONE.................................734 453-2300
Victor Vojcek, *CEO*
Lou Burr, *President*
Jason Atkinson, *COO*
James Joo, *Plant Mgr*
Alex Bibeau, *Purch Agent*
▲ **EMP:** 200
SQ FT: 246,000
SALES (est): 136.7MM **Privately Held**
SIC: 3541 Machine tools, metal cutting type

(G-12675)
LOCAL MOBILE SERVICES LLC
40500 Ann Arbor Rd E (48170-4483)
PHONE.................................313 963-1917
Melba Vinson, *Principal*
EMP: 3
SALES (est): 110.1K **Privately Held**
SIC: 7372 Application computer software

(G-12676)
LOCHINVAR LLC
45900 Port St (48170-6052)
PHONE.................................734 454-4480
Jack Myers, *Vice Pres*
Simon Gaines, *Manager*
Dan Walker, *Administration*
EMP: 20
SALES (corp-wide): 3.1B **Publicly Held**
WEB: www.lochinvar.com
SIC: 5074 5091 3443 Water heaters, except electric; swimming pools, equipment & supplies; fabricated plate work (boiler shop)
HQ: Lochinvar Llc
300 Maddox Simpson Pkwy
Lebanon TN 37090

(G-12677)
LOCPAC INC
13505 N Haggerty Rd (48170-4251)
PHONE.................................734 453-2300
Victor Vojcek, *CEO*
Lou Burr, *President*
Tammy Meehan, *General Mgr*
Jason Atkinson, *COO*
Thomas Horne, *CFO*
EMP: 50
SQ FT: 35,000
SALES: 4.4MM
SALES (corp-wide): 136.7MM **Privately Held**
SIC: 7389 3479 Packaging & labeling services; painting of metal products
PA: Loc Performance Products, Inc.
13505 N Haggerty Rd
Plymouth MI 48170
734 453-2300

(G-12678)
LRS INC
9448 Northern Ave (48170-4048)
PHONE.................................734 416-5050
Lawrence R Schafer, *Ch of Bd*
John Schafer, *President*
Mary C Schafer, *Corp Secy*
Shawn Snyder, *Sales Staff*
Ryan Howerter, *Marketing Staff*
EMP: 6 **EST:** 1967
SALES: 600K **Privately Held**
WEB: www.lrs.com
SIC: 3544 Dies & die holders for metal cutting, forming, die casting

(G-12679)
LSR INCORPORATED
11050 N Beck Rd (48170-3327)
PHONE.................................734 455-6530
Larry Runnion, *President*
EMP: 10
SALES (est): 500K **Privately Held**
SIC: 0782 3499 Landscape contractors; giftware, copper goods

(G-12680)
M-52 SAND & GRAVEL LLC
8483 Ann Arbor Rd W (48170-5101)
PHONE.................................734 453-3695
Rick Perlongo, *Principal*
Richard Perlongo, *Principal*
EMP: 6 **EST:** 2009
SALES (est): 510.9K **Privately Held**
SIC: 1442 Construction sand & gravel

(G-12681)
MAGNESIUM PRODUCTS AMERICA INC (HQ)
Also Called: Meridian Lightweight Tech
47805 Galleon Dr (48170-2434)
PHONE.................................734 416-8600
Erick Showalter, *President*
Wayne Oliver, *VP Finance*
▲ **EMP:** 360
SQ FT: 160,000
SALES (est): 174.6MM
SALES (corp-wide): 138.8MM **Privately Held**
WEB: www.meridian-mag.com
SIC: 3364 3369 3714 Magnesium & magnesium-base alloy die-castings; nonferrous foundries; motor vehicle parts & accessories
PA: Mlth Holdings Inc
25 Mcnab St
Strathroy ON N7G 4
519 246-9600

(G-12682)
MAJESKE MACHINE INC
44650 Pinetree Dr (48170-3841)
PHONE.................................319 273-8905
Gerald Majeske Jr, *President*
EMP: 19
SALES: 1MM **Privately Held**
SIC: 3545 Precision tools, machinists'

(G-12683)
MANUFACTURING PRODUCTS & SVCS
260 Ann Arbor Rd W (48170-2222)
PHONE.................................734 927-1964
Paul Degrazi, *President*
EMP: 10
SALES (est): 700K **Privately Held**
SIC: 3465 3711 4225 7389 Automotive stampings; automobile assembly, including specialty automobiles; general warehousing & storage; commodity inspection; industrial & commercial equipment inspection service

(G-12684)
MARJO PLASTICS COMPANY INC
1081 Cherry (48170-1304)
PHONE.................................734 455-4130
Fred D Hovorka, *President*
EMP: 4 **EST:** 1948
SQ FT: 3,600
SALES (est): 769.8K **Privately Held**
SIC: 3312 Tool & die steel

(G-12685)
MASTER AUTOMATIC MCH CO INC (PA)
40485 Schoolcraft Rd (48170-2706)
PHONE.................................734 414-0500
John D Evasic Jr, *Ch of Bd*
Mark Evasic, *President*
Jennifer Zinn, *President*
William Evasic, *Exec VP*
Bill Evasic, *Vice Pres*
EMP: 148 **EST:** 1942
SQ FT: 100,000
SALES (est): 30.2MM **Privately Held**
WEB: www.masterautomatic.com
SIC: 3451 Screw machine products

(G-12686)
MATERIALISE USA LLC
44650 Helm Ct (48170-6061)
PHONE.................................734 259-6445
Wilifried Vancrean, *CEO*
Bryan Crutchfield, *Managing Dir*
Kerry Schwartz, *Production*

▲ = Import ▼ = Export
◆ = Import/Export

GEOGRAPHIC SECTION

Plymouth - Wayne County (G-12714)

Evan Kirby, *Engineer*
Alyssa Ricker, *Engineer*
EMP: 60
SQ FT: 1,200
SALES (est): 16.1MM
SALES (corp-wide): 125.5MM **Privately Held**
WEB: www.materialise.com
SIC: 5734 2759 Computer software & accessories; laser printing
PA: Materialise
Technologielaan 15
Leuven 3001
163 966-11

(G-12687)
MC REA CORPORATION
40422 Cove Ct (48170-2684)
PHONE..................................734 420-2116
Raymond Fredrickson, *President*
EMP: 6
SQ FT: 10,000
SALES (est): 625.1K **Privately Held**
SIC: 3548 Spot welding apparatus, electric

(G-12688)
MCCOIG MATERIALS LLC
40500 Ann Arbor Rd E (48170-4483)
P.O. Box 6349 (48170-0353)
PHONE..................................734 414-6179
Reaburn King, *Vice Pres*
Kathy Hayes, *Controller*
Nancy Skaggs, *Accountant*
EMP: 40 **EST:** 2012
SALES (est): 7.3MM **Privately Held**
SIC: 3273 Ready-mixed concrete

(G-12689)
MEMTECH INC (PA)
9033 General Dr (48170-4680)
PHONE..................................734 455-8550
Dale Manor, *President*
Amy Prater-Manor, *Project Engr*
Carl Evans, *Admin Sec*
EMP: 11
SALES (est): 1MM **Privately Held**
WEB: www.memtechbrush.com
SIC: 3053 5085 8711 5033 Gaskets & sealing devices; seals, industrial; engineering services; roofing, siding & insulation; miscellaneous fabricated wire products; metal doors, sash & trim

(G-12690)
MERIDIAN LIGHTWEIGHT TECH INC
47805 Galleon Dr Ste B (48170-2434)
PHONE..................................248 663-8100
Eric Showalter, *CEO*
Jeffrey L Moyer, *Vice Pres*
Tony Papa, *Vice Pres*
EMP: 5 **EST:** 2013
SALES (est): 277.3K
SALES (corp-wide): 279.8MM **Privately Held**
SIC: 1081 8641 Metal mining services; environmental protection organization
HQ: Meridian Lightweight Technologies Holdings Inc
25 Mcnab St
Strathroy ON N7G 4
519 246-9600

(G-12691)
METALDYNE SINTERED COMPONENTS
47603 Halyard Dr (48170-2429)
PHONE..................................734 207-6200
Thomas A Amato, *CEO*
Ben Schmidt, *Vice Pres*
Mark Blaufuss, *CFO*
EMP: 13
SALES (est): 2.1MM **Privately Held**
SIC: 3714 Motor vehicle parts & accessories

(G-12692)
MICHIGAN TAPE INC
41016 Concept Dr (48170-4252)
PHONE..................................734 582-9800
Fred J Perenic, *President*
EMP: 9
SALES (est): 987.6K **Privately Held**
SIC: 2672 Tape, pressure sensitive: made from purchased materials

(G-12693)
MILLER MACHINE INC
41250 Joy Rd (48170-4697)
PHONE..................................734 455-5333
Raymond Miller, *President*
Gary Robert, *Vice Pres*
EMP: 4
SQ FT: 3,000
SALES: 448.5K **Privately Held**
SIC: 3599 Machine shop, jobbing & repair

(G-12694)
MILLER TECHNICAL SERVICES INC
Also Called: M T S
47801 W Anchor Ct (48170-6018)
PHONE..................................734 207-3159
Patrick Miller, *CEO*
Mike Zamaria, *President*
John Toigo, *COO*
▲ **EMP:** 15
SQ FT: 35,000
SALES (est): 3.1MM **Privately Held**
WEB: www.mtsmedicalmfg.com
SIC: 3842 Wheelchairs

(G-12695)
MOOG INC
Also Called: Moog Fcs
47495 Clipper St (48170-2470)
PHONE..................................734 738-5862
John Clawson, *General Mgr*
Drew Steele, *Principal*
Joe Morrill, *Director*
EMP: 20
SALES (corp-wide): 2.9B **Publicly Held**
WEB: www.moog.com
SIC: 7373 3674 Computer integrated systems design; semiconductors & related devices
PA: Moog Inc.
400 Jamison Rd
Elma NY 14059
716 805-2604

(G-12696)
MPG INC
47659 Halyard Dr (48170-2429)
PHONE..................................734 207-6200
Thomas V Chambers, *President*
George Thomas, *President*
Witkow Edward, *COO*
Tina Kozak, *COO*
Beverly Mathews, *COO*
▲ **EMP:** 6500
SQ FT: 50,000
SALES (est): 1.1MM **Privately Held*
WEB: www.metaldyne.com
SIC: 3499 Aerosol valves, metal; aquarium accessories, metal; doors, safe & vault: metal

(G-12697)
MYCRONA INC
14777 Keel St (48170-6001)
PHONE..................................734 453-9348
EMP: 15
SQ FT: 8,000
SALES (est): 1.3MM **Privately Held**
SIC: 5084 7699 3823 Whol & Services Industrial Measuring Equipment

(G-12698)
NATIONAL CONCRETE PRODUCTS CO
939 S Mill St (48170-4320)
PHONE..................................734 453-8448
Jack E Cook, *President*
James J Manson, *Vice Pres*
Robert Terwin, *Treasurer*
EMP: 35 **EST:** 1959
SQ FT: 75,000
SALES (est): 5.1MM **Privately Held**
SIC: 3272 Pipe, concrete or lined with concrete

(G-12699)
NATIONAL WHOLESALE PRTG CORP
41290 Joy Rd (48170-4697)
PHONE..................................734 416-8400
Brian L Marr, *President*
EMP: 9
SQ FT: 7,500

SALES (est): 1.4MM **Privately Held**
SIC: 2752 7331 Commercial printing, offset; direct mail advertising services

(G-12700)
NEEDLES N PINS INC
754 S Main St (48170-2047)
PHONE..................................734 459-0625
Rl Laird, *Owner*
EMP: 6
SALES (est): 835.9K **Privately Held**
WEB: www.needlesnpinsembroidery.com
SIC: 3552 Embroidery machines

(G-12701)
NORTH AMRCN MASUREMENT SYSTEMS
44549 Clare Blvd (48170-3802)
PHONE..................................734 646-3458
David Hickel, *Principal*
EMP: 3 **EST:** 2010
SALES (est): 246.9K **Privately Held**
SIC: 3829 Measuring & controlling devices

(G-12702)
OILES AMERICA CORPORATION
44099 Plymouth Oaks Blvd (48170-6527)
PHONE..................................734 414-7400
Terry Wright, *QC Mgr*
Mickey Rosiu, *Branch Mgr*
EMP: 80 **Privately Held**
WEB: www.oiles.com
SIC: 3714 Motor vehicle parts & accessories
HQ: Oiles America Corporation
4510 Enterprise Dr Nw
Concord NC 28027
704 784-4500

(G-12703)
OPTRAND INC
46155 Five Mile Rd (48170-2424)
PHONE..................................734 451-3480
Marek T Wlodarczyk, *President*
EMP: 13
SQ FT: 10,000
SALES (est): 830K **Privately Held**
WEB: www.optrand.com
SIC: 3229 Glass fiber products

(G-12704)
ORTHOTOOL LLC (PA)
50325 Ann Arbor Rd W (48170-6333)
PHONE..................................734 455-8103
John Chiatalas, *CEO*
David Hellar, *COO*
James B Stiehl, *Chief Mktg Ofcr*
EMP: 4
SQ FT: 200
SALES (est): 511.7K **Privately Held**
SIC: 3143 3144 3149 5047 Orthopedic shoes, men's; orthopedic shoes, women's; orthopedic shoes, children's; orthopedic equipment & supplies

(G-12705)
ORTHOVIEW LLC
44650 Helm Ct (48170-6061)
PHONE..................................800 318-0923
John Chambers, *CEO*
William Peterson, *General Mgr*
EMP: 3
SALES (est): 372.8K **Privately Held**
SIC: 8011 7372 Orthopedic physician; application computer software

(G-12706)
PACKAGING CORPORATION AMERICA
Pca/Plymouth 364
936 N Sheldon Rd (48170-1016)
PHONE..................................734 453-6262
Willie Lathon, *Cust Mgr*
Kavanagh Gary, *Executive*
EMP: 100
SALES (corp-wide): 7B **Publicly Held**
WEB: www.packagingcorp.com
SIC: 2653 Boxes, corrugated: made from purchased materials
PA: Packaging Corporation Of America
1 N Field Ct
Lake Forest IL 60045
847 482-3000

(G-12707)
PALM INDUSTRIES LLC
9135 General Ct (48170-4621)
PHONE..................................248 444-7921
Kay Jolene, *Principal*
EMP: 6
SALES (est): 384.3K **Privately Held**
SIC: 3999 Manufacturing industries

(G-12708)
PARKER-HANNIFIN CORPORATION
Cylinder Division
900 Plymouth Rd (48170-1896)
PHONE..................................734 455-1700
Donald P Szmania, *Branch Mgr*
Robert Jensen,
EMP: 54
SALES (corp-wide): 14.3B **Publicly Held**
WEB: www.parker.com
SIC: 3594 Fluid power pumps & motors
PA: Parker-Hannifin Corporation
6035 Parkland Blvd
Cleveland OH 44124
216 896-3000

(G-12709)
PATRIOT MANUFACTURING LLC (PA)
Also Called: Americam Solutions
45345 Five Mile Rd (48170-2426)
P.O. Box 970, Belleville (48112-0970)
PHONE..................................734 259-2059
Dan Schlamb,
EMP: 3
SALES (est): 602.8K **Privately Held**
SIC: 3999 3545 Barber & beauty shop equipment; machine tool accessories

(G-12710)
PENNISULAR PACKAGING LLC
13505 N Haggerty Rd (48170-4251)
PHONE..................................313 304-4724
Wesley Charles, *President*
EMP: 4
SQ FT: 5,000
SALES (est): 195.1K **Privately Held**
SIC: 3325 Steel foundries

(G-12711)
PENROSE THERAPEUTIX LLC
46701 Commerce Center Dr (48170-2475)
PHONE..................................847 370-0303
Umrai Gill, *Mng Member*
James Jaber,
EMP: 5
SQ FT: 1,000
SALES (est): 336.4K **Privately Held**
SIC: 2834 Proprietary drug products

(G-12712)
PERCEPTRON INC (PA)
47827 Halyard Dr (48170-2461)
PHONE..................................734 414-6100
Jay W Freeland, *Ch of Bd*
David L Watza, *President*
Laura Pecoraro, *Vice Pres*
Richard J Van Valkenburg, *Vice Pres*
Troy Bourassa, *Project Mgr*
▲ **EMP:** 165
SQ FT: 70,000
SALES: 76.8MM **Publicly Held**
WEB: www.perceptron.com
SIC: 3827 3829 Optical instruments & lenses; measuring & controlling devices

(G-12713)
PERIBAMBINI SERVICES LLC
13505 N Haggerty Rd (48170-4251)
PHONE..................................318 466-2881
Dominique Charles, *President*
EMP: 6
SALES (est): 227.4K **Privately Held**
SIC: 2211 Luggage fabrics, cotton

(G-12714)
PHILLIPS SERVICE INDS INC (PA)
Also Called: PSI
14492 N Sheldon Rd # 300 (48170-2493)
PHONE..................................734 853-5000
W Scott Phillips, *President*
William T Phillips, *Chairman*
Robert Phillips, *Vice Pres*
Dave Madgwick, *Opers Mgr*

Phil Peters, *Foreman/Supr*
EMP: 12
SQ FT: 170,000
SALES (est): 67.8MM **Privately Held**
WEB: www.psi-online.com
SIC: 7699 7694 7629 3452 Pumps & pumping equipment repair; valve repair, industrial; electric motor repair; circuit board repair; bolts, nuts, rivets & washers

(G-12715)
PIERBURG INSTRUMENTS
47519 Halyard Dr (48170-2438)
PHONE.................................734 414-9600
Juergen Neugebauer, *President*
Waltraud Zimmer, *Vice Pres*
EMP: 200 **EST:** 1963
SQ FT: 27,560
SALES (est): 11.4MM
SALES (corp-wide): 242.1K **Privately Held**
SIC: 3823 3829 3824 Industrial instrmnts msrmnt display/control process variable; measuring & controlling devices; fluid meters & counting devices
HQ: Avl Michigan Holding Corporation
 47519 Halyard Dr
 Plymouth MI 48170

(G-12716)
PINE TECH INC (PA)
14941 Cleat St (48170-6015)
PHONE.................................989 426-0006
Lawrence H Markey Jr, *President*
Keith A Iverson, *Treasurer*
EMP: 44
SQ FT: 6,000
SALES (est): 3.8MM **Privately Held**
SIC: 2421 2431 2426 Furniture dimension stock, softwood; kiln drying of lumber; millwork; hardwood dimension & flooring mills

(G-12717)
PIOLAX CORPORATION
47075 Five Mile Rd (48170-3765)
PHONE.................................734 668-6005
Fred Beauregard, *Manager*
EMP: 15 **Privately Held**
WEB: www.piolaxusa.com
SIC: 5013 3572 Automotive supplies & parts; disk drives, computer
HQ: Piolax Corporation
 139 Etowah Industrial Ct
 Canton GA 30114
 770 479-2227

(G-12718)
PLASTIPAK HOLDINGS INC (PA)
41605 Ann Arbor Rd E (48170-4304)
P.O. Box 701575 (48170-0967)
PHONE.................................734 455-3600
William C Young, *President*
Sharon Hedgecock, *President*
Reed Newland, *Counsel*
Greg Dean, *Vice Pres*
Tim Eppinga, *Vice Pres*
◆ **EMP:** 15
SQ FT: 37,500
SALES (est): 1.3B **Privately Held**
SIC: 3089 Blow molded finished plastic products

(G-12719)
PLASTIPAK PACKAGING INC (HQ)
Also Called: Multi-Financial
41605 Ann Arbor Rd E (48170-4304)
P.O. Box 701575 (48170-0967)
PHONE.................................734 455-3600
William C Young, *President*
Frank Pollack, *President*
Jim Kulp, *COO*
Gerry Cornell, *Vice Pres*
Richard Darr, *Vice Pres*
◆ **EMP:** 150 **EST:** 1967
SQ FT: 37,500
SALES (est): 1.2B
SALES (corp-wide): 1.3B **Privately Held**
WEB: www.plastipak.com
SIC: 3085 Plastics bottles
PA: Plastipak Holdings, Inc.
 41605 Ann Arbor Rd E
 Plymouth MI 48170
 734 455-3600

(G-12720)
PLYMOUTH PLATING WORKS INC
42200 Joy Rd (48170-4636)
PHONE.................................734 453-1560
Donald E Webb, *President*
Dale E Webb, *Vice Pres*
EMP: 10 **EST:** 1923
SQ FT: 18,000
SALES (est): 1.1MM **Privately Held**
SIC: 3471 Electroplating of metals or formed products

(G-12721)
PLYMOUTH-CANTON CMNTY CRIER (PA)
Also Called: Comma
821 Penniman Ave (48170-1621)
PHONE.................................734 453-6900
W Edward Wendover, *President*
EMP: 30 **EST:** 1974
SQ FT: 10,000
SALES (est): 1.9MM **Privately Held**
SIC: 2711 Newspapers: publishing only, not printed on site

(G-12722)
PLYMOUTH-CANTON CMNTY CRIER
Also Called: Comma
306 S Main St Ste 100 (48170-1604)
PHONE.................................734 453-6900
W Edward Wendover, *President*
Bill Joyner, *Manager*
EMP: 20
SALES (corp-wide): 1.9MM **Privately Held**
SIC: 2791 2711 Typesetting; newspapers
PA: Plymouth-Canton Community Crier Inc
 821 Penniman Ave
 Plymouth MI 48170
 734 453-6900

(G-12723)
POOF-SLINKY LLC
Also Called: Alex Brands
45605 Helm St (48170-6025)
P.O. Box 701394 (48170-0964)
PHONE.................................734 454-9552
Mike Schmitt, *Plant Mgr*
EMP: 30
SQ FT: 18,050
SALES (corp-wide): 100.1MM **Privately Held**
WEB: www.poof-slinky.com
SIC: 3944 Games, toys & children's vehicles
HQ: Poof-Slinky, Llc
 40 Lane Rd
 Fairfield NJ 07004
 734 454-9552

(G-12724)
POWER PROCESS PIPING INC (PA)
45780 Port St (48170-6049)
PHONE.................................734 451-0130
Graham Williams, *CEO*
Steve Fielder, *Superintendent*
Scott Simmers, *Corp Secy*
Art Espey, *COO*
Jerry L Palmer, *Vice Pres*
EMP: 250 **EST:** 1974
SQ FT: 30,000
SALES (est): 102.3MM **Privately Held**
WEB: www.ppphq.com
SIC: 3498 1711 Fabricated pipe & fittings; plumbing, heating, air-conditioning contractors

(G-12725)
PSI HYDRAULICS
14492 N Sheldon Rd # 374 (48170-2493)
PHONE.................................734 261-4160
William T Phillips, *President*
Eugene G Lawrie, *COO*
B J De Boe, *Vice Pres*
Mark W Jahnke, *CFO*
EMP: 200
SALES (est): 25.2MM
SALES (corp-wide): 67.8MM **Privately Held**
SIC: 3452 7629 7699 Bolts, nuts, rivets & washers; electrical repair shops; pumps & pumping equipment repair; valve repair, industrial
PA: Phillips Service Industries, Inc.
 14492 N Sheldon Rd # 300
 Plymouth MI 48170
 734 853-5000

(G-12726)
PYXIS TECHNOLOGIES LLC
45911 Port St (48170-6010)
PHONE.................................734 414-0261
Todd Kuehn,
Jeffrey Wickens,
▲ **EMP:** 43 **EST:** 2000
SQ FT: 51,000
SALES (est): 18MM **Privately Held**
WEB: www.pyxistechnologies.com
SIC: 3599 Machine shop, jobbing & repair

(G-12727)
QUARTERS LLC
1415 Sheridan St (48170-1532)
PHONE.................................313 510-5555
Leonard Daitch, *Mng Member*
EMP: 4
SALES (est): 420.8K **Privately Held**
SIC: 3581 Automatic vending machines

(G-12728)
R & D ENTERPRISES INC
46900 Port St (48170-6035)
PHONE.................................248 349-7077
George Sheriff, *CEO*
Richard D Cox, *CEO*
Diane Cox, *CFO*
Yvonne Cox, *Treasurer*
◆ **EMP:** 50
SQ FT: 58,000
SALES (est): 10.3MM **Privately Held**
WEB: www.rdent.net
SIC: 3443 3519 3429 Heat exchangers: coolers (after, inter), condensers, etc.; parts & accessories, internal combustion engines; manufactured hardware (general)

(G-12729)
R S V P INC
833 Penniman Ave Ste A (48170-2862)
PHONE.................................734 455-7229
Tanja Von Kulajta, *President*
EMP: 6
SQ FT: 1,000
SALES (est): 436K **Privately Held**
SIC: 5947 2759 Gift shop; invitations: printing

(G-12730)
RB OIL ENTERPRISES LLC
Plymouth Mi (48170)
PHONE.................................734 354-0700
Abe Rababeh, *Mng Member*
Yasseen Rababeh,
EMP: 4
SALES (est): 510K **Privately Held**
SIC: 3559 7699 Automotive maintenance equipment; miscellaneous automotive repair services

(G-12731)
RBD CREATIVE
705 S Main St Ste 220 (48170-5436)
PHONE.................................313 259-5507
Stan Dickson, *Principal*
Rebecca Haase, *CFO*
EMP: 5
SALES (est): 307.7K **Privately Held**
SIC: 2759 Publication printing

(G-12732)
RBT MFG LLC
Also Called: Replacement Brush Tables
9033 General Dr (48170-4680)
PHONE.................................800 691-8204
Jeff Fettig, *Sales Mgr*
Greg Gach,
EMP: 3 **EST:** 2017
SALES (est): 149.6K **Privately Held**
SIC: 3991 Brushes, household or industrial

(G-12733)
RECARO NORTH AMERICA INC (HQ)
49200 Halyard Dr (48170-2481)
PHONE.................................734 254-5000
Kai T Weisskopf, *President*
Bill Pierchala, *Controller*
Hendrik Ockenga, *Director*
◆ **EMP:** 80
SQ FT: 110,000
SALES (est): 102.2MM **Privately Held**
WEB: www.recaronorthamerica.com
SIC: 2531 8711 Seats, automobile; engineering services

(G-12734)
RESINATE MATERIALS GROUP INC
46701 Commerce Center Dr C (48170-2475)
PHONE.................................800 891-2955
Brian D Phillips, *CEO*
Brian J Chermside, *COO*
Rick Tabor, *Exec VP*
Cayla Allen, *Marketing Staff*
Adam Emerson, *Lab Dir*
EMP: 16
SQ FT: 5,500
SALES (est): 4.1MM **Privately Held**
SIC: 2821 Plastics materials & resins

(G-12735)
REX M TUBBS
Also Called: Engraving Connection
1205 S Main St (48170-2215)
PHONE.................................734 459-3180
Rex M Tubbs, *Owner*
EMP: 5
SQ FT: 3,500
SALES (est): 240K **Privately Held**
WEB: www.engravecon.com
SIC: 7389 5944 3069 Engraving service; jewelry, precious stones & precious metals; custom compounding of rubber materials

(G-12736)
RIPPER VENTURES LLC
14708 Keel St (48170-6004)
PHONE.................................248 808-2325
Kimberly Ripper, *President*
David Ripper,
EMP: 6
SALES (est): 355K **Privately Held**
SIC: 3949 Gymnasium equipment

(G-12737)
RIVIAN AUTOMOTIVE INC (PA)
13250 N Haggerty Rd (48170-4206)
PHONE.................................734 855-4350
Robert J Scaringe, *CEO*
Matt Tall, *VP Mfg*
Tyler Nuss, *Purch Mgr*
Vikram Appia, *Engineer*
Curt McNamara, *Engineer*
EMP: 100 **EST:** 2015
SQ FT: 40,000
SALES (est): 50.1MM **Privately Held**
SIC: 3711 Automobile assembly, including specialty automobiles

(G-12738)
RIVIAN AUTOMOTIVE INC
41100 Plymouth Rd 4ne (48170-3799)
PHONE.................................408 483-1987
EMP: 4
SALES (corp-wide): 50.1MM **Privately Held**
SIC: 3711 Automobile assembly, including specialty automobiles
PA: Rivian Automotive, Inc.
 13250 N Haggerty Rd
 Plymouth MI 48170
 734 855-4350

(G-12739)
RIVIAN AUTOMOTIVE LLC (HQ)
13250 N Haggerty Rd (48170-4206)
PHONE.................................734 855-4350
Robert Scaringe, *CEO*
Ryan Green, *CFO*
Amy Taylor, *Controller*
Neil Sitron, *General Counsel*
◆ **EMP:** 90 **EST:** 2015
SQ FT: 40,000

SALES (est): 2.1MM
SALES (corp-wide): 50.1MM **Privately Held**
SIC: 3711 3714 Motor vehicles & car bodies; motor vehicle parts & accessories
PA: Rivian Automotive, Inc.
  13250 N Haggerty Rd
  Plymouth MI 48170
  734 855-4350

(G-12740)
RMT ACQUISITION COMPANY LLC (PA)
Also Called: Rmt Woodworth
45755 Five Mile Rd (48170-2476)
PHONE.................................248 353-4229
Terry Woodworth, *CEO*
Kelly Block, *Controller*
EMP: 6
SALES (est): 1MM **Privately Held**
SIC: 3398 Metal heat treating

(G-12741)
ROBERT BOSCH LLC
15000 N Haggerty Rd (48170-3698)
PHONE.................................734 979-3000
Stefan Mischo, *Vice Pres*
Manthan Pandit, *Vice Pres*
Elaine Arnold, *Engineer*
Kevin Maurer, *Sales Staff*
Sam Messina, *Manager*
EMP: 1200
SALES (corp-wide): 294.8MM **Privately Held**
WEB: www.boschservice.com
SIC: 3714 3694 5013 5064 Motor vehicle engines & parts; motor vehicle brake systems & parts; motor vehicle electrical equipment; motors, starting: automotive & aircraft; distributors, motor vehicle engine; automotive supplies & parts; automotive engines & engine parts; automotive brakes; radios, motor vehicle; packaging machinery; deburring machines
HQ: Robert Bosch Llc
  2800 S 25th Ave
  Broadview IL 60155
  248 876-1000

(G-12742)
ROBERT BOSCH LLC
39775 Five Mile Rd (48170-2708)
PHONE.................................734 979-3412
EMP: 441
SALES (corp-wide): 294.8MM **Privately Held**
SIC: 3714 Motor vehicle parts & accessories
HQ: Robert Bosch Llc
  2800 S 25th Ave
  Broadview IL 60155
  248 876-1000

(G-12743)
ROCK TOOL & MACHINE CO INC
45145 Five Mile Rd (48170-2596)
PHONE.................................734 455-9840
Robert Oak, *President*
Laura Frehrenvach, *CFO*
Jonathon Plemmons, *CFO*
Glenn Simms, *Treasurer*
Clay Kessler, *Admin Sec*
▲ **EMP:** 44 **EST:** 1969
SQ FT: 27,000
SALES (est): 10.9MM **Privately Held**
WEB: www.rocktool.com
SIC: 3541 3549 3423 Deburring machines; machine tool replacement & repair parts, metal cutting types; assembly machines, including robotic; hand & edge tools

(G-12744)
ROCK-WAY LLC
40500 Ann Arbor Rd E R (48170-4483)
PHONE.................................734 357-2112
John Formentin,
Ace Wykoff,
EMP: 3
SALES (est): 237K **Privately Held**
SIC: 3532 Rock crushing machinery, stationary

(G-12745)
ROFIN-SINAR TECHNOLOGIES LLC (HQ)
40984 Concept Dr (48170-4252)
PHONE.................................734 416-0206
John R Ambroseo, *President*
Noemi Otero Carbon, *Engineer*
Karen Decker, *Software Dev*
EMP: 10
SQ FT: 52,128
SALES (est): 519.6MM
SALES (corp-wide): 1.9B **Publicly Held**
WEB: www.rofin-inc.com
SIC: 3699 3845 Laser systems & equipment; electromedical equipment
PA: Coherent, Inc.
  5100 Patrick Henry Dr
  Santa Clara CA 95054
  408 764-4000

(G-12746)
RUBBER STAMPS UNLIMITED INC
334 S Harvey St Ste 1 (48170-2270)
PHONE.................................734 451-7300
Maryellen Lewandowski, *President*
William Lewandowski, *Vice Pres*
EMP: 11
SQ FT: 1,500
SALES (est): 1MM **Privately Held**
WEB: www.thestampmaker.com
SIC: 3953 5999 5099 Embossing seals & hand stamps; rubber stamps; rubber stamps

(G-12747)
SAMES KREMLIN INC (DH)
Also Called: Exel Industries Group
45001 Five Mile Rd (48170-2587)
PHONE.................................734 979-0100
Jean Patry, *CEO*
Ryan Gates, *Vice Pres*
Steven Carter, *Opers Mgr*
Ken Coleman, *Production*
Cynthia Overton, *Purch Agent*
▲ **EMP:** 114
SQ FT: 52,000
SALES (est): 45.5MM
SALES (corp-wide): 889.5K **Privately Held**
SIC: 5084 5231 3492 Paint spray equipment, industrial; paint & painting supplies; fluid power valves & hose fittings
HQ: Sames Kremlin
  13 Chemin De Malacher
  Meylan 38240
  476 416-060

(G-12748)
SAMES KREMLIN INC
45001 Five Mile Rd (48170-2587)
PHONE.................................734 979-0100
Todd O'Neill, *Treasurer*
EMP: 15
SQ FT: 52,000
SALES (corp-wide): 889.5K **Privately Held**
SIC: 5084 3561 5231 Paint spray equipment, industrial; pumps & pumping equipment; paint & painting supplies
HQ: Sames Kremlin Inc.
  45001 Five Mile Rd
  Plymouth MI 48170
  734 979-0100

(G-12749)
SAMPO COMPANY LLC
41218 Greenbriar Ln (48170-2624)
PHONE.................................734 664-9761
Thomas Keranen,
EMP: 3
SALES (est): 90.2K **Privately Held**
SIC: 3999 Manufacturing industries

(G-12750)
SAVANNA INC
Also Called: Rmt Woodworth
45755 Five Mile Rd (48170-2476)
PHONE.................................734 254-0566
Bob Bosquez, *Plant Mgr*
EMP: 45 **Privately Held**
SIC: 3398 Metal heat treating
PA: Savanna, Inc.
  20941 East St
  Southfield MI 48033

(G-12751)
SELECT DENTAL GROUPCOM
47299 Five Mile Rd (48170-3764)
PHONE.................................734 459-3200
Moufida Khalife, *Principal*
EMP: 7
SALES (est): 940.3K **Privately Held**
SIC: 3843 Enamels, dentists'

(G-12752)
SGO CORPORATE CENTER LLC (PA)
Also Called: Image360-Plymouth
47581 Galleon Dr (48170-2466)
PHONE.................................248 596-8626
Michael Marcantonio,
EMP: 10
SQ FT: 66,000
SALES: 4.2MM **Privately Held**
SIC: 3993 Signs & advertising specialties

(G-12753)
SIGN & GRAPHICS OPERATIONS LLC
Also Called: Signs By Tomorrow
47585 Galleon Dr (48170-2466)
PHONE.................................248 596-8626
Laura Pierce-Marutz,
EMP: 45
SQ FT: 60,000
SALES: 5.2MM
SALES (corp-wide): 44.2MM **Privately Held**
SIC: 3993 Signs & advertising specialties
PA: Alliance Franchise Brands Llc
  47585 Galleon Dr
  Plymouth MI 48170
  248 596-8600

(G-12754)
SIGNALX TECHNOLOGIES LLC
41100 Plymouth Rd (48170-3799)
PHONE.................................248 935-4237
Garrett Marsh, *Software Engr*
Michael Albright,
Aaron Grzymkowski,
John Niezgoski,
EMP: 11
SALES: 1.7MM **Privately Held**
SIC: 7379 7372 Computer related consulting services; prepackaged software

(G-12755)
SIMOLEX RUBBER CORPORATION
14505 Keel St (48170-6002)
PHONE.................................734 453-4500
Bob Dungarani, *President*
EMP: 15
SQ FT: 15,000
SALES (est): 2.4MM **Privately Held**
WEB: www.simolex.com
SIC: 3069 Molded rubber products

(G-12756)
SKF USA INC
46815 Port St (48170-6060)
PHONE.................................734 414-6585
Steve Robinson, *Project Mgr*
Bernie Kotera, *Mfg Staff*
Nestor Burgermeister, *Purch Mgr*
Brett Lyles, *Engineer*
Lokesh Nagarajan, *Engineer*
EMP: 75
SALES (corp-wide): 9.5B **Privately Held**
WEB: www.skfusa.com
SIC: 3562 3053 8734 Ball & roller bearings; gaskets & sealing devices; testing laboratories
HQ: Skf Usa Inc.
  890 Forty Foot Rd
  Lansdale PA 19446
  267 436-6000

(G-12757)
SKYWAY PRECISION INC (PA)
Also Called: B & D Sales and Service
41225 Plymouth Rd (48170-6123)
PHONE.................................734 454-3550
Bill Bonnell, *President*
Elias Garcia, *Plant Mgr*
Matthew Byers, *Sales Staff*
Pamela Bissell, *Manager*
Alondra Martinez, *Admin Asst*
◆ **EMP:** 165
SQ FT: 84,000
SALES (est): 45.3MM **Privately Held**
WEB: www.skywayprecision.com
SIC: 3599 Machine shop, jobbing & repair

(G-12758)
SOLUTIONS IN STONE INC
41980 Ann Arbor Rd E (48170-4371)
PHONE.................................734 453-4444
Michael Doherty, *President*
EMP: 5
SALES (est): 364.4K **Privately Held**
WEB: www.solutionsinstone.com
SIC: 3281 Granite, cut & shaped

(G-12759)
SPECIAL PROJECTS INC
45901 Helm St (48170-6025)
PHONE.................................734 455-7130
Kenneth E Yanez, *President*
Kyle Yanez, *Corp Comm Staff*
Dave Buyak, *Manager*
Albert Yanez, *Admin Sec*
Debra Herrington, *Admin Asst*
EMP: 32
SALES (est): 7.6MM **Privately Held**
WEB: www.specproj.com
SIC: 3711 3441 Automobile bodies, passenger car, not including engine, etc.; fabricated structural metal

(G-12760)
STARDOCK SYSTEMS INC (PA)
15090 N Beck Rd Ste 300 (48170-2413)
PHONE.................................734 927-0677
Bradley Wardell, *President*
Kris Kwilas, *President*
Angela Marshall, *COO*
Derek Paxton, *Vice Pres*
Jeff Sanders, *QC Mgr*
EMP: 50
SQ FT: 30,000
SALES (est): 8.5MM **Privately Held**
WEB: www.stardock.net
SIC: 7372 7371 Prepackaged software; custom computer programming services

(G-12761)
SUMITOMO ELECTRIC CARBIDE INC
14496 N Sheldon Rd # 230 (48170-2265)
PHONE.................................734 451-0200
Gary McWilliams, *Manager*
EMP: 10 **Privately Held**
WEB: www.sumicarbide.com
SIC: 2819 Carbides
HQ: Sumitomo Electric Carbide Inc
  1001 E Business Center Dr
  Mount Prospect IL 60056
  847 635-0044

(G-12762)
SUN PLASTICS COATING COMPANY
Also Called: Sun Coating Co
42105 Postiff Ave (48170-4688)
PHONE.................................734 453-0822
Joseph Tate, *President*
Mark Tate, *Vice Pres*
Andrew Tate, *Production*
Sandy Tate, *Technology*
EMP: 18
SQ FT: 38,000
SALES (est): 3.3MM **Privately Held**
WEB: www.suncoating.com
SIC: 3479 Coating of metals & formed products

(G-12763)
SUPERIOR CONTROLS INC
Also Called: Redviking
46247 Five Mile Rd (48170-2421)
PHONE.................................734 454-0500
Randall Brodzik, *President*
Mark Sobkow, *Vice Pres*
Michael Glynn, *Engineer*
Kevin Butler, *Treasurer*
Julie Krisko, *Human Res Mgr*
EMP: 195
SQ FT: 45,000

Plymouth - Wayne County (G-12764) — GEOGRAPHIC SECTION

SALES: 45MM **Privately Held**
WEB: www.superiorcontrols.net
SIC: 3613 3823 8711 3829 Control panels, electric; controllers for process variables, all types; consulting engineer; electrical or electronic engineering; dynamometer instruments; relays & industrial controls; machine tool accessories

(G-12764)
T & L TRANSPORT INC
13801 Westbrook Rd (48170-2405)
PHONE.................................313 350-1535
Thomas Marciniak, *Owner*
EMP: 17
SALES: 2MM **Privately Held**
SIC: 3537 Trucks, tractors, loaders, carriers & similar equipment

(G-12765)
TAYLOR MACHINE PRODUCTS INC
176 S Harvey St (48170-1616)
PHONE.................................734 287-3550
Charles W Jones, *Ch of Bd*
EMP: 130
SALES (est): 14.4MM **Privately Held**
SIC: 3451 Screw machine products

(G-12766)
TECH TOOL SUPPLY LLC
9060 General Dr (48170-4624)
PHONE.................................734 207-7700
Brent Hagood, *Mng Member*
Austin Dodson, *Technical Staff*
EMP: 6
SALES (est): 840K **Privately Held**
SIC: 3823 Digital displays of process variables

(G-12767)
TECHNOTRIM INC
40600 Ann Arbor Rd E (48170-4675)
PHONE.................................734 254-5243
Brian Grady, *Ch of Bd*
Lynda Watters, *Controller*
EMP: 1500
SALES (est): 228.8MM **Privately Held**
SIC: 2399 Seat covers, automobile
HQ: Adient Inc.
49200 Halyard Dr
Plymouth MI 48170
734 254-5000

(G-12768)
TEMPRO INDUSTRIES INC
47808 Galleon Dr (48170-2468)
PHONE.................................734 451-5900
Sarah M Fedor, *President*
Matthew Fedor, *Treasurer*
EMP: 15
SQ FT: 13,500
SALES (est): 860K **Privately Held**
SIC: 2396 3498 Automotive & apparel trimmings; tube fabricating (contract bending & shaping)

(G-12769)
TENNECO INC
44099 Plymouth Oaks Blvd (48170-6527)
PHONE.................................734 254-1122
EMP: 3
SALES (corp-wide): 11.7B **Publicly Held**
SIC: 3714 Motor vehicle parts & accessories
PA: Tenneco Inc.
500 N Field Dr
Lake Forest IL 60045
847 482-5000

(G-12770)
THUNDERDOME MEDIA LLC
Also Called: Functional Hand Strength
6218 Valleyfield Dr (48170-7620)
P.O. Box 4429, Ann Arbor (48106-4429)
PHONE.................................800 978-0206
John Wood,
EMP: 4
SALES: 300K **Privately Held**
SIC: 3949 Sporting & athletic goods

(G-12771)
TITANIUM INDUSTRIES INC
14505 Keel St Ste B (48170-6002)
PHONE.................................973 983-1185
Lynn Brace, *Manager*
EMP: 6 **Privately Held**
SIC: 3462 3542 5051 Flange, valve & pipe fitting forgings, ferrous; metal deposit forming machines; iron & steel (ferrous) products
PA: Titanium Industries, Inc.
18 Green Pond Rd Ste 1
Rockaway NJ 07866

(G-12772)
TNT-EDM INC
47689 E Anchor Ct (48170-2455)
PHONE.................................734 459-1700
Tom Mullen, *Principal*
Troy Lockhart, *QC Mgr*
Todd Gardiner, *CFO*
Debbie Reed, *Personnel*
Sam Shegitz, *Prgrmr*
EMP: 25
SQ FT: 76,000
SALES (est): 5.9MM **Privately Held**
WEB: www.tntedm.com
SIC: 3544 Forms (molds), for foundry & plastics working machinery

(G-12773)
TOLEDO MOLDING & DIE INC
Also Called: Development Office
47912 Halyard Dr (48170-2494)
PHONE.................................734 233-6338
Mark Hellie, *Engineer*
Don Harbaugh, *Branch Mgr*
EMP: 7
SALES (corp-wide): 3MM **Privately Held**
SIC: 3823 5013 Fluidic devices, circuits & systems for process control; automotive supplies & parts
HQ: Toledo Molding & Die, Inc.
1429 Coining Dr
Toledo OH 43612
419 470-3950

(G-12774)
TOMAS PLASTICS INC
9833 Tennyson Dr (48170-3643)
PHONE.................................734 455-4706
Frank Tomaszycki, *President*
EMP: 13
SQ FT: 7,200
SALES (est): 1.2MM **Privately Held**
SIC: 3089 Injection molding of plastics

(G-12775)
TOOLCO INC
47709 Galleon Dr (48170-2466)
PHONE.................................734 453-9911
William Tustian, *President*
Rob Tustian, *Plant Mgr*
Greg Cavanaugh, *QC Mgr*
Terry Decamillo, *Engineer*
Karen Dillon, *Office Mgr*
EMP: 35
SQ FT: 16,000
SALES (est): 5MM **Privately Held**
SIC: 3544 Special dies & tools; wire drawing & straightening dies

(G-12776)
TOWER AUTOMOTIVE OPERATIONS I
43955 Plymouth Oaks Blvd (48170-2557)
P.O. Box 701580 (48170-0967)
PHONE.................................734 414-3100
Todd Lee, *General Mgr*
Fred Effinger, *Engineer*
EMP: 200
SALES (corp-wide): 2.2B **Privately Held**
SIC: 3465 Automotive stampings
HQ: Tower Automotive Operations Usa I, Llc
17672 N Laurel Park Dr 400e
Livonia MI 48152

(G-12777)
TRAILER TECH REPAIR INC
Also Called: Trailer Tech One
13101 Eckles Rd (48170-4245)
PHONE.................................734 354-6680
Paul Storey, *President*
EMP: 6
SALES (est): 967.7K **Privately Held**
SIC: 3711 Truck tractors for highway use, assembly of

(G-12778)
TRAM INC (HQ)
47200 Port St (48170-6082)
PHONE.................................734 254-8500
Masayuki Morita, *CEO*
Yoshihei Iida, *Ch of Bd*
Yutaka Yamauchi, *President*
Annie Raba, *Business Mgr*
Koichi Kihira, *Vice Pres*
▲ EMP: 135
SQ FT: 50,000
SALES (est): 268.8MM **Privately Held**
SIC: 3714 3643 Motor vehicle electrical equipment; current-carrying wiring devices

(G-12779)
TRI-POWER MANUFACTURING INC
9229 General Dr Ste B (48170-4672)
PHONE.................................734 414-8084
Marilyn Tringali, *CEO*
Nick Tringali, *Vice Pres*
EMP: 8
SALES (est): 950K **Privately Held**
SIC: 3541 Machine tools, metal cutting type

(G-12780)
TRIN INC
47200 Port St (48170-6082)
PHONE.................................260 587-9282
Theresa Ream, *Mfg Mgr*
Kosuke Naritomi, *Engineer*
Karen Slaughter, *Engineer*
Matt Leslie, *Human Res Mgr*
Nozomu Yamada, *Branch Mgr*
EMP: 7 **Privately Held**
SIC: 3714 Motor vehicle parts & accessories
HQ: Trin, Inc
803 H L Thompson Jr Dr
Ashley IN 46705
260 587-9282

(G-12781)
TROY DESIGN & MANUFACTURING CO (HQ)
14425 N Sheldon Rd (48170-2407)
PHONE.................................734 738-2300
John L Lowery, *President*
Tim Jagoda, *Vice Pres*
Jim Hartsuff, *Purch Mgr*
Ed Strach, *Comptroller*
Jerry Schwartz, *Program Mgr*
▲ EMP: 187 EST: 1981
SQ FT: 115,000
SALES (est): 130.4MM
SALES (corp-wide): 160.3B **Publicly Held**
SIC: 3465 Automotive stampings
PA: Ford Motor Company
1 American Rd
Dearborn MI 48126
313 322-3000

(G-12782)
TRUANS CANDIES INC (PA)
4251 Fleming Way (48170-6361)
PHONE.................................313 281-0185
Mark A Truan, *President*
EMP: 11 EST: 1930
SQ FT: 15,000
SALES (est): 1.3MM **Privately Held**
WEB: www.truanscandiesonline.com
SIC: 2064 5441 Candy bars, including chocolate covered bars; chocolate candy, except solid chocolate; candy

(G-12783)
TRUMPF INC
47711 Clipper St (48170-3591)
PHONE.................................734 354-9770
Tim Morris, *Technical Mgr*
EMP: 50
SALES (corp-wide): 4.2B **Privately Held**
WEB: www.us.trumpf.com
SIC: 3699 Laser welding, drilling & cutting equipment
HQ: Trumpf, Inc.
111 Hyde Rd
Farmington CT 06032
860 255-6000

(G-12784)
USUI INTERNATIONAL CORPORATION (HQ)
44780 Helm St (48170-6026)
PHONE.................................734 354-3626
William Atteberry, *President*
Dennis Chiu, *Vice Pres*
Iyoshi Watanabe, *Vice Pres*
Timothy Sircy, *Treasurer*
◆ EMP: 30
SALES: 206.3MM **Privately Held**
SIC: 3714 3317 Motor vehicle parts & accessories; steel pipe & tubes

(G-12785)
VARN INTERNATIONAL INC
14909 N Beck Rd (48170-2411)
PHONE.................................734 781-4600
William B Miller, *President*
EMP: 6
SALES (est): 631.9K **Privately Held**
SIC: 2899 3555 Chemical preparations; type & type making machinery & equipment

(G-12786)
VARROC LIGHTING SYSTEMS INC (HQ)
Also Called: USA Hq Michigan
47828 Halyard Dr (48170-2454)
PHONE.................................734 446-4400
Stephane Vedie, *President*
Jorge Cornejo, *Vice Pres*
Enrique Galvan, *Opers Staff*
John Kovalik, *Mfg Staff*
Ed Baetzold, *Engineer*
▲ EMP: 100
SALES (est): 678.7MM **Privately Held**
SIC: 3751 Motorcycles, bicycles & parts

(G-12787)
VELESCO PHRM SVCS INC (PA)
46701 Commerce Center Dr (48170-2475)
PHONE.................................734 527-9125
David Barnes, *CEO*
EMP: 15
SQ FT: 2,300
SALES (est): 3.9MM **Privately Held**
SIC: 3559 2834 Pharmaceutical machinery; druggists' preparations (pharmaceuticals)

(G-12788)
VENTURA INDUSTRIES INC
46301 Port St (48170-6043)
PHONE.................................734 357-0114
Gary Winkler, *President*
Nicholas Mustola, *Engineer*
EMP: 40 EST: 1966
SQ FT: 22,000
SALES (est): 4.3MM **Privately Held**
SIC: 3728 Aircraft assemblies, subassemblies & parts

(G-12789)
VICO COMPANY
41555 Ann Arbor Rd E (48170-4300)
PHONE.................................734 453-3777
Curt Schultz, *President*
▲ EMP: 6
SQ FT: 6,000
SALES (est): 470K **Privately Held**
SIC: 3299 Sand lime products

(G-12790)
VICO PRODUCTS CO (PA)
41555 Ann Arbor Rd E (48170-4397)
PHONE.................................734 453-3777
Curt R Schultz, *President*
Caryn Williams, *Vice Pres*
Joaquin Davis, *Program Mgr*
▲ EMP: 110 EST: 1943
SQ FT: 88,000
SALES (est): 26.6MM **Privately Held**
WEB: www.vico.com
SIC: 3452 Bolts, metal; screws, metal; pins

(G-12791)
WEBASTO CONVERTIBLES USA INC (DH)
Also Called: Webasto-Group
14988 Pilot Dr (48170-3672)
PHONE.................................734 582-5900
Mark Denny, *CEO*
Dr Holger Engelmann, *Ch of Bd*

Axel Schulmeyer, *President*
Wisam Aljoher, *Engineer*
Stephen Chesna, *CFO*
▲ **EMP:** 130
SQ FT: 144,000
SALES (est): 30.6MM
SALES (corp-wide): 411.9K **Privately Held**
SIC: 3714 Tops, motor vehicle
HQ: Webasto Roof Systems Inc.
 1757 Northfield Dr
 Rochester Hills MI 48309
 248 997-5100

(G-12792)
WEBASTO CONVERTIBLES USA INC
14967 Pilot Dr (48170-3674)
PHONE..................734 582-5900
Mark Denny, *Branch Mgr*
EMP: 3
SALES (corp-wide): 411.9K **Privately Held**
SIC: 3559 Automotive related machinery
HQ: Webasto Convertibles Usa Inc.
 14988 Pilot Dr
 Plymouth MI 48170

(G-12793)
WESTROCK COMPANY
11333 General Dr (48170-4337)
PHONE..................734 453-6700
Jeff Bettelom, *Branch Mgr*
EMP: 50
SALES (corp-wide): 14.8B **Publicly Held**
SIC: 2653 Boxes, corrugated: made from purchased materials
PA: Westrock Company
 1000 Abernathy Rd Ste 125
 Atlanta GA 30328
 770 448-2193

(G-12794)
WHITING CORPORATION
48961 Thoreau Dr (48170-3341)
PHONE..................734 451-0400
EMP: 3
SALES (corp-wide): 102.5MM **Privately Held**
SIC: 3536 5084 3535 Mfg Hoists/Cranes/Monorails Whol Industrial Equipment Mfg Conveyors/Equipment
HQ: Whiting Corporation
 26000 S Whiting Way Ste 1
 Monee IL 60449
 708 587-2000

(G-12795)
YALE TOOL & ENGRAVING INC
1471 Gold Smith (48170-1082)
PHONE..................734 459-7171
Frank A Bauss, *President*
Robert B Zalobsky, *President*
Daniel J Damiani, *Vice Pres*
Janice P Zalobsky, *Admin Sec*
EMP: 8
SQ FT: 5,100
SALES: 591.9K **Privately Held**
WEB: www.yaletool.com
SIC: 3599 3479 Machine shop, jobbing & repair; etching & engraving

(G-12796)
YANFENG US AUTOMOTIVE
49200 Halyard Dr (48170-2481)
PHONE..................734 254-5000
Nelli Shmidt, *Engineer*
Alan Mumby, *Branch Mgr*
Mariana Birlan, *Program Mgr*
Lisa Johnson, *Technology*
Mukesh Kumar, *IT/INT Sup*
EMP: 240
SALES (corp-wide): 55MM **Privately Held**
SIC: 3089 Injection molding of plastics
HQ: Yanfeng Us Automotive Interior Systems I Llc
 41935 W 12 Mile Rd
 Novi MI 48377
 248 319-7333

Pontiac
Oakland County

(G-12797)
21ST CENTURY NEWSPAPERS INC
Also Called: Homes For Sale
28 W Huron St (48342-2100)
PHONE..................586 469-4510
Justin Wilcox, *Manager*
EMP: 100
SALES (corp-wide): 697.5MM **Privately Held**
WEB: www.macombdaily.com
SIC: 2711 Newspapers, publishing & printing
HQ: 21st Century Newspapers, Inc.
 19176 Hall Rd Ste 200
 Clinton Township MI 48038
 586 469-4510

(G-12798)
ACCESSORIES WHOLESALE INC
Also Called: Accessories R US
555 Friendly St (48341-2650)
PHONE..................248 755-7465
Claudia Tomina, *President*
Mitch Gappy, *Partner*
Sahir Gappy, *Partner*
EMP: 14
SQ FT: 32,000
SALES: 9.2MM **Privately Held**
SIC: 3679 Antennas, receiving

(G-12799)
AIRLITE SYNTHETICS MFG INC
342 Irwin Ave (48341-2949)
PHONE..................248 335-8131
Ronald Herman, *President*
Sharon Herman, *Corp Secy*
Eric Herman, *Vice Pres*
EMP: 10 **EST:** 1974
SQ FT: 36,400
SALES (est): 1.1MM **Privately Held**
SIC: 2299 Pillow fillings: curled hair, cotton waste, moss, hemp tow; quilt fillings: curled hair, cotton waste, moss, hemp tow

(G-12800)
AKZO NOBEL COATINGS INC
120 Franklin Rd (48342-2220)
P.O. Box 669 (48341)
PHONE..................248 451-6231
Richard Gray, *General Mgr*
Satyam Naik, *Prdtn Mgr*
Kelly Shimmell, *Production*
Nancy Corrion-Powers, *Human Res Mgr*
EMP: 100
SALES (corp-wide): 11.3B **Privately Held**
WEB: www.nam.sikkens.com
SIC: 2851 2869 Paints & allied products; industrial organic chemicals
HQ: Akzo Nobel Coatings Inc.
 8220 Mohawk Dr
 Strongsville OH 44136
 440 297-5100

(G-12801)
AKZO NOBEL COATINGS INC
Also Called: Deco Finishes
117 Brush St (48341-2215)
PHONE..................248 637-0400
Dave Bupler, *Principal*
Cor Degrauw, *Administration*
EMP: 25
SALES (corp-wide): 11.3B **Privately Held**
WEB: www.nam.sikkens.com
SIC: 2851 8731 Wood stains; commercial physical research
HQ: Akzo Nobel Coatings Inc.
 8220 Mohawk Dr
 Strongsville OH 44136
 440 297-5100

(G-12802)
ALUMINUM BLANKING CO INC
Also Called: Abco
360 W Sheffield Ave (48340-1879)
PHONE..................248 338-4422
Marvin Hole, *CEO*
Eric Hole, *President*
Laura Anderson, *Exec VP*
Chris Morris, *Human Res Mgr*
Enoch Davis, *Technology*
▲ **EMP:** 80
SQ FT: 160,000
SALES (est): 21.2MM **Privately Held**
WEB: www.albl.com
SIC: 3469 3446 3444 3353 Metal stampings; architectural metalwork; sheet metalwork; aluminum sheet, plate & foil; copper rolling & drawing; secondary non-ferrous metals

(G-12803)
AMERICAN ASSEMBLERS INC
40 W Howard St Ste 222 (48342-1282)
PHONE..................248 334-9777
Gerald Shohan, *President*
Sandy Clemons, *Manager*
EMP: 6
SQ FT: 2,000
SALES (est): 796.5K **Privately Held**
SIC: 3544 Industrial molds

(G-12804)
AMERIPAK INC
591 Bradford St (48341-3112)
PHONE..................248 858-9000
Aaron Martin, *President*
EMP: 12
SQ FT: 5,000
SALES (est): 1.6MM **Privately Held**
WEB: www.ameripakpackaging.com
SIC: 3086 Packaging & shipping materials, foamed plastic

(G-12805)
AUTOLIV ASP INC
Also Called: Autoliv Technical Center-W
856 Featherstone St (48342-1723)
PHONE..................248 761-0081
Bruce Nara, *Program Mgr*
EMP: 155
SALES (corp-wide): 8.6B **Publicly Held**
SIC: 3714 Motor vehicle parts & accessories
HQ: Autoliv Asp, Inc.
 1000 W 3300 S
 Ogden UT 84401
 248 475-9000

(G-12806)
AUTOMOTIVE MEDIA LLC
Also Called: I.M. Branded
2020 Ring Rd (48341-3189)
PHONE..................248 537-8500
Jim Whitehead, *President*
Kristie Shepard, *Project Mgr*
Ryan Helme, *Purch Mgr*
Jeff Morche, *Engineer*
Jennifer Zaraga, *Accounting Mgr*
EMP: 125
SQ FT: 20,000
SALES: 30MM **Privately Held**
WEB: www.innovativemediallc.com
SIC: 2752 Commercial printing, lithographic

(G-12807)
BMAX USA LLC
777 Enterprise Dr Ste 100 (48341-3169)
PHONE..................248 794-4176
Rani Plaut, *CEO*
EMP: 30 **EST:** 2014
SQ FT: 10,000
SALES: 5MM
SALES (corp-wide): 257K **Privately Held**
SIC: 3542 Electroforming machines
PA: Ipulse
 78 Rue La Condamine
 Paris
 609 816-406

(G-12808)
CHEROKEE INDUSTRIES INC
28 N Saginaw St Ste 911 (48342-2142)
PHONE..................248 333-1343
Yvonne Miller, *President*
EMP: 4
SALES (est): 290K **Privately Held**
SIC: 2671 Packaging paper & plastics film, coated & laminated

(G-12809)
CLAMP INDUSTRIES INCORPORATED
342 Irwin Ave (48341-2949)
PHONE..................248 335-8131
Eric Herman, *Principal*
EMP: 12 **EST:** 1995
SQ FT: 35,000
SALES (est): 708.4K **Privately Held**
SIC: 2299 Textile mill waste & remnant processing

(G-12810)
CLYDES FRAME & WHEEL SERVICE
725 Cesar E Chavez Ave (48340-2464)
PHONE..................248 338-0323
Charles Spurgeon, *President*
Charlene Spurgeon, *Treasurer*
EMP: 12
SQ FT: 17,000
SALES: 1.6MM **Privately Held**
SIC: 7539 4959 5012 3715 Automotive repair shops; snowplowing; trailers for trucks, new & used; truck trailers

(G-12811)
CREATIVE DESIGNS & SIGNS INC
146 Cesar E Chavez Ave (48342-2047)
PHONE..................248 334-5580
Albert F Lalonde, *President*
Jody C La Londe, *Vice Pres*
EMP: 5
SQ FT: 12,000
SALES (est): 609.7K **Privately Held**
SIC: 3993 Signs, not made in custom sign painting shops

(G-12812)
CUPCAKE STATION
47 Peggy Ave (48341-1921)
PHONE..................248 334-7927
Kerry Johnson, *Principal*
EMP: 3
SALES (est): 232.1K **Privately Held**
SIC: 2051 Bread, cake & related products

(G-12813)
DAILY OAKLAND PRESS (DH)
48 W Huron St (48342-2101)
P.O. Box 436009 (48343-6009)
PHONE..................248 332-8181
Jerry Bammel, *President*
Greg Mazanec, *Publisher*
Matt Mowery, *Editor*
EMP: 365
SQ FT: 77,600
SALES: 38.3MM
SALES (corp-wide): 697.5MM **Privately Held**
WEB: www.theoaklandpress.com
SIC: 2711 2791 2752 Newspapers, publishing & printing; typesetting; commercial printing, lithographic
HQ: 21st Century Newspapers, Inc.
 19176 Hall Rd Ste 200
 Clinton Township MI 48038
 586 469-4510

(G-12814)
DATACOVER INC
1735 Highwood W (48340-1264)
PHONE..................844 875-4076
Justin Powers, *CEO*
Roberto Loftin, *CEO*
EMP: 4
SQ FT: 6,000
SALES (est): 286K **Privately Held**
SIC: 3089 Boxes, plastic; cases, plastic

(G-12815)
DEL PUEBLO TORTILLAS
511 N Perry St (48342-2452)
PHONE..................248 858-9835
Rosalia A Narvaez, *Owner*
EMP: 3 **EST:** 1975
SQ FT: 1,500
SALES (est): 154.5K **Privately Held**
SIC: 2099 Tortillas, fresh or refrigerated

Pontiac - Oakland County (G-12816)

(G-12816)
DETROIT STEEL TREATING COMPANY
1631 Highwood E (48340-1236)
PHONE 248 334-7436
Raymond D Fox, *President*
Helene Fox, *Treasurer*
Janet Fox, *Admin Sec*
EMP: 32 **EST:** 1923
SQ FT: 18,000
SALES (est): 6MM **Privately Held**
WEB: www.sunsteeltreating.com
SIC: 3398 3544 3471 3423 Metal heat treating; special dies, tools, jigs & fixtures; plating & polishing; hand & edge tools; industrial furnaces & ovens

(G-12817)
DIAMOND CASE HOLDINGS LLC
1590 Highwood E Ste A (48340-1239)
PHONE 800 293-2496
Jeff Cunningham,
▲ **EMP:** 9
SALES (est): 1.2MM **Privately Held**
SIC: 3544 Special dies, tools, jigs & fixtures

(G-12818)
DONE RIGHT ENGRAVING INC
Also Called: Done Right Enterprises
119 N Saginaw St (48342-2113)
PHONE 248 332-3133
Kathleen Trombly, *CEO*
Steven C Trombly, *President*
Kevin Ollila, *General Mgr*
Bruce D Trombly, *Vice Pres*
EMP: 5 **EST:** 1972
SQ FT: 23,500
SALES (est): 642.7K **Privately Held**
WEB: www.donerightsigns.com
SIC: 7336 3479 Silk screen design; etching & engraving

(G-12819)
EASTERN OIL COMPANY (PA)
Also Called: Bipco
590 S Paddock St (48341-3236)
PHONE 248 333-1333
Mike Skuratovich, *CEO*
Theodore R Plafchan, *President*
Carol L Plafchan, *Vice Pres*
Aaron Spencer, *Prdtn Mgr*
Erin Viers, *Accountant*
EMP: 40
SQ FT: 26,000
SALES (est): 25.1MM **Privately Held**
WEB: www.easternoil.com
SIC: 5172 2992 5087 3471 Lubricating oils & greases; lubricating oils & greases; service establishment equipment; plating & polishing; chemical preparations

(G-12820)
ELAN DESIGNS INC
238 S Telegraph Rd (48341-1933)
PHONE 248 682-3000
Elan Bauer, *President*
EMP: 4
SQ FT: 2,400
SALES: 230K **Privately Held**
SIC: 2434 2431 Wood kitchen cabinets; millwork

(G-12821)
ELECTROLUX PROFESSIONAL INC
Also Called: Aerus Electrolux
214 S Telegraph Rd (48341-1933)
PHONE 248 338-4320
EMP: 5
SALES (corp-wide): 13.7B **Privately Held**
SIC: 5722 5064 3635 Vacuum cleaners; vacuum cleaners; household vacuum cleaners
HQ: Electrolux Professional, Inc.
   20445 Emerald Pkwy
   Cleveland OH 44135
   216 898-1800

(G-12822)
ENERGY POWERCELL LLC
750 South Blvd E (48341-3129)
PHONE 248 585-1000
Subhash Dhar, *CEO*
Fabio Albano,
EMP: 20
SALES (est): 4.8MM **Privately Held**
SIC: 3691 Storage batteries

(G-12823)
ERAE AMS AMERICA CORP
2011 Centerpoint Pkwy (48341-3148)
PHONE 419 386-8876
James Kim, *CEO*
JB Yoon, *CFO*
EMP: 17
SQ FT: 155,000 **Privately Held**
SIC: 6719 3714 Investment holding companies, except banks; drive shafts, motor vehicle

(G-12824)
ERAE AMS USA MANUFACTURING LLC
Also Called: Branch Office
2011 Centerpoint Pkwy (48341-3148)
PHONE 248 770-6969
James Kim, *President*
Joongbeom Yoon, *CFO*
EMP: 17
SQ FT: 160,000
SALES (est): 2.1MM **Privately Held**
SIC: 3559 Automotive related machinery

(G-12825)
FREIBORNE INDUSTRIES INC
15 W Silverdome Indus Par (48342-2994)
PHONE 248 333-2490
Kevin Gill, *CEO*
Scott Herkes, *President*
Maureen Gill, *Chairman*
Keith Sturgeon, *Plant Mgr*
Brian Knapp, *Accounts Exec*
EMP: 20
SQ FT: 24,000
SALES (est): 5.7MM **Privately Held**
WEB: www.freiborne.com
SIC: 2819 Phosphates, except fertilizers: defluorinated & ammoniated

(G-12826)
GENERAL MOTORS LLC
895 Joslyn Ave (48340-2920)
PHONE 248 874-1737
EMP: 190
SALES (corp-wide): 155.9B **Publicly Held**
SIC: 3711 3714 Mfg Motor Vehicle/Car Bodies Mfg Motor Vehicle Parts/Accessories
HQ: General Motors Llc
   300 Renaissance Ctr L1
   Detroit MI 48243
   313 556-5000

(G-12827)
GENERAL MOTORS LLC
2000 Centerpoint Pkwy (48341-3146)
PHONE 248 456-5000
Kim Konesny, *Engineer*
John Tamm, *Branch Mgr*
EMP: 21 **Publicly Held**
SIC: 5511 3714 6153 6141 Automobiles, new & used; motor vehicle parts & accessories; short-term business credit; personal credit institutions; automobile finance leasing; fire, marine & casualty insurance
HQ: General Motors Llc
   300 Renaissance Ctr L1
   Detroit MI 48243

(G-12828)
GENERAL MOTORS LLC
1251 Joslyn Ave (48340-2064)
PHONE 248 857-3500
Stephanie Malave, *Branch Mgr*
EMP: 700 **Publicly Held**
SIC: 5511 5012 3711 Automobiles, new & used; automobiles & other motor vehicles; motor vehicles & car bodies
HQ: General Motors Llc
   300 Renaissance Ctr L1
   Detroit MI 48243

(G-12829)
GONZALEZ PROD SYSTEMS INC
1670 Highwood E (48340-1235)
PHONE 248 745-1200
Gary Gonzalez, *Owner*
EMP: 120
SALES (corp-wlde): 57.7MM **Privately Held**
WEB: www.gonzprodsys.com
SIC: 3535 Conveyors & conveying equipment
PA: Gonzalez Production Systems, Inc.
   1670 Highwood E
   Pontiac MI 48340
   248 548-6010

(G-12830)
GRAND TRUNK RR
777 Cesar E Chavez Ave (48340-2466)
PHONE 248 452-4881
EMP: 5 **EST:** 2011
SALES (est): 685.5K **Privately Held**
SIC: 3161 Trunks

(G-12831)
GVN GROUP CORP (PA)
Also Called: Sharpertek
486 S Opdyke Rd (48341-3119)
PHONE 248 340-0342
Gus Nasrala, *President*
Ghassan Nasrallah, *General Mgr*
Tim Bartlett, *Accounts Mgr*
▲ **EMP:** 30
SQ FT: 33,000
SALES: 2.5MM **Privately Held**
SIC: 3699 Cleaning equipment, ultrasonic, except medical & dental

(G-12832)
HEAT TREATING SVCS CORP AMER (PA)
217 Central Ave (48341-2924)
P.O. Box 430269 (48343-0269)
PHONE 248 858-2230
Stephen R Hynes, *President*
Tara Kranz, *Corp Secy*
Brad Hynes, *Vice Pres*
Ken Rogghe, *Engineer*
Liz Mauricio, *Human Res Mgr*
EMP: 40
SQ FT: 36,000
SALES (est): 22.7MM **Privately Held**
WEB: www.htsmi.com
SIC: 3398 Metal heat treating

(G-12833)
HEAT TREATING SVCS CORP AMER
915 Cesar E Chavez Ave (48340-2374)
PHONE 248 332-1510
Bob Culbreath, *Principal*
EMP: 30
SALES (corp-wide): 22.7MM **Privately Held**
WEB: www.htsmi.com
SIC: 3398 Metal heat treating
PA: Heat Treating Services Corporation Of America
   217 Central Ave
   Pontiac MI 48341
   248 858-2230

(G-12834)
HERITAGE NEWSPAPERS
28 W Huron St (48342-2100)
PHONE 586 783-0300
EMP: 3
SALES (est): 145K **Privately Held**
SIC: 2711 Newspapers, publishing & printing

(G-12835)
HIGHWOOD DIE & ENGINEERING INC
1353 Highwood Blvd (48340-1925)
PHONE 248 338-1807
Marilyn Miller, *President*
Mike Miller, *Treasurer*
Jodi Sheridan, *Admin Sec*
EMP: 30
SQ FT: 20,000
SALES (est): 11.6MM **Privately Held**
SIC: 3469 3544 Stamping metal for the trade; special dies, tools, jigs & fixtures

(G-12836)
INTEGRATED MARKETING SVCS LLC
Also Called: IMS
125 E Columbia Ave (48340-2715)
PHONE 248 625-7444
Larry Orlando, *General Mgr*
Robert C Schaffer, *Mng Member*
Robert Schaffer, *Mng Member*
EMP: 15 **EST:** 1999
SALES (est): 2.6MM **Privately Held**
WEB: www.4ims.net
SIC: 3823 Water quality monitoring & control systems

(G-12837)
IRVIN ACQUISITION LLC (HQ)
2600 Centerpoint Pkwy (48341-3172)
PHONE 248 451-4100
Vincent Johnson,
EMP: 14
SALES (est): 554.2MM
SALES (corp-wide): 1.6B **Privately Held**
SIC: 2396 Automotive & apparel trimmings
PA: Piston Group, L.L.C.
   3000 Town Ctr Ste 3250
   Southfield MI 48075
   248 226-3976

(G-12838)
IRVIN AUTOMOTIVE PRODUCTS LLC (DH)
2600 Centerpoint Pkwy (48341-3172)
PHONE 248 451-4100
Timothy Mann, *Vice Pres*
Jason Kennedy, *CIO*
Joseph Finn,
▲ **EMP:** 150
SQ FT: 70,000
SALES (est): 7.7MM
SALES (corp-wide): 1.6B **Privately Held**
WEB: www.irvinautomotive.com
SIC: 2396 Automotive & apparel trimmings
HQ: Irvin Acquisition Llc
   2600 Centerpoint Pkwy
   Pontiac MI 48341
   248 451-4100

(G-12839)
JAC HOLDING CORPORATION (DH)
3937 Campus Dr (48341-3124)
PHONE 248 874-1800
Jack Falcon, *CEO*
Mike Wood, *COO*
Noel Ranka, *Vice Pres*
Mike Vanloon, *CFO*
◆ **EMP:** 5
SALES (est): 269.7MM
SALES (corp-wide): 608.8MM **Privately Held**
SIC: 3089 Injection molding of plastics
HQ: Argonaut Private Equity Fund Iii, Lp
   7030 S Yale Ave Ste 810
   Tulsa OK 74136
   918 392-9600

(G-12840)
JAC PRODUCTS INC
3937 Campus Dr (48341-3124)
PHONE 248 874-1800
Don Cline, *Branch Mgr*
Eric Kromer, *Technology*
EMP: 70
SALES (corp-wide): 608.8MM **Privately Held**
WEB: www.jacproducts.com
SIC: 3089 3714 Injection molding of plastics; motor vehicle parts & accessories
HQ: Jac Products, Inc.
   225 S Industrial Dr
   Saline MI 48176
   734 944-8844

(G-12841)
JOMAR PERFORMANCE PRODUCTS LLC
211 N Cass Ave (48342-1005)
PHONE 248 322-3080
John J Ansteth, *Mng Member*
Geraldine Ansteth,
Jonathan Best,
EMP: 4
SQ FT: 3,600
SALES (est): 611.2K **Privately Held**
WEB: www.jomarperformance.com
SIC: 3714 Motor vehicle parts & accessories

GEOGRAPHIC SECTION

(G-12842) JOY INDUSTRIES INC
117 Turk St (48341-3068)
PHONE...............................248 334-4062
Norman Beaubien, *President*
EMP: 10
SALES (est): 1MM **Privately Held**
WEB: www.joyindustries.com
SIC: 7692 Automotive welding

(G-12843) JUNK MAN LLC
111 Vernon Dr (48342-2559)
PHONE...............................248 459-7359
Jaquan Whittaker,
EMP: 5
SALES: 426K **Privately Held**
SIC: 3711 Wreckers (tow truck), assembly of

(G-12844) KODIAK MANUFACTURING CO INC
318 Irwin Ave (48341-2947)
PHONE...............................248 335-5552
James Warrick, *President*
Julie Ozias, *Manager*
EMP: 9
SQ FT: 5,000
SALES (est): 1.4MM **Privately Held**
SIC: 3599 Machine shop, jobbing & repair

(G-12845) LORYCO INC
51920 Woodward Ave Ste B (48342-5035)
PHONE...............................248 674-4673
Justin Ballard, *President*
EMP: 5
SALES: 700K **Privately Held**
SIC: 3492 Hose & tube fittings & assemblies, hydraulic/pneumatic

(G-12846) LPM SUPPLY INC
Also Called: Ladlas Prince
28 N Saginaw St Ste 801 (48342-2148)
PHONE...............................248 333-9440
Amos O Ajani, *Principal*
EMP: 4 **EST:** 2012
SALES (est): 268.6K **Privately Held**
SIC: 3494 Valves & pipe fittings

(G-12847) MANTA GROUP LLC
Also Called: Pk Global Logistics
35 W Huron St Ste 10 (48342-2120)
PHONE...............................248 325-8264
Reginald B Kelley Sr,
EMP: 5
SALES (est): 828.5K **Privately Held**
SIC: 3296 Mineral wool

(G-12848) MERRIFIELD MCHY SOLUTIONS INC
1651 Highwood E (48340-1236)
PHONE...............................248 494-7335
Richard Rohn, *Principal*
Fred Gravelle, *Finance Mgr*
Barbara Lewis, *Sales Staff*
Nicholas Merrifield, *Info Tech Dir*
EMP: 34
SALES (est): 3.3MM **Privately Held**
SIC: 3545 5084 Machine tool accessories; industrial machinery & equipment

(G-12849) METALWORKING LUBRICANTS CO (PA)
25 W Silverdome Indus Par (48342-2994)
P.O. Box 214379, Auburn Hills (48321-4379)
PHONE...............................248 332-3500
Robert F Tomlinson, *Ch of Bd*
Kim Onnie, *General Mgr*
Adam Bujoll, *Vice Pres*
Dr Nilda Grenier, *Vice Pres*
Sandra Ruggles, *Mfg Staff*
▲ **EMP:** 243
SQ FT: 26,000
SALES (est): 221.8MM **Privately Held**
WEB: www.mwlco.com
SIC: 5172 2869 2843 2992 Lubricating oils & greases; phosphoric acid esters; emulsifiers, except food & pharmaceutical; cutting oils, blending: made from purchased materials; rust arresting compounds, animal or vegetable oil base

(G-12850) MIS ASSOCIATES INC
Also Called: Data Cover .com
1735 Highwood W (48340-1264)
PHONE...............................844 225-8156
Roberto LIftin, *President*
Roberto Loftin, *President*
EMP: 5
SQ FT: 4,000
SALES (est): 1.2MM **Privately Held**
SIC: 5112 2865 5085 Office supplies; laserjet supplies; color lakes or toners; ink, printers

(G-12851) MORNING STAR PUBLISHING CO
Also Called: Northern Star
48 W Huron St (48342-2101)
PHONE...............................989 732-5125
Kevin Jones, *Manager*
EMP: 12
SALES (corp-wide): 697.5MM **Privately Held**
SIC: 2711 Newspapers, publishing & printing
HQ: Morning Star Publishing Company
  311 E Superior St Ste A
  Alma MI 48801
  989 779-6000

(G-12852) NORTHERN STAIRCASE CO INC
630 Cesar E Chavez Ave (48342-1057)
PHONE...............................248 836-0652
Patrick Donovan, *President*
James Steinhaus, *Vice Pres*
EMP: 13
SQ FT: 18,000
SALES (est): 1.7MM **Privately Held**
SIC: 2431 Staircases & stairs, wood

(G-12853) O TP INDUSTRIAL SOLUTIONS
895 Joslyn Ave (48340-2920)
PHONE...............................248 745-5503
Sarah Whetstone, *Principal*
EMP: 3 **EST:** 2010
SALES (est): 204K **Privately Held**
SIC: 3568 Power transmission equipment

(G-12854) OVSHINSKY TECHNOLOGIES LLC
1 N Saginaw St (48342-2111)
PHONE...............................248 390-3564
Guy Wicker,
EMP: 4
SALES (est): 88.6K **Privately Held**
SIC: 8731 3674 3559 Natural resource research; solar cells; semiconductor manufacturing machinery

(G-12855) PEPSI-COLA METRO BTLG CO INC
960 Featherstone St (48342-1827)
PHONE...............................248 335-3528
Jennifer Mayer, *Financial Exec*
Jeff Bickerman, *Manager*
Kurt Norman, *Manager*
Joel Phillips, *Manager*
EMP: 115
SALES (corp-wide): 64.6B **Publicly Held**
WEB: www.joy-of-cola.com
SIC: 2086 Carbonated soft drinks, bottled & canned
HQ: Pepsi-Cola Metropolitan Bottling Company, Inc.
  1111 Westchester Ave
  White Plains NY 10604
  914 767-6000

(G-12856) PONTIAC ELECTRIC MOTOR WORKS
224 W Sheffield Ave (48340-1854)
PHONE...............................248 332-4622
Peter A Polk, *President*
Joan E Polk, *Corp Secy*
Anthony Polk, *Vice Pres*
EMP: 5
SQ FT: 2,400
SALES (est): 1.9MM **Privately Held**
WEB: www.electric-motor-works.com
SIC: 5063 7694 Motors, electric; electric motor repair

(G-12857) PRESS ROOM EQP SLS & SVC CO
244 W Sheffield Ave (48340-1854)
PHONE...............................248 334-1880
Rick Hole, *President*
Scott Hole, *Vice Pres*
EMP: 6
SQ FT: 6,000
SALES (est): 765.9K **Privately Held**
SIC: 5084 3542 Industrial machinery & equipment; machine tools, metal forming type

(G-12858) PRIMO CRAFTS
1304 University Dr (48342-1974)
PHONE...............................248 373-3229
Brian F Mc Carthy, *Owner*
EMP: 8
SQ FT: 3,500
SALES: 190K **Privately Held**
SIC: 2759 Screen printing

(G-12859) PRINTWAND INC
Also Called: Company Folders
22 W Huron St (48342-2192)
PHONE...............................248 738-7225
Vladimir Gendelman, *CEO*
EMP: 8
SQ FT: 5,000
SALES (est): 929.9K **Privately Held**
WEB: www.printwand.com
SIC: 7311 2752 Advertising agencies; commercial printing, lithographic

(G-12860) RAQ LLC
392 S Sanford St (48342-3448)
PHONE...............................313 473-7271
Jon Sader, *Mng Member*
EMP: 13 **EST:** 2013
SQ FT: 7,500
SALES: 104.9K **Privately Held**
SIC: 3449 Custom roll formed products

(G-12861) RESOURCE RCOVERY SOLUTIONS INC
100 W Sheffield Ave (48340-1850)
PHONE...............................248 454-3442
Andrew Quigley, *President*
EMP: 7
SQ FT: 15,000
SALES (est): 846.5K **Privately Held**
SIC: 3339 5093 Primary nonferrous metals; nonferrous metals scrap; metal scrap & waste materials

(G-12862) RIVORE METALS LLC
500 South Blvd E Ste 200 (48341-3143)
PHONE...............................248 397-8724
EMP: 22
SALES (corp-wide): 21.5MM **Privately Held**
SIC: 3914 Silverware & plated ware
PA: Rivore Metals Llc
  850 Stephenson Hwy # 200
  Troy MI 48083
  800 248-1250

(G-12863) S & B ROOFING SERVICES INC
Also Called: General Roofing Services
184 W Sheffield Ave (48340-1852)
PHONE...............................248 334-5372
Fax: 248 334-5897
EMP: 95
SQ FT: 20,000
SALES (est): 4.2MM
SALES (corp-wide): 227.3MM **Privately Held**
SIC: 1761 1542 1521 3444 Roofing/Siding Contr/Nonresidential Cnstn/Single-Family House Cnst/Mfg Sheet Metalwork
HQ: General Roofing Services, Inc.
  3300 S Parker Rd Ste 500
  Aurora CO 80014

(G-12864) SALK COMMUNICATIONS INC
Also Called: Salk Sound
40 W Howard St Ste 204 (48342-1284)
PHONE...............................248 342-7109
Jim Salk, *Owner*
▲ **EMP:** 3
SALES (est): 385.4K **Privately Held**
SIC: 3651 Loudspeakers, electrodynamic or magnetic

(G-12865) SHOULDERS LLC
487 N Perry St (48342-2451)
PHONE...............................248 843-1536
Sherina Nelson,
EMP: 3 **EST:** 2017
SQ FT: 300
SALES (est): 82.5K **Privately Held**
SIC: 8322 7349 2326 Homemakers' service; hospital housekeeping; medical & hospital uniforms, men's

(G-12866) SLADES PRINTING COMPANY INC
1502 Baldwin Ave (48340-1106)
PHONE...............................248 334-6257
Richard L Slade, *President*
EMP: 12
SQ FT: 3,520
SALES: 250K **Privately Held**
SIC: 2752 Commercial printing, offset

(G-12867) SLC METER LLC
595 Bradford St (48341-3112)
PHONE...............................248 625-0667
Ryan Eichbrecht, *Vice Pres*
John F Traynor,
EMP: 17
SALES (est): 3.2MM **Privately Held**
SIC: 3824 Water meters

(G-12868) SMEDE-SON STEEL AND SUP CO INC
1097 Cesar E Chavez Ave (48340-2344)
PHONE...............................248 332-0300
Dale Crondak, *Owner*
EMP: 6
SALES (corp-wide): 18.8MM **Privately Held**
WEB: www.smedeson.com
SIC: 3441 Fabricated structural metal
PA: Smede-Son Steel And Supply Company, Inc.
  12584 Inkster Rd
  Redford MI 48239
  313 937-8300

(G-12869) SOUTHERN AUTO WHOLESALERS INC
597 N Saginaw St (48342-1468)
PHONE...............................248 335-5555
Thomas M Tyson, *President*
Denise Faust, *Manager*
▲ **EMP:** 15
SQ FT: 6,800
SALES (est): 3.8MM **Privately Held**
WEB: www.southernautomotive.com
SIC: 3621 3694 3643 3625 Motors, electric; motors, starting: automotive & aircraft; ignition apparatus, internal combustion engines; alternators, automotive; electric switches; electric controls & control accessories, industrial; electromechanical counters; motor vehicle supplies & new parts

Pontiac - Oakland County (G-12870)

(G-12870)
TIANHAI ELECTRIC N AMER INC (DH)
70 E Silverdome Indus Par (48342-2986)
PHONE...............................248 987-2100
Jun Lan, *President*
John Nye, *Vice Pres*
Matt Tenfelde, *Vice Pres*
Michael Kosnik, *Purch Agent*
Dawn Neill, *Buyer*
▲ **EMP:** 86
SQ FT: 30,000
SALES (est): 72MM
SALES (corp-wide): 1.3MM **Privately Held**
SIC: 3714 Motor vehicle parts & accessories
HQ: Henan Thb Electronics Co., Ltd.
No.003, Songjiang Road, Economic Technology Development Zone
Hebi 45803
392 328-9122

(G-12871)
TRANS TUBE INC
34 W Sheffield Ave (48340-1846)
PHONE...............................248 334-5720
Leslie Dale Walter, *President*
Daisy P Walter, *Corp Secy*
EMP: 14
SQ FT: 60,000
SALES (est): 1.3MM **Privately Held**
SIC: 3317 Steel pipe & tubes

(G-12872)
UNIQUE FOOD MANAGEMENT INC
Also Called: Randy's Catering
248 S Telegraph Rd (48341-1933)
PHONE...............................248 738-9393
Rosa Randolph, *President*
Jim Lang, *Vice Pres*
Lou Hawkins, *Admin Sec*
EMP: 38
SALES (est): 6.9MM **Privately Held**
WEB: www.randyscatering.com
SIC: 2099 Food preparations

(G-12873)
UNITED FBRCNTS STRAINRITE CORP
Also Called: Oakland Engineering Filtration
481 N Saginaw St Ste A (48342-1453)
PHONE...............................800 487-3136
William Okay, *Opers Mgr*
Ed Bush, *Sales Mgr*
Alan Roberts, *Sales Staff*
Janet Allen, *Manager*
Monica Harris, *Manager*
EMP: 25
SALES (corp-wide): 21.9MM **Privately Held**
WEB: www.ufstrainrite.com
SIC: 3569 Filters, general line: industrial
HQ: United Fabricants Strainrite Corporation
65 First Flight Dr
Auburn ME 04210
207 376-1600

(G-12874)
WENZ & GIBBENS ENTERPRISES
Also Called: City Sign Company
101 E Walton Blvd (48340-1266)
PHONE...............................248 333-7938
Gerald Gibbens, *President*
Dave Wenz, *Vice Pres*
EMP: 7 **EST:** 1959
SQ FT: 2,400
SALES (est): 876.8K **Privately Held**
SIC: 3993 1799 Signs & advertising specialties; sign installation & maintenance

(G-12875)
WILLIAMS INTERNATIONAL CO LLC (PA)
Also Called: Willc
2000 Centerpoint Pkwy (48341-3146)
PHONE...............................248 624-5200
Jim Devlin, *Vice Pres*
Frank Smith, *Vice Pres*
Anna Rodriguez, *Production*
Dan Hartley, *Buyer*
Nathan Buford, *Engineer*

▲ **EMP:** 277
SALES (est): 248.4MM **Privately Held**
WEB: www.williams-int.com
SIC: 3724 3764 Turbines, aircraft type; engines & engine parts, guided missile

(G-12876)
WOODWORTH INC (PA)
500 Centerpoint Pkwy N (48341-3171)
PHONE...............................248 481-2354
Terry R Woodworth, *President*
Dennis Deciechi, *Vice Pres*
Matt Woodworth, *Vice Pres*
Robert Woodworth, *Shareholder*
EMP: 35
SQ FT: 380,000
SALES (est): 15.1MM **Privately Held**
WEB: www.woodworthinc.com
SIC: 3398 Metal heat treating

(G-12877)
XALT ENERGY LLC
750 South Blvd E (48341-3129)
PHONE...............................248 409-5419
EMP: 4
SALES (corp-wide): 11B **Privately Held**
SIC: 3691 Storage batteries
HQ: Xalt Energy, Llc
2700 S Saginaw Rd
Midland MI 48640

Port Austin
Huron County

(G-12878)
PORT AUSTIN LEVEL & TL MFG CO
130 Arthur St (48467-6703)
P.O. Box 365 (48467-0365)
PHONE...............................989 738-5291
Robert Upthegrove, *President*
Robert B Upthegrove, *President*
Mary Jaworski, *Admin Sec*
EMP: 15
SQ FT: 30,000
SALES (est): 2.2MM **Privately Held**
SIC: 3423 3829 Hand & edge tools; measuring & controlling devices

Port Huron
St. Clair County

(G-12879)
1365267 ONTARIO INC
Also Called: Jailbird Designs
2014 Holland Ave (48060-1406)
PHONE...............................888 843-5245
Tom Woodland, *CEO*
EMP: 5
SALES (corp-wide): 1.6MM **Privately Held**
SIC: 2759 2395 Screen printing; emblems, embroidered
PA: 1365267 Ontario Inc
380 High St E
Strathroy ON N7G 3
519 457-7755

(G-12880)
ABLE SOLUTIONS LLC
2030 10th St (48060-6217)
PHONE...............................810 216-6106
Paul Horn, *President*
EMP: 8
SQ FT: 1,608
SALES (est): 708K **Privately Held**
SIC: 2842 3089 5169 Specialty cleaning preparations; holders: paper towel, grocery bag, etc.: plastic; specialty cleaning & sanitation preparations

(G-12881)
AFX INDUSTRIES LLC (DH)
Also Called: Afx/Trim
1411 3rd St Ste G (48060-5480)
PHONE...............................810 966-4650
Bill Schroers,
Drew Knight,
Paul Riganelli,
Brad Watson,
▲ **EMP:** 5

SQ FT: 91,000
SALES (est): 169.5MM
SALES (corp-wide): 440.5MM **Privately Held**
WEB: www.afxindustries.com
SIC: 3111 5531 Industrial leather products; automotive parts
HQ: Exco Inc.
1007 N Orange St
Wilmington DE 19801
905 477-3065

(G-12882)
AGI CCAA INC
Also Called: Arctic Glacier
1755 Yeager St (48060-2594)
PHONE...............................715 355-0856
Don Aregoni, *Branch Mgr*
EMP: 4
SALES (corp-wide): 2.4B **Publicly Held**
SIC: 2097 Manufactured ice
HQ: Agi Ccaa Inc
625 Henry Ave
Winnipeg MB R3A 0
204 772-2473

(G-12883)
AINSWORTH ELECTRIC INC
3200 Dove Rd Ste A (48060-7489)
PHONE...............................810 984-5768
Richard R Ainsworth, *President*
Cynthia Ainsworth, *Corp Secy*
▲ **EMP:** 20
SQ FT: 10,000
SALES (est): 4.1MM **Privately Held**
WEB: www.ainsworthelectric.com
SIC: 1731 7629 3621 5063 General electrical contractor; generator repair; generator sets: gasoline, diesel or dual-fuel; generators

(G-12884)
ALD THERMAL TREATMENT INC
2656 24th St (48060-6419)
PHONE...............................810 357-0693
Jim Kassan, *Vice Pres*
Michael Heifner, *Production*
Randy Jerome, *Purch Agent*
Enrique Lopez, *Sales Staff*
Matthew Hoffman, *Technology*
▲ **EMP:** 174
SQ FT: 78,424
SALES (est): 45.2MM
SALES (corp-wide): 1B **Privately Held**
WEB: www.aldtt.net
SIC: 3398 Metal heat treating
HQ: Metallurg, Inc.
435 Devon Park Dr Ste 200
Wayne PA 19087
610 293-2501

(G-12885)
ALTAGAS MARKETING (US) INC
1411 3rd St Ste A (48060-5480)
PHONE...............................810 887-4105
David M Harris, *President*
Deborah S Stein, *Senior VP*
Nicholas Galotti, *Vice Pres*
Steven W Warsinske, *Vice Pres*
Shaun Toivanen, *Treasurer*
EMP: 7
SALES (est): 316.8K
SALES (corp-wide): 3.2B **Privately Held**
SIC: 4923 1321 Gas transmission & distribution; natural gasoline production
PA: Altagas Ltd
355 4 Ave Sw Suite 1700
Calgary AB T2P 0
403 691-7575

(G-12886)
ALTAGAS POWER HOLDINGS US INC (DH)
1411 3rd St Ste A (48060-5480)
PHONE...............................810 887-4105
David M Harris, *President*
Deborah S Stein, *Senior VP*
Nicholas Galotti, *Vice Pres*
Steven W Warsinske, *Vice Pres*
Shaun Toivanen, *Treasurer*
EMP: 7
SALES (est): 5.7MM
SALES (corp-wide): 3.2B **Privately Held**
SIC: 1321 4923 Natural gasoline production; gas transmission & distribution

(G-12887)
ALTAGAS RNWABLE ENRGY COLO LLC
1411 3rd St Ste A (48060-5480)
PHONE...............................810 987-2200
David Harris, *Principal*
Deborah S Stein, *Principal*
Luanne Eikhoff, *CPA*
Christopher J Doyle, *Admin Sec*
EMP: 3 **EST:** 2011
SALES (est): 172.9K **Privately Held**
SIC: 3621 Windmills, electric generating

(G-12888)
ALUDYNE EAST MICHIGAN LLC
Also Called: Chassis Co. of Michigan, LLC
2223 Dove St (48060-6738)
PHONE...............................810 987-7633
Andreas Weller, *Mng Member*
Michael Beyer,
Eric Rouchy,
▲ **EMP:** 80
SALES (est): 20.6MM
SALES (corp-wide): 1.3B **Privately Held**
WEB: www.smwauto.com
SIC: 3714 Motor vehicle parts & accessories
HQ: Aludyne International, Inc
300 Galleria Ofcntr Ste 5
Southfield MI 48034

(G-12889)
ALUDYNE US LLC
3150 Dove St (48060-6766)
PHONE...............................810 987-1112
EMP: 100
SALES (corp-wide): 1.3B **Privately Held**
WEB: www.smwauto.com
SIC: 3465 3714 3549 Body parts, automobile: stamped metal; motor vehicle parts & accessories; metalworking machinery
HQ: Aludyne Us Llc
12700 Stephens Rd
Warren MI 48089

(G-12890)
ALUDYNE US LLC
Also Called: Chasix
2347 Dove St (48060-6715)
PHONE...............................810 966-9350
EMP: 100
SALES (corp-wide): 1.3B **Privately Held**
SIC: 3465 Body parts, automobile: stamped metal
HQ: Aludyne Us Llc
12700 Stephens Rd
Warren MI 48089

(G-12891)
ANCHOR RECYCLING INC
2829 Goulden St (48060-6975)
PHONE...............................810 984-5545
EMP: 9
SALES (est): 980.1K **Privately Held**
SIC: 2611 4953 Pulp Mill Refuse System

(G-12892)
ARCTIC GLACIER GRAYLING INC
1755 Yeager St (48060-2594)
PHONE...............................810 987-7100
Robert Nagy, *President*
Keith McMahon, *Vice Pres*
EMP: 12
SQ FT: 12,000
SALES (est): 1.5MM **Privately Held**
SIC: 2097 Manufactured ice

(G-12893)
ARCTIC GLACIER INC
1755 Yeager St (48060-2594)
PHONE...............................734 485-0430
David Blind, *Vice Pres*
Kerry Chamberlin,
▲ **EMP:** 50
SALES (est): 5.4MM **Privately Held**
SIC: 5199 2097 Ice, manufactured or natural; manufactured ice

(G-12894)
ARCTIC GLACIER PA INC
1755 Yeager St (48060-2594)
PHONE...............................610 494-8200
John Stratman, *Executive*

GEOGRAPHIC SECTION

Port Huron - St. Clair County (G-12921)

EMP: 50
SALES (est): 3.9MM
SALES (corp-wide): 1MM **Privately Held**
SIC: 2097 Manufactured ice
PA: Arctic Glacier Income Fund
625 Henry Ave
Winnipeg MB R3A 0
204 772-2473

(G-12895)
AUTO ANODICS INC
2407 16th St (48060-6196)
PHONE....................810 984-5600
Max Andrew Wiener, *Vice Pres*
Lisa Wiener, *Vice Pres*
EMP: 50
SQ FT: 56,000
SALES (est): 6.1MM **Privately Held**
WEB: www.autoanodics.com
SIC: 3471 Plating of metals or formed products; anodizing (plating) of metals or formed products

(G-12896)
B & L INDUSTRIES INC
2121 16th St (48060-6175)
P.O. Box 611011 (48061-1011)
PHONE....................810 987-9121
Richard Foster, *President*
Margaret J Foster, *Vice Pres*
EMP: 18
SQ FT: 10,000
SALES (est): 3MM **Privately Held**
SIC: 3444 Sheet metalwork

(G-12897)
BAKER & BAKER
2835 W Water St (48060-7744)
PHONE....................810 982-2763
Donald Ebaker, *Principal*
EMP: 3
SALES (est): 119K **Privately Held**
SIC: 2051 Cakes, bakery; except frozen

(G-12898)
BARRY ELECTRIC-ROVILL CO
1431 White St (48060-5736)
PHONE....................810 985-8960
Vicki Smith, *President*
EMP: 5
SQ FT: 1,500
SALES: 200K **Privately Held**
SIC: 7694 Electric motor repair

(G-12899)
BIOPRO INC
2929 Lapeer Rd (48060-2558)
PHONE....................810 982-7777
Patrick E Pringle, *President*
Jeffrey Hendrix, *Sales Dir*
Jason Pringle, *Mktg Coord*
Gayle Richards, *Mktg Coord*
Mary J Burns, *Manager*
EMP: 27
SQ FT: 26,000
SALES (est): 5.2MM **Privately Held**
WEB: www.bioproimplants.com
SIC: 3842 5999 Prosthetic appliances; orthopedic & prosthesis applications

(G-12900)
BLACK RIVER MANUFACTURING INC (PA)
2625 20th St (48060-6443)
PHONE....................810 982-9812
Jarold Hawks, *President*
Andrew Lacy, *Production*
Debbie Rabidue, *Finance Mgr*
Jason Keil, *Info Tech Mgr*
EMP: 45 EST: 1977
SQ FT: 3,000
SALES (est): 22.5MM **Privately Held**
SIC: 3714 3451 3441 3061 Motor vehicle engines & parts; transmission housings or parts, motor vehicle; screw machine products; fabricated structural metal; mechanical rubber goods

(G-12901)
BLACK RIVER MANUFACTURING INC
2401 20th St (48060-6406)
PHONE....................810 982-9812
Debbie Keil, *Branch Mgr*
EMP: 100
SALES (corp-wide): 22.5MM **Privately Held**
SIC: 3714 Motor vehicle engines & parts
PA: Black River Manufacturing Inc
2625 20th St
Port Huron MI 48060
810 982-9812

(G-12902)
BLUE WATER BIOPRODUCTS LLC
3735 Dove Rd (48060-7444)
PHONE....................586 453-9219
Kurt Kurple, *Mng Member*
EMP: 3 EST: 2010
SALES (est): 262K **Privately Held**
SIC: 3086 2821 Plastics foam products; polyurethane resins

(G-12903)
BME INC
3763 Lapeer Rd Ste E (48060-4523)
PHONE....................810 937-2974
Brett May, *President*
EMP: 5
SALES: 1.7MM **Privately Held**
SIC: 3569 3531 Assembly machines, non-metalworking; construction machinery

(G-12904)
BOWMAN PRINTING INC
Also Called: Sir Speedy
600 Huron Ave (48060-3702)
PHONE....................810 982-8202
Lisa Bowman, *President*
Cary Bowman, *Vice Pres*
EMP: 4
SQ FT: 3,000
SALES (est): 874.7K **Privately Held**
WEB: www.bowmanprinting.com
SIC: 2752 Commercial printing, lithographic

(G-12905)
BUILT RITE TOOL AND ENGRG LLC
1605 Beard St (48060-6420)
PHONE....................810 966-5133
Scott Smith, *Mng Member*
Keith Smith,
EMP: 3
SALES (est): 330K **Privately Held**
WEB: www.builtritetool.com
SIC: 3089 Injection molding of plastics

(G-12906)
CHANGE HEALTHCARE TECH LLC
1530 Pine Grove Ave Ste 7 (48060-3370)
PHONE....................810 985-0029
Pat Macy, *Manager*
EMP: 5
SALES (corp-wide): 214.3B **Publicly Held**
WEB: www.per-se.com
SIC: 3663 Satellites, communications
HQ: Change Healthcare Technologies, Llc
5995 Windward Pkwy
Alpharetta GA 30005

(G-12907)
CIPA USA INC (PA)
Also Called: Auto & Truck Components, Co.
3350 Griswold Rd (48060-4742)
PHONE....................810 982-3555
Rick Leveille, *President*
Paul J Leveille, *Exec VP*
▲ EMP: 40
SQ FT: 105,000
SALES (est): 9.9MM **Privately Held**
WEB: www.cipausa.com
SIC: 3714 Motor vehicle parts & accessories

(G-12908)
CITY OF PORT HURON
Also Called: Waste and Water Trtmnt Plant
100 Merchant St (48060-4004)
PHONE....................810 984-9775
Randy Studaker, *Manager*
EMP: 25 **Privately Held**
WEB: www.fmi.com
SIC: 3589 Water treatment equipment, industrial

PA: City Of Port Huron
100 Mcmorran Blvd Rm City
Port Huron MI 48060
810 984-9727

(G-12909)
COMMUNITY MARKETING GROUP LLC
1419 15th St (48060-5604)
PHONE....................810 966-9982
Trina Avedisian, *Principal*
EMP: 3
SALES (est): 132.1K **Privately Held**
SIC: 2711 Newspapers, publishing & printing

(G-12910)
COOPER & COOPER SALES INC
851 W Pointe (48060-4454)
P.O. Box 611107 (48061-1107)
PHONE....................810 327-6247
Steve G Cooper, *CEO*
Diane M Cooper, *President*
Grant Cooper, *Vice Pres*
EMP: 5
SALES: 3MM **Privately Held**
WEB: www.coopertube.com
SIC: 3441 Fabricated structural metal

(G-12911)
DICKS SIGNS
2560 40th St (48060-2571)
PHONE....................810 987-9002
Dick Darling, *Owner*
EMP: 5
SALES (est): 276.6K **Privately Held**
SIC: 3993 7532 Signs & advertising specialties; truck painting & lettering

(G-12912)
DOMTAR INDUSTRIES INC
Also Called: Domtar Gypsum
1700 Washington Ave (48060-3400)
P.O. Box 5003 (48061-5003)
PHONE....................810 982-0191
Mark Bessette, *Vice Pres*
Michelle L Morris, *Purchasing*
Timothy Wight, *Technical Mgr*
Philip Jerman, *Engineer*
EMP: 73
SALES (est): 37.5MM **Privately Held**
SIC: 2621 Paper mills

(G-12913)
DUNN PAPER INC (HQ)
218 Riverview St (48060-2996)
PHONE....................810 984-5521
Brent Earnshaw, *President*
Wade Kemnitz, *COO*
Greg Howe, *Exec VP*
Rob Emigh, *Vice Pres*
Kevin French, *Plant Mgr*
◆ EMP: 10
SQ FT: 165,000
SALES (est): 139.6MM **Privately Held**
WEB: www.dunnpaper.com
SIC: 2671 2672 Paper coated or laminated for packaging; coated & laminated paper
PA: Dunn Paper Holdings, Inc.
218 Riverview St
Port Huron MI 48060
810 984-5521

(G-12914)
DUNN PAPER HOLDINGS INC (PA)
218 Riverview St (48060-2976)
PHONE....................810 984-5521
Brent Earnshaw, *President*
Richard Voss, *Vice Pres*
Gerry Konop, *Opers Staff*
Sharon Brown, *Senior Buyer*
Gregory Howe, *CFO*
EMP: 3
SQ FT: 165,000
SALES (est): 139.6MM **Privately Held**
SIC: 2621 2672 Paper mills; coated & laminated paper

(G-12915)
E B EDDY PAPER INC
Also Called: Domtar Eddy Specialty Papers
1700 Washington Ave (48060-3462)
P.O. Box 5003 (48061-5003)
PHONE....................810 982-0191

John Williams, *CEO*
Gilles Pharand, *Vice Pres*
John Harnish, *Safety Mgr*
Charlie Dees, *Director*
Al Martin, *Director*
EMP: 324
SQ FT: 525,000
SALES (est): 96.5MM
SALES (corp-wide): 177.9K **Privately Held**
WEB: www.domtar.com
SIC: 2621 Packaging paper; specialty papers; offset paper; fine paper
HQ: Domtar Inc
395 Boul De Maisonneuve O Bureau 200
Montreal QC H3A 1
514 848-5555

(G-12916)
EISSMANN AUTO PORT HURON LLC (DH)
2440 20th St (48060-6436)
PHONE....................810 216-6300
Brian Tinney, *Co-President*
Joerg Schultz, *Co-President*
Lucas Butterstein, *CFO*
Lindsay Ken, *Administration*
▲ EMP: 180 EST: 2014
SALES (est): 17MM
SALES (corp-wide): 547.3MM **Privately Held**
SIC: 2396 Automotive trimmings, fabric
HQ: Eissmann Automotive North America, Inc.
599 Ed Gardner Dr
Pell City AL 35125
205 338-4044

(G-12917)
EXPERT MACHINE & TOOL INC
2424 Lapeer Rd (48060-2528)
PHONE....................810 984-2323
Micheal J Biga, *President*
EMP: 9
SQ FT: 8,000
SALES (est): 1.1MM **Privately Held**
SIC: 3544 Special dies & tools; jigs & fixtures

(G-12918)
FLOW GAS MISTURE SOLUTIONS INC
Also Called: Fgm Solutions
901 Huron Ave Ste 4 (48060-3700)
PHONE....................810 216-9004
Timothy Storm, *Director*
EMP: 3 EST: 2015
SQ FT: 400
SALES: 750K **Privately Held**
SIC: 3632 Household refrigerators & freezers

(G-12919)
FORT GRTIOT CBNETS COUNTER LLC
3390 Ravenswood Rd (48060-4662)
PHONE....................810 364-1924
Jeain Lenn, *Owner*
Jean Lenn,
EMP: 11
SALES: 500K **Privately Held**
SIC: 2434 Wood kitchen cabinets

(G-12920)
FUEL WOODFIRE GRILL LLC
213 Huron Ave (48060-3821)
PHONE....................810 479-4933
Mike Taylor, *Principal*
EMP: 7
SALES (est): 1.1MM **Privately Held**
SIC: 2869 Fuels

(G-12921)
GB DYNAMICS INC
1620 Kearney St (48060-3420)
PHONE....................313 400-3570
Jonathan Granger, *CEO*
Keith Gardner, *CFO*
EMP: 20
SALES (est): 632.1K **Privately Held**
SIC: 4789 2869 Cargo loading & unloading services; fuels

Port Huron - St. Clair County (G-12922)

(G-12922)
GEARTEC INC
1105 24th St (48060-4849)
P.O. Box 5006 (48061-5006)
PHONE..................................810 987-4700
John O Wirtz, *President*
Bruce Patchel, *Finance*
EMP: 6
SQ FT: 24,000
SALES (est): 399K **Privately Held**
SIC: 3566 7389 Reduction gears & gear units for turbines, except automotive;

(G-12923)
GRAPHTEK INC
Also Called: Michigan Industrial Pdts Co
2301 16th St (48060-6401)
PHONE..................................810 985-4545
Robert Hartnett, *President*
Molly McTague, *Marketing Staff*
Stephanie Janis, *Director*
EMP: 6 **EST:** 1975
SQ FT: 13,000
SALES (est): 1.1MM **Privately Held**
WEB: www.graphtek.com
SIC: 2992 Lubricating oils & greases

(G-12924)
GREENE MANUFACTURING TECH LLC
Also Called: Greene Group Industries
2600 20th St (48060-6444)
PHONE..................................810 982-9720
Jay Scheid, *Project Mgr*
Mark Ward, *Mng Member*
Dawn Sawicki-Franz, *Admin Asst*
EMP: 130
SALES (est): 25.7MM **Privately Held**
SIC: 3499 3559 Friction material, made from powdered metal; electronic component making machinery

(G-12925)
HOLD-IT INC
2301 16th St (48060-6401)
P.O. Box 611391 (48061-1391)
PHONE..................................810 984-4213
Debra Sullivan, *President*
Hope Sexton, *Admin Sec*
Bonnie Steece, *Administration*
EMP: 7
SALES: 480K **Privately Held**
WEB: www.hold-it.com
SIC: 3069 Grips or handles, rubber

(G-12926)
HP PELZER AUTO SYSTEMS INC
2415 Dove St (48060-6716)
PHONE..................................810 987-4444
Tim Hockney, *Branch Mgr*
EMP: 49
SALES (corp-wide): 74.8MM **Privately Held**
SIC: 3559 5013 3714 3296 Automotive related machinery; automotive supplies & parts; motor vehicle parts & accessories; mineral wool
HQ: Hp Pelzer Automotive Systems, Inc.
1175 Crooks Rd
Troy MI 48084

(G-12927)
HP PELZER AUTOMOTIVE SYSTEMS
2630 Dove St (48060-6719)
PHONE..................................810 987-0725
Janet Goldsbey, *Principal*
Donald Reddy, *Manager*
▲ **EMP:** 40
SALES (est): 6.5MM
SALES (corp-wide): 74.8MM **Privately Held**
SIC: 3711 Automobile bodies, passenger car, not including engine, etc.
HQ: Hp Pelzer Automotive Systems, Inc.
1175 Crooks Rd
Troy MI 48084

(G-12928)
HURON INDUSTRIES INC
2301 16th St (48060-6401)
P.O. Box 610104 (48061-0104)
PHONE..................................810 984-4213
Verna Boukamp, *President*
Debra Sullivan, *Purchasing*
John W Boukamp, *Treasurer*
▼ **EMP:** 5
SQ FT: 5,000
SALES (est): 500K **Privately Held**
SIC: 2992 2891 2911 Lubricating oils; sealants; greases, lubricating

(G-12929)
IMPRINT HOUSE LLC
1113 Military St (48060-5418)
PHONE..................................810 985-8203
Ted Smith, *Owner*
EMP: 4
SALES (est): 322.4K **Privately Held**
WEB: www.theimprinthouse.com
SIC: 5199 2396 2395 2759 Advertising specialties; screen printing on fabric articles; embroidery products, except schiffli machine; business forms: printing

(G-12930)
INTERNATIONAL AUTOMOTIVE COMPO
1905 Beard St (48060-6440)
PHONE..................................810 987-8500
Domenic Calagna, *Business Mgr*
Derek Klink, *Materials Mgr*
Chad Schisler, *Maint Spvr*
Greg Delano, *QC Mgr*
EMP: 450 **Privately Held**
WEB: www.iaaawards.com
SIC: 2396 3714 3429 Automotive trimmings, fabric; motor vehicle parts & accessories; manufactured hardware (general)
HQ: International Automotive Components Group North America, Inc.
28333 Telegraph Rd
Southfield MI 48034

(G-12931)
JABARS COMPLEMENTS LLC
Also Called: Chefshell Catering
2639 24th St (48060-6418)
PHONE..................................810 966-8371
Mark Wrubel, *Managing Prtnr*
Michelle Wrubel, *Managing Prtnr*
EMP: 7 **EST:** 1988
SQ FT: 1,100
SALES (est): 550K **Privately Held**
WEB: www.jabars.com
SIC: 2035 5812 Pickles, sauces & salad dressings; eating places

(G-12932)
JGR PLASTICS LLC
Also Called: Prism
2040 International Way (48060-7471)
PHONE..................................810 990-1957
Adam Smith, *Project Engr*
Darrell Witham, *Project Engr*
Theresa Knapp, *Human Res Mgr*
Rhonda Wallace, *Accounts Mgr*
Gerry Phillips, *Mng Member*
EMP: 50
SQ FT: 18,000
SALES (est): 13MM **Privately Held**
WEB: www.prismplastics.com
SIC: 3089 Injection molding of plastics

(G-12933)
KARAMON SALES COMPANY
1816 N Woodland Dr (48060-1939)
PHONE..................................810 984-1750
Ken Karamon, *Owner*
EMP: 3
SALES: 130K **Privately Held**
SIC: 3559 Robots, molding & forming plastics

(G-12934)
KIMBERLY-CLARK CORPORATION
2609 Electric Ave Ste C (48060-6589)
PHONE..................................810 985-1830
EMP: 4
SALES (corp-wide): 18.4B **Publicly Held**
SIC: 2621 2676 Sanitary tissue paper; infant & baby paper products
PA: Kimberly-Clark Corporation
351 Phelps Dr
Irving TX 75038
972 281-1200

(G-12935)
KNOWLTON ENTERPRISES INC (PA)
Also Called: Party Time Ice Co
1755 Yeager St (48060-2594)
PHONE..................................810 987-7100
Norman F Knowlton, *President*
Charles J Knowlton, *Vice Pres*
Bill Rock, *Plant Mgr*
EMP: 55
SALES (est): 5.3MM **Privately Held**
WEB: www.knowltonenterprises.com
SIC: 2097 Block ice; ice cubes

(G-12936)
M C WARD INC
4100 Griswold Rd (48060-7495)
PHONE..................................810 982-9720
Mark C Ward, *President*
EMP: 50
SALES (est): 5.6MM **Privately Held**
WEB: www.brittmfg.com
SIC: 3544 Industrial molds

(G-12937)
MAG AUTOMOTIVE LLC
2555 20th St (48060-6450)
PHONE..................................586 446-7000
EMP: 9 **Privately Held**
SIC: 3559 Automotive related machinery
HQ: Mag Automotive Llc
6015 Center Dr
Sterling Heights MI 48312
586 446-7000

(G-12938)
MAJOR INDUSTRIES LTD
511 Fort St Rm 445 (48060-3934)
PHONE..................................810 985-9372
Algong Lee, *President*
Todd Goldman, *Vice Pres*
▲ **EMP:** 62
SQ FT: 700
SALES (est): 5.9MM **Privately Held**
SIC: 3312 Tool & die steel & alloys

(G-12939)
MAPAL INC (HQ)
4032 Dove Rd (48060-7442)
PHONE..................................810 364-8020
Dieter Kress, *President*
Bryant Riddle, *Regional Mgr*
Don Lynch, *Vice Pres*
Greg Kolowich, *Engineer*
Jerrold J Zuzolo, *CFO*
◆ **EMP:** 60
SQ FT: 45,000
SALES (est): 17.5MM
SALES (corp-wide): 717.5K **Privately Held**
WEB: www.mapal.com
SIC: 3545 Cutting tools for machine tools
PA: Mapal Fabrik Fur Prazisionswerkzeuge Dr. Kress Kg
Obere Bahnstr. 13
Aalen 73431
736 158-50

(G-12940)
METER OF AMERICA INC
920 Military St 1 (48060-5415)
PHONE..................................810 216-6074
Jacob P Danik, *Principal*
EMP: 9 **EST:** 1999
SALES (est): 1.1MM **Privately Held**
SIC: 3339 Antifriction bearing metals, lead-base

(G-12941)
MICHIGAN MANUFACTURED PDTS INC
Also Called: M M P
3605 32nd St (48060-6900)
PHONE..................................586 770-2584
Kevin M Daniel, *Mng Member*
▲ **EMP:** 3
SQ FT: 15,000
SALES: 450K **Privately Held**
SIC: 3544 3089 Industrial molds; injection molding of plastics

(G-12942)
MICHIGAN METAL COATINGS CO
2015 Dove St (48060-6738)
PHONE..................................810 966-9240
Yasutaka Hasegawa, *President*
EMP: 53
SALES: 12MM **Privately Held**
WEB: www.michiganmetalcoatings.net
SIC: 3479 Coating of metals & formed products
PA: Mc Systems Inc.
4-1, Tomifunecho, Nakagawa-Ku
Nagoya AIC 454-0

(G-12943)
MNP CORPORATION
2305 Beard St (48060-6438)
PHONE..................................810 982-8996
Cary Camphausen, *Prdtn Mgr*
Bruce Miller, *Manager*
EMP: 11
SALES (corp-wide): 232.6MM **Privately Held**
WEB: www.mnp.com
SIC: 3541 3545 3544 Machine tool replacement & repair parts, metal cutting types; machine tool accessories; special dies, tools, jigs & fixtures
PA: Mnp Corporation
44225 Utica Rd
Utica MI 48317
586 254-1320

(G-12944)
MODERN TECH MACHINING LLC
3735 Lapeer Rd Ste C (48060-7728)
PHONE..................................810 531-7992
Rob Budgell, *President*
EMP: 5
SALES (est): 569.7K **Privately Held**
SIC: 3451 Screw machine products

(G-12945)
MUELLER BRASS CO
2199 Lapeer Ave (48060-4155)
P.O. Box 5021 (48061-5021)
PHONE..................................810 987-7770
Doug Westbrook, *Manager*
EMP: 51
SALES (corp-wide): 2.5B **Publicly Held**
WEB: www.muellerbrass.com
SIC: 3366 3351 Brass foundry; pipe, brass & bronze
HQ: Mueller Brass Co.
8285 Tournament Dr # 150
Memphis TN 38125
901 753-3200

(G-12946)
MUELLER BRASS FORGING CO INC
2199 Lapeer Ave (48060-4155)
PHONE..................................810 987-7770
James H Rourke, *President*
Kent A Mc Kee, *CFO*
James E Browne, *Asst Sec*
EMP: 90
SQ FT: 60,000
SALES (est): 17.3MM
SALES (corp-wide): 2.5B **Publicly Held**
WEB: www.muellerbrass.com
SIC: 3463 Aluminum forgings
HQ: Mueller Brass Co.
8285 Tournament Dr # 150
Memphis TN 38125
901 753-3200

(G-12947)
MUELLER INDUSTRIAL REALTY CO
2199 Lapeer Ave (48060-4155)
PHONE..................................810 987-7770
William H Hensley, *VP Legal*
James R Rourke, *Vice Pres*
Karl J Bambas, *Vice Pres*
Kent A McKee, *Treasurer*
Earl W Bunkers, *VP Finance*
EMP: 300
SALES (est): 32.2MM
SALES (corp-wide): 2.5B **Publicly Held**
WEB: www.muellerbrass.com
SIC: 3312 Rods, iron & steel: made in steel mills

GEOGRAPHIC SECTION
Port Huron - St. Clair County (G-12976)

HQ: Mueller Brass Co.
  8285 Tournament Dr # 150
  Memphis TN 38125
  901 753-3200

(G-12948)
MURTECH ENERGY SERVICES LLC
3097 Aberdeen Ct (48060-2348)
PHONE.................................810 653-5681
Marilyn I Murray,
EMP: 4
SALES (est): 360K Privately Held
SIC: 3564 3585 Blowers & fans; air conditioning equipment, complete

(G-12949)
NOF METAL COATINGS N AMER INC
2015 Dove St (48060-6738)
PHONE.................................810 966-9240
George Palek, Branch Mgr
EMP: 4 Privately Held
WEB: www.geomet.net
SIC: 2899 Chemical preparations
HQ: Nof Metal Coatings North America Inc.
  275 Industrial Pkwy
  Chardon OH 44024
  440 285-2231

(G-12950)
NORTHERN PURE ICE CO L L C
Also Called: Ice Makers
1755 Yeager St (48060-2594)
PHONE.................................989 344-2088
Robert Reutter, Principal
Charles J Knowlton, Principal
EMP: 12
SALES (est): 580K Privately Held
SIC: 2097 Ice cubes; block ice

(G-12951)
O E M COMPANY INC
3495 24th St (48060-6809)
PHONE.................................810 985-9070
Larry Fletcher, President
Everette Fletcher, Vice Pres
EMP: 25
SALES (est): 2.2MM Privately Held
WEB: www.oemcompanyinc.com
SIC: 7692 Automotive welding

(G-12952)
OXMASTER INC (PA)
1105 24th St (48060-4849)
PHONE.................................810 987-7600
John O Wirtz, CEO
EMP: 2
SALES (est): 4.1MM Privately Held
WEB: www.oxmaster.com
SIC: 3559 Automotive related machinery

(G-12953)
P J WALLBANK SPRINGS INC
2121 Beard St (48060-6422)
PHONE.................................810 987-2992
Melvyn J Wallbank, President
Rob Cronce, Engineer
Timothy Roelens, Engineer
Randy Grewe, Info Tech Mgr
EMP: 85
SQ FT: 66,000
SALES (est): 19.8MM Privately Held
WEB: www.pjws.com
SIC: 3493 Steel springs, except wire

(G-12954)
P M R INDUSTRIES INC
2311 16th St (48060-6401)
PHONE.................................810 989-5020
Timothy Colein, President
Robert Colein, Vice Pres
EMP: 14 EST: 1967
SQ FT: 10,000
SALES (est): 1.9MM Privately Held
SIC: 3542 3541 3599 Forging machinery & hammers; cutoff machines (metalworking machinery); machine shop, jobbing & repair

(G-12955)
PARKSIDE SPEEDY PRINT INC
1319 Military St (48060-5422)
P.O. Box 610396 (48061-0396)
PHONE.................................810 985-8484
James Paulus, President
Donna Paulus, Vice Pres
EMP: 6
SQ FT: 1,500
SALES (est): 450.9K Privately Held
SIC: 2752 2791 2789 Lithographing on metal; typesetting; bookbinding & related work

(G-12956)
PLASTIC DRESS-UP SERVICE INC
2735 20th St (48060-6452)
PHONE.................................586 727-7878
Ronald Jacques, President
EMP: 21
SALES (est): 3.5MM Privately Held
WEB: www.plasticdressup.com
SIC: 3089 Injection molding of plastics

(G-12957)
PLASTIC PLAQUE INC
1635 Poplar St (48060-3329)
P.O. Box 610964 (48061-0964)
PHONE.................................810 982-9591
Charles W Fead, Ch of Bd
William F Fead, President
EMP: 9
SQ FT: 8,000
SALES (est): 1MM Privately Held
SIC: 3082 Unsupported plastics profile shapes

(G-12958)
PORT HURON BUILDING SUPPLY CO
Also Called: Do It Best
3555 Electric Ave (48060-6621)
PHONE.................................810 987-2666
Fax: 810 987-4531
EMP: 12
SQ FT: 25,000
SALES (est): 1.2MM Privately Held
SIC: 5251 3271 3273 3272 Ret Hardware Mfg Concrete Block/Brick Mfg Ready-Mixed Concrete Mfg Concrete Products

(G-12959)
R D M ENTERPRISES CO INC
4045 Griswold Rd (48060-4752)
PHONE.................................810 985-4721
Alvin Rinke, President
EMP: 8
SQ FT: 11,000
SALES (est): 800K Privately Held
WEB: www.rdmenterprises.net
SIC: 3465 3544 Body parts, automobile: stamped metal; die sets for metal stamping (presses)

(G-12960)
RAE MANUFACTURING COMPANY
1327 Cedar St (48060-6176)
PHONE.................................810 987-9170
EMP: 16
SQ FT: 10,000
SALES (est): 3.5MM Privately Held
SIC: 3452 3443 3541 5072 Mfg Bolts/Screws/Rivets Mfg Fabricated Plate Wrk Mfg Machine Tool-Cutting Whol Hardware Mfg Screw Machine Prdts

(G-12961)
RAE PRECISION PRODUCTS INC
1327 Cedar St (48060-6176)
PHONE.................................810 987-9170
EMP: 5
SALES (est): 167.6K Privately Held
SIC: 3599 Mfg Industrial Machinery

(G-12962)
RAY SCOTT INDUSTRIES INC
3921 32nd St (48060-6950)
PHONE.................................248 535-2528
Raymond H Bunton, President
EMP: 9 EST: 2017
SALES (est): 360.5K Privately Held
SIC: 3089 7389 Injection molded finished plastic products; printers' services: folding, collating

(G-12963)
ROSS PALLET CO
3360 Petit St (48060-4737)
PHONE.................................810 966-4945
John Ross, Mng Member
Dennis Ross,
EMP: 8
SALES (est): 634.6K Privately Held
SIC: 2448 Pallets, wood

(G-12964)
SBR PRINTING USA INC
2101 Cypress St (48060-6080)
PHONE.................................810 388-9441
Terry Kraft, President
▲ EMP: 12
SALES (est): 1.8MM Privately Held
SIC: 2752 Commercial printing, offset

(G-12965)
SHAWMUT CORPORATION
Also Called: Shawmut Mills
2770 Dove St (48060-6719)
PHONE.................................810 987-2222
Jason Planck, Plant Mgr
Jamie Reaume, Warehouse Mgr
Nick Astianelli, Engineer
Alex Morris, Engineer
Monica Cadarit, Branch Mgr
EMP: 120
SALES (corp-wide): 185.1MM Privately Held
WEB: www.darlexx.com
SIC: 2295 2672 3083 2671 Laminating of fabrics; coated & laminated paper; laminated plastics plate & sheet; packaging paper & plastics film, coated & laminated
PA: Shawmut Llc
  208 Manley St
  West Bridgewater MA 02379
  508 588-3300

(G-12966)
SIGNS PLUS (PA)
1604 Stone St (48060-3344)
PHONE.................................810 987-7446
Deanna Vanlerberghe, Owner
EMP: 10
SALES (est): 746.6K Privately Held
SIC: 3993 1799 Signs, not made in custom sign painting shops; sign installation & maintenance

(G-12967)
SMITH MEAT PACKING INC
2043 International Way (48060-7471)
PHONE.................................810 985-5900
Anthony Peters, President
EMP: 30
SQ FT: 24,000
SALES (est): 13.7MM Privately Held
SIC: 2011 Meat packing plants

(G-12968)
SMR AUTOMOTIVE SYSTEMS USA INC
2611 16th St (48060-6456)
PHONE.................................810 937-2456
Cindy Grimson, Branch Mgr
EMP: 10
SALES (corp-wide): 1B Privately Held
SIC: 3231 Products of purchased glass
HQ: Smr Automotive Systems Usa Inc.
  1855 Busha Hwy
  Marysville MI 48040
  810 364-4141

(G-12969)
STONE SHOP INC
2920 Wright St (48060-8529)
PHONE.................................248 852-4700
Gary Vermander, President
Kenneth Vermander, Vice Pres
EMP: 11 EST: 1960
SALES (est): 1.3MM Privately Held
SIC: 3281 Stone, quarrying & processing of own stone products; marble, building: cut & shaped

(G-12970)
TAPEX AMERICAN CORPORATION
Also Called: Formex International Div
2626 20th St (48060-6444)
P.O. Box 610233 (48061-0233)
PHONE.................................810 987-4722
Norman Catlos, President
EMP: 15
SQ FT: 80,000
SALES (est): 2.6MM Privately Held
WEB: www.tapex.net
SIC: 2241 3399 Cords, fabric; metal fasteners

(G-12971)
TIMES HERALD COMPANY (HQ)
911 Military St (48060-5414)
PHONE.................................810 985-7171
Timothy Dowd, President
Eric Ahrens, Vice Pres
EMP: 17 EST: 1910
SQ FT: 150,000
SALES: 26.6MM
SALES (corp-wide): 2.9B Publicly Held
SIC: 2711 2752 2791 Newspapers, publishing & printing; commercial printing, lithographic; typesetting
PA: Gannett Co., Inc.
  7950 Jones Branch Dr
  Mc Lean VA 22102
  703 854-6000

(G-12972)
TOOLING CNCEPTS DESIGN NOT INC
Also Called: Tooling Solutions Plus
3921 32nd St (48060-6950)
PHONE.................................810 444-9807
Jerry Eschenburg, Branch Mgr
EMP: 11
SALES (est): 1MM Privately Held
SIC: 3089 5013 Injection molding of plastics; tools & equipment, automotive
PA: Tooling Concepts & Design, Inc (Not Inc)
  34357 Jefferson Ave
  Harrison Township MI 48045

(G-12973)
TPI INDUSTRIES LLC
2770 Dove St (48060-6719)
PHONE.................................810 987-2222
EMP: 3
SALES (corp-wide): 185.1MM Privately Held
SIC: 2295 Laminating of fabrics
HQ: Tpi Industries, Llc
  265 Ballard Rd
  Middletown NY 10941
  845 692-2820

(G-12974)
US FARATHANE HOLDINGS CORP
2133 Petit St (48060-6433)
PHONE.................................248 754-7000
John Lojewski, Manager
EMP: 250
SALES (corp-wide): 876MM Privately Held
SIC: 3089 Injection molding of plastics; thermoformed finished plastic products; casting of plastic
PA: U.S. Farathane Holdings Corp.
  11650 Park Ct
  Shelby Township MI 48315
  586 726-1200

(G-12975)
WARWICK MAS & EQUIPMENT CO
1621 Pine Grove Ave (48060-3325)
PHONE.................................810 966-3431
Garry Warwick, Owner
Brian Linne, Manager
EMP: 3
SALES (est): 115.3K Privately Held
SIC: 3842 Surgical appliances & supplies

(G-12976)
WIRCO MANUFACTURING LLC
2550 20th St (48060-6493)
PHONE.................................810 984-5576
Ronald W Scafe, President

Port Huron - St. Clair County (G-12977)

▼ EMP: 10
SALES: 1MM Privately Held
SIC: 3465 Automotive stampings

(G-12977)
WIRCO PRODUCTS INC
2550 20th St (48060-6493)
PHONE..............................810 984-5576
Ronald W Scafe, President
Joe Piechotte, COO
EMP: 13
SQ FT: 20,000
SALES (est): 6.4MM Privately Held
WEB: www.wircoproducts.com
SIC: 3465 Body parts, automobile: stamped metal

(G-12978)
WIRTZ MANUFACTURING CO INC (PA)
1105 24th St (48060-4894)
P.O. Box 5006 (48061-5006)
PHONE..............................810 987-7600
John O Wirtz, President
Cary Bowman, Manager
Garry Hale, CTO
Rob Wirtz, Planning
▲ EMP: 100 EST: 1932
SALES (est): 40.1MM Privately Held
WEB: www.wirtzusa.com
SIC: 3559 Automotive related machinery

(G-12979)
YEN GROUP LLC
2340 Dove St (48060-6740)
PHONE..............................810 201-6457
David Yen,
Andrew Cesarski,
Jane Chang,
Benjamin Yen,
EMP: 15
SALES (est): 911.8K Privately Held
SIC: 3599 Crankshafts & camshafts, machining

Portage
Kalamazoo County

(G-12980)
A-1 SIGNS
2318 Winters Dr (49002-1642)
PHONE..............................269 488-9411
Richard Raschke, Owner
EMP: 3
SALES: 200K Privately Held
WEB: www.aonesigns.com
SIC: 5999 7336 3993 Banners; commercial art & graphic design; signs & advertising specialties

(G-12981)
AMERICA INK AND TECHNOLOGY
8975 Shaver Rd (49024-6156)
PHONE..............................269 345-4657
Brady Garrison, President
EMP: 6
SALES (est): 660K Privately Held
SIC: 2893 Printing ink

(G-12982)
AUSTIN COMPANY
9764 Portage Rd (49002-7251)
PHONE..............................269 329-1181
Dan Healy, Project Mgr
Steve Vanwormer, Manager
EMP: 15 EST: 2013
SALES (est): 3.4MM Privately Held
SIC: 3644 Raceways

(G-12983)
BAKEWELL COMPANY
2725 E Milham Ave (49002-1740)
PHONE..............................269 459-8030
Erin Hill, Principal
EMP: 5
SALES (est): 296K Privately Held
SIC: 2051 Bakery: wholesale or wholesale/retail combined

(G-12984)
BERCHTOLD CORPORATION
1651 W Centre Ave (49024-6312)
PHONE..............................269 329-2001
EMP: 3
SALES (est): 167.8K
SALES (corp-wide): 13.6B Publicly Held
SIC: 3841 3842 Surgical instruments & apparatus; saws, surgical; bone drills; suction therapy apparatus; implants, surgical
PA: Stryker Corporation
2825 Airview Blvd
Portage MI 49002
269 385-2600

(G-12985)
BJ SPORTS INC
453 W Kilgore Rd (49002-0500)
PHONE..............................269 342-2415
Jim Kakabeeke, President
EMP: 18
SQ FT: 3,000
SALES (est): 2MM Privately Held
WEB: www.bjsports.com
SIC: 3949 Hockey equipment & supplies, general; lacrosse equipment & supplies, general

(G-12986)
BOSKAGE COMMERCE PUBLICATIONS
510 E Milham Ave (49002-1439)
PHONE..............................269 673-7242
Scott Taylor, Owner
EMP: 5
SALES (est): 553.9K Privately Held
WEB: www.boskage.com
SIC: 2731 4731 Books: publishing only; freight transportation arrangement

(G-12987)
BOWMAN ENTERPRISES INC
Also Called: Great Deals Magazine
1905 Lakeview Dr (49002-6926)
P.O. Box 1862 (49081-1862)
PHONE..............................269 720-1946
John M Bowman, President
EMP: 6
SQ FT: 1,000
SALES (est): 71.9K Privately Held
SIC: 2721 7311 Magazines: publishing & printing; advertising agencies
HQ: Clipper Magazine, Llc
3708 Hempland Rd
Mountville PA 17554
717 569-5100

(G-12988)
BUSINESS CARDS PLUS INC
8785 Portage Indus Dr (49024-6148)
P.O. Box 644 (49081-0644)
PHONE..............................269 327-7727
Vaughn Leonard, President
Kevin Laurin, Engineer
Tom Dillon, Technology
EMP: 58
SQ FT: 14,000
SALES (est): 7.3MM Privately Held
WEB: www.businesscardsplus.com
SIC: 2752 Commercial printing, offset

(G-12989)
COLONIAL ENGINEERING INC (PA)
6400 Corporate Ave (49002-9399)
PHONE..............................269 323-2495
Mark F Bainbridge, President
Carroll J Haas, Principal
Patrick Beebe, Vice Pres
▲ EMP: 14
SQ FT: 15,000
SALES (est): 3.3MM Privately Held
WEB: www.colonialengineering.com
SIC: 3089 5085 3494 Fittings for pipe, plastic; industrial supplies; valves & pipe fittings

(G-12990)
CUSTOM DESIGN INC
4481 Commercial Ave (49002-9743)
PHONE..............................269 323-8561
Tim Bickings, President
Jim Heldt, General Mgr
EMP: 40
SQ FT: 30,000
SALES (est): 6.5MM Privately Held
SIC: 3544 Forms (molds), for foundry & plastics working machinery

(G-12991)
DYNAMIC AUTO TEST ENGINEERING
Also Called: Datec
1017 W Kilgore Rd (49024-5815)
PHONE..............................269 342-1334
EMP: 5
SQ FT: 7,500
SALES (est): 300K Privately Held
SIC: 7549 3825 Automotive Services Mfg Electrical Measuring Instruments

(G-12992)
ELIASON CORPORATION (DH)
Also Called: Doors4
9229 Shaver Rd (49024-6799)
PHONE..............................269 327-7003
Chris Herrick, Regional Mgr
Tom Mack, Opers Staff
Mason Deluca, Production
Patrick McMullen, CFO
Jim Lascala, Sales Staff
◆ EMP: 86 EST: 1952
SQ FT: 52,000
SALES (est): 21.4MM
SALES (corp-wide): 7.9B Privately Held
WEB: www.eliasoncorp.com
SIC: 3442 3089 Metal doors; plastic containers, except foam
HQ: Eliason Holdings Corporation
9229 Shaver Rd
Portage MI 49024
269 327-7003

(G-12993)
ERBSLOEH ALUM SOLUTIONS INC
Also Called: Wkw Extrusion
6565 S Sprinkle Rd (49002-9717)
PHONE..............................269 323-2565
Jon H Bowers, President
Meredith Warnicke, Finance Mgr
Bryan Farwell, Manager
▲ EMP: 290 EST: 1928
SQ FT: 300,000
SALES (est): 41.8MM
SALES (corp-wide): 144.1K Privately Held
WEB: www.bowers-mfg.com
SIC: 3471 3354 3353 3444 Anodizing (plating) of metals or formed products; buffing for the trade; aluminum extruded products; aluminum sheet, plate & foil; sheet metalwork
HQ: Wkw Erbsloeh North America, Llc
103 Parkway E
Pell City AL 35125
205 338-4242

(G-12994)
EVE SALONSPA
7117 S Westnedge Ave 3b (49002-4201)
PHONE..............................269 327-4811
Ben Boyer, Principal
EMP: 4
SALES (est): 555.3K Privately Held
SIC: 2844 Manicure preparations

(G-12995)
FEDEX OFFICE & PRINT SVCS INC
5730 S Westnedge Ave (49002-1470)
PHONE..............................269 344-7445
EMP: 20
SALES (corp-wide): 69.6B Publicly Held
WEB: www.kinkos.com
SIC: 7334 2791 2789 Photocopying & duplicating services; typesetting; bookbinding & related work
HQ: Fedex Office And Print Services, Inc.
7900 Legacy Dr
Plano TX 75024
800 463-3339

(G-12996)
FEMA CORPORATION OF MICHIGAN
1716 Vanderbilt Ave (49024-6069)
PHONE..............................269 323-1369
Robert T Banfield, President
Mike Johnson, Engineer
Paul Stevens, Engineer
EMP: 200
SQ FT: 49,000
SALES (est): 46.6MM Privately Held
WEB: www.fema-corp.com
SIC: 3679 3728 Solenoids for electronic applications; aircraft parts & equipment

(G-12997)
FRED OSWALTS PINS UNLTD
2610 Hill An Brook Dr (49024-5621)
PHONE..............................269 342-1387
Nancy Olds, Principal
EMP: 3
SALES (est): 172.6K Privately Held
SIC: 3452 Pins

(G-12998)
GEORGE JENSEN
Also Called: Jensen Security Systems
2228 Beethoven Ave (49024-6610)
PHONE..............................269 329-1543
George Jensen, Owner
EMP: 3
SALES (est): 213.5K Privately Held
SIC: 5999 3699 Alarm signal systems; security devices

(G-12999)
GREAT LAKES CHEMICAL SERVICES
616 W Centre Ave (49024-5308)
PHONE..............................269 372-6886
John Braganini, President
Edward Overbeck, Vice Pres
Kelly Carr, Controller
Joel Gasidlo, Wholesale
Charles Holley, Accounts Exec
EMP: 40
SALES (est): 9.7MM Privately Held
SIC: 2819 Chemicals, high purity: refined from technical grade

(G-13000)
HIGH PRFMCE MET FINSHG INC
1821 Vanderbilt Ave (49024-6010)
PHONE..............................269 327-8897
Patrick Greene, President
Kevin Greene, Vice Pres
Bruce E Justin, Treasurer
EMP: 10
SQ FT: 30,000
SALES: 500K Privately Held
SIC: 3471 Finishing, metals or formed products; plating of metals or formed products

(G-13001)
HOWMEDICA OSTEONICS CORP
1901 Romence Road Pkwy (49002-3672)
PHONE..............................269 389-8959
EMP: 9
SALES (corp-wide): 13.6B Publicly Held
SIC: 3842 Surgical appliances & supplies
HQ: Howmedica Osteonics Corp.
325 Corporate Dr
Mahwah NJ 07430
201 831-5000

(G-13002)
INTEGRA MOLD INC
10746 S Westnedge Ave (49002-7353)
PHONE..............................269 327-4337
Alan Blood, President
Michael Blood, Corp Secy
EMP: 5
SALES: 200K Privately Held
SIC: 3089 Injection molding of plastics

(G-13003)
JOHNSON CONTROLS INC
5164 S Sprinkle Rd (49002-2055)
PHONE..............................269 226-4748
EMP: 4 Privately Held
SIC: 2531 Seats, automobile
HQ: Johnson Controls, Inc.
5757 N Green Bay Ave
Milwaukee WI 53209
414 524-1200

GEOGRAPHIC SECTION

Portage - Kalamazoo County (G-13031)

(G-13004)
KALAMAZOO MACHINE TOOL CO INC
6700 Quality Way (49002-9756)
PHONE 269 321-8860
James R Larson, *President*
▲ **EMP:** 5
SQ FT: 10,000
SALES (est): 942.3K **Privately Held**
WEB: www.kmtsaw.com
SIC: 3541 Machine tools, metal cutting type

(G-13005)
KALAMAZOO STRIPPING DERUSTING
3921 E Centre Ave (49002-5855)
PHONE 269 323-1340
Anthony Pienta, *President*
Kathy Paul, *Opers Mgr*
EMP: 13
SQ FT: 22,000
SALES (est): 1.6MM **Privately Held**
SIC: 3471 Finishing, metals or formed products

(G-13006)
KAUFMAN ENTERPRISES INC (PA)
Also Called: Allegra Print & Imaging No 38
6054 Lovers Ln (49002-3026)
PHONE 269 324-0040
Victor W Kaufman, *President*
Brian Kaufman, *Principal*
EMP: 9
SQ FT: 3,500
SALES: 1MM **Privately Held**
SIC: 2752 Commercial printing, offset

(G-13007)
LEVANNES INC
8840 Portage Indus Dr (49024-6151)
PHONE 269 327-4484
Theodere Stender, *President*
Tony Stender, *Vice Pres*
EMP: 12
SQ FT: 13,000
SALES: 1.4MM **Privately Held**
WEB: www.levannes.com
SIC: 3544 Forms (molds), for foundry & plastics working machinery

(G-13008)
LIBERTY MANUFACTURING COMPANY
Also Called: Liberty Molds
8631 Portage Indus Dr (49024-6174)
PHONE 269 327-0997
Bill Berghuis, *President*
Brian Scott, *General Mgr*
Pat Stevens, *Principal*
Todd Charlton, *Vice Pres*
Mark Israels, *Engineer*
▲ **EMP:** 30
SALES (est): 5.3MM **Privately Held**
SIC: 3544 Industrial molds

(G-13009)
LINK TECHNOLOGY INC
Also Called: Silverglide Surgical Tech,
4100 E Milham Ave (49002-9704)
PHONE 269 324-8212
EMP: 10
SQ FT: 500
SALES (est): 780K **Privately Held**
SIC: 3841 Mfg Surgical/Medical Instruments

(G-13010)
LIVBIG LLC
Also Called: Submerge Camera
1821 Vanderbilt Ave Ste A (49024-6010)
PHONE 888 519-8290
EMP: 6
SALES: 1MM **Privately Held**
SIC: 5946 7335 5941 3663 Ret Cameras/Photo Supply Commercial Photography Ret Sport Goods/Bicycles Mfg Radio/Tv Comm Equip Photo Portrait Studio

(G-13011)
LLOMEN INC
Also Called: Super Book
5346 Ivanhoe Ct (49002-1555)
P.O. Box 20353, Kalamazoo (49019-1353)
PHONE 269 345-3555
Barbera Menlen, *President*
EMP: 8
SALES: 460K **Privately Held**
SIC: 2741 Miscellaneous publishing

(G-13012)
LUBE-TECH INC
Also Called: Great Lakes Lube-Tech
3960 Arbutus Trl (49024-1065)
P.O. Box 51301, Kalamazoo (49005-1301)
PHONE 269 329-1269
John J Cugnetti, *President*
Sharyn E Cugnetti, *Corp Secy*
EMP: 6
SALES (est): 533.2K **Privately Held**
SIC: 2992 5084 Re-refining lubricating oils & greases; petroleum industry machinery

(G-13013)
MANN + HUMMEL INC (DH)
6400 S Sprinkle Rd (49002-9706)
PHONE 269 329-3900
Alfred Weber, *President*
Nicolaas Zerbst, *Internal Med*
▲ **EMP:** 1
SQ FT: 60,000
SALES (est): 273.1MM
SALES (corp-wide): 4.5B **Privately Held**
SIC: 3559 3585 Plastics working machinery; dehumidifiers electric, except portable
HQ: Mann+Hummel Gmbh
    Schwieberdinger Str. 126
    Ludwigsburg 71636
    714 198-0

(G-13014)
MANN + HUMMEL USA INC (DH)
6400 S Sprinkle Rd (49002-9706)
PHONE 269 329-3900
Alfred Weber, *CEO*
Frank B Jehle, *President*
Emese Weissenbacher, *CFO*
Mareike Zahn, *Human Res Mgr*
▲ **EMP:** 19
SQ FT: 133,000
SALES (est): 899MM
SALES (corp-wide): 4.5B **Privately Held**
SIC: 3089 3714 Injection molding of plastics; motor vehicle parts & accessories
HQ: Mann + Hummel Holding Gmbh
    Schwieberdinger Str. 126
    Ludwigsburg 71636
    714 198-0

(G-13015)
MDG COMMERCIAL KITCHEN LLC
2312 Hemlock Ave (49024-1275)
PHONE 269 207-1344
Michael Grusell, *Owner*
EMP: 6 **EST:** 2010
SALES: 425K **Privately Held**
SIC: 3263 Commercial tableware or kitchen articles, fine earthenware

(G-13016)
METROPOLITAN INDUS LITHOGRAPHY
Also Called: Portage Printing
1116 W Centre Ave (49024-5391)
PHONE 269 323-9333
Craig Vestal, *President*
Dan Cyr, *Production*
EMP: 6
SALES (est): 880.9K **Privately Held**
WEB: www.portageprinting.com
SIC: 2752 2791 2789 Commercial printing, offset; typesetting; bookbinding & related work

(G-13017)
MV METAL PDTS & SOLUTIONS LLC (PA)
3585 Bellflower Dr (49024-3974)
PHONE 269 471-7715
Brian Spear, *Director*
EMP: 529
SALES (est): 131.5MM **Privately Held**
SIC: 3364 Nonferrous die-castings except aluminum

(G-13018)
NELSON HARDWARE
Also Called: Do It Best
9029 Portage Rd (49002-6419)
PHONE 269 327-3583
Bill Rowe, *President*
Jean Rowe Truitt, *Admin Sec*
EMP: 8
SQ FT: 10,000
SALES (est): 868.4K **Privately Held**
SIC: 5251 3498 Hardware; fabricated pipe & fittings

(G-13019)
NORTH AMERICAN COLOR INC
5960 S Sprinkle Rd (49002-9712)
PHONE 269 323-0552
Lawrence Leto Jr, *President*
B Jane Leto, *Vice Pres*
Tim Leto, *Plant Mgr*
Miranda Kucemba, *Manager*
Steve Pijaszek, *Senior Mgr*
EMP: 27 **EST:** 1981
SQ FT: 35,000
SALES (est): 4.9MM **Privately Held**
WEB: www.nac-mi.com
SIC: 2796 2752 Color separations for printing; commercial printing, lithographic

(G-13020)
ORTUS ENTERPRISES LLC
2527 Rolling Hill Ave (49024-6640)
PHONE 269 491-1447
EMP: 3 **EST:** 2009
SALES (est): 190K **Privately Held**
SIC: 3086 3965 5082 Mfg Plastic Foam Products Mfg Fasteners/Buttons/Pins Whol Construction/Mining Equipment

(G-13021)
PERSPECTIVE ENTERPRISES INC
7829 S Sprinkle Rd Ste A (49002-9013)
P.O. Box 670 (49081-0670)
PHONE 269 327-0869
Norman Root, *President*
Melisa Root, *Vice Pres*
Sharron Root, *Admin Sec*
EMP: 6
SQ FT: 4,200
SALES: 1MM **Privately Held**
WEB: www.perspectiveent.com
SIC: 3841 3713 Surgical & medical instruments; specialty motor vehicle bodies

(G-13022)
PETERMAN MOBILE CONCRETE INC (PA)
Also Called: Peterman Concrete Co
333 Peterman Ln (49002-5158)
PHONE 269 324-1211
Frank Peterman, *President*
Jim Peterman, *Vice Pres*
Scott Peterman, *Vice Pres*
Helen Peterman, *Treasurer*
EMP: 30
SALES (est): 6MM **Privately Held**
SIC: 3273 Ready-mixed concrete

(G-13023)
PRECISION PRINTER SERVICES INC
9185 Portage Indus Dr (49024-6193)
PHONE 269 384-5725
Roy Gooch, *President*
Patricia Gooch, *Principal*
EMP: 19
SQ FT: 7,000
SALES (est): 3.4MM **Privately Held**
WEB: www.precisionprinterservices.com
SIC: 3861 5734 7378 Toners, prepared photographic (not made in chemical plants); computer & software stores; printers & plotters: computers; computer maintenance & repair; computer peripheral equipment repair & maintenance

(G-13024)
PRINTING SERVICES
8815 S Sprinkle Rd (49002-6588)
P.O. Box 2646 (49081-2646)
PHONE 269 321-9826
Steven Huntington, *Owner*
Matthew Huntington, *Sales Staff*
Jason Huntington, *Manager*
EMP: 4
SQ FT: 1,600
SALES (est): 503K **Privately Held**
WEB: www.pservices.net
SIC: 2752 Commercial printing, offset; photo-offset printing

(G-13025)
QSV PHARMA LLC
3585 Bellflower Dr (49024-3974)
PHONE 269 324-2358
Kamesh Venugopal, *Principal*
EMP: 4
SALES (est): 324.1K **Privately Held**
SIC: 2834 Pharmaceutical preparations

(G-13026)
R L HUME AWARD CO
2226 Kalarama Ave (49024-3226)
PHONE 269 324-3063
Rick Hume, *CEO*
EMP: 3
SQ FT: 2,700
SALES (est): 260.8K **Privately Held**
WEB: www.award-1.com
SIC: 3299 3499 3993 Plaques: clay, plaster or papier mache; trophies, metal, except silver; signs & advertising specialties

(G-13027)
RATHCO SAFETY SUPPLY INC
6742 Lovers Ln (49002-3669)
PHONE 269 323-0153
Russell Rathburn, *President*
Sally Rathburn, *Corp Secy*
EMP: 30
SQ FT: 17,000
SALES: 4.3MM **Privately Held**
SIC: 3993 5063 Signs, not made in custom sign painting shops; signaling equipment, electrical

(G-13028)
RUBBAIR LLC
9229 Shaver Rd (49024-6763)
PHONE 269 327-7003
Patrick McMullen, *CFO*
EMP: 4
SALES (est): 163.5K
SALES (corp-wide): 7.9B **Privately Held**
SIC: 3442 Metal doors, sash & trim
HQ: Chase Industries, Inc.
    10021 Commerce Park Dr
    West Chester OH 45246
    513 860-5565

(G-13029)
S & K TOOL & DIE COMPANY INC
4401 Environmental Dr (49002-9307)
PHONE 269 345-2174
Philip Best, *President*
EMP: 16
SQ FT: 5,500
SALES (est): 2.6MM **Privately Held**
SIC: 3544 Forms (molds), for foundry & plastics working machinery

(G-13030)
S2 GAMES LLC
950 Trade Centre Way # 200 (49002-0487)
PHONE 269 344-8020
Marc Deforest, *CEO*
Joe Gray, *Manager*
Pu Liu, *Director*
EMP: 95
SALES (est): 5.2MM **Privately Held**
SIC: 7372 Prepackaged software

(G-13031)
SANITOR MFG CO
1221 W Centre Ave (49024-5384)
P.O. Box 2433 (49081-2433)
PHONE 269 327-3001
David J Dietrich, *President*
Katherine Morris, *Treasurer*
Jeanne Kirkendall, *Human Resources*

(PA)=Parent Co (HQ)=Headquarters (DH)=Div Headquarters
✿ = New Business established in last 2 years

Portage - Kalamazoo County (G-13032) — GEOGRAPHIC SECTION

Diane Dietrich, *Admin Sec*
▼ **EMP:** 17 **EST:** 1931
SQ FT: 24,000
SALES (est): 4MM **Privately Held**
WEB: www.sanitorusa.com
SIC: 2621 Toweling tissue, paper; sanitary tissue paper

(G-13032)
SELECT PRODUCTS LIMITED
Also Called: Select Hinges
9770 Shaver Rd (49024-6732)
PHONE.................................269 323-4433
Robert Cronk, *Vice Pres*
Aaron McElrath, *Regl Sales Mgr*
Chris Orme, *Regl Sales Mgr*
Kimberly Payne, *Sales Staff*
EMP: 30
SQ FT: 24,000
SALES (est): 2.2MM **Privately Held**
WEB: www.select-hinges.com
SIC: 3429 Door opening & closing devices, except electrical; furniture builders' & other household hardware

(G-13033)
SOLUTIONSNOWBIZ
8675 Portage Rd Ste 7 (49002-5700)
PHONE.................................269 321-5062
EMP: 4
SALES (est): 173.5K **Privately Held**
SIC: 8742 2759 Marketing consulting services; publication printing

(G-13034)
STAINLESS FABG & ENGRG INC
Also Called: SFE
9718 Portage Rd (49002-7251)
P.O. Box 627 (49081-0627)
PHONE.................................269 329-6142
Laura Goff, *President*
Mike Keeler, *Vice Pres*
EMP: 7
SQ FT: 22,000
SALES (est): 1.2MM **Privately Held**
WEB: www.sfe-inc.us
SIC: 3444 Sheet metalwork

(G-13035)
STAR CRANE HIST SVC OF KLMAZOO
8722 Portage Indus Dr (49024-6149)
PHONE.................................269 321-8882
Craig Derks, *President*
Scott De Kryger, *Vice Pres*
Larry Derks, *Vice Pres*
EMP: 5
SALES (est): 389.9K **Privately Held**
SIC: 7699 3536 7389 Industrial machinery & equipment repair; cranes & monorail systems; hoists; crane & aerial lift service

(G-13036)
STRYKER AUSTRALIA LLC (HQ)
2825 Airview Blvd (49002-1802)
PHONE.................................269 385-2600
EMP: 3
SALES (est): 1.8MM
SALES (corp-wide): 13.6B **Publicly Held**
SIC: 3841 3842 Surgical instruments & apparatus; saws, surgical; bone drills; suction therapy apparatus; implants, surgical
PA: Stryker Corporation
2825 Airview Blvd
Portage MI 49002
269 385-2600

(G-13037)
STRYKER CORPORATION
Stryker Instruments
6300 S Sprinkle Rd (49002-9705)
PHONE.................................269 389-3741
William Berry, *Vice Pres*
Alex Crawford, *Sales Staff*
Anton Kharin, *Sales Staff*
Lonny Carpenter, *Manager*
Sherrie Sessa, *Manager*
EMP: 42
SALES (corp-wide): 13.6B **Publicly Held**
SIC: 3842 3841 Personal safety equipment; surgical appliances & supplies; surgical & medical instruments
PA: Stryker Corporation
2825 Airview Blvd
Portage MI 49002
269 385-2600

(G-13038)
STRYKER CORPORATION (PA)
2825 Airview Blvd (49002-1802)
PHONE.................................269 385-2600
Kevin A Lobo, *Ch of Bd*
Viju Menon, *President*
Timothy J Scannell, *President*
Spencer Stiles, *President*
Steve Hill, *General Mgr*
EMP: 30 **EST:** 1941
SALES: 13.6B **Publicly Held**
WEB: www.stryker.com
SIC: 3841 3842 2599 Surgical instruments & apparatus; saws, surgical; bone drills; suction therapy apparatus; implants, surgical; hospital beds

(G-13039)
STRYKER CORPORATION
Stryker Craniomaxillofacial
750 Trade Centre Way # 200 (49002-0480)
PHONE.................................269 324-5346
Ramie Yesh, *Opers Staff*
Dipika Shukla, *Engineer*
Andrew Pierce, *Manager*
Kimber Atteberry, *Manager*
EMP: 195
SALES (corp-wide): 13.6B **Publicly Held**
SIC: 3841 Surgical & medical instruments
PA: Stryker Corporation
2825 Airview Blvd
Portage MI 49002
269 385-2600

(G-13040)
STRYKER CORPORATION
Also Called: Stryker Medical A Div Stryker
3800 E Centre Ave (49002-5826)
PHONE.................................269 329-2100
Curt Hartman, *Branch Mgr*
EMP: 312
SALES (corp-wide): 13.6B **Publicly Held**
SIC: 3841 3842 2599 Surgical instruments & apparatus; implants, surgical; hospital beds
PA: Stryker Corporation
2825 Airview Blvd
Portage MI 49002
269 385-2600

(G-13041)
STRYKER CORPORATION
Stryker Corp - Shared Svcs
1901 Romence Road Pkwy (49002-3672)
PHONE.................................269 389-2300
Lonny Carpenter, *Branch Mgr*
EMP: 129
SALES (corp-wide): 13.6B **Publicly Held**
SIC: 3841 Surgical instruments & apparatus; medical instruments & equipment, blood & bone work
PA: Stryker Corporation
2825 Airview Blvd
Portage MI 49002
269 385-2600

(G-13042)
STRYKER CORPORATION
Also Called: Stryker Instrs A Div Stryker
4100 E Milham Ave (49002-9303)
PHONE.................................269 323-1027
James N Heath, *Manager*
Allan Golston, *Director*
EMP: 38
SALES (corp-wide): 13.6B **Publicly Held**
SIC: 3842 3841 Personal safety equipment; surgical appliances & supplies; surgical & medical instruments
PA: Stryker Corporation
2825 Airview Blvd
Portage MI 49002
269 385-2600

(G-13043)
STRYKER CUSTOMS BROKERS LLC
1901 Romence Road Pkwy (49002-3672)
PHONE.................................269 389-2300
T Dembski-Brandl,
David Furgason,
EMP: 19
SALES (est): 769K
SALES (corp-wide): 13.6B **Publicly Held**
SIC: 3842 Implants, surgical
PA: Stryker Corporation
2825 Airview Blvd
Portage MI 49002
269 385-2600

(G-13044)
STRYKER FAR EAST INC (HQ)
2825 Airview Blvd (49002-1802)
PHONE.................................269 385-2600
Kevin A Lobo, *President*
William R Jellison, *Vice Pres*
Katherine A Owen, *Vice Pres*
EMP: 21
SALES (est): 51.7MM
SALES (corp-wide): 13.6B **Publicly Held**
SIC: 3841 3842 2599 8049 Surgical instruments & apparatus; saws, surgical; bone drills; suction therapy apparatus; implants, surgical; hospital beds; physical therapist
PA: Stryker Corporation
2825 Airview Blvd
Portage MI 49002
269 385-2600

(G-13045)
SUMMIT POLYMERS INC (PA)
Also Called: Technical Center
6715 S Sprinkle Rd (49002-9707)
PHONE.................................269 324-9330
James Haas, *President*
Dan Brown, *General Mgr*
Gregory Goodman, *Vice Pres*
Mark Hammer, *Vice Pres*
Phillip Holley, *Prdtn Mgr*
▲ **EMP:** 185
SQ FT: 70,000
SALES (est): 444.7MM **Privately Held**
WEB: www.summitpolymers.com
SIC: 3089 Injection molding of plastics

(G-13046)
SUMMIT POLYMERS INC
6615 S Sprinkle Rd (49002-9709)
PHONE.................................269 324-9320
Kay Salyer, *Manager*
EMP: 5
SALES (corp-wide): 444.7MM **Privately Held**
SIC: 3089 Automotive parts, plastic
PA: Summit Polymers, Inc.
6715 S Sprinkle Rd
Portage MI 49002
269 324-9330

(G-13047)
SUMMIT POLYMERS INC
Also Called: Plant 1
4750 Executive Dr (49002-9388)
PHONE.................................269 323-1301
Roy Hudson, *Materials Mgr*
Joel Krygier, *QC Mgr*
Tim Eccles, *Engineer*
Dennis Edwards, *Engineer*
Pat Michael, *Engineer*
EMP: 300
SALES (corp-wide): 444.7MM **Privately Held**
WEB: www.summitpolymers.com
SIC: 3089 3083 Injection molding of plastics; laminated plastics plate & sheet
PA: Summit Polymers, Inc.
6715 S Sprinkle Rd
Portage MI 49002
269 324-9330

(G-13048)
TENANTS TOLERANCE TOOLING
3704 Wedgwood Dr (49024-5529)
PHONE.................................269 349-6907
EMP: 3
SQ FT: 50,000
SALES: 500K **Privately Held**
SIC: 3599 3545 3544 Mfg Industrial Machinery Mfg Machine Tool Accessories Mfg Dies/Tools/Jigs/Fixtures

(G-13049)
THERMO FISHER SCIENTIFIC INC
4169 Commercial Ave (49002-9701)
PHONE.................................800 346-4364
Richard Gibbs, *Sales Associate*
Steve Grabosky, *Marketing Mgr*
EMP: 10
SALES (corp-wide): 24.3B **Publicly Held**
SIC: 3826 Analytical instruments
PA: Thermo Fisher Scientific Inc.
168 3rd Ave
Waltham MA 02451
781 622-1000

(G-13050)
TINDALL PACKAGING INC
9718 Portage Rd (49002-7251)
PHONE.................................269 649-1163
Marianne Tindall, *President*
EMP: 5
SALES (est): 729.9K **Privately Held**
WEB: www.tindallpackaging.com
SIC: 3565 7699 8742 3523 Packaging machinery; industrial machinery & equipment repair; manufacturing management consultant; farm machinery & equipment

(G-13051)
UNIFAB CORPORATION
Also Called: Unifab Cages
5260 Lovers Ln (49002-1560)
PHONE.................................269 382-2803
Mick Madden, *President*
Robert Thayer, *Mfg Mgr*
EMP: 23 **EST:** 1940
SQ FT: 40,000
SALES (est): 4.9MM **Privately Held**
WEB: www.unifabcorporation.com
SIC: 3444 3496 Sheet metalwork; cages, wire

(G-13052)
UNITED KENNEL CLUB INC
100 E Kilgore Rd (49002-0506)
PHONE.................................269 343-9020
Wayne Cavanaugh, *President*
Mark Threlfaoo, *Vice Pres*
EMP: 50
SQ FT: 16,500
SALES (est): 6.2MM **Privately Held**
WEB: www.ukcdogs.com
SIC: 2721 0752 7997 Magazines: publishing only, not printed on site; pedigree record services, pet & animal specialties; membership sports & recreation clubs

(G-13053)
USA SUMMIT PLAS SILAO 1 LLC (HQ)
6715 S Sprinkle Rd (49002-9707)
PHONE.................................269 324-9330
Andrea Haas, *President*
James Haas, *President*
John Meyer, *CFO*
Reed Kendell, *Asst Sec*
EMP: 4 **EST:** 2011
SALES (est): 12.4MM
SALES (corp-wide): 444.7MM **Privately Held**
SIC: 3089 Injection molding of plastics
PA: Summit Polymers, Inc.
6715 S Sprinkle Rd
Portage MI 49002
269 324-9330

(G-13054)
W SOULE & CO (PA)
Also Called: W Soule & Co Service Group
7125 S Sprinkle Rd (49002-9437)
P.O. Box 2169, Kalamazoo (49003-2169)
PHONE.................................269 324-7001
John Soule, *President*
Kevin Waterstradt, *Vice Pres*
Josh Hoikka, *Project Mgr*
Matt Sparks, *Project Mgr*
Brett Walters, *Project Mgr*
EMP: 100 **EST:** 1920
SQ FT: 5,100
SALES (est): 81.3MM **Privately Held**
WEB: www.wsoule.com
SIC: 1711 3444 Process piping contractor; sheet metal specialties, not stamped

(G-13055)
WEST MICHIGAN STAMP & SEAL
10330 Portage Rd (49002-7279)
PHONE.................................269 323-1913
Mark Terpstra, *President*
EMP: 3

GEOGRAPHIC SECTION

SALES (est): 244.8K Privately Held
SIC: 3953 3479 Embossing seals & hand stamps; etching & engraving

(G-13056)
WKW ROOF RAIL SYSTEMS LLC
6565 S Sprinkle Rd (49002-9717)
PHONE..................................205 338-4242
Deborah Grant,
▲ EMP: 75
SALES (est): 10.6MM
SALES (corp-wide): 144.1K Privately Held
SIC: 3462 Automotive forgings, ferrous: crankshaft, engine, axle, etc.
HQ: Wkw Erbsloeh North America Holding, Inc.
103 Parkway E
Pell City AL 35125

(G-13057)
WL MOLDING OF MICHIGAN LLC
8212 Shaver Rd (49024-5440)
PHONE..................................269 327-3075
Nigam Tripathi,
EMP: 60
SQ FT: 43,000
SALES (est): 16.7MM Privately Held
WEB: www.wlmolding.com
SIC: 3089 Molding primary plastic

(G-13058)
WMH FLUIDPOWER INC (PA)
Also Called: W M H Fluidpower
862 Lenox Ave (49024-5490)
PHONE..................................269 327-7011
Dave Gruss, President
William Beaupre, Vice Pres
Bill Elhart, Accounts Mgr
Kathy Martin, Sales Staff
Bill Frye, Manager
EMP: 14
SQ FT: 10,000
SALES (est): 7.6MM Privately Held
WEB: www.wmh.com
SIC: 5084 3492 3728 3594 Hydraulic systems equipment & supplies; pneumatic tools & equipment; control valves, fluid power: hydraulic & pneumatic; hose & tube fittings & assemblies, hydraulic/pneumatic; aircraft parts & equipment; fluid power pumps & motors; turbines & turbine generator sets

(G-13059)
WOODEN MOON STUDIO
10334 Portage Rd (49002-7279)
PHONE..................................269 329-3229
EMP: 3
SALES (est): 247.6K Privately Held
SIC: 3993 Mfg Signs/Advertising Specialties

Portland
Ionia County

(G-13060)
ADL SYSTEMS INC
5596 E Grand River Ave (48875)
P.O. Box 256 (48875-0256)
PHONE..................................517 647-7543
Albert L Vroman, Ch of Bd
Ryan Vroman, President
Rodney P Vroman, President
Patricia Vroman, Corp Secy
Daniel Vroman, Vice Pres
EMP: 3 EST: 1973
SQ FT: 12,000
SALES (est): 567.9K Privately Held
SIC: 3272 Concrete products, precast; tanks, concrete

(G-13061)
ARCHER-DANIELS-MIDLAND COMPANY
Also Called: ADM
401 E Grand River Ave (48875-1403)
P.O. Box 260 (48875-0260)
PHONE..................................517 647-4155
Tony Kolarik, Branch Mgr
EMP: 35
SALES (corp-wide): 64.3B Publicly Held
WEB: www.admworld.com
SIC: 2041 2047 Flour & other grain mill products; dog & cat food
PA: Archer-Daniels-Midland Company
77 W Wacker Dr Ste 4600
Chicago IL 60601
312 634-8100

(G-13062)
GREAT LAKES PUBLISHING INC
212 Kent St Ste 6 (48875-1480)
PHONE..................................517 647-4444
Ken Kramer, President
EMP: 9
SQ FT: 2,000
SALES (est): 881.9K Privately Held
WEB: www.greatlakespub.com
SIC: 2741 6531 Telephone & other directory publishing; real estate agents & managers

(G-13063)
MICHIGAN STEEL AND TRIM INC
349 N Water St (48875-1060)
P.O. Box 346 (48875-0346)
PHONE..................................517 647-4555
EMP: 5 EST: 2014
SALES (est): 363.7K Privately Held
SIC: 1761 2952 Roofing contractor; roofing materials

(G-13064)
MOODY SIGN CO
14470 Howe Rd (48875-9303)
PHONE..................................517 626-6404
Daniel Moody, Owner
EMP: 3
SALES (est): 127.4K Privately Held
SIC: 3993 Signs & advertising specialties

(G-13065)
PORTLAND PLASTICS CO
3 Industrial Dr (48875)
P.O. Box 436 (48875-0436)
PHONE..................................517 647-4115
Robert Tait, President
Steve Macksoob, Vice Pres
▲ EMP: 20
SQ FT: 57,000
SALES (est): 800K Privately Held
SIC: 3087 2891 2851 Custom compound purchased resins; adhesives & sealants; paints & allied products

(G-13066)
PRESSWELD MANUFACTURING CO
Also Called: Royal Rod Co
11290 Charlotte Hwy (48875-8400)
PHONE..................................734 675-8282
EMP: 3
SQ FT: 2,000
SALES: 100K Privately Held
SIC: 3949 3429 Mfg Sporting/Athletic Goods Mfg Hardware

(G-13067)
SEBEWA SAND & GRAVEL LLC
11858 Keefer Hwy (48875-9710)
PHONE..................................517 647-4296
Dale Hanson, Principal
EMP: 3
SALES (est): 150.6K Privately Held
SIC: 1442 Construction sand & gravel

(G-13068)
THK RHYTHM AUTO MICH CORP
902 Lyons Rd (48875-1000)
PHONE..................................517 647-4121
Akihiro Teramachi, President
EMP: 250
SALES (est): 213.7K Privately Held
SIC: 3714 Motor vehicle parts & accessories
PA: Thk Co., Ltd.
2-12-10, Shibaura
Minato-Ku TKY 108-0

Posen
Presque Isle County

(G-13069)
HINCKA LOGGING LLC
6464 Lake Augusta Hwy (49776-9765)
P.O. Box 218 (49776-0218)
PHONE..................................989 766-8893
Clarence Hincka Sr,
Fernades Clarence, Admin Sec
EMP: 5
SALES (est): 605K Privately Held
SIC: 2411 Logging camps & contractors

(G-13070)
MAPLE RIDGE COMPANIES INC
9528 S Bolton Rd (49776-9625)
PHONE..................................989 356-4807
Gerald J Kamysiak, President
EMP: 20
SQ FT: 30,000
SALES (est): 1.9MM Privately Held
WEB: www.bicyclestand.com
SIC: 3999 0811 Novelties, bric-a-brac & hobby kits; Christmas tree farm

(G-13071)
R & R FOREST PRODUCTS INC
8622 M 65 (49776-9767)
PHONE..................................989 766-8227
Richard Romel, President
Mark J Romel, Vice Pres
Susanne Romel, Admin Sec
EMP: 4
SALES (est): 459.7K Privately Held
SIC: 2411 Poles, posts & pilings: untreated wood

Potterville
Eaton County

(G-13072)
21ST CENTURY PLASTICS CORP (PA)
300 Wright Pkwy (48876)
P.O. Box 188 (48876-0188)
PHONE..................................517 645-2695
Greg Dobie, President
Craig Wright, Vice Pres
Kate Nowicki, Accounting Dir
▲ EMP: 65
SQ FT: 68,000
SALES: 17MM Privately Held
SIC: 3089 Injection molding of plastics

(G-13073)
CROSS COUNTRY HOMES
Also Called: Harbor Sales
5117 Windsor Hwy (48876-8762)
PHONE..................................517 694-0778
Willard Lievense, President
EMP: 3
SALES: 3MM Privately Held
SIC: 2451 Mobile homes

(G-13074)
KAMPS INC
4400 Shance Hwy (48876)
PHONE..................................517 645-2800
Tony Sokoloski, Branch Mgr
EMP: 12
SALES (corp-wide): 157.4MM Privately Held
WEB: www.kampspallets.com
SIC: 2448 2449 Pallets, wood; wood containers
PA: Kamps, Inc.
2900 Peach Ridge Ave Nw
Grand Rapids MI 49534
616 453-9676

(G-13075)
PROFILE INC
345 Wright Indus Pkwy (48876)
PHONE..................................517 224-8012
Peter Roginski, Sales Mgr
EMP: 40 EST: 2012
SALES (est): 1.3MM Privately Held
SIC: 3469 Metal stampings

Powers
Menominee County

(G-13076)
✸ 702 CEDAR RIVER LBR INC
W4249 Us Hwy 2 (49874)
P.O. Box 340 (49874-0340)
PHONE..................................906 497-5365
Donald S Leboeuf, President
Donald S Le Boeuf, President
Cathy Phelps, Vice Pres
Greg Le Boeuf, Marketing Staff
EMP: 45
SQ FT: 3,000
SALES (est): 5.1MM Privately Held
WEB: www.cedarriverlumber.com
SIC: 2421 2452 2491 Planing mills; custom sawmill; prefabricated wood buildings; wood preserving

(G-13077)
GATIEN FARM & FOREST PDTS LLC
N16323 River Road J.5 (49874-9629)
PHONE..................................906 497-5541
Lisa Gatien,
EMP: 3
SALES: 350K Privately Held
SIC: 2421 Sawmills & planing mills, general

(G-13078)
OGDEN NEWSPAPERS INC
Also Called: Powers Printing
W3985 2nd St (49874-9601)
PHONE..................................906 497-5652
Jeff Schwaller, Principal
EMP: 4 Privately Held
WEB: www.miningjournal.net
SIC: 2711 Newspapers: publishing only, not printed on site
HQ: The Ogden Newspapers Inc
1500 Main St
Wheeling WV 26003
304 233-0100

(G-13079)
U P MACHINE & ENGINEERING CO
Also Called: U.P. Machine
N15930 Main St (49874-9610)
P.O. Box 400 (49874-0400)
PHONE..................................906 497-5278
Cal Land, President
Jesse Land, Business Mgr
Jeff Land, Vice Pres
Cindy Meiner, Office Mgr
EMP: 25 EST: 1963
SQ FT: 23,000
SALES: 3MM Privately Held
SIC: 3599 Machine shop, jobbing & repair

Prescott
Ogemaw County

(G-13080)
IDEAL WHOLESALE INC
Also Called: K & D Wholesale & Embroidery
3430 Henderson Lake Rd (48756-9338)
PHONE..................................989 873-5850
Keith Dupuis, President
Darlene Dupuis, Vice Pres
EMP: 4
SALES (est): 706.8K Privately Held
SIC: 5199 5092 5136 5137 Gifts & novelties; toys & hobby goods & supplies; men's & boys' sportswear & work clothing; women's & children's sportswear & swimsuits; schiffli machine embroideries; embroidery products, except schiffli machine

(G-13081)
SWANSONS EXCAVATING INC
2733 Greenwood Rd (48756-9143)
PHONE..................................989 873-4419
Richard E Swanson, President
EMP: 4
SQ FT: 5,000

Presque Isle - Presque Isle County (G-13082)

GEOGRAPHIC SECTION

SALES: 200K **Privately Held**
SIC: 3273 1794 Ready-mixed concrete; excavation work

Presque Isle
Presque Isle County

(G-13082)
AUSTIN POWDER COMPANY
11351 E Grand Lake Rd (49777-8383)
PHONE..................989 595-2400
EMP: 12
SALES (corp-wide): 418.2MM **Privately Held**
SIC: 2892 Mfg Explosives
HQ: Austin Powder Company
25800 Science Park Dr # 300
Cleveland OH 44122
216 464-2400

(G-13083)
LAFARGE NORTH AMERICA INC
11351 E Grand Lake Rd (49777-8383)
PHONE..................989 595-3820
Nicole Heberling, *General Mgr*
Dave Nelson, *Branch Mgr*
EMP: 175
SALES (corp-wide): 27.6B **Privately Held**
WEB: www.lafargenorthamerica.com
SIC: 3241 Cement, hydraulic
HQ: Lafarge North America Inc.
8700 W Bryn Mawr Ave
Chicago IL 60631
773 372-1000

Prudenville
Roscommon County

(G-13084)
AMERICAN VAULT SERVICE (PA)
2063 Norway Ln (48651-9506)
PHONE..................989 366-8657
James W Stender, *Owner*
EMP: 4
SALES: 600K **Privately Held**
SIC: 5087 3544 7261 Caskets; welding positioners (jigs); crematory

(G-13085)
MAPLE VALLEY TRUSS CO
4287 E West Branch Rd (48651-9441)
PHONE..................989 389-4267
Richard Gurzenda, *President*
EMP: 20
SQ FT: 11,800
SALES (est): 2.9MM **Privately Held**
SIC: 2439 Trusses, except roof: laminated lumber; trusses, wooden roof

(G-13086)
VIKING OIL LLC
Also Called: Performance Plus
55 W Houghton Lake Dr (48651)
PHONE..................989 366-4772
John Mendynk, *Manager*
EMP: 5
SALES (corp-wide): 50K **Privately Held**
SIC: 3599 Oil filters, internal combustion engine, except automotive
PA: Viking Oil, Llc
6228 Crystal Beach Rd Nw
Rapid City MI

Pullman
Allegan County

(G-13087)
PAUL F HESTER
Also Called: Organized Crime Entertainment
954 Maple St (49450-9684)
PHONE..................616 302-6039
Paul Hester, *Owner*
Joshua Carter, *Principal*
Brian Haff, *Principal*
Kendall Moore, *Principal*
EMP: 13

SALES (est): 324.9K **Privately Held**
SIC: 2741 7922 7389 Music book & sheet music publishing; booking agency, theatrical; concert management service; recording studio, noncommercial records; music recording producer

Quincy
Branch County

(G-13088)
ALUMIRAMP INC
855 E Chicago Rd (49082-9450)
PHONE..................517 639-5103
Linda Burke, *President*
Jenifer Bruke, *Vice Pres*
Barbara Anderson, *Art Dir*
EMP: 10
SALES (est): 1.1MM **Privately Held**
WEB: www.alumiramp.com
SIC: 3448 Ramps: prefabricated metal

(G-13089)
BAADE FABRICATING & ENGRG
210 S Ray Quincy Rd (49082-9523)
PHONE..................517 639-4536
Jon R Baade, *President*
Judy Baade, *Treasurer*
EMP: 5 **EST:** 1967
SQ FT: 12,000
SALES (est): 252.8K **Privately Held**
SIC: 3599 Machine shop, jobbing & repair

(G-13090)
BRECO LLC
57 Cole St (49082)
P.O. Box 216 (49082-0216)
PHONE..................517 317-2211
Ken Holroyd,
EMP: 7
SALES (est): 1MM **Privately Held**
SIC: 3599 Machine & other job shop work; machine shop, jobbing & repair

(G-13091)
CCO HOLDINGS LLC
1 W Chicago St (49082-1103)
PHONE..................517 639-1060
EMP: 3
SALES (corp-wide): 43.6B **Publicly Held**
SIC: 5064 4841 3663 3651 Electrical appliances, television & radio; cable & other pay television services; radio & TV communications equipment; household audio & video equipment
HQ: Cco Holdings, Llc
400 Atlantic St
Stamford CT 06901
203 905-7801

(G-13092)
CONAGRA BRANDS INC
4551 Squires Rd (49082-9601)
PHONE..................402 240-8210
John Hennessy, *Branch Mgr*
EMP: 30
SALES (corp-wide): 9.5B **Publicly Held**
WEB: www.conagra.com
SIC: 2099 Food preparations
PA: Conagra Brands, Inc.
222 Mdse Mart Plz
Chicago IL 60654
312 549-5000

(G-13093)
CPS LLC
Also Called: Commercial Painting Services
11 E Chicago St (49082-1101)
PHONE..................517 639-1464
Ian Bernard, *Project Mgr*
EMP: 12
SQ FT: 7,000
SALES: 1.2MM **Privately Held**
SIC: 1721 1761 3531 Industrial painting; commercial painting; roofing contractor; surfacers, concrete grinding

(G-13094)
EAB FABRICATION INC
64 Cole St (49082-1032)
P.O. Box 72 (49082-0072)
PHONE..................517 639-7080
Edwin A Bowerman, *President*

Thelma Bowerman, *Corp Secy*
Sandy Coffee, *Human Res Mgr*
EMP: 50
SQ FT: 20,000
SALES (est): 13.3MM **Privately Held**
SIC: 3441 Fabricated structural metal

(G-13095)
LSP INC
Also Called: Lsp Dock Systems
855 E Chicago Rd (49082-9450)
PHONE..................517 639-3815
Jenifer Burke, *Principal*
EMP: 21
SALES (est): 5.2MM **Privately Held**
SIC: 3531 Marine related equipment

(G-13096)
MARSH BROTHERS INC
9800 Youngs Rd (49082-9605)
PHONE..................517 869-2653
Dan Marsh, *President*
George Calvin Marsh, *Vice Pres*
EMP: 15
SQ FT: 15,000
SALES (est): 2MM **Privately Held**
WEB: www.marshbrothersonline.com
SIC: 7699 3732 5551 Marine engine repair; boat building & repairing; outboard motors

(G-13097)
MUNIMULA INC
548 Squires Rd (49082-8423)
PHONE..................517 605-5343
Pauline K Munn, *CEO*
Barbara Anderson, *Graphic Designe*
EMP: 3 **EST:** 2011
SALES (est): 197.4K **Privately Held**
SIC: 3089 Plastic kitchenware, tableware & houseware

(G-13098)
SPEEDRACK PRODUCTS GROUP LTD
42 Cole St (49082-1032)
PHONE..................517 639-8781
Corrine Towns, *Branch Mgr*
EMP: 141
SALES (corp-wide): 35.6MM **Privately Held**
WEB: www.speedrack.net
SIC: 3449 Miscellaneous metalwork
PA: Speedrack Products Group, Ltd.
7903 Venture Ave Nw
Sparta MI 49345
616 887-0002

(G-13099)
STAR OF WEST MILLING COMPANY
14 Church St (49082-1096)
PHONE..................517 639-3165
James Hargett, *Branch Mgr*
Tom Saltsgiver, *Maintence Staff*
EMP: 25
SALES (corp-wide): 380.1MM **Privately Held**
SIC: 2041 Flour & other grain mill products
PA: Star Of The West Milling Company
121 E Tuscola St
Frankenmuth MI 48734
989 652-9971

(G-13100)
SUN GRO HORTICULTURE DIST INC
1150 E Chicago Rd (49082-9585)
PHONE..................517 639-3115
Daniel Johnson, *Manager*
Dan D Johnson, *Director*
EMP: 70 **Privately Held**
WEB: www.sungro.com
SIC: 2875 0781 Potting soil, mixed; horticultural counseling services
PA: Sun Gro Horticulture Distribution Inc.
770 Silver St
Agawam MA 01001

Quinnesec
Dickinson County

(G-13101)
PASTY OVEN INC (PA)
W7279 Us Highway 2 (49876-9709)
P.O. Box 100 (49876-0100)
PHONE..................906 774-2328
Gene Carollo, *President*
▲ **EMP:** 7
SQ FT: 2,400
SALES: 1.1MM **Privately Held**
SIC: 2038 Ethnic foods, frozen

(G-13102)
SPECIALTY MINERALS INC
Also Called: Minerals Technology
W6705 Us Highway 2 (49876)
P.O. Box 1047, Iron Mountain (49801-8047)
PHONE..................906 779-9138
Varis Kukainis, *Manager*
EMP: 11 **Publicly Held**
WEB: www.specialtyminerals.com
SIC: 2819 Industrial inorganic chemicals
HQ: Specialty Minerals Inc.
622 3rd Ave Fl 38
New York NY 10017
212 878-1800

(G-13103)
UP TRUCK CENTER INC
4920 Menominee St (49876)
P.O. Box 261 (49876-0261)
PHONE..................906 774-0098
Thomas Sullivan, *President*
Beth Sullivan, *Admin Sec*
◆ **EMP:** 22
SQ FT: 26,650
SALES: 3.5MM **Privately Held**
WEB: www.uptruckcenter.com
SIC: 5511 5531 7692 Trucks, tractors & trailers: new & used; truck equipment & parts; automotive welding

(G-13104)
VERSO PAPER HOLDING LLC
W6791 Us Highway 2 (49876)
P.O. Box 211, Norway (49870-0211)
PHONE..................906 779-3200
Mike Sussman, *Manager*
Jeff Maule, *Manager*
Mark Mielcarek, *Info Tech Dir*
Donald Davy, *Network Enginr*
George Curran, *Executive*
EMP: 10 **Publicly Held**
WEB: www.versopaper.com
SIC: 2671 2611 2621 Paper coated or laminated for packaging; pulp mills; paper mills
HQ: Verso Paper Holding Llc
8540 Gander Creek Dr
Miamisburg OH 45342
877 855-7243

(G-13105)
VERSO PAPER HOLDING LLC
W6705 Us Highway 2 (49876)
PHONE..................906 396-2358
Mike Sussman, *Branch Mgr*
EMP: 490 **Publicly Held**
SIC: 2671 Paper coated or laminated for packaging
HQ: Verso Paper Holding Llc
8540 Gander Creek Dr
Miamisburg OH 45342
877 855-7243

(G-13106)
VERSO QUINNESEC LLC
W6791 Us Highway 2 (49876)
P.O. Box 221, Norway (49870-0221)
PHONE..................877 447-2737
David J Paterson,
EMP: 8
SALES (est): 2.3MM **Publicly Held**
SIC: 2621 Paper mills
PA: Verso Corporation
8540 Gander Creek Dr
Miamisburg OH 45342

GEOGRAPHIC SECTION

Ray - Macomb County (G-13135)

(G-13107)
VERSO QUINNESEC REP LLC
W6705 Us Highway 2 (49876)
PHONE..................................906 779-3200
John Valas, *Credit Staff*
EMP: 4 **Publicly Held**
SIC: 2621 Paper mills
HQ: Verso Quinnesec Rep Llc
8540 Gander Creek Dr
Miamisburg OH 45342
901 369-4100

(G-13108)
VERTIGO
1006 Lake Ave (49876)
PHONE..................................910 381-8925
Matthew Meyers, *President*
Amy Larson, *Vice Pres*
Chris Larson, *Vice Pres*
EMP: 3
SALES (est): 119.7K **Privately Held**
SIC: 3441 Tower sections, radio & television transmission

Rapid City
Kalkaska County

(G-13109)
KNUST MASONRY
6092 Aarwood Rd Nw (49676-9483)
PHONE..................................231 322-2587
Rick Knust, *Owner*
EMP: 7
SALES: 450K **Privately Held**
SIC: 3241 1741 Masonry cement; masonry & other stonework

(G-13110)
PETROLEUM ENVIRONMENTAL TECH
5681 Rapid City Rd Nw (49676-8420)
PHONE..................................231 258-0400
Larry Thompson, *President*
Terry Thompson, *Vice Pres*
EMP: 3
SQ FT: 3,000
SALES (est): 405.2K **Privately Held**
SIC: 2899 8742 Chemical preparations; management consulting services

Rapid River
Delta County

(G-13111)
CREATIVE COMPOSITES INC
7637 Us Highway 2 (49878-9791)
PHONE..................................906 474-9941
Brad McPhee, *President*
Stepnaie Lockhart, *Office Mgr*
EMP: 30
SQ FT: 8,500
SALES (est): 6.7MM **Privately Held**
WEB: www.isp360.net
SIC: 3446 8711 Architectural metalwork; engineering services

(G-13112)
DUANE F PROEHL INC
11064 T.65 Rd (49878-9313)
PHONE..................................906 474-6630
Duane F Proehl, *President*
Ruth Proehl, *Admin Sec*
EMP: 5
SALES: 400K **Privately Held**
SIC: 2411 Logging

(G-13113)
POMEROY FOREST PRODUCTS INC
9577 Ee.25 Rd (49878-9103)
PHONE..................................906 474-6780
Mark Pomeroy, *President*
Vicky Pomeroy, *Admin Sec*
EMP: 9 **EST:** 1977
SALES (est): 1MM **Privately Held**
SIC: 2411 Logging

(G-13114)
RAPID RIVER RUSTIC INC (PA)
Also Called: Rapid River Loghome
9211 County 511 22 And (49878)
P.O. Box 10 (49878-0010)
PHONE..................................906 474-6404
Ivan R Malnar, *President*
Jodi Malnar, *Corp Secy*
EMP: 50
SALES (est): 5.6MM **Privately Held**
WEB: www.rapidriverrustic.com
SIC: 2421 2499 3496 2439 Lumber stacking or sticking; fencing, wood; miscellaneous fabricated wire products; structural wood members; logging

(G-13115)
ROBERT MCINTYRE LOGGING
6427 E Maple Rdg Rd (49878)
PHONE..................................906 446-3158
EMP: 3
SALES (est): 225.9K **Privately Held**
SIC: 2411 Logging

(G-13116)
TRI-FORESTRY
10222 15.25 Rd (49878-9281)
PHONE..................................906 474-9379
Ed Rivers, *Partner*
James Spriks, *Partner*
EMP: 3
SALES (est): 211.4K **Privately Held**
SIC: 2411 Logging camps & contractors

(G-13117)
WILLIAMS MILLING & MOULDING IN
10304 Bay Shore Dr (49878-9796)
PHONE..................................906 474-9222
Gene Williams, *Principal*
EMP: 5
SALES (est): 370.6K **Privately Held**
SIC: 2041 Flour & other grain mill products

Ravenna
Muskegon County

(G-13118)
DAN DRUMMOND
Also Called: Drummond Meat Processing
1830 S Slocum Rd (49451-9114)
PHONE..................................231 853-6200
Dan Drummond, *Owner*
EMP: 3
SQ FT: 3,220
SALES (est): 200K **Privately Held**
SIC: 5421 2011 Meat markets, including freezer provisioners; meat packing plants

(G-13119)
DYNAMIC CUSTOM MACHINING LLC
12745 Neil Rd (49451-9458)
PHONE..................................231 853-8648
EMP: 3 **EST:** 2007
SALES (est): 210K **Privately Held**
SIC: 3599 Mfg Industrial Machinery

(G-13120)
GRIPTRAC INC
Also Called: Gilbert & Riplo Company
4865 S Ravenna Rd (49451-9174)
PHONE..................................231 853-2284
Fred Riplo, *President*
▲ **EMP:** 18
SQ FT: 10,000
SALES (est): 4.2MM **Privately Held**
WEB: www.griptrac.com
SIC: 3523 3441 7692 Combines (harvester-threshers); fabricated structural metal; welding repair

(G-13121)
JERRYS WELDING INC
11210 Ellis Rd (49451-9443)
PHONE..................................231 853-6494
Jerry Ruch, *President*
Robert Ruch, *Vice Pres*
EMP: 5
SQ FT: 1,800
SALES (est): 725.3K **Privately Held**
SIC: 7692 Welding repair

(G-13122)
JOHNSON LOGGING FIREWOO
8473 Apple Ave (49451-9731)
PHONE..................................231 578-5833
Anthony Johnson, *Principal*
EMP: 3 **EST:** 2010
SALES (est): 197.5K **Privately Held**
SIC: 2411 Logging

(G-13123)
LIBERTY PRODUCTS INC
Also Called: Stud Boy Traction
3073 Mortimer St (49451-9566)
P.O. Box 338 (49451-0338)
PHONE..................................231 853-2323
Ronald Pattyn, *President*
Robert Baker, *Vice Pres*
▲ **EMP:** 19
SQ FT: 12,000
SALES (est): 3.8MM **Privately Held**
WEB: www.studboytraction.com
SIC: 3799 Snowmobiles

(G-13124)
METAL TECHNOLOGIES INC
Also Called: Ravenna Ductile Iron
3800 Adams Rd (49451-9450)
P.O. Box 397 (49451-0397)
PHONE..................................231 853-0300
Jeff Bromenschenkel, *Manager*
EMP: 170
SALES (corp-wide): 293.2MM **Privately Held**
SIC: 3321 Gray iron castings
PA: Metal Technologies Of Indiana, Inc.
1401 S Grandstaff Dr
Auburn IN 46706
260 925-4717

(G-13125)
METCALF MACHINE INC
6439 Rollenhagen Rd (49451-9428)
PHONE..................................616 837-8128
Pat Metcalf, *President*
EMP: 3 **EST:** 1974
SQ FT: 6,000
SALES (est): 290K **Privately Held**
SIC: 3714 Axles, motor vehicle; wheels, motor vehicle

(G-13126)
RAVENNA CASTING CENTER INC
3800 Adams Rd (49451-9450)
P.O. Box 397 (49451-0397)
PHONE..................................231 853-0300
Rick James, *CEO*
Keith Turner, *COO*
EMP: 200
SALES: 17.7MM
SALES (corp-wide): 293.2MM **Privately Held**
SIC: 3714 3321 Motor vehicle parts & accessories; ductile iron castings
PA: Metal Technologies Of Indiana, Inc.
1401 S Grandstaff Dr
Auburn IN 46706
260 925-4717

(G-13127)
RAVENNA PATTERN & MFG
Also Called: RAVENNA HYDRAULICS
13101 Apple Ave (49451-9755)
P.O. Box 219 (49451-0219)
PHONE..................................231 853-2264
Joshua Emery, *President*
Neil Emery, *Vice Pres*
Michael Emery, *Engineer*
Andy Emery, *Manager*
EMP: 40 **EST:** 1962
SQ FT: 37,000
SALES (est): 4.4MM **Privately Held**
WEB: www.ravennapattern.com
SIC: 3544 3543 Industrial molds; industrial patterns

(G-13128)
ROGERS PRINTING INC
3350 Main St (49451-9400)
P.O. Box 215 (49451-0215)
PHONE..................................231 853-2244
Tom Rogers, *CEO*
Jeff Selk, *Vice Pres*
Rick Feist, *CFO*
Morgan Goddard, *Accounts Mgr*
Fran Raddatz, *Office Mgr*
EMP: 133 **EST:** 1888
SQ FT: 40,000
SALES (est): 39.9MM **Privately Held**
WEB: www.rogersprinting.net
SIC: 2752 2759 2732 Commercial printing, offset; commercial printing; book printing

(G-13129)
SWANSON GRADING & BRINING INC
11561 Heights Ravenna Rd (49451-9243)
P.O. Box 211 (49451-0211)
PHONE..................................231 853-2289
John W Swanson II, *President*
EMP: 70
SQ FT: 1,000
SALES: 9.3MM **Privately Held**
SIC: 2035 Pickles, sauces & salad dressings

(G-13130)
SWANSON PICKLE CO INC
11561 Heights Ravenna Rd (49451-9243)
P.O. Box 211 (49451-0211)
PHONE..................................231 853-2289
John Swanson, *President*
Donald Swanson, *Chairman*
Katie Hensley, *Finance*
David Swanson, *Shareholder*
Paul Swanson, *Admin Sec*
EMP: 20
SQ FT: 6,000
SALES: 4.2MM **Privately Held**
SIC: 2035 Cucumbers, pickles & pickle salting

Ray
Macomb County

(G-13131)
A-OK PRECISION PROTOTYPE INC
59539 Romeo Plank Rd (48096-3529)
PHONE..................................586 758-3430
Robert D Watson, *President*
Mary Nepper, *Admin Sec*
EMP: 15 **EST:** 1970
SQ FT: 12,000
SALES (est): 2.4MM **Privately Held**
WEB: www.aokprecision.com
SIC: 3565 Packaging machinery

(G-13132)
CUSTOM EMBROIDERY & SEWING
63289 North Ave (48096-2708)
PHONE..................................586 749-7669
Tracy Lecluyse, *Owner*
EMP: 3
SALES (est): 202K **Privately Held**
SIC: 2395 Embroidery products, except schiffli machine

(G-13133)
GLEASON HOLBROOK MFG CO
22401 28 Mile Rd (48096-3204)
PHONE..................................586 749-5519
Daniel E Gleason, *President*
Thomas Gleason, *Vice Pres*
EMP: 10 **EST:** 1964
SQ FT: 21,700
SALES (est): 765.6K **Privately Held**
SIC: 3544 Special dies & tools

(G-13134)
MARBLE GRINDING & POLISHING
57885 Romeo Plank Rd (48096-4145)
PHONE..................................586 321-0543
Giuseppe Fanone, *Executive*
EMP: 3
SALES (est): 195.1K **Privately Held**
SIC: 3471 Polishing, metals or formed products

(G-13135)
PARAMOUNT SOLUTIONS INC
59285 Elizabeth Ln (48096-3552)
PHONE..................................586 914-0708
Linda Kuskowski, *Owner*
Danny Kuskowski, *Vice Pres*

Reading
Hillsdale County

(G-13136)
DICKAREN INC
6491 Reading Rd (49274-9710)
PHONE...................................517 283-2444
Dick Heffelfinger, *President*
Karen Heffelfinger, *Admin Sec*
EMP: 3
SALES: 100K **Privately Held**
SIC: 7692 Welding repair

(G-13137)
ROLL TECH INC
104 Enterprise St (49274-9587)
P.O. Box 419 (49274-0419)
PHONE...................................517 283-3811
Michael Clark, *President*
EMP: 20
SALES (est): 1.6MM **Privately Held**
WEB: www.roll-tech.com
SIC: 3544 Special dies, tools, jigs & fixtures

(G-13138)
ROLLEIGH INC
104 Enterprise St (49274-9587)
P.O. Box 419 (49274-0419)
PHONE...................................517 283-3811
Michael L Clark, *President*
William R Clark, *Vice Pres*
Matt Clark Jr, *Shareholder*
EMP: 12
SQ FT: 8,000
SALES (est): 2.4MM **Privately Held**
WEB: www.rolleigh.com
SIC: 3544 Dies, steel rule; industrial molds

(G-13139)
WILCO TOOLING & MFG LLC
105 Enterprise St (49274)
P.O. Box 183 (49274-0183)
PHONE...................................517 901-0147
Jeff Wilson, *Mng Member*
EMP: 13
SQ FT: 16,000
SALES: 850K **Privately Held**
SIC: 3545 Machine tool accessories

Redford
Wayne County

(G-13140)
AAA INDUSTRIES INC
24500 Capitol (48239-2446)
PHONE...................................313 255-0420
Mark Yessian, *President*
Charles Torosian, *Vice Pres*
EMP: 32 **EST:** 1962
SQ FT: 13,600
SALES (est): 5.3MM **Privately Held**
WEB: www.aaaind.com
SIC: 3451 3452 3541 Screw machine products; bolts, nuts, rivets & washers; machine tools, metal cutting type

(G-13141)
AC COVERS INC
Also Called: A/C Covers
25544 5 Mile Rd (48239-3229)
PHONE...................................313 541-7770
Constance Kowalczyk, *President*
John A Kowalczyk, *Treasurer*
EMP: 10
SALES: 1.2MM **Privately Held**
SIC: 3564 Blowers & fans

(G-13142)
ADVERTISING ACCENTS INC
18845 Denby (48240-2040)
PHONE...................................313 937-3890
Tom Krause, *President*
EMP: 20
SQ FT: 4,000
SALES (est): 3.6MM **Privately Held**
SIC: 5199 2261 Advertising specialties; screen printing of cotton broadwoven fabrics

(G-13143)
AQUA-GEL CORPORATION
12700 Marion (48239-2653)
PHONE...................................313 538-9240
Linda Hart, *President*
Bryan Hart, *Corp Secy*
Michael Hart, *Manager*
EMP: 3 **EST:** 1972
SQ FT: 2,500
SALES (est): 346.6K **Privately Held**
SIC: 2841 Soap & other detergents

(G-13144)
ARGUS CORPORATION (PA)
12540 Beech Daly Rd (48239-2469)
PHONE...................................313 937-2900
Fred Ransford, *President*
EMP: 40
SQ FT: 135,000
SALES: 25.1MM **Privately Held**
WEB: www.arguscorporation.com
SIC: 3544 Special dies & tools

(G-13145)
ATHLETIC UNIFORM LETTERING
26114 W 6 Mile Rd (48240-2217)
PHONE...................................313 533-9071
Joseph J Copperstone, *President*
EMP: 5
SQ FT: 3,600
SALES (est): 500.6K **Privately Held**
SIC: 2396 Screen printing on fabric articles

(G-13146)
AUTOMATED MEDIA INC
12171 Beech Daly Rd (48239-2482)
PHONE...................................313 662-0185
Gerald A Gentile, *President*
Nancy Williamson, *Vice Pres*
EMP: 85
SQ FT: 12,000
SALES (est): 11.4MM **Privately Held**
WEB: www.auto-med.com
SIC: 7372 5734 7378 Application computer software; computer peripheral equipment; computer maintenance & repair

(G-13147)
BEIRUT BAKERY INC
25706 Schoolcraft (48239-2631)
PHONE...................................313 533-4422
Alex Wakim, *President*
Iskandar Wakim, *President*
Hala Wakim, *Corp Secy*
Milad Wakim, *Vice Pres*
EMP: 14 **EST:** 1979
SQ FT: 2,500
SALES: 550K **Privately Held**
WEB: www.beirutbakery.com
SIC: 2051 5149 Bakery: wholesale or wholesale/retail combined; bakery products

(G-13148)
BEST PRODUCTS INC
14208 Sarasota (48239-2889)
PHONE...................................313 538-7414
Jim Gonzales, *CEO*
EMP: 22
SQ FT: 12,500
SALES: 2.7MM **Privately Held**
SIC: 3714 3826 Motor vehicle parts & accessories; analytical instruments

(G-13149)
BIG D LLC
26038 Grand River Ave (48240-1439)
PHONE...................................248 787-2724
Vadim Yelizarov, *CEO*
EMP: 4 **EST:** 2017
SALES (est): 170.4K **Privately Held**
SIC: 2759 Screen printing

(G-13150)
BOOMS STONE COMPANY
12275 Dixie (48239-2490)
PHONE...................................313 531-3000
Richard Booms, *President*
BSC Mary, *Admin Sec*
▲ **EMP:** 60
SQ FT: 42,000
SALES (est): 8.3MM **Privately Held**
WEB: www.boomsstone.com
SIC: 3281 Cut stone & stone products

(G-13151)
C R STITCHING
26150 5 Mile Rd 1c (48239-3244)
PHONE...................................313 538-1660
Cynthia Moll, *Owner*
EMP: 4
SQ FT: 1,800
SALES (est): 215.6K **Privately Held**
SIC: 2395 Embroidery & art needlework

(G-13152)
CHEMEISTERS INC
26202 W 7 Mile Rd (48240-1849)
PHONE...................................313 538-5550
Gordon Schultz, *President*
Sandra O'Shea, *Vice Pres*
Janice A Schultz, *Admin Sec*
EMP: 7 **EST:** 1977
SQ FT: 7,400
SALES (est): 650K **Privately Held**
WEB: www.chemeistersusa.com
SIC: 2842 Rug, upholstery, or dry cleaning detergents or spotters

(G-13153)
CLASSIC PLATING INC
12600 Farley (48239-2643)
PHONE...................................313 532-1440
Susan Barbret, *President*
J R Morgan, *Vice Pres*
Mike Morgan, *Vice Pres*
Steve Morgan, *Vice Pres*
EMP: 8
SQ FT: 17,195
SALES (est): 1.1MM **Privately Held**
SIC: 3471 Electroplating of metals or formed products

(G-13154)
CREATIVE SOLUTIONS GROUP INC
Also Called: Csg Storage Facility
12285 Dixie (48239-2491)
PHONE...................................734 425-2257
Kori Valentine, *Accounts Exec*
Don Holms, *Manager*
Don Holmes, *Manager*
Jack McCoy, *Manager*
EMP: 4
SALES (corp-wide): 30.2MM **Privately Held**
WEB: www.csgnow.com
SIC: 7389 2542 Advertising, promotional & trade show services; partitions & fixtures, except wood
PA: Creative Solutions Group, Inc.
  1250 N Crooks Rd
  Clawson MI 48017
  248 288-9700

(G-13155)
DAIMAY NORTH AMERICA AUTO INC
24450 Plymouth Rd (48239)
PHONE...................................313 533-9860
EMP: 3 **Privately Held**
SIC: 3694 Automotive Services
HQ: Daimay North America Automotive, Inc.
  24400 Plymouth Rd
  Redford MI 48239
  313 533-9680

(G-13156)
DAIMAY NORTH AMERICA AUTO INC (HQ)
24400 Plymouth Rd (48239-1617)
PHONE...................................313 533-9680
Jay Wang, *President*
Allen Reinwasser, *Engineer*
Joseph Greco, *Director*
EMP: 50
SQ FT: 2,500
SALES: 26.7MM
SALES (corp-wide): 146.7MM **Privately Held**
WEB: www.daimaynorthamerica.com
SIC: 3714 Motor vehicle parts & accessories
PA: Zhejiang Zhoushan Daimay Investment Co., Ltd.
  No.174, Gongsheng Road, Dongsha Town, Daishan County
  Zhoushan 31621
  580 709-1161

(G-13157)
DETROIT DIESEL CORPORATION
12200 Telegraph Rd (48239)
PHONE...................................313 592-8256
EMP: 15
SALES (corp-wide): 193.7B **Privately Held**
SIC: 3519 3714 7538 Mfg Intrnl Cmbstn Engine Mfg Motor Vehicle Parts General Auto Repair
HQ: Detroit Diesel Corporation
  13400 W Outer Dr
  Detroit MI 48239
  313 592-5000

(G-13158)
DETROIT TECH INNOVATION LLC
Also Called: Dti
25036 W 6 Mile Rd (48240-2101)
PHONE...................................734 259-4168
Baojian Liao, *General Mgr*
EMP: 8 **EST:** 2013
SQ FT: 2,000
SALES (est): 818.5K **Privately Held**
SIC: 3559 Automotive related machinery

(G-13159)
DOG BROWN MANUFACTURING LLC
24800 Plymouth Rd (48239-1633)
PHONE...................................313 255-1400
Darin Dudek, *Principal*
EMP: 3
SALES (est): 409.7K **Privately Held**
SIC: 3999 Manufacturing industries

(G-13160)
FAMILY MACHINISTS
20456 Lexington (48240-1149)
PHONE...................................734 340-1848
Darrell Riesenberger, *President*
EMP: 4
SALES (est): 139.1K **Privately Held**
SIC: 3599 Machine shop, jobbing & repair

(G-13161)
FARBER CONCESSIONS INC
Also Called: Detroit Popcorn Company
14950 Telegraph Rd (48239-3457)
PHONE...................................313 387-1600
David Barber, *President*
Evan Singer, *Vice Pres*
Chris Deneen, *Manager*
EMP: 25 **EST:** 1942
SQ FT: 70,000
SALES (est): 6.1MM **Privately Held**
WEB: www.detroitpopcorn.com
SIC: 5046 7359 2038 2087 Commercial cooking & food service equipment; equipment rental & leasing; snacks, including onion rings, cheese sticks, etc.; beverage bases, concentrates, syrups, powders & mixes; cane sugar refining; frozen fruits & vegetables

(G-13162)
FRANKLIN FASTENER COMPANY
12701 Beech Daly Rd (48239-2472)
PHONE...................................313 537-8900
James M Sampson, *President*
Andrew W Hayes, *Vice Pres*
Norma E Sampson, *Admin Sec*
▼ **EMP:** 31 **EST:** 1953
SQ FT: 26,500
SALES (est): 7.6MM **Privately Held**
SIC: 3496 3469 3429 3452 Miscellaneous fabricated wire products; metal stampings; manufactured hardware (general); bolts, nuts, rivets & washers; automotive stampings

(G-13163)
GEORGE W TRAPP CO (PA)
15000 Fox (48239-2794)
PHONE...................................313 531-7180

GEOGRAPHIC SECTION

Redford - Wayne County (G-13193)

Richard E Trapp, *President*
EMP: 27 **EST:** 1930
SQ FT: 36,000
SALES (est): 4MM **Privately Held**
WEB: www.trappdoors.com
SIC: 3442 Sash, door or window: metal

(G-13164)
HART ACQUISITION COMPANY LLC
12700 Marion (48239-2653)
PHONE.................................313 537-0490
Keith Thornton, *CFO*
Scott Weyandt,
EMP: 30
SQ FT: 50,000
SALES (est): 1MM **Privately Held**
SIC: 3444 Casings, sheet metal

(G-13165)
HART PRECISION PRODUCTS INC
12700 Marion (48239-2695)
PHONE.................................313 537-0490
Darlene Hart Weyandt, *President*
Beatrice Hart, *Corp Secy*
Scott Weyandt, *Director*
EMP: 50 **EST:** 1953
SQ FT: 35,000
SALES (est): 11.7MM **Privately Held**
WEB: www.hart-precision.com
SIC: 3728 3537 Aircraft parts & equipment; tractors, used in plants, docks, terminals, etc.: industrial

(G-13166)
INSTALLATIONS INC
25257 W 8 Mile Rd (48240-1003)
PHONE.................................313 532-9000
Pearl Baltes, *President*
Lawrence S Baltes, *Corp Secy*
Steven Baltes, *VP Sales*
EMP: 15 **EST:** 1978
SQ FT: 10,000
SALES (est): 3.1MM **Privately Held**
WEB: www.bulletresistbarriers.com
SIC: 3089 1799 Flat panels, plastic; home/office interiors finishing, furnishing & remodeling

(G-13167)
J&J MACHINE PRODUCTS CO INC
12734 Inkster Rd (48239-3003)
PHONE.................................313 534-8024
Myra Lane Juhnke, *Ch of Bd*
Stephanie Dougherty, *President*
David W Juhnke, *President*
Michael Dougherty, *Vice Pres*
EMP: 20
SQ FT: 20,000
SALES (est): 3.4MM **Privately Held**
SIC: 3451 5072 Screw machine products; bolts, nuts & screws

(G-13168)
LPS-2 INC
24755 5 Mile Rd Ste 100 (48239-3665)
PHONE.................................313 538-0181
Michael Dorsey, *President*
EMP: 5
SALES (est): 385K **Privately Held**
SIC: 3955 Print cartridges for laser & other computer printers

(G-13169)
LUBE ZONE LLC
9977 Telegraph Rd (48239-1421)
PHONE.................................313 543-2910
Mohamad Debek,
EMP: 3
SALES (est): 290.1K **Privately Held**
SIC: 2911 Oils, lubricating

(G-13170)
M & D DISTRIBUTION INC
25550 Grand River Ave (48240-1427)
PHONE.................................313 592-1467
William McEvoy, *President*
Donald Diaz, *Vice Pres*
EMP: 7
SQ FT: 9,000
SALES: 1MM **Privately Held**
SIC: 3631 Indoor cooking equipment

(G-13171)
MCNICHOLS POLSG & ANODIZING (PA)
12139 Woodbine (48239-2417)
PHONE.................................313 538-3470
G Rose Smith, *President*
Diana L Tibbits, *Admin Sec*
EMP: 16
SQ FT: 10,000
SALES (est): 2.2MM **Privately Held**
WEB: www.mcnicholsanodizing.com
SIC: 3471 Anodizing (plating) of metals or formed products; polishing, metals or formed products; buffing for the trade

(G-13172)
MCNICHOLS POLSG & ANODIZING
12139 Wormer (48239-2422)
PHONE.................................313 538-3470
Diane Tibbits, *Manager*
EMP: 8
SALES (corp-wide): 2.2MM **Privately Held**
WEB: www.mcnicholsanodizing.com
SIC: 3471 Anodizing (plating) of metals or formed products; polishing, metals or formed products; buffing for the trade
PA: Mcnichols Polishing & Anodizing Inc
12139 Woodbine
Redford MI 48239
313 538-3470

(G-13173)
METRO STAMPING & MFG CO
26955 Fullerton (48239-2592)
PHONE.................................313 538-6464
Robert H Leonard, *President*
Richard M Leonard, *Treasurer*
Carol J Doak, *Shareholder*
EMP: 15
SQ FT: 14,000
SALES (est): 1.8MM **Privately Held**
WEB: www.metrostamp.com
SIC: 3469 Metal stampings

(G-13174)
METRO TURN INC
12081 Farley (48239-2471)
PHONE.................................313 937-1904
Mike Lauderdack, *Owner*
EMP: 5
SALES: 150K **Privately Held**
SIC: 3599 Machine shop, jobbing & repair

(G-13175)
MOLDEX CRANK SHAFT INC
12255 Wormer (48239-2424)
PHONE.................................313 561-7676
Joseph Flower, *President*
EMP: 5
SQ FT: 18,000
SALES (est): 410K **Privately Held**
SIC: 3714 Crankshaft assemblies, motor vehicle

(G-13176)
NOVI TOOL & MACHINE COMPANY
Also Called: Novi Matic Valves
12202 Woodbine (48239-2420)
PHONE.................................313 532-0900
David Sumara, *President*
EMP: 60
SQ FT: 4,000
SALES (est): 5.3MM **Privately Held**
SIC: 3541 3494 3547 3498 Cutoff machines (metalworking machinery); valves & pipe fittings; rolling mill machinery; fabricated pipe & fittings; fluid power valves & hose fittings; industrial valves

(G-13177)
ONEIDA TOOL CORPORATION
12700 Inkster Rd (48239-3099)
PHONE.................................313 537-0770
John Darnbrook, *President*
Ed Dambrook, *Vice Pres*
Anthony Antinozzzi, *Technology*
EMP: 42
SQ FT: 12,000
SALES (est): 5.6MM **Privately Held**
SIC: 3599 3545 Machine shop, jobbing & repair; machine tool accessories

(G-13178)
PATTON PRINTING INC
24625 Capitol (48239-2448)
PHONE.................................313 535-9099
Edward Sabroski, *President*
EMP: 3
SQ FT: 10,000
SALES (est): 370.9K **Privately Held**
SIC: 2752 Commercial printing, offset

(G-13179)
PECK ENGINEERING INC
12660 Farley (48239-2643)
PHONE.................................313 534-2950
George Thomas, *President*
David Post, *Vice Pres*
EMP: 14 **EST:** 1952
SALES (est): 2.1MM **Privately Held**
SIC: 3069 Molded rubber products

(G-13180)
PEGASUS INDUSTRIES INC
12380 Beech Daly Rd (48239-2433)
PHONE.................................313 937-0770
Kenneth P Zecman, *President*
Kris Zecman, *Principal*
Kurt Zecman, *Principal*
Lynn Wright, *Controller*
EMP: 17
SALES (est): 3.3MM **Privately Held**
SIC: 3544 Industrial molds

(G-13181)
PET TREATS PLUS
14141 Marion (48239-2843)
PHONE.................................313 533-1701
Fax: 313 533-4031
EMP: 10
SALES (est): 852.8K **Privately Held**
SIC: 2048 Mfg Prepared Feeds

(G-13182)
PISTON AUTOMOTIVE LLC (HQ)
12723 Telegraph Rd Ste 1 (48239-1489)
PHONE.................................313 541-8674
Robert Ajersch, *President*
Robert Holloway, *President*
Vincent Johnson, *Chairman*
Amit Singhi, *COO*
Frank W Ervin III, *Vice Pres*
◆ **EMP:** 300 **EST:** 1997
SQ FT: 260,000
SALES (est): 1B
SALES (corp-wide): 1.6B **Privately Held**
WEB: www.pistongroup.com
SIC: 3714 Motor vehicle parts & accessories
PA: Piston Group, L.L.C.
3000 Town Ctr Ste 3250
Southfield MI 48075
248 226-3976

(G-13183)
PLASTICRAFTS INC
25675 W 8 Mile Rd (48240-1007)
PHONE.................................313 532-1900
Rajni Dhawan, *President*
Anil Dhawan, *Vice Pres*
▲ **EMP:** 5
SQ FT: 14,840
SALES (est): 628.6K **Privately Held**
SIC: 3993 3089 Signs, not made in custom sign painting shops; plastic containers, except foam; kitchenware, plastic; organizers for closets, drawers, etc.: plastic

(G-13184)
POSITIVE TOOL & ENGINEERING CO
26025 W 7 Mile Rd (48240-1846)
PHONE.................................313 532-1674
Robert J Hewitt, *President*
EMP: 4 **EST:** 1960
SQ FT: 3,200
SALES (est): 578.3K **Privately Held**
SIC: 3544 Special dies & tools; jigs & fixtures

(G-13185)
PREEMINENCE INC
12889 Leverne (48239-2732)
PHONE.................................313 737-7920
Angelo Austin, *President*
EMP: 4 **EST:** 2015

SALES (est): 299K **Privately Held**
SIC: 5999 3999 5149 Toiletries, cosmetics & perfumes; candles; flavourings & fragrances

(G-13186)
QUALITY TOOL & GEAR INC
12693 Marlin Dr (48239-2765)
PHONE.................................734 266-1500
Domenico Pelle, *President*
Angelo Berlase, *Vice Pres*
Fred Pelle, *Vice Pres*
Joe Pelle, *Opers Mgr*
Kathy Diovardi, *Office Mgr*
EMP: 25
SQ FT: 23,000
SALES (est): 4.7MM **Privately Held**
WEB: www.qualitytoolandgear.com
SIC: 3599 Machine shop, jobbing & repair

(G-13187)
RATIO MACHINING INC
12214 Woodbine (48239-2420)
PHONE.................................313 531-5155
Matthew Spease, *President*
EMP: 4
SALES (est): 410K **Privately Held**
SIC: 3599 Machine shop, jobbing & repair

(G-13188)
ROYAL CABINETS
15730 Telegraph Rd (48239-3530)
PHONE.................................313 541-1190
Hamze Chehade, *Owner*
EMP: 4
SALES (est): 452.1K **Privately Held**
SIC: 2434 Wood kitchen cabinets

(G-13189)
RTG PRODUCTS INC
15924 Centralia (48239-3821)
PHONE.................................734 323-8916
Thomas Kappler, *Principal*
EMP: 5
SALES (est): 620K **Privately Held**
SIC: 3612 Transformers, except electric

(G-13190)
RUSAS PRINTING CO INC
26770 Grand River Ave (48240-1529)
P.O. Box 2609, Detroit (48202-0609)
PHONE.................................313 952-2977
Donald Frank Rusas, *President*
EMP: 8
SQ FT: 20,000
SALES (est): 1.1MM **Privately Held**
WEB: www.rusasprinting.com
SIC: 2759 Commercial printing

(G-13191)
SHIPPING CONTAINER CORPORATION
26000 Capitol (48239-2402)
PHONE.................................313 937-2411
Joseph Anton Mooter, *President*
Bob Schuelke, *General Mgr*
EMP: 20
SQ FT: 20,000
SALES: 2.7MM **Privately Held**
SIC: 2653 Boxes, corrugated: made from purchased materials

(G-13192)
SMEDE-SON STEEL AND SUP CO INC (PA)
12584 Inkster Rd (48239-2569)
PHONE.................................313 937-8300
Albert A Huyser, *President*
Anthony Huyser, *Vice Pres*
Teri Zaborowski, *Exec Dir*
Barbara Huyser, *Admin Sec*
EMP: 55 **EST:** 1954
SQ FT: 6,000
SALES (est): 18.8MM **Privately Held**
WEB: www.smedeson.com
SIC: 3441 5251 Fabricated structural metal; builders' hardware

(G-13193)
SPRAY BOOTH PRODUCTS INC
26211 W 7 Mile Rd (48240-1850)
PHONE.................................313 766-4400
Kenneth Mikols, *President*
Tami Zellner, *Office Mgr*
EMP: 34

Redford - Wayne County (G-13194)

GEOGRAPHIC SECTION

SALES (est): 4.1MM **Privately Held**
SIC: **1711** 3053 5084 Mechanical contractor; packing: steam engines, pipe joints, air compressors, etc.; industrial machinery & equipment

(G-13194)
STEEL INDUSTRIES INC
12600 Beech Daly Rd (48239-2455)
PHONE.................................313 535-8505
Drew F Baker, *President*
Drew Baker, *Exec VP*
Mark Wejroch, *Vice Pres*
Frank Witte, *Plant Mgr*
Dee Varga, *Human Res Dir*
◆ **EMP**: 175
SQ FT: 217,000
SALES (est): 57.5MM
SALES (corp-wide): 278.3MM **Privately Held**
WEB: www.steelindustriesinc.com
SIC: **3398** 3312 Metal heat treating; forgings, iron & steel
PA: Ameriforge Group Inc.
945 Bunker Hill Rd # 500
Houston TX 77024
713 393-4200

(G-13195)
STELLAR FORGE PRODUCTS INC (PA)
13050 Inkster Rd (48239-3047)
PHONE.................................313 535-7631
Diran D Arslanian, *President*
Anto Arslanian, *Vice Pres*
Bruce D Franz, *Admin Sec*
▲ **EMP**: 12
SQ FT: 8,000
SALES (est): 2.2MM **Privately Held**
SIC: **3544** Special dies & tools

(G-13196)
STERLING TRUCK AND WSTN STAR (DH)
Also Called: Sterling Trucking
13400 W Outer Dr (48239-1309)
PHONE.................................313 592-4200
Jim Hebe, *President*
John Merrifield, *Senior VP*
▼ **EMP**: 50
SALES (est): 10.1MM
SALES (corp-wide): 191.6B **Privately Held**
SIC: **3537** Trucks, tractors, loaders, carriers & similar equipment
HQ: Daimler Trucks North America Llc
4555 N Channel Ave
Portland OR 97217
503 745-8000

(G-13197)
SUPERIOR CASKET CO
26789 Fullerton (48239-2553)
PHONE.................................313 592-3190
Anthony Ferro, *President*
Mark Ferro, *Vice Pres*
Mary Ferro, *Admin Sec*
EMP: 20 **EST**: 1971
SQ FT: 13,000
SALES (est): 3MM **Privately Held**
SIC: **3995** Burial caskets

(G-13198)
SY FUEL INC
27360 Grand River Ave (48240-1609)
PHONE.................................313 531-5894
Jim Hamade, *Principal*
EMP: 3
SALES (est): 381.2K **Privately Held**
SIC: **2869** Fuels

(G-13199)
T-SHIRT WORLD
25351 Grand River Ave (48240-1406)
PHONE.................................313 387-2023
Sam Malla, *Owner*
EMP: 3
SALES (est): 238.7K **Privately Held**
SIC: **2254** Shirts & t-shirts (underwear), knit

(G-13200)
TALENT INDUSTRIES INC
12950 Inkster Rd (48239-3000)
PHONE.................................313 531-4700
William L Randall, *President*

John Robert, *Corp Secy*
Rick Robert, *Vice Pres*
EMP: 15 **EST**: 1956
SQ FT: 7,500
SALES (est): 2.8MM **Privately Held**
SIC: **3544** Special dies & tools

(G-13201)
THERMA-TECH ENGINEERING INC
Also Called: A. R. Lintern Division
24900 Capitol (48239-2449)
PHONE.................................313 537-5330
Ron O'Dell, *President*
Dave Poma, *Plant Mgr*
Terri Boyle, *Buyer*
Maryanne Camp, *VP Sales*
Doug Riddell, *Sales Mgr*
EMP: 30
SALES (est): 4.5MM **Privately Held**
SIC: **8711** 3714 Engineering services; defrosters, motor vehicle; heaters, motor vehicle

(G-13202)
TOPS ALL CLAMPS INC
Also Called: Htc Tops All Clamps
26627 W 8 Mile Rd (48240-1142)
PHONE.................................313 533-7500
Dennis Jackson, *President*
Sheryl Jackson, *Corp Secy*
EMP: 4
SQ FT: 6,000
SALES: 1MM **Privately Held**
WEB: www.htc-topsallclamps.com
SIC: **3429** 5084 3544 3494 Clamps, couplings, nozzles & other metal hose fittings; industrial machinery & equipment; special dies, tools, jigs & fixtures; valves & pipe fittings; plumbing fixture fittings & trim

(G-13203)
ULTIMATE MANUFACTURING INC
12125 Dixie (48239-2464)
PHONE.................................313 538-6212
Graham Clements, *President*
Karen Kellner, *Corp Secy*
EMP: 7
SQ FT: 11,000
SALES (est): 888.7K **Privately Held**
SIC: **3499** Metal ladders

(G-13204)
ULTRALIGHT PROSTHETICS INC
24781 5 Mile Rd (48239-3632)
PHONE.................................313 538-8500
Jeffery Giacinto, *President*
Joseph Giacinto, *Treasurer*
EMP: 5
SQ FT: 1,100
SALES (est): 645.4K **Privately Held**
WEB: www.ultralightprosthetics.com
SIC: **3842** Limbs, artificial; prosthetic appliances

(G-13205)
V & S DETROIT GALVANIZING LLC
12600 Arnold (48239-2637)
PHONE.................................313 535-2600
Tim Woll, *Principal*
Tom Bottorff, *Plant Mgr*
Don Houston, *Opers Mgr*
EMP: 10
SALES (est): 1.1MM **Privately Held**
SIC: **3479** Galvanizing of iron, steel or end-formed products

(G-13206)
VOIGT & SCHWEITZER LLC
12600 Arnold (48239-2637)
PHONE.................................313 535-2600
Ken Tokarz, *Manager*
EMP: 45
SALES (corp-wide): 819.3MM **Privately Held**
WEB: www.hotdipgalvanizing.com
SIC: **3479** Hot dip coating of metals or formed products
HQ: Voigt & Schweitzer Llc
987 Buckeye Park Rd
Columbus OH 43207
614 449-8281

(G-13207)
VOIGT SCHWTZER GALVANIZERS INC
12600 Arnold (48239-2637)
PHONE.................................313 535-2600
Werner Niehaus, *President*
Brian Miller, *Vice Pres*
Maia Johnson, *Admin Sec*
EMP: 70
SQ FT: 50,000
SALES (est): 4.6MM
SALES (corp-wide): 819.3MM **Privately Held**
WEB: www.hotdipgalvanizing.com
SIC: **3479** Hot dip coating of metals or formed products; galvanizing of iron, steel or end-formed products
HQ: Voigt & Schweitzer Llc
987 Buckeye Park Rd
Columbus OH 43207
614 449-8281

(G-13208)
W T & M INC
Also Called: Walker Tool & Manufacturing
12635 Arnold (48239-2636)
PHONE.................................313 533-7888
Donald W Hoyt, *President*
Katherine M Hoyt, *Principal*
Nick Cosentino, *Vice Pres*
Kathy Cosentino, *Admin Sec*
EMP: 8
SQ FT: 17,000
SALES (est): 941.2K **Privately Held**
WEB: www.wtm.com
SIC: **3599** Machine shop, jobbing & repair

(G-13209)
Z TECHNOLOGIES CORPORATION
26500 Capitol (48239-2506)
PHONE.................................313 937-0710
Ellis L Breskman, *President*
Louis Breskman, *Vice Pres*
Wayne Hall, *Plant Mgr*
Todd Belcher, *QC Mgr*
▲ **EMP**: 25
SQ FT: 60,000
SALES (est): 8.3MM **Privately Held**
SIC: **2891** 3479 2851 Sealants; coating of metals & formed products; paints & paint additives; epoxy coatings

Reed City
Osceola County

(G-13210)
BCT-2017 INC
Also Called: Ben Tek
710 E Church Ave (49677-9194)
PHONE.................................231 832-3114
Bill Cooper, *Manager*
EMP: 30
SALES (corp-wide): 2.7MM **Privately Held**
WEB: www.bentek.com
SIC: **3599** Machine shop, jobbing & repair
PA: Bct-2017, Inc.
710 E Church Ave
Reed City MI 49677
231 832-3114

(G-13211)
BCT-2017 INC (PA)
Also Called: Bentek
710 E Church Ave (49677-9194)
P.O. Box 1117, Big Rapids (49307-0307)
PHONE.................................231 832-3114
Thomas C Benedict, *President*
EMP: 24
SQ FT: 22,000
SALES (est): 2.7MM **Privately Held**
WEB: www.bentek.com
SIC: **3599** Machine shop, jobbing & repair

(G-13212)
CONINE PUBLISHING COMPANY
Also Called: Osceola Addition
211 W Upton Ave Ste B (49677-1236)
PHONE.................................231 832-5566
EMP: 3

SALES (corp-wide): 27.2MM **Privately Held**
SIC: **2711** Newspapers-Publishing/Printing
PA: The Conine Publishing Company
115 N Michigan Ave
Big Rapids MI 49307
231 796-4831

(G-13213)
GENERAL MILLS INC
128 E Slosson Ave (49677-1229)
PHONE.................................231 832-3285
Carol McKernan, *Train & Dev Mgr*
David Towner, *Manager*
EMP: 40
SALES (corp-wide): 16.8B **Publicly Held**
WEB: www.generalmills.com
SIC: **2026** 2041 Yogurt; flour mixes
PA: General Mills, Inc.
1 General Mills Blvd
Minneapolis MN 55426
763 764-7600

(G-13214)
H & H WILDLIFE DESGN & FURNG I (PA)
5704 220th Ave (49677-8217)
PHONE.................................231 832-7002
Mark Marlette, *President*
EMP: 11
SALES (est): 1.1MM **Privately Held**
SIC: **3999** Furs

(G-13215)
HYDROLAKE INC
420 S Roth St Ste A (49677-9115)
P.O. Box 88 (49677-0088)
PHONE.................................231 825-2233
Mike Bigford, *Principal*
EMP: 7 **Privately Held**
SIC: **2499** Poles, wood
HQ: Hydrolake, Inc.
6151 W Gerwoude Dr
Mc Bain MI 49657
231 825-2233

(G-13216)
JC METAL FABRICATING INC
21831 9 Mile Rd (49677-8466)
PHONE.................................231 629-0425
John Cook, *President*
EMP: 15
SALES (est): 2.7MM **Privately Held**
SIC: **3444** Sheet metalwork

(G-13217)
KRAFTUBE INC
925 E Church Ave (49677-9196)
PHONE.................................231 832-5562
John Kinnally, *President*
Kevin Kinnally, *President*
Scott Gray, *Engineer*
Todd Reitzel, *Engineer*
Daryl Stitt, *Maintence Staff*
▲ **EMP**: 145 **EST**: 1946
SQ FT: 100,000
SALES (est): 32.7MM **Privately Held**
WEB: www.kraftube.com
SIC: **3444** 3441 3585 3544 Furnace casings, sheet metal; fabricated structural metal; refrigeration & heating equipment; die sets for metal stamping (presses)

(G-13218)
KRAUTER FOREST PRODUCTS LLC
21224 Sylvan Rd (49677-7911)
PHONE.................................815 317-6561
EMP: 15 **EST**: 2010
SALES (est): 1MM **Privately Held**
SIC: **2448** Operates A Manufacturer Of Forest Products Specializing In Wood Pallets

(G-13219)
LC MATERIALS
Also Called: Lc Redi Mix
955 E Church Ave (49677-9196)
PHONE.................................231 832-5460
Denny Daniels, *Manager*
EMP: 9
SALES (corp-wide): 8MM **Privately Held**
SIC: **3273** Ready-mixed concrete

PA: Lc Materials
805 W 13th St
Cadillac MI 49601
231 825-2473

(G-13220)
MARTINREA INDUSTRIES INC
Reed City Tool and Die
603 E Church Ave (49677-9102)
PHONE.................................231 832-5504
Rod Weck, *Plant Mgr*
Ardy Rasmussen, *Purchasing*
Chris Raymond, *QC Dir*
Bruce Killenbeck, *Engineer*
Chad Comstock, *Sales Engr*
EMP: 110
SQ FT: 85,000
SALES (corp-wide): 2.7B **Privately Held**
WEB: www.reedcitytool.com
SIC: 3317 3089 3544 3542 Steel pipe & tubes; plastic processing; special dies, tools, jigs & fixtures; machine tools; metal forming type
HQ: Martinrea Industries, Inc.
10501 Mi State Road 52
Manchester MI 48158
734 428-2400

(G-13221)
NABCO INC (DH)
660 Commerce Dr (49677-9300)
PHONE.................................231 832-2001
Lyle Lodholtz, *Division Mgr*
Ron Johnson, *Manager*
EMP: 9
SQ FT: 92,000
SALES (est): 41.2MM
SALES (corp-wide): 10.5B **Publicly Held**
SIC: 5063 5013 3694 3625 Motor controls, starters & relays: electric; alternators; engine electrical equipment; relays & industrial controls

(G-13222)
REED CITY GROUP LLC
603 E Church Ave (49677-9102)
PHONE.................................231 832-7500
John Barnett, *CEO*
Rod Weck, *Chief Mktg Ofcr*
Thomas Miller, *Marketing Staff*
▲ **EMP:** 97
SQ FT: 82,000
SALES (est): 17.5MM **Privately Held**
SIC: 3089 Injection molding of plastics

(G-13223)
THORN CREEK LUMBER LLC
9676 S Hawkins Rd (49677-8702)
PHONE.................................231 832-1600
David Miller, *President*
John Kaufman,
James Miller,
EMP: 8
SALES (est): 690K **Privately Held**
SIC: 2421 Sawmills & planing mills, general

(G-13224)
TUBELITE INC
4878 Mackinaw Trl (49677-9186)
PHONE.................................800 866-2227
Ken Werbowy, *President*
Gary Johnson, *Vice Pres*
Terry Britt, *Manager*
EMP: 13
SALES (corp-wide): 1.4B **Publicly Held**
WEB: www.tubeliteinc.com
SIC: 3449 Miscellaneous metalwork
HQ: Tubelite Inc.
3056 Walker Ridge Dr Nw G
Walker MI 49544

(G-13225)
UTILITY SUPPLY AND CNSTR CO (PA)
420 S Roth St Ste A (49677-9115)
PHONE.................................231 832-2297
Michael Bigford, *President*
Franklin C Wheatlake, *Principal*
Brad Hilliard, *Vice Pres*
Dan Melkey, *Vice Pres*
Kent Lawrence, *Engineer*
EMP: 3

SALES (est): 197.9MM **Privately Held**
SIC: 2411 2491 2631 5063 Logging; wood preserving; coated & treated board; electrical supplies

(G-13226)
UUSI LLC
Also Called: Nartron
5000 N Us 131 (49677)
PHONE.................................231 832-5513
Norman Rautiola,
▲ **EMP:** 42
SQ FT: 210,000
SALES (est): 10.9MM **Privately Held**
WEB: www.nartron.com
SIC: 3674 Semiconductors & related devices

(G-13227)
YOPLAIT USA
128 E Slosson Ave (49677-1229)
P.O. Box 33 (49677-0033)
PHONE.................................231 832-3285
Dave Towner, *President*
EMP: 15
SALES (est): 2.2MM **Privately Held**
SIC: 2026 Fluid milk

Reese
Tuscola County

(G-13228)
ADVANCED MCRONUTRIENT PDTS INC
Also Called: A M P
2405 W Vassar Rd (48757-9340)
PHONE.................................989 752-2138
Robert Bowen, *President*
John Bowen, *Vice Pres*
Terry Hart, *Plant Mgr*
Mark Whitfield, *CFO*
◆ **EMP:** 30
SALES (est): 5.9MM
SALES (corp-wide): 7.2MM **Privately Held**
SIC: 2873 Fertilizers: natural (organic), except compost
PA: Cameron Chemicals, Inc.
4530 Prof Cir Ste 201
Virginia Beach VA 23455
757 487-0656

(G-13229)
CCO HOLDINGS LLC
9989 Saginaw St (48757-9567)
PHONE.................................989 863-4023
EMP: 3
SALES (corp-wide): 43.6B **Publicly Held**
SIC: 5064 4841 3663 3651 Electrical appliances, television & radio; cable & other pay television services; radio & TV communications equipment; household audio & video equipment
HQ: Cco Holdings, Llc
400 Atlantic St
Stamford CT 06901
203 905-7801

(G-13230)
GREENIA CUSTOM WOODWORKING INC
2380 W Vassar Rd (48757-9300)
PHONE.................................989 868-9790
Thomas Greenia, *President*
Kathleen Greenia, *Vice Pres*
EMP: 20
SQ FT: 60,000
SALES (est): 4.1MM **Privately Held**
SIC: 5211 5031 2434 1751 Millwork & lumber; lumber, plywood & millwork; building materials, exterior; building materials, interior; wood kitchen cabinets; carpentry work

(G-13231)
REIS CUSTOM CABINETS
1398 S Bradford Rd (48757-9541)
PHONE.................................586 791-4925
Randy Reis, *Owner*
Tamala Reis, *Manager*
EMP: 4

SALES: 210K **Privately Held**
SIC: 2541 5712 5211 Cabinets, lockers & shelving; cabinet work, custom; cabinets, kitchen

(G-13232)
ROHLOFF BUILDERS INC
Also Called: Oak Tree Cabinet & Woodworking
9916 Saginaw St (48757-9401)
P.O. Box 158 (48757-0158)
PHONE.................................989 868-3191
Steve Rohloff, *President*
EMP: 47
SQ FT: 3,840
SALES (est): 4.8MM **Privately Held**
SIC: 2434 Wood kitchen cabinets

(G-13233)
STELLAR SCENTS
8110 W Caro Rd (48757-9225)
PHONE.................................989 868-3477
Robert Rembisz, *Principal*
EMP: 3
SALES (est): 220.1K **Privately Held**
SIC: 2844 Toilet preparations

(G-13234)
T & L PRODUCTS
2586 S Bradleyville Rd (48757-9214)
PHONE.................................989 868-4428
Thomas W Kabat, *Owner*
EMP: 6 **EST:** 1990
SALES (est): 470K **Privately Held**
SIC: 5088 3429 Marine supplies; marine hardware

(G-13235)
VOORHEIS HAUSBECK EXCAVATING
2695 W Vassar Rd (48757-9352)
P.O. Box 375 (48757-0375)
PHONE.................................989 752-9666
Donald N Voorheis, *President*
Dave Hausbeck, *Owner*
EMP: 18
SQ FT: 2,000
SALES (est): 892K **Privately Held**
SIC: 1794 3273 Excavation & grading, building construction; ready-mixed concrete

(G-13236)
WILFRED SWARTZ & SWARTZ G
11465 Holland Rd (48757-9309)
PHONE.................................989 652-6322
Wilfred Swartz, *Manager*
EMP: 4
SALES (est): 275.7K **Privately Held**
SIC: 3993 Signs & advertising specialties

Remus
Mecosta County

(G-13237)
BANDIT INDUSTRIES INC
6750 W Millbrook Rd (49340-9662)
PHONE.................................989 561-2270
Jerry M Morey, *President*
Dianne C Morey, *Vice Pres*
Jamie Morey, *Parts Mgr*
Richard Curtiss, *CFO*
Rosie Ebbinghaus, *Human Res Dir*
◆ **EMP:** 400
SQ FT: 12,000
SALES (est): 179.3MM **Privately Held**
WEB: www.banditchippers.com
SIC: 3531 5082 Chippers: brush, limb & log; logging & forestry machinery & equipment

(G-13238)
BRIAN A BROOMFIELD
Also Called: B&B Dumpsters
14776 10th Ave (49340-9787)
PHONE.................................989 309-0709
Brian A Broomfield, *Principal*
EMP: 4
SALES (est): 267.1K **Privately Held**
SIC: 3443 Dumpsters, garbage

(G-13239)
LEPRINO FOODS COMPANY
311 N Sheridan Ave (49340-9114)
P.O. Box 208 (49340-0208)
PHONE.................................989 967-3635
Marianne Thomsen, *Plt & Fclts Mgr*
EMP: 60
SALES (corp-wide): 1.7B **Privately Held**
WEB: www.leprinofoods.com
SIC: 2022 Natural cheese
PA: Leprino Foods Company
1830 W 38th Ave
Denver CO 80211
303 480-2600

(G-13240)
LOR PRODUCTS INC
2962 16 Mile Rd (49340-9516)
PHONE.................................989 382-9020
Duane Martin, *President*
Christina Martin, *Admin Sec*
EMP: 7
SALES (est): 673.7K **Privately Held**
SIC: 3449 Miscellaneous metalwork

(G-13241)
SMORACY LLC
6750 W Millbrook Rd (49340-9662)
PHONE.................................989 561-2270
Jerry M Morey,
EMP: 7
SALES (est): 951.2K **Privately Held**
SIC: 3599 Custom machinery

(G-13242)
TRELAN MANUFACTURING
498 8 Mile Rd (49340-9316)
PHONE.................................989 561-2280
Nell Schumacher, *President*
EMP: 20
SQ FT: 45,000
SALES (est): 5.4MM **Privately Held**
WEB: www.trelan.com
SIC: 3531 Chippers: brush, limb & log

(G-13243)
USM ACQUISITION LLC (HQ)
Also Called: United States Marble
7839 Costabella Ave (49340-9585)
PHONE.................................989 561-2293
Rick Foster, *President*
Kirstie Green, *Vice Pres*
EMP: 70 **EST:** 1967
SQ FT: 95,000
SALES (est): 25.8MM
SALES (corp-wide): 113.8MM **Privately Held**
WEB: www.usmarble.com
SIC: 3281 Marble, building: cut & shaped

Republic
Marquette County

(G-13244)
ANTILLA LOGGING INC
7794 State Highway M95 (49879-9041)
PHONE.................................906 376-2374
Oscar Antilla, *President*
Joan Antilla, *Vice Pres*
David Antilla, *Treasurer*
EMP: 6
SALES (est): 748.4K **Privately Held**
SIC: 2411 Logging camps & contractors

(G-13245)
DILLON CHARLES LOGGING & CNSTR
Also Called: Dillon Forest Products
2666 State Highway M95 (49879-9210)
P.O. Box 94 (49879-0094)
PHONE.................................906 376-8470
Charles Dillon, *President*
EMP: 6
SALES: 1.5MM **Privately Held**
SIC: 2411 Pulpwood camp not operating a pulp mill at same site

(G-13246)
NORTHERN SPECIALTY CO
146 Evergreen St (49879-9105)
PHONE.................................906 376-8165
Fax: 906 376-8165
EMP: 3

Republic - Marquette County (G-13247)

SQ FT: 1,620
SALES (est): 300K **Privately Held**
SIC: **5199** 2752 Whol Advertising Specialties

(G-13247)
WILLIAM S WIXTROM
Also Called: Wixtrom Lumber Co
2131 County Road 601 (49879)
PHONE..................................906 376-8247
William S Wixtrom, *Owner*
EMP: 4 EST: 1963
SQ FT: 12,000
SALES (est): 385.5K **Privately Held**
SIC: **2421** 5031 2431 2426 Sawmills & planing mills, general; lumber: rough, dressed & finished; millwork; hardwood dimension & flooring mills

Richland
Kalamazoo County

(G-13248)
EILEEN SMELTZER
Also Called: Chaubrei Gardens
8227 N 30th St (49083-9743)
PHONE..................................269 629-8056
Eileen Smeltzer, *Owner*
EMP: 5
SALES (est): 325K **Privately Held**
WEB: www.chaubreigardens.com
SIC: **3999** Artificial flower arrangements

(G-13249)
FUSION FLEXO LLC (PA)
6330 Canterwood Dr (49083-8431)
PHONE..................................269 685-5827
Brian Anderson, *CEO*
EMP: 9
SALES (est): 2.8MM **Privately Held**
SIC: **2796** Photoengraving plates, linecuts or halftones

(G-13250)
JAMIESON FABRICATION UNLIMITED
8530 M 89 (49083-8205)
PHONE..................................269 760-1473
Andrew Jamieson, *Owner*
EMP: 3
SALES (est): 297.2K **Privately Held**
SIC: **3999** Manufacturing industries

(G-13251)
MAIN STREET PORTRAITS
7586 Foxwood (49083-9460)
PHONE..................................269 321-3310
EMP: 3
SALES (est): 229.5K **Privately Held**
SIC: **2759** 7221 Visiting cards (including business): printing; photographic studios, portrait

(G-13252)
PARKER-HANNIFIN CORPORATION
Pneumatic North America
8676 M 89 (49083-9580)
PHONE..................................269 629-5000
Russell Evans, *Engineer*
Craig Hoyt, *Engineer*
Travis McCulley, *Engineer*
Timothy Miller, *Engineer*
Rick Prather, *Engineer*
EMP: 350
SALES (corp-wide): 14.3B **Publicly Held**
WEB: www.parker.com
SIC: **3494** 3613 3612 3593 Valves & pipe fittings; switchgear & switchboard apparatus; transformers, except electric; fluid power cylinders & actuators; blowers & fans; fluid power valves & hose fittings
PA: Parker-Hannifin Corporation
6035 Parkland Blvd
Cleveland OH 44124
216 896-3000

(G-13253)
PRINTEX PRINTING & GRAPHICS
8988 E D Ave (49083-8442)
PHONE..................................269 629-0122
James Berry, *Owner*

Marlene Berry, *Principal*
EMP: 5
SQ FT: 1,400
SALES: 260K **Privately Held**
SIC: **2752** Commercial printing, offset

(G-13254)
RICHLAND MACHINE & PUMP CO
9854 M 89 (49083-9645)
PHONE..................................269 629-4344
Jerome Bohl Jr, *CEO*
Joseph Bohl, *CFO*
EMP: 9
SQ FT: 13,000
SALES (est): 1.2MM **Privately Held**
SIC: **3599** 7699 Machine shop, jobbing & repair; industrial machinery & equipment repair

(G-13255)
SHEPHERD SPECIALITY PAPERS INC (PA)
10211 M 89 Ste 230 (49083-8308)
P.O. Box 346 (49083-0346)
PHONE..................................269 629-8001
Joel M Shepherd III, *President*
Dina Waddell, *General Mgr*
Dina K Waddell, *Admin Sec*
◆ EMP: 9
SQ FT: 75,000
SALES (est): 3.9MM **Privately Held**
SIC: **2679** Paper products, converted

(G-13256)
STEDMAN CORP
10301 M 89 (49083-9347)
PHONE..................................269 629-5930
William Hannapel, *President*
EMP: 5
SQ FT: 6,000
SALES: 300K **Privately Held**
WEB: www.stedmancorp.com
SIC: **3651** 5736 Microphones; musical instrument stores

Richmond
Macomb County

(G-13257)
A2Z OUTSIDE SERVICES INC
33922 Armada Ridge Rd (48062-5314)
PHONE..................................586 430-1143
Ronald Ward, *President*
EMP: 3
SALES: 250K **Privately Held**
SIC: **3271** 0783 Blocks, concrete: landscape or retaining wall; removal services, bush & tree

(G-13258)
ADVANTAGE DESIGN AND TOOL
35800 Big Hand Rd (48062-4204)
PHONE..................................586 801-7413
Michelle Kerner, *President*
Joseph Torregrossa, *Vice Pres*
EMP: 7
SALES (est): 545.6K **Privately Held**
SIC: **3544** 3545 Jigs & fixtures; gauges (machine tool accessories)

(G-13259)
ALLWOOD BUILDING COMPONENTS
35377 Division Rd (48062-1301)
P.O. Box 547 (48062-0547)
PHONE..................................586 727-2731
Eric O Lundquist, *President*
Irvin Strickstein, *Admin Sec*
EMP: 65
SQ FT: 26,000
SALES (est): 8.3MM **Privately Held**
SIC: **2439** Trusses, except roof: laminated lumber

(G-13260)
B & H PLASTIC CO INC
66725 S Forest Ave (48062)
P.O. Box 117 (48062-0117)
PHONE..................................586 727-7100
Hiram J S Badia, *President*
Judith Badia, *Vice Pres*
EMP: 10

SQ FT: 9,000
SALES (est): 565.6K **Privately Held**
SIC: **3089** Injection molded finished plastic products

(G-13261)
DOUGLAS GAGE INC
69681 Lowe Plank Rd (48062-5345)
PHONE..................................586 727-2089
Kenneth Loria, *President*
Douglas Clark, *President*
EMP: 14
SQ FT: 6,000
SALES (est): 1.5MM **Privately Held**
WEB: www.douglasgage.net
SIC: **3545** Gauges (machine tool accessories)

(G-13262)
EMPIRE HARDCHROME
33450 Bordman Rd (48062-2306)
PHONE..................................810 392-3122
William Hall, *Principal*
EMP: 3
SALES (est): 126.8K **Privately Held**
SIC: **3471** Chromium plating of metals or formed products

(G-13263)
GIOVANNIS APPTZING FD PDTS INC
37775 32 Mile Rd (48062)
P.O. Box 26 (48062-0026)
PHONE..................................586 727-9355
Philip Ricossa, *President*
Giovanni Ricossa, *Vice Pres*
▲ EMP: 19
SQ FT: 1,700
SALES (est): 3.3MM **Privately Held**
WEB: www.gioapp.com
SIC: **2099** Food preparations

(G-13264)
GREAT LAKES PHOTO INC
29080 Armada Ridge Rd (48062-4509)
PHONE..................................586 784-5446
Mark Ezzo, *President*
Victoria Ezzo, *Vice Pres*
Cheryl Ezzo, *Admin Sec*
EMP: 4
SQ FT: 3,300
SALES: 300K **Privately Held**
SIC: **7221** 2732 School photographer; books: printing & binding

(G-13265)
KROGER CO
66900 Gratiot Ave (48062-1913)
PHONE..................................586 727-4946
Joe Shortal, *Manager*
EMP: 110
SQ FT: 3,300
SALES (corp-wide): 121.1B **Publicly Held**
WEB: www.kroger.com
SIC: **5411** 5912 2051 Supermarkets, chain; drug stores & proprietary stores; bread, cake & related products
PA: The Kroger Co
1014 Vine St Ste 1000
Cincinnati OH 45202
513 762-4000

(G-13266)
MIRKWOOD PROPERTIES INC
Also Called: Miller Transit Mix
35555 Division Rd (48062-1387)
PHONE..................................586 727-3363
Terry Miller, *President*
Gayl Miller, *Corp Secy*
Alan Miller, *Vice Pres*
EMP: 5
SQ FT: 2,400
SALES (est): 972.7K **Privately Held**
SIC: **6512** 3273 Commercial & industrial building construction; ready-mixed concrete

(G-13267)
NEW IMAGE DENTAL P C
35000 Division Rd Ste 4 (48062-1566)
PHONE..................................586 727-1100
Daryl Thomas Peraino, *Principal*
EMP: 8
SALES (est): 640.4K **Privately Held**
SIC: **3843** Enamels, dentists'

(G-13268)
PRINT ALL
69347 N Main St (48062-1144)
PHONE..................................586 430-4383
Eric Gordon, *Principal*
Michelle Aiken, *CFO*
EMP: 9
SALES (est): 327K **Privately Held**
SIC: **2752** Commercial printing, lithographic

(G-13269)
PROSPER-TECH MACHINE & TL LLC
69160 Skinner Dr (48062-1538)
PHONE..................................586 727-8800
Heidi Devroy, *Mng Member*
Robert Devroy,
EMP: 11
SALES: 1.1MM **Privately Held**
SIC: **3544** 3599 Special dies, tools, jigs & fixtures; industrial molds; machine shop, jobbing & repair

(G-13270)
RICHMOND MEAT PACKERS INC
Also Called: King Koal Barbecue Equipment
68104 S Main St (48062-1332)
P.O. Box 246 (48062-0246)
PHONE..................................586 727-1450
Joannes Evans, *President*
Corinne Evans, *Corp Secy*
EMP: 3
SQ FT: 6,000
SALES (est): 340K **Privately Held**
SIC: **5421** 5812 3631 5147 Meat markets, including freezer provisioners; caterers; barbecues, grills & braziers (outdoor cooking); meats, fresh

(G-13271)
SPEEDWAY LLC
67371 Gratiot Ave (48062-1917)
PHONE..................................586 727-2638
June Welsh, *Manager*
EMP: 10 **Publicly Held**
WEB: www.speedwaynet.com
SIC: **1311** Crude petroleum production
HQ: Speedway Llc
500 Speedway Dr
Enon OH 45323
937 864-3000

(G-13272)
THREADED PRODUCTS CO
68750 Oak St (48062-1267)
P.O. Box 160 (48062-0160)
PHONE..................................586 727-3435
Kevin Flanigan, *President*
Daneil W Sedor, *Corp Secy*
EMP: 20
SALES (est): 3.8MM **Privately Held**
SIC: **3321** 3366 Pressure pipe & fittings, cast iron; bushings & bearings, brass (nonmachined)

Riley
St. Clair County

(G-13273)
DRW SYSTEMS CARBIDE LLC
12618 Masters Rd (48041-2304)
PHONE..................................810 392-3526
David Rushing, *Principal*
EMP: 5
SALES (est): 324.9K **Privately Held**
SIC: **2819** Carbides

River Rouge
Wayne County

(G-13274)
CARMEUSE LIME INC
Also Called: Carmeuse Lime & Stone
25 Marion Ave (48218-1469)
P.O. Box 18118 (48218-0118)
PHONE..................................313 849-9268
Thomas A Buck, *CEO*
Jeffrey Bittner, *General Mgr*
Hugh Crosmun, *Engineer*

GEOGRAPHIC SECTION

Riverview - Wayne County (G-13300)

Greg Kolodziej, *Project Engr*
Kevin Miller, *Accountant*
EMP: 49
SQ FT: 900
SALES (corp-wide): 177.9K **Privately Held**
SIC: 1422 Crushed & broken limestone
HQ: Carmeuse Lime, Inc.
11 Stanwix St Fl 21
Pittsburgh PA 15222
412 995-5500

(G-13275)
DONNA JEROY
Also Called: Classic Printing & Graphics
10460 W Jefferson Ave (48218-1334)
PHONE...................313 554-2722
Donna Stewart, *Owner*
EMP: 3
SALES: 100K **Privately Held**
SIC: 2759 Commercial printing

(G-13276)
FABRICON PRODUCTS INC (PA)
1721 W Pleasant St (48218-1099)
P.O. Box 18358 (48218-0358)
PHONE...................313 841-8200
Bruce L Dinda, *President*
Beverly Dechant, *Human Res Mgr*
▲ **EMP:** 16 EST: 1997
SQ FT: 150,000
SALES: 6MM **Privately Held**
WEB: www.fabriconproducts.com
SIC: 2671 Packaging paper & plastics film, coated & laminated

(G-13277)
FRITZ ENTERPRISES INC
23550 Pennsylvania Rd (48218)
PHONE...................734 283-7272
Al Seguin, *Branch Mgr*
EMP: 17
SALES (corp-wide): 72MM **Privately Held**
SIC: 3312 Blast furnaces & steel mills
PA: Fritz Enterprises, Inc.
1650 W Jefferson Ave
Trenton MI 48183
734 692-4231

(G-13278)
INTERNTNAL PRCAST SLUTIONS LLC
60 Haltiner St (48218-1259)
PHONE...................313 843-0073
Loris Collavino, *CEO*
Don Little, *President*
Anil Mehta, *Vice Pres*
Paul Phillips, *Vice Pres*
EMP: 100
SALES (est): 30.5MM
SALES (corp-wide): 57.5MM **Privately Held**
SIC: 3272 Concrete products, precast
PA: Prestressed Systems Incorporated
4955 Walker Rd
Windsor ON N9A 6
519 737-1216

(G-13279)
NICHOLSON TERMINAL & DOCK CO (PA)
380 E Great Lakes St (48218-2606)
P.O. Box 18066 (48218-0066)
PHONE...................313 842-4300
Daniel Deane, *President*
Thomas Deane, *Vice Pres*
Patrick Sutka, *Treasurer*
Brendan Deane, *Asst Sec*
▲ **EMP:** 150
SALES (est): 13.6MM **Privately Held**
WEB: www.nicholson-terminal.com
SIC: 4491 3731 4225 7692 Marine terminals; shipbuilding & repairing; general warehousing; welding repair; sheet metalwork; fabricated plate work (boiler shop)

(G-13280)
PRAXAIR INC
300 E Great Lakes St (48218-2606)
PHONE...................313 849-4200
Bill Pakeswill Hardy, *Principal*
EMP: 50 **Privately Held**
SIC: 2813 Industrial gases
HQ: Praxair, Inc.
10 Riverview Dr
Danbury CT 06810
203 837-2000

(G-13281)
TELEGRAM NEWSPAPER
Also Called: Ecorse Telegram Newspaper
10748 W Jefferson Ave (48218-1232)
P.O. Box 29085, Ecorse (48229-0085)
PHONE...................313 928-2955
Gina Wilson, *Owner*
EMP: 3
SALES (est): 167.1K **Privately Held**
SIC: 2711 Commercial printing & newspaper publishing combined; newspapers, publishing & printing

(G-13282)
UNITED STATES GYPSUM COMPANY
10090 W Jefferson Ave (48218-1363)
PHONE...................313 624-4232
Michael Inman, *Engineer*
Kevin Rennie, *Branch Mgr*
EMP: 10
SALES (corp-wide): 8.2B **Privately Held**
SIC: 3275 Gypsum products
HQ: United States Gypsum Company
550 W Adams St Ste 1300
Chicago IL 60661
312 606-4000

(G-13283)
US GYPSUM CO
10090 W Jefferson Ave (48218-1363)
PHONE...................313 842-5800
Jim Sherwin, *Principal*
EMP: 8
SALES (est): 1.3MM **Privately Held**
SIC: 3275 Gypsum products

Riverdale
Gratiot County

(G-13284)
DANIEL D SLATER
Also Called: Log Cabin Lumber
10361 W Van Buren Rd (48877-9708)
PHONE...................989 833-7135
Daniel E Slater, *Owner*
EMP: 4
SQ FT: 5,700
SALES: 700K **Privately Held**
SIC: 5031 5211 2431 2421 Lumber: rough, dressed & finished; lumber & other building materials; millwork; sawmills & planing mills, general

Riverside
Berrien County

(G-13285)
MONTE PACKAGE COMPANY LLC
3752 Riverside Rd (49084-5101)
P.O. Box 128 (49084-0128)
PHONE...................269 849-1722
Anthony Monte, *President*
EMP: 40
SALES (est): 2.1MM
SALES (corp-wide): 11.6B **Privately Held**
SIC: 2449 2653 Fruit crates, wood: wirebound; vegetable crates, wood: wirebound; boxes, corrugated: made from purchased materials
PA: Bunzl Public Limited Company
York House, 45 Seymour Street
London W1H 7
207 725-5000

(G-13286)
RIVERSIDE ELECTRIC SERVICE INC
3864 Riverside Rd (49084-5100)
P.O. Box 32 (49084-0032)
PHONE...................269 849-1222
Walter Sewcyck, *President*
Paul T Sewcyck, *Treasurer*
EMP: 8
SQ FT: 3,000
SALES (est): 1MM **Privately Held**
SIC: 7694 5063 Electric motor repair; motors, electric

(G-13287)
TPS LLC
Also Called: Lindberg/Mph
3827 Riverside Rd (49084-5103)
P.O. Box 131 (49084-0131)
PHONE...................269 849-2700
Jason Edgerton, *Engineer*
Donald Kublick, *Engineer*
Joel Shingledecker, *Manager*
EMP: 60
SALES (corp-wide): 95.3MM **Privately Held**
WEB: www.spx.com
SIC: 3567 Industrial furnaces & ovens
HQ: Tps, Llc
2821 Old Route 15
New Columbia PA 17856
570 538-7200

Riverview
Wayne County

(G-13288)
A A A WIRE ROPE & SPLICING INC
12650 Sibley Rd (48193-4597)
P.O. Box 2153 (48193-1153)
PHONE...................734 283-1765
Robert Matthews, *President*
Louise Blessing, *Admin Sec*
EMP: 12 EST: 1965
SQ FT: 10,000
SALES (est): 3.6MM **Privately Held**
SIC: 3496 Miscellaneous fabricated wire products

(G-13289)
ALL CITY ELECTRIC MOTOR REPAIR
18750 Fort St Apt 15 (48193-7407)
PHONE...................734 284-2268
Mark Watson, *President*
Kelly Watson, *Vice Pres*
EMP: 4
SQ FT: 5,500
SALES: 790K **Privately Held**
SIC: 7694 Electric motor repair

(G-13290)
AMERICAN STEEL WORKS INC
12615 Nixon Ave (48193-4517)
PHONE...................734 282-0300
Robert P Schneider, *President*
Yvonne Schneider, *Admin Sec*
EMP: 10
SQ FT: 25,000
SALES (est): 1.6MM **Privately Held**
SIC: 7699 3441 Industrial equipment services; fabricated structural metal

(G-13291)
B COMPANY INC
14773 Parkview St (48193-7637)
PHONE...................734 283-7080
Steve Beutner, *President*
Scott Beutner, *Exec VP*
◆ **EMP:** 10
SALES (est): 850K **Privately Held**
SIC: 3651 5065 Home entertainment equipment, electronic; electronic parts & equipment

(G-13292)
CONTROL MANUFACTURING CORP
18601 Krause St (48193-4276)
P.O. Box 2008 (48193-1008)
PHONE...................734 283-4300
Harold J Raines, *President*
Don W Fielder, *Corp Secy*
EMP: 32
SQ FT: 37,000
SALES: 1.6MM **Privately Held**
SIC: 3564 Air purification equipment

(G-13293)
DFC INC
Also Called: Denesczuk Firebrick Company
17651 Yorkshire Dr (48193-8166)
PHONE...................734 285-6749
Gail Denesczuk, *President*
Ted Denesczuk, *Vice Pres*
EMP: 5
SALES (est): 607.1K **Privately Held**
SIC: 3567 1711 Industrial furnaces & ovens; boiler & furnace contractors

(G-13294)
FAR ASSOCIATES INC
11801 Longsdorf St (48193-4250)
PHONE...................734 282-1881
Frederick J Rotter, *President*
Randall Gibbs, *Vice Pres*
EMP: 8
SQ FT: 6,300
SALES (est): 1.2MM **Privately Held**
WEB: www.one2find.com
SIC: 3599 Machine shop, jobbing & repair

(G-13295)
HEAVY DUTY RADIATOR LLC
Also Called: Detroit Radiator
18235 Krause St (48193-4259)
PHONE...................800 525-0011
David Bitel, *General Mgr*
Eric Bitel, *Accountant*
EMP: 34
SALES (est): 10.7MM **Privately Held**
SIC: 3714 Motor vehicle parts & accessories

(G-13296)
HERITAGE SERVICES COMPANY INC
18582 Jefferson (48193-4266)
PHONE...................734 282-4566
EMP: 3 EST: 1987
SQ FT: 7,000
SALES (est): 260K **Privately Held**
SIC: 3089 Mfg Plastic Products

(G-13297)
HOMESPUN FURNITURE INC
18540 Fort St (48193-7442)
PHONE...................734 284-6277
Ronald Snider, *President*
Scott Hamelin, *General Mgr*
Gary Ogden, *Vice Pres*
Karen Ogden, *Treasurer*
Lynn Snider, *Admin Sec*
EMP: 17
SQ FT: 20,000
SALES (est): 2MM **Privately Held**
WEB: www.homespunfurniture.com
SIC: 5712 5713 7641 7389 Furniture stores; carpets; reupholstery; interior decorating; upholstered household furniture; floor laying & floor work

(G-13298)
INDUSTRIAL WOOD FAB & PACKG CO (PA)
18620 Fort St (48193-7443)
PHONE...................734 284-4808
Richard E Ott, *President*
EMP: 3
SQ FT: 65,000
SALES: 2MM **Privately Held**
WEB: www.industrialwoodfab.com
SIC: 2449 4783 Boxes, wood: wirebound; barrels, wood: coopered; packing & crating

(G-13299)
JONES CHEMICAL INC
18000 Payne St (48193-4252)
PHONE...................734 283-0677
Jeff Jones, *President*
EMP: 9
SALES (est): 923.1K **Privately Held**
SIC: 2899 Chemical preparations

(G-13300)
LLC ASH STEVENS (HQ)
18655 Krause St (48193-4260)
PHONE...................734 282-3370
Stephen A Munk, *President*
Dr James M Hamby, *Vice Pres*
Rashida Najmi, *Vice Pres*
Sandeep Oke, *Vice Pres*

Vikram Duggal, *VP Human Rcs*
EMP: 70
SQ FT: 47,000
SALES (est): 18.4MM
SALES (corp-wide): 518.1MM **Privately Held**
WEB: www.ashstevens.com
SIC: 2834 Pharmaceutical preparations
PA: Piramal Enterprises Limited
Agastya Corporate Park, Building Anant, Opposite Fire Brigade,
Mumbai MH 40007
223 095-6666

(G-13301)
MATERIALS PROCESSING INC
Also Called: M P I Coating
17423 Jefferson (48193-4205)
PHONE..................................734 282-1888
Emmett Windisch III, *President*
Joanne Frid, *Foreman/Supr*
Scott Boyd, *Maint Spvr*
Gary Keranen, *CFO*
Jason Jackson, *Accounting Mgr*
◆ **EMP:** 80 **EST:** 1981
SQ FT: 900,000
SALES (est): 12.9MM **Privately Held**
SIC: 4225 4226 2891 2851 General warehousing & storage; special warehousing & storage; adhesives & sealants; paints & allied products

(G-13302)
NORTH AMERICAN AUTO INDS INC
Also Called: Noram Autobody Parts
18238 Fort St (48193-7439)
PHONE..................................734 288-3877
David Baird, *President*
EMP: 7
SQ FT: 12,000
SALES: 1.5MM **Privately Held**
SIC: 5015 3465 Automotive parts & supplies, used; body parts, automobile: stamped metal

(G-13303)
P & A CONVEYOR SALES INC
18999 Quarry St (48193-4552)
P.O. Box 2145 (48193-1145)
PHONE..................................734 285-7970
Donny Joe Strong, *President*
EMP: 6
SQ FT: 27,000
SALES (est): 2MM **Privately Held**
SIC: 3535 5084 Conveyors & conveying equipment; conveyor systems

(G-13304)
PERRY TOOL COMPANY INC
12329 Hale St (48193-4562)
PHONE..................................734 283-7393
William L Perry, *President*
Donna Perry, *Corp Secy*
EMP: 5
SQ FT: 4,500
SALES (est): 763.8K **Privately Held**
SIC: 3545 Gauges (machine tool accessories); tools & accessories for machine tools

(G-13305)
SIGN A RAMA CANTON
Also Called: Sign-A-Rama
18073 Ray St (48193-7424)
PHONE..................................734 844-9068
Fax: 734 981-8758
EMP: 3
SALES (est): 251.9K **Privately Held**
SIC: 3993 Signsadv Specs

(G-13306)
WEST SHORE SIGNS INC
18600 Krause St (48193-4247)
PHONE..................................734 324-7076
Janice Renier, *President*
EMP: 3
SALES (est): 180K **Privately Held**
WEB: www.westshoresigns.com
SIC: 7532 7699 3993 Truck painting & lettering; boat repair; signs & advertising specialties

(G-13307)
WSI INDUSTRIAL SERVICES INC (PA)
18555 Fort St (48193-7436)
PHONE..................................734 942-9300
Philip Rye, *President*
Thomas Redmond, *Exec VP*
Craig Colmer, *Vice Pres*
Jerry Tolstyka, *Treasurer*
EMP: 45
SQ FT: 13,000
SALES (est): 13.6MM **Privately Held**
WEB: www.wsiind.com
SIC: 3471 Cleaning & descaling metal products

Rives Junction
Jackson County

(G-13308)
HACKER MACHINE INC
Also Called: Hmi
11200 Broughwell Rd (49277-9671)
PHONE..................................517 569-3348
Charles Hacker, *President*
EMP: 16 **EST:** 1973
SQ FT: 26,000
SALES: 2.5MM **Privately Held**
SIC: 3714 3544 Motor vehicle engines & parts; special dies & tools

(G-13309)
METTER FLOORING LLC
Also Called: Metter Flooring and Cnstr
2531 W Territorial Rd (49277-9709)
PHONE..................................517 914-2004
David Metter,
EMP: 4
SALES (est): 250.5K **Privately Held**
SIC: 2426 3315 1799 1542 Hardwood dimension & flooring mills; chain link fencing; fence construction; commercial & office building, new construction

(G-13310)
RIVES MANUFACTURING INC
4000 Rives Eaton Rd (49277-9650)
P.O. Box 98 (49277-0098)
PHONE..................................517 569-3380
Richard R Stahl, *President*
Vincent P Stahl, *Vice Pres*
EMP: 34
SQ FT: 50,000
SALES (est): 12.1MM **Privately Held**
WEB: www.rivesmfg.com
SIC: 3496 3441 Miscellaneous fabricated wire products; fabricated structural metal

Rochester
Oakland County

(G-13311)
ADVANCED COMPOSITE TECH INC
417 E 2nd St (48307-2007)
PHONE..................................248 709-9097
Peer Larson, *Director*
EMP: 7
SALES (corp-wide): 1.3MM **Privately Held**
SIC: 3089 2221 2396 Automotive parts, plastic; automotive fabrics, manmade fiber; automotive & apparel trimmings
PA: Advanced Composite Technology, Inc.
4200 N Atlantic Blvd
Auburn Hills MI

(G-13312)
ADVERTSING NTWRK SOLUTIONS INC (PA)
Also Called: American Newspaper Solutions
530 Pine St Ste F (48307-1482)
PHONE..................................248 475-7881
Jerry Bellanger, *CEO*
Doug Marchal, *Vice Pres*
Richard Decook, *CFO*
EMP: 6
SALES: 12MM **Privately Held**
WEB: www.adnetworksolutions.com
SIC: 3993 Advertising novelties

(G-13313)
APPLIED & INTEGRATED MFG INC
Also Called: Aim
280 Mill St Ste 8 (48307-6712)
PHONE..................................248 370-8950
Jayanth Yale, *CEO*
EMP: 6
SALES (est): 18.5K **Privately Held**
SIC: 3569 Robots, assembly line: industrial & commercial

(G-13314)
AURUM DESIGN INC
Also Called: Aurum Design Jewelry
400 S Main St (48307-2031)
PHONE..................................248 651-9040
Daren Schurman, *Owner*
EMP: 6
SQ FT: 2,043
SALES (est): 890.4K **Privately Held**
WEB: www.aurumdesign.com
SIC: 3911 5944 Jewelry, precious metal; jewelry stores

(G-13315)
BIZCARD XPRESS
229 N Alice Ave (48307-1811)
PHONE..................................248 288-4800
EMP: 4 **EST:** 2012
SALES (est): 246K **Privately Held**
SIC: 2752 Commercial printing, lithographic

(G-13316)
BUSINESS PRESS INC
Also Called: American Speedy Printing
917 N Main St (48307-1436)
PHONE..................................248 652-8855
William Davies, *President*
EMP: 4
SQ FT: 2,000
SALES (est): 617.8K **Privately Held**
SIC: 2752 2791 2789 2761 Commercial printing, offset; typesetting; bookbinding & related work; manifold business forms

(G-13317)
COSELLA DORKEN PRODUCTS INC
1795 Chase Dr (48307-1799)
PHONE..................................888 433-5824
EMP: 3
SALES (est): 252K **Privately Held**
SIC: 3272 Concrete products

(G-13318)
CPR III INC
Also Called: Preferred Engineering
380 South St (48307-2240)
P.O. Box 81458 (48308-1458)
PHONE..................................248 652-2900
Charles P Ring III, *President*
Paul Kidwell, *Vice Pres*
EMP: 12
SQ FT: 10,000
SALES (est): 2.3MM **Privately Held**
WEB: www.cpriii.com
SIC: 3825 Test equipment for electronic & electrical circuits

(G-13319)
DS AUTOMOTION LLC
280 Mill St Ste C (48307-6713)
PHONE..................................248 370-8950
Jay Yale, *CEO*
EMP: 5
SALES: 250K **Privately Held**
SIC: 3799 Recreational vehicles

(G-13320)
FAMS T-SHIRTS AND DESIGNS
120 E University Dr (48307-2044)
PHONE..................................248 841-1086
Zack Hayes, *Owner*
EMP: 3
SALES (est): 153.7K **Privately Held**
SIC: 2759 Screen printing

(G-13321)
FEDEX OFFICE & PRINT SVCS INC
133 S Main St (48307-2032)
PHONE..................................248 651-2679
EMP: 6
SALES (corp-wide): 69.6B **Publicly Held**
WEB: www.kinkos.com
SIC: 7334 2711 Photocopying & duplicating services; commercial printing & newspaper publishing combined
HQ: Fedex Office And Print Services, Inc.
7900 Legacy Dr
Plano TX 75024
800 463-3339

(G-13322)
GORANG INDUSTRIES INC
Also Called: Wheel Truing Brake Shoe Co
305 South St (48307-2241)
P.O. Box 80636 (48308-0636)
PHONE..................................248 651-9010
Michael Gorang, *President*
Sue Gorang, *Vice Pres*
EMP: 4
SQ FT: 4,600
SALES: 500K **Privately Held**
SIC: 3743 Brakes, air & vacuum: railway

(G-13323)
GRIT OBSTACLE TRAINING LLP
1389 Kentfield Dr (48307-6048)
PHONE..................................248 829-0414
Jason Verbrugghe, *Partner*
EMP: 3
SALES: 150K **Privately Held**
SIC: 7991 7372 Physical fitness facilities; application computer software

(G-13324)
HARMAN CORPORATION (PA)
360 South St (48307-6632)
P.O. Box 80665 (48308-0665)
PHONE..................................248 651-4477
Jeff Harman, *President*
Ron Harman, *Vice Pres*
John Johnston, *Plant Mgr*
Ted Fisher, *Opers Mgr*
Mark Maurer, *Controller*
▲ **EMP:** 35
SQ FT: 65,500
SALES (est): 5MM **Privately Held**
WEB: www.brandlabs.us
SIC: 3089 3643 Blow molded finished plastic products; current-carrying wiring devices

(G-13325)
HELRO CORPORATION
326 Albertson St (48307-1409)
P.O. Box 80732 (48308-0732)
PHONE..................................248 650-8500
Jeffrey Russell, *President*
Kim Russell, *Admin Sec*
▼ **EMP:** 8
SQ FT: 10,000
SALES: 1MM **Privately Held**
WEB: www.helro.com
SIC: 3291 Wheels, abrasive

(G-13326)
HOME BAKERY
300 S Main St (48307-2030)
PHONE..................................248 651-4830
Larry Morevick, *President*
EMP: 30
SQ FT: 3,600
SALES (est): 1MM **Privately Held**
SIC: 5461 2051 Cakes; bread, cake & related products

(G-13327)
HOUSEART LLC
386 South St (48307-2240)
PHONE..................................248 651-8124
Melanie King, *Manager*
Ginger Finley,
▼ **EMP:** 4
SQ FT: 2,000
SALES (est): 464.7K **Privately Held**
SIC: 3612 5251 5063 Doorbell transformers, electric; hardware; lighting fixtures

(G-13328)
IMAGES UNLIMITED LLC
361 South St Ste A (48307-2259)
PHONE..................................248 608-8685
John Meyer,
EMP: 4 **EST:** 1996
SQ FT: 1,400
SALES (est): 451.6K **Privately Held**
SIC: 3993 Signs & advertising specialties

GEOGRAPHIC SECTION — Rochester Hills - Oakland County

(G-13329)
INNOVATIVE WELD SOLUTIONS LLC
1022 Miners Run (48306-4590)
PHONE..................937 545-7695
Venkat Ananthanarayanan, *Principal*
EMP: 8
SQ FT: 8,000
SALES (est): 199.6K **Privately Held**
SIC: 8733 3691 8711 8731 Scientific research agency; storage batteries; engineering services; commercial physical research; business consulting

(G-13330)
INTERPRO TECHNOLOGY INC
722 W University Dr (48307-1851)
PHONE..................248 650-8695
Kevin Ouellette, *Owner*
Sandra McGuffie, *Owner*
Thomas Perry, *Officer*
EMP: 13
SQ FT: 5,800
SALES (est): 1.9MM **Privately Held**
WEB: www.interpro-tech.com
SIC: 7372 Application computer software

(G-13331)
JENDA CONTROLS INC
363 South St Apt B (48307-2274)
PHONE..................248 656-0090
David Lewinski, *President*
EMP: 20
SALES (est): 1.4MM **Privately Held**
SIC: 3625 Electric controls & control accessories, industrial

(G-13332)
KING PHARMACEUTICALS LLC
1200 Parkdale Rd (48307-1744)
PHONE..................248 650-6400
Steve Samet, *Branch Mgr*
EMP: 62
SALES (corp-wide): 53.6B **Publicly Held**
SIC: 2834 Pharmaceutical preparations
HQ: King Pharmaceuticals Llc
501 5th St
Bristol TN 37620

(G-13333)
MARY PANTELY ASSOCIATES
2710 Ledgewood Ct (48306-2381)
PHONE..................248 723-8771
Mary Pantely, *Owner*
EMP: 3
SALES (est): 129.1K **Privately Held**
WEB: www.marypantely.com
SIC: 2721 Magazines: publishing & printing

(G-13334)
METALMITE CORPORATION
194 S Elizabeth St (48307-2027)
PHONE..................248 651-9415
Tom Gendich, *President*
Michael Gendich Jr, *President*
Bob Supernaw, *Plant Supt*
Steve Shelton, *Manager*
Ryan Matz, *Supervisor*
EMP: 18
SQ FT: 10,000
SALES (est): 3.4MM **Privately Held**
WEB: www.metalmite.com
SIC: 3599 3544 Machine shop, jobbing & repair; special dies, tools, jigs & fixtures

(G-13335)
MOON RIVER SOAP CO LLC
339 East St Ste 100 (48307-7400)
PHONE..................248 930-9467
Elizabeth Aprea, *Mng Member*
Carlos Aprea,
EMP: 5 **EST:** 2009
SALES: 130K **Privately Held**
SIC: 2841 Soap & other detergents

(G-13336)
NORBORD PANELS USA INC
410 W University Dr # 210 (48307-1938)
PHONE..................248 608-0387
Peter Wijnbergen, *President*
David Van Maele, *Asst Treas*
EMP: 2000
SALES: 600MM
SALES (corp-wide): 2.4B **Privately Held**
SIC: 2493 Flakeboard
PA: Norbord Inc
1 Toronto St Suite 600
Toronto ON M5C 2
416 365-0705

(G-13337)
NOVAVAX INC
870 Parkdale Rd (48307-1740)
PHONE..................248 656-5336
EMP: 4 **Publicly Held**
WEB: www.novavax.com
SIC: 2836 Vaccines & other immunizing products
PA: Novavax, Inc.
21 Firstfield Rd
Gaithersburg MD 20878

(G-13338)
OAKLAND SAIL INC
Also Called: OAKLAND POST
61 Oakland Ctr (48309-4409)
PHONE..................248 370-4268
Holly Gilbert, *President*
EMP: 25
SALES (est): 34.3K **Privately Held**
SIC: 2711 Newspapers, publishing & printing

(G-13339)
ODT SYSTEMS INC
Also Called: Odt Research
741 Ridgewood Rd (48306-2651)
PHONE..................248 953-9512
Thiago D Olson, *President*
EMP: 12
SALES (est): 641.4K **Privately Held**
SIC: 3795 Tanks & tank components

(G-13340)
OLIVE VINEGAR
205 S Main St Ste C (48307-2066)
PHONE..................248 923-2310
Nicole Loffredo, *General Mgr*
EMP: 4
SALES (est): 231.9K **Privately Held**
SIC: 2099 Vinegar

(G-13341)
ONESTREAM SOFTWARE CORP
425 S Main St Ste 203 (48307-6729)
P.O. Box 81605 (48308-1605)
PHONE..................248 841-1356
Thomas Shae, *President*
Craig Colby, *Vice Pres*
Eric Davidson, *Vice Pres*
Robert Powers, *CTO*
EMP: 9 **EST:** 2009
SQ FT: 1,200
SALES (est): 844.3K **Privately Held**
SIC: 7372 Business oriented computer software

(G-13342)
ONESTREAM SOFTWARE LLC (PA)
362 S St Rochester (48307)
P.O. Box 81605 (48308-1605)
PHONE..................248 342-1541
Marcus Hartwell, *Business Mgr*
Ken Hohenstein, *Vice Pres*
John Von Allmen, *CFO*
Kelsey Ryan, *HR Admin*
Randy Cramp, *Sales Mgr*
EMP: 10
SQ FT: 2,100
SALES (est): 3.4MM **Privately Held**
SIC: 7372 Business oriented computer software

(G-13343)
OPTIMIZERX CORPORATION (PA)
400 Water St Ste 200 (48307-2090)
PHONE..................248 651-6568
William J Febbo, *CEO*
Gus D Halas, *Ch of Bd*
Miriam J Paramore, *President*
Terence J Hamilton, *Senior VP*
Douglas P Baker, *CFO*
EMP: 5
SALES (est): 21.2MM **Publicly Held**
SIC: 7372 Business oriented computer software

(G-13344)
PAR STERILE PRODUCTS LLC
Also Called: Par Pharmaceutical
870 Parkdale Rd (48307-1740)
PHONE..................248 651-9081
Brian Boesch, *Vice Pres*
Ron Dibrango, *Project Mgr*
Robyn Duby, *Project Mgr*
Adianez Miranda-Colon, *Project Mgr*
Suresh Bhamidi, *Opers Mgr*
EMP: 128 **Privately Held**
SIC: 2834 Pharmaceutical preparations
HQ: Par Sterile Products, Llc
6 Ram Ridge Rd
Chestnut Ridge NY 10977

(G-13345)
PARKEDALE PHARMACEUTICALS INC
1200 Parkdale Rd (48307-1744)
PHONE..................248 650-6400
Matthew Lepore, *President*
Brian McMahon, *Treasurer*
Susan Grant, *Admin Sec*
EMP: 51 **EST:** 1997
SALES (est): 17.4MM
SALES (corp-wide): 53.6B **Publicly Held**
WEB: www.kingpharm.com
SIC: 2834 Pharmaceutical preparations
PA: Pfizer Inc.
235 E 42nd St
New York NY 10017
212 733-2323

(G-13346)
PFIZER INC
1200 Parkdale Rd (48307-1744)
PHONE..................248 650-6400
Donald Ferry, *Branch Mgr*
EMP: 10
SALES (corp-wide): 53.6B **Publicly Held**
SIC: 2834 Pharmaceutical preparations
PA: Pfizer Inc.
235 E 42nd St
New York NY 10017
212 733-2323

(G-13347)
PRACTICAL POWER
202 South St (48307-2238)
PHONE..................866 385-2961
Mark Bunting, *President*
EMP: 4
SALES (est): 611K **Privately Held**
SIC: 3679 Power supplies, all types: static

(G-13348)
ROCHESTER CIDER MILL
5215 N Rochester Rd (48306-2737)
PHONE..................248 651-4224
Thomas Barkham, *Owner*
EMP: 3
SQ FT: 10,890
SALES (est): 172.4K **Privately Held**
SIC: 2099 5149 Cider, nonalcoholic; juices

(G-13349)
RYAN REYNOLDS GOLF SHOP LLC
112 Walnut Blvd Unit 307 (48307-2317)
PHONE..................269 629-9311
Ryan Reynolds, *Owner*
EMP: 4 **EST:** 2011
SALES (est): 233.6K **Privately Held**
SIC: 3949 Golf equipment

(G-13350)
SALES DRIVEN SERVICES LLC
Also Called: Raybend
3128 Walt Blvd Ste 216 (48309)
PHONE..................586 854-9494
Jon Reesman, *President*
Joseph Mauro, *Mng Member*
▲ **EMP:** 5
SQ FT: 15,000
SALES (est): 1.1MM **Privately Held**
SIC: 3561 5084 Pumps, domestic: water or sump; water pumps (industrial)

(G-13351)
SAMPSON TOOL INCORPORATED
383 South St (48307-2241)
PHONE..................248 651-3313
William C Reese, *President*
EMP: 5 **EST:** 1976
SQ FT: 4,200
SALES (est): 691.6K **Privately Held**
SIC: 3544 Special dies & tools

(G-13352)
SOLARONICS INC
704 Woodward Ave (48307-1170)
P.O. Box 80217 (48308-0217)
PHONE..................248 651-5333
Richard F Rush Jr, *CEO*
Richard F Rush III, *COO*
Robert C Rush, *Vice Pres*
Jim Herr, *Project Mgr*
Justin Davis, *Purch Mgr*
▲ **EMP:** 35
SQ FT: 50,000
SALES (est): 14.3MM **Privately Held**
WEB: www.solaronicsusa.com
SIC: 3567 3589 3433 Radiant heating systems, industrial process; cooking equipment, commercial; heating equipment, except electric

(G-13353)
STONE FOR YOU
111 W 2nd St Ste A (48307-6738)
PHONE..................248 651-9940
Costin Dragnea, *President*
EMP: 6 **EST:** 2011
SALES (est): 426.7K **Privately Held**
SIC: 3441 Fabricated structural metal

(G-13354)
SU-DAN PLASTICS INC
4693 Gallagher Rd (48306-1501)
PHONE..................248 651-6035
Mike Brockway, *Manager*
EMP: 281
SALES (corp-wide): 24.6MM **Privately Held**
SIC: 3089 3544 Injection molding of plastics; industrial molds
PA: Su-Dan Plastics, Inc.
190 Northpointe Dr
Lake Orion MI 48359
248 651-6035

(G-13355)
TRANS INDUSTRIES PLASTICS LLC (PA)
Also Called: KY Holdings
414 East St (48307-2016)
PHONE..................248 310-0008
William Gruits,
EMP: 20
SQ FT: 60,000
SALES (est): 2.2MM **Privately Held**
SIC: 3089 Injection molding of plastics

(G-13356)
US ENERGIA LLC
Also Called: Energy Products & Services
400 Water St Ste 250 (48307-2091)
PHONE..................248 669-1462
Jeff Moss, *President*
EMP: 80
SALES (est): 3.7MM **Privately Held**
SIC: 8711 3613 Engineering services; control panels, electric

Rochester Hills — Oakland County

(G-13357)
360 GROUP AU PTY LTD
2990 Technology Dr (48309-3588)
PHONE..................586 219-2005
Robert Weins, *President*
EMP: 6
SQ FT: 50,000
SALES (est): 259K **Privately Held**
SIC: 3728 Aircraft parts & equipment

(G-13358)
A RAYMOND CORP N AMER INC (HQ)
2350 Austin Ave Ste 200 (48309-3679)
PHONE..................248 853-2500
Earl Brown, *CEO*
Jason Reznar, *Mfg Mgr*
Donald Dunbar, *Safety Mgr*
James Lewis, *Purch Mgr*

Michelle Patterson, *Buyer*
EMP: 23
SALES (est): 350.7MM
SALES (corp-wide): 177.9K **Privately Held**
SIC: 5085 3469 6719 Fasteners & fastening equipment; metal stampings; investment holding companies, except banks
PA: A Raymond Et Compagnie
113 Cours Berriat
Grenoble
476 210-233

(G-13359)
A RAYMOND CORP N AMER INC
2350 Austin Ave Ste 100 (48309-3679)
PHONE....................810 964-7994
EMP: 4
SALES (corp-wide): 177.9K **Privately Held**
SIC: 3492 Fluid power valves & hose fittings
HQ: A. Raymond Corporate North America, Inc.
2350 Austin Ave Ste 200
Rochester Hills MI 48309
248 853-2500

(G-13360)
A RAYMOND TINNERMAN AUTO INC
2900 Technology Dr (48309-3588)
PHONE....................248 537-3147
Don Brown, *Branch Mgr*
EMP: 11
SALES (corp-wide): 177.9K **Privately Held**
SIC: 3312 Rail joints or fastenings
HQ: A. Raymond Tinnerman Automotive, Inc.
3091 Research Dr
Rochester Hills MI 48309
248 260-2121

(G-13361)
A RAYMOND TINNERMAN MEXICO
3091 Research Dr (48309-3581)
PHONE....................248 537-3404
Daniel Dolan,
EMP: 1
SALES: 1MM
SALES (corp-wide): 177.9K **Privately Held**
SIC: 3965 Fasteners
HQ: A. Raymond Tinnerman Automotive, Inc.
3091 Research Dr
Rochester Hills MI 48309
248 260-2121

(G-13362)
ACCURATE GAUGE & MFG INC (PA)
Also Called: A G
2943 Technology Dr (48309-3589)
PHONE....................248 853-2400
Raymond Velthuysen, *President*
Nancy Cream, *CFO*
Sue Mullins, *Manager*
Clint Velthuysen, *Technology*
EMP: 60
SQ FT: 64,000
SALES (est): 30.4MM **Privately Held**
SIC: 3599 3586 3568 Machine shop, jobbing & repair; measuring & dispensing pumps; power transmission equipment

(G-13363)
ADCO CIRCUITS INC (PA)
2868 Bond St (48309-3514)
PHONE....................248 853-6620
Archie J Damman III, *President*
Andrew Nichols, *Editor*
Marc J Damman, *Vice Pres*
Kevin Barrett, *Plant Mgr*
Jennifer Brown, *Production*
▲ **EMP:** 145
SQ FT: 55,000
SALES (est): 26.9MM **Privately Held**
WEB: www.adcocircuits.com
SIC: 3679 Electronic circuits

(G-13364)
ADDUXI
2791 Research Dr (48309-3575)
PHONE....................248 564-2000
Xavier Ovize, *CEO*
Mathieu Chapellier, *Project Engr*
▲ **EMP:** 20
SALES: 3.4MM **Privately Held**
SIC: 3089 Automotive parts, plastic

(G-13365)
ADVANCE GRAPHIC SYSTEMS INC
1806 Rochester Indl Dr (48309-3337)
PHONE....................248 656-8000
James E Hall, *President*
EMP: 50
SQ FT: 47,800
SALES (est): 10.7MM
SALES (corp-wide): 457.2MM **Privately Held**
WEB: www.advancegraphic.net
SIC: 2791 2759 2752 2396 Typesetting; commercial printing; commercial printing, lithographic; automotive & apparel trimmings; signs, not made in custom sign painting shops
HQ: Federal Heath Sign Company, Llc
2300 St Hwy 121
Euless TX 76039

(G-13366)
ADVANCED AUTOMATION GROUP LLC
1685 W Hamlin Rd (48309-3312)
PHONE....................248 299-8100
Shaotang Chen,
▲ **EMP:** 5
SALES (est): 1.2MM **Privately Held**
SIC: 3625 Motor controls & accessories

(G-13367)
AIR AND LIQUID SYSTEMS INC
1680 S Livernois Rd (48307-3381)
PHONE....................248 656-3610
James E Miller, *President*
Melissa Pollmann, *Purchasing*
Gordon Urquhart, *Engineer*
Melissa Harding, *Sales Staff*
Daniel Whyman, *Sales Staff*
▲ **EMP:** 44
SQ FT: 25,000
SALES: 25MM **Privately Held**
WEB: www.alsys.biz
SIC: 3564 Air purification equipment

(G-13368)
AMERICAN AXLE & MFG INC
Also Called: AAM Technical Center
2965 Technology Dr (48309-3589)
PHONE....................248 299-2900
Daniel Sagady, *Vice Pres*
Charles Stuart, *Engineer*
EMP: 24
SALES (corp-wide): 7.2B **Publicly Held**
WEB: www.aam.com
SIC: 3714 Motor vehicle parts & accessories
HQ: American Axle & Manufacturing, Inc.
1 Dauch Dr
Detroit MI 48211

(G-13369)
APPLIED AUTOMATION TECH INC
1688 Star Batt Dr (48309-3705)
PHONE....................248 656-4930
Ray Karadayi, *President*
Aat PM, *Program Mgr*
▲ **EMP:** 20
SQ FT: 9,800
SALES: 1MM **Privately Held**
SIC: 3695 8243 Computer software tape & disks: blank, rigid & floppy; software training, computer

(G-13370)
ARGON GROUP LLC
1021 Olympia Dr (48306-3785)
PHONE....................248 370-0003
Sheila Fox, *Principal*
EMP: 3
SALES (est): 135.6K **Privately Held**
SIC: 2813 Argon

(G-13371)
ASSEMBLY ALTERNATIVES INC
501 Longford Dr (48309-2416)
PHONE....................248 362-1616
Herman Walker, *CEO*
Richard F Schafer, *President*
EMP: 7
SALES (est): 1.3MM **Privately Held**
WEB: www.aaiusa.net
SIC: 3672 Printed circuit boards

(G-13372)
AVON BROACH & PROD CO LLC
1089 John R Rd (48307-3207)
P.O. Box 80310, Rochester (48308-0310)
PHONE....................248 650-8080
George M Buhaj, *President*
▲ **EMP:** 26
SQ FT: 30,000
SALES (est): 4.2MM **Privately Held**
WEB: www.avonbroach.com
SIC: 3599 3545 Machine shop, jobbing & repair; broaches (machine tool accessories)

(G-13373)
AVON CABINETS ATKINS
2596 Hessel Ave (48307-4824)
PHONE....................248 237-1103
Brian Gatkins, *Principal*
EMP: 3
SALES (est): 278.5K **Privately Held**
SIC: 2434 Wood kitchen cabinets

(G-13374)
AVON PLASTIC PRODUCTS INC
2890 Technology Dr (48309-3586)
PHONE....................248 852-1000
Edward J Gorski, *President*
EMP: 55
SQ FT: 24,000
SALES (est): 7.3MM **Privately Held**
SIC: 3089 3714 Injection molding of plastics; motor vehicle parts & accessories

(G-13375)
BARCLAY PHARMACY
75 Barclay Cir Ste 114 (48307-5803)
PHONE....................248 852-4600
Jignesh Patel, *Owner*
EMP: 3
SALES (est): 345K **Privately Held**
SIC: 2834 Pharmaceutical preparations

(G-13376)
BERKLEY SCREW MACHINE PDTS INC
2100 Royce Haley Dr (48309-3703)
PHONE....................248 853-0044
Kenneth Haley, *President*
Patricia M Lewis, *Corp Secy*
Royce Haley Jr, *Vice Pres*
Tim Jones, *Mfg Spvr*
Amy Cuthbertson, *Manager*
EMP: 41
SQ FT: 30,000
SALES (est): 10.3MM **Privately Held**
WEB: www.bmproducts.com
SIC: 3451 3429 Screw machine products; manufactured hardware (general)

(G-13377)
BERNAL LLC
Also Called: Cerutti Bernal
2960 Technology Dr (48309-3588)
PHONE....................248 299-3600
Kenneth Smott, *CEO*
Frank Penksa, *VP Mfg*
John Vanderham, *Purchasing*
Robert Moore, *Engineer*
Joseph Rinker, *Engineer*
▲ **EMP:** 60
SQ FT: 42,000
SALES (est): 12.1MM
SALES (corp-wide): 78.2MM **Privately Held**
WEB: www.bernal.com
SIC: 3544 3554 Special dies & tools; paper industries machinery
PA: Auxo Investment Partners, Llc
146 Monroe Center St Nw # 1125
Grand Rapids MI 49503
616 200-4454

(G-13378)
BOS AUTOMOTIVE PRODUCTS INC (HQ)
2956 Waterview Dr (48309-3484)
PHONE....................248 289-6072
Stefan Grein, *Ch of Bd*
Ivan Jones, *President*
▲ **EMP:** 40
SQ FT: 20,000
SALES (est): 18.1MM
SALES (corp-wide): 985.8MM **Privately Held**
WEB: www.bos.de
SIC: 3714 Motor vehicle parts & accessories
PA: Bos Gmbh & Co. Kg
Ernst-Heinkel-Str. 2
Ostfildern 73760
711 936-00

(G-13379)
BUHLER TECHNOLOGIES LLC
1030 W Hamlin Rd (48309-3354)
P.O. Box 70212 (48307-0004)
PHONE....................248 652-1546
Dirk Bloser, *Managing Dir*
Gerd R Biller, *Principal*
Rick Brown, *COO*
Oliver Fries, *Vice Pres*
Melissa Cooper, *CFO*
EMP: 15
SALES (est): 2.4MM
SALES (corp-wide): 30.7MM **Privately Held**
SIC: 3492 3569 Control valves, fluid power: hydraulic & pneumatic; filters
PA: Buhler Technologies Gmbh
Harkortstr. 29
Ratingen
210 249-890

(G-13380)
BURTON PRESS CO INC
2156 Avon Industrial Dr (48309-3610)
PHONE....................248 853-0212
Edward Lapierre, *President*
EMP: 5
SQ FT: 1,500
SALES (est): 370K **Privately Held**
WEB: www.burtonpress.com
SIC: 3542 3549 Presses: hydraulic & pneumatic, mechanical & manual; metalworking machinery

(G-13381)
BUSHINGS INC
1967 Rochester Indus Dr (48309-3344)
PHONE....................248 650-0603
Thomas Jacob, *President*
Rob Wolf, *Vice Pres*
Rodney Wolf, *Vice Pres*
Kenneth Maust, *Data Proc Exec*
Kenneth Wayne Maust, *Admin Sec*
◆ **EMP:** 15 **EST:** 1942
SALES (est): 2.5MM **Privately Held**
WEB: www.bushingsinc.com
SIC: 3069 3714 Bushings, rubber; motor vehicle parts & accessories

(G-13382)
BYK USA INC
2932 Waterview Dr (48309-3484)
PHONE....................203 265-2086
Louis Martin, *Branch Mgr*
EMP: 20
SALES (corp-wide): 385.1K **Privately Held**
SIC: 3087 Custom compound purchased resins
HQ: Byk Usa Inc.
524 S Cherry St
Wallingford CT 06492
203 265-2086

(G-13383)
C M S SALES COMPANY INC
2700 Frankson Ave (48307-4635)
PHONE....................248 853-7446
Cheryl A Dennis, *President*
Michael W Dennis, *Treasurer*
EMP: 3
SQ FT: 2,500
SALES (est): 370K **Privately Held**
SIC: 5085 3993 Signmaker equipment & supplies; signs & advertising specialties

GEOGRAPHIC SECTION
Rochester Hills - Oakland County (G-13410)

(G-13384)
CANADIAN AMRCN RSTORATION SUPS (PA)
Also Called: C.A.R.S.
2600 Bond St (48309-3509)
PHONE..................................248 853-8900
Larry Wallie, *President*
Dave Pini, *Vice Pres*
▲ EMP: 28 EST: 1976
SQ FT: 15,000
SALES (est): 8.7MM **Privately Held**
WEB: www.carsinc.com
SIC: 5013 2396 5531 Automotive supplies & parts; automotive trimmings, fabric; automotive parts; automotive accessories

(G-13385)
CARLSON ENTERPRISES INC
Also Called: Cookie Bouquet
922 S Rochester Rd (48307-2742)
PHONE..................................248 656-1442
Connie Carlson, *President*
Tom Carlson, *Vice Pres*
EMP: 6
SALES (est): 230K **Privately Held**
SIC: 5461 5947 2051 Cookies; gift baskets; bread, cake & related products

(G-13386)
CARTER FUEL SYSTEMS LLC
3255 W Hamlin Rd (48309-3231)
PHONE..................................248 371-8392
Rick Rhoades, *Director*
EMP: 5
SALES (corp-wide): 1B **Privately Held**
SIC: 3714 Fuel pumps, motor vehicle
HQ: Carter Fuel Systems, Llc
    101 E Industrial Blvd
    Logansport IN 46947
    574 722-6141

(G-13387)
CASE DIAMOND LINEAR
1809 Rochester Indus Ct (48309-3336)
PHONE..................................800 293-2496
EMP: 3
SALES (est): 91.5K **Privately Held**
SIC: 3544 Special dies, tools, jigs & fixtures

(G-13388)
CELLULAR CONCEPTS CO INC
Also Called: Cell-Con
3667 Merriweather Ln (48306-3642)
PHONE..................................313 371-4800
George Simon II, *President*
▲ EMP: 25
SQ FT: 70,000
SALES (est): 3.7MM
SALES (corp-wide): 12.1MM **Privately Held**
WEB: www.cellcon.com
SIC: 3541 Numerically controlled metal cutting machine tools
HQ: U. S. Equipment Co.
    3667 Merriweather Ln
    Rochester Hills MI 48306
    313 526-8300

(G-13389)
CLYMER MANUFACTURING COMPANY
1605 W Hamlin Rd (48309-3312)
PHONE..................................248 853-5555
Todd Wilms, *President*
EMP: 7 EST: 1951
SQ FT: 7,700
SALES (est): 964.3K **Privately Held**
WEB: www.clymertool.com
SIC: 3545 Cutting tools for machine tools

(G-13390)
COLE WAGNER CABINETRY
2511 Leach Rd (48309-3556)
PHONE..................................248 852-2406
Cole Wagner,
EMP: 15
SALES (est): 304.7K **Privately Held**
SIC: 2434 Wood kitchen cabinets

(G-13391)
COMBUSTION RESEARCH CORP
2516 Leach Rd (48309-3555)
PHONE..................................248 852-3611
Winifred Johnson, *CEO*
Sharon Demeritt, *President*
Paul Demeritt, *Vice Pres*
Vail Demeritt, *Mfg Staff*
◆ EMP: 20
SQ FT: 25,000
SALES (est): 4.6MM **Privately Held**
WEB: www.combustionresearch.com
SIC: 3585 3564 Heating equipment, complete; blowers & fans

(G-13392)
COMMONWEALTH SERVICE SLS CORP
1715 W Hamlin Rd (48309-3368)
PHONE..................................313 581-8050
John S Seraphin, *President*
Victoria Seraphin, *Admin Sec*
EMP: 5
SALES (est): 590.3K **Privately Held**
SIC: 7694 5063 Electric motor repair; motors, electric

(G-13393)
COMPUNETICS SYSTEMS INC
3235 Fulham Dr (48309-4388)
P.O. Box 108, Howell (48844-0108)
PHONE..................................248 531-0015
David Gore, *President*
Jeff Drabek, *Vice Pres*
EMP: 6 EST: 1996
SQ FT: 2,700
SALES (est): 3MM **Privately Held**
WEB: www.compuneticssystems.com
SIC: 3577 Bar code (magnetic ink) printers

(G-13394)
CONNER STEEL PRODUCTS (PA)
2295 Star Ct (48309-3625)
PHONE..................................248 852-5110
David Barnhart, *Partner*
Gunther George, *Partner*
EMP: 7
SALES (est): 1.4MM **Privately Held**
WEB: www.connersteelproducts.com
SIC: 3469 3444 3443 Stamping metal for the trade; sheet metalwork; fabricated plate work (boiler shop)

(G-13395)
CONTEMPORARY AMPEREX CORP
Also Called: Catl USA
2114 Austin Ave (48309-3667)
PHONE..................................248 289-6200
Jian Wang, *President*
Qim Wang, *Manager*
EMP: 8
SQ FT: 3,000
SALES (est): 1.4MM **Privately Held**
SIC: 3691 5013 Storage batteries; automotive batteries

(G-13396)
CONTITECH NORTH AMERICA INC
2044 Austin Ave (48309-3665)
PHONE..................................248 312-3050
Dave Rudyk, *General Mgr*
EMP: 15
SALES (corp-wide): 50.8B **Privately Held**
SIC: 3061 Mechanical rubber goods
HQ: Contitech North America, Inc.
    703 S Clvlnd Massillon Rd
    Fairlawn OH 44333

(G-13397)
CRANE TECHNOLOGIES GROUP INC
Also Called: Michigan Crane Parts & Svc Co
1954 Rochester Indus Dr (48309-3343)
PHONE..................................248 652-8700
Charles J Bauss, *Ch of Bd*
Dorothy Bauss, *President*
David Bauss, *Vice Pres*
Bobby Miller, *Engineer*
Travis Dunny, *Project Engr*
▲ EMP: 33
SQ FT: 38,000
SALES (est): 6MM **Privately Held**
WEB: www.cranetechnologies.com
SIC: 7389 5084 3536 Crane & aerial lift service; cranes, industrial; cranes, industrial plant

(G-13398)
CROSSCON INDUSTRIES LLC
2889 Bond St (48309-3515)
PHONE..................................248 852-5888
Don Shi, *Mng Member*
▲ EMP: 14
SALES (est): 2.3MM **Privately Held**
SIC: 3694 Automotive electrical equipment

(G-13399)
CS EXPRESS INC
2181 Siboney Ct (48309-3748)
PHONE..................................248 425-1726
Ann Soos, *President*
EMP: 4
SALES (est): 169.1K **Privately Held**
SIC: 2741 Miscellaneous publishing

(G-13400)
D2T AMERICA INC
2870 Technology Dr (48309-3586)
PHONE..................................248 680-9001
Philippe Lacassandra, *President*
▲ EMP: 10
SQ FT: 10,000
SALES (est): 2.5MM
SALES (corp-wide): 707.4MM **Privately Held**
WEB: www.d2t.com
SIC: 5045 5013 3829 3825 Computer software; automotive hardware; measuring & controlling devices; instruments to measure electricity; industrial instrmnts msrmnt display/control process variable; motor vehicle parts & accessories
HQ: Fev Software And Testing Solutions
    Fev S A
    Trappes 78190
    130 130-707

(G-13401)
DAMICK ENTERPRISES
1801 Rochester Indus Ct (48309-3336)
PHONE..................................248 652-7500
Frank Sikorski, *President*
Mike Janes, *Vice Pres*
Dale Janes, *Treasurer*
EMP: 15
SQ FT: 8,300
SALES (est): 2.6MM **Privately Held**
WEB: www.damick.net
SIC: 3599 Electrical discharge machining (EDM)

(G-13402)
DATASPEED INC (PA)
2736 Research Dr (48309)
PHONE..................................248 879-0528
Paul Fleck, *President*
Paul Mc Cown, *CFO*
EMP: 18
SALES (est): 5MM **Privately Held**
SIC: 3699 Automotive driving simulators (training aids), electronic

(G-13403)
DEFENSE COMPANY OF AMERICA
324 Fordcroft Dr (48309-1145)
PHONE..................................248 763-6509
Amy Carlton, *Principal*
EMP: 3
SALES (est): 186.9K **Privately Held**
SIC: 3812 Defense systems & equipment

(G-13404)
DELFINGEN US INC (DH)
3985 W Hamlin Rd (48309-3233)
PHONE..................................716 215-0300
Bernard Streit, *President*
Emanuel Klinklin, *Chief*
Vince Anderson, *Business Mgr*
Dave Hutton, *Business Mgr*
Clement Dousteyssier, *Project Mgr*
◆ EMP: 25
SQ FT: 38,000
SALES (est): 28.4MM
SALES (corp-wide): 3.1MM **Privately Held**
SIC: 3089 Extruded finished plastic products
HQ: Delfingen Us- Holding, Inc
    3985 W Hamlin Rd
    Rochester Hills MI 48309
    248 519-0534

(G-13405)
DELFINGEN US- HOLDING INC (DH)
Also Called: Delfingen Industry
3985 W Hamlin Rd (48309-3233)
PHONE..................................248 519-0534
Bernard Streit, *President*
Dean Talbot, *Business Mgr*
Mark Blanke, *CFO*
Lynn Amaro, *Accountant*
Eddie Munoz, *Supervisor*
▲ EMP: 1
SQ FT: 5,000
SALES: 75MM
SALES (corp-wide): 3.1MM **Privately Held**
SIC: 3089 Extruded finished plastic products; injection molded finished plastic products
HQ: Delfingen Industry
    Delfingen
    Anteuil 25340
    381 907-300

(G-13406)
DELFINGEN US-CENTRAL AMER INC
3985 W Hamlin Rd (48309-3233)
PHONE..................................248 230-3500
Gerald Streit, *CEO*
Bernard Streit, *President*
Mark Blanke, *CFO*
Leilani Santos, *Controller*
Emmanuel Klinklin, *Admin Sec*
EMP: 1
SALES: 49MM
SALES (corp-wide): 3.1MM **Privately Held**
SIC: 3089 Extruded finished plastic products
HQ: Delfingen Us- Holding, Inc
    3985 W Hamlin Rd
    Rochester Hills MI 48309
    248 519-0534

(G-13407)
DELL MARKING SYSTEMS INC
6841 N Rochester Rd 250c (48306-4375)
PHONE..................................248 547-7750
Michael A Grattan, *President*
▼ EMP: 9
SQ FT: 7,000
SALES (est): 1.3MM **Privately Held**
WEB: www.dellid.com
SIC: 2899 Ink or writing fluids

(G-13408)
DETROIT WILBERT CREMATION SERV
3658 Samuel Ave (48309-4252)
PHONE..................................248 853-0559
Chris Gordon, *Principal*
EMP: 3
SALES (est): 240.4K **Privately Held**
SIC: 3272 Burial vaults, concrete or precast terrazzo

(G-13409)
DL ENGINEERING & TECH INC
Also Called: Rytam Technolgy
1749 W Hamlin Rd (48309-3373)
PHONE..................................248 852-6900
David Lubera, *President*
EMP: 6
SQ FT: 8,500
SALES (est): 1MM **Privately Held**
SIC: 3089 Injection molded finished plastic products

(G-13410)
DURA BRAKE SYSTEMS LLC
2791 Research Dr (48309-3575)
PHONE..................................248 299-7500
EMP: 3

Rochester Hills - Oakland County (G-13411)

SALES (est): 37.7K
SALES (corp-wide): 4.1B **Privately Held**
WEB: www.duraauto.com
SIC: **3714** Motor vehicle parts & accessories
HQ: Dura Automotive Systems, Llc
1780 Pond Run
Auburn Hills MI 48326

(G-13411)
DURA CABLES NORTH LLC
2791 Research Dr (48309-3575)
PHONE.................................248 299-7500
EMP: 3
SALES (est): 22.2K
SALES (corp-wide): 4.1B **Privately Held**
WEB: www.duraauto.com
SIC: **3714** Motor vehicle parts & accessories
HQ: Dura Automotive Systems, Llc
1780 Pond Run
Auburn Hills MI 48326

(G-13412)
DURA CABLES SOUTH LLC
2791 Research Dr (48309-3575)
PHONE.................................248 299-7500
EMP: 3
SALES (est): 21.7K
SALES (corp-wide): 4.1B **Privately Held**
WEB: www.duraauto.com
SIC: **3714** Motor vehicle parts & accessories
HQ: Dura Automotive Systems, Llc
1780 Pond Run
Auburn Hills MI 48326

(G-13413)
DURA GLOBAL TECHNOLOGIES INC
2791 Research Dr (48309-3575)
PHONE.................................248 299-7500
EMP: 4
SALES (est): 34.5K
SALES (corp-wide): 4.1B **Privately Held**
WEB: www.duraauto.com
SIC: **3714** Motor vehicle parts & accessories
HQ: Dura Automotive Systems, Llc
1780 Pond Run
Auburn Hills MI 48326

(G-13414)
DURA SHIFTER LLC
2791 Research Dr (48309-3575)
PHONE.................................248 299-7500
EMP: 3
SALES (est): 27K
SALES (corp-wide): 4.1B **Privately Held**
WEB: www.duraauto.com
SIC: **3714** Motor vehicle parts & accessories
HQ: Dura Automotive Systems, Llc
1780 Pond Run
Auburn Hills MI 48326

(G-13415)
ECO PAPER
1150 W Hamlin Rd (48309-3356)
PHONE.................................248 652-3601
EMP: 5
SALES (est): 482.3K **Privately Held**
SIC: **2653** Mfg Corrugated/Solid Fiber Boxes

(G-13416)
EISSMANN AUTO PORT HURON LLC
2655 Product Dr (48309-3808)
PHONE.................................248 829-4990
Joerg Schultz, *Managing Dir*
EMP: 50
SALES (corp-wide): 547.3MM **Privately Held**
SIC: **2396** Automotive trimmings, fabric
HQ: Eissmann Automotive Port Huron Llc
2440 20th St
Port Huron MI 48060
810 216-6300

(G-13417)
ELITE ENGINEERING INC
Also Called: Eflex Sytems
210 W Tienken Rd (48306-4404)
PHONE.................................517 304-3354
Dan McKierman, *President*

George Jewell, *Vice Pres*
Todd Schlueter, *Program Mgr*
Richard Kubina, *Sr Software Eng*
Rachel Glomski, *Software Dev*
EMP: 15
SQ FT: 11,000
SALES (est): 3MM **Privately Held**
SIC: **8711** 7371 3577 Consulting engineer; computer software development; computer peripheral equipment

(G-13418)
ENTREPRENEURIAL PURSUITS
Also Called: Jan Fan
2727 Product Dr (48309-3810)
PHONE.................................248 829-6903
John Hamernik, *President*
Mark Goatley, *Vice Pres*
EMP: 4
SALES (est): 469.4K **Privately Held**
SIC: **3564** Blowing fans: industrial or commercial

(G-13419)
ENVISICS LLC (PA)
2021 Austin Ave (48309)
PHONE.................................248 802-4461
Jamison Christmas,
John Nowinski,
EMP: 9
SALES (est): 4.4MM **Privately Held**
SIC: **3812** Search & navigation equipment

(G-13420)
EPTECH INC
541 Oakhill Ct (48309-1737)
PHONE.................................586 254-2722
Emrick Papp, *President*
EMP: 3
SALES (est): 99.8K **Privately Held**
SIC: **3599** Machine shop, jobbing & repair

(G-13421)
EWS LEGACY LLC (PA)
2119 Austin Ave (48309-3668)
PHONE.................................248 853-6363
Robert Brzustewicz, *General Mgr*
Bob Brewster, *Vice Pres*
Tomoji Yamamoto, *Vice Pres*
Bob Campbell, *Mfg Mgr*
Thomas Roach, *QC Mgr*
▲ EMP: 47
SQ FT: 53,000
SALES (est): 46.8MM **Privately Held**
WEB: www.empirewc.com
SIC: **3641** 3613 3357 3643 Electric lamps; switchgear & switchboard apparatus; nonferrous wiredrawing & insulating; current-carrying wiring devices; electronic computers; noncurrent-carrying wiring services

(G-13422)
F I D CORPORATION
Also Called: Epcon
3424 Charlwood Dr (48306-3619)
PHONE.................................248 373-7005
Felix Nedorezov, *President*
Nina Nedorezov, *Vice Pres*
EMP: 18
SQ FT: 2,000
SALES: 1.5MM **Privately Held**
SIC: **3829** 8742 Aircraft & motor vehicle measurement equipment; business consultant

(G-13423)
FANUC AMERICA CORPORATION (HQ)
3900 W Hamlin Rd (48309-3253)
PHONE.................................248 377-7000
Richard E Schneider, *Ch of Bd*
Mike Cicco, *President*
Justin Bodily, *District Mgr*
Josh Holtsberry, *District Mgr*
Gary Kowalski, *District Mgr*
◆ EMP: 500
SQ FT: 370,000
SALES (est): 530.7MM **Privately Held**
WEB: www.fanucrobotics.com
SIC: **3559** 3548 3569 3542 Metal finishing equipment for plating, etc.; electric welding equipment; robots, assembly line: industrial & commercial; robots for metal forming: pressing, extruding, etc.

(G-13424)
FIDIA CO
3098 Research Dr (48309-3580)
PHONE.................................248 680-0700
Giuseppe Morfino, *President*
Jorge Correa, *Vice Pres*
Andy Taylor, *Regl Sales Mgr*
Doug Michael, *Manager*
▲ EMP: 15
SALES (est): 3.3MM
SALES (corp-wide): 53.1MM **Privately Held**
SIC: **3625** 7699 Numerical controls; industrial equipment services
PA: Fidia Spa
Corso Lombardia 11
San Mauro Torinese TO 10099
011 222-7111

(G-13425)
FLEXTRONICS AUTOMOTIVE USA INC (DH)
2120 Austin Ave (48309-3667)
PHONE.................................248 853-5724
Mike McNamara, *CEO*
Franois Barbier, *President*
Doug Britt, *President*
Paul Humphries, *President*
Mike De Irala, *Exec VP*
▲ EMP: 100
SQ FT: 68,000
SALES (est): 442.2MM
SALES (corp-wide): 26.2B **Privately Held**
WEB: www.saturnee.com
SIC: **3625** 3714 3643 Control circuit relays, industrial; solenoid switches (industrial controls); switches, electronic applications; motor vehicle parts & accessories; vacuum brakes, motor vehicle; fuel systems & parts, motor vehicle; oil strainers, motor vehicle; current-carrying wiring devices

(G-13426)
FOAMPARTNER AMERICAS INC
Also Called: Otto Bock
2923 Technology Dr (48309-3589)
PHONE.................................248 243-3100
Olaf Vorwald, *CEO*
Peter Gansen, *President*
Hans Georg Nader, *Vice Pres*
Nancy Feeney, *Controller*
▲ EMP: 7
SALES (est): 4.2MM
SALES (corp-wide): 1.8B **Privately Held**
SIC: **2821** Plastics materials & resins
HQ: Foampartner Germany Gmbh
Max-Nader-Str. 15
Duderstadt 37115
552 784-80

(G-13427)
FORMFAB LLC
3044 Research Dr (48309-3580)
PHONE.................................248 844-3676
Norman P Caetano, *President*
Darryl Melone, *Engineer*
EMP: 25
SQ FT: 15,900
SALES (est): 5.5MM **Privately Held**
WEB: www.formfabllc.com
SIC: **3317** 3498 3714 3544 Steel pipe & tubes; fabricated pipe & fittings; air conditioner parts, motor vehicle; forms (molds), for foundry & plastics working machinery

(G-13428)
FRASER FAB AND MACHINE INC
1696 Star Batt Dr (48309-3705)
PHONE.................................248 852-9050
David Hartig, *President*
James Hartig, *Treasurer*
EMP: 24 EST: 1967
SQ FT: 13,000
SALES (est): 4.3MM **Privately Held**
SIC: **3599** 7692 3535 Machine shop, jobbing & repair; welding repair; conveyors & conveying equipment

(G-13429)
FUTURISTIC ARTWEAR INC
787 Majestic (48306-3572)
PHONE.................................248 680-0200
Michael Cannon, *President*

EMP: 20
SQ FT: 16,000
SALES (est): 2.1MM **Privately Held**
SIC: **2759** Screen printing

(G-13430)
G P DURA
2791 Research Dr (48309-3575)
PHONE.................................248 299-7500
EMP: 3
SALES (est): 25.3K
SALES (corp-wide): 4.1B **Privately Held**
WEB: www.duraauto.com
SIC: **3714** Motor vehicle parts & accessories
HQ: Dura Automotive Systems, Llc
1780 Pond Run
Auburn Hills MI 48326

(G-13431)
GATES CORPORATION
Also Called: Worldwide Power Transm Div
2975 Waterview Dr (48309-4600)
PHONE.................................248 260-2300
Robert Willig, *Manager*
Tom Lovin, *Manager*
EMP: 100
SALES (corp-wide): 3.3B **Publicly Held**
WEB: www.gates.com
SIC: **3052** 8731 3568 3714 Rubber belting; commercial physical research; power transmission equipment; motor vehicle parts & accessories; manufactured hardware (general)
HQ: The Gates Corporation
1144 15th St Ste 1400
Denver CO 80202
303 744-1911

(G-13432)
GENERAL DYNAMICS GLBL IMG TECH (DH)
2909 Waterview Dr (48309-4600)
PHONE.................................248 293-2929
Scott Butler, *President*
▲ EMP: 1284 EST: 2012
SALES (est): 228.8MM
SALES (corp-wide): 36.1B **Publicly Held**
WEB: www.axsys.com
SIC: **3827** 3861 Optical instruments & apparatus; photographic equipment & supplies; aerial cameras
HQ: General Dynamics Government Systems Corporation
2941 Fairview Park Dr
Falls Church VA 22042
703 876-3000

(G-13433)
GENERAL DYNAMICS GLBL IMG TECH
2909 Waterview Dr (48309-4600)
PHONE.................................248 293-2929
Janet Soller, *Branch Mgr*
EMP: 15
SALES (corp-wide): 36.1B **Publicly Held**
SIC: **3728** 3829 Aircraft parts & equipment; manufactured hardware (general)
HQ: General Dynamics Global Imaging Technologies, Inc.
2909 Waterview Dr
Rochester Hills MI 48309
248 293-2929

(G-13434)
GENERAL DYNAMICS MISSION
2909 Waterview Dr (48309-4600)
PHONE.................................530 271-2500
EMP: 1284
SALES (corp-wide): 36.1B **Publicly Held**
SIC: **3827** 3861 Optical instruments & apparatus; photographic equipment & supplies; aerial cameras
HQ: General Dynamics Mission Systems, Inc.
12450 Fair Lakes Cir # 200
Fairfax VA 22033
703 263-2800

(G-13435)
GRANITE PRECISION TOOL CORP
2257 Star Ct (48309-3625)
PHONE.................................248 299-8317
Richard Przybylowicz, *President*

EMP: 9
SQ FT: 1,600
SALES (est): 1.2MM **Privately Held**
SIC: 3544 Special dies & tools

(G-13436)
GST AUTOLEATHER INC (PA)
2920 Waterview Dr (48309-3484)
PHONE..................248 436-2300
Randy Johnson, *CEO*
Timothy Brennan, *President*
Eric Evans, *President*
Timothy Lieckfelt, *Vice Pres*
Phillip Reise, *Treasurer*
EMP: 12
SALES: 500MM **Privately Held**
SIC: 2396 Automotive trimmings, fabric

(G-13437)
H S DIE & ENGINEERING INC
Also Called: H S Express
1720 Star Batt Dr (48309-3707)
PHONE..................248 373-4048
Jeffrey Hearn, *Manager*
EMP: 11
SALES (corp-wide): 69.1MM **Privately Held**
WEB: www.hsdie.com
SIC: 3442 Molding, trim & stripping; window & door frames
PA: H. S. Die & Engineering, Inc.
O-215 Lake Michigan Dr Nw
Grand Rapids MI 49534
616 453-5451

(G-13438)
HAMLIN TOOL & MACHINE CO INC
1671 E Hamlin Rd (48307-3624)
PHONE..................248 651-6302
Patrick Pihjalic, *President*
Thom Chuminatto, *General Mgr*
Stan Damer, *QC Mgr*
Nigel Barnett, *VP Sales*
Anna Zambiski, *Director*
EMP: 100
SQ FT: 55,000
SALES (est): 19.9MM **Privately Held**
WEB: www.hamlintool.com
SIC: 3714 3465 Motor vehicle parts & accessories; automotive stampings

(G-13439)
HANWHA TECHM USA LLC
1857 Enterprise Dr (48309-3802)
PHONE..................248 588-1242
Jeonsu Jang,
▲ EMP: 7 EST: 2013
SQ FT: 3,600
SALES (est): 7.4MM **Privately Held**
SIC: 3549 Assembly machines, including robotic
PA: Hanwha Corporation
86 Cheonggyecheon-Ro, Jung-Gu
Seoul 04541

(G-13440)
HI-LEX AMERICA INCORPORATED
Also Called: Hi-Lex Automotive Centre
2911 Research Dr (48309-3579)
PHONE..................248 844-0096
Ken Repke, *Engineer*
Robert Canham, *Accounts Exec*
Nick Gerasimidis, *Accounts Exec*
Suzanne Beauchamp, *Manager*
EMP: 100 **Privately Held**
WEB: www.hci.hi-lex.com
SIC: 3714 3496 3643 Motor vehicle parts & accessories; cable, uninsulated wire: made from purchased wire; current-carrying wiring devices
HQ: Hi-Lex America, Incorporated
5200 Wayne Rd
Battle Creek MI 49037
269 968-0781

(G-13441)
HI-TECH MOLD & ENGINEERING INC
1758 Northfield Dr (48309-3818)
PHONE..................248 844-0722
EMP: 20
SALES (corp-wide): 58.8MM **Privately Held**
SIC: 3544 Mfg Plastic Injection Molds & Dies
PA: Hi-Tech Mold & Engineering, Inc.
2775 Commerce Dr
Rochester Hills MI 48309
248 852-6600

(G-13442)
HI-TECH MOLD & ENGINEERING INC
1744 Northfield Dr (48309-3818)
PHONE..................248 844-9159
EMP: 15
SALES (corp-wide): 53.4MM **Privately Held**
SIC: 3544 Forms (molds), for foundry & plastics working machinery; dies, plastics forming
PA: Hi-Tech Mold & Engineering, Inc.
2775 Commerce Dr
Rochester Hills MI 48309
248 852-6600

(G-13443)
HI-TECH MOLD & ENGINEERING INC (PA)
2775 Commerce Dr (48309-3815)
PHONE..................248 852-6600
Robert Schulte, *President*
Siegfried Schulte, *Chairman*
Terry Sanders, *COO*
Ken Dilas, *QC Mgr*
Bruno Mariani, *Engineer*
▲ EMP: 37
SQ FT: 140,000
SALES (est): 53.4MM **Privately Held**
WEB: www.hitechmold.com
SIC: 3544 Forms (molds), for foundry & plastics working machinery; dies, plastics forming

(G-13444)
HIRSCHMANN AUTO N AMER LLC
2927 Waterview Dr (48309-4600)
PHONE..................248 495-2677
Volker Buth, *CEO*
EMP: 3
SALES (est): 276.5K
SALES (corp-wide): 2.6MM **Privately Held**
SIC: 3678 Electronic connectors
HQ: Hirschmann Automotive Gmbh
Oberer Paspelsweg 6-8
Rankweil 6830
552 230-70

(G-13445)
HOSPITAL CURTAIN SOLUTIONS INC
2285 Star Ct (48309-3625)
PHONE..................248 293-9785
Karen Serio, *President*
Arthur Serio III, *Vice Pres*
EMP: 3
SQ FT: 1,000
SALES: 700K **Privately Held**
SIC: 2391 Curtains, window: made from purchased materials

(G-13446)
HOT MELT TECHNOLOGIES INC
Also Called: H M T
1723 W Hamlin Rd (48309-3368)
P.O. Box 80067, Rochester (48308-0067)
PHONE..................248 853-2011
Bryan J Tanury, *President*
Ester C Tanury, *Vice Pres*
Rosalyn Wilson, *Production*
Ed Spearing, *Engineer*
Colin Holzman, *Electrical Engi*
▼ EMP: 30
SQ FT: 18,000
SALES (est): 14.3MM **Privately Held**
WEB: www.hotmelt-tech.com
SIC: 5084 3569 3565 Industrial machinery & equipment; packaging machinery & equipment; assembly machines, non-metalworking; packaging machinery

(G-13447)
HYDRAULIC SYSTEMS TECHNOLOGY
1156 Whispering Knoll Ln (48306-4176)
PHONE..................248 656-5810
Perry Decuir, *President*
EMP: 5
SALES (est): 982.9K **Privately Held**
WEB: www.hstpress.com
SIC: 5013 5065 3625 8734 Motor vehicle supplies & new parts; electronic parts & equipment; motor controls & accessories; product testing laboratories

(G-13448)
HYDRO-CRAFT INC
1821 Rochster Indus Dr (48309-3336)
PHONE..................248 652-8100
Peter Blumbergs, *Branch Mgr*
EMP: 25
SALES (corp-wide): 57.8K **Privately Held**
WEB: www.hydro-craft.com
SIC: 3429 3541 3714 3594 Manufactured hardware (general); machine tools, metal cutting type; motor vehicle parts & accessories; fluid power pumps & motors; fabricated plate work (boiler shop); machine tool attachments & accessories
PA: Hydro-Craft, Inc.
320 Sunpac Ct Ste 100
Henderson NV 89011
702 566-8798

(G-13449)
INDUSTRIAL AUTOMATION LLC (PA)
2968 Waterview Dr (48309-3484)
PHONE..................248 598-5900
Holly Dolphin, *General Mgr*
Jeff Kotila, *General Mgr*
Paul Rotole, *Sales Engr*
Justin Barbe, *Program Mgr*
Andrew Arnott, *Manager*
◆ EMP: 80
SQ FT: 15,000
SALES (est): 25.8MM **Privately Held**
SIC: 3549 5084 Metalworking machinery; industrial machinery & equipment

(G-13450)
INOVISION INC
2610 Bond St (48309-3509)
PHONE..................248 299-1915
EMP: 29 **Privately Held**
SIC: 7372 Prepackaged software
PA: Inovision Software Solutions, Inc.
50561 Chesterfield Rd
Chesterfield MI 48051

(G-13451)
INZI CONTROLS DETROIT LLC
2950 Technology Dr (48309-3588)
PHONE..................334 282-4237
Gyuwan Kim, *President*
▲ EMP: 3
SALES: 6.7MM **Privately Held**
SIC: 3714 Motor vehicle parts & accessories
HQ: Inzi Controls Alabama, Inc.
375 Alabama Highway 203
Elba AL 36323

(G-13452)
JAMES W LIESS CO INC
3410 Baroque Ct (48306-3704)
PHONE..................248 547-9160
EMP: 4
SALES (corp-wide): 469.7K **Privately Held**
SIC: 3536 Man/Ret Gantries
PA: James W Liess Co Inc
3628 Thornwood Dr
Auburn Hills MI 48326
248 373-1510

(G-13453)
JENOPTIK AUTOMOTIVE N AMER LLC
Also Called: Hommel Movomatic
1500 W Hamlin Rd (48309-3365)
PHONE..................248 853-5888
Hans-Peter Schumacher, *CEO*
Andreas Blind, *Vice Pres*
David Matynowski, *Vice Pres*
Brian Chiaz, *Engineer*
Kurt Andrews, *Finance*
◆ EMP: 121
SQ FT: 100,000
SALES (est): 22.8MM
SALES (corp-wide): 955.4MM **Privately Held**
WEB: www.dphgage.com
SIC: 3827 Optical instruments & lenses
HQ: Jenoptik North America, Inc.
16490 Innovation Dr
Jupiter FL 33478

(G-13454)
KAMAX INC (HQ)
Also Called: Kamax L.P.
1606 Star Batt Dr (48309-3705)
PHONE..................248 879-0200
David Winn, *Vice Pres*
Jay Dusenberry, *Vice Pres*
Thomas Hoppenstedt, *Vice Pres*
Dan Schram, *Foreman/Supr*
Angie Culpert, *Senior Buyer*
◆ EMP: 255 EST: 1935
SQ FT: 162,000
SALES (est): 146.2MM
SALES (corp-wide): 900.9MM **Privately Held**
SIC: 3452 Bolts, metal
PA: Kamax Holding Gmbh & Co. Kg
Dr.-Rudolf-Kellermann-Str. 2
Homberg (Ohm) 35315
663 379-0

(G-13455)
KATHREIN AUTOMOTIVE N AMER INC
Also Called: Kathrein Automotive USA
3967 W Hamlin Rd (48309-3233)
PHONE..................248 230-2951
Andreas Fuchs, *CEO*
EMP: 6
SALES (est): 944.6K
SALES (corp-wide): 50.8B **Privately Held**
SIC: 3694 Automotive electrical equipment
HQ: Continental Advanced Antenna Gmbh
Romerring 1
Hildesheim 31137
512 199-8140

(G-13456)
KORENS
1685 W Hamlin Rd (48309-3312)
PHONE..................248 817-5188
Tae Jin Kim, *Administration*
EMP: 5 EST: 2013
SALES (est): 326.6K **Privately Held**
SIC: 3069 Rubber automotive products

(G-13457)
KOSTAL KONTAKT SYSTEME INC
Also Called: Kostal Group
1350 W Hamlin Rd (48309-3361)
PHONE..................248 284-7600
Holger Lettmann, *CEO*
Steve Verzyl, *Research*
Anna Mueller, *CFO*
Jake Harlick, *Financial Analy*
Kristin Pavliscak, *Accounts Mgr*
▲ EMP: 200
SALES (est): 31.2MM
SALES (corp-wide): 1B **Privately Held**
SIC: 3678 Electronic connectors
PA: Leopold Kostal Gmbh & Co. Kg
An Der Bellmerei 10
Ludenscheid 58513
235 116-0

(G-13458)
LEAR CORPORATION
3000 Research Dr (48309-3580)
PHONE..................248 299-7100
Bret Eadertsher, *Branch Mgr*
EMP: 377
SALES (corp-wide): 21.1B **Publicly Held**
WEB: www.lear.com
SIC: 3714 Motor vehicle parts & accessories
PA: Lear Corporation
21557 Telegraph Rd
Southfield MI 48033
248 447-1500

Rochester Hills - Oakland County (G-13459)

(G-13459)
LEAR CORPORATION
Also Called: Rochester Hills Facility
2930 W Auburn Rd (48309-3505)
PHONE..............................248 853-3122
EMP: 25
SALES (corp-wide): 21.1B **Publicly Held**
SIC: 3111 Leather tanning & finishing
PA: Lear Corporation
  21557 Telegraph Rd
  Southfield MI 48033
  248 447-1500

(G-13460)
LETICA CORPORATION (DH)
52585 Dequindre Rd (48307-2321)
P.O. Box 5005, Rochester (48308-5005)
PHONE..............................248 652-0557
Anton Letica, *CEO*
Gerald Curtis, *QC Mgr*
◆ EMP: 150
SQ FT: 92,584
SALES: 450MM **Publicly Held**
WEB: www.letica.com
SIC: 2656 3089 Sanitary food containers; plastic containers, except foam

(G-13461)
LITEX INC (PA)
2774 Product Dr (48309-3809)
PHONE..............................248 852-0661
Thomas J Parsons, *President*
EMP: 5
SQ FT: 4,900
SALES: 9.1MM **Privately Held**
WEB: www.litex.com
SIC: 3442 Sash, door or window: metal

(G-13462)
LUMEN NORTH AMERICA INC
2850 Commerce Dr (48309-3816)
PHONE..............................248 289-6100
Jonathan Evans, *President*
Michael Waterson, *Vice Pres*
EMP: 3
SALES (est): 145.6K **Privately Held**
SIC: 3559 Automotive related machinery

(G-13463)
M P I INTERNATIONAL INC (PA)
2129 Austin Ave (48309-3668)
PHONE..............................608 764-5416
Mike Bryant, *CEO*
Robert Kuth, *Vice Pres*
Larry Schieve, *Opers Mgr*
Carlos Luca, *Mfg Staff*
Hubert Schneider, *Engineer*
EMP: 86
SALES (est): 252MM **Privately Held**
SIC: 3462 3714 3469 Automotive forgings, ferrous: crankshaft, engine, axle, etc.; motor vehicle transmissions, drive assemblies & parts; metal stampings

(G-13464)
M&S PRINTMEDIA INC
732 Brookwood Ln E (48309-1542)
P.O. Box 81728, Rochester (48308-1728)
PHONE..............................248 601-1200
Rich R Sommerfield Jr, *President*
Richard Sommerfield, *Vice Pres*
Jeanne Sommerfield, *Treasurer*
EMP: 3
SALES: 500K **Privately Held**
WEB: www.msprintmedia.com
SIC: 2759 Screen printing

(G-13465)
MACAUTO U S A INC
3360 Crestwater Ct (48309-2781)
PHONE..............................248 499-8208
EMP: 3
SALES (est): 161.2K **Privately Held**
SIC: 3089 Automotive parts, plastic

(G-13466)
MACKELLAR ASSOCIATES INC
Also Called: Burro Graphics
1729 Northfield Dr (48309-3819)
PHONE..............................248 335-4440
Duane Christoff, *Branch Mgr*
EMP: 11
SQ FT: 2,000
SALES (corp-wide): 6MM **Privately Held**
WEB: www.mackellar.com
SIC: 7336 3993 2396 2395 Art design services; silk screen design; signs & advertising specialties; automotive & apparel trimmings; pleating & stitching
PA: Mackellar Associates, Inc.
  1729 Northfield Dr
  Rochester Hills MI 48309
  248 335-4440

(G-13467)
MANUFACTURING CTRL SYSTEMS INC
1928 Star Batt Dr Ste C (48309-3722)
PHONE..............................248 853-7400
Joseph L Steimel, *President*
Nancy Steimel, *Vice Pres*
EMP: 7
SALES (est): 2.3MM **Privately Held**
SIC: 3625 8711 Industrial controls: push button, selector switches, pilot; electrical or electronic engineering

(G-13468)
MATHEW PARMELEE
Also Called: Parma Diversified Technologies
707 W Hamlin Rd (48307-3434)
PHONE..............................248 894-4955
Mathew Parmelee, *Partner*
Ken Schafer, *Partner*
EMP: 4
SALES (est): 750K **Privately Held**
SIC: 8299 3599 Musical instrument lessons; machine shop, jobbing & repair

(G-13469)
MAXUM LLC
600 Oliver Dr (48309)
P.O. Box 70025, Rochester (48307-0001)
PHONE..............................248 726-7110
James Pamey,
EMP: 6
SALES (est): 790.7K **Privately Held**
SIC: 3599 Industrial machinery

(G-13470)
MCKENNA ENTERPRISES INC
3128 Walton Blvd (48309-1265)
PHONE..............................248 375-3388
Kevin McKenna, *Manager*
EMP: 5
SALES (est): 548.8K **Privately Held**
SIC: 2674 Shipping & shopping bags or sacks

(G-13471)
MELCO ENGRAVING INC
1800 Production Dr (48309-3350)
PHONE..............................248 656-9000
Melvyn O Dowd, *President*
EMP: 3
SQ FT: 6,900
SALES (est): 430K **Privately Held**
SIC: 2759 Engraving

(G-13472)
METAL MERCHANTS OF MICHIGAN
2691 Leach Rd (48309-3558)
PHONE..............................248 293-0621
Robert Allen, *CEO*
EMP: 50
SALES (est): 3.2MM **Privately Held**
SIC: 3444 Concrete forms, sheet metal

(G-13473)
MICROTAP USA INC
1854 Star Batt Dr (48309-3709)
PHONE..............................248 852-8277
H Roger Rowley, *President*
EMP: 3
SALES (est): 370.7K **Privately Held**
SIC: 3541 Machine tools, metal cutting type

(G-13474)
MID-WEST WIRE PRODUCTS INC
1109 Brompton Rd (48309-4384)
PHONE..............................248 548-3200
Richard Geralds, *CEO*
William Klein, *President*
George Buchanan, *Vice Pres*
Christopher Wozniacki, *Vice Pres*
▼ EMP: 80
SQ FT: 80,000
SALES (est): 13.6MM **Privately Held**
WEB: www.midwestwire.com
SIC: 3496 Miscellaneous fabricated wire products

(G-13475)
MIS CONTROLS INC
2890 Technology Dr (48309-3586)
PHONE..............................586 339-3900
Naji Gebara, *President*
EMP: 11
SALES (est): 1.8MM **Privately Held**
SIC: 3281 Switchboard panels, slate

(G-13476)
MOTOR PARTS INC OF MICHIGAN
2751 Commerce Dr (48309-3815)
PHONE..............................248 852-1522
Earl Moede, *President*
EMP: 21
SQ FT: 18,600
SALES (est): 5.4MM **Privately Held**
SIC: 3714 Motor vehicle engines & parts

(G-13477)
MPI PRODUCTS HOLDINGS LLC (DH)
2129 Austin Ave (48309-3668)
PHONE..............................248 237-3007
Steven Crain, *President*
Mike Putz, *CFO*
EMP: 5 EST: 2012
SALES (est): 155.4MM
SALES (corp-wide): 435.7MM **Privately Held**
SIC: 3448 Prefabricated metal components
HQ: Mpi Global Holdings Corp.
  2129 Austin Ave
  Rochester Hills MI 48309
  248 237-3007

(G-13478)
MPI PRODUCTS LLC (DH)
2129 Austin Ave (48309-3668)
PHONE..............................248 237-3007
Frans Boos, *Vice Pres*
Steve Fitzgerald, *Engineer*
Michael Putz, *CFO*
Wendy Pennewell, *Controller*
Larry Rouhib, *Accounting Mgr*
▼ EMP: 20
SQ FT: 14,000
SALES (est): 206.9MM
SALES (corp-wide): 435.7MM **Privately Held**
SIC: 3469 Metal stampings
HQ: Mpi Products Holdings Llc
  2129 Austin Ave
  Rochester Hills MI 48309
  248 237-3007

(G-13479)
NATIONAL PACKAGING CORPORATION
1150 W Hamlin Rd (48309-3356)
PHONE..............................248 652-3600
William Icikson, *President*
Ester Icikson, *Vice Pres*
EMP: 12 EST: 1978
SQ FT: 40,000
SALES (est): 2MM **Privately Held**
SIC: 5113 2653 Corrugated & solid fiber boxes; corrugated & solid fiber boxes

(G-13480)
NEXIQ TECHNOLOGIES INC
2950 Waterview Dr (48309-4601)
PHONE..............................248 293-8200
Jack Michael, *President*
David Shock, *Manager*
EMP: 12
SALES (est): 1.4MM **Privately Held**
SIC: 7372 Application computer software

(G-13481)
NORGREN AUTOMTN SOLUTIONS LLC
2871 Bond St (48309-3515)
PHONE..............................586 463-3000
Timothy Key, *President*
EMP: 163
SALES (corp-wide): 2.4B **Privately Held**
SIC: 3549 Metalworking machinery
HQ: Norgren Automation Solutions, Llc
  1325 Woodland Dr
  Saline MI 48176
  734 429-4989

(G-13482)
NORTHERN CLASSICS TRUCKS INC
3136 Norton Lawn (48307-5034)
PHONE..............................586 254-2835
EMP: 4
SALES: 300K **Privately Held**
SIC: 3714 Mfg Motor Vehicle Parts/Accessories

(G-13483)
NORTHERN STAMPINGS INC (PA)
Also Called: Nsi
1853 Rochester Indus Ct (48309-3336)
PHONE..............................586 598-6969
Charles Johnson, *President*
Austin Fletcher, *Opers Mgr*
EMP: 10
SQ FT: 5,000
SALES (est): 4.5MM **Privately Held**
WEB: www.northernstampings.com
SIC: 3469 Stamping metal for the trade

(G-13484)
NORTHVILLE CIRCUITS INC
Also Called: N. C. I.
1689 W Hamlin Rd (48309-3312)
PHONE..............................248 853-3232
Frederick P Freeland, *President*
EMP: 8 EST: 1979
SQ FT: 2,616
SALES: 420K **Privately Held**
SIC: 3672 8711 3824 Printed circuit boards; engineering services; fluid meters & counting devices

(G-13485)
NORTHWEST GRAPHIC SERVICES
Also Called: Northwest Advertising
145 S Livernois Rd 277 (48307-1837)
PHONE..............................248 349-9480
Tom Graham, *CEO*
EMP: 7
SALES (est): 924.9K **Privately Held**
SIC: 7311 2752 Advertising consultant; commercial printing, lithographic

(G-13486)
NYLUBE PRODUCTS COMPANY LLC (PA)
Also Called: Nylube Products Div
2299 Star Ct (48309-3625)
PHONE..............................248 852-6500
Shirley Edwards, *Treasurer*
Frank R Edwards,
Frank M Edwards,
▲ EMP: 25 EST: 1936
SQ FT: 30,000
SALES (est): 4.9MM **Privately Held**
WEB: www.nylube.com
SIC: 3646 3534 Commercial indusl & institutional electric lighting fixtures; elevators & equipment

(G-13487)
ONYX MANUFACTURING INC
1663 Star Batt Dr (48309-3706)
PHONE..............................248 687-8611
Raymond Wisniewski, *President*
Stephen Roach III, *Vice Pres*
EMP: 7
SALES (est): 620K **Privately Held**
SIC: 7373 3569 3711 8711 Computer-aided manufacturing (CAM) systems service; computer-aided design (CAD) systems service; robots, assembly line: industrial & commercial; automobile assembly, including specialty automobiles; machine tool design;

(G-13488)
ORACLE SYSTEMS CORPORATION
1365 N Fairview Ln (48306-4133)
PHONE..............................248 614-5139
Thomas Robb, *Branch Mgr*

GEOGRAPHIC SECTION

Rochester Hills - Oakland County (G-13513)

EMP: 252
SALES (corp-wide): 39.5B **Publicly Held**
WEB: www.forcecapital.com
SIC: 7372 Prepackaged software
HQ: Oracle Systems Corporation
500 Oracle Pkwy
Redwood City CA 94065
650 506-7000

(G-13489)
OSCO INC
2937 Waterview Dr (48309-4600)
PHONE 248 852-7310
Jane L Johnson, *President*
Terry Hill, *Engineer*
Chris Pilchak, *Engineer*
Charles Gilliland, *Sales Staff*
EMP: 25
SQ FT: 30,000
SALES (est): 7.3MM **Privately Held**
WEB: www.oscosystems.com
SIC: 3089 Plastic containers, except foam

(G-13490)
PARSON ADHESIVES INC (PA)
3345 W Auburn Rd Ste 107 (48309-5501)
PHONE 248 299-5585
Pete Shah, *Vice Pres*
Chuck Parekh,
▲ **EMP:** 7
SALES (est): 7.1MM **Privately Held**
WEB: www.parsonadhesives.com
SIC: 2891 Adhesives

(G-13491)
PATENT LCNSING CLRINGHOUSE LLC
2791 Research Dr (48309-3575)
PHONE 248 299-7500
EMP: 3
SALES (est): 22.3K
SALES (corp-wide): 4.1B **Privately Held**
WEB: www.duraauto.com
SIC: 3714 Motor vehicle parts & accessories
HQ: Dura Automotive Systems, Llc
1780 Pond Run
Auburn Hills MI 48326

(G-13492)
PGF TECHNOLOGY GROUP INC
2993 Technology Dr (48309-3589)
PHONE 248 852-2800
Naji Gebara, *CEO*
Ghassan Gebara, *President*
EMP: 35
SQ FT: 38,000
SALES (est): 9MM **Privately Held**
WEB: www.pgftech.com
SIC: 3672 3714 Printed circuit boards; automotive wiring harness sets

(G-13493)
PHOTO-TRON CORP
1854 Star Batt Dr (48309-3709)
PHONE 248 852-5200
Roger Rowley, *President*
EMP: 6 **EST:** 1978
SQ FT: 3,000
SALES: 350K **Privately Held**
WEB: www.photo-tron.com
SIC: 3679 Electronic circuits

(G-13494)
PITTSBURGH GLASS WORKS LLC
Also Called: Pgw
3255 W Hamlin Rd (48309-3231)
PHONE 248 371-1700
Joe Stas, *President*
Patricia Philiph, *Manager*
Barb Shaddock, *Manager*
EMP: 200 **Privately Held**
SIC: 3211 2851 2893 2821 Flat glass; paints & allied products; printing ink; plastics materials & resins; alkalies & chlorine; motor vehicle supplies & new parts
HQ: Pittsburgh Glass Works, Llc
323 N Shore Dr Ste 600
Pittsburgh PA 15212

(G-13495)
PLAS-TEC INC
1926 Northfield Dr (48309-3823)
PHONE 248 853-7777
Daniel Loscher, *President*
Nelly Loscher, *Corp Secy*
Paul Loscher, *Vice Pres*
EMP: 8
SQ FT: 15,000
SALES: 900K **Privately Held**
WEB: www.plas-tec-inc.com
SIC: 3544 Special dies & tools; jigs & fixtures

(G-13496)
PLYMOUTH TECHNOLOGY INC
2700 Bond St (48309-3512)
PHONE 248 537-0081
Amanda Christides, *President*
Angela McConachie, *Controller*
Stacey Miller, *Human Resources*
Todd Betts, *Sales Staff*
Tim Omara, *Sales Staff*
▲ **EMP:** 13
SQ FT: 3,000
SALES (est): 8.2MM **Privately Held**
WEB: www.plymouthtechnology.com
SIC: 5074 1629 3589 Water softeners; railroad & subway construction; water filters & softeners, household type

(G-13497)
PRECISION MASTERS INC (PA)
Also Called: Maple Mold Technologies
1985 Northfield Dr (48309-3824)
PHONE 248 853-0308
Doug Bachan, *President*
Kristie Francis, *Controller*
Suzanne Howard, *Accountant*
Christy Francis, *Manager*
Adam Japar, *Manager*
▲ **EMP:** 30
SQ FT: 16,000
SALES (est): 12.8MM **Privately Held**
WEB: www.maplemold.com
SIC: 3544 Industrial molds

(G-13498)
PRECISION PARTS HOLDINGS INC
2129 Austin Ave (48309-3668)
PHONE 248 853-9010
John Lutsi, *Ch of Bd*
Michael Bryant, *President*
Michael Niemic, *Treasurer*
Karen Tuleta, *Admin Sec*
EMP: 1163
SALES (est): 4.8MM
SALES (corp-wide): 757.8MM **Privately Held**
SIC: 3465 3469 3544 Automotive stampings; metal stampings; die sets for metal stamping (presses)
PA: First Atlantic Capital, Ltd.
477 Madison Ave Ste 330
New York NY 10022
212 207-0300

(G-13499)
QUAD PRECISION TOOL CO INC
1763 W Hamlin Rd (48309-3373)
PHONE 248 608-2400
Robert Klein, *President*
Joseph Smyles, *President*
Chris Sneary, *Vice Pres*
William Bedeski, *Treasurer*
EMP: 16
SQ FT: 15,000
SALES (est): 2.4MM **Privately Held**
WEB: www.quadprecisiontool.com
SIC: 3544 Special dies & tools

(G-13500)
QUALCOMM INCORPORATED
359 Jonathan Dr (48307-5262)
PHONE 248 853-2017
EMP: 350
SALES (corp-wide): 24.2B **Publicly Held**
SIC: 3674 Integrated circuits, semiconductor networks, etc.
PA: Qualcomm Incorporated
5775 Morehouse Dr
San Diego CA 92121
858 587-1121

(G-13501)
QUASAR INDUSTRIES INC (PA)
1911 Northfield Dr (48309-3824)
PHONE 248 844-7190
Denise Higgins, *President*
L Ann Peterson, *Corp Secy*
EMP: 120 **EST:** 1967
SQ FT: 40,000
SALES (est): 18.5MM **Privately Held**
WEB: www.quasarindustries.net
SIC: 3544 3599 Forms (molds), for foundry & plastics working machinery; machine shop, jobbing & repair

(G-13502)
QUASAR INDUSTRIES INC
2687 Commerce Dr (48309-3813)
PHONE 248 852-0300
Wayne Miller, *Manager*
EMP: 111
SALES (corp-wide): 18.5MM **Privately Held**
WEB: www.quasarindustries.net
SIC: 3599 3544 Machine shop, jobbing & repair; electrical discharge machining (EDM); forms (molds), for foundry & plastics working machinery
PA: Quasar Industries, Inc.
1911 Northfield Dr
Rochester Hills MI 48309
248 844-7190

(G-13503)
RAVAL USA INC
1939 Northfield Dr (48309-3824)
PHONE 248 260-4050
AVI Livne, *President*
Denise Chodzko, *Plant Mgr*
Sasha Zabel, *Accountant*
▲ **EMP:** 16
SQ FT: 30,000
SALES (est): 3.1MM
SALES (corp-wide): 57.1MM **Privately Held**
SIC: 3714 Gas tanks, motor vehicle
PA: Raval A.C.S. Ltd.
11 Hakotzer
Beer Sheva 84889
895 211-00

(G-13504)
RAYCONNECT INC
2350 Austin Ave Ste 100 (48309-3679)
PHONE 248 265-4000
Earl Brown, *President*
Mick Benedict, *Engineer*
Matt Lutzke, *Engineer*
Robert Tolitsky, *Engineer*
Tim O'Neal, *CFO*
▲ **EMP:** 60
SQ FT: 64,000
SALES (est): 14.6MM
SALES (corp-wide): 177.9K **Privately Held**
WEB: www.rayconnect.com
SIC: 3999 Atomizers, toiletry
HQ: Araymond France
Fixation Fr Agrafe Fr 113 Et 115
Grenoble 38000
476 210-233

(G-13505)
REAGAN TESTING TOOLS
2171 Avon Industrial Dr (48309-3611)
PHONE 248 894-3423
Dave Reagan, *Owner*
EMP: 3
SQ FT: 1,600
SALES (est): 137.5K **Privately Held**
SIC: 3544 Special dies & tools

(G-13506)
ROCHESTER PALLET
2641 W Auburn Rd (48309-4014)
PHONE 248 266-1094
James Lee Miles, *Principal*
EMP: 4
SALES (est): 201.4K **Privately Held**
SIC: 2448 Pallets, wood & wood with metal

(G-13507)
ROCHESTER SPORTS LLC
Also Called: Soccer World's
1900 S Rochester Rd (48307-3534)
PHONE 248 608-6000
Terry Sana, *Owner*
EMP: 12
SALES (est): 2MM **Privately Held**
WEB: www.rochesterphysicaltherapy.com
SIC: 3949 Sporting & athletic goods

(G-13508)
S & J INC
Also Called: Aria Furniture
1860 Star Batt Dr (48309-3709)
PHONE 248 299-0822
Steven Scott, *President*
Jennifer Scott, *Vice Pres*
EMP: 7
SQ FT: 8,000
SALES: 700K **Privately Held**
WEB: www.ariafurniture.com
SIC: 2521 Wood office furniture

(G-13509)
SAARSTEEL INCORPORATED
445 S Livernois Rd # 222 (48307-2576)
PHONE 248 608-0849
Frank Hartgers, *Principal*
▼ **EMP:** 4
SALES (est): 639.9K **Privately Held**
SIC: 3325 Steel foundries

(G-13510)
SANYO MACHINE AMERICA CORP
950 S Rochester Rd (48307-2742)
PHONE 248 651-5911
Masatake Horiba, *President*
Frank Kramarczyk, *President*
Rick Wood, *Facilities Mgr*
David McLaughlin, *Engineer*
Hiro Nomura, *Sales Mgr*
▲ **EMP:** 75
SQ FT: 164,000
SALES (est): 15.1MM **Privately Held**
WEB: www.sanyo-machine.com
SIC: 3548 3569 Spot welding apparatus, electric; assembly machines, non-metalworking

(G-13511)
SCHAENZLE TOOL AND DIE INC
1785 E Hamlin Rd (48307-3625)
PHONE 248 656-0596
Horst W Schaenzle, *President*
Elizabeth Schaenzle, *Vice Pres*
EMP: 5
SQ FT: 7,000
SALES (est): 701.5K **Privately Held**
SIC: 3544 Special dies & tools

(G-13512)
SCIEMETRIC INC (HQ)
1670 Star Batt Dr (48309-3705)
PHONE 248 509-2209
Nathan Sheaff, *CEO*
Don Silverman, *CFO*
Cyndi Gould, *Controller*
Greg Len, *Sales Mgr*
EMP: 13
SQ FT: 4,000
SALES (est): 2.5MM
SALES (corp-wide): 23.6MM **Privately Held**
WEB: www.sciemetric.com
SIC: 3825 7371 Instruments to measure electricity; computer software development
PA: Sciemetric Instruments Inc
359 Terry Fox Dr Suite 100
Kanata ON K2K 2
613 254-7054

(G-13513)
SLW AUTOMOTIVE INC (DH)
Also Called: Slpt Global Pump Group
1955 W Hamlin Rd (48309-3338)
PHONE 248 464-6200
Dean Luo, *President*
Dennis Koenig, *Chief Engr*
◆ **EMP:** 107
SQ FT: 10,000
SALES (est): 32MM
SALES (corp-wide): 93.8MM **Privately Held**
SIC: 3714 Fuel pumps, motor vehicle
HQ: Ningbo Shenglong Automotive Powertrain System Co., Ltd.
No.788, Jinda Road, Industrial Zone, Yinzhou District
Ningbo 31510
574 881-6700

Rochester Hills - Oakland County

(G-13514)
SMART AUTOMATION SYSTEMS INC (PA)
950 S Rochester Rd (48307-2742)
PHONE 248 651-5911
Takeshi Horiba, *Ch of Bd*
Masatake Horiba, *President*
Robert Schuhrke, *Mfg Mgr*
Kazuyoshi Hara, *Director*
▲ **EMP:** 6
SQ FT: 68,000
SALES (est): 4MM **Privately Held**
SIC: 3711 Automobile assembly, including specialty automobiles

(G-13515)
SMARTEYE CORPORATION
2637 Bond St (48309-3510)
PHONE 248 853-4495
James L De Lange, *President*
Don Dollens, *Sales Dir*
Michael Baxter, *Manager*
EMP: 19
SALES (est): 2MM **Privately Held**
WEB: www.smarteyecorporation.com
SIC: 3823 Computer interface equipment for industrial process control

(G-13516)
SPECIAL MOLD ENGINEERING INC (PA)
Also Called: Rochester Grinding
1900 Production Dr (48309-3352)
PHONE 248 652-6600
Marta Macdonald, *President*
Dina J De Weese, *Corp Secy*
Darin Macdonald, *Vice Pres*
David Macdonald, *Vice Pres*
G Keith Macdonald, *Vice Pres*
EMP: 20
SQ FT: 40,000
SALES (est): 9.6MM **Privately Held**
WEB: www.specialmold.com
SIC: 3544 3443 3089 5122 Industrial molds; fabricated plate work (boiler shop); injection molded finished plastic products; pharmaceuticals

(G-13517)
SSB HOLDINGS INC
Also Called: Comtrex
2619 Bond St (48309-3510)
PHONE 586 755-1660
Chain S Sandhu, *President*
Jatinder-Bir S Sandhu, *CFO*
EMP: 26
SQ FT: 120,000
SALES (est): 5MM **Privately Held**
SIC: 3089 3087 Extruded finished plastic products; custom compound purchased resins

(G-13518)
STANT USA CORP
1955 Enterprise Dr (48309-3804)
PHONE 765 827-8104
EMP: 50
SALES (corp-wide): 28B **Privately Held**
SIC: 3714 Motor vehicle parts & accessories
HQ: Stant Usa Corp.
1620 Columbia Ave
Connersville IN 47331

(G-13519)
STYLERITE LABEL CORPORATION (PA)
2140 Avon Industrial Dr (48309-3610)
PHONE 248 853-7977
Andrea Pescijones, *President*
Dick Pesci, *Principal*
Coleen Platz, *Plant Mgr*
Dan Jones, *Opers Staff*
Brigitte Baldwin, *Accounting Mgr*
EMP: 32
SQ FT: 26,000
SALES (est): 3.3MM **Privately Held**
WEB: www.styleritelabel.com
SIC: 2759 Labels & seals: printing

(G-13520)
SU-DAN PLASTICS INC
1949 Rochester Indus Dr (48309-3344)
PHONE 248 651-6035
EMP: 12
SQ FT: 26,000
SALES (est): 1.7MM **Privately Held**
SIC: 3089 3544 Mfg Plastic Products Mfg Dies/Tools/Jigs/Fixtures

(G-13521)
SU-TEC INC
Also Called: Alpha Engineered Refrigeration
1852 Star Batt Dr (48309-3709)
PHONE 248 852-4711
Howard Dibble, *Principal*
EMP: 15
SQ FT: 17,000
SALES (est): 2.5MM **Privately Held**
WEB: www.alphaengref.com
SIC: 3585 Refrigeration equipment, complete

(G-13522)
TA SYSTEMS INC
1842 Rochester Indus Dr (48309-3337)
PHONE 248 656-5150
Tim Gale, *President*
Patrick Burke, *Vice Pres*
Jim Barclay, *Purch Agent*
Jason Clos, *Purchasing*
Mike Sadler, *Engineer*
EMP: 90
SQ FT: 45,000
SALES (est): 25.2MM **Privately Held**
WEB: www.ta-systems.com
SIC: 3549 Assembly machines, including robotic

(G-13523)
TACS AUTOMATION LLC (PA)
Also Called: Transporation Automation Conve
1856 Star Batt Dr (48309-3709)
P.O. Box 180289, Utica (48318-0289)
PHONE 586 446-8828
Kevin Quaglia, *President*
Michael Scott, *Vice Pres*
Sherly Waldowski, *Controller*
◆ **EMP:** 14 **EST:** 2007
SQ FT: 12,000
SALES: 8.5MM **Privately Held**
SIC: 3535 Robotic conveyors

(G-13524)
TESCA USA INC
2638 Bond St (48309-3509)
PHONE 586 991-0744
Christopher Glinka, *General Mgr*
David J Glinka, *Vice Pres*
Chris Glinka, *Sales Staff*
EMP: 43
SQ FT: 34,300
SALES (est): 6.1MM **Privately Held**
WEB: www.cmaincorp.com
SIC: 2396 3089 3465 3714 Automotive trimmings, fabric; injection molding of plastics; automotive stampings; automotive wiring harness sets

(G-13525)
THREE-DIMENSIONAL SERVICES INC
Also Called: 3-Dimensional Service
2547 Product Dr (48309-3806)
PHONE 248 852-1333
Douglas Peterson, *President*
Vince Brown, *Counsel*
Alan R Peterson, *Vice Pres*
Gary Malega, *Plant Mgr*
Wes Wehner, *QC Mgr*
EMP: 200
SQ FT: 54,000
SALES (est): 25.1MM **Privately Held**
SIC: 7539 8711 3545 Machine shop, automotive; engineering services; machine tool accessories

(G-13526)
THUNDER TECHNOLOGIES LLC
1618 Star Batt Dr (48309-3705)
PHONE 248 844-4875
Andrew Kalinowski, *Sales Staff*
Kim Kalinowski, *Mktg Dir*
Marc Kalinowski,
EMP: 12
SALES (est): 2.6MM **Privately Held**
SIC: 3069 3599 3052 Sheets, hard rubber; flexible metal hose, tubing & bellows; rubber & plastics hose & beltings

(G-13527)
TOMS SIGN SERVICE
Also Called: Tom's Sign
2926 Grant Rd (48309-3623)
PHONE 248 852-3550
Tom Tioran, *Owner*
EMP: 9
SALES (est): 453.1K **Privately Held**
SIC: 3993 Signs & advertising specialties

(G-13528)
TORSION CONTROL PRODUCTS INC
1900 Northfield Dr (48309-3823)
PHONE 248 537-1900
Timothy A Thane, *President*
Michael Mackool, *Vice Pres*
Michael Youngerman, *Vice Pres*
EMP: 19
SQ FT: 11,300
SALES: 20MM
SALES (corp-wide): 3.5B **Publicly Held**
WEB: www.torsioncontrol.com
SIC: 3714 8711 Transmission housings or parts, motor vehicle; engineering services
PA: The Timken Company
4500 Mount Pleasant St Nw
North Canton OH 44720
234 262-3000

(G-13529)
TOTAL PLASTICS RESOURCES LLC
1661 Northfield Dr (48309-3825)
PHONE 248 299-9500
Vince R BR, *Manager*
EMP: 10
SALES (corp-wide): 863.9MM **Privately Held**
WEB: www.totalplastics.com
SIC: 5162 3089 Plastics sheets & rods; plastic processing
HQ: Total Plastics Resources Llc
2810 N Burdick St Ste A
Kalamazoo MI 49004
269 344-0009

(G-13530)
TOWING & EQUIPMENT MAGAZINE
1700 W Hamlin Rd Ste 100 (48309-3346)
PHONE 248 601-1385
Jim McNeely, *President*
Kristofer Petruska, *Sales Staff*
EMP: 8
SALES (est): 658.2K **Privately Held**
SIC: 2721 Magazines: publishing only, not printed on site

(G-13531)
TRICO PRODUCTS CORPORATION (HQ)
3255 W Hamlin Rd (48309-3231)
PHONE 248 371-1700
James Wiggins, *CEO*
Frank Arellano, *Transportation*
Norma Resendez, *Purch Agent*
Mike Currie, *Engineer*
Lauren Pilette, *Marketing Mgr*
◆ **EMP:** 150
SQ FT: 75,000
SALES (est): 332.6MM **Privately Held**
WEB: www.tricoproducts.com
SIC: 3069 3082 8734 8731 Tubing, rubber; tubes, unsupported plastic; testing laboratories; commercial physical research; windshield wiper systems, motor vehicle
PA: Ktri Holdings, Inc.
127 Public Sq Ste 5110
Cleveland OH 44114
216 371-1700

(G-13532)
TROY MILLWORK INC
1841 Northfield Dr (48309-3822)
PHONE 248 852-8383
Terrence T Cruice, *President*
Terrance T Cruice, *President*
EMP: 8
SQ FT: 5,600
SALES (est): 1.2MM **Privately Held**
SIC: 2431 Millwork

(G-13533)
U S EQUIPMENT CO (HQ)
Also Called: Roto Flo
3667 Merriweather Ln (48306-3642)
PHONE 313 526-8300
Paul Simon, *Ch of Bd*
George Simon II, *President*
April Simon, *VP Sales*
▲ **EMP:** 25 **EST:** 1946
SALES (est): 3.7MM
SALES (corp-wide): 12.1MM **Privately Held**
WEB: www.usequipment.com
SIC: 3541 5084 7629 Numerically controlled metal cutting machine tools; industrial machinery & equipment; electrical repair shops
PA: U. S. Group, Inc.
3667 Merriweather Ln
Rochester Hills MI 48306
313 372-7900

(G-13534)
U S GROUP INC (PA)
3667 Merriweather Ln (48306-3642)
PHONE 313 372-7900
Paul Simon, *Chairman*
George Simon, *Vice Pres*
▼ **EMP:** 3
SQ FT: 70,000
SALES (est): 12.1MM **Privately Held**
WEB: www.usgroup.com
SIC: 5084 3599 Industrial machinery & equipment; machine shop, jobbing & repair

(G-13535)
UNIQUE FABRICATING INC
2817 Bond St (48309-3515)
PHONE 248 853-2333
Douglas Stahl, *President*
EMP: 35
SQ FT: 22,000
SALES (corp-wide): 174.9MM **Publicly Held**
WEB: www.uniquefab.com
SIC: 3053 3086 Gaskets, all materials; plastics foam products
HQ: Unique Fabricating Na, Inc.
800 Standard Pkwy
Auburn Hills MI 48326
248 853-2333

(G-13536)
UNIVERSAL TUBE INC
2607 Bond St (48309-3510)
PHONE 248 853-5100
Karl Konen, *Exec VP*
Robert Hammond, *Vice Pres*
Rick Webb, *Safety Mgr*
Rebecca Tyszkowski, *Human Res Mgr*
Sherri Coffen, *Manager*
▲ **EMP:** 160
SQ FT: 75,200
SALES (est): 35.5MM **Privately Held**
SIC: 3498 Tube fabricating (contract bending & shaping)

(G-13537)
URGENT PLASTIC SERVICES INC (PA)
2777 Product Dr (48309-3810)
PHONE 248 852-8999
Douglas Peterson, *President*
Jeffrey Peterson, *General Mgr*
Alan R Peterson, *Vice Pres*
Alan Peteson, *Vice Pres*
Jeffrey Felker, *Plant Mgr*
EMP: 3
SQ FT: 54,000
SALES (est): 14.7MM **Privately Held**
SIC: 3089 Injection molded finished plastic products

(G-13538)
US ENERGY SYSTEMS INC
Also Called: Uses
1761 John R Rd (48307-5704)
PHONE 248 765-7995
EMP: 3
SALES (est): 141.3K **Privately Held**
SIC: 3999 Mfg Misc Products

GEOGRAPHIC SECTION

(G-13539)
VALIANT SPECIALTIES INC
301 Hacker St Unit 3 (48307-2636)
PHONE..................................248 656-1001
James Riley, *President*
EMP: 4
SQ FT: 1,500
SALES: 60K **Privately Held**
SIC: 7692 Welding repair

(G-13540)
WARA CONSTRUCTION COMPANY LLC
2927 Waterview Dr (48309-4600)
PHONE..................................248 299-2410
EMP: 99
SQ FT: 7,500
SALES (est): 1.9MM **Privately Held**
SIC: 1382 1389 4212 8711 Oil/Gas Exploration Svcs Oil/Gas Field Services Oil/Gas Field Services Local Trucking Operator Engineering Services

(G-13541)
WARREN SCRW PRODUCTS INC
1733 Mead Rd (48306-3567)
PHONE..................................586 994-0342
EMP: 3
SALES (est): 145.6K **Privately Held**
SIC: 3451 Screw machine products

(G-13542)
WEB LITHO INC
560 John R Rd (48307-2349)
PHONE..................................586 803-9000
Fax: 586 268-5046
EMP: 8
SQ FT: 12,000
SALES (est): 1.6MM **Privately Held**
SIC: 2752 Lithographic Commercial Printing

(G-13543)
WEBASTO ROOF SYSTEMS INC (DH)
Also Called: Webasto Roofing
1757 Northfield Dr (48309-3819)
PHONE..................................248 997-5100
Andre Schoenekaes, *CEO*
Tim Thompson, *Materials Mgr*
Susan Pedlar, *Buyer*
Marissa Elwart, *Engineer*
Ralph Gigliotti, *Engineer*
▲ **EMP:** 260
SQ FT: 94,000
SALES (est): 102.2MM
SALES (corp-wide): 411.9K **Privately Held**
WEB: www.webasto.com
SIC: 3714 3441 Sun roofs, motor vehicle; fabricated structural metal
HQ: Webasto Se
    Kraillinger Str. 5
    Stockdorf 82131
    898 579-40

(G-13544)
WEBASTO ROOF SYSTEMS INC
Also Called: Webasto Sunroofs
2700 Product Dr (48309-3809)
PHONE..................................248 299-2000
Fred Olson, *President*
EMP: 550
SQ FT: 74,000
SALES (corp-wide): 411.9K **Privately Held**
WEB: www.webasto.com
SIC: 3469 Metal stampings
HQ: Webasto Roof Systems Inc.
    1757 Northfield Dr
    Rochester Hills MI 48309
    248 997-5100

(G-13545)
WEBASTO ROOF SYSTEMS INC
Also Called: Webasto Assembly
1757 Northfield Dr (48309-3819)
PHONE..................................248 997-5100
Michelle Mitchel, *Manager*
EMP: 12

SALES (corp-wide): 411.9K **Privately Held**
WEB: www.webasto.com
SIC: 3469 3714 3441 Metal stampings; motor vehicle parts & accessories; fabricated structural metal
HQ: Webasto Roof Systems Inc.
    1757 Northfield Dr
    Rochester Hills MI 48309
    248 997-5100

(G-13546)
WEC GROUP LLC
1850 Northfield Dr (48309-3821)
PHONE..................................248 260-4252
Greg Wolf, *Mng Member*
EMP: 19
SALES: 6MM **Privately Held**
SIC: 2396 Automotive & apparel trimmings

(G-13547)
WILLIAMS BUSINESS SERVICES
551 Brittany Ct (48309-2613)
PHONE..................................248 280-0073
Kari Williams, *President*
Dawn Chatman, *Owner*
EMP: 3
SQ FT: 1,350
SALES: 600K **Privately Held**
WEB: www.marwoodmetal.com
SIC: 3444 Sheet metalwork

(G-13548)
WIRIC CORPORATION
2781 Bond St (48309-3513)
PHONE..................................248 598-5297
Philip H Warburton, *President*
◆ **EMP:** 36
SQ FT: 18,000
SALES (est): 10.7MM **Privately Held**
SIC: 3714 3694 Automotive wiring harness sets; automotive electrical equipment

(G-13549)
YASKAWA AMERICA INC
2050 Austin Ave (48309-3665)
PHONE..................................248 668-8800
Glenn Jackson, *Branch Mgr*
EMP: 11 **Privately Held**
SIC: 3549 Assembly machines, including robotic
HQ: Yaskawa America, Inc.
    2121 Norman Dr
    Waukegan IL 60085
    847 887-7000

(G-13550)
YASKAWA AMERICA INC
2050 Austin Ave (48309-3665)
PHONE..................................248 668-8800
EMP: 6
SALES (corp-wide): 3.3B **Privately Held**
SIC: 3569 Mfg Robotic Assembly Systems
HQ: Yaskawa America, Inc.
    2121 Norman Dr
    Waukegan IL 60085
    847 887-7000

(G-13551)
YATES CIDER MILL INC
1990 E Avon Rd (48307-6815)
PHONE..................................248 651-8300
Leslie J Posey, *President*
Karen Posey, *Admin Sec*
EMP: 7 **EST:** 1863
SQ FT: 9,800
SALES (est): 914K **Privately Held**
WEB: www.yatescidermill.com
SIC: 2099 0175 5431 5441 Cider, nonalcoholic; apple orchard; fruit stands or markets; candy, nut & confectionery stores; doughnuts

Rock
Delta County

(G-13552)
AFFORDABLE NEON ENT
17498 State Highway M35 (49880-9437)
PHONE..................................906 356-6168
EMP: 3

SALES (est): 163.5K **Privately Held**
SIC: 2813 Mfg Industrial Gases

(G-13553)
K2 ENGINEERING INC
14444 State Highway M35 (49880)
PHONE..................................906 356-6303
Jed Koski, *President*
Robert Koski, *Vice Pres*
EMP: 3
SQ FT: 5,000
SALES (est): 317.2K **Privately Held**
SIC: 3531 Forestry related equipment

(G-13554)
KANERVA FOREST PRODUCTS INC
15096 Autumn Ln (49880-9525)
P.O. Box 55 (49880-0055)
PHONE..................................906 356-6061
Terry Kanerva, *President*
EMP: 8
SALES: 97K **Privately Held**
SIC: 2411 Logging camps & contractors

Rockford
Kent County

(G-13555)
ACCRA-WIRE CONTROLS INC (PA)
Also Called: A W C
10891 Northland Dr Ne (49341-8627)
PHONE..................................616 866-3434
Johnnie Jones, *President*
EMP: 10
SQ FT: 34,668
SALES: 1.4MM **Privately Held**
WEB: www.accrainc.com
SIC: 3496 Miscellaneous fabricated wire products

(G-13556)
AIR SUPPLY COMPANY INC
7459 9 Mile Rd Ne (49341-8466)
PHONE..................................616 874-7751
Richard Gates, *President*
Angela Gates, *Vice Pres*
EMP: 3
SQ FT: 4,000
SALES (est): 784.1K **Privately Held**
SIC: 3053 7699 Packing: steam engines, pipe joints, air compressors, etc.; compressor repair

(G-13557)
ALLOY EXCHANGE INC (PA)
300 Rockford Park Dr Ne (49341-7818)
PHONE..................................616 863-0640
Robert W Corl III, *President*
Greg Thebo, *VP Opers*
Becky Mitchell, *Controller*
EMP: 15
SQ FT: 56,000
SALES (est): 3.9MM **Privately Held**
WEB: www.alloyexchangeinc.com
SIC: 3082 Unsupported plastics profile shapes

(G-13558)
AXIS MOLD WORKS INC
8005 Childsdale Ave Ne (49341-7459)
PHONE..................................616 866-2222
Dan Adams, *President*
John Liefferrs, *Vice Pres*
EMP: 17
SALES (est): 3.2MM **Privately Held**
SIC: 3544 Industrial molds

(G-13559)
BOLD AMMO & GUNS INC
Also Called: Bold Services
5083 Natchez Ct Ne (49341-9308)
PHONE..................................616 826-0913
Terrance Debold, *Principal*
Willam Baker, *Opers Staff*
Sheri Plakos-Debold, *Admin Sec*
EMP: 5
SQ FT: 400

SALES (est): 211.8K **Privately Held**
SIC: 3482 0781 3544 0783 Small arms ammunition; landscape services; special dies, tools, jigs & fixtures; removal services, bush & tree

(G-13560)
BYRNE ELEC SPECIALISTS INC (PA)
320 Byrne Industrial Dr (49341-1083)
PHONE..................................616 866-3461
Norman R Byrne, *President*
Rosemary Byrne, *Vice Pres*
Patrick Huver, *Engineer*
Kristen Hummel, *Marketing Staff*
George Fabis, *Technology*
▲ **EMP:** 203
SQ FT: 52,000
SALES (est): 55.8MM **Privately Held**
SIC: 3679 Harness assemblies for electronic use: wire or cable

(G-13561)
BYRNE ELEC SPECIALISTS INC
725 Byrne Industrial Dr (49341-1089)
PHONE..................................616 866-3461
Norman R Byrne, *Branch Mgr*
EMP: 5
SALES (est): 607.8K
SALES (corp-wide): 55.8MM **Privately Held**
SIC: 3679 Harness assemblies for electronic use: wire or cable
PA: Byrne Electrical Specialists, Inc.
    320 Byrne Industrial Dr
    Rockford MI 49341
    616 866-3461

(G-13562)
BYRNE TOOL & DIE INC
316 Byrne Industrial Dr (49341-1083)
PHONE..................................616 866-4479
Norman R Byrne, *CEO*
Dan Hosford, *General Mgr*
Jill Maksimowski, *Accountant*
EMP: 15
SQ FT: 10,000
SALES: 2.7MM **Privately Held**
WEB: www.byrne-electrical.com
SIC: 3599 3544 Machine shop, jobbing & repair; special dies, tools, jigs & fixtures

(G-13563)
CANNONSBURG WOOD PRODUCTS INC
10251 Northland Dr Ne (49341-9730)
P.O. Box 678 (49341-0678)
PHONE..................................616 866-4459
Dave Powers Sr, *President*
EMP: 20
SQ FT: 5,000
SALES (est): 3MM **Privately Held**
WEB: www.cannonsburgwoodproducts.com
SIC: 2448 Pallets, wood

(G-13564)
CTC ACQUISITION COMPANY LLC (HQ)
Also Called: Grand Rapids Controls Company
825 Northland Dr Ne (49341-7655)
PHONE..................................616 884-7100
Scott Todd, *Warehouse Mgr*
Penny Gohn, *Purchasing*
Dave Bach, *Engineer*
Emily Foster, *Engineer*
Eric Pierman, *Engineer*
▲ **EMP:** 101
SQ FT: 82,000
SALES (est): 7.1MM **Privately Held**
WEB: www.grcontrols.com
SIC: 3625 3679 Actuators, industrial; flow actuated electrical switches; harness assemblies for electronic use: wire or cable
PA: C. T. Charlton & Associates, Inc.
    24000 Greater Mack Ave
    Saint Clair Shores MI 48080
    586 775-2900

(G-13565)
D & D BUFFING & POLISHING
6270 12 Mile Rd Ne (49341-9704)
PHONE..................................616 866-1015
Dan Heiss, *President*
EMP: 3

Rockford - Kent County (G-13566) — GEOGRAPHIC SECTION

SALES (est): 178.4K **Privately Held**
SIC: 3471 Polishing, metals or formed products

(G-13566)
DERBY FABG SOLUTIONS LLC
Also Called: Aftech
687 Byrne Industrial Dr (49341-1085)
PHONE 616 866-1650
EMP: 80
SALES (corp-wide): 28.1MM **Privately Held**
SIC: 3089 3086 2499 3069 Injection molding of plastics; plastics foam products; cork & cork products; rubber hardware; gaskets, all materials
PA: Derby Fabricating Solutions, Llc
4500 Produce Rd
Louisville KY 40218
502 964-9135

(G-13567)
DISTINCTIVE MACHINE CORP
300 Byrne Industrial Dr B (49341-1423)
PHONE 616 433-4111
Gary Berkenpas, *President*
Jeff Tait, *Vice Pres*
EMP: 21
SQ FT: 8,300
SALES (est): 5MM **Privately Held**
WEB: www.distinctive-machine.com
SIC: 3599 Machine shop, jobbing & repair

(G-13568)
EZ VENT LLC
8235 Belding Rd Ne (49341-9628)
PHONE 616 874-2787
Nichole Nelson, *Opers Mgr*
Robert Fortin, *Mng Member*
EMP: 6
SALES: 48K **Privately Held**
WEB: www.glsdsn.com
SIC: 2741 5031 Directories: publishing & printing; windows

(G-13569)
FOREST ELDERS PRODUCTS INC
10367 Northland Dr Ne (49341-9730)
P.O. Box 557, Cedar Springs (49319-0557)
PHONE 616 866-9317
Jerry Elder, *President*
Chad Elder, *Vice Pres*
EMP: 15
SQ FT: 6,000
SALES (est): 2.4MM **Privately Held**
SIC: 2421 2426 Lumber: rough, sawed or planed; hardwood dimension & flooring mills

(G-13570)
H R P MOTOR SPORTS INC
8775 Belding Rd Ne (49341-9361)
PHONE 616 874-6338
Brad Hulings, *President*
Stacie Hulings, *Webmaster*
EMP: 3
SQ FT: 9,000
SALES (est): 440.4K **Privately Held**
SIC: 3714 5599 5013 Motor vehicle parts & accessories; snowmobiles; motor vehicle supplies & new parts

(G-13571)
HERMANS BOY
220 Northland Dr Ne (49341-1042)
PHONE 616 866-2900
Floyd Havemeier, *Owner*
EMP: 7
SQ FT: 4,500
SALES (est): 568.9K **Privately Held**
WEB: www.hermansboy.com
SIC: 5441 5499 5149 2095 Candy, nut & confectionery stores; coffee; coffee, green or roasted; coffee roasting (except by wholesale grocers)

(G-13572)
HY-TEST INC
9341 Courtland Dr Ne (49351-1002)
PHONE 616 866-5500
Blake Krueger, *President*
EMP: 5
SALES (est): 515K
SALES (corp-wide): 2.2B **Publicly Held**
WEB: www.wolverineworldwide.com
SIC: 3143 Boots, dress or casual: men's
PA: Wolverine World Wide, Inc.
9341 Courtland Dr Ne
Rockford MI 49351
616 866-5500

(G-13573)
ITW DAHTI SEATING
206 Byrne Industrial Dr (49341-1075)
PHONE 616 866-1323
Eric Wiederhoeft, *Plant Mgr*
Rob Bratty, *Engineer*
Randy Sayers, *Engineer*
Rick Vandekopple, *Project Engr*
Michelle Coleman, *Controller*
▼ **EMP:** 22
SALES (est): 3.3MM **Privately Held**
SIC: 2531 Public building & related furniture

(G-13574)
JOYCE ZAHRADNIK
Also Called: Altec Financial
8321 Kreuter Rd Ne (49341-9032)
PHONE 616 874-3350
Joyce Zahradnik, *Owner*
EMP: 3
SQ FT: 100
SALES (est): 365.9K **Privately Held**
SIC: 7389 3499 Financial services; novelties & giftware, including trophies

(G-13575)
K & T TOOL AND DIE INC
7805 Childsdale Ave Ne (49341-7487)
PHONE 616 884-5900
Witt Kurtz, *President*
Rick Kurtz, *President*
EMP: 11
SQ FT: 24,000
SALES: 2.4MM **Privately Held**
SIC: 3544 Special dies & tools; jigs & fixtures

(G-13576)
KARLA-VON CERAMICS INC
Also Called: Karlavon Ceramics
10580 Northland Dr Ne (49341-8010)
PHONE 616 866-0563
Dolores Herrema, *President*
Veronica Woznika, *Vice Pres*
EMP: 3
SQ FT: 4,800
SALES: 60K **Privately Held**
SIC: 3269 5719 Art & ornamental ware, pottery; pottery

(G-13577)
KNAPE INDUSTRIES INC
10701 Northland Dr Ne (49341-8008)
PHONE 616 866-1651
William Knape, *President*
Herbert F Knape, *Chairman*
◆ **EMP:** 20
SQ FT: 34,000
SALES: 1MM **Privately Held**
SIC: 3479 Painting of metal products

(G-13578)
MARREL CORPORATION
4750 14 Mile Rd Ne (49341-8427)
PHONE 616 863-9155
Vincent Revol, *President*
Brenda Toppel, *Office Mgr*
▲ **EMP:** 5
SQ FT: 20,000
SALES (est): 1.7MM
SALES (corp-wide): 832.2K **Privately Held**
WEB: www.marrel.com
SIC: 5084 3711 Hydraulic systems equipment & supplies; motor vehicles & car bodies
HQ: Marrel
Lieu Dit Zone Industrielle
Andrezieux-Boutheon 42160
477 362-961

(G-13579)
MI BREW LLC
Also Called: Hideout Brewing Company, The
321 Northland Dr Ne (49341-1025)
PHONE 616 361-9658
Nicholas Humphrey, *President*
Scott Colson, *Treasurer*
EMP: 17
SALES: 600K **Privately Held**
SIC: 2084 2082 Wines; ale (alcoholic beverage)

(G-13580)
MJB CONCEPTS INC
Also Called: MJB Creative Concepts
113 Courtland St (49341-1031)
PHONE 616 866-1470
Mark Bivins, *President*
EMP: 4
SQ FT: 3,200
SALES (est): 335.2K **Privately Held**
SIC: 2395 2759 5094 Embroidery & art needlework; engraving; trophies

(G-13581)
MOTOR CITY AEROSPACE
10500 Harvard Ave Ne (49341-8471)
PHONE 616 916-5473
Russell Golemba, *Owner*
EMP: 20
SALES (est): 930.7K **Privately Held**
SIC: 3728 Aircraft parts & equipment

(G-13582)
NEWKIRK AND ASSOCIATES INC
Also Called: Whiteboard Depot
9767 Shaw Creek Ct Ne (49341-9777)
PHONE 616 863-9899
Chris Newkirk, *President*
EMP: 5
SALES (est): 659K **Privately Held**
WEB: www.whiteboarddepot.com
SIC: 2599 Boards: planning, display, notice

(G-13583)
NORTHLAND TOOL & DIE INC
10399 Northland Dr Ne (49341-9730)
PHONE 616 866-4451
Richard Cossin, *President*
David Cossin, *Vice Pres*
Perri Cossin, *Vice Pres*
EMP: 25
SQ FT: 18,500
SALES (est): 4MM **Privately Held**
WEB: www.ntdusa.com
SIC: 3544 Special dies & tools

(G-13584)
NORTHPORT MANUFACTURING INC
Also Called: Best Tackle Manufacturing Co
8553 Browmyer Ct Ne (49341-9382)
PHONE 616 874-6455
Lon Hilliker, *President*
William Dommer, *Vice Pres*
EMP: 3
SQ FT: 2,200
SALES (est): 100K **Privately Held**
SIC: 3949 Fishing tackle, general

(G-13585)
PETERSON JIG & FIXTURE INC (PA)
Also Called: Precision Jig & Fixture
301 Rockford Park Dr Ne (49341-7817)
PHONE 616 866-8296
David Schuiling, *President*
Anthony Calain, *QC Mgr*
Scott Hansen, *QC Mgr*
Nicholas Ketelaar, *Design Engr*
Gene Burley, *VP Bus Dvlpt*
EMP: 45
SQ FT: 20,000
SALES (est): 10.7MM **Privately Held**
WEB: www.pjfinc.com
SIC: 3544 Special dies & tools; jigs: inspection, gauging & checking

(G-13586)
RIVERVIEW PRODUCTS INC
201 Byrne Industrial Dr (49341-1078)
PHONE 616 866-1305
Christopher J Martin, *President*
EMP: 5
SQ FT: 10,000
SALES (est): 841.6K **Privately Held**
SIC: 3469 Stamping metal for the trade

(G-13587)
ROCKFORD CONTRACT MFG
Also Called: Wizard Electronics
198 Rollingwood Dr (49341-1192)
P.O. Box 207 (49341-0207)
PHONE 616 304-3837
Paul Michael Magnan, *President*
EMP: 5
SQ FT: 5,200
SALES (est): 492.9K **Privately Held**
SIC: 3679 Electronic circuits

(G-13588)
ROCKFORD MOLDING & TRIM
8317 Woodcrest Dr Ne (49341-8507)
PHONE 616 874-8997
Richard Kirchhoff, *President*
EMP: 4
SALES (est): 189.3K **Privately Held**
SIC: 3089 Molding primary plastic

(G-13589)
SAUCONY INC
Wolverine Children's Group
9341 Courtland Dr Ne (49351-1002)
PHONE 616 866-5500
EMP: 3
SALES (corp-wide): 2.2B **Publicly Held**
SIC: 3149 Children's footwear, except athletic
HQ: Saucony, Inc.
500 Totten Pond Rd Ste 1
Waltham MA 02451
617 824-6000

(G-13590)
SHORE-MATE PRODUCTS LLC
Also Called: Manning Marine
9260 Belding Rd Ne (49341-9386)
PHONE 616 874-5438
Ryan Earl, *Sales Staff*
Kenneth Spencer,
EMP: 3
SQ FT: 42,000
SALES (est): 452.4K **Privately Held**
SIC: 3536 3448 Boat lifts; docks: prefabricated metal

(G-13591)
SS SERVICES
2431 13 Mile Rd Ne (49341-8021)
PHONE 616 866-6453
Steve Staniulis, *Principal*
EMP: 3
SALES (est): 327.7K **Privately Held**
SIC: 3531 Backhoes

(G-13592)
TAMARACK UPHL & INTERIORS
Also Called: Langerak Upholstery
9024 Algoma Ave Ne (49341-8043)
PHONE 616 866-2922
Thomas H Langerak, *President*
EMP: 4 **EST:** 1939
SALES (est): 250K **Privately Held**
SIC: 7641 2512 5714 Reupholstery; upholstered household furniture; draperies; upholstery materials

(G-13593)
THOMPSON WELL DRILLING
12300 Stultz St Ne (49341-9535)
PHONE 616 754-5032
Daniel Thompson, *Owner*
Dan Thompson, *Contractor*
EMP: 6 **EST:** 1965
SQ FT: 2,500
SALES (est): 469.4K **Privately Held**
SIC: 1381 1781 Drilling oil & gas wells; water well drilling

(G-13594)
TRENDWELL ENERGY CORPORATION
10 E Bridge St Ste 200 (49341-1296)
P.O. Box 560 (49341-0560)
PHONE 616 866-5024
Thomas H Mall, *CEO*
Todd R Mall, *President*
Angela Adams, *Vice Pres*
Steve Rapanos, *Manager*
David Heinz, *Executive*
EMP: 15
SQ FT: 2,000

GEOGRAPHIC SECTION

SALES: 10MM **Privately Held**
WEB: www.trendwellenergy.com
SIC: **1311** Crude petroleum production; natural gas production

(G-13595)
UNIVERSAL PRODUCTS INC
210 Rockford Park Dr Ne (49341-7827)
P.O. Box 369, Howard City (49329-0369)
PHONE...............................231 937-5555
Kenneth Koster, *President*
Dale Cederquist, *Vice Pres*
William Herberg, *Vice Pres*
▲ EMP: 41
SQ FT: 26,500
SALES (est): 14.1MM **Privately Held**
SIC: **3089** Injection molded finished plastic products

(G-13596)
WESTERN ADHESIVE INC
6768 Kitson Dr Ne (49341-9423)
PHONE...............................616 874-5869
David Trebilcock, *President*
EMP: 10
SALES: 500K **Privately Held**
SIC: **2891** Adhesives

(G-13597)
WOLVERINE PROCUREMENT INC
Also Called: Wolverine Worldwide
175 S Main St (49341-1221)
PHONE...............................616 866-9521
Pgskin Leather, *Vice Pres*
EMP: 50
SALES (corp-wide): 2.2B **Publicly Held**
SIC: **3143** 3144 3131 Men's footwear, except athletic; women's footwear, except athletic; footwear cut stock
HQ: Wolverine Procurement, Inc.
9341 Ne Courland Dr
Rockford MI 49341
616 866-5500

(G-13598)
WOLVERINE PROCUREMENT INC (HQ)
9341 Ne Courland Dr (49341)
PHONE...............................616 866-5500
Gordon Baird, *President*
Gail Kirchhoff, *Marketing Staff*
▲ EMP: 10
SALES (est): 45.4MM
SALES (corp-wide): 2.2B **Publicly Held**
SIC: **3143** 3021 Men's footwear, except athletic; rubber & plastics footwear
PA: Wolverine World Wide, Inc.
9341 Courtland Dr Ne
Rockford MI 49351
616 866-5500

(G-13599)
WOLVERINE SLIPPER GROUP INC (HQ)
9341 Courtland Dr Ne Hb1141 (49351-1002)
PHONE...............................616 866-5500
Blake W Krueger, *President*
John Estes, *Vice Pres*
Kenneth A Grady, *Admin Sec*
Cherrelle Jones, *Admin Asst*
EMP: 6
SALES (est): 20.2MM
SALES (corp-wide): 2.2B **Publicly Held**
SIC: **3142** House slippers
PA: Wolverine World Wide, Inc.
9341 Courtland Dr Ne
Rockford MI 49351
616 866-5500

(G-13600)
WOLVERINE WORLD WIDE INC (PA)
Also Called: Wolverine Worldwide
9341 Courtland Dr Ne (49351-0001)
PHONE...............................616 866-5500
Blake W Krueger, *Ch of Bd*
Chris Hufnagel, *President*
Ken Syrba, *Chairman*
James D Zwiers, *Exec VP*
Amy M Klimek, *Senior VP*
◆ EMP: 227 EST: 1883
SQ FT: 225,000
SALES: 2.2B **Publicly Held**
WEB: www.wolverineworldwide.com
SIC: **3143** 3149 3144 3111 Men's footwear, except athletic; athletic shoes, except rubber or plastic; women's footwear, except athletic; leather tanning & finishing

(G-13601)
WOLVERINE WORLD WIDE INC
9343 Courtland Dr Ne (49351-0003)
PHONE...............................616 863-3983
Mylinh Truong, *Database Admin*
EMP: 3
SALES (corp-wide): 2.2B **Publicly Held**
SIC: **3143** Men's footwear, except athletic
PA: Wolverine World Wide, Inc.
9341 Courtland Dr Ne
Rockford MI 49351
616 866-5500

(G-13602)
WOLVERINE WORLD WIDE INC
Also Called: Wolverine Leathers
123 N Main St (49341-1079)
PHONE...............................616 866-5500
Stephen Lyons, *CEO*
EMP: 7
SALES (corp-wide): 2.2B **Publicly Held**
WEB: www.wolverineworldwide.com
SIC: **3143** Men's footwear, except athletic
PA: Wolverine World Wide, Inc.
9341 Courtland Dr Ne
Rockford MI 49351
616 866-5500

Rockwood
Wayne County

(G-13603)
AIS AUTOMATION SYSTEMS INC
20950 Woodruff Rd (48173-9791)
PHONE...............................734 365-2384
Paul Brazier, *President*
EMP: 14
SQ FT: 24,000
SALES (est): 5.5MM **Privately Held**
SIC: **3549** Assembly machines, including robotic

(G-13604)
GIBRALTAR CANVAS INC
28599 N Gibraltar Rd (48173-9733)
PHONE...............................734 675-4891
Jeffery A Bickerstaff, *President*
EMP: 3
SALES (est): 200K **Privately Held**
SIC: **2394** 5162 Liners & covers, fabric: made from purchased materials; plastics products

(G-13605)
INDUSTRIAL FABRICATING INC
28233 W Fort St (48173)
PHONE...............................734 676-2710
Robert E Joaquin, *President*
Joel Joaquin, *Vice Pres*
EMP: 10
SQ FT: 30,000
SALES (est): 1.8MM **Privately Held**
SIC: **3441** Fabricated structural metal

(G-13606)
LAFRONTERA TORTILLAS INC
32845 Cleveland St (48173-9602)
PHONE...............................734 231-1701
Orfanidia Garza, *President*
Lito Garza, *General Mgr*
Karina Garza, *Accounting Mgr*
EMP: 4
SALES (est): 437.7K **Privately Held**
SIC: **2099** Tortillas, fresh or refrigerated

(G-13607)
LET LOVE RULE
21391 Russell St (48173-9749)
PHONE...............................734 749-7435
EMP: 5 EST: 2015
SALES (est): 550.4K **Privately Held**
SIC: **2759** Screen printing

(G-13608)
MILLPLEX MACHINE PRODUCTS INC
23539 W Ditner Dr (48173-1235)
PHONE...............................734 497-0763
Randolph Weaver, *President*
Judy Weaver, *Vice Pres*
EMP: 3
SALES: 100K **Privately Held**
SIC: **3599** Machine shop, jobbing & repair

(G-13609)
N A SUEZ
Also Called: SUEZ N.A.
34004 W Jefferson Ave (48173-9639)
PHONE...............................734 379-3855
David Dupuis, *Branch Mgr*
EMP: 7
SALES (corp-wide): 94.7MM **Privately Held**
SIC: **2899** Water treating compounds
HQ: Suez Water Indiana Llc
461 From Rd Ste F400
Paramus NJ 07652
201 767-9300

(G-13610)
PENSTONE INC
31605 Gossett Dr (48173-9700)
PHONE...............................734 379-3160
EMP: 20
SQ FT: 57,640
SALES (est): 2.2MM
SALES (corp-wide): 355.2MM **Privately Held**
SIC: **3231** 3429 Mfg Products-Purchased Glass Mfg Hardware
PA: Ishizaki Honten Co.,Ltd.
1-2-15, Yanoshimmachi, Aki-Ku
Hiroshima HIR 736-0
828 201-600

(G-13611)
R J MARSHALL COMPANY
21220 Huron River Dr (48173-9601)
PHONE...............................734 379-4044
Bill Miller, *Manager*
EMP: 24
SALES (corp-wide): 20.3MM **Privately Held**
WEB: www.rjmarshallco.com
SIC: **2899** 3295 Fire retardant chemicals; minerals, ground or treated
PA: The R J Marshall Company
26776 W 12 Mile Rd # 201
Southfield MI 48034
248 353-4100

Rodney
Mecosta County

(G-13612)
CHIPPEWA STONE & GRAVEL INC
15240 110th Ave (49342-9757)
PHONE...............................231 867-5757
Walter Hazen, *President*
Deb Wiersma, *Office Mgr*
EMP: 4
SQ FT: 400
SALES (est): 432.4K **Privately Held**
SIC: **1442** Gravel mining

Rogers City
Presque Isle County

(G-13613)
CADILLAC PRODUCTS INC
Rogers City Plant
4858 Williams Rd (49779-9606)
PHONE...............................989 766-2294
Steven Harris, *Branch Mgr*
Art Ditullio, *Info Tech Dir*
Jerome Balingit, *Technician*
Neil Young, *Maintence Staff*
EMP: 83
SALES (corp-wide): 168.4MM **Privately Held**
SIC: **3089** 2621 2673 5199 Automotive parts, plastic; paper mills; bags: plastic, laminated & coated; fabrics, yarns & knit goods; motor vehicle parts & accessories; unsupported plastics film & sheet
PA: Cadillac Products, Inc.
5800 Crooks Rd Ste 100
Troy MI 48098
248 813-8200

(G-13614)
CARMEUSE LIME & STONE INC
1035 Calcite Rd (49779-1900)
PHONE...............................989 734-2131
Ivy Cook, *Branch Mgr*
Alan Pines, *Maintence Staff*
EMP: 9
SALES (corp-wide): 177.9K **Privately Held**
SIC: **1422** Crushed & broken limestone
HQ: Carmeuse Lime & Stone, Inc.
11 Stanwix St Fl 21
Pittsburgh PA 15222
412 995-5500

(G-13615)
E H TULGESTKA & SONS INC
1160 Hwy F 21 S (49779)
P.O. Box 169 (49779-0169)
PHONE...............................989 734-2129
Erhardt Tulgestka Sr, *President*
Christopher Tulgestka, *Treasurer*
Nancy Tulgestka, *Admin Sec*
EMP: 15
SQ FT: 1,000
SALES (est): 2.6MM **Privately Held**
SIC: **2411** 2421 4213 Logging camps & contractors; sawmills & planing mills, general; trucking, except local

(G-13616)
LEES READY MIX INC
3232 Birchwood Dr (49779-1551)
PHONE...............................989 734-7666
EMP: 4 EST: 1985
SQ FT: 3,000
SALES: 500K **Privately Held**
SIC: **3273** Mfg Ready-Mixed Concrete

(G-13617)
NOWAKS WINDOW DOOR & CAB CO
4003 Us Highway 23 S (49779-9648)
PHONE...............................989 734-2808
Shirley Nowak, *President*
Donald White, *Vice Pres*
EMP: 8 EST: 1951
SQ FT: 6,000
SALES (est): 1.6MM **Privately Held**
SIC: **5211** 2431 Windows, storm: wood or metal; windows, wood; doors, wood

(G-13618)
O-N MINERALS MICHIGAN COMPANY
Also Called: Carmeuse Lime & Stone
1035 Calcite Rd (49779-1900)
PHONE...............................989 734-2131
EMP: 3
SALES (corp-wide): 177.9K **Privately Held**
SIC: **1422** Crushed & broken limestone
HQ: O-N Minerals (Michigan) Company
11 Stanwix St Fl 21
Pittsburgh PA 15222
412 995-5500

(G-13619)
O-N MINERALS MICHIGAN COMPANY (PA)
Also Called: Division Oglebay Norton Co
1035 Calcite Rd (49779-1900)
PHONE...............................989 734-2131
Michelle Harris, *President*
Joe Chevreaux, *Plant Mgr*
Darryl Hubble, *Buyer*
Dean Roof, *Project Engr*
Dave Altman, *Supervisor*
EMP: 200
SQ FT: 2,000

Rogers City - Presque Isle County (G-13620)

SALES (est): 58.1MM **Privately Held**
SIC: **1411** 1422 5032 Limestone, dimension-quarrying; dolomite, dimension-quarrying; crushed & broken limestone; limestone

(G-13620)
PERSONS INC
285 S Bradley Hwy Ste 2 (49779-2141)
PHONE..................989 734-3835
Richard M Lewandowski, *Principal*
EMP: 4
SALES (est): 439.7K **Privately Held**
SIC: **2992** Oils & greases, blending & compounding

(G-13621)
PRESQUE ISLE NEWSPAPERS INC
Also Called: Advance
104 S 3rd St (49779-1710)
P.O. Box 50 (49779-0050)
PHONE..................989 734-2105
Richard Lamb, *President*
Cella Bade, *Adv Mgr*
EMP: 10 **EST:** 1878
SQ FT: 3,250
SALES (est): 651.9K **Privately Held**
SIC: **2711** 2741 Job printing & newspaper publishing combined; shopping news: publishing only, not printed on site

(G-13622)
SCHLEBEN FOREST PRODUCTS INC
Also Called: Schleben Rhinold Forest Pdts
3302 S Ward Branch Rd (49779-9678)
PHONE..................989 734-2858
EMP: 4
SALES (est): 520K **Privately Held**
SIC: **5099** 2421 5031 Whol Durable Goods Sawmill/Planing Mill Whol Lumber/Plywood/Millwork

Romeo
Macomb County

(G-13623)
ALCO PLASTICS INC (PA)
160 E Pond Dr (48065-4902)
PHONE..................586 752-4527
Daniel J Conway, *President*
Joshua Hautamaki, *General Mgr*
Cathy Conway, *Vice Pres*
Darren Oreilly, *Opers Staff*
Derrick Miller, *QC Mgr*
EMP: 100
SQ FT: 66,000
SALES (est): 20.5MM **Privately Held**
WEB: www.alcoplastics.com
SIC: **3089** Injection molding of plastics

(G-13624)
AWCCO USA INCORPORATED
171 Shafer Dr (48065-4913)
PHONE..................586 336-9135
Arthur Capon, *President*
Miriam Capon, *CFO*
Karen Kloska, *Office Mgr*
Perry Kloska, *Manager*
EMP: 6 **EST:** 2011
SQ FT: 14,000
SALES (est): 961K **Privately Held**
SIC: **3321** 7373 3369 Gray iron castings; computer-aided design (CAD) systems service; computer-aided manufacturing (CAM) systems service; nonferrous foundries

(G-13625)
CAMMAND MACHINING LLC
101 Shafer Dr (48065-4913)
PHONE..................586 752-0366
Jim More, *Manager*
Clarence A Meltzer Jr,
Jeff Bond,
EMP: 13
SQ FT: 7,500
SALES: 1.2MM **Privately Held**
SIC: **3544** Special dies, tools, jigs & fixtures

(G-13626)
D & N BENDING CORP (PA)
Also Called: D & N Casting
150 Shafer Dr (48065-4907)
PHONE..................586 752-5511
Brian Murray, *President*
Steve Murray, *Vice Pres*
▲ **EMP:** 34
SQ FT: 12,000
SALES (est): 50.7MM **Privately Held**
WEB: www.dnbend.com
SIC: **3465** Moldings or trim, automobile: stamped metal

(G-13627)
D & N GAGE INC
161 E Pond Dr (48065-4903)
PHONE..................586 336-2110
Dan Schweiger, *President*
Lori Schweiger, *Manager*
EMP: 10
SALES (est): 2.3MM **Privately Held**
SIC: **3829** Gauges, motor vehicle: oil pressure, water temperature; instrument board gauges, automotive: computerized

(G-13628)
FRAN TECHNOLOGY LLC
132 Shafer Dr (48065-4907)
PHONE..................586 336-4085
Joseph Juszczyk, *Principal*
EMP: 3
SALES (est): 294.6K **Privately Held**
SIC: **3599** Machine shop, jobbing & repair

(G-13629)
HENSHAW INC
100 Shafer Dr (48065-4907)
PHONE..................586 752-0700
Dave Clark, *CEO*
Franco Cimaroli, *Manager*
EMP: 38
SQ FT: 42,000
SALES (est): 9.5MM **Privately Held**
WEB: www.henshawelectric.com
SIC: **8711** 3823 3613 Industrial engineers; industrial instrmnts msrmnt display/control process variable; switchgear & switchboard apparatus

(G-13630)
I S P COATINGS CORP
130 Shafer Dr (48065-4902)
PHONE..................586 752-5020
John Malinich, *President*
EMP: 30
SQ FT: 15,000
SALES (est): 7MM **Privately Held**
WEB: www.ispcc.us
SIC: **3479** Coating of metals & formed products; painting, coating & hot dipping

(G-13631)
KRIEWALL ENTERPRISES INC
140 Shafer Dr (48065-4907)
PHONE..................586 336-0600
Edwin C Kriewall, *CEO*
Theresa Chase, *President*
Sandra Kriewall, *Vice Pres*
Todd Kriewall, *Sales Executive*
EMP: 20
SQ FT: 10,000
SALES (est): 3.4MM **Privately Held**
WEB: www.keiprototype.com
SIC: **3599** 3444 3469 3999 Machine shop, jobbing & repair; sheet metalwork; metal stampings; barber & beauty shop equipment; manufactured hardware (general); fabricated structural metal

(G-13632)
LITTLE BUILDINGS INC
161 Shafer Dr (48065-4913)
PHONE..................586 752-7100
James Sudomier, *President*
Linda Sudomier, *Vice Pres*
Nicole Fitch, *Admin Asst*
EMP: 7
SQ FT: 8,800
SALES (est): 1.1MM **Privately Held**
WEB: www.littlebuildingsinc.com
SIC: **3448** 2452 Buildings, portable: prefabricated metal; prefabricated wood buildings

(G-13633)
MC PHERSON INDUSTRIAL CORP
Also Called: Quality Chaser Co Div
120 E Pond Dr (48065-4902)
P.O. Box 496 (48065-0496)
PHONE..................586 752-5555
Keith Mc Pherson, *President*
Urlsa Mc Pherson, *Corp Secy*
EMP: 51
SQ FT: 8,000
SALES (est): 7.4MM **Privately Held**
WEB: www.qualitychaser.com
SIC: **3545** 3541 Thread cutting dies; machine tools, metal cutting type

(G-13634)
P & K TECHNOLOGIES INC
111 Shafer Dr (48065-4913)
PHONE..................586 336-9545
Paul Kasper, *President*
EMP: 3
SQ FT: 3,200
SALES (est): 512.5K **Privately Held**
SIC: **3089** Injection molding of plastics

(G-13635)
PETROLEUM RESOURCES INC (PA)
134 W Saint Clair St (48065-4656)
P.O. Box 466 (48065-0466)
PHONE..................586 752-7856
Ernest G Moeller Jr, *President*
Stanley N Masoner, *Principal*
Michael E Moeller, *Principal*
Charles A Brennecker Jr, *Vice Pres*
EMP: 6 **EST:** 1962
SALES (est): 3.9MM **Privately Held**
SIC: **1311** Crude petroleum production

(G-13636)
RAMTEC CORP
409 E Saint Clair St (48065-5270)
PHONE..................586 752-9270
Mark Nichols, *President*
Johnny Nichols, *Vice Pres*
EMP: 10
SALES (est): 1MM **Privately Held**
WEB: www.ramtech-phone.com
SIC: **3599** 7389 Electrical discharge machining (EDM); grinding, precision: commercial or industrial

(G-13637)
ROMEO PRINTING COMPANY INC
225 N Main St (48065-4617)
PHONE..................586 752-9003
Jon Malzahn, *President*
Christine Malzahn, *Vice Pres*
Ted Czajka, *Director*
Bill Parker, *Director*
EMP: 4
SQ FT: 2,360
SALES: 400K **Privately Held**
SIC: **2752** 2759 Commercial printing, offset; letterpress printing

(G-13638)
SEAL SUPPORT SYSTEMS INC (DH)
Also Called: Seal Pots
141 Shafer Dr (48065-4913)
PHONE..................586 331-7251
Juan Johnson, *General Mgr*
EMP: 30
SQ FT: 7,250
SALES (est): 6.4MM
SALES (corp-wide): 11B **Privately Held**
WEB: www.sealpotsinc.com
SIC: **3443** 2891 Heat exchangers, condensers & components; heat exchangers, plate type; heat exchangers: coolers (after, inter), condensers, etc.; adhesives & sealants
HQ: Eagleburgmann Industries Lp
10035 Brookriver Dr
Houston TX 77040
713 939-9515

(G-13639)
STARTECH SERVICES INC
111 E Pond Dr (48065-4903)
PHONE..................586 752-2460
Len Robare, *President*

Carrie Zink, *Vice Pres*
EMP: 3
SALES (est): 174.2K **Privately Held**
SIC: **7336** 3465 Graphic arts & related design; automotive stampings

(G-13640)
TK MOLD & ENGINEERING INC
131 Shafer Dr (48065-4913)
PHONE..................586 752-5840
Thomas W Barr, *Principal*
Tom Barr, *Manager*
Sam Viviano, *Manager*
◆ **EMP:** 34
SALES (est): 6.3MM **Privately Held**
WEB: www.tkmoldeng.com
SIC: **3544** Industrial molds

(G-13641)
WHITCOMB AND SONS SIGN CO INC
Also Called: Whitcomb Sign
315 E Lafayette St (48065-5239)
PHONE..................586 752-3576
Lawrence Whitcomb, *President*
Leslie Whitcomb, *Vice Pres*
EMP: 5
SQ FT: 5,500
SALES (est): 554.4K **Privately Held**
SIC: **7336** 3993 Graphic arts & related design; electric signs

(G-13642)
WRANOSKY & SONS INC
105 S Main St (48065-5125)
PHONE..................586 336-9761
Gary John Wranosky, *Principal*
EMP: 8
SALES (est): 1MM **Privately Held**
SIC: **3423** Carpenters' hand tools, except saws: levels, chisels, etc.

(G-13643)
ZF PASSIVE SAFETY SYSTEMS US
Also Called: TRW Oss
14761 E32 Mile Rd (48065)
PHONE..................586 752-1409
Julieta Santacruz, *Branch Mgr*
EMP: 50
SALES (corp-wide): 216.2K **Privately Held**
SIC: **3714** Motor vehicle parts & accessories
HQ: Zf Passive Safety Systems Us Inc.
4505 26 Mile Rd
Washington MI 48094
586 232-7200

Romulus
Wayne County

(G-13644)
A S AUTO LIGHTS INC
15326 Oakwood Dr (48174-3610)
PHONE..................734 941-1164
EMP: 3 **EST:** 2015
SALES (est): 123.3K **Privately Held**
SIC: **3647** Motor vehicle lighting equipment

(G-13645)
A Y SAND AND GRAVEL
27416 Ecorse Rd (48174-2427)
PHONE..................313 779-4825
Zena Farhat, *Principal*
EMP: 3
SALES (est): 134.8K **Privately Held**
SIC: **1442** Construction sand & gravel

(G-13646)
A123 SYSTEMS LLC
Also Called: A123 Systems Rmulus Operations
38100 Ecorse Rd (48174-5306)
PHONE..................734 772-0600
Leonard Kastamo, *Design Engr*
John Patel, *CFO*
Michael O'Kronley, *Exec Dir*
Sam Trinch, *Officer*
EMP: 222
SALES (corp-wide): 2.9B **Privately Held**
SIC: **3691** Storage batteries

GEOGRAPHIC SECTION

Romulus - Wayne County (G-13672)

HQ: A123 Systems Llc
27101 Cabaret Dr
Novi MI 48377
248 412-9249

(G-13647)
ABRASIVE SERVICES INCORPORATED
29040 Northline Rd (48174-2836)
PHONE..................................734 941-2144
Steve Belinc, *Owner*
EMP: 5 **EST:** 2007
SALES (est): 406K **Privately Held**
SIC: 3471 3541 4812 4813 Electroplating & plating; buffing & polishing machines; cellular telephone services; data telephone communications

(G-13648)
AE GROUP LLC
Also Called: Aerostar Manufacturing
28275 Northline Rd (48174-2829)
PHONE..................................734 942-0615
John Shipley, *Buyer*
Nathan Ortner, *Engineer*
Lonnie Hampton, *Controller*
Sheila Ossowski, *Accounting Mgr*
Robert Johnson, *VP Sales*
▲ **EMP:** 150
SQ FT: 50,000
SALES (est): 35.8MM **Privately Held**
WEB: www.aerostarmfg.com
SIC: 3599 Machine shop, jobbing & repair

(G-13649)
AIR CONDITIONING PRODUCTS CO (PA)
30350 Ecorse Rd (48174-3595)
PHONE..................................734 326-0050
Philip K Mebus Jr, *President*
Christopher Mebus, *President*
Ed Kirstein, *Engineer*
Tim Fleitz, *Sales Mgr*
Peter Kay, *Exec Dir*
▲ **EMP:** 100
SQ FT: 110,000
SALES (est): 18.3MM **Privately Held**
WEB: www.acpshutters.com
SIC: 3444 3354 2431 Ventilators, sheet metal; aluminum extruded products; millwork

(G-13650)
ALLIANCE POLYMERS AND SVCS LLC
Also Called: APS Elastomers
30735 Cypress Rd Ste 400 (48174-3541)
PHONE..................................734 710-6700
Stephane Morin,
Roger Huarng,
▲ **EMP:** 2
SALES (est): 5.4MM **Privately Held**
SIC: 2821 4225 Thermoplastic materials; general warehousing

(G-13651)
APPROVED AIRCRAFT ACCESSORIES
Also Called: Aero Test
29300 Goddard Rd (48174-2704)
P.O. Box 666, Taylor (48180-0666)
PHONE..................................734 946-9000
Gail A Yancheck, *President*
Jerry Helgeson, *Vice Pres*
Jerry Wicker, *Mfg Staff*
EMP: 9
SQ FT: 7,500
SALES (est): 1.2MM **Privately Held**
WEB: www.aerotest.com
SIC: 3724 4581 Aircraft engines & engine parts; airports, flying fields & services

(G-13652)
ASTRO LITE WINDOW COMPANY INC
Also Called: Astro Lite Window Co Factory
28615 Beverly Rd (48174-2405)
PHONE..................................734 326-2455
Herb Francis, *Opers-Prdtn-Mfg*
EMP: 25
SALES (corp-wide): 5.9MM **Privately Held**
SIC: 3211 Window glass, clear & colored

PA: Astro Lite Window Company Inc
22900 Ecorse Rd
Taylor MI 48180
313 291-5900

(G-13653)
AZTEC MANUFACTURING CORP
15378 Oakwood Dr (48174-3653)
PHONE..................................734 942-7433
Francis Lopez, *President*
Rick Johnson, *Corp Secy*
Robert Reyna, *Supervisor*
Gil Ruicci, *Shareholder*
▲ **EMP:** 130
SQ FT: 73,300
SALES (est): 25.3MM **Privately Held**
WEB: www.aztecmfgcorp.com
SIC: 3714 Motor vehicle parts & accessories

(G-13654)
B & K BUFFING INC
29040 Northline Rd (48174-2836)
PHONE..................................734 941-2144
Steve Belinc, *President*
Gerald Krohn, *Vice Pres*
EMP: 6
SQ FT: 3,200
SALES (est): 312K **Privately Held**
SIC: 3471 Buffing for the trade; finishing, metals or formed products; polishing, metals or formed products

(G-13655)
BAWDEN INDUSTRIES INC
29909 Beverly Rd (48174-2031)
PHONE..................................734 721-6414
John Bawden, *President*
EMP: 12
SQ FT: 4,500
SALES (est): 1.2MM **Privately Held**
SIC: 3544 Dies & die holders for metal cutting, forming, die casting

(G-13656)
BENLEE INC (PA)
30383 Ecorse Rd (48174-3521)
PHONE..................................586 791-1830
Gregory Brown, *CEO*
William B Wolok, *President*
David Gibb, *CFO*
EMP: 35
SALES (est): 6MM **Privately Held**
WEB: www.benlee.com
SIC: 3715 7538 5511 7539 Truck trailers; general truck repair; trucks, tractors & trailers: new & used; automotive repair shops

(G-13657)
BIOBEST USA INC
11700 Metro Airport Ste (48174)
PHONE..................................734 626-5693
Richard Ward, *CEO*
EMP: 4
SALES (est): 592.3K **Privately Held**
SIC: 2879 Pesticides, agricultural or household

(G-13658)
BIRCLAR ELECTRIC AND ELEC LLC
12060 Wayne Rd (48174-3776)
PHONE..................................734 941-7400
Tim Martindale, *CEO*
James Fitzwater, *Division Mgr*
Emily Tucker, *Buyer*
Jim Bunker, *Supervisor*
Ed Dodson, *Supervisor*
EMP: 18
SALES (est): 3.8MM **Privately Held**
WEB: www.birclar.com
SIC: 7694 Electric motor repair

(G-13659)
BODYCOTE THERMAL PROC INC
38100 Jay Kay Dr (48174-4000)
PHONE..................................313 442-2387
Walter D'Souza, *Branch Mgr*
EMP: 3
SALES (corp-wide): 935.8MM **Privately Held**
SIC: 3398 Brazing (hardening) of metal

HQ: Bodycote Thermal Processing, Inc.
12700 Park Central Dr # 700
Dallas TX 75251
214 904-2420

(G-13660)
CARTEX CORPORATION
Also Called: Dynaflex
15573 Oakwood Dr (48174-3656)
PHONE..................................734 857-5961
Stephen Murphy, *Branch Mgr*
EMP: 80
SQ FT: 41,000
SALES (corp-wide): 1.9B **Privately Held**
WEB: www.woodbridgegroup.com
SIC: 7532 2821 Top & body repair & paint shops; plastics materials & resins
HQ: Cartex Corporation
1515 Equity Dr 100
Troy MI 48084
610 759-1650

(G-13661)
CASTINO CORPORATION (PA)
16777 Wahrman St (48174-3633)
PHONE..................................734 941-7200
Robert L Castino Jr, *President*
EMP: 40 **EST:** 1981
SQ FT: 25,000
SALES (est): 8.9MM **Privately Held**
WEB: www.castino.com
SIC: 3089 Injection molding of plastics

(G-13662)
CENTRAL OHIO PAPER & PACKG INC
Also Called: Breckenridge Paper & Packaging
9675 Harrison Ste 100-101 (48174-2526)
P.O. Box 16, Taylor (48180-0016)
PHONE..................................734 955-9960
James Ostermyer, *Branch Mgr*
EMP: 4 **Privately Held**
WEB: www.breckpack.com
SIC: 2671 Paper coated or laminated for packaging
PA: Central Ohio Paper & Packaging, Inc.
2350 University Dr E
Huron OH 44839

(G-13663)
COLFRAN INDUSTRIAL SALES INC
38127 Ecorse Rd (48174-1349)
PHONE..................................734 595-8920
Carl Stevens, *President*
EMP: 17
SALES (est): 1.9MM **Privately Held**
SIC: 5169 3341 Industrial chemicals; secondary nonferrous metals

(G-13664)
CONTROL ELECTRONICS
29231 Northline Rd (48174-2835)
PHONE..................................734 941-5008
John Mayor, *President*
EMP: 34
SALES (est): 1.9MM **Privately Held**
SIC: 3679 Electronic components

(G-13665)
CRYSTAL CUT TOOL INC
10360 Harrison (48174-2635)
PHONE..................................734 494-5076
Wayne Robinson, *President*
Wesley Wiley, *Corp Secy*
EMP: 7
SQ FT: 6,000
SALES (est): 1MM **Privately Held**
WEB: www.crystalcuttool.com
SIC: 3545 Diamond cutting tools for turning, boring, burnishing, etc.

(G-13666)
DETROIT TARPAULIN REPR SP INC
6760 Metro Plex Dr (48174-2012)
PHONE..................................734 955-8200
Guy D Sullins, *President*
Lou Stephenson, *Principal*
Roy Sullins, *Principal*
Thomas Stephenson, *Vice Pres*
Donald Sullins, *Vice Pres*
▲ **EMP:** 24 **EST:** 1945
SQ FT: 32,000

SALES (est): 3.4MM **Privately Held**
SIC: 2394 5013 Tarpaulins, fabric: made from purchased materials; automotive trim

(G-13667)
DST INDUSTRIES INC (HQ)
Also Called: Diversified Services Tech
34364 Goddard Rd (48174-3451)
PHONE..................................734 941-0300
Brenda Lewo, *President*
Joe Lewo, *Principal*
Don Snell, *COO*
Michael Krohn, *Project Mgr*
Mark Krench, *Purchasing*
◆ **EMP:** 225
SQ FT: 125,000
SALES (est): 29.8MM
SALES (corp-wide): 31.1MM **Privately Held**
WEB: www.dstindustries.com
SIC: 3465 Fenders, automobile: stamped or pressed metal
PA: J. L. International, Inc.
34364 Goddard Rd
Romulus MI 48174
734 941-0300

(G-13668)
E & W CABINET & COUNTER
8925 Hannan Rd (48174-1318)
PHONE..................................734 895-7497
Walter Froehlich, *Owner*
EMP: 3
SQ FT: 7,000
SALES: 150K **Privately Held**
SIC: 2434 Vanities, bathroom: wood

(G-13669)
EAGLE RIDGE PAPER LTD
15355 Oakwood Dr (48174-3611)
PHONE..................................248 376-9503
EMP: 3
SALES (corp-wide): 22.6MM **Privately Held**
SIC: 2621 Printing paper
HQ: Eagle Ridge Paper Ltd.
100 S Anaheim Blvd # 250
Anaheim CA 92805
714 780-1799

(G-13670)
ELEPHANT HEAD LLC
35465 Goddard Rd (48174-1436)
PHONE..................................734 256-4555
Melvin Johnson, *CEO*
EMP: 8
SQ FT: 3,500
SALES (est): 168.8K **Privately Held**
SIC: 2396 5999 7389 Screen printing on fabric articles; banners, flags, decals & posters; advertising, promotional & trade show services

(G-13671)
ELKINS MACHINE & TOOL CO INC
27482 Northline Rd (48174-2826)
PHONE..................................734 941-0266
Mike Nicastro, *Opers Staff*
Radu Stingu, *Opers Staff*
Anca Stingu, *Engineer*
Ken Buzo, *Controller*
Jerry Verhoven, *Sales Staff*
EMP: 30
SALES (corp-wide): 6.4MM **Privately Held**
WEB: www.elkinsmachine.com
SIC: 3599 3451 Amusement park equipment; screw machine products
PA: Elkins Machine & Tool Co Inc
27510 Northline Rd
Romulus MI 48174
734 941-0266

(G-13672)
ELKINS MACHINE & TOOL CO INC (PA)
27510 Northline Rd (48174-2826)
PHONE..................................734 941-0266
Tim Swoish, *President*
Rick Sollars, *Vice Pres*
Jerry Verhoven, *Opers Mgr*
Ryan Parker, *Administration*
EMP: 33
SQ FT: 11,500

(PA)=Parent Co (HQ)=Headquarters (DH)=Div Headquarters
✪ = New Business established in last 2 years

Romulus - Wayne County (G-13673)

GEOGRAPHIC SECTION

SALES (est): 6.4MM **Privately Held**
WEB: www.elkinsmachine.com
SIC: 3599 3451 3469 Machine shop, jobbing & repair; screw machine products; metal stampings

(G-13673)
EQ RESOURCE RECOVERY INC (HQ)
36345 Van Born Rd (48174-4057)
PHONE 734 727-5500
Jeffrey R Feeler, *President*
Simon Bell, *Vice Pres*
Eric Gerratt, *Treasurer*
Wayne Ipsen, *Admin Sec*
EMP: 3
SQ FT: 15,000
SALES (est): 7.1MM
SALES (corp-wide): 565.9MM **Publicly Held**
SIC: 2869 Solvents, organic
PA: Us Ecology, Inc.
  101 S Capitol Blvd # 1000
  Boise ID 83702
  208 331-8400

(G-13674)
EUCLID MACHINE & MFG CO
29030 Northline Rd (48174-2836)
PHONE 734 941-1080
Robert Kluba, *President*
Brian Kluba, *Vice Pres*
Dolores Kluba, *Admin Sec*
EMP: 12 EST: 1978
SQ FT: 7,200
SALES (est): 951.6K **Privately Held**
WEB: www.euclidgages.com
SIC: 3599 Machine shop, jobbing & repair

(G-13675)
FASTENTECH INC
Also Called: Fabristeel Romulus Div
7845 Middlebelt Rd # 200 (48174-2174)
PHONE 313 299-8500
Richard Ward, *Branch Mgr*
EMP: 3
SALES (corp-wide): 3.4B **Privately Held**
SIC: 3452 Nuts, metal
HQ: Fastentech, Inc.
  8500 Normandale Lake Blvd
  Minneapolis MN 55437
  952 921-2090

(G-13676)
FEDERAL SCREW WORKS (PA)
34846 Goddard Rd (48174-3400)
PHONE 734 941-4211
Thomas Zurschmiede, *CEO*
W T Zurschmiede Jr, *Ch of Bd*
Robert F Zurschmiede, *Exec VP*
Jan Buckler, *Vice Pres*
Jeffrey M Harness, *Vice Pres*
◆ EMP: 15
SQ FT: 12,000
SALES (est): 2.4K **Privately Held**
WEB: www.federalscrew.com
SIC: 3444 3592 3452 Studs & joists, sheet metal; pistons & piston rings; bolts, metal

(G-13677)
FEDERAL SCREW WORKS
Also Called: Romulus Nut Division
34846 Goddard Rd (48174-3400)
PHONE 734 941-4211
R F Zurschmiede, *President*
EMP: 127
SALES (corp-wide): 2.4K **Privately Held**
WEB: www.federalscrew.com
SIC: 3357 3452 Building wire & cable, nonferrous; nuts, metal
PA: Federal Screw Works
  34846 Goddard Rd
  Romulus MI 48174
  734 941-4211

(G-13678)
FINTEX LLC
8900 Inkster Rd (48174-2695)
PHONE 734 946-3100
David Purcell, *Manager*
Mike Rapp, *Executive*
Kent M Desjardins,
▲ EMP: 28

SALES (est): 4.4MM **Privately Held**
SIC: 3471 Electroplating of metals or formed products

(G-13679)
FUTURE TOOL AND MACHINE INC
28900 Goddard Rd (48174-2700)
PHONE 734 946-2100
Leslee Franzel, *CEO*
Larry Franzel, *President*
Raymond Wojt, *QC Mgr*
EMP: 45
SQ FT: 50,000
SALES (est): 6MM **Privately Held**
WEB: www.futuretool.com
SIC: 3599 Machine shop, jobbing & repair

(G-13680)
GLOBAL AUTOMOTIVE PRODUCTS INC
Also Called: Gap
38100 Jay Kay Dr (48174-4000)
P.O. Box 891, Melville NY (11747-0891)
PHONE 734 589-6179
Paul Foertsch, *COO*
▲ EMP: 24 EST: 2013
SQ FT: 72,000
SALES (est): 3.4MM **Privately Held**
SIC: 3089 Automotive parts, plastic

(G-13681)
GM POWERTRAIN-ROMULUS ENGINE
36880 Ecorse Rd (48174-1395)
PHONE 734 595-5203
Ralph Pierce, *Manager*
EMP: 5
SALES (est): 1.3MM **Privately Held**
SIC: 3519 Internal combustion engines

(G-13682)
GMA INDUSTRIES INC
38127 Ecorse Rd (48174-1349)
PHONE 734 595-7300
Carl Stevens, *President*
Coleen Stevens, *Corp Secy*
Donald Wood, *Plant Mgr*
Erin Jameson, *Opers Staff*
Eric Zalewski, *Engineer*
▲ EMP: 20
SQ FT: 26,000
SALES (est): 3.7MM **Privately Held**
WEB: www.gmaind.com
SIC: 3291 Steel shot abrasive; grit, steel; aluminum oxide (fused) abrasives

(G-13683)
GROUP B INDUSTRIES INC
15399 Oakwood Dr (48174-3655)
PHONE 734 941-6640
Bonnie Burry, *President*
EMP: 6
SQ FT: 9,600
SALES (est): 594.8K **Privately Held**
WEB: www.groupbind.com
SIC: 3544 Special dies, tools, jigs & fixtures

(G-13684)
H & J MFG CONSULTING SVCS CORP
15771 S Huron River Dr (48174-3668)
PHONE 734 941-8314
Bill Junge, *President*
EMP: 7
SQ FT: 28,000
SALES (est): 590K **Privately Held**
WEB: www.hjmfg.com
SIC: 3479 2842 Painting of metal products; specialty cleaning, polishes & sanitation goods

(G-13685)
HOME CITY ICE COMPANY
15475 Oakwood Dr (48174-3655)
PHONE 734 955-9094
Greg Hug, *Branch Mgr*
EMP: 50
SALES (corp-wide): 234.4MM **Privately Held**
WEB: www.homecityice.com
SIC: 2097 Ice cubes

PA: The Home City Ice Company
  6045 Bridgetown Rd Ste 1
  Cincinnati OH 45248
  513 574-1800

(G-13686)
HUYS ELECTRODES INC
6810 Metro Plex Dr # 200 (48174-2062)
PHONE 215 723-4897
Barry R Clymer, *Principal*
EMP: 6
SALES (est): 1MM **Privately Held**
SIC: 3448 Prefabricated metal components

(G-13687)
INTERNATIONAL PAINT STRIPPING (PA)
15300 Oakwood Dr (48174-3610)
PHONE 734 942-0500
Joseph Kochanoski, *President*
Mark Kochanoski, *Vice Pres*
Carol Kochanoski, *Treasurer*
EMP: 18 EST: 1982
SQ FT: 21,200
SALES (est): 2.1MM **Privately Held**
SIC: 3471 Cleaning & descaling metal products

(G-13688)
INTERNATIONAL PAINT STRIPPING
15326 Oakwood Dr (48174-3610)
PHONE 734 942-0500
Joseph Kochananoski, *President*
EMP: 16
SALES (corp-wide): 2.1MM **Privately Held**
SIC: 3471 Cleaning & descaling metal products
PA: International Paint Stripping Inc
  15300 Oakwood Dr
  Romulus MI 48174
  734 942-0500

(G-13689)
J C GOSS COMPANY
15500 Oakwood Dr (48174-3670)
PHONE 313 259-3520
Richard H Dancy Jr, *President*
Robert Brobst, *General Mgr*
Robert Dancy, *Vice Pres*
EMP: 3
SALES: 750K **Privately Held**
WEB: www.jcgoss.com
SIC: 2394 Tarpaulins, fabric: made from purchased materials; canopies, fabric: made from purchased materials; cloth, drop (fabric): made from purchased materials; tents: made from purchased materials

(G-13690)
J L INTERNATIONAL INC (PA)
Also Called: Pft Industries
34364 Goddard Rd (48174-3451)
PHONE 734 941-0300
Brenda Lewo, *President*
EMP: 200
SQ FT: 125,000
SALES (est): 31.1MM **Privately Held**
SIC: 3714 5065 Motor vehicle parts & accessories; telephone equipment

(G-13691)
JADE MFG INC
36535 Grant St (48174-1443)
P.O. Box 864, Dearborn (48121-0864)
PHONE 734 942-1462
James M Egyed, *President*
Diane B Egyed, *Corp Secy*
EMP: 6
SQ FT: 3,500
SALES (est): 928K **Privately Held**
WEB: www.jademfg.com
SIC: 3493 Coiled flat springs

(G-13692)
JOHN JOHNSON COMPANY
Also Called: Detroit Cover
15500 Oakwood Dr (48174-3670)
PHONE 313 496-0600
Richard H Dancy Jr, *President*
Robert B Dancy, *Vice Pres*
▲ EMP: 90

SALES (est): 14.1MM **Privately Held**
SIC: 2221 Upholstery, tapestry & wall covering fabrics

(G-13693)
JOINT CLUTCH & GEAR SVC INC (PA)
30200 Cypress Rd (48174-3538)
PHONE 734 641-7575
Gary R Scherz, *Exec VP*
Jason Sierocki, *Vice Pres*
James Quarles, *Vice Pres*
David L Scherz, *Vice Pres*
Stanley C Drabik, *CFO*
EMP: 25
SQ FT: 20,000
SALES (est): 5.9MM **Privately Held**
WEB: www.jointclutchandgear.com
SIC: 5013 5531 3714 Truck parts & accessories; automobile & truck equipment & parts; motor vehicle parts & accessories

(G-13694)
JUST COVER IT UP
34754 Lynn Dr (48174-1565)
PHONE 734 247-4729
Ann McCauley, *Principal*
EMP: 4
SALES (est): 415.4K **Privately Held**
SIC: 2448 Cargo containers, wood & wood with metal

(G-13695)
KANAWHA SCALES & SYSTEMS INC
28500 Eureka Rd (48174-2858)
PHONE 734 947-4030
Ron Lliitle, *President*
EMP: 14
SALES (corp-wide): 54.4MM **Privately Held**
SIC: 5046 7699 3822 3596 Scales, except laboratory; scale repair service; auto controls regulating residntl & coml environmt & applncs; scales & balances, except laboratory
PA: Kanawha Scales & Systems, Inc.
  111 Jacobson Dr
  Poca WV 25159
  304 755-8321

(G-13696)
KERR CORPORATION
Also Called: Kerr Manufacturing
28200 Wick Rd (48174-2600)
PHONE 734 946-7800
Dina Graham, *Safety Mgr*
Lawrence Girling, *Branch Mgr*
Clifford Ruddle, *Products*
EMP: 240
SALES (corp-wide): 19.8B **Publicly Held**
WEB: www.kerrdental.com
SIC: 3843 Dental materials; dental laboratory equipment; impression material, dental; dental hand instruments
HQ: Kerr Corporation
  1717 W Collins Ave
  Orange CA 92867
  714 516-7400

(G-13697)
KIRMIN DIE & TOOL INC
36360 Ecorse Rd (48174-4159)
PHONE 734 722-9210
Tom Mulanka, *President*
Casimira Buraczewski, *Corp Secy*
EMP: 30
SQ FT: 21,000
SALES (est): 5MM **Privately Held**
SIC: 3465 3544 Automotive stampings; special dies & tools

(G-13698)
KRMC LLC
Also Called: Kut-Rite Manufacturing Company
27456 Northline Rd (48174-2826)
P.O. Box 1417, Taylor (48180-5817)
PHONE 734 955-9311
Ralph O Neri,
Rich Sollars,
Ray Swoish,
Tim Swoish,
Jennifer Temple,
▲ EMP: 9 EST: 1947

GEOGRAPHIC SECTION
Romulus - Wayne County (G-13725)

SQ FT: 65,000
SALES (est): 1.8MM **Privately Held**
WEB: www.kutritemfg.com
SIC: 3291 3545 3541 Wheels, abrasive; machine tool accessories; machine tools, metal cutting type

(G-13699)
LASER MFG INC
Also Called: Sealmaster/Michigan
27989 Van Born Rd (48174-2368)
PHONE..................313 292-2299
Michael Laser, *President*
EMP: 7
SQ FT: 20,000
SALES (est): 1.4MM **Privately Held**
WEB: www.sealmasterdetroit.com
SIC: 2951 Asphalt paving mixtures & blocks

(G-13700)
LEPAGES 2000 INC
Also Called: Conros
12900 S Huron River Dr (48174-1157)
P.O. Box 307, Taylor (48180-0307)
PHONE..................416 357-0041
Sunir Chandaria, *President*
Brian Tobias, *Vice Pres*
Ajay RAO, *CFO*
Shernee Chandaria, *Treasurer*
Sheena Chandaria, *Admin Sec*
▲ **EMP:** 6
SQ FT: 3,300
SALES (est): 27MM
SALES (corp-wide): 2.1MM **Privately Held**
SIC: 5112 2653 2672 Business forms; corrugated & solid fiber boxes; adhesive papers, labels or tapes: from purchased material
PA: Conros Group Ltd
  125 Bermondsey Rd
  North York ON M4A 1
  416 757-6700

(G-13701)
LEWKOWICZ CORPORATION
Also Called: Landis Machine Shop
36425 Grant St (48174-1112)
PHONE..................734 941-0411
Mark Lewkowicz, *President*
Candace Lewkowicz, *Vice Pres*
Larry Martin, *Assistant*
EMP: 10
SQ FT: 7,200
SALES: 490K **Privately Held**
SIC: 3599 3366 Machine shop, jobbing & repair; castings (except die): brass

(G-13702)
LINCOLN PARK BORING CO
28089 Wick Rd (48174-2622)
PHONE..................734 946-8300
Richard N Yesue, *President*
Gary C Yesue, *Vice Pres*
Gary Yesue, *Vice Pres*
Nancy M Yesue, *Treasurer*
Nancy Jesue, *Executive*
▲ **EMP:** 30
SQ FT: 60,000
SALES: 8MM **Privately Held**
WEB: www.lincolnparkboring.com
SIC: 3599 Machine shop, jobbing & repair

(G-13703)
MAGNUM TOOLSCOM LLC
30690 Cypress Rd (48174-3599)
PHONE..................734 595-4600
Sean Green, *Sales Dir*
Jason Pask, *Manager*
Daniel B Martin,
Ashley Riopelle,
▲ **EMP:** 11
SQ FT: 96,000
SALES (est): 2.5MM **Privately Held**
SIC: 5082 3531 Construction & mining machinery; construction machinery

(G-13704)
MBM FABRICATORS CO INC
36333 Northline Rd (48174-3645)
PHONE..................734 941-0100
Donald A Makins, *President*
Joe Leslie, *General Mgr*
Piper Myers, *General Mgr*
Ernest Peterson, *Foreman/Supr*

EMP: 215 **EST:** 1962
SQ FT: 38,619
SALES (est): 29MM **Privately Held**
WEB: www.mbmfab.com
SIC: 1791 3441 Structural steel erection; fabricated structural metal

(G-13705)
METAL IMPROVEMENT COMPANY LLC
Also Called: Advanced Material Process
30100 Cypress Rd (48174-3591)
PHONE..................734 728-8600
Scott Riddle, *Engineer*
Perry Celsi, *Manager*
EMP: 55
SALES (corp-wide): 2.4B **Publicly Held**
WEB: www.mic-houston.com
SIC: 3398 Shot peening (treating steel to reduce fatigue)
HQ: Metal Improvement Company, Llc
  80 E Rte 4 Ste 310
  Paramus NJ 07652
  201 843-7800

(G-13706)
METREX RESEARCH LLC
28210 Wick Rd (48174-2639)
PHONE..................734 947-6700
Tobin Johnson, *Manager*
EMP: 75
SALES (corp-wide): 19.8B **Publicly Held**
SIC: 2819 3845 8731 Industrial inorganic chemicals; electromedical equipment; commercial physical research
HQ: Metrex Research, Llc
  1717 W Collins Ave
  Orange CA 92867
  714 516-7788

(G-13707)
METRO MACHINE WORKS INC
11977 Harrison (48174-2799)
PHONE..................734 941-4571
Eric Beckeman, *President*
Timothy R Zink, *President*
Roger Stewart, *Vice Pres*
Tim Zink, *Vice Pres*
Dave Jones, *Purchasing*
EMP: 60 **EST:** 1919
SQ FT: 27,000
SALES (est): 12.8MM **Privately Held**
WEB: www.metromachineworks.net
SIC: 3724 7692 3545 3511 Turbines, aircraft type; welding repair; machine tool accessories; turbines & turbine generator sets; metal heat treating

(G-13708)
MICHIGAN ATF HOLDINGS LLC (HQ)
Also Called: Header Products
11850 Wayne Rd (48174-1447)
PHONE..................734 941-2220
Kimberly Bottenhorn, *Director*
John J Glazier Jr,
▲ **EMP:** 70
SALES (est): 22.9MM
SALES (corp-wide): 108MM **Privately Held**
SIC: 3965 Buckles & buckle parts
PA: Atf Inc.
  3550 W Pratt Ave
  Lincolnwood IL 60712
  847 677-1300

(G-13709)
MILLENNIUM TECHNOLOGY II INC
Also Called: Damar Tool Manufacturing
28888 Goddard Rd Ste 200 (48174-2752)
PHONE..................734 479-4440
EMP: 14
SQ FT: 12,000
SALES (est): 3MM **Privately Held**
SIC: 3545 Mfg Machine Tool Accessories

(G-13710)
MULTI MCHNING CAPABILITIES INC
27482 Northline Rd # 100 (48174-2826)
PHONE..................734 955-5592
Richard Sollars Jr, *President*
Tim Swoish, *Vice Pres*
Dave Camilleri, *Plant Mgr*

Radu Stingu, *Manager*
EMP: 5
SALES (est): 744.5K **Privately Held**
SIC: 3599 Machine shop, jobbing & repair

(G-13711)
NATIONAL METAL SALES INC
27400 Northline Rd (48174-2826)
PHONE..................734 942-3000
William Molnar Jr, *CEO*
Robert Molnar, *President*
EMP: 9
SALES (est): 1.2MM **Privately Held**
SIC: 3441 Fabricated structural metal

(G-13712)
NELMS TECHNOLOGIES INC
15385 Pine (48174-3659)
PHONE..................734 955-6500
Edwin Nelms, *Ch of Bd*
Mark Nelms, *Vice Pres*
EMP: 86
SALES (est): 9.2MM **Privately Held**
SIC: 3592 3451 Valves; screw machine products

(G-13713)
NITTO INC
36663 Van Born Rd Ste 360 (48174-4160)
PHONE..................732 276-1039
EMP: 4 **Privately Held**
SIC: 3714 Motor vehicle parts & accessories
HQ: Nitto, Inc.
  1990 Rutgers Blvd
  Lakewood NJ 08701
  732 901-7905

(G-13714)
NITTO INC
Also Called: Nitto Denko Automotive
36663 Van Born Rd Ste 360 (48174-4160)
PHONE..................734 729-7800
Denny Pedri, *Vice Pres*
EMP: 14 **Privately Held**
SIC: 3069 Rubber automotive products
HQ: Nitto, Inc.
  1990 Rutgers Blvd
  Lakewood NJ 08701
  732 901-7905

(G-13715)
NOR-DIC TOOL COMPANY INC
6577 Beverly Plz (48174-3513)
PHONE..................734 326-3610
Edward Christie, *President*
Lisa Swinton, *Corp Secy*
Kurt Christie, *Vice Pres*
EMP: 11
SQ FT: 52,000
SALES (est): 2MM **Privately Held**
SIC: 3469 1799 Stamping metal for the trade; welding on site

(G-13716)
OAK MOUNTAIN INDUSTRIES
14770 5 M Center Dr (48174-2869)
PHONE..................734 941-7000
Mike Lafferty, *General Mgr*
Cindy Bevlukvo, *Manager*
EMP: 3 **EST:** 2009
SALES (est): 306.8K **Privately Held**
SIC: 3999 Manufacturing industries

(G-13717)
OSBORNE CONCRETE CO
37500 Northline Rd (48174-1180)
PHONE..................734 941-3008
John D Osborne Sr, *President*
EMP: 6 **EST:** 1965
SQ FT: 17,000
SALES (est): 1.2MM **Privately Held**
SIC: 3273 Ready-mixed concrete

(G-13718)
PACKAGING SPECIALTIES INC (HQ)
Also Called: Manhattan Container
8111 Middlebelt Rd (48174-2134)
PHONE..................586 473-6703
Kurt Tabor, *President*
Brian Bazick, *Vice Pres*
Claredine Tabor, *Treasurer*
▲ **EMP:** 30

SALES (est): 9.9MM
SALES (corp-wide): 517.7MM **Privately Held**
WEB: www.packspec.net
SIC: 2653 2652 2671 2657 Boxes, corrugated: made from purchased materials; partitions, corrugated: made from purchased materials; sheets, corrugated: made from purchased materials; setup paperboard boxes; packaging paper & plastics film, coated & laminated; folding paperboard boxes; paperboard mills; nailed wood boxes & shook
PA: Welch Packaging Group, Inc.
  1020 Herman St
  Elkhart IN 46516
  574 295-2460

(G-13719)
PARAGON TOOL COMPANY
36130 Ecorse Rd (48174-4103)
PHONE..................734 326-1702
Raymond F Wasielewski, *President*
Raymond A Wasielewski, *President*
EMP: 7 **EST:** 1953
SQ FT: 3,500
SALES: 450K **Privately Held**
SIC: 3541 Machine tools, metal cutting: exotic (explosive, etc.)

(G-13720)
PENN AUTOMOTIVE INC
Also Called: Romulus Division
7845 Middlebelt Rd # 200 (48174-2174)
PHONE..................313 299-8500
Robert Wiese, *Admin Sec*
EMP: 55
SALES (corp-wide): 483.7MM **Privately Held**
WEB: www.fabristeel.com
SIC: 3429 Manufactured hardware (general)
HQ: Penn Automotive, Inc.
  5331 Dixie Hwy
  Waterford MI 48329
  248 599-3700

(G-13721)
PENTEL TOOL & DIE INC
26531 King Rd (48174-9430)
PHONE..................734 782-9500
EMP: 6
SQ FT: 7,200
SALES: 786.3K **Privately Held**
SIC: 3544 Mfg Dies Tools Jigs & Fixtures

(G-13722)
PLASTIPAK PACKAGING INC
36445 Van Born Rd Ste 200 (48174-4051)
PHONE..................734 467-7519
Fax: 734 467-7547
▲ **EMP:** 14 **EST:** 2001
SALES (est): 986.6K **Privately Held**
SIC: 3085 Mfg Plastic Bottles

(G-13723)
PLUM BROTHERS LLC
Also Called: Klassic Tool Crib
9350 Harrison (48174-2503)
PHONE..................734 947-8100
Tom Brotz,
EMP: 6
SALES (est): 600K **Privately Held**
WEB: www.klassictoolcrib.com
SIC: 3546 Power-driven handtools

(G-13724)
PRECISION MTL HDLG EQP LLC
36663 Van Born Rd Ste 350 (48174-4160)
PHONE..................734 351-7350
Shaun Kastarek, *Branch Mgr*
EMP: 56
SALES (corp-wide): 20.3MM **Privately Held**
SIC: 3441 Fabricated structural metal
HQ: Precision Material Handling Equipment, Llc
  26700 Princeton St
  Inkster MI 48141
  313 789-8101

(G-13725)
R & L MACHINE PRODUCTS INC
15995 S Huron River Dr (48174-3668)
PHONE..................734 992-2574
Robert Fitzpatrick, *President*

EMP: 5
SQ FT: 6,500
SALES (est): 722.6K **Privately Held**
SIC: 3469 Machine parts, stamped or pressed metal

(G-13726)
RAINBOW TAPE & LABEL INC
11600 Wayne Rd (48174-1462)
P.O. Box 74453 (48174-0453)
PHONE.................................734 941-6090
Richard Walters, *President*
Thelma Walters, *Corp Secy*
David R Walters, *Systems Staff*
EMP: 21
SQ FT: 14,000
SALES (est): 2.6MM **Privately Held**
WEB: www.rainbowtapeandlabel.com
SIC: 2754 Labels: gravure printing

(G-13727)
RELIABLE FREIGHT FWDG INC
30300 Cypress Rd (48174-3594)
PHONE.................................734 595-6165
Andrew F Gomolak, *President*
EMP: 8
SALES: 950K **Privately Held**
SIC: 2721 Periodicals

(G-13728)
RELIANCE TOOL COMPANY INC
39110 Pennsylvania Rd (48174-9722)
PHONE.................................734 946-9130
Stanley Piesiak, *President*
EMP: 3
SQ FT: 5,000
SALES: 300K **Privately Held**
SIC: 3544 Special dies & tools

(G-13729)
RITE WAY PRINTING
5821 Essex St (48174-1839)
PHONE.................................734 721-2746
Arthur Tabbs, *Principal*
EMP: 3
SALES (est): 202.8K **Privately Held**
SIC: 2752 Commercial printing, lithographic

(G-13730)
RM MACHINE & MOLD
30399 Ecorse Rd (48174-3521)
PHONE.................................734 721-8800
William Zablocki, *Principal*
EMP: 8
SALES (est): 1.1MM **Privately Held**
SIC: 3544 Industrial molds

(G-13731)
SAINT-GOBAIN DELAWARE CORP
Also Called: St Gobain Abrasives
27588 Northline Rd (48174-2826)
PHONE.................................734 941-1300
Michael Tracy, *Branch Mgr*
EMP: 7
SALES (corp-wide): 215.9MM **Privately Held**
SIC: 3291 Abrasive products
HQ: Saint-Gobain Delaware Corporation
750 E Swedesford Rd
Valley Forge PA 19482

(G-13732)
SATURN ELECTRONICS CORP
28450 Northline Rd (48174-2832)
PHONE.................................734 941-8100
Nagji Sutariya, *President*
Raj Sutariya, *Vice Pres*
Yash Sutariya, *Vice Pres*
Yash Suteriya, *Safety Mgr*
Sultana Ahmed, *Engineer*
▲ EMP: 200
SQ FT: 89,000
SALES (est): 36.3MM **Privately Held**
WEB: www.saturnelectronics.com
SIC: 3672 Circuit boards, television & radio printed

(G-13733)
SERTA RESTOKRAFT MAT CO INC
38025 Jay Kay Dr (48174-5083)
PHONE.................................734 727-9000
Lawrence Kraft, *President*
Bob Malin, *Vice Pres*
Steve Sterling, *Vice Pres*
David Williamsen, *Asst Controller*
▲ EMP: 110 EST: 1931
SALES (est): 22.2MM **Privately Held**
SIC: 2515 Mattresses, innerspring or box spring; box springs, assembled

(G-13734)
SPARTAN BARRICADING
27730 Ecorse Rd (48174-2429)
PHONE.................................313 292-2488
Fax: 313 292-2366
EMP: 4
SALES (est): 260K **Privately Held**
SIC: 1799 3499 Trade Contractor Mfg Misc Fabricated Metal Products

(G-13735)
SUPERIOR MATERIALS LLC
39001 W Huron River Dr (48174-1104)
PHONE.................................734 941-2479
EMP: 104
SALES (corp-wide): 23.8MM **Privately Held**
SIC: 5211 3273 Cement; ready-mixed concrete
PA: Superior Materials, Llc
30701 W 10 Mile Rd
Farmington Hills MI 48336

(G-13736)
UNITED BRASS MANUFACTURERS INC (PA)
Also Called: DACA DIV
35030 Goddard Rd (48174-3444)
P.O. Box 74095 (48174-0095)
PHONE.................................734 941-0700
James R Donahey, *President*
Raymond Frisbie, *Corp Secy*
EMP: 52 EST: 1950
SQ FT: 120,000
SALES (est): 9.5MM **Privately Held**
SIC: 3432 3463 Plumbers' brass goods: drain cocks, faucets, spigots, etc.; nonferrous forgings

(G-13737)
UNITED BRASS MANUFACTURERS INC
Also Called: Machine Division
39000 W Huron River Dr (48174-1105)
PHONE.................................734 942-9224
Charles Droullard, *Manager*
EMP: 45
SALES (corp-wide): 9.5MM **Privately Held**
SIC: 3463 3432 Nonferrous forgings; plumbers' brass goods: drain cocks, faucets, spigots, etc.
PA: United Brass Manufacturers, Inc.
35030 Goddard Rd
Romulus MI 48174
734 941-0700

(G-13738)
VACUUM ORNA METAL COMPANY INC
11380 Harrison (48174-2722)
PHONE.................................734 941-9100
Jan Reydon, *Vice Pres*
EMP: 21
SQ FT: 40,000
SALES (est): 3.2MM **Privately Held**
SIC: 3089 3471 3429 Injection molding of plastics; electroplating & plating; manufactured hardware (general)

(G-13739)
WESTSIDE POWDER COAT LLC
35777 Genron Ct (48174-3654)
PHONE.................................734 729-1667
Joseph Seror, *President*
EMP: 4 EST: 2012
SALES (est): 590.8K **Privately Held**
SIC: 3399 Powder, metal

(G-13740)
WHITE AUTOMATION & TOOL CO
28888 Goddard Rd Ste 100 (48174-2752)
PHONE.................................734 947-9822
Gary White, *President*
Donna Nemeth, *Corp Secy*
Allen White, *Vice Pres*
EMP: 12
SQ FT: 7,200
SALES (est): 1.5MM **Privately Held**
SIC: 3544 Special dies & tools

(G-13741)
WOLVERINE CRANE & SERVICE INC
30777 Beverly Rd Ste 150 (48174-2052)
PHONE.................................734 467-9066
Rich Kelps, *President*
Jerry Nastale, *Manager*
EMP: 10 **Privately Held**
WEB: www.wolverinecrane.com
SIC: 3536 7699 Cranes, overhead traveling; industrial equipment services
PA: Wolverine Crane & Service Inc
2557 Thornwood St Sw
Grand Rapids MI 49519

(G-13742)
WOODBRIDGE HOLDINGS INC
Also Called: Woodbridge Group
15573 Oakwood Dr (48174-3656)
PHONE.................................734 942-0458
Tom Dowdall, *Opers Mgr*
Jill De Bala, *Controller*
EMP: 165
SALES (corp-wide): 1.9B **Privately Held**
SIC: 3086 2531 Plastics foam products; public building & related furniture
HQ: Woodbridge Holdings Inc.
1515 Equity Dr Ste 100
Troy MI 48084
248 288-0100

(G-13743)
WORLDTEK INDUSTRIES LLC
36310 Eureka Rd (48174-3652)
PHONE.................................734 494-5204
Jeff Payne, *VP Bus Dvlpt*
Sharon Thibodeau, *Officer*
Michael Crooks,
Mary Kay Yackel,
EMP: 42 EST: 2010
SQ FT: 100,000
SALES (est): 11.4MM **Privately Held**
WEB: worldtek-industries.com
SIC: 3599 Machine shop, jobbing & repair

(G-13744)
YANFENG US AUTOMOTIVE
9800 Inkster Rd (48174-2616)
PHONE.................................734 946-0600
EMP: 20
SALES (corp-wide): 55MM **Privately Held**
SIC: 3089 Plastic containers, except foam
HQ: Yanfeng Us Automotive Interior Systems Ii Llc
5757 N Green Bay Ave
Milwaukee WI 53209
205 477-4225

(G-13745)
YAPP USA AUTO SYSTEMS INC
36320 Eureka Rd (48174-3652)
PHONE.................................248 404-8796
Erik Grant, *Director*
EMP: 9
SALES (corp-wide): 1.1B **Privately Held**
SIC: 3089 3714 Automotive parts, plastic; fuel systems & parts, motor vehicle
HQ: Yapp Usa Automotive Systems, Inc.
300 Abc Blvd
Gallatin TN 37066

(G-13746)
ZYNP INTERNATIONAL CORP
Also Called: Zyongyuan International
27501 Hldbrndt Rd Ste 300 (48174)
PHONE.................................734 947-1000
Frank Yang, *CEO*
▲ EMP: 25
SALES (est): 6.9MM
SALES (corp-wide): 229.9MM **Privately Held**
WEB: www.zynp.com
SIC: 3714 Motor vehicle parts & accessories
PA: Zynp Corporation
No.69, Huaihe Avenue, Industrial Agglomeration Zone
Mengzhou 45475

Roscommon
Roscommon County

(G-13747)
ACE CONSULTING & MGT INC
Also Called: Northline Express
10386 S Leline Rd (48653-9782)
PHONE.................................989 821-7040
Robert Cochran, *President*
Kathy Olson,
▲ EMP: 30
SQ FT: 24,000
SALES: 6.1MM **Privately Held**
WEB: www.northlineexpress.com
SIC: 3317 Steel pipe & tubes

(G-13748)
C & S SECURITY INC
138 Argus Ct (48653-8905)
PHONE.................................989 821-5759
Jamie Cullip, *President*
EMP: 4
SALES (est): 436.7K **Privately Held**
WEB: www.cssecurity.com
SIC: 3429 Handcuffs & leg irons

(G-13749)
JW PENNINGTON LLC
Also Called: JW Pennington
5503 W Higgins Lake Dr (48653-9520)
P.O. Box 272, Portland (48875-0272)
PHONE.................................989 965-2736
Jason Pennington, *Principal*
EMP: 3
SALES (est): 488.4K **Privately Held**
SIC: 3537 Trucks, tractors, loaders, carriers & similar equipment

(G-13750)
LEAR CORPORATION
10161 N Roscommon Rd (48653-9296)
P.O. Box 488 (48653-0488)
PHONE.................................989 275-5794
EMP: 200
SALES (corp-wide): 20.4B **Publicly Held**
SIC: 3714 Mfg Motor Vehicle Parts/Accessories
PA: Lear Corporation
21557 Telegraph Rd
Southfield MI 48033
248 447-1500

(G-13751)
NORTH CENTRAL WELDING CO
Also Called: Nucraft Metal Products
402 Southline Rd (48653-7652)
PHONE.................................989 275-8054
Lee Wiltse, *President*
Dale Wiltse, *Vice Pres*
Ronald Wiltse, *Vice Pres*
EMP: 20
SQ FT: 20,000
SALES: 2.2MM **Privately Held**
SIC: 3443 3536 Fabricated plate work (boiler shop); hoists, cranes & monorails

(G-13752)
NORTHERN MICH ENDOCRINE PLLC
103 Misty Meadow Ct (48653-7676)
PHONE.................................989 281-1125
Bashar Kiami, *Principal*
EMP: 3
SALES (est): 256.9K **Privately Held**
SIC: 2435 Hardwood veneer & plywood

(G-13753)
R & L FRYE
Also Called: Cross Country Ski Headquarters
9435 N Cut Rd (48653-9339)
PHONE.................................989 821-6661
Robert Frye, *Owner*
EMP: 3 EST: 1971
SQ FT: 2,914
SALES (est): 574K **Privately Held**
WEB: www.skibones.com
SIC: 5941 5699 3089 Skiing equipment; sports apparel; injection molded finished plastic products

GEOGRAPHIC SECTION

Roseville - Macomb County (G-13779)

(G-13754)
SCOTTS ENTERPRISES INC
Also Called: Scott's Wood Products
554 W Federal Hwy (48653-9700)
P.O. Box 739 (48653-0739)
PHONE.................................989 275-5011
Mark Scott, *President*
EMP: 30 **EST:** 1973
SQ FT: 5,000
SALES (est): 4.1MM **Privately Held**
WEB: www.scottsent.com
SIC: 2449 2448 2653 2441 Rectangular boxes & crates, wood; pallets, wood; corrugated & solid fiber boxes; nailed wood boxes & shook

(G-13755)
TRAVEL INFORMATION SERVICES
101 E Federal Hwy (48653-9318)
PHONE.................................989 275-8042
Charles E Mires, *President*
Charles Scott Mires, *Vice Pres*
Linda S Mires, *Vice Pres*
EMP: 15
SALES (est): 2MM **Privately Held**
WEB: www.travelbrochure.com
SIC: 4724 2759 5199 Tourist agency arranging transport, lodging & car rental; commercial printing; general merchandise, non-durable

Rose City
Ogemaw County

(G-13756)
ADMIN INDUSTRIES LLC
3049 Beechwood Rd (48654-9562)
PHONE.................................989 685-3438
Eric Carlson, *Mng Member*
Stephanie Carlson,
EMP: 10
SQ FT: 5,600
SALES (est): 1.3MM **Privately Held**
SIC: 3999 3443 3444 3441 Dock equipment & supplies, industrial; fabricated plate work (boiler shop); sheet metalwork; fabricated structural metal

(G-13757)
AMERICAN PLASTIC TOYS INC
3059 Beechwood Rd (48654-9562)
PHONE.................................989 685-2455
Ken Hebert, *Branch Mgr*
EMP: 90
SALES (est): 7.3MM
SALES (corp-wide): 48.5MM **Privately Held**
WEB: www.aptoys.net
SIC: 3944 5092 Games, toys & children's vehicles; toys
PA: American Plastic Toys, Inc.
799 Ladd Rd
Walled Lake MI 48390
248 624-4881

(G-13758)
AMERICAN PLEASURE PRODUCTS INC
2823 E Industrial Dr (48654-9478)
PHONE.................................989 685-8484
Robert Brodie, *President*
Michael Gilligan, *Corp Secy*
EMP: 9 **EST:** 1967
SALES: 750K **Privately Held**
SIC: 3732 Pontoons, except aircraft & inflatable

(G-13759)
ASSEMBLY CONCEPTS INC
Also Called: Aci
2651 S M 33 (48654)
P.O. Box 589 (48654-0589)
PHONE.................................989 685-2603
Michael Quigley, *President*
Patti Quigley, *Vice Pres*
EMP: 20
SQ FT: 5,000
SALES (est): 1.9MM **Privately Held**
SIC: 3544 3599 Special dies, tools, jigs & fixtures; machine shop, jobbing & repair

(G-13760)
ATF INC
Also Called: Header Products
285 Casemaster Dr (48654-9676)
P.O. Box 366 (48654-0366)
PHONE.................................989 685-2468
Leslie Quigley, *Manager*
Michael Brennan, *Technology*
EMP: 35
SALES (corp-wide): 108MM **Privately Held**
WEB: www.headerproducts.com
SIC: 3499 3714 3451 Stabilizing bars (cargo), metal; motor vehicle parts & accessories; screw machine products
HQ: Michigan Atf Holdings, Llc
11850 Wayne Rd
Romulus MI 48174
734 941-2220

(G-13761)
DELT FORGE INC
2816 E Industrial Dr (48654-9478)
PHONE.................................989 685-2118
Edward Hock, *President*
Thomas Rose, *Vice Pres*
EMP: 3
SQ FT: 2,400
SALES (est): 289.8K **Privately Held**
SIC: 3462 Railroad wheels, axles, frogs or other equipment: forged

(G-13762)
LITES ALTERNATIVE INC
Also Called: Litesalternative
2643 S M 33 (48654)
PHONE.................................989 685-3476
Michael Quigly, *President*
EMP: 10
SQ FT: 7,000
SALES (est): 1.1MM **Privately Held**
WEB: www.litesalternative.com
SIC: 3089 Windows, plastic

(G-13763)
MASONS LUMBER & HARDWARE INC
Also Called: Do It Best
2493 S M 33 (48654)
PHONE.................................989 685-3999
Gloria Neubecker, *President*
Randy Mason, *Treasurer*
EMP: 7
SQ FT: 16,000
SALES (est): 805.6K **Privately Held**
SIC: 5251 5211 2452 Hardware; lumber & other building materials; log cabins, prefabricated, wood

(G-13764)
MERIT ENERGY COMPANY
749 E Hughes Lake Rd (48654-9638)
PHONE.................................989 685-3446
Bill Gayden, *Principal*
EMP: 3
SALES (est): 178.7K **Privately Held**
SIC: 1311 Crude petroleum production

Rosebush
Isabella County

(G-13765)
SUMMIT-REED CITY INC
4147 E Monroe St (48878-5008)
P.O. Box 365, Mount Pleasant (48804-0365)
PHONE.................................989 433-5716
Jeff Wilson, *Manager*
EMP: 20
SALES (corp-wide): 75.7MM **Privately Held**
SIC: 4225 1311 General warehousing; crude petroleum & natural gas
PA: Summit-Reed City, Inc.
1315 S Mission Rd
Mount Pleasant MI 48858
989 772-2028

Roseville
Macomb County

(G-13766)
A-1 FABRICATION INC
16601 Eastland St (48066-2089)
PHONE.................................586 775-8392
Nazih Hussein, *President*
EMP: 3
SALES (est): 587.9K **Privately Held**
SIC: 3441 Fabricated structural metal

(G-13767)
ACAL UNIVERSAL GRINDING CO
Also Called: Acal Precision Products
20200 Cornillie Dr (48066-1746)
PHONE.................................586 296-3900
Joseph Elsesser, *President*
Gregg Blind, *Sales Staff*
Thomas Elsesser, *Executive*
EMP: 16 **EST:** 1945
SQ FT: 15,400
SALES (est): 2.7MM **Privately Held**
WEB: www.acalprecision.com
SIC: 3599 Machine shop, jobbing & repair

(G-13768)
ADVANCE PRECISION GRINDING CO
29739 Groesbeck Hwy (48066-1940)
PHONE.................................586 773-1330
William A Kemp, *President*
William Kemp Jr, *Vice Pres*
EMP: 6 **EST:** 1974
SQ FT: 16,000
SALES (est): 490K **Privately Held**
SIC: 3599 Machine shop, jobbing & repair

(G-13769)
AERO BOX COMPANY
20101 Cornillie Dr (48066-1766)
PHONE.................................586 415-0000
Gary Corte, *Manager*
EMP: 4 **EST:** 1986
SALES (est): 490K **Privately Held**
SIC: 2653 Boxes, corrugated: made from purchased materials

(G-13770)
AERO GRINDING INC (PA)
Also Called: Centerless Grinder Repair Div
28300 Groesbeck Hwy (48066-2382)
PHONE.................................586 774-6450
William Magee, *Vice Pres*
EMP: 60
SQ FT: 30,000
SALES (est): 16.6MM **Privately Held**
WEB: www.aerogrinding.com
SIC: 5084 3599 7629 Machine tools & metalworking machinery; machine shop, jobbing & repair; electrical repair shops

(G-13771)
AERO GRINDING INC
Also Called: Grind Repair
28240 Groesbeck Hwy (48066-2389)
PHONE.................................586 774-6450
Roland Di Mattia, *Owner*
EMP: 4
SALES (corp-wide): 16.6MM **Privately Held**
WEB: www.aerogrinding.com
SIC: 3599 5084 Machine shop, jobbing & repair; industrial machinery & equipment
PA: Aero Grinding, Inc.
28300 Groesbeck Hwy
Roseville MI 48066
586 774-6450

(G-13772)
AMERICAN BEVERAGE EQUIPMENT CO
27560 Groesbeck Hwy (48066-2759)
PHONE.................................586 773-0094
James Testori, *President*
Lawrence Marchorni, *Vice Pres*
Christopher Pochmara, *Vice Pres*
Josephine Testori, *Vice Pres*
Judy Pochmara, *Admin Sec*
▲ **EMP:** 20 **EST:** 1930
SQ FT: 12,000
SALES (est): 2.4MM **Privately Held**
SIC: 3432 5074 Faucets & spigots, metal & plastic; plumbers' brass goods & fittings

(G-13773)
APOLLO PLATING INC
15765 Sturgeon St (48066-1879)
PHONE.................................586 777-0070
James E Grimes, *CEO*
EMP: 153 **EST:** 1970
SQ FT: 50,000
SALES (est): 10.5MM **Privately Held**
WEB: www.apolloplatinginc.com
SIC: 3471 Buffing for the trade; polishing, metals or formed products

(G-13774)
ARIN INC
29139 Calahan Rd (48066-1850)
PHONE.................................586 779-3410
Carol Gee-Romanoski, *President*
Carol Gee Romanoski, *President*
Geraldine Kipke, *Vice Pres*
Elizabeth Mewton, *Safety Mgr*
Niels Smeehuyzen, *Director*
EMP: 19 **EST:** 1959
SQ FT: 24,000
SALES (est): 3.6MM **Privately Held**
WEB: www.arininc.com
SIC: 3699 Laser welding, drilling & cutting equipment

(G-13775)
ARMARTIS MANUFACTURING INC
20815 Kraft Blvd (48066-2232)
PHONE.................................248 308-9622
Christof Traidl, *CEO*
EMP: 50
SQ FT: 34,000
SALES (est): 1.8MM **Privately Held**
SIC: 3711 Universal carriers, military, assembly of

(G-13776)
BAY ELECTRONICS INC
20805 Kraft Blvd (48066-2232)
P.O. Box 397 (48066-0397)
PHONE.................................586 296-0900
Daniel J Olsen, *President*
Dan Olsen, *Safety Mgr*
Jane Gerds, *Production*
Chrissy Balsamo, *Administration*
EMP: 49
SQ FT: 11,000
SALES (est): 8.6MM **Privately Held**
WEB: www.bayelectronics.com
SIC: 3625 3679 Industrial electrical relays & switches; harness assemblies for electronic use: wire or cable

(G-13777)
BEACON PARK FINISHING LLC
15765 Sturgeon St (48066-1816)
PHONE.................................248 318-4286
EMP: 13
SALES (est): 1.9MM **Privately Held**
SIC: 3471 Plating & polishing

(G-13778)
BRECKERS ABC TOOL COMPANY INC
15919 E 12 Mile Rd (48066-1846)
PHONE.................................586 779-1122
George Buhler Jr, *President*
Dave Ashley, *Accounts Mgr*
EMP: 17
SQ FT: 7,200
SALES (est): 4.3MM **Privately Held**
SIC: 3545 Cutting tools for machine tools

(G-13779)
CADILLAC PRODUCTS INC
Also Called: Cadillac Products Auto Co
29784 Little Mack Ave (48066-2239)
PHONE.................................586 774-1700
Eric Ebenhoeh, *General Mgr*
Mike Moritz, *Engineer*
Jim Williams, *Marketing Mgr*
EMP: 100
SALES (corp-wide): 168.4MM **Privately Held**
SIC: 3714 2673 3081 Motor vehicle parts & accessories; plastic bags: made from purchased materials; polyethylene film

Roseville - Macomb County (G-13780)

PA: Cadillac Products, Inc.
5800 Crooks Rd Ste 100
Troy MI 48098
248 813-8200

(G-13780)
CDP ENVIRONMENTAL INC
Also Called: Curbs and Dampers
16517 Eastland St (48066-2032)
PHONE..................586 776-7890
John Gabridge, *President*
Frank Brunell, *Vice Pres*
EMP: 25
SQ FT: 8,000
SALES (est): 2.7MM **Privately Held**
SIC: 3444 Sheet metalwork

(G-13781)
CLANCY EXCAVATING CO
Also Called: Clancy Crushed Concrete
29950 Little Mack Ave (48066-2272)
PHONE..................586 294-2900
Robert J Clancy, *President*
Gerald Clancy, *Vice Pres*
EMP: 9 **EST:** 1963
SQ FT: 2,000
SALES (est): 1.1MM **Privately Held**
SIC: 1611 3272 1794 Highway & street paving contractor; concrete products; excavation & grading, building construction

(G-13782)
CMN FABRICATION INC
32580 Kelly Rd (48066-1059)
PHONE..................586 294-1941
Nick Saliga, *President*
Leslie Saliga, *Vice Pres*
EMP: 7
SALES (est): 413.2K **Privately Held**
SIC: 3444 Sheet metal specialties, not stamped

(G-13783)
COLORTECH GRAPHICS INC
28700 Hayes Rd (48066-2316)
PHONE..................586 779-7800
Alleyne Kelly, *President*
Daniel P Kelly, *Vice Pres*
Daniel Kelly, *Vice Pres*
Audrene Apostolos, *Purchasing*
David Matyas, *Marketing Staff*
EMP: 65
SQ FT: 31,000
SALES (est): 17.1MM **Privately Held**
WEB: www.colortechgraphics.com
SIC: 2752 Commercial printing, offset

(G-13784)
COMFORT MATTRESS CO
Also Called: King Coil
30450 Little Mack Ave (48066-1707)
PHONE..................586 293-4000
Pete Hage, *President*
Paul Christlieb, *Plant Mgr*
Thomas Kelley, *Director*
▲ **EMP:** 75
SQ FT: 65,000
SALES (est): 9.4MM **Privately Held**
WEB: www.kingcoil.com
SIC: 2515 Mattresses, innerspring or box spring

(G-13785)
CONCRETE MANUFACTURING INC
29100 Groesbeck Hwy (48066-1922)
PHONE..................586 777-3320
Elvira M Bizzocchi, *President*
EMP: 5
SALES (est): 456.6K **Privately Held**
SIC: 2891 3272 Cement, except linoleum & tile; concrete products

(G-13786)
CONWAY DETROIT CORPORATION
Also Called: National Bronze Mfg Co
28070 Hayes Rd (48066-5049)
PHONE..................586 552-8413
Frederick Conway, *President*
William Austerberry, *Vice Pres*
▲ **EMP:** 20 **EST:** 1911
SQ FT: 26,000
SALES (est): 14.1MM **Privately Held**
WEB: www.nationalbronze.com
SIC: 5051 3366 Metals service centers & offices; machinery castings: copper or copper-base alloy

(G-13787)
COPYRITE PRINTING INC
30503 Gratiot Ave (48066-1775)
PHONE..................586 774-0006
Bernard Palo, *President*
Bob Clinton, *Sales Staff*
EMP: 5
SALES (est): 887.9K **Privately Held**
WEB: www.copyriteprinting.net
SIC: 2752 Commercial printing, offset

(G-13788)
CURBS & DAMPER PRODUCTS INC
16525 Eastland St (48066-2032)
PHONE..................586 776-7890
John W Gabridge, *President*
Frank Brunell, *Vice Pres*
Jason Gabridge, *Vice Pres*
EMP: 16
SQ FT: 10,000
SALES (est): 2.7MM **Privately Held**
WEB: www.curbsanddampers.com
SIC: 3444 3442 Hoods, range: sheet metal; metal doors, sash & trim

(G-13789)
DAYCO PRODUCTS LLC
16000 Common Rd (48066-1822)
PHONE..................248 404-6537
James Barrett, *Business Mgr*
Brent Charles, *Branch Mgr*
Gary Baruth, *Manager*
Felix Buccellato, *Manager*
EMP: 168
SALES (corp-wide): 178.8MM **Privately Held**
SIC: 3052 Rubber hose; plastic hose; rubber belting; plastic belting
HQ: Dayco Products, Llc
1650 Research Dr Ste 200
Troy MI 48083

(G-13790)
DECCA PATTERN CO INC
29778 Little Mack Ave (48066-2239)
PHONE..................586 775-8450
Frederick Stemmler Jr, *President*
Carmen J Neaton, *Treasurer*
EMP: 4 **EST:** 1949
SQ FT: 6,400
SALES (est): 467.1K **Privately Held**
SIC: 3543 Industrial patterns

(G-13791)
DENIM BABY LLC
30606 Sandhurst Ct # 207 (48066-7750)
PHONE..................313 539-5309
Theresa Y Edwards, *Administration*
EMP: 3
SALES (est): 121.9K **Privately Held**
SIC: 2211 Denims

(G-13792)
DETRIOT CHOPPERS INC
29455 Gratiot Ave (48066-4142)
PHONE..................586 498-8909
Robert Gallo, *President*
EMP: 6 **EST:** 2012
SQ FT: 6,000
SALES (est): 600K **Privately Held**
SIC: 3751 Motorcycles & related parts

(G-13793)
DETROIT EDGE TOOL COMPANY
Michigan Flame Hardening
28370 Groesbeck Hwy (48066-2384)
PHONE..................586 776-3727
Ken Hoffman, *Manager*
EMP: 4
SALES (est): 597.2K
SALES (corp-wide): 34.1MM **Privately Held**
SIC: 3398 Metal heat treating
PA: Detroit Edge Tool Company
6570 E Nevada St
Detroit MI 48234
313 366-4120

(G-13794)
DETROIT EDGE TOOL COMPANY
Also Called: Kirby Grinding
28370 Groesbeck Hwy (48066-2384)
PHONE..................586 776-1598
Samuel Olarte, *Manager*
EMP: 30
SALES (corp-wide): 34.1MM **Privately Held**
WEB: www.detroitedge.com
SIC: 3545 3599 3541 Machine knives, metalworking; machine & other job shop work; machine tools, metal cutting type
PA: Detroit Edge Tool Company
6570 E Nevada St
Detroit MI 48234
313 366-4120

(G-13795)
DIETECH NORTH AMERICA LLC
Also Called: Dietech NA
16630 Eastland St (48066-2087)
PHONE..................586 771-8580
J Christopher Kantgias,
Dennis M Alderson,
David A Pascoe,
EMP: 100
SQ FT: 72,009
SALES (est): 15.8MM **Privately Held**
WEB: www.dietechna.com
SIC: 3544 Dies & die holders for metal cutting, forming, die casting

(G-13796)
DNL FABRICATION LLC
28514 Hayes Rd (48066-2314)
PHONE..................586 872-2656
Kevin Verkest, *Engineer*
Lyn M Classy,
EMP: 17
SALES (est): 3.2MM **Privately Held**
SIC: 3549 Wiredrawing & fabricating machinery & equipment, ex. die

(G-13797)
DOMINION TECH GROUP INC
Also Called: Sturgeon Controls
15736 Sturgeon St (48066-1817)
PHONE..................586 773-3303
Edward Lashier Jr, *President*
Norman Garant, *Controller*
Rick Kozlowski, *Project Leader*
Sharon Lashier, *Admin Sec*
◆ **EMP:** 185
SQ FT: 203,000
SALES (est): 49.6MM **Privately Held**
WEB: www.dominiontec.com
SIC: 3549 Assembly machines, including robotic

(G-13798)
EASY SCRUB LLC
16629 Bettmar St (48066-3225)
PHONE..................586 565-1777
Glen Moore, *President*
EMP: 4 **EST:** 2016
SALES (est): 192.6K **Privately Held**
SIC: 3589 Commercial cleaning equipment

(G-13799)
ELCO INC
30660 Edison Dr (48066-7338)
PHONE..................586 778-6858
David K Miller, *President*
Valerie Czarnomski, *Vice Pres*
EMP: 3
SQ FT: 5,000
SALES: 350K **Privately Held**
WEB: www.elco-inc.com
SIC: 3321 3363 3599 Gray & ductile iron foundries; aluminum die-castings; machine & other job shop work

(G-13800)
ELRINGKLINGER AUTO MFG INC
30233 Groesbeck Hwy (48066-1548)
PHONE..................586 445-3050
EMP: 3
SALES (est): 309.3K
SALES (corp-wide): 1.9B **Privately Held**
SIC: 3465 Mfg Automotive Stampings
HQ: Elringklinger Automotive Manufacturing, Inc.
23300 Northwestern Hwy
Southfield MI 48075
248 727-6600

(G-13801)
END PRODUCT RESULTS LLC
Also Called: Golden Dental Solutions
27115 Gratiot Ave Ste B (48066-2900)
PHONE..................586 585-1210
Theresa Thompson, *Office Mgr*
Jackie Golden, *Mng Member*
EMP: 10
SALES (est): 915.7K **Privately Held**
SIC: 3843 Dental equipment & supplies

(G-13802)
EUROPEAN CABINET MFG CO
30665 Groesbeck Hwy (48066-1546)
PHONE..................586 445-8909
Giulio Zaccagnini, *President*
Ben Lograsso, *Vice Pres*
Carlo Zaccagnini, *Treasurer*
▲ **EMP:** 30
SQ FT: 14,000
SALES (est): 5.7MM **Privately Held**
SIC: 3469 2511 2434 2541 Metal stampings; wood household furniture; wood kitchen cabinets; wood partitions & fixtures; wood television & radio cabinets

(G-13803)
FEDEX OFFICE & PRINT SVCS INC
Also Called: Fedex Office Print & Ship Ctr
31980 Gratiot Ave (48066-4586)
PHONE..................586 296-4890
EMP: 25
SALES (corp-wide): 69.6B **Publicly Held**
WEB: www.kinkos.com
SIC: 7334 7336 2791 2789 Photocopying & duplicating services; commercial art & graphic design; typesetting; bookbinding & related work
HQ: Fedex Office And Print Services, Inc.
7900 Legacy Dr
Plano TX 75024
800 463-3339

(G-13804)
FLAT IRON LLC
27251 Gratiot Ave (48066-2967)
PHONE..................248 268-1668
Ryan Wargner, *President*
EMP: 3 **EST:** 2015
SALES (est): 198.3K **Privately Held**
SIC: 2869 Casing fluids for curing fruits, spices, tobacco, etc.

(G-13805)
G & G WOOD & SUPPLY INC
29920 Little Mack Ave (48066-2272)
PHONE..................586 293-0450
Mario Grillo, *President*
EMP: 18
SQ FT: 8,000
SALES (est): 1.7MM **Privately Held**
SIC: 2439 5712 6512 2541 Trusses, except roof: laminated lumber; cabinet work, custom; commercial & industrial building operation; wood partitions & fixtures; wood kitchen cabinets

(G-13806)
G & L POWERUP INC
Also Called: Batteries Plus
31044 Gratiot Ave (48066-4510)
PHONE..................586 200-2169
Gregory Beltowski, *Principal*
EMP: 4
SALES (est): 390.9K **Privately Held**
SIC: 5531 3691 5063 3641 Batteries, automotive & truck; batteries, rechargeable; light bulbs & related supplies; electric light bulbs, complete; primary batteries, dry & wet

(G-13807)
GFM LLC (DH)
Also Called: Gfm Corp.
29685 Calahan Rd (48066-1807)
PHONE..................586 777-4542
Senthil Kumar, *CEO*
Dave Papak, *President*
Alina Kozlowski, *Purch Mgr*
Paula Speller, *Human Res Mgr*
EMP: 48
SQ FT: 60,000

GEOGRAPHIC SECTION

Roseville - Macomb County (G-13834)

SALES: 15MM
SALES (corp-wide): 205.8MM **Privately Held**
SIC: 3465 Automotive stampings
HQ: Lgb Usa Inc.
15585 Sturgeon St
Roseville MI 48066
586 777-4542

(G-13808)
GLOBAL ROLLFORMING SYSTEMS LLC
Also Called: Global Automotive Systems
15500 E 12 Mile Rd (48066-1804)
PHONE..................586 218-5100
Lynne Tillman, *Principal*
Torben V Staden,
EMP: 5
SALES (est): 1.2MM
SALES (corp-wide): 4.1B **Privately Held**
SIC: 3469 Metal stampings
HQ: Global Automotive Systems, Llc
1780 Pond Run
Auburn Hills MI 48326
248 299-7500

(G-13809)
GORDINIER ELECTRONICS CORP
16380 E 13 Mile Rd (48066-1557)
PHONE..................586 778-0426
James A Gordinier, *President*
Ann Patricia Gordinier, *Vice Pres*
EMP: 5
SQ FT: 10,000
SALES: 350K **Privately Held**
WEB: www.gordinier.com
SIC: 3823 Industrial instrmnts msrmnt display/control process variable

(G-13810)
GRAPHICS EAST INC
16005 Sturgeon St (48066-1827)
PHONE..................586 598-1500
Michael J Easthope, *President*
John Griffin, *CFO*
Tom Tennant, *Accounts Exec*
Yvonne Busby-Dean, *Sales Staff*
EMP: 35
SQ FT: 28,000
SALES (est): 7.3MM **Privately Held**
WEB: www.graphicseast.com
SIC: 2752 Commercial printing, offset

(G-13811)
GREAT LAKES PAPER STOCK CORP
Also Called: Glr
30835 Groesbeck Hwy (48066-1510)
PHONE..................586 779-1310
Sandy Rosen, *CEO*
Michael Bassirpour, *President*
Ilene Rosen Bischer, *Vice Pres*
Michael Mione, *CFO*
Shannon Semik, *Controller*
EMP: 80
SQ FT: 100,000
SALES (est): 46.8MM **Privately Held**
WEB: www.greatlakesrecycling.com
SIC: 5093 3341 2611 Waste paper; metal scrap & waste materials; plastics scrap; secondary nonferrous metals; pulp mills

(G-13812)
GREIF INC
20101 Cornillie Dr (48066-1766)
PHONE..................586 415-0000
George Petzelt, *Branch Mgr*
Doug Duda, *Executive*
EMP: 40
SALES (corp-wide): 3.8B **Publicly Held**
WEB: www.greif.com
SIC: 2655 Fiber cans, drums & similar products
PA: Greif, Inc.
425 Winter Rd
Delaware OH 43015
740 549-6000

(G-13813)
GRIPPE MACHINING AND MFG CO
15642 Common Rd (48066-1826)
PHONE..................586 778-3150
Salvatore Militello, *President*
Angeline Militello, *Vice Pres*
EMP: 18 **EST**: 1954
SQ FT: 17,500
SALES (est): 3MM **Privately Held**
SIC: 3449 Miscellaneous metalwork

(G-13814)
H & M MACHINING INC
29625 Parkway (48066-1927)
PHONE..................586 778-5028
David Glaza, *President*
EMP: 19 **EST**: 1979
SQ FT: 18,000
SALES (est): 3MM **Privately Held**
SIC: 3544 7692 Jigs & fixtures; welding repair

(G-13815)
HEATEX WAREHOUSE LLC (PA)
16174 Common Rd (48066-1814)
PHONE..................586 773-0770
Joseph Deponio Jr,
Peter Nicholas,
▲ **EMP**: 6
SQ FT: 25,000
SALES (est): 4.2MM **Privately Held**
SIC: 3714 Radiators & radiator shells & cores, motor vehicle

(G-13816)
HOWARD FINISHING LLC
15765 Sturgeon St (48066-1816)
PHONE..................586 777-0070
James E Grimes, *Branch Mgr*
EMP: 80
SALES (corp-wide): 26.1MM **Privately Held**
SIC: 3471 Electroplating & plating
PA: Howard Finishing, Llc
32565 Dequindre Rd
Madison Heights MI 48071
248 588-9050

(G-13817)
HUSKY LLC
Also Called: Husky Precision
28100 Hayes Rd (48066-5049)
PHONE..................586 774-6148
Richard Seleno,
Glen Schleicher,
EMP: 15
SQ FT: 10,500
SALES (est): 2.3MM **Privately Held**
WEB: www.huskymachine.com
SIC: 3599 Machine shop, jobbing & repair

(G-13818)
INDUSTRIAL DUCTS SYSTEMS INC
Also Called: IDS
30015 Groesbeck Hwy (48066-1508)
PHONE..................586 498-3993
Glen Croft, *President*
Miechelle Croft, *Vice Pres*
Marilyn Rogers, *Manager*
EMP: 5
SALES (est): 927.8K **Privately Held**
SIC: 3444 Sheet metalwork

(G-13819)
INDUSTRIAL STAMPING & MFG CO
16590 E 13 Mile Rd (48066-1507)
PHONE..................586 772-8430
Marvin J Tomlan, *President*
Zulema Fernandez, *Technology*
EMP: 20 **EST**: 1956
SQ FT: 45,000
SALES (est): 5.3MM **Privately Held**
WEB: www.industrialstamping.com
SIC: 3469 Metal stampings

(G-13820)
INTERNATIONAL ABRASIVES INC
27980 Groesbeck Hwy (48066-2757)
PHONE..................586 778-8490
George F Barnett, *President*
Gloria Barnett, *Manager*
◆ **EMP**: 4
SQ FT: 7,500
SALES (est): 449.1K **Privately Held**
SIC: 3291 Abrasive products

(G-13821)
INTERNATIONAL CASTING CORP
28178 Hayes Rd (48066-2346)
PHONE..................586 293-8220
Doug Smith, *Branch Mgr*
EMP: 12
SALES (corp-wide): 3.8MM **Privately Held**
SIC: 3325 3322 Steel foundries; malleable iron foundries
PA: International Casting Corporation
37087 Green St
New Baltimore MI 48047
586 293-8220

(G-13822)
IRON FETISH METALWORKS INC
Also Called: Ifm
30233 Groesbeck Hwy (48066-1548)
PHONE..................586 776-8311
Karen Arondoski, *President*
Jeffrey Maxwell, *Exec VP*
EMP: 15
SQ FT: 14,110
SALES: 600K **Privately Held**
WEB: www.ifmetalworks.com
SIC: 7692 3441 3446 Welding repair; fabricated structural metal; architectural metalwork

(G-13823)
J & E MANUFACTURING COMPANY
16470 E 13 Mile Rd (48066-1501)
PHONE..................586 777-5614
John Babiarz, *President*
Evelyn Babiarz, *Corp Secy*
EMP: 7
SQ FT: 3,000
SALES (est): 761K **Privately Held**
SIC: 3599 Machine shop, jobbing & repair

(G-13824)
JOSEPH M HOFFMAN INC (PA)
16560 Industrial St (48066-1944)
PHONE..................586 774-8500
Joseph M Hoffman, *President*
Fred C Pike, *Corp Secy*
EMP: 17 **EST**: 1960
SQ FT: 8,000
SALES (est): 1.4MM **Privately Held**
SIC: 3479 Name plates: engraved, etched, etc.

(G-13825)
KOMARNICKI TOOL & DIE COMPANY
29650 Parkway (48066-1928)
PHONE..................586 776-9300
Joseph R Komarnicki, *President*
EMP: 50
SQ FT: 11,000
SALES: 10MM **Privately Held**
SIC: 3544 Special dies & tools

(G-13826)
LGB USA INC (HQ)
15585 Sturgeon St (48066-1816)
PHONE..................586 777-4542
EMP: 4 **EST**: 2012
SALES (est): 15MM
SALES (corp-wide): 205.8MM **Privately Held**
SIC: 3465 Automotive stampings
PA: L.G.Balakrishnan & Bros Limited
6/16/13 Krishnarayapuram Road
Coimbatore TN 64100
422 253-2325

(G-13827)
M & J MANUFACTURING INC
28184 Groesbeck Hwy (48066-2389)
PHONE..................586 778-6322
Michael Belkowski, *President*
EMP: 5
SQ FT: 5,000
SALES (est): 625.3K **Privately Held**
SIC: 3499 Machine bases, metal

(G-13828)
MACHINING & FABRICATING INC
30546 Groesbeck Hwy (48066-1567)
PHONE..................586 773-9288
Robert C Gielghem, *President*
Sarah Shields, *Admin Sec*
EMP: 24
SQ FT: 9,600
SALES: 2.5MM **Privately Held**
SIC: 3545 Tools & accessories for machine tools

(G-13829)
MARSACK SAND & GRAVEL INC
20900 E 14 Mile Rd (48066-1169)
PHONE..................586 293-4414
Thomas Marsack, *President*
Gary Marsack, *Vice Pres*
Ken Marsack, *Treasurer*
Edward Marsack, *Admin Sec*
EMP: 12 **EST**: 1928
SQ FT: 2,650
SALES (est): 790K **Privately Held**
SIC: 1442 Construction sand & gravel

(G-13830)
MARTIN TOOL & MACHINE INC
29739 Groesbeck Hwy (48066-1940)
PHONE..................586 775-1800
Edward Kunnath, *President*
William A Kemp, *Admin Sec*
EMP: 5
SQ FT: 7,200
SALES: 1.5MM **Privately Held**
WEB: www.martintoolmachine.com
SIC: 3544 Special dies & tools

(G-13831)
MATHESON
26415 Gratiot Ave (48066-5108)
PHONE..................586 498-8315
Robert Wayne, *Manager*
EMP: 3
SALES (est): 151.2K **Privately Held**
SIC: 2813 Industrial gases

(G-13832)
MCKECHNIE VHCL CMPNNTS USA INC
Also Called: McKechnie Tooling and Engrg
27087 Gratiot Ave 2 (48066-2947)
PHONE..................218 894-1218
Jeanie Johnson, *Principal*
David Kolstad, *Principal*
Steve Palmer, *Principal*
Brent Fischmann, *Manager*
EMP: 22 **Privately Held**
WEB: www.mvcna.com
SIC: 3089 3544 3083 2821 Molding primary plastic; thermoformed finished plastic products; special dies, tools, jigs & fixtures; laminated plastics plate & sheet; plastics materials & resins
HQ: Mckechnie Vehicle Components Usa, Inc.
27087 Gratiot Ave Fl 2
Roseville MI 48066
586 491-2600

(G-13833)
MCKECHNIE VHCL CMPNNTS USA INC (HQ)
Also Called: Mvc
27087 Gratiot Ave Fl 2 (48066-2947)
PHONE..................586 491-2600
Mike Torakis, *CEO*
Mike Auten, *Vice Pres*
Tim Coots, *Vice Pres*
Jeffrey E Palazzolo, *CFO*
EMP: 14
SQ FT: 10,000
SALES (est): 41MM **Privately Held**
WEB: www.mvcna.com
SIC: 3089 Automotive parts, plastic; plastic processing

(G-13834)
METAL STMPING SPPORT GROUP LLC
Also Called: Air Feeds/Roll Feeds
16660 E 13 Mile Rd (48066-1556)
PHONE..................586 777-7440
Eric Werner,
Sherry Barkatt,
James Hewines,
EMP: 11

SALES (est): 2.2MM **Privately Held**
SIC: **3469** 3549 Machine parts, stamped or pressed metal; metalworking machinery

(G-13835)
MICROPHOTO INCORPORATED
30499 Edison Dr (48066-1577)
PHONE..................................586 772-1999
Richard Wade, *President*
Brian Wade, *Vice Pres*
Craig Ban Mill, *Director*
EMP: 20
SQ FT: 17,000
SALES (est): 5.9MM **Privately Held**
WEB: www.microphoto.net
SIC: **3569** Filters & strainers, pipeline

(G-13836)
MIDWEST GEAR & TOOL INC
15700 Common Rd (48066-1893)
PHONE..................................586 779-1300
Craig Ross, *President*
EMP: 48
SQ FT: 5,000
SALES (est): 1.7MM **Privately Held**
SIC: **3462** Gears, forged steel

(G-13837)
MIDWEST MOLD SERVICES INC
29900 Hayes Rd (48066-1820)
PHONE..................................586 888-8800
John Hill, *President*
▲ EMP: 26
SQ FT: 37,000
SALES (est): 7.2MM **Privately Held**
SIC: **3544** Industrial molds

(G-13838)
MIDWEST RESIN INC
15320 Common Rd (48066-1802)
PHONE..................................586 803-3417
William Hughes, *President*
Michael Ouimet, *Vice Pres*
Robert Limeright, *Treasurer*
Chris Ouimet, *Accounts Mgr*
Todd Grabel, *Sales Staff*
EMP: 5
SQ FT: 10,000
SALES (est): 1.2MM **Privately Held**
SIC: **2821** Plastics materials & resins

(G-13839)
MOON ROOF CORPORATION AMERICA (PA)
Also Called: MRC Manufacturing
28117 Groesbeck Hwy (48066-2344)
PHONE..................................586 772-8730
Quirino D Alessandro, *CEO*
William Schauffer, *President*
Paul Torres, *Vice Pres*
EMP: 23
SQ FT: 62,000
SALES (est): 14.1MM **Privately Held**
SIC: **3089** Automotive parts, plastic; injection molding of plastics

(G-13840)
MOON ROOF CORPORATION AMERICA
30750 Edison Dr (48066-1554)
PHONE..................................586 552-1901
Mike Spencer, *Branch Mgr*
EMP: 50
SALES (corp-wide): 14.1MM **Privately Held**
SIC: **3089** Injection molding of plastics
PA: Moon Roof Corporation Of America
28117 Groesbeck Hwy
Roseville MI 48066
586 772-8730

(G-13841)
MP TOOL & ENGINEERING COMPANY
15850 Common Rd (48066-1895)
PHONE..................................586 772-7730
Longine V Morawski, *President*
Lukas Morawski, *General Mgr*
Lawrence Marawski, *Vice Pres*
John Piccinino, *QA Dir*
Robert Shea, *Sales Staff*
EMP: 30 **EST:** 1946
SQ FT: 24,000
SALES (est): 5.9MM **Privately Held**
WEB: www.mptool.com
SIC: **3545** 3559 Tools & accessories for machine tools; metal finishing equipment for plating, etc.

(G-13842)
MST STEEL CORP
30360 Edison Dr (48066-1543)
PHONE..................................586 359-2648
John Dobek, *Manager*
EMP: 15
SALES (corp-wide): 300MM **Privately Held**
SIC: **3548** Welding apparatus
PA: Mst Steel Corp.
24417 Groesbeck Hwy
Warren MI 48089
586 773-5460

(G-13843)
MVC HOLDINGS LLC (PA)
27087 Gratiot Ave Fl 2 (48066-2947)
PHONE..................................586 491-2600
Michael Torakis, *CEO*
Linda Torakis, *President*
Timothy Coots, *Mfg Staff*
Jeffrey Palazzolo, *Treasurer*
EMP: 14
SALES (est): 56.1MM **Privately Held**
SIC: **3714** 3465 3429 3471 Motor vehicle wheels & parts; automotive stampings; manufactured hardware (general); plating & polishing

(G-13844)
NATIONAL CONEY ISLAND CHILI CO
Also Called: National Chili
27947 Groesbeck Hwy (48066-5221)
PHONE..................................313 365-5611
James Giftos, *President*
Paul Neiman, *General Mgr*
John Dallas, *Vice Pres*
EMP: 15 **EST:** 1963
SQ FT: 16,000
SALES (est): 2.2MM **Privately Held**
SIC: **2032** Chili with or without meat: packaged in cans, jars, etc.

(G-13845)
NBC TRUCK EQUIPMENT INC (PA)
Also Called: Fleet Truck Service
28130 Groesbeck Hwy (48066-2389)
PHONE..................................586 774-4900
E William Roland Jr, *President*
Daniel A Sabedra Jr, *Vice Pres*
George Wimbrow, *Vice Pres*
Janet M Roland, *Admin Sec*
EMP: 50
SQ FT: 34,000
SALES (est): 16.4MM **Privately Held**
WEB: www.nbctruckequip.com
SIC: **5013** 5012 3713 3441 Truck parts & accessories; truck bodies; truck & bus bodies; fabricated structural metal

(G-13846)
NEW CONCEPTS SOFTWARE INC
28490 Bohn St (48066-2487)
P.O. Box 688 (48066-0688)
PHONE..................................586 776-2855
Julius M Boleyn, *President*
Deborah L Boleyn, *Treasurer*
EMP: 4
SALES (est): 100K **Privately Held**
WEB: www.ncsoftware.com
SIC: **7372** 7371 Prepackaged software; custom computer programming services

(G-13847)
NEW DIMENSION LASER INC
29540 Calahan Rd (48066-1853)
PHONE..................................586 415-6041
EMP: 4
SALES (est): 557.9K **Privately Held**
SIC: **3541** Mfg Electrical Equipment/Supplies

(G-13848)
NORTH COAST STUDIOS INC
29181 Calahan Rd (48066-1850)
PHONE..................................586 359-6630
Steven J Burns, *President*
EMP: 10
SQ FT: 12,000
SALES: 1MM **Privately Held**
SIC: **3999** Stage hardware & equipment, except lighting

(G-13849)
PARADIGM ENGINEERING INC
Also Called: Detail Standard Company
16470 E 13 Mile Rd (48066-1501)
PHONE..................................586 776-5910
Peter Manetta, *President*
EMP: 6
SALES (est): 200K **Privately Held**
WEB: www.detailstandard.com
SIC: **5084** 3469 Industrial machine parts; machine parts, stamped or pressed metal

(G-13850)
PARAMOUNT BAKING COMPANY
29790 Little Mack Ave (48066-2256)
PHONE..................................313 690-4844
Joseph Hanna, *President*
EMP: 16 **EST:** 1965
SQ FT: 9,859
SALES (est): 3.4MM **Privately Held**
SIC: **2051** Breads, rolls & buns

(G-13851)
PAUL MURPHY PLASTICS CO (PA)
Also Called: Murphy Software Company
15301 E 11 Mile Rd (48066-2780)
PHONE..................................586 774-4880
J Murphy, *President*
Paul Murphy, *Treasurer*
Julianne Murphy, *Admin Sec*
EMP: 34 **EST:** 1963
SQ FT: 31,000
SALES (est): 6.2MM **Privately Held**
SIC: **3089** 3442 3272 3131 Plastic processing; metal doors, sash & trim; concrete products; footwear cut stock; laminated plastics plate & sheet

(G-13852)
PAUL W MARINO GAGES INC
Also Called: Alufix Services Inspection
30744 Groesbeck Hwy (48066-1511)
P.O. Box 3755, Center Line (48015-0755)
PHONE..................................586 772-2400
Paul W Marino, *President*
Linda Marino, *Vice Pres*
▲ EMP: 25
SQ FT: 40,000
SALES (est): 9.1MM **Privately Held**
WEB: www.pmargage.com
SIC: **3441** Fabricated structural metal

(G-13853)
PENINSULAR INC
Also Called: Peninsular Cylinder Company
27650 Groesbeck Hwy (48066-2759)
PHONE..................................586 775-7211
Brent Paterson, *President*
David Vondett, *Materials Mgr*
James Czegledi, *Engineer*
Sharon Garnett, *Engineer*
Jorge Montemayor, *Regl Sales Mgr*
EMP: 50 **EST:** 1949
SQ FT: 20,000
SALES (est): 10.5MM **Privately Held**
WEB: www.peninsularcylinders.com
SIC: **3443** 3593 3537 3429 Cylinders, pressure: metal plate; fluid power cylinders & actuators; industrial trucks & tractors; manufactured hardware (general)

(G-13854)
PENTECH INDUSTRIES INC
15645 Sturgeon St (48066-1816)
PHONE..................................586 445-1070
David Vernier, *President*
EMP: 32 **EST:** 2001
SQ FT: 9,400
SALES (est): 5.8MM **Privately Held**
WEB: www.pentechind.com
SIC: **3541** Machine tools, metal cutting type

(G-13855)
PIPER INDUSTRIES INC
15930 Common Rd (48066-1812)
P.O. Box 41 (48066-0041)
PHONE..................................586 771-5100
Walter A Wosik, *President*
Marshall Wosik, *Sales Mgr*
Amanda Wosik, *Accounts Mgr*
▲ EMP: 100 **EST:** 1946
SQ FT: 40,000
SALES (est): 18.5MM **Privately Held**
WEB: www.piperindustries.com
SIC: **3494** 3594 3492 3451 Pipe fittings; fluid power pumps & motors; fluid power valves & hose fittings; screw machine products

(G-13856)
PROPHOTONIX LIMITED
Also Called: Stilson Die-Draulic
15935 Sturgeon St (48066-1818)
PHONE..................................586 778-1100
Tom Graskewicz, *Manager*
EMP: 30
SQ FT: 50,000
SALES (corp-wide): 20.4MM **Publicly Held**
WEB: www.stockeryale.com
SIC: **3542** 3594 3544 3537 Machine tools, metal forming type; fluid power pumps & motors; special dies, tools, jigs & fixtures; industrial trucks & tractors
PA: Prophotonix Limited
13 Red Roof Ln Ste 200
Salem NH 03079
603 893-8778

(G-13857)
PROTO-TEK MANUFACTURING INC
16094 Common Rd (48066-1814)
PHONE..................................586 772-2663
Richard Hansen, *President*
EMP: 20
SQ FT: 12,800
SALES (est): 3.3MM **Privately Held**
SIC: **3544** 3599 Jigs & fixtures; machine shop, jobbing & repair

(G-13858)
R & R BROACH INC
29680 Parkway (48066-1928)
PHONE..................................586 779-2227
Patrick W Considine, *President*
EMP: 5
SQ FT: 5,000
SALES (est): 510.7K **Privately Held**
SIC: **3599** Machine shop, jobbing & repair

(G-13859)
RCO AEROSPACE PRODUCTS LLC
15725 E 12 Mile Rd (48066-1844)
PHONE..................................586 774-8400
Michael Carollo, *CEO*
EMP: 55
SALES: 28MM
SALES (corp-wide): 172.7MM **Privately Held**
SIC: **2531** Public building & related furniture
PA: Rco Engineering, Inc.
29200 Calahan Rd
Roseville MI 48066
586 774-0100

(G-13860)
RCO ENGINEERING INC
15725 E 12 Mile Rd (48066-1844)
PHONE..................................586 620-4133
Jeff Simek, *Principal*
EMP: 65
SALES (corp-wide): 172.7MM **Privately Held**
SIC: **3714** 3089 3325 3365 Motor vehicle parts & accessories; injection molded finished plastic products; steel foundries; aluminum foundries; employment agencies; public building & related furniture
PA: Rco Engineering, Inc.
29200 Calahan Rd
Roseville MI 48066
586 774-0100

GEOGRAPHIC SECTION
Roseville - Macomb County (G-13888)

(G-13861)
REID INDUSTRIES INC
28440 Groesbeck Hwy (48066-2329)
PHONE..................................586 776-2070
Michael McCuish, *President*
EMP: 3
SQ FT: 6,400
SALES (est): 332.7K **Privately Held**
SIC: 3544 3545 Special dies, tools, jigs & fixtures; machine tool attachments & accessories

(G-13862)
ROBERT & SON BLACK OX SPECIAL
30665 Edison Dr (48066-1583)
PHONE..................................586 778-7633
Tim Roberts, *President*
Matt Roberts, *Manager*
EMP: 8
SQ FT: 8,000
SALES (est): 1MM **Privately Held**
SIC: 3471 Electroplating of metals or formed products

(G-13863)
ROYAL OAK NAME PLATE COMPANY
16560 Industrial St (48066-1997)
PHONE..................................586 774-8500
Joseph M Hoffman, *President*
Linda Hoffman, *Vice Pres*
Fred C Pike, *Treasurer*
EMP: 12
SQ FT: 14,500
SALES (est): 1.3MM
SALES (corp-wide): 1.4MM **Privately Held**
WEB: www.ronp.com
SIC: 3479 3993 Name plates: engraved, etched, etc.; signs & advertising specialties
PA: Joseph M Hoffman Inc
16560 Industrial St
Roseville MI 48066
586 774-8500

(G-13864)
RPS TOOL AND ENGINEERING INC (PA)
16149 Common Rd (48066-1813)
PHONE..................................586 298-6590
Richard May, *President*
Don Watson, *General Mgr*
Scott Constantine, *Vice Pres*
Ryan Furtah, *Program Mgr*
Kevin May, *Program Mgr*
EMP: 33 **EST:** 2011
SALES (est): 5.7MM **Privately Held**
SIC: 3089 8711 Injection molding of plastics; engineering services

(G-13865)
SALINE MANUFACTURING INC
15890 Sturgeon Ct (48066-1823)
PHONE..................................586 294-4701
Bruce Steffens, *President*
EMP: 15
SQ FT: 15,000
SALES (est): 4MM **Privately Held**
SIC: 3443 Trash racks, metal plate

(G-13866)
SAMCO INDUSTRIES LLC
15985 Sturgeon St (48066-1818)
PHONE..................................586 447-3900
Sam Munaco,
EMP: 15
SALES: 950K **Privately Held**
SIC: 3914 Silverware & plated ware

(G-13867)
SEAMAN INDUSTRIES INC
16500 E 13 Mile Rd (48066-1507)
P.O. Box 35 (48066-0035)
PHONE..................................586 776-9620
Robert Trailer, *President*
Helen Trailer, *Admin Sec*
EMP: 3
SQ FT: 6,500
SALES (est): 470.4K **Privately Held**
SIC: 3714 Motor vehicle parts & accessories

(G-13868)
SHILOH MANUFACTURING LLC
Also Called: Plant 28
28101 Grsbeck Hwy Rsville Roseville (48066)
PHONE..................................586 873-2835
Luai Kahli, *Plant Mgr*
EMP: 13 **Publicly Held**
SIC: 3465 3469 3544 Automotive stampings; metal stampings; special dies, tools, jigs & fixtures
HQ: Shiloh Manufacturing, Llc
880 Steel Dr
Valley City OH 44280
330 558-2693

(G-13869)
SIGNATURE GLASS INC
26415 Gratiot Ave (48066-5108)
P.O. Box 66399 (48066-6399)
PHONE..................................586 447-9000
Dennis J Kocis II, *President*
EMP: 3
SALES (est): 209.6K **Privately Held**
SIC: 3231 Products of purchased glass

(G-13870)
SKIP PRINTING AND DUP CO
Also Called: Skip Printing Co.
28032 Groesbeck Hwy (48066-2345)
PHONE..................................586 779-2640
Robert Sauers III, *President*
Gail S Sauers, *Treasurer*
Tricia Bower, *Technology*
EMP: 8
SQ FT: 2,010
SALES: 1MM **Privately Held**
SIC: 2752 7336 2791 Commercial printing, offset; graphic arts & related design; typesetting, computer controlled

(G-13871)
SODECIA AUTO DETROIT CORP
Also Called: AZ Automotive
15260 Common Rd (48066-1810)
PHONE..................................586 759-2200
Mitch Leeman, *Manager*
Rosa Gardner, *Manager*
EMP: 300
SQ FT: 28,400 **Privately Held**
WEB: www.azautomotive.com
SIC: 3465 Body parts, automobile: stamped metal
HQ: Sodecia Automotive Detroit Corp.
969 Chicago Rd
Troy MI 48083
586 759-2200

(G-13872)
SONIC EDM LLC
29970 Calahan Rd (48066-1889)
PHONE..................................248 379-2888
Louis Oudin, *Mng Member*
Carol Oudin,
EMP: 3
SALES: 300K **Privately Held**
WEB: www.sonicedm.com
SIC: 3462 Automotive forgings, ferrous: crankshaft, engine, axle, etc.

(G-13873)
SPARTAN GRINDING INC
28186 Hayes Rd (48066-2390)
PHONE..................................586 774-1970
Richard Smith, *President*
EMP: 11 **EST:** 1914
SQ FT: 5,000
SALES (est): 2MM
SALES (corp-wide): 18.2MM **Privately Held**
WEB: www.spartangrinding.com
SIC: 3599 Machine shop, jobbing & repair
PA: Wolverine Bronze Company
28178 Hayes Rd
Roseville MI 48066
586 776-8180

(G-13874)
STATE WIDE GRINDING CO
27980 Groesbeck Hwy (48066-2757)
PHONE..................................586 778-5700
George H Barnett, *President*
Gloria Barnett, *Office Mgr*
EMP: 9 **EST:** 1977
SQ FT: 10,000
SALES: 1.3MM **Privately Held**
SIC: 3599 Machine shop, jobbing & repair

(G-13875)
STILSON PRODUCTS LLC
28400 Groesbeck Hwy (48066-2329)
PHONE..................................586 778-1100
Jeff Smith,
EMP: 30
SALES (est): 4.2MM **Privately Held**
WEB: www.stilsonproducts.com
SIC: 3542 Machine tools, metal forming type

(G-13876)
T E C BORING
15645 Sturgeon St (48066-1816)
PHONE..................................586 443-5437
Michael Crusoe, *Administration*
EMP: 4
SALES (est): 406.9K **Privately Held**
SIC: 3541 Drilling & boring machines

(G-13877)
TBL FABRICATIONS INC
28178 Hayes Rd (48066-2346)
PHONE..................................586 294-2087
Douglas Smith, *President*
Richard Smith, *Vice Pres*
Dennis Mascioli, *Treasurer*
EMP: 20
SQ FT: 30,000
SALES: 5.5MM
SALES (corp-wide): 18.2MM **Privately Held**
WEB: www.wolverinebronze.com
SIC: 3441 Building components, structural steel
PA: Wolverine Bronze Company
28178 Hayes Rd
Roseville MI 48066
586 776-8180

(G-13878)
THERMAL DESIGNS & MANUFACTURNG
16660 E 13 Mile Rd (48066-1556)
PHONE..................................586 773-5231
L Garnick, *Owner*
EMP: 30
SALES (est): 1.9MM **Privately Held**
SIC: 1761 7692 3567 3444 Sheet metalwork; welding repair; industrial furnaces & ovens; sheet metalwork

(G-13879)
TRI-COUNTY FAB INC
16153 Common Rd (48066-1813)
PHONE..................................586 443-5130
David Kuffer, *President*
Steve Stopinski, *Vice Pres*
EMP: 4
SQ FT: 10,000
SALES (est): 571.9K **Privately Held**
SIC: 3441 Fabricated structural metal

(G-13880)
TRI-WAY MANUFACTURING INC
Also Called: TRI-WAY MOLD & ENGINEERING
15363 E 12 Mile Rd (48066-1834)
PHONE..................................586 776-0700
John J Burke, *President*
Robert Zerrafa, *Vice Pres*
Tammy Leonard, *Admin Sec*
▲ **EMP:** 30 **EST:** 1976
SQ FT: 20,800
SALES: 6.6MM **Privately Held**
WEB: www.tri-waymold.com
SIC: 3599 3089 3544 Electrical discharge machining (EDM); injection molded finished plastic products; special dies, tools, jigs & fixtures

(G-13881)
TRIANGLE PRINTING INC
30520 Gratiot Ave (48066-1728)
PHONE..................................586 293-7530
Jeff Lawson, *President*
Cathy Lawson, *Vice Pres*
EMP: 6
SQ FT: 1,500
SALES (est): 826K **Privately Held**
SIC: 2752 Commercial printing, offset

(G-13882)
TRUE INDUSTRIAL CORPORATION (PA)
Also Called: CENTERLINE DIE & ENGINEERING
15300 E 12 Mile Rd (48066-1835)
PHONE..................................586 771-3500
Gregory L Kiesgen, *CEO*
Gary A Kiesgen, *President*
Emil Cook, *Purch Agent*
Amanda Savon, *Controller*
Gary Marshall, *Info Tech Mgr*
▲ **EMP:** 57
SQ FT: 42,300
SALES: 12MM **Privately Held**
SIC: 3544 Die sets for metal stamping (presses)

(G-13883)
TURRIS ITALIAN FOODS INC (PA)
16695 Common Rd (48066-1901)
PHONE..................................586 773-6010
Anthony P Turri Jr, *President*
John Sadowsky, *General Mgr*
Mary Derlicki, *Corp Secy*
John Turri, *COO*
Joe Morano, *Vice Pres*
▲ **EMP:** 89
SQ FT: 24,000
SALES: 17.7MM
SALES (corp-wide): 18MM **Privately Held**
WEB: www.turrisitalianfoods.com
SIC: 2038 2098 Ethnic foods, frozen; macaroni & spaghetti

(G-13884)
U S TARGET INC
16472 Common Rd (48066-5903)
PHONE..................................586 445-3131
Mark Polakowski, *President*
EMP: 3 **EST:** 1975
SQ FT: 4,000
SALES (est): 301.9K **Privately Held**
WEB: www.ustargetonline.com
SIC: 3949 Targets, archery & rifle shooting

(G-13885)
ULTIMATION INDUSTRIES LLC
15935 Sturgeon St (48066-1818)
PHONE..................................586 771-1881
Jacqueline Canny, *CEO*
Carol Barker, *Accounting Mgr*
EMP: 45
SALES (est): 12MM **Privately Held**
SIC: 3535 Conveyors & conveying equipment

(G-13886)
ULTRA STITCH EMBROIDERY
16627 Eastland St (48066-2089)
PHONE..................................586 498-5600
Marilyn Jolet, *Owner*
Robert Jolet, *Owner*
EMP: 10
SALES (est): 510K **Privately Held**
SIC: 2395 Embroidery & art needlework

(G-13887)
UPTON INDUSTRIES INC
Also Called: Ualoy
30435 Groesbeck Hwy Ste 2 (48066-1599)
PHONE..................................586 771-1200
William I Minoletti, *President*
Kenneth Minoletti, *COO*
Jerry Bogan, *Project Engr*
Cheryl Carrothers, *Admin Asst*
EMP: 20
SQ FT: 35,000
SALES (est): 4.9MM **Privately Held**
WEB: www.uptonindustries.com
SIC: 3567 3559 Industrial furnaces & ovens; metal finishing equipment for plating, etc.

(G-13888)
VERSI-TECH INCORPORATED
Also Called: Versa Tech Technologies
29901 Calahan Rd (48066-1892)
PHONE..................................586 944-2230
Ron Schroeder, *Principal*
EMP: 10
SQ FT: 16,500

Roseville - Macomb County (G-13889)

SALES (est): 2.1MM
SALES (corp-wide): 36.3MM **Privately Held**
WEB: www.mid-westforge.com
SIC: 3599 Machine shop, jobbing & repair
PA: Mid-West Forge Corporation
  17301 Saint Clair Ave
  Cleveland OH 44110
  216 481-3030

(G-13889)
VIRTEC MANUFACTURING LLC
28302 Hayes Rd (48066-2317)
PHONE..................................313 590-2367
Charles Palms, *Mng Member*
Kevin Kosciolek, *Mng Member*
Jeff Miller, *Mng Member*
EMP: 10
SQ FT: 14,200
SALES (est): 938K **Privately Held**
SIC: 7692 7389 Automotive welding; metal cutting services

(G-13890)
WESTGOOD MANUFACTURING CO (PA)
15211 E 11 Mile Rd (48066-2789)
PHONE..................................586 771-3970
Edna Westerman, *President*
Lisa Spear, *Treasurer*
EMP: 20 EST: 1957
SQ FT: 11,000
SALES (est): 2.3MM **Privately Held**
SIC: 3544 3451 Special dies, tools, jigs & fixtures; screw machine products

(G-13891)
WOLVERINE BRONZE COMPANY (PA)
Also Called: Wb
28178 Hayes Rd (48066-2391)
PHONE..................................586 776-8180
Richard A Smith, *President*
Dennis Mascioli, *Corp Secy*
Douglas Smith, *Vice Pres*
William P Smith, *VP Mfg*
Bill Smith Jr, *Plant Mgr*
EMP: 60 EST: 1956
SQ FT: 90,000
SALES (est): 18.2MM **Privately Held**
WEB: www.wolverinebronze.com
SIC: 3365 3364 3322 Aluminum & aluminum-based alloy castings; brass & bronze die-castings; malleable iron foundries

(G-13892)
WOLVERINE PLATING CORPORATION
29456 Groesbeck Hwy (48066-1969)
PHONE..................................586 771-5000
Rick Keith, *President*
Tim Slater, *COO*
Kenneth Wrobel, *Vice Pres*
Kenneth M Wrobel, *Vice Pres*
Thomas Braciszewski, *VP Opers*
▲ EMP: 50 EST: 1956
SALES (est): 14MM **Privately Held**
WEB: www.wolvpltg.com
SIC: 3471 Electroplating of metals or formed products

(G-13893)
ZUCKERO & SONS INC
27450 Groesbeck Hwy (48066-2715)
PHONE..................................586 772-3377
David Zuckero, *President*
Michael Zuckero, *Vice Pres*
Sarah Zuckero, *VP Finance*
EMP: 40
SQ FT: 15,000
SALES (est): 7.3MM **Privately Held**
WEB: www.zuckero.com
SIC: 2541 Cabinets, except refrigerated: show, display, etc.: wood

Rothbury
Oceana County

(G-13894)
BARBER STEEL FOUNDRY CORP
2625 W Winston Rd (49452-9777)
PHONE..................................231 894-1830
EMP: 18
SALES (est): 4.9MM
SALES (corp-wide): 4.3B **Publicly Held**
SIC: 3324 Steel investment foundries
HQ: Wabtec Corporation
  1001 Airbrake Ave
  Wilmerding PA 15148

(G-13895)
S & N MACHINE & FABRICATING
Also Called: S&N Fabricating
7989 S Michigan Ave (49452-7949)
PHONE..................................231 894-2658
Steven Putnam, *President*
Nancy Putnam, *Treasurer*
EMP: 16
SALES (est): 3.3MM **Privately Held**
WEB: www.sn-machine.com
SIC: 3449 3444 3441 Miscellaneous metalwork; sheet metalwork; fabricated structural metal

(G-13896)
WELLMASTER CONSULTING INC
2658 W Winston Rd (49452-9777)
PHONE..................................231 893-9266
EMP: 13
SQ FT: 19,000
SALES (est): 1.9MM **Privately Held**
SIC: 1389 Oil/Gas Field Services

Royal Oak
Oakland County

(G-13897)
360OFME INC
225 S Main St Ste 200 (48067-2656)
P.O. Box 4449, Traverse City (49685-4449)
PHONE..................................844 360-6363
EMP: 6
SQ FT: 1,850
SALES (est): 148.8K **Privately Held**
SIC: 7372 Prepackaged Software Services

(G-13898)
AAM PWDER METAL COMPONENTS INC
Also Called: Cloyes-Renold
2727 W 14 Mile Rd (48073-1712)
PHONE..................................248 597-3800
David Schaefer, *Manager*
EMP: 11
SALES (corp-wide): 7.2B **Publicly Held**
WEB: www.cloyes.com
SIC: 3714 Motor vehicle parts & accessories
HQ: Aam Powder Metal Components, Inc.
  615 W Walnut St
  Paris AR 72855
  479 963-2105

(G-13899)
ALCO PRINTING SERVICES INC
4921 Delemere Ave (48073-1016)
PHONE..................................248 280-1124
Alex M Watson, *President*
EMP: 3 EST: 1977
SQ FT: 3,000
SALES: 190K **Privately Held**
SIC: 2752 Commercial printing, offset

(G-13900)
ALLMET INDUSTRIES INC
5030 Leafdale Blvd (48073-1011)
PHONE..................................248 280-4600
Rodney R Floyd, *President*
Sheralyn M Floyd, *Vice Pres*
EMP: 5
SQ FT: 4,500
SALES (est): 579.2K **Privately Held**
WEB: www.allmetindustries.com
SIC: 3599 Machine shop, jobbing & repair

(G-13901)
AMERICAN INDUSTRIAL GAUGE INC
Also Called: Standard Spring
4839 Leafdale Blvd (48073-1008)
PHONE..................................248 280-0048
John M Payne, *President*
EMP: 5
SQ FT: 2,800
SALES (est): 124.1K **Privately Held**
SIC: 3545 Gauges (machine tool accessories); tools & accessories for machine tools

(G-13902)
ANGLER STRATEGIES LLC
2815 Benjamin Ave (48073-3088)
PHONE..................................248 439-1420
Sean Dunlop, *Principal*
EMP: 3
SALES (est): 115.7K **Privately Held**
SIC: 2711 Newspapers

(G-13903)
APIS NORTH AMERICA LLC
938 N Washington Ave (48067-1740)
PHONE..................................800 470-8970
Lynn Johnson, *President*
EMP: 3
SALES: 1.3MM
SALES (corp-wide): 9.3MM **Privately Held**
SIC: 7372 8243 8748 Application computer software; software training, computer; systems analysis & engineering consulting services
PA: Apis Informationstechnologien Gmbh
  Gewerbepark A 13
  Worth A.D.Donau 93086
  948 294-150

(G-13904)
ARBOR PRESS LLC
Also Called: Arboroakland Group
4303 Normandy Ct (48073-2266)
PHONE..................................248 549-0150
Niels Winther, *CEO*
Ken Dause, *Partner*
Paul Cartwright, *Vice Pres*
Jim Duprey, *Vice Pres*
Michael Penkala, *Purchasing*
EMP: 58
SQ FT: 30,000
SALES (est): 18.5MM **Privately Held**
WEB: www.thinkarbor.com
SIC: 2752 8742 8299 Commercial printing, offset; marketing consulting services; educational services

(G-13905)
ARCHITECTURAL PRODUCTS INC
4850 Coolidge Hwy B (48073-1022)
PHONE..................................248 585-8272
Ronald Crossley, *President*
EMP: 5 EST: 1967
SALES (est): 824.9K **Privately Held**
SIC: 2431 Millwork

(G-13906)
ASP HHI HOLDINGS INC (DH)
2727 W 14 Mile Rd (48073-1712)
PHONE..................................248 597-3800
Mike Johnson, *CFO*
EMP: 11
SALES (est): 328.8MM
SALES (corp-wide): 7.2B **Publicly Held**
SIC: 3714 Motor vehicle parts & accessories

(G-13907)
BERLINE GROUP INC
423 N Main St Ste 300 (48067-1884)
PHONE..................................248 203-0492
James Berline, *CEO*
Michelle Horowitz, *President*
EMP: 30
SQ FT: 10,000
SALES (est): 6.6MM **Privately Held**
SIC: 7311 3993 Advertising agencies; signs & advertising specialties

(G-13908)
BLUE DE-SIGNS LLC
4605 Briarwood Ave (48073-1734)
PHONE..................................248 808-2583
Sasha Nedelkoski, *Mng Member*
EMP: 5
SALES: 320K **Privately Held**
SIC: 3993 Signs & advertising specialties

(G-13909)
BONAL INTERNATIONAL INC (PA)
1300 N Campbell Rd Ste A (48067-1573)
PHONE..................................248 582-0900
Paul Y Hebel, *Vice Ch Bd*
Thomas E Hebel, *President*
Harold Hebel, *CFO*
Brian F York, *Treasurer*
Gregory Merritt, *VP Sales*
EMP: 14
SQ FT: 13,500
SALES: 2MM **Privately Held**
WEB: www.bonal.com
SIC: 3829 Stress, strain & flaw detecting/measuring equipment

(G-13910)
BONAL TECHNOLOGIES INC
1300 N Campbell Rd (48067-1573)
PHONE..................................248 582-0900
Thomas E Hebel, *Ch of Bd*
A George Hebel III, *Ch of Bd*
Greg Merritt, *Vice Pres*
Brian F York, *Treasurer*
Paul Pieprzyk, *Accounts Exec*
EMP: 17
SQ FT: 11,600
SALES: 1.3MM
SALES (corp-wide): 2MM **Privately Held**
WEB: www.pulsepuddle.com
SIC: 3829 3544 Stress, strain & flaw detecting/measuring equipment; special dies, tools, jigs & fixtures
PA: Bonal International, Inc.
  1300 N Campbell Rd Ste A
  Royal Oak MI 48067
  248 582-0900

(G-13911)
BROLLYTIME INC
306 S Washington Ave # 400 (48067-3845)
PHONE..................................312 854-7606
Greg Edson, *President*
EMP: 10
SALES (est): 787K **Privately Held**
SIC: 3991 3999 2399 Brushes, household or industrial; umbrellas, canes & parts; pet collars, leashes, etc.: non-leather

(G-13912)
C S L INC
Also Called: Sir Speedy
1323 E 11 Mile Rd (48067-2051)
PHONE..................................248 549-4434
Cynthia K Leigh, *President*
Scott Leigh, *Vice Pres*
EMP: 7
SQ FT: 5,000
SALES (est): 820K **Privately Held**
SIC: 2752 Commercial printing, lithographic

(G-13913)
CHANGE DYNAMIX INC
4327 Delemere Ct (48073-1809)
PHONE..................................248 671-6700
Robert Capinjola, *CEO*
Steve Akers, *CTO*
EMP: 7
SQ FT: 4,000
SALES: 800K **Privately Held**
SIC: 7372 Application computer software

(G-13914)
CHELSEA GRINDING COMPANY
2417 Vinsetta Blvd (48073-3337)
PHONE..................................517 796-0343
EMP: 41 EST: 1953
SQ FT: 11,500
SALES (est): 3.5MM **Privately Held**
SIC: 3599 Machine Shop
PA: Das Group, Inc.
  2417 Vinsetta Blvd
  Royal Oak MI 48073
  248 670-2718

GEOGRAPHIC SECTION

Royal Oak - Oakland County (G-13945)

(G-13915)
CRAWFORD ASSOCIATES INC
Also Called: Creative Graphic Concepts
4526 Fernlee Ave (48073-1782)
PHONE..................248 549-9494
Gregg Kaitner, *President*
Chris Kaitner, *Corp Secy*
EMP: 6 **EST:** 1976
SQ FT: 3,200
SALES (est): 620.6K **Privately Held**
SIC: 2396 Screen printing on fabric articles

(G-13916)
CREATIVE ARTS STUDIO ROYAL OAK
114 W 4th St (48067-3805)
PHONE..................248 544-2234
Kristen Ashare, *Owner*
David Fredenberg, *Co-Owner*
▲ **EMP:** 10
SALES: 250K **Privately Held**
SIC: 3269 Art & ornamental ware, pottery

(G-13917)
DAS GROUP INC (PA)
2417 Vinsetta Blvd (48073-3337)
PHONE..................248 670-2718
Doug Steward, *President*
EMP: 4
SQ FT: 25,000
SALES (est): 3.3MM **Privately Held**
SIC: 3599 3549 Machine shop, jobbing & repair; assembly machines, including robotic

(G-13918)
DETROIT STEEL GROUP INC
916 S Washington Ave (48067-3216)
PHONE..................248 298-2900
Terry Boyette, *President*
EMP: 6
SQ FT: 2,000
SALES (est): 1.9MM **Privately Held**
SIC: 5051 3312 Steel; blast furnaces & steel mills

(G-13919)
DIXON & RYAN CORPORATION
4343 Normandy Ct Ste A (48073-2201)
PHONE..................248 549-4000
Mark D Ryan, *President*
Richard Dixon, *Vice Pres*
EMP: 10 **EST:** 1929
SQ FT: 6,500
SALES (est): 1.9MM **Privately Held**
SIC: 7699 3545 3544 Professional instrument repair services; machine tool accessories; special dies, tools, jigs & fixtures

(G-13920)
E I DU PONT DE NEMOURS & CO
1412 W Windemere Ave (48073-5219)
PHONE..................248 549-4794
Peter Merritt, *Manager*
EMP: 339
SALES (corp-wide): 30.6B **Publicly Held**
WEB: www.dupont.com
SIC: 2879 Agricultural chemicals
HQ: E. I. Du Pont De Nemours And Company
974 Centre Rd Bldg 735
Wilmington DE 19805
302 485-3000

(G-13921)
EMATRIX ENERGY SYSTEMS INC
4706 Delemere Blvd (48073-1776)
PHONE..................248 797-2149
EMP: 3
SALES (est): 348.9K **Privately Held**
SIC: 3691 Storage batteries

(G-13922)
EMATRIX ENERGY SYSTEMS INC
4425 Fernlee Ave (48073-1722)
PHONE..................248 629-9111
Idan Kovent, *President*
Matthew Griffith, *Admin Secy*
EMP: 4
SQ FT: 2,900
SALES (est): 169.6K **Privately Held**
SIC: 3691 Batteries, rechargeable

(G-13923)
EMMA SOGOIAN INC
4336 Normandy Ct (48073-2265)
PHONE..................248 549-8690
Emma Sogoian, *President*
Kal P Sogoian, *Vice Pres*
Alexander J Jemal Jr, *Admin Sec*
EMP: 29
SQ FT: 20,000
SALES (est): 3.9MM **Privately Held**
SIC: 3599 3714 Machine shop, jobbing & repair; motor vehicle parts & accessories

(G-13924)
EMPIRE PRINTING
400 E Lincoln Ave Ste A (48067-2766)
PHONE..................248 547-9223
Asgar Ismailji, *Partner*
Salma Ismailji, *Partner*
EMP: 4
SALES (est): 370K **Privately Held**
SIC: 2752 Commercial printing, offset

(G-13925)
ENGINERED COMBUSTN SYSTEMS LLC
4240 Delemere Ct (48073-1808)
PHONE..................248 549-1703
Adam Rusek, *Engineer*
David Beebe,
EMP: 7
SQ FT: 5,000
SALES (est): 1.7MM **Privately Held**
WEB: www.engineeredcombustionsystems.com
SIC: 3823 Combustion control instruments

(G-13926)
EPATH LOGIC INC
418 N Main St 200 (48067-1813)
PHONE..................313 375-5375
Michael Germain, *President*
EMP: 6
SALES (est): 370.2K **Privately Held**
SIC: 7372 Application computer software

(G-13927)
EXCLUSIVE IMAGERY INC
1505 E 11 Mile Rd (48067-2027)
PHONE..................248 436-2999
Ceaser Yaldo, *Co-Owner*
EMP: 7 **EST:** 2007
SQ FT: 10,000
SALES: 1MM **Privately Held**
SIC: 2752 7336 3479 2396 Commercial printing, offset; poster & decal printing, lithographic; commercial art & graphic design; etching & engraving; screen printing on fabric articles

(G-13928)
FORMTECH INDS HOLDINGS LLC
2727 W 14 Mile Rd (48073-1712)
PHONE..................248 597-3800
Charles W Moore, *CFO*
EMP: 5
SALES (est): 490.7K **Privately Held**
SIC: 3714 Motor vehicle parts & accessories

(G-13929)
GAYLES CHOCOLATES LIMITED
417 S Washington Ave (48067-3823)
P.O. Box 1873, Sedona AZ (86339-1873)
PHONE..................248 398-0001
Gayle Harte, *President*
▲ **EMP:** 23
SQ FT: 5,000
SALES (est): 1.8MM **Privately Held**
WEB: www.gayleschocolates.com
SIC: 5441 2064 2066 Confectionery produced for direct sale on the premises; candy; chocolate candy, except solid chocolate; chocolate & cocoa products

(G-13930)
GOODYEAR TIRE & RUBBER COMPANY
29444 Woodward Ave (48073-0903)
PHONE..................248 336-0135
EMP: 6
SALES (corp-wide): 15.4B **Publicly Held**
SIC: 5531 3011 Automotive tires; inner tubes, all types
PA: The Goodyear Tire & Rubber Company
200 E Innovation Way
Akron OH 44316
330 796-2121

(G-13931)
H A KING CO INC (PA)
5038 Leafdale Blvd (48073-1011)
PHONE..................248 280-0006
Alfred W Rich, *President*
EMP: 6 **EST:** 1927
SQ FT: 3,500
SALES (est): 1.8MM **Privately Held**
WEB: www.ha-king.com
SIC: 3069 Molded rubber products

(G-13932)
HHI FORGING LLC (DH)
2727 W 14 Mile Rd (48073-1712)
PHONE..................248 284-2900
George Thanopoulos,
EMP: 32 **EST:** 2005
SALES (est): 253.9MM
SALES (corp-wide): 7.2B **Publicly Held**
SIC: 3462 Automotive forgings, ferrous: crankshaft, engine, axle, etc.
HQ: Hephaestus Holdings, Llc
39475 W 13 Mile Rd # 105
Novi MI 48377
248 479-2700

(G-13933)
HHI FORM TECH LLC
2727 W 14 Mile Rd (48073-1712)
PHONE..................248 597-3800
George Thanopoulos, *Mng Member*
Matt Nosewicz,
▲ **EMP:** 500
SALES (est): 154.3MM
SALES (corp-wide): 1.9B **Privately Held**
SIC: 3462 Automotive & internal combustion engine forgings
PA: Kps Capital Partners, Lp
485 Lexington Ave Fl 31
New York NY 10017
212 338-5100

(G-13934)
HHI FORMTECH INDUSTRIES LLC
2727 W 14 Mile Rd (48073-1712)
PHONE..................248 597-3800
R Harris, *COO*
Richard J Larkin, *Exec VP*
Charles Moore, *CFO*
▼ **EMP:** 600
SALES (est): 151.8MM **Privately Held**
WEB: www.formtech2.com
SIC: 3462 Iron & steel forgings

(G-13935)
IMAGE PRINTING INC
1902 Crooks Rd (48073-4048)
PHONE..................248 585-4080
Donald F Edgerly, *President*
Sandra Edgerly, *Admin Sec*
EMP: 4
SQ FT: 4,200
SALES (est): 532.4K **Privately Held**
SIC: 2752 Commercial printing, offset; letters, circular or form; lithographed

(G-13936)
INTERNATIONAL MECH DESIGN
Also Called: I M D
2015 Bellaire Ave (48067-1516)
PHONE..................248 546-5740
Frank D Ascenzo, *President*
EMP: 21
SQ FT: 11,000
SALES: 722.2K **Privately Held**
WEB: www.inter-mech-design.com
SIC: 3545 3544 8711 Machine tool accessories; special dies, tools, jigs & fixtures; industrial engineers

(G-13937)
J & C INDUSTRIES INC
4520 Fernlee Ave (48073-1782)
PHONE..................248 549-4866
Jimmy Jones, *President*
Craig Allen Jones, *Vice Pres*
EMP: 5
SQ FT: 4,000
SALES (est): 360.2K **Privately Held**
SIC: 3544 Special dies, tools, jigs & fixtures

(G-13938)
JD HEMP INC
Also Called: Signs By Tomorrow
31930 Woodward Ave (48073-0939)
PHONE..................248 549-0095
Diana Hemp, *President*
Jack Hemp, *Vice Pres*
EMP: 5
SQ FT: 2,000
SALES: 520K **Privately Held**
SIC: 3993 Signs & advertising specialties

(G-13939)
JONES PRECISION JIG GRINDING
4520 Fernlee Ave (48073-1782)
PHONE..................248 549-4866
Jimmy Jones, *President*
EMP: 4
SQ FT: 4,000
SALES (est): 534.1K **Privately Held**
SIC: 3599 Machine shop, jobbing & repair

(G-13940)
JROP LLC
404 E 4th St Ste 110 (48067-2757)
PHONE..................800 404-9494
Carl Redding,
EMP: 10 **EST:** 2017
SALES (est): 150.4K **Privately Held**
SIC: 7549 7372 Towing, mobile homes; application computer software

(G-13941)
KLEIBERIT ADHESIVES USA INC
4305 Beverly Ct (48073-6349)
PHONE..................248 709-9308
EMP: 3
SALES (est): 123.2K **Privately Held**
SIC: 2891 Adhesives

(G-13942)
KOPPY CORPORATION (PA)
Also Called: Sigma Stamping Division
415 S West St Ste 200 (48067-2521)
PHONE..................248 373-1900
Ronald E Prater, *President*
Karen Prater, *Exec Dir*
EMP: 75 **EST:** 1938
SQ FT: 144,000
SALES (est): 15.9MM **Privately Held**
SIC: 3544 3542 Special dies & tools; jigs & fixtures; machine tools, metal forming type; punching, shearing & bending machines

(G-13943)
KYRIE ENTERPRISES LLC
Also Called: Kp Sogoian
4336 Normandy Ct (48073-2265)
PHONE..................248 549-8690
Kevin Colvin Jr, *Web Dvlpr*
Kevin L Colvin,
Michelle Colvin,
EMP: 25 **EST:** 2010
SALES (est): 2.8MM **Privately Held**
SIC: 3089 7538 Automotive parts, plastic; engine repair

(G-13944)
LMI TECHNOLOGIES INC
29488 Woodward Ave # 331 (48073-0903)
PHONE..................248 298-2839
Cathy Lim, *Human Res Mgr*
Glenn Hennin, *Branch Mgr*
EMP: 8
SALES (corp-wide): 1.8B **Privately Held**
SIC: 3577 Magnetic ink & optical scanning devices
HQ: Lmi Technologies, Inc
29488 Woodward Ave # 331
Royal Oak MI 48073
248 298-2839

(G-13945)
MAC LEAN-FOGG COMPANY
Also Called: Mac Lean Fasteners
3200 W 14 Mile Rd (48073-1609)
PHONE..................248 280-0880
Al Fabian, *General Mgr*
Ryan Heslin, *Materials Mgr*
Ana Menjak, *QC Mgr*

Guy Bennett, *Engineer*
Robert Janowski, *Engineer*
EMP: 150
SQ FT: 78,607
SALES (corp-wide): 1.2B **Privately Held**
WEB: www.maclean-fogg.com
SIC: 3678 3452 3714 Electronic connectors; bolts, nuts, rivets & washers; motor vehicle parts & accessories
PA: Mac Lean-Fogg Company
1000 Allanson Rd
Mundelein IL 60060
847 566-0010

(G-13946)
MANUFCTURING ASSEMBLY INTL LLC
Also Called: International Mfg & Assembly
2521 Torquay Ave (48073-1014)
PHONE 248 549-4700
Gilles Teste,
▲ **EMP:** 15
SQ FT: 51,000
SALES (est): 3.4MM **Privately Held**
SIC: 3465 Body parts, automobile: stamped metal

(G-13947)
MARQUETTE CASTINGS LLC
123 W 5th St (48067-2527)
PHONE 248 798-8035
K Steckling, *Principal*
EMP: 3 **EST:** 2016
SALES (est): 228.5K **Privately Held**
SIC: 3272 Concrete products

(G-13948)
MAYO WELDING & FABRICATING CO
5061 Delemere Ave (48073-1004)
PHONE 248 435-2730
James Suratt, *President*
David Suratt, *Business Mgr*
EMP: 7
SQ FT: 6,200
SALES: 500K **Privately Held**
SIC: 7692 3446 3444 3443 Welding repair; architectural metalwork; sheet metalwork; fabricated plate work (boiler shop); fabricated structural metal

(G-13949)
MCCLURES PICKLES LLC
212 Royal Ave (48073-5118)
PHONE 248 837-9323
EMP: 4
SALES (est): 290K **Privately Held**
SIC: 2035 Mfg Pickles/Sauces/Dressing

(G-13950)
MEDIAFORM LLC
623 E 6th St (48067-2851)
P.O. Box 550 (48068-0550)
PHONE 248 548-0260
Chris George, *Mng Member*
Noel George,
EMP: 20
SQ FT: 5,000
SALES (est): 2.4MM **Privately Held**
WEB: www.mediaformusa.com
SIC: 3083 Laminated plastic sheets

(G-13951)
MICHIGAN SOY PRODUCTS COMPANY
1213 N Main St (48067-1364)
PHONE 248 544-7742
Ken Lin, *President*
EMP: 6
SQ FT: 1,600
SALES (est): 687.9K **Privately Held**
SIC: 2075 Soybean oil mills

(G-13952)
MIND FUEL LLC
2120 N Connecticut Ave (48073-4212)
PHONE 248 414-5296
Jeffrey Sierra, *Principal*
EMP: 3
SALES (est): 152.7K **Privately Held**
SIC: 2869 Fuels

(G-13953)
NATIONAL SOAP COMPANY INC
1911 Bellaire Ave (48067-1514)
PHONE 248 545-8180
Gerald Carafelly, *President*
Carol Carafelly, *Corp Secy*
EMP: 4
SQ FT: 5,000
SALES: 160K **Privately Held**
WEB: www.nationalsoap.com
SIC: 5087 2841 Janitors' supplies; soap: granulated, liquid, cake, flaked or chip; detergents, synthetic organic or inorganic alkaline

(G-13954)
NORTH END ELECTRIC COMPANY
2000 Bellaire Ave (48067-1517)
PHONE 248 398-8187
Robert M Watt, *President*
EMP: 3
SQ FT: 2,400
SALES (est): 432.2K **Privately Held**
SIC: 7694 7699 5063 5084 Electric motor repair; pumps & pumping equipment repair; motors, electric; pumps & pumping equipment

(G-13955)
PANTHER JAMES LLC
Also Called: Drought
28822 Woodward Ave (48067-0941)
PHONE 248 850-7522
Caitlin James, *Mng Member*
EMP: 4
SALES (est): 181.9K **Privately Held**
SIC: 2033 5499 Vegetable juices: fresh; beverage stores

(G-13956)
PETNET SOLUTIONS INC
3601 W 13 Mile Rd (48073-6712)
PHONE 865 218-2000
Eric Bishop, *Branch Mgr*
EMP: 4
SALES (corp-wide): 95B **Privately Held**
SIC: 2835 Radioactive diagnostic substances
HQ: Petnet Solutions, Inc.
810 Innovation Dr
Knoxville TN 37932
865 218-2000

(G-13957)
PILKINGTON NORTH AMERICA INC
1920 Bellaire Ave (48067-1515)
PHONE 248 542-8300
EMP: 15 **Privately Held**
SIC: 3211 Mfg Flat Glass
HQ: Pilkington North America, Inc.
811 Madison Ave Fl 1
Toledo OH 43604
419 247-4955

(G-13958)
PRIMEWAY INC
4250 Normandy Ct (48067-2263)
PHONE 248 583-6922
Kevin Walby, *President*
EMP: 12
SQ FT: 12,000
SALES (est): 2.1MM **Privately Held**
SIC: 2521 Wood office furniture

(G-13959)
PRIORAT IMPORTERS CORPORATION
815 Baldwin Ave (48067-4207)
PHONE 248 217-4608
Craig Bell,
EMP: 3
SALES (est): 126.9K **Privately Held**
SIC: 2079 2099 Olive oil; honey, strained & bottled

(G-13960)
PYRAMID TOOL COMPANY INC
4512 Fernlee Ave (48073-1782)
PHONE 248 549-0602
John R Roberts, *President*
EMP: 3
SQ FT: 2,000
SALES: 200K **Privately Held**
SIC: 3545 Cutting tools for machine tools; tools & accessories for machine tools

(G-13961)
RALEIGH & RON CORPORATION (PA)
Also Called: Oakridge Supermarket
2560 Crooks Rd (48073-3352)
P.O. Box 71028, Madison Heights (48071-0028)
PHONE 248 280-2820
Ron Kohler, *President*
Raleigh Wilburn, *Vice Pres*
EMP: 100
SQ FT: 15,500
SALES (est): 32.1MM **Privately Held**
SIC: 5411 2051 Grocery stores, independent; bread, cake & related products

(G-13962)
RAM METER INC (HQ)
1815 Bellaire Ave Ste B (48067-1578)
PHONE 248 362-0990
Jerry Marsoupian, *CEO*
Ram Meter, *Sales Staff*
EMP: 13
SQ FT: 25,000
SALES: 4MM
SALES (corp-wide): 30.7MM **Privately Held**
WEB: www.rammeter.com
SIC: 5065 3825 3829 Electronic parts & equipment; instruments to measure electricity; measuring & controlling devices
PA: Hughes Corporation
16900 Foltz Pkwy
Strongsville OH 44149
440 238-2550

(G-13963)
RAYS ICE CREAM CO INC
4233 Coolidge Hwy (48073-1696)
PHONE 248 549-5256
Dale B Stevens, *President*
Thomas Stevens, *President*
EMP: 20 **EST:** 1958
SQ FT: 4,300
SALES (est): 2.7MM **Privately Held**
WEB: www.raysicecream.com
SIC: 2024 5812 2099 2038 Ice cream, bulk; ice cream stands or dairy bars; food preparations; frozen specialties

(G-13964)
RECYCLING RIZZO SERVICES LLC
Also Called: Royal Oak Recycling
414 E Hudson Ave (48067-3740)
PHONE 248 541-4020
Charles Rizzo Jr, *CEO*
Wade Stevenson, *CFO*
EMP: 70
SALES (est): 4.4MM
SALES (corp-wide): 12.4MM **Privately Held**
SIC: 4953 2611 Recycling, waste materials; pulp mills, mechanical & recycling processing; pulp manufactured from waste or recycled paper
PA: Gfl Environmental Real Property Inc
26999 Central Park Blvd # 200
Southfield MI 48076
888 877-4996

(G-13965)
REVOLUTIONS SIGNS DESIGNS LLC
2429 N Connecticut Ave (48073-4214)
PHONE 248 439-0727
Mark Mulcahy, *Mng Member*
EMP: 5 **EST:** 2009
SQ FT: 800
SALES (est): 297K **Privately Held**
SIC: 3993 Signs & advertising specialties

(G-13966)
ROCKET PRINT COPY SHIP CENTER
605 S Washington Ave (48067-3827)
PHONE 248 336-3636
Vaughn Masropian, *Principal*
EMP: 6
SALES (est): 417.2K **Privately Held**
SIC: 2752 Commercial printing, offset

(G-13967)
ROYAL OAK & BIRMINGHAM TENT (PA)
Also Called: Birmingham Royal Oak Tent Awng
2625 W 14 Mile Rd (48073-1710)
PHONE 248 542-5552
Carol Genereau,
EMP: 15
SQ FT: 2,100
SALES (est): 1.5MM **Privately Held**
SIC: 2394 1799 Awnings, fabric: made from purchased materials; awning installation

(G-13968)
ROYAL OAK MILLWORK COMPANY LLC
226 E Hudson Ave (48067-3700)
PHONE 248 547-1210
Stephen Kassab, *Principal*
EMP: 3
SALES (est): 351.6K **Privately Held**
SIC: 2599 Cabinets, factory

(G-13969)
RPB SAFETY LLC
2807 Samoset Rd (48073-1726)
PHONE 866 494-4599
Philip Ivory,
▲ **EMP:** 25
SALES (est): 14.5MM **Privately Held**
SIC: 5084 1731 3842 Safety equipment; safety & security specialization; respiratory protection equipment, personal

(G-13970)
SIGNS & DESIGNS INC
30414 Woodward Ave (48073-0913)
PHONE 248 549-4850
Phyllis R Sherwin, *President*
EMP: 3
SALES (est): 274.6K **Privately Held**
WEB: www.signs-n-designs.com
SIC: 3993 Signs, not made in custom sign painting shops

(G-13971)
SODIUS CORPORATION
418 N Main St Ste 200 (48067-1813)
PHONE 720 507-7078
Jean - Philippe Lerat, *CEO*
Thomas Capelle, *President*
EMP: 3
SALES: 2.5MM
SALES (corp-wide): 2.2MM **Privately Held**
SIC: 7372 Application computer software
PA: Sodius
34 Boulevard Marechal Alphonse Juin
Nantes 44100

(G-13972)
SPARKS EXHBITS ENVRNMENTS CORP
600 E 11 Mile Rd (48067-1998)
PHONE 248 291-0007
Mee Ryan, *Manager*
EMP: 3 **Privately Held**
SIC: 3999 7389 Advertising display products; trade show arrangement
HQ: Sparks Exhibits & Environments Corp.
2828 Charter Rd
Philadelphia PA 19154
215 676-1100

(G-13973)
STERLING OIL & CHEMICAL CO (PA)
702 E 11 Mile Rd (48067-1964)
PHONE 248 298-2973
Graham T Eddleston, *President*
Laura Eddleston, *Treasurer*
EMP: 1
SQ FT: 1,100
SALES (est): 1.2MM **Privately Held**
SIC: 2992 Oils & greases, blending & compounding

(G-13974)
STUDIO OF FINE ARTS INC
Also Called: Yaw Gallery
4921 Leafdale Blvd (48073-1020)
PHONE 313 280-1177
James J Yaw, *President*

GEOGRAPHIC SECTION

Nancy Yaw, *Vice Pres*
EMP: 3
SQ FT: 13,000
SALES (est): 420K **Privately Held**
WEB: www.yawgallery.com
SIC: 5199 2499 Art goods & supplies; picture & mirror frames, wood

(G-13975)
SWEET EARTH
313 S Main St (48067-2613)
PHONE...................................248 850-8031
Ryan Robertson, *Owner*
EMP: 4
SALES (est): 169.4K **Privately Held**
SIC: 2026 Yogurt

(G-13976)
TREE TECH
820 S Washington Ave (48067-3286)
PHONE...................................248 543-2166
Charles Seidel, *Partner*
Chuck Seidel, *Partner*
James Seidel, *Partner*
EMP: 4
SALES (est): 270K **Privately Held**
SIC: 2499 Kitchen, bathroom & household ware: wood

(G-13977)
UNDERGROUND BEV BRANDS LLC
800 N Rembrandt Ave (48067-2016)
PHONE...................................248 336-9383
EMP: 3
SALES (est): 80.4K **Privately Held**
SIC: 2086 Mfg Bottled/Canned Soft Drinks

(G-13978)
UNITED RESIN INC (PA)
4359 Normandy Ct (48073-2266)
PHONE...................................800 521-4757
Jane Wyer, *President*
John B Los, *Vice Pres*
EMP: 21
SQ FT: 20,000
SALES (est): 3.5MM **Privately Held**
SIC: 2821 Epoxy resins

(G-13979)
UP NORTH SPICES INC
612 E 4th St (48067-2802)
PHONE...................................419 346-4155
Eva WEI Qingchun, *CEO*
EMP: 3
SALES (est): 91.3K **Privately Held**
SIC: 2034 Dehydrated fruits, vegetables, soups

(G-13980)
V & M CORPORATION (PA)
Also Called: Royal Oak Waste Ppr Met No 2
414 E Hudson Ave (48067-3740)
PHONE...................................248 541-4020
Habib Mamou, *President*
Ed Mamou, *Vice Pres*
Diane White, *Treasurer*
Evan Barrett, *Sales Mgr*
Sharon Schypinski, *Admin Sec*
EMP: 42
SQ FT: 70,000
SALES (est): 23.1MM **Privately Held**
SIC: 5093 4953 3341 2611 Waste paper; metal scrap & waste materials; refuse systems; secondary nonferrous metals; pulp mills

(G-13981)
VERSICOR LLC
333 W 7th St (48067-2513)
PHONE...................................734 306-9137
Christina Coplen, *President*
EMP: 10
SQ FT: 1,400
SALES (est): 1MM **Privately Held**
SIC: 3829 Measuring & controlling devices

(G-13982)
ZFERRAL INC
Also Called: Ambassador Software
333 W 7th St Ste 310 (48067-2510)
PHONE...................................248 792-3472
Jeffrey Epstein, *CEO*
Zach Taylor, *Vice Pres*
Corey Fields, *Engineer*
Dave Haberkorn, *Finance Mgr*

Lindsey Benninger, *Sales Staff*
EMP: 4 **EST:** 2010
SALES (est): 270.3K
SALES (corp-wide): 2.2B **Privately Held**
SIC: 7372 Business oriented computer software
HQ: Intrado Corporation
11808 Miracle Hills Dr
Omaha NE 68154

Rudyard
Chippewa County

(G-13983)
BLACK CREEK TIMBER LLC
18026 S Sullivan Creek Rd (49780-9212)
PHONE...................................517 202-2169
Kristen Claus, *President*
EMP: 3 **EST:** 2016
SALES (est): 55.6K **Privately Held**
SIC: 0851 3559 2421 2431 Forestry services; kilns, lumber; custom sawmill; kiln drying of lumber; floor baseboards, wood

(G-13984)
KAMPERS WOODFIRE COMPANY INC
14696 S Tilson Rd (49780-9365)
PHONE...................................906 478-7902
Charles Kamper, *President*
Fred Kamper, *Vice Pres*
EMP: 3 **EST:** 1975
SALES (est): 500K **Privately Held**
SIC: 3433 1521 Stoves, wood & coal burning; new construction, single-family houses

(G-13985)
POSTMA BROTHERS MAPLE SYRUP
10702 W Ploegstra Rd (49780-9345)
PHONE...................................906 478-3051
Greg Postma, *Principal*
EMP: 6
SALES (est): 422.6K **Privately Held**
SIC: 2099 Maple syrup

(G-13986)
RMG FAMILY SUGAR BUSH INC
11866 W Thompson Rd (49780-9372)
PHONE...................................906 478-3038
Joy Ross, *President*
Michael J Ross, *Vice Pres*
Mike Ross, *Vice Pres*
EMP: 4
SALES (est): 363.4K **Privately Held**
WEB: www.rmgmaple.com
SIC: 2099 Maple syrup

Ruth
Huron County

(G-13987)
BISCHER READY-MIX INC (PA)
6121 Purdy Rd (48470-9720)
PHONE...................................989 479-3267
Melvin Bischer, *President*
Janet Bischer, *Corp Secy*
EMP: 7
SALES (est): 1.2MM **Privately Held**
SIC: 3273 1442 Ready-mixed concrete; gravel mining

(G-13988)
D & M CABINET SHOP INC
5230 Purdy Rd (48470-9769)
PHONE...................................989 479-9271
Douglas Klee, *President*
Marilyn Klee, *Corp Secy*
EMP: 6
SQ FT: 8,000
SALES: 700K **Privately Held**
WEB: www.dandmcabinet.com
SIC: 2434 2521 5211 Wood kitchen cabinets; wood office furniture; cabinets, kitchen

(G-13989)
RUTH DRAIN TILE INC
4551 Ruth Rd (48470-9780)
PHONE...................................989 864-3406
Margaret D Goniwiecha, *President*
John Goniwiecha, *Vice Pres*
EMP: 5
SQ FT: 2,000
SALES (est): 639K **Privately Held**
SIC: 3273 3272 Ready-mixed concrete; precast terrazo or concrete products

Saginaw
Saginaw County

(G-13990)
3DFX INTERACTIVE INC
1813 Mackinaw St (48602-3031)
PHONE...................................918 938-8967
Deanna Nixon, *CEO*
Jackson Nixon, *CEO*
Zachary Nixon,
David Weiner,
EMP: 45
SALES (est): 1.2MM **Privately Held**
SIC: 7372 7373 7371 3511 Operating systems computer software; turnkey vendors, computer systems; computer software systems analysis & design, custom; computer software development & applications; turbines & turbine generator set units, complete; windmills, electric generating; personal computers (microcomputers)

(G-13991)
ACCURATE CARBIDE TOOL CO INC
5655 N Westervelt Rd (48604-1200)
PHONE...................................989 755-0429
Marshall J Longtain, *President*
EMP: 13 **EST:** 1947
SQ FT: 7,200
SALES (est): 2.3MM **Privately Held**
WEB: www.accuratecarbide.com
SIC: 3545 Cutting tools for machine tools; machine tool attachments & accessories

(G-13992)
ADVANCE TECH SOLUTIONS LLC
Also Called: Remote Tank Monitors
1348 Delta Dr (48638-4610)
PHONE...................................989 928-1806
Peter Giles,
Jerry Ruthruff,
EMP: 6
SQ FT: 10,000
SALES: 800K **Privately Held**
SIC: 3824 Liquid meters

(G-13993)
AIRTIFICIAL INTELLIGENT ROBOTS
3175 Christy Way S Ste 5 (48603-2210)
PHONE...................................989 799-6669
Jaine Calaramunt, *President*
Salvabor Montaner, *Vice Pres*
EMP: 6
SQ FT: 3,000
SALES (est): 1MM
SALES (corp-wide): 18.1MM **Privately Held**
WEB: www.maprotest.com
SIC: 3569 Assembly machines, non-metalworking
HQ: Airtificial Intelligent Robots Sau Poligono La Guera, Sector 11c, Par Burgo De Osma-Ciudad De Osma 42300

(G-13994)
AL-FE HEAT TREATING INC
1300 Leon Scott Ct (48601-1204)
PHONE...................................989 752-2819
Matt Jones, *Manager*
EMP: 38
SALES (corp-wide): 81.9MM **Privately Held**
WEB: www.al-fe.com
SIC: 3398 Metal heat treating

HQ: Al-Fe Heat Treating, Llc
6920 Pointe Inverness Way # 140
Fort Wayne IN 46804
260 747-9422

(G-13995)
ALLIED TOOL AND MACHINE CO
3545 Janes Ave (48601-6369)
P.O. Box 1407 (48605-1407)
PHONE...................................989 755-5384
Bruce Dankert, *President*
Thomas Shabluk, *Vice Pres*
Scott Slominski, *Vice Pres*
Carrie Stedry, *Treasurer*
EMP: 23
SQ FT: 20,000
SALES (est): 6.1MM **Privately Held**
SIC: 3549 3544 Assembly machines, including robotic; special dies & tools

(G-13996)
ARTISANS CSTM MMORY MATTRESSES
Also Called: Artisans Mattresses
2200 S Hamilton St Ste 3 (48602-1277)
PHONE...................................989 793-3208
Dale Humbert, *President*
EMP: 15
SQ FT: 5,000
SALES: 500K **Privately Held**
WEB: www.artisansmattress.com
SIC: 2515 5712 3732 3714 Mattresses & foundations; furniture stores; boat building & repairing; motor vehicle parts & accessories

(G-13997)
B K CORPORATION
5675 Dixie Hwy (48601-5828)
PHONE...................................989 777-2111
Robert Webber, *President*
Jeff Maslin, *Partner*
Scott Johnson, *CFO*
Mark Kloha, *Human Res Dir*
Cindi Cole, *Receptionist*
EMP: 7
SALES (est): 849K **Privately Held**
SIC: 3559 Special industry machinery

(G-13998)
B&P LITTLEFORD DAY LLC
1000 Hess Ave (48601-3729)
PHONE...................................989 757-1300
EMP: 80
SALES (est): 8.9MM **Privately Held**
SIC: 3552 3559 3554 3556 Mfg Special Industrial Machinery For Process Industries Including Food Chemical Plastics Pharmaceuticals Textile & Paper

(G-13999)
B&P LITTLEFORD LLC (PA)
Also Called: B&P Process Eqp & Systems
1000 Hess Ave (48601-3729)
PHONE...................................989 757-1300
Laurence S Slovin, *President*
Robert Lytkowski, *Vice Pres*
Chasen Clement, *Project Mgr*
Joni Harshman, *Buyer*
Dan Lemke, *Buyer*
◆ **EMP:** 40 **EST:** 1959
SQ FT: 80,000
SALES (est): 18.8MM **Privately Held**
WEB: www.bpprocess.com
SIC: 3559 3542 3531 Chemical machinery & equipment; machine tools, metal forming type; construction machinery

(G-14000)
BANNER ENGINEERING & SALES INC
Also Called: Joseph M. Day Company
1840 N Michigan Ave Ste 1 (48602-5567)
PHONE...................................989 755-0584
J Michael Day, *Owner*
Kyle Gradowski, *General Mgr*
Jim Glidden, *Project Mgr*
EMP: 17
SQ FT: 12,000
SALES: 3.7MM **Privately Held**
WEB: www.banner-day.com
SIC: 3556 5074 3823 3433 Bakery machinery; gas burners; oil burners; boilers, hot water heating; industrial process control instruments; heating equipment, except electric

Saginaw - Saginaw County (G-14001)

(G-14001)
BARRETT SIGNS
321 Lyon St (48602-1522)
PHONE..................989 792-7446
Steve Jordan, *Owner*
EMP: 11
SALES: 950K **Privately Held**
SIC: 3993 Signs & advertising specialties

(G-14002)
BEAM INDUSTRIES INC
3521 State St (48602-3267)
PHONE..................989 799-4044
Anthony Essex, *Administration*
EMP: 3
SALES (est): 164K **Privately Held**
SIC: 3999 Manufacturing industries

(G-14003)
BECKERT & HIESTER INC (PA)
2025 Carman Dr (48602-2915)
P.O. Box 1885 (48605-1885)
PHONE..................989 793-2420
Bruce A Beckert, *President*
O Wendell Hiester, *Vice Pres*
EMP: 4
SQ FT: 2,000
SALES (est): 480K **Privately Held**
WEB: www.bhdustcollectors.com
SIC: 3564 5075 Dust or fume collecting equipment, industrial; dust collecting equipment

(G-14004)
BELL ENGINEERING INC
735 S Outer Dr (48601-6598)
PHONE..................989 753-3127
Richard L Bell, *President*
Dottie M Bell, *Vice Pres*
Jim Buckles,
EMP: 25
SQ FT: 25,000
SALES (est): 4.1MM **Privately Held**
SIC: 3599 Machine shop, jobbing & repair

(G-14005)
BELL ENGINEERING LLC
735 S Outer Dr (48601-6598)
PHONE..................989 753-3127
Kenneth Bess, *President*
EMP: 17 **EST:** 2016
SALES (est): 954.8K **Privately Held**
SIC: 3599 Machine shop, jobbing & repair

(G-14006)
BERNIER CAST METALS INC
2626 Hess Ave (48601-7498)
PHONE..................989 754-7571
Joshua Bernier, *President*
Noelle Dickerson, *Manager*
EMP: 8
SQ FT: 20,800
SALES (est): 1.7MM **Privately Held**
WEB: www.bernierinc.com
SIC: 3365 3321 3366 Aluminum & aluminum-based alloy castings; gray & ductile iron foundries; castings (except die): brass; castings (except die): bronze; castings (except die): copper & copper-base alloy

(G-14007)
BIERI HEARING INSTRUMENTS INC (PA)
Also Called: Bieri Digital Hearing Center
2650 Mccarty Rd (48603-2554)
PHONE..................989 793-2701
Catherine Bieri Ryan, *President*
Marie Bieri, *Vice Pres*
EMP: 10
SALES (est): 1.2MM **Privately Held**
SIC: 5999 3845 Hearing aids; audiological equipment, electromedical

(G-14008)
BLUEWATER THERMAL SOLUTIONS
Also Called: Saginaw
2240 Veterans Mem Pkwy (48601-1268)
PHONE..................989 753-7770
Michael Wellham, *President*
Ben Crawford, *COO*
Keith Beasley, *CFO*
EMP: 8
SALES (est): 1.4MM **Privately Held**
SIC: 3398 Metal heat treating
HQ: Bwt Llc
201 Brookfield Pkwy
Greenville SC 29607

(G-14009)
CARAUSTAR INDUSTRIES INC
Also Called: Caraustar Saginaw Plant
3265 Commerce Centre Dr (48601-9696)
PHONE..................989 793-4820
Marie Hall, *Human Res Mgr*
Roger McDougall, *Branch Mgr*
EMP: 25
SALES (corp-wide): 3.8B **Publicly Held**
SIC: 2655 Fiber cans, drums & similar products
HQ: Caraustar Industries, Inc.
5000 Austell Powder Sprin
Austell GA 30106
770 948-3101

(G-14010)
CARPENTERS CABINETS
5066 Dixie Hwy (48601-5454)
PHONE..................989 777-1070
Matt Johnson, *Owner*
EMP: 4
SQ FT: 7,000
SALES (est): 350K **Privately Held**
SIC: 2541 Table or counter tops, plastic laminated; cabinets, lockers & shelving

(G-14011)
CARROLLTON CONCRETE MIX INC
2924 Carrollton Rd (48604-2397)
PHONE..................989 753-7737
Hans Langschwager, *President*
Fred Langschwager, *Corp Secy*
EMP: 4
SALES (est): 487K **Privately Held**
SIC: 3273 Ready-mixed concrete

(G-14012)
CARROLLTON PAVING CO
2924 Carrollton Rd (48604-2305)
PHONE..................989 752-7139
Hans Langschwager, *President*
Fred P Lanschwager, *Treasurer*
John H Lanschwagner, *Admin Sec*
EMP: 10
SQ FT: 20,000
SALES (est): 584.2K **Privately Held**
SIC: 1771 3273 1446 Blacktop (asphalt) work; driveway contractor; curb construction; ready-mixed concrete; industrial sand

(G-14013)
CENTENNIAL TECHNOLOGIES INC
1335 Agricola Dr (48604-9247)
PHONE..................989 752-6167
James F Hammis, *President*
Carolyn Hammis, *Treasurer*
Linda Jackson, *Clerk*
EMP: 25 **EST:** 1976
SQ FT: 24,000
SALES (est): 5.3MM **Privately Held**
WEB: www.centennialtech.com
SIC: 3544 3559 Extrusion dies; foundry machinery & equipment

(G-14014)
CENTRAL MICH KNWRTH SGINAW LLC
3046 Commerce Centre Dr (48601-9697)
PHONE..................989 754-4500
Jesse Berger, *President*
EMP: 8 **EST:** 2010
SALES (est): 1.2MM **Privately Held**
SIC: 3713 4492 Truck bodies & parts; towing & tugboat service

(G-14015)
CESERE ENTERPRISES INC
Also Called: Napolitano Bakery
2614 State St (48602-3994)
PHONE..................989 799-3350
Leo A Cesere, *President*
Ann S Cesere, *Vice Pres*
EMP: 13
SQ FT: 3,100
SALES (est): 660.3K **Privately Held**
SIC: 2051 Breads, rolls & buns; bakery: wholesale or wholesale/retail combined

(G-14016)
CHARLES LANGE
Also Called: Cignys Bridgeport
5763 Dixie Hwy (48605-5916)
PHONE..................989 777-0110
Charles Lange, *Owner*
Ron Weidenmiller, *Purchasing*
Jeff Shelagowski, *Engineer*
Terry Nagy, *Administration*
EMP: 8 **EST:** 2010
SALES (est): 1MM **Privately Held**
SIC: 3537 Industrial trucks & tractors

(G-14017)
CHR W LLC
Also Called: Mid-Michigan Truss Components
2795 Harrison St (48604-2314)
P.O. Box 407, Carrollton (48724-0407)
PHONE..................989 755-4000
Jeff Ross,
EMP: 20
SALES (est): 3.1MM **Privately Held**
SIC: 2499 Decorative wood & woodwork

(G-14018)
CIGNYS INC
68 Williamson St (48601-3246)
PHONE..................989 753-1411
Don Mastromatteo, *Vice Pres*
Dan Rutkowski, *Engineer*
Elaine Moore, *Admin Asst*
◆ **EMP:** 3 **EST:** 2001
SALES (est): 601.3K
SALES (corp-wide): 19MM **Privately Held**
WEB: www.saginawproducts.com
SIC: 3535 Conveyors & conveying equipment
PA: Saginaw Products Corporation
68 Williamson St
Saginaw MI 48601
989 753-1411

(G-14019)
CITY OF SAGINAW
Also Called: Traffic Engineering
1741 S Jefferson Ave (48601-2849)
PHONE..................989 759-1670
Randy Chesney, *Manager*
EMP: 11 **Privately Held**
WEB: www.saginaw-mi.com
SIC: 3669 Traffic signals, electric
PA: City Of Saginaw
1315 S Washington Ave
Saginaw MI 48601
989 759-1400

(G-14020)
CLICK CARE LLC
2650 Mcleod Dr N (48604-2850)
PHONE..................989 792-1544
William Richter,
Derrick Richardson,
Michelle Richter,
EMP: 4 **EST:** 2013
SALES (est): 172.9K **Privately Held**
SIC: 7372 7373 Utility computer software; systems software development services

(G-14021)
COTTAGE BAKERY
4940 Hepburn Rd (48603-2927)
PHONE..................989 790-8135
Louann Dise, *Principal*
EMP: 4 **EST:** 1989
SALES (est): 178.3K **Privately Held**
SIC: 2051 Bread, cake & related products

(G-14022)
COUNTRY REGISTER OF MICH INC
3790 Manistee St (48603-3143)
PHONE..................989 793-4211
William Howell, *President*
Marlene Howell, *Vice Pres*
EMP: 7
SALES: 200K **Privately Held**
SIC: 2741 Miscellaneous publishing

(G-14023)
CUMMINS INC
722 N Outer Dr (48601-6236)
PHONE..................989 752-5200
Thomas Lidletei, *Manager*
EMP: 30
SALES (corp-wide): 23.7B **Publicly Held**
WEB: www.bridgewaypower.com
SIC: 5084 7538 3519 Engines & parts, diesel; diesel engine repair: automotive; internal combustion engines
PA: Cummins Inc.
500 Jackson St
Columbus IN 47201
812 377-5000

(G-14024)
CUSTOM FOODS INC
634 Kendrick St (48602-1237)
PHONE..................989 249-8061
John J Hausbeck, *President*
Mary Hausbeck, *Vice Pres*
EMP: 20 **EST:** 1997
SQ FT: 2,000
SALES (est): 2.9MM **Privately Held**
SIC: 2035 2099 Pickles, vinegar; food preparations

(G-14025)
DELTA STEEL INC
1410 Webber St (48601-3438)
P.O. Box 3231 (48605-3231)
PHONE..................989 752-5129
Elizabeth Maczik, *President*
Arlene Maczik, *Vice Pres*
Ron Markey, *Production*
EMP: 7 **EST:** 1975
SQ FT: 7,000
SALES (est): 2MM **Privately Held**
WEB: www.deltasteelinc.com
SIC: 3441 Fabricated structural metal

(G-14026)
DETROIT NEWSPAPER PARTNR LP
Also Called: Detroit Free Press
2654 N Outer Dr Ste 4 (48601-6012)
PHONE..................989 752-3023
EMP: 6
SALES (corp-wide): 6B **Publicly Held**
SIC: 2711 Newspapers-Publishing/Printing
HQ: Detroit Newspaper Partnership, L.P.
160 W Fort St
Detroit MI 48226
313 222-2300

(G-14027)
DIAL TENT & AWNING CO
5330 Davis Rd (48604-9497)
PHONE..................989 793-0741
Mark Rieffel, *President*
EMP: 15 **EST:** 1936
SQ FT: 14,000
SALES (est): 1.5MM **Privately Held**
SIC: 7359 2394 Tent & tarpaulin rental; awnings, fabric: made from purchased materials; liners & covers, fabric: made from purchased materials

(G-14028)
DONS WELDING
2461 Bellevue St (48601-6716)
PHONE..................989 792-0287
Keith Falkenhagen, *Owner*
EMP: 3
SQ FT: 2,400
SALES (est): 150K **Privately Held**
SIC: 7692 Welding repair

(G-14029)
DR & HI MOLD & MACHINE IN
4506 S Washington Rd (48601-5751)
PHONE..................989 746-9290
Fax: 989 746-0081
EMP: 3
SALES (est): 506.2K **Privately Held**
SIC: 3544 Mfg Dies/Tools/Jigs/Fixtures

(G-14030)
DUPERON CORPORATION
1200 Leon Scott Ct (48601-1273)
PHONE..................800 383-8479
Tammy L Bernier, *President*
Terry L Duperon, *Chairman*
Julie Wilson, *Project Mgr*

GEOGRAPHIC SECTION

Saginaw - Saginaw County (G-14057)

Larry Shelahowski, *Research*
Jan Lafave, *Engineer*
▲ **EMP:** 60
SQ FT: 72,000
SALES (est): 15.2MM **Privately Held**
WEB: www.duperon.com
SIC: 3569 Filters

(G-14031)
DURO-LAST INC (PA)
Also Called: Duro-Last Roofing
525 E Morley Dr (48601)
PHONE.....................800 248-0280
Tom Saeli, *CEO*
Troy Jenison, *Regional Mgr*
Charles Smith, *Regional Mgr*
Shawn Sny, *Exec VP*
Jason Tunney, *Exec VP*
▼ **EMP:** 280
SQ FT: 74,480
SALES: 207.6MM **Privately Held**
WEB: www.duro-last.com
SIC: 2295 Resin or plastic coated fabrics

(G-14032)
DURO-LAST INC
525 W Morley Dr (48601-9485)
PHONE.....................800 248-0280
EMP: 70
SALES (corp-wide): 207.6MM **Privately Held**
WEB: www.duro-last.com
SIC: 2295 Resin or plastic coated fabrics
PA: Duro-Last, Inc.
    525 E Morley Dr
    Saginaw MI 48601
    800 248-0280

(G-14033)
DURO-LAST INC
525 W Morley Dr (48601-9485)
P.O. Box 3301 (48605-3301)
PHONE.....................800 248-0280
Tom Hollingworth, *President*
EMP: 100
SALES (corp-wide): 207.6MM **Privately Held**
WEB: www.duro-last.com
SIC: 2295 Resin or plastic coated fabrics
PA: Duro-Last, Inc.
    525 E Morley Dr
    Saginaw MI 48601
    800 248-0280

(G-14034)
ELDERBERRY STEAM ENGINES
5215 Pheasant Run Dr # 5 (48638-6349)
PHONE.....................989 245-0652
EMP: 3 **EST:** 2016
SALES (est): 130.5K **Privately Held**
SIC: 3511 Steam engines

(G-14035)
ERIE MARKING INC
Also Called: Erie Custom Signs
1017 S Wheeler St (48602-1112)
PHONE.....................989 754-8360
Lisa R Shabluk, *President*
Michael R Sahbluk, *Treasurer*
EMP: 14
SQ FT: 12,000
SALES: 1.3MM **Privately Held**
SIC: 3993 5099 Signs, not made in custom sign painting shops; signs, except electric

(G-14036)
FARMER BROS CO
3691 Fashion Square Blvd # 6 (48603-2466)
PHONE.....................989 791-7985
EMP: 12
SALES (corp-wide): 595.9MM **Publicly Held**
SIC: 2095 Roasted coffee
PA: Farmer Bros. Co.
    1912 Farmer Brothers Dr
    Northlake TX 76262
    888 998-2468

(G-14037)
FERGUSON ENTERPRISES INC
Also Called: Johnson Contrls Authorized Dlr
3944 Fortune Blvd (48603-2253)
PHONE.....................989 790-2220
Casey Bradley, *Branch Mgr*
EMP: 20
SALES (corp-wide): 20.7B **Privately Held**
WEB: www.ferguson.com
SIC: 5074 5085 5051 3498 Plumbing fittings & supplies; valves & fittings; pipe & tubing, steel; pipe fittings, fabricated from purchased pipe
HQ: Ferguson Enterprises, Llc
    12500 Jefferson Ave
    Newport News VA 23602
    757 874-7795

(G-14038)
FRANKENMUTH WELDING & FABG
4765 E Holland Rd (48601-9463)
PHONE.....................989 754-9457
Micheal Schreiber, *President*
Daniel Vesterfelt, *President*
EMP: 7
SALES (est): 1.4MM **Privately Held**
SIC: 3449 3444 7692 Miscellaneous metalwork; sheet metalwork; welding repair

(G-14039)
FRED CARTER
6 Benton Rd (48602-1952)
PHONE.....................989 799-7176
Fred Carter, *Owner*
EMP: 4 **EST:** 2001
SALES (est): 210.4K **Privately Held**
SIC: 2841 Soap & other detergents

(G-14040)
FRITO-LAY NORTH AMERICA INC
100 S Outer Dr (48601-6330)
PHONE.....................989 754-0435
Robert Licht, *Manager*
EMP: 45
SALES (corp-wide): 64.6B **Publicly Held**
WEB: www.fritolay.com
SIC: 5145 2052 Snack foods; pretzels
HQ: Frito-Lay North America, Inc.
    7701 Legacy Dr
    Plano TX 75024

(G-14041)
FULLERTON TOOL COMPANY INC
121 Perry St (48602-1496)
P.O. Box 2008 (48605-2008)
PHONE.....................989 799-4550
Morgan L Curry Jr, *CEO*
Patrick Curry, *President*
Richard Curry, *Vice Pres*
Bruce Miller, *CFO*
EMP: 130
SQ FT: 27,000
SALES (est): 35.4MM **Privately Held**
WEB: www.fullertontool.com
SIC: 3545 Files, machine tool; milling machine attachments (machine tool accessories); reamers, machine tool

(G-14042)
GENERAL MACHINE SERVICE INC
494 E Morley Dr (48601-9402)
PHONE.....................989 752-5161
Stephen G Slachta, *President*
EMP: 35
SQ FT: 25,000
SALES: 4.5MM **Privately Held**
SIC: 3599 Machine shop, jobbing & repair

(G-14043)
GENERAL MOTORS COMPANY
1629 N Washington Ave (48601-1211)
PHONE.....................989 757-1576
Cameron Morford, *Engineer*
John Lancaster, *Branch Mgr*
Craig Jablonski, *Manager*
EMP: 26 **Publicly Held**
SIC: 3325 Steel foundries
PA: General Motors Company
    300 Renaissance Ctr L1
    Detroit MI 48243

(G-14044)
GENERAL MOTORS LLC
3900 N Towerline Rd (48601)
PHONE.....................989 757-0528
Howard Wachner, *Fire Chief*
Ray Wright, *Manager*
EMP: 486 **Publicly Held**
SIC: 3321 3325 3334 Gray & ductile iron foundries; steel foundries; primary aluminum
HQ: General Motors Llc
    300 Renaissance Ctr L1
    Detroit MI 48243

(G-14045)
GLASTENDER INC (PA)
5400 N Michigan Rd (48604-9700)
PHONE.....................989 752-4275
Todd Hall, *President*
Jon D Hall Sr, *President*
Mark Norris, *Vice Pres*
Jeff Stack, *Production*
Ginger Stoneback, *Project Engr*
◆ **EMP:** 180 **EST:** 1969
SQ FT: 187,000
SALES (est): 57.5MM **Privately Held**
WEB: www.glastender.com
SIC: 3589 2542 3585 Dishwashing machines, commercial; bar fixtures, except wood; refrigeration & heating equipment

(G-14046)
GLS DIOCESAN REPORTS (PA)
Also Called: Catholic Weekly
1520 Court St (48602-4067)
PHONE.....................989 793-7661
Mark Myczkowiak, *President*
Christine Brass, *Corp Secy*
Elaine Raymond, *Director*
Sister Elaine Raymond, *Director*
EMP: 7
SQ FT: 2,000
SALES: 291K **Privately Held**
SIC: 2711 Newspapers: publishing only, not printed on site

(G-14047)
GODFREY & WING INC
2240 Veterans Mem Pkwy (48601-1268)
PHONE.....................330 562-1440
Nick Chapman, *Manager*
EMP: 8
SALES (corp-wide): 19.3MM **Privately Held**
SIC: 3479 Coating of metals with plastic or resins
PA: Godfrey & Wing Inc.
    220 Campus Dr
    Aurora OH 44202
    330 562-1440

(G-14048)
GOMBAR CORP
Also Called: Print Shop, The
5645 State St Ste B (48603-3691)
P.O. Box 6893 (48608-6893)
PHONE.....................989 793-9427
Ben Gombar, *President*
Linda Gombar, *Vice Pres*
Dan Samolewski, *Graphic Designe*
EMP: 8
SQ FT: 2,000
SALES (est): 500K **Privately Held**
SIC: 2752 2791 2789 Commercial printing, offset; typesetting; bookbinding & related work

(G-14049)
GOSEN TOOL & MACHINE INC
2054 Brettrager Dr (48601-9790)
PHONE.....................989 777-6493
Jeff Gosen, *President*
Steve Gosen, *Vice Pres*
Bill Gosen, *Treasurer*
EMP: 15
SQ FT: 8,000
SALES (est): 1.1MM **Privately Held**
WEB: www.gosentoolandmachine.com
SIC: 3599 3441 Machine shop, jobbing & repair; fabricated structural metal

(G-14050)
GOWER CORPORATION
2840 Universal Dr (48603-2411)
PHONE.....................989 249-5938
Gregg A Gower, *President*
EMP: 6
SQ FT: 2,400
SALES (est): 430K **Privately Held**
SIC: 7694 5063 Electric motor repair; rewinding stators; motors, electric; motor controls, starters & relays: electric

(G-14051)
GRAMINEX LLC (PA)
95 Midland Rd (48638-5770)
PHONE.....................989 797-5502
Harold Baldauf, *Mng Member*
Alexander Grantz, *Security Dir*
Cynthia May,
EMP: 5
SALES (est): 3.4MM **Privately Held**
WEB: www.gmtfinechemicalssa.com
SIC: 3559 Pharmaceutical machinery

(G-14052)
GREGORY M BOESE
Also Called: Boese Equipment Co
2929 River St (48601-4343)
PHONE.....................989 754-2990
Gregory M Boese, *Owner*
EMP: 12
SQ FT: 30,000
SALES (est): 2.4MM **Privately Held**
SIC: 5083 5084 3599 Harvesting machinery & equipment; hydraulic systems equipment & supplies; custom machinery

(G-14053)
HAMILTON ELECTRIC CO
3175 Pierce Rd (48604-9755)
PHONE.....................989 799-6291
Mark Doyle, *President*
Sherry Raymond, *Admin Sec*
EMP: 16
SQ FT: 1,700
SALES (est): 3.2MM **Privately Held**
WEB: www.hamiltonelec.com
SIC: 7694 5063 Electric motor repair; motors, electric

(G-14054)
HAUSBECK PICKLE COMPANY (PA)
1626 Hess Ave (48601-3970)
PHONE.....................989 754-4721
Tim Hausbeck, *CEO*
Timothy Hausbeck, *President*
Joe Hausbeck, *Vice Pres*
John Joseph Hausbeck, *Vice Pres*
Joshua Hernandez, *Production*
◆ **EMP:** 60
SQ FT: 60,000
SALES: 27.3MM **Privately Held**
WEB: www.hausbeck.com
SIC: 2035 Pickled fruits & vegetables; cucumbers, pickles & pickle salting

(G-14055)
HAWK DESIGN INC
Also Called: Print Express Office Products
7760 Gratiot Rd (48609-5043)
PHONE.....................989 781-1152
Michael Slasinski, *President*
Leanne Slasinski, *Principal*
Steve Slasinski, *Vice Pres*
EMP: 4
SQ FT: 2,750
SALES (est): 685.1K **Privately Held**
SIC: 8711 5943 2752 Engineering services; office forms & supplies; commercial printing, offset

(G-14056)
HENRY MACHINE SHOP
1553 E Moore Rd (48601-9352)
PHONE.....................989 777-8495
Earl Urbanke, *Owner*
EMP: 3 **EST:** 1968
SALES (est): 279.9K **Privately Held**
SIC: 3089 Automotive parts, plastic

(G-14057)
HI-TECH OPTICAL INC
3139 Christy Way S (48603-2226)
P.O. Box 1443 (48605-1443)
PHONE.....................989 799-9390
Tom Ryan, *President*
Dean Sheehan, *Regl Sales Mgr*
Brian Schneider, *Manager*
Rebecca Younk, *Admin Asst*
EMP: 25
SQ FT: 4,000

(G-14058)
HI-TECH STEEL TREATING INC
2720 Roberts St (48601-3197)
PHONE..................800 835-8294
James A Stone, *President*
George Clauss, *Vice Pres*
Charles Parsell, *Treasurer*
Chris Muscott, *Controller*
Nick Horenziak, *Admin Sec*
EMP: 55
SQ FT: 50,000
SALES (est): 13.2MM **Privately Held**
WEB: www.hitechsteel.com
SIC: 3398 Metal heat treating

Prior entry (continuing):
SALES (est): 5.4MM **Privately Held**
WEB: www.hi-techoptical.com
SIC: 5048 3851 5661 5699 Frames, ophthalmic; lenses, ophthalmic; lens coating, ophthalmic; shoe stores; customized clothing & apparel; surgical appliances & supplies; optical goods

(G-14059)
HMG AGENCY
4352 Bay Rd Ste 131 (48603-1206)
PHONE..................989 443-3819
Loreal Hartwell,
EMP: 15
SALES (est): 366K **Privately Held**
SIC: 2741

(G-14060)
HOLCIM (US) INC
900 N Adams St (48604-1248)
PHONE..................989 755-7515
Filiberto Ruiz, *President*
EMP: 13
SALES (corp-wide): 27.6B **Privately Held**
SIC: 3241 5032 Portland cement; cement
HQ: Holcim (Us) Inc.
  8700 W Bryn Mawr Ave
  Chicago IL 60631
  773 372-1000

(G-14061)
HONEYWELL INTERNATIONAL INC
5153 Hampton Pl (48604-9576)
PHONE..................989 792-8707
Shelly Crannell, *Administration*
EMP: 22
SALES (corp-wide): 41.8B **Publicly Held**
WEB: www.honeywell.com
SIC: 3724 Aircraft engines & engine parts
PA: Honeywell International Inc.
  300 S Tryon St
  Charlotte NC 28202
  973 455-2000

(G-14062)
HOWARD STRUCTURAL STEEL INC
807 Veterans Mem Pkwy (48601-1498)
PHONE..................989 752-3000
Kenneth Hioward Westlund Jr, *President*
James Englehardt, *Vice Pres*
Sharon K Westlund, *Admin Sec*
EMP: 25
SQ FT: 20,000
SALES (est): 9.3MM **Privately Held**
WEB: www.howard-steel.com
SIC: 3441 1791 3535 5033 Building components, structural steel; structural erection; conveyors & conveying equipment; roofing, asphalt & sheet metal; siding, except wood

(G-14063)
HOWES CUSTOM COUNTER TOPS
3270 Bay Rd (48603-2413)
PHONE..................989 498-4044
Denny Howes, *Owner*
EMP: 3 **EST:** 2000
SALES (est): 178.4K **Privately Held**
SIC: 2541 5211 1799 Counters or counter display cases, wood; cabinets, kitchen; counter top installation

(G-14064)
INVISION BOATWORKS LLC
5700 Becker Rd (48601-9644)
PHONE..................989 754-3341
Jeff Schroeder,
Janet Wendland,
EMP: 3
SALES: 100K **Privately Held**
SIC: 3732 Boat building & repairing

(G-14065)
J & B PRODUCTS LTD
Also Called: Ultra Derm Systems
2201 S Michigan Ave (48602-1293)
PHONE..................989 792-6119
Joseph Bommarito, *CEO*
Linda Bommarito, *President*
▼ **EMP:** 15
SQ FT: 22,000
SALES (est): 3.5MM **Privately Held**
WEB: www.itehex.com
SIC: 3648 Lighting equipment

(G-14066)
JCP LLC
Also Called: Johnson Carbide Products
1422 S 25th St (48601-6601)
PHONE..................989 754-7496
James Foulds, *Mng Member*
◆ **EMP:** 28
SALES (est): 2.6MM **Privately Held**
SIC: 3823 Industrial instrmnts msrmnt display/control process variable

(G-14067)
JORDAN ADVERTISING INC
Also Called: Barrett Advertising
321 Lyon St (48602-1522)
PHONE..................989 792-7446
Steven D Jordan, *President*
EMP: 11
SQ FT: 10,000
SALES (est): 1MM **Privately Held**
SIC: 3993 Signs & advertising specialties

(G-14068)
K2 STONEWORKS LLC
5195 Dixie Hwy (48605-5569)
PHONE..................989 790-3250
Jeff Koski, *Owner*
EMP: 3 **EST:** 2014
SALES (est): 128.7K **Privately Held**
SIC: 3281 Marble, building: cut & shaped; granite, cut & shaped; limestone, cut & shaped

(G-14069)
KAPEX MANUFACTURING LLC
3130 Christy Way N Ste 3 (48603-2258)
P.O. Box 5589 (48603-0589)
PHONE..................989 928-4993
Timothy Tapert,
James Kowalczyk,
EMP: 7 **EST:** 1964
SQ FT: 10,000
SALES: 2MM **Privately Held**
SIC: 3544 3549 3559 Special dies, tools, jigs & fixtures; metalworking machinery; plastics working machinery

(G-14070)
KATYS KARDS
1200 Court St (48602-4142)
PHONE..................989 793-4094
Kim Clarke, *Owner*
EMP: 4
SALES: 200K **Privately Held**
SIC: 2771 5947 Greeting cards; greeting cards

(G-14071)
KERNEL BURNER
6171 Tittabawassee Rd (48603-9627)
PHONE..................989 792-2808
Gerald Savage, *Principal*
EMP: 6
SALES (est): 724.4K **Privately Held**
SIC: 3567 Electrical furnaces, ovens & heating devices, exc. induction

(G-14072)
KLC ENTERPRISES INC
4765 E Holland Rd (48601-9463)
PHONE..................989 753-0496
Scott Counts, *President*
Susan Auernhammer, *Corp Secy*
Donald S Counts, *VP Mfg*
Donald Counts, *VP Mfg*
Kathy Tucker, *Buyer*
EMP: 14
SQ FT: 10,000
SALES (est): 1.1MM **Privately Held**
WEB: www.goklc.com
SIC: 3829 Measuring & controlling devices

(G-14073)
KLOPP GROUP LLC
Also Called: B.K. Vending
3535 Bay Rd Ste 3 (48603-2464)
PHONE..................877 256-4528
Brian Klopp, *Mng Member*
EMP: 6
SALES: 650K **Privately Held**
SIC: 2064 Candy & other confectionery products

(G-14074)
KUKA ASSEMBLY AND TEST CORP (DH)
5675 Dixie Hwy (48601-5828)
P.O. Box 1968 (48605-1968)
PHONE..................989 220-3088
Scott Orendach, *President*
Lev Mondrusov, *Vice Pres*
Joe Burgess, *Project Mgr*
Scott Green, *Project Mgr*
Brian Hoy, *Mfg Mgr*
▲ **EMP:** 160 **EST:** 1948
SQ FT: 120,000
SALES (est): 35.8MM
SALES (corp-wide): 37.7B **Privately Held**
SIC: 3829 3549 Testing equipment: abrasion, shearing strength, etc.; assembly machines, including robotic
HQ: Kuka Ag
  Zugspitzstr. 140
  Augsburg 86165
  821 797-50

(G-14075)
KUREK TOOL INC
4735 Dixie Hwy (48601-4259)
PHONE..................989 777-5300
Joann Kurek, *President*
EMP: 11
SQ FT: 7,000
SALES (est): 1.5MM **Privately Held**
WEB: www.kurektool.com
SIC: 3544 3545 Special dies & tools; machine tool accessories

(G-14076)
LAFARGE NORTH AMERICA INC
1701 N 1st St (48601-1063)
PHONE..................989 399-1005
David Johns, *Accounts Mgr*
Frances Sargent, *Branch Mgr*
EMP: 27
SALES (corp-wide): 27.6B **Privately Held**
SIC: 3241 Cement, hydraulic
HQ: Lafarge North America Inc.
  8700 W Bryn Mawr Ave
  Chicago IL 60631
  773 372-1000

(G-14077)
LAFARGE NORTH AMERICA INC
900 N Adams St (48604-1248)
PHONE..................989 755-7515
Lester Johnson, *Engineer*
Rick Oswald, *Manager*
Ryan Kapalla, *Supervisor*
EMP: 3
SALES (corp-wide): 27.6B **Privately Held**
WEB: www.lafargenorthamerica.com
SIC: 3241 Cement, hydraulic
HQ: Lafarge North America Inc.
  8700 W Bryn Mawr Ave
  Chicago IL 60631
  773 372-1000

(G-14078)
LINEAR MOTION LLC
Also Called: Thomson Aerospace & Defense
628 N Hamilton St (48602-4301)
PHONE..................989 759-8300
Nathan Hendrix, *President*
Craig Palmer, *President*
▲ **EMP:** 170
SALES (est): 38.2MM **Privately Held**
WEB: www.linearmotion.com
SIC: 3728 Aircraft parts & equipment
HQ: Umbragroup Spa
  Via Valter Baldaccini 1
  Foligno PG 06034
  074 234-81

(G-14079)
LOGGERS BREWING CO
1215 S River Rd (48609-5208)
PHONE..................989 401-3085
EMP: 4
SALES (est): 75.4K **Privately Held**
SIC: 2082 5084 Beer (alcoholic beverage); brewery products manufacturing machinery, commercial

(G-14080)
M CURRY CORPORATION
Also Called: Endurance Carbide
4475 Marlea Dr (48601-7203)
P.O. Box 269, Bridgeport (48722-0269)
PHONE..................989 777-7950
Patrick H Curry, *President*
Brian Hammond, *Vice Pres*
Gary Browne, *Plant Supt*
Steve Prabucki, *Engineer*
EMP: 26 **EST:** 1961
SQ FT: 18,000
SALES (est): 3.8MM **Privately Held**
SIC: 3545 3544 Drill bushings (drilling jig); gauges (machine tool accessories); punches, forming & stamping; special dies & tools

(G-14081)
MARKETING VI GROUP INC
Also Called: Sir Speedy
4414 Bay Rd Ste 1 (48603-5222)
PHONE..................989 793-3933
Carol Henthorn, *President*
EMP: 7
SQ FT: 2,500
SALES (est): 880.8K **Privately Held**
SIC: 2752 2796 2791 Commercial printing, lithographic; platemaking services; typesetting

(G-14082)
MARSHALL TOOL SERVICE INC
2700 Iowa Ave (48601-5459)
P.O. Box 480, Bridgeport (48722-0480)
PHONE..................989 777-3137
Steven McDonald, *President*
Steven Brown, *Vice Pres*
EMP: 9
SALES (est): 997.1K **Privately Held**
SIC: 3599 5251 Machine shop, jobbing & repair; tools

(G-14083)
MASTERS TOOL & DIE INC
4485 Marlea Dr (48601-7203)
PHONE..................989 777-2450
Charles Smith, *President*
EMP: 6
SQ FT: 5,000
SALES (est): 951.5K **Privately Held**
SIC: 3544 Jigs & fixtures

(G-14084)
MCCRAY PRESS
2710 State St (48602-3736)
PHONE..................989 792-8681
Robert D Mc Cray, *Partner*
Flora E McCray, *Partner*
EMP: 25
SALES (est): 1.9MM **Privately Held**
WEB: www.mccraypress.com
SIC: 3089 2672 Laminating of plastic; coated & laminated paper

(G-14085)
MEAN ERECTORS INC
1928 Wilson Ave (48638-6704)
PHONE..................989 737-3285
Todd B Culver, *President*
EMP: 30
SALES: 1MM **Privately Held**
SIC: 1791 3312 Iron work, structural; structural shapes & pilings, steel

(G-14086)
MEANS INDUSTRIES INC (HQ)
3715 E Washington Rd (48601-9623)
PHONE..................989 754-1433
Jeremy Holt, *President*
Ed Shemanski, *Vice Pres*
Edward Shemanski, *Vice Pres*
Thomas Essenmacher, *Plant Mgr*
Jim Pastori, *Purchasing*
◆ **EMP:** 175
SQ FT: 40,000

▲ = Import ▼ = Export
◆ = Import/Export

SALES (est): 164.2MM
SALES (corp-wide): 2.4B **Privately Held**
WEB: www.meansindustries.com
SIC: 3714 3465 Transmission housings or parts, motor vehicle; automotive stampings
PA: Amsted Industries Incorporated
180 N Stetson Ave # 1800
Chicago IL 60601
312 645-1700

(G-14087)
MEANS INDUSTRIES INC
1860 S Jefferson Ave (48601-2824)
PHONE.................................989 754-3300
Bill Shaw, *Branch Mgr*
EMP: 99
SALES (corp-wide): 2.4B **Privately Held**
WEB: www.meansindustries.com
SIC: 3465 3469 Body parts, automobile: stamped metal; metal stampings
HQ: Means Industries, Inc.
3715 E Washington Rd
Saginaw MI 48601
989 754-1433

(G-14088)
MENU PULSE INC
1901 Kollen St (48602-2730)
PHONE.................................989 708-1207
Andrew Lay, *President*
EMP: 7
SALES (est): 290.6K
SALES (corp-wide): 292.3K **Privately Held**
SIC: 8742 7372 Marketing consulting services; application computer software
PA: Lay Enterprises, Inc
1901 Kollen St
Saginaw MI
989 708-1207

(G-14089)
MERRILL TECHNOLOGIES GROUP
Also Called: Merrill Aviation & Defense
1023 S Wheeler St (48602-1112)
PHONE.................................989 921-1490
Robert Yackel, *Branch Mgr*
EMP: 20
SALES (corp-wide): 60MM **Privately Held**
SIC: 3724 3728 8734 Aircraft engines & engine parts; aircraft parts & equipment; testing laboratories; product certification, safety or performance
PA: Merrill Technologies Group, Inc.
400 Florence St
Saginaw MI 48602
989 791-6676

(G-14090)
MERRILL TECHNOLOGIES GROUP INC (PA)
Also Called: Merrill Tool Holding Company
400 Florence St (48602-1203)
PHONE.................................989 791-6676
Robert Yackel, *CEO*
Gary Yackel, *Chairman*
Rob Schmaltz, *Business Mgr*
Mary K Yackel, *Corp Secy*
Jeffery J Yackel, *Vice Pres*
▲ **EMP:** 70
SQ FT: 100,000
SALES (est): 60MM **Privately Held**
WEB: www.merrilltg.com
SIC: 3443 3599 8734 8711 Fabricated plate work (boiler shop); machine & other job shop work; testing laboratories; engineering services; aircraft engines & engine parts

(G-14091)
MICHIGAN SATELLITE
Also Called: Future Vision
3215 Christy Way S (48603-2245)
PHONE.................................989 792-6666
John Dawson, *President*
EMP: 50
SALES (est): 3.8MM **Privately Held**
SIC: 3663 1731 Space satellite communications equipment; electrical work

(G-14092)
MICRON PRECISION MACHINING INC (PA)
225 E Morley Dr (48601-9482)
PHONE.................................989 759-1030
Darrin Krogman, *President*
EMP: 32 **EST:** 2000
SQ FT: 4,000
SALES (est): 4.6MM **Privately Held**
WEB: www.micronpm.com
SIC: 3599 Machine shop, jobbing & repair

(G-14093)
MICRON PRECISION MACHINING INC
2824 Universal Dr (48603-2411)
PHONE.................................989 790-2425
Darrin Krogman, *Branch Mgr*
EMP: 6
SALES (corp-wide): 4.6MM **Privately Held**
SIC: 3599 Machine shop, jobbing & repair
PA: Micron Precision Machining Inc.
225 E Morley Dr
Saginaw MI 48601
989 759-1030

(G-14094)
MID-STATE DISTRIBUTORS INC
3137 Boardwalk Dr (48603-2325)
PHONE.................................989 793-1820
Robert L Frank, *Manager*
EMP: 3
SALES (est): 378.7K
SALES (corp-wide): 3.3MM **Privately Held**
SIC: 2511 Wood household furniture
PA: A. T. Frank Company, Inc.
3135 Boardwalk Dr
Saginaw MI
989 497-1900

(G-14095)
MIDWEST MARKETING INC
Also Called: Sweney-Kern Manufacturing
105 Lyon St (48602-1565)
P.O. Box 6858 (48608-6858)
PHONE.................................989 793-9393
Randy Kern, *President*
Diane Sweney, *Vice Pres*
EMP: 7
SQ FT: 21,000
SALES (est): 2.5MM **Privately Held**
WEB: www.sweney-kern.com
SIC: 2048 Bird food, prepared

(G-14096)
MISTEQUAY GROUP LTD
1212 N Niagara St (48602-4742)
PHONE.................................989 752-7700
Ken Jones, *Branch Mgr*
EMP: 48 **Privately Held**
SIC: 3544 Special dies & tools
PA: Mistequay Group Ltd.
1156 N Niagara St
Saginaw MI 48602

(G-14097)
MISTEQUAY GROUP LTD (PA)
Also Called: Mistequay NDT Center
1156 N Niagara St (48602-4741)
PHONE.................................989 752-7700
James Paas, *President*
Wayne Bamberg, *Mfg Spvr*
Craig Cory, *Engineer*
Gary Steele, *CFO*
Diane Shark, *Cust Mgr*
▲ **EMP:** 13
SQ FT: 22,500
SALES (est): 38.1MM **Privately Held**
WEB: www.mistequaygroup.com
SIC: 3544 3714 3812 3545 Special dies, tools, jigs & fixtures; motor vehicle parts & accessories; search & navigation equipment; machine tool accessories

(G-14098)
MKR FABRICATING INC
Also Called: Companions' Cuisine
810 N Towerline Rd (48601-9466)
PHONE.................................989 753-8100
Rob Webb, *President*
Jennifer Eaton, *Principal*
Jake Mattes, *Principal*
Meghann Webb, *Principal*
Robert Hickey, *Vice Pres*
EMP: 18
SALES (est): 4.9MM **Privately Held**
WEB: www.mkrfab.com
SIC: 3441 Fabricated structural metal

(G-14099)
MORNING STAR
306 E Remington St (48601-2508)
PHONE.................................989 755-2660
Charles Bird, *Owner*
EMP: 4
SALES (est): 270.8K **Privately Held**
SIC: 2741 2711 Miscellaneous publishing; newspapers, publishing & printing

(G-14100)
MOTION INDUSTRIES INC
D.P. Brown of Detroit
1646 Champagne Dr N (48604-9202)
PHONE.................................989 771-0200
Dave Kennedy, *General Mgr*
Carol Plaza, *Opers Mgr*
EMP: 9
SALES (corp-wide): 18.7B **Publicly Held**
WEB: www.dpbrownofdetroit.com
SIC: 5063 5085 3535 Power transmission equipment, electric; industrial supplies; conveyors & conveying equipment
HQ: Motion Industries, Inc.
1605 Alton Rd
Birmingham AL 35210
205 956-1122

(G-14101)
NATIONAL PATTERN INC
5900 Sherman Rd (48604-1199)
PHONE.................................989 755-6274
C Gregory Larson, *President*
Debbie Fisher, *Purchasing*
Greg Larson, *Financial Exec*
▲ **EMP:** 33
SQ FT: 25,000
SALES (est): 4.5MM **Privately Held**
WEB: www.nationalpattern.com
SIC: 3543 Industrial patterns

(G-14102)
NATIONAL ROOFG & SHTMTL CO INC
200 Lee St (48602-1443)
PHONE.................................989 964-0557
Brian Ora, *Branch Mgr*
EMP: 80
SALES (corp-wide): 16.8MM **Privately Held**
WEB: www.nr-sm.com
SIC: 1761 3444 Roofing contractor; sheet metal specialties, not stamped
PA: National Roofing And Sheet Metal Co., Inc.
4130 Flint Asphalt Dr
Burton MI 48529
810 742-7373

(G-14103)
NATIONWIDE NETWORK INC (PA)
Also Called: Nationwide Intelligence
3401 Peale Dr (48602-3472)
P.O. Box 1922 (48605-1922)
PHONE.................................989 793-0123
David Oppermann, *President*
EMP: 30
SALES (est): 1.5MM **Privately Held**
WEB: www.newref.com
SIC: 7389 4724 7929 2721 Convention & show services; travel agencies; entertainment service; periodicals: publishing only

(G-14104)
NEXTEER AUTOMOTIVE CORPORATION
Also Called: Nexteer Saginaw
3900 E Holland Rd (48601-9494)
PHONE.................................989 757-5000
Manuel Grimaldo, *Opers Mgr*
Mike Kettler, *Opers Mgr*
Eric Hunter, *Maint Spvr*
Ray Parker, *Production*
Aldo Gonzalez, *Purch Dir*
EMP: 300 **Privately Held**
WEB: www.delphiauto.com
SIC: 5531 3711 3545 3714 Automobile & truck equipment & parts; motor vehicles & car bodies; tools & accessories for machine tools; steering mechanisms, motor vehicle
HQ: Nexteer Automotive Corporation
1272 Doris Rd
Auburn Hills MI 48326

(G-14105)
NEXTEER AUTOMOTIVE CORPORATION
Nexteer Saginaw Prototype Ctr
2975 Nodular Dr (48601-9264)
PHONE.................................989 754-1920
Robert Remenar, *Branch Mgr*
EMP: 409 **Privately Held**
WEB: www.delphiauto.com
SIC: 3714 Motor vehicle parts & accessories
HQ: Nexteer Automotive Corporation
1272 Doris Rd
Auburn Hills MI 48326

(G-14106)
NEXTEER AUTOMOTIVE CORPORATION
Also Called: Nexteer - Saginaw Plant 7
3900 E Holland Rd (48601-9494)
PHONE.................................989 757-5000
Robert Remenar, *Branch Mgr*
EMP: 824 **Privately Held**
WEB: www.delphiauto.com
SIC: 3714 Gears, motor vehicle
HQ: Nexteer Automotive Corporation
1272 Doris Rd
Auburn Hills MI 48326

(G-14107)
NEXTEER AUTOMOTIVE CORPORATION
Also Called: Nexteer - Saginaw Plant 5
3900 E Holland Rd (48601-9494)
PHONE.................................989 757-5000
Robert Remenar, *Branch Mgr*
EMP: 500 **Privately Held**
WEB: www.delphiauto.com
SIC: 3714 Axles, motor vehicle
HQ: Nexteer Automotive Corporation
1272 Doris Rd
Auburn Hills MI 48326

(G-14108)
NEXTEER AUTOMOTIVE CORPORATION
Also Called: Nexteer - Plant 6
3900 E Holland Rd (48601-9494)
PHONE.................................989 757-5000
Roger Johnson, *Engineer*
Andrew Stewart, *Branch Mgr*
EMP: 1000 **Privately Held**
WEB: www.delphiauto.com
SIC: 3714 Motor vehicle parts & accessories
HQ: Nexteer Automotive Corporation
1272 Doris Rd
Auburn Hills MI 48326

(G-14109)
NEXTEER AUTOMOTIVE CORPORATION
Also Called: Nexteer - Saginaw Plant 4
3900 E Holland Rd (48601-9494)
PHONE.................................989 757-5000
Robert Remenar, *Branch Mgr*
EMP: 510 **Privately Held**
WEB: www.delphiauto.com
SIC: 3714 Axles, motor vehicle
HQ: Nexteer Automotive Corporation
1272 Doris Rd
Auburn Hills MI 48326

(G-14110)
NEXTEER AUTOMOTIVE CORPORATION
Also Called: Nexteer - Saginaw Plant 3
3900 E Holland Rd (48601-9494)
PHONE.................................989 757-5000
Dragi Kuzmanovski, *Opers Mgr*
EMP: 510 **Privately Held**
WEB: www.delphiauto.com
SIC: 3714 Motor vehicle parts & accessories

HQ: Nexteer Automotive Corporation
1272 Doris Rd
Auburn Hills MI 48326

(G-14111)
NEXTEER AUTOMOTIVE CORPORATION
Nexteer Plant 8
3900 E Holland Rd (48601-9494)
PHONE................................989 757-5000
Todd Banning, *Plant Mgr*
EMP: 100 **Privately Held**
SIC: 3714 Motor vehicle parts & accessories
HQ: Nexteer Automotive Corporation
1272 Doris Rd
Auburn Hills MI 48326

(G-14112)
NEXTEER AUTOMOTIVE CORPORATION
Also Called: Nexteer - Plant 6 E-Bike
3900 E Holland Rd (48601-9494)
PHONE................................989 757-5000
John Riester, *Director*
EMP: 50 **Privately Held**
SIC: 3714 Motor vehicle parts & accessories
HQ: Nexteer Automotive Corporation
1272 Doris Rd
Auburn Hills MI 48326

(G-14113)
NEXTEER AUTOMOTIVE CORPORATION
Also Called: Nexteer - Saginaw Plant 1
3900 E Holland Rd (48601-9494)
PHONE................................989 757-5000
Robert Remenar, *Branch Mgr*
EMP: 210 **Privately Held**
WEB: www.delphiauto.com
SIC: 3714 Power steering equipment, motor vehicle
HQ: Nexteer Automotive Corporation
1272 Doris Rd
Auburn Hills MI 48326

(G-14114)
NEXTEER AUTOMOTIVE CORPORATION
Nexteer - Saginaw Plant 18
5153 Hess Rd (48601)
PHONE................................989 757-5000
Robert Remenar, *Branch Mgr*
EMP: 409 **Privately Held**
WEB: www.delphiauto.com
SIC: 3714 Motor vehicle steering systems & parts
HQ: Nexteer Automotive Corporation
1272 Doris Rd
Auburn Hills MI 48326

(G-14115)
NEXTEER AUTOMOTIVE GROUP LTD
3900 E Holland Rd (48601-9494)
PHONE................................989 757-5000
Zhao Guibin, *CEO*
Bresson Laurent Robert, *President*
Perkins Joseph Michael, *Vice Pres*
Jeremy Bierlein, *Engineer*
Joshua Golimbieski, *Engineer*
EMP: 1835
SALES (est): 350.9K **Privately Held**
SIC: 3714 Motor vehicle steering systems & parts
HQ: Nexteer Automotive Corporation
1272 Doris Rd
Auburn Hills MI 48326

(G-14116)
NORTHERN SIERRA CORPORATION
5450 East Rd (48601-9748)
PHONE................................989 777-4784
Ross A Lake, *President*
EMP: 5
SQ FT: 10,500
SALES (est): 734.3K **Privately Held**
SIC: 3543 Industrial patterns

(G-14117)
ORACLE BREWING COMPANY
122 N Michigan Ave (48602-4234)
PHONE................................989 401-7446
EMP: 5
SALES (est): 310.8K **Privately Held**
SIC: 2082 Malt beverages

(G-14118)
PAN-TECK CORPORATION
248 Stoneham Rd (48638-6222)
PHONE................................989 792-2422
William T Nicholson, *President*
James Nicholson, *Vice Pres*
Mary Catherine Nicholson, *Treasurer*
EMP: 6
SALES (est): 892.9K **Privately Held**
SIC: 3569 Lubricating systems, centralized

(G-14119)
PAPER MACHINE SERVICE INDS (PA)
3075 Shattuck Rd Ste 801 (48603-3299)
PHONE................................989 695-2646
Mark R Baluha, *Owner*
EMP: 12
SQ FT: 15,000
SALES (est): 2MM **Privately Held**
WEB: www.psimarine.com
SIC: 3554 Paper industries machinery

(G-14120)
PEPSI BEVERAGES CO
100 S Outer Dr (48601-6330)
PHONE................................989 754-0435
Mike Fraser, *Principal*
EMP: 5
SALES (est): 98.5K **Privately Held**
SIC: 2086 Carbonated soft drinks, bottled & canned

(G-14121)
PEPSI-COLA METRO BTLG CO INC
736 N Outer Dr (48601-6236)
PHONE................................989 755-1020
Matt Chapelain, *Branch Mgr*
Roxane Pavlawk, *Admin Asst*
EMP: 80
SALES (corp-wide): 64.6B **Publicly Held**
WEB: www.joy-of-cola.com
SIC: 2086 5078 Carbonated soft drinks, bottled & canned; beverage coolers
HQ: Pepsi-Cola Metropolitan Bottling Company, Inc.
1111 Westchester Ave
White Plains NY 10604
914 767-6000

(G-14122)
PILKINGTON NORTH AMERICA INC
1400 Weiss St (48602-5278)
PHONE................................989 754-2956
Dan Corl, *Manager*
EMP: 18 **Privately Held**
WEB: www.low-eglass.com
SIC: 3211 Flat glass
HQ: Pilkington North America, Inc.
811 Madison Ave Fl 3
Toledo OH 43604
419 247-3731

(G-14123)
PLASTATECH ENGINEERING LTD (PA)
725 E Morley Dr (48601)
PHONE................................989 754-6500
John C Burt, *Ch of Bd*
Tom Saeli, *President*
Mark Rose, *General Mgr*
Shawn Sny, *Exec VP*
Jason Tunney, *Exec VP*
EMP: 82
SQ FT: 125,000
SALES (est): 22.6MM **Privately Held**
WEB: www.plastatech.com
SIC: 2295 Laminating of fabrics

(G-14124)
PLASTATECH ENGINEERING LTD
825 W Morley Dr (48601-9493)
PHONE................................989 754-6500

Kathy Allen, *President*
EMP: 32
SALES (est): 2.1MM
SALES (corp-wide): 22.6MM **Privately Held**
WEB: www.plastatech.com
SIC: 2295 Laminating of fabrics
PA: Plastatech Engineering, Ltd.
725 E Morley Dr
Saginaw MI 48601
989 754-6500

(G-14125)
POOR BOY WOODWORKS INC
1903 S Michigan Ave (48602-1232)
PHONE................................989 799-9440
Matt Hunter, *President*
Christian Schumaker, *Principal*
EMP: 3
SALES (est): 1.6MM **Privately Held**
SIC: 2431 Millwork

(G-14126)
PSI MARINE INC
Also Called: Tideslide Mooring Products
3075 Shattuck Rd Ste 801 (48603-3299)
PHONE................................989 695-2646
Mark Baluha, *COO*
▼ **EMP:** 12
SQ FT: 5,000
SALES: 1.4MM **Privately Held**
WEB: www.papermachine.com
SIC: 3441 3531 4491 Fabricated structural metal for ships; marine related equipment; docks, piers & terminals

(G-14127)
R & R READY-MIX INC (PA)
6050 Melbourne Rd (48604-9710)
PHONE................................989 753-3862
Russell A Willett, *President*
Richard Willett, *Corp Secy*
EMP: 15
SALES (est): 4MM **Privately Held**
SIC: 3273 Ready-mixed concrete

(G-14128)
R & S CUTTER GRIND INC
2870 Universal Dr (48603-2411)
PHONE................................989 791-3100
Richard Terry, *President*
Alan McNalley, *Manager*
EMP: 6
SQ FT: 3,700
SALES (est): 984.5K **Privately Held**
SIC: 3599 7699 Grinding castings for the trade; industrial tool grinding

(G-14129)
R A TOWNSEND COMPANY
2845 Mccarty Rd (48603-2442)
PHONE................................989 498-7000
Therese M Muszynski, *Branch Mgr*
EMP: 7
SALES (corp-wide): 31.1MM **Privately Held**
SIC: 3088 Plastics plumbing fixtures
PA: R. A. Townsend Company
1100 N Bagley St
Alpena MI 49707
989 354-3105

(G-14130)
RANGER TOOL & DIE CO
317 S Westervelt Rd (48604-1330)
PHONE................................989 754-1403
John Kuhnle, *President*
Tom Schick, *Vice Pres*
Brian Keidel, *Director*
EMP: 30
SQ FT: 16,000
SALES (est): 4.6MM **Privately Held**
WEB: www.ranger-tool.com
SIC: 3544 7692 3469 Special dies & tools; welding repair; metal stampings

(G-14131)
RAPID GRINDING & MACHINE CO
3500 Janes Ave (48601-6321)
PHONE................................989 753-1744
EMP: 3
SQ FT: 3,500
SALES (est): 358.3K **Privately Held**
SIC: 3541 3599 Mfg Machine Tools-Cutting Mfg Industrial Machinery

(G-14132)
REIMOLD PRINTING CORPORATION
Also Called: Cuadvantage Mktg Solutions
5171 Blackbeak Dr (48604-9704)
PHONE................................989 799-0784
Ronald Reimold, *President*
Michael White, *Owner*
Mary Reimold, *Corp Secy*
Mike Hatfield, *Representative*
EMP: 9 **EST:** 1964
SQ FT: 5,000
SALES (est): 1.3MM **Privately Held**
SIC: 2752 Commercial printing, offset

(G-14133)
RHINEVAULT OLSEN MACHINE & TL
2533 Carrollton Rd (48604-2455)
PHONE................................989 753-4363
Glen Olsen, *President*
Michael Olsen, *Vice Pres*
EMP: 6 **EST:** 1932
SQ FT: 5,000
SALES: 480K **Privately Held**
SIC: 3545 Tools & accessories for machine tools

(G-14134)
RPC COMPANY
Also Called: A H Webster
1708 N Michigan Ave (48602-5343)
P.O. Box 1944 (48605-1944)
PHONE................................989 752-3618
George Roe, *President*
Cindy Jones, *Manager*
EMP: 10 **EST:** 1935
SQ FT: 8,000
SALES (est): 2.4MM **Privately Held**
SIC: 5136 5699 2759 2284 Sportswear, men's & boys'; work clothing, men's & boys'; work clothing; commercial printing; embroidery thread

(G-14135)
S F S CARBIDE TOOL
Also Called: Service File Sharpening
4480 Marlea Dr (48601-7203)
P.O. Box 394, Clawson (48017-0394)
PHONE................................989 777-3890
Robert White, *Owner*
EMP: 5
SALES (est): 408.9K **Privately Held**
SIC: 3545 7699 5251 Cutting tools for machine tools; knife, saw & tool sharpening & repair; tools

(G-14136)
SAFETY-KLEEN SYSTEMS INC
3899 Wolf Rd (48601-9256)
PHONE................................989 753-3261
Steve Tratt, *Branch Mgr*
EMP: 20
SALES (corp-wide): 3.3B **Publicly Held**
SIC: 7359 3559 Equipment rental & leasing; degreasing machines, automotive & industrial
HQ: Safety-Kleen Systems, Inc.
2600 N Central Expy # 400
Richardson TX 75080
972 265-2000

(G-14137)
SAGINAW BEARING COMPANY
1400 Agricola Dr (48604-9771)
PHONE................................989 752-3169
Robert L Pieschke Sr, *President*
Curtis J Olsen, *Vice Pres*
EMP: 10 **EST:** 1920
SQ FT: 18,000
SALES (est): 1.6MM **Privately Held**
WEB: www.saginawbearing.com
SIC: 3568 Bearings, bushings & blocks

(G-14138)
SAGINAW CONTROL & ENGRG INC (PA)
Also Called: SCE
95 Midland Rd (48638-5791)
PHONE................................989 799-6871
Harold C Baldauf, *Ch of Bd*
Frederick H May Jr, *President*
John Garner, *Prdtn Mgr*
David Baldauf, *Treasurer*
Janet Baldauf, *Admin Sec*

GEOGRAPHIC SECTION

Saginaw - Saginaw County (G-14164)

▲ EMP: 300 EST: 1963
SALES (est): 87.8MM **Privately Held**
SIC: 3699 3444 Electrical equipment & supplies; sheet metalwork

(G-14139)
SAGINAW INDUSTRIES LLC
1622 Champagne Dr N (48604-9202)
PHONE.................................989 752-5514
James Kruske, *President*
Harold Boehler, *Vice Pres*
Don Hamilton, *Manager*
EMP: 16 EST: 1998
SQ FT: 4,800
SALES (est): 3.9MM **Privately Held**
SIC: 3553 Pattern makers' machinery, woodworking

(G-14140)
SAGINAW MACHINE SYSTEMS INC
Also Called: SMS
800 N Hamilton St (48602-4354)
PHONE.................................989 753-8465
James Buckley, *President*
Theodore D Birkmeier, *Vice Pres*
Pamela K Baran, *CFO*
Gary Rottman, *Manager*
▲ EMP: 66 EST: 1854
SQ FT: 70,000
SALES (est): 12.8MM
SALES (corp-wide): 16.7MM **Privately Held**
WEB: www.saginawmachine.com
SIC: 3829 3548 3541 Measuring & controlling devices; arc welders, transformer-rectifier; resistance welders, electric; welding & cutting apparatus & accessories; drilling & boring machines
PA: Sms Holding Co., Inc
   800 N Hamilton St
   Saginaw MI 48602
   989 753-8465

(G-14141)
SAGINAW PRODUCTS CORPORATION (PA)
Also Called: Cignys
68 Williamson St (48601-3246)
PHONE.................................989 753-1411
James Kendall, *President*
Elaine D Rapanos, *Owner*
Kirk Peterson, *Vice Pres*
Steve Chapman, *Production*
Eric Federspiel, *Production*
▲ EMP: 38 EST: 1920
SQ FT: 70,000
SALES: 19MM **Privately Held**
WEB: www.saginawproducts.com
SIC: 3535 3423 3537 3562 Conveyors & conveying equipment; jacks: lifting, screw or ratchet (hand tools); industrial trucks & tractors; casters; actuators, industrial; machine shop, jobbing & repair

(G-14142)
SAGINAW PRODUCTS CORPORATION
5763 Dixie Hwy (48601-5916)
PHONE.................................989 753-1411
EMP: 60
SALES (corp-wide): 19MM **Privately Held**
SIC: 3599 Machine shop, jobbing & repair
PA: Saginaw Products Corporation
   68 Williamson St
   Saginaw MI 48601
   989 753-1411

(G-14143)
SAGINAW PRODUCTS CORPORATION
Also Called: Cignys
1320 S Graham Rd (48609-8832)
PHONE.................................989 753-1411
Matthew Ware, *Manager*
EMP: 60
SALES (corp-wide): 19MM **Privately Held**
SIC: 3599 Machine shop, jobbing & repair
PA: Saginaw Products Corporation
   68 Williamson St
   Saginaw MI 48601
   989 753-1411

(G-14144)
SAGINAW ROCK PRODUCTS CO
1701 N 1st St (48601-1063)
P.O. Box 3245 (48605-3245)
PHONE.................................989 754-6589
Frances A Sargent, *President*
Marc Short, *General Mgr*
William Webber, *Admin Sec*
◆ EMP: 30
SQ FT: 5,000
SALES (est): 5.3MM **Privately Held**
SIC: 3273 5032 1442 Ready-mixed concrete; aggregate; sand, construction; gravel; stone, crushed or broken; construction sand & gravel

(G-14145)
SANDLOT SPORTS
2900 Universal Dr (48603-2414)
PHONE.................................989 835-9696
Adam McCauley, *Branch Mgr*
EMP: 8
SALES (corp-wide): 919.8K **Privately Held**
SIC: 5949 2759 Sewing & needlework; screen printing
PA: Sandlot Sports
   600 N Euclid Ave
   Bay City MI 48706
   989 391-9684

(G-14146)
SEVERANCE TOOL INDUSTRIES INC (PA)
3790 Orange St (48601-5549)
P.O. Box 1866 (48605-1866)
PHONE.................................989 777-5500
Robert Severence Jr, *Ch of Bd*
John Pease, *President*
Paul De Wyse, *Sales Executive*
EMP: 20 EST: 1930
SQ FT: 43,148
SALES (est): 2.6MM **Privately Held**
WEB: www.severancetool.com
SIC: 3545 Cutting tools for machine tools

(G-14147)
SEVERANCE TOOL INDUSTRIES INC
2150 Iowa Ave (48601-5521)
PHONE.................................989 777-5500
Robert Severance, *President*
EMP: 4
SALES (corp-wide): 2.6MM **Privately Held**
WEB: www.severancetool.com
SIC: 3545 Cutting tools for machine tools
PA: Severance Tool Industries Inc.
   3790 Orange St
   Saginaw MI 48601
   989 777-5500

(G-14148)
SHAY WATER CO INC
320 W Bristol St (48602-4610)
P.O. Box 1926 (48605-1926)
PHONE.................................989 755-3221
James Shay, *President*
EMP: 20 EST: 1929
SQ FT: 10,000
SALES (est): 4.1MM **Privately Held**
SIC: 2899 7389 Distilled water; coffee service

(G-14149)
SIGN IMAGE INC
8155 Gratiot Rd (48609-4876)
PHONE.................................989 781-5229
John Eggers, *President*
EMP: 10
SALES (est): 908.4K **Privately Held**
WEB: www.signimage.com
SIC: 3993 7319 Electric signs; display advertising service

(G-14150)
SMS HOLDING CO INC (PA)
Also Called: SMS Group
800 N Hamilton St (48602-4354)
PHONE.................................989 753-8465
Paul Chen, *President*
James Buckley, *President*
David Jay Albert, *Vice Pres*
William Spievak, *Vice Pres*
Pamela Baran, *CFO*
EMP: 190
SQ FT: 100,000
SALES (est): 16.7MM **Privately Held**
SIC: 3541 Drilling & boring machines

(G-14151)
SOLUTIONS 4 AUTOMATION INC
2124 S Michigan Ave (48602-1233)
PHONE.................................989 790-2778
Gary Seibert, *President*
Brad Federspiel, *Treasurer*
Troy Osbourne, *Admin Sec*
EMP: 12
SQ FT: 20,000
SALES (est): 4.2MM **Privately Held**
SIC: 3569 Liquid automation machinery & equipment

(G-14152)
SPATZ BAKERY INC
1120 State St (48602-5438)
P.O. Box 6303 (48608-6303)
PHONE.................................989 755-5551
Joseph Spatz, *President*
EMP: 11
SQ FT: 4,000
SALES (est): 1.7MM **Privately Held**
SIC: 2051 Bread, all types (white, wheat, rye, etc): fresh or frozen

(G-14153)
SPAULDING MACHINE CO INC
5366 East Rd (48601-9748)
PHONE.................................989 777-0694
Lucile Brettrager, *Corp Secy*
EMP: 25
SQ FT: 5,600
SALES (est): 3.7MM **Privately Held**
SIC: 3599 7692 Machine shop, jobbing & repair; welding repair

(G-14154)
SPAULDING MFG INC
5366 East Rd (48601-9748)
PHONE.................................989 777-4550
Edward Brettrager, *President*
Michelle Desonia, *Principal*
Lucille Brettrager, *Corp Secy*
Cindy Cherry, *Parts Mgr*
Jason Bowman, *Design Engr*
EMP: 25
SALES (est): 6.4MM **Privately Held**
WEB: www.spauldingmfg.com
SIC: 3531 Road construction & maintenance machinery

(G-14155)
SPECIALTY MANUFACTURING INC
2210 Midland Rd (48603-3440)
PHONE.................................989 790-9011
Kathleen Thompson, *President*
Amanda Schiedner, *Vice Pres*
Kristi Wiechmann, *Vice Pres*
Tony Rowe, *Plant Mgr*
Jordan Cooper, *Engineer*
EMP: 45
SQ FT: 25,000
SALES (est): 10MM **Privately Held**
WEB: www.smimfg.com
SIC: 2822 Silicone rubbers

(G-14156)
SPORTS JUNCTION (PA)
5605 State St (48603-3682)
PHONE.................................989 791-5900
Arthur W Tolfree Jr, *Partner*
David A Bedford, *Partner*
EMP: 7
SQ FT: 3,000
SALES (est): 872.7K **Privately Held**
SIC: 5699 5941 2759 2395 Sports apparel; team sports equipment; baseball equipment; basketball equipment; football equipment; screen printing; embroidery products, except schiffli machine

(G-14157)
STANDING COMPANY
Also Called: Standing Wheelchair Company
5848 Dixie Hwy (48601-5967)
PHONE.................................989 746-9100
David J Maczik, *President*
Eddie Cox, *Mktg Coord*
EMP: 14
SQ FT: 4,800
SALES (est): 2.1MM **Privately Held**
SIC: 3842 Wheelchairs

(G-14158)
STEERING SOLUTIONS CORPORATION (DH)
3900 E Holland Rd (48601-9494)
PHONE.................................989 757-5000
Mike Richardson, *CEO*
◆ EMP: 32
SALES (est): 8.3MM **Privately Held**
SIC: 3714 Motor vehicle parts & accessories

(G-14159)
SVRC INDUSTRIES INC (PA)
Also Called: Saginaw Vly Rehabilitation Ctr
203 S Washington Ave # 310 (48607-1208)
PHONE.................................989 280-3038
Dean Emerson, *President*
Matthew Muempfer, *Vice Pres*
Deborah Snyder, *Vice Pres*
Rose Jurek, *Director*
EMP: 50
SQ FT: 42,000
SALES: 10.2MM **Privately Held**
WEB: www.svrcindustries.com
SIC: 8331 7349 8299 3089 Vocational rehabilitation agency; building & office cleaning services; educational services; automotive parts, plastic

(G-14160)
SWEENEY METALWORKING LLC
4450 Marlea Dr (48601)
P.O. Box 605, Bridgeport (48722-0605)
PHONE.................................989 401-6531
Doug Sweeney, *Mng Member*
EMP: 12
SQ FT: 13,000
SALES (est): 1.8MM **Privately Held**
SIC: 3544 Special dies, tools, jigs & fixtures

(G-14161)
SWEET CREATIONS
1375 Lathrup Ave (48638-4736)
PHONE.................................989 327-1157
Ronald Stanley, *Principal*
EMP: 4
SALES (est): 229.5K **Privately Held**
SIC: 2053 Cakes, bakery: frozen

(G-14162)
SWS - TRIMAC INC
Also Called: Special Welding Services
5225 Davis Rd (48604-9419)
PHONE.................................989 791-4595
Gordon McIntosh, *President*
Jennifer Wooten, *Manager*
EMP: 33
SQ FT: 20,000
SALES: 4MM **Privately Held**
WEB: www.sws-trimac.com
SIC: 8711 7692 3599 Engineering services; welding repair; machine shop, jobbing & repair

(G-14163)
TEAMTECH MOTORSPORTS SAFETY
6285 Bay Rd Ste 7 (48604-8798)
P.O. Box 5586 (48603-0586)
PHONE.................................989 792-4880
Curt Tucker, *President*
EMP: 8
SQ FT: 4,000
SALES (est): 968.5K **Privately Held**
WEB: www.teamtechmotorsports.com
SIC: 2399 3714 3728 3429 Seat belts, automobile & aircraft; motor vehicle parts & accessories; aircraft parts & equipment; aircraft hardware; marine hardware; scientific research agency; motor vehicle supplies & new parts

(G-14164)
TIP TOP SCREW MANUFACTURI
725 W Morley Dr (48601-8405)
P.O. Box 2491 (48605-2491)
PHONE.................................989 739-5157
EMP: 3
SALES (est): 230K **Privately Held**
SIC: 3999 Manufacturing industries

Saginaw - Saginaw County (G-14165)

(G-14165)
TOW-LINE TRAILERS
Also Called: Tow-Line Trailer Sales
4854 E Holland Rd (48601-9463)
PHONE 989 752-0055
Freda Hewitt, *Owner*
EMP: 7
SQ FT: 2,400
SALES (est): 1MM **Privately Held**
SIC: 5599 3715 5511 Utility trailers; truck trailers; trucks, tractors & trailers: new & used

(G-14166)
TREIB INC (PA)
Also Called: Central Metalizing & Machine
850 S Outer Dr (48601-6504)
PHONE 989 752-4821
Kenneth Treib, *President*
David Treib, *Corp Secy*
Robert Treib, *Vice Pres*
EMP: 14
SQ FT: 2,500
SALES (est): 10.4MM **Privately Held**
WEB: www.treib.com
SIC: 3599 7542 5541 Machine shop, jobbing & repair; carwash, automatic; filling stations, gasoline

(G-14167)
TRI-CITY VINYL INC
640 E Morley Dr (48601-9401)
P.O. Box 3301 (48605-3301)
PHONE 989 401-7992
John C Burt, *Ch of Bd*
Mark Irwin, *Plant Mgr*
EMP: 25 **EST:** 1975
SQ FT: 35,000
SALES (est): 2.8MM **Privately Held**
WEB: www.tricityvinyl.com
SIC: 2295 Resin or plastic coated fabrics

(G-14168)
TSUNAMI INC
Also Called: Easy Printing Center
6235 Gratiot Rd (48638-5987)
PHONE 989 497-5200
Robert C Hansens, *President*
Richard M Welzein, *President*
EMP: 6
SQ FT: 4,000
SALES: 630K **Privately Held**
SIC: 2752 Commercial printing, offset

(G-14169)
TUPES OF SAGINAW INC
2858 Enterprise Ct (48603-2408)
P.O. Box 5989 (48603-0989)
PHONE 989 799-1550
James R Kaylor, *President*
Sharon A Kaylor, *Admin Sec*
EMP: 15 **EST:** 1933
SQ FT: 18,000
SALES (est): 4.5MM **Privately Held**
SIC: 5084 5169 5083 7692 Welding machinery & equipment; safety equipment; oxygen; acetylene; farm equipment parts & supplies; welding repair; welding apparatus

(G-14170)
TURN ONE INC
1260 S Beyer Rd (48601-9437)
PHONE 989 652-2778
Jeff Roethlisberger, *President*
EMP: 3
SALES (est): 310.2K **Privately Held**
SIC: 3714 Motor vehicle steering systems & parts

(G-14171)
TURNER BUSINESS FORMS INC (PA)
Also Called: Tbf Graphics
19 Slatestone Dr (48603-2890)
PHONE 989 752-5540
Gregory J Turner, *President*
Gregory S Turner, *COO*
EMP: 25
SQ FT: 18,000
SALES: 2.9MM **Privately Held**
WEB: www.tbfgraphics.com
SIC: 2752 5112 2791 2789 Commercial printing, offset; business forms; typesetting; bookbinding & related work; commercial printing

(G-14172)
U S GRAPHITE INC (PA)
1620 E Holland Ave (48601-2999)
PHONE 989 755-0441
Richard Gledhill, *President*
John Schmitzer, *General Mgr*
Sarah Witgen, *Human Res Dir*
Victor Monroe, *Director*
▲ **EMP:** 119
SQ FT: 290,000
SALES (est): 17.7MM **Privately Held**
WEB: www.usgraphite.net
SIC: 3624 3568 3053 Carbon & graphite products; power transmission equipment; gaskets, packing & sealing devices

(G-14173)
UNIVERSAL / DEVLIEG INC
1270 Agricola Dr (48604-9702)
PHONE 989 752-3077
Sherry Carpenter, *President*
EMP: 10 **EST:** 2014
SQ FT: 10,000
SALES (est): 1.5MM **Privately Held**
SIC: 3545 Cutting tools for machine tools

(G-14174)
UNIVERSAL/DEVLIEG LLC
1270 Agricola Dr (48604-9702)
PHONE 989 752-7700
R James Paas,
Sherry R Carpenter,
James Shinners,
▲ **EMP:** 10
SQ FT: 22,500
SALES (est): 2.5MM **Privately Held**
SIC: 3545 Tool holders

(G-14175)
VALLEY GLASS CO INC
2424 Midland Rd (48603-3444)
PHONE 989 790-9342
Thomas J Witkowski, *President*
EMP: 8
SQ FT: 5,600
SALES (est): 1.3MM **Privately Held**
SIC: 1793 5231 3231 3211 Glass & glazing work; glass; products of purchased glass; flat glass

(G-14176)
VALLEY GROUP OF COMPANIES
Also Called: Valley Services
548 Shattuck Rd Ste B (48604-2468)
PHONE 989 799-9669
EMP: 11
SQ FT: 7,000
SALES (est): 1.1MM **Privately Held**
SIC: 1799 1742 3625 Trade Contractor Drywall/Insulating Contractor Mfg Relays/Industrial Controls

(G-14177)
VALLEY STEEL COMPANY
1322 King St (48602-1403)
P.O. Box 1386 (48605-1386)
PHONE 989 799-2600
Tom Maczik, *President*
Lois Maczik, *Vice Pres*
Gary E Maczik, *Admin Sec*
EMP: 15 **EST:** 1982
SQ FT: 20,000
SALES (est): 3.6MM **Privately Held**
SIC: 3441 Fabricated structural metal

(G-14178)
VARGAS & SONS
125 S Park Ave (48607-1547)
PHONE 989 754-4636
Albert Vargas Jr, *Owner*
Mike Vargas, *VP Mktg*
EMP: 10
SALES (est): 430K **Privately Held**
SIC: 2051 Bread, cake & related products

(G-14179)
VERDONI PRODUCTIONS INC
Also Called: Hispanic Visions
5090 Overhill Dr (48603-1750)
PHONE 989 790-0845
Ricardo Verdoni, *President*
Clarillen Verdoni, *Treasurer*
EMP: 5 **EST:** 1977
SQ FT: 7,000
SALES: 250K **Privately Held**
SIC: 7812 8742 2741 2721 Audio-visual program production; video tape production; management consulting services; marketing consulting services; newsletter publishing; technical manuals: publishing only, not printed on site; magazines: publishing only, not printed on site

(G-14180)
WALKER TELECOMMUNICATIONS
1375 S Center Rd (48638-6321)
PHONE 989 274-7384
Roy Walker, *Owner*
EMP: 5
SALES (est): 256.5K **Privately Held**
SIC: 3699 1731 Electrical equipment & supplies; voice, data & video wiring contractor

(G-14181)
WEIGHMAN ENTERPRISES INC
Also Called: Dornbos Printing Impressions
1131 E Genesee Ave (48607-1746)
PHONE 989 755-2116
Ron Weighman, *President*
EMP: 6
SQ FT: 8,600
SALES (est): 853.8K **Privately Held**
SIC: 2752 2796 2759 Commercial printing, offset; letterpress plates, preparation of; commercial printing

(G-14182)
WENDLING SHEET METAL INC
2633 Carrollton Rd (48604-2401)
PHONE 989 753-5286
Kevin Wendling, *President*
Stephanie Patrzik, *Principal*
Chad Wojciecho, *Vice Pres*
EMP: 35
SQ FT: 25,600
SALES: 7.6MM **Privately Held**
SIC: 3444 Sheet metalwork

(G-14183)
WILBERT SAGINAW VAULT CORP (PA)
2810 Hess Ave (48601-7416)
P.O. Box 1346 (48605-1346)
PHONE 989 753-3065
Jack Swihart, *President*
Lori J Davis, *COO*
Cynthia Swihart, *Vice Pres*
EMP: 3 **EST:** 1929
SQ FT: 25,000
SALES (est): 1.9MM **Privately Held**
SIC: 3272 7261 Burial vaults, concrete or precast terrazzo; crematory

(G-14184)
WRIGHT-K TECHNOLOGY INC
Also Called: Wright-K Spare Parts and Svcs
2025 E Genesee Ave (48601-2499)
PHONE 989 752-2588
Constance Kostrzewa, *Ch of Bd*
John Sivey, *President*
Jim Nicoson, *Engineer*
Jerry Vermeesch, *Manager*
Brandon Donaghy, *Info Tech Mgr*
EMP: 35
SQ FT: 65,180
SALES: 8MM **Privately Held**
WEB: www.wright-k.com
SIC: 8711 3549 3541 Designing: ship, boat, machine & product; assembly machines, including robotic; drilling machine tools (metal cutting)

(G-14185)
ZF ACTIVE SAFETY US INC
2828 E Genesee Ave (48601)
PHONE 248 863-2412
EMP: 126
SALES (corp-wide): 216.2K **Privately Held**
SIC: 3714 Motor vehicle parts & accessories
HQ: Zf Active Safety Us Inc.
12001 Tech Center Dr
Livonia MI 48150
734 812-6979

Sagola
Dickinson County

(G-14186)
FLEMING FABRICATION MACHINING
W9295 Bice Creek Ln (49881-9729)
PHONE 906 542-3573
Martin Fleming, *Owner*
EMP: 3
SALES (est): 449.1K **Privately Held**
SIC: 3531 Construction machinery

(G-14187)
MINERICK LOGGING INC
N10670 State Highway M95 (49881-9730)
P.O. Box 99 (49881-0099)
PHONE 906 542-3583
Robert Minerick, *President*
Margaret Minerick, *Corp Secy*
Phillip Minerick, *Vice Pres*
EMP: 26
SQ FT: 10,000
SALES (est): 4.1MM **Privately Held**
SIC: 2411 Pulpwood camp not operating a pulp mill at same site

(G-14188)
SAGOLA HARDWOODS INC
N10640 State Highway M95 (49881-9730)
P.O. Box 99 (49881-0099)
PHONE 906 542-7200
Margaret Minerick, *President*
Robert Minerick, *Vice Pres*
Kim Olson, *Office Mgr*
EMP: 56
SALES (est): 7.7MM **Privately Held**
SIC: 2421 Sawmills & planing mills, general

Saint Charles
Saginaw County

(G-14189)
ABLE WELDING INC
5265 S Graham Rd (48655-8523)
PHONE 989 865-9611
Bernard Schultz Sr, *President*
EMP: 5
SQ FT: 5,200
SALES: 350K **Privately Held**
SIC: 7692 3471 Welding repair; plating & polishing

(G-14190)
BLACKLEDGE TOOL INC
305 Entrepreneur Dr (48655-8644)
P.O. Box 117 (48655-0117)
PHONE 989 865-8393
Clark Blackledge, *President*
Kay Blackledge, *Bookkeeper*
EMP: 5
SALES (est): 656.7K **Privately Held**
SIC: 3544 3599 Special dies & tools; machine shop, jobbing & repair

(G-14191)
D & K PATTERN INC
12021 Beaver Rd (48655-9681)
P.O. Box 58 (48655-0058)
PHONE 989 865-9955
Kenneth J Braun, *President*
EMP: 3
SQ FT: 3,500
SALES (est): 436.3K **Privately Held**
SIC: 3543 Foundry patternmaking

(G-14192)
EAGLE CREEK MFG & SALES
6753 S Steel Rd (48655-9732)
PHONE 989 643-7521
Roger Miller, *Owner*
Sharon Miller, *Co-Owner*
EMP: 7
SQ FT: 4,000
SALES: 225K **Privately Held**
SIC: 3451 Screw machine products

GEOGRAPHIC SECTION

Saint Clair - St. Clair County (G-14219)

(G-14193)
JUNGNITSCH BROS LOGGING
15250 W Townline Rd (48655-9760)
PHONE..................989 233-8091
Scott Jungnitsch, *Principal*
EMP: 3
SALES (est): 284.2K **Privately Held**
SIC: 2411 Logging

(G-14194)
KELLY INDUSTRIAL SERVICE CORP
Also Called: Hot Powder Coating
11975 Beaver Rd (48655-9687)
P.O. Box 237 (48655-0237)
PHONE..................989 865-6111
Kelly Bellenbaum, *President*
Kristina Bellenbaum, *Admin Sec*
EMP: 3
SQ FT: 3,800
SALES (est): 458K **Privately Held**
SIC: 3599 Machine shop, jobbing & repair

(G-14195)
M J MECHANICAL INC
Also Called: Mj Mechanical Services
11787 Prior Rd (48655-9559)
PHONE..................989 865-9633
Matthew Berent, *President*
EMP: 20
SALES (est): 4.3MM **Privately Held**
WEB: www.mj-mechanical.com
SIC: 3444 Sheet metalwork

(G-14196)
MICHIGAN PALLET INC (PA)
Also Called: Lewiston Forest Products
1225 N Saginaw St (48655-1024)
P.O. Box 97 (48655-0097)
PHONE..................989 865-9915
Paul Kamps, *President*
Rich Newill, *Supervisor*
EMP: 15
SQ FT: 13,000
SALES (est): 2.8MM **Privately Held**
SIC: 2448 Pallets, wood

(G-14197)
MTI PRECISION MACHINING INC
Also Called: Method Tool
11980 Beaver Rd (48655-9687)
P.O. Box 205 (48655-0205)
PHONE..................989 865-9880
Stuart Yntema, *President*
Robert Milbrandt, *Supervisor*
EMP: 11
SALES: 930K
SALES (corp-wide): 16.1MM **Privately Held**
SIC: 3544 Special dies, tools, jigs & fixtures
PA: Tpi Powder Metallurgy, Inc.
  12030 Beaver Rd
  Saint Charles MI 48655
  989 865-9921

(G-14198)
POREX TECHNOLOGIES CORPORATION
Also Called: Filtrona Porous Technologies
5301 S Graham Rd (48655-8522)
PHONE..................989 865-8200
Julie Hill, *Manager*
EMP: 25
SALES (corp-wide): 108MM **Privately Held**
SIC: 3842 3082 Surgical appliances & supplies; unsupported plastics profile shapes
PA: Porex Technologies Corp.
  1625 Ashton Park Dr Ste A
  South Chesterfield VA 23834
  804 524-4983

(G-14199)
PRECISION JIG GRINDING INC
165 Entrepreneur Dr (48655-9600)
P.O. Box 208 (48655-0208)
PHONE..................989 865-7953
John Sievert, *President*
Dawn Sievert, *Treasurer*
EMP: 5
SQ FT: 3,000
SALES (est): 385K **Privately Held**
SIC: 3541 Jig boring & grinding machines

(G-14200)
RIVERSIDE BLOCK CO INC
1024 N Saginaw St (48655-1022)
PHONE..................989 865-9951
Michael Mendyk, *President*
Penny Mendyk, *Treasurer*
EMP: 4 **EST:** 1946
SQ FT: 9,000
SALES (est): 508K **Privately Held**
SIC: 3273 Ready-mixed concrete

(G-14201)
ST CHARLES HARDWOOD MICHIGAN
10500 Mckeighan Rd (48655-8637)
P.O. Box 96 (48655-0096)
PHONE..................989 865-9299
Gary Tarr, *President*
Lorraine Lewenberger, *Corp Secy*
Linda Tarr, *Vice Pres*
EMP: 19
SALES (est): 1.4MM **Privately Held**
SIC: 2421 1629 Sawmills & planing mills, general; land clearing contractor

(G-14202)
TK ENTERPRISES INC
1225 N Saginaw St (48655-1024)
PHONE..................989 865-9915
Paul M Kamps, *President*
EMP: 40 **EST:** 1967
SQ FT: 70,000
SALES (est): 1.9MM **Privately Held**
SIC: 2448 2449 Pallets, wood; skids, wood; fruit crates, wood: wirebound; vegetable crates, wood: wirebound

(G-14203)
TPI POWDER METALLURGY INC (PA)
12030 Beaver Rd (48655-8639)
P.O. Box 69 (48655-0069)
PHONE..................989 865-9921
Stuart H Yntema Jr, *President*
Stuart Yntema Jr, *President*
Steven B Yntema, *Admin Sec*
EMP: 70 **EST:** 1967
SQ FT: 20,000
SALES (est): 16.1MM **Privately Held**
SIC: 3499 Fire- or burglary-resistive products

Saint Clair
St. Clair County

(G-14204)
AQPE LLC
561 N Riverside Ave (48079-5415)
PHONE..................810 329-9259
Timothy J Burns, *President*
EMP: 3
SQ FT: 1,000
SALES: 150K **Privately Held**
SIC: 8742 3089 Management consulting services; plastic processing

(G-14205)
AURIA ST CLAIR LLC
2001 Christian B Haas Dr (48079-4297)
PHONE..................810 329-8400
Brian Pour, *CEO*
Dennis Hillman, *Engineer*
Donna Schultz, *Manager*
EMP: 31
SALES: 50MM
SALES (corp-wide): 571K **Privately Held**
WEB: www.iaaawards.com
SIC: 3714 Motor vehicle parts & accessories
HQ: Auria Solutions Usa Inc.
  26999 Central Park Blvd # 300
  Southfield MI 48076
  734 456-2800

(G-14206)
BIEWER LUMBER LLC (PA)
Also Called: Pine River Group
812 S Riverside Ave (48079-5393)
P.O. Box 497 (48079-0497)
PHONE..................810 326-3930
Craig Little, *General Mgr*
Kevin Pierce, *Superintendent*
Tim Biewer, *Vice Pres*
Lea Shivers, *Safety Dir*
Aaron Breitmeyer, *Plant Mgr*
▲ **EMP:** 30
SQ FT: 5,000
SALES (est): 120.2MM **Privately Held**
WEB: www.biewerlumber.com
SIC: 2491 Structural lumber & timber, treated wood; pilings, treated wood

(G-14207)
CARGILL INCORPORATED
916 S Riverside Ave (48079-5335)
PHONE..................810 329-2736
Ike Venker, *Manager*
EMP: 284
SALES (corp-wide): 114.7B **Privately Held**
WEB: www.cargill.com
SIC: 2899 5169 Salt; salts, industrial
PA: Cargill, Incorporated
  15407 Mcginty Rd W
  Wayzata MN 55391
  952 742-7575

(G-14208)
CASTING INDUSTRIES INC
315 Whiting St (48079-4981)
P.O. Box 668, Saint Clair Shores (48080-0668)
PHONE..................586 776-5700
Fred E Kilgus, *President*
EMP: 17 **EST:** 1974
SQ FT: 3,500
SALES: 4MM **Privately Held**
WEB: www.castinginc.net
SIC: 3321 3365 Gray iron castings; aluminum & aluminum-based alloy castings

(G-14209)
CENTRACORE LLC (PA)
315 Whiting St (48079-4981)
P.O. Box 668, Saint Clair Shores (48080-0668)
PHONE..................586 776-5700
Gary Ray, *Engineer*
Frederick E Kilgus, *Mng Member*
▲ **EMP:** 12
SALES (est): 3.7MM **Privately Held**
SIC: 3365 3559 Aerospace castings, aluminum; aluminum & aluminum-based alloy castings; automotive related machinery

(G-14210)
CENTRACORE DE MEXICO LLC
315 Whiting St (48079-4981)
PHONE..................586 776-5700
Todd Kilgus, *Principal*
EMP: 20
SALES (est): 882.6K **Privately Held**
SIC: 3363 Aluminum die-castings

(G-14211)
CORSON FABRICATING LLC
1701 Sinclair St Ste B (48079-5906)
PHONE..................810 326-0532
Gary Corrigan,
Michael Gibson,
EMP: 15
SALES (est): 2.1MM **Privately Held**
SIC: 1791 3449 Structural steel erection; bars, concrete reinforcing: fabricated steel

(G-14212)
CRAIG ASSEMBLY INC
1111 Fred W Moore Hwy (48079-4967)
PHONE..................810 326-1374
Werner Deggim, *CEO*
Thomas Geiser, *President*
Russel Hutchins, *Vice Pres*
Tom Geiser, *Plant Mgr*
Michael Bucher, *Engineer*
▲ **EMP:** 150
SQ FT: 30,000
SALES: 30MM
SALES (corp-wide): 1.2B **Privately Held**
WEB: www.craigassembly.com
SIC: 3492 3089 5013 Fluid power valves & hose fittings; injection molded finished plastic products; seat belts
PA: Norma Group Se
  Edisonstr. 4
  Maintal 63477
  618 140-30

(G-14213)
DANA LIMITED
Also Called: Thermal Products
2020 Christian B Haas Dr (48079-5701)
PHONE..................810 329-2500
Ridhan Riyal, *Engineer*
John Geddes, *Asst Treas*
Vic Avram, *Sales Staff*
Bob Albrecht, *Branch Mgr*
Tim Williams, *Program Mgr*
EMP: 100 **Publicly Held**
WEB: www.intelligentcooling.com
SIC: 3714 Motor vehicle parts & accessories
HQ: Dana Limited
  3939 Technology Dr
  Maumee OH 43537

(G-14214)
DANA THERMAL PRODUCTS LLC
Power Technologies Group
2020 Christian B Haas Dr (48079-5701)
PHONE..................810 329-2500
David Dumas, *Production*
EMP: 60 **Publicly Held**
SIC: 3714 Motor vehicle parts & accessories
HQ: Dana Thermal Products, Llc
  3939 Technology Dr
  Maumee OH 43537

(G-14215)
DANA THERMAL PRODUCTS LLC
Also Called: Long Manufacturing
2020 Christian B Haas Dr (48079-5701)
PHONE..................810 329-2500
Tim Cajac, *Manager*
EMP: 170 **Publicly Held**
SIC: 3714 Motor vehicle parts & accessories
HQ: Dana Thermal Products, Llc
  3939 Technology Dr
  Maumee OH 43537

(G-14216)
DECKER GEAR INC (PA)
1500 Glendale St (48079-5100)
PHONE..................810 388-1500
Louise Decker, *President*
Rick Decker, *President*
EMP: 18
SQ FT: 5,400
SALES (est): 1.7MM **Privately Held**
WEB: www.deckergear.com
SIC: 3566 3599 3462 Gears, power transmission, except automotive; machine shop, jobbing & repair; gear & chain forgings

(G-14217)
ENGINEERED PLASTIC COMPONENTS
2000 Christian B Haas Dr (48079-5701)
PHONE..................810 326-1650
Miky Hartman, *Manager*
EMP: 120 **Privately Held**
WEB: www.epciowa.com
SIC: 3089 Injection molding of plastics
PA: Engineered Plastic Components, Inc.
  4500 Westown Pkwy Ste 277
  West Des Moines IA 50266

(G-14218)
ENGINEERED PLASTIC COMPONENTS
2015 S Range Rd (48079-4120)
PHONE..................810 326-3010
Stuart Duncan, *Branch Mgr*
EMP: 128 **Privately Held**
SIC: 3089 Injection molding of plastics
PA: Engineered Plastic Components, Inc.
  4500 Westown Pkwy Ste 277
  West Des Moines IA 50266

(G-14219)
EPC-COLUMBIA INC
2000 Christian B Haas Dr (48079-5701)
PHONE..................810 326-1650
Reza Kargarzadeh, *President*
EMP: 80
SALES (est): 1.2MM **Privately Held**
SIC: 3089 Injection molding of plastics

Saint Clair - St. Clair County (G-14220)

PA: Engineered Plastic Components, Inc.
4500 Westown Pkwy Ste 277
West Des Moines IA 50266

(G-14220)
FLIGHT MOLD & ENGINEERING INC
1940 Fred W Moore Hwy (48079-4701)
PHONE................................810 329-2900
Robert A Ward, *President*
EMP: 30
SQ FT: 17,500
SALES (est): 5.9MM **Privately Held**
WEB: www.flightmoldeng.com
SIC: 3089 Injection molding of plastics

(G-14221)
HEILEMAN SONS SIGNS & LTG SVCS
Also Called: Heileman Sons Signs & Ltg Ser
4797 Gratiot Ave (48079-1518)
PHONE................................810 364-2900
Richard H Heileman, *President*
Dan Heileman, *Vice Pres*
Gary Heileman, *Vice Pres*
Timothy Heileman, *Vice Pres*
Diane Heileman, *Vice Pres*
EMP: 9
SQ FT: 3,000
SALES: 600K **Privately Held**
WEB: www.heilemansigns.com
SIC: 3993 Signs & advertising specialties

(G-14222)
HODGES & IRVINE INC
1900 Sinclair St (48079-5513)
P.O. Box 197 (48079-0197)
PHONE................................810 329-4787
Roger Powers, *President*
Valeria Shatzel, *Systems Dir*
John Jeffrey Hodges, *Director*
EMP: 18 **EST:** 1940
SQ FT: 4,000
SALES (est): 2.2MM **Privately Held**
WEB: www.hodgesandirvine.com
SIC: 2754 2789 2759 2752 Job printing, gravure; bookbinding & related work; commercial printing; commercial printing, lithographic

(G-14223)
JGS MACHINING LLC
4455 Davis Rd (48079-2807)
PHONE................................810 329-4210
John Sams, *Mng Member*
EMP: 5
SQ FT: 3,500
SALES (est): 804.8K **Privately Held**
SIC: 3829 Testing equipment: abrasion, shearing strength, etc.

(G-14224)
JOHN A BIEWER CO OF ILLINOIS
812 S Riverside Ave (48079-5393)
P.O. Box 497 (48079-0497)
PHONE................................810 326-3930
Richard N Biewer, *President*
Brian B Biewer, *Corp Secy*
Timothy Biewer, *Vice Pres*
EMP: 25 **EST:** 1982
SQ FT: 5,000
SALES (est): 2.5MM
SALES (corp-wide): 120.2MM **Privately Held**
WEB: www.biewerlumber.com
SIC: 2491 Structural lumber & timber, treated wood
PA: Biewer Lumber, Llc
812 S Riverside Ave
Saint Clair MI 48079
810 326-3930

(G-14225)
JOHN A BIEWER LUMBER COMPANY (PA)
812 S Riverside Ave (48079-5393)
P.O. Box 497 (48079-0497)
PHONE................................810 329-4789
Richard Biewer, *President*
Richard N Biewer, *President*
Brian B Biewer, *Corp Secy*
Timothy Biewer, *Vice Pres*
▲ **EMP:** 300
SQ FT: 5,000
SALES (est): 53.8MM **Privately Held**
SIC: 2491 Structural lumber & timber, treated wood; pilings, treated wood

(G-14226)
LOGAN PATTERN & ENGRG CO LLC
5149 Bowman Rd (48079-3311)
PHONE................................810 364-9298
J Douglas Logan,
EMP: 3 **EST:** 1950
SALES (est): 478.2K **Privately Held**
SIC: 3543 Industrial patterns

(G-14227)
MARVEL TOOL & MACHINE COMPANY
1096 River Rd (48079-2800)
P.O. Box 90 (48079-0090)
PHONE................................810 329-2781
Richard Pierce, *President*
Elizabeth Ward-Pierce, *Vice Pres*
EMP: 3
SALES: 300K **Privately Held**
SIC: 3544 Special dies & tools

(G-14228)
MEMORIES MANOR
613 N Riverside Ave (48079-5417)
PHONE................................810 329-2800
Janine Zimmer, *Principal*
EMP: 4
SALES (est): 303.4K **Privately Held**
SIC: 2782 Scrapbooks

(G-14229)
MICHIGAN PRECISION SWISS PRTS
Also Called: MPS
2145 Wadhams Rd (48079-3808)
P.O. Box 376 (48079-0376)
PHONE................................810 329-2270
David D Murphy, *CEO*
Cheryl Pryor, *CFO*
Gerald D Meldrum, *Treasurer*
EMP: 45
SQ FT: 38,000
SALES (est): 10.4MM **Privately Held**
WEB: www.mpswiss.com
SIC: 3451 Screw machine products

(G-14230)
NORMA GROUP CRAIG ASSEMBLY
1219 Fred Moore Hwy (48079)
PHONE................................810 326-1374
EMP: 5
SALES (est): 214K **Privately Held**
SIC: 3678 Electronic connectors

(G-14231)
PIER ONE POLYMERS INCORPORATED
Also Called: Bh Polymers
2011 Christian B Haas Dr (48079-4297)
PHONE................................810 326-1456
Michael D Pier, *President*
Shawna Brasty, *Exec VP*
Jason Macuga, *CFO*
▲ **EMP:** 11
SQ FT: 7,800
SALES (est): 8MM **Privately Held**
SIC: 2821 Plastics materials & resins

(G-14232)
READYSETMAIL
64 S Range Rd 8 (48079-1526)
P.O. Box 238, Marysville (48040-0238)
PHONE................................810 982-1924
Jean Chapdelaine, *Owner*
EMP: 3
SALES (est): 259.4K **Privately Held**
WEB: www.readysetmail.com
SIC: 3273 Ready-mixed concrete

(G-14233)
REELING SYSTEMS LLC
Also Called: Dirkes Industries
5323 Gratiot Ave (48079-1426)
P.O. Box 265, Marysville (48040-0265)
PHONE................................810 364-3900
Chris Graham,
EMP: 9
SQ FT: 16,000
SALES (est): 1.7MM **Privately Held**
WEB: www.reelingsystems.com
SIC: 3357 3563 Nonferrous wiredrawing & insulating; spraying outfits: metals, paints & chemicals (compressor)

(G-14234)
RIVERSIDE TANK & MFG CORP
1230 Clinton Ave (48079-4958)
P.O. Box 67 (48079-0067)
PHONE................................810 329-7143
Fred Cartwright, *President*
Vicki Cartwright, *Admin Sec*
▼ **EMP:** 25
SQ FT: 20,000
SALES (est): 4.9MM **Privately Held**
WEB: www.riversidetank.com
SIC: 3443 3714 Tanks for tank trucks, metal plate; motor vehicle parts & accessories

(G-14235)
TITANIUM PRODUCTS CORP
2855 E Mill Creek Rd (48079-4753)
PHONE................................810 326-4325
Roger Romatz, *President*
Christina Romatz, *Corp Secy*
EMP: 3
SQ FT: 3,500
SALES: 400K **Privately Held**
SIC: 7692 Welding repair

(G-14236)
WACHTEL TOOL & BROACH INC
6676 Fred W Moore Hwy (48079-4401)
PHONE................................586 758-0110
Klaus Wachtel, *President*
Susan Wachtel, *Admin Sec*
EMP: 9
SQ FT: 2,500
SALES (est): 1MM **Privately Held**
SIC: 3545 Broaches (machine tool accessories)

(G-14237)
WRIGHT PLASTIC PRODUCTS CO LLC
2021 Christian B Haas Dr (48079-4297)
PHONE................................810 326-3000
Skip Hines, *Accounts Mgr*
Tom Arquette, *Branch Mgr*
EMP: 55
SALES (corp-wide): 38.5MM **Privately Held**
SIC: 3089 3544 5162 Injection molded finished plastic products; forms (molds), for foundry & plastics working machinery; plastics products
PA: Wright Plastic Products Co L.L.C.
201 E Condensery Rd
Sheridan MI 48884
989 291-3211

Saint Clair Shores
Macomb County

(G-14238)
ALEXANDER AND HORNUNG INC
Also Called: BROOKSIDE FOODS
20643 Stephens St (48080-1047)
PHONE................................586 771-9880
Bernie Polen, *President*
Joe Casasanta, *Vice Pres*
Tom Eckert, *Vice Pres*
Thomas Trombley, *Engineer*
Tim Houghton, *Marketing Staff*
◆ **EMP:** 100 **EST:** 1954
SQ FT: 100,000
SALES: 39.1MM **Privately Held**
WEB: www.alexander-hornung.com
SIC: 2013 Sausages & other prepared meats

(G-14239)
ALLIANCE TOOL AND MACHINE CO
21418 Timberidge St (48082-2257)
PHONE................................586 427-6411
EMP: 10 **EST:** 1944
SQ FT: 4,200
SALES (est): 1.1MM **Privately Held**
SIC: 3544 Mfg Dies/Tools/Jigs/Fixtures

(G-14240)
AMERICAN GRAPHICS INC
Also Called: American Speedy Printing
27413 Harper Ave (48081-1921)
PHONE................................586 774-8880
Donald Girodat, *President*
Sandra Girodat, *Vice Pres*
EMP: 8
SQ FT: 2,500
SALES (est): 1.1MM **Privately Held**
SIC: 2752 Commercial printing, offset

(G-14241)
C H M GRAPHICS & LITHO INC
20220 Stephens St (48080-1033)
PHONE................................586 777-4550
Kathleen Campbell, *President*
Philip Mousseau, *Vice Pres*
EMP: 4
SALES (est): 278.1K **Privately Held**
SIC: 2752 7336 Commercial printing, offset; commercial art & graphic design

(G-14242)
CAL CHEMICAL MANUFACTURING CO
605 Shore Club Dr (48080-1559)
PHONE................................586 778-7006
EMP: 5 **EST:** 1962
SQ FT: 2,250
SALES (est): 150K **Privately Held**
SIC: 2842 Mfg Cleaning Compounds

(G-14243)
DEL PRINTING INC
19724 E 9 Mile Rd (48080-1687)
PHONE................................586 445-3044
Joanne Leblanc, *President*
Perry Leblanc, *Vice Pres*
EMP: 10
SQ FT: 10,000
SALES (est): 1.6MM **Privately Held**
WEB: www.delprinting.com
SIC: 2759 Commercial printing

(G-14244)
DISRUPTTECH LLC
22631 Bayview Dr (48081-2465)
PHONE................................248 225-8383
Mark Colonese, *Mng Member*
EMP: 4 **EST:** 2016
SALES (est): 211.7K **Privately Held**
SIC: 3312 3571 8711 Stainless steel; electronic computers; consulting engineer

(G-14245)
ELITE WOODWORKING LLC
Also Called: Detroit Woodworking
22960 W Industrial Dr B (48080-1182)
PHONE................................586 204-5882
Amy Lee, *Office Mgr*
Daniel J Connell, *Mng Member*
EMP: 50
SALES (est): 88.4K **Privately Held**
SIC: 2434 Wood kitchen cabinets

(G-14246)
EMBROIDERY & MUCH MORE LLC
27419 Harper Ave (48081-1921)
PHONE................................586 771-3832
Linda Bologna, *Human Res Mgr*
EMP: 10
SALES (est): 874.4K **Privately Held**
WEB: www.embroiderymore.com
SIC: 2395 5699 Embroidery products, except schiffli machine; pleating & tucking, for the trade; sports apparel

(G-14247)
ETHELS EDIBLES LLC
Also Called: Ethel's Baking Co.
22314 Harper Ave (48080-1818)
PHONE................................586 552-5110
Jill Bommarito,
EMP: 11
SALES (est): 1.5MM **Privately Held**
SIC: 2051 Cakes, bakery: except frozen

GEOGRAPHIC SECTION

Saint Clair Shores - Macomb County (G-14275)

(G-14248)
FINGER FIT CO
24410 Harper Ave (48080-1237)
P.O. Box 692 (48080-0692)
PHONE.................................734 522-2935
Tom Lillie, *President*
EMP: 3
SQ FT: 1,200
SALES (est): 341.4K **Privately Held**
WEB: www.fingerfit.com
SIC: 3915 5944 Jewelers' findings & materials; jewelry stores

(G-14249)
FISHER & COMPANY INCORPORATED (PA)
Also Called: Fisher Dynamics
33300 Fisher Dr (48082)
PHONE.................................586 746-2000
Alfred J Fisher III, *Chairman*
Alfred J Fisher III, *Chairman*
James Babiasz, *Vice Pres*
Joseph E Blake, *Vice Pres*
Alfred J Fisher IV, *Vice Pres*
◆ **EMP:** 450
SQ FT: 135,000
SALES (est): 477.8MM **Privately Held**
WEB: www.fisherco.com
SIC: 2531 Seats, automobile

(G-14250)
FISHER & COMPANY INCORPORATED
Also Called: Fisher Safety Structures
33200 Fisher Dr (48082-1071)
PHONE.................................586 746-2280
Alfred J Fisher IV, *Division Pres*
Sandra Kenney, *Manager*
EMP: 47
SALES (corp-wide): 477.8MM **Privately Held**
SIC: 3714 Motor vehicle parts & accessories
PA: Fisher & Company, Incorporated
33300 Fisher Dr
Saint Clair Shores MI 48082
586 746-2000

(G-14251)
FISHER DYNAMICS CORPORATION
33180 Fisher Dr (48082-1005)
PHONE.................................586 746-2000
EMP: 28 **EST:** 2014
SALES (est): 264.6K
SALES (corp-wide): 477.8MM **Privately Held**
SIC: 2531 Seats, automobile
PA: Fisher & Company, Incorporated
33300 Fisher Dr
Saint Clair Shores MI 48082
586 746-2000

(G-14252)
FOURTH SEACOAST PUBLISHING CO
Also Called: Quick Caller, The
25300 Little Mack Ave (48081-3369)
P.O. Box 145 (48080-0145)
PHONE.................................586 779-5570
Thomas Buysse, *President*
Sharon Roman, *Sales Staff*
Carlos Valdez, *Manager*
EMP: 7
SQ FT: 1,300
SALES (est): 822.9K **Privately Held**
WEB: www.fourthseacoast.com
SIC: 2741 4731 Directories: publishing only, not printed on site; freight transportation arrangement

(G-14253)
FULL SPEKTREM LLC
21925 Harper Ave (48080-2217)
PHONE.................................313 910-1920
Alan Zimmer, *President*
EMP: 4 **EST:** 2010
SALES (est): 378.1K **Privately Held**
SIC: 2851 5033 Paints & allied products; asphalt felts & coating

(G-14254)
GENERAL MEDIA LLC
Also Called: Used Car News
24114 Harper Ave (48080-1234)
P.O. Box 80800 (48080-5800)
PHONE.................................586 541-0075
Shannon Colby, *Natl Sales Mgr*
Lynda Thomas, *Mng Member*
EMP: 22
SALES (est): 1.6MM **Privately Held**
WEB: www.usedcarnews.com
SIC: 2711 Newspapers, publishing & printing

(G-14255)
GREENLIGHT HOME INSPECTION SVC
23340 Westbury St (48080-2540)
PHONE.................................313 885-5616
Philip Hutchings, *Principal*
EMP: 5
SALES (est): 281.4K **Privately Held**
SIC: 1389 Construction, repair & dismantling services

(G-14256)
HARDY & SONS SIGN SERVICE INC
22340 Harper Ave (48080-1818)
PHONE.................................586 779-8018
Carolyn Hardy, *President*
David Hardy, *Treasurer*
EMP: 5
SALES (est): 500K **Privately Held**
SIC: 3993 Electric signs

(G-14257)
K&K STAMPING COMPANY
23015 W Industrial Dr (48080-1187)
PHONE.................................586 443-7900
Joseph J Koch, *President*
Richard N Koch, *Vice Pres*
▲ **EMP:** 50
SQ FT: 45,000
SALES (est): 9.9MM **Privately Held**
WEB: www.kandk.com
SIC: 3465 3544 3469 Body parts, automobile: stamped metal; special dies & tools; metal stampings

(G-14258)
KURTH BAYARD CO
20628 Alger St (48080-3711)
PHONE.................................586 771-5174
Bayard Kurth III, *President*
Brenden Kurth, *Admin Sec*
EMP: 17
SALES (est): 500K **Privately Held**
SIC: 3993 Displays, paint process

(G-14259)
LANDRA PRSTHTICS ORTHOTICS INC
29840 Harper Ave (48082-2608)
PHONE.................................586 294-7188
Steven Landra, *Branch Mgr*
EMP: 5
SALES (corp-wide): 908.9K **Privately Held**
SIC: 3842 5047 8082 8099 Prosthetic appliances; medical & hospital equipment; home health care services; medical services organization
PA: Landra Prosthetics And Orthotics, Inc.
14725 Northline Rd
Southgate MI 48195
734 281-8144

(G-14260)
LORD LABORATORIES
Also Called: Tech Engineering International
20416 Sunnydale St (48081-3449)
PHONE.................................586 447-8955
Sean Gosselin, *Owner*
EMP: 3
SALES (est): 150K **Privately Held**
SIC: 2992 8711 Oils & greases, blending & compounding; engineering services

(G-14261)
MARK FOUR CAM INC
22926 W Industrial Dr (48080-1131)
PHONE.................................586 204-5906
Edward A Gieche, *President*
Ronald Dooley, *Treasurer*
Alan Imboden, *Admin Sec*
EMP: 8
SQ FT: 9,500
SALES (est): 1MM **Privately Held**
SIC: 3544 Forms (molds), for foundry & plastics working machinery

(G-14262)
MARKS FUEL DOCK
24200 Jefferson Ave (48080-1577)
PHONE.................................586 445-8525
Mark Conely, *Principal*
EMP: 4 **EST:** 2009
SALES (est): 260.7K **Privately Held**
SIC: 2869 Fuels

(G-14263)
METALS PRESERVATION GROUP LLC
20420 Stephens St (48080-3186)
PHONE.................................586 944-2720
Joseph Louisell, *President*
EMP: 17 **EST:** 2013
SQ FT: 9,000
SALES (est): 5MM **Privately Held**
SIC: 5199 2842 Packaging materials; rust removers

(G-14264)
MICROFORM TOOL COMPANY INC
20601 Stephens St (48080-1047)
PHONE.................................586 776-4840
Thomas Alschbach, *President*
Margaret Alschbach, *Admin Sec*
EMP: 4 **EST:** 1961
SQ FT: 4,000
SALES (est): 924.6K **Privately Held**
WEB: www.microformtool.com
SIC: 3541 Machine tools, metal cutting type

(G-14265)
NORTH SAILS GROUP LLC
Also Called: North Sails-Detroit
22600 Greater Mack Ave (48080-2015)
PHONE.................................586 776-1330
Fax: 586 776-2762
EMP: 4 **Privately Held**
SIC: 2394 Mfg Canvas/Related Products
HQ: North Sails Group, Llc
125 Old Gate Ln Ste 7
Milford CT 06460
203 874-7548

(G-14266)
OPENSYSTEMS PUBLISHING LLC (PA)
Also Called: Compact PCI Systems
30233 Jefferson Ave (48082-1787)
PHONE.................................586 415-6500
Micheal Hopper, *President*
Patrick Hopper, *Vice Pres*
Arthur Swift, *Vice Pres*
Rebecca Barker, *Accounts Mgr*
Eric Henry, *Accounts Mgr*
EMP: 13
SQ FT: 1,200
SALES (est): 1.7MM **Privately Held**
WEB: www.embedded-computing.com
SIC: 2721 Periodicals: publishing only

(G-14267)
PRACTICAL SOLAR
23276 Doremus St (48080-2710)
PHONE.................................586 864-6686
Franklin Scruggs, *Owner*
EMP: 3
SALES (est): 136.5K **Privately Held**
SIC: 2371 Fur goods

(G-14268)
PRINT PLUS INC
Also Called: Reproductions Resource
28324 Elmdale St (48081-1483)
PHONE.................................586 888-8000
John Blumline, *President*
EMP: 4
SALES (est): 551.3K **Privately Held**
SIC: 2752 Commercial printing, offset

(G-14269)
PRINTING BUYING SERVICE
Also Called: Printing Buying Services
28108 Roy St (48081-1632)
PHONE.................................586 907-2011
Mike Mandell, *Owner*
EMP: 4 **EST:** 1980
SALES (est): 258.8K **Privately Held**
SIC: 2752 Commercial printing, lithographic

(G-14270)
SPECTRUM WIRELESS (USA) INC
27601 Little Mack Ave (48081-1833)
P.O. Box 538 (48080-0538)
PHONE.................................586 693-7525
Gordon Mayhew, *President*
EMP: 4
SQ FT: 2,000
SALES (est): 765K **Privately Held**
SIC: 3663 Radio & TV communications equipment

(G-14271)
TECHNOLOGY NETWORK SVCS INC (PA)
Also Called: Tech Enterprises
31375 Harper Ave (48082-2453)
PHONE.................................586 294-7771
Sam Agosta, *President*
EMP: 12
SQ FT: 2,400
SALES: 1MM **Privately Held**
WEB: www.techenterprise.com
SIC: 5045 5065 5044 5087 Computers; facsimile equipment; telephone equipment; photocopy machines; shredders, industrial & commercial; business oriented computer software; custom computer programming services

(G-14272)
THOMAS KENYON INC
Also Called: Sir Speedy
22704 Harper Ave (48080-1823)
PHONE.................................248 476-8130
Thomas Kenyon, *President*
Joyce Kenyon, *Corp Secy*
EMP: 5
SQ FT: 2,600
SALES (est): 794.7K **Privately Held**
SIC: 2752 7338 2791 2789 Commercial printing, lithographic; secretarial & court reporting; typesetting; bookbinding & related work; commercial printing

(G-14273)
TRIN-MAC COMPANY INC
24825 Little Mack Ave # 200 (48080-3224)
PHONE.................................586 774-1900
Dan Mc Closkey, *President*
EMP: 4 **EST:** 1973
SQ FT: 4,000
SALES: 1MM **Privately Held**
WEB: www.trin-mac.com
SIC: 1799 3369 Sandblasting of building exteriors; nonferrous foundries

(G-14274)
TRISCO CHEMICAL CO
Also Called: Trisco Products
21125 Yale St (48081-1870)
PHONE.................................586 779-8260
Sharon Povlitz, *President*
Greg Povlitz, *Vice Pres*
EMP: 3 **EST:** 1934
SALES: 300K **Privately Held**
WEB: www.scubadiving.com
SIC: 2869 Embalming fluids

(G-14275)
VINYL GRAPHIX INC
24731 Harper Ave (48080-1256)
PHONE.................................586 774-1188
Charles Bird, *President*
Diane Bird, *Admin Sec*
EMP: 5
SALES (est): 521.5K **Privately Held**
WEB: www.vinylgraphix.com
SIC: 7336 3993 Art design services; signs & advertising specialties

Saint Clair Shores - Macomb County (G-14276) — GEOGRAPHIC SECTION

(G-14276)
WARTIAN LOCK COMPANY
20525 E 9 Mile Rd (48080-1798)
PHONE.................................586 777-2244
George Wartian, *President*
Loretta Banek, *Treasurer*
▲ EMP: 9 EST: 1948
SQ FT: 36,000
SALES (est): 1.2MM **Privately Held**
WEB: www.lockcodes.com
SIC: 3429 3462 Door locks, bolts & checks; keys & key blanks; door opening & closing devices, except electrical; keys, locks & related hardware; iron & steel forgings

(G-14277)
YATES INDUSTRIES INC (PA)
Also Called: Yates Cylinders
23050 E Industrial Dr (48080-1177)
PHONE.................................586 778-7680
William H Yates III, *President*
Bill Yates, *General Mgr*
Crystal Brock, *Vice Pres*
Mark Cook, *Vice Pres*
Robert Martin, *Plant Mgr*
▲ EMP: 56
SQ FT: 100,000
SALES (est): 16.1MM **Privately Held**
SIC: 3593 7699 3594 3053 Fluid power cylinders, hydraulic or pneumatic; hydraulic equipment repair; fluid power pumps & motors; gaskets, packing & sealing devices; engineering services

Saint Helen
Roscommon County

(G-14278)
GAGE WELL DRILLING INC
9609 Artesia Beach Rd (48656-9524)
PHONE.................................989 389-4372
Daniel Sentell, *President*
EMP: 5
SALES (est): 630K **Privately Held**
SIC: 1381 1781 Drilling oil & gas wells; water well drilling

Saint Ignace
Mackinac County

(G-14279)
ST IGNACE NEWS
Also Called: Town Crier
359 Reagon St (49781-1144)
P.O. Box 277 (49781-0277)
PHONE.................................906 643-9150
Wesley Maurer Jr, *Owner*
EMP: 13
SQ FT: 4,500
SALES (est): 719.6K **Privately Held**
WEB: www.stignacenews.com
SIC: 2711 Commercial printing & newspaper publishing combined

Saint Johns
Clinton County

(G-14280)
COG MARKETERS LTD
Also Called: Agriculture Liquid Fertilizers
3026 W M 21 (48879-8746)
PHONE.................................989 224-4117
Galynn Beer, *Sales Mgr*
Jeff Luiken, *Branch Mgr*
Troy Bancroft, *Manager*
EMP: 26
SALES (corp-wide): 42.1MM **Privately Held**
SIC: 2874 Phosphatic fertilizers
PA: Cog Marketers, Ltd.
  3055 W M 21
  Saint Johns MI 48879
  989 227-3827

(G-14281)
COG MARKETERS LTD
Also Called: Argo Liquid
3055 W M 21 (48879-8745)
PHONE.................................989 224-4117
EMP: 16
SALES (corp-wide): 42.1MM **Privately Held**
SIC: 2875 Fertilizers, mixing only
PA: Cog Marketers, Ltd.
  3055 W M 21
  Saint Johns MI 48879
  989 227-3827

(G-14282)
CUSTOM EMBROIDERY PLUS LLC (PA)
304 N Lansing St (48879-1424)
PHONE.................................989 227-9432
Cory Gartside,
Kirk Gartside,
EMP: 6
SALES: 675K **Privately Held**
WEB: www.ceplusonline.com
SIC: 2395 Embroidery & art needlework

(G-14283)
GOODRICH BROTHERS INC
3060 County Farm Rd (48879-9278)
PHONE.................................989 224-4944
EMP: 9
SALES (corp-wide): 7.2MM **Privately Held**
SIC: 2431 Mfg Millwork
PA: Goodrich Brothers, Inc.
  11409 E Bluewater Hwy
  Pewamo MI 48873
  989 593-2104

(G-14284)
INNOVATIVE POLYMERS INC
Also Called: Innovtive Polymers Rampf Group
208 Kuntz St (48879-1172)
PHONE.................................989 224-9500
Mike Molitor, *President*
Matt Buckland, *Mfg Mgr*
◆ EMP: 13
SQ FT: 12,000
SALES (est): 3.4MM
SALES (corp-wide): 1.4MM **Privately Held**
WEB: www.innovative-polymers.com
SIC: 2821 2851 Polyurethane resins; polyurethane coatings
HQ: Rampf Group, Inc.
  49037 Wixom Tech Dr
  Wixom MI 48393
  248 295-0223

(G-14285)
JET SPEED PRINTING COMPANY
313 N Clinton Ave (48879-1505)
PHONE.................................989 224-6475
James Pratl, *President*
EMP: 6
SQ FT: 2,800
SALES (est): 708.7K **Privately Held**
SIC: 2752 Commercial printing, offset

(G-14286)
LUPAUL INDUSTRIES INC (PA)
Also Called: Mercury Stamping Div
310 E Steel St (48879-1302)
PHONE.................................517 783-3223
J Michael Smith, *President*
Jim Drake, *Corp Secy*
M Jank, *Vice Pres*
M Moran, *Vice Pres*
EMP: 15 EST: 1940
SQ FT: 23,000
SALES (est): 5.1MM **Privately Held**
WEB: www.lupaul.com
SIC: 3544 3469 3496 Special dies & tools; metal stampings; miscellaneous fabricated wire products

(G-14287)
MACO TOOL & ENGINEERING INC
210 Spring St (48879-1534)
PHONE.................................989 224-6723
Mark Hoover, *President*
Mary Walker, *Treasurer*
EMP: 30 EST: 1971
SQ FT: 23,000
SALES: 4MM **Privately Held**
WEB: www.macotool.com
SIC: 3544 Special dies & tools

(G-14288)
MAHLE INDUSTRIES INCORPORATED
916 W State St Ste B (48879-1469)
PHONE.................................989 224-5423
Richard Dennis, *Branch Mgr*
EMP: 120
SQ FT: 100,000
SALES (corp-wide): 504.6K **Privately Held**
WEB: www.glacier-vandervell.com
SIC: 3714 Motor vehicle parts & accessories
HQ: Mahle Industries, Incorporated
  23030 Mahle Dr
  Farmington Hills MI 48335
  248 305-8200

(G-14289)
MICHIGAN GRAPHICS & SIGNS
1110 E Steel Rd (48879-1185)
PHONE.................................989 224-1936
Bruce Delong, *Owner*
Conne Delong, *Co-Owner*
EMP: 4
SALES (est): 293.2K **Privately Held**
SIC: 3993 5999 Signs, not made in custom sign painting shops; banners, flags, decals & posters

(G-14290)
MICHIGAN POLYMER RECLAIM INC
Also Called: Mpr, Visitmpr
107 E Walker Rd (48879-8526)
PHONE.................................989 227-0497
John C Stehlik, *President*
Paul Marsh, *Engineer*
EMP: 12
SQ FT: 30,000
SALES (est): 2.4MM **Privately Held**
SIC: 2821 Plastics materials & resins

(G-14291)
OLYMPIAN TOOL LLC
604 N Us Highway 27 (48879-1125)
P.O. Box 416 (48879-0416)
PHONE.................................989 224-4817
Todd Deitrich, *President*
Robert Frostick, *Officer*
EMP: 25
SQ FT: 20,000
SALES (est): 5.5MM **Privately Held**
WEB: www.olympiantool.com
SIC: 3544 3545 Special dies & tools; machine tool accessories

(G-14292)
OMNI TECHNICAL SERVICES INC
Also Called: Omni Ergonomics
203 E Tolles Dr (48879-1166)
P.O. Box 37, Owosso (48867-0037)
PHONE.................................989 227-8900
John Schafer, *CEO*
Jack Roth, *Vice Pres*
EMP: 25 EST: 1978
SQ FT: 45,000
SALES (est): 3.2MM **Privately Held**
WEB: www.omni-tsi.com
SIC: 8711 3496 Mechanical engineering; conveyor belts

(G-14293)
SAYLOR-BEALL MANUFACTURING CO
400 N Kibbee St (48879-1602)
PHONE.................................989 224-2371
Bruce C Mc Fee, *President*
Mary George, *Purchasing*
▲ EMP: 254
SQ FT: 52,500
SALES (est): 75.3MM **Privately Held**
WEB: www.saylor-beall.com
SIC: 3563 Air & gas compressors including vacuum pumps

(G-14294)
SCHNEIDER FABRICATION INC
3200 W M 21 (48879-8723)
PHONE.................................989 224-6937
Gary G Schneider, *President*
EMP: 7
SALES (est): 1.1MM **Privately Held**
SIC: 3441 Fabricated structural metal

(G-14295)
SEARLES CONSTRUCTION INC (PA)
1213 N Us 127 (48879)
PHONE.................................989 224-3297
Lillian Searles, *Ch of Bd*
Leon Searles, *President*
▲ EMP: 4 EST: 1951
SQ FT: 1,000
SALES (est): 4.4MM **Privately Held**
SIC: 1442 1794 Construction sand & gravel; excavation & grading, building construction

(G-14296)
ST JOHNS COMPUTER MACHINING
Also Called: Saint Johns Computer Machining
501 E Steel St (48879-1171)
PHONE.................................989 224-7664
Michael J Jorae, *President*
Bernadette Hayes, *Office Mgr*
Renee Jorae, *Admin Sec*
EMP: 6
SQ FT: 2,400
SALES (est): 692.5K **Privately Held**
SIC: 3312 3599 Tool & die steel & alloys; machine shop, jobbing & repair

(G-14297)
STONY CREEK ESSENTIAL OILS
6718 W Centerline Rd (48879-9572)
PHONE.................................989 227-5500
Doug Irrer, *General Mgr*
Thomas Irrer, *Principal*
EMP: 6
SALES (est): 902.3K **Privately Held**
SIC: 2899 5169 Oils & essential oils; oil additives

(G-14298)
UNCLE JOHNS CIDER MILL INC
8614 N Us Highway 27 (48879-9425)
PHONE.................................989 224-3686
John Beck, *CEO*
Michael John Beck, *President*
Carolyn Beck, *Vice Pres*
EMP: 70
SQ FT: 4,900
SALES (est): 4.8MM **Privately Held**
WEB: www.ujcidermill.com
SIC: 0175 5431 2099 2051 Apple orchard; fruit stands or markets; cider, non-alcoholic; bread, cake & related products; canned fruits & specialties; groceries & related products

(G-14299)
UNIFIED SCREENING AND CRUSHING
305 E Walker Rd (48879-8574)
PHONE.................................888 464-9473
Tom Lencsch, *Mng Member*
Chrell Hoffman, *Manager*
EMP: 11
SQ FT: 17,000
SALES (est): 3MM
SALES (corp-wide): 15.6MM **Privately Held**
WEB: www.twincitywire.com
SIC: 3496 3535 Miscellaneous fabricated wire products; conveyors & conveying equipment
PA: Unified Screening & Crushing - Mn, Inc.
  3350 Highway 149
  Eagan MN 55121
  651 454-8835

Saint Joseph
Berrien County

(G-14300)
AMERICAN SOC AG BLGCAL ENGNERS
2950 Niles Rd (49085-8607)
PHONE.....................................269 429-0300
Darrin Drollinger, *President*
Mark Zielke, *CFO*
Beth Settles, *Administration*
EMP: 24 **EST:** 1907
SQ FT: 17,000
SALES: 2.7MM **Privately Held**
WEB: www.asabe.org
SIC: 8621 2731 Engineering association; book publishing

(G-14301)
B & L PATTERN COMPANY
191 Hawthorne Ave Apt B (49085-2643)
PHONE.....................................269 982-0214
William Husek, *President*
Patricia Husek, *Admin Sec*
EMP: 3
SQ FT: 4,800
SALES (est): 210K **Privately Held**
SIC: 3543 3544 Industrial patterns; industrial molds

(G-14302)
BLACK DRAGON LLC
4024 Niles Rd (49085-9602)
PHONE.....................................269 277-4874
Paul Peterson, *Mng Member*
EMP: 3 **EST:** 2015
SALES: 85K **Privately Held**
SIC: 2084 Wines

(G-14303)
C I M PRODUCT
822 Highland Ave (49085-2512)
PHONE.....................................269 983-5348
Thomas Johnson, *President*
EMP: 7
SALES (est): 997.2K **Privately Held**
SIC: 3199 Harness or harness parts

(G-14304)
CASCADE TOOL & DIE INC
4035 Lincoln Ave (49085-9539)
PHONE.....................................269 429-2210
Phillip Bielinski, *President*
Sheri Bielinski, *Vice Pres*
EMP: 3
SALES (est): 410.9K **Privately Held**
SIC: 3544 Special dies & tools

(G-14305)
CUSTOM PRODUCTS INC
Also Called: Custometal Products
180 Kerth St (49085-2630)
P.O. Box 950 (49085-0950)
PHONE.....................................269 983-9500
Dan Kirksey, *President*
Ronald Bowman, *Admin Sec*
EMP: 12
SQ FT: 45,000
SALES (est): 2MM **Privately Held**
WEB: www.custometalproducts.com
SIC: 3444 Sheet metal specialties, not stamped; machine guards, sheet metal; metal housings, enclosures, casings & other containers

(G-14306)
DESIGNERS SHEET METAL INC
205 Palladium Dr (49085-9552)
PHONE.....................................269 429-4133
Bruce E Ringer, *President*
EMP: 5
SQ FT: 6,000
SALES (est): 342.3K **Privately Held**
SIC: 1761 3444 Sheet metalwork; sheet metalwork

(G-14307)
DRIVEN-4 LLC
2900 S State St Ste 2w (49085-2476)
PHONE.....................................269 281-7567
James Danforth, *Mng Member*
Alfredo Bellio, *Mng Member*
Bala Shetty, *Mng Member*
Carl Wendtland, *Mng Member*
EMP: 4
SALES (est): 186.9K **Privately Held**
SIC: 7372 7373 7371 Prepackaged software; computer integrated systems design; computer software systems analysis & design, custom

(G-14308)
EDGEWATER AUTOMATION LLC
481 Renaissance Dr (49085-2176)
PHONE.....................................269 983-1300
Richard Blake, *President*
Seth V Ark, *Business Mgr*
Seth Vander, *Business Mgr*
Chad Henry, *Project Mgr*
Darrel Kettring, *Project Mgr*
▲ **EMP:** 55
SQ FT: 35,000
SALES: 23.7MM **Privately Held**
WEB: www.edgewaterautomation.com
SIC: 3549 Wiredrawing & fabricating machinery & equipment, ex. die

(G-14309)
EMPIRE MACHINE COMPANY
350 Palladium Dr (49085-9128)
PHONE.....................................269 684-3713
Lazell Davis, *President*
EMP: 18 **EST:** 1967
SQ FT: 21,000
SALES: 1MM **Privately Held**
WEB: www.mainspringpress.com
SIC: 3544 Special dies & tools

(G-14310)
F P ROSBACK CO
125 Hawthorne Ave (49085-2636)
PHONE.....................................269 983-2582
Lawrence H Fish, *Ch of Bd*
Larry Bowman, *President*
Ronald Bowman, *Vice Pres*
Randy Fish, *Chief Engr*
Chuck Shotton, *Info Tech Mgr*
▲ **EMP:** 20
SQ FT: 124,256
SALES (est): 6.2MM **Privately Held**
WEB: www.rosbackcompany.com
SIC: 3555 Bookbinding machinery

(G-14311)
FUZZYBUTZ
306 State St Ste A (49085-2292)
PHONE.....................................269 983-9663
Rick Schaut, *Principal*
EMP: 6
SALES (est): 557.3K **Privately Held**
SIC: 2253 T-shirts & tops, knit

(G-14312)
GHOST MFG LLC (PA)
480 Ansley Dr (49085-3673)
PHONE.....................................269 281-0489
Dan Wagner, *Opers Staff*
Rudolf Ronto,
EMP: 3 **EST:** 2012
SALES (est): 563.3K **Privately Held**
SIC: 3843 Dental equipment & supplies

(G-14313)
GREAT LAKES ELECTRIC LLC
Also Called: Gle Solar Energy
1776 Hilltop Rd (49085-2305)
PHONE.....................................269 408-8276
Zheng Zhang, *General Mgr*
EMP: 6
SALES: 50K **Privately Held**
SIC: 3625 3433 Motor controls & accessories; solar heaters & collectors

(G-14314)
HANSON COLD STORAGE CO (PA)
Also Called: Hanson Logistics
2900 S State St Ste 4e (49085-2467)
PHONE.....................................269 982-1390
Gregory P Hanson, *President*
Andrew B Janson, *President*
Matt Luckas, *President*
Justin Hanson, *General Mgr*
Dave Murphy, *General Mgr*
EMP: 16 **EST:** 1954
SQ FT: 400,000
SALES (est): 31.9MM **Privately Held**
WEB: www.hansoncoldstorage.com
SIC: 4222 4225 2097 Storage, frozen or refrigerated goods; warehousing, cold storage or refrigerated; general warehousing & storage; manufactured ice

(G-14315)
HANSON INTERNATIONAL INC (PA)
Also Called: Hanson Mold Division
3500 Hollywood Rd (49085-9581)
P.O. Box 8 (49085-0008)
PHONE.....................................269 429-5555
Merlin Hanson, *Ch of Bd*
Daniel Bernson, *President*
Ken Patzkowski, *Vice Pres*
Gene Stemm, *Vice Pres*
Dan Florian, *Maint Spvr*
EMP: 3
SQ FT: 3,000
SALES: 1.3MM **Privately Held**
WEB: www.hansonmold.com
SIC: 3544 Special dies & tools; industrial molds

(G-14316)
HANSON INTERNATIONAL INC
Hanson Mold
3500 Hollywood Rd (49085-9581)
PHONE.....................................269 429-5555
Keith V Weide, *General Mgr*
Thomas Reule, *Vice Pres*
Gene Stemm, *Vice Pres*
Tim Tyler, *Vice Pres*
Heath Weich, *Engineer*
EMP: 100
SALES (corp-wide): 1.3MM **Privately Held**
WEB: www.hansonmold.com
SIC: 3363 3549 3544 Aluminum die-castings; marking machines, metalworking; special dies, tools, jigs & fixtures
PA: Hanson International, Inc.
3500 Hollywood Rd
Saint Joseph MI 49085
269 429-5555

(G-14317)
HOFFMANN DIE CAST LLC
229 Kerth St (49085-2623)
PHONE.....................................269 983-1102
Michael Oros, *President*
Jim Selmer, *Vice Pres*
Jeff Yakim, *Plant Mgr*
Tom Redding, *Chief Engr*
William E Criswell, *Finance Dir*
EMP: 108
SQ FT: 100,000
SALES (est): 4.1MM **Privately Held**
WEB: www.hoffmanndc.com
SIC: 3363 3364 3369 3365 Aluminum die-castings; zinc & zinc-base alloy die-castings; nonferrous foundries; aluminum foundries

(G-14318)
INDUSTRIAL FABRIC PRODUCTS INC
Also Called: Tarps Now
4133 M 139 (49085-8689)
P.O. Box 667, Stevensville (49127-0667)
PHONE.....................................269 932-4440
Michael Dill, *President*
◆ **EMP:** 4
SQ FT: 46,000
SALES: 3.1MM **Privately Held**
SIC: 2394 Canvas awnings & canopies; canvas covers & drop cloths; shades, canvas; made from purchased materials

(G-14319)
JOURNAL DISPOSITION CORP
Also Called: IPC Communication Services
2180 Maiden Ln (49085-9596)
PHONE.....................................269 428-2054
Richard Butterworth, *Principal*
EMP: 5
SALES (corp-wide): 329.5MM **Privately Held**
SIC: 2752 Periodicals, lithographed
HQ: Journal Disposition Corporation
2180 Maiden Ln
Saint Joseph MI 49085
888 563-3220

(G-14320)
KAY MANUFACTURING COMPANY
3491 S Lakeshore Dr (49085-8289)
PHONE.....................................269 408-8344
Scott Dekker, *Vice Pres*
EMP: 20
SALES (est): 2.6MM **Privately Held**
SIC: 3714 Motor vehicle parts & accessories

(G-14321)
KISMET STRATEGIC SOURCING PART
717 Sint Jseph Dr Ste 270 (49085)
PHONE.....................................269 932-4990
Scott Lange,
EMP: 5
SALES (est): 464.9K **Privately Held**
WEB: www.kismetssp.com
SIC: 3571 Personal computers (microcomputers)

(G-14322)
LAFARGE NORTH AMERICA INC
200 Upton Dr (49085-1148)
PHONE.....................................269 983-6333
Rick Moore, *Manager*
EMP: 5
SALES (corp-wide): 27.6B **Privately Held**
WEB: www.lafargenorthamerica.com
SIC: 3273 Ready-mixed concrete
HQ: Lafarge North America Inc.
8700 W Bryn Mawr Ave
Chicago IL 60631
773 372-1000

(G-14323)
LAZY BALLERINA WINERY LLC (PA)
315 State St (49085-1247)
PHONE.....................................269 363-6218
Melanie Owen,
Lauren Kniebes,
EMP: 6
SALES (est): 1MM **Privately Held**
SIC: 2084 Wines

(G-14324)
LECO CORPORATION (PA)
Also Called: Tem-Press Division
3000 Lakeview Ave (49085-2319)
PHONE.....................................269 983-5531
Carl S Warren, *President*
B John Hawkins, *President*
Larry S O'Brien, *President*
Elizabeth S Warren, *President*
Larry O'Brien, *General Mgr*
◆ **EMP:** 500
SQ FT: 300,000
SALES (est): 192MM
SALES (corp-wide): 179MM **Privately Held**
WEB: www.pier33.com
SIC: 3821 3826 3825 3823 Laboratory apparatus, except heating & measuring; chemical laboratory apparatus; analytical instruments; instruments to measure electricity; industrial instrmnts msrmnt display/control process variable; porcelain electrical supplies

(G-14325)
LECO CORPORATION
Leco Plating Division
3000 Lakeview Ave (49085-2319)
PHONE.....................................269 982-2230
Vern Keson, *Branch Mgr*
EMP: 17
SALES (corp-wide): 179MM **Privately Held**
WEB: www.pier33.com
SIC: 3821 4493 3826 3825 Laboratory apparatus, except heating & measuring; chemical laboratory apparatus; boat yards, storage & incidental repair; marine basins; analytical instruments; instruments to measure electricity; industrial instrmnts msrmnt display/control process variable; porcelain electrical supplies
PA: Leco Corporation
3000 Lakeview Ave
Saint Joseph MI 49085
269 983-5531

Saint Joseph - Berrien County (G-14326)

GEOGRAPHIC SECTION

(G-14326)
LEISURE STUDIOS INC
3909 Stonegate Park (49085-9130)
PHONE..................269 428-5299
William Carle, *President*
EMP: 150
SQ FT: 2,500
SALES (est): 11.3MM **Privately Held**
SIC: 3496 Miscellaneous fabricated wire products

(G-14327)
LIBERTY STEEL FABRICATING INC
Also Called: Liberty 3d Technologies
350 Palladium Dr (49085-9128)
PHONE..................269 556-9792
Andrew Gantenbein, *President*
Matt Baggett, *Opers Mgr*
John Bournay, *Finance*
Debbie Wishart, *Human Res Mgr*
Pete Ciula, *Sales Engr*
EMP: 50
SALES: 8MM **Privately Held**
WEB: www.libsteel.com
SIC: 3541 3444 3443 Machine tool replacement & repair parts, metal cutting types; sheet metalwork; fabricated plate work (boiler shop)

(G-14328)
MASTER WOODWORKS
2916 Veronica Ct (49085-2373)
PHONE..................269 240-3262
John Ott, *Owner*
EMP: 6
SALES (est): 238K **Privately Held**
SIC: 2421 Sawmills & planing mills, general

(G-14329)
MOXIES BOUTIQUE LLC
321 State St (49085-1247)
PHONE..................269 983-4273
Monica Bolin, *Administration*
EMP: 5 EST: 2015
SALES (est): 213.7K **Privately Held**
SIC: 2339 Women's & misses' athletic clothing & sportswear

(G-14330)
NELSON SPECIALTIES COMPANY
211 Hilltop Rd (49085-2300)
PHONE..................269 983-1878
Keith Nelson, *CEO*
Mike Nelson, *President*
Lisa Eyerly, *Corp Secy*
Dorwin Nelson, *Vice Pres*
Kathy Heine, *Senior Buyer*
EMP: 14
SQ FT: 10,784
SALES (est): 2.5MM **Privately Held**
WEB: www.nelson-specialties.com
SIC: 3679 Electronic circuits

(G-14331)
NEOGEN CORPORATION
Also Called: Steven Schadler
2620 S Cleveland Ave # 100 (49085-3021)
PHONE..................800 327-5487
Tina German, *Research*
Jeanne Strine, *Manager*
Cornelia Schafer, *Administration*
EMP: 3
SALES (corp-wide): 414.1MM **Publicly Held**
SIC: 2835 In vitro & in vivo diagnostic substances
PA: Neogen Corporation
   620 Lesher Pl
   Lansing MI 48912
   517 372-9200

(G-14332)
NORTH PIER BREWING COMPANY LLC
3266 Estates Dr (49085-3428)
PHONE..................312 545-0446
Jeff Fettig, *Principal*
EMP: 3 EST: 2015
SALES (est): 75.4K **Privately Held**
SIC: 2082 Malt beverages

(G-14333)
NUWAVE TECHNOLOGY PARTNERS LLC
Also Called: Nuwave Medical Solutions
2231 Mount Curve Ave (49085-2023)
PHONE..................269 342-4400
Rob Fowler, *Principal*
EMP: 6 **Privately Held**
SIC: 3661 7371 Telephone & telegraph apparatus; custom computer programming services
PA: Nuwave Technology Partners, Llc
   5268 Azo Dr
   Kalamazoo MI 49048

(G-14334)
PAXTON MEDIA GROUP LLC
Also Called: Herald Palladium, The
3450 Hollywood Rd (49085-9155)
P.O. Box 128 (49085-0128)
PHONE..................269 429-2400
David Holgate, *Branch Mgr*
EMP: 100
SALES (corp-wide): 244.2MM **Privately Held**
WEB: www.jonesborosun.com
SIC: 2711 4833 Newspapers, publishing & printing; television broadcasting stations
PA: Paxton Media Group, Llc
   100 Television Ln
   Paducah KY 42003
   270 575-8630

(G-14335)
PEERLESS CANVAS PRODUCTS INC
2355 Niles Rd (49085-2813)
PHONE..................269 429-0600
Paul Kosachuk, *Principal*
EMP: 4
SQ FT: 3,200
SALES (est): 382.1K **Privately Held**
SIC: 2394 Convertible tops, canvas or boat: from purchased materials; awnings, fabric: made from purchased materials

(G-14336)
PRINTEK INC (PA)
3515 Lakeshore Dr Ste 1 (49085-2952)
PHONE..................269 925-3200
Thomas C Yeager, *President*
Julie Payovich, *Exec VP*
Scott Barnett, *Vice Pres*
EMP: 110
SQ FT: 70,000
SALES (est): 19.6MM **Privately Held**
WEB: www.printek.com
SIC: 3577 Printers, computer; printers & plotters

(G-14337)
RESISTANCE WELDING MACHNE & AC
255 Palladium Dr (49085-9552)
PHONE..................269 428-4770
Clifton Adams, *President*
Tim Duer, *Sales Engr*
David Mangold, *Sales Staff*
▲ EMP: 19
SQ FT: 6,000
SALES (est): 3.4MM **Privately Held**
SIC: 3463 3544 3548 Nonferrous forgings; special dies & tools; spot welding apparatus, electric

(G-14338)
ROBERT BOSCH LLC
Also Called: Bosch Chassis St Joseph Plant
3737 Red Arrow Hwy (49085-9208)
PHONE..................269 429-3221
Steve Pear, *Opers Mgr*
Christine Gerlach, *Controller*
Ron Lumfden, *Manager*
Dave Anderson, *Lab Dir*
EMP: 12
SALES (corp-wide): 294.8MM **Privately Held**
WEB: www.boschservice.com
SIC: 3714 3594 3321 3322 Motor vehicle brake systems & parts; motor vehicle steering systems & parts; fluid power pumps & motors; gray & ductile iron foundries; malleable iron foundries
HQ: Robert Bosch Llc
   2800 S 25th Ave
   Broadview IL 60155
   248 876-1000

(G-14339)
SONOCO PRODUCTS COMPANY
500 Renaissance Dr # 102 (49085-2175)
PHONE..................269 408-0182
EMP: 92
SALES (corp-wide): 5.3B **Publicly Held**
SIC: 2631 Paperboard mills
PA: Sonoco Products Company
   1 N 2nd St
   Hartsville SC 29550
   843 383-7000

(G-14340)
SOPER MANUFACTURING COMPANY
3638 Bacon School Rd (49085-9634)
PHONE..................269 429-5245
John Soper IV, *President*
John Globensky, *Admin Sec*
EMP: 28 EST: 1946
SQ FT: 35,000
SALES (est): 3.9MM **Privately Held**
SIC: 3369 3544 3363 Zinc & zinc-base alloy castings, except die-castings; special dies, tools, jigs & fixtures; aluminum die-castings

(G-14341)
STAR SHADE CUTTER CO
2028 Washington Ave (49085-2421)
PHONE..................269 983-2403
Michael Gast, *President*
Albert K Gast, *Vice Pres*
EMP: 4
SQ FT: 2,800
SALES: 500K **Privately Held**
WEB: www.starshade.com
SIC: 3552 Textile machinery

(G-14342)
STEELE SUPPLY CO
3413 Hill St (49085-2621)
PHONE..................269 983-0920
Thomas D Steele, *President*
EMP: 8
SALES (est): 2.9MM **Privately Held**
WEB: www.steeles.com
SIC: 5047 3841 3842 Diagnostic equipment, medical; surgical & medical instruments; surgical appliances & supplies

(G-14343)
TELIC CORPORATION
581 Upton Dr (49085-1092)
P.O. Box 67, Sodus (49126-0067)
PHONE..................219 406-2164
Frank Minton, *President*
EMP: 3
SQ FT: 10,000
SALES (est): 1.8MM **Privately Held**
WEB: www.teliccorporation.com
SIC: 3761 Guided missiles & space vehicles

(G-14344)
TUTEUR INC
Also Called: Oscar's Printing
1721 Lakeshore Dr (49085-1637)
PHONE..................269 983-1246
Edwin Stubelt, *President*
EMP: 8 EST: 1973
SQ FT: 1,400
SALES: 1MM **Privately Held**
WEB: www.oscarsprinting.com
SIC: 2752 Commercial printing, offset

(G-14345)
TWIN CITIES ORTHOTIC & PROSTHE
3538 Magnolia Ln (49085-8265)
PHONE..................269 428-2910
EMP: 4
SQ FT: 1,500
SALES (est): 389.6K **Privately Held**
SIC: 3842 Mfg Braces & Artificial Limbs

(G-14346)
TWIN CITY ENGRAVING COMPANY
Also Called: Premier Promotions
1232 Broad St (49085-1213)
P.O. Box 85 (49085-0085)
PHONE..................269 983-0601
Jeffrey Jones, *President*
Jerold Jones, *Vice Pres*
EMP: 8 EST: 1938
SQ FT: 21,000
SALES (est): 835.9K **Privately Held**
WEB: www.premierpromos.com
SIC: 7389 5199 4225 2796 Engraving service; embroidering of advertising on shirts, etc.; advertising, promotional & trade show services; advertising specialties; general warehousing; platemaking services; automotive & apparel trimmings; pleating & stitching

(G-14347)
UNITED FR SURVL ST JOSEPH RECY
2215 Wilson Ct (49085-1833)
PHONE..................269 983-3820
Tim Schroeder, *President*
Gale Cutler, *Vice Pres*
Jackie Taglia, *Treasurer*
John Taglia, *Med Doctor*
John Tielemeier, *Director*
EMP: 30
SALES (est): 2.6MM **Privately Held**
SIC: 2611 Pulp mills, mechanical & recycling processing

(G-14348)
VALLEY TRUCK PARTS INC
305 Palladium Dr (49085-9128)
PHONE..................269 429-9953
Doug Stutz, *Manager*
EMP: 3
SALES (corp-wide): 72.4MM **Privately Held**
WEB: www.valleytruckparts.com
SIC: 3714 Motor vehicle parts & accessories
PA: Valley Truck Parts, Inc.
   1900 Chicago Dr Sw
   Wyoming MI 49519
   616 241-5431

(G-14349)
VENTURE MANUFACTURING INC
3542 Crestview Rd (49085-8902)
PHONE..................269 429-6337
William Warren, *President*
Donald Warren, *Vice Pres*
EMP: 7
SALES: 600K **Privately Held**
SIC: 3544 Special dies & tools

(G-14350)
WALSWORTH PUBLISHING CO INC
Also Called: Walsworth Print Group
2180 Maiden Ln (49085-9596)
PHONE..................269 428-2054
Mike Wells, *Manager*
EMP: 300
SALES (corp-wide): 329.5MM **Privately Held**
SIC: 2741 Yearbooks: publishing & printing
PA: Walsworth Publishing Company, Inc.
   306 N Kansas Ave
   Marceline MO 64658
   660 376-3543

(G-14351)
WEB PRINTING & MKTG CONCEPTS
Also Called: Xpress Printing
4086 Red Arrow Hwy (49085-9209)
PHONE..................269 983-4646
Walter Buesing, *President*
Joanne Buesing, *Admin Sec*
EMP: 8
SQ FT: 6,400
SALES: 878.6K **Privately Held**
SIC: 2752 5112 5199 Commercial printing, offset; business forms; advertising specialties

GEOGRAPHIC SECTION

Saline - Washtenaw County (G-14379)

(G-14352)
WHIRLPOOL CORPORATION
500 Renaissance Dr # 102 (49085-2174)
PHONE.................................269 923-7441
Gary Bormann, *Counsel*
Karen Schiltz, *Buyer*
Raymond Smith, *Senior Engr*
Robert Mink, *Branch Mgr*
Teresa Jenkins, *Manager*
EMP: 175
SALES (corp-wide): 21B **Publicly Held**
SIC: 3633 Household laundry machines, including coin-operated
PA: Whirlpool Corporation
2000 N M 63
Benton Harbor MI 49022
269 923-5000

(G-14353)
WHIRLPOOL CORPORATION
303 Upton Dr (49085-1149)
PHONE.................................269 923-6057
Damon Chang, *Buyer*
Joe Lopresti, *Buyer*
Michael Goslee, *Engineer*
Thomas Latack, *Engineer*
Dave Gushwa, *Senior Engr*
EMP: 175
SALES (corp-wide): 21B **Publicly Held**
WEB: www.whirlpoolcorp.com
SIC: 3633 Household laundry equipment
PA: Whirlpool Corporation
2000 N M 63
Benton Harbor MI 49022
269 923-5000

(G-14354)
WOLVERINE METAL STAMPING INC (PA)
3600 Tennis Ct (49085-9502)
PHONE.................................269 429-6600
Eric Jackson, *President*
Richard Frederick, *Purch Agent*
Bruce Weber, *CFO*
Chris Champion, *Manager*
Kevin Jeans, *Manager*
▲ **EMP:** 90 **EST:** 1967
SQ FT: 104,000
SALES (est): 29MM **Privately Held**
WEB: www.wms-inc.com
SIC: 3469 3443 Stamping metal for the trade; fabricated plate work (boiler shop)

(G-14355)
WORLDWIDE MARKETING SERVICES
Also Called: Owens Classic International
1776 Hilltop Rd (49085-2305)
PHONE.................................269 556-2000
Peter J Marr, *President*
Tracy Marr, *Vice Pres*
Bobbi Jo Hahm, *Controller*
◆ **EMP:** 21
SQ FT: 6,000
SALES (est): 5.5MM **Privately Held**
WEB: www.autofloormat.com
SIC: 5013 3713 Automotive supplies & parts; truck bodies & parts; truck tops

(G-14356)
Y M C A FAMILY CENTER
Also Called: YMCA
3665 Hollywood Rd (49085-9581)
PHONE.................................269 428-9622
Daniel Astyn, *Director*
Mike Ahearn, *Director*
EMP: 4
SALES: 2.1MM **Privately Held**
SIC: 7999 3949 Recreation center; exercise equipment

Saint Louis
Gratiot County

(G-14357)
AMERICAN SOFT TRIM INC
Also Called: Owosso Soft Trim
300 Woodside Dr (48880-1148)
PHONE.................................989 681-0037
Mark Dupuie, *President*
EMP: 25 **EST:** 1988
SQ FT: 15,000
SALES (est): 2.1MM **Privately Held**
WEB: www.americansofttrim.com
SIC: 2211 Upholstery fabrics, cotton

(G-14358)
AMERICAST LLC
107 Enterprize Dr (48880-1059)
PHONE.................................989 681-4800
Dan Bishop,
EMP: 6
SQ FT: 12,000
SALES: 400K **Privately Held**
SIC: 3261 Bathroom accessories/fittings, vitreous china or earthenware

(G-14359)
APEX MARINE INC
300 Woodside Dr (48880-1148)
PHONE.................................989 681-4300
Mark Dupuie, *President*
Kyle Acker, *Engineer*
Brad Dupuie, *Engineer*
Scott Dosson, *Sales Engr*
Ron Sincissen, *Sales Staff*
▼ **EMP:** 65
SQ FT: 25,000
SALES (est): 20.6MM **Privately Held**
SIC: 3069 Pontoons, rubber

(G-14360)
CENTRAL MICHIGAN TANK RENTAL
9701 Gruett Rd (48880-9732)
PHONE.................................989 681-5963
EMP: 4
SQ FT: 3,600
SALES (est): 270K **Privately Held**
SIC: 1389 Oil/Gas Field Services

(G-14361)
CRIPPEN MANUFACTURING COMPANY
400 Woodside Dr (48880-1057)
P.O. Box 128, Alma (48801-0128)
PHONE.................................989 681-4323
Jim Gascho, *President*
Mark Wilk, *Mfg Staff*
Earl Fritz, *Manager*
▼ **EMP:** 30 **EST:** 1988
SALES (est): 5.4MM **Privately Held**
WEB: www.crippenmfg.com
SIC: 3523 3841 3829 3535 Cleaning machines for fruits, grains & vegetables; surgical & medical instruments; measuring & controlling devices; conveyors & conveying equipment; abrasive products

(G-14362)
CRYSTAL PURE WATER INC
1211 Michigan Ave (48880-1023)
PHONE.................................989 681-3547
Joe Earegood, *President*
EMP: 3
SQ FT: 2,400
SALES (est): 170K **Privately Held**
SIC: 2086 5499 Pasteurized & mineral waters, bottled & canned; water: distilled mineral or spring

(G-14363)
EXTREME FITNESS GYM
116 N Mill St (48880-1521)
P.O. Box 24 (48880-0024)
PHONE.................................989 681-8339
EMP: 7
SALES (est): 70.3K **Privately Held**
SIC: 8099 2759 Nutrition services; screen printing

(G-14364)
JER-DEN PLASTICS INC (PA)
750 Woodside Dr (48880-1051)
P.O. Box 240 (48880-0240)
PHONE.................................989 681-4303
Dennis J Howe, *President*
Jerry Sprague Sr, *Vice Pres*
Steve McNeal, *Design Engr*
EMP: 40
SQ FT: 35,000
SALES (est): 7.5MM **Privately Held**
WEB: www.jer-denplastics.com
SIC: 3089 Injection molding of plastics

(G-14365)
KEN LUNEACK CONSTRUCTION INC (PA)
Also Called: Bear Truss & Components
721 E Washington St (48880-1986)
P.O. Box 239 (48880-0239)
PHONE.................................989 681-5774
Paul B Luneack, *President*
Pam Luneack, *CFO*
EMP: 168
SQ FT: 60,000
SALES (est): 40.1MM **Privately Held**
WEB: www.beartruss.net
SIC: 2439 Trusses, wooden roof; trusses, except roof: laminated lumber

(G-14366)
MOMENTUM INDUSTRIES INC
100 Woodside Dr (48880-1144)
PHONE.................................989 681-5735
Dean Sharick, *President*
EMP: 20
SQ FT: 15,000
SALES (est): 2.2MM **Privately Held**
WEB: www.momentumind.com
SIC: 3544 7389 3599 Special dies & tools; grinding, precision: commercial or industrial; custom machinery

(G-14367)
NORTH STATE SALES
6298 N State Rd (48880-9207)
PHONE.................................989 681-2806
Roger Anna, *Owner*
EMP: 8
SALES: 500K **Privately Held**
WEB: www.northstatesales-online.com
SIC: 2434 Wood kitchen cabinets

(G-14368)
PLASTI - PAINT INC (PA)
801 Woodside Dr (48880-1054)
P.O. Box 280 (48880-0280)
PHONE.................................989 285-2280
David D Roslund, *President*
Charles Brandenburg, *Plant Mgr*
Terri Rhoades, *Manager*
EMP: 119
SALES (est): 19.2MM **Privately Held**
WEB: www.plastipaint.com
SIC: 3479 Coating of metals & formed products; painting, coating & hot dipping

(G-14369)
POWELL FABRICATION & MFG INC
740 E Monroe Rd (48880-9200)
PHONE.................................989 681-2158
Duane Powell, *Principal*
▼ **EMP:** 34
SQ FT: 33,000
SALES (est): 11.8MM **Privately Held**
WEB: www.powellfab.com
SIC: 3559 3441 Chemical machinery & equipment; fabricated structural metal

(G-14370)
TIENDA SAN RAFAEL LLC
321 N Mill St (48880-1546)
PHONE.................................989 681-2020
EMP: 3
SALES (est): 211.3K **Privately Held**
SIC: 2032 Mfg Canned Specialties

Saline
Washtenaw County

(G-14371)
ACADIA GROUP LLC
Also Called: Allegra Print & Imaging
1283 Industrial Dr (48176-9434)
PHONE.................................734 944-1404
Patrick M Mahoney, *Corp Secy*
Jason McLean, *Accounts Mgr*
Francis Olegario, *Accounts Mgr*
Deare Mahoney,
EMP: 30 **EST:** 1973
SQ FT: 27,000
SALES (est): 3.2MM **Privately Held**
WEB: www.allegra.net
SIC: 2752 7334 Commercial printing, offset; photocopying & duplicating services

(G-14372)
ACCU PRODUCTS INTERNATIONAL
7836 Bethel Church Rd (48176-9732)
PHONE.................................734 429-9571
John M Kosmalski, *President*
Patricia Kosmalski, *Vice Pres*
▲ **EMP:** 5
SALES (est): 840K **Privately Held**
WEB: www.accuproducts.com
SIC: 3545 5961 Precision measuring tools; tools & hardware, mail order

(G-14373)
AKERVALL TECHNOLOGIES INC (PA)
Also Called: Sisu Mouthguards
1512 Woodland Dr (48176-1632)
PHONE.................................800 444-0570
Liz Akervall, *CEO*
Jan Akervall, *Corp Secy*
Kathy Capelli, *COO*
Ben Bloomfield, *Project Mgr*
Lisa Edwards, *Project Mgr*
EMP: 12
SALES (est): 3MM **Privately Held**
SIC: 3843 Dental equipment & supplies

(G-14374)
AMERICAN FARM PRODUCTS INC
1382 Industrial Dr Ste 4 (48176-9487)
PHONE.................................734 484-4180
William R Absalom, *President*
Bill Lindhorst, *Sales Mgr*
Lawrence R Jones, *Manager*
Arlin Koglin, *Manager*
EMP: 10 **EST:** 1982
SQ FT: 2,000
SALES (est): 1.7MM **Privately Held**
SIC: 2869 Enzymes

(G-14375)
AMERICAN SOY PRODUCTS INC
Also Called: A S P
1474 Woodland Dr (48176-1282)
PHONE.................................734 429-2310
Hiroyasu Iwatsuki, *CEO*
Ron Roller, *President*
James Fox, *VP Opers*
Sue Denison, *Purchasing*
Cassandra Stephenson, *Purchasing*
▲ **EMP:** 70
SQ FT: 65,000
SALES (est): 18.8MM **Privately Held**
WEB: www.americansoy.com
SIC: 2099 Food preparations

(G-14376)
ANN ARBOR JOURNAL
106 W Michigan Ave (48176-1325)
PHONE.................................734 429-7380
Michelle Rogers, *Manager*
EMP: 3
SALES (est): 74.7K **Privately Held**
SIC: 2711 Newspapers

(G-14377)
ANN ARBOR PLASTICS INC
815 Woodland Dr (48176-1259)
PHONE.................................734 944-0800
K Anthony Glinke, *President*
Lori Stefanski, *Office Mgr*
EMP: 8
SQ FT: 18,000
SALES: 2MM **Privately Held**
WEB: www.aaplastics.com
SIC: 3089 5162 Injection molding of plastics; blow molded finished plastic products; plastics sheets & rods

(G-14378)
ARCON VERNOVA INC
271 Old Creek Dr (48176-1686)
PHONE.................................734 904-1895
Thomas M Curran, *President*
EMP: 5
SALES (est): 403K **Privately Held**
SIC: 3559 Special industry machinery

(G-14379)
B C & A CO
1270 Barnes Ct (48176-9589)
PHONE.................................734 429-3129

Saline - Washtenaw County (G-14380)

Bruce D Clyde, *President*
David Clyde, *Vice Pres*
Connie Petrinovic, *Opers Mgr*
John Cameron, *Engineer*
EMP: 40
SQ FT: 28,000
SALES (est): 8.2MM **Privately Held**
WEB: www.plastechsinc.com
SIC: 3089 Injection molding of plastics

(G-14380)
C & M TOOL LLC
1235 Industrial Dr Ste 7 (48176-1742)
PHONE 734 944-3355
Richard Leonte, *Office Mgr*
Pavel Leonte, *Mng Member*
EMP: 7
SQ FT: 3,000
SALES: 750K **Privately Held**
SIC: 3544 Special dies & tools

(G-14381)
CATALINA SOFTWARE
3103 Overlook Ct (48176-9559)
PHONE 734 429-3550
Peter R Fodor, *Principal*
EMP: 5
SALES (est): 335.5K **Privately Held**
SIC: 7372 Prepackaged software

(G-14382)
COBREX LTD
5880 Braun Rd (48176-8903)
PHONE 734 429-9758
Rex Smith, *President*
Judith Smith, *Treasurer*
EMP: 4
SALES (est): 416.1K **Privately Held**
SIC: 2759 3993 Screen printing; signs & advertising specialties

(G-14383)
CONDAT CORPORATION
250 S Industrial Dr (48176-9397)
PHONE 734 944-4994
Brad Sulkey, *CEO*
Roberto Castillo, *Regl Sales Mgr*
◆ **EMP:** 30
SALES (est): 9.9MM
SALES (corp-wide): 52.8MM **Privately Held**
WEB: www.condatcorp.com
SIC: 2992 5169 5172 Oils & greases, blending & compounding; rustproofing chemicals; lubricating oils & greases
PA: Condat Sa
     Condat
     Chasse-Sur-Rhone 38670
     478 738-641

(G-14384)
CRESCIVE DIE AND TOOL INC
Also Called: MTI-Saline
905 Woodland Dr (48176-1625)
P.O. Box 70 (48176-0070)
PHONE 734 482-0303
Joe Ponteri, *CEO*
Mike Wilson, *CFO*
EMP: 60 **EST:** 1998
SALES (est): 25.6MM **Privately Held**
WEB: www.crescive.com
SIC: 3465 Automotive stampings

(G-14385)
DAVCO MANUFACTURING LLC
1600 Woodland Dr (48176-1629)
PHONE 734 429-5665
Kevin Rucinski, *COO*
Steven Emery, *Project Mgr*
Eric Chernenkoff, *Info Tech Mgr*
EMP: 60
SALES (est): 8.2MM **Privately Held**
SIC: 5013 3714 3443 Motor vehicle supplies & new parts; motor vehicle parts & accessories; fabricated plate work (boiler shop)

(G-14386)
DAVCO TECHNOLOGY LLC
1600 Woodland Dr (48176-1629)
P.O. Box 487 (48176-0487)
PHONE 734 429-5665
Mark Bera, *President*
◆ **EMP:** 52
SQ FT: 54,000
SALES (est): 13.3MM
SALES (corp-wide): 11.1B **Privately Held**
WEB: www.davcotec.com
SIC: 3714 Fuel systems & parts, motor vehicle
PA: Penske Corporation
     2555 S Telegraph Rd
     Bloomfield Hills MI 48302
     248 648-2000

(G-14387)
ELECTROCRAFT MICHIGAN INC
1705 Woodland Dr Ste 101 (48176-1606)
P.O. Box 7746, Ann Arbor (48107-7746)
PHONE 603 516-1297
Jim Elsmer, *President*
EMP: 16
SQ FT: 8,000
SALES (est): 2.5MM **Privately Held**
SIC: 3625 Motor starters & controllers, electric

(G-14388)
EVJUMP SOLAR INC
149 Sheffield (48176-1020)
PHONE 734 277-5075
Arthur Harmala, *President*
EMP: 3
SALES (est): 257.3K **Privately Held**
SIC: 3674 Semiconductors & related devices

(G-14389)
FAURECIA INTERIOR SYSTEMS INC
Also Called: Faurecia Intr Systems Saline
7700 E Michigan Ave (48176-1721)
PHONE 734 429-0030
Sebastien Guery, *Manager*
EMP: 50
SALES (corp-wide): 38.2MM **Privately Held**
WEB: www.detroit.faurecia.com
SIC: 3714 Motor vehicle parts & accessories
HQ: Faurecia Interior Systems, Inc.
     2500 Executive Hills Dr
     Auburn Hills MI 48326
     248 724-5100

(G-14390)
FINKBEINER L & D FEED & FARM
114 W Michigan Ave (48176-2207)
PHONE 734 429-9777
Dennis Finkbeiner, *Owner*
Lyn Finkbeiner, *Co-Owner*
EMP: 3
SALES (est): 164K **Privately Held**
SIC: 0119 2048 Sunflower farm; milo farm; feed premixes

(G-14391)
FLATOUT INC
Also Called: Flatout Bakery
1422 Woodland Dr (48176-1633)
PHONE 734 944-5445
Stacey Marsh, *CEO*
Michael Marsh, *President*
Kathy Capelli, *Controller*
James McDonald, *Human Res Mgr*
Kevin Clark, *VP Sales*
▲ **EMP:** 80
SQ FT: 34,000
SALES (est): 16.9MM
SALES (corp-wide): 1.2B **Publicly Held**
WEB: www.delections.com
SIC: 2051 Bakery: wholesale or wholesale/retail combined
HQ: T.Marzetti Company
     380 Polaris Pkwy Ste 400
     Westerville OH 43082
     614 846-2232

(G-14392)
GANNONS GENERAL CONTRACT
9216 Yorkshire Dr (48176-9442)
PHONE 734 429-5859
Thomas Gannon, *Owner*
EMP: 12
SALES (est): 731.7K **Privately Held**
SIC: 3479 Painting, coating & hot dipping

(G-14393)
GENTILE PACKAGING MACHINERY CO
8300 Boettner Rd (48176-9828)
PHONE 734 429-1177
Aliseo Gentile, *President*
Anthony Gentile, *Vice Pres*
Cathy Gentile, *Treasurer*
EMP: 5
SQ FT: 1,500
SALES (est): 1MM **Privately Held**
SIC: 3565 Packaging machinery

(G-14394)
HEAR CLEAR INC
311 Castlebury Dr (48176-1473)
PHONE 734 525-8467
David R Wizgird, *Principal*
EMP: 4
SALES (est): 339.7K **Privately Held**
SIC: 3613 Regulators, power

(G-14395)
IMPERIAL INDUSTRIES INC
815 Woodland Dr (48176-1259)
PHONE 734 397-1400
Wendell G Lewellen, *President*
Wendell G Lewellen III, *Vice Pres*
Jeanne H Lewellen, *Admin Sec*
EMP: 16 **EST:** 1945
SQ FT: 28,000
SALES (est): 3.1MM **Privately Held**
WEB: www.imperialindustriesinc.com
SIC: 3089 3643 3559 Plastic containers, except foam; current-carrying wiring devices; sewing machines & hat & zipper making machinery

(G-14396)
INVERTECH INC
1404 Industrial Dr Ste 1 (48176-9495)
PHONE 734 944-4400
Lance Ennis, *Principal*
EMP: 14
SALES (est): 2MM **Privately Held**
SIC: 3829 Gas detectors

(G-14397)
KYOCERA UNIMERCO TOOLING INC
Also Called: Unimerco Group A/S
6620 State Rd (48176-9274)
PHONE 734 944-4433
Jeremy Parrish, *Finance Dir*
▲ **EMP:** 48
SQ FT: 50,000
SALES (est): 18.5MM **Publicly Held**
WEB: www.kyocera-unimerco.us
SIC: 5084 7699 3545 Machine tools & accessories; knife, saw & tool sharpening & repair; cutting tools for machine tools
HQ: Kyocera Unimerco A/S
     Drejervej 2
     Sunds 7451
     962 923-00

(G-14398)
LIEBHERR AEROSPACE SALINE INC
1465 Woodland Dr (48176-1627)
PHONE 734 429-7225
Alex Vlielander, *President*
Steven Fracassa, *Engineer*
Cristian Fodor, *Manager*
Derek Hampel, *Manager*
Jim Will, *Manager*
▲ **EMP:** 145
SQ FT: 100,000
SALES (est): 41.4MM
SALES (corp-wide): 13.1B **Privately Held**
SIC: 4581 7699 3728 Aircraft servicing & repairing; aircraft & heavy equipment repair services; aircraft flight instrument repair; antique repair & restoration, except furniture, automobiles; alighting (landing gear) assemblies, aircraft
PA: Liebherr-International S.A.
     Rue Hans-Liebherr 7
     Bulle FR 1630
     269 133-111

(G-14399)
MCNAUGHTON & GUNN INC (PA)
960 Woodland Dr (48176-1634)
P.O. Box 10 (48176-0010)
PHONE 734 429-5411
Julie McFarland, *President*
Julie Mc Farland, *President*
Robert L Mc Naughton, *President*
Ruth Spaulding, *Production*
Marc Moore, *Regl Sales Mgr*
▼ **EMP:** 112
SQ FT: 82,000
SALES (est): 21.7MM **Privately Held**
WEB: www.mcnaughton-gunn.com
SIC: 2732 2789 Books: printing & binding; bookbinding & related work

(G-14400)
MECTRON ENGINEERING CO INC
400 S Industrial Dr (48176-9497)
PHONE 734 944-8777
James L Hanna, *President*
Mark L Hanna, *COO*
Scott Corrunker, *Vice Pres*
Carol A Hanna, *Vice Pres*
Kathy Gram, *Controller*
▲ **EMP:** 38
SQ FT: 39,000
SALES (est): 8.8MM **Privately Held**
WEB: www.mectron.net
SIC: 3826 Analytical instruments

(G-14401)
MIKAN CORPORATION
Also Called: Akki Products
1271 Industrial Dr Ste 3 (48176-8400)
P.O. Box 381 (48176-0381)
PHONE 734 944-9447
Margaret G Stevens, *President*
Michael G Stevens, *Vice Pres*
EMP: 10
SQ FT: 7,800
SALES (est): 1.6MM **Privately Held**
WEB: www.mikancorp.com
SIC: 3955 7378 5045 5112 Print cartridges for laser & other computer printers; computer peripheral equipment repair & maintenance; computers, peripherals & software; printers, computer; stationery & office supplies

(G-14402)
MITOVATION INC
1280 Wedgewood Cir (48176-9276)
PHONE 734 395-1635
Mark Morsfield, *CEO*
Maik Huttemann,
Thomas Sanderson,
EMP: 3
SALES (est): 208.5K **Privately Held**
SIC: 3841 7389 Surgical & medical instruments;

(G-14403)
MMI ENGINEERED SOLUTIONS INC (HQ)
Also Called: Drayton Plains Tool Company
1715 Woodland Dr (48176-1614)
PHONE 734 429-4664
Doug Callahan, *President*
Jane Clawson-Palfi, *Opers Staff*
Paul Larson, *CFO*
David Inman, *Controller*
Cal Dawson, *IT/INT Sup*
▲ **EMP:** 86 **EST:** 1983
SQ FT: 80,000
SALES (est): 29.2MM **Privately Held**
WEB: www.moldedmaterials.com
SIC: 3089 8711 Injection molding of plastics; engineering services

(G-14404)
MOGULTECH LLC
1454 Judd Rd (48176-8819)
P.O. Box 561 (48176-0561)
PHONE 734 944-5053
Jeff Stockwell, *Mng Member*
Lori Stockwell,
EMP: 5
SALES (est): 640.4K **Privately Held**
SIC: 3599 Machine shop, jobbing & repair

GEOGRAPHIC SECTION
Sandusky - Sanilac County (G-14433)

(G-14405)
NA PUBLISHING INC
6564 State Rd (48176-8707)
P.O. Box 926 (48176-0926)
PHONE..................................734 302-6500
Jeff Moyer, *President*
Joe Mills, *Managing Dir*
Richard Joseph Mills, *Managing Dir*
EMP: 45
SQ FT: 3,200
SALES (est): 5.3MM **Privately Held**
SIC: 2731 7374 Books: publishing & printing; data processing service
PA: Image Data Conversion, Llc
6564 State Rd
Saline MI 48176

(G-14406)
NORGREN AUTOMTN SOLUTIONS LLC (DH)
Also Called: I.S.I. Automation Products
1325 Woodland Dr (48176-1626)
PHONE..................................734 429-4989
Tim Key, *President*
Frank Alex, *CFO*
▲ EMP: 200 EST: 1996
SQ FT: 90,000
SALES (est): 44.8MM
SALES (corp-wide): 2.4B **Privately Held**
SIC: 3549 Assembly machines, including robotic
HQ: Norgren, Inc.
5400 S Delaware St
Littleton CO 80120
303 794-5000

(G-14407)
PHOENIX PACKAGING CORPORATION
600 W Michigan Ave Ste A (48176-7600)
PHONE..................................734 944-3916
Christopher Molloy, *President*
Patricia Molloy, *Vice Pres*
EMP: 4
SALES (est): 1.1MM **Privately Held**
SIC: 5113 2653 3089 Corrugated & solid fiber boxes; boxes, solid fiber: made from purchased materials; pallets, plastic

(G-14408)
PLASTECHS LLC
1270 Barnes Ct (48176-9589)
PHONE..................................734 429-3129
Connie Petrinovic, *Opers Mgr*
Nigam Tripathi,
EMP: 3
SALES (est): 97.8K **Privately Held**
SIC: 3089 Injection molding of plastics

(G-14409)
PRINTING SERVICES INC
Also Called: Allegra Printing & Imaging
1283 Industrial Dr (48176-9434)
PHONE..................................734 944-1404
Patrick Mahoney, *President*
Deare Mahoney, *Corp Secy*
EMP: 20
SALES (est): 2.4MM **Privately Held**
SIC: 2752 Commercial printing, offset

(G-14410)
R & B PLASTICS MACHINERY LLC
1605 Woodland Dr (48176-1638)
PHONE..................................734 429-9421
Tom Redies, *Vice Pres*
Dave Johnson, *Engineer*
James Sheely, *VP Bus Dvlpt*
Jake Losee, *Manager*
Larry Weber, *Director*
◆ EMP: 38
SQ FT: 80,000
SALES: 11MM **Privately Held**
WEB: www.rbplasticsmachinery.com
SIC: 3559 3544 Plastics working machinery; industrial molds

(G-14411)
RALRUBE INC
8423 Boettner Rd (48176-9829)
PHONE..................................734 429-0033
Robert Skandalaris, *President*
EMP: 6
SQ FT: 8,000
SALES (est): 873.2K **Privately Held**
SIC: 2899 Chemical preparations

(G-14412)
REPORTER PAPERS INC
106 W Michigan Ave (48176-1325)
PHONE..................................734 429-5428
Jim Williams, *President*
EMP: 16
SALES (est): 442.6K **Privately Held**
SIC: 2711 Newspapers

(G-14413)
SALINE LECTRONICS INC
710 N Maple Rd (48176-1294)
PHONE..................................734 944-1972
Mario Sciberras, *President*
Matthew Turner, *Vice Pres*
Desiree Molnar, *Buyer*
▲ EMP: 122
SQ FT: 110,000
SALES (est): 64.6MM **Privately Held**
WEB: www.lectronics.net
SIC: 3672 Printed circuit boards

(G-14414)
SANS SERIF INC
75 E Henry St (48176-1362)
PHONE..................................734 944-1190
Vivian Bradbury, *President*
Susan Kenyon, *Vice Pres*
EMP: 5
SQ FT: 900
SALES (est): 280K **Privately Held**
WEB: www.sansserif.com
SIC: 2791 7336 Typesetting; commercial art & graphic design

(G-14415)
SHAUN JACKSON DESIGN INC
Also Called: Higher Ground
134 S Industrial Dr (48176-9493)
P.O. Box 130500, Ann Arbor (48113-0500)
PHONE..................................734 975-7500
Mark Zadvinskis, *President*
Jaron Patterson, *Accounts Mgr*
Brian Poore, *Accounts Mgr*
EMP: 4
SQ FT: 1,500
SALES (est): 2.1MM **Privately Held**
WEB: www.sjdesign.com
SIC: 7389 3161 Design, commercial & industrial; traveling bags

(G-14416)
STONY LAKE CORPORATION
5115 Saline Waterworks Rd (48176-9703)
PHONE..................................734 944-9426
Gerald Tubbs, *Principal*
EMP: 4
SALES (est): 203K **Privately Held**
SIC: 2082 Beer (alcoholic beverage)

(G-14417)
SVN INC
Also Called: Lookingbus
6763 Heatheridge Dr (48176-9230)
PHONE..................................734 707-7131
Nirit Glazer, *CEO*
Zvi Zuler, *Principal*
EMP: 4
SALES (est): 167.1K **Privately Held**
SIC: 2899 Food contamination testing or screening kits

(G-14418)
TOWNSHIP OF SALINE
205 E Michigan Ave (48176-1554)
PHONE..................................734 429-4440
Marilyn Gordon, *Branch Mgr*
EMP: 10
SALES (est): 1.2MM **Privately Held**
SIC: 3711 9224 7389 Fire department vehicles (motor vehicles), assembly of; fire protection; personal service agents, brokers & bureaus
PA: Township Of Saline
4725 Willow Rd
Saline MI
734 429-7722

(G-14419)
TRANSTECHBIO INC
5001 Quincy Ct (48176-9597)
PHONE..................................734 994-4728
Jian Zong, *President*
EMP: 8 EST: 1990
SALES (est): 1.1MM **Privately Held**
SIC: 2836 Blood derivatives

(G-14420)
VERTIGEE CORPORATION
1722 Wildwood Trl (48176-1655)
PHONE..................................313 999-1020
Stephen Farr, *CEO*
Jean Fideler, *Admin Sec*
EMP: 7
SALES (est): 168K **Privately Held**
SIC: 7372 Prepackaged software

(G-14421)
WINDSOR MOLD USA INC
Also Called: Windsor Mold Saline
1294 Beach Ct (48176-9185)
P.O. Box 32523, Detroit (48232-0523)
PHONE..................................734 944-5080
Keith Henry, *President*
Greg Mahoney, *Corp Secy*
EMP: 50 EST: 2013
SQ FT: 73,000
SALES (est): 13.1MM
SALES (corp-wide): 796K **Privately Held**
SIC: 3799 Trailers & trailer equipment
PA: 873740 Ontario Inc
1628 Durham Pl
Windsor ON N8W 2
519 258-3475

(G-14422)
YOUNG CABINETRY INC
1400 E Michigan Ave (48176-1733)
P.O. Box 782 (48176-0782)
PHONE..................................734 316-2896
EMP: 3
SALES (est): 65K **Privately Held**
SIC: 2434 Wood kitchen cabinets

Sand Lake
Kent County

(G-14423)
HIGH GRADE MATERIALS COMPANY
16180 Northland Dr (49343-8856)
PHONE..................................616 696-9540
James Sturris, *Manager*
EMP: 25
SALES (corp-wide): 28.3MM **Privately Held**
SIC: 3273 Ready-mixed concrete
PA: High Grade Materials Company
9266 Snows Lake Rd
Greenville MI 48838
616 754-5545

(G-14424)
MELLEMAS CUT STONE
16610 Findley Dr (49343-9256)
PHONE..................................616 984-2493
Greg Mellema, *Principal*
EMP: 6 EST: 2010
SALES (est): 425.7K **Privately Held**
SIC: 3281 Cut stone & stone products

(G-14425)
R & C REDI-MIX INC
Also Called: Ensley Sand & Gravel
11991 Elm St (49343)
P.O. Box 185, Grant (49327-0185)
PHONE..................................616 636-5650
Raymond Oppenhuizen Jr, *President*
EMP: 9
SQ FT: 2,800
SALES (est): 1.2MM **Privately Held**
SIC: 3273 Ready-mixed concrete

(G-14426)
R & S PROPELLER INC
Also Called: R & S Propeller Repair
212 S 3rd St (49343-9203)
PHONE..................................616 636-8202
Judith A Rowland, *President*
EMP: 10
SALES (est): 787.4K **Privately Held**
SIC: 3449 Miscellaneous metalwork

(G-14427)
RC METAL PRODUCTS INC
4365 21 Mile Rd (49343-9473)
P.O. Box 129, Grandville (49468-0129)
PHONE..................................616 696-1694
Richard Crooks, *President*
EMP: 9
SQ FT: 7,000
SALES: 1MM **Privately Held**
SIC: 3443 Metal parts

Sandusky
Sanilac County

(G-14428)
ASCO LP
Also Called: Numatics
360 Thelma St (48471-1415)
PHONE..................................810 648-9141
EMP: 195
SALES (corp-wide): 17.4B **Publicly Held**
SIC: 3491 Industrial valves
HQ: Asco, L.P.
160 Park Ave
Florham Park NJ 07932
800 972-2726

(G-14429)
BADER & CO
Also Called: Tri-County Equip-Sandusky
989 W Sanilac Rd (48471-9789)
PHONE..................................810 648-2404
Dan Wadsworth, *President*
EMP: 25
SALES (est): 3.6MM **Privately Held**
SIC: 3523 7699 5261 Farm machinery & equipment; lawn mower repair shop; lawnmowers & tractors

(G-14430)
BAY-HOUSTON TOWING COMPANY
Also Called: Michigan Peak Company
875 E Sanilac Rd (48471-8790)
P.O. Box 312 (48471-0312)
PHONE..................................810 648-2210
David Newman, *Vice Pres*
Kevin Wormwood, *Plant Mgr*
EMP: 30
SALES (corp-wide): 17.9MM **Privately Held**
WEB: www.bayhouston.com
SIC: 4212 1499 2875 5083 Local trucking, without storage; peat grinding; fertilizers, mixing only; landscaping equipment; hand & edge tools
PA: Bay-Houston Towing Company
2243 Milford St
Houston TX 77098
713 529-3755

(G-14431)
CINNABAR ENGINEERING INC
116 Orval St (48471-1411)
PHONE..................................810 648-2444
R Weston Caughlan, *President*
EMP: 14
SQ FT: 15,000
SALES (est): 2.1MM **Privately Held**
WEB: www.cinnabarengineering.com
SIC: 3714 5013 Motor vehicle parts & accessories; automotive supplies & parts

(G-14432)
DAWSON MANUFACTURING
180 Dawson St (48471-1034)
PHONE..................................269 639-4213
EMP: 3 EST: 2016
SALES (est): 130K **Privately Held**
SIC: 2891 Adhesives & sealants

(G-14433)
ELDON PUBLISHING LLC
Also Called: Tribune Recorder
43 S Elk St (48471-1353)
PHONE..................................810 648-5282
William Dixon,
EMP: 4
SQ FT: 800
SALES: 227.2K **Privately Held**
SIC: 2711 Newspapers, publishing & printing

Sandusky - Sanilac County (G-14434)

(G-14434)
GREAT NORTHERN PUBLISHING INC
Also Called: Buyers Guide
356 E Sanilac Rd (48471-1151)
P.O. Box 72 (48471-0072)
PHONE 810 648-4000
Jane Vanderpoel, *President*
EMP: 25
SALES (est): 1.5MM
SALES (corp-wide): 697.5MM **Privately Held**
WEB: www.greatnorthernpublishing.com
SIC: 2741 Shopping news: publishing & printing
HQ: 21st Century Newspapers, Inc.
19176 Hall Rd Ste 200
Clinton Township MI 48038
586 469-4510

(G-14435)
INDUSTRIAL ATOMATED DESIGN LLC
245 S Stoutenburg Rd (48471-8649)
PHONE 810 648-9200
Brian Park, *Administration*
Vance Upper,
EMP: 20 **EST:** 1999
SQ FT: 11,005
SALES (est): 5.3MM **Privately Held**
WEB: www.iadesigns.net
SIC: 3569 Robots, assembly line: industrial & commercial

(G-14436)
J R C INC (PA)
Also Called: Bargain Hunter
356 E Sanilac Rd (48471-1151)
P.O. Box 72 (48471-0072)
PHONE 810 648-4000
Jane Vanderpoel, *Principal*
Eric Levine, *Advt Staff*
EMP: 14
SQ FT: 10,000
SALES (est): 1.1MM **Privately Held**
WEB: www.sanilaccountynews.com
SIC: 2711 2752 Newspapers, publishing & printing; commercial printing, offset

(G-14437)
JENSEN BRIDGE & SUPPLY COMPANY (PA)
400 Stoney Creek Dr (48471-1043)
P.O. Box 151 (48471-0151)
PHONE 810 648-3000
Roger A Loding, *President*
Edward D Giroux, *Vice Pres*
EMP: 25
SQ FT: 52,000
SALES (est): 8.1MM **Privately Held**
WEB: www.jensenbridge.com
SIC: 3444 5039 5211 Culverts, sheet metal; prefabricated structures; lumber & other building materials

(G-14438)
K PRINTING PUBLIC RELATIONS CO
42 Austin St (48471-1245)
PHONE 810 648-4410
Denise Kelley, *Owner*
EMP: 3
SQ FT: 1,800
SALES (est): 225.1K **Privately Held**
WEB: www.clearidea.com
SIC: 2752 8743 Commercial printing, offset; public relations & publicity

(G-14439)
KNOERR FARMS
1700 E Custer Rd (48471-9119)
PHONE 989 670-2199
Doug Knoerr, *Owner*
EMP: 3
SALES: 950K **Privately Held**
SIC: 3523 Driers (farm): grain, hay & seed

(G-14440)
NELSON MANUFACTURING INC
1240 W Sanilac Rd Ste A (48471-9654)
PHONE 810 648-0065
Brian Nelson, *President*
Debra Nelson, *Vice Pres*
EMP: 7
SALES (est): 1MM **Privately Held**
WEB: www.nelsonmanufacturing.com
SIC: 3469 3312 Machine parts, stamped or pressed metal; structural shapes & pilings, steel

(G-14441)
PRODUCTION DEV SYSTEMS LLC
245 Campbell Rd (48471-1427)
PHONE 810 648-2111
EMP: 15 **EST:** 2014
SALES (est): 2.9MM **Privately Held**
SIC: 3599 Mfg Industrial Machinery

(G-14442)
SANDUSKY CONCRETE & SUPPLY
376 E Sanilac Rd (48471-1158)
PHONE 810 648-2627
William Burgess Jr, *President*
John Bungart, *Vice Pres*
Curt Backus, *Treasurer*
Jeff Walkup, *Office Mgr*
Alex Galligan, *Admin Sec*
EMP: 4 **EST:** 1946
SQ FT: 2,500
SALES (est): 824K **Privately Held**
SIC: 5032 5211 3171 3272 Concrete mixtures; sand, construction; gravel; concrete & cinder block; sand & gravel; cement; purses, women's; septic tanks, concrete

(G-14443)
SANILAC DRAIN AND TILE CO
61 Orval St (48471-1410)
PHONE 810 648-4100
Robert Hall, *President*
Deanna Stone, *Admin Sec*
EMP: 6
SQ FT: 5,000
SALES (est): 600K **Privately Held**
SIC: 3272 Concrete products used to facilitate drainage

(G-14444)
STOUTENBURG INC
Also Called: Breiten Lumber
121 Campbell Rd (48471-1412)
PHONE 810 648-4400
Clinton A Stoutenburg, *President*
Gary Bright, *Plant Mgr*
EMP: 20
SQ FT: 300,000
SALES (est): 2.1MM **Privately Held**
SIC: 2448 Pallets, wood

(G-14445)
THUMB BIOENERGY LLC
155 Orval St (48471-1491)
PHONE 810 404-2466
James Hastings, *Principal*
Alex Ritter, *Prdtn Mgr*
EMP: 7
SALES (est): 787.9K **Privately Held**
SIC: 2869 High purity grade chemicals, organic

(G-14446)
VIBRACOUSTIC USA INC
Also Called: Trelleborg Automotive
180 Dawson St (48471-1034)
PHONE 810 648-2100
Brad Glenn, *General Mgr*
Bill Tobin, *Branch Mgr*
EMP: 300
SQ FT: 280,000
SALES (corp-wide): 2.4B **Privately Held**
SIC: 3061 Automotive rubber goods (mechanical)
HQ: Vibracoustic Usa, Inc.
400 Aylworth Ave
South Haven MI 49090
269 637-2116

(G-14447)
VIBRACOUSTIC USA INC
370 Industrial St (48471-1493)
PHONE 810 648-2100
Bill Tobin, *Branch Mgr*
EMP: 6
SALES (corp-wide): 2.4B **Privately Held**
SIC: 3061 Mechanical rubber goods
HQ: Vibracoustic Usa, Inc.
400 Aylworth Ave
South Haven MI 49090
269 637-2116

Sanford
Midland County

(G-14448)
BRIGGS CONTRACTING
62 E Saginaw Rd (48657-9250)
P.O. Box 319 (48657-0319)
PHONE 989 687-7331
Gary L Briggs, *Owner*
Anne Briggs, *Corp Secy*
EMP: 7 **EST:** 1966
SQ FT: 3,200
SALES (est): 1.1MM **Privately Held**
SIC: 1442 Construction sand & gravel

(G-14449)
DOUGLASS SAFETY SYSTEMS LLC
2655 N Meridian Rd Ste 6 (48657-9008)
PHONE 989 687-7600
David Dorr, *Sales Staff*
Matt Dumond, *Sales Staff*
Jim Reed, *Sales Staff*
Douglas Engwis, *Mng Member*
EMP: 7
SALES (est): 1.4MM **Privately Held**
SIC: 5084 3052 3842 3429 Safety equipment; fire hose, rubber; clothing, fire resistant & protective; nozzles, fire fighting

(G-14450)
FARM COUNTRY FRZ CUSTARD & KIT
Also Called: Sanford Whippy Dip
2890 N Meridian Rd (48657-9542)
PHONE 989 687-6700
Dean Davis, *President*
EMP: 5
SALES (est): 353.4K **Privately Held**
SIC: 2024 Ice cream & frozen desserts

(G-14451)
MARK MOLD AND ENGINEERING
773 W Beamish Rd (48657-9489)
P.O. Box 407 (48657-0407)
PHONE 989 687-9786
Mark Reynaert, *Owner*
EMP: 10
SQ FT: 3,500
SALES: 250K **Privately Held**
SIC: 3544 Special dies & tools

Saranac
Ionia County

(G-14452)
ADVERTISER PUBLISHING CO INC
Also Called: Ionia County Shoppers Guide
13 N Bridge St (48881-5122)
P.O. Box 46 (48881-0046)
PHONE 616 642-9411
John Brown, *President*
Carol Benjamin, *Admin Sec*
EMP: 6
SQ FT: 2,800
SALES (est): 665K **Privately Held**
WEB: www.ioniacountyshoppersguide.com
SIC: 2741 Guides: publishing only, not printed on site

(G-14453)
AMW MACHINE CONTROL INC
6963 Cherrywood Ln (48881-7701)
PHONE 616 642-9514
Mark Williams, *President*
EMP: 4
SALES (est): 483.2K **Privately Held**
SIC: 3531 Construction machinery

(G-14454)
DYNAMIC WOOD PRODUCTS INC
9385 Potters Rd (48881-9661)
PHONE 616 897-8114
Donald Braam, *President*
Jeffrey Braam, *Vice Pres*
Craig Braam, *Treasurer*
EMP: 4
SALES (est): 278.1K **Privately Held**
WEB: www.stantonmfg.com
SIC: 2521 Wood office furniture

(G-14455)
SARANAC TANK INC
100 W Main St (48881-5117)
P.O. Box 26 (48881-0026)
PHONE 616 642-9481
Gregory Grieves, *President*
Vickey Grieves, *Corp Secy*
EMP: 7
SQ FT: 5,000
SALES (est): 495K **Privately Held**
SIC: 3443 7699 Tanks, standard or custom fabricated: metal plate; tank repair

(G-14456)
US GUYS DEER PROCESSING LLC
7661 Bluewater Hwy (48881-9453)
PHONE 616 642-0967
Meisha Russell, *Office Mgr*
Darin Wilber, *Mng Member*
EMP: 3
SALES (est): 223.4K **Privately Held**
SIC: 2011 Meat packing plants

(G-14457)
WHOLESALE TICKET CO INC
41 Parsonage St (48881-9825)
P.O. Box 33 (48881-0033)
PHONE 616 642-9476
Edward Brown, *President*
Deb Brown, *Vice Pres*
EMP: 12 **EST:** 1976
SQ FT: 3,200
SALES (est): 1.5MM **Privately Held**
WEB: www.wholesaleticket.com
SIC: 2752 2759 Commercial printing, offset; letterpress printing

Saugatuck
Allegan County

(G-14458)
ENAGON LLC
3381 Blue Star Hwy (49453-9724)
PHONE 269 455-5110
Terry Ebels, *Mng Member*
EMP: 7
SALES (est): 2MM **Privately Held**
SIC: 3541 Milling machines

(G-14459)
KAECHELE INC
Also Called: Commercial Record/Resorter
3217 Blue Star Hwy (49453-9723)
P.O. Box 246 (49453-0246)
PHONE 269 857-2570
Mike Wilcox, *President*
EMP: 3
SALES (est): 137.9K **Privately Held**
SIC: 2711 Newspapers: publishing only, not printed on site

(G-14460)
N D R ENTERPRISES INC
Also Called: Macatawa Bay Boat Works
297 S Maple St (49453-9795)
PHONE 269 857-4556
Jonathan Reuf, *President*
EMP: 6
SQ FT: 8,000
SALES (est): 418K **Privately Held**
WEB: www.mbbw.com
SIC: 3732 Boat building & repairing

GEOGRAPHIC SECTION

Sault Sainte Marie
Chippewa County

(G-14461)
BELTONE SKORIC HEARNG AID CNTR
240 W Portage Ave (49783-1922)
PHONE..................906 379-0606
EMP: 7 EST: 2015
SALES (est): 94.1K Privately Held
SIC: 7629 3842 Lamp repair & mounting; absorbent cotton, sterilized

(G-14462)
CANUSA LLC
Also Called: Quarter To 5
2510 Ashmun St (49783-3745)
PHONE..................906 259-0800
Kristina Thibault, *Principal*
Eric Thibault, *Principal*
EMP: 14
SALES (est): 835.8K Privately Held
SIC: 3131 Quarters

(G-14463)
CUSTOM RUSTIC FLAGS LLC
1018 Bingham Ave (49783-2971)
PHONE..................906 203-6935
Adam Knackstadt,
EMP: 3 EST: 2018
SALES (est): 103.3K Privately Held
SIC: 2499 Decorative wood & woodwork

(G-14464)
GENE BROW & SONS INC
2754 W 20th St (49783-9459)
PHONE..................906 635-0859
EMP: 10
SALES (est): 1MM Privately Held
SIC: 3273 Mfg Ready-Mixed Concrete

(G-14465)
GREAT LAKES FINE CABINETRY
844 E 3 Mile Rd (49783-9305)
PHONE..................906 493-5780
Philip Winkel, *President*
Rick Bouwma, *Vice Pres*
EMP: 5
SQ FT: 5,000
SALES (est): 240K Privately Held
SIC: 2434 1751 Wood kitchen cabinets; cabinet & finish carpentry

(G-14466)
J A S VENEER & LUMBER INC
1300 W 12th St (49783-1356)
PHONE..................906 635-0710
Jack A Schikofsky, *President*
Mike Schikofsky, *Vice Pres*
EMP: 25
SQ FT: 33,000
SALES (est): 4.5MM Privately Held
SIC: 2435 Veneer stock, hardwood

(G-14467)
K & K RACING LLC
Also Called: K & K Motorsports
1877 Timber Wolf Ln (49783-9442)
PHONE..................906 322-1276
Walt Komarnizki, *Owner*
Walter Komarnizki, *Owner*
Rebecca Komarnizki, *Corp Secy*
EMP: 15
SALES (est): 250K Privately Held
SIC: 3799 Recreational vehicles

(G-14468)
MALEPORTS SAULT PRTG CO INC
314 Osborn Blvd (49783-1820)
P.O. Box 323 (49783-0323)
PHONE..................906 632-3369
Ronald T Maleport, *President*
Cindy Albon, *Corp Secy*
Michael Maleport, *Vice Pres*
EMP: 20
SQ FT: 12,500
SALES (est): 1.8MM Privately Held
WEB: www.saultprinting.com
SIC: 5112 5044 5021 2752 Office supplies; office equipment; office furniture; commercial printing, offset; bookbinding & related work; commercial printing

(G-14469)
NORTHLAND MAINTENANCE CO INC
Also Called: Northland Maintenace
2366 E 3 Mile Rd (49783-9378)
PHONE..................906 253-9161
James Menard, *CEO*
Noah Menard, *Admin Sec*
EMP: 3
SALES (est): 198.5K Privately Held
SIC: 3492 5085 Fluid power valves & hose fittings; valves & fittings

(G-14470)
PRECISION EDGE SRGCAL PDTS LLC (PA)
415 W 12th Ave (49783-2607)
PHONE..................906 632-5600
John Truckey, *President*
Scott Nagy, *Opers Mgr*
Patt Blanchard, *Human Res Mgr*
Stacey Swanson, *Accounts Mgr*
EMP: 73
SQ FT: 35,000
SALES: 24.7MM Privately Held
WEB: www.precisionedge.com
SIC: 3841 Surgical & medical instruments

(G-14471)
R & B ELECTRONICS INC (PA)
1520 Industrial Park Dr (49783-1474)
PHONE..................906 632-1542
Debra Rogers, *President*
Jim Cloudman, *Engineer*
Wayne Olsen, *CFO*
Robert Kerley, *Manager*
Cindy Peller, *Executive*
EMP: 51
SQ FT: 12,160
SALES: 4.4MM Privately Held
WEB: www.rbesoo.com
SIC: 3728 Aircraft assemblies, subassemblies & parts

(G-14472)
ROGERS BEEF FARMS
6917 S Nicolet Rd (49783-9609)
PHONE..................906 632-1584
Dan Rogers, *Principal*
EMP: 6
SALES (est): 353.5K Privately Held
SIC: 2011 Beef products from beef slaughtered on site

(G-14473)
SAULT TRIBE NEWS
Also Called: Communications Dept
531 Ashmun St (49783-1926)
PHONE..................906 632-6398
Aaron Payment, *Chairman*
Allan Kamuda, *Director*
Cory Wilson, *Deputy Dir*
EMP: 12
SALES (est): 564.7K Privately Held
WEB: www.communicationsdept.com
SIC: 2711 Newspapers, publishing & printing

(G-14474)
SOO WELDING INC
934 E Portage Ave (49783-2444)
P.O. Box 1583 (49783-7583)
PHONE..................906 632-8241
Charles M Fabry, *President*
Jody Fabry, *Admin Sec*
EMP: 12 EST: 1927
SQ FT: 3,000
SALES (est): 4MM Privately Held
SIC: 5051 7692 3599 5085 Steel; pipe & tubing, steel; welding repair; machine shop, jobbing & repair; welding supplies

(G-14475)
SUPERIOR MAR & ENVMTL SVCS LLC
3779 S Riverside Dr (49783-9505)
PHONE..................906 253-9448
Christina Sams, *Partner*
Thomas L Farnquist, *Partner*
Jenny Oliver, *Principal*
Sandra Sawyer, *Principal*
Kenny Wagner, *Principal*
EMP: 4
SALES (est): 242.4K Privately Held
SIC: 4493 4492 1389 7389 Marine basins; marine towing services; running, cutting & pulling casings, tubes & rods; divers, commercial; marine reporting

(G-14476)
TN MICHIGAN LLC
Also Called: Hoover Precision Products
1390 Industrial Park Dr (49783-1452)
PHONE..................906 632-7310
Sharon Lajoie, *Purchasing*
Terry Adams,
EMP: 55
SALES (est): 6.1MM Privately Held
SIC: 3562 Ball & roller bearings
PA: Tsubaki Nakashima Co.,Ltd.
   19, Shakudo
   Katsuragi NAR 639-2

(G-14477)
VAN SLOTEN ENTERPRISES INC (PA)
Also Called: Northern Sand & Gravel
1320 W 3 Mile Rd (49783-9251)
P.O. Box 365 (49783-0365)
PHONE..................906 635-5151
Raymond Van Sloten, *President*
Gerald Van Sloten, *Vice Pres*
Allan Van Sloten, *Treasurer*
Gladys Norris, *Admin Sec*
EMP: 17 EST: 1963
SQ FT: 1,800
SALES: 3.5MM Privately Held
SIC: 3273 1442 3272 Ready-mixed concrete; common sand mining; gravel mining; concrete products

(G-14478)
VITAL SIGNS MICHIGAN INC
751 Peck St (49783-1520)
P.O. Box 1598 (49783-7598)
PHONE..................906 632-7602
Mark Wilton, *President*
Misty Wilton, *Corp Secy*
Benjamin Winberg, *Assistant VP*
Chad Wilton, *Vice Pres*
EMP: 4
SALES: 250K Privately Held
SIC: 7389 3993 Lettering & sign painting services; electric signs

(G-14479)
WENDRICKS TRUSS INC
6142 S Mackinac Trl (49783)
P.O. Box 463 (49783-0463)
PHONE..................906 635-8822
Steve Hagan, *Manager*
EMP: 10
SALES (est): 951.1K
SALES (corp-wide): 7.3MM Privately Held
WEB: www.wendrickstruss.com
SIC: 2439 Trusses, wooden roof
PA: Wendricks Truss, Inc.
   W5728 Old Us 2 Road No 43
   Hermansville MI 49847
   906 498-7709

(G-14480)
YOOPER WD WRKS RESTORATION LLC
Also Called: Yooper Wood Works & Designs
312 Barbeau St (49783-2404)
PHONE..................906 203-0056
Walter Komarnizk, *Mng Member*
EMP: 4
SALES (est): 91.2K Privately Held
SIC: 2491 2426 Wood preserving; carvings, furniture: wood

Sawyer
Berrien County

(G-14481)
ARLINGTON METALS CORPORATION
13100 Arlington Dr (49125-9376)
P.O. Box 284 (49125-0284)
PHONE..................269 426-3371
Rob Woredehoff, *Opers-Prdtn-Mfg*
EMP: 68
SALES (est): 4.4MM
SALES (corp-wide): 107.6MM Privately Held
WEB: www.arlingtonmetals.com
SIC: 7389 3312 5051 Metal cutting services; blast furnaces & steel mills; metals service centers & offices
PA: Arlington Metals Corporation
   11355 Franklin Ave
   Franklin Park IL 60131
   847 451-9100

(G-14482)
BURKHOLDER EXCAVATING INC
4898 Weechik Rd (49125-9255)
PHONE..................269 426-4227
Scott Burkholder, *CEO*
EMP: 6
SALES (est): 540K Privately Held
WEB: www.burkholderpaving.com
SIC: 1389 Excavating slush pits & cellars

(G-14483)
CC INDUSTRIES LLC
Also Called: Corvette Central
13550 Three Oaks Rd (49125-9328)
P.O. Box 16 (49125-0016)
PHONE..................269 426-3342
Dan Baber, *CFO*
Gerald E Kohn,
◆ EMP: 100
SQ FT: 40,000
SALES (est): 17.9MM Privately Held
WEB: www.corvettecentral.com
SIC: 5013 5531 3714 Automotive supplies & parts; automobile & truck equipment & parts; motor vehicle parts & accessories

(G-14484)
CENTER OF WORLD WOODSHOP INC
13400 Red Arrow Hwy (49125-9308)
P.O. Box 354, New Troy (49119-0354)
PHONE..................269 469-5687
Terry Hanover, *President*
Lorraine Hanover, *General Mgr*
Rabecca Gloe, *Corp Secy*
EMP: 9
SALES: 458K Privately Held
WEB: www.centeroftheworld.net
SIC: 2511 Wood household furniture

(G-14485)
INFUSCO COFFEE ROASTERS LLC
5846 Sawyer Rd (49125-9387)
PHONE..................269 213-5282
Richard Siri,
EMP: 8 EST: 2011
SQ FT: 1,800
SALES (est): 632.4K Privately Held
SIC: 2095 3556 Roasted coffee; roasting machinery: coffee, peanut, etc.

(G-14486)
KEY CASTING COMPANY INC (PA)
13145 Red Arrow Hwy (49125-9175)
P.O. Box 246 (49125-0246)
PHONE..................269 426-3800
Dale R Ender, *President*
Joyce Ender, *Corp Secy*
EMP: 8
SQ FT: 12,000
SALES (est): 1.3MM Privately Held
SIC: 3363 3364 3544 Aluminum die-castings; zinc & zinc-base alloy die-castings; special dies & tools

Sawyer - Berrien County (G-14487)

(G-14487)
QUALI TONE CORPORATION
Also Called: Quali Tone Pwdr Cating Sndblst
13092 Red Arrow Hwy (49125-9174)
PHONE.................................269 426-3664
Anthony Pitone, *President*
Joseph Pitone, *Vice Pres*
EMP: 18
SQ FT: 23,000
SALES (est): 2.5MM **Privately Held**
SIC: 3479 3471 Painting, coating & hot dipping; plating & polishing

(G-14488)
RMCS WINGS ENTERPRISE
12421 Flynn Rd (49125-9251)
PHONE.................................269 426-3559
Roger Sinner, *Partner*
Chad Sinner, *Partner*
Melissa Sinner, *Partner*
EMP: 3
SALES (est): 109.6K **Privately Held**
SIC: 3999 Lawn ornaments

Schoolcraft
Kalamazoo County

(G-14489)
C2DX INC
555 E Eliza St Ste A (49087-8831)
PHONE.................................269 409-0068
Kevin McLeod, *CEO*
Ian Bund, *Director*
Brook Critchfield, *Director*
Ron Frisbie, *Director*
Jack Kelley, *Director*
EMP: 10
SALES (est): 685.6K **Privately Held**
SIC: 5047 3841 Medical equipment & supplies; surgical & medical instruments

(G-14490)
CANADIAN HARVEST LP (DH)
16369 Us Highway 131 S (49087-9150)
PHONE.................................952 835-6429
Scott Gordon, *General Mgr*
Nathan French, *CFO*
EMP: 6
SALES (est): 20.3MM
SALES (corp-wide): 355.8K **Privately Held**
SIC: 2099 Food preparations
HQ: J. Rettenmaier & Sohne Gmbh + Co. Kg
Holzmuhle 1
Rosenberg 73494
796 715-20

(G-14491)
CHEM LINK INC
353 E Lyons St (49087-9478)
P.O. Box 9 (49087-0009)
PHONE.................................269 679-4440
John E Thomas, *President*
Randy Copeland, *Division Mgr*
Don Webb, *Plant Mgr*
Jeremy Howard, *Opers Mgr*
Jim Sonntag, *Maint Spvr*
EMP: 70
SQ FT: 50,000
SALES (est): 50MM
SALES (corp-wide): 12.3MM **Privately Held**
SIC: 2891 Adhesives
HQ: Soprema, Inc.
310 Quadral Dr
Wadsworth OH 44281
330 334-0066

(G-14492)
COMMAND ELECTRONICS INC
15670 Morris Indus Dr (49087-9628)
PHONE.................................269 679-4011
Cary Campagna, *President*
▲ **EMP:** 48 **EST:** 1969
SQ FT: 26,000
SALES (est): 8.6MM **Privately Held**
WEB: www.commandelectronics.com
SIC: 3646 3613 Commercial indusl & institutional electric lighting fixtures; control panels, electric

(G-14493)
CONCEPT MOLDS INC
12273 N Us Highway 131 (49087-8902)
PHONE.................................269 679-2100
Chris Williams, *President*
Lane Smous, *COO*
Dan Northup, *Vice Pres*
Kima Bogema, *CFO*
Jason Sparks, *Technical Staff*
EMP: 34
SQ FT: 25,000
SALES (est): 6.5MM **Privately Held**
WEB: www.conceptmolds.com
SIC: 3544 Industrial molds

(G-14494)
CRAFT PRECISION INC
610 E Eliza St (49087-8740)
PHONE.................................269 679-5121
Steve Sutton, *President*
EMP: 40
SQ FT: 10,000
SALES (est): 2.4MM **Privately Held**
WEB: www.craftprecision.com
SIC: 3599 Machine shop, jobbing & repair

(G-14495)
INTERFIBE CORPORATION (PA)
16369 Us Highway 131 S (49087-9150)
PHONE.................................269 327-6141
John Karnemaat, *President*
Christopher Sullivan, *Corp Secy*
Terry L Mleczewski, *Vice Pres*
EMP: 15
SQ FT: 80,000
SALES (est): 12.1MM **Privately Held**
WEB: www.interfibe.com
SIC: 2821 Plastics materials & resins

(G-14496)
J L MILLING INC
15262 Industrial Dr (49087-9612)
PHONE.................................269 679-5769
Linda Schuring, *President*
Jerry Schuring, *Treasurer*
EMP: 10
SQ FT: 10,000
SALES (est): 2.3MM **Privately Held**
SIC: 2951 Asphalt paving mixtures & blocks

(G-14497)
J RETTENMAIER USA LP (DH)
16369 Us Highway 131 S (49087-9150)
PHONE.................................269 679-2340
Thorsten W Willmann, *General Mgr*
Aaron Hart, *Business Mgr*
Lee Rockstead, *Plant Mgr*
Elaine Thomas, *Plant Mgr*
Jeff Hampton, *Opers Mgr*
▲ **EMP:** 152
SQ FT: 250,000
SALES: 12MM
SALES (corp-wide): 355.8K **Privately Held**
WEB: www.jrsusa.com
SIC: 2823 Cellulosic manmade fibers
HQ: J. Rettenmaier & Sohne Gmbh + Co. Kg
Holzmuhle 1
Rosenberg 73494
796 715-20

(G-14498)
KALAMAZOO CHUCK MFG SVC CTR CO
11825 S Shaver Rd (49087-9403)
PHONE.................................269 679-2325
Duane Burnham, *President*
EMP: 10 **EST:** 1998
SALES (est): 1.5MM **Privately Held**
WEB: www.kalamazoochuck.com
SIC: 3545 Chucks: drill, lathe or magnetic (machine tool accessories)

(G-14499)
METAL MECHANICS INC
350 S 14th St (49087)
P.O. Box 447 (49087-0447)
PHONE.................................269 679-2525
Thomas Dailey, *President*
Barbara Dailey, *Principal*
James Dailey, *Principal*
Elizabeth Delisle, *Vice Pres*
Jim Delisle, *Prdtn Mgr*
EMP: 14 **EST:** 1950
SQ FT: 10,000
SALES (est): 2.7MM **Privately Held**
WEB: www.metalmechanics.com
SIC: 3599 3542 Machine shop, jobbing & repair; presses: hydraulic & pneumatic, mechanical & manual

(G-14500)
NEW CONCEPT PRODUCTS INC
Also Called: Hole Chief
277 E Lyons St (49087-9772)
PHONE.................................269 679-5970
Kelly Molenaar, *Principal*
EMP: 8
SALES (est): 1.1MM **Privately Held**
SIC: 3599 7539 Machine shop, jobbing & repair; machine shop, automotive

(G-14501)
ST MARYS CEMENT INC (US)
640 South St (49087-9166)
PHONE.................................269 679-5253
Fax: 269 679-5254
EMP: 4 **Privately Held**
SIC: 3271 5032 Mfg Concrete Block/Brick Whol Brick/Stone Material
HQ: St. Marys Cement Inc. (U.S.)
9333 Dearborn St
Detroit MI 48209
313 842-4600

(G-14502)
SUNOPTA INGREDIENTS INC
16369 Us Highway 131 S (49087-9150)
PHONE.................................502 587-7999
Fax: 502 587-8999
EMP: 26
SALES (corp-wide): 1.2B **Privately Held**
SIC: 8731 2099 2087 Commercial Physical Research Mfg Food Preparations Mfg Flavor Extracts/Syrup
HQ: Sunopta Ingredients Inc.
7301 Ohms Ln Ste 600
Edina MN 55439
831 685-6506

Scotts
Kalamazoo County

(G-14503)
CHIP SYSTEMS INTERNATIONAL
10953 Norscott St (49088-5107)
P.O. Box 68 (49088-0068)
PHONE.................................269 626-8000
Jeff Dudley, *President*
Michael Dudley, *Corp Secy*
Jill Wilson, *Vice Pres*
▲ **EMP:** 10
SQ FT: 30,000
SALES (est): 1.8MM **Privately Held**
WEB: www.chipsystemsintl.com
SIC: 3589 3569 3535 Shredders, industrial & commercial; centrifuges, industrial; belt conveyor systems, general industrial use

(G-14504)
COLE CARTER INC
Also Called: Pease Packing
8713 38th St S (49088-9338)
PHONE.................................269 626-8891
David Pease, *President*
EMP: 9
SQ FT: 11,250
SALES (est): 850.2K **Privately Held**
SIC: 2011 0291 Meat packing plants; livestock farm, general

(G-14505)
KRISTUS INC
Also Called: Airpower America
8370 Greenfield Shores Dr (49088-8727)
PHONE.................................269 321-3330
Barry Kearns, *President*
Ben Ipema, *Vice Pres*
Joe Kearns, *Manager*
▲ **EMP:** 10
SQ FT: 10,000
SALES (est): 2.6MM **Privately Held**
WEB: www.liquivac.com
SIC: 3561 Pumps & pumping equipment

(G-14506)
ROBERTS MOVABLE WALLS INC
9611 32nd St S (49088-9751)
PHONE.................................269 626-0227
Lane Mottor, *President*
EMP: 3
SALES (est): 257.5K **Privately Held**
SIC: 2653 Corrugated boxes, partitions, display items, sheets & pad

(G-14507)
SCOTTS HOOK & CLEAVER INC
Also Called: Pease Packing
8713 38th St S (49088-9338)
PHONE.................................269 626-8891
Robert M Gibson, *President*
EMP: 25 **EST:** 2013
SALES (est): 104.6K **Privately Held**
SIC: 2011 Meat by-products from meat slaughtered on site

Scottville
Mason County

(G-14508)
BAUER SHEET METAL & FABG INC
703 W 1st St (49454-9640)
PHONE.................................231 757-4993
Ronald Sejat, *Branch Mgr*
EMP: 4
SALES (est): 465K
SALES (corp-wide): 8.8MM **Privately Held**
SIC: 3444 Sheet metal specialties, not stamped
PA: Bauer Sheet Metal & Fabricating, Inc.
1550 Evanston Ave
Muskegon MI 49442
231 773-3244

(G-14509)
KELDER LLC
979 W 1st St (49454-8520)
P.O. Box 83 (49454-0083)
PHONE.................................231 757-3000
Jeff Barnett, *President*
EMP: 4
SALES (est): 421.9K **Privately Held**
SIC: 3272 Concrete structural support & building material

(G-14510)
PADDLESPORTS WAREHOUSE INC
467 W Us Highway 10 31 (49454-9301)
PHONE.................................231 757-9051
Edward Spyker, *President*
◆ **EMP:** 7
SALES (est): 1.2MM **Privately Held**
SIC: 5091 2499 5551 Canoes; oars & paddles, wood; canoe & kayak dealers

(G-14511)
WOLF LOG HOME BUILDINGS
Also Called: Ws Woodworks
880 W Us Highway 10 31 (49454-9303)
PHONE.................................231 757-7000
Phil Wolf, *Partner*
EMP: 3
SALES (est): 200K **Privately Held**
SIC: 2452 Log cabins, prefabricated, wood

Sears
Osceola County

(G-14512)
MORGAN COMPOSTING INC (PA)
Also Called: Compassionate Soils
4353 Us Highway 10 (49679-8706)
PHONE.................................231 734-2451
Brad Morgan, *President*
Jeremie Morgan, *Principal*
Justin Morgan, *Vice Pres*
Nickole Taylor, *Admin Asst*
EMP: 2

GEOGRAPHIC SECTION

SALES: 9.5MM **Privately Held**
WEB: www.morgancomposting.com
SIC: 2875 Compost; potting soil, mixed

(G-14513)
MORGAN COMPOSTING INC
Also Called: Morgan Farm and Gardens
4281 Us Highway 10 (49679-8706)
PHONE..................................231 734-2790
Brad Morgan, *President*
EMP: 38
SALES (corp-wide): 9.5MM **Privately Held**
WEB: www.morgancomposting.com
SIC: 2875 Compost; potting soil, mixed
PA: Morgan Composting, Inc.
4353 Us Highway 10
Sears MI 49679
231 734-2451

Sebewaing
Huron County

(G-14514)
DARWIN SNELLER
8677 Kilmanagh Rd (48759-9725)
PHONE..................................989 977-3718
Darwin Sneller, *Owner*
Roger Gremel, *Owner*
EMP: 4 **EST:** 1983
SALES (est): 154.8K **Privately Held**
SIC: 2046 2063 2051 2048 Wet corn milling; granulated sugar from sugar beets; bread, all types (white, wheat, rye, etc); fresh or frozen; alfalfa or alfalfa meal, prepared as animal feed; soybeans

(G-14515)
GREAT LAKES PALLET INC
714 N Beck St (48759-1120)
P.O. Box 537 (48759-0537)
PHONE..................................989 883-9220
Renda Joworski, *President*
EMP: 5
SQ FT: 4,000
SALES: 500K **Privately Held**
SIC: 2448 Pallets, wood

(G-14516)
MICHIGAN SUGAR COMPANY
763 N Beck St (48759-1119)
P.O. Box 626 (48759-0626)
PHONE..................................989 883-3200
Kelly Scheffler, *Plant Mgr*
Gary Hamlin, *Branch Mgr*
Mike Matthews, *Maintence Staff*
EMP: 80
SQ FT: 375,000
SALES (corp-wide): 600MM **Privately Held**
SIC: 2063 2061 Beet sugar; raw cane sugar
PA: Michigan Sugar Company
122 Uptown Dr Unit 300
Bay City MI 48708
989 686-0161

(G-14517)
NITZ VALVE HARDWARE INC
8610 Unionville Rd (48759-9568)
P.O. Box 654 (48759-0654)
PHONE..................................989 883-9500
Vincent Nitz, *President*
James Leppek, *Sales Staff*
EMP: 11
SQ FT: 3,500
SALES (est): 1.7MM **Privately Held**
SIC: 3494 Valves & pipe fittings

(G-14518)
SEBEWAING CONCRETE PDTS INC
8552 Unionville Rd (48759-9568)
PHONE..................................989 883-3860
Terry Wissner, *President*
Christina Wissner, *Corp Secy*
Scott Wissner, *Vice Pres*
EMP: 11
SQ FT: 3,500
SALES (est): 1.4MM **Privately Held**
SIC: 3273 Ready-mixed concrete

(G-14519)
SEBEWAING TOOL AND ENGRG CO
Also Called: Sebewaing Flow Control
415 Union St (48759-1054)
P.O. Box 685 (48759-0685)
PHONE..................................989 883-2000
Shawn Marshall, *President*
Dan Healey, *Mfg Mgr*
◆ **EMP:** 40
SQ FT: 40,000
SALES: 4.9MM **Privately Held**
WEB: www.sebewaingtool.com
SIC: 3599 Machine shop, jobbing & repair

(G-14520)
TRUCKSFORSALECOM
Also Called: Ellenbaum Truck Sales
8440 Unionville Rd (48759-9567)
PHONE..................................989 883-3382
John Elenbaum, *President*
John Ellenbaum, *Owner*
Rhonda Ellenbaum, *Vice Pres*
▼ **EMP:** 8
SALES (est): 1.4MM **Privately Held**
WEB: www.trucksforsale.com
SIC: 3596 5521 Truck (motor vehicle) scales; used car dealers

(G-14521)
VENTURE TOOL & METALIZING
42 E Main St (48759-1555)
PHONE..................................989 883-9121
John F Sigmund, *Owner*
EMP: 5
SQ FT: 15,000
SALES: 150K **Privately Held**
SIC: 3599 Machine shop, jobbing & repair

Seney
Schoolcraft County

(G-14522)
SUPERIOR COUNTRY WOOD TRUSS
Railroad St (49883)
P.O. Box 35 (49883-0035)
PHONE..................................906 499-3354
P J Kosta, *Manager*
EMP: 7
SALES (corp-wide): 654K **Privately Held**
SIC: 2439 Trusses, except roof: laminated lumber; trusses, wooden roof
PA: Superior Country Wood Truss, Inc.
1207 Morrison St
Germfask MI

Shelby
Oceana County

(G-14523)
BECKMAN BROTHERS INC
3455 W Baker Rd (49455)
P.O. Box 268 (49455-0268)
PHONE..................................231 861-2031
Robert Beckman, *President*
EMP: 20 **EST:** 1946
SALES (est): 2.8MM **Privately Held**
WEB: www.beckmanbros.com
SIC: 3273 Ready-mixed concrete

(G-14524)
CHERRY CENTRAL COOPERATIVE INC
Also Called: Oceana Foods
168 Lincoln St (49455-1277)
P.O. Box 156 (49455-0156)
PHONE..................................231 861-2141
Carl Schuchardt, *QC Mgr*
Jeff Tucker, *Branch Mgr*
EMP: 85
SALES (corp-wide): 133MM **Privately Held**
WEB: www.cherrycentral.com
SIC: 2033 2034 Fruits: packaged in cans, jars, etc.; fruit pie mixes & fillings: packaged in cans, jars, etc.; fruit juices: packaged in cans, jars, etc.; dehydrated fruits, vegetables, soups
PA: Cherry Central Cooperative, Inc.
1771 N Us 31 S
Traverse City MI 49685
231 946-1860

(G-14525)
GEORGE KOTZIAN
Also Called: Kotzian Ironworks
1461 S 44th Ave (49455-9226)
PHONE..................................231 861-6520
George Kotzian, *Owner*
Joyce Kotzian, *Principal*
Brett Kotzian, *Vice Pres*
EMP: 4
SQ FT: 4,000
SALES (est): 281.8K **Privately Held**
SIC: 3541 Milling machines

(G-14526)
JARVIS SAW MILL INC
Also Called: Jarvis Sawmill
1570 S 112th Ave (49455-9782)
PHONE..................................231 861-2078
Robert Mayo, *President*
EMP: 8 **EST:** 1960
SQ FT: 2,000
SALES: 1MM **Privately Held**
SIC: 2448 2426 Pallets, wood; furniture stock & parts, hardwood

(G-14527)
JERSHON INC
980 Industrial Park Dr (49455-8234)
P.O. Box 337 (49455-0337)
PHONE..................................231 861-2900
Rodney Kurzer, *President*
EMP: 7
SALES (est): 1.1MM **Privately Held**
WEB: www.jershon.com
SIC: 3499 Ladder assemblies, combination workstand: metal

(G-14528)
KELLEY LABORATORIES INC
Also Called: Beechem Labs
617 Industrial Park Dr (49455-9584)
P.O. Box 188 (49455-0188)
PHONE..................................231 861-6257
Larry P Kelley, *President*
EMP: 15 **EST:** 1939
SQ FT: 3,900
SALES (est): 1MM **Privately Held**
WEB: www.rippoffs.com
SIC: 2869 2851 Solvents, organic; lacquers, varnishes, enamels & other coatings

(G-14529)
KELLEY MACHINING INC
647 Industrial Park Dr (49455-9584)
P.O. Box 309 (49455-0309)
PHONE..................................231 861-0951
Art Kelley, *President*
Chad Kelley, *Vice Pres*
Rick Hartley,
EMP: 8
SQ FT: 6,000
SALES (est): 676.4K **Privately Held**
WEB: www.kelleymachining.com
SIC: 3599 Machine shop, jobbing & repair

(G-14530)
KOTZIAN TOOL INC
6971 W Shelby Rd (49455-9385)
PHONE..................................231 861-5377
Brett Kotzian, *President*
Joyce Kotzian, *Corp Secy*
Mike Usiak, *Vice Pres*
EMP: 10
SQ FT: 5,000
SALES (est): 600K **Privately Held**
SIC: 3599 Custom machinery

(G-14531)
OCEANA FOODS INC
168 Lincoln St (49455-1277)
P.O. Box 156 (49455-0156)
PHONE..................................231 861-2141
Richard Bogard, *Principal*
Jeff Tucker, *Site Mgr*
Mark McAuliffe, *Buyer*
Carrie Tanner, *Manager*
▲ **EMP:** 38 **EST:** 1989
SALES (est): 7.1MM **Privately Held**
WEB: www.lakesidefoods.com
SIC: 2033 Fruits: packaged in cans, jars, etc.

(G-14532)
OCEANA FOREST PRODUCTS INC
2033 Loop Rd (49455-9751)
PHONE..................................231 861-6115
Steven Aslakson, *President*
EMP: 7
SALES: 500K **Privately Held**
SIC: 2421 Sawmills & planing mills, general

(G-14533)
PACE GRINDING INC
8647 W Shelby Rd (49455-8043)
PHONE..................................231 861-0448
Ron Klein, *President*
Dennis Klein, *Vice Pres*
EMP: 3
SQ FT: 5,000
SALES (est): 331K **Privately Held**
SIC: 3545 Cutting tools for machine tools

(G-14534)
PETERSON FARMS INC
3104 W Baseline Rd (49455-9633)
P.O. Box 115 (49455-0115)
PHONE..................................231 861-6333
Aaron L Peterson, *CEO*
Earl L Peterson, *Ch of Bd*
Lorraine Odle Dp, *President*
Linda A Peterson, *Corp Secy*
Sarah M Peterson-Schlkebir, *Vice Pres*
◆ **EMP:** 400
SQ FT: 800,000
SALES (est): 153.7MM **Privately Held**
SIC: 2037 0723 2033 Fruits, quick frozen & cold pack (frozen); fruit (fresh) packing services; fruit juices: fresh

(G-14535)
SCHMIEDING SAW MILL INC
Also Called: Schmieding Sawmill
1820 S 124th Ave (49455-9765)
PHONE..................................231 861-4189
Richard A Schmieding, *Partner*
David A Schmieding, *Partner*
Ilene Schmieding, *Partner*
EMP: 3
SQ FT: 6,000
SALES: 450K **Privately Held**
SIC: 2448 Pallets, wood; skids, wood

(G-14536)
SILVER STREET INCORPORATED
Also Called: Mediatechnologies
892 Industrial Park Dr (49455-8235)
P.O. Box 159 (49455-0159)
PHONE..................................231 861-2194
Craig Hardy, *President*
Randy Seaver, *Corp Secy*
Chris Flahive, *Engineer*
Sarah Hardy, *CFO*
Jamie Ritter, *Marketing Staff*
▲ **EMP:** 45 **EST:** 1979
SQ FT: 30,000
SALES (est): 10MM **Privately Held**
SIC: 2499 2521 Decorative wood & woodwork; wood office furniture

(G-14537)
WILL LENT HORSESHOE CO
5800 W Woodrow Rd (49455-8052)
PHONE..................................231 861-5033
William Lent, *Owner*
EMP: 3
SALES: 250K **Privately Held**
WEB: www.willlent.com
SIC: 3462 Horseshoes

Shelby Township
Macomb County

(G-14538)
ACCU-RITE INDUSTRIES LLC (PA)
51047 Oro Dr (48315-2912)
PHONE..................................586 247-0060

Shelby Township - Macomb County (G-14539)   GEOGRAPHIC SECTION

Kirko Mickovski, *President*
John Loudon, *Vice Pres*
Craig Hawkins, *Program Mgr*
Ray Vanlith, *Program Mgr*
EMP: 30
SQ FT: 8,500
SALES (est): 4.1MM **Privately Held**
WEB: www.accu-rite.com
SIC: 3549 Metalworking machinery

(G-14539)
ACCU-TECH MANUFACTURING INC
51559 Oro Dr (48315-2932)
PHONE......................586 532-4000
Louis Rahhal, *President*
Christy Mc Keogh, *Vice Pres*
Theodore Wiley, *Treasurer*
EMP: 25
SQ FT: 10,000
SALES (est): 3.9MM **Privately Held**
SIC: 3599 Machine shop, jobbing & repair

(G-14540)
ACG SERVICES INC
51512 Schoenherr Rd (48315-2754)
PHONE......................586 232-4698
Nancy Marsack, *Principal*
EMP: 4
SALES (est): 580.5K **Privately Held**
SIC: 3545 3544 Collets (machine tool accessories); subpresses, metalworking

(G-14541)
ACUMEN TECHNOLOGIES INC
51445 Celeste (48315-2905)
PHONE......................586 566-8600
Clifford S Willner, *President*
Cliff Willner, *President*
Russell Dibbel, *Vice Pres*
EMP: 12
SQ FT: 11,000
SALES (est): 3.4MM **Privately Held**
WEB: www.acumen-tech.com
SIC: 3569 5085 Lubrication equipment, industrial; industrial supplies

(G-14542)
ADVANCE CYLINDER PRODUCTS LLC
50300 Rizzo Dr (48315-3251)
PHONE......................586 991-2445
Michael Simmons,
Richard Wirsing,
Rossan Wolfbaur,
EMP: 3
SALES (est): 372.3K **Privately Held**
WEB: www.advancedinduction.com
SIC: 3612 Transformers, except electric

(G-14543)
AHD LLC
50649 Central Indus Dr (48315-3119)
PHONE......................586 922-6511
Vishal Bhagat,
EMP: 6
SALES (est): 395.5K **Privately Held**
SIC: 3511 Hydraulic turbine generator set units, complete

(G-14544)
ALCOCK PRINTING INC
Also Called: American Speedy Printing
46723 Van Dyke Ave (48317-4376)
PHONE......................586 731-4366
Michael Alcock, *President*
Holly Alcock, *Vice Pres*
EMP: 3
SQ FT: 1,600
SALES (est): 476.8K **Privately Held**
SIC: 2752 Commercial printing, offset

(G-14545)
ALL SEASON ENCLOSURES
2760 Marissa Way (48316-1297)
PHONE......................248 650-8020
Robert J Pelzel, *Executive Asst*
EMP: 8
SALES (est): 882.8K **Privately Held**
SIC: 3448 Screen enclosures

(G-14546)
ANDROID INDUSTRIES-WIXOM LLC
50150 Ryan Rd (48317-1035)
PHONE......................248 255-5434
Greg Nichols, *Branch Mgr*
EMP: 10
SALES (corp-wide): 559.5MM **Privately Held**
SIC: 3714 Motor vehicle parts & accessories
HQ: Android Industries-Wixom Llc
4444 W Maple Dr
Auburn Hills MI 48326
248 732-0000

(G-14547)
ANTENNA TECHNOLOGIES INC
56716 Mound Rd (48316-4942)
PHONE......................586 697-5626
Thomas N Mueller, *President*
▲ **EMP:** 3
SQ FT: 2,000
SALES (est): 442.8K **Privately Held**
SIC: 3663 Antennas, transmitting & communications

(G-14548)
ARCHITECTURAL DESIGN WDWRK INC
52976 Van Dyke Ave (48316-3548)
PHONE......................586 726-9050
Robert J Roose, *President*
EMP: 3
SQ FT: 6,000
SALES (est): 625.8K **Privately Held**
WEB: www.adwonline.net
SIC: 5211 1751 2431 Doors, wood or metal, except storm; window & door (prefabricated) installation; interior & ornamental woodwork & trim

(G-14549)
ARISTO-COTE INC
11655 Park Ct (48315-3109)
PHONE......................586 447-9049
EMP: 70 **Privately Held**
SIC: 3479 Painting, coating & hot dipping
PA: Aristo-Cote, Inc.
24951 Henry B Joy Blvd
Harrison Township MI 48045

(G-14550)
ATLANTIC PRECISION PDTS INC
51234 Filomena Dr (48315-2942)
PHONE......................586 532-9420
Rosa Slongo, *President*
Norma Gorski, *Vice Pres*
Jennifer Kurtzhals, *QC Mgr*
Jennifer Morris, *QC Mgr*
Rob Pryomski, *Engineer*
EMP: 15
SALES (est): 5.4MM **Privately Held**
SIC: 3089 1446 3021 Molding primary plastic; molding sand mining; shoes, rubber or plastic molded to fabric

(G-14551)
AVON MACHINING LLC
Also Called: Avon Gear
11968 Investment Dr (48315-1794)
PHONE......................586 884-2200
Matt Korth, *President*
Mike Nowinski, *Maint Spvr*
Richard Kitchen, *Engineer*
Chad Fietsam, *CFO*
▲ **EMP:** 100
SQ FT: 110,000
SALES: 22MM
SALES (corp-wide): 178.1MM **Privately Held**
WEB: www.agcoga.com
SIC: 3462 3011 3465 Gears, forged steel; truck or bus inner tubes; body parts, automobile: stamped metal
PA: Speyside Equity Fund I Lp
430 E 86th St
New York NY 10028
212 994-0308

(G-14552)
AVON MACHINING HOLDINGS INC
11968 Investment Dr (48315-1794)
PHONE......................586 884-2200

Chad Fietsam, *CEO*
Matt Korth, *President*
EMP: 125
SQ FT: 100,000
SALES: 35MM
SALES (corp-wide): 178.1MM **Privately Held**
SIC: 6719 3462 3011 3465 Investment holding companies, except banks; gears, forged steel; truck or bus inner tubes; body parts, automobile: stamped metal
PA: Speyside Equity Fund I Lp
430 E 86th St
New York NY 10028
212 994-0308

(G-14553)
B & M BENDING & FORGING INC
47601 Shelby Rd (48317-3164)
PHONE......................586 731-3332
Ken Brooks, *President*
Charles Moll, *Vice Pres*
EMP: 3
SQ FT: 15,000
SALES: 1.4MM **Privately Held**
SIC: 3542 Bending machines

(G-14554)
B T I INDUSTRIES
49820 Oakland Dr (48315-3943)
PHONE......................586 532-8411
Edward Bohmier, *Principal*
Samantha Bohmier, *Accounts Mgr*
EMP: 15
SALES (est): 1.7MM **Privately Held**
SIC: 3999 Barber & beauty shop equipment

(G-14555)
BROWN-CAMPBELL COMPANY (PA)
Also Called: Brown-Campbell Steel
11800 Investment Dr (48315-1794)
PHONE......................586 884-2180
John D Campbell Sr, *Ch of Bd*
Murdoch Campbell, *President*
Scott Triner, *Plant Mgr*
Tracy Garrett, *Purch Mgr*
Kevin Collins, *Engineer*
◆ **EMP:** 10 **EST:** 1954
SALES (est): 65.3MM **Privately Held**
WEB: www.brown-campbell.com
SIC: 5051 3446 Steel; stairs, staircases, stair treads: prefabricated metal

(G-14556)
C H INDUSTRIES INC
Also Called: C.H. Industries
50699 Central Indus Dr (48315-3119)
PHONE......................586 997-1717
Ryan Haas, *Mng Member*
Sue Hibberd,
EMP: 10
SQ FT: 18,000
SALES: 1.3MM **Privately Held**
WEB: www.chindustries.net
SIC: 3721 Aircraft

(G-14557)
CARLO JOHN INC
Also Called: National Asphalt Products
12345 23 Mile Rd (48315-2619)
PHONE......................586 254-3800
Brian Stlouis, *Branch Mgr*
EMP: 30
SALES (corp-wide): 24.3MM **Privately Held**
WEB: www.carlocompanies.com
SIC: 2951 Asphalt paving mixtures & blocks
PA: Carlo John Inc
20848 Hall Rd
Clinton Township MI 48038

(G-14558)
CBS TOOL INC
51601 Oro Dr (48315-2934)
PHONE......................586 566-5945
Bruce Dettloff, *President*
Robert Legato, *Vice Pres*
EMP: 10 **EST:** 1998
SQ FT: 10,000
SALES: 1.8MM **Privately Held**
SIC: 3541 3544 Machine tools, metal cutting type; special dies, tools, jigs & fixtures

(G-14559)
CENTURY PLASTICS LLC (DH)
Also Called: Cie USA
15030 23 Mile Rd (48315-3010)
PHONE......................586 566-3900
Joe Carroll, *President*
Mark Simon, *COO*
Brian Enjaian, *CFO*
Jeff Reid, *Sales Executive*
Bill Hoover, *Manager*
▲ **EMP:** 111
SQ FT: 14,000
SALES (est): 77.9MM
SALES (corp-wide): 118.8MM **Privately Held**
WEB: www.centuryplastics.net
SIC: 3089 Injection molding of plastics

(G-14560)
CENTURY PLASTICS INC
15030 23 Mile Rd (48315-3010)
PHONE......................586 566-3900
Shirley Frank, *President*
Steve Hensley, *Plant Mgr*
Christopher Wolber, *Warehouse Mgr*
Laura Franklin, *QC Mgr*
Kevin Curtis, *Engineer*
EMP: 8 **EST:** 2015
SALES (est): 184.1K **Privately Held**
SIC: 2821 Molding compounds, plastics

(G-14561)
CHAMPION LABORATORIES INC
51180 Celeste (48315-2938)
PHONE......................586 247-9044
John Evans, *President*
EMP: 60
SALES (corp-wide): 553.7MM **Privately Held**
WEB: www.champlabs.com
SIC: 3714 Filters: oil, fuel & air, motor vehicle
HQ: Champion Laboratories, Inc.
200 S 4th St
Albion IL 62806
618 445-6011

(G-14562)
CINCINNATI TYROLIT INC
4636 Regency Dr (48316-1533)
PHONE......................513 458-8121
Fritz Corradi, *President*
▲ **EMP:** 190
SQ FT: 225,000
SALES (est): 15.1MM
SALES (corp-wide): 797.8MM **Privately Held**
SIC: 3291 Wheels, grinding: artificial
PA: Tyrolit - Schleifmittelwerke Swarovski K.G.
SwarovskistraBe 33
Schwaz 6130
524 260-60

(G-14563)
CLARK BROTHERS INSTRUMENT CO
56680 Mound Rd (48316-4906)
PHONE......................586 781-7000
Thomas F Wright Sr, *President*
Thomas F Wright Jr, *Vice Pres*
▲ **EMP:** 18
SQ FT: 17,600
SALES (est): 4.8MM **Privately Held**
WEB: www.clarkbrothers.net
SIC: 3824 Vehicle instruments

(G-14564)
COLONIAL PLASTICS INCORPORATED
Also Called: Colonial Group
51734 Filomena Dr (48315-2948)
PHONE......................586 469-4944
Cathy Roberts, *President*
EMP: 36
SQ FT: 46,000
SALES (est): 10.3MM **Privately Held**
SIC: 3089 Injection molding of plastics

GEOGRAPHIC SECTION

Shelby Township - Macomb County (G-14593)

(G-14565)
COMPLETE HOME ADV MEDIA/PROMO
Also Called: Rabaut Printing Co
15018 Technology Dr (48315-3950)
PHONE....................586 254-9555
Mark B Rabaut, *President*
Claudia Rabaut, *Corp Secy*
EMP: 5 **EST:** 1981
SQ FT: 4,000
SALES: 800K **Privately Held**
SIC: 2752 Commercial printing, offset

(G-14566)
CONNECT WITH US LLC
4311 Kingmont Dr (48317-1139)
PHONE....................586 262-4359
Greg Newman, *CEO*
Robert Santoro, *Partner*
Gregory L Newman, *Administration*
EMP: 20
SALES: 1.7MM **Privately Held**
SIC: 3679 Harness assemblies for electronic use: wire or cable

(G-14567)
CONTINENTAL PLASTICS CO
50900 Birch Rd (48315-3205)
PHONE....................586 294-4600
Joan Luckino, *Ch of Bd*
Anthony Catenacci, *President*
Russell Thomas, *COO*
Pat Luckino, *Human Res Dir*
Frances Luckino Catenacci, *Admin Sec*
▲ **EMP:** 520 **EST:** 1957
SQ FT: 206,000
SALES (est): 60.4MM **Privately Held**
WEB: www.contplastics.com
SIC: 3052 Automobile hose, plastic

(G-14568)
COOK SIGN PLUS
48534 Van Dyke Ave (48317-3266)
PHONE....................586 254-7000
Dan Cook, *President*
EMP: 5
SALES: 300K **Privately Held**
SIC: 3993 Signs, not made in custom sign painting shops

(G-14569)
COSWORTH LLC
52685 Shelby Pkwy (48315-1778)
PHONE....................586 353-5403
Kenneth Gembel, *Branch Mgr*
EMP: 20
SALES (corp-wide): 71.1MM **Privately Held**
SIC: 3519 Internal combustion engines
HQ: Cosworth, Llc
  5355 W 86th St
  Indianapolis IN 46268
  844 278-6941

(G-14570)
CRAFT INDUSTRIES INC
13231 23 Mile Rd (48315-2713)
PHONE....................586 726-4300
Thomas J Carter, *President*
Stefan Wanczyk, *Vice Pres*
EMP: 700
SQ FT: 62,640
SALES (est): 72.5MM
SALES (corp-wide): 565.7MM **Privately Held**
SIC: 3548 3569 3544 3541 Resistance welders, electric; assembly machines, non-metalworking; special dies, tools, jigs & fixtures; machine tools, metal cutting type
PA: Utica Enterprises, Inc.
  5750 New King Dr Ste 200
  Troy MI 48098
  586 726-4300

(G-14571)
CRYSTAL LAKE APARTMENTS FAMILY (PA)
2001 Crystal Lake Dr (48316-2818)
PHONE....................586 731-3500
Antonio Lo Chirco, *Partner*
Michael Lo Chirco, *General Ptnr*
▲ **EMP:** 35
SQ FT: 1,200

(G-14572)
DAVIS GIRLS
54421 Iroquois Ln (48315-1174)
PHONE....................586 781-6865
Gwendolyn Zollner, *Partner*
EMP: 3
SALES (est): 209.1K **Privately Held**
SIC: 2389 Apparel & accessories

(G-14573)
DDKS INDUSTRIES LLC
14954 Technology Dr (48315-3949)
PHONE....................586 323-5909
David Kelley, *General Mgr*
Kimberly S Kelley, *Mng Member*
▲ **EMP:** 6
SQ FT: 5,500
SALES (est): 248K **Privately Held**
WEB: www.ddksindustries.com
SIC: 3594 3599 Fluid power pumps & motors; crankshafts & camshafts, machining

(G-14574)
DELAND MANUFACTURING INC
50674 Central Indus Dr (48315-3116)
PHONE....................586 323-2350
Dennis L Wygocki, *President*
Diane J Wygocki, *Treasurer*
Cindy Ballard, *Manager*
EMP: 20 **EST:** 1966
SQ FT: 35,500
SALES (est): 3.4MM **Privately Held**
SIC: 3599 3544 Machine shop, jobbing & repair; special dies, tools, jigs & fixtures

(G-14575)
DIESEL PERFORMANCE PRODUCTS
Also Called: K A L Enterprises
7459 Flickinger Dr (48317-2333)
PHONE....................586 726-7478
Keith Long, *President*
Mary Long, *Vice Pres*
EMP: 8 **EST:** 2000
SALES (est): 1.1MM **Privately Held**
SIC: 3714 Motor vehicle parts & accessories

(G-14576)
DIGITAL FINISHING CORP
14050 Simone Dr (48315-3235)
PHONE....................586 427-6003
Norman Lin, *President*
Doug Stankey, *General Mgr*
▲ **EMP:** 4
SALES (est): 405.8K **Privately Held**
SIC: 3579 Binding machines, plastic & adhesive

(G-14577)
DIGITAL PRINTING & GRAPHICS
50711 Wing Dr (48315-3269)
PHONE....................586 566-9499
Sheldon Wildeman, *Owner*
EMP: 4
SQ FT: 5,000
SALES (est): 388.7K **Privately Held**
WEB: www.dpgprinting.com
SIC: 2752 Commercial printing, offset

(G-14578)
DIGITAL PRINTING SOLUTIONS LLC
48688 Eagle Butte Ct (48315-4268)
PHONE....................586 566-4910
Larry Schehr Sr, *Principal*
EMP: 4
SALES (est): 340.5K **Privately Held**
SIC: 2752 Commercial printing, lithographic

(G-14579)
DIRKSEN SCREW PRODUCTS CO (PA)
14490 23 Mile Rd (48315-2916)
PHONE....................586 247-5400
Clifford S Dirksen, *CEO*
Mike Potter, *Plant Mgr*
Bruce Weston, *Plant Mgr*
Peter Cicci, *QC Mgr*
Martin Lewis, *Engineer*
▲ **EMP:** 50 **EST:** 1939
SQ FT: 80,000
SALES (est): 21.1MM **Privately Held**
WEB: www.dirksenscrew.com
SIC: 3452 3451 3356 Bolts, nuts, rivets & washers; screw machine products; non-ferrous rolling & drawing

(G-14580)
DUBETSKY K9 ACADEMY LLC
50699 Central Indus Dr (48315-3119)
PHONE....................586 997-1717
Dan T Moore,
Bryan Dubetsky,
EMP: 11
SALES (est): 369.2K **Privately Held**
SIC: 3544 Special dies, tools, jigs & fixtures

(G-14581)
DUGGAN MANUFACTURING LLC
50150 Ryan Rd (48317-1028)
PHONE....................586 254-7400
Tony Pinho, *President*
Roger Hill, *Prdtn Mgr*
Brian Brody, *Program Mgr*
Mark Burrows, *Manager*
Gary Shenkosky, *Manager*
▼ **EMP:** 150
SQ FT: 70,000
SALES (est): 35.4MM **Privately Held**
SIC: 3469 Stamping metal for the trade

(G-14582)
DUGGANS LIMITED LLC
50150 Ryan Rd Ste 15 (48317-1035)
PHONE....................586 254-7400
Anthony Pinho,
EMP: 13 **EST:** 2000
SQ FT: 7,000
SALES (est): 1.1MM **Privately Held**
SIC: 3469 Metal stampings

(G-14583)
DYNAMITE MACHINING INC
51149 Filomena Dr (48315-2940)
PHONE....................586 247-8230
Scott R Laskowski, *President*
EMP: 8
SQ FT: 10,000
SALES (est): 1MM **Privately Held**
SIC: 3599 Machine shop, jobbing & repair

(G-14584)
E D M CUT-RITE INC
51445 Oro Dr (48315-2932)
PHONE....................586 566-0100
Craig Sizemore, *President*
EMP: 19
SQ FT: 8,300
SALES (est): 3.4MM **Privately Held**
SIC: 3599 Electrical discharge machining (EDM); machine shop, jobbing & repair

(G-14585)
EAGLE MANUFACTURING CORP
Also Called: Eaglematic
52113 Shelby Pkwy (48315-1778)
PHONE....................586 323-0303
Brent Short, *President*
EMP: 18 **EST:** 1960
SQ FT: 30,000
SALES (est): 3.7MM **Privately Held**
SIC: 3089 Injection molding of plastics

(G-14586)
ELITE MOLD & ENGINEERING INC
Also Called: Elite Medical Molding
51548 Filomena Dr (48315-2946)
PHONE....................586 873-1770
Joseph Mandeville, *President*
Kristen Chase, *Office Mgr*
Mark Fletcher, *Manager*
Eugene McCaffrey, *Manager*
EMP: 25
SQ FT: 17,400
SALES (est): 5.4MM **Privately Held**
WEB: www.elitemold.com
SIC: 3544 Dies, plastics forming; industrial molds

(G-14587)
ELITE PLASTIC PRODUCTS INC
51354 Filomena Dr (48315-2944)
PHONE....................586 247-5800
Robert Mandeville, *President*
Joseph Mandeville, *Vice Pres*
Scott Downey, *Purch Agent*
EMP: 30
SQ FT: 24,000
SALES (est): 9.7MM **Privately Held**
WEB: www.teameliteonline.com
SIC: 3089 3714 Injection molding of plastics; motor vehicle parts & accessories

(G-14588)
ENTERPRISE PLASTICS LLC
51354 Filomena Dr (48315-2944)
PHONE....................586 665-1030
Michael Flores, *CEO*
Salvatore Cassisi, *President*
EMP: 15 **EST:** 1999
SQ FT: 36,000
SALES (est): 400K **Privately Held**
SIC: 3089 Injection molded finished plastic products

(G-14589)
EPIC EQUIPMENT & ENGRG INC
52301 Shelby Pkwy (48315-1778)
PHONE....................586 314-0020
Mark Milewicz, *President*
Steve Wilkins, *Vice Pres*
Eric Szlachtowicz, *Plant Mgr*
Ken Herzog, *Design Engr*
David Gardiner, *Controller*
EMP: 85
SQ FT: 50,000
SALES (est): 23.3MM
SALES (corp-wide): 32.8MM **Privately Held**
SIC: 3599 Custom machinery
PA: Bpg International Finance Co Llc
  4760 Fulton St E Ste 201
  Ada MI 49301
  616 855-1480

(G-14590)
EPOXY PRO FLR CTNGS RSTORATION
51947 Filomena Dr (48315-2950)
PHONE....................248 990-8890
Kevin O'Connor, *Partner*
EMP: 5
SALES (est): 345.9K **Privately Held**
SIC: 2851 Epoxy coatings

(G-14591)
FABRICATIONS UNLIMITED INC (PA)
45757 Cornwall St (48317-4709)
PHONE....................313 567-9616
Lee Perrell, *President*
Fred Martin, *Vice Pres*
Patricia Perrell, *Admin Sec*
EMP: 7
SALES (est): 1.2MM **Privately Held**
SIC: 3443 Tanks, standard or custom fabricated: metal plate

(G-14592)
FEC INC
Also Called: FEC Automation Systems
51341 Celeste (48315-2943)
PHONE....................586 580-2622
Ronald Jaeger, *President*
Benny La Rocca, *Managing Dir*
Paul Gomez, *Engineer*
Brad Gomez, *Info Tech Mgr*
▲ **EMP:** 30 **EST:** 1983
SQ FT: 43,000
SALES (est): 9.6MM **Privately Held**
WEB: www.fec-usa.com
SIC: 3569 Assembly machines, non-metalworking

(G-14593)
FIGLAN WELDING
7548 22 Mile Rd (48317-2308)
PHONE....................586 739-6837
Catheline Figlan, *Partner*
Alan Figlan, *Partner*
EMP: 3
SALES (est): 367.4K **Privately Held**
SIC: 7692 Welding repair

Shelby Township - Macomb County (G-14594)

(G-14594)
FLUE SENTINEL LLC
8123 Janis St (48317-5315)
PHONE...................586 739-4373
EMP: 6
SALES (est): 527.7K
SALES (corp-wide): 1.2B **Privately Held**
SIC: 3429 Mfg Electric Fireplace Damper
HQ: Field Controls, L.L.C.
2630 Airport Rd
Kinston NC 28504
252 208-7300

(G-14595)
G&G INDUSTRIES INC
50665 Corporate Dr (48315-3100)
PHONE...................586 726-6000
Bruce M Gantner, *President*
Henry Opie, *General Mgr*
Craig Gantner, *Vice Pres*
Richard Flavell, *Plant Mgr*
Kurt Ortwein, *Info Tech Mgr*
▲ **EMP:** 47
SQ FT: 18,000
SALES (est): 8MM **Privately Held**
WEB: www.gandgindustries.com
SIC: 7532 3545 3429 Upholstery & trim shop, automotive; precision measuring tools; manufactured hardware (general)

(G-14596)
GLOBAL ENGINEERING INC
50685 Rizzo Dr (48315-3227)
PHONE...................586 566-0423
Mark Koerner, *President*
Bernd Koerner, *Vice Pres*
Barry York, *Vice Pres*
EMP: 23
SQ FT: 23,000
SALES (est): 4.2MM **Privately Held**
WEB: www.globaleng.com
SIC: 3545 3544 Machine tool accessories; special dies, tools, jigs & fixtures

(G-14597)
GRAPHIC CMMNCTIONS DESIGN SVCS
Also Called: Graphic Communications
50671 Wing Dr (48315-3263)
PHONE...................586 566-5200
Dennis A Wrobleski, *President*
EMP: 3 EST: 1980
SQ FT: 2,400
SALES (est): 344.2K **Privately Held**
WEB: www.graphiccom.com
SIC: 3993 Signs & advertising specialties

(G-14598)
GREAT HARVEST BREAD CO
48923 Hayes Rd (48315-4400)
PHONE...................586 566-9500
Steve Troszak, *Owner*
EMP: 5
SALES (est): 169.7K **Privately Held**
SIC: 5461 2051 Bread; bread, cake & related products

(G-14599)
HARRISON STEEL LLC
50390 Utica Dr (48315-3290)
PHONE...................586 247-1230
John Chirikas,
Mark Jacobs,
Rick Nicolay,
EMP: 6
SQ FT: 75,000
SALES (est): 658.4K **Privately Held**
SIC: 3312 5051 Slabs, steel; steel

(G-14600)
HI-TECH FURNACE SYSTEMS INC
13179 W Star Dr (48315-2736)
PHONE...................586 566-0600
Robert Kornfeld, *President*
Richard Mueller, *Vice Pres*
▲ **EMP:** 13
SQ FT: 11,000
SALES (est): 4.1MM **Privately Held**
WEB: www.hi-techfurnace.com
SIC: 3567 8711 Heating units & devices, industrial: electric; engineering services

(G-14601)
HUNTLER INDUSTRIES INC
Also Called: Visionary Landscaping
51532 Schoenherr Rd (48315-2727)
PHONE...................586 566-7684
Kipp Rammler, *President*
Steve Dhondt, *Vice Pres*
EMP: 27
SQ FT: 4,500
SALES (est): 3.8MM **Privately Held**
SIC: 2891 Sealants

(G-14602)
HYDRAULIC PRESS SERVICE
4175 22 Mile Rd (48317-1503)
PHONE...................586 859-7099
EMP: 5
SALES (est): 83.8K **Privately Held**
SIC: 2711 Newspapers

(G-14603)
IANNA FAB INC
5575 22 Mile Rd (48317-1531)
PHONE...................586 739-2410
Daniel D Iannamico, *President*
John Iannamico, *Admin Sec*
EMP: 6 EST: 1976
SQ FT: 4,800
SALES: 400K **Privately Held**
SIC: 7692 Automotive welding

(G-14604)
IN LINE TUBE INC
Also Called: Inline Tube
15066 Technology Dr (48315-3950)
PHONE...................586 532-1338
James Kryta, *President*
▲ **EMP:** 10
SQ FT: 1,600
SALES (est): 2MM **Privately Held**
SIC: 3714 Motor vehicle parts & accessories

(G-14605)
INTERGRTED DSPNSE SLUTIONS LLC
Also Called: IDS
14310 Industrial Ctr Dr (48315-3292)
PHONE...................586 554-7404
Jan Pitzer, *Mng Member*
Thomas Murray, *Mng Member*
EMP: 10
SQ FT: 12,000
SALES (est): 1.3MM
SALES (corp-wide): 6.7MM **Privately Held**
SIC: 3728 Countermeasure dispensers, aircraft
PA: Hosco, Inc
28026 Oakland Oaks Ct
Wixom MI 48393
248 912-1750

(G-14606)
J & J SPRING CO INC
14100 23 Mile Rd (48315-2910)
PHONE...................586 566-7600
Richard E McGuire, *President*
Cheryl McGuire, *Vice Pres*
EMP: 15 EST: 1952
SQ FT: 14,500
SALES (est): 3MM **Privately Held**
WEB: www.jandjspring.com
SIC: 3493 3495 3465 Torsion bar springs; coiled flat springs; flat springs, sheet or strip stock; wire springs; automotive stampings

(G-14607)
J & J SPRING ENTERPRISES LLC
14100 23 Mile Rd (48315-2910)
PHONE...................586 566-7600
Joseph Kattula,
EMP: 8
SALES (est): 1.2MM **Privately Held**
SIC: 3495 Wire springs

(G-14608)
JAC PRODUCTS INC
12000 Shelby Tech Dr (48315-1789)
PHONE...................586 254-1534
Mark Jakson, *General Mgr*
EMP: 8
SALES (corp-wide): 608.8MM **Privately Held**
SIC: 3714 Motor vehicle parts & accessories
HQ: Jac Products, Inc.
225 S Industrial Dr
Saline MI 48176
734 944-8844

(G-14609)
JBL SYSTEMS INC
51935 Filomena Dr (48315-2950)
PHONE...................586 802-6700
James Bogaski, *President*
Cori Fiscelli, *Technology*
EMP: 7
SQ FT: 5,000
SALES (est): 1.2MM **Privately Held**
WEB: www.jblsys.com
SIC: 3544 Die sets for metal stamping (presses)

(G-14610)
JEMAR TOOL INC
51268 Fischer Park Dr (48316-4402)
PHONE...................586 726-6960
Martin Kalisch, *President*
▲ **EMP:** 23
SQ FT: 15,000
SALES (est): 1.1MM **Privately Held**
WEB: www.jemartool.com
SIC: 3544 Special dies & tools

(G-14611)
JOLICO/J-B TOOL INC
4325 22 Mile Rd (48317-1507)
PHONE...................586 739-5555
Patricia Wieland, *President*
W Michael Wieland, *Admin Sec*
EMP: 42
SQ FT: 55,000
SALES (est): 6.8MM **Privately Held**
WEB: www.jolico.com
SIC: 3544 3599 Special dies & tools; jigs & fixtures; machine shop, jobbing & repair

(G-14612)
JOLICOR MANUFACTURING SERVICES
13357 W Star Dr (48315-2701)
PHONE...................586 323-5090
John Livingstone, *President*
Elizabeth Livingstone, *Vice Pres*
EMP: 12
SQ FT: 10,500
SALES (est): 2.3MM **Privately Held**
SIC: 4953 3089 Recycling, waste materials; plastic processing

(G-14613)
JVIS - USA LLC (PA)
52048 Shelby Pkwy (48315-1787)
PHONE...................586 884-5700
Jack Furey, *Vice Pres*
Mike Alexander, *CFO*
Michael Alexander, *VP Finance*
Jason Murar, *Mng Member*
EMP: 18 EST: 2006
SQ FT: 100,000
SALES (est): 381.6MM **Privately Held**
SIC: 3089 Automotive parts, plastic

(G-14614)
JVIS INTERNATIONAL LLC (HQ)
Also Called: Jvis - USA
52048 Shelby Pkwy (48315-1787)
PHONE...................586 739-9542
Jason Murar, *CEO*
Tim Bradley,
▲ **EMP:** 76
SQ FT: 650,000
SALES (est): 236.2MM
SALES (corp-wide): 381.6MM **Privately Held**
SIC: 3089 Automotive parts, plastic
PA: Jvis - Usa, Llc
52048 Shelby Pkwy
Shelby Township MI 48315
586 884-5700

(G-14615)
KUKA ROBOTICS CORPORATION
Also Called: Kuka Omnimove
51870 Shelby Pkwy (48315-1787)
PHONE...................586 795-2000
Leroy Rodgers, *President*
Bryan Cermak, *Admin Sec*
EMP: 45
SALES (est): 88.4K
SALES (corp-wide): 37.7B **Privately Held**
WEB: www.kukarobotics.com
SIC: 3549 Metalworking machinery
HQ: Kuka Systems North America Llc
6600 Center Dr
Sterling Heights MI 48312
586 795-2000

(G-14616)
KUKA SYSTEMS NORTH AMERICA LLC
13231 23 Mile Rd (48315-2713)
PHONE...................586 726-4300
Lawrence Drake, *President*
EMP: 4
SALES (corp-wide): 37.7B **Privately Held**
SIC: 3549 Assembly machines, including robotic
HQ: Kuka Systems North America Llc
6600 Center Dr
Sterling Heights MI 48312
586 795-2000

(G-14617)
KWIK TECH INC
9068 Lone Pine Ct (48317-1444)
PHONE...................586 268-6201
Sophie Sondey, *President*
EMP: 20
SQ FT: 7,600
SALES (est): 2.8MM **Privately Held**
WEB: www.kwiktech.net
SIC: 3544 3545 Special dies & tools; tools & accessories for machine tools; gauges (machine tool accessories)

(G-14618)
L & H DIVERSIFIED MFG USA LLC
51559 Oro Dr (48315-2932)
P.O. Box 183667 (48318-3667)
PHONE...................586 615-4873
Marcus Murray, *Mng Member*
Mark Shows,
Conston Taylor,
EMP: 4
SALES (est): 310K **Privately Held**
SIC: 3549 Assembly machines, including robotic

(G-14619)
LABEL TECH INC
51322 Oro Dr (48315-2928)
P.O. Box 94048, Washington (48094-4048)
PHONE...................586 247-6444
Barbara Schemanske, *President*
EMP: 10
SQ FT: 10,000
SALES (est): 1MM **Privately Held**
SIC: 2759 5112 5045 Labels & seals: printing; inked ribbons; office supplies; computer software

(G-14620)
LAFATA CABINET SHOP (PA)
Also Called: La Fata Cabinets
50905 Hayes Rd (48315-3237)
PHONE...................586 247-6536
Peter La Fata, *President*
Giovanni Lafata, *Vice Pres*
Anthony Russo, *Sales Mgr*
Brian Beckeman, *Sales Staff*
EMP: 32 EST: 1962
SQ FT: 35,000
SALES (est): 16.8MM **Privately Held**
WEB: www.lafata.com
SIC: 5211 2434 2541 Cabinets, kitchen; wood kitchen cabinets; cabinets, except refrigerated: show, display, etc.: wood

(G-14621)
LAKEPOINT ELEC
56812 Mound Rd (48316-4943)
PHONE...................586 983-2510
Paul Olivieri, *Owner*
EMP: 7 EST: 2007
SALES (est): 1MM **Privately Held**
SIC: 3699 Electrical equipment & supplies

GEOGRAPHIC SECTION — Shelby Township - Macomb County

(G-14622)
LASTEK INDUSTRIES LLC
50515 Corporate Dr (48315-3103)
PHONE..........................586 739-6666
Christopher Krystek,
Janusz Lachowski,
EMP: 5
SQ FT: 9,000
SALES: 6.5MM **Privately Held**
SIC: 3699 Welding machines & equipment, ultrasonic

(G-14623)
LDB PLASTICS INC
50845 Rizzo Dr (48315-3249)
PHONE..........................586 566-9698
Renae A Syrowik, *President*
Daniel J Syrowik, *Exec VP*
Daniel Syrowik, *Exec VP*
Billy L Duncan, *Vice Pres*
▼ **EMP:** 7
SQ FT: 9,200
SALES (est): 665.5K **Privately Held**
WEB: www.ldbplastics.com
SIC: 3089 Injection molding of plastics

(G-14624)
LEADER CORPORATION (PA)
51644 Filomena Dr (48315-2947)
PHONE..........................586 566-7114
Michael Arcari, *President*
Brenda Arcari, *Vice Pres*
EMP: 35 **EST:** 1958
SQ FT: 14,500
SALES: 5.7MM **Privately Held**
WEB: www.leader-corp.com
SIC: 3545 3541 3823 Gauges (machine tool accessories); jig boring & grinding machines; industrial instrmnts msrmnt display/control process variable

(G-14625)
LEADING EDGE ENGINEERING INC
14498 Oakwood Dr (48315-1526)
PHONE..........................586 786-0382
Anthony J Solomon, *President*
EMP: 14
SQ FT: 10,000
SALES (est): 2.5MM **Privately Held**
SIC: 3599 8711 Custom machinery; industrial engineers

(G-14626)
LEWMAR CUSTOM DESIGNS INC
56588 Scotland Blvd (48316-5045)
P.O. Box 70674, Rochester Hills (48307-0013)
PHONE..........................586 677-5135
EMP: 4
SALES: 35K **Privately Held**
SIC: 2389 Mfg Apparel/Accessories

(G-14627)
LIBERTY TRANSIT MIX LLC
7520 23 Mile Rd (48315-4422)
PHONE..........................586 254-2212
Cheryl A Menlen, *President*
EMP: 3
SALES (est): 100.5K **Privately Held**
SIC: 3272 Concrete stuctural support & building material

(G-14628)
LUBE - POWER INC
50146 Utica Dr (48315-3293)
PHONE..........................586 247-6500
Dale McNeill, *President*
Brian Lightcap, *Vice Pres*
Jim Thorpe, *Prdtn Mgr*
Mark Gehres, *Purch Mgr*
Leah-Marie Couwlier, *Buyer*
◆ **EMP:** 83
SQ FT: 70,784
SALES: 36.6MM **Privately Held**
WEB: www.lubepower.com
SIC: 3569 5084 8711 Lubrication equipment, industrial; hydraulic systems equipment & supplies; consulting engineer

(G-14629)
M P C AWARDS
52130 Van Dyke Ave (48316-3527)
PHONE..........................586 254-4660
Beth George, *Owner*
EMP: 6
SQ FT: 2,000
SALES (est): 405.5K **Privately Held**
SIC: 3914 3999 5999 7389 Trophies; plaques, picture, laminated; trophies & plaques; engraving service

(G-14630)
MACOMB NORTH CLINTON ADVISOR
Also Called: Advisor The
48075 Van Dyke Ave (48317-3258)
PHONE..........................586 731-1000
Frank Sheaper, *Owner*
Wayne Oehmke, *Principal*
EMP: 50
SALES (est): 954.3K **Privately Held**
SIC: 2711 Newspapers

(G-14631)
MACOMB STAIRS INC
51032 Oro Dr (48315-2966)
PHONE..........................586 226-2800
Tom Vitale, *President*
Vince E Vitale, *Vice Pres*
Rhonda Yaroch, *Director*
James A Vitale, *Admin Sec*
EMP: 18
SQ FT: 16,000
SALES: 3.4MM **Privately Held**
WEB: www.macombstairs.com
SIC: 2431 Staircases & stairs, wood; moldings & baseboards, ornamental & trim

(G-14632)
MAGNA SEATING AMERICA INC
Also Called: Shelby Foam Systems
6200 26 Mile Rd (48316-5000)
PHONE..........................586 816-1400
EMP: 5
SALES (corp-wide): 40.8B **Privately Held**
SIC: 3714 Motor vehicle parts & accessories
HQ: Magna Seating Of America, Inc.
30020 Cabot Dr
Novi MI 48377

(G-14633)
MARK SCHWAGER INC
13170 W Star Dr (48315-2736)
P.O. Box 183335 (48318-3335)
PHONE..........................248 275-1978
Mark Schwager, *President*
▲ **EMP:** 3
SALES: 400K **Privately Held**
SIC: 5162 3089 Plastics materials & basic shapes; injection molded finished plastic products; injection molding of plastics

(G-14634)
MARY BOGGS BAGGS
Also Called: Belts & Ties By Mary Boggs
5218 Robert St (48316-4142)
PHONE..........................586 731-2513
Mary A Boggs, *Partner*
EMP: 3 **EST:** 1982
SALES (est): 160K **Privately Held**
SIC: 3161 3171 Luggage; handbags, women's

(G-14635)
MASTER MODEL & FIXTURE INC
51731 Oro Dr (48315-2934)
PHONE..........................586 532-1153
Brian Grasso, *President*
EMP: 10
SQ FT: 12,000
SALES (est): 1.5MM **Privately Held**
SIC: 3544 Industrial molds

(G-14636)
MAYA PLASTICS INC
13179 W Star Dr (48315-2736)
P.O. Box 183817, Utica (48318-3817)
PHONE..........................586 997-6000
EMP: 40
SQ FT: 10,800
SALES (est): 4.6MM **Privately Held**
SIC: 3089 Mfg Injection Molding Of Plastics

(G-14637)
MEGA PRECAST INC
14670 23 Mile Rd (48315-3000)
PHONE..........................586 477-5959
Amedeo Piccinini, *President*
EMP: 13
SALES (est): 1.9MM **Privately Held**
SIC: 3272 Concrete products

(G-14638)
METAL FORMING & COINING CORP
51810 Danview Tech Ct (48315)
PHONE..........................586 731-2003
Dave Huber, *Manager*
EMP: 4
SALES (est): 815.2K
SALES (corp-wide): 26.9MM **Privately Held**
WEB: www.mfccorp.com
SIC: 3462 Iron & steel forgings
PA: Metal Forming & Coining Corp
1007 Illinois Ave
Maumee OH 43537
419 897-9530

(G-14639)
METALFORM INDUSTRIES LLC
52830 Tuscany Grv (48315-2081)
PHONE..........................248 462-0056
Craig Scott,
EMP: 5
SALES (est): 636.6K **Privately Held**
SIC: 8711 8742 3569 3544 Machine tool design; management engineering; assembly machines, non-metalworking; special dies, tools, jigs & fixtures

(G-14640)
METRIC HYDRULIC COMPONENTS LLC
13870 Cavaliere Dr (48315-2961)
PHONE..........................586 786-6990
Jerry Pizzimenti, *Principal*
EMP: 10
SALES (est): 1.5MM **Privately Held**
WEB: www.metrichydraulics.com
SIC: 3823 Fluidic devices, circuits & systems for process control

(G-14641)
MISSION CRITICAL FIREARMS LLC
48380 Van Dyke Ave (48317-3277)
PHONE..........................586 232-5185
Edward Pireh, *President*
EMP: 4
SALES: 1.3MM **Privately Held**
SIC: 5941 7389 5169 2892 Firearms; personal service agents, brokers & bureaus; explosives; plastic explosives; law enforcement equipment & supplies

(G-14642)
MLC WINDOW CO INC (PA)
Also Called: Mlcwindows & Doors
2001 Crystal Lake Dr (48315-2818)
PHONE..........................586 731-3500
Michael Lochirco, *President*
▲ **EMP:** 30
SQ FT: 1,000
SALES (est): 3.4MM **Privately Held**
SIC: 2431 Storm windows, wood

(G-14643)
MOBILITY INNOVATIONS LLC
51277 Celeste (48315-2941)
PHONE..........................586 843-3816
James Morrison, *CEO*
EMP: 5
SALES (est): 210.2K **Privately Held**
SIC: 3711 Motor vehicles & car bodies

(G-14644)
MODELS & TOOLS INC
51400 Bellestri Ct (48315-2749)
PHONE..........................586 580-6900
Randal Bellestri, *CEO*
Philip Neale, *Exec VP*
Tom Timmerman, *Purch Mgr*
Rick Faubert, *CFO*
Karissa Cooper, *Sales Staff*
EMP: 180 **EST:** 1974
SQ FT: 115,000
SALES: 35MM **Privately Held**
WEB: www.modelsandtools.com
SIC: 3544 Special dies & tools

(G-14645)
MODULAR DATA SYSTEMS INC
53089 Bellamine Dr (48316-2101)
PHONE..........................586 739-5870
Gerald J Wolschlager, *President*
Robert Luxa, *Vice Pres*
Judy Wolschlager, *Admin Sec*
EMP: 10 **EST:** 1970
SALES: 750K **Privately Held**
WEB: www.modulardata.com
SIC: 3824 Electromechanical counters

(G-14646)
MOLD SPECIALTIES INC
51232 Oro Dr (48315-2903)
PHONE..........................586 247-4660
Reiner Buchholtz, *President*
EMP: 8
SQ FT: 3,000
SALES (est): 993.7K **Privately Held**
SIC: 3544 Industrial molds

(G-14647)
MOLLER GROUP NORTH AMERICA INC (DH)
Also Called: Megaplast North America
13877 Teresa Dr (48315-2929)
PHONE..........................586 532-0860
Peter Von Moller, *President*
▲ **EMP:** 12
SALES (est): 45.5MM
SALES (corp-wide): 257.2K **Privately Held**
SIC: 3089 Injection molding of plastics
HQ: Mollertech International Gmbh
Kupferhammer
Bielefeld 33649
521 447-70

(G-14648)
MOLLERTECH LLC
13877 Teresa Dr (48315-2929)
PHONE..........................586 532-0860
Steve Jordan, *President*
Kristine Nowowiecki, *Vice Pres*
Chuck Gietzen, *Opers Mgr*
Slobodan Jovanovich, *Purch Mgr*
Kevin Adams, *Manager*
▲ **EMP:** 125 **EST:** 1998
SQ FT: 80,000
SALES (est): 24.5MM
SALES (corp-wide): 257.2K **Privately Held**
SIC: 3089 Injection molding of plastics
HQ: Moller Group North America, Inc.
13877 Teresa Dr
Shelby Township MI 48315
586 532-0860

(G-14649)
MOORE SIGNS INVESTMENTS INC
5220 Rail View Ct Apt 245 (48316-5703)
P.O. Box 836, Mount Clemens (48046-0836)
PHONE..........................586 783-9339
Frank Declerck, *President*
EMP: 25 **EST:** 1919
SQ FT: 12,000
SALES (est): 2MM **Privately Held**
SIC: 3993 Signs & advertising specialties

(G-14650)
MSINC
50463 Wing Dr (48315-3261)
P.O. Box 183335, Utica (48318-3335)
PHONE..........................248 275-1978
Mark Schwager, *Principal*
Noelle Schwager, *CFO*
▲ **EMP:** 6
SALES (est): 769.8K **Privately Held**
SIC: 3089 Injection molding of plastics

(G-14651)
NETWORK MACHINERY INC
54407 Woodcreek Blvd (48315-1433)
PHONE..........................586 992-2459
Gary Sredzinski, *President*
Garry Sredzinski, *Principal*
Matthew Czajka, *Accounts Mgr*
EMP: 5

Shelby Township - Macomb County (G-14652)

SALES (est): 824.6K **Privately Held**
WEB: www.networkmachinery.com
SIC: 3825 Network analyzers

(G-14652)
NEW LINE INC
Also Called: New Line Laminate Design
15164 Commercial Dr (48315-3982)
PHONE.................586 228-4820
Giovanni Ferrazzo, *President*
EMP: 8
SQ FT: 6,000
SALES: 500K **Privately Held**
SIC: 2434 3469 2519 Wood kitchen cabinets; kitchen fixtures & equipment, porcelain enameled; fiberglass & plastic furniture

(G-14653)
NITRO EDM AND MACHINING INC
50606 Sabrina Dr (48315-2957)
PHONE.................586 247-8035
Vince Dinezio, *President*
EMP: 3
SQ FT: 4,500
SALES (est): 436.4K **Privately Held**
SIC: 3599 Machine shop, jobbing & repair

(G-14654)
NORTH AMERICAN CONTROLS INC
13955 Teresa Dr (48315-2930)
PHONE.................586 532-7140
Antonio Sciacca, *President*
Edward E Page III, *CFO*
Stephen Deninson, *Admin Sec*
▼ **EMP:** 37
SQ FT: 17,000
SALES (est): 8.4MM **Privately Held**
WEB: www.nacontrols.com
SIC: 3829 Measuring & controlling devices

(G-14655)
NORTH AMERICAN MCH & ENGRG CO
Also Called: North American Machine & Engrg
13290 W Star Dr (48315-2741)
PHONE.................586 726-6700
James R Howes, *President*
EMP: 5 **EST:** 1981
SQ FT: 6,000
SALES: 1.5MM **Privately Held**
WEB: www.nameco1.com
SIC: 7699 5084 3599 Industrial machinery & equipment repair; industrial machinery & equipment; machine shop, jobbing & repair

(G-14656)
NORTHERN METALCRAFT INC
50490 Corporate Dr (48315-3104)
PHONE.................586 997-9630
Joseph Toepfner, *President*
Nikolaus Kolling, *Vice Pres*
Elisabeth Hammer, *Treasurer*
Karin Schwalbe, *Persnl Dir*
EMP: 15
SQ FT: 26,000
SALES: 1.5MM **Privately Held**
WEB: www.northernmetalcraft.com
SIC: 3465 Automotive stampings

(G-14657)
NORTHROP GRUMMAN INNOVATION
Also Called: Atk Lc
2845 Plymouth Dr (48316-4890)
PHONE.................313 424-9411
Aaron Kicinski, *Administration*
EMP: 70 **Publicly Held**
SIC: 3764 Propulsion units for guided missiles & space vehicles
HQ: Northrop Grumman Innovation Systems, Inc.
45101 Warp Dr
Dulles VA 20166
703 406-5000

(G-14658)
ORTHOTIC SHOP INC
14200 Industrial Ctr Dr (48315-3259)
PHONE.................800 309-0412
Matthew Behnke, *President*

Reena Sezz, *Marketing Mgr*
EMP: 3
SALES (est): 330K **Privately Held**
SIC: 3842 Orthopedic appliances

(G-14659)
PARAGON READY MIX INC (PA)
48000 Hixson Ave (48317-2731)
PHONE.................586 731-8000
Steve Simpson, *President*
Jason Piper, *Technical Staff*
EMP: 35
SALES (est): 6.3MM **Privately Held**
SIC: 3273 Ready-mixed concrete

(G-14660)
PASLIN COMPANY
52550 Shelby Pkwy (48315-1778)
PHONE.................248 953-8419
Richard Stathakis, *Superintendent*
EMP: 200 **Privately Held**
SIC: 3548 3544 3535 Electric welding equipment; jigs & fixtures; conveyors & conveying equipment
HQ: The Paslin Company
25303 Ryan Rd
Warren MI 48091
586 758-0200

(G-14661)
PEAKE ASPHALT INC
48181 Ryan Rd (48317-2882)
PHONE.................586 254-4567
Mariah Peake, *Manager*
EMP: 15
SALES: 30MM **Privately Held**
SIC: 2951 Asphalt paving mixtures & blocks

(G-14662)
PEG-MASTER BUSINESS FORMS INC
Also Called: Michigan Printing Impressions
15018 Technology Dr (48315-3950)
PHONE.................586 566-8694
Linda Ianni, *President*
EMP: 9
SALES (est): 1.1MM **Privately Held**
SIC: 2752 2791 2761 2759 Commercial printing, offset; typesetting; manifold business forms; commercial printing

(G-14663)
PERMAN INDUSTRIES LLC
51523 Celeste (48315-2923)
PHONE.................586 991-5600
EMP: 15
SALES (est): 241.5K **Privately Held**
SIC: 3599 Mfg Industrial Machinery

(G-14664)
PERSICO USA INC
50450 Wing Dr (48315-3288)
PHONE.................248 299-5100
Pierino Persico, *President*
Alison Traver, *Purchasing*
Leo Centofanti, *Controller*
◆ **EMP:** 68
SALES: 10.5MM **Privately Held**
SIC: 3423 Soldering tools

(G-14665)
PHILLIPS ENTERPRISES INC
Also Called: Banner Sign Specialties
51245 Filomena Dr (48315-2942)
PHONE.................586 615-6208
Mark Phillips, *President*
Dianna Phillips, *Vice Pres*
EMP: 46
SQ FT: 6,000
SALES (est): 8MM **Privately Held**
SIC: 3993 Signs & advertising specialties

(G-14666)
PINK PIN LADY LLC
47768 Barclay Ct (48317-3678)
PHONE.................586 731-1532
Jacqueline Nash, *Principal*
EMP: 4
SALES (est): 287.5K **Privately Held**
SIC: 3452 Pins

(G-14667)
PIONEER PLASTICS INC
51650 Oro Dr (48315-2933)
PHONE.................586 262-0159
Darin Steven Morisette, *Principal*
EMP: 24
SALES (corp-wide): 3.3MM **Privately Held**
SIC: 2295 Resin or plastic coated fabrics
PA: Pioneer Plastics, Inc.
2295 Bart Ave
Warren MI 48091
586 262-0159

(G-14668)
PLASTIC TRENDS INC
Also Called: Royal Building Products
56400 Mound Rd (48316-4904)
PHONE.................586 232-4167
Jon Houghton, *President*
Chad Hall, *Natl Sales Mgr*
◆ **EMP:** 95
SQ FT: 265,000
SALES (est): 30.9MM **Publicly Held**
WEB: www.plastictrends.com
SIC: 3432 Plumbing fixture fittings & trim
HQ: Axiall Corporation
1000 Abernathy Rd # 1200
Atlanta GA 30328
304 455-2200

(G-14669)
POLYMER PROCESS DEV LLC
11969 Shelby Tech Dr (48315-1788)
PHONE.................586 464-6400
Perry Giese, *President*
Robert Brisley, *Vice Pres*
Bret Bailey, *VP Opers*
Dan Smith, *Project Engr*
Mark Gula, *Controller*
EMP: 72 **EST:** 1996
SALES (est): 15.4MM **Privately Held**
WEB: www.ppdllc.com
SIC: 3089 3231 Injection molding of plastics; products of purchased glass

(G-14670)
PPG INDUSTRIES INC
Also Called: PPG 5624
13651 23 Mile Rd (48315-2906)
PHONE.................586 566-3789
EMP: 5
SALES (corp-wide): 15.3B **Publicly Held**
WEB: www.ppg.com
SIC: 2851 Paints & allied products
PA: Ppg Industries, Inc.
1 Ppg Pl
Pittsburgh PA 15272
412 434-3131

(G-14671)
PRISM PLASTICS INC
50581 Sabrina Dr (48315-2963)
PHONE.................810 292-6300
Stan Nosakowski, *Branch Mgr*
EMP: 25
SALES (corp-wide): 225.3B **Publicly Held**
SIC: 3089 Injection molding of plastics
HQ: Prism Plastics, Inc.
52111 Sierra Dr
Chesterfield MI 48047
810 292-6300

(G-14672)
PROGRESSIVE CUTTER GRINDING CO
14207 Rick Dr (48315-2935)
PHONE.................586 580-2367
Jorgo Villa, *President*
EMP: 7
SALES (est): 904.9K **Privately Held**
SIC: 3599 Grinding castings for the trade

(G-14673)
PROTODESIGN INC
50495 Corporate Dr Ste 10 (48315-3132)
PHONE.................586 739-4340
Tony Sajkowski, *President*
John Zimmer, *Mfg Spvr*
Linda Labarbera, *Mfg Staff*
Johnathan Zimmer, *QC Mgr*
Kristi Krathwohl, *Planning*
EMP: 20
SQ FT: 10,000

SALES (est): 4.4MM **Privately Held**
WEB: www.teampdi.com
SIC: 3672 Printed circuit boards

(G-14674)
PROTOTYPE CAST MFG INC (PA)
Also Called: Pcmi Manufacturing Integration
51292 Danview Tech Ct (48315)
PHONE.................586 739-0180
William Edney, *President*
Bill Edney, *Vice Pres*
▲ **EMP:** 8
SQ FT: 10,000
SALES: 8MM **Privately Held**
WEB: www.prototypecast.com
SIC: 3363 3599 Aluminum die-castings; machine & other job shop work

(G-14675)
QUANTUM GRAPHICS INC
50720 Corporate Dr (48315-3105)
PHONE.................586 566-5656
Michael Burton, *President*
Gerard Buczek, *Vice Pres*
Steve Burton, *Vice Pres*
EMP: 24
SQ FT: 26,380
SALES (est): 4.2MM **Privately Held**
WEB: www.quantumgrphinc.com
SIC: 2759 Screen printing

(G-14676)
QUICK BUILT
51450 Oro Dr (48315-2931)
PHONE.................586 286-2900
EMP: 3
SALES (est): 315.5K **Privately Held**
SIC: 3599 Machine shop, jobbing & repair

(G-14677)
R S C PRODUCTIONS
Also Called: Contemporary Bride
7811 24 Mile Rd (48316-2509)
PHONE.................586 532-9200
Riccardo Coletti, *President*
EMP: 6
SALES (est): 431.9K **Privately Held**
WEB: www.cbride.com
SIC: 7389 2741 Advertising, promotional & trade show services; miscellaneous publishing

(G-14678)
RASSEY INDUSTRIES INC
50375 Central Indus Dr (48315-3114)
PHONE.................586 803-9500
Louis N Rassey, *President*
Edward A Rassey, *Vice Pres*
Cat Arcori, *Project Mgr*
Amy Devries, *Purch Agent*
▲ **EMP:** 22
SQ FT: 36,000
SALES (est): 5MM **Privately Held**
WEB: www.rassey.com
SIC: 3714 3599 Motor vehicle parts & accessories; machine shop, jobbing & repair

(G-14679)
REW INDUSTRIES INC
51572 Danview Tech Ct (48315)
PHONE.................586 803-1150
Russell Willauer, *President*
EMP: 30
SQ FT: 12,000
SALES (est): 5.3MM **Privately Held**
WEB: www.rewindustries.com
SIC: 3469 Stamping metal for the trade

(G-14680)
ROCHESTER TUBE PRODUCTS LTD
Also Called: Rochester Tube Products Rtp
51366 Fischer Park Dr (48316-4402)
PHONE.................586 726-4816
A Neil Preston, *CEO*
Cheryl Kassin, *Purch Mgr*
Jennie Preston, *Marketing Staff*
Cheryl A Kassin, *Manager*
B D Fischer, *Director*
EMP: 25 **EST:** 1973
SQ FT: 29,000
SALES (est): 6.3MM **Privately Held**
WEB: www.rochestertube.com
SIC: 3498 Tube fabricating (contract bending & shaping)

GEOGRAPHIC SECTION

(G-14681)
ROLFS JEWELERS LTD
52930 Van Dyke Ave (48316-3547)
PHONE.................................586 739-3906
Scott Rolf, *Owner*
EMP: 3
SALES (est): 226K **Privately Held**
SIC: 3911 Jewelry, precious metal

(G-14682)
ROSS CABINETS II INC
50169 Hayes Rd (48315-3229)
PHONE.................................586 752-7750
Antonio Verelli, *President*
Anthony Verelli, *President*
EMP: 50
SALES (est): 7.5MM **Privately Held**
SIC: 2541 2517 2434 Cabinets, lockers & shelving; wood television & radio cabinets; wood kitchen cabinets

(G-14683)
RSLS CORP
51084 Filomena Dr (48315-2937)
PHONE.................................248 726-0675
Russell Carter, *President*
EMP: 5
SALES (est): 533.8K **Privately Held**
SIC: 2396 3993 Screen printing on fabric articles; letters for signs, metal

(G-14684)
S N D STEEL FABRICATION INC
11611 Park Ct (48315-3109)
PHONE.................................586 997-1500
Milivoje Djordjevic, *President*
Zoran Djordjevic, *Vice Pres*
EMP: 18 **EST:** 1979
SQ FT: 24,000
SALES (est): 3.2MM **Privately Held**
SIC: 3443 Weldments

(G-14685)
SBTI COMPANY
Also Called: Smith Bros. Tool Company
50600 Corporate Dr (48315-3107)
PHONE.................................586 726-5756
Hodges Tennyson Smith, *President*
Jere Rush, *President*
EMP: 55 **EST:** 1981
SQ FT: 130,000
SALES (est): 13.7MM **Privately Held**
SIC: 3543 3544 3545 Industrial patterns; special dies, tools, jigs & fixtures; machine tool accessories

(G-14686)
SCENARIO SYSTEMS LTD
50466 Rizzo Dr (48315-3275)
PHONE.................................586 532-1320
Edward Strehl, *President*
Gary Pizzimenti, *Vice Pres*
EMP: 7
SQ FT: 36,000
SALES (est): 399.3K **Privately Held**
SIC: 3499 Welding tips, heat resistant: metal

(G-14687)
SCHWAB INDUSTRIES INC
Also Called: Plant 2
50750 Rizzo Dr (48315-3274)
PHONE.................................586 566-8090
Brian Gibson, *Manager*
EMP: 10
SQ FT: 70,000
SALES (corp-wide): 20MM **Privately Held**
SIC: 3714 Motor vehicle parts & accessories
PA: Schwab Industries, Inc.
50850 Rizzo Dr
Shelby Township MI 48315
586 566-8090

(G-14688)
SCHWAB INDUSTRIES INC (PA)
50850 Rizzo Dr (48315-3248)
PHONE.................................586 566-8090
Reiner Koerner, *President*
EMP: 125
SQ FT: 110,000

SALES (est): 20MM **Privately Held**
SIC: 3544 3469 3465 3291 Die sets for metal stamping (presses); ornamental metal stampings; fenders, automobile: stamped or pressed metal; steel wool

(G-14689)
SENSORDATA TECHNOLOGIES INC
50207 Hayes Rd (48315-3230)
PHONE.................................586 739-4254
Sherif Gindy, *President*
Michael Parker, *Vice Pres*
Arsim Hidic, *Purchasing*
EMP: 15
SQ FT: 2,000
SALES: 1.5MM **Privately Held**
WEB: www.sensdata.com
SIC: 3829 Measuring & controlling devices

(G-14690)
SGL TECHNIC INC
Also Called: Sgl Carbon Group
2156 Willow Cir (48316-1054)
PHONE.................................248 540-9508
William J Raven, *Manager*
EMP: 4
SALES (corp-wide): 1.2B **Privately Held**
WEB: www.polycarbon.com
SIC: 3295 Graphite, natural: ground, pulverized, refined or blended
HQ: Sgl Technic Llc
28176 Avenue Stanford
Valencia CA 91355
661 257-0500

(G-14691)
SHAYN ALLEN MARQUETRY
14009 Simone Dr (48315-3234)
PHONE.................................586 991-0445
Shayn Smith, *Partner*
EMP: 4
SALES (est): 300K **Privately Held**
SIC: 2431 2434 Floor baseboards, wood; wood kitchen cabinets

(G-14692)
SHELBY ANTOLIN INC
52888 Shelby Pkwy (48315-1778)
PHONE.................................734 395-0328
Joseph McCluskey, *General Mgr*
Catherine Ivan, *Finance Mgr*
EMP: 12
SQ FT: 350,000
SALES: 209K
SALES (corp-wide): 33.3MM **Privately Held**
SIC: 3714 Motor vehicle parts & accessories
HQ: Grupo Antolin North America, Inc.
1700 Atlantic Blvd
Auburn Hills MI 48326
248 373-1749

(G-14693)
SHELBY SIGNARAMA TOWNSHIP
51084 Filomena Dr (48315-2937)
PHONE.................................586 843-3702
Russell Carter, *President*
EMP: 4
SALES: 200K **Privately Held**
SIC: 3993 7336 Signs & advertising specialties; commercial art & graphic design

(G-14694)
SIGNS365COM LLC
51245 Filomena Dr (48315-2942)
PHONE.................................800 265-8830
Dianna Phillips, *Administration*
EMP: 6
SALES (est): 1.1MM **Privately Held**
SIC: 2759 5131 3993 Screen printing; flags & banners; signs & advertising specialties

(G-14695)
SMITH BROTHERS TOOL COMPANY
50600 Corporate Dr (48315-3107)
PHONE.................................586 726-5756
Karl Lapeer, *Ch of Bd*
Jere Rush, *Vice Pres*
Carl Russo, *Vice Pres*
Christopher Gessner, *Admin Sec*

EMP: 53
SQ FT: 36,984
SALES (est): 11.4MM **Privately Held**
SIC: 3544 Special dies & tools

(G-14696)
SMS ELOTHERM NORTH AMERICA LLC
13129 23 Mile Rd (48315-2711)
PHONE.................................586 469-8324
Roddey Liekhus, *Manager*
Johannn Rinnhofer,
Martin Schulteis,
EMP: 9
SALES (est): 1MM **Privately Held**
SIC: 3567 Induction heating equipment

(G-14697)
SNYDER CORPORATION
13231 23 Mile Rd (48315-2713)
PHONE.................................586 726-4300
Thomas J Carter, *Ch of Bd*
Stefan Wanczyk, *President*
EMP: 42
SQ FT: 62,640
SALES (est): 3.1MM
SALES (corp-wide): 565.7MM **Privately Held**
SIC: 3541 Machine tools, metal cutting type
PA: Utica Enterprises, Inc.
5750 New King Dr Ste 200
Troy MI 48098
586 726-4300

(G-14698)
SOLUTION STEEL TREATING LLC
51689 Oro Dr (48315-2934)
PHONE.................................586 247-9250
Steve Hawkins,
Jeff Flannery,
Edward Lowmaster,
Stephen Spohn,
EMP: 16 **EST:** 2000
SQ FT: 8,300
SALES (est): 3.4MM **Privately Held**
SIC: 3398 Metal heat treating

(G-14699)
SPARTAN AUTOMATION INC
50508 Central Indus Dr (48315-3116)
PHONE.................................586 206-7231
Gerald Hughes, *President*
EMP: 5
SALES (est): 570K **Privately Held**
WEB: www.spartanautomation.net
SIC: 3559 Automotive related machinery

(G-14700)
SPEC TECHNOLOGIES INC
Also Called: Spec Check
51455 Schoenherr Rd (48315-2734)
PHONE.................................586 726-0000
Rick Schneider, *President*
Wayne Russell, *Vice Pres*
Amy Schneider, *Vice Pres*
Robert O'Neill, *CFO*
Robert O'Neal, *Controller*
EMP: 60
SQ FT: 40,000
SALES: 8MM **Privately Held**
WEB: www.gospec.com
SIC: 3599 7549 Machine & other job shop work; inspection & diagnostic service, automotive

(G-14701)
SPI LLC
Also Called: Sterling
51370 Celeste (48315-2902)
PHONE.................................586 566-5870
Pat King, *QC Mgr*
Werner Kleinert,
Donald Barnhart,
Michael Kleinert,
Walt Patzker,
EMP: 30
SQ FT: 30,000
SALES: 5.5MM **Privately Held**
WEB: www.spicerax.com
SIC: 3089 Injection molded finished plastic products

(G-14702)
SPRING DESIGN AND MFG INC
14105 Industrial Ctr Dr D (48315-3260)
PHONE.................................586 566-9741
John Gehart, *President*
EMP: 50
SALES (est): 7.9MM **Privately Held**
SIC: 3495 Wire springs

(G-14703)
SUMMIT PLASTIC MOLDING INC
51340 Celeste (48315-2902)
PHONE.................................586 262-4500
Raymond Kalinowski, *President*
Nick Gedeon, *Sales Mgr*
▲ **EMP:** 45
SQ FT: 15,000
SALES (est): 12.3MM **Privately Held**
WEB: www.summitplasticmolding.com
SIC: 3089 Molding primary plastic; injection molded finished plastic products

(G-14704)
SUMMIT PLASTIC MOLDING II INC (PA)
51340 Celeste (48315-2902)
PHONE.................................586 262-4500
Raymond Kalinowski, *President*
▲ **EMP:** 18
SQ FT: 15,000
SALES (est): 3.7MM **Privately Held**
SIC: 3089 Molding primary plastic; injection molded finished plastic products

(G-14705)
SUMMIT SERVICES INC
51340 Celeste (48315-2902)
PHONE.................................586 977-8300
Raymond Kalinowski, *President*
EMP: 25 **EST:** 1982
SQ FT: 18,000
SALES (est): 4MM **Privately Held**
SIC: 3544 Industrial molds

(G-14706)
SUPERIOR CUTTER GRINDING INC
54631 Franklin Dr (48316-1622)
PHONE.................................586 781-2365
Gene L Ursu, *President*
EMP: 6 **EST:** 1962
SQ FT: 3,000
SALES (est): 300K **Privately Held**
SIC: 3599 Grinding castings for the trade

(G-14707)
TAKE US-4-GRANITE INC
13000 23 Mile Rd (48315-2702)
PHONE.................................586 803-1305
Matthew S Anderson, *President*
Michael Naiorano, *Corp Secy*
EMP: 7
SALES (est): 600K **Privately Held**
SIC: 1411 Granite dimension stone

(G-14708)
TELSONIC ULTRASONICS INC (DH)
14120 Industrial Ctr Dr (48315-3276)
PHONE.................................586 802-0033
Jochen Bacher, *President*
Nicole Bacher, *Accounting Mgr*
James Jaworski, *Sales Staff*
▲ **EMP:** 24
SQ FT: 20,000
SALES (est): 4.4MM
SALES (corp-wide): 392.5K **Privately Held**
WEB: www.telsonic.com
SIC: 3541 3699 Ultrasonic metal cutting machine tools; cleaning equipment, ultrasonic, except medical & dental; welding machines & equipment, ultrasonic
HQ: Telsonic Ag
Industriestrasse 6b
Bronschhofen SG 9552
719 139-888

(G-14709)
TI-COATING INC
50500 Corporate Dr (48315-3102)
PHONE.................................586 726-1900
Charles Zichichi, *Ch of Bd*
Rosemarie Zichichi, *Ch of Bd*
William C Zichichi, *President*

Shelby Township - Macomb County (G-14710)

GEOGRAPHIC SECTION

Leo Manoogian, *Safety Mgr*
Leonard Jankowski, *Sales Staff*
EMP: 47 EST: 1975
SQ FT: 32,000
SALES (est): 6.4MM **Privately Held**
WEB: www.ticoating.com
SIC: 3479 3559 Coating of metals & formed products; chemical machinery & equipment

(G-14710)
TRANSFORM AUTOMOTIVE LLC
52400 Shelby Pkwy (48315-1778)
PHONE.................................586 826-8500
Karl Yates, *Manager*
EMP: 99
SALES (corp-wide): 2.4B **Privately Held**
SIC: 3714 Motor vehicle parts & accessories
HQ: Transform Automotive, Llc
7026 Sterling Ponds Ct
Sterling Heights MI 48312
586 826-8500

(G-14711)
TROY INDUSTRIES INC
13300 W Star Dr (48315-2700)
PHONE.................................586 739-7760
Stojan Stojanovski, *President*
Christopher Amidon, *IT/INT Sup*
EMP: 10 **EST:** 1977
SQ FT: 7,000
SALES (est): 1MM **Privately Held**
SIC: 3541 Machine tools, metal cutting type

(G-14712)
TURBOSOCKS PERFORMANCE
50765 Cedargrove Rd (48317-1105)
PHONE.................................586 864-3252
Nate Poole, *Principal*
EMP: 3
SALES (est): 184.4K **Privately Held**
SIC: 2252 Socks

(G-14713)
TWIN MOLD AND ENGINEERING LLC
51738 Filomena Dr (48315-2948)
PHONE.................................586 532-8558
Jason Van Laere, *Owner*
Jamie Smith, *Owner*
EMP: 29
SQ FT: 10,000
SALES (est): 8.3MM **Privately Held**
WEB: www.twinmold.com
SIC: 3544 Industrial molds

(G-14714)
US FARATHANE HOLDINGS CORP (PA)
Also Called: U.S. Farathane Corp
11650 Park Ct (48315-3108)
PHONE.................................586 726-1200
Andy Greenlee, *President*
Carl Ammerman, *General Mgr*
Chris Wooten, *General Mgr*
Cyril J Edwards Jr, *Chairman*
Rodney Turton, *Purchasing*
◆ **EMP:** 480
SQ FT: 68,000
SALES (est): 876MM **Privately Held**
SIC: 3089 Injection molding of plastics; thermoformed finished plastic products; casting of plastic

(G-14715)
US FARATHANE HOLDINGS CORP
11650 Park Ct Bldg B (48315-3108)
PHONE.................................248 754-7000
EMP: 265
SALES (corp-wide): 876MM **Privately Held**
SIC: 3089 Automotive parts, plastic
PA: U.S. Farathane Holdings Corp.
11650 Park Ct
Shelby Township MI 48315
586 726-1200

(G-14716)
VAN LOON INDUSTRIES INC
51583 Filomena Dr (48315-2946)
PHONE.................................586 532-8530
Thomas J V Loon, *President*

Diana V Loon, *Vice Pres*
Christine Dixson, *Admin Sec*
EMP: 25
SQ FT: 12,000
SALES (est): 5.1MM **Privately Held**
WEB: www.vligroup.com
SIC: 3469 3444 3443 Metal stampings; sheet metalwork; fabricated plate work (boiler shop)

(G-14717)
VEIGEL NORTH AMERICA LLC
Also Called: Mobility Products and Design
51277 Celeste (48315-2941)
P.O. Box 182160 (48318-2160)
PHONE.................................586 843-3816
James Morrison, *Partner*
Chris Williams, *Engineer*
EMP: 10
SQ FT: 11,000
SALES (est): 1.3MM **Privately Held**
SIC: 3711 Automobile assembly, including specialty automobiles

(G-14718)
VENDCO LLC
50613 Central Indus Dr (48315-3119)
PHONE.................................800 764-8245
Kurt Briggs,
▲ **EMP:** 3
SALES (est): 250K **Privately Held**
SIC: 5087 3556 Vending machines & supplies; food products machinery

(G-14719)
VINCE JOES FRT MKT - SHLBY INC
55178 Van Dyke Ave (48316-5302)
PHONE.................................586 786-9230
Vincenzo Victalv, *President*
Salvo Munaco, *Manager*
EMP: 24
SALES (est): 4.3MM **Privately Held**
SIC: 2035 Pickled fruits & vegetables

(G-14720)
VISION FUELS LLC
51969 Van Dyke Ave (48316-4455)
PHONE.................................586 997-3286
EMP: 3
SALES (est): 204.1K **Privately Held**
SIC: 2869 Fuels

(G-14721)
WEBER ELECTRIC MFG CO
Also Called: Wemco
2465 23 Mile Rd (48316-3805)
PHONE.................................586 323-9000
Salvatore P Munaco, *President*
▲ **EMP:** 35
SQ FT: 20,000
SALES (est): 7MM **Privately Held**
WEB: www.wemco-usa.com
SIC: 3549 Wiredrawing & fabricating machinery & equipment, ex. die

(G-14722)
WHATS YOUR MIX MENCHIES LLC
2168 Scarboro Ct (48316-1266)
PHONE.................................248 840-1668
Louis Messina, *Principal*
EMP: 5 **EST:** 2012
SALES (est): 457.1K **Privately Held**
SIC: 3273 Ready-mixed concrete

(G-14723)
WORLD CLASS EQUIPMENT COMPANY
Also Called: Wcec
51515 Celeste (48315-2923)
PHONE.................................586 331-2121
Mark Matheson, *President*
Jeff Hinsperger, *Vice Pres*
Jerry Stein, *Buyer*
Joe Phillips, *Sales Engr*
EMP: 11 **EST:** 2012
SALES: 2.5MM **Privately Held**
SIC: 3599 8711 Machine shop, jobbing & repair; machine tool design

(G-14724)
XPRESS PACKAGING SOLUTIONS LLC
11655 Park Ct (48315-3109)
PHONE.................................231 629-0463
Matt Murray, *CEO*
EMP: 4
SALES (est): 245K **Privately Held**
SIC: 2655 Fiber shipping & mailing containers

(G-14725)
YOUR HOMETOWN SHOPPER LLC
Also Called: Creative Kids Publication
55130 Shelby Rd Ste A (48316-1176)
PHONE.................................586 412-8500
Pamela J Meadows,
EMP: 10
SQ FT: 2,500
SALES: 1.5MM **Privately Held**
WEB: www.yourhometownshopper.com
SIC: 7311 2711 7331 Advertising agencies; newspapers: publishing only, not printed on site; mailing service

Shepherd
Isabella County

(G-14726)
CCO HOLDINGS LLC
257 W Wright Ave (48883-2502)
PHONE.................................989 567-0151
EMP: 3
SALES (corp-wide): 43.6B **Publicly Held**
SIC: 5064 4841 3663 3651 Electrical appliances, television & radio; cable & other pay television services; radio & TV communications equipment; household audio & video equipment
HQ: Cco Holdings, Llc
400 Atlantic St
Stamford CT 06901
203 905-7801

(G-14727)
CONTOUR ENGINEERING INC
2305 E Coe Rd (48883-9575)
PHONE.................................989 828-6526
Kurt Willoughby, *President*
EMP: 10
SQ FT: 12,000
SALES (est): 1.5MM **Privately Held**
WEB: www.contourengineering.com
SIC: 3089 3469 Thermoformed finished plastic products; patterns on metal

(G-14728)
HIGHLAND PLASTICS INC
525 N 2nd St (48883-9026)
P.O. Box 99 (48883-0099)
PHONE.................................989 828-4400
Stephen Simmons, *President*
Jeremy Becker, *Plant Mgr*
Matt Seidel, *Purch Agent*
EMP: 42
SQ FT: 56,000
SALES: 15MM **Privately Held**
WEB: www.highlandplasticsinc.com
SIC: 3082 Unsupported plastics profile shapes

(G-14729)
JOAM INC
9495 S Green Rd (48883-7500)
PHONE.................................989 828-5749
Daniel Cottle, *CEO*
EMP: 3
SALES (est): 250K **Privately Held**
SIC: 3537 Industrial trucks & tractors

(G-14730)
PAUL JEFFREY KENNY
Also Called: Kenny Machining
1345 E Pleasant Valley Rd (48883-9528)
PHONE.................................989 828-6109
Paul Jeffrey Kenny, *Owner*
EMP: 8
SQ FT: 4,000
SALES: 490K **Privately Held**
SIC: 3599 Machine shop, jobbing & repair

(G-14731)
TOTAL CHIPS COMPANY INC
11285 S Winn Rd (48883-9544)
PHONE.................................989 866-2610
Ben C Nestle, *President*
Edward Morey, *Vice Pres*
EMP: 10
SQ FT: 6,000
SALES (est): 1MM **Privately Held**
SIC: 2411 2421 Logging; sawmills & planing mills, general

Sheridan
Montcalm County

(G-14732)
CUSTOM VINYL SIGNS & DESIGNS
3018 Log Cabin Trl (48884-9417)
PHONE.................................989 261-7446
Sheila Elderidge, *Owner*
Tom Elderidge, *Owner*
EMP: 3 **EST:** 1998
SALES: 140K **Privately Held**
SIC: 3993 Signs & advertising specialties

(G-14733)
PATRIOT PYROTECHNICS
5735 S Townhall Rd B (48884-9630)
PHONE.................................989 831-7788
Bill Collins, *Owner*
EMP: 4
SALES (est): 257.7K **Privately Held**
SIC: 2899 Fireworks

(G-14734)
PRECISION TOOL & MACHINE INC
154 E Condensery Rd (48884-9647)
PHONE.................................989 291-3365
John Roy, *President*
Heather Hardy, *Manager*
EMP: 5
SQ FT: 4,500
SALES: 250K **Privately Held**
SIC: 3599 Machine shop, jobbing & repair

(G-14735)
TOMMY JOE REED
Also Called: A & J Pallets
6551 S Townhall Rd (48884-9757)
PHONE.................................989 291-5768
Tommy J Reed, *Owner*
Joseph Reed, *Owner*
EMP: 5
SQ FT: 1,536
SALES (est): 248.8K **Privately Held**
SIC: 2448 Pallets, wood

(G-14736)
WRIGHT PLASTIC PRODUCTS CO LLC (PA)
201 E Condensery Rd (48884-9654)
PHONE.................................989 291-3211
Bob Luce, *Mng Member*
Dina Calcagno Masek,
Timothy Masek,
▲ **EMP:** 91 **EST:** 1973
SQ FT: 79,000
SALES: 38.5MM **Privately Held**
SIC: 3089 Injection molding of plastics

Sherwood
Branch County

(G-14737)
WOODCRAFTERS
Also Called: Woodcrafters Custom Furniture
855 Athens Rd (49089-9701)
PHONE.................................517 741-7423
Bill Shoop, *Partner*
Cal Shoop, *Partner*
EMP: 4 **EST:** 1962
SQ FT: 10,000
SALES: 125K **Privately Held**
WEB: www.woodcrafterscustomwoodworking.com
SIC: 2431 2511 Staircases, stairs & railings; wood household furniture

Sidney
Montcalm County

(G-14738)
CCO HOLDINGS LLC
2894 W Sidney Rd (48885-9751)
PHONE.................................989 328-4187
EMP: 3
SALES (corp-wide): 43.6B Publicly Held
SIC: 5064 4841 3663 3651 Electrical appliances, television & radio; cable & other pay television services; radio & TV communications equipment; household audio & video equipment
HQ: Cco Holdings, Llc
    400 Atlantic St
    Stamford CT 06901
    203 905-7801

Sidney
Oakland County

(G-14739)
FFT SIDNEY LLC
Also Called: Conform Automotive
1630 Ferguson Ct (48025)
PHONE.................................248 647-0400
Steven Phillips, *CEO*
John Anderson, *CFO*
EMP: 14 EST: 2013
SALES (est): 9.4MM Privately Held
SIC: 3442 3714 Moldings & trim, except automobile: metal; motor vehicle parts & accessories
PA: Detroit Technologies, Inc.
    32500 Telg Rd Ste 207
    Bingham Farms MI 48025

Six Lakes
Montcalm County

(G-14740)
HIGH GRADE MATERIALS COMPANY
3261 W Fleck Rd (48886-9738)
PHONE.................................989 365-3010
Ben Reynolds, *Manager*
EMP: 12
SALES (corp-wide): 28.3MM Privately Held
SIC: 3273 Ready-mixed concrete
PA: High Grade Materials Company
    9266 Snows Lake Rd
    Greenville MI 48838
    616 754-5545

Snover
Sanilac County

(G-14741)
ADVANCED AUTO TRENDS INC
3279 Washington St (48472-9601)
PHONE.................................810 672-9203
Rick Koshorek, *QC Mgr*
Pete Koprowski, *Branch Mgr*
Mike Robinson, *Info Tech Mgr*
EMP: 35
SALES (corp-wide): 29.6MM Privately Held
WEB: www.advancedautotrends.com
SIC: 3089 Injection molded finished plastic products
PA: Advanced Auto Trends, Inc.
    2230 Metamora Rd
    Oxford MI 48371
    248 628-6111

(G-14742)
ALBRECHT SAND & GRAVEL CO
3790 W Sanilac Rd (48472-9703)
PHONE.................................810 672-9272
Robert G Albrecht, *President*
Karen Downing, *Corp Secy*
EMP: 35
SQ FT: 1,000
SALES: 6.5MM Privately Held
SIC: 1442 Gravel mining

(G-14743)
ARCHER-DANIELS-MIDLAND COMPANY
Also Called: ADM
1337 W Elevator St (48472)
P.O. Box 8 (48472-0008)
PHONE.................................810 672-9221
Gary Flynn, *Branch Mgr*
EMP: 3
SALES (corp-wide): 64.3B Publicly Held
WEB: www.admworld.com
SIC: 2041 5153 Flour & other grain mill products; grain elevators
PA: Archer-Daniels-Midland Company
    77 W Wacker Dr Ste 4600
    Chicago IL 60601
    312 634-8100

(G-14744)
TWIN ASH FRMS ORGANIC PROC LLC
4175 Mushroom Rd (48472-9718)
P.O. Box 147 (48472-0147)
PHONE.................................810 404-1943
Teresa Berden Clarkson,
EMP: 4
SALES: 350K Privately Held
SIC: 2869 7349 Industrial organic chemicals; building maintenance services

Sodus
Berrien County

(G-14745)
HOME CITY ICE COMPANY
2875 S Pipestone Rd (49126-9717)
PHONE.................................269 926-2490
Joe Heck, *Branch Mgr*
EMP: 27
SALES (corp-wide): 234.4MM Privately Held
SIC: 2097 Manufactured ice
PA: The Home City Ice Company
    6045 Bridgetown Rd Ste 1
    Cincinnati OH 45248
    513 574-1800

(G-14746)
PRECISION MACHINING
2809 Yore Ave (49126-9716)
PHONE.................................269 925-5321
Emil Widmann, *Owner*
EMP: 3
SQ FT: 6,000
SALES (est): 206.4K Privately Held
SIC: 3544 Special dies & tools; industrial molds

(G-14747)
SODUS HARD CHROME INC
3085 Yore Ave (49126-9761)
PHONE.................................269 925-2077
Edward Thomas Sosnowski, *President*
Sally Sosnowski, *Vice Pres*
EMP: 15
SQ FT: 40,800
SALES (est): 1.3MM Privately Held
WEB: www.sodushardchrome.com
SIC: 7389 3471 Grinding, precision: commercial or industrial; chromium plating of metals or formed products

South Boardman
Kalkaska County

(G-14748)
ADVANCED ENERGY SERVICES LLC
Also Called: Advanced Energy Svc
5894 Puffer Rd Sw (49680-9723)
P.O. Box 85 (49680-0085)
PHONE.................................231 369-2602
Gary Provins, *President*
Jeffery Welch, *Vice Pres*
Steve Ordway, *Safety Dir*
Chris Diepenhorst, *CFO*
Randall Parsons,
EMP: 60
SQ FT: 50,000
SALES (est): 34MM Privately Held
WEB: www.advancedenergyservices.com
SIC: 1381 Drilling oil & gas wells

South Branch
Ogemaw County

(G-14749)
MATTHEWS MILL INC
6400 E County Line Rd (48761-9637)
P.O. Box 282 (48761-0282)
PHONE.................................989 257-3271
George Matthews Sr, *President*
George Matthews Jr, *Vice Pres*
Leroy Matthews, *Vice Pres*
Lisa Matthews, *Admin Sec*
EMP: 10
SALES (est): 2.2MM Privately Held
SIC: 2421 2448 Sawmills & planing mills, general; wood pallets & skids

(G-14750)
QUIGLEY LUMBER INC
5874 Heath Rd (48761-9515)
P.O. Box 141 (48761-0141)
PHONE.................................989 257-5116
James F Quigley, *President*
EMP: 9
SQ FT: 2,160
SALES: 1.5MM Privately Held
SIC: 2421 2426 Lumber: rough, sawed or planed; hardwood dimension & flooring mills

South Haven
Van Buren County

(G-14751)
ALBEMARLE CORPORATION
1421 Kalamazoo St (49090-1945)
PHONE.................................269 637-8474
Randy Andrews, *General Mgr*
Jason Fisher, *Opers Mgr*
Jessica Schneider, *Safety Mgr*
Janice Rissley, *Sales Executive*
Mike Annette, *Director*
EMP: 125 Publicly Held
WEB: www.stabrom.com
SIC: 2819 Industrial inorganic chemicals
PA: Albemarle Corporation
    4250 Congress St Ste 900
    Charlotte NC 28209

(G-14752)
AMERICAN TWISTING COMPANY (PA)
Also Called: AM Twist
1675 Stieve Dr (49090-9167)
P.O. Box 391 (49090-0391)
PHONE.................................269 637-8581
Thomas F Phelps Sr, *President*
Jeanne Phelps, *Vice Pres*
Thomas E Phelps Jr, *Treasurer*
Mark Rydecki, *Sales Staff*
Denise Tranker, *Manager*
▲ EMP: 26
SQ FT: 104,000
SALES (est): 4MM Privately Held
WEB: www.americantwisting.com
SIC: 2298 2621 2396 Twine, cord & cordage; cord, braided; cable, fiber; paper mills; automotive & apparel trimmings

(G-14753)
ANDERSEN BOAT WORKS
815 Wells St (49090-8643)
P.O. Box 856, Saugatuck (49453-0856)
PHONE.................................616 836-2502
Dave Andersen, *President*
EMP: 6
SALES (est): 658.5K Privately Held
SIC: 3732 Boat building & repairing

(G-14754)
APOGEE TECHNOLOGIES INC
170 Veterans Blvd 3 (49090-8630)
PHONE.................................269 639-1616
Gerald W Portman, *President*
Julie Portman, *Corp Secy*
EMP: 14
SALES (est): 1.5MM Privately Held
WEB: www.apogeemems.com
SIC: 2211 Scrub cloths

(G-14755)
B & K MACHINE PRODUCTS INC
100 Aylworth Ave (49090-1637)
P.O. Box 187 (49090-0187)
PHONE.................................269 637-3001
Gary Plankenhorn, *President*
Rich Ransom, *Vice Pres*
Paula Plankenhorn, *Treasurer*
EMP: 30
SALES (est): 3.9MM Privately Held
SIC: 3599 Machine shop, jobbing & repair

(G-14756)
CLASSIC STONE CREATIONS INC
1301 M 43 Ste 3 (49090-7506)
PHONE.................................269 637-9497
Kevin Coady, *President*
EMP: 8 EST: 1997
SQ FT: 1,600
SALES (est): 715.9K Privately Held
WEB: www.classicstonecreations.com
SIC: 3281 Table tops, marble

(G-14757)
COASTAL CONCIERGE
1210 Phoenix St Ste 9 (49090-7914)
PHONE.................................269 639-1515
Julie Vincent, *Owner*
EMP: 4
SALES (est): 479K Privately Held
SIC: 2842 Cleaning or polishing preparations

(G-14758)
DO-IT CORPORATION
1201 Blue Star Mem Hwy (49090)
P.O. Box 592 (49090-0592)
PHONE.................................269 637-1121
Mark T Mc Clendon, *President*
Jeff Wilson, *Mfg Staff*
Tracey Radtke, *Purch Mgr*
Lincoln Osbon, *Sales Mgr*
Dale Novotny, *IT/INT Sup*
◆ EMP: 65
SQ FT: 50,000
SALES (est): 12MM Privately Held
WEB: www.do-it.com
SIC: 3089 Clothes hangers, plastic

(G-14759)
FOODTOOLS INC
190 Veterans Blvd (49090-8630)
PHONE.................................269 637-9969
David Thompson, *Opers Staff*
Todd Schubert, *Regl Sales Mgr*
Douglas Petrovich, *Manager*
EMP: 30
SALES (corp-wide): 11.1MM Privately Held
WEB: www.foodtools.com
SIC: 3556 Slicers, commercial, food
PA: Foodtools Consolidated, Inc.
    315 Laguna St
    Santa Barbara CA 93101
    805 962-8383

(G-14760)
GAC
1301 M 43 (49090-7506)
PHONE.................................269 639-3010
Bill Pater, *Owner*
▲ EMP: 25
SALES (est): 2.7MM Privately Held
SIC: 3713 Truck bodies & parts

(G-14761)
GRAND STRATEGY LLC
15038 73rd St (49090-8976)
PHONE.................................269 637-8330
Gregory L Fones, *President*
John Jackoboice,
Jeffrey G Muth,
Edward Perdue,
EMP: 4
SQ FT: 1,500
SALES: 2.5MM Privately Held
SIC: 2211 Towels, dishcloths & washcloths: cotton

South Haven - Van Buren County (G-14762)

(G-14762)
HAVEN SPORTS MANUFACTURING LLC
67294 Becky Ln (49090-8311)
PHONE.....................269 639-8782
EMP: 3
SALES (est): 140K Privately Held
SIC: 3999 Mfg Misc Products

(G-14763)
LOOPE ENTERPRISES INC
Also Called: South Haven Packaging
73475 8th Ave (49090-9769)
PHONE.....................269 639-1567
Brian Loope, *President*
EMP: 12 EST: 2012
SQ FT: 55,000
SALES (est): 1MM Privately Held
SIC: 2653 Boxes, corrugated: made from purchased materials

(G-14764)
LOVEJOY INC
200 Lovejoy Ave (49090-1652)
PHONE.....................269 637-3017
Mark Goodrich, *Branch Mgr*
EMP: 55
SALES (corp-wide): 3.5B Publicly Held
WEB: www.lovejoy-inc.com
SIC: 3568 Couplings, shaft: rigid, flexible, universal joint, etc.; pulleys, power transmission
HQ: Lovejoy, Inc.
    2655 Wisconsin Ave
    Downers Grove IL 60515
    630 852-0500

(G-14765)
LOVEJOY CURTIS LLC (DH)
200 Lovejoy Ave (49090-1652)
PHONE.....................269 637-5132
John R Szarka, *President*
Hansal N Patel, *Admin Sec*
Ryan Hartong,
EMP: 2
SALES (est): 2.1MM
SALES (corp-wide): 3.5B Publicly Held
SIC: 3568 Couplings, shaft: rigid, flexible, universal joint, etc.
HQ: Lovejoy, Inc.
    2655 Wisconsin Ave
    Downers Grove IL 60515
    630 852-0500

(G-14766)
NATIONAL APPLIANCE PARTS CO
Also Called: Napco
900 Indiana Ave (49090)
P.O. Box 474 (49090-0474)
PHONE.....................269 639-1469
Sandra Keathley, *Vice Pres*
▲ EMP: 17
SALES (est): 2.8MM Privately Held
SIC: 3567 Heating units & devices, industrial: electric

(G-14767)
PETTER INVESTMENTS INC
Also Called: Riveer Environmental, The
233 Veterans Blvd (49090-8632)
PHONE.....................269 637-1997
Mathew Petter, *President*
Doug Petter, *Vice Pres*
▲ EMP: 15
SQ FT: 7,000
SALES (est): 8.1MM Privately Held
SIC: 3569 3531 5082 Filters; construction machinery; pavers

(G-14768)
PRECISION MACHINE CO S HAVEN
435 66th St (49090-9545)
PHONE.....................269 637-2372
Carl L Brenner, *President*
EMP: 8 EST: 1973
SALES: 1.9MM Privately Held
SIC: 3451 Screw machine products

(G-14769)
RODS PRINTS & PROMOTIONS
67654 M 43 (49090-8752)
PHONE.....................269 639-8814
Rodney Brinks, *Owner*
EMP: 3
SALES: 49K Privately Held
SIC: 2759 Screen printing

(G-14770)
SHERMAN DAIRY PRODUCTS CO INC
Also Called: Sherman Dairy Bar
1601 Phoenix St (49090-7156)
P.O. Box 529 (49090-0529)
PHONE.....................269 637-8251
Robert V Eisenman, *President*
Jeanine Eisenman, *Vice Pres*
EMP: 15
SALES (est): 2.4MM Privately Held
WEB: www.shermanicecream.com
SIC: 2024 Ice cream, bulk; ice cream, packaged: molded, on sticks, etc.; sherbets, dairy based; yogurt desserts, frozen

(G-14771)
SOUTH HAVEN COIL INC (HQ)
05585 Blue Star Mem Hwy (49090-8189)
P.O. Box 2008, Kalamazoo (49003-2008)
PHONE.....................269 637-5201
Randall M Webber, *Ch of Bd*
Brenda Balfour, *Manager*
Melvin Cole, *Maintence Staff*
EMP: 30 EST: 1957
SQ FT: 18,000
SALES (est): 7.9MM
SALES (corp-wide): 34MM Privately Held
WEB: www.southhavencoil.com
SIC: 3677 Coil windings, electronic
PA: Humphrey Products Company
    5070 E N Ave
    Kalamazoo MI 49048
    269 381-5500

(G-14772)
SOUTH HAVEN FINISHING INC
1610 Stieve Dr (49090-9167)
PHONE.....................269 637-2047
Eric Ellison, *President*
EMP: 25
SQ FT: 12,000
SALES (est): 3.5MM Privately Held
WEB: www.southhavenfinishing.com
SIC: 3471 3398 Finishing, metals or formed products; polishing, metals or formed products; buffing for the trade; cleaning, polishing & finishing; metal heat treating

(G-14773)
SOUTH HAVEN PACKAGING INC
73475 8th Ave (49090-9769)
PHONE.....................269 639-1567
Randy Mohler, *President*
EMP: 15
SQ FT: 31,000
SALES (est): 4MM
SALES (corp-wide): 29.8MM Privately Held
SIC: 2653 Boxes, corrugated: made from purchased materials
PA: Kindlon Enterprises, Inc
    2300 Raddant Rd Ste B
    Aurora IL 60502
    708 367-4000

(G-14774)
SOUTH HAVEN TRIBUNE
308 Kalamazoo St (49090-1308)
PHONE.....................269 637-1104
Becky Burkert, *General Mgr*
Jim Pezzuto, *Superintendent*
EMP: 4
SALES (est): 190K Privately Held
WEB: www.southhaventribune.com
SIC: 2711 Newspapers: publishing only, not printed on site

(G-14775)
SPENCER MANUFACTURING INC
165 Veterans Dr (49090-8650)
PHONE.....................269 637-9459
Brian Spencer, *President*
Peggy Spencer, *Corp Secy*
Ken Wattrick, *Manager*
Amy Dannenberg, *Technology*
EMP: 15
SQ FT: 26,000
SALES (est): 4.5MM Privately Held
WEB: www.spencermfginc.com
SIC: 3711 Fire department vehicles (motor vehicles), assembly of

(G-14776)
SYSTEM COMPONENTS INC
1635 Stieve Dr (49090-9167)
PHONE.....................269 637-2191
Eugen Gawreliuk, *President*
Mary Gawreliuk, *Vice Pres*
▲ EMP: 40 EST: 1965
SQ FT: 40,000
SALES: 10MM Privately Held
WEB: www.sci-couplings.com
SIC: 3568 Couplings, shaft: rigid, flexible, universal joint, etc.

(G-14777)
TAYLOR CONTROLS INC
10529 Blue Star Mem Hwy (49090-9401)
P.O. Box 362 (49090-0362)
PHONE.....................269 637-8521
Terry L Taylor, *President*
EMP: 14
SQ FT: 5,400
SALES: 745.8K Privately Held
SIC: 3297 3822 3823 3443 Cement: high temperature, refractory (nonclay); thermostats & other environmental sensors; industrial instrmnts msrmnt display/control process variable; fabricated plate work (boiler shop)

(G-14778)
TRELLEBORG CORPORATION (HQ)
200 Veterans Blvd Ste 3 (49090-8663)
PHONE.....................269 639-9891
Torgney Astrom, *President*
Jeannette Goh, *President*
Jose De, *Managing Dir*
Richard Hodgson, *Vice Pres*
Rosman Jahja, *Vice Pres*
◆ EMP: 1
SALES (est): 1.1B
SALES (corp-wide): 3.7B Privately Held
SIC: 1021 3341 1031 1044 Copper ore mining & preparation; secondary precious metals; zinc ores mining; silver ores mining; liquid storage; gold ores mining
PA: Trelleborg Ab
    Johan Kocksgatan 10
    Trelleborg 231 4
    410 670-00

(G-14779)
USMFG INC
1500 Kalamazoo St (49090-1944)
PHONE.....................262 993-9197
Paul Kline, *Manager*
EMP: 5
SALES (corp-wide): 197.6MM Privately Held
SIC: 3325 Steel foundries
HQ: Usmfg, Inc.
    28400 Northwestern Hwy # 2
    Southfield MI 48034
    269 637-6392

(G-14780)
VIBRACOUSTIC NORTH AMERICA L P (HQ)
400 Aylworth Ave (49090-1707)
PHONE.....................269 637-2116
Mehdi Ilkhani, *President*
Ronald S Guest, *General Ptnr*
Leesa Smith, *General Ptnr*
Sergus R Thomas, *General Ptnr*
John Prince, *Vice Pres*
◆ EMP: 20
SALES (est): 124.4MM
SALES (corp-wide): 2.4B Privately Held
SIC: 2821 3714 3053 3061 Plastics materials & resins; motor vehicle parts & accessories; gaskets, packing & sealing devices; mechanical rubber goods
PA: Vibracoustic Ag
    Europaplatz 4
    Darmstadt 64293
    615 139-640

(G-14781)
VIBRACOUSTIC USA INC (HQ)
Also Called: Trelleborg Automotive
400 Aylworth Ave (49090-1707)
PHONE.....................269 637-2116
Kelly Reynolds, *President*
Bob Prostko, *Managing Dir*
Hakan Cirag, *Vice Pres*
Evelyn Wu, *Purch Mgr*
Joakim Hansson, *Purchasing*
▲ EMP: 165
SQ FT: 60,000
SALES (est): 250.2MM
SALES (corp-wide): 2.4B Privately Held
WEB: www.trelleborg.com
SIC: 3061 3625 Automotive rubber goods (mechanical); noise control equipment
PA: Vibracoustic Ag
    Europaplatz 4
    Darmstadt 64293
    615 139-640

(G-14782)
VOCHASKA ENGINEERING
66935 County Road 388 (49090-9320)
PHONE.....................269 637-5670
Vern A Vochaska, *Owner*
EMP: 4
SQ FT: 6,656
SALES (est): 550K Privately Held
SIC: 7539 3441 7692 Machine shop, automotive; fabricated structural metal; welding repair

(G-14783)
WARNER VINEYARDS INC
515 Williams St (49090-2513)
PHONE.....................269 637-6900
Patrick Warner, *Branch Mgr*
EMP: 3
SALES (corp-wide): 522.8K Privately Held
SIC: 2084 Wines
PA: Warner Vineyards Inc
    706 S Kalamazoo St
    Paw Paw MI 49079
    269 657-3165

(G-14784)
WINN ARCHERY EQUIPMENT CO
13757 64th St (49090-8155)
PHONE.....................269 637-2658
Geary Garvison, *President*
Rosanne Garvison, *Corp Secy*
EMP: 3
SQ FT: 1,285
SALES (est): 389.5K Privately Held
WEB: www.winnarchery.com
SIC: 3949 5941 Archery equipment, general; sporting goods & bicycle shops

South Lyon
Oakland County

(G-14785)
AKTV8 LLC
10056 Colonial Indus Dr (48178-9154)
PHONE.....................517 775-1270
EMP: 7 EST: 2015
SALES (est): 798.4K Privately Held
SIC: 3679 Electronic switches

(G-14786)
BEEBE FUEL SYSTEMS INC
6351 Wilderness Dr (48178-7038)
PHONE.....................248 437-3322
Dale Belsley, *Principal*
EMP: 3
SALES (est): 221.5K Privately Held
SIC: 2869 Fuels

(G-14787)
BROWNIE SIGNS LLC
8791 Earhart Rd (48178-7015)
PHONE.....................248 437-0800
Brad Braun,
EMP: 4
SALES: 320K Privately Held
SIC: 3993 Neon signs

GEOGRAPHIC SECTION
South Range - Houghton County (G-14818)

(G-14788)
CAMBRIDGE SHARPE INC
8325 N Rushton Rd (48178-9119)
PHONE..................................248 613-5562
Richard E Sharpe, *President*
EMP: 100
SQ FT: 100,000
SALES: 15MM **Privately Held**
SIC: 2096 3714 Potato chips & similar snacks; motor vehicle parts & accessories

(G-14789)
CLIPS COUPONS OF ANN ARBO
9477 Silverside (48178-8809)
PHONE..................................248 437-9294
William Bunn, *Owner*
EMP: 4
SALES (est): 215.9K **Privately Held**
SIC: 3993 Signs & advertising specialties

(G-14790)
EMERY DESIGN & WOODWORK LLC
8277 Tower Rd (48178-9683)
PHONE..................................734 709-1687
Jacquelyn Emery, *Principal*
EMP: 4 **EST:** 2010
SALES (est): 288.5K **Privately Held**
SIC: 2431 Millwork

(G-14791)
EXPRESS CARE OF SOUTH LYON
501 S Lafayette St (48178-1490)
PHONE..................................248 437-6919
Travis Curry, *Owner*
EMP: 4
SALES (est): 287.8K **Privately Held**
SIC: 1382 Oil & gas exploration services

(G-14792)
GALE TOOL CO INC
10801 N Rushton Rd (48178-9135)
PHONE..................................248 437-4610
Robert Gale, *President*
EMP: 3
SQ FT: 1,800
SALES (est): 320K **Privately Held**
SIC: 3312 Tool & die steel & alloys

(G-14793)
GREEN INDUSTRIES INC
515 N Mill St (48178-1262)
PHONE..................................248 446-8900
David W Green, *President*
EMP: 12
SQ FT: 10,000
SALES: 846.8K **Privately Held**
SIC: 3451 Screw machine products

(G-14794)
INTEGRATED PRACTICE SERVICE
111 S Lafayette St # 609 (48178-9924)
PHONE..................................248 646-7009
Jeff Burton, *Principal*
EMP: 5
SALES (est): 128.9K **Privately Held**
SIC: 7372 Prepackaged software

(G-14795)
INTERNATIONAL MACHINING SVC
Also Called: Imservice
12622 10 Mile Rd (48178-9141)
P.O. Box 142 (48178-0142)
PHONE..................................248 486-3600
Fred Smith, *President*
EMP: 4 **EST:** 2000
SALES (est): 320K **Privately Held**
WEB: www.imsrv.com
SIC: 3599 7371 Machine shop, jobbing & repair; custom computer programming services

(G-14796)
IXL GRAPHICS INC
23265 Country Club Dr (48178-9815)
PHONE..................................313 350-2800
August Anthony Grebinski, *President*
EMP: 2
SALES (est): 2.5MM **Privately Held**
SIC: 2759 7389 Advertising literature: printing;

(G-14797)
KEMARI LLC
11986 Ruth St (48178-9128)
PHONE..................................248 348-7407
Mack Dobbie,
Richard Englert,
Kent Symanzik,
EMP: 3
SALES (est): 126.6K **Privately Held**
SIC: 7372 7389 Prepackaged software;

(G-14798)
KILLER PAINT BALL
509 S Lafayette St (48178-1490)
PHONE..................................248 491-0088
EMP: 7 **EST:** 2000
SALES (est): 416.3K **Privately Held**
SIC: 3949 Mfg Sporting/Athletic Goods

(G-14799)
KOLCO INDUSTRIES INC
10078 Colonial Indus Dr (48178-9154)
PHONE..................................248 486-1690
Chris Koltz, *President*
EMP: 6
SALES: 700K **Privately Held**
SIC: 3559 Automotive related machinery

(G-14800)
LGA RETAIL INC
22770 Spy Glass Hill Dr (48178-9433)
PHONE..................................248 910-1918
EMP: 4 **EST:** 2017
SALES (est): 270.9K **Privately Held**
SIC: 3571 Personal computers (microcomputers)

(G-14801)
MICHIGAN SEAMLESS TUBE LLC
Also Called: Blue Diamond
400 Mcmunn St (48178-1379)
PHONE..................................248 486-0100
Joel Hawthorne, *CEO*
Ted Fairley, *Vice Pres*
Cassie Furey, *Engineer*
Mark Baugous, *Design Engr*
Kathy Sobiesiak, *Credit Staff*
▲ **EMP:** 280
SQ FT: 440,000
SALES (est): 134.9MM
SALES (corp-wide): 472.4MM **Privately Held**
WEB: www.michiganseamlesstube.com
SIC: 3317 Tubes, seamless steel
PA: Specialty Steel Works Incorporated
1412 150th St
Hammond IN 46327
877 289-2277

(G-14802)
MIRROR IMAGE INC
3700 5 Mile Rd (48178-9696)
PHONE..................................248 446-8440
Alfonso Bologna, *President*
EMP: 3
SALES: 350K **Privately Held**
SIC: 3211 Flat glass

(G-14803)
MULTIFORM STUDIOS LLC
12012 Doane Rd (48178-8801)
PHONE..................................248 437-5964
James Leacock, *Principal*
EMP: 5
SQ FT: 4,000
SALES (est): 529.4K **Privately Held**
WEB: www.multiformstudios.com
SIC: 2531 Public building & related furniture

(G-14804)
MYKIN INC
Also Called: Midnight Scoop
10081 Colonial Indus Dr (48178-9153)
PHONE..................................248 667-8030
Michael Chou, *President*
▲ **EMP:** 12
SQ FT: 15,000
SALES: 5MM **Privately Held**
SIC: 3069 2822 5122 Custom compounding of rubber materials; rubber automotive products; synthetic rubber; butadiene-acrylonitrile, nitrile rubbers, NBR; medical rubber goods

(G-14805)
NIMS PRECISION MACHINING INC
9493 Pontiac Trl (48178-7020)
PHONE..................................248 446-1053
Joann Nims, *President*
Myrom Nims, *Vice Pres*
EMP: 4
SALES: 100K **Privately Held**
WEB: www.nims-precision.com
SIC: 3599 Machine shop, jobbing & repair

(G-14806)
NOIR MEDICAL TECHNOLOGIES LLC
Also Called: Noir Manufacturing
10125 Colonial Indus Dr (48178-9151)
PHONE..................................248 486-3760
A Brooks Gleichert, *Partner*
Michael Smiglewski, *Mfg Staff*
Marc Gleichert, *Purch Dir*
EMP: 15
SALES (est): 1.8MM
SALES (corp-wide): 5MM **Privately Held**
WEB: www.noir-medical.com
SIC: 3851 3842 Glasses, sun or glare; surgical appliances & supplies
PA: Noir Medical Technologies Llc
4975 Technical Dr
Milford MI 48381
734 769-5565

(G-14807)
NOPRAS TECHNOLOGIES INC
13513 Windmoor Dr (48178-8145)
PHONE..................................248 486-6684
EMP: 4
SALES (est): 187K **Privately Held**
SIC: 5912 5122 2834 Drug stores & proprietary stores; toothbrushes, except electric; pharmaceutical preparations

(G-14808)
PALM INDUSTRIES LLC
4285 Clair Dr (48178-9633)
PHONE..................................248 444-7922
Paul Pattee, *Mng Member*
Dawn Pattee, *Mng Member*
EMP: 3
SALES: 347K **Privately Held**
SIC: 3999 3559 Airplane models, except toy; models, except toy; automotive related machinery

(G-14809)
PHOENIX INDUCTION CORPORATION
10132 Colonial Indus Dr (48178-9150)
PHONE..................................248 486-7377
Marc Senters, *President*
Robert Van Aken, *Vice Pres*
EMP: 10
SQ FT: 6,000
SALES (est): 2MM **Privately Held**
SIC: 3567 5075 Induction heating equipment; furnaces, heating: electric; fans, heating & ventilation equipment

(G-14810)
PITNEY BOWES INC
23594 Prescott Ln W (48178-8240)
PHONE..................................203 356-5000
David Appicelli, *Principal*
EMP: 60
SALES (corp-wide): 3.5B **Publicly Held**
SIC: 3579 Mailing machines
PA: Pitney Bowes Inc.
3001 Summer St Ste 3
Stamford CT 06905
203 356-5000

(G-14811)
RAINMAKER FOOD SOLUTIONS LLC
22857 Saint Andrews Dr (48178-9444)
PHONE..................................313 530-1321
Christopher J Mattina, *Mng Member*
EMP: 6
SQ FT: 3,000
SALES (est): 500.1K **Privately Held**
SIC: 2096 Potato chips & similar snacks

(G-14812)
SERVICE IRON WORKS INC
245 S Mill St (48178-1813)
PHONE..................................248 446-9750
Kerry Holmes, *President*
Cindee Ahn, *Principal*
Bob Harteg, *Principal*
Claudia Needham, *Principal*
Stan Zasuwa, *Principal*
EMP: 25
SQ FT: 60,000
SALES (est): 8.4MM **Privately Held**
WEB: www.serviceiron.com
SIC: 3441 3312 Fabricated structural metal; blast furnaces & steel mills

(G-14813)
SUN STEEL TREATING INC
550 N Mill St (48178-1263)
P.O. Box 759 (48178-0759)
PHONE..................................877 471-0844
William Niedzwiecki, *Principal*
Chris Baer, *Buyer*
EMP: 67 **EST:** 1958
SQ FT: 40,000
SALES: 10MM **Privately Held**
SIC: 3398 Annealing of metal

(G-14814)
TRIUNFAR INDUSTRIES INC
10813 Bouldercrest Dr (48178-8200)
PHONE..................................313 790-5592
Anthony Morales II, *CEO*
EMP: 4
SALES (est): 170.5K **Privately Held**
SIC: 3999 Manufacturing industries

(G-14815)
TUTHILL FARMS & COMPOSTING
10505 Tuthill Rd (48178-9338)
PHONE..................................248 437-7354
Sandra Tuthill, *President*
James Tuthill, *Vice Pres*
EMP: 3
SALES (est): 417.7K **Privately Held**
WEB: www.tuthillfarms.com
SIC: 2875 0211 0251 Compost; beef cattle feedlots; broiler, fryer & roaster chickens

(G-14816)
UNIVERSAL HEATING AND COOLING
6301 Pontiac Trl (48178-9647)
PHONE..................................734 216-5826
Mark Willets, *President*
Shirley Willetts, *Vice Pres*
EMP: 3
SALES: 100K **Privately Held**
SIC: 3585 Heating & air conditioning combination units

South Range
Houghton County

(G-14817)
KEWEENAW BREWING COMPANY LLC
10 4th St (49963-5102)
P.O. Box 7 (49963-0007)
PHONE..................................906 482-1937
Richard J Gray, *Branch Mgr*
EMP: 9
SALES (corp-wide): 2.6MM **Privately Held**
SIC: 2082 Beer (alcoholic beverage)
PA: Keweenaw Brewing Company, Llc
408 Shelden Ave
Houghton MI 49931
906 482-5596

(G-14818)
NORTHERN HARDWOODS OPER CO LLC
45807 Hwy M 26 (49963)
PHONE..................................860 632-3505
Theodore P Rossi, *Mng Member*
Andrew E Becker,
EMP: 70
SQ FT: 4,500

South Range - Houghton County (G-14819)

SALES (est): 7.1MM **Privately Held**
SIC: **2421** 5031 Sawmills & planing mills, general; lumber, plywood & millwork

(G-14819)
SOUTH RANGE BOTTLING WORKS INC
23 Champion St (49963-5108)
P.O. Box 9 (49963-0009)
PHONE....................906 370-2295
Margaret Hayrynen, *President*
Scott Hayrynen, *Trustee*
Randall Hayrynen, *Vice Pres*
EMP: 3 EST: 1963
SQ FT: 5,000
SALES (est): 743K **Privately Held**
SIC: **5149** 2086 Soft drinks; bottled & canned soft drinks

South Rockwood
Monroe County

(G-14820)
BRADYS FENCE COMPANY INC
11093 Armstrong Rd (48179-9762)
PHONE....................313 492-8804
Mark Brady, *President*
EMP: 4
SALES (est): 394.9K **Privately Held**
SIC: **1799** 3089 3446 5039 Fence construction; fences, gates & accessories: plastic; fences or posts, ornamental iron or steel; wire fence, gates & accessories

(G-14821)
GREAT LAKES AGGREGATES LLC (PA)
Also Called: Sylvania Minerals
5699 Ready Rd (48179-9592)
PHONE....................734 379-0311
Chris Kinney, *President*
Keith Childress, *QC Mgr*
Bill Begley, *Manager*
Tom Downs, *Manager*
Daniel Clark,
EMP: 71
SALES (est): 76.1MM **Privately Held**
WEB: www.greatlakesagg.com
SIC: **1422** Lime rock, ground

(G-14822)
ROCKWOOD QUARRY LLC (PA)
5699 Ready Rd (48179-9592)
P.O. Box 406 (48179-0406)
PHONE....................734 783-7415
Jim Friel, *Mng Member*
Jamie Jacobs,
Chris Peyerk,
EMP: 125
SALES (est): 14.4MM **Privately Held**
SIC: **3281** Stone, quarrying & processing of own stone products

Southfield
Oakland County

(G-14823)
ABC GROUP HOLDINGS INC (DH)
Also Called: ABC Group Sale & Marketing
24133 Northwestern Hwy (48075-2568)
PHONE....................248 352-3706
Mike Schmidt, *President*
Ray Tinoli, *Vice Pres*
James Augustine, *Treasurer*
◆ EMP: 1 EST: 2001
SALES (est): 160.8MM
SALES (corp-wide): 28B **Privately Held**
SIC: **3089** Blow molded finished plastic products; injection molded finished plastic products
HQ: Abc Group Limited
2 Norelco Dr
North York ON M9L 2
416 246-1782

(G-14824)
AIN PLASTICS
23235 Telegraph Rd (48033-4127)
P.O. Box 5116 (48086-5116)
PHONE....................248 356-4000
Michael Dantonio, *President*
EMP: 14
SALES (est): 2.3MM **Privately Held**
SIC: **3089** Plastic processing

(G-14825)
AIR-MATIC PRODUCTS COMPANY INC (PA)
22218 Telegraph Rd (48033-4263)
PHONE....................248 356-4200
Jeffrey W Smolek, *President*
EMP: 25 EST: 1950
SQ FT: 44,000
SALES (est): 3.6MM **Privately Held**
WEB: www.air-matic.com
SIC: **3451** Screw machine products

(G-14826)
AKTIS ENGRG SOLUTIONS INC
17340 W 12 Mile Rd Ste 20 (48076-2122)
PHONE....................313 450-2420
Sandeep Nair, *President*
Shuvendu Mishra, *Manager*
EMP: 2
SQ FT: 350
SALES (est): 2MM **Privately Held**
SIC: **3089** 8711 Automotive parts, plastic; designing: ship, boat, machine & product
PA: Aktis Engineering Solutions Private Limited
I Floor Jnr Plaza
Bengaluru KA 56006

(G-14827)
ALLEGRA PRINT & IMAGING
28810 Northwestern Hwy (48034-1831)
PHONE....................248 354-1313
Gerald Christensen, *Principal*
EMP: 4
SALES (est): 527.1K **Privately Held**
SIC: **2752** Commercial printing, offset

(G-14828)
ALPHA 21 LLC
22400 Telegraph Rd Ste A (48033-6800)
PHONE....................248 352-7330
Walter Hutchinson, *Mng Member*
Arnold Weingart,
EMP: 4
SQ FT: 2,700
SALES (est): 724.5K **Privately Held**
WEB: www.alpha21.com
SIC: **2796** 7336 Color separations for printing; art design services

(G-14829)
ALTA DISTRIBUTION LLC
21650 W 11 Mile Rd (48076-3715)
PHONE....................313 363-1682
Kenneth Allen,
EMP: 10
SALES (est): 311.4K **Privately Held**
SIC: **3999** 5047 Manufacturing industries; medical & hospital equipment

(G-14830)
ALTA VISTA TECHNOLOGY LLC
24700 Northwestern Hwy (48075-2315)
PHONE....................248 733-4504
Scott Jackson, *President*
Hollie Murray, *Vice Pres*
David Valade, *Vice Pres*
EMP: 12
SALES (est): 453.6K **Privately Held**
SIC: **7372** Application computer software

(G-14831)
ALUDYNE INC (HQ)
300 Galleria Ofcntr Ste 5 (48034-4700)
PHONE....................248 728-8642
Andreas Weller, *President*
Julie Samson, *Vice Pres*
Len Bogus, *Vice Pres*
Alexandre Debrye, *Vice Pres*
Michael Dorah, *Vice Pres*
EMP: 200 EST: 2012
SQ FT: 28,000
SALES (est): 1B
SALES (corp-wide): 1.3B **Privately Held**
SIC: **3714** Motor vehicle parts & accessories
PA: Uc Holdings, Inc.
300 Galleria Officentre
Southfield MI 48034
248 728-8642

(G-14832)
ALUDYNE COLUMBUS LLC (DH)
Also Called: Dmi Columbus, LLC
300 Galleria Ofcntr Ste 5 (48034-4700)
P.O. Box 4201, Columbus GA (31914-0201)
PHONE....................248 728-8642
Julie Samson, *Finance Dir*
Andreas Weller,
Michael Beyer,
▲ EMP: 482
SALES (est): 93.2MM
SALES (corp-wide): 1.3B **Privately Held**
SIC: **3714** Motor vehicle parts & accessories
HQ: Aludyne North America Inc.
300 Galleria Ofcntr Ste 5
Southfield MI 48034
248 728-8642

(G-14833)
ALUDYNE INTERNATIONAL INC (DH)
Also Called: Concord International, Inc.
300 Galleria Ofcntr Ste 5 (48034-4700)
PHONE....................248 728-8642
EMP: 1
SQ FT: 28,000
SALES (est): 88.4MM
SALES (corp-wide): 1.3B **Privately Held**
WEB: www.concordintl.com
SIC: **3465** Body parts, automobile: stamped metal
HQ: Aludyne, Inc.
300 Galleria Ofcntr Ste 5
Southfield MI 48034
248 728-8642

(G-14834)
ALUDYNE MONTAGUE LLC (DH)
Also Called: Chassix - Dmi Montague
300 Galleria Ofcntr Ste 5 (48034-4700)
PHONE....................248 479-6455
Andreas Weller, *CEO*
Michael Beyer, *CFO*
Mary Twa, *Training Spec*
Harvey Pruitt, *Maintence Staff*
▲ EMP: 600
SQ FT: 320,000
SALES (est): 163.1MM
SALES (corp-wide): 1.3B **Privately Held**
SIC: **3714** Motor vehicle parts & accessories
HQ: Aludyne North America Inc.
300 Galleria Ofcntr Ste 5
Southfield MI 48034
248 728-8642

(G-14835)
ALUDYNE NORTH AMERICA INC (DH)
300 Galleria Ofcntr Ste 5 (48034-4700)
PHONE....................248 728-8642
Andreas Weller, *CEO*
Safi Hamid, *Vice Pres*
Eric Rouchy, *Vice Pres*
Michael Beyer, *CFO*
▲ EMP: 5
SQ FT: 28,000
SALES (est): 459.1MM
SALES (corp-wide): 1.3B **Privately Held**
WEB: www.divmi.com
SIC: **3714** Motor vehicle parts & accessories
HQ: Aludyne, Inc.
300 Galleria Ofcntr Ste 5
Southfield MI 48034
248 728-8642

(G-14836)
AMERICAN AXLE & MFG INC
Also Called: AAM Southfield
4000 Town Ctr Ste 500 (48075-1419)
PHONE....................248 522-4500
Chris Lautzenhiser, *Manager*
Jeff Dean, *Associate*
EMP: 100

SALES (corp-wide): 7.2B **Publicly Held**
WEB: www.berlin.citation.net
SIC: **3321** 3599 Gray iron castings; machine & other job shop work
HQ: American Axle & Manufacturing, Inc.
1 Dauch Dr
Detroit MI 48211

(G-14837)
AMERICAN WLDG & PRESS REPR INC
26500 W 8 Mile Rd (48033-5924)
PHONE....................248 358-2050
William A Sheffer, *President*
EMP: 10
SQ FT: 18,000
SALES (est): 1.9MM **Privately Held**
SIC: **7699** 7692 7629 3542 Industrial machinery & equipment repair; welding repair; electrical repair shops; machine tools, metal forming type

(G-14838)
ANGSTROM USA LLC (HQ)
2000 Town Ctr Ste 1100 (48075-1251)
PHONE....................313 295-0100
Nagesh Palakurthi, *CEO*
Rajenesh Banga, *Vice Pres*
Jayanth Karnam, *Plant Mgr*
Lalitha Dadiraju, *Controller*
Sandra Bradford, *Ch Credit Ofcr*
◆ EMP: 25
SALES (est): 41.8MM **Privately Held**
WEB: www.angstrom-usa.com
SIC: **5531** 3317 Automotive parts: tubes, seamless steel

(G-14839)
ANSO PRODUCTS
21380 Telegraph Rd (48033-4217)
PHONE....................248 357-2300
Tom Timmins, *President*
EMP: 5
SALES (est): 237K **Privately Held**
SIC: **2522** 5021 5932 Office furniture, except wood; office & public building furniture; office furniture & store fixtures, secondhand

(G-14840)
ARTISTIC PRINTING INC
26040 W 12 Mile Rd (48034-1783)
PHONE....................248 356-1004
Roy Swinea Jr, *President*
EMP: 4
SQ FT: 1,500
SALES: 450K **Privately Held**
SIC: **2752** 2759 Commercial printing, offset; laser printing

(G-14841)
ASIMCO INTERNATIONAL INC
1000 Town Ctr Ste 1050 (48075-1261)
PHONE....................248 213-5200
Gary W Riley, *President*
▲ EMP: 9 EST: 1997
SQ FT: 7,000
SALES (est): 30.5MM **Privately Held**
SIC: **5013** 3679 Automotive supplies & parts; recording & playback apparatus, including phonograph
HQ: Asimco Technologies, Inc.
1000 Town Ctr Ste 1050
Southfield MI 48075
248 213-5200

(G-14842)
ASP GREDE ACQUISITIONCO LLC (DH)
1 Towne Sq Ste 550 (48076-3710)
PHONE....................248 727-1800
David C Dauch, *Ch of Bd*
EMP: 4
SALES (est): 675.3MM
SALES (corp-wide): 7.2B **Publicly Held**
SIC: **3714** 3711 Motor vehicle parts & accessories; motor vehicles & car bodies
HQ: Asp Grede Intermediate Holdings Llc
1 Dauch Dr
Detroit MI 48211
313 758-2000

GEOGRAPHIC SECTION
Southfield - Oakland County (G-14867)

(G-14843)
ASP HHI INTERMEDIATE HOLDINGS (DH)
1 Towne Sq Ste 550 (48076-3710)
PHONE..................................248 727-1800
David C Dauch, *Ch of Bd*
EMP: 5
SALES (est): 328.8MM
SALES (corp-wide): 7.2B **Publicly Held**
SIC: 3711 3714 Motor vehicles & car bodies; motor vehicle parts & accessories
HQ: Asp Hhi Intermediate Holdings, Inc.
1 Towne Sq Ste 550
Southfield MI 48076
248 727-1800

(G-14844)
ASP HHI INTRMDATE HOLDINGS INC (DH)
1 Towne Sq Ste 550 (48076-3710)
PHONE..................................248 727-1800
David C Dauch, *Ch of Bd*
EMP: 3
SALES (est): 530.3MM
SALES (corp-wide): 7.2B **Publicly Held**
SIC: 3714 3711 Motor vehicle parts & accessories; motor vehicles & car bodies
HQ: Asp Hhi Holdings, Inc.
2727 W 14 Mile Rd
Royal Oak MI 48073
248 597-3800

(G-14845)
AURIA SOLUTIONS USA INC (DH)
26999 Central Park Blvd # 300 (48076-4178)
PHONE..................................734 456-2800
Brian Pour, *President*
Qiuming Yang, *Exec VP*
Tom Allard, *Vice Pres*
Lorenzo Tonndorf, *Vice Pres*
Paul Anderson, *Engineer*
EMP: 19
SALES (est): 898.6MM
SALES (corp-wide): 571K **Privately Held**
SIC: 3714 Motor vehicle parts & accessories
HQ: Auria Solutions Ltd.
Highway Point Gorsey Lane
Birmingham W MIDLANDS
167 546-4999

(G-14846)
AUTO ELECTRIC INTERNATIONAL
22211 Telegraph Rd (48033-4221)
PHONE..................................248 354-2082
Fax: 248 355-1237
▲ **EMP:** 12
SQ FT: 5,000
SALES (est): 2.2MM **Privately Held**
SIC: 3694 Mfg Engine Electrical Equipment

(G-14847)
AUTOMOTIVE LLC
300 Galleria Office Ctr (48034)
PHONE..................................248 712-1175
Pierre Dubeauclard, *President*
◆ **EMP:** 140 **EST:** 1999
SQ FT: 147,000
SALES (est): 9.9MM
SALES (corp-wide): 1.3B **Privately Held**
WEB: www.automotivecorporation.com
SIC: 3714 Motor vehicle parts & accessories
HQ: Aludyne Us Llc
12700 Stephens Rd
Warren MI 48089

(G-14848)
B & B PRETZELS INC
Also Called: Auntie Anne's
19155 Addison Dr (48075-2404)
PHONE..................................248 358-1655
Ernest Boyce, *President*
Carol Ann Boyce, *Vice Pres*
EMP: 24
SQ FT: 1,040
SALES: 800K **Privately Held**
SIC: 5461 2099 Pretzels; food preparations

(G-14849)
BAKE STATION BAKERIES MICH INC
26000 W 8 Mile Rd (48033-5916)
PHONE..................................248 352-9000
Steven Katz, *President*
EMP: 28 **EST:** 2007
SALES: 4.7MM **Privately Held**
SIC: 2052 Bakery products, dry

(G-14850)
BASF CORPORATION
Also Called: Coatings & Refinish Division
26701 Telegraph Rd (48033-2442)
PHONE..................................248 827-4670
McKenzy Ridner, *Marketing Staff*
Phil Lemon, *Branch Mgr*
Tim Elkins, *Manager*
Rock McNeil, *Manager*
Thomas Sisk, *Manager*
EMP: 101
SALES (corp-wide): 71.7B **Privately Held**
WEB: www.basf.com
SIC: 2869 Industrial organic chemicals
HQ: Basf Corporation
100 Park Ave
Florham Park NJ 07932
973 245-6000

(G-14851)
BEHRMANN PRINTING COMPANY INC
21063 Bridge St (48033-4088)
PHONE..................................248 799-7771
Ivan Behrmann, *President*
Steve Behrmann, *Corp Secy*
Scott Behrmann, *Vice Pres*
Jim Behrman, *Marketing Staff*
EMP: 15 **EST:** 1968
SQ FT: 20,000
SALES (est): 2.2MM **Privately Held**
WEB: www.behrmannprinting.com
SIC: 2752 2759 2796 Commercial printing, offset; commercial printing; embossing on paper; platemaking services

(G-14852)
BERCI PRINTING SERVICES INC
22400 Telegraph Rd Ste B (48033-6800)
PHONE..................................248 350-0206
John Berci, *President*
EMP: 4
SQ FT: 6,300
SALES (est): 644.7K **Privately Held**
SIC: 2752 2759 Commercial printing, offset; letterpress printing

(G-14853)
BIO-VAC INC
21316 Bridge St (48033-4900)
PHONE..................................248 350-2150
Lee Allen Stouse, *President*
Anthony Crivella, *Vice Pres*
Tom Parasiliti, *Prdtn Mgr*
Winchester Rice, *Supervisor*
Charles Crivella, *Admin Sec*
EMP: 40
SQ FT: 16,000
SALES (est): 417.2K **Privately Held**
SIC: 3479 3841 Coating of metals & formed products; surgical instruments & apparatus

(G-14854)
BLUEWATER TECH GROUP INC (PA)
Also Called: Bluewater Visual Services
24050 Northwestern Hwy (48075-2567)
PHONE..................................248 356-4399
John Tracy, *CEO*
Suzanne Schoeneberger, *President*
Tobi Tungl, *President*
Brian Sieloff, *General Mgr*
Robert Bolzman, *Business Mgr*
EMP: 125
SQ FT: 58,000
SALES (est): 35.9MM **Privately Held**
WEB: www.bluewatertech.com
SIC: 3651 5064 7622 7359 Household audio & video equipment; electrical entertainment equipment; video repair; audiovisual equipment & supply rental

(G-14855)
BRADLEY-THOMPSON TOOL COMPANY
22108 W 8 Mile Rd (48033-4494)
PHONE..................................248 352-1466
Michael D Huard, *President*
Jeff Sutter, *Vice Pres*
Sherry Hamilton, *Purch Agent*
Brian Wehrs, *QC Mgr*
EMP: 30 **EST:** 1952
SQ FT: 19,000
SALES (est): 6MM **Privately Held**
WEB: www.bradleythompsontool.com
SIC: 3544 3728 Special dies & tools; jigs & fixtures; aircraft assemblies, subassemblies & parts

(G-14856)
BRAND ORTHOPEDIC & SHOE SVCS
21701 W 11 Mile Rd Ste 2 (48076-3713)
PHONE..................................248 352-0000
Mark Brand, *President*
EMP: 4
SALES (est): 310.7K **Privately Held**
SIC: 3842 Orthopedic appliances

(G-14857)
BRIANS FOODS LLC
21444 Bridge St (48033-4031)
PHONE..................................248 739-5280
Steve Katz, *Mng Member*
Brian Jacobs, *Mng Member*
EMP: 8 **EST:** 2013
SALES (est): 344.5K **Privately Held**
SIC: 2099 Food preparations

(G-14858)
BRILLION IRON WORKS INC (DH)
1 Towne Sq Ste 550 (48076-3710)
P.O. Box 127, Brillion WI (54110-0127)
PHONE..................................248 727-1800
Douglas J Grimm, *President*
John Longhurst, *Accounts Mgr*
◆ **EMP:** 136
SQ FT: 580,000
SALES (est): 93.3MM
SALES (corp-wide): 7.2B **Publicly Held**
WEB: www.brillionironworks.com
SIC: 3321 Gray iron castings; ductile iron castings

(G-14859)
BUDD MAGNETIC PRODUCTS INC
22525 Telegraph Rd (48033-4106)
PHONE..................................248 353-2533
Robert W Budd, *President*
Gladys Budd, *Corp Secy*
Vincent Gilles, *Vice Pres*
EMP: 6
SQ FT: 6,000
SALES (est): 654.7K **Privately Held**
SIC: 3537 Trucks, tractors, loaders, carriers & similar equipment

(G-14860)
BUSCHE SOUTHFIELD INC
Also Called: Busche Performance Group
26290 W 8 Mile Rd (48033-3650)
PHONE..................................248 357-5180
Nick Busche, *CEO*
▲ **EMP:** 150
SQ FT: 136,000
SALES (est): 22.8MM
SALES (corp-wide): 360.5MM **Privately Held**
WEB: www.3pointmachine.com
SIC: 7539 3559 Machine shop, automotive; automotive maintenance equipment
PA: Shipston Group U.S., Inc.
22122 Telegraph Rd
Southfield MI 48033
603 929-6825

(G-14861)
BUSINESS DESIGN SOLUTIONS INC (PA)
Also Called: American Cmmnities Media Group
17360 W 12 Mile Rd # 201 (48076-2117)
PHONE..................................248 672-8007
Dimitri Lebedinskiy, *President*
EMP: 7
SALES (est): 559.2K **Privately Held**
SIC: 2752 Catalogs, lithographed; business form & card printing, lithographic

(G-14862)
CADILLAC ASPHALT LLC
21521 Hilltop Ste 23 (48033)
PHONE..................................248 215-0416
EMP: 21
SALES (corp-wide): 47.3MM **Privately Held**
SIC: 2951 Asphalt paving mixtures & blocks
PA: Cadillac Asphalt, L.L.C.
2575 S Haggerty Rd # 100
Canton MI 48188
734 397-2050

(G-14863)
CAMRYN INDUSTRIES LLC (HQ)
21624 Melrose Ave (48075-7905)
PHONE..................................248 663-5850
Jim Comer,
▲ **EMP:** 150
SALES (est): 33.7K
SALES (corp-wide): 35.5K **Privately Held**
SIC: 2821 Molding compounds, plastics
PA: Comer Holdings Llc
21624 Melrose Ave
Southfield MI 48075
248 663-5700

(G-14864)
CDM MACHINE CO
23009 Lake Ravines Dr (48033-3453)
PHONE..................................313 538-9100
Calvin Davidson, *President*
EMP: 18
SALES (est): 2.4MM **Privately Held**
WEB: www.cdm-machine.com
SIC: 3541 Machine tools, metal cutting type

(G-14865)
CHARIDIMOS INC
Also Called: Athena Foods
23100 Telegraph Rd (48033-4155)
PHONE..................................248 827-7733
Charidimos A Sitaras, *President*
Jim Sitaras, *Manager*
EMP: 8
SQ FT: 3,600
SALES (est): 888.1K **Privately Held**
SIC: 2032 Italian foods: packaged in cans, jars, etc.

(G-14866)
CHEMICO SYSTEMS INC (PA)
Also Called: Chemico Mays
25200 Telg Rd Ste 120 (48034)
PHONE..................................248 723-3263
Leon C Richardson, *President*
David Macleod, *Vice Pres*
Harry Seifert, *Vice Pres*
Paul Sinko, *Treasurer*
EMP: 20
SALES (est): 23.3MM **Privately Held**
WEB: www.chemicosystems.com
SIC: 7699 2819 Industrial equipment cleaning; chemicals, high purity: refined from technical grade

(G-14867)
CITATION CAMDEN CAST CTR LLC
1 Towne Sq Ste 550 (48076-3710)
PHONE..................................248 727-1800
John E Utley, *Ch of Bd*
Steven M Palm, *President*
William T Kirk, *Engineer*
Ben Sherard, *Controller*
Nancy Roberts, *Finance*
EMP: 233 **EST:** 1973
SQ FT: 150,000
SALES (est): 18.3MM
SALES (corp-wide): 7.2B **Publicly Held**
SIC: 3321 Ductile iron castings
HQ: Grede Ii Llc
20750 Civic Center Dr # 100
Southfield MI 48076
248 727-1800

Southfield - Oakland County (G-14868)

(G-14868)
CITATION LOST FOAM PTTRNS LLC
1 Towne Sq Ste 550 (48076-3710)
PHONE.................................248 727-1800
David C Dauch, *Ch of Bd*
EMP: 33 **EST:** 2009
SALES (est): 1.5MM
SALES (corp-wide): 7.2B **Publicly Held**
SIC: 3711 3714 Motor vehicles & car bodies; motor vehicle parts & accessories
HQ: Grede Ii Llc
  20750 Civic Center Dr # 100
  Southfield MI 48076
  248 727-1800

(G-14869)
CLARITY COMM ADVISORS INC
Also Called: Clarity Voice
2 Corporate Dr Ste 250 (48076-3716)
PHONE.................................248 327-4390
Gary A Goerke, *President*
EMP: 22
SALES (est): 3.4MM **Privately Held**
SIC: 3661 Telegraph or telephone carrier & repeater equipment

(G-14870)
COLOR CONNECTION
29487 Northwestern Hwy (48034)
PHONE.................................248 351-0920
Albert Scaglione, *President*
Amelia Scaglione, *Admin Sec*
EMP: 6
SALES (est): 457.6K **Privately Held**
SIC: 2752 2791 2789 Commercial printing, offset; typesetting; bookbinding & related work

(G-14871)
COMAU LLC (DH)
Also Called: Comau Pico
21000 Telegraph Rd (48033-4280)
PHONE.................................248 353-8888
Brendan Blenner-Hassett, *CEO*
Mauro Fenzi, *Ch of Bd*
Andrew Lloyd, *COO*
Nick Altrock, *Project Mgr*
Michael Donnelly, *Project Mgr*
◆ **EMP:** 400 **EST:** 1980
SQ FT: 198,000
SALES (est): 520.5MM
SALES (corp-wide): 126.4B **Privately Held**
SIC: 3548 3829 3545 Resistance welders, electric; testing equipment: abrasion, shearing strength, etc.; gauges (machine tool accessories); tools & accessories for machine tools
HQ: Comau Spa
  Via Rivalta 30
  Grugliasco TO 10095
  011 004-9111

(G-14872)
CONTRACT PEOPLE CORPORATION
29444 Northwestern Hwy (48034-1029)
P.O. Box 3112 (48037-3112)
PHONE.................................248 304-9900
Terry A Wallace, *President*
EMP: 10
SQ FT: 1,200
SALES (est): 840K **Privately Held**
WEB: www.bugeyes.com
SIC: 7363 3679 8731 8711 Employee leasing service; electronic circuits; commercial physical research; engineering services

(G-14873)
CONTROLLED POWER TECH INC
2000 Town Ctr Ste 1800 (48075-1165)
PHONE.................................248 825-0100
Nicholas Pascoe, *President*
Taylor Hansen, *Vice Pres*
EMP: 80
SALES (est): 2.6MM **Privately Held**
SIC: 3621 Motors & generators

(G-14874)
COVISINT CORPORATION (HQ)
26533 Evergreen Rd # 500 (48076-4234)
PHONE.................................248 483-2000
Mark J Barrenechea, *CEO*
Muhi Majzoub, *Exec VP*
Douglas M Parker, *Senior VP*
Amin Aziz, *Vice Pres*
Nilesh Dayal, *Vice Pres*
EMP: 82
SQ FT: 33,786
SALES: 70.2MM
SALES (corp-wide): 2.8B **Privately Held**
WEB: www.compuware.com
SIC: 7374 7372 Data processing service; prepackaged software
PA: Open Text Corporation
  275 Frank Tompa Dr
  Waterloo ON N2L 0
  519 888-7111

(G-14875)
CUSTOM GIANT LLC
16216 Lamplighter Ct # 1025 (48075-3534)
PHONE.................................313 799-2085
Darnell Wilson, *Mng Member*
EMP: 4
SALES (est): 120K **Privately Held**
SIC: 5651 2329 Unisex clothing stores; riding clothes:, men's, youths' & boys'

(G-14876)
D&E INCORPORATED
20542 Oldham Rd (48076-4026)
PHONE.................................313 673-3284
Damious Eason, *President*
EMP: 4
SALES (est): 203.2K **Privately Held**
SIC: 2211 7389 Osnaburgs;

(G-14877)
DABIR SURFACES INC
24585 Evergreen Rd (48075-5503)
PHONE.................................248 796-0802
Dave Dziobia, *President*
EMP: 3
SALES (corp-wide): 1B **Publicly Held**
SIC: 3842 Surgical appliances & supplies
HQ: Dabir Surfaces, Inc.
  7447 W Wilson Ave
  Harwood Heights IL 60706
  708 867-6777

(G-14878)
DANDO CHEMICALS US LLC
28560 Sutherland St (48076-7342)
PHONE.................................248 629-9434
Yipeng Wang, *Principal*
Yi Zhong,
▲ **EMP:** 8
SALES (est): 1.1MM **Privately Held**
SIC: 2819 Industrial inorganic chemicals

(G-14879)
DENSO INTERNATIONAL AMER INC (HQ)
24777 Denso Dr (48033-5244)
PHONE.................................248 350-7500
Hikaru Sugi, *President*
Kazumasa Kimura, *COO*
Bill Foy, *Vice Pres*
Stephen Milam, *Vice Pres*
Koji Mori, *Vice Pres*
◆ **EMP:** 700
SQ FT: 43,000
SALES (est): 3.3B **Privately Held**
WEB: www.densocorp-na.com
SIC: 3714 Motor vehicle engines & parts

(G-14880)
DETROIT CHILI CO INC (PA)
21400 Telegraph Rd (48033-4245)
PHONE.................................248 440-5933
Tim S Keros, *President*
EMP: 4 **EST:** 1969
SQ FT: 900
SALES (est): 451.8K **Privately Held**
SIC: 2038 Frozen specialties

(G-14881)
DETROIT JEWISH NEWS LTD PARTNR (PA)
Also Called: Jewish News, The
29200 Northwestern Hwy # 110 (48034-1013)
PHONE.................................248 354-6060
Arthur Horwitz, *Partner*
EMP: 58
SALES (est): 3.2MM **Privately Held**
SIC: 2711 Newspapers: publishing only, not printed on site; newspapers, publishing & printing

(G-14882)
DIVERSIFIED TUBE LLC
21056 Bridge St (48033-4087)
PHONE.................................313 790-7348
Cassaundra Bing, *Mng Member*
EMP: 10
SALES (est): 1MM **Privately Held**
SIC: 3317 Steel pipe & tubes

(G-14883)
DLHBOWLES INC
20755 Greenfield Rd # 806 (48075-5403)
PHONE.................................248 569-0652
Dan McNary, *VP Sales*
EMP: 10
SALES (corp-wide): 252.6MM **Privately Held**
SIC: 8711 3089 3082 Engineering services; injection molding of plastics; tubes, unsupported plastic
PA: Dlhbowles, Inc.
  2422 Leo Ave Sw
  Canton OH 44706
  330 478-2503

(G-14884)
DMI EDON LLC (DH)
300 Gllria Ofc Ctr Ste 50 (48034)
PHONE.................................248 728-8642
Stephen M Bay, *COO*
Shankar Kiru, *CFO*
Chris Connely,
▲ **EMP:** 4
SALES (est): 8.1MM
SALES (corp-wide): 1.3B **Privately Held**
SIC: 3714 Motor vehicle parts & accessories
HQ: Aludyne North America Inc.
  300 Galleria Ofcntr Ste 5
  Southfield MI 48034
  248 728-8642

(G-14885)
DMP SIGN COMPANY
20732 Negaunee St (48033-3526)
PHONE.................................248 996-9281
EMP: 3
SALES (est): 55.7K **Privately Held**
SIC: 3993 Signs & advertising specialties

(G-14886)
DOULTON & CO
19541 Cherry Hill St (48076-5316)
PHONE.................................248 258-6977
EMP: 3
SALES (est): 140K **Privately Held**
SIC: 3589 Mfg Service Industry Machinery

(G-14887)
DUNNS WELDING INC
22930 Lahser Rd (48033-4408)
PHONE.................................248 356-3866
Thomas P Dunn, *President*
Peter Dunn, *Vice Pres*
Margaret Dunn, *Treasurer*
Judee Dunn, *Manager*
EMP: 6
SQ FT: 9,600
SALES: 60K **Privately Held**
WEB: www.dunnswelding.com
SIC: 3441 1799 7692 Fabricated structural metal; welding on site; welding repair

(G-14888)
DURR INC (HQ)
26801 Northwestern Hwy (48033-6251)
PHONE.................................734 459-6800
Bruno Welsch, *President*
Ken Chandler, *Vice Pres*
Norbert Klapper, *Vice Pres*
Oliver Gary, *Plant Mgr*
Kathy Malone, *Project Mgr*
▲ **EMP:** 1
SQ FT: 270,000
SALES: 461.4MM
SALES (corp-wide): 4.4B **Privately Held**
SIC: 3559 3567 Metal finishing equipment for plating, etc.; incinerators, metal: domestic or commercial
PA: Durr Ag
  Carl-Benz-Str. 34
  Bietigheim-Bissingen 74321
  714 278-0

(G-14889)
DURR SYSTEMS INC (DH)
Also Called: Pfs - Pnt Fnal Assmbly Systems
26801 Northwestern Hwy (48033-6251)
PHONE.................................248 450-2000
Ralf W Dieter, *CEO*
Varun Gupta, *General Mgr*
Dave Ciuffoletti, *Vice Pres*
Geunter Dielmann, *Vice Pres*
Nathan Dow, *Project Mgr*
◆ **EMP:** 300
SQ FT: 270,000
SALES (est): 162.4MM
SALES (corp-wide): 4.4B **Privately Held**
WEB: www.durr.com
SIC: 3559 3567 Metal finishing equipment for plating, etc.; incinerators, metal: domestic or commercial

(G-14890)
DURR SYSTEMS INC
Also Called: APT Division
26801 Northwestern Hwy (48033-6251)
PHONE.................................248 745-8500
Werner Baumgartner, *Principal*
EMP: 150
SALES (corp-wide): 4.4B **Privately Held**
SIC: 3559 Metal finishing equipment for plating, etc.
HQ: Durr Systems, Inc
  26801 Northwestern Hwy
  Southfield MI 48033
  248 450-2000

(G-14891)
DYNA TECH
27050 W 8 Mile Rd (48033-3568)
PHONE.................................248 358-3962
Stewart Rich, *Principal*
EMP: 4
SALES (est): 338.6K **Privately Held**
SIC: 2891 Adhesives & sealants

(G-14892)
EARBYTE INC
Also Called: Antelope Audio
19785 W 12 Mile Rd 61 (48076-2584)
PHONE.................................734 418-8661
Egor Lavine, *CEO*
EMP: 3
SALES (est): 167.6K **Privately Held**
SIC: 3651 5999 Audio electronic systems; audio-visual equipment & supplies

(G-14893)
EATON CORPORATION
Eaton Fuel Vapor Systems Div
26201 Northwestern Hwy (48076-3926)
PHONE.................................248 226-6347
Michael Stefaniak, *Business Mgr*
Chuck Molnar, *Vice Pres*
Manuel Ballina, *Purchasing*
Clark Fortune, *Chief Engr*
Kaylah Berndt, *Engineer*
EMP: 530 **Privately Held**
WEB: www.eaton.com
SIC: 5993 3566 3822 Tobacco stores & stands; speed changers, drives & gears; auto controls regulating residntl & coml environmt & applncs
HQ: Eaton Corporation
  1000 Eaton Blvd
  Cleveland OH 44122
  440 523-5000

(G-14894)
EATON CORPORATION
Also Called: Vehicles
26101 Northwestern Hwy (48076-3925)
PHONE.................................248 226-6200
Brian O'Neil, *Engineer*
Cindy Shane, *Manager*
Charles Hart, *Master*
EMP: 25 **Privately Held**
SIC: 3714 Motor vehicle parts & accessories
HQ: Eaton Corporation
  1000 Eaton Blvd
  Cleveland OH 44122
  440 523-5000

GEOGRAPHIC SECTION

Southfield - Oakland County (G-14919)

(G-14895)
EATON INOAC COMPANY (DH)
26101 Northwestern Hwy (48076-3925)
PHONE..................................248 226-6200
Gustavo M Decruz, *President*
▲ EMP: 20
SQ FT: 7,650
SALES (est): 23.6MM **Privately Held**
SIC: 3089 Blow molded finished plastic products; injection molding of plastics
HQ: Eaton Corporation
1000 Eaton Blvd
Cleveland OH 44122
440 523-5000

(G-14896)
ECJ PROCESSING
17379 Park Ln (48076-7716)
PHONE..................................248 540-2336
EMP: 3
SALES (est): 252.6K **Privately Held**
SIC: 3471 Plating & polishing

(G-14897)
ECOCLEAN INC (HQ)
26801 Northwestern Hwy (48033-6251)
PHONE..................................248 450-2000
Andreas Reger, *President*
Ralf Dienel, *VP Opers*
Dale Biros, *Design Engr*
Steve Heinrich, *CFO*
Brolan Conkey, *Manager*
▲ EMP: 121
SQ FT: 45,000
SALES (est): 26MM **Privately Held**
WEB: www.durrautomation.com
SIC: 3452 3677 Washers; filtration devices, electronic

(G-14898)
ELRINGKLINGER AUTO MFG INC (HQ)
Also Called: Elringklinger North Amer Inc
23300 Northwestern Hwy (48075-3350)
PHONE..................................248 727-6600
Stefan Wolf, *CEO*
Stephan Maier, *General Mgr*
Reiner Drews, *COO*
Walter E Misch, *Vice Pres*
Thomas Jessulat, *CFO*
▲ EMP: 20 EST: 1945
SQ FT: 27,000
SALES (est): 28MM
SALES (corp-wide): 1.9B **Privately Held**
SIC: 3465 Automotive stampings
PA: Elringklinger Ag
Max-Eyth-Str. 2
Dettingen An Der Erms 72581
712 372-40

(G-14899)
ENGINEERING SERVICE OF AMERICA
Also Called: Engineering Systems Intl
21556 Telegraph Rd (48033-6815)
P.O. Box 7 (48037-0007)
PHONE..................................248 357-3800
James A Karchon, *President*
Dennis M Karchon, *Asst Sec*
EMP: 60
SQ FT: 22,600
SALES (est): 5.6MM **Privately Held**
SIC: 8711 3714 Designing; ship, boat, machine & product; motor vehicle parts & accessories

(G-14900)
EPPERT CONCRETE PRODUCTS INC
30725 Longcrest St (48076-7603)
PHONE..................................248 647-1800
EMP: 3
SALES: 120K **Privately Held**
SIC: 3272 Mfg Concrete Products

(G-14901)
EVELYN ROBERTSON LETT
Also Called: Evelyn's Bakery and Catering
27125 Everett St (48076-5128)
PHONE..................................248 569-8746
Evelyn R Lett, *Principal*
EMP: 6
SALES (est): 105K **Privately Held**
SIC: 5812 2051 Caterers; bread, cake & related products

(G-14902)
FAMEK INC
Also Called: Stringo
2000 Town Ctr Ste 1830 (48075-1151)
PHONE..................................734 895-6794
Goran Fahlen, *Director*
▲ EMP: 1
SALES (est): 1MM **Privately Held**
SIC: 3711 Scout cars (motor vehicles), assembly of

(G-14903)
FARAGO & ASSOCIATES LLC
29200 Northwestern Hwy # 114 (48034-1055)
PHONE..................................248 546-7070
Peter J Farago, *Mng Member*
Bruce Macdonald,
Mike Schofding,
Scott Schofding,
EMP: 17
SALES (est): 2.3MM **Privately Held**
WEB: www.faragoassoc.com
SIC: 2721 Magazines: publishing only, not printed on site

(G-14904)
FAURECIA
26555 Evergreen Rd # 1700 (48076-4257)
PHONE..................................248 917-1702
▲ EMP: 4
SALES (est): 438.8K **Privately Held**
SIC: 3714 Motor vehicle parts & accessories

(G-14905)
FEDERAL GROUP USA INC
Also Called: Federal Group, The
21126 Bridge St (48033-4032)
PHONE..................................248 545-5000
Robert Levy, *President*
▲ EMP: 11 EST: 1980
SALES (est): 3.8MM **Privately Held**
WEB: www.thefedgroup.com
SIC: 5072 3321 3324 3363 Bolts; nuts (hardware); screws; gray iron castings; commercial investment castings, ferrous; aluminum die-castings; castings, except die-castings, precision

(G-14906)
FEDERAL-MOGUL CHASSIS LLC (HQ)
Also Called: Federal-Mogul Motorparts
27300 W 11 Mile Rd (48034-6147)
PHONE..................................248 354-7700
Brad Norton, *CEO*
Rainer Jueckstock, *Co-CEO*
Michelle E Taigman, *Senior VP*
Jerome Rouquet, *CFO*
Marco Desanto, *Ch Credit Ofcr*
EMP: 14 EST: 2013
SALES (est): 3MM
SALES (corp-wide): 11.7B **Publicly Held**
SIC: 3711 Chassis, motor vehicle
PA: Tenneco Inc.
500 N Field Dr
Lake Forest IL 60045
847 482-5000

(G-14907)
FEDERAL-MOGUL IGNITION LLC (HQ)
26555 Northwestern Hwy (48033-2199)
PHONE..................................248 354-7700
David A Bozynski, *President*
▲ EMP: 14
SQ FT: 400,000
SALES (est): 31.9MM
SALES (corp-wide): 11.7B **Publicly Held**
SIC: 3053 Gaskets & sealing devices
PA: Tenneco Inc.
500 N Field Dr
Lake Forest IL 60045
847 482-5000

(G-14908)
FEDERAL-MOGUL MOTORPARTS LLC (HQ)
27300 W 11 Mile Rd (48034-6147)
P.O. Box 981469, El Paso TX (79998-1469)
PHONE..................................248 354-7700
Daniel A Ninivaggi, *CEO*
Carl Icahn, *President*
Sonya Usman, *Human Resources*
Lacee Lang, *Corp Comm Staff*
Troy Edwards, *IT/INT Sup*
EMP: 109
SALES (est): 76.9MM
SALES (corp-wide): 11.7B **Publicly Held**
SIC: 3711 Automobile assembly, including specialty automobiles
PA: Tenneco Inc.
500 N Field Dr
Lake Forest IL 60045
847 482-5000

(G-14909)
FEDERAL-MOGUL PISTON RINGS INC (HQ)
26555 Northwestern Hwy (48033-2199)
PHONE..................................248 354-7700
David Krohn, *President*
Gerard Chochoy, *Senior VP*
Renlf Dalleur, *Senior VP*
Janice Maiden, *Senior VP*
Sunit Kapur, *Vice Pres*
▲ EMP: 15 EST: 1978
SALES (est): 273.3MM
SALES (corp-wide): 11.7B **Publicly Held**
SIC: 3592 3053 3369 Pistons & piston rings; gaskets & sealing devices; gaskets, all materials; nonferrous foundries
PA: Tenneco Inc.
500 N Field Dr
Lake Forest IL 60045
847 482-5000

(G-14910)
FEDERAL-MOGUL POWERTRAIN LLC (HQ)
27300 W 11 Mile Rd (48034-6147)
PHONE..................................248 354-7700
Rainer Jueckstock, *CEO*
David A Bozynski, *President*
Robert L Katz, *Vice Pres*
Robert C Rozycki, *Vice Pres*
▲ EMP: 8
SALES (est): 178.2MM
SALES (corp-wide): 11.7B **Publicly Held**
SIC: 3053 5013 Gaskets & sealing devices; automotive supplies & parts
PA: Tenneco Inc.
500 N Field Dr
Lake Forest IL 60045
847 482-5000

(G-14911)
FEDERAL-MOGUL PRODUCTS US LLC (HQ)
26555 Northwestern Hwy (48033-2199)
PHONE..................................248 354-7700
David A Bozynski, *President*
Alice Hutchens, *Purchasing*
Mark Bauer, *Director*
▲ EMP: 2600 EST: 1977
SQ FT: 500,000
SALES (est): 254.5MM
SALES (corp-wide): 11.7B **Publicly Held**
SIC: 3714 Ball joints, motor vehicle
PA: Tenneco Inc.
500 N Field Dr
Lake Forest IL 60045
847 482-5000

(G-14912)
FEDERAL-MOGUL VALVE TRAIN INTE (HQ)
27300 W 11 Mile Rd (48034-6147)
PHONE..................................248 354-7700
Daniel Ninivaggi, *Co-CEO*
Rainer Jueckstock, *Co-CEO*
Rajesh Shah, *CFO*
EMP: 36 EST: 2014
SALES (est): 90.8MM
SALES (corp-wide): 11.7B **Publicly Held**
SIC: 3592 Valves, engine
PA: Tenneco Inc.
500 N Field Dr
Lake Forest IL 60045
847 482-5000

(G-14913)
FEDERAL-MOGUL WORLD WIDE LLC (HQ)
26555 Northwestern Hwy (48033-2199)
PHONE..................................248 354-7700
Richard Snell, *President*
EMP: 3
SALES (est): 847.5K
SALES (corp-wide): 11.7B **Publicly Held**
SIC: 3714 Motor vehicle parts & accessories
PA: Tenneco Inc.
500 N Field Dr
Lake Forest IL 60045
847 482-5000

(G-14914)
FEDERL-MGUL DUTCH HOLDINGS INC
26555 Northwestern Hwy (48033-2146)
PHONE..................................248 354-7700
Brian J Kesseler, *CEO*
EMP: 85
SALES (est): 638.1K
SALES (corp-wide): 11.7B **Publicly Held**
SIC: 3053 Gaskets, packing & sealing devices
PA: Tenneco Inc.
500 N Field Dr
Lake Forest IL 60045
847 482-5000

(G-14915)
FEDEX OFFICE & PRINT SVCS INC
28844 Northwestern Hwy (48034-1831)
PHONE..................................248 355-5670
EMP: 32
SALES (corp-wide): 69.6B **Publicly Held**
WEB: www.kinkos.com
SIC: 7334 2791 2789 2759 Photocopying & duplicating services; typesetting; bookbinding & related work; commercial printing
HQ: Fedex Office And Print Services, Inc.
7900 Legacy Dr
Plano TX 75024
800 463-3339

(G-14916)
FUTURE REPRODUCTIONS INC
21477 Bridge St Ste L (48033-4079)
PHONE..................................248 350-2060
Kathryn Warras, *President*
Steve Warras, *Vice Pres*
Laura Carnali, *Manager*
EMP: 12 EST: 1976
SQ FT: 13,500
SALES (est): 1.5MM **Privately Held**
WEB: www.futurereproductions.com
SIC: 2752 2791 2789 Commercial printing, offset; typesetting; bookbinding & related work

(G-14917)
FXI INC
Also Called: Foamex
26777 Centrl Pk Blvd # 100 (48076-4163)
PHONE..................................248 553-1039
Don Phillips, *Manager*
EMP: 12 **Privately Held**
SIC: 3086 Packaging & shipping materials, foamed plastic
HQ: Fxi, Inc.
1400 N Providence Rd # 2000
Media PA 19063

(G-14918)
GASKET HOLDINGS INC
26555 Northwestern Hwy (48033-2146)
PHONE..................................248 354-7700
Brian J Kesseler, *CEO*
EMP: 5
SALES (est): 448.8K
SALES (corp-wide): 11.7B **Publicly Held**
SIC: 3053 Gaskets & sealing devices
PA: Tenneco Inc.
500 N Field Dr
Lake Forest IL 60045
847 482-5000

(G-14919)
GFL ENVRONMENTAL REAL PROPERTY (PA)
Also Called: Rizzo Environmental Services
26999 Central Park Blvd # 200 (48076-4174)
PHONE..................................888 877-4996
Wade Stevenson, *CFO*
Carl Geyer, *Manager*
Charles Rizzo Jr,
EMP: 31 EST: 2013

SALES (est): 12.4MM **Privately Held**
SIC: **2611** Pulp mills, mechanical & recycling processing

(G-14920)
GLOBAL FLEET SALES LLC
24725 W 12 Mile Rd # 114 (48034-8345)
PHONE..................................248 327-6483
Kevin R Whitcraft, *President*
Carol Grakul, *Vice Pres*
Alexander Brenneisen, *CFO*
Mark I Whitcraft, *Treasurer*
▼ EMP: 8
SQ FT: 1,350
SALES (est): 19.2MM **Privately Held**
WEB: www.globalfleetsales.net
SIC: **5012** 8711 3621 Automobiles & other motor vehicles; engineering services; generators & sets, electric

(G-14921)
GLOBAL INFORMATION SYSTEMS
29777 Telg Rd Ste 2450 (48034)
PHONE..................................248 223-9800
Prasad Devabhaktuni, *Principal*
Praneet Venkata, *Office Mgr*
EMP: 100
SALES (est): 9.3MM **Privately Held**
WEB: www.gissite.com
SIC: **7372** Prepackaged software

(G-14922)
GLORIA C WILLIAMS
Also Called: Immaculate Enterprises
17310 Westland Ave (48075-7628)
P.O. Box 47652, Oak Park (48237-5352)
PHONE..................................313 220-2735
Gloria C Williams, *Owner*
EMP: 3
SALES (est): 160K **Privately Held**
SIC: **1799** 1389 8742 Construction site cleanup; construction, repair & dismantling services; construction project management consultant

(G-14923)
GREDE FOUNDRIES INC (PA)
4000 Town Ctr Ste 500 (48075-1419)
PHONE..................................248 440-9500
W Stewart Davis, *Ch of Bd*
Thomas F Walker Sr, *President*
Raymond F Lowery, *CFO*
Burleigh E Jacobs, *Chm Emeritus*
◆ EMP: 150
SQ FT: 23,000
SALES (est): 368.3MM **Privately Held**
WEB: www.grede.com
SIC: **3321** Gray iron castings; ductile iron castings

(G-14924)
GREDE HOLDINGS LLC (DH)
20750 Civic Center Dr # 100 (48076-4152)
PHONE..................................248 440-9500
Douglas J Grimm, *President*
Todd Heavin, *COO*
William R Goodin, *Vice Pres*
Anthony Lovell, *Vice Pres*
Paul Suber, *Vice Pres*
EMP: 25
SQ FT: 24,000
SALES (est): 530MM
SALES (corp-wide): 7.2B **Publicly Held**
SIC: **3321** Gray iron castings; ductile iron castings
HQ: Asp Grede Acquisitionco Llc
1 Towne Sq Ste 550
Southfield MI 48076
248 727-1800

(G-14925)
GREDE II LLC (DH)
20750 Civic Center Dr # 100 (48076-4152)
PHONE..................................248 727-1800
Douglas J Grimm, *President*
Stephen Busby, *Vice Pres*
Louis Lavorata, *CFO*
▲ EMP: 35
SQ FT: 24,000
SALES (est): 298.6MM
SALES (corp-wide): 7.2B **Publicly Held**
WEB: www.citationcorp.com
SIC: **3321** Ductile iron castings; gray iron castings

(G-14926)
GREDE LLC (DH)
20750 Civic Center Dr # 100 (48076-4152)
PHONE..................................248 440-9500
Douglas J Grimm, *CEO*
Louis Lavorata, *CFO*
▲ EMP: 365
SQ FT: 23,000
SALES (est): 147.3MM
SALES (corp-wide): 7.2B **Publicly Held**
SIC: **3321** Gray iron castings; ductile iron castings

(G-14927)
GREDE MACHINING LLC
1 Towne Sq Ste 550 (48076-3710)
PHONE..................................248 727-1800
David C Dauch, *Ch of Bd*
EMP: 37
SALES (est): 1.8MM
SALES (corp-wide): 7.2B **Publicly Held**
SIC: **3714** 3711 Motor vehicle parts & accessories; motor vehicles & car bodies
HQ: Grede Ii Llc
20750 Civic Center Dr # 100
Southfield MI 48076
248 727-1800

(G-14928)
GREDE OMAHA LLC
Also Called: Omaha Plant
1 Towne Sq Ste 550 (48076-3710)
PHONE..................................248 727-1800
David C Dauch, *Ch of Bd*
EMP: 33
SALES (est): 1.5MM
SALES (corp-wide): 7.2B **Publicly Held**
SIC: **3711** 3714 Motor vehicles & car bodies; motor vehicle parts & accessories
HQ: Grede Ii Llc
20750 Civic Center Dr # 100
Southfield MI 48076
248 727-1800

(G-14929)
GREDE RADFORD LLC
1 Towne Sq Ste 550 (48076-3710)
PHONE..................................248 727-1800
David C Dauch, *Ch of Bd*
EMP: 33
SALES (est): 1.5MM
SALES (corp-wide): 7.2B **Publicly Held**
SIC: **3711** 3714 Motor vehicles & car bodies; motor vehicle parts & accessories
HQ: Grede Ii Llc
20750 Civic Center Dr # 100
Southfield MI 48076
248 727-1800

(G-14930)
GREDE WSCNSIN SUBSIDIARIES LLC
Also Called: Citation Berlin
20750 Civic Center Dr # 100 (48076-4152)
PHONE..................................248 727-1800
Mike Dowling, *President*
Douglas J Grimm, *Chairman*
Todd Heavin, *Senior VP*
Todd A Heavin, *Senior VP*
Louis Lavorata, *Senior VP*
▼ EMP: 350
SQ FT: 229,864
SALES (est): 1.1MM
SALES (corp-wide): 7.2B **Publicly Held**
WEB: www.berlin.citation.net
SIC: **3321** Gray iron castings; ductile iron castings
HQ: Grede Ii Llc
20750 Civic Center Dr # 100
Southfield MI 48076
248 727-1800

(G-14931)
GREENGLOW PRODUCTS LLC
21170 Bridge St (48033-4032)
P.O. Box 760164, Lathrup Village (48076-0164)
PHONE..................................248 827-1451
Barry Fleischer, *Mng Member*
EMP: 6
SALES (est): 729.3K **Privately Held**
SIC: **2851** Paints & allied products

(G-14932)
GRIGG GRAPHIC SERVICES INC
Also Called: Bridge Street Design & Mktg
20982 Bridge St (48033-4033)
PHONE..................................248 356-5005
Stuart W Grigg, *President*
Dawn Sinclair, *Manager*
Dawn Bender, *Supervisor*
Kate Walsh, *Graphic Designe*
EMP: 18
SQ FT: 7,500
SALES (est): 3MM **Privately Held**
WEB: www.grigg.com
SIC: **2752** 7336 Commercial printing, offset; graphic arts & related design

(G-14933)
GSC RIII - GREDE LLC
1 Towne Sq Ste 550 (48076-3710)
PHONE..................................248 727-1800
David C Dauch, *Ch of Bd*
EMP: 4
SALES (est): 560.1MM
SALES (corp-wide): 7.2B **Publicly Held**
SIC: **3714** 3711 Motor vehicle parts & accessories; motor vehicles & car bodies
HQ: Asp Grede Acquisitionco Llc
1 Towne Sq Ste 550
Southfield MI 48076
248 727-1800

(G-14934)
GUYOUNG TECH USA INC (HQ)
26555 Evergreen Rd # 1515 (48076-4206)
PHONE..................................248 746-4261
Moo Chan Lee, *President*
▲ EMP: 41
SALES (est): 55.3MM **Privately Held**
SIC: **3465** Automotive stampings

(G-14935)
HALLWELL GAMES LLC
18444 W 10 Mile Rd (48075-2653)
P.O. Box 361147, Grosse Pointe Farms (48236-5147)
PHONE..................................586 879-3404
Yvonne Bendross-Kimble,
Sharnella Clark,
Jonathan Kimble,
EMP: 3
SQ FT: 500
SALES (est): 109.8K **Privately Held**
SIC: **3944** Board games, children's & adults'

(G-14936)
HELPING HANDS THERAPY
23999 Northwestern Hwy (48075-2578)
PHONE..................................313 492-6007
Tina Williams,
EMP: 5
SALES (est): 198.4K **Privately Held**
SIC: **3845** Electromedical equipment

(G-14937)
HONEYWELL INTERNATIONAL INC
20500 Ste 4004 (48076)
PHONE..................................248 827-6460
Scott Ferriman, *Manager*
EMP: 8
SALES (corp-wide): 41.8B **Publicly Held**
WEB: www.honeywell.com
SIC: **3714** Motor vehicle parts & accessories
PA: Honeywell International Inc.
300 S Tryon St
Charlotte NC 28202
973 455-2000

(G-14938)
HOUSEY PHRM RES LABS LLC
16800 W 12 Mile Rd (48076-2108)
PHONE..................................248 663-7000
Gerard Housey, *President*
EMP: 7
SALES (est): 1MM **Privately Held**
SIC: **2834** Pharmaceutical preparations

(G-14939)
HYDRO KING INCORPORATED
Also Called: Detroit Recker Sales
21384 Mcclung Ave (48075-3297)
PHONE..................................313 835-8700
Rick Farrell, *President*
Betty Farrell, *Vice Pres*
EMP: 10
SALES (est): 700K **Privately Held**
SIC: **3799** Towing bars & systems

(G-14940)
IAC CREATIVE LLC
Also Called: International Autmtv Compnents
28333 Telegraph Rd (48034-1953)
PHONE..................................248 455-7000
Richard Sine, *Superintendent*
David Pipper, *Principal*
Maureen Blazer-Adams, *Business Mgr*
Gina Brines, *Business Mgr*
Tanya Geffrard, *Business Mgr*
EMP: 10
SALES (est): 730.5K **Privately Held**
SIC: **2759** Commercial printing
HQ: International Automotive Components Group North America, Inc.
28333 Telegraph Rd
Southfield MI 48034

(G-14941)
IAC MEXICO HOLDINGS INC (DH)
28333 Telegraph Rd (48034-1953)
PHONE..................................248 455-7000
Manfred Gingl, *CEO*
Robert Cook, *General Mgr*
David Heseltine, *General Mgr*
Christoffer Hansson, *Business Mgr*
Eileen Kiddell, *Business Mgr*
EMP: 6
SALES (est): 1.4MM **Privately Held**
SIC: **3089** Automotive parts, plastic

(G-14942)
IDEMITSU CHEMICALS USA CORP
3000 Town Ctr Ste 2820 (48075-1203)
PHONE..................................248 355-0666
Kazuto Hasaimoto, *President*
▲ EMP: 8
SQ FT: 3,600
SALES (est): 2.4MM **Privately Held**
SIC: **3082** 5169 5162 Unsupported plastics profile shapes; chemicals & allied products; plastics materials & basic shapes
PA: Idemitsu Kosan Co.,Ltd.
3-1-1, Marunouchi
Chiyoda-Ku TKY 100-0

(G-14943)
IDEMITSU LUBRICANTS AMER CORP
3000 Town Ctr Ste 2820 (48075-1203)
PHONE..................................248 355-0666
Bob Hashmi, *Division Mgr*
Masanori Enomoto, *Principal*
Jason Couch, *Prdtn Mgr*
Shari Lawler, *Human Resources*
Ricky Adkins, *Manager*
EMP: 15 **Privately Held**
WEB: www.apolloamerica.com
SIC: **2992** 5162 Lubricating oils & greases; plastics materials & basic shapes
HQ: Idemitsu Lubricants America Corporation
701 Port Rd
Jeffersonville IN 47130

(G-14944)
IDP INC
21300 W 8 Mile Rd (48075-5638)
PHONE..................................248 352-0044
Isaac Benezra, *President*
▲ EMP: 26
SALES (est): 4.9MM **Privately Held**
SIC: **2431** Door frames, wood

(G-14945)
INDUSTRIAL BAG & SPC INC
17800 Northland Park Ct # 107 (48075-4304)
PHONE..................................248 559-5550
Kenneth M Borin, *President*
Phillip Quartana, *Vice Pres*
EMP: 15
SQ FT: 3,500

GEOGRAPHIC SECTION

Southfield - Oakland County (G-14971)

SALES: 850K **Privately Held**
WEB: www.industrialbag.com
SIC: 2393 2394 Bags & containers, except sleeping bags: textile; duffle bags, canvas: made from purchased materials; liners & covers, fabric: made from purchased materials

(G-14946)
INDUSTRIAL EXPRMENTAL TECH LLC
Also Called: Iet
21556 Telegraph Rd (48033-4247)
PHONE 248 948-1100
James Karchon, *Mng Member*
EMP: 30
SALES (est): 1.4MM **Privately Held**
SIC: 3599 Machine shop, jobbing & repair

(G-14947)
INFORMA BUSINESS MEDIA INC
Also Called: Wards Automotive International
3000 Town Ctr Ste 2750 (48075-1245)
PHONE 248 357-0800
Roger Powers, *President*
Alan Binder, *Editor*
EMP: 48
SALES (corp-wide): 3B **Privately Held**
SIC: 2721 Magazines: publishing only, not printed on site
HQ: Informa Business Media, Inc.
605 3rd Ave
New York NY 10158
212 204-4200

(G-14948)
INTERNATIONAL AUTOMOTIVE COMPO (DH)
Also Called: IAC Group
28333 Telegraph Rd (48034-1953)
PHONE 248 455-7000
Natale Nat REA, *President*
Prayag Thakkar, *General Mgr*
Chaelynne Hernandez, *Business Mgr*
Joe Mordarski, *Business Mgr*
Janis Acosta, *Exec VP*
◆ **EMP:** 800
SALES (est): 7.7B **Privately Held**
WEB: www.iaaawards.com
SIC: 3089 Automotive parts, plastic
HQ: International Automotive Components Group
Rue Lou Hemmer 4
Sandweiler
267 504-22

(G-14949)
JAIMES LIQUIDATION INC
19270 W 8 Mile Rd (48075-5722)
PHONE 248 356-8600
Rudolph Taylor, *President*
Michael Redding, *Data Proc Dir*
Bill Barr, *Admin Sec*
EMP: 11 **EST:** 1979
SALES (est): 1.4MM **Privately Held**
SIC: 3441 Joists, open web steel: long-span series

(G-14950)
JANESVILLE LLC
Also Called: Janesville Acoustics
29200 Northwestern Hwy # 400 (48034-1068)
PHONE 248 948-1811
Shannon White, *Mng Member*
EMP: 300
SALES (est): 6.7MM
SALES (corp-wide): 573.9MM **Privately Held**
SIC: 3086 Insulation or cushioning material, foamed plastic
HQ: Motus Pivot, Inc.
88 E 48th St
Holland MI 49423
616 610-0064

(G-14951)
JASON INCORPORATED
Janesville Acoustics
29200 Northwestern Hwy (48034-1013)
P.O. Box 349, Norwalk OH (44857-0349)
PHONE 248 948-1811
Srivas Prasad, *General Mgr*
Matthew Oberski, *Vice Pres*
EMP: 30

SALES (corp-wide): 612.9MM **Publicly Held**
WEB: www.jasoninc.com
SIC: 3086 Insulation or cushioning material, foamed plastic
HQ: Jason Incorporated
833 E Michigan St Ste 900
Milwaukee WI 53202
414 277-9300

(G-14952)
JERRYS QUALITY QUICK PRINT
Also Called: American Speedy Printing
28810 Northwestern Hwy (48034-1831)
PHONE 248 354-1313
Gerald Christensen, *President*
EMP: 7
SQ FT: 2,800
SALES (est): 1MM **Privately Held**
SIC: 2752 Commercial printing, offset

(G-14953)
JUVENEX INC
26222 Telegraph Rd (48033-5318)
PHONE 248 436-2866
▲ **EMP:** 10
SALES (est): 796.3K **Privately Held**
SIC: 2037 Mfg Frozen Fruits/Vegetables

(G-14954)
KEYSTONE PRODUCTS LLC
24445 Northwestern Hwy # 101 (48075-2436)
PHONE 248 363-5552
Richard Ballentine, *Principal*
EMP: 6
SQ FT: 4,000
SALES (est): 212.2K **Privately Held**
SIC: 3999 Christmas tree ornaments, except electrical & glass

(G-14955)
KIRK ENTERPRISES INC
20905 Telegraph Rd (48033-6816)
PHONE 248 357-5070
Fax: 248 357-1430
EMP: 6 **EST:** 1971
SQ FT: 7,500
SALES: 720K **Privately Held**
SIC: 3613 Mfg Electric Control Panels

(G-14956)
KNIGHT TONYA
Also Called: Knights Glass Block Windows
17390 W 8 Mile Rd (48075-4301)
PHONE 313 255-3434
Tonya Knight, *Owner*
EMP: 6
SQ FT: 2,732
SALES (est): 384.8K **Privately Held**
SIC: 1793 3231 5231 Glass & glazing work; products of purchased glass; glass

(G-14957)
KTR DENTAL LAB & PDTS LLC
17040 W 12 Mile Rd # 150 (48076-2131)
PHONE 248 224-9158
Robert Stern,
Sylvan Stern, *Advisor*
EMP: 10 **EST:** 2009
SQ FT: 2,000
SALES: 1MM **Privately Held**
SIC: 3843 8072 Dental equipment & supplies; dental laboratories

(G-14958)
LACHMAN ENTERPRISES INC
Also Called: Lachman & Company
20955 Telegraph Rd (48033-4240)
PHONE 248 948-9944
Carrie Lachman, *President*
EMP: 6 **EST:** 1893
SQ FT: 6,000
SALES: 800K **Privately Held**
WEB: www.4-awards.com
SIC: 5094 5947 3499 7389 Trophies; gift, novelty & souvenir shop; novelties & giftware, including trophies; balloons, novelty & toy

(G-14959)
LAVANWAY SIGN CO INC
22124 Telegraph Rd (48033-4213)
PHONE 248 356-1600
Lawrence K Lavanway Jr, *President*
Brad Warden, *Vice Pres*

Michael Kean, *Project Mgr*
EMP: 8
SQ FT: 11,000
SALES (est): 1.3MM **Privately Held**
WEB: www.lavanwaysigns.com
SIC: 3993 Signs, not made in custom sign painting shops

(G-14960)
LEAR CORP EEDS AND INTERIORS (DH)
21557 Telegraph Rd (48033-4248)
PHONE 248 447-1500
Robert Rossiter, *President*
Sherry Burgess, *Treasurer*
▼ **EMP:** 10
SALES (est): 2.1MM
SALES (corp-wide): 21.1B **Publicly Held**
SIC: 3714 Motor vehicle parts & accessories

(G-14961)
LEAR CORPORATION
21557 Telg Rd Ste 300 (48033)
PHONE 313 852-7800
Tony Tucker, *Branch Mgr*
EMP: 663
SALES (corp-wide): 21.1B **Publicly Held**
WEB: www.lear.com
SIC: 3714 Motor vehicle parts & accessories
PA: Lear Corporation
21557 Telegraph Rd
Southfield MI 48033
248 447-1500

(G-14962)
LEAR CORPORATION (PA)
21557 Telegraph Rd (48033-4248)
PHONE 248 447-1500
Raymond E Scott, *President*
Terrence B Larkin, *Exec VP*
Amy A Doyle, *Vice Pres*
◆ **EMP:** 281
SALES: 21.1B **Publicly Held**
WEB: www.lear.com
SIC: 3714 2531 2396 3643 Motor vehicle electrical equipment; instrument board assemblies, motor vehicle; automotive wiring harness sets; motor vehicle body components & frame; seats, automobile; automotive & apparel trimmings; current-carrying wiring devices

(G-14963)
LEAR EUROPEAN OPERATIONS CORP
21557 Telegraph Rd (48033-4248)
PHONE 248 447-1500
Robert E Rossiter, *Ch of Bd*
EMP: 5
SALES (est): 350.3K
SALES (corp-wide): 21.1B **Publicly Held**
WEB: www.lear.com
SIC: 2531 3714 Seats, automobile; motor vehicle electrical equipment; instrument board assemblies, motor vehicle; automotive wiring harness sets; motor vehicle body components & frame
PA: Lear Corporation
21557 Telegraph Rd
Southfield MI 48033
248 447-1500

(G-14964)
LEAR MEXICAN SEATING CORP (HQ)
21557 Telegraph Rd (48033-4248)
P.O. Box 17709, El Paso TX (79917-7709)
PHONE 248 447-1500
Matthew J Simoncini, *CEO*
Jeffrey H Vanneste, *President*
William P McLaughlin, *Vice Pres*
Shari L Burgess, *Treasurer*
Terrence B Larkin, *Admin Sec*
▲ **EMP:** 2
SALES (est): 1.3MM
SALES (corp-wide): 21.1B **Publicly Held**
WEB: www.lear.com
SIC: 2531 Seats, automobile
PA: Lear Corporation
21557 Telegraph Rd
Southfield MI 48033
248 447-1500

(G-14965)
LEAR OPERATIONS CORPORATION (HQ)
21557 Telegraph Rd (48033-4248)
P.O. Box 5008 (48086-5008)
PHONE 248 447-1500
Robert Rossiter, *President*
Sherri Burgess, *Treasurer*
◆ **EMP:** 1
SALES (est): 427.3MM
SALES (corp-wide): 21.1B **Publicly Held**
SIC: 3089 Plastic processing
PA: Lear Corporation
21557 Telegraph Rd
Southfield MI 48033
248 447-1500

(G-14966)
LEAR TRIM LP (PA)
21557 Telegraph Rd (48033-4248)
P.O. Box 17709, El Paso TX (79917-7709)
PHONE 248 447-1500
Conrad Mallett, *Director*
EMP: 8
SALES (est): 4.5MM **Privately Held**
SIC: 3714 Motor vehicle parts & accessories

(G-14967)
LEXMARK INTERNATIONAL INC
2 Towne Sq Ste 150 (48076-3762)
PHONE 248 352-0616
EMP: 14
SALES (corp-wide): 2.5B **Privately Held**
SIC: 3577 Mfg Computer Peripheral Equipment
PA: Lexmark International, Inc.
740 W New Circle Rd
Lexington KY 40511
859 232-2000

(G-14968)
LIFE IS DIGITAL LLC
17180 Revere St (48076-1214)
PHONE 734 252-6449
Matthew Eleweke, *President*
Roderick Walker, *Vice Pres*
EMP: 3
SALES (est): 111.3K **Privately Held**
SIC: 7372 Application computer software

(G-14969)
LINDE GAS NORTH AMERICA LLC
21421 Hilltop St Ste 1 (48033-4009)
PHONE 630 857-6460
Kirk Phelps, *Area Mgr*
EMP: 5 **Privately Held**
SIC: 2813 Oxygen, compressed or liquefied; nitrogen; argon; hydrogen
HQ: Linde Gas North America Llc
200 Somerset Corp Blvd # 7000
Bridgewater NJ 08807

(G-14970)
LUMIGEN INC
22900 W 8 Mile Rd (48033-4302)
PHONE 248 351-5600
Scott Garrett, *President*
A Paul Schaap, *General Mgr*
Hashem Akhavan-Tafti PHD, *Research*
Gary T Priestap, *Director*
EMP: 40
SQ FT: 45,000
SALES (est): 9MM
SALES (corp-wide): 19.8B **Publicly Held**
WEB: www.lumigen.com
SIC: 3826 Analytical instruments
PA: Danaher Corporation
2200 Penn Ave Nw Ste 800w
Washington DC 20037
202 828-0850

(G-14971)
M A S INFORMATION AGE TECH
23132 Lake Ravines Dr (48033-6531)
PHONE 248 352-0162
Michael Steele, *President*
EMP: 5
SQ FT: 1,200
SALES: 100K **Privately Held**
SIC: 3651 Home entertainment equipment, electronic

Southfield - Oakland County (G-14972)

(G-14972)
M&M MFG INC
29765 Briarbank Ct (48034-4623)
PHONE..................................248 356-6543
Mike Marmorstein, *President*
EMP: 8
SALES (est): 810K **Privately Held**
SIC: 3714 Filters: oil, fuel & air, motor vehicle

(G-14973)
MARSHALL-GRUBER COMPANY LLC (HQ)
Also Called: Gruber Supplies & Accessories
26776 W 12 Mile Rd (48034-7807)
PHONE..................................248 353-4100
The Rj Marshall Com, *Principal*
◆ EMP: 10 EST: 2014
SALES (est): 6.2MM
SALES (corp-wide): 20.3MM **Privately Held**
SIC: 3545 5085 3255 Machine tool attachments & accessories; industrial supplies; industrial tools; clay refractories
PA: The R J Marshall Company
26776 W 12 Mile Rd # 201
Southfield MI 48034
248 353-4100

(G-14974)
MAXITROL COMPANY (PA)
23555 Telegraph Rd (48033-4176)
P.O. Box 2230 (48037-2230)
PHONE..................................248 356-1400
Bonnie Kern-Koskela, *Ch of Bd*
Larry Koskela, *COO*
David H Holcomb, *Vice Pres*
Brian O'Sullivan, *Vice Pres*
John Schlachter, *Vice Pres*
▲ EMP: 75 EST: 1946
SQ FT: 31,000
SALES (est): 54.8MM **Privately Held**
WEB: www.maxitrol.com
SIC: 3625 3823 3494 3612 Relays & industrial controls; temperature instruments: industrial process type; pressure measurement instruments, industrial; controllers for process variables, all types; valves & pipe fittings; transformers, except electric; temperature controls, automatic; appliance regulators; gas burner, automatic controls

(G-14975)
MC DONALD COMPUTER CORPORATION
21411 Civic Center Dr # 100 (48076-3910)
PHONE..................................248 350-9290
James B Mc Donald, *President*
Neil Stevenson, *Vice Pres*
Mary Hassell, *Office Mgr*
EMP: 11
SQ FT: 5,200
SALES (est): 745.8K **Privately Held**
WEB: www.myloaninfo.com
SIC: 7374 7372 Data processing service; business oriented computer software

(G-14976)
MCNICHOLS CONVEYOR COMPANY
21411 Civic Center Dr # 204 (48076-3950)
PHONE..................................248 357-6077
Robert Iwrey, *President*
EMP: 10 EST: 1926
SALES (est): 1.6MM **Privately Held**
WEB: www.mcnicholsconveyor.com
SIC: 3535 Conveyors & conveying equipment

(G-14977)
MEJENTA SYSTEMS INC
Also Called: Npo Synergy Donor Management
30233 Southfield Rd # 113 (48076-1304)
PHONE..................................248 434-2583
Nirmaia Nallabhantu, *President*
Sreekrishna Vinjamoori, *Vice Pres*
EMP: 22
SQ FT: 1,300
SALES (est): 1.5MM **Privately Held**
SIC: 7374 7372 7373 7371 Data processing & preparation; educational computer software; application computer software; systems software development services; computer software systems analysis & design, custom; computer software development & applications; consulting engineer

(G-14978)
METALDYNE PRFMCE GROUP INC (HQ)
1 Towne Sq Ste 550 (48076-3710)
PHONE..................................248 727-1800
George Thanopoulos, *CEO*
Kevin Penn, *Ch of Bd*
Douglas Grimm, *President*
Russell Bradley, *Exec VP*
Thomas M Dono Jr, *Exec VP*
EMP: 43 EST: 2005
SQ FT: 25,000
SALES: 2.7B
SALES (corp-wide): 7.2B **Publicly Held**
SIC: 3714 Motor vehicle transmissions, drive assemblies & parts
PA: American Axle & Manufacturing Holdings, Inc.
1 Dauch Dr
Detroit MI 48211
313 758-2000

(G-14979)
METALDYNE TBLAR COMPONENTS LLC
1 Towne Sq Ste 550 (48076-3710)
P.O. Box 185, Hamburg (48139-0185)
PHONE..................................248 727-1800
Joseph Nowak, *President*
Scott Ferriman, *Vice Pres*
Bob Kirkendall, *Vice Pres*
Timothy Wadhams, *Treasurer*
Pat Senak, *Controller*
EMP: 212 EST: 1945
SQ FT: 60,000
SALES (est): 31.2K
SALES (corp-wide): 7.2B **Publicly Held**
SIC: 3714 3498 3441 Manifolds, motor vehicle; exhaust systems & parts, motor vehicle; fabricated pipe & fittings; fabricated structural metal
HQ: Metaldyne Powertrain Components, Inc.
1 Dauch Dr
Detroit MI 48211
313 758-2000

(G-14980)
MEXICAN FOOD SPECIALTIES INC
Also Called: Don Marcos Tortillas
21084 Bridge St (48033-4087)
PHONE..................................734 779-2370
Mark A Gutierrez, *President*
Daniel Gutierrez, *Vice Pres*
Deya Gutierrez, *Treasurer*
EMP: 5
SQ FT: 4,000
SALES (est): 2.3MM **Privately Held**
SIC: 2099 5141 Tortillas, fresh or refrigerated; food brokers

(G-14981)
MICHIGAN METALS AND MFG INC
29100 Northwestern Hwy (48034-1046)
P.O. Box 252684, West Bloomfield (48325-2684)
PHONE..................................248 910-7674
Isaac Lakritz, *President*
Richard Freedland, *Vice Pres*
Larry A Berry, *VP Finance*
EMP: 4
SALES (est): 200K **Privately Held**
SIC: 3295 Minerals, ground or treated

(G-14982)
MICRO FOCUS SOFTWARE INC
Also Called: Novell
26677 W 12 Mile Rd Ste 1 (48034-1514)
PHONE..................................248 353-8010
Mark Conley, *Branch Mgr*
EMP: 566
SALES (corp-wide): 1B **Privately Held**
SIC: 7372 Prepackaged software
PA: Micro Focus Software Inc.
1800 Novell Pl
Provo UT 84606
801 861-7000

(G-14983)
MINERAL COSMETICS INC
Also Called: European Skin Care & Cosmetics
21314 Hilltop St (48033-4063)
PHONE..................................248 542-7733
Robert S Glancz, *President*
Lucy Selezer, *Vice Pres*
EMP: 6
SALES (est): 420K **Privately Held**
SIC: 2844 Cosmetic preparations

(G-14984)
MIX FACTORY ONE LLC
27380 W 9 Mile Rd (48033-3470)
PHONE..................................248 799-9390
V Johnson, *Mng Member*
EMP: 6
SALES (est): 526.2K **Privately Held**
SIC: 3273 Ready-mixed concrete

(G-14985)
MKP ENTERPRISES INC
Also Called: Alternatives In Advertising
19785 W 12 Mile Rd 338 (48076-2584)
PHONE..................................248 809-2525
Madelyn Phillips, *President*
Mike Phillips, *Vice Pres*
Erik Phillips, *Natl Sales Mgr*
EMP: 4
SALES (est): 365.8K **Privately Held**
SIC: 7389 7319 2752 Advertising, promotional & trade show services; distribution of advertising material or sample services; commercial printing, offset

(G-14986)
MOBIMOGUL INC
29193 Northwestern Hwy (48034-1011)
PHONE..................................313 575-2795
Marcus Huddleston, *CEO*
Gary Curry, *CFO*
EMP: 4
SQ FT: 1,000
SALES (est): 305.9K **Privately Held**
SIC: 3663 Radio & TV communications equipment

(G-14987)
MORRIS ASSOCIATES INC
Also Called: Milliken and Company
24007 Telegraph Rd (48033-3031)
PHONE..................................248 355-9055
Zeno R Windley, *President*
Chris Allen, *Regional Mgr*
Troy Hodges, *Regional Mgr*
Lei Qian, *Business Mgr*
Brad Smith, *Vice Pres*
EMP: 26
SQ FT: 17,000
SALES (est): 4.6MM **Privately Held**
SIC: 3711 5131 Automobile assembly, including specialty automobiles; piece goods & notions

(G-14988)
N O F METAL COATINGS N AMER
26877 Northwestern Hwy (48033-2141)
PHONE..................................248 228-8610
Shin Masuda, *President*
EMP: 3 EST: 2011
SALES (est): 137.9K **Privately Held**
SIC: 3479 Coating of metals & formed products

(G-14989)
NEMAK COMMERCIAL SERVICES INC
2 Towne Sq Ste 300 (48076-3761)
PHONE..................................248 350-3999
Clifford Munson, *President*
EMP: 32 EST: 2000
SALES (est): 10.5MM **Privately Held**
SIC: 3334 Primary aluminum
HQ: Nemak Mexico, S.A.
Libramiento Arco Vial Km. 3.8
Garcia N.L. 66001

(G-14990)
NEMO CAPITAL PARTNERS LLC (PA)
28819 Franklin Rd Ste 130 (48034-1656)
PHONE..................................248 213-9899
Ali Safiedine, *CEO*
Faisal Ghazi, *Vice Pres*
Christopher Ruma, *Vice Pres*
Alan Agemy, *Controller*
EMP: 15
SALES (est): 9.5MM **Privately Held**
SIC: 7372 Operating systems computer software

(G-14991)
NEXT LEVEL MEDIA INC
Also Called: Azon Elite Summaries
15989 Addison St (48075-6902)
PHONE..................................248 762-7043
Kalon Willis, *CEO*
EMP: 5
SALES (est): 163.9K **Privately Held**
SIC: 2731 Textbooks: publishing only, not printed on site

(G-14992)
NOVARES US ENG COMPONENTS INC
29200 Northwestern Hwy (48034-1013)
PHONE..................................248 799-8949
Russ Bush, *General Mgr*
Christopher Corbett, *Manager*
EMP: 60
SALES (corp-wide): 102.8MM **Privately Held**
WEB: www.miniatureprecisioncomponents.com
SIC: 3089 Injection molded finished plastic products
HQ: Novares Us Engine Components, Inc.
820 Wisconsin St
Walworth WI 53184
262 275-5791

(G-14993)
NV LABS INC
Also Called: Reforma
20777 East St (48033-3603)
PHONE..................................248 358-9022
Vesna Deljosevic, *President*
Suzana Margilaj, *Manager*
Gary Cunitz,
EMP: 15
SQ FT: 20,000
SALES (est): 821.3K **Privately Held**
SIC: 2844 Toilet preparations

(G-14994)
P & O SERVICES INC
24293 Telg Rd Ste 140 (48033)
PHONE..................................248 809-3072
Zia Rahman, *President*
EMP: 5 EST: 2014
SQ FT: 1,800
SALES: 566.9K **Privately Held**
SIC: 3842 Prosthetic appliances

(G-14995)
P G K ENTERPRISES LLC
23450 Telegraph Rd (48033-4157)
PHONE..................................248 535-4411
Paul Kokx, *Administration*
EMP: 5
SALES (est): 365.1K **Privately Held**
SIC: 2411 Wheelstock, hewn

(G-14996)
PACIFIC INSIGHT ELEC CORP
25650 W 11 Mile Rd # 100 (48034-2253)
PHONE..................................248 344-2569
Cindy Walter, *Sales Staff*
Martin Baker, *Branch Mgr*
EMP: 21
SALES (corp-wide): 1B **Publicly Held**
SIC: 3674 Modules, solid state
HQ: Pacific Insight Electronics Corp
1155 Insight Dr
Nelson BC V1L 5
250 354-1155

GEOGRAPHIC SECTION

Southfield - Oakland County (G-15024)

(G-14997)
PETERSON AMERICAN CORPORATION (PA)
Also Called: Peterson Spring-Tech Pdts Ctr
21200 Telegraph Rd (48033-4243)
PHONE.................................248 799-5400
Dan Sceli, *CEO*
Edward Franks, *Division Mgr*
Travis Bell, *General Mgr*
Craig Gray, *General Mgr*
Rick Sbrocca, *General Mgr*
▲ **EMP:** 50 **EST:** 1932
SQ FT: 45,000
SALES (est): 290.5MM **Privately Held**
WEB: www.pspring.com
SIC: 3495 Wire springs

(G-14998)
PHOENIX DATA INCORPORATED
Also Called: Phoenix Data Systems
28588 Northwestern Hwy # 280 (48034-1840)
PHONE.................................248 281-0054
Bernard R Mannisto, *President*
Michael Salinger, *Director*
EMP: 17
SQ FT: 2,500
SALES (est): 1.9MM **Privately Held**
WEB: www.goaims.com
SIC: 7372 Application computer software

(G-14999)
PISTON GROUP LLC (PA)
3000 Town Ctr Ste 3250 (48075-1216)
PHONE.................................248 226-3976
Vincent Johnson, *CEO*
Amit Singhi, *COO*
EMP: 2
SALES (est): 1.6B **Privately Held**
SIC: 3714 Motor vehicle parts & accessories

(G-15000)
PLATFORM COMPUTING INC
2000 Town Ctr Ste 1900 (48075-1152)
PHONE.................................248 359-7825
Russ McKee, *Branch Mgr*
EMP: 4
SALES (corp-wide): 92.2MM **Privately Held**
SIC: 7372 Prepackaged software
HQ: Platform Computing, Inc.
  4400 N 1st St
  San Jose CA
  408 392-4900

(G-15001)
POLYMER INC (PA)
Also Called: United Paint & Chemical
24671 Telegraph Rd (48033-3035)
PHONE.................................248 353-3035
John G Piceu Jr, *CEO*
J Geoffrey Piceu, *Vice Pres*
▲ **EMP:** 99 **EST:** 1953
SQ FT: 65,000
SALES (est): 21.1MM **Privately Held**
SIC: 2851 5231 Paints: oil or alkyd vehicle or water thinned; undercoatings, paint; paint

(G-15002)
PPG INDUSTRIES INC
Also Called: PPG 5625
23361 Telegraph Rd (48033-4119)
PHONE.................................248 357-4817
Dan Braurer, *Branch Mgr*
EMP: 24
SALES (corp-wide): 15.3B **Publicly Held**
WEB: www.ppg.com
SIC: 2851 Paints & allied products
PA: Ppg Industries, Inc.
  1 Ppg Pl
  Pittsburgh PA 15272
  412 434-3131

(G-15003)
PRESTIGE PET PRODUCTS INC
Also Called: Hacht Sales
30410 Balewood St (48076-1566)
PHONE.................................248 615-1526
James R Hacht, *President*
▲ **EMP:** 5
SALES (est): 360K **Privately Held**
WEB: www.prestigepet.com
SIC: 2047 0742 Dog & cat food; veterinary services, specialties

(G-15004)
PRESTOLITE WIRE LLC (DH)
200 Galleria Officentre (48034-4708)
PHONE.................................248 355-4422
Gregory Ulewicz, *President*
Michael Murphy, *VP Bus Dvlpt*
John Cattell,
Martin Halle,
▲ **EMP:** 25
SQ FT: 6,000
SALES (est): 295.8MM **Privately Held**
WEB: www.prestolite.com
SIC: 3694 Battery cable wiring sets for internal combustion engines

(G-15005)
PRINTING BY MARC
25960 Franklin Pointe Dr (48034-1538)
PHONE.................................248 355-0848
Rose Hechler, *Owner*
Mark Hechler, *Co-Owner*
▲ **EMP:** 4
SALES (est): 239.4K **Privately Held**
SIC: 2752 Commercial printing, lithographic

(G-15006)
QP ACQUISITION 2 INC
2000 Town Ctr Ste 2450 (48075-1208)
PHONE.................................248 594-7432
Wallace L Rueckel, *President*
Jason G Runco, *Treasurer*
EMP: 20 **EST:** 1997
SQ FT: 10,000
SALES (est): 1.5MM
SALES (corp-wide): 533.3MM **Privately Held**
SIC: 3714 7532 3465 2711 Sun roofs, motor vehicle; customizing services, non-factory basis; moldings or trim, automobile: stamped metal; newspapers, publishing & printing; motel, franchised; leaf springs: automobile, locomotive, etc.
PA: Questor Partners Fund Ii, L.P.
  101 Southfield Rd 2
  Birmingham MI 48009
  248 593-1930

(G-15007)
QUANTAM SOLUTIONS LLC
18877 W 10 Mile Rd # 108 (48075-2613)
PHONE.................................248 395-2200
Larry Freimark, *President*
EMP: 7
SALES (est): 138.4K **Privately Held**
SIC: 3572 Computer storage devices

(G-15008)
QUANTUM LABS LLC
24555 Southfield Rd (48075-2738)
PHONE.................................248 262-7731
EMP: 3
SALES (est): 104K **Privately Held**
SIC: 3572 Mfg Computer Storage Devices

(G-15009)
R J MARSHALL COMPANY (PA)
26776 W 12 Mile Rd # 201 (48034-7807)
PHONE.................................248 353-4100
Richard Marshall, *CEO*
Joan E Marshall, *Exec VP*
Daniel Mahlmeister, *Vice Pres*
Tim Price, *Vice Pres*
David Pierce, *Research*
▲ **EMP:** 19 **EST:** 1979
SQ FT: 6,000
SALES (est): 20.3MM **Privately Held**
WEB: www.rjmarshallco.com
SIC: 3295 5169 Minerals, ground or otherwise treated; chemicals & allied products

(G-15010)
RAR GROUP INC
Also Called: Pinnacle Printing & Promotions
21421 Hilltop St Ste 12 (48033-4009)
PHONE.................................248 353-2266
Richard M Reinman, *President*
Ann Reinman, *Admin Sec*
EMP: 6
SQ FT: 3,100
SALES (est): 624K **Privately Held**
WEB: www.pinnacle-printing.com
SIC: 2752 Commercial printing, offset

(G-15011)
REAL LOVE PRINTWEAR
28475 Greenfield Rd # 212 (48076-3034)
PHONE.................................248 327-7181
Lisa Love, *Principal*
EMP: 4 **EST:** 2012
SQ FT: 300
SALES (est): 219.6K **Privately Held**
SIC: 2752 5699 7389 5947 Commercial printing, lithographic; customized clothing & apparel; designers, apparel; apparel designers, commercial; gift, novelty & souvenir shop; women's apparel, mail order

(G-15012)
RENA DRANE ENTERPRISES INC
24150 Philip Dr (48075-7720)
PHONE.................................248 796-2765
Sharena Dixon, *President*
EMP: 3
SQ FT: 1,800
SALES (est): 83.9K **Privately Held**
SIC: 3999 5065 7371 7389 Hair & hair-based products; electronic parts & equipment; software programming applications; apparel designers, commercial

(G-15013)
RENAISSANCE MEDIA LLC
Also Called: Detroit Jewish New
29200 Northwstrn Hwy 11 (48034)
PHONE.................................248 354-6060
Arthur M Horwitz,
Kevin Browett,
EMP: 70
SALES (est): 8.1MM **Privately Held**
WEB: www.thejewishnews.com
SIC: 2721 Magazines: publishing only, not printed on site

(G-15014)
REVSTONE INDUSTRIES LLC
2000 Town Ctr Ste 2100 (48075-1130)
PHONE.................................248 351-8800
S Mitchell, *Office Mgr*
EMP: 12 **Privately Held**
SIC: 2821 Plastics materials & resins
PA: Revstone Industries, Llc
  2008 Cypress St Ste 100
  Paris KY 40361

(G-15015)
RICHARD LARABEE
Also Called: Richard Reproductions
22132 W 9 Mile Rd (48033-6007)
PHONE.................................248 827-7755
Richard Larabee, *Owner*
Marcia Larabee, *Co-Owner*
EMP: 5 **EST:** 1972
SQ FT: 4,000
SALES (est): 417.1K **Privately Held**
SIC: 2752 2791 Commercial printing, offset; typesetting

(G-15016)
RMT ACQUISITION COMPANY LLC
Also Called: Rmt Woodworth
20941 East St (48033-5934)
PHONE.................................248 353-5487
EMP: 3
SALES (est): 280.1K
SALES (corp-wide): 1.3MM **Privately Held**
SIC: 3398 Metal Heat Treating
PA: Rmt Acquisition Company, Llc
  45755 Five Mile Rd
  Plymouth MI 48170
  248 353-4229

(G-15017)
ROSE BUSINESS FORMS COMPANY
Also Called: Rose Printing Services
22008 W 8 Mile Rd (48033-4495)
P.O. Box 129, Fowlerville (48836-0129)
PHONE.................................734 424-5200
William R Rose, *President*
Frank C Cassise, *Vice Pres*
EMP: 20 **EST:** 1976
SQ FT: 30,000
SALES (est): 4.5MM **Privately Held**
WEB: www.rpsvs.com
SIC: 5112 2752 Business forms; commercial printing, offset

(G-15018)
ROYAL LUX MAGAZINE
25055 Champlaign Dr (48034-1203)
PHONE.................................248 602-6565
Johnson Shantel, *Principal*
EMP: 3 **EST:** 2015
SALES (est): 78.6K **Privately Held**
SIC: 2711 Newspapers

(G-15019)
SABA SOFTWARE INC
26999 Centrl Pk Blvd # 210 (48076-4174)
PHONE.................................248 228-7300
Nguyen Huong, *Opers Staff*
Sridhar Guduguntla, *Manager*
EMP: 26
SALES (corp-wide): 177MM **Privately Held**
WEB: www.saba.com
SIC: 7372 Application computer software
PA: Saba Software, Inc.
  4120 Dublin Blvd Ste 200
  Dublin CA 94568
  877 722-2101

(G-15020)
SAGE AUTOMOTIVE INTERIORS INC
24007 Telegraph Rd (48033-3031)
PHONE.................................248 355-9055
Steve Morris, *Branch Mgr*
EMP: 14 **Privately Held**
SIC: 2399 Seat covers, automobile
HQ: Sage Automotive Interiors Inc
  3 Research Dr Ste 300
  Greenville SC 29607

(G-15021)
SAMS SUIT FCTRY & ALTERATION
25040 Southfield Rd (48075-1902)
PHONE.................................248 424-8666
Abbas Sarmad, *Managing Prtnr*
EMP: 12
SALES (est): 1.2MM **Privately Held**
SIC: 2329 Riding clothes:, men's, youths' & boys'

(G-15022)
SAVANNA INC (PA)
Also Called: Rmt Woodworth Heat Treating
20941 East St (48033-5934)
PHONE.................................248 353-8180
Terry R Woodworth, *President*
Tom Villerot, *General Mgr*
Rick Woodworth, *COO*
Scott Berry, *Director*
▲ **EMP:** 80
SALES (est): 12.2MM **Privately Held**
SIC: 3398 Metal heat treating

(G-15023)
SC INDUSTRIES INC (PA)
Also Called: Mdhearingaid
24151 Telg Rd Ste 100 (48033)
PHONE.................................312 366-3899
Sreekant Cherukuri, *President*
Sreenivas Cherukuri, *COO*
Jason McKinney, *Vice Pres*
EMP: 14
SALES (est): 1.7MM **Privately Held**
SIC: 3842 Hearing aids

(G-15024)
SCHENCK USA CORP
26801 Northwestern Hwy (48033-6251)
PHONE.................................248 377-2100
Mark Hass, *Branch Mgr*
EMP: 40
SALES (corp-wide): 4.4B **Privately Held**
SIC: 3545 3423 3829 3541 Balancing machines (machine tool accessories); hand & edge tools; testing equipment: abrasion, shearing strength, etc.; pointing & burring machines; deburring machines; assembly machines, including robotic
HQ: Schenck Usa Corp.
  535 Acorn St
  Deer Park NY 11729
  631 242-4010

Southfield - Oakland County (G-15025) — GEOGRAPHIC SECTION

(G-15025)
SEAL ALL ALUMINUM PDTS CORP
23200 Ranch Hill Dr E (48033-3181)
PHONE................................248 585-6061
EMP: 3 **EST:** 1961
SQ FT: 2,000
SALES: 125K **Privately Held**
SIC: 3442 3444 7699 Mfg Metal Doors/Sash/Trim Mfg Sheet Metalwork Repair Services

(G-15026)
SELECT STEEL FABRICATORS INC
23281 Telegraph Rd (48033-4127)
PHONE................................248 945-9582
Philip F Baker, *President*
Melody Baker, *Vice Pres*
EMP: 15
SQ FT: 22,000
SALES: 2MM **Privately Held**
SIC: 3541 3545 Machine tools, metal cutting type; machine tool accessories

(G-15027)
SHOP IV SBUSID INV GREDE LLC
1 Towne Sq Ste 550 (48076-3710)
PHONE................................248 727-1800
David C Dauch, *Ch of Bd*
EMP: 388 **EST:** 2010
SALES (est): 95.9K
SALES (corp-wide): 7.2B **Publicly Held**
SIC: 3711 3714 Motor vehicles & car bodies; motor vehicle parts & accessories
HQ: Asp Grede Acquisitionco Llc
1 Towne Sq Ste 550
Southfield MI 48076
248 727-1800

(G-15028)
SIMPLY DIVINE BAKING LLC
25162 Coral Gables St (48033-2403)
P.O. Box 225 (48037-0225)
PHONE................................313 903-2881
Adrienne Smiley, *Principal*
EMP: 4
SALES (est): 244.7K **Privately Held**
SIC: 2051 Bread, cake & related products

(G-15029)
SISTAHS BRAID TOO
17600 W 8 Mile Rd Ste 3 (48075-4316)
PHONE................................248 552-6202
Crystal Dewitt, *Owner*
EMP: 3
SALES (est): 258.9K **Privately Held**
SIC: 2241 Narrow fabric mills

(G-15030)
SKOKIE CASTINGS LLC
1 Towne Sq Ste 550 (48076-3710)
PHONE................................248 727-1800
EMP: 76 **EST:** 2010
SALES (est): 1.1MM
SALES (corp-wide): 7.2B **Publicly Held**
SIC: 3714 Motor vehicle parts & accessories
HQ: Grede Ii Llc
20750 Civic Center Dr # 100
Southfield MI 48076
248 727-1800

(G-15031)
SPEYSIDE REAL ESTATE LLC
26555 Northwestern Hwy (48033-2146)
PHONE................................248 354-7700
Brian J Kesseler, *CEO*
EMP: 10
SALES (est): 84.3K
SALES (corp-wide): 11.7B **Publicly Held**
SIC: 3053 Gaskets & sealing devices
PA: Tenneco Inc.
500 N Field Dr
Lake Forest IL 60045
847 482-5000

(G-15032)
SROSE PUBLISHING COMPANY
29100 Pointe O Woods Pl # 207 (48034-1227)
PHONE................................248 208-7073
Sylvia Rose, *President*
EMP: 3
SALES (est): 170.8K **Privately Held**
SIC: 2741 Miscellaneous publishing

(G-15033)
STARTECH-SOLUTIONS LLC
26300 Telg Rd Ste 101 (48033)
PHONE................................248 419-0650
Kevin Williams, *Vice Pres*
Joe Williams, *Vice Pres*
Joyce A Williams,
EMP: 6 **EST:** 2015
SQ FT: 2,000
SALES (est): 470.9K **Privately Held**
SIC: 3429 3577 3651 4813 Security cable locking system; data conversion equipment, media-to-media: computer; household audio & video equipment; telephone/video communications; video & audio equipment

(G-15034)
STERLING LABORATORIES INC
19270 W 8 Mile Rd (48075-5722)
PHONE................................248 233-1190
Herschel S Wright, *President*
EMP: 3
SALES: 100K **Privately Held**
SIC: 2841 Soap & other detergents

(G-15035)
STERLING SCALE COMPANY (PA)
20955 Boening Dr (48075-5738)
PHONE................................248 358-0590
E Donald Dixon, *President*
James Dixon, *Vice Pres*
J Schultz, *QC Mgr*
Keith Bonka, *Manager*
Donald Dixon, *Manager*
EMP: 4 **EST:** 1961
SQ FT: 12,000
SALES (est): 3.9MM **Privately Held**
SIC: 3596 7699 7359 Industrial scales; scale repair service; equipment rental & leasing

(G-15036)
SUN COMMUNITIES INC (PA)
27777 Franklin Rd Ste 200 (48034-8205)
PHONE................................248 208-2500
Gary A Shiffman, *Ch of Bd*
Susan Loren, *General Mgr*
Nicole Cooley, *Business Mgr*
Jonathan M Colman, *Exec VP*
Melinda Graulau, *Vice Pres*
EMP: 106
SALES: 1.1B **Publicly Held**
WEB: www.suncommunities.com
SIC: 6798 2451 Real estate investment trusts; mobile homes

(G-15037)
SUPER VIDEO SERVICE CENTER
26561 W 12 Mile Rd # 102 (48034-5693)
PHONE................................248 358-4794
Carl Friedlander, *CEO*
Allen Friedlander, *Vice Pres*
EMP: 5
SQ FT: 1,000
SALES (est): 678.7K **Privately Held**
SIC: 3652 7812 7359 Master records or tapes, preparation of; video tape production; video cassette recorder & accessory rental

(G-15038)
SUPERIOR INDUSTRIES INTL INC (PA)
26600 Telg Rd Ste 400 (48033)
PHONE................................248 352-7300
Timothy C McQuay, *Ch of Bd*
Majdi B Abulaban, *President*
Joanne M Finnorn, *Senior VP*
Parveen Kakar, *Senior VP*
James Sistek, *Senior VP*
▲ **EMP:** 250
SALES: 1.5B **Publicly Held**
WEB: www.superiorindustries.com
SIC: 3714 Motor vehicle wheels & parts

(G-15039)
SUPERIOR INDUSTRIES N AMER LLC
26600 Telegraph Rd # 400 (48033-5300)
PHONE................................248 352-7300
Steven J Borick, *Ch of Bd*
▲ **EMP:** 46
SALES (est): 364.8K
SALES (corp-wide): 1.5B **Publicly Held**
SIC: 3714 Motor vehicle wheels & parts
HQ: Superior Industries International Holdings, Llc
7800 Woodley Ave
Van Nuys CA 91406
818 781-4973

(G-15040)
SURE-WELD & PLATING RACK CO (PA)
Also Called: Sure-Plating Rack Co
21680 W 8 Mile Rd (48075-5637)
PHONE................................248 304-9430
EMP: 5 **EST:** 1947
SQ FT: 25,000
SALES (est): 1.2MM **Privately Held**
SIC: 3444 3479 Mfg Metal Industrial Material Handling Racks & Stands & Plastic Coating Metal

(G-15041)
SUSE LLC
Also Called: Suse Linux
26677 W 12 Mile Rd Ste 1 (48034-1514)
PHONE................................248 353-8010
EMP: 10
SALES (corp-wide): 17.7MM **Privately Held**
SIC: 7372 Prepackaged software
PA: Suse Llc
1800 Novell Pl
Provo UT 84606
206 217-7500

(G-15042)
SYNDEVCO INC
24205 Telegraph Rd (48033-7915)
P.O. Box 265 (48037-0265)
PHONE................................248 356-2839
William M Straith, *Ch of Bd*
Thomas W Straith, *President*
Tom Straith, *Vice Pres*
Ron Grobbel, *CFO*
Ronald M Grobbel, *Treasurer*
EMP: 15
SQ FT: 22,000
SALES: 3.3MM **Privately Held**
WEB: www.syndevco.com
SIC: 3612 3643 Transformers, except electric; connectors & terminals for electrical devices

(G-15043)
TAYLOR COMMUNICATIONS INC
24800 Denso Dr Ste 140 (48033-7448)
PHONE................................248 304-4800
Doug McDougall, *Principal*
EMP: 16
SALES (corp-wide): 2.8B **Privately Held**
SIC: 2754 8741 Business forms: gravure printing; management services
HQ: Taylor Communications, Inc.
1725 Roe Crest Dr
North Mankato MN 56003
507 625-2828

(G-15044)
TENNECO INC
Also Called: Federal-Mogul
27300 W 11 Mile Rd (48034-6147)
PHONE................................248 354-7700
Rod Davis, *Opers Staff*
Jennifer Hoenig, *Purch Mgr*
Arthur Fong, *Engineer*
Edmo Soares, *Engineer*
Hans Lipp, *Manager*
EMP: 10
SALES (corp-wide): 11.7B **Publicly Held**
SIC: 3462 3559 3674 Automotive & internal combustion engine forgings; degreasing machines, automotive & industrial; computer logic modules
PA: Tenneco Inc.
500 N Field Dr
Lake Forest IL 60045
847 482-5000

(G-15045)
TENNECO INC
26555 Northwestern Hwy (48033-2146)
P.O. Box 77539, Detroit (48277-0539)
PHONE................................248 354-7700
EMP: 4
SALES (corp-wide): 11.7B **Publicly Held**
SIC: 3714 Motor vehicle parts & accessories
PA: Tenneco Inc.
500 N Field Dr
Lake Forest IL 60045
847 482-5000

(G-15046)
TOSHIBA AMER BUS SOLUTIONS INC
29100 Northwstn Hwy 300 (48034)
PHONE................................248 427-8100
Anthony Pusino, *Principal*
EMP: 10 **Privately Held**
SIC: 3577 Computer peripheral equipment
HQ: Toshiba America Business Solutions, Inc.
25530 Commercentre Dr
Lake Forest CA 92630
949 462-6000

(G-15047)
TOTAL TOXICOLOGY LABS LLC
24525 Southfield Rd (48075-2740)
PHONE................................248 352-7171
Martin Bluth, *Director*
EMP: 6
SALES (est): 562.6K **Privately Held**
SIC: 3821 Time interval measuring equipment, electric (lab type)

(G-15048)
TRACTECH INC (DH)
26201 Northwestern Hwy (48076-3926)
PHONE................................248 226-6800
Carl Pittner, *President*
EMP: 45
SALES (est): 8.5MM **Privately Held**
SIC: 3714 3713 3568 Motor vehicle parts & accessories; truck & bus bodies; power transmission equipment
HQ: Eaton Corporation
1000 Eaton Blvd
Cleveland OH 44122
440 523-5000

(G-15049)
TRISTONE FLOWTECH USA INC (DH)
2000 Town Ctr Ste 660 (48075-1199)
PHONE................................248 560-1724
Gokhan Tektas, *Managing Dir*
Jon Hagan, *Managing Dir*
Kimberly Mohr, *Finance*
EMP: 5
SQ FT: 215,000
SALES: 100MM
SALES (corp-wide): 1.7B **Privately Held**
SIC: 3714 Motor vehicle parts & accessories
HQ: Tristone Flowtech Germany Gmbh
Unterschweinstiege 2-14
Frankfurt Am Main 60549
699 043-0010

(G-15050)
TRUARX INC
2000 Town Ctr Ste 2050 (48075-1131)
PHONE................................248 538-7809
EMP: 15
SQ FT: 2,100
SALES (est): 1MM
SALES (corp-wide): 2.2B **Privately Held**
SIC: 7372 Prepackaged Software Services
HQ: Anxebusiness, Llc
2000 Town Ctr Ste 2050
Southfield MI 48076
248 263-3400

(G-15051)
TYSON FRESH MEATS INC
I B P Smoked Meat Division
26999 Central Park Blvd (48076-4174)
PHONE................................248 213-1000
Ron Spangler, *Principal*
EMP: 100
SALES (corp-wide): 42.4B **Publicly Held**
SIC: 2011 Meat packing plants

GEOGRAPHIC SECTION
Southgate - Wayne County (G-15080)

HQ: Tyson Fresh Meats, Inc.
800 Stevens Port Dr
Dakota Dunes SD 57049
605 235-2061

(G-15052)
UC HOLDINGS INC (PA)
300 Galleria Officentre (48034-4700)
PHONE.................................248 728-8642
Andreas Weller, *CEO*
EMP: 100
SQ FT: 10,000
SALES (est): 1.3B **Privately Held**
SIC: 3714 Motor vehicle engines & parts

(G-15053)
ULTRA PRINTING
22850 Inkster Rd (48033-3409)
P.O. Box 206 (48037-0206)
PHONE.................................248 352-7238
EMP: 3 **EST:** 2003
SALES (est): 180K **Privately Held**
SIC: 2752 Lithographic Commercial Printing

(G-15054)
UNITED PAINT AND CHEMICAL CORP
24671 Telegraph Rd (48033-3035)
PHONE.................................248 353-3035
John G Piceu, *CEO*
EMP: 60 **EST:** 1953
SQ FT: 60,000
SALES (est): 8MM
SALES (corp-wide): 21.1MM **Privately Held**
SIC: 2851 Paints: oil or alkyd vehicle or water thinned; undercoatings, paint
PA: Polymer, Inc.
24671 Telegraph Rd
Southfield MI 48033
248 353-3035

(G-15055)
UNIVERSAL WARRANTY CORPOR
300 Galleria Officentre (48034-4700)
PHONE.................................248 263-6900
Rose Soper, *President*
Hj Bolar, *Principal*
EMP: 3 **EST:** 2010
SALES (est): 197.2K **Privately Held**
SIC: 3498 Tube fabricating (contract bending & shaping)

(G-15056)
URBAN SPECIALTY APPAREL INC
29540 Southfield Rd # 102 (48076-2047)
PHONE.................................248 395-9500
Ronald Jones, *President*
EMP: 13
SALES (est): 1.9MM **Privately Held**
SIC: 2834 Pharmaceutical preparations

(G-15057)
USMFG INC (HQ)
28400 Northwestern Hwy # 2 (48034-8348)
PHONE.................................269 637-6392
Bernd Blondin, *CEO*
EMP: 1 **EST:** 2013
SQ FT: 1,000
SALES (est): 1.5MM
SALES (corp-wide): 197.6MM **Privately Held**
SIC: 3339 Precious metals
PA: Mfg Metall- Und Ferrolegierungsges.
Mbh Hafner, Blondin & Tidou
Rudolf-Diesel-Str. 9
Meerbusch 40670
215 969-630

(G-15058)
VEONEER INC (PA)
26360 American Dr (48034-6116)
PHONE.................................248 223-0600
Jan Carlson, *Ch of Bd*
Nishant Batra, *Exec VP*
Art Blanchford, *Exec VP*
Thomas Jonsson, *Exec VP*
Steve Rode, *Exec VP*
EMP: 600
SALES: 2.2B **Publicly Held**
SIC: 3694 3714 Automotive electrical equipment; motor vehicle parts & accessories

(G-15059)
VEONEER US INC (HQ)
26360 American Dr (48034-6116)
PHONE.................................248 223-8074
Steve Rode, *CEO*
EMP: 132
SALES (est): 630MM
SALES (corp-wide): 2.2B **Publicly Held**
SIC: 3694 3674 Automotive electrical equipment; semiconductors & related devices
PA: Veoneer, Inc.
26360 American Dr
Southfield MI 48034
248 223-0600

(G-15060)
VEONEER US INC
Also Called: Veoneer Southfield
26360 American Dr (48034-6116)
PHONE.................................248 223-0600
Veronica Sheredy, *Buyer*
Paul Chwalebny, *Project Engr*
Amol Shelar, *Associate*
EMP: 496
SALES (corp-wide): 2.2B **Publicly Held**
SIC: 3694 Automotive electrical equipment
HQ: Veoneer Us, Inc.
26360 American Dr
Southfield MI 48034
248 223-8074

(G-15061)
VISUAL PRODUCTIONS INC
24050 Northwestern Hwy (48075-2567)
PHONE.................................248 356-4399
Tom Battaglia, *President*
EMP: 50
SALES (est): 4MM **Privately Held**
SIC: 8748 7359 3993 Business consulting; equipment rental & leasing; signs & advertising specialties

(G-15062)
VIVA BEVERAGES LLC
Also Called: Quick Beverages
27777 Franklin Rd # 1640 (48034-8265)
PHONE.................................248 746-7044
Harry Bigelow, *President*
Robert Nistico, *President*
Gary Shiffman, *Mng Member*
Ron Ferber,
Lon Kufman,
▼ **EMP:** 54
SQ FT: 1,800
SALES (est): 12.9MM **Privately Held**
SIC: 5149 2086 Beverages, except coffee & tea; carbonated beverages, nonalcoholic: bottled & canned

(G-15063)
VIVIAN ENTERPRISES LLC
Also Called: Bagel Brothers Cafe
29111 Telegraph Rd (48034-7603)
PHONE.................................248 792-9925
Matthew Shouneyia, *Mng Member*
Johnny Shouneyia,
EMP: 32
SALES: 300K **Privately Held**
SIC: 5812 7372 Cafe; application computer software

(G-15064)
W T BERESFORD CO
26400 Lahser Rd Ste 408 (48033-2604)
PHONE.................................248 350-2900
Chris Beresford, *President*
Thomas Beresford, *Vice Pres*
William T Beresford, *Vice Pres*
▲ **EMP:** 8 **EST:** 1975
SQ FT: 3,436
SALES (est): 2.2MM **Privately Held**
WEB: www.beresfordco.com
SIC: 3089 Identification cards, plastic

(G-15065)
WALLACE STUDIOS LLC
17260 Madison St (48076-1274)
PHONE.................................248 917-2459
Ashley Wallace,
EMP: 3

SALES (est): 207.7K **Privately Held**
SIC: 2721 7336 Comic books: publishing & printing; commercial art & graphic design

(G-15066)
WIN SCHULER FOODS INC
27777 Franklin Rd # 1520 (48034-8261)
PHONE.................................248 262-3450
Robert P Nunez, *President*
Tom Bitterman, *COO*
EMP: 2
SQ FT: 1,800
SALES (est): 4MM **Privately Held**
SIC: 2022 5145 Cheese, natural & processed; snack foods

(G-15067)
X-CEL INDUSTRIES INC
21121 Telegraph Rd (48033-4253)
PHONE.................................248 226-6000
James M Richard Jr, *President*
James Kendall, *General Mgr*
Carl Hawkins, *Plant Mgr*
Kristin Barlow, *Materials Mgr*
Raymond Dobring, *Controller*
▲ **EMP:** 110
SQ FT: 110,000
SALES (est): 12MM **Privately Held**
WEB: www.xcelpaint.com
SIC: 3479 Coating of metals & formed products

(G-15068)
XPO NLM
600 Galleria Officentre S (48034)
PHONE.................................866 251-3651
Bradley S Jacobs, *CEO*
EMP: 4
SALES (est): 555.1K **Privately Held**
SIC: 3799 Transportation equipment

(G-15069)
YOUNG DIVERSIFIED INDUSTRIES
21015 Bridge St (48033-4088)
PHONE.................................248 353-1867
Richard Young, *President*
EMP: 6
SQ FT: 3,500
SALES (est): 600K **Privately Held**
SIC: 3714 Motor vehicle parts & accessories

(G-15070)
ZIMMERMANN ENGINEERING CO INC
24260 Telegraph Rd (48033-3056)
PHONE.................................248 358-0044
Paul Zimmermann, *President*
Donald Zimmermann, *Treasurer*
EMP: 5 **EST:** 1945
SALES (est): 675.6K **Privately Held**
SIC: 3451 3545 Screw machine products; cutting tools for machine tools

Southgate
Wayne County

(G-15071)
1ST CLASS EMBROIDERY LLC
Also Called: First Class Silkscreening EMB
11205 Morningview (48195-7306)
PHONE.................................734 282-7745
Henry Forbes, *Mng Member*
EMP: 3
SALES (est): 280K **Privately Held**
SIC: 2396 Screen printing on fabric articles

(G-15072)
A LA DON SEASONINGS
16201 Allen Rd Apt 145 (48195-7900)
P.O. Box 571, Taylor (48180-0571)
PHONE.................................734 532-7862
Donaldson Richmond, *Principal*
EMP: 3
SALES: 10K **Privately Held**
SIC: 2099 Food preparations

(G-15073)
ABTECH INSTALLATION & SVC INC
Also Called: Ems Equipment Management Svcs
11900 Reeck Rd Ste 100 (48195-2229)
PHONE.................................800 548-2381
Sorinel Andronic, *President*
Tony Andronic, *Vice Pres*
EMP: 28
SQ FT: 18,000
SALES (est): 1.6MM **Privately Held**
SIC: 3825 Semiconductor test equipment; test equipment for electronic & electric measurement; digital test equipment, electronic & electrical circuits

(G-15074)
AZTECNOLOGY LLC
15677 Noecker Way Ste 100 (48195-2272)
PHONE.................................734 857-2045
Ken Jones, *Mng Member*
Pauline Kemke,
EMP: 8
SALES (est): 2MM **Privately Held**
SIC: 3679 Electronic circuits

(G-15075)
CLASSIC ACCENTS INC
13631 Brest St (48195-1702)
P.O. Box 1181 (48195-0181)
PHONE.................................734 284-7661
Peter Brevoort, *President*
▲ **EMP:** 3
SALES (est): 414.9K **Privately Held**
WEB: www.classicaccents.net
SIC: 3613 Switchgear & switchboard apparatus

(G-15076)
DAILY FANTASY KING
15425 Glenhurst (48195-8530)
PHONE.................................734 238-2622
William Lauterbach, *Principal*
EMP: 3
SALES (est): 151.5K **Privately Held**
SIC: 2711 Newspapers, publishing & printing

(G-15077)
GT FOODS INC
13467 Pullman St (48195-1168)
PHONE.................................734 934-2729
Brian Sharkey, *Principal*
EMP: 3
SALES (est): 168.9K **Privately Held**
SIC: 2099 Food preparations

(G-15078)
HALSAN INC
Also Called: International Minute Press
15315 Dix Toledo Rd (48195-2693)
PHONE.................................734 285-5420
Harold Wendt, *President*
Sandra Wendt, *Vice Pres*
EMP: 4
SALES (est): 514.3K **Privately Held**
WEB: www.pickimp.com
SIC: 2752 2791 2789 Commercial printing, offset; typesetting; bookbinding & related work

(G-15079)
L & M HARDWOOD & SKIDS LLC
15361 Goddard Rd (48195-2218)
PHONE.................................734 281-3043
Debra Mosley,
EMP: 4
SQ FT: 5,000
SALES (est): 663.9K **Privately Held**
SIC: 2448 5031 Skids, wood; lumber: rough, dressed & finished

(G-15080)
LANDRA PRSTHTICS ORTHOTICS INC (PA)
14725 Northline Rd (48195-2407)
PHONE.................................734 281-8144
Steve Landra, *CEO*
EMP: 6
SALES (est): 908.9K **Privately Held**
SIC: 3842 Limbs, artificial; prosthetic appliances

Southgate - Wayne County

(G-15081)
MICHIGAN VEHICLE SOLUTIONS LLC
16600 Fort St (48195-1440)
PHONE..................734 720-7649
Richard Oliver, *Principal*
EMP: 3
SALES (est): 297.4K **Privately Held**
SIC: 3465 Body parts, automobile: stamped metal; moldings or trim, automobile: stamped metal

(G-15082)
PEPSICO INC
12862 Reeck Rd (48195-2270)
PHONE..................734 374-9841
EMP: 3
SALES (est): 237.6K **Privately Held**
SIC: 2086 Carbonated soft drinks, bottled & canned

(G-15083)
STAN KELL INC
Also Called: Field House
12045 Dix Toledo Rd (48195-1714)
PHONE..................734 283-0005
Charlotte Stanley, *President*
Diane Kell, *Vice Pres*
EMP: 3
SALES (est): 316.1K **Privately Held**
SIC: 2599 Bar, restaurant & cafeteria furniture

(G-15084)
STOP & GO NO 10 INC
13785 Allen Rd (48195-3001)
PHONE..................734 281-7500
Chuck Mayzer, *President*
EMP: 6
SALES (est): 648.9K **Privately Held**
SIC: 3563 Air & gas compressors

(G-15085)
TRADE SPECIFIC SOLUTIONS LLC
13092 Superior St (48195-1204)
PHONE..................734 752-7124
Greg Boland, *Principal*
EMP: 4
SALES: 20K **Privately Held**
SIC: 3444 Metal roofing & roof drainage equipment

Spalding
Menominee County

(G-15086)
EARL ST JOHN FOREST PRODUCTS
N16226 Birch St (49886)
P.O. Box 130 (49886-0130)
PHONE..................906 497-5667
Earl St John Jr, *President*
Edgar A Larche, *Admin Sec*
EMP: 35 **EST:** 1962
SQ FT: 10,000
SALES (est): 9MM **Privately Held**
SIC: 2411 Logging

(G-15087)
TDRN INC
N16187 N Balsam Lane I.5 (49886-9702)
P.O. Box 189 (49886-0189)
PHONE..................906 497-5510
Cynthia Parrish, *President*
EMP: 7
SQ FT: 7,200
SALES (est): 1.9MM **Privately Held**
SIC: 3599 Machine shop, jobbing & repair

Sparta
Kent County

(G-15088)
BESSEY TOOL & DIE INC
617 10 Mile Rd Nw (49345-9459)
PHONE..................616 887-8820
Steven Bessey, *President*
Rocky Johnston, *Vice Pres*
Marlene Bessey, *Treasurer*
EMP: 18
SQ FT: 26,000
SALES (est): 4MM **Privately Held**
SIC: 3544 Special dies & tools

(G-15089)
CASCADE DIE CASTING GROUP INC
Great Lakes Division
9983 Sparta Ave Nw (49345-9786)
PHONE..................616 887-1771
John Koetje, *Principal*
Michael Simpson, *Production*
Art Hamrick, *Regl Sales Mgr*
Jeremy Rochow, *Technology*
EMP: 80
SALES (corp-wide): 83.8MM **Privately Held**
WEB: www.cascade-cdc.com
SIC: 3364 3365 3363 Zinc & zinc-base alloy die-castings; aluminum foundries; aluminum die-castings
HQ: Cascade Die Casting Group Inc
7441 Division Ave S A1
Grand Rapids MI 49548
616 281-1774

(G-15090)
CELIA CORPORATION (PA)
Also Called: General Formulations
309 S Union St (49345-1529)
P.O. Box 158 (49345-0158)
PHONE..................616 887-7387
Celia Said, *President*
James Clay, *Vice Pres*
▲ **EMP:** 2 **EST:** 1953
SQ FT: 200,000
SALES (est): 62.9MM **Privately Held**
WEB: www.generalformulations.com
SIC: 2672 2759 2893 7389 Adhesive backed films, foams & foils; screen printing; labels & seals: printing; printing ink; laminating service

(G-15091)
CELIA CORPORATION
Also Called: Continental Ideification Pdts
140 E Averill St (49345-1516)
P.O. Box 98 (49345-0098)
PHONE..................616 887-7341
David Douma, *Branch Mgr*
EMP: 100
SALES (corp-wide): 62.9MM **Privately Held**
WEB: www.generalformulations.com
SIC: 2752 2796 2675 2672 Decals, lithographed; platemaking services; die-cut paper & board; coated & laminated paper; automotive & apparel trimmings; pleating & stitching
PA: Celia Corporation
309 S Union St
Sparta MI 49345
616 887-7387

(G-15092)
COACH HOUSE IRON INC
1005 9 Mile Rd Nw Ste 1 (49345-7202)
PHONE..................616 785-8967
Michael Bergstrom, *President*
Herb Bergstrom, *Vice Pres*
EMP: 7
SQ FT: 9,000
SALES (est): 450K **Privately Held**
SIC: 3312 Blast furnaces & steel mills

(G-15093)
CONTROL SYSTEMS & SERVICE
392 E Division St Ste A (49345-1377)
PHONE..................616 887-2738
Mark Allen, *Owner*
EMP: 3
SALES (est): 130K **Privately Held**
WEB: www.webs-2-u.com
SIC: 3822 Hardware for environmental regulators

(G-15094)
FEDERAL-MOGUL POWERTRAIN INC
200 Maple St (49345-1563)
PHONE..................616 887-8231
Richard Van Eck, *Branch Mgr*
Kristapher Mixell, *Director*
EMP: 180
SALES (corp-wide): 11.7B **Publicly Held**
SIC: 3321 3053 3714 3592 Gray & ductile iron foundries; gaskets & sealing devices; motor vehicle parts & accessories; carburetors, pistons, rings, valves
HQ: Federal-Mogul Powertrain Llc
27300 W 11 Mile Rd
Southfield MI 48034

(G-15095)
GREAT AMERICAN PUBLISHING CO
75 Applewood Dr Ste A (49345-1741)
P.O. Box 128 (49345-0128)
PHONE..................616 887-9008
Matt Mc Callum, *President*
Kim Warren, *Editor*
David Fairbourn, *Manager*
Sally Ostman, *Manager*
Matt Milkovich, *Assoc Editor*
EMP: 43
SALES (est): 1.6MM **Privately Held**
WEB: www.fruitgrowersnews.com
SIC: 2711 Newspapers, publishing & printing

(G-15096)
HANDY WACKS CORPORATION (PA)
100 E Averill St (49345-1516)
P.O. Box 129 (49345-0129)
PHONE..................616 887-8268
Henry B Fairchild III, *President*
Paul Steffens, *Prdtn Mgr*
Marcia Fairchild, *Treasurer*
Sue Harrison, *Cust Mgr*
Chris Roberts, *Sales Staff*
♦ **EMP:** 40 **EST:** 1935
SQ FT: 44,000
SALES (est): 11.4MM **Privately Held**
SIC: 2621 Paper mills

(G-15097)
HANDY WACKS CORPORATION
100 E Averill St (49345-1516)
P.O. Box 129 (49345-0129)
PHONE..................616 887-8268
Fran Bryant, *Manager*
EMP: 45
SALES (corp-wide): 11.4MM **Privately Held**
SIC: 2631 Coated paperboard
PA: Handy Wacks Corporation
100 E Averill St
Sparta MI 49345
616 887-8268

(G-15098)
HART ENTERPRISES USA INC
400 Apple Jack Ct (49345-1708)
PHONE..................616 887-0400
Alan Taylor, *President*
Robert Striebel, *Vice Pres*
EMP: 78
SQ FT: 35,000
SALES (est): 14.4MM **Privately Held**
WEB: www.hartneedles.com
SIC: 3841 Surgical & medical instruments

(G-15099)
JLORE WELDING
8810 W Sunset Pnes (49345-8274)
PHONE..................989 402-7201
Jonathon Lore, *Principal*
EMP: 8 **EST:** 2018
SALES (est): 88.7K **Privately Held**
SIC: 7692 Welding repair

(G-15100)
K & K MFG INC
951 9 Mile Rd Nw (49345-9428)
PHONE..................616 784-4286
Timothy W Kidder, *President*
Patricia V Kidder, *Vice Pres*
Jennifer Kidder, *Cust Mgr*
Steve Kidder, *Sales Staff*
Lori Auterson, *Office Mgr*
▲ **EMP:** 9
SQ FT: 12,000
SALES (est): 1.6MM **Privately Held**
WEB: www.kkmfg.com
SIC: 5531 5013 3465 Automotive parts; automotive supplies & parts; automotive stampings

(G-15101)
LEGGETT PLATT COMPONENTS INC
Also Called: Moiron Branch 0918
7701 Venture Ave Nw (49345-8369)
PHONE..................616 784-7000
Paul Haverkate, *Manager*
EMP: 100
SALES (corp-wide): 4.2B **Publicly Held**
SIC: 3498 Tube fabricating (contract bending & shaping)
HQ: Leggett & Platt Components Company, Inc.
115 N Industrial Rd
Tupelo MS 38801
662 844-4224

(G-15102)
MICHIGAN APPLE PACKERS COOP
10740 Peach Tree (49345)
P.O. Box 305 (49345-0305)
PHONE..................616 887-9933
Robert Steffens, *President*
Jeff Berenbrock, *Treasurer*
EMP: 4 **EST:** 1996
SQ FT: 5,000
SALES (est): 246.7K **Privately Held**
SIC: 2033 Apple sauce: packaged in cans, jars, etc.

(G-15103)
OLD ORCHARD BRANDS LLC
1991 12 Mile Rd Nw (49345-9757)
P.O. Box 66 (49345-0066)
PHONE..................616 887-1745
Mark Saur, *President*
Tony Woody, *General Mgr*
Jeffrey Pochop, *Business Mgr*
Craig Lampright, *Vice Pres*
Gregory V Mangione, *Vice Pres*
♦ **EMP:** 95
SQ FT: 140,000
SALES (est): 48.5MM
SALES (corp-wide): 402MM **Privately Held**
WEB: www.OldOrchard.com
SIC: 2033 2037 Fruit juices: packaged in cans, jars, etc.; frozen fruits & vegetables
HQ: Industries Lassonde Inc
755 Rue Principale
Rougemont QC J0L 1
450 469-4926

(G-15104)
P-S BUSINESS ACQUISITION INC (HQ)
Also Called: Pak-Sak Industries
122 S Aspen St (49345-1442)
PHONE..................616 887-8837
James Wood, *Manager*
EMP: 21
SALES (est): 9.4MM
SALES (corp-wide): 97MM **Privately Held**
SIC: 2673 Plastic bags: made from purchased materials
PA: Packaging Personified, Inc.
246 Kehoe Blvd
Carol Stream IL 60188
630 653-1655

(G-15105)
PACKAGING PERSONIFIED INC
122 S Aspen St (49345-1442)
PHONE..................616 887-8837
Dominic Imburgia, *President*
Dan Inburgia, *General Mgr*
EMP: 120
SALES (corp-wide): 97MM **Privately Held**
WEB: www.packagingpersonified.com
SIC: 2673 Garment bags (plastic film): made from purchased materials
PA: Packaging Personified, Inc.
246 Kehoe Blvd
Carol Stream IL 60188
630 653-1655

(G-15106)
PRINT METRO INC
98 E Division St (49345-1395)
P.O. Box 268 (49345-0268)
PHONE..................616 887-1723
Tom Kastelz, *Principal*

GEOGRAPHIC SECTION

Spring Lake - Ottawa County (G-15132)

EMP: 8
SALES (est): 345K Privately Held
SIC: 2752 Photo-offset printing

(G-15107)
PRO COATINGS INC
233 1/2 Prospect St (49345-1459)
P.O. Box 419 (49345-0419)
PHONE..................................616 887-8808
Nathan Ronald Rider, *President*
EMP: 12
SQ FT: 10,000
SALES (est): 2.4MM Privately Held
SIC: 2851 Paints & paint additives; varnishes

(G-15108)
RON FISK HARDWOODS INC (PA)
10700 Low Lake Dr Ne (49345-9430)
PHONE..................................616 887-3826
Dan Fisk, *Corp Secy*
Larry Fisk, *Vice Pres*
Wayne Bills, *Vice Pres*
EMP: 2 EST: 1975
SQ FT: 1,000
SALES: 1.9MM Privately Held
SIC: 2426 Hardwood dimension & flooring mills

(G-15109)
SCHANTZ LLC
9 Loomis St (49345-1117)
PHONE..................................616 887-0517
Ron Schantz,
EMP: 8
SALES (est): 410.4K Privately Held
SIC: 2048 5191 Prepared feeds; animal feeds

(G-15110)
SPARTA OUTLETS
470 E Division St (49345-1339)
PHONE..................................616 887-6010
Ken Miller, *Owner*
John Foley, *Co-Owner*
EMP: 4
SALES (est): 347.3K Privately Held
SIC: 3629 Electrical industrial apparatus

(G-15111)
SPARTA WASH & STORAGE LLC
510 S State St (49345-1547)
PHONE..................................616 887-1034
Mark Sinkelstein, *CEO*
Bryan Bailey, *Manager*
EMP: 6
SQ FT: 2,170
SALES (est): 538.8K Privately Held
SIC: 3589 4225 Car washing machinery; warehousing, self-storage

(G-15112)
SPEC TOOL COMPANY (PA)
389 E Div St (49345)
P.O. Box 127 (49345-0127)
PHONE..................................888 887-1717
Lee Hiler, *President*
Rick Diekevers, *Opers Mgr*
Barry Hartwell, *Engineer*
Steve Bosch, *Finance Mgr*
Carol Forward, *Human Res Dir*
EMP: 54
SQ FT: 15,000
SALES (est): 17.1MM Privately Held
WEB: www.spec-tool.com
SIC: 3599 Machine shop, jobbing & repair

(G-15113)
SPEEDRACK PRODUCTS GROUP LTD (PA)
Also Called: Integrted Systems Group Div of
7903 Venture Ave Nw (49345-9427)
PHONE..................................616 887-0002
Ron Ducharme, *CEO*
Michael Roney, *President*
Timothy Bastic, *Vice Pres*
John Kettman, *Vice Pres*
H Will Baird III, *CFO*
▼ EMP: 35
SQ FT: 16,800
SALES (est): 35.6MM Privately Held
WEB: www.speedrack.net
SIC: 3449 Miscellaneous metalwork

(G-15114)
STORAGE CONTROL SYSTEMS INC (PA)
Also Called: Gas Control Systems
100 Applewood Dr (49345-1711)
P.O. Box 304 (49345-0304)
PHONE..................................616 887-7994
Jim Schaefer, *President*
Todd Johnson, *Sales Staff*
Darius Warne, *Sales Staff*
Andrew Klipa, *Marketing Staff*
▲ EMP: 21
SQ FT: 34,000
SALES (est): 9.4MM Privately Held
WEB: www.storagecontrol.com
SIC: 3829 Measuring & controlling devices

(G-15115)
STRUCTURAL STANDARDS INC
465 Apple Jack Ct (49345-1708)
PHONE..................................616 813-1798
Scott Johnson, *President*
EMP: 18
SQ FT: 4,800
SALES (est): 4.4MM Privately Held
SIC: 3441 Fabricated structural metal

(G-15116)
TESA TAPE INC
324 S Union St (49345-1530)
PHONE..................................616 887-3107
Deb Szczepanski, *Principal*
Al Tramper, *Opers Mgr*
EMP: 90
SQ FT: 140,000
SALES (corp-wide): 11.8B Privately Held
WEB: www.tesatape.com
SIC: 2672 3842 3644 2671 Tape, pressure sensitive: made from purchased materials; surgical appliances & supplies; noncurrent-carrying wiring services; packaging paper & plastics film, coated & laminated
HQ: Tesa Tape, Inc.
    5825 Carnegie Blvd
    Charlotte NC 28209
    704 554-0707

(G-15117)
TIP TOP DRILLING LLC
8274 Alpine Ave (49345-9413)
PHONE..................................616 291-8006
Aaron Dekubber,
Jessica Dekubber,
EMP: 4
SQ FT: 10,000
SALES: 1.1MM Privately Held
SIC: 1381 Directional drilling oil & gas wells

Spring Arbor
Jackson County

(G-15118)
AMERICAN SALES CO
Also Called: American Resources Group
3215 Chapel Rd (49283-8703)
P.O. Box 424 (49283-0424)
PHONE..................................517 750-4070
Charles Tomasello, *Owner*
Jeremy Burton, *Sls & Mktg Exec*
EMP: 3
SALES (est): 251K Privately Held
SIC: 2211 5199 Apparel & outerwear fabrics, cotton; coutil, cotton; general merchandise, non-durable

(G-15119)
ARBOR STONE
6718 Spring Arbor Rd (49283-9737)
PHONE..................................517 750-1340
Robert L Gray, *Owner*
EMP: 3
SQ FT: 6,000
SALES (est): 150K Privately Held
WEB: www.arborstoneproperties.com
SIC: 3272 5032 5211 5989 Precast terrazo or concrete products; concrete & cinder building products; concrete & cinder block; coal; coal

(G-15120)
B & B CUSTOM AND PROD WLDG
10391 Spring Arbor Rd (49283-9621)
PHONE..................................517 524-7121
Bill Burk, *President*
Debbie Burk, *Treasurer*
EMP: 10
SQ FT: 6,000
SALES: 300K Privately Held
SIC: 1799 3599 Welding on site; machine & other job shop work

(G-15121)
DIVERSIFIED PRECISION PDTS INC
6999 Spring Arbor Rd (49283-9737)
P.O. Box 488 (49283-0488)
PHONE..................................517 750-2310
Stephen J Lazaroff, *President*
Deborah Lazaroff, *Vice Pres*
Linda Farrow, *Treasurer*
EMP: 35
SQ FT: 18,000
SALES (est): 6.7MM Privately Held
WEB: www.diversifiedprecision.com
SIC: 3541 7389 Grinding machines, metalworking; grinding, precision: commercial or industrial

(G-15122)
FABRICATION CONCEPTS LLC
Also Called: Fire Fabrication & Supply
347 E Main St (49283-9617)
P.O. Box 225 (49283-0225)
PHONE..................................517 750-4742
Brian Fletcher, *Controller*
Bruce Ulrich, *Executive*
EMP: 14
SQ FT: 30,000
SALES (est): 4.8MM Privately Held
SIC: 3569 Sprinkler systems, fire: automatic

(G-15123)
KEL TOOL INC
6999 Spring Arbor Rd (49283-9737)
PHONE..................................517 750-4515
Stephen Lazaroff, *President*
James Lazaroff, *Vice Pres*
Janet Lazaroff, *Treasurer*
EMP: 3
SQ FT: 8,000
SALES (est): 294.9K Privately Held
SIC: 3545 Cutting tools for machine tools

(G-15124)
LAB TOOL AND ENGINEERING CORP
7755 King Rd (49283-9777)
P.O. Box 400 (49283-0400)
PHONE..................................517 750-4131
Randall Ball, *CEO*
Joan Croad, *Vice Pres*
Phyllis Ball, *Admin Sec*
EMP: 29
SQ FT: 20,000
SALES (est): 4.3MM Privately Held
SIC: 3544 3549 3714 3545 Special dies & tools; assembly machines, including robotic; motor vehicle parts & accessories; machine tool accessories; metal stampings

(G-15125)
LOMAR MACHINE & TOOL CO
7755 King Rd (49283-9777)
PHONE..................................517 750-4089
EMP: 12
SALES (corp-wide): 26.6MM Privately Held
SIC: 3599 Machine shop, jobbing & repair
PA: Lomar Machine & Tool Co.
    135 Main St
    Horton MI 49246
    517 563-8136

(G-15126)
MICRO FORM INC
180 Teft Rd (49283-9688)
P.O. Box 130 (49283-0130)
PHONE..................................517 750-3660
David Kane, *President*
Suzanne Kane, *Vice Pres*
EMP: 4
SQ FT: 7,200
SALES (est): 93.1K Privately Held
SIC: 3545 Precision tools, machinists'; cutting tools for machine tools; gauges (machine tool accessories)

(G-15127)
R J DESIGNERS INC
Also Called: Fritz Advertising Company
8032 Spring Arbor Rd (49283-9764)
P.O. Box 397 (49283-0397)
PHONE..................................517 750-1990
Rhonda Pickrell, *President*
EMP: 8
SQ FT: 4,000
SALES: 650K Privately Held
SIC: 3993 5039 7312 Electric signs; architectural metalwork; billboard advertising

(G-15128)
SPRING ARBOR COATINGS LLC
Also Called: Sac
190 W Main St (49283-9669)
P.O. Box 582 (49283-0582)
PHONE..................................517 750-2903
Pete Schira, *General Mgr*
Charles Winters, *Treasurer*
Dan Craig, *Mng Member*
Chris Parrott,
EMP: 60 EST: 2006
SQ FT: 25,000
SALES (est): 7.3MM
SALES (corp-wide): 863.9MM Privately Held
SIC: 3471 Electroplating & plating
HQ: Hatch Stamping Company Llc
    635 E Industrial Dr
    Chelsea MI 48118
    734 475-8628

(G-15129)
WARDCRAFT INDUSTRIES LLC
1 Wardcraft Dr (49283-9757)
PHONE..................................517 750-9100
James Snyder, *President*
Aquanita Johnson, *Controller*
Greg Chmielewski, *Manager*
EMP: 29
SQ FT: 217,800
SALES (est): 941.1K Privately Held
SIC: 3544 3535 Special dies, tools, jigs & fixtures; unit handling conveying systems

Spring Lake
Ottawa County

(G-15130)
A & A MANUFACTURING CO
19033 174th Ave (49456-9708)
PHONE..................................616 846-1730
Jim Fairbanks, *CEO*
Alex C Marciniak, *Partner*
Lawrence Marciniak, *Partner*
EMP: 5
SQ FT: 4,400
SALES (est): 723.7K Privately Held
WEB: www.aa-mfg.com
SIC: 3711 3469 3544 Chassis, motor vehicle; metal stampings; special dies, tools, jigs & fixtures

(G-15131)
ACTIVE MANUFACTURING CORP
17127 Hickory St (49456-9712)
PHONE..................................616 842-0800
Jeff Braak, *President*
Jeff Berry, *Corp Secy*
▲ EMP: 30
SQ FT: 44,000
SALES (est): 6.5MM Privately Held
WEB: www.proenterpriz.com
SIC: 3599 Machine shop, jobbing & repair

(G-15132)
ALMOND PRODUCTS INC
17150 148th Ave (49456-9514)
PHONE..................................616 844-1813
John De Maria, *Ch of Bd*
Joy Ponce, *Vice Pres*
Mike Ponce, *Plant Mgr*
Lisa Chapman, *Engineer*

Spring Lake - Ottawa County (G-15133)

Christopher Stebbins, *Engineer*
EMP: 85
SQ FT: 33,000
SALES (est): 18.8MM **Privately Held**
WEB: www.almondproducts.com
SIC: 3479 3471 Painting of metal products; anodizing (plating) of metals or formed products

(G-15133)
AMERICAN FABRICATED PDTS INC
16910 148th Ave (49456-9570)
PHONE 616 607-8785
Andy Bush, *President*
Kevin Gagnon, *General Mgr*
EMP: 15 **EST:** 2008
SALES (est): 3.3MM **Privately Held**
SIC: 3444 3469 3537 3711 Sheet metalwork; metal stampings; containers (metal), air cargo; pallets, metal; military motor vehicle assembly

(G-15134)
BT ENGINEERING LLC
223 River St (49456-2050)
PHONE 734 417-2218
Jessica Boria,
Karl Brakora,
EMP: 4
SALES: 10K **Privately Held**
SIC: 3699 Electrical equipment & supplies

(G-15135)
CANVAS KINGS
16506 144th Ave (49456-9283)
PHONE 616 846-6220
Robert King, *Owner*
EMP: 3
SALES (est): 217.1K **Privately Held**
SIC: 2394 Canvas awnings & canopies; canvas covers & drop cloths

(G-15136)
CONCEPT METAL PRODUCTS INC (PA)
Also Called: Concept Metals Group
16928 148th Ave (49456-9570)
PHONE 231 799-3202
John Walton, *CEO*
Paul Horstman, *President*
Graham Howe, *President*
Nick Gentry, *Engineer*
Gretchen Abernathy, *Controller*
EMP: 70
SALES (est): 19.8MM **Privately Held**
SIC: 3449 Miscellaneous metalwork

(G-15137)
CRAFT STEEL PRODUCTS INC
16885 148th Ave (49456-8861)
PHONE 616 935-7575
Chris Kieffer, *Principal*
EMP: 22
SQ FT: 17,500
SALES (est): 4.9MM **Privately Held**
WEB: www.craftsteel.com
SIC: 3568 3469 Bearings, plain; metal stampings

(G-15138)
DETROIT CITY DISTILLERY LLC
15295 Concord Dr (49456-2184)
PHONE 734 904-3073
Paul McCormick, *Principal*
EMP: 3 **EST:** 2017
SALES (est): 111.3K **Privately Held**
SIC: 2085 Distilled & blended liquors

(G-15139)
DYNAMIC WOOD SOLUTIONS
18518 Trimble Ct (49456-9725)
PHONE 616 935-7727
Gary Moody, *President*
Abbott Chris, *Partner*
Ryan Gardner, *Partner*
EMP: 8
SALES (est): 1.5MM **Privately Held**
SIC: 2499 Decorative wood & woodwork

(G-15140)
ELEGANCE OF SEASON
209 N Buchanan St (49456-1707)
PHONE 616 296-1059
Julie Gomez, *Principal*
EMP: 8
SALES (est): 568K **Privately Held**
WEB: www.eleganceoftheseasons.com
SIC: 2051 Bakery: wholesale or wholesale/retail combined

(G-15141)
FALCON CORPORATION
Also Called: Falcon Tool & Die
14510 Cleveland St (49456-9151)
PHONE 616 842-7071
Gerald J Johnston, *President*
David L Peppin, *President*
Ron Kobryn, *Engineer*
EMP: 40 **EST:** 1964
SQ FT: 11,000
SALES (est): 8.3MM **Privately Held**
SIC: 3544 Special dies & tools; jigs & fixtures

(G-15142)
FOCAL POINT METAL FAB LLC
17354 Teunis Dr (49456-9727)
PHONE 616 844-7670
Matt Campau, *Mng Member*
EMP: 5
SALES (est): 771.4K **Privately Held**
SIC: 3499 Fabricated metal products

(G-15143)
G A RICHARDS PLANT TWO
701 E Savidge St (49456-2430)
PHONE 616 850-8528
Kevin Mesler, *President*
EMP: 4
SALES (est): 692.2K **Privately Held**
SIC: 3444 Sheet metalwork

(G-15144)
GARRISON DENTAL SOLUTIONS LLC (PA)
150 Dewitt Ln (49456-1921)
PHONE 616 842-2035
Tom Garrison, *Vice Pres*
Edward Sumrell, *Opers Staff*
Mickey Morris, *QC Mgr*
Alex Hull, *Project Engr*
Nicole Abbott, *Controller*
EMP: 24 **EST:** 1997
SALES (est): 4.2MM **Privately Held*
WEB: www.composi-tight.com
SIC: 3843 Dental equipment

(G-15145)
GAZELLE PROTOTYPE LLC
18683 Trimble Ct (49456-8822)
PHONE 616 844-1820
Willard Van Harn,
Roma Van Harn,
EMP: 5
SALES (est): 550K **Privately Held**
WEB: www.gazelleprototype.com
SIC: 3082 Unsupported plastics profile shapes

(G-15146)
GRAFLEX INC
15276 Oak Point Dr (49456-2180)
PHONE 616 842-3654
Richard Fletemeyer, *President*
EMP: 10
SQ FT: 20,000
SALES (est): 1.5MM **Privately Held**
WEB: www.graflex.com
SIC: 3089 3541 Molding primary plastic; machine tools, metal cutting type

(G-15147)
GRAND RIVER POLISHING CO CORP
19191 174th Ave (49456-9700)
PHONE 616 846-1420
Larry R Scott, *President*
EMP: 23
SQ FT: 7,500
SALES: 1.2MM
SALES (corp-wide): 4.2B **Publicly Held**
SIC: 3471 Polishing, metals or formed products; buffing for the trade
PA: Leggett & Platt, Incorporated
1 Leggett Rd
Carthage MO 64836
417 358-8131

(G-15148)
GREAT LAKES CORDAGE INC
Also Called: Great Lakes American
17045 148th Ave (49456-9580)
PHONE 616 842-4455
Jeffrey S Bovid, *President*
Lu Bethke, *Technology*
▲ **EMP:** 14
SALES (est): 2MM **Privately Held**
SIC: 2298 Cordage & twine

(G-15149)
GREAT LAKES TOLL SERVICES
17354 Teunis Dr Ste D (49456-9727)
PHONE 616 847-1868
John Memmott, *President*
▲ **EMP:** 4
SQ FT: 8,600
SALES: 450K **Privately Held**
SIC: 2893 Printing ink

(G-15150)
HART CONCRETE LLC
540 Maple St (49456-9070)
PHONE 231 873-2183
Steven Freed,
EMP: 8
SQ FT: 3,000
SALES: 1.2MM **Privately Held**
SIC: 3273 Ready-mixed concrete

(G-15151)
HERMAN MILLER
17170 Hickory St (49456-9783)
PHONE 616 296-3422
Mary Stnroos, *Principal*
EMP: 12 **EST:** 2011
SALES (est): 1.6MM
SALES (corp-wide): 2.5B **Publicly Held**
SIC: 2521 Wood office furniture
PA: Herman Miller, Inc.
855 E Main Ave
Zeeland MI 49464
616 654-3000

(G-15152)
HERMAN MILLER INC
18558 171st Ave (49456-9784)
P.O. Box 302, Zeeland (49464-0302)
PHONE 616 846-0280
Kim Hookstra, *Branch Mgr*
EMP: 5
SALES (corp-wide): 2.5B **Publicly Held**
WEB: www.hermanmiller.com
SIC: 2521 Wood office furniture
PA: Herman Miller, Inc.
855 E Main Ave
Zeeland MI 49464
616 654-3000

(G-15153)
INDUSTRIAL MTAL IDNTFCTION INC
Also Called: I M I
17796 North Shore Dr (49456-9102)
PHONE 616 847-0060
David Engel, *President*
EMP: 5
SALES: 500K **Privately Held**
SIC: 3999 2759 Identification tags, except paper; screen printing

(G-15154)
INTEGRICOAT INC
16928 148th Ave (49456-9570)
PHONE 616 935-7878
Graham Howe, *President*
EMP: 20
SQ FT: 22,000
SALES (est): 2.3MM **Privately Held**
WEB: www.integricoat.com
SIC: 3479 Coating of metals & formed products

(G-15155)
INTERIOR CONCEPTS CORPORATION
18525 Trimble Ct (49456-9794)
PHONE 616 842-5550
Donald Ott, *Ch of Bd*
Jeff Ott, *Regional Mgr*
Russell Nagel, *COO*
Rust Napel, *Vice Pres*
Scott Bradfield, *Engineer*
▼ **EMP:** 43
SQ FT: 72,000
SALES (est): 9.4MM **Privately Held**
WEB: www.interiorconcepts.com
SIC: 2522 2521 Office furniture, except wood; wood office furniture

(G-15156)
JOHNSON CONTROLS INC
15115 Leonard Rd (49456-9215)
PHONE 616 847-2766
Tom Postumas, *Manager*
EMP: 25 **Privately Held**
SIC: 2531 7699 Seats, automobile; boiler & heating repair services
HQ: Johnson Controls, Inc.
5757 N Green Bay Ave
Milwaukee WI 53209
414 524-1200

(G-15157)
JSJ CORPORATION
Also Called: Counter Point Furniture Pdts
17237 Van Wagoner Rd (49456-9702)
PHONE 616 847-7000
EMP: 159
SALES (corp-wide): 596.1MM **Privately Held**
SIC: 2521 Mfg Wood Office Furniture
PA: Jsj Corporation
700 Robbins Rd
Grand Haven MI 49417
616 842-6350

(G-15158)
LAUREN PLASTICS LLC
17155 Van Wagoner Rd (49456-9793)
PHONE 330 339-3373
Lisa Huntsman, *President*
Dave Gingrich, *CFO*
Michael Klunder, *Accounting Mgr*
EMP: 40
SALES: 6.7MM
SALES (corp-wide): 150.6MM **Privately Held**
SIC: 2821 Plastics materials & resins
PA: Lauren International, Ltd.
2228 Reiser Ave Se
New Philadelphia OH 44663
330 339-3373

(G-15159)
LUDVANWALL INC
Also Called: Vander Wall Bros
19156 174th Ave (49456-9722)
P.O. Box 473 (49456-0473)
PHONE 616 842-4500
Dale Vanderwall, *President*
Dale Vander Wall, *President*
Paul Vander Wall, *Vice Pres*
EMP: 20
SQ FT: 20,000
SALES (est): 3MM **Privately Held**
SIC: 3271 5211 Blocks, concrete or cinder: standard; brick

(G-15160)
MARQUIS INDUSTRIES INC
Also Called: Michigan Brass Division
17310 Teunis Dr (49456-9727)
PHONE 616 842-2810
Douglas L Pimm, *President*
Carla Hower, *VP Finance*
Jeremy Hower, *Manager*
▲ **EMP:** 18
SQ FT: 9,000
SALES (est): 3.3MM **Privately Held**
WEB: www.michiganbrass.com
SIC: 3432 5074 Plumbers' brass goods: drain cocks, faucets, spigots, etc.; plumbing & hydronic heating supplies

(G-15161)
MEDALLION INSTRUMENTATION
17150 Hickory St (49456-9712)
PHONE 616 847-3700
Nick Hoiles, *Managing Dir*
Martin Payne, *Principal*
▲ **EMP:** 135
SQ FT: 80,000
SALES (est): 57.9MM **Privately Held**
WEB: www.medallionis.com
SIC: 3714 3824 Motor vehicle parts & accessories; fluid meters & counting devices

GEOGRAPHIC SECTION

Springfield - Calhoun County (G-15188)

(G-15162)
MICHIGAN ADHESIVE MFG INC
Also Called: Seal Bond
14851 Michael Ln (49456-9566)
PHONE.................................616 850-0507
Scott Carmichael, *President*
Jim Gillhespy, *Vice Pres*
Kelly Barnes, *Sales Staff*
Gerard Tejeda, *Manager*
Patrick Young, *Technology*
◆ **EMP:** 30
SQ FT: 10,000
SALES (est): 16.6MM **Privately Held**
WEB: www.michiganadhesive.com
SIC: 2891 Adhesives & sealants

(G-15163)
MICHIGAN SHIPPERS SUPPLY INC (PA)
17369 Taft Rd (49456-9711)
P.O. Box 315, Ferrysburg (49409-0315)
PHONE.................................616 935-6680
Stephen D Wooldridge, *President*
EMP: 12 **EST:** 1959
SALES (est): 2.6MM **Privately Held**
WEB: www.michiganshippers.com
SIC: 5084 2672 3953 Industrial machinery & equipment; adhesive papers, labels or tapes: from purchased material; marking devices

(G-15164)
MLP MFG INC
18630 Trimble Ct (49456-8822)
P.O. Box 231 (49456-0231)
PHONE.................................616 842-8767
Michael L Palkowski, *CEO*
Kirk Palkowski, *President*
EMP: 30
SQ FT: 31,000
SALES (est): 2.7MM **Privately Held**
SIC: 3444 Sheet metal specialties, not stamped

(G-15165)
MULTI-LAB LLC
Also Called: Keur Industries Acquisition Co
18784 174th Ave (49456-9760)
PHONE.................................616 846-6990
Mark Deal, *Mng Member*
EMP: 18 **EST:** 1974
SQ FT: 20,000
SALES: 1MM **Privately Held**
WEB: www.keurind.com
SIC: 3821 Autoclaves, laboratory

(G-15166)
NEW RULES MARKETING INC
Also Called: Duratran Company, The
540 Oak St (49456-9157)
PHONE.................................800 962-3119
Casey Ford, *President*
Kelly Bailey, *Principal*
Nick Ford, *Principal*
Jennifer Krampe, *Principal*
Lacey Riggs, *Principal*
EMP: 25
SALES (est): 2.5MM **Privately Held**
WEB: www.duratran.com
SIC: 8742 3993 Marketing consulting services; signs & advertising specialties

(G-15167)
OLECO INC (PA)
Also Called: Global Technologies
18683 Trimble Ct (49456-8822)
PHONE.................................616 842-6790
Jeff Olds, *CEO*
Stanley Richentstien Jr, *Vice Pres*
Timothy Ellis, *Opers Staff*
EMP: 50
SQ FT: 20,000
SALES (est): 9.9MM **Privately Held**
SIC: 3699 Electrical equipment & supplies

(G-15168)
PHOENIX FIXTURES LLC (AZ)
16910 148th Ave (49456-9570)
PHONE.................................616 847-0895
EMP: 2
SALES: 1.2MM **Privately Held**
SIC: 2542 Mfg Office & Store Fixtures

(G-15169)
PLIANT PLASTICS CORP (PA)
17000 Taft Rd (49456-9705)
PHONE.................................616 844-0300
Tom Devoursney, *President*
Jeff McMartin, *Plant Mgr*
Michael Dowker, *Human Res Mgr*
▲ **EMP:** 63 **EST:** 1966
SALES (est): 22.4MM **Privately Held**
WEB: www.pliantplastics.com
SIC: 3089 Injection molding of plastics

(G-15170)
PLIANT PLASTICS CORP
17024 Taft Rd (49456-9705)
PHONE.................................616 844-3215
Daniel Bloom, *Branch Mgr*
EMP: 10
SALES (corp-wide): 22.4MM **Privately Held**
SIC: 3089 Injection molding of plastics
PA: Pliant Plastics Corp.
  17000 Taft Rd
  Spring Lake MI 49456
  616 844-0300

(G-15171)
PROTEIN MAGNET CORP
15450 Oak Dr (49456-2148)
PHONE.................................616 844-1545
Glorilyn Castagna, *Principal*
EMP: 3
SALES (est): 159.8K **Privately Held**
SIC: 2077 Animal & marine fats & oils

(G-15172)
REYERS COMPANY INC
Also Called: Reyers Advertising
700 E Savidge St (49456-1959)
PHONE.................................616 414-5530
Harlan Reyers, *President*
Sharon Reyers, *Corp Secy*
EMP: 10
SQ FT: 12,000
SALES (est): 1MM **Privately Held**
SIC: 2771 2789 5021 5044 Greeting cards; bookbinding & related work; office & public building furniture; office equipment; shopping center, property operation only

(G-15173)
ROOMS OF GRAND RAPIDS LLC
17971 N Fruitport Rd (49456-1569)
PHONE.................................616 260-1452
Katherine M Cather, *Mng Member*
EMP: 12
SALES (est): 636.3K **Privately Held**
SIC: 7021 2211 2511 Furnished room rental; furniture denim; wood bedroom furniture

(G-15174)
SAC PLASTICS INC
17259 Hickory St (49456-9703)
PHONE.................................616 846-0820
Richard Lattin, *President*
Mike Lawton, *General Mgr*
Beverly Lattin, *Vice Pres*
EMP: 9
SQ FT: 25,400
SALES (est): 1.6MM **Privately Held**
WEB: www.sacplastics.com
SIC: 3089 Injection molding of plastics

(G-15175)
SCHAP SPECIALTY MACHINE INC (PA)
17309 Taft Rd Ste A (49456-8809)
PHONE.................................616 846-6530
William Schap, *President*
Dave Clow, *General Mgr*
Wanda Martin, *General Mgr*
John Deppe, *Project Mgr*
Jeremy Vanderwall, *Project Mgr*
EMP: 20
SQ FT: 16,000
SALES (est): 3.3MM **Privately Held**
WEB: www.schapmachine.com
SIC: 3829 3569 Aircraft & motor vehicle measurement equipment; assembly machines, non-metalworking

(G-15176)
SHAPE CORP
17155 Van Wagoner Rd (49456-9793)
PHONE.................................616 846-8700
Robert Currier, *President*
EMP: 7
SALES (corp-wide): 565.6MM **Privately Held**
SIC: 3449 Custom roll formed products
PA: Shape Corp.
  1900 Hayes St
  Grand Haven MI 49417
  616 846-8700

(G-15177)
SHAPE CORP
Also Called: Shape Stampings
16933 144th Ave (49456)
P.O. Box 515 (49456-0515)
PHONE.................................616 842-2825
Robert Dornbos, *Branch Mgr*
EMP: 73
SALES (corp-wide): 565.6MM **Privately Held**
SIC: 3449 3469 Miscellaneous metalwork; metal stampings
PA: Shape Corp.
  1900 Hayes St
  Grand Haven MI 49417
  616 846-8700

(G-15178)
SINTEL INC
18437 171st Ave (49456-9731)
PHONE.................................616 842-6960
Nicholas Kulkarni, *CEO*
Nicholas Lardo, *CFO*
Russ Andreas, *Sales Engr*
Kevin Smith, *Supervisor*
EMP: 105
SQ FT: 120,000
SALES (est): 24.3MM **Privately Held**
WEB: www.sintelinc.com
SIC: 3444 3469 Sheet metal specialties, not stamped; stamping metal for the trade

(G-15179)
SPARKS BELTING COMPANY INC
17237 Van Wagoner Rd (49456-9702)
PHONE.................................800 451-4537
Bob Johnson, *Regional Mgr*
EMP: 9
SALES (corp-wide): 550.2MM **Privately Held**
SIC: 3535 Conveyors & conveying equipment
HQ: Sparks Belting Company, Inc.
  3800 Stahl Dr Se
  Grand Rapids MI 49546

(G-15180)
STRAIGHT LINE DESIGN
18055 174th Ave (49456-9767)
PHONE.................................616 296-0920
Randy Ruter, *Mng Member*
EMP: 4
SALES (est): 499.4K **Privately Held**
SIC: 2434 7389 Wood kitchen cabinets; design services

(G-15181)
SUNDOWN SHEET METAL INC
16929 148th Ave (49456-9570)
P.O. Box 272 (49456-0272)
PHONE.................................616 846-7674
Greg North, *President*
EMP: 4
SQ FT: 6,400
SALES (est): 760.9K **Privately Held**
SIC: 3312 Structural shapes & pilings, steel

(G-15182)
SUPREME DOMESTIC INTL SLS CORP
18686 172nd Ave (49456-9720)
PHONE.................................616 842-6550
Gregory Olson, *President*
EMP: 3
SALES (est): 152.4K **Privately Held**
SIC: 3451 Screw machine products

(G-15183)
SUPREME MACHINED PDTS CO INC (PA)
18686 172nd Ave (49456-9720)
PHONE.................................616 842-6550
Gregory Olson, *President*
Bruce Rice, *General Mgr*
Mike Workman, *Purch Mgr*
Julie Kelly, *Buyer*
Joshua Datte, *QC Mgr*
▲ **EMP:** 140
SALES (est): 35.9MM **Privately Held**
WEB: www.supreme1.com
SIC: 3451 Screw machine products

(G-15184)
SUPREME MACHINED PDTS CO INC
18686 172nd Ave (49456-9720)
PHONE.................................616 842-6550
Dale Mosher, *Branch Mgr*
EMP: 40
SALES (est): 3.7MM
SALES (corp-wide): 35.9MM **Privately Held**
WEB: www.supreme1.com
SIC: 3451 Screw machine products
PA: Supreme Machined Products Company, Inc.
  18686 172nd Ave
  Spring Lake MI 49456
  616 842-6550

(G-15185)
TELCO TOOLS
510 Elm St (49456-7900)
PHONE.................................616 296-0253
Richard Beaudreault, *Vice Pres*
▲ **EMP:** 10
SALES (est): 944.5K **Privately Held**
SIC: 3544 3546 Special dies & tools; power-driven handtools

(G-15186)
WEBER PRECISION GRINDING INC
18438 171st Ave (49456-9717)
P.O. Box 484 (49456-0484)
PHONE.................................616 842-1634
Michael J Bonevelle, *President*
Pamela J Bonevelle, *Admin Sec*
EMP: 6 **EST:** 1943
SQ FT: 3,700
SALES: 300K **Privately Held**
WEB: www.webergrinding.com
SIC: 7699 3545 Knife, saw & tool sharpening & repair; machine tool accessories

Springfield
Calhoun County

(G-15187)
BACK MACHINE SHOP LLC
685 20th St N (49037-7431)
PHONE.................................269 963-7061
Tom Back, *Engineer*
Dan Back,
EMP: 7
SQ FT: 3,400
SALES: 550K **Privately Held**
SIC: 3599 7699 Machine shop, jobbing & repair; industrial equipment services

(G-15188)
BEECH & RICH INC
525 20th St N (49037-7897)
PHONE.................................269 968-8012
James E Beech, *President*
Kadra Parker, *Business Mgr*
Scott Lowery, *Opers Staff*
Jeanita Hegner, *Purchasing*
Glenn Lussier, *Sales Dir*
EMP: 20
SQ FT: 50,000
SALES (est): 2.3MM **Privately Held**
WEB: www.beechandrich.com
SIC: 1721 3471 3479 Industrial painting; sand blasting of metal parts; coating of metals & formed products

Springfield - Calhoun County (G-15189)

(G-15189)
CHRISTMAN SCREENPRINT INC
2822 Wilbur St (49037-7954)
PHONE......................................800 962-9330
David Christman, *President*
Dana Christman, *Corp Secy*
Michael Christman, *Vice Pres*
Mike Christman, *Vice Pres*
Kathy Mrozinski, *Sales Staff*
EMP: 14 **EST:** 1917
SQ FT: 12,000
SALES (est): 2.1MM **Privately Held**
WEB: www.christmanscreenprint.com
SIC: 2752 5699 Commercial printing, offset; T-shirts, custom printed

(G-15190)
DARE PRODUCTS INC
860 Betterly Rd (49037-8392)
P.O. Box 157, Battle Creek (49016-0157)
PHONE......................................269 965-2307
Robert M Wilson Jr, *President*
Steven A Wilson, *Vice Pres*
▲ **EMP:** 35
SALES: 11MM **Privately Held**
WEB: www.dareproducts.com
SIC: 3644 3229 3699 3089 Insulators & insulation materials, electrical; pressed & blown glass; electrical equipment & supplies; injection molded finished plastic products; miscellaneous fabricated wire products

(G-15191)
GAGE COMPANY
Also Called: Gage Printing
4550 Wayne Rd (49037-7347)
PHONE......................................269 965-4279
Michael Fatt, *President*
Linda Fatt, *Corp Secy*
EMP: 13
SQ FT: 5,500
SALES (est): 1.5MM **Privately Held**
SIC: 2752 Commercial printing, offset

(G-15192)
GHS CORPORATION
Also Called: Ghs Strings
2813 Wilbur St (49037-7990)
PHONE......................................269 968-3351
Russell S McFee, *President*
Robert D McFee, *Admin Sec*
◆ **EMP:** 255 **EST:** 1981
SQ FT: 25,000
SALES (est): 81.5K **Privately Held**
WEB: www.ghsstrings.com
SIC: 3931 3679 Guitars & parts, electric & nonelectric; electronic circuits

(G-15193)
GHS CORPORATION (PA)
Also Called: D'Angelico Strings
2813 Wilbur St (49037-7990)
PHONE......................................800 388-4447
Russell S McFee, *President*
Constance McFee, *Marketing Staff*
Robert D McFee, *Admin Sec*
EMP: 31 **EST:** 1964
SALES (est): 5.8MM **Privately Held**
SIC: 3931 Strings, musical instrument

(G-15194)
JN NEWMAN CONSTRUCTION LLC
Also Called: Newman Construction
2869 W Dickman Rd (49037-7962)
PHONE......................................269 968-1290
Joseph Newman,
Patricia Newman,
EMP: 8
SQ FT: 3,500
SALES (est): 968.7K **Privately Held**
WEB: www.newmanconstruction.com
SIC: 1522 1521 1389 1542 Residential construction; single-family housing construction; new construction, single-family houses; construction, repair & dismantling services; nonresidential construction

(G-15195)
KEYES-DAVIS COMPANY
74 14th St N (49037-8216)
P.O. Box 1557, Battle Creek (49016-1557)
PHONE......................................269 962-7505
Robert Barker, *President*
Mardell Barker, *Treasurer*
EMP: 20 **EST:** 1901
SQ FT: 28,500
SALES: 1.2MM **Privately Held**
WEB: www.keyesdavis.com
SIC: 3999 3469 Identification plates; identification tags, except paper; metal stampings

(G-15196)
LAKELAND ASPHALT CORPORATION
548 Avenue A (49037-7834)
PHONE......................................269 964-1720
Raymond Carr, *President*
Chris Carr, *General Mgr*
John Carr, *Principal*
Rosemary Carr, *Vice Pres*
Thomas Carr, *Executive*
EMP: 23 **EST:** 1947
SQ FT: 1,000
SALES (est): 6.9MM **Privately Held**
SIC: 2951 Asphalt paving mixtures & blocks

(G-15197)
LINCOLNS WELDING
256 30th St N (49037-7980)
PHONE......................................269 964-1858
Lynn T Lincoln, *Owner*
EMP: 3
SQ FT: 3,500
SALES (est): 110K **Privately Held**
SIC: 7692 Welding repair

(G-15198)
MARKETPLUS SOFTWARE INC (PA)
Also Called: Owl Leasing
2821 Wilbur St (49037-7953)
P.O. Box 2422, Battle Creek (49016-2422)
PHONE......................................269 968-4240
Russell Mc Fee, *President*
Constance Mc Fee, *Principal*
EMP: 10
SALES (est): 990.5K **Privately Held**
WEB: www.mcfeetech.com
SIC: 7372 7359 Prepackaged software; equipment rental & leasing

(G-15199)
PALLET MAN
555 Upton Ave (49037-8383)
PHONE......................................269 274-8825
Byron Jones, *Principal*
EMP: 4
SALES (est): 223.3K **Privately Held**
SIC: 2448 Pallets, wood & wood with metal

(G-15200)
PERFORMCOAT OF MICHIGAN LLC
319 Mcintyre Ln (49037-7686)
PHONE......................................269 282-7030
Christian Kunz,
EMP: 10
SALES (est): 917.3K **Privately Held**
SIC: 3479 Coating of metals & formed products

(G-15201)
PRO CONNECTIONS LLC
Also Called: McMillan Printing
4550 Wayne Rd (49037-7347)
PHONE......................................269 962-4219
Colleen Brunt, *Owner*
EMP: 3
SQ FT: 17,000
SALES (est): 419K **Privately Held**
WEB: www.proconnections.us
SIC: 2759 4225 Commercial printing; mini-warehouse, warehousing

(G-15202)
PULVERDRYER USA LLC
126 Avenue C (49037-8240)
P.O. Box 248, Augusta (49012-0248)
PHONE......................................269 552-5290
Lee New, *President*
Wayne Case,
Robert Graving,
EMP: 30
SQ FT: 10,000
SALES (est): 5.6MM **Privately Held**
WEB: www.pulverdryerusa.com
SIC: 3567 Driers & redriers, industrial process

(G-15203)
SIGNS & DESIGNS INC
260 30th St N (49037-7980)
PHONE......................................269 968-8909
Jerry Ure, *President*
EMP: 4
SQ FT: 2,500
SALES (est): 386.1K **Privately Held**
WEB: www.signsndesigns.com
SIC: 3993 Signs, not made in custom sign painting shops

(G-15204)
SPRINGFIELD LANDSCAPE MTLS
700 20th St N (49037-7473)
PHONE......................................269 965-6748
Fax: 269 969-0122
EMP: 6
SALES (est): 690K **Privately Held**
SIC: 3271 5032 5999 5083 Concrete Block And Brick, Nsk

(G-15205)
SPRINGFIELD MACHINE AND TL INC
257 30th St N (49037-7911)
PHONE......................................269 968-8223
Cheryl Thornton, *President*
Glen Thornton, *Vice Pres*
Allan Thornton, *Treasurer*
EMP: 8
SALES (est): 1.4MM **Privately Held**
SIC: 3599 Machine shop, jobbing & repair

(G-15206)
TRAFFIC SIGNS INC
341 Helmer Rd N (49037-7777)
PHONE......................................269 964-7511
Cristy Merkle, *President*
Robert Wolfe, *President*
EMP: 8
SQ FT: 16,000
SALES (est): 500K **Privately Held**
WEB: www.trafficsignsinc.com
SIC: 3993 Electric signs

(G-15207)
TRI K CYLINDER SERVICE INC
4539 Wayne Rd (49037-7348)
PHONE......................................269 965-3981
Kurk Sparks, *President*
EMP: 4
SALES (est): 450K **Privately Held**
SIC: 3471 Plating of metals or formed products

Springport
Jackson County

(G-15208)
CHALLENGER COMMUNICATIONS LLC
7241 Monroe Rd (49284-9471)
PHONE......................................517 680-0125
Eugene Sorgi, *Partner*
Gene Sorgi, *Partner*
EMP: 15
SALES (est): 1.8MM **Privately Held**
SIC: 4899 3699 Communication services; electrical equipment & supplies

(G-15209)
COCHRAN CORPORATION
120 Mill St (49284-9534)
P.O. Box 219 (49284-0219)
PHONE......................................517 857-2211
Anthony Cochran, *President*
Andy Cochran, *Manager*
EMP: 18
SQ FT: 45,000
SALES: 3.3MM **Privately Held**
SIC: 3599 7699 Machine shop, jobbing & repair; industrial machinery & equipment repair

(G-15210)
DOWDING TOOL PRODUCTS LLC
8950 Narrow Lake Rd (49284-9311)
PHONE......................................517 541-2795
Maurice Dowding,
EMP: 15 **EST:** 2011
SALES (est): 2.3MM **Privately Held**
SIC: 3444 Sheet metalwork

(G-15211)
JP CASTINGS INC
Also Called: Specialty Castings
211 Mill St (49284-9479)
P.O. Box 129 (49284-0129)
PHONE......................................517 857-3660
EMP: 27
SALES (est): 3.6MM **Privately Held**
SIC: 3321 Gray/Ductile Iron Foundry

(G-15212)
MASSIVE MINERAL MIX LLC
21110 29 1/2 Mile Rd (49284-9403)
PHONE......................................517 857-4544
Jack Hadley, *Principal*
EMP: 4 **EST:** 2010
SALES (est): 310.2K **Privately Held**
SIC: 3273 Ready-mixed concrete

Spruce
Alcona County

(G-15213)
CHIPPEWA FARM SUPPLY LLC
6701 N Us Highway 23 (48762-9706)
PHONE......................................989 471-5523
Myron Martin, *President*
EMP: 8
SQ FT: 25,000
SALES (est): 662.1K **Privately Held**
SIC: 0723 2048 5191 Feed milling custom services; poultry feeds; stock feeds, dry; fertilizers & agricultural chemicals

(G-15214)
WITSON QUALITY TOOLS LLC
5601 F 41 (48762-9719)
PHONE......................................989 471-2317
EMP: 3
SALES (est): 359K **Privately Held**
SIC: 3599 Machine shop, jobbing & repair

Standish
Arenac County

(G-15215)
AIRPARK PLASTICS LLC
Also Called: Vantage Plastics
1415 W Cedar St (48658-9527)
PHONE......................................989 846-1029
Paul Aultman, *President*
George Aultman,
EMP: 15
SALES: 10.7MM **Privately Held**
WEB: www.vantageplastics.com
SIC: 3089 Thermoformed finished plastic products
PA: P.R.A. Company
1415 W Cedar St
Standish MI 48658

(G-15216)
ARQUETTE CONCRETE & SUPPLY (PA)
4374 Airpark Dr (48658-9447)
P.O. Box 178 (48658-0178)
PHONE......................................989 846-4131
Norman Willett, *President*
EMP: 6 **EST:** 1945
SALES (est): 511.7K **Privately Held**
SIC: 3273 5231 5211 Ready-mixed concrete; paint; brick; cement; concrete & cinder block

(G-15217)
COMPETITIVE MACHINING INC
4245 Airpark Dr (48658-9447)
P.O. Box 1097 (48658-1097)
PHONE......................................989 846-6069
Laura Puzzuoli, *President*

Robert Eddins, *Vice Pres*
EMP: 14
SQ FT: 11,000
SALES (est): 2.6MM **Privately Held**
SIC: 3599 Machine shop, jobbing & repair

(G-15218)
FORWARD DISTRIBUTING INC
219 N Front St (48658-9428)
PHONE..................................989 846-4501
Terry McTaggart, *President*
Dave Gould, *Vice Pres*
EMP: 40 **EST:** 1995
SALES (est): 2MM
SALES (corp-wide): 188.1MM **Privately Held**
WEB: www.trmctaggart.com
SIC: 1382 Oil & gas exploration services
PA: Forward Corporation
219 N Front St
Standish MI 48658
989 846-4501

(G-15219)
GLOBE TECHNOLOGIES CORPORATION
1109 W Cedar St (48658-9535)
P.O. Box 1070 (48658-1070)
PHONE..................................989 846-9591
Norman W Van Wormer Sr, *Ch of Bd*
▲ **EMP:** 35
SQ FT: 45,000
SALES (est): 7.2MM **Privately Held**
SIC: 3469 Spinning metal for the trade

(G-15220)
JOES TABLES LLC
2700 W Huron Rd (48658-9169)
PHONE..................................989 846-4970
Joseph R Guoan,
EMP: 6
SQ FT: 18,000
SALES: 500K **Privately Held**
SIC: 2531 Picnic tables or benches, park

(G-15221)
MAGLINE INC (PA)
1205 W Cedar St (48658-9563)
PHONE..................................800 624-5463
D Brian Law, *CEO*
Sam Cina, *President*
Michael A Kirby, *President*
George Lehnerer, *Treasurer*
Matt Laplant, *Info Tech Mgr*
◆ **EMP:** 110 **EST:** 1945
SQ FT: 110,000
SALES (est): 26.7MM **Privately Held**
WEB: www.magliner.com
SIC: 3537 Trucks, tractors, loaders, carriers & similar equipment; dollies (hand or power trucks), industrial except mining

(G-15222)
MAGLINE INC
Also Called: Standish Magline
1205 W Cedar St (48658-9563)
PHONE..................................800 624-5463
Mike Kirby, *Branch Mgr*
EMP: 70
SQ FT: 40,000
SALES (corp-wide): 26.7MM **Privately Held**
WEB: www.magliner.com
SIC: 3537 3535 Trucks, tractors, loaders, carriers & similar equipment; conveyors & conveying equipment
PA: Magline, Inc.
1205 W Cedar St
Standish MI 48658
800 624-5463

(G-15223)
MAGLINE INTERNATIONAL LLC
1205 W Cedar St (48658-9563)
PHONE..................................989 512-1000
D Brian Law,
Bruce W Law,
EMP: 7
SQ FT: 1,500
SALES (est): 1MM **Privately Held**
SIC: 3537 Trucks, tractors, loaders, carriers & similar equipment; dollies (hand or power trucks), industrial except mining

(G-15224)
MISTEQUAY GROUP LTD
1015 W Cedar St (48658-9421)
PHONE..................................989 846-1000
Ken Jones, *Plant Mgr*
Laura Littleton, *Sales Staff*
EMP: 60 **Privately Held**
SIC: 6159 3769 3714 Machinery & equipment finance leasing; guided missile & space vehicle parts & auxiliary equipment; motor vehicle parts & accessories
PA: Mistequay Group Ltd.
1156 N Niagara St
Saginaw MI 48602

(G-15225)
POOLES MEAT PROCESSING
3084 Grove Street Rd (48658-9215)
P.O. Box 867 (48658-0867)
PHONE..................................989 846-6348
Gary L Poole, *President*
Kathleen Poole, *Vice Pres*
EMP: 4 **EST:** 1950
SQ FT: 50,000
SALES (est): 276.1K **Privately Held**
SIC: 2011 0751 Meat packing plants; slaughtering: custom livestock services

(G-15226)
PRA COMPANY (PA)
Also Called: Vantage Plastics
1415 W Cedar St (48658-9527)
PHONE..................................989 846-1029
Paul Aultman, *President*
George Aultman, *Director*
Karl Bauman, *Director*
EMP: 88
SQ FT: 77,000
SALES (est): 21.6MM **Privately Held**
WEB: www.vantageplastics.com
SIC: 3089 3069 Thermoformed finished plastic products; rubberized fabrics

Stanton
Montcalm County

(G-15227)
AFFORDABLE OEM AUTOLIGHTING
3068 W Klees Rd (48888-9717)
PHONE..................................989 400-6106
Keith Howard, *Principal*
EMP: 3
SALES (est): 163.3K **Privately Held**
SIC: 3648 Lighting equipment

(G-15228)
BUCK STOP LURE COMPANY INC
3600 N Grow Rd (48888-9648)
P.O. Box 636 (48888-0636)
PHONE..................................989 762-5091
Dawn Phenix, *President*
EMP: 4
SQ FT: 20,000
SALES (est): 469.7K **Privately Held**
WEB: www.buckstopscents.com
SIC: 3949 Hunting equipment

(G-15229)
DOUBLE SIX SPORTS COMPLEX
4860 N Sheridan Rd (48888)
PHONE..................................989 762-5342
EMP: 10
SALES (est): 449.6K **Privately Held**
SIC: 3949 Mfg Sporting/Athletic Goods

(G-15230)
VS PRODUCTS
2075 Lakeside Dr (48888-9109)
PHONE..................................989 831-4861
Daryl Williams, *Owner*
EMP: 3
SALES (est): 79.9K **Privately Held**
SIC: 7692 Welding repair

Stanwood
Mecosta County

(G-15231)
AVIAN CONTROL TECHNOLOGIES LLC
6800 Mayfair Dr (49346-9600)
PHONE..................................231 349-9050
Bruce Vergote,
EMP: 5
SALES: 150K **Privately Held**
SIC: 3499 Barricades, metal

(G-15232)
BRYAN K SERGENT
19383 10 Mile Rd (49346-8861)
PHONE..................................231 670-2106
Bryan Sergent, *Principal*
EMP: 3
SALES (est): 192.7K **Privately Held**
SIC: 2411 Logging

(G-15233)
CUSTOM ANYTHING LLC
7547 River Ridge Rd (49346-8969)
P.O. Box 930194, Wixom (48393-0194)
PHONE..................................231 282-1981
Donald Williams,
EMP: 3
SALES (est): 231.5K **Privately Held**
SIC: 3479 Metal coating & allied service

(G-15234)
JRJ ENERGY SERVICES LLC
7302 Northland Dr (49346-8742)
P.O. Box 338 (49346-0338)
PHONE..................................231 823-2171
John R Johnson, *General Mgr*
EMP: 120
SALES (est): 29.3MM **Privately Held**
SIC: 1389 Construction, repair & dismantling services

Stephenson
Menominee County

(G-15235)
FORTE INDUSTRIES MILL INC
N8076 Us Highway 41 (49887-9008)
P.O. Box 279 (49887-0279)
PHONE..................................906 753-6256
Charles Duffrin, *President*
Richard Duffrin, *Vice Pres*
◆ **EMP:** 18
SQ FT: 8,000
SALES: 2.5MM **Privately Held**
SIC: 2421 2436 2435 2426 Sawmills & planing mills, general; softwood veneer & plywood; hardwood veneer & plywood; hardwood dimension & flooring mills

(G-15236)
KELLS SAWMILL INC
N8780 County Road 577 (49887-8333)
PHONE..................................906 753-2778
Allen Majkrzak, *President*
Laurel Majkrzak, *Corp Secy*
EMP: 6 **EST:** 1956
SALES: 178K **Privately Held**
SIC: 2499 2421 2411 Surveyors' stakes, wood; sawmills & planing mills, general; logging

(G-15237)
MENOMINEE CNTY JURNL PRINT SP
S322 Menominee St (49887-5106)
P.O. Box 247 (49887-0247)
PHONE..................................906 753-2296
Gilbert G Grinsteiner, *Owner*
EMP: 10 **EST:** 1956
SALES: 400K **Privately Held**
SIC: 2711 2752 Commercial printing & newspaper publishing combined; commercial printing, lithographic

(G-15238)
MINERALS PROCESSING CORP
Also Called: Field Office
N9373 River Rd (49887-8132)
PHONE..................................906 753-9602
Stephanie Malec, *CFO*
Tom Quigley, *Branch Mgr*
EMP: 20 **Privately Held**
SIC: 3354 Aluminum extruded products
PA: Minerals Processing Corporation
314 W Superior St Ste 310
Duluth MN 55802

(G-15239)
ROSARY WORKSHOP
5209 W 16 5 Ln (49887)
PHONE..................................906 788-4846
Margot Blair, *Owner*
EMP: 5
SALES (est): 160.6K **Privately Held**
WEB: www.rosaryworkshop.com
SIC: 8661 3961 Religious organizations; rosaries & small religious articles, except precious metal

(G-15240)
RULEAU BROTHERS INC (PA)
Also Called: Door County White Fish
W521 Stephenson S Dr (49887)
P.O. Box 337 (49887-0337)
PHONE..................................906 753-4767
Robert Ruleau, *President*
Kathleen Ruleau, *Corp Secy*
Robert Kuntze, *Manager*
▼ **EMP:** 30
SALES: 2MM **Privately Held**
SIC: 0912 2092 2091 Finfish; fresh or frozen packaged fish; fish, salted; fish, smoked

(G-15241)
TERRY HEIDEN
Also Called: Heiden Lumber & Fencing
N8745 Us Highway 41 (49887)
PHONE..................................906 753-6248
Terry Heiden, *Owner*
EMP: 4
SQ FT: 7,700
SALES (est): 372.6K **Privately Held**
SIC: 2421 Sawmills & planing mills, general

Sterling
Arenac County

(G-15242)
ALMARC TUBE CO INC
129 Main St (48659-9564)
P.O. Box 15 (48659-0015)
PHONE..................................989 654-2660
Marc D Ffranklin, *President*
Alton D Franklin, *Vice Pres*
EMP: 3 **EST:** 1976
SQ FT: 7,500
SALES (est): 378.6K **Privately Held**
SIC: 3498 Tube fabricating (contract bending & shaping)

(G-15243)
BURMEISTER ENGINEERING
230 Fritz Rd (48659-9404)
PHONE..................................989 654-2537
Arthur Burmeister, *Owner*
EMP: 3
SALES (est): 131.6K **Privately Held**
SIC: 3599 8711 Machine shop, jobbing & repair; designing: ship, boat, machine & product

(G-15244)
MAPLE RIDGE HARDWOODS INC
Also Called: East Michigan Lumber
2270 Dobler Rd (48659-9442)
PHONE..................................989 873-5305
Douglas Devereaux, *President*
Tom Barbier, *Principal*
Todd Southworth, *Principal*
Peter Barbier, *Treasurer*
EMP: 50

Sterling Heights
Macomb County

(G-15245)
A G SIMPSON (USA) INC
6700 18 1/2 M (48314)
PHONE..............................586 268-4817
Paul Sobocan, *Branch Mgr*
EMP: 90
SALES (corp-wide): 365.5MM **Privately Held**
SIC: 3465 Body parts, automobile: stamped metal
HQ: A. G. Simpson (Usa), Inc.
  6640 Sterling Dr S
  Sterling Heights MI 48312
  586 268-5844

(G-15246)
A G SIMPSON (USA) INC
6700 18 1/2 (48314)
PHONE..............................586 268-4817
Paul Sobocan, *Branch Mgr*
EMP: 10
SALES (corp-wide): 365.5MM **Privately Held**
SIC: 3465 Body parts, automobile: stamped metal
HQ: A. G. Simpson (Usa), Inc.
  6640 Sterling Dr S
  Sterling Heights MI 48312
  586 268-5844

(G-15247)
A G SIMPSON (USA) INC (HQ)
6640 Sterling Dr S (48312-5845)
PHONE..............................586 268-5844
Joe Loparco, *President*
Joe Leon, *Vice Pres*
Rob Dinatale, *Exec Dir*
Adele Leandro, *Admin Sec*
EMP: 30
SQ FT: 126,000
SALES (est): 23.4MM
SALES (corp-wide): 365.5MM **Privately Held**
SIC: 3465 Body parts, automobile: stamped metal
PA: J2 Management Corp
  200 Yorkland Blvd Suite 800
  Toronto ON M2J 5
  416 438-6650

(G-15248)
ABB MOTORS AND MECHANICAL INC
Also Called: Baldor Electric Motors
5993 Progress Dr (48312-2621)
PHONE..............................586 978-9800
John Parker, *Opers Mgr*
Mark Lough, *Accounts Mgr*
Art Hossman, *Branch Mgr*
EMP: 15
SALES (corp-wide): 36.4B **Privately Held**
WEB: www.baldor.com
SIC: 3621 4225 Motors & generators; general warehousing & storage
HQ: Abb Motors And Mechanical Inc.
  5711 Rs Boreham Jr St
  Fort Smith AR 72901
  479 646-4711

(G-15249)
ABSOLUTE LSER WLDG SLTIONS LLC
6545 19 Mile Rd (48314-2116)
PHONE..............................586 932-2597
David Gall,
EMP: 17
SALES (est): 1.5MM **Privately Held**
SIC: 7692 Welding repair

(G-15250)
ACCUTEK MOLD & ENGINEERING
35815 Stanley Dr (48312-2663)
PHONE..............................586 978-1335
Luciano Pierobon, *President*
Marco Pierobon, *Vice Pres*
EMP: 12
SALES: 1MM **Privately Held**
SIC: 3312 Tool & die steel

(G-15251)
ACP TECHNOLOGIES LLC
7205 Sterling Ponds Ct (48312-5813)
PHONE..............................586 322-3511
Thomas Holcombe, *CEO*
Dennis Wend, *President*
D Chris Boyer, *Shareholder*
Donald P Malone, *Shareholder*
EMP: 6 **EST:** 2017
SQ FT: 1,000
SALES (est): 251.5K **Privately Held**
SIC: 3624 2821 Fibers, carbon & graphite; molding compounds, plastics

(G-15252)
ACUMENT GLOBAL TECH INC (DH)
6125 18 Mile Rd (48314-4205)
PHONE..............................586 254-3900
Patrick Paige, *President*
Lynn Stanton, *Business Mgr*
John Clark, *Exec VP*
Andreas Frobese, *Opers Mgr*
Donny Williams, *Maint Spvr*
▲ **EMP:** 45
SQ FT: 10,000
SALES (est): 2.6B
SALES (corp-wide): 30.9MM **Privately Held**
WEB: www.acument.com
SIC: 3965 5072 Fasteners; hardware
HQ: Fontana America Incorporated
  6125 18 Mile Rd
  Sterling Heights MI 48314
  586 997-5600

(G-15253)
ACUMENT GLOBAL TECH INC
Manufacturing Division
6125 18 Mile Rd (48314-4205)
PHONE..............................586 254-3900
Michael Dunn, *Manager*
EMP: 423
SALES (corp-wide): 30.9MM **Privately Held**
SIC: 3452 Bolts, nuts, rivets & washers
HQ: Acument Global Technologies, Inc.
  6125 18 Mile Rd
  Sterling Heights MI 48314
  586 254-3900

(G-15254)
ADVANCED SCREENPRINTING
35957 Mound Rd Ste 2 (48310-4779)
PHONE..............................586 979-4412
Dale Wrubel, *Owner*
EMP: 3 **EST:** 2009
SALES (est): 234.6K **Privately Held**
SIC: 2759 Screen printing

(G-15255)
AERO EMBEDDED TECHNOLOGIES INC
Also Called: In-Tronics
6580 Cotter Ave (48314-2148)
PHONE..............................586 251-2980
Peter G Vanheusden, *President*
EMP: 4
SALES (est): 1.1MM **Privately Held**
SIC: 3672 Printed circuit boards

(G-15256)
AG DAVIS GAGE & ENGRG CO (PA)
Also Called: AG Davis
6533 Sims Dr (48313-3724)
PHONE..............................586 977-9000
Edwin G Chapman, *President*
Greg Chapman, *Vice Pres*
Gregory Chapman, *Vice Pres*
Bill Lewis, *Engineer*
Michelle Beckman, *CFO*
EMP: 30
SQ FT: 20,000
SALES (est): 3.9MM **Privately Held**
WEB: www.agdavis.com
SIC: 3545 5084 3825 3823 Gauges (machine tool accessories); industrial machinery & equipment; instruments to measure electricity; industrial instrmnts msrmnt display/control process variable; laboratory apparatus & furniture; relays & industrial controls

(G-15257)
AM SPECIALTIES INC
5985 Wall St (48312-1074)
PHONE..............................586 795-9000
EMP: 3 **EST:** 2018
SALES (est): 108.3K **Privately Held**
SIC: 3465 Automotive stampings

(G-15258)
AM SPECIALTIES INC
5985 Wall St (48312-1074)
PHONE..............................586 795-9000
Alan G Klinger, *President*
Brian Jeffers, *Supervisor*
EMP: 19
SQ FT: 11,000
SALES (est): 1.9MM **Privately Held**
SIC: 3714 Radiators & radiator shells & cores, motor vehicle

(G-15259)
AMERICAN RHNMTALL VEHICLES LLC
7205 Sterling (48312)
PHONE..............................703 221-9288
Matthew Warnick, *Mng Member*
EMP: 3
SALES (est): 146K **Privately Held**
SIC: 3795 Tanks & tank components

(G-15260)
AMPLAS COMPOUNDING LLC
6675 Sterling Dr N (48312-4559)
PHONE..............................586 795-2555
Geraldine Beaupre, *President*
Darin Beaupre, *Exec VP*
EMP: 15
SQ FT: 63,000
SALES (est): 3.4MM
SALES (corp-wide): 6MM **Privately Held**
WEB: www.amplascompounding.com
SIC: 3089 2821 3087 Plastic processing; plastics materials & resins; custom compound purchased resins
PA: Delta Polymers Co.
  6685 Sterling Dr N
  Sterling Heights MI 48312
  586 795-2900

(G-15261)
AMX CORP
38780 Hartwell Dr (48312-1327)
P.O. Box 759, Novi (48376-0759)
PHONE..............................469 624-8000
Dave Hill, *Principal*
EMP: 3 **EST:** 2016
SALES (est): 97.2K **Privately Held**
SIC: 3625 Relays & industrial controls

(G-15262)
APHASE II INC (PA)
6120 Center Dr (48312-2614)
PHONE..............................586 977-0790
Edward Bluthardt, *President*
Rob Bluthardt, *Vice Pres*
Don Parrett, *Vice Pres*
EMP: 92
SQ FT: 36,771
SALES: 10.9MM **Privately Held**
WEB: www.aphaseii.com
SIC: 8711 3465 Engineering services; automotive stampings

(G-15263)
APPLIED TECHNOLOGY GROUP
Also Called: D E S Group
7205 Sterling Ponds Ct (48312-5813)
PHONE..............................586 286-6442
Ronald Plaza,
EMP: 3
SALES (est): 125.5K **Privately Held**
SIC: 3714 Motor vehicle parts & accessories

(G-15264)
ART GLASS INC
44045 Donley Dr (48314-2637)
PHONE..............................586 731-8627
Arthur Dolenga, *President*
EMP: 3
SALES: 200K **Privately Held**
SIC: 8748 3559 Business consulting; glass making machinery: blowing, molding, forming, etc.

(G-15265)
ASMUS SEASONING INC
36625 Metro Ct Ste A (48312-1060)
PHONE..............................586 939-4505
Marvin Asmus Jr, *President*
Tom Fritz, *Vice Pres*
EMP: 11
SALES (est): 2.2MM **Privately Held**
SIC: 2099 5149 Seasonings & spices; spices & seasonings

(G-15266)
ASTRA ASSOCIATES INC
Also Called: Mid-West Instrument Company
6500 Dobry Dr (48314-1424)
PHONE..............................586 254-6500
Frederick Lueck, *President*
Ellen I Lueck, *Corp Secy*
James F Lueck, *Vice Pres*
Michael A Lueck, *Vice Pres*
Stanley Daalder, *Sales Staff*
EMP: 45
SQ FT: 35,000
SALES (est): 10.8MM **Privately Held**
WEB: www.midwestinstrument.com
SIC: 3823 3829 3822 3643 Differential pressure instruments, industrial process type; measuring & controlling devices; auto controls regulating residntl & coml environmt & applncs; current-carrying wiring devices

(G-15267)
AUTOMOTIVE COMPONENT MFG (PA)
Also Called: Acm
36155 Mound Rd (48310-4736)
PHONE..............................705 549-7406
Robert Hall, *President*
Doug Ewen, *Vice Pres*
EMP: 3
SALES (est): 30.3MM **Privately Held**
SIC: 3559 Automotive related machinery

(G-15268)
AUTOMOTIVE TECHNOLOGY LLC
6015 Center Dr (48312-2667)
PHONE..............................586 446-7000
Brian Prina, *President*
Robert Dudek, *Treasurer*
EMP: 221
SALES (est): 14.7MM **Privately Held**
SIC: 3559 Automotive related machinery
HQ: M-Sko Ias Holdings, Inc.
  1395 Brickell Ave Ste 800
  Miami FL 33131
  786 871-2904

(G-15269)
B & B HOLDINGS GROESBECK LLC
Also Called: Krh Industries, LLC
42450 R Mancini Dr (48314-3265)
PHONE..............................586 554-7600
Stephanie Serra-Bartolotta,
EMP: 12
SALES (est): 356.9K **Privately Held**
SIC: 1799 7389 3542 Welding on site; metal cutting services; punching, shearing & bending machines

(G-15270)
BAE SYSTEMS LAND ARMAMENTS LP
34201 Van Dyke Ave (48312-4648)
PHONE..............................586 596-4123
Joe Hoffman, *Buyer*
Esma Elmazaj, *Engineer*
Neil Gavrich, *Engineer*
Kent Williams, *Project Engr*
Tracie Opaitz, *Finance*
EMP: 15

GEOGRAPHIC SECTION
Sterling Heights - Macomb County (G-15297)

SALES (corp-wide): 21.6B **Privately Held**
WEB: www.udlp.com
SIC: 3795 Tanks & tank components
HQ: Bae Systems Land & Armaments L.P.
2000 15th St N Fl 11
Arlington VA 22201
703 907-8250

(G-15271)
BAIRD INVESTMENTS LLC (PA)
Also Called: Jaan Technolgies
43333 Westview Dr (48313-2170)
PHONE................................586 665-0154
Jacqueline Baird, *Mng Member*
Steven Baird, *Program Mgr*
EMP: 4
SALES: 1.3MM **Privately Held**
SIC: 3569 Assembly machines, non-metal-working

(G-15272)
BARNES INTERNATIONAL
40848 Brightside Ct (48310-6953)
PHONE................................586 978-2880
EMP: 3
SALES (est): 170K **Privately Held**
SIC: 1446 Industrial Sand Mining

(G-15273)
BATTERIES SHACK
44478 Mound Rd (48314-1330)
PHONE................................586 580-2893
Anas Tela, *Owner*
EMP: 3
SALES (est): 251.5K **Privately Held**
SIC: 3691 Storage batteries

(G-15274)
BIRMINGHAM JEWELRY INC
34756 Dequindre Rd (48310-5279)
PHONE................................586 939-5100
Gregory Pilibosian, *President*
Reba Pilibosian, *Vice Pres*
EMP: 5
SQ FT: 5,000
SALES: 1MM **Privately Held**
WEB: www.birminghamjewelry.com
SIC: 3911 5992 Jewelry, precious metal; flowers, fresh

(G-15275)
BITNER TOOLING TECHNOLOGIES
6650 Burroughs Ave (48314-2135)
PHONE................................586 803-1100
Curtis Lansbury, *President*
EMP: 15
SQ FT: 26,000
SALES (est): 1.5MM
SALES (corp-wide): 12MM **Privately Held**
WEB: www.natool.com
SIC: 3545 Cutting tools for machine tools; drill bits, metalworking
PA: North American Tool Corporation
215 Elmwood Ave
South Beloit IL 61080
815 389-2300

(G-15276)
BOLMAN DIE SERVICES INC
7515 19 Mile Rd (48314-3222)
PHONE................................810 919-2262
Scott Bolman, *President*
EMP: 10
SALES (est): 55K **Privately Held**
SIC: 3544 Special dies & tools; punches, forming & stamping

(G-15277)
BRANSON ULTRASONICS CORP
6590 Sims Dr (48313-3751)
PHONE................................586 276-0150
Ryan McEntee, *Manager*
EMP: 11
SALES (corp-wide): 17.4B **Publicly Held**
SIC: 3699 Cleaning equipment, ultrasonic, except medical & dental
HQ: Branson Ultrasonics Corporation
41 Eagle Rd Ste 1
Danbury CT 06810
203 796-0400

(G-15278)
C & C MANUFACTURING INC
35455 Stanley Dr (48312-2657)
PHONE................................586 268-3650
Joseph Colella, *President*
Paul Cusmasno, *Vice Pres*
Joseph Alnaraie, *Project Mgr*
Andy Simonds, *Opers Mgr*
EMP: 11
SQ FT: 6,500
SALES: 750K **Privately Held**
SIC: 3354 Aluminum extruded products

(G-15279)
CAMCAR LLC (DH)
6125 18 Mile Rd (48314-4205)
PHONE................................586 254-3900
Richard Dauch, *President*
David Harlow, *Vice Pres*
Keith Kim, *Vice Pres*
Mary Sigler, *Vice Pres*
Michael Claassen, *VP Engrg*
EMP: 3 EST: 2005
SALES: 6.8MM
SALES (corp-wide): 30.9MM **Privately Held**
SIC: 3452 5072 Bolts, nuts, rivets & washers; bolts, nuts & screws
HQ: Acument Global Technologies, Inc.
6125 18 Mile Rd
Sterling Heights MI 48314
586 254-3900

(G-15280)
CAPITAL INDUCTION INC
6505 Diplomat Dr (48314-1421)
PHONE................................586 322-1444
Larry Misner, *President*
Claire Tomlinson, *Admin Sec*
▼ EMP: 10
SQ FT: 13,000
SALES (est): 1.3MM **Privately Held**
WEB: www.capitalinduction.com
SIC: 3567 Induction heating equipment

(G-15281)
CAPLER MFG
6664 Sterling Dr N (48312-4558)
PHONE................................586 264-7851
Tomas Capler, *Manager*
EMP: 7
SALES (est): 98.1K **Privately Held**
SIC: 3999 Manufacturing industries

(G-15282)
CARROLL PRODUCTS INC
44056 Phoenix Dr (48314-1463)
PHONE................................586 254-6300
Harold Wolf, *President*
EMP: 30
SQ FT: 28,000
SALES: 10MM **Privately Held**
SIC: 2673 Plastic bags: made from purchased materials

(G-15283)
CASADEI STRUCTURAL STEEL INC
Also Called: Casadei Steel
40675 Mound Rd (48310-2263)
P.O. Box 70 (48311-0070)
PHONE................................586 698-2898
Bruno Casadei, *President*
Robert Casadei, *Vice Pres*
Tony Babcock, *Project Mgr*
Michelle Corsini, *Human Resources*
Donna Kotcher, *Technology*
EMP: 35
SQ FT: 150,000
SALES: 18MM **Privately Held**
SIC: 3441 Fabricated structural metal

(G-15284)
CENTRAL ON LINE DATA SYSTEMS
34200 Mound Rd (48310-6613)
PHONE................................586 939-7000
F V McBrien, *President*
Ronald Lech, *Vice Pres*
Agnes A Moroun, *Admin Sec*
EMP: 6
SQ FT: 42,600
SALES (est): 628.7K
SALES (corp-wide): 273.6MM **Privately Held**
SIC: 3661 7622 Telephone & telegraph apparatus; communication equipment repair
PA: Centra Inc.
12225 Stephens Rd
Warren MI 48089
586 939-7000

(G-15285)
CERTIFIED REDUCER RBLDRS INC
6480 Sims Dr (48313-3700)
PHONE................................248 585-0883
Michael P Ruger, *President*
Robert L Wenzel, *Corp Secy*
EMP: 15 EST: 1979
SQ FT: 6,000
SALES (est): 2.3MM **Privately Held**
WEB: www.certifiedreducer.net
SIC: 7699 3566 Industrial machinery & equipment repair; speed changers, drives & gears

(G-15286)
CHALKER TOOL & GAUGE INC
35425 Beattie Dr (48312-2613)
PHONE................................586 977-8660
Patrick Chalker, *President*
Bonnie Chalker, *Shareholder*
EMP: 11
SQ FT: 7,920
SALES (est): 1.6MM **Privately Held**
SIC: 3599 Machine shop, jobbing & repair

(G-15287)
CHARDAM GEAR COMPANY INC
40805 Mound Rd (48310-2258)
PHONE................................586 795-8900
Miike Brzoska, *President*
Eric Schmidt, *Superintendent*
Kay Becker, *Vice Pres*
Dough Perzyk, *Vice Pres*
Edward Kozlowski, *Shareholder*
EMP: 87 EST: 1946
SQ FT: 12,000
SALES (est): 19.5MM **Privately Held**
WEB: www.chardam.com
SIC: 3728 3462 Aircraft parts & equipment; iron & steel forgings; aircraft forgings, ferrous

(G-15288)
CHRYSLER GROUP LLC
Also Called: Chrysler Sterling Test Center
7150 Metropolitan Pkwy (48312-1040)
PHONE................................586 977-4900
Fax: 586 977-4913
EMP: 100
SALES (corp-wide): 90.3MM **Privately Held**
SIC: 3711 Mfg Motor Vehicle/Car Bodies
HQ: Chrysler Group Llc
1000 Chrysler Dr
Auburn Hills MI 48326
248 512-2950

(G-15289)
CIRCLE ENGINEERING INC
5495 Gatewood Dr (48310-2226)
PHONE................................586 978-8120
William J Sammut, *President*
John Sammut, *Admin Sec*
EMP: 9
SQ FT: 10,500
SALES (est): 1.4MM **Privately Held**
WEB: www.circleeng.com
SIC: 3544 Special dies & tools

(G-15290)
CLASSIC TOOL & BORING INC
5970 Wall St (48312-1069)
PHONE................................586 795-8967
Lou Gavrilovski, *President*
EMP: 9
SQ FT: 11,000
SALES: 790K **Privately Held**
SIC: 3599 Machine shop, jobbing & repair

(G-15291)
COLD FORMING TECHNOLOGY INC
44476 Phoenix Dr (48314-1467)
PHONE................................586 254-4600
John T Donnelly, *Ch of Bd*
James A Ferrett, *Vice Pres*
Suren B RAO, *Vice Pres*
▲ EMP: 19
SQ FT: 7,200
SALES (est): 3.5MM **Privately Held**
WEB: www.coldformingtechnology.com
SIC: 3542 Machine tools, metal forming type

(G-15292)
COMMERCIAL GRAPHICS INC
42704 Mound Rd (48314-3254)
PHONE................................586 726-8150
Tracy Simmons, *President*
EMP: 8
SALES (est): 1.4MM **Privately Held**
SIC: 2752 Commercial printing, offset

(G-15293)
COMPUTER MAIL SERVICES INC (PA)
44648 Mound Rd (48314-1322)
PHONE................................248 352-6700
Lih-Tah Wong, *President*
Daniel J Deward, *Vice Pres*
Alan Sitek, *Vice Pres*
Richard Wongsonegoro, *Vice Pres*
EMP: 12
SQ FT: 4,000
SALES (est): 1.7MM **Privately Held**
WEB: www.cmslink.com
SIC: 7372 4822 7371 Business oriented computer software; electronic mail; computer software development

(G-15294)
COMPUTER SCIENCES CORPORATION
6000 17 Mile Rd (48313-4541)
PHONE................................586 825-5043
Mark Dieterle, *Branch Mgr*
EMP: 170
SALES (corp-wide): 20.7B **Publicly Held**
WEB: www.csc.com
SIC: 7373 7372 Systems integration services; prepackaged software
HQ: Computer Sciences Corporation
1775 Tysons Blvd Ste 1000
Tysons VA 22102
703 245-9675

(G-15295)
CONNELY COMPANY
36155 Mound Rd (48310-4736)
PHONE................................586 977-0700
Fax: 586 977-6836
EMP: 3
SALES (est): 247.5K **Privately Held**
SIC: 3999 Mfg Misc Products

(G-15296)
CONTINENTAL ELECTRICAL PDTS
5971 Product Dr (48312-4561)
PHONE................................248 589-2758
Joan Cotsonika, *President*
EMP: 3 EST: 2011
SALES (est): 449.7K **Privately Held**
SIC: 3613 Cubicles (electric switchboard equipment)

(G-15297)
CONTROL ONE INC
6460 Sims Dr Ste A (48313-3721)
PHONE................................586 979-6106
Fax: 586 979-6109
EMP: 9
SQ FT: 10,000
SALES (est): 780K **Privately Held**
SIC: 3625 1731 1799 Mfg Relays/Industrial Controls Electrical Contractor Trade Contractor

Sterling Heights - Macomb County (G-15298)

(G-15298)
CONTROL TECHNIQUE INCORPORATED
Also Called: C T I
41200 Technology Park Dr (48314-4102)
PHONE...................................586 997-3200
Richard C Mueller, *President*
Jim Shereda, *Vice Pres*
Martin R Shereda, *Vice Pres*
Angie Mueller, *Shareholder*
EMP: 75
SQ FT: 40,000
SALES: 38.4MM **Privately Held**
SIC: 3613 Control panels, electric

(G-15299)
CONVEX MOLD INC
35360 Beattie Dr (48312-2610)
PHONE...................................586 978-0808
Joseph Bolton, *President*
EMP: 7 **EST:** 1967
SQ FT: 7,600
SALES (est): 723.4K
SALES (corp-wide): 5.3B **Publicly Held**
SIC: 3544 7699 Industrial molds; tool repair services
HQ: Sebro Plastics, Inc.
29200 Wall St
Wixom MI 48393
248 348-4121

(G-15300)
COPLAS INC
Also Called: Coplas-Tiercon
6700 18 1/2 Mile Rd (48314-3206)
PHONE...................................586 739-8940
Joseph P Leon, *CEO*
Kermit Welch, *Manager*
EMP: 9
SALES (est): 1MM
SALES (corp-wide): 365.5MM **Privately Held**
SIC: 2821 Molding compounds, plastics
HQ: A. G. Simpson (Usa), Inc.
6640 Sterling Dr S
Sterling Heights MI 48312
586 268-5844

(G-15301)
COTSON FABRICATING INC
5971 Product Dr (48312-4561)
PHONE...................................248 589-2758
Joan Cotsonika, *President*
Philip Calvert, *General Mgr*
Cindy Calvert, *Vice Pres*
EMP: 23
SQ FT: 11,500
SALES (est): 5.4MM **Privately Held**
SIC: 3449 Bars, concrete reinforcing: fabricated steel

(G-15302)
COUSINS MANUFACTURING INC
43734 Merrill Rd (48314-2172)
PHONE...................................586 323-6033
Glenn Roberts, *President*
EMP: 3
SALES (est): 373.8K **Privately Held**
WEB: www.cousinscurrie.com
SIC: 3599 Custom machinery

(G-15303)
CREATIVE AWARDS
42830 Mound Rd (48314-3256)
PHONE...................................586 739-4999
Joe Weigand, *Principal*
EMP: 3
SALES (est): 190.7K **Privately Held**
SIC: 5999 2759 Trophies & plaques; screen printing

(G-15304)
CUTVERSION TECHNOLOGIES CORP
13335 15 Mile Rd Ste 313 (48312-4210)
PHONE...................................586 634-1339
Alan Watt, *President*
EMP: 3
SALES: 950K **Privately Held**
SIC: 3714 Motor vehicle parts & accessories

(G-15305)
CYPRIUM INDUCTION LLC
42770 Mound Rd (48314-3254)
PHONE...................................586 884-4982
James Link,
Christina Liccardello,
EMP: 5
SALES (est): 993.8K **Privately Held**
SIC: 3398 3567 Annealing of metal; induction heating equipment

(G-15306)
D & F CORPORATION
42455 Merrill Rd (48314-3268)
PHONE...................................586 254-5300
William Y Gard, *Ch of Bd*
Paul D Gard, *President*
Van Smith, *Vice Pres*
Tammy Szymanski, *Human Res Mgr*
John Verbeek, *Accounts Mgr*
EMP: 60
SQ FT: 83,000
SALES (est): 11.6MM **Privately Held**
WEB: www.d-f.com
SIC: 3544 3559 3999 3545 Jigs: inspection, gauging & checking; forms (molds), for foundry & plastics working machinery; automotive related machinery; models, general, except toy; machine tool accessories

(G-15307)
DAG LTD LLC
34400 Mound Rd (48310-5757)
PHONE...................................586 276-9310
Dale Hadel, *Mng Member*
▲ **EMP:** 15
SALES (est): 380.8K **Privately Held**
SIC: 3479 2399 Name plates: engraved, etched, etc.; emblems, badges & insignia

(G-15308)
DELTA MOLDED PRODUCTS
Also Called: Delta Trading Co
42754 Mound Rd (48314-3254)
PHONE...................................586 731-9595
Shaheen Mohuddin, *Owner*
EMP: 3
SALES (est): 180K **Privately Held**
SIC: 3089 Molding primary plastic

(G-15309)
DELTA POLYMERS CO (PA)
6685 Sterling Dr N (48312-4559)
PHONE...................................586 795-2900
Delmer Beaupre, *President*
Brian Beaupre, *President*
Darin Beaupre, *Vice Pres*
▲ **EMP:** 28
SQ FT: 96,000
SALES (est): 6MM **Privately Held**
WEB: www.deltapoly.com
SIC: 2821 Molding compounds, plastics

(G-15310)
DEMMAK INDUSTRIES LLC
Also Called: Iridium Manufacturing
43714 Utica Rd (48314-2361)
PHONE...................................586 884-6441
Walter Demock, *Mng Member*
EMP: 6 **EST:** 2002
SALES (est): 275.4K **Privately Held**
SIC: 3599 Machine shop, jobbing & repair

(G-15311)
DETROIT BORING & MCH CO LLC
42818 Mound Rd (48314-3256)
PHONE...................................586 604-6506
William E Noll,
EMP: 4
SALES: 250K **Privately Held**
SIC: 3541 Machine tools, metal cutting type

(G-15312)
DETROIT HOIST & CRANE CO L L C
Also Called: Brandenburg
6650 Sterling Dr N (48312-4558)
PHONE...................................586 268-2600
Ulrich Vorpahl, *President*
Gregory Kanasty, *Sales Mgr*
Piyush Parikh, *Admin Sec*
▲ **EMP:** 35
SQ FT: 60,000
SALES (est): 10.6MM **Privately Held**
WEB: www.detroithoist.com
SIC: 3536 Hoists

(G-15313)
DETROIT NEWS INC
Also Called: Detroit News, The
6200 Metropolitan Pkwy (48312-1022)
P.O. Box 8001 (48311-8001)
PHONE...................................313 222-6400
Michael Quinn, *Vice Pres*
EMP: 4
SQ FT: 360,000
SALES (corp-wide): 4.2B **Privately Held**
SIC: 2711 2752 Newspapers, publishing & printing; commercial printing, lithographic
HQ: The Detroit News Inc
160 W Fort St
Detroit MI 48226
313 222-2300

(G-15314)
DETROIT NEWSPAPER PARTNR LP
6200 Metropolitan Pkwy (48312-1022)
PHONE...................................586 826-7187
Keith Pierce, *Vice Pres*
Brian Nasiadko, *Engineer*
Debbie Janda, *Manager*
EMP: 1000
SALES (corp-wide): 2.9B **Publicly Held**
WEB: www.dnps.com
SIC: 2711 2752 Commercial printing & newspaper publishing combined; advertising posters, lithographed
HQ: Detroit Newspaper Partnership, L.P.
160 W Fort St
Detroit MI 48226
313 222-2300

(G-15315)
DETRONIC INDUSTRIES INC (PA)
35800 Beattie Dr (48312-2620)
P.O. Box 608 (48311-0608)
PHONE...................................586 268-6392
James D Carne, *President*
Marilyn A Carne, *Corp Secy*
Ryan M Carne, *Vice Pres*
Bill Birta, *Purch Agent*
Eric Otto, *QC Mgr*
EMP: 80 **EST:** 1958
SQ FT: 55,510
SALES (est): 23.2MM **Privately Held**
WEB: www.detronic.com
SIC: 3444 Sheet metal specialties, not stamped

(G-15316)
DIAGNOSTIC INSTRUMENTS INC
Also Called: Spot Imaging Solutions
6540 Burroughs Ave (48314-2133)
PHONE...................................586 731-6000
Patrick Merlo, *President*
Linda Merlo, *Corp Secy*
Philip Merlo, *Vice Pres*
John Torongo, *Project Mgr*
Michael Szymula, *Production*
EMP: 26
SQ FT: 13,000
SALES (est): 5.9MM **Privately Held**
WEB: www.diaginc.com
SIC: 3827 3851 Optical instruments & lenses; ophthalmic goods

(G-15317)
DIHYDRO SERVICES INC
40833 Brentwood Dr (48310-2215)
PHONE...................................586 978-0900
Dann Hutchins, *President*
EMP: 23
SQ FT: 6,000
SALES (est): 4.9MM **Privately Held**
WEB: www.dihydro.com
SIC: 3589 Water treatment equipment, industrial

(G-15318)
DIVERSIFIED MFG & ASSEMBLY LLC (PA)
Also Called: Dma
5545 Bridgewood Dr (48310-2219)
PHONE...................................586 272-2431
Tommy Longest, *President*
EMP: 10
SALES (est): 1.7MM **Privately Held**
SIC: 3714 Rear axle housings, motor vehicle

(G-15319)
DM TOOL & FAB INC
6101 18 1/2 Mile Rd (48314-3116)
PHONE...................................586 726-8390
Americo Valente, *President*
Theresa Rinker, *Executive*
EMP: 70
SQ FT: 10,000
SALES (est): 14.9MM **Privately Held**
WEB: www.dmfabrication.com
SIC: 3544 3542 Industrial molds; machine tools, metal forming type

(G-15320)
DOBDAY MANUFACTURING CO INC
42750 Merrill Rd (48314-3244)
PHONE...................................586 254-6777
Desmond I Dobday, *President*
EMP: 20 **EST:** 1965
SQ FT: 8,000
SALES (est): 1.1MM **Privately Held**
WEB: www.dobday.com
SIC: 3599 3545 Machine shop, jobbing & repair; machine tool accessories

(G-15321)
DU VAL INDUSTRIES LLC
6410 19 Mile Rd (48314-2109)
PHONE...................................586 737-2710
Theodore Elward,
Kimberly Elward,
Brett Kurily,
EMP: 21
SQ FT: 11,600
SALES (est): 3.4MM **Privately Held**
SIC: 3544 Industrial molds
PA: Pacific Tool & Engineering Ltd.
6410 19 Mile Rd
Sterling Heights MI 48314
586 737-2710

(G-15322)
DUO ROBOTIC SOLUTIONS INC
36715 Metro Ct (48312-1011)
PHONE...................................586 883-7559
Dominique Girard, *President*
EMP: 10
SQ FT: 9,200
SALES: 2MM
SALES (corp-wide): 4.2MM **Privately Held**
SIC: 3549 Assembly machines, including robotic
PA: Duo Machinery Equipment(Shanghai)Co., Lt D.
No.66 Fulian 3th Rd, Baoshan Dist
Shanghai 20043
216 538-5822

(G-15323)
DURA HOG INC
Also Called: Fitzpatrick Manufacturing
33637 Sterling Ponds Blvd (48312-5810)
PHONE...................................586 825-0066
Michael Fitzpatrick, *President*
Barbara Fitzpatrick, *Admin Sec*
EMP: 4
SALES (est): 472.8K **Privately Held**
WEB: www.dura-hog.com
SIC: 3599 Machine shop, jobbing & repair

(G-15324)
E Q R 2 INC
Also Called: Imagamerica
44479 Phoenix Dr (48314-1468)
PHONE...................................586 731-3383
Mike Resnick, *President*
Bev Resnick, *Vice Pres*
Matt Resnick, *Admin Sec*
EMP: 5
SQ FT: 1,600
SALES: 750K **Privately Held**
SIC: 2395 2396 Embroidery & art needlework; automotive & apparel trimmings

GEOGRAPHIC SECTION

(G-15325)
EAGLE MACHINE PRODUCTS COMPANY
35440 Stanley Dr (48312-2656)
PHONE..................................586 268-2460
Vasel Nicaj, *President*
EMP: 5
SQ FT: 10,000
SALES: 300K **Privately Held**
SIC: 3599 Machine shop, jobbing & repair

(G-15326)
EAGLE MASKING FABRICATION INC
6633 Diplomat Dr (48314-1423)
PHONE..................................586 992-3080
Christopher J Sinicki, *President*
Timothy C Hicks, *Corp Secy*
EMP: 6
SALES: 500K **Privately Held**
WEB: www.eaglemasking.com
SIC: 3544 Industrial molds

(G-15327)
EAGLE THREAD VERIFIER LLC
40631 Firesteel Dr (48313-4219)
PHONE..................................586 764-8218
Gordon Taylor, *Mng Member*
EMP: 8
SALES (est): 146.4K **Privately Held**
SIC: 3714 5013 Motor vehicle parts & accessories; automotive supplies & parts

(G-15328)
EAGLE TOOL GROUP LLC
42724 Mound Rd (48314-3254)
P.O. Box 143, Bloomfield Hills (48303-0143)
PHONE..................................586 997-0800
John Hascall,
EMP: 10
SALES (est): 699.1K **Privately Held**
WEB: www.clamp-it.com
SIC: 3423 Ironworkers' hand tools

(G-15329)
EAST PENN MANUFACTURING CO
Also Called: Deka Batteries & Cables
6023 Progress Dr (48312-2621)
PHONE..................................586 979-5300
Jeff Pruett, *Principal*
EMP: 11
SALES (corp-wide): 2.8B **Privately Held**
SIC: 3691 Storage batteries
PA: East Penn Manufacturing Co.
102 Deka Rd
Lyon Station PA 19536
610 682-6361

(G-15330)
ELMHIRST INDUSTRIES INC
7630 19 Mile Rd (48314-3221)
PHONE..................................586 731-8663
John Elmhirst, *President*
Jennifer Howard, *Vice Pres*
EMP: 45
SQ FT: 28,500
SALES: 6MM **Privately Held**
WEB: www.elmhirst.net
SIC: 3545 3543 3469 Machine tool accessories; industrial patterns; metal stampings

(G-15331)
EMERSON ELECTRIC CO
6590 Sims Dr (48313-3751)
PHONE..................................586 268-3104
Jeff Welker, *Project Mgr*
Scott Menko, *Engineer*
EMP: 23
SALES (corp-wide): 17.4B **Publicly Held**
SIC: 3823 Industrial instrmnts msrmnt display/control process variable
PA: Emerson Electric Co.
8000 West Florissant Ave
Saint Louis MO 63136
314 553-2000

(G-15332)
EMITTED ENERGY INC (PA)
6559 Diplomat Dr (48314-1421)
PHONE..................................855 752-3347
Gordon Pesola, *President*
David Kember, *Vice Pres*

Roy Ray, *Vice Pres*
Lisa Powell, *Sales Staff*
EMP: 12
SALES (est): 2.1MM **Privately Held**
SIC: 3641 3823 Electric lamps & parts for specialized applications; industrial process control instruments

(G-15333)
ETHNIC ARTWORK INC
Also Called: E.a Graphics
42111 Van Ave (48314)
P.O. Box 595 (48311-0595)
PHONE..................................586 726-1400
Robert W Artymovich, *President*
Elaine Artymovich, *Corp Secy*
Rich Artymovich, *VP Sales*
EMP: 18
SQ FT: 18,000
SALES (est): 2.3MM **Privately Held**
SIC: 2396 Screen printing on fabric articles

(G-15334)
EURO-CRAFT INTERIORS INC
6611 Diplomat Dr (48314-1423)
PHONE..................................586 254-9130
Gaspare Vitale, *President*
Vince Vitale, *Vice Pres*
Maria Vitale, *Treasurer*
EMP: 18
SQ FT: 6,000
SALES (est): 2.5MM **Privately Held**
WEB: www.eurocraftinteriors.com
SIC: 2434 Wood kitchen cabinets

(G-15335)
EXPERI-METAL INC
6385 Wall St (48312-1079)
PHONE..................................586 977-7800
Valiena A Allison, *President*
Bernard McConnell, *Production*
Janene Legree, *Buyer*
Gary Sears, *Draft/Design*
David Maschke, *Engineer*
EMP: 144
SQ FT: 285,000
SALES (est): 42.4MM **Privately Held**
WEB: www.experi-metal.com
SIC: 3544 3444 3469 Special dies, tools, jigs & fixtures; sheet metalwork; stamping metal for the trade

(G-15336)
FAS N NEDSCHROEF AMER INC
6635 19 Mile Rd (48314-2117)
PHONE..................................586 795-1220
Josh Swim, *Managing Dir*
Marc Van Opstal, *Finance Dir*
EMP: 3
SALES (est): 179.1K **Privately Held**
SIC: 5943 3965 Office forms & supplies; fasteners

(G-15337)
FCA US LLC
Also Called: Chrysler International Sales
38111 Van Dyke Ave (48211-1138)
PHONE..................................586 978-0067
James Bauer, *Manager*
EMP: 75
SALES (corp-wide): 126.4B **Privately Held**
SIC: 5511 3711 Automobiles, new & used; motor vehicles & car bodies
HQ: Fca Us Llc
1000 Chrysler Dr
Auburn Hills MI 48326

(G-15338)
FENIXX TECHNOLOGIES LLC
6633 Diplomat Dr (48314-1423)
PHONE..................................586 254-6000
Sylwia Okruta, *Executive*
Lawrence J Schaller,
EMP: 7
SQ FT: 36,000
SALES (est): 1.2MM **Privately Held**
SIC: 3444 Sheet metalwork

(G-15339)
FETTES MANUFACTURING CO
35855 Stanley Dr (48312-2663)
PHONE..................................586 939-8500
James E McKown, *President*
Tony Schodowski, *Purch Mgr*
Jean Camilletti, *Manager*

Bill Bueche, *Director*
EMP: 44
SQ FT: 25,000
SALES (est): 8.7MM **Privately Held**
WEB: www.fettesmfg.com
SIC: 3451 Screw machine products

(G-15340)
FIBRO LAEPPLE TECHNOLOGY INC
33286 Sterling Ponds Blvd (48312-5808)
PHONE..................................248 591-4494
Guido Setzkorn, *Principal*
Zivko Nikolic, *Vice Pres*
EMP: 4
SQ FT: 16,500
SALES: 43.7K
SALES (corp-wide): 522.3MM **Privately Held**
SIC: 3535 Robotic conveyors
HQ: Fibro Lapple Technology Gmbh
August-Lapple-Weg
HaBmersheim 74855
626 673-0

(G-15341)
FISHER & COMPANY INCORPORATED
Also Called: Fisher Dynamics Metal Forming
6550 Progress Dr (48312-2618)
PHONE..................................586 746-2000
Jeff Thomson, *Manager*
EMP: 80
SALES (corp-wide): 477.8MM **Privately Held**
SIC: 3469 Perforated metal, stamped
PA: Fisher & Company, Incorporated
33300 Fisher Dr
Saint Clair Shores MI 48082
586 746-2000

(G-15342)
FLEX BUILDING SYSTEMS LLC
42400 Merrill Rd (48314-3238)
P.O. Box 180149, Utica (48318-0149)
PHONE..................................586 803-6000
Matthew Winget, *President*
Allen Grajek, *CFO*
EMP: 5
SQ FT: 150,000
SALES (est): 236.7K **Privately Held**
SIC: 2451 Mobile buildings: for commercial use

(G-15343)
FLUID INNOVATIONS INC
43730 Merrill Rd (48314-2172)
P.O. Box 152, Lakeville (48366-0152)
PHONE..................................810 241-0990
Mark Crowell, *President*
EMP: 6
SQ FT: 2,800
SALES (est): 672.4K **Privately Held**
SIC: 3549 Assembly machines, including robotic

(G-15344)
FORMAX PRECISION GEAR INC
6047 18 Mile Rd (48314-4264)
PHONE..................................586 323-9067
Thomas Rosa, *President*
Jack Higgins, *Vice Pres*
EMP: 24
SALES (est): 2.7MM **Privately Held**
SIC: 3462 Gear & chain forgings

(G-15345)
FORMS TRAC ENTERPRISES INC
37827 Brookwood Dr (48312-1915)
PHONE..................................248 524-0006
Harold Hoover, *Owner*
EMP: 4
SALES (est): 309.9K **Privately Held**
SIC: 2761 Manifold business forms

(G-15346)
FOUR STAR TOOLING & ENGRG INC
40550 Brentwood Dr (48310-2208)
PHONE..................................586 264-4090
Stan Bilek, *President*
Grace Dzierzanowski, *Vice Pres*
John Bilek, *Admin Sec*
EMP: 8

SQ FT: 36,000
SALES (est): 1.5MM **Privately Held**
SIC: 3469 3544 Stamping metal for the trade; special dies & tools

(G-15347)
FREE RNGE NTRALS DOG TRATS INC
44648 Mound Rd (48314-1322)
PHONE..................................586 737-0797
EMP: 17 **EST**: 2010
SALES (est): 2.4MM **Privately Held**
SIC: 2047 Dog food

(G-15348)
FRICIA ENTERPRISES INC
Also Called: Industrial Metal Coating Co
6070 18 Mile Rd (48314-4202)
PHONE..................................586 977-1900
Philip A Oliver, *President*
Concetta Oliver, *Admin Sec*
EMP: 9
SALES (est): 1.4MM **Privately Held**
WEB: www.industrialmetalcoating.com
SIC: 3479 Coating of metals & formed products

(G-15349)
FRIENDSHIP INDUSTRIES INC (PA)
6520 Arrow Dr (48314-1412)
PHONE..................................586 323-0033
Herman Spiess, *President*
Cynthia Spiess, *Vice Pres*
EMP: 20
SQ FT: 18,000
SALES (est): 2.9MM **Privately Held**
SIC: 3549 3499 Metalworking machinery; stabilizing bars (cargo), metal

(G-15350)
FRIENDSHIP INDUSTRIES INC
6521 Arrow Dr (48314-1413)
PHONE..................................586 997-1325
Blake Francis, *Manager*
EMP: 10
SALES (corp-wide): 2.9MM **Privately Held**
SIC: 3549 Metalworking machinery
PA: Friendship Industries, Inc.
6520 Arrow Dr
Sterling Heights MI 48314
586 323-0033

(G-15351)
FUSION FABRICATING AND MFG LLC
42380 Mound Rd (48314-3147)
PHONE..................................586 739-1970
Gene Rundell,
Rusty Korhonen,
EMP: 3
SQ FT: 1,500
SALES (est): 250K **Privately Held**
SIC: 3441 Fabricated structural metal

(G-15352)
FUSION LASER SERVICES
42412 Mound Rd (48314-3149)
PHONE..................................586 739-7716
Ted Chudzik, *Principal*
EMP: 3
SALES (est): 391.3K **Privately Held**
SIC: 3699 Laser systems & equipment

(G-15353)
G TECH SALES LLC
6601 Burroughs Ave (48314-2132)
PHONE..................................586 803-9393
Lawrence Gniatczyk,
EMP: 4
SALES (est): 358.8K **Privately Held**
WEB: www.gtechsales.net
SIC: 3711 5012 Motor vehicles & car bodies; automobile auction

(G-15354)
GEARX LLC
35502 Mound Rd (48310-4722)
PHONE..................................248 766-6903
Madhu Naidu,
EMP: 3
SALES (est): 84.3K **Privately Held**
SIC: 3999 3462 Barber & beauty shop equipment; gears, forged steel

Sterling Heights - Macomb County (G-15355)

GEOGRAPHIC SECTION

(G-15355)
GEMINI SALES ORG LLC
2156 Keystone Dr (48310-2849)
PHONE..................................248 765-1118
Mark Merola, *Principal*
EMP: 3
SALES: 100K **Privately Held**
WEB: www.ipsglobal.com
SIC: 2759 Commercial printing

(G-15356)
GENERAL DYNAMICS LAND
6000 17 Mile Rd (48313-4500)
PHONE..................................586 825-4805
Tom Morococo, *Engineer*
Phil Reske, *Engineer*
Dave Cafagna, *Project Engr*
John Gonias, *Branch Mgr*
Jeff Lamb, *Program Mgr*
EMP: 500
SQ FT: 80,000
SALES (corp-wide): 36.1B **Publicly Held**
WEB: www.gdls.com
SIC: 3482 Small arms ammunition
HQ: General Dynamics Land Systems Inc.
   38500 Mound Rd
   Sterling Heights MI 48310
   586 825-4000

(G-15357)
GENERAL DYNAMICS LAND
Also Called: Shelby Operations 1
38500 Mound Rd (48310-3200)
P.O. Box 2125, Warren (48090-2125)
PHONE..................................586 825-8400
Michael Clancy, *Branch Mgr*
EMP: 5
SALES (corp-wide): 36.1B **Publicly Held**
WEB: www.gdls.com
SIC: 3795 Amphibian tanks, military
HQ: General Dynamics Land Systems Inc.
   38500 Mound Rd
   Sterling Heights MI 48310
   586 825-4000

(G-15358)
GENERAL MOTORS LLC
6200 19 Mile Rd (48314-2103)
PHONE..................................586 731-2743
EMP: 11 **Publicly Held**
SIC: 5511 3714 Ret New/Used Automobiles
HQ: General Motors Llc
   300 Renaissance Ctr L 1
   Detroit MI 48243

(G-15359)
GENERALERAL DYNAMICS
8235 San Marco Blvd (48313-4764)
PHONE..................................601 877-6436
EMP: 4
SALES (est): 149.8K **Privately Held**
SIC: 3795 Tanks & tank components

(G-15360)
GENIX LLC (PA)
Also Called: G P Technologies
43665 Utica Rd (48314-2359)
PHONE..................................248 419-0231
Edward Kim, *Mng Member*
Marc Santucci,
EMP: 10
SQ FT: 10,000
SALES (est): 6.7MM **Privately Held**
SIC: 3559 3599 Automotive related machinery; custom machinery

(G-15361)
GLOBAL WHOLESALE & MARKETING
Also Called: Polsorb Sales
6566 Burroughs Ave (48314-2133)
PHONE..................................248 910-8302
EMP: 4
SQ FT: 1,100
SALES: 50K **Privately Held**
SIC: 2842 Mfg Polish/Sanitation Goods

(G-15362)
GM GDLS DEFENSE GROUP LLC (DH)
38500 Mound Rd (48310-3260)
PHONE..................................586 825-4000
J Keith Zerebecki, *President*
Mark Roulet, *Vice Pres*
Geo Zarins, *Plant Mgr*
Julie Farina Percy,
▲ **EMP:** 6
SALES (est): 678.8K
SALES (corp-wide): 36.1B **Publicly Held**
SIC: 3711 8711 Motor vehicles & car bodies; consulting engineer
HQ: General Dynamics Land Systems Inc.
   38500 Mound Rd
   Sterling Heights MI 48310
   586 825-4000

(G-15363)
GMR STONE PRODUCTS LLC
Also Called: Gmr Quality Stone
36955 Metro Ct (48312-1015)
PHONE..................................586 739-2700
Craig Griffin,
▲ **EMP:** 12
SALES (est): 2.1MM **Privately Held**
SIC: 3281 Cut stone & stone products

(G-15364)
GREAT LKES INDUS FRNC SVCS INC
6780 19 1/2 Mile Rd (48314-1403)
PHONE..................................586 323-9200
Charles Hatala, *President*
Tammy Hatala, *Vice Pres*
EMP: 15
SQ FT: 4,000
SALES (est): 4.2MM **Privately Held**
WEB: www.glifs.com
SIC: 3567 7699 Heating units & devices, industrial: electric; industrial equipment services

(G-15365)
GUARDIAN AUTOMOTIVE CORP
Also Called: Automotive Moulding
35555 Mound Rd (48310-4724)
PHONE..................................586 757-7800
Chris Harrison, *Manager*
Javier Garcia, *Director*
EMP: 140
SQ FT: 67,000
SALES (corp-wide): 40.6B **Privately Held**
SIC: 3465 3442 3429 Moldings or trim, automobile: stamped metal; metal doors, sash & trim; manufactured hardware (general)
HQ: Guardian Automotive Corporation
   23751 Amber Ave
   Warren MI 48089
   586 757-7800

(G-15366)
HART INDUSTRIES LLC
43718 Utica Rd (48314-2361)
PHONE..................................313 588-1837
Lisa Brown,
Paul Hartigan,
EMP: 13
SALES (est): 695.5K **Privately Held**
SIC: 3599 Machine & other job shop work

(G-15367)
HEGENSCHEIDT-MFD CORPORATION
6255 Center Dr (48312-2667)
PHONE..................................586 274-4900
David Phillips, *Vice Pres*
Jerry Olshove, *Site Mgr*
Rock Smith, *Purch Mgr*
Martin Pielach, *Engineer*
Sue Gonzales, *Administration*
▲ **EMP:** 21
SQ FT: 30,000
SALES (est): 6MM
SALES (corp-wide): 212.8K **Privately Held**
WEB: www.hegenscheidtmfd.com
SIC: 3541 Machine tools, metal cutting type
HQ: Hegenscheidt-Mfd Gmbh
   Hegenscheidt-Platz
   Erkelenz 41812
   243 186-0

(G-15368)
HORSTMAN INC
Also Called: Milair
44215 Phoenix Dr (48314-1466)
PHONE..................................586 737-2100
Larry Humphrey, *President*
James Kuhns, *Vice Pres*
Andy Godshaw, *Engineer*
Debra Edwards, *Program Mgr*
Phillip Sugg, *Program Mgr*
EMP: 32
SALES (est): 214.3K **Privately Held**
SIC: 3714 3795 3711 Axle housings & shafts, motor vehicle; tanks & tank components; ambulances (motor vehicles), assembly of

(G-15369)
HTI CYBERNETICS INC (PA)
6701 Center Dr (48312-2627)
PHONE..................................586 826-8346
Arno Rabin, *CEO*
Dennis Dawes, *Vice Pres*
Dennis Sims, *Vice Pres*
Joseph Keppler, *CFO*
Erika Allen, *Sales Mgr*
EMP: 45
SQ FT: 48,750
SALES (est): 12.7MM **Privately Held**
WEB: www.hticyber.com
SIC: 3542 3548 3549 3545 Bending machines; resistance welders, electric; metalworking machinery; machine tool accessories; special dies, tools, jigs & fixtures; automotive related machinery

(G-15370)
IMPCO TECHNOLOGIES INC
Also Called: Impco Industrial Eng Systems
7100 15 Mile Rd (48312-4522)
PHONE..................................586 264-1200
Wendy Spencer, *Human Res Mgr*
Kenn Panasiewicz, *Manager*
EMP: 39
SALES (corp-wide): 270.2MM **Privately Held**
WEB: www.impcotechnologies.com
SIC: 3714 3519 Fuel systems & parts, motor vehicle; internal combustion engines
HQ: Impco Technologies, Inc.
   3030 S Susan St
   Santa Ana CA 92704
   714 656-1200

(G-15371)
IMPEL INDUSTRIES INC
44494 Phoenix Dr (48314-1467)
PHONE..................................586 254-5800
Tom Patzer, *President*
Ed Bohmier, *Vice Pres*
Suzan Patzer, *Treasurer*
Jessica Bowker, *Manager*
EMP: 45
SQ FT: 18,000
SALES (est): 8.8MM **Privately Held**
WEB: www.impelind.com
SIC: 3542 Sheet metalworking machines

(G-15372)
INDICON CORPORATION (PA)
6125 Center Dr (48312-2667)
PHONE..................................586 274-0505
Paul Duhaime, *President*
Andrew T Conti, *Corp Secy*
John Spavale, *Project Leader*
EMP: 225
SQ FT: 52,500
SALES (est): 46.6MM **Privately Held**
WEB: www.indicon.com
SIC: 3613 3625 Control panels, electric; relays & industrial controls

(G-15373)
INDUSTRIAL FRNC INTERIORS INC
Also Called: I F I
35160 Stanley Dr (48312-2650)
PHONE..................................586 977-9600
Clyde Bennett, *President*
Clyde J Bennett, *President*
EMP: 5
SQ FT: 8,000
SALES (est): 855.8K **Privately Held**
WEB: www.ifi-inc.com
SIC: 3567 Heating units & devices, industrial: electric

(G-15374)
INNOVTIVE DESIGN SOLUTIONS INC
Also Called: IDS
6801 15 Mile Rd (48312-4517)
PHONE..................................248 583-1010
Robert Ford, *President*
Shawn Haley, *Vice Pres*
Jamie Lopiccolo, *Purch Mgr*
▲ **EMP:** 120
SALES (est): 35.1MM
SALES (corp-wide): 2.4B **Publicly Held**
WEB: www.idselectronics.com
SIC: 3571 Electronic computers
HQ: Lippert Components, Inc.
   3501 County Road 6 E
   Elkhart IN 46514
   574 312-7480

(G-15375)
INTEC AUTOMATED CONTROLS INC
44440 Phoenix Dr (48314-1467)
PHONE..................................586 532-8881
Jeff Spada, *President*
Scott Krueger, *Vice Pres*
Greg Spada, *Mfg Mgr*
Jim Hude, *Engineer*
Derek Kage, *Engineer*
EMP: 50
SQ FT: 3,600
SALES (est): 13MM **Privately Held**
SIC: 3613 Control panels, electric

(G-15376)
INTERNATIONAL AUTOMOTIVE COMPO
6600 15 Mile Rd (48312-4512)
PHONE..................................586 795-7800
EMP: 273 **Privately Held**
WEB: www.iaaawards.com
SIC: 3089 Automotive parts, plastic
HQ: International Automotive Components Group North America, Inc.
   28333 Telegraph Rd
   Southfield MI 48034

(G-15377)
ISBY INDUSTRY LLC
14534 Redford Dr (48312-5763)
PHONE..................................313 269-4213
Zahria Isby, *Administration*
EMP: 4
SALES (est): 149.4K **Privately Held**
SIC: 3914 Loving cups, stainless steel

(G-15378)
J G KERN ENTERPRISES INC
44044 Merrill Rd (48314-1440)
PHONE..................................586 531-9472
Joseph G Kern, *Ch of Bd*
Brian Kern, *President*
Daniel Hampu, *Engineer*
Connie Grabowski, *Treasurer*
Beverly Bartlett, *Manager*
▲ **EMP:** 62
SQ FT: 152,000
SALES (est): 15.1MM **Privately Held**
SIC: 3714 3566 Motor vehicle parts & accessories; gears, power transmission, except automotive

(G-15379)
J W FROEHLICH INC
7305 19 Mile Rd (48314-3217)
PHONE..................................586 580-0025
▲ **EMP:** 5
SQ FT: 4,000
SALES (est): 988.2K
SALES (corp-wide): 484.2K **Privately Held**
SIC: 3549 Assembly machines, including robotic
HQ: Jw Froehlich Maschinenfabrik Gmbh
   Kohlhammerstr. 18-24
   Leinfelden-Echterdingen 70771
   711 797-660

(G-15380)
JDL ENTERPRISES INC (PA)
36425 Maas Dr (48312-2832)
PHONE..................................586 977-8863
John Dominka, *President*
Sue Krajenke, *Manager*
EMP: 13

SALES: 1.2MM **Privately Held**
WEB: www.jdlent.com
SIC: 3491 3541 3823 3494 Industrial valves; machine tools, metal cutting type; industrial instrmnts msrmnt display/control process variable; valves & pipe fittings

(G-15381)
JOE DAVIS CRUSHING INC
42101 Bobjean St (48314-3126)
PHONE..................................586 757-3612
Joe Davis, *President*
Bonnie Davis, *Corp Secy*
EMP: 6 **EST:** 1952
SQ FT: 3,000
SALES (est): 670K **Privately Held**
SIC: 3241 Cement, hydraulic

(G-15382)
JOHNSON CONTROLS INC
6111 Sterling Dr N (48312-4549)
PHONE..................................586 826-8845
Alfred Loosvelt, *President*
EMP: 153 **Privately Held**
SIC: 3714 Motor vehicle body components & frame
HQ: Johnson Controls, Inc.
5757 N Green Bay Ave
Milwaukee WI 53209
414 524-1200

(G-15383)
JVRF UNIFIED INC
13854 Lakeside Cir 503-O (48313-1316)
PHONE..................................248 973-2006
Daniel Lewis, *CEO*
Chanel Lewis, *President*
EMP: 8
SALES: 1.1MM **Privately Held**
SIC: 3993 Electric signs

(G-15384)
K & K DIE INC
40700 Enterprise Dr (48314-3760)
PHONE..................................586 268-8812
Manfred Kunath, *President*
Christian Kunath, *Vice Pres*
Mike Scavone, *Program Mgr*
EMP: 50 **EST:** 1974
SQ FT: 56,000
SALES (est): 10.4MM **Privately Held**
WEB: www.kandkdie.com
SIC: 3469 Metal stampings

(G-15385)
K & K PRECISION TOOL LLC
43765 Trillium Dr (48314-1954)
PHONE..................................586 294-1030
Kathleen Kelly,
EMP: 3
SALES: 800K **Privately Held**
SIC: 3544 Special dies & tools

(G-15386)
K-B TOOL CORPORATION
5985 Wall St (48312-1074)
PHONE..................................586 795-9003
Alan G Klinger, *President*
EMP: 9
SQ FT: 11,000
SALES (est): 1.3MM **Privately Held**
SIC: 3544 Special dies & tools; jigs & fixtures

(G-15387)
KATH KHEMICALS LLC
6050 19 Mile Rd (48314-2101)
PHONE..................................586 275-2646
Emmett Jones, *President*
Rita K Holston, *Vice Pres*
▲ **EMP:** 12
SALES (est): 2.3MM **Privately Held**
SIC: 2842 Specialty cleaning, polishes & sanitation goods

(G-15388)
KAYLER MOLD & ENGINEERING
7370 19 Mile Rd (48314-3214)
PHONE..................................586 739-0699
Candee B Boschman, *President*
EMP: 5
SQ FT: 1,800
SALES (est): 1.1MM **Privately Held**
WEB: www.kaylermold.com
SIC: 2821 Plastics materials & resins

(G-15389)
KINDER PRODUCTS UNLIMITED LLC
6471 Metro Pkwy (48312-1027)
PHONE..................................586 557-3453
Andrew Blake,
Paul Blake,
Peter Blake,
Gino Roncelli,
EMP: 5
SALES (est): 229.7K **Privately Held**
SIC: 2833 Vitamins, natural or synthetic: bulk, uncompounded

(G-15390)
KNIGHT KRAFT INC
44476 Phoenix Dr (48314-1467)
P.O. Box 180168, Utica (48318-0168)
PHONE..................................586 726-6821
Michael Dyda, *President*
EMP: 11
SQ FT: 2,400
SALES (est): 2.1MM **Privately Held**
SIC: 3548 Spot welding apparatus, electric

(G-15391)
KROPP WOODWORKING INC
6812 19 1/2 Mile Rd (48314-1404)
PHONE..................................586 997-3000
Paul Kropp, *Principal*
EMP: 3
SALES (est): 435.8K **Privately Held**
WEB: www.kroppwoodworking.com
SIC: 2431 Millwork

(G-15392)
KUKA SYSTEMS NORTH AMERICA LLC (DH)
Also Called: Kuka Aerospace
6600 Center Dr (48312-2666)
PHONE..................................586 795-2000
Lawrence A Drake, *President*
Charlie Pierce, *Project Mgr*
Baida Davish, *Purch Dir*
Nick Schultz, *Buyer*
Jon Pierre Vos, *Purchasing*
▲ **EMP:** 400 **EST:** 1935
SQ FT: 320,000
SALES (est): 572MM
SALES (corp-wide): 37.7B **Privately Held**
WEB: www.kukausa.com
SIC: 3549 Assembly machines, including robotic
HQ: Kuka Systems Gmbh
Blucherstr. 144
Augsburg 86165
821 797-0

(G-15393)
KUKA US HOLDING COMPANY LLC (DH)
Also Called: Kuka Robotics
6600 Center Dr (48312-2666)
PHONE..................................586 795-2000
Joseph Gemma, *President*
Bryan Cermak, *Corp Secy*
Scott Flood, *Vice Pres*
Pat Duda, *Engineer*
Glenn Quedens, *Engineer*
▲ **EMP:** 17
SALES (est): 40MM
SALES (corp-wide): 37.7B **Privately Held**
WEB: www.kuka-robotics.com
SIC: 5084 3549 Industrial machinery & equipment; assembly machines, including robotic
HQ: Kuka Deutschland Gmbh
Zugspitzstr. 140
Augsburg 86165
821 797-4000

(G-15394)
KUSTOM CREATIONS INC
6665 Burroughs Ave (48314-2132)
PHONE..................................586 997-4141
Harvey Ledesma, *President*
EMP: 7
SALES (est): 876.5K **Privately Held**
WEB: www.kustomcreations.net
SIC: 7539 3449 Automotive repair shops; miscellaneous metalwork

(G-15395)
LANDMARK ENERGY DEVELOPMENT CO
14738 Rice Dr (48313-2940)
PHONE..................................586 457-0200
George J Nosis, *CEO*
EMP: 3
SALES (est): 169.1K **Privately Held**
SIC: 3646 Commercial indusl & institutional electric lighting fixtures

(G-15396)
LESNAU PRINTING COMPANY
6025 Wall St (48312-1075)
PHONE..................................586 795-9200
Robert A Lesnau, *President*
Paul Lesnau, *Vice Pres*
Michael Lesnau, *Treasurer*
EMP: 18 **EST:** 1948
SQ FT: 45,000
SALES (est): 3.3MM **Privately Held**
WEB: www.lesnauprinting.com
SIC: 2752 2759 Commercial printing, offset; letterpress printing

(G-15397)
LETNAN INDUSTRIES INC
Also Called: Rh Spies Group
6520 Arrow Dr (48314-1412)
PHONE..................................586 726-1155
Cynthia Spiess, *CEO*
Erica Francis, *President*
Herman Spiess, *President*
Christina Vloch, *President*
Richard Thornbro, *Project Engr*
◆ **EMP:** 24 **EST:** 1964
SQ FT: 19,000
SALES (est): 5.1MM **Privately Held**
WEB: www.letnanind.com
SIC: 3549 Assembly machines, including robotic

(G-15398)
LIBERTY TOOL INC
44404 Phoenix Dr (48314-1467)
PHONE..................................586 726-2449
Chris Maier, *President*
Shannon Maler, *Purchasing*
EMP: 22
SQ FT: 11,000
SALES (est): 5MM **Privately Held**
WEB: www.liberty-tool.com
SIC: 3541 3599 3544 3728 Machine tools, metal cutting type; machine shop, jobbing & repair; special dies, tools, jigs & fixtures; aircraft parts & equipment

(G-15399)
LIGHT ROBOTICS AUTOMATION INC
43252 Merrill Rd (48314-2162)
PHONE..................................586 254-6655
EMP: 3
SALES (est): 320K **Privately Held**
SIC: 3569 Mfg Robotic Groupers

(G-15400)
LIGHTHOUSE ELEC PROTECTION LLC
7314 19 Mile Rd (48314-3214)
PHONE..................................586 932-2690
Scott Reisfield, *Chief Mktg Ofcr*
Scott Lowes, *Mng Member*
EMP: 8
SQ FT: 6,500
SALES (est): 468.5K **Privately Held**
SIC: 3699 Electrical equipment & supplies

(G-15401)
LOC PERFORMANCE PRODUCTS INC
33852 Sterling Ponds Blvd (48312-5808)
PHONE..................................734 453-2300
Anthony Militello, *Manager*
EMP: 5
SALES (corp-wide): 136.7MM **Privately Held**
SIC: 3541 Machine tools, metal cutting type
PA: Loc Performance Products, Inc.
13505 N Haggerty Rd
Plymouth MI 48170
734 453-2300

(G-15402)
LOCAL PRINTERS INC
40594 Brentwood Dr (48310-2208)
PHONE..................................586 795-1290
Thomas R Holdsworth, *President*
EMP: 4
SQ FT: 3,000
SALES (est): 490K **Privately Held**
SIC: 5112 2752 Business forms; computer paper; mimeograph paper; commercial printing, offset

(G-15403)
LUCKMARR PLASTICS INC
Also Called: L M Group
35735 Stanley Dr (48312-2661)
PHONE..................................586 978-8498
Luciano Pierobon, *President*
John Cochrain, *General Mgr*
Kurt Hahn, *General Mgr*
Virgil Nicaise, *General Mgr*
Marco Pierobon, *Vice Pres*
EMP: 65
SQ FT: 36,000
SALES: 10MM **Privately Held**
SIC: 3089 3544 3469 Injection molding of plastics; special dies, tools, jigs & fixtures; metal stampings

(G-15404)
M & M MACHINING INC
42876 Mound Rd (48314-3256)
P.O. Box 191 (48311-0191)
PHONE..................................586 997-9910
Marco Lachapelle, *President*
Michelle Lachapelle, *Vice Pres*
EMP: 5 **EST:** 1996
SQ FT: 2,450
SALES: 160K **Privately Held**
SIC: 3599 Amusement park equipment; machine shop, jobbing & repair

(G-15405)
M & M THREAD & ASSEMBLY INC
42716 Mound Rd (48314-3254)
PHONE..................................248 583-9696
James Milonoff, *President*
Eugene Wojtowicz, *Vice Pres*
Kandis Milonoff, *Treasurer*
EMP: 8 **EST:** 1961
SQ FT: 22,000
SALES: 246.5K **Privately Held**
SIC: 3545 Thread cutting dies

(G-15406)
MACOMB COUNTY REPUBLICAN PARTY
41800 Prunum Dr (48314-4001)
PHONE..................................586 662-3703
Roger Lonsway, *Principal*
EMP: 3
SALES (est): 122.7K **Privately Held**
SIC: 2711 Newspapers, publishing & printing

(G-15407)
MAG AUTOMOTIVE LLC (DH)
6015 Center Dr (48312-2667)
PHONE..................................586 446-7000
Debbie Lueker, *Accounts Mgr*
Brian Prina,
Paul Chen,
Robert Dudek,
EMP: 99
SALES: 183.2MM **Privately Held**
SIC: 3559 Automotive related machinery
HQ: Mag Us Holding Inc.
6015 Center Dr
Sterling Heights MI 48312
586 446-7000

(G-15408)
MAG-POWERTRAIN
6015 Center Dr (48312-2667)
PHONE..................................586 446-7000
Bob Dudek, *Principal*
Ronald Quaile, *Marketing Staff*
William Thee, *Corp Counsel*
Debbie Lueker, *Admin Sec*
Shauna Chaityn, *Administration*
▲ **EMP:** 12 **EST:** 2008
SALES (est): 2.1MM **Privately Held**
SIC: 3541 Drilling & boring machines

Sterling Heights - Macomb County (G-15409)   GEOGRAPHIC SECTION

(G-15409)
MAGNA POWERTRAIN USA INC
Sterling Heights Division
6363 E 14 Mile Rd (48312-5804)
PHONE..................................586 264-8180
Tim Beckwith, *Branch Mgr*
EMP: 150
SALES (corp-wide): 40.8B **Privately Held**
SIC: 3714 Motor vehicle parts & accessories
HQ: Magna Powertrain Usa, Inc.
1870 Technology Dr
Troy MI 48083
248 680-4900

(G-15410)
MAN U TEC INC
Also Called: Manutec
6522 Diplomat Dr (48314-1420)
PHONE..................................586 262-4085
James Kaleniecki, *President*
Jeremy Kaleniecki, *Director*
Stacey Castillo, *Admin Sec*
EMP: 8
SQ FT: 4,000
SALES (est): 1.2MM **Privately Held**
SIC: 3599 Machine shop, jobbing & repair

(G-15411)
MANNINO TILE & MARBLE INC
Also Called: Tile Installation
38790 Hartwell Dr (48312-1327)
PHONE..................................586 978-3390
Rodney J Mannino, *President*
Kenzie Mannino, *Admin Sec*
EMP: 15
SALES: 1MM **Privately Held**
SIC: 3253 Ceramic wall & floor tile

(G-15412)
MASTER PRECISION TOOL CORP
7362 19 Mile Rd (48314-3214)
PHONE..................................586 739-3240
Douglas De Wolfe, *President*
Chuck Busuisto, *Vice Pres*
Charles Busuito, *Sales Staff*
Doug Dewolfe, *Manager*
EMP: 19 **EST:** 1978
SQ FT: 7,800
SALES (est): 3MM **Privately Held**
SIC: 3544 Punches, forming & stamping

(G-15413)
MATUSCHEK WELDING PRODUCTS INC
42378 Yearego Dr (48314-3267)
PHONE..................................586 991-2434
Gregory Barbeau, *General Mgr*
Joanne Silamianos, *Office Mgr*
Lawrence Wright, *Manager*
EMP: 3
SALES (est): 347.9K
SALES (corp-wide): 15.9MM **Privately Held**
SIC: 7692 Welding repair
PA: Matuschek MeBtechnik Gmbh
Werner-Heisenberg-Str. 14
Alsdorf 52477
240 467-60

(G-15414)
MAYCO INTERNATIONAL LLC (PA)
Also Called: Njt Enterprises LLC
42400 Merrill Rd (48314-3238)
P.O. Box 180149, Utica (48318-0149)
PHONE..................................586 803-6000
Allen L Grajek, *CFO*
Marria Saroli, *Controller*
Nick Demiro, *Mng Member*
Tim Bradley,
▲ **EMP:** 750
SQ FT: 700,000
SALES: 350MM **Privately Held**
SIC: 3089 Injection molding of plastics

(G-15415)
MB AEROSPACE STERLING HTS INC (PA)
38111 Comm Dr (48312)
PHONE..................................586 977-9200
Craig Gallagher, *CEO*
Kevin Johnston, *President*
John Kozma, *Vice Pres*
Luke Jones, *Program Mgr*
Pete Tsilimingras, *Program Mgr*
▲ **EMP:** 63
SQ FT: 30,000
SALES (est): 19.2MM **Privately Held**
WEB: www.norbertind.com
SIC: 3599 Machine shop, jobbing & repair

(G-15416)
METALSA STRUCTURAL PDTS INC
Also Called: Metalsa SA De Cv
40117 Mitchell Dr (48313-4507)
PHONE..................................248 669-3704
EMP: 3 **Privately Held**
SIC: 3714 Motor vehicle parts & accessories
HQ: Metalsa Structural Products, Inc.
29545 Hudson Dr
Novi MI 48377

(G-15417)
METRO PRINTS INC
5580 Gatewood Dr Ste 103 (48310-2228)
PHONE..................................586 979-9690
Terry Hillker, *Principal*
EMP: 14
SALES (est): 1.8MM **Privately Held**
SIC: 2752 Commercial printing, lithographic

(G-15418)
METTLE CRAFT MANUFACTURING LLC
3223 15 Mile Rd (48310-5348)
PHONE..................................586 306-8962
Katie Bigelow, *Principal*
Kathryn Bigelow, *Principal*
Danielle Deshard, *Principal*
Heidi Devroy, *Principal*
EMP: 5
SALES (est): 179.9K **Privately Held**
SIC: 3999 Manufacturing industries

(G-15419)
MGR MOLDS INC
6450 Cotter Ave (48314-2146)
PHONE..................................586 254-6020
Robert Walter, *President*
◆ **EMP:** 15
SQ FT: 12,822
SALES (est): 2.5MM **Privately Held**
WEB: www.mgrmold.com
SIC: 3544 3089 Industrial molds; injection molded finished plastic products

(G-15420)
MIBA HYDRAMECHANICA CORP
6625 Cobb Dr (48312-2625)
PHONE..................................586 264-3094
Werner Kollment, *President*
Clemens Honeder, *Managing Dir*
Emily Neiswonger, *Opers Mgr*
Bruce Rigard, *Opers Mgr*
Paul Sloan, *Safety Mgr*
◆ **EMP:** 58
SQ FT: 26,080
SALES (est): 21.6MM
SALES (corp-wide): 735.9K **Privately Held**
WEB: www.mibahmc.com
SIC: 3499 Friction material, made from powdered metal
HQ: Miba Aktiengesellschaft
Dr. Mitterbauer-StraBe 3
Laakirchen 4663
761 325-410

(G-15421)
MICHIGAN RBR & GASKET CO INC
Also Called: M R G
7447 19 Mile Rd (48314-3219)
PHONE..................................586 323-4100
Chris Hunt, *President*
EMP: 20
SALES (est): 2.8MM **Privately Held**
SIC: 3053 Gasket materials

(G-15422)
MICROPRECISION CLEANING
6145 Wall St (48312-1058)
PHONE..................................586 997-6960
Larry Roads, *President*
Dave Baumgarten, *General Mgr*
EMP: 20
SALES (est): 1.2MM **Privately Held**
SIC: 3541 Deburring machines

(G-15423)
MIDWAY GROUP LLC
Also Called: Protocon Rm
6227 Metropolitan Pkwy (48312-1023)
PHONE..................................586 264-5380
Edward C Levy Jr, *President*
Gary Lowell, *President*
Robert Scholz, *Vice Pres*
S E Weiner, *Vice Pres*
EMP: 30
SALES (est): 3.9MM
SALES (corp-wide): 368.1MM **Privately Held**
SIC: 3273 Ready-mixed concrete
PA: Edw. C. Levy Co.
9300 Dix
Dearborn MI 48120
313 429-2200

(G-15424)
MIDWEST TUBE FABRICATORS INC
36845 Metro Ct (48312-1013)
PHONE..................................586 264-9898
James Mc Carthy, *President*
Debi Cavanaugh, *General Mgr*
Victoria Mc Carthy, *Vice Pres*
Pat Macmillan, *Opers Mgr*
Kim Mills, *Bookkeeper*
▲ **EMP:** 24
SQ FT: 5,500
SALES (est): 6.8MM **Privately Held**
SIC: 3498 Tube fabricating (contract bending & shaping)

(G-15425)
MILAIR LLC
44215 Phoenix Dr (48314-1466)
PHONE..................................513 576-0123
Bruce J Burton,
EMP: 6
SALES: 5MM **Privately Held**
SIC: 3585 3621 3433 Air conditioning equipment, complete; air conditioning units, complete: domestic or industrial; motors & generators; heating equipment, except electric

(G-15426)
MOLDING CONCEPTS INC
6700 Sims Dr (48313-3727)
PHONE..................................586 264-6990
Mark Mies, *President*
EMP: 20
SQ FT: 10,000
SALES (est): 3.2MM **Privately Held**
WEB: www.moldingconcepts.com
SIC: 3089 Injection molded finished plastic products; injection molding of plastics

(G-15427)
MOR-TECH DESIGN INC (PA)
6503 19 1/2 Mile Rd (48314-1407)
PHONE..................................586 254-7982
David Clark, *President*
Christopher McEvoy, *Design Engr*
Nicholas Cadarean, *Treasurer*
EMP: 38
SQ FT: 12,000
SALES (est): 6.2MM **Privately Held**
WEB: www.mortechdesign.com
SIC: 3542 8711 Machine tools, metal forming type; mechanical engineering

(G-15428)
MOR-TECH MANUFACTURING INC
6503 19 1/2 Mile Rd (48314-1407)
PHONE..................................586 254-7982
David Clark, *President*
EMP: 38 **EST:** 1997
SALES (est): 209.8K
SALES (corp-wide): 6.2MM **Privately Held**
SIC: 3542 8711 Machine tools, metal forming type; mechanical engineering
PA: Mor-Tech Design, Inc.
6503 19 1/2 Mile Rd
Sterling Heights MI 48314
586 254-7982

(G-15429)
MSE FABRICATION LLC
6624 Burroughs Ave (48314-2135)
PHONE..................................586 991-6138
Neil Wiebe,
Margaret Wiebe,
EMP: 12
SQ FT: 130,000
SALES (est): 1.5MM **Privately Held**
SIC: 3444 Sheet metalwork

(G-15430)
MYRON ZUCKER INC
36825 Metro Ct (48312-1013)
PHONE..................................586 979-9955
Donna L Zobel, *President*
Mary Anderson, *Buyer*
Thomas J Carbone, *Treasurer*
Lauren Loudon, *Info Tech Mgr*
▼ **EMP:** 9
SQ FT: 8,000
SALES (est): 1.6MM **Privately Held**
WEB: www.myronzucker.com
SIC: 3559 Semiconductor manufacturing machinery

(G-15431)
N/C PRODUCTION & GRINDING INC
43758 Merrill Rd (48314-2172)
PHONE..................................586 731-2150
Scott Carter, *President*
EMP: 4
SQ FT: 5,600
SALES (est): 548.9K **Privately Held**
SIC: 3599 Machine shop, jobbing & repair

(G-15432)
NATIONAL CASE CORPORATION
42710 Mound Rd (48314-3254)
PHONE..................................586 726-1710
Peter Klenner, *President*
EMP: 5
SQ FT: 3,000
SALES (est): 430K **Privately Held**
WEB: www.nationalcase.net
SIC: 2542 3089 2441 2394 Carrier cases & tables, mail: except wood; boxes, plastic; packing cases, wood: nailed or lock corner; tarpaulins, fabric: made from purchased materials

(G-15433)
NATIONWIDE DESIGN INC
6605 Burroughs Ave (48314-2132)
P.O. Box 385, Howell (48844-0385)
PHONE..................................586 254-5493
EMP: 16
SQ FT: 14,000
SALES (est): 225K **Privately Held**
SIC: 3714 3711 Mfg Automotive Parts & Body Prototypes

(G-15434)
NIEDDU DRAPERY MFG
35532 Mound Rd (48310-4722)
PHONE..................................586 977-0065
Paul Nieddu, *Principal*
EMP: 3
SALES (est): 234.9K **Privately Held**
SIC: 2391 Draperies, plastic & textile: from purchased materials

(G-15435)
NIKOLIC INDUSTRIES INC
43252 Merrill Rd (48314-2162)
PHONE..................................586 254-4810
Martha Nikolic, *President*
Veliko Nikolic, *Vice Pres*
Vera Bozinovski, *Info Tech Mgr*
EMP: 20
SQ FT: 12,000
SALES (est): 2.7MM **Privately Held**
WEB: www.nikolicindustries.com
SIC: 3599 Machine shop, jobbing & repair

(G-15436)
NISSHINBO AUTOMOTIVE MFG INC
6100 19 Mile Rd (48314-2102)
PHONE..................................586 997-1000
Yukhiko Konno, *President*
EMP: 85 **Privately Held**
SIC: 3714 3441 Motor vehicle brake systems & parts; fabricated structural metal

GEOGRAPHIC SECTION
Sterling Heights - Macomb County (G-15464)

HQ: Nisshinbo Automotive Manufacturing Inc.
14187 Nisshinbo Dr
Covington GA 30014
770 787-2002

(G-15437)
NORBERT INDUSTRIES INC
38111 Commerce Dr (48312-1082)
PHONE.................................586 977-9200
Ken Brubaker, *Manager*
EMP: 7
SALES (corp-wide): 21.3MM **Privately Held**
WEB: www.norbertind.com
SIC: **3599** Machine shop, jobbing & repair
PA: Mb Aerospace Sterling Heights, Inc.
38111 Comm Dr
Sterling Heights MI 48312
586 977-9200

(G-15438)
NORTHERN PLASTICS INC
6137 Product Dr (48312-4565)
PHONE.................................586 979-7737
Philip K Truscott, *President*
EMP: 11
SALES (est): 2MM **Privately Held**
SIC: **3089** Plastic processing

(G-15439)
OLIVE VINEGAR
44230 Apple Blossom Dr (48314-1028)
PHONE.................................586 484-4700
EMP: 3
SALES (est): 118.1K **Privately Held**
SIC: **2099** Vinegar

(G-15440)
OLIVER INDUSTRIES INC
Also Called: Industrial Metal Finishing Co
6070 18 Mile Rd (48314-4202)
PHONE.................................586 977-7750
Concetta F Oliver, *President*
Philip A Oliver, *Vice Pres*
EMP: 26
SQ FT: 50,000
SALES (est): 2.2MM **Privately Held**
SIC: **3471** Finishing, metals or formed products

(G-15441)
PACIFIC TOOL & ENGINEERING LTD (PA)
6410 19 Mile Rd (48314-2109)
PHONE.................................586 737-2710
Ted Elward II, *President*
Kim Elward, *Shareholder*
EMP: 4
SQ FT: 11,600
SALES (est): 3.4MM **Privately Held**
SIC: **3544** Industrial molds

(G-15442)
PALM SWEETS LLC
Also Called: Palm Sweets Bakery & Cafe
3605 15 Mile Rd (48310-5356)
PHONE.................................586 554-7979
Suha Toma, *Principal*
Nuha Toma, *Administration*
EMP: 25
SALES (est): 979.1K **Privately Held**
SIC: **2051** Cakes, bakery: except frozen

(G-15443)
PEPSICO INC
6600 17 Mile Rd (48313-4501)
PHONE.................................586 276-4102
Erica Young, *Admin Asst*
EMP: 4 **EST:** 2017
SALES (est): 149.6K **Privately Held**
SIC: **2086** Carbonated soft drinks, bottled & canned

(G-15444)
PHOENIX COUNTERTOPS LLC
7322 19 Mile Rd (48313-3214)
PHONE.................................586 254-1450
Franklin A Holtz,
Nate Alazzolo,
EMP: 7
SQ FT: 6,000
SALES (est): 939.3K **Privately Held**
SIC: **2541** Counter & sink tops

(G-15445)
PHOTOGRAPHIC SUPPORT INC
Also Called: PSI Automotive Support Group
6210 Product Dr (48312-4566)
PHONE.................................586 264-9957
William F Beaudin Jr, *President*
Mark Linz, *Vice Pres*
Lymm Beaudin, *Admin Sec*
EMP: 5
SQ FT: 25,000
SALES: 500K **Privately Held**
SIC: **3599** Machine shop, jobbing & repair

(G-15446)
PLASTIC MOLDING DEVELOPMENT
42400 Yearego Dr (48314-3262)
PHONE.................................586 739-4500
Gary Kitts, *President*
Albie Kitts, *Vice Pres*
EMP: 4
SQ FT: 25,000
SALES (est): 770.1K **Privately Held**
WEB: www.plastic-molding-development.com
SIC: **3089** Injection molding of plastics

(G-15447)
PORTABLE FACTORY
7205 Sterling Ponds Ct (48312-5813)
PHONE.................................586 883-6843
Sorin Coman, *President*
Chris Wolfe, *CFO*
EMP: 10
SALES (est): 868.5K **Privately Held**
SIC: **3694** **8711** Automotive electrical equipment; engineering services

(G-15448)
POWER PRECISION INDUSTRIES INC
43545 Utica Rd (48314-2358)
PHONE.................................586 997-0600
Gary Churchill, *President*
Clarence Churchill, *Vice Pres*
Martha Churchill, *Admin Sec*
Benjamin Churchill, *Admin Asst*
EMP: 7
SQ FT: 28,000
SALES (est): 1.2MM **Privately Held**
WEB: www.power-analysis.com
SIC: **3599** Machine shop, jobbing & repair

(G-15449)
PRECISION LASER & MFG LLC
Also Called: Iza Design and Manufacturing
5690 18 Mile Rd (48314-4108)
PHONE.................................519 733-8422
Peter Friesen, *CEO*
EMP: 4
SALES (corp-wide): 5.6MM **Privately Held**
SIC: **3713** **8748** Truck beds; systems analysis & engineering consulting services
HQ: Precision Laser & Mfg Llc
80 Motivation Dr
Lawrenceburg TN 38464

(G-15450)
PREMIER PROTOTYPE INC
7775 18 1/2 Mile Rd (48314-3675)
PHONE.................................586 323-6114
Jim Elmhirst, *President*
Emily Meza, *General Mgr*
Betty Elmhirst, *Vice Pres*
EMP: 50
SQ FT: 26,500
SALES (est): 8.8MM **Privately Held**
WEB: www.premierprototype.com
SIC: **3469** **3441** Metal stampings; fabricated structural metal for bridges

(G-15451)
PREST SALES CO
14963 Park View Ct (48313-5771)
PHONE.................................586 566-6900
Gerald Prest, *President*
Vallen L Prest, *Vice Pres*
Vallen Prest, *Vice Pres*
Renee L Prest, *Treasurer*
EMP: 3
SALES: 700K **Privately Held**
WEB: www.prestsales.com
SIC: **5199** **2759** Advertising specialties; commercial printing

(G-15452)
PRO PRECISION INC
14178 Randall Dr (48313-3557)
PHONE.................................586 247-6160
Robert M Proszkowski, *President*
EMP: 8
SQ FT: 10,000
SALES: 800K **Privately Held**
WEB: www.proprecision.com
SIC: **3541** Numerically controlled metal cutting machine tools

(G-15453)
PROFICIENT PRODUCTS INC
6283 Millett Ave (48312-2645)
PHONE.................................586 977-8630
Joe Robinson, *President*
John Robinson, *Corp Secy*
EMP: 5 **EST:** 1977
SQ FT: 8,900
SALES (est): 900K **Privately Held**
WEB: www.proficientproducts.com
SIC: **3544** Forms (molds), for foundry & plastics working machinery

(G-15454)
PROTO GAGE INC
Also Called: Manufacturing Center
5972 Product Dr (48312-4560)
PHONE.................................586 978-2783
Michael Stanton, *President*
Jeff Potter, *Purch Mgr*
Christine Hayden, *Director*
EMP: 70
SALES (corp-wide): 20.1MM **Privately Held**
WEB: www.protogage.com
SIC: **3544** Special dies & tools
PA: Gage Proto Inc
35320 Beattie Dr
Sterling Heights MI 48312
586 979-1172

(G-15455)
PROTOTYPE CAST MFG INC
42872 Mound Rd (48314-3256)
PHONE.................................586 615-8524
William Edney, *Branch Mgr*
EMP: 5
SALES (corp-wide): 8MM **Privately Held**
WEB: www.prototypecast.com
SIC: **3363** Aluminum die-castings
PA: Prototype Cast Manufacturing, Inc.
51292 Danview Tech Ct
Shelby Township MI 48315
586 739-0180

(G-15456)
PULL-BUOY INC
6515 Cotter Ave (48314-2149)
PHONE.................................586 997-0900
Kurt Carbonero, *President*
Fred L Carbonero, *Admin Sec*
▲ **EMP:** 8
SQ FT: 15,000
SALES (est): 1MM **Privately Held**
WEB: www.gymcloset.com
SIC: **3949** Gymnasium equipment

(G-15457)
PURE HERBS LTD
33410 Sterling Ponds Blvd (48312-5808)
PHONE.................................586 446-8200
Eugene Watkins, *President*
EMP: 16
SQ FT: 16,000
SALES (est): 2.1MM **Privately Held**
WEB: www.pureherbs.com
SIC: **2087** Extracts, flavoring

(G-15458)
QUAKER CHEMICAL CORPORATION
41111 Van Dyke Ave (48314-3654)
PHONE.................................586 826-6454
Jennifer Rzeszewski, *Manager*
EMP: 3
SALES (corp-wide): 867.5MM **Publicly Held**
SIC: **7537** **3492** Automotive transmission repair shops; fluid power valves & hose fittings
PA: Quaker Chemical Corporation
1 Quaker Park
Conshohocken PA 19428
610 832-4000

(G-15459)
QUALITY INSPECTIONS INC
7563 19 Mile Rd (48314-3222)
PHONE.................................586 323-6135
Norman Soeder, *President*
Jim Lama, *Vice Pres*
EMP: 4
SALES: 495K **Privately Held**
SIC: **3711** Automobile bodies, passenger car, not including engine, etc.

(G-15460)
QUANTUM MOLD & ENGINEERING LLC
35700 Stanley Dr (48312-2660)
PHONE.................................586 276-0100
Jason B Bojan, *Owner*
Matt Tarnowsky, *Accounts Mgr*
Tony Andren,
EMP: 11
SQ FT: 10,000
SALES (est): 2.6MM **Privately Held**
SIC: **3559** **3544** Plastics working machinery; special dies, tools, jigs & fixtures

(G-15461)
RAVE COMPUTER ASSOCIATION INC
7171 Sterling Ponds Ct (48312-5813)
PHONE.................................586 939-8230
Frederick Darter, *CEO*
Tony Scicluna, *Vice Pres*
Tad Bilby, *Engineer*
Tony Miller, *Accounts Mgr*
Mollie Minsel, *Accounts Mgr*
EMP: 25
SQ FT: 35,000
SALES (est): 22.2MM **Privately Held**
WEB: www.rave.net
SIC: **5045** **5065** **3571** **3572** Computers; electronic parts; electronic computers; computer storage devices

(G-15462)
RAYCO MANUFACTURING INC
5520 Bridgewood Dr (48310-2217)
PHONE.................................586 795-2884
Douglas Cole, *President*
EMP: 14
SQ FT: 6,400
SALES (est): 3.1MM **Privately Held**
SIC: **3545** **3829** Precision tools, machinists'; measuring & controlling devices

(G-15463)
REKLEIN PLASTICS INCORPORATED
Also Called: Resin Services
42130 Mound Rd (48314-3152)
PHONE.................................586 739-8850
Americo Valente, *President*
Joe Frank, *Engineer*
EMP: 8 **EST:** 1975
SQ FT: 14,750
SALES (est): 1.5MM **Privately Held**
WEB: www.resinservices-reklein.com
SIC: **3089** **3086** **2821** Panels, building: plastic; plastics foam products; plastics materials & resins

(G-15464)
RELIANT INDUSTRIES INC
6119 15 Mile Rd (48312-4503)
PHONE.................................586 275-0479
Donald Zack, *President*
David Winfield, *Vice Pres*
EMP: 20
SQ FT: 18,000
SALES (est): 4MM **Privately Held**
SIC: **3469** **3465** Stamping metal for the trade; automotive stampings

Sterling Heights - Macomb County (G-15465)

(G-15465)
RESIN SERVICES INC
5959 18 1/2 Mile Rd (48314-3114)
PHONE...................586 254-6770
Americo Valente, *President*
EMP: 10
SQ FT: 12,000
SALES: 2MM **Privately Held**
WEB: www.resinservices.com
SIC: 2821 Epoxy resins

(G-15466)
RESPONSE WELDING INC
40785 Brentwood Dr (48310-2214)
PHONE...................586 795-8090
Robert Shepherd, *President*
Mike Sobosky, *Train & Dev Mgr*
EMP: 6
SALES: 800K **Privately Held**
SIC: 7692 Automotive welding

(G-15467)
REX PRINTING COMPANY
7472 19 Mile Rd (48314-3218)
PHONE...................586 323-4002
Theresa M Noechel, *President*
Michael Donahue, *Vice Pres*
EMP: 6
SQ FT: 20,000
SALES (est): 875.9K **Privately Held**
SIC: 2752 Commercial printing, offset

(G-15468)
RICHCOAT LLC
40573 Brentwood Dr (48310-2210)
PHONE...................586 978-1311
Timothy Richardson,
Jeffery M Scott,
EMP: 23
SQ FT: 14,000
SALES (est): 1.6MM **Privately Held**
SIC: 3479 3471 Coating of metals & formed products; plating & polishing

(G-15469)
RICHELIEU AMERICA LTD (HQ)
Also Called: Chair City Supply
7021 Sterling Ponds Ct (48312-5809)
PHONE...................586 264-1240
Richard Lord, *President*
Marion Kloibhofer, *General Mgr*
Randy Roach, *General Mgr*
Joselin Proteau, *Chairman*
Antoine Auclair, *Vice Pres*
◆ **EMP:** 35
SALES: 1B
SALES (corp-wide): 772.8MM **Privately Held**
SIC: 5072 5031 2435 Builders' hardware; kitchen cabinets; panels, hardwood plywood
PA: Richelieu Hardware Ltd
7900 Boul Henri-Bourassa O Bureau 200
Saint-Laurent QC H4S 1
514 336-4144

(G-15470)
RING SCREW LLC (DH)
6125 18 Mile Rd (48314-4205)
PHONE...................586 997-5600
Patrick Paige, *Mng Member*
▲ **EMP:** 83
SALES (est): 64.6MM
SALES (corp-wide): 30.9MM **Privately Held**
SIC: 3532 3452 Stamping mill machinery (mining machinery); bolts, nuts, rivets & washers
HQ: Acument Global Technologies, Inc.
6125 18 Mile Rd
Sterling Heights MI 48312
586 254-3900

(G-15471)
RITE TOOL COMPANY INC
36740 Metro Ct (48312-1010)
PHONE...................586 264-1900
Steven Berger, *President*
EMP: 9
SALES (est): 1.2MM **Privately Held**
WEB: www.loop-ventures.com
SIC: 3599 Machine shop, jobbing & repair

(G-15472)
RITE WAY ASPHALT INC
Also Called: Patch Master Services
6699 16 Mile Rd Ste B (48312-1004)
PHONE...................586 264-1020
EMP: 5 **EST:** 1987
SALES: 500K **Privately Held**
SIC: 2951 Mfg Asphalt Mixtures/Blocks

(G-15473)
RIVAS INC (PA)
12146 Monsbrook Dr (48312-1343)
PHONE...................586 566-0326
Evangelina Young, *CEO*
Bill Young, *President*
Peer Larson, *Vice Pres*
Randy Meder, *Vice Pres*
Yvette Young, *Treasurer*
▲ **EMP:** 60
SQ FT: 32,000
SALES (est): 10.1MM **Privately Held**
WEB: www.rivasinc.com
SIC: 3714 Motor vehicle parts & accessories

(G-15474)
RJ ACQUISITION CORP
Also Called: Rj USA
5585 Gatewood Dr (48310-2227)
PHONE...................586 268-2300
Giacomo Iuculano, *CEO*
Roco Vella, *General Mgr*
▲ **EMP:** 23 **EST:** 1955
SQ FT: 17,500
SALES: 4MM
SALES (corp-wide): 48.9MM **Privately Held**
SIC: 3469 Machine parts, stamped or pressed metal
PA: R.J. Srl
Via Per Caluso 31
San Giorgio Canavese TO 10090
012 445-211

(G-15475)
RK TOOL INC (PA)
44443 Phoenix Dr Ste B (48314-1468)
PHONE...................586 731-5640
Robert Keyes, *President*
Judith Keyes, *Principal*
EMP: 4
SQ FT: 3,500
SALES: 688K **Privately Held**
SIC: 3544 Special dies, tools, jigs & fixtures

(G-15476)
ROBOVENT PRODUCTS GROUP INC (HQ)
37900 Mound Rd (48310-4132)
PHONE...................586 698-1800
John Reid, *President*
John Botti, *Research*
Missy Carr-Dudas, *Hum Res Coord*
Frank Cea-It, *Marketing Staff*
Fred Hughes, *Manager*
◆ **EMP:** 35
SQ FT: 50,000
SALES (est): 30MM
SALES (corp-wide): 3.6MM **Privately Held**
SIC: 3564 5075 Air cleaning systems; air pollution control equipment & supplies
PA: Air Filtration Holdings, Llc
900 N Michigan Ave # 1800
Chicago IL 60611
312 649-5666

(G-15477)
ROCKSTAR DIGITAL INC
Also Called: Rockstar Group
6520 Cotter Ave (48314-2148)
PHONE...................888 808-5868
Robinder Dhillon, *President*
Shubhpreet Dhillon, *Shareholder*
EMP: 12 **EST:** 2013
SQ FT: 8,000
SALES (est): 3.5MM **Privately Held**
SIC: 3993 3672 Signs & advertising specialties; printed circuit boards

(G-15478)
RONAL INDUSTRIES INC
6615 19 Mile Rd (48314-2117)
PHONE...................248 616-9691
Dolores Fishman, *CEO*
Joe Busch, *President*
EMP: 15 **EST:** 1967
SQ FT: 17,200
SALES (est): 5.8MM **Privately Held**
WEB: www.ronalind.com
SIC: 3795 3564 3599 Specialized tank components, military; blowers & fans; air intake filters, internal combustion engine, except auto

(G-15479)
ROSE-A-LEE TECHNOLOGIES INC
Also Called: Ral Technologies
6550 Sims Dr (48313-3751)
PHONE...................586 799-4555
Patricia Elmhirst, *President*
Jennifer Howard, *Vice Pres*
EMP: 3 **EST:** 2013
SQ FT: 10,000
SALES (est): 291.7K **Privately Held**
SIC: 3469 3714 Metal stampings; motor vehicle body components & frame

(G-15480)
ROTTMAN MANUFACTURING GROUP
35566 Mound Rd (48310-4722)
PHONE...................586 693-5676
Raymond Rottmann, *Principal*
EMP: 4
SALES (est): 191.7K **Privately Held**
SIC: 3999 Manufacturing industries

(G-15481)
RUCCI FORGED WHEELS INC (PA)
Also Called: Forgetek
2003 E 14 Mile Rd (48310-5905)
PHONE...................248 577-3500
Andy Franko, *CEO*
Nick Abouna, *President*
EMP: 5
SQ FT: 10,000
SALES (est): 944.5K **Privately Held**
SIC: 3312 Wheels

(G-15482)
RUSTIC CKING DSIGNS STRLNG HTS
5352 Northlawn Dr (48310-6623)
PHONE...................586 795-4897
Jeffrey Lowry, *Owner*
Andrea Lowry, *CFO*
EMP: 3
SALES (est): 236.7K **Privately Held**
SIC: 3556 Ovens, bakery

(G-15483)
SAINT-GOBAIN SEKURIT USA INC (DH)
35801 Mound Rd (48310-4731)
PHONE...................586 264-1072
Christopher McRae, *Finance*
EMP: 10
SQ FT: 8,600
SALES (est): 950.8K
SALES (corp-wide): 215.9MM **Privately Held**
SIC: 3211 Flat glass
HQ: Saint-Gobain Glass Corporation
20 Moores Rd
Malvern PA 19355
484 595-9430

(G-15484)
SANKUER COMPOSITE TECH INC
36850 Metro Ct (48312-1012)
PHONE...................586 264-1880
Patrick Sankuer, *President*
Timothy Doty II, *Director*
EMP: 17 **EST:** 2012
SALES (est): 2.4MM **Privately Held**
SIC: 3624 Fibers, carbon & graphite

(G-15485)
SAS AUTOMOTIVE USA INC (HQ)
Also Called: Sas Automotive Systems
42555 Merrill Rd (48314-3241)
PHONE...................248 606-1152
Wolfgang Braun, *CEO*
Raymond Chizmadia, *Engineer*
Francisco Alcalde, *CFO*
▲ **EMP:** 40
SQ FT: 110,000
SALES: 15MM
SALES (corp-wide): 3.4B **Privately Held**
SIC: 3714 3711 Motor vehicle parts & accessories; automobile assembly, including specialty automobiles
PA: Sas Autosystemtechnik Gmbh & Co. Kg
Siemensallee 84
Karlsruhe 76187
721 350-550

(G-15486)
SCHROTH ENTERPRISES INC
40736 Brentwood Dr (48310-2212)
PHONE...................586 939-0770
James L Schroth, *Manager*
EMP: 10
SALES (corp-wide): 3.4MM **Privately Held**
SIC: 3496 Woven wire products
PA: Schroth Enterprises Inc
95 Tonnacour Pl
Grosse Pointe Farms MI 48236
586 759-4240

(G-15487)
SCOTTS COMPANY LLC
6575 Arrow Dr (48314-1413)
PHONE...................586 254-6849
Mike Brelinski, *Branch Mgr*
EMP: 60
SALES (corp-wide): 2.6B **Publicly Held**
WEB: www.scottscompany.com
SIC: 2873 Fertilizers: natural (organic), except compost
HQ: The Scotts Company Llc
14111 Scottslawn Rd
Marysville OH 43040
937 644-0011

(G-15488)
SELECTOR SPLINE PRODUCTS CO
6576 Diplomat Dr (48314-1420)
PHONE...................586 254-4020
Thomas P Tabaka, *President*
Gregory J Shalagan, *Vice Pres*
EMP: 10
SQ FT: 5,000
SALES (est): 1.1MM **Privately Held**
WEB: www.selectorspline.com
SIC: 3545 Precision tools, machinists'; gauges (machine tool accessories)

(G-15489)
SEOUL INTERNATIONAL INC
40622 Mound Rd (48310-2240)
PHONE...................586 275-2494
Anthony Chang, *President*
EMP: 4
SALES (est): 450.4K **Privately Held**
SIC: 3911 Jewelry, precious metal

(G-15490)
SERAPID INC
Also Called: Serapid Scenic Technologies
34100 Mound Rd (48310-6612)
PHONE...................586 274-0774
Said Lounis, *President*
Bruce Downer, *Project Mgr*
Denis Pronin, *Project Mgr*
William Goolsby, *Mfg Mgr*
Eric Mackey, *Materials Mgr*
▲ **EMP:** 18
SQ FT: 13,000
SALES (est): 4.6MM **Privately Held**
SIC: 3625 5072 Actuators, industrial; chains

(G-15491)
SERRA SPRING & MFG LLC
7515 19 Mile Rd (48314-3222)
PHONE...................586 932-2202
Sarah Balkisson, *CEO*
EMP: 5
SQ FT: 17,000
SALES: 1MM **Privately Held**
SIC: 3495 5051 5719 Mechanical springs, precision; stampings; metal; lighting, lamps & accessories

GEOGRAPHIC SECTION

Sterling Heights - Macomb County (G-15518)

(G-15492)
SESCO PRODUCTS GROUP INC
40549 Brentwood Dr (48310-2210)
PHONE..................586 979-4400
John C Coe, *President*
EMP: 70
SQ FT: 20,000
SALES (est): 6.3MM
SALES (corp-wide): 25.6MM **Privately Held**
WEB: www.cpec.com
SIC: 3545 Machine tool attachments & accessories
PA: Coe Press Equipment Corporation
40549 Brentwood Dr
Sterling Heights MI 48310
586 979-4400

(G-15493)
SET ENTERPRISES INC (PA)
38600 Van Dy (48312)
PHONE..................586 573-3600
Sidney Taylor, *President*
Wayne McVeigh, *Engineer*
Jeff Patterson, *Manager*
Antoinette Turner, *Manager*
Donna Taylor, *Exec Dir*
EMP: 20
SALES (est): 69.7MM **Privately Held**
SIC: 7389 3465 3544 3312 Metal cutting services; automotive stampings; special dies, tools, jigs & fixtures; blast furnaces & steel mills

(G-15494)
SET ENTERPRISES OF MI INC (HQ)
38600 Van Dyke Ave # 325 (48312-1170)
PHONE..................586 573-3600
Sid Etaylor, *Chairman*
Ken Pachla, *CFO*
EMP: 140
SQ FT: 4,000
SALES (est): 43.9MM
SALES (corp-wide): 69.7MM **Privately Held**
WEB: www.michsteel.com
SIC: 3444 3544 7692 3469 Metal housings, enclosures, casings & other containers; special dies, tools, jigs & fixtures; welding repair; metal stampings
PA: Set Enterprises, Inc.
38600 Van Dy
Sterling Heights MI 48312
586 573-3600

(G-15495)
SHELBY AUTO TRIM INC
Also Called: Shelby Trim Auto Uphl Cnvrtibl
40430 Mound Rd (48310-2243)
PHONE..................586 939-9090
Daniel A Kreucher, *President*
Teresa Kreucher, *Corp Secy*
EMP: 12
SQ FT: 10,000
SALES (est): 890K **Privately Held**
WEB: www.shelbytrim.com
SIC: 7532 2394 Upholstery & trim shop, automotive; convertible tops, canvas or boat: from purchased materials

(G-15496)
SHELER CORPORATION
37885 Commerce Dr (48312-1001)
PHONE..................586 979-8560
Gary L Burnash, *President*
Eddie Raffoul, *Sales Staff*
EMP: 18
SQ FT: 8,000
SALES (est): 770K **Privately Held**
WEB: www.shelercorp.com
SIC: 3567 Induction heating equipment

(G-15497)
SHUERT INDUSTRIES INC
Also Called: Shuert Technologies
6600 Dobry Dr (48314-1425)
PHONE..................586 254-4590
Lyle Shuert, *Ch of Bd*
Matthew C Shuert, *President*
Joyce Shuert, *Corp Secy*
Paul G Shuert, *Vice Pres*
Sharon Hammond, *Purch Mgr*
▼ **EMP:** 200 EST: 1960
SQ FT: 250,000
SALES (est): 68MM **Privately Held**
WEB: www.shuert.com
SIC: 3089 Thermoformed finished plastic products

(G-15498)
SIGNZ LLC
40307 Denbigh Dr (48310-6942)
PHONE..................586 940-9891
Mohammad Qureshi, *Opers Staff*
Zahida Qureshi, *Mng Member*
EMP: 3
SALES: 75K **Privately Held**
SIC: 3993 Neon signs

(G-15499)
SINK RITE DIE COMPANY
6170 Wall St (48312-1071)
PHONE..................586 268-0000
Alfred C Harris, *President*
Sandra Harris, *Corp Secy*
Kirk Harris, *Vice Pres*
EMP: 13
SQ FT: 16,000
SALES (est): 2.2MM **Privately Held**
SIC: 3544 Special dies & tools

(G-15500)
SME HOLDINGS LLC
Also Called: Sterling Manufacturing & Engrg
6750 19 Mile Rd (48314-2112)
PHONE..................586 254-5310
Bill Davis,
EMP: 25
SALES (est): 892.5K **Privately Held**
SIC: 3545 Precision measuring tools

(G-15501)
SMEKO INC
6750 19 Mile Rd (48314-2112)
PHONE..................586 254-5310
EMP: 25
SQ FT: 18,000
SALES (est): 5.9MM **Privately Held**
SIC: 3545 3544 Mfg Machine Tool Accessories Mfg Dies/Tools/Jigs/Fixtures

(G-15502)
SODECIA AUTO DETROIT CORP
Also Called: Sodecia North America
42600 Merrill Rd (48314-3242)
PHONE..................586 759-2200
Rob Gilkes, *Branch Mgr*
EMP: 50 **Privately Held**
WEB: www.azautomotive.com
SIC: 3465 Body parts, automobile: stamped metal
HQ: Sodecia Automotive Detroit Corp.
969 Chicago Rd
Troy MI 48083
586 759-2200

(G-15503)
SOFTWARE ADVANTAGE CONSULTING
8814 Pemberton Dr (48312-1967)
PHONE..................586 264-5632
David P Miller, *President*
EMP: 4
SALES: 125K **Privately Held**
SIC: 7379 7372 Computer related consulting services; application computer software

(G-15504)
SPARTAN TOOL SALES INC
13715 Heritage Rd (48312-6531)
PHONE..................586 268-1556
Bill Ozinian, *President*
Judy Ozinian, *Vice Pres*
EMP: 15
SALES (est): 2MM **Privately Held**
WEB: www.spartantoolsales.com
SIC: 3545 Gauges (machine tool accessories)

(G-15505)
SPECULAR LLC
6210 Product Dr (48312-4566)
PHONE..................248 680-1720
Marc Radecky, *Partner*
EMP: 3
SALES: 250K **Privately Held**
SIC: 3479 Painting of metal products

(G-15506)
SPLINE SPECIALIST INC
7346 19 Mile Rd (48314-3214)
PHONE..................586 731-4569
Thomas Kassin, *President*
EMP: 4 EST: 1994
SALES (est): 477.3K **Privately Held**
SIC: 3542 Spline rolling machines

(G-15507)
SSI TECHNOLOGY INC
35715 Stanley Dr (48312-2661)
PHONE..................248 582-0600
Robert A Bloom, *President*
Gary Kippe, *President*
Lou Zagone, *Mfg Staff*
EMP: 55
SQ FT: 12,500
SALES (est): 19MM **Privately Held**
WEB: www.ssi-tek.com
SIC: 3829 3629 3823 3625 Aircraft & motor vehicle measurement equipment; gauges, motor vehicle: oil pressure, water temperature; power conversion units, a.c. to d.c.: static-electric; industrial instrmnts msrmnt display/control process variable; relays & industrial controls

(G-15508)
STAHLS INC (PA)
Also Called: Groupe Stahl
6353 E 14 Mile Rd (48312-5804)
P.O. Box 628, Saint Clair Shores (48080-0628)
PHONE..................800 478-2457
Ted Stahl, *CEO*
Rich Ellsworth, *Vice Pres*
Tammy Duffiney, *Purchasing*
Jon Deimel, *CFO*
Brent Kisha, *Sales Staff*
◆ **EMP:** 65
SQ FT: 71,000
SALES (est): 30.5MM **Privately Held**
WEB: www.stahls.com
SIC: 2891 5045 3585 2399 Adhesives; computers, peripherals & software; computer software; evaporative condensers, heat transfer equipment; emblems, badges & insignia: from purchased materials; pleating & stitching; finishing plants, manmade fiber & silk fabrics

(G-15509)
STANDARD COMPONENTS LLC
Also Called: SCI Consulting
44208 Phoenix Dr (48314-1465)
PHONE..................586 323-9700
James Wilkins Jr, *President*
David Jackson, *Vice Pres*
Joe Lucent, *Vice Pres*
John Kalist, *Plant Supt*
Mike Gottschling, *QC Mgr*
▼ **EMP:** 58
SQ FT: 35,000
SALES (est): 14.7MM **Privately Held**
WEB: www.scigage.com
SIC: 3544 Special dies & tools

(G-15510)
STECHSCHULTE/WEGERLY AG LLC
Also Called: Endura Coatings
42250 Yearego Dr (48314-3260)
PHONE..................586 739-0101
Michael Stechschulte,
EMP: 17
SQ FT: 10,000
SALES (est): 2.7MM **Privately Held**
WEB: www.enduracoatings.com
SIC: 3479 Coating of metals & formed products

(G-15511)
STERLING DIAGNOSTICS INC
36645 Metro Ct (48312-1009)
P.O. Box 817 (48311-0817)
PHONE..................586 979-2141
Eli Santa Maria, *President*
Lou Maria, *Vice Pres*
Dave Callender, *CFO*
EMP: 14
SQ FT: 5,000
SALES (est): 2.5MM **Privately Held**
WEB: www.sterlingdiagnostics.com
SIC: 2819 Inorganic acids, except nitric & phosphoric; lithium compounds, inorganic

(G-15512)
STERLING METAL WORKS LLC
Also Called: Liberty Cast Products
35705 Beattie Dr (48312-2619)
PHONE..................586 977-9577
Amy Jeric, *Office Mgr*
Rajiv Pithadia, *Mng Member*
EMP: 5
SQ FT: 11,200
SALES (est): 2MM **Privately Held**
SIC: 3365 3366 Aluminum & aluminum-based alloy castings; copper foundries

(G-15513)
STONEBRIDGE INDUSTRIES INC
Also Called: Mayco Plastics
42400 Merrill Rd (48314-3238)
PHONE..................586 323-0348
Ed Wright, *President*
Robert Roberts, *COO*
Mark Blaufuss, *CFO*
▲ **EMP:** 771 EST: 1996
SALES (est): 77.3MM **Privately Held**
WEB: www.mayco-mi.com
SIC: 3496 3462 3451 Miscellaneous fabricated wire products; iron & steel forgings; screw machine products
PA: Kirtland Capital Partners L.P.
3201 Entp Pkwy Ste 200
Beachwood OH 44122

(G-15514)
STRIVE ORTHTICS PRSTHETICS LLC
Also Called: Strive O&P
41400 Dequindre Rd # 105 (48314-3763)
PHONE..................586 803-4325
Matthew McEwin, *Principal*
EMP: 3 EST: 2017
SALES (est): 231.2K **Privately Held**
SIC: 3842 Orthopedic appliances

(G-15515)
SUMMIT PLASTIC MOLDING II INC
5985 Wall St (48312-1074)
PHONE..................586 977-8300
Raymond Kalinowski, *Branch Mgr*
EMP: 6
SALES (est): 437.3K **Privately Held**
SIC: 3089 Molding primary plastic; injection molding of plastics
PA: Summit Plastic Molding Ii, Inc.
51340 Celeste
Shelby Township MI 48315

(G-15516)
SUPERIOR MOLD SERVICES INC
6100 15 Mile Rd (48312-4502)
PHONE..................586 264-9570
Gordon Bishop, *President*
Cheyrl Conn, *Controller*
EMP: 16
SQ FT: 13,000
SALES: 2.5MM **Privately Held**
WEB: www.superiorairflow.com
SIC: 3544 Forms (molds), for foundry & plastics working machinery

(G-15517)
SWEET & SWEETER INC
Also Called: Sweet & Sweeter By Linda
4059 17 Mile Rd (48310-6837)
PHONE..................586 977-9338
Fouad Juka, *President*
EMP: 4
SALES (est): 179.8K **Privately Held**
SIC: 5461 2051 Cakes; cakes, pies & pastries

(G-15518)
T J K INC
Also Called: Sir Speedy
39370 Bella Vista Dr (48313-5214)
PHONE..................586 731-9639
Timothy J Knapps, *President*
Bob Richardson, *Telecomm Dir*
Barbara Knapps, *Admin Sec*
EMP: 5
SQ FT: 2,400

Sterling Heights - Macomb County (G-15519)

SALES: 480K **Privately Held**
WEB: www.tjk.com
SIC: **2752** 2791 2789 2759 Commercial printing, lithographic; typesetting; bookbinding & related work; commercial printing; secretarial & court reporting

(G-15519)
TAPESTRY INC
14000 Lakeside Cir (48313-1320)
PHONE..............................631 724-8066
Rose Lichocki, *Sales Associate*
EMP: 15
SALES (corp-wide): 6B **Publicly Held**
WEB: www.coach.com
SIC: **3171** Handbags, women's
PA: Tapestry, Inc.
10 Hudson Yards
New York NY 10001
212 594-1850

(G-15520)
TARUS PRODUCTS INC (PA)
38100 Commerce Dr (48312-1006)
PHONE..............................586 977-1400
Douglas J Greig, *President*
Carolyn Greig, *Vice Pres*
Steve Ponke, *Purchasing*
Lee Barkhaus, *Manager*
Brad Kleinow, *Manager*
▲ EMP: 100
SQ FT: 128,000
SALES (est): 24.4MM **Privately Held**
WEB: www.tarus.com
SIC: **3541** Electrical discharge erosion machines

(G-15521)
TD INDUSTRIAL COVERINGS INC
Also Called: T D I C
6220 18 1/2 Mile Rd (48314-3111)
PHONE..............................586 731-2080
Tommaso Dandreta, *CEO*
Sharon D'Andreta-Walle, *President*
Mark Dandreta, *President*
Phillipa Dandreta, *Corp Secy*
▲ EMP: 85
SQ FT: 34,000
SALES (est): 11.5MM **Privately Held**
WEB: www.tdic.com
SIC: **2394** Canvas covers & drop cloths

(G-15522)
TENNESSEE FABRICATORS LLC
35900 Mound Rd (48310-4730)
PHONE..............................615 793-4444
Brian Jardine, *Mng Member*
Lanny Jardine,
Nicholas Jardine,
Nancy Wade,
EMP: 8 EST: 2013
SALES (est): 765.8K **Privately Held**
SIC: **3449** Bars, concrete reinforcing: fabricated steel

(G-15523)
TEST PRODUCTS INCORPORATED
41255 Technology Park Dr (48314-4102)
PHONE..............................586 997-9600
David Bruszewski, *President*
Richard Gillies, *Vice Pres*
Dave Coatney, *Safety Mgr*
Rob Treend, *Purch Mgr*
Bob Ramseyer, *Engineer*
EMP: 30
SQ FT: 18,000
SALES (est): 8MM **Privately Held**
WEB: www.testprod.com
SIC: **3825** Test equipment for electronic & electric measurement

(G-15524)
THREAD-CRAFT INC
43643 Utica Rd (48314-2359)
P.O. Box 220 (48311-0220)
PHONE..............................586 323-1116
Dennis Johnson, *President*
John Fauer, *Purchasing*
Derek Polsdorfer, *Regl Sales Mgr*
Celeste Johnson, *Info Tech Mgr*
▲ EMP: 70 EST: 1958
SQ FT: 27,000

SALES: 8.5MM **Privately Held**
SIC: **3599** 3545 Machine shop, jobbing & repair; machine tool accessories

(G-15525)
TOOL-CRAFT INDUSTRIES INC
6101 Product Dr (48312-4565)
PHONE..............................248 549-0077
Chester A Wilson Jr, *President*
EMP: 18
SQ FT: 8,160
SALES (est): 3.5MM **Privately Held**
SIC: **3545** 5084 Cutting tools for machine tools; industrial machinery & equipment

(G-15526)
TOTAL HEALTH COLON CARE
38245 Mound Rd E (48310-3466)
PHONE..............................586 268-5444
Diane Simmons, *Owner*
EMP: 3
SALES (est): 278.9K **Privately Held**
WEB: www.totalhealthcoloncare.com
SIC: **3842** 8099 Hydrotherapy equipment; health & allied services

(G-15527)
TRANSFORM AUTOMOTIVE LLC (DH)
7026 Sterling Ponds Ct (48312-5809)
PHONE..............................586 826-8500
Teds Ens, *President*
Thomas Meier, *Vice Pres*
Shannon Schneider, *QC Mgr*
Willey Zhang, *Engineer*
Steven Swieczkowski, *Manager*
▲ EMP: 102
SQ FT: 75,000
SALES (est): 49.2MM
SALES (corp-wide): 2.4B **Privately Held**
WEB: www.transformauto.com
SIC: **3714** Motor vehicle transmissions, drive assemblies & parts
HQ: Means Industries, Inc.
3715 E Washington Rd
Saginaw MI 48601
989 754-1433

(G-15528)
TRANSPAK INC
Also Called: GP Strategies C/O Transpak
34400 Mound Rd (48310-5757)
PHONE..............................586 264-2064
Fax: 586 795-2126
EMP: 40
SQ FT: 25,000
SALES (est): 3.4MM **Privately Held**
SIC: **4225** 5013 3714 3086 General Warehse/Storage Whol Auto Parts/Supplies Mfg Motor Vehicle Parts Mfg Plastic Foam Prdts

(G-15529)
TRI-STAR TOOLING LLC
Also Called: Tri-Star Engineering
35640 Beattie Dr (48312-2616)
PHONE..............................586 978-0435
Richard Ignagni, *Mng Member*
Rick Ignagni, *Software Engr*
EMP: 13
SQ FT: 11,300
SALES (est): 2MM **Privately Held**
WEB: www.tristarengineering.com
SIC: **3544** 3543 7389 Industrial molds; jigs & fixtures; industrial patterns; inspection & testing services

(G-15530)
TRIPLE TOOL
40715 Brentwood Dr (48310-2214)
PHONE..............................586 795-1785
Ursula Czachor, *Owner*
EMP: 15
SALES (est): 1.1MM **Privately Held**
SIC: **5251** 3542 Tools; machine tools, metal forming type

(G-15531)
TUNKERS INC
Also Called: Tunkers-Mastech
36200 Mound Rd (48310-4737)
PHONE..............................734 744-5990
Olaf Tuenkers, *President*
Gary Gavioli, *Vice Pres*
Christian Heyer, *Vice Pres*
George Owens, *Opers Mgr*

Todd Moriarty, *Sales Engr*
▲ EMP: 25
SALES (est): 5MM
SALES (corp-wide): 177.9K **Privately Held**
SIC: **3711** Automobile assembly, including specialty automobiles
HQ: Tunkers Maschinenbau Gmbh
Am Rosenkothen 4-12
Ratingen 40880
210 245-170

(G-15532)
UMIX DISSOULTION CORP
6050 15 Mile Rd (48312-4500)
PHONE..............................586 446-9950
Tak Mimura, *President*
▲ EMP: 8
SALES (est): 997.6K **Privately Held**
SIC: **3423** 7389 Hand & edge tools; hand tool designers
PA: Umix Co., Ltd.
2-37-1, Kasugakitamachi
Hirakata OSK 573-0

(G-15533)
UNITED MACHINING INC (DH)
6300 18 1/2 Mile Rd (48314-3112)
PHONE..............................586 323-4300
Edward G Frackowiak, *CEO*
▲ EMP: 180
SQ FT: 62,000
SALES (est): 29.2MM
SALES (corp-wide): 526.8MM **Privately Held**
WEB: www.unitedmachining.com
SIC: **3714** Motor vehicle parts & accessories
HQ: Wescast Industries Inc
150 Savannah Oaks Dr
Brantford ON N3V 1
519 750-0000

(G-15534)
UNIVERSAL TL EQP & CONTRLS INC
Also Called: Utec
42409 Van Dyke Ave (48314-3200)
PHONE..............................586 268-4380
Stephanie Serra-Bartolotta, *President*
Bill Bartolotta, *Vice Pres*
Courtney Rushing, *Admin Asst*
EMP: 98
SQ FT: 200,000
SALES (est): 17.5MM **Privately Held**
SIC: **3569** Robots, assembly line: industrial & commercial

(G-15535)
US FARATHANE HOLDINGS CORP
38000 Mound Rd (48310-3461)
PHONE..............................586 726-1200
Steve Macdko, *Principal*
EMP: 150
SALES (corp-wide): 876MM **Privately Held**
SIC: **3089** Injection molding of plastics
PA: U.S. Farathane Holdings Corp.
11650 Park Ct
Shelby Township MI 48315
586 726-1200

(G-15536)
US FARATHANE HOLDINGS CORP
6543 Arrow Dr (48314-1413)
PHONE..............................586 991-6922
Karl Brunsman, *Principal*
EMP: 30
SALES (corp-wide): 876MM **Privately Held**
SIC: **3714** Motor vehicle parts & accessories
PA: U.S. Farathane Holdings Corp.
11650 Park Ct
Shelby Township MI 48315
586 726-1200

(G-15537)
US FARATHANE HOLDINGS CORP
Also Called: US Farathane Merrill Plant
42155 Merrill Rd (48314-3233)
PHONE..............................586 685-4000

John Lojewski, *Principal*
Jim Curtis, *Safety Mgr*
Kevin Baxter, *Info Tech Mgr*
EMP: 50
SALES (corp-wide): 876MM **Privately Held**
SIC: **3089** Injection molding of plastics
PA: U.S. Farathane Holdings Corp.
11650 Park Ct
Shelby Township MI 48315
586 726-1200

(G-15538)
VAN PELT CORPORATION (PA)
Also Called: Service Steel Company
36155 Mound Rd (48310-4736)
PHONE..............................313 365-3600
Roger Van Pelt, *CEO*
A Joyce Pelt, *Chairman*
Charles Debeau, *Vice Pres*
Chuck Debeau, *Vice Pres*
Scott Streeter, *Maint Spvr*
▲ EMP: 8 EST: 1920
SQ FT: 83,000
SALES (est): 30.5MM **Privately Held**
WEB: www.servicesteel.com
SIC: **3441** 5051 Fabricated structural metal; metals service centers & offices

(G-15539)
VILLAGE CABINET SHOPPE INC
37975 Commerce Dr (48312-1003)
PHONE..............................586 264-6464
Richard Breitenbeck, *President*
Kelly Breitenbeck, *Admin Sec*
EMP: 9 EST: 1971
SQ FT: 5,000
SALES: 1.1MM **Privately Held**
SIC: **1751** 2434 2541 Cabinet building & installation; wood kitchen cabinets; counter & sink tops

(G-15540)
VINCE KRSTEVSKI
Also Called: Vancho Tool and Engineering
43450 Merrill Rd (48314-2166)
PHONE..............................586 739-7600
Vince Krstevski, *Owner*
EMP: 4
SQ FT: 7,100
SALES: 300K **Privately Held**
SIC: **3599** Machine shop, jobbing & repair

(G-15541)
VISOR FRAMES LLC
6400 Sterling Dr N Ste B (48312-4514)
PHONE..............................586 864-6058
Salvatore Dinello, *Mng Member*
EMP: 10
SALES (est): 655.2K **Privately Held**
SIC: **3465** Body parts, automobile: stamped metal

(G-15542)
WALKER WIRE (ISPAT) INC
42744 Mound Rd (48314-3254)
PHONE..............................248 399-4800
EMP: 4
SALES (est): 370.1K **Privately Held**
SIC: **3398** Metal Heat Treating

(G-15543)
WAPC HOLDINGS INC
Also Called: Weave Alloy Products Company
40736 Brentwood Dr (48310-2212)
PHONE..............................586 939-0770
Timothy Brownfield, *President*
EMP: 10 EST: 1954
SQ FT: 12,000
SALES (est): 2MM **Privately Held**
SIC: **3315** Wire, ferrous/iron

(G-15544)
WARREN BROACH & MACHINE CORP
6541 Diplomat Dr (48314-1421)
PHONE..............................586 254-7080
James McMahon, *President*
Donald Mc Mahon, *President*
Bill Foth, *General Mgr*
William Foth, *General Mgr*
Michael Beaudoin, *Site Mgr*
EMP: 18
SQ FT: 14,000

GEOGRAPHIC SECTION

Stevensville - Berrien County (G-15572)

SALES (est): 2.9MM **Privately Held**
WEB: www.warrenbroach.com
SIC: 3545 3541 Broaches (machine tool accessories); machine tools, metal cutting type

(G-15545)
WEBO DETROIT CORP
6221 Progress Dr (48312-2621)
PHONE.................................586 268-8900
Mark Verbrueggen, *President*
EMP: 13
SALES (est): 512.4K **Privately Held**
SIC: 3599 Machine shop, jobbing & repair

(G-15546)
WING PATTERN INC
6145 Wall St Ste D (48312-1058)
PHONE.................................248 588-1121
Thomas Booser, *President*
James Booser, *Vice Pres*
EMP: 5
SALES (est): 150K **Privately Held**
SIC: 3553 3543 Pattern makers' machinery, woodworking; industrial patterns

(G-15547)
WYATT SERVICES INC
6425 Sims Dr (48313-3722)
PHONE.................................586 264-8000
Jean M Wyatt, *President*
Bill Wyatt, *Vice Pres*
Billy C Wyatt Jr, *Vice Pres*
Mark Andrews, *Plant Mgr*
Debbie Andrews, *Finance*
EMP: 18
SQ FT: 18,000
SALES (est): 3.7MM **Privately Held**
WEB: www.wyattservices.net
SIC: 3398 Metal heat treating

(G-15548)
ZF ACTIVE SAFETY US INC
42315 R Mancini Dr (48314-3265)
PHONE.................................586 899-2807
Mike Obrien, *Manager*
EMP: 250
SALES (corp-wide): 216.2K **Privately Held**
SIC: 3714 Motor vehicle engines & parts
HQ: Zf Active Safety Us Inc.
12001 Tech Center Dr
Livonia MI 48150
734 812-6979

Sterling Hts
Macomb County

(G-15549)
DIVERSIFIED MFG & ASSEMBLY LLC
5545 Bridgewood Dr (48310-2219)
PHONE.................................313 758-4797
EMP: 3
SALES (est): 370.2K **Privately Held**
SIC: 3672 Mfg Printed Circuit Boards

(G-15550)
INTL GIUSEPPES OILS & VINEGARS
38033 Opatik Ct (48312-1408)
PHONE.................................586 698-2754
Joseph Cucinello, *Principal*
EMP: 3 **EST:** 2010
SALES (est): 189.8K **Privately Held**
SIC: 2099 Vinegar

Stevensville
Berrien County

(G-15551)
ACCU DIE & MOLD INC
7473 Red Arrow Hwy (49127-9248)
PHONE.................................269 465-4020
Daniel Reifschneider, *President*
EMP: 39

SALES (est): 7.3MM **Privately Held**
WEB: www.accu-die.com
SIC: 3544 Forms (molds), for foundry & plastics working machinery; industrial molds

(G-15552)
ACCUSPEC GRINDING INC (PA)
2660 Lawrence St (49127-1252)
P.O. Box 121 (49127-0121)
PHONE.................................269 556-1410
Joseph Ondraka, *CEO*
Jeffery J Ondraka, *President*
Anette Ondraka, *Exec VP*
EMP: 28
SQ FT: 35,000
SALES (est): 3.4MM **Privately Held**
WEB: www.accuspec-inc.com
SIC: 3451 Screw machine products

(G-15553)
ALPHA RESOURCES LLC
3090 Johnson Rd (49127-1270)
P.O. Box 199 (49127-0199)
PHONE.................................269 465-5559
Philip T Lunsford, *President*
Joyce Lunsford, *Corp Secy*
◆ **EMP:** 43
SQ FT: 70,000
SALES (est): 15.3MM **Privately Held**
WEB: www.alpharesources.com
SIC: 5049 3255 3821 3313 Laboratory equipment, except medical or dental; clay refractories; laboratory apparatus & furniture; electrometallurgical products

(G-15554)
ALUDYNE INC
2800 Yasdick Dr (49127-1241)
PHONE.................................269 556-9236
Clint Connelly, *Plant Mgr*
EMP: 14
SALES (corp-wide): 1.3B **Privately Held**
SIC: 3363 Aluminum die-castings
HQ: Aludyne, Inc.
300 Galleria Ofcntr Ste 5
Southfield MI 48034
248 728-8642

(G-15555)
ALUDYNE WEST MICHIGAN LLC
2800 Yasdick Dr (49127-1241)
PHONE.................................248 728-8642
Pierre Dubeauclard,
Michael Beyer,
▲ **EMP:** 11
SALES (est): 35.9MM
SALES (corp-wide): 1.3B **Privately Held**
WEB: www.concordintl.com
SIC: 3714 Motor vehicle parts & accessories
HQ: Aludyne International, Inc
300 Galleria Ofcntr Ste 5
Southfield MI 48034

(G-15556)
ANSTEY FOUNDRY CO INC
2788 Lawrence St (49127-1254)
P.O. Box 255 (49127-0255)
PHONE.................................269 429-3229
Thomas J Anstey, *President*
Donald J Anstey, *Vice Pres*
James G Anstey, *Vice Pres*
Richard J Anstey, *Vice Pres*
Janet Anstey, *Admin Sec*
EMP: 22 **EST:** 1945
SQ FT: 15,000
SALES (est): 2.9MM **Privately Held**
SIC: 3398 3321 Metal heat treating; gray iron castings

(G-15557)
BLENDCO LLC
5000 Advance Way (49127-9544)
PHONE.................................269 350-2914
Leigh Ann Sayen,
EMP: 12
SALES (est): 2.8MM **Privately Held**
SIC: 2047 Dog & cat food

(G-15558)
BRIDGVILLE PLASTICS INC
7380 Jericho Rd (49127-9209)
PHONE.................................269 465-6516
Thomas Moneta, *President*
Carol Moneta, *Vice Pres*

Angie Meltinos, *Admin Asst*
EMP: 16
SQ FT: 10,000
SALES (est): 4.8MM **Privately Held**
WEB: www.bridgville.com
SIC: 3089 Injection molding of plastics

(G-15559)
CARSON WOOD SPECIALTIES INC
7526 Jericho Rd (49127-9723)
PHONE.................................269 465-6091
Thomas Carson, *President*
Charlene Carson, *Co-Owner*
EMP: 5
SALES (est): 785.5K **Privately Held**
SIC: 5031 5211 2431 2434 Lumber, plywood & millwork; lumber products; doors & door parts & trim, wood; wood kitchen cabinets; chairs, table & arm

(G-15560)
CUSTOM TOOL AND DIE CO
7059 Red Arrow Hwy (49127-9681)
PHONE.................................269 465-9130
Harry Reinhardt, *President*
Heinrich Reinhardt, *Shareholder*
EMP: 45 **EST:** 1967
SQ FT: 13,350
SALES (est): 8.3MM **Privately Held**
WEB: www.ctd1.com
SIC: 3544 Dies & die holders for metal cutting, forming, die casting; special dies & tools

(G-15561)
D M P E
5790 Saint Joseph Ave (49127-1237)
PHONE.................................269 428-5070
EMP: 5
SALES (est): 552.7K **Privately Held**
SIC: 3714 Motor vehicle engines & parts

(G-15562)
DANE SYSTEMS LLC
Also Called: Jr Automation Technologies
7275 Red Arrow Hwy (49127-9734)
PHONE.................................269 465-3263
Bryan Jones, *Principal*
Scot Lindemann, *Co-CEO*
Barry Kohn, *CFO*
Bryan V Dorpowski, *Controller*
▲ **EMP:** 87
SQ FT: 45,000
SALES (est): 21.3MM
SALES (corp-wide): 230.4MM **Privately Held**
WEB: www.danesys.com
SIC: 3549 Assembly machines, including robotic
PA: Jr Technology Group, Llc
13365 Tyler St
Holland MI 49424
616 399-2168

(G-15563)
DEE-BLAST CORPORATION (PA)
Also Called: Air Source
5992 Oelke Park St (49127-1233)
P.O. Box 517 (49127-0517)
PHONE.................................269 428-2400
Michael A Johnson, *President*
David Tompkins, *Chairman*
Kevin Edmundson, *QC Mgr*
Patterson Todd, *Sales Staff*
Marlene E Johnson, *Admin Sec*
EMP: 10
SQ FT: 24,000
SALES (est): 4.6MM **Privately Held**
WEB: www.dee-blast.com
SIC: 3569 5084 3469 2542 Blast cleaning equipment, dustless; industrial machinery & equipment; metal stampings; partitions & fixtures, except wood

(G-15564)
DISCOVERY GOLD CORP
4472 Winding Ln (49127-9330)
PHONE.................................269 429-7002
Steve Flechner, *Owner*
EMP: 3 **EST:** 2015
SALES (est): 96.4K **Privately Held**
SIC: 1499 Miscellaneous nonmetallic minerals

(G-15565)
DURA MOLD INC
3390 W Linco Rd (49127-9725)
PHONE.................................269 465-3301
Franz Bock, *President*
▲ **EMP:** 55
SQ FT: 22,000
SALES: 15MM **Privately Held**
WEB: www.duramold.com
SIC: 3544 Special dies & tools

(G-15566)
E Z TOOL INC
4796 Roosevelt Rd (49127-9522)
PHONE.................................269 429-0070
Larry Engler, *President*
Susan Engler, *Admin Sec*
EMP: 3 **EST:** 1966
SQ FT: 5,000
SALES: 700K **Privately Held**
WEB: www.ez-tool.com
SIC: 3544 Special dies & tools

(G-15567)
FALCON LAKESIDE MFG INC
4999 Advance Way (49127-9544)
PHONE.................................269 429-6193
Francis Sant, *Principal*
Jennifer Sill, *Principal*
EMP: 24
SALES (est): 4.5MM **Privately Held**
SIC: 3544 Dies & die holders for metal cutting, forming, die casting

(G-15568)
GREAT LAKES WIRE PACKAGING LLC
Also Called: Third Coast Manufacturing
4232 N Roosevelt Rd (49127-9527)
P.O. Box 164 (49127-0164)
PHONE.................................269 428-7220
Matt Fisher,
Matthew Fisher,
EMP: 3
SQ FT: 11,000
SALES (est): 307.5K **Privately Held**
SIC: 3449 Miscellaneous metalwork

(G-15569)
GRIFFIN TOOL INC
2951 Johnson Rd (49127-1216)
P.O. Box 528 (49127-0528)
PHONE.................................269 429-4077
Greg Griffin, *President*
Griffin Christol, *Vice Pres*
Steven Scudder, *Draft/Design*
EMP: 25
SQ FT: 11,000
SALES (est): 5.7MM **Privately Held**
WEB: www.griffintool.com
SIC: 3544 Special dies & tools

(G-15570)
HARBOR ISLE PLASTICS LLC
2337 W Marquette Woods Rd (49127-9587)
PHONE.................................269 465-6004
Ewald Lehmann,
Peter Bartschke,
Mark Lehmann,
▲ **EMP:** 30
SQ FT: 110,000
SALES (est): 8.2MM **Privately Held**
WEB: www.allstar-plastics.com
SIC: 3089 Injection molding of plastics

(G-15571)
HARRIS TOOLING
6230 Jericho Rd (49127-9236)
PHONE.................................269 465-5870
Robert Harris, *Owner*
EMP: 3
SQ FT: 3,600
SALES (est): 216.3K **Privately Held**
SIC: 3544 Special dies & tools; jigs & fixtures

(G-15572)
JOHN LAMANTIA CORPORATION
Also Called: Lamantia Machine Company
4825 Roosevelt Rd (49127-9522)
P.O. Box 320 (49127-0320)
PHONE.................................269 428-8100
Anthony Lamantia, *President*

Stevensville - Berrien County (G-15573)

EMP: 6
SQ FT: 5,500
SALES (est): 750K **Privately Held**
SIC: 3469 3544 8711 Metal stampings; special dies & tools; consulting engineer

(G-15573)
KLAUS NIXDORF
Also Called: Flour Shop Bakery & Pizza, The
1727 W John Beers Rd (49127-9403)
PHONE.................................269 429-3259
Klaus Nixdorf, *Owner*
EMP: 21
SQ FT: 2,700
SALES (est): 646K **Privately Held**
SIC: 5461 5812 2051 Cakes; pizzeria, independent; bread, cake & related products

(G-15574)
LAKESHORE MARBLE COMPANY INC
4410 N Roosevelt Rd (49127-9100)
P.O. Box 132 (49127-0132)
PHONE.................................269 429-8241
James Chartrand, *President*
Thad Chartrand, *Vice Pres*
Matthew Chartrand, *Treasurer*
EMP: 32
SQ FT: 20,000
SALES (est): 3.6MM **Privately Held**
WEB: www.bravobuildingco.com
SIC: 3281 3431 2434 3088 Marble, building: cut & shaped; building stone products; metal sanitary ware; wood kitchen cabinets; plastics plumbing fixtures; plastics materials & resins

(G-15575)
LAKESHORE MOLD AND DIE LLC
2355 W Marquette Woods Rd (49127-9587)
PHONE.................................269 429-6764
Todd Nitz, *Mng Member*
Sherri Nitz,
EMP: 5
SQ FT: 12,000
SALES: 1MM **Privately Held**
SIC: 3544 Industrial molds; forms (molds), for foundry & plastics working machinery

(G-15576)
LAKESIDE MANUFACTURING CO
4999 Advance Way (49127-9544)
PHONE.................................269 429-6193
Lawrence Holben, *President*
Alvin Ziebart, *Vice Pres*
Henry Kraklau Jr, *Director*
EMP: 35 EST: 1967
SQ FT: 34,000
SALES (est): 4.6MM **Privately Held**
WEB: www.lakesidemfgco.com
SIC: 3599 3544 Machine shop, jobbing & repair; special dies & tools

(G-15577)
MEIJER INC
5019 Red Arrow Hwy (49127-1013)
PHONE.................................269 556-2400
Rob Vassar, *Principal*
Cory Hedman, *Director*
John Spaulding, *Director*
Maggie Poquette, *Planning*
Karen Versaille, *Technician*
EMP: 11
SALES (corp-wide): 10.7B **Privately Held**
SIC: 3421 Table & food cutlery, including butchers'
HQ: Meijer, Inc.
2929 Walker Ave Nw
Grand Rapids MI 49544
616 453-6711

(G-15578)
MEMCON NORTH AMERICA LLC
6000 Red Arrow Hwy Unit I (49127-1166)
PHONE.................................269 281-0478
Martin Gilbert, *President*
Simon Blackwell, *Administration*
EMP: 10
SALES (est): 1MM **Privately Held**
SIC: 3613 5063 Switchgear & switchboard apparatus; switchboards

(G-15579)
R J FLOOD PROFESSIONAL CO
2691 Orchard Ln (49127-9382)
PHONE.................................269 930-3608
Robert Flood, *Principal*
EMP: 4
SALES (est): 452.3K **Privately Held**
SIC: 3553 Cabinet makers' machinery

(G-15580)
SCIENTIFIC NOTEBOOK COMPANY
3295 W Linco Rd (49127-9240)
P.O. Box 238 (49127-0238)
PHONE.................................269 429-8285
Ben Gallup, *President*
Patrick Gallup, *Vice Pres*
EMP: 14
SQ FT: 25,000
SALES: 2MM **Privately Held**
WEB: www.snco.us
SIC: 2678 Notebooks: made from purchased paper

(G-15581)
SLAUGHTER INSTRUMENT COMPANY
4356 N Roosevelt Rd (49127-9527)
PHONE.................................269 428-7471
Charles Eversole, *President*
EMP: 12
SQ FT: 8,100
SALES: 500K **Privately Held**
WEB: www.slaughtercoinc.com
SIC: 3841 Surgical instruments & apparatus

(G-15582)
STANDARD TOOL & DIE INC
2950 Johnson Rd (49127-1217)
P.O. Box 608 (49127-0608)
PHONE.................................269 465-6004
Peter Bartschke, *CEO*
Mark Lehmann, *President*
▲ EMP: 65
SQ FT: 54,000
SALES (est): 14.9MM **Privately Held**
WEB: www.standardtool.net
SIC: 3544 Dies & die holders for metal cutting, forming, die casting

(G-15583)
SUPREME CASTING INC
3389 W Linco Rd (49127-9725)
PHONE.................................269 465-5757
William Bancroft, *President*
Elizabeth Kohn, *Corp Secy*
Robert Kohn, *Engineer*
Carrie Aleman, *Office Mgr*
Robert Bancroft, *Shareholder*
EMP: 60
SQ FT: 56,000
SALES: 16.1MM **Privately Held**
WEB: www.supremecasting.com
SIC: 3363 3365 Aluminum die-castings; aluminum foundries

(G-15584)
TOGREENCLEANCOM
4791 S Cedar Trl (49127-9546)
PHONE.................................269 428-4812
Janice Bussone, *Principal*
EMP: 3
SALES (est): 120K **Privately Held**
SIC: 3471 Cleaning & descaling metal products

(G-15585)
TRI-M-MOLD INC
3390 W Linco Rd (49127-9725)
PHONE.................................269 465-3301
Manfred Moneta, *President*
Carol Moneta, *Vice Pres*
Tom Moneta, *Vice Pres*
EMP: 51
SQ FT: 22,000
SALES: 4MM **Privately Held**
SIC: 3544 Special dies & tools

(G-15586)
Z-BRITE METAL FINISHING INC
6979 Stvnsville Baroda Rd (49127-9781)
PHONE.................................269 422-2191
Gary F Zavoral Sr, *President*
Gary Zavoral, *President*
Patricia Zoral, *Principal*
EMP: 17
SALES (est): 2.3MM **Privately Held**
SIC: 3559 Metal finishing equipment for plating, etc.

(G-15587)
ZAV-TECH METAL FINISHING
6979 Stvnsville Baroda Rd (49127-9781)
P.O. Box 576 (49127-0576)
PHONE.................................269 422-2559
Chad Zavoral, *Partner*
EMP: 6 EST: 1996
SALES (est): 575.4K **Privately Held**
SIC: 3471 Finishing, metals or formed products

Stockbridge
Ingham County

(G-15588)
DAVID GAUSS LOGGING
4635 Cooper Rd (49285-9752)
PHONE.................................517 851-8102
Mary Gauss, *Principal*
EMP: 3 EST: 2012
SALES (est): 135K **Privately Held**
SIC: 2411 Logging

(G-15589)
KENDALL MICROTECH INC
3436 Parman Rd (49285-9514)
P.O. Box 296 (49285-0296)
PHONE.................................517 565-3802
Steven Kendall, *President*
Sharon Kendall, *Treasurer*
▼ EMP: 3
SALES (est): 210K **Privately Held**
SIC: 3315 Steel wire & related products

(G-15590)
LINCOLN WELDING COMPANY
4445 Brogan Rd (49285-9467)
PHONE.................................313 292-2299
Richard Aquino, *President*
Donna Aquino, *Admin Sec*
EMP: 4
SQ FT: 9,550
SALES (est): 230K **Privately Held**
SIC: 3441 Fabricated structural metal

(G-15591)
MAIN STREET PRINTING
119 W Main St (49285-9483)
PHONE.................................517 851-3816
Mclhael Fletcher, *Principal*
EMP: 3 EST: 2010
SALES (est): 199.5K **Privately Held**
SIC: 2759 Commercial printing

(G-15592)
PRO POLYMERS INC
4974 Bird Dr (49285-9476)
PHONE.................................734 222-8820
Peter Unger, *CEO*
▲ EMP: 8 EST: 1996
SQ FT: 22,000
SALES (est): 1MM **Privately Held**
SIC: 2821 Plastics materials & resins

(G-15593)
STOCKBRIDGE MANUFACTURING CO
4859 E Main St (49285-9153)
P.O. Box 189 (49285-0189)
PHONE.................................517 851-7865
Camiel Thorrez, *President*
Phillip Thorrez, *Vice Pres*
Camiel E Thorrez, *VP Mfg*
EMP: 22
SQ FT: 27,000
SALES (est): 4.5MM
SALES (corp-wide): 21.8MM **Privately Held**
WEB: www.stockbridgemfginc.com
SIC: 3451 Screw machine products
PA: C. Thorrez Industries, Inc.
4909 W Michigan Ave
Jackson MI 49201
517 750-3160

Sturgis
St. Joseph County

(G-15594)
ABBOTT LABORATORIES
Abbott Nutrition
901 N Centerville Rd (49091-9302)
PHONE.................................269 651-0600
Tj Hathaway, *Project Mgr*
Colin McCarthy, *Facilities Mgr*
Steve Vanmol, *Manager*
EMP: 420
SALES (corp-wide): 30.5B **Publicly Held**
WEB: www.abbott.com
SIC: 2834 Druggists' preparations (pharmaceuticals)
PA: Abbott Laboratories
100 Abbott Park Rd
Abbott Park IL 60064
224 667-6100

(G-15595)
ACM PLASTIC PRODUCTS INC
507 Saint Joseph St (49091-1345)
P.O. Box 580 (49091-0580)
PHONE.................................269 651-7888
Maurice K Walters, *President*
Chuck Walters, *Vice Pres*
▲ EMP: 64
SQ FT: 70,000
SALES (est): 10.6MM **Privately Held**
SIC: 3089 Blow molded finished plastic products; injection molding of plastics

(G-15596)
AMERICRAFT CARTON INC
305 W South St (49091-2100)
P.O. Box 570 (49091-0570)
PHONE.................................269 651-2365
Eric Hansen, *General Mgr*
John Hart, *Safety Mgr*
Bob Easterday, *Sales Dir*
Daniel Barnell, *Manager*
Steve Palmer, *CIO*
EMP: 70
SALES (corp-wide): 194.1MM **Privately Held**
WEB: www.americraft.com
SIC: 2657 Folding paperboard boxes
PA: Americraft Carton, Inc.
7400 State Line Rd # 206
Prairie Village KS 66208
913 387-3700

(G-15597)
AUSTIN ENGINEERING
1221 N Clay St (49091-1183)
PHONE.................................269 659-6335
EMP: 3 EST: 2000
SQ FT: 5,000
SALES (est): 190K **Privately Held**
SIC: 7692 Trade Contractor

(G-15598)
BOGEN CONCRETE INC
26959 Bogen Rd (49091-8713)
PHONE.................................269 651-6751
Mark R Bogen, *President*
Dennis French, *Opers Mgr*
EMP: 7
SALES (est): 1.3MM **Privately Held**
WEB: www.bogenconcrete.com
SIC: 3273 Ready-mixed concrete

(G-15599)
BURR OAK TOOL INC (PA)
Also Called: Burr Oak Tool
405 W South St (49091-2192)
PHONE.................................269 651-9393
Brian McConell, *President*
Newell Franks, *Chairman*
David Clark, *Vice Pres*
Stacie Ogg, *Senior Buyer*
David L Franks, *Treasurer*
◆ EMP: 186 EST: 1944
SQ FT: 250,000
SALES: 4.8MM **Privately Held**
SIC: 3999 3443 3317 Atomizers, toiletry; finned tubes, for heat transfer; tubes, seamless steel

GEOGRAPHIC SECTION

Sturgis - St. Joseph County (G-15626)

(G-15600)
COLLIER ENTERPRISE III
Also Called: Tough Coatings
1510 Sunnyfield Rd (49091-9761)
P.O. Box 1056, Paradise CA (95967-1056)
PHONE.................................269 503-3402
Cori Gerken,
EMP: 5
SALES (est): 261.3K **Privately Held**
SIC: 1752 3953 7389 Floor laying & floor work; stencils, painting & marking;

(G-15601)
CON-DE MANUFACTURING INC
Also Called: Midwest Fire Protection
26436 Us Highway 12 (49091-9705)
P.O. Box 366 (49091-0366)
PHONE.................................269 651-3756
Jim Reilly, *President*
Dave Yunker, *Corp Secy*
EMP: 5 **EST:** 1961
SQ FT: 6,500
SALES (est): 616K **Privately Held**
SIC: 3448 3499 1799 5999 Docks: prefabricated metal; ladders, portable: metal; dock equipment installation, industrial; fire extinguishers; safety supplies & equipment

(G-15602)
CRONKHITE FARMS TRUCKING LLC
33135 Deer Park Rd (49091)
PHONE.................................269 489-5225
Scott Cronkhite, *Mng Member*
EMP: 3
SALES (est): 267.6K **Privately Held**
SIC: 2452 Farm & agricultural buildings, prefabricated wood

(G-15603)
DAVE BRAND
Also Called: Red Rose Flooring Shop
26541 Us 12 (49091-9703)
PHONE.................................269 651-4693
Dave Brand, *Owner*
EMP: 5
SQ FT: 2,500
SALES: 250K **Privately Held**
SIC: 5713 2591 7217 Carpets; window blinds; carpet & upholstery cleaning

(G-15604)
GATEHOUSE MEDIA LLC
Sturgis Journal
209 John St (49091-1459)
P.O. Box 660 (49091-0660)
PHONE.................................269 651-5407
Corky Emrick, *Editor*
Candice Phelps, *Regional Mgr*
Shelly Fox, *Sales Staff*
Dan Tolleson, *Manager*
EMP: 42
SALES (corp-wide): 1.5B **Privately Held**
WEB: www.gatehousemedia.com
SIC: 2711 Newspapers, publishing & printing
HQ: Gatehouse Media, Llc
  175 Sullys Trl Fl 3
  Pittsford NY 14534
  585 598-0030

(G-15605)
GRAV CO LLC
400 Norwood St (49091-2132)
P.O. Box 599 (49091-0599)
PHONE.................................269 651-5467
Brent Sheehan,
EMP: 10 **EST:** 1948
SQ FT: 35,000
SALES: 1.2MM **Privately Held**
WEB: www.graviflo.com
SIC: 2842 3559 Specialty cleaning preparations; cleaning or polishing preparations; metal finishing equipment for plating, etc.

(G-15606)
GRAVEL FLOW INC (PA)
400 Norwood St (49091-2179)
P.O. Box 2168, Kalamazoo (49003-2168)
PHONE.................................269 651-5467
R Scott Davidson, *President*
EMP: 4
SQ FT: 10,000
SALES (est): 980.5K **Privately Held**
SIC: 5085 3559 Industrial supplies; metal finishing equipment for plating, etc.

(G-15607)
INDUSTRIAL CONTROL SYSTEMS LLC
70380 M 66 (49091-9433)
P.O. Box 718 (49091-0718)
PHONE.................................269 689-3241
Thomas Tison, *Mng Member*
EMP: 5
SALES (est): 368.2K **Privately Held**
SIC: 1381 Drilling oil & gas wells

(G-15608)
JIM DETWEILER
64177 Rommel Rd (49091-9363)
PHONE.................................269 467-7728
James Detweiler, *Principal*
EMP: 3
SALES (est): 248.3K **Privately Held**
SIC: 2411 Logging

(G-15609)
JOHNSON PRECISION MOLD & ENGRG
1001 Haines Blvd (49091-9685)
PHONE.................................269 651-2553
Randal Lee Johnson, *President*
Mark Bingaman, *Engineer*
Shirley Johnson, *Admin Sec*
EMP: 9
SALES (est): 1.2MM **Privately Held**
WEB: www.johnsonmold.com
SIC: 3544 3599 Industrial molds; forms (molds), for foundry & plastics working machinery; machine & other job shop work

(G-15610)
KRONTZ GENERAL MACHINE & TOOL
412 W Congress St (49091-1617)
PHONE.................................269 651-5882
Roger Krontz, *President*
William Krontz, *Vice Pres*
EMP: 4
SQ FT: 29,000
SALES (est): 598.3K **Privately Held**
SIC: 3599 Machine shop, jobbing & repair

(G-15611)
LAKE FABRICATORS INC
Also Called: Unique Truck Accessories
1000 N Clay St (49091-1011)
P.O. Box 7067 (49091-7067)
PHONE.................................269 651-1935
Stanley Lake, *President*
Greg Chamberlain, *VP Opers*
EMP: 25
SQ FT: 20,000
SALES (est): 4.7MM **Privately Held**
WEB: www.uniquetruckaccessories.com
SIC: 3469 Boxes: tool, lunch, mail, etc.: stamped metal

(G-15612)
LCA MOLD & ENGINEERING INC
1200 W Lafayette St (49091-1093)
PHONE.................................269 651-1193
William Luttmann, *President*
Doug Cossairt, *Treasurer*
Bob Anderson, *Admin Sec*
EMP: 8 **EST:** 1999
SQ FT: 3,000
SALES (est): 410K **Privately Held**
SIC: 3544 Special dies & tools

(G-15613)
LITHO PRINTERS INC
620 N Centerville Rd (49091-9602)
PHONE.................................269 651-7309
Mark Wentzel, *President*
Jill Wentzel, *Vice Pres*
EMP: 10 **EST:** 1964
SQ FT: 5,500
SALES: 350K **Privately Held**
WEB: www.lithoprinters.com
SIC: 2752 Commercial printing, offset

(G-15614)
LUTTMANN PRECISION MOLD INC
1200 W Lafayette St (49091-1093)
PHONE.................................269 651-1193
William R Luttmann, *President*
Jason Hopkins, *Engineer*
EMP: 42
SQ FT: 18,000
SALES (est): 6.4MM **Privately Held**
SIC: 3089 Injection molding of plastics

(G-15615)
MARTIN PRODUCTS COMPANY INC
66635 M 66 N (49091)
P.O. Box 269 (49091-0269)
PHONE.................................269 651-1721
Daniel Martin, *President*
EMP: 12
SQ FT: 16,000
SALES: 1MM **Privately Held**
SIC: 2499 3479 Picture & mirror frames, wood; painting, coating & hot dipping

(G-15616)
MAYER TOOL & ENGINEERING INC
1404 N Centerville Rd (49091-9699)
P.O. Box 8 (49091-0008)
PHONE.................................269 651-1428
John Mayer, *President*
Patrick Rouffey, *President*
Pat Roussey, *Plant Mgr*
Caralee A Mayer, *Treasurer*
Deborah Mayer, *Asst Sec*
▲ **EMP:** 37 **EST:** 1975
SALES (est): 6.9MM **Privately Held**
WEB: www.mayertool.com
SIC: 3544 Forms (molds), for foundry & plastics working machinery; industrial molds

(G-15617)
MICHIANA CORRUGATED PDTS CO
110 N Franks Ave (49091-1582)
P.O. Box 790 (49091-0790)
PHONE.................................269 651-5225
Eric Jones, *President*
Matt Miller, *Executive*
EMP: 24
SQ FT: 53,000
SALES (est): 5.5MM **Privately Held**
WEB: www.michianacorrugated.com
SIC: 2653 Boxes, corrugated: made from purchased materials

(G-15618)
MICHIGAN ROLLER INC
1113 N Clay St (49091-1012)
PHONE.................................269 651-2304
Jesse Fogleman, *President*
Mary Fogleman, *Corp Secy*
EMP: 5 **EST:** 1974
SQ FT: 6,000
SALES: 400K **Privately Held**
WEB: www.michiganroller.com
SIC: 3069 5084 Printers' rolls & blankets: rubber or rubberized fabric; printing trades machinery, equipment & supplies

(G-15619)
MICHIGAN TOOL WORKS LLC
618 N Centerville Rd (49091-9602)
P.O. Box 158 (49091-0158)
PHONE.................................269 651-5139
Robert Morgan,
Peter Stemen,
EMP: 20
SALES (est): 4.2MM **Privately Held**
SIC: 3599 Machine shop, jobbing & repair

(G-15620)
MIDWEST PLASTIC ENGINEERING
1501 Progress St (49091-8301)
P.O. Box 320 (49091-0320)
PHONE.................................269 651-5223
Dennis E Baker, *President*
Judith A Baker, *Corp Secy*
▲ **EMP:** 100
SALES (est): 22.2MM **Privately Held**
WEB: www.midwestplastic.com
SIC: 3089 3544 Injection molded finished plastic products; forms (molds), for foundry & plastics working machinery

(G-15621)
MIDWEST TOOL AND CUTLERY CO (PA)
1210 Progress St (49091-9386)
P.O. Box 160 (49091-0160)
PHONE.................................269 651-2476
Stephen Deter, *President*
David Schmick, *Vice Pres*
Roger Rynberg, *Plant Mgr*
Andrew Jones, *Purch Agent*
Scott Musser, *Engineer*
▼ **EMP:** 80 **EST:** 1960
SQ FT: 26,000
SALES (est): 16.2MM **Privately Held**
WEB: www.midwestsnips.com
SIC: 3545 3421 Machine tool accessories; scissors, shears, clippers, snips & similar tools

(G-15622)
MORGAN OLSON LLC (HQ)
1801 S Nottawa St (49091-8723)
PHONE.................................269 659-0200
Michael Ownbey, *President*
Larry Palmer, *Business Mgr*
Dan Desrochers, *Exec VP*
David Halladay, *Vice Pres*
Bernie Supianoski, *Project Mgr*
◆ **EMP:** 700
SQ FT: 384,000
SALES: 33MM
SALES (corp-wide): 1.2B **Privately Held**
WEB: www.morganolson.com
SIC: 3713 Truck bodies (motor vehicles)
PA: J. B. Poindexter & Co., Inc
  600 Travis St Ste 200
  Houston TX 77002
  713 655-9800

(G-15623)
NEO MANUFACTURING INC
Also Called: Neo Trailers
21900 Us Highway 12 (49091-9295)
PHONE.................................269 503-7630
Wade Wolf,
EMP: 18
SQ FT: 40,000
SALES (est): 4.7MM **Privately Held**
SIC: 3715 Truck trailers

(G-15624)
OAK PRESS SOLUTIONS INC
504 Wade Rd (49091-9765)
PHONE.................................269 651-8513
Newell A Franks II, *Ch of Bd*
David L Franks, *President*
Brian P McConnell, *Vice Pres*
◆ **EMP:** 50
SQ FT: 136,000
SALES (est): 8.7MM **Privately Held**
SIC: 3542 Presses: forming, stamping, punching, sizing (machine tools)

(G-15625)
OWENS PRODUCTS INC
1107 Progress St (49091-9375)
P.O. Box 670 (49091-0670)
PHONE.................................269 651-2300
Gary Kirtley, *CEO*
John Youga, *Plant Mgr*
Susan Ford, *Bookkeeper*
Bob Mansmith, *Marketing Staff*
▼ **EMP:** 40 **EST:** 1992
SQ FT: 35,000
SALES: 8.4MM
SALES (corp-wide): 11.9MM **Privately Held**
WEB: www.owensproducts.com
SIC: 3714 Motor vehicle body components & frame
PA: Owens-Classic Inc
  1000 Progress St
  Sturgis MI 49091
  269 651-2300

(G-15626)
PARMA TUBE CORP
1008 Progress St (49091-9375)
PHONE.................................269 651-2351
Mark A Roberts, *President*

Sturgis - St. Joseph County (G-15627)

Joe Reed, *Project Mgr*
Steve Toner, *Sales Engr*
Bill Wetzel, *Supervisor*
EMP: 48
SQ FT: 60,000
SALES (est): 11.5MM **Privately Held**
WEB: www.parmatube.com
SIC: 3317 7692 3498 Steel pipe & tubes; welding repair; fabricated pipe & fittings

(G-15627)
PDC (PA)
69701 White St (49091-2187)
PHONE 269 651-9975
Rick Pennzoni, *President*
Rick Savage, *Vice Pres*
▲ **EMP:** 13
SQ FT: 6,000
SALES: 1.5MM **Privately Held**
WEB: www.displayco.com
SIC: 2541 Display fixtures, wood; showcases, except refrigerated: wood

(G-15628)
PENGUIN LLC
Also Called: Penguin-Iceberg Enterprises
1855 W Chicago Rd (49091-8736)
P.O. Box 7039 (49091-7039)
PHONE 269 651-9488
Christine Parker, *Safety Mgr*
John Carter, *Exec Dir*
Tracy Bernstein, *Senior Editor*
Howard Green,
Richard Fox,
▲ **EMP:** 110
SQ FT: 100,000
SALES (est): 19MM
SALES (corp-wide): 50.1MM **Privately Held**
WEB: www.icebergenterprises.com
SIC: 3089 Blow molded finished plastic products; injection molding of plastics
PA: Iceberg Enterprises, Llc
2700 S River Rd Ste 303
Des Plaines IL 60018
847 685-9500

(G-15629)
PENGUIN MOLDING LLC
1855 W Chicago Rd (49091-8736)
PHONE 847 297-0560
Eileen Kreit, *Publisher*
Sarah McGrath, *Vice Pres*
Caitlin Gomez, *Accounts Mgr*
Todd Jones, *Regl Sales Mgr*
Elyse Marshall, *Director*
EMP: 12
SALES (est): 1.4MM **Privately Held**
SIC: 3089 Molding primary plastic

(G-15630)
PRAIRIE WOOD PRODUCTS INC
506 Prairie St (49091-2180)
PHONE 269 659-1163
Mike Melvin, *President*
Carolyn Melvin, *Corp Secy*
EMP: 17
SALES (est): 2.6MM **Privately Held**
SIC: 2448 Wood pallets & skids

(G-15631)
PRECISION SPEED EQUIPMENT INC
1400 W Lafayette St (49091-8905)
P.O. Box 7036 (49091-7036)
PHONE 269 651-4303
Robert Griffioen, *President*
Josephine Griffioen, *Vice Pres*
Tom Beal, *Engineer*
Rod Telsworth, *Info Tech Mgr*
▲ **EMP:** 125
SQ FT: 22,000
SALES (est): 21MM **Privately Held**
WEB: www.pse-usa.com
SIC: 3822 Appliance controls except air-conditioning & refrigeration; flame safety controls for furnaces & boilers; ignition controls for gas appliances & furnaces, automatic; gas burner, automatic controls

(G-15632)
REHAU INCORPORATED
1110 N Clay St (49091-1013)
PHONE 269 651-7845
Bruce Claridge, *Manager*
Iweta Ostgorg, *Analyst*
EMP: 50 **Privately Held**
WEB: www.rehauna.com
SIC: 3069 3543 3083 Molded rubber products; industrial patterns; laminated plastics plate & sheet
PA: Rehau Incorporated
1501 Edwards Ferry Rd Ne
Leesburg VA 20176

(G-15633)
SE-KURE CONTROLS INC
1139 Haines Blvd (49091-9619)
PHONE 269 651-9351
Roger Leyden, *President*
David Robinson, *Production*
Eric Goold, *Director*
EMP: 30
SALES (corp-wide): 12MM **Privately Held**
WEB: www.displaysecurity.com
SIC: 3842 3699 3231 Personal safety equipment; security control equipment & systems; products of purchased glass
PA: Se-Kure Controls Inc.
3714 Runge St
Franklin Park IL 60131
847 288-1111

(G-15634)
SE-KURE DOMES & MIRRORS INC
1139 Haines Blvd (49091-9619)
PHONE 269 651-9351
Roger Leyden, *Principal*
EMP: 30
SALES (est): 1.5MM **Privately Held**
SIC: 7382 3231 Security systems services; mirrored glass

(G-15635)
STURGIS ELECTRIC MOTOR SERVICE
703 N Centerville Rd (49091-9603)
P.O. Box 255 (49091-0255)
PHONE 269 651-2955
Allen White, *Owner*
EMP: 4
SQ FT: 4,500
SALES (est): 486.3K **Privately Held**
SIC: 7694 Electric motor repair

(G-15636)
STURGIS MOLDED PRODUCTS CO
Also Called: Smp
70343 Clark Rd (49091-9755)
PHONE 269 651-9381
Mark D Weishaar, *President*
Bud Clark, *Senior VP*
Chris Emery, *Vice Pres*
Christopher Emery, *Vice Pres*
Paul G Feaman, *Vice Pres*
EMP: 200
SQ FT: 145,000
SALES (est): 72.5MM **Privately Held**
WEB: www.smpco.com
SIC: 3089 3544 Injection molding of plastics; special dies, tools, jigs & fixtures

(G-15637)
STURGIS TOOL AND DIE INC
817 Broadus St (49091-1373)
P.O. Box 368 (49091-0368)
PHONE 269 651-5435
Robert M Zimmerman, *President*
Ronald S Zimmerman, *Vice Pres*
Steve Zimmerman, *VP Sales*
EMP: 25 **EST:** 1966
SQ FT: 26,000
SALES (est): 4.3MM **Privately Held**
SIC: 3544 Dies & die holders for metal cutting, forming, die casting; special dies & tools

(G-15638)
SUMMIT POLYMERS INC
Also Called: Syntech Plant
1211 Progress St (49091-9386)
PHONE 269 651-1643
Christopher Hiscox, *Engineer*
Brent Yager, *Manager*
EMP: 293
SALES (corp-wide): 444.7MM **Privately Held**
WEB: www.summitpolymers.com
SIC: 3089 3083 Thermoformed finished plastic products; laminated plastics plate & sheet
PA: Summit Polymers, Inc.
6715 S Sprinkle Rd
Portage MI 49002
269 324-9330

(G-15639)
VCI INC (PA)
Also Called: Basin Material Handling
1500 Progress St (49091-8301)
P.O. Box 7034 (49091-7034)
PHONE 269 659-3676
Eugene R Harrison, *President*
Rusty Smith, *Vice Pres*
▲ **EMP:** 90
SQ FT: 100,000
SALES (est): 36.2MM **Privately Held**
WEB: www.vciusa.com
SIC: 3537 3441 Platforms, stands, tables, pallets & similar equipment; skid boxes, metal; building components, structural steel

(G-15640)
VCI INC
1301 W Dresser Dr (49091-9387)
PHONE 269 659-3676
Eugene Harrison, *President*
EMP: 50
SALES (corp-wide): 36.2MM **Privately Held**
SIC: 3441 Building components, structural steel
PA: Vci, Inc.
1500 Progress St
Sturgis MI 49091
269 659-3676

(G-15641)
WEIDERMAN MOTORSPORTS
28386 Witt Lake Rd (49091-8805)
PHONE 269 689-0264
Matt Weiderman, *Principal*
EMP: 3 **EST:** 2010
SALES (est): 289.3K **Privately Held**
SIC: 3713 Car carrier bodies

Sumner
Gratiot County

(G-15642)
HUBSCHER & SON INC
8189 W Washington Rd (48889-8716)
PHONE 989 875-2151
Oscar Rulapaugh, *Manager*
EMP: 6
SALES (corp-wide): 2.6MM **Privately Held**
SIC: 1442 Gravel mining
PA: Hubscher & Son Inc.
1101 N Franklin Ave
Mount Pleasant MI 48858
989 773-5369

(G-15643)
SPIKE BROS NATURES TREASURES
11230 W Saint Charles Rd (48889-9702)
PHONE 989 833-5443
Annette Sandy, *Owner*
EMP: 3
SALES (est): 127.3K **Privately Held**
SIC: 3999 Honeycomb foundations (beekeepers' supplies)

Sunfield
Eaton County

(G-15644)
ALLEN TOOL
110 Jackson St (48890-9711)
P.O. Box 138 (48890-0138)
PHONE 517 566-2200
Tom Allen, *Owner*
EMP: 5
SALES (est): 182.9K **Privately Held**
SIC: 3469 5051 Machine parts, stamped or pressed metal; miscellaneous nonferrous products

(G-15645)
AUTOMOTIVE MANUFACTURING
101 Main St (48890)
P.O. Box 148 (48890-0148)
PHONE 517 566-8174
Michael Frey, *Owner*
EMP: 5
SALES (est): 300K **Privately Held**
SIC: 3089 7389 Injection molding of plastics; design services

(G-15646)
GREAT LAKES TREATMENT CORP
5630 E Eaton Hwy (48890-9730)
PHONE 517 566-8008
Kerry J Haynor, *President*
Janice Powell, *Office Mgr*
EMP: 4
SALES (est): 653.7K **Privately Held**
WEB: www.greatlakeswatertmt.com
SIC: 2899 Water treating compounds

Superior Township
Washtenaw County

(G-15647)
EFESTO LLC
3400 Woodhill Cir (48198-9650)
PHONE 734 913-0428
EMP: 3
SALES: 3MM **Privately Held**
SIC: 3599 Mfg Industrial Machinery

(G-15648)
VANOVA TECHNOLOGIES LLC
5403 Waldenhill Ct (48198-9654)
PHONE 734 476-7204
Viktoras Brandtneris,
Roy Clarke,
Ibrahim Oraiqat,
EMP: 3
SALES (est): 199K **Privately Held**
SIC: 3559 7389 Electroplating machinery & equipment;

Suttons Bay
Leelanau County

(G-15649)
BLACK & RED INC
Also Called: Chateau De Leelanau Vineyard
5046 S West Bay Shore Dr 4a (49682-9721)
PHONE 231 271-8888
Joanne Smart, *President*
Roberta Kurtz, *Corp Secy*
EMP: 9 **EST:** 1990
SALES (est): 417.9K **Privately Held**
SIC: 0174 2084 Citrus fruits; wine cellars, bonded: engaged in blending wines

(G-15650)
BLACK STAR FARMS LLC (PA)
Also Called: Suttons Bay Tasting Room
10844 E Revold Rd (49682-9703)
PHONE 231 271-4970
Chris Lopez, *General Mgr*
Michael Lahti, *CFO*
Sherri Fenton, *Comms Dir*
Kimberly Zacharias, *Mktg Coord*
Kari Merz, *Manager*
▲ **EMP:** 17
SALES (est): 1.7MM **Privately Held**
WEB: www.blackstarfarms.com
SIC: 2084 7011 0752 Wines; brandy; bed & breakfast inn; boarding services, horses: racing & non-racing; training services, horses (except racing horses)

(G-15651)
BUSINESS HELPER LLC
117 W Broadway (49682-5101)
P.O. Box 414 (49682-0414)
PHONE 231 271-4404

GEOGRAPHIC SECTION

Tawas City - Iosco County (G-15679)

Jackie Morrison, *Owner*
Mary Bush, *Mng Member*
EMP: 5
SQ FT: 2,000
SALES: 80K **Privately Held**
WEB: www.shopleelanaufirst.com
SIC: 2752 4822 4731 4783 Commercial printing, offset; facsimile transmission services; freight transportation arrangement; packing goods for shipping; artists' supplies & materials; office forms & supplies

(G-15652)
HANG ON EXPRESS
316 N Saint Joseph St (49682-5104)
P.O. Box 907 (49682-0907)
PHONE 231 271-0202
Hang Vang, *Owner*
Maika Hang, *Co-Owner*
EMP: 4
SALES: 150K **Privately Held**
SIC: 2741 Miscellaneous publishing

(G-15653)
L MAWBY LLC
Also Called: Mawby, L Vineyards
4519 S Elm Valley Rd (49682-9473)
PHONE 231 271-3522
Peter Laing, *Opers Mgr*
Lawrence Mawby,
EMP: 3
SQ FT: 6,000
SALES (est): 300.3K **Privately Held**
WEB: www.lmawby.com
SIC: 2084 Wines

(G-15654)
POWELL & CRISP PLANKTERS LLC
109 W Fourth St (49682-9732)
P.O. Box 960 (49682-0960)
PHONE 231 271-6769
EMP: 3 **EST:** 2000
SALES: 100K **Privately Held**
SIC: 3732 Boatbuilding/Repairing

(G-15655)
SHADY LANE ORCHARDS INC
Also Called: Shady Lane Cellars
9580 E Shady Ln (49682-9440)
PHONE 231 935-1620
Adam Atchwell, *General Mgr*
▲ **EMP:** 10
SALES (est): 1.4MM **Privately Held**
WEB: www.shadylanecellars.com
SIC: 5921 2084 Wine; wines

(G-15656)
SUTTONS BAY CIDERS
10530 E Hilltop Rd (49682-9420)
PHONE 734 646-3196
Madelynn Korzon, *Principal*
EMP: 7
SALES (est): 555.6K **Privately Held**
SIC: 2084 Wines

(G-15657)
WILLOW VINEYARDS INC
10702 E Hilltop Rd (49682-9419)
PHONE 231 271-4810
Joe Crampton, *Vice Pres*
John Crampton, *Vice Pres*
EMP: 52
SALES (est): 4.2MM **Privately Held**
SIC: 2084 Wines

(G-15658)
WINERY AT BLACK STAR FARMS LLC
10844 E Revold Rd (49682-9703)
PHONE 231 271-4882
Lee Lutes,
Kermit Campbell,
Donald Coe,
William Hjorth,
EMP: 20
SQ FT: 15,000
SALES (est): 1.8MM **Privately Held**
SIC: 2084 Wines

Swartz Creek
Genesee County

(G-15659)
AHLUSION LLC
8048 Miller Rd (48473-1340)
PHONE 888 277-0001
Alyssa Foo,
EMP: 9 **EST:** 2011
SALES (est): 1.1MM **Privately Held**
SIC: 2869 Perfumes, flavorings & food additives

(G-15660)
AIR PUMP VALVE CORPORATION
6503 Linden Rd (48473-8982)
P.O. Box 806, Grand Blanc (48480-0806)
PHONE 810 655-6444
Cheryl W Haedt, *President*
EMP: 3
SALES (est): 379.7K **Privately Held**
SIC: 3823 Level & bulk measuring instruments, industrial process

(G-15661)
ASSENMACHER LIGHTWEIGHT CYCLES (PA)
Also Called: Assenmachers Hill Road Cyclery
8053 Miller Rd (48473-1333)
PHONE 810 635-7844
Matthew Assenmacher, *Owner*
Barbara Assenmacher, *Co-Owner*
EMP: 5
SQ FT: 6,000
SALES (est): 1MM **Privately Held**
WEB: www.assenmachers.com
SIC: 5941 3751 Bicycle & bicycle parts; frames, motorcycle & bicycle; bicycles & related parts

(G-15662)
BIG MONEY MAGAZINE
5490 Wyndemere Sq (48473-8906)
PHONE 810 655-0621
Robert Natzel, *Principal*
EMP: 3
SALES (est): 141.4K **Privately Held**
SIC: 2721 Magazines: publishing & printing

(G-15663)
BILL DAUP SIGNS INC
7389 Ponderosa Dr (48473-9453)
PHONE 810 235-4080
EMP: 4
SQ FT: 3,000
SALES: 390K **Privately Held**
SIC: 3993 1799 Mfg And Maintenance Of Signs

(G-15664)
BROADBLADE PRESS
11314 Miller Rd (48473-8570)
PHONE 810 635-3156
Stan Perkins, *Owner*
EMP: 3
SALES (est): 110K **Privately Held**
SIC: 2731 Book publishing

(G-15665)
D O W ASPHALT PAVING LLC
10421 Calkins Rd (48473-9757)
PHONE 810 743-2633
James Weisberg, *President*
Robert Ward,
EMP: 18
SALES (est): 1.6MM **Privately Held**
SIC: 1771 2951 1611 Blacktop (asphalt) work; asphalt paving mixtures & blocks; surfacing & paving

(G-15666)
FIRESIDE COFFEE COMPANY INC
3239 S Elms Rd (48473-7928)
PHONE 810 635-9196
Carol Davis, *President*
Mike Davis, *Vice Pres*
EMP: 12
SQ FT: 4,800
SALES: 1.2MM **Privately Held**
WEB: www.firesidecoffee.com
SIC: 2095 5149 Instant coffee; groceries & related products

(G-15667)
HOUGEN MANUFACTURING INC
3001 Hougen Dr (48473-7935)
P.O. Box 2005, Flint (48501-2005)
PHONE 810 635-7111
Randall Hougen, *CEO*
Gregory Phillips, *President*
Mary Chrastek, *General Mgr*
Victor Hougen, *Vice Pres*
Dan Piggott, *Plant Mgr*
◆ **EMP:** 130 **EST:** 1959
SQ FT: 80,000
SALES (est): 89.9MM **Privately Held**
WEB: www.hougen.com
SIC: 5084 3545 3546 3541 Machine tools & metalworking machinery; drill bits, metalworking; broaches (machine tool accessories); power-driven handtools; machine tools, metal cutting type

(G-15668)
J C WALKER & SONS CORP
Also Called: Michigan Playground Safety
3115 S Elms Rd (48473-7927)
PHONE 248 752-8165
Jack Walker, *President*
Laura Walker, *Corp Secy*
EMP: 3 **EST:** 1997
SALES (est): 372.9K **Privately Held**
WEB: www.jcwalkerandsons.com
SIC: 1799 5091 3949 Playground construction & equipment installation; sporting & recreation goods; playground equipment

(G-15669)
NAGEL PAPER INC
6437 Lennon Rd (48473-7916)
PHONE 989 753-4405
Marcus J Baker, *President*
James L Baker, *CFO*
Linda Elaine Baker, *Admin Sec*
▲ **EMP:** 20 **EST:** 1924
SQ FT: 35,000
SALES (est): 5.4MM **Privately Held**
WEB: www.npbc.com
SIC: 2655 Tubes, fiber or paper: made from purchased material

(G-15670)
WREATHS BY HEATHER RE NEE
4377 Staunton Dr (48473-8278)
PHONE 810 874-3119
Heather Ramsey, *Principal*
EMP: 3 **EST:** 2015
SALES (est): 121.1K **Privately Held**
SIC: 3999 Wreaths, artificial

Sylvan Lake
Oakland County

(G-15671)
AVIAN ENTERPRISES LLC (PA)
Also Called: Avian Control
2000 Pontiac Dr (48320-1758)
PHONE 888 366-0709
Jon Stone, *President*
Steven Stone, *Exec VP*
Kenneth Stone, *Vice Pres*
EMP: 20 **EST:** 2013
SQ FT: 100,000
SALES (est): 1.8MM **Privately Held**
SIC: 2879 Agricultural chemicals

(G-15672)
STONE SOAP COMPANY INC
2000 Pontiac Dr (48320-1758)
PHONE 248 706-1000
Kenneth Stone, *Ch of Bd*
Steven Stone, *Exec VP*
Jackie Elchemmas, *Plant Mgr*
Jon Stone, *Controller*
Dan Kramer, *Manager*
▲ **EMP:** 50 **EST:** 1932
SQ FT: 150,000
SALES (est): 14.8MM **Privately Held**
SIC: 2841 2844 Soap & other detergents; cosmetic preparations

(G-15673)
WMV INCORPORATED
2187 Orchard Lake Rd # 205 (48320-1779)
PHONE 248 333-1380
Aron Lorenz, *President*
▲ **EMP:** 3
SQ FT: 1,500
SALES: 535K **Privately Held**
SIC: 3531 Finishers & spreaders (construction equipment)

(G-15674)
WORLD WIDE CABINETS INC
2655 Orchard Lake Rd # 101 (48320-1571)
PHONE 248 683-2680
Ralph Campbell, *President*
EMP: 10
SQ FT: 4,000
SALES: 870K **Privately Held**
WEB: www.worldwidecabinets.com
SIC: 2434 Wood kitchen cabinets

Tawas City
Iosco County

(G-15675)
ADVANCE MACHINE CORP
612 9th Ave (48763-9532)
P.O. Box 789 (48764-0789)
PHONE 989 362-9192
Gary Schulman, *President*
Kellee Chomin, *Manager*
EMP: 5
SQ FT: 9,000
SALES (est): 370K **Privately Held**
SIC: 3599 Machine shop, jobbing & repair

(G-15676)
PLASTIC TRIM INC
905 Cedar St (48763-9200)
PHONE 937 429-1100
Bill Carroll, *President*
▲ **EMP:** 400
SALES (est): 49.5MM **Privately Held**
SIC: 3089 Extruded finished plastic products; injection molding of plastics

(G-15677)
R E GLANCY INC (PA)
124 W M 55 (48763-9251)
P.O. Box 418 (48764-0418)
PHONE 989 362-0997
Michael Glancy, *President*
Rhoda Moelter, *Corp Secy*
Robert E Glancy Jr, *Vice Pres*
EMP: 20 **EST:** 1963
SALES (est): 1.6MM **Privately Held**
SIC: 1422 Limestones, ground

(G-15678)
R E GLANCY INC
5278 Turner Rd (48763-9403)
P.O. Box 418 (48764-0418)
PHONE 989 876-6030
EMP: 3
SALES (corp-wide): 3.4MM **Privately Held**
SIC: 1442 1422 Portable Gravel Plants Mining Construction Sand & Gravel & Limestone
PA: R E Glancy Inc
124 W M 55
Tawas City MI 48763
989 362-0997

(G-15679)
STRAITS CORPORATION (PA)
616 Oak St (48763-9338)
PHONE 989 684-5088
Michael D Seward, *CEO*
Charles A Pinkerton III, *President*
Michael J Biber, *Treasurer*
Katie Look, *Controller*
William F Bartlett, *Manager*
EMP: 12 **EST:** 1953
SQ FT: 15,200
SALES: 21.7MM **Privately Held**
SIC: 4011 0211 2491 5712 Railroads, line-haul operating; beef cattle feedlots; wood preserving; furniture stores

Tawas City - Iosco County (G-15680) — GEOGRAPHIC SECTION

(G-15680)
STRAITS OPERATIONS COMPANY
616 Oak St (48763-9338)
PHONE 989 684-5088
Charles A Pinkerton III, *President*
Michael Biber, *Treasurer*
EMP: 9
SALES: 2MM
SALES (corp-wide): 21.7MM **Privately Held**
SIC: 2491 Wood preserving
PA: The Straits Corporation
616 Oak St
Tawas City MI 48763
989 684-5088

(G-15681)
STRAITS SERVICE CORPORATION
616 Oak St (48763-9338)
PHONE 989 684-5088
Charles A Pinkerton III, *President*
EMP: 14
SQ FT: 14,000
SALES: 880K
SALES (corp-wide): 21.7MM **Privately Held**
SIC: 2491 Wood preserving
PA: The Straits Corporation
616 Oak St
Tawas City MI 48763
989 684-5088

(G-15682)
STRAITS WOOD TREATING INC (HQ)
616 Oak St (48763-9338)
PHONE 989 684-5088
Charles A Pinkerton III, *President*
James P Pitz, *Vice Pres*
EMP: 1
SALES: 4.7MM
SALES (corp-wide): 21.7MM **Privately Held**
SIC: 2491 Wood preserving
PA: The Straits Corporation
616 Oak St
Tawas City MI 48763
989 684-5088

(G-15683)
TAWAS PLATING COMPANY
510 Industrial Ave (48763-9110)
P.O. Box 419 (48764-0419)
PHONE 989 362-2011
Kevin T Jungquist, *President*
Deborah K Jungquist, *Corp Secy*
Diane Knight, *Vice Pres*
Harold J Knight, *Vice Pres*
Lynette Knight, *Vice Pres*
EMP: 58
SQ FT: 30,000
SALES (est): 6.1MM **Privately Held**
WEB: www.tawasplating.com
SIC: 3471 Plating of metals or formed products

(G-15684)
TAWAS POWDER COATING INC
510 Industrial Ave (48763-9110)
P.O. Box 419 (48764-0419)
PHONE 989 362-2011
Harold Knight, *President*
EMP: 40
SQ FT: 18,000
SALES (est): 3.5MM **Privately Held**
SIC: 3479 Coating of metals & formed products

Taylor
Wayne County

(G-15685)
AJM PACKAGING CORPORATION
Also Called: Roblaw Industries
21130 Trolley Indus Dr (48180-1871)
PHONE 313 291-6500
Keith Stillson, *Administration*
EMP: 50
SALES (corp-wide): 351.1MM **Privately Held**
WEB: www.ajmpack.com
SIC: 2674 2679 Paper bags: made from purchased materials; plates, pressed & molded pulp: from purchased material
PA: A.J.M. Packaging Corporation
E-4111 Andover Rd
Bloomfield Hills MI 48302
248 901-0040

(G-15686)
AMERICAN SPEEDY PRINTING CTRS
20320 Ecorse Rd (48180-1953)
PHONE 313 928-5820
Jeff Reynolds, *Owner*
EMP: 6
SALES (est): 420K **Privately Held**
SIC: 2752 Commercial printing, offset

(G-15687)
AMERICANE SUGAR REFINING LLC (PA)
Also Called: Amcane Sugar
21010 Trolley Indus Dr (48180-1841)
PHONE 313 299-1300
Gregory F Kozak, *Mng Member*
Karen Malnar, *Mng Member*
◆ **EMP:** 4
SALES (est): 86.6MM **Privately Held**
SIC: 2062 Cane sugar refining

(G-15688)
ANDEX LASER INC
12222 Universal Dr (48180-4074)
PHONE 734 947-9840
Robert Anderson, *President*
Kevin Dexter, *Vice Pres*
EMP: 5
SALES (est): 958K **Privately Held**
SIC: 3699 Laser welding, drilling & cutting equipment; laser systems & equipment

(G-15689)
ANGSTROM AUTOMOTIVE GROUP LLC (PA)
26980 Trolley Indus Dr (48180-1424)
PHONE 313 295-0100
Nagesh Palakurthi,
EMP: 1
SALES (est): 70.8MM **Privately Held**
SIC: 3714 7389 7692 Axle housings & shafts, motor vehicle; ball joints, motor vehicle; drive shafts, motor vehicle; cloth cutting, bolting or winding; automotive welding

(G-15690)
ATLAS OIL TRANSPORTATION INC
24501 Ecorse Rd (48180-1641)
PHONE 800 878-2000
Sam Simon, *CEO*
Michael Evans, *President*
Edwin 'skip' Herbert, *Exec VP*
Robert Kenyon, *Exec VP*
Satish Kalala, *Vice Pres*
EMP: 11
SALES (est): 1.1MM **Privately Held**
SIC: 1389 Acidizing wells

(G-15691)
AUTOMOTIVE TRIM TECHNOLOGIES
12400 Universal Dr (48180-6837)
PHONE 734 947-0344
Gino Martino Jr, *CEO*
Diane Goodreau, *Engineer*
▲ **EMP:** 20
SQ FT: 5,000
SALES (est): 1.9MM **Privately Held**
SIC: 2396 Automotive trimmings, fabric

(G-15692)
AVANTI PRESS INC
22701 Trolley Industrial (48180-1895)
PHONE 313 961-0022
EMP: 35
SALES (corp-wide): 14.2MM **Privately Held**
WEB: www.avantipress.com
SIC: 2771 Greeting cards
PA: Avanti Press, Inc.
155 W Congress St Ste 200
Detroit MI 48226
800 228-2684

(G-15693)
B & D THREAD ROLLING INC
Also Called: B & D Cold Heading
25000 Brest (48180-4042)
PHONE 734 728-7070
Dennis Doyle, *President*
Tom Glinski, *Engineer*
Scott Sanderson, *CFO*
Lucy Doyle, *Treasurer*
Ted Schiebold, *Sales Mgr*
▲ **EMP:** 62
SQ FT: 110,000
SALES (est): 27MM **Privately Held**
WEB: www.bdthreadrolling.com
SIC: 3444 3452 Studs & joists, sheet metal; bolts, metal

(G-15694)
B G INDUSTRIES INC
6835 Monroe Blvd (48180-1815)
PHONE 313 292-5355
Gerald Cummings, *President*
EMP: 14
SQ FT: 50,000
SALES (est): 1.4MM **Privately Held**
SIC: 3599 Machine shop, jobbing & repair

(G-15695)
BALOGH
14102 Jackson St (48180-5349)
PHONE 734 283-3972
Timothy Balogh, *Principal*
EMP: 3
SALES (est): 217.7K **Privately Held**
SIC: 3661 Telephone & telegraph apparatus

(G-15696)
BJERKE FORGINGS INC
20257 Ecorse Rd (48180-1956)
P.O. Box 250, Allen Park (48101-0250)
PHONE 313 382-2600
Dale E Bjerke, *President*
EMP: 594
SALES (est): 46.2MM **Privately Held**
WEB: www.bjerkeforgings.com
SIC: 3312 3462 Blast furnaces & steel mills; iron & steel forgings

(G-15697)
C L RIECKHOFF COMPANY INC (PA)
26265 Northline Rd (48180-4412)
PHONE 734 946-8220
Charles Rieckhoff, *President*
John Rieckhoff, *Plant Mgr*
Dan Rieckhoff, *Project Mgr*
Al Shriver, *Project Mgr*
▲ **EMP:** 120 **EST:** 1963
SQ FT: 60,000
SALES (est): 25MM **Privately Held**
SIC: 3444 1761 Sheet metalwork; siding contractor

(G-15698)
CAMPBELL SOUP COMPANY
21740 Trlley Indus Dr D (48180-1874)
PHONE 313 295-6884
Gordon McCarty, *Branch Mgr*
EMP: 10
SALES (corp-wide): 8.1B **Publicly Held**
SIC: 5461 2038 2033 2052 Bakeries; frozen specialties; canned fruits & specialties; cookies & crackers; bread, cake & related products; potato chips & similar snacks
PA: Campbell Soup Company
1 Campbell Pl
Camden NJ 08103
856 342-4800

(G-15699)
CATTLEMANS MEAT COMPANY
Also Called: Cattlemans Fresh Mt & Fish Mkt
11400 Telegraph Rd (48180-4078)
PHONE 734 287-8260
David S Rohtbart, *President*
Benjamin D Govaere, *Senior VP*
Markus Rohtbart, *Treasurer*
EMP: 275
SQ FT: 56,500
SALES: 18.4MM **Privately Held**
SIC: 2013 5421 Prepared beef products from purchased beef; meat markets, including freezer provisioners

(G-15700)
CITY OF TAYLOR
Also Called: Public Works Dept
25605 Northline Rd (48180-7908)
PHONE 734 374-1372
James Katona, *Exec Dir*
EMP: 50 **Privately Held**
SIC: 3991 4959 4212 Street sweeping brooms, hand or machine; sanitary services; local trucking, without storage
PA: City Of Taylor
23555 Goddard Rd
Taylor MI 48180
734 374-1474

(G-15701)
CLASSIC JERKY COMPANY
21655 Trolley Indus Dr (48180-1811)
PHONE 313 357-9904
Debbie Rightmer, *President*
Jeff Sigouin, *Managing Dir*
Pedro Kanegae, *CFO*
▼ **EMP:** 75 **EST:** 2015
SALES (est): 257.6K
SALES (corp-wide): 146MM **Privately Held**
SIC: 2013 Snack sticks, including jerky: from purchased meat
PA: Link Snacks, Inc.
1 Snack Food Ln
Minong WI 54859
715 466-2234

(G-15702)
CO-PIPE PRODUCTS INC
20501 Goddard Rd (48180-4352)
PHONE 734 287-1000
Jenny Coco, *CEO*
Rocky Coco, *President*
Nina Coco, *Manager*
Monica Marshall, *Manager*
EMP: 45 **EST:** 1930
SALES (est): 7.9MM **Privately Held**
WEB: www.copipe.com
SIC: 3272 Sewer pipe, concrete

(G-15703)
COLONIAL TOOL SALES & SVC LLC
Also Called: Advanced Cutting Tool Systems
12344 Delta St (48180-6832)
PHONE 734 946-2733
Dina Dicarlo, *Purchasing*
Paul Thrasher,
Brett Froats,
▲ **EMP:** 10
SQ FT: 28,000
SALES (est): 1.8MM **Privately Held**
WEB: www.colonialtool.com
SIC: 3545 Cutting tools for machine tools

(G-15704)
COMMERCIAL GROUP INC (PA)
Also Called: Commercial Group Lifting Pdts
12801 Universal Dr (48180-6844)
PHONE 313 931-6100
Garland Knight, *President*
Scottie Knight, *COO*
Tony Zomparelli, *Vice Pres*
Sonja Chumura, *Purch Agent*
Jim Karshina, *CFO*
▼ **EMP:** 47 **EST:** 1956
SQ FT: 220,000
SALES (est): 53.5MM **Privately Held**
WEB: www.commercial-group.com
SIC: 5085 5051 3496 3537 Industrial supplies; rope, wire (not insulated); cable, wire; cable, uninsulated wire: made from purchased wire; wire chain; industrial trucks & tractors; elevators & moving stairways

(G-15705)
CUT ALL WATER JET CUTTING INC
25944 Northline Rd (48180-4413)
PHONE 734 946-7880
Patrick Spence, *President*
EMP: 8
SQ FT: 6,000

▲ = Import ▼ = Export
◆ = Import/Export

GEOGRAPHIC SECTION

Taylor - Wayne County (G-15732)

SALES (est): 1.3MM **Privately Held**
SIC: 3599 Machine shop, jobbing & repair

(G-15706)
DEARBORN MID-WEST COMPANY LLC (PA)
20334 Superior Rd (48180-6301)
PHONE.................................734 288-4400
Jeff Homenik, *President*
C Bagierek, *Vice Pres*
Yasser Haidar-Ahmad, *Project Mgr*
Marius Vlad, *Project Mgr*
Mike Olson, *Engineer*
▲ EMP: 150
SALES: 176.4MM **Privately Held**
SIC: 3535 Conveyors & conveying equipment

(G-15707)
DOLPHIN MANUFACTURING INC
12650 Universal Dr (48180-6839)
PHONE.................................734 946-6322
Alvin R Fritz, *President*
Derek Fritz, *General Mgr*
Teresa Fritz, *Treasurer*
EMP: 25 EST: 1982
SQ FT: 33,000
SALES (est): 5.3MM **Privately Held**
SIC: 3714 3728 3544 3429 Motor vehicle engines & parts; aircraft parts & equipment; special dies, tools, jigs & fixtures; manufactured hardware (general)

(G-15708)
DOWNRIVER CRUSHED CONCRETE
20538 Pennsylvania Rd (48180-5331)
PHONE.................................734 283-1833
Larry Roy, *Owner*
EMP: 8
SALES (est): 638.1K **Privately Held**
SIC: 3273 1442 Ready-mixed concrete; construction sand & gravel

(G-15709)
DOWNRIVER DEBURRING INC
20248 Lorne St (48180-1970)
PHONE.................................313 388-2640
Bryan Neely, *President*
EMP: 4
SQ FT: 4,600
SALES: 250K **Privately Held**
SIC: 3471 Plating & polishing

(G-15710)
DUKE DE JONG LLC
12680 Delta St (48180-6833)
PHONE.................................734 403-1708
Hillary Carter, *Plant Mgr*
Michael De Jong, *Opers Staff*
Jeff Rhoades, *Technical Staff*
▲ EMP: 5
SQ FT: 20,000
SALES (est): 1.4MM
SALES (corp-wide): 183.7K **Privately Held**
SIC: 3556 Roasting machinery: coffee, peanut, etc.
HQ: J.M. De Jong Duke Automatenfabriek B.V.
Bruningsstraat 1
Sliedrecht 3364
184 496-769

(G-15711)
DURA-PACK INC
Also Called: Dura Pack
7641 Holland Rd (48180-1450)
PHONE.................................313 299-9600
Tim Harrison, *President*
Linda Harrison, *Corp Secy*
▲ EMP: 20
SQ FT: 25,000
SALES (est): 6MM **Privately Held**
SIC: 3565 5046 Packaging machinery; scales, except laboratory

(G-15712)
EDGEWELL PERSONAL CARE COMPANY
12103 Delta St (48180-4082)
PHONE.................................866 462-8669
Alan Hoskins, *Branch Mgr*
EMP: 3
SALES (corp-wide): 2.2B **Publicly Held**
SIC: 3421 Razor blades & razors
PA: Edgewell Personal Care Company
1350 Tmberlake Manor Pkwy
Chesterfield MO 63017
314 594-1900

(G-15713)
EFTEC NORTH AMERICA LLC (PA)
20219 Northline Rd (48180-4786)
PHONE.................................248 585-2200
Shawn Kelly, *Project Mgr*
Rodney Lowe, *Project Mgr*
Mark Korytkowski, *QA Dir*
Debbie Haliczer, *Human Res Mgr*
Uwe Bonkat,
▲ EMP: 90
SQ FT: 50,000
SALES (est): 86.3MM **Privately Held**
WEB: www.eftec.com
SIC: 2891 8731 3296 2899 Adhesives & sealants; commercial physical research; mineral wool; chemical preparations; paints & allied products

(G-15714)
ELDEN CYLINDER TESTING INC
9465 Inkster Rd (48180-3044)
PHONE.................................734 946-6900
Denis J Hurley III, *President*
Brian Hurley, *General Mgr*
EMP: 20 EST: 2001
SALES: 1.5MM **Privately Held**
WEB: www.eldencylindertesting.com
SIC: 3443 Cylinders, pressure: metal plate

(G-15715)
ELDEN INDUSTRIES CORPORATION
9465 Inkster Rd (48180-3044)
PHONE.................................734 946-6900
Dennis J Hurley III, *President*
Brian Hurley, *General Mgr*
Lorie Ouellette, *Office Mgr*
EMP: 15
SQ FT: 13,000
SALES (est): 1.6MM **Privately Held**
SIC: 7692 8734 3369 2295 Cracked casting repair; testing laboratories; nonferrous foundries; coated fabrics, not rubberized

(G-15716)
EPIC FINE ARTS COMPANY INC (HQ)
21001 Van Born Rd (48180-1340)
PHONE.................................313 274-7400
Eugene Gargaro, *President*
EMP: 5
SALES (est): 37.6MM
SALES (corp-wide): 8.3B **Publicly Held**
SIC: 3993 3432 Advertising artwork; faucets & spigots, metal & plastic
PA: Masco Corporation
17450 College Pkwy
Livonia MI 48152
313 274-7400

(G-15717)
EXCEL SCREW MACHINE TOOLS
20300 Lorne St (48180-1969)
PHONE.................................313 383-4200
Rita Baumler, *President*
Kevin Baumler, *Corp Secy*
Gerald Baumler, *Vice Pres*
EMP: 9
SQ FT: 5,100
SALES (est): 430K **Privately Held**
SIC: 3545 Pushers

(G-15718)
F & F INDUSTRIES INC
Also Called: Unirak
7620 Telegraph Rd (48180-2237)
PHONE.................................313 278-7600
Dan Deradoorian, *President*
Eric Gonda, *Vice Pres*
Kevin Gonda, *Treasurer*
Alan Gliese, *Admin Sec*
EMP: 26
SQ FT: 20,000
SALES (est): 243.4K **Privately Held**
SIC: 2542 Pallet racks: except wood

(G-15719)
F F INDUSTRIES
7620 Telegraph Rd (48180-2237)
PHONE.................................313 291-7600
Eric Joseph Gonda, *Administration*
EMP: 7
SALES (est): 1MM **Privately Held**
SIC: 2542 Pallet racks: except wood

(G-15720)
FASTIME RACING ENGINES & PARTS
12254 Universal Dr (48180-4074)
PHONE.................................734 947-1600
Christine Smith, *Owner*
Clayton Smith, *Principal*
EMP: 4
SALES (est): 409.2K **Privately Held**
SIC: 3714 Motor vehicle parts & accessories

(G-15721)
FAURECIA EMISSIONS CONTL TECH
24850 Northline Rd (48180-4594)
PHONE.................................734 947-1688
Richard Belcher, *Branch Mgr*
EMP: 443
SALES (corp-wide): 38.2MM **Privately Held**
WEB: www.emcontechnologies.com
SIC: 3714 Motor vehicle parts & accessories
HQ: Faurecia Emissions Control Technologies Usa, Llc
950 W 450 S
Columbus IN 47201

(G-15722)
FEDEX OFFICE & PRINT SVCS INC
23077 Eureka Rd (48180-5255)
PHONE.................................734 374-0225
EMP: 15
SALES (corp-wide): 69.6B **Publicly Held**
WEB: www.kinkos.com
SIC: 7334 7338 2791 2789 Photocopying & duplicating services; secretarial & court reporting; typesetting; bookbinding & related work; commercial printing; commercial printing, lithographic
HQ: Fedex Office And Print Services, Inc.
7900 Legacy Dr
Plano TX 75024
800 463-3339

(G-15723)
FORD MOTOR COMPANY
21001 Van Born Rd (48180-1340)
PHONE.................................910 381-7998
Minyang Jiang, *Branch Mgr*
EMP: 22
SALES (corp-wide): 160.3B **Publicly Held**
SIC: 5511 3713 Automobiles, new & used; truck & bus bodies
PA: Ford Motor Company
1 American Rd
Dearborn MI 48126
313 322-3000

(G-15724)
G & R MACHINE TOOL INC
20410 Superior Rd (48180-5362)
PHONE.................................734 641-6560
Susana N Kornijenko, *President*
Jorge Kornijenko, *Vice Pres*
Ralph Sulek, *Vice Pres*
Lucy Sulek, *Treasurer*
EMP: 6
SALES (est): 1.1MM **Privately Held**
SIC: 3999 Military insignia

(G-15725)
GENERAL DYNAMICS CORPORATION
Also Called: Wireless Svcs Div Navy A Force
25435 Brest (48180-6811)
PHONE.................................615 427-5768
Steve Baier, *Manager*
EMP: 40
SALES (corp-wide): 36.1B **Publicly Held**
SIC: 3812 Aircraft/aerospace flight instruments & guidance systems
PA: General Dynamics Corporation
11011 Sunset Hills Rd
Reston VA 20190
703 876-3000

(G-15726)
GREAT FRESH FOODS CO LLC
Also Called: Clean Planet Foods
21740 Trolley Industrial (48180-1875)
PHONE.................................586 846-3521
Shawn Spencer, *President*
Jack Aronson, *Mng Member*
David Koslosky, *Director*
EMP: 16
SALES (est): 2.3MM **Privately Held**
SIC: 2013 Cooked meats from purchased meat

(G-15727)
GREENSEED LLC
26980 Trolley Indus Dr (48180-1424)
PHONE.................................313 295-0100
EMP: 5 EST: 2008
SQ FT: 30,000
SALES (est): 390K **Privately Held**
SIC: 3463 Nonferrous Forgings

(G-15728)
HANCOCK ENTERPRISES INC
Also Called: Corky's Bar and Restaurant
20655 Northline Rd (48180-4797)
PHONE.................................734 287-8840
John Hancock Jr, *CEO*
Bob Joly, *President*
Cindy Joly, *Corp Secy*
Robert Joly, *Manager*
▲ EMP: 65
SQ FT: 80,000
SALES (est): 14.7MM **Privately Held**
SIC: 3444 3354 Metal roofing & roof drainage equipment; aluminum extruded products

(G-15729)
J & B PRECISION INC
5886 Pelham Rd (48180-1391)
PHONE.................................313 565-3431
Gerald Bartoszek, *President*
Stanley Bartoszek, *Chairman*
EMP: 6
SQ FT: 5,000
SALES (est): 961.3K **Privately Held**
SIC: 3545 Precision tools, machinists'

(G-15730)
JAMISON INDUSTRIES INC
12669 Delta St (48180-6835)
PHONE.................................734 946-3088
Eugene Jamison Jr, *President*
Matt J Jamison, *General Mgr*
Sharon Jamison, *Corp Secy*
EMP: 12
SQ FT: 10,000
SALES (est): 2.2MM **Privately Held**
SIC: 3599 Machine shop, jobbing & repair

(G-15731)
JOHNSON MATTHEY NORTH AMER INC
12600 Universal Dr (48180-6839)
PHONE.................................734 946-9856
Robert Bullen-Smith, *General Mgr*
Tim Stevenson, *Chairman*
Paul Evans, *Vice Pres*
Martin Anderson, *Safety Mgr*
Andrew McClure, *Mfg Staff*
EMP: 1
SALES (est): 2.1MM
SALES (corp-wide): 13.8B **Privately Held**
SIC: 3341 Gold smelting & refining (secondary)
HQ: Matthey Johnson Holdings Inc
435 Devon Park Dr Ste 600
Wayne PA 19087
610 971-3000

(G-15732)
KAMPS INC
20310 Pennsylvania Rd (48180-6370)
PHONE.................................734 281-3300
Kim Collura, *Manager*
EMP: 24
SALES (corp-wide): 157.4MM **Privately Held**
SIC: 2448 Pallets, wood

Taylor - Wayne County (G-15733) GEOGRAPHIC SECTION

PA: Kamps, Inc.
2900 Peach Ridge Ave Nw
Grand Rapids MI 49534
616 453-9676

(G-15733)
KRUSH INDUSTRIES INC
12729 Universal Dr (48180-6843)
PHONE..................................248 238-2296
Kyle T Rushing, *President*
EMP: 4 **EST:** 2010
SQ FT: 3,600
SALES: 250K **Privately Held**
SIC: 3569 Robots, assembly line: industrial & commercial

(G-15734)
LEAR CORPORATION
Also Called: United Technologies
26575 Northline Rd (48180-4479)
PHONE..................................734 946-1600
Roger Vail, *Plant Mgr*
Alex Farhart, *Project Mgr*
Monika Redmond, *Engineer*
Dragos Serbanescu, *Engineer*
EMP: 120
SALES (corp-wide): 21.1B **Publicly Held**
WEB: www.lear.com
SIC: 3714 Motor vehicle parts & accessories
PA: Lear Corporation
21557 Telegraph Rd
Southfield MI 48033
248 447-1500

(G-15735)
LEONARD & RANDY INC
20555 Northline Rd (48180-4779)
PHONE..................................734 287-9500
Randy Sides, *President*
Leonard Sides, *Vice Pres*
Crystal Bryant, *Admin Sec*
EMP: 8
SALES (est): 1.1MM **Privately Held**
SIC: 3715 4212 Semitrailers for truck tractors; steel hauling, local

(G-15736)
MA MA LA ROSA FOODS INC
12100 Universal Dr (48180-4000)
PHONE..................................734 946-7878
James D Larosa, *President*
Michael Franchi, *Vice Pres*
Kevin Zevchak, *Sales Mgr*
Sandy Cherry, *Manager*
EMP: 14
SQ FT: 15,000
SALES (est): 4MM **Privately Held**
WEB: www.mamalarosafoods.com
SIC: 2045 Pizza doughs, prepared: from purchased flour

(G-15737)
MASCO DE PUERTO RICO INC
21001 Van Born Rd (48180-1340)
PHONE..................................313 274-7400
Richard Manoogian, *CEO*
EMP: 4
SALES (est): 223.4K
SALES (corp-wide): 8.3B **Publicly Held**
WEB: www.masco.com
SIC: 3432 Plumbing fixture fittings & trim
PA: Masco Corporation
17450 College Pkwy
Livonia MI 48152
313 274-7400

(G-15738)
MEL PRINTING CO INC
Also Called: Mel Media Group
6000 Pardee Rd (48180-1316)
PHONE..................................313 928-5440
Michael Filkovich, *President*
August Grebinski, *Vice Pres*
Joyce Hunter, *Vice Pres*
Michelle Martinez, *Prdtn Mgr*
Tiffany Topor, *Manager*
EMP: 26
SQ FT: 10,000
SALES (est): 7.4MM **Privately Held**
WEB: www.melprinting.com
SIC: 2752 2796 2789 2732 Commercial printing, offset; platemaking services; bookbinding & related work; book printing

(G-15739)
MESSENGER PRINTING SERVICE
20136 Ecorse Rd (48180-1957)
PHONE..................................313 381-0300
Robert Herriman, *President*
EMP: 24
SQ FT: 4,200
SALES (est): 2.8MM **Privately Held**
WEB: www.messengerprinting.com
SIC: 2752 Commercial printing, offset

(G-15740)
METRIE INC
27025 Trolley Indus Dr (48180-1423)
PHONE..................................313 299-1860
Larry Boldt, *Manager*
Sherry Andrews, *Info Tech Mgr*
EMP: 18
SALES (corp-wide): 183.4MM **Privately Held**
SIC: 2431 Millwork
HQ: Metrie Inc.
2200 140th Ave E Ste 600
Sumner WA 98390
253 470-5050

(G-15741)
MI CUSTOM SIGNS LLC
20109 Northline Rd (48180-4726)
PHONE..................................734 946-7446
Ken Moreno, *Sales Staff*
Rene R Pare,
EMP: 10
SALES (est): 320.2K **Privately Held**
SIC: 3993 Signs, not made in custom sign painting shops

(G-15742)
MICHIGAN INDUSTRIAL TRIM INC (PA)
12400 Universal Dr (48180-6837)
P.O. Box 1676 (48180-6676)
PHONE..................................734 947-0344
Gino Martino, *CEO*
Renee Perez, *Controller*
EMP: 17
SQ FT: 12,000
SALES (est): 1.3MM **Privately Held**
WEB: www.mitproto.com
SIC: 2399 Automotive covers, except seat & tire covers

(G-15743)
MICHIGAN POLY SUPPLIES INC
26060 Northline Rd (48180-6510)
PHONE..................................734 282-5554
Lalit Sood, *President*
EMP: 3
SALES (est): 552.6K **Privately Held**
SIC: 2676 2673 5113 Towels, napkins & tissue paper products; trash bags (plastic film): made from purchased materials; plastic bags: made from purchased materials; cups, disposable plastic & paper

(G-15744)
MIDWEST FABRICATING INC
26465 Northline Rd (48180-4479)
PHONE..................................734 921-3914
Joyce Smith, *CEO*
Steve Smith, *President*
EMP: 5
SQ FT: 8,000
SALES (est): 500K **Privately Held**
SIC: 3441 7539 7692 Fabricated structural metal; machine shop, automotive; automotive welding

(G-15745)
MODERN CAM AND TOOL CO
27272 Wick Rd (48180-3097)
PHONE..................................734 946-9800
Scott A Bitters, *President*
EMP: 8
SQ FT: 6,750
SALES (est): 580.8K **Privately Held**
WEB: www.moderncam.com
SIC: 3545 Cams (machine tool accessories)

(G-15746)
MONOGRAMS & MORE INC
Also Called: Impressions Specialty Advg
8914 Telegraph Rd (48180-8399)
PHONE..................................313 299-3140
Louise A Leveque, *President*
Marlene Zerkel, *Vice Pres*
EMP: 35
SQ FT: 8,700
SALES (est): 4.6MM **Privately Held**
WEB: www.impressionsco.com
SIC: 2395 2759 5199 Embroidery & art needlework; screen printing; advertising specialties

(G-15747)
MOTOR CITY METAL FAB INC
24340 Northline Rd (48180-4586)
PHONE..................................734 345-1001
Sheri Zimmerman, *Principal*
▼ **EMP:** 20
SALES (est): 549.2K **Privately Held**
SIC: 3479 Coating of metals & formed products

(G-15748)
MOTOWN HARLEY-DAVIDSON INC
Also Called: Biker Bobs Hrly-Dvidson Motown
14100 Telegraph Rd (48180-8208)
PHONE..................................734 947-4647
Robert A Demattia, *President*
A Jason Breckenridge, *Vice Pres*
Steven Chapin, *Vice Pres*
Paul Rzepka, *CFO*
Mary Davis, *Admin Sec*
EMP: 68 **EST:** 1997
SQ FT: 55,000
SALES (est): 14.7MM **Privately Held**
WEB: www.bikerbobshd.com
SIC: 5571 7694 Motorcycles; motor repair services

(G-15749)
NEWELL BRANDS INC
20033 Eureka Rd (48180-5372)
PHONE..................................734 284-2528
Donna Root, *Vice Pres*
Tim Hollingsworth, *Branch Mgr*
EMP: 6
SALES (corp-wide): 8.6B **Publicly Held**
SIC: 3911 Jewelry, precious metal
PA: Newell Brands Inc.
221 River St Ste 13
Hoboken NJ 07030
201 610-6600

(G-15750)
OAKWOOD ENERGY MANAGEMENT INC (HQ)
Also Called: Oakwood Expansion
9755 Inkster Rd (48180-3048)
PHONE..................................734 947-7700
Richard Audi II, *President*
Mike Wimberly, *Exec Dir*
▲ **EMP:** 175
SQ FT: 41,000
SALES (est): 14.1MM
SALES (corp-wide): 178.3MM **Privately Held**
SIC: 3479 3544 3441 3089 Painting, coating & hot dipping; special dies & tools; fabricated structural metal; injection molded finished plastic products
PA: Oakwood Metal Fabricating Co.
1100 Oakwood Blvd
Dearborn MI 48124
313 561-7740

(G-15751)
OAKWOOD METAL FABRICATING CO
Oakwood Plastic Division
9755 Inkster Rd (48180-3048)
PHONE..................................734 947-7740
Tony Shackelford, *QC Mgr*
Matthew Gerwolls, *Marketing Staff*
Stan Keennarv, *Manager*
Sharon Harper, *Administration*
EMP: 300
SALES (est): 21MM
SALES (corp-wide): 178.3MM **Privately Held**
SIC: 3465 Automotive stampings

PA: Oakwood Metal Fabricating Co.
1100 Oakwood Blvd
Dearborn MI 48124
313 561-7740

(G-15752)
OLDCASTLE BUILDINGENVELOPE INC
26471 Nrthline Cmmerce Dr (48180-7951)
PHONE..................................734 947-9670
EMP: 19
SALES (corp-wide): 23.7B **Privately Held**
SIC: 3231 5231 Mfg Products-Purchased Glass Ret Paint/Glass/Wallpaper
HQ: Oldcastle Buildingenvelope, Inc.
5005 Lbj Fwy Ste 1050
Dallas TX 75244
214 273-3400

(G-15753)
PERFECT DISH LLC
21867 Kings Pte Blvd (48180)
P.O. Box 84 (48180-0084)
PHONE..................................313 784-3976
Antionette Arnold,
EMP: 5
SALES: 240K **Privately Held**
SIC: 2599 Food wagons, restaurant

(G-15754)
PPG INDUSTRIES INC
22673 Northline Rd (48180-4661)
PHONE..................................734 287-2110
Dan Coski, *Branch Mgr*
EMP: 4
SALES (corp-wide): 15.3B **Publicly Held**
WEB: www.ppg.com
SIC: 2851 Paints & allied products
PA: Ppg Industries, Inc.
1 Ppg Pl
Pittsburgh PA 15272
412 434-3131

(G-15755)
PRECISION FRAMING SYSTEMS INC
Also Called: Pfs
21001 Van Born Rd (48180-1340)
PHONE..................................704 588-6680
EMP: 50
SALES (est): 4.9MM
SALES (corp-wide): 7.6B **Publicly Held**
SIC: 2439 2435 Mfg Wood House Frames Wood Trusses
PA: Masco Corporation
17450 College Pkwy
Livonia MI 48152
313 274-7400

(G-15756)
PRIME INDUSTRIES INC
12350 Universal Dr (48180-4070)
P.O. Box 1890 (48180-5990)
PHONE..................................734 946-8588
EMP: 20
SQ FT: 8,000
SALES (est): 1.8MM **Privately Held**
SIC: 3541 3545 3544 Mfg Machine Tools-Cutting Mfg Machine Tool Accessories Mfg Dies/Tools/Jigs/Fixtures

(G-15757)
PRINTING SYSTEMS INC
12005 Beech Daly Rd (48180-3936)
PHONE..................................734 946-5111
Edwin G Stevens, *President*
Mark Stevens, *Vice Pres*
Ronda Wilson, *Director*
EMP: 6
SALES (est): 1.7MM **Privately Held**
SIC: 2752 Commercial printing, lithographic

(G-15758)
PRINTWELL ACQUISITION CO INC
Also Called: Printwell Printing
26975 Northline Rd (48180-4408)
PHONE..................................734 941-6300
Paul Borg, *Ch of Bd*
James Callender, *Vice Pres*
Dave Schacht, *Opers Mgr*
Shawn Borg, *CFO*
Kevin R Donley, *VP Sales*
▲ **EMP:** 97

GEOGRAPHIC SECTION   Tecumseh - Lenawee County (G-15786)

SQ FT: 18,000
SALES (est): 26.4MM **Privately Held**
WEB: www.printwell.com
SIC: 2789 7331 2759 Bookbinding & related work; direct mail advertising services; commercial printing

(G-15759)
PROTO MANUFACTURING INC
12350 Universal Dr (48180-4070)
PHONE 734 946-0974
Michael Brauss, *President*
Daniel Gorzen, *Vice Pres*
Brian Simpson, *Electrical Engi*
EMP: 25
SQ FT: 20,000
SALES: 6.7MM **Privately Held**
WEB: www.protoxrd.com
SIC: 3826 Analytical instruments

(G-15760)
QUANTA CONTAINERS LLC (PA)
15801 Huron St (48180-5281)
PHONE 734 282-3044
Vincent Concessi, *Mng Member*
EMP: 6
SALES: 5MM **Privately Held**
SIC: 2655 Fiber cans, drums & containers

(G-15761)
RAINBOW PIZZA INC
Also Called: New Delray Baking Co
14702 Allen Rd (48180-5383)
PHONE 734 246-4250
Fax: 734 753-5867
EMP: 8
SALES (est): 666K **Privately Held**
SIC: 2051 5461 Bakery & Ret Bakery Goods

(G-15762)
REVAK PRECISION GRINDING INC
20188 Lorne St (48180-1941)
PHONE 313 388-2626
Steve Hernandez, *President*
EMP: 4
SQ FT: 1,500
SALES: 200K **Privately Held**
SIC: 3599 Machine shop, jobbing & repair

(G-15763)
RHINO STRAPPING PRODUCTS INC
24341 Brest (48180-6848)
PHONE 734 442-4040
Gary Galliers, *President*
EMP: 12
SQ FT: 30,000
SALES: 3MM **Privately Held**
SIC: 3053 3493 3965 Gaskets & sealing devices; flat springs, sheet or strip stock; buckles & buckle parts

(G-15764)
SERVOTECH INDUSTRIES INC (PA)
25580 Brest (48180-4065)
PHONE 734 697-5555
Hamid Servati, *President*
EMP: 10
SQ FT: 10,000
SALES (est): 1MM **Privately Held**
SIC: 3599 3714 3444 3441 Machine shop, jobbing & repair; motor vehicle parts & accessories; sheet metalwork; fabricated structural metal

(G-15765)
SFS LLC
Also Called: Specialty Fabrication Services
12621 Universal Dr (48180-6842)
PHONE 734 947-4377
Kathy Rose, *Mng Member*
EMP: 5
SQ FT: 8,000
SALES (est): 481.5K **Privately Held**
SIC: 3599 Bellows, industrial: metal

(G-15766)
SILK REFLECTIONS
22018 Haig St (48180-3652)
PHONE 313 292-1150
Susan Ann Gray, *Partner*
Fred Gray, *Partner*
EMP: 4
SALES (est): 322.5K **Privately Held**
SIC: 2399 Hand woven & crocheted products

(G-15767)
SMI AMERICAN INC
6835 Monroe Blvd (48180-1815)
PHONE 313 438-0096
Vince Schiller, *Principal*
EMP: 4 EST: 2013
SALES (est): 295.4K **Privately Held**
SIC: 3441 Fabricated structural metal

(G-15768)
SMS GROUP INC
Also Called: Acutus Gladwin Industries
15200 Huron St (48180-6032)
PHONE 734 246-8230
Greg Merta, *General Mgr*
Daniel De Shetler, *Production*
EMP: 55
SALES (corp-wide): 144.1K **Privately Held**
SIC: 3569 Assembly machines, non-metalworking
HQ: Sms Group Inc.
    100 Sandusky St
    Pittsburgh PA 15212
    412 231-1200

(G-15769)
SMW MFG INC
25575 Brest (48180-6846)
PHONE 517 596-3300
Bob Danford, *Manager*
EMP: 36
SALES (corp-wide): 60MM **Privately Held**
SIC: 3599 Machine shop, jobbing & repair
PA: Smw Mfg, Inc.
    8707 Samuel Barton Dr
    Van Buren Twp MI 48111
    517 596-3300

(G-15770)
SPECIALTY ENG COMPONENTS LLC (PA)
25940 Northline Rd (48180-4413)
PHONE 734 955-6500
Mark E Nelms, *Mng Member*
Charles Pipis,
▲ EMP: 100 EST: 1946
SQ FT: 60,000
SALES (est): 16.7MM **Privately Held**
WEB: www.wathomas.com
SIC: 3714 Motor vehicle engines & parts

(G-15771)
SPEEDWAY LLC
Also Called: Speedway 8863
21943 Ecorse Rd (48180-1832)
PHONE 313 291-3710
Kay Lowery, *Manager*
EMP: 8 **Publicly Held**
WEB: www.speedwaynet.com
SIC: 1311 Crude petroleum production
HQ: Speedway Llc
    500 Speedway Dr
    Enon OH 45323
    937 864-3000

(G-15772)
SRG GLOBAL INC
12620 Delta St (48180-6833)
PHONE 586 757-7800
Joe Hoban, *Plant Mgr*
Kyle Wolfe, *Mfg Staff*
Brian Phillips, *Production*
Meredith Sorrow, *Production*
Shamieka Williams, *Production*
EMP: 15
SALES (corp-wide): 40.6B **Privately Held**
SIC: 2396 Automotive & apparel trimmings
HQ: Srg Global, Inc.
    800 Stephenson Hwy
    Troy MI 48083

(G-15773)
SUPERIOR FLUID SYSTEMS
7804 Beech Daly Rd (48180-1533)
PHONE 734 246-4550
Duane Brow, *Mng Member*
EMP: 9
SALES (est): 1.3MM **Privately Held**
SIC: 3498 Piping systems for pulp paper & chemical industries

(G-15774)
SUPERIOR SPINDLE SERVICES LLC
25377 Brest (48180-4054)
PHONE 734 946-4646
Kenneth Kirchner, *CEO*
Ray Baldwin, *President*
Pamela Egnatowski, *Purch Mgr*
Ronald Jaeger, *CFO*
EMP: 14
SALES (est): 2.4MM **Privately Held**
SIC: 2241 Spindle banding

(G-15775)
T-MACH INDUSTRIES LLC
7941 Margaret St (48180-2409)
PHONE 734 673-6964
Ronald Mason,
EMP: 3
SALES: 120K **Privately Held**
SIC: 3829 Measuring & controlling devices

(G-15776)
TAPOOS LLC
21813 Hunter Cir S (48180-6362)
PHONE 619 319-4872
Fahad Aslam,
EMP: 5
SALES (est): 130.5K **Privately Held**
SIC: 2741

(G-15777)
TOTAL MGT RECLAMATION SVCS LLC
8400 Beech Daly Rd (48180-2031)
P.O. Box 152, Newport (48166-0152)
PHONE 734 384-3500
Shannon Salter, *President*
EMP: 8
SALES: 1.3MM **Privately Held**
SIC: 3341 3462 Recovery & refining of nonferrous metals; automotive forgings, ferrous: crankshaft, engine, axle, etc.

(G-15778)
VINEWOOD METALCRAFT INC
9501 Inkster Rd (48180-3044)
P.O. Box 186 (48180-0186)
PHONE 734 946-8733
Claud M Mick Jr, *President*
Fred Mick, *President*
Mark Caudell, *Engineer*
Katie Gietl, *Controller*
Jim Gietl, *Sales Mgr*
EMP: 25
SQ FT: 23,000
SALES (est): 4.8MM **Privately Held**
SIC: 3469 Stamping metal for the trade

(G-15779)
W A THOMAS COMPANY
25940 Northline Rd (48180-4413)
PHONE 734 955-6500
Micheal Akowitz, *Principal*
Mark Nelms, *Principal*
EMP: 3
SALES (est): 300K **Privately Held**
SIC: 2273 3471 3312 Carpets & rugs; plating of metals or formed products; tool & die steel & alloys

(G-15780)
W B MASON CO INC
25299 Brest (48180-6850)
PHONE 734 947-6370
EMP: 52
SALES (corp-wide): 773MM **Privately Held**
SIC: 5943 5712 2752 Office forms & supplies; office furniture; commercial printing, lithographic
PA: W. B. Mason Co., Inc.
    59 Center St
    Brockton MA 02301
    781 794-8800

(G-15781)
WALLSIDE INC
Also Called: Wallside Window Factory
27000 Trolley Indus Dr (48180-1422)
PHONE 313 292-4400
Stanford Blanck, *President*
Stuart Blanck, *Treasurer*
Katy Cook, *Human Res Mgr*
Dave Ball, *Supervisor*
Mary Mertz, *Account Dir*
EMP: 10
SQ FT: 75,000
SALES (est): 3.6MM **Privately Held**
WEB: www.wallside.com
SIC: 1751 3442 Window & door (prefabricated) installation; metal doors, sash & trim

(G-15782)
WINDSOR MCH & STAMPING 2009
Also Called: W M G
26655 Northline Rd (48180-4481)
PHONE 734 941-7320
Paul Brancaccio, *VP Opers*
Sal Di Stefano, *Plant Mgr*
Wendell Zhen, *Materials Mgr*
Laura Richie, *QC Mgr*
Mary Manners, *Branch Mgr*
EMP: 64
SALES (corp-wide): 18.2MM **Privately Held**
SIC: 3714 Motor vehicle parts & accessories
PA: Windsor Machine & Stamping (2009) Ltd
    2187 Huron Church Rd Unit 340a
    Windsor ON N9C 2
    519 737-7155

(G-15783)
WORTHINGTON STEEL OF MICHIGAN (HQ)
11700 Worthington Dr (48180-4390)
PHONE 734 374-3260
John Christie, *President*
Dale T Brinkman, *Admin Sec*
▲ EMP: 31
SQ FT: 361,000
SALES (est): 291.6MM
SALES (corp-wide): 3.7B **Publicly Held**
WEB: www.worthingtonindustries.com
SIC: 3316 3312 Cold finishing of steel shapes; blast furnaces & steel mills
PA: Worthington Industries, Inc.
    200 W Old Wlson Bridge Rd
    Worthington OH 43085
    614 438-3210

Tecumseh
Lenawee County

(G-15784)
CLASSIC CABINETS INTERIORS LLC (PA)
118 W Chicago Blvd (49286-1553)
PHONE 517 423-2600
Charles Barnes, *Ch of Bd*
Amie Pelham, *Mng Member*
EMP: 4
SALES: 2.5MM **Privately Held**
SIC: 2434 Wood kitchen cabinets

(G-15785)
COMSTAR AUTOMOTIVE USA LLC
900 Industrial Dr (49286-9701)
PHONE 517 266-2445
Praveen Chakrapani, *Vice Pres*
▲ EMP: 10
SQ FT: 12,500
SALES (est): 2MM **Privately Held**
SIC: 3711 Automobile assembly, including specialty automobiles

(G-15786)
CREEK PLASTICS LLC
508 Mohawk St (49286-9301)
PHONE 517 423-1003
Jason Derby, *President*
Eric Harbaugh, *Vice Pres*
Frank Willett, *Treasurer*
Barry Hartmann, *Sales Staff*
Scott Kolanek, *Admin Sec*
EMP: 10
SALES (est): 1.4MM **Privately Held**
SIC: 3084 Plastics pipe

Tecumseh - Lenawee County (G-15787)

(G-15787)
DIGGYPOD INC
301 Industrial Dr (49286-9788)
PHONE................................734 429-3307
Tim Simpson, *President*
EMP: 7
SQ FT: 1,250
SALES (est): 1.1MM **Privately Held**
WEB: www.quickprintink.com
SIC: 2741 Miscellaneous publishing

(G-15788)
DIVERSE MANUFACTURING SOLTION
805 S Maumee St (49286-2053)
P.O. Box 400 (49286-0400)
PHONE................................517 423-6691
EMP: 3
SALES (est): 173.6K **Privately Held**
SIC: 3999 Manufacturing industries

(G-15789)
DMS MANUFACTURING SOLUTIONS
800 S Maumee St (49286-2061)
PHONE................................517 423-6691
James Roberts, *Principal*
EMP: 8
SALES (est): 950.5K **Privately Held**
SIC: 3999 Manufacturing industries

(G-15790)
DOCTOR FLUE INC
1610 Dinius Rd (49286-9713)
PHONE................................517 423-2832
Kevon Binder, *President*
Valerie Binder, *Vice Pres*
EMP: 3
SALES (est): 227.1K **Privately Held**
SIC: 7349 3429 Chimney cleaning; fireplace equipment, hardware: andirons, grates, screens

(G-15791)
DPRINTER INC
Also Called: D' Printer Inc-Shop
6197 N Adrian Hwy (49286-9797)
PHONE................................517 423-6554
David Hawkins, *President*
Jaina R Brown, *Vice Pres*
EMP: 4
SQ FT: 2,800
SALES: 350K **Privately Held**
SIC: 2752 2791 2789 Commercial printing, offset; typesetting; bookbinding & related work

(G-15792)
ERVIN INDUSTRIES INC
Also Called: Ervin Development Center
200 Industrial Dr (49286-9787)
PHONE................................517 423-5477
Tim Mostowy, *Engineer*
Ron Bates, *Manager*
EMP: 30
SALES (corp-wide): 200MM **Privately Held**
WEB: www.ervinindustries.com
SIC: 8731 3291 Commercial physical research; abrasive products
PA: Ervin Industries, Inc.
3893 Research Park Dr
Ann Arbor MI 48108
734 769-4600

(G-15793)
EXTRUNET AMERICA INC
903 Industrial Dr (49286-9701)
PHONE................................517 301-4504
Helmut Linsgeseder, *President*
▲ **EMP:** 9
SQ FT: 12,000
SALES (est): 1.8MM **Privately Held**
SIC: 3355 Extrusion ingot, aluminum: made in rolling mills

(G-15794)
GLOV ENTERPRISES LLC
412 S Maumee St (49286-2055)
PHONE................................517 423-9700
Louis Farkas, *Partner*
Geneva Beall, *Office Mgr*
Gordon Young, *Mng Member*
Moritz Vonmoeller,
EMP: 74

SALES: 12MM **Privately Held**
SIC: 3089 8711 7389 Injection molding of plastics; engineering services; design services;

(G-15795)
GLYCON CORP
Also Called: Great Lakes Feedscrews
912 Industrial Dr (49286-9701)
PHONE................................517 423-8356
Jeffrey A Kuhman, *President*
Jeff Howard, *Plant Mgr*
Trevor Stornant, *Engineer*
Brian Warner, *Project Engr*
H Lee Prettyman, *Administration*
EMP: 30 **EST:** 1976
SQ FT: 22,000
SALES (est): 6.9MM **Privately Held**
WEB: www.glycon.com
SIC: 3559 3544 3452 3443 Plastics working machinery; special dies, tools, jigs & fixtures; bolts, nuts, rivets & washers; fabricated plate work (boiler shop)

(G-15796)
HAMBLIN COMPANY
109 E Logan St (49286-1558)
P.O. Box 350 (49286-0350)
PHONE................................517 423-7491
Raymond J Hamblin, *President*
Madlyn C Hamblin, *Vice Pres*
EMP: 35
SQ FT: 3,800
SALES (est): 5.6MM **Privately Held**
WEB: www.hamblin-inc.com
SIC: 2752 2796 2789 2759 Commercial printing, offset; platemaking services; bookbinding & related work; commercial printing; die-cut paper & board

(G-15797)
HERALD PUBLISHING COMPANY
Also Called: Tecumseh Herald
110 E Logan St (49286-1559)
P.O. Box 218 (49286-0218)
PHONE................................517 423-2174
James C Lincoln, *President*
Dorothy Lincoln, *Vice Pres*
EMP: 20 **EST:** 1957
SQ FT: 9,000
SALES (est): 2.9MM **Privately Held**
WEB: www.tecumsehherald.com
SIC: 2752 2711 Commercial printing, lithographic; newspapers

(G-15798)
IDIDIT INC
610 S Maumee St (49286-2051)
PHONE................................517 424-0577
Ken Callison, *CEO*
Jane Callison, *President*
Ted W Keating, *General Mgr*
Scott Callison, *Vice Pres*
Matt Woerner, *Plant Mgr*
EMP: 38
SQ FT: 32,000
SALES (est): 7.8MM **Privately Held**
WEB: www.ididitinc.com
SIC: 3714 5531 5013 Motor vehicle steering systems & parts; automotive parts; automotive supplies & parts

(G-15799)
KIRCHHOFF AUTO TECUMSEH INC
5550 Occidental Hwy (49286)
PHONE................................517 490-9965
Robert Lambright, *Manager*
EMP: 15
SALES (corp-wide): 1.8B **Privately Held**
SIC: 3465 Automotive stampings
HQ: Kirchhoff Automotive Tecumseh Inc.
1200 E Chicago Blvd
Tecumseh MI 49286
517 423-2400

(G-15800)
KIRCHHOFF AUTO TECUMSEH INC (DH)
1200 E Chicago Blvd (49286-9674)
PHONE................................517 423-2400
Allan Power, *President*
▲ **EMP:** 258
SQ FT: 300,000

SALES (est): 86.5MM
SALES (corp-wide): 1.8B **Privately Held**
WEB: www.lenaweestamping.com
SIC: 3465 Body parts, automobile: stamped metal
HQ: Kirchhoff Automotive Gmbh
Stefanstr. 2
Iserlohn 58638
237 182-000

(G-15801)
LIBRA PRECISION MACHINING INC
Also Called: Libra Manufacturing
5353 N Rogers Hwy (49286-9535)
PHONE................................517 423-1365
Fax: 517 423-2531
EMP: 12
SQ FT: 11,500
SALES: 1MM **Privately Held**
SIC: 3599 Mfg Industrial Machinery

(G-15802)
MILACRON LLC
5550 S Occidental Rd (49286-8749)
PHONE................................517 424-8981
EMP: 20
SALES (corp-wide): 1.2B **Privately Held**
SIC: 3549 Metalworking machinery
HQ: Milacron Llc
10200 Alliance Rd Ste 200
Blue Ash OH 45242

(G-15803)
NATIONAL AIRCRAFT SERVICE INC
9133 Tecumseh Clinton Hwy (49286-1128)
PHONE................................517 423-7589
Wesley M Plattner, *President*
Rod Guth, *Vice Pres*
EMP: 12
SQ FT: 8,000
SALES (est): 2.1MM **Privately Held**
WEB: www.nasisystems.com
SIC: 3728 3585 Aircraft parts & equipment; refrigeration & heating equipment

(G-15804)
PEGASUS MOLD & DIE INC
415 E Russell Rd (49286-7502)
PHONE................................517 423-2009
Deborah Loveland, *President*
EMP: 6 **EST:** 1979
SQ FT: 5,100
SALES (est): 771.8K **Privately Held**
SIC: 3544 Special dies, tools, jigs & fixtures

(G-15805)
PENTAMERE WINERY
131 E Chicago Blvd Ste 1 (49286-1570)
P.O. Box 96 (49286-0096)
PHONE................................517 423-9000
Edward Gerten, *Managing Prtnr*
Daniel Measel, *Partner*
EMP: 10
SALES (est): 783.1K **Privately Held**
WEB: www.pentamerewinery.com
SIC: 2084 Wines

(G-15806)
RARE TOOL INC
300 E Russell Rd (49286-2058)
PHONE................................517 423-5000
Jack Reeck, *President*
Gary Anderson, *Corp Secy*
EMP: 17
SQ FT: 10,000
SALES (est): 3.1MM **Privately Held**
SIC: 3544 Special dies, tools, jigs & fixtures

(G-15807)
ROBERTS TOOL COMPANY
800 S Maumee St (49286-2061)
P.O. Box 400 (49286-0400)
PHONE................................517 423-6691
Allen Roberts, *President*
James D Roberts, *Vice Pres*
Dave Campbell, *Purchasing*
EMP: 10
SQ FT: 2,500
SALES (est): 2.4MM **Privately Held**
WEB: www.robertstoolco.com
SIC: 3089 Automotive parts, plastic

(G-15808)
ROESCH MAUFACTURING CO LLC
Also Called: Roesch Manufacturing
904 Industrial Dr (49286-9701)
PHONE................................517 424-6300
George Edward Roesch,
Candice Roesch,
Karalyn Roesch,
Ross Roesch,
EMP: 7
SQ FT: 8,000
SALES: 300K **Privately Held**
WEB: www.roeschmfg.com
SIC: 3545 5084 3546 3423 Machine tool accessories; industrial machinery & equipment; power-driven handtools; hand & edge tools

(G-15809)
SPECTRUM PRINTERS INC
400 E Russell Rd Ste 1 (49286-7501)
PHONE................................517 423-5735
Andy Van Staveren, *President*
Joshua Ketola, *President*
Rick Nadeau, *Vice Pres*
Gale Shaver, *Accounts Exec*
Cindy Dumeyer, *Manager*
EMP: 33
SQ FT: 24,000
SALES (est): 5.6MM **Privately Held**
WEB: www.spectrumprinters.com
SIC: 2752 2791 2789 Commercial printing, offset; typesetting; bookbinding & related work

(G-15810)
T & D MACHINE INC
2485 E Monroe Rd (49286-8737)
PHONE................................517 423-0778
Debra Fowle, *Partner*
Terry Fowle, *Partner*
EMP: 3
SQ FT: 4,800
SALES (est): 79.7K **Privately Held**
WEB: www.tdmachineinc.net
SIC: 3542 3451 Machine tools, metal forming type; screw machine products

(G-15811)
TECUMSEH PACKG SOLUTIONS INC (PA)
Also Called: Tecumseh Division
707 S Evans St (49286-1919)
P.O. Box 427 (49286-0427)
PHONE................................517 423-2126
William C Akers II, *President*
Michael Akey II, *Vice Pres*
James F Akers, *Admin Sec*
EMP: 50 **EST:** 2006
SQ FT: 100,000
SALES (est): 8.8MM **Privately Held**
SIC: 2653 Boxes, corrugated: made from purchased materials

(G-15812)
TECUMSEH SIGNALS LLC
805 S Maumee St (49286-2053)
P.O. Box 583 (49286-0583)
PHONE................................517 301-2064
Tim Wertz, *Mng Member*
EMP: 3
SQ FT: 1,600
SALES: 750K **Privately Held**
SIC: 3669 Signaling apparatus, electric

(G-15813)
TOTAL MOLDING SOLUTIONS INC
416 E Cummins St (49286-2063)
PHONE................................517 424-5900
Rajiv Naik, *President*
EMP: 30
SQ FT: 45,000
SALES (est): 5.5MM **Privately Held**
SIC: 2821 Molding compounds, plastics

(G-15814)
TURKEY CREEK INC
Also Called: Tc Sports
7279 Smith Rd (49286-9658)
PHONE................................517 451-5221
Jill Felbaum, *President*
Troy De Jonghe, *Vice Pres*
EMP: 19

GEOGRAPHIC SECTION

SQ FT: 29,900
SALES (est): 2.2MM **Privately Held**
WEB: www.tc-sports.com
SIC: **3949** 3523 Sporting & athletic goods; farm machinery & equipment

(G-15815)
UNILOY INC
5550 S Occidental Rd B (49286-8749)
PHONE..................................514 424-8900
Brian Marston, *CEO*
Tom McDonald, *Vice Pres*
Dave Skala, *Vice Pres*
Jodie Garcia, *Purch Mgr*
Michael Kippnick, *Technical Mgr*
EMP: 60
SALES (est): 8MM **Privately Held**
SIC: **3559** Plastics working machinery

(G-15816)
VAN-ROB USA HOLDINGS (HQ)
Also Called: Kirchhoff Automotive Companies
1200 E Chicago Blvd (49286-9674)
PHONE..................................517 423-2400
EMP: 20
SALES (est): 12.6MM
SALES (corp-wide): 1.8B **Privately Held**
SIC: **3559** Automotive related machinery
PA: Kirchhoff Automotive Holding Gmbh & Co.Kg
Stefanstr. 2
Iserlohn 58638
237 182-000

Tekonsha
Calhoun County

(G-15817)
CCO HOLDINGS LLC
114 N Main St (49092-5100)
PHONE..................................517 583-4125
EMP: 3
SALES (corp-wide): 43.6B **Publicly Held**
SIC: **5064** 4841 3663 3651 Electrical appliances, television & radio; cable & other pay television services; radio & TV communications equipment; household audio & video equipment
HQ: Cco Holdings, Llc
400 Atlantic St
Stamford CT 06901
203 905-7801

(G-15818)
DOUGLAS CORP
103 S Main St (49092-9480)
P.O. Box 310 (49092-0310)
PHONE..................................517 767-4112
Terry T Hampton, *President*
Joannie N Nitz, *Manager*
Cat Pluchino, *Director*
EMP: 18
SQ FT: 20,000
SALES (est): 1.4MM **Privately Held**
SIC: **7699** 3479 7629 2851 Pumps & pumping equipment repair; industrial machinery & equipment repair; painting, coating & hot dipping; electrical repair shops; paints & allied products; inorganic pigments

(G-15819)
JORGENSEN STL MCH & FAB INC
166 Spires Pkwy (49092-9351)
P.O. Box 315 (49092-0315)
PHONE..................................517 767-4600
Matthew Jorgensen, *President*
EMP: 14
SALES (est): 3MM **Privately Held**
SIC: **3599** 3714 Machine shop, jobbing & repair; motor vehicle parts & accessories

(G-15820)
MARKING MACHINE CO
286 Spires Pkwy (49092-9347)
P.O. Box 159 (49092-0159)
PHONE..................................517 767-4155
Dan Kempton, *President*
Carol Kimball, *Corp Secy*
EMP: 10 **EST:** 1950
SQ FT: 20,000
SALES (est): 968K **Privately Held**
WEB: www.markingmachine.com
SIC: **2759** 3549 Engraving; marking machines, metalworking

(G-15821)
RANDALL FOODS INC
401 S Main St (49092-9255)
PHONE..................................517 767-3247
Denise Maurer, *Human Res Mgr*
Randy Waltz, *Manager*
EMP: 16
SALES (corp-wide): 3.1MM **Privately Held**
WEB: www.randallbeans.com
SIC: **5411** 2033 2032 Grocery stores; canned fruits & specialties; beans, baked with meat: packaged in cans, jars, etc.
PA: Randall Foods Inc.
312 Walnut St Ste 1600
Cincinnati OH 45202
513 793-6525

Temperance
Monroe County

(G-15822)
ACCUWORX LLC (PA)
7156 Sulier Dr (48182-9510)
PHONE..................................734 847-6115
Angela Lehmann, *Accountant*
Jeff Loch, *Mng Member*
Rachel Lienemann, *Program Mgr*
Tim Warring, *Program Mgr*
Larry Carter,
EMP: 35
SALES: 6MM **Privately Held**
SIC: **3599** Custom machinery

(G-15823)
BEL-KUR INC
Also Called: Ttg Automation
7297 Express Rd (48182-9592)
PHONE..................................734 847-0651
Jeffery J Kuhr, *President*
Pat Kuhr, *Vice Pres*
Kevin Kuhr, *Purch Dir*
EMP: 40
SQ FT: 12,000
SALES (est): 9.2MM
SALES (corp-wide): 48.7MM **Privately Held**
WEB: www.bel-kur.com
SIC: **3544** 3549 7692 8711 Special dies & tools; industrial molds; metalworking machinery; welding repair; engineering services
PA: Tooling Technology, Llc
51223 Quadrate Dr
Macomb MI 48042
937 381-9211

(G-15824)
BURROW INDUSTRIES INC
7380 Express Rd (48182-9597)
P.O. Box 359 (48182-0359)
PHONE..................................734 847-1842
Oliver F Burrow, *President*
Mark Burrow, *Vice Pres*
Ryan Held, *Engineer*
Dean Portratz, *Sales Staff*
▼ EMP: 13
SQ FT: 12,400
SALES (est): 2.1MM **Privately Held**
WEB: www.burrowindustries.com
SIC: **3599** Machine & other job shop work; machine shop, jobbing & repair

(G-15825)
CORRUGATED OPTIONS LLC
2163 Briar Ln (48182-1572)
PHONE..................................734 850-1300
EMP: 3
SALES (est): 207.4K **Privately Held**
SIC: **2653** Mfg Corrugated/Solid Fiber Boxes

(G-15826)
CORTZ INDUSTRIES
9411 Summerfield Rd (48182-9760)
PHONE..................................734 856-5091
Thomas Meissner, *Principal*
EMP: 3
SALES (est): 243.4K **Privately Held**
SIC: **3599** Machine shop, jobbing & repair

(G-15827)
ELLIS MACHINE & TOOL CO INC
7168 Sulier Dr (48182-9510)
PHONE..................................734 847-4113
Michael Ellis, *President*
James Ellis, *Office Mgr*
Barbara Ellis, *Admin Sec*
EMP: 3
SQ FT: 4,000
SALES (est): 270K **Privately Held**
SIC: **3544** Special dies & tools

(G-15828)
FISCHER TOOL & DIE CORP (PA)
7155 Industrial Dr Ste A (48182-9172)
PHONE..................................734 847-4788
Michael J Fischer, *CEO*
Jj Fischer, *President*
Jeff Warner, *Engineer*
Connie Fleury, *Accounting Mgr*
Sean Ball, *Manager*
▲ EMP: 95
SQ FT: 45,000
SALES (est): 16.6MM **Privately Held**
WEB: www.fischertool.com
SIC: **3544** Special dies & tools

(G-15829)
FUSION MFG SOLUTIONS LLC
7193 Sulier Dr (48182-9510)
PHONE..................................734 224-7216
Mike Kujda, *General Mgr*
Mark Mallory, *Mfg Mgr*
EMP: 8
SALES (est): 1.1MM **Privately Held**
SIC: **3599** Machine shop, jobbing & repair

(G-15830)
H E L P PRINTERS INC
9673 Lewis Ave (48182-9358)
PHONE..................................734 847-0554
Carol R Lutman, *President*
Wayne Gamble, *Vice Pres*
EMP: 4
SALES: 350K **Privately Held**
WEB: www.helpprinters.com
SIC: **2752** 2759 Commercial printing, offset; promotional printing

(G-15831)
HI TECH MECHANICAL SVCS LLC
Also Called: Honeywell Authorized Dealer
7070 Crabb Rd (48182-9552)
PHONE..................................734 847-1831
William Murry,
EMP: 6
SALES (est): 805.1K **Privately Held**
SIC: **3599** 1731 1711 Machine shop, jobbing & repair; electrical work; plumbing, heating, air-conditioning contractors

(G-15832)
I D PRO EMBROIDERY LLC
1287 W Sterns Rd (48182-1504)
PHONE..................................734 847-6650
EMP: 4
SQ FT: 2,000
SALES (est): 326.6K **Privately Held**
SIC: **2395** Custom Embroidery / Screen Printing

(G-15833)
LAKE ERIE MED SURGICAL SUP INC (PA)
7560 Lewis Ave (48182-9539)
P.O. Box 1267, Holland OH (43528-1267)
PHONE..................................734 847-3847
Michael W Holmes, *President*
Joeseph Braker, *Principal*
Robert Holmes, *Vice Pres*
Jeannie Sieren, *Treasurer*
Carol Holmes, *Admin Sec*
EMP: 22
SQ FT: 13,000
SALES (est): 16.4MM **Privately Held**
SIC: **5047** 3826 3841 Medical & hospital equipment; analytical instruments; surgical & medical instruments

(G-15834)
LOONAR STN TWO THE 2 OR 2ND
6656 Lewis Ave Ste 5 (48182-1201)
PHONE..................................419 720-1222
EMP: 4
SALES (est): 399.2K **Privately Held**
SIC: **5051** 2221 3999 Pipe & tubing, steel; upholstery, tapestry & wall covering fabrics; tobacco pipes, pipestems & bits

(G-15835)
M & N CONTROLS INC
7180 Sulier Dr (48182-9510)
PHONE..................................734 850-2127
Michael J Nagy, *President*
EMP: 8
SQ FT: 2,000
SALES (est): 710K **Privately Held**
SIC: **3613** Control panels, electric

(G-15836)
MATRIX NORTH AMERCN CNSTR INC
6945 Crabb Rd (48182-9547)
PHONE..................................734 847-4605
Eric Foster, *Branch Mgr*
EMP: 104
SALES (corp-wide): 1.4B **Publicly Held**
SIC: **7699** 3443 3441 Tank repair & cleaning services; fabricated plate work (boiler shop); fabricated structural metal
HQ: Matrix North American Construction, Inc.
5100 E Skelly Dr Ste 100
Tulsa OK 74135

(G-15837)
MET-L-TEC LLC (PA)
7310 Express Rd (48182-9514)
PHONE..................................734 847-7004
Aaron Soldenwagner, *Engineer*
Paul Schmidt, *Mng Member*
Paul J Schmitz III,
EMP: 31 **EST:** 1971
SQ FT: 15,000
SALES (est): 7.2MM **Privately Held**
WEB: www.met-l-tec.com
SIC: **3544** 3559 Special dies & tools; forms (molds), for foundry & plastics working machinery; metal finishing equipment for plating, etc.

(G-15838)
MICHIGAN TUBE SWAGERS & FAB (PA)
Also Called: MTS Seating
7100 Industrial Dr (48182-9105)
PHONE..................................734 847-3875
Paul Swy, *President*
Barton Kulish, *President*
Leroy Laplante, *General Mgr*
Matt Smart, *Prdtn Mgr*
Chris Clark, *Maint Spvr*
◆ EMP: 370 **EST:** 1955
SQ FT: 218,000
SALES (est): 70MM **Privately Held**
WEB: www.mtsseating.com
SIC: **2521** Wood office furniture

(G-15839)
MTS BURGESS LLC
1244 W Dean Rd (48182-3800)
P.O. Box 489 (48182-0416)
PHONE..................................734 847-2937
Charles Stahl, *General Mgr*
Joe Restivo, *CFO*
Peter Swy, *Treasurer*
Phillip Swy, *Mng Member*
Jeremy Burgess,
▼ EMP: 100
SALES (est): 12.3MM
SALES (corp-wide): 70MM **Privately Held**
WEB: www.mtsseating.com
SIC: **2514** Chairs, household: metal
PA: Michigan Tube Swagers And Fabricators, Inc.
7100 Industrial Dr
Temperance MI 48182
734 847-3875

Temperance - Monroe County

(G-15840)
PANTLESS JAMS LLC
6937 Maplewood Dr (48182-1326)
PHONE.................................419 283-8470
Jessica Hopkins, *Principal*
EMP: 3
SALES (est): 116.3K **Privately Held**
SIC: 2033 Jams, jellies & preserves: packaged in cans, jars, etc.

(G-15841)
REFLECTION MEDICAL INC
3200 W Temperance Rd B (48182-2415)
PHONE.................................734 850-0777
Cindy A Liley, *President*
EMP: 4
SALES (est): 643.4K **Privately Held**
SIC: 3842 Wheelchairs

(G-15842)
ROLLED ALLOYS INC (PA)
125 W Sterns Rd (48182-9567)
P.O. Box 310 (48182-0310)
PHONE.................................800 521-0332
Thomas Nichol, *Principal*
▲ **EMP:** 92 **EST:** 1953
SQ FT: 83,000
SALES (est): 269.4MM **Privately Held**
WEB: www.rolledalloys.com
SIC: 5051 3369 3341 3317 Steel; nonferrous foundries; secondary nonferrous metals; steel pipe & tubes; chemical preparations; paints & allied products

(G-15843)
ROYAL STEWART ENTERPRISES
Also Called: Kustom Kaps
7355 Lewis Ave Ste B (48182-1465)
P.O. Box 273 (48182-0273)
PHONE.................................734 224-7994
Richard Stewart, *Partner*
Tim Stewart, *Partner*
▲ **EMP:** 5
SQ FT: 2,400
SALES (est): 508.1K **Privately Held**
WEB: www.royalstewartenterprises.com
SIC: 2395 2759 Embroidery products, except schiffli machine; emblems, embroidered; screen printing

(G-15844)
SPECIALTY HARDWOOD MOLDINGS
1244 W Dean Rd (48182-3800)
PHONE.................................734 847-3997
EMP: 10
SALES (est): 1MM **Privately Held**
SIC: 2431 Mfg Millwork

(G-15845)
TEMPERANCE DISTILLING COMPANY
Also Called: Zippers
177 Reed Dr (48182-8900)
PHONE.................................734 847-5262
Ted Fason, *CEO*
Molly Pearson, *Vice Pres*
EMP: 15 **EST:** 1998
SQ FT: 2,200
SALES (est): 3.9MM **Privately Held**
WEB: www.bpncdistillery.com
SIC: 2085 Applejack (alcoholic beverage)

(G-15846)
UNIQUE TOOL & MFG CO INC
100 Reed Dr (48182-8900)
PHONE.................................734 850-1050
Allan J Chabler, *Principal*
Jim Nalepa, *Engineer*
Rhonda Shaw, *Accountant*
Loraine Paul, *Technology*
Andy Thurlow, *Technology*
EMP: 11 **EST:** 1963
SALES (est): 432.8K **Privately Held**
SIC: 3544 Special dies, tools, jigs & fixtures

(G-15847)
WESTOOL CORPORATION
7383 Sulier Dr (48182-9510)
PHONE.................................734 847-2520
Greg West, *President*
Brooke Smith, *Office Mgr*
▲ **EMP:** 23
SQ FT: 25,000
SALES (est): 5.2MM **Privately Held**
WEB: www.westools.com
SIC: 3544 Special dies & tools

Three Oaks
Berrien County

(G-15848)
C & K HARDWOODS LLC
7325 Elm Valley Rd (49128-8503)
PHONE.................................269 231-0048
Greg Kerigan, *Ch of Bd*
Thomas Carson, *President*
Jennifer Hickory, *Treasurer*
Charlene Carson, *Admin Sec*
EMP: 7
SQ FT: 15,000
SALES (est): 300K **Privately Held**
SIC: 2431 Millwork

(G-15849)
H & K MACHINE COMPANY INC
7451 Us Highway 12 (49128-9166)
PHONE.................................269 756-7339
Fax: 269 756-7501
EMP: 5
SQ FT: 10,000
SALES (est): 500K **Privately Held**
SIC: 3451 Mfg Screw Machine Products

(G-15850)
SHEPHERD HARDWARE PRODUCTS INC
6961 Us Highway 12 (49128-9556)
P.O. Box 394 (49128-0394)
PHONE.................................269 756-3830
Marvin W Ross, *President*
R C Gluth, *Treasurer*
Robert W Webb, *Admin Sec*
▲ **EMP:** 95
SQ FT: 200,000
SALES (est): 15.4MM **Privately Held**
WEB: www.shepherdhardware.com
SIC: 3429 5072 Manufactured hardware (general); casters & glides

(G-15851)
THREE OAKS ENGRAVING & ENGRG
14381 Three Oaks Rd (49128-9716)
PHONE.................................269 469-2124
John Schmidt, *President*
EMP: 5
SALES (est): 291.2K **Privately Held**
SIC: 3479 Engraving jewelry silverware, or metal

(G-15852)
TO WILLOW HARBOR VINEYARD
3223 Kaiser Rd (49128-8543)
PHONE.................................269 369-3900
Kristie Kelleher, *Principal*
EMP: 4
SALES (est): 252.2K **Privately Held**
SIC: 2084 Wines

Three Rivers
St. Joseph County

(G-15853)
AMERICAN AXLE & MFG INC
Also Called: Three Rivers Driveline Fcilty
1 Manufacturing Dr (49093-8907)
PHONE.................................269 278-0211
David Anderson, *Engineer*
Robert Middleton, *Engineer*
Sean Skinner, *Engineer*
Greg Yezback, *Manager*
Patrick York, *Info Tech Mgr*
EMP: 600
SALES (corp-wide): 7.2B **Publicly Held**
WEB: www.aam.com
SIC: 3714 Axles, motor vehicle
HQ: American Axle & Manufacturing, Inc.
1 Dauch Dr
Detroit MI 48211

(G-15854)
AMERICAN METAL FAB INC
Also Called: A M F
55515 Franklin Dr (49093-9692)
PHONE.................................269 279-5108
John Crowell, *President*
Jason Crowell, *Vice Pres*
Gerald S Eplee, *Vice Pres*
Dennis Sutfin, *Project Mgr*
Randy Mobley, *QC Mgr*
EMP: 60
SQ FT: 100,000
SALES (est): 13.3MM **Privately Held**
WEB: www.americanmetalfab.com
SIC: 3444 3469 2531 3443 Sheet metal specialties, not stamped; metal stampings; seats, automobile; fabricated plate work (boiler shop)

(G-15855)
AQUATIC CO
Lasco Bathware
888 W Broadway St (49093-1900)
PHONE.................................269 279-7461
Sarah Mercer, *Human Res Mgr*
Jim Dreher, *Branch Mgr*
EMP: 97
SALES (corp-wide): 443.5MM **Privately Held**
SIC: 3088 Hot tubs, plastic or fiberglass; shower stalls, fiberglass & plastic
HQ: Aquatic Co.
1700 N Delilah St
Corona CA 92879

(G-15856)
ARMSTRONG FLUID HANDLING INC
221 Armstrong Blvd (49093-2374)
PHONE.................................269 279-3600
David Armstrong, *President*
Steve Gibson, *Treasurer*
Tom Morris, *Admin Sec*
▲ **EMP:** 205
SQ FT: 6,000
SALES (est): 24.4MM
SALES (corp-wide): 107.6MM **Privately Held**
WEB: www.armstrongcompressedair.com
SIC: 3594 Fluid power pumps
PA: Armstrong International, Inc.
816 Maple St
Three Rivers MI 49093
269 273-1415

(G-15857)
ARMSTRONG HOT WATER INC (HQ)
221 Armstrong Blvd (49093-2374)
PHONE.................................269 278-1413
Larry Daugherty, *President*
Stephen Gibson, *Treasurer*
Matt Bradford, *Sales Staff*
Thomas J Morris, *Admin Sec*
▲ **EMP:** 32
SALES (est): 5.3MM
SALES (corp-wide): 107.6MM **Privately Held**
WEB: www.armstrongcompressedair.com
SIC: 3433 5074 Boilers, low-pressure heating: steam or hot water; sanitary ware, china or enameled iron
PA: Armstrong International, Inc.
816 Maple St
Three Rivers MI 49093
269 273-1415

(G-15858)
ARMSTRONG INTERNATIONAL INC (PA)
816 Maple St (49093-2345)
PHONE.................................269 273-1415
Douglas Bloss, *CEO*
Patrick Armstrong, *Ch of Bd*
Rex Cummings, *General Mgr*
Shelly Wheeler, *Project Mgr*
David Armstrong, *Opers Staff*
▲ **EMP:** 220 **EST:** 1895
SQ FT: 149,000
SALES (est): 107.6MM **Privately Held**
WEB: www.armstrongcompressedair.com
SIC: 3491 Steam traps; pressure valves & regulators, industrial; regulators (steam fittings)

(G-15859)
CELIA DEBOER
14791 Hoffman Rd (49093-9703)
PHONE.................................269 279-9102
Celia Deboer, *Owner*
EMP: 10
SALES (est): 714.9K **Privately Held**
SIC: 2951 Asphalt paving mixtures & blocks

(G-15860)
DENNY GRICE INC
Also Called: R & H Machine Products
702 Webber Ave (49093-8911)
P.O. Box 32, Marcellus (49067-0032)
PHONE.................................269 279-6113
Denny Grice, *President*
Troy Wilde, *Sales Engr*
EMP: 16 **EST:** 1967
SQ FT: 10,000
SALES (est): 3.1MM **Privately Held**
WEB: www.rh-machine.net
SIC: 3451 Screw machine products

(G-15861)
FASTENER COATINGS INC
1111 River St (49093-1151)
PHONE.................................269 279-5134
Douglas Garvey, *CEO*
Joy Garvey, *President*
Beverly Garvey, *Corp Secy*
EMP: 15
SQ FT: 10,000
SALES (est): 1.6MM **Privately Held**
WEB: www.fastenercoatings.com
SIC: 3479 Coating of metals & formed products

(G-15862)
FLINT GROUP US LLC
111 Day Dr (49093-2100)
PHONE.................................269 279-5161
Carol Dobrowolski, *Purch Mgr*
Joseph Doornbos, *Branch Mgr*
Jim Cotton, *Manager*
EMP: 63
SQ FT: 58,000
SALES (corp-wide): 177.9K **Privately Held**
SIC: 3069 2759 Printers' rolls & blankets: rubber or rubberized fabric; commercial printing
HQ: Flint Group Us Llc
17177 N Laurel Park Dr # 300
Livonia MI 48152
734 781-4600

(G-15863)
GAR-V MANUFACTURING INC
1111 River St (49093-1199)
PHONE.................................269 279-5134
Joy Garvey, *President*
EMP: 7
SQ FT: 20,000
SALES (est): 789.1K **Privately Held**
WEB: www.gar-v.com
SIC: 3469 Stamping metal for the trade

(G-15864)
H B D M INC (PA)
207 Portage Ave (49093-1529)
P.O. Box 15 (49093-0015)
PHONE.................................269 273-1976
Herman A F Beuter, *President*
EMP: 1 **EST:** 1967
SALES (est): 1.2MM **Privately Held**
SIC: 3544 Special dies & tools

(G-15865)
H B D M INC
1149 Millard St (49093-9567)
P.O. Box 15 (49093-0015)
PHONE.................................269 273-1976
Ford Brewder, *Manager*
EMP: 12
SALES (corp-wide): 1.2MM **Privately Held**
SIC: 3544 Special dies & tools
PA: H B D M Inc
207 Portage Ave
Three Rivers MI 49093
269 273-1976

GEOGRAPHIC SECTION

(G-15866)
INTERNATIONAL PAPER COMPANY
1321 3rd St (49093-2726)
PHONE.....................................269 273-8461
Bob Wenker, *Vice Pres*
Scott Dillon, *Manager*
EMP: 150
SQ FT: 260,000
SALES (corp-wide): 23.3B **Publicly Held**
WEB: www.internationalpaper.com
SIC: 2621 Paper mills
PA: International Paper Company
6400 Poplar Ave
Memphis TN 38197
901 419-9000

(G-15867)
KADANT JOHNSON LLC (HQ)
Also Called: Kadant Johnson Inc.
805 Wood St (49093-1053)
PHONE.....................................269 278-1715
Greg Wedel, *President*
Jeff Fruehauf, *Manager*
Gene Troyer, *Manager*
Steve Candelaria, *Supervisor*
Dennis Moon, *Info Tech Mgr*
◆ **EMP:** 150 **EST:** 1930
SQ FT: 130,000
SALES (est): 216.2MM
SALES (corp-wide): 633.7MM **Publicly Held**
WEB: www.kadant.com
SIC: 3494 8711 1389 3052 Steam fittings & specialties; construction & civil engineering; construction, repair & dismantling services; rubber hose
PA: Kadant Inc.
1 Technology Park Dr # 210
Westford MA 01886
978 776-2000

(G-15868)
KDF FLUID TREATMENT INC
1500 Kdf Dr (49093-9287)
PHONE.....................................269 273-3300
Issa Al-Kahrusy, *CEO*
John B Heskett, *President*
Dorothy M Heskett, *Chairman*
Denise Al-Kahrusy, *Vice Pres*
Donna Smith, *Treasurer*
EMP: 10
SQ FT: 5,000
SALES (est): 1MM **Privately Held**
WEB: www.kdfft.com
SIC: 3569 Filters; filter elements, fluid, hydraulic line; filters, general line: industrial

(G-15869)
MARCO ROLLO INC
Also Called: Mid-American Rubber Co
415 W Cushman St (49093-2431)
PHONE.....................................269 279-5246
Troy Browder, *CEO*
Cleo A Miller, *Vice Pres*
Cleo Miller, *VP Sales*
EMP: 15 **EST:** 1980
SQ FT: 20,000
SALES (est): 2.5MM **Privately Held**
SIC: 3069 Rubber rolls & roll coverings; printers' rolls & blankets: rubber or rubberized fabric

(G-15870)
METAL TECHNOLOGIES INDIANA INC
Also Called: Metal Technologies Trg
429 4th St (49093-1697)
PHONE.....................................269 278-1765
Douglas Monroe, *Manager*
Scott Outman, *Manager*
Ron Niemi, *Maintence Staff*
EMP: 170
SALES (corp-wide): 293.2MM **Privately Held**
SIC: 3321 Gray iron castings
PA: Metal Technologies Of Indiana, Inc.
1401 S Grandstaff Dr
Auburn IN 46706
260 925-4717

(G-15871)
MORTON BUILDINGS INC
59924 S Us Highway 131 (49093-8579)
PHONE.....................................616 696-4747
Mike Martin, *Principal*
EMP: 18
SALES (corp-wide): 463.7MM **Privately Held**
WEB: www.mortonbuildings.com
SIC: 3448 5039 1796 Prefabricated metal buildings; prefabricated structures; installing building equipment
PA: Morton Buildings, Inc.
252 W Adams St
Morton IL 61550
800 447-7436

(G-15872)
PETERSON AMERICAN CORP
Also Called: Peterson Spring Cima
16805 Heimbach Rd (49093-9622)
PHONE.....................................269 279-7421
Dean Decker, *Manager*
EMP: 59
SALES (corp-wide): 290.5MM **Privately Held**
WEB: www.pspring.com
SIC: 3429 3495 Clamps & couplings, hose; wire springs
PA: Peterson American Corporation
21200 Telegraph Rd
Southfield MI 48033
248 799-5400

(G-15873)
PETERSON AMERICAN CORPORATION
Peterson Spring Packg & Dist
16805 Heimbach Rd (49093-9622)
PHONE.....................................269 279-7421
Kristin Peterson, *Manager*
EMP: 14
SQ FT: 12,000
SALES (corp-wide): 290.5MM **Privately Held**
WEB: www.pspring.com
SIC: 3495 Wire springs
PA: Peterson American Corporation
21200 Telegraph Rd
Southfield MI 48033
248 799-5400

(G-15874)
PRECISION WIRE FORMS INC (PA)
1100 W Broadway St (49093-8701)
P.O. Box 29 (49093-0029)
PHONE.....................................269 279-0053
Francoise Beuter, *President*
▲ **EMP:** 37 **EST:** 1997
SQ FT: 34,000
SALES (est): 7.5MM **Privately Held**
WEB: www.wire-forms.com
SIC: 3496 Miscellaneous fabricated wire products

(G-15875)
PROGRESSIVE PAPER CORP
Also Called: Castel Leasing
1111 3rd St (49093-1926)
P.O. Box 308 (49093-0308)
PHONE.....................................269 279-6320
EMP: 8
SQ FT: 250,000
SALES: 1.6MM **Privately Held**
SIC: 2679 Mfg Custom Paper Converters

(G-15876)
REPUBLIC ROLLER CORPORATION
205 S Us Highway 131 (49093-9295)
P.O. Box 330 (49093-0330)
PHONE.....................................269 273-9591
Daniel Meeth, *President*
Rohit Shah, *Vice Pres*
Sherrie Holden, *Treasurer*
Gene Lempert, *Analyst*
EMP: 25
SQ FT: 80,000
SALES (est): 4.4MM **Privately Held**
WEB: www.republicroller.com
SIC: 3069 Rubber rolls & roll coverings

(G-15877)
SIMPSONS ENTERPRISES INC
55255 Franklin Dr (49093-9685)
PHONE.....................................269 279-7237
James W Simpson, *President*
Gerald A Simpson, *Treasurer*
EMP: 45
SQ FT: 40,000
SALES (est): 6.6MM **Privately Held**
SIC: 3544 3543 Industrial molds; forms (molds), for foundry & plastics working machinery; industrial patterns

(G-15878)
TAMARA TOOL INC
1234 William R Monroe Blv (49093-8626)
PHONE.....................................269 273-1463
Robert L Hempel Jr, *President*
Kathryn Hempel, *Vice Pres*
EMP: 10
SQ FT: 12,000
SALES (est): 600K **Privately Held**
SIC: 3544 Special dies & tools

(G-15879)
THREE RIVERS COFFEE COMPANY
1501 Kdf Dr (49093-9287)
PHONE.....................................269 244-0083
James Welton, *CEO*
EMP: 3
SALES (est): 91.3K **Privately Held**
SIC: 2095 Roasted coffee

(G-15880)
THREE RIVERS COMMERCIAL NEWS
Also Called: Penny Saver
124 N Main St (49093-1559)
P.O. Box 130 (49093-0130)
PHONE.....................................269 279-7488
Richard Milliman II, *President*
Penelope Faber Milliman, *Vice Pres*
Ann M Milliman, *Treasurer*
Teresa J Fitzwater, *Admin Sec*
EMP: 20
SQ FT: 15,500
SALES (est): 1.2MM **Privately Held**
WEB: www.threeriversnews.com
SIC: 2711 Newspapers, publishing & printing
PA: Milliman Communications Inc
4601 W Saginaw Hwy Apt 2
Lansing MI 48917
517 327-8407

(G-15881)
TRIM PAC INC
315 7th Ave (49093-1132)
P.O. Box 118 (49093-0118)
PHONE.....................................269 279-9498
Dan Fuller, *President*
Greg Ellis, *Vice Pres*
EMP: 5
SQ FT: 6,000
SALES: 800K **Privately Held**
SIC: 2679 2675 2631 Paper products, converted; die-cut paper & board; chip board

(G-15882)
TRIPLE CREEK SHIRTS AND MORE
54 N Main St (49093-1532)
P.O. Box 223 (49093-0223)
PHONE.....................................269 273-5154
Mandy Murphy, *Owner*
EMP: 4 **EST:** 2014
SALES (est): 240.9K **Privately Held**
SIC: 2759 Screen printing

(G-15883)
X-L MACHINE CO INC
20481 M 60 (49093-8000)
PHONE.....................................269 279-5128
James King, *President*
▲ **EMP:** 47 **EST:** 1977
SQ FT: 8,000
SALES (est): 9.5MM **Privately Held**
SIC: 3544 Special dies & tools
HQ: Burke E. Porter Machinery Company
730 Plymouth Ave Ne
Grand Rapids MI 49505
616 234-1200

Tipton
Lenawee County

(G-15884)
MICHIGAN CHESE PRTEIN PDTS LLC
10015 Wisner Hwy (49287-9704)
PHONE.....................................517 403-5247
Gregg Hardy, *CEO*
EMP: 142
SQ FT: 265,000
SALES (est): 4.9MM **Privately Held**
SIC: 2022 Cheese, natural & processed

Toivola
Houghton County

(G-15885)
THOMAS CHEAL
Also Called: Cheal Woodworking
40240 Aspen Rd (49965-9393)
PHONE.....................................906 288-3487
Thomas Cheal, *Owner*
EMP: 4
SALES (est): 170K **Privately Held**
WEB: www.chealwoodworking.com
SIC: 2431 Moldings & baseboards, ornamental & trim

Traverse City
Grand Traverse County

(G-15886)
5 BY 5 LLC
333 W Grandview Pkwy (49684-2289)
PHONE.....................................855 369-6757
Troy Hill, *President*
Rishon Kimber, *President*
Travis McDougall, *Vice Pres*
EMP: 10
SALES: 10MM **Privately Held**
SIC: 1389 Pipe testing, oil field service

(G-15887)
ACE WELDING & MACHINE INC
1505 Premier St (49686-4391)
PHONE.....................................231 941-9664
Terry Walters, *President*
Beth Walters, *Manager*
EMP: 12 **EST:** 1950
SQ FT: 6,000
SALES: 400K **Privately Held**
WEB: www.acewelding.com
SIC: 7692 3441 3444 Welding repair; fabricated structural metal; forming machine work, sheet metal

(G-15888)
ACOUSTIC TAP ROOM
119 N Maple St (49684-2238)
PHONE.....................................231 714-5028
EMP: 3
SALES (est): 66.8K **Privately Held**
SIC: 5813 2082 Beer garden (drinking places); malt beverages

(G-15889)
ACTIVE BRACE AND LIMB LLC (PA)
5123 N Royal Dr (49684-9201)
PHONE.....................................231 932-8702
Mark Bishop, *Officer*
Jerry Pierce,
Scott Mosher,
EMP: 14
SALES (est): 1.8MM **Privately Held**
SIC: 3842 Orthopedic appliances

(G-15890)
ACTRON STEEL INC
2341 Molon Dr (49684-9101)
P.O. Box 966 (49685-0966)
PHONE.....................................231 947-3981
Ronald Watson, *President*
Brian Moore, *Vice Pres*
EMP: 36
SQ FT: 43,450

Traverse City - Grand Traverse County (G-15891) — GEOGRAPHIC SECTION

SALES (est): 17.4MM **Privately Held**
SIC: 5051 3441 3469 3412 Steel; fabricated structural metal; metal stampings; metal barrels, drums & pails; dumpsters, garbage

(G-15891)
ALCOTEC WIRE CORPORATION (DH)
2750 Aero Park Dr (49686-9263)
PHONE..................................800 228-0750
Tom Svaboda, *President*
George Townsend, *CFO*
Brian Harrison, *Regl Sales Mgr*
Bob Gulas, *Sales Staff*
Aaron Heine, *Sales Staff*
▲ **EMP:** 85
SQ FT: 180,000
SALES (est): 37.1MM
SALES (corp-wide): 3.6B **Publicly Held**
WEB: www.alcotec.com
SIC: 3355 8711 3548 Aluminum wire & cable; engineering services; welding apparatus
HQ: The Esab Group Inc
  2800 Airport Rd
  Denton TX 76207
  800 372-2123

(G-15892)
ALFIE EMBROIDERY INC
2425 Switch Dr Ste A (49684-4342)
PHONE..................................231 935-1488
Bonnie Alfonso, *President*
Marty Beaudoin, *Vice Pres*
Mike Alfonso, *Treasurer*
Carol Nickerson, *Admin Sec*
EMP: 12
SALES (est): 1.3MM **Privately Held**
WEB: www.alfiewear.com
SIC: 2395 Embroidery products, except schiffli machine; embroidery & art needlework

(G-15893)
ALL TOOL SALES INC
Also Called: All Integrated Solutions
812 Hughes Dr (49686-8255)
P.O. Box 5816 (49696-5816)
PHONE..................................231 941-4302
Jeff Diller, *Branch Mgr*
EMP: 12 **Publicly Held**
SIC: 5072 5085 3452 Hardware; industrial supplies; bolts, nuts, rivets & washers
HQ: All Tool Sales, Inc.
  8625 Industrial Dr
  Franksville WI 53126
  262 637-7447

(G-15894)
ALLESK ENTERPRISES INC (PA)
Also Called: Allegra Printing
1224 Centre St (49686-3406)
PHONE..................................231 941-5770
Roger Leask, *President*
EMP: 7
SQ FT: 1,860
SALES: 3.2MM **Privately Held**
SIC: 2752 2759 Commercial printing, offset; commercial printing

(G-15895)
APW
1801 Garfield Rd N (49696-1101)
PHONE..................................231 922-1863
EMP: 3 **EST:** 2015
SALES (est): 198K **Privately Held**
SIC: 3644 Noncurrent-carrying wiring services

(G-15896)
ARBOR OPERATING LLC
333 W Grandview Pkwy # 4 (49684-2289)
PHONE..................................231 941-2237
Terry L Beia, *Mng Member*
James Eichstadt,
EMP: 5
SALES (est): 717.8K **Privately Held**
SIC: 1382 Oil & gas exploration services

(G-15897)
ASTELLAS PHARMA US INC
807 Airport Access Rd # 209 (49686-3594)
PHONE..................................231 947-3630
Todd Oosterhouse, *Branch Mgr*

EMP: 3 **Privately Held**
WEB: www.ambisome.com
SIC: 2834 Pharmaceutical preparations
HQ: Astellas Pharma Us, Inc.
  1 Astellas Way
  Northbrook IL 60062
  800 888-7704

(G-15898)
ASTRO BUILDING PRODUCTS INC (HQ)
221 W South Airport Rd (49686-4876)
PHONE..................................231 941-0324
Fred C Deschler, *President*
Michael Deschler, *Vice Pres*
John Everest, *Vice Pres*
Merry McCray, *Treasurer*
Scott Schoech, *Admin Sec*
EMP: 5
SQ FT: 19,000
SALES (est): 1.9MM
SALES (corp-wide): 30.6B **Privately Held**
WEB: www.astrobp.com
SIC: 5211 3442 5033 5031 Siding; metal doors, sash & trim; storm doors or windows, metal; shutters, door or window: metal; siding, except wood; lumber, plywood & millwork
PA: Crh Public Limited Company
  Stonemasons Way
  Dublin D16 K
  140 410-00

(G-15899)
ATLANTIC BOAT BROKERS
801 S Garfield Ave (49686-3429)
PHONE..................................231 941-8050
Jerry Stauffer, *Principal*
EMP: 4
SALES (est): 413.9K **Privately Held**
SIC: 3714 Motor vehicle parts & accessories

(G-15900)
ATTITUDE & EXPERIENCE INC
Also Called: A & E Sign
1230 S M 37 (49685-8506)
PHONE..................................231 946-7446
Jason Orton, *President*
Jeffrey Orton, *Vice Pres*
EMP: 12
SQ FT: 3,600
SALES (est): 1.7MM **Privately Held**
SIC: 5099 3993 Signs, except electric; signs & advertising specialties

(G-15901)
AUXIER & ASSOCIATES LLC
Also Called: Signs Now
1702 Barlow St Ste A (49684-4723)
PHONE..................................231 486-0641
Elis Auxier,
EMP: 5
SALES (est): 435.8K **Privately Held**
SIC: 3993 Signs & advertising specialties

(G-15902)
AUXIER & ASSOCIATES LLC
741 Woodmere Ave (49684-3348)
PHONE..................................231 933-7446
William Auxier, *President*
EMP: 8
SQ FT: 1,500
SALES (est): 490K **Privately Held**
SIC: 3993 Signs, not made in custom sign painting shops; electric signs

(G-15903)
BANNERGALAXYCOM LLC
2322 Cass Rd (49684-9147)
PHONE..................................231 941-8200
Paul Britten,
▲ **EMP:** 3
SALES (est): 244.8K **Privately Held**
SIC: 2399 5999 Banners, made from fabric; banners

(G-15904)
BAUM SPORTS INC
360 Knollwood Dr (49686-1859)
PHONE..................................231 922-2125
Steve Baum, *President*
EMP: 3
SALES (est): 232.7K **Privately Held**
SIC: 3949 Sporting & athletic goods

(G-15905)
BAY AREA TOOL LLC
466 Hughes Dr (49696-8255)
PHONE..................................231 946-3500
John Bergman, *Partner*
Mike Doriot, *Partner*
EMP: 4
SQ FT: 8,000
SALES (est): 443.5K **Privately Held**
SIC: 3544 Special dies, tools, jigs & fixtures

(G-15906)
BAY BREAD CO
601 Randolph St (49684-2246)
PHONE..................................231 922-8022
Stacey Wilcox, *President*
Steven Wilcox, *Vice Pres*
EMP: 19
SALES: 824K **Privately Held**
SIC: 2051 5812 Bread, all types (white, wheat, rye, etc): fresh or frozen; lunchrooms & cafeterias

(G-15907)
BAY MOTOR PRODUCTS INC
3100 Cass Rd Ste 1 (49684-6963)
P.O. Box 982 (49685-0982)
PHONE..................................231 941-0411
Andrew Robitshek, *President*
Dave Bleich, *Opers Mgr*
Greg Hill, *Engineer*
EMP: 40
SQ FT: 18,500
SALES: 7MM **Privately Held**
SIC: 3621 Motors, electric

(G-15908)
BAY SUPPLY & MARKETING INC
520 Us Highway 31 S (49685-8018)
PHONE..................................231 943-3249
Charles Benson, *President*
EMP: 7
SQ FT: 10,000
SALES (est): 1.1MM **Privately Held**
SIC: 5199 2399 2395 2396 Advertising specialties; flags, fabric; banners, made from fabric; embroidery products, except schiffli machine; screen printing on fabric articles

(G-15909)
BAYGEO INC
Also Called: Bay Geophysical, Inc.
528 Hughes Dr (49696-8255)
PHONE..................................231 941-7660
Phil Vanhollebeke, *President*
Ronald Carr, *Vice Pres*
Pam Hornak, *Treasurer*
Greg Southworth, *Manager*
EMP: 25
SALES (est): 3.8MM **Privately Held**
WEB: www.baygeo.com
SIC: 8748 8999 1382 Environmental consultant; earth science services; oil & gas exploration services; geological exploration, oil & gas field; geophysical exploration, oil & gas field; seismograph surveys

(G-15910)
BAYVIEW SIGN & DESIGN
618 W Eighth St (49684-3109)
PHONE..................................231 922-7759
David Opatik, *Owner*
EMP: 3
SALES (est): 120K **Privately Held**
SIC: 3993 Signs & advertising specialties

(G-15911)
BIG DIPPER DOUGH CO INC
2819 Cass Rd Ste E4 (49684-7138)
P.O. Box 1838 (49685-1838)
PHONE..................................231 883-6035
Austin Groesser, *Mng Member*
Daniel Fuller,
EMP: 5
SQ FT: 2,000
SALES: 70.1K **Privately Held**
SIC: 2045 Doughs, frozen or refrigerated: from purchased flour

(G-15912)
BIMBO BAKERIES USA INC
Also Called: Sara Lee Bakery Outlet
1668 Northern Star Dr (49696-9242)
PHONE..................................231 922-3296
Susan Larose, *Manager*
EMP: 3 **Privately Held**
SIC: 2053 5461 Frozen bakery products, except bread; bakeries
HQ: Bimbo Bakeries Usa, Inc
  255 Business Center Dr # 200
  Horsham PA 19044
  215 347-5500

(G-15913)
BLOOM INDUSTRIES LLC
726 Hastings St Ste A (49686-3461)
PHONE..................................616 890-8029
EMP: 6
SALES (corp-wide): 680.6K **Privately Held**
SIC: 3999 Barber & beauty shop equipment
PA: Bloom Industries Llc
  2218 Ashcreek Ct Nw
  Grand Rapids MI 49534
  616 453-2946

(G-15914)
BLUE WATER SAIL & CANVAS INC
Also Called: Doyle Sailmakers
10531 E Carter Rd (49684-5434)
PHONE..................................231 941-5224
William Buchbinder, *President*
EMP: 3
SALES (est): 204.8K **Privately Held**
SIC: 2394 Canvas boat seats

(G-15915)
BLUESHIFT MOTORCYCLES LLC
13919 S West Bay Shore Dr G01 (49684-6216)
PHONE..................................231 946-8772
EMP: 3
SALES (est): 240.6K **Privately Held**
SIC: 3751 Mfg Motorcycles/Bicycles

(G-15916)
BORIDE ENGINEERED ABR INC
2615 Aero Park Dr (49686-9101)
PHONE..................................231 929-2121
Larry Tiefenbach, *President*
Mark Klug, *Mfg Mgr*
Ernie Fryer, *Safety Mgr*
Jeff Ziesmer, *QC Mgr*
Betsi Burns, *Manager*
EMP: 15
SALES (est): 583K **Privately Held**
SIC: 3541 Grinding, polishing, buffing, lapping & honing machines

(G-15917)
BOSTWICK ENTERPRISES INC (PA)
Also Called: Wilbert Burial Vault Co
3575 Veterans Dr (49684-4512)
PHONE..................................231 946-8613
Alan Bostwick, *President*
EMP: 12
SALES (est): 1.7MM **Privately Held**
SIC: 3272 Burial vaults, concrete or precast terrazzo

(G-15918)
BOTSG INC
Also Called: Boride Engineered Abrasives
2615 Aero Park Dr (49686-9101)
PHONE..................................231 929-2121
Larry Tiefenbach, *President*
Kenneth Osborne, *Vice Pres*
John Sak, *Vice Pres*
▲ **EMP:** 54
SQ FT: 22,000
SALES (est): 9.4MM **Privately Held**
WEB: www.boride-eng-abr.com
SIC: 3291 3281 Abrasive products; cut stone & stone products

GEOGRAPHIC SECTION
Traverse City - Grand Traverse County (G-15945)

(G-15919)
BOWERS HARBOR VINYRD & WINERY
Also Called: 45th Parallel
2896 Bowers Harbor Rd (49686-9735)
PHONE...................................231 223-7615
Spencer Stegenga, *President*
Linda Stegenga, *Corp Secy*
Kristy McClellan, *Opers Staff*
Justin Leshinsky, *Sales Staff*
EMP: 8
SALES (est): 824.8K **Privately Held**
WEB: www.bowersharbor.com
SIC: 2084 5812 Wines; eating places

(G-15920)
BRITTEN INC
2322 Cass Rd (49684-9147)
PHONE...................................231 941-8200
Paul Britten, *President*
Rylan Ash, *Project Mgr*
Danielle Dlattner, *Asst Controller*
Casey Gelow, *Accounts Exec*
Courtney Look, *Accounts Exec*
EMP: 240
SALES (est): 4.1MM **Privately Held**
SIC: 2399 3993 2796 2396 Banners, pennants & flags; banners, made from fabric; signs & advertising specialties; platemaking services; automotive & apparel trimmings; architectural metalwork; sheet metalwork

(G-15921)
BRITTEN METALWORKS LLC
1661 Northern Star Dr (49696-9243)
PHONE...................................231 421-1615
Aul Briten, *President*
Mark A Augustine,
EMP: 9
SQ FT: 11,000
SALES (est): 723.8K **Privately Held**
SIC: 7692 3465 Automotive welding; automotive stampings

(G-15922)
BRITTEN POP LLC
2322 Cass Rd (49684-9147)
PHONE...................................800 426-9496
Paul Britten,
EMP: 3
SALES (est): 190.7K **Privately Held**
SIC: 2399 Banners, made from fabric

(G-15923)
BRYS ESTATE VINEYARD & WINERY
3309 Blue Water Rd (49686-8561)
PHONE...................................231 223-9303
Cornel Olivier, *Manager*
Taylor Lopiccolo, *Manager*
EMP: 3
SALES (est): 265.8K **Privately Held**
SIC: 2084 Wines

(G-15924)
BURNETTE FOODS INC
2955 Kroupa Rd (49686-9731)
PHONE...................................231 223-4282
Jim Horton, *President*
Donald Shea, *Vice Pres*
Clint Warren, *Manager*
EMP: 23
SQ FT: 28,000
SALES (est): 3.9MM **Privately Held**
SIC: 5148 4222 0723 2099 Fruits, fresh; warehousing, cold storage or refrigerated; fruit crops market preparation services; food preparations

(G-15925)
BUSINESS NEWS
Also Called: Eyes Media
129 E Front St 200 (49684-2508)
PHONE...................................231 929-7919
Luke Haase, *President*
Gayle Neu, *Editor*
Cyndi Csapo, *Advt Staff*
EMP: 4
SALES: 650K **Privately Held**
WEB: www.tcbusinessnews.com
SIC: 2711 Newspapers, publishing & printing

(G-15926)
C R T & ASSOCIATES INC
806 Hastings St Ste H (49686-3400)
PHONE...................................231 946-1680
Doug Hamar, *Principal*
EMP: 5
SALES (est): 338K **Privately Held**
WEB: www.crt-a.com
SIC: 7372 Prepackaged software

(G-15927)
CABINETS BY ROBERT INC
Also Called: Cbr Industries
2774 Garfield Rd N Ste C (49686-5090)
PHONE...................................231 947-3261
Gary Godziebiewski, *President*
Chuck Goudey, *Foreman/Supr*
Robert Godziebiewski, *Shareholder*
EMP: 10
SQ FT: 3,600
SALES (est): 1.9MM **Privately Held**
SIC: 2434 Wood kitchen cabinets

(G-15928)
CAKE CONNECTION TC LLC
5730 Cherry Blossom Dr (49685-8369)
PHONE...................................231 943-3531
Sherry Keech, *Principal*
EMP: 5
SALES (est): 111.1K **Privately Held**
SIC: 5461 2051 Cakes; cakes, bakery: except frozen

(G-15929)
CANDLE FACTORY GRAND TRAVERSE
Also Called: Home Elements
301 W Grandview Pkwy (49684-2365)
P.O. Box 807 (49685-0807)
PHONE...................................231 946-2280
John Teichman, *Owner*
EMP: 12 **EST:** 1971
SALES (est): 1.1MM **Privately Held**
WEB: www.candles.net
SIC: 5719 3999 Housewares; candles

(G-15930)
CARBON IMPACT INC
2628 Garfield Rd N Ste 38 (49686-5089)
PHONE...................................231 929-8152
Pierre Pujos, *President*
EMP: 34
SQ FT: 2,000
SALES (est): 2.6MM **Privately Held**
WEB: www.carbonimpact.com
SIC: 3949 Arrows, archery

(G-15931)
CENTURN MACHINE & TOOL INC
6185 E Traverse Hwy (49684-8397)
PHONE...................................231 947-4773
James Balesh, *President*
Arlene Balesh, *Vice Pres*
EMP: 7
SQ FT: 2,000
SALES (est): 768.7K **Privately Held**
SIC: 3544 Special dies, tools, jigs & fixtures

(G-15932)
CENTURY INC (PA)
Also Called: Century-Sun Metal Treating
2410 W Aero Park Ct (49686-9102)
PHONE...................................231 947-6400
William G Janis, *President*
Charlie Janis, *General Mgr*
Wayne Gibson, *Vice Pres*
Pat Lott, *Opers Mgr*
Joshua Farrell, *Prdtn Mgr*
▲ **EMP:** 170 **EST:** 1966
SQ FT: 76,000
SALES (est): 72.1MM **Privately Held**
WEB: www.centinc.com
SIC: 3544 3398 3399 3559 Special dies, tools, jigs & fixtures; metal heat treating; powder, metal; plastics working machinery; machine tools, metal forming type

(G-15933)
CENTURY INC
Century Rollforming
2410 W Aero Park Ct (49686-9102)
PHONE...................................231 946-7500
Chris Darelston, *Branch Mgr*
EMP: 8

SALES (corp-wide): 72.1MM **Privately Held**
WEB: www.centinc.com
SIC: 3544 3545 Special dies, tools, jigs & fixtures; tools & accessories for machine tools
PA: Century, Inc.
2410 W Aero Park Ct
Traverse City MI 49686
231 947-6400

(G-15934)
CENTURY INC
Also Called: Century-Sun Metal Treating
2411 W Aero Park Ct (49686-9102)
PHONE...................................231 941-7800
James Black, *Manager*
EMP: 100
SALES (corp-wide): 72.1MM **Privately Held**
WEB: www.centinc.com
SIC: 3544 3398 3399 Special dies, tools, jigs & fixtures; metal heat treating; powder, metal
PA: Century, Inc.
2410 W Aero Park Ct
Traverse City MI 49686
231 947-6400

(G-15935)
CERNY INDUSTRIES LLC
Also Called: Strata Design
1645 Park Dr (49686-4701)
P.O. Box 6250 (49696-6250)
PHONE...................................231 929-2140
Tyler Cerny,
EMP: 25
SQ FT: 32,000
SALES (est): 3.3MM **Privately Held**
WEB: www.stratamail.com
SIC: 2522 Cabinets, office: except wood

(G-15936)
CHATEAU GRAND TRAVERS LTD
Also Called: Grand Traverse Vineyards
12239 Center Rd (49686-8558)
PHONE...................................231 223-7355
Edward L O'Keefe Jr, *CEO*
Edward L O'Keefe III, *President*
EMP: 4
SQ FT: 10,000
SALES (est): 2.1MM **Privately Held**
WEB: www.cgtinn.com
SIC: 2084 Wines
PA: O'keefe Centre Ltd
12239 Center Rd
Traverse City MI 49686
231 223-7355

(G-15937)
CHATEAU OPERATIONS LTD
Also Called: Chateau Chantal
15900 Rue De Vin (49686-9379)
PHONE...................................231 223-4110
Robert Begin, *CEO*
Elizabeth Burger, *General Mgr*
Elizabeth Berger, *Opers Mgr*
Terrie McClelland, *Controller*
Christine Raymond, *Marketing Mgr*
▲ **EMP:** 34
SQ FT: 11,000
SALES (est): 3.9MM **Privately Held**
WEB: www.chateauchantal.com
SIC: 0172 2084 5921 7011 Grapes; wines; wine; bed & breakfast inn

(G-15938)
CHERRY CENTRAL COOPERATIVE INC (PA)
1771 N Us 31 S (49685-8748)
P.O. Box 988 (49685-0988)
PHONE...................................231 946-1860
Steve Eiseler, *President*
Robert McMullin, *Principal*
George Wright, *Corp Secy*
Rick Luther, *COO*
Roy Hackert, *Vice Pres*
◆ **EMP:** 30
SQ FT: 15,000
SALES: 133MM **Privately Held**
WEB: www.cherrycentral.com
SIC: 2033 Canned fruits & specialties

(G-15939)
CHERRY CONE LLC
240 E Front St (49684-2526)
PHONE...................................231 944-1036
Joe Welsh,
EMP: 5
SQ FT: 1,965
SALES (est): 381.3K **Privately Held**
SIC: 2052 Cones, ice cream

(G-15940)
CHERRY GROWERS INC
Also Called: Cherry Growers Plant 2
9440 S Center Hwy (49684-9557)
PHONE...................................231 947-2502
EMP: 5
SALES (est): 250.3K
SALES (corp-wide): 24MM **Privately Held**
SIC: 2037 2033 Freezer Plant
PA: Cherry Growers, Inc.
6331 Us Highway 31
Grawn MI 48009
231 276-9241

(G-15941)
CIMA ENERGY LP
125 S Park St Ste 450 (49684-3605)
PHONE...................................231 941-0633
Stephen Trippe, *Manager*
EMP: 4 **Privately Held**
SIC: 1311 Crude petroleum & natural gas
PA: Cima Energy, Lp
100 Waugh Dr Ste 500
Houston TX 77007

(G-15942)
CLARK MANUFACTURING COMPANY
2485 Aero Park Dr (49686-9119)
PHONE...................................231 946-5110
Robert Milliron, *President*
Cameron Fuller, *Vice Pres*
Brian Walter, *Vice Pres*
Wendy Gauthier, *Accountant*
EMP: 100 **EST:** 1975
SQ FT: 60,000
SALES (est): 18.6MM **Privately Held**
WEB: www.clarkmfg.com
SIC: 3599 Machine shop, jobbing & repair

(G-15943)
COCA-COLA REFRESHMENTS USA INC
1031 Hastings St (49686-3444)
PHONE...................................231 947-4150
Charlie Raymond, *Manager*
EMP: 55
SALES (corp-wide): 31.8B **Publicly Held**
WEB: www.cokecce.com
SIC: 2086 Bottled & canned soft drinks
HQ: Coca-Cola Refreshments Usa, Inc.
2500 Windy Ridge Pkwy Se
Atlanta GA 30339
770 989-3000

(G-15944)
COGNISYS INC
459 Hughes Dr (49696-8255)
PHONE...................................231 943-2425
Paul Dezeeuw, *President*
Matt Cardwell, *Admin Sec*
EMP: 5 **EST:** 2008
SALES: 1MM **Privately Held**
SIC: 3861 5963 Photographic instruments, electronic; direct selling establishments

(G-15945)
CONE DRIVE OPERATIONS INC (HQ)
Also Called: Cone Drive Gearing Solutions
240 E Twelfth St (49684-3269)
P.O. Box 272 (49685-0272)
PHONE...................................231 946-8410
Kurt Gamelin, *CEO*
Vicki Lardie, *General Mgr*
Michael King, *Vice Pres*
Tom Peters, *Opers Staff*
Shayne Gatzke, *Mfg Staff*
◆ **EMP:** 150
SQ FT: 135,000

Traverse City - Grand Traverse County (G-15946)

SALES (est): 37.6MM
SALES (corp-wide): 3.5B **Publicly Held**
WEB: www.conedrive.com
SIC: 3566 Speed changers (power transmission equipment), except auto
PA: The Timken Company
4500 Mount Pleasant St Nw
North Canton OH 44720
234 262-3000

(G-15946)
COOPER PUBLISHING GROUP LLC
251 Knollwood Dr (49686-1856)
PHONE 231 933-9958
Joanne Cooper,
Irving Butch Cooper,
EMP: 5
SQ FT: 3,000
SALES: 320K **Privately Held**
SIC: 2731 Textbooks: publishing only, not printed on site

(G-15947)
COPY CENTRAL INC
Also Called: Printing Place, The
314 E Eighth St (49684-2540)
PHONE 231 941-2298
Mark Bonter, *President*
Pam Bonter, *Admin Sec*
EMP: 7
SQ FT: 4,000
SALES (est): 621.5K **Privately Held**
SIC: 7334 7374 2752 3993 Blueprinting service; computer processing services; offset & photolithographic printing; signs & advertising specialties; typesetting; bookbinding & related work

(G-15948)
CORE ENERGY LLC
1011 Noteware Dr (49686-8184)
PHONE 231 946-2419
Robert Mannes, *CEO*
Rick Pardini, *Vice Pres*
Bob Tipsword, *Opers Mgr*
Randy Odell, *Foreman/Supr*
Anna Heiges, *Asst Controller*
EMP: 6
SALES (est): 1.4MM **Privately Held**
WEB: www.coreenergy.net
SIC: 1382 Oil & gas exploration services

(G-15949)
COX MACHINE LLC
2823 Cass Rd Ste F1 (49684-7139)
PHONE 269 953-5446
Nathan Cox, *Principal*
EMP: 3
SALES (est): 108.4K **Privately Held**
SIC: 3599 Machine shop, jobbing & repair; machine & other job shop work; electrical discharge machining (EDM)

(G-15950)
CPM ACQUISITION CORP
2412 W Aero Park Ct (49686-9102)
PHONE 231 947-6400
EMP: 9 **Privately Held**
WEB: www.betaraven.com
SIC: 3523 3355 Farm machinery & equipment; extrusion ingot, aluminum: made in rolling mills
HQ: Cpm Acquisition Corp.
2975 Airline Cir
Waterloo IA 50703
319 232-8444

(G-15951)
CPM ACQUISITION CORP
Also Called: CPM Century Extrusion
2412 W Aero Park Ct (49686-9102)
PHONE 231 947-6400
Cliff Anderson, *President*
▲ **EMP:** 85
SALES (est): 14.4MM **Privately Held**
SIC: 3451 Screw machine products

(G-15952)
CRM INC
495 W South Airport Rd (49686-4842)
PHONE 231 947-0304
Clare Ray, *President*
Mark Ray, *Vice Pres*
Lance Kretschmer, *Engineer*
EMP: 90
SQ FT: 42,000
SALES (est): 12.4MM **Privately Held**
SIC: 3479 Painting of metal products

(G-15953)
CROWN EQUIPMENT CORPORATION
Also Called: Crown Lift Trucks
903 Lynch Dr Ste 103 (49686-4800)
PHONE 616 530-3000
Eric McNutt, *Manager*
EMP: 6
SALES (corp-wide): 3.4B **Privately Held**
SIC: 3537 Lift trucks, industrial: fork, platform, straddle, etc.
PA: Crown Equipment Corporation
44 S Washington St
New Bremen OH 45869
419 629-2311

(G-15954)
D & D SIGNS INC
2694 Garfield Rd N Ste 25 (49686-5177)
PHONE 231 941-0340
Dana Thompson, *President*
Donna Thompson, *Vice Pres*
EMP: 3
SQ FT: 2,400
SALES: 300K **Privately Held**
WEB: www.ddsigns.com
SIC: 3993 Signs & advertising specialties

(G-15955)
D C NORRIS NORTH AMERICA LLC
2375 Traversefield Dr (49686-9266)
PHONE 231 935-1519
Dick Smith, *Vice Pres*
Brian Irwin, *Project Engr*
EMP: 4
SALES (est): 129.6K **Privately Held**
SIC: 5084 3556 1799 5999 Food product manufacturing machinery; food products machinery; food service equipment installation; alcoholic beverage making equipment & supplies

(G-15956)
DIAMONDBCK-DRECTIONAL DRLG LLC
Also Called: Directional Drilling Contrs
2122 S M 37 (49685-8061)
P.O. Box 6156 (49696-6156)
PHONE 231 943-3000
EMP: 15
SALES (est): 2MM **Privately Held**
SIC: 1381 Oil/Gas Well Drilling

(G-15957)
DOUG MURDICKS FUDGE INC
4500 N Us Highway 31 N (49686-3761)
PHONE 231 938-2330
Doug Murdick, *Owner*
EMP: 6
SALES (corp-wide): 851.4K **Privately Held**
WEB: www.murdocksfudge.com
SIC: 2064 5441 Fudge (candy); candy
PA: Doug Murdick's Fudge Inc
116 E Front St
Traverse City MI 49684
231 947-4841

(G-15958)
DTE GAS & OIL COMPANY
Also Called: MCN Oil & Gas
10691 E Carter Rd Ste 201 (49684-5499)
PHONE 231 995-4000
Richard Redmond, *President*
EMP: 45 **EST:** 1992
SQ FT: 15,000
SALES (est): 2.1MM **Privately Held**
SIC: 1382 Oil & gas exploration services

(G-15959)
DUTCHMAN MFG CO LLC
6185 E Traverse Hwy Ste B (49684-8397)
PHONE 734 922-5803
Thomas Van Fossen, *Administration*
EMP: 9
SALES (est): 852.6K **Privately Held**
SIC: 3494 3492 3491 Valves & pipe fittings; fluid power valves & hose fittings; industrial valves

(G-15960)
EDWARD G HINKELMAN
Also Called: World Trade Press
616 E Eighth St Ste 7 (49686-2505)
PHONE 707 778-1124
Edward Hinkelman, *Owner*
◆ **EMP:** 10
SQ FT: 6,300
SALES (est): 977.8K **Privately Held**
WEB: www.worldtradepress.com
SIC: 2741 Miscellaneous publishing

(G-15961)
ELECTRO-OPTICS TECHNOLOGY INC (PA)
Also Called: Eot
3340 Parkland Ct (49686-8723)
P.O. Box 987 (49685-0987)
PHONE 231 935-4044
David Scerbak, *President*
Michael Torrance, *Vice Pres*
Lisa S Long, *Purchasing*
Bill Bradley, *Engineer*
Joseph Mambourg, *Engineer*
▲ **EMP:** 70
SQ FT: 15,000
SALES (est): 10.6MM **Privately Held**
WEB: www.eotech.com
SIC: 3827 Optical instruments & lenses

(G-15962)
ELMERS CRANE AND DOZER INC (PA)
Also Called: Elmers Construction Engrg
3600 Rennie School Rd (49685-9170)
P.O. Box 6150 (49696-6150)
PHONE 231 943-3443
Russell L Broad, *President*
Max Bott, *Division Mgr*
Tanya Broad, *Vice Pres*
Todd Broad, *Vice Pres*
Troy Broad, *Vice Pres*
EMP: 150
SQ FT: 12,000
SALES (est): 48.8MM **Privately Held**
SIC: 1771 1794 1611 3273 Driveway, parking lot & blacktop contractors; excavation work; highway & street paving contractor; ready-mixed concrete; asphalt paving mixtures & blocks; construction sand & gravel

(G-15963)
EMERSON GEOPHYSICAL LLC
3819 4 Mile Rd N (49686-9344)
PHONE 231 943-1400
Mitchell Pasinski, *Mng Member*
EMP: 20
SALES (est): 416.2K **Privately Held**
SIC: 1382 Seismograph surveys

(G-15964)
ENSIGN EMBLEM LTD (PA)
Also Called: Ensign Technical Services
1746 Keane Dr (49696-8257)
PHONE 231 946-7703
Gayle M Zreliak, *President*
John Matthews, *COO*
Toni Butkovich, *Opers Mgr*
Mary Giscart, *Human Res Mgr*
Tom Paquette, *Natl Sales Mgr*
EMP: 85
SQ FT: 20,000
SALES (est): 13.4MM **Privately Held**
WEB: www.ensignemblem.com
SIC: 2395 Embroidery products, except schiffli machine

(G-15965)
ENVIRONMENTAL PROTECTION INC
1567 W South Airport Rd # 1 (49686-4702)
PHONE 231 943-2265
Daniel S Rohe, *President*
Brad Dearment, *General Mgr*
EMP: 19
SALES (est): 3.4MM **Privately Held**
SIC: 8748 3081 8731 Environmental consultant; polyethylene film; environmental research

(G-15966)
ESSILOR LABORATORIES AMER INC
Also Called: Twin City Optical
2323 W Aero Park Ct (49686-9102)
PHONE 231 922-0344
Richard Gross, *Branch Mgr*
EMP: 31
SALES (corp-wide): 1.4MM **Privately Held**
WEB: www.crizal.com
SIC: 5049 3851 Optical goods; ophthalmic goods
HQ: Essilor Laboratories Of America, Inc.
13515 N Stemmons Fwy
Dallas TX 75234
972 241-4141

(G-15967)
EXPRESS PUBLICATIONS INC
Also Called: Northern Express Publications
129 E Front St 200 (49684-2658)
P.O. Box 209 (49685-0209)
PHONE 231 947-8787
Robert Downes, *President*
Katy McCain, *Sales Staff*
EMP: 10
SQ FT: 1,200
SALES (est): 501.2K **Privately Held**
SIC: 2711 Newspapers: publishing only, not printed on site

(G-15968)
FASTSIGNS INTERNATIONAL INC
1420 Trade Center Dr (49696-8917)
PHONE 231 941-0300
Judy Prewitt, *Manager*
EMP: 4
SALES (corp-wide): 25.8MM **Privately Held**
SIC: 3993 Signs & advertising specialties
PA: Fastsigns International, Inc.
2542 Highlander Way
Carrollton TX 75006
888 285-5935

(G-15969)
FEDERAL SCREW WORKS
2270 Traversefield Dr (49686-9251)
PHONE 231 922-9500
W T Zurschiede Jr, *Chairman*
Scott Rozema, *Accountant*
EMP: 8
SALES (corp-wide): 2.4K **Privately Held**
WEB: www.federalscrew.com
SIC: 3452 3325 Bolts, metal; steel foundries
PA: Federal Screw Works
34846 Goddard Rd
Romulus MI 48174
734 941-4211

(G-15970)
FEDERATED OIL & GAS PRPTS INC
12719 S West Bay Shore Dr # 5 (49684-5489)
P.O. Box 946 (49685-0946)
PHONE 231 929-4466
Joseph Kostrzewa, *Chairman*
EMP: 6
SQ FT: 1,500
SALES (est): 860K **Privately Held**
SIC: 1311 Crude petroleum production; natural gas production

(G-15971)
FOOD FOR THOUGHT INC
7738 N Long Lake Rd (49685-8226)
PHONE 231 326-5444
Gregory Young, *President*
EMP: 20
SALES (est): 2.3MM **Privately Held**
WEB: www.wildjam.com
SIC: 2033 Fruits & fruit products in cans, jars, etc.

(G-15972)
FOREWORD MAGAZINE INC
425 Boardman Ave (49684-2562)
PHONE 231 933-3699
Victoria Sutherland, *CEO*
Michelle Schingler, *Editor*
Bill Harper, *Chief*

GEOGRAPHIC SECTION

Traverse City - Grand Traverse County (G-16000)

Matt Sutherland, *Production*
EMP: 10 **EST:** 1998
SALES (est): 1.3MM **Privately Held**
WEB: www.forewordmagazine.com
SIC: 2721 2731 Magazines: publishing only, not printed on site; book publishing

(G-15973)
FORKARDT INC
Also Called: Forkardt North America
2155 Traversefield Dr (49686-8699)
PHONE.................................231 995-8300
Richard L Simons, *President*
Bill Sepanik, *General Mgr*
Charlie Carmoney, *Opers Mgr*
Don Kochanowski, *Engineer*
Allen Pivitt, *Engineer*
EMP: 35 **EST:** 1969
SALES (est): 7.1MM **Privately Held**
SIC: 3545 Machine tool accessories

(G-15974)
FULTZ MANUFACTURING INC
1631 Park Dr Ste A (49686-4772)
PHONE.................................231 947-5801
Charles Fultz, *President*
Dennis Bartlett, *General Mgr*
Jacqueline Fultz, *Admin Sec*
EMP: 7
SQ FT: 19,000
SALES (est): 871.2K **Privately Held**
WEB: www.fultzmfg.com
SIC: 2493 Reconstituted wood products

(G-15975)
G F INC
Also Called: Glynn, Mark, Builder
1032 Woodmere Ave Ste B (49686-4265)
PHONE.................................231 946-5330
Angela Glynn, *President*
Mark Glynn, *General Mgr*
Jim Swartout, *Vice Pres*
EMP: 16
SQ FT: 8,000
SALES (est): 1MM **Privately Held**
SIC: 2431 Millwork

(G-15976)
GARY CORK INCORPORATED (PA)
Also Called: Snap Quickprint
806 S Garfield Ave Ste B (49686-2400)
PHONE.................................231 946-1061
Gary Cork, *President*
EMP: 7 **EST:** 1979
SQ FT: 1,200
SALES (est): 1MM **Privately Held**
SIC: 2752 7334 Commercial printing, offset; photocopying & duplicating services

(G-15977)
GENESEE VALLEY PETROLEUM
523 Cottage Arbor Ln # 5 (49684-3010)
P.O. Box 1067 (49685-1067)
PHONE.................................231 946-8630
Peter Zirnhelt, *Owner*
EMP: 3
SALES (est): 211.2K **Privately Held**
WEB: www.geneseelandtrust.org
SIC: 1321 Liquefied petroleum gases (natural) production

(G-15978)
GEOMEMBRANE RESEARCH
1567 W South Airport Rd (49686-4702)
PHONE.................................231 943-2266
Daniel S Rohe, *Principal*
EMP: 3
SALES (est): 155.7K **Privately Held**
SIC: 2821 Plastics materials & resins

(G-15979)
GET IN GAME MARKETING LLC
Also Called: Threads
2322 Cass Rd (49684-9147)
PHONE.................................231 846-1976
Joshua Ludka, *Mng Member*
EMP: 8
SALES (est): 231.9K **Privately Held**
SIC: 2399 Banners, pennants & flags

(G-15980)
GODIN TOOL INC
466 Hughes Dr (49696-8255)
P.O. Box 6246 (49696-6246)
PHONE.................................231 946-2210
Allen F Godin, *President*
EMP: 7
SALES (est): 570K **Privately Held**
WEB: www.godintool.com
SIC: 3541 Machine tools, metal cutting type

(G-15981)
GOODWILL INDS NTHRN MICH INC
Also Called: Goodwill Inn
1329 S Division St (49684-4427)
PHONE.................................231 922-4890
Lois Lannin, *Branch Mgr*
EMP: 9
SALES (corp-wide): 15.9MM **Privately Held**
SIC: 5932 8331 2431 8322 Used merchandise stores; sheltered workshop; millwork; meal delivery program; settlement house
PA: Goodwill Industries Of Northern Michigan, Inc.
2279 S Airport Rd W
Traverse City MI 49684
231 922-4805

(G-15982)
GRAND TRAVERSE CANVAS WORKS
3975 3 Mile Rd N (49686-9164)
PHONE.................................231 947-3140
Mary Wodzien, *President*
Larry Wodzien, *Vice Pres*
EMP: 12
SQ FT: 6,000
SALES (est): 1.4MM **Privately Held**
SIC: 2394 7641 Awnings, fabric: made from purchased materials; convertible tops, canvas or boat: from purchased materials; reupholstery

(G-15983)
GRAND TRAVERSE CONTINUOUS INC
1661 Park Dr (49686-4701)
PHONE.................................231 941-5400
Walter Gallagher, *President*
EMP: 22
SQ FT: 10,000
SALES (est): 2.9MM **Privately Held**
WEB: www.gtcontinuous.com
SIC: 2761 2759 2752 Manifold business forms; commercial printing; commercial printing, lithographic

(G-15984)
GRAND TRAVERSE CRANE CORP
3876 Blair Townhall Rd (49685-9196)
PHONE.................................231 943-7787
Craig Derks, *President*
Nathan Derks, *Business Mgr*
Scott Dekryger, *Corp Secy*
Larry Derks, *Vice Pres*
Megan Derks, *Human Resources*
EMP: 4 **EST:** 1964
SQ FT: 23,000
SALES (est): 719.4K **Privately Held**
SIC: 7699 3536 Industrial equipment services; cranes, overhead traveling; hoists

(G-15985)
GRAND TRAVERSE GARAGE DOORS
823 W Commerce Dr (49685-5806)
PHONE.................................231 943-9897
John Long, *Manager*
EMP: 22
SQ FT: 4,000
SALES (est): 2.1MM
SALES (corp-wide): 2.4MM **Privately Held**
SIC: 3429 5211 7699 1751 Door locks, bolts & checks; door & window products; door & window repair; carpentry work
PA: Cadillac Garage Door, Inc
8888 E 34 Rd Ste A
Cadillac MI 49601
231 775-3239

(G-15986)
GRAND TRAVERSE MACHINE CO
1247 Boon St (49686-4349)
PHONE.................................231 946-8006
Mike Alfonso, *President*
Scott Larigan, *Business Mgr*
Dave Rahe, *Vice Pres*
Darry Rosinski, *QC Mgr*
Chris Laundry, *Prgrmr*
EMP: 65
SQ FT: 21,400
SALES (est): 11.1MM **Privately Held**
SIC: 3599 Machine shop, jobbing & repair

(G-15987)
GRAND TRAVERSE REELS INC
Also Called: Grand Traverse Container
1050 Business Park Dr (49686-8372)
PHONE.................................231 946-1057
Thomas Schofield, *President*
Mike Chereskin, *Vice Pres*
Vince Balog, *Treasurer*
EMP: 104
SQ FT: 80,000
SALES (est): 25.1MM **Privately Held**
WEB: www.gtcontainer.com
SIC: 2653 Boxes, corrugated: made from purchased materials

(G-15988)
GRAND TRAVERSE STAMPING CO
1677 Park Dr (49686-4750)
PHONE.................................231 929-4215
Fred Militz, *President*
Kenneth A Batterbee, *Principal*
Robert J Fair Jr, *Principal*
Richard J Lauer, *Principal*
John J Murray, *Corp Secy*
EMP: 13
SALES (est): 2MM **Privately Held**
SIC: 3714 Motor vehicle electrical equipment

(G-15989)
GRAND TRAVERSE TOOL INC
396 Hughes Dr (49696-8255)
PHONE.................................231 929-4743
Jeff Gothrup, *President*
EMP: 5
SQ FT: 2,000
SALES (est): 250K **Privately Held**
WEB: www.grandtraversetool.com
SIC: 2821 Molding compounds, plastics

(G-15990)
GRAND TRVRSE CULINARY OILS LLC
2780 Cass Rd (49684-7860)
PHONE.................................231 590-2180
William Koucky,
EMP: 3
SQ FT: 9,600
SALES (est): 212.8K **Privately Held**
SIC: 2076 Vegetable oil mills

(G-15991)
GREAT LAKES BATH & BODY INC
110 E Front St (49684-2509)
P.O. Box 924 (49685-0924)
PHONE.................................231 421-9160
Lynn Rodenroth, *Principal*
EMP: 4
SALES (est): 294.8K **Privately Held**
SIC: 7532 2841 Body shop, automotive; detergents, synthetic organic or inorganic alkaline

(G-15992)
GREAT LAKES FORGE INC
Also Called: Grand Traverse Forging & Steel
2465 N Aero Pk Ct (49686-9262)
PHONE.................................231 947-4931
Peter Jones, *President*
Greg Behrens, *Vice Pres*
Shelly Shively, *QC Mgr*
Helen Zakrzewski, *Manager*
▲ **EMP:** 9
SQ FT: 22,000
SALES: 2.5MM **Privately Held**
WEB: www.glforge.com
SIC: 3462 Iron & steel forgings

(G-15993)
GREAT LAKES STAINLESS INC
1305 Stepke Ct (49685-9331)
PHONE.................................231 943-7648
Terry Berden, *CEO*
Michael De Bruyn, *President*
Peter Berden, *Vice Pres*
Rayma Berden, *Treasurer*
EMP: 30
SQ FT: 50,000
SALES: 11.7MM **Privately Held**
WEB: www.grandtraverserefrigeration.com
SIC: 3441 Fabricated structural metal

(G-15994)
GREAT LAKES WELD LLC
889 S East Silver Lake Rd (49685-9340)
PHONE.................................231 943-4180
Shawn Boyd, *Owner*
EMP: 5
SALES (est): 156.5K **Privately Held**
SIC: 7692 7699 Welding repair; cash register repair

(G-15995)
H AND M LUBE DBA JLUBE
529 W Fourteenth St (49684-4042)
PHONE.................................231 929-1197
Moses Nasser, *Managing Prtnr*
EMP: 4
SALES (est): 435.7K **Privately Held**
SIC: 2992 Lubricating oils & greases

(G-15996)
H M DAY SIGNS INC
233 E Twelfth St (49684-3215)
PHONE.................................231 946-7132
Harry M Day Jr, *President*
Patricia Day, *Treasurer*
EMP: 6
SALES: 600K **Privately Held**
SIC: 7374 3993 1799 Computer graphics service; signs & advertising specialties; neon signs; sign installation & maintenance

(G-15997)
HILLSHIRE BRANDS COMPANY
2314 Sybrant Rd (49685-9151)
PHONE.................................231 947-2100
Randy Tucker, *Branch Mgr*
EMP: 600
SALES (corp-wide): 42.4B **Publicly Held**
SIC: 2099 Food preparations
HQ: The Hillshire Brands Company
400 S Jefferson St Fl 1
Chicago IL 60607
312 614-6000

(G-15998)
HOBART BROTHERS COMPANY
Also Called: Maxal Hobart Brothers
1631 International Dr (49686-8964)
PHONE.................................231 933-1234
Sundaran Magarajan, *President*
EMP: 10
SALES (corp-wide): 14.7B **Publicly Held**
SIC: 3548 3537 Welding apparatus; industrial trucks & tractors
HQ: Hobart Brothers Llc
101 Trade Sq E
Troy OH 45373
937 332-5439

(G-15999)
HOWARD ENERGY CO INC (PA)
125 S Park St Ste 250 (49684-3601)
P.O. Box 949 (49685-0949)
PHONE.................................231 995-7850
Mike Palmer, *General Mgr*
Patrick McGuire, *Controller*
Richard Newell, *Admin Sec*
EMP: 28
SQ FT: 12,000
SALES (est): 6.5MM **Privately Held**
SIC: 1382 4924 4922 Oil & gas exploration services; natural gas distribution; storage, natural gas

(G-16000)
HSS INDUSTRIES INC
2464 Cass Rd (49684-9148)
P.O. Box 2060 (49685-2060)
PHONE.................................231 946-6101
Herman Hinsenkamp, *President*
Darren Hinsenkamp, *Vice Pres*

Traverse City - Grand Traverse County (G-16001)

Diane Hinsenkamp, *Info Tech Mgr*
▲ **EMP:** 20 **EST:** 1982
SQ FT: 16,000
SALES (est): 3.2MM **Privately Held**
WEB: www.hsspostal.com
SIC: 2542 Locker boxes, postal service: except wood; cabinets: show, display or storage: except wood

(G-16001)
IDEL LLC
1315 Woodmere Ave (49686-4308)
PHONE 231 929-3195
Leonard Korson,
EMP: 7
SQ FT: 7,500
SALES (est): 647.4K **Privately Held**
SIC: 3544 Special dies & tools

(G-16002)
ILLINOIS TOOL WORKS INC
Also Called: I T W Workholding
2155 Traversefield Dr (49686-8699)
P.O. Box 547 (49685-0547)
PHONE 231 947-5755
Chuck Delonghi, *Manager*
EMP: 60
SALES (corp-wide): 14.7B **Publicly Held**
WEB: www.itwchucks.com
SIC: 3545 Machine tool accessories
PA: Illinois Tool Works Inc.
155 Harlem Ave
Glenview IL 60025
847 724-7500

(G-16003)
ILLINOIS TOOL WORKS INC
Forkardt North America
2155 Traversefield Dr (49686-8699)
PHONE 231 947-5755
EMP: 6
SALES (corp-wide): 14.3B **Publicly Held**
SIC: 3545 Mfg Machine Tool Accessories
PA: Illinois Tool Works Inc.
155 Harlem Ave
Glenview IL 60025
847 724-7500

(G-16004)
INNOVA EXPLORATION INC
333 W Grandview Pkwy # 502 (49684-2289)
P.O. Box 129 (49685-0129)
PHONE 231 929-3985
Ron Budrose, *President*
Gail Hooper, *Office Mgr*
Jared Bowen, *Associate*
EMP: 3
SALES (est): 519.2K **Privately Held**
WEB: www.innova-exploration.com
SIC: 1382 Oil & gas exploration services

(G-16005)
INSTANT FRAMER
322 S Union St (49684-2535)
PHONE 231 947-8908
Ken Meyer, *Owner*
EMP: 4
SALES (est): 497.9K **Privately Held**
SIC: 2752 Commercial printing, lithographic

(G-16006)
INSTEP PEDORTHICS LLC
4338 Manhattan E (49685-9620)
PHONE 810 285-9109
EMP: 3
SALES (est): 180.3K **Privately Held**
SIC: 3842 Braces, orthopedic

(G-16007)
INTERACTIVE AERIAL INC
1135 Woodmere Ave Ste A (49686-4218)
PHONE 231 715-1422
Christian Smith, *CEO*
Pierce Thomas, *COO*
Christopher Schmidt, *Chief Engr*
Justin Bensten, *Development*
Justin Bentsen, *CIO*
EMP: 5 **EST:** 2016
SQ FT: 2,000
SALES (est): 245.8K **Privately Held**
SIC: 3812 Aircraft/aerospace flight instruments & guidance systems

(G-16008)
JADE TOOL INC
891 Duell Rd (49686-4859)
PHONE 231 946-7710
John A Korson, *President*
Dora Korson, *Corp Secy*
Don Dowker, *Engineer*
Jason Kent, *Engineer*
Dave Terbrack, *Engineer*
EMP: 25
SQ FT: 6,150
SALES (est): 4.1MM **Privately Held**
WEB: www.jadetool.com
SIC: 3545 Tool holders; boring machine attachments (machine tool accessories); tools & accessories for machine tools

(G-16009)
JANTEC INCORPORATED
1777 Northern Star Dr (49696-9244)
PHONE 231 941-4339
Ronald Sommerfield, *President*
Robert Leusby, *Vice Pres*
Andy Richards, *Financial Exec*
Penny Sommerfield, *Executive Asst*
EMP: 20 **EST:** 1979
SQ FT: 20,000
SALES (est): 5.5MM **Privately Held**
WEB: www.jantec.com
SIC: 3535 Conveyors & conveying equipment

(G-16010)
JENKINS GROUP INC
Also Called: Axiom Business Book Awards
1129 Woodmere Ave Ste B (49686-4275)
PHONE 231 933-4954
Jerrold Jenkins, *CEO*
Jim Kalajian, *President*
▲ **EMP:** 10
SQ FT: 2,400
SALES (est): 2MM **Privately Held**
WEB: www.jenkinsgroup.com
SIC: 2731 2732 Book publishing; book printing

(G-16011)
JENTEES CUSTOM SCREEN PRTG LLC
Also Called: Jentees Custom Logo Gear
515 Wellington St (49686-2660)
PHONE 231 929-3610
Mark Jensen,
EMP: 10
SQ FT: 4,000
SALES (est): 859.9K **Privately Held**
SIC: 2759 Screen printing

(G-16012)
JEREMY JELINEK (PA)
8389 E Lakeview Hills Rd (49684-7513)
PHONE 231 313-7124
Jeremy Jelinek, *Owner*
EMP: 6
SALES: 150K **Privately Held**
SIC: 3999 Honeycomb foundations (beekeepers' supplies)

(G-16013)
JKR VENTURES LLC
Also Called: Super Bowl 50 Book
1129 Woodmere Ave Ste B (49686-4275)
PHONE 734 645-2320
Peter Racine, *Partner*
EMP: 3
SALES (est): 102.6K
SALES (corp-wide): 2.7B **Publicly Held**
SIC: 2731 Book publishing
PA: Graham Holdings Company
1300 17th St N Ste 1700
Arlington VA 22209
703 345-6300

(G-16014)
JOHNSON-CLARK PRINTERS INC
Also Called: Prepress Services
1224 Centre St (49686-3491)
PHONE 231 947-6898
Sandy Henschell, *President*
Wayne Miller, *Vice Pres*
EMP: 10 **EST:** 1949
SQ FT: 9,000
SALES (est): 1.2MM **Privately Held**
WEB: www.jcprinters.com
SIC: 2752 2759 Commercial printing, offset; letterpress printing

(G-16015)
JORDAN EXPLORATION CO LLC
1503 Garfield Rd N (49696-1111)
PHONE 231 935-4220
Benjamin Brower, *Vice Pres*
Bill Quinlan, *VP Opers*
Tom Robb, *Opers Mgr*
William Quinlan, *Production*
Jessica Fellows, *Accountant*
EMP: 15
SALES (est): 3.6MM **Privately Held**
WEB: www.jordanex.com
SIC: 1311 Crude petroleum production; natural gas production

(G-16016)
KEENAN ENTERPRISES INC
3866 Jupiter Cresent Dr (49685-9335)
PHONE 231 943-0516
Dennis Keenan, *President*
EMP: 3
SALES (est): 396.4K **Privately Held**
SIC: 3544 Special dies, tools, jigs & fixtures

(G-16017)
KELLY OIL & GAS INC
303 S Union St Ofc C (49684-5775)
PHONE 231 929-0591
Robert K Robinson, *President*
Colleen Heron, *Corp Secy*
Madeline Robinson, *Vice Pres*
EMP: 8
SQ FT: 1,200
SALES (est): 993.5K **Privately Held**
SIC: 1311 Crude petroleum & natural gas

(G-16018)
KENNAMETAL INC
2879 Aero Park Dr (49686-8494)
PHONE 231 946-2100
Doug Grove, *Mfg Mgr*
Kelly Stachnik, *Materials Mgr*
Larry Hagberg, *Engineer*
Michael Omallei, *Branch Mgr*
Lindsey Agruda, *Manager*
EMP: 90
SALES (corp-wide): 2.3B **Publicly Held**
WEB: www.kennametal.com
SIC: 3545 Cutting tools for machine tools
PA: Kennametal Inc.
600 Grant St Ste 5100
Pittsburgh PA 15219
412 248-8000

(G-16019)
KWIKIE INC
Also Called: Traverse City Print & Copy
700 Boon St (49686-4301)
PHONE 231 946-9942
Anthony Casciani, *President*
Kathleen Casciani, *Vice Pres*
Carmen Casciani, *Treasurer*
EMP: 6
SQ FT: 1,800
SALES (est): 325K **Privately Held**
WEB: www.tcprint-copy.com
SIC: 2752 7334 Commercial printing, offset; photocopying & duplicating services

(G-16020)
LACO INC
1561 Laitner Dr (49696-8878)
PHONE 231 929-3300
▲ **EMP:** 30 **EST:** 1855
SQ FT: 42,000
SALES (est): 2.8MM **Privately Held**
SIC: 3991 Mfg Brooms/Brushes

(G-16021)
LAND SERVICES INCORPORATED
Also Called: L S I
401 W Front St Ste 7 (49684-2259)
PHONE 231 947-9400
Joseph M Holt, *President*
Susan Wiersema, *Admin Asst*
EMP: 3
SQ FT: 1,000
SALES (est): 294.9K **Privately Held**
WEB: www.landservicesinc.com
SIC: 1389 Fishing for tools, oil & gas field

(G-16022)
LEAD SCREWS INTERNATIONAL INC
2101 Precision Dr (49686-9239)
PHONE 262 786-1500
David L Busch, *President*
▼ **EMP:** 35
SQ FT: 45,000
SALES (est): 7.1MM
SALES (corp-wide): 1.6B **Privately Held**
WEB: www.lsitvc.com
SIC: 3545 Precision tools, machinists'
HQ: Dynatect Manufacturing, Inc.
2300 S Calhoun Rd
New Berlin WI 53151
262 786-1500

(G-16023)
LEAR CORPORATION
710 Carver St (49686-3202)
PHONE 231 947-0160
Cathy Griffin, *Manager*
EMP: 150
SALES (corp-wide): 21.1B **Publicly Held**
WEB: www.lear.com
SIC: 3714 Motor vehicle parts & accessories
PA: Lear Corporation
21557 Telegraph Rd
Southfield MI 48033
248 447-1500

(G-16024)
LEELANAU INDUSTRIES INC
6052 E Traverse Hwy (49684-7949)
P.O. Box 4120 (49685-4120)
PHONE 231 947-0372
Tonya Otten, *President*
Dave Derosihia, *General Mgr*
Rob Krinnock, *QC Mgr*
Tom Fraser, *Engineer*
Robert Kausler, *Sales Staff*
EMP: 31 **EST:** 1980
SQ FT: 40,000
SALES (est): 6MM **Privately Held**
WEB: www.leeindinc.com
SIC: 3599 Machine shop, jobbing & repair

(G-16025)
LEFT FOOT CHARLEY
806 Reads Run (49685)
PHONE 231 995-0500
Ryan Olbrick, *Owner*
Meridith Lauzon, *Opers Mgr*
Melissa Fischer, *Manager*
EMP: 15 **EST:** 2007
SALES (est): 1.1MM **Privately Held**
SIC: 2084 Wine cellars, bonded: engaged in blending wines; wines

(G-16026)
LINN ENERGY INC
226 E Sixteenth St Ste A (49684-4117)
PHONE 231 922-7302
Joel Lee, *Manager*
EMP: 50
SALES (corp-wide): 1.9MM **Publicly Held**
SIC: 1311 Natural gas production; crude petroleum production
HQ: Linn Energy, Inc.
600 Travis St
Houston TX 77002
281 840-4000

(G-16027)
LOBO SIGNS INC
Also Called: Nu Art Designs Sign Fabg
322 E Welch Ct (49686-4873)
PHONE 231 941-7739
Carla Chappell, *CEO*
Chad Albaugh, *President*
Michael J Albaugh, *Vice Pres*
EMP: 20
SQ FT: 2,000
SALES (est): 4MM **Privately Held**
WEB: www.nuartsigns.com
SIC: 3993 Signs & advertising specialties

(G-16028)
LOUIES MEATS INC
2040 Cass Rd (49684-8839)
PHONE 231 946-4811

GEOGRAPHIC SECTION

Traverse City - Grand Traverse County (G-16059)

Anthony Alpers, *President*
EMP: 15
SALES (est): 2.2MM **Privately Held**
SIC: **2013** Sausages & related products, from purchased meat

(G-16029)
M-22 CHALLENGE
121 E Front St Ste 104 (49684-2570)
PHONE.................................231 392-2212
Matt Wiesen, *Principal*
EMP: 4
SALES (est): 576.4K **Privately Held**
SIC: **3949** Sporting & athletic goods

(G-16030)
MACK OIL CORPORATION
7721 Outer Dr S (49685-9029)
PHONE.................................231 590-5903
John W Mack, *President*
Michael Mack, *Vice Pres*
Robert Mack, *Admin Sec*
EMP: 5
SQ FT: 1,300
SALES (est): 520K **Privately Held**
SIC: **1311** Crude petroleum production; natural gas production

(G-16031)
MANUFAX INC
1324 Barlow St Ste D (49686-4396)
PHONE.................................231 929-3226
Kurt Hansemann, *President*
Randy L Shaw, *Vice Pres*
Randy Shaw, *Vice Pres*
EMP: 6
SQ FT: 4,000
SALES (est): 490K **Privately Held**
SIC: **3544** Dies, plastics forming

(G-16032)
MARI VILLA VINEYARDS
8175 Center Rd (49686-1669)
PHONE.................................231 935-4513
Alex Lagina, *General Mgr*
EMP: 3 EST: 2011
SALES (est): 103.6K **Privately Held**
SIC: **0172** 2084 Grapes; wines

(G-16033)
MARTEC LAND SERVICES INC
3335 S Arprt Rd W Ste A5 (49684)
PHONE.................................231 929-3971
Randy Marshall, *President*
EMP: 10
SALES (est): 653.9K **Privately Held**
SIC: **1382** Oil & gas exploration services

(G-16034)
MAVERICK EXPLORATION PROD INC
3301 Veterans Dr Ste 107 (49684-4564)
PHONE.................................231 929-3923
Dwight Gookin, *President*
Rita Gookin, *Admin Sec*
EMP: 4
SQ FT: 700
SALES (est): 158K **Privately Held**
SIC: **1382** Oil & gas exploration services

(G-16035)
MIDWEST AIR PRODUCTS CO INC
281 Hughes Dr (49696-8255)
P.O. Box 5319 (49696-5319)
PHONE.................................231 941-5865
Rick Whiteherse, *Owner*
Jamie M Shellenbarger, *Manager*
▼ EMP: 20
SQ FT: 21,100
SALES (est): 4.7MM **Privately Held**
SIC: **3564** Air purification equipment

(G-16036)
MIDWEST DEFENSE CORP
15543 Birch Dr (49686-9730)
PHONE.................................231 590-6857
Patrick Karpowski, *President*
EMP: 3
SALES: 30K **Privately Held**
SIC: **3999** 7389 Manufacturing industries;

(G-16037)
MILLER EXPLORATION COMPANY (PA)
3104 Logan Valley Rd (49684-4772)
P.O. Box 348 (49685-0348)
PHONE.................................231 941-0004
John W Elias, *President*
Kelly E Miller, *President*
Deanna L Cannon, *CFO*
Lew P Murray, *Executive*
EMP: 10
SQ FT: 10,500
SALES (est): 1.4MM **Privately Held**
WEB: www.mexp.com
SIC: **1311** 2911 Crude petroleum & natural gas; crude petroleum production; natural gas production; petroleum refining

(G-16038)
MILLER INVESTMENT COMPANY LLC
10850 E Traverse Hwy # 5595 (49684-1325)
P.O. Box 348 (49685-0348)
PHONE.................................231 933-3233
Kelly E Miller, *CEO*
Curtiss R Yeite, *CFO*
EMP: 6
SALES (est): 450.3K **Privately Held**
SIC: **6531** 1389 Real estate listing services; cementing oil & gas well casings

(G-16039)
MIRACLE PETROLEUM LLC
2780 Garfield Rd N (49686-5004)
P.O. Box 6320 (49696-6320)
PHONE.................................231 946-8090
Sally Somsel, *Manager*
Gene Farber,
Edward Gage,
EMP: 6
SALES: 120K **Privately Held**
SIC: **1382** Oil & gas exploration services

(G-16040)
MODZEL SCREEN PRINTING
1017 Washington St (49686-2734)
PHONE.................................231 941-0911
William Modzel, *Owner*
Sally Modzel, *Co-Owner*
EMP: 3
SQ FT: 2,000
SALES: 150K **Privately Held**
SIC: **2759** 7336 Screen printing; graphic arts & related design

(G-16041)
MOLD MATTER
1650 Barlow St (49686-4721)
PHONE.................................231 933-6653
George Jorkasky, *Principal*
EMP: 5
SALES (est): 616.4K **Privately Held**
SIC: **3544** Industrial molds

(G-16042)
MONITEC SERVICES INCORPORATED
4459 Lakeview Trl (49696-9464)
PHONE.................................231 943-2227
EMP: 3
SALES (est): 29.2K **Privately Held**
SIC: **3669** 7629 Mfg Communications Equipment Electrical Repair

(G-16043)
MOOMERS HOMEMADE ICE CREAM LLC
7263 N Long Lake Rd (49685-7495)
PHONE.................................231 941-4122
Nancy Plummer, *CEO*
John Plummer, *Mng Member*
Becky Plummer,
Robert Plummer,
EMP: 20
SQ FT: 1,700
SALES (est): 2.6MM **Privately Held**
WEB: www.moomers.com
SIC: **2024** 5812 5143 Ice cream & ice milk; ice cream stands or dairy bars; ice cream & ices

(G-16044)
MOPEGA LLC
238 E Front St (49684-2526)
P.O. Box 7047 (49696-7047)
PHONE.................................231 631-2580
Pierre Pujoy, *Mng Member*
EMP: 5
SQ FT: 2,000
SALES (est): 500K **Privately Held**
SIC: **5651** 2389 Unisex clothing stores; disposable garments & accessories

(G-16045)
MP6 LLC
2488 Cass Rd (49684-9148)
PHONE.................................231 409-7530
Vicki Paulus, *Principal*
Rick Flees,
EMP: 6
SALES (est): 1.2MM **Privately Held**
SIC: **3089** Injection molding of plastics

(G-16046)
NATURAL GAS COMPRESS (PA)
2480 Aero Park Dr (49686-9180)
PHONE.................................231 941-0107
A J Yuncker, *President*
Bill Jenkins, *Vice Pres*
Mark Riitola, *VP Opers*
Penni Schratz, *Human Res Dir*
Annette Jacobson, *Sales Staff*
EMP: 25 EST: 2001
SALES (est): 7.5MM **Privately Held**
WEB: www.natgascomp.com
SIC: **3563** Air & gas compressors

(G-16047)
NATURES EDGE STONE PRODU
1776 Southpeak Dr (49685-8719)
PHONE.................................231 943-3440
Ronald Hagelstein, *Owner*
EMP: 5
SALES (est): 591.1K **Privately Held**
SIC: **2541** Counter & sink tops

(G-16048)
NEW MIX 96
856 E Eighth St (49686-2100)
PHONE.................................231 941-0963
EMP: 3
SALES (est): 179.8K **Privately Held**
SIC: **3273** Mfg Ready-Mixed Concrete

(G-16049)
NORMIC INDUSTRIES INC
1733 Park Dr (49686-4788)
PHONE.................................231 947-8860
George Kausler, *President*
Robert Kausler, *Vice Pres*
Jeffry Palisin, *Vice Pres*
Dennis Runwick, *Chief Mktg Ofcr*
Stacey Pezzetti, *Shareholder*
EMP: 24
SQ FT: 14,000
SALES (est): 3.3MM **Privately Held**
WEB: www.normicind.com
SIC: **3479** 3993 Etching & engraving; name plates: engraved, etched, etc.; signs & advertising specialties

(G-16050)
NORTHERN MICH SUPPORTIVE HSING
250 E Front St (49684-3602)
PHONE.................................231 929-1309
EMP: 5
SALES (est): 605.9K **Privately Held**
SIC: **2435** Mfg Hardwood Veneer/Plywood

(G-16051)
NORTHERN MICHIGAN GLASS LLC
1101 Hammond Rd W (49686-9241)
PHONE.................................231 941-0050
Jeff Fogo, *Mng Member*
Linda Mc Daniel, *Manager*
Michael Braden,
EMP: 20
SQ FT: 13,000
SALES (est): 3.4MM **Privately Held**
SIC: **1793** 1761 3449 1542 Glass & glazing work; skylight installation; curtain wall, metal; curtain walls for buildings, steel; store front construction

(G-16052)
NORTHERN MICHIGAN PUBLISHING
2438 Potter Rd E (49696-8599)
PHONE.................................231 946-7878
Joshua Mitchell, *Owner*
James Mitchell, *Principal*
EMP: 4
SALES (est): 154.9K **Privately Held**
SIC: **2741** Miscellaneous publishing

(G-16053)
NPI WIRELESS (PA)
3054 Cass Rd (49684-8800)
P.O. Box 879 (49685-0879)
PHONE.................................231 922-9273
Frank Noverr, *President*
EMP: 44 EST: 1972
SQ FT: 8,000
SALES (est): 4.1MM **Privately Held**
WEB: www.noverr.com
SIC: **2711** 2741 2752 5999 Newspapers, publishing & printing; directories, telephone: publishing & printing; catalogs, lithographed; telephone equipment & systems; radio, television & electronic stores

(G-16054)
OIL ENERGY CORP (PA)
954 Businemi Pk Dr Ste 5 (49686)
PHONE.................................231 933-3600
T D Provins, *CEO*
EMP: 10
SALES (est): 2MM **Privately Held**
SIC: **1382** Oil & gas exploration services

(G-16055)
OILGEAR COMPANY (DH)
1424 International Dr (49686-8751)
PHONE.................................231 929-1660
Craig Lafave, *President*
Chris Howie, *Vice Pres*
Marc Langs, *CFO*
John Dunn, *Manager*
▲ EMP: 70
SALES: 50MM
SALES (corp-wide): 44.1MM **Privately Held**
WEB: www.oilgear.com
SIC: **3594** 3492 Fluid power pumps; motors: hydraulic, fluid power or air; control valves, fluid power: hydraulic & pneumatic
HQ: Texas Hydraulics, Inc.
3410 Range Rd
Temple TX 76504
254 778-4701

(G-16056)
OKEEFE CENTRE LTD (PA)
Also Called: Chateau Grand Traverse
12239 Center Rd (49686-8558)
PHONE.................................231 223-7355
Edward Okeefe, *CEO*
Edward O'Keefe The Third,
▲ EMP: 4
SQ FT: 15,000
SALES (est): 2.1MM **Privately Held**
WEB: www.cgtwines.com
SIC: **2084** Wines

(G-16057)
OLD MISSION GAZETTE
12875 Bluff Rd (49686-8447)
PHONE.................................231 590-4715
Jane Boursaw, *Principal*
EMP: 4
SALES (est): 217.1K **Privately Held**
SIC: **2711** Newspapers

(G-16058)
OLD MISSION MULTIGRAIN LLC
1515 Chimney Ridge Dr (49686-9233)
PHONE.................................231 366-4121
Pearl Brown,
Peter Brown,
EMP: 9
SQ FT: 2,000
SALES (est): 380K **Privately Held**
SIC: **2051** Bakery: wholesale or wholesale/retail combined

(G-16059)
OMEGA RESOURCES INC
415 S Union St Fl 1-2 (49684-2536)
PHONE.................................231 941-4838

Traverse City - Grand Traverse County (G-16060)

Terry L Beia, *President*
Jeff A Coon, *Corp Secy*
EMP: 3
SQ FT: 1,000
SALES (est): 307.6K
SALES (corp-wide): 1.9MM **Privately Held**
SIC: 1311 Crude petroleum production; natural gas production
PA: Management Holdings Co Inc
 415 S Union St
 Traverse City MI 49684
 231 933-0033

(G-16060)
OPTI TEMP INC
1500 International Dr (49686-8752)
P.O. Box 5246 (49696-5246)
PHONE.................................231 946-2931
Dan Dorn, *CEO*
James A Childs, *President*
EMP: 45
SQ FT: 22,500
SALES (est): 7.1MM **Privately Held**
WEB: www.optitemp.com
SIC: 3585 Refrigeration & heating equipment

(G-16061)
OPTION ENERGY LLC
102 E River Rd (49696-8222)
PHONE.................................269 329-4317
Jon Rockwood,
EMP: 15
SQ FT: 15,000
SALES: 275MM **Privately Held**
SIC: 4924 1311 4931 1711 Natural gas distribution; natural gas production; ; solar energy contractor

(G-16062)
PAGE COMPONENTS CORPORATION
15 Whispering Woods Dr (49696-1158)
PHONE.................................231 922-3600
Scott Page, *President*
Edmund Page, *Vice Pres*
Dorlene Page, *Treasurer*
EMP: 15
SQ FT: 11,500
SALES: 3.9MM **Privately Held**
SIC: 3469 3465 Metal stampings; automotive stampings

(G-16063)
PDM INDUSTRIES INC
1124 Stepke Ct (49685-9331)
PHONE.................................231 943-9601
Roger Werly, *President*
Rod Werly, *Vice Pres*
EMP: 23
SALES (est): 3.1MM **Privately Held**
WEB: www.pdmind.com
SIC: 3479 3089 Coating of metals with plastic or resins; coating of metals & formed products; molding primary plastic

(G-16064)
PEPSI-COLA METRO BTLG CO INC
2550 Cass Rd (49684-9149)
PHONE.................................231 946-0452
Magaret Addis, *Manager*
Chris McManus, *Manager*
Jerry Howard, *Executive*
Danielle Bott, *Administration*
EMP: 40
SALES (corp-wide): 64.6B **Publicly Held**
WEB: www.joy-of-cola.com
SIC: 2086 Carbonated soft drinks, bottled & canned
HQ: Pepsi-Cola Metropolitan Bottling Company, Inc.
 1111 Westchester Ave
 White Plains NY 10604
 914 767-6000

(G-16065)
PERFORMANCE TOOL INC
731 Mizar Ct (49685-8764)
PHONE.................................231 943-9338
Kevin Lindsay, *President*
Vicki Lindsay, *Corp Secy*
Brian Popp, *Vice Pres*
EMP: 3
SQ FT: 2,400
SALES (est): 385K **Privately Held**
WEB: www.performancetool.com
SIC: 3599 Custom machinery

(G-16066)
PERSONALIZED EMBROIDERY CO
645 Clyde Lee Dr (49696-8651)
PHONE.................................208 263-1267
Mary Carboneau, *Owner*
EMP: 3
SALES (est): 161.8K **Privately Held**
SIC: 2395 Embroidery products, except schiffli machine

(G-16067)
PHOENIX TECHNOLOGY SVCS USA
Also Called: Nevis Energy
327 E Welch Ct Ste A (49686-5449)
PHONE.................................231 995-0100
EMP: 16
SALES (corp-wide): 67.5MM **Privately Held**
SIC: 1381 Drilling Oil And Gas Wells, Nsk
HQ: Phoenix Technology Services Usa Inc
 12329 Cutten Rd
 Houston TX 77043
 713 337-0600

(G-16068)
PHOTODON LLC
2682 Garfield Rd N (49686-5087)
PHONE.................................847 377-1185
Mandy Peterson, *Principal*
Donald W Basch,
▲ **EMP:** 6
SALES (est): 570K **Privately Held**
WEB: www.photodon.com
SIC: 5734 3575 5999 7389 Computer peripheral equipment; computer terminals, monitors & components; cleaning equipment & supplies;

(G-16069)
PICKLE PRINT & MARKETING LLC
525 W Fourteenth St D (49684-4061)
PHONE.................................231 668-4148
Marcus Christian, *Principal*
EMP: 3
SALES (est): 176.6K **Privately Held**
SIC: 2752 Commercial printing, lithographic

(G-16070)
PLASCON INC
2375 Traversefield Dr (49686-9266)
P.O. Box 6231 (49696-6231)
PHONE.................................231 935-1580
David Peterson, *President*
Brett Milliman, *COO*
Matt Keller, *Vice Pres*
Todd Cote, *QA Dir*
Jeff Klug, *CFO*
▲ **EMP:** 43
SALES (est): 12MM **Privately Held**
WEB: www.plasconinc.com
SIC: 2821 Plastics materials & resins

(G-16071)
PLASCON FILMS INC
2375 Traversefield Dr (49686-9266)
P.O. Box 6231 (49696-6231)
PHONE.................................231 935-1580
David Peterson, *President*
EMP: 13
SALES (est): 950K **Privately Held**
SIC: 2821 Plastics materials & resins

(G-16072)
PLASCON PACKAGING INC
2375 Traversefield Dr (49686-9266)
P.O. Box 6231 (49696-6231)
PHONE.................................231 935-1580
David E Peterson, *President*
EMP: 3
SALES (est): 360.9K **Privately Held**
SIC: 2821 Plastics materials & resins

(G-16073)
PLASPORT INC
2375 Traversefield Dr (49686-9266)
P.O. Box 6231 (49696-6231)
PHONE.................................231 935-1580
David E Peterson, *President*
▲ **EMP:** 7
SALES (est): 1.2MM **Privately Held**
SIC: 2673 Bags: plastic, laminated & coated

(G-16074)
PLASTIC SOLUTIONS LLC
1300 Stepke Ct (49685)
PHONE.................................231 824-7350
Dan C McGrew, *Agent*
Dan McGrew, *Agent*
EMP: 5
SALES (est): 407.8K **Privately Held**
SIC: 3089 Molding primary plastic

(G-16075)
POWERPLUS MOUTHGUARD
10850 E Traverse Hwy (49684-1364)
PHONE.................................231 357-2167
Michael Hutchison, *CEO*
EMP: 3
SALES (est): 174.7K **Privately Held**
SIC: 3949 Protective sporting equipment

(G-16076)
PRESIDIUM ENERGY LLC
3760 N Us Highway 31 S B (49684-4497)
P.O. Box 2128 (49685-2128)
PHONE.................................231 933-6373
John Miller, *Mng Member*
Mark Erickson,
EMP: 3
SALES (est): 330K **Privately Held**
SIC: 1311 Crude petroleum production

(G-16077)
PRESS ON JUICE
305 Knollwood Dr (49686-1858)
PHONE.................................231 409-9971
Kristin Rockwood, *Principal*
EMP: 4
SALES (est): 139.5K **Privately Held**
SIC: 2741 Miscellaneous publishing

(G-16078)
PRISM PUBLICATIONS INC
Also Called: Traverse Nthrn Michigans Mag
125 S Park St Ste 155 (49684-3601)
PHONE.................................231 941-8174
Deborah Wyatt Fellows, *President*
Theresa Baehr, *Prdtn Dir*
Ann Gatrell, *Accounts Exec*
Jill Hayes, *Accounts Exec*
Cyndi Ludka, *Accounts Exec*
EMP: 23
SQ FT: 3,000
SALES (est): 3.1MM **Privately Held**
WEB: www.traversemagazine.com
SIC: 2721 Magazines: publishing only, not printed on site

(G-16079)
PRO IMAGE DESIGN
331 W South Airport Rd (49686-4841)
PHONE.................................231 322-8052
Alan Hubbard, *Owner*
Tara Hubbard, *Co-Owner*
EMP: 4
SALES (est): 507.8K **Privately Held**
WEB: www.proimagedesign.net
SIC: 3993 Electric signs

(G-16080)
PRODUCTION INDUSTRIES II INC
3535 Rennie School Rd (49685-9171)
PHONE.................................231 352-7500
Charles C Frost, *President*
EMP: 11
SALES (est): 2.9MM **Privately Held**
WEB: www.prodind.com
SIC: 3568 Belting, chain
PA: Frost Links
 2900 Northridge Dr Nw
 Grand Rapids MI 49544
 616 785-9030

(G-16081)
PROGRESS PRINTERS INC
1445 Woodmere Ave (49686-4309)
PHONE.................................231 947-5311
James M Novak, *President*
EMP: 25 **EST:** 1949
SQ FT: 7,000
SALES (est): 3.6MM
SALES (corp-wide): 6.4MM **Privately Held**
WEB: www.progress-printers.com
SIC: 2752 Commercial printing, offset
PA: Mitchell Graphics, Inc.
 2363 Mitchell Park Dr
 Petoskey MI 49770
 231 347-4635

(G-16082)
PROMETHIENT INC
2382 Cass Rd (49684-9147)
PHONE.................................231 525-0500
William Myers, *CEO*
EMP: 7
SALES (est): 1MM **Privately Held**
SIC: 3674 Semiconductors & related devices

(G-16083)
PUBSOF CHICAGO LLC
1766 Lake Pointe Dr (49686-4782)
PHONE.................................312 448-8282
Jeffrey Kane,
EMP: 5
SQ FT: 2,700
SALES (est): 506.8K **Privately Held**
SIC: 3229 5023 5399 7389 Art, decorative & novelty glassware; decorative home furnishings & supplies; mirrors & pictures, framed & unframed; catalog showrooms; show card & poster painting

(G-16084)
PYRINAS LLC
10574 Waterford Rd (49684-6235)
PHONE.................................810 422-7535
Nathan Bildeaux,
▲ **EMP:** 4 **EST:** 2016
SQ FT: 1,000
SALES (est): 250K **Privately Held**
SIC: 3433 8711 Solar heaters & collectors; engineering services

(G-16085)
QSDG MANUFACTURING LLC
1576 International Dr (49686-8752)
PHONE.................................231 941-1222
Frederick E Reynolds, *President*
EMP: 17
SALES (est): 1.9MM **Privately Held**
SIC: 3999 Barber & beauty shop equipment

(G-16086)
QUALITY TIME COMPONENTS
343 Hughes Dr (49696-8255)
PHONE.................................231 947-1071
Mike Wallace, *President*
Keith Hart, *General Mgr*
EMP: 13
SQ FT: 15,000
SALES (est): 2MM **Privately Held**
WEB: www.qualitytc.com
SIC: 3873 Watches, clocks, watchcases & parts

(G-16087)
QUANTUM SAILS DESIGN GROUP LLC (PA)
1576 International Dr (49686-8752)
PHONE.................................231 941-1222
Frederick Reynolds, *President*
▼ **EMP:** 11
SALES (est): 6MM **Privately Held**
SIC: 3732 Sailboats, building & repairing

(G-16088)
R M YOUNG COMPANY
2801 Aero Park Dr (49686-9171)
PHONE.................................231 946-3980
Thomas Young, *President*
Robert Young, *Chairman*
Michael Young, *Vice Pres*
EMP: 34
SQ FT: 19,200
SALES (est): 8.4MM **Privately Held**
WEB: www.rmyoung.com
SIC: 3829 Meteorological instruments

GEOGRAPHIC SECTION

Traverse City - Grand Traverse County (G-16117)

(G-16089)
RAINBOW SEAMLESS SYSTEMS INC (PA)
4107 Manor Wood Dr S (49685-8768)
PHONE.....................................231 933-8888
Michael Collins, *President*
Matthew Collins, *Principal*
Patrick Collins, *Principal*
Skye Vedrode, *Office Mgr*
EMP: 10
SQ FT: 1,500
SALES: 700K **Privately Held**
WEB: www.rainbowseamless.com
SIC: 3444 1761 Gutters, sheet metal; gutter & downspout contractor

(G-16090)
RARE EARTH HARDWOODS INC
Also Called: Extreem Laser Dynamics
5800 Denali Dr (49684-8445)
PHONE.....................................231 946-0043
Richard Paid, *President*
Deborah Paid, *Vice Pres*
▲ **EMP:** 14
SALES (est): 2.3MM **Privately Held**
WEB: www.rare-earth-hardwoods.com
SIC: 2426 5031 5211 Flooring, hardwood; lumber: rough, dressed & finished; millwork & lumber

(G-16091)
RAVENWOOD
503 Devonshire Ct (49686-5408)
PHONE.....................................231 421-5682
Lisa Berry, *President*
EMP: 4
SALES: 600K **Privately Held**
SIC: 2844 Toilet preparations

(G-16092)
RAYMOND S ROSS
9740 E Avondale Ln (49684-5201)
PHONE.....................................231 922-0235
Fax: 231 922-0235
EMP: 3
SALES (est): 100K **Privately Held**
SIC: 2741 Misc Publishing

(G-16093)
REILCHZ INC
Also Called: Cheese Lady The
600 W Front St (49684-2210)
PHONE.....................................231 421-9600
Christina Zinn, *President*
EMP: 5
SALES: 390K **Privately Held**
SIC: 5149 5451 7213 3269 Specialty food items; cheese; linen supply; cookware: stoneware, coarse earthenware & pottery

(G-16094)
RIGHT BRAIN BREWERY
1837 Carlisle Rd (49696-9156)
PHONE.....................................231 922-9662
Russ Springsteen, *President*
EMP: 4 **EST:** 2001
SALES (est): 14K **Privately Held**
SIC: 2041 Corn grits & flakes, for brewers' use

(G-16095)
RIVERSIDE ENERGY MICHIGAN LLC
10691 E Carter Rd Ste 201 (49684-5499)
PHONE.....................................231 995-4000
Rob Gerhard, *CEO*
Rob Symons, *CFO*
EMP: 30
SQ FT: 15,000
SALES (est): 775.7K **Privately Held**
SIC: 1389 Gas compressing (natural gas) at the fields

(G-16096)
RJG TECHNOLOGIES INC (PA)
3111 Park Dr (49686-4713)
PHONE.....................................231 947-3111
Matt Groleau, *CEO*
Michael Groleau, *Vice Pres*
Rodney Groleau, *Treasurer*
Judith Groleau, *Admin Sec*
EMP: 101
SQ FT: 21,000
SALES (est): 21.8MM **Privately Held**
WEB: www.rjginc.com
SIC: 3823 3625 Industrial instrmnts msrmnt display/control process variable; relays & industrial controls

(G-16097)
ROWE & ASSOCIATES
13685 S West Bay Shore Dr # 115 (49684-6200)
PHONE.....................................231 932-9716
Karen Irish, *Owner*
EMP: 3
SALES (est): 308.5K **Privately Held**
SIC: 1382 7389 Oil & gas exploration services; brokers' services

(G-16098)
SAVOY EXPLORATION INC
Also Called: Savoy Energy
920 Hastings St Ste A (49686-3443)
P.O. Box 1560 (49685-1560)
PHONE.....................................231 941-9552
Thomas C Pangborn, *CEO*
Cheryl A De Young, *Corp Secy*
EMP: 7
SQ FT: 3,200
SALES (est): 1.3MM **Privately Held**
WEB: www.savoyenergy.com
SIC: 1382 Oil & gas exploration services

(G-16099)
SCHMUDE OIL INC
2150 Ste B S Airport Rd W (49684)
P.O. Box 1008 (49685-1008)
PHONE.....................................231 947-4410
Dennis Schmude, *President*
Mary Jo Schmude, *Admin Sec*
EMP: 4
SQ FT: 1,560
SALES (est): 1.3MM **Privately Held**
SIC: 1382 Oil & gas exploration services

(G-16100)
SENECA ENTERPRISES LLC
Also Called: Rf System Lab
1745 Barlow St Ste A (49686-4745)
PHONE.....................................231 943-1171
Sean Oconnor, *General Mgr*
Joel Riling, *General Mgr*
Evan Miller, *Sales Staff*
Marcie Rau, *Sales Staff*
Sonja Morton, *Office Mgr*
EMP: 9
SALES (est): 1.7MM **Privately Held**
SIC: 3825 3827 Instruments to measure electricity; optical instruments & lenses

(G-16101)
SHEREN PLUMBING & HEATING INC
3801 Rennie School Rd (49685-8245)
PHONE.....................................231 943-7916
Jerry Sheren, *President*
Don Kastenschmidt, *Manager*
EMP: 40
SQ FT: 5,500
SALES (est): 1.9MM
SALES (corp-wide): 2.1B **Publicly Held**
WEB: www.sherenplumbingheating.com
SIC: 1711 3444 Plumbing contractors; warm air heating & air conditioning contractor; ventilation & duct work contractor; sheet metalwork
PA: Comfort Systems Usa, Inc.
675 Bering Dr Ste 400
Houston TX 77057
713 830-9600

(G-16102)
SHORELINE FRUIT LLC (PA)
10850 E Traverse Hwy (49684-1364)
P.O. Box 987 (49685-0987)
PHONE.....................................231 941-4336
John M Sommavilla, *CEO*
Corey Geer, *CFO*
Anne Moeller, *Controller*
Charlene Bowen, *Human Res Dir*
Tom Berg, *Marketing Staff*
◆ **EMP:** 81
SALES (est): 32MM **Privately Held**
SIC: 2034 Fruits, dried or dehydrated, except freeze-dried

(G-16103)
SIGNPLICITY SIGN SYSTEMS INC
1555 S M 37 (49685-8505)
P.O. Box 168 (49685-0168)
PHONE.....................................231 943-3800
Simon Wolf, *President*
Kevin Vann, *Director*
EMP: 5
SALES (est): 631.5K **Privately Held**
SIC: 3993 Signs, not made in custom sign painting shops

(G-16104)
SILIKIDS INC
153 1/2 E Front St Ste B (49684-2508)
P.O. Box 2443 (49685-2443)
PHONE.....................................866 789-7454
Hilary Abbott, *Corp Comm Staff*
▲ **EMP:** 8
SALES (est): 1MM **Privately Held**
SIC: 3089 Plastics products

(G-16105)
SKILLED MANUFACTURING INC (PA)
Also Called: SMI Automotive
3680 Cass Rd (49684-9153)
PHONE.....................................231 941-0290
Dodd Russell, *President*
Jerry A Carlson, *Vice Pres*
Thomas Lawson, *Vice Pres*
W D Russell, *Vice Pres*
Jerry Warren, *Plant Mgr*
▲ **EMP:** 145
SQ FT: 100,000
SALES (est): 39.1MM **Privately Held**
WEB: www.skilledmfg.com
SIC: 3714 Motor vehicle parts & accessories

(G-16106)
SKILLED MANUFACTURING INC
Also Called: SMI- Aerospace
2440 Aero Park Dr (49686-9180)
PHONE.....................................231 941-0032
Dennis Tyler, *Branch Mgr*
EMP: 50
SALES (corp-wide): 39.1MM **Privately Held**
WEB: www.skilledmfg.com
SIC: 3714 Motor vehicle parts & accessories
PA: Skilled Manufacturing, Inc.
3680 Cass Rd
Traverse City MI 49684
231 941-0290

(G-16107)
SLEEP DIAGNOSIS NORTHERN MICH
550 Munson Ave Ste 202 (49686-3580)
PHONE.....................................231 935-9275
David Walker, *Owner*
EMP: 6
SALES (est): 481.7K **Privately Held**
SIC: 3821 Laboratory measuring apparatus

(G-16108)
SOCKS & ASSOCIATES DEVELOPMENT
516 Hidden Ridge Dr (49686-1867)
PHONE.....................................231 421-5150
John R Socks, *Principal*
EMP: 4
SALES (est): 315.4K **Privately Held**
SIC: 2252 Socks

(G-16109)
SOMOCO INC
13685 S West Bay Shore Dr (49684-6200)
PHONE.....................................231 946-0200
Robert E Tucker Jr, *President*
Gary L Gottschalk, *Vice Pres*
David Rataj, *Treasurer*
Cynthia Buit, *Admin Sec*
EMP: 20
SQ FT: 2,700
SALES: 15.1K **Privately Held**
SIC: 1311 Crude petroleum production; natural gas production

(G-16110)
SRW INC
10691 E Carter Rd Ste 201 (49684-5499)
PHONE.....................................989 732-8884
John Stegman, *Manager*
EMP: 5
SALES (corp-wide): 3.2MM **Privately Held**
SIC: 1381 1389 Drilling oil & gas wells; oil field services
PA: Srw, Inc.
175 Thompson Rd Ste A
Bad Axe MI 48413
989 269-8528

(G-16111)
STEXLEY-BRAKE LLC
Also Called: Tape Wrangler
164 Carpenter Hill Rd (49686-6108)
PHONE.....................................231 421-3092
Wendy H Steele, *Mng Member*
Rick Steele,
EMP: 3
SQ FT: 5,000
SALES: 200K **Privately Held**
SIC: 3089 5099 Injection molding of plastics; brass goods

(G-16112)
STONE HOUSE BREAD LLC (PA)
4200 Us Highway 31 S (49685-9301)
PHONE.....................................231 933-8864
Jeffery McMullen,
EMP: 35
SQ FT: 5,000
SALES (est): 5.6MM **Privately Held**
WEB: www.stonehousebread.com
SIC: 2051 5461 Bakery: wholesale or wholesale/retail combined; bread

(G-16113)
STONE HOUSE BREAD INC
4200 Us Highway 31 S (49685-9301)
PHONE.....................................231 933-8864
Robert Pisor, *President*
Ellen Pisor, *Corp Secy*
EMP: 20
SQ FT: 1,700
SALES: 500K **Privately Held**
SIC: 2051 2052 5461 5149 Breads, rolls & buns; cookies & crackers; bakeries; groceries & related products

(G-16114)
STROMBERG-CARLSON PRODUCTS INC
2323 Traversefield Dr (49686-9266)
P.O. Box 266 (49685-0266)
PHONE.....................................231 947-8600
Robert C Brammer Jr, *President*
Charles Brammer, *Vice Pres*
Robert Brammer, *Human Res Dir*
▲ **EMP:** 15 **EST:** 1959
SQ FT: 35,000
SALES (est): 4MM **Privately Held**
WEB: www.strombergcarlson.com
SIC: 3429 5561 3714 Manufactured hardware (general); recreational vehicle dealers; motor vehicle parts & accessories

(G-16115)
SUGAR KISSED CUPCAKES LLC
127 E Front St (49684-2508)
PHONE.....................................231 421-9156
Christina Burke, *Mng Member*
EMP: 7
SALES (est): 392.9K **Privately Held**
SIC: 2024 Non-dairy based frozen desserts

(G-16116)
SUNEK CO
3125 Buttermilk Loop (49686-5443)
PHONE.....................................231 421-5317
Kin Cook, *CEO*
EMP: 14
SALES (est): 716.4K **Privately Held**
SIC: 2431 Door frames, wood

(G-16117)
SUPERIOR COLLISION INC
9419 Westwood Dr (49685-8814)
PHONE.....................................231 946-4983
Mike Coil, *President*

Michael Coyle, *Manager*
EMP: 6
SALES (est): 671.7K **Privately Held**
SIC: 7532 3479 Body shop, automotive; collision shops, automotive; rust proofing (hot dipping) of metals & formed products

(G-16118)
T E TECHNOLOGY INC
1590 Keane Dr (49696-8257)
PHONE..................231 929-3966
Richard J Buist, *President*
Paul G Lau, *Vice Pres*
Michael J Nagy, *Vice Pres*
◆ **EMP:** 29
SQ FT: 11,600
SALES: 7.5MM **Privately Held**
WEB: www.tetech.com
SIC: 3674 3829 3822 8711 Thermoelectric devices, solid state; measuring & controlling devices; auto controls regulating residntl & coml environmt & applncs; consulting engineer

(G-16119)
TCWC LLC (HQ)
Also Called: Traverse City Whiskey Co.
201 E Fourteenth St (49684-3222)
PHONE..................231 922-8292
Christopher Fredrickson, *President*
EMP: 10 **EST:** 2011
SQ FT: 12,500
SALES (est): 723.9K **Privately Held**
SIC: 2085 Bourbon whiskey

(G-16120)
TETRADYN LTD
9833 E Cherry Bend Rd (49684-7607)
PHONE..................202 415-7295
Martin Dudziak, *Principal*
EMP: 8
SALES (est): 543.3K **Privately Held**
SIC: 3674 3812 8731 Radiation sensors; detection apparatus: electronic/magnetic field, light/heat; biotechnical research, commercial

(G-16121)
THERMO FISHER SCIENTIFIC INC
6270 S West Bay Shore Dr (49684-9209)
PHONE..................231 932-0242
Bob Walton, *Branch Mgr*
EMP: 3
SALES (corp-wide): 24.3B **Publicly Held**
WEB: www.thermo.com
SIC: 3826 Analytical instruments
PA: Thermo Fisher Scientific Inc.
168 3rd Ave
Waltham MA 02451
781 622-1000

(G-16122)
THOMPSON SURGICAL INSTRS INC
10170 E Cherry Bend Rd (49684-6843)
PHONE..................231 922-0177
Daniel K Farley, *President*
Chris Martin, *Engineer*
Travis Witulski, *Design Engr*
Peggy Janis, *Accounts Mgr*
EMP: 20 **EST:** 1947
SALES (est): 4.1MM **Privately Held**
SIC: 3841 8011 Surgical & medical instruments; offices & clinics of medical doctors

(G-16123)
THOMPSON SURGICAL INSTRS INC
10341 E Cherry Bend Rd (49684-5241)
PHONE..................231 922-5169
EMP: 4
SALES (est): 474.8K **Privately Held**
SIC: 3841 Surgical & medical instruments

(G-16124)
TILE CRAFT INC (PA)
1430 Trade Center Dr (49696-8917)
P.O. Box 2004 (49685-2004)
PHONE..................231 929-7207
Dale Censer, *President*
Thomas Denton, *Purch Mgr*
▲ **EMP:** 17
SQ FT: 3,500
SALES: 2MM **Privately Held**
SIC: 1743 3281 Tile installation, ceramic; marble, building: cut & shaped

(G-16125)
TOOL NORTH INC
2475 N Aero Park Ct (49686-9262)
PHONE..................231 941-1150
Kenneth G Berg, *President*
Gary H Barg, *Vice Pres*
Gary Barg, *Vice Pres*
Timothy G Berg, *Vice Pres*
Jon Lejeune, *Vice Pres*
EMP: 24
SQ FT: 34,000
SALES (est): 7.9MM **Privately Held**
WEB: www.toolnorth.com
SIC: 3569 3544 Assembly machines, non-metalworking; special dies, tools, jigs & fixtures

(G-16126)
TRAVERSE CITY HELICOPTERS LLC (HQ)
Also Called: Tc Flying Adventures
1190 Airport Access Rd B (49686-3582)
PHONE..................231 668-6000
Paul Chauvette, *Manager*
Josh McCoy, *Manager*
Michael Terfther,
Robert F Barnes,
EMP: 1
SALES (est): 1.1MM
SALES (corp-wide): 1.7MM **Privately Held**
SIC: 3721 Helicopters
PA: Rfb Aviation Enterprises Llc
1190 Airport Access Rd
Traverse City MI 49686
231 668-6000

(G-16127)
TRAVERSE CITY PIE COMPANY LLC
2911 Garfield Rd N (49686-5007)
PHONE..................231 929-7437
Mike Busley,
Tim Rice,
EMP: 10
SQ FT: 4,500
SALES: 750K **Privately Held**
SIC: 2051 Cakes, pies & pastries

(G-16128)
TRAVERSE CITY PRODUCTS INC
501 Hughes Dr (49696-8255)
PHONE..................231 946-4414
Herman J Thomas Jr, *President*
Martin B Cotanche, *Treasurer*
Doug Lucas, *Manager*
Jay Langler, *Supervisor*
Robin Pegouske, *Admin Sec*
EMP: 90
SQ FT: 35,000
SALES (est): 24.2MM **Privately Held**
WEB: www.tcproducts.net
SIC: 3465 3356 Automotive stampings; nonferrous rolling & drawing

(G-16129)
TRAVERSE CY RECORD- EAGLE INC
Also Called: Traverse City Record-Eagle
120 W Front St (49684-2202)
P.O. Box 632 (49685-0632)
PHONE..................231 946-2000
Ann Reed, *President*
EMP: 5
SALES (est): 472.1K **Privately Held**
WEB: www.traversebiz.com
SIC: 2711 2752 Newspapers: publishing only, not printed on site; commercial printing, lithographic
HQ: Community Newspaper Group, Llc
3500 Colonnade Pkwy # 600
Birmingham AL 35243

(G-16130)
TRIMET INDUSTRIES INC
829 Duell Rd (49686-4859)
PHONE..................231 929-9100
Mark Ludwig, *Principal*
Robert Leppo, *Principal*
Kirk Schuch, *Principal*
Doug Austin, *Manager*
EMP: 20
SQ FT: 9,000
SALES (est): 4.7MM **Privately Held**
SIC: 3441 Fabricated structural metal

(G-16131)
TWIN BAY DOCK AND PRODUCTS
982 E Commerce Dr Ste B (49685-6956)
PHONE..................231 943-8420
Robert Serschen, *President*
Walter Drabek, *Vice Pres*
Tom Drabek, *Vice Pres*
Joyce Serschen, *Admin Sec*
EMP: 6
SALES (est): 722.3K **Privately Held**
SIC: 3448 Docks: prefabricated metal

(G-16132)
TYSON
2314 Sybrant Rd (49684-9151)
PHONE..................231 922-3214
EMP: 3
SALES (est): 117.7K **Privately Held**
SIC: 2011 Meat packing plants

(G-16133)
TYSON FOODS INC
845 Bertina Ln (49686-8629)
PHONE..................231 929-2456
EMP: 277
SALES (corp-wide): 42.4B **Publicly Held**
SIC: 2011 Meat packing plants
PA: Tyson Foods, Inc.
2200 W Don Tyson Pkwy
Springdale AR 72762
479 290-4000

(G-16134)
UNITED ENGINEERED TOOLING
Also Called: United Tool
1974 Cass Hartman Ct (49685-9133)
PHONE..................231 947-3650
Dietrich Heyde, *President*
Shawn McClellan, *General Mgr*
EMP: 24 **EST:** 1978
SQ FT: 7,800
SALES (est): 5.2MM **Privately Held**
WEB: www.unitedtool.com
SIC: 3599 Machine shop, jobbing & repair

(G-16135)
UNITED SHIELD INTL LLC
1462 International Dr (49686-8751)
PHONE..................231 933-1179
Paul Banducci, *President*
Terry Hand, *Managing Dir*
▲ **EMP:** 40
SALES (est): 10MM **Privately Held**
WEB: www.unitedshield.net
SIC: 3949 Protective sporting equipment

(G-16136)
VEGA MANUFACTURING LLC
Also Called: Boxer Tactical
526 W Fourteenth St # 150 (49684-4051)
PHONE..................231 668-6365
William Johnson, *President*
EMP: 3
SALES (est): 326.4K **Privately Held**
SIC: 2329 2387 2392 2326 Men's & boys' sportswear & athletic clothing; hunting coats & vests, men's; apparel belts; bags, garment storage: except paper or plastic film; industrial garments, men's & boys'

(G-16137)
VILLAGE PRESS INC
Also Called: Vp Demand Creation Services
2779 Aero Park Dr (49686-9100)
P.O. Box 968 (49685-0968)
PHONE..................231 946-3712
Robert Goff, *Principal*
Neil Knopf, *Editor*
Steve Smith, *Editor*
Judy Sines, *Accounts Mgr*
Debbie Wakefield, *Accounts Mgr*
EMP: 9
SALES (est): 1.4MM **Privately Held**
SIC: 2741 Miscellaneous publishing

(G-16138)
VILLAGE SHOP INC
2779 Aero Park Dr (49686-9101)
P.O. Box 968 (49685-0968)
PHONE..................231 946-3712
Robert Goff, *President*
▲ **EMP:** 65
SQ FT: 35,000
SALES (est): 5.5MM **Privately Held**
WEB: www.villagepress.com
SIC: 2721 2752 2791 2789 Magazines: publishing & printing; commercial printing, offset; typesetting; bookbinding & related work

(G-16139)
VISUAL IDENTIFICATION PRODUCTS
Also Called: Market Novelty Products
1733 Park Dr (49686-4703)
PHONE..................231 941-7272
EMP: 3
SALES (est): 173.9K **Privately Held**
SIC: 3873 5411 Assemble Decorative Wall Clocks

(G-16140)
W BAY CUPCAKES
524 W Thirteenth St (49684-4014)
PHONE..................231 632-2010
Breanna Thomas, *Principal*
EMP: 4
SALES (est): 173.4K **Privately Held**
SIC: 2051 Bread, cake & related products

(G-16141)
W NEWS
300 E Front St (49684-2596)
PHONE..................231 946-4446
EMP: 3
SALES (est): 111.9K **Privately Held**
SIC: 2711 Newspapers-Publishing/Printing

(G-16142)
WEPCO ENERGY LLC (PA)
250 E Front St Ste 402 (49684-3603)
P.O. Box 849 (49685-0849)
PHONE..................231 932-8615
Ed Walker,
Richard Ellis,
EMP: 3
SALES (est): 142.5K **Privately Held**
SIC: 1311 1382 Crude petroleum & natural gas production; oil & gas exploration services

(G-16143)
WEST BAY EXPLORATION COMPANY (PA)
13685 S West Bay Shore Dr (49684-1399)
PHONE..................231 946-3529
Robert E Tucker Jr, *President*
Tim Baker, *Vice Pres*
Gary L Gottschalk, *Vice Pres*
Harry Graham, *Vice Pres*
David Rataj, *Treasurer*
EMP: 15
SALES: 429K **Privately Held**
SIC: 1311 Crude petroleum production; natural gas production

(G-16144)
WEST BAY GEOPHYSICAL INC
13685 W Bay Shr 116 (49684-6200)
PHONE..................231 946-3529
Robert E Tucker Jr, *President*
Gary Gottschalk, *Vice Pres*
David Rataj, *Treasurer*
Cynthia Buit, *Admin Sec*
EMP: 13
SQ FT: 286
SALES: 5.2MM
SALES (corp-wide): 429K **Privately Held**
WEB: www.westbayexploration.com
SIC: 1382 Seismograph surveys
PA: West Bay Exploration Company
13685 S West Bay Shore Dr
Traverse City MI 49684
231 946-3529

GEOGRAPHIC SECTION

Troy - Oakland County (G-16170)

(G-16145)
WHEELOCK & SON WELDING SHOP
Also Called: Wheelock & Sons Welding
9954 N Long Lake Rd (49685-9635)
PHONE..................................231 947-6557
Addison Wheelock Jr, *Owner*
Randolph Wheelock, *Co-Owner*
Bonny Wheelock, *Manager*
Jamie Wheelock, *Manager*
EMP: 8
SQ FT: 6,900
SALES (est): 1.2MM **Privately Held**
SIC: 3448 7692 Docks: prefabricated metal; welding repair

(G-16146)
WILLIAM SHAW INC
Also Called: Sky Electric Northern Michigan
402 Wadsworth St (49684-3116)
PHONE..................................231 536-3569
William Rodney Shaw, *President*
Daniel A Bruce, *Admin Sec*
EMP: 18
SQ FT: 3,000
SALES (est): 3MM **Privately Held**
SIC: 3569 Filters & strainers, pipeline

(G-16147)
WINSTANLEY ASSOCIATES LLC
Also Called: Kiosks By Winstanley
2670 Garfield Rd N Ste 19 (49686-5172)
PHONE..................................231 946-3552
Gordon H Winstanley,
Sally Winstanley,
EMP: 7
SQ FT: 5,000
SALES (est): 664.8K **Privately Held**
WEB: www.kbw.net
SIC: 7373 3577 Computer integrated systems design; computer peripheral equipment

(G-16148)
WMC LIEVENSE COMPANY
Also Called: World Magnetics
810 Hastings St (49686-3441)
PHONE..................................231 946-3800
Jim Lievense, *President*
Lynn Hedeman, *Vice Pres*
Janice Blackburn, *Admin Sec*
▲ **EMP:** 27
SQ FT: 15,100
SALES (est): 7MM **Privately Held**
WEB: www.worldmagnetics.com
SIC: 3829 3679 Pressure & vacuum indicators, aircraft engine; recording & playback heads, magnetic

Trenary
Alger County

(G-16149)
ANYWHERE WELDING
N3550 Et Rd (49891-9572)
PHONE..................................906 250-7217
Kelsey McMaster, *Principal*
EMP: 8
SALES (est): 88.7K **Privately Held**
SIC: 7692 Welding repair

(G-16150)
FM RESEARCH MANAGEMENT LLC
1958 Eben Trenary Rd (49891)
PHONE..................................906 360-5833
Jeffery Millin, *CEO*
EMP: 4
SALES (est): 172.3K **Privately Held**
SIC: 2821 Plastics materials & resins

(G-16151)
HOLMQUIST FEED MILL
Also Called: Trenary Wood Products
232 N Main St (49891)
P.O. Box 208 (49891-0208)
PHONE..................................906 446-3325
Sharon Boyer, *Owner*
EMP: 7
SQ FT: 3,171
SALES (est): 919.1K **Privately Held**
WEB: www.trenarywoodproducts.com
SIC: 2048 5191 2429 Livestock feeds; animal feeds; shingles, wood: sawed or hand split

Trenton
Wayne County

(G-16152)
AUTOSPORT DEVELOPMENT LLC
2331 Toledo St (48183-4715)
PHONE..................................734 675-1620
David Moxlow, *President*
Jim Schiesel,
EMP: 8
SALES (est): 734.1K **Privately Held**
WEB: www.autosportdevelopment.com
SIC: 3599 Amusement park equipment

(G-16153)
EASTMAN CHEMICAL COMPANY
5100 W Jefferson Ave (48183-4729)
PHONE..................................734 672-7823
EMP: 6
SALES (est): 666.3K **Privately Held**
SIC: 2821 Plastics materials & resins

(G-16154)
FRITZ ENTERPRISES (HQ)
Also Called: Fritz Products Inc
1650 W Jefferson Ave (48183-2136)
PHONE..................................734 283-7272
Leonard Fritz, *President*
Eric Fritz, *Admin Sec*
EMP: 4
SALES (est): 2.2MM
SALES (corp-wide): 72MM **Privately Held**
WEB: www.fritzinc.com
SIC: 3312 3295 1442 Hot-rolled iron & steel products; minerals, ground or treated; construction sand & gravel
PA: Fritz Enterprises, Inc.
1650 W Jefferson Ave
Trenton MI 48183
734 692-4231

(G-16155)
HURON VALLEY STEEL CORPORATION (PA)
1650 W Jefferson Ave (48183-2136)
PHONE..................................734 479-3500
Eric R Fritz, *President*
Ronald Dalton, *President*
David Wallace, *Senior VP*
Ron Dalton, *Vice Pres*
Mark Gaffney, *Vice Pres*
◆ **EMP:** 110 **EST:** 1961
SQ FT: 7,000
SALES (est): 135.2MM **Privately Held**
WEB: www.hvsc.net
SIC: 5093 3341 3559 Nonferrous metals scrap; zinc smelting & refining (secondary); aluminum smelting & refining (secondary); recycling machinery

(G-16156)
PFIZER INC
3495 Margarette Dr (48183-2309)
PHONE..................................734 671-9315
Robert Camilleri, *Branch Mgr*
EMP: 5
SALES (corp-wide): 53.6B **Publicly Held**
WEB: www.pfizerinc.com
SIC: 2834 Pharmaceutical preparations
PA: Pfizer Inc.
235 E 42nd St
New York NY 10017
212 733-2323

(G-16157)
SOLUTIA INC
5100 W Jefferson Ave (48183-4729)
PHONE..................................734 676-4400
Gary Williams, *Branch Mgr*
EMP: 500 **Publicly Held**
SIC: 2821 2824 3231 2819 Plastics materials & resins; organic fibers, noncellulosic; products of purchased glass; industrial inorganic chemicals
HQ: Solutia Inc.
575 Maryville Centre Dr
Saint Louis MO 63141
423 229-2000

(G-16158)
STANS AFFORDABLE VIDEOGRAPHY
4290 Ponderosa St (48183-3986)
PHONE..................................734 671-2975
Stanley Keda, *Principal*
EMP: 3
SALES (est): 246K **Privately Held**
SIC: 3695 Video recording tape, blank

(G-16159)
TRENTON FORGING COMPANY
5523 Hoover St (48183-4791)
PHONE..................................734 675-1620
David M Moxlow, *President*
Renee Moxlow, *Treasurer*
Jim Schiesel, *Controller*
Stephanie Cobb, *Human Res Mgr*
David Montiy, *Manager*
EMP: 92
SQ FT: 35,000
SALES (est): 33MM **Privately Held**
WEB: www.trentonforging.com
SIC: 3462 Iron & steel forgings

(G-16160)
TRENTON HEARTHSIDE SHOP INC
Also Called: Hearthside Fireplace & Bbq Sp
2447 3rd St (48183-2719)
PHONE..................................734 558-5860
Dean Barill, *Owner*
EMP: 3
SQ FT: 3,700
SALES (est): 223.5K **Privately Held**
WEB: www.hearthsidefire.com
SIC: 5719 3631 Fireplaces & wood burning stoves; fireplace equipment & accessories; barbecues, grills & braziers (outdoor cooking)

(G-16161)
TRENTON JEWELERS LTD
2355 West Rd (48183-3617)
PHONE..................................734 676-0188
Wayne H McDermitt, *President*
Wayne McDwight, *President*
Jenea McDermitt, *Manager*
EMP: 7
SQ FT: 2,400
SALES (est): 790.5K **Privately Held**
WEB: www.trentonjewelers.com
SIC: 5944 3915 7631 Jewelry, precious stones & precious metals; watches; jewelers' findings & materials; jewelry repair services; watch repair

Trout Creek
Ontonagon County

(G-16162)
CALDERWOOD WD PDTS & SVCS LLC
9968 Calderwood Rd (49967-5106)
P.O. Box 131 (49967-0131)
PHONE..................................906 852-3232
Fred Sliger,
EMP: 5
SALES (est): 100K **Privately Held**
SIC: 2439 Structural wood members

(G-16163)
GUSTAFSON LOGGING
10857 N Agate Rd (49967-9201)
PHONE..................................906 250-2482
Gary Gustafson, *Owner*
EMP: 3
SQ FT: 2,380
SALES: 570K **Privately Held**
SIC: 2411 Logging camps & contractors

Troy
Oakland County

(G-16164)
A ME VERTICAL INCORPORATED
675 E Big Beaver Rd (48083-1418)
PHONE..................................248 720-0245
David Easterbrook, *Principal*
Bryan Talaga, *VP Sales*
EMP: 4
SALES (est): 78.5K **Privately Held**
SIC: 2591 Blinds vertical

(G-16165)
ACCELERATED PRESS INC
1337 Piedmont Dr (48083-1918)
PHONE..................................248 524-1850
Gaylord Vince, *President*
EMP: 7
SQ FT: 3,800
SALES (est): 1.2MM **Privately Held**
WEB: www.acceleratedpress.com
SIC: 2752 7334 Commercial printing, offset; photocopying & duplicating services

(G-16166)
ACE CANVAS & TENT CO
465 Stephenson Hwy (48083-1130)
PHONE..................................313 842-3011
Michael A Caruso, *President*
EMP: 10 **EST:** 1974
SQ FT: 8,000
SALES (est): 786.5K **Privately Held**
SIC: 7359 2394 7699 Tent & tarpaulin rental; tents: made from purchased materials; tent repair shop

(G-16167)
ACE ELECTRONICS LLC MICHIGAN
401 Minnesota Dr (48083-4698)
PHONE..................................443 327-6100
Nish Patel, *Human Res Dir*
EMP: 6
SALES (est): 950K **Privately Held**
SIC: 3679 Electronic components

(G-16168)
ADS LLC
Also Called: A D S Environmental Srvs
1100 Owendale Dr Ste K (48083-1914)
PHONE..................................248 740-9593
Larry Greene, *Manager*
EMP: 6
SALES (corp-wide): 2.4B **Publicly Held**
SIC: 3823 8748 8711 Flow instruments, industrial process type; business consulting; engineering services
HQ: Ads Llc
340 The Bridge St Ste 204
Huntsville AL 35806
256 430-3366

(G-16169)
ADVANCED FEEDLINES LLC
Also Called: Dallas Industries
103 Park Dr (48083-2770)
PHONE..................................248 583-9400
Joseph A Gentilia, *President*
Larry Slater, *Purchasing*
Robert W Klotz, *Treasurer*
Dave Laws, *Sales Mgr*
Warren Gideon, *Regl Sales Mgr*
EMP: 54 **EST:** 1959
SALES (est): 12.5MM **Privately Held**
WEB: www.dallasindustries.com
SIC: 3542 5084 3549 3545 Machine tools, metal forming type; industrial machinery & equipment; metalworking machinery; machine tool accessories

(G-16170)
ADVANCED-CABLE LLC
1179 Chicago Rd (48083-4239)
PHONE..................................586 491-3073
Deanna Zwiesele,
EMP: 10 **EST:** 2012
SALES (est): 1.5MM **Privately Held**
SIC: 5065 3669 Electronic parts; visual communication systems

Troy - Oakland County (G-16171)

(G-16171)
AFFILIATED TROY DERMATOLOGIST
4600 Investment Dr (48098-6365)
PHONE..................248 267-5020
Marcia Cardelli, *Partner*
Louis Sobol, *Otolaryngology*
EMP: 15
SALES (est): 2.8MM **Privately Held**
SIC: 2834 8011 Dermatologicals; offices & clinics of medical doctors

(G-16172)
AFFINITY TOOL WORKS LLC
1161 Rankin Dr (48083-2825)
PHONE..................248 588-0395
Sam Ursell, *President*
Mike Ursell,
▲ **EMP:** 5
SALES (est): 1MM **Privately Held**
SIC: 3423 Hand & edge tools

(G-16173)
AIP GROUP INC
2041 E Square Lake Rd # 100 (48085-3897)
PHONE..................248 828-4400
Meiling Ngai, *Chairman*
Adrian Donev, *VP Opers*
Maggie Flood, *Technology*
Nanci Murphy, *Assistant*
EMP: 6
SALES (est): 493.2K **Privately Held**
WEB: www.aiponline.net
SIC: 2754 Business forms: gravure printing

(G-16174)
AJAX MATERIALS CORPORATION (DH)
Also Called: Detroit Asphalt Paving Company
1957 Crooks Rd A (48084-5504)
P.O. Box 7058 (48084)
PHONE..................248 244-3300
James A Jacob, *President*
Wally Cabral, *Foreman/Supr*
EMP: 4
SQ FT: 10,000
SALES (est): 6.2MM
SALES (corp-wide): 301.7MM **Privately Held**
SIC: 2951 Asphalt & asphaltic paving mixtures (not from refineries)
HQ: Ajax Paving Industries, Inc.
1957 Crooks Rd A
Troy MI 48084
248 244-3300

(G-16175)
AJAX PAVING INDUSTRIES INC (HQ)
1957 Crooks Rd A (48084-5504)
P.O. Box 7058 (48007-7058)
PHONE..................248 244-3300
Herbert H Jacob, *Ch of Bd*
James A Jacob, *President*
Christie Alvaro, *General Mgr*
Brian Pittman, *Superintendent*
Steven E Jacob, *Principal*
EMP: 200
SQ FT: 10,000
SALES (est): 307.5MM
SALES (corp-wide): 301.7MM **Privately Held**
WEB: www.ajaxpaving.com
SIC: 1611 2951 3273 3272 Highway & street paving contractor; concrete construction: roads, highways, sidewalks, etc.; resurfacing contractor; asphalt & asphaltic paving mixtures (not from refineries); ready-mixed concrete; concrete products
PA: Hhj Holdings, Limited
1957 Crooks Rd A
Troy MI 48084
248 652-9716

(G-16176)
AK STEEL CORPORATION
5440 Corporate Dr Ste 125 (48098-2619)
P.O. Box 1699, Dearborn (48121-1699)
PHONE..................513 425-2707
Tom Sullivan, *Purch Agent*
Hasan Emlemdi, *Engineer*
Paul Janavicius, *Engineer*
Stephen Feldmeier, *Project Engr*
Amber Morris, *Sales Staff*
EMP: 30 **Publicly Held**
WEB: www.ketnar.org
SIC: 3312 Blast furnaces & steel mills
HQ: Ak Steel Corporation
9227 Centre Pointe Dr
West Chester OH 45069
513 425-4200

(G-16177)
AKZO NOBEL COATINGS INC
1845 Maxwell Dr Ste 100 (48084-4506)
PHONE..................248 637-0400
EMP: 21
SALES (corp-wide): 11.3B **Privately Held**
SIC: 2851 Paints & allied products
HQ: Akzo Nobel Coatings Inc.
8220 Mohawk Dr
Strongsville OH 44136
440 297-5100

(G-16178)
AKZO NOBEL COATINGS INC
27 Brush St (48084)
PHONE..................248 451-6231
John Lindeman, *Manager*
EMP: 30
SALES (corp-wide): 11.3B **Privately Held**
WEB: www.nam.sikkens.com
SIC: 2851 Paints & allied products
HQ: Akzo Nobel Coatings Inc.
8220 Mohawk Dr
Strongsville OH 44136
440 297-5100

(G-16179)
AKZO NOBEL COATINGS INC
2373 John R Rd Ste A (48083-2567)
PHONE..................248 528-0715
Kevin Hales, *Manager*
EMP: 8
SALES (corp-wide): 11.3B **Privately Held**
WEB: www.nam.sikkens.com
SIC: 2851 Paints & allied products
HQ: Akzo Nobel Coatings Inc.
8220 Mohawk Dr
Strongsville OH 44136
440 297-5100

(G-16180)
AKZO NOBEL COATINGS INC
Sikkens Car Refinishes
1696 Maxwell Dr (48084-4505)
PHONE..................312 544-7000
Tim Loden, *Manager*
EMP: 20
SALES (corp-wide): 11.3B **Privately Held**
SIC: 2851 Paints & allied products
HQ: Akzo Nobel Coatings Inc.
8220 Mohawk Dr
Strongsville OH 44136
440 297-5100

(G-16181)
AL-CRAFT DESIGN & ENGRG INC (PA)
Also Called: Al-Craft Industries
710 Minnesota Dr (48083-6204)
PHONE..................248 589-3827
John Graham, *CEO*
Jane Nido, *President*
Lisa Schroeder, *Accounting Mgr*
EMP: 5
SQ FT: 32,000
SALES (est): 3.9MM **Privately Held**
WEB: www.al-craft.com
SIC: 3544 3543 Special dies, tools, jigs & fixtures; industrial patterns

(G-16182)
ALBAH MANUFACTURING TECH CORP
1985 Ring Dr (48083-4229)
P.O. Box 441637, Detroit (48244-1637)
PHONE..................519 972-7222
Amma C Adomako, *President*
Kofi Adomako, *Vice Pres*
EMP: 25
SQ FT: 12,000
SALES (est): 1.2MM **Privately Held**
WEB: www.albah.com
SIC: 3479 Coating, rust preventive

(G-16183)
ALEX AND ANI LLC
2800 W Big Beaver Rd (48084-3206)
PHONE..................248 649-7348
EMP: 3 **Privately Held**
SIC: 3915 3911 Jewelers' materials & lapidary work; jewelry, precious metal
PA: Alex And Ani, Llc
2000 Chapel View Blvd # 360
Cranston RI 02920

(G-16184)
ALEX DELVECCHIO ENTPS INC
1343 Piedmont Dr (48083-1918)
P.O. Box 1256 (48099-1256)
PHONE..................248 619-9600
Alex J Delvecchio Jr, *President*
EMP: 20 **EST:** 1986
SQ FT: 5,000
SALES: 1.6MM **Privately Held**
WEB: www.theimprintshop.com
SIC: 5199 3993 Advertising specialties; signs, not made in custom sign painting shops; name plates: except engraved, etched, etc.: metal

(G-16185)
ALEXANDER J BONGIORNO INC
101 W Big Beavr Rd # 135 (48084-5353)
PHONE..................248 689-7766
Alexander J Bongiorno, *President*
David Anthony Bongiorno, *Office Mgr*
EMP: 5 **EST:** 1959
SQ FT: 1,565
SALES: 633.2K **Privately Held**
SIC: 3911 5944 Jewelry, precious metal; jewelry stores

(G-16186)
ALFMEIER FRIEDRICHS & RATH LLC
340 E Big Beaver Rd # 135 (48083-1218)
PHONE..................248 526-1650
Derek Loader, *Principal*
EMP: 6
SALES (corp-wide): 22K **Privately Held**
WEB: www.alfmeier.com
SIC: 3714 Fuel systems & parts, motor vehicle
HQ: Alfmeier Friedrichs & Rath Llc
120 Elcon Dr
Greenville SC 29605

(G-16187)
ALHERN-MARTIN INDUS FRNC CO
2155 Austin Dr (48083-2237)
PHONE..................248 689-6363
James J Van Etten, *President*
James Vanetten, *General Mgr*
Scott Jones, *Vice Pres*
EMP: 20
SQ FT: 10,000
SALES (est): 5.2MM **Privately Held**
WEB: www.alhern-martin.com
SIC: 5074 3567 3433 Heating equipment (hydronic); heating units & devices, industrial: electric; heating equipment, except electric

(G-16188)
ALL ACCESS NAME TAGS
1435 Rochester Rd (48083-6016)
PHONE..................866 955-8247
Timothy Hourigan, *Principal*
Erin Dawkins, *Mktg Dir*
EMP: 3
SQ FT: 4,000
SALES (est): 322.7K **Privately Held**
SIC: 2759 Tags: printing

(G-16189)
ALL WELDING AND FABG CO INC
1882 Woodslee Dr (48083-2207)
PHONE..................248 689-0986
Thomas Cameron, *President*
EMP: 18 **EST:** 1981
SQ FT: 18,000
SALES (est): 1.9MM **Privately Held**
SIC: 7692 Welding repair

(G-16190)
ALLAN TOOL & MACHINE CO INC (PA)
1822 E Maple Rd (48083-4240)
PHONE..................248 585-2910
Jeffrey M Scott, *President*
Bob Boyce, *Manager*
Don Prucha, *Info Tech Dir*
Marian Neumann, *Admin Sec*
▲ **EMP:** 85
SQ FT: 45,000
SALES (est): 22.5MM **Privately Held**
WEB: www.allantool.com
SIC: 3451 3471 Screw machine products; anodizing (plating) of metals or formed products

(G-16191)
ALLOYING SURFACES INC
Also Called: Surfalloy
1346 Wheaton Dr (48083-1989)
PHONE..................248 524-9200
William H Bagley, *President*
Janet E Bagley, *Vice Pres*
EMP: 4
SQ FT: 5,000
SALES: 1MM **Privately Held**
WEB: www.surfalloy.com
SIC: 3325 3313 3341 2851 Alloy steel castings, except investment; alloys, additive, except copper: not made in blast furnaces; secondary nonferrous metals; paints & allied products; inorganic pigments

(G-16192)
ALTAIR ENGINEERING INC (PA)
1820 E Big Beaver Rd (48083-2031)
PHONE..................248 614-2400
James R Scapa, *Ch of Bd*
Jorge Alarcon, *Engineer*
Yuvraj Kumar, *Engineer*
Jason Sucharski, *Engineer*
Pritam Deshpande, *Accounts Mgr*
EMP: 200
SQ FT: 132,900
SALES: 396.3MM **Publicly Held**
WEB: www.altair.com
SIC: 7372 8711 Prepackaged software; engineering services

(G-16193)
ALUMALIGHT LLC
1307 E Maple Rd Ste E (48083-6023)
P.O. Box 944, Birmingham (48012-0944)
PHONE..................248 457-9302
Bill Tocco, *General Mgr*
Michael Stenback, *Mng Member*
EMP: 20
SQ FT: 10,000
SALES (est): 4.1MM **Privately Held**
SIC: 3646 Commercial indusl & institutional electric lighting fixtures

(G-16194)
AMALGAMATIONS LTD
6181 Elmoor Dr (48098-1896)
P.O. Box 127 (48099-0127)
PHONE..................248 879-7345
Sharon Meyer, *President*
EMP: 5
SALES (est): 320K **Privately Held**
SIC: 3961 3911 Costume jewelry, ex. precious metal & semiprecious stones; jewelry, precious metal

(G-16195)
AMERI-SERV GROUP
2855 Coolidge Hwy Ste 112 (48084-3215)
PHONE..................734 426-9700
EMP: 13 **EST:** 1999
SALES (est): 1.8MM **Privately Held**
SIC: 3565 7629 Air Vac Machinery Service And Repair

(G-16196)
AMERICAN JOURNAL HLTH PROM INC
55 E Long Lake Rd 466 (48085-4738)
P.O. Box 1254 (48099-1254)
PHONE..................248 682-0707
Michael P O'Donnell, *President*
Leslie M Nye, *Vice Pres*
EMP: 4

GEOGRAPHIC SECTION

SALES (est): 343.2K **Privately Held**
WEB: www.healthpromotionjournal.com
SIC: 2721 8742 Trade journals: publishing only, not printed on site; management consulting services

(G-16197)
AMERICAN MSC INC
2451 Elliott Dr (48083-4503)
PHONE.....................248 589-7770
John Behler, *Manager*
EMP: 60 **Privately Held**
SIC: 3493 Automobile springs
HQ: American Msc Inc.
2401 Elliott Dr
Troy MI 48083
248 589-7770

(G-16198)
AMERICAN MSC INC (HQ)
2401 Elliott Dr (48083-4503)
PHONE.....................248 589-7770
Ichiro Murata, *Ch of Bd*
Norimoto Usui, *Exec VP*
Brian Peters, *Info Tech Mgr*
▲ **EMP:** 50
SQ FT: 50,000
SALES (est): 8.3MM **Privately Held**
SIC: 3493 3999 Automobile springs; atomizers, toiletry

(G-16199)
AMS CO LTD
Also Called: AMS America
3221 W Big Beaver Rd # 117 (48084-2803)
PHONE.....................248 712-4435
Jin Chae Lee, *Office Mgr*
EMP: 4 **Privately Held**
SIC: 8711 3699 Engineering services; automotive driving simulators (training aids), electronic
PA: Ams Co., Ltd.
5/F Dukam Bldg., Garak-Dong
Seoul

(G-16200)
AMTECH ELECTROCIRCUITS INC
Also Called: Amelectro
701 Minnesota Dr (48083-6203)
PHONE.....................248 583-1801
Jay Patel, *President*
Dev Patel, *General Mgr*
Vasu R Patel, *Corp Secy*
EMP: 8
SQ FT: 15,000
SALES (est): 2.5MM **Privately Held**
WEB: www.amelectro.com
SIC: 3672 Printed circuit boards

(G-16201)
ANCOR INFORMATION MGT LLC (PA)
Also Called: Utilitec
1911 Woodslee Dr (48083-2236)
PHONE.....................248 740-8866
Gary Zabislik, *General Mgr*
Lindsay Morgan, *Business Mgr*
Tom Schneider, *Vice Pres*
Heather Regier, *Project Mgr*
Erin Romo, *Project Mgr*
EMP: 100
SALES (est): 31.2MM **Privately Held**
SIC: 7374 7371 7374 7259 7331 Data processing service; custom computer programming services; laser printing; direct mail advertising services

(G-16202)
ANDERTON EQUITY LLC (PA)
3001 W Big Beaver Rd # 310 (48084-3101)
PHONE.....................248 430-6650
EMP: 0
SALES (est): 40.5MM **Privately Held**
SIC: 6719 3465 Investment holding companies, except banks; body parts, automobile: stamped metal

(G-16203)
ANTOLIN INTERIORS USA INC
600 Wilshire Dr (48084-1625)
PHONE.....................248 567-4000
Michelle Bronstein, *Purch Mgr*
Benito Wong, *Accounts Mgr*
Jeff Jermyn, *Branch Mgr*
EMP: 4
SALES (corp-wide): 33.3MM **Privately Held**
SIC: 3714 Motor vehicle parts & accessories
HQ: Antolin Interiors Usa, Inc.
1700 Atlantic Blvd
Auburn Hills MI 48326
248 373-1749

(G-16204)
APB INC
Also Called: Allegra Print & Imaging
3334 Rochester Rd (48083-5426)
PHONE.....................248 528-2990
Stuart Glasier, *President*
Gerald Savalle, *Opers Mgr*
EMP: 7
SQ FT: 1,300
SALES (est): 600K **Privately Held**
WEB: www.apb.com
SIC: 2752 2791 2789 2759 Commercial printing, offset; typesetting; bookbinding & related work; commercial printing

(G-16205)
APOLLO TRICK TITANIUM INC
321 Elmwood Dr (48083-2754)
P.O. Box 428, Holt (48842-0428)
PHONE.....................517 694-7449
Regis A Gully, *President*
EMP: 17
SQ FT: 9,000
SALES (est): 2.5MM **Privately Held**
WEB: www.tricktitanium.com
SIC: 3369 Titanium castings, except die-casting

(G-16206)
APROTECH POWERTRAIN LLC (PA)
2150 Butterfield Dr (48084-3427)
PHONE.....................248 649-9200
Karyl Kyser, *Materials Mgr*
Danny Nichols, *Mng Member*
James Jones, *Exec Dir*
Larry George, *Director*
▼ **EMP:** 24
SALES (est): 8.4MM **Privately Held**
SIC: 3612 Vibrators, interrupter

(G-16207)
APTIV CORPORATION (HQ)
Also Called: Delphi
5820 Innovation Dr (48098-2824)
PHONE.....................248 813-2000
Rodney O'Neal, *President*
Duane Swanson, *Project Mgr*
Kyle Cooper, *Engineer*
Biao Huang, *Engineer*
Rohan Kalurkar, *Engineer*
EMP: 600
SALES (est): 2.7B
SALES (corp-wide): 16.6B **Privately Held**
SIC: 3714 Motor vehicle parts & accessories
PA: Aptiv Plc
Queensway House Hilgrove Street
Jersey JE1 1
163 422-4000

(G-16208)
APTIV HOLDINGS (US) LLC (HQ)
5820 Innovation Dr (48098-2824)
PHONE.....................248 813-2000
Rodney O'Neal, *President*
EMP: 22
SALES (est): 648.9MM
SALES (corp-wide): 16.6B **Privately Held**
SIC: 3714 Motor vehicle parts & accessories
PA: Aptiv Plc
Queensway House Hilgrove Street
Jersey JE1 1
163 422-4000

(G-16209)
APTIV MEXICAN HOLDINGS US LLC (HQ)
5820 Innovation Dr (48098-2824)
PHONE.....................248 813-2000
EMP: 4
SALES (est): 2.1MM
SALES (corp-wide): 16.6B **Privately Held**
SIC: 3714 Motor vehicle parts & accessories

(G-16210)
APTIV PLC
5725 Innovation Dr (48098-2852)
PHONE.....................248 813-2000
EMP: 3
SALES (corp-wide): 16.6B **Privately Held**
SIC: 3714 Motor vehicle parts & accessories
PA: Aptiv Plc
Queensway House Hilgrove Street
Jersey JE1 1
163 422-4000

(G-16211)
APTIV SERVICES 2 US INC (HQ)
5820 Innovation Dr (48098-2824)
PHONE.....................248 813-2000
Thierry Rossigneux, *President*
B Jill Steps, *Vice Pres*
Charlie Gross, *Engineer*
William Tanis, *Engineer*
Donald J Callahan, *Treasurer*
◆ **EMP:** 39 **EST:** 2011
SALES (est): 27.1MM
SALES (corp-wide): 16.6B **Privately Held**
WEB: www.fciconnect.com
SIC: 3694 Automotive electrical equipment
PA: Aptiv Plc
Queensway House Hilgrove Street
Jersey JE1 1
163 422-4000

(G-16212)
APTIV SERVICES 3 (US) LLC
Also Called: Delphi
5725 Innovation Dr (48098-2852)
PHONE.....................248 813-2000
Taylor Isselhard, *Manager*
Virginia Snyder,
◆ **EMP:** 8
SALES (est): 170K **Privately Held**
SIC: 3714 Motor vehicle parts & accessories

(G-16213)
APTIV SERVICES US LLC
Delphi
5725 Innovation Dr (48098-2852)
PHONE.....................248 813-2000
Brian Frost, *Finance*
Julie Carmany, *Manager*
Trisha Zickmund, *Manager*
EMP: 80
SALES (corp-wide): 16.6B **Privately Held**
WEB: www.delphiauto.com
SIC: 3714 Motor vehicle parts & accessories
HQ: Aptiv Services Us, Llc
5725 Innovation Dr
Troy MI 48098

(G-16214)
APTIV SERVICES US LLC (HQ)
Also Called: Delphi Product & Svc Solutions
5725 Innovation Dr (48098-2852)
P.O. Box 5053, Southfield (48086-5053)
PHONE.....................248 813-2000
Kevin P Clark, *President*
Jeffrey J Owens, *President*
Majdi B Abulaban, *Senior VP*
Kevin M Butler, *Senior VP*
Michael Gassen, *Vice Pres*
◆ **EMP:** 277
SALES (est): 3.7B
SALES (corp-wide): 16.6B **Privately Held**
SIC: 3714 Motor vehicle parts & accessories
PA: Aptiv Plc
Queensway House Hilgrove Street
Jersey JE1 1
163 422-4000

(G-16215)
APTIV TRADE MGT SVCS US LLC
5820 Innovation Dr (48098-2824)
PHONE.....................248 813-2000
EMP: 3
SALES (est): 190.7K
SALES (corp-wide): 16.6B **Privately Held**
SIC: 3714 Motor vehicle parts & accessories
PA: Aptiv Plc
Queensway House Hilgrove Street
Jersey JE1 1
163 422-4000

(G-16216)
ARCHITECTURAL BLDG PDTS INC
1441 E Maple Rd Ste 360 (48083-4006)
PHONE.....................248 680-1563
Steve Dickerson, *Manager*
EMP: 5
SALES (est): 350.5K **Privately Held**
SIC: 3259 Architectural clay products

(G-16217)
ART IN TRANSIT INC
1260 Rankin Dr Ste F (48083-2845)
PHONE.....................248 585-5566
Gregory Love, *President*
Maureen Love, *Vice Pres*
EMP: 3
SQ FT: 3,100
SALES (est): 379.2K **Privately Held**
WEB: www.artintransit.com
SIC: 2796 7336 Embossing plates for printing; commercial art & graphic design

(G-16218)
ART OF CUSTOM FRAMING INC
3863 Rochester Rd (48083-5245)
PHONE.....................248 435-3726
Denise Bashi, *President*
Art Bashi, *Vice Pres*
EMP: 8
SALES (est): 530K **Privately Held**
SIC: 2499 8412 Picture & mirror frames, wood; art gallery

(G-16219)
ART OF SHAVING - FL LLC
2800 W Big Beavr Rd Fl 2 (48084-3206)
PHONE.....................248 649-5872
Moira Gallo, *Branch Mgr*
EMP: 4
SALES (corp-wide): 67.6B **Publicly Held**
SIC: 5999 2844 3421 5122 Hair care products; toilet preparations; razor blades & razors; razor blades
HQ: The Art Of Shaving - Fl Llc
6100 Blue Lagoon Dr # 150
Miami FL 33126

(G-16220)
ARTIC TECHNOLOGIES INTL
3456 Rochester Rd (48083-5210)
PHONE.....................248 689-9884
Tim A Gargagliano, *President*
Kathryn L Gargagliano, *VP Opers*
EMP: 6
SQ FT: 6,000
SALES (est): 454.4K **Privately Held**
WEB: www.artictech.com
SIC: 7373 3577 Systems software development services; computer peripheral equipment

(G-16221)
ARVIN INTL HOLDINGS LLC (HQ)
2135 W Maple Rd (48084-7121)
PHONE.....................248 435-1000
John A Crable, *President*
▲ **EMP:** 6
SALES (est): 2MM **Publicly Held**
SIC: 3714 Motor vehicle parts & accessories

(G-16222)
ARVINMERITOR INC
2135 W Maple Rd (48084-7121)
PHONE.....................248 435-1000
Larry Dowers, *General Mgr*
Danny Comer, *District Mgr*
Bart Hakenewert, *District Mgr*
Jose Ramos, *Counsel*
Perry Lipe, *Vice Pres*
EMP: 27
SALES (est): 4.2MM **Publicly Held**
SIC: 3493 3625 3465 3714 Automobile springs; actuators, industrial; automotive stampings; drive shafts, motor vehicle

Troy - Oakland County (G-16223) — GEOGRAPHIC SECTION

PA: Meritor, Inc.
2135 W Maple Rd
Troy MI 48084

(G-16223)
ARVINMERITOR OE LLC (HQ)
2135 W Maple Rd (48084-7121)
PHONE.....................................248 435-1000
Carmen De Stefano, *Business Mgr*
Charles G McClure Jr, *Mng Member*
▲ EMP: 1
SALES (est): 79.6MM **Publicly Held**
SIC: 3714 Motor vehicle parts & accessories

(G-16224)
ASSEMBLY TECHNOLOGIES INTL
Also Called: American Beauty Tools
1937 Barrett Dr (48084-5372)
PHONE.....................................248 280-2810
Eric Soderlund, *President*
Diane Zielke, *Purchasing*
◆ EMP: 15
SQ FT: 13,000
SALES (est): 3.3MM **Privately Held**
WEB: www.americanbeautytools.com
SIC: 5084 3423 7699 Welding machinery & equipment; soldering irons or coppers; welding equipment repair

(G-16225)
ASSET HEALTH INC
2250 Butterfield Dr # 100 (48084-3404)
PHONE.....................................248 822-2870
David Wilson, *CEO*
Mihaela Mazzenga, *District Mgr*
Mike Creal, *Vice Pres*
Charlie Estey, *Vice Pres*
Matthew Duggan, *Human Res Mgr*
EMP: 26
SALES (est): 4MM **Privately Held**
WEB: www.assethealth.com
SIC: 7372 Application computer software

(G-16226)
ATLAS WELDING ACCESSORIES INC
501 Stephenson Hwy (48083-1166)
P.O. Box 969 (48099-0969)
PHONE.....................................248 588-4666
Betty Honhart, *President*
Keith Honhart, *Vice Pres*
John Honhart, *Treasurer*
Anne Honhart, *CIO*
EMP: 52 EST: 1939
SQ FT: 44,000
SALES (est): 9.1MM **Privately Held**
WEB: www.atlasweld.com
SIC: 3423 3548 5084 Hand & edge tools; welding & cutting apparatus & accessories; welding machinery & equipment; safety equipment

(G-16227)
ATMO-SEAL INC
Also Called: Atmo-Seal Enginering
1091 Wheaton Dr (48083-1928)
PHONE.....................................248 528-9640
Everett O Carter, *President*
Tammy Jenkins, *Production*
Loran Sherwood, *Engineer*
EMP: 8
SALES (est): 2.2MM **Privately Held**
WEB: www.atmoseal-eng.com
SIC: 3823 8711 Industrial process measurement equipment; analyzers, industrial process type; annunciators, relay & solid state types; infrared instruments, industrial process type; engineering services

(G-16228)
ATOS SYNTEL INC (HQ)
525 E Big Beaver Rd # 300 (48083-1364)
PHONE.....................................248 619-2800
Rakesh Khanna, *President*
Ramakumar Singampalli, *Senior VP*
Ram Singampalli, *Vice Pres*
Dhiraj Achwale, *Project Mgr*
Harish Gangadharan, *Project Mgr*
EMP: 143
SQ FT: 6,430
SALES: 923.8MM
SALES (corp-wide): 166.6MM **Privately Held**
WEB: www.syntelinc.com
SIC: 7372 8748 7371 Prepackaged software; systems analysis & engineering consulting services; computer software development
PA: Atos Se
River Ouest
Bezons 95870
964 450-614

(G-16229)
AUDIO TECHNOLOGIES INC
Also Called: Premier Sound
1713 Larchwood Dr Ste B (48083-2233)
PHONE.....................................586 323-3890
David Cenkner, *President*
Sandra Cenkner, *Vice Pres*
EMP: 4
SQ FT: 900
SALES: 350K **Privately Held**
SIC: 3651 1731 Household audio & video equipment; sound equipment specialization

(G-16230)
AVALON TOOLS INC
1910 Barrett Dr (48084-5371)
PHONE.....................................248 269-0001
Robert Beatty, *President*
Sheryl Beatty, *Vice Pres*
EMP: 5
SQ FT: 2,000
SALES (est): 33.9K **Privately Held**
SIC: 3546 Power-driven handtools

(G-16231)
AXIS TMS CORP
Also Called: Blusys
780 W Maple Rd Ste A (48084-5374)
P.O. Box 328, Royal Oak (48068-0328)
PHONE.....................................248 509-2440
Anel Ceric, *President*
Nick Nader Sr, *CFO*
EMP: 21
SALES (est): 80K **Privately Held**
SIC: 7371 3669 Computer software development; intercommunication systems, electric

(G-16232)
AXLETECH INTL HOLDINGS LLC
1400 Rochester Rd (48083-6014)
PHONE.....................................248 658-7200
Bill Gryzenia, *CEO*
Brandon Meek, *Buyer*
Joe La Cola, *Engineer*
Bakhus Isaac, *CFO*
David Exelby, *Administration*
EMP: 99
SQ FT: 200,000
SALES (est): 3.2MM **Privately Held**
SIC: 3714 Rear axle housings, motor vehicle

(G-16233)
BARRETT PAVING MATERIALS INC
Also Called: Troy Mixing Plant
2040 Barrett Dr (48084-5373)
PHONE.....................................248 362-0850
Charlie Sweet, *Manager*
EMP: 225
SALES (corp-wide): 83.5MM **Privately Held**
WEB: www.barrettpaving.com
SIC: 2951 5032 Concrete, bituminous; asphalt mixture
HQ: Barrett Paving Materials Inc.
3 Becker Farm Rd Ste 307
Roseland NJ 07068
973 533-1001

(G-16234)
BCI GROUP INC
Also Called: Print Max
1717 Stutz Dr (48084-4509)
P.O. Box 130 (48099-0130)
PHONE.....................................248 925-2000
Nick Caaracci, *President*
EMP: 30
SQ FT: 4,000
SALES (est): 4.6MM **Privately Held**
WEB: www.ccdresellers.com
SIC: 2752 2761 Commercial printing, offset; manifold business forms

(G-16235)
BECKER OREGON INC
635 Executive Dr (48083-4576)
PHONE.....................................248 588-7480
Kyle Scott, *CEO*
EMP: 20
SQ FT: 16,000
SALES: 1.3MM **Privately Held**
SIC: 3842 Braces, orthopedic

(G-16236)
BECKER ORTHOPEDIC APPLIANCE CO (PA)
635 Executive Dr (48083-4576)
PHONE.....................................248 588-7480
Rudolf Becker, *Ch of Bd*
Ingrid Becker, *Corp Secy*
John Lesner, *Plant Mgr*
Beatrice Janka, *Engineer*
Francis Duignan, *CFO*
▲ EMP: 65 EST: 1934
SQ FT: 36,000
SALES (est): 24.4MM **Privately Held**
WEB: www.beckerortho.com
SIC: 3842 5999 Limbs, artificial; orthopedic & prosthesis applications

(G-16237)
BERGHOF GROUP NORTH AMER INC
1500 W Big Beavr Rd 2nd (48084-3522)
PHONE.....................................313 720-6884
William Doell, *Director*
EMP: 10
SALES (est): 531.8K
SALES (corp-wide): 2.6MM **Privately Held**
SIC: 3559 Automotive maintenance equipment
PA: Berghof Gmbh
Harretstr. 1
Eningen Unter Achalm 72800
712 189-40

(G-16238)
BERMAR ASSOCIATES INC
433 Minnesota Dr (48083-4698)
P.O. Box 99430 (48099-9430)
PHONE.....................................248 589-2460
Janet Roncelli, *President*
Dan Gorney, *Vice Pres*
EMP: 10 EST: 1969
SQ FT: 10,900
SALES (est): 1.5MM **Privately Held**
WEB: www.bermarassociates.com
SIC: 3089 Injection molded finished plastic products; injection molding of plastics

(G-16239)
BESWICK CORPORATION
2591 Elliott Dr (48083-4605)
PHONE.....................................248 589-0562
Keith Banish, *President*
Arlene Beswick, *Vice Pres*
▲ EMP: 10
SQ FT: 10,000
SALES (est): 1.8MM **Privately Held**
SIC: 3444 3569 Sheet metalwork; filters & strainers, pipeline

(G-16240)
BILLIE TIMES LTD
1008 Alameda Blvd (48085-6733)
PHONE.....................................248 813-9114
Kenneth Cheatham, *Principal*
EMP: 3 EST: 2015
SALES (est): 77.7K **Privately Held**
SIC: 2711 Newspapers

(G-16241)
BLACK BOX CORPORATION
1287 Rankin Dr (48083-6007)
PHONE.....................................248 743-1320
Rick Gannon, *President*
Dan Costanzo, *Opers Mgr*
Matt Mogge, *Accounts Mgr*
EMP: 7 **Privately Held**
SIC: 3577 4899 Computer peripheral equipment; data communication services
HQ: Black Box Corporation
1000 Park Dr
Lawrence PA 15055
724 746-5500

(G-16242)
BNP MEDIA INC (PA)
2401 W Big Beaver Rd # 700 (48084-3333)
P.O. Box 2600 (48007-2600)
PHONE.....................................248 362-3700
Harper Henderson, *President*
Pamela Hugill, *Publisher*
Amy Vodraska, *Publisher*
Eric Fish, *Editor*
Dave Johnson, *Editor*
EMP: 202
SQ FT: 45,000
SALES (est): 156.9MM **Privately Held**
WEB: www.bnpmedia.com
SIC: 2721 Trade journals: publishing only, not printed on site

(G-16243)
BOLLHOFF RIVNUT
800 Kirts Blvd Ste 500 (48084-4879)
PHONE.....................................248 269-0475
Cindy Husk, *Manager*
EMP: 6
SALES (est): 492.9K **Privately Held**
SIC: 3452 Bolts, nuts, rivets & washers

(G-16244)
BONTAZ CENTRE USA INC
1099 Chicago Rd (48083-4204)
PHONE.....................................248 588-8113
Yves Bontaz, *CEO*
Christopher Bontaz, *Treasurer*
Donna Swagert, *Human Res Dir*
▲ EMP: 15
SQ FT: 40,000
SALES (est): 1.7MM
SALES (corp-wide): 3MM **Privately Held**
SIC: 3694 Engine electrical equipment
HQ: Bontaz Centre
Zone Industrielle Des Valignons
Marnaz 74460
450 960-025

(G-16245)
BORGWARNER PDS ANDERSON LLC
5455 Corporate Dr Ste 116 (48098-2620)
PHONE.....................................248 641-3045
EMP: 4
SALES (corp-wide): 9.8B **Publicly Held**
SIC: 3714 Mfg Motor Vehicle Parts/Accessories
HQ: Borgwarner Pds (Anderson), L.L.C.
13975 Borgwarner Dr
Noblesville IN 46060

(G-16246)
BRINSTON ACQUISITION LLC
Also Called: New World Systems
840 W Long Lake Rd (48098-6356)
PHONE.....................................248 269-1000
Angie Ostrom, *Business Mgr*
Christopher Vargo, *Business Mgr*
John Derby, *Project Mgr*
Steve Doinidis, *Project Mgr*
Doraine Fitzgerald, *Project Mgr*
EMP: 45
SALES (est): 61.8K
SALES (corp-wide): 935.2MM **Publicly Held**
SIC: 7372 Prepackaged software
PA: Tyler Technologies, Inc.
5101 Tennyson Pkwy
Plano TX 75024
972 713-3700

(G-16247)
BRISTOL-MYERS SQUIBB COMPANY
2460 Waltham Dr (48085-3550)
PHONE.....................................248 528-2476
Michael Dibartolomeo, *Branch Mgr*
EMP: 89
SALES (corp-wide): 22.5B **Publicly Held**
WEB: www.bms.com
SIC: 2834 Pharmaceutical preparations
PA: Bristol-Myers Squibb Company
430 E 29th St Fl 14
New York NY 10016
212 546-4000

GEOGRAPHIC SECTION

Troy - Oakland County (G-16273)

(G-16248)
BUSINESS NEWS PUBLISHING
2401 W Big Beaver Rd # 700
(48084-3306)
PHONE.....................248 362-3700
Taggart Henderson, *CEO*
Sean Bogle, *Natl Sales Mgr*
EMP: 300
SALES (est): 11.4MM **Privately Held**
SIC: 2711 Newspapers: publishing only, not printed on site

(G-16249)
C & C GRINDING CORP
1685 Austin Dr (48083-2208)
PHONE.....................248 689-1979
Carl Lee Mancier, *President*
Cheryl Mancier, *Admin Sec*
EMP: 4
SQ FT: 3,200
SALES (est): 459.6K **Privately Held**
SIC: 3599 Grinding castings for the trade

(G-16250)
C I I LTD
354 Indusco Ct (48083-4643)
PHONE.....................248 585-9905
Shrikant Mehta, *President*
Neena Metha, *Vice Pres*
EMP: 6
SALES (est): 630K **Privately Held**
SIC: 3911 Jewelry, precious metal

(G-16251)
C2 IMAGING LLC
Also Called: Tepel Brothers
1725 John R Rd (48083-2512)
PHONE.....................248 743-2903
Jim Tepel, *President*
EMP: 105
SALES (corp-wide): 128.5MM **Privately Held**
SIC: 2759 Commercial printing
HQ: C2 Imaging, Llc
201 Plaza Two
Jersey City NJ 07311

(G-16252)
CADILLAC COFFEE COMPANY
194 E Maple Rd (48083-2714)
PHONE.....................800 438-6900
Guy Gehlert, *Branch Mgr*
EMP: 8
SALES (corp-wide): 98.8MM **Privately Held**
SIC: 2095 Coffee roasting (except by wholesale grocers)
PA: Cadillac Coffee Company
7221 Innovation Blvd
Fort Wayne IN 46818
248 545-2266

(G-16253)
CADILLAC PRODUCTS INC (PA)
5800 Crooks Rd Ste 100 (48098-2830)
P.O. Box 5004 (48007-5004)
PHONE.....................248 813-8200
Robert J Williams Sr, *Ch of Bd*
Michael P Williams II, *President*
Robert J Williams Jr, *President*
Eric Ebenhoeh, *Plant Mgr*
Mike Terrill, *Plant Mgr*
▲ **EMP:** 450 **EST:** 1942
SQ FT: 25,000
SALES (est): 168.4MM **Privately Held**
SIC: 3714 3081 2673 3089 Motor vehicle parts & accessories; polyethylene film; plastic bags: made from purchased materials; thermoformed finished plastic products

(G-16254)
CADILLAC PRODUCTS PACKAGING CO (PA)
5800 Crooks Rd (48098-2830)
PHONE.....................248 879-5000
Robert J Williams Jr, *CEO*
Jamie Kreger, *Purchasing*
Tim Rosso, *Controller*
EMP: 250
SALES (est): 95.9MM **Privately Held**
SIC: 3081 Packing materials, plastic sheet

(G-16255)
CADILLAC PRSENTATION SOLUTIONS
1195 Equity Dr (48084-7108)
PHONE.....................248 288-9777
Kurt Streng, *President*
Kristen Streng, *Treasurer*
Tom Krebaum, *Sales Staff*
Kerry Streng, *Shareholder*
William Streng, *Shareholder*
▲ **EMP:** 43 **EST:** 1951
SQ FT: 45,000
SALES (est): 6.5MM **Privately Held**
WEB: www.cadlp.com
SIC: 2782 2759 2675 2396 Looseleaf binders & devices; commercial printing; die-cut paper & board; automotive & apparel trimmings

(G-16256)
CAMDEX INC
2330 Alger Dr (48083-2001)
PHONE.....................248 528-2300
Robert A Leich, *President*
Eugene Leich, *Vice Pres*
EMP: 5
SQ FT: 5,000
SALES (est): 610K **Privately Held**
WEB: www.camdexloader.com
SIC: 3489 Ordnance & accessories

(G-16257)
CAPCO AUTOMOVITE
82 Park Dr (48083-2723)
PHONE.....................248 616-8888
Anthony Candella, *Principal*
EMP: 3
SALES (est): 188.8K **Privately Held**
SIC: 3465 Hub caps, automobile: stamped metal

(G-16258)
CARLEX GLASS AMERICA LLC
1209 E Big Beaver Rd (48083-1905)
PHONE.....................248 824-8800
Yosuke Yamao, *Manager*
EMP: 600 **Privately Held**
SIC: 3211 Flat glass
HQ: Carlex Glass America, Llc
7200 Centennial Blvd
Nashville TN 37209

(G-16259)
CARLSON METAL PRODUCTS INC
2335 Alger Dr (48083-2052)
PHONE.....................248 528-1931
John Martin, *President*
Julie Martin, *Treasurer*
Dean McKean, *Manager*
Paul Stoll, *Manager*
EMP: 30 **EST:** 1971
SQ FT: 17,000
SALES (est): 5.3MM **Privately Held**
WEB: www.carlsonmetal.com
SIC: 3444 Sheet metal specialties, not stamped

(G-16260)
CARO CARBIDE CORPORATION
553 Robbins Dr (48083-4559)
PHONE.....................248 588-4252
Richard Cieszkowski, *President*
EMP: 21
SQ FT: 10,000
SALES (est): 3.9MM **Privately Held**
WEB: www.carocarbide.com
SIC: 3545 Cutting tools for machine tools

(G-16261)
CARTEX CORPORATION (DH)
1515 Equity Dr 100 (48084-7129)
PHONE.....................610 759-1650
Hugh W Sloan Jr, *President*
Robert Magee, *Exec VP*
Carol Dickson, *Vice Pres*
Richard Jocsak, *Treasurer*
Marie Claude Manseau, *Admin Sec*
EMP: 7
SQ FT: 108,000
SALES (est): 19.3MM
SALES (corp-wide): 1.9B **Privately Held**
WEB: www.woodbridgegroup.com
SIC: 3069 Foam rubber

HQ: Woodbridge Holdings Inc.
1515 Equity Dr Ste 100
Troy MI 48084
248 288-0100

(G-16262)
CENTRAL SCREW PRODUCTS COMPANY
Also Called: CSP Truck
1070 Maplelawn Dr (48084-5332)
PHONE.....................313 893-9100
Arnot B Heller II, *President*
Elizabeth Feldt, *Info Tech Mgr*
▲ **EMP:** 15 **EST:** 1924
SQ FT: 12,000
SALES (est): 3.8MM **Privately Held**
WEB: www.centralscrewproducts.com
SIC: 3451 Screw machine products

(G-16263)
CHAMPION HOME BUILDERS INC (HQ)
755 W Big Beaver Rd # 1000 (48084-4908)
PHONE.....................248 614-8200
John N Lawless, *CEO*
John Copeletti, *General Mgr*
Lj Lewis, *General Mgr*
Chris Miller, *General Mgr*
Dave Busche, *Business Mgr*
EMP: 75 **EST:** 1953
SQ FT: 16,000
SALES (est): 2.6B
SALES (corp-wide): 1.3B **Publicly Held**
WEB: www.championaz.com
SIC: 1521 2451 New construction, single-family houses; mobile homes, except recreational
PA: Skyline Champion Corporation
2520 Bypass Rd
Elkhart IN 46514
574 294-6521

(G-16264)
CHECK TECHNOLOGY SOLUTIONS LLC
1800 Stephenson Hwy (48083-2148)
PHONE.....................248 680-2323
Robert Check, *CEO*
▲ **EMP:** 50
SQ FT: 40,000
SALES (est): 13.2MM **Privately Held**
WEB: www.seatheater.com
SIC: 3585 3714 Heating equipment, complete; motor vehicle parts & accessories

(G-16265)
CHELSEA-MEGAN HOLDING INC
Also Called: Compound Technology
1121 Rochester Rd (48083-6012)
PHONE.....................248 307-9160
Willis Engle, *President*
EMP: 15
SQ FT: 38,000
SALES (est): 4MM **Privately Held**
SIC: 2821 Plastics materials & resins

(G-16266)
CHICL LLC
Also Called: Chicago Miniature Optoelectron
1708 Northwood Dr (48084-5521)
PHONE.....................859 294-5590
Steve Imgham, *CEO*
William Drexles, *CFO*
▲ **EMP:** 1399
SQ FT: 15,000
SALES (est): 182.9MM **Privately Held**
WEB: www.cml-it.com
SIC: 3641 Electric lamps
PA: Revstone Industries, Llc
2008 Cypress St Ste 100
Paris KY 40361

(G-16267)
CHOR INDUSTRIES INC
500 Robbins Dr (48083-4514)
PHONE.....................248 585-3323
David M Chor, *President*
Ellen Chor, *Vice Pres*
EMP: 20
SQ FT: 19,000

SALES (est): 2.1MM **Privately Held**
WEB: www.chorindustries.com
SIC: 3471 Finishing, metals or formed products; electroplating of metals or formed products

(G-16268)
CITY ANIMATION CO (PA)
Also Called: Neway Manufacturing
57 Park Dr (48083-2753)
PHONE.....................248 589-0600
Eric Schultz, *CEO*
Brian Cybul, *CFO*
Mary Eickholt, *Admin Sec*
EMP: 50 **EST:** 1960
SQ FT: 22,000
SALES (est): 11.2MM **Privately Held**
WEB: www.cityanimation.com
SIC: 5099 3993 7359 7812 Video & audio equipment; signs & advertising specialties; audio-visual equipment & supply rental; video tape production; machine tools, metal cutting type

(G-16269)
CLASSIC STONE MBL & GRAN INC
2340 Alger Dr (48083-2001)
PHONE.....................248 588-1599
Adrian Bejan, *Administration*
EMP: 6
SALES (est): 421.7K **Privately Held**
SIC: 1799 3281 5032 Counter top installation; granite, cut & shaped; marble building stone

(G-16270)
CLASSIC SYSTEMS LLC
Also Called: Classic Design
1100 Piedmont Dr (48083-1944)
PHONE.....................248 588-2738
Abe Kandel, *President*
William Herd, *Vice Pres*
James Kaczmarek, *Vice Pres*
Jim Kaczmarek, *Vice Pres*
Greg Fullmer, *Engineer*
EMP: 110
SALES (est): 25.3MM **Privately Held**
SIC: 8711 3569 Engineering services; robots, assembly line: industrial & commercial
PA: Mba Tech, Inc.
1100 Piedmont Dr
Troy MI 48083

(G-16271)
COBRA MAUFACTURING
1147 Rankin Dr (48083-6006)
PHONE.....................248 585-1606
Wayne Pabisz, *President*
EMP: 10
SQ FT: 3,760
SALES (est): 1.4MM **Privately Held**
SIC: 3423 Hand & edge tools

(G-16272)
COLOR SOURCE GRAPHICS INC
Also Called: Woodward Printing Co
1925 W Maple Rd Ste A (48084-7116)
PHONE.....................248 458-2040
Craig Sobolewski, *President*
EMP: 4 **EST:** 1975
SQ FT: 5,000
SALES (est): 380K **Privately Held**
WEB: www.colorsourcegraphics.com
SIC: 2752 Commercial printing, offset

(G-16273)
COMBINE INTERNATIONAL INC (PA)
Also Called: Artistic
354 Indusco Ct (48083-4643)
PHONE.....................248 585-9900
Shrikant C Mehta, *President*
Bharat Dave, *Purch Agent*
Roger D Parsons, *CFO*
Cyril Valimattom, *CFO*
Eva Shaya, *Sales Staff*
▲ **EMP:** 225
SQ FT: 35,000
SALES (est): 30.8MM **Privately Held**
WEB: www.combine.com
SIC: 3911 5094 Jewelry, precious metal; pearls

Troy - Oakland County (G-16274)

(G-16274)
COMMANDO LOCK COMPANY LLC
395 Elmwood Dr (48083-2754)
PHONE....................248 709-7901
Patrick Smith, *Sales Mgr*
Kim Marsh,
▲ EMP: 10
SALES (est): 864.6K **Privately Held**
SIC: 3429 Locks or lock sets

(G-16275)
COMPLETE DATA PRODUCTS INC (PA)
5755 New King Dr (48098-2649)
PHONE....................248 651-8602
Tom Carswell, *President*
Neal Doshi, *Partner*
Nirav Doshi, *Partner*
EMP: 4
SALES (est): 3.8MM **Privately Held**
WEB: www.carswelldata.com
SIC: 5112 7372 7371 7373 Business forms; computer & photocopying supplies; application computer software; business oriented computer software; computer software development; systems software development services

(G-16276)
COMPUNETICS INCORPORATED
2500 Rochester Ct (48083-5200)
PHONE....................248 524-6376
Donald R Bernier, *President*
Bruce R Shaw, *Vice Pres*
EMP: 20 EST: 1971
SQ FT: 21,000
SALES (est): 2.6MM **Privately Held**
WEB: www.compuneticsinc.com
SIC: 8711 3674 Engineering services; microprocessors

(G-16277)
CONTINENTAL AUTO SYSTEMS INC
Siemens VDO North America
4685 Investment Dr (48098-6335)
PHONE....................248 267-9408
Beyza Sarioglu, *Engineer*
Keith Robinson, *Branch Mgr*
Patrick Lang, *Manager*
Scott Thomason, *Senior Mgr*
Ralf Woods, *Director*
EMP: 50
SALES (corp-wide): 50.8B **Privately Held**
SIC: 3714 5013 3621 Motor vehicle parts & accessories; motor vehicle supplies & new parts; motors & generators
HQ: Continental Automotive Systems, Inc.
1 Continental Dr
Auburn Hills MI 48326
248 393-5300

(G-16278)
CONTINENTAL STRL PLAS INC
1805 Larchwood Dr (48083-2226)
PHONE....................248 593-9500
Robert Simon, *Vice Pres*
Daniel Arney, *Opers Mgr*
Mike King, *Maint Spvr*
Steve Zachrich, *Engrg Dir*
John Griswold, *QC Mgr*
EMP: 20 **Privately Held**
SIC: 3089 Plastic processing
HQ: Continental Structural Plastics, Inc.
255 Rex Blvd
Auburn Hills MI 48326
248 237-7800

(G-16279)
CONTOUR METROLOGICAL & MFG INC
Also Called: C M M
488 Oliver Dr (48084-5426)
PHONE....................248 273-1111
Kevin McMahon, *President*
Nick Parlove, *Engineer*
EMP: 17
SQ FT: 15,000
SALES: 5MM **Privately Held**
WEB: www.cmmoptic.com
SIC: 3827 Optical instruments & lenses

(G-16280)
CONTROL POWER-RELIANCE LLC (HQ)
Also Called: C P R
310 Executive Dr 314 (48083-4532)
PHONE....................248 583-1020
J Edgar Myles, *President*
Janet Trammel, *Controller*
EMP: 9
SALES (est): 1.1MM
SALES (corp-wide): 8.4MM **Privately Held**
WEB: www.cp-r.com
SIC: 3829 Measuring & controlling devices
PA: J. E. Myles, Inc.
310 Executive Dr
Troy MI 48083
248 583-1020

(G-16281)
CONTROLLED POWER COMPANY (PA)
1955 Stephenson Hwy Ste G (48083-2183)
PHONE....................248 528-3700
Christian Tazzia, *President*
Dave Gerds, *Vice Pres*
Mark Hunt, *Vice Pres*
Chris Tazzia, *Vice Pres*
Chris Tassia, *VP Opers*
▼ EMP: 113
SQ FT: 90,000
SALES: 17.3MM **Privately Held**
SIC: 3612 3629 3677 8711 Rectifier transformers; power conversion units, a.c. to d.c.: static-electric; electronic coils, transformers & other inductors; engineering services

(G-16282)
COPELAND-GIBSON PRODUCTS CORP
1025 E Maple Rd (48083-2814)
PHONE....................248 740-4400
Raymond E Howard, *President*
Nancy Howard, *Vice Pres*
Dave Barrett, *Engineer*
Charles Howard, *Treasurer*
Ann Howard, *Admin Sec*
EMP: 12
SQ FT: 6,500
SALES (est): 1.1MM **Privately Held**
WEB: www.copeland-gibson.com
SIC: 7389 3053 Metal cutting services; gaskets & sealing devices

(G-16283)
CORPORATE ELECTRONIC STY INC
Also Called: Colorpoint Print.com
2708 American Dr (48083-4625)
PHONE....................248 583-7070
Bonnie Mc Donald, *President*
James W Mc Donald II, *Vice Pres*
Kelley McDonald, *Mktg Dir*
EMP: 75
SQ FT: 17,940
SALES (est): 12.3MM **Privately Held**
SIC: 2759 2791 2752 Thermography; typesetting; commercial printing, lithographic

(G-16284)
COSMA INTERNATIONAL AMER INC (HQ)
Also Called: Cosma Engineering
750 Tower Dr (48098-2863)
PHONE....................248 631-1100
Don Walker, *CEO*
Elizabeth Maccabe, *Vice Pres*
Watson Minnette, *Research*
Jamie Ledford, *Engineer*
Ryan Warpup, *Engineer*
▲ EMP: 300
SALES (est): 576.9MM
SALES (corp-wide): 40.8B **Privately Held**
SIC: 3714 Motor vehicle parts & accessories
PA: Magna International Inc
337 Magna Dr
Aurora ON L4G 7
905 726-2462

(G-16285)
CREATIVE PERFORMANCE RACG LLC
Also Called: Cpr Racing
120 Birchwood Dr (48083-1711)
PHONE....................248 250-6187
Goran Bogdanovic,
EMP: 6 EST: 1997
SQ FT: 4,000
SALES: 300K **Privately Held**
WEB: www.cprracing.com
SIC: 3714 3559 Automotive wiring harness sets; automotive related machinery

(G-16286)
CREATIVE PRINT CREW LLC
1119 Rochester Rd (48083-6013)
PHONE....................248 629-9404
Joseph Gatt, *Owner*
EMP: 4
SALES (est): 472.1K **Privately Held**
SIC: 2752 Commercial printing, offset

(G-16287)
CREWBOTIQ LLC
755 W Big Beaver Rd # 2020 (48084-4925)
PHONE....................248 939-4229
Michelle Mopkins, *President*
EMP: 20
SALES (est): 242K **Privately Held**
SIC: 3822 Auto controls regulating residntl & coml environmt & applncs

(G-16288)
CRUUX LLC
4897 River Bank Ct (48085-4896)
PHONE....................248 515-8411
In Seok OH,
MI Jeong OH,
EMP: 4
SALES: 20K **Privately Held**
SIC: 3499 7389 Magnetic shields, metal;

(G-16289)
CUSTOM ENGINEERING & DESIGN
3448 Rowland Ct (48083-5677)
PHONE....................248 680-1435
Dennis Nowicki, *President*
EMP: 6
SQ FT: 3,200
SALES (est): 823.9K **Privately Held**
SIC: 3625 Relays & industrial controls

(G-16290)
CUSTOM PRINTING OF MICHIGAN
1659 Rochester Rd (48083-1829)
PHONE....................248 585-9222
Mark Grimske, *President*
EMP: 12
SQ FT: 7,000
SALES (est): 770K **Privately Held**
SIC: 2752 Commercial printing, offset

(G-16291)
CYBERLOGIC TECHNOLOGIES INC
755 W Big Beaver Rd # 2020 (48084-4925)
PHONE....................248 631-2200
Kemal Turedi, *Ch of Bd*
Pawel T Mikulski, *President*
EMP: 30
SALES (est): 2.4MM **Privately Held**
WEB: www.cyberlogic.com
SIC: 7372 Prepackaged software

(G-16292)
D & M TRUCK TOP CO INC
2354 Dorchester Dr N # 108 (48084-3722)
PHONE....................248 792-7972
Aaron Greenspon, *President*
Cynthia Greenspon, *Admin Sec*
EMP: 8
SQ FT: 15,800
SALES (est): 570K **Privately Held**
SIC: 3714 Tops, motor vehicle

(G-16293)
D FIND CORPORATION
1955 Rolling Woods Dr (48098-6606)
P.O. Box 1715 (48099-1715)
PHONE....................248 641-2858
Varsha Baxi, *President*
Indra Baxi, *Vice Pres*
▲ EMP: 4
SQ FT: 4,500
SALES: 400K **Privately Held**
SIC: 1731 3089 8742 Access control systems specialization; injection molded finished plastic products; marketing consulting services

(G-16294)
DAEWON AMERICA INC
1450 W Long Lake Rd # 175 (48098-6353)
PHONE....................334 364-1630
Heeyong Bang, *President*
Duk OH, *CFO*
EMP: 3
SQ FT: 300
SALES (est): 203.5K **Privately Held**
SIC: 3694 Ignition coils, automotive

(G-16295)
DAIEK PRODUCTS INC
Also Called: Daiek Door Sytem
1725 Blaney Dr (48084)
PHONE....................248 816-1360
David E Daiek, *President*
▲ EMP: 12
SQ FT: 8,400
SALES (est): 1.6MM **Privately Held**
WEB: www.daiekproducts.com
SIC: 3442 5031 3089 Metal doors; doors & windows; fiberglass doors

(G-16296)
DAYCO LLC (PA)
1650 Research Dr Ste 200 (48083-2143)
PHONE....................248 404-6500
Joel E Wiegert, *CEO*
Michael Omotoso, *Business Mgr*
Gordon Hensley, *Vice Pres*
Chris Buddington, *Engineer*
Ben McEachern, *Engineer*
EMP: 8
SALES (est): 178.8MM **Privately Held**
SIC: 3568 Power transmission equipment

(G-16297)
DAYCO INCORPORATED (HQ)
1650 Research Dr Ste 200 (48083-2143)
PHONE....................248 404-6500
Joel E Wiegert, *CEO*
Chris Werth, *Manager*
EMP: 5
SALES (est): 178.8MM **Privately Held**
SIC: 3465 Body parts, automobile: stamped metal
PA: Dayco, Llc
1650 Research Dr Ste 200
Troy MI 48083
248 404-6500

(G-16298)
DAYCO PRODUCTS LLC
Also Called: Mark 4 Automotive
1650 Research Dr Ste 200 (48083-2143)
PHONE....................248 404-6506
Jim Orchard, *Principal*
EMP: 91
SALES (corp-wide): 178.8MM **Privately Held**
WEB: www.mark-iv.com
SIC: 3052 8711 Automobile hose, plastic; automobile hose, rubber; plastic belting; rubber belting; engineering services
HQ: Dayco Products, Llc
1650 Research Dr Ste 200
Troy MI 48083

(G-16299)
DAYCO PRODUCTS LLC (DH)
1650 Research Dr Ste 200 (48083-2143)
PHONE....................248 404-6500
John T Bohenick, *CEO*
Doug Bowen, *President*
John Kinnick, *President*
Al Devore, *Vice Pres*
Dan Engler, *Vice Pres*
EMP: 277

GEOGRAPHIC SECTION

SALES (est): 178.8MM **Privately Held**
WEB: www.mark-iv.com
SIC: **3568** Power transmission equipment

(G-16300)
DEBRON INDUSTRIAL ELEC INC
Also Called: Debron Indus Elctronicschitran
591 Executive Dr (48083-4507)
PHONE..................................248 588-7220
Ronald J Bernot, *President*
David A Conover, *Vice Pres*
Josh Schell, *Manager*
EMP: 25
SQ FT: 17,200
SALES (est): 6.3MM **Privately Held**
WEB: www.debron-electronics.com
SIC: **3679** 8711 3672 3825 Electronic circuits; electrical or electronic engineering; printed circuit boards; test equipment for electronic & electric measurement; electrodes used in industrial process measurement; motor vehicle parts & accessories

(G-16301)
DELCO ELEC OVERSEAS CORP (HQ)
5820 Innovation Dr (48098-2824)
PHONE..................................248 813-2000
EMP: 4
SALES (est): 184.1K
SALES (corp-wide): 16.6B **Privately Held**
WEB: www.delphiauto.com
SIC: **3714** Motor vehicle parts & accessories
PA: Aptiv Plc
   Queensway House Hilgrove Street
   Jersey JE1 1
   163 422-4000

(G-16302)
DELPHI
5725 Innovation Dr (48098-2852)
PHONE..................................248 813-2000
Luiz R Corrallo, *President*
Kevin P Clark, *COO*
Majdi B Abulaban, *Senior VP*
Jessica L Holscott, *Vice Pres*
Mark J Murphy, *CFO*
EMP: 4
SALES (est): 564.6K **Privately Held**
SIC: **3714** Motor vehicle parts & accessories

(G-16303)
DELPHI AUTOMOTIVE SYSTEMS
5820 Innovation Dr (48098-2824)
PHONE..................................248 813-2000
Diane Kaye, *Principal*
EMP: 4
SALES (est): 103.1K
SALES (corp-wide): 16.6B **Privately Held**
WEB: www.delphiauto.com
SIC: **3714** Motor vehicle parts & accessories
PA: Aptiv Plc
   Queensway House Hilgrove Street
   Jersey JE1 1
   163 422-4000

(G-16304)
DELPHI POWERTRAIN CORPORATION
5820 Innovation Dr (48098-2824)
PHONE..................................248 813-2000
EMP: 3
SALES (est): 95.9K
SALES (corp-wide): 1.5MM **Privately Held**
SIC: **3714** Motor vehicle parts & accessories
PA: Delphi Technologies Plc
   Queensway House, Hilgrove Street
   Jersey
   163 423-4422

(G-16305)
DELPHI POWERTRAIN SYSTEMS LLC
1624 Meijer Dr (48084-7141)
P.O. Box 5052 (48007-5052)
PHONE..................................248 280-8340
Saal Ramos, *Analyst*
EMP: 15
SALES (corp-wide): 1.5MM **Privately Held**
WEB: www.delphiauto.com
SIC: **3714** Motor vehicle parts & accessories
HQ: Delphi Powertrain Systems, Llc
   5825 Innovation Dr
   Troy MI 48098
   248 813-2000

(G-16306)
DELPHI POWERTRAIN SYSTEMS LLC (HQ)
5825 Innovation Dr (48098-2824)
PHONE..................................248 813-2000
Kevin P Clark, *President*
Rock Lindsay, *Senior Buyer*
EMP: 1 EST: 2017
SALES (est): 2.7MM
SALES (corp-wide): 1.5MM **Privately Held**
SIC: **3714** Motor vehicle parts & accessories
PA: Delphi Technologies Plc
   Queensway House, Hilgrove Street
   Jersey
   163 423-4422

(G-16307)
DELPHI POWERTRAIN SYSTEMS LLC
5820 Innovation Dr (48098-2824)
PHONE..................................248 813-1549
David Helton, *Engineer*
Lucia V Moretti, *Mktg Dir*
Frank Ordonez, *Branch Mgr*
Katrina Guttrich, *Executive Asst*
Melody Allen, *Admin Asst*
EMP: 41
SALES (corp-wide): 1.5MM **Privately Held**
WEB: www.delphiauto.com
SIC: **3714** Motor vehicle parts & accessories
HQ: Delphi Powertrain Systems, Llc
   5825 Innovation Dr
   Troy MI 48098
   248 813-2000

(G-16308)
DELPHI POWERTRAIN SYSTEMS LLC
5725 Innovation Dr (48098-2852)
PHONE..................................248 813-2000
Guy Hachey, *Manager*
EMP: 209
SALES (corp-wide): 1.5MM **Privately Held**
WEB: www.delphiauto.com
SIC: **3714** Motor vehicle parts & accessories
HQ: Delphi Powertrain Systems, Llc
   5825 Innovation Dr
   Troy MI 48098
   248 813-2000

(G-16309)
DELPHI POWERTRAIN SYSTEMS LLC
1624 Meijer Dr (48084-7141)
P.O. Box 7079 (48007-7079)
PHONE..................................248 280-8319
Elli Minert, *Branch Mgr*
EMP: 100
SALES (corp-wide): 1.5MM **Privately Held**
WEB: www.delphidiesel.com
SIC: **3714** Motor vehicle parts & accessories
HQ: Delphi Powertrain Systems, Llc
   5825 Innovation Dr
   Troy MI 48098
   248 813-2000

(G-16310)
DELPHI POWERTRAIN SYSTEMS LLC
1624 Meijer Dr (48084-7141)
PHONE..................................800 521-4784
Mark Mason, *Manager*
EMP: 23
SALES (corp-wide): 1.5MM **Privately Held**
WEB: www.delphiauto.com
SIC: **3714** Motor vehicle parts & accessories
HQ: Delphi Powertrain Systems, Llc
   5825 Innovation Dr
   Troy MI 48098
   248 813-2000

(G-16311)
DELPHI PWERTRAIN INTL SVCS LLC
5820 Innovation Dr (48098-2824)
PHONE..................................248 813-2000
Rodney O'Neal, *President*
EMP: 3
SALES (est): 102.1K
SALES (corp-wide): 1.5MM **Privately Held**
SIC: **3714** Motor vehicle parts & accessories
PA: Delphi Technologies Plc
   Queensway House, Hilgrove Street
   Jersey
   163 423-4422

(G-16312)
DELPHI PWRTRAIN TECH GEN PRTNR
5820 Innovation Dr (48098-2824)
PHONE..................................248 813-2000
EMP: 3 EST: 2017
SALES (est): 95.9K
SALES (corp-wide): 1.5MM **Privately Held**
SIC: **3714** Motor vehicle parts & accessories
PA: Delphi Technologies Plc
   Queensway House, Hilgrove Street
   Jersey
   163 423-4422

(G-16313)
DEPOR INDUSTRIES INC (HQ)
1902 Northwood Dr (48084-5523)
PHONE..................................248 362-3900
David E Berry, *Ch of Bd*
James W Cooper, *Vice Pres*
Rick McIntosh, *Prdtn Mgr*
Amelia Bradford, *Production*
Dennis Brady, *Manager*
▲ EMP: 3 EST: 1972
SALES (est): 5.9MM
SALES (corp-wide): 80.5MM **Privately Held**
WEB: www.deporindustries.net
SIC: **3479** Coating, rust preventive
PA: The Magni Group Inc
   390 Park St Ste 300
   Birmingham MI 48009
   248 647-4500

(G-16314)
DETROIT LEGAL NEWS PUBG LLC
1409 Allen Dr Ste B (48083-4003)
PHONE..................................248 577-6100
Brad Thompson, *Mng Member*
Suzanne Favaley,
Chad T Parks,
Richard Swiftney,
EMP: 25
SALES (est): 1.8MM **Privately Held**
WEB: www.oaklandlegalnews.com
SIC: **2711** 8111 2791 Newspapers, publishing & printing; legal services; typesetting

(G-16315)
DGA PRINTING INC
Also Called: Sterling Printing & Graphics
567 Robbins Dr (48083-4515)
PHONE..................................586 979-2244
Deborah Majchrzak, *President*
Gary Majchrzak, *Vice Pres*
EMP: 4
SQ FT: 2,000
SALES (est): 640.9K **Privately Held**
WEB: www.spgraphics.net
SIC: **2752** Commercial printing, offset

(G-16316)
DIANAMIC ABRASIVE PRODUCTS
2566 Industrial Row Dr (48084-7035)
PHONE..................................248 280-1185
George J Collins, *President*
Steven Vafeas, *Vice Pres*
Vasiliki Collins, *Admin Sec*
EMP: 12
SQ FT: 13,500
SALES (est): 1.4MM **Privately Held**
WEB: www.dianamic.com
SIC: **3291** 3545 Wheels, abrasive; wheel turning equipment, diamond point or other

(G-16317)
DICK AND JANE BAKING CO LLC
755 W Big Beaver Rd # 2020 (48084-4925)
PHONE..................................248 519-2418
Richard Held, *Mng Member*
Robert Fell,
Mike Lukas,
EMP: 4
SALES (est): 863.5K **Privately Held**
SIC: **5149** 2052 Bakery products; cookies & crackers

(G-16318)
DICKS SPORTING GOODS INC
750 W 14 Mile Rd (48083-4200)
PHONE..................................248 581-8028
EMP: 3
SALES (corp-wide): 8.4B **Publicly Held**
SIC: **1311** Crude petroleum & natural gas
PA: Dick's Sporting Goods, Inc.
   345 Court St
   Coraopolis PA 15108
   724 273-3400

(G-16319)
DIEOMATIC INCORPORATED (DH)
Also Called: Benco Manufacturing
750 Tower Dr Mail 7000 Mail Code (48098)
PHONE..................................319 668-2031
Tommy Skudutis, *President*
Brian Duivesteyn, *Principal*
Richard J Smith, *Treasurer*
Arthur L Lee, *Admin Sec*
EMP: 85
SALES (est): 297.8MM
SALES (corp-wide): 40.8B **Privately Held**
SIC: **3714** Motor vehicle parts & accessories
HQ: Cosma International Of America, Inc.
   750 Tower Dr
   Troy MI 48098
   248 631-1100

(G-16320)
DIGITAL PERFORMANCE TECH
3221 W Big Beaver Rd (48084-2803)
PHONE..................................877 983-4230
Lisa Klein, *CEO*
EMP: 11
SALES (est): 232.1K **Privately Held**
SIC: **8742** 3823 Maintenance management consultant; data loggers, industrial process type

(G-16321)
DISPLAY STRUCTURES INC
288 Robbins Dr (48083-4512)
PHONE..................................810 991-0801
Diane Dearing, *President*
Steve Dearing, *Vice Pres*
EMP: 16
SQ FT: 17,820
SALES: 991.2K **Privately Held**
WEB: www.displaystructuresinc.com
SIC: **3993** Displays & cutouts, window & lobby

(G-16322)
DONGAH AMERICA INC
Also Called: DTR Logistics
1807 E Maple Rd (48083-4212)
PHONE..................................248 918-5810
S H Kim, *President*
Jae Kim, *Engineer*
Rose Lloyd, *Manager*
Rose Lloyd-Rose, *Manager*
Duck Hwang, *Director*
◆ EMP: 40
SQ FT: 93,000
SALES (est): 10MM **Privately Held**
SIC: **3465** Body parts, automobile: stamped metal
PA: Dtr Automotive Corporation
   12 Cheoyongsaneop 2-Gil, Onsan-Eup, Ulju-Gun
   Ulsan 44993

Troy - Oakland County (G-16323)

(G-16323)
DPH LLC
Also Called: Delphi
5820 Innovation Dr (48098-2824)
PHONE.................................248 813-2000
Robert Brust,
◆ **EMP**: 1000
SALES (est): 121.1MM
SALES (corp-wide): 16.6B **Privately Held**
WEB: www.delphiauto.com
SIC: 3714 Motor vehicle parts & accessories
PA: Aptiv Plc
   Queensway House Hilgrove Street
   Jersey JE1 1
   163 422-4000

(G-16324)
DPH HOLDINGS CORP (HQ)
Also Called: Delphi
5725 Innovation Dr (48098-2852)
PHONE.................................248 813-2000
Rodney O'Neal, *CEO*
Majdi B Abulaban, *Senior VP*
Kevin M Butler, *Senior VP*
Liam Butterworth, *Senior VP*
Kevin P Clark, *Senior VP*
◆ **EMP**: 215
SQ FT: 264,000
SALES (est): 928.7MM
SALES (corp-wide): 16.6B **Privately Held**
WEB: www.delphiauto.com
SIC: 3714 Motor vehicle parts & accessories
PA: Aptiv Plc
   Queensway House Hilgrove Street
   Jersey JE1 1
   163 422-4000

(G-16325)
DPH-DAS GLOBAL (HOLDINGS) LLC
5820 Innovation Dr (48098-2824)
PHONE.................................248 813-2000
Bette Walker, *Principal*
Lindsey Williams, *Pub Rel Mgr*
Luis Herrera, *Info Tech Mgr*
▲ **EMP**: 1000
SALES (est): 73.2MM
SALES (corp-wide): 16.6B **Privately Held**
SIC: 3714 Motor vehicle parts & accessories
PA: Aptiv Plc
   Queensway House Hilgrove Street
   Jersey JE1 1
   163 422-4000

(G-16326)
DPH-DAS LLC
5820 Innovation Dr (48098-2824)
PHONE.................................248 813-2000
J T Battenberg III,
◆ **EMP**: 7695
SALES (est): 228.8MM
SALES (corp-wide): 16.6B **Privately Held**
SIC: 3714 Motor vehicle parts & accessories
PA: Aptiv Plc
   Queensway House Hilgrove Street
   Jersey JE1 1
   163 422-4000

(G-16327)
DRACO MFG INC
629 Minnesota Dr (48083-6202)
PHONE.................................248 585-0320
James McArthur, *President*
Deborah Amundson, *Treasurer*
▼ **EMP**: 7
SQ FT: 7,200
SALES (est): 617K **Privately Held**
WEB: www.dracomfg.com
SIC: 3599 Machine shop, jobbing & repair

(G-16328)
DREAL INC
5820 Innovation Dr (48098-2824)
PHONE.................................248 813-2000
EMP: 3
SALES (est): 11.6K
SALES (corp-wide): 16.6B **Privately Held**
WEB: www.delphiauto.com
SIC: 3714 Motor vehicle parts & accessories
PA: Aptiv Plc
   Queensway House Hilgrove Street
   Jersey JE1 1
   163 422-4000

(G-16329)
DUN MOR EMBROIDERY & DESIGNS
Also Called: Dun Mor Design
360 E Maple Rd Ste O (48083-2707)
PHONE.................................248 577-1155
Linda Dunmore, *President*
Rich Dunmore, *Vice Pres*
EMP: 10
SQ FT: 5,000
SALES (est): 680K **Privately Held**
SIC: 2395 Emblems, embroidered

(G-16330)
DYNAMIC JIG GRINDING CORP
Also Called: Dynamic Precision Tool & Mfg
985 Troy Ct (48083-2728)
PHONE.................................248 589-3110
John A Eckhout, *President*
Sue Eckhout, *Officer*
EMP: 20
SQ FT: 15,000
SALES (est): 3.7MM **Privately Held**
WEB: www.dynamicjig.com
SIC: 3599 3545 3544 Machine shop, jobbing & repair; machine tool accessories; special dies, tools, jigs & fixtures

(G-16331)
DYNETICS INC
1100 Owendale Dr (48083-1914)
PHONE.................................248 619-1681
Alix Reinhalter, *Branch Mgr*
EMP: 4
SALES (corp-wide): 315.4MM **Privately Held**
SIC: 3465 Body parts, automobile: stamped metal
PA: Dynetics, Inc.
   1002 Explorer Blvd Nw
   Huntsville AL 35806
   256 964-4000

(G-16332)
E & C MANUFACTURING LLC
2125 Butterfield Dr # 200 (48084-3410)
PHONE.................................248 330-0400
Barry Connelly, *Mng Member*
Stephen J Paver Jr,
EMP: 13
SALES (est): 650K **Privately Held**
SIC: 5047 3599 Hospital equipment & furniture; machine & other job shop work

(G-16333)
EAGLE FASTENERS INC
Also Called: Efi Custom Injection Molding
185 Park Dr (48083-2770)
PHONE.................................248 577-1441
Theresa C Srock, *President*
James P Srock, *Vice Pres*
Joseph C Srock, *Vice Pres*
▲ **EMP**: 12
SQ FT: 23,000
SALES (est): 2.1MM **Privately Held**
WEB: www.eaglefasteners.com
SIC: 3089 Injection molding of plastics

(G-16334)
EASI LLC
340 E Big Beaver Rd (48083-1218)
PHONE.................................248 712-2750
Kevin Smith, *Engineer*
Hushedar Mehta, *Branch Mgr*
EMP: 33
SALES (corp-wide): 13.4B **Privately Held**
SIC: 3822 Energy cutoff controls, residential or commercial types
HQ: Easi, Llc
   7301 Parkway Dr
   Hanover MD 21076
   717 553-7700

(G-16335)
EDON CONTROLS INC
2891 Industrial Row Dr (48084-7041)
PHONE.................................248 280-0420
Norman N Fender, *President*
Christine Fender, *Vice Pres*
EMP: 7
SQ FT: 10,000
SALES (est): 1.3MM **Privately Held**
WEB: www.edoncontrols.com
SIC: 3625 Industrial electrical relays & switches

(G-16336)
ELBA INC
Also Called: Elba Laboratories
1925 W Maple Rd Ste B (48084-7116)
PHONE.................................248 288-6098
Michael Froehlich, *President*
▲ **EMP**: 32
SQ FT: 22,000
SALES (est): 4.3MM **Privately Held**
WEB: www.elba-labs.com
SIC: 2834 Pharmaceutical preparations

(G-16337)
ELDOR AUTOMOTIVE N AMER INC
100 W Big Beavr Rd # 200 (48084-5206)
PHONE.................................248 878-9193
EMP: 9
SALES (est): 1MM
SALES (corp-wide): 57.2K **Privately Held**
SIC: 3694 Ignition coils, automotive
HQ: Eldor Corporation Spa
   Via Don Paolo Berra 18
   Orsenigo CO 22030
   031 636-111

(G-16338)
ELECTRICAL DESIGN AND CTRL CO
2200 Stephenson Hwy (48083-2153)
PHONE.................................248 743-2400
Shay Friedman, *CEO*
EMP: 50 EST: 1958
SQ FT: 29,000
SALES (est): 2.7MM
SALES (corp-wide): 6.1MM **Privately Held**
WEB: www.edandc.com
SIC: 8711 3613 Consulting engineer; control panels, electric
HQ: Dascan Industrial Controls, Inc.
   803 W Big Beaver Rd # 355
   Troy MI 48084
   248 269-7747

(G-16339)
ELECTRICAL PRODUCT SALES INC
2611 Elliott Dr (48083-4637)
PHONE.................................248 583-6100
Richard Stone, *President*
EMP: 12
SQ FT: 10,000
SALES (est): 1MM **Privately Held**
WEB: www.electricalproducts.com
SIC: 3643 Current-carrying wiring devices

(G-16340)
ELSA ENTERPRISES INC
Also Called: Rocky Mountain Chocolate
2800 W Big Beaver Rd # 124 (48084-3206)
PHONE.................................248 816-1454
Alan Rosen, *President*
EMP: 6
SALES (est): 650K **Privately Held**
SIC: 5441 2064 Candy; chocolate candy, except solid chocolate

(G-16341)
ELUMIGEN LLC
820 Kirts Blvd Ste 300 (48084-4836)
PHONE.................................855 912-0477
Gerry Fedele, *President*
Mounir El-Mourad, *Financial Analy*
EMP: 8
SALES (est): 332.7K
SALES (corp-wide): 21.1B **Publicly Held**
SIC: 3641 Electric light bulbs, complete
PA: Lear Corporation
   21557 Telegraph Rd
   Southfield MI 48033
   248 447-1500

(G-16342)
EMHART TEKNOLOGIES LLC
Also Called: STANLEY ENGINEERED FASTENING
2500 Meijer Dr (48084-7146)
PHONE.................................248 677-9693
◆ **EMP**: 100
SALES (est): 10.2MM
SALES (corp-wide): 11.1B **Publicly Held**
SIC: 3999 1541 8742 Mfg Misc Products Industrial Building Construction Management Consulting Services
PA: Stanley Black & Decker, Inc.
   1000 Stanley Dr
   New Britain CT 06053
   860 225-5111

(G-16343)
EMHART TEKNOLOGIES LLC
Also Called: Stanley Engineered Fastening
2400 Meijer Dr Bldg 2 (48084-7110)
PHONE.................................800 783-6427
James Puscas, *VP Sales*
EMP: 11
SALES (corp-wide): 13.9B **Publicly Held**
SIC: 3541 Machine tools, metal cutting type
HQ: Emhart Teknologies Llc
   480 Myrtle St
   New Britain CT 06053
   800 783-6427

(G-16344)
ENDLICH STUDIOS LLC
2950 Bywater Dr (48085-7002)
PHONE.................................248 524-9671
EMP: 3
SALES (est): 306.6K **Privately Held**
SIC: 3823 Mfg Process Control Instruments

(G-16345)
ENERGY PRODUCTS INC
Also Called: Energy Products Service Dept
315 Indusco Ct (48083-4646)
PHONE.................................248 866-5622
Dave Budde, *Branch Mgr*
EMP: 9 **Privately Held**
WEB: www.energyprod.com
SIC: 5063 5084 7699 3625 Storage batteries, industrial; industrial machinery & equipment; battery service & repair; relays & industrial controls; automotive repair shops; motors & generators
PA: Energy Products, Inc.
   1551 E Lincoln Ave # 101
   Madison Heights MI 48071

(G-16346)
ENGINEERING TECH ASSOC INC (PA)
Also Called: E T A
1133 E Maple Rd Ste 200 (48083-2853)
PHONE.................................248 729-3010
Abraham N Keisoglou, *President*
Arthur Tang, *Vice Pres*
Divesh Mittal, *Engineer*
Abhishek Shrawan, *Project Engr*
Sujeet Thokade, *Project Engr*
EMP: 60
SQ FT: 10,000
SALES (est): 19.1MM **Privately Held**
SIC: 7371 8711 7372 Computer software development; engineering services; prepackaged software

(G-16347)
ENGINRED PLSTIC COMPONENTS INC
Also Called: Wilbert Plastic Services
100 W Big Beavr Rd # 200 (48084-5206)
PHONE.................................248 825-4508
EMP: 85 **Privately Held**
SIC: 3089 Injection molding of plastics
PA: Engineered Plastic Components, Inc.
   4500 Westown Pkwy Ste 11
   West Des Moines IA 50266

(G-16348)
ENTERTAINMENT PUBLICATIONS INC
1401 Crooks Rd Ste 150 (48084-7106)
PHONE.................................248 404-1000
Kimberly Bohn, *President*
Nancy McCabe, *Principal*
Lawrence Bridgeland, *Opers Spvr*
Diane Werre, *Opers Staff*
Tony Molino, *Mfg Staff*
EMP: 284
SALES (est): 74.7MM **Privately Held**
SIC: 2731 Book publishing

GEOGRAPHIC SECTION

Troy - Oakland County (G-16375)

(G-16349)
ENVIROLITE LLC (PA)
1700 W Big Beaver Rd # 150 (48084-3550)
PHONE..................................248 792-3184
Brad Patterson, *Mfg Staff*
Vatche Tazian, *Mng Member*
Brian Naumann, *Manager*
▲ **EMP:** 15
SQ FT: 7,000
SALES (est): 24.2MM **Privately Held**
SIC: 5199 5999 3086 Foams & rubber; foam & foam products; plastics foam products

(G-16350)
ENVIRONMENTAL CATALYSTS LLC
5820 Innovation Dr (48098-2824)
PHONE..................................248 813-2000
EMP: 3
SALES (est): 9.8K
SALES (corp-wide): 16.6B **Privately Held**
WEB: www.delphiauto.com
SIC: 3714 Motor vehicle parts & accessories
PA: Aptiv Plc
Queensway House Hilgrove Street
Jersey JE1 1
163 422-4000

(G-16351)
EQUITABLE ENGINEERING CO INC
1840 Austin Dr (48083-2204)
P.O. Box 1159 (48099-1159)
PHONE..................................248 689-9700
Randy J Pasko, *Vice Pres*
Randall Pasko, *Engineer*
Glenn R Pasko, *CFO*
EMP: 20 **EST:** 1951
SQ FT: 21,000
SALES: 2.3MM **Privately Held**
WEB: www.equitable-eng.com
SIC: 3462 7699 3829 3812 Gears, forged steel; industrial equipment services; measuring & controlling devices; search & navigation equipment; power transmission equipment; machine tool accessories

(G-16352)
ETHNICEMEDIA LLC
Also Called: Ethnicemeida
338 Thistle Ln (48098-4644)
PHONE..................................248 762-8904
Saravanan Govindaraj,
EMP: 4 **EST:** 2014
SALES: 50K **Privately Held**
SIC: 2741 7371 7389 Directories: publishing & printing; software programming applications;

(G-16353)
EURIDIUM SOLUTIONS LLC
55 E Long Lake Rd Ste 243 (48085-4738)
P.O. Box 99610 (48099-9610)
PHONE..................................248 535-7005
Lee A Holly, *Mng Member*
EMP: 6
SQ FT: 2,000
SALES: 2MM **Privately Held**
WEB: www.euridium.com
SIC: 3312 Coated or plated products

(G-16354)
EVANS COATINGS L L C
1330 Souter Dr (48083-2839)
PHONE..................................248 583-9890
David Evans, *Mng Member*
Mike Evans,
EMP: 9
SALES: 890K **Privately Held**
SIC: 3479 Coating of metals & formed products

(G-16355)
EXO-S US LLC
1500 W Big Beaver Rd 101c (48084-3522)
PHONE..................................248 614-9707
EMP: 5
SALES (corp-wide): 49.5MM **Privately Held**
SIC: 3089 Mfg Plastic Products
HQ: Exo-S Us Llc
6505 N State Road 9
Howe IN 46746
260 562-4100

(G-16356)
EXONE AMERICAS LLC (HQ)
2341 Alger Dr (48083-2052)
PHONE..................................248 740-1580
John H Gemmill, *CFO*
Terry Senish, *Manager*
▲ **EMP:** 6
SALES (est): 884.9K
SALES (corp-wide): 64.6MM **Publicly Held**
SIC: 2754 Job printing, gravure
PA: The Exone Company
127 Industry Blvd
North Huntingdon PA 15642
724 863-9663

(G-16357)
EXTRUSION PUNCH & TOOL INC
2326 Alger Dr (48083-2001)
PHONE..................................248 689-3300
Roger D Michels, *CEO*
Greg Ornazian, *President*
EMP: 25 **EST:** 1980
SQ FT: 8,000
SALES (est): 3.2MM **Privately Held**
SIC: 3599 3544 3494 Machine shop, jobbing & repair; special dies, tools, jigs & fixtures; valves & pipe fittings

(G-16358)
FAB-ALL MANUFACTURING INC
645 Executive Dr (48083-4536)
PHONE..................................248 585-6700
Josef F Hubert, *President*
EMP: 99 **EST:** 1978
SQ FT: 36,000
SALES (est): 4.8MM **Privately Held**
SIC: 3465 Automotive stampings

(G-16359)
FAIR INDUSTRIES LLC
3260 Talbot Dr (48083-5092)
PHONE..................................248 740-7841
Michael J Kuron, *President*
Edward J Apfel, *Vice Pres*
EMP: 130 **EST:** 1979
SALES: 50MM **Privately Held**
WEB: www.fairindustries.com
SIC: 3548 3541 3544 Resistance welders, electric; spot welding apparatus, electric; arc welders, transformer-rectifier; boring mills; milling machines; special dies, tools, jigs & fixtures

(G-16360)
FATIGUE DYNAMICS INC
5250 Cardinal Dr (48098-2466)
PHONE..................................248 641-9487
Milton N Weber, *President*
Brian D Weber, *Corp Secy*
Gordon Sorenson, *Vice Pres*
EMP: 3
SQ FT: 2,500
SALES: 300K **Privately Held**
WEB: www.fdinc.com
SIC: 3829 Fatigue testing machines, industrial: mechanical

(G-16361)
FEDEX OFFICE & PRINT SVCS INC
4050 Rochester Rd (48085-4923)
PHONE..................................248 680-0280
Mike Goodwin, *Manager*
EMP: 18
SALES (corp-wide): 69.6B **Publicly Held**
WEB: www.kinkos.com
SIC: 7334 2791 2789 2759 Photocopying & duplicating services; typesetting; bookbinding & related work; commercial printing
HQ: Fedex Office And Print Services, Inc.
7900 Legacy Dr
Plano TX 75024
800 463-3339

(G-16362)
FISHER & COMPANY INCORPORATED
1625 W Maple Rd (48084-7118)
PHONE..................................248 280-0808
Mark Waggener, *VP Finance*
Faiz Jergees, *Branch Mgr*
EMP: 6
SALES (corp-wide): 477.8MM **Privately Held**
SIC: 2531 Seats, automobile
PA: Fisher & Company, Incorporated
33300 Fisher Dr
Saint Clair Shores MI 48082
586 746-2000

(G-16363)
FISHER & COMPANY INCORPORATED
1625 W Maple Rd (48084-7118)
PHONE..................................248 280-0808
Jeff Thompson, *Branch Mgr*
EMP: 140
SALES (corp-wide): 477.8MM **Privately Held**
SIC: 3465 3469 Automotive stampings; metal stampings
PA: Fisher & Company, Incorporated
33300 Fisher Dr
Saint Clair Shores MI 48082
586 746-2000

(G-16364)
FISHER & COMPANY INCORPORATED
1625 W Marble Rd (48084)
PHONE..................................586 746-2101
Jeff Thompson, *Branch Mgr*
EMP: 57
SALES (corp-wide): 477.8MM **Privately Held**
SIC: 3714 Motor vehicle parts & accessories
PA: Fisher & Company, Incorporated
33300 Fisher Dr
Saint Clair Shores MI 48082
586 746-2000

(G-16365)
FITZ MANUFACTURING INC
324 Robbins Dr (48083-4558)
PHONE..................................248 589-1780
Patrick J Fitzpatrick, *President*
Bobbie Fitzpatrick, *Corp Secy*
Clayton Burnett, *Sales Staff*
Robert Laskos, *Sales Staff*
EMP: 15 **EST:** 1977
SQ FT: 18,000
SALES (est): 2.5MM **Privately Held**
SIC: 3545 Precision tools, machinists'

(G-16366)
FITZ-RITE PRODUCTS INC
1122 Naughton Dr (48083-1930)
PHONE..................................248 528-8440
W Dean Fitzpatrick, *President*
Peter Petrash, *Marketing Staff*
EMP: 20
SQ FT: 15,500
SALES (est): 3.6MM **Privately Held**
WEB: www.fitzrite.com
SIC: 3625 5084 3545 3544 Numerical controls; industrial machinery & equipment; machine tool accessories; special dies, tools, jigs & fixtures

(G-16367)
FLIPSNACK LLC
2701 Troy Center Dr # 255 (48084-4753)
PHONE..................................650 741-1328
Gabriel Ciordas,
EMP: 36
SALES: 900K **Privately Held**
SIC: 2741 Miscellaneous publishing

(G-16368)
FLORIDA PRODUCTION ENGRG INC
Also Called: Fpe
550 Stephenson Hwy # 360 (48083-1109)
PHONE..................................248 588-4870
Brad Gotts, *President*
Jason Jutte, *President*
EMP: 10
SALES (corp-wide): 351.5MM **Privately Held**
WEB: www.fpe-inc.com
SIC: 2821 Plastics materials & resins
HQ: Florida Production Engineering, Inc.
2 E Tower Cir
Ormond Beach FL 32174
386 677-2566

(G-16369)
FORM G TECH CO
1291 Rochester Rd (48083-2879)
PHONE..................................248 583-3610
Shkelqim Lumani, *President*
▲ **EMP:** 53
SQ FT: 32,000
SALES: 100K **Privately Held**
WEB: www.formgtech.com
SIC: 3312 Tool & die steel & alloys; tool & die steel

(G-16370)
FORTIS ENERGY SERVICES INC (PA)
3001 W Big Beaver Rd # 525 (48084-3100)
PHONE..................................248 283-7100
George Molski, *President*
Warren Jensen, *Opers Mgr*
Randy Martinez, *Opers Mgr*
Susan Censoni, *VP Finance*
Chris Zanon, *Sales Staff*
EMP: 57
SALES (est): 45.6MM **Privately Held**
WEB: www.arrowenergyservices.com
SIC: 1381 3625 3621 Drilling oil & gas wells; noise control equipment; motors & generators

(G-16371)
FOSTERS VENTURES LLC
Also Called: Signs & More
1371 Souter Dr (48083-2840)
PHONE..................................248 519-7446
Larry Foster,
Molly Smith,
EMP: 11
SALES (est): 860K **Privately Held**
SIC: 3993 Signs & advertising specialties

(G-16372)
FOUR-WAY TOOL AND DIE INC (PA)
239 Indusco Ct (48083-4679)
PHONE..................................248 585-8255
Lawrence Erickson, *President*
Helen Erickson, *Corp Secy*
David Erickson, *Asst Treas*
EMP: 30
SQ FT: 17,000
SALES (est): 3.4MM **Privately Held**
SIC: 3544 3643 Special dies & tools; current-carrying wiring devices

(G-16373)
FOUR-WAY TOOL AND DIE INC
Also Called: Try Square Design
217 Indusco Ct (48083-4645)
PHONE..................................248 585-8255
Lawrence Erickson, *Principal*
EMP: 30
SQ FT: 6,000
SALES (corp-wide): 3.4MM **Privately Held**
SIC: 3544 Special dies, tools, jigs & fixtures
PA: Four-Way Tool And Die Inc
239 Indusco Ct
Troy MI 48083
248 585-8255

(G-16374)
FRACO PRODUCTS LTD
5225 Renshaw Dr (48085-4071)
PHONE..................................248 667-9260
Scott Guilbault, *Manager*
EMP: 4
SALES (corp-wide): 950K **Privately Held**
SIC: 3272 Concrete products
HQ: Produits Fraco Ltee, Les
91 Ch Des Patriotes
Saint-Mathias-Sur-Richelieu QC J3L 6
514 990-7750

(G-16375)
FSP INC
Also Called: Five Star Products
1270 Rankin Dr Ste B (48083-2843)
PHONE..................................248 585-0760
Charles E Wallace, *President*

Neil Wallace, *Corp Secy*
Richard Holmes, *Executive*
EMP: 14
SQ FT: 10,000
SALES (est): 2MM **Privately Held**
WEB: www.fivestar-tooling.com
SIC: 3545 Cutting tools for machine tools; tool holders

(G-16376)
G T JERSEYS LLC
997 Rochester Rd Ste C (48083-6025)
PHONE.................................248 588-3231
Virginia Thackaberry, *Mng Member*
EMP: 5
SQ FT: 2,800
SALES (est): 650K **Privately Held**
SIC: 7336 7299 2211 5699 Silk screen design; chart & graph design; stitching, custom; chenilles; tufted textile; uniforms

(G-16377)
GAGE RITE PRODUCTS INC
356 Executive Dr (48083-4532)
PHONE.................................248 588-7796
Art Jadach, *President*
EMP: 12
SQ FT: 10,300
SALES (est): 2.2MM **Privately Held**
WEB: www.gagerite.com
SIC: 3545 Precision tools, machinists'

(G-16378)
GALLAGHER-KAISER CORPORATION (PA)
777 Chicago Rd Ste 1 (48083-4234)
PHONE.................................313 368-3100
Robert S Kaiser, *CEO*
Tracy E Roberts, *COO*
Kenneth M Krause, *CFO*
Mary Herbert, *Controller*
◆ **EMP:** 75 **EST:** 1952
SQ FT: 100,000
SALES (est): 54MM **Privately Held**
WEB: www.gkcorp.com
SIC: 3444 1761 3567 3564 Booths, spray; prefabricated sheet metal; sheet metalwork; paint baking & drying ovens; air purification equipment; dust or fume collecting equipment, industrial

(G-16379)
GARDNER SIGNS INC
1087 Naughton Dr (48083-1911)
PHONE.................................248 689-9100
Scott Gardner, *Manager*
EMP: 10
SALES (corp-wide): 3.7MM **Privately Held**
WEB: www.gardnersigns.com
SIC: 3993 Electric signs; neon signs
PA: Gardner Signs, Inc.
3800 Airport Hwy
Toledo OH 43615
419 385-6669

(G-16380)
GAZETTE NEWSPAPERS INC
Also Called: Troy Somerset Gazette
6966 Crooks Rd Ste 22 (48098-1798)
P.O. Box 482 (48099-0482)
PHONE.................................248 524-4868
Claire Weber, *President*
Cynthia K Mett, *Editor*
EMP: 6
SQ FT: 1,800
SALES: 750K **Privately Held**
WEB: www.troy-somersetgazette.com
SIC: 2711 2791 Newspapers: publishing only, not printed on site; typesetting

(G-16381)
GENERAL BROACH & ENGRG INC
5750 New King Dr Ste 200 (48098-2611)
PHONE.................................586 726-4300
Stefan Wandzyk, *President*
Sharon Van Doren, *Production*
EMP: 34
SQ FT: 62,640
SALES (est): 4.4MM
SALES (corp-wide): 565.7MM **Privately Held**
SIC: 3541 3545 3599 Broaching machines; broaches (machine tool accessories); machine shop, jobbing & repair
PA: Utica Enterprises, Inc.
5750 New King Dr Ste 200
Troy MI 48098
586 726-4300

(G-16382)
GESTAMP NORTH AMERICA INC (HQ)
2701 Troy Center Dr # 150 (48084-4753)
PHONE.................................248 743-3400
Jeffrey Wilson, *President*
Guillermo Alvarez, *General Mgr*
Kevin Stobbs, *General Mgr*
John Craig, *Vice Pres*
Aritz Iturbe, *Vice Pres*
▲ **EMP:** 188
SALES (est): 953.1MM
SALES (corp-wide): 120.9MM **Privately Held**
SIC: 3714 Motor vehicle parts & accessories
PA: Acek Desarrollo Y Gestion Industrial Sl.
Calle Alfonso Xii 16
Madrid 28014
913 791-999

(G-16383)
GETRAG TRANSMISSIONS CORP
1235 E Big Beaver Rd (48083-1905)
PHONE.................................586 620-1300
Mihir Kotecha, *CEO*
Tobias Hagenmeyer, *President*
John McDonald, *COO*
Kumar Jesudas, *Buyer*
Nikolaus Andriaschko, *Engineer*
EMP: 129
SALES (est): 21.7MM
SALES (corp-wide): 2.6MM **Privately Held**
SIC: 3714 Gears, motor vehicle
PA: Thi Holdings Gmbh
Eberhardstr. 65
Stuttgart 70173
711 230-8680

(G-16384)
GHSP INC
Also Called: Electronics Tech Center
560 Kirts Blvd Ste 111 (48084-4141)
PHONE.................................248 581-0890
Kathi Lewis, *COO*
EMP: 75
SALES (corp-wide): 550.2MM **Privately Held**
SIC: 3714 Motor vehicle parts & accessories
HQ: Ghsp, Inc.
1250 S Beechtree St
Grand Haven MI 49417
616 842-5500

(G-16385)
GOODPACK
2820 W Maple Rd Ste 128 (48084-7047)
PHONE.................................248 458-0041
EMP: 4
SALES (est): 270K **Privately Held**
SIC: 2655 Mfg Fiber Cans/Drums

(G-16386)
GRAPHIC RESOURCE GROUP INC
Also Called: Grg
528 Robbins Dr (48083-4514)
PHONE.................................248 588-6100
Deborah Pyc, *CEO*
Chester Allen Pyc, *President*
Lynn Caron, *Vice Pres*
Chad Dewey, *Accounts Mgr*
Shane Collom, *Accounts Exec*
▲ **EMP:** 21
SQ FT: 11,500
SALES: 8.7MM **Privately Held**
WEB: www.graphicresource.com
SIC: 7336 7312 3577 5199 Graphic arts & related design; outdoor advertising services; poster advertising, outdoor; graphic displays, except graphic terminals; gifts & novelties; advertising specialties; marketing consulting services

(G-16387)
GREG LINSKA SALES INC
2987 Hill Dr (48085-3715)
PHONE.................................248 765-6354
Greg Linska, *President*
EMP: 2
SQ FT: 1,250
SALES: 1.6MM **Privately Held**
WEB: www.greglinskasales.com
SIC: 3089 Identification cards, plastic

(G-16388)
HA AUTOMOTIVE SYSTEMS INC (PA)
1300 Coolidge Hwy (48084-7018)
PHONE.................................248 781-0001
William Chen, *President*
EMP: 15
SALES (est): 2.5MM **Privately Held**
SIC: 3647 Motor vehicle lighting equipment

(G-16389)
HALLOWEEN EVENTS
Also Called: Fear Finder, The
36393 Dequindre Rd (48083-2480)
PHONE.................................248 332-7884
Edward Terebus, *President*
Jacqueline Terebus, *Vice Pres*
EMP: 3
SALES (est): 320K **Privately Held**
SIC: 2721 Magazines: publishing & printing

(G-16390)
HALTERMANN CARLESS US INC
901 Wilshire Dr Ste 570 (48084-1665)
PHONE.................................248 422-6548
Daniel Haamann, *Principal*
EMP: 3
SALES (est): 81.8K **Privately Held**
SIC: 2899 Chemical preparations
HQ: Haltermann Carless Deutschland Gmbh
Schlengendeich 17
Hamburg 21107
403 331-80

(G-16391)
HANHO AMERICA CO LTD
Also Called: Hha
100 E Big Beaver Rd # 845 (48083-1204)
PHONE.................................248 422-6921
Hyun Dong Lee, *Administration*
EMP: 7
SALES (est): 795.7K **Privately Held**
SIC: 3714 Motor vehicle parts & accessories
PA: Hanho Industrial Co.,Ltd.
148-32 Guil-Gil, Naenam-Myeon
Gyeongju 38195

(G-16392)
HBPO NORTH AMERICA INC
Also Called: Mahale
700 Tower Dr (48098-2808)
PHONE.................................248 823-7076
Tibor Wesseling, *President*
Diana Mannino, *President*
Eric Leroy, *Engineer*
Marty Thibert, *Manager*
Christian Krasenbrink, *Director*
EMP: 125 **EST:** 1999
SALES (est): 26.2MM
SALES (corp-wide): 10.4MM **Privately Held**
SIC: 3465 8711 Body parts, automobile: stamped metal; engineering services
HQ: Hbpo Gmbh
Rixbecker Str. 111
Lippstadt 59557
294 128-380

(G-16393)
HEAD OVER HEELS
164 E Maple Rd Ste G (48083-2700)
PHONE.................................248 435-2954
Sarah Hyland, *Owner*
EMP: 3
SALES (est): 187.7K **Privately Held**
SIC: 3999 Hair curlers, designed for beauty parlors

(G-16394)
HELLER INC
1225 Equity Dr (48084-7107)
PHONE.................................248 288-5000
Rolf Klenk, *President*
Karen Muchitsch, *Principal*
Hans Geiblinger, *Engineer*
Vince Gunkel, *Engineer*
Xu Weiyang, *Engineer*
EMP: 50
SQ FT: 32,000
SALES (est): 6.6MM **Privately Held**
WEB: www.heller.us
SIC: 3541 Machine tools, metal cutting type

(G-16395)
HEXAGON ENTERPRISES INC
256 Minnesota Dr (48083-4667)
P.O. Box 1320 (48099-1320)
PHONE.................................248 583-0550
Lou Cudin, *President*
Patrick O Berry, *Vice Pres*
EMP: 20
SQ FT: 8,000
SALES (est): 2.7MM **Privately Held**
SIC: 3452 5085 Nuts, metal; fasteners, industrial: nuts, bolts, screws, etc.

(G-16396)
HHJ HOLDINGS LIMITED (PA)
1957 Crooks Rd A (48084-5504)
PHONE.................................248 652-9716
James Friel, *Controller*
Rodney Cyrowski,
EMP: 10
SQ FT: 10,000
SALES (est): 308MM **Privately Held**
SIC: 1611 2951 Highway & street paving contractor; asphalt & asphaltic paving mixtures (not from refineries)

(G-16397)
HMS MFG CO (PA)
1230 E Big Beaver Rd (48083-1904)
PHONE.................................248 689-3232
Janet Sofy, *President*
Brian Wood, *General Mgr*
David Sofy, *Corp Secy*
Nancy Negohosian, *Vice Pres*
Matt Norton, *Engineer*
▲ **EMP:** 70
SQ FT: 6,000
SALES: 75MM **Privately Held**
WEB: www.hmsmfg.com
SIC: 3089 Injection molded finished plastic products

(G-16398)
HMS PRODUCTS CO
1200 E Big Beaver Rd (48083-1982)
PHONE.................................248 689-8120
David Sofy, *President*
David A Sofy, *Vice Pres*
Michael Vandaele, *General Mgr*
Chris Lawson, *District Mgr*
Nancy A Negohosian, *Vice Pres*
▲ **EMP:** 80
SQ FT: 39,000
SALES (est): 20MM **Privately Held**
WEB: www.hmsproducts.com
SIC: 3535 3549 3542 Conveyors & conveying equipment; metalworking machinery; machine tools, metal forming type

(G-16399)
HONHART MID-NITE BLACK CO
501 Stephenson Hwy (48083-1134)
PHONE.................................248 588-1515
Betty Honhart, *President*
Keith Honhart, *Vice Pres*
John Honhart, *Treasurer*
EMP: 20
SQ FT: 8,000
SALES (est): 1.8MM **Privately Held**
SIC: 3471 6512 Plating of metals or formed products; commercial & industrial building operation

(G-16400)
HORIBA INSTRUMENTS INC
2890 John R Rd (48083-2353)
PHONE.................................248 689-9000
Ken Mitira, *Office Mgr*
EMP: 93 **Privately Held**

GEOGRAPHIC SECTION
Troy - Oakland County (G-16425)

SIC: 3823 Industrial process measurement equipment; analyzers, industrial process type; controllers for process variables, all types
HQ: Horiba Instruments Incorporated
9755 Research Dr
Irvine CA 92618
949 250-4811

(G-16401)
HORIZON GLOBAL CORPORATION (PA)
2600 W Big Beaver Rd # 555 (48084-3337)
PHONE.................................248 593-8820
Terrence G Gohl, *CEO*
Meghan Joki, *Business Mgr*
Paddy Enright, *Vice Pres*
Jamie G Pierson, *CFO*
Brian Whittman, *VP Finance*
EMP: 110
SALES: 849.9MM **Publicly Held**
SIC: 3714 3711 5531 Trailer hitches, motor vehicle; motor vehicle electrical equipment; wreckers (tow truck), assembly of; automobile & truck equipment & parts

(G-16402)
HORN CORPORATION
Also Called: Eclipse Tanning
1263 Rochester Rd (48083-2879)
PHONE.................................248 583-7789
Matthew Horn, *President*
Jamie Horn, *Vice Pres*
EMP: 26
SQ FT: 5,200
SALES (est): 1.6MM **Privately Held**
SIC: 2752 5943 Commercial printing, lithographic; stationery stores

(G-16403)
HOUR MEDIA LLC (PA)
Also Called: Hour Detroit Magazine
5750 New King Dr Ste 100 (48098-2696)
PHONE.................................248 691-1800
David Christensen, *Partner*
Ed Peabody, *General Mgr*
Mike Muszall, *Vice Pres*
Jon Reynolds, *Prdtn Dir*
Sofia Pinkhasova, *Research*
EMP: 50
SQ FT: 4,000
SALES (est): 27MM **Privately Held**
SIC: 2721 Magazines: publishing only, not printed on site

(G-16404)
HP INC
560 Kirts Blvd Ste 120 (48084-4141)
PHONE.................................248 614-6600
Adam T Schwerin, *Principal*
EMP: 7
SALES (corp-wide): 58.4B **Publicly Held**
SIC: 3571 Personal computers (microcomputers)
PA: Hp, Inc.
1501 Page Mill Rd
Palo Alto CA 94304
650 857-1501

(G-16405)
HP PELZER AUTO SYSTEMS INC (DH)
Also Called: Adler Pelzer Group
1175 Crooks Rd (48084-7136)
PHONE.................................248 280-1010
John Pendleton, *CEO*
Stuart McRobbie, *COO*
Nick Fennewald, *Prdtn Mgr*
Lori Post, *Materials Mgr*
Alejandro Chavez Martinez, *Research*
▲ **EMP:** 45
SALES (est): 338MM
SALES (corp-wide): 74.8MM **Privately Held**
SIC: 3061 2273 Automotive rubber goods (mechanical); carpets & rugs
HQ: Adler Pelzer Holding Gmbh
Kabeler Str. 4
Hagen 58099
230 266-8159

(G-16406)
HSP EPI ACQUISITION LLC (PA)
Also Called: Entertainment
1401 Crooks Rd Ste 150 (48084-7106)
PHONE.................................248 404-1520
Lowell Potiker, *Mng Member*
EMP: 62
SQ FT: 81,000
SALES (est): 173.1MM **Privately Held**
SIC: 2731 Books: publishing only

(G-16407)
HYPERTEK CORPORATION
575 E Big Beaver Rd # 170 (48083-1361)
P.O. Box 4327 (48099-4327)
PHONE.................................248 619-0395
Louis Sarna, *President*
Geoffrey Sarna, *Vice Pres*
EMP: 3
SALES (est): 307.2K **Privately Held**
WEB: www.hypertek.net
SIC: 7372 7374 Application computer software; computer graphics service

(G-16408)
I-9 ADVANTAGE
101 W Big Beaver Rd 14 (48084-5253)
PHONE.................................800 724-8546
Dawn Hurd, *Opers Staff*
EMP: 4
SALES (est): 313.2K **Privately Held**
SIC: 7372 Prepackaged software

(G-16409)
IKEA CHIP LLC
2609 Crooks Rd Ste 235 (48084-4714)
PHONE.................................877 218-9931
Hao Ivy, *Mng Member*
EMP: 9
SALES (est): 617.3K **Privately Held**
SIC: 4213 1542 8748 2426 Automobiles, transport & delivery; custom builders, non-residential; business consulting; carvings, furniture: wood

(G-16410)
ILLINOIS TOOL WORKS INC
ITW Global Automotive
2002 Stephenson Hwy (48083-2151)
PHONE.................................248 589-2500
Sandra Bielewski, *General Mgr*
Steven Bonnell, *Principal*
Mike Omastiak, *Plant Mgr*
Tyler Terrell, *Project Mgr*
Rita Worsham, *Opers Mgr*
EMP: 100
SALES (corp-wide): 14.7B **Publicly Held**
SIC: 3089 5013 3043 3711 Automotive parts, plastic; automotive engines & engine parts; dies & die holders for metal cutting, forming, die casting; dies, plastics forming; automobile assembly, including specialty automobiles; automotive stampings; tapping machines
PA: Illinois Tool Works Inc.
155 Harlem Ave
Glenview IL 60025
847 724-7500

(G-16411)
ILUMISYS INC
Also Called: Toggled
164 Indusco Ct (48083-4641)
PHONE.................................844 864-4533
Dave Simon, *President*
▲ **EMP:** 4
SALES (est): 924.1K
SALES (corp-wide): 396.3MM **Publicly Held**
SIC: 3641 Electric lamps
PA: Altair Engineering Inc.
1820 E Big Beaver Rd
Troy MI 48083
248 614-2400

(G-16412)
IMPERIAL ENGINEERING INC
1173 Combermere Dr (48083-2701)
PHONE.................................248 588-2022
Norbert Kubicki, *President*
Joyce Kubicki, *Corp Secy*
EMP: 3 **EST:** 1972
SQ FT: 7,000
SALES (est): 356.9K **Privately Held**
SIC: 3544 Special dies & tools

(G-16413)
IMPRESSION CENTER CO
224 Minnesota Dr (48083-4667)
PHONE.................................248 989-8080
Daniel Goehmann, *President*
Jenifer Goehmann, *Admin Sec*
EMP: 4
SQ FT: 2,000
SALES: 200K **Privately Held**
SIC: 2759 Imprinting; screen printing

(G-16414)
INDEPNDNCE TLING SOLUTIONS LLC
1200 Rochester Rd (48083-2833)
PHONE.................................586 274-2300
Tony Parete, *General Mgr*
Beth McReynolds, *Vice Pres*
Lloyd Brown, *Mng Member*
EMP: 23
SQ FT: 16,400
SALES (est): 1.7MM **Privately Held**
SIC: 3545 Tools & accessories for machine tools
PA: Waltonen Engineering, Inc.
31330 Mound Rd
Warren MI 48092

(G-16415)
INDIANA NEWSPAPERS LLC
Also Called: Gannett National Newspaper Sls
340 E Big Beaver Rd Ste 1 (48083-1218)
PHONE.................................248 680-9905
Jim Chauvin, *Branch Mgr*
James P Chauvin, *Branch Mgr*
EMP: 35
SALES (corp-wide): 2.9B **Publicly Held**
SIC: 2711 Newspapers, publishing & printing
HQ: Indiana Newspapers Llc
130 S Meridian St
Indianapolis IN 46225
317 444-4000

(G-16416)
INDRATECH LLC (PA)
1212 E Maple Rd (48083-2817)
PHONE.................................248 377-1877
Surendre Khambete,
EMP: 70
SALES (est): 17.5MM **Privately Held**
WEB: www.indratech-us.com
SIC: 2515 Mattresses & foundations

(G-16417)
INFORMATION BUILDERS INC
Also Called: I Way Software
1301 W Long Lake Rd # 150 (48098-6336)
PHONE.................................248 641-8820
Sharon Kohler, *Opers Mgr*
Joseph Beaubien, *Engineer*
Dan Burnette, *Engineer*
Robert Szczerba, *Engineer*
Bill Dykema, *Senior Engr*
EMP: 40
SALES (corp-wide): 258.7MM **Privately Held**
WEB: www.informationbuilders.com
SIC: 7372 Prepackaged software
PA: Information Builders, Inc.
2 Penn Plz Fl 28
New York NY 10121
212 736-4433

(G-16418)
INNOVATIVE SUPPORT SVCS INC
Also Called: ISS
1270 Souter Dr (48083-2837)
PHONE.................................248 585-3600
William Herndon, *President*
EMP: 25
SQ FT: 3,500
SALES (est): 1.8MM **Privately Held**
WEB: www.isscnc.com
SIC: 7629 3625 3823 3577 Electronic equipment repair; motor controls & accessories; industrial instrmnts msrmnt display/control process variable; computer peripheral equipment

(G-16419)
INOAC USA INC (PA)
1515 Equity Dr Ste 200 (48084-7129)
PHONE.................................248 619-7031
Toyohiko Okina, *CEO*
Charles Little, *President*
Carl D Malz, *President*
Soichi Inoue, *Chairman*
Del Felter, *Vice Pres*
▲ **EMP:** 31
SALES (est): 342.6MM **Privately Held**
SIC: 3085 3714 Plastics bottles; motor vehicle parts & accessories

(G-16420)
INTELLITECH SYSTEMS INC
303 Evaline Dr (48085-5510)
PHONE.................................586 219-3737
Chadi Shaya, *President*
EMP: 6
SALES: 450K **Privately Held**
SIC: 7929 3651 Entertainment service; home entertainment equipment, electronic

(G-16421)
INTERNTONAL INNOVATIVE SYSTEMS
Also Called: Christian Pages
36551 Dequindre Rd (48083-2481)
P.O. Box 817 (48099-0817)
PHONE.................................248 524-2222
Robert A Hover, *President*
Peter Hover, *Treasurer*
EMP: 3
SALES (est): 244.8K **Privately Held**
WEB: www.christianpages.com
SIC: 2759 7311 5063 5191 Advertising literature: printing; advertising agencies; electrical apparatus & equipment; garden supplies

(G-16422)
INTEVA PRODUCTS LLC
Also Called: Scheduling
1401 Crooks Rd (48084-7106)
PHONE.................................248 655-8886
Martin Nunnold, *General Mgr*
Renee Haley, *Project Mgr*
EMP: 10
SALES (corp-wide): 4.1B **Privately Held**
SIC: 3714 Motor vehicle parts & accessories
HQ: Inteva Products, Llc
1401 Crooks Rd
Troy MI 48084

(G-16423)
INTEVA PRODUCTS LLC
Also Called: Inteva - Troy Engineering Ctr
2305 Crooks Rd (48084)
PHONE.................................248 655-8886
Joe Long, *Branch Mgr*
EMP: 14
SALES (corp-wide): 4.1B **Privately Held**
SIC: 3714 Motor vehicle parts & accessories
HQ: Inteva Products, Llc
1401 Crooks Rd
Troy MI 48084

(G-16424)
INTEVA PRODUCTS LLC (HQ)
1401 Crooks Rd (48084-7106)
PHONE.................................248 655-8886
Lon Offenbacher, *President*
Robert Baker, *General Mgr*
Carolyn Bohlken, *Regional Mgr*
Deroy Bryant, *Vice Pres*
Steven Galle, *Vice Pres*
◆ **EMP:** 400
SQ FT: 200,000
SALES (est): 3.8B
SALES (corp-wide): 4.1B **Privately Held**
WEB: www.intevaproducts.com
SIC: 3714 5085 Motor vehicle parts & accessories; industrial supplies
PA: The Renco Group Inc
1 Rockefeller Plz Fl 29
New York NY 10020
212 541-6000

(G-16425)
INTEVA PRODUCTS USA LLC
1401 Crooks Rd (48084-7106)
PHONE.................................248 655-8886
Lon Offenbacher, *President*
William Dircks, *Exec VP*
Steven Galle, *Vice Pres*
Jan Griffiths, *Vice Pres*

Thomas Munley, *Vice Pres*
EMP: 4 **EST:** 2010
SALES (est): 176.4K
SALES (corp-wide): 4.1B **Privately Held**
SIC: 3714 Motor vehicle parts & accessories
HQ: Inteva Products, Llc
1401 Crooks Rd
Troy MI 48084

(G-16426)
INTUITIVE CIRCUITS LLC
3928 Wardlow Ct (48083-6808)
PHONE..................................248 588-4400
Chris Oesterling,
EMP: 3
SALES: 400K **Privately Held**
SIC: 3679 Electronic circuits

(G-16427)
IWIS ENGINE SYSTEMS LP
340 E Big Beaver Rd # 155 (48083-1269)
PHONE..................................248 247-3178
Johannes Winklhoser, *Mng Member*
Scott E Tarter,
▲ **EMP:** 5
SALES (est): 723.4K
SALES (corp-wide): 426.2MM **Privately Held**
SIC: 3462 Automotive forgings, ferrous: crankshaft, engine, axle, etc.
PA: Joh. Winklhofer Beteiligungs Gmbh & Co. Kg
Albert-RoBhaupter-Str. 53
Munchen 81369
897 690-90

(G-16428)
J & M INTERNATIONAL CORP
1200 Rochester Rd (48083-2833)
PHONE..................................248 588-8108
EMP: 3
SALES (est): 200K **Privately Held**
SIC: 7389 2791 Business Services Typesetting Services

(G-16429)
J & M REPRODUCTIONS CORP
1200 Rochester Rd (48083-2833)
P.O. Box 2065, Howell (48844-2065)
PHONE..................................248 588-8100
John Milanowski, *President*
▼ **EMP:** 40
SQ FT: 35,000
SALES (est): 6.4MM **Privately Held**
WEB: www.jmrepro.com
SIC: 2752 7334 Commercial printing, offset; photocopying & duplicating services; blueprinting service

(G-16430)
J E MYLES INC (PA)
Also Called: Myles Group
310 Executive Dr (48083-4587)
PHONE..................................248 583-1020
J Edgar Myles, *President*
J Scott Myles, *Vice Pres*
EMP: 23 **EST:** 1957
SQ FT: 24,700
SALES (est): 8.4MM **Privately Held**
WEB: www.jemyles.com
SIC: 5085 8734 3829 Pistons & valves; valves & fittings; filters, industrial; power transmission equipment & apparatus; product testing laboratory, safety or performance; measuring & controlling devices

(G-16431)
J2 LICENSING INC (PA)
351 Executive Dr (48083-4533)
PHONE..................................586 307-3400
John P Debay, *President*
▲ **EMP:** 3
SQ FT: 4,500
SALES (est): 1.7MM **Privately Held**
SIC: 2759 2396 2395 Letterpress & screen printing; automotive & apparel trimmings; pleating & stitching

(G-16432)
JASLIN ASSEMBLY INC
4537 Harold Dr (48085-5703)
PHONE..................................248 528-3024
EMP: 6

SALES (est): 473.9K **Privately Held**
SIC: 3496 Electronic Cable Assembly

(G-16433)
JAY/ENN CORPORATION
Also Called: Jay Enn
33943 Dequindre Rd (48083-4632)
PHONE..................................248 588-2393
Burton J Kirsten, *President*
Nathan Jakey, *Corp Secy*
Jeffrey Baroli, *Vice Pres*
Heather Lang, *Office Mgr*
EMP: 65 **EST:** 1970
SQ FT: 38,000
SALES (est): 15.1MM **Privately Held**
WEB: www.jayenn.com
SIC: 3543 3823 8711 3544 Industrial patterns; industrial instrmnts msrmnt display/control process variable; designing: ship, boat, machine & product; special dies, tools, jigs & fixtures

(G-16434)
JB PRODUCTS INC
143 Indusco Ct (48083-4644)
PHONE..................................248 549-1900
Larry Brown, *President*
▲ **EMP:** 8
SQ FT: 14,500
SALES (est): 1.4MM **Privately Held**
WEB: www.jbproductsinc.com
SIC: 2821 Plastics materials & resins

(G-16435)
JBS TRANSPORT LLC
1834 Kirkton Dr (48083-1725)
PHONE..................................248 636-5546
Donna Jones, *CEO*
EMP: 3 **EST:** 2016
SALES (est): 125.5K **Privately Held**
SIC: 3715 Truck trailers

(G-16436)
JEMMS-CASCADE INC
238 Executive Dr (48083-4530)
PHONE..................................248 526-8100
Donald E Galat, *President*
EMP: 11
SQ FT: 5,000
SALES (est): 1.5MM **Privately Held**
WEB: www.jemms-cascade.com
SIC: 3546 Power-driven handtools

(G-16437)
JET BOX CO INC
1822 Thunderbird (48084-5479)
PHONE..................................248 362-1260
Lynda K Zardus, *Ch of Bd*
Kathryn L Woch, *President*
Robert Louis Zardus, *Vice Pres*
EMP: 18
SQ FT: 23,000
SALES (est): 4.9MM **Privately Held**
SIC: 2653 Boxes, corrugated: made from purchased materials

(G-16438)
JL GEISLER SIGN COMPANY
1017 Naughton Dr (48083-1911)
PHONE..................................586 574-1800
Jane Geisler, *President*
Gary Geisler, *Vice Pres*
Tammy Kelly, *Vice Pres*
Corinne Skawski, *Office Mgr*
EMP: 13 **EST:** 1966
SQ FT: 8,000
SALES: 1.4MM **Privately Held**
WEB: www.jlgeisler.com
SIC: 3993 3953 5112 Signs, not made in custom sign painting shops; marking devices; office supplies

(G-16439)
JO-MAR INDUSTRIES INC
2876 Elliott Dr (48083-4635)
PHONE..................................248 588-9625
Richard J Roth, *President*
▼ **EMP:** 16
SQ FT: 12,400
SALES (est): 987.6K **Privately Held**
SIC: 3544 Special dies & tools

(G-16440)
JOMESA NORTH AMERICA INC
2095 E Big Beaver Rd (48083-2356)
PHONE..................................248 457-0023

Polly Hongisto, *Principal*
EMP: 5 **EST:** 2013
SALES (est): 623.8K **Privately Held**
SIC: 3569 Filters, general line: industrial

(G-16441)
JUST GIRLS LLC
Also Called: Justgirls Boutique
6907 Orchard Lake Rd (48098)
PHONE..................................248 952-1967
Jill Oleski, *Mng Member*
EMP: 6 **EST:** 2010
SALES (est): 787.1K **Privately Held**
SIC: 2369 Children's culottes & shorts; coat & legging sets: girls' & children's; pantsuits: girls', children's & infants'

(G-16442)
K-VALUE INSULATION LLC
4956 Butler Dr (48083-3526)
P.O. Box 4481 (48099-4481)
PHONE..................................248 688-5816
Anthony Noel,
EMP: 4
SALES (est): 509.6K **Privately Held**
SIC: 3292 Pipe covering (heat insulating material), except felt

(G-16443)
KARJO TRUCKING INC
1890 E Maple Rd (48083-4240)
PHONE..................................248 597-3700
Mike Karjo, *President*
▲ **EMP:** 10
SALES (est): 1.1MM **Privately Held**
SIC: 2448 Cargo containers, wood & metal combination

(G-16444)
KAUTEX INC (HQ)
750 Stephenson Hwy # 200 (48083-1103)
PHONE..................................248 616-5100
Vicente Perez-Lucerga, *President*
Hanno Neizer, *COO*
Klaus Konig, *Exec VP*
John H Bracken, *Vice Pres*
Mira Eigler, *Vice Pres*
▲ **EMP:** 900
SALES (est): 3.6B
SALES (corp-wide): 13.9B **Publicly Held**
WEB: www.textronautotrim.com
SIC: 3714 Instrument board assemblies, motor vehicle
PA: Textron Inc.
40 Westminster St
Providence RI 02903
401 421-2800

(G-16445)
KEIPER LLC
2600 Bellingham Dr # 100 (48083-2014)
PHONE..................................248 655-5100
Andrew Ason, *CEO*
Joe Peters,
▲ **EMP:** 200
SALES (est): 16.4MM **Privately Held**
WEB: www.keiper.net
SIC: 3089 Automotive parts, plastic
PA: Adient Public Limited Company
25-28 North Wall Quay
Dublin

(G-16446)
KIRCHHOFF AUTOMOTIVE USA INC
2600 Bellingham Dr # 400 (48083-2014)
PHONE..................................248 247-3740
Josh Forquer, *Vice Pres*
EMP: 10
SALES (est): 34.1K
SALES (corp-wide): 1.8B **Privately Held**
SIC: 7538 3465 General automotive repair shops; body parts, automobile: stamped metal
PA: Kirchhoff Automotive Holding Gmbh & Co.Kg
Stefanstr. 2
Iserlohn 58638
237 182-000

(G-16447)
KM AND I
3155 W Big Beaver Rd # 111 (48084-3006)
PHONE..................................248 792-2782
William Cantwell, *President*
EMP: 5

SALES (est): 310K **Privately Held**
SIC: 3089 Plastic processing

(G-16448)
KORCAST PRODUCTS INCORPORATED (PA)
Also Called: Kor-Cast Products
1725 Larchwood Dr (48083-2224)
PHONE..................................248 740-2340
Larry Bremner, *President*
EMP: 4
SQ FT: 4,500
SALES (est): 1.3MM **Privately Held**
WEB: www.moderncountertop.com
SIC: 2541 1799 Cabinets, except refrigerated: show, display, etc.: wood; counters or counter display cases, wood; counter top installation

(G-16449)
KORCAST PRODUCTS INCORPORATED
Also Called: Modern Kitchen & Bath
1725 Larchwood Dr (48083-2224)
PHONE..................................248 740-2340
Larry Bremner, *Branch Mgr*
EMP: 9
SALES (corp-wide): 1.3MM **Privately Held**
WEB: www.moderncountertop.com
SIC: 2541 1799 3281 Cabinets, except refrigerated: show, display, etc.: wood; counters or counter display cases, wood; kitchen & bathroom remodeling; cut stone & stone products
PA: Korcast Products Incorporated
1725 Larchwood Dr
Troy MI 48083
248 740-2340

(G-16450)
KOSTAL OF AMERICA INC
Also Called: Kostal North America
350 Stephenson Hwy (48083-1119)
PHONE..................................248 284-6500
Andreas Kostal, *Chairman*
Brendan Walsh, *Mfg Staff*
Petra Frey, *Purch Mgr*
Tim Oconnor, *Purch Mgr*
Juan Serrano, *Purch Mgr*
▲ **EMP:** 170 **EST:** 1987
SQ FT: 78,000
SALES (est): 37.5MM
SALES (corp-wide): 889.5K **Privately Held**
SIC: 7389 3714 3643 3613 Design, commercial & industrial; motor vehicle parts & accessories; current-carrying wiring devices; switchgear & switchboard apparatus
PA: Kostal Beteiligungsges. Mbh
Wiesenstr. 47
Ludenscheid 58507
235 116-0

(G-16451)
KRAMER INTERNATIONAL INC
5750 New King Dr Ste 200 (48098-2611)
PHONE..................................586 726-4300
Paul Rhodes, *Vice Pres*
EMP: 9
SALES (est): 994.1K **Privately Held**
SIC: 3322 Malleable iron foundries

(G-16452)
KUNSTSTOFF TECHNIK SCHERER
3150 Livernois Rd Ste 275 (48083-5034)
PHONE..................................734 944-5080
Tom Kozyra, *President*
▲ **EMP:** 55
SQ FT: 75,000
SALES (est): 13.5MM **Privately Held**
SIC: 3089 Plastic processing

(G-16453)
L PERRIGO COMPANY
101 W Big Beaver Rd (48084-5253)
PHONE..................................248 687-1036
EMP: 78 **Privately Held**
SIC: 2834 Analgesics
HQ: L Perrigo Company
515 Eastern Ave
Allegan MI 49010
269 673-8451

(G-16454)
L S MACHINING INC
1250 Rankin Dr Ste E (48083-2844)
PHONE..................................248 583-7277
Lyle A Stuemke, *President*
Guyann Stuemke, *Vice Pres*
EMP: 5 **EST:** 1978
SQ FT: 4,800
SALES (est): 480K **Privately Held**
SIC: 3599 3544 Machine shop, jobbing & repair; special dies, tools, jigs & fixtures

(G-16455)
LA FORCE INC
289 Robbins Dr (48083-4513)
PHONE..................................248 588-5601
Kevin Letto, *Branch Mgr*
EMP: 9
SALES (corp-wide): 156.3MM **Privately Held**
WEB: www.laforceinc.com
SIC: 5031 5072 3442 Lumber, plywood & millwork; hardware; metal doors, sash & trim
PA: La Force, Inc.
1060 W Mason St
Green Bay WI 54303
920 497-7100

(G-16456)
LAMACS INC
360 E Maple Rd Ste I (48083-2707)
PHONE..................................248 643-9210
William L Haines Jr, *President*
Peggy Donnelly, *Vice Pres*
EMP: 4
SALES: 600K **Privately Held**
SIC: 2399 5136 Emblems, badges & insignia: from purchased materials; uniforms, men's & boys'

(G-16457)
LANE TOOL AND MFG CORP
1830 Brinston Dr (48083-2215)
PHONE..................................248 528-1606
Kevin Harper, *President*
Chris Harper, *Treasurer*
Michael Harper, *Manager*
Scott Harper, *Admin Sec*
EMP: 9
SQ FT: 6,000
SALES (est): 1.4MM **Privately Held**
WEB: www.lanetool.net
SIC: 3544 Jigs & fixtures; dies, steel rule

(G-16458)
LAVALIER CORP
Also Called: Tape Master
900 Rochester Rd (48083-6009)
PHONE..................................248 616-8880
EMP: 30 **EST:** 1976
SQ FT: 29,000
SALES (est): 6.6MM **Privately Held**
SIC: 3545 3544 Machine tool accessories; special dies, tools, jigs & fixtures

(G-16459)
LAWRENCE SURFACE TECH INC
1895 Crooks Rd (48084-5382)
PHONE..................................248 609-9001
Bret Evans, *President*
Byron Beattie, *Personnel*
EMP: 2 **EST:** 2012
SQ FT: 2,500
SALES: 15MM
SALES (corp-wide): 31.5MM **Privately Held**
SIC: 3471 Decorative plating & finishing of formed products
PA: Ningbo Huaxiang Import & Export Co., Ltd.
Zhen'an Road, Xizhou Town, Xiangshan County
Ningbo 31501
574 874-9303

(G-16460)
LEGENDARY MILLWORK INC
2655 Elliott Dr (48083-4637)
PHONE..................................248 588-5663
Doug Massey, *President*
Matthew Snarski, *Vice Pres*
EMP: 4
SQ FT: 10,000
SALES: 2MM **Privately Held**
WEB: www.legendarymillwork.net
SIC: 2431 Millwork

(G-16461)
LG CHEM MICHIGAN INC
3221 W Big Beaver Rd (48084-2803)
PHONE..................................248 291-2385
EMP: 3 **Privately Held**
SIC: 3691 Storage batteries
HQ: Lg Chem Michigan Inc.
1 Lg Way
Holland MI 49423
616 494-7100

(G-16462)
LG CHEM MICHIGAN INC
Also Called: Lg Chem Michigan Inc Tech Ctr
1857 Technology Dr (48083-4244)
PHONE..................................248 307-1800
Denise Gray, *Branch Mgr*
EMP: 4 **Privately Held**
SIC: 3691 Storage batteries
HQ: Lg Chem Michigan Inc.
1 Lg Way
Holland MI 49423
616 494-7100

(G-16463)
LG ELECTRONICS USA INC
1835 Technology Dr (48083-4244)
PHONE..................................248 268-5100
Joshua Harvey, *Transportation*
Brian Bogdan, *Engineer*
Michael Goldfarb, *Sales Staff*
Renaud Smith, *Sales Staff*
Sarah Cho, *Manager*
EMP: 140 **Privately Held**
SIC: 3651 5064 Household audio & video equipment; electrical appliances, major
HQ: Lg Electronics U.S.A., Inc.
1000 Sylvan Ave
Englewood Cliffs NJ 07632
201 816-2000

(G-16464)
LG ELECTRONICS VEHICLE COMPONE
1835 Technology Dr Bldg E (48083-4244)
PHONE..................................248 268-5851
Kenneth Cheng, *President*
EMP: 190 **Privately Held**
SIC: 3694 Automotive electrical equipment
HQ: Lg Electronics Vehicle Components U.S.A., Llc
1400 E 10 Mile Rd Ste 100
Hazel Park MI 48030
248 268-5851

(G-16465)
LONERO ENGINEERING CO INC
2050 Stephenson Hwy (48083-2151)
P.O. Box 935 (48099-0935)
PHONE..................................248 689-9120
Vincent J Lonero, *President*
Tod F Lonero, *Vice Pres*
Shawn Luteran, *Engineer*
Scott Galer, *Senior Engr*
Phil Varvatos, *CFO*
EMP: 30 **EST:** 1951
SQ FT: 18,000
SALES (est): 5.5MM **Privately Held**
WEB: www.hegenscheidt.com
SIC: 3544 Jigs & fixtures; dies & die holders for metal cutting, forming, die casting

(G-16466)
LUMA LASER AND MEDI SPA
700 E Big Beaver Rd Ste C (48083-1435)
PHONE..................................248 817-5499
EMP: 3
SALES (est): 152.8K **Privately Held**
SIC: 3842 7231 8011 Cosmetic restorations; cosmetologist; plastic surgeon

(G-16467)
M & M SERVICES INC
1844 Woodslee Dr (48083-2207)
PHONE..................................248 619-9861
Marion J Kras, *President*
Pam Givens, *Officer*
EMP: 9
SQ FT: 7,000
SALES: 750K **Privately Held**
SIC: 3544 3599 Special dies & tools; machine & other job shop work

(G-16468)
MAC-TECH TOOLING CORPORATION
1874 Larchwood Dr (48083-2225)
PHONE..................................248 743-1400
William Macinnis, *President*
Curtis Macinnis, *President*
Amy McCaffrey, *Vice Pres*
EMP: 9
SQ FT: 5,500
SALES (est): 1.1MM **Privately Held**
SIC: 7699 3545 Tool repair services; cutting tools for machine tools

(G-16469)
MACAUTO USA INC
2654 Elliott Dr (48083-4633)
PHONE..................................248 556-5256
Wu Miller, *Branch Mgr*
EMP: 8 **Privately Held**
SIC: 3089 Automotive parts, plastic
HQ: Macauto Usa, Inc.
80 Excel Dr
Rochester NY 14621
585 342-2060

(G-16470)
MAGNA CAR TOP SYSTEMS AMER INC
1200 Chicago Rd (48083-4230)
PHONE..................................248 619-8133
Rich Machnik, *Branch Mgr*
EMP: 15
SALES (corp-wide): 40.8B **Privately Held**
SIC: 2394 Convertible tops, canvas or boat: from purchased materials
HQ: Magna Car Top Systems Of America, Inc.
2725 Commerce Pkwy
Auburn Hills MI 48326
248 836-4500

(G-16471)
MAGNA ELECTRONICS INC
1465 Combermere Dr (48083-2745)
PHONE..................................810 606-0444
Rajeev Joshi, *Branch Mgr*
EMP: 25
SALES (corp-wide): 40.8B **Privately Held**
SIC: 3699 Electrical equipment & supplies
HQ: Magna Electronics Inc.
2050 Auburn Rd
Auburn Hills MI 48326

(G-16472)
MAGNA EXTERIORS AMERICA INC (HQ)
Also Called: Decoma Admark
750 Tower Dr (48098-2863)
PHONE..................................248 631-1100
Donald J Walker, *CEO*
Guenther Apfalter, *President*
Grahame Burrow, *General Mgr*
Tom J Skudutis, *COO*
Marc Neeb, *Exec VP*
◆ **EMP:** 800
SALES (est): 942.2MM
SALES (corp-wide): 40.8B **Privately Held**
SIC: 3714 3544 8711 Motor vehicle body components & frame; forms (molds), for foundry & plastics working machinery; engineering services
PA: Magna International Inc
337 Magna Dr
Aurora ON L4G 7
905 726-2462

(G-16473)
MAGNA EXTRORS INTRORS AMER INC
750 Tower Dr (48098-2863)
PHONE..................................248 729-2400
Marc Neeb, *Exec VP*
Stephen Sloan, *Vice Pres*
Todd Curtis, *Materials Mgr*
Ken Besedich, *Engineer*
Scott Morris, *Engineer*
EMP: 185
SALES (corp-wide): 40.8B **Privately Held**
WEB: www.magnaint.com
SIC: 3714 Motor vehicle parts & accessories

HQ: Magna Exteriors Of America, Inc.
750 Tower Dr
Troy MI 48098
248 631-1100

(G-16474)
MAGNA INTERNATIONAL AMER INC (HQ)
750 Tower Dr 7000 (48098-2863)
PHONE..................................248 729-2400
Donald Walker, *President*
Marc Neeb, *President*
Vincent J Galifi, *Exec VP*
Swamy Kotagiri, *Exec VP*
Jeffrey O Palmer, *Exec VP*
EMP: 146
SALES (est): 1.7B
SALES (corp-wide): 40.8B **Privately Held**
SIC: 3714 Motor vehicle parts & accessories
PA: Magna International Inc
337 Magna Dr
Aurora ON L4G 7
905 726-2462

(G-16475)
MAGNA POWERTRAIN AMERICA INC (HQ)
1870 Technology Dr (48083-4232)
PHONE..................................248 597-7811
Donald J Walker, *CEO*
Nirmal Datta, *General Mgr*
Tom Rucker, *General Mgr*
Ginno Imperial, *Mfg Mgr*
David Dorigo, *Mfg Staff*
▲ **EMP:** 150
SALES (est): 41.6MM
SALES (corp-wide): 40.8B **Privately Held**
SIC: 3714 Motor vehicle parts & accessories
PA: Magna International Inc
337 Magna Dr
Aurora ON L4G 7
905 726-2462

(G-16476)
MAGNA POWERTRAIN USA INC (DH)
Also Called: Magna Powertrain Troy
1870 Technology Dr (48083-4232)
PHONE..................................248 680-4900
Jake Hirsch, *President*
Trey Becker, *Engineer*
Emanuel Ramirez, *Engineer*
Joe Robinson, *Engineer*
Kim Sikorski, *Human Res Mgr*
▲ **EMP:** 94
SQ FT: 31,000
SALES (est): 784.6MM
SALES (corp-wide): 40.8B **Privately Held**
SIC: 3714 Motor vehicle engines & parts
HQ: Magna Powertrain Inc
50 Casmir Crt
Concord ON
905 532-2100

(G-16477)
MAGNA POWERTRAIN USA INC
1875 Research Dr (48083-2191)
PHONE..................................248 524-1397
Graciela Alarcon, *Human Resources*
EMP: 300
SALES (corp-wide): 40.8B **Privately Held**
SIC: 3714 Motor vehicle engines & parts
HQ: Magna Powertrain Usa, Inc.
1870 Technology Dr
Troy MI 48083
248 680-4900

(G-16478)
MAGNA STEYR LLC
Also Called: Magna Steyr North America
1965 Research Dr Ste 100 (48083-2137)
PHONE..................................248 740-0214
Ian R Simmons, *Exec Dir*
August Hofbauer,
Mark Lukasiak,
Michael J Scott,
Derek Trice,
▲ **EMP:** 170 **EST:** 2000
SQ FT: 10,400
SALES (est): 22MM
SALES (corp-wide): 40.8B **Privately Held**
WEB: www.magnasteyr.com
SIC: 3711 Motor vehicles & car bodies

Troy - Oakland County (G-16479) — GEOGRAPHIC SECTION

PA: Magna International Inc
337 Magna Dr
Aurora ON L4G 7
905 726-2462

(G-16479)
MAGNETOOL INC
505 Elmwood Dr (48083-2755)
PHONE.................................248 588-5400
Albert T Churchill, *President*
▲ **EMP:** 28 **EST:** 1951
SQ FT: 30,000
SALES (est): 3MM **Privately Held**
WEB: www.magnetool.com
SIC: 3542 Magnetic forming machines

(G-16480)
MAHLE BEHR MFG MGT INC
2700 Daley Dr (48083-1949)
PHONE.................................248 735-3623
Wilm Uhlenbecker, *Vice Pres*
EMP: 12600 **EST:** 2015
SALES: 2B
SALES (corp-wide): 504.6K **Privately Held**
SIC: 5013 3714 Automotive supplies & parts; air conditioner parts, motor vehicle
PA: M A H L E - S T I F T U N G
Gesellschaft Mit Beschrankter Haftung
Leibnizstr. 35
Stuttgart 70193
711 656-6169

(G-16481)
MAHLE BEHR TROY INC (DH)
Also Called: Behr Climate Systems
2700 Daley Dr (48083-1949)
PHONE.................................248 743-3700
Jennifer Mensing, *Principal*
Hans Lange, *Director*
▲ **EMP:** 150
SQ FT: 115,800
SALES (est): 80.8MM
SALES (corp-wide): 504.6K **Privately Held**
SIC: 3585 3714 Air conditioning, motor vehicle; radiators & radiator shells & cores, motor vehicle
HQ: Mahle Behr Usa Inc.
2700 Daley Dr
Troy MI 48083
248 743-3700

(G-16482)
MAHLE BEHR TROY INC
5820 Innovation Dr (48098-2824)
PHONE.................................248 735-3623
EMP: 80
SALES (corp-wide): 504.6K **Privately Held**
SIC: 3714 Motor vehicle parts & accessories
HQ: Mahle Behr Troy Inc.
2700 Daley Dr
Troy MI 48083
248 743-3700

(G-16483)
MAHLE BEHR USA INC (DH)
2700 Daley Dr (48083-1949)
PHONE.................................248 743-3700
Wilm Uhlenbecker, *President*
Dean Arneson, *Vice Pres*
Mailend Delind, *Finance*
▲ **EMP:** 500
SQ FT: 10,000
SALES (est): 1.4B
SALES (corp-wide): 504.6K **Privately Held**
SIC: 3714 Radiators & radiator shells & cores, motor vehicle; air conditioner parts, motor vehicle engines & parts
HQ: Mahle Gmbh
Pragstr. 26-46
Stuttgart 70376
711 501-0

(G-16484)
MAKS INCORPORATED
Also Called: Multi Tech Systems
1150 Rankin Dr (48083-6003)
PHONE.................................248 733-9771
Mohamed Khalil, *President*
Sanaa Khalil, *Vice Pres*
EMP: 45

SQ FT: 17,500
SALES (est): 5.7MM **Privately Held**
SIC: 8711 3679 Electrical or electronic engineering; electronic circuits

(G-16485)
MARELLI TENNESSEE USA LLC
Also Called: Magneti Mrlli Sspnsons USA LLC
1389 Wheaton Dr (48083-1933)
PHONE.................................248 680-8872
E L Duarte,
EMP: 5004
SALES (est): 747.4K **Privately Held**
SIC: 3714 Shock absorbers, motor vehicle
HQ: Magneti Marelli Holding Usa Llc
3900 Automation Ave
Auburn Hills MI 48326

(G-16486)
MARIAH INDUSTRIES INC (PA)
1407 Allen Dr Ste E (48083-4009)
PHONE.................................248 237-0404
Samone Delagarza, *President*
Maria Christina Sammon, *Bd of Directors*
◆ **EMP:** 23
SQ FT: 42,000
SALES (est): 5.1MM **Privately Held**
WEB: www.mariah-industries.com
SIC: 3714 Motor vehicle parts & accessories

(G-16487)
MARK CARBIDE CO
1830 Brinston Dr (48083-2215)
PHONE.................................248 545-0606
William Blanc, *President*
EMP: 7 **EST:** 1952
SALES (est): 866.6K **Privately Held**
SIC: 3544 Special dies & tools

(G-16488)
MARSHAL E HYMAN AND ASSOCIATES
3250 W Big Beaver Rd # 529 (48084-2902)
PHONE.................................248 643-0642
Marshal Hyman, *President*
EMP: 9 **EST:** 2001
SALES (est): 1MM **Privately Held**
WEB: www.marshalhyman.com
SIC: 3942 8111 Dolls, except stuffed toy animals; legal services

(G-16489)
MASTER HANDYMAN PRESS INC
Also Called: America's Master Handyman
1224 Rankin Dr (48083-6004)
PHONE.................................248 616-0810
Glenn Haege, *President*
EMP: 3
SQ FT: 4,440
SALES: 150K **Privately Held**
WEB: www.masterhandyman.com
SIC: 2731 Books: publishing only

(G-16490)
MASTER MACHINING INC
1960 Thunderbird (48084-5466)
PHONE.................................248 454-9890
James Armstrong, *President*
Denise Armstrong, *Treasurer*
EMP: 14
SQ FT: 6,000
SALES (est): 2.7MM **Privately Held**
WEB: www.mastermachining.com
SIC: 3599 Machine shop, jobbing & repair

(G-16491)
MED-KAS HYDRAULICS INC
1419 John R Rd (48083-5861)
P.O. Box 1163 (48099-1163)
PHONE.................................248 585-3220
Thomas Medici, *President*
Terry Medici, *Vice Pres*
Tina Crean, *Sales Staff*
EMP: 15 **EST:** 1964
SQ FT: 27,000
SALES (est): 3.2MM **Privately Held**
WEB: www.med-kas.com
SIC: 3714 3594 Hydraulic fluid power pumps for auto steering mechanism; fluid power pumps & motors

(G-16492)
MEIKI CORPORATION
200 E Big Beaver Rd (48083-1208)
PHONE.................................248 680-4638
Tony Galluci, *Branch Mgr*
EMP: 3 **Privately Held**
SIC: 3086 5084 Packaging & shipping materials, foamed plastic; industrial machinery & equipment
HQ: Meiki Corporation
3450 Bonita Rd Ste 107
Chula Vista CA 91910
619 422-5872

(G-16493)
MERITOR INC (PA)
2135 W Maple Rd (48084-7121)
PHONE.................................248 435-1000
Jeffrey A Craig, *CEO*
Joseph Plomin, *President*
Chris Villavarayan, *President*
Ken Hogan, *General Mgr*
Scott Burckhard, *District Mgr*
◆ **EMP:** 250
SALES: 4.3B **Publicly Held**
WEB: www.arvinmeritor.com
SIC: 3493 3625 3465 3714 Automobile springs; actuators, industrial; automotive stampings; drive shafts, motor vehicle

(G-16494)
MERITOR HEAVY VHCL SYSTEMS LLC (HQ)
2135 W Maple Rd (48084-7121)
PHONE.................................248 435-1000
Jeffrey A Craig, *CEO*
Carl Anderson, *Vice Pres*
Lee French, *Technical Mgr*
Patrick McNally, *Engineer*
Kevin Nowlan, *CFO*
▲ **EMP:** 172
SALES (est): 33.4MM **Publicly Held**
WEB: www.meritor.com
SIC: 3711 Military motor vehicle assembly

(G-16495)
MERITOR INDUS AFTERMARKET LLC
Also Called: Axletech, LLC
1400 Rochester Rd (48083-6014)
PHONE.................................248 658-7345
Bill Gryzenia, *CEO*
Jonathan Ball, *CFO*
EMP: 6
SALES (est): 884.3K **Publicly Held**
SIC: 3462 3714 Railroad wheels, axles, frogs or other equipment: forged; axles, motor vehicle
HQ: Meritor Industrial Products, Llc
1400 Rochester Rd
Troy MI 48083
248 658-7200

(G-16496)
MERITOR INDUS INTL HLDINGS LLC
Also Called: Axletech Distribution Center
1400 Rochester Rd (48083-6014)
PHONE.................................248 658-7345
EMP: 8 **Publicly Held**
SIC: 3694 Distributors, motor vehicle engine
HQ: Meritor Industrial Products, Llc
1400 Rochester Rd
Troy MI 48083
248 658-7200

(G-16497)
MERITOR INDUSTRIAL PDTS LLC (HQ)
Also Called: Meritor Indus Intl Hldings LLC
1400 Rochester Rd (48083-6014)
PHONE.................................248 658-7200
Bill Gryzenia, *CEO*
▲ **EMP:** 10
SQ FT: 16,000
SALES (est): 72.9MM **Publicly Held**
SIC: 3714 Motor vehicle parts & accessories

(G-16498)
MERITOR INTL HOLDINGS LLC (HQ)
2135 W Maple Rd (48084-7121)
PHONE.................................248 435-1000
EMP: 5 **EST:** 2017
SALES (est): 1.9MM **Publicly Held**
SIC: 3714 Motor vehicle parts & accessories

(G-16499)
METAVATION LLC (HQ)
900 Wilshire Dr Ste 270 (48084-1600)
PHONE.................................248 351-1000
John M Hrit, *Mng Member*
◆ **EMP:** 40
SALES (est): 94MM **Privately Held**
SIC: 3714 Motor vehicle parts & accessories

(G-16500)
METHOD TECHNOLOGY SERVICE LLC (PA)
100 W Big Beavr Rd # 200 (48084-5206)
PHONE.................................312 622-7697
Ritu Anand, *Business Mgr*
Alka Gautam, *Business Anlyst*
Vikram Verma,
Natasha Verma,
EMP: 25
SQ FT: 2,000
SALES (est): 2.9MM **Privately Held**
SIC: 8711 7372 7371 Engineering services; application computer software; software programming applications

(G-16501)
METRO PRINTING SERVICE INC
Also Called: Metro Promotional Specialties
1950 Barrett Dr (48084-5371)
PHONE.................................248 545-4444
William J Brown, *CEO*
William R Brown, *President*
Peter Betto, *Mktg Coord*
Mindy L Brown, *Admin Sec*
◆ **EMP:** 7
SALES (est): 837.1K **Privately Held**
SIC: 5199 2752 Advertising specialties; commercial printing, offset

(G-16502)
METRO TECHNOLOGIES LTD
1462 E Big Beaver Rd (48083-1950)
PHONE.................................248 528-9240
Alfred J Hook, *President*
Patricia Hook, *Corp Secy*
EMP: 60
SQ FT: 20,000
SALES (est): 9.6MM **Privately Held**
WEB: www.mtl-troy.com
SIC: 3543 3544 Industrial patterns; special dies, tools, jigs & fixtures

(G-16503)
MICHAEL-STEPHENS COMPANY
1206 E Maple Rd (48083-2817)
PHONE.................................248 583-7767
Michael King, *President*
Mitch Mitchell, *Rector*
EMP: 8
SALES (est): 936.3K **Privately Held**
WEB: www.sealkits.com
SIC: 3053 Gaskets, packing & sealing devices

(G-16504)
MICHIGAN CARBIDE COMPANY INC
1263 Souter Dr (48083-2838)
PHONE.................................586 264-8780
Rick Kosky, *President*
EMP: 14
SQ FT: 10,000
SALES (est): 3.5MM **Privately Held**
WEB: www.michigancarbide.com
SIC: 3291 Tungsten carbide abrasive

(G-16505)
MICHIGAN DRILL CORPORATION (PA)
1863 Larchwood Dr (48083-2243)
P.O. Box 7012 (48007-7012)
PHONE.................................248 689-5050
Richard Kandarian, *President*
Hyman Ash, *Vice Pres*

▲ = Import ▼=Export
◆ =Import/Export

GEOGRAPHIC SECTION

Troy - Oakland County (G-16533)

Randy Tucker, *Opers Mgr*
John Marion, *Site Mgr*
Mark Linari, *Sales Staff*
▲ **EMP:** 18
SQ FT: 10,500
SALES (est): 19.1MM **Privately Held**
WEB: www.michigandrill.com
SIC: 3545 3544 Machine tool accessories; special dies, tools, jigs & fixtures

(G-16506)
MICROCIDE INC
2209 Niagara Dr (48083-5933)
PHONE..................................248 526-9663
John Lopes, *President*
EMP: 5
SALES (est): 1MM **Privately Held**
WEB: www.microcideinc.com
SIC: 2844 2869 Mouthwashes; industrial organic chemicals

(G-16507)
MICRODENTAL LABORATORIES INC (PA)
500 Stephenson Hwy (48083-1118)
PHONE..................................877 711-8778
Marjorie Coll, *Principal*
Wayne Coll, *Principal*
EMP: 3
SALES (est): 5.7MM **Privately Held**
SIC: 3843 Dental equipment & supplies

(G-16508)
MIDWEST ACORN NUT COMPANY (PA)
256 Minnesota Dr (48083-4671)
PHONE..................................800 422-6887
Monica E Kopsch, *President*
Brian Smith, *Vice Pres*
Kevin Marcy, *Warehouse Mgr*
Karen Smith, *Purchasing*
Rich Duff, *QC Mgr*
EMP: 20 **EST:** 1948
SQ FT: 10,000
SALES (est): 4.2MM **Privately Held**
WEB: www.midwestacornnut.com
SIC: 3452 Nuts, metal

(G-16509)
MITSUBISHI STEEL MFG CO LTD
Also Called: Mssc
2040 Crooks Rd Ste A (48084-5520)
PHONE..................................248 502-8000
Anita Turner, *Branch Mgr*
EMP: 30 **Privately Held**
SIC: 3714 Motor vehicle engines & parts
PA: Mitsubishi Steel Mfg. Co., Ltd.
  4-16-13, Tsukishima
  Chuo-Ku TKY 104-0

(G-16510)
MMI COMPANIES LLC
1094 Naughton Dr (48083-1910)
PHONE..................................248 528-1680
Susan Sharpe, *Finance*
Thomas Rickel, *Mng Member*
Mark Rickel, *Program Mgr*
Joseph Kosmolski,
EMP: 21
SQ FT: 21,000
SALES (est): 4MM **Privately Held**
SIC: 3089 Injection molding of plastics

(G-16511)
MODEL-MATIC INC
1094 Naughton Dr (48083-1910)
PHONE..................................248 528-1680
Stanley M Kosmalski, *President*
Joseph Kosmalski, *Vice Pres*
Wilma Kosmalski, *Admin Sec*
EMP: 10
SQ FT: 28,000
SALES (est): 1.4MM **Privately Held**
WEB: www.model-matic.com
SIC: 3544 3714 Industrial molds; motor vehicle parts & accessories

(G-16512)
MORE SIGNATURE CAKES LLC
Also Called: Thomas Cake Shop
5065 Livernois Rd (48098-3201)
PHONE..................................248 266-0504
EMP: 4
SALES (est): 161.5K **Privately Held**
SIC: 2051 Cakes, bakery: except frozen; cakes, pies & pastries

(G-16513)
MOUND STEEL & SUPPLY INC
1450 Rochester Rd (48083-6014)
PHONE..................................248 852-6630
David Simko, *President*
Frank Ianelli, *Admin Sec*
EMP: 12
SQ FT: 4,000
SALES (est): 2.3MM **Privately Held**
SIC: 5211 3441 Lumber & other building materials; fabricated structural metal

(G-16514)
MPT DRIVELINE SYSTEMS
1870 Technology Dr (48083-4232)
PHONE..................................248 680-3786
Teri Freeburn, *Opers Mgr*
Trey Becker, *Engineer*
Rick Woodard, *Engineer*
EMP: 4 **EST:** 2013
SALES (est): 458.1K **Privately Held**
SIC: 3714 Motor vehicle parts & accessories

(G-16515)
MSSC INC (HQ)
2040 Crooks Rd Ste A (48084-5520)
PHONE..................................248 502-8000
Gerald Anderson, *President*
Mohit Agarwal, *Engineer*
Shane Black, *Engineer*
Jeffrey Check, *Engineer*
Michele McKinley, *Finance*
▲ **EMP:** 33
SQ FT: 8,000
SALES (est): 19.3MM **Privately Held**
WEB: www.arvinmeritor.com
SIC: 3714 Motor vehicle body components & frame

(G-16516)
MULTIFINISH-USA INC
1389 Wheaton Dr Ste 300 (48083-1929)
PHONE..................................248 528-1154
Debra Sevon, *Principal*
▲ **EMP:** 7 **EST:** 2008
SALES (est): 600K **Privately Held**
SIC: 3541 Buffing & polishing machines

(G-16517)
MUSTANG AERONAUTICS INC
1990 Heide Dr (48083-5314)
PHONE..................................248 649-6818
Christopher Tieman, *President*
Teri Underhill, *Manager*
EMP: 5
SQ FT: 8,000
SALES (est): 867.9K **Privately Held**
WEB: www.mustangaero.com
SIC: 3721 Aircraft

(G-16518)
N A SODECIA INC
Also Called: Sodecia Group
969 Chicago Rd (48083-4227)
PHONE..................................586 879-8969
Rui Montero, *CEO*
Gary Easterly, *Vice Pres*
Sheryl McGowan, *Treasurer*
▲ **EMP:** 300
SQ FT: 180,000
SALES (est): 27.5MM **Privately Held**
SIC: 3465 Body parts, automobile: stamped metal
HQ: Sodecia Automotive Detroit Corp.
  969 Chicago Rd
  Troy MI 48083
  586 759-2200

(G-16519)
N S INTERNATIONAL LTD (HQ)
600 Wilshire Dr (48084-1625)
PHONE..................................248 251-1600
Teruyuki Matsui, *CEO*
Joe Kallenbach, *Prdtn Mgr*
Joe Bleau, *Facilities Mgr*
Mark Riege, *Purchasing*
John Armstrong, *Engineer*
▲ **EMP:** 106
SALES (est): 64.4MM **Privately Held**
SIC: 5013 3672 3812 Automotive supplies & parts; motorcycle parts; printed circuit boards; detection apparatus: electronic/magnetic field, light/heat

(G-16520)
NATIONAL INDUSTRIAL SUP CO INC
Also Called: N I S
1201 Rochester Rd (48083-2834)
PHONE..................................248 588-1828
Kathreen Harper, *President*
Charles W Brett, *Corp Secy*
Kevin Brett, *Vice Pres*
Mary Dingman, *Vice Pres*
Charles Brett, *CFO*
EMP: 12
SQ FT: 10,000
SALES (est): 4MM **Privately Held**
WEB: www.nischain.com
SIC: 3496 5085 Woven wire products; industrial fittings

(G-16521)
ND INDUSTRIES INC
1819 Thunderbird (48084-5402)
PHONE..................................248 288-0000
Glen Gregg, *General Mgr*
Tom Lipinski, *Vice Pres*
Mitch Symonds, *Prdtn Mgr*
Dave Snow, *Research*
Desiree Snyder, *Research*
EMP: 25
SALES (corp-wide): 81.5MM **Privately Held**
WEB: www.ndindustries.com
SIC: 3549 Wiredrawing & fabricating machinery & equipment, ex. die
PA: Nd Industries, Inc.
  1000 N Crooks Rd
  Clawson MI 48017
  248 288-0000

(G-16522)
ND INDUSTRIES INC
Also Called: Vibra-Tite
1893 Barrett Dr (48084-5378)
PHONE..................................248 288-0000
Richard Wallace, *President*
Cavin Ciaciuch, *Technician*
EMP: 20
SALES (corp-wide): 81.5MM **Privately Held**
WEB: www.ndindustries.com
SIC: 3479 5072 Coating of metals & formed products; miscellaneous fasteners
PA: Nd Industries, Inc.
  1000 N Crooks Rd
  Clawson MI 48017
  248 288-0000

(G-16523)
NESTLE PURINA PETCARE COMPANY
600 Executive Dr (48083-4537)
P.O. Box 7027 (48083)
PHONE..................................888 202-4554
EMP: 27
SALES (corp-wide): 92B **Privately Held**
SIC: 2047 Dog & cat food
HQ: Nestle Purina Petcare Company
  1 Checkerboard Sq
  Saint Louis MO 63164
  314 982-1000

(G-16524)
NIHIL ULTRA CORPORATION
55 E Long Lake Rd (48085-4738)
PHONE..................................413 723-3218
Saikat Ghosh, *Principal*
EMP: 4 **EST:** 2010
SALES (est): 291.4K **Privately Held**
SIC: 3674 Light emitting diodes

(G-16525)
NITTO SEIKO CO LTD
1301 Rankin Dr (48083-6008)
PHONE..................................248 588-0133
Masami Zaiki, *President*
▲ **EMP:** 25 **Privately Held**
SIC: 3399 Metal fasteners
PA: Nitto Seiko Co.,Ltd.
  20, Umegahata, Inokuracho
  Ayabe KYO 623-0

(G-16526)
NOACK VENTURES LLC
Also Called: Alba Plastics
1407 Allen Dr Ste G (48083-4009)
PHONE..................................248 583-0311
Mike Daley, *Principal*
EMP: 4
SALES (est): 300K **Privately Held**
WEB: www.albaplastics.com
SIC: 3089 Plastic processing

(G-16527)
NORTHSTAR SOURCING LLC
1399 Combermere Dr (48083)
PHONE..................................313 782-4749
John Koussa, *Mng Member*
Mike Bayoff,
EMP: 7 **EST:** 2017
SQ FT: 40,000
SALES (est): 8MM **Privately Held**
SIC: 2621 Paper mills

(G-16528)
NTVB MEDIA INC (PA)
Also Called: National Television Book Co
213 Park Dr (48083-2726)
PHONE..................................248 583-4190
Andrew V De Angelis, *President*
Robin Block-Taylor, *Vice Pres*
Larry Mackenzie, *CFO*
EMP: 50 **EST:** 1981
SQ FT: 22,000
SALES (est): 99.5MM **Privately Held**
WEB: www.nationalbook.com
SIC: 2752 Commercial printing, offset

(G-16529)
NUBREED NUTRITION INC
318 John R Rd Ste 310 (48083-4542)
PHONE..................................734 272-7395
John Kazmar, *President*
EMP: 4 **EST:** 2013
SALES (est): 112.1K **Privately Held**
SIC: 8049 2075 Nutrition specialist; soybean protein concentrates & isolates

(G-16530)
NVENT THERMAL LLC
900 Wilshire Dr Ste 150 (48084-1600)
PHONE..................................248 273-3359
Dwight Hansell, *Manager*
EMP: 70
SALES (corp-wide): 352.2K **Privately Held**
WEB: www.tycothermal.com
SIC: 3678 Electronic connectors
HQ: Nvent Thermal Llc
  899 Broadway St
  Redwood City CA 94063
  650 474-7414

(G-16531)
OAKWOOD VENEER COMPANY
1830 Stephenson Hwy Ste A (48083-2173)
PHONE..................................248 720-0288
Peter Rodgers, *President*
◆ **EMP:** 18
SQ FT: 44,000
SALES (est): 2.8MM **Privately Held**
WEB: www.oakwoodveneer.com
SIC: 2499 Veneer work, inlaid

(G-16532)
ODIN DEFENSE INDUSTRIES INC
2145 Crooks Rd Ste 210 (48084-5539)
PHONE..................................248 434-5072
Joseph Caradonna, *Principal*
EMP: 5
SALES (est): 202K **Privately Held**
SIC: 3999 Manufacturing industries

(G-16533)
OERLIKON METCO (US) INC
1972 Meijer Dr (48084-7143)
PHONE..................................248 288-0027
Kevin Luer, *Manager*
EMP: 50
SALES (corp-wide): 2.6B **Privately Held**
SIC: 5084 3356 3341 2819 Textile machinery & equipment; nonferrous rolling & drawing; secondary nonferrous metals; industrial inorganic chemicals; inorganic pigments
HQ: Oerlikon Metco (Us) Inc.
  1101 Prospect Ave
  Westbury NY 11590
  516 334-1300

Troy - Oakland County (G-16534) — GEOGRAPHIC SECTION

(G-16534)
OFFICE EXPRESS INC
Also Called: Oex, Inc.
1280 E Big Beaver Rd A (48083-1946)
PHONE..................................248 307-1850
Anna Sinagra, *CEO*
Jeff Eusebio, *President*
Kevin Monreal, *Accountant*
Mike Carr, *Accounts Mgr*
Jim George, *Accounts Mgr*
EMP: 22
SQ FT: 10,000
SALES (est): 8.3MM **Privately Held**
WEB: www.officeexpressnow.com
SIC: 5112 2752 5943 Stationery & office supplies; commercial printing, offset; stationery stores

(G-16535)
ORACLE AMERICA INC
Also Called: Sun Microsystems
755 W Big Beavr Rd # 245 (48084-4900)
PHONE..................................248 273-1934
Russ Cuthrell, *Branch Mgr*
EMP: 3
SALES (corp-wide): 39.5B **Publicly Held**
SIC: 7372 Prepackaged software
HQ: Oracle America, Inc.
  500 Oracle Pkwy
  Redwood City CA 94065
  650 506-7000

(G-16536)
ORACLE SYSTEMS CORPORATION
3290 W Big Beaver Rd # 300 (48084-2903)
PHONE..................................248 816-8050
Debbie Macdonald, *Opers Staff*
Richard Lawshaw, *Manager*
Sanjay Sil, *Manager*
Victor Capton, *Info Tech Mgr*
Srivatsan Santhanam, *Info Tech Mgr*
EMP: 175
SALES (corp-wide): 39.5B **Publicly Held**
WEB: www.forcecapital.com
SIC: 7372 Prepackaged software
HQ: Oracle Systems Corporation
  500 Oracle Pkwy
  Redwood City CA 94065
  650 506-7000

(G-16537)
ORBIS CORPORATION
999 Chicago Rd (48083-4227)
PHONE..................................248 616-3232
Dan Roovers, *Exec VP*
Jack Fillmore, *Branch Mgr*
EMP: 114
SALES (corp-wide): 1.8B **Privately Held**
WEB: www.orbiscorporation.com
SIC: 3089 Synthetic resin finished products
HQ: Orbis Corporation
  1055 Corporate Center Dr
  Oconomowoc WI 53066
  262 560-5000

(G-16538)
ORTHO-CLINICAL DIAGNOSTICS INC
2128 Lancer Dr (48084-1308)
PHONE..................................248 797-8087
EMP: 176
SALES (corp-wide): 594.4MM **Privately Held**
SIC: 2835 Blood derivative diagnostic agents
PA: Ortho-Clinical Diagnostics, Inc.
  1001 Route 202
  Raritan NJ 08869
  908 218-8000

(G-16539)
OTTER COMPANY
2687 Amberly Ln (48084-2694)
PHONE..................................248 566-3235
Michael Otter, *Principal*
▲ **EMP:** 3
SALES (est): 208.8K **Privately Held**
SIC: 2339 Women's & misses' outerwear

(G-16540)
P G S INC
Also Called: Precision Global Systems
1600 E Big Beaver Rd (48083-2002)
PHONE..................................248 526-3800
Stephanie Najarian, *CEO*
Richard T Najarian, *President*
EMP: 185 **EST:** 1983
SQ FT: 175,000
SALES (est): 26MM **Privately Held**
WEB: www.pgsinc.net
SIC: 7389 7549 5013 3714 Inspection & testing services; inspection & diagnostic service, automotive; motor vehicle supplies & new parts; differentials & parts, motor vehicle; motor vehicle transmissions, drive assemblies & parts; axle housings & shafts, motor vehicle

(G-16541)
PALMER PAINT PRODUCTS INC
1291 Rochester Rd (48083-2879)
P.O. Box 1058 (48099-1058)
PHONE..................................248 588-4500
Beverly A Geisler, *President*
Garrett J Hess, *Vice Pres*
▲ **EMP:** 82 **EST:** 1932
SQ FT: 54,000
SALES (est): 15.8MM **Privately Held**
WEB: www.palmerpaint.com
SIC: 2851 Paints: oil or alkyd vehicle or water thinned; lacquers, varnishes, enamels & other coatings

(G-16542)
PERCEPTIVE MACHINING INC
297 Elmwood Dr (48083-4801)
PHONE..................................248 577-0380
Don Merckling, *President*
EMP: 3
SQ FT: 3,500
SALES: 250K **Privately Held**
WEB: www.perceptivemachining.com
SIC: 3599 Machine shop, jobbing & repair

(G-16543)
PERFORMANCE FUELS SYSTEMS INC
3108 Newport Ct (48084-1323)
PHONE..................................248 202-1789
Al Petrulis, *Administration*
EMP: 3
SALES (est): 202.7K **Privately Held**
SIC: 2869 Fuels

(G-16544)
PERSPECTIVES CUSTOM CABINETRY
Also Called: Perspectives Cabinetry
1401 Axtell Dr (48084-7002)
PHONE..................................248 288-4100
John A Morgan, *President*
EMP: 29
SQ FT: 22,000
SALES (est): 4.2MM **Privately Held**
WEB: www.perspectivescabinetry.com
SIC: 2511 2434 Wood household furniture; vanities, bathroom: wood

(G-16545)
PETER-LACKE USA LLC (DH)
865 Stephenson Hwy (48083-1142)
PHONE..................................248 588-9400
John Bilson, *COO*
David Peter, *Mng Member*
▲ **EMP:** 9
SQ FT: 21,000
SALES (est): 67.9MM
SALES (corp-wide): 896.9K **Privately Held**
SIC: 2851 Paints & paint additives
HQ: Peter-Lacke Holding Gmbh
  Engerstr. 3-5
  Herford 32051
  522 192-9170

(G-16546)
PHOENIX PRESS INCORPORATED
Also Called: Phoenix Innovate
1775 Bellingham Dr (48083-2056)
PHONE..................................248 435-8040
Geoffrey Vercnocke, *President*
Kirk Vercnocke, *Corp Secy*
Paul King, *Exec VP*
Mark Gaskill, *Vice Pres*
Angelika Niemczyk, *Marketing Staff*
EMP: 35
SQ FT: 14,000
SALES (est): 11.7MM **Privately Held**
WEB: www.phoenixpress.net
SIC: 2752 8742 Commercial printing, offset; marketing consulting services

(G-16547)
PHOENIX WIRE CLOTH INC
Also Called: Phoenix Safety Systems
585 Stephenson Hwy (48083-1134)
P.O. Box 610 (48099-0610)
PHONE..................................248 585-6350
Toll Free:.......................................877 -
Richard J Holmes, *President*
John D Holmes, *Chairman*
William D Holmes, *Vice Pres*
▲ **EMP:** 30 **EST:** 1885
SQ FT: 60,000
SALES (est): 6.7MM **Privately Held**
WEB: www.phoenixwirecloth.com
SIC: 3496 3446 5051 Mesh, made from purchased wire; architectural metalwork; wire

(G-16548)
PIPELINE PACKAGING
1421 Piedmont Dr (48083-1952)
PHONE..................................248 743-0248
EMP: 4
SALES (est): 338K **Privately Held**
SIC: 3053 Mfg Gaskets/Packing/Sealing Devices

(G-16549)
PITSS AMERICA LLC
570 Kirts Blvd Ste 207 (48083-4112)
PHONE..................................248 740-0935
Anna Daugherty, *Marketing Staff*
Ashwani Braj, *Software Dev*
Jeremy Stahl, *Software Dev*
Martin Disterheft,
EMP: 21
SALES (est): 3MM **Privately Held**
SIC: 7372 Prepackaged software

(G-16550)
PLASTIC OMNIUM INC
2710 Bellingham Dr # 400 (48083-2045)
PHONE..................................248 458-0772
Brian Crawford, *Project Mgr*
Ange Chay, *Purchasing*
Cedric Gesnouin, *Director*
EMP: 5
SALES (est): 319.9K **Privately Held**
SIC: 3011 Tires & inner tubes

(G-16551)
PLASTIC OMNIUM AUTO EXTERIORS (DH)
2710 Bellingham Dr # 400 (48083-2045)
PHONE..................................248 458-0700
Marc Cornet,
Laurent Burrell,
Bruno Courtet,
Mike Sias,
▲ **EMP:** 327
SALES (est): 275.4MM
SALES (corp-wide): 10.4MM **Privately Held**
SIC: 3089 Automotive parts, plastic
HQ: Plastic Omnium Auto Exteriors
  19 Avenue Jules Carteret
  Lyon 7e Arrondissement
  140 876-400

(G-16552)
PLASTIC OMNIUM AUTO INERGY LLC
2585 W Maple Rd (48084-7114)
PHONE..................................248 743-5700
Bill Starrs, *Manager*
EMP: 20
SALES (corp-wide): 10.4MM **Privately Held**
SIC: 3714 Motor vehicle parts & accessories
HQ: Plastic Omnium Auto Inergy (Usa) Llc
  2710 Bellingham Dr
  Troy MI 48083
  248 743-5700

(G-16553)
PLASTIC OMNIUM AUTO INERGY LLC (DH)
2710 Bellingham Dr (48083-2045)
PHONE..................................248 743-5700
Adeline Mickeler, *Exec VP*
Mark Sullivan, *Mng Member*
▲ **EMP:** 468
SALES (est): 1B
SALES (corp-wide): 10.4MM **Privately Held**
SIC: 3714 Fuel systems & parts, motor vehicle
HQ: Plastic Omnium Auto Exteriors
  19 Avenue Jules Carteret
  Lyon 7e Arrondissement
  140 876-400

(G-16554)
PORITE USA CO LTD
1295 Combermere Dr (48083-2734)
PHONE..................................248 597-9988
Dr Bong Sun, *President*
▲ **EMP:** 5
SALES (est): 873.2K **Privately Held**
SIC: 3566 Gears, power transmission, except automotive
PA: Porite Corporation
  2-121, Nisshincho, Kita-Ku
  Saitama STM 331-0

(G-16555)
POWER SEAL INTERNATIONAL LLC
250 Park Dr (48083-2772)
PHONE..................................248 537-1103
Rick Rowe, *Mng Member*
Cherry Vegella, *Mng Member*
EMP: 20
SQ FT: 16,000
SALES (est): 3.9MM **Privately Held**
WEB: www.powerseal1.com
SIC: 3069 Molded rubber products

(G-16556)
PPG COATING SERVICES (HQ)
Also Called: Crown Group Co., The
5875 New King Ct (48098-2692)
PHONE..................................586 575-9800
Eric Vermillion, *General Mgr*
Jim Keena, *COO*
Frank Knoth, *Vice Pres*
Ron Orlow, *QC Mgr*
Chris Wypych, *QC Mgr*
EMP: 11
SQ FT: 14,000
SALES (est): 174.1MM
SALES (corp-wide): 15.3B **Publicly Held**
SIC: 3479 Coating of metals & formed products
PA: Ppg Industries, Inc.
  1 Ppg Pl
  Pittsburgh PA 15272
  412 434-3131

(G-16557)
PPG INDUSTRIES INC
5875 New King Ct (48098-2692)
PHONE..................................248 641-2000
Richard Rurak, *Branch Mgr*
EMP: 19
SALES (corp-wide): 15.3B **Publicly Held**
SIC: 3211 3231 3229 2812 Flat glass; strengthened or reinforced glass; windshields, glass: made from purchased glass; glass fiber products; fiber optics strands; alkalies & chlorine; chlorine, compressed or liquefied; caustic soda, sodium hydroxide; plastics materials & resins; paints & paint additives
PA: Ppg Industries, Inc.
  1 Ppg Pl
  Pittsburgh PA 15272
  412 434-3131

(G-16558)
PPI LLC
5868 Hilmore Dr (48085-3330)
PHONE..................................248 841-7721
Johnathan Egle, *Branch Mgr*
EMP: 3
SALES (corp-wide): 4MM **Privately Held**
SIC: 3812 Aircraft/aerospace flight instruments & guidance systems

GEOGRAPHIC SECTION

Troy - Oakland County (G-16586)

PA: Ppi, Llc
23514 Groesbeck Hwy
Warren MI 48089
586 772-7736

(G-16559)
PRECISION COMPONENTS
324 Robbins Dr (48083-4558)
PHONE.................................248 588-5650
Bobbie Fitzgerald, *Owner*
Bobbie Fitzpatrick, *Treasurer*
Tom Coleman, *Sales Executive*
EMP: 13
SQ FT: 18,000
SALES (est): 933.8K **Privately Held**
WEB: www.pctooling.com
SIC: 3545 End mills

(G-16560)
PRECISION EXTRACTION CORP
Also Called: Precision Extraction Solutions
2468 Industrial Row Dr (48084-7005)
PHONE.................................855 420-0020
EMP: 4
SALES (est): 667.6K **Privately Held**
SIC: 3556 Juice extractors, fruit & vegetable: commercial type

(G-16561)
PRECISION RESOURCE INC
3250 W Big Beaver Rd # 231 (48084-2900)
PHONE.................................248 478-3704
Paul Mosser, *Branch Mgr*
EMP: 3
SALES (corp-wide): 260.1MM **Privately Held**
WEB: www.precisionresource.com
SIC: 3469 Stamping metal for the trade
PA: Precision Resource, Inc.
25 Forest Pkwy
Shelton CT 06484
203 925-0012

(G-16562)
PREMIUM AIR SYSTEMS INC
1051 Naughton Dr (48083-1911)
PHONE.................................248 680-8800
Leonard A Framalin, *President*
Elsie Stewart, *Mfg Staff*
Mark Findora, *Manager*
EMP: 62
SQ FT: 15,000
SALES (est): 9.8MM **Privately Held**
WEB: www.premiumair.net
SIC: 1711 3312 Warm air heating & air conditioning contractor; refrigeration contractor; blast furnaces & steel mills

(G-16563)
PROBUS TECHNICAL SERVICES INC
2424 Crooks Rd Apt 21 (48084-5337)
PHONE.................................876 226-5692
Guruprasad Srihari, *CEO*
EMP: 10
SALES (est): 226.8K **Privately Held**
SIC: 8742 3999 Industrial & labor consulting services; barber & beauty shop equipment

(G-16564)
PROCHIMIR INC
200 E Big Beaver Rd Mi (48083-1208)
PHONE.................................248 457-4538
EMP: 3
SALES (est): 99K **Privately Held**
SIC: 3674 Thin film circuits

(G-16565)
PRODUCT ASSEMBLY GROUP LLC
Also Called: Pag
1080 Naughton Dr (48083-1910)
PHONE.................................586 549-8601
Douglass Goad, *President*
Jonathan Paquin,
EMP: 6
SQ FT: 4,000
SALES (est): 1.1MM **Privately Held**
SIC: 3714 Motor vehicle parts & accessories

(G-16566)
PRODUCTION SPRING LLC
1151 Allen Dr (48083-4002)
PHONE.................................248 583-0036
Roderick Frazier, *Owner*
Jenny Evans, *Manager*
Zachary Savas,
EMP: 40 EST: 1980
SQ FT: 31,000
SALES (est): 7.5MM **Privately Held**
WEB: www.production-spring.com
SIC: 3469 Stamping metal for the trade

(G-16567)
PROFESSIONAL RUG WORKS INC
1020 Livernois Rd (48083-2710)
PHONE.................................248 577-1400
John Raible, *President*
EMP: 3
SALES (est): 406.9K **Privately Held**
SIC: 2273 Carpets & rugs

(G-16568)
PROS-TECH INC
1717 Stephenson Hwy (48083-2149)
PHONE.................................248 680-2800
Keith Girardot, *President*
Martin Hillbom, *Treasurer*
EMP: 13
SALES (est): 2MM **Privately Held**
WEB: www.prostechctr.com
SIC: 3842 Prosthetic appliances

(G-16569)
PROTOFAB CORPORATION
2835 Daley Dr (48083-1940)
PHONE.................................248 689-3730
William H Hart Sr, *President*
EMP: 9
SQ FT: 1,600
SALES (est): 1.6MM **Privately Held**
SIC: 3444 Sheet metal specialties, not stamped

(G-16570)
PURE & SIMPLE SOLUTIONS LLC
Also Called: Casa D'Oro
1187 Souter Dr (48083-2821)
PHONE.................................248 398-4600
Douglas P Blunden,
▲ EMP: 28
SQ FT: 12,500
SALES (est): 2.8MM **Privately Held**
WEB: www.italiangoldcharms.com
SIC: 3911 5094 Bracelets, precious metal; jewelry

(G-16571)
QUAD ELECTRONICS INC (PA)
Also Called: Cablcon
359 Robbins Dr (48084-4561)
PHONE.................................800 969-9220
Clay Pace, *President*
Bryan Kadrich, *Principal*
Gerald Demski, *Vice Pres*
John Foley, *Warehouse Mgr*
Jessica Wilson, *Purch Mgr*
▲ EMP: 75
SQ FT: 29,000
SALES (est): 24.1MM **Privately Held**
WEB: www.cablcon.com
SIC: 3357 5063 Nonferrous wiredrawing & insulating; electrical apparatus & equipment

(G-16572)
QUAD/GRAPHICS INC
3250 W Big Beaver Rd # 127 (48084-2900)
PHONE.................................248 637-9950
John Stano, *Manager*
EMP: 4
SALES (corp-wide): 4.1B **Publicly Held**
WEB: www.qg.com
SIC: 2752 Commercial printing, lithographic
PA: Quad/Graphics Inc.
N61w23044 Harrys Way
Sussex WI 53089
414 566-6000

(G-16573)
QUIRKROBERTS PUBLISHING LTD
Also Called: Young Ideas Enterprises
6219 Seminole Dr (48085-1127)
P.O. Box 71 (48099-0071)
PHONE.................................248 879-2598
Linda Hodgdon, *President*
EMP: 8 EST: 1985
SALES (est): 885.1K **Privately Held**
SIC: 2731 8748 Books: publishing only; educational consultant

(G-16574)
R H K TECHNOLOGY INC
Also Called: Sonic Alert
1233 Chicago Rd (48083-4231)
PHONE.................................248 577-5426
Adam Kollin, *President*
Lindsey Dokianos, *Accounts Mgr*
Michael Donovan, *Sales Staff*
Allen G Vallei, *Sales Staff*
Craig Wall, *Marketing Staff*
▲ EMP: 42
SALES (est): 11.1MM **Privately Held**
WEB: www.sonicalert.com
SIC: 3826 3669 Analytical instruments; signaling apparatus, electric

(G-16575)
RAFALSKI CPA
1607 E Big Beaver Rd # 103 (48083-2028)
PHONE.................................248 689-1685
David Rafalski, *Principal*
EMP: 4
SALES (est): 240K **Privately Held**
SIC: 1381 8721 Drilling oil & gas wells; accounting, auditing & bookkeeping

(G-16576)
RAJASON INTERNATIONAL CORP
1207 Hartland Dr (48083-5431)
PHONE.................................248 506-4456
Ajit Singh Chana, *President*
Balwinder Chana, *General Mgr*
Sewa Singh Chana, *Corp Secy*
◆ EMP: 3
SALES: 100K
SALES (corp-wide): 3.4MM **Privately Held**
WEB: www.rajasontools.com
SIC: 3069 Rubber automotive products
PA: Rajason Tools Inc
11664 County Rd 42
Windsor ON N8N 2
519 979-1263

(G-16577)
REVSTONE INDUSTRIES LLC
900 Wilshire Dr Ste 270 (48084-1600)
P.O. Box 1720, Birmingham (48012-1720)
PHONE.................................248 351-1000
Scott Hofmeister, *Branch Mgr*
EMP: 12 **Privately Held**
SIC: 2821 3086 3341 Plastics materials & resins; plastics foam products; secondary nonferrous metals
PA: Revstone Industries, Llc
2008 Cypress St Ste 100
Paris KY 40361

(G-16578)
REXAIR HOLDINGS INC
50 W Big Beavr Rd Ste 350 (48084-5203)
PHONE.................................248 643-7222
F Philip Handy, *CEO*
◆ EMP: 2
SALES (est): 2.2MM
SALES (corp-wide): 8.6B **Publicly Held**
SIC: 3635 Household vacuum cleaners
HQ: Jarden Llc
221 River St
Hoboken NJ 07030

(G-16579)
REXAIR LLC (PA)
Also Called: Rainbow Cleaning System
50 W Big Beaver Rd # 350 (48084-5203)
PHONE.................................248 643-7222
Paul T Vidovich, *CEO*
James Williams, *President*
Jim Williams, *Counsel*
Barry Brim, *Project Mgr*
Alyson Rock, *Project Mgr*
◆ EMP: 2
SQ FT: 142,290
SALES (est): 126MM **Privately Held**
WEB: www.rainbow.net
SIC: 3635 Household vacuum cleaners

(G-16580)
RINGMASTER SOFTWARE CORP
631 E Big Beaver Rd # 109 (48083-1419)
PHONE.................................802 383-1050
Susan Dorn, *President*
Michael Rooney, *Exec VP*
EMP: 10
SALES (est): 442.9K **Privately Held**
WEB: www.ringmastersw.com
SIC: 7372 Prepackaged software

(G-16581)
RIVORE METALS LLC (PA)
850 Stephenson Hwy # 200 (48083-1151)
PHONE.................................800 248-1250
Reanna Peyton, *Vice Pres*
Kosta Marselis,
EMP: 54
SALES (est): 21.5MM **Privately Held**
SIC: 3914 5051 Carving sets, stainless steel; copper

(G-16582)
ROCKWELL AUTOMATION INC
1441 W Long Lake Rd # 150 (48098-4403)
PHONE.................................248 696-1200
Beth Glaspie, *Engineer*
Don Werner, *Branch Mgr*
Todd Montpas, *Manager*
Larry Smentowski, *Manager*
Chris Yasso, *Manager*
EMP: 60 **Publicly Held**
SIC: 3625 7389 Relays & industrial controls; personal service agents, brokers & bureaus
PA: Rockwell Automation, Inc.
1201 S 2nd St
Milwaukee WI 53204

(G-16583)
ROSE MOBILE COMPUTER REPR LLC
Also Called: Rose Computer Consulting
200 E Big Beaver Rd (48083-1208)
PHONE.................................248 653-0865
Adam Rosenman, *CEO*
EMP: 10 EST: 2012
SALES: 2.5MM **Privately Held**
SIC: 7378 7372 7379 Computer maintenance & repair; application computer software; computer related consulting services

(G-16584)
ROSS DECCO COMPANY
Also Called: Detroit Coil
1250 Stephenson Hwy (48083-1115)
PHONE.................................248 764-1845
Don Jamisom, *President*
▲ EMP: 46
SALES: 7.2MM
SALES (corp-wide): 45.5MM **Privately Held**
SIC: 3625 Relays & industrial controls
PA: Ross Operating Valve Company
1250 Stephenson Hwy
Troy MI 48083
248 764-1800

(G-16585)
RUSH MACHINING INC
256 Minnesota Dr (48083-4667)
PHONE.................................248 583-0550
Brian Smith, *Vice Pres*
Patrick O Berry, *Vice Pres*
Colleen Gagnon, *Treasurer*
EMP: 12
SQ FT: 8,000
SALES: 1.5MM **Privately Held**
SIC: 3452 5085 Nuts, metal; fasteners, industrial: nuts, bolts, screws, etc.

(G-16586)
S & N AZIZA INC
Also Called: Eastern Graphics & Printing
6974 Brunswick Dr (48085-1269)
PHONE.................................248 879-9396
Steve Aziza, *President*
Samir Daya, *Vice Pres*
Nadwa Aziza, *Admin Sec*

Troy - Oakland County (G-16587) GEOGRAPHIC SECTION

EMP: 4
SQ FT: 4,688
SALES: 500K Privately Held
SIC: 2752 Commercial printing, offset

(G-16587)
S C JOHNSON & SON INC
Also Called: S C Johnson Wax
3001 W Big Beaver Rd # 402
(48084-3101)
PHONE..................248 822-2174
Calvin Comeau, Manager
EMP: 15
SALES (corp-wide): 3.6B Privately Held
WEB: www.scjohnson.com
SIC: 2842 2844 Floor waxes; shampoos, rinses, conditioners: hair
PA: S. C. Johnson & Son, Inc.
1525 Howe St
Racine WI 53403
262 260-2000

(G-16588)
SADIA ENTERPRISES INC
Also Called: Prairie Pride Carrier
3373 Rochester Rd (48083-5427)
PHONE..................248 854-4666
EMP: 7
SALES (est): 28.6K Privately Held
SIC: 3537 4789 Lift trucks, industrial: fork, platform, straddle, etc.; pipeline terminal facilities, independently operated

(G-16589)
SAE INTERNATIONAL
755 W Big Beaver Rd # 1600
(48084-4906)
PHONE..................248 273-2455
Jack Pokrzywa, Branch Mgr
EMP: 20
SALES (corp-wide): 73.5MM Privately Held
SIC: 8699 2741 Automobile owners' association; technical manual & paper publishing
PA: Sae International
400 Commonwealth Dr
Warrendale PA 15086
724 776-4841

(G-16590)
SAINT GOBAIN GLASS CORPORATION
1651 W Big Beaver Rd (48084-3501)
PHONE..................248 816-0060
EMP: 3
SALES (corp-wide): 207.6MM Privately Held
SIC: 3211 Mfg Automotive Glass
HQ: Saint Gobain Glass Corporation
750 S Swedesford Rd
Valley Forge PA 19355

(G-16591)
SALEEN SPECIAL VEHICLES INC
1225 E Maple Rd (48083-2818)
PHONE..................909 978-6700
▲ EMP: 297
SQ FT: 184,000
SALES (est): 38.1MM Privately Held
SIC: 3711 Mfg Motor Vehicle/Car Bodies

(G-16592)
SAMUEL SON & CO (USA) INC
Samuel Mdwest A Div Samuel Son
580 Kirts Blvd Ste 300 (48084-4138)
PHONE..................414 486-1556
Mark Magro, Sales Staff
Tom Sennett, Branch Mgr
Bill McAlister, Administration
EMP: 52
SALES (corp-wide): 1.8B Privately Held
SIC: 5051 3316 3441 3312 Steel; aluminum bars, rods, ingots, sheets, pipes, plates, etc.; cold-rolled strip or wire; fabricated structural metal; blast furnaces & steel mills
HQ: Samuel, Son & Co. (Usa) Inc.
1401 Davey Rd Ste 300
Woodridge IL 60517
630 783-2900

(G-16593)
SANDMAN INC
5877 Livernois Rd Ste 103 (48098-3100)
PHONE..................248 652-3432
Joel Garrett, President
Thomas Powell, Treasurer
EMP: 6
SALES: 1MM Privately Held
WEB: www.sandman.net
SIC: 1442 Construction sand mining

(G-16594)
SAVE ON EVERYTHING INC (PA)
1000 W Maple Rd Ste 200 (48084-5368)
PHONE..................248 362-9119
Michael Gauthier, President
Heather Uballe, COO
Eric Birtch, Vice Pres
Bill Davis, Vice Pres
David Leale, Sales Associate
EMP: 55
SQ FT: 24,000
SALES (est): 14.6MM Privately Held
WEB: www.saveoneverything.com
SIC: 2759 Coupons: printing

(G-16595)
SBZ CORPORATION
3001 W Big Beaver Rd # 402
(48084-3101)
PHONE..................248 649-1166
Laurence Holder, President
Wendy Wood, Business Mgr
EMP: 4
SALES (est): 100K Privately Held
SIC: 2819 Industrial inorganic chemicals

(G-16596)
SECO HOLDING CO INC
Also Called: Carboloy
2805 Bellingham Dr (48083-2046)
PHONE..................248 528-5200
Bruce E Belden, President
▲ EMP: 600
SQ FT: 650,000
SALES (est): 46.9MM
SALES (corp-wide): 11.1B Privately Held
SIC: 3545 Cutting tools for machine tools
HQ: Seco Tools Ab
Bjornbacksvagen 10
Fagersta 737 3
223 400-00

(G-16597)
SERVICE & TECHNICAL ASSOC LLC
318 John R Rd Ste 323 (48083-4542)
PHONE..................248 233-3761
Jeffery Jones, Mng Member
EMP: 12 EST: 2005
SALES (est): 942.2K Privately Held
SIC: 3823 Industrial instrmnts msrmnt display/control process variable

(G-16598)
SHADKO ENTERPRISES INC
1701 Lexington Dr (48084-5711)
PHONE..................248 816-1712
Leposava Shadko, President
EMP: 4
SALES (est): 62.7K Privately Held
SIC: 3462 Chains, forged steel

(G-16599)
SIEMENS AG
777 Chicago Rd (48083-4234)
PHONE..................248 307-3400
Richard Preston, Accounts Mgr
Len Restivo, Manager
EMP: 3
SALES (est): 177.5K Privately Held
SIC: 3674 1711 Semiconductors & related devices; plumbing, heating, air-conditioning contractors

(G-16600)
SIGN CONCEPTS CORPORATION
Also Called: Asi Signage Innovation
1119 Wheaton Dr (48083-6701)
PHONE..................248 680-8970
Craig Breeden, President
Ian Hillgartner, Business Mgr
Philip Miller, Corp Secy
John Watkins, Vice Pres
Debbie Klein, Project Mgr
EMP: 18 EST: 1980
SQ FT: 15,000
SALES: 2.1MM Privately Held
SIC: 3993 Signs, not made in custom sign painting shops

(G-16601)
SIGNPROCO INC
Also Called: Signarama Troy Metro Detroit
1017 Naughton Dr (48083-1911)
PHONE..................248 585-6880
Robert Chapa, President
EMP: 15
SQ FT: 2,500
SALES (est): 2.3MM Privately Held
SIC: 3993 Signs, not made in custom sign painting shops

(G-16602)
SIGNS & LASER ENGRAVING
1221 E 14 Mile Rd (48083-4656)
PHONE..................248 577-6191
Elton Topalli, Owner
EMP: 6
SALES (est): 416.1K Privately Held
SIC: 3993 Signs & advertising specialties

(G-16603)
SILKROUTE GLOBAL INC
950 Stephenson Hwy (48083-1113)
PHONE..................248 854-3409
Amjad Hussain, President
Steve Hanna, Project Mgr
Adam Moy, CTO
Indar Rathore, Technical Staff
Devin Duden, Sr Software Eng
EMP: 50
SQ FT: 67,000
SALES (est): 6MM Privately Held
SIC: 7371 7372 Computer software development; prepackaged software; application computer software; business oriented computer software

(G-16604)
SINERAMICS INCORPORATED
2062 Chancery Dr (48085-1028)
PHONE..................248 879-0812
James P Edler, President
Derrick Edler, Vice Pres
Patrick Edler, Vice Pres
EMP: 3
SQ FT: 10,000
SALES (est): 300K Privately Held
WEB: www.sineramics.com
SIC: 3251 Ceramic glazed brick, clay

(G-16605)
SIXTEEN CROOKS BP FUEL
2989 Crooks Rd (48084-4715)
PHONE..................248 643-7272
Saif Jameel, Principal
EMP: 4
SALES (est): 302.2K Privately Held
SIC: 2869 Fuels

(G-16606)
SIZMEK DSP INC
Also Called: Rocket Fuel
101 W Big Beaver Rd (48084-5253)
PHONE..................313 516-4482
EMP: 5
SALES (corp-wide): 463.4MM Privately Held
SIC: 3999 Advertising display products
HQ: Sizmek Dsp, Inc.
2000 Seaport Blvd Ste 400
Redwood City CA 94063

(G-16607)
SKYPERSONIC LLC (PA)
1667 Picadilly Dr (48084-1499)
PHONE..................248 648-4822
EMP: 6
SALES (est): 1.8MM Privately Held
SIC: 3861 Photographic equipment & supplies

(G-16608)
SNAP JAWS MANUFACTURING INC
33215 Dequindre Rd (48083-4628)
PHONE..................248 588-1099
John Fitzpatrick, President
EMP: 7
SQ FT: 5,000
SALES (est): 1MM Privately Held
WEB: www.snapjaw.com
SIC: 3541 3545 Numerically controlled metal cutting machine tools; machine tool attachments & accessories

(G-16609)
SODECIA AUTO DETROIT CORP (DH)
Also Called: Sodecia Group
969 Chicago Rd (48083-4227)
PHONE..................586 759-2200
Rui Montero, CEO
Don Bilyea, Vice Pres
Vince Accardo, Purch Agent
Aloisio Monteiro, Purchasing
Kevin Rodriguez, Engineer
◆ EMP: 200
SALES (est): 254MM Privately Held
WEB: www.azautomotive.com
SIC: 3465 Body parts, automobile: stamped metal
HQ: Sodecia - ParticipaCOes Sociais. Sgps, S.A.
Rua Do Espido, 164f
Maia 4470-
220 101-900

(G-16610)
SOLIDBODY TECHNOLOGY COMPANY
Also Called: Commando Lock Company
395 Elmwood Dr (48083-2754)
PHONE..................248 709-7901
Patrick Smith, President
EMP: 4 EST: 2013
SALES: 240K Privately Held
SIC: 3429 Padlocks

(G-16611)
SOMANETICS
1653 E Maple Rd (48083-4208)
PHONE..................248 689-3050
Marcela Bordusanu, Principal
EMP: 13
SALES (est): 1.3MM Privately Held
SIC: 3845 Electromedical equipment

(G-16612)
SORT-TEK INSPTN SYSTEMS INC
1784 Larchwood Dr (48083-2223)
PHONE..................248 273-5200
Patricia Richards, President
Patrick Richards, Vice Pres
EMP: 18
SALES: 1.3MM Privately Held
SIC: 3714 Motor vehicle parts & accessories

(G-16613)
SOURCEHUB LLC
1875 Stephenson Hwy (48083-2150)
PHONE..................800 246-1844
William Nick, President
Robert Long, Vice Pres
▲ EMP: 2
SQ FT: 23,475
SALES (est): 1.7MM Privately Held
WEB: www.sourcehubllc.com
SIC: 5085 3423 Industrial supplies; hand & edge tools

(G-16614)
SOUTH HILL SAND AND GRAVEL (PA)
5877 Livernois Rd Ste 103 (48098-3100)
PHONE..................248 828-1726
Joel Garrett, President
EMP: 1
SQ FT: 2,000
SALES: 2.5MM Privately Held
SIC: 1442 Gravel mining

(G-16615)
SPECTRUM GRAPHICS INC
301 Park Dr (48083-2778)
P.O. Box 428, Clawson (48017-0428)
PHONE..................248 589-2795
Ted Saski, President
EMP: 12
SQ FT: 18,000

GEOGRAPHIC SECTION
Troy - Oakland County (G-16641)

SALES (est): 1.6MM **Privately Held**
WEB: www.spectrumgraphic.com
SIC: 2759 Screen printing

(G-16616)
SPEED INDUSTRY LLC
1668 Thorncroft Dr (48084-4610)
PHONE..................248 458-1335
Jan Niemi, *Principal*
EMP: 3
SALES (est): 218.9K **Privately Held**
SIC: 3999 Manufacturing industries

(G-16617)
SRG GLOBAL INC (DH)
800 Stephenson Hwy (48083-1120)
PHONE..................248 509-1100
Kevin Baird, *President*
Terry Derousse, *Plant Mgr*
Tom Bell, *Opers Mgr*
Brandon Lorenz, *Opers Mgr*
Terry Nonte, *Safety Mgr*
EMP: 169
SALES (est): 1.4B
SALES (corp-wide): 40.6B **Privately Held**
SIC: 2396 Automotive & apparel trimmings
HQ: Guardian Industries, Llc
2300 Harmon Rd
Auburn Hills MI 48326
248 340-1800

(G-16618)
SRG GLOBAL COATINGS INC (DH)
800 Stephenson Hwy (48083-1120)
PHONE..................248 509-1100
Dave Prater, *CEO*
Timothy Prest, *Superintendent*
Kenny Abernathy, *Engineer*
Willie Sturgill, *Engineer*
Ashley Lorano, *Human Resources*
◆ EMP: 230 EST: 1946
SQ FT: 25,000
SALES (est): 954.1MM
SALES (corp-wide): 40.6B **Privately Held**
WEB: www.srob.com
SIC: 3089 3494 2522 3826 Blow molded finished plastic products; injection molded finished plastic products; thermoformed finished plastic products; valves & pipe fittings; office furniture, except wood; analytical instruments; instruments to measure electricity
HQ: Guardian Industries, Llc
2300 Harmon Rd
Auburn Hills MI 48326
248 340-1800

(G-16619)
STAPELS MANUFACTURING LLC
Also Called: Wes Stabeck Industries, LLC
2612 Elliott Dr (48083-4633)
PHONE..................248 577-5570
Mark Stapels,
Nicholas Stapels,
EMP: 14
SQ FT: 15,000
SALES (est): 2.9MM **Privately Held**
WEB: www.stabeck.com
SIC: 3545 Machine tool accessories

(G-16620)
STARLIGHT TECHNOLOGIES INC
2055 Applewood Dr (48085-7032)
PHONE..................248 250-9607
Andrew Tong, *President*
EMP: 6
SALES (est): 620K **Privately Held**
SIC: 3694 Harness wiring sets, internal combustion engines

(G-16621)
STEGMAN TOOL CO INC
1985 Ring Dr (48083-4229)
PHONE..................248 588-4634
Robert J Begeny, *President*
Roger Paquette, *Director*
Victoria Begeny, *Shareholder*
EMP: 25 EST: 1957
SQ FT: 20,000
SALES (est): 7MM **Privately Held**
WEB: www.stegmantool.com
SIC: 3369 8711 Castings, except die-castings, precision; sanitary engineers

(G-16622)
STERLING SOFTWARE INC
525 E Big Beaver Rd # 204 (48083-1363)
PHONE..................248 528-6500
Ganesh Yarapatineni, *President*
EMP: 2
SALES (est): 4.9MM **Privately Held**
SIC: 7372 Prepackaged software

(G-16623)
STORM SEAL CO INC
2789 Rochester Rd (48083-1920)
PHONE..................248 689-1900
Edward A Barrington, *President*
Mark Barrington, *President*
EMP: 6 EST: 1954
SQ FT: 3,000
SALES (est): 988.6K **Privately Held**
SIC: 3442 5211 Storm doors or windows, metal; lumber & other building materials

(G-16624)
STYLE CRAFT PROTOTYPE INC
1820 Brinston Dr (48083-2215)
PHONE..................248 619-9048
Michael Muszynski, *President*
Eric Huntley, *Vice Pres*
Reinhart Egbert, *Treasurer*
EMP: 16
SALES (est): 4.4MM **Privately Held**
SIC: 3465 Body parts, automobile: stamped metal

(G-16625)
SUNERA TECHNOLOGIES INC (PA)
631 E Big Beaver Rd # 105 (48083-1420)
PHONE..................248 524-0222
Srikanth Pakala, *CEO*
Pavan Keesara, *Vice Pres*
Neetha Pai, *Vice Pres*
Vinil Vadi, *CTO*
Ashish Kar, *Officer*
EMP: 26
SQ FT: 2,500
SALES (est): 15.2MM **Privately Held**
WEB: www.suneratech.com
SIC: 7379 7372 Computer related consulting services; application computer software

(G-16626)
SUNGWOO HITECH CO LTD
3321 W Big Beaver Rd # 303 (48084)
PHONE..................248 509-0445
Mun Yong Lee, *President*
Hyejung Yun, *Corp Secy*
Jin Seok Park, *Director*
EMP: 3
SALES (est): 286.9K **Privately Held**
SIC: 3559 Automotive related machinery

(G-16627)
SUPERIOR MANUFACTURING CORP (PA)
Also Called: ABC Industrial Supply
431 Stephenson Hwy (48083-1130)
PHONE..................313 935-1550
Aaron Chernow, *President*
David Chernow, *Vice Pres*
EMP: 15
SALES (est): 2MM **Privately Held**
SIC: 2842 Degreasing solvent

(G-16628)
SURFACE ACTIVATION TECH LLC
Also Called: Sat Plating LLC
1837 Thunderbird (48084-5402)
PHONE..................248 273-0037
John Wallace, *President*
William Wallace, *General Mgr*
Brad Radke, *Plant Mgr*
Anastasia Plonkey, *Admin Mgr*
EMP: 4
SALES (est): 590K **Privately Held**
SIC: 2899 Plating compounds

(G-16629)
SYSTEMS DUPLICATING CO INC
358 Robbins Dr (48083-4558)
PHONE..................248 585-7590
Charles A De Vito Sr, *President*
Bernice De Vito, *Corp Secy*
EMP: 10
SQ FT: 5,000
SALES (est): 1.5MM **Privately Held**
WEB: www.sdci.net
SIC: 2752 Commercial printing, offset

(G-16630)
T M SHEA PRODUCTS INC
1950 Austin Dr (48083-2205)
PHONE..................800 992-5233
Thomas M Shea, *President*
Monica Spaulding, *Vice Pres*
Debbie Junaud, *Executive*
EMP: 10
SQ FT: 14,800
SALES (est): 2MM **Privately Held**
WEB: www.tmshea.com
SIC: 2542 3993 Fixtures, store: except wood; signs & advertising specialties

(G-16631)
TARRS TREE SERVICE INC
2009 Milverton Dr (48083-2535)
PHONE..................248 528-3313
Linda Tarr, *President*
Gary Tarr, *Vice Pres*
EMP: 17
SALES (est): 1MM **Privately Held**
SIC: 2411 Logging

(G-16632)
TATA AUTOCOMP SYSTEMS LIMITED
Also Called: Mechanical Engineer
200 E Big Beaver Rd # 145 (48083-1208)
PHONE..................248 680-4608
EMP: 4
SALES (corp-wide): 176.4MM **Privately Held**
SIC: 3714 Motor vehicle parts & accessories
PA: Tata Autocomp Systems Limited
Taco House, Plot No- 20/B Fpn085,
V.G. Damle Path,
Pune MH 41100
202 665-0103

(G-16633)
TE CONNECTIVITY CORPORATION
900 Wilshire Dr Ste 150 (48084-1600)
PHONE..................248 273-3344
Dwight Hansell, *Manager*
EMP: 198
SALES (corp-wide): 13.9B **Privately Held**
SIC: 3678 Electronic connectors
HQ: Te Connectivity Corporation
1050 Westlakes Dr
Berwyn PA 19312
610 893-9800

(G-16634)
TEBIS AMERICA INC
400 E Big Beaver Rd # 200 (48083-1260)
PHONE..................248 524-0430
David Klotz, *President*
Gerardo Mueller, *Human Res Mgr*
Vernon Benson, *Accounts Mgr*
Cindy Davidson, *Sales Staff*
John Kowalczyk, *Sales Staff*
EMP: 23
SALES (est): 3.1MM
SALES (corp-wide): 57.6MM **Privately Held**
WEB: www.tebis.com
SIC: 7372 Prepackaged software
PA: Tebis Technische Informationssysteme Ag
Einsteinstr. 39
Planegg 82152
898 180-30

(G-16635)
TEDSON INDUSTRIES INC
1408 Allen Dr (48083-4013)
PHONE..................248 588-9230
Steven Marek, *President*
Elyse Marek, *Admin Sec*
EMP: 19
SQ FT: 20,000
SALES (est): 2MM **Privately Held**
SIC: 3543 Industrial patterns

(G-16636)
TENNANT & ASSOCIATES INC
1700 Stutz Dr Ste 61 (48084-4502)
PHONE..................248 643-6140
Mary Tennant, *President*
Terrence J Tennant, *Treasurer*
EMP: 5
SQ FT: 4,200
SALES (est): 509.2K **Privately Held**
SIC: 2396 5131 Furniture trimmings, fabric; piece goods & notions

(G-16637)
TESLA INC
Also Called: Tesla Motors
2850 W Big Beaver Rd (48084-3205)
PHONE..................248 205-3206
EMP: 3
SALES (corp-wide): 21.4B **Publicly Held**
SIC: 3711 Motor vehicles & car bodies
PA: Tesla, Inc.
3500 Deer Creek Rd
Palo Alto CA 94304
650 681-5000

(G-16638)
THORESON-MC COSH INC
1885 Thunderbird (48084-5472)
PHONE..................248 362-0960
David Klatt, *President*
▼ EMP: 30 EST: 1940
SQ FT: 26,000
SALES: 5.1MM **Privately Held**
WEB: www.thoresonmccosh.com
SIC: 3559 3634 3567 3537 Plastics working machinery; electric housewares & fans; industrial furnaces & ovens; industrial trucks & tractors; conveyors & conveying equipment; prefabricated metal buildings

(G-16639)
THYSSENKRUPP AUTOMOTIVE SALES
Also Called: Thyssenkrupp Components
3331 W Big Beaver Rd # 300 (48084-2815)
PHONE..................248 530-2991
Michelle Bosway, *Branch Mgr*
EMP: 18
SALES (corp-wide): 39.8B **Privately Held**
SIC: 5013 3714 Motor vehicle supplies & new parts; motor vehicle parts & accessories
HQ: Thyssenkrupp Automotive Sales & Technical Center, Inc.
3155 W Big Beaver Rd # 260
Troy MI 48084

(G-16640)
THYSSENKRUPP AUTOMOTIVE SALES (DH)
3155 W Big Beaver Rd # 260 (48084-3002)
P.O. Box 2601 (48007-2601)
PHONE..................248 530-2902
Craig Shetler, *President*
Jeff Fischer, *President*
Richard J Trahey, *Director*
Angela Briglia, *Admin Asst*
◆ EMP: 35
SQ FT: 8,000
SALES (est): 125.4MM
SALES (corp-wide): 39.8B **Privately Held**
SIC: 5013 3714 Motor vehicle supplies & new parts; motor vehicle parts & accessories
HQ: Thyssenkrupp North America, Inc.
111 W Jackson Blvd # 2400
Chicago IL 60604
312 525-2800

(G-16641)
THYSSENKRUPP BILSTEIN AMER INC
3155 W Big Beaver Rd # 125 (48084-3002)
PHONE..................248 530-2900
Axel Boehne, *Branch Mgr*
EMP: 13

Troy - Oakland County (G-16642)

GEOGRAPHIC SECTION

SALES (corp-wide): 39.8B **Privately Held**
SIC: **3714** 5013 Shock absorbers, motor vehicle; springs, shock absorbers & struts
HQ: Thyssenkrupp Bilstein Of America, Inc.
8685 Bilstein Blvd
Hamilton OH 45015
513 881-7600

(G-16642)
TI GROUP AUTO SYSTEMS LLC
Also Called: Fuel Systems
100 W Big Beaver Rd (48084-5206)
PHONE..................248 494-5000
EMP: 50
SALES (corp-wide): 3.9B **Privately Held**
SIC: 3714 Fuel pumps, motor vehicle
HQ: Ti Group Automotive Systems, Llc
2020 Taylor Rd
Auburn Hills MI 48326
248 296-8000

(G-16643)
TILCO INC
401 Elmwood Dr (48083-4802)
P.O. Box 1803, Birmingham (48012-1803)
PHONE..................248 644-0901
Stephen R Tille, *President*
Melissa Tille, *Admin Sec*
EMP: 9 **EST:** 1997
SQ FT: 8,200
SALES: 560K **Privately Held**
SIC: 3841 5199 Surgical & medical instruments; advertising specialties

(G-16644)
TIMOTHY J TADE INC (PA)
Also Called: Tade Publishing Group
4798 Butler Dr (48085-3525)
P.O. Box 4803 (48099-4803)
PHONE..................248 552-8583
Thomas James Lynch, *President*
Susan Marie Lynch, *Treasurer*
EMP: 6
SQ FT: 1,450
SALES (est): 665.8K **Privately Held**
WEB: www.tadesite.com
SIC: 2721 2741 4813 Trade journals: publishing only, not printed on site; miscellaneous publishing;

(G-16645)
TKS INDUSTRIAL COMPANY (HQ)
901 Tower Dr Ste 300 (48098-2817)
PHONE..................248 786-5000
Bob Booth, *Exec VP*
Karl Safranek, *Electrical Engi*
Jonathan Carender, *Accounts Mgr*
Irving Shiffman, *MIS Mgr*
▲ **EMP:** 40
SQ FT: 6,000
SALES (est): 37.7MM **Privately Held**
WEB: www.tks-america.com
SIC: 1721 3559 Interior commercial painting contractor; metal finishing equipment for plating, etc.

(G-16646)
TMB TRENDS INC
100 W Big Beaver Rd (48084-5206)
PHONE..................866 445-2344
Tatiana Mabika, *Principal*
EMP: 4
SALES (est): 98K **Privately Held**
SIC: 3171 7389 Women's handbags & purses;

(G-16647)
TORAY RESIN COMPANY (DH)
2800 Livernois Rd D115 (48083-1215)
PHONE..................248 269-8800
Takashi Endo, *President*
Shinichi Tachibana, *Principal*
Mark Barton, *Vice Pres*
▲ **EMP:** 100
SQ FT: 5,800
SALES (est): 24.3MM **Privately Held**
SIC: 2821 Plastics materials & resins
HQ: Toray Holding (U.S.A.), Inc.
461 5th Ave Fl 9
New York NY 10017
212 697-8150

(G-16648)
TOTAL FLOW PRODUCTS INC
1197 Rochester Rd Ste N (48083-6031)
PHONE..................248 588-4490
Stephen Sanchez, *President*
EMP: 5
SQ FT: 3,000
SALES (est): 837.2K **Privately Held**
WEB: www.totalflowproducts.com
SIC: 3593 Fluid power cylinders, hydraulic or pneumatic

(G-16649)
TOTAL PACKAGING SOLUTIONS LLC
775 W Big Beavr Rd # 2020 (48084)
PHONE..................248 519-2376
Elizabeth Dzuris,
EMP: 3
SQ FT: 200
SALES (est): 309.6K **Privately Held**
SIC: 7389 2393 Packaging & labeling services; textile bags

(G-16650)
TOYODA GOSEI NORTH AMER CORP (HQ)
1400 Stephenson Hwy (48083-1189)
PHONE..................248 280-2100
Hiromi Ikehata, *President*
Todd Braund, *General Mgr*
Mak Endo, *General Mgr*
Pierre Lessard, *General Mgr*
Michael Olesko, *General Mgr*
◆ **EMP:** 216
SQ FT: 36,000
SALES: 913.1MM **Privately Held**
WEB: www.tggroupna.com
SIC: 3069 3089 Weather strip, sponge rubber; automotive parts, plastic

(G-16651)
TROY ORTHOPEDIC ASSOCIATES PLC
1350 Kirts Blvd Ste 160 (48084-4852)
PHONE..................248 244-9426
Craig W Roodbeen, *Partner*
Nicholas Dutcheshen, *Med Doctor*
EMP: 3
SALES (est): 273K **Privately Held**
SIC: 3842 Trusses, orthopedic & surgical

(G-16652)
TRUCK TRAILER TRANSIT INC
1400 Rochester Rd (48083-6014)
PHONE..................313 516-7151
Ralph David Lawrence, *President*
▲ **EMP:** 25 **EST:** 1982
SQ FT: 40,000
SALES (est): 3.5MM **Privately Held**
WEB: www.tttonline.com
SIC: 3714 Motor vehicle brake systems & parts

(G-16653)
TRUE FABRICATIONS & MACHINE
1731 Thorncroft Dr (48084-4613)
PHONE..................248 288-0140
Steve Stelkic, *President*
Neil Stelkic, *Vice Pres*
EMP: 10
SQ FT: 14,000
SALES: 1MM **Privately Held**
WEB: www.truefabrications.com
SIC: 3443 3541 Fabricated plate work (boiler shop); numerically controlled metal cutting machine tools

(G-16654)
TRUING SYSTEMS INC
1060 Chicago Rd (48083-4298)
PHONE..................248 588-9060
Ronald Stempin, *President*
David Stempin, *Vice Pres*
EMP: 17
SQ FT: 3,000
SALES (est): 3.1MM **Privately Held**
WEB: www.truingsystems.com
SIC: 3545 Diamond dressing & wheel crushing attachments

(G-16655)
TRUTRON CORPORATION
274 Executive Dr (48083-4530)
PHONE..................248 583-9166
Lisa J Kingsley, *President*
▼ **EMP:** 35
SQ FT: 14,029
SALES (est): 5.3MM **Privately Held**
WEB: www.trutron.com
SIC: 3544 Special dies & tools

(G-16656)
TUBULAR PDT SOLUTIONS NA LLC
Also Called: Tps North America LLC
700 E Big Beaver Rd Ste F (48083-1435)
PHONE..................248 388-4664
Andrew Raczkowski,
EMP: 3 **EST:** 2016
SALES (est): 125.7K **Privately Held**
SIC: 3429 Motor vehicle hardware

(G-16657)
TUOCAI AMERICA LLC
5700 Crooks Rd Ste 222 (48098-2809)
PHONE..................248 346-5910
Frank Yang,
EMP: 8
SALES (est): 340K **Privately Held**
SIC: 2899 Metal treating compounds

(G-16658)
TUWAY AMERICAN GROUP INC
Also Called: Tu Way
3155 W Big Beaver Rd # 104 (48084-3006)
PHONE..................248 205-9999
Gertrude Koester, *CEO*
Douglas Koester, *President*
Judy Piatek, *Accountant*
▲ **EMP:** 147 **EST:** 1947
SQ FT: 1,000
SALES (est): 19.3MM **Privately Held**
WEB: www.tuway.com
SIC: 2392 Mops, floor & dust

(G-16659)
TYDE GROUP WORLDWIDE LLC
5700 Crooks Rd Ste 207 (48098-2809)
PHONE..................248 879-7656
Steven Dow, *Principal*
EMP: 9
SALES (est): 125.7MM
SALES (corp-wide): 16.9B **Privately Held**
SIC: 3592 Carburetors
PA: Sun Capital Partners, Inc.
5200 Town Center Cir # 600
Boca Raton FL 33486
561 962-3400

(G-16660)
TYGRUS LLC
1134 E Big Beaver Rd (48083-1934)
PHONE..................248 218-0347
Art McWood, *Exec VP*
Larry Carlson, *CTO*
Daniel Jenuwine, *Exec Dir*
Patrick Scalera, *Director*
EMP: 5
SQ FT: 500
SALES (est): 690.5K **Privately Held**
SIC: 2869 Industrial organic chemicals

(G-16661)
UFI FILTERS USA INC
50 W Big Beavr Rd Ste 440 (48084-5290)
PHONE..................248 376-0441
EMP: 4
SALES (corp-wide): 507.8K **Privately Held**
SIC: 3714 Mfg Motor Vehicle Parts/Accessories
HQ: Ufi Filters Usa, Inc.
110 Firestone Pt
Duluth GA 48084

(G-16662)
UFI FILTERS USA INC
50 W Big Beavr Rd Ste 440 (48084-5290)
PHONE..................248 376-0441
Richard Hubbell, *President*
Matt Tenbusch, *Sales Staff*
Richard Belf, *Manager*
Andrea Prando, *Prgrmr*
▲ **EMP:** 12
SQ FT: 2,600
SALES: 10MM
SALES (corp-wide): 417.8K **Privately Held**
SIC: 3714 Filters: oil, fuel & air, motor vehicle
HQ: Ufi Filters Spa
Via Europa 26
Porto Mantovano MN 46047
037 638-6812

(G-16663)
UNITED GLOBAL SOURCING INC (PA)
Also Called: Ugs
5607 New King Dr Ste 100 (48098-2660)
PHONE..................248 952-5700
Kenneth Eisenbraun, *Ch of Bd*
Kevin De Hart, *President*
Roger Gregory, *Vice Pres*
Pam S Payne, *Vice Pres*
Pam Payne, *Vice Pres*
▲ **EMP:** 18
SQ FT: 9,900
SALES (est): 5.8MM **Privately Held**
WEB: www.unitedgs.com
SIC: 3334 2491 Primary aluminum; flooring, treated wood block

(G-16664)
UNITED SYSTEMS
Also Called: Western Press
525 Elmwood Dr (48083-2755)
P.O. Box 353, Clawson (48017-0353)
PHONE..................248 583-9670
David A Thomas, *Owner*
David Thomas, *Principal*
EMP: 8
SQ FT: 4,600
SALES: 2MM **Privately Held**
SIC: 1799 3599 Welding on site; custom machinery

(G-16665)
UNIVERSAL TOOL INC
552 Robbins Dr (48083-4514)
PHONE..................248 733-9800
William Nordness, *President*
Todd Ballard, *Vice Pres*
▼ **EMP:** 7
SALES (est): 1MM **Privately Held**
SIC: 3545 Sockets (machine tool accessories)

(G-16666)
US FARATHANE HOLDINGS CORP
Also Called: Chemcast
750 W Maple Rd (48084-5315)
PHONE..................586 978-2800
Greg Schaff, *Principal*
Brian Winowski, *Technology*
EMP: 64
SALES (corp-wide): 876MM **Privately Held**
SIC: 3089 Injection molding of plastics
PA: U.S. Farathane Holdings Corp.
11650 Park Ct
Shelby Township MI 48315
586 726-1200

(G-16667)
USA CARBIDE
1395 Wheaton Dr Ste 500 (48083-1926)
PHONE..................248 817-5137
Ralph D Schiller III, *Administration*
EMP: 3
SALES (est): 88.7K **Privately Held**
SIC: 2819 Carbides

(G-16668)
USA TODAY ADVERTISING
2800 Livernois Rd Ste 600 (48083-1231)
PHONE..................248 680-6530
Marcia Bollard, *Principal*
EMP: 4
SALES (est): 228.7K **Privately Held**
SIC: 2711 Newspapers, publishing & printing

(G-16669)
UTICA BODY & ASSEMBLY INC (HQ)
5750 New King Dr Ste 200 (48098-2611)
PHONE..................586 726-4330

Thomas J Carter, *President*
Stefan Wanczyk, *Vice Pres*
EMP: 20
SQ FT: 62,640
SALES (est): 6.6MM
SALES (corp-wide): 565.7MM **Privately Held**
SIC: 3549 8711 3541 Assembly machines, including robotic; designing: ship, boat, machine & product; machine tools, metal cutting type
PA: Utica Enterprises, Inc.
5750 New King Dr Ste 200
Troy MI 48098
586 726-4300

(G-16670)
UTICA ENTERPRISES INC (PA)
Also Called: Utica Laeser Systems
5750 New King Dr Ste 200 (48098-2611)
PHONE 586 726-4300
Thomas J Carter, *Ch of Bd*
Stefan Wanczyk, *President*
Dennis Lucas, *Vice Pres*
Miriam Millan, *Purch Mgr*
James Bates, *Technical Mgr*
▲ **EMP:** 200
SQ FT: 160,000
SALES (est): 565.7MM **Privately Held**
SIC: 3548 3549 3545 3544 Welding apparatus; assembly machines, including robotic; broaches (machine tool accessories); special dies & tools; designing: ship, boat, machine & product; machine tools, metal cutting type; broaching machines

(G-16671)
UTICA INTERNATIONAL INC (HQ)
5750 New King Dr Ste 200 (48098-2611)
PHONE 586 726-4330
Thomas J Carter, *Ch of Bd*
Stefan Wanczyk, *President*
EMP: 200
SALES (est): 50.2MM
SALES (corp-wide): 565.7MM **Privately Held**
WEB: www.dct-inc.com
SIC: 3549 3548 3544 Assembly machines, including robotic; electric welding equipment; special dies, tools, jigs & fixtures
PA: Utica Enterprises, Inc.
5750 New King Dr Ste 200
Troy MI 48098
586 726-4300

(G-16672)
UTLEY BROTHERS INC
Also Called: Heritage Business Cards
567 Robbins Dr (48083-4515)
P.O. Box 1469 (48099-1469)
PHONE 248 585-1700
Duane Harrison, *President*
Andrew Harrison, *Vice Pres*
Patricia R Harrison, *Treasurer*
Lainie Seibold, *Customer Svc Re*
EMP: 38 EST: 1945
SQ FT: 23,200
SALES (est): 7.7MM **Privately Held**
WEB: www.utleybros.com
SIC: 2752 2759 5112 Business form & card printing, lithographic; thermography; stationery & office supplies

(G-16673)
V E S T INC
3250 W Big Beaver Rd # 440 (48084-2902)
PHONE 248 649-9550
Shruti Raina, *President*
EMP: 7 EST: 1997
SALES (est): 1MM **Privately Held**
WEB: www.vestusa.com
SIC: 7372 Prepackaged software

(G-16674)
V S AMERICA INC
1000 John R Rd Ste 111 (48083-4317)
PHONE 248 585-6715
Oliver Diehm, *President*
Elizabeth Roberson, *Office Mgr*
▲ **EMP:** 2
SQ FT: 1,000
SALES: 9.4MM
SALES (corp-wide): 32.6MM **Privately Held**
WEB: www.vs-america.com
SIC: 7692 Welding repair
PA: Vs Guss Ag
Parallelstr. 17
Solingen 42719
212 384-0

(G-16675)
VALEO FRICTION MATERIALS INC (DH)
Also Called: Valeo Wiper Systems
150 Stephenson Hwy (48083-1116)
PHONE 248 619-8300
Lionel Brenac, *President*
Eric Amiot, *Business Mgr*
Octavio Zavala, *Engineer*
Luc Charlemagne, *Treasurer*
Viral Patel, *Manager*
▲ **EMP:** 4
SQ FT: 40,000
SALES (est): 10.9MM
SALES (corp-wide): 177.9K **Privately Held**
SIC: 3714 Clutches, motor vehicle

(G-16676)
VALEO NORTH AMERICA INC
Also Called: Valeo Service Center
150 Stephenson Hwy (48083-1116)
PHONE 248 619-8300
James Schwyn, *General Mgr*
Bruce Clutton, *General Mgr*
Mark Coykendall, *Vice Pres*
Jean-Sebastie Delfosse, *Project Mgr*
Dennis Linson, *Project Mgr*
EMP: 200
SALES (corp-wide): 177.9K **Privately Held**
WEB: www.valeoinc.com
SIC: 3625 7336 8731 Switches, electric power; art design services; commercial physical research
HQ: Valeo North America, Inc.
150 Stephenson Hwy
Troy MI 48083

(G-16677)
VALEO NORTH AMERICA INC (HQ)
Also Called: Valeo Wiper Systems
150 Stephenson Hwy (48083-1116)
PHONE 248 619-8300
Francoise Colpron, *President*
◆ **EMP:** 74
SQ FT: 437,000
SALES (est): 1.1B
SALES (corp-wide): 177.9K **Privately Held**
SIC: 3714 Motor vehicle electrical equipment; heaters, motor vehicle; windshield wiper systems, motor vehicle; air conditioner parts, motor vehicle
PA: Valeo
43 Rue Bayen
Paris 17e Arrondissement
140 687-476

(G-16678)
VALEO RADAR SYSTEMS INC (HQ)
150 Stephenson Hwy (48083-1116)
PHONE 248 619-8300
James Schwyn, *President*
Nicolas Retailleau, *CFO*
EMP: 10
SALES (est): 79.7MM
SALES (corp-wide): 177.9K **Privately Held**
WEB: www.valeoraytheon.com
SIC: 5731 3714 Radio, television & electronic stores; motor vehicle electrical equipment
PA: Valeo
43 Rue Bayen
Paris 17e Arrondissement
140 687-476

(G-16679)
VALEO SWITCHES & DETE (DH)
150 Stephenson Hwy (48083-1116)
PHONE 248 619-8300
James Schwyn, *President*
▲ **EMP:** 42
SALES (est): 209.8MM
SALES (corp-wide): 177.9K **Privately Held**
SIC: 3714 Motor vehicle parts & accessories

(G-16680)
VEHMA INTERNATIONAL AMER INC
1230 Chicago Rd (48083-4230)
PHONE 248 585-4800
Simon Bennett, *Manager*
EMP: 200
SALES (corp-wide): 40.8B **Privately Held**
SIC: 8711 3714 Designing: ship, boat, machine & product; motor vehicle parts & accessories
HQ: Vehma International Of America, Inc.
750 Tower Dr 4000
Troy MI 48098
248 631-2800

(G-16681)
VEHMA INTERNATIONAL AMER INC (DH)
Also Called: Cosma Engineering
750 Tower Dr 4000 (48098-2863)
PHONE 248 631-2800
Frank Gabbianelli, *General Mgr*
Swamy Kotagiri, *Exec VP*
Arthur L Lee, *Vice Pres*
Gerd Brusius, *Vice Pres*
John Goodrow, *Vice Pres*
◆ **EMP:** 100
SQ FT: 115,000
SALES (est): 47.6MM
SALES (corp-wide): 40.8B **Privately Held**
SIC: 3714 Motor vehicle parts & accessories
HQ: Cosma International Of America, Inc.
750 Tower Dr
Troy MI 48098
248 631-1100

(G-16682)
VELCRO USA INC
Velcro Automotives Division
1210 Souter Dr (48083-6020)
PHONE 248 583-6060
Fax: 248 585-7861
EMP: 7 **Privately Held**
SIC: 3713 Sales Office
HQ: Velcro Usa Inc.
95 Sundial Ave
Manchester NH 03103
603 669-4880

(G-16683)
VERSATUBE CORPORATION
4755 Rochester Rd Ste 200 (48085-4963)
PHONE 248 524-0299
Eugene Goodman, *President*
Sandra Goodman, *Admin Sec*
▲ **EMP:** 12 EST: 1959
SQ FT: 180,000
SALES (est): 2.4MM **Privately Held**
WEB: www.versatubecorp.com
SIC: 3465 3469 3599 Moldings or trim, automobile: stamped metal; metal stampings; tubing, flexible metallic

(G-16684)
VIBRATION CONTROLS TECH LLC
2075 W Big Beaver Rd # 500 (48084-3407)
PHONE 248 822-8010
Joseph B Anderson,
EMP: 5
SALES (est): 400K **Privately Held**
SIC: 3822 Damper operators: pneumatic, thermostatic, electric

(G-16685)
VIRTUAL ADVANTAGE LLC
3290 W Big Beavr Rd # 310 (48084-2910)
PHONE 877 772-6886
Ryan Robison,
EMP: 5
SALES: 950K **Privately Held**
SIC: 7372 Prepackaged software

(G-16686)
VIRTUAL TECHNOLOGY INC
1345 Wheaton Dr (48083-1994)
PHONE 248 528-6565
Michael Dolik, *General Mgr*
EMP: 12
SQ FT: 20,000
SALES (est): 1.7MM **Privately Held**
SIC: 3572 5045 Computer storage devices; computer peripheral equipment

(G-16687)
VISALUS SCIENCES
340 E Big Beaver Rd # 280 (48083-1218)
PHONE 877 847-2587
EMP: 4
SALES (est): 170.2K
SALES (corp-wide): 2.4B **Publicly Held**
SIC: 2023 Dietary supplements, dairy & non-dairy based
HQ: Partylite, Inc.
59 Armstrong Rd
Plymouth MA 02360
203 661-1926

(G-16688)
WCSCARTS LLC (PA)
Also Called: World Class Shopping Carts
900 Wilshire Dr Ste 202 (48084-1600)
P.O. Box 3355, Rocklin CA (95677-8468)
PHONE 248 901-0965
Ross Vincent, *Mng Member*
▲ **EMP:** 14
SALES: 10MM **Privately Held**
SIC: 3496 Grocery carts, made from purchased wire

(G-16689)
WESTERN INTERNATIONAL INC
Also Called: Western Global
1707 Northwood Dr (48084-5524)
PHONE 866 814-2470
Tomasz Majcherski, *General Mgr*
James Truan, *General Mgr*
Barry Truan, *Vice Pres*
Greg Cornell, *Opers Staff*
Malcolm Gash, *Engineer*
▲ **EMP:** 33
SQ FT: 26,000
SALES (est): 11.4MM **Privately Held**
SIC: 3443 5084 4225 5051 Fuel tanks (oil, gas, etc.): metal plate; industrial machinery & equipment; general warehousing & storage; metals service centers & offices

(G-16690)
WEYV INC
1820 E Big Beaver Rd (48083-2031)
PHONE 248 614-2400
Srinivasa Palepu, *Controller*
EMP: 10 EST: 2017
SALES (est): 287.1K
SALES (corp-wide): 396.3MM **Publicly Held**
SIC: 2741
PA: Altair Engineering Inc.
1820 E Big Beaver Rd
Troy MI 48083
248 614-2400

(G-16691)
WILLCO EXTRUSION LLC
1107 Naughton Dr (48083-1932)
PHONE 248 817-2373
Pamela L Mytnik, *Principal*
EMP: 3
SALES (est): 515.1K **Privately Held**
SIC: 3089 Plastic processing

(G-16692)
WITZENMANN USA LLC (PA)
1201 Stephenson Hwy (48083-1105)
PHONE 248 588-6033
Keith Shivnen, *Mng Member*
◆ **EMP:** 179
SQ FT: 60,000
SALES (est): 32.3MM **Privately Held**
WEB: www.witzenmann-usa.com
SIC: 3449 Miscellaneous metalwork

Troy - Oakland County

(G-16693)
WKW ERBSLOEH N AMER HOLDG INC
3310 W Big Beaver Rd (48084-2809)
PHONE.....................205 338-4242
Arne Kramer, *Branch Mgr*
EMP: 58
SALES (corp-wide): 144.1K **Privately Held**
SIC: 3714 Motor vehicle parts & accessories
HQ: Wkw Erbsloeh North America Holding, Inc.
103 Parkway E
Pell City AL 35125

(G-16694)
WOLVERINE CARBIDE & TOOL INC
684 Robbins Dr (48083-4563)
PHONE.....................248 247-3888
Derek J Stevens, *President*
Randall Grunewald, *General Mgr*
Thomas Dharte, *Vice Pres*
Gregory J Stevens, *Vice Pres*
Arthur Keysaer, *Plant Supt*
EMP: 59
SQ FT: 19,400
SALES (est): 9.1MM **Privately Held**
WEB: www.wolverinecarbide.com
SIC: 3544 Special dies, tools, jigs & fixtures

(G-16695)
WOLVERINE CARBIDE DIE COMPANY
2613 Industrial Row Dr (48084-7081)
PHONE.....................248 280-0300
Nicholas Stavropoulos, *President*
Gus Stavropoulos, *President*
Mark Stavropoulos, *Vice Pres*
Maria Stavropoulos, *Admin Sec*
EMP: 40 EST: 1965
SQ FT: 30,000
SALES (est): 6.7MM **Privately Held**
SIC: 3599 3541 3544 3316 Electrical discharge machining (EDM); machine tools, metal cutting type; grinding machines, metalworking; special dies & tools; cold finishing of steel shapes

(G-16696)
WOODBRIDGE GROUP INC
2400 Meijer Dr (48084-7110)
PHONE.....................269 324-8993
Dennis Baer, *President*
Guy Didio, *Engineer*
Randy Haffey, *Human Res Dir*
Cedra Upshaw, *Director*
EMP: 1
SALES (est): 1.9MM **Privately Held**
SIC: 3312 Chemicals & other products derived from coking

(G-16697)
WOODBRIDGE HOLDINGS INC (HQ)
1515 Equity Dr Ste 100 (48084-7129)
PHONE.....................248 288-0100
Hugh W Sloan Jr, *President*
Taleen Nigosian Baldwi, *Business Mgr*
Brad Hasenfratz, *Business Mgr*
Terry Campbell, *COO*
Robert Magee, *Exec VP*
▲ EMP: 6
SQ FT: 20,000
SALES (est): 609.9MM
SALES (corp-wide): 1.9B **Privately Held**
SIC: 2531 3086 Seats, automobile; plastics foam products
PA: Woodbridge Foam Corporation
4240 Sherwoodtowne Blvd Suite 300
Mississauga ON L4Z 2
905 896-3626

(G-16698)
WOODBRIDGE SALES & ENGRG INC (DH)
1515 Equity Dr (48084-7129)
PHONE.....................248 288-0100
Bob Magee, *President*
Richard Jocsak, *Treasurer*
EMP: 120

SALES (est): 57.9MM
SALES (corp-wide): 1.9B **Privately Held**
SIC: 5162 5013 2821 Plastics products; automotive supplies & parts; plastics materials & resins
HQ: Woodbridge Holdings Inc.
1515 Equity Dr Ste 100
Troy MI 48084
248 288-0100

(G-16699)
WORLD CLASS STEEL & PROC INC
2673 American Dr (48083-4619)
PHONE.....................586 585-1734
Jay Tlumak, *President*
EMP: 4
SALES (est): 4MM **Privately Held**
SIC: 3999 5051 Advertising curtains; steel

(G-16700)
WRIGHT COMMUNICATIONS INC
1229 Chicago Rd (48083-4231)
P.O. Box 71276, Madison Heights (48071-0276)
PHONE.....................248 585-3838
Kevin Wright, *President*
Bill Wright, *Treasurer*
EMP: 15
SQ FT: 2,500
SALES (est): 2.3MM **Privately Held**
WEB: www.wrightdigital.net
SIC: 5045 2721 Printers, computer; periodicals

(G-16701)
X-BAR AUTOMATION INC
961 Elmsford Dr (48083-2803)
PHONE.....................248 616-9890
Michael O'Hagan, *President*
Daniel Selonke, *Corp Secy*
Thomas McQuarter, *Vice Pres*
Dave Jerore, *Production*
Craig Speakman, *Executive*
EMP: 25
SQ FT: 12,500
SALES (est): 7.7MM **Privately Held**
SIC: 3613 Control panels, electric

(G-16702)
YAREMA DIE & ENGINEERING CO (PA)
300 Minnesota Dr (48083-4610)
PHONE.....................248 585-2830
Lester Fisher, *President*
George W Lukowski, *Chairman*
James Yarema, *Vice Chairman*
EMP: 100
SQ FT: 43,272
SALES (est): 22.3MM **Privately Held**
WEB: www.yarema.com
SIC: 3544 3465 Die sets for metal stamping (presses); moldings or trim, automobile: stamped metal

(G-16703)
YAREMA DIE & ENGINEERING CO
1855 Stephenson Hwy (48083-2150)
PHONE.....................248 689-5777
Dan Cooper, *Principal*
EMP: 40
SALES (corp-wide): 22.2MM **Privately Held**
SIC: 3469 3499 Stamping metal for the trade; boxes for packing & shipping, metal
PA: Yarema Die & Engineering Co.
300 Minnesota Dr
Troy MI 48083
248 585-2830

(G-16704)
YTI OFFICE EXPRESS LLC
1280 E Big Beaver Rd A (48083-1946)
PHONE.....................866 996-8952
Devin Durrell, *Mng Member*
Michael Carr,
EMP: 5
SQ FT: 12,000
SALES (est): 364.2K **Privately Held**
SIC: 5712 5112 2752 Office furniture; stationery & office supplies; commercial printing, offset

(G-16705)
ZHONGLI NORTH AMERICA INC
449 Executive Dr (48083-4535)
PHONE.....................248 733-9300
Yaunpeng Dai, *President*
Yacong Dai, *Treasurer*
Rita Rohan, *Office Mgr*
▲ EMP: 94
SALES (est): 16.7MM
SALES (corp-wide): 7.3MM **Privately Held**
SIC: 3714 Motor vehicle engines & parts
PA: Shanghai Zhongli Investment Development Co., Ltd.
Rm.250, No.375, Pingshun Rd.
Shanghai 20043

(G-16706)
ZIEBART INTERNATIONAL CORP (PA)
1290 E Maple Rd (48083-2817)
PHONE.....................248 588-4100
Thomas E Wolfe, *President*
Daniel C Baker, *Exec VP*
William Patterson, *Senior VP*
Michael W Riley, *Senior VP*
Thomas A Wolfe, *Senior VP*
▼ EMP: 130
SQ FT: 35,000
SALES (est): 32.6MM **Privately Held**
WEB: www.ziebart.com
SIC: 7549 6794 5013 2842 Lubrication service, automotive; sun roof installation, automotive; franchises, selling or licensing; automotive supplies; specialty cleaning, polishes & sanitation goods; adhesives & sealants; paints & allied products

(G-16707)
ZKW LIGHTING SYSTEMS USA INC
100 W Big Beavr Rd # 300 (48084-5283)
PHONE.....................248 525-4600
Stefan Hauptmann, *Manager*
EMP: 9 EST: 2014
SALES (est): 787.5K **Privately Held**
SIC: 3647 Automotive lighting fixtures

Turner
Arenac County

(G-16708)
BAY CITY CRANE INC
3951 Allen Rd (48765-9502)
PHONE.....................989 867-4292
Brian Tressler, *CEO*
Gary Tressler, *Corp Secy*
EMP: 4
SQ FT: 7,800
SALES (est): 181.5K **Privately Held**
SIC: 3599 Machine shop, jobbing & repair

Tustin
Osceola County

(G-16709)
C & L CONCRETE
20994 200th Ave (49688-8134)
PHONE.....................231 829-3386
EMP: 3 EST: 2005
SALES: 50K **Privately Held**
SIC: 1422 Crushed/Broken Limestone

(G-16710)
COE CREEK PORTABLE SAWMILL
22033 230th Ave (49688-8077)
PHONE.....................231 829-3035
Tim Seguin, *Principal*
EMP: 6
SALES (est): 698.7K **Privately Held**
SIC: 2421 Sawmills & planing mills, general

(G-16711)
NELSONS SAW MILL INC
8482 N Raymond Rd (49688-9603)
PHONE.....................231 829-5220
Steve Nelson, *President*

Michael Nelson, *Vice Pres*
Robert Nelson, *Treasurer*
EMP: 5
SALES (est): 610K **Privately Held**
SIC: 2421 Resawing lumber into smaller dimensions

Twin Lake
Muskegon County

(G-16712)
GREAT LAKES LOG & FIREWD CO
11405 Russell Rd (49457-9469)
PHONE.....................231 206-4073
Dennis Blankenship, *President*
Sharon Blankenship, *Vice Pres*
EMP: 4
SALES: 1.5MM **Privately Held**
SIC: 2411 5099 5734 Logging camps & contractors; firewood; word processing equipment & supplies

(G-16713)
KENNETH A GOULD
2790 W Raymond Rd (49457-9127)
PHONE.....................231 828-4705
Kenneth Gould, *Principal*
EMP: 3
SALES (est): 225.6K **Privately Held**
SIC: 2411 Logging

(G-16714)
S&M LOGGING LLC
6141 16th St (49457-9709)
PHONE.....................231 821-0588
Mark Sundberg, *Principal*
EMP: 3
SALES (est): 204.4K **Privately Held**
SIC: 2411 Logging

(G-16715)
TOP FORM INC
4165 River Rd (49457-8759)
PHONE.....................815 653-9616
Bruce Bates, *President*
EMP: 4
SALES (est): 563.2K **Privately Held**
SIC: 2541 Counter & sink tops

Ubly
Huron County

(G-16716)
GEMINI PLASTICS INC
4385 Garfield St (48475-9553)
PHONE.....................989 658-8557
John Moll, *President*
EMP: 250
SALES (est): 173.8K **Privately Held**
SIC: 3086 6531 Plastics foam products; real estate agents & managers
PA: Gemini Group, Inc.
175 Thompson Rd Ste A
Bad Axe MI 48413

(G-16717)
GEMINI PLASTICS DE MEXICO INC
4385 Garfield St (48475-9553)
PHONE.....................989 658-8557
David Hyzer, *Principal*
EMP: 1
SALES (est): 6.2MM **Privately Held**
SIC: 3089 Extruded finished plastic products
PA: Gemini Group, Inc.
175 Thompson Rd Ste A
Bad Axe MI 48413

(G-16718)
LANNY BENSINGER
Also Called: Paul Bunyon Saw Mill
1491 E Morrison Rd (48475-8803)
PHONE.....................989 658-2590
Lanny Bensinger, *Owner*
EMP: 3
SALES (est): 241.7K **Privately Held**
SIC: 2448 Pallets, wood

GEOGRAPHIC SECTION

Utica - Macomb County (G-16744)

(G-16719)
MAURER MEAT PROCESSORS INC
4075 Purdy Rd (48475-9744)
PHONE................................989 658-8185
Jim Maurer, *President*
EMP: 40
SQ FT: 7,500
SALES (est): 3.4MM Privately Held
SIC: 2011 Meat packing plants

(G-16720)
PEPRO ENTERPRISES INC
Also Called: Valley Enterprises
2147 Leppek Rd (48475-9790)
PHONE................................989 658-3200
EMP: 96 Privately Held
SIC: 3089 Mfg Plastic Products
HQ: Pepro Enterprises, Inc.
    2147 Leppek Rd
    Ubly MI 48475
    989 658-3200

(G-16721)
PEPRO ENTERPRISES INC (HQ)
Also Called: Gemini Plastics
4385 Garfield St (48475-9553)
PHONE................................989 658-3200
Lyn Drake, *President*
Michelle Gunderman, *Safety Mgr*
Scott Stanger, *Purchasing*
Rick Spurlock, *Sales Staff*
▲ EMP: 180 EST: 1977
SQ FT: 100,000
SALES (est): 108.6MM Privately Held
SIC: 3089 Extruded finished plastic products; plastic processing

(G-16722)
QUALITY WOOD PRODUCTS INC
3399 Bay Cy Frestville Rd (48475)
PHONE................................989 658-2160
Rick Vogel, *President*
EMP: 10
SALES: 750K Privately Held
SIC: 2431 Millwork

(G-16723)
REGENCY PLASTICS - UBLY INC (HQ)
4147 N Ubly Rd (48475-9578)
PHONE................................989 658-8504
William Roberts, *President*
Frank Peplinski, *Corp Secy*
Chris Fluegge, *Technology*
Jackie Braun, *Executive*
EMP: 100
SQ FT: 42,000
SALES (est): 80MM Privately Held
SIC: 3089 3714 Blow molded finished plastic products; motor vehicle parts & accessories

(G-16724)
TRU FLO CARBIDE INC
3999 N Ubly Rd (48475-9764)
P.O. Box 276 (48475-0276)
PHONE................................989 658-8515
Brian Gunn, *President*
EMP: 60
SQ FT: 15,000
SALES (est): 5.2MM Privately Held
SIC: 3544 3545 3444 Special dies & tools; machine tool accessories; sheet metalwork

(G-16725)
VALLEY ENTERPRISES UBLY INC
Ubly Logistics Center
4175 N Ubly Rd (48475)
PHONE................................989 269-6272
Lynette G Drake, *President*
EMP: 11 Privately Held
SIC: 2431 Interior & ornamental woodwork & trim
HQ: Valley Enterprises Ubly Inc.
    2147 Leppek Rd
    Ubly MI 48475

(G-16726)
VALLEY ENTERPRISES UBLY INC (HQ)
2147 Leppek Rd (48475-9790)
PHONE................................989 658-3200

Lynette Drake, *President*
Shari Quinn, *Exec VP*
Jeffrey Rochefort, *Vice Pres*
Dave Chumbler, *Opers Mgr*
Dawn Hurlburt, *Treasurer*
▲ EMP: 121
SQ FT: 80,000
SALES (est): 25.9MM Privately Held
SIC: 3089 Automotive parts, plastic

Union
Cass County

(G-16727)
ADMAT MANUFACTURING INC
16744 Us Highway 12 (49130-9224)
PHONE................................269 641-7453
Donald K Miller, *President*
Jeffrita L Colglazier, *Vice Pres*
Rosemary Miller, *Treasurer*
EMP: 15 EST: 1961
SQ FT: 15,700
SALES (est): 2.3MM Privately Held
SIC: 3429 3469 Manufactured hardware (general); stamping metal for the trade

(G-16728)
GARYS CUSTOM MEATS
Also Called: Gary's Custom Meat Processing
16237 Mason St (49130-9606)
P.O. Box 456 (49130-0456)
PHONE................................269 641-5683
Gary Lorenz, *Owner*
Jode Lorenz, *Corp Secy*
EMP: 4
SQ FT: 2,800
SALES (est): 259.4K Privately Held
SIC: 2011 Meat packing plants

(G-16729)
HARMAN LUMBER & SUPPLY INC
Also Called: Harman Builders
15479 Us Highway 12 Ste 7 (49130-9742)
PHONE................................269 641-5424
William M Harman, *President*
Delores Harman, *Admin Sec*
EMP: 5
SQ FT: 10,000
SALES (est): 422.5K Privately Held
SIC: 2452 1521 Log cabins, prefabricated, wood; new construction, single-family houses

(G-16730)
HIBSHMAN SCREW MCH PDTS INC
69351 Union Rd S (49130-9760)
P.O. Box 138 (49130-0138)
PHONE................................269 641-7525
William M Hibshman, *President*
Gary A Vanderbeek, *Vice Pres*
Shane Harris, *Sales Mgr*
▲ EMP: 50 EST: 1967
SQ FT: 27,000
SALES (est): 9MM Privately Held
WEB: www.hibshman.com
SIC: 3451 3469 Screw machine products; metal stampings

Union City
Branch County

(G-16731)
ARCOSA SHORING PRODUCTS INC (HQ)
8530 M 60 (49094-9345)
PHONE................................517 741-4300
Ken Groenewold, *President*
▲ EMP: 34
SALES (est): 25MM
SALES (corp-wide): 1.4B Publicly Held
SIC: 3731 3743 3531 Barges, building & repairing; freight cars & equipment; concrete plants
PA: Arcosa, Inc.
    500 N Akard St Ste 400
    Dallas TX 75201
    972 942-6500

(G-16732)
COUNTRYSIDE QUALITY MEATS LLC
1184 Adolph Rd (49094-9757)
PHONE................................517 741-4275
Dave Leonard, *Manager*
EMP: 4
SALES (est): 346.7K Privately Held
SIC: 2011 Meat packing plants

(G-16733)
ENER-TEC INC
306 Railroad St (49094-1216)
P.O. Box 85 (49094-0085)
PHONE................................517 741-5015
Larry Shroyer, *President*
Susan Shroyer, *Admin Sec*
EMP: 18
SQ FT: 1,500
SALES (est): 2.2MM Privately Held
WEB: www.ener-tec.com
SIC: 3589 Water treatment equipment, industrial; sewage & water treatment equipment

(G-16734)
GLOVE COATERS INCORPORATED
8380 M 60 (49094-9634)
P.O. Box 5 (49094-0005)
PHONE................................517 741-8402
Gene Tassie, *President*
▲ EMP: 20 EST: 1961
SQ FT: 6,000
SALES: 1MM Privately Held
SIC: 3089 Casting of plastic

(G-16735)
MILLWORKS ENGINEERING INC
Also Called: Craft Room
584 W Girard Rd (49094-9797)
PHONE................................517 741-5511
Vern Coffman, *Ch of Bd*
Marvin Herman, *Vice Pres*
Leon Edwards, *VP Sales*
◆ EMP: 10
SQ FT: 15,000
SALES (est): 221.6K Privately Held
WEB: www.thecraftroom.com
SIC: 2499 Picture frame molding, finished

(G-16736)
TRINITY INDUSTRIES INC
Also Called: GME
594 M 60 (49094-8740)
P.O. Box 98 (49094-0098)
PHONE................................517 741-4300
Joe Zylman, *Manager*
EMP: 60
SALES (corp-wide): 2.5B Publicly Held
WEB: www.gme-shields.com
SIC: 3599 Machine shop, jobbing & repair
PA: Trinity Industries, Inc.
    2525 N Stemmons Fwy
    Dallas TX 75207
    214 631-4420

Union Pier
Berrien County

(G-16737)
COLLINS CAVIAR COMPANY
9595 Union Pier Rd (49129-9411)
PHONE................................269 469-4576
Rachel Collins, *Principal*
EMP: 5
SALES (est): 317.6K Privately Held
SIC: 2092 Fresh or frozen packaged fish

(G-16738)
PLUM TREE
16337 Red Arrow Hwy (49129-9320)
P.O. Box 601 (49129-0601)
PHONE................................269 469-5980
Tim Rodeghier, *Partner*
Pat Rodeghier, *Partner*
EMP: 3
SQ FT: 1,000
SALES (est): 144.5K Privately Held
SIC: 5932 2511 2512 5999 Antiques; wood household furniture; upholstered household furniture; art dealers

(G-16739)
THOMASINE D JONES LLC
9974 Town Line Rd (49129)
PHONE................................773 726-1404
Thomasine Jones, *Manager*
Millicent Davis,
EMP: 3
SALES (est): 116.1K Privately Held
SIC: 2299 Textile goods

Utica
Macomb County

(G-16740)
21ST CENTURY GRAPHIC TECH LLC
8344 Hall Rd Ste 210 (48317-5554)
PHONE................................586 463-9599
Steve Buckler, *VP Opers*
Arthur Zysk,
Ron Bracali,
EMP: 5
SQ FT: 1,200
SALES (est): 600K Privately Held
WEB: www.21cgt.com
SIC: 7372 7371 Prepackaged software; custom computer programming services

(G-16741)
DOLLS BY MAURICE INC
45207 Cass Ave (48317-5601)
PHONE................................586 739-5147
Ruth Charnesky, *President*
Maurice Charnesky, *Vice Pres*
EMP: 3
SQ FT: 1,200
SALES (est): 160K Privately Held
SIC: 3942 5945 5092 Dolls, except stuffed toy animals; dolls & accessories; dolls

(G-16742)
HL MANUFACTURING INC
45399 Utica Park Blvd (48315-5903)
PHONE................................586 731-2800
Perry Gibbs, *President*
EMP: 19
SQ FT: 7,000
SALES (est): 4MM Privately Held
SIC: 3911 3961 Jewelry, precious metal; costume jewelry

(G-16743)
J D RUSSELL COMPANY
44865 Utica Rd (48317-5474)
P.O. Box 183471, Shelby Township (48318-3471)
PHONE................................586 254-8500
Dan Caffey, *General Mgr*
Brad Danna, *Vice Pres*
Kimberly Creamer, *Sales Staff*
EMP: 25
SALES (corp-wide): 40.2MM Privately Held
WEB: www.jdrussellco.com
SIC: 3494 3446 Expansion joints pipe; architectural metalwork
PA: The J D Russell Company
    4075 N Highway Dr
    Tucson AZ 85705
    520 742-6194

(G-16744)
MNP CORPORATION (PA)
Also Called: STEEL AND WIRE
44225 Utica Rd (48317-5464)
P.O. Box 189002 (48318-9002)
PHONE................................586 254-1320
Terri Chapman, *CEO*
Thomas Klein, *President*
Randy Feger, *General Mgr*
Chad Clifford, *Vice Pres*
Dave Cornovich, *Vice Pres*
▲ EMP: 600
SQ FT: 500,000
SALES: 232.6MM Privately Held
WEB: www.mnp.com
SIC: 3452 5051 5072 3714 Bolts, metal; screws, metal; washers, metal; steel; wire; bolts; screws; washers (hardware); miscellaneous fasteners; motor vehicle parts & accessories

Van Buren Twp
Wayne County

(G-16745)
A DESIGN LINE EMBROIDERY LLC
10669 Belleville Rd (48111-1385)
PHONE.................................734 697-3545
Caroline Manley, *Sales Staff*
Janet Manley,
EMP: 3 **EST:** 2000
SQ FT: 1,200
SALES: 330K **Privately Held**
WEB: www.adesignline.com
SIC: 2395 Embroidery & art needlework

(G-16746)
AEL/SPAN LLC (PA)
41775 Ecorse Rd Ste 100 (48111-5165)
PHONE.................................734 957-1600
John Henderson, *President*
EMP: 40
SQ FT: 185,000
SALES (est): 56.8MM **Privately Held**
SIC: 4225 3625 General warehousing & storage; switches, electronic applications

(G-16747)
BAYLOFF STMPED PDTS DTROIT INC (PA)
5910 Belleville Rd (48111-1120)
PHONE.................................734 397-9116
Richard Bayer, *President*
Trent Vondrasek, *General Mgr*
Christopher Bayer, *Vice Pres*
Jamie Dixson, *Vice Pres*
Megan Bailey, *Production*
▲ **EMP:** 100 **EST:** 1948
SALES (est): 26.9MM **Privately Held**
WEB: www.bayloff.com
SIC: 3469 Stamping metal for the trade

(G-16748)
BELL INDUCTION HEATING INC
41241 Edison Lake Rd (48111)
P.O. Box 112, Belleville (48112-0112)
PHONE.................................734 697-0133
John P Dolski, *President*
John Dolski Jr, *Vice Pres*
Alta Dolski, *Treasurer*
EMP: 6
SQ FT: 5,000
SALES (est): 422.8K **Privately Held**
SIC: 3398 Brazing (hardening) of metal

(G-16749)
BLADE WELDING SERVICE INC
10910 Hannan Rd (48111-4321)
PHONE.................................734 941-4253
Tom Blade, *President*
Lodema Blade, *Vice Pres*
EMP: 5
SALES (est): 340K **Privately Held**
SIC: 7692 3694 3496 3444 Welding repair; engine electrical equipment; miscellaneous fabricated wire products; sheet metalwork

(G-16750)
CASCADE EQUIPMENT COMPANY
43412 N Interstate 94 Ser (48111-2468)
P.O. Box 587, Belleville (48112-0587)
PHONE.................................734 697-7870
Timo Ruuskanen, *President*
EMP: 4
SQ FT: 6,000
SALES: 800K **Privately Held**
SIC: 3589 7699 Car washing machinery; aircraft & heavy equipment repair services

(G-16751)
CENTURY FUEL PRODUCTS
51225 Martz Rd (48111-2565)
PHONE.................................734 728-0300
▲ **EMP:** 11 **EST:** 2012
SALES (est): 1.6MM **Privately Held**
SIC: 2869 Fuels

(G-16752)
CONSTELLIUM AUTOMOTIVE USA LLC (DH)
6331 Schooner St (48111-5366)
PHONE.................................734 879-9700
Pierre Vareille, *CEO*
Jeremy Leach, *President*
Nicolas Brun, *Vice Pres*
Didier Fontaine, *CFO*
Fabienne Le Tadic, *VP Mktg*
EMP: 155
SALES (est): 62.5MM
SALES (corp-wide): 6.5B **Privately Held**
SIC: 3334 3341 Primary aluminum; aluminum smelting & refining (secondary)
HQ: Constellium Singen Gmbh
Alusingenplatz 1
Singen (Hohentwiel) 78224
773 180-0

(G-16753)
CONTRACT WELDING AND FABG INC
385 Sumpter Rd (48111-2932)
P.O. Box 68, Belleville (48112-0068)
PHONE.................................734 699-5561
Harry Tinsley, *President*
Toni Golden, *Principal*
Thomas Tinsley, *Vice Pres*
EMP: 30 **EST:** 1980
SQ FT: 16,000
SALES (est): 10.6MM **Privately Held**
WEB: www.contractwelding.com
SIC: 3443 7692 3532 3531 Bins, prefabricated metal plate; welding repair; mining machinery; construction machinery; metal stampings; metal cans

(G-16754)
COUNTERPOINT BY HLF
44001 Van Born Rd (48111-1149)
PHONE.................................734 699-7100
Bob Bechthel, *Owner*
Charles Hood, *Owner*
EMP: 80
SALES (est): 4.4MM **Privately Held**
SIC: 2521 2531 2522 2426 Wood office furniture; public building & related furniture; office furniture, except wood; hardwood dimension & flooring mills

(G-16755)
D B MATTSON CO
44505 Harmony Ln (48111-2409)
PHONE.................................734 697-8056
Donald B Mattson, *Owner*
EMP: 3 **EST:** 1976
SALES: 120K **Privately Held**
SIC: 3599 Custom machinery

(G-16756)
D L R MANUFACTURING INC
44205 Yost Rd (48111-1125)
PHONE.................................734 394-0690
Dennis Hennells, *President*
EMP: 6
SQ FT: 3,200
SALES: 500K **Privately Held**
SIC: 3599 Machine shop, jobbing & repair

(G-16757)
DENSO INTERNATIONAL AMER INC
Denso Manufacturing TN
8652 Haggerty Rd Ste 220 (48111-1848)
PHONE.................................248 359-4177
Juan Garcia, *Branch Mgr*
EMP: 5 **Privately Held**
SIC: 3625 3694 Starter, electric motor; alternators, automotive
HQ: Denso International America, Inc.
24777 Denso Dr
Southfield MI 48033
248 350-7500

(G-16758)
DIE SERVICES INTERNATIONAL LLC
45000 Van Born Rd (48111-1152)
PHONE.................................734 699-3400
Steven Rowe, *Exec VP*
Larry Traynor, *Project Mgr*
Tiffany Ringrose, *Admin Asst*
▲ **EMP:** 65 **EST:** 2010
SALES (est): 14.2MM **Privately Held**
SIC: 3545 Machine tool accessories

(G-16759)
DIE-NAMIC INC
7565 Haggerty Rd (48111-1601)
PHONE.................................734 710-3200
Robert J Bologna, *President*
Jeff Carmack, *Vice Pres*
Chris Hayes, *Controller*
Ron Bologna, *Sales Mgr*
EMP: 115 **EST:** 1978
SQ FT: 87,050
SALES (est): 16.5MM **Privately Held**
WEB: www.die-namic.com
SIC: 3544 Special dies & tools

(G-16760)
EXEDY-DYNAX AMERICA CORP
8601 Haggerty Rd (48111-1607)
PHONE.................................734 397-6556
Koji Akita, *President*
Matthew Shelton, *Administration*
EMP: 11
SALES (est): 1.5MM **Privately Held**
SIC: 3714 Clutches, motor vehicle

(G-16761)
GENTLE MACHINE TOOL & DIE
13600 Martinsville Rd (48111-2890)
PHONE.................................734 699-2013
Aaron R Gentle, *President*
William Majnaric, *Corp Secy*
EMP: 6 **EST:** 1940
SQ FT: 12,000
SALES (est): 763.7K **Privately Held**
SIC: 3599 Machine shop, jobbing & repair

(G-16762)
H L F FURNITURE INCORPORATED
44001 Van Born Rd (48111-1149)
PHONE.................................734 697-3000
Robert B Bechtel, *President*
Harold Becker Jr, *Exec VP*
Charles Hood Jr, *Treasurer*
EMP: 50
SQ FT: 63,000
SALES (est): 8.5MM **Privately Held**
WEB: www.hlffurniture.com
SIC: 2521 5712 2541 2511 Wood office filing cabinets & bookcases; wood office desks & tables; furniture stores; wood partitions & fixtures; wood household furniture

(G-16763)
HERMAN MILLER INC
9000 Haggerty Rd (48111-1632)
PHONE.................................616 654-3716
Abe Carrillo, *Manager*
EMP: 3
SALES (corp-wide): 2.5B **Publicly Held**
WEB: www.hermanmiller.com
SIC: 2521 Wood office furniture
PA: Herman Miller, Inc.
855 E Main Ave
Zeeland MI 49464
616 654-3000

(G-16764)
HONEY TREE
9624 Belleville Rd (48111-1365)
PHONE.................................734 697-1000
Al George, *Manager*
EMP: 6
SALES (est): 251.8K **Privately Held**
SIC: 2099 Food preparations

(G-16765)
INDUSTRIAL COMPUTER & CONTROLS
43774 Bemis Rd (48111-8765)
PHONE.................................734 697-4152
Louis G Kovach II, *President*
EMP: 10
SQ FT: 3,500
SALES (est): 973.6K **Privately Held**
SIC: 3625 3621 Relays & industrial controls; motors & generators

(G-16766)
JOHNSON CONTROLS INC
41873 Ecorse Rd (48111-5227)
PHONE.................................313 842-3479
Denise Stinson, *Branch Mgr*
EMP: 200 **Privately Held**
SIC: 3585 Refrigeration & heating equipment
HQ: Johnson Controls, Inc.
5757 N Green Bay Ave
Milwaukee WI 53209
414 524-1200

(G-16767)
KAGE GROUP LLC
Also Called: Esgar Products
13835 Basswood Cir (48111-2018)
PHONE.................................734 604-5052
Kudakwashe Garaba,
EMP: 30
SALES: 1.1MM **Privately Held**
SIC: 2819 8748 Sodium compounds or salts, inorg., ex. refined sod. chloride; business consulting

(G-16768)
KREBS TOOL INC
611 Savage Rd (48111-2954)
P.O. Box 398, Belleville (48112-0398)
PHONE.................................734 697-8611
Allan D Krebs, *President*
Jeff Krebs, *Vice Pres*
EMP: 5
SQ FT: 6,000
SALES (est): 606.7K **Privately Held**
WEB: www.krebstool.com
SIC: 3545 Cutting tools for machine tools

(G-16769)
L & W INC
Also Called: L&W Engineering Co Plant 1
6771 Haggerty Rd (48111-5271)
PHONE.................................734 397-8085
Kevin Pires, *Manager*
EMP: 228
SALES (corp-wide): 2.2B **Privately Held**
SIC: 3465 3469 3441 Automotive stampings; metal stampings; fabricated structural metal
HQ: L & W, Inc.
17757 Woodland Dr
New Boston MI 48164
734 397-6300

(G-16770)
L & W INC
Also Called: L & W Engineering Co Plant 2
6201 Haggerty Rd (48111-1137)
PHONE.................................734 397-2212
Al Henry, *Branch Mgr*
EMP: 350
SALES (corp-wide): 2.2B **Privately Held**
SIC: 3465 3443 Automotive stampings; bins, prefabricated metal plate
HQ: L & W, Inc.
17757 Woodland Dr
New Boston MI 48164
734 397-6300

(G-16771)
MAYSER USA INC
6200 Schooner St (48111-5312)
PHONE.................................734 858-1290
William Fournier, *CEO*
Julius Rummel, *CFO*
Scott Behr, *Sales Engr*
Clay Mitchem, *Manager*
EMP: 85
SALES (est): 18.4MM **Privately Held**
SIC: 3714 5013 Motor vehicle parts & accessories; motor vehicle supplies & new parts

(G-16772)
MICHIGAN PAVING AND MTLS CO
1785 Rawsonville Rd (48111-1242)
PHONE.................................734 485-1717
Alan Sandell, *Branch Mgr*
EMP: 33
SALES (corp-wide): 30.6B **Privately Held**
SIC: 2951 1611 Asphalt paving mixtures & blocks; highway & street construction
HQ: Michigan Paving And Materials Company
2575 S Haggerty Rd # 100
Canton MI 48188
734 397-2050

GEOGRAPHIC SECTION

(G-16773)
MIRRAGE LTD
8300 Belleville Rd
P.O. Box 607, Belleville (48112-0607)
PHONE..................734 697-6447
Mr Raymond Price, *President*
Linda Price, *Admin Sec*
EMP: 17
SALES (est): 940K **Privately Held**
SIC: 3479 Coating of metals & formed products

(G-16774)
MOUNTAIN MACHINE LLC
7850 Rawsonville Rd (48111-2344)
PHONE..................734 480-2200
Brian Napier, *Asst Director*
Stephen Ortner,
EMP: 16
SALES (est): 1MM **Privately Held**
SIC: 3559 3451 3599 Automotive related machinery; screw machine products; machine & other job shop work; machine shop, jobbing & repair; custom machinery

(G-16775)
NEAPCO DRIVELINES LLC
Belleville Plant
6735 Haggerty Rd (48111-5271)
PHONE..................734 447-1316
Scott Kalkofen, *Branch Mgr*
EMP: 400
SALES (corp-wide): 2.9B **Privately Held**
SIC: 3714 Transmission housings or parts, motor vehicle
HQ: Neapco Drivelines, Llc
    6735 Haggerty Rd
    Van Buren Twp MI 48111

(G-16776)
NEAPCO DRIVELINES LLC (DH)
6735 Haggerty Rd (48111-5271)
PHONE..................734 447-1300
Kenneth L Hopkins, *CEO*
Robert W Hawkey, *President*
Gary Hughes, *Regional Mgr*
J Robert Mangini, *COO*
Tim Goode, *Vice Pres*
▲ **EMP:** 105
SALES (est): 149.7MM
SALES (corp-wide): 2.9B **Privately Held**
SIC: 3714 Transmission housings or parts, motor vehicle

(G-16777)
PACIFIC OIL RESOURCES INC
44141 Yost Rd (48111-1153)
PHONE..................734 397-1120
James K Dowling Jr, *President*
Tim Dowling, *Officer*
EMP: 22
SALES: 1.5MM **Privately Held**
SIC: 2911 5172 Oils, fuel; fuel oil

(G-16778)
PAICH RAILWORKS INC
41275 Van Born Rd (48111-1147)
PHONE..................734 397-2424
Mike Paich, *President*
Michael B Paich, *Vice Pres*
EMP: 6
SQ FT: 5,000
SALES (est): 985.9K **Privately Held**
SIC: 3312 Rails, steel or iron

(G-16779)
PISTON AUTOMOTIVE LLC
8500 Haggerty Rd (48111-1821)
PHONE..................313 541-8789
Robert Ajersch, *General Mgr*
EMP: 70
SALES (corp-wide): 1.6B **Privately Held**
SIC: 3714 Motor vehicle parts & accessories
HQ: Piston Automotive, L.L.C.
    12723 Telegraph Rd Ste 1
    Redford MI 48239
    313 541-8674

(G-16780)
PLANT DF
41133 Van Born Rd Ste 205 (48111-1199)
PHONE..................734 397-0397
▲ **EMP:** 25 **EST:** 2008
SALES (est): 1.4MM **Privately Held**
SIC: 2273 Mfg Carpets/Rugs

(G-16781)
R E B TOOL INC
Also Called: REB Tool Company
5910 Belleville Rd (48111-1120)
PHONE..................734 397-9116
Richard Bayer, *President*
▲ **EMP:** 120
SALES (est): 12.4MM **Privately Held**
WEB: www.rebtool.com
SIC: 3544 Special dies & tools; jigs & fixtures

(G-16782)
REPUBLIC DIE & TOOL CO
45000 Van Born Rd (48111-1152)
P.O. Box 339, Belleville (48112-0339)
PHONE..................734 699-3400
John C Lasko, *President*
Charles B Zimmerman, *Admin Sec*
EMP: 50 **EST:** 1947
SQ FT: 250,000
SALES (est): 5.1MM **Privately Held**
SIC: 3544 Special dies & tools

(G-16783)
SMW MFG INC (PA)
8707 Samuel Barton Dr (48111-1600)
PHONE..................517 596-3300
Stan Dzierwa, *President*
Mike Kavanaugh, *Materials Mgr*
David Marton, *Mfg Staff*
EMP: 58
SALES (est): 60MM **Privately Held**
SIC: 3599 Machine shop, jobbing & repair

(G-16784)
SPAN AMERICA DETROIT INC
41775 Ecorse Rd Ste 100 (48111-5165)
PHONE..................734 957-1600
Birindra Singh Jind, *President*
EMP: 37
SQ FT: 100,000
SALES (est): 2.8MM **Privately Held**
SIC: 4226 3465 Special warehousing & storage; automotive stampings

(G-16785)
STATEWIDE BORING AND MCH INC
6401 Haggerty Rd (48111-5116)
PHONE..................734 397-5950
Michael William Thomas, *President*
EMP: 30
SQ FT: 34,100
SALES (est): 5MM **Privately Held**
SIC: 3599 Machine shop, jobbing & repair

(G-16786)
TAYLOR SCREW PRODUCTS COMPANY
16894 Haggerty Rd (48111-6008)
P.O. Box 549, Belleville (48112-0549)
PHONE..................734 697-8018
Kathleen Kondzer, *President*
Kim Kondzer, *Vice Pres*
EMP: 7 **EST:** 1974
SQ FT: 6,000
SALES (est): 2MM **Privately Held**
WEB: www.taylorscrewproducts.com
SIC: 3451 Screw machine products

(G-16787)
THE ENVELOPE PRINTERY INC (PA)
8979 Samuel Barton Dr (48111-1600)
PHONE..................734 398-7700
David Hamilton, *President*
Ken Hamilton, *Vice Pres*
John Marks, *Plant Engr*
EMP: 77
SQ FT: 73,258
SALES (est): 15.2MM **Privately Held**
WEB: www.envelopeprintery.com
SIC: 2677 2759 2791 2752 Envelopes; envelopes: printing; typesetting; commercial printing, lithographic

(G-16788)
TRI-DIM FILTER CORPORATION
11800 Hannan Rd (48111-1438)
PHONE..................734 229-0877
Frank Janke, *Branch Mgr*
EMP: 11

SALES (corp-wide): 4.5B **Privately Held**
WEB: www.tridim.com
SIC: 3564 Filters, air: furnaces, air conditioning equipment, etc.
HQ: Tri-Dim Filter Corporation
    93 Industrial Dr
    Louisa VA 23093
    540 967-2600

(G-16789)
VIHI LLC (HQ)
1 Village Center Dr (48111-5711)
PHONE..................734 710-2277
EMP: 4
SALES (est): 2.3MM
SALES (corp-wide): 2.9B **Publicly Held**
SIC: 3714 Motor vehicle parts & accessories
PA: Visteon Corporation
    1 Village Center Dr
    Van Buren Twp MI 48111
    800 847-8366

(G-16790)
VISTEON CORPORATION (PA)
1 Village Center Dr (48111-5711)
PHONE..................800 847-8366
Sachin S Lawande, *President*
Sunil K Bilolikar, *Senior VP*
Markus J Schupfner, *Senior VP*
Stephanie S Marianos, *Vice Pres*
Robert R Vallance, *Vice Pres*
EMP: 277
SALES: 2.9B **Publicly Held**
WEB: www.visteon.com
SIC: 3714 Motor vehicle engines & parts

(G-16791)
VISTEON ELECTRONICS CORP
1 Village Center Dr (48111-5711)
PHONE..................800 847-8366
Timothy D Leuliette, *CEO*
EMP: 7
SALES (est): 866.5K
SALES (corp-wide): 2.9B **Publicly Held**
WEB: www.visteon.com
SIC: 3714 Motor vehicle parts & accessories
PA: Visteon Corporation
    1 Village Center Dr
    Van Buren Twp MI 48111
    800 847-8366

(G-16792)
VISTEON GLOBAL ELECTRONICS INC (HQ)
1 Village Center Dr (48111-5711)
PHONE..................800 847-8366
Martin T Thall, *President*
Robert R Krakowiak, *Treasurer*
Jennifer Pretzel, *Treasurer*
Heidi A Sepanik, *Admin Sec*
Peter M Ziparo, *Admin Sec*
EMP: 5
SALES (est): 5.7MM
SALES (corp-wide): 2.9B **Publicly Held**
SIC: 3714 Motor vehicle parts & accessories
PA: Visteon Corporation
    1 Village Center Dr
    Van Buren Twp MI 48111
    800 847-8366

(G-16793)
VISTEON GLOBAL ELECTRONICS INC
Also Called: Glcc Tech Center
1 Village Center Dr (48111-5711)
PHONE..................734 710-5000
Timothy Blumer, *Manager*
EMP: 3
SALES (corp-wide): 2.9B **Publicly Held**
SIC: 3714 Motor vehicle parts & accessories
HQ: Visteon Global Electronics, Inc.
    1 Village Center Dr
    Van Buren Twp MI 48111
    800 847-8366

(G-16794)
VISTEON INTL HOLDINGS INC (HQ)
Also Called: Visteon International Business
1 Village Center Dr (48111-5711)
PHONE..................734 710-2000

Brian P Casey, *Treasurer*
EMP: 11
SALES (est): 19.4MM
SALES (corp-wide): 2.9B **Publicly Held**
SIC: 3711 Motor vehicles & car bodies
PA: Visteon Corporation
    1 Village Center Dr
    Van Buren Twp MI 48111
    800 847-8366

(G-16795)
VISTEON SYSTEMS LLC (HQ)
1 Village Center Dr (48111-5711)
PHONE..................800 847-8366
Sachin Lawande, *CEO*
EMP: 26
SALES (est): 1.6MM
SALES (corp-wide): 2.9B **Publicly Held**
SIC: 3714 Motor vehicle engines & parts
PA: Visteon Corporation
    1 Village Center Dr
    Van Buren Twp MI 48111
    800 847-8366

(G-16796)
WELLINGTON INDUSTRIES INC (PA)
39555 S I 94 Servce Dr (48111-2877)
PHONE..................734 942-1060
Marvin Tyghem, *Ch of Bd*
Blaise Flack, *CFO*
▲ **EMP:** 150
SQ FT: 134,000
SALES (est): 92.5MM **Privately Held**
WEB: www.wellingtonind.com
SIC: 3465 Body parts, automobile: stamped metal

(G-16797)
WELLINGTON INDUSTRIES INC
39635 S I 94 Servce Dr (48111-2858)
PHONE..................734 403-6112
Blaise Flack, *CFO*
EMP: 50
SALES (corp-wide): 92.5MM **Privately Held**
SIC: 3465 7692 Automotive stampings; automotive welding
PA: Wellington Industries, Inc.
    39555 S I 94 Servce Dr
    Van Buren Twp MI 48111
    734 942-1060

(G-16798)
WELLINGTON-ALMONT LLC (HQ)
39555 S Interstate 94 Ser (48111-2858)
PHONE..................734 942-1060
Marvin Tyghem,
Purnima Mistry,
EMP: 100
SQ FT: 150,000
SALES (est): 15.3MM
SALES (corp-wide): 92.5MM **Privately Held**
SIC: 3465 Body parts, automobile: stamped metal
PA: Wellington Industries, Inc.
    39555 S I 94 Servce Dr
    Van Buren Twp MI 48111
    734 942-1060

Vandalia
Cass County

(G-16799)
BERGEN R C HELICOPTERS LLC
16672 M 60 (49095-9772)
PHONE..................269 445-2060
Chris Bergen,
EMP: 6
SQ FT: 3,600
SALES: 250K **Privately Held**
SIC: 3599 Machine shop, jobbing & repair

(G-16800)
CONNELLS RESTORATION & SEALAN
16011 Hoffman St (49095-9530)
PHONE..................269 370-0805
Robert Connell, *Administration*

Vandalia - Cass County (G-16801)

EMP: 3
SALES (est): 135.6K **Privately Held**
SIC: 2891 Sealants

(G-16801)
LA EAST INC
Also Called: Middlebury Trailers
62702 Woodland Dr (49095-9745)
PHONE..............................269 476-7170
James Bergan, *President*
Georgia Vangilder, *Corp Secy*
EMP: 55
SALES (est): 1MM **Privately Held**
SIC: 3731 Cargo vessels, building & repairing

(G-16802)
NORTH AMERICAN AQUA ENVMTL LLC
17397 Black St (49095-9559)
P.O. Box 130 (49095-0130)
PHONE..............................269 476-2092
Olafur Olafsson, *Mng Member*
Barb Olafsson,
EMP: 10
SALES: 500K **Privately Held**
SIC: 3589 8999 8744 Water treatment equipment, industrial; natural resource preservation service;

Vanderbilt
Otsego County

(G-16803)
BUNKER & SONS SAWMILL LLC
119 Alexander Rd (49795-9707)
PHONE..............................989 983-2715
Jim Bunker, *Mng Member*
Cathy Bunker,
Daniel Bunker,
EMP: 7
SALES (est): 530K **Privately Held**
SIC: 2448 Pallets, wood

(G-16804)
ELL TRON MANUFACTURING CO (PA)
11893 Old 27 Hwy N (49795-9713)
P.O. Box 416 (49795-0416)
PHONE..............................989 983-3181
Kay Anderson, *President*
Louis Holm, *Principal*
Craig Vantielen, *Vice Pres*
Lisa Holm, *Treasurer*
Charissa Matewicz, *Sales Executive*
▲ EMP: 30 EST: 1972
SQ FT: 4,625
SALES: 2.9MM **Privately Held**
WEB: www.elltron.com
SIC: 3089 Injection molding of plastics

(G-16805)
ELL TRON MANUFACTURING CO
10957 Old 27 Hwy N (49795-9320)
PHONE..............................989 983-3181
Kay Holms, *Vice Pres*
EMP: 5
SALES (corp-wide): 2.9MM **Privately Held**
WEB: www.elltron.com
SIC: 3089 Injection molding of plastics
PA: Ell Tron Manufacturing Co.
11893 Old 27 Hwy N
Vanderbilt MI 49795
989 983-3181

(G-16806)
MAYVILLE ENGINEERING CO INC
1444 Alexander Rd (49795-9709)
PHONE..............................989 748-6031
EMP: 197
SQ FT: 50,000
SALES (corp-wide): 354.5MM **Publicly Held**
SIC: 3498 Tube fabricating (contract bending & shaping)
PA: Mayville Engineering Co Inc
715 South St
Mayville WI 53050
920 387-4500

(G-16807)
MAYVILLE ENGINEERING CO INC
8276 Yuill Rd (49795-9528)
P.O. Box 426 (49795-0426)
PHONE..............................989 983-3911
Greg Rippey, *Branch Mgr*
EMP: 35
SALES (corp-wide): 354.5MM **Publicly Held**
SIC: 3714 Motor vehicle parts & accessories
PA: Mayville Engineering Co Inc
715 South St
Mayville WI 53050
920 387-4500

(G-16808)
NORTHERN MICH RESIDENTIAL SVCS
9571 Rajasi Cir (49795-9350)
PHONE..............................231 547-6144
John Pfluecke, *Principal*
EMP: 3
SALES: 1.9K **Privately Held**
SIC: 2435 Hardwood veneer & plywood

(G-16809)
QUIGLEY CO
8276 Mill St (49795-9701)
PHONE..............................989 983-3911
Carol Quigley, *Owner*
EMP: 45
SALES (est): 2.1MM **Privately Held**
WEB: www.quigley.com
SIC: 3714 Motor vehicle engines & parts

Vassar
Tuscola County

(G-16810)
ADVANCE VEHICLE ASSEMBLY INC
555 E Huron Ave (48768-1831)
PHONE..............................989 823-3800
Asaf Cohen, *Principal*
EMP: 10
SQ FT: 50,000
SALES (est): 453.4K **Privately Held**
SIC: 3711 Truck & tractor truck assembly

(G-16811)
ASTECH INC
5512 Scotch Rd (48768-9235)
P.O. Box 158 (48768-0158)
PHONE..............................989 823-7211
Alan Bukach, *President*
Rick Wark, *Shareholder*
EMP: 49
SQ FT: 40,000
SALES (est): 9.7MM **Privately Held**
WEB: www.astechinc.net
SIC: 3624 3325 3369 3341 Carbon & graphite products; steel foundries; nonferrous foundries; secondary nonferrous metals

(G-16812)
LARSEN GRAPHICS INC
1065 E Huron Ave (48768-1816)
P.O. Box 1641 (48768-0641)
PHONE..............................989 823-3000
Harold Larsen, *President*
Rita Whalen, *Accounting Mgr*
EMP: 21
SQ FT: 17,000
SALES (est): 2.5MM **Privately Held**
WEB: www.larsengraphics.com
SIC: 2759 2752 2791 2396 Screen printing; commercial printing, lithographic; typesetting; automotive & apparel trimmings

(G-16813)
LOUIS J WICKINGS
4650 Waltan Rd (48768-8903)
PHONE..............................989 823-8765
Louis Wickings, *Principal*
EMP: 3 EST: 2010
SALES (est): 201.9K **Privately Held**
SIC: 2241 Wicking

(G-16814)
QUALITY STEEL
4021 W Saginaw Rd (48768-9577)
PHONE..............................989 823-1524
EMP: 3
SALES (est): 101.7K **Privately Held**
SIC: 3599 Machine shop, jobbing & repair

(G-16815)
TUSCOLA COUNTY ADVERTISER INC
Also Called: Cass River Trader East
5881 Frankenmuth Rd (48768-9401)
PHONE..............................989 823-8651
EMP: 12
SALES (corp-wide): 40.6MM **Privately Held**
SIC: 2741 7313 Miscellaneous publishing; newspaper advertising representative
PA: Tuscola County Advertiser, Inc.
344 N State St
Caro MI 48723
989 673-3181

(G-16816)
VASSAR WELDING & MACHINE CO
769 Birch Rd (48768-9238)
PHONE..............................989 823-8266
EMP: 3
SQ FT: 8,184
SALES (est): 170K **Privately Held**
SIC: 3599 Mfg Industrial Machinery

(G-16817)
WARNER DOOR
397 Division St (48768-1246)
PHONE..............................989 823-8397
Mark Warner, *Owner*
EMP: 3
SQ FT: 1,750
SALES: 300K **Privately Held**
SIC: 2426 5211 Carvings, furniture: wood; flooring, hardwood; millwork & lumber

(G-16818)
WATERMAN TOOL & MACHINE CORP
1032 E Huron Ave (48768-1818)
P.O. Box 1674 (48768-0674)
PHONE..............................989 823-8181
Francis Longuski, *President*
Elaine Zink, *Office Mgr*
EMP: 12
SQ FT: 7,290
SALES (est): 1.6MM **Privately Held**
SIC: 3544 Special dies & tools

(G-16819)
WEBER STEEL INC
Also Called: Weber Steel & Body
3000 Bradford Rd (48768-9467)
PHONE..............................989 868-4162
James Scherzer, *President*
Albert Scherzer, *Vice Pres*
EMP: 10
SQ FT: 25,000
SALES (est): 1.4MM **Privately Held**
SIC: 3599 5251 Machine shop, jobbing & repair; hardware

(G-16820)
WILSON STAMPING & MFG INC
603 State Rd (48768-9248)
P.O. Box 219 (48768-0219)
PHONE..............................989 823-8521
Fax: 989 823-3206
EMP: 3 EST: 1956
SQ FT: 20,000
SALES (est): 280K **Privately Held**
SIC: 3519 3585 Mfg Internal Combustion Engines Mfg Refrigeration/Heating Equipment

Vermontville
Eaton County

(G-16821)
HAIGHS MAPLE SYRUP & SUPS LLC
11756 Scipio Hwy (49096-9433)
PHONE..............................517 202-6975

Larry Haigh, *Branch Mgr*
EMP: 10
SALES (corp-wide): 2.2MM **Privately Held**
SIC: 2099 Maple syrup
PA: Haighs Maple Syrup And Supplies Llc
6903 S Lacey Lake Rd
Bellevue MI 49021
269 763-2210

(G-16822)
MERITT TOOL & DIE
2354 N Pease Rd (49096-9502)
PHONE..............................517 726-1452
Eugene Miller, *Owner*
EMP: 6
SQ FT: 1,500
SALES: 500K **Privately Held**
SIC: 3599 Machine shop, jobbing & repair

(G-16823)
PRECISION TOOL INC
519 Allegan Rd (49096-9700)
P.O. Box 189 (49096-0189)
PHONE..............................517 726-1060
James Noe, *President*
Benjamin Pierce, *Vice Pres*
EMP: 20
SALES: 1.9MM **Privately Held**
SIC: 3599 Machine shop, jobbing & repair

(G-16824)
TERRELL ASSOC SIGNS & DISP
8939 Spore St (49096-8541)
PHONE..............................517 726-0455
Kelly Terrell, *Owner*
EMP: 3
SQ FT: 2,000
SALES (est): 120K **Privately Held**
SIC: 3993 5999 Signs & advertising specialties; banners, flags, decals & posters

Vestaburg
Montcalm County

(G-16825)
ADVANCED FARM EQUIPMENT LLC
5773 N Crystal Rd (48891-9706)
PHONE..............................989 268-5711
Greg Merrihew,
EMP: 16
SQ FT: 2,500
SALES (est): 3.8MM **Privately Held**
SIC: 3523 Farm machinery & equipment

(G-16826)
M-A METALS INC
7470 N Crystal Rd (48891-8754)
P.O. Box 216 (48891-0216)
PHONE..............................989 268-5080
Fax: 989 268-5080
EMP: 7
SQ FT: 7,300
SALES (est): 410K **Privately Held**
SIC: 3599 Mfg Industrial Machinery

(G-16827)
OLES MEAT PROCESSING
11800 S Winn Rd (48891-9600)
PHONE..............................989 866-6442
Kris Olejniczak, *Principal*
EMP: 3
SALES (est): 151.8K **Privately Held**
SIC: 2011 Meat packing plants

(G-16828)
ROSE ACRES PALLETS LLC
4769 N Bollinger Rd (48891-9732)
PHONE..............................989 268-3074
Allen Beachy, *Principal*
EMP: 4
SALES (est): 469.1K **Privately Held**
SIC: 2448 Pallets, wood & wood with metal

(G-16829)
ROSE ACRES TALLETS
9932 E Kendaville Rd (48891-9738)
PHONE..............................989 268-3074
Melvin River, *Office Mgr*
EMP: 3
SALES (est): 138.3K **Privately Held**
SIC: 2448 Wood pallets & skids

Vicksburg
Kalamazoo County

(G-16830)
A & O MOLD AND ENG INC
301 N 4th St (49097-1045)
PHONE 269 649-0600
Douglas Northup, *President*
Doug Northup, *President*
Dave Ellison, *Vice Pres*
Steve Harden, *Vice Pres*
Tom Rice, *Vice Pres*
▲ **EMP:** 45
SQ FT: 15,000
SALES (est): 8.9MM **Privately Held**
WEB: www.aomold.com
SIC: 3544 Industrial molds

(G-16831)
BRIDGE ORGANICS COMPANY
311 W Washington St (49097-1200)
PHONE 269 649-4200
Edward J Hessler, *President*
Max Bruer, *Vice Pres*
Brad Hewitt, *Vice Pres*
Harold Karnes, *Vice Pres*
Tom Nanninga, *Vice Pres*
◆ **EMP:** 30
SQ FT: 9,400
SALES (est): 3.4MM **Privately Held**
WEB: www.bridgeorganics.com
SIC: 2899 Chemical preparations

(G-16832)
CAL MANUFACTURING COMPANY INC
5500 E V Ave (49097-8315)
P.O. Box 180 (49097-0180)
PHONE 269 649-2942
Barbara Morren, *CEO*
Cheryl Benson, *Business Mgr*
EMP: 6
SQ FT: 15,500
SALES (est): 1.2MM **Privately Held**
SIC: 7692 Welding repair

(G-16833)
CENTRAL ELEVATOR CO INC (PA)
18 Baur Ln (49097-8782)
PHONE 269 329-0705
Suzanne M Schulz, *President*
Bertha Lindsley, *Vice Pres*
EMP: 12
SQ FT: 5,000
SALES (est): 1.1MM **Privately Held**
SIC: 7699 3534 Elevators: inspection, service & repair; elevators & equipment

(G-16834)
EIMO TECHNOLOGIES INC (DH)
Also Called: Eimo Americas
14320 Portage Rd (49097-7716)
P.O. Box 156 (49097-0156)
PHONE 269 649-0545
Gary Hallam, *Business Mgr*
Michael Nuyen, *Mfg Spvr*
Marco Garcia, *Production*
Brian Jackson, *Design Engr*
Leslie Fryer, *Controller*
▲ **EMP:** 20
SQ FT: 60,000
SALES (est): 25.3MM **Privately Held**
WEB: vicksburg.eimoam.com
SIC: 3089 3544 Injection molded finished plastic products; industrial molds
HQ: Nissha Usa, Inc.
1051 Perimeter Dr Ste 600
Schaumburg IL 60173
847 413-2665

(G-16835)
EIMO TECHNOLOGIES INC
Tooling & Technology Center
14300 Portage Rd (49097-7716)
PHONE 269 649-5031
Mark Key, *Branch Mgr*
EMP: 75 **Privately Held**
SIC: 3544 Industrial molds

HQ: Eimo Technologies, Inc.
14320 Portage Rd
Vicksburg MI 49097
269 649-0545

(G-16836)
IMERYS PERLITE USA INC
Also Called: Harborlite
1950 E W Ave (49097-9777)
P.O. Box 100 (49097-0100)
PHONE 269 649-1352
William G Blunt, *President*
Mark Miller, *Manager*
EMP: 10
SQ FT: 7,000
SALES (corp-wide): 3MM **Privately Held**
WEB: www.worldminerals.com
SIC: 3295 Minerals, ground or treated
HQ: Imerys Perlite Usa, Inc.
1732 N 1st St Ste 450
San Jose CA 95112

(G-16837)
KEN GORSLINE WELDING (PA)
2210 E Vw Ave (49097-7735)
PHONE 269 649-0650
Ken Gorsline, *Owner*
EMP: 4
SQ FT: 6,000
SALES (est): 150K **Privately Held**
SIC: 3441 Fabricated structural metal

(G-16838)
KEPCO INC
Also Called: Kalamazoo Electropolishing Co
145 N Leja Dr (49097-1192)
PHONE 269 649-5800
Bill Hochstetler, *President*
Paula Hochstetler, *Vice Pres*
EMP: 20
SQ FT: 20,000
SALES (est): 2.1MM **Privately Held*
WEB: www.kepcoinc.com
SIC: 3471 Polishing, metals or formed products

(G-16839)
MINIATURE CUSTOM MFG LLC
170 N Leja Dr (49097-1192)
PHONE 269 998-1277
Steve Shoemaker, *Owner*
▲ **EMP:** 12 **EST:** 2011
SALES (est): 1.2MM **Privately Held**
SIC: 3089 Injection molding of plastics

(G-16840)
OZLAND ENTERPRISES INC
603 W Prairie St (49097-1177)
PHONE 269 649-0706
Michael D Oswalt, *President*
Julia Oswalt, *Corp Secy*
EMP: 3
SQ FT: 1,700
SALES (est): 422.9K **Privately Held**
WEB: www.ozlandent.com
SIC: 2759 5083 Calendars: printing; poultry & livestock equipment

(G-16841)
PRINTER INK WAREHOUSECOM LLC
Also Called: Ink-Refills-Ink.com
109 E Prairie St (49097-1256)
PHONE 269 649-5492
Joe Briggs,
Fred M Medich,
▲ **EMP:** 9
SQ FT: 5,500
SALES (est): 1MM **Privately Held**
WEB: www.ink-refills-ink.com
SIC: 2752 Commercial printing, lithographic

(G-16842)
RONNINGEN RESEARCH AND DEV CO
Also Called: Emergent Technologies Co
6700 E Yz Ave (49097-8374)
P.O. Box 70 (49097-0070)
PHONE 269 649-0520
Darrel Myers, *CEO*
EMP: 175
SQ FT: 50,000

SALES (est): 31MM **Privately Held**
SIC: 3544 8711 3089 Industrial molds; designing: ship, boat, machine & product; injection molded finished plastic products

(G-16843)
SCHMIDT GRINDING
202 E Raymond St (49097-1458)
PHONE 269 649-4604
Jeff Schmidt, *Owner*
EMP: 4 **EST:** 2001
SALES (est): 376.9K **Privately Held**
SIC: 3479 Metal coating & allied service

(G-16844)
STEWART SUTHERLAND INC
5411 E V Ave (49097-8387)
P.O. Box 162 (49097-0162)
PHONE 269 649-0530
John C Stewart, *President*
William Moran, *Vice Pres*
Patricia Stewart, *Vice Pres*
Tom Farrell, *Sales Mgr*
Kristen McGruder, *Manager*
▲ **EMP:** 145 **EST:** 1958
SQ FT: 90,000
SALES (est): 56.3MM **Privately Held**
WEB: www.ssbags.com
SIC: 2671 2674 2672 Waxed paper: made from purchased material; paper bags: made from purchased materials; coated & laminated paper

(G-16845)
SUMMIT POLYMERS INC
115 S Leja Dr (49097-1193)
PHONE 269 649-4900
Chuck Devries, *General Mgr*
Adam Kline, *Mfg Mgr*
Amy Clary, *Purchasing*
Cale Munson, *Purchasing*
Richard Gippert, *Engineer*
EMP: 174
SALES (corp-wide): 444.7MM **Privately Held**
WEB: www.summitpolymers.com
SIC: 2821 Plastics materials & resins
PA: Summit Polymers, Inc.
6715 S Sprinkle Rd
Portage MI 49002
269 324-9330

Vulcan
Dickinson County

(G-16846)
UNITED ABRASIVE INC (PA)
19100 Industrial Dr (49892-8825)
P.O. Box 98 (49892-0098)
PHONE 906 563-9249
William R Paupore Jr, *Ch of Bd*
William R Paupore III, *President*
EMP: 13 **EST:** 1960
SQ FT: 35,000
SALES (est): 1MM **Privately Held**
SIC: 3291 5085 3829 2819 Abrasive products; industrial supplies; measuring & controlling devices; industrial inorganic chemicals

(G-16847)
VULCAN WOOD PRODUCTS INC
N1549 Sturgeon Mill Rd (49892-8679)
P.O. Box 125, Norway (49870-0125)
PHONE 906 563-8995
Jeff Goudreau, *President*
Bob Kordus, *Vice Pres*
EMP: 15
SALES: 1.5MM **Privately Held**
WEB: www.vulcanwoodproducts.com
SIC: 2411 Fuel wood harvesting

Wakefield
Gogebic County

(G-16848)
COPPERWOOD RESOURCES INC
310 E Us Highway 2 (49968-1000)
PHONE 906 229-3115
Denis Miville-Deschenes, *President*

Timothy Lynott, *Manager*
EMP: 12
SALES (est): 251K **Privately Held**
SIC: 1021 Copper ore mining & preparation

(G-16849)
D & D DRIERS TIMBER PRODUCT
115 E Old Us 2 (49968-9217)
PHONE 906 224-7251
Mike Drier, *President*
EMP: 5
SALES (est): 550.6K **Privately Held**
SIC: 3469 Machine parts, stamped or pressed metal

(G-16850)
EXTREME TOOL AND ENGRG INC (PA)
999 Production Dr (49968-9210)
PHONE 906 229-9100
Mike Zacharias, *President*
Chris Longhini, *Vice Pres*
Jeff Zeller, *Mfg Dir*
Mike Haupert, *Production*
Chuck Hampston, *Project Engr*
▲ **EMP:** 80
SQ FT: 30,000
SALES (est): 15.5MM **Privately Held**
WEB: www.extremetool.com
SIC: 3544 Industrial molds

(G-16851)
EXTREME TOOL AND ENGRG INC
703 Chippawa Dr (49968-9222)
PHONE 906 229-9100
Mike Zacharias, *Branch Mgr*
EMP: 8
SALES (est): 876.9K
SALES (corp-wide): 15.5MM **Privately Held**
SIC: 3089 Injection molding of plastics
PA: Extreme Tool And Engineering, Inc.
999 Production Dr
Wakefield MI 49968
906 229-9100

(G-16852)
GA DALBECK LOGGING LLC
205 N County Road 519 (49968-9580)
PHONE 906 364-3300
George A Dalbeck, *Mng Member*
EMP: 12 **EST:** 2010
SALES (est): 30.9K **Privately Held**
SIC: 2411 Logging camps & contractors

(G-16853)
MILJEVICH CORPORATION
511 Putnam St (49968-1021)
PHONE 906 229-5367
Kathleen Miljevich, *President*
Michael Miljevich, *Vice Pres*
Loralee Radowski, *Treasurer*
EMP: 17
SALES (est): 2.1MM **Privately Held**
SIC: 2411 Logging camps & contractors

(G-16854)
MLC OF WAKEFIELD INC
893 Cemetery Rd (49968-9443)
PHONE 906 224-1120
Brian Miljevich, *President*
EMP: 11
SQ FT: 4,000
SALES: 1.5MM **Privately Held**
SIC: 2421 Sawmills & planing mills, general

(G-16855)
RANDALLS BAKERY
Also Called: Roger Randall Bakery
505 Sunday Lake St (49968-1339)
PHONE 906 224-5401
Roger B Randall, *Owner*
Anamarie Randall, *Owner*
EMP: 9 **EST:** 1943
SQ FT: 1,250
SALES (est): 312K **Privately Held**
SIC: 5461 2051 Bakeries; bread, cake & related products

Wakefield - Gogebic County (G-16856)

(G-16856)
WAKEFIELD NEWS
405 Sunday Lake St (49968-1399)
PHONE..................................906 224-9561
Henry Backman, *Owner*
EMP: 3 **EST:** 1890
SQ FT: 3,200
SALES (est): 190.3K **Privately Held**
SIC: 2711 5943 Commercial printing & newspaper publishing combined; office forms & supplies

Waldron
Hillsdale County

(G-16857)
DAVID BOYD
Also Called: Boyd and Son Logging
8800 Camden Rd (49288-9770)
PHONE..................................517 567-2302
David Boyd, *Owner*
EMP: 3
SALES (est): 274.9K **Privately Held**
SIC: 2411 Logging

(G-16858)
GERKEN MATERIALS INC
Also Called: Hillsdale Sand and Gravel
11671 Tripp Rd (49288-9762)
PHONE..................................517 567-4406
Denny Fackler, *Manager*
EMP: 3
SALES (corp-wide): 80.7MM **Privately Held**
SIC: 1442 Gravel mining
PA: Gerken Materials, Inc.
9072 County Road 424
Napoleon OH 43545
419 533-2421

Wales
St. Clair County

(G-16859)
JEFFREY ALAN MFG & ENGRG LLC
8625 Lapeer Rd (48027-1617)
P.O. Box 9, Goodells (48027-0009)
PHONE..................................810 325-1119
Evelyn Sutphen,
EMP: 3
SALES (est): 192.1K **Privately Held**
SIC: 3599 Machine shop, jobbing & repair

(G-16860)
SIMPSON INDUSTRIAL SVCS LLC
9020 Green Rd (48027-2401)
P.O. Box 12, Goodells (48027-0012)
PHONE..................................810 392-2717
Susan Dungan, *Mng Member*
EMP: 6
SQ FT: 5,000
SALES (est): 969.2K **Privately Held**
SIC: 3531 3536 Cranes; hoists, cranes & monorails

Walker
Kent County

(G-16861)
ALTUS INDUSTRIES INC
3731 Northridge Dr Nw # 1 (49544-9140)
PHONE..................................616 233-9530
Craig Vanderheide, *President*
Diane Schmitt, *General Mgr*
Eric Kahkonen, *Vice Pres*
Jeff Mirbaha, *Buyer*
Angie Gort, *Technology*
▲ **EMP:** 15 **EST:** 2001
SQ FT: 7,500
SALES (est): 5.8MM **Privately Held**
WEB: www.altus-inc.com
SIC: 2522 Office furniture, except wood

(G-16862)
CHALLENGE MFG COMPANY
3200 Fruit Ridge Ave Nw (49544-9707)
PHONE..................................616 735-6530
Douglas Bradley, *Branch Mgr*
EMP: 10
SALES (corp-wide): 763MM **Privately Held**
SIC: 3465 Automotive stampings
PA: Challenge Mfg. Company, Llc
3200 Fruit Ridge Ave Nw
Walker MI 49544
616 735-6500

(G-16863)
CHALLENGE MFG COMPANY LLC
2969 3 Mile Rd Nw (49534-1321)
P.O. Box 141637, Grand Rapids (49514-1637)
PHONE..................................616 735-6500
Doug Bradley, *Vice Pres*
EMP: 12
SALES (corp-wide): 763MM **Privately Held**
SIC: 3465 Body parts, automobile: stamped metal
PA: Challenge Mfg. Company, Llc
3200 Fruit Ridge Ave Nw
Walker MI 49544
616 735-6500

(G-16864)
CHALLENGE MFG COMPANY LLC (PA)
3200 Fruit Ridge Ave Nw (49544-9707)
PHONE..................................616 735-6500
Bruce Vor Broker, *President*
Douglas N Bradley, *Vice Pres*
Boyd Vor Broker, *Vice Pres*
Keith O''brien, *Vice Pres*
Leonard J Rinke Jr, *Vice Pres*
▲ **EMP:** 500
SQ FT: 251,000
SALES (est): 763MM **Privately Held**
SIC: 3465 Automotive stampings

(G-16865)
DIE TECH SERVICES INC
2457 Waldorf Ct Nw (49544-1472)
PHONE..................................616 363-6604
Kelly C Darby, *President*
Casey Darby, *President*
Ron Bourque, *Vice Pres*
Kelly Darby, *Vice Pres*
Kate Murphy, *Human Res Mgr*
EMP: 48
SQ FT: 27,000
SALES (est): 5.9MM **Privately Held**
WEB: www.dietechservices.com
SIC: 7361 3544 Labor contractors (employment agency); special dies, tools, jigs & fixtures; welding positioners (jigs)

(G-16866)
HAVILAND CONTOURED PLASTICS
2168 Avastar Pkwy Nw (49544-1928)
PHONE..................................616 361-6691
E Bernard Haviland, *President*
▲ **EMP:** 4
SALES (est): 398.6K **Privately Held**
SIC: 3052 Plastic hose; vacuum cleaner hose, plastic

(G-16867)
HERALD PUBLISHING COMPANY LLC (HQ)
Also Called: Advance Central Services Mich
3102 Walker Ridge Dr Nw (49544-9125)
PHONE..................................616 222-5400
Michael Ply, *Vice Pres*
John Markham, *Accounts Exec*
Craig Brown, *Sales Staff*
Geralyn Balardo, *Manager*
Ann Keeler, *Manager*
EMP: 44
SALES (est): 15.9MM
SALES (corp-wide): 5.5B **Privately Held**
SIC: 2711 Newspapers, publishing & printing
PA: Advance Publications, Inc.
1 World Trade Ctr Fl 43
New York NY 10007
718 981-1234

(G-16868)
HUNDERMAN & SONS REDI-MIX INC
1050 Maynard Ave Sw (49534-7030)
PHONE..................................616 453-5999
Elmer Hunderman, *President*
Ben Hunderman, *Principal*
EMP: 8
SALES (est): 1.3MM **Privately Held**
SIC: 3273 Ready-mixed concrete

(G-16869)
KENTWOOD PACKAGING CORPORATION
2102 Avastar Pkwy Nw (49544-1928)
PHONE..................................616 698-9000
Thomas A Boluyt, *President*
Leonard R Vining, *Principal*
Jack Skoog, *Vice Pres*
Sharon Mesker, *Accountant*
Tom Boluyt, *Human Res Mgr*
▲ **EMP:** 60 **EST:** 1977
SQ FT: 70,000
SALES (est): 20.2MM **Privately Held**
WEB: www.kentwoodpackaging.com
SIC: 2653 3496 2821 2631 Boxes, corrugated: made from purchased materials; miscellaneous fabricated wire products; plastics materials & resins; paperboard mills

(G-16870)
KRUPP INDUSTRIES LLC (PA)
Also Called: Universal Spiral Air
2735 West River Dr Nw (49544-2013)
PHONE..................................616 475-5905
David C Krupp,
EMP: 38
SQ FT: 18,000
SALES (est): 17.1MM **Privately Held**
SIC: 3444 Ducts, sheet metal

(G-16871)
NBHX TRIM USA CORPORATION
3056 Wlker Ridge Ct Ste D (49544)
PHONE..................................616 785-9400
Tim Isley, *Branch Mgr*
EMP: 15
SALES (corp-wide): 2.1B **Privately Held**
SIC: 3714 Motor vehicle parts & accessories
HQ: Nbhx Trim Usa Corporation
1020 7 Mile Rd Nw
Comstock Park MI 49321
616 785-9400

(G-16872)
OLIVER PACKAGING AND EQP CO
3236 Wilson Dr Nw (49534-7505)
PHONE..................................616 356-2950
Jerry Bennish, *President*
Jamie Blanchard, *President*
Mark Kreiss, *Regional Mgr*
Chadd Floria, *Vice Pres*
Vance Matz, *Engineer*
▲ **EMP:** 61
SALES (est): 21.1MM
SALES (corp-wide): 2.9B **Privately Held**
WEB: www.oliverquality.com
SIC: 2675 3556 2672 Die-cut paper & board; bakery machinery; adhesive papers, labels or tapes: from purchased material
HQ: Oliver Products Company
445 6th St Nw
Grand Rapids MI 49504
616 456-7711

(G-16873)
PIPP MOBIL STORA SYSTE HOLDI C
2966 Wilson Dr Nw (49534-7592)
PHONE..................................616 735-9100
Craig J Umans, *President*
Erik E Maurer, *Chairman*
Allen Jarboe, *CFO*
Keith Tolger, *CFO*
Richard C Tuttle, *Treasurer*
EMP: 150
SALES (est): 12.3MM **Privately Held**
SIC: 5719 2542 Closet organizers & shelving units; fixtures: display, office or store: except wood

(G-16874)
PLASAN CARBON COMPOSITES INC (DH)
3195 Wilson Dr Nw (49534-7565)
PHONE..................................616 965-9450
James Staargaard, *President*
Dalton Blackwell, *Vice Pres*
Gregory Nicholson, *Vice Pres*
Melanie Kramer, *Buyer*
David Pape, *Research*
▲ **EMP:** 130
SQ FT: 49,000
SALES (est): 29.7MM
SALES (corp-wide): 788.8K **Privately Held**
SIC: 3714 Motor vehicle parts & accessories
HQ: Plasan Sasa Ltd.
Kibbutz
Sasa 13870
468 090-00

(G-16875)
PLASAN NORTH AMERICA INC
3236 Wilson Dr Nw Ste B (49534-7506)
P.O. Box 169, Bennington VT (05201-0169)
PHONE..................................616 559-0032
Azriel Biberstain, *Vice Pres*
Dalton Blackwell, *Vice Pres*
Megan Pell, *Program Mgr*
◆ **EMP:** 80
SALES (est): 27.5MM
SALES (corp-wide): 15MM **Privately Held**
SIC: 3795 Specialized tank components, military
HQ: Plasan Us, Inc.
3236 Wilson Dr Nw Ste B
Walker MI 49534

(G-16876)
PLASAN US INC (HQ)
3236 Wilson Dr Nw Ste B (49534-7506)
PHONE..................................616 559-0032
Adrienne Stevens, *President*
Daniel Hartzler, *Engineer*
Azriel Biberstain, *CFO*
Mary Beth Bennett, *Controller*
EMP: 16
SALES (est): 30.4MM
SALES (corp-wide): 15MM **Privately Held**
SIC: 2655 8711 Cans, composite: foil-fiber & other: from purchased fiber; engineering services
PA: Plasan Holdings Usa, Inc.
139 Shields Dr
Bennington VT 05201
802 445-1700

(G-16877)
QUALITY EDGE INC (DH)
Also Called: Qe
2712 Walkent Dr Nw (49544-1439)
PHONE..................................616 735-3833
Craig Rasmussen, *President*
Scott Rasmussen, *President*
Rick Simkins, *CFO*
Eric McCarty, *Controller*
◆ **EMP:** 80
SQ FT: 180,000
SALES (est): 19.7MM **Privately Held**
WEB: www.quality-edge.com
SIC: 3442 Metal doors, sash & trim
HQ: Marubeni-Itochu Steel America Inc.
150 E 42nd St Fl 7
New York NY 10017
212 660-6000

(G-16878)
QUIKRETE COMPANIES INC
Also Called: Quickrete
20 N Park St Nw (49544-6906)
P.O. Box 89, Comstock Park (49321-0089)
PHONE..................................616 784-5790
Jeremy Burt, *Site Mgr*
Noel Nixon, *Branch Mgr*
EMP: 30 **Privately Held**
SIC: 3272 Dry mixture concrete
HQ: The Quikrete Companies Llc
5 Concourse Pkwy Ste 1900
Atlanta GA 30328
404 634-9100

GEOGRAPHIC SECTION

(G-16879)
TECH GROUP GRAND RAPIDS INC
3116 N Wilson Ct Nw (49534-7566)
PHONE.................................616 643-6001
Eric M Green, *President*
George L Miller, *Senior VP*
Daniel Malone, *Vice Pres*
Mike Treadaway, *Vice Pres*
Brian Meines, *Engineer*
EMP: 325
SALES (est): 12.1MM
SALES (corp-wide): 1.7B **Publicly Held**
SIC: 3089 Injection molding of plastics
PA: West Pharmaceutical Services, Inc.
530 Herman O West Dr
Exton PA 19341
610 594-2900

(G-16880)
TUBELITE INC (HQ)
3056 Walker Ridge Dr Nw G (49544-9133)
PHONE.................................800 866-2227
Steve Green, *President*
W Robert Keyes, *Chairman*
Glen Barfknecht, *Vice Pres*
Tim Salach, *Vice Pres*
John Williamson, *Plant Supt*
EMP: 91
SQ FT: 250,000
SALES (est): 37.6MM
SALES (corp-wide): 1.4B **Publicly Held**
WEB: www.tubeliteinc.com
SIC: 3449 3442 3444 3354 Miscellaneous metalwork; window & door frames; sheet metalwork; aluminum extruded products
PA: Apogee Enterprises, Inc.
4400 W 78th St Ste 520
Minneapolis MN 55435
952 835-1874

(G-16881)
VISTA MANUFACTURING INC
Also Called: Facements
3110 Wilson Dr Nw (49534-7564)
PHONE.................................616 719-5520
Rick Nykamp, *President*
Ric Nykamp, *President*
Paul Knapp, *Vice Pres*
Dave Steil, *Vice Pres*
EMP: 50
SALES (est): 10.9MM **Privately Held**
SIC: 2542 Office & store showcases & display fixtures

(G-16882)
WEST MICHIGAN GAGE INC
4055 Rmmbrnce Rd Nw Ste 1 (49534)
PHONE.................................616 735-0585
Mike Zajac, *Principal*
Al Smith, *Principal*
Tina McLouth, *Admin Asst*
EMP: 14
SALES (est): 2.9MM **Privately Held**
WEB: www.wmgage.com
SIC: 2599 3714 3545 Factory furniture & fixtures; motor vehicle parts & accessories; machine tool accessories

(G-16883)
WRIGHT SEALANT RESTORATION INC
3848 Sydney Ct Nw (49534-3647)
PHONE.................................616 453-5914
Andrew Wright, *Principal*
EMP: 4 **EST:** 2012
SALES (est): 263.4K **Privately Held**
SIC: 2891 Sealants

Walkerville
Oceana County

(G-16884)
ARBRE FARMS CORPORATION
6362 N 192nd Ave (49459-8601)
PHONE.................................231 873-3337
C O Johnson, *President*
Dylan Marks, *Vice Pres*
Samantha Harjes, *QC Mgr*
Samantha Oesch, *HR Admin*
Andy Akins, *Manager*
▼ **EMP:** 300

SALES (est): 71.3MM **Privately Held**
SIC: 2099 0191 Food preparations; general farms, primarily crop

Wallace
Menominee County

(G-16885)
ADVANCED BLNDING SOLUTIONS LLC
W5649 County Road 342 (49893-9375)
P.O. Box 37 (49893-0037)
PHONE.................................920 664-1469
Keith Hanson, *Project Engr*
Nick Rhode, *Administration*
EMP: 29
SALES (est): 6.7MM **Privately Held**
SIC: 3089 Plastic processing

(G-16886)
KOPACH FILTER LLC
N3840 R 2 Ln (49893-9642)
PHONE.................................906 863-8611
James R Parrett, *Principal*
EMP: 8
SALES (est): 560.1K **Privately Held**
SIC: 3999 Manufacturing industries

(G-16887)
PAL-TEC INC
14 Ln W5886 (49893)
PHONE.................................906 788-4229
Larry Palzewic, *President*
Barbara Palzewic, *Corp Secy*
EMP: 6
SALES (est): 250K **Privately Held**
SIC: 3325 Steel foundries

(G-16888)
SUPERIOR SYNCHRONIZED SYS
W4365 Pinewoods Loop 12 (49893-9750)
PHONE.................................906 863-7824
Keith Hanson, *President*
Michael Reasner, *Vice Pres*
EMP: 60
SQ FT: 30,000
SALES (est): 2MM **Privately Held**
SIC: 3715 Truck trailers

Walled Lake
Oakland County

(G-16889)
AERO INC
1010 W West Maple Rd (48390-2935)
PHONE.................................248 669-4085
Francis R Geisler III, *President*
EMP: 18
SQ FT: 21,000
SALES (est): 4MM **Privately Held**
SIC: 3441 Fabricated structural metal

(G-16890)
AMERICAN PLASTIC TOYS INC (PA)
799 Ladd Rd (48390-3025)
PHONE.................................248 624-4881
David B Littleton, *Ch of Bd*
John W Gessert, *President*
Jim Grau, *Treasurer*
Ruth W Littleton, *Admin Sec*
◆ **EMP:** 300 **EST:** 1962
SQ FT: 284,000
SALES: 48.5MM **Privately Held**
WEB: www.aptoys.net
SIC: 3944 Craft & hobby kits & sets; automobiles & trucks, toy; dollhouses & furniture; doll carriages & carts

(G-16891)
BASIC RUBBER AND PLASTICS CO (PA)
8700 Boulder Ct (48390-4104)
PHONE.................................248 360-7400
David C Smith, *President*
Deb Isaacson, *General Mgr*
Thomas P Smith, *Vice Pres*
Randy Klann, *Mfg Staff*
Mike Clemons, *Engineer*
EMP: 31

SQ FT: 35,000
SALES (est): 5.6MM **Privately Held**
WEB: www.basicrubber.com
SIC: 3053 3069 3083 3061 Gaskets, all materials; sponge rubber & sponge rubber products; laminated plastics plate & sheet; mechanical rubber goods

(G-16892)
C F LONG & SONS INC
1555 E West Maple Rd (48390-3770)
P.O. Box 837 (48390-0837)
PHONE.................................248 624-1562
Craig Long, *President*
Ronald C Long, *Corp Secy*
John D Long, *Vice Pres*
EMP: 15
SQ FT: 3,000
SALES (est): 2.7MM **Privately Held**
SIC: 3273 5032 Ready-mixed concrete; concrete & cinder block; concrete mixtures; sand, construction; gravel

(G-16893)
ERIN INDUSTRIES INC (PA)
902 N Pontiac Trl (48390-3234)
PHONE.................................248 669-2050
Steve A Atwell, *President*
Steven A Atwell, *President*
Bruce A Robertson, *Vice Pres*
Mary E Bradburn, *Treasurer*
EMP: 23 **EST:** 1975
SQ FT: 20,000
SALES (est): 2.9MM **Privately Held**
SIC: 3498 5013 Tube fabricating (contract bending & shaping); automotive supplies & parts

(G-16894)
GREAT LAKES POWDER COATING LLC
1020 Decker Rd (48390-3218)
PHONE.................................248 522-6222
Dewain Diacono, *Mng Member*
EMP: 16 **EST:** 2009
SQ FT: 55,000
SALES: 1.9MM **Privately Held**
SIC: 3479 3444 Coating of metals & formed products; sheet metalwork

(G-16895)
HUSKY ENVELOPE PRODUCTS INC (PA)
1225 E West Maple Rd (48390-3764)
P.O. Box 868 (48390-0868)
PHONE.................................248 624-7070
William Reske, *President*
Robert Muehl, *Vice Pres*
Brian Tabaczka, *CFO*
Brian S Tabaczka, *Treasurer*
Linda Johnson, *Sales Staff*
EMP: 90 **EST:** 1984
SQ FT: 50,000
SALES (est): 23.6MM **Privately Held**
WEB: www.huskyenvelope.com
SIC: 2677 2759 Envelopes; commercial printing

(G-16896)
LAWSON MANUFACTURING INC
920 Ladd Rd (48390-3028)
PHONE.................................248 624-1818
Lillian Lawson, *President*
Edward Lawson, *Vice Pres*
EMP: 12
SQ FT: 4,300
SALES (est): 1.9MM **Privately Held**
WEB: www.lawsonaerator.com
SIC: 3599 Machine shop, jobbing & repair

(G-16897)
LOKOL LLC
1011 Decker Rd (48390-3219)
PHONE.................................586 615-1727
Jacob Rosen, *Mng Member*
Michael Goodwin, *Mng Member*
Peter Rosen, *Mng Member*
EMP: 3 **EST:** 2015
SALES (est): 106.7K **Privately Held**
SIC: 7372 Application computer software

(G-16898)
MEGA PRINTING INC
1600 W West Maple Rd D (48390-1915)
PHONE.................................248 624-6065
Mark Grimm, *President*

Ed Grimm, *Vice Pres*
EMP: 4
SQ FT: 1,800
SALES (est): 200K **Privately Held**
WEB: www.printingtechnologies.com
SIC: 2752 7334 Commercial printing, offset; photocopying & duplicating services

(G-16899)
MTU ONSITE ENERGY CORPORATION
1424 Crimson Way (48390-2146)
PHONE.................................805 879-3499
EMP: 3
SALES (est): 157.1K **Privately Held**
SIC: 3621 Motors & generators

(G-16900)
NATIONWIDE ENVLOPE SPCLSTS INC (PA)
1225 E West Maple Rd (48390-3764)
PHONE.................................248 354-5500
Alex Sova, *President*
Tom Lewis, *Manager*
EMP: 13
SQ FT: 2,500
SALES (est): 2.1MM **Privately Held**
WEB: www.nespn.com
SIC: 2752 Commercial printing, offset

(G-16901)
PARAMOUNT TECHNOLOGIES INC
1374 E West Maple Rd (48390-3765)
PHONE.................................248 960-0909
Salim A Khalife, *CEO*
EMP: 25
SQ FT: 8,500
SALES (est): 4.3MM **Privately Held**
WEB: www.paramounttechnologies.com
SIC: 7372 Business oriented computer software

(G-16902)
RICHARDSON ACQSTIONS GROUP INC
Also Called: V-Line Precision Products
961 Decker Rd (48390-3217)
PHONE.................................248 624-2272
Mason Richardson, *President*
Thomas Leblanc, *General Mgr*
Robin Carano, *Plant Mgr*
EMP: 25
SALES (est): 1.6MM **Privately Held**
SIC: 3541 Drilling & boring machines

(G-16903)
SHAIS LDSCPG SNOW PLOWING LLC
995 N Pontiac Trl (48390-7055)
PHONE.................................248 234-3663
Shai Grossman, *Principal*
EMP: 5 **EST:** 2016
SALES (est): 69.9K **Privately Held**
SIC: 0782 3991 4959 Lawn & garden services; street sweeping brooms, hand or machine; snowplowing

(G-16904)
TZAMCO INC (PA)
1060 W West Maple Rd (48390-2935)
PHONE.................................248 624-7710
Nancy Amberger, *CEO*
Dave Pratt, *President*
◆ **EMP:** 50 **EST:** 1941
SQ FT: 100,000
SALES (est): 14.2MM **Privately Held**
WEB: www.dedoes.com
SIC: 3559 Paint making machinery

Warren
Macomb County

(G-16905)
A & B TUBE BENDERS INC (PA)
13465 E 9 Mile Rd (48089-2697)
PHONE.................................586 773-0440
Joseph REA, *President*
Mary REA, *Vice Pres*
Salvatore REA, *Vice Pres*
Agnes REA, *Treasurer*
Nadalie REA, *Admin Sec*

Warren - Macomb County (G-16906)   GEOGRAPHIC SECTION

EMP: 30 EST: 1960
SQ FT: 37,850
SALES (est): 5MM **Privately Held**
SIC: 3429 3498 3732 3317 Marine hardware; tube fabricating (contract bending & shaping); boat building & repairing; steel pipe & tubes

(G-16906)
A & B TUBE BENDERS INC
23133 Schoenherr Rd (48089-4262)
PHONE..............................586 773-0440
Diane Ashmore, *Branch Mgr*
EMP: 5
SALES (corp-wide): 5MM **Privately Held**
SIC: 3498 Fabricated pipe & fittings
PA: A & B Tube Benders, Inc.
    13465 E 9 Mile Rd
    Warren MI 48089
    586 773-0440

(G-16907)
A & M DISTRIBUTORS
31239 Mound Rd (48092-4736)
PHONE..............................586 755-9045
David Agno, *Principal*
EMP: 4
SALES (est): 354.2K **Privately Held**
WEB: www.amdistributors.com
SIC: 2951 Asphalt paving mixtures & blocks

(G-16908)
A A TANKS CO
25110 Thomas Dr (48091-1336)
PHONE..............................586 427-7700
Tom Martin, *Owner*
Jeffery Martin, *Partner*
Jim Pudlo, *Partner*
EMP: 6 EST: 2000
SALES (est): 1.5MM **Privately Held**
WEB: www.aatanks.com
SIC: 3443 Tanks, standard or custom fabricated: metal plate

(G-16909)
A S I INSTRUMENTS INC
12900 E 10 Mile Rd (48089-2045)
PHONE..............................586 756-1222
Chris Chiodo, *President*
David Chiodo, *Opers Staff*
EMP: 6
SQ FT: 6,700
SALES (est): 1.2MM **Privately Held**
WEB: www.asi-instruments.com
SIC: 3829 Measuring & controlling devices

(G-16910)
AAA WATERJET AND MACHINING INC
23720 Hoover Rd (48089-1944)
PHONE..............................586 759-3736
Cynthia Barna, *President*
Glenn L Barna, *Vice Pres*
EMP: 4
SALES: 500K **Privately Held**
SIC: 3499 Fabricated metal products

(G-16911)
ABC BORING CO INC
30600 Ryan Rd (48092-4953)
PHONE..............................586 751-2580
Dave Duhaime, *President*
EMP: 40
SQ FT: 25,000
SALES (est): 6.7MM **Privately Held**
SIC: 3541 Boring mills

(G-16912)
ABC MACHINING & FABRICATING
6737 E 8 Mile Rd (48091-2989)
PHONE..............................586 758-0680
Robert Kay, *President*
EMP: 11 EST: 1962
SQ FT: 11,000
SALES: 1.5MM **Privately Held**
SIC: 3599 Machine shop, jobbing & repair

(G-16913)
ACCUTRONIC INCORPORATED
11281 E 9 Mile Rd (48089-2530)
PHONE..............................586 756-2510
Roy Lyon, *President*
EMP: 3 EST: 1961

SQ FT: 4,000
SALES (est): 399.1K **Privately Held**
SIC: 3599 Electrical discharge machining (EDM)

(G-16914)
ACE FINISHING INC
13195 E 8 Mile Rd (48089-3299)
PHONE..............................586 777-1390
James K Oleksik, *CEO*
John R Oleksik, *President*
Greg Wirth, *Treasurer*
EMP: 7 EST: 1935
SQ FT: 30,000
SALES: 1.3MM **Privately Held**
WEB: www.acefinishing.com
SIC: 3471 Electroplating of metals or formed products; finishing, metals or formed products

(G-16915)
ACHS METAL PRODUCTS INC
22238 Schoenherr Rd (48089-5400)
PHONE..............................586 772-2734
Richard Achs, *President*
Barbara Achs, *Vice Pres*
John Achs, *Vice Pres*
Michael Achs, *Vice Pres*
Patrick Achs, *Vice Pres*
EMP: 5
SALES (est): 599K **Privately Held**
SIC: 7692 Welding repair

(G-16916)
ACME CASTING ENTERPRISES INC
2565 John B Ave (48091-4244)
PHONE..............................586 755-0300
Jon Dooge, *President*
Eric Kriebel, *Vice Pres*
EMP: 4 EST: 1954
SQ FT: 12,250
SALES: 2MM **Privately Held**
SIC: 5051 3543 Castings, rough: iron or steel; foundry patternmaking

(G-16917)
ACME HOLDING COMPANY
Also Called: Acme Abrasive Co.
24200 Marmon Ave (48089-3808)
PHONE..............................586 759-3332
Robert Beebe, *President*
Colleen McFall, *Admin Asst*
EMP: 24
SALES (est): 5MM **Privately Held**
SIC: 3291 Pumice & pumicite abrasive

(G-16918)
ADEMCO INC
Also Called: ADI Global Distribution
24749 Forterra Dr (48089-4376)
PHONE..............................586 759-1455
Roger Black, *Branch Mgr*
EMP: 6
SALES (corp-wide): 4.8B **Publicly Held**
SIC: 5063 3669 3822 Electrical apparatus & equipment; emergency alarms; auto controls regulating residntl & coml environmt & applncs
HQ: Ademco Inc.
    1985 Douglas Dr N
    Golden Valley MN 55422
    800 468-1502

(G-16919)
ADVANCE MOTOR REBUILDERS INC
22850 Groesbeck Hwy (48089-4240)
PHONE..............................586 222-9583
Jerome Poma, *President*
EMP: 3
SQ FT: 4,200
SALES (est): 339.6K **Privately Held**
SIC: 3714 Rebuilding engines & transmissions, factory basis

(G-16920)
ADVANCED RUBBER & PLASTIC (PA)
3035 Otis Ave (48091-2325)
PHONE..............................586 754-7398
Frank D Aquino, *President*
Karin Barachkov, *Corp Secy*
EMP: 6

SALES: 1MM **Privately Held**
SIC: 3069 3089 5085 Molded rubber products; injection molding of plastics; rubber goods, mechanical

(G-16921)
AIR SUPPLY INC
Also Called: A S I
21300 Groesbeck Hwy (48089-4920)
PHONE..............................586 773-6600
Ronald Dicicco, *President*
Dean Huber, *Corp Secy*
EMP: 6
SQ FT: 18,000
SALES (est): 827.6K **Privately Held**
SIC: 3842 Respirators

(G-16922)
AJAX METAL PROCESSING INC
22105 Hoover Rd (48089-2566)
PHONE..............................586 497-7000
Robert Holland, *Plant Mgr*
EMP: 15
SQ FT: 20,000
SALES (corp-wide): 30.3MM **Privately Held**
WEB: www.ajaxmetal.com
SIC: 3398 Annealing of metal
PA: Ajax Metal Processing, Inc.
    4651 Bellevue St
    Detroit MI 48207
    313 267-2100

(G-16923)
AJAX TRAILERS INC (PA)
2089 E 10 Mile Rd (48091-1306)
PHONE..............................586 757-7676
Michael G Paulina, *President*
Justin McMaster, *Sales Staff*
EMP: 14 EST: 1941
SQ FT: 16,800
SALES: 1.5MM **Privately Held**
WEB: www.ajaxtrailers.com
SIC: 3715 7539 5599 3792 Truck trailers; trailer repair; utility trailers; travel trailers & campers

(G-16924)
ALTERNATIVE COMPONENTS LLC (PA)
24055 Mound Rd (48091-2039)
PHONE..............................586 755-9177
Adam Clifton, *President*
Michelle Swallow, *Business Mgr*
Ty Oberlin, *Engineer*
John Miller, *Administration*
EMP: 33
SQ FT: 26,000
SALES (est): 7.8MM **Privately Held**
WEB: www.alternativecomponents.com
SIC: 3498 Coils, pipe: fabricated from purchased pipe

(G-16925)
ALTRA INDUSTRIAL MOTION CORP
Formsprag Clutch
23601 Hoover Rd (48089-1986)
P.O. Box 778 (48090-0778)
PHONE..............................586 758-5000
Naytoe Aye, *Business Mgr*
Andy Zielaskowski, *Purch Mgr*
Kevin Ackerman, *Engineer*
Ben Blondin, *Engineer*
Donald Morris, *Engineer*
EMP: 90
SALES (corp-wide): 1.1B **Publicly Held**
WEB: www.altramotion.com
SIC: 3568 Clutches, except vehicular
PA: Altra Industrial Motion Corp.
    300 Granite St Ste 201
    Braintree MA 02184
    781 917-0600

(G-16926)
ALUDYNE INC
24155 Wahl St (48089-2057)
PHONE..............................248 506-1692
EMP: 3
SALES (corp-wide): 1.3B **Privately Held**
SIC: 3363 Aluminum die-castings
HQ: Aludyne, Inc.
    300 Galleria Ofcntr Ste 5
    Southfield MI 48034
    248 728-8642

(G-16927)
ALUDYNE US LLC (DH)
12700 Stephens Rd (48089-4334)
PHONE..............................586 782-0200
Michael Dorah, *Vice Pres*
Eric Rouchy, *Vice Pres*
Vicki Mitchell, *Purch Agent*
Khan Lee, *Engineer*
Michael Beyer, *CFO*
▲ EMP: 132
SQ FT: 85,000
SALES (est): 31.9MM
SALES (corp-wide): 1.3B **Privately Held**
WEB: www.smwauto.com
SIC: 3714 Motor vehicle parts & accessories

(G-16928)
ALUDYNE US LLC
23300 Blackstone Ave (48089-4206)
PHONE..............................248 728-8642
EMP: 10
SALES (corp-wide): 1.3B **Privately Held**
SIC: 3465 Body parts, automobile: stamped metal
HQ: Aludyne Us Llc
    12700 Stephens Rd
    Warren MI 48089

(G-16929)
AMERICAN BLOWER SUPPLY INC
Also Called: American Fan & Blower
14219 E 10 Mile Rd (48089-2162)
PHONE..............................586 771-7337
Randall Morrow, *President*
▲ EMP: 15
SALES (est): 3.9MM **Privately Held**
SIC: 5085 3444 Industrial supplies; sheet metalwork

(G-16930)
AMERICAN GRAPHITE CORPORATION
21756 Dequindre Rd (48091-2102)
PHONE..............................586 757-3540
Kenneth R Smith, *President*
EMP: 6
SQ FT: 5,000
SALES: 800K **Privately Held**
SIC: 3624 Carbon & graphite products

(G-16931)
AMERICAN METAL PROCESSING CO
22720 Nagel St (48089-3725)
PHONE..............................586 757-7144
Gerald Pinkos, *President*
George Baloi, *QC Mgr*
Dennis Pinkos, *Admin Sec*
▲ EMP: 33 EST: 1945
SQ FT: 30,000
SALES (est): 7.1MM **Privately Held**
WEB: www.ampht.com
SIC: 3398 Metal heat treating

(G-16932)
AMERY TAPE & LABEL CO INC
4145 E 10 Mile Rd (48091-1508)
P.O. Box 1914 (48090-1914)
PHONE..............................586 759-3230
Ted Kowalski, *President*
EMP: 8
SQ FT: 7,000
SALES: 390K **Privately Held**
SIC: 2759 Labels & seals: printing

(G-16933)
ANDROID INDUSTRIES-STERLING (HQ)
Also Called: Ai Warren
27767 George Merrelli Dr (48092-2792)
PHONE..............................586 486-5616
Darrel Reece, *Principal*
EMP: 25
SALES (est): 8.5MM
SALES (corp-wide): 559.5MM **Privately Held**
SIC: 3711 Motor vehicles & car bodies
PA: Android Industries, L.L.C.
    2155 Executive Hills Dr
    Auburn Hills MI 48326
    248 454-0500

GEOGRAPHIC SECTION
Warren - Macomb County (G-16961)

(G-16934)
ANGELOS CRUSHED CONCRETE INC (PA)
26300 Sherwood Ave (48091-4168)
PHONE.................................586 756-1070
Angelo Iafrate Jr, *President*
Dominic Iafrate, *Vice Pres*
EMP: 4
SQ FT: 25,000
SALES (est): 684.5K **Privately Held**
SIC: 2951 3273 5032 Asphalt & asphaltic paving mixtures (not from refineries); ready-mixed concrete; concrete mixtures

(G-16935)
ANTICIPATED PLASTICS INC
24392 Gibson Dr (48089-4310)
PHONE.................................586 427-9450
Glenn Pesti, *President*
Brian Pesti, *Plant Mgr*
EMP: 10
SQ FT: 8,000
SALES (est): 1.2MM **Privately Held**
SIC: 3089 Injection molding of plastics

(G-16936)
APEX BROACHING SYSTEMS INC
22862 Hoover Rd (48089-2568)
PHONE.................................586 758-2626
Leonard Bantleon Jr, *President*
Lisa Thomas, *Corp Secy*
Phil House, *Opers Mgr*
James See, *Opers Mgr*
EMP: 12
SQ FT: 10,000
SALES (est): 2.1MM **Privately Held**
WEB: www.apbsi.com
SIC: 3541 3545 Broaching machines; machine tool accessories

(G-16937)
APPLIED VISUAL CONCEPTS LLC
Also Called: Ceiling Scenes
24680 Mound Rd (48091-2036)
PHONE.................................866 440-6888
Mark Jenzen,
▼ **EMP:** 6
SALES: 100K **Privately Held**
WEB: www.appliedvisualconcepts.com
SIC: 2759 Commercial printing

(G-16938)
ARM TOOLING SYSTEMS INC
2453 John B Ave (48091-4242)
PHONE.................................586 759-5677
Martin Merrell, *President*
Roger A Murrell, *Vice Pres*
Ronald E Murrell, *Vice Pres*
EMP: 11
SQ FT: 3,000
SALES (est): 3.4MM **Privately Held**
SIC: 5084 5251 3545 Machine tools & metalworking machinery; tools; measuring tools & machines, machinists' metalworking type

(G-16939)
ARTED CHROME PLATING
24657 Mound Rd (48091-2043)
PHONE.................................586 758-0050
EMP: 5
SALES (est): 504.7K **Privately Held**
SIC: 3471 Plating/Polishing Service

(G-16940)
ARTISAN BREAD CO LLC
Also Called: Bosco's Pizza Co.
25000 Guenther (48091-1375)
PHONE.................................586 756-0100
Donnie Smith, *President*
Donnie King, *President*
Wes Morris, *President*
Dennis Letherby, *CFO*
EMP: 26 **EST:** 2000
SALES (est): 7.9MM
SALES (corp-wide): 42.4B **Publicly Held**
SIC: 2099 2052 Pizza, refrigerated: except frozen; pretzels
PA: Tyson Foods, Inc.
 2200 W Don Tyson Pkwy
 Springdale AR 72762
 479 290-4000

(G-16941)
AS PROPERTY MANAGEMENT INC
Also Called: Admiral Box Company
25133 Thomas Dr (48091-1397)
PHONE.................................586 427-8000
Steven J Stanton, *President*
Annette Stanton, *Admin Sec*
EMP: 10
SQ FT: 20,000
SALES (est): 1.9MM **Privately Held**
WEB: www.admiralboxco.com
SIC: 2449 Rectangular boxes & crates, wood

(G-16942)
ASE INDUSTRIES INC
Also Called: AUTOMATION SERVICE EQUIPMENT
23850 Pinewood St (48091-4763)
PHONE.................................586 754-7480
Carl Lepera, *President*
Robert Curtis, *Vice Pres*
EMP: 55
SQ FT: 45,000
SALES: 6.9MM **Privately Held**
WEB: www.aseind.com
SIC: 3599 3535 1796 7699 Custom machinery; conveyors & conveying equipment; machinery installation; industrial machinery & equipment repair

(G-16943)
ASPRA WORLD INC
25160 Easy St (48089-4129)
PHONE.................................248 872-7030
Shalu Sinha,
Sameer Sinha,
▲ **EMP:** 100
SQ FT: 8,300
SALES (est): 14MM **Privately Held**
WEB: www.aspraworld.com
SIC: 3714 Motor vehicle parts & accessories

(G-16944)
ASSI FUEL INC
8309 E 8 Mile Rd (48089-2955)
PHONE.................................586 759-4759
Samir Assi, *Principal*
EMP: 5 **EST:** 2013
SALES (est): 255.9K **Privately Held**
SIC: 2869 Fuels

(G-16945)
ATLAS TILE & STONE LLC
31134 Dequindre Rd (48092-3722)
PHONE.................................586 264-7720
John Derosa,
EMP: 5
SALES (est): 380K **Privately Held**
WEB: www.atlastileandstone.com
SIC: 3281 Cut stone & stone products

(G-16946)
B & B MOLD & ENGINEERING INC
25185 Easy St (48089-4132)
PHONE.................................586 773-6664
Gerald Kuhl, *President*
EMP: 5 **EST:** 1975
SQ FT: 7,500
SALES: 325K **Privately Held**
SIC: 3544 Special dies & tools; industrial molds

(G-16947)
B & L PLATING CO INC
21353 Edom Ave (48089-4953)
PHONE.................................586 778-9300
Eugene O Pirrami, *President*
Grace M Pirrami, *Admin Sec*
EMP: 6 **EST:** 1970
SQ FT: 5,000
SALES (est): 669K **Privately Held**
WEB: www.blplating.com
SIC: 3471 Plating of metals or formed products

(G-16948)
B & N PLASTICS INC
8100 E 9 Mile Rd (48089-2362)
PHONE.................................586 758-0030
EMP: 7
SQ FT: 8,400
SALES: 390K **Privately Held**
SIC: 3089 Mfg Plastic Products

(G-16949)
B-J INDUSTRIES INC
14440 Barber Ave (48088-4833)
PHONE.................................586 778-7200
Brian Drzewiecki, *President*
James Drzewiecki, *Treasurer*
Ann D Drzewiecki, *Admin Sec*
EMP: 5 **EST:** 1966
SQ FT: 5,000
SALES (est): 635.5K **Privately Held**
SIC: 3599 Machine shop, jobbing & repair

(G-16950)
BAE INDUSTRIES INC (HQ)
26020 Sherwood Ave (48091-1252)
PHONE.................................586 754-3000
Jesse Lopez, *President*
Dutch Jones, *Exec VP*
Stephen Bruck, *Vice Pres*
Mark Doetsch, *Vice Pres*
Eric Downs, *Engineer*
▲ **EMP:** 163
SQ FT: 90,000
SALES (est): 37MM **Privately Held**
WEB: www.baeind.com
SIC: 3465 3469 Body parts, automobile: stamped metal; metal stampings
PA: Marisa Industries, Inc.
 1426 Pacific Dr
 Auburn Hills MI 48326
 248 475-9600

(G-16951)
BAILEY ROLL FORM COMPANY INC
13446 E 9 Mile Rd (48089-2616)
PHONE.................................586 777-4890
Diane Bailey, *President*
EMP: 8 **EST:** 1962
SQ FT: 6,400
SALES (est): 1MM **Privately Held**
SIC: 3544 Dies & die holders for metal cutting, forming, die casting

(G-16952)
BAR PROCESSING CORPORATION
22534 Groesbeck Hwy (48089-2680)
PHONE.................................734 782-4454
Aeiph King, *Manager*
Matt Holody, *Manager*
EMP: 75
SALES (corp-wide): 39.9MM **Privately Held**
SIC: 3471 3444 3316 3312 Finishing, metals or formed products; polishing, metals or formed products; sheet metalwork; cold finishing of steel shapes; blast furnaces & steel mills
HQ: Bar Processing Corporation
 26601 W Huron River Dr
 Flat Rock MI 48134
 734 782-4454

(G-16953)
BAUER PRECISION TOOL CO
Also Called: East Side Gear
8670 E 9 Mile Rd (48089-2453)
PHONE.................................586 758-7370
Anton Bauer, *President*
Melba Bauer, *Corp Secy*
Jim Bauer, *Manager*
EMP: 5
SQ FT: 4,000
SALES (est): 36.3K **Privately Held**
SIC: 3544 Special dies, tools, jigs & fixtures

(G-16954)
BELLE ISLE AWNING CO INC
13701 E 9 Mile Rd (48089-2766)
PHONE.................................586 294-6050
William J Belluomo, *President*
Gail Wilk, *Sales Staff*
EMP: 35 **EST:** 1930
SQ FT: 14,000
SALES (est): 3.4MM **Privately Held**
WEB: www.belleisleawning.com
SIC: 5999 2394 Canvas products; awnings; canvas & related products

(G-16955)
BERKLEY PHARMACY LLC
28577 Schoenherr Rd (48088-4330)
PHONE.................................586 573-8300
Munice Patel, *Owner*
Chirag Modi, *Manager*
EMP: 11
SALES (est): 1.8MM **Privately Held**
SIC: 2064 2834 Cough drops, except pharmaceutical preparations; pharmaceutical preparations

(G-16956)
BEST BLOCK COMPANY (PA)
Also Called: Best Alloys
22001 Groesbeck Hwy (48089-4228)
PHONE.................................586 772-7000
Robert Pachota, *President*
David Pachota, *Vice Pres*
Michael Pachota, *Treasurer*
EMP: 40
SQ FT: 60,000
SALES (est): 19MM **Privately Held**
SIC: 5211 3271 3272 0782 Concrete & cinder block; blocks, concrete or cinder: standard; concrete products; lawn & garden services

(G-16957)
BEST INDUSTRIAL GROUP INC
7256 Murthum Ave (48092-1251)
PHONE.................................586 826-8800
John Edgell Sr, *President*
John Edgell II, *Vice Pres*
Dorothy Korgol, *Vice Pres*
Anita Edgell, *Treasurer*
EMP: 14
SQ FT: 8,000
SALES: 2MM **Privately Held**
WEB: www.bestindustrialgroup.com
SIC: 5084 1796 3535 Conveyor systems; machinery installation; conveyors & conveying equipment

(G-16958)
BIG BOY RESTAURANTS INTL LLC (PA)
Also Called: Big Boy Restaurant Management
4199 Marcy St (48091-1733)
PHONE.................................586 759-6000
Keith E Sirois, *CEO*
Linda Grady, *Bookkeeper*
Kelly Osegueda, *Marketing Staff*
Frank Alessandrini, *Manager*
Paul W Black,
EMP: 200
SQ FT: 200,000
SALES (est): 81.9MM **Privately Held**
SIC: 5812 2099 Restaurant, family: chain; food preparations

(G-16959)
BILCO TOOL CORPORATION
30076 Dequindre Rd (48092-1899)
PHONE.................................586 574-9300
Gerald Ivey, *President*
Raymond Ivey, *Vice Pres*
Pam Klassen, *Office Mgr*
EMP: 9 **EST:** 1970
SQ FT: 9,500
SALES (est): 1.3MM **Privately Held**
WEB: www.bilcotool.com
SIC: 3544 3545 Jigs & fixtures; gauges (machine tool accessories)

(G-16960)
BIMBO BAKERIES USA INC
26800 Schoenherr Rd (48089-5902)
PHONE.................................586 772-0055
Darrin Walters, *Manager*
EMP: 50 **Privately Held**
SIC: 2051 Bread, cake & related products
HQ: Bimbo Bakeries Usa, Inc
 255 Business Center Dr # 200
 Horsham PA 19044
 215 347-5500

(G-16961)
BIOSAN LABORATORIES INC
1950 Tobsal Ct (48091-1351)
PHONE.................................586 755-8970
Leonard A Rossmoore, *President*
Randy Lauinger, *Controller*
EMP: 15 **EST:** 1973
SQ FT: 10,000

Warren - Macomb County (G-16962)   GEOGRAPHIC SECTION

SALES: 2.6MM **Privately Held**
WEB: www.biosan.com
SIC: **8731** 2835 3829 2836 Biological research; microbiology & virology diagnostic products; measuring & controlling devices; biological products, except diagnostic

(G-16962)
BORDER CITY TOOL AND MFG CO
23325 Blackstone Ave (48089-2675)
PHONE.................................586 758-5574
Don Rothburn, *President*
EMP: 20
SQ FT: 8,000
SALES (est): 4.6MM **Privately Held**
WEB: www.bordercitytool.com
SIC: **3531** Construction machinery

(G-16963)
BOSCH AUTO SVC SOLUTIONS INC (HQ)
28635 Mound Rd (48092-5509)
PHONE.................................586 574-2332
Vickie Gamble, *Auditor*
Guy Garrett, *Sales Staff*
Brian Echtinaw, *Manager*
Jacqueline McCraw, *Manager*
Michael Reimer, *Manager*
▲ **EMP:** 168
SALES (est): 106.3MM
SALES (corp-wide): 294.8MM **Privately Held**
SIC: **7549** 3714 Inspection & diagnostic service, automotive; motor vehicle parts & accessories
PA: R O B E R T B O S C H S T I F T U N G Gesellschaft Mit Beschrankter Haftung
Heidehofstr. 31
Stuttgart 70184
711 460-840

(G-16964)
BOSCH AUTO SVC SOLUTIONS INC
5775 Enterprise Ct (48092-3463)
PHONE.................................586 574-1820
Bob Wiegand, *Principal*
EMP: 40
SALES (corp-wide): 294.8MM **Privately Held**
WEB: www.spx.com
SIC: **3443** Cooling towers, metal plate
HQ: Bosch Automotive Service Solutions Inc.
28635 Mound Rd
Warren MI 48092
586 574-2332

(G-16965)
BRAUER CLAMPS USA
25269 Mound Rd (48091-3857)
PHONE.................................586 427-5304
Mark Matzka, *President*
▲ **EMP:** 150
SALES (est): 9.9MM **Privately Held**
SIC: **3429** Manufactured hardware (general)

(G-16966)
BREAK-A-BEAM
25257 Mound Rd (48091-3857)
PHONE.................................586 758-7790
Tom Matzka, *CEO*
Mark Matzka, *President*
EMP: 18
SALES (est): 2.6MM **Privately Held**
WEB: www.break-a-beam.com
SIC: **5085** 3643 Bearings; current-carrying wiring devices

(G-16967)
BRIDGEWATER INTERIORS LLC
7500 Tank Ave (48092-2707)
PHONE.................................586 582-0882
Alison Sanders, *Manager*
EMP: 600 **Privately Held**
SIC: **2531** Seats, automobile
HQ: Bridgewater Interiors, L.L.C.
4617 W Fort St
Detroit MI 48209
313 842-3300

(G-16968)
BROACHING DIAMOND SERVICE LLC
3560 E 10 Mile Rd (48091-3717)
PHONE.................................586 757-5131
Kevin Peacock, *President*
EMP: 3 **EST:** 2016
SALES (est): 169.4K **Privately Held**
SIC: **3566** Speed changers, drives & gears

(G-16969)
BRUMLEY TOOLS INC
26520 Burg Rd (48089-1043)
PHONE.................................586 260-8326
Phillip Brumley, *CEO*
EMP: 3
SQ FT: 500
SALES (est): 189K **Privately Held**
WEB: www.brumleytools.com
SIC: **3999** Dock equipment & supplies, industrial

(G-16970)
C & G NEWS INC
Also Called: Shelby Utica News, The
13650 E 11 Mile Rd (48089-1422)
PHONE.................................586 498-8000
Gil Demers, *President*
Greg Demers, *Vice Pres*
Michelle Moran, *Production*
Lisa Damon, *Accounts Exec*
Laura Gayan, *Accounts Exec*
EMP: 80
SALES (est): 3.4MM **Privately Held**
WEB: www.candgnews.com
SIC: **2711** Commercial printing & newspaper publishing combined; newspapers: publishing only, not printed on site

(G-16971)
C & G PUBLISHING INC
Also Called: Advertiser, The
13650 E 11 Mile Rd (48089-1422)
PHONE.................................586 498-8000
Gregory A Demers, *President*
Charlotte Demers, *Principal*
Gilbert Demers, *Principal*
Michelle Moran, *Editor*
Nick Mordowanec, *Editor*
EMP: 80
SQ FT: 10,000
SALES (est): 5.1MM **Privately Held**
SIC: **2711** Newspapers: publishing only, not printed on site

(G-16972)
C E C CONTROLS COMPANY INC (HQ)
14555 Barber Ave (48088-6002)
PHONE.................................586 779-0222
Robert Scheper, *President*
Chris Street, *Project Mgr*
Matt Wezensky, *Purchasing*
Dean Fransen, *Engineer*
Richard Waskowitz, *Engineer*
◆ **EMP:** 94
SQ FT: 40,000
SALES: 35.3MM
SALES (corp-wide): 10B **Privately Held**
SIC: **3823** Industrial instrmnts msrmnt display/control process variable
PA: John Wood Group Plc
15 Justice Mill Lane
Aberdeen AB12
122 485-1000

(G-16973)
C R B CRANE & SERVICE CO (PA)
3751 E 10 Mile Rd (48091-3722)
PHONE.................................586 757-1222
Craig R Benedict, *President*
Patricia Benedict, *Vice Pres*
EMP: 7
SQ FT: 12,000
SALES (est): 548.6K **Privately Held**
WEB: www.crbcrane.com
SIC: **3536** 5084 7699 Cranes, overhead traveling; cranes, industrial; industrial equipment services

(G-16974)
C T MACHINING INC
23031 Roseberry Ave (48089-2214)
PHONE.................................586 772-0320

Charles T Corder, *President*
EMP: 6
SQ FT: 4,600
SALES (est): 667.3K **Privately Held**
SIC: **3599** Machine shop, jobbing & repair

(G-16975)
CADILLAC PLATING CORPORATION
23849 Groesbeck Hwy (48089-6004)
PHONE.................................586 771-9191
Nick Salvati, *President*
Mahmood Ahmed, *Vice Pres*
John Kitchen, *Vice Pres*
EMP: 80 **EST:** 1957
SQ FT: 80,000
SALES (est): 11.2MM **Privately Held**
WEB: www.cadillacplating.com
SIC: **3471** Electroplating of metals or formed products

(G-16976)
CANDELA PRODUCTS INC
Also Called: Dramatic Graphics
24760 Romano St (48091-3377)
PHONE.................................248 541-2547
Robert Loiko, *President*
Mary Ann Loiko, *Corp Secy*
EMP: 3
SQ FT: 3,500
SALES: 150K **Privately Held**
SIC: **3999** 5137 5094 Candles; women's & children's clothing; jewelry

(G-16977)
CERATIZIT USA INC
11355 Stephens Rd (48089-1802)
PHONE.................................586 759-2280
Tim Tisler, *President*
▲ **EMP:** 200
SQ FT: 75,000
SALES (est): 46.7MM
SALES (corp-wide): 23.8MM **Privately Held**
SIC: **3545** 2819 Cutting tools for machine tools; industrial inorganic chemicals
PA: Ceratizit Sa
Route De Holzem 101
Mamer 8232
312 085-1

(G-16978)
CG LIQUIDATION INCORPORATED (HQ)
2111 Walter P Reuther Dr (48091-6108)
PHONE.................................586 575-9800
William P Baer, *CEO*
Frank Knoth, *President*
Ken Stallons, *President*
Mitchell Berends, *Business Mgr*
Glen Ford, *VP Business*
▲ **EMP:** 25
SQ FT: 14,000
SALES (est): 70.5MM
SALES (corp-wide): 15.3B **Publicly Held**
SIC: **3479** 3471 Painting of metal products; plating & polishing
PA: Ppg Industries, Inc.
1 Ppg Pl
Pittsburgh PA 15272
412 434-3131

(G-16979)
CHASSIX BLACKSTONE OPERAT
23300 Blackstone Ave (48089-4206)
PHONE.................................586 782-7311
EMP: 4
SALES (est): 539.6K **Privately Held**
SIC: **3714** Motor vehicle parts & accessories

(G-16980)
CHEMICO SYSTEMS INC
6250 Chicago Rd (48092)
PHONE.................................586 986-2343
Kurt Sladick, *Branch Mgr*
EMP: 4
SALES (corp-wide): 23.3MM **Privately Held**
WEB: www.chemicosystems.com
SIC: **2819** Chemicals, high purity: refined from technical grade

PA: Chemico Systems, Inc.
25200 Telg Rd Ste 120
Southfield MI 48034
248 723-3263

(G-16981)
CLARK GRAPHIC SERVICE INC
Also Called: Clark Graphics
21914 Schmeman Ave (48089-3296)
PHONE.................................586 772-4900
Judy A Clark, *CEO*
Charles H Clark, *CEO*
Steve Belote, *VP Opers*
Frank J Canu, *Treasurer*
Tammy Weaver, *Office Mgr*
EMP: 70 **EST:** 1966
SQ FT: 55,000
SALES (est): 17.1MM **Privately Held**
WEB: www.clarkgraphic.com
SIC: **2752** 2791 2789 Commercial printing, offset; typesetting; bookbinding & related work

(G-16982)
CLASSIC CAR PORT & CANOPIES
11800 E 9 Mile Rd (48089-2588)
PHONE.................................586 759-5490
Russ Dibartoloneo, *President*
Lisa Redd, *Administration*
EMP: 15
SALES (est): 1MM **Privately Held**
SIC: **3448** Prefabricated metal buildings

(G-16983)
CLASSIC WELDING INC
21500 Ryan Rd (48091-4669)
PHONE.................................586 758-2400
John Stoianov, *President*
Agnita Stoianov, *Vice Pres*
EMP: 10
SQ FT: 3,000
SALES: 500K **Privately Held**
WEB: www.classicwelding.com
SIC: **7692** Automotive welding

(G-16984)
CLUTCH MASTERS INC
7065 E 8 Mile Rd (48091-2906)
PHONE.................................586 759-1300
Paul Dathe, *President*
EMP: 3
SALES: 150K **Privately Held**
SIC: **3714** Motor vehicle parts & accessories

(G-16985)
COLD HEADING CO (HQ)
21777 Hoover Rd (48089-2544)
PHONE.................................586 497-7000
Derek J Stevens, *Ch of Bd*
James R Joliet, *President*
William Buban, *Vice Pres*
Thomas Dharte, *Vice Pres*
Drayke Dondero, *Vice Pres*
◆ **EMP:** 74 **EST:** 1912
SQ FT: 602,000
SALES (est): 111.1MM
SALES (corp-wide): 55.6MM **Privately Held**
WEB: www.coldheading.com
SIC: **3452** 8711 Bolts, metal; engineering services
PA: Beachlawn Inc.
21777 Hoover Rd
Warren MI 48089
586 497-7000

(G-16986)
COLD HEADING CO
22155 Hoover Rd (48089-2566)
PHONE.................................586 497-7016
Jim Yacks, *Plant Mgr*
EMP: 63
SALES (corp-wide): 55.6MM **Privately Held**
WEB: www.coldheading.com
SIC: **3452** 3316 Bolts, metal; cold finishing of steel shapes
HQ: The Cold Heading Co
21777 Hoover Rd
Warren MI 48089
586 497-7000

GEOGRAPHIC SECTION

Warren - Macomb County (G-17015)

(G-16987)
COLLEGE PARK INDUSTRIES INC
27955 College Park Dr (48088-4877)
P.O. Box 1227 (48090-1227)
PHONE.................................586 294-7950
Michael Schey, *President*
Martin Sternberg, *President*
Kevin Lheureux, *Engineer*
Aaron Taszreak, *Engineer*
Ryan Wahl, *Senior Engr*
EMP: 45
SQ FT: 7,500
SALES (est): 9.6MM **Privately Held**
WEB: www.college-park.com
SIC: 3842 Limbs, artificial

(G-16988)
COMMERCIAL TRCK TRANSF SIGNS
4133 E 10 Mile Rd (48091-1508)
PHONE.................................586 754-7100
Debra Cunningham, *President*
Sharon Salcpa, *Admin Sec*
EMP: 4 **EST:** 1957
SQ FT: 4,500
SALES (est): 480.4K **Privately Held**
SIC: 2752 Decals, lithographed

(G-16989)
COMPANY PRODUCTS INC
11800 Commerce St (48089-3878)
PHONE.................................586 757-6160
Karl Strang, *President*
David B Mills, *Corp Secy*
EMP: 8 **EST:** 1945
SQ FT: 7,000
SALES (est): 1.3MM **Privately Held**
WEB: www.companyproducts.com
SIC: 3639 3544 Sewing machines & attachments, domestic; special dies, tools, jigs & fixtures

(G-16990)
CONDOR MANUFACTURING INC
11800 E 9 Mile Rd (48089-2588)
PHONE.................................586 427-4715
Daniel C Confer, *President*
Sheri Confer, *Corp Secy*
Mary Ann Adhikari, *Controller*
EMP: 25 **EST:** 1950
SQ FT: 25,000
SALES (est): 4MM **Privately Held**
SIC: 3451 Screw machine products

(G-16991)
CONQUEST MANUFACTURING LLC
28408 Lorna Ave (48092-3937)
PHONE.................................586 576-7600
Tim McCarthy, *Mfg Staff*
James D Miller, *Mng Member*
▲ **EMP:** 55 **EST:** 1998
SQ FT: 100,000
SALES (est): 14MM **Privately Held**
WEB: www.ductconnection.com
SIC: 3443 3444 5039 Ducting, metal plate; sheet metalwork; air ducts, sheet metal

(G-16992)
CONTINENTAL COMMUNITIES
3127 Maple St (48091-4253)
PHONE.................................586 757-7412
Mark Kruger, *President*
EMP: 3
SALES (est): 304.7K **Privately Held**
SIC: 2451 Mobile homes

(G-16993)
COOK INDUSTRIES INC
23515 Pinewood St (48091-3121)
PHONE.................................586 754-4070
Carlos Cook, *President*
EMP: 9
SQ FT: 11,000
SALES (est): 1.1MM **Privately Held**
SIC: 3599 Machine shop, jobbing & repair

(G-16994)
COUNTRYSIDE FOODS LLC (HQ)
Also Called: I & K Distributors
26661 Bunert Rd (48089-3650)
PHONE.................................586 447-3500
Robert Fishbein, *President*
Greg Huff, *Business Mgr*
Raymond Feldmeier, *Vice Pres*
Jeff Racheter, *Vice Pres*
Carl Warschausky, *CFO*
EMP: 350
SQ FT: 60,000
SALES (est): 119.4MM
SALES (corp-wide): 805.3MM **Privately Held**
WEB: www.bernea.com
SIC: 5141 2099 Groceries, general line; salads, fresh or refrigerated; pizza, refrigerated: except frozen; noodles, uncooked: packaged with other ingredients
PA: Lipari Foods Operating Company Llc
26661 Bunert Rd
Warren MI 48089
586 447-3500

(G-16995)
CUSTOM FAB INC
24440 Gibson Dr (48089-4311)
PHONE.................................586 755-7260
Gregory E Simmons, *President*
Michael Nixon, *Vice Pres*
EMP: 6
SQ FT: 8,500
SALES (est): 828.9K **Privately Held**
SIC: 1761 3444 Sheet metalwork; sheet metalwork

(G-16996)
D & W MANAGEMENT COMPANY INC
Also Called: All Type Truck and Trlr Repr
23660 Sherwood Ave (48091-5365)
PHONE.................................586 758-2284
Lynn Christel, *President*
Roger J Christel, *Admin Sec*
EMP: 50
SQ FT: 50,000
SALES (est): 3.7MM **Privately Held**
SIC: 7538 7539 3792 3713 General truck repair; trailer repair; automotive springs, rebuilding & repair; brake repair, automotive; travel trailers & campers; truck & bus bodies

(G-16997)
D K ENTERPRISES INC
Also Called: A & S Silver Brazing Co
21942 Dequindre Rd (48091-2107)
PHONE.................................586 756-7350
Dan Kalich, *President*
EMP: 4 **EST:** 1962
SQ FT: 3,000
SALES (est): 350K **Privately Held**
SIC: 7692 3567 Brazing; induction heating equipment

(G-16998)
D W HINES MANUFACTURING CORP
21887 Schoenherr Rd (48089-2856)
PHONE.................................586 775-1200
Donald W Hines, *President*
William Hines, *Vice Pres*
Joan M Hines, *Admin Sec*
EMP: 4
SQ FT: 7,000
SALES: 210K **Privately Held**
SIC: 3599 Machine shop, jobbing & repair

(G-16999)
DART MACHINERY LTD
2097 Bart Ave (48091-3206)
PHONE.................................248 362-1188
Richard A Maskin, *President*
Gary St Denis, *Principal*
Tricia Kortes, *CFO*
Matt Genette, *Manager*
Jason Hahn, *Supervisor*
▲ **EMP:** 85
SALES (est): 15MM **Privately Held**
SIC: 3599 Machine shop, jobbing & repair

(G-17000)
DETROIT RADIANT PRODUCTS CO
Also Called: Re-Verber-Ray
21400 Hoover Rd (48089-3162)
PHONE.................................586 756-0950
Joseph B Wortman, *President*
Angela Taormina, *Exec VP*
Joseph A Wortman, *Vice Pres*
Pj Wortman, *Plant Mgr*
Michelle Kostusyk, *Sales Staff*
▲ **EMP:** 45
SQ FT: 98,000
SALES (est): 15.1MM **Privately Held**
WEB: www.detroitradiant.com
SIC: 3433 Room heaters, gas

(G-17001)
DEXTER ROLL FORM COMPANY
30150 Ryan Rd (48092-6005)
PHONE.................................586 573-6930
Robert Rinaldi, *President*
Kathleen Rinaldi, *Vice Pres*
EMP: 6 **EST:** 1962
SQ FT: 6,000
SALES (est): 807.3K **Privately Held**
WEB: www.dexterrollform.com
SIC: 3547 3544 Rolling mill machinery; special dies, tools, jigs & fixtures

(G-17002)
DIAMOND BROACH COMPANY
3560 E 10 Mile Rd (48091-1392)
PHONE.................................586 757-5131
Ronald Fauquier, *President*
Patricia Fauquier, *Vice Pres*
EMP: 6
SQ FT: 3,000
SALES (est): 648.3K **Privately Held**
SIC: 3545 Broaches (machine tool accessories)

(G-17003)
DMI EDON LLC
12700 Stephens Rd (48089-4334)
PHONE.................................586 782-7311
EMP: 3
SALES (corp-wide): 1.3B **Privately Held**
SIC: 3714 Motor vehicle parts & accessories
HQ: Dmi Edon, Llc
300 Gllria Ofc Ctr Ste 50
Southfield MI 48034

(G-17004)
DOUGH & SPICE INC
2150 E 10 Mile Rd (48091-1381)
PHONE.................................586 756-6100
Steve Antoon, *President*
EMP: 5 **EST:** 1999
SQ FT: 500
SALES (est): 800K **Privately Held**
SIC: 2045 Prepared flour mixes & doughs

(G-17005)
DOUGH MASTERS
23412 Dequindre Rd (48091-1822)
PHONE.................................248 585-0600
George Kakouros, *Principal*
EMP: 30 **EST:** 2009
SALES (est): 2.4MM **Privately Held**
SIC: 2051 Bakery: wholesale or wholesale/retail combined

(G-17006)
DPR MANUFACTURING & SVCS INC
23675 Mound Rd (48091-5315)
PHONE.................................586 757-1421
Westliegh De Guvera, *President*
Emmett De Guvera, *Vice Pres*
EMP: 20
SQ FT: 20,000
SALES (est): 2.6MM **Privately Held**
SIC: 3312 Stainless steel

(G-17007)
DUNNE-RITE PERFORMANCE INC
26063 Newport Ave (48089-1326)
PHONE.................................616 828-0908
Jeffrey H Dunne, *President*
EMP: 10
SALES (est): 2.1MM **Privately Held**
SIC: 3465 Body parts, automobile: stamped metal

(G-17008)
DUPLICAST CORPORATION
24583 Gibson Dr (48089-2072)
PHONE.................................586 756-5900
Thomas Doyle, *President*
EMP: 7 **EST:** 1959
SQ FT: 10,000
SALES: 800K **Privately Held**
WEB: www.duplicast.com
SIC: 3366 Copper foundries

(G-17009)
DURAMIC ABRASIVE PRODUCTS INC
24135 Gibson Dr (48089-2068)
PHONE.................................586 755-7220
William Steele, *President*
John Kennedy, *Vice Pres*
▲ **EMP:** 30 **EST:** 1960
SQ FT: 26,000
SALES (est): 3.9MM **Privately Held**
WEB: www.duramic.com
SIC: 3291 Wheels, abrasive

(G-17010)
DURR SYSTEMS INC
Also Called: Durr Systems Fap
12755 E 9 Mile Rd (48089-2621)
PHONE.................................586 755-7500
John Christman, *Branch Mgr*
EMP: 20
SALES (corp-wide): 4.4B **Privately Held**
SIC: 3535 Conveyors & conveying equipment
HQ: Durr Systems, Inc
26801 Northwestern Hwy
Southfield MI 48033
248 450-2000

(G-17011)
DWM HOLDINGS INC
24874 Groesbeck Hwy (48089-4726)
PHONE.................................586 541-0013
Ryan Macvoy, *President*
Kelly Guffey, *Risk Mgmt Dir*
EMP: 95
SQ FT: 50,000
SALES: 28MM **Privately Held**
SIC: 3317 Seamless pipes & tubes

(G-17012)
E & E SPECIAL PRODUCTS LLC
7200 Miller Dr (48092-4727)
P.O. Box 808 (48090-0808)
PHONE.................................586 978-3377
Doris Gormley, *General Mgr*
Steve Hirzel, *General Mgr*
Patrick Miloser, *Vice Pres*
Kathy Messina, *Info Tech Mgr*
Paul M Hirzel,
EMP: 19
SALES (est): 3.8MM **Privately Held**
SIC: 3545 5084 Machine tool attachments & accessories; machine tools & accessories

(G-17013)
E AND J ADVERTISING LLC
Also Called: Compass Graphix
32806 Ryan Rd (48092-4350)
PHONE.................................586 977-3500
Ed Babbie, *Mng Member*
EMP: 3
SALES (est): 139.3K **Privately Held**
SIC: 2752 3993 Commercial printing, lithographic; signs & advertising specialties

(G-17014)
E R TOOL COMPANY INC
3720 E 10 Mile Rd Ste A (48091-6019)
PHONE.................................586 757-1159
Edward Ruth, *President*
EMP: 7
SQ FT: 3,800
SALES (est): 820.4K **Privately Held**
SIC: 3599 Machine shop, jobbing & repair

(G-17015)
EASTERN MICHIGAN INDUSTRIES
23850 Ryan Rd (48091-1931)
PHONE.................................586 757-4140
Derrick Kemppainen, *President*
EMP: 23
SALES (est): 5.4MM **Privately Held**
WEB: www.emifab.com
SIC: 3441 Fabricated structural metal

(G-17016)
EDE CO
26969 Ryan Rd (48091-4077)
PHONE.....................................586 756-7555
David E Turowski, *President*
Edward R Turowski, *Vice Pres*
EMP: 5
SQ FT: 20,000
SALES (est): 663.5K **Privately Held**
SIC: 3444 Pipe, sheet metal

(G-17017)
ELECTRA CABLE & COMMUNICATION
24846 Forterra Dr (48089-4367)
PHONE.....................................586 754-3479
Mark Machowicz, *Owner*
EMP: 4 **Privately Held**
SIC: 3694 Automotive electrical equipment
PA: Electra Cable & Communication Inc
24844 Marine Ave
Eastpointe MI 48021

(G-17018)
ENGRAVE A REMEMBRANCE INC
28555 Flanders Ave (48088-4315)
PHONE.....................................586 772-7480
Anthony J Russo, *President*
EMP: 5
SALES: 150K **Privately Held**
WEB: www.engrave-a-remembrance.com
SIC: 3231 Cut & engraved glassware: made from purchased glass

(G-17019)
EQUIVALENT BASE CO
Also Called: Prompt Pattern
4175 E 10 Mile Rd (48091-1508)
PHONE.....................................586 759-2030
Michael Healy, *President*
EMP: 17
SALES (est): 4.4MM **Privately Held**
SIC: 3599 Machine shop, jobbing & repair

(G-17020)
ESSEX BRASS CORPORATION
23500 Pinewood St (48091-3198)
P.O. Box 629 (48090-0629)
PHONE.....................................586 757-8200
David B Nagel, *President*
Thomas Phillips, *Prdtn Mgr*
Gary Motyl, *Foreman/Supr*
Christine Snooks, *Sales Mgr*
▲ **EMP:** 17
SQ FT: 24,000
SALES: 1.9MM **Privately Held**
WEB: www.essexbrass.com
SIC: 3569 3824 3599 Lubrication equipment, industrial; gauges for computing pressure temperature corrections; grease cups, metal; oil cups, metal

(G-17021)
ESSEX WELD USA INC
24445 Forterra Dr (48089-4379)
PHONE.....................................519 776-9153
John Friesen, *President*
Abe Friesen, *Vice Pres*
Tony Van Noggeren, *Controller*
EMP: 40
SQ FT: 1,200
SALES: 5.9MM
SALES (corp-wide): 19.2MM **Privately Held**
SIC: 3496 Miscellaneous fabricated wire products
PA: Essex Weld Solutions Ltd
340 Allen Ave
Essex ON N8M 3
519 776-9153

(G-17022)
ETCS INC
21275 Mullin Ave (48089-3086)
PHONE.....................................586 268-4870
Ravi Kapur, *President*
Sameer Agnihotri, *Project Mgr*
Priya Kapur, *Program Mgr*
▲ **EMP:** 17
SALES (est): 3.6MM **Privately Held**
WEB: www.etcs.net
SIC: 3545 8711 3679 7361 Tools & accessories for machine tools; engineering services; recording & playback apparatus, including phonograph; placement agencies

(G-17023)
EVEREST ENERGY FUND L L C
30078 Schoenherr Rd # 150 (48088-3179)
PHONE.....................................586 445-2300
Rai Bhargava,
Vincent J Brennan,
EMP: 8
SQ FT: 6,000
SALES (est): 641.8K **Privately Held**
SIC: 1321 3569 Natural gasoline production; filters & strainers, pipeline

(G-17024)
EVERFRESH BEVERAGES INC
6600 E 9 Mile Rd (48091-2673)
PHONE.....................................586 755-9500
Nick A Caporella, *Ch of Bd*
Joseph G Caporella, *President*
EMP: 60
SALES (est): 11.9MM
SALES (corp-wide): 1B **Publicly Held**
WEB: www.natbev.com
SIC: 2033 2086 Fruit juices: packaged in cans, jars, etc.; fruit juices: concentrated, hot pack; fruit drinks (less than 100% juice): packaged in cans, etc.; water, pasteurized: packaged in cans, bottles, etc.
HQ: Newbevco, Inc.
1 N University Dr
Plantation FL 33324

(G-17025)
EXCELLENT DESIGNS SWIMWEAR
5751 E 13 Mile Rd (48092-1504)
PHONE.....................................586 977-9140
Patricia Karalla, *President*
EMP: 25
SQ FT: 6,000
SALES (est): 2.5MM **Privately Held**
WEB: www.exelnt.com
SIC: 2339 2389 5699 Bathing suits: women's, misses' & juniors'; theatrical costumes; costumes, masquerade or theatrical; bathing suits

(G-17026)
EXPRESS COAT CORPORATION
27350 Gloede Dr (48088-4870)
PHONE.....................................586 773-2682
Lawrence H Werner, *President*
Lawrence E Werner Jr, *Chairman*
EMP: 30 **EST:** 1967
SQ FT: 15,700
SALES: 1.8MM **Privately Held**
WEB: www.expresscoat.com
SIC: 3479 Painting of metal products

(G-17027)
EXPRESS MACHINE & TOOL CO
2204 E 9 Mile Rd (48091-2144)
PHONE.....................................586 758-5080
Wolfgang Koellhofer, *President*
EMP: 3 **EST:** 1978
SQ FT: 3,000
SALES (est): 322.7K **Privately Held**
SIC: 3599 7692 3545 3544 Machine shop, jobbing & repair; welding repair; machine tool accessories; special dies, tools, jigs & fixtures

(G-17028)
F J LUCIDO & ASSOCIATES (PA)
Also Called: Lucido, F J & Associates
29400 Van Dyke Ave (48093-2320)
PHONE.....................................586 574-3577
Frank J Lucido Jr, *President*
Bonnie Lucido, *Vice Pres*
EMP: 50
SALES (est): 14.9MM **Privately Held**
SIC: 5013 7361 3544 Automotive supplies & parts; employment agencies; special dies, tools, jigs & fixtures

(G-17029)
FCA US LLC
Also Called: Warren Stamping Plant
22800 Mound Rd (48091-5401)
PHONE.....................................586 497-3630
Craig Corrington, *Manager*
Brian Bush, *Manager*
EMP: 2000
SALES (corp-wide): 126.4B **Privately Held**
SIC: 3465 3711 Automotive stampings; motor vehicles & car bodies
HQ: Fca Us Llc
1000 Chrysler Dr
Auburn Hills MI 48326

(G-17030)
FCA US LLC
Warren Truck Assembly Plant
21500 Mound Rd (48091-4840)
PHONE.....................................586 497-2500
Robert Bowers, *Manager*
EMP: 670
SALES (corp-wide): 126.4B **Privately Held**
SIC: 3714 Motor vehicle parts & accessories
HQ: Fca Us Llc
1000 Chrysler Dr
Auburn Hills MI 48326

(G-17031)
FCA US LLC
Also Called: ITM
6565 E 8 Mile Rd (48091-2949)
PHONE.....................................248 576-5741
Mukul Kumar, *Manager*
EMP: 300
SALES (corp-wide): 126.4B **Privately Held**
SIC: 3711 Motor vehicles & car bodies
HQ: Fca Us Llc
1000 Chrysler Dr
Auburn Hills MI 48326

(G-17032)
FEDERAL INDUSTRIAL SVCS INC (PA)
11223 E 8 Mile Rd (48089-3070)
PHONE.....................................586 427-6383
Steve Hadwin, *President*
EMP: 10
SQ FT: 4,000
SALES (est): 1.3MM **Privately Held**
SIC: 3398 Shot peening (treating steel to reduce fatigue)

(G-17033)
FINI FINISH METAL FINISHING
24657 Mound Rd (48091-2043)
PHONE.....................................586 758-0050
Ronald Borawski, *President*
EMP: 13
SALES (est): 1.6MM **Privately Held**
SIC: 3471 Plating of metals or formed products

(G-17034)
FLEX SLOTTER INC
3462 E 10 Mile Rd (48091-1309)
PHONE.....................................586 756-6444
Steven T Perlik, *President*
Christopher Perlik, *Treasurer*
EMP: 6
SQ FT: 2,800
SALES (est): 400K **Privately Held**
SIC: 3599 Machine shop, jobbing & repair

(G-17035)
FLEX-N GATE SHELBY LLC
5663 E 9 Mile Rd (48091-2562)
PHONE.....................................586 759-8092
David Ekblad, *Mng Member*
EMP: 200
SQ FT: 125,000
SALES (est): 30MM **Privately Held**
SIC: 3089 Automotive parts, plastic

(G-17036)
FLEX-N-GATE LLC
Also Called: Ventra Plastics
5663 E 9 Mile Rd (48091-2562)
PHONE.....................................800 398-1496
Kevin Hamilton, *Principal*
Mike Elliott, *Engineer*
Paul Geiger, *Engineer*
Gerald Gromacki, *Engineer*
Tom Vigrass, *Engineer*
▲ **EMP:** 150
SALES (est): 60.1MM
SALES (corp-wide): 3.3B **Privately Held**
WEB: www.flex-n-gate.com
SIC: 3714 Motor vehicle parts & accessories
PA: Flex-N-Gate Llc
1306 E University Ave
Urbana IL 61802
217 384-6600

(G-17037)
FLEX-N-GATE CORPORATION
Also Called: Flex-N-Gate Forming Tech
26269 Groesbeck Hwy (48089-4150)
PHONE.....................................586 773-0800
Shahid Khan, *CEO*
David Decaussin, *Maint Spvr*
Mike Kay, *Mfg Staff*
Karrie Szalony, *VP Sales*
Mark Kiefer, *Accounts Mgr*
EMP: 31
SALES (corp-wide): 3.3B **Privately Held**
WEB: www.flex-n-gate.com
SIC: 3714 Motor vehicle parts & accessories
PA: Flex-N-Gate Llc
1306 E University Ave
Urbana IL 61802
217 384-6600

(G-17038)
FLEX-N-GATE DETROIT LLC
5663 E 9 Mile Rd (48091-2562)
PHONE.....................................586 759-8092
David Ekblad, *CFO*
Steve Wachowski, *Accounts Mgr*
EMP: 400
SQ FT: 300,000
SALES (est): 61.7MM
SALES (corp-wide): 3.3B **Privately Held**
SIC: 3089 Automotive parts, plastic
PA: Flex-N-Gate Llc
1306 E University Ave
Urbana IL 61802
217 384-6600

(G-17039)
FLEX-N-GATE MICHIGAN LLC
Also Called: Veltri Tooling Company
5663 E 9 Mile Rd (48091-2562)
PHONE.....................................586 759-8900
Dave Papak, *President*
Andre Sopena, *Buyer*
Kelly Hill, *Accountant*
Kevin Williams, *Accounts Mgr*
Jeff Lawrenson, *Program Mgr*
▲ **EMP:** 22
SALES (est): 5.2MM
SALES (corp-wide): 3.3B **Privately Held**
SIC: 3714 Bumpers & bumperettes, motor vehicle
PA: Flex-N-Gate Llc
1306 E University Ave
Urbana IL 61802
217 384-6600

(G-17040)
FLEX-N-GATE STAMPING LLC
27027 Groesbeck Hwy (48089-1538)
PHONE.....................................810 772-1514
Thomas Orr, *Administration*
EMP: 15
SALES (corp-wide): 3.3B **Privately Held**
SIC: 3444 3496 Sheet metalwork; miscellaneous fabricated wire products
HQ: Flex-N-Gate Stamping, Llc
5663 E 9 Mile Rd
Warren MI 48091

(G-17041)
FLEX-N-GATE STAMPING LLC (HQ)
5663 E 9 Mile Rd (48091-2562)
PHONE.....................................586 759-8900
Dan Sabelli, *Program Mgr*
Kip Taylor, *Program Mgr*
Shahid Khan,
▲ **EMP:** 34

GEOGRAPHIC SECTION
Warren - Macomb County (G-17068)

SALES (est): 11.3MM
SALES (corp-wide): 3.3B **Privately Held**
WEB: www.flex-n-gate.com
SIC: 3444 3496 Sheet metalwork; miscellaneous fabricated wire products
PA: Flex-N-Gate Llc
 1306 E University Ave
 Urbana IL 61802
 217 384-6600

(G-17042)
FORDSELL MACHINE PRODUCTS CO
30400 Ryan Rd (48092-1997)
PHONE.................................586 751-4700
David H Redfield, *President*
Barry Marshall, *Vice Pres*
Jean Hicks, *Treasurer*
EMP: 43 EST: 1946
SQ FT: 20,000
SALES (est): 9.4MM **Privately Held**
WEB: www.fordsell.com
SIC: 3451 Screw machine products

(G-17043)
FORMSPRAG LLC
Also Called: Marland Clutch
23601 Hoover Rd (48089-3994)
PHONE.................................586 758-5000
Carl Christenson, *CEO*
Richard Powers, *Engineer*
Jeff Sharp, *Engineer*
David Stoltze, *Manager*
Amy Chan, *Administration*
▲ EMP: 105
SQ FT: 79,000
SALES (est): 24.1MM
SALES (corp-wide): 1.1B **Publicly Held**
WEB: www.altramotion.com
SIC: 3568 Clutches, except vehicular
PA: Altra Industrial Motion Corp.
 300 Granite St Ste 201
 Braintree MA 02184
 781 917-0600

(G-17044)
FORST-USA INCORPORATED
23640 Hoover Rd (48089-1944)
PHONE.................................586 759-9380
▲ EMP: 4
SALES (est): 450K **Privately Held**
SIC: 3541 Mfg Machine Tools-Cutting

(G-17045)
FRANK TERLECKI COMPANY INC
Also Called: Creative Store Fixtures
4129 Kendall Rd (48091-1900)
PHONE.................................586 759-5770
Frank Terlecki, *President*
EMP: 10
SQ FT: 9,000
SALES (est): 1.4MM **Privately Held**
SIC: 2599 Factory furniture & fixtures

(G-17046)
FUTURAMIC TOOL & ENGRG CO (PA)
24680 Gibson D (48089)
PHONE.................................586 758-2200
Mark Jurcak, *President*
Chris Schanta, *Plant Mgr*
Robert Oliver, *Project Mgr*
Gregory Hammond, *Purchasing*
Scott Adams, *QC Mgr*
EMP: 145 EST: 1955
SQ FT: 120,000
SALES (est): 41.9MM **Privately Held**
WEB: www.futuramic.com
SIC: 3544 Jigs & fixtures; special dies & tools

(G-17047)
FUTURE MILL INC
25450 Ryan Rd (48091-1326)
PHONE.................................586 754-8088
Stephen Fitzpatrick, *President*
Lynda Fitzpatrick, *Vice Pres*
EMP: 7
SQ FT: 12,000
SALES (est): 874.2K **Privately Held**
SIC: 3599 Chemical milling job shop

(G-17048)
G & G STEEL FABRICATING CO
31154 Dequindre Rd (48092-3722)
PHONE.................................586 979-4112
Olimpio Giacomantonio, *President*
EMP: 5
SQ FT: 8,000
SALES (est): 804.2K **Privately Held**
SIC: 3312 1791 Structural shapes & pilings, steel; structural steel erection

(G-17049)
GAGE EAGLE SPLINE INC
2357 E 9 Mile Rd (48091-2162)
PHONE.................................586 776-7240
Vincent V Spica III, *President*
EMP: 54 EST: 1960
SQ FT: 2,800
SALES (est): 4.4MM
SALES (corp-wide): 8MM **Privately Held**
WEB: www.invospline.com
SIC: 3545 3829 3544 3462 Gauges (machine tool accessories); measuring & controlling devices; special dies, tools, jigs & fixtures; iron & steel forgings
PA: Invo Spline Inc
 2357 E 9 Mile Rd
 Warren MI 48091
 586 757-8840

(G-17050)
GCH TOOL GROUP INC
13265 E 8 Mile Rd (48089-3275)
PHONE.................................586 777-6250
Daniel Geddes, *President*
Chrissy Tidrick, *General Mgr*
Dennis Nicholas, *Principal*
Jeff Carter, *Vice Pres*
Joe Giacalone, *Vice Pres*
▲ EMP: 28
SQ FT: 25,000
SALES (est): 8.3MM **Privately Held**
SIC: 3546 Grinders, portable: electric or pneumatic

(G-17051)
GENERAL MOTORS COMPANY
7015 Edward Cole Blvd (48093-1809)
PHONE.................................586 218-9240
Jim Robeson, *Branch Mgr*
Cristina Learman, *Manager*
EMP: 300 **Publicly Held**
SIC: 5511 3714 7371 Automobiles, new & used; motor vehicle parts & accessories; custom programming services
PA: General Motors Company
 300 Renaissance Ctr L1
 Detroit MI 48243

(G-17052)
GENERAL MOTORS LLC
7111 E 11 Mile Rd (48092-2709)
PHONE.................................931 486-1914
Sue Rimas, *Manager*
EMP: 10 **Publicly Held**
WEB: www.saturnbp.com
SIC: 3679 Electronic circuits
HQ: General Motors Llc
 300 Renaissance Ctr L1
 Detroit MI 48243

(G-17053)
GENERAL MOTORS LLC
7111 E 11 Mile Rd (48092-2709)
P.O. Box 1500, Spring Hill TN (37174-1500)
PHONE.................................931 486-5049
Ken Knight, *Branch Mgr*
EMP: 15 **Publicly Held**
WEB: www.saturnbp.com
SIC: 5511 3714 Automobiles, new & used; motor vehicle parts & accessories
HQ: General Motors Llc
 300 Renaissance Ctr L1
 Detroit MI 48243

(G-17054)
GENERAL STRUCTURES INC
23171 Groesbeck Hwy (48089-4249)
PHONE.................................586 774-6105
Douglas W Macvoy, *President*
Cathy Lee, *Partner*
Mary Szydzik, *Partner*
John Turrell, *Sales Mgr*
David Pauwels, *Sales Staff*
EMP: 37

SALES (est): 4.4MM
SALES (corp-wide): 11.6MM **Privately Held**
WEB: www.polemfg.com
SIC: 3648 3354 3317 3355 Lighting equipment; aluminum extruded products; steel pipe & tubes; aluminum rolling & drawing
PA: United Lighting Standards, Inc.
 23171 Groesbeck Hwy
 Warren MI 48089
 586 774-5650

(G-17055)
GENEX WINDOW INC
23110 Sherwood Ave (48091-2025)
PHONE.................................586 754-2917
Geno Hodzic, *President*
EMP: 4
SQ FT: 5,000
SALES (est): 829.6K **Privately Held**
WEB: www.genexwindows.com
SIC: 3089 5211 Windows, plastic; door & window products

(G-17056)
GENTRY SERVICES OF ALABAMA
31943 Red Run Dr (48093-1143)
PHONE.................................248 321-6368
James Gentry, *CEO*
EMP: 5
SALES (est): 117.2K **Privately Held**
SIC: 7372 Application computer software; business oriented computer software

(G-17057)
GFL ENVRONMENTAL REAL PROPERTY
25601 Flanders Ave (48089-1405)
PHONE.................................586 774-1360
Pietro Rizzo, *Branch Mgr*
EMP: 3
SALES (corp-wide): 12.4MM **Privately Held**
SIC: 2611 Pulp mills, mechanical & recycling processing
PA: Gfl Environmental Real Property Inc
 26999 Central Park Blvd # 200
 Southfield MI 48076
 888 877-4996

(G-17058)
GLS INDUSTRIES LLC (PA)
Also Called: Global Logistics Services
7111 E 11 Mile Rd (48092-2709)
PHONE.................................586 255-9221
EMP: 2
SALES (est): 2.4MM **Privately Held**
SIC: 3089 Fittings for pipe, plastic

(G-17059)
GLS INDUSTRIES LLC
8333 E 11 Mile Rd (48093-2875)
PHONE.................................586 255-9221
EMP: 20
SALES (corp-wide): 2.4MM **Privately Held**
SIC: 3089 Fittings for pipe, plastic
PA: Gls Industries Llc
 7111 E 11 Mile Rd
 Warren MI 48092
 586 255-9221

(G-17060)
GNU SOFTWARE DEVELOPMENT INC
14156 E 11 Mile Rd (48091-1468)
PHONE.................................586 778-9182
EMP: 8
SALES (est): 620K **Privately Held**
SIC: 7372 Prepackaged Software Services

(G-17061)
GOLLNICK TOOL CO
24300 Marmon Ave (48089-3874)
PHONE.................................586 755-0100
Arden Gollnick, *Owner*
Kevin Bohannon, *Manager*
EMP: 5 EST: 1954
SQ FT: 7,000
SALES: 400K **Privately Held**
SIC: 3544 Special dies & tools

(G-17062)
GRANDADS SWEET TEA LLC
26532 Joe Dr (48091-3954)
PHONE.................................313 320-4446
Ricky McQueen, *Mng Member*
Mark Baldwin,
Darrell Goolsby,
Charles Richardson,
EMP: 4 EST: 2008
SALES: 38K **Privately Held**
SIC: 2086 Tea, iced: packaged in cans, bottles, etc.

(G-17063)
GREAT LAKES TIRE LLC
12225 Stephens Rd (48089-2010)
PHONE.................................586 939-7000
Hal Briand, *President*
EMP: 80
SQ FT: 120,000
SALES (est): 7.6MM
SALES (corp-wide): 273.6MM **Privately Held**
SIC: 3011 Retreading materials, tire
PA: Centra Inc.
 12225 Stephens Rd
 Warren MI 48089
 586 939-7000

(G-17064)
GREAT LAKES TOOL LLC
24027 Ryan Rd (48091-1644)
PHONE.................................586 759-5253
Stanley Sznitka, *Mng Member*
EMP: 10
SQ FT: 8,000
SALES: 900K **Privately Held**
SIC: 3545 Machine tool accessories

(G-17065)
GREENDALE SCREW PDTS CO INC
11500 Hupp Ave (48089-3720)
PHONE.................................586 759-8100
Bernard J Damman, *President*
John Taylor, *Engineer*
George Bardel, *Plant Engr*
Angelia Moore, *Office Mgr*
Sarra Damman, *Executive Asst*
EMP: 40
SQ FT: 20,000
SALES: 5MM **Privately Held**
WEB: www.greendalescrewproducts.com
SIC: 3451 Screw machine products

(G-17066)
GREENFIELD CABINETRY INC
23811 Ryan Rd (48091-1932)
PHONE.................................586 759-3300
Joseph Salet, *President*
Audrey Salet, *Admin Sec*
▲ EMP: 12
SQ FT: 10,000
SALES (est): 2MM **Privately Held**
SIC: 2522 2541 2542 5031 Cabinets, office: except wood; table or counter tops, plastic laminated; partitions & fixtures, except wood; kitchen cabinets

(G-17067)
GRINDING PRODUCTS COMPANY INC
11084 E 9 Mile Rd (48089-2493)
PHONE.................................586 757-2118
Clyde Olivero, *President*
Clifford Olivero, *Vice Pres*
EMP: 12 EST: 1950
SQ FT: 11,500
SALES: 1.2MM **Privately Held**
SIC: 3599 Machine shop, jobbing & repair

(G-17068)
GROSSE TOOL AND MACHINE CO
23080 Groesbeck Hwy (48089-2690)
PHONE.................................586 773-6770
Douglas Mack, *President*
Walter Grosse, *Vice Pres*
Mathias Kirsch, *Treasurer*
Kristi Barnett, *Cust Mgr*
Kurt Mack, *Admin Sec*
EMP: 25 EST: 1965
SQ FT: 15,000

Warren - Macomb County (G-17069)

SALES: 2.4MM **Privately Held**
WEB: www.grossetool.com
SIC: **3369** 3544 Castings, except die-castings, precision; special dies, tools, jigs & fixtures

(G-17069)
GRUPO ANTOLIN MICHIGAN INC
25800 Sherwood Ave (48091-4160)
PHONE..................989 635-5080
Jesus Tompirez, *Branch Mgr*
EMP: 50
SALES (corp-wide): 33.3MM **Privately Held**
SIC: **3714** 3429 Motor vehicle body components & frame; motor vehicle hardware
HQ: Grupo Antolin Michigan, Inc.
6300 Euclid St
Marlette MI 48453
989 635-5055

(G-17070)
GUARDIAN AUTOMOTIVE CORP (DH)
Also Called: Guardian Automotive Trim
23751 Amber Ave (48089-6000)
PHONE..................586 757-7800
Daniel J Davis, *CEO*
Kevin Myers, *Senior VP*
Joseph Abbruzzi, *Vice Pres*
Rick Cassiday, *Vice Pres*
Chuck Wilson, *Vice Pres*
▲ **EMP:** 70 **EST:** 1949
SQ FT: 25,000
SALES (est): 392MM
SALES (corp-wide): 40.6B **Privately Held**
SIC: **3089** 3465 Extruded finished plastic products; molding primary plastic; moldings or trim, automobile: stamped metal

(G-17071)
GUELPH TOOL SALES INC
24150 Gibson Dr (48089-4308)
PHONE..................586 755-3333
Robert Ireland, *President*
Chris McMahon, *Sales Staff*
EMP: 500
SALES (est): 59.8MM
SALES (corp-wide): 218.9MM **Privately Held**
WEB: www.guelphtool.com
SIC: **3465** 8744 Body parts, automobile: stamped metal; facilities support services
PA: Guelph Manufacturing Group Inc
39 Royal Rd
Guelph ON N1H 1
519 822-5401

(G-17072)
GYB LLC
31065 Ryan Rd (48092-1332)
PHONE..................586 218-3222
Raymond Ouillette Jr, *Mng Member*
EMP: 10 **EST:** 2015
SALES (est): 674.9K **Privately Held**
SIC: **3647** Motor vehicle lighting equipment

(G-17073)
H & G TOOL COMPANY
30700 Ryan Rd (48092-1995)
PHONE..................586 573-7040
Donald Hunt, *President*
EMP: 12
SQ FT: 8,000
SALES: 580K **Privately Held**
SIC: **3545** 3541 Tools & accessories for machine tools; machine tools, metal cutting type

(G-17074)
H & L TOOL & ENGINEERING INC
23701 Blackstone Ave (48089-4217)
PHONE..................586 755-2806
Bill Lapierre, *President*
Tom Bhavsar, *Accountant*
Bill La Pierre, *Manager*
EMP: 6
SQ FT: 2,500
SALES (est): 770.7K **Privately Held**
SIC: **3599** Machine shop, jobbing & repair

(G-17075)
HANWHA AZDEL INC
2200 Centerwood Dr (48091-5867)
PHONE..................810 629-2496
Erich Vorenkamp, *Branch Mgr*
EMP: 12 **Privately Held**
SIC: **3083** 3089 Thermoplastic laminates: rods, tubes, plates & sheet; spouting, plastic & glass fiber reinforced
HQ: Hanwha Azdel, Inc.
2000 Enterprise Dr
Forest VA 24551
434 385-6524

(G-17076)
HAPPY CANDY
2325 John B Ave (48091-4240)
PHONE..................248 629-9819
EMP: 3
SALES (est): 120.9K **Privately Held**
SIC: **5145** 2064 Confectionery; candy & other confectionery products

(G-17077)
HARPER MACHINE TOOL INC
21410 Ryan Rd (48091-4667)
PHONE..................586 756-0140
John Crawford, *President*
Carol Crawford, *Vice Pres*
EMP: 5
SQ FT: 2,300
SALES (est): 634.4K **Privately Held**
SIC: **3544** Special dies & tools

(G-17078)
HB STUBBS COMPANY LLC
27027 Mound Rd (48092-2615)
P.O. Box 910, Birmingham (48012-0910)
PHONE..................586 574-9700
Jeff Laverty, *Administration*
EMP: 13
SALES (est): 1.3MM **Privately Held**
SIC: **3993** Signs & advertising specialties

(G-17079)
HEMCO MACHINE CO INC
6785 Chicago Rd (48092-1659)
PHONE..................586 264-8911
Ralph W Ascroft, *President*
Sandy Ascroft, *Treasurer*
EMP: 5
SQ FT: 20,000
SALES (est): 750K **Privately Held**
WEB: www.hemcomachine.com
SIC: **3714** 5531 Motor vehicle engines & parts; automotive & home supply stores

(G-17080)
HENKEL US OPERATIONS CORP
23343 Sherwood Ave (48091-2097)
PHONE..................586 759-5555
Joe Dunn, *Business Mgr*
Linda Chase, *Vice Pres*
Juliane Hefel, *Vice Pres*
Dale Tuscany, *Plant Mgr*
Corey Peck, *Project Mgr*
EMP: 125
SQ FT: 19,000
SALES (corp-wide): 22.7B **Privately Held**
SIC: **2819** 2899 Industrial inorganic chemicals; chemical preparations
HQ: Henkel Us Operations Corporation
1 Henkel Way
Rocky Hill CT 06067
860 571-5100

(G-17081)
HI-TECH COATINGS INC (DH)
24600 Industrial Hwy (48089-4346)
PHONE..................586 759-3559
Kenneth Pape, *Ch of Bd*
Fred Pape, *President*
EMP: 50
SQ FT: 44,000
SALES (est): 6.1MM
SALES (corp-wide): 33.8MM **Privately Held**
SIC: **3471** Plating & polishing

(G-17082)
HUDSON INDUSTRIES INC
Also Called: Xtol
24623 Ryan Rd (48091-3386)
PHONE..................800 459-1077
Bryan Hudson, *CEO*
EMP: 5

SQ FT: 1,500
SALES (est): 167.6K **Privately Held**
SIC: **3599** 3229 3714 Oil filters, internal combustion engine, except automotive; lenses, lantern, flashlight, headlight, etc.: glass; windshield wiper systems, motor vehicle

(G-17083)
HYDRO-LOGIC INC
24832 Romano St (48091-3379)
PHONE..................586 757-7477
Ronald Reed, *President*
Paul Mazetti, *Vice Pres*
EMP: 35
SQ FT: 9,500
SALES (est): 5.7MM **Privately Held**
WEB: www.hydro-logic.com
SIC: **3625** 3613 Relays & industrial controls; switchgear & switchboard apparatus

(G-17084)
HYDRONIC COMPONENTS INC
Also Called: Hci
7243 Miller Dr Ste 200 (48092-4746)
PHONE..................586 268-1640
Joseph Martin, *Ch of Bd*
Michael Puysse, *Manager*
Mark Waligora, *Manager*
◆ **EMP:** 10
SALES (est): 1.7MM **Privately Held**
WEB: www.hciterminator.com
SIC: **3491** Industrial valves

(G-17085)
INALFA ROOF SYSTEMS INC
12500 E 9 Mile Rd (48089-2634)
PHONE..................586 758-6620
Donna Montgomery, *Info Tech Mgr*
Russell Anglebrandt, *Director*
EMP: 230
SALES (corp-wide): 7.3MM **Privately Held**
SIC: **3714** Motor vehicle parts & accessories
HQ: Inalfa Roof Systems, Inc.
1370 Pacific Dr
Auburn Hills MI 48326
248 371-3060

(G-17086)
INALFA/SSI ROOF SYSTEMS LLC
12500 E 9 Mile Rd (48089-2634)
PHONE..................586 758-6620
Les Morrell, *Mng Member*
▲ **EMP:** 100
SALES (est): 12.9MM
SALES (corp-wide): 7.3MM **Privately Held**
WEB: www.ach-aci.com
SIC: **3465** 3544 3469 Automotive stampings; special dies, tools, jigs & fixtures; metal stampings
HQ: Inalfa Roof Systems, Inc.
1370 Pacific Dr
Auburn Hills MI 48326
248 371-3060

(G-17087)
INDEPENDENT DIE ASSOCIATION
Also Called: I.D.A.
14689 E 11 Mile Rd (48088-4887)
PHONE..................586 773-9000
Greg Smith, *President*
Francis M Smith, *President*
EMP: 6
SQ FT: 3,000
SALES (est): 621.5K **Privately Held**
WEB: www.independent-die.com
SIC: **3544** Special dies & tools

(G-17088)
INDUCTION PROCESSING INC
24872 Gibson Dr (48089-4315)
PHONE..................586 756-5101
Albert Schult, *President*
Katherine Schult, *Vice Pres*
EMP: 16
SQ FT: 7,200
SALES (est): 2.2MM **Privately Held**
SIC: **3398** Metal heat treating

(G-17089)
INDUCTION SERVICES INC
24800 Mound Rd (48091-5334)
PHONE..................586 754-1640
David De Arment, *President*
Mike Miles, *QC Mgr*
EMP: 40 **EST:** 1956
SQ FT: 33,000
SALES (est): 9.2MM **Privately Held**
WEB: www.inductionservicesinc.com
SIC: **3398** Metal burning

(G-17090)
INDUSTRIAL BORING COMPANY
23175 Blackstone Ave (48089-2688)
PHONE..................586 756-9110
Jay Kaip, *President*
Donna M Kaip, *Corp Secy*
Paul Kaip, *Vice Pres*
EMP: 3
SQ FT: 4,000
SALES: 130K **Privately Held**
SIC: **3541** Drilling & boring machines

(G-17091)
INDUSTRIAL CONVERTING INC
21650 Hoover Rd (48089-3158)
PHONE..................586 757-8820
Kenneth Bugno, *President*
Tom Polsuk, *Vice Pres*
EMP: 13
SQ FT: 2,500
SALES: 600K **Privately Held**
WEB: www.industrialconvertinginc.com
SIC: **3544** 3053 Dies & die holders for metal cutting, forming, die casting; dies, steel rule; gaskets, packing & sealing devices

(G-17092)
INNOVATE INDUSTRIES INC
5600 Enterprise Ct (48092-3474)
PHONE..................586 558-8990
Norb Spinski, *CEO*
EMP: 4 **EST:** 1965
SQ FT: 8,000
SALES (est): 639.9K **Privately Held**
SIC: **3444** 3448 Sheet metalwork; panels for prefabricated metal buildings

(G-17093)
INNOVATIVE THERMAL SYSTEMS LLC
21400 Hoover Rd (48089-3162)
PHONE..................586 920-2900
EMP: 6 **EST:** 2014
SALES (est): 63.9K **Privately Held**
SIC: **3999** 8711 Barber & beauty shop equipment; engineering services

(G-17094)
INTEGRATED INTERIORS INC
21221 Hoover Rd (48089-3164)
PHONE..................586 756-4840
Lawrence Barnes, *President*
Bob Barnes, *Vice Pres*
Stephanie Morrison, *CFO*
Laurie Gottman, *Office Mgr*
Dave Pendley,
EMP: 17
SQ FT: 18,000
SALES (est): 2.1MM **Privately Held**
WEB: www.integratedinteriors.com
SIC: **3296** Acoustical board & tile, mineral wool

(G-17095)
INTER CITY NEON INC
23920 Amber Ave (48089-4203)
P.O. Box 3762, Center Line (48015-0762)
PHONE..................586 754-6020
Walter Schafer, *President*
Joyce Schafer, *Corp Secy*
Donna Holkey, *Office Mgr*
EMP: 8 **EST:** 1948
SQ FT: 6,400
SALES (est): 961.2K **Privately Held**
WEB: www.intercityneon.com
SIC: **3993** Neon signs

(G-17096)
INVECAST CORPORATION
25737 Sherwood Ave (48091-4159)
PHONE..................586 755-4050
Gregory P Kurze, *President*

GEOGRAPHIC SECTION

Warren - Macomb County (G-17124)

Judy Riley, *Office Mgr*
EMP: 25
SQ FT: 16,000
SALES (est): 5.2MM **Privately Held**
SIC: 3324 3369 3325 Commercial investment castings, ferrous; nonferrous foundries; steel foundries

(G-17097)
INVO SPLINE INC (PA)
2357 E 9 Mile Rd (48091-2162)
PHONE..................................586 757-8840
Vincent Spica III, *President*
Terry Spear, *Accountant*
Brenda Smith, *Administration*
EMP: 30 **EST**: 1947
SQ FT: 20,000
SALES (est): 8MM **Privately Held**
WEB: www.invospline.com
SIC: 3545 3599 3829 3566 Gauges (machine tool accessories); machine shop, jobbing & repair; measuring & controlling devices; speed changers, drives & gears; special dies, tools, jigs & fixtures; iron & steel forgings

(G-17098)
IRON CAPITAL OF AMERICA CO
21550 Groesbeck Hwy (48089-3133)
PHONE..................................586 771-5840
Jerry Noto, *President*
Bud Baxters, *General Mgr*
EMP: 5
SQ FT: 6,000
SALES (est): 440K **Privately Held**
SIC: 3446 Architectural metalwork

(G-17099)
IROQUOIS ASSEMBLY SYSTEMS INC
23220 Pinewood St (48091-4753)
PHONE..................................586 771-5734
Reinhard Eschbach, *President*
EMP: 10
SALES (est): 2MM **Privately Held**
SIC: 3559 Automotive related machinery

(G-17100)
IROQUOIS INDUSTRIES INC (PA)
24400 Hoover Rd (48089-1970)
PHONE..................................586 771-5734
Reinhard Eschbach, *President*
Al Godin, *General Mgr*
Kurt Lang, *Business Mgr*
Jim Carleton, *Vice Pres*
Mark Thompson, *Vice Pres*
◆ **EMP**: 85
SQ FT: 455,384
SALES (est): 56.8MM **Privately Held**
WEB: www.iroquoisind.com
SIC: 3465 Automotive stampings

(G-17101)
IROQUOIS INDUSTRIES INC
25101 Groesbeck Hwy (48089-1425)
PHONE..................................586 756-6922
Kathleen Hunt, *Branch Mgr*
EMP: 35
SALES (corp-wide): 56.8MM **Privately Held**
WEB: www.iroquoisind.com
SIC: 4225 3469 General warehousing; metal stampings
PA: Iroquois Industries, Inc.
24400 Hoover Rd
Warren MI 48089
586 771-5734

(G-17102)
IROQUOIS INDUSTRIES INC
23750 Regency Park Dr (48089-2649)
PHONE..................................586 353-1410
Ryan Hart-Bachbrook, *President*
EMP: 31
SALES (corp-wide): 56.8MM **Privately Held**
SIC: 3465 Body parts, automobile: stamped metal
PA: Iroquois Industries, Inc.
24400 Hoover Rd
Warren MI 48089
586 771-5734

(G-17103)
J & J BURNING CO
Also Called: J & J Burning and Fabg Co
24622 Mound Rd (48091-2094)
PHONE..................................586 758-7619
Timothy Farrar, *President*
Gary Farrar, *Vice Pres*
EMP: 50
SQ FT: 50,000
SALES (est): 17MM **Privately Held**
WEB: www.jjburning.com
SIC: 3441 Fabricated structural metal

(G-17104)
J & L MFG CO (PA)
23334 Schoenherr Rd (48089-2672)
PHONE..................................586 445-9530
John L Metzger Sr, *President*
Lance L Metzger, *Vice Pres*
Kelly Harris, *Buyer*
Scott Wigglesworth, *Purchasing*
Betty Lynn Wills, *Controller*
EMP: 24
SQ FT: 7,000
SALES (est): 4.2MM **Privately Held**
WEB: www.jnlmfg.com
SIC: 3444 3469 3465 Sheet metalwork; metal stampings; automotive stampings

(G-17105)
J AND N FABRICATIONS INC
30130 Ryan Rd (48092-3337)
PHONE..................................586 751-6350
Nick Kuzatko Sr, *President*
Nick Kuzatko Jr, *Vice Pres*
Carol Kuzatko, *Admin Sec*
EMP: 6
SQ FT: 13,000
SALES (est): 1.1MM **Privately Held**
SIC: 3444 Sheet metal specialties, not stamped

(G-17106)
J C MANUFACTURING COMPANY
23900 Ryan Rd (48091-4556)
PHONE..................................586 757-2713
Dan Crawford, *President*
Ann Crawford, *Admin Sec*
EMP: 4 **EST**: 1946
SQ FT: 7,040
SALES (est): 617.2K **Privately Held**
SIC: 3544 3599 3541 Special dies & tools; electrical discharge machining (EDM); die sinking machines

(G-17107)
J L SCHROTH CO
24074 Gibson Dr (48089-2001)
PHONE..................................586 759-4240
Richrad Davidson, *President*
Robert A Connelly, *Vice Pres*
EMP: 4
SALES (est): 665.6K
SALES (corp-wide): 3.4MM **Privately Held**
WEB: www.jlschroth.com
SIC: 3053 Gaskets, packing & sealing devices
PA: Schroth Enterprises Inc
95 Tonnacour Pl
Grosse Pointe Farms MI 48236
586 759-4240

(G-17108)
J M L CONTRACTING & SALES INC
5649 E 8 Mile Rd (48091-2844)
PHONE..................................586 756-4133
Jay M Lifshay, *President*
EMP: 10
SALES (est): 1MM **Privately Held**
WEB: www.jmlsheetmetal.com
SIC: 1761 3444 3353 3351 Sheet metalwork; sheet metalwork; aluminum sheet, plate & foil; copper rolling & drawing

(G-17109)
J M MOLD TECHNOLOGIES INC
25185 Easy St (48089-4132)
PHONE..................................586 773-6664
Marion Danak, *President*
Johnny Bossio, *Vice Pres*
EMP: 12
SQ FT: 7,200

SALES (est): 1.7MM **Privately Held**
SIC: 3544 Industrial molds

(G-17110)
J&J FREON REMOVAL
32344 Newcastle Dr (48093-1257)
PHONE..................................586 264-6379
Jack Movsesian, *Principal*
EMP: 4 **EST**: 2009
SALES (est): 368.4K **Privately Held**
SIC: 2869 Freon

(G-17111)
JAIMES CUPCAKE HAVEN
26142 Fairfield Ave (48089-4520)
PHONE..................................586 596-6809
Jamie Keller, *Principal*
EMP: 4 **EST**: 2011
SALES (est): 233.2K **Privately Held**
SIC: 2051 Bread, cake & related products

(G-17112)
JAX SERVICES LLC
25343 Masch Ave (48091-5025)
PHONE..................................586 703-3212
Austin Fletcher, *CEO*
EMP: 5
SALES (est): 218.4K **Privately Held**
SIC: 3569 8721 7291 8711 Robots, assembly line: industrial & commercial; billing & bookkeeping service; tax return preparation services; consulting engineer

(G-17113)
JDL ENTERPRISES INC
7200 Miller Dr (48092-4727)
PHONE..................................586 977-8863
Kathy Shaver, *Manager*
EMP: 8
SALES (corp-wide): 1.2MM **Privately Held**
WEB: www.jdlent.com
SIC: 3491 3541 Industrial valves; machine tools, metal cutting type
PA: Jdl Enterprises Inc
36425 Maas Dr
Sterling Heights MI 48312
586 977-8863

(G-17114)
JHS GRINDING LLC
24700 Mound Rd (48091-5332)
PHONE..................................586 427-6006
Rudy Lipski, *Mng Member*
Coutnie Heikkinen,
Jody Sparks,
EMP: 35
SQ FT: 25,000
SALES (est): 4.8MM **Privately Held**
WEB: www.jhsgrinding.com
SIC: 3599 Machine shop, jobbing & repair

(G-17115)
JMS PRINTING SVC LLC
Also Called: International Minute Press
14147 Edison Dr (48088-3755)
PHONE..................................734 414-6203
Tim Higgins, *President*
EMP: 8
SALES (est): 370.2K **Privately Held**
SIC: 2752 Commercial printing, lithographic

(G-17116)
JOHN SAMS TOOL CO
14478 E 9 Mile Rd (48089-2756)
PHONE..................................586 776-3560
John Samohin, *President*
Denetrios Samoin, *Vice Pres*
Alexander Samohin, *Shareholder*
EMP: 5
SQ FT: 4,000
SALES: 400K **Privately Held**
SIC: 3599 Machine shop, jobbing & repair

(G-17117)
JORDAN TOOL CORPORATION
Also Called: Victoria Tool & Machine Div
11801 Commerce St (48089-3937)
PHONE..................................586 755-6700
Donna Pilarski, *President*
Jimmy Pilarski, *Vice Pres*
Tami Roberts, *Office Mgr*
EMP: 35
SQ FT: 22,500

SALES (est): 5.8MM **Privately Held**
WEB: www.jordantool.com
SIC: 3544 7389 Special dies & tools; grinding, precision: commercial or industrial

(G-17118)
KC JONES BRAZING INC
2845 E 10 Mile Rd (48091-1359)
PHONE..................................586 755-4900
Rick Stewart, *President*
EMP: 6
SQ FT: 2,500
SALES (est): 528.6K **Privately Held**
SIC: 7692 Brazing

(G-17119)
KC JONES PLATING CO (PA)
2845 E 10 Mile Rd (48091-1359)
PHONE..................................586 755-4900
Robert H Burger, *CEO*
Lenard Berman, *Admin Sec*
◆ **EMP**: 25 **EST**: 1957
SQ FT: 36,000
SALES: 21.4MM **Privately Held**
WEB: www.kcjplating.com
SIC: 3471 3479 Electroplating of metals or formed products; coating of metals & formed products

(G-17120)
KEO CUTTERS INC
25040 Easy St (48089-4100)
PHONE..................................586 771-2050
Eli Crotzer, *President*
EMP: 50
SQ FT: 45,000
SALES (est): 9.9MM
SALES (corp-wide): 724.3MM **Privately Held**
WEB: www.keocutters.com
SIC: 3545 Machine tool accessories
HQ: Arch Global Precision Llc
2600 S Telg Rd Ste 180
Bloomfield Hills MI 48302
734 266-6900

(G-17121)
KRAFT-WRAP INC
21650 Hoover Rd (48089-3158)
PHONE..................................586 755-2050
Kenneth Bugno, *President*
Patricia Bugno, *Treasurer*
Margaret Bugno, *Admin Sec*
EMP: 11
SQ FT: 14,000
SALES (est): 1.5MM **Privately Held**
WEB: www.kraftwrap.com
SIC: 2653 3081 2655 Boxes, corrugated: made from purchased materials; unsupported plastics film & sheet; fiber cans, drums & similar products

(G-17122)
KRINGER INDUSTRIAL CORPORATION
24435 Forterra Dr (48089-4379)
PHONE..................................519 818-3509
EMP: 10
SALES: 100K **Privately Held**
SIC: 3086 7389 Mfg Plastic Foam Products

(G-17123)
L & M MACHINING & MFG INC
14200 E 10 Mile Rd (48089-2163)
PHONE..................................586 498-7110
Jan Linthorst, *President*
Lawrence Morath, *Principal*
EMP: 5
SALES (est): 530K **Privately Held**
SIC: 3599 Machine shop, jobbing & repair

(G-17124)
L D S SHEET METAL INC
21831 Schoenherr Rd (48089-2857)
PHONE..................................313 892-2624
Kirk Lambert, *President*
Matt Lambert, *Vice Pres*
EMP: 5
SQ FT: 6,000
SALES (est): 931.7K **Privately Held**
WEB: www.ldssheetmetal.com
SIC: 3444 Metal ventilating equipment; guard rails, highway: sheet metal

Warren - Macomb County (G-17125) — GEOGRAPHIC SECTION

(G-17125)
LAY MANUFACTURING INC
31614 Iroquois Dr (48088-7011)
PHONE..................313 369-1627
Paul Lay, *President*
EMP: 7
SQ FT: 44,000
SALES (est): 853.4K **Privately Held**
SIC: 3452 Nuts, metal; bolts, metal

(G-17126)
LEEWARD TOOL INC
23781 Blackstone Ave (48089-4217)
PHONE..................586 754-7200
Fax: 586 756-2434
EMP: 5
SALES (est): 526.5K **Privately Held**
SIC: 3544 Mfg Dies/Tools/Jigs/Fixtures

(G-17127)
LEONARD MACHINE TOOL SYSTEMS
22800 Hoover Rd (48089-2568)
PHONE..................586 757-8040
Leonard Bantleon, *President*
Leonard Bantle, *President*
Rhonda Martinez, *Project Engr*
Lisa Thomas, *Treasurer*
David Hunter, *Manager*
EMP: 20
SQ FT: 26,000
SALES (est): 3.9MM **Privately Held**
WEB: www.lmtsi.com
SIC: 3549 3544 Metalworking machinery; special dies, tools, jigs & fixtures

(G-17128)
LEONI WIRING SYSTEMS INC
Also Called: Lws - Design Center Detroit
30500 Van Dyke Ave # 300 (48093-2110)
PHONE..................586 782-4444
EMP: 10
SALES (corp-wide): 5.8B **Privately Held**
WEB: www.leoniwiring.com
SIC: 3679 Electronic circuits
HQ: Leoni Wiring Systems, Inc.
3100 N Campbell Ave # 101
Tucson AZ 85719

(G-17129)
LOC INDUSTRIES INC
13001 Stephens Rd (48089-2009)
PHONE..................586 759-8412
David Schrage, *President*
Derek Kowalski, *Engineer*
EMP: 3
SALES (est): 507K **Privately Held**
SIC: 2791 Hand composition typesetting

(G-17130)
LOGAN TOOL AND ENGINEERING
23919 Blackstone Ave (48089-4200)
PHONE..................586 755-3555
John R Ugo, *President*
EMP: 7
SQ FT: 4,000
SALES (est): 850.1K **Privately Held**
SIC: 3599 Machine shop, jobbing & repair

(G-17131)
LORNA ICR LLC
Also Called: I C R
28601 Lorna Ave (48092-3931)
PHONE..................586 582-1500
Brian Bauers, *Manager*
Jerry McDonald, *Manager*
Anne Popelier, *Manager*
Colette Schneider, *Manager*
EMP: 5
SALES (est): 116.8K **Privately Held**
SIC: 7694 7699 8742 Motor repair services; cash register repair; automation & robotics consultant

(G-17132)
LUMERICA CORPORATION
21400 Hoover Rd (48089-3162)
PHONE..................248 543-8085
Justin Palm, *President*
▼ **EMP:** 15
SQ FT: 15,000
SALES (est): 2.6MM **Privately Held**
SIC: 3648 Lighting equipment

(G-17133)
LYONS TOOL & ENGINEERING INC
13720 E 9 Mile Rd (48089-2767)
PHONE..................586 200-3003
Mary A Lyons, *President*
Steven J Botwin, *Vice Pres*
William J Lyons, *Vice Pres*
Nancy M Skerchock, *Admin Sec*
EMP: 20 **EST:** 1960
SQ FT: 10,000
SALES (est): 1.6MM **Privately Held**
WEB: www.lyonstoolandengineering.com
SIC: 3544 3545 3462 Special dies & tools; machine tool accessories; iron & steel forgings

(G-17134)
LYTE POLES INCORPORATED
24874 Groesbeck Hwy (48089-4726)
PHONE..................586 771-4610
Ryan Macvoy, *President*
Jessica Schultz, *Partner*
Justin Hodge, *COO*
Justin Snowden, *Engineer*
Jeff Aliotta, *Finance*
EMP: 90
SALES (est): 4.7MM **Privately Held**
SIC: 3646 Commercial indusl & institutional electric lighting fixtures

(G-17135)
MACOMB TUBE FABRICATING CO
13403 E 9 Mile Rd (48089-2658)
PHONE..................586 445-6770
Walter Magreta, *General Mgr*
EMP: 15
SQ FT: 12,000
SALES (est): 2.7MM **Privately Held**
WEB: www.macombtube.com
SIC: 3498 Tube fabricating (contract bending & shaping)

(G-17136)
MADISON ELECTRIC COMPANY (PA)
Also Called: Madison Electronics
31855 Van Dyke Ave (48093-1047)
PHONE..................586 825-0200
Brett Schneider, *President*
Scott Leemaster, *Vice Pres*
Phil Snider, *Vice Pres*
Richard Sonenklar, *Vice Pres*
Jon Waitz, *Vice Pres*
EMP: 63 **EST:** 1914
SQ FT: 93,000
SALES (est): 158.4MM **Privately Held**
WEB: www.madisonelectric.com
SIC: 5063 3679 Electrical construction materials; electrical supplies; lighting fixtures; harness assemblies for electronic use: wire or cable

(G-17137)
MAGNA MODULAR SYSTEMS LLC
Also Called: Aim Systems Warren
14253 Frazho Rd (48089-1476)
PHONE..................586 279-2000
Keith McMahon, *General Mgr*
EMP: 225
SALES (corp-wide): 40.8B **Privately Held**
SIC: 3714 Motor vehicle body components & frame
HQ: Magna Modular Systems Llc
1800 Nathan Dr
Toledo OH 43611
419 324-3387

(G-17138)
MAGNUMM CORPORATION (PA)
3839 E 10 Mile Rd (48091-1358)
PHONE..................586 427-9420
Martin L Abel, *President*
Joseph M Lane, *Chairman*
◆ **EMP:** 13
SALES (est): 21.3MM **Privately Held**
SIC: 3714 3599 Thermostats, motor vehicle; bellows, industrial: metal

(G-17139)
MARIAS HOUSE MADE SALSA
23425 Blackstone Ave (48089-4211)
PHONE..................313 733-8406
EMP: 3
SALES (est): 139.5K **Privately Held**
SIC: 2099 Dips, except cheese & sour cream based

(G-17140)
MARIX SPECIALTY WELDING CO
3822 Kiefer Ave (48091-3765)
PHONE..................586 754-9685
Henry R Di Laura, *President*
David Jackf, *Supervisor*
EMP: 25
SQ FT: 12,000
SALES: 4MM **Privately Held**
SIC: 3443 Metal parts

(G-17141)
MARTINREA HOT STAMPINGS INC
14401 Frazho Rd (48089-1512)
PHONE..................859 509-3031
EMP: 50
SALES (corp-wide): 2.8B **Privately Held**
SIC: 3465 Mfg Automotive Stampings
HQ: Martinrea Hot Stampings, Inc.
19200 Glendale St
Detroit MI 48223
313 272-8400

(G-17142)
MARYSVILLE HYDROCARBONS LLC
30078 Schoenherr Rd # 150 (48088-3179)
PHONE..................586 445-2300
Rai Bhergava, *Branch Mgr*
EMP: 3
SALES (corp-wide): 9.8B **Publicly Held**
SIC: 2911 Petroleum refining
HQ: Marysville Hydrocarbons Llc
2510 Busha Hwy
Marysville MI 48040
586 445-2300

(G-17143)
MATERION BRUSH INC
Also Called: Materion Brush Prfmce Alloys
27555 College Park Dr (48088-4875)
PHONE..................586 443-4925
David Moore, *Branch Mgr*
EMP: 18
SALES (corp-wide): 1.2B **Publicly Held**
WEB: www.brushwellman.com
SIC: 4225 3351 3341 3339 General warehousing; copper rolling & drawing; secondary nonferrous metals; primary nonferrous metals; primary copper
HQ: Materion Brush Inc.
6070 Parkland Blvd Ste 1
Mayfield Heights OH 44124
216 486-4200

(G-17144)
MB AEROSPACE WARREN LLC
Also Called: Gentz Aero
25250 Easy St (48089-4130)
PHONE..................586 772-2500
Roger Bartolomei, *General Mgr*
Bill Evans II, *Senior VP*
John Kozma, *Vice Pres*
Denise Pecherski, *Buyer*
Tom Pabin, *VP Finance*
EMP: 210
SQ FT: 132,000
SALES (est): 81.6MM **Privately Held**
SIC: 3769 3443 3444 3724 Guided missile & space vehicle parts & auxiliary equipment; fabricated plate work (boiler shop); sheet metalwork; aircraft engines & engine parts; metal heat treating
HQ: Mb Aerospace Us Holdings, Inc.
25250 Easy St
Warren MI 48089
586 772-2500

(G-17145)
MCCORMICK & COMPANY INC
28650 Dequindre Rd (48092-2467)
PHONE..................586 558-8424
Khanitha Sookanit, *Branch Mgr*
EMP: 104
SALES (corp-wide): 5.4B **Publicly Held**
SIC: 2099 Spices, including grinding; seasonings: dry mixes; gravy mixes, dry; sauces: dry mixes
PA: Mccormick & Company Incorporated
24 Schilling Rd Ste 1
Hunt Valley MD 21031
410 771-7301

(G-17146)
MCKEON PRODUCTS INC (PA)
Also Called: Mack's Ear Plugs
25460 Guenther (48091-6801)
PHONE..................586 427-7560
Devin Benner, *CEO*
Jake Herman, *Natl Sales Mgr*
Emily Hilsabeck, *Sales Staff*
Susan Elwood, *VP Mktg*
Dominic Rosiek, *Manager*
▲ **EMP:** 50
SQ FT: 21,000
SALES (est): 9.3MM **Privately Held**
WEB: www.macksearplugs.com
SIC: 3842 3949 3851 Ear plugs; sporting & athletic goods; ophthalmic goods

(G-17147)
MELODY DIGIGLIO
Also Called: McBf
8088 E 9 Mile Rd (48089-2320)
PHONE..................586 754-4405
Melody Digiglio, *Owner*
Frank Digiglio, *Principal*
EMP: 16
SQ FT: 15,000
SALES (est): 1.2MM **Privately Held**
SIC: 5023 2591 1799 Window furnishings; drapery hardware & blinds & shades; window treatment installation

(G-17148)
METAL MART USA INC
31164 Dequindre Rd (48092-3722)
PHONE..................586 977-5820
Bruno Tome, *CEO*
John Vandermark, *CEO*
EMP: 6 **EST:** 1997
SQ FT: 10,000
SALES (est): 2.7MM **Privately Held**
WEB: www.metalmartusa.com
SIC: 5051 3441 Steel; fabricated structural metal

(G-17149)
METALLURGICAL PROCESSING LLC
Also Called: Metallurgical Processing Co.
23075 Warner Ave (48091-1919)
PHONE..................586 758-3100
Jeff Pyne, *President*
James L Schroth, *President*
Kevin Brown, *Vice Pres*
Robert A Connelly, *Vice Pres*
Ronald Abbott, *Supervisor*
EMP: 20 **EST:** 1954
SQ FT: 30,000
SALES: 5.4MM
SALES (corp-wide): 3.4MM **Privately Held**
SIC: 3398 Metal heat treating
PA: Schroth Enterprises Inc
95 Tonnacour Pl
Grosse Pointe Farms MI 48236
586 759-4240

(G-17150)
METRO BROACH INC
2160 E 9 Mile Rd (48091-2145)
PHONE..................586 758-2340
Clyde Hishok, *CEO*
Josephine Hishok, *President*
EMP: 10 **EST:** 1980
SQ FT: 14,000
SALES (est): 750K **Privately Held**
SIC: 3599 Machine shop, jobbing & repair

(G-17151)
MICA TEC INC
Also Called: Jon F Canty
21325 Hoover Rd (48089-3156)
PHONE..................586 758-4404
Jon F Canty, *President*
Nadine Canty, *Info Tech Mgr*
EMP: 6
SQ FT: 11,900
SALES (est): 1.1MM **Privately Held**
WEB: www.micatec.net
SIC: 2522 Cabinets, office: except wood

GEOGRAPHIC SECTION

(G-17152)
MICHIGAN COUNTER TOPS COMPANY
Also Called: Futura Custom Kitchen
2929 John B Ave (48091-4200)
PHONE.................................313 369-1511
Frank D Scalzi, *President*
Richard Scalzi, *Vice Pres*
Donna Wojcik, *Admin Sec*
EMP: 11 **EST:** 1975
SQ FT: 30,000
SALES (est): 1.1MM **Privately Held**
WEB: www.michiganmarble.com
SIC: 2434 Wood kitchen cabinets

(G-17153)
MICHIGAN METAL FABRICATORS
24575 Hoover Rd (48089-1930)
PHONE.................................586 754-0421
John Sweet, *President*
Richard Sweet, *Vice Pres*
Kenneth Sweet, *Treasurer*
EMP: 8 **EST:** 1949
SQ FT: 9,000
SALES: 225K **Privately Held**
SIC: 3443 3444 Weldments; sheet metalwork

(G-17154)
MICHIGAN SLOTTING COMPANY INC
22214 Schoenherr Rd (48089-5458)
PHONE.................................586 772-1270
Fax: 586 772-6013
EMP: 4
SQ FT: 3,200
SALES (est): 280K **Privately Held**
SIC: 3599 Mfg Industrial Machinery

(G-17155)
MIDWEST BRAKE BOND CO
Also Called: Sommer Co.
26255 Groesbeck Hwy (48089-1587)
PHONE.................................586 775-3000
James L Taylor Jr, *President*
Joan Coyle, *Vice Pres*
Joyce Johnston, *Treasurer*
Sue Vansteel, *Accounting Mgr*
Kur Leibol, *Sales Staff*
EMP: 27
SALES (est): 6.8MM **Privately Held**
WEB: www.midwestbrake.com
SIC: 3714 Motor vehicle brake systems & parts; transmission housings or parts, motor vehicle

(G-17156)
MIKE MANUFACTURING CORPORATION (PA)
7214 Murthum Ave (48092-1251)
PHONE.................................586 759-1140
Gerald Schumacher, *President*
EMP: 3
SQ FT: 30,000
SALES (est): 881.9K **Privately Held**
WEB: www.mikemanufacturing.com
SIC: 3444 3441 3354 Awnings, sheet metal; fabricated structural metal; aluminum extruded products

(G-17157)
MITSUBISHI CHLS PERF PLYRS INC
Also Called: McPp-Detroit, LLC
24060 Hoover Rd (48091-1942)
PHONE.................................586 755-1660
Keith Thomas, *Plant Mgr*
EMP: 40 **Privately Held**
SIC: 2821 2822 Plastics materials & resins; synthetic rubber
HQ: Mitsubishi Chemical Performance Polymers, Inc.
2001 Hood Rd
Greer SC 29650
864 879-5487

(G-17158)
MMI ENGINEERED SOLUTIONS INC
12700 Stephens Rd (48089-4334)
PHONE.................................734 429-5130
Paul Larson, *CFO*
EMP: 50 **Privately Held**
SIC: 3089 8711 Injection molding of plastics; engineering services
HQ: Mmi Engineered Solutions, Inc.
1715 Woodland Dr
Saline MI 48176
734 429-4664

(G-17159)
MOBILE MINI INC
21900 Hoover Rd (48089-2557)
PHONE.................................586 759-4916
Brendan Clark, *Branch Mgr*
EMP: 15
SALES (corp-wide): 593.2MM **Publicly Held**
WEB: www.mobilemini.com
SIC: 3448 Buildings, portable: prefabricated metal
PA: Mobile Mini, Inc.
4646 E Van Buren St # 400
Phoenix AZ 85008
480 894-6311

(G-17160)
MOTION SYSTEMS INCORPORATED
21335 Schoenherr Rd (48089-3332)
PHONE.................................586 774-5666
William Ericson, *President*
Greg Ericson, *General Mgr*
◆ **EMP:** 15
SQ FT: 10,000
SALES (est): 2.6MM **Privately Held**
SIC: 3429 3462 Pulleys metal; gears, forged steel

(G-17161)
MOTOR CITY NATURALS LLC
24201 Hoover Rd (48089-1973)
PHONE.................................313 329-4071
Maddy Frechette,
Nick Parker,
EMP: 7
SQ FT: 7,800
SALES: 300K **Privately Held**
SIC: 2834 Vitamin, nutrient & hematinic preparations for human use

(G-17162)
MULTI GRINDING INC
6877 Miller Dr (48092-1674)
PHONE.................................586 268-7388
Joseph Groves, *President*
Margaret Groves, *Treasurer*
EMP: 24 **EST:** 1982
SALES (est): 3.4MM **Privately Held**
WEB: www.multigrinding.com
SIC: 3599 Grinding castings for the trade

(G-17163)
MURRAY EQUIPMENT COMPANY INC (PA)
6737 E 8 Mile Rd (48091-2905)
PHONE.................................313 869-4444
Robert W Murray, *President*
James J Murray Jr, *Chairman*
Joseph Fillippi, *Admin Sec*
EMP: 12 **EST:** 1946
SQ FT: 11,000
SALES (est): 2MM **Privately Held**
SIC: 3568 3625 Power transmission equipment; relays & industrial controls

(G-17164)
N-P GRINDING INC
3700 E 10 Mile Rd (48091-3721)
PHONE.................................586 756-6262
Mark Hampton, *President*
EMP: 4 **EST:** 1967
SQ FT: 6,000
SALES (est): 444.7K **Privately Held**
SIC: 3599 Machine shop, jobbing & repair

(G-17165)
NAAMS LLC
25141 Easy St (48089-4132)
PHONE.................................586 285-5684
John Djurasaj, *Mng Member*
EMP: 15
SALES: 2MM **Privately Held**
SIC: 3549 Metalworking machinery

(G-17166)
NATIONAL MANUFACTURING INC
25426 Ryan Rd (48091-1326)
PHONE.................................586 755-8983
Nelida Mari, *President*
EMP: 5
SALES (est): 59.4K **Privately Held**
SIC: 3111 Industrial leather products; accessory products, leather

(G-17167)
NINE MILE DEQUINDRE FUEL STOP
1940 E 9 Mile Rd (48091-2109)
PHONE.................................586 757-7721
Kristen Deuben, *Principal*
EMP: 3
SALES (est): 235.5K **Privately Held**
SIC: 2869 Fuels

(G-17168)
NITRO-VAC HEAT TREAT INC
23080 Dequindre Rd (48091-1898)
PHONE.................................586 754-4350
Felix Stomber, *President*
Phyllis La Prairie, *Vice Pres*
William F Stomber, *Vice Pres*
Cheryl Trombley, *Admin Sec*
EMP: 11
SQ FT: 5,400
SALES (est): 1.9MM **Privately Held**
WEB: www.heattreatonline.com
SIC: 3398 Brazing (hardening) of metal

(G-17169)
NOLANS TOP TIN INC
8428 Republic Ave (48089-1716)
PHONE.................................586 899-3421
Nolan Brown, *Principal*
EMP: 4
SALES (est): 507.4K **Privately Held**
SIC: 3356 Tin

(G-17170)
NOR-COTE INC
11425 Timken Ave (48089-3863)
PHONE.................................586 756-1200
Stanley C Grouse, *President*
Barbara A Grouse, *Corp Secy*
Christopher Grouse, *Vice Pres*
EMP: 45 **EST:** 1954
SQ FT: 43,000
SALES (est): 8.6MM **Privately Held**
WEB: www.nor-coteinc.com
SIC: 3471 5051 3398 Plating & polishing; metals service centers & offices; annealing of metal

(G-17171)
NORBROOK PLATING INC
11400 E 9 Mile Rd (48089-2583)
PHONE.................................586 755-4110
F Preston Kemp, *President*
Ken Otto, *Corp Secy*
Kathleen Kemp, *Vice Pres*
EMP: 27 **EST:** 1953
SQ FT: 30,000
SALES (est): 3.5MM **Privately Held**
WEB: www.norbrookplating.com
SIC: 3471 Plating of metals or formed products; buffing for the trade; polishing, metals or formed products

(G-17172)
NORTH AMERICAN ASPHALT
11720 Susan Ave (48093-8338)
PHONE.................................586 754-0014
Daniel Bergen, *Principal*
EMP: 3
SALES (est): 220K **Privately Held**
SIC: 2951 Asphalt paving mixtures & blocks

(G-17173)
NORTH AMERICAN GRAPHICS INC
24487 Gibson Dr (48089-2030)
PHONE.................................586 486-1110
John Mertz, *President*
EMP: 21
SQ FT: 10,000
SALES (est): 3MM **Privately Held**
WEB: www.nagtype.com
SIC: 2791 2796 2752 Typesetting; platemaking services; commercial printing, lithographic

(G-17174)
NOVATRON CORPORATION (PA)
6000 Rinke Ave (48091-5350)
PHONE.................................609 815-2100
Saul Epstein, *CEO*
Charles Debeau, *President*
Karen Phillips, *Chairman*
Fred Kolacki, *Vice Pres*
James P Wheeler, *CFO*
EMP: 150
SQ FT: 38,000
SALES (est): 17.9MM **Privately Held**
WEB: www.novatroncorp.com
SIC: 3829 3812 Instrument board gauges, automotive: computerized; nautical instruments

(G-17175)
NOVUS CORPORATION
Also Called: Archangel's Jewelry
3077 Chard Ave (48092-3526)
PHONE.................................248 545-8600
Steven Arcangeli, *President*
EMP: 50
SALES (est): 5.2MM **Privately Held**
WEB: www.novuscorp.org
SIC: 3911 5944 5932 7631 Jewelry, precious metal; jewelry, precious stones & precious metals; pawnshop; jewelry repair services

(G-17176)
OAKLEY INDUSTRIES SUB ASSEMBLY
25295 Guenther Ste 200 (48091-6020)
PHONE.................................586 754-5555
Bill Lethig, *Maint Spvr*
Doanald Amthor, *Branch Mgr*
EMP: 100
SALES (corp-wide): 130.1MM **Privately Held**
SIC: 3714 3559 Motor vehicle wheels & parts; rubber working machinery, including tires
PA: Oakley Industries Sub Assembly Division, Inc.
4333 Matthew
Flint MI 48507
810 720-4444

(G-17177)
OPUS MACH LLC
31845 Denton Dr (48092-4719)
PHONE.................................586 270-5170
Dee Kapur, *CEO*
Dave Bruford, *Vice Pres*
Tom Dennis, *Engineer*
Darren Ebertowski, *Manager*
Allan Sharp,
EMP: 7
SQ FT: 36,000
SALES: 700K **Privately Held**
SIC: 3544 8711 Industrial molds; engineering services

(G-17178)
OSHKOSH DEFENSE LLC
27600 Donald Ct (48092-5908)
PHONE.................................586 576-8301
Yancey Williams, *Branch Mgr*
EMP: 36
SALES (corp-wide): 7.7B **Publicly Held**
SIC: 3531 3715 3711 Mixers, concrete; truck trailers; military motor vehicle assembly
HQ: Oshkosh Defense, Llc
2307 Oregon St
Oshkosh WI 54902
920 235-9150

(G-17179)
PAINT WORK INCORPORATED
2088 Riggs Ave (48091-3771)
PHONE.................................586 759-6640
Elisabeth Weldhaddow, *President*
Mark Shamblin, *Vice Pres*
EMP: 10 **EST:** 1968
SQ FT: 8,000

Warren - Macomb County (G-17180)   GEOGRAPHIC SECTION

SALES: 600K **Privately Held**
SIC: **3479** Painting of metal products; coating of metals & formed products

(G-17180)
PARTON & PREBLE INC
23507 Groesbeck Hwy (48089-2694)
PHONE..................................586 773-6000
Orville S Parton, *President*
Bruce Parton, *Vice Pres*
Shirley Parton, *Treasurer*
Louise Wilson, *Admin Sec*
EMP: 40 **EST:** 1959
SQ FT: 50,000
SALES (est): 11.1MM **Privately Held**
SIC: **3312** 3444 3443 3441 Plate, steel; sheet metalwork; fabricated plate work (boiler shop); fabricated structural metal

(G-17181)
PASLIN COMPANY
23655 Hoover Rd (48089-1986)
PHONE..................................586 755-1693
Danny Pasque, *Owner*
EMP: 40 **Privately Held**
WEB: www.paslin.com
SIC: **3545** Machine tool accessories
HQ: The Paslin Company
    25303 Ryan Rd
    Warren MI 48091
    586 758-0200

(G-17182)
PASLIN COMPANY (HQ)
25303 Ryan Rd (48091-3778)
PHONE..................................586 758-0200
Kirk Goins, *CEO*
Ronald Pasque, *Vice Pres*
Steve Ayris, *Purch Mgr*
Michael Murphy, *QC Mgr*
Therese Polk, *Corp Comm Staff*
▲ **EMP:** 750 **EST:** 1937
SQ FT: 700,000
SALES (est): 228.8MM **Privately Held**
WEB: www.paslin.com
SIC: **3548** 3544 3545 Electric welding equipment; jigs & fixtures; machine tool accessories
PA: Zhejiang Wanfeng Technology Development Co., Ltd. Engineering Center
    Wanfeng Technology Park, Xinchang
    Shaoxing
    575 865-0700

(G-17183)
PASLIN COMPANY
Also Called: Paslin Controls Group
3400 E 10 Mile Rd (48091-3787)
PHONE..................................586 755-3606
Michael Keith, *Project Mgr*
Tim Dory, *Manager*
EMP: 20 **Privately Held**
WEB: www.paslin.com
SIC: **7389** 3548 Design services; welding apparatus
HQ: The Paslin Company
    25303 Ryan Rd
    Warren MI 48091
    586 758-0200

(G-17184)
PATIO LAND MFG INC
Also Called: Russ Parke Awnings
8407 E 9 Mile Rd (48089-2460)
PHONE..................................586 758-5660
Russell K Parke, *President*
Joann Parke, *Vice Pres*
EMP: 7
SQ FT: 3,000
SALES (est): 1MM **Privately Held**
SIC: **3444** 5999 Awnings, sheet metal; awnings

(G-17185)
PGM PRODUCTS INC
21034 Ryan Rd (48091-2740)
PHONE..................................586 757-4400
Ramo A Salerno Sr, *President*
Denise Marschner, *Admin Sec*
EMP: 10
SALES: 715.3K **Privately Held**
SIC: **3452** 7699 Bolts, nuts, rivets & washers; industrial machinery & equipment repair

(G-17186)
PIONEER METAL FINISHING LLC
13251 Stephens Rd (48089-4377)
PHONE..................................877 721-1100
▲ **EMP:** 4 **EST:** 2014
SALES (est): 193.2K **Privately Held**
SIC: **3559** Metal finishing equipment for plating, etc.

(G-17187)
PIONEER PLASTICS INC (PA)
Also Called: Pioneer Molding
2295 Bart Ave (48091-3207)
PHONE..................................586 262-0159
Rajeev Gandhi, *President*
Vinita Gandhi, *Owner*
EMP: 21
SQ FT: 40,000
SALES: 3.3MM **Privately Held**
SIC: **3089** Automotive parts, plastic; injection molding of plastics

(G-17188)
POLYTEC FOHA INC (HQ)
7020 Murthum Ave (48092-3831)
PHONE..................................586 978-9386
Howard Lipman, *President*
Sieglinde Kaiser, *Vice Pres*
Steffen Richter, *Human Res Dir*
Nicholas Sturrock, *Human Res Mgr*
Paul Rettenbacher, *Relations*
▲ **EMP:** 19
SQ FT: 70,000
SALES (est): 5.9MM
SALES (corp-wide): 728.5MM **Privately Held**
WEB: www.polytec-foha.com
SIC: **5013** 3429 3089 Automotive supplies & parts; furniture builders' & other household hardware; plastic containers, except foam
PA: Polytec Holding Ag
    Polytec-Str. 1
    HOrsching 4063
    722 170-10

(G-17189)
PPG INDUSTRIES INC
Also Called: PPG 5628
13344 E 11 Mile Rd (48089-1367)
PHONE..................................586 755-2011
Jason Macauley, *Branch Mgr*
EMP: 24
SALES (corp-wide): 15.3B **Publicly Held**
WEB: www.ppg.com
SIC: **2851** Paints & allied products
PA: Ppg Industries, Inc.
    1 Ppg Pl
    Pittsburgh PA 15272
    412 434-3131

(G-17190)
PPI LLC (PA)
Also Called: Ppi Aerospace
23514 Groesbeck Hwy (48089-4246)
PHONE..................................586 772-7736
Paul Clark, *President*
Kirk Thams, *Principal*
Scott Thams, *Principal*
EMP: 45
SQ FT: 80,000
SALES: 4MM **Privately Held**
SIC: **3471** Plating of metals or formed products

(G-17191)
PRAXAIR INC
30600 Dequindre Rd (48092-4819)
PHONE..................................586 751-7400
Randy Schraier, *Branch Mgr*
Jerry Fiorani, *Executive*
Connie Menichi, *Regional*
EMP: 15
SQ FT: 25,201 **Privately Held**
SIC: **2813** 5169 Industrial gases; industrial gases
HQ: Praxair, Inc.
    10 Riverview Dr
    Danbury CT 06810
    203 837-2000

(G-17192)
PRECISION HONING
2029 Riggs Ave (48091-3772)
PHONE..................................586 757-0304
John Canning, *President*

EMP: 4 **EST:** 1998
SALES (est): 579.8K **Privately Held**
SIC: **3541** Machine tool replacement & repair parts, metal cutting types

(G-17193)
PRECISION MOLD & ENGINEERING
13143 E 9 Mile Rd (48089-2620)
PHONE..................................586 774-2421
David Loehr, *President*
Walter Loehr, *Treasurer*
Julie Patterson, *Manager*
Janet Loehr, *Admin Sec*
▲ **EMP:** 20
SQ FT: 16,500
SALES (est): 3.8MM **Privately Held**
WEB: www.precisionmold.com
SIC: **3544** 3089 Industrial molds; injection molding of plastics

(G-17194)
PRECISION PACKING CORPORATION
2145 Centerwood Dr (48091-5866)
PHONE..................................586 756-8700
Anthony Pappas, *President*
John Whitefoot, *Vice Pres*
Michael Pappas, *Treasurer*
Terry Daubenmeyer, *Admin Sec*
EMP: 30
SQ FT: 12,600
SALES (est): 5.6MM **Privately Held**
SIC: **2891** 3492 3053 Sealants; fluid power valves & hose fittings; gaskets, packing & sealing devices

(G-17195)
PREMIER MALT PRODUCTS INC
25760 Groesbeck Hwy # 103 (48089-1589)
P.O. Box 898, Saddle Brook NJ (07663-0898)
PHONE..................................586 443-3355
M Stuart Andreas, *President*
Vicky Cohn, *Marketing Mgr*
▼ **EMP:** 25 **EST:** 1933
SQ FT: 1,440
SALES (est): 2MM **Privately Held**
WEB: www.premiermalt.com
SIC: **2082** 5149 Malt syrups; malt extract; sugar, honey, molasses & syrups

(G-17196)
PRESTIGE STAMPING LLC
23513 Groesbeck Hwy (48089-6001)
PHONE..................................586 773-2700
Christopher Rink, *CEO*
Jeffrey Rink, *Sales Staff*
EMP: 120
SQ FT: 105,000
SALES (est): 28.2MM
SALES (corp-wide): 78.2MM **Privately Held**
WEB: www.prestigestamping.com
SIC: **3452** 3465 Washers, metal; automotive stampings
PA: Auxo Investment Partners, Llc
    146 Monroe Center St Nw # 1125
    Grand Rapids MI 49503
    616 200-4454

(G-17197)
PRESTIGE WAREHOUSE & ASSEMBLY
26155 Groesbeck Hwy (48089-4149)
PHONE..................................586 777-1820
William Fritts, *President*
Perry Russo, *Principal*
Tom Nichols, *Vice Pres*
▲ **EMP:** 35
SQ FT: 50,000
SALES (est): 3.5MM **Privately Held**
SIC: **3714** Motor vehicle parts & accessories

(G-17198)
PROCESS SYSTEMS INC (HQ)
23633 Pinewood St (48091-3196)
PHONE..................................586 757-5711
Thomas Ruthman, *President*
Radu Paveluc, *Plant Mgr*
Paul Boles, *Sales Staff*
▲ **EMP:** 54

SALES (est): 9.4MM
SALES (corp-wide): 45.4MM **Privately Held**
WEB: www.psi4pumps.com
SIC: **2448** 3561 3564 5084 Wood pallets & skids; industrial pumps & parts; blowers & fans; pumps & pumping equipment; pumps & pumping equipment repair; fabricated plate work (boiler shop)
PA: Ruthman Pump And Engineering, Inc
    1212 Streng St
    Cincinnati OH 45223
    513 559-1901

(G-17199)
PRODUCTION HONING COMPANY INC
24101 Wahl St (48089-2057)
PHONE..................................586 757-1800
Nowell Conte, *President*
Helen D Conte, *Corp Secy*
Timothy McCarthy, *Opers Staff*
EMP: 4
SQ FT: 12,000
SALES (est): 500K **Privately Held**
WEB: www.productionhoning.com
SIC: **3599** Machine shop, jobbing & repair

(G-17200)
PROGRESSIVE METAL MFG CO (PA)
3100 E 10 Mile Rd (48091-3713)
PHONE..................................248 546-2827
Eric Borman, *President*
Julie Borman, *Chairman*
Lewis Buko, *Engineer*
Jonathon Frohlich, *Engineer*
Janet Six, *Marketing Staff*
EMP: 25 **EST:** 1962
SQ FT: 55,000
SALES: 22.8MM **Privately Held**
WEB: www.pmmco.com
SIC: **3537** Trucks, tractors, loaders, carriers & similar equipment

(G-17201)
PROMPT PATTERN INC
4175 E 10 Mile Rd (48091-1508)
PHONE..................................586 759-2030
Michael J Healy, *President*
EMP: 20
SALES (est): 2.9MM **Privately Held**
SIC: **3543** 3369 3366 3365 Industrial patterns; nonferrous foundries; copper foundries; aluminum foundries; malleable iron foundries

(G-17202)
PROMPT PLASTICS
5524 E 10 Mile Rd (48091-3899)
PHONE..................................586 307-8525
Greg Keoenig, *Owner*
EMP: 4
SALES (est): 333.9K **Privately Held**
SIC: **3089** Plastics products

(G-17203)
PROPER AROSPC & MACHINING LLC
13870 E 11 Mile Rd (48089-1471)
PHONE..................................586 779-8787
Mark A Rusch,
EMP: 6
SALES: 950K **Privately Held**
SIC: **3499** Fabricated metal products

(G-17204)
PROPER GROUP INTERNATIONAL INC
Also Called: Proper Polymers
14575 E 11 Mile Rd (48088-4861)
PHONE..................................586 552-5267
EMP: 175 **Privately Held**
SIC: **3089** Vulcanized fiber plates, sheets, rods or tubes
PA: Proper Group International, Inc.
    13870 E 11 Mile Rd
    Warren MI 48089

(G-17205)
PROPER GROUP INTERNATIONAL INC (PA)
Also Called: Proper Tooling
13870 E 11 Mile Rd (48089-1471)
PHONE..................................586 779-8787

GEOGRAPHIC SECTION

Warren - Macomb County (G-17233)

Geoff O'Brien, *President*
Mark Rusch, *CFO*
Thomas Bullard, *Manager*
Ronald Truett, *Maintence Staff*
▲ **EMP:** 6
SALES (est): 125MM **Privately Held**
SIC: 3089 Automotive parts, plastic

(G-17206)
PROPER POLYMERS - ANDERSON LLC
13870 E 11 Mile Rd (48089-1471)
PHONE................................586 408-9120
Mark A Rusch, *Mng Member*
EMP: 3
SALES (est): 97.8K **Privately Held**
SIC: 3089 Injection molding of plastics

(G-17207)
PROPER POLYMERS - WARREN LLC (PA)
Also Called: PME - Croswell
13870 E 11 Mile Rd (48089-1471)
PHONE................................586 552-5267
EMP: 27 **EST:** 2007
SALES (est): 12.3MM **Privately Held**
SIC: 3089 Air mattresses, plastic

(G-17208)
PROPER POLYMERS - WARREN LLC
14575 E 11 Mile Rd (48088-4861)
PHONE................................586 552-5267
Brian Szczepaniak, *Branch Mgr*
EMP: 27
SALES (corp-wide): 12.3MM **Privately Held**
SIC: 3089 Air mattresses, plastic
PA: Proper Polymers - Warren, Llc
13870 E 11 Mile Rd
Warren MI 48089
586 552-5267

(G-17209)
PROPER POLYMERS-PULASKI LLC
13870 E 11 Mile Rd (48089-1471)
PHONE................................931 371-3147
EMP: 51
SALES (corp-wide): 14.1MM **Privately Held**
SIC: 3089 Injection molding of plastics
PA: Proper Polymers-Pulaski, Llc
102 Magneti Marelli Dr
Pulaski TN 38478
931 371-3147

(G-17210)
PROTECTO HORSE EQUIPMENT INC
22722 Dequindre Rd (48091-2103)
P.O. Box 215, Clawson (48017-0215)
PHONE................................586 754-4820
Al G Terwilliger, *President*
Myra T Terwilliger, *Vice Pres*
▲ **EMP:** 5 **EST:** 1967
SQ FT: 7,000
SALES: 500K **Privately Held**
WEB: www.protectohorse.com
SIC: 3199 Saddles or parts

(G-17211)
PUNCHCRAFT MCHNING TOOLING LLC
Also Called: Warren Mfg Facility
30500 Ryan Rd (48092-1902)
PHONE................................586 573-4840
Doug Grimm, *Mng Member*
▲ **EMP:** 45
SQ FT: 25,000
SALES (est): 9.6MM
SALES (corp-wide): 7.2B **Publicly Held**
WEB: www.metaldyne.com
SIC: 5084 3544 Machine tools & accessories; special dies & tools
HQ: Metaldyne Powertrain Components, Inc.
1 Dauch Dr
Detroit MI 48211
313 758-2000

(G-17212)
QUANTUM DIGITAL VENTURES LLC
24680 Mound Rd (48091-2036)
PHONE................................248 292-5686
Nicole Walsh, *Marketing Staff*
Dirk Grizzle,
Jaime Merrywether,
Lee Skandalaris,
EMP: 20
SQ FT: 15,000
SALES (est): 3.5MM **Privately Held**
SIC: 2752 Promotional printing, lithographic

(G-17213)
R & M MACHINE INC
23895 Regency Park Dr (48089-2677)
PHONE................................586 754-8447
Randy Tunison, *President*
EMP: 18
SQ FT: 14,000
SALES (est): 3.2MM **Privately Held**
SIC: 3599 Machine shop, jobbing & repair

(G-17214)
R+R MFG/ENG INC
21448 Mullin Ave (48089-3083)
PHONE................................586 758-4420
Joseph Duguay, *President*
EMP: 5 **EST:** 1974
SQ FT: 8,000
SALES (est): 601K **Privately Held**
SIC: 3599 Machine shop, jobbing & repair

(G-17215)
RADAR MEXICAN INVESTMENTS LLC
27101 Groesbeck Hwy (48089-4162)
PHONE................................586 779-0300
Ramzi Hermiz, *CEO*
David Zmyslowski, *President*
Mark Zmyslowski, *Vice Pres*
EMP: 5
SQ FT: 75,000
SALES (est): 224.8K **Publicly Held**
SIC: 3469 3465 Metal stampings; automotive stampings
PA: Shiloh Industries, Inc.
880 Steel Dr
Valley City OH 44280

(G-17216)
RADAR TOOL & MANUFACTURING CO
23201 Blackstone Ave (48089-4209)
PHONE................................586 759-2800
Fred Deckert, *President*
Mark Deckert, *Vice Pres*
Paul Deckert, *Treasurer*
Karen Robinson, *Admin Sec*
EMP: 8 **EST:** 1945
SQ FT: 9,200
SALES (est): 370K **Privately Held**
SIC: 3544 Special dies & tools

(G-17217)
RAYOMAR ENTERPRISES INC
28600 Norwood Ave (48092-5631)
PHONE................................313 415-9102
Richard Rayos, *President*
Kevin Donnenwerth, *Vice Pres*
EMP: 3
SALES (est): 120K **Privately Held**
SIC: 3965 3429 Fasteners; metal fasteners

(G-17218)
REHMANN INDUSTRIES INC
23051 Roseberry Ave (48089-2214)
PHONE................................810 748-7793
Robert F Rehmann, *President*
▲ **EMP:** 15
SQ FT: 9,600
SALES (est): 1.5MM **Privately Held**
SIC: 3599 Machine shop, jobbing & repair

(G-17219)
REIF CARBIDE TOOL CO INC
11055 E 9 Mile Rd (48089-2454)
P.O. Box 862 (48090-0862)
PHONE................................586 754-1890
Fred John Reif, *President*
James Dennis, *Exec VP*
Vincent F Locicero, *Admin Sec*
EMP: 15
SQ FT: 10,000
SALES (est): 1.1MM **Privately Held**
WEB: www.reifcarbidetool.com
SIC: 3545 5084 Cutting tools for machine tools; tools & accessories for machine tools; industrial machinery & equipment

(G-17220)
RENS LLC
Also Called: Maxi-Grip
24871 Gibson Dr (48089-4323)
PHONE................................586 756-6777
Daniel Martin, *Principal*
Jack McCray, *Principal*
EMP: 14
SQ FT: 11,000
SALES (est): 2.5MM **Privately Held**
SIC: 3544 Jigs & fixtures

(G-17221)
RIZK NATIONAL INDUSTRIES INC
24422 Ryan Rd (48091-1654)
PHONE................................586 757-4700
George Rizk, *President*
EMP: 23
SQ FT: 30,000
SALES: 1MM **Privately Held**
SIC: 3612 3694 Autotransformers, electric (power transformers); battery charging generators, automobile & aircraft

(G-17222)
ROCAR PRECISION INC
31207 Stricker Dr (48088-7344)
PHONE................................586 226-2711
Roger Kunko, *President*
EMP: 4 **EST:** 1977
SALES (est): 601.4K **Privately Held**
WEB: www.rocarprecision.com
SIC: 3599 Machine shop, jobbing & repair

(G-17223)
ROGER ZATKOFF COMPANY
Also Called: Zatkoff Gasket Division
31773 Denton Dr (48092-4718)
PHONE................................586 264-3593
Art Stietz, *Manager*
EMP: 27
SALES (corp-wide): 126.3MM **Privately Held**
WEB: www.zatkoff.com
SIC: 3053 Gaskets & sealing devices
PA: Roger Zatkoff Company
23230 Industrial Park Dr
Farmington Hills MI 48335
248 478-2400

(G-17224)
ROYAL CONTAINER SERVICES INC (PA)
22510 Hoover Rd (48089-2575)
PHONE................................586 775-7600
Claudette Schnoblen, *President*
Brandi Brown, *Vice Pres*
EMP: 2
SALES (est): 1.1MM **Privately Held**
SIC: 3089 Garbage containers, plastic

(G-17225)
ROYAL FLEX-N-GATE OAK LLC
5663 E 9 Mile Rd (48091-2562)
PHONE................................248 549-3800
Perry Silvaggi, *General Mgr*
Malcolm Koresh, *Controller*
Kevin Hamilton, *Mng Member*
Timothy Graham,
James Zsebok,
▲ **EMP:** 350
SQ FT: 250,000
SALES (est): 46.6MM
SALES (corp-wide): 3.3B **Privately Held**
WEB: www.chromecraft.com
SIC: 3469 3465 Metal stampings; body parts, automobile: stamped metal
PA: Flex-N-Gate Llc
1306 E University Ave
Urbana IL 61802
217 384-6600

(G-17226)
ROYCE CORPORATION
23042 Sherwood Ave (48091-2024)
PHONE................................586 758-1500
Glen B Brown, *President*
EMP: 5
SQ FT: 8,000
SALES (est): 719.6K **Privately Held**
SIC: 3714 Motor vehicle parts & accessories

(G-17227)
SALERNO TOOL WORKS INC
21034 Ryan Rd (48091-2740)
PHONE................................586 755-5000
Ramo A Salerno Sr, *President*
Ramo A Salerno Jr, *Vice Pres*
Rhonda Salerno, *Admin Sec*
EMP: 8 **EST:** 1964
SQ FT: 7,000
SALES (est): 740K **Privately Held**
SIC: 3545 Precision tools, machinists'

(G-17228)
SAN MARINO IRON COMPANY
21401 Hoover Rd (48089-3161)
PHONE................................313 526-9255
Vincenzo Ciavaglia, *Owner*
▼ **EMP:** 3 **EST:** 1972
SQ FT: 3,000
SALES (est): 659.6K **Privately Held**
WEB: www.sanmarinoiron.com
SIC: 3446 Railings, prefabricated metal

(G-17229)
SAS GLOBAL CORPORATION (PA)
21601 Mullin Ave (48089-3008)
PHONE................................248 414-4470
Robert Wark, *President*
Tim Foley, *Vice Pres*
Thomas Mahfet, *Vice Pres*
Phil Lizak, *Plant Mgr*
Jim Gillis, *Project Mgr*
◆ **EMP:** 110
SQ FT: 185,000
SALES (est): 45.1MM **Privately Held**
WEB: www.cladtec.com
SIC: 3441 3479 5051 Fabricated structural metal; coating of metals & formed products; metals service centers & offices; steel

(G-17230)
SAS GLOBAL CORPORATION
Also Called: Sure Alloy Steel
21601 Mullin Ave (48089-3008)
PHONE................................248 414-4470
Brian Henkel, *Vice Pres*
Chuck Stage, *Purchasing*
Eric Cheever, *Project Engr*
Rob Wark, *Sales Staff*
EMP: 35
SALES (corp-wide): 45.1MM **Privately Held**
WEB: www.cladtec.com
SIC: 5051 3548 3441 Steel; welding & cutting apparatus & accessories; fabricated structural metal
PA: Sas Global Corporation
21601 Mullin Ave
Warren MI 48089
248 414-4470

(G-17231)
SAWING LOGZ LLC
28634 Milton Ave (48092-2368)
PHONE................................586 883-5649
Jeff Shelby, *President*
EMP: 9
SALES (est): 752.9K **Privately Held**
SIC: 2421 Sawmills & planing mills, general

(G-17232)
SCHIMMELMANNS TOOL
32408 Dequindre Rd (48092-1005)
PHONE................................586 795-0538
James Schimmelmanns, *Owner*
EMP: 3
SALES (est): 246.6K **Privately Held**
SIC: 3423 Hand & edge tools

(G-17233)
SCHULTZ BINDERY INC
14495 E 8 Mile Rd (48089-3433)
PHONE................................586 771-0777
Thomas Schultz, *President*
EMP: 17
SQ FT: 23,000

Warren - Macomb County (G-17234)

SALES (est): 1.9MM **Privately Held**
SIC: 2789 2675 Pamphlets, binding; die-cut paper & board

(G-17234)
SCHWARTZ MACHINE CO
4441 E 8 Mile Rd (48091-2798)
PHONE..............................586 756-2300
Robert C Schwartz, *Ch of Bd*
Kenneth Sabo, *President*
James C Harm, *Admin Sec*
EMP: 45 EST: 1951
SQ FT: 36,000
SALES (est): 6.8MM **Privately Held**
WEB: www.schwartzmachine.com
SIC: 3599 Machine shop, jobbing & repair

(G-17235)
SCREENTEK IMAGING
12934 E 10 Mile Rd (48089-2045)
PHONE..............................586 759-4850
Dominic Ciaravino, *Owner*
EMP: 3
SALES (est): 150K **Privately Held**
SIC: 2759 Screen printing

(G-17236)
SD OIL ENTERPRISES INC
28851 Hoover Rd (48093-4102)
PHONE..............................248 688-1419
Vikas Tandan, *Principal*
EMP: 3
SALES (est): 90.1K **Privately Held**
SIC: 1311 Crude petroleum & natural gas

(G-17237)
SELECT DISTRIBUTORS LLC
2324 Morrissey Ave (48091-3271)
PHONE..............................586 510-4647
EMP: 11
SQ FT: 1,600
SALES (est): 907.2K **Privately Held**
SIC: 2086 3999 5074 Mfg Soft Drinks Mfg Misc Products Whol Plumbing Equip/Supp

(G-17238)
SHEPTIME MUSIC
27035 Lorraine Ave (48093-4443)
PHONE..............................586 806-9058
Sean Shepard, *Owner*
EMP: 12
SALES (est): 459.3K **Privately Held**
SIC: 2731 7389 Book music: publishing & printing;

(G-17239)
SHILOH MANUFACTURING LLC
Also Called: Plant 27
27101 Groesbeck Hwy (48089-4162)
PHONE..............................586 779-0300
Jim Dakims, *Manager*
EMP: 100 **Publicly Held**
WEB: www.radarind.com
SIC: 3469 3465 Metal stampings; automotive stampings
HQ: Shiloh Manufacturing, Llc
880 Steel Dr
Valley City OH 44280
330 558-2693

(G-17240)
SKYBLADE FAN COMPANY
24501 Hoover Rd (48089-1930)
PHONE..............................586 806-5107
Jonathon Jones, *VP Opers*
EMP: 5 EST: 2012
SALES (est): 376.3K **Privately Held**
SIC: 3564 Blowing fans: industrial or commercial; air cleaning systems: exhaust fans: industrial or commercial

(G-17241)
SMO INTERNATIONAL INC
Also Called: Bigdaddybeauty.com
31745 Mound Rd (48092-1611)
PHONE..............................248 275-1091
Dennis Smolinski, *President*
▲ EMP: 13
SALES: 420K **Privately Held**
SIC: 2844 5122 Toilet preparations; drugs & drug proprietaries

(G-17242)
SMS MODERN HARD CHROME LLC
Also Called: SMS-Mhc
12880 E 9 Mile Rd (48089-2664)
PHONE..............................586 445-0330
Charles Nicholl, *President*
Arthur Nicholl, *Vice Pres*
Art Nicholl, *VP Opers*
Joanne Gallinagh, *Purch Mgr*
Samuel R Nicholl,
▲ EMP: 80 EST: 1939
SQ FT: 50,000
SALES (est): 10.5MM
SALES (corp-wide): 144.1K **Privately Held**
SIC: 3471 3599 Electroplating of metals or formed products; plating of metals or formed products; grinding castings for the trade
HQ: Sms Group Gmbh
Eduard-Schloemann-Str. 4
Dusseldorf 40237
211 881-0

(G-17243)
SMS TECHNICAL SERVICES
12880 E 9 Mile Rd (48089-2664)
PHONE..............................586 445-0330
Doug Dunworth, *Administration*
EMP: 8
SALES (est): 190.3K **Privately Held**
SIC: 3569 General industrial machinery

(G-17244)
SONUS ENGINEERED SOLUTIONS LLC
23031 Sherwood Ave (48091-2044)
PHONE..............................586 427-3838
Tim Droege, *President*
Edin Jakupovic, *Mfg Staff*
Richard Krause, *Mfg Staff*
Rachael Carmichael, *Buyer*
Kevin Jordan, *CFO*
◆ EMP: 110
SQ FT: 120,000
SALES (est): 24.2MM **Privately Held**
WEB: www.de.wocogroup.com
SIC: 3089 Plastic containers, except foam

(G-17245)
SPECILTY VHCL ACQUISITION CORP
Also Called: ASC
6115 E 13 Mile Rd (48092-2050)
PHONE..............................586 446-4701
Joe Bione, *CEO*
Heinz Prechter, *Principal*
Marcus Shelley, *Controller*
▲ EMP: 40
SQ FT: 38,000
SALES (est): 3.3MM
SALES (corp-wide): 121.4MM **Privately Held**
SIC: 8748 2394 Systems analysis or design; convertible tops, canvas or boat: from purchased materials
PA: Hancock Park Associates Ii, L.P.
10350 Santa Monica Blvd # 295
Los Angeles CA 90025
310 228-6900

(G-17246)
SPENCE INDUSTRIES INC
23888 Dequindre Rd (48091-1823)
PHONE..............................586 758-3800
Charles Dillon, *President*
EMP: 4
SQ FT: 2,500
SALES (est): 160K **Privately Held**
WEB: www.jo-plug.com
SIC: 3545 Gauges (machine tool accessories)

(G-17247)
SPINA ELECTRIC COMPANY
26801 Groesbeck Hwy (48089-1583)
PHONE..............................586 771-8080
John Spina, *President*
Paul Spina, *President*
Albert Spina, *Chairman*
Timothy Spina, *Treasurer*
Rick Gudenau, *Sales Mgr*
EMP: 35 EST: 1948
SQ FT: 29,000
SALES (est): 30.2MM **Privately Held**
WEB: www.spinaelectric.com
SIC: 5063 7694 7629 Motors, electric; electric motor repair; electrical repair shops

(G-17248)
SPINA WIND LLC
26801 Groesbeck Hwy (48089-4160)
PHONE..............................586 771-8080
John Spina,
Timothy Spina,
EMP: 5
SALES (est): 950K **Privately Held**
SIC: 3621 Windmills, electric generating

(G-17249)
SPM INDUSTRIES INC
2455 E 10 Mile Rd (48091-3704)
PHONE..............................586 758-1100
Frank C Bellisario, *President*
Ronald A Di Mambro, *Vice Pres*
EMP: 100 EST: 1972
SQ FT: 20,000
SALES (est): 13.2MM **Privately Held**
WEB: www.spmindustries.com
SIC: 3599 Machine shop, jobbing & repair

(G-17250)
SPRINGER PUBLISHING CO INC (PA)
Also Called: New Center News
31201 Chicago Rd S A101 (48093-5500)
PHONE..............................586 939-6800
William L Springer IL, *President*
Mary Gatsch, *Publisher*
Lenita Parillon, *Accountant*
Shaun Duffy, *Sales Staff*
EMP: 18 EST: 1933
SQ FT: 2,400
SALES (est): 1.8MM **Privately Held**
SIC: 2711 Newspapers: publishing only, not printed on site

(G-17251)
SPX CORPORATION
Miller Special Tool Division
28635 Mound Rd (48092-5509)
PHONE..............................586 574-2332
Mr Tanvir Arfi, *President*
EMP: 200
SALES (corp-wide): 1.5B **Publicly Held**
WEB: www.spx.com
SIC: 3443 Cooling towers, metal plate
PA: Spx Corporation
13320a Balntyn Corp Pl
Charlotte NC 28277
980 474-3700

(G-17252)
SPX CORPORATION
SPX Service Solutions
28635 Mines Rd (48092)
PHONE..............................586 574-2332
Cynthia Broich, *Purch Mgr*
EMP: 200
SALES (corp-wide): 1.5B **Publicly Held**
WEB: www.spx.com
SIC: 3443 Fabricated plate work (boiler shop)
PA: Spx Corporation
13320a Balntyn Corp Pl
Charlotte NC 28277
980 474-3700

(G-17253)
STANDARD PRINTING OF WARREN
13647 E 10 Mile Rd (48089-4799)
PHONE..............................586 771-3770
William Ventimiglia Jr, *President*
EMP: 5
SQ FT: 6,100
SALES (est): 470K **Privately Held**
SIC: 2752 2759 Commercial printing, offset; letterpress printing

(G-17254)
STATE BUILDING PRODUCT INC
21751 Schmeman Ave (48089-3219)
PHONE..............................586 772-8878
Andrew Stark, *CEO*
Troy Frank, *President*
Peter Stark, *President*
Eric Griswold, *CFO*
Jodi Kurzyniec, *Controller*
EMP: 45
SQ FT: 144,500
SALES: 21MM **Privately Held**
WEB: www.statebp.com
SIC: 3444 Studs & joists, sheet metal

(G-17255)
STEEL MILL COMPONENTS INC
22522 Hoover Rd (48089-2575)
PHONE..............................586 920-2595
Robert Appleyard, *Manager*
EMP: 16
SALES (est): 2MM **Privately Held**
SIC: 3312 Blast furnaces & steel mills
PA: Steel Mill Components, Inc.
17000 Ecorse Rd
Allen Park MI 48101

(G-17256)
STEEL PROCESSING COMPANY INC
23605 Groesbeck Hwy (48089-4254)
PHONE..............................586 772-3310
Robert O Rink, *General Mgr*
Christopher P Rink, *Vice Pres*
EMP: 15
SQ FT: 35,000
SALES (est): 2.5MM **Privately Held**
SIC: 3398 Tempering of metal

(G-17257)
SUNDANCE BEVERAGES INC
Also Called: Sundance Beverage Company
6600 E 9 Mile Rd (48091-2673)
PHONE..............................586 755-9470
Nick A Caporella, *Ch of Bd*
Eric Hellman, *Plant Mgr*
Marc Llewellyn, *Production*
Douglas Wells, *Production*
Jon Skiba, *Administration*
EMP: 41
SALES (est): 10.6MM
SALES (corp-wide): 1B **Publicly Held**
WEB: www.natbev.com
SIC: 2086 Fruit drinks (less than 100% juice): packaged in cans, etc.
PA: National Beverage Corp.
8100 Sw 10th St Ste 4000
Plantation FL 33324
954 581-0922

(G-17258)
SUPER STEEL TREATING INC
6227 Rinke Ave (48091-2070)
PHONE..............................586 755-9140
Terence D Farrar, *President*
Don Huldin, *Principal*
Charles H Farrar, *Vice Pres*
Lillie Ball, *Purch Agent*
Maureen Farrar, *Treasurer*
▲ EMP: 65
SQ FT: 300,000
SALES (est): 19.1MM **Privately Held**
WEB: www.supersteeltreating.com
SIC: 3398 Annealing of metal

(G-17259)
SYNCREONUS INC
12350 E 9 Mile Rd (48089-2647)
PHONE..............................586 754-4100
Brian Enright, *Branch Mgr*
EMP: 5 **Privately Held**
SIC: 3446 Architectural metalwork
HQ: Syncreon.Us Inc.
2851 High Meadow Cir # 250
Auburn Hills MI 48326
248 377-4700

(G-17260)
TADEY FRANK R RADIAN TOOL CO
23823 Blackstone Ave (48089-4218)
PHONE..............................586 754-7422
Kris Tadey, *CEO*
Ann Tadey, *Corp Secy*
EMP: 4
SQ FT: 3,200
SALES (est): 448.9K **Privately Held**
SIC: 3544 Special dies, tools, jigs & fixtures

(G-17261)
TAMBRA INVESTMENTS INC
Also Called: Real Time Diagnostics
23247 Pinewood St (48091-4754)
PHONE..............................866 662-7897

GEOGRAPHIC SECTION

Warren - Macomb County (G-17290)

Michael D Evans, *CEO*
Brent Devooght, *CFO*
Nicole Simpson, *Director*
EMP: 3
SALES (est): 511.7K **Privately Held**
SIC: 3841 Surgical instruments & apparatus

(G-17262)
TANK TRUCK SERVICE & SALES INC (PA)
25150 Dequindre Rd (48091-1384)
PHONE 586 757-6500
James H Lawler, *President*
David M Lawler, *Vice Pres*
Karen Lawler, *Treasurer*
Jeff Lawer, *Manager*
EMP: 32
SQ FT: 18,000
SALES (est): 13.2MM **Privately Held**
SIC: 3541 3795 Machine tool replacement & repair parts, metal cutting types; tanks & tank components

(G-17263)
TARPON AUTOMATION & DESIGN CO
26692 Groesbeck Hwy (48089-1591)
PHONE 586 774-8020
Robert Legeret, *President*
Robert Legeret Jr, *Sales Mgr*
Vanderdonck Scott, *Director*
EMP: 50
SQ FT: 31,000
SALES: 10MM **Privately Held**
WEB: www.tarponautomation.com
SIC: 3549 Assembly machines, including robotic

(G-17264)
TECHNICAL ROTARY SERVICES INC
14020 Hovey Ave (48089-1457)
PHONE 586 772-6755
Craig Barker, *President*
EMP: 7
SQ FT: 6,000
SALES: 1MM **Privately Held**
WEB: www.precisionrotarytables.com
SIC: 3545 Rotary tables

(G-17265)
TEXAS METAL INDUSTRIES INC
2305 E 9 Mile Rd (48091-2162)
PHONE 586 261-0090
Cary Carter, *President*
▼ **EMP:** 3
SQ FT: 10,000
SALES: 100K **Privately Held**
SIC: 7692 Welding repair

(G-17266)
TONY S DIE MACHINE COMPANY
24358 Groesbeck Hwy (48089-4718)
PHONE 586 773-7379
Douglas Wolfbauer, *Partner*
Doug Wolfbauer, *Partner*
Robert Wolfbauer, *Partner*
Dave Kohler, *Plant Mgr*
EMP: 11
SQ FT: 44,000
SALES (est): 1.1MM **Privately Held**
SIC: 3544 Industrial molds; jigs & fixtures

(G-17267)
TRI COUNTY PRECISION GRINDING
Also Called: Tri-County Precision Grinding
21960 Schmeman Ave (48089-3281)
PHONE 586 776-6600
Lee Roy Hall, *President*
Ellen L Hall, *Treasurer*
EMP: 15
SQ FT: 17,300
SALES (est): 2.5MM **Privately Held**
SIC: 3599 Machine shop, jobbing & repair

(G-17268)
TRI-STATE FLAME HARDENING CO
27150 Gloede Dr (48088-6031)
PHONE 586 776-0035
Larry May, *President*
EMP: 3 **EST:** 1976
SQ FT: 6,200
SALES (est): 581.6K **Privately Held**
WEB: www.tristateflame.com
SIC: 3398 Metal heat treating

(G-17269)
TROY LASER & FAB LLC
23720 Dequindre Rd (48091-3236)
PHONE 586 510-4570
Sheila Brooks, *Office Mgr*
Nicodim Haragos,
Jason Gabor,
EMP: 3 **EST:** 2008
SQ FT: 2,000
SALES: 450K **Privately Held**
SIC: 3699 Laser welding, drilling & cutting equipment

(G-17270)
TRUEMNER ENTERPRISES INC
25418 Ryan Rd (48091-1326)
PHONE 586 756-6470
Dale Truemner, *President*
Mary Truemner, *Vice Pres*
EMP: 7 **EST:** 1900
SQ FT: 5,000
SALES (est): 450K **Privately Held**
SIC: 3566 Gears, power transmission, except automotive; reduction gears & gear units for turbines, except automotive

(G-17271)
TSS INC
Also Called: TSS
21000 Hoover Rd (48089-3153)
PHONE 586 427-0070
Ismael Mosa Sasha, *President*
Abe Basha, *Vice Pres*
Mike Mustedanagic, *Mfg Staff*
Bobby Jones, *Art Dir*
Ryan Caldwell, *Graphic Designe*
▲ **EMP:** 20
SQ FT: 2,400
SALES (est): 4.1MM **Privately Held**
SIC: 3993 Signs, not made in custom sign painting shops; electric signs

(G-17272)
TUBE-CO INC
23094 Schoenherr Rd (48089-2668)
PHONE 586 775-0244
Melissa Shevela, *President*
EMP: 7 **EST:** 1962
SQ FT: 15,000
SALES (est): 1.8MM **Privately Held**
SIC: 3498 Tube fabricating (contract bending & shaping)

(G-17273)
UNITED LIGHTING STANDARDS INC (PA)
23171 Groesbeck Hwy (48089-6002)
PHONE 586 774-5650
Bob Wesch, *COO*
Cheryl Kowalski, *Warehouse Mgr*
Chris Ewert, *Manager*
Shelby Ross, *Personnel Assit*
Christopher McKenna,
EMP: 66
SQ FT: 57,500
SALES (est): 11.6MM **Privately Held**
WEB: www.polemfg.com
SIC: 3446 Architectural metalwork

(G-17274)
UNITED MFG NETWRK INC
14500 E 11 Mile Rd (48089-1557)
PHONE 586 321-7887
Gerald Sitek,
EMP: 4 **EST:** 2013
SALES (est): 307.3K **Privately Held**
SIC: 3541 3999 Grinding machines, metalworking; custom pulverizing & grinding of plastic materials

(G-17275)
US BORING INC
24895 Mound Rd Ste D (48091-5398)
PHONE 586 756-7511
EMP: 4
SQ FT: 5,000
SALES (est): 370K **Privately Held**
SIC: 3544 Mfg Dies/Tools/Jigs/Fixtures

(G-17276)
VAC-MET INC
7236 Murthum Ave (48092-1296)
PHONE 586 264-8100
Robert F Gunow Jr, *President*
EMP: 20
SQ FT: 14,000
SALES (est): 4.7MM **Privately Held**
WEB: www.vac-met.com
SIC: 3398 Brazing (hardening) of metal

(G-17277)
VAN DYKE FUELL
21715 Van Dyke Ave (48089-2321)
PHONE 586 758-0120
Mike Sweiss, *Manager*
EMP: 3
SALES (est): 327.4K **Privately Held**
SIC: 2869 Fuels

(G-17278)
VARIABLE MACHINING & TOOL INC
21443 Groesbeck Hwy (48089-3136)
PHONE 586 778-8803
Michael Bonneau, *President*
Cindy Bonneau, *Treasurer*
EMP: 3
SALES (est): 424.7K **Privately Held**
SIC: 3541 Grinding machines, metalworking

(G-17279)
VARIETY FOODS INC (PA)
7001 Chicago Rd (48092-1615)
PHONE 586 268-4900
James Champane Jr, *CEO*
Dean Champane, *President*
Chris Champane, *Vice Pres*
George Champane, *Treasurer*
EMP: 27 **EST:** 1928
SQ FT: 55,000
SALES (est): 5.4MM **Privately Held**
SIC: 2068 2099 2096 Salted & roasted nuts & seeds; food preparations; potato chips & other potato-based snacks

(G-17280)
VEET AXELSON LIBERTY INDUSTRY
14322 E 9 Mile Rd (48089-5032)
PHONE 586 776-3000
Robert Veet, *Owner*
EMP: 10
SALES (est): 621.2K **Privately Held**
SIC: 3599 Machine shop, jobbing & repair

(G-17281)
VEET INDUSTRIES INC
Also Called: Axelson-Veet-Liberty Inds
14322 E 9 Mile Rd (48089-5032)
PHONE 586 776-3000
Robert C Veit, *President*
EMP: 10 **EST:** 1921
SQ FT: 240,000
SALES (est): 1.1MM **Privately Held**
SIC: 3714 3549 3728 Motor vehicle parts & accessories; metalworking machinery; aircraft parts & equipment

(G-17282)
VENTRA GREENWICH HOLDINGS CORP
Also Called: Ventra Greenwich Tooling Co
5663 E 9 Mile Rd (48091-2562)
PHONE 586 759-8900
Tom Orr, *Director*
EMP: 4
SALES (est): 245.2K **Privately Held**
SIC: 3541 Machine tools, metal cutting type

(G-17283)
VERTICAL TECHNOLOGIES LLC
12901 Stephens Rd (48089-4333)
PHONE 586 619-0141
Bruce Burns, *Mfg Staff*
Tim McShane, *Sales Mgr*
Brian Burns,
EMP: 26
SQ FT: 48,000
SALES (est): 5.7MM **Privately Held**
WEB: www.verticaltechnologies.org
SIC: 3544 Special dies & tools

(G-17284)
VIROTECH BIOMATERIALS INC
8260 Dartmouth Dr (48093-2815)
PHONE 313 421-1648
WEI Song, *President*
EMP: 5
SALES (est): 304K **Privately Held**
SIC: 3841 7389 Medical instruments & equipment, blood & bone work;

(G-17285)
WARREN ABRASIVES INC
25800 Groesbeck Hwy (48089-4143)
P.O. Box 530, Roseville (48066-0530)
PHONE 586 772-0002
EMP: 14
SQ FT: 12,000
SALES: 840K **Privately Held**
SIC: 3291 Manufacturor Of Abrasive Grinding Wheels

(G-17286)
WARREN CHASSIX
23300 Blackstone Ave (48089-4206)
PHONE 248 728-8700
Warren Chassix, *Principal*
Julien Brasseur, *Engineer*
EMP: 8
SALES (est): 1.9MM **Privately Held**
SIC: 3714 Motor vehicle parts & accessories

(G-17287)
WARREN INDUSTRIAL WELDING CO (PA)
24275 Hoover Rd (48089-1973)
PHONE 586 756-0230
Gregory Lee, *President*
Lester Hall, *Assistant VP*
EMP: 18
SQ FT: 10,000
SALES (est): 2MM **Privately Held**
WEB: www.warrenindustrial.com
SIC: 7692 Welding repair

(G-17288)
WARREN SCREW PRODUCTS INC
13201 Stephens Rd (48089-4340)
PHONE 586 757-1280
Chris Kaspari, *CEO*
Carl Kaspari III, *President*
Steven G Kaspari, *Vice Pres*
Sue Ann Wessel, *Controller*
EMP: 110 **EST:** 1957
SQ FT: 140,000
SALES (est): 31.3MM **Privately Held**
SIC: 3451 3714 Screw machine products; motor vehicle parts & accessories

(G-17289)
WARRIOR SPORTS INC (DH)
Also Called: Brine
32125 Hollingsworth Ave (48092-3804)
PHONE 800 968-7845
David K Morrow, *President*
Grant Smith, *Mfg Staff*
Kevin Klucka, *Senior Buyer*
Constantino Velazquez, *Engineer*
Fredrick Sohm, *CFO*
▲ **EMP:** 96
SQ FT: 120,000
SALES (est): 46.7MM
SALES (corp-wide): 3.2B **Privately Held**
SIC: 3949 3149 Hockey equipment & supplies, general; lacrosse equipment & supplies, general; athletic shoes, except rubber or plastic
HQ: New Balance Athletics, Inc.
100 Guest St Fl 5
Boston MA 02135
617 783-4000

(G-17290)
WELDALOY PRODUCTS COMPANY
24011 Hoover Rd (48089-1931)
PHONE 586 758-5550
Jim Smietana, *CEO*
Richard E Warren, *Chairman*
Michelle McCullough, *Vice Pres*
Dayakara Perubandi, *Vice Pres*
David Raska, *Vice Pres*
▲ **EMP:** 58 **EST:** 1946
SQ FT: 33,000

Warren - Macomb County (G-17291)

GEOGRAPHIC SECTION

SALES (est): 18.4MM **Privately Held**
WEB: www.weldaloy.com
SIC: 3449 3463 Miscellaneous metalwork; nonferrous forgings

(G-17291)
WELDMET INDUSTRIES INC
21799 Schmeman Ave (48089-3219)
PHONE..................586 773-0533
Andrew Stark, *President*
EMP: 5
SQ FT: 9,000
SALES: 1MM **Privately Held**
SIC: 3544 Special dies, tools, jigs & fixtures

(G-17292)
WELFORM ELECTRODES INC
2147 Kenney Ave (48091-1379)
PHONE..................586 755-1184
Charles S Beach, *President*
C Edward Slade, *Vice Pres*
EMP: 60
SQ FT: 12,700
SALES (est): 11.9MM **Privately Held**
WEB: www.welform.com
SIC: 3699 3823 3548 Electrical welding equipment; industrial instrmnts msrmnt display/control process variable; welding apparatus

(G-17293)
WICO METAL PRODUCTS COMPANY (PA)
23500 Sherwood Ave (48091-5363)
PHONE..................586 755-9600
Richard A Brodie, *President*
Mike Bennett, *Exec VP*
Mike Piatt, *Vice Pres*
Derek Burkhart, *Plant Mgr*
Dennis Vennard, *Plant Mgr*
▲ EMP: 150
SQ FT: 100,000
SALES (est): 42.8MM **Privately Held**
WEB: www.wicometal.com
SIC: 3465 3469 3452 3429 Automotive stampings; metal stampings; bolts, nuts, rivets & washers; manufactured hardware (general)

(G-17294)
WITHERS CORPORATION
23801 Mound Rd (48091-5319)
PHONE..................586 758-2750
Kathleen M Withers, *President*
Mike Withers, *Vice Pres*
Brian Withers, *Treasurer*
EMP: 20
SQ FT: 22,000
SALES (est): 3MM **Privately Held**
SIC: 3544 Special dies & tools

(G-17295)
WOCHEN-POST
Also Called: German/American Newspaper Age
12200 E 13 Mile Rd # 140 (48093-3093)
PHONE..................248 641-9944
Knuth Beth, *Owner*
EMP: 20
SALES (est): 547.2K **Privately Held**
SIC: 2711 Newspapers, publishing & printing

(G-17296)
WOLVERINE DIE CAST LTD PTNSHP
22550 Nagel St (48089-3755)
PHONE..................586 757-1900
Michael Karadimas, *Partner*
William Selecman, *Partner*
EMP: 40
SQ FT: 22,000
SALES: 5MM **Privately Held**
WEB: www.wolverinediecast.com
SIC: 3363 3364 3365 Aluminum die-castings; zinc & zinc-base alloy die-castings; aluminum foundries

(G-17297)
WORKBLADES INC
21535 Groesbeck Hwy (48089-4921)
PHONE..................586 778-0060
Edward P Bard, *President*
Edward P Bard Jr, *Vice Pres*
EMP: 22

SQ FT: 21,000
SALES (est): 4.1MM **Privately Held**
WEB: www.workbladesinc.com
SIC: 3545 3425 Cutting tools for machine tools; saw blades & handsaws

(G-17298)
WRIGHT & FILIPPIS INC
13384 E 11 Mile Rd (48089-1367)
PHONE..................586 756-4020
Les Van Kuren, *Manager*
Les Kuren, *Manager*
EMP: 17
SALES (corp-wide): 51.4MM **Privately Held**
WEB: www.firsttoserve.com
SIC: 3842 5999 7352 Surgical appliances & supplies; convalescent equipment & supplies; medical equipment rental
PA: Wright & Filippis, Inc.
2845 Crooks Rd
Rochester Hills MI 48309
248 829-8292

(G-17299)
WSP MANAGEMENT LLC
23600 Schoenherr Rd (48089-4272)
PHONE..................586 447-2750
Gregory Depolo, *President*
EMP: 3
SALES (est): 268.1K **Privately Held**
SIC: 3451 Screw machine products

(G-17300)
XC LLC
24060 Hoover Rd (48089-1942)
PHONE..................586 755-1660
Chain S Sandhu,
EMP: 25
SQ FT: 110,000
SALES (est): 3.1MM **Privately Held**
WEB: www.comtrex-inc.com
SIC: 2821 Molding compounds, plastics

(G-17301)
XMCO INC
Also Called: KONIAG DEVELOPMENT COMPANY LLC
5501 Entp Ct Ste 400 (48092)
PHONE..................586 558-8510
Linda Czajka, *President*
Ann Lee, *Publisher*
Billy Gragg, *General Mgr*
Neva Carter, *Editor*
Thomas Panamaroff, *Chairman*
EMP: 58
SALES: 11.1MM
SALES (corp-wide): 323.8MM **Privately Held**
WEB: www.xmcoinc.com
SIC: 2731 Book publishing
HQ: Koniag Government Services, Llc
3800 Centerpoint Dr # 502
Anchorage AK 99503
907 561-2668

Washington
Macomb County

(G-17302)
ARTFUL SCRAPBOOKING & RUBBER
7220 Smale St (48094-2750)
PHONE..................586 651-1577
Pam Planitz, *Owner*
EMP: 4
SALES (est): 245.8K **Privately Held**
SIC: 2782 Scrapbooks

(G-17303)
ENGINEERED CONTROL SYSTEMS INC
Also Called: E C S
12700 31 Mile Rd (48095-1418)
PHONE..................509 483-6215
Charles Veniez, *President*
Joe Awad, *Vice Pres*
Steven Eisner, *Vice Pres*
Kurt Hans, *Vice Pres*
John Pachman, *Project Engr*
EMP: 30

SALES (est): 6.4MM
SALES (corp-wide): 137.1MM **Privately Held**
WEB: www.ecs-systems.com
SIC: 3669 8711 Burglar alarm apparatus, electric; fire alarm apparatus, electric; engineering services
PA: Cornerstone Detention Products, Inc.
14000 Al Highway 20
Madison AL 35756
256 355-2396

(G-17304)
GREEN AGE PRODUCTS & SVCS LLC
Also Called: Green Age Organics
64155 Van Dyke Rd Ste 238 (48095-2580)
PHONE..................586 207-5724
Harold W Parslow Jr,
EMP: 13
SQ FT: 12,500
SALES (est): 2.3MM **Privately Held**
WEB: www.greenageproducts.com
SIC: 5084 3599 Industrial machinery & equipment; custom machinery

(G-17305)
INNOVATIVE MOLD INC
Also Called: I M I
12500 31 Mile Rd (48095-1466)
PHONE..................586 752-2996
George Kasper, *President*
Dave Kasper, *Vice Pres*
Natalie Gaval, *Admin Sec*
Kimberly Podlesney, *Administration*
EMP: 22
SQ FT: 9,500
SALES (est): 4.7MM **Privately Held**
WEB: www.innovativemoldinc.com
SIC: 3544 Forms (molds), for foundry & plastics working machinery; industrial molds

(G-17306)
LOW COST SURCING SOLUTIONS LLC
Also Called: Lcss Worldwide
57253 Willow Way Ct (48094-4220)
P.O. Box 80672, Rochester (48308-0672)
PHONE..................248 535-7721
Douglas Stahl, *Mng Member*
▲ EMP: 4
SQ FT: 15,000
SALES (est): 283.4K **Privately Held**
SIC: 3469 3199 Metal stampings; harness or harness parts

(G-17307)
MARCEAU ENTERPRISES INC
Also Called: Puroclean Restoration Services
11517 Laurel Woods Dr (48094-3764)
PHONE..................586 697-8100
EMP: 3
SALES (est): 119.9K **Privately Held**
SIC: 7342 2273 Disinfecting services; carpets & rugs

(G-17308)
NORCROSS VISCOSITY CONTROLS
12427 31 Mile Rd (48095-1419)
PHONE..................586 336-0700
EMP: 3
SALES (est): 207.8K **Privately Held**
SIC: 3823 Industrial instrmnts msrmnt display/control process variable

(G-17309)
PILGRIM PRINTING
64007 Van Dyke Rd Ste 1 (48095-2854)
PHONE..................586 752-9664
Tom Hoffmann, *President*
EMP: 3
SALES (est): 240K **Privately Held**
SIC: 2759 Commercial printing

(G-17310)
POTTERYLAND INC
7045 Emerson (48094-2719)
PHONE..................586 781-4425
Gary Adam, *President*
Colleen M Adam, *Treasurer*
EMP: 4 EST: 1956
SQ FT: 500

SALES: 320K **Privately Held**
WEB: www.potteryland-online.com
SIC: 3999 Lawn ornaments

(G-17311)
STOP & GO TRANSPORTATION LLC
13425 Amberglen Dr (48094-3152)
PHONE..................313 346-7114
EMP: 3
SALES (est): 103.3K **Privately Held**
SIC: 2911 Petroleum refining

(G-17312)
T & C TOOL & SALES INC
60950 Van Dyke Rd (48094-3902)
PHONE..................586 677-8390
Thomas Beard, *President*
EMP: 10
SQ FT: 6,000
SALES (est): 1.6MM **Privately Held**
SIC: 3544 Special dies & tools; jigs & fixtures

(G-17313)
VERELLEN ORCHARDS
Also Called: Verellen Orchards & Cider Mill
63260 Van Dyke Rd (48095-2569)
PHONE..................586 752-2989
William Verellen, *Owner*
EMP: 3
SALES (est): 296.4K **Privately Held**
SIC: 0175 0171 0172 2099 Apple orchard; strawberry farm; grapes; cider, nonalcoholic; fruit & vegetable markets

(G-17314)
WG SWEIS INVESTMENTS LLC
Also Called: Cold Stone Creamery
57155 Covington Dr (48094-3160)
PHONE..................313 477-8433
Gassab Sweis,
William Sweis,
EMP: 30
SQ FT: 1,300
SALES: 70K **Privately Held**
SIC: 2024 Ice cream & frozen desserts

(G-17315)
ZF ACTIVE SAFETY US INC
Also Called: TRW Atmtive Stering Suspension
4585 26 Mile Rd (48094-2600)
PHONE..................586 232-7200
Derrick Lemons, *Engineer*
Andrew Smydra, *Engineer*
Joe Gaus, *Branch Mgr*
Dennis Fryzel, *Administration*
EMP: 650
SALES (corp-wide): 216.2M **Privately Held**
SIC: 3714 Motor vehicle parts & accessories
HQ: Zf Active Safety Us Inc.
12001 Tech Center Dr
Livonia MI 48150
734 855-2542

(G-17316)
ZF PASSIVE SAFETY
Also Called: North American Oss Operations
4505 26 Mile Rd (48094-2600)
PHONE..................586 232-7200
Jim Biermann, *Purch Mgr*
Annmarie McMillan, *Engrg Mgr*
Dwayne Cook, *Engineer*
Thomas Ruhlman, *Design Engr*
Elizabeth Landry, *Human Res Mgr*
EMP: 333
SALES (corp-wide): 216.2M **Privately Held**
SIC: 3679 3469 3089 Electronic switches; metal stampings; plastic processing
HQ: Zf Active Safety & Electronics Us Llc
12001 Tech Center Dr
Livonia MI 48150
734 855-2600

(G-17317)
ZF PASSIVE SAFETY SYSTEMS US
4505 26 Mile Rd (48094-2600)
PHONE..................586 781-5511
Julieta Santacruz, *Manager*
EMP: 325

SALES (corp-wide): 216.2K Privately Held
SIC: 3714 Motor vehicle parts & accessories
HQ: Zf Passive Safety Systems Us Inc.
4505 26 Mile Rd
Washington MI 48094
586 232-7200

(G-17318)
ZF PASSIVE SAFETY US INC
4505 26 Mile Rd (48094-2600)
PHONE..................586 232-7200
EMP: 3
SALES (corp-wide): 216.2K Privately Held
SIC: 3714 Motor vehicle parts & accessories
HQ: Zf Passive Safety Us Inc.
12001 Tech Center Dr
Livonia MI 48150
734 855-2600

(G-17319)
ZF PASSIVE SFETY SYSTEMS US IN (DH)
4505 26 Mile Rd (48094-2600)
PHONE..................586 232-7200
Joe Gaus, *President*
Darcy Miller, *Program Mgr*
Kathleen Darga, *Executive Asst*
▲ EMP: 1473
SALES (est): 5.5MM
SALES (corp-wide): 216.2K Privately Held
SIC: 3714 Motor vehicle parts & accessories
HQ: Zf Trw Automotive Holdings Corp.
12001 Tech Center Dr
Livonia MI 48150
734 855-2600

Washington Township
Macomb County

(G-17320)
YAKEL ENTERPRISES LLC
Also Called: Favi Entertainment
8679 26 Mile Rd Ste 305 (48094-2967)
PHONE..................586 943-5885
Jeff Yakel, *COO*
Jeremy Yakel, *Mng Member*
Karen Yakel, *Manager*
▲ EMP: 7 EST: 2007
SQ FT: 5,000
SALES (est): 1.4MM Privately Held
SIC: 3577 Computer peripheral equipment

Waterford
Oakland County

(G-17321)
ABC CUSTOM CHROME INC
3370 Warren Dr (48329-3547)
PHONE..................248 674-4333
EMP: 3
SQ FT: 3,700
SALES (est): 314.9K Privately Held
SIC: 3471 Plating/Polishing Service

(G-17322)
ARCHITECTURAL PLANNERS INC
Also Called: API Plan Design Build
5101 Williams Lake Rd (48329-3555)
PHONE..................248 674-1340
Keith Lutz, *President*
Alisha Robinson, *CFO*
EMP: 26
SQ FT: 2,500
SALES (est): 3.7MM Privately Held
SIC: 1542 2431 8712 Commercial & office building, new construction; shopping center construction; restaurant construction; religious building construction; millwork; architectural services

(G-17323)
ARROW PRINTING LLC
5457 Elizabeth Lake Rd (48327-2752)
PHONE..................248 738-2222
Kevin Armstrong,
Lawrence Keivit,
EMP: 3
SQ FT: 1,300
SALES (est): 432.7K Privately Held
SIC: 2752 7336 2759 2789 Commercial printing, offset; art design services; silk screen design; commercial printing; bookbinding & related work

(G-17324)
BABY PALLET
1367 Forest Bay Dr (48328-4293)
PHONE..................248 210-3851
Emilie Roper, *Principal*
EMP: 4 EST: 2014
SALES (est): 254.5K Privately Held
SIC: 2448 Pallets, wood & wood with metal

(G-17325)
BLUE FIRE MANUFACTURING LLC
5405 Perry Dr (48329-3462)
PHONE..................248 714-7166
Timothy Harris, *Mng Member*
EMP: 20
SALES (est): 2MM Privately Held
SIC: 3089 3469 3321 Automotive parts, plastic; metal stampings; gray iron castings

(G-17326)
BROADSWORD SOLUTIONS CORP
3795 Dorothy Ln (48329-1110)
PHONE..................248 341-3367
Jeffrey Dalton, *President*
Jill Mannaioni, *Partner*
Rob Macdonald, *Marketing Staff*
Darian Poinseta, *Sr Consultant*
Michelle Rauch, *Sr Consultant*
EMP: 12
SALES (est): 645.5K Privately Held
WEB: www.broadsword.com
SIC: 7372 Business oriented computer software

(G-17327)
BROADTEQ INCORPORATED
5119 Highland Rd Ste 386 (48327-1915)
PHONE..................248 794-9323
Jeff Vancamp, *President*
EMP: 3
SALES (est): 156.3K Privately Held
SIC: 3823 Industrial instrmnts msrmnt display/control process variable

(G-17328)
C T & T INC
Also Called: Waterfall Jewelers
5619 Dixie Hwy (48329-1619)
PHONE..................248 623-9422
Thomas F Brown Jr, *President*
Christine Strong, *Treasurer*
Deanna Meyers, *Sales Staff*
Heather Howie, *Manager*
John Strong, *Shareholder*
EMP: 12
SALES (est): 1.8MM Privately Held
WEB: www.waterfalljewelers.com
SIC: 5944 7631 3911 Jewelry, precious stones & precious metals; watches; diamond setter; jewelry repair services; jewelry, precious metal

(G-17329)
CONNOLLY
5805 Pontiac Lake Rd (48327-2118)
PHONE..................248 683-7985
D Connolly, *Principal*
EMP: 5
SALES (est): 264.2K Privately Held
SIC: 3699 Electrical equipment & supplies

(G-17330)
CUSTOM FIREPLACE DOORS INC
3809 Lakewood Dr (48329-3952)
PHONE..................248 673-3121
Stuart R Taylor, *President*
Bruce M Taylor, *Treasurer*
EMP: 10
SQ FT: 6,000
SALES (est): 760K Privately Held
WEB: www.cfd-inc.com
SIC: 3429 Fireplace equipment, hardware: andirons, grates, screens

(G-17331)
CYGNET FINANCIAL PLANNING INC
Also Called: Cygnet Financial Freedom House
4139 W Walton Blvd Ste D (48329-4187)
P.O. Box 301000 (48330-1000)
PHONE..................248 673-2900
Ted Lakkides, *President*
Brian Lakkides, *Vice Pres*
EMP: 9
SALES (est): 32.6K Privately Held
SIC: 8742 7372 Financial consultant; application computer software

(G-17332)
D & D PRODUCTION INC
2500 Williams Dr (48328-1868)
PHONE..................248 334-2112
Scott Kather, *President*
Kraig Kather, *Vice Pres*
EMP: 10 EST: 1972
SQ FT: 5,000
SALES (est): 1.4MM Privately Held
WEB: www.ddproductioninc.com
SIC: 3546 3541 Saws, portable & handheld: power driven; machine tools, metal cutting type

(G-17333)
DALTON INDUSTRIES LLC
2800 Alliance Ste B (48328-1800)
PHONE..................248 673-0755
Terry Eichbrecht, *General Mgr*
Steve Tolliver, *Mktg Dir*
Craig Johnson, *Marketing Staff*
▲ EMP: 50
SQ FT: 80,000
SALES (est): 14.8MM Privately Held
WEB: www.daltonind.com
SIC: 3547 3599 Rolling mill machinery; machine shop, jobbing & repair

(G-17334)
DIVERSIFIED DAVITCO LLC
2569 Dixie Hwy (48328-1705)
PHONE..................248 681-9197
Alan Crudele,
EMP: 12
SALES (est): 1.9MM Privately Held
SIC: 2842 5087 Window cleaning preparations; cleaning & maintenance equipment & supplies

(G-17335)
DONALD E ROGERS ASSOCIATES
Also Called: D E Rogers & Assoc.
2627 Williams Dr (48328-1872)
PHONE..................248 673-9878
Donald Kather, *Principal*
EMP: 6
SQ FT: 3,000
SALES (est): 660K Privately Held
SIC: 3541 Machine tool replacement & repair parts, metal cutting types

(G-17336)
DOUGLAS WATER CONDITIONING (PA)
7234 Cooley Lake Rd (48327-4188)
PHONE..................248 363-8383
Douglas R Lanni, *President*
Jerry Tiefenback, *Vice Pres*
Stephen Wolfe, *Vice Pres*
EMP: 27
SALES (est): 5.1MM Privately Held
WEB: www.douglaswater.com
SIC: 3589 5999 7389 5084 Water treatment equipment, industrial; water purification equipment; water softener service; industrial machinery & equipment

(G-17337)
DOVETAILS INC
5600 Williams Lake Rd B (48329-3283)
PHONE..................248 674-8777
Kevin Evanson, *Owner*
Ralph Rexroat, *Treasurer*
Denice Evanson, *Admin Sec*
EMP: 11
SQ FT: 6,500
SALES (est): 1.5MM Privately Held
WEB: www.dovetailsinc.net
SIC: 2431 Millwork

(G-17338)
DOWNEYS POTATO CHIPS-WATERFORD
Also Called: Downey's & Design
4709 Highland Rd (48328-1136)
PHONE..................248 673-3636
Rosemary Hogarth, *President*
Richard Downey, *President*
Donald Hogarth, *Corp Secy*
Rebecca Hogarth, *Vice Pres*
Elizabeth Wieland, *Vice Pres*
EMP: 5
SALES (est): 577.2K Privately Held
SIC: 2096 5499 2099 Potato chips & other potato-based snacks; gourmet food stores; food preparations

(G-17339)
DRAYTON IRON & METAL INC (PA)
5229 Williams Lake Rd (48329-3557)
PHONE..................248 673-1269
Lloyd L Spurgeon, *President*
Eddie E Spurgeon, *Vice Pres*
Tom Spurgeon, *Treasurer*
EMP: 14
SALES (est): 2.7MM Privately Held
WEB: www.draytonhall.org
SIC: 5093 3273 Ferrous metal scrap & waste; ready-mixed concrete

(G-17340)
EAGLE GRAPHICS AND DESIGN
2040 Airport Rd (48327-1204)
PHONE..................248 618-0000
Arthur T Lucero, *President*
Arthur Lucero, *President*
Edward Lucero, *Vice Pres*
Aaron Lucero, *Treasurer*
Patricia Lucero, *Admin Sec*
EMP: 5
SQ FT: 3,500
SALES: 300K Privately Held
SIC: 3993 Signs, not made in custom sign painting shops

(G-17341)
EARTHWORM CSTNGS UNLIMITED LLC
1179 Sylvertis Dr (48328-2042)
PHONE..................248 882-3329
Dean Weston, *CEO*
Beverly Beaudoin, *Mng Member*
Ruth Beaudoin, *Mng Member*
Jared Weston, *Mng Member*
EMP: 18 EST: 2013
SQ FT: 10,000
SALES: 370K Privately Held
SIC: 2873 Fertilizers: natural (organic), except compost

(G-17342)
ENGINEERING INTERESTS INC
5600 Williams Lake Rd F (48329-3283)
PHONE..................248 461-6706
Dean Weston, *President*
Tracy Gutek, *President*
EMP: 4
SALES (est): 589.1K Privately Held
SIC: 4971 3563 Water distribution or supply systems for irrigation; air & gas compressors

(G-17343)
FANTASTIC IMAGES SIGNS
1032 W Huron St (48328-3730)
PHONE..................248 683-5556
Keith H Mc Auliff, *President*
EMP: 3 EST: 1997
SALES (est): 234.4K Privately Held
SIC: 3993 Signs & advertising specialties

(G-17344)
FORCE DYNAMICS INC
2627 Williams Dr (48328-1872)
PHONE..................248 673-9878
Kraig Kather, *President*

Scott Kather, *Vice Pres*
EMP: 3
SALES (est): 321.6K **Privately Held**
SIC: 3829 Measuring & controlling devices

(G-17345)
FORSTERS AND SONS OIL CHANGE
4773 Dixie Hwy (48329-3523)
P.O. Box 300815, Drayton Plains (48330-0815)
PHONE 248 618-6860
Matt Perry, *President*
EMP: 12
SQ FT: 2,000
SALES (est): 1.1MM **Privately Held**
SIC: 1389 Oil field services

(G-17346)
GONZALEZ WELDING
1385 Hira St (48328-1519)
PHONE 248 469-3016
EMP: 8
SALES (est): 88.7K **Privately Held**
SIC: 7692 Welding repair

(G-17347)
GR INNOVATIONS LLC
6650 Highland Rd (48327-1660)
PHONE 248 618-3813
EMP: 3
SALES (est): 418.9K **Privately Held**
SIC: 3545 Mfg Machine Tool Accessories

(G-17348)
HANGER PRSTHETCS & ORTHO INC
4000 Highland Rd Ste 108 (48328-2163)
PHONE 248 683-5070
Eric Oertel, *Manager*
EMP: 4
SALES (corp-wide): 1B **Publicly Held**
SIC: 3842 Orthopedic appliances
HQ: Hanger Prosthetics & Orthotics, Inc.
10910 Domain Dr Ste 300
Austin TX 78758
512 777-3800

(G-17349)
HDP INC
4670 Hatchery Rd Ste C (48329-3633)
PHONE 248 674-4967
Steven F Lowe,
EMP: 3
SALES: 500K **Privately Held**
SIC: 3519 Internal combustion engines

(G-17350)
HEAT TREATING SVCS CORP AMER
Also Called: Heating Treating Services
2501 Williams Dr (48328-1869)
PHONE 248 253-9560
Tony Patterson, *Branch Mgr*
EMP: 35
SALES (corp-wide): 22.7MM **Privately Held**
WEB: www.htsmi.com
SIC: 3398 Metal heat treating
PA: Heat Treating Services Corporation Of America
217 Central Ave
Pontiac MI 48341
248 858-2230

(G-17351)
INFRA CORPORATION
5454 Dixie Hwy (48329-1615)
P.O. Box 300997 (48330-0997)
PHONE 248 623-0400
Bryan A McGraw, *President*
Cindy McGraw, *CFO*
EMP: 10
SQ FT: 12,000
SALES: 850K **Privately Held**
WEB: www.infracorporation.com
SIC: 3541 3569 3613 3914 Drilling machine tools (metal cutting); assembly machines, non-metalworking; control panels, electric; stainless steel ware

(G-17352)
JOHNNIE ON SPOT INC
Also Called: Johnnie On Spot Printing Co
2149 Deer Run Trl (48329-2383)
PHONE 248 673-2233
John Lawler, *President*
EMP: 3
SALES (est): 332.3K **Privately Held**
WEB: www.johnnieonthespot.com
SIC: 7389 2752 Printing broker; commercial printing, lithographic

(G-17353)
K & K SALES ASSOC LLC
3661 Dorothy Ln (48329-1108)
PHONE 248 623-7378
James Kiley, *President*
EMP: 4
SALES (est): 362.3K **Privately Held**
SIC: 3465 Body parts, automobile: stamped metal

(G-17354)
KENNEDYS IRISH PUB INC
1055 W Huron St (48328-3731)
PHONE 248 681-1050
William Kennedy, *Owner*
EMP: 3
SALES (est): 234.3K **Privately Held**
SIC: 5813 2599 Cocktail lounge; bar, restaurant & cafeteria furniture

(G-17355)
KEVIN LARKIN INC
Also Called: Lake Superior Soap Co
2611 Woodbourne Dr (48329-2479)
PHONE 248 736-8203
EMP: 4
SALES: 77K **Privately Held**
SIC: 3999 Mfg Misc Products

(G-17356)
L E Q INC
Also Called: Architrave Woodworking
5600 Williams Lake Rd B (48329-3283)
PHONE 248 257-5466
Marilyn Nehring, *Principal*
EMP: 5 **EST:** 2015
SALES (est): 219.4K **Privately Held**
SIC: 2431 Millwork

(G-17357)
MICHIGAN VUE MAGAZINE
5865 Crescent Rd (48327-2626)
PHONE 248 681-2410
Hily Trevethan, *Owner*
EMP: 3 **EST:** 1996
SALES: 190K **Privately Held**
WEB: www.michiganvue.com
SIC: 2721 Magazines: publishing only, not printed on site

(G-17358)
MIDLAND SILICON COMPANY LLC
3840 Island Park Dr (48329-1906)
PHONE 248 674-3736
James May, *CEO*
Virago Capital,
EMP: 11
SQ FT: 1,000
SALES: 3.5MM **Privately Held**
SIC: 3479 Coating of metals with silicon

(G-17359)
MIDWEST QUALITY BEDDING INC
Also Called: Mattress Mart
1384 Glenview Dr (48327-2978)
PHONE 614 504-5971
John Fogt, *Vice Pres*
EMP: 14
SALES (est): 2.3MM **Privately Held**
SIC: 2515 Mattresses & bedsprings

(G-17360)
NETCON ENTERPRISES INC
5085 Williams Lake Rd A (48329-3573)
PHONE 248 673-7855
Gary L Leonard, *President*
Stacy Behrens, *General Mgr*
Terrence P Mirabito, *Vice Pres*
Corinne Dropiewski, *Purchasing*
Terry Mirabito, *VP Sales*
EMP: 25

SQ FT: 10,000
SALES: 1MM **Privately Held**
WEB: www.netconinc.net
SIC: 3679 Harness assemblies for electronic use: wire or cable

(G-17361)
OAKLAND MACHINE COMPANY
4865 Highland Rd Ste G (48328-1171)
PHONE 248 674-2201
William H Weber, *President*
Peggy Madsen, *Office Mgr*
EMP: 10
SQ FT: 10,000
SALES (est): 1.5MM **Privately Held**
WEB: www.oaklandmachine.com
SIC: 3599 Machine shop, jobbing & repair

(G-17362)
OMTRON INC
2560 Silverside Rd (48328-1760)
PHONE 248 673-3896
Kenneth Richardson, *President*
EMP: 5
SQ FT: 2,200
SALES (est): 678.5K **Privately Held**
WEB: www.omtron.com
SIC: 3679 Electronic circuits

(G-17363)
OPENINGS INC
Also Called: Total Door An Openings
6145 Delfield Dr (48329-1388)
PHONE 248 623-6899
Leon Yulkowski, *Partner*
Jeanne Kitchen, *Controller*
Brian Butler, *Manager*
▲ **EMP:** 50
SQ FT: 200,000
SALES (est): 9.3MM **Privately Held**
WEB: www.totaldoor.com
SIC: 3442 Metal doors

(G-17364)
ORRI CORP
5385 Perry Dr (48329-3460)
PHONE 248 618-1104
Lori Doa, *President*
Angelo Doa, *Vice Pres*
▲ **EMP:** 16 **EST:** 2001
SALES (est): 1.7MM **Privately Held**
SIC: 3496 3552 Cable, uninsulated wire: made from purchased wire; heddles for loom harnesses, wire

(G-17365)
PAUL HORN AND ASSOCIATES
2525 Sylvan Shores Dr (48328-3934)
PHONE 248 682-8490
EMP: 3
SALES: 1MM **Privately Held**
SIC: 3564 5075 Mfg Air Blowoff & Antistatic Equip & Whol Air Blowoff & Antistatic Equip

(G-17366)
PENN AUTOMOTIVE INC (DH)
Also Called: Profile Steel and Wire
5331 Dixie Hwy (48329-1612)
P.O. Box 380643, Clinton Township (48038-0069)
PHONE 248 599-3700
Jeff Lewis, *Vice Pres*
Cathy Tinnley, *Accountant*
Judy McLauckin, *Bookkeeper*
Eric Wolk, *Manager*
Elliott Israel, *Admin Sec*
▲ **EMP:** 280
SALES (est): 46.6MM
SALES (corp-wide): 483.7MM **Privately Held**
WEB: www.fabristeel.com
SIC: 3965 5085 3429 Fasteners; fasteners & fastening equipment; metal fasteners
HQ: Penn Engineering & Manufacturing Corp.
5190 Old Easton Rd
Danboro PA 18916
215 766-8853

(G-17367)
PENN ENGINEERING & MFG CORP
5331 Dixie Hwy (48329-1612)
PHONE 313 299-8500

Mark Petty, *President*
EMP: 280
SALES (corp-wide): 483.7MM **Privately Held**
SIC: 3965 5085 3429 Fasteners; fasteners & fastening equipment; metal fasteners
HQ: Penn Engineering & Manufacturing Corp.
5190 Old Easton Rd
Danboro PA 18916
215 766-8853

(G-17368)
PERPETUAL MEASUREMENT INC
3185 Seebaldt Ave (48329-4152)
PHONE 248 343-2952
Todd A Wyatt, *President*
EMP: 4
SALES: 600K **Privately Held**
SIC: 3823 Industrial process measurement equipment

(G-17369)
PIFERS AIRMOTIVE INC
1660 Airport Rd (48327-1301)
PHONE 248 674-0909
Richard S Pifer, *President*
Lois M Pifer, *Vice Pres*
EMP: 6 **EST:** 1970
SQ FT: 4,500
SALES: 300K **Privately Held**
WEB: www.pifersinc.com
SIC: 3728 Aircraft assemblies, subassemblies & parts

(G-17370)
PPG INDUSTRIES INC
Also Called: PPG 5629
497 Elizabeth Lake Rd (48328-3302)
PHONE 248 683-8052
Joe Brunet, *Branch Mgr*
EMP: 24
SALES (corp-wide): 15.3B **Publicly Held**
WEB: www.ppg.com
SIC: 2851 Paints & allied products
PA: Ppg Industries, Inc.
1 Ppg Pl
Pittsburgh PA 15272
412 434-3131

(G-17371)
PRECISION LABEL SPECIALIST
4887 Highland Rd (48328-1141)
PHONE 248 673-5010
Ronald Gardner, *President*
▼ **EMP:** 3
SALES: 1.2MM **Privately Held**
SIC: 2759 Labels & seals: printing

(G-17372)
PROFESSIONAL INSTANT PRINTING
949 W Huron St (48328-3727)
PHONE 248 335-1117
John R Allen, *President*
EMP: 3
SQ FT: 600
SALES (est): 368.6K **Privately Held**
SIC: 2752 Commercial printing, lithographic

(G-17373)
RUELLE INDUSTRIES INC
5425 Perry Dr Ste 108 (48329-4826)
PHONE 248 618-0333
Patrick Ruelle, *President*
EMP: 3
SALES (est): 253.7K **Privately Held**
SIC: 3544 Special dies, tools, jigs & fixtures

(G-17374)
SAFETY TECHNOLOGY INTL INC (PA)
Also Called: Safety Technology Intl
2306 Airport Rd (48327-1209)
PHONE 248 673-9898
Margie Gobler, *President*
John F Taylor, *Vice Pres*
Robert Petrach, *Mfg Mgr*
Jamie Paul, *Sls & Mktg Exec*
Michael Mikaelian, *Natl Sales Mgr*
▲ **EMP:** 35

GEOGRAPHIC SECTION

Wayland - Allegan County (G-17402)

SQ FT: 20,000
SALES (est): 8.7MM **Privately Held**
WEB: www.sti-usa.com
SIC: 3669 Burglar alarm apparatus, electric

(G-17375)
SAFETY TECHNOLOGY INTL INC
Also Called: S T I
3777 Airport Rd (48329-1355)
PHONE..................................248 673-9898
Margie Gobler, *President*
EMP: 3
SALES (corp-wide): 8.7MM **Privately Held**
SIC: 3669 Burglar alarm apparatus, electric
PA: Safety Technology International, Inc.
2306 Airport Rd
Waterford MI 48327
248 673-9898

(G-17376)
SIGNS NOW
5425 Perry Dr Ste 110 (48329-4826)
PHONE..................................248 623-4966
Tom Kiihr, *Owner*
EMP: 3
SALES (est): 243.1K **Privately Held**
SIC: 3993 Signs & advertising specialties

(G-17377)
SILENT CALL CORPORATION
Also Called: Silent Call Communications
5095 Williams Lake Rd (48329-3553)
PHONE..................................248 673-7353
George J Elwell, *President*
Bob Wood, *General Mgr*
▲ EMP: 11
SQ FT: 4,000
SALES (est): 1.9MM **Privately Held**
SIC: 5999 3699 Audio-visual equipment & supplies; accelerating waveguide structures

(G-17378)
SUNBURST SHUTTERS
5499 Perry Dr Ste M (48329-4827)
PHONE..................................248 674-4600
Steve Hill, *Manager*
EMP: 6
SALES (est): 472.2K **Privately Held**
SIC: 5211 5023 2591 Door & window products; venetian blinds; window blinds

(G-17379)
SUPREME TOOL & MACHINE INC
5409 Perry Dr (48329-3462)
PHONE..................................248 673-8408
Mark E Beyer, *President*
Dawn M Beyer, *Vice Pres*
EMP: 10
SQ FT: 4,000
SALES (est): 1.9MM **Privately Held**
WEB: www.supremetoolinc.com
SIC: 3544 3599 Special dies & tools; machine shop, jobbing & repair

(G-17380)
T F BOYER INDUSTRIES INC
5489 Perry Dr Ste C (48329-4832)
PHONE..................................248 674-8420
Thomas F Boyer, *President*
EMP: 6 EST: 1977
SQ FT: 5,500
SALES (est): 510K **Privately Held**
SIC: 2521 Bookcases, office: wood; cabinets, office: wood

(G-17381)
TOTAL DOOR II INC
6145 Delfield Dr (48329-1388)
PHONE..................................866 781-2069
Patricia Yulkowski, *President*
EMP: 50
SALES (est): 1.2MM **Privately Held**
SIC: 3442 Metal doors

(G-17382)
VAN HORN BROS INC (PA)
Also Called: Van Horn Concrete
3700 Airport Rd (48329-1303)
PHONE..................................248 623-4830
Richard B Clark, *Ch of Bd*
Gale Wigner, *Vice Pres*
Kenneth Clark, *Treasurer*
EMP: 30 EST: 1959
SQ FT: 2,000
SALES (est): 8.9MM **Privately Held**
WEB: www.vanhornconcrete.com
SIC: 3273 Ready-mixed concrete

(G-17383)
VAN HORN BROS INC
Also Called: Van Horn Concrete
3770 Airport Rd (48329-1303)
PHONE..................................248 623-6000
Richard B Clark, *President*
Gale Wigner, *Vice Pres*
EMP: 30
SALES (est): 4.7MM
SALES (corp-wide): 8.9MM **Privately Held**
WEB: www.vanhornconcrete.com
SIC: 3273 Ready-mixed concrete
PA: Van Horn Bros., Inc.
3700 Airport Rd
Waterford MI 48329
248 623-4830

(G-17384)
VHB-123 CORPORATION
3770 Airport Rd (48329-1303)
PHONE..................................248 623-4830
Kenneth Clark, *Manager*
EMP: 4
SALES (est): 398.4K **Privately Held**
SIC: 3273 Ready-mixed concrete

(G-17385)
WHITESELL FRMED COMPONENTS INC
Fabristeel Taylor
5331 Dixie Hwy (48329-1612)
PHONE..................................313 299-1178
EMP: 75
SALES (corp-wide): 50MM **Privately Held**
SIC: 3452 3544 Mfg Bolts/Screws/Rivets Mfg Dies/Tools/Jigs/Fixtures
PA: Whitesell Formed Components, Inc.
5331 Dixie Hwy
Waterford MI 48329
313 299-8500

(G-17386)
WILLIAMS INTERNATIONAL CO LLC
Also Called: Flight Department
7201 Astro Dr N (48327-1003)
PHONE..................................248 762-8713
Robert Lambert, *Branch Mgr*
EMP: 131
SALES (corp-wide): 248.4MM **Privately Held**
SIC: 3724 3764 Turbines, aircraft type; engines & engine parts, guided missile
PA: Williams International Co Llc
2000 Centerpoint Pkwy
Pontiac MI 48341
248 624-5200

(G-17387)
WOLVERINE WATER WORKS INC
Also Called: Wolverine Waterworks
2469 Airport Rd (48327-1213)
PHONE..................................248 673-4310
Ron Gobler, *President*
Juli Philips, *Manager*
EMP: 4
SALES (est): 528.1K **Privately Held**
WEB: www.wolverinewater.com
SIC: 3569 3594 Assembly machines, non-metalworking; fluid power pumps & motors

(G-17388)
ZIMBELL HOUSE PUBLISHING LLC
1093 Irwin Dr (48327-2020)
P.O. Box 1172, Union Lake (48387-1172)
PHONE..................................248 909-0143
Evelyn M Zimmer, *Mng Member*
EMP: 5
SALES (est): 93.5K **Privately Held**
SIC: 2741 Miscellaneous publishing

Watersmeet
Gogebic County

(G-17389)
RUBBER ROPE PRODUCTS COMPANY
25760 Old Hwy 2e 2 E (49969)
PHONE..................................906 358-4133
Sharon J Rehling, *President*
Fay Diethert, *President*
C William Rehling, *Admin Sec*
EMP: 9
SALES (est): 1.1MM **Privately Held**
SIC: 3732 Non-motorized boat, building & repairing

Watervliet
Berrien County

(G-17390)
CUSTOM BUILT BRUSH COMPANY
7390 Dan Smith Rd (49098-9740)
PHONE..................................269 463-3171
G Jack Clark, *President*
Carol Lenz, *Admin Sec*
EMP: 12
SQ FT: 26,000
SALES (est): 1.2MM **Privately Held**
WEB: www.custombuiltbrush.com
SIC: 3991 Brushes, household or industrial

(G-17391)
DRAPERY WORKROOM
5864 N County Line Rd (49098-9798)
PHONE..................................269 463-5633
Eileen Kolosowsky, *Owner*
James Kolosowsky Jr, *Manager*
EMP: 5
SQ FT: 1,500
SALES (est): 284.5K **Privately Held**
SIC: 2211 Draperies & drapery fabrics, cotton

(G-17392)
FINE TOOL JOURNAL LLC
Also Called: Brown Auction Services
9325 Dwight Boyer Rd (49098-9732)
P.O. Box 737 (49098-0737)
PHONE..................................269 463-8255
Jim Gehring, *Mng Member*
EMP: 3 EST: 2013
SALES (est): 208.4K **Privately Held**
SIC: 2711 7389 Newspapers, publishing & printing; auctioneers, fee basis

(G-17393)
JARVIS CONCRETE PRODUCTS INC
7584 Red Arrow Hwy (49098-8552)
P.O. Box 658 (49098-0658)
PHONE..................................269 463-3000
Eugene Jarvis, *President*
James Jarvis, *President*
EMP: 4
SQ FT: 6,000
SALES: 250K **Privately Held**
SIC: 3272 Burial vaults, concrete or precast terrazzo; steps, prefabricated concrete

(G-17394)
TRI CITY RECORD LLC
138 N Main St (49098-9787)
P.O. Box 7, Vandalia (49095-0007)
PHONE..................................269 463-6397
Karl Bayer, *Mng Member*
Anne Bayer,
EMP: 4
SALES (est): 245.3K **Privately Held**
WEB: www.tricityrecord.com
SIC: 2711 Job printing & newspaper publishing combined; newspapers, publishing & printing

Watton
Baraga County

(G-17395)
SANTTI BROTHERS INC
26339 Ford Rd (49970-9016)
PHONE..................................906 355-2347
Donald Santti, *President*
EMP: 5
SALES (est): 496K **Privately Held**
SIC: 2411 Logging camps & contractors

Wayland
Allegan County

(G-17396)
A AND J INDUSTRIES
4066 Division St Ste C (49348-9752)
PHONE..................................616 877-4845
Betty Bartholomew, *Owner*
EMP: 3
SALES: 350K **Privately Held**
SIC: 3842 Gloves, safety

(G-17397)
ADVANTAGE HOUSING INC
3555 12th St (49348-9133)
PHONE..................................269 792-6291
Jiten Shah, *CEO*
Mike Mead, *President*
EMP: 8
SQ FT: 3,040
SALES: 12MM **Privately Held**
SIC: 5271 2451 Mobile homes; mobile homes

(G-17398)
AZTEC PRODUCING CO INC
3312 12th St (49348-9545)
PHONE..................................269 792-0505
Marcelino Candia, *Bd of Directors*
EMP: 3
SALES (est): 306K **Privately Held**
SIC: 1311 Crude petroleum & natural gas

(G-17399)
BAY VALLEY FOODS LLC
652 W Elm St (49348-1088)
PHONE..................................269 792-2277
Dave Carter, *Manager*
EMP: 120
SALES (corp-wide): 5.8B **Publicly Held**
SIC: 2023 2043 2026 Cream substitutes; dietary supplements, dairy & non-dairy based; cereal breakfast foods; fluid milk
HQ: Bay Valley Foods, LLC
3200 Riverside Dr Ste A
Green Bay WI 54301
800 558-4700

(G-17400)
BEST MFG TOOLING SOLUTIONS LTD
1158 Morren Ct (49348-8944)
PHONE..................................616 877-0504
Brian Schaidt, *President*
EMP: 5
SALES: 1MM **Privately Held**
SIC: 3559 Automotive related machinery

(G-17401)
BLAIN MACHINING INC
1115 142nd Ave Ste 1 (49348-8966)
PHONE..................................616 877-0426
Kevin Blain, *President*
EMP: 7
SQ FT: 5,000
SALES (est): 997.1K **Privately Held**
SIC: 3599 Machine shop, jobbing & repair

(G-17402)
BUCK-SPICA EQUIPMENT LTD
Also Called: Bakery Equipment/Design
631 W Cherry St (49348-1012)
PHONE..................................269 792-2251
Gerald Rose, *President*
Dan Rose, *Vice Pres*
Jon Rose, *Vice Pres*
EMP: 10
SQ FT: 15,000

Wayland - Allegan County (G-17403)

SALES (est): 1.8MM **Privately Held**
SIC: 2499 Bakers' equipment, wood

(G-17403)
DAILY BREWS GOURMET COFFE
128 S Main St (49348-1209)
PHONE.................269 792-2739
Kathleen Patrick, *Executive Asst*
EMP: 4
SALES (est): 277.4K **Privately Held**
SIC: 2711 Newspapers, publishing & printing

(G-17404)
DIGITRACE MACHINE WORKS LTD
Also Called: Digitrace Limited
1158 Morren Ct (49348-8944)
PHONE.................616 877-4818
Lawrance Schaidt, *President*
Tom Woodward, *General Mgr*
Brian Schaidt, *Vice Pres*
EMP: 32 **EST:** 1996
SQ FT: 20,000
SALES: 5MM **Privately Held**
SIC: 3599 Machine shop, jobbing & repair

(G-17405)
ECLIPSE TOOL & DIE INC
4713 Circuit Ct Ste A (49348-8992)
PHONE.................616 877-3717
Calvin De Good, *President*
Paul Bogardus III, *Vice Pres*
Brian Merdzinski, *Plant Mgr*
Scott Degood, *Purchasing*
Chad Davis, *QC Mgr*
EMP: 50
SQ FT: 52,900
SALES: 10.7MM **Privately Held**
WEB: www.eclipsetd.com
SIC: 3544 Special dies & tools

(G-17406)
MAYVILLE ENGINEERING CO INC
4714 Circuit Ct (49348-8908)
PHONE.................616 877-2073
Missy Moederzoon, *Principal*
EMP: 99
SALES (corp-wide): 354.5MM **Publicly Held**
SIC: 3498 Tube fabricating (contract bending & shaping)
PA: Mayville Engineering Co Inc
715 South St
Mayville WI 53050
920 387-4500

(G-17407)
MOBILE PALLET SERVICE INC (PA)
858 S Main St (49348-1323)
PHONE.................269 792-4200
Michael Kamps, *President*
Steve Kamps, *Vice Pres*
Nathan Kamps, *Treasurer*
EMP: 47
SQ FT: 37,000
SALES (est): 6.9MM **Privately Held**
WEB: www.mobilepalletservice.com
SIC: 7699 5031 2448 Pallet repair; pallets, wood; wood pallets & skids

(G-17408)
OMEGA STEEL INCORPORATED
1232 Ingle Rd Ste A (49348-8964)
PHONE.................616 877-3782
Roger Sorensen, *President*
Sally Sorensen, *Admin Sec*
EMP: 4
SALES (est): 605.4K **Privately Held**
SIC: 3312 Plate, sheet & strip, except coated products

(G-17409)
PLASMA-TEC INC
1119 Morren Ct (49348-8944)
PHONE.................616 455-2593
Laurence A Wysong, *CEO*
Christopher Wysong, *President*
Bryan Degroot, *General Mgr*
Mike Schroeder, *Vice Pres*
EMP: 25 **EST:** 1981
SQ FT: 18,000
SALES (est): 6.4MM **Privately Held**
WEB: www.plasma-tec.com
SIC: 3599 3479 3561 3511 Machine shop, jobbing & repair; coating of metals & formed products; pumps & pumping equipment; turbines & turbine generator sets

(G-17410)
RECCO PRODUCTS INC
702 S Main St (49348-1319)
P.O. Box 443 (49348-0443)
PHONE.................269 792-2243
Brandon Cooper, *CEO*
Brian Cooper, *Vice Pres*
Jesse Schenkoske, *Design Engr*
Laura Cooper, *CFO*
EMP: 36
SALES (est): 11.4MM **Privately Held**
WEB: www.recco.net
SIC: 3569 Filters, general line: industrial; filters

(G-17411)
RHINO SEED & LANDSCAPE SUP LLC (PA)
1093 129th Ave (49348-9542)
PHONE.................800 482-3130
Scott Hilbert,
▲ **EMP:** 40
SQ FT: 25,000
SALES (est): 7.9MM **Privately Held**
SIC: 2499 5191 Mulch, wood & bark; seeds: field, garden & flower

(G-17412)
ROCKWELL AUTOMATION INC
1121 133rd Ave (49348-9535)
PHONE.................269 792-9137
Bruce Merrill, *Branch Mgr*
EMP: 67 **Publicly Held**
SIC: 3625 Relays & industrial controls
PA: Rockwell Automation, Inc.
1201 S 2nd St
Milwaukee WI 53204

(G-17413)
SAND TRAXX
12956 Valley Dr (49348-9088)
PHONE.................616 460-5137
William J Berzley, *Principal*
EMP: 3 **EST:** 2010
SALES (est): 158.8K **Privately Held**
SIC: 3674 Semiconductors & related devices

(G-17414)
SAWMILL ESTATES
Also Called: Kmg Prestige
1185 Eagle Dr (49348-1714)
PHONE.................269 792-7500
Jennifer Troud, *Manager*
EMP: 9
SALES (est): 530K **Privately Held**
SIC: 2421 Sawmills & planing mills, general

(G-17415)
SEBRIGHT PRODUCTS INC
Also Called: Bright Technologies
2631 12th St (49348)
PHONE.................269 792-6229
Mark Schwartz, *Branch Mgr*
EMP: 30
SALES (corp-wide): 18.3MM **Privately Held**
SIC: 3589 Sewage & water treatment equipment
PA: Sebright Products, Inc.
127 N Water St
Hopkins MI 49328
269 793-7183

(G-17416)
SERVO INNOVATIONS LLC
2560 Patterson Rd (49348-9458)
PHONE.................269 792-9279
Troy Diller, *Owner*
EMP: 8
SQ FT: 864
SALES: 690K **Privately Held**
WEB: www.servoinnovations.com
SIC: 3825 Standards & calibrating equipment, laboratory

(G-17417)
STAMPEDE DIE CORP
Also Called: Stampede Die & Engineering
1142 Electric Ave (49348-8901)
PHONE.................616 877-0100
Lee Vandyk, *President*
Adam Swann, *Vice Pres*
EMP: 75
SQ FT: 40,000
SALES (est): 23.3MM **Privately Held**
SIC: 3544 Special dies & tools

(G-17418)
UNITED COLLISION
125 Railroad St (49348-1051)
PHONE.................269 792-7274
Jansen Jerry, *Principal*
EMP: 3
SALES (est): 395.1K **Privately Held**
SIC: 3711 Motor vehicles & car bodies

(G-17419)
WELDING FABRICATING INC
3989 9th St (49348-9742)
PHONE.................616 877-4345
Terry Senneker, *President*
EMP: 3
SALES (est): 160K **Privately Held**
SIC: 7692 Welding repair

(G-17420)
WEST MICHIGAN FORKLIFT INC
4155 12th St (49348-9589)
PHONE.................616 262-4949
EMP: 4
SALES (est): 600.5K **Privately Held**
SIC: 3537 Forklift trucks

Wayne
Wayne County

(G-17421)
ALLIED SUPPORT SYSTEMS
Also Called: Unistrut
4205 Elizabeth St (48184-2162)
PHONE.................734 721-4040
Mark Goodman, *Branch Mgr*
EMP: 3 **EST:** 2001
SALES (est): 407.4K **Privately Held**
SIC: 3999 Manufacturing industries

(G-17422)
ALLIED TUBE & CONDUIT CORP
4205 Elizabeth St (48184-2162)
PHONE.................734 721-4040
Chucks Neahls, *Manager*
EMP: 250
SQ FT: 300,000 **Publicly Held**
WEB: www.alliedtube.com
SIC: 3644 Noncurrent-carrying wiring services
HQ: Allied Tube & Conduit Corporation
16100 Lathrop Ave
Harvey IL 60426
708 339-1610

(G-17423)
AMERICAN JETWAY CORPORATION
34136 Myrtle St (48184-1729)
PHONE.................734 721-5930
Gordon Jones, *President*
Charles Quint, *President*
Janice Germann, *COO*
Bill Dick, *Vice Pres*
Robert Litner, *Safety Dir*
◆ **EMP:** 78
SQ FT: 36,000
SALES (est): 37.7MM **Privately Held**
WEB: www.americanjetway.com
SIC: 2842 2899 Specialty cleaning preparations; fuel tank or engine cleaning chemicals

(G-17424)
ASSOCIATED NEWSPAPERS MICHIGAN
35128 W Michigan Ave (48184-1614)
P.O. Box 6320, Plymouth (48170-0316)
PHONE.................734 467-1900
Dave Willett, *Owner*
EMP: 5

SALES (est): 243.6K **Privately Held**
SIC: 2711 Newspapers

(G-17425)
AXCHEM INC
38070 Van Born Rd (48184-1577)
PHONE.................734 641-9842
Donald Kay, *Manager*
EMP: 3 **EST:** 2010
SALES (est): 239.5K **Privately Held**
SIC: 2819 Industrial inorganic chemicals

(G-17426)
B AND D THD ROLLING FAS INDUS
36820 Van Born Rd (48184-1555)
P.O. Box 275 (48184-0275)
PHONE.................734 728-7070
Tom Glinski, *Vice Pres*
Jessica Shinkonis, *QC Mgr*
Brenda Lott, *Sales Mgr*
Larry Thomason, *Cust Mgr*
Tim Quick, *Telecom Exec*
EMP: 9
SALES (est): 945.2K **Privately Held**
SIC: 3452 Bolts, nuts, rivets & washers

(G-17427)
BACKDRAFT BREWING COMPANY
Also Called: Fire Acadamy
35122 W Michigan Ave (48184-1614)
PHONE.................734 722-7639
Michael Reddy, *Partner*
George Riley, *Partner*
EMP: 100
SQ FT: 8,000
SALES: 17MM **Privately Held**
SIC: 2082 5812 5813 Beer (alcoholic beverage); eating places; drinking places

(G-17428)
COMPLEX STEEL & WIRE CORP
36254 Annapolis St (48184-2094)
P.O. Box 446 (48184-0446)
PHONE.................734 326-1600
Vincent Fedell, *President*
▼ **EMP:** 15
SQ FT: 45,000
SALES (est): 3.2MM **Privately Held**
WEB: www.complexsteel.com
SIC: 3441 Fabricated structural metal

(G-17429)
CUL-MAC INDUSTRIES INC
Also Called: Tech Group
3720 Venoy Rd (48184-1837)
PHONE.................734 728-9700
William Mc Laughlin, *President*
Scott Crigchton, *Vice Pres*
Dean Tabin, *Sales Staff*
EMP: 50 **EST:** 1981
SQ FT: 120,000
SALES (est): 20.1MM **Privately Held**
WEB: www.cul-mac.com
SIC: 2841 2842 Soap: granulated, liquid, cake, flaked or chip; disinfectants, household or industrial plant

(G-17430)
FRENCHYS SKIRTING INC
34111 Michigan Ave (48184-1738)
PHONE.................734 721-3013
Eddy Fournier, *President*
Daniel Fournier, *Vice Pres*
Serge Fournier, *Treasurer*
Lina Fournier, *Admin Sec*
EMP: 4 **EST:** 1972
SQ FT: 6,000
SALES (est): 485.1K **Privately Held**
SIC: 3444 1799 Sheet metalwork; building site preparation

(G-17431)
GENERAL ELECTRIC COMPANY
38303 Michigan Ave (48184-1042)
PHONE.................734 728-1472
Chad Russell, *Manager*
EMP: 64
SALES (corp-wide): 121.6B **Publicly Held**
SIC: 4911 3699 Electric services; electrical equipment & supplies

▲ = Import ▼ = Export
◆ = Import/Export

PA: General Electric Company
41 Farnsworth St
Boston MA 02210
617 443-3000

(G-17432)
IMPERIAL PRESS INC
36024 W Michigan Ave (48184-1671)
PHONE..................734 728-5430
Charles Rushlow, *President*
EMP: 5
SQ FT: 1,650
SALES (est): 602K **Privately Held**
SIC: 2752 Commercial printing, offset

(G-17433)
KOENIG FUEL & SUPPLY CO
5501 Cogswell Rd (48184-1504)
P.O. Box 6349, Plymouth (48170-0353)
PHONE..................313 368-1870
Dave Folkerson, *Principal*
EMP: 5
SALES (est): 564.3K **Privately Held**
SIC: 3273 5983 Ready-mixed concrete; fuel oil dealers

(G-17434)
KWIK-SITE CORPORATION
5555 Treadwell St (48184-1599)
PHONE..................734 326-1500
Irving N Rubin, *President*
Ivan Jimenez, *Corp Secy*
EMP: 10
SQ FT: 10,000
SALES (est): 1.1MM **Privately Held**
WEB: www.kwiksitecorp.com
SIC: 3827 Lens mounts; gun sights, optical

(G-17435)
L A S LEASING INC
36253 Michigan Ave (48184-1652)
PHONE..................734 727-5148
Lisa Russo, *President*
EMP: 12
SQ FT: 15,000
SALES (est): 1.2MM **Privately Held**
SIC: 3537 Industrial trucks & tractors

(G-17436)
LENAWEE INDUSTRIAL PNT SUP INC (PA)
Also Called: Stage 5 Coatings
5645 Cogswell Rd (48184-1544)
PHONE..................734 729-8080
Kevin Stricker, *President*
Robert Wipe, *Principal*
EMP: 6
SQ FT: 20,000
SALES (est): 1.5MM **Privately Held**
WEB: www.lenaweepaint.com
SIC: 2851 Paints & allied products

(G-17437)
LOTTERY INFO
8432 Hannan Rd (48184-1558)
P.O. Box 87361, Canton (48187-0361)
PHONE..................734 326-0097
Warren Haley, *Owner*
EMP: 8
SALES (est): 573.4K **Privately Held**
WEB: www.lotteryinfoinc.com
SIC: 2732 Pamphlets: printing & binding, not published on site

(G-17438)
MOGUL MINDS LLC
3019 S Wayne Rd 23 (48184-1218)
PHONE..................682 217-9506
Jordan Cobb,
EMP: 3
SALES (est): 65.8K **Privately Held**
SIC: 7336 2759 Commercial art & graphic design; commercial printing

(G-17439)
MORKIN AND SOWARDS INC
38058 Van Born Rd (48184-1577)
PHONE..................734 729-4242
James Sowards, *President*
EMP: 12
SQ FT: 22,000
SALES (est): 2.6MM **Privately Held**
SIC: 3441 Fabricated structural metal

(G-17440)
OPIO LLC
35000 Van Born Rd (48184-2458)
PHONE..................313 433-1098
Bilal Hashwi, *President*
EMP: 10
SALES: 11.1MM **Privately Held**
SIC: 7372 4121 Application computer software; taxicabs

(G-17441)
REALM
34950 Van Born Rd (48184-2731)
PHONE..................313 706-4401
Larry Sheffield, *President*
EMP: 4
SALES (est): 408.9K **Privately Held**
WEB: www.realm.com
SIC: 5084 3699 Robots, industrial; teaching machines & aids, electronic

(G-17442)
RINGMASTERS MFG LLC
36502 Van Born Rd (48184-1510)
PHONE..................734 729-6110
Robert Krysiak,
Sharon Haverstock,
Michael Klingenberg,
EMP: 42
SALES (est): 8.1MM **Privately Held**
SIC: 3462 Iron & steel forgings

(G-17443)
SPORTS INC
34904 W Michigan Ave (48184-1766)
PHONE..................734 728-1313
Jeff Auer, *Owner*
EMP: 3
SALES (est): 359.6K **Privately Held**
SIC: 2759 5651 5941 5999 Screen printing; family clothing stores; sporting goods & bicycle shops; trophies & plaques

(G-17444)
TORTILLAS TITA LLC
3763 Commerce Ct (48184-2803)
PHONE..................734 756-7646
Martha Jaramillo, *Administration*
EMP: 6
SALES (est): 535.6K **Privately Held**
SIC: 2099 Tortillas, fresh or refrigerated

(G-17445)
UNISTRUT INTERNATIONAL CORP
Also Called: Unistrut Diversified Products
4205 Elizabeth St (48184-2091)
PHONE..................734 721-4040
J Piwok, *Plant Mgr*
EMP: 250 **Publicly Held**
SIC: 3441 Fabricated structural metal
HQ: Unistrut International Corporation
16100 Lathrop Ave
Harvey IL 60426
800 882-5543

Webberville
Ingham County

(G-17446)
APPLEGATE INSUL SYSTEMS INC (PA)
1000 Highview Dr (48892-9007)
PHONE..................517 521-3545
Aaron Applegate, *CEO*
Terry Applegate, *President*
Randy Beckett, *General Mgr*
Bob Thorp, *General Mgr*
Tracey Johnson, *Purch Mgr*
▼ **EMP:** 25
SQ FT: 30,000
SALES (est): 20.9MM **Privately Held**
SIC: 2499 2493 2823 2421 Mulch or sawdust products, wood; insulation & roofing material, reconstituted wood; cellulosic manmade fibers; sawmills & planing mills, general; recycling, waste materials

(G-17447)
CAR-MIN-VU FARM
2965 E Howell Rd (48892-9215)
PHONE..................517 749-9112
Carl Minnis, *Partner*
EMP: 2
SALES (est): 762.6K **Privately Held**
SIC: 2241 Narrow fabric mills

(G-17448)
CONTROLS FOR INDUSTRIES INC
5279 Royce Rd (48892-9760)
PHONE..................517 468-3385
David M Jackson, *President*
Dan Jackson, *Vice Pres*
Thomas Jackson, *Vice Pres*
EMP: 11
SALES: 300K **Privately Held**
SIC: 3625 Relays & industrial controls

(G-17449)
FORMRITE INC
2060 Elm Rd (48892)
P.O. Box 12 (48892-0012)
PHONE..................517 521-1373
Joseph Bonadeo, *President*
EMP: 5
SALES (est): 257.1K **Privately Held**
SIC: 3443 Chutes, metal plate

(G-17450)
GNUTTI CARLO USA INC
1101 Highview Dr (48892-9290)
PHONE..................517 223-1059
Paolo Groff, *CEO*
EMP: 292
SALES (corp-wide): 103.8MM **Privately Held**
SIC: 5084 3519 3699 8742 Welding machinery & equipment; diesel, semi-diesel or duel-fuel engines, including marine; welding machines & equipment, ultrasonic; management consulting services
HQ: Gnutti Carlo Usa, Inc.
1310 Francis St W
Jacksonville AL 36265
256 435-2200

(G-17451)
J AMERICA LLC (HQ)
Also Called: J. America Retail Products
1200 Mason Ct (48892-9021)
PHONE..................517 521-2525
Marius Brie, *Controller*
Peter Ruhala, *Mng Member*
Stephanie Vavricka, *Technology*
Jeff Fenech,
Jeff Radway,
◆ **EMP:** 50
SQ FT: 26,500
SALES: 1MM
SALES (corp-wide): 50.1MM **Privately Held**
SIC: 2329 2396 2395 Men's & boys' sportswear & athletic clothing; automotive & apparel trimmings; screen printing on fabric articles; embroidery products, except schiffli machine
PA: Vetta, Llc
1200 Mason Ct
Webberville MI 48892
517 521-2525

(G-17452)
MS PLASTIC WELDERS LLC
1101 Highview Dr (48892-9290)
PHONE..................517 223-1059
Volker Amann, *President*
Andreas Kriegler, *Vice Pres*
Mark Pucel, *Vice Pres*
Christine Greck, *Treasurer*
▲ **EMP:** 26
SQ FT: 32,000
SALES (est): 5.7MM **Privately Held**
SIC: 3699 Welding machines & equipment, ultrasonic

(G-17453)
SA AUTOMOTIVE LTD (PA)
1307 Highview Dr (48892-9300)
PHONE..................517 521-4205
Philip Zuehlke, *CFO*
Ed Shepler, *Manager*
Paul Crawford,
Shahriar Hedayat,
▲ **EMP:** 175
SQ FT: 63,000
SALES (est): 63.3MM **Privately Held**
SIC: 3089 Automotive parts, plastic

(G-17454)
SAKAIYA COMPANY AMERICA LTD
901 Highview Dr (48892-9270)
PHONE..................517 521-5633
Akira Sakaitani, *President*
Toshi Kazuma, *General Mgr*
Ken Sakaitani, *Treasurer*
Tetsuro Kobayashi, *Admin Sec*
▲ **EMP:** 30
SQ FT: 29,000
SALES (est): 5.8MM **Privately Held**
SIC: 3465 Moldings or trim, automobile: stamped metal

(G-17455)
VETTA LLC (PA)
1200 Mason Ct (48892-9021)
PHONE..................517 521-2525
Peter Ruhala, *Mng Member*
EMP: 6
SALES (est): 50.1MM **Privately Held**
SIC: 2329 Men's & boys' sportswear & athletic clothing

Weidman
Isabella County

(G-17456)
DYNAMIC MANUFACTURING LLC
5059 W Weidman Rd (48893-9718)
P.O. Box 39 (48893-0039)
PHONE..................989 644-8109
Fax: 989 644-6697
▼ **EMP:** 20 **EST:** 2010
SQ FT: 12,000
SALES (est): 2.4MM **Privately Held**
SIC: 3524 Mfg Lawn/Garden Equipment

(G-17457)
HARDCRETE INC
3610 N Rolland Rd (48893-9241)
PHONE..................989 644-5543
Ed Oneil, *Owner*
EMP: 6 **EST:** 2000
SALES: 500K **Privately Held**
SIC: 3273 Ready-mixed concrete

(G-17458)
LOR MANUFACTURING CO INC
7131 W Drew Rd (48893-9634)
PHONE..................866 644-8622
Lawrence O Rescoe, *President*
David Price, *Research*
Fred Bland, *Electrical Engi*
Blake Sisco, *Technology*
EMP: 8
SALES (est): 1.4MM **Privately Held**
WEB: www.lormfg.com
SIC: 3625 3663 3593 Electric controls & control accessories, industrial; radio & TV communications equipment; fluid power cylinders & actuators

(G-17459)
MAEDER BROS INC
Also Called: Maeder Bros Saw Mill
5016 W Weidman Rd (48893-9718)
PHONE..................989 644-2235
Richard Maeder, *President*
Gerald Maeder, *Shareholder*
Jane Atkinson, *Admin Sec*
EMP: 20
SALES: 2.8MM **Privately Held**
SIC: 2421 5211 Lumber: rough, sawed or planed; millwork & lumber

(G-17460)
MAEDER BROS QLTY WD PLLETS INC
5180 W Weidman Rd (48893-9718)
PHONE..................989 644-3500
Richard Maeder, *President*
Gerald Maeder, *Shareholder*
Jane Atkinson, *Admin Sec*
EMP: 13

Weidman - Isabella County (G-17461)   **GEOGRAPHIC SECTION**

SALES (est): 2.9MM **Privately Held**
SIC: **2421** Sawmills & planing mills, general

(G-17461)
PWGG
1040 Pueblo Pass (48893-9322)
PHONE...................................989 506-9402
James B Gutierrez, *Principal*
EMP: 12
SALES (est): 641.3K **Privately Held**
SIC: **2499** Wood products

(G-17462)
UNIFIED BRANDS INC
Also Called: Randell
525 S Coldwater Rd (48893-9609)
PHONE...................................989 644-3331
Jim Ervin, *Engineer*
Brian Simon, *Engineer*
Mark Upton, *Manager*
EMP: 20
SALES (corp-wide): 6.9B **Publicly Held**
SIC: **3469** Metal stampings
HQ: Unified Brands, Inc.
2016 Gees Mill Rd Ne
Conyers GA 30013
601 372-3903

Wellston
Manistee County

(G-17463)
NORMAN TOWNSHIP
Also Called: Norman Township Fire Dept
17201 6th St (49689-9347)
P.O. Box 143 (49689-0143)
PHONE...................................231 848-4495
Brook Schaffer, *Manager*
EMP: 21 **Privately Held**
SIC: **3569** Firefighting apparatus & related equipment
PA: Norman Township
1738 Maple St
Wellston MI 49689
231 848-4138

West Bloomfield
Oakland County

(G-17464)
ALLEGRA NETWORK LLC
7015 Cooley Lake Rd (48324-3902)
PHONE...................................248 360-1290
Tim Venus, *President*
Karen Venus, *President*
Bill Medlen, *Principal*
EMP: 10
SALES (est): 1.2MM **Privately Held**
SIC: **2752** Commercial printing, offset

(G-17465)
APPLIED COMPUTER TECHNOLOGIES
4301 Orchard Lake Rd # 160 (48323-1604)
PHONE...................................248 388-0211
EMP: 10
SALES (est): 760K **Privately Held**
SIC: **7372** Automotive Industry Consultant

(G-17466)
BLACK SKI WEEKEND LLC
7650 Cooley Lk Rd Ste 955 (48324)
PHONE...................................313 879-7150
Shed Amin, *Mng Member*
EMP: 2
SALES: 1MM **Privately Held**
SIC: **4724** 7372 Travel agencies; application computer software

(G-17467)
CALSONICKANSEI NORTH AMER INC
7460 Honeysuckle Rd (48324-2428)
PHONE...................................248 848-4727
EMP: 3
SALES (corp-wide): 8.1B **Privately Held**
SIC: **3694** Engine Electrical Equipment, Nsk
HQ: Cna Inc.
1 Calsonic Way
Shelbyville TN 37160
931 684-4490

(G-17468)
CARTALIGN RESEARCH CO
2667 Birch Harbor Ln (48324-1905)
PHONE...................................248 681-6689
Michael Goldstein, *Owner*
Arna Goldstein, *CFO*
EMP: 3
SALES (est): 252.3K **Privately Held**
SIC: **3651** Audio electronic systems

(G-17469)
CAUSEY CONSULTING LLC
6689 Orchard Lake Rd # 242 (48322-3404)
PHONE...................................248 671-4979
Michael Causey, *CEO*
EMP: 9 EST: 2013
SALES (est): 2.4MM **Privately Held**
SIC: **8748** 3669 4899 7389 Telecommunications consultant; emergency alarms; data communication services;

(G-17470)
CENTER CUPCAKES
6271 Bromley Ct (48322-3242)
PHONE...................................248 302-6503
EMP: 4
SALES (est): 320.9K **Privately Held**
SIC: **3331** Primary Copper Producer

(G-17471)
CROWN STEEL RAIL CO (PA)
6347 Northfield Rd (48322-2435)
P.O. Box 2703, Birmingham (48012-2703)
PHONE...................................248 593-7100
Roger S Trunsky, *President*
Barbara Trunsky, *Vice Pres*
Leonard H Trunsky, *Treasurer*
▲ EMP: 8 EST: 1980
SALES (est): 3.6MM **Privately Held**
SIC: **5088** 3312 Railroad equipment & supplies; railroad crossings, steel or iron

(G-17472)
D J ROTUNDA ASSOCIATES INC
2634 Peterboro Ct (48323-3121)
PHONE...................................586 772-3350
Donald D Rotunda, *President*
EMP: 5
SQ FT: 5,300
SALES (est): 750K **Privately Held**
SIC: **2752** 2759 Commercial printing, offset; advertising literature: printing

(G-17473)
DANIF INDUSTRIES INC
4289 Stoddard Rd (48323-3259)
PHONE...................................248 539-0295
EMP: 3
SALES (est): 158.9K **Privately Held**
SIC: **3999** Mfg Misc Products

(G-17474)
DETROIT AUTO SPECIALTIES INC
6960 Orchard Lake Rd # 301 (48322-4527)
PHONE...................................248 496-3856
Gary F Wyner, *President*
▲ EMP: 4 EST: 1977
SQ FT: 1,100
SALES (est): 155.3K **Privately Held**
SIC: **3429** Animal traps, iron or steel; motor vehicle hardware

(G-17475)
DETROIT EVRLASTING DEZIGNS INC
3648 Valleyview Ln (48323-3362)
PHONE...................................248 790-0850
Humam Alwan, *CEO*
EMP: 3
SALES (est): 25K **Privately Held**
SIC: **2759** Commercial printing

(G-17476)
ENERGY EFFICIENT LTG LLC EEL
3297 Wdview Lk Rd Ste 200 (48323)
PHONE...................................586 214-5557
Derryl Reed,
EMP: 4

SALES (est): 176.5K **Privately Held**
SIC: **1731** 3641 Electronic controls installation; lighting contractor; general electrical contractor; electric lamps; lamps, fluorescent, electric

(G-17477)
GENESIS SAND AND GRAVEL INC
6689 Orchard Lake Rd # 219 (48322-3404)
PHONE...................................313 587-8530
Jason Coleman, *Principal*
EMP: 3 EST: 2009
SALES (est): 146.5K **Privately Held**
SIC: **1442** Construction sand & gravel

(G-17478)
GENIX LLC
3151 Walnut Lake Rd (48323-3446)
PHONE...................................248 761-3030
EMP: 108
SALES (corp-wide): 6.7MM **Privately Held**
SIC: **3559** Ammunition & explosives, loading machinery
PA: Genix, Llc
43665 Utica Rd
Sterling Heights MI 48314
248 419-0231

(G-17479)
HARVEY S FREEMAN
Also Called: Independent Engineering Co
4159 Ladysmith St (48323-3108)
PHONE...................................248 852-2222
Harvey S Freeman, *Owner*
EMP: 20 EST: 1949
SALES (est): 1.7MM **Privately Held**
SIC: **3569** 3714 3563 3549 Assembly machines, non-metalworking; motor vehicle parts & accessories; air & gas compressors; metalworking machinery; industrial trucks & tractors; conveyors & conveying equipment

(G-17480)
HYDRO GIANT 4 INC
7480 Haggerty Rd (48322-1067)
PHONE...................................248 661-0034
Martin Yono, *President*
EMP: 12
SALES (est): 112K
SALES (corp-wide): 3.4MM **Privately Held**
SIC: **0782** 3524 Garden services; lawn & garden equipment
PA: Hg Management, Inc.
21651 W 8 Mile Rd
Detroit MI 48219
313 693-4916

(G-17481)
IGAN MICH PUBLISHING LLC
7025 Dandison Blvd (48324-2828)
PHONE...................................248 877-4649
Udo Neumann, *Principal*
EMP: 4
SALES (est): 175.2K **Privately Held**
SIC: **2711** Newspapers, publishing & printing

(G-17482)
JANICE MORSE INC
Also Called: Designs Unlimited
3160 Haggerty Rd Ste N (48323-2002)
PHONE...................................248 624-7300
Janice Morse, *President*
EMP: 24
SALES (est): 3.1MM **Privately Held**
WEB: www.designsunlimitedonline.com
SIC: **3083** 2511 2434 Plastic finished products, laminated; wood household furniture; vanities, bathroom: wood

(G-17483)
MARO PRECISION TOOL COMPANY
Also Called: Triple R Precision Boring Co
5041 Pheasant Cv (48323-2082)
PHONE...................................734 261-3100
Laurence S Rothenberg, *President*
Sol Rothenberg, *Vice Pres*
Alan Rothenberg, *Treasurer*
EMP: 18 EST: 1956
SQ FT: 11,000

SALES (est): 2.5MM **Privately Held**
WEB: www.marotool.com
SIC: **3545** Precision tools, machinists'

(G-17484)
METRO REBAR INC
4275 Middlebelt Rd (48323-3220)
PHONE...................................248 851-5894
Kenneth W Dudzinski, *President*
EMP: 6
SQ FT: 10,000
SALES (est): 1.4MM **Privately Held**
SIC: **3449** Bars, concrete reinforcing: fabricated steel

(G-17485)
MH INDUSTRIES LTD
Also Called: Detroit Washer & Specials
6960 Orchard Lake Rd # 301 (48322-4515)
PHONE...................................734 261-7560
Gary Wyner, *President*
Mike Eastman, *Manager*
EMP: 1
SALES: 5MM **Privately Held**
WEB: www.mhindustries.com
SIC: **3411** 3465 Metal cans; automotive stampings

(G-17486)
MICRO LOGIC
4710 Rolling Ridge Rd (48323-3342)
PHONE...................................248 432-7209
Sheldon Wolberg, *Administration*
EMP: 3
SALES (est): 207.6K **Privately Held**
SIC: **3672** Printed circuit boards

(G-17487)
MOHYI LABS LLC
2649 Cove Ln (48323-3601)
PHONE...................................248 973-7321
John Mohyi,
EMP: 6 EST: 2012
SALES (est): 284.9K **Privately Held**
SIC: **3721** Research & development on aircraft by the manufacturer

(G-17488)
MY PERMIT PAL INC
5030 Meadowbrook Dr (48322-1570)
PHONE...................................248 432-2699
Franci Silver, *President*
Carolann Goode, *Senior VP*
Robert Goode, *Shareholder*
Larry Silver, *Shareholder*
EMP: 4
SALES (est): 248.8K **Privately Held**
SIC: **3264** Magnets, permanent: ceramic or ferrite

(G-17489)
NAKED FUEL JUICE BAR
6718 Orchard Lake Rd (48322-3491)
PHONE...................................248 325-9735
EMP: 3
SALES (est): 194K **Privately Held**
SIC: **2869** Fuels

(G-17490)
NANEVA INC
5832 Naneva Ct (48322-2516)
PHONE...................................248 561-6425
David Mayer, *President*
EMP: 3
SALES (est): 133.4K **Privately Held**
SIC: **3695** Computer software tape & disks: blank, rigid & floppy

(G-17491)
NATIONAL CREDIT CORPORATION (PA)
7091 Orchard Lake Rd # 300 (48322-3654)
PHONE...................................734 459-8100
Fax: 248 855-6246
EMP: 10 EST: 1962
SALES (est): 20.4MM **Privately Held**
SIC: **6153** 6512 3949 6111 S-Term Bus Credit Instn Nonresdentl Bldg Operatr Mfg Sport/Athletic Goods Federal Credit Agency

GEOGRAPHIC SECTION

West Branch - Ogemaw County (G-17521)

(G-17492)
OPERATIONS RESEARCH TECH LLC
4050 Hanover Ct (48323-1815)
PHONE..................................248 626-8960
Steven A Semenuk,
Steven Semenuk,
EMP: 3
SALES: 100K **Privately Held**
SIC: 3559 3841 Automotive related machinery; surgical & medical instruments

(G-17493)
PHILLIPS-MEDISIZE LLC
Also Called: Detroit Sales Office
5706 Stonington Ct (48322-1432)
PHONE..................................248 592-2144
Caesar Weston, *Branch Mgr*
EMP: 10
SALES (corp-wide): 40.6B **Privately Held**
WEB: www.phillipsplastics.com
SIC: 3089 Injection molded finished plastic products
HQ: Pantheon Topco, Inc.
7 Long Lake Dr
Phillips WI 54555
715 386-4320

(G-17494)
RIVER RAISIN MODELS
6160 Upper Straits Blvd (48324-2870)
PHONE..................................248 366-9621
Daniel J Navarre, *Partner*
John W Hartmeyer, *Partner*
James Kindraka, *Partner*
EMP: 3
SALES: 100K **Privately Held**
WEB: www.riverraisinmodels.com
SIC: 3999 5945 Railroad models, except toy; hobby, toy & game shops

(G-17495)
SHERWOOD STUDIOS INC (PA)
Also Called: Sherwood Furniture
6644 Orchard Lake Rd (48322-3402)
PHONE..................................248 855-1600
Mark Morganroth, *President*
◆ **EMP:** 30
SQ FT: 23,000
SALES: 2.7MM **Privately Held**
WEB: www.sherwoodstudiosinc.com
SIC: 2512 7389 Upholstered household furniture; interior design services

(G-17496)
SHUTTERBOOTH
2441 Burleigh St (48324-3623)
PHONE..................................586 747-4110
EMP: 3
SALES (est): 218.8K **Privately Held**
SIC: 3442 Shutters, door or window: metal

(G-17497)
SINGH SENIOR LIVING LLC (PA)
Also Called: Walton Wood
7125 Orchard Lake Rd # 200 (48322-3615)
P.O. Box 255005 (48325-5005)
PHONE..................................248 865-1600
Rhonda Stewart, *Financial Analy*
Steven Tyshka, *Mng Member*
Chris Grabowski, *Manager*
Jessica Bartol, *Director*
Lindsay Charlefour, *Director*
EMP: 32
SALES (est): 17.4MM **Privately Held**
SIC: 2512 Living room furniture: upholstered on wood frames

(G-17498)
STANECKI INC (PA)
Also Called: Don-Lors Electronics
7550 Walnut Lake Rd (48323-2146)
PHONE..................................734 432-9900
Jason Stanecki, *President*
Anita Collins, *General Mgr*
Aaron Germaine, *General Mgr*
Jeremy Strickland, *General Mgr*
Tom Pomeroy, *Vice Pres*
EMP: 52
SQ FT: 4,800
SALES (est): 40.2MM **Privately Held**
WEB: www.donlors.com
SIC: 3663 Antennas, transmitting & communications

(G-17499)
STARTECH-SOLUTIONS LLC
6689 Orchard Lake Rd # 267 (48322-3404)
PHONE..................................248 419-0650
Joseph Williams, *Mng Member*
Joyce Williams, *Director*
Kevin Williams,
EMP: 5
SALES (est): 438.9K **Privately Held**
WEB: www.startechsolutions.org
SIC: 7373 1731 5099 7629 Computer integrated systems design; voice, data & video wiring contractor; video & audio equipment; telecommunication equipment repair (except telephones); radio receiver networks; telephone/video communications

(G-17500)
TANDIS LLC
6357 Branford Dr (48322-1098)
PHONE..................................248 345-3448
Igor Dykhno, *President*
EMP: 4
SALES (est): 213K **Privately Held**
SIC: 3699 Electron beam metal cutting, forming or welding machines

(G-17501)
TOPORS PICKLE CO INC
5407 Pocono Dr (48323-2339)
PHONE..................................313 237-0288
Larry Topor, *President*
Clara Topor, *Treasurer*
EMP: 6
SQ FT: 30,000
SALES: 750K **Privately Held**
SIC: 2035 Cucumbers, pickles & pickle salting; pickled fruits & vegetables

(G-17502)
TRU-FIT INTERNATIONAL INC
Also Called: Raydiance
5799 W Maple Rd Ste 167 (48322-4458)
PHONE..................................248 855-8845
Lisa Lano, *President*
EMP: 4
SALES (est): 378.6K **Privately Held**
SIC: 3999 Wigs, including doll wigs, toupees or wiglets

(G-17503)
TWIST
6331 Haggerty Rd (48322-5031)
PHONE..................................248 859-2169
Scott Simonovic, *Principal*
EMP: 6 EST: 2012
SALES (est): 486.3K **Privately Held**
SIC: 2026 Yogurt

(G-17504)
UNIQUE REPRODUCTIONS INC
5470 Carol Run S (48322-2110)
PHONE..................................248 788-2887
EMP: 4
SALES (est): 315.2K **Privately Held**
SIC: 2759 Commercial Printing

West Branch
Ogemaw County

(G-17505)
ADAPT
105 W Houghton Ave (48661-1286)
PHONE..................................989 343-9755
Vijay Kumar, *Owner*
EMP: 3
SALES (est): 224.9K **Privately Held**
SIC: 3999 Manufacturing industries; computer-aided design (CAD) systems service

(G-17506)
ASSOCIATE MFG INC
3977 S M 30 (48661-9106)
PHONE..................................989 345-0025
Jeff Dunlap, *President*
Jeff A Dunlap, *Manager*
EMP: 4 EST: 2004
SALES (est): 402.4K **Privately Held**
SIC: 3543 Industrial patterns

(G-17507)
BRANCH WEST CONCRETE PRODUCTS
3350 Rau Rd (48661-8723)
P.O. Box 336 (48661-0336)
PHONE..................................989 345-0794
Alan Gildner, *President*
Doris Gildner, *Corp Secy*
Rodger Gildner, *Vice Pres*
EMP: 10
SQ FT: 3,500
SALES (est): 1.7MM **Privately Held**
SIC: 3271 3273 1442 Blocks, concrete or cinder: standard; ready-mixed concrete; gravel mining

(G-17508)
BUNTING SAND & GRAVEL PRODUCTS
3247 Cook Rd (48661-9318)
P.O. Box 217 (48661-0217)
PHONE..................................989 345-2373
Robert A Resteiner, *President*
EMP: 20
SQ FT: 800
SALES (est): 5.6MM **Privately Held**
SIC: 1442 Construction sand mining

(G-17509)
JMC CUSTOM CABINETRY
960 W Houghton Ave (48661-1234)
PHONE..................................989 345-0475
EMP: 3
SALES (est): 244.9K **Privately Held**
SIC: 2434 Wood kitchen cabinets

(G-17510)
LAHTI FABRICATION INC
651 Columbus Ave (48661-8704)
PHONE..................................989 343-0420
Goerge O Lahti, *President*
George O Lahti, *President*
EMP: 14 EST: 1997
SQ FT: 5,000
SALES (est): 2.2MM **Privately Held**
WEB: www.lahtifab.com
SIC: 3444 Sheet metal specialties, not stamped

(G-17511)
LAY PRECISION MACHINE INC
620 Parkway Dr (48661-9201)
PHONE..................................989 726-5022
Kyle Hawley, *President*
Melinda Hawley, *Vice Pres*
EMP: 9 EST: 2017
SALES (est): 363.1K **Privately Held**
SIC: 3724 Aircraft engines & engine parts

(G-17512)
LINE X OF WESTBRANCH
155 N 4th St (48661-1217)
PHONE..................................989 345-7800
Craig Schwartz, *Owner*
EMP: 3
SALES (est): 200K **Privately Held**
SIC: 3714 Pickup truck bed liners

(G-17513)
MJ-HICK INC
2367 S M 76 (48661-9380)
PHONE..................................989 345-7610
Mark Hickey, *President*
EMP: 8 EST: 1995
SQ FT: 1,500
SALES (est): 990K **Privately Held**
WEB: www.balsm.com
SIC: 6531 7692 Real estate managers; welding repair

(G-17514)
OGEMAW COUNTY HERALD INC (PA)
Also Called: Northland Ad-Liner
215 W Houghton Ave (48661-1219)
P.O. Box 247 (48661-0247)
PHONE..................................989 345-0044
Robert E Perlberg, *President*
Ed Perlberg, *Admin Sec*
EMP: 23 EST: 1974
SALES (est): 1.6MM **Privately Held**
WEB: www.ogemawherald.com
SIC: 2711 2791 2789 2759 Newspapers: publishing only, not printed on site; typesetting; bookbinding & related work; commercial printing; commercial printing, lithographic

(G-17515)
PBG MICHIGAN LLC
610 Parkway Dr (48661-9201)
PHONE..................................989 345-2595
EMP: 4
SALES (est): 266.9K **Privately Held**
SIC: 2086 Bottled & canned soft drinks

(G-17516)
PEPSI-COLA METRO BTLG CO INC
610 Parkway Dr (48661-9205)
PHONE..................................989 345-2595
Brian Secorski, *Manager*
EMP: 30
SALES (corp-wide): 64.6B **Publicly Held**
WEB: www.joy-of-cola.com
SIC: 2086 Carbonated soft drinks, bottled & canned
HQ: Pepsi-Cola Metropolitan Bottling Company, Inc.
1111 Westchester Ave
White Plains NY 10604
914 767-6000

(G-17517)
PVH CORP
Also Called: Van Heusen
2990 Cook Rd Ste 104 (48661-9389)
PHONE..................................989 345-7939
EMP: 4
SALES (corp-wide): 8.2B **Publicly Held**
SIC: 2321 Mfg Men's/Boy's Furnishings
PA: Pvh Corp.
200 Madison Ave Bsmt 1
New York NY 10016
212 381-3500

(G-17518)
R & J QUALITY SCREENPRINTING
Also Called: R & J Screen Printing
266 S M 33 (48661-9799)
PHONE..................................989 345-8614
Robin Shite, *Owner*
EMP: 3
SQ FT: 1,392
SALES (est): 273K **Privately Held**
SIC: 2759 Screen printing

(G-17519)
ROSE TOOL & DIE INC
640 S Valley St (48661-9292)
P.O. Box 218 (48661-0218)
PHONE..................................989 343-1015
Les Fetters, *President*
Patti Fetters, *Admin Sec*
EMP: 22
SQ FT: 11,000
SALES (est): 4.8MM **Privately Held**
SIC: 3545 Machine tool accessories

(G-17520)
SANDVIK INC
510 Griffin Rd (48661-9251)
PHONE..................................989 345-6138
Gary Roberts, *Manager*
Heath Sinn, *Manager*
Jennifer Keeler, *Analyst*
EMP: 3
SALES (est): 199.6K **Privately Held**
SIC: 3341 Secondary nonferrous metals

(G-17521)
SAPPINGTON CRUDE OIL INC
123 N 6th St (48661-1263)
P.O. Box 279 (48661-0279)
PHONE..................................989 345-1052
Walter Sappington, *President*
Dianne M Sappington, *Corp Secy*
EMP: 8 EST: 1975
SQ FT: 2,400
SALES (est): 1.6MM **Privately Held**
SIC: 1311 1389 Crude petroleum production; natural gas production; servicing oil & gas wells

West Branch - Ogemaw County (G-17522)

(G-17522)
SAPPINGTON HENRY MACHINE & TL
222 Thomas St (48661-1102)
PHONE..................989 345-0711
Mary Ellen Good, *President*
Teresa Panigay, *President*
Rose Marie Joye, *Vice Pres*
Josephine Sappington, *Treasurer*
EMP: 20 **EST:** 1945
SALES (est): 1MM **Privately Held**
SIC: 1389 3599 Oil field services; haulage, oil field; roustabout service; machine shop, jobbing & repair

(G-17523)
SUNRISE PRINT CMMNICATIONS INC
118 W Houghton Ave (48661-1276)
PHONE..................989 345-4475
Chris Dack, *Principal*
EMP: 11
SALES (est): 1.6MM **Privately Held**
WEB: www.sunriseprint.com
SIC: 2752 Commercial printing, offset

(G-17524)
SUPER SIDEBAR INC
1396 Autumn Trl (48661-9097)
PHONE..................989 709-0048
Anthony Schmitt, *President*
▲ **EMP:** 3
SALES (est): 177.7K **Privately Held**
SIC: 2086 5046 Bottled & canned soft drinks; restaurant equipment & supplies

(G-17525)
TAYLOR BUILDING PRODUCTS INC (PA)
631 N 1st St (48661-1058)
P.O. Box 457 (48661-0457)
PHONE..................989 345-5110
Nick Cangialosi, *President*
Carol Valley, *VP Mfg*
Barb Krogulecki, *Controller*
Lori Halm, *Director*
▼ **EMP:** 72
SQ FT: 212,000
SALES (est): 17.6MM **Privately Held**
SIC: 3442 Metal doors; garage doors, overhead: metal

(G-17526)
TR TIMBER CO
502 E State Rd (48661-9762)
PHONE..................989 345-5350
Todd Rosebrugh, *Vice Pres*
Rebeka Rosebrugh, *Treasurer*
Tony Rosebrugh, *Treasurer*
Tamara Grezeszak, *Admin Sec*
Amanda Podojak, *Admin Sec*
EMP: 17
SQ FT: 4,000
SALES (est): 2MM **Privately Held**
SIC: 2411 Logging

(G-17527)
WALTER SAPPINGTON
Also Called: Sappington Machine & Tool
483 N 1st St (48661-1119)
PHONE..................989 345-1052
Walter Sappington, *Owner*
EMP: 3
SALES (est): 184.5K **Privately Held**
SIC: 3599 7692 3714 Machine shop, jobbing & repair; welding repair; motor vehicle parts & accessories

(G-17528)
WEST BRANCH WOOD TREATING INC
3800 S M 30 (48661-9170)
PHONE..................989 343-0066
Eugene Zapczynski, *Principal*
EMP: 4
SALES (est): 339.9K **Privately Held**
SIC: 2491 Wood preserving

(G-17529)
WHITING PETROLEUM CORPORATION
2251 Simmons Rd (48661-9365)
PHONE..................989 345-7903
Brian Osborne, *Manager*
EMP: 6
SALES (corp-wide): 2B **Publicly Held**
SIC: 1382 Oil & gas exploration services
PA: Whiting Petroleum Corporation
1700 Broadway Ste 2300
Denver CO 80290
303 837-1661

(G-17530)
WRIGHT BRACE & LIMB INC
611 Court St Ste 102 (48661-8820)
PHONE..................989 343-0300
Joseph Michael Wright, *President*
EMP: 3
SQ FT: 1,800
SALES (est): 345.1K **Privately Held**
SIC: 3842 Limbs, artificial; abdominal supporters, braces & trusses

West Olive
Ottawa County

(G-17531)
BBC COMMUNICATIONS INC
6463 Lakeshore Dr (49460-9743)
PHONE..................616 399-0432
Marilyn Benson, *President*
EMP: 4
SALES (est): 220.7K **Privately Held**
WEB: www.bbcworks.com
SIC: 3651 Household audio & video equipment

(G-17532)
BUNDEZE LLC
9717 Cottontail St (49460-8507)
PHONE..................248 343-9179
Aaron Schradin,
Todd Ireland,
Miles Smith,
EMP: 4 **EST:** 2013
SALES (est): 250K **Privately Held**
SIC: 2298 Slings, rope

(G-17533)
OLIVE ENGINEERING COMPANY
14354 Blair St W (49460)
P.O. Box 1624, Holland (49422-1624)
PHONE..................616 399-1756
William Wiswedel, *Owner*
EMP: 3
SQ FT: 2,400
SALES (est): 271.7K **Privately Held**
SIC: 3544 Jigs & fixtures

(G-17534)
PINNACLE MOLD & MACHINE INC
9900 Lake Michigan Dr (49460-9645)
PHONE..................616 892-9018
Don Morren, *President*
EMP: 4
SQ FT: 5,000
SALES (est): 410.8K **Privately Held**
SIC: 3544 Dies, plastics forming

(G-17535)
SKYLINE WINDOW CLEANING INC
Also Called: Skyline Fall Protection
9790 Winans St (49460-8906)
PHONE..................616 813-0536
Rick Ensing, *President*
Matthew Ensing, *Vice Pres*
EMP: 8
SQ FT: 2,600
SALES: 2.3MM **Privately Held**
SIC: 3842 5999 Personal safety equipment; safety supplies & equipment

(G-17536)
WELLARD INC
Also Called: Logodance, Inc.
10377 Mesic Dr (49460-9639)
PHONE..................312 752-0155
Ann Wellard, *Principal*
EMP: 3
SALES (est): 236.6K **Privately Held**
SIC: 8742 7389 2759 Marketing consulting services; embroidering of advertising on shirts, etc.; screen printing

Westland
Wayne County

(G-17537)
A-1 AWNING COMPANY
27618 Warren Rd (48185-2655)
PHONE..................734 421-0680
Stefan Bilak, *Owner*
EMP: 3
SQ FT: 6,000
SALES (est): 221.4K **Privately Held**
SIC: 3444 1521 Awnings, sheet metal; single-family housing construction

(G-17538)
ACME CARBIDE DIE INC (PA)
6202 E Executive Dr (48185-5694)
PHONE..................734 722-2303
Allen Schmitt, *President*
Sharon K Schmitt, *Corp Secy*
EMP: 20
SQ FT: 12,200
SALES (est): 2MM **Privately Held**
WEB: www.acmecarbide.com
SIC: 3544 3545 3444 Die sets for metal stamping (presses); machine tool accessories; sheet metalwork

(G-17539)
AERO MARINE INC
1517 N Wayne Rd (48185-7739)
PHONE..................734 721-6241
Scott Hebron, *President*
Randall C Hebron, *Vice Pres*
EMP: 3 **EST:** 1960
SQ FT: 3,600
SALES: 200K **Privately Held**
WEB: www.aeromarine.com
SIC: 3599 Machine & other job shop work

(G-17540)
ALTO MANUFACTURING INC
38338 Abruzzi Dr (48185-3282)
PHONE..................734 641-8800
Rudolph Ureste, *President*
Paul Ureste, *Vice Pres*
John Kraly, *Admin Sec*
EMP: 12 **EST:** 1948
SQ FT: 10,000
SALES: 1.5MM **Privately Held**
WEB: www.altomfg.com
SIC: 3541 Machine tool replacement & repair parts, metal cutting types

(G-17541)
AMERICAN GEAR & ENGRG CO INC
38200 Abruzzi Dr (48185-3280)
PHONE..................734 595-6400
Jeffrey L Emerson, *President*
Gerry Kmet, *Plant Mgr*
Tammy Adams, *Manager*
EMP: 40
SQ FT: 28,500
SALES (est): 9.5MM **Privately Held**
SIC: 3566 3545 3541 Gears, power transmission, except automotive; machine tool accessories; cutting tools for machine tools; machine tool replacement & repair parts, metal cutting types

(G-17542)
APOLLO BROACH INC
39001 Webb Ct (48185-7606)
PHONE..................734 467-5750
Kenneth Ahlgren Jr, *President*
Cheri Ahlgren, *Corp Secy*
John Knecht Jr, *Vice Pres*
EMP: 9
SQ FT: 10,500
SALES (est): 1MM **Privately Held**
WEB: www.apollobroach.com
SIC: 3545 Broaches (machine tool accessories)

(G-17543)
ARTCRAFT PATTERN WORKS INC
6430 Commerce Dr (48185-5677)
PHONE..................734 729-0022
Blair Mc Kendrick, *President*
Maria Mc Kendrick, *Corp Secy*
EMP: 15 **EST:** 1946
SQ FT: 8,000
SALES (est): 3MM **Privately Held**
WEB: www.artcraftgages.com
SIC: 3545 8711 8742 Gauges (machine tool accessories); designing: ship, boat, machine & product; quality assurance consultant

(G-17544)
ATM INTERNATIONAL SERVICES LLC
8351 N Wayne Rd (48185-1351)
PHONE..................734 524-9771
Fouad Dabaja,
EMP: 14
SALES (est): 1.8MM **Privately Held**
SIC: 3578 Automatic teller machines (ATM)

(G-17545)
AYOTTE CSTM MSCAL ENGRVNGS LLC
36688 Rolf St (48186-4071)
PHONE..................734 595-1901
Benjamin Ayotte,
EMP: 5
SALES (est): 308.2K **Privately Held**
SIC: 2741 Music book & sheet music publishing; music books: publishing & printing; music books: publishing only, not printed on site; music, sheet: publishing & printing

(G-17546)
B C I COLLET INC
6125 E Executive Dr (48185-1932)
P.O. Box 85718 (48185-0718)
PHONE..................734 326-1222
Richard T Baruk, *President*
David Baruk, *Vice Pres*
EMP: 25 **EST:** 1941
SQ FT: 11,000
SALES (est): 4.1MM **Privately Held**
WEB: www.bcicollet.com
SIC: 3545 Collets (machine tool accessories); pushers; tools & accessories for machine tools

(G-17547)
CDS SPECIALTY COATINGS LLC
1667 Rose Ln (48186-8632)
PHONE..................734 244-6708
Curtis Tamlin, *Mng Member*
Yvette Tamlin,
EMP: 7
SALES: 230K **Privately Held**
SIC: 3471 Plating & polishing

(G-17548)
CROSS TECHNOLOGIES GROUP INC
Also Called: Cross Chemical Company
1210 Manufacturers Dr (48186-4064)
PHONE..................734 895-8084
Mark Brown, *President*
Dennis Kendall Sr, *Vice Pres*
Robert Dyla, *Treasurer*
▲ **EMP:** 15
SQ FT: 25,000
SALES: 6.8MM **Privately Held**
WEB: www.crosschemical.com
SIC: 2899 Metal treating compounds

(G-17549)
DISCOUNT JEWELRY CENTER INC
8339 N Wayne Rd (48185-1351)
PHONE..................734 266-8200
Jay Benjamin, *President*
Brad Smith, *Vice Pres*
EMP: 5
SQ FT: 1,000
SALES: 700K **Privately Held**
SIC: 5944 3911 7631 Jewelry, precious stones & precious metals; jewelry, precious metal; jewelry repair services

(G-17550)
DNR INC (PA)
38475 Webb Dr (48185-1975)
PHONE..................734 722-4000
Dale V Roberts, *President*
Guy Roberts, *Vice Pres*
EMP: 18
SQ FT: 10,200

SALES: 1.2MM **Privately Held**
SIC: 3471 Tumbling (cleaning & polishing) of machine parts

(G-17551)
DOUBLE H MFG INC
6171 Commerce Dr (48185-7629)
PHONE 734 729-3450
Frank J Hradil, *President*
Olive Crysler, *Vice Pres*
EMP: 21
SQ FT: 20,000
SALES (est): 5.3MM **Privately Held**
WEB: www.doublehmfg.com
SIC: 3519 Engines, diesel & semi-diesel or dual-fuel

(G-17552)
EMBROIDERY SHOPPE LLC
39017 Cherry Hill Rd (48186-3250)
PHONE 734 595-7612
Jean Napolitano,
EMP: 7
SQ FT: 2,800
SALES: 800K **Privately Held**
WEB: www.theembroideryshoppe.com
SIC: 5699 2395 Uniforms; embroidery & art needlework

(G-17553)
ENRINITY SUPPLEMENTS INC
6480 Commerce Dr (48185-5677)
PHONE 734 322-4966
Udayan Chokshi, *President*
Parimal Bhatt, *Shareholder*
EMP: 8
SQ FT: 10,000
SALES: 500K **Privately Held**
SIC: 2023 Dietary supplements, dairy & non-dairy based

(G-17554)
ERNEST INDUSTRIES ACQUISITION, (PA)
Also Called: Ernest Industries Company
39133 Webb Dr (48185-1986)
PHONE 734 595-9500
EMP: 20
SALES (est): 8MM **Privately Held**
WEB: www.ernestind.com
SIC: 3469 3315 3317 3824 Metal stampings; welded steel wire fabric; welded pipe & tubes; mechanical & electro-mechanical counters & devices

(G-17555)
FEDEX OFFICE & PRINT SVCS INC
7677 N Wayne Rd (48185-2014)
PHONE 734 522-7322
EMP: 14
SALES (corp-wide): 69.6B **Publicly Held**
WEB: www.kinkos.com
SIC: 7334 2791 2789 2752 Photocopying & duplicating services; typesetting; bookbinding & related work; commercial printing, lithographic
HQ: Fedex Office And Print Services, Inc.
    7900 Legacy Dr
    Plano TX 75024
    800 463-3339

(G-17556)
FLEETWOOD TOOL & GAGE INC
39050 Webb Ct (48185-7606)
PHONE 734 326-6737
Jurgen Schnepel, *CEO*
David Schnepel, *President*
EMP: 15
SQ FT: 10,000
SALES (est): 2.7MM **Privately Held**
WEB: www.fleetwoodtool.com
SIC: 3599 Machine shop, jobbing & repair

(G-17557)
FLINT GROUP LLC
6380 Commerce Dr (48185-9120)
PHONE 734 641-3062
John Louzon, *Opers Mgr*
Hogen Susan, *Accounts Mgr*
Jim Oconnell, *Sales Staff*
Jeff Sherwood, *Marketing Mgr*
Howard Flint, *Branch Mgr*
EMP: 4

SALES (corp-wide): 177.9K **Privately Held**
SIC: 2893 Printing ink
HQ: Flint Group, Llc
    19401 Rogers Dr
    Rogers MN 55374
    763 559-5911

(G-17558)
FLODRAULIC GROUP INCORPORATED
Also Called: Rhm Fluid Power
375 Manufacturers Dr (48186-4038)
PHONE 734 326-5400
Mark Jackson, *General Mgr*
Matthew Verona, *General Mgr*
Frank Bowles, *Engineer*
Richard Czajka, *Sales Staff*
EMP: 65
SALES (est): 2.5B **Privately Held**
SIC: 5084 3569 Hydraulic systems equipment & supplies; compressors, except air conditioning; filter elements, fluid, hydraulic line; jacks, hydraulic
PA: Flodraulic Group Incorporated
    3539 N 700 W
    Greenfield IN 46140
    317 890-3700

(G-17559)
G & L TOOL INC
Also Called: G & L Tool & Die
5874 E Executive Dr (48185-9115)
PHONE 734 728-1990
David Jackson, *President*
James Hill, *Vice Pres*
EMP: 14
SQ FT: 6,950
SALES (est): 2.2MM **Privately Held**
SIC: 3544 Special dies & tools

(G-17560)
G&J PRODUCTS & SERVICES
8219 Roselawn St (48185-1613)
PHONE 734 522-2984
John Mendler, *Owner*
EMP: 6
SALES (est): 406.7K **Privately Held**
SIC: 2511 Camp furniture: wood

(G-17561)
GENERATION TOOL INC
307 Manufacturers Dr (48186-4038)
PHONE 734 641-6937
Michael E Rotter, *President*
EMP: 6
SQ FT: 10,000
SALES (est): 1.1MM **Privately Held**
WEB: www.generationtools.com
SIC: 3559 3544 Automotive related machinery; jigs & fixtures

(G-17562)
GLOBAL GEAR INC
6049 E Executive Dr (48185-1932)
PHONE 734 979-0888
Jun Zheng, *CEO*
Peng Fei, *Vice Pres*
EMP: 30 **EST:** 2017
SQ FT: 6,000
SALES: 100K **Privately Held**
SIC: 3462 Gear & chain forgings

(G-17563)
GREAT LAKES AIR PRODUCTS INC
1515 S Nwburgh Rd Ste 100 (48186)
PHONE 734 326-7080
Patricia J Larson, *President*
Larry Larson, *Vice Pres*
Ben Traver, *Sales Engr*
Brian Larson, *Marketing Staff*
Pat Larson, *Manager*
▲ EMP: 48
SQ FT: 20,100
SALES (est): 12.7MM **Privately Held**
WEB: www.glair.com
SIC: 3585 Compressors for refrigeration & air conditioning equipment

(G-17564)
GREENS WELDING & REPAIR CO
1507 S Wayne Rd (48186-5436)
PHONE 734 721-5434

Laina Green, *President*
Al Green, *Vice Pres*
Larry Green, *Treasurer*
EMP: 3
SQ FT: 5,000
SALES: 150K **Privately Held**
SIC: 3444 3599 7692 5051 Sheet metalwork; machine shop, jobbing & repair; welding repair; metals service centers & offices; fabricated plate work (boiler shop)

(G-17565)
GRINDING SPECIALISTS INC
38310 Abruzzi Dr (48185-3282)
PHONE 734 729-1775
Dennis Johnson, *President*
Cindy Johnson, *Vice Pres*
EMP: 20
SQ FT: 12,000
SALES (est): 2.8MM **Privately Held**
WEB: www.gsi1.com
SIC: 3599 3317 Grinding castings for the trade; welded pipe & tubes

(G-17566)
GT TECHNOLOGIES INC (PA)
Also Called: Defiance Group, The
5859 E Executive Dr (48185-1932)
PHONE 734 467-8371
Paul Schwarzbaum, *President*
John Brune, *Vice Pres*
Jim Porcaro, *Vice Pres*
Jennifer George, *Purch Mgr*
Theresa Brenner, *Senior Buyer*
◆ EMP: 40
SALES (est): 102.9MM **Privately Held**
SIC: 8711 3714 3545 3089 Designing: ship, boat, machine & product; motor vehicle engines & parts; machine tool attachments & accessories; injection molded finished plastic products

(G-17567)
H & A PHARMACY II LLC
2379 S Venoy Rd (48186-4662)
PHONE 313 995-4552
Hassan Saaad, *Mng Member*
EMP: 3
SALES (est): 81.8K **Privately Held**
SIC: 2834 Tablets, pharmaceutical

(G-17568)
HELIUM HOME BASE LLC
2600 Nichols Ct (48186-9376)
PHONE 734 895-3608
David Jenkins, *Principal*
EMP: 3
SALES (est): 149.1K **Privately Held**
SIC: 2813 Helium

(G-17569)
HIGH-STAR CORPORATION
Also Called: Engineering and Mfg Svcs
6171 Commerce Dr (48185-5683)
PHONE 734 743-1503
Son Do, *CEO*
◆ EMP: 5
SQ FT: 6,000
SALES (est): 250K **Privately Held**
SIC: 3541 3469 8711 Lathes, metal cutting & polishing; numerically controlled metal cutting machine tools; metal stampings; designing: ship, boat, machine & product

(G-17570)
HILL SCREW MACHINE PRODUCTS
8463 Hugh St (48185-1840)
PHONE 734 427-8237
William F Hill, *President*
John Fowler, *Vice Pres*
EMP: 8
SQ FT: 12,000
SALES (est): 798.7K **Privately Held**
WEB: www.colescrew.com
SIC: 3451 Screw machine products

(G-17571)
INTRA CORPORATION (PA)
885 Manufacturers Dr (48186-4036)
PHONE 734 326-7030
John Battista Sr, *CEO*
John Battista Jr, *President*
Eric Headrick, *Plant Mgr*
Clifford Norris, *Plant Mgr*

John Pfeiffer, *Purch Agent*
▲ EMP: 105
SQ FT: 55,000
SALES (est): 24.7MM **Privately Held**
WEB: www.intra-corp.net
SIC: 3829 Measuring & controlling devices

(G-17572)
JADE SCIENTIFIC INC (PA)
39103 Warren Rd (48185-1928)
PHONE 734 207-3775
Jheri Len Smolin, *President*
Michael Smolin, *President*
Charles Holleran, *Owner*
Micky Jones, *Sales Staff*
Jodi Moss, *Sales Staff*
EMP: 11
SQ FT: 9,500
SALES (est): 8.8MM **Privately Held**
WEB: www.jadesci.com
SIC: 5049 5169 3821 2869 Analytical instruments; laboratory equipment, except medical or dental; scientific instruments; chemicals & allied products; laboratory equipment: fume hoods, distillation racks, etc.; worktables, laboratory; laboratory chemicals, organic; industrial inorganic chemicals; microscopes, electron & proton

(G-17573)
JEDTCO CORP
5899 E Executive Dr (48185-5696)
PHONE 734 326-3010
Nancy Siwik, *President*
Michael Siwik, *Corp Secy*
S Ann Elliott, *Vice Pres*
EMP: 22 **EST:** 1971
SALES (est): 3.8MM **Privately Held**
SIC: 3069 Custom compounding of rubber materials; molded rubber products

(G-17574)
JET INDUSTRIES INC
38379 Abruzzi Dr (48185-3283)
PHONE 734 641-0900
Debra Kansier, *President*
Maureen Trainor, *Senior VP*
Daniel Trainor, *Vice Pres*
▲ EMP: 24
SQ FT: 7,500
SALES: 1.5MM **Privately Held**
SIC: 3714 3494 Exhaust systems & parts, motor vehicle; mufflers (exhaust), motor vehicle; valves & pipe fittings

(G-17575)
JOKAB SAFETY NORTH AMERICA INC (PA)
6471 Commerce Dr (48185-9127)
PHONE 888 282-2123
Brian Sukarukoff, *Principal*
▲ EMP: 13
SALES (est): 1.6MM **Privately Held**
WEB: www.jokabsafetyna.com
SIC: 3499 Fire- or burglary-resistive products

(G-17576)
KAH
Also Called: Universal Laundry Machinery
38700 Webb Dr (48185-1978)
PHONE 734 727-0478
Mark Hubbard, *President*
Ted Jaeckel, *Controller*
▲ EMP: 3
SALES (est): 747.9K **Privately Held**
WEB: www.univlaundry.com
SIC: 3582 Commercial laundry equipment

(G-17577)
LINK TOOL & MFG CO LLC
Also Called: Linktool Group
39115 Warren Rd (48185-1928)
PHONE 734 710-0010
Mark Petty, *President*
EMP: 80
SQ FT: 28,000
SALES (est): 13.3MM
SALES (corp-wide): 483.7MM **Privately Held**
WEB: www.linktoolmfg.com
SIC: 3544 Extrusion dies

Westland - Wayne County (G-17578)

HQ: Penn Engineering & Manufacturing Corp.
5190 Old Easton Rd
Danboro PA 18916
215 766-8853

(G-17578)
MASTER COAT LLC
6120 Commerce Dr (48185-9119)
PHONE..................734 405-2340
Leonard Stephenson,
EMP: 12
SQ FT: 33,000
SALES: 1MM **Privately Held**
SIC: 3479 Coating of metals & formed products

(G-17579)
METRO CAST CORPORATION
6170 Commerce Dr (48185-9119)
PHONE..................734 728-0210
Constantin Bodea, *President*
Ramon Escobar, *Officer*
EMP: 6
SQ FT: 14,000
SALES (est): 1MM **Privately Held**
WEB: www.metrocastcorp.com
SIC: 3272 Concrete products

(G-17580)
MIKES CABINET SHOP INC
Also Called: MCS Custom Design
37100 Enterprise Dr (48186-4028)
PHONE..................734 722-1800
Tony Chalhoub, *Opers Staff*
Mikhail Chalhoub, *Branch Mgr*
EMP: 6
SALES (corp-wide): 729.7K **Privately Held**
SIC: 2434 Wood kitchen cabinets
PA: Mike's Cabinet Shop, Inc.
27031 W 7 Mile Rd
Redford MI
313 533-5800

(G-17581)
MONARCH PRINT AND MAIL LLC
1461 Selma St (48186-4024)
PHONE..................734 620-8378
Scott Wolkhamer, *Principal*
EMP: 4
SALES (est): 114.4K **Privately Held**
SIC: 2752 Commercial printing, offset

(G-17582)
NATIONAL BLOCK COMPANY
Also Called: National Ready-Mix
39000 Ford Rd (48185-1998)
PHONE..................734 721-4050
Marty Eisenstein, *President*
James Gendron, *Vice Pres*
Brenda Birman, *Controller*
Amy Hollinshead, *Human Resources*
EMP: 25
SQ FT: 4,800
SALES (est): 5.7MM **Privately Held**
WEB: www.nationalblock.com
SIC: 3273 3271 5211 3272 Ready-mixed concrete; blocks, concrete or cinder: standard; cement; masonry materials & supplies; concrete products

(G-17583)
NEW GENESIS ENTERPRISE INC
37774 Willow Ln Apt S2 (48185-3326)
PHONE..................313 220-0365
David Lyles, *CEO*
EMP: 13
SALES (est): 65.4K **Privately Held**
SIC: 7929 2741 Entertainment service; miscellaneous publishing

(G-17584)
NORTHFIELD MANUFACTURING INC
38549 Webb Dr (48185-1983)
PHONE..................734 729-2890
Dennis Tynan, *CEO*
Scott Tynan, *President*
Dave Sylvester, *COO*
Christopher Tynan, *Vice Pres*
EMP: 45
SQ FT: 30,000
SALES (est): 9.4MM **Privately Held**
WEB: www.northfieldfoundry.com
SIC: 3325 Alloy steel castings, except investment

(G-17585)
NYX LLC
Also Called: Nyx Cherryhill Division
1000 Manufacturers Dr (48186-4064)
PHONE..................734 467-7200
Dennis Dunlop, *Manager*
EMP: 150
SALES (corp-wide): 607.1MM **Privately Held**
WEB: www.nyxinc.com
SIC: 3089 Injection molding of plastics
PA: Nyx, Llc
36111 Schoolcraft Rd
Livonia MI 48150
734 462-2385

(G-17586)
PARKER ENGINEERING AMER CO LTD
38147 Abruzzi Dr (48185-3279)
PHONE..................734 326-7630
John M Cole, *President*
EMP: 13
SALES (est): 633.3K **Privately Held**
SIC: 3563 Robots for industrial spraying, painting, etc.

(G-17587)
PENGUIN JUICE CO (PA)
39002 Webb Ct (48185-7606)
PHONE..................734 467-6991
Jack D Pauley, *President*
Victoria Kohlstrand, *Corp Secy*
Linda Pauley, *Vice Pres*
▲ **EMP:** 15
SQ FT: 11,150
SALES (est): 1.9MM **Privately Held**
SIC: 2087 5149 Beverage bases, concentrates, syrups, powders & mixes; fruit juices: concentrated for fountain use; syrups, drink; extracts, flavoring; beverage concentrates

(G-17588)
PLASMA PROS
8179 Parkside Dr (48185-4607)
PHONE..................734 354-6737
EMP: 3
SALES (est): 229.3K **Privately Held**
SIC: 2836 Mfg Biological Products

(G-17589)
PLASTIPAK PACKAGING INC
1351 N Hix Rd (48185-3258)
PHONE..................734 326-6184
William C Young, *President*
EMP: 123
SALES (corp-wide): 1.3B **Privately Held**
WEB: www.plastipak.com
SIC: 3089 3085 Pallets, plastic; plastics bottles
HQ: Plastipak Packaging, Inc.
41605 Ann Arbor Rd E
Plymouth MI 48170
734 455-3600

(G-17590)
PLYMOUTH BRAZING INC
6140 N Hix Rd (48185-1962)
PHONE..................734 453-6274
Dallas Gibson, *President*
Jason Tell, *Vice Pres*
Diane Gibson, *Office Mgr*
Rob McComb, *Manager*
Debbie Snider, *Manager*
EMP: 65
SQ FT: 32,000
SALES (est): 3MM **Privately Held**
WEB: www.plymouthbrazing.com
SIC: 7692 Brazing

(G-17591)
PROMAX ENGINEERING LLC
6035 E Executive Dr (48185-1932)
PHONE..................734 979-0888
John Zheng, *General Mgr*
Jun Zheng,
▲ **EMP:** 110
SALES (est): 14.9MM **Privately Held**
WEB: www.promax-eng.com
SIC: 2531 Seats, automobile

(G-17592)
PROVIDENCE WORLDWIDE LLC
39005 Webb Dr (48185-1979)
PHONE..................313 586-4144
Jeff Bucher,
EMP: 20
SQ FT: 33,000
SALES: 471.1K **Privately Held**
SIC: 3444 Metal housings, enclosures, casings & other containers

(G-17593)
R & A TOOL & ENGINEERING CO
39127 Ford Rd (48185-1985)
PHONE..................734 981-2000
Richard L Raymond, *President*
Gregory J Raymond, *Vice Pres*
Robert P Raymond, *Vice Pres*
Ron Raymond, *Vice Pres*
▲ **EMP:** 30 EST: 1945
SQ FT: 26,000
SALES (est): 6.2MM **Privately Held**
WEB: www.randatool.com
SIC: 3545 3544 Tools & accessories for machine tools; dies & die holders for metal cutting, forming, die casting

(G-17594)
RED SPOT WESTLAND INC
550 Edwin St (48186-3801)
PHONE..................734 729-1913
Charles D Storms, *President*
Madelyn Kraemer, *Admin Sec*
▲ **EMP:** 110
SQ FT: 85,000
SALES (est): 15.5MM **Privately Held**
WEB: www.redspot.com
SIC: 2851 Paints & paint additives; lacquers, varnishes, enamels & other coatings
HQ: Red Spot Paint & Varnish Co Inc
1107 E Louisiana St
Evansville IN 47711
812 428-9100

(G-17595)
RELIANCE METAL PRODUCTS INC
1157 Mfrs Dr Ste B (48186)
PHONE..................734 641-3334
Thomas P Malysz, *President*
▲ **EMP:** 7
SALES: 1MM **Privately Held**
SIC: 3469 Machine parts, stamped or pressed metal

(G-17596)
RELIANCE RUBBER INDUSTRIES INC
38230 N Executive Dr (48185-1972)
PHONE..................734 641-4100
Gordhan Akbari, *President*
EMP: 9
SQ FT: 11,000
SALES (est): 1.1MM **Privately Held**
SIC: 3061 Mechanical rubber goods

(G-17597)
ROBMAR PRECISION MFG INC
38189 Abruzzi Dr (48185-3279)
PHONE..................734 326-2664
Greg S Doss, *President*
Robert King, *Vice Pres*
EMP: 26
SQ FT: 12,000
SALES (est): 4.5MM **Privately Held**
WEB: www.robmar.com
SIC: 3599 Machine shop, jobbing & repair

(G-17598)
SAAD FUELS INC
8755 N Middlebelt Rd (48185-1812)
PHONE..................734 425-2829
Sleiman Saad, *Principal*
EMP: 3
SALES (est): 252.2K **Privately Held**
SIC: 2869 Fuels

(G-17599)
SOMERS STEEL
6221 Commerce Dr (48185-5678)
PHONE..................734 729-3700
Cheryl Frey, *Branch Mgr*
EMP: 3
SQ FT: 10,000
SALES: 495K **Privately Held**
SALES (corp-wide): 22.4MM **Privately Held**
WEB: www.somersforge.com
SIC: 3462 Iron & steel forgings
HQ: Folkes Forgings Limited
Haywood Forge
Halesowen W MIDLANDS B62 8

(G-17600)
SPECTRUM METAL PRODUCTS INC
38289 Abruzzi Dr (48185-3281)
PHONE..................734 595-7600
Paul Massimilla, *President*
Dolores Massimilla, *Vice Pres*
EMP: 7
SQ FT: 6,800
SALES: 700K **Privately Held**
SIC: 3444 Sheet metalwork

(G-17601)
SURE-FIT GLOVE & SAFETY
38241 Abruzzi Dr (48185-3281)
P.O. Box 85546 (48185-0546)
PHONE..................734 729-4960
Robert Elrod, *Partner*
EMP: 3
SQ FT: 400
SALES (est): 370K **Privately Held**
WEB: www.surefitglove.com
SIC: 3842 Clothing, fire resistant & protective

(G-17602)
TECRA SYSTEMS INC (PA)
6005 E Executive Dr (48185-1932)
PHONE..................248 888-1116
Giridhar Gondi, *President*
Rod Lowe, *Minister*
Chip Culley, *Vice Pres*
SAI Parvataneni, *Vice Pres*
Giri Vinnakota, *Programmer Anys*
EMP: 28
SQ FT: 2,500
SALES (est): 5.7MM **Privately Held**
WEB: www.tecra.com
SIC: 7372 7379 7371 Prepackaged software; data processing consultant; computer software development

(G-17603)
THERMAL ONE INC (PA)
Also Called: Special Div
39026 Webb Ct (48185-7606)
PHONE..................734 721-8500
Ted Gaderick, *CEO*
Robert Gaderick, *Vice Pres*
EMP: 15
SALES (est): 3.3MM **Privately Held**
SIC: 3398 Metal heat treating

(G-17604)
TOP NOTCH COOKIES & CAKES INC
1849 Knolson St (48185-3256)
PHONE..................734 467-9550
Theresa Wheelock, *President*
Greg Wheelock, *Vice Pres*
EMP: 8
SALES: 500K **Privately Held**
SIC: 2052 2051 5461 Cookies; cakes, bakery: except frozen; bread, all types (white, wheat, rye, etc): fresh or frozen; bakeries

(G-17605)
TRI-STAR TOOL & MACHINE CO
613 Manufacturers Dr (48186-4036)
PHONE..................734 729-5700
Kenneth Pelland, *President*
Winifred Pelland, *Corp Secy*
EMP: 10
SQ FT: 13,600
SALES (est): 1.6MM **Privately Held**
SIC: 3599 3544 Machine shop, jobbing & repair; jigs & fixtures

(G-17606)
TRU-BORE MACHINE TOOL CO INC
6262 E Executive Dr (48185-1940)
PHONE..................734 729-9590
Jon Horgas, *President*
EMP: 8

GEOGRAPHIC SECTION

SQ FT: 4,000
SALES (est): 638.1K **Privately Held**
WEB: www.tru-bore.com
SIC: 3599 Machine shop, jobbing & repair

(G-17607)
US FARATHANE HOLDINGS CORP
39200 Ford Rd (48185-9131)
PHONE.................................586 978-2800
Mike Sermo, *Principal*
EMP: 70
SALES (corp-wide): 876MM **Privately Held**
SIC: 3089 Plastic hardware & building products
PA: U.S. Farathane Holdings Corp.
11650 Park Ct
Shelby Township MI 48315
586 726-1200

(G-17608)
VITRO AUTOMOTRIZ SA DE CV
Also Called: V V P Auto Glass
1515 S Newburgh Rd Unit B (48186-4077)
PHONE.................................734 727-5001
Carolyn Rowland, *Opers Mgr*
Horacio Trujillo, *Marketing Mgr*
Luis Corona, *Branch Mgr*
Doug Harts, *CTO*
EMP: 15 **Privately Held**
SIC: 3231 5013 Doors, glass: made from purchased glass; automobile glass
HQ: Vitro Automotriz, S.A. De C.V.
Carretera A Garcia Km. 10.3
Villa De Garcia N.L. 66000

(G-17609)
WARFIELD ELECTRIC COMPANY INC
5920 N Hix Rd (48185-7674)
PHONE.................................734 722-4044
Ed Hazelrigg, *Manager*
EMP: 5
SALES (corp-wide): 6MM **Privately Held**
SIC: 7694 Rewinding stators; rebuilding motors, except automotive; coil winding service
PA: Warfield Electric Company, Inc.
175 Industry Ave
Frankfort IL 60423
815 469-4094

(G-17610)
WEBB PARTNERS INC
39140 Webb Dr (48185-7628)
PHONE.................................734 727-0560
David Lagrow, *President*
Cynthia Lagrow, *CFO*
EMP: 25
SQ FT: 230,000
SALES (est): 4.3MM **Privately Held**
WEB: www.magnum-mfg.com
SIC: 3599 Machine shop, jobbing & repair

(G-17611)
WEST SIDE FLAMEHARDENING INC
38200 N Executive Dr (48185-1972)
PHONE.................................734 729-1665
Michael Seror, *President*
EMP: 13
SQ FT: 10,500
SALES: 790K **Privately Held**
WEB: www.westsideflamehardening.com
SIC: 3398 Brazing (hardening) of metal

(G-17612)
WESTSIDE TOOL & GAGE LLC
5682 Morley St (48185-1911)
PHONE.................................734 728-9520
William Jakel,
EMP: 3
SALES: 150K **Privately Held**
SIC: 3545 Gauges (machine tool accessories)

Weston
Lenawee County

(G-17613)
SILBOND CORPORATION
9901 Sand Creek Hwy (49289)
PHONE.................................517 436-3171
Larry Brown, *COO*
John Gruber, *CFO*
Timothy Walz, *Controller*
◆ **EMP:** 50
SALES (est): 24.5MM **Privately Held**
WEB: www.silbond.com
SIC: 2819 Industrial inorganic chemicals

Westphalia
Clinton County

(G-17614)
GROSS MACHINE SHOP
319 E Main St (48894-5113)
P.O. Box 65 (48894-0065)
PHONE.................................989 587-4021
Gerard A Gross, *Partner*
Gerard Gross, *Partner*
Michael Gross, *Partner*
EMP: 4 **EST:** 1937
SALES (est): 499.9K **Privately Held**
WEB: www.spectrumbusiness.com
SIC: 3599 Machine shop, jobbing & repair

Wetmore
Alger County

(G-17615)
MICHAEL GRAVES LOGGING
N3293 Buckhorn Rd (49895-9035)
PHONE.................................906 387-2852
EMP: 3
SALES (est): 210.3K **Privately Held**
SIC: 2411 Logging

(G-17616)
MODERN WOODSMITH LLC
E9998 State Highway M28 (49895-9567)
PHONE.................................906 387-5577
Timothy Flynn,
EMP: 5
SALES (est): 580K **Privately Held**
WEB: www.themodernwoodsmith.com
SIC: 5031 2431 Kitchen cabinets; millwork

Wheeler
Gratiot County

(G-17617)
PATCH WORKS FARMS INC
Also Called: Double B'S Steel and Mfg
9710 E Monroe Rd (48662-9772)
PHONE.................................989 430-3610
Greg Baxter, *General Mgr*
William Butcher, *Principal*
Chuck Baxter, *Manager*
EMP: 4
SALES (est): 190.9K **Privately Held**
SIC: 3599 3291 Custom machinery; abrasive metal & steel products

White Cloud
Newaygo County

(G-17618)
ACAT GLOBAL LLC
66 N North St (49349-8832)
PHONE.................................231 437-5000
Joe Moch, *Branch Mgr*
EMP: 10
SALES (corp-wide): 2.4MM **Privately Held**
SIC: 3621 Rotary converters (electrical equipment)
PA: Acat Global, Llc
5339 M 66 N
Charlevoix MI 49720
231 330-2553

(G-17619)
ARROW DIE & MOLD REPAIR
8527 E Wilderness Trl (49349-9127)
PHONE.................................231 689-1829
Roger Mollema, *Owner*
EMP: 4
SQ FT: 6,000
SALES: 200K **Privately Held**
SIC: 3089 Injection molded finished plastic products

(G-17620)
BP LUBRICANTS USA INC
201 N Webster St (49349-9678)
PHONE.................................231 689-0002
Pam Myers, *Human Res Mgr*
Dave Herin, *Accounts Mgr*
Richard Moen, *Branch Mgr*
Nesrin Sheppard, *Manager*
EMP: 47
SALES (corp-wide): 298.7B **Privately Held**
WEB: www.lubecon.com
SIC: 5171 2992 Petroleum bulk stations & terminals; lubricating oils & greases
HQ: Bp Lubricants Usa Inc.
1500 Valley Rd
Wayne NJ 07470
973 633-2200

(G-17621)
E POWER REMOTE LTD
Also Called: Services Unlimited
223 N Webster St (49349-9678)
P.O. Box 951 (49349-0951)
PHONE.................................231 689-5448
Craig L Myers, *President*
Lyle G Myers, *Chairman*
EMP: 3
SALES (est): 426.4K **Privately Held**
SIC: 3569 1542 1541 Lubricating equipment; commercial & office building contractors; industrial buildings & warehouses

(G-17622)
GREAT LAKES ALLIED LLC
87 N Benson St (49349-9485)
PHONE.................................231 924-5794
Gary Anderson,
Pam Anderson,
◆ **EMP:** 8
SQ FT: 10,000
SALES (est): 1.4MM **Privately Held**
WEB: www.greatlakesallied.com
SIC: 5084 3559 5999 5941 Materials handling machinery; ; cleaning equipment & supplies; golf goods & equipment; truck equipment & parts

(G-17623)
HARBISONWALKER INTL INC
1301 E 8th St (49349-9746)
PHONE.................................231 689-6641
Jim Maile, *Plant Engr*
Paul Eno, *Branch Mgr*
Gerald Tuin, *Maintence Staff*
EMP: 120
SALES (corp-wide): 703.8MM **Privately Held**
WEB: www.rhiamerica.com
SIC: 3255 3297 Clay refractories; nonclay refractories
HQ: Harbisonwalker International, Inc.
1305 Cherrington Pkwy # 100
Moon Township PA 15108

(G-17624)
HERITAGE FORESTRY LLC
3729 N Evergreen Dr (49349-9414)
PHONE.................................231 689-5721
James Ryan Coon, *Principal*
EMP: 3
SALES (est): 231.6K **Privately Held**
SIC: 2411 Logging

(G-17625)
LUBECON SYSTEMS INC
Also Called: Lubetronics
201 N Webster St (49349-9678)
PHONE.................................231 689-0002
Lyle G Myers, *President*
Helen Myers, *Admin Sec*
EMP: 65
SQ FT: 8,000
SALES: 6.6MM
SALES (corp-wide): 298.7B **Privately Held**
SIC: 5084 5172 2992 Industrial machinery & equipment; lubricating oils & greases; lubricating oils & greases
HQ: Castrol Industrial North America Inc.
150 W Warrenville Rd
Naperville IL 60563
877 641-1600

(G-17626)
M 37 CONCRETE PRODUCTS INC
Also Called: Elmer's
1231 E 16th St M (49349-9748)
PHONE.................................231 689-1785
Mark C Holbrook, *Manager*
EMP: 9
SALES (est): 447.3K
SALES (corp-wide): 6.9MM **Privately Held**
SIC: 5032 5211 3273 3272 Concrete & cinder building products; concrete building products; lumber & other building materials; concrete & cinder block; ready-mixed concrete; concrete products
PA: M 37 Concrete Products Inc
767 E Sherman Blvd
Muskegon MI 49444
231 733-8247

(G-17627)
WHITE CLOUD MFG CO
19 N Charles St (49349)
PHONE.................................231 689-6087
Jack Benedict, *President*
Fred K Benedict, *Vice Pres*
EMP: 7
SQ FT: 12,000
SALES (est): 581.9K **Privately Held**
SIC: 3366 Bronze foundry

White Lake
Oakland County

(G-17628)
AMERICAN MARINE SHORE CONTROL
Also Called: American Marine SC
6777 Highland Rd (48383-2844)
PHONE.................................248 887-7855
Richard A Mini Jr, *President*
Ken Lunsford, *Admin Sec*
EMP: 12
SQ FT: 3,000
SALES (est): 1.2MM **Privately Held**
WEB: www.americanmarinesc.com
SIC: 3999 Dock equipment & supplies, industrial

(G-17629)
AMICUS SOFTWARE
11231 Sugden Lake Rd (48386)
PHONE.................................313 417-9550
Ted Williford, *Owner*
Janie Williford, *Co-Owner*
Brad Affolder, *Marketing Staff*
EMP: 7
SQ FT: 500
SALES: 500K **Privately Held**
WEB: www.amicussoftware.com
SIC: 7371 7372 Computer software development; prepackaged software

(G-17630)
BILL ELDRIDGE ASSOCIATES
331 Rosario Ln (48386-4401)
PHONE.................................248 698-3705
Bill Eldridge, *Owner*
EMP: 3
SALES (est): 170K **Privately Held**
SIC: 3949 Sporting & athletic goods

(G-17631)
COLLAGECOM LLC
1471 Lynwood Ln (48383-3056)
P.O. Box 1684, Brighton (48116-5484)
PHONE.................................248 971-0538

White Lake - Oakland County (G-17632)

GEOGRAPHIC SECTION

Kevin Borders,
Joe Golden,
EMP: 7
SALES (est): 643.9K **Privately Held**
SIC: 7372 Application computer software

(G-17632)
DEFENSE MATERIAL RECAPITALIZAT
9164 Elizabeth Lake Rd (48386-2415)
PHONE..................248 698-9333
Rodney Giles, *Administration*
EMP: 3 **EST:** 2017
SALES (est): 184.5K **Privately Held**
SIC: 3812 Defense systems & equipment

(G-17633)
GENERL-LCTRICAL-MECHANICAL INC
Also Called: G-E-M
10415 Highland Rd (48386-1810)
PHONE..................248 698-1110
Vernon G Hooper, *President*
Louis Hooper, *Vice Pres*
Robin Hooper, *Admin Sec*
EMP: 8
SQ FT: 14,800
SALES: 1MM **Privately Held**
WEB: www.g-e-m-inc.com
SIC: 3613 3599 Control panels, electric; machine shop, jobbing & repair

(G-17634)
MACK INDUSTRIES MICHIGAN INC
8265 White Lake Rd (48386-1157)
PHONE..................248 620-7400
Howard J Mack, *President*
Richard W Mack, *Vice Pres*
EMP: 173
SALES (est): 26MM **Privately Held**
SIC: 3272 Concrete products, precast

(G-17635)
OFFICE UPDATING
2275 Reidsview E (48383-3936)
PHONE..................248 770-4769
Dennis Irelan, *Owner*
EMP: 3
SALES: 250K **Privately Held**
SIC: 2522 Office desks & tables: except wood

(G-17636)
OXBOWINDO
10195 Highland Rd (48386-1856)
PHONE..................248 698-9400
Todd Burmeister, *President*
EMP: 20
SQ FT: 35,000
SALES (est): 1.9MM **Privately Held**
WEB: www.oxbowindo.com
SIC: 2431 Windows, wood

(G-17637)
P D Q SIGNS INC
9578 Buckingham St (48386-1526)
PHONE..................248 669-8600
Steve Olive, *Owner*
EMP: 3
SALES (est): 273K **Privately Held**
SIC: 3993 Signs, not made in custom sign painting shops

(G-17638)
SLIP DEFENSE INC
10279 Lakeside Dr (48386-2241)
PHONE..................248 366-4423
Brian Greenstein, *Principal*
EMP: 3
SALES (est): 155K **Privately Held**
SIC: 3812 Defense systems & equipment

(G-17639)
SOLTIS PLASTICS CORP
10479 Highland Rd (48386-1810)
PHONE..................248 698-1440
Joseph A Soltis, *President*
Gregory Soltis, *Vice Pres*
EMP: 6 **EST:** 1957
SQ FT: 8,000
SALES: 215K **Privately Held**
WEB: www.soltisplastics.com
SIC: 3089 Injection molding of plastics

(G-17640)
TIME FOR BLINDS INC
9633 Highland Rd (48386-2315)
PHONE..................248 363-9174
Mark F Sause, *President*
EMP: 6
SQ FT: 5,000
SALES (est): 610K **Privately Held**
SIC: 2591 5719 Blinds vertical; mini blinds; window furnishings; vertical blinds; window shades

(G-17641)
UNLIMITED MARINE INC
7775 Highland Rd (48383-2947)
PHONE..................248 249-0222
Douglas M Henn, *President*
EMP: 7 **EST:** 2010
SALES (est): 457.8K **Privately Held**
SIC: 3732 4959 4226 Boat building & repairing; snowplowing; special warehousing & storage

(G-17642)
VULCANMASTERS WELDING INC
2094 Hampton St (48386-1536)
PHONE..................313 843-5043
Roger Pappas, *President*
Scott Weaver, *Vice Pres*
EMP: 16
SALES (est): 1.3MM **Privately Held**
WEB: www.vulcanmayerswelding.com
SIC: 7692 Welding repair

White Pigeon
St. Joseph County

(G-17643)
A N M PRODUCTS
10645 Silver Creek Rd (49099-8402)
PHONE..................269 483-1228
EMP: 3 **EST:** 2003
SALES: 400K **Privately Held**
SIC: 3441 Structural Metal Fabrication

(G-17644)
ARTISTIC CARTON COMPANY
Also Called: White Pigeon Paper Co
15781 River St (49099-9410)
P.O. Box 277 (49099-0277)
PHONE..................269 483-7601
David Dibiaggio, *Branch Mgr*
Donita Slack, *Manager*
EMP: 100
SALES (corp-wide): 61.5MM **Privately Held**
WEB: www.artisticcarton.com
SIC: 2631 Boxboard
PA: Artistic Carton Company
1975 Big Timber Rd
Elgin IL 60123
847 741-0247

(G-17645)
BANKS HARDWOODS INC (PA)
Also Called: Banks Hardwoods Florida
69937 M 103 (49099-9449)
PHONE..................269 483-2323
Spencer Lutz, *President*
Stephen G Banks, *President*
Mark Bojanich, *Plant Mgr*
Steve Newburry, *Safety Mgr*
James F Clarke, *CFO*
▼ **EMP:** 100
SQ FT: 2,500
SALES (est): 22.5MM **Privately Held**
WEB: www.bankshardwoods.com
SIC: 2421 5031 2426 Kiln drying of lumber; lumber: rough, dressed & finished; hardwood dimension & flooring mills

(G-17646)
CCO HOLDINGS LLC
350 W Chicago Rd (49099-8135)
PHONE..................269 464-3454
EMP: 4
SALES (corp-wide): 43.6B **Publicly Held**
SIC: 5064 4841 3663 3651 Electrical appliances, television & radio; cable & other pay television services; radio & TV communications equipment; household audio & video equipment
HQ: Cco Holdings, Llc
400 Atlantic St
Stamford CT 06901
203 905-7801

(G-17647)
EMERALD MFG
69223 S Kalamazoo St (49099-9414)
PHONE..................269 483-2676
Damian Oconnor, *Principal*
EMP: 3
SALES (est): 276.4K **Privately Held**
SIC: 3999 Manufacturing industries

(G-17648)
FIRST CHOICE OF ELKHART INC
10888 Us Highway 12 (49099-9124)
PHONE..................269 483-2010
Misty Campagna, *President*
Rebecca Smith, *Vice Pres*
EMP: 6
SQ FT: 10,000
SALES (est): 2.1MM **Privately Held**
WEB: www.firstchoiceautohaul.com
SIC: 3743 Freight cars & equipment

(G-17649)
GRAY BROS STAMPING & MCH INC
424 W Chicago Rd (49099-9111)
P.O. Box 338 (49099-0338)
PHONE..................269 483-7615
James Reilly, *President*
Donald C Grant, *Vice Pres*
Adele Gray, *Vice Pres*
James Gray, *Vice Pres*
Phyllis Gray, *Vice Pres*
EMP: 35 **EST:** 1948
SQ FT: 51,000
SALES (est): 5MM **Privately Held**
WEB: www.graybrosstmp.com
SIC: 3469 3498 3544 Stamping metal for the trade; tube fabricating (contract bending & shaping); special dies & tools

(G-17650)
GRAY BROTHERS MFG INC
424 W Chicago Rd (49099-9111)
P.O. Box 338 (49099-0338)
PHONE..................269 483-7615
James Gray, *President*
James Riley, *Corp Secy*
Phyllis Gray, *Vice Pres*
James Reilly, *Finance*
EMP: 30
SALES (est): 2.7MM **Privately Held**
WEB: www.graybrosmfg.com
SIC: 3498 3469 3444 3441 Fabricated pipe & fittings; metal stampings; sheet metalwork; fabricated structural metal

(G-17651)
HAGEN CEMENT PRODUCTS INC
17149 Us Highway 12 (49099-9779)
P.O. Box 606 (49099-0606)
PHONE..................269 483-9641
Sidney Hagen, *President*
Scott Hagen, *Vice Pres*
Terry Hagen, *Treasurer*
Jean Hagen, *Admin Sec*
EMP: 9
SQ FT: 7,000
SALES (est): 1.7MM **Privately Held**
SIC: 3271 5032 Blocks, concrete or cinder: standard; brick, stone & related material; brick, except refractory; sand, construction; gravel

(G-17652)
MAINE ORNAMENTAL LLC
Also Called: Deckorators
68956 Us Highway 131 (49099-8156)
PHONE..................800 556-8449
John Teller, *Principal*
▲ **EMP:** 19
SALES: 3.5MM
SALES (corp-wide): 4.4B **Publicly Held**
WEB: www.postcaps.com
SIC: 2499 5031 3496 Fencing, wood; lumber: rough, dressed & finished; miscellaneous fabricated wire products
HQ: Universal Consumer Products, Inc.
2801 E Beltline Ave Ne
Grand Rapids MI 49525

(G-17653)
MERHOW ACQUISITION LLC
Also Called: Merhow Industries
617 S Miller Rd (49099-8423)
PHONE..................269 483-0010
Mark Walter, *Controller*
Melissa Hahn, *Sales Staff*
Dennis Marcott,
EMP: 100
SQ FT: 72,000
SALES: 15MM **Privately Held**
SIC: 3715 Trailers or vans for transporting horses

(G-17654)
MORRIS EXCAVATING INC
69067 S Kalamazoo St (49099-9414)
P.O. Box 308 (49099-0308)
PHONE..................269 483-7773
John Morris, *President*
EMP: 10
SQ FT: 28,000
SALES (est): 1.8MM **Privately Held**
SIC: 1794 1611 1623 1442 Excavation work; concrete construction: roads, highways, sidewalks, etc.; underground utilities contractor; gravel mining

(G-17655)
QUADRA MANUFACTURING INC (PA)
Also Called: Big Foot
305 Us Highway 131 S (49099-9131)
PHONE..................269 483-9633
Eugene Lehman, *President*
Roger Miller, *General Mgr*
Clinton Lehman, *Opers Mgr*
Toby Moore, *Purch Dir*
Bob Slack, *Engineer*
EMP: 28
SQ FT: 10,000
SALES (est): 4.2MM **Privately Held**
WEB: www.quadraleveler.com
SIC: 3799 Trailers & trailer equipment

(G-17656)
UNIVERSAL CONSUMER PDTS INC
Also Called: Ucp
68956 Us Highway 131 (49099-8156)
PHONE..................616 365-4201
Larry Beck, *Purch Agent*
Ryan Hossman, *Manager*
EMP: 65
SALES (corp-wide): 4.4B **Publicly Held**
WEB: www.ufpinc.com
SIC: 3089 Fences, gates & accessories: plastic
HQ: Universal Consumer Products, Inc.
2801 E Beltline Ave Ne
Grand Rapids MI 49525

(G-17657)
WARREN MANUFACTURING
68635 Suszek Rd (49099-9029)
PHONE..................269 483-0603
Ken Warren, *President*
Barbara Warren, *Vice Pres*
EMP: 8
SALES: 380K **Privately Held**
SIC: 3599 5084 Machine shop, jobbing & repair; industrial machinery & equipment

White Pine
Ontonagon County

(G-17658)
PM POWER GROUP INC
29639 Willow Rd (49971-5001)
PHONE..................906 885-7100
Brant Zettl, *President*
Zachary Halkola, *COO*
EMP: 7
SALES (est): 425.4K **Privately Held**
SIC: 8742 1731 3331 Administrative services consultant; general electrical contractor; primary copper

GEOGRAPHIC SECTION

(G-17659)
WHITE PINE COPPER REFINERY INC
29784 Willow Rd (49971-5001)
P.O. Box 38 (49971-0038)
PHONE..................................906 885-7100
Mark Pierpont, *Bd of Directors*
▲ EMP: 1
SALES (est): 9.8MM **Privately Held**
SIC: 3341 Copper smelting & refining (secondary)

Whitehall
Muskegon County

(G-17660)
ALCOA HOWMET
1 Misco Dr (49461-1755)
PHONE..................................231 894-5686
Michael A Pepper, *President*
Dirk Bauer, *Vice Pres*
Jack Bodner, *Vice Pres*
Boyd Mueller, *Vice Pres*
Paul Myron, *Vice Pres*
EMP: 11 EST: 2012
SALES (est): 1.3MM **Privately Held**
SIC: 3353 Aluminum sheet, plate & foil

(G-17661)
ARCONIC INC
Also Called: Arconic Howmet 10 Plant
3850 White Lake Dr (49461-9345)
PHONE..................................231 981-3002
EMP: 12
SALES (corp-wide): 14B **Publicly Held**
SIC: 3334 Primary aluminum
PA: Arconic Inc.
    201 Isabella St Ste 200
    Pittsburgh PA 15212
    412 553-1950

(G-17662)
ARCONIC INC
1 Misco Dr (49461-1755)
PHONE..................................231 894-5686
Gail Cole, *Vice Pres*
Leon Brown, *Production*
Bill Dewitt, *Engineer*
Randall Diehm, *Engineer*
Annette Hilton, *Engineer*
EMP: 5
SALES (corp-wide): 14B **Publicly Held**
SIC: 3334 3353 1099 Primary aluminum; aluminum sheet & strip; coils, sheet aluminum; plates, aluminum; foil, aluminum; bauxite mining
PA: Arconic Inc.
    201 Isabella St Ste 200
    Pittsburgh PA 15212
    412 553-1950

(G-17663)
CONRAD MACHINE COMPANY
1525 Warner St (49461-1826)
PHONE..................................231 893-7455
Earl Conrad, *Ch of Bd*
Thomas Conrad, *President*
Doug Conrad, *Vice Pres*
▲ EMP: 10 EST: 1947
SQ FT: 6,800
SALES (est): 1.2MM **Privately Held**
WEB: www.conradmachine.com
SIC: 3555 Printing presses

(G-17664)
CONSUMERS CONCRETE CORPORATION
2259 Holton Whitehall Rd (49461-9115)
PHONE..................................231 894-2705
Mike Woodward, *Manager*
EMP: 13
SALES (corp-wide): 102.9MM **Privately Held**
WEB: www.consumersconcrete.com
SIC: 3273 Ready-mixed concrete
PA: Consumers Concrete Corporation
    3508 S Sprinkle Rd
    Kalamazoo MI 49001
    269 342-0136

(G-17665)
ERDMAN MACHINE CO
8529 Silver Creek Rd (49461-9125)
PHONE..................................231 894-1010
Scott Erdman, *President*
Ken Lahey, *Vice Pres*
Nancy Erdman, *Production*
EMP: 35
SQ FT: 20,000
SALES (est): 5.7MM **Privately Held**
WEB: www.erdmanmachine.com
SIC: 3545 Machine tool accessories

(G-17666)
FORM ALL TOOL COMPANY
803 S Mears Ave (49461-1521)
P.O. Box 413 (49461-0413)
PHONE..................................231 894-6303
Thomas J Peterson, *President*
Cynthia Lombard, *Corp Secy*
EMP: 14
SQ FT: 4,185
SALES (est): 997.3K **Privately Held**
SIC: 3451 Screw machine products

(G-17667)
FRETTY MEDIA LLC
Also Called: Barrels of Yum
201 W Obell St (49461-1742)
PHONE..................................231 894-8055
Peter Fretty, *Mng Member*
Zackery Fretty, *Mng Member*
EMP: 6
SALES (est): 408K **Privately Held**
SIC: 2064 Candy & other confectionery products

(G-17668)
HILITE INTERNATIONAL INC
Also Called: Acutex Division
2001 Peach St (49461-1844)
PHONE..................................231 894-3200
Ron Overway, *President*
Tom Buckingham, *Vice Pres*
Thomas Buckingham, *Vice Pres*
Richard Smith, *Vice Pres*
Charlie Afton, *Engineer*
EMP: 230
SALES (corp-wide): 43.3B **Privately Held**
WEB: www.hiliteinternational.com
SIC: 3492 3594 3593 Fluid power valves & hose fittings; fluid power pumps & motors; fluid power cylinders & actuators
HQ: Hilite International, Inc.
    1671 S Broadway St
    Carrollton TX 75006
    972 242-2116

(G-17669)
HOWMET CORPORATION (DH)
Also Called: Alcoa Power & Propulsion
1 Misco Dr (49461-1799)
PHONE..................................231 894-5686
David L Squier, *President*
Marklin Lasker, *Senior VP*
James R Stanley, *Senior VP*
Roland A Paul, *Vice Pres*
B Dennis Albrechtsen, *VP Mfg*
◆ EMP: 30
SQ FT: 10,000
SALES (est): 1.7B
SALES (corp-wide): 14B **Publicly Held**
WEB: www.alcoa.com
SIC: 3324 3542 5051 3479 Commercial investment castings, ferrous; machine tools, metal forming type; ferroalloys; ingots; coating of metals & formed products
HQ: Howmet Holdings Corporation
    1 Misco Dr
    Whitehall MI 49461
    231 894-5686

(G-17670)
HOWMET CORPORATION
Alcoa Howmet Ti-Ingot
555 Benston Rd (49461-1899)
PHONE..................................231 894-7183
Allen Zwierzchowski, *President*
Don Larsen, *Manager*
EMP: 57
SALES (corp-wide): 14B **Publicly Held**
SIC: 3324 Commercial investment castings, ferrous

HQ: Howmet Corporation
    1 Misco Dr
    Whitehall MI 49461
    231 894-5686

(G-17671)
HOWMET CORPORATION
Also Called: Arconic Power & Propulsion RES
1500 Warner St (49461-1895)
PHONE..................................231 894-7290
Adam Sylvester, *Engineer*
Boyd Mueller, *Manager*
EMP: 170
SALES (corp-wide): 14B **Publicly Held**
SIC: 3324 Commercial investment castings, ferrous
HQ: Howmet Corporation
    1 Misco Dr
    Whitehall MI 49461
    231 894-5686

(G-17672)
HOWMET CORPORATION
Alcoa Howmet, Ti-Cast
1600 Warner St (49461-1897)
PHONE..................................231 981-3269
Brian Plummer, *Engineer*
Trezelle Jenkins, *Manager*
EMP: 220
SALES (corp-wide): 14B **Publicly Held**
SIC: 3324 Commercial investment castings, ferrous
HQ: Howmet Corporation
    1 Misco Dr
    Whitehall MI 49461
    231 894-5686

(G-17673)
HOWMET CORPORATION
3850 White Lake Dr (49461-9345)
PHONE..................................231 981-3000
James Vresics, *Manager*
EMP: 14
SALES (corp-wide): 14B **Publicly Held**
SIC: 3479 Coating of metals & formed products
HQ: Howmet Corporation
    1 Misco Dr
    Whitehall MI 49461
    231 894-5686

(G-17674)
HOWMET CORPORATION
Also Called: Alcoa Howmet, Thermatech
555 Benston Rd (49461-1899)
PHONE..................................231 894-5686
Laura Carpenter, *Manager*
EMP: 135
SALES (corp-wide): 14B **Publicly Held**
SIC: 3353 Aluminum sheet, plate & foil
HQ: Howmet Corporation
    1 Misco Dr
    Whitehall MI 49461
    231 894-5686

(G-17675)
HOWMET CORPORATION
Also Called: Alcoa Howmet, Wthl, Casting Op
1 Misco Dr (49461-1799)
PHONE..................................231 894-5686
Dan Grozskiewicz, *Manager*
EMP: 135
SALES (corp-wide): 14B **Publicly Held**
SIC: 3353 Aluminum sheet, plate & foil
HQ: Howmet Corporation
    1 Misco Dr
    Whitehall MI 49461
    231 894-5686

(G-17676)
HOWMET HOLDINGS CORPORATION (HQ)
1 Misco Dr (49461-1799)
PHONE..................................231 894-5686
Mario Longhi, *CEO*
Raymond B Mitchell, *President*
James R Stanley, *Vice Pres*
▲ EMP: 1
SALES (est): 1.8B
SALES (corp-wide): 14B **Publicly Held**
SIC: 3324 3542 5051 3479 Commercial investment castings, ferrous; machine tools, metal forming type; ferroalloys; ingots; coating of metals & formed products

PA: Arconic Inc.
    201 Isabella St Ste 200
    Pittsburgh PA 15212
    412 553-1950

(G-17677)
MAS INC
2100 Cogswell Dr (49461-1852)
PHONE..................................231 894-0409
EMP: 9
SALES (est): 1MM **Privately Held**
SIC: 3728 Aircraft parts & equipment

(G-17678)
TROPHY CENTER WEST MICHIGAN
8060 Whitehall Rd (49461-9496)
PHONE..................................231 893-1686
Pamela Semelbauer, *Owner*
EMP: 6
SQ FT: 50,000
SALES (est): 515.6K **Privately Held**
SIC: 2261 2395 5999 7389 Screen printing of cotton broadwoven fabrics; embroidery & art needlework; trophies & plaques; engraving service; sporting goods & bicycle shops

(G-17679)
VIKING TOOL & ENGINEERING INC
2780 Colby Rd (49461-9254)
PHONE..................................231 893-0031
Warren Hutchins, *President*
Richard Seaver, *Vice Pres*
Rick Seaver, *Vice Pres*
Fred Danz, *Program Mgr*
Tom Burrous, *Manager*
◆ EMP: 33 EST: 1964
SQ FT: 17,500
SALES (est): 6.6MM **Privately Held**
SIC: 3544 Special dies & tools; dies, plastics forming

(G-17680)
WHITE LAKE BEACON INC
432 E Spring St (49461-1153)
P.O. Box 98 (49461-0098)
PHONE..................................231 894-5356
Richard Lound, *President*
Greg Means, *Publisher*
Dan Heller, *Sales Staff*
Katy Teitgen, *Internal Med*
EMP: 6
SALES (est): 190.9K **Privately Held**
SIC: 2711 Newspapers, publishing & printing

(G-17681)
WHITE LAKE EXCAVATING INC
2571 Holton Whitehall Rd (49461-9169)
PHONE..................................231 894-6918
Tom Waruszewski, *President*
EMP: 13
SQ FT: 6,280
SALES (est): 3.1MM **Privately Held**
SIC: 3531 5032 3272 1794 Asphalt plant, including gravel-mix type; gravel; concrete products; cast stone, concrete; excavation work; gravel or dirt road construction; surfacing & paving; paving stones; sand & gravel

(G-17682)
WHITEHALL PRODUCTS LLC
1625 Warner St (49461-1827)
PHONE..................................231 894-2688
Jeremy Santose, *Materials Mgr*
Megan Nelson, *Production*
Tim Swainston, *Purch Agent*
Nicholas Hesse, *Natl Sales Mgr*
Marybeth Taylor, *Natl Sales Mgr*
▲ EMP: 75
SQ FT: 110,000
SALES (est): 17.1MM **Privately Held**
WEB: www.whitehallproducts.com
SIC: 3599 3993 3365 3524 Weather vanes; signs & advertising specialties; aluminum foundries; lawn & garden equipment

Whitmore Lake
Washtenaw County

(G-17683)
A&E MACHINE & FABRICATION INC
7540 Wheeler Rd (48189-9696)
PHONE....................740 820-4701
Adam Mdoll, *Branch Mgr*
EMP: 8
SALES (est): 1.1MM **Privately Held**
SIC: 3599 Machine shop, jobbing & repair
PA: A&E Machine And Fabrication, Inc.
384 State Route 335
Beaver OH 45613

(G-17684)
ACTION ASPHALT LLC
11224 Lemen Rd Ste A (48189-8104)
PHONE....................734 449-8565
Daniel James Gee, *President*
EMP: 16
SQ FT: 10,000
SALES: 1.5MM **Privately Held**
SIC: 3479 1771 Coating of metals & formed products; blacktop (asphalt) work

(G-17685)
AERO AUTO STUD SPECIALISTS INC
10769 Plaza Dr (48189-9737)
P.O. Box 140, New Hudson (48165-0330)
PHONE....................248 437-2171
David L Stanton Jr, *President*
Michael J Stanton, *Vice Pres*
EMP: 20 EST: 1960
SQ FT: 20,000
SALES (est): 4.5MM **Privately Held**
SIC: 3452 Rivets, metal; bolts, metal

(G-17686)
AL DENTE INC
9815 Main St (48189-9438)
PHONE....................734 449-8522
Monique Deschaine, *President*
EMP: 27
SQ FT: 6,000
SALES (est): 4.7MM **Privately Held**
WEB: www.aldentepasta.com
SIC: 2099 Pasta, uncooked: packaged with other ingredients

(G-17687)
AMERICAN MODELS
11770 Green Oak Indus Dr (48189-9064)
PHONE....................248 437-6800
Ronald Bashista, *Owner*
▲ EMP: 5
SALES (est): 473.4K **Privately Held**
WEB: www.american-flyer.com
SIC: 3944 5945 Trains & equipment, toy: electric & mechanical; hobby, toy & game shops

(G-17688)
APPLIED MOLECULES LLC
11042 Hi Tech Dr (48189-9133)
PHONE....................810 355-1475
Paul Snowwhite, *Principal*
EMP: 3
SQ FT: 2,500
SALES: 900K **Privately Held**
SIC: 2891 8731 Adhesives & sealants; commercial research laboratory

(G-17689)
BALANCE TECHNOLOGY INC (PA)
Also Called: Bti Precision Measurement Tstg
7035 Jomar Dr (48189)
PHONE....................734 769-2100
Thomas P Plunkett, *President*
▲ EMP: 100
SQ FT: 53,000
SALES (est): 20.3MM **Privately Held**
WEB: www.balancetechnology.com
SIC: 3829 3825 3823 3821 Testing equipment: abrasion, shearing strength, etc.; vibration meters, analyzers & calibrators; instruments to measure electricity; industrial instrmnts msrmnt display/control process variable; laboratory apparatus & furniture; hand & edge tools

(G-17690)
BLANK SLATE CREAMERY LLC
4090 Lori Lynn Ln (48189-9018)
PHONE....................734 218-3242
Janice Sigler, *Principal*
EMP: 4
SALES (est): 195.1K **Privately Held**
SIC: 2021 Creamery butter

(G-17691)
BTI MEASUREMENT TSTG SVCS LLC (PA)
7035 Jomar Dr (48189)
PHONE....................734 769-2100
Stephen Simon, *Manager*
Thomas P Plunkett,
EMP: 6 EST: 2015
SALES (est): 1.1MM **Privately Held**
SIC: 3829 Testing equipment: abrasion, shearing strength, etc.

(G-17692)
CONCEPT ALLOYS INC
11234 Lemen Rd (48189-8115)
PHONE....................734 449-9680
Robert Biermann, *President*
Tim Peters, *Principal*
▲ EMP: 6
SALES: 1.5MM **Privately Held**
WEB: www.conceptalloys.com
SIC: 3356 Nonferrous rolling & drawing

(G-17693)
CONTROLLED MAGNETICS INC
10766 Plaza Dr (48189-9737)
PHONE....................734 449-7225
Michael J Jagiela, *President*
Steven T Krause, *Admin Sec*
EMP: 10
SQ FT: 5,000
SALES (est): 2.1MM **Privately Held**
WEB: www.controlledmagnetics.com
SIC: 3612 Autotransformers, electric (power transformers)

(G-17694)
CREATIVE AUTOMATION INC
1175 E N Territorial Rd (48189-9253)
PHONE....................734 780-3175
Bernd Walter, *President*
Florence Walter, *Admin Sec*
▲ EMP: 25
SQ FT: 45,000
SALES (est): 7MM **Privately Held**
WEB: www.cautomation.com
SIC: 3549 Assembly machines, including robotic

(G-17695)
DISTILLERY 9 LLC
8040 Apple Creek Ct (48189-9039)
PHONE....................517 990-2929
Nicole Barczak, *Principal*
EMP: 3
SALES (est): 117.7K **Privately Held**
SIC: 2085 Distilled & blended liquors

(G-17696)
EJW CONTRACT INC
7930 Forest Creek Ct (48189-9142)
PHONE....................616 293-5181
Erin Wallis, *President*
Steven Gottbreht, *Treasurer*
EMP: 2
SALES: 3MM **Privately Held**
SIC: 2511 Wood household furniture

(G-17697)
ENERGY DESIGN SVC SYSTEMS LLC
7050 Jomar Dr (48189)
PHONE....................810 227-3377
David Ely, *CEO*
John Santulli, *Vice Pres*
Kyle Leighton, *Manager*
Simon Ren, *Director*
Laurie Anderson, *Executive Asst*
EMP: 11
SALES (est): 1.4MM **Privately Held**
SIC: 3646 3648 8711 5063 Commercial indusl & institutional electric lighting fixtures; lighting equipment; engineering services; electrical apparatus & equipment

(G-17698)
ENGINEERED PRFMCE MTLS CO LLC
Also Called: EPM
11228 Lemen Rd Ste A (48189-9194)
PHONE....................734 904-4023
Phil Young, *Engineer*
EMP: 4
SALES (est): 141.5K **Privately Held**
WEB: www.epm-us.com
SIC: 3357 Nonferrous wiredrawing & insulating

(G-17699)
EXTREME MACHINE INC
10068 Industrial Dr (48189-9180)
PHONE....................810 231-0521
Michael Barackman, *President*
EMP: 52
SQ FT: 31,000 **Privately Held**
SIC: 3599 3519 3714 Machine & other job shop work; parts & accessories, internal combustion engines; transmission housings or parts, motor vehicle
PA: Extreme Machine, Inc.
10034 Industrial Dr
Whitmore Lake MI 48189

(G-17700)
EXTREME MACHINE INC (PA)
10034 Industrial Dr (48189-9180)
PHONE....................810 231-0521
Michael Barackman, *President*
Kim Barackman, *Vice Pres*
Lester Vincent, *Vice Pres*
Dennis Courter, *Plant Mgr*
Randall Stull, *Production*
EMP: 63
SQ FT: 31,000
SALES (est): 11.8MM **Privately Held**
WEB: www.extreme-machine.com
SIC: 3599 3519 8711 3714 Machine shop, jobbing & repair; internal combustion engines; engineering services; transmissions, motor vehicle

(G-17701)
GARY L MELCHI INC
11275 Merrill Rd (48189-9754)
P.O. Box 1331, Ann Arbor (48106-1331)
PHONE....................810 231-0262
Gary L Melchi, *Principal*
EMP: 3
SALES (est): 144.8K **Privately Held**
SIC: 3643 Lightning arrestors & coils

(G-17702)
HIGH EFFCNCY PWR SOLUTIONS INC
11060 Hi Tech Dr (48189-9133)
PHONE....................800 833-7094
Henry Grell Jr, *President*
Dean K Brown, *President*
Robert Rose, *Principal*
EMP: 9
SALES (est): 871.9K **Privately Held**
SIC: 3679 Electronic loads & power supplies

(G-17703)
METAL FINISHING QUOTECOM LLC
10799 Plaza Dr (48189-9737)
PHONE....................248 890-1096
Mark Miller, *Principal*
EMP: 3
SALES (est): 124.8K **Privately Held**
SIC: 3471 Cleaning, polishing & finishing

(G-17704)
MICHIGAN CNC TOOL INC
Also Called: Machine Shop
11710 Green Oak Indus Dr (48189-9064)
P.O. Box 626, Lakeland (48143-0626)
PHONE....................734 449-9590
John Dziuban, *CEO*
EMP: 15
SQ FT: 11,500
SALES (est): 2.3MM **Privately Held**
SIC: 3541 Machine tool replacement & repair parts, metal cutting types

(G-17705)
OSMI INC
777 Eight Mile Rd (48189-9190)
PHONE....................561 504-3924
Pierre Tremblay, *Plant Supt*
Jim Knicley, *Manager*
EMP: 18
SALES (corp-wide): 11.4MM **Privately Held**
SIC: 3297 Nonclay refractories
PA: Osmi, Inc.
7777 Glades Rd Ste 200
Boca Raton FL 33434
561 330-9300

(G-17706)
PRECISE POWER SYSTEMS LLC
10520 Plaza Dr (48189-9156)
PHONE....................248 709-4750
Frank Taube, *Mng Member*
EMP: 8
SALES (est): 319.7K **Privately Held**
SIC: 3625 Marine & navy auxiliary controls

(G-17707)
STELLAR MATERIALS INTL LLC
777 Eight Mile Rd (48189-9190)
PHONE....................561 504-3924
David Mintz, *President*
EMP: 45
SQ FT: 82,000
SALES (est): 22MM **Privately Held**
SIC: 3297 Cement refractories

(G-17708)
VCONVERTER CORPORATION (PA)
10505 Plaza Dr Ste C (48189-8109)
PHONE....................248 388-0549
Mark W Midgley, *CEO*
Don Nowland, *President*
Cheryl Lampman, *Accounting Mgr*
Jared Dunham, *Program Mgr*
Michael O'Brien, *Manager*
EMP: 59
SQ FT: 60,000
SALES: 25MM **Privately Held**
SIC: 3567 Industrial furnaces & ovens

Whittemore
Iosco County

(G-17709)
NEARS INC
Also Called: Near's Septic
425 N M 65 (48770-9426)
P.O. Box 185 (48770-0185)
PHONE....................989 756-2203
Eugene Near, *President*
Sarah Crafford, *Corp Secy*
Albert Near, *Vice Pres*
EMP: 3 EST: 1976
SQ FT: 2,000
SALES (est): 535.5K **Privately Held**
SIC: 3272 Septic tanks, concrete

Williamsburg
Grand Traverse County

(G-17710)
CHERRY BLOSSOM
8365 Park Rd (49690-9590)
PHONE....................231 342-3635
Chris Hubbell, *Owner*
EMP: 3 EST: 2010
SALES (est): 285.1K **Privately Held**
SIC: 2099 Food preparations

(G-17711)
DOUBLE CHECK TOOLS SERVICE
6937 M 72 E (49690-9446)
PHONE....................231 947-1632

Jim Munn, *Manager*
EMP: 7
SALES (est): 336.6K **Privately Held**
SIC: 1389 Oil field services

(G-17712)
GRACE METAL PRODS INC
6322 Yuba Rd (49690-9525)
PHONE....................................231 264-8133
Dan Morrison, *President*
EMP: 4
SALES (est): 260.9K **Privately Held**
SIC: 3423 Hand & edge tools

(G-17713)
GREAT LAKES TRIM INC
6183 S Railway Cmn (49690-8545)
PHONE....................................231 267-3000
Tom Crandall, *President*
Jeff Crandall, *Vice Pres*
EMP: 60
SQ FT: 20,000
SALES (est): 11.4MM **Privately Held**
WEB: www.greatlakestrim.com
SIC: 3465 3429 3442 Moldings or trim, automobile: stamped metal; manufactured hardware (general); metal doors, sash & trim

(G-17714)
KDK DOWNHOLE TOOLING LLC
6671 M 72 E (49690-9360)
PHONE....................................231 590-3137
Kenneth Flannery, *Principal*
EMP: 3
SALES (est): 287.9K **Privately Held**
SIC: 1389 Construction, repair & dismantling services

(G-17715)
NORTHERN MICH WDDING OFFCIANTS
4617 Bartlett Rd (49690-9325)
PHONE....................................231 938-1683
Crystal Yarlott, *Principal*
EMP: 3
SALES (est): 179.8K **Privately Held**
SIC: 2435 Hardwood veneer & plywood

(G-17716)
NORTHERN MICHIGAN SAWMILL
4593 Hampshire Dr (49690-9633)
PHONE....................................231 409-1314
Vincenzo Festa, *Principal*
EMP: 3
SALES (est): 178K **Privately Held**
SIC: 2421 Sawmills & planing mills, general

(G-17717)
NORTHWOODS SODA AND SYRUP CO
Also Called: Northwoods Soda & Syrup
5450 N Broomhead Rd (49690-9708)
PHONE....................................231 267-5853
William Fosdick, *President*
Maureen Fosdick, *Vice Pres*
EMP: 3
SQ FT: 3,000
SALES (est): 675K **Privately Held**
SIC: 2087 Syrups, drink

(G-17718)
NOWAK CABINETS INC
11744 S Us Highway 31 (49690-9449)
PHONE....................................231 264-8603
Joseph Nowak, *Owner*
EMP: 8
SALES (est): 839.1K **Privately Held**
SIC: 2434 Wood kitchen cabinets

(G-17719)
PHOENIX OPERATING COMPANY INC
4480b Mount Hope Rd (49690-9209)
PHONE....................................231 929-7171
Jeffrey Critchfield, *President*
EMP: 8
SALES (est): 1.1MM **Privately Held**
SIC: 1389 Oil field services; gas field services

(G-17720)
SAINT-GOBAIN PRFMCE PLAS CORP
Also Called: Twin Bay Medical
11590 S Us Highway 31 (49690-9434)
PHONE....................................231 264-0101
Albert Werth, *Branch Mgr*
Al Werth, *Branch Mgr*
EMP: 15
SALES (corp-wide): 215.9MM **Privately Held**
SIC: 3841 Surgical & medical instruments
HQ: Saint-Gobain Performance Plastics Corporation
31500 Solon Rd
Solon OH 44139
440 836-6900

(G-17721)
THOMAS A DESPRES INC
Also Called: Cold Saw Precision
4229 Williamston Ct (49690-8627)
PHONE....................................313 633-9648
Thomas A Despres, *President*
Dolores Despres, *Corp Secy*
EMP: 15
SQ FT: 27,000
SALES (est): 1.7MM **Privately Held**
WEB: www.coldsawprecision.com
SIC: 3599 Machine shop, jobbing & repair

(G-17722)
TOP OF LINE CRANE SERVICE LLC
6925 M 72 E (49690-9446)
P.O. Box 101 (49690-0101)
PHONE....................................231 267-5326
Carl Baker, *Mng Member*
EMP: 7
SALES (est): 348K **Privately Held**
SIC: 3531 Cranes

(G-17723)
TOWNLINE CIDERWORKS LLC
11595 S Us Highway 31 (49690-9434)
PHONE....................................231 883-5330
Brian Altonen,
EMP: 3
SQ FT: 4,260
SALES (est): 110.5K **Privately Held**
SIC: 2084 Wines

(G-17724)
WIPER SHAKER LLC
6650 E Railway Cmn (49690-8558)
PHONE....................................231 668-2418
Marty Lagina, *Principal*
EMP: 3
SALES (est): 256.3K **Privately Held**
SIC: 3714 Windshield wiper systems, motor vehicle

Williamston
Ingham County

(G-17725)
AOA PRODUCTIONS LLC
2447 N Williamston Rd (48895-9462)
PHONE....................................517 256-0820
Lloyd Williams, *Principal*
EMP: 4
SALES (est): 193.7K **Privately Held**
SIC: 3569 Robots, assembly line: industrial & commercial

(G-17726)
BECK MOBILE CONCRETE LLC
2303 E Grand River Rd (48895-9158)
P.O. Box 354 (48895-0354)
PHONE....................................517 655-4996
Kevin Beck,
EMP: 4
SALES (est): 950K **Privately Held**
SIC: 3273 3272 Ready-mixed concrete; concrete products, precast

(G-17727)
BEKUM AMERICA CORPORATION
1140 W Grand River Ave (48895-1394)
P.O. Box 567 (48895-0567)
PHONE....................................517 655-4331
Martin Stark, *Ch of Bd*
Gottfried Mehnert, *Ch of Bd*
Chuck Flammer, *Business Mgr*
Steven D London, *Exec VP*
Charles Downer, *Buyer*
▲ **EMP:** 102
SQ FT: 120,000
SALES (est): 32.2MM
SALES (corp-wide): 26.1MM **Privately Held**
WEB: www.bekumamerica.com
SIC: 3559 3544 Plastics working machinery; special dies, tools, jigs & fixtures
PA: Bekum - Maschinenfabriken Gesellschaft Mit Beschrankter Haftung
Kitzingstr. 15-19
Berlin 12277
307 490-0

(G-17728)
CARDINAL FABRICATING INC
3394 Corwin Rd (48895-9711)
P.O. Box 69 (48895-0069)
PHONE....................................517 655-2155
Michael G Kavanagh, *President*
Stephen Zynda, *Principal*
Brad Tostevin, *Vice Pres*
EMP: 20 **EST:** 1970
SQ FT: 13,000
SALES (est): 3.3MM **Privately Held**
SIC: 3441 Fabricated structural metal

(G-17729)
D & G EQUIPMENT INC (PA)
Also Called: John Deere Authorized Dealer
2 Industrial Park Dr (48895-1600)
PHONE....................................517 655-4606
Elden E Gustafson, *Owner*
Jolene Gustafson, *Treasurer*
EMP: 124
SQ FT: 7,000
SALES (est): 22.7MM **Privately Held**
WEB: www.dgequipment.com
SIC: 5999 5261 7629 3648 Farm equipment & supplies; lawn & garden supplies; electrical repair shops; outdoor lighting equipment; construction & mining machinery

(G-17730)
GEOTECH ENVIRONMENTAL EQP INC
1099 W Grnd Riv 6 (48895)
PHONE....................................517 655-5616
David Bean, *Manager*
EMP: 7
SALES (corp-wide): 18.3MM **Privately Held**
WEB: www.geotechenv.com
SIC: 3823 Water quality monitoring & control systems
PA: Geotech Environmental Equipment, Inc.
2650 E 40th Ave
Denver CO 80205
303 320-4764

(G-17731)
JAMES AVE CATERING
1311 James Ave (48895-9702)
PHONE....................................517 655-4532
Colleen Gilmore, *Principal*
EMP: 4 **EST:** 2010
SALES (est): 210.1K **Privately Held**
SIC: 2051 Cakes, bakery: except frozen

(G-17732)
JBJ PRODUCTS AND MACHINERY
125 Industrial Park Dr (48895-1656)
PHONE....................................517 655-4734
John Palazzolo, *President*
James Palazzolo, *Vice Pres*
Jim Palazzolo, *Vice Pres*
Robert Palazzolo, *Treasurer*
EMP: 5
SQ FT: 2,000
SALES (est): 875K **Privately Held**
SIC: 3599 Machine shop, jobbing & repair

(G-17733)
M C MOLDS INC
125 Industrial Park Dr (48895-1656)
PHONE....................................517 655-5481
Robert J Palazzolo, *President*
William Russell, *Corp Secy*
Dave Keesaer, *Vice Pres*
Edward Fitzgerald, *Supervisor*
EMP: 39
SQ FT: 12,000
SALES (est): 10MM **Privately Held**
SIC: 3089 3544 3542 Blow molded finished plastic products; special dies, tools, jigs & fixtures; machine tools, metal forming type

(G-17734)
MACHINE CONTROL TECHNOLOGY
4033 Vanneter Rd (48895-9172)
PHONE....................................517 655-3506
Jay Merkle, *President*
EMP: 5
SQ FT: 10,000
SALES (est): 313.4K **Privately Held**
SIC: 7373 3541 7699 5084 Systems integration services; grinding machines, metalworking; industrial machinery & equipment repair; machine tools & accessories

(G-17735)
MODERN METAL PROCESSING CORP
3448 Corwin Rd (48895-9711)
P.O. Box 22 (48895-0022)
PHONE....................................517 655-4402
Chester Wesolek, *President*
Carolyn Wesolek, *Corp Secy*
Edward Wesolek, *Vice Pres*
Shelly Wesolek, *Accountant*
EMP: 5
SQ FT: 15,000
SALES (est): 867.8K **Privately Held**
WEB: www.modernmetalprocessing.com
SIC: 3398 Brazing (hardening) of metal

(G-17736)
PERFORMANCE PRINT AND MKTG
Also Called: Proforma
1907 Burkley Rd (48895-9755)
PHONE....................................517 896-9682
EMP: 3 **EST:** 2011
SALES (est): 13.8K **Privately Held**
SIC: 2752 Commercial printing, lithographic

(G-17737)
PRO BOTTLE LLC
Also Called: Vade Nutrition
805 Linn Rd (48895-9363)
PHONE....................................248 345-9224
Joe Johnson, *Mng Member*
Megan Johnson,
▲ **EMP:** 3
SQ FT: 1,200
SALES: 500K **Privately Held**
SIC: 2834 Vitamin preparations

(G-17738)
R N FINK MANUFACTURING CO
1530 Noble Rd (48895-9354)
P.O. Box 245 (48895-0245)
PHONE....................................517 655-4351
Raymond N Fink, *Ch of Bd*
Eric Fink, *President*
Judy Jones, *Purch Mgr*
Dan Feldpausch, *Finance Mgr*
Dan Fulbush, *Admin Sec*
▼ **EMP:** 30
SQ FT: 47,489
SALES (est): 4.3MM **Privately Held**
WEB: www.rnfink.com
SIC: 3085 Plastics bottles

(G-17739)
ROYAL STONE LLC
3014 Dietz Rd (48895-9214)
PHONE....................................248 343-6232
Mike Funk, *Corp Secy*
Greg Hitchcock, *Vice Pres*
James Palazeti,
EMP: 25
SALES: 3.3MM **Privately Held**
SIC: 3272 3281 Cast stone, concrete; concrete products, precast; cut stone & stone products

Williamston - Ingham County (G-17740) — GEOGRAPHIC SECTION

(G-17740)
SEELEY INC
Also Called: Midway Rotary Die Solutions
811 Progress Ct (48895-1658)
PHONE 517 655-5631
Richard B Seeley, *President*
Elizabeth L Seeley, *Vice Pres*
Mike Graham, *Controller*
Mike Fitchett, *Accounts Mgr*
Teresa Cook, *Marketing Staff*
EMP: 40
SQ FT: 100,000
SALES (est): 6.1MM **Privately Held**
WEB: www.midwayengravers.com
SIC: 2754 Rotary photogravure printing

(G-17741)
VERTICAL SOLUTIONS COMPANY
1436 E Grand River Rd (48895-9336)
P.O. Box 247 (48895-0247)
PHONE 517 655-8164
Bonnie Vant, *President*
▼ **EMP:** 5
SQ FT: 8,000
SALES (est): 1MM **Privately Held**
WEB: www.verticalsolutions.net
SIC: 3534 Elevators & equipment

(G-17742)
WILLIAMSTON PRODUCTS INC (PA)
Also Called: Wpi
845 Progress Ct (48895-1658)
PHONE 517 655-2131
Frank Remesch, *President*
Nigam Tripathi, *Principal*
Aashir Patel, *Vice Pres*
Ron Phillips, *Vice Pres*
Ed Carpenter, *CFO*
▲ **EMP:** 65
SQ FT: 36,000
SALES (est): 142.9MM **Privately Held**
WEB: www.wpius.com
SIC: 3089 Automotive parts, plastic

(G-17743)
WILLIAMSTON PRODUCTS INC
1560 Noble Rd (48895-9354)
PHONE 517 655-2273
Frank J Remesch, *Branch Mgr*
EMP: 50 **Privately Held**
SIC: 3089 Automotive parts, plastic
PA: Williamston Products, Inc.
845 Progress Ct
Williamston MI 48895

Willis
Washtenaw County

(G-17744)
KEVIN BUTZIN RECYCLING INC
9292 Oakville Waltz Rd (48191-9604)
PHONE 734 587-3710
Christina Butzin, *CEO*
Kevin Butzin, *Vice Pres*
EMP: 4
SALES (est): 571.2K **Privately Held**
SIC: 2611 Pulp mills, mechanical & recycling processing

(G-17745)
UNITED MILL & CABINET COMPANY
8842 Bunton Rd (48191-9619)
P.O. Box 339 (48191-0339)
PHONE 734 482-1981
Dennis Ruppert, *CEO*
Mark Boatwright, *President*
Marjorie Boatwright, *Chairman*
Karen Stalmack, *Finance*
EMP: 10
SQ FT: 19,900
SALES (est): 1.4MM **Privately Held**
SIC: 2431 5211 Millwork; lumber & other building materials

Winn
Isabella County

(G-17746)
BOXER EQUIPMENT/MORBARK INC
8507 S Winn Rd (48896)
P.O. Box 1000 (48896-1000)
PHONE 989 866-2381
Jim Shoemaker Jr, *President*
Eldon Sprague, *Safety Dir*
Ben Schanck, *Production*
Dennis O'Hara, *Controller*
Brian Pickelman, *Human Res Dir*
EMP: 3
SALES (est): 359.3K
SALES (corp-wide): 115.5MM **Privately Held**
SIC: 3599 3553 3549 3523 Machine shop, jobbing & repair; woodworking machinery; metalworking machinery; farm machinery & equipment
PA: Morbark, Llc
8507 S Winn Rd
Winn MI 48896
989 866-2381

(G-17747)
MORBARK LLC (PA)
8507 S Winn Rd (48896)
P.O. Box 1000 (48896-1000)
PHONE 989 866-2381
Dan Ruskin, *CEO*
John Foote, *Vice Pres*
Miland Robinson, *Vice Pres*
Brett Godwin, *Engineer*
John Schoenfeld, *Engineer*
♦ **EMP:** 413
SQ FT: 1,500,000
SALES (est): 115.5MM **Privately Held**
WEB: www.morbark.net
SIC: 3599 3553 3549 3523 Machine shop, jobbing & repair; woodworking machinery; metalworking machinery; farm machinery & equipment

Wixom
Oakland County

(G-17748)
3CON CORPORATION
47295 Cartier Dr (48393-2874)
PHONE 248 859-5440
Hannes Auer, *CEO*
Raymond Costello, *President*
Roman Pumpernick, *COO*
♦ **EMP:** 25
SQ FT: 32,000
SALES: 3.5MM
SALES (corp-wide): 51.5MM **Privately Held**
SIC: 3694 Automotive electrical equipment; motor generator sets, automotive
PA: 3con Anlagenbau Gmbh
Kleinfeld 16
Ebbs 6341
537 342-111

(G-17749)
3M COMPANY
30975 Century Dr (48393-2064)
PHONE 248 926-2500
Richard Marshall, *General Mgr*
EMP: 40
SALES (corp-wide): 32.7B **Publicly Held**
WEB: www.wdi.wendtgroup.com
SIC: 3542 Machine tools, metal forming type
PA: 3m Company
3m Center
Saint Paul MN 55144
651 733-1110

(G-17750)
ACCEL PERFORMANCE GROUP LLC
Also Called: Accel DFI
29387 Lorie Ln (48393-3684)
PHONE 248 380-2780
J Alameddine, *Branch Mgr*
EMP: 10
SALES (corp-wide): 133MM **Privately Held**
WEB: www.mrgasket.com
SIC: 3714 Motor vehicle parts & accessories
HQ: Accel Performance Group Llc
6100 Oak Tree Blvd # 200
Independence OH 44131

(G-17751)
ACROMAG INCORPORATED (PA)
30765 S Wixom Rd (48393-2417)
P.O. Box 437 (48393-0379)
PHONE 248 624-1541
John G Venious, *Ch of Bd*
Deb Baron, *General Mgr*
John Venious, *Exec VP*
Bret Stephenson, *Opers Mgr*
Reg Crawford, *Purch Agent*
EMP: 57 **EST:** 1957
SQ FT: 33,480
SALES (est): 12.5MM **Privately Held**
SIC: 3823 3829 3672 3625 Industrial process control instruments; controllers for process variables, all types; measuring & controlling devices; printed circuit boards; relays & industrial controls; computer peripheral equipment

(G-17752)
ADEMCO INC
Also Called: ADI Global Distribution
47247 Cartier Dr (48393-2874)
PHONE 248 926-5510
Mike Sampson, *Manager*
EMP: 20
SALES (corp-wide): 4.8B **Publicly Held**
WEB: www.adilink.com
SIC: 5063 3669 3822 Electrical apparatus & equipment; emergency alarms; auto controls regulating residntl & coml environmt & applncs
HQ: Ademco Inc.
1985 Douglas Dr N
Golden Valley MN 55422
800 468-1502

(G-17753)
ADEPT PLASTIC FINISHING INC
30540 Beck Rd (48393-2882)
PHONE 248 863-5930
David J Connell, *President*
Shane Gibson, *Principal*
EMP: 14
SALES (est): 803.7K **Privately Held**
SIC: 3089 Injection molding of plastics

(G-17754)
AFC-HOLCROFT LLC (HQ)
Also Called: Pacific Industrial Furnace Div
49630 Pontiac Trl (48393-2009)
PHONE 248 624-8191
William Disler, *President*
Michael Hull, *CFO*
▲ **EMP:** 100 **EST:** 1962
SQ FT: 63,000
SALES (est): 36.4MM
SALES (corp-wide): 19.5MM **Privately Held**
SIC: 3567 Industrial furnaces & ovens
PA: Atmosphere Group Inc.
49630 Pontiac Trl
Wixom MI 48393
248 624-8191

(G-17755)
AG PRECISION GAGE INC
28317 Beck Rd Ste E6 (48393-4729)
PHONE 248 374-0063
John Baldwin, *President*
Joe Schmidt, *Exec VP*
EMP: 4
SALES (est): 600K **Privately Held**
WEB: www.agprecisiongage.com
SIC: 3674 Strain gages, solid state

(G-17756)
AICHELIN HEAT TREATMENT SYST
49630 Pontiac Trl (48393-2009)
PHONE 734 459-9850
Udo Prenner, *President*
▲ **EMP:** 7
SALES (est): 1.5MM
SALES (corp-wide): 809.5MM **Privately Held**
WEB: www.aichelinusa.com
SIC: 3567 Industrial furnaces, ovens & heating devices, exc. induction
HQ: Aichelin Holding Gmbh
Fabriksgasse 3
MOdling 2340
223 623-6460

(G-17757)
ALLFI ROBOTICS INC
Also Called: Robotic System Integration
48829 West Rd (48393-3556)
P.O. Box 255, Walled Lake (48390-0255)
PHONE 586 248-1198
Samuel Song, *President*
♦ **EMP:** 3
SQ FT: 6,000
SALES (est): 2MM **Privately Held**
SIC: 3569 3541 Robots, assembly line: industrial & commercial; cutoff machines (metalworking machinery); drilling machine tools (metal cutting)

(G-17758)
ALTAIR SYSTEMS INC
30553 S Wixom Rd Ste 400 (48393-4420)
PHONE 248 668-0116
EMP: 15
SQ FT: 15,000
SALES (est): 780K **Privately Held**
SIC: 3625 3823 Mfg Relays/Industrial Controls Mfg Process Control Instruments

(G-17759)
AMADA MIYACHI AMERICA INC
Miyachi Unitek
50384 Dennis Ct (48393-2025)
PHONE 248 313-3078
Paul Brackell, *Branch Mgr*
EMP: 3 **Privately Held**
SIC: 3548 Welding apparatus
HQ: Amada Miyachi America, Inc.
1820 S Myrtle Ave
Monrovia CA 91016

(G-17760)
AMERICAN AGGREGATES MICH INC (HQ)
Also Called: Natural Aggregate
51445 W 12 Mile Rd (48393-3100)
P.O. Box H, New Hudson (48165-0337)
PHONE 248 348-8511
Edward C Levy Jr, *President*
EMP: 16
SALES (est): 19.2MM
SALES (corp-wide): 368.1MM **Privately Held**
SIC: 1442 Sand mining; gravel mining
PA: Edw. C. Levy Co.
9300 Dix
Dearborn MI 48120
313 429-2200

(G-17761)
APOLLO IDEMITSU CORPORATION
48325 Alpha Dr Ste 200 (48393-3451)
PHONE 248 675-4345
EMP: 7 **Privately Held**
SIC: 2992 Lubricating oils & greases
HQ: Apollo Idemitsu Corporation
1831 16th St
Sacramento CA 95811
916 443-0890

(G-17762)
ATLANTIC SHUTTER
29797 Beck Rd (48393-2834)
PHONE 248 668-6408
Jack Lawless, *Principal*
EMP: 6
SALES (est): 801.3K **Privately Held**
SIC: 3442 Shutters, door or window: metal

(G-17763)
ATMOSPHERE GROUP INC (PA)
49630 Pontiac Trl (48393-2009)
PHONE 248 624-8191
William M Keough, *Ch of Bd*
Gary G Dawson, *CFO*
Mark R Lezotte, *Admin Sec*
EMP: 4 **EST:** 1977
SQ FT: 40,000

▲ = Import ▼ = Export
♦ = Import/Export

GEOGRAPHIC SECTION

Wixom - Oakland County (G-17790)

SALES (est): 19.5MM **Privately Held**
SIC: **3567** 3398 Industrial furnaces & ovens; metal heat treating

(G-17764)
ATMOSPHERE HEAT TREATING INC
30760 Century Dr (48393-2063)
PHONE.................................248 960-4700
William Keough, *Ch of Bd*
James Haase, *President*
Wallace James, *Vice Pres*
Gary Dauson, *CFO*
EMP: 19
SQ FT: 41,000
SALES (est): 4.1MM **Privately Held**
WEB: www.atmosphere-online.com
SIC: **3398** Metal heat treating

(G-17765)
ATS ASSEMBLY AND TEST INC (HQ)
1 Ats Dr (48393-2446)
PHONE.................................937 222-3030
David McAusland, *Ch of Bd*
John Donaldson, *Safety Mgr*
▲ **EMP:** 277
SQ FT: 140,000
SALES (est): 150.5MM
SALES (corp-wide): 947.9MM **Privately Held**
WEB: www.assembly-testww.com
SIC: **3599** Machine shop, jobbing & repair
PA: Ats Automation Tooling Systems Inc
730 Fountain St Suite 2b
Cambridge ON N3H 4
519 653-6500

(G-17766)
ATS ASSEMBLY AND TEST INC
Advanced Assembly Automation
1 Ats Dr (48393-2446)
PHONE.................................937 222-3030
Bill Budde, *Director*
EMP: 395
SALES (corp-wide): 947.9MM **Privately Held**
WEB: www.assembly-testww.com
SIC: **3569** 3825 Assembly machines, non-metalworking; instruments to measure electricity
HQ: Ats Assembly And Test, Inc.
1 Ats Dr
Wixom MI 48393
937 222-3030

(G-17767)
AUBIO LIFE SCIENCES LLC
50164 Pontiac Trl Unit 7 (48393-2079)
P.O. Box 13025, Scottsdale AZ (85267-3025)
PHONE.................................561 289-1888
Scott Woolley, *Mng Member*
EMP: 3
SQ FT: 2,500
SALES (est): 266.6K **Privately Held**
SIC: **2865** 5149 Color pigments, organic; natural & organic foods

(G-17768)
AUSTEMPER INC (HQ)
30760 Century Dr (48393-2063)
PHONE.................................586 293-4554
Lee C Price, *President*
Gary Dawson, *CFO*
EMP: 48
SQ FT: 30,000
SALES (est): 5.2MM
SALES (corp-wide): 19.5MM **Privately Held**
WEB: www.austemperinc.com
SIC: **3398** Metal heat treating
PA: Atmosphere Group Inc.
49630 Pontiac Trl
Wixom MI 48393
248 624-8191

(G-17769)
AXSYS INC
29627 West Tech Dr (48393-3561)
PHONE.................................248 926-8810
Steven Braykovich, *President*
Roy Howard, *Vice Pres*
George Lineman, *Engineer*
EMP: 24
SQ FT: 8,000
SALES (est): 6.9MM **Privately Held**
WEB: www.axsys.net
SIC: **5045** 3843 7373 Computer software; dental equipment; furnaces, laboratory, dental; computer-aided design (CAD) systems service

(G-17770)
B C MANUFACTURING INC
29431 Lorie Ln (48393-3686)
PHONE.................................248 344-0101
Louis Conrad, *President*
EMP: 10
SALES (est): 1.3MM **Privately Held**
SIC: **3544** Special dies & tools

(G-17771)
BEAR FACTORY LLC
46968 Liberty Dr (48393-3693)
PHONE.................................248 437-4930
▲ **EMP:** 14
SALES (est): 1.3MM **Privately Held**
WEB: www.thebearfactory.com
SIC: **3942** Stuffed toys, including animals

(G-17772)
BELASH INC
Also Called: Simplicabinets
2111 N Wixom Rd (48393-4249)
PHONE.................................248 379-4444
Kawkab Matti, *Principal*
EMP: 2
SALES (est): 2.1MM **Privately Held**
SIC: **2434** Wood kitchen cabinets

(G-17773)
BENNY GAGE INC
Also Called: Zero Gage Division
4875 Product Dr Ste A (48393-2050)
PHONE.................................734 455-3080
Benny Dorenzo Jr, *President*
John Vogel, *Admin Sec*
EMP: 33
SALES (est): 3.8MM **Privately Held**
WEB: www.zerogage.com
SIC: **3545** 5084 3823 Gauges (machine tool accessories); industrial machinery & equipment; industrial instrmnts msrmnt display/control process variable

(G-17774)
BLADE INDUSTRIAL PRODUCTS INC
29289 Lorie Ln (48393-3682)
PHONE.................................248 773-7400
Joseph Smotherman, *President*
Joseph Mancos, *Vice Pres*
EMP: 7
SALES (est): 1.1MM **Privately Held**
SIC: **3069** 3089 2499 3053 Rubber hardware; injection molded finished plastic products; cork & cork products; gaskets, packing & sealing devices

(G-17775)
BLADES ENTERPRISES LLC
47570 Avante Dr (48393-3617)
PHONE.................................734 449-4479
Sue Merchant, *Finance Mgr*
Edward Blades, *Mng Member*
Daniel Blades,
EMP: 10
SALES (est): 1.5MM **Privately Held**
SIC: **3312** Tool & die steel & alloys

(G-17776)
BLINDS AND DESIGNS INC
29988 Anthony Dr (48393-3609)
PHONE.................................770 971-5524
Neil S Lullove, *President*
Arlene Lullove, *Vice Pres*
EMP: 100
SQ FT: 31,000
SALES (est): 8MM **Privately Held**
SIC: **2591** Window blinds; micro blinds; mini blinds

(G-17777)
BORAL BUILDING PRODUCTS INC (DH)
Also Called: Tapco Group, The
29797 Beck Rd (48393-2834)
PHONE.................................248 668-6400
Brian Below, *President*
Lynn Turner, *Treasurer*
Mike Mildenhall, *Admin Sec*
EMP: 117
SQ FT: 50,000
SALES (est): 18.5MM **Privately Held**
SIC: **8711** 3542 3089 3531 Building construction consultant; sheet metalworking machines; shutters, plastic; construction machinery; sheet metalwork; hand & edge tools

(G-17778)
BROWN JIG GRINDING CO
Also Called: Bjg
28005 Oakland Oaks Ct (48393-3342)
PHONE.................................248 349-7744
Michael Brown, *President*
EMP: 12 **EST:** 1966
SQ FT: 12,000
SALES (est): 1.9MM **Privately Held**
WEB: www.brownjig.com
SIC: **3599** Machine shop, jobbing & repair

(G-17779)
BRUNT ASSOCIATES INC
47689 Avante Dr (48393-3697)
PHONE.................................248 960-8295
Denis P Brunt, *President*
Brian J Brunt, *Vice Pres*
Steve Fromm, *Project Mgr*
Ralph Rexroat, *Project Engr*
Denise Maciok, *Office Mgr*
EMP: 50
SQ FT: 30,000
SALES (est): 6.6MM **Privately Held**
WEB: www.bruntassociates.com
SIC: **2431** 1751 Millwork; carpentry work

(G-17780)
C E C CONTROLS COMPANY INC
50208 Pontiac Trl (48393-2023)
PHONE.................................248 926-5701
Christopher Byrne, *Manager*
EMP: 7
SALES (corp-wide): 10B **Privately Held**
SIC: **3823** Industrial instrmnts msrmnt display/control process variable
HQ: C E C Controls Company, Inc.
14555 Barber Ave
Warren MI 48088
586 779-0222

(G-17781)
CCS DESIGN LLC
49620 Martin Dr (48393-2400)
PHONE.................................248 313-9178
Christopher C Sciacca, *Principal*
▲ **EMP:** 3
SALES: 220K **Privately Held**
SIC: **7389** 3559 8742 Design services; automotive related machinery; automation & robotics consultant

(G-17782)
CENTRAL CONVEYOR COMPANY LLC (DH)
52800 Pontiac Trl (48393-1928)
PHONE.................................248 446-0118
James Puscas, *CEO*
Larry Estes, *CEO*
John Allman, *General Mgr*
Daniel Zinger, *General Mgr*
Steve Cleary, *Superintendent*
▲ **EMP:** 70
SQ FT: 85,000
SALES (est): 145.9MM **Privately Held**
WEB: www.centralconveyor.com
SIC: **3535** Conveyors & conveying equipment
HQ: U.S. Tsubaki Holdings, Inc.
301 E Marquardt Dr
Wheeling IL 60090
847 459-9500

(G-17783)
CHAIN INDUSTRIES INC (PA)
51035 Grand River Ave (48393-3329)
PHONE.................................248 348-7722
James M Chain, *President*
Timothy Doherty, *Vice Pres*
Russell Holman, *Vice Pres*
▲ **EMP:** 25
SQ FT: 33,000
SALES (est): 7.8MM **Privately Held**
WEB: www.chainoil.com
SIC: **3324** 6798 Steel investment foundries; real estate investment trusts

(G-17784)
CHAMPION SCREW MACHINE SVCS
Also Called: Champion Screw Machine Engrg
30419 Beck Rd (48393-2841)
PHONE.................................248 624-4545
Katherine L Coffman, *President*
Susan Gorniak, *Vice Pres*
EMP: 3
SALES (est): 448K
SALES (corp-wide): 5.4MM **Privately Held**
WEB: www.championscrew.com
SIC: **3541** Screw machines, automatic
PA: Champion Screw Machine Engineering, Inc.
30419 Beck Rd
Wixom MI 48393
248 624-4545

(G-17785)
CHAMPION SCREW MCH ENGRG INC (PA)
30419 Beck Rd (48393-2841)
PHONE.................................248 624-4545
Katharine L Coffman, *President*
Susan Gorniak, *Vice Pres*
Kevin Coffman, *Treasurer*
Jim Merritt, *Sales Mgr*
Tim Ruloff, *Sales Staff*
EMP: 15
SQ FT: 23,000
SALES (est): 5.4MM **Privately Held**
WEB: www.championscrew.com
SIC: **5084** 3541 Machine tools & accessories; industrial machine parts; screw machines, automatic

(G-17786)
CHASE NEDROW MANUFACTURING INC
150 Landrow Dr (48393-2057)
P.O. Box 930313 (48393-0313)
PHONE.................................248 669-9886
James A Chase, *President*
Brian Nedrow, *Vice Pres*
Leon Cudnohufsky, *Sales Mgr*
EMP: 30
SQ FT: 20,000
SALES (est): 5.7MM **Privately Held**
SIC: **3297** Cement refractories

(G-17787)
CLASSIC PRECISION INC
28016 Oakland Oaks Ct (48393-3341)
PHONE.................................248 349-8811
Lawrence J Waligorski, *President*
Richard Przywara, *Vice Pres*
Jo Ann Przywara, *Treasurer*
Denise Waligorski, *Admin Sec*
EMP: 20
SQ FT: 12,000
SALES (est): 3.1MM **Privately Held**
SIC: **3599** Machine shop, jobbing & repair

(G-17788)
COMFORT BLINDS
1081 Yorick Path (48393-4523)
PHONE.................................248 926-9300
Michael Keenan, *Principal*
EMP: 4
SALES (est): 371.8K **Privately Held**
SIC: **2431** Blinds (shutters), wood

(G-17789)
COMPLETE CUTTING TL & MFG INC
47577 Avante Dr (48393-3618)
PHONE.................................248 662-9811
Wendell Branton, *President*
Denise Branton, *Corp Secy*
EMP: 4
SQ FT: 2,000
SALES (est): 564.4K **Privately Held**
SIC: **3545** Cutting tools for machine tools

(G-17790)
COUNTER REACTION LLC
46915 Liberty Dr (48393-3602)
PHONE.................................248 624-7900

Wixom - Oakland County (G-17791)

Craig Fry, *Mng Member*
Ed Bear,
Jim Grover,
Mike Harris,
▲ **EMP:** 7
SALES: 3.2MM **Privately Held**
SIC: 3821 Laboratory furniture

(G-17791)
CPM SERVICES GROUP INC
47924 West Rd (48393-3669)
P.O. Box 301, Walled Lake (48390-0301)
PHONE.................................248 624-5100
Kevin Wadsworth, *President*
EMP: 4
SQ FT: 5,300
SALES: 600K **Privately Held**
WEB: www.cpmsg.com
SIC: 7331 2752 Mailing service; commercial printing, offset

(G-17792)
CREATIVE MACHINE COMPANY
50140 Pontiac Trl (48393-2019)
PHONE.................................248 669-4230
Gordon K Boring, *President*
EMP: 20 **EST:** 1980
SALES (est): 4.2MM **Privately Held**
SIC: 3599 Custom machinery; machine shop, jobbing & repair

(G-17793)
CUSTOM ELECTRIC MFG LLC
48941 West Rd (48393-3555)
PHONE.................................248 305-7700
Bob Edwards, *President*
Jim Strauss, *Project Engr*
EMP: 20
SALES (est): 906.9K
SALES (corp-wide): 11.1B **Privately Held**
SIC: 3567 Heating units & devices, industrial: electric
PA: Sandvik Ab
  Hogbovagen 45
  Sandviken 811 3
  262 600-00

(G-17794)
DISCRAFT INC
51000 Grand River Ave (48393-3326)
PHONE.................................248 624-2250
James F Kenner, *President*
Gail E Mc Coll, *Corp Secy*
Mike Wagner, *Research*
Scott Aikens, *Sales Staff*
Erich Sitler, *Sales Staff*
▲ **EMP:** 25
SALES (est): 4.8MM **Privately Held**
WEB: www.discraft.com
SIC: 3949 Sporting & athletic goods

(G-17795)
DISTINCTIVE APPLIANCES DISTRG
51155 Grand River Ave (48393-3330)
PHONE.................................248 380-2007
Michel Benoit, *President*
Nadia Amiel, *Vice Pres*
Nathan Raveed, *Manager*
▲ **EMP:** 10
SQ FT: 30,740
SALES (est): 2.7MM
SALES (corp-wide): 45.1MM **Privately Held**
SIC: 3634 Housewares, excluding cooking appliances & utensils
PA: Distinctive Appliances Inc
  2025 Rue Cunard
  Montreal QC H7S 2
  450 687-6311

(G-17796)
DS SALES INC
Also Called: Premier International
46903 West Rd (48393-3654)
P.O. Box 88, Fenton (48430-0088)
PHONE.................................248 960-6411
David S Strach, *President*
EMP: 4
SQ FT: 15,200
SALES (est): 1.5MM **Privately Held**
SIC: 3069 Foam rubber

(G-17797)
EAGLE INDUSTRIES INC (PA)
30926 Century Dr (48393-2064)
PHONE.................................248 624-4266
John R Bull Jr, *President*
Mike Obrien, *Opers Mgr*
Greg Feiten, *CFO*
John Stefanko, *Accountant*
Donna Yelinek, *Human Res Mgr*
▲ **EMP:** 45
SQ FT: 42,000
SALES (est): 36.7MM **Privately Held**
SIC: 3086 Packaging & shipping materials, foamed plastic

(G-17798)
EBERSPAECHER NORTH AMERICA INC
30220 Oak Creek Dr (48393-2430)
PHONE.................................517 303-1775
Rodney Endsley, *Production*
Jeff Paquin, *Branch Mgr*
Patrick Hampton, *Manager*
EMP: 50
SALES (corp-wide): 5.2B **Privately Held**
WEB: www.eberspacher.com
SIC: 3714 4225 Exhaust systems & parts, motor vehicle; general warehousing
HQ: Eberspaecher North America, Inc.
  29101 Haggerty Rd
  Novi MI 48377
  248 994-7010

(G-17799)
ECOTRONS LLC
28287 Beck Rd Ste D5 (48393-4700)
PHONE.................................248 891-6965
Matt Liao, *Mng Member*
EMP: 4
SALES: 300K **Privately Held**
SIC: 3714 Motor vehicle parts & accessories

(G-17800)
ELECTROJET INC
50164 Pontiac Trl Unit 5 (48393-2079)
PHONE.................................734 272-4709
Kyle Schwulst, *CEO*
▲ **EMP:** 6
SALES (est): 1MM **Privately Held**
SIC: 3625 Control equipment, electric

(G-17801)
ELOPAK INC
46962 Liberty Dr (48393-3693)
PHONE.................................248 486-4600
Robert B Gillis, *President*
Nils Erik Aaby, *Vice Pres*
Gunnar Engen, *Vice Pres*
Thomas Marchioni, *Treasurer*
▲ **EMP:** 130
SQ FT: 175,000
SALES (est): 18.9MM **Privately Held**
SIC: 3565 Carton packing machines
HQ: Elopak-Americas, Inc.
  46962 Liberty Dr
  Wixom MI 48393
  248 486-4600

(G-17802)
ELOPAK-AMERICAS INC (DH)
46962 Liberty Dr (48393-3693)
PHONE.................................248 486-4600
Robert B Gillis, *President*
Mils-Erik Aaby, *Vice Pres*
Gunnar Engen, *Vice Pres*
Stan Odroniec, *Vice Pres*
Shane Carey, *Plant Mgr*
♦ **EMP:** 129
SQ FT: 175,000
SALES (est): 23.3MM **Privately Held**
SIC: 3565 Carton packing machines
HQ: Elopak As
  Industriveien 30
  Spikkestad 3430
  312 710-00

(G-17803)
ENA NORTH AMERICA CORPORATION
51150 Century Ct (48393-2077)
PHONE.................................248 926-0011
Cheol SOO Shin, *Ch of Bd*
Hobum Shin, *Vice Pres*
▲ **EMP:** 15
SQ FT: 32,000
SALES: 14MM **Privately Held**
SIC: 5013 3052 Automotive supplies & parts; rubber & plastics hose & beltings
PA: Ena Industry Co., Ltd.
  71 Gongdan 1-Ro, Jillyang-Eup
  Gyeongsan 38459

(G-17804)
ENERGY MANUFACTURING INC
47654 West Rd (48393-3663)
P.O. Box 24, Walled Lake (48390-0024)
PHONE.................................248 360-0065
Martin Sause, *President*
EMP: 3
SALES: 600K **Privately Held**
SIC: 3053 Gaskets & sealing devices

(G-17805)
ENGAI
27056 Pinewood Dr Apt 203 (48393-3294)
PHONE.................................313 605-8220
Rodney Endsley, *Production*
EMP: 3
SALES (est): 127.8K **Privately Held**
SIC: 2741 Miscellaneous publishing

(G-17806)
ESOC INC
Also Called: Environmental Safe Oil Change
48553 West Rd (48393-3537)
PHONE.................................248 624-7992
Ram Bedi, *President*
Michele Collins, *Business Mgr*
Charles Bullock, *Manager*
EMP: 10
SALES (est): 1.3MM **Privately Held**
SIC: 3559 5084 Automotive maintenance equipment; industrial machinery & equipment

(G-17807)
EXATEC LLC
31220 Oak Creek Dr (48393-2432)
PHONE.................................248 926-4200
Mr Ciemens Kaiser, *CEO*
Dominic McMahon, *General Mgr*
Michael Haag, *Technology*
▲ **EMP:** 40
SQ FT: 100,000
SALES (est): 8.4MM **Privately Held**
WEB: www.exatec.biz
SIC: 3231 Windshields, glass: made from purchased glass

(G-17808)
EXCEL MEDICAL PRODUCTS INC
28011 Grand Oaks Ct (48393-3340)
PHONE.................................810 714-4775
Adam Cole, *President*
Brian Stern, *Project Mgr*
EMP: 15
SQ FT: 12,000
SALES (est): 2.9MM **Privately Held**
WEB: www.angioplast.com
SIC: 3089 Injection molded finished plastic products

(G-17809)
FARO TECHNOLOGIES INC
46998 Magellan Ste 100 (48393-4723)
PHONE.................................248 669-8620
Sungho Moon, *Marketing Staff*
Bill Anderson, *Branch Mgr*
EMP: 10
SALES (corp-wide): 403.6MM **Publicly Held**
SIC: 3541 Machine tool replacement & repair parts, metal cutting types
PA: Faro Technologies, Inc.
  250 Technology Park
  Lake Mary FL 32746
  407 333-9911

(G-17810)
FIREBOLT GROUP INC (PA)
Also Called: Firebolt Igniting Brand Prfmce
28059 Center Oaks Ct (48393-3347)
PHONE.................................248 624-8880
Philip Ochtman, *CEO*
Brian Sciackitano, *COO*
Alex Topsfield, *Project Mgr*
Tony Lobaito, *Opers Staff*
Joel Sharp, *Engineer*
▲ **EMP:** 11
SQ FT: 4,800
SALES (est): 2.3MM **Privately Held**
SIC: 3993 Signs & advertising specialties

(G-17811)
FLAGG DISTRIBUTION LLC
48155 West Rd Ste 6 (48393-4740)
PHONE.................................248 926-0510
Warren A Flagg Jr, *President*
EMP: 11
SALES (est): 1.3MM **Privately Held**
SIC: 2434 Wood kitchen cabinets

(G-17812)
FORTIS SLTIONS GROUP CENTL LLC (PA)
Also Called: A & M Label
28505 Automation Blvd (48393-3154)
PHONE.................................248 437-5200
James Listerman, *Ch of Bd*
Pauline Listerman, *President*
John O Wynne Jr, *Principal*
Pat Watson, *Director*
EMP: 90 **EST:** 1971
SQ FT: 30,000
SALES (est): 10.6MM **Privately Held**
WEB: www.amlabel.com
SIC: 2759 2796 Flexographic printing; platemaking services

(G-17813)
FORTUNE TOOL & MACHINE INC
29650 Beck Rd (48393-2822)
PHONE.................................248 669-9119
Donna Dancik, *President*
Michael Dancik, *Vice Pres*
EMP: 22
SQ FT: 8,000
SALES (est): 2.1MM **Privately Held**
SIC: 7699 3544 3541 Industrial machinery & equipment repair; special dies, tools, jigs & fixtures; machine tools, metal cutting type

(G-17814)
FRIMO INC (DH)
50685 Century Ct (48393-2066)
PHONE.................................248 668-3160
Jeff Daily, *President*
Wolfgang Kleingunther, *Engineer*
Mike Myers, *Design Engr*
Trish Kirkman, *Controller*
Dominique Modiquet, *Sales Mgr*
▲ **EMP:** 190
SQ FT: 25,000
SALES (est): 37.8MM
SALES (corp-wide): 177.9K **Privately Held**
WEB: www.frimo.com
SIC: 3544 Special dies & tools
HQ: Frimo Group Gmbh
  Hansaring 1
  Lotte 49504
  540 488-60

(G-17815)
GATHERALL BINDERY INC
46980 Liberty Dr (48393-3601)
PHONE.................................248 669-6850
Mark A Culley, *President*
Brian C Johnson, *Treasurer*
Brian Johnson, *Treasurer*
EMP: 9
SQ FT: 3,000
SALES (est): 780K **Privately Held**
WEB: www.gatherall.net
SIC: 2789 Binding only: books, pamphlets, magazines, etc.

(G-17816)
GENERAL MILL SUPPLY COMPANY
50690 General Mill Dr (48393-2085)
PHONE.................................248 668-0800
Stuart Rotenberg, *President*
Robert Rotenberg, *Corp Secy*
Joshua Rotenberg, *Accounts Exec*
EMP: 35
SQ FT: 65,000
SALES (est): 16.4MM **Privately Held**
SIC: 5093 2611 Metal scrap & waste materials; waste paper; plastics scrap; pulp mills

GEOGRAPHIC SECTION

(G-17817)
GENERAL TAPE LABEL LIQUIDATING
Also Called: A & M Label
28505 Automation Blvd (48393-3154)
PHONE..................................248 437-5200
James Listerman, *Ch of Bd*
Pauline Listerman, *President*
Pat Watson, *President*
EMP: 67 **EST:** 1949
SQ FT: 22,000
SALES (est): 6.2MM
SALES (corp-wide): 10.6MM **Privately Held**
WEB: www.gentape.com
SIC: 5085 2759 5169 2671 Adhesives, tape & plasters; labels & seals: printing; chemicals & allied products; packaging paper & plastics film, coated & laminated
PA: Fortis Solutions Group Central Llc
28505 Automation Blvd
Wixom MI 48393
248 437-5200

(G-17818)
GLOBAL RETOOL GROUP AMER LLC
50660 Century Ct (48393-2066)
PHONE..................................248 289-5820
Andreas Quak, *President*
Stacey Nathanson, *Office Admin*
EMP: 15
SQ FT: 46,000
SALES: 5.8MM
SALES (corp-wide): 47.9MM **Privately Held**
SIC: 3545 Machine tool accessories
HQ: Wema Vogtland Technology Gmbh
Schenkendorfstr. 14
Plauen 08525
374 159-20

(G-17819)
GREAT LAKES RUBBER CO
30573 Anderson Ct (48393-2817)
P.O. Box 930199 (48393-0199)
PHONE..................................248 624-5710
Don Demallie, *President*
Martha C Welch, *Vice Pres*
Donald Demallie, *Marketing Mgr*
EMP: 70
SQ FT: 21,000
SALES (est): 10.5MM
SALES (corp-wide): 175.1MM **Privately Held**
WEB: www.greatlakesrubberco.com
SIC: 3069 Molded rubber products
PA: Mac Valves, Inc.
30569 Beck Rd
Wixom MI 48393
248 624-7700

(G-17820)
GRESHAM DRIVING AIDS INC (PA)
30800 S Wixom Rd (48393-2418)
P.O. Box 930334 (48393-0334)
PHONE..................................248 624-1533
William J Dillon, *President*
Mark Boehme, *Human Res Mgr*
Craig Wigginton, *Sales Staff*
Alan Anderson, *Manager*
Rich Campbell, *Manager*
EMP: 21
SQ FT: 7,000
SALES (est): 1.7MM **Privately Held**
WEB: www.greshamdrivingaids.com
SIC: 3842 Technical aids for the handicapped

(G-17821)
HALLMARK TOOL AND GAGE CO INC
51200 Pontiac Trl (48393-2043)
PHONE..................................248 669-4010
George H Richards, *President*
Scott A Richards, *Vice Pres*
EMP: 37
SQ FT: 22,353
SALES: 6.4MM **Privately Held**
SIC: 3544 3599 Special dies & tools; jigs & fixtures; machine shop, jobbing & repair

(G-17822)
HAMATON INC
47815 West Rd Ste D-109 (48393-4741)
PHONE..................................248 308-3856
EMP: 3
SALES (est): 256.8K **Privately Held**
SIC: 3714 Motor vehicle parts & accessories

(G-17823)
HANK THORN CO
Also Called: Van F Belknap Company
29164 Wall St (48393-3524)
PHONE..................................248 348-7800
Mayford W Thorn, *President*
Julie Acosta, *Corp Secy*
Dan Thorpe, *Technical Staff*
Glenda Reaves,
EMP: 18
SQ FT: 12,000
SALES (est): 5.6MM **Privately Held**
WEB: www.belknaptools.com
SIC: 5072 3546 3545 3423 Hand tools; power handtools; power-driven handtools; machine tool accessories; hand & edge tools

(G-17824)
HARMON SIGN INC (PA)
Also Called: Planet Neon
28054 Center Oaks Ct A (48393-3363)
PHONE..................................248 348-8150
Jeffrey Kasper, *President*
Daniel C Kasper, *Vice Pres*
Scott Brady, *Sales Staff*
EMP: 5
SQ FT: 7,500
SALES (est): 1.6MM **Privately Held**
SIC: 3993 3599 Neon signs; custom machinery

(G-17825)
HAWK TOOL AND MACHINE INC
29183 Lorie Ln (48393-3680)
P.O. Box 930351 (48393-0351)
PHONE..................................248 349-0121
George L Hawkins, *President*
EMP: 18
SALES (est): 3.1MM **Privately Held**
WEB: www.hawktool.com
SIC: 3599 Machine shop, jobbing & repair

(G-17826)
HEXAGON METROLOGY INC
Also Called: Brown & Sharpe Precision Ctr
48443 Alpha Dr Ste 100 (48393-3463)
PHONE..................................248 662-1740
Tim Cronyn, *Branch Mgr*
EMP: 80
SALES (corp-wide): 4.3B **Privately Held**
SIC: 3823 Industrial instrmnts msrmnt display/control process variable
HQ: Hexagon Metrology, Inc.
250 Circuit Dr
North Kingstown RI 02852
401 886-2000

(G-17827)
HONEYWELL INTERNATIONAL INC
49116 Wixom Tech Dr (48393-3563)
PHONE..................................248 926-4800
Tom Menard, *Business Mgr*
George Eberlein, *Manager*
EMP: 75
SALES (corp-wide): 41.8B **Publicly Held**
WEB: www.honeywell.com
SIC: 3491 7382 5075 1711 Valves, automatic control; security systems services; warm ajr heating & air conditioning; plumbing, heating, air-conditioning contractors
PA: Honeywell International Inc.
300 S Tryon St
Charlotte NC 28202
973 455-2000

(G-17828)
HOSCO INC (PA)
28026 Oakland Oaks Ct (48393-3341)
PHONE..................................248 912-1750
Jan Pitzer, *Vice Pres*
EMP: 19

SALES (est): 6.7MM **Privately Held**
SIC: 3599 3498 3451 Flexible metal hose, tubing & bellows; pipe fittings, fabricated from purchased pipe; pipe sections fabricated from purchased pipe; screw machine products

(G-17829)
HOSCO FITTINGS LLC
28026 Oakland Oaks Ct (48393-3341)
PHONE..................................248 912-1750
Tom Murray, *Mng Member*
Mike Vincent, *Supervisor*
EMP: 24
SQ FT: 22,000
SALES: 9MM **Privately Held**
SIC: 3492 Fluid power valves & hose fittings

(G-17830)
HURON TOOL & GAGE CO INC
28005 Oakland Oaks Ct (48393-3342)
PHONE..................................313 381-1900
EMP: 5
SQ FT: 5,000
SALES: 300K **Privately Held**
SIC: 3544 3545 Mfg Metalworking Dies & Tools

(G-17831)
HURON VLLEYS HRSE BLNKET HDQTR
28525 Beck Rd Unit 102 (48393-4742)
PHONE..................................248 859-2398
Bread Kraust, *Principal*
EMP: 4
SALES (est): 197.2K **Privately Held**
SIC: 2399 Horse blankets

(G-17832)
HUSSMANN CORPORATION
46974 Liberty Dr (48393-3601)
PHONE..................................248 668-0790
Ray Lima, *Manager*
EMP: 98 **Privately Held**
SIC: 3585 Refrigeration & heating equipment
HQ: Hussmann Corporation
12999 St Charles Rock Rd
Bridgeton MO 63044
314 291-2000

(G-17833)
INDEPENDENT MFG SOLUTIONS CORP
46918 Liberty Dr (48393-3600)
PHONE..................................248 960-3550
EMP: 23 **EST:** 2005
SQ FT: 13,500
SALES: 20MM **Privately Held**
SIC: 3561 3562 3569 3621 Mfg Pumps/Pumping Equip Mfg Ball/Roller Bearings Mfg General Indstl Mach Mfg Motors/Generators Elementary/Secondary Sch

(G-17834)
INNOVTIVE SRGCAL SOLUTIONS LLC
Also Called: Sentio
50461 Pontiac Trl (48393-2028)
PHONE..................................248 595-0420
Christopher Wybo, *President*
EMP: 12 **EST:** 2007
SALES (est): 1.4MM
SALES (corp-wide): 81.5B **Publicly Held**
SIC: 3845 Laser systems & equipment, medical
HQ: Depuy Synthes Products, Inc.
325 Paramount Dr
Raynham MA 02767
508 880-8100

(G-17835)
INTEGRAL VISION INC (PA)
Also Called: Integral Vision-Aid
49113 Wixom Tech Dr (48393-3559)
PHONE..................................248 668-9230
Charles J Drake, *Ch of Bd*
Max A Coon, *Vice Ch Bd*
Mark R Doede, *President*
Vincent Shunsky, *Treasurer*
David Blatt, *Manager*
▲ **EMP:** 9
SQ FT: 14,000

SALES (est): 577.5K **Publicly Held**
WEB: www.commonvisionblox.com
SIC: 3827 3823 Optical test & inspection equipment; industrial instrmnts msrmnt display/control process variable

(G-17836)
INTEGRITY BEVERAGE INC
28004 Center Oaks Ct # 102 (48393-3360)
PHONE..................................248 348-1010
Dan Abrams, *President*
Tim Sunder, *CFO*
Sunder Tim, *Technology*
EMP: 30
SQ FT: 20,000
SALES (est): 3.6MM **Privately Held**
WEB: www.integritybev.com
SIC: 2033 Fruit juices: concentrated, hot pack

(G-17837)
JCU INTERNATIONAL INC
51004 Century Ct (48393-2087)
PHONE..................................248 313-6630
Keiji Ozawa, *CEO*
EMP: 5
SALES (est): 1MM **Privately Held**
SIC: 3559 Chemical machinery & equipment

(G-17838)
JEM JIG GRINDING INC
29450 Haas Rd (48393-3022)
PHONE..................................248 486-7006
EMP: 3
SALES (est): 246.5K **Privately Held**
SIC: 3599 Mfg Industrial Machinery

(G-17839)
JTEKT TOYODA AMERICAS CORP
51300 Pontiac Trl (48393-2045)
PHONE..................................847 506-2415
EMP: 13 **Privately Held**
SIC: 3541 Machine tools, metal cutting type
HQ: Jtekt Toyoda Americas Corporation
316 W University Dr
Arlington Heights IL 60004
847 253-0340

(G-17840)
KENNEDY INDUSTRIES INC
Also Called: K.I.S.M.
4925 Holtz Dr (48393-2094)
P.O. Box 930079 (48393-0079)
PHONE..................................248 684-1200
Jeffrey Nachtweih, *President*
Shirley Schmitz, *Corp Secy*
Marcus Hemeyer, *Vice Pres*
Bryan Davidson, *Project Mgr*
Spencer Hasbrouck, *Sales Staff*
EMP: 70
SQ FT: 19,600
SALES: 30MM **Privately Held**
WEB: www.kennedyind.com
SIC: 7699 5085 3594 Pumps & pumping equipment repair; industrial machinery & equipment repair; valves & fittings; valves, pistons & fittings; fluid power pumps

(G-17841)
KIEKERT USA INC
50695 Varsity Ct (48393-2067)
PHONE..................................248 960-4100
Mike Hietbrink, *Branch Mgr*
EMP: 75
SALES (corp-wide): 65.9B **Privately Held**
SIC: 3714 Motor vehicle parts & accessories
HQ: Kiekert Usa, Inc.
46941 Liberty Dr
Wixom MI 48393
248 960-4100

(G-17842)
KIEKERT USA INC (DH)
Also Called: Keykert
46941 Liberty Dr (48393-3603)
PHONE..................................248 960-4100
Guido Hanel, *CEO*
Mike Hietbrink, *General Mgr*
Karl Lambertz, *General Mgr*
Matthias Berg, *Exec VP*
Guglielmo Guastella, *Exec VP*

Wixom - Oakland County (G-17843)

▲ EMP: 119
SQ FT: 40,000
SALES (est): 32.3MM
SALES (corp-wide): 65.9B **Privately Held**
WEB: www.keykertusa.com
SIC: 3714 Motor vehicle body components & frame
HQ: Kiekert Ag
Hoseler Platz 2
Heiligenhaus 42579
205 615-0

(G-17843)
KORD INDUSTRIAL INC
47845 Anna Ct (48393-3688)
PHONE..................................248 374-8900
Edward J Bowler, *President*
Kathy Mercier, *Sales Staff*
EMP: 8
SQ FT: 10,800
SALES: 2.5MM **Privately Held**
WEB: www.kordindustrial.com
SIC: 5084 3492 Hydraulic systems equipment & supplies; hose & tube fittings & assemblies, hydraulic/pneumatic

(G-17844)
LANCER TOOL CO
29289 Lorie Ln (48393-3682)
PHONE..................................248 380-8830
EMP: 12 EST: 1969
SQ FT: 8,500
SALES (est): 1.8MM **Privately Held**
SIC: 3545 Mfg Precision Machine Tools

(G-17845)
LEONARDOS MARBLE & GRANITE
29000 S Wixom Rd (48393-3418)
PHONE..................................248 468-2900
Leonard Rapaj, *President*
Dale Tuckett, *General Mgr*
EMP: 10
SQ FT: 8,000
SALES (est): 2.2MM **Privately Held**
SIC: 3281 Granite, cut & shaped

(G-17846)
LESCO DESIGN & MFG CO INC
28243 Beck Rd Ste B1 (48393-4722)
PHONE..................................248 596-9301
Lance Kaufman, *President*
Ken Zane, *Office Mgr*
EMP: 375
SALES (corp-wide): 99.3MM **Privately Held**
WEB: www.lescodesign.com
SIC: 3496 Conveyor belts
PA: Lesco Design & Manufacturing Company, Inc.
1120 Fort Pickens Rd
La Grange KY 40031
502 222-7101

(G-17847)
LYMAN THORNTON
2317 Gage St (48393-4229)
PHONE..................................248 762-8433
Lyman Thornton, *Owner*
EMP: 2
SALES: 1MM **Privately Held**
SIC: 3822 8748 5084 Auto controls regulating residntl & coml environmt & applncs; environmental consultant; pollution control equipment, water (environmental)

(G-17848)
LYON SAND & GRAVEL CO
Also Called: Div Edw C Levy Co
51455 W 12 Mile Rd (48393-3100)
PHONE..................................248 348-8511
Mike Taylor, *Manager*
EMP: 60
SQ FT: 8,510
SALES (corp-wide): 4.4MM **Privately Held**
WEB: www.edwclevy.net
SIC: 1442 Gravel mining
PA: Lyon Sand & Gravel Co
9300 Dix
Dearborn MI 48120
313 843-7200

(G-17849)
LYONS TOOL AND MFG CORP
47840 Anna Ct (48393-3687)
PHONE..................................248 344-9644
Michael J Murray, *President*
EMP: 20 EST: 1951
SQ FT: 12,000
SALES (est): 3.3MM **Privately Held**
SIC: 3451 Screw machine products

(G-17850)
M C CARBIDE TOOL CO
28565 Automation Blvd (48393-3154)
PHONE..................................248 486-9590
Mark Boksha, *President*
Myron Boksha, *Vice Pres*
EMP: 14 EST: 1970
SQ FT: 23,000
SALES (est): 2.2MM **Privately Held**
SIC: 3545 3568 3541 Cutting tools for machine tools; power transmission equipment; machine tools, metal cutting type

(G-17851)
MAC VALVE ASIA INC (HQ)
30569 Beck Rd (48393-2842)
PHONE..................................248 624-7700
Robert Neff, *President*
EMP: 3
SALES (est): 532.6K
SALES (corp-wide): 175.1MM **Privately Held**
SIC: 3492 3494 3491 Control valves, fluid power: hydraulic & pneumatic; valves & pipe fittings; industrial valves
PA: Mac Valves, Inc.
30569 Beck Rd
Wixom MI 48393
248 624-7700

(G-17852)
MAC VALVES INC (PA)
Also Called: M A C
30569 Beck Rd (48393-2842)
P.O. Box 111 (48393-0679)
PHONE..................................248 624-7700
Robert Neff, *President*
Jay Diehl, *President*
Robert H Neff, *President*
Jennifer Diamond, *Vice Pres*
Douglas Mc Cuiston, *Vice Pres*
▲ EMP: 740 EST: 1948
SQ FT: 108,000
SALES (est): 175.1MM **Privately Held**
WEB: www.macvalves.com
SIC: 3492 3494 3491 Control valves, fluid power: hydraulic & pneumatic; valves & pipe fittings; industrial valves

(G-17853)
MASON TOOL AND GAGE INC
28800 Wall St (48393-3518)
P.O. Box 930165 (48393-0165)
PHONE..................................248 344-0412
Joseph Mason, *President*
Aaron Mason, *Vice Pres*
EMP: 3
SQ FT: 3,000
SALES (est): 521.6K **Privately Held**
SIC: 3599 Machine shop, jobbing & repair

(G-17854)
METHODS MACHINE TOOLS INC
50531 Varsity Ct (48393-2081)
PHONE..................................248 624-8601
Kevin Davidson, *Opers Mgr*
Lisa Kiser, *Purch Agent*
Mike Kocsis, *Project Engr*
Sean Mayer, *Accounts Mgr*
Thomas Saur, *Branch Mgr*
EMP: 20
SALES (corp-wide): 115.9MM **Privately Held**
SIC: 3541 Machine tools, metal cutting type
PA: Methods Machine Tools, Inc.
65 Union Ave
Sudbury MA 01776
978 443-5388

(G-17855)
MIDWEST SALES ASSOCIATES INC
Also Called: Michael Schafer and Associates
29445 Beck Rd Ste A103 (48393-2880)
PHONE..................................248 348-9600
Michael Schafer, *President*
EMP: 5
SALES (est): 754.8K **Privately Held**
WEB: www.midwestsalesassociates.com
SIC: 3678 3699 Electronic connectors; electrical equipment & supplies

(G-17856)
MINTH NORTH AMERICA INC
Also Called: Pti International
51331 Pontiac Trl (48393-2046)
PHONE..................................248 259-7468
Howard Boyer, *CEO*
Ed Viksne, *Engineer*
Joy Zheng, *Treasurer*
Luis Sommer, *Accounts Mgr*
Steve Fleming, *Program Mgr*
EMP: 95
SQ FT: 15,000
SALES (est): 17MM **Privately Held**
SIC: 8711 3465 Consulting engineer; body parts, automobile: stamped metal
HQ: Minth Group Us Holding Inc
51331 Pontiac Trl
Wixom MI
248 848-8530

(G-17857)
MODERN MILLWORK INC
29020 S Wixom Rd Ste 100 (48393-3467)
P.O. Box 930347 (48393-0347)
PHONE..................................248 347-4777
Jeffery K Weinger, *President*
Sandy Stcharles, *Office Mgr*
EMP: 10 EST: 1979
SQ FT: 14,000
SALES (est): 1.5MM **Privately Held**
WEB: www.modernmillworkinc.com
SIC: 2431 Millwork

(G-17858)
MOHAWK INDUSTRIES INC
28435 Automation Blvd A (48393-3160)
PHONE..................................248 486-4075
Mike Seigle, *Manager*
EMP: 9
SALES (corp-wide): 9.9B **Publicly Held**
SIC: 2273 Finishers of tufted carpets & rugs
PA: Mohawk Industries, Inc.
160 S Industrial Blvd
Calhoun GA 30701
706 629-7721

(G-17859)
MOLLEWOOD EXPORT INC
Also Called: Pak-Rite Michigan
46921 Enterprise Ct (48393-4728)
PHONE..................................248 624-1885
Scott De Henau, *President*
EMP: 23
SQ FT: 25,000
SALES (est): 5.4MM **Privately Held**
WEB: www.pak-rite.com
SIC: 4783 2441 2449 3089 Packing goods for shipping; nailed wood boxes & shook; rectangular boxes & crates, wood; prefabricated plastic buildings

(G-17860)
MOTOR CITY WASH WORKS INC
48285 Frank St (48393-4712)
PHONE..................................248 313-0272
Lionel G Belanger, *President*
▲ EMP: 45
SALES (est): 9.4MM **Privately Held**
SIC: 3589 Car washing machinery

(G-17861)
NATIONAL INTGRATED SYSTEMS INC
29241 Beck Rd (48393-3679)
PHONE..................................734 927-3030
Jay Park, *President*
Cheryl Magewick, *Project Mgr*
Aaron Domke, *Accounts Mgr*
Russell Gregg, *Accounts Mgr*
Daniel Plucinski, *Info Tech Mgr*
▲ EMP: 12
SALES (est): 2.5MM **Privately Held**
SIC: 2542 Racks, merchandise display or storage: except wood

(G-17862)
NAVTECH LLC
47906 West Rd (48393-3669)
PHONE..................................248 427-1080
Rozlynn Ilkhani-Pour,
Mehdi Ilkhani-Pour,
EMP: 8
SQ FT: 5,000
SALES (est): 590K **Privately Held**
SIC: 2821 Plastics materials & resins

(G-17863)
NEDROW REFRACTORIES CO
150 Landrow Dr (48393-2057)
P.O. Box 930313 (48393-0313)
PHONE..................................248 669-2500
James A Chase, *President*
Nedrow Brian, *Vice Pres*
Barbara A Nedrow Sitzler, *Vice Pres*
Brian T Nedrow, *Treasurer*
Brad Nedrow, *Accounts Mgr*
EMP: 30
SQ FT: 8,000
SALES (est): 2.4MM **Privately Held**
WEB: www.chasenedrow.com
SIC: 7699 3297 Industrial machinery & equipment repair; nonclay refractories

(G-17864)
NEWTECH 3 INC
28373 Beck Rd Ste H7 (48393-4735)
P.O. Box 441123, Detroit (48244-1123)
PHONE..................................248 912-0807
Jack Long, *President*
EMP: 25
SALES: 35.8K **Privately Held**
SIC: 3714 Automotive wiring harness sets

(G-17865)
NGK SPARK PLUGS (USA) INC (DH)
Also Called: NGK Spark Plugs USA
46929 Magellan (48393-3699)
PHONE..................................248 926-6900
Goro Ogawa, *CEO*
Shin Odo, *President*
Todd Cullums, *General Mgr*
Hideyuki Koiso, *Vice Pres*
Ryosuke Furuhashi, *Project Mgr*
▲ EMP: 150
SQ FT: 18,000
SALES (est): 132.1MM **Privately Held**
WEB: www.ngksparkplugs.com
SIC: 3643 3264 Current-carrying wiring devices; porcelain parts for electrical devices, molded
HQ: Ngk Spark Plugs (U.S.A.) Holding, Inc.
1011 Centre Rd
Wilmington DE 19805
302 288-0131

(G-17866)
NORDSON CORPORATION
28775 Beck Rd (48393-3637)
PHONE..................................734 459-8600
EMP: 60
SALES (corp-wide): 2.2B **Publicly Held**
SIC: 3823 3586 3563 3531 Industrial flow & liquid measuring instruments; measuring & dispensing pumps; air & gas compressors; construction machinery; valves & pipe fittings; industrial valves
PA: Nordson Corporation
28601 Clemens Rd
Westlake OH 44145
440 892-1580

(G-17867)
NORMAN INDUSTRIES INC
Also Called: Nordic Label
47850 West Rd (48393-3667)
PHONE..................................248 669-6213
Carl C Norman III, *President*
Kenneth Diacono, *Principal*
Craig C Norman, *Treasurer*
EMP: 5
SQ FT: 4,600
SALES (est): 749.7K **Privately Held**
SIC: 2754 Labels: gravure printing

GEOGRAPHIC SECTION

(G-17868)
NORTHERN MICH AGGREGATES LLC
Also Called: Ledgestone
51445 W12 Mile Rd (48393)
P.O. Box 678, Alpena (49707-0678)
PHONE..................989 354-3502
S Evan Weiner, *President*
Edward C Levy Jr, *Chairman*
Robert P Scholz, *CFO*
EMP: 10
SALES (est): 655.7K **Privately Held**
SIC: 1411 Limestone, dimension-quarrying
PA: Levy Indiana Slag Co.
  9300 Dix
  Dearborn MI 48120

(G-17869)
NORTHERN PROCESSES & SALES LLC
49700 Martin Dr (48393-2402)
PHONE..................248 669-3918
Richard Shefferly, *Mng Member*
EMP: 8
SQ FT: 3,000
SALES: 1MM **Privately Held**
WEB: www.northernprocessessales.com
SIC: 5085 3569 Industrial supplies; assembly machines, non-metalworking

(G-17870)
NTZ MICRO FILTRATION LLC
28221 Beck Rd Ste A1 (48393-4701)
PHONE..................248 449-8700
John Billinghurst, *General Mgr*
Pierre Nieuwland, *Mng Member*
▲ **EMP:** 15
SQ FT: 2,000
SALES (est): 3.1MM
SALES (corp-wide): 379.8MM **Privately Held**
WEB: www.ntzfilter.com
SIC: 3569 Filters, general line: industrial
HQ: Ntz International Holding B.V.
  Sydneystraat 37
  Rotterdam 3047
  102 383-818

(G-17871)
O & S TOOL AND MACHINE INC
50400 Dennis Ct Unit B (48393-2048)
PHONE..................248 926-8045
Ray Orlando, *President*
Joanne Orlando, *Corp Secy*
EMP: 9
SQ FT: 3,200
SALES (est): 585.6K **Privately Held**
SIC: 3599 Machine shop, jobbing & repair

(G-17872)
OAKS CONCRETE PRODUCTS INC
51744 Pontiac Trl (48393-1906)
PHONE..................248 684-5004
Lanzy Fuchs, *Marketing Staff*
▲ **EMP:** 19
SALES (est): 3.3MM
SALES (corp-wide): 121.2MM **Privately Held**
SIC: 3272 Concrete products
PA: Brampton Brick Limited
  225 Wanless Dr
  Brampton ON L7A 1
  905 840-1011

(G-17873)
OERLIKON BLZERS CATING USA INC
Also Called: Wixom Coating Center
46947 West Rd (48393-3654)
PHONE..................248 960-9055
David Lindsey, *Branch Mgr*
EMP: 20
SALES (corp-wide): 2.6B **Privately Held**
WEB: www.balzers.com
SIC: 3479 Coating of metals & formed products
HQ: Oerlikon Balzers Coating Usa Inc.
  1700 E Golf Rd Ste 200
  Schaumburg IL 60173
  847 619-5141

(G-17874)
OPS SOLUTIONS LLC (PA)
48443 Alpha Dr Ste 175 (48393-3464)
PHONE..................248 374-8000
Paul Ryznar, *CEO*
Eve Ryznar, *Manager*
William Coe,
John Morelli,
Will Sommerville,
◆ **EMP:** 27
SQ FT: 10,000
SALES: 6.8MM **Privately Held**
SIC: 7372 Application computer software

(G-17875)
PARAGON MODEL AND TOOL INC
Also Called: Paragon Tool
46934 Magellan (48393-3699)
PHONE..................248 960-1223
S Lee Brithinee, *President*
EMP: 7
SALES (est): 1MM **Privately Held**
WEB: www.paragonwixom.com
SIC: 3599 Custom machinery

(G-17876)
PEAK EDM INC
28221 Beck Rd Ste A2 (48393-4701)
PHONE..................248 380-0871
Robert Palmer, *President*
Lonnie Jewell, *Vice Pres*
EMP: 8
SQ FT: 3,100
SALES: 1.7MM **Privately Held**
WEB: www.peakedm.com
SIC: 5084 3699 Machine tools & accessories; electrical equipment & supplies

(G-17877)
PEPSI BEVERAGES COMPANY
Also Called: Pepsico
28345 Beck Rd (48393-4733)
PHONE..................248 596-9028
Robert Henebry, *Branch Mgr*
Robert Halstead, *Manager*
EMP: 44
SALES (corp-wide): 64.6B **Publicly Held**
SIC: 2086 Carbonated soft drinks, bottled & canned
HQ: Pepsi Beverages Company
  110 S Byhalia Rd
  Collierville TN 38017
  901 853-5736

(G-17878)
POWER CLEANING SYSTEMS INC
28294 Beck Rd (48393-3623)
PHONE..................248 347-7727
Richard H Mc Carthy, *President*
Pamela Mc Carthy, *Vice Pres*
Rick McCarthy, *Opers Staff*
EMP: 5
SALES: 900K **Privately Held**
WEB: www.powercleaningsystems.com
SIC: 5087 3699 Cleaning & maintenance equipment & supplies; cleaning equipment, ultrasonic, except medical & dental

(G-17879)
PRECISE TOOL & CUTTER INC
51143 Pontiac Trl (48393-2042)
PHONE..................248 684-8480
Nash Sinishtaj, *President*
EMP: 5
SQ FT: 2,000
SALES (est): 705.6K **Privately Held**
SIC: 3599 Machine shop, jobbing & repair

(G-17880)
PRO-MOTION TECH GROUP LLC
29755 Beck Rd (48393-2834)
PHONE..................248 668-3100
Lynn Matson, *CEO*
Asher McGhee, *Project Mgr*
Nicole Pauly, *Project Mgr*
Spencer Knisely, *Chief Mktg Ofcr*
▲ **EMP:** 60
SQ FT: 65,000
SALES (est): 22.9MM **Privately Held**
SIC: 3993 5063 Signs & advertising specialties; wire & cable

(G-17881)
PURITAN AUTOMATION LLC
28389 Beck Rd Ste J2 (48393-4732)
PHONE..................248 668-1114
Jeremy Sanger, *CEO*
Briget Sawallich, *Controller*
EMP: 15
SQ FT: 15,000
SALES: 2MM **Privately Held**
WEB: www.puritanautomation.com
SIC: 3545 3569 Precision tools, machinists'; assembly machines, non-metalworking

(G-17882)
QUALITY CAVITY INC
47955 Anna Ct (48393-3690)
PHONE..................248 344-9995
Dennis J Craig, *President*
Barbara Craig, *Vice Pres*
EMP: 10
SQ FT: 7,000
SALES (est): 1.5MM **Privately Held**
SIC: 3599 3312 Machine & other job shop work; tool & die steel

(G-17883)
QUALITY ENGINEERING COMPANY
30194 S Wixom Rd (48393-3440)
PHONE..................248 351-9000
Abraham Varkovitzky, *President*
Bill Iordanou, *Vice Pres*
Lou Iordanou, *Vice Pres*
▲ **EMP:** 15 **EST:** 1981
SQ FT: 43,700
SALES: 8.3MM **Privately Held**
SIC: 8711 3714 8742 8744 Engineering services; motor vehicle parts & accessories; productivity improvement consultant; facilities support services

(G-17884)
RECOGNITION ROBOTICS INC
29445 Beck Rd Ste A106 (48393-2880)
PHONE..................440 590-0499
Simon Melikian, *President*
EMP: 6
SALES (corp-wide): 11.8MM **Privately Held**
SIC: 3569 8742 Robots, assembly line: industrial & commercial; automation & robotics consultant
PA: Recognition Robotics, Inc.
  151 Innovation Dr
  Elyria OH 44035
  440 590-0499

(G-17885)
RGM NEW VENTURES INC (PA)
Also Called: Barracuda Mfg
48230 West Rd (48393-3675)
P.O. Box 930439 (48393-0439)
PHONE..................248 624-5050
Bob Muse, *President*
Martin Agrest, *Vice Pres*
Herb Kindt, *Opers Staff*
▲ **EMP:** 60 **EST:** 1964
SQ FT: 42,000
SALES (est): 8MM **Privately Held**
SIC: 3229 2511 3231 Pressed & blown glass; wood household furniture; mirrored glass

(G-17886)
ROCKWELL MEDICAL INC (PA)
30142 S Wixom Rd (48393-3440)
PHONE..................248 960-9009
John P McLaughlin, *Ch of Bd*
Robert L Chioini, *President*
Jim McCarthy, *Senior VP*
Anne Boardman, *Vice Pres*
Paul E McGarry, *Vice Pres*
EMP: 193
SQ FT: 68,500
SALES: 63.3MM **Publicly Held**
WEB: www.rockwellmed.com
SIC: 3845 Dialyzers, electromedical

(G-17887)
S & M MACHINING COMPANY
47590 Avante Dr (48393-3617)
PHONE..................248 348-0310
Scott W McFarland, *Owner*
EMP: 4
SQ FT: 3,500
SALES: 600K **Privately Held**
SIC: 3599 Amusement park equipment

(G-17888)
S MAIN COMPANY LLC
Also Called: The South Main Company
50489 Pontiac Trl (48393-2028)
P.O. Box 3464, Farmington (48333-3464)
PHONE..................248 960-1540
Edmund J Swain,
Peter Bracco,
Mark Mosher,
EMP: 25 **EST:** 1997
SQ FT: 10,000
SALES (est): 3.7MM **Privately Held**
WEB: www.southmain.net
SIC: 3613 Panel & distribution boards & other related apparatus

(G-17889)
S&S PRECISION LLC
1378 Cherrystone Ct (48393-1612)
PHONE..................248 266-4770
Robert Sexton,
EMP: 3
SALES (est): 149.8K **Privately Held**
SIC: 3089 5013 5169 Automotive parts, plastic; automotive supplies & parts; compressed gas

(G-17890)
SCODELLER CONSTRUCTION INC
51722 Grand River Ave (48393-2303)
PHONE..................248 374-1102
Peter D Scodeller, *President*
EMP: 95
SQ FT: 4,000
SALES (est): 18.1MM **Privately Held**
SIC: 2891 1771 Sealing compounds for pipe threads or joints; concrete repair

(G-17891)
SEBRO PLASTICS INC (DH)
29200 Wall St (48393-3526)
PHONE..................248 348-4121
Joseph Bolton, *Vice Pres*
▲ **EMP:** 50
SQ FT: 18,500
SALES (est): 7.1MM
SALES (corp-wide): 5.3B **Publicly Held**
SIC: 3089 Injection molding of plastics
HQ: Sonoco-Crellin International, Inc.
  87 Center St
  Chatham NY 12037
  518 392-2000

(G-17892)
SEKISUI PLASTICS US A INC
28345 Beck Rd Ste 406 (48393-4745)
PHONE..................248 308-3000
EMP: 10
SALES (est): 753K **Privately Held**
SIC: 3086 5199 Packaging & shipping materials, foamed plastic; packaging materials
PA: Sekisui Plastics U.S. A., Inc.
  110 Clifton Way Dr
  Mount Pleasant TN 38474

(G-17893)
SEMICNDCTOR HYBRID ASSMBLY INC
Also Called: S H A
49113 Wixom Tech Dr (48393-3559)
P.O. Box 930835 (48393-0835)
PHONE..................248 668-9050
Yassin Burgol, *President*
Hisham Burgol, *Vice Pres*
EMP: 10
SQ FT: 5,500
SALES (est): 2.3MM **Privately Held**
WEB: www.shainc.net
SIC: 3672 Printed circuit boards

(G-17894)
SLM SOLUTIONS NA INC
48561 Alpha Dr Ste 300 (48393-3458)
PHONE..................248 243-5400
Andreas Frahm, *President*
Mark Hoefing, *Exec VP*
Michael Hansen, *Engineer*
Kristal Kilgore, *Marketing Mgr*
EMP: 24

Wixom - Oakland County (G-17895)

GEOGRAPHIC SECTION

SALES (est): 3.4MM **Privately Held**
SIC: **3699** Laser welding, drilling & cutting equipment

(G-17895)
SQUIRES INDUSTRIES INC
Also Called: Petronis Industries
29181 Beck Rd (48393-3642)
PHONE..................................248 449-6092
Edwin L Squires Jr, *President*
EMP: 30
SQ FT: 8,000
SALES (est): 2.1MM **Privately Held**
SIC: **3599** Machine shop, jobbing & repair

(G-17896)
STATIC CONTROLS CORP
30460 S Wixom Rd (48393-2410)
PHONE..................................248 926-4400
Robert Gassman, *President*
William Yonish, *Owner*
Judith Yonish, *Admin Sec*
▲ EMP: 22 EST: 1968
SQ FT: 26,500
SALES (est): 4.3MM **Privately Held**
WEB: www.scccontrols.com
SIC: **3625** 5999 5065 Industrial controls: push button, selector switches, pilot; electronic parts & equipment; electronic parts

(G-17897)
STERLING EDGE INC
50230 Dennis Ct (48393-2024)
PHONE..................................248 438-6034
Albert L Robitaille, *President*
David Brochu, *Vice Pres*
Chris Sellers, *VP Opers*
EMP: 6
SQ FT: 3,000
SALES (est): 1.6MM **Privately Held**
WEB: www.sterlingedge.com
SIC: **3545** Cutting tools for machine tools

(G-17898)
STT USA INC
47815 West Rd Ste D-101 (48393-4741)
PHONE..................................248 522-9655
Calvin Hashisaka, *President*
Takafumi Sugasawa, *Vice Pres*
Shigetaka Mori, *Director*
Hirohisa Takata, *Director*
EMP: 5
SQ FT: 2,400
SALES (est): 132.8K **Privately Held**
SIC: **2992** Lubricating oils & greases
PA: Stt Inc.
2-6-1, Tatenodai
Hadano KNG 257-0

(G-17899)
SUMMIT CUTTING TOOLS AND MFG
50210 Dennis Ct (48393-2023)
PHONE..................................248 859-2625
Jennifer Dreyer, *Owner*
EMP: 3
SALES (est): 240.8K **Privately Held**
SIC: **3999** Manufacturing industries

(G-17900)
SUNSET SPORTSWEAR INC
676 Shady Maple Dr (48393-4308)
PHONE..................................248 437-7611
Jeffrey C Wixom, *President*
EMP: 10
SALES (est): 1MM **Privately Held**
WEB: www.sunsetsportswear.com
SIC: **2396** Screen printing on fabric articles

(G-17901)
SUPERABRASIVES INC
28047 Grand Oaks Ct (48393-3340)
PHONE..................................248 348-7670
Charles Halprin, *President*
Linda Halrin, *CFO*
Michael J Sidley, *Treasurer*
Mark Elliott, *Sales Staff*
▲ EMP: 30
SQ FT: 25,000
SALES (est): 5.9MM **Privately Held**
WEB: www.superabrasives.com
SIC: **3541** 3291 Grinding machines, metalworking; abrasive products

(G-17902)
SURE CONVEYORS INC
48155 West Rd Ste 6 (48393-4740)
PHONE..................................248 926-2100
EMP: 9
SALES (est): 1.3MM **Privately Held**
SIC: **3535** Conveyors & conveying equipment

(G-17903)
TACTICAL SIMPLICITY LLC
Also Called: Detroit Bullet Works
2817 Beck Rd Ste E-16 (48393)
PHONE..................................248 410-4523
Christopher Jones,
EMP: 2 EST: 2012
SALES: 1.4MM **Privately Held**
SIC: **3482** Small arms ammunition

(G-17904)
TANFASTER INC
813 Saint Charles Pl (48393-1853)
P.O. Box 930073 (48393-0073)
PHONE..................................248 669-3312
EMP: 3
SALES (est): 270.6K **Privately Held**
SIC: **3648** Mfg Lighting Equipment

(G-17905)
TAPCO HOLDINGS INC (DH)
Also Called: Mid America Building Pdts Div
29797 Beck Rd (48393-2834)
PHONE..................................248 668-6400
Allen Gurney, *Vice Pres*
Jack Wallace III, *Vice Pres*
Matt Greenberg, *Purchasing*
Barb Rakowski, *Sales Staff*
EMP: 117
SQ FT: 50,000
SALES (est): 18.5MM **Privately Held**
WEB: www.atlanticshuttersystems.com
SIC: **3542** 3089 3531 3444 Sheet metalworking machines; shutters, plastic; construction machinery; sheet metalwork; hand & edge tools; millwork

(G-17906)
TAYLOR TURNING INC
29632 West Tech Dr (48393-3561)
PHONE..................................248 960-7920
Russell J Taylor, *President*
EMP: 25
SQ FT: 11,500
SALES (est): 29.8MM **Privately Held**
SIC: **3544** 3545 Special dies & tools; machine tool accessories

(G-17907)
TECART INDUSTRIES INC
28059 Center Oaks Ct (48393-3347)
PHONE..................................248 624-8880
Kimberly Perrigan, *CEO*
H Halstead Scudder, *President*
Keith Tofan, *Manager*
▲ EMP: 26
SQ FT: 34,000
SALES (est): 4MM **Privately Held**
WEB: www.tecartinc.com
SIC: **3993** Electric signs

(G-17908)
TEPSO GEN-X PLASTICS LLC
28525 Beck Rd Unit 111 (48393-4742)
PHONE..................................248 869-2130
Pere Vazquez, *Vice Pres*
Carles Marti, *CFO*
Troy Isaacson, *Mng Member*
EMP: 8
SALES: 4.5MM
SALES (corp-wide): 876MM **Privately Held**
WEB: www.gen-x-eng.com
SIC: **3089** Automotive parts, plastic
HQ: U.S. Farathane, S.A. De C.V.
Carretera A Huinala Km 1.5
Apodaca N.L. 66634

(G-17909)
TESTEK LLC
28320 Lakeview Dr (48393-3157)
PHONE..................................248 573-4980
Harish Patel, *CEO*
Mona Patel, *President*
Shilpa Patel, *CFO*
Matt Poursaba, *Regl Sales Mgr*
▲ EMP: 90
SQ FT: 120,000
SALES (est): 32.6MM **Privately Held**
WEB: www.testek.com
SIC: **3829** 3699 8711 Physical property testing equipment; electrical equipment & supplies; engineering services

(G-17910)
TOMCO FABRICATING & ENGRG INC
50853 Century Ct (48393-2066)
PHONE..................................248 669-2900
Donald Henry, *President*
Joan Henry, *Treasurer*
EMP: 10
SQ FT: 7,800
SALES: 2MM **Privately Held**
SIC: **3599** Machine shop, jobbing & repair

(G-17911)
TOOL & DIE SYSTEMS INC
30529 Anderson Ct (48393-2877)
PHONE..................................248 446-1499
Steven Claserner, *President*
Thomas Collopy, *Vice Pres*
EMP: 3
SALES: 700K **Privately Held**
SIC: **3544** Special dies & tools

(G-17912)
TOSHIBA AMERICA ELECTRONIC
48679 Alpha Dr Ste 120 (48393-3455)
PHONE..................................248 347-2608
Mark Downing, *Branch Mgr*
EMP: 4 **Privately Held**
SIC: **3674** Semiconductors & related devices
HQ: Toshiba America Electronic Components Inc
5231 California Ave
Irvine CA 92617
949 462-7700

(G-17913)
TOX PRESSO TECHNIK
28287 Beck Rd Ste D12 (48393-4706)
PHONE..................................248 374-1877
Eugene Rapp, *Owner*
EMP: 4
SALES (est): 270.3K **Privately Held**
SIC: **3542** Sheet metalworking machines

(G-17914)
TRAFFIC SFETY CTRL SYSTEMS INC
Also Called: TRAFFIC & SAFETY
48584 Downing St (48393-3501)
PHONE..................................248 348-0570
Keith E Hay, *President*
Deborah Cantlon, *Exec VP*
Anthony Jaworowski, *Electrical Engi*
Dan Hubert, *Technician*
EMP: 25
SQ FT: 9,000
SALES: 9.9MM **Privately Held**
WEB: www.trafficandsafety.com
SIC: **5065** 3559 1799 7382 Security control equipment & systems; parking facility equipment & supplies; parking facility equipment installation; security systems services

(G-17915)
TRAILER TECH HOLDINGS LLC
Also Called: Kentucky Trailer Technologies
48282 Frank St (48393-4711)
PHONE..................................248 960-9700
Gary A Smith, *President*
Larry Roy, *Exec VP*
Al Fosmoen, *Purchasing*
◆ EMP: 50
SQ FT: 35,000
SALES (est): 13.2MM
SALES (corp-wide): 6.8B **Publicly Held**
SIC: **3715** Semitrailers for truck tractors
HQ: R. C. Tway Company
7201 Logistics Dr
Louisville KY 40258
502 637-2551

(G-17916)
TRIBAR MANUFACTURING LLC
30517 Anderson Ct (48393-2817)
P.O. Box 930359 (48393-0359)
PHONE..................................248 669-0077
Dave Connell, *Manager*
EMP: 40
SALES (corp-wide): 55.3MM **Privately Held**
SIC: **3089** 2789 2759 Coloring & finishing of plastic products; bookbinding & related work; commercial printing
HQ: Tribar Manufacturing, L.L.C.
2211 Grand Commerce Dr
Howell MI 48855

(G-17917)
TRIBAR MANUFACTURING LLC
Also Called: Adept Plastic Finishing
29883 Beck Rd (48393-2835)
PHONE..................................248 374-5870
EMP: 4
SALES (corp-wide): 55.3MM **Privately Held**
SIC: **3089** Coloring & finishing of plastic products
HQ: Tribar Manufacturing, L.L.C.
2211 Grand Commerce Dr
Howell MI 48855

(G-17918)
TRIBAR TECHNOLOGIES INC (PA)
48668 Alpha Dr (48393-3445)
PHONE..................................248 516-1600
EMP: 350
SALES (est): 55.3MM **Privately Held**
SIC: **3089** Automotive parts, plastic

(G-17919)
TRIBAR TECHNOLOGIES INC
48668 Alpha Dr (48393-3445)
PHONE..................................248 516-1600
Jeff Wilson, *CEO*
EMP: 2200
SALES: 145MM **Privately Held**
SIC: **3089** Automotive parts, plastic

(G-17920)
TRIJICON INC (PA)
49385 Shafer Ct (48393-2869)
P.O. Box 930059 (48393-0059)
PHONE..................................248 960-7700
Stephen Bindon, *President*
John Rupp, *President*
Michelle Mahoney, *General Mgr*
Dave Sikorski, *Vice Pres*
Jeannie Stone, *Vice Pres*
EMP: 145 EST: 1971
SQ FT: 42,000
SALES (est): 29.9MM **Privately Held**
WEB: www.trijicon.com
SIC: **3827** Gun sights, optical; telescopic sights

(G-17921)
TRISPEC PRECISION PRODUCTS INC
47580 Avante Dr (48393-3617)
PHONE..................................248 308-3231
John Cavalier, *President*
EMP: 3
SQ FT: 3,500
SALES: 300K **Privately Held**
SIC: **3544** 7699 3541 Special dies & tools; industrial machinery & equipment repair; machine tools, metal cutting type

(G-17922)
USA SWITCH INC (PA)
49030 Pontiac Trl Ste 100 (48393-2586)
PHONE..................................248 960-8500
Thomas P Petrillo, *President*
▲ EMP: 13
SQ FT: 20,000
SALES (est): 1MM **Privately Held**
WEB: www.asnu-usa.com
SIC: **3694** Engine electrical equipment

(G-17923)
V & V INDUSTRIES INC
Also Called: 2v Industries
48553 West Rd (48393-3537)
PHONE..................................248 624-7943
Ram Bedi, *President*

GEOGRAPHIC SECTION

Wyandotte - Wayne County (G-17949)

Bill Edgar, *President*
Matthew Roberts, *General Mgr*
Uma Bedi, *Chairman*
Vijay Bedi, *Vice Pres*
EMP: 15
SQ FT: 27,800
SALES (est): 3.9MM **Privately Held**
WEB: www.2vindustries.com
SIC: 2899 8999 Metal treating compounds; chemical consultant

(G-17924)
VELESCO PHRM SVCS INC
28036 Oakland Oaks Ct (48393-3348)
PHONE 734 545-0696
Dave Barnes, *Branch Mgr*
EMP: 7 **Privately Held**
SIC: 3559 2834 Pharmaceutical machinery; druggists' preparations (pharmaceuticals)
PA: Velesco Pharmaceutical Services, Inc.
46701 Commerce Center Dr
Plymouth MI 48170

(G-17925)
VENTURA AEROSPACE LLC
51170 Grand River Ave A (48393-3361)
PHONE 734 357-0114
Brad Blanchard, *President*
Jack Akey, *Sales Staff*
EMP: 45
SALES (est): 9.3MM **Privately Held**
WEB: www.venturaaerospace.net
SIC: 3728 3494 3433 Aircraft assemblies, subassemblies & parts; valves & pipe fittings; heating equipment, except electric

(G-17926)
VENTURE GRAFIX LLC
47757 West Rd Ste C-105 (48393-4739)
PHONE 248 449-1330
Michael J Cortis,
EMP: 7
SQ FT: 5,000
SALES (est): 400K **Privately Held**
SIC: 7319 3993 Display advertising service; electric signs

(G-17927)
WAGON AUTOMOTIVE INC
28025 Oakland Oaks Ct (48393-3342)
PHONE 248 262-2020
Ben Orler, *General Mgr*
▲ **EMP:** 76
SQ FT: 78,000
SALES (est): 8.4MM
SALES (corp-wide): 138.8MM **Privately Held**
WEB: www.wagonautomotive.com
SIC: 3441 Fabricated structural metal
PA: Modineer Co.
2190 Industrial Dr
Niles MI 49120
269 683-2550

(G-17928)
WEST SIDE MFG FABRICATION INC
28776 Wall St (48393-3516)
PHONE 248 380-6640
Glenn D Viazanko, *President*
EMP: 12
SQ FT: 12,000
SALES (est): 1.6MM **Privately Held**
WEB: www.westsidemanufacturing.net
SIC: 3444 7692 Sheet metalwork; welding repair

(G-17929)
WETZEL TOOL & ENGINEERING INC
46952 Liberty Dr (48393-3693)
PHONE 248 960-0430
Wieland H Wetzel, *President*
Frank Myers, *Foreman/Supr*
Hanna Wetzel, *Purchasing*
Hannelore C Wetzel, *Office Mgr*
EMP: 11
SQ FT: 10,000
SALES (est): 798.6K **Privately Held**
SIC: 3544 Special dies & tools

(G-17930)
WFL MILLTURN TECHNOLOGIES INC
48152 West Rd (48393-3673)
PHONE 440 729-0896
Nobert Jungreip Mayr, *President*
Ben Baggerly, *Sales Mgr*
◆ **EMP:** 3
SQ FT: 1,000
SALES: 500K
SALES (corp-wide): 726.3K **Privately Held**
SIC: 3541 Machine tools, metal cutting type
HQ: Wfl Millturn Technologies Gmbh & Co. Kg
WahringerstraBe 36
Linz 4030
732 691-30

(G-17931)
WIXOM MOVING BOXES LLC
27046 Sprucewood Dr # 204 (48393-3280)
PHONE 248 613-5078
EMP: 3
SALES (est): 131.9K **Privately Held**
SIC: 2211 5111 Cotton Broadwoven Fabric Mill Whol Printing/Writing Paper

(G-17932)
XILINX INC
28345 Beck Rd Ste 400 (48393-4745)
PHONE 248 344-0786
EMP: 4
SALES (corp-wide): 3B **Publicly Held**
SIC: 3672 3674 7372 Printed circuit boards; microcircuits, integrated (semiconductor); application computer software
PA: Xilinx, Inc.
2100 All Programable
San Jose CA 95124
408 559-7778

(G-17933)
YOUNGTRONICS LLC
49197 Wixom Tech Dr Ste A (48393-3572)
PHONE 248 896-5790
Rupesh Srivastava, *CEO*
Kumar Arbind, *General Mgr*
Nick Horlock, *Manager*
EMP: 10
SALES (est): 2MM **Privately Held**
SIC: 3569 Assembly machines, non-metalworking

Wolverine
Cheboygan County

(G-17934)
JAROCHE BROTHERS INC
Also Called: M & J Forest Products
4250 Secord Rd (49799-9718)
PHONE 231 525-8100
EMP: 10
SALES (est): 1.3MM **Privately Held**
SIC: 2421 2426 Sawmill/Planing Mill Hardwood Dimension/Floor Mill

Wolverine Lake
Oakland County

(G-17935)
CASTANO PLASTICS INC
2337 Solano Dr (48390-2460)
PHONE 248 624-3724
Blanca Castano, *President*
John Castano, *Admin Sec*
EMP: 7
SQ FT: 29,800
SALES: 600K **Privately Held**
WEB: www.castanoplastics.com
SIC: 3089 Injection molding of plastics

(G-17936)
HERITAGE HONE & GAGE INC
1155 Ladd Rd (48390-3068)
PHONE 248 926-8449
Douglas Spitery, *President*
EMP: 3

SALES: 200K **Privately Held**
SIC: 3599 Machine shop, jobbing & repair

Woodhaven
Wayne County

(G-17937)
AMERICAN WIND & SOLAR LLC
18638 Van Horn Rd Apt 11 (48183-3818)
PHONE 734 904-8490
John A Lay,
EMP: 3
SALES (est): 230.9K **Privately Held**
SIC: 3674 Semiconductors & related devices

(G-17938)
CIRCLE S PRODUCTS INC (PA)
16415 Carter Rd (48183-2254)
PHONE 734 675-2960
John Scharboneau, *President*
Carolyn Scharboneau, *Treasurer*
▼ **EMP:** 7
SALES (est): 1.7MM **Privately Held**
WEB: www.dryflo.com
SIC: 3441 7389 Fabricated structural metal;

(G-17939)
DIEZ GROUP LLC (PA)
Also Called: Integrated Terminals
25325 Hall Rd (48183-5101)
PHONE 734 675-1700
April Diez, *CEO*
Gerald Diez Jr, *President*
Michael Roualet, *Vice Pres*
EMP: 59
SQ FT: 250,000
SALES: 15MM **Privately Held**
SIC: 3316 3353 5051 Cold finishing of steel shapes; aluminum sheet, plate & foil; metals service centers & offices

(G-17940)
PARKER MACHINE & ENGINEERING
25028 Research Way (48183-5107)
PHONE 734 692-4600
Robert W Parker, *President*
EMP: 4
SQ FT: 5,000
SALES: 300K **Privately Held**
SIC: 3599 Machine shop, jobbing & repair

(G-17941)
PIPPA CUSTOM DESIGN PRINTING
22025 King Rd (48183-1026)
PHONE 734 552-1598
Nancy L Weil, *Principal*
EMP: 4 **EST:** 2010
SALES (est): 374.6K **Privately Held**
SIC: 2752 Commercial printing, lithographic

(G-17942)
YAMATO INTERNATIONAL CORP
22036 Commerce Dr (48183-5105)
PHONE 734 675-6055
Yutaka Hasegawa, *President*
Minal Patel, *Purch Agent*
Mikio Sato, *Treasurer*
Marcia Lavassaur, *IT/INT Sup*
▲ **EMP:** 22
SQ FT: 14,000
SALES (est): 4.5MM **Privately Held**
WEB: www.yamatousa.com
SIC: 2672 Tape, pressure sensitive: made from purchased materials
PA: Yamato Co.,Ltd.
9-10, Nihombashiodemmacho
Chuo-Ku TKY 103-0

Woodland
Barry County

(G-17943)
THOMAS LOGGING LLC
11777 Reflection Dr (48897-9662)
PHONE 269 838-2020

Brian Thomas, *Principal*
EMP: 3
SALES (est): 150K **Privately Held**
SIC: 2411 Logging

Wyandotte
Wayne County

(G-17944)
ABBOTT LABORATORIES
1609 Biddle Ave (48192-3729)
PHONE 734 324-6666
Tom Soblesky, *Manager*
EMP: 30
SALES (corp-wide): 30.5B **Publicly Held**
WEB: www.abbott.com
SIC: 2834 Druggists' preparations (pharmaceuticals)
PA: Abbott Laboratories
100 Abbott Park Rd
Abbott Park IL 60064
224 667-6100

(G-17945)
ABBVIE INC
1609 Biddle Ave (48192-3729)
PHONE 734 324-6650
Miles D White, *Ch of Bd*
Martin McMillan, *QC Mgr*
EMP: 6
SALES (corp-wide): 32.7B **Publicly Held**
SIC: 2834 Druggists' preparations (pharmaceuticals)
PA: Abbvie Inc.
1 N Waukegan Rd
North Chicago IL 60064
847 932-7900

(G-17946)
ARROW MOTOR & PUMP INC
629 Cent St (48192)
PHONE 734 285-7860
Nancy Prohaska, *President*
EMP: 30
SQ FT: 11,500
SALES (est): 180MM **Privately Held**
WEB: www.arrowmotor.com
SIC: 7694 5063 7699 5084 Electric motor repair; motors, electric; pumps & pumping equipment repair; pumps & pumping equipment

(G-17947)
BASF CORPORATION
40 James Desana Dr (48192-4691)
PHONE 734 324-6963
EMP: 101
SALES (corp-wide): 71.7B **Privately Held**
SIC: 2869 Industrial organic chemicals
HQ: Basf Corporation
100 Park Ave
Florham Park NJ 07932
973 245-6000

(G-17948)
BASF CORPORATION
BASF Cellasto
1609 Biddle Ave (48192-3729)
PHONE 734 324-6000
Erin Wagner, *Buyer*
Michael Krupa, *Technical Mgr*
Majiid Khalatbari, *Research*
Joe Lengyel, *Design Engr*
Jim Lyon, *Marketing Mgr*
EMP: 200
SALES (corp-wide): 71.7B **Privately Held**
SIC: 2869 2843 Industrial organic chemicals; surface active agents
HQ: Basf Corporation
100 Park Ave
Florham Park NJ 07932
973 245-6000

(G-17949)
BASF CORPORATION
1609 Biddle Ave (48192-3729)
PHONE 734 324-6100
Greg Pflum, *Branch Mgr*
EMP: 1200
SALES (corp-wide): 71.7B **Privately Held**
SIC: 2869 Industrial organic chemicals

Wyandotte - Wayne County (G-17950)

HQ: Basf Corporation
100 Park Ave
Florham Park NJ 07932
973 245-6000

(G-17950)
CADON PLATING & COATINGS LLC
3715 11th St (48192-6496)
PHONE.................................734 282-8100
Craig L Stormer,
Allen Ensign,
Tom Klein,
Gerald Lorenz,
William Sheets,
EMP: 80
SQ FT: 85,000
SALES (est): 11.2MM **Privately Held**
WEB: www.cadonplating.com
SIC: 3471 Plating of metals or formed products

(G-17951)
CAP COLLET & TOOL CO INC
4082 6th St (48192-7104)
PHONE.................................734 283-4040
Jerry Potter, *President*
John D Potter Jr, *President*
EMP: 11
SQ FT: 32,000
SALES: 750K **Privately Held**
WEB: www.capcollet.com
SIC: 3545 3451 Chucks: drill, lathe or magnetic (machine tool accessories); screw machine products

(G-17952)
CJM MAINTENANCE
18322 Koester St (48193-7471)
PHONE.................................734 285-0247
Christopher McFarlane, *Owner*
EMP: 3
SALES (est): 323.6K **Privately Held**
SIC: 3524 0782 Grass catchers, lawn mower; lawn services

(G-17953)
CONCEPP TECHNOLOGIES
1609 Biddle Ave (48192-3729)
PHONE.................................734 324-6750
EMP: 11
SALES (corp-wide): 9.8MM **Privately Held**
SIC: 2821 Polypropylene resins
PA: Concepp Technologies Incorporated
454 Rue Edouard
Granby QC
450 378-9093

(G-17954)
DETROIT TUBULAR RIVET INC (PA)
1213 Grove St (48192-7045)
P.O. Box 279 (48192-0279)
PHONE.................................734 282-7979
Gerald Keast, *President*
Gary Sadonis, *Vice Pres*
EMP: 54
SQ FT: 55,000
SALES (est): 7.1MM **Privately Held**
WEB: www.dtrrivets.com
SIC: 3452 Rivets, metal

(G-17955)
DIGITALMUNI LLC
2245 Eureka Rd (48192-6018)
PHONE.................................248 237-4077
Joseph Murnane, *Mng Member*
Gerry Morgan,
EMP: 3
SALES (est): 242.8K **Privately Held**
SIC: 2741 Miscellaneous publishing

(G-17956)
ECORSE MCHY SLS & RBLDRS INC
Also Called: Ecorse Precision Products
4621 13th St (48192)
PHONE.................................313 383-2100
Ivan Doverspike, *President*
EMP: 25
SQ FT: 25,000
SALES (est): 7.9MM **Privately Held**
WEB: www.ecorse.com
SIC: 3491 8711 3541 Automatic regulating & control valves; engineering services; machine tools, metal cutting type

(G-17957)
ELECTRO OPTICS MFG INC
4459 13th St (48192-7004)
PHONE.................................734 283-3000
Kathryn Chambers, *CEO*
Russell Chambers, *President*
EMP: 10
SQ FT: 20,000
SALES: 804.6K **Privately Held**
WEB: www.electroopticsmfg.com
SIC: 3469 Stamping metal for the trade

(G-17958)
EQUIPMENT MATERIAL SALES LLC
671 Grove St (48192-6833)
PHONE.................................734 284-8711
Mike Malcho, *Mng Member*
Lorraine Malcho,
EMP: 3
SQ FT: 6,000
SALES: 250K **Privately Held**
SIC: 5999 5084 3629 Auction rooms (general merchandise); industrial machine parts; electronic generation equipment

(G-17959)
GEE & MISSLER INC
744 Vinewood St (48192-5007)
PHONE.................................734 284-1224
Elmer M Gee, *President*
EMP: 20 EST: 1945
SQ FT: 7,500
SALES (est): 2.6MM **Privately Held**
SIC: 1711 3444 Mechanical contractor; sheet metalwork

(G-17960)
HESS PRINTING
201 Elm St Apt A (48192-5962)
PHONE.................................734 285-4377
Rachel Hess, *Principal*
EMP: 4
SALES (est): 503.4K **Privately Held**
SIC: 2752 Commercial printing, offset

(G-17961)
HPS FABRICATIONS INC
4410 13th St (48192-7005)
PHONE.................................734 282-2285
Robert Lang, *CEO*
Gerald Page, *President*
Mitch Saari, *Purch Mgr*
EMP: 15
SQ FT: 12,000
SALES (est): 3MM **Privately Held**
SIC: 3444 Sheet metalwork

(G-17962)
II ENTERPRISES INC
555 Grove St (48192-6837)
P.O. Box 526 (48192-0526)
PHONE.................................734 285-6030
William Iverson, *President*
Anthony Sawicki, *COO*
Thomas Iverson, *Vice Pres*
Bill Roy, *Opers Mgr*
Bethany Iverson, *Treasurer*
▲ **EMP:** 10
SALES (est): 2MM **Privately Held**
SIC: 3559 4225 Glass making machinery: blowing, molding, forming, etc.; general warehousing

(G-17963)
JCI JONES CHEMICALS INC
18000 Payne Ave (48192)
P.O. Box 2208, Riverview (48193-1208)
PHONE.................................734 283-0677
D W Skidmore, *Branch Mgr*
EMP: 25
SALES (corp-wide): 179MM **Privately Held**
WEB: www.jcichem.com
SIC: 2812 5169 2819 Alkalies & chlorine; industrial chemicals; industrial inorganic chemicals
PA: Jci Jones Chemicals, Inc.
1765 Ringling Blvd # 200
Sarasota FL 34236
941 330-1537

(G-17964)
KULICK ENTERPRISES INC
4082 Biddle Ave (48192-7116)
PHONE.................................734 283-6999
Robert Kulick, *President*
EMP: 4
SALES (est): 340K **Privately Held**
WEB: www.kulickenterprises.com
SIC: 3444 Sheet metal specialties, not stamped

(G-17965)
LAKE SHORE SERVICES INC
4354 Biddle Ave (48192-7304)
PHONE.................................734 285-7007
Robert Lemay, *President*
Jennifer McConnell, *Business Mgr*
EMP: 15
SQ FT: 10,000
SALES: 1.4MM **Privately Held**
SIC: 7692 3441 Welding repair; fabricated structural metal

(G-17966)
MADDEN ENTERPRISES INC
Also Called: American Speedy Printing
3557 Fort St (48192-6315)
PHONE.................................734 284-5330
Janell Madden, *President*
EMP: 5 EST: 1977
SALES (est): 753.5K **Privately Held**
SIC: 2752 Commercial printing, offset

(G-17967)
MECHANICAL SHEET METAL CO
723 Walnut St (48192-4338)
PHONE.................................734 284-1006
David Karl, *President*
Daniel Karl, *Treasurer*
EMP: 10
SQ FT: 4,000
SALES (est): 1.7MM **Privately Held**
SIC: 3444 Sheet metalwork

(G-17968)
MERCURY MANUFACTURING COMPANY
Also Called: Apg - Splcty Vlve McHined Pdts
1212 Grove St (48192-7099)
PHONE.................................734 285-5150
Janice Wiegand, *President*
Jan Wiegand, *COO*
Roy Craig, *Engineer*
▲ **EMP:** 68 EST: 1964
SQ FT: 53,000
SALES (est): 16.9MM **Privately Held**
WEB: www.mercurymfg.com
SIC: 3451 3491 Screw machine products; pressure valves & regulators, industrial
PA: Alpha Precision Group, Llc
95 Mason Run Rd
Ridgway PA 15853
814 773-3191

(G-17969)
MR LUBE INC
6915 Airport Hwy (48192)
PHONE.................................313 615-6161
Mohamed Hameed, *Principal*
EMP: 4 EST: 2011
SALES (est): 349.7K **Privately Held**
SIC: 2992 Lubricating oils

(G-17970)
ORION BUS ACCNTING SLTIONS LLC
1611 Ford Ave (48192-2303)
PHONE.................................248 893-1060
Jeff Smith, *Mng Member*
Jim Steele,
EMP: 4
SALES: 400K **Privately Held**
WEB: www.orionbas.com
SIC: 8721 7372 Accounting services, except auditing; business oriented computer software

(G-17971)
RAPP & SON INC (PA)
3767 11th St (48192-6431)
PHONE.................................734 283-1000
Roy W Rapp Jr, *President*
Roy W Rapp III, *Vice Pres*
Cheryl L Rapp, *Admin Sec*
EMP: 162 EST: 1939
SALES (est): 11.8MM **Privately Held**
SIC: 3724 3812 3769 3678 Engine mount parts, aircraft; search & navigation equipment; guided missile & space vehicle parts & auxiliary equipment; electronic connectors; motor vehicle parts & accessories

(G-17972)
RICKS COVE INC
467 Biddle Ave (48192-2703)
PHONE.................................734 283-7505
Michael D Martin, *President*
EMP: 3
SALES (est): 170K **Privately Held**
SIC: 3732 Boat building & repairing

(G-17973)
ROCKERY
1175 Eureka Rd Uppr (48192-5690)
PHONE.................................734 281-4629
Joseph Piteo, *Owner*
EMP: 4
SALES (est): 226.8K **Privately Held**
SIC: 2085 Cocktails, alcoholic

(G-17974)
S S GRAPHICS INC
Also Called: Signoutfitters.com
4176 6th St (48192-7106)
PHONE.................................734 246-4420
Russ Kissel, *President*
Russ Kissle, *President*
Scott Smiddy, *Vice Pres*
EMP: 9
SQ FT: 7,500
SALES: 1MM **Privately Held**
WEB: www.ssnautical.com
SIC: 3993 Signs, not made in custom sign painting shops

(G-17975)
SIGNS ETC
1439 Fort St (48192-3036)
PHONE.................................734 941-6991
Jeff Pettry, *President*
Teresa Pettry, *Manager*
EMP: 3 EST: 1997
SQ FT: 1,200
SALES: 150K **Privately Held**
WEB: www.signsetcweb.com
SIC: 3993 Signs, not made in custom sign painting shops

(G-17976)
STEWART PRINTING COMPANY INC
2715 Fort St (48192-4820)
PHONE.................................734 283-8440
Louis George, *President*
Cindy Scott, *Manager*
EMP: 8 EST: 1950
SQ FT: 2,000
SALES: 200K **Privately Held**
SIC: 2752 Commercial printing, offset

(G-17977)
STROHS
3162 Biddle Ave (48192-5916)
PHONE.................................734 285-5480
Julie Volante, *Owner*
EMP: 3
SALES (est): 194.4K **Privately Held**
SIC: 2024 Ice cream, bulk

(G-17978)
TRI-TECH ENGINEERING INC
3663 11th St (48192-6406)
PHONE.................................734 283-3700
George Balint, *President*
David Isham, *Treasurer*
EMP: 21
SQ FT: 13,000

GEOGRAPHIC SECTION

Wyoming - Kent County (G-18006)

SALES (est): 4.5MM **Privately Held**
WEB: www.tri-techeng.com
SIC: 3593 7699 Fluid power cylinders, hydraulic or pneumatic; hydraulic equipment repair

(G-17979)
VINYL INDUSTRIAL PAINTS INC
1401 Sycamore St (48192-5513)
PHONE..................................734 284-3536
Mose Thomas Muscat Jr, *Owner*
Patricia Muscat, *Corp Secy*
EMP: 3
SQ FT: 5,500
SALES (est): 395.6K **Privately Held**
SIC: 2851 Paints & paint additives

(G-17980)
VIRTUAL EMERGENCY SERVICES LLC
1400 Biddle Ave (48192-3706)
PHONE..................................734 324-2299
Keith A Murray,
EMP: 10
SQ FT: 1,800
SALES: 700K **Privately Held**
SIC: 8322 7372 8748 Emergency social services; application computer software; business consulting

(G-17981)
WAYNE COUNTY LABORATORY
797 Central St (48192-7307)
PHONE..................................734 285-5215
Jim Berry, *Counsel*
Kelli Barg, *Department Mgr*
Walter Syrkowski, *Director*
EMP: 6
SALES (est): 1MM **Privately Held**
SIC: 3589 Sewage & water treatment equipment

(G-17982)
WYANDOTTE COLLET AND TOOL INC
4070 5th St (48192-7102)
PHONE..................................734 283-8055
Victor Forsman, *President*
Phillip A Robinson III, *Vice Pres*
EMP: 14 EST: 1970
SQ FT: 6,000
SALES (est): 1.2MM **Privately Held**
SIC: 3545 3599 Collets (machine tool accessories); pushers; sockets (machine tool accessories); machine shop, jobbing & repair

Wyoming
Kent County

(G-17983)
2K TOOL LLC
3025 Madison Ave Se (49548-1209)
PHONE..................................616 452-4927
Heidi Smith, *President*
Amanda Smith, *Admin Asst*
Kevin Smith,
EMP: 8
SQ FT: 8,500
SALES (est): 1.3MM **Privately Held**
WEB: www.2ktool.com
SIC: 3544 Industrial molds

(G-17984)
ADVANCED ALTRNTIVE SLTIONS LLC
2600 De Laat Ave Sw (49519-2360)
PHONE..................................616 607-6956
Aaron Esquivel,
EMP: 3
SALES (est): 135.4K **Privately Held**
SIC: 7389 1389 8711 ; testing, measuring, surveying & analysis services; building construction consultant
PA: New American Media, Inc.
2600 De Laat Ave Sw
Wyoming MI 49519

(G-17985)
ALL-TECH INC (PA)
Also Called: All-Tech Engineering
1030 58th St Sw (49509-9365)
PHONE..................................616 406-0681
Bruce Bunker, *President*
David Steffen, *General Mgr*
Brian Ames, *Engineer*
Ron Goldwater, *Project Engr*
Brett Lame, *Project Engr*
EMP: 46
SQ FT: 32,000
SALES (est): 10.6MM **Privately Held**
WEB: www.alltech-eng.com
SIC: 3599 Machine shop, jobbing & repair

(G-17986)
AMI ENTERTAINMENT NETWORK INC
4147 Estrn Ave Se Ste 200 (49508)
PHONE..................................877 762-6765
EMP: 5
SALES (corp-wide): 3.8B **Privately Held**
SIC: 3999 Coin-operated amusement machines
HQ: Ami Entertainment Network, Inc.
925 Canal St
Bristol PA 19007
215 826-1400

(G-17987)
ASSURAMED INC
Also Called: Edgepark Medical Supplies
3576 R B Chaffee Mem Se (49548)
PHONE..................................616 419-2020
Kurt Packer, *Branch Mgr*
EMP: 3
SALES (corp-wide): 145.5B **Publicly Held**
SIC: 3841 Hypodermic needles & syringes
HQ: Assuramed, Inc.
1810 Summit Commerce Park
Twinsburg OH 44087
330 963-6998

(G-17988)
BOLD ENDEAVORS LLC
Also Called: Boldsocks
5752 Barcroft Cir Sw (49418-9394)
PHONE..................................616 389-3902
Ryan Preisner, *Manager*
EMP: 7
SALES (est): 734.4K **Privately Held**
SIC: 2252 Socks

(G-17989)
BOSS ELECTRO STATIC INC
3974 Linden Ave Se (49548-3432)
PHONE..................................616 575-0577
Kathi S Lynch, *President*
Michael Lynch, *Vice Pres*
▲ EMP: 22
SQ FT: 30,000
SALES (est): 2.2MM **Privately Held**
WEB: www.bosselectrostatic.com
SIC: 3479 1721 Etching & engraving; painting & paper hanging

(G-17990)
BUSTER MATHIS FOUNDATION
Also Called: Soul of The City Classics Socc
4409 Carol Ave Sw (49519-4519)
PHONE..................................616 843-4433
Buster Mathis, *President*
Joe Gonnella, *Principal*
Robert Woonacott, *Principal*
EMP: 4
SALES (est): 214.4K **Privately Held**
SIC: 8331 3542 3545 1522 Job training & vocational rehabilitation services; robots for metal forming: pressing, extruding, etc.; measuring tools & machines, machinists' metalworking type; residential construction; sports promotion

(G-17991)
CHAMBERS INDUSTRIAL TECH INC
2220 Byron Center Ave Sw (49519-1652)
PHONE..................................616 249-8190
Anna Chambers, *President*
Chad Chambers, *General Mgr*
Richard Chambers, *Vice Pres*
Nate V Kamp, *Manager*
▲ EMP: 8
SALES: 400K **Privately Held**
SIC: 3089 Injection molding of plastics

(G-17992)
CONCRETE PIPE NORTHERN
2701 Chicago Dr Sw (49519-1604)
PHONE..................................616 608-6025
Lee Watt, *Principal*
Jamie England, *Cust Mgr*
Tim Gohn, *Sales Staff*
Robin Denman, *Marketing Staff*
EMP: 3
SALES (est): 323.9K **Privately Held**
SIC: 3272 Concrete products

(G-17993)
CONSUMERS CONCRETE CORP
1505 Burlingame Ave Sw (49509-1001)
PHONE..................................616 243-3651
Tom Thomas, *President*
Steve Thomas, *Vice Pres*
Mike Kline, *Plant Mgr*
EMP: 20 EST: 1945
SQ FT: 12,000
SALES (est): 2.4MM
SALES (corp-wide): 102.9MM **Privately Held**
WEB: www.consumersconcrete.com
SIC: 3271 3272 Blocks, concrete or cinder: standard; concrete products
PA: Consumers Concrete Corporation
3508 S Sprinkle Rd
Kalamazoo MI 49001
269 342-0136

(G-17994)
CONTROL DEKK LLC
4035 Oak Valley Ct Sw (49519-3775)
PHONE..................................616 828-4862
Len Logsdon, *Mng Member*
Jared Dekker,
Jordan Dekker,
EMP: 4
SALES: 7K **Privately Held**
SIC: 3448 Greenhouses: prefabricated metal

(G-17995)
DAVIS DENTAL LABORATORY
5830 Crossroads Cmmrce (49519-9572)
PHONE..................................616 261-9191
Bob Ditta, *President*
Kim Jones, *Vice Pres*
EMP: 5
SALES (est): 548.6K **Privately Held**
SIC: 8072 3842 Crown & bridge production; surgical appliances & supplies

(G-17996)
DETAIL TECHNOLOGIES LLC
5900 Crssrds Cmmrce Pkwy (49519)
PHONE..................................616 261-1313
Christopher Ostosh, *CEO*
Josh Schwab, *Vice Pres*
EMP: 48
SQ FT: 20,000
SALES (est): 8.9MM **Privately Held**
SIC: 3599 Electrical discharge machining (EDM)

(G-17997)
EJ USA INC
5075 Clyde Park Ave Sw (49509-5119)
PHONE..................................616 538-2040
Mike Warmouth, *Manager*
EMP: 14 **Privately Held**
WEB: www.ejiw.com
SIC: 3321 Manhole covers, metal
HQ: Ej Usa, Inc.
301 Spring St
East Jordan MI 49727
800 874-4100

(G-17998)
EL INFORMADOR LLC
2000 28th St Sw Ste 4 (49519-2609)
P.O. Box 9625 (49509-0625)
PHONE..................................616 272-1092
Alma Molina, *Mng Member*
EMP: 6
SALES (est): 147.3K **Privately Held**
SIC: 2711 7371 Newspapers; computer software development & applications

(G-17999)
ELECTRO CHEMICAL FINISHING CO (PA)
2610 Remico St Sw (49519-2408)
PHONE..................................616 531-0670
Terry Vollmer, *President*
Don Post, *President*
Eric Romero, *COO*
Dan Trapp, *VP Admin*
Steve Hulst, *Safety Mgr*
EMP: 15 EST: 1977
SQ FT: 64,000
SALES (est): 21.4MM **Privately Held**
WEB: www.ecfinc.com
SIC: 3471 3479 Electroplating of metals or formed products; coating of metals & formed products

(G-18000)
ENGINE GURU LLC
6709 18th Ave (49509)
PHONE..................................616 430-3114
Kyle Miller, *President*
EMP: 3
SALES: 150K **Privately Held**
SIC: 3519 Engines, diesel & semi-diesel or dual-fuel

(G-18001)
FHC HOLDING COMPANY (PA)
Also Called: F H C
2509 29th St Sw (49519-2468)
P.O. Box 9100, Grand Rapids (49509-0100)
PHONE..................................616 538-3231
Robert W Holt Jr, *CEO*
Thomas R Butterworth, *President*
Robert Holt, *Project Mgr*
Larry Lind, *Project Mgr*
EMP: 4
SQ FT: 18,000
SALES: 16MM **Privately Held**
SIC: 1711 3498 3444 Warm air heating & air conditioning contractor; fabricated pipe & fittings; sheet metalwork

(G-18002)
FISK PRECISION TECH LLC
3403 Lousma Dr Se (49548-2265)
PHONE..................................616 514-1415
Amy Steketee, *Principal*
EMP: 5
SALES (est): 694.4K **Privately Held**
SIC: 3545 Precision measuring tools

(G-18003)
GIPSON FABRICATIONS
2151 Chicago Dr Sw (49519-1214)
PHONE..................................616 245-7331
Joe Weber, *General Mgr*
John Gipson, *Principal*
EMP: 8 EST: 2010
SALES (est): 1.1MM **Privately Held**
SIC: 3842 Welders' hoods

(G-18004)
GOLDEN EAGLE PALLETS LLC
1701 Clyde Park Ave Sw (49509-1500)
PHONE..................................616 233-0970
Manuel Juarez, *Principal*
EMP: 13
SALES (est): 1.8MM **Privately Held**
SIC: 2448 Pallets, wood; pallets, wood & wood with metal

(G-18005)
GRAND RAPIDS GRAPHIX
3853 Llewellyn Ct Sw (49519-3128)
PHONE..................................616 359-2383
Adam Lamos, *Partner*
Joseph Brunet, *Partner*
EMP: 4
SALES (est): 227.1K **Privately Held**
SIC: 2759 7389 Screen printing;

(G-18006)
GRT AVIONICS INC
3133 Madison Ave Se Ste B (49548-1277)
PHONE..................................616 245-7700
Greg Toman, *President*
EMP: 5 EST: 2004
SALES (est): 525.8K **Privately Held**
SIC: 3699 Electrical equipment & supplies

Wyoming - Kent County (G-18007)

(G-18007)
HALDEX BRAKE PRODUCTS CORP
5801 Weller Ct Sw Ste D (49509-9601)
PHONE..................................616 827-9641
Chuck Zimmer, *Branch Mgr*
EMP: 116
SALES (corp-wide): 528.7MM **Privately Held**
SIC: 3714 Air brakes, motor vehicle
HQ: Haldex Brake Products Corporation
10930 N Pomona Ave
Kansas City MO 64153
816 891-2470

(G-18008)
HASKELL OFFICE
3770 Hagen Dr Se (49548-2343)
PHONE..................................616 988-0880
Alan Robins, *Owner*
EMP: 6
SALES: 950K **Privately Held**
SIC: 2522 Office furniture, except wood

(G-18009)
HEYS FABRICATION AND MCH CO
3059 Hillcroft Ave Sw (49548-1034)
PHONE..................................616 247-0065
Rick Heys, *CEO*
EMP: 16
SALES (est): 3.5MM **Privately Held**
SIC: 3441 Fabricated structural metal

(G-18010)
HIGHLIGHT INDUSTRIES INC
2694 Prairie St Sw (49519-2461)
PHONE..................................616 531-2464
Kurt Riemenschneider, *President*
Alan Martens, *Vice Pres*
Karen Riemenschneider, *Vice Pres*
Randy Himstra, *Plant Mgr*
Christina Agema, *Engineer*
▲ EMP: 69
SQ FT: 57,000
SALES (est): 21.2MM **Privately Held**
WEB: www.highlightindustries.com
SIC: 3565 Wrapping machines

(G-18011)
HME INC
Also Called: Hme Silverfox
1950 Byron Center Ave Sw (49519-1223)
PHONE..................................616 534-1463
Jim Monterusso, *CEO*
Rex Troost, *Principal*
Ken Lenz, *Vice Pres*
Rod McNeil, *Vice Pres*
Veronica Lisowski, *HR Admin*
EMP: 120
SQ FT: 140,000
SALES: 67.9MM
SALES (corp-wide): 72.4MM **Privately Held**
SIC: 3713 3546 3537 3536 Truck & bus bodies; power-driven handtools; industrial trucks & tractors; hoists, cranes & monorails; motor vehicles & car bodies
PA: Valley Truck Parts, Inc.
1900 Chicago Dr Sw
Wyoming MI 49519
616 241-5431

(G-18012)
JACKSONS INDUSTRIAL MFG
2662 Prairie St Sw (49519-2461)
PHONE..................................616 531-1820
Gerald Grooters, *CEO*
Susan Latham, *President*
Barbara Grooters, *Vice Pres*
EMP: 10
SQ FT: 25,000
SALES: 700K **Privately Held**
SIC: 3561 Pumps & pumping equipment

(G-18013)
KALAMAZOO PACKG SYSTEMS LLC
900 47th St Sw Ste J (49509-5142)
P.O. Box 88141, Grand Rapids (49518-0141)
PHONE..................................616 534-2600
Richard Wietczak, *President*
EMP: 10
SALES (est): 581K **Privately Held**
SIC: 3565 5084 Packing & wrapping machinery; industrial machinery & equipment

(G-18014)
KEVCO METAL SURFACE PREP
138 39th St Sw (49548-3104)
PHONE..................................616 538-1377
EMP: 3 EST: 2009
SALES (est): 212.8K **Privately Held**
SIC: 3471 Plating/Polishing Service

(G-18015)
LEWIS WELDING INC
274 Mart St Sw (49548-1000)
PHONE..................................616 452-9226
Lyman Lewis, *President*
Becky Broton, *Purchasing*
EMP: 20
SQ FT: 5,200
SALES (est): 2.8MM **Privately Held**
SIC: 7692 Welding repair

(G-18016)
LIGHT METALS CORPORATION
Also Called: LMC
2740 Prairie St Sw (49519-6098)
PHONE..................................616 538-3030
George T Boylan, *President*
Lance Auyer, *Business Mgr*
Jeff Boylan, *Vice Pres*
Linus Schwartz, *Foreman/Supr*
David Moore, *Production*
▼ EMP: 270 EST: 1944
SQ FT: 170,000
SALES (est): 52.8MM **Privately Held**
WEB: www.light-metals.com
SIC: 3354 3444 Aluminum extruded products; sheet metalwork

(G-18017)
LINDE GAS NORTH AMERICA LLC
Also Called: Lifegas
3535 R B Chaffee Mem Dr (49548)
PHONE..................................616 475-0203
Paul Stanton, *Branch Mgr*
EMP: 19 **Privately Held**
SIC: 2813 Nitrogen; oxygen, compressed or liquefied
HQ: Linde Gas North America Llc
200 Somerset Corp Blvd # 7000
Bridgewater NJ 08807

(G-18018)
LOUIS PADNOS IRON AND METAL CO
500 44th St Sw (49548-4127)
PHONE..................................616 301-7900
EMP: 16
SALES (corp-wide): 520.8MM **Privately Held**
SIC: 4491 3599 5093 Waterfront terminal operation; machine shop, jobbing & repair; metal scrap & waste materials
PA: Louis Padnos Iron And Metal Company
185 W 8th St
Holland MI 49423
616 396-6521

(G-18019)
LOWING PRODUCTS LLC
1500 Whiting St Sw (49509-1056)
PHONE..................................616 530-7440
David Lowing,
Adam Boeskool,
Matthew Lowing,
Stephen Paulsen,
EMP: 4
SQ FT: 18,000
SALES (est): 159.5K **Privately Held**
SIC: 3599 Tubing, flexible metallic

(G-18020)
MICHIGAN TURKEY PRODUCERS (PA)
2140 Chicago Dr Sw (49519-1215)
PHONE..................................616 245-2221
Dan Lennon, *President*
Brian Boerigter, *CFO*
EMP: 450
SQ FT: 192,000
SALES (est): 113.3MM **Privately Held**
WEB: www.miturkey.com
SIC: 2015 Turkey processing & slaughtering

(G-18021)
NATIONAL NAIL CORP (PA)
Also Called: West Michigan Nail & Wire Co
2964 Clydon Ave Sw (49519-2497)
PHONE..................................616 538-8000
Roger C Bruins, *Ch of Bd*
Scott Baker, *President*
Chip Manger, *President*
Richard Bilton, *General Mgr*
John P Krugman, *Corp Secy*
◆ EMP: 150
SQ FT: 130,000
SALES (est): 30MM **Privately Held**
SIC: 3315 3442 Nails, steel: wire or cut; storm doors or windows, metal

(G-18022)
NATIONAL PRINTING SERVICES
5360 Pine Slope Dr Sw (49519-9641)
PHONE..................................616 813-0758
Ken Filary, *Sales Staff*
EMP: 4 EST: 2014
SALES (est): 178.1K **Privately Held**
SIC: 2752 Commercial printing, offset

(G-18023)
NU-TRAN LLC
2947 Buchanan Ave Sw (49548-1043)
PHONE..................................616 350-9575
Chanh Nguyen, *Owner*
EMP: 8
SALES: 170K **Privately Held**
SIC: 2421 2511 2541 Building & structural materials, wood; wood household furniture; table or counter tops, plastic laminated

(G-18024)
P & F ENTERPRISES LLC
Also Called: Screen Vaccine
4095 Oak Valley Ave Sw (49519-3755)
PHONE..................................616 340-1265
Paul Fitzpatrick,
Jeffrey Phenix,
EMP: 3
SALES (est): 182.9K **Privately Held**
SIC: 2842 7389 Specialty cleaning preparations;

(G-18025)
P D P LLC
Also Called: Peninsula Prestress Company
2675 Chicago Dr Sw (49519-1677)
PHONE..................................616 437-9618
Paul A Marsh, *Mng Member*
David Marsh, *Mng Member*
EMP: 15 EST: 2012
SALES (est): 2.5MM **Privately Held**
SIC: 3273 Ready-mixed concrete

(G-18026)
PERCOR MANUFACTURING INC
4203 Roger B Chaffee Mem (49548-3476)
PHONE..................................616 554-1668
Alan Niemeyer, *President*
EMP: 14 EST: 2000
SQ FT: 12,000
SALES (est): 3MM **Privately Held**
WEB: www.percormfg.com
SIC: 3312 Tubes, steel & iron

(G-18027)
PINNACLE TOOL INCORPORATED
1150 Gezon Pkwy Sw (49509-9582)
PHONE..................................616 257-2700
Tim Hitson, *President*
Dick Gerke, *Vice Pres*
Brian Rieth, *Engineer*
Jamie Vanbeek, *Project Engr*
John Botner, *Sales Staff*
▲ EMP: 37 EST: 2008
SQ FT: 41,000
SALES (est): 7.9MM **Privately Held**
SIC: 3469 Machine parts, stamped or pressed metal

(G-18028)
PLEXICASE INC
2431 Clyde Park Ave Sw (49509-1935)
PHONE..................................616 246-6400
Steven Ries, *President*
Robert R Ries, *President*
Paul Geelhoed, *Treasurer*
EMP: 5
SALES (est): 834.4K **Privately Held**
WEB: www.plexicase.com
SIC: 3089 Thermoformed finished plastic products

(G-18029)
PRECISION AUTOMOTIVE MCH SP
2320 Chicago Dr Sw (49519-1219)
PHONE..................................616 534-6946
Arnie Snyder, *Mng Member*
EMP: 5
SALES (est): 155.8K **Privately Held**
SIC: 3599 Machine shop, jobbing & repair

(G-18030)
RIETH-RILEY CNSTR CO INC
2100 Chicago Dr Sw (49519-1215)
PHONE..................................616 248-0920
Chad Loney, *Branch Mgr*
EMP: 23
SALES (corp-wide): 205.9MM **Privately Held**
WEB: www.reithriley.com
SIC: 1611 2951 Surfacing & paving; asphalt paving mixtures & blocks
PA: Rieth-Riley Construction Co., Inc.
3626 Elkhart Rd
Goshen IN 46526
574 875-5183

(G-18031)
RIM GUARD INC
1575 Gezon Pkwy Sw Ste E (49509-9381)
PHONE..................................616 608-7745
Philip Globig, *President*
Robert P Koch, *Admin Sec*
EMP: 2
SQ FT: 144
SALES (est): 1.5MM **Privately Held**
WEB: www.rimguard.biz
SIC: 2879 Agricultural chemicals

(G-18032)
RIVERSIDE CNC LLC
3331 Lousma Dr Se (49548-2251)
PHONE..................................616 246-6000
Bryan Roodvoets, *Principal*
EMP: 5
SALES (est): 475.4K **Privately Held**
SIC: 3541 3674 Milling machines; vertical turning & boring machines (metalworking); strain gages, solid state

(G-18033)
SUCCESS BY DESIGN INC
3741 Linden Ave Se (49548-3474)
PHONE..................................800 327-0057
Steve Landheer, *President*
Bill Rutherford, *Mktg Dir*
Amy Cole, *Graphic Designe*
EMP: 14
SQ FT: 21,000
SALES (est): 2MM **Privately Held**
WEB: www.successbydesign.com
SIC: 2732 Book printing

(G-18034)
SWEETWATER BREW LLC
1760 44th St Sw (49519-6441)
PHONE..................................616 805-5077
EMP: 4 EST: 2016
SALES (est): 75.4K **Privately Held**
SIC: 2082 Malt beverages

(G-18035)
TOUCHSTONE SYSTEMS & SVCS INC
1817 Porter St Sw (49519-1765)
PHONE..................................616 532-0060
Jayma Kamerling, *President*
EMP: 8
SQ FT: 6,500
SALES: 800K **Privately Held**
WEB: www.touchstone-testing.com
SIC: 8748 3679 3676 Testing services; electronic circuits; electronic loads & power supplies; electronic crystals; electronic switches; electronic resistors

GEOGRAPHIC SECTION

Ypsilanti - Washtenaw County (G-18060)

(G-18036)
TRIANGLE WINDOW FASHIONS INC
2625 Buchanan Ave Sw A (49548-1056)
PHONE.................................616 538-9676
Carol Limber, *President*
Mark Weih, *Vice Pres*
Jennifer Barnes, *Sales Staff*
Steven Skalandis, *Sales Staff*
Savanna Weih, *Manager*
EMP: 20 **EST:** 1969
SQ FT: 7,200
SALES (est): 3.4MM Privately Held
WEB: www.trianglewindowfashions.com
SIC: 2391 2591 5023 Draperies, plastic & textile: from purchased materials; blinds vertical; window shades; window furnishings

(G-18037)
TYGHT DEFENSE
4409 Carol Ave Sw (49519-4519)
PHONE.................................616 427-3760
Buster Mathis, *Principal*
EMP: 3
SALES (est): 161.4K Privately Held
SIC: 3812 Defense systems & equipment

(G-18038)
ULTRA-TECH PRINTING CO
5851 Crossrds Cmmrce Pkwy (49519)
PHONE.................................616 249-0500
Thomas Gunn, *President*
Charles Piette, *VP Opers*
Jody Hul, *Sales Staff*
EMP: 16
SQ FT: 25,000
SALES (est): 3.1MM Privately Held
WEB: www.utprinting.com
SIC: 2752 2759 Commercial printing, offset; commercial printing

(G-18039)
UNDERCAR PRODUCTS GROUP INC
4247 Eastern Ave Se (49508-3400)
PHONE.................................616 719-4571
Mike Schmidt, *President*
James Augustine, *Treasurer*
▲ **EMP:** 450 **EST:** 1992
SQ FT: 440,000
SALES (est): 95MM
SALES (corp-wide): 28B Privately Held
SIC: 3089 Injection molding of plastics
HQ: Abc Group Holdings Inc.
24133 Northwestern Hwy
Southfield MI 48075
248 352-3706

(G-18040)
VALLEY TRUCK PARTS INC (PA)
1900 Chicago Dr Sw (49519-1211)
PHONE.................................616 241-5431
Jack Goodale, *President*
Rex Troost, *Vice Pres*
EMP: 100
SQ FT: 15,000
SALES (est): 72.4MM Privately Held
WEB: www.valleytruckparts.com
SIC: 5013 5015 5012 7539 Automotive supplies & parts; automotive parts & supplies, used; trucks, commercial; automotive repair shops; truck & tractor truck assembly; armature rewinding shops

(G-18041)
VIKING SPAS INC
Also Called: Destiny River
2725 Prairie St Sw (49519-2458)
PHONE.................................616 248-7800
Tom Veneklase, *President*
Paul Kantor, *Exec VP*
John Gallagher, *Vice Pres*
Cary Glonek, *Vice Pres*
Pat Mester, *Controller*
▼ **EMP:** 12 **EST:** 1998
SQ FT: 30,000
SALES (est): 2.3MM Privately Held
WEB: www.vikingspas.com
SIC: 3999 Hot tubs

(G-18042)
WAL-VAC INC
900 47th St Sw Ste A (49509-5142)
PHONE.................................616 241-6717
David Mol, *President*
Thom Courtright, *President*
EMP: 3
SQ FT: 8,500
SALES: 250K Privately Held
WEB: www.walvac.com
SIC: 5087 5722 3635 7629 Vacuum cleaning systems; household appliance stores; household vacuum cleaners; vacuum cleaner repair

(G-18043)
WILD MITTEN LLC
2037 Holliday Dr Sw (49519-4234)
PHONE.................................616 795-1610
Joshua Kruis, *Principal*
EMP: 3 **EST:** 2014
SALES (est): 136.4K Privately Held
SIC: 2082 Malt beverages

(G-18044)
WOLVERINE GLASS PRODUCTS INC
3400 Wentworth Dr Sw (49519-6108)
PHONE.................................616 538-0100
Mark McGan, *President*
Mark Mc Gann, *President*
Tim Ogarek, *Vice Pres*
Bryan McGann, *Plant Mgr*
Chelsie Cowles, *Accounts Mgr*
▲ **EMP:** 20
SALES (est): 3.6MM Privately Held
WEB: www.wolverineglass.com
SIC: 3231 Products of purchased glass

Yale
St. Clair County

(G-18045)
C ROY INC
Also Called: Yale Bologna
444 Roy Dr (48097-3461)
PHONE.................................810 387-3975
Richard Roy, *CEO*
Brian Lossing, *Vice Pres*
Jennifer Lossing, *Treasurer*
EMP: 20
SQ FT: 2,000
SALES (est): 1.9MM Privately Held
SIC: 2011 Meat packing plants

(G-18046)
MARGATE INDUSTRIES INC
129 N Main St (48097-2840)
PHONE.................................810 387-4300
William H Hopton, *President*
David A Widlak, *Vice Pres*
EMP: 4
SQ FT: 70,000
SALES: 1.5MM Privately Held
SIC: 3471 Finishing, metals or formed products

(G-18047)
TARTAN INDUSTRIES INC
2 1st St (48097-2800)
PHONE.................................810 387-4255
Dennis Hughes, *President*
Tim Hughes, *Manager*
EMP: 8
SALES (est): 550K Privately Held
WEB: www.tartanindustries.com
SIC: 3441 3544 Fabricated structural metal; special dies, tools, jigs & fixtures

(G-18048)
YALE EXPOSITOR
21 S Main St (48097-3317)
P.O. Box 158 (48097-0158)
PHONE.................................810 387-2300
Arthur Brown, *Owner*
Bonnie Brown, *Co-Owner*
EMP: 5 **EST:** 1874
SQ FT: 1,320
SALES (est): 258.8K Privately Held
SIC: 2711 2752 Newspapers, publishing & printing; commercial printing, lithographic

Ypsilanti
Washtenaw County

(G-18049)
734 BREWING COMPANY INC
15 E Cross St (48198-2841)
PHONE.................................734 649-6453
Patrick Echlin, *President*
EMP: 3
SALES (est): 91.3K Privately Held
SIC: 2082 Beer (alcoholic beverage)

(G-18050)
ALPHA PACKAGING MICHIGAN INC
Also Called: Quality Container
1236 Watson St (48198-9114)
PHONE.................................314 427-4300
David Spence, *President*
Dan Creston, *COO*
Gary Seeman, *CFO*
◆ **EMP:** 83
SQ FT: 105,000
SALES (est): 29MM Privately Held
WEB: www.qualitycontainer.com
SIC: 3085 Plastics bottles
HQ: Alpha Plastics Inc.
1555 Page Industrial Blvd
Saint Louis MO 63132
314 427-4300

(G-18051)
AMERICAN BROACH & MACHINE CO
Also Called: American Gear Tools
575 S Mansfield St (48197-5157)
PHONE.................................734 961-0300
Xingyuan Long, *Ch of Bd*
Mike Castro, *President*
Mike Casto, *President*
Feng Mao, *Principal*
Sha Tian, *Principal*
◆ **EMP:** 46 **EST:** 1919
SQ FT: 75,000
SALES (est): 10.7MM Privately Held
WEB: www.americanbroach.com
SIC: 3541 3545 Broaching machines; tools & accessories for machine tools

(G-18052)
ARBOR WOODS MFG HOME COMMUNITY
1993 Arbor Woods Blvd (48198-9496)
PHONE.................................734 482-4305
Steven Fisher, *Partner*
Frances Hoffman, *Manager*
EMP: 3
SALES (est): 310K Privately Held
SIC: 2451 6513 Mobile homes; apartment building operators

(G-18053)
AUNT MILLIES BAKERIES INC (HQ)
5331 W Michigan Ave (48197-4900)
PHONE.................................734 528-1475
Tom Miskowski, *Manager*
EMP: 27 **EST:** 1985
SALES: 5MM
SALES (corp-wide): 535.8MM Privately Held
WEB: www.perfectionpastries.com
SIC: 2051 4225 4215 Bread, all types (white, wheat, rye, etc): fresh or frozen; general warehousing & storage; courier services, except by air
PA: Perfection Bakeries, Inc.
350 Pearl St
Fort Wayne IN 46802
260 424-8245

(G-18054)
B & W TOOL CO
Also Called: St Lawrence Boring
1160 Watson St (48198-9202)
PHONE.................................734 485-2540
David Stiles, *President*
Tom Brown, *Vice Pres*
EMP: 6
SQ FT: 12,000
SALES: 400K Privately Held
WEB: www.davestiles.com
SIC: 3599 Machine shop, jobbing & repair

(G-18055)
BARRETT PAVING MATERIALS INC
5800 Cherry Hill Rd (48198-9631)
PHONE.................................734 985-9480
Dan Dennaro, *Principal*
John Kristin, *Manager*
Barbara Lixey, *Manager*
EMP: 25
SALES (corp-wide): 83.5MM Privately Held
WEB: www.barrettpaving.com
SIC: 1611 2951 1771 Surfacing & paving; asphalt paving mixtures & blocks; concrete work
HQ: Barrett Paving Materials Inc.
3 Becker Farm Rd Ste 307
Roseland NJ 07068
973 533-1001

(G-18056)
BOSAL INDUSTRIES-GEORGIA INC (HQ)
Also Called: Bosal International North Amer
1476 Seaver Way (48197-8300)
PHONE.................................734 547-7022
Rene De Wit, *President*
Steve Steeden, *President*
Philip De Bruyn, *Regional Mgr*
Mark Henshaw, *Business Mgr*
Kris Swinnen, *Vice Pres*
◆ **EMP:** 50
SQ FT: 100,000
SALES (est): 50MM
SALES (corp-wide): 599.8MM Privately Held
SIC: 3714 Exhaust systems & parts, motor vehicle
PA: Bosal Nederland B.V.
Kamerlingh Onnesweg 5
Vianen Ut 4131
347 362-911

(G-18057)
BREASCO LLC
3840 Carpenter Rd (48197-9635)
PHONE.................................734 961-9020
Carol Worthing, *Partner*
Carole Worthing,
EMP: 6
SALES (est): 600K Privately Held
WEB: www.breasco.com
SIC: 3315 Steel wire & related products

(G-18058)
BURRELL TRI-COUNTY VAULTS INC
1106 E Michigan Ave (48198-5881)
P.O. Box 981112 (48198-1112)
PHONE.................................734 483-2024
Douglas Stark, *President*
Leonard Stark, *Admin Sec*
EMP: 12
SQ FT: 13,000
SALES: 750K Privately Held
WEB: www.btvinc.com
SIC: 3272 5087 5211 Burial vaults, concrete or precast terrazzo; caskets; concrete & cinder block

(G-18059)
CAFLOR INDUSTRIES LLC
2375 Parkwood (48198-7830)
PHONE.................................734 604-1168
Cesar A Flores, *Mng Member*
EMP: 9
SQ FT: 10,000
SALES: 920K Privately Held
SIC: 3999 Atomizers, toiletry

(G-18060)
CITY PRINTING CO OF YPSILANTI
411 W Cross St (48197-2404)
PHONE.................................734 482-8490
David Peasley, *President*
EMP: 3
SQ FT: 3,000
SALES (est): 325.4K Privately Held
SIC: 2752 2759 Commercial printing, offset; letterpress printing

Ypsilanti - Washtenaw County (G-18061)

(G-18061)
CORNER BREWERY LLC
720 Norris St (48198-2825)
PHONE..................734 480-2739
Renee Greff, *President*
EMP: 25
SALES (est): 1.4MM **Privately Held**
WEB: www.cornerbrewery.com
SIC: 2082 5812 Beer (alcoholic beverage); American restaurant; restaurant, family: independent

(G-18062)
CROWN INDUSTRIAL SERVICES INC (PA)
Also Called: Crown Tumbling
2480 Airport Dr (48198-8038)
P.O. Box 970197 (48197-0026)
PHONE..................734 483-7270
Kimberly Bullock, *President*
Jeffrey Bullock, *Corp Secy*
Mark Beck, *Vice Pres*
Jeffery Bullock, *VP Human Res*
Dave McCliment, *Sales Staff*
EMP: 47 **EST:** 1994
SQ FT: 150,000
SALES (est): 17.4MM **Privately Held**
SIC: 3471 Tumbling (cleaning & polishing) of machine parts

(G-18063)
CTMF INC
924 Minion St (48198-5811)
P.O. Box 970197 (48197-0026)
PHONE..................734 482-3086
Jeffery Bullock, *President*
Kimberly Bullock, *Corp Secy*
EMP: 50
SALES (est): 5MM **Privately Held**
SIC: 3559 Metal finishing equipment for plating, etc.

(G-18064)
DATA OPTICS INC
Also Called: Ann Arbor Optical Company
115 Holmes Rd (48198-3020)
PHONE..................734 483-8228
David M Shindell, *President*
Mary L Coffey, *Vice Pres*
EMP: 3 **EST:** 1966
SQ FT: 5,500
SALES (est): 125K **Privately Held**
WEB: www.dataoptics.com
SIC: 3827 3829 Optical test & inspection equipment; measuring & controlling devices

(G-18065)
DESIGN SAFETY ENGINEERING INC
305 Elm St (48197-2723)
PHONE..................734 483-2033
Bruce Main, *President*
EMP: 3
SALES (est): 210K **Privately Held**
WEB: www.designsafe.com
SIC: 7372 8711 Prepackaged software; consulting engineer

(G-18066)
DISRUPTIVE EATING LLC
2874 Washtenaw Rd (48197-1507)
PHONE..................734 262-0560
Priya Dass, *Manager*
Mamta Tiwari,
EMP: 4 **EST:** 2016
SQ FT: 4,000
SALES (est): 116.1K **Privately Held**
SIC: 2099 Sauces: gravy, dressing & dip mixes

(G-18067)
DOAN CONSTRUCTION CO (PA)
Also Called: Doan Companies
3670 Carpenter Rd (48197-9614)
PHONE..................734 971-4678
Dennis Doan, *CEO*
Matt Doan, *President*
Jim McInnis, *General Mgr*
Kevin Hoatlin, *CFO*
Jim Hart, *Manager*
EMP: 19 **EST:** 1970
SQ FT: 3,000
SALES (est): 30.5MM **Privately Held**
WEB: www.doancompanies.com
SIC: 8741 3273 Construction management; ready-mixed concrete

(G-18068)
EASTERN MICHIGAN UNIVERSITY
Also Called: Eastern Echo School Newspaper
18b Goddard Hall (48197-2215)
PHONE..................734 487-1010
George Borel Jr, *Editor*
Catherine Hill, *Director*
EMP: 80
SALES (corp-wide): 240.6MM **Privately Held**
WEB: www.emich.edu
SIC: 2711 8221 Newspapers; university
PA: Eastern Michigan University
202 Welch Hall
Ypsilanti MI 48197
734 487-2031

(G-18069)
ELECTRONICS FOR IMAGING INC
1260 James L Hart Pkwy (48197-7194)
PHONE..................734 641-3062
Brad Scott, *Branch Mgr*
EMP: 75
SALES (corp-wide): 1B **Privately Held**
SIC: 3577 Printers & plotters
HQ: Electronics For Imaging, Inc.
6750 Dumbarton Cir
Fremont CA 94555
650 357-3500

(G-18070)
EMBRACE PREMIUM VODKA LLC
515 Ferris St (48197-5303)
PHONE..................616 617-5602
Carlos Robinson, *President*
EMP: 1
SALES: 20MM **Privately Held**
SIC: 2085 7389 Vodka (alcoholic beverage);

(G-18071)
EMBROIDERY PRODUCTS LLC
12 S Huron St (48197-5488)
PHONE..................734 483-0293
Zachary Clipper, *Managing Prtnr*
Angela Johnson, *CFO*
EMP: 3
SALES (est): 35.8K **Privately Held**
SIC: 2395 5699 Embroidery products, except schiffli machine; customized clothing & apparel

(G-18072)
ENSURE TECHNOLOGIES INC
135 S Prospect St Ste 100 (48198-7914)
PHONE..................734 668-8800
John Dunlop, *President*
Mary Shindell, *Partner*
▲ **EMP:** 15 **EST:** 1997
SQ FT: 5,200
SALES (est): 2.7MM **Privately Held**
WEB: www.ensuretech.com
SIC: 3577 7382 Computer peripheral equipment; security systems services

(G-18073)
FINISHING SERVICES INC
877 Ann St (48197-2474)
PHONE..................734 484-1700
Mitchell Marsh, *President*
James Nelson, *Corp Secy*
Matthew T Marsh, *Vice Pres*
▲ **EMP:** 105
SQ FT: 23,000
SALES (est): 11.1MM
SALES (corp-wide): 17.6MM **Privately Held**
WEB: www.finishingservices.com
SIC: 3471 3479 Electroplating of metals or formed products; coating of metals & formed products
PA: Marsh Plating Corporation
103 N Grove St
Ypsilanti MI 48198
734 483-5767

(G-18074)
FORD MOTOR COMPANY
10300 Textile Rd (48197-9200)
PHONE..................734 484-8000
Mark Willis, *Manager*
EMP: 2000
SALES (corp-wide): 160.3B **Publicly Held**
WEB: www.ford.com
SIC: 5511 3694 3677 3625 Automobiles, new & used; engine electrical equipment; electronic coils, transformers & other inductors; relays & industrial controls; motors & generators; pumps & pumping equipment
PA: Ford Motor Company
1 American Rd
Dearborn MI 48126
313 322-3000

(G-18075)
GEAR GEAR INC
129 Bell St (48197-5519)
PHONE..................517 861-7757
EMP: 3
SALES (est): 225.3K **Privately Held**
SIC: 3566 Speed changers, drives & gears

(G-18076)
HEIKKINEN PRODUCTIONS INC
1410 W Michigan Ave (48197-5129)
P.O. Box 980401 (48198-0401)
PHONE..................734 485-4020
Daniel Heikkinen, *President*
Mary H Heikkinen, *Vice Pres*
EMP: 3
SALES (est): 440K **Privately Held**
SIC: 5136 5137 2395 Sportswear, men's & boys'; women's & children's sportswear & swimsuits; embroidery & art needlework

(G-18077)
HURON ADVERTISING COMPANY INC
Also Called: Huron Sign Co
663 S Mansfield St (48197-5156)
P.O. Box 980423 (48198-0423)
PHONE..................734 483-2000
William J Short III, *President*
Barbara Hagadorn, *Corp Secy*
Dave Rudd, *Foreman/Supr*
Kevin Short, *VP Sales*
Tom Short, *Supervisor*
EMP: 20 **EST:** 1966
SQ FT: 24,000
SALES (est): 2.5MM **Privately Held**
WEB: www.huronsign.com
SIC: 1799 3993 Sign installation & maintenance; electric signs

(G-18078)
IHA VSCLAR ENDVSCLAR SPCALISTS
5325 Elliott Dr Ste 104 (48197-8633)
PHONE..................734 712-8150
Mark Lepage MD, *CEO*
EMP: 8 **EST:** 2014
SALES (est): 764.1K **Privately Held**
SIC: 3845 8011 Endoscopic equipment, electromedical; cardiologist & cardio-vascular specialist

(G-18079)
IMAGILLATION INC
Also Called: Hikking Production Embroidery
133 W Michigan Ave Ste 2 (48197-5550)
PHONE..................734 481-0140
David W Heikkinen, *President*
Linda Hikking, *Corp Secy*
EMP: 4
SALES (est): 410.7K **Privately Held**
SIC: 3999 Music boxes

(G-18080)
INFINITY TECH & AROSPC INC
2901 Tyler Rd (48198-6126)
PHONE..................734 480-9001
Mark Andrews, *President*
Rhonda Andrews, *Principal*
EMP: 3
SALES (est): 340.1K **Privately Held**
SIC: 3365 Aerospace castings, aluminum

(G-18081)
INTEGRATED SENSING SYSTEMS INC (PA)
Also Called: Issys
391 Airport Industrial Dr (48198-7812)
PHONE..................734 547-9896
Nader Najafi, *President*
Mike Bolt, *Engineer*
Annette Gannon, *Marketing Mgr*
Christopher Battle, *Technician*
Bob Nuss, *Maintence Staff*
EMP: 30
SQ FT: 16,000
SALES (est): 3.4MM **Privately Held**
WEB: www.mems-issys.com
SIC: 3829 Measuring & controlling devices

(G-18082)
INTERCLEAN EQUIPMENT LLC
709 James L Hart Pkwy (48197-9791)
PHONE..................734 961-3300
Dan Bickersteth, *CEO*
Greg Harvey, *Vice Pres*
Scott Hessling, *Purch Mgr*
Chris Leineke, *Sales Engr*
Janet Stanke, *Sales Staff*
◆ **EMP:** 35
SQ FT: 20,000
SALES (est): 10MM **Privately Held**
WEB: www.interclean.com
SIC: 3589 7542 Car washing machinery; truck wash

(G-18083)
LADDER CAROLINA COMPANY INC
12 E Forest Ave (48198-2803)
P.O. Box 981307 (48198-1307)
PHONE..................734 482-5946
Robert F Nissly, *President*
David Nissly, *Treasurer*
EMP: 12 **EST:** 1953
SQ FT: 75,000
SALES (est): 889.3K **Privately Held**
WEB: www.carolinaladder.com
SIC: 2499 Ladders, wood

(G-18084)
LE FORGES PIPE & FAB INC
64 Wiard Rd (48198-4233)
PHONE..................734 482-2100
Eric Le Forge, *President*
EMP: 4
SQ FT: 8,000
SALES (est): 648.2K **Privately Held**
SIC: 7692 Welding repair

(G-18085)
LENCO BORING INC
1620 Beverly Ave (48198-9211)
PHONE..................734 483-8880
EMP: 3
SALES: 300K **Privately Held**
SIC: 3599 Mfg Machine Shop Jobbing & Repair

(G-18086)
LYNN NOYES INDUSTRIES INC
2714 Ambassador Dr (48198-1029)
PHONE..................313 841-3130
Aloysius Gauszka, *President*
Karen Crimmins, *Vice Pres*
EMP: 3 **EST:** 1945
SALES (est): 309.1K **Privately Held**
SIC: 3111 Industrial leather products

(G-18087)
MAGNUM FABRICATING
1754 E Michigan Ave (48198-6008)
PHONE..................734 484-5800
EMP: 4
SALES (est): 321.8K **Privately Held**
SIC: 3499 3441 Fabricated metal products; fabricated structural metal

(G-18088)
MARSH PLATING CORPORATION (PA)
103 N Grove St (48198-2906)
PHONE..................734 483-5767
David Marsh, *Principal*
David Willox, *Vice Pres*
Mitch Marsh, *Plant Mgr*
Tim Gschwender, *Opers Mgr*
John Watson, *Production*

GEOGRAPHIC SECTION
Zeeland - Ottawa County (G-18116)

▲ EMP: 80 EST: 1959
SQ FT: 80,000
SALES (est): 17.6MM **Privately Held**
WEB: www.marshplating.com
SIC: 3471 3511 3441 Electroplating of metals or formed products; hydraulic turbine generator set units, complete; fabricated structural metal

(G-18089)
MASTER MIX COMPANY
Also Called: Mastermix
612 S Mansfield St (48197-5167)
PHONE.................................734 487-7870
Frederick McCants, *President*
EMP: 15
SALES (est): 2.2MM **Privately Held**
WEB: www.mastermixco.com
SIC: 3479 2891 Coating, rust preventive; adhesives

(G-18090)
MICHIGAN LADDER COMPANY LLC
12 E Forest Ave (48198-2803)
P.O. Box 981307 (48198-1307)
PHONE.................................734 482-5946
Tom Harrison, *President*
Chuck Ratcliff, *Purch Mgr*
▲ EMP: 15 EST: 1901
SQ FT: 75,000
SALES (est): 3.2MM **Privately Held**
WEB: www.michiganladder.com
SIC: 2499 5082 Ladders, wood; ladders

(G-18091)
MISHIGAMA BREWING COMPANY
124 Pearl St (48197-2663)
PHONE.................................734 547-5840
William Anhut, *Principal*
EMP: 3
SALES (est): 137.2K **Privately Held**
SIC: 5921 2082 Beer (packaged); malt beverages

(G-18092)
MSW PRINT AND IMAGING
3901 Bestech Rd (48197-9815)
PHONE.................................734 544-1626
Scott Katke, *Owner*
EMP: 10 EST: 2009
SALES (est): 1.1MM **Privately Held**
SIC: 2752 Commercial printing, offset

(G-18093)
OFFICE DESIGN & FURN LLC
Also Called: Office Ways
417 S Huron St (48197-5424)
PHONE.................................734 217-2717
Fred W Crandal III, *President*
EMP: 3
SQ FT: 500
SALES: 973.9K **Privately Held**
SIC: 2522 5712 Office furniture, except wood; office furniture

(G-18094)
PIERIAN PRESS INC
3196 Maple Dr (48197-3788)
PHONE.................................734 434-4074
Carroll Edward Wall, *President*
Edward Prezbiemda, *Vice Pres*
Mary Wall, *Sales Staff*
EMP: 4
SQ FT: 8,000
SALES (est): 200K **Privately Held**
WEB: www.pierianpress.com
SIC: 2731 2741 2721 Books: publishing only; miscellaneous publishing; periodicals

(G-18095)
PREMIUMS PLUS MORE
2080 Whittaker Rd 222 (48197-8238)
PHONE.................................734 485-2423
John Shook, *Owner*
EMP: 1
SQ FT: 2,500
SALES: 1.3MM **Privately Held**
SIC: 5199 2759 Advertising specialties; commercial printing

(G-18096)
PRINTING PLUS INC
Also Called: Q P S Printing
989 James L Hart Pkwy (48197-9791)
PHONE.................................734 482-1680
Kim Craddick, *President*
EMP: 4
SQ FT: 1,500
SALES (est): 441.5K **Privately Held**
WEB: www.qpsprinting.com
SIC: 2752 2789 Commercial printing, offset; bookbinding & related work

(G-18097)
PROTO TOOL & GAGE INC
300 S Ford Blvd (48198-6067)
PHONE.................................734 487-0830
Keith Stephens, *President*
Clark M Brown, *Corp Secy*
Ken Martenka, *Vice Pres*
EMP: 3
SQ FT: 5,400
SALES (est): 473.3K **Privately Held**
SIC: 3599 7692 3545 Machine shop, jobbing & repair; welding repair; machine tool accessories

(G-18098)
QC AMERICAN LLC
575 S Mansfield St (48197-5157)
PHONE.................................734 961-0300
Fran Mao, *Managing Dir*
▲ EMP: 4
SALES: 650K
SALES (corp-wide): 459.2MM **Privately Held**
SIC: 3545 Cutting tools for machine tools
PA: Qinchuan Machine Tool & Tool Group Share Co., Ltd.
No.22, Jiangtan Rd.
Baoji 72100
917 367-0665

(G-18099)
QUANTUM COMPLIANCE SYSTEMS
2111 Golfside Rd Ste B (48197-1146)
PHONE.................................734 930-0009
Patricia L Brooks, *President*
EMP: 60
SQ FT: 12,000
SALES (est): 5.3MM **Privately Held**
WEB: www.qcs-facts.com
SIC: 7371 7372 Computer software development; prepackaged software

(G-18100)
SENSITILE SYSTEMS LLC
1735 Holmes Rd (48198-4155)
PHONE.................................313 872-6314
Vanika Lath, *CFO*
Abhinand Lath, *Mng Member*
▲ EMP: 30
SQ FT: 36,000
SALES (est): 6.2MM **Privately Held**
WEB: www.sensitile.com
SIC: 2421 Building & structural materials, wood

(G-18101)
SMOOCHES BLEND BAR LLC ✪
636 Onandago St (48198-6179)
PHONE.................................734 756-7152
Brianne Richards, *Mng Member*
EMP: 5 EST: 2019
SALES: 70K **Privately Held**
SIC: 2844 Cosmetic preparations

(G-18102)
STANDARD PRINTING
120 E Cross St (48198-2878)
PHONE.................................734 483-0339
John Harrington,
EMP: 6
SQ FT: 2,000
SALES (est): 801.5K **Privately Held**
SIC: 2752 2759 Commercial printing, offset; letterpress printing

(G-18103)
SUEMATEK
Also Called: Research and Development
4255 Lilac Ln (48197-4682)
PHONE.................................517 614-2235
Pierre Ferdinand Poudeu Poudeu, *CEO*
Alan Olvera, *COO*
Alvine Ngounou, *CFO*
EMP: 3 EST: 2017
SALES (est): 69.5K **Privately Held**
SIC: 8731 3674 8733 Energy research; electronic research; photovoltaic devices, solid state; solid state electronic devices; physical research, noncommercial

(G-18104)
SUPERIOR TEXT LLC
151 Airport Industrial Dr (48198-7811)
PHONE.................................866 482-8762
Luke Oskvarek, *Controller*
Minette Perigard, *Accountant*
Michael Ehinger, *Mng Member*
John Cristiano, *Manager*
EMP: 15
SALES (est): 4.2MM **Privately Held**
WEB: www.superiortext.com
SIC: 5192 2732 Books; textbooks: printing & binding, not publishing

(G-18105)
THA SHOPP LLC
162 S Ford Blvd (48198-6068)
PHONE.................................734 231-9991
Malik McCullough, *President*
Torrence Amos, *Vice Pres*
George Nartin, *Vice Pres*
EMP: 3
SALES (est): 136.2K **Privately Held**
SIC: 2326 Service apparel (baker, barber, lab, etc.), washable: men's

(G-18106)
TRITON GLOBAL SOURCES INC
2111 Golfside Rd (48197-1145)
P.O. Box 130603, Ann Arbor (48113-0603)
PHONE.................................734 668-7107
Eric He, *Vice Pres*
Wen Huang, *CFO*
▲ EMP: 4
SALES (est): 420K **Privately Held**
WEB: www.w8w.com
SIC: 3321 3324 3363 3369 Ductile iron castings; gray iron castings; commercial investment castings, ferrous; aluminum die-castings; zinc & zinc-base alloy castings, except die-castings

(G-18107)
VGKIDS INC
884 Railroad St Ste C (48197-3503)
PHONE.................................734 485-5128
James Marks, *Owner*
Aaron Bobzien, *Manager*
EMP: 17
SQ FT: 6,000
SALES (est): 1.3MM **Privately Held**
WEB: www.vgkids.com
SIC: 2759 Screen printing

(G-18108)
X-RAY AND SPECIALTY INSTRS
Also Called: Xsi
1980 E Michigan Ave (48198-6010)
PHONE.................................734 485-6300
Daniel Gorzen, *President*
Lisa Teets, *Vice Pres*
EMP: 4
SQ FT: 2,500
SALES: 200K **Privately Held**
WEB: www.xsiinc.com
SIC: 3826 Analytical instruments

Zeeland
Ottawa County

(G-18109)
ACTIVE TOOLING LLC
6017 Chicago Dr (49464-9515)
PHONE.................................616 875-8111
Tim Van Dam, *Vice Pres*
Troy Karsemeyer, *Controller*
Gary Lubbers, *Mng Member*
EMP: 13
SALES (est): 1.5MM **Privately Held**
SIC: 3545 Tool holders

(G-18110)
ALLIED ENGINEERING INC
3424 88th Ave Ste 6 (49464-8534)
PHONE.................................616 748-7990
Michael Johnson, *President*
Kurt Vugteveen, *Vice Pres*
EMP: 4
SQ FT: 2,400
SALES: 600K **Privately Held**
SIC: 3465 Automotive stampings

(G-18111)
ALLROUT INC
3382 Production Ct (49464-8528)
PHONE.................................616 748-7696
Jeff Robinson, *President*
Mike Viletstre, *Vice Pres*
EMP: 6
SALES: 900K **Privately Held**
WEB: www.allrout.com
SIC: 3823 Computer interface equipment for industrial process control

(G-18112)
ARTEX LABEL & GRAPHICS INC
740 Case Karsten Dr (49464-9693)
P.O. Box 331 (49464-0331)
PHONE.................................616 748-9655
Terry Gruppen, *President*
Josh Gruppen, *Opers Staff*
Kim Williams, *Purch Agent*
Wayne Romeyn, *Accounts Mgr*
Jan Wiersma, *Accounts Exec*
EMP: 30
SQ FT: 22,000
SALES (est): 7.2MM **Privately Held**
WEB: www.artexlabel.com
SIC: 2679 Labels, paper: made from purchased material

(G-18113)
ARTISAN MEDICAL DISPLAYS LLC
Also Called: Medical ACC & Reseach Co
219 N Church St (49464-1245)
PHONE.................................616 748-8950
Kris Wickens, *Business Mgr*
Jordan Vander Kolk, *Mng Member*
▼ EMP: 35
SQ FT: 14,100
SALES (est): 5.2MM **Privately Held**
WEB: www.medacc.com
SIC: 3841 Surgical & medical instruments

(G-18114)
ASTRO WOOD STAKE INC
6017 Chicago Dr (49464-9515)
PHONE.................................616 875-8118
Gary Lubbers, *President*
Troy Karsemeyer, *Marketing Staff*
Carol Karsemeyer, *Office Mgr*
EMP: 8
SQ FT: 30,000
SALES (est): 988.1K **Privately Held**
WEB: www.astrowoodstake.com
SIC: 2499 Surveyors' stakes, wood

(G-18115)
AUGUST LIGHTING INC
Also Called: Custom Frame Coatings
10030 Stanton St (49464-9446)
PHONE.................................616 895-4951
Scott August, *President*
EMP: 3
SQ FT: 10,000
SALES: 179K **Privately Held**
SIC: 3479 Coating of metals & formed products

(G-18116)
BAUMANN TOOL & DIE
232 E Roosevelt Ave (49464-1240)
PHONE.................................616 772-6768
David Baumann, *Partner*
Lester Baumann, *Partner*
Ron Laduke, *Plant Mgr*
Chad Levalley, *Plant Mgr*
EMP: 6 EST: 1980
SQ FT: 13,500
SALES (est): 630K **Privately Held**
WEB: www.baumanntd.com
SIC: 3544 Forms (molds), for foundry & plastics working machinery

Zeeland - Ottawa County (G-18117)

(G-18117)
BENNETT WOOD SPECIALTIES INC
Also Called: Carlton, Robert Hanger Company
109 N Carlton St (49464-1303)
P.O. Box 279 (49464-0279)
PHONE..................................616 772-6683
Joe Bennett, *President*
Norraine Bennett, *Admin Sec*
▲ **EMP:** 15 **EST:** 1906
SQ FT: 25,000
SALES (est): 1.1MM **Privately Held**
WEB: www.robertcarltonhangers.com
SIC: 2441 2541 Cases, wood; wood partitions & fixtures

(G-18118)
BERRY GLOBAL INC
200 N Franklin St (49464-1075)
PHONE..................................616 772-4635
Steve McDonough, *President*
EMP: 400 **Publicly Held**
WEB: www.6sens.com
SIC: 3081 3089 Plastic film & sheet; bottle caps, molded plastic
HQ: Berry Global, Inc.
101 Oakley St
Evansville IN 47710
812 424-2904

(G-18119)
BESSER COMPANY USA
Also Called: Besser Lithibar
201 W Washington Ave # 202 (49464-1085)
P.O. Box 2008, Holland (49422-2008)
PHONE..................................616 399-5215
Kevin Curtis, *President*
Larry Dutkiewicz, *Controller*
Sandra V Munster, *Office Mgr*
▲ **EMP:** 20
SQ FT: 93,000
SALES (est): 4.4MM
SALES (corp-wide): 243.4MM **Privately Held**
SIC: 3536 3537 Hoists; industrial trucks & tractors; pallet loaders & unloaders; palletizers & depalletizers
PA: Besser Company
801 Johnson St
Alpena MI 49707
989 354-4111

(G-18120)
BIOTEC INCORPORATED
652 E Main Ave (49464-1399)
PHONE..................................616 772-2133
Harold Tai, *CEO*
Charles De Pree, *President*
EMP: 60
SQ FT: 20,000
SALES (est): 9.8MM **Privately Held**
SIC: 3843 2434 Cabinets, dental; dental tools; wood kitchen cabinets

(G-18121)
BLACK RIVER PALLET COMPANY
410 E Roosevelt Ave (49464-1342)
PHONE..................................616 772-6211
Larry Slagh, *President*
EMP: 25 **EST:** 1962
SQ FT: 16,000
SALES (est): 3.3MM **Privately Held**
SIC: 2448 2449 Pallets, wood; wood containers

(G-18122)
BLACK SWAMP PERCUSSION LLC
11114 James St (49464-9125)
PHONE..................................800 557-0988
Jamel Taylor, *Prdtn Mgr*
Kristi Warren, *Bookkeeper*
Eric Sooy,
Julie Sooy,
▲ **EMP:** 8
SQ FT: 9,000
SALES (est): 1.2MM **Privately Held**
WEB: www.blackswamp.com
SIC: 3931 5736 Guitars & parts, electric & nonelectric; musical instrument stores

(G-18123)
BREMER AUTHENTIC INGREDIENTS
420 100th Ave (49464-2061)
PHONE..................................616 772-9100
Dan Nagelkerke, *General Mgr*
Tim Malefyt, *Purch Mgr*
Joan Broersma, *Bookkeeper*
EMP: 7
SALES (est): 151.5K **Privately Held**
SIC: 2499 Bakers' equipment, wood

(G-18124)
CHARTER HOUSE HOLDINGS LLC
200 N Franklin St Ste B (49464-1075)
PHONE..................................616 399-6000
Charles Reid, *Principal*
◆ **EMP:** 186
SQ FT: 72,000
SALES (est): 41.6MM **Privately Held**
WEB: www.gotochi.com
SIC: 3999 Advertising display products

(G-18125)
CONCEPT TOOL & DIE INC
9371 Henry Ct (49464-9216)
PHONE..................................616 875-4600
Michael Cooper, *President*
Daniel Cooper, *Vice Pres*
EMP: 4
SQ FT: 1,000
SALES (est): 340K **Privately Held**
SIC: 3544 Dies & die holders for metal cutting, forming, die casting

(G-18126)
CONTOUR TOOL & ENGINEERING INC
2425 104th Ave (49464-6800)
PHONE..................................616 772-6360
Timothy Rietsma, *President*
Mike Rietsma, *Vice Pres*
EMP: 8
SQ FT: 12,000
SALES (est): 1MM **Privately Held**
SIC: 3544 Special dies, tools, jigs & fixtures

(G-18127)
CORLETT-TURNER CO
2500 104th Ave (49464-9824)
PHONE..................................616 772-9082
Jesse Massengill, *President*
Lyn Gunderman, *QC Mgr*
Gerald Van Nuil, *Engineer*
Harry Armstrong, *Treasurer*
Roger Klynstra, *Admin Sec*
EMP: 90
SQ FT: 58,000
SALES (est): 17.8MM **Privately Held**
WEB: www.corlett-turner.com
SIC: 3451 Screw machine products

(G-18128)
CULTURED LOVE LLC
2752 Meadow Dr (49464-9025)
PHONE..................................703 362-5991
Jodie Krumpe, *Administration*
EMP: 3
SALES (est): 216.9K **Privately Held**
SIC: 2035 Sauerkraut, bulk

(G-18129)
CUSTOM ARCHITECTURAL PRODUCTS
430 100th Ave (49464-2061)
PHONE..................................616 748-1905
Dave Quist, *Manager*
EMP: 6 **Privately Held**
SIC: 3441 Fabricated structural metal
PA: Custom Architectural Products Inc
4155 Yorkshire Ct
Hudsonville MI 49426

(G-18130)
CUSTOM TOOLING SYSTEMS INC
3331 80th Ave (49464-9583)
PHONE..................................616 748-9880
John Bouwkamp, *President*
Sean Devoe, *QC Mgr*
Todd Kane, *Treasurer*
Tammy Scharphorn, *Office Mgr*
EMP: 60
SQ FT: 50,000
SALES (est): 10.8MM **Privately Held**
WEB: www.ctooling.com
SIC: 3544 Special dies & tools

(G-18131)
D & D TOOL INC
218 E Harrison Ave (49464-1207)
PHONE..................................616 772-2416
Paul Dannenberg, *President*
Jill Dannenberg, *Vice Pres*
EMP: 6
SQ FT: 3,750
SALES (est): 838.2K **Privately Held**
SIC: 3599 Machine shop, jobbing & repair

(G-18132)
DUN-RITE MACHINE CO
4526 Adams St (49464-9318)
PHONE..................................616 688-5266
Mike Zuverink, *Owner*
▲ **EMP:** 8
SALES (est): 200K **Privately Held**
SIC: 3599 Machine shop, jobbing & repair

(G-18133)
EAGLE DESIGN & TECHNOLOGY INC
55 E Roosevelt Ave (49464-1235)
PHONE..................................616 748-1022
Bruce Okkema, *President*
Rick Huizenga, *Shareholder*
EMP: 29
SQ FT: 22,000
SALES (est): 9.1MM **Privately Held**
SIC: 2821 Plastics materials & resins

(G-18134)
EMPIRE COMPANY LLC (DH)
8181 Logistics Dr (49464-9378)
P.O. Box 17 (49464-0017)
PHONE..................................800 253-9000
Thomas H Highley, *President*
Doug Sawyer, *Division Mgr*
Robin Sobota, *General Mgr*
Richard Carlson, *Vice Pres*
Stephen R Grossman, *Vice Pres*
◆ **EMP:** 137
SQ FT: 220,000
SALES (est): 140.2MM
SALES (corp-wide): 227.6MM **Privately Held**
WEB: www.empireco.com
SIC: 5031 2431 Lumber: rough, dressed & finished; millwork: molding, all materials; staircases, stairs & railings

(G-18135)
ENVIRNMNTAL PLLET SLUTIONS INC
9500 Henry Ct Ste 350 (49464-8945)
PHONE..................................616 283-1784
Bryant Vanoverloop, *Principal*
EMP: 4
SALES (est): 590.8K **Privately Held**
SIC: 2448 Pallets, wood

(G-18136)
EXTOL INC (PA)
Also Called: Affinity Solutions
651 Case Karsten Dr (49464-8729)
PHONE..................................616 741-0231
Ross Van Klompenberg, *President*
Andrew Van Klompenberg, *Vice Pres*
Dakota Werley, *Project Mgr*
Don Wire, *Project Mgr*
Mike Peters, *Mfg Staff*
◆ **EMP:** 90
SQ FT: 53,000
SALES (est): 23.2MM **Privately Held**
SIC: 3559 Automotive related machinery

(G-18137)
FILLER SPECIALTIES INC
440 100th Ave (49464-2061)
PHONE..................................616 772-9235
Norman Slagh, *President*
Barbara Slagh, *Vice Pres*
Vern Slagh, *Vice Pres*
◆ **EMP:** 20
SQ FT: 9,000
SALES (est): 4.9MM **Privately Held**
WEB: www.filler-specialties.com
SIC: 3565 Bottling machinery: filling, capping, labeling

(G-18138)
GENTEX CORPORATION (PA)
600 N Centennial St (49464-1374)
PHONE..................................616 772-1800
James Wallace, *Ch of Bd*
Steve Downing, *President*
Brad Bosma, *Vice Pres*
Bill Tonar, *Vice Pres*
Kurt Wassink, *Vice Pres*
EMP: 250
SALES: 1.8B **Publicly Held**
WEB: www.gentex.com
SIC: 3231 3714 3669 Mirrors, truck & automobile: made from purchased glass; motor vehicle parts & accessories; smoke detectors

(G-18139)
GENTEX CORPORATION
9001 Riley St (49464)
PHONE..................................616 772-1800
Kevin Nash, *Vice Pres*
EMP: 49
SALES (corp-wide): 1.8B **Publicly Held**
SIC: 3231 Mirrors, truck & automobile: made from purchased glass
PA: Gentex Corporation
600 N Centennial St
Zeeland MI 49464
616 772-1800

(G-18140)
GENTEX CORPORATION
58 E Riley St (49464-9610)
PHONE..................................616 772-1800
Dan Suman, *Branch Mgr*
EMP: 150
SALES (corp-wide): 1.8B **Publicly Held**
WEB: www.gentex.com
SIC: 3231 3669 Mirrors, truck & automobile: made from purchased glass; smoke detectors
PA: Gentex Corporation
600 N Centennial St
Zeeland MI 49464
616 772-1800

(G-18141)
GENTEX CORPORATION
675 N State St (49464-1232)
PHONE..................................616 772-1800
Derek Blaskowski, *Manager*
EMP: 175
SALES (corp-wide): 1.8B **Publicly Held**
WEB: www.gentex.com
SIC: 3231 Mirrors, truck & automobile: made from purchased glass
PA: Gentex Corporation
600 N Centennial St
Zeeland MI 49464
616 772-1800

(G-18142)
GENTEX CORPORATION
10985 Chicago Dr (49464-8101)
PHONE..................................616 392-7195
Scott Edwards, *Vice Pres*
Gary Bryan, *Mfg Staff*
Dave Christian, *QC Dir*
Scott Chamberlain, *VP Mktg*
Lisa Lantz, *Advt Staff*
EMP: 150
SALES (corp-wide): 1.8B **Publicly Held**
WEB: www.gentex.com
SIC: 3669 1731 Fire alarm apparatus, electric; fire detection systems, electric; smoke detectors; fire detection & burglar alarm systems specialization
PA: Gentex Corporation
600 N Centennial St
Zeeland MI 49464
616 772-1800

(G-18143)
GENTEX CORPORATION
310 E Riley St (49464-9789)
PHONE..................................616 772-1800
Rosalie McCormick, *Manager*
EMP: 200
SALES (corp-wide): 1.8B **Publicly Held**
SIC: 3231 Mirrors, truck & automobile: made from purchased glass
PA: Gentex Corporation
600 N Centennial St
Zeeland MI 49464
616 772-1800

GEOGRAPHIC SECTION

Zeeland - Ottawa County (G-18169)

(G-18144)
GIBRALTAR INC
421 N Centennial St (49464-1371)
PHONE..................................616 748-4857
Paul Koning, *CEO*
◆ **EMP:** 38
SQ FT: 70,000
SALES (est): 8.2MM **Privately Held**
WEB: www.gibraltarinc.com
SIC: 3499 Furniture parts, metal

(G-18145)
HARP COLUMN LLC
304 E Central Ave (49464-1706)
P.O. Box 441 (49464-0441)
PHONE..................................215 564-3232
Kimberly Rowe,
Alison Reese,
EMP: 3
SALES (est): 137.5K **Privately Held**
SIC: 2721 Magazines: publishing only, not printed on site

(G-18146)
HEKMAN FURNITURE COMPANY (HQ)
Also Called: Hekman Contract Division
860 E Main Ave (49464-1365)
PHONE..................................616 748-2660
Jack Miller, *CEO*
Dan Masters, *President*
Alan Forist, *CFO*
Mike Hall, *Sales Mgr*
James Rupp, *Sales Staff*
▲ **EMP:** 20
SQ FT: 200,000
SALES (est): 10.3MM
SALES (corp-wide): 99.1MM **Privately Held**
WEB: www.hekman.com
SIC: 2511 Wood household furniture
PA: Howard Miller Company
860 E Main Ave
Zeeland MI 49464
616 772-9131

(G-18147)
HERMAN MILLER INC (PA)
855 E Main Ave (49464-1372)
P.O. Box 302 (49464-0302)
PHONE..................................616 654-3000
John Edelman, *CEO*
Michael A Volkema, *Ch of Bd*
Andrea Owen, *President*
Gregory J Bylsma, *President*
Steven C Gane, *President*
◆ **EMP:** 277 **EST:** 1905
SQ FT: 750,800
SALES: 2.5B **Publicly Held**
WEB: www.hermanmiller.com
SIC: 2521 2522 2541 2542 Wood office furniture; office furniture, except wood; wood partitions & fixtures; partitions & fixtures, except wood; public building & related furniture

(G-18148)
HIGHPOINT FINSHG SOLUTIONS INC
541 E Roosevelt Ave (49464-1378)
PHONE..................................616 772-4425
James Davis, *President*
EMP: 70
SQ FT: 4,000
SALES: 3MM **Privately Held**
SIC: 3471 Electroplating of metals or formed products

(G-18149)
HIL-MAN AUTOMATION LLC
260 E Roosevelt Ave (49464-1261)
PHONE..................................616 741-9099
Rick Mannes, *President*
EMP: 13
SALES (est): 2.4MM **Privately Held**
WEB: www.hil-manautomation.com
SIC: 3451 Screw machine products

(G-18150)
HILLSHIRE BRANDS COMPANY
Bil Mar Foods
8300 96th Ave (49464-9177)
PHONE..................................616 875-8131
Ross Myers, *Plant Mgr*
Gary Dewitt, *Branch Mgr*
Vonda Jewett, *Manager*
Mark Huyser, *Director*
EMP: 602
SALES (corp-wide): 42.4B **Publicly Held**
SIC: 2013 2099 2015 Sausages & other prepared meats; food preparations; poultry slaughtering & processing
HQ: The Hillshire Brands Company
400 S Jefferson St Fl 1
Chicago IL 60607
312 614-6000

(G-18151)
HMI LIQUIDATING COMPANY INC
855 E Main Ave (49464-1366)
PHONE..................................616 654-5055
Daniel King, *President*
EMP: 3
SALES (est): 428.9K **Privately Held**
SIC: 2522 2599 Office furniture, except wood; hospital furniture, except beds

(G-18152)
HOLLAND AWNING CO (PA)
Also Called: Big Red Resources
10875 Chicago Dr (49464-8126)
PHONE..................................616 772-2052
Steven Schaftenaar, *CEO*
Doug Buma, *President*
Scott Smith, *Vice Pres*
Todd Stockdale, *Vice Pres*
▲ **EMP:** 80 **EST:** 1946
SQ FT: 162,000
SALES (est): 53.9MM **Privately Held**
WEB: www.ifrinc.com
SIC: 2394 Tents: made from purchased materials

(G-18153)
HOLLAND LITHO SERVICE INC
Also Called: Holland Litho Printing Service
10972 Chicago Dr (49464-8100)
PHONE..................................616 392-4644
Jerry Baarman, *President*
Brian Baarman, *Exec VP*
Rick Baarman, *Vice Pres*
Tamas Baarman, *Vice Pres*
Eric Hunt, *Engineer*
EMP: 100 **EST:** 1957
SQ FT: 40,000
SALES (est): 20.2MM **Privately Held**
WEB: www.hollandlitho.com
SIC: 2752 Commercial printing, offset

(G-18154)
HOWARD MILLER COMPANY (PA)
Also Called: Howard Miller Clock Company
860 E Main Ave (49464-1365)
PHONE..................................616 772-9131
Philip Miller, *Ch of Bd*
Howard C Miller, *President*
Dennis Palasek, *Vice Pres*
Paul Van Noord, *Mfg Staff*
Steve Richel, *Engineer*
▲ **EMP:** 300 **EST:** 1946
SQ FT: 50,000
SALES (est): 99.1MM **Privately Held**
WEB: www.howardmiller.com
SIC: 3873 3829 3823 Clocks, except timeclocks; measuring & controlling devices; industrial instrmnts msrmnt display/control process variable

(G-18155)
HUIZENGA & SONS INC
Also Called: Huizenga Redi-Mix
10075 Gordon St (49464-1491)
PHONE..................................616 772-6241
Phil Huizenga, *President*
EMP: 20
SQ FT: 16,320
SALES: 1.5MM **Privately Held**
SIC: 3273 Ready-mixed concrete

(G-18156)
HUIZENGA GRAVEL COMPANY INC (PA)
10075 Gordon St (49464-1491)
PHONE..................................616 772-6241
Phil Huizenga, *President*
Bruce Huizenga, *Vice Pres*
EMP: 18
SQ FT: 15,000
SALES: 4.5MM **Privately Held**
SIC: 1442 Construction sand & gravel

(G-18157)
ILLINOIS TOOL WORKS INC
ITW Drawform
500 N Fairview Rd (49464-9419)
PHONE..................................616 772-1910
Michael Olsen, *Production*
Ben V Sloten, *Purch Mgr*
Tom Crum, *Engineer*
Brandon Dykstra, *Engineer*
Brian Lackey, *Engineer*
EMP: 280
SALES (corp-wide): 14.7B **Publicly Held**
SIC: 3469 Stamping metal for the trade
PA: Illinois Tool Works Inc.
155 Harlem Ave
Glenview IL 60025
847 724-7500

(G-18158)
INDUSTRIAL WOODWORKING CORP
9380 Pentatech Dr (49464-9090)
P.O. Box 286 (49464-0286)
PHONE..................................616 741-9663
Bradford Davis, *President*
Greg Raczok, *Vice Pres*
Larry Kelly, *Engineer*
Dave Stumpfig, *Lab Dir*
▼ **EMP:** 44
SQ FT: 22,000
SALES (est): 6.6MM **Privately Held**
WEB: www.industrialwoodworking.com
SIC: 2511 5047 Wood household furniture; hospital equipment & furniture

(G-18159)
INFORMATION STN SPECIALISTS
Also Called: ISS
3368 88th Ave (49464-9674)
P.O. Box 51 (49464-0051)
PHONE..................................616 772-2300
William W Baker, *President*
Linda Folland, *Treasurer*
Margaret Baker, *Admin Sec*
EMP: 10
SQ FT: 2,400
SALES: 2MM **Privately Held**
WEB: www.issinfosite.com
SIC: 3663 Radio & TV communications equipment

(G-18160)
INNOTEC CORP (PA)
Also Called: Innotec Automation
441 E Roosevelt Ave (49464-1278)
PHONE..................................616 772-5959
Michael Lanser, *President*
Bryan Lanser, *Vice Pres*
▲ **EMP:** 90
SQ FT: 12,000
SALES (est): 22.9MM **Privately Held**
WEB: www.innotecgroup.com
SIC: 3469 3679 Metal stampings; electronic circuits

(G-18161)
JSK SPECIALTIES
11007 Chicago Dr Ste 34 (49464-9186)
PHONE..................................616 218-2416
EMP: 3
SALES (est): 314.6K **Privately Held**
SIC: 3599 Machine shop, jobbing & repair

(G-18162)
MEAD JOHNSON & COMPANY LLC
725 E Main Ave (49464-1368)
PHONE..................................616 748-7100
Vernon Hyde, *Warehouse Mgr*
Marcus Jordan, *Engineer*
Frieda Kaiser, *Engineer*
Adam Vogt, *Engineer*
Michele Lyons, *Human Res Mgr*
EMP: 27
SALES (corp-wide): 16.1B **Privately Held**
SIC: 2099 Food preparations
HQ: Mead Johnson & Company, Llc
2400 W Lloyd Expy
Evansville IN 47712
812 429-5000

(G-18163)
MICHIGAN TURKEY PRODUCERS
9983 Polk St (49464-9778)
PHONE..................................616 875-1838
Daniel Lennon, *Branch Mgr*
EMP: 8
SALES (corp-wide): 113.3MM **Privately Held**
WEB: www.miturkey.com
SIC: 2015 Turkey processing & slaughtering
PA: Michigan Turkey Producers Cooperative, Inc.
2140 Chicago Dr Sw
Wyoming MI 49519
616 245-2221

(G-18164)
MICHIGAN WOOD FIBERS LLC
9426 Henry Ct (49464-8944)
PHONE..................................616 875-2241
Charles Weaver, *President*
Nathan Weaver, *General Mgr*
EMP: 9
SQ FT: 40,000
SALES (est): 1.8MM **Privately Held**
WEB: www.michiganwoodfibers.com
SIC: 2499 5083 Mulch, wood & bark; landscaping equipment

(G-18165)
MIDWAY MACHINE TECH INC
555 N State St (49464-1230)
PHONE..................................616 772-0808
Jerry Geertman, *President*
Terry Geertman, *Exec VP*
EMP: 25
SQ FT: 19,000
SALES (est): 6.5MM **Privately Held**
WEB: www.midwaymachine.com
SIC: 3599 Machine shop, jobbing & repair

(G-18166)
MILCARE INC (HQ)
855 E Main Ave (49464-1366)
PHONE..................................616 654-8000
David Reid, *President*
EMP: 350
SQ FT: 63,400
SALES: 29.4MM
SALES (corp-wide): 2.5B **Publicly Held**
SIC: 2531 Public building & related furniture
PA: Herman Miller, Inc.
855 E Main Ave
Zeeland MI 49464
616 654-3000

(G-18167)
MOODY BIBLE INST OF CHICAGO
Also Called: Wgnb
3764 84th Ave (49464-9706)
P.O. Box 40 (49464-0040)
PHONE..................................616 772-7300
Jack Haveman, *Branch Mgr*
EMP: 4
SALES (corp-wide): 111.9MM **Privately Held**
WEB: www.moody.edu
SIC: 3663 Radio & TV communications equipment
PA: The Moody Bible Institute Of Chicago
820 N La Salle Dr
Chicago IL 60610
312 329-4000

(G-18168)
NEPHEW FABRICATION INC
10752 Polk St (49464-9779)
PHONE..................................616 875-2121
Mike Nephew, *President*
Adel Nephew, *Vice Pres*
EMP: 4
SQ FT: 1,200
SALES (est): 558.8K **Privately Held**
SIC: 3599 1799 Machine & other job shop work; welding on site

(G-18169)
NOVO BUILDING PRODUCTS LLC (HQ)
8181 Logistics Dr (49464-9378)
PHONE..................................800 253-9000

Tom B Highley, *CEO*
Meriden Smucker, *President*
EMP: 2
SALES (est): 227.6MM **Privately Held**
SIC: 2431 Staircases & stairs, wood; doors & door parts & trim, wood; moldings, wood: unfinished & prefinished
PA: Blue Wolf Capital Partners Llc
165 Broadway Fl 52
New York NY 10006
212 488-1340

(G-18170)
ODL INCORPORATED (PA)
Also Called: O D L
215 E Roosevelt Ave (49464-1239)
PHONE..................................616 772-9111
Jeffrey Mulder, *CEO*
Dave Killoran, *Ch of Bd*
Jim Oren, *Vice Pres*
Ivan Samalot, *Vice Pres*
Bryan Bultema, *VP Opers*
▲ **EMP:** 301 **EST:** 1951
SQ FT: 14,000
SALES (est): 164.1MM **Privately Held**
WEB: www.odl.com
SIC: 2431 Doors & door parts & trim, wood

(G-18171)
ODL INCORPORATED
100 Mulder Rd (49464-8001)
PHONE..................................616 772-9111
Jim Allardyce, *Senior Engr*
Gave Kiallol, *Branch Mgr*
EMP: 400
SALES (corp-wide): 164.1MM **Privately Held**
WEB: www.odl.com
SIC: 2431 Millwork
PA: Odl, Incorporated
215 E Roosevelt Ave
Zeeland MI 49464
616 772-9111

(G-18172)
ODOR GONE INC
2849 Air Park Dr (49464-9412)
PHONE..................................888 636-7292
Kathy Pittsley, *President*
Mark Pittsley, *Vice Pres*
EMP: 10 **EST:** 1996
SALES (est): 840K **Privately Held**
WEB: www.ultraodorsgone.com
SIC: 2842 5169 Sanitation preparations, disinfectants & deodorants; aromatic chemicals

(G-18173)
PI OPTIMA INC
Also Called: Industrial Machining Services
2734 84th Ave (49464-9594)
PHONE..................................616 772-2138
Nelson Zeerip, *President*
EMP: 13
SQ FT: 7,500
SALES (est): 1.8MM **Privately Held**
WEB: www.indmachining.com
SIC: 3599 Machine shop, jobbing & repair; custom machinery

(G-18174)
PI OPTIMA MANUFACTURING LLC
2734 84th Ave (49464-9594)
PHONE..................................616 931-9750
Jason Beecham,
Kyle Snyder,
EMP: 10
SALES (est): 637.5K **Privately Held**
SIC: 3999 Manufacturing industries

(G-18175)
PLASCORE INC
581 E Roosevelt Ave (49464-1379)
PHONE..................................616 772-1220
Fritz Huebner, *Branch Mgr*
EMP: 13
SALES (corp-wide): 83MM **Privately Held**
SIC: 3354 Aluminum extruded products
PA: Plascore, Inc.
615 N Fairview Rd
Zeeland MI 49464
616 772-1220

(G-18176)
PLASCORE INC
500a E Roosevelt Ave (49464-1344)
PHONE..................................616 772-1220
Dave Vander Ploeg, *Principal*
EMP: 62
SALES (corp-wide): 83MM **Privately Held**
WEB: www.plascore.com
SIC: 3086 3083 Plastics foam products; laminated plastics plate & sheet
PA: Plascore, Inc.
615 N Fairview Rd
Zeeland MI 49464
616 772-1220

(G-18177)
PRIMERA PLASTICS INC (PA)
Also Called: Primera Pathways
3424 Production Ct (49464-8546)
PHONE..................................616 748-6248
Noel Cuellar, *President*
Bambi Hollingsworth, *Opers Staff*
Lucas Smith, *Production*
Trea Raymond, *Buyer*
Nick Rose, *Engineer*
EMP: 80
SQ FT: 60,000
SALES (est): 17.3MM **Privately Held**
WEB: www.primera-inc.com
SIC: 3089 Injection molding of plastics

(G-18178)
PRO-CAM SERVICES LLC
323 E Roosevelt Ave (49464-1339)
PHONE..................................616 748-4200
Thomas E Bassett II,
Malinda Bassett,
EMP: 8 **EST:** 1995
SALES (est): 700K **Privately Held**
SIC: 3599 Machine shop, jobbing & repair

(G-18179)
PRODUCTS ENGINEERED DALEY
913 Mid Bluff Dr (49464-8704)
PHONE..................................616 748-0162
EMP: 3 **EST:** 2007
SALES (est): 50K **Privately Held**
SIC: 3589 Mfg Service Industry Machinery

(G-18180)
PROGRESSIVE PANEL SYSTEMS
8095 Riley St (49464-8517)
PHONE..................................616 748-1384
Stanley Sluiter, *President*
Steve Sluiter, *Corp Secy*
Scott Sluiter, *Vice Pres*
Alex Sluiter, *Engineer*
Bruce Jorgensen, *Sales Mgr*
EMP: 15
SQ FT: 22,500
SALES (est): 2.3MM **Privately Held**
WEB: www.progressivesystem.com
SIC: 3448 8711 Trusses & framing: prefabricated metal; acoustical engineering

(G-18181)
PROTO-TEC INC
260 N Church St (49464-1244)
PHONE..................................616 772-9511
Kalvin Vanden Bosch, *President*
EMP: 10
SQ FT: 8,600
SALES (est): 1.4MM **Privately Held**
WEB: www.proto-tec.com
SIC: 3089 3544 Injection molded finished plastic products; special dies, tools, jigs & fixtures

(G-18182)
QUALITY MARINE ELECTRONICS LLC
10692 Chicago Dr (49464-9184)
PHONE..................................616 566-2101
Goran Majdandzic,
EMP: 3
SQ FT: 3,000
SALES (est): 330K **Privately Held**
SIC: 3531 5551 Marine related equipment; marine supplies & equipment

(G-18183)
R M N MACHINING & FABRICATING
3252 88th Ave (49464-9640)
PHONE..................................616 772-4111
Stan Osterbaan, *President*
Gail Osterbaan, *Vice Pres*
EMP: 3
SQ FT: 1,500
SALES (est): 300K **Privately Held**
SIC: 3599 Machine shop, jobbing & repair

(G-18184)
R-BO CO INC
150 W Washington Ave (49464-1102)
PHONE..................................616 748-9733
Larry Rigterink, *President*
▲ **EMP:** 32
SQ FT: 32,000
SALES (est): 3.5MM **Privately Held**
SIC: 3469 3646 3645 3441 Metal stampings; commercial indusl & institutional electric lighting fixtures; residential lighting fixtures; fabricated structural metal; wood household furniture

(G-18185)
ROWLAND MOLD & MACHINE INC
9395 Henry Ct (49464-9216)
PHONE..................................616 875-5400
Tim Rowland, *President*
EMP: 8
SQ FT: 48,000
SALES: 1MM **Privately Held**
SIC: 3544 Industrial molds

(G-18186)
SKYLARK MACHINE INC
501 E Roosevelt Ave (49464-1343)
PHONE..................................616 931-1010
Mark Hulst, *President*
Dave Kooiker, *Vice Pres*
EMP: 8
SQ FT: 3,000
SALES (est): 530.5K **Privately Held**
WEB: www.skylarkmachine.com
SIC: 3544 3599 Jigs & fixtures; machine shop, jobbing & repair

(G-18187)
SPURT INDUSTRIES LLC
Also Called: CST
5204 Adams St (49464-9005)
PHONE..................................616 688-5575
Tom Turner, *Mng Member*
EMP: 6
SQ FT: 1,200
SALES (est): 1.1MM **Privately Held**
WEB: www.compostsoiltech.com
SIC: 2875 Compost

(G-18188)
STONE PLASTICS AND MFG INC
8245 Riley St Ste 100 (49464-8568)
PHONE..................................616 748-9740
Mark J Mason, *President*
Brian Dropiewski, *Design Engr*
Trevor Bussies, *Program Mgr*
Nicholas Neumann, *Technology*
Richard Griggs, *IT/INT Sup*
▲ **EMP:** 120
SQ FT: 136
SALES (est): 101.9MM **Privately Held**
SIC: 5162 3089 Plastics products; injection molding of plastics

(G-18189)
SYMBIOTE INC
300 N Centennial St (49464-1312)
PHONE..................................616 772-1790
Travis Randolph, *President*
Robert Kubasiak, *General Mgr*
Sandra Randolph, *Vice Pres*
Savad Som, *Production*
Mike Doucette, *Engineer*
▲ **EMP:** 47
SALES: 8MM **Privately Held**
WEB: www.symbiote.com
SIC: 3535 3821 2599 3446 Conveyors & conveying equipment; laboratory apparatus & furniture; factory furniture & fixtures; architectural metalwork

(G-18190)
TYSON FOODS /HR
8300 96th Ave (49464-9177)
PHONE..................................616 875-2311
Denise Brown, *Principal*
Mark Huyser, *Plant Mgr*
EMP: 3
SALES (est): 279.7K **Privately Held**
SIC: 2015 Poultry slaughtering & processing

(G-18191)
VAN ENK WOODCRAFTERS LLC
500 E Washington Ave # 50 (49464-1385)
P.O. Box 79 (49464-0079)
PHONE..................................616 931-0090
Ben Van Enk, *Mng Member*
David Van Enk, *Mng Member*
EMP: 16
SQ FT: 21,000
SALES (est): 1.3MM **Privately Held**
SIC: 2431 Millwork

(G-18192)
VENTURA MANUFACTURING INC (PA)
471 E Roosevelt Ave # 100 (49464-1257)
PHONE..................................616 772-7405
France Allen, *President*
Michael Allen, *Mfg Staff*
Kris Dibble, *Mfg Staff*
Joshua Driscoll, *Mfg Staff*
Terry Gort, *Mfg Staff*
◆ **EMP:** 109
SQ FT: 95,000
SALES (est): 42.1MM **Privately Held**
WEB: www.venturamfg.com
SIC: 3315 Steel wire & related products

(G-18193)
VERTELLUS HLTH SPCLTY PDTS LLC
Also Called: Vertellus Specialty Materials
215 N Centennial St (49464-1309)
PHONE..................................616 772-2193
◆ **EMP:** 6
SALES (est): 610K **Privately Held**
SIC: 2899 Mfg Chemical Preparations

(G-18194)
VERTELLUS LLC
Also Called: Vertellus Zeeland
215 N Centennial St (49464-1309)
PHONE..................................616 772-2193
Tod Hammond, *Manager*
EMP: 150
SALES (corp-wide): 488.3MM **Privately Held**
SIC: 2869 Industrial organic chemicals
HQ: Vertellus Llc
1500 S Tibbs Ave
Indianapolis IN 46241
317 247-8141

(G-18195)
VORTEC
201 W Washington Ave # 110 (49464-1086)
PHONE..................................616 292-2401
Matthew D Potts, *Administration*
EMP: 8
SALES (est): 810K **Privately Held**
SIC: 3544 Special dies, tools, jigs & fixtures

(G-18196)
WESTERN REFLECTIONS LLC
215 E Roosevelt Ave (49464-1239)
PHONE..................................616 772-9111
Jeff Mulder, *Mng Member*
▲ **EMP:** 50
SALES (est): 5.6MM
SALES (corp-wide): 164.1MM **Privately Held**
SIC: 2431 Millwork
PA: Odl, Incorporated
215 E Roosevelt Ave
Zeeland MI 49464
616 772-9111

(G-18197)
WOODWARD INC
Fuel Systems Division
700 N Centennial St (49464-1369)
PHONE..................................616 772-9171

Bill Meoy, *Principal*
Debra Hamelink, *VP Mfg*
Miklos Kovach, *Project Mgr*
Tim Diekema, *Facilities Mgr*
Tom Anys, *Engineer*
EMP: 400
SALES (corp-wide): 2.3B **Publicly Held**
WEB: www.woodward.com
SIC: 7699 3824 3812 Aircraft & heavy equipment repair services; fluid meters & counting devices; search & navigation equipment
PA: Woodward, Inc.
   1081 Woodward Way
   Fort Collins CO 80524
   970 482-5811

(G-18198)
WOODWARD FST INC
700 N Centennial St (49464-1369)
PHONE..................................616 772-9171
Thomas A Gendron, *Ch of Bd*
James R Rulseh, *President*
John D Cohn, *Senior VP*
Halil Kinaci, *Purch Dir*
EMP: 230
SALES (est): 53.3MM
SALES (corp-wide): 2.3B **Publicly Held**
SIC: 3724 Aircraft engines & engine parts
PA: Woodward, Inc.
   1081 Woodward Way
   Fort Collins CO 80524
   970 482-5811

(G-18199)
ZEELAND BIO-BASED PRODUCTS LLC
2525 84th Ave (49464-9501)
P.O. Box 290 (49464-0290)
PHONE..................................616 748-1831
Robert D Meeuwsen,
EMP: 9
SALES: 950K **Privately Held**
SIC: 2075 Soybean oil mills

(G-18200)
ZEELAND COMPONENT SALES LLC
138 W Washington Ave (49464-1120)
P.O. Box 222 (49464-0222)
PHONE..................................616 399-8614
Douglas Lincicum,
EMP: 5
SALES (est): 748.1K **Privately Held**
SIC: 3531 5999 Subgraders (construction equipment); batteries, non-automotive

(G-18201)
ZEELAND FARM SERVICES INC (PA)
Also Called: Zeeland Freight Services
2525 84th Ave (49464-9501)
P.O. Box 290 (49464-0290)
PHONE..................................616 772-9042
Cliff Meeuwsen, *President*
Robb Meeusen, *Vice Pres*
Arlen Meeuwsen, *Vice Pres*
Eric Musen, *Vice Pres*
Brian Terborg, *Vice Pres*
◆ **EMP:** 130 **EST:** 1950
SQ FT: 40,000
SALES (est): 38.7MM **Privately Held**
SIC: 2075 5153 4212 Soybean oil mills; grains; dump truck haulage; steel hauling, local

(G-18202)
ZEELAND PRINT SHOP CO
145 E Main Ave (49464-1735)
PHONE..................................616 772-6636
Brian Van Hoven, *President*
EMP: 6 **EST:** 1932
SQ FT: 2,400
SALES (est): 958K **Privately Held**
SIC: 2752 Commercial printing, offset

(G-18203)
ZEELAND RECORD CO
16 S Elm St (49464-1751)
PHONE..................................616 772-2131
Paul Van Koevering, *President*
Kraig Van Koevering, *Corp Secy*
Kurt Van Koevering, *Vice Pres*
EMP: 6
SQ FT: 12,000

SALES (est): 1MM **Privately Held**
SIC: 2759 Commercial printing

SIC INDEX

Standard Industrial Classification Alphabetical Index

SIC NO	PRODUCT

A

3291 Abrasive Prdts
2891 Adhesives & Sealants
3563 Air & Gas Compressors
3585 Air Conditioning & Heating Eqpt
3721 Aircraft
3724 Aircraft Engines & Engine Parts
3728 Aircraft Parts & Eqpt, NEC
2812 Alkalies & Chlorine
3363 Aluminum Die Castings
3354 Aluminum Extruded Prdts
3365 Aluminum Foundries
3355 Aluminum Rolling & Drawing, NEC
3353 Aluminum Sheet, Plate & Foil
3826 Analytical Instruments
2077 Animal, Marine Fats & Oils
2389 Apparel & Accessories, NEC
2387 Apparel Belts
3446 Architectural & Ornamental Metal Work
7694 Armature Rewinding Shops
3292 Asbestos products
2952 Asphalt Felts & Coatings
3822 Automatic Temperature Controls
3581 Automatic Vending Machines
3465 Automotive Stampings
2396 Automotive Trimmings, Apparel Findings, Related Prdts

B

2673 Bags: Plastics, Laminated & Coated
2674 Bags: Uncoated Paper & Multiwall
3562 Ball & Roller Bearings
2836 Biological Prdts, Exc Diagnostic Substances
1221 Bituminous Coal & Lignite: Surface Mining
2782 Blankbooks & Looseleaf Binders
3312 Blast Furnaces, Coke Ovens, Steel & Rolling Mills
3564 Blowers & Fans
3732 Boat Building & Repairing
3452 Bolts, Nuts, Screws, Rivets & Washers
2732 Book Printing, Not Publishing
2789 Bookbinding
2731 Books: Publishing & Printing
3131 Boot & Shoe Cut Stock & Findings
2342 Brassieres, Girdles & Garments
2051 Bread, Bakery Prdts Exc Cookies & Crackers
3251 Brick & Structural Clay Tile
3991 Brooms & Brushes
3995 Burial Caskets
2021 Butter

C

3578 Calculating & Accounting Eqpt
2064 Candy & Confectionery Prdts
2033 Canned Fruits, Vegetables & Preserves
2032 Canned Specialties
2394 Canvas Prdts
3624 Carbon & Graphite Prdts
3955 Carbon Paper & Inked Ribbons
3592 Carburetors, Pistons, Rings & Valves
2273 Carpets & Rugs
2823 Cellulosic Man-Made Fibers
3241 Cement, Hydraulic
3253 Ceramic Tile
2043 Cereal Breakfast Foods
2022 Cheese
1479 Chemical & Fertilizer Mining
2899 Chemical Preparations, NEC
2067 Chewing Gum
3261 China Plumbing Fixtures & Fittings
2066 Chocolate & Cocoa Prdts
2111 Cigarettes
2257 Circular Knit Fabric Mills
3255 Clay Refractories
1241 Coal Mining Svcs
3479 Coating & Engraving, NEC
2095 Coffee
3316 Cold Rolled Steel Sheet, Strip & Bars
3582 Commercial Laundry, Dry Clean & Pressing Mchs
2759 Commercial Printing
2754 Commercial Printing: Gravure
2752 Commercial Printing: Lithographic
3646 Commercial, Indl & Institutional Lighting Fixtures
3669 Communications Eqpt, NEC
3577 Computer Peripheral Eqpt, NEC
3572 Computer Storage Devices
3575 Computer Terminals
3271 Concrete Block & Brick
3272 Concrete Prdts
3531 Construction Machinery & Eqpt
1442 Construction Sand & Gravel
2679 Converted Paper Prdts, NEC
3535 Conveyors & Eqpt
2052 Cookies & Crackers
3366 Copper Foundries
1021 Copper Ores
2298 Cordage & Twine
2653 Corrugated & Solid Fiber Boxes
3961 Costume Jewelry & Novelties
2261 Cotton Fabric Finishers
2211 Cotton, Woven Fabric
3466 Crowns & Closures
1311 Crude Petroleum & Natural Gas
1423 Crushed & Broken Granite
1422 Crushed & Broken Limestone
1429 Crushed & Broken Stone, NEC
3643 Current-Carrying Wiring Devices
2391 Curtains & Draperies
3087 Custom Compounding Of Purchased Plastic Resins
3281 Cut Stone Prdts
3421 Cutlery
2865 Cyclic-Crudes, Intermediates, Dyes & Org Pigments

D

3843 Dental Eqpt & Splys
2835 Diagnostic Substances
2675 Die-Cut Paper & Board
3544 Dies, Tools, Jigs, Fixtures & Indl Molds
1411 Dimension Stone
2047 Dog & Cat Food
3942 Dolls & Stuffed Toys
2591 Drapery Hardware, Window Blinds & Shades
2381 Dress & Work Gloves
2034 Dried Fruits, Vegetables & Soup
1381 Drilling Oil & Gas Wells

E

3263 Earthenware, Whiteware, Table & Kitchen Articles
3634 Electric Household Appliances
3641 Electric Lamps
3694 Electrical Eqpt For Internal Combustion Engines
3629 Electrical Indl Apparatus, NEC
3699 Electrical Machinery, Eqpt & Splys, NEC
3845 Electromedical & Electrotherapeutic Apparatus
3313 Electrometallurgical Prdts
3677 Electronic Coils & Transformers
3679 Electronic Components, NEC
3571 Electronic Computers
3678 Electronic Connectors
3676 Electronic Resistors
3471 Electroplating, Plating, Polishing, Anodizing & Coloring
3534 Elevators & Moving Stairways
3431 Enameled Iron & Metal Sanitary Ware
2677 Envelopes
2892 Explosives

F

2241 Fabric Mills, Cotton, Wool, Silk & Man-Made
3499 Fabricated Metal Prdts, NEC
3498 Fabricated Pipe & Pipe Fittings
3443 Fabricated Plate Work
3069 Fabricated Rubber Prdts, NEC
3441 Fabricated Structural Steel
2399 Fabricated Textile Prdts, NEC
2295 Fabrics Coated Not Rubberized
3523 Farm Machinery & Eqpt
3965 Fasteners, Buttons, Needles & Pins
2875 Fertilizers, Mixing Only
2655 Fiber Cans, Tubes & Drums
2091 Fish & Seafoods, Canned & Cured
2092 Fish & Seafoods, Fresh & Frozen
3211 Flat Glass
2087 Flavoring Extracts & Syrups
2045 Flour, Blended & Prepared
2041 Flour, Grain Milling
3824 Fluid Meters & Counters
3593 Fluid Power Cylinders & Actuators
3594 Fluid Power Pumps & Motors
3492 Fluid Power Valves & Hose Fittings
2657 Folding Paperboard Boxes
3556 Food Prdts Machinery
2099 Food Preparations, NEC
3149 Footwear, NEC
2053 Frozen Bakery Prdts
2037 Frozen Fruits, Juices & Vegetables
2038 Frozen Specialties
2371 Fur Goods
2599 Furniture & Fixtures, NEC

G

3944 Games, Toys & Children's Vehicles
3524 Garden, Lawn Tractors & Eqpt
3053 Gaskets, Packing & Sealing Devices
2369 Girls' & Infants' Outerwear, NEC
3221 Glass Containers
3231 Glass Prdts Made Of Purchased Glass
1041 Gold Ores
3321 Gray Iron Foundries
2771 Greeting Card Publishing
3769 Guided Missile/Space Vehicle Parts & Eqpt, NEC
3764 Guided Missile/Space Vehicle Propulsion Units & parts
3761 Guided Missiles & Space Vehicles
2861 Gum & Wood Chemicals
3275 Gypsum Prdts

H

3423 Hand & Edge Tools
3425 Hand Saws & Saw Blades
3171 Handbags & Purses
3429 Hardware, NEC
2426 Hardwood Dimension & Flooring Mills
2435 Hardwood Veneer & Plywood
2353 Hats, Caps & Millinery
3433 Heating Eqpt
3536 Hoists, Cranes & Monorails
2252 Hosiery, Except Women's
2392 House furnishings: Textile
3142 House Slippers
3639 Household Appliances, NEC
3651 Household Audio & Video Eqpt
3631 Household Cooking Eqpt
2519 Household Furniture, NEC
3633 Household Laundry Eqpt
3632 Household Refrigerators & Freezers
3635 Household Vacuum Cleaners

I

2097 Ice
2024 Ice Cream
2819 Indl Inorganic Chemicals, NEC
3823 Indl Instruments For Meas, Display & Control
3569 Indl Machinery & Eqpt, NEC
3567 Indl Process Furnaces & Ovens
3537 Indl Trucks, Tractors, Trailers & Stackers
2813 Industrial Gases
2869 Industrial Organic Chemicals, NEC
3543 Industrial Patterns
1446 Industrial Sand
3491 Industrial Valves
2816 Inorganic Pigments
3825 Instrs For Measuring & Testing Electricity
3519 Internal Combustion Engines, NEC
3462 Iron & Steel Forgings
1011 Iron Ores

J

3915 Jewelers Findings & Lapidary Work
3911 Jewelry: Precious Metal

K

2253 Knit Outerwear Mills
2254 Knit Underwear Mills
2259 Knitting Mills, NEC

L

3821 Laboratory Apparatus & Furniture
1031 Lead & Zinc Ores
3952 Lead Pencils, Crayons & Artist's Mtrls
2386 Leather & Sheep Lined Clothing
3151 Leather Gloves & Mittens
3199 Leather Goods, NEC
3111 Leather Tanning & Finishing
3648 Lighting Eqpt, NEC
3996 Linoleum & Hard Surface Floor Coverings, NEC

SIC INDEX

SIC NO	PRODUCT
2085	Liquors, Distilled, Rectified & Blended
2411	Logging
2992	Lubricating Oils & Greases
3161	Luggage

M

SIC NO	PRODUCT
2098	Macaroni, Spaghetti & Noodles
3545	Machine Tool Access
3541	Machine Tools: Cutting
3542	Machine Tools: Forming
3599	Machinery & Eqpt, Indl & Commercial, NEC
3322	Malleable Iron Foundries
2083	Malt
2082	Malt Beverages
2761	Manifold Business Forms
3999	Manufacturing Industries, NEC
3953	Marking Devices
2515	Mattresses & Bedsprings
3829	Measuring & Controlling Devices, NEC
3586	Measuring & Dispensing Pumps
2011	Meat Packing Plants
3568	Mechanical Power Transmission Eqpt, NEC
2833	Medicinal Chemicals & Botanical Prdts
2329	Men's & Boys' Clothing, NEC
2325	Men's & Boys' Separate Trousers & Casual Slacks
2321	Men's & Boys' Shirts
2311	Men's & Boys' Suits, Coats & Overcoats
2322	Men's & Boys' Underwear & Nightwear
2326	Men's & Boys' Work Clothing
3143	Men's Footwear, Exc Athletic
3412	Metal Barrels, Drums, Kegs & Pails
3411	Metal Cans
3442	Metal Doors, Sash, Frames, Molding & Trim
3497	Metal Foil & Leaf
3398	Metal Heat Treating
2514	Metal Household Furniture
1081	Metal Mining Svcs
1099	Metal Ores, NEC
3469	Metal Stampings, NEC
3549	Metalworking Machinery, NEC
2026	Milk
2023	Milk, Condensed & Evaporated
2431	Millwork
3296	Mineral Wool
3295	Minerals & Earths: Ground Or Treated
3532	Mining Machinery & Eqpt
3496	Misc Fabricated Wire Prdts
2741	Misc Publishing
3449	Misc Structural Metal Work
1499	Miscellaneous Nonmetallic Mining
2451	Mobile Homes
3061	Molded, Extruded & Lathe-Cut Rubber Mechanical Goods
3716	Motor Homes
3714	Motor Vehicle Parts & Access
3711	Motor Vehicles & Car Bodies
3751	Motorcycles, Bicycles & Parts
3621	Motors & Generators
3931	Musical Instruments

N

SIC NO	PRODUCT
1321	Natural Gas Liquids
2711	Newspapers: Publishing & Printing
2873	Nitrogenous Fertilizers
3297	Nonclay Refractories
3644	Noncurrent-Carrying Wiring Devices
3364	Nonferrous Die Castings, Exc Aluminum
3463	Nonferrous Forgings
3369	Nonferrous Foundries: Castings, NEC
3357	Nonferrous Wire Drawing
3299	Nonmetallic Mineral Prdts, NEC
1481	Nonmetallic Minerals Svcs, Except Fuels

O

SIC NO	PRODUCT
2522	Office Furniture, Except Wood
3579	Office Machines, NEC
1382	Oil & Gas Field Exploration Svcs
1389	Oil & Gas Field Svcs, NEC
3533	Oil Field Machinery & Eqpt
3851	Ophthalmic Goods
3827	Optical Instruments
3489	Ordnance & Access, NEC
3842	Orthopedic, Prosthetic & Surgical Appliances/Splys

P

SIC NO	PRODUCT
3565	Packaging Machinery
2851	Paints, Varnishes, Lacquers, Enamels
2671	Paper Coating & Laminating for Packaging
2672	Paper Coating & Laminating, Exc for Packaging
3554	Paper Inds Machinery
2621	Paper Mills
2631	Paperboard Mills
2542	Partitions & Fixtures, Except Wood
2951	Paving Mixtures & Blocks
3951	Pens & Mechanical Pencils
2844	Perfumes, Cosmetics & Toilet Preparations
2721	Periodicals: Publishing & Printing
3172	Personal Leather Goods
2879	Pesticides & Agricultural Chemicals, NEC
2911	Petroleum Refining
2834	Pharmaceuticals
3652	Phonograph Records & Magnetic Tape
2874	Phosphatic Fertilizers
3861	Photographic Eqpt & Splys
2035	Pickled Fruits, Vegetables, Sauces & Dressings
3085	Plastic Bottles
3086	Plastic Foam Prdts
3083	Plastic Laminated Plate & Sheet
3084	Plastic Pipe
3088	Plastic Plumbing Fixtures
3089	Plastic Prdts
3082	Plastic Unsupported Profile Shapes
3081	Plastic Unsupported Sheet & Film
2821	Plastics, Mtrls & Nonvulcanizable Elastomers
2796	Platemaking & Related Svcs
2395	Pleating & Stitching For The Trade
3432	Plumbing Fixture Fittings & Trim, Brass
3264	Porcelain Electrical Splys
1474	Potash, Soda & Borate Minerals
2096	Potato Chips & Similar Prdts
3269	Pottery Prdts, NEC
2015	Poultry Slaughtering, Dressing & Processing
3546	Power Hand Tools
3612	Power, Distribution & Specialty Transformers
3448	Prefabricated Metal Buildings & Cmpnts
2452	Prefabricated Wood Buildings & Cmpnts
7372	Prepackaged Software
2048	Prepared Feeds For Animals & Fowls
3229	Pressed & Blown Glassware, NEC
3692	Primary Batteries: Dry & Wet
3399	Primary Metal Prdts, NEC
3339	Primary Nonferrous Metals, NEC
3334	Primary Production Of Aluminum
3331	Primary Smelting & Refining Of Copper
3672	Printed Circuit Boards
2893	Printing Ink
3555	Printing Trades Machinery & Eqpt
2531	Public Building & Related Furniture
2611	Pulp Mills
3561	Pumps & Pumping Eqpt

R

SIC NO	PRODUCT
3663	Radio & T V Communications, Systs & Eqpt, Broadcast/Studio
3671	Radio & T V Receiving Electron Tubes
3743	Railroad Eqpt
3273	Ready-Mixed Concrete
2493	Reconstituted Wood Prdts
3695	Recording Media
3625	Relays & Indl Controls
3645	Residential Lighting Fixtures
3547	Rolling Mill Machinery & Eqpt
3351	Rolling, Drawing & Extruding Of Copper
3356	Rolling, Drawing-Extruding Of Nonferrous Metals
3021	Rubber & Plastic Footwear
3052	Rubber & Plastic Hose & Belting

S

SIC NO	PRODUCT
2068	Salted & Roasted Nuts & Seeds
2656	Sanitary Food Containers
2676	Sanitary Paper Prdts
2013	Sausages & Meat Prdts
2421	Saw & Planing Mills
3596	Scales & Balances, Exc Laboratory
2397	Schiffli Machine Embroideries
3451	Screw Machine Prdts
3812	Search, Detection, Navigation & Guidance Systs & Instrs
3341	Secondary Smelting & Refining Of Nonferrous Metals
3674	Semiconductors
3589	Service Ind Machines, NEC
2652	Set-Up Paperboard Boxes
3444	Sheet Metal Work
3731	Shipbuilding & Repairing
2079	Shortening, Oils & Margarine
3993	Signs & Advertising Displays
2262	Silk & Man-Made Fabric Finishers
2221	Silk & Man-Made Fiber
1044	Silver Ores
3914	Silverware, Plated & Stainless Steel Ware
3484	Small Arms
3482	Small Arms Ammunition
2841	Soap & Detergents
2086	Soft Drinks
2436	Softwood Veneer & Plywood
2075	Soybean Oil Mills
2842	Spec Cleaning, Polishing & Sanitation Preparations
3559	Special Ind Machinery, NEC
2429	Special Prdt Sawmills, NEC
3566	Speed Changers, Drives & Gears
3949	Sporting & Athletic Goods, NEC
2678	Stationery Prdts
3511	Steam, Gas & Hydraulic Turbines & Engines
3325	Steel Foundries, NEC
3324	Steel Investment Foundries
3317	Steel Pipe & Tubes
3493	Steel Springs, Except Wire
3315	Steel Wire Drawing & Nails & Spikes
3691	Storage Batteries
3259	Structural Clay Prdts, NEC
2439	Structural Wood Members, NEC
2063	Sugar, Beet
2061	Sugar, Cane
2062	Sugar, Cane Refining
2843	Surface Active & Finishing Agents, Sulfonated Oils
3841	Surgical & Medical Instrs & Apparatus
3613	Switchgear & Switchboard Apparatus
2824	Synthetic Organic Fibers, Exc Cellulosic
2822	Synthetic Rubber (Vulcanizable Elastomers)

T

SIC NO	PRODUCT
3795	Tanks & Tank Components
3661	Telephone & Telegraph Apparatus
2393	Textile Bags
2269	Textile Finishers, NEC
2299	Textile Goods, NEC
3552	Textile Machinery
2284	Thread Mills
2296	Tire Cord & Fabric
3011	Tires & Inner Tubes
2131	Tobacco, Chewing & Snuff
3799	Transportation Eqpt, NEC
3792	Travel Trailers & Campers
3713	Truck & Bus Bodies
3715	Truck Trailers
2791	Typesetting

V

SIC NO	PRODUCT
3494	Valves & Pipe Fittings, NEC
2076	Vegetable Oil Mills
3647	Vehicular Lighting Eqpt

W

SIC NO	PRODUCT
3873	Watch & Clock Devices & Parts
3548	Welding Apparatus
7692	Welding Repair
2046	Wet Corn Milling
2084	Wine & Brandy
3495	Wire Springs
2331	Women's & Misses' Blouses
2335	Women's & Misses' Dresses
2339	Women's & Misses' Outerwear, NEC
2337	Women's & Misses' Suits, Coats & Skirts
3144	Women's Footwear, Exc Athletic
2341	Women's, Misses' & Children's Underwear & Nightwear
2441	Wood Boxes
2449	Wood Containers, NEC
2511	Wood Household Furniture
2512	Wood Household Furniture, Upholstered
2434	Wood Kitchen Cabinets
2521	Wood Office Furniture
2448	Wood Pallets & Skids
2499	Wood Prdts, NEC
2491	Wood Preserving
2517	Wood T V, Radio, Phono & Sewing Cabinets
2541	Wood, Office & Store Fixtures
3553	Woodworking Machinery
2231	Wool, Woven Fabric

X

SIC NO	PRODUCT
3844	X-ray Apparatus & Tubes

Y

SIC NO	PRODUCT
2281	Yarn Spinning Mills
2282	Yarn Texturizing, Throwing, Twisting & Winding Mills

SIC INDEX

Standard Industrial Classification Numerical Index

SIC NO	PRODUCT

10 metal mining
1011 Iron Ores
1021 Copper Ores
1031 Lead & Zinc Ores
1041 Gold Ores
1044 Silver Ores
1081 Metal Mining Svcs
1099 Metal Ores, NEC

12 coal mining
1221 Bituminous Coal & Lignite: Surface Mining
1241 Coal Mining Svcs

13 oil and gas extraction
1311 Crude Petroleum & Natural Gas
1321 Natural Gas Liquids
1381 Drilling Oil & Gas Wells
1382 Oil & Gas Field Exploration Svcs
1389 Oil & Gas Field Svcs, NEC

14 mining and quarrying of nonmetallic minerals, except fuels
1411 Dimension Stone
1422 Crushed & Broken Limestone
1423 Crushed & Broken Granite
1429 Crushed & Broken Stone, NEC
1442 Construction Sand & Gravel
1446 Industrial Sand
1474 Potash, Soda & Borate Minerals
1479 Chemical & Fertilizer Mining
1481 Nonmetallic Minerals Svcs, Except Fuels
1499 Miscellaneous Nonmetallic Mining

20 food and kindred products
2011 Meat Packing Plants
2013 Sausages & Meat Prdts
2015 Poultry Slaughtering, Dressing & Processing
2021 Butter
2022 Cheese
2023 Milk, Condensed & Evaporated
2024 Ice Cream
2026 Milk
2032 Canned Specialties
2033 Canned Fruits, Vegetables & Preserves
2034 Dried Fruits, Vegetables & Soup
2035 Pickled Fruits, Vegetables, Sauces & Dressings
2037 Frozen Fruits, Juices & Vegetables
2038 Frozen Specialties
2041 Flour, Grain Milling
2043 Cereal Breakfast Foods
2045 Flour, Blended & Prepared
2046 Wet Corn Milling
2047 Dog & Cat Food
2048 Prepared Feeds For Animals & Fowls
2051 Bread, Bakery Prdts Exc Cookies & Crackers
2052 Cookies & Crackers
2053 Frozen Bakery Prdts
2061 Sugar, Cane
2062 Sugar, Cane Refining
2063 Sugar, Beet
2064 Candy & Confectionery Prdts
2066 Chocolate & Cocoa Prdts
2067 Chewing Gum
2068 Salted & Roasted Nuts & Seeds
2075 Soybean Oil Mills
2076 Vegetable Oil Mills
2077 Animal, Marine Fats & Oils
2079 Shortening, Oils & Margarine
2082 Malt Beverages
2083 Malt
2084 Wine & Brandy
2085 Liquors, Distilled, Rectified & Blended
2086 Soft Drinks
2087 Flavoring Extracts & Syrups
2091 Fish & Seafoods, Canned & Cured
2092 Fish & Seafoods, Fresh & Frozen
2095 Coffee
2096 Potato Chips & Similar Prdts
2097 Ice
2098 Macaroni, Spaghetti & Noodles
2099 Food Preparations, NEC

21 tobacco products
2111 Cigarettes
2131 Tobacco, Chewing & Snuff

22 textile mill products
2211 Cotton, Woven Fabric
2221 Silk & Man-Made Fiber
2231 Wool, Woven Fabric
2241 Fabric Mills, Cotton, Wool, Silk & Man-Made
2252 Hosiery, Except Women's
2253 Knit Outerwear Mills
2254 Knit Underwear Mills
2257 Circular Knit Fabric Mills
2259 Knitting Mills, NEC
2261 Cotton Fabric Finishers
2262 Silk & Man-Made Fabric Finishers
2269 Textile Finishers, NEC
2273 Carpets & Rugs
2281 Yarn Spinning Mills
2282 Yarn Texturizing, Throwing, Twisting & Winding Mills
2284 Thread Mills
2295 Fabrics Coated Not Rubberized
2296 Tire Cord & Fabric
2298 Cordage & Twine
2299 Textile Goods, NEC

23 apparel and other finished products made from fabrics and similar material
2311 Men's & Boys' Suits, Coats & Overcoats
2321 Men's & Boys' Shirts
2322 Men's & Boys' Underwear & Nightwear
2325 Men's & Boys' Separate Trousers & Casual Slacks
2326 Men's & Boys' Work Clothing
2329 Men's & Boys' Clothing, NEC
2331 Women's & Misses' Blouses
2335 Women's & Misses' Dresses
2337 Women's & Misses' Suits, Coats & Skirts
2339 Women's & Misses' Outerwear, NEC
2341 Women's, Misses' & Children's Underwear & Nightwear
2342 Brassieres, Girdles & Garments
2353 Hats, Caps & Millinery
2369 Girls' & Infants' Outerwear, NEC
2371 Fur Goods
2381 Dress & Work Gloves
2386 Leather & Sheep Lined Clothing
2387 Apparel Belts
2389 Apparel & Accessories, NEC
2391 Curtains & Draperies
2392 House furnishings: Textile
2393 Textile Bags
2394 Canvas Prdts
2395 Pleating & Stitching For The Trade
2396 Automotive Trimmings, Apparel Findings, Related Prdts
2397 Schiffli Machine Embroideries
2399 Fabricated Textile Prdts, NEC

24 lumber and wood products, except furniture
2411 Logging
2421 Saw & Planing Mills
2426 Hardwood Dimension & Flooring Mills
2429 Special Prdt Sawmills, NEC
2431 Millwork
2434 Wood Kitchen Cabinets
2435 Hardwood Veneer & Plywood
2436 Softwood Veneer & Plywood
2439 Structural Wood Members, NEC
2441 Wood Boxes
2448 Wood Pallets & Skids
2449 Wood Containers, NEC
2451 Mobile Homes
2452 Prefabricated Wood Buildings & Cmpnts
2491 Wood Preserving
2493 Reconstituted Wood Prdts
2499 Wood Prdts, NEC

25 furniture and fixtures
2511 Wood Household Furniture
2512 Wood Household Furniture, Upholstered
2514 Metal Household Furniture
2515 Mattresses & Bedsprings
2517 Wood TV, Radio, Phono & Sewing Cabinets
2519 Household Furniture, NEC
2521 Wood Office Furniture
2522 Office Furniture, Except Wood
2531 Public Building & Related Furniture
2541 Wood, Office & Store Fixtures
2542 Partitions & Fixtures, Except Wood
2591 Drapery Hardware, Window Blinds & Shades
2599 Furniture & Fixtures, NEC

26 paper and allied products
2611 Pulp Mills
2621 Paper Mills
2631 Paperboard Mills
2652 Set-Up Paperboard Boxes
2653 Corrugated & Solid Fiber Boxes
2655 Fiber Cans, Tubes & Drums
2656 Sanitary Food Containers
2657 Folding Paperboard Boxes
2671 Paper Coating & Laminating for Packaging
2672 Paper Coating & Laminating, Exc for Packaging
2673 Bags: Plastics, Laminated & Coated
2674 Bags: Uncoated Paper & Multiwall
2675 Die-Cut Paper & Board
2676 Sanitary Paper Prdts
2677 Envelopes
2678 Stationery Prdts
2679 Converted Paper Prdts, NEC

27 printing, publishing, and allied industries
2711 Newspapers: Publishing & Printing
2721 Periodicals: Publishing & Printing
2731 Books: Publishing & Printing
2732 Book Printing, Not Publishing
2741 Misc Publishing
2752 Commercial Printing: Lithographic
2754 Commercial Printing: Gravure
2759 Commercial Printing
2761 Manifold Business Forms
2771 Greeting Card Publishing
2782 Blankbooks & Looseleaf Binders
2789 Bookbinding
2791 Typesetting
2796 Platemaking & Related Svcs

28 chemicals and allied products
2812 Alkalies & Chlorine
2813 Industrial Gases
2816 Inorganic Pigments
2819 Indl Inorganic Chemicals, NEC
2821 Plastics, Mtrls & Nonvulcanizable Elastomers
2822 Synthetic Rubber (Vulcanizable Elastomers)
2823 Cellulosic Man-Made Fibers
2824 Synthetic Organic Fibers, Exc Cellulosic
2833 Medicinal Chemicals & Botanical Prdts
2834 Pharmaceuticals
2835 Diagnostic Substances
2836 Biological Prdts, Exc Diagnostic Substances
2841 Soap & Detergents
2842 Spec Cleaning, Polishing & Sanitation Preparations
2843 Surface Active & Finishing Agents, Sulfonated Oils
2844 Perfumes, Cosmetics & Toilet Preparations
2851 Paints, Varnishes, Lacquers, Enamels
2861 Gum & Wood Chemicals
2865 Cyclic-Crudes, Intermediates, Dyes & Org Pigments
2869 Industrial Organic Chemicals, NEC
2873 Nitrogenous Fertilizers
2874 Phosphatic Fertilizers
2875 Fertilizers, Mixing Only
2879 Pesticides & Agricultural Chemicals, NEC
2891 Adhesives & Sealants
2892 Explosives
2893 Printing Ink
2899 Chemical Preparations, NEC

29 petroleum refining and related industries
2911 Petroleum Refining
2951 Paving Mixtures & Blocks
2952 Asphalt Felts & Coatings
2992 Lubricating Oils & Greases

30 rubber and miscellaneous plastics products
3011 Tires & Inner Tubes
3021 Rubber & Plastic Footwear
3052 Rubber & Plastic Hose & Belting
3053 Gaskets, Packing & Sealing Devices
3061 Molded, Extruded & Lathe-Cut Rubber Mechanical

SIC INDEX

SIC NO	PRODUCT

Goods
3069 Fabricated Rubber Prdts, NEC
3081 Plastic Unsupported Sheet & Film
3082 Plastic Unsupported Profile Shapes
3083 Plastic Laminated Plate & Sheet
3084 Plastic Pipe
3085 Plastic Bottles
3086 Plastic Foam Prdts
3087 Custom Compounding Of Purchased Plastic Resins
3088 Plastic Plumbing Fixtures
3089 Plastic Prdts

31 leather and leather products

3111 Leather Tanning & Finishing
3131 Boot & Shoe Cut Stock & Findings
3142 House Slippers
3143 Men's Footwear, Exc Athletic
3144 Women's Footwear, Exc Athletic
3149 Footwear, NEC
3151 Leather Gloves & Mittens
3161 Luggage
3171 Handbags & Purses
3172 Personal Leather Goods
3199 Leather Goods, NEC

32 stone, clay, glass, and concrete products

3211 Flat Glass
3221 Glass Containers
3229 Pressed & Blown Glassware, NEC
3231 Glass Prdts Made Of Purchased Glass
3241 Cement, Hydraulic
3251 Brick & Structural Clay Tile
3253 Ceramic Tile
3255 Clay Refractories
3259 Structural Clay Prdts, NEC
3261 China Plumbing Fixtures & Fittings
3263 Earthenware, Whiteware, Table & Kitchen Articles
3264 Porcelain Electrical Splys
3269 Pottery Prdts, NEC
3271 Concrete Block & Brick
3272 Concrete Prdts
3273 Ready-Mixed Concrete
3275 Gypsum Prdts
3281 Cut Stone Prdts
3291 Abrasive Prdts
3292 Asbestos products
3295 Minerals & Earths: Ground Or Treated
3296 Mineral Wool
3297 Nonclay Refractories
3299 Nonmetallic Mineral Prdts, NEC

33 primary metal industries

3312 Blast Furnaces, Coke Ovens, Steel & Rolling Mills
3313 Electrometallurgical Prdts
3315 Steel Wire Drawing & Nails & Spikes
3316 Cold Rolled Steel Sheet, Strip & Bars
3317 Steel Pipe & Tubes
3321 Gray Iron Foundries
3322 Malleable Iron Foundries
3324 Steel Investment Foundries
3325 Steel Foundries, NEC
3331 Primary Smelting & Refining Of Copper
3334 Primary Production Of Aluminum
3339 Primary Nonferrous Metals, NEC
3341 Secondary Smelting & Refining Of Nonferrous Metals
3351 Rolling, Drawing & Extruding Of Copper
3353 Aluminum Sheet, Plate & Foil
3354 Aluminum Extruded Prdts
3355 Aluminum Rolling & Drawing, NEC
3356 Rolling, Drawing-Extruding Of Nonferrous Metals
3357 Nonferrous Wire Drawing
3363 Aluminum Die Castings
3364 Nonferrous Die Castings, Exc Aluminum
3365 Aluminum Foundries
3366 Copper Foundries
3369 Nonferrous Foundries: Castings, NEC
3398 Metal Heat Treating
3399 Primary Metal Prdts, NEC

34 fabricated metal products, except machinery and transportation equipment

3411 Metal Cans
3412 Metal Barrels, Drums, Kegs & Pails
3421 Cutlery
3423 Hand & Edge Tools
3425 Hand Saws & Saw Blades
3429 Hardware, NEC
3431 Enameled Iron & Metal Sanitary Ware
3432 Plumbing Fixture Fittings & Trim, Brass
3433 Heating Eqpt
3441 Fabricated Structural Steel
3442 Metal Doors, Sash, Frames, Molding & Trim
3443 Fabricated Plate Work
3444 Sheet Metal Work
3446 Architectural & Ornamental Metal Work
3448 Prefabricated Metal Buildings & Cmpnts
3449 Misc Structural Metal Work
3451 Screw Machine Prdts
3452 Bolts, Nuts, Screws, Rivets & Washers
3462 Iron & Steel Forgings
3463 Nonferrous Forgings
3465 Automotive Stampings
3466 Crowns & Closures
3469 Metal Stampings, NEC
3471 Electroplating, Plating, Polishing, Anodizing & Coloring
3479 Coating & Engraving, NEC
3482 Small Arms Ammunition
3484 Small Arms
3489 Ordnance & Access, NEC
3491 Industrial Valves
3492 Fluid Power Valves & Hose Fittings
3493 Steel Springs, Except Wire
3494 Valves & Pipe Fittings, NEC
3495 Wire Springs
3496 Misc Fabricated Wire Prdts
3497 Metal Foil & Leaf
3498 Fabricated Pipe & Pipe Fittings
3499 Fabricated Metal Prdts, NEC

35 industrial and commercial machinery and computer equipment

3511 Steam; Gas & Hydraulic Turbines & Engines
3519 Internal Combustion Engines, NEC
3523 Farm Machinery & Eqpt
3524 Garden, Lawn Tractors & Eqpt
3531 Construction Machinery & Eqpt
3532 Mining Machinery & Eqpt
3533 Oil Field Machinery & Eqpt
3534 Elevators & Moving Stairways
3535 Conveyors & Eqpt
3536 Hoists, Cranes & Monorails
3537 Indl Trucks, Tractors, Trailers & Stackers
3541 Machine Tools: Cutting
3542 Machine Tools: Forming
3543 Industrial Patterns
3544 Dies, Tools, Jigs, Fixtures & Indl Molds
3545 Machine Tool Access
3546 Power Hand Tools
3547 Rolling Mill Machinery & Eqpt
3548 Welding Apparatus
3549 Metalworking Machinery, NEC
3552 Textile Machinery
3553 Woodworking Machinery
3554 Paper Inds Machinery
3555 Printing Trades Machinery & Eqpt
3556 Food Prdts Machinery
3559 Special Indl Machinery, NEC
3561 Pumps & Pumping Eqpt
3562 Ball & Roller Bearings
3563 Air & Gas Compressors
3564 Blowers & Fans
3565 Packaging Machinery
3566 Speed Changers, Drives & Gears
3567 Indl Process Furnaces & Ovens
3568 Mechanical Power Transmission Eqpt, NEC
3569 Indl Machinery & Eqpt, NEC
3571 Electronic Computers
3572 Computer Storage Devices
3575 Computer Terminals
3577 Computer Peripheral Eqpt, NEC
3578 Calculating & Accounting Eqpt
3579 Office Machines, NEC
3581 Automatic Vending Machines
3582 Commercial Laundry, Dry Clean & Pressing Mchs
3585 Air Conditioning & Heating Eqpt
3586 Measuring & Dispensing Pumps
3589 Service Ind Machines, NEC
3592 Carburetors, Pistons, Rings & Valves
3593 Fluid Power Cylinders & Actuators
3594 Fluid Power Pumps & Motors
3596 Scales & Balances, Exc Laboratory
3599 Machinery & Eqpt, Indl & Commercial, NEC

36 electronic and other electrical equipment and components, except computer

3612 Power, Distribution & Specialty Transformers
3613 Switchgear & Switchboard Apparatus
3621 Motors & Generators
3624 Carbon & Graphite Prdts
3625 Relays & Indl Controls
3629 Electrical Indl Apparatus, NEC
3631 Household Cooking Eqpt
3632 Household Refrigerators & Freezers
3633 Household Laundry Eqpt
3634 Electric Household Appliances
3635 Household Vacuum Cleaners
3639 Household Appliances, NEC
3641 Electric Lamps
3643 Current-Carrying Wiring Devices
3644 Noncurrent-Carrying Wiring Devices
3645 Residential Lighting Fixtures
3646 Commercial, Indl & Institutional Lighting Fixtures
3647 Vehicular Lighting Eqpt
3648 Lighting Eqpt, NEC
3651 Household Audio & Video Eqpt
3652 Phonograph Records & Magnetic Tape
3661 Telephone & Telegraph Apparatus
3663 Radio & T V Communications, Systs & Eqpt, Broadcast/Studio
3669 Communications Eqpt, NEC
3671 Radio & T V Receiving Electron Tubes
3672 Printed Circuit Boards
3674 Semiconductors
3676 Electronic Resistors
3677 Electronic Coils & Transformers
3678 Electronic Connectors
3679 Electronic Components, NEC
3691 Storage Batteries
3692 Primary Batteries: Dry & Wet
3694 Electrical Eqpt For Internal Combustion Engines
3695 Recording Media
3699 Electrical Machinery, Eqpt & Splys, NEC

37 transportation equipment

3711 Motor Vehicles & Car Bodies
3713 Truck & Bus Bodies
3714 Motor Vehicle Parts & Access
3715 Truck Trailers
3716 Motor Homes
3721 Aircraft
3724 Aircraft Engines & Engine Parts
3728 Aircraft Parts & Eqpt, NEC
3731 Shipbuilding & Repairing
3732 Boat Building & Repairing
3743 Railroad Eqpt
3751 Motorcycles, Bicycles & Parts
3761 Guided Missiles & Space Vehicles
3764 Guided Missile/Space Vehicle Propulsion Units & parts
3769 Guided Missile/Space Vehicle Parts & Eqpt, NEC
3792 Travel Trailers & Campers
3795 Tanks & Tank Components
3799 Transportation Eqpt, NEC

38 measuring, analyzing and controlling instruments; photographic, medical an

3812 Search, Detection, Navigation & Guidance Systs & Instrs
3821 Laboratory Apparatus & Furniture
3822 Automatic Temperature Controls
3823 Indl Instruments For Meas, Display & Control
3824 Fluid Meters & Counters
3825 Instrs For Measuring & Testing Electricity
3826 Analytical Instruments
3827 Optical Instruments
3829 Measuring & Controlling Devices, NEC
3841 Surgical & Medical Instrs & Apparatus
3842 Orthopedic, Prosthetic & Surgical Appliances/Splys
3843 Dental Eqpt & Splys
3844 X-ray Apparatus & Tubes
3845 Electromedical & Electrotherapeutic Apparatus
3851 Ophthalmic Goods
3861 Photographic Eqpt & Splys
3873 Watch & Clock Devices & Parts

39 miscellaneous manufacturing industries

3911 Jewelry: Precious Metal
3914 Silverware, Plated & Stainless Steel Ware
3915 Jewelers Findings & Lapidary Work
3931 Musical Instruments
3942 Dolls & Stuffed Toys
3944 Games, Toys & Children's Vehicles
3949 Sporting & Athletic Goods, NEC
3951 Pens & Mechanical Pencils
3952 Lead Pencils, Crayons & Artist's Mtrls
3953 Marking Devices
3955 Carbon Paper & Inked Ribbons
3961 Costume Jewelry & Novelties
3965 Fasteners, Buttons, Needles & Pins
3991 Brooms & Brushes
3993 Signs & Advertising Displays
3995 Burial Caskets

SIC INDEX

SIC NO	PRODUCT
3996	Linoleum & Hard Surface Floor Coverings, NEC
3999	Manufacturing Industries, NEC

73 business services

SIC NO	PRODUCT
7372	Prepackaged Software

76 miscellaneous repair services

SIC NO	PRODUCT
7692	Welding Repair
7694	Armature Rewinding Shops

SIC SECTION

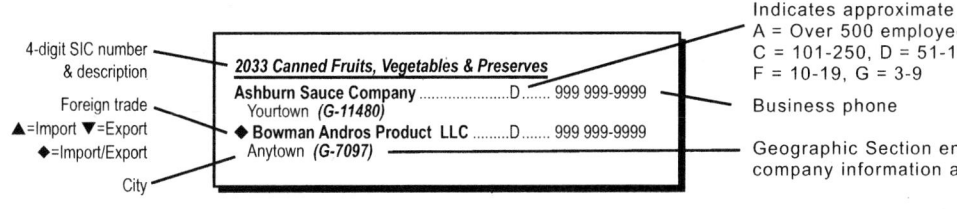

- 4-digit SIC number & description
- Foreign trade ▲=Import ▼=Export ◆=Import/Export
- City
- Indicates approximate employment figure A = Over 500 employees, B = 251-500 C = 101-250, D = 51-100, E = 20-50 F = 10-19, G = 3-9
- Business phone
- Geographic Section entry number where full company information appears.

See footnotes for symbols and codes identification.

- The SIC codes in this section are from the latest Standard Industrial Classification manual published by the U.S. Government's Office of Management and Budget. For more information regarding SICs, see the Explanatory Notes.
- Companies may be listed under multiple classifications.

10 METAL MINING

1011 Iron Ores
Cleveland-Cliffs Inc ....A 906 475-3547
  Ishpeming *(G-8343)*
Constine Inc ....E 989 723-6043
  Owosso *(G-12284)*
Empire Iron Mining Partnership ....A 906 475-3600
  Palmer *(G-12381)*
Tilden Mining Company LC ....A 906 475-3400
  Ishpeming *(G-8354)*

1021 Copper Ores
Copperwood Resources Inc ....F 906 229-3115
  Wakefield *(G-16848)*
Eagle Mine LLC ....B 906 339-7000
  Champion *(G-2602)*
◆ Trelleborg Corporation ....G 269 639-9891
  South Haven *(G-14778)*

1031 Lead & Zinc Ores
Lee Industries Inc ....E 231 777-2537
  Muskegon *(G-11365)*
National Zinc Processors Inc ....F 269 926-1161
  Benton Harbor *(G-1535)*
◆ Trelleborg Corporation ....G 269 639-9891
  South Haven *(G-14778)*

1041 Gold Ores
◆ Trelleborg Corporation ....G 269 639-9891
  South Haven *(G-14778)*

1044 Silver Ores
◆ Trelleborg Corporation ....G 269 639-9891
  South Haven *(G-14778)*

1081 Metal Mining Svcs
Battjes Boring Inc ....G 616 363-1969
  Grand Rapids *(G-6205)*
Makaveli Cnstr & Assoc Inc ....G 810 892-3412
  Detroit *(G-4217)*
Meridian Lightweight Tech Inc ....G 248 663-8100
  Plymouth *(G-12690)*
Minerals Processing Corp ....G 906 352-4024
  Menominee *(G-10751)*
URS Energy & Construction Inc ....C 989 642-4190
  Hemlock *(G-7464)*

1099 Metal Ores, NEC
Arconic Inc ....G 231 894-5686
  Whitehall *(G-17662)*

12 COAL MINING

1221 Bituminous Coal & Lignite: Surface Mining
◆ Lotus International Company ....A 734 245-0140
  Canton *(G-2394)*
Silver Slate LLC ....E 248 486-3989
  Milford *(G-10985)*

1241 Coal Mining Svcs
Peak Manufacturing Inc ....E 517 769-6900
  Pleasant Lake *(G-12553)*

13 OIL AND GAS EXTRACTION

1311 Crude Petroleum & Natural Gas
A1 Utility Contractor Inc ....D 989 324-8581
  Evart *(G-4877)*
Aztec Producing Co Inc ....G 269 792-0505
  Wayland *(G-17398)*
Bailer and De Shaw ....G 989 684-3610
  Kawkawlin *(G-8970)*
Black River Oil Corp ....G 231 723-6502
  Manistee *(G-10416)*
Blarney Castle Inc ....G 231 864-3111
  Bear Lake *(G-1376)*
Christian Oil Company ....F 269 673-2218
  Allegan *(G-152)*
Cima Energy LP ....G 231 941-0633
  Traverse City *(G-15941)*
Columbus Oil & Gas LLC ....G 810 385-9140
  Burtchville *(G-2140)*
Dart Energy Corporation ....F 231 885-1665
  Mesick *(G-10769)*
Devonian Energy Inc ....G 989 732-9400
  Gaylord *(G-5855)*
Dicks Sporting Goods Inc ....G 248 581-8028
  Troy *(G-16318)*
DTE Energy Co ....F 616 632-2663
  Grand Rapids *(G-6362)*
▼ DTE Energy Company ....E 313 235-4000
  Detroit *(G-4019)*
DTE Energy Trust II ....G 313 235-8822
  Detroit *(G-4021)*
Federated Oil & Gas Prpts Inc ....G 231 929-4466
  Traverse City *(G-15970)*
Force Energy Inc ....G 989 732-0724
  Gaylord *(G-5858)*
Goodale Enterprises LLC ....G 616 453-7690
  Grand Rapids *(G-6448)*
Jackhill Oil Company ....G 734 994-6599
  Ann Arbor *(G-509)*
Jordan Exploration Co LLC ....F 231 935-4220
  Traverse City *(G-16015)*
Kelly Oil & Gas Inc ....G 231 929-0591
  Traverse City *(G-16017)*
Lease Management Inc ....G 989 773-5948
  Mount Pleasant *(G-11202)*
Linn Energy Inc ....E 231 922-7302
  Traverse City *(G-16026)*
Mack Oil Corporation ....G 231 590-5903
  Traverse City *(G-16030)*
McNic Oil & Gas Properties ....G 313 256-5500
  Detroit *(G-4223)*
Merit Energy Company ....G 989 685-3446
  Rose City *(G-13764)*
Merit Energy Company LLC ....E 231 258-6401
  Kalkaska *(G-8950)*
Michael R Burzynski ....G 989 732-1820
  Gaylord *(G-5881)*
Michigan Reef Development ....G 989 288-2172
  Durand *(G-4609)*
Miller Exploration Company ....F 231 941-0004
  Traverse City *(G-16037)*
Oil City Venture Inc ....G 989 832-8071
  Midland *(G-10899)*
Omega Resources Inc ....G 231 941-4838
  Traverse City *(G-16059)*
Omimex Energy Inc ....F 231 845-7358
  Ludington *(G-10077)*
Omimex Energy Inc ....G 517 628-2820
  Mason *(G-10650)*
Option Energy LLC ....F 269 329-4317
  Traverse City *(G-16061)*
Petroleum Resources Inc ....G 586 752-7856
  Romeo *(G-13635)*
Presidium Energy LLC ....G 231 933-6373
  Traverse City *(G-16076)*
Refinery Corporation America ....G 877 881-0336
  Harper Woods *(G-7303)*
Sappington Crude Oil Inc ....G 989 345-1052
  West Branch *(G-17521)*
SD Oil Enterprises Inc ....G 248 688-1419
  Warren *(G-17236)*
Shell Oil Company ....G 248 693-0036
  Lake Orion *(G-9160)*
Somoco Inc ....E 231 946-0200
  Traverse City *(G-16109)*
Southwestern Mich Dust Ctrl ....F 269 521-7638
  Bloomingdale *(G-1814)*
Speedway LLC ....F 586 727-2638
  Richmond *(G-13271)*
Speedway LLC ....G 313 291-3710
  Taylor *(G-15771)*
Speedway LLC ....F 231 775-8101
  Cadillac *(G-2278)*
Summit-Reed City Inc ....E 989 433-5716
  Rosebush *(G-13765)*
Tolas Oil Gas Exploration Co ....G 989 772-2599
  Mount Pleasant *(G-11233)*
Trendwell Energy Corporation ....F 616 866-5024
  Rockford *(G-13594)*
Tronox Incorporated ....G 231 328-4986
  Merritt *(G-10765)*
Wepco Energy LLC ....G 231 932-8615
  Traverse City *(G-16142)*
West Bay Exploration Company ......F 231 946-3529
  Traverse City *(G-16143)*
William R Hall Kimberly ....G 989 426-4605
  Gladwin *(G-5939)*

1321 Natural Gas Liquids
Altagas Marketing (us) Inc ....G 810 887-4105
  Port Huron *(G-12885)*
Altagas Power Holdings US Inc ......G 810 887-4105
  Port Huron *(G-12886)*
Everest Energy Fund L L C ....G 586 445-2300
  Warren *(G-17023)*
Genesee Valley Petroleum ....G 231 946-8630
  Traverse City *(G-15977)*
Tronox Incorporated ....G 231 328-4986
  Merritt *(G-10765)*

1381 Drilling Oil & Gas Wells
5 Star Drctional Drlg Svcs Ind ....G 231 263-2050
  Kingsley *(G-9069)*
Advanced Energy Services LLC ......D 231 369-2602
  South Boardman *(G-14748)*
Alexander Directional Boring ....G 989 362-9506
  East Tawas *(G-4686)*
Alpha Directional Boring ....G 586 405-0171
  Davisburg *(G-3624)*
Arrow Drilling Services LLC ....E 231 258-4596
  Kalkaska *(G-8936)*
Bigard & Huggard Drilling Inc ....D 989 775-6608
  Mount Pleasant *(G-11178)*
Bob Fleming Well Drilling ....G 248 627-3511
  Ortonville *(G-12195)*
Crystal Flash Inc ....G 269 781-8221
  Marshall *(G-10565)*
Diamondbck-Drctional Drlg LLC .....F 231 943-3000
  Traverse City *(G-15956)*

13 OIL AND GAS EXTRACTION — SIC SECTION

Eis Inc .... F 734 266-6500
 Livonia *(G-9722)*
Energy Acquisition Corp .... F 517 339-0249
 Holt *(G-7911)*
Fortis Energy Services Inc .... E 231 258-4596
 Bloomfield Hills *(G-1766)*
Fortis Energy Services Inc .... D 248 283-7100
 Troy *(G-16370)*
Gage Well Drilling Inc .... G 989 389-4372
 Saint Helen *(G-14278)*
GTM Steamer Service Inc .... G 989 732-7678
 Gaylord *(G-5863)*
Industrial Control Systems LLC ...... G 269 689-3241
 Sturgis *(G-15607)*
Key Energy Services Inc .... E 231 258-9637
 Kalkaska *(G-8947)*
Michiwest Energy Inc .... G 989 772-2107
 Mount Pleasant *(G-11206)*
Newton Well Service Inc .... G 269 945-5084
 Hastings *(G-7422)*
Phoenix Technology Svcs USA .... F 231 995-0100
 Traverse City *(G-16067)*
R M Brewer & Son Inc .... G 517 531-3022
 Parma *(G-12393)*
Rafalski CPA .... G 248 689-1685
 Troy *(G-16575)*
RC Directional Boring Inc .... F 517 545-4887
 Howell *(G-8088)*
▲ S and P Drctnal Boring Svc LLC ...... G 989 832-7716
 Midland *(G-10910)*
Smith Well & Pump .... G 269 721-3118
 Battle Creek *(G-1250)*
Srw Inc .... F 989 732-8884
 Traverse City *(G-16110)*
Srw Inc .... F 989 269-8528
 Bad Axe *(G-1071)*
Stovall Well Drilling Co .... G 616 364-4144
 Grand Rapids *(G-6894)*
Thompson Well Drilling .... G 616 754-5032
 Rockford *(G-13593)*
Tip Top Drilling LLC .... G 616 291-8006
 Sparta *(G-15117)*
Walters Plumbing Company .... F 269 962-6250
 Battle Creek *(G-1266)*

1382 Oil & Gas Field Exploration Svcs

Arbor Operating LLC .... G 231 941-2237
 Traverse City *(G-15896)*
Baker Hghes Olfld Oprtions LLC ..... F 989 773-7992
 Mount Pleasant *(G-11175)*
Baygeo Inc .... E 231 941-7660
 Traverse City *(G-15909)*
Beckman Production Svcs Inc .... E 989 539-7126
 Harrison *(G-7309)*
Bobcat Oil & Gas Inc .... G 989 426-4375
 Gladwin *(G-5924)*
▼ CMS Enterprises Company .... C 517 788-0550
 Jackson *(G-8413)*
Core Energy LLC .... G 231 946-2419
 Traverse City *(G-15948)*
Dart Energy Corporation .... F 231 885-1665
 Mesick *(G-10769)*
Dcr Services & Cnstr Inc .... F 313 297-6544
 Detroit *(G-3962)*
Don Yohe Enterprises Inc .... F 586 784-5556
 Armada *(G-718)*
DTE Gas & Oil Company .... E 231 995-4000
 Traverse City *(G-15958)*
Dynamic Development Inc .... G 231 723-8318
 Manistee *(G-10419)*
Emerson Geophysical LLC .... E 231 943-1400
 Traverse City *(G-15963)*
Energy Exploration .... G 248 579-6531
 Novi *(G-11884)*
Express Care of South Lyon .... G 248 437-6919
 South Lyon *(G-14791)*
Forward Distributing Inc .... E 989 846-4501
 Standish *(G-15218)*
Geostar Corporation .... E 989 773-7050
 Mount Pleasant *(G-11194)*
Howard Energy Co Inc .... E 231 995-7850
 Traverse City *(G-15999)*
HRF Exploration & Prod LLC .... F 989 732-6950
 Gaylord *(G-5865)*
Innova Exploration Inc .... G 231 929-3985
 Traverse City *(G-16004)*
J R Productions Inc .... G 989 732-2905
 Gaylord *(G-5867)*
John T Stoliker Enterprises .... G 586 727-1402
 Columbus *(G-3379)*

Loneys Welding & Excvtg Inc .... G 231 328-4408
 Merritt *(G-10764)*
Maness Petroleum Corp .... G 989 773-5475
 Mount Pleasant *(G-11203)*
Martec Land Services Inc .... F 231 929-3971
 Traverse City *(G-16033)*
Maverick Exploration Prod Inc .... G 231 929-3923
 Traverse City *(G-16034)*
Meridian Energy Corporation .... F 517 339-8444
 Haslett *(G-7397)*
Miller Energy Inc .... F 269 352-5960
 Kalamazoo *(G-8828)*
Miracle Petroleum LLC .... G 231 946-8090
 Traverse City *(G-16039)*
Muzyl Oil Corp .... G 989 732-8100
 Gaylord *(G-5884)*
OIL Energy Corp .... F 231 933-3600
 Traverse City *(G-16054)*
Patrick Exploration Company .... G 517 787-6633
 Jackson *(G-8547)*
Penin Oil & Gas Compan Michiga .. G 616 676-2090
 Ada *(G-26)*
Pinnacle Energy LLC .... G 248 623-6091
 Clarkston *(G-2945)*
Rowe & Associates .... G 231 932-9716
 Traverse City *(G-16097)*
Savoy Exploration Inc .... G 231 941-9552
 Traverse City *(G-16098)*
Schmude Oil Inc .... G 231 947-4410
 Traverse City *(G-16099)*
Sturak Brothers Inc .... G 269 345-2929
 Kalamazoo *(G-8900)*
Unoco Exploration Co .... G 231 829-3235
 Leroy *(G-9539)*
Wara Construction Company LLC . D 248 299-2410
 Rochester Hills *(G-13540)*
Ward-Williston Company .... F 248 594-6622
 Bloomfield *(G-1737)*
Wepco Energy LLC .... G 231 932-8615
 Traverse City *(G-16142)*
West Bay Geophysical Inc .... F 231 946-3529
 Traverse City *(G-16144)*
Western Land Services Inc .... D 231 843-8878
 Ludington *(G-10088)*
Whiting Petroleum Corporation ...... G 989 345-7903
 West Branch *(G-17529)*
Wolverine Gas and Oil Corp .... E 616 458-1150
 Grand Rapids *(G-6998)*

1389 Oil & Gas Field Svcs, NEC

1st Choice Trckg & Rentl Inc .... G 231 258-0417
 Kalkaska *(G-8935)*
5 By 5 LLC .... F 855 369-6757
 Traverse City *(G-15886)*
917 Chittock Street LLC .... F 866 945-0269
 Jackson *(G-9331)*
Acme Septic Tank Co .... F 989 684-3852
 Kawkawlin *(G-8969)*
Advanced Altrntive Sltions LLC ...... G 616 607-6956
 Wyoming *(G-17984)*
Ally Servicing LLC .... F 248 948-7702
 Detroit *(G-3859)*
Atlas Oil Transportation Inc .... F 800 878-2000
 Taylor *(G-15690)*
B & H Cementing Services Inc .... G 989 773-5975
 Mount Pleasant *(G-11172)*
B & H Tractor & Truck Inc .... G 989 773-5975
 Mount Pleasant *(G-11173)*
Bach Services & Mfg Co LLC .... E 231 263-2777
 Kingsley *(G-9070)*
Badger Pipe & Piling LLC .... F 989 965-0126
 Harrison *(G-7308)*
Baker Hghes Olfld Oprtions LLC .... G 989 772-1600
 Mount Pleasant *(G-11174)*
Baker Hghes Olfld Oprtions LLC .... F 989 773-7992
 Mount Pleasant *(G-11175)*
Baker Hughes A GE Company LLC . G 989 506-2167
 Mount Pleasant *(G-11176)*
Baker Hughes A GE Company LLC . G 989 732-2082
 Gaylord *(G-5849)*
Beckman Production Svcs Inc .... D 231 258-9524
 Kalkaska *(G-8939)*
Beckman Production Svcs Inc .... E 989 539-7126
 Harrison *(G-7309)*
Beckman Production Svcs Inc .... G 231 885-1665
 Mesick *(G-10766)*
Beckman Production Svcs Inc .... E 989 732-9341
 Gaylord *(G-5850)*
Bruno Wojcik .... G 989 785-5555
 Atlanta *(G-730)*

Burkholder Excavating Inc .... G 269 426-4177
 Sawyer *(G-14482)*
Central Mich Cmenting Svcs LLC .. G 989 775-0940
 Mount Pleasant *(G-11184)*
Central Michigan Tank Rental .... G 989 681-5963
 Saint Louis *(G-14360)*
Coil Drilling Technologies Inc .... G 989 773-6504
 Mount Pleasant *(G-11190)*
Columbus Oil & Gas LLC .... G 810 385-9140
 Burtchville *(G-2140)*
Concrete Lifters Inc .... G 616 669-0400
 Jenison *(G-8622)*
Cross Country Oilfld Svcs Inc .... G 337 366-3840
 Metamora *(G-10774)*
D & W Flow Testing Inc .... G 231 258-4926
 Kalkaska *(G-8940)*
Dama Tool & Gauge Company .... F 616 842-9631
 Norton Shores *(G-11747)*
Double Check Tools Service .... G 231 947-1632
 Williamsburg *(G-17711)*
DTE Energy Resources Inc .... C 313 297-4203
 Detroit *(G-4020)*
▼ DTE Energy Resources Inc .... D 734 302-4800
 Ann Arbor *(G-426)*
Eastport Group Inc .... F 989 732-0030
 Johannesburg *(G-8649)*
El Paso LLC .... G 231 587-0704
 Mancelona *(G-10389)*
Exodus Pressure Control .... G 231 258-8001
 Kalkaska *(G-8942)*
Field Tech Services Inc .... G 989 786-7046
 Lewiston *(G-9548)*
Fiore Construction .... G 517 404-0000
 Howell *(G-8041)*
Forsters and Sons Oil Change .... F 248 618-6860
 Waterford *(G-17345)*
Gas Recovery Systems LLC .... F 248 305-7774
 Northville *(G-11693)*
Gloria C Williams .... G 313 220-2735
 Southfield *(G-14922)*
Go Frac LLC .... E 817 731-0301
 Detroit *(G-4094)*
Grace Contracting Services LLC ... G 906 630-4680
 Mc Millan *(G-10685)*
Great Lakes Compression Inc .... E 989 786-3788
 Lewiston *(G-9549)*
Great Lakes Wellhead Inc .... G 231 943-9100
 Grawn *(G-7098)*
Greenlight Home Inspection Svc ... G 313 885-5616
 Saint Clair Shores *(G-14255)*
GTM Steamer Service Inc .... G 989 732-7678
 Gaylord *(G-5863)*
Guided Per Bus & Prof Svcs LLC ... G 248 567-2121
 Livonia *(G-9762)*
Harmonie International LLC .... E 248 737-9933
 Farmington Hills *(G-5017)*
Hobys Contracting .... G 989 631-4263
 Bentley *(G-1477)*
Integrity Sltons Feld Svcs Inc .... F 303 263-9522
 East Lansing *(G-4664)*
Jet Subsurface Rod Pumps Corp ... G 989 732-7513
 Gaylord *(G-5869)*
Jn Newman Construction LLC .... G 269 968-1290
 Springfield *(G-15194)*
JO Well Service and Tstg Inc .... G 989 772-4221
 Mount Pleasant *(G-11200)*
Jones Ray Well Servicing Inc .... E 989 832-8071
 Midland *(G-10877)*
Jr Larry Dudley .... G 313 721-3600
 Detroit *(G-4166)*
Jrj Energy Services LLC .... C 231 823-2171
 Stanwood *(G-15234)*
◆ Kadant Johnson LLC .... C 269 278-1715
 Three Rivers *(G-15867)*
Kdk Downhole Tooling LLC .... G 231 590-3137
 Williamsburg *(G-17714)*
Land Services Incorporated .... G 231 947-9400
 Traverse City *(G-16021)*
Lapeer Fuel Ventures Inc .... G 810 664-8770
 Lapeer *(G-9466)*
Lease Management Inc .... G 989 773-5948
 Mount Pleasant *(G-11202)*
Lgc Global Inc .... E 313 989-4141
 Detroit *(G-4202)*
Loshaw Bros Inc .... G 989 732-7263
 Gaylord *(G-5875)*
Maximum Oilfield Service Inc .... E 989 731-0099
 Elmira *(G-4791)*
McConnell & Scully Inc .... E 517 568-4104
 Homer *(G-7945)*

Melix Services Inc..................G....... 248 387-9303
Hamtramck *(G-7244)*
Meridian Contg & Excvtg LLC..................G....... 734 476-5933
Commerce Township *(G-3431)*
Michigan Wireline Service..................F....... 989 772-5075
Mount Pleasant *(G-11205)*
Mid State Oil Tools Inc..................E....... 989 773-4114
Mount Pleasant *(G-11207)*
Mikes Steamer Service Inc..................E....... 231 258-8500
Kalkaska *(G-8954)*
Miller Investment Company LLC..................G....... 231 933-3233
Traverse City *(G-16038)*
Northern A 1 Services Inc..................E....... 231 258-9961
Kalkaska *(G-8955)*
Northern Tank Truck Service..................G....... 989 732-7531
Gaylord *(G-5885)*
Oil Exchange 6 Inc..................G....... 734 641-4310
Inkster *(G-8230)*
Pelhams Construction LLC..................G....... 517 549-8276
Jonesville *(G-8666)*
Penin Oil & Gas Compan Michiga..................G....... 616 676-2090
Ada *(G-26)*
Phoenix Operating Company Inc..................G....... 231 929-7171
Williamsburg *(G-17719)*
Pioneer Oil Tools Inc..................G....... 989 644-6999
Mount Pleasant *(G-11218)*
Premier Casing Crews Inc..................G....... 989 775-7436
Mount Pleasant *(G-11220)*
Rcs Services Company LLC..................F....... 989 732-7999
Johannesburg *(G-8650)*
Red Carpet Capital Inc..................G....... 248 952-8583
Orchard Lake *(G-12169)*
Reid Contractors Inc..................G....... 906 632-2936
Dafter *(G-3620)*
Riverside Energy Michigan LLC..................E....... 231 995-4000
Traverse City *(G-16095)*
Rock Industries Inc..................E....... 248 338-2800
Bloomfield Hills *(G-1796)*
Rowsey Construction & Dev LLC..................G....... 313 675-2464
Detroit *(G-4348)*
Saginaw Valley Inst Mtls Inc..................G....... 989 496-2307
Midland *(G-10911)*
Sappington Crude Oil Inc..................G....... 989 345-1052
West Branch *(G-17521)*
Sappington Henry Machine & Tl..................E....... 989 345-0711
West Branch *(G-17522)*
Schunk Oil Field Service Inc..................G....... 517 676-8900
Mason *(G-10654)*
Seal Right Services Inc..................G....... 231 357-5595
Buckley *(G-2131)*
Sledgehammer Construction Inc..................G....... 313 478-5648
Detroit *(G-4365)*
Soli-Bond Inc..................G....... 989 684-9611
Bay City *(G-1359)*
Srw Inc..................F....... 989 732-8884
Traverse City *(G-16110)*
Srw Inc..................F....... 989 269-8528
Bad Axe *(G-1071)*
Stovall Well Drilling Co..................G....... 616 364-4144
Grand Rapids *(G-6894)*
Superior Inspection Svc..................G....... 231 258-9400
Kalkaska *(G-8959)*
Superior Mar & Envmtl Svcs LLC..................G....... 906 253-9448
Sault Sainte Marie *(G-14475)*
Target Oil Tools LLC..................G....... 231 258-4960
Kalkaska *(G-8960)*
Team Services LLC..................E....... 231 258-9130
Kalkaska *(G-8961)*
Team Spooling Services LLC..................G....... 231 258-9130
Kalkaska *(G-8962)*
Tims Underbody..................G....... 231 347-9146
Petoskey *(G-12477)*
TNT Well Service Ltd..................G....... 989 939-7098
Gaylord *(G-5896)*
Top Shelf Painter Inc..................G....... 586 465-0867
Fraser *(G-5739)*
Trend Services Company..................G....... 231 258-9951
Kalkaska *(G-8965)*
Tuscola Energy..................G....... 989 894-5815
Bay City *(G-1364)*
Uncle Eds Oil Shoppes Inc..................G....... 269 962-0999
Battle Creek *(G-1262)*
Unoco Exploration Co..................G....... 231 829-3235
Leroy *(G-9539)*
Verbio North America Corp..................G....... 866 306-4777
Livonia *(G-9989)*
Wara Construction Company LLC..................D....... 248 299-2410
Rochester Hills *(G-13540)*
Wellmaster Consulting Inc..................F....... 231 893-9266
Rothbury *(G-13896)*
Woder Construction Inc..................E....... 989 731-6371
Gaylord *(G-5900)*

14 MINING AND QUARRYING OF NONMETALLIC MINERALS, EXCEPT FUELS

1411 Dimension Stone

Doug Wirt Enterprises Inc..................G....... 989 684-5777
Bay City *(G-1305)*
▲ Levy Indiana Slag Co..................F....... 313 843-7200
Dearborn *(G-3733)*
Manigg Enterprises Inc..................F....... 989 356-4986
Alpena *(G-296)*
▲ Michigan Tile and Marble Co..................E....... 313 931-1700
Detroit *(G-4244)*
Northern Mich Aggregates LLC..................F....... 989 354-3502
Wixom *(G-17868)*
O-N Minerals Michigan Company..................C....... 989 734-2131
Rogers City *(G-13619)*
▲ Surface Encounters LLC..................D....... 586 566-7557
Macomb *(G-10164)*
Take Us-4-Granite Inc..................G....... 586 803-1305
Shelby Township *(G-14707)*
TNT Marble and Stone Inc..................G....... 248 887-8237
Hartland *(G-7394)*

1422 Crushed & Broken Limestone

Aggregate and Developing LLC..................G....... 269 217-5492
Allegan *(G-146)*
C & L Concrete..................G....... 231 829-3386
Tustin *(G-16709)*
Carmeuse Lime Inc..................E....... 906 484-2201
Cedarville *(G-2566)*
Carmeuse Lime Inc..................E....... 313 849-9268
River Rouge *(G-13274)*
Carmeuse Lime & Stone Inc..................G....... 989 734-2131
Rogers City *(G-13614)*
Carmeuse Lime & Stone Inc..................D....... 906 283-3456
Gulliver *(G-7211)*
Eggers Excavating LLC..................F....... 989 695-5205
Freeland *(G-5756)*
F G Cheney Limestone Co..................G....... 269 763-9541
Bellevue *(G-1454)*
Falcon Trucking Company..................E....... 989 656-2831
Bay Port *(G-1373)*
Flint Lime Industries Inc..................G....... 313 843-6050
Detroit *(G-4064)*
▲ Genesee Cut Stone & Marble Co..................E....... 810 743-1800
Flint *(G-5437)*
Grand Rapids Gravel Company..................F....... 616 538-9000
Grand Rapids *(G-6454)*
Great Lakes Aggregates LLC..................D....... 734 379-0311
South Rockwood *(G-14821)*
O N Minerals..................G....... 906 484-2201
Cedarville *(G-2569)*
O-N Minerals Michigan Company..................D....... 906 484-2201
Cedarville *(G-2570)*
O-N Minerals Michigan Company..................G....... 989 734-2131
Rogers City *(G-13618)*
O-N Minerals Michigan Company..................G....... 906 484-2201
Cedarville *(G-2571)*
O-N Minerals Michigan Company..................C....... 989 734-2131
Rogers City *(G-13619)*
Osborne Materials Company..................E....... 906 493-5211
Drummond Island *(G-4566)*
R E Glancy Inc..................E....... 989 362-0997
Tawas City *(G-15677)*
R E Glancy Inc..................G....... 989 876-6030
Tawas City *(G-15678)*
State Crushing Inc..................G....... 248 332-6210
Auburn Hills *(G-1002)*
Stoneco Inc..................E....... 734 587-7125
Maybee *(G-10673)*
Waanders Concrete Co..................E....... 269 673-6352
Allegan *(G-190)*

1423 Crushed & Broken Granite

▲ Genesee Cut Stone & Marble Co..................E....... 810 743-1800
Flint *(G-5437)*
Graniteonecom Inc..................G....... 616 452-8372
Grand Rapids *(G-6472)*

1429 Crushed & Broken Stone, NEC

American Aggregate Inc..................G....... 269 683-6160
Niles *(G-11594)*
Sandys Contracting..................G....... 810 629-2259
Fenton *(G-5237)*

1442 Construction Sand & Gravel

A & E Agg Inc..................F....... 248 547-4711
Berkley *(G-1577)*
A Lindberg & Sons Inc..................E....... 906 485-5705
Ishpeming *(G-8342)*
A Y Sand and Gravel..................G....... 313 779-4825
Romulus *(G-13645)*
Afgco Sand & Gravel Co Inc..................G....... 810 798-3293
Almont *(G-250)*
Aggregtes Excvtg Logistics LLC..................G....... 231 737-4949
Muskegon *(G-11264)*
Albrecht Sand & Gravel Co..................E....... 810 672-9272
Snover *(G-14742)*
Alpena Aggregate Inc..................F....... 989 595-2511
Alpena *(G-273)*
American Aggregate Inc..................G....... 269 683-6160
Niles *(G-11594)*
American Aggregates Mich Inc..................F....... 248 348-8511
Wixom *(G-17760)*
Bailey Sand & Gravel Co..................F....... 517 750-4889
Jackson *(G-8387)*
Barber Creek Sand & Gravel..................F....... 616 675-7619
Kent City *(G-8987)*
Bdk Group Northern Mich Inc..................E....... 574 875-5183
Charlevoix *(G-2609)*
Bechtel Sand & Gravel..................G....... 810 346-2041
Brown City *(G-2046)*
Bently Sand & Gravel..................G....... 810 629-6172
Fenton *(G-5189)*
Bischer Ready-Mix Inc..................G....... 989 479-3267
Ruth *(G-13987)*
Bouchey and Sons Inc..................G....... 989 588-4118
Farwell *(G-5158)*
Branch West Concrete Products..................F....... 989 345-0794
West Branch *(G-17507)*
Brewer Sand & Gravel Inc..................G....... 616 393-8990
Holland *(G-7577)*
Briggs Contracting..................G....... 989 687-7331
Sanford *(G-14448)*
Bunting Sand & Gravel Products..................E....... 989 345-2373
West Branch *(G-17508)*
Carr Brothers and Sons Inc..................E....... 517 629-3549
Albion *(G-117)*
Carr Brothers and Sons Inc..................F....... 517 531-3358
Albion *(G-118)*
Cheboygan Cement Products Inc..................E....... 231 627-5631
Cheboygan *(G-2677)*
Chippewa Stone & Gravel Inc..................G....... 231 867-5757
Rodney *(G-13612)*
Cliffs Sand & Gravel Inc..................G....... 989 422-3463
Houghton Lake *(G-7989)*
Crandell Bros Trucking Co..................E....... 517 543-2930
Charlotte *(G-2644)*
Delhi Leasing Inc..................G....... 517 694-8578
Holt *(G-7910)*
Downriver Crushed Concrete..................G....... 734 283-1833
Taylor *(G-15708)*
Elmers Crane and Dozer Inc..................C....... 231 943-3443
Traverse City *(G-15962)*
Falcon Trucking Company..................G....... 313 843-7200
Dearborn *(G-3704)*
Falcon Trucking Company..................E....... 989 656-2831
Bay Port *(G-1373)*
Falcon Trucking Company..................F....... 248 634-9471
Davisburg *(G-3633)*
Fenton Sand & Gravel Inc..................G....... 810 750-4293
Fenton *(G-5213)*
Fidelis Contracting LLC..................G....... 313 361-1000
Detroit *(G-4057)*
Finch Sand & Gravel LLC..................G....... 734 439-1044
Milan *(G-10937)*
Flushing Sand and Gravel..................G....... 810 577-8260
Flint *(G-5431)*
Frisbie Sand & Gravel..................G....... 269 432-3379
Colon *(G-3372)*
Fritz Enterprises..................G....... 734 283-7272
Trenton *(G-16154)*
Fuoss Gravel Company..................F....... 989 725-2084
Owosso *(G-12292)*
Fyke Washed Sand Gravel..................G....... 248 547-4714
Berkley *(G-1583)*
Gale Briggs Inc..................G....... 517 543-1320
Charlotte *(G-2651)*
Genesis Sand and Gravel Inc..................G....... 313 587-8530
West Bloomfield *(G-17477)*
Genoak Materials Inc..................G....... 810 742-0050
Burton *(G-2155)*

SIC

14 MINING AND QUARRYING OF NONMETALLIC MINERALS, EXCEPT FUELS

Genoak Materials Inc ....C 248 634-8276
 Holly (G-7880)
Gerken Materials Inc ....G 517 567-4406
 Waldron (G-16858)
Grand Rapids Gravel Company ....F 616 538-9000
 Belmont (G-1462)
Grand Rapids Gravel Company ....F 616 538-9000
 Grand Rapids (G-6454)
Grifco Inc ....G 989 352-7965
 Lakeview (G-9173)
Halliday Sand & Gravel Inc ....E 989 422-3463
 Houghton Lake (G-7990)
Heritage Resources Inc ....G 616 554-9888
 Caledonia (G-2298)
High Grade Materials Company ....E 616 754-5545
 Greenville (G-7138)
Hubscher & Son Inc ....G 989 773-5369
 Mount Pleasant (G-11196)
Hubscher & Son Inc ....G 989 875-2151
 Sumner (G-15642)
Huizenga Gravel Company Inc ....F 616 772-6241
 Zeeland (G-18156)
Huizenga Gravel Company Inc ....F 616 457-1030
 Jenison (G-8629)
Ironwood Ready Mix & Trucking ....G 906 932-4531
 Ironwood (G-8331)
J T Express Ltd ....G 810 724-6471
 Brown City (G-2052)
Jack Millikin Inc ....G 989 348-8411
 Grayling (G-7109)
Jeff Brown Sand & Gravel ....G 517 445-2700
 Clayton (G-3008)
John R Sand & Gravel Co Inc ....G 810 678-3715
 Metamora (G-10777)
Kasson Sand & Gravel Co Inc ....F 231 228-5455
 Maple City (G-10461)
Ken Measel Supply Inc ....G 810 798-3293
 Almont (G-260)
Koenig Sand & Gravel LLC ....G 248 628-2711
 Oxford (G-12354)
Kurtz Gravel Company Inc ....E 810 787-6543
 Farmington Hills (G-5040)
Lafarge North America Inc ....F 703 480-3600
 Dundee (G-4591)
Lc Materials ....E 231 839-4319
 Lake City (G-9091)
Lc Materials ....G 231 825-2473
 Cadillac (G-2260)
Lyon Sand & Gravel Co ....G 313 843-7200
 Dearborn (G-3734)
Lyon Sand & Gravel Co ....D 248 348-8511
 Wixom (G-17848)
M-52 Sand & Gravel LLC ....G 734 453-3695
 Plymouth (G-12680)
M-57 Aggregate Company ....G 810 639-7516
 Montrose (G-11103)
Maple Valley Concrete Products ....G 517 852-1900
 Nashville (G-11460)
Marsack Sand & Gravel Inc ....F 586 293-4414
 Roseville (G-13829)
Mbcd Inc ....E 517 484-4426
 Lansing (G-9395)
Michiana Aggregate Inc ....G 269 695-7669
 Niles (G-11626)
Michigan Aggr Sand/Gravel Haul ....F 231 258-8237
 Kalkaska (G-8952)
Miller Sand & Gravel Company ....G 269 672-5601
 Hopkins (G-7959)
Modern Industries Inc ....E 810 767-3330
 Flint (G-5469)
Morris Excavating Inc ....F 269 483-7773
 White Pigeon (G-17654)
Mottes Materials Inc ....E 906 265-9955
 Iron River (G-8316)
Natural Aggregates Corporation ....F 248 685-1502
 Milford (G-10975)
Newark Gravel Company ....F 810 796-3072
 Dryden (G-4570)
Nivers Sand Gravel ....F 231 743-6126
 Marion (G-10492)
Nugent Sand Company Inc ....E 231 755-1686
 Norton Shores (G-11785)
Parker Excvtg Grav & Recycle ....F 616 784-1681
 Comstock Park (G-3505)
R and Js Gravel ....G 906 663-4571
 Bessemer (G-1606)
R E Glancy Inc ....G 989 876-6010
 Tawas City (G-15678)
R H Huhtala Aggregates Inc ....G 906 524-7758
 Lanse (G-9200)

Round Lake Sand & Gravel Inc ....G 517 467-4458
 Addison (G-38)
Ruppe Manufacturing Company ....E 906 932-3540
 Ironwood (G-8339)
◆ Saginaw Rock Products Co ....E 989 754-6589
 Saginaw (G-14144)
Sand Products Wisconsin LLC ....G 231 722-6691
 Muskegon (G-11418)
Sandman Inc ....G 248 652-3432
 Troy (G-16593)
Schultz Sand Gravel LLC ....G 269 720-7225
 Plainwell (G-12544)
▲ Searles Construction Inc ....G 989 224-3297
 Saint Johns (G-14295)
Sebewa Sand & Gravel LLC ....G 517 647-4296
 Portland (G-13067)
Simmons Gravel Co ....G 616 754-7073
 Greenville (G-7153)
Snider Construction Inc ....G 231 537-4851
 Levering (G-9546)
South Flint Gravel Inc ....G 810 232-8911
 Holly (G-7897)
South Hill Sand and Gravel ....G 248 828-1726
 Troy (G-16614)
South Hill Sand and Gravel ....G 248 685-7020
 Milford (G-10986)
South Kent Gravel Inc ....E 269 795-3500
 Middleville (G-10807)
Southwest Gravel Inc ....G 269 673-4665
 Allegan (G-188)
Stansley Mineral Resources Inc ....G 517 456-6310
 Clinton (G-3025)
Summers Road Gravel & Dev LLC ....G 810 798-8533
 Almont (G-268)
Technisand Inc ....D 269 465-5833
 Benton Harbor (G-1554)
Tip Top Gravel Co Inc ....G 616 897-8342
 Ada (G-31)
Top OMichigan Reclaimers Inc ....G 989 705-7983
 Gaylord (G-5897)
Tri County Sand and Stone Inc ....G 231 331-6549
 Alden (G-137)
Tri-City Aggregates Inc ....E 248 634-8276
 Holly (G-7900)
Trillacorpe/Bk LLC ....G 248 433-0585
 Bingham Farms (G-1662)
Trp Enterprises Inc ....G 810 329-4027
 East China (G-4625)
Van Sloten Enterprises Inc ....F 906 635-5151
 Sault Sainte Marie (G-14477)
Vermeulen & Associates Inc ....G 616 291-1255
 Grand Rapids (G-6966)
Waanders Concrete Co ....G 269 673-6352
 Allegan (G-190)
Weber Sand and Gravel Inc ....F 248 373-0900
 Lake Orion (G-9169)

1446 Industrial Sand

Atlantic Precision Pdts Inc ....F 586 532-9420
 Shelby Township (G-14550)
Barnes International ....G 586 978-2880
 Sterling Heights (G-15272)
Cabot Corporation ....E 989 495-2113
 Midland (G-10821)
Carrollton Paving Co ....F 989 752-7139
 Saginaw (G-14012)
Eggers Excavating LLC ....F 989 695-5205
 Freeland (G-5756)
Fairmount Santrol Inc ....E 800 255-7263
 Benton Harbor (G-1497)
Sand Products Corporation ....G 906 292-5432
 Moran (G-11108)
Sargent Sand Co ....G 989 792-8734
 Midland (G-10912)
Standard Sand Corporation ....G 616 538-3667
 Grand Haven (G-6083)

1474 Potash, Soda & Borate Minerals

Cargill Incorporated ....D 810 989-7242
 Hersey (G-7471)
Mosiac Potash Hersey LLC ....G 231 832-3755
 Hersey (G-7474)

1479 Chemical & Fertilizer Mining

Morton Salt Inc ....F 231 398-0758
 Manistee (G-10431)

1481 Nonmetallic Minerals Svcs, Except Fuels

Aquila Resources Inc ....G 906 352-4024
 Menominee (G-10724)
Bourque H James & Assoc Inc ....G 906 635-9191
 Brimley (G-2013)
Detroit Salt Company LC ....E 313 554-0456
 Detroit (G-4001)

1499 Miscellaneous Nonmetallic Mining

Bay-Houston Towing Company ....E 810 648-2210
 Sandusky (G-14430)
Discovery Gold Corp ....G 269 429-7002
 Stevensville (G-15564)
Eggers Excavating LLC ....F 989 695-5205
 Freeland (G-5756)
J M Longyear Heirs Inc ....G 906 228-7960
 Marquette (G-10535)
Markham Peat Corp ....F 800 851-7230
 Lakeview (G-9175)
Michigan Gypsum Co ....F 989 792-8734
 Midland (G-10885)

20 FOOD AND KINDRED PRODUCTS

2011 Meat Packing Plants

A & R Packing Co Inc ....E 734 422-2060
 Livonia (G-9618)
Alto Meat Processing ....G 616 868-6080
 Alto (G-322)
Bellinger Packing ....F 989 838-2274
 Ashley (G-726)
Bernthal Packing Inc ....E 989 652-2648
 Frankenmuth (G-5583)
Berry & Sons-Rababeh ....G 313 259-6925
 Detroit (G-3901)
Bert Hazekamp & Son Inc ....C 231 773-8302
 Muskegon (G-11279)
Berthiaume Slaughter House ....G 989 879-4921
 Pinconning (G-12506)
Boars Head Provisions Co Inc ....B 941 955-0994
 Holland (G-7572)
Bob Evans Farms Inc ....D 517 437-3349
 Hillsdale (G-7518)
Boyers Meat Processing Inc ....G 734 495-1342
 Canton (G-2355)
C Roy Inc ....E 810 387-3975
 Yale (G-18045)
Cargill Incorporated ....F 608 868-5150
 Owosso (G-12281)
Carol Packing House ....G 989 673-2688
 Caro (G-2466)
Clemens Food Group LLC ....G 517 278-2500
 Coldwater (G-3295)
Clemens Welcome Center ....G 517 278-2500
 Coldwater (G-3296)
Cole Carter Inc ....G 269 626-8891
 Scotts (G-14504)
Cornbelt Beef Corporation ....E 313 237-0087
 Oak Park (G-12054)
Countryside Quality Meats LLC ....G 517 741-4275
 Union City (G-16732)
Dan Drummond ....G 231 853-6200
 Ravenna (G-13118)
Erlas Inc ....D 989 872-2191
 Cass City (G-2514)
Fillmore Beef Company Inc ....G 616 396-6693
 Holland (G-7631)
Flemings Meat Processing ....G 810 679-3668
 Croswell (G-3596)
Gainors Meat Packing Inc ....G 989 269-8161
 Bad Axe (G-1061)
Garys Custom Meats ....G 269 641-5683
 Union (G-16728)
Gibbies Deer Processing ....F 231 924-6042
 Fremont (G-5774)
Hormel Foods Corporation ....C 616 454-0418
 Grand Rapids (G-6516)
Jbs Packerland Inc ....E 269 685-6886
 Plainwell (G-12526)
Jbs Plainwell Inc ....C 269 685-6886
 Plainwell (G-12527)
Kellys Catering ....G 231 796-5414
 Big Rapids (G-1635)
Kent Quality Foods Inc ....C 616 459-4595
 Hudsonville (G-8161)
L&J Packaging ....G 269 782-2628
 Dowagiac (G-4546)

Lake Odessa Meat Processing G 616 374-8392
Lake Odessa *(G-9116)*
Lloyd Johnson Livestock Inc G 906 786-4878
Escanaba *(G-4840)*
Makkedah Mt Proc & Bulk Fd Str G 231 873-2113
Hart *(G-7376)*
Maurer Meat Processors Inc E 989 658-8185
Ubly *(G-16719)*
Michigan Meat Processing F 906 786-7010
Escanaba *(G-4845)*
Michigan Veal Inc F 616 669-6688
Hudsonville *(G-8169)*
Mmm Meat LLC F 616 669-6140
Hudsonville *(G-8171)*
Mypac Inc G 616 896-9359
Hudsonville *(G-8172)*
Nagel Meat Processing F 517 568-5035
Homer *(G-7947)*
Northwest Market G 517 787-5005
Jackson *(G-8543)*
Oles Meat Processing G 989 866-6442
Vestaburg *(G-16827)*
Packerland Packing Co G 269 685-6886
Plainwell *(G-12533)*
Pooles Meat Processing G 989 846-6348
Standish *(G-15225)*
Prime Cuts of Jackson LLC E 517 768-8090
Jackson *(G-8557)*
Rays Game G 810 346-2628
Brown City *(G-2056)*
Ricks Meat Processing LLC G 517 628-2263
Eaton Rapids *(G-4733)*
Rogers Beef Farms G 906 632-1584
Sault Sainte Marie *(G-14472)*
Safari Meats Llc G 313 539-3367
Oak Park *(G-12097)*
Scotts Hook & Cleaver Inc E 269 626-8891
Scotts *(G-14507)*
Smith & Sons Meat Proc Inc G 989 772-6048
Mount Pleasant *(G-11227)*
Smith - Sons ME G 989 772-6048
Mount Pleasant *(G-11228)*
Smith Meat Packing Inc E 810 985-5900
Port Huron *(G-12967)*
Spillson Ltd G 734 384-0284
Monroe *(G-11068)*
Standard Provision LLC G 989 354-4975
Alpena *(G-313)*
Tolmans Processing G 616 875-8598
Hudsonville *(G-8183)*
Tyson G 231 922-3214
Traverse City *(G-16132)*
Tyson Foods Inc B 231 929-2456
Traverse City *(G-16133)*
Tyson Fresh Meats Inc D 248 213-1000
Southfield *(G-15051)*
US Guys Deer Processing LLC G 616 642-0967
Saranac *(G-14456)*
Vin-Lee-Ron Meat Packing LLC E 574 353-1386
Cassopolis *(G-2538)*
◆ **Wolverine Packing Co** D 313 259-7500
Detroit *(G-4446)*

2013 Sausages & Meat Prdts

A & R Packing Co Inc E 734 422-2060
Livonia *(G-9618)*
◆ **Alexander and Hornung Inc** D 586 771-9880
Saint Clair Shores *(G-14238)*
Bernthal Packing Inc E 989 652-2648
Frankenmuth *(G-5583)*
Bert Hazekamp & Son Inc C 231 773-8302
Muskegon *(G-11279)*
Big O Smokehouse F 616 891-5555
Caledonia *(G-2289)*
Boars Head Provisions Co Inc B 941 955-0994
Holland *(G-7572)*
Cattlemans Meat Company B 734 287-8260
Taylor *(G-15699)*
▼ **Classic Jerky Company** D 313 357-9904
Taylor *(G-15701)*
Clemens Food Group LLC G 517 278-2500
Coldwater *(G-3295)*
Darling Ingredients Inc E 269 751-0560
Hamilton *(G-7231)*
Deerings Jerky Co LLC G 231 590-5687
Interlochen *(G-8239)*
Detroit Sausage Co Inc F 313 259-0555
Detroit *(G-4002)*
Dina Mia Kitchens Inc F 906 265-9082
Iron River *(G-8308)*
Erlas Inc D 989 872-2191
Cass City *(G-2514)*
Great Fresh Foods Co LLC F 586 846-3521
Taylor *(G-15726)*
Heinzerling Enterprises Inc G 734 529-9100
Dundee *(G-4586)*
Hillshire Brands Company A 616 875-8131
Zeeland *(G-18150)*
Ilowski Sausage Company Inc G 810 329-9117
East China *(G-4622)*
Johnston Meat Processing G 810 378-5455
Peck *(G-12419)*
Kellys Catering G 231 796-5414
Big Rapids *(G-1635)*
Kent Quality Foods Inc C 616 459-4595
Hudsonville *(G-8161)*
Kerns Sausages Inc E 989 652-2684
Frankenmuth *(G-5590)*
Kgdh LLC G 989 652-9041
Frankenmuth *(G-5591)*
Koegel Meats Inc C 810 238-3685
Flint *(G-5456)*
Kowalski Companies Inc C 313 873-8200
Detroit *(G-4182)*
Krzysiak Family Restaurant D 989 894-5531
Bay City *(G-1326)*
L&J Packaging G 269 782-2628
Dowagiac *(G-4546)*
Louies Meats Inc F 231 946-4811
Traverse City *(G-16028)*
Macomb Smoked Meats LLC D 313 842-2375
Dearborn *(G-3735)*
Marquette Meats In City LLC G 906 226-8333
Marquette *(G-10545)*
Mello Meats Inc F 800 852-5019
Auburn Hills *(G-945)*
Pioneer Meats LLC F 248 862-1988
Birmingham *(G-1698)*
Quincy Street Inc C 616 399-3330
Holland *(G-7781)*
Smigelski Properties LLC G 989 255-6252
Alpena *(G-312)*
T Wigley Inc F 313 831-6881
Detroit *(G-4394)*
Vandco Incorporated E 906 482-1550
Hancock *(G-7258)*
Viaus Super Market G 906 786-1950
Escanaba *(G-4866)*
Winter Sausage Mfg Co Inc E 586 777-9080
Eastpointe *(G-4713)*
Zicks Specialty Meats Inc G 269 471-7121
Berrien Springs *(G-1602)*

2015 Poultry Slaughtering, Dressing & Processing

Cargill Incorporated F 608 868-5150
Owosso *(G-12281)*
Cargill Americas Inc D 810 989-7689
New Haven *(G-11522)*
Detroit Smoke House LLC G 313 622-9714
Ecorse *(G-4743)*
Farmers Egg Cooperative G 517 649-8957
Charlotte *(G-2648)*
Hillshire Brands Company A 616 875-8131
Zeeland *(G-18150)*
Michigan Turkey Producers B 616 245-2221
Wyoming *(G-18020)*
Michigan Turkey Producers G 616 875-1838
Zeeland *(G-18163)*
Michigan Turkey Producers F 616 245-2221
Grand Rapids *(G-6676)*
Tyson Foods /Hr G 616 875-2311
Zeeland *(G-18190)*

2021 Butter

Blank Slate Creamery LLC G 734 218-3242
Whitmore Lake *(G-17690)*
Brinks Family Creamery LLC G 231 826-0099
Mc Bain *(G-10680)*
Browndog Creamery LLC G 248 361-3759
Northville *(G-11681)*
Greenville Ventr Partners LLC E 616 303-2400
Greenville *(G-7137)*
Inverness Dairy Inc E 231 627-4655
Cheboygan *(G-2681)*
Michigan Milk Producers Assn E 269 435-2835
Constantine *(G-3539)*
Michigan Milk Producers Assn E 248 474-6672
Novi *(G-11947)*
Michigan Milk Producers Assn D 989 834-2221
Ovid *(G-12273)*
Moo-Ville Inc E 517 852-9003
Nashville *(G-11462)*
Purple Cow Creamery G 616 494-1933
Holland *(G-7778)*

2022 Cheese

Agropur Inc D 616 538-3822
Grand Rapids *(G-6154)*
Baracoa Dips G 616 643-3204
Grand Rapids *(G-6204)*
Country Home Creations Inc E 810 244-7348
Flint *(G-5405)*
Evergreen Lane Farm LLC G 269 543-9900
Fennville *(G-5171)*
Farm Country Cheese House F 989 352-7779
Lakeview *(G-9172)*
Greenville Ventr Partners LLC E 616 303-2400
Greenville *(G-7137)*
Kraft Heinz G 616 940-2260
Grand Rapids *(G-6589)*
Krafts & Thingz G 810 689-2457
Chesterfield *(G-2799)*
Leprino Foods Company D 989 967-3635
Remus *(G-13239)*
Leprino Foods Company C 616 895-5800
Allendale *(G-221)*
Liberty Dairy Company C 800 632-5552
Evart *(G-4885)*
Litehouse Inc C 616 897-5911
Lowell *(G-10034)*
Michigan Chese Prtein Pdts LLC C 517 403-5247
Tipton *(G-15884)*
Reilly Craft Creamery LLC G 313 300-9859
Detroit *(G-4338)*
White Lotus Farms Inc G 734 904-1379
Ann Arbor *(G-698)*
Williams Cheese Co E 989 697-4492
Linwood *(G-9599)*
Win Schuler Foods Inc G 248 262-3450
Southfield *(G-15066)*
Zingermans Creamery LLC F 734 929-0500
Ann Arbor *(G-709)*

2023 Milk, Condensed & Evaporated

▼ **Artjen Complexus Usa LLC** G 519 919-0814
Detroit *(G-3881)*
Bay Valley Foods LLC C 269 792-2277
Wayland *(G-17399)*
Castle Remedies Inc F 734 973-8990
Ann Arbor *(G-394)*
▲ **Continental Dar Facilities LLC** D 616 837-7641
Coopersville *(G-3552)*
Dairy Farmers America Inc E 517 265-5045
Adrian *(G-57)*
Enrinity Supplements Inc G 734 322-4966
Westland *(G-17553)*
Gerber Products Company E 231 928-2076
Fremont *(G-5772)*
Gerber Products Company C 231 928-2000
Fremont *(G-5773)*
Green Room Michigan LLC F 248 289-3288
Farmington Hills *(G-5015)*
Greenville Ventr Partners LLC E 616 303-2400
Greenville *(G-7137)*
Kerry Inc D 616 871-9940
Detroit *(G-4175)*
Michigan Milk Producers Assn E 248 474-6672
Novi *(G-11947)*
Michigan Milk Producers Assn D 989 834-2221
Ovid *(G-12273)*
Michigan Milk Producers Assn E 269 435-2835
Constantine *(G-3539)*
Verndale Products Inc E 313 834-4190
Detroit *(G-4426)*
Visalus Sciences G 877 847-2587
Troy *(G-16687)*

2024 Ice Cream

Alinosi French Ice Cream Co G 313 527-3195
Detroit *(G-3855)*
Berkley Frosty Freeze Inc G 248 336-2634
Berkley *(G-1581)*
Blossom Berry G 517 775-6978
Novi *(G-11838)*
Cold Stone Creamery G 313 886-4020
Grosse Pointe Park *(G-7192)*
Comstock Creamery LLC G 269 929-7693
Kalamazoo *(G-8712)*

Employee Codes: A=Over 500 employees, B=251-500
C=101-250, D=51-100, E=20-50, F=10-19, G=3-9
2020 Harris Michigan
Industrial Directory
699

20 FOOD AND KINDRED PRODUCTS SIC SECTION

Corner Cone G 810 412-4433
Davison *(G-3644)*

Custard Corner Inc G 734 771-4396
Grosse Ile *(G-7168)*

Dairy Freezzz Too LLC G 248 629-6666
Madison Heights *(G-10226)*

Dairy Queen F 616 235-0102
Grand Rapids *(G-6333)*

Deans Ice Cream Inc F 269 685-6641
Plainwell *(G-12522)*

Farm Country Frz Custard & Kit G 989 687-6700
Sanford *(G-14450)*

Frosty Cove G 231 343-6643
Muskegon *(G-11328)*

Froyo Pinckney LLC G 248 310-4465
Pinckney *(G-12498)*

Guernsey Dairy Stores Inc C 248 349-1466
Northville *(G-11696)*

Hattiegirl Ice Cream Foods LLC G 877 444-3738
Detroit *(G-4118)*

▼ House of Flavors Inc C 231 845-7369
Ludington *(G-10066)*

Hudsonvlle Crmry Ice Cream LLC E 616 546-4005
Holland *(G-7684)*

Independent Dairy Inc E 734 241-6016
Monroe *(G-11041)*

International Brands Inc G 248 644-2701
Bloomfield Hills *(G-1775)*

Loven Spoonful G 517 522-3953
Grass Lake *(G-7089)*

Moo-Ville Inc E 517 852-9003
Nashville *(G-11462)*

Moomers Homemade Ice Cream LLC E 231 941-4122
Traverse City *(G-16043)*

PGI of Saugatuck Inc E 269 561-2000
Fennville *(G-5176)*

Plainwell Ice Cream Co F 269 685-8586
Plainwell *(G-12537)*

Pump House G 616 647-5481
Grand Rapids *(G-6795)*

Quality Dairy Company E 517 367-2400
Lansing *(G-9417)*

Rays Ice Cream Co Inc E 248 549-5256
Royal Oak *(G-13963)*

Reilly Craft Creamery LLC G 313 300-9859
Detroit *(G-4338)*

Sherman Dairy Products Co Inc F 269 637-8251
South Haven *(G-14770)*

Shetler Family Dairy LLC F 231 258-8216
Kalkaska *(G-8958)*

Strohs G 734 285-5480
Wyandotte *(G-17977)*

Stuarts of Novi G 248 615-2955
Novi *(G-12007)*

Sugar Kissed Cupcakes LLC G 231 421-9156
Traverse City *(G-16115)*

Sweet Tmpttons Ice Cream Prlor G 616 842-8108
Grand Haven *(G-6088)*

Swirlberry G 734 779-0830
Livonia *(G-9949)*

That French Place F 231 437-6037
Charlevoix *(G-2633)*

WG Sweis Investments LLC E 313 477-8433
Washington *(G-17314)*

Whats Scoop G 616 662-6423
Hudsonville *(G-8187)*

2026 Milk

Bay Valley Foods LLC C 269 792-2277
Wayland *(G-17399)*

Bloomberry G 586 212-9510
East China *(G-4621)*

▲ C F Burger Creamery Co D 313 584-4040
Detroit *(G-3925)*

Calder Bros Dairy Inc E 313 381-8858
Lincoln Park *(G-9575)*

Chocolate Vault Llc G 517 688-3388
Horton *(G-7963)*

Country Dairy Inc D 231 861-4636
New ERA *(G-11520)*

Country Fresh LLC C 734 261-7980
Livonia *(G-9691)*

Cream Cup Dairy G 231 889-4158
Kaleva *(G-8931)*

Dairy Farmers America Inc E 517 265-5045
Adrian *(G-57)*

Fruit Fro Yo G 517 580-3967
Okemos *(G-12124)*

General Mills Inc E 231 832-3285
Reed City *(G-13213)*

Greenville Ventr Partners LLC E 616 303-2400
Greenville *(G-7137)*

Inverness Dairy Inc E 231 627-4655
Cheboygan *(G-2681)*

Langs Inc G 248 634-6048
Holly *(G-7884)*

Liberty Dairy Company C 800 632-5552
Evart *(G-4885)*

Melody Farms LLC E 734 261-7980
Livonia *(G-9837)*

Michigan Milk Producers Assn D 989 834-2221
Ovid *(G-12273)*

Michigan Milk Producers Assn E 269 435-2835
Constantine *(G-3539)*

Michigan Milk Producers Assn E 248 474-6672
Novi *(G-11947)*

◆ Old Europe Cheese Inc D 269 925-5003
Benton Harbor *(G-1536)*

Quality Dairy Company E 517 367-2400
Lansing *(G-9417)*

Rocky Mtn Choclat Fctry Inc D 810 606-8550
Grand Blanc *(G-5981)*

Shetler Family Dairy LLC F 231 258-8216
Kalkaska *(G-8958)*

Sugar Berry G 517 321-0177
Lansing *(G-9324)*

Sweet Earth G 248 850-8031
Royal Oak *(G-13975)*

Twist G 248 859-2169
West Bloomfield *(G-17503)*

Yogurtown Inc G 313 908-9376
Dearborn *(G-3775)*

Yoplait USA F 231 832-3285
Reed City *(G-13227)*

2032 Canned Specialties

American Spoon Foods Inc E 231 347-9030
Petoskey *(G-12440)*

◆ Amway International Inc E 616 787-1000
Ada *(G-7)*

Charidimos Inc G 248 827-7733
Southfield *(G-14865)*

Detroit Chili Co Inc G 313 521-6323
Detroit *(G-3975)*

Global Restaurant Group Inc F 313 271-2777
Dearborn *(G-3716)*

Kraft Heinz Foods Company B 616 396-6557
Holland *(G-7713)*

National Coney Island Chili Co F 313 365-5611
Roseville *(G-13844)*

Onion Crock of Michigan Inc G 616 458-2922
Grand Rapids *(G-6731)*

Paul J Baroni Co G 906 337-3920
Calumet *(G-2331)*

Randall Foods Inc F 517 767-3247
Tekonsha *(G-15821)*

SBR LLC E 313 350-8799
Harper Woods *(G-7304)*

Tienda San Rafael LLC G 989 681-2020
Saint Louis *(G-14370)*

Turchetti Spaghetti Co LLC G 616 706-4766
Hart *(G-7380)*

2033 Canned Fruits, Vegetables & Preserves

Almar Orchards LLC E 810 659-6568
Flushing *(G-5531)*

American Spoon Foods Inc E 231 347-9030
Petoskey *(G-12440)*

Birds Eye Foods Inc C 269 561-8211
Fennville *(G-5170)*

Blakes Orchard Inc G 586 784-5343
Armada *(G-717)*

Brownwood Acres Foods Inc F 231 599-3101
Eastport *(G-4714)*

◆ Burnette Foods Inc D 231 264-8116
Elk Rapids *(G-4776)*

Burnette Foods Inc D 269 621-3181
Hartford *(G-7382)*

Burnette Foods Inc E 231 536-2284
East Jordan *(G-4626)*

Burnette Foods Inc C 231 861-2151
New ERA *(G-11519)*

Campbell Soup Company F 313 295-6884
Taylor *(G-15698)*

Campbell Soup Company D 248 336-8486
Ferndale *(G-5265)*

◆ Cherry Central Cooperative Inc E 231 946-1860
Traverse City *(G-15938)*

Cherry Central Cooperative Inc D 231 861-2141
Shelby *(G-14524)*

◆ Cherry Growers Inc C 231 276-9241
Birmingham *(G-1676)*

Cherry Growers Inc G 231 947-2502
Traverse City *(G-15940)*

Cherry Hut Products LLC G 231 882-4431
Benzonia *(G-1574)*

Cherry Republic Inc D 231 334-3150
Glen Arbor *(G-5940)*

Country Mill Farms LLC E 517 543-1019
Charlotte *(G-2642)*

Crazy Joes Enterprises LLC G 906 395-1522
Baraga *(G-1100)*

Everfresh Beverages Inc D 586 755-9500
Warren *(G-17024)*

Fairview Farms G 269 449-0500
Berrien Springs *(G-1595)*

Food For Thought Inc E 231 326-5444
Traverse City *(G-15971)*

◆ Gray & Company C 231 873-5628
Hart *(G-7372)*

▼ Great Lakes Packing Co E 231 264-5561
Kewadin *(G-9039)*

Hopeful Harvest Foods Inc G 248 967-1500
Oak Park *(G-12073)*

I Jams LLC G 248 756-1380
Keego Harbor *(G-8980)*

◆ Indian Summer Cooperative Inc C 231 845-6248
Ludington *(G-10067)*

Integrity Beverage Inc E 248 348-1010
Wixom *(G-17836)*

J House LLC G 313 220-4449
Grosse Pointe Farms *(G-7185)*

Jt Foods Inc G 810 772-9035
Owosso *(G-12297)*

Knouse Foods Cooperative Inc D 269 657-5524
Paw Paw *(G-12406)*

Kraft Heinz Foods Company B 616 447-0481
Grand Rapids *(G-6590)*

Kraft Heinz Foods Company B 616 396-6557
Holland *(G-7713)*

La Rozinas Inc G 906 779-2181
Iron Mountain *(G-8287)*

M Forche Farms Inc F 517 447-3488
Blissfield *(G-1718)*

Materne North America Corp E 231 346-6600
Grawn *(G-7099)*

▼ McClures Pickles LLC E 248 837-9323
Detroit *(G-4221)*

Michigan Apple Packers Coop G 616 887-9933
Sparta *(G-15102)*

Mitten Fruit Company LLC G 269 585-8541
Kalamazoo *(G-8829)*

Mizkan America Inc F 616 794-0226
Belding *(G-1425)*

Mpc Company Inc G 269 927-3371
Benton Harbor *(G-1534)*

New ERA Canning Company C 231 861-2151
New ERA *(G-11521)*

Northville Cider Mill Inc E 248 349-3181
Northville *(G-11715)*

▲ Oceana Foods Inc E 231 861-2141
Shelby *(G-14531)*

◆ Old Orchard Brands LLC D 616 887-1745
Sparta *(G-15103)*

◆ Packers Canning Co Inc D 269 624-4681
Lawton *(G-9513)*

Panther James LLC G 248 850-7522
Royal Oak *(G-13955)*

Pantless Jams LLC G 419 283-8470
Temperance *(G-15840)*

◆ Peterson Farms Inc B 231 861-6333
Shelby *(G-14534)*

Randall Foods Inc F 517 767-3247
Tekonsha *(G-15821)*

Rice Juice Company Inc G 906 774-1733
Iron Mountain *(G-8298)*

Society of Saint John Inc G 906 289-4484
Eagle Harbor *(G-4618)*

St Julian Wine Company Inc E 269 657-5568
Paw Paw *(G-12414)*

Thomas Cooper G 231 599-2251
Ellsworth *(G-4789)*

Twin City Foods Inc C 616 374-4002
Lake Odessa *(G-9120)*

Uncle Johns Cider Mill Inc D 989 224-3686
Saint Johns *(G-14298)*

Welch Foods Inc A Cooperative D 269 624-4141
Lawton *(G-9516)*

2034 Dried Fruits, Vegetables & Soup

American Spoon Foods Inc ....E....... 231 347-9030
  Petoskey *(G-12440)*
Apple Quest Inc ....C...... 616 299-4834
  Conklin *(G-3528)*
Cherry Central Cooperative Inc ....D....... 231 861-2141
  Shelby *(G-14524)*
◆ Graceland Fruit Inc ....C...... 231 352-7181
  Frankfort *(G-5602)*
◆ Shoreline Fruit LLC ....D....... 231 941-4336
  Traverse City *(G-16102)*
▼ Smeltzer Companies Inc ....C...... 231 882-4421
  Frankfort *(G-5606)*
Up North Spices Inc ....G....... 419 346-4155
  Royal Oak *(G-13979)*

2035 Pickled Fruits, Vegetables, Sauces & Dressings

American Spoon Foods Inc ....E....... 231 347-9030
  Petoskey *(G-12440)*
Barlows Gourmet Products Inc ....G....... 248 245-0393
  Holly *(G-7870)*
Bessinger Pickle Co Inc ....G....... 989 876-8008
  Au Gres *(G-743)*
Brede Inc ....G....... 313 273-1079
  Detroit *(G-3914)*
Crazy Joes Enterprises LLC ....G....... 906 395-1522
  Baraga *(G-1100)*
Cultured Love LLC ....G....... 703 362-5991
  Zeeland *(G-18128)*
Custom Foods Inc ....E....... 989 249-8061
  Saginaw *(G-14024)*
DForte Inc ....F....... 269 657-6996
  Paw Paw *(G-12402)*
Dimitri Mansour ....G....... 248 684-4545
  Milford *(G-10961)*
Dina Mia Kitchens Inc ....F....... 906 265-9082
  Iron River *(G-8308)*
Flamm Pickle and Packaging Co .....F....... 269 461-6916
  Eau Claire *(G-4739)*
Garden Fresh Gourmet LLC ....E....... 866 725-7239
  Ferndale *(G-5289)*
◆ Gielow Pickles Inc ....C....... 810 359-7680
  Lexington *(G-9557)*
Gourmet Holdings LLC ....G....... 313 432-2121
  Grosse Pointe *(G-7179)*
◆ Great Lakes Food Center LLC ....E....... 248 397-8166
  Madison Heights *(G-10261)*
Harrison Packing Co Inc ....F....... 269 381-3837
  Kalamazoo *(G-8761)*
Harrison Packing Co Inc ....G....... 989 427-5535
  Edmore *(G-4751)*
◆ Hausbeck Pickle Company ....D....... 989 754-4721
  Saginaw *(G-14054)*
Hopeful Harvest Foods Inc ....G....... 248 967-1500
  Oak Park *(G-12073)*
◆ Indian Summer Cooperative Inc .....C....... 231 845-6248
  Ludington *(G-10067)*
Jabars Complements LLC ....G....... 810 966-8371
  Port Huron *(G-12931)*
Kaiser Foods Inc ....F....... 989 879-2087
  Pinconning *(G-12508)*
Knouse Foods Cooperative Inc ....D....... 269 657-5524
  Paw Paw *(G-12406)*
Litehouse Inc ....C....... 616 897-5911
  Lowell *(G-10034)*
McClures Pickles LLC ....G....... 248 837-9323
  Royal Oak *(G-13949)*
▲ Mr Chips Inc ....G....... 989 879-3555
  Pinconning *(G-12510)*
Swanson Grading & Brining Inc .....D....... 231 853-2289
  Ravenna *(G-13129)*
Swanson Pickle Co Inc ....E....... 231 853-2289
  Ravenna *(G-13130)*
Topors Pickle Co Inc ....G....... 313 237-0288
  West Bloomfield *(G-17501)*
Vince Joes Frt Mkt - Shlby Inc ....E....... 586 786-9230
  Shelby Township *(G-14719)*

2037 Frozen Fruits, Juices & Vegetables

All American Whse & Cold Stor ......E....... 313 865-3870
  Detroit *(G-3856)*
◆ Cherry Growers Inc ....C....... 231 276-9241
  Birmingham *(G-1676)*
Cherry Growers Inc ....G....... 231 947-2502
  Traverse City *(G-15940)*
Clarkson Smoothie Inc ....G....... 248 620-8005
  Clarkston *(G-2911)*
Clio Smoothie LLC ....G....... 810 691-9620
  Fenton *(G-5195)*
Coloma Frozen Foods Inc ....D....... 269 849-0500
  Coloma *(G-3356)*
Dole Packaged Foods LLC ....E....... 269 423-6375
  Decatur *(G-3803)*
Farber Concessions Inc ....E....... 313 387-1600
  Redford *(G-13161)*
◆ Graceland Fruit Inc ....C....... 231 352-7181
  Frankfort *(G-5602)*
Hart Freeze Pack LlC ....F....... 231 873-2175
  Hart *(G-7373)*
Jar-ME LLC ....G....... 313 319-7765
  Detroit *(G-4158)*
▲ Juvenex Inc ....F....... 248 436-2866
  Southfield *(G-14953)*
MI Frozen Food LLC ....G....... 231 357-4334
  Manistee *(G-10430)*
◆ Old Orchard Brands LLC ....D....... 616 887-1745
  Sparta *(G-15103)*
◆ Peterson Farms Inc ....B....... 231 861-6333
  Shelby *(G-14534)*
Potatoe Ball LLC ....G....... 313 483-0901
  Clinton Township *(G-3197)*
Sill Farms & Market Inc ....E....... 269 674-3755
  Lawrence *(G-9508)*
▼ Smeltzer Companies Inc ....C....... 231 882-4421
  Frankfort *(G-5606)*
Smoothies ....G....... 231 498-2374
  Kewadin *(G-9040)*
Standale Smoothie LLC ....G....... 810 691-9625
  Fenton *(G-5239)*
Super Fluids LLC ....G....... 313 409-6522
  Detroit *(G-4386)*
Twin City Foods Inc ....C....... 616 374-4002
  Lake Odessa *(G-9120)*
Welch Foods Inc A Cooperative ......D....... 269 624-4141
  Lawton *(G-9516)*

2038 Frozen Specialties

Achatzs Hand Made Pie Co ....D....... 586 749-2882
  Chesterfield *(G-2731)*
Campbell Soup Company ....F....... 313 295-6884
  Taylor *(G-15698)*
Campbell Soup Company ....D....... 248 336-8486
  Ferndale *(G-5265)*
Cole King Foods ....E....... 313 872-0220
  Detroit *(G-3943)*
Coles Quality Foods Inc ....E....... 231 722-1651
  Muskegon *(G-11295)*
Detroit Chili Co Inc ....G....... 248 440-5933
  Southfield *(G-14880)*
DForte Inc ....F....... 269 657-6996
  Paw Paw *(G-12402)*
Dina Mia Kitchens Inc ....F....... 906 265-9082
  Iron River *(G-8308)*
Farber Concessions Inc ....E....... 313 387-1600
  Redford *(G-13161)*
Frandale Sub Shop ....F....... 616 446-6311
  Allendale *(G-217)*
◆ Kellogg Company ....A....... 269 961-2000
  Battle Creek *(G-1211)*
Kring Pizza Inc ....G....... 586 792-0049
  Harrison Township *(G-7336)*
▲ Mid America Commodities LLC .....G....... 810 936-0108
  Linden *(G-9594)*
▲ Pasty Oven Inc ....F....... 906 774-2328
  Quinnesec *(G-13101)*
Paul J Baroni Co ....G....... 906 337-3920
  Calumet *(G-2331)*
▲ Pierino Frozen Foods Inc ....E....... 313 928-0950
  Lincoln Park *(G-9583)*
Pinnacle Foods Group LLC ....B....... 810 724-6144
  Imlay City *(G-8210)*
Rays Ice Cream Co Inc ....E....... 248 549-5256
  Royal Oak *(G-13963)*
▲ Turris Italian Foods Inc ....D....... 586 773-6010
  Roseville *(G-13883)*
Twin City Foods Inc ....C....... 616 374-4002
  Lake Odessa *(G-9120)*

2041 Flour, Grain Milling

▲ Advanced Food Technologies Inc ....D....... 616 574-4144
  Grand Rapids *(G-6148)*
Archer-Daniels-Midland Company ....C....... 269 968-2900
  Battle Creek *(G-1147)*
Archer-Daniels-Midland Company ....G....... 810 672-9221
  Snover *(G-14743)*
Archer-Daniels-Midland Company ....F....... 517 627-4017
  Grand Ledge *(G-6101)*
Archer-Daniels-Midland Company ....E....... 517 647-4155
  Portland *(G-13061)*
Cake Flour ....G....... 231 571-3054
  Norton Shores *(G-11743)*
Chelsea Milling Company ....B....... 734 475-1361
  Chelsea *(G-2704)*
Citizens LLC ....G....... 517 541-1449
  Charlotte *(G-2640)*
Dorothy Dawson Food Products .....E....... 517 788-9830
  Jackson *(G-8435)*
Freeport Milling ....G....... 616 765-8421
  Freeport *(G-5764)*
General Mills Inc ....E....... 231 832-3285
  Reed City *(G-13213)*
General Mills Inc ....G....... 269 337-0288
  Kalamazoo *(G-8750)*
▲ Ittner Bean & Grain Inc ....F....... 989 662-4461
  Auburn *(G-753)*
◆ Kellogg Company ....A....... 269 961-2000
  Battle Creek *(G-1211)*
Kelloggs Corporation ....F....... 616 219-6100
  Grand Rapids *(G-6572)*
◆ King Milling Company ....D....... 616 897-9264
  Lowell *(G-10033)*
Knappen Milling Company ....E....... 269 731-4141
  Augusta *(G-1053)*
Mennel Milling Co of Mich Inc ....C....... 269 782-5175
  Dowagiac *(G-4550)*
◆ Purity Foods Inc ....F....... 517 448-7440
  Hudson *(G-8140)*
Right Brain Brewery ....G....... 231 922-9662
  Traverse City *(G-16094)*
▼ Star of West Milling Company ......D....... 989 652-9971
  Frankenmuth *(G-5596)*
Star of West Milling Company ....E....... 517 639-3165
  Quincy *(G-13099)*
Star of West Milling Company ....G....... 989 872-5847
  Cass City *(G-2522)*
Williams Milling & Moulding In .....G....... 906 474-9222
  Rapid River *(G-13117)*

2043 Cereal Breakfast Foods

Bay Valley Foods LLC ....C....... 269 792-2277
  Wayland *(G-17399)*
General Mills Inc ....D....... 763 764-7600
  Kalamazoo *(G-8749)*
Hearthside Food Solutions LLC ......C....... 616 871-6240
  Kentwood *(G-9009)*
Hearthside Food Solutions LLC ......B....... 616 574-2000
  Kentwood *(G-9010)*
◆ K-Two Inc ....F....... 269 961-2000
  Battle Creek *(G-1206)*
Kellogg (thailand) Limited ....G....... 269 969-8937
  Battle Creek *(G-1208)*
Kellogg Chile Inc ....G....... 269 961-2000
  Battle Creek *(G-1209)*
Kellogg Company ....B....... 269 961-2000
  Battle Creek *(G-1210)*
Kellogg Company ....B....... 810 653-5625
  Davison *(G-3655)*
Kellogg Company ....B....... 269 961-9387
  Mulliken *(G-11239)*
Kellogg Company ....B....... 269 964-8525
  Battle Creek *(G-1212)*
Kellogg Company ....G....... 269 969-8107
  Battle Creek *(G-1213)*
Kellogg Company ....B....... 901 373-6115
  Battle Creek *(G-1214)*
Kellogg Company ....A....... 269 961-6693
  Battle Creek *(G-1216)*
Kellogg Company ....C....... 269 961-2000
  Battle Creek *(G-1217)*
Kellogg Company ....D....... 269 961-2000
  Battle Creek *(G-1215)*
◆ Kellogg Company ....A....... 269 961-2000
  Battle Creek *(G-1211)*
▼ Kellogg USA Inc ....C....... 269 961-2000
  Battle Creek *(G-1219)*
Michaelenes Inc ....G....... 248 625-0156
  Clarkston *(G-2938)*
Post Foods LLC ....C....... 269 966-1000
  Battle Creek *(G-1236)*
◆ Roskam Baking Company ....C....... 616 574-5757
  Grand Rapids *(G-6839)*
Rothbury Farms Inc ....A....... 616 574-5757
  Grand Rapids *(G-6844)*
Snackwerks of Michigan LLC ....F....... 269 719-8282
  Battle Creek *(G-1251)*
Treehouse Private Brands Inc ....C....... 269 968-6181
  Battle Creek *(G-1260)*

20 FOOD AND KINDRED PRODUCTS

2045 Flour, Blended & Prepared

▲ Advanced Food Technologies Inc ....D...... 616 574-4144
Grand Rapids *(G-6148)*
Bektrom Foods Inc ....F...... 734 241-3796
Monroe *(G-11021)*
Big Dipper Dough Co Inc ....G...... 231 883-6035
Traverse City *(G-15911)*
Dawn Food Products Inc ....C...... 517 789-4400
Jackson *(G-8428)*
Dawn Food Products Inc ....C...... 800 654-4843
Grand Rapids *(G-6337)*
◆ Dawn Food Products Inc ....C...... 517 789-4400
Jackson *(G-8429)*
◆ Dawn Foods Inc ....C...... 517 789-4400
Jackson *(G-8430)*
Dawn Foods International Corp..........C...... 517 789-4400
Jackson *(G-8431)*
▲ Dominos Pizza LLC..........................C...... 734 930-3030
Ann Arbor *(G-424)*
Dorothy Dawson Food Products.........E...... 517 788-9830
Jackson *(G-8435)*
Dough & Spice Inc ....G...... 586 756-6100
Warren *(G-17004)*
Ezbake Technologies LLC ....G...... 817 430-1621
Fenton *(G-5206)*
Fry Krisp Food Products Inc ....F...... 517 784-8531
Jackson *(G-8452)*
MA MA La Rosa Foods Inc ....F...... 734 946-7878
Taylor *(G-15736)*
Pizza Crust Company Inc ....F...... 517 482-3368
Lansing *(G-9257)*

2046 Wet Corn Milling

Cargill Incorporated..........................F...... 608 868-5150
Owosso *(G-12281)*
Darwin Sneller...................................G...... 989 977-3718
Sebewaing *(G-14514)*
Schuette Farms ....G...... 989 550-0563
Elkton *(G-4783)*
Synex Wolverine LLC ....G...... 989 689-3161
Edenville *(G-4748)*

2047 Dog & Cat Food

Archer-Daniels-Midland Company ....E...... 517 647-4155
Portland *(G-13061)*
Blendco LLC ....F...... 269 350-2914
Stevensville *(G-15557)*
Free Rnge Ntrals Dog Trats Inc ....F...... 586 737-0797
Sterling Heights *(G-15347)*
▲ Happy Howies Inc ....F...... 313 537-7200
Detroit *(G-4116)*
Harvey Richard John ....G...... 269 781-5801
Marshall *(G-10571)*
Nestle Purina Petcare Company..........E...... 888 202-4554
Troy *(G-16523)*
▲ Prestige Pet Products Inc ....G...... 248 615-1526
Southfield *(G-15003)*
Three Dogs One Cat ....D...... 313 285-8371
Detroit *(G-4399)*
Vita Plus Corporation ....F...... 989 665-0013
Gagetown *(G-5803)*
Wysong Medical Corporation ....E...... 989 631-0009
Midland *(G-10925)*

2048 Prepared Feeds For Animals & Fowls

▲ Active Feed Company ....D...... 989 453-2472
Pigeon *(G-12485)*
Armada Grain Co ....E...... 586 784-5911
Armada *(G-714)*
Bake N Cakes LP ....G...... 517 337-2253
Lansing *(G-9345)*
Belle Feeds ....G...... 269 628-1231
Paw Paw *(G-12397)*
Big Jon Sports Inc ....G...... 231 275-1010
Interlochen *(G-8236)*
Cargill Incorporated..........................F...... 608 868-5150
Owosso *(G-12281)*
Chippewa Farm Supply LLC ....G...... 989 471-5523
Spruce *(G-15213)*
Corunna Mills Feed LLC ....G...... 989 743-3110
Corunna *(G-3580)*
Custom Blend Feeds Inc ....G...... 810 798-3265
Bruce Twp *(G-2081)*
Darling Ingredients Inc ....C...... 517 279-9731
Coldwater *(G-3301)*
Darling Ingredients Inc ....D...... 313 928-7400
Melvindale *(G-10695)*
Darling Ingredients Inc ....E...... 269 751-0560
Hamilton *(G-7231)*

Darwin Sneller...................................G...... 989 977-3718
Sebewaing *(G-14514)*
Endres Processing LLC ....D...... 616 878-4230
Byron Center *(G-2189)*
Endres Processing Michigan LLC ....F...... 269 965-0427
Battle Creek *(G-1177)*
Finkbeiner L & D Feed & Farm..........G...... 734 429-9777
Saline *(G-14390)*
Hatfield Enterprises ....G...... 616 677-5215
Marne *(G-10508)*
Hearthside Food Solutions LLC ....C...... 616 871-6240
Kentwood *(G-9009)*
▲ Heath Manufacturing Company.........D...... 616 997-8181
Coopersville *(G-3561)*
Holmquist Feed Mill ....G...... 906 446-3325
Trenary *(G-16151)*
John A Van Den Bosch Co ....E...... 616 848-2000
Holland *(G-7695)*
Kemin Industries Inc ....F...... 248 869-3080
Plymouth *(G-12663)*
Kent Nutrition Group Inc ....F...... 517 676-9544
Mason *(G-10643)*
Mac Baits ....G...... 616 392-2553
Holland *(G-7730)*
Mar-Vo Mineral Company Inc ....G...... 517 523-2669
Hillsdale *(G-7529)*
Markham Peat Corp ....F...... 800 851-7230
Lakeview *(G-9175)*
Mathie Energy Supply Co Inc ....G...... 517 625-3646
Morrice *(G-11120)*
Meal and More Incorporated ....E...... 517 625-3186
Morrice *(G-11121)*
Mid McHgan Feed Ingrdients LLC ......G...... 989 236-5014
Middleton *(G-10794)*
Midwest Marketing Inc......................G...... 989 793-9393
Saginaw *(G-14095)*
N F P Inc ....G...... 989 631-0009
Midland *(G-10896)*
Pet Treats Plus ....F...... 313 533-1701
Redford *(G-13181)*
Purina Mills LLC ....E...... 517 322-0200
Lansing *(G-9319)*
Quality Liquid Feeds Inc ....G...... 616 784-2930
Comstock Park *(G-3511)*
Schantz LLC ....G...... 616 887-0517
Sparta *(G-15109)*
Vita Plus Corporation ....F...... 989 665-0013
Gagetown *(G-5803)*
Wysong Corporation ....G...... 989 631-0009
Midland *(G-10924)*
Wysong Medical Corporation ....E...... 989 631-0009
Midland *(G-10925)*

2051 Bread, Bakery Prdts Exc Cookies & Crackers

Achatzs Hand Made Pie Co................D...... 586 749-2882
Chesterfield *(G-2731)*
Aldos Bakery Inc ....G...... 810 744-9123
Flint *(G-5374)*
Almar Orchards LLC ....E...... 810 659-6568
Flushing *(G-5531)*
Apple Valley Natural Foods................C...... 269 471-3234
Berrien Springs *(G-1592)*
Aunt Millies Bakeries ....G...... 989 356-6688
Alpena *(G-278)*
Aunt Millies Bakeries Inc ....E...... 734 528-1475
Ypsilanti *(G-18053)*
Baker & Baker ....G...... 810 982-2763
Port Huron *(G-12897)*
Bakewell Company ....G...... 269 459-8030
Portage *(G-12983)*
Barneys Bakery ....G...... 989 895-5466
Bay City *(G-1281)*
Bay Bread Co ....F...... 231 922-8022
Traverse City *(G-15906)*
Beirut Bakery Inc ....F...... 313 533-4422
Redford *(G-13147)*
Big Boy Restaurants Intl LLC ....D...... 586 263-6220
Clinton Township *(G-3067)*
Bimbo Bakeries Usa Inc ....F...... 734 953-5741
Livonia *(G-9665)*
Bimbo Bakeries Usa Inc ....E...... 906 786-4042
Escanaba *(G-4819)*
Bimbo Bakeries Usa Inc ....E...... 989 667-0551
Bay City *(G-1291)*
Bimbo Bakeries Usa Inc ....E...... 586 772-0055
Warren *(G-16960)*
Bimbo Bakeries Usa Inc ....B...... 616 252-2709
Grand Rapids *(G-6222)*

Bimbo Bakeries Usa Inc ....E...... 810 239-8070
Flint *(G-5390)*
Bread of Life Bakery & Cafe..............F...... 906 663-4005
Bessemer *(G-1603)*
Brothers Baking Company ....E...... 269 663-8591
Edwardsburg *(G-4761)*
Cake Connection Tc LLC....................G...... 231 943-3531
Traverse City *(G-15928)*
Cambridge Foods LLC ....G...... 248 348-3800
Northville *(G-11682)*
Campbell Soup Company ....F...... 313 295-6884
Taylor *(G-15698)*
Campbell Soup Company ....D...... 248 336-8486
Ferndale *(G-5265)*
Care2share Baking Company ....G...... 810 280-0307
Attica *(G-739)*
Carlson Enterprises Inc ....E...... 248 656-1442
Rochester Hills *(G-13385)*
Cesere Enterprises Inc ....F...... 989 799-3350
Saginaw *(G-14015)*
Chewys Gourmet Kitchen LLC ....G...... 313 757-2595
Detroit *(G-3934)*
Classroom Farming Ltd.....................G...... 810 247-8410
Owosso *(G-12283)*
Coles Quality Foods Inc ....C...... 231 722-1651
Grand Rapids *(G-6288)*
Coles Quality Foods Inc ....C...... 231 722-1651
Muskegon *(G-11295)*
Cottage Bakery ....G...... 989 790-8135
Saginaw *(G-14021)*
Country Mill Farms LLC ....E...... 517 543-1019
Charlotte *(G-2642)*
Creme Curls Bakery Inc ....C...... 616 669-6230
Hudsonville *(G-8151)*
Cupcake Station ....G...... 248 334-7927
Pontiac *(G-12812)*
Dakota Cupcake Factory ....G...... 810 694-7198
Grand Blanc *(G-5964)*
Darwin Sneller...................................G...... 989 977-3718
Sebewaing *(G-14514)*
Divine Dessert ....G...... 313 278-3322
Dearborn Heights *(G-3782)*
Doll Face Chef LLC ....G...... 248 495-8280
Bloomfield Hills *(G-1760)*
Donutville...G...... 616 396-1160
Holland *(G-7610)*
Dorothy Dawson Food Products.........E...... 517 788-9830
Jackson *(G-8435)*
Dough Masters ....E...... 248 585-0600
Warren *(G-17005)*
Dunkin Donuts & Baskin-Robbins ......E...... 989 835-8412
Midland *(G-10856)*
Elegance of Season ....G...... 616 296-1059
Spring Lake *(G-15140)*
Embassy Distributing Company.........G...... 248 926-0590
Commerce Township *(G-3404)*
Ethels Edibles LLC ....F...... 586 552-5110
Saint Clair Shores *(G-14247)*
Evelyn Robertson Lett.......................G...... 248 569-8746
Southfield *(G-14901)*
Farmington Bakery ....G...... 248 442-2360
Farmington *(G-4899)*
▲ Flatout Inc ....D...... 734 944-5445
Saline *(G-14391)*
For The Love of Cupcakes ....G...... 906 399-3004
Bark River *(G-1119)*
G M Paris Bakery Inc ....E...... 734 425-2060
Livonia *(G-9746)*
Gr Baking Company ....F...... 616 245-3446
Grand Rapids *(G-6449)*
Grace Extended.................................G...... 616 502-2078
Grand Haven *(G-6020)*
Great Harvest Bread Co ....G...... 586 566-9500
Shelby Township *(G-14598)*
Home Bakery ....E...... 248 651-4830
Rochester *(G-13326)*
Hostess Cake ITT Contntl Bkg...........G...... 231 775-4629
Cadillac *(G-2253)*
Italian BTR Bread Sticks Bky ....G...... 313 893-4945
Detroit *(G-4152)*
Jaimes Cupcake Haven ....G...... 586 596-6809
Warren *(G-17111)*
James Ave Catering ....G...... 517 655-4532
Williamston *(G-17731)*
Jorgensens Inc..................................E...... 989 831-8338
Greenville *(G-7140)*
Josefs French Pastry Shop Co ....E...... 313 881-5710
Grosse Pointe Woods *(G-7204)*
Jt Bakers ....G...... 989 424-5102
Clare *(G-2874)*

SIC SECTION 20 FOOD AND KINDRED PRODUCTS

Julian Brothers Inc ...E ... 248 588-0280
Clawson (G-2981)
◆ Keebler Company ...B ... 269 961-2000
Battle Creek (G-1207)
Kellers Farm Bakery ...G ... 734 753-4360
Belleville (G-1446)
◆ Kellogg Company ...A ... 269 961-2000
Battle Creek (G-1211)
Klaus Nixdorf ...E ... 269 429-3259
Stevensville (G-15573)
Knickerbocker Baking Inc ...E ... 248 541-2110
Madison Heights (G-10291)
Kroger Co ...C ... 586 727-4946
Richmond (G-13265)
Linwood Bakery ...G ... 989 697-4430
Linwood (G-9598)
Looney Baker of Livonia Inc ...E ... 734 425-8569
Livonia (G-9818)
Mackenzies Bakery ...E ... 269 343-8440
Kalamazoo (G-8814)
Magic Treatz LLC ...G ... 248 989-9956
Oak Park (G-12080)
Marias Italian Bakery Inc ...F ... 734 981-1200
Canton (G-2396)
Marie Minnie Bakers Inc ...C ... 734 522-1100
Livonia (G-9823)
Metropolitan Baking Company ...D ... 313 875-7246
Detroit (G-4234)
Milano Bakery Inc ...E ... 313 833-3500
Detroit (G-4249)
Miles Cake Candy Supplies ...G ... 586 783-9252
Clinton Township (G-3176)
More Signature Cakes LLC ...G ... 248 266-0504
Troy (G-16512)
National Bakery ...G ... 313 891-7803
Detroit (G-4262)
New Martha Washington Bakery ...G ... 313 872-1988
Detroit (G-4268)
New Yasmeen Detroit Inc ...E ... 313 582-6035
Dearborn (G-3744)
New York Bagel Baking Co ...F ... 248 548-2580
Ferndale (G-5305)
Old Mission Multigrain LLC ...G ... 231 366-4121
Traverse City (G-16058)
Palm Sweets LLC ...E ... 586 554-7979
Sterling Heights (G-15442)
Paramount Baking Company ...F ... 313 690-4844
Roseville (G-13850)
Perfection Bakeries Inc ...D ... 269 343-1217
Kalamazoo (G-8847)
Perfection Bakeries Inc ...D ... 810 653-2378
Davison (G-3658)
Perfection Bakeries Inc ...D ... 517 278-2370
Coldwater (G-3319)
Perfection Bakeries Inc ...F ... 231 779-5365
Cadillac (G-2269)
Perfection Bakeries Inc ...E ... 517 750-1818
Jackson (G-8550)
Rainbow Pizza Inc ...G ... 734 246-4250
Taylor (G-15761)
Raleigh & Ron Corporation ...D ... 248 280-2820
Royal Oak (G-13961)
Randalls Bakery ...G ... 906 224-5401
Wakefield (G-16855)
Roma Bakery & Imported Foods ...E ... 517 485-9466
Lansing (G-9419)
◆ Roskam Baking Company ...C ... 616 574-5757
Grand Rapids (G-6839)
Roskam Baking Company ...D ... 616 574-5757
Grand Rapids (G-6840)
Roskam Baking Company ...C ... 616 574-5757
Grand Rapids (G-6841)
Roskam Baking Company ...C ... 616 554-9160
Grand Rapids (G-6842)
Roskam Baking Company ...B ... 616 574-5757
Grand Rapids (G-6843)
Rothbury Farms Inc ...A ... 616 574-5757
Grand Rapids (G-6844)
▲ Russos Bakery Inc ...F ... 586 791-7320
Clinton Township (G-3218)
▲ Savory Foods Inc ...D ... 616 241-2583
Grand Rapids (G-6851)
Schnitzelstein Baking Co ...G ... 616 988-2316
Grand Rapids (G-6853)
Schuette Farms ...G ... 989 550-0563
Elkton (G-4783)
▲ Shatila Food Products Inc ...E ... 313 934-1520
Dearborn (G-3758)
Simply Divine Baking LLC ...G ... 313 903-2881
Southfield (G-15028)
Sophias Bakery Inc ...F ... 313 582-6992
Detroit (G-4367)
Spartannash Company ...C ... 517 629-6313
Albion (G-132)
Spartannash Company ...D ... 517 278-8963
Coldwater (G-3333)
Spatz Bakery Inc ...F ... 989 755-5551
Saginaw (G-14152)
Stone House Bread LLC ...E ... 231 933-8864
Traverse City (G-16112)
Stone House Bread Inc ...E ... 231 933-8864
Traverse City (G-16113)
Supreme Baking Company ...E ... 313 894-0222
Detroit (G-4389)
Sweet & Sweeter Inc ...G ... 586 977-9338
Sterling Heights (G-15517)
Sweet Mellisas Cupcakes ...G ... 616 889-3998
Lowell (G-10043)
Sweet Potato Sensations Inc ...G ... 313 532-7996
Detroit (G-4391)
Sweetheart Bakery Inc ...D ... 313 839-6330
Detroit (G-4392)
Sweetheart Bakery of Michigan ...D ... 586 795-1660
Harper Woods (G-7306)
Sweetwaters Donut Mill ...F ... 269 979-1944
Battle Creek (G-1256)
Telo ...G ... 810 845-8051
Fenton (G-5242)
Top Notch Cookies & Cakes Inc ...G ... 734 467-9550
Westland (G-17604)
Traverse City Pie Company LLC ...F ... 231 929-7437
Traverse City (G-16127)
Uncle Johns Cider Mill Inc ...D ... 989 224-3686
Saint Johns (G-14298)
Vargas & Sons ...F ... 989 754-4636
Saginaw (G-14178)
W Bay Cupcakes ...G ... 231 632-2010
Traverse City (G-16140)
Walmart Inc ...B ... 517 541-1481
Charlotte (G-2670)
Way Bakery ...C ... 517 787-6720
Jackson (G-8605)
▼ West Thomas Partners LLC ...E ... 616 430-7585
Grand Rapids (G-6989)
White Lotus Farms Inc ...G ... 734 904-1379
Ann Arbor (G-698)
Wow Factor Tables and Events ...G ... 248 550-5922
Howell (G-8122)
Zingermans Bakehouse Inc ...D ... 734 761-2095
Ann Arbor (G-708)

2052 Cookies & Crackers

Among Friends LLC ...F ... 734 997-9720
Ann Arbor (G-354)
Artisan Bread Co LLC ...E ... 586 756-0100
Warren (G-16940)
Bake Station Bakeries Mich Inc ...E ... 248 352-9000
Southfield (G-14849)
Bimbo Bakeries Usa Inc ...B ... 616 252-2709
Grand Rapids (G-6222)
Campbell Soup Company ...F ... 313 295-6884
Taylor (G-15698)
Campbell Soup Company ...D ... 248 336-8486
Ferndale (G-5265)
Cherry Cone LLC ...G ... 231 944-1036
Traverse City (G-15939)
Cherry Republic Inc ...D ... 231 334-3150
Glen Arbor (G-5940)
Chewys Gourmet Kitchen LLC ...G ... 313 757-2595
Detroit (G-3934)
Dick and Jane Baking Co LLC ...G ... 248 519-2418
Troy (G-16317)
Frito-Lay North America Inc ...E ... 989 754-0435
Saginaw (G-14040)
Karemor Inc ...G ... 517 323-3042
Lansing (G-9303)
◆ Keebler Company ...B ... 269 961-2000
Battle Creek (G-1207)
Keebler Company ...D ... 231 445-0335
Cheboygan (G-2684)
◆ Kellogg Company ...A ... 269 961-2000
Battle Creek (G-1211)
Kellogg North America Company ...A ... 269 961-2000
Battle Creek (G-1218)
Krumbsnatcher Enterprises LLC ...F ... 313 408-6802
Detroit (G-4184)
▲ Lotte USA Incorporated ...F ... 269 963-6664
Battle Creek (G-1223)
Ludwicks Frozen Donuts Inc ...F ... 616 453-6880
Grand Rapids (G-6635)
Marias Italian Bakery Inc ...F ... 734 981-1200
Canton (G-2396)
Nautical Knots ...G ... 231 206-0400
Grand Haven (G-6058)
Pepperidge Farm Incorporated ...G ... 734 953-6729
Livonia (G-9885)
Roma Bakery & Imported Foods ...E ... 517 485-9466
Lansing (G-9419)
▲ Savory Foods Inc ...D ... 616 241-2583
Grand Rapids (G-6851)
▲ Shatila Food Products Inc ...E ... 313 934-1520
Dearborn (G-3758)
Stone House Bread Inc ...E ... 231 933-8864
Traverse City (G-16113)
Supreme Baking Company ...E ... 313 894-0222
Detroit (G-4389)
Sweet Potato Sensations Inc ...G ... 313 532-7996
Detroit (G-4391)
Sweetie Pie Pantry ...G ... 517 669-9300
Dewitt (G-4466)
Syd Enterprises ...G ... 517 719-2740
Howell (G-8104)
Top Notch Cookies & Cakes Inc ...G ... 734 467-9550
Westland (G-17604)

2053 Frozen Bakery Prdts

Bakers Rhapsody ...G ... 269 767-1368
Dowagiac (G-4535)
Bimbo Bakeries Usa Inc ...G ... 231 922-3296
Traverse City (G-15912)
Bimbo Bakeries Usa Inc ...B ... 616 252-2709
Grand Rapids (G-6222)
◆ Dawn Foods Inc ...C ... 517 789-4400
Jackson (G-8430)
Jakes Cakes Inc ...G ... 734 522-2103
Garden City (G-5831)
Julian Brothers Inc ...E ... 248 588-0280
Clawson (G-2981)
Ludwicks Frozen Donuts Inc ...F ... 616 453-6880
Grand Rapids (G-6635)
Marie Minnie Bakers Inc ...C ... 734 522-1100
Livonia (G-9823)
Pepperidge Farm Incorporated ...G ... 734 953-6729
Livonia (G-9885)
▲ Savory Foods Inc ...D ... 616 241-2583
Grand Rapids (G-6851)
Sweet Creations ...G ... 989 327-1157
Saginaw (G-14161)

2061 Sugar, Cane

Michigan Sugar Company ...D ... 989 883-3200
Sebewaing (G-14516)
Michigan Sugar Company ...D ... 989 673-2223
Caro (G-2473)

2062 Sugar, Cane Refining

◆ Americane Sugar Refining LLC ...G ... 313 299-1300
Taylor (G-15687)
Farber Concessions Inc ...E ... 313 387-1600
Redford (G-13161)
Michigan Sugar Company ...C ... 989 673-3126
Caro (G-2472)

2063 Sugar, Beet

Darwin Sneller ...G ... 989 977-3718
Sebewaing (G-14514)
Michigan Sugar Company ...C ... 989 673-3126
Caro (G-2472)
Michigan Sugar Company ...D ... 989 883-3200
Sebewaing (G-14516)
Michigan Sugar Company ...D ... 810 679-2241
Croswell (G-3601)
▲ Michigan Sugar Company ...D ... 989 686-0161
Bay City (G-1333)
Michigan Sugar Company ...D ... 989 673-2223
Caro (G-2473)
Schuette Farms ...G ... 989 550-0563
Elkton (G-4783)

2064 Candy & Confectionery Prdts

American Gourmet Snacks LLC ...G ... 989 892-4856
Essexville (G-4867)
Berkley Pharmacy LLC ...F ... 586 573-8300
Warren (G-16955)
Chocolate Vault Llc ...G ... 517 688-3388
Horton (G-7963)
Comstock Creamery LLC ...G ... 269 929-7693
Kalamazoo (G-8712)

S I C

Employee Codes: A=Over 500 employees, B=251-500
C=101-250, D=51-100, E=20-50, F=10-19, G=3-9
2020 Harris Michigan
Industrial Directory
703

20 FOOD AND KINDRED PRODUCTS

D A U P Corp .... G 906 477-1148
  Naubinway (G-11465)
Detroit Fd Entrprnrship Acdemy .... F 248 894-8941
  Detroit (G-3984)
Detroit Fudge Company Inc .... G 734 369-8573
  Ann Arbor (G-417)
Donckers Candies & Gifts .... G 906 226-6110
  Marquette (G-10526)
Doug Murdicks Fudge Inc .... G 231 938-2330
  Traverse City (G-15957)
Elsa Enterprises Inc .... G 248 816-1454
  Troy (G-16340)
Fretty Media LLC .... G 231 894-8055
  Whitehall (G-17667)
▲ Gayles Chocolates Limited .... E 248 398-0001
  Royal Oak (G-13929)
Gerbers Home Made Sweets .... G 231 348-3743
  Charlevoix (G-2615)
Gki Foods LLC .... D 248 486-0055
  Brighton (G-1931)
Happy Candy .... G 248 629-9819
  Warren (G-17076)
Junkless Foods Inc .... G 616 560-7895
  Kalamazoo (G-8782)
Klopp Group LLC .... G 877 256-4528
  Saginaw (G-14073)
Liquid Otc LLC .... G 248 214-7771
  Commerce Township (G-3422)
▲ Lotte USA Incorporated .... F 269 963-6664
  Battle Creek (G-1223)
Maas Enterprises Michigan LLC .... G 616 875-8099
  Holland (G-7729)
Marshalls Trail Inc .... F 231 436-5082
  Mackinaw City (G-10099)
Morley Brands LLC .... D 586 468-4300
  Clinton Township (G-3180)
Mr Peel Inc .... G 734 266-2022
  Livonia (G-9853)
Nassau Candy Midwest L L C .... D 734 464-2787
  Livonia (G-9859)
Original Murdicks Fudge Co .... E 906 847-3530
  Mackinac Island (G-10097)
▲ R & J Almonds Inc .... F 810 767-6887
  Flint (G-5489)
Rocky Mtn Choclat Fctry Inc .... D 810 606-8550
  Grand Blanc (G-5981)
Rps Bar .... G 810 235-8876
  Flint (G-5496)
▲ Sanders Candy LLC .... D 800 651-7263
  Clinton Township (G-3221)
Simply Suzanne LLC .... G 917 364-4549
  Detroit (G-4363)
Sugar Free Specialties LLC .... F 616 734-6999
  Comstock Park (G-3517)
Sweet Essentials LLC .... G 248 398-7933
  Berkley (G-1589)
Truans Candies Inc .... F 313 281-0185
  Plymouth (G-12782)
Vineyards Gourmet .... G 269 468-4778
  Coloma (G-3366)
W2 Inc .... G 517 764-3141
  Jackson (G-8602)
White River Sugar Bush .... G 231 861-4860
  Hesperia (G-7480)

2066 Chocolate & Cocoa Prdts

Alinosi French Ice Cream Co .... G 313 527-3195
  Detroit (G-3855)
▲ Gayles Chocolates Limited .... E 248 398-0001
  Royal Oak (G-13929)
Heather N Holly .... G 989 832-6460
  Midland (G-10869)
Kemnitz Fine Candies .... G 734 453-0480
  Plymouth (G-12665)
Kilwins Qulty Confections Inc .... G 231 347-3800
  Petoskey (G-12452)
Marshalls Trail Inc .... F 231 436-5082
  Mackinaw City (G-10099)
Original Murdicks Fudge Co .... E 906 847-3530
  Mackinac Island (G-10097)
Rocky Mtn Choclat Fctry Inc .... D 810 606-8550
  Grand Blanc (G-5981)
Rocky Mtn Choclat Fctry Inc .... G 989 624-4784
  Birch Run (G-1669)
▲ Sanders Candy LLC .... D 800 651-7263
  Clinton Township (G-3221)
Sugar Free Specialties LLC .... F 616 734-6999
  Comstock Park (G-3517)

2067 Chewing Gum

▲ Lotte USA Incorporated .... F 269 963-6664
  Battle Creek (G-1223)

2068 Salted & Roasted Nuts & Seeds

Kar Nut Products Company LLC .... C 248 588-1903
  Madison Heights (G-10288)
Knpc Holdco LLC .... G 248 588-1903
  Madison Heights (G-10292)
◆ Koeze Company .... E 616 724-2601
  Grand Rapids (G-6588)
Nutco Inc .... E 800 872-4006
  Detroit (G-4280)
St Laurent Brothers Inc .... E 989 893-7522
  Bay City (G-1360)
Variety Foods Inc .... E 586 268-4900
  Warren (G-17279)

2075 Soybean Oil Mills

Cargill Incorporated .... F 608 868-5150
  Owosso (G-12281)
Ferguson Landscaping .... G 248 761-1005
  Oak Park (G-12067)
Michigan Soy Products Company .... G 248 544-7742
  Royal Oak (G-13951)
Nubreed Nutrition Inc .... G 734 272-7395
  Troy (G-16529)
Zeeland Bio-Based Products LLC .... G 616 748-1831
  Zeeland (G-18199)
◆ Zeeland Farm Services Inc .... C 616 772-9042
  Zeeland (G-18201)

2076 Vegetable Oil Mills

Darling Ingredients Inc .... D 313 928-7400
  Melvindale (G-10695)
Darling Ingredients Inc .... E 269 751-0560
  Hamilton (G-7231)
Go Beyond Healthy LLC .... G 407 255-0314
  Grand Rapids (G-6445)
Grand Trvrse Culinary Oils LLC .... G 231 590-2180
  Traverse City (G-15990)

2077 Animal, Marine Fats & Oils

Asao LLC .... F 734 522-6333
  Livonia (G-9653)
Darling Ingredients Inc .... D 313 928-7400
  Melvindale (G-10695)
Darling Ingredients Inc .... F 989 752-4340
  Carrollton (G-2485)
Darling Ingredients Inc .... C 517 279-9731
  Coldwater (G-3301)
Darling Ingredients Inc .... E 269 751-0560
  Hamilton (G-7231)
Evergreen Grease Service Inc .... G 517 264-9913
  Adrian (G-63)
Kellys Recycling Service Inc .... G 313 389-7870
  Detroit (G-4174)
Michigan Protein Inc .... G 616 696-7854
  Cedar Springs (G-2558)
Protein Magnet Corp .... G 616 844-1545
  Spring Lake (G-15171)

2079 Shortening, Oils & Margarine

Asao LLC .... F 734 522-6333
  Livonia (G-9653)
Cozart Producers .... G 810 736-1046
  Flint (G-5406)
Frank Smith .... G 313 443-8882
  Detroit (G-4072)
Michigan Biodiesel LLC .... G 269 427-0804
  Kalamazoo (G-8823)
Mount of Olive Oil Company .... G 989 928-9030
  Mayville (G-10675)
Priorat Importers Corporation .... G 248 217-4608
  Royal Oak (G-13959)
Stamatopolos & Sons .... G 734 369-2995
  Ann Arbor (G-644)

2082 Malt Beverages

127 Brewing .... G 517 258-1346
  Jackson (G-8368)
5 Mile Brewing Company LLC .... G 313 348-1628
  Detroit (G-3825)
51 North Brewing .... G 248 690-7367
  Lake Orion (G-9121)
734 Brewing Company Inc .... G 734 649-6453
  Ypsilanti (G-18049)
▲ Abaco Partners LLC .... C 616 532-1700
  Kentwood (G-8997)
Acoustic Tap Room .... G 231 714-5028
  Traverse City (G-15888)
Apple Blossom Winery LLC .... F 269 668-3724
  Kalamazoo (G-8679)
Atwater In Park .... G 313 344-5104
  Grosse Pointe Park (G-7191)
Austin Brothers Beer Co LLC .... G 909 213-4194
  Alpena (G-279)
Backdraft Brewing Company .... D 734 722-7639
  Wayne (G-17427)
Bells Brewery Inc .... F 269 382-1402
  Kalamazoo (G-8695)
◆ Bells Brewery Inc .... E 269 382-2338
  Galesburg (G-5806)
Bells Brewery Inc .... G 906 233-5000
  Escanaba (G-4816)
Biere De Mac Brew Works LLC .... G 616 862-8018
  Mackinaw City (G-10098)
Black Bottom Brewing Co Inc .... G 313 205-5493
  Detroit (G-3905)
Blackrocks Brewery LLC .... G 906 273-1333
  Marquette (G-10520)
Blackrocks Brewery LLC .... G 906 273-1333
  Marquette (G-10521)
Brew Detroit LLC .... F 313 974-7366
  Detroit (G-3915)
▲ Canal Street Brewing Co LLC .... D 616 776-1195
  Grand Rapids (G-6253)
Clarkston Courts LLC .... C 248 383-8444
  Clarkston (G-2913)
Corner Brewery LLC .... E 734 480-2739
  Ypsilanti (G-18061)
Detroit Cycle Pub LLC .... G 231 286-5257
  Macomb (G-10116)
Detroit Rivertwn Brewing Co LL .... C 313 877-9205
  Detroit (G-4000)
Draught Horse Group LLC .... G 231 631-5218
  New Hudson (G-11538)
Eastside Spot Inc .... G 906 226-9431
  Marquette (G-10528)
Fabiano Bros Dev - Wscnsin LLC .... G 989 509-0200
  Bay City (G-1313)
Frankenmuth Brewery LLC .... C 989 262-8300
  Frankenmuth (G-5585)
Frankenmuth Brewing Company .... D 989 262-8300
  Frankenmuth (G-5586)
Ghost Island Brewery .... G 219 242-4800
  New Buffalo (G-11515)
Gpbc Inc .... C 734 741-7325
  Ann Arbor (G-475)
Harville Associates Inc .... G 313 839-5712
  Harper Woods (G-7301)
Im A Beer Hound .... G 517 331-0528
  Lansing (G-9296)
James Joy LLC .... G 989 317-6629
  Farwell (G-5162)
Jolly Pumpkin Artisan Ales LLC .... G 734 426-4962
  Dexter (G-4496)
▲ Keweenaw Brewing Company LLC .. F 906 482-5596
  Houghton (G-7973)
Keweenaw Brewing Company LLC ...... G 906 482-1937
  South Range (G-14817)
Knickerbocker .... G 616 345-5642
  Grand Rapids (G-6586)
Kraftbrau Brewery Inc .... G 269 384-0288
  Kalamazoo (G-8803)
Loggers Brewing Co .... G 989 401-3085
  Saginaw (G-14079)
Lucky Girl Brwing - Cross Rads .... G 630 723-4285
  Paw Paw (G-12407)
M4 CIC LLC .... G 734 436-8507
  Ann Arbor (G-539)
Marquette Distillery .... G 906 869-4933
  Marquette (G-10543)
MI Brew LLC .... F 616 361-9658
  Rockford (G-13579)
Michigan Beer Growler Company .... G 248 385-3773
  Beverly Hills (G-1619)
Midland Brewing Co LLC .... G 989 631-3041
  Midland (G-10887)
Mishigama Brewing Company .... G 734 547-5840
  Ypsilanti (G-18091)
Mitten Brewing Company LLC .... G 616 608-5612
  Grand Rapids (G-6691)
▲ Mor-Dall Enterprises Inc .... G 269 558-4915
  Marshall (G-10584)
Mount Pleasant Brewing Company .... G 989 400-4666
  Mount Pleasant (G-11210)

SIC SECTION
20 FOOD AND KINDRED PRODUCTS

Mountain Town Stn Brew Pub LLC .... C 989 775-2337
Mount Pleasant *(G-11211)*
Mug Shots Burgers and Brews .... G 616 895-2337
Allendale *(G-225)*
New Holland Brewery .... F 616 298-7727
Holland *(G-7756)*
New Holland Brewery .... G 616 202-7200
Grand Rapids *(G-6716)*
▲ New Holland Brewing Co LLC .... C 616 355-2941
Holland *(G-7757)*
North Pier Brewing Company LLC .... G 312 545-0446
Saint Joseph *(G-14332)*
Northern Oak Brewery Inc .... F 248 634-7515
Holly *(G-7889)*
Null Taphouse .... G 734 792-9124
Dexter *(G-4501)*
One Beer At A Time LLC .... E 616 719-1604
Grand Rapids *(G-6730)*
Oracle Brewing Company .... G 989 401-7446
Saginaw *(G-14117)*
Oracle Brewing Company LLC .... G 989 401-7446
Breckenridge *(G-1845)*
Ore Dock Brewing Company LLC .... G 906 228-8888
Marquette *(G-10550)*
Paddle Hard Distributing LLC .... G 513 309-1192
Grayling *(G-7115)*
Plow Point Brewing Co .... G 734 562-9102
Chelsea *(G-2717)*
▼ Premier Malt Products Inc .... E 586 443-3355
Warren *(G-17195)*
Rare Bird Holdings LLC .... G 616 335-9463
Holland *(G-7785)*
Rochester Mlls Prod Brewry LLC .... G 248 377-3130
Auburn Hills *(G-993)*
S B C Holdings Inc .... F 313 446-2000
Detroit *(G-4350)*
Saugatuck Brewing Co Inc .... E 269 857-7222
Douglas *(G-4532)*
Shorts Brewing Company LLC .... D 231 498-2300
Elk Rapids *(G-4780)*
Stony Lake Corporation .... G 734 944-9426
Saline *(G-14416)*
Stroh Companies Inc .... F 313 446-2000
Detroit *(G-4380)*
Sweetwater Brew LLC .... G 616 805-5077
Wyoming *(G-18034)*
Wild Mitten LLC .... G 616 795-1610
Wyoming *(G-18043)*
Woodward Avenue Brewers .... E 248 894-7665
Ferndale *(G-5330)*

2083 Malt

Apple Blossom Winery LLC .... F 269 668-3724
Kalamazoo *(G-8679)*

2084 Wine & Brandy

▲ 45 North Vineyard & Winery .... F 231 271-1188
Lake Leelanau *(G-9098)*
▲ Andretta & Associates Inc .... F 586 557-6226
Macomb *(G-10107)*
Aurora Cellars 2015 LLC .... F 231 994-3188
Lake Leelanau *(G-9099)*
B Nektar LLC .... G 313 999-5157
Ferndale *(G-5264)*
Black & Red Inc .... G 231 271-8888
Suttons Bay *(G-15649)*
Black Dragon LLC .... G 269 277-4874
Saint Joseph *(G-14302)*
▲ Black Star Farms LLC .... F 231 271-4970
Suttons Bay *(G-15650)*
Blustone Partners LLC .... F 231 256-0146
Lake Leelanau *(G-9101)*
Bowers Harbor Vinyrd & Winery .... G 231 223-7615
Traverse City *(G-15919)*
Brys Estate Vineyard & Winery .... G 231 223-9303
Traverse City *(G-15923)*
Cellar 849 Winery .... G 734 254-0275
Plymouth *(G-12594)*
Chateau Aronautique Winery LLC .... G 517 569-2132
Jackson *(G-8407)*
Chateau Grand Travers Ltd .... G 231 223-7355
Traverse City *(G-15936)*
▲ Chateau Operations Ltd .... E 231 223-4110
Traverse City *(G-15937)*
▲ CHI Co/Tabor Hill Winery .... D 269 422-1161
Buchanan *(G-2113)*
CHI Co/Tabor Hill Winery .... G 269 465-6566
Bridgman *(G-1861)*
Circus Procession LLC .... G 616 834-8048
Holland *(G-7591)*
Cody Kresta Vineyard & Winery .... G 269 668-3800
Mattawan *(G-10663)*
Dablon Vineyards LLC .... G 269 422-2846
Baroda *(G-1123)*
Dunn Beverage Intl LLC .... G 269 420-1547
Battle Creek *(G-1176)*
End of Road Winery LLC .... G 906 450-1541
Germfask *(G-5901)*
Evergreen Winery LLC .... G 989 392-2044
Bay City *(G-1311)*
Fenton Winery Brewery .... G 810 373-4194
Fenton *(G-5214)*
Flying Otter Winery LLC .... G 517 424-7107
Adrian *(G-65)*
Fontaine Chateau .... G 231 256-0000
Lake Leelanau *(G-9103)*
Garden Bay Winery LLC .... G 906 361-0318
Cooks *(G-3546)*
Garden Bay Winery LLC .... G 906 361-6136
Menominee *(G-10737)*
▲ Great Lakes Wine & Spirits LLC .... C 313 278-5400
Highland Park *(G-7506)*
Great Meadhall Brewing Co LLC .... G 269 427-0827
Bangor *(G-1091)*
Harbor Sprng Vnyrds Winery LLC .... G 231 242-4062
Harbor Springs *(G-7283)*
▲ Hickory Creek Winery LLC .... G 269 422-1100
Buchanan *(G-2120)*
Howells Mainstreet Winery .... G 517 545-9463
Howell *(G-8053)*
L Mawby LLC .... G 231 271-3522
Suttons Bay *(G-15653)*
Lawton Ridge Winery LLC .... G 269 372-9463
Kalamazoo *(G-8806)*
Lazy Ballerina Winery LLC .... G 269 363-6218
Saint Joseph *(G-14323)*
Lazy Ballerina Winery LLC .... F 269 759-8486
Bridgman *(G-1870)*
▲ Leelanau Wine Cellars Ltd .... G 231 386-5201
Ann Arbor *(G-527)*
Left Foot Charley .... F 231 995-0500
Traverse City *(G-16025)*
Leighs Garden Winery Inc .... G 906 553-7799
Escanaba *(G-4839)*
Lemon Creek Winery Ltd .... G 616 844-1709
Grand Haven *(G-6048)*
Lemon Creek Winery Ltd .... E 269 471-1321
Berrien Springs *(G-1597)*
Little Man Winery LLC .... G 616 292-3983
Holland *(G-7726)*
Mari Villa Vineyards .... G 231 935-4513
Traverse City *(G-16032)*
MI Brew LLC .... F 616 361-9658
Rockford *(G-13579)*
Modern Craft Winery LLC .... G 989 876-4948
Au Gres *(G-747)*
Nate Ronald .... E 269 424-3777
Dowagiac *(G-4556)*
Nicholass Black River Vineyar .... G 231 436-5770
Mackinaw City *(G-10100)*
▲ Nicholass Black River Vineyar .... G 231 625-9060
Cheboygan *(G-2687)*
Northville Cider Mill Inc .... E 248 349-3181
Northville *(G-11715)*
Northville Winery .... F 248 320-6507
Northville *(G-11718)*
▲ OKeefe Centre Ltd .... G 231 223-7355
Traverse City *(G-16056)*
Pentamere Winery .... F 517 423-9000
Tecumseh *(G-15805)*
R C M S Inc .... G 269 422-1617
Baroda *(G-1130)*
Schramms Mead .... G 248 439-5000
Ferndale *(G-5317)*
▲ Shady Lane Orchards Inc .... F 231 935-1620
Suttons Bay *(G-15655)*
Spotted Dog Winery .... G 734 944-9463
Ann Arbor *(G-642)*
St Julian Wine Company Inc .... F 734 529-3700
Dundee *(G-4601)*
St Julian Wine Company Inc .... E 269 657-5568
Paw Paw *(G-12414)*
St Julian Wine Company Inc .... G 989 652-3281
Frankenmuth *(G-5595)*
Stoney Acres Winery .... G 989 356-1041
Alpena *(G-317)*
Suttons Bay Ciders .... G 734 646-3196
Suttons Bay *(G-15656)*
To Willow Harbor Vineyard .... G 269 369-3900
Three Oaks *(G-15852)*
Townline Ciderworks LLC .... G 231 883-5330
Williamsburg *(G-17723)*
Vander Mill LLC .... D 616 259-8828
Grand Rapids *(G-6960)*
Veritas Vineyard LLC .... G 517 474-9026
Albion *(G-135)*
Veritas Vineyard LLC .... G 517 592-4663
Brooklyn *(G-2043)*
Veritas Vineyard LLC .... E 517 962-2427
Jackson *(G-8600)*
Vineyard 2121 LLC .... F 269 429-0555
Benton Harbor *(G-1561)*
Vipers Den Winery LLC .... G 734 644-0213
Detroit *(G-4429)*
Virtue Cider .... G 269 455-0526
Fennville *(G-5179)*
Warner Vineyards Inc .... G 269 657-3165
Paw Paw *(G-12417)*
Warner Vineyards Inc .... G 269 637-6900
South Haven *(G-14783)*
Weathervane Vinyards Inc .... G 231 228-4800
Cedar *(G-2543)*
Willow Vineyards Inc .... D 231 271-4810
Suttons Bay *(G-15657)*
Wine Cellar Visions LLC .... G 517 332-1026
East Lansing *(G-4682)*
Winery At Black Star Farms LLC .... E 231 271-4882
Suttons Bay *(G-15658)*

2085 Liquors, Distilled, Rectified & Blended

Ann Arbor Distilling Co .... G 734 769-6075
Ann Arbor *(G-357)*
Artesian Distillers .... G 616 252-1700
Grand Rapids *(G-6184)*
Beverage Solution Technolgies .... G 616 252-1700
Grand Rapids *(G-6215)*
Bier Barrel Distillery LLC .... G 616 633-8601
Comstock Park *(G-3464)*
Detroit City Distillery LLC .... F 313 338-3760
Detroit *(G-3977)*
Detroit City Distillery LLC .... G 734 904-3073
Spring Lake *(G-15138)*
Distillery 9 LLC .... G 517 990-2929
Whitmore Lake *(G-17695)*
Embrace Premium Vodka LLC .... G 616 617-5602
Ypsilanti *(G-18070)*
Les Cheneaux Distillers Inc .... G 906 748-0505
Cedarville *(G-2568)*
▲ Liquid Manufacturing LLC .... C 810 220-2802
Ann Arbor *(G-530)*
Long Road Distillers LLC .... G 616 356-1770
Grand Rapids *(G-6630)*
Mammoth Distilling LLC .... G 773 841-4242
Central Lake *(G-2592)*
Michigrain Distillery .... G 517 580-8624
Lansing *(G-9400)*
Proof & Union LLC .... G 312 919-0191
Grand Rapids *(G-6790)*
▲ RGI Brands LLC .... F 312 253-7400
Bloomfield Hills *(G-1794)*
Rockery .... G 734 281-4629
Wyandotte *(G-17973)*
Sunlite Market Inc .... G 586 792-9870
Clinton Township *(G-3236)*
Tcwc LLC .... F 231 922-8292
Traverse City *(G-16119)*
Temperance Distilling Company .... F 734 847-5262
Temperance *(G-15845)*
▲ Two James Spirits LLC .... G 313 964-4800
Detroit *(G-4411)*
Valentine Distilling .... G 248 629-9951
Ferndale *(G-5327)*
Valentine Distilling Co .... G 646 286-2690
Ferndale *(G-5328)*

2086 Soft Drinks

Absopure Water Company LLC .... B 734 459-8000
Plymouth *(G-12560)*
American Bottling Company .... D 810 564-1432
Mount Morris *(G-11157)*
American Bottling Company .... D 616 396-1281
Holland *(G-7556)*
American Bottling Company .... E 616 392-2124
Holland *(G-7557)*
American Bottling Company .... E 989 731-5392
Gaylord *(G-5848)*
American Bottling Company .... E 231 775-7393
Cadillac *(G-2227)*
American Bottling Company .... D 517 622-8605
Grand Ledge *(G-6100)*

SIC

20 FOOD AND KINDRED PRODUCTS SIC SECTION

- **Aqua Fine Inc** G 616 392-7843 Holland *(G-7560)*
- **Arbor Springs Water Company** E 734 668-8270 Ann Arbor *(G-365)*
- **Binks Coca-Cola Bottling Co** E 906 786-4144 Escanaba *(G-4820)*
- **Binks Coca-Cola Bottling Co** F 906 774-3202 Iron Mountain *(G-8277)*
- **Bottling Group Inc** G 517 545-2624 Howell *(G-8017)*
- **Coca-Cola Bottling Co** G 313 868-2167 Highland Park *(G-7502)*
- **Coca-Cola Company** B 269 657-3171 Paw Paw *(G-12399)*
- **Coca-Cola Company** C 734 397-2700 Belleville *(G-1443)*
- **Coca-Cola Refreshments USA Inc** D 989 895-8537 Bay City *(G-1296)*
- **Coca-Cola Refreshments USA Inc** D 231 947-4150 Traverse City *(G-15943)*
- **Coca-Cola Refreshments USA Inc** D 616 458-4536 Grand Rapids *(G-6285)*
- **Coca-Cola Refreshments USA Inc** E 231 347-3242 Petoskey *(G-12445)*
- **Coca-Cola Refreshments USA Inc** D 269 657-8538 Paw Paw *(G-12400)*
- **Coca-Cola Refreshments USA Inc** D 810 237-4000 Flint *(G-5398)*
- **Coca-Cola Refreshments USA Inc** C 313 897-2176 Detroit *(G-3942)*
- **Coca-Cola Refreshments USA Inc** C 517 322-2349 Lansing *(G-9283)*
- **Coca-Cola Refreshments USA Inc** C 313 897-5000 Farmington Hills *(G-4964)*
- **Coke Bottle** G 810 424-3352 Flint *(G-5399)*
- **Crystal Falls Springs Inc** G 906 875-3191 Crystal Falls *(G-3608)*
- **Crystal Pure Water Inc** G 989 681-3547 Saint Louis *(G-14362)*
- **Detroit Bubble Tea Company** G 248 239-1131 Ferndale *(G-5273)*
- **Diehls Orchard & Cider Mill** G 248 634-8981 Holly *(G-7876)*
- **Dr Pepper Snapple Group** G 616 393-5800 Holland *(G-7611)*
- **Ellis Infinity LLC** G 313 570-0840 Detroit *(G-4033)*
- **Everfresh Beverages Inc** D 586 755-9500 Warren *(G-17024)*
- **Faygo Beverages Inc** B 313 925-1600 Detroit *(G-4052)*
- **Florida Coca-Cola Bottling Co** F 906 495-2261 Kincheloe *(G-9051)*
- **Global Restaurant Group Inc** F 313 271-2777 Dearborn *(G-3716)*
- **Grandads Sweet Tea LLC** G 313 320-4446 Warren *(G-17062)*
- **Hancock Bottling Co Inc** F 906 482-3701 Hancock *(G-7251)*
- **Hill Brothers** G 616 784-2767 Grand Rapids *(G-6513)*
- **Jbt Bottling LLC** G 269 377-4905 Kalamazoo *(G-8777)*
- **Jumpin Johnnys Inc** G 989 832-0160 Midland *(G-10878)*
- **Keurig Dr Pepper Inc** G 231 775-7393 Cadillac *(G-2257)*
- **Keurig Dr Pepper Inc** D 313 937-3500 Detroit *(G-4176)*
- ▲ **Liquid Manufacturing LLC** C 810 220-2802 Ann Arbor *(G-530)*
- ▲ **Michigan Btlg & Cstm Pack Co** D 313 846-1717 Detroit *(G-4239)*
- **Minute Maid Co** G 269 657-3171 Paw Paw *(G-12410)*
- **Newberry Bottling Co Inc** G 906 293-5189 Newberry *(G-11582)*
- **Northville Cider Mill Inc** E 248 349-3181 Northville *(G-11715)*
- **Pbg Michigan LLC** G 989 345-2595 West Branch *(G-17515)*
- **Pepsi** G 231 627-2290 Cheboygan *(G-2690)*
- **Pepsi Beverages Co** G 989 754-0435 Saginaw *(G-14120)*
- **Pepsi Beverages Company** E 248 596-9028 Wixom *(G-17877)*
- **Pepsi Bottling Group** G 810 966-8060 Kimball *(G-9046)*
- **Pepsi Bottling Group** F 517 546-2777 Howell *(G-8077)*
- **Pepsi Cola Botling Co Houghton** F 906 482-0161 Houghton *(G-7980)*
- **Pepsi-Cola Metro Btlg Co Inc** D 517 321-0231 Lansing *(G-9254)*
- **Pepsi-Cola Metro Btlg Co Inc** C 248 335-3528 Pontiac *(G-12855)*
- **Pepsi-Cola Metro Btlg Co Inc** E 989 345-2595 West Branch *(G-17516)*
- **Pepsi-Cola Metro Btlg Co Inc** E 231 946-0452 Traverse City *(G-16064)*
- **Pepsi-Cola Metro Btlg Co Inc** D 989 755-1020 Saginaw *(G-14121)*
- **Pepsi-Cola Metro Btlg Co Inc** D 517 546-2777 Howell *(G-8078)*
- **Pepsi-Cola Metro Btlg Co Inc** D 269 226-6400 Kalamazoo *(G-8846)*
- **Pepsi-Cola Metro Btlg Co Inc** D 810 232-3925 Flint *(G-5479)*
- **Pepsi-Cola Metro Btlg Co Inc** D 616 285-8200 Grand Rapids *(G-6747)*
- **Pepsi-Cola Metro Btlg Co Inc** E 517 279-8436 Coldwater *(G-3318)*
- **Pepsi-Cola Metro Btlg Co Inc** E 313 832-0910 Detroit *(G-4296)*
- **Pepsi-Cola Metro Btlg Co Inc** E 231 798-1274 Norton Shores *(G-11788)*
- **Pepsi-Cola Metro Btlg Co Inc** E 810 987-2181 Kimball *(G-9047)*
- **Pepsi-New Bern-Howell-151** G 517 546-7542 Howell *(G-8079)*
- **Pepsico Inc** G 734 374-9841 Southgate *(G-15082)*
- **Pepsico Inc** G 586 276-4102 Sterling Heights *(G-15443)*
- **Pure Water Tech of Mid-MI** G 888 310-9848 Grand Blanc *(G-5979)*
- **Refreshment Product Svcs Inc** G 906 475-7003 Negaunee *(G-11474)*
- **S B C Holdings Inc** F 313 446-2000 Detroit *(G-4350)*
- **Select Distributors LLC** F 586 510-4647 Warren *(G-17237)*
- **South Range Bottling Works Inc** G 906 370-2295 South Range *(G-14819)*
- **St Julian Wine Company Inc** G 989 652-3281 Frankenmuth *(G-5595)*
- **Stroh Companies Inc** F 313 446-2000 Detroit *(G-4380)*
- **Sundance Beverages Inc** E 586 755-9470 Warren *(G-17257)*
- ▲ **Super Sidebar Inc** G 989 709-0048 West Branch *(G-17524)*
- **Underground Bev Brands LLC** G 248 336-9383 Royal Oak *(G-13977)*
- ▼ **Viva Beverages LLC** D 248 746-7044 Southfield *(G-15062)*
- **Warner Vineyards Inc** G 269 657-3165 Paw Paw *(G-12417)*

2087 Flavoring Extracts & Syrups

- **Coca-Cola Refreshments USA Inc** C 517 322-2349 Lansing *(G-9283)*
- ▲ **Coffee Beanery Ltd** E 810 733-1020 Flushing *(G-5533)*
- **Contract Flavors Inc** F 616 454-5950 Grand Rapids *(G-6304)*
- **Farber Concessions Inc** E 313 387-1600 Redford *(G-13161)*
- ▼ **Glcc Co** E 269 657-3167 Paw Paw *(G-12404)*
- **Jogue Inc** F 248 349-1501 Northville *(G-11703)*
- ◆ **Jogue Inc** E 734 207-0100 Plymouth *(G-12654)*
- **Jogue Inc** G 313 921-4802 Detroit *(G-4163)*
- ◆ **John L Hinkle Holding Co Inc** E 269 344-3640 Kalamazoo *(G-8780)*
- ◆ **Kalsec Inc** B 269 349-9711 Kalamazoo *(G-8799)*
- **Leonard Fountain Spc Inc** D 313 891-4141 Detroit *(G-4199)*
- **Leroy Worden** G 231 325-3837 Beulah *(G-1610)*
- **National Product Co** G 269 344-3640 Kalamazoo *(G-8834)*
- **Northville Laboratories Inc** F 248 349-1500 Northville *(G-11716)*
- **Northwoods Soda and Syrup Co** G 231 267-5853 Williamsburg *(G-17717)*
- ▲ **Penguin Juice Co** F 734 467-6991 Westland *(G-17587)*
- **Pure Herbs Ltd** F 586 446-8200 Sterling Heights *(G-15457)*
- **Real Flavors LLC** F 855 443-9685 Bay City *(G-1349)*
- **Refreshment Product Svcs Inc** G 906 475-7003 Negaunee *(G-11474)*
- **Sensient Flavors LLC** G 989 479-3211 Harbor Beach *(G-7270)*
- **Sensient Technologies Corp** D 989 479-3211 Harbor Beach *(G-7271)*
- **Sunopta Ingredients Inc** E 502 587-7999 Schoolcraft *(G-14502)*
- **Watkins Products** G 586 774-3187 Eastpointe *(G-4712)*
- **Wild Flavors Inc** E 269 216-2603 Kalamazoo *(G-8925)*

2091 Fish & Seafoods, Canned & Cured

- **Big O Smokehouse** F 616 891-5555 Caledonia *(G-2289)*
- **Gustafson Smoked Fish** G 906 292-5424 Moran *(G-11107)*
- ▼ **Ruleau Brothers Inc** E 906 753-4767 Stephenson *(G-15240)*
- **Sea Fare Foods Inc** E 313 568-0223 Detroit *(G-4357)*

2092 Fish & Seafoods, Fresh & Frozen

- **Collins Caviar Company** G 269 469-4576 Union Pier *(G-16737)*
- ▼ **Ruleau Brothers Inc** E 906 753-4767 Stephenson *(G-15240)*
- **Sea Fare Foods Inc** E 313 568-0223 Detroit *(G-4357)*

2095 Coffee

- **Becharas Bros Coffee Co** E 313 869-4700 Detroit *(G-3897)*
- **Cadillac Coffee Company** G 800 438-6900 Troy *(G-16252)*
- **Caffina Coffee Co** G 313 584-3584 Dearborn *(G-3683)*
- ▲ **Coffee Beanery Ltd** E 810 733-1020 Flushing *(G-5533)*
- **Coffee Express Co** F 734 459-4900 Plymouth *(G-12599)*
- **Cozy Cup Coffee Company Llc** G 989 984-7619 Oscoda *(G-12207)*
- **Farmer Bros Co** F 989 791-7985 Saginaw *(G-14036)*
- **Fireside Coffee Company Inc** F 810 635-9196 Swartz Creek *(G-15666)*
- **Good Sense Coffee LLC** G 810 355-2349 Brighton *(G-1932)*
- **Hermans Boy** G 616 866-2900 Rockford *(G-13571)*
- **Infusco Coffee Roasters LLC** G 269 213-5282 Sawyer *(G-14485)*
- **Inter State Foods Inc** F 517 372-5500 Lansing *(G-9237)*
- ◆ **Koeze Company** E 616 724-2601 Grand Rapids *(G-6588)*
- **La Colombe Torrefaction** G 231 798-9853 Norton Shores *(G-11769)*
- **Prospectors LLC** G 616 634-8260 Grand Rapids *(G-6792)*
- **Rowster Coffee Inc** E 616 780-7777 Grand Rapids *(G-6846)*
- **Stickmann Baeckerei** G 269 205-2444 Middleville *(G-10809)*
- **Three Rivers Coffee Company** G 269 244-0083 Three Rivers *(G-15879)*
- **Treat of Day LLC** F 616 706-1717 Grand Rapids *(G-6936)*

2096 Potato Chips & Similar Prdts

- **Better Made Snack Foods Inc** C 313 925-4774 Detroit *(G-3902)*
- **Cambridge Sharpe Inc** D 248 613-5562 South Lyon *(G-14788)*
- **Campbell Soup Company** F 313 295-6884 Taylor *(G-15698)*
- **Campbell Soup Company** D 248 336-8486 Ferndale *(G-5265)*

SIC SECTION
20 FOOD AND KINDRED PRODUCTS

▲ Dedinas & Franzak Entps Inc .... D 616 784-6095
Grand Rapids *(G-6342)*
Detroit Frnds Potato Chips LLC .... G 313 924-0085
Detroit *(G-3985)*
Downeys Potato Chips-Waterford .... G 248 673-3636
Waterford *(G-17338)*
▼ Grandpapas Inc .... E 313 891-6830
Detroit *(G-4099)*
▲ Great Lkes Fstida Holdings Inc .... F 616 241-0400
Grand Rapids *(G-6481)*
Hacienda Mexican Foods LLC .... D 313 895-8823
Detroit *(G-4110)*
Hacienda Mexican Foods LLC .... F 313 843-7007
Detroit *(G-4111)*
Manos Authentic LLC .... G 800 242-2796
Clinton Township *(G-3167)*
▲ Mexamerica Foods LLC .... E 814 781-1447
Grand Rapids *(G-6665)*
Pepsi-Cola Metro Btlg Co Inc .... D 517 272-2800
Lansing *(G-9410)*
Rainmaker Food Solutions LLC .... G 313 530-1321
South Lyon *(G-14811)*
Uncle Rays LLC .... G 313 739-6035
Detroit *(G-4413)*
▲ Uncle Rays LLC .... D 313 834-0800
Detroit *(G-4414)*
Variety Foods Inc .... E 586 268-4900
Warren *(G-17279)*

2097 Ice

Agi Ccaa Inc .... G 715 355-0856
Port Huron *(G-12882)*
Arctic Glacier Grayling Inc .... F 810 987-7100
Port Huron *(G-12892)*
▲ Arctic Glacier Inc .... E 734 485-0430
Port Huron *(G-12893)*
Arctic Glacier PA Inc .... E 610 494-8200
Port Huron *(G-12894)*
Arctic Glacier Texas Inc .... G 517 999-3500
Lansing *(G-9340)*
Daneks Goodtime Ice Co Inc .... G 989 725-5920
Owosso *(G-12287)*
Gold Coast Ice Makers LLC .... G 231 845-2745
Ludington *(G-10060)*
Hanson Cold Storage Co .... F 269 982-1390
Saint Joseph *(G-14314)*
Home City Ice Company .... E 269 926-2490
Sodus *(G-14745)*
Home City Ice Company .... E 734 955-9094
Romulus *(G-13685)*
Imlay City High Pressure .... G 810 395-7459
Capac *(G-2448)*
Kelly Bros Inc .... G 989 723-4543
Owosso *(G-12298)*
Knowlton Enterprises Inc .... D 810 987-7100
Port Huron *(G-12935)*
Lansing Ice and Fuel Company .... F 517 372-3850
Lansing *(G-9240)*
Michigan Pure Ice Co LLC .... G 231 420-9896
Indian River *(G-8220)*
Northern Pure Ice Co L L C .... F 989 344-2088
Port Huron *(G-12950)*
U S Ice Corp .... E 313 862-3344
Detroit *(G-4412)*

2098 Macaroni, Spaghetti & Noodles

Asian Noodle LLC .... G 989 316-2380
Bay City *(G-1277)*
Dina Mia Kitchens Inc .... F 906 265-9082
Iron River *(G-8308)*
Eden Foods Inc .... F 313 921-2053
Detroit *(G-4027)*
Greenfield Noodle Specialty Co .... F 313 873-2212
Detroit *(G-4103)*
Krzysiak Family Restaurant .... D 989 894-5531
Bay City *(G-1326)*
La Rozinas Inc .... G 906 779-2181
Iron Mountain *(G-8287)*
Northside Noodle .... G 906 779-2181
Iron Mountain *(G-8294)*
▲ Pierino Frozen Foods Inc .... E 313 928-0950
Lincoln Park *(G-9583)*
Tomukun Noodle Bar .... G 734 995-8668
Ann Arbor *(G-679)*
▲ Turris Italian Foods Inc .... D 586 773-6010
Roseville *(G-13883)*

2099 Food Preparations, NEC

18th Street Deli Inc .... G 313 921-7710
Hamtramck *(G-7243)*
A La Don Seasonings .... G 734 532-7862
Southgate *(G-15072)*
Ace Vending Service Inc .... E 616 243-7983
Grand Rapids *(G-6135)*
Al Dente Inc .... E 734 449-8522
Whitmore Lake *(G-17686)*
American Classics Corp .... G 231 843-0523
Ludington *(G-10048)*
▲ American Soy Products Inc .... D 734 429-2310
Saline *(G-14375)*
Among Friends LLC .... F 734 997-9720
Ann Arbor *(G-354)*
◆ Amway International Inc .... E 616 787-1000
Ada *(G-7)*
▼ Arbre Farms Corporation .... B 231 873-3337
Walkerville *(G-16884)*
Artisan Bread Co LLC .... E 586 756-0100
Warren *(G-16940)*
Aseltine Cider Company Inc .... G 616 784-7676
Comstock Park *(G-3460)*
Asmus Seasoning Inc .... F 586 939-4505
Sterling Heights *(G-15265)*
Azz On Fire LLC .... G 248 470-3742
Detroit *(G-3889)*
B & B Pretzels Inc .... E 248 358-1655
Southfield *(G-14848)*
Bektrom Foods Inc .... G 734 241-3711
Monroe *(G-11022)*
Better Made Snack Foods Inc .... C 313 925-4774
Detroit *(G-3902)*
Big Boy Restaurants Intl LLC .... C 586 759-6000
Warren *(G-16958)*
Bimbo Bakeries Usa Inc .... B 616 252-2709
Grand Rapids *(G-6222)*
Blakes Orchard Inc .... G 586 784-5343
Armada *(G-717)*
Bliss & Vinegar LLC .... G 616 970-0732
Grand Rapids *(G-6231)*
Brians Foods LLC .... G 248 739-5280
Southfield *(G-14857)*
Buddies Foods LLC .... E 586 776-4036
Fraser *(G-5632)*
Burnette Foods Inc .... E 231 223-4282
Traverse City *(G-15924)*
Butterball Farms Inc .... C 616 243-0105
Grand Rapids *(G-6247)*
Canadian Harvest LP .... G 952 835-6429
Schoolcraft *(G-14490)*
Champion Foods LLC .... B 734 753-3663
New Boston *(G-11499)*
Cherry Blossom .... G 231 342-3635
Williamsburg *(G-17710)*
▲ Coffee Beanery Ltd .... E 810 733-1020
Flushing *(G-5533)*
Conagra Brands Inc .... E 402 240-8210
Quincy *(G-13092)*
Conagra Foods .... G 616 392-2359
Holland *(G-7597)*
Country Home Creations Inc .... E 810 244-7348
Flint *(G-5405)*
Countryside Foods LLC .... B 586 447-3500
Warren *(G-16994)*
Custom Foods Inc .... E 989 249-8061
Saginaw *(G-14024)*
Daniel Olson .... G 269 816-1838
Jones *(G-8651)*
▲ Dedinas & Franzak Entps Inc .... D 616 784-6095
Grand Rapids *(G-6342)*
Del Pueblo Tortillas .... G 248 858-9835
Pontiac *(G-12815)*
Dexter Cider Mill Inc .... G 734 475-6419
Chelsea *(G-2707)*
DForte Inc .... F 269 657-6996
Paw Paw *(G-12402)*
Disruptive Eating LLC .... G 734 262-0560
Ypsilanti *(G-18066)*
Dorothy Dawson Food Products .... E 517 788-9830
Jackson *(G-8435)*
Downeys Potato Chips-Waterford .... G 248 673-3636
Waterford *(G-17338)*
◆ Eden Foods Inc .... C 517 456-7424
Clinton *(G-3019)*
El Milagro of Michigan .... G 616 452-6625
Grand Rapids *(G-6371)*
Frandale Sub Shop .... F 616 446-6311
Allendale *(G-217)*
▲ Giovannis Apptzing Fd Pdts Inc .... F 586 727-9355
Richmond *(G-13263)*
▲ Global Quality Ingredients Inc .... G 651 337-2028
Onsted *(G-12153)*
Gourmet Kitchen Qiuyang LLC .... G 517 332-8866
East Lansing *(G-4659)*
Grand Rapids Salsa .... G 616 780-1801
Grand Rapids *(G-6463)*
Grandpa Hanks Maple Syrup LLC .... G 231 826-4494
Falmouth *(G-4893)*
Green Zebra Foods Incorporated .... G 248 291-7339
Grosse Pointe Park *(G-7194)*
Gt Foods Inc .... G 734 934-2729
Southgate *(G-15077)*
Hacienda Mexican Foods LLC .... F 313 843-7007
Detroit *(G-4111)*
Haighs Maple Syrup & Sups LLC .... F 517 202-6975
Vermontville *(G-16821)*
Herman Hillbillies Farm LLC .... G 906 201-0760
Lanse *(G-9192)*
Hill Brothers .... G 616 784-2767
Grand Rapids *(G-6513)*
Hillshire Brands Company .... A 231 947-2100
Traverse City *(G-15997)*
Hillshire Brands Company .... A 616 875-8131
Zeeland *(G-18150)*
Home Style Foods Inc .... F 313 874-3250
Detroit *(G-4126)*
Honey Tree .... G 734 697-1000
Van Buren Twp *(G-16764)*
Indian Summer Cooperative Inc .... E 231 873-7504
Hart *(G-7374)*
International Noodle Co Inc .... G 248 583-2479
Madison Heights *(G-10277)*
Intl Giuseppes Oils & Vinegars .... G 586 698-2754
Sterling Hts *(G-15550)*
Intl Giuseppes Oils & Vinegars .... G 586 263-4200
Clinton Township *(G-3144)*
J B Dough Co .... G 269 944-4160
Benton Harbor *(G-1514)*
Jaspers Sugar Bush LLC .... G 906 639-2588
Carney *(G-2463)*
Jogue Inc .... F 248 349-1501
Northville *(G-11703)*
◆ Jogue Inc .... E 734 207-0100
Plymouth *(G-12654)*
◆ Kalamazoo Holdings Inc .... G 269 349-9711
Kalamazoo *(G-8789)*
◆ Kalsec Inc .... B 269 349-9711
Kalamazoo *(G-8799)*
Kerry Foods .... G 616 871-9940
Grand Rapids *(G-6582)*
Knouse Foods Cooperative Inc .... D 269 657-5524
Paw Paw *(G-12406)*
Kraft Heinz Foods Company .... B 616 396-6557
Holland *(G-7713)*
Kring Pizza Inc .... G 586 792-0049
Harrison Township *(G-7336)*
L & J Enterprises Inc .... G 586 995-4153
Metamora *(G-10778)*
L & J Products K Huntington .... G 810 919-3550
Brighton *(G-1947)*
L & P LLC .... F 231 733-1415
Muskegon *(G-11360)*
La Jalisciense Inc .... F 313 237-0008
Farmington Hills *(G-5041)*
Lafrontera Tortillas Inc .... G 734 231-1701
Rockwood *(G-13606)*
Las Brazas Tortillas .... G 616 886-0737
Holland *(G-7720)*
Lesley Elizabeth Inc .... G 810 667-0706
Lapeer *(G-9469)*
▲ Lesley Elizabeth Inc .... F 810 667-0706
Lapeer *(G-9470)*
Levi Ohman Micah .... G 612 251-1293
Marquette *(G-10540)*
Litehouse Inc .... C 616 897-5911
Lowell *(G-10034)*
Marias House Made Salsa .... G 313 733-8406
Warren *(G-17139)*
Marshalls Trail Inc .... F 231 436-5082
Mackinaw City *(G-10099)*
▼ McClures Pickles LLC .... E 248 837-9323
Detroit *(G-4221)*
McCormick & Company Inc .... C 586 558-8424
Warren *(G-17145)*
Mead Johnson & Company LLC .... E 616 748-7100
Zeeland *(G-18162)*
▲ Mexamerica Foods LLC .... E 814 781-1447
Grand Rapids *(G-6665)*
Mexican Food Specialties Inc .... G 734 779-2370
Southfield *(G-14980)*
Michigan Celery Promotion Coop .... E 616 669-1250
Hudsonville *(G-8168)*

S I C

Employee Codes: A=Over 500 employees, B=251-500
C=101-250, D=51-100, E=20-50, F=10-19, G=3-9
2020 Harris Michigan
Industrial Directory
707

20 FOOD AND KINDRED PRODUCTS

Michigan Dessert Corporation .... E 248 544-4574
  Oak Park (G-12085)
Milton Chili Company Inc .... G 248 585-0300
  Madison Heights (G-10307)
Mizkan America Inc .... F 616 794-0226
  Belding (G-1425)
N F P Inc .... G 989 631-0009
  Midland (G-10896)
▲ Natural American Foods Inc .... E 517 467-2065
  Onsted (G-12155)
Natures Select Inc .... G 616 956-1105
  Grand Rapids (G-6712)
New Moon Noodle Incorporated .... E 269 962-8820
  Battle Creek (G-1232)
Olive Vinegar .... G 248 923-2310
  Rochester (G-13340)
Olive Vinegar .... G 586 484-4700
  Sterling Heights (G-15439)
Onion Crock of Michigan Inc .... G 616 458-2922
  Grand Rapids (G-6731)
Otsuka America Foods Inc .... G 231 383-3124
  Frankfort (G-5604)
Parshallville Cider Mill .... G 810 629-9079
  Fenton (G-5229)
Parsons Centennial Farm LLC .... G 231 547-2038
  Charlevoix (G-2625)
Pepperidge Farm Incorporated .... G 734 953-6729
  Livonia (G-9885)
▲ Pierino Frozen Foods Inc .... E 313 928-0950
  Lincoln Park (G-9583)
Porters Orchards Farm Market .... F 810 636-7156
  Goodrich (G-5956)
Postma Brothers Maple Syrup .... G 906 478-3051
  Rudyard (G-13985)
Priorat Importers Corporation .... G 248 217-4608
  Royal Oak (G-13959)
Questor Partners Fund II LP .... G 248 593-1930
  Birmingham (G-1699)
Rays Ice Cream Co Inc .... E 248 549-5256
  Royal Oak (G-13963)
Ridge Cider .... G 231 674-2040
  Grant (G-7082)
Rmg Family Sugar Bush Inc .... G 906 478-3038
  Rudyard (G-13986)
Rochester Cider Mill .... G 248 651-4224
  Rochester (G-13348)
Russo Bros Inc .... E 906 485-5250
  Ishpeming (G-8353)
Safie Specialty Foods Co Inc .... E 586 598-8282
  Chesterfield (G-2836)
▲ Savory Foods Inc .... D 616 241-2583
  Grand Rapids (G-6851)
Sensient Flavors LLC .... G 989 479-3211
  Harbor Beach (G-7270)
Sensient Technologies Corp .... D 989 479-3211
  Harbor Beach (G-7271)
Shady Nook Farms .... G 989 236-7240
  Middleton (G-10795)
Sleeping Bear Apiaries Ltd .... F 231 882-4456
  Beulah (G-1612)
Spartan Central Kitchen .... G 616 878-8940
  Grand Rapids (G-6877)
St Laurent Brothers Inc .... G 989 893-7522
  Bay City (G-1360)
Stephen Haas .... G 906 475-4826
  Negaunee (G-11477)
Steves Backroom LLC .... F 313 527-7240
  Dearborn (G-3763)
Subway Restaurant .... G 248 625-5739
  Clarkston (G-2960)
Sunopta Ingredients Inc .... E 502 587-7999
  Schoolcraft (G-14502)
Tortillas Tita LLC .... G 734 756-7646
  Wayne (G-17444)
Twin City Foods Inc .... C 616 374-4002
  Lake Odessa (G-9120)
Twinlab Holdings Inc .... G 800 645-5626
  Grand Rapids (G-6943)
Uncle Johns Cider Mill Inc .... D 989 224-3686
  Saint Johns (G-14298)
Union Commissary LLC .... F 248 795-2483
  Clarkston (G-2963)
Unique Food Management Inc .... E 248 738-9393
  Pontiac (G-12872)
Variety Foods Inc .... E 586 268-4900
  Warren (G-17279)
Verellen Orchards .... G 586 752-2989
  Washington (G-17313)
Villanuevo Soledad .... E 989 770-4309
  Burt (G-2139)

West Brothers LLC .... G 734 457-0083
  Monroe (G-11084)
White River Sugar Bush .... G 231 861-4860
  Hesperia (G-7480)
Windmill Hill Farm LLC .... G 810 378-5972
  Croswell (G-3606)
Wysong Medical Corporation .... E 989 631-0009
  Midland (G-10925)
Yates Cider Mill Inc .... G 248 651-8300
  Rochester Hills (G-13551)

21 TOBACCO PRODUCTS

2111 Cigarettes

R J Reynolds Tobacco Company .... G 616 949-3740
  Kentwood (G-9027)

2131 Tobacco, Chewing & Snuff

Akston Hughes Intl LLC .... F 989 448-2322
  Gaylord (G-5847)
D & T Smoke LLC .... G 586 263-6888
  Clinton Township (G-3097)
Smoker Butts .... G 586 362-2451
  Fraser (G-5725)

22 TEXTILE MILL PRODUCTS

2211 Cotton, Woven Fabric

▲ Ace-Tex Enterprises Inc .... E 313 834-4000
  Detroit (G-3839)
Allender & Company .... G 248 398-5776
  Ferndale (G-5258)
American Sales Co .... G 517 750-4070
  Spring Arbor (G-15118)
American Soft Trim LLC .... G 989 681-0037
  Saint Louis (G-14357)
Apogee Technologies Inc .... F 269 639-1616
  South Haven (G-14754)
Bearcub Outfitters LLC .... F 231 439-9500
  Petoskey (G-12441)
Canvas Co Inc .... G 231 276-3083
  Interlochen (G-8238)
Canvas Innovations LLC .... G 616 393-4400
  Holland (G-7584)
Carry-All Products Inc .... F 616 399-8080
  Holland (G-7585)
D&E Incorporated .... G 313 673-3284
  Southfield (G-14876)
Denim Baby LLC .... G 313 539-5309
  Roseville (G-13791)
Detroit Denim LLC .... G 313 626-9216
  Detroit (G-3979)
Drapery Workroom .... G 269 463-5633
  Watervliet (G-17391)
◆ Floracraft Corporation .... C 231 845-5127
  Ludington (G-10059)
G T Jerseys LLC .... G 248 588-3231
  Troy (G-16376)
Grand Strategy LLC .... G 269 637-8330
  South Haven (G-14761)
Great Lakes Canvas Co .... G 954 439-3090
  Fennville (G-5172)
Great Lkes Tex Restoration LLC .... G 989 448-8600
  Gaylord (G-5861)
Joan Arnoudse .... G 616 364-9075
  Grand Rapids (G-6561)
Mackarynn Inc .... E 616 263-9743
  Cedar Springs (G-2557)
▲ Nanosystems Inc .... F 734 274-0020
  Ann Arbor (G-570)
Peribambini Services LLC .... G 318 466-2881
  Plymouth (G-12713)
Rooms of Grand Rapids LLC .... F 616 260-1452
  Spring Lake (G-15173)
Simco Automotive Trim .... D 800 372-3172
  Macomb (G-10161)
Street Denim & Co .... G 313 837-1200
  Detroit (G-4379)
Window Designs Inc .... F 616 396-5295
  Holland (G-7859)
Wixom Moving Boxes LLC .... G 248 613-5078
  Wixom (G-17931)

2221 Silk & Man-Made Fiber

Advanced Composite Tech Inc .... G 248 709-9097
  Rochester (G-13311)
Airhug LLC .... G 734 262-0431
  Canton (G-2346)

Bay City Fiberglass Inc .... G 989 751-9622
  Bay City (G-1285)
C & J Fabrication Inc .... G 586 791-6269
  Clinton Township (G-3071)
▲ Fulcrum Composites Inc .... G 989 636-1025
  Midland (G-10863)
Glassline Incorporated .... F 734 453-2728
  Plymouth (G-12628)
▲ J America Licensed Pdts Inc .... G 517 655-8800
  Fowlerville (G-5571)
JAC Custom Pouches Inc .... E 269 782-3190
  Dowagiac (G-4544)
▲ John Johnson Company .... D 313 496-0600
  Romulus (G-13692)
Loonar Stn Two The 2 or 2nd .... G 419 720-1222
  Temperance (G-15834)
Nickels Boat Works Inc .... F 810 767-4050
  Flint (G-5472)
P I W Corporation .... G 989 448-2501
  Gaylord (G-5887)
Performance Sailing Inc .... F 586 790-7500
  Clinton Township (G-3193)
Sassy Fabrics Inc .... G 810 694-0440
  Grand Blanc (G-5982)
Takata Americas .... E 336 547-1600
  Auburn Hills (G-1012)
West Michigan Canvas Company ...... G 616 355-7855
  Holland (G-7855)
Window Designs Inc .... F 616 396-5295
  Holland (G-7859)

2231 Wool, Woven Fabric

Stonehedge Farm .... G 231 536-2779
  East Jordan (G-4646)
West Michigan Alpacas .... G 616 990-0556
  Holland (G-7854)

2241 Fabric Mills, Cotton, Wool, Silk & Man-Made

▲ B Erickson Manufacturing Ltd .... F 810 765-1144
  Marine City (G-10470)
Car-Min-Vu Farm .... G 517 749-9112
  Webberville (G-17447)
▲ Global Strapping LLC .... G 517 545-4900
  Howell (G-8044)
Louis J Wickings .... G 989 823-8765
  Vassar (G-16813)
Nitto Inc .... G 248 449-2300
  Novi (G-11954)
Permacel Corporation .... G 248 347-2843
  Novi (G-11973)
Rhino Products Inc .... F 269 674-8309
  Lawrence (G-9507)
Sistahs Braid Too .... G 248 552-6202
  Southfield (G-15029)
Superior Spindle Services LLC .... F 734 946-4646
  Taylor (G-15774)
Tapex American Corporation .... F 810 987-4722
  Port Huron (G-12970)

2252 Hosiery, Except Women's

5 Water Socks LLC .... G 248 735-1730
  Northville (G-11674)
Argyle Socks LLC .... G 269 615-0097
  Kalamazoo (G-8683)
Bold Endeavors LLC .... G 616 389-3902
  Wyoming (G-17988)
Grandview Foot & Ankle .... G 989 584-3916
  Carson City (G-2489)
Skechers USA Inc .... F 989 624-9336
  Birch Run (G-1672)
Socks & Associates Development ..... G 231 421-5150
  Traverse City (G-16108)
Socks Galore Wholesale Inc .... G 248 545-7625
  Oak Park (G-12099)
Socks Kick LLC .... G 231 222-2402
  East Jordan (G-4645)
▲ Soyad Brothers Textile Corp .... E 586 755-5700
  Fraser (G-5726)
Turbosocks Performance .... G 586 864-3252
  Shelby Township (G-14712)
Warmerscom .... G 800 518-0938
  Byron Center (G-2216)

2253 Knit Outerwear Mills

Fuzzybutz .... G 269 983-9663
  Saint Joseph (G-14311)
M Den On Main .... G 734 761-1030
  Ann Arbor (G-537)

SIC SECTION — 23 APPAREL AND OTHER FINISHED PRODUCTS MADE FROM FABRICS AND SIMILAR MATERIAL

▲ Sb3 LLC .... G 877 978-6286
  Ada *(G-29)*
Wickedglow Industries Inc .... G 586 776-4132
  Mount Clemens *(G-11154)*

2254 Knit Underwear Mills
T-Shirt World .... G 313 387-2023
  Redford *(G-13199)*

2257 Circular Knit Fabric Mills
▲ Circular Motion LLC .... G 989 779-9040
  Mount Pleasant *(G-11188)*

2259 Knitting Mills, NEC
▲ Star Textile Inc .... E 888 527-5700
  Madison Heights *(G-10361)*

2261 Cotton Fabric Finishers
Adco Specialties Inc .... G 616 452-6882
  Grand Rapids *(G-6143)*
Advanced Printwear Inc .... G 248 585-4412
  Madison Heights *(G-10182)*
Advertising Accents Inc .... E 313 937-3890
  Redford *(G-13142)*
Allgraphics Corp .... G 248 994-7373
  Farmington Hills *(G-4928)*
Baumans Running Center Inc .... G 810 238-5981
  Flint *(G-5385)*
Charlevoix Screen Masters Inc .... G 231 547-5111
  Charlevoix *(G-2612)*
Great Put On Inc .... G 810 733-8021
  Flint *(G-5442)*
Hilton Screeners Inc .... G 810 653-0711
  Davison *(G-3654)*
Inkpressions LLC .... E 248 461-2555
  Commerce Township *(G-3416)*
Janet Kelly .... F 231 775-2313
  Cadillac *(G-2256)*
Meridian Screen Prtg & Design .... G 517 351-2525
  Okemos *(G-12130)*
Perrin Screen Printing Inc .... D 616 785-9900
  Comstock Park *(G-3507)*
Pro Shop The/P S Graphics .... G 517 448-8490
  Hudson *(G-8139)*
Prong Horn .... G 616 456-1903
  Grand Rapids *(G-6789)*
Sign of The Loon Gifts Inc .... G 231 436-5155
  Mackinaw City *(G-10101)*
Slick Shirts Screen Printing .... F 517 371-3600
  Lansing *(G-9424)*
Trophy Center West Michigan .... G 231 893-1686
  Whitehall *(G-17678)*

2262 Silk & Man-Made Fabric Finishers
Armada Printwear Inc .... G 586 784-5553
  Armada *(G-715)*
Creative Promotions .... G 734 854-2292
  Lambertville *(G-9181)*
◆ Stahls Inc .... D 800 478-2457
  Sterling Heights *(G-15508)*

2269 Textile Finishers, NEC
Karms LLC .... G 810 229-0829
  Brighton *(G-1946)*

2273 Carpets & Rugs
Apparelmaster-Muskegon Inc .... E 231 728-5406
  Muskegon *(G-11271)*
Classic Designs Cstm Area Rugs .... G 616 530-0740
  Grandville *(G-7026)*
▼ Custom Marine Carpet .... G 269 684-1922
  Niles *(G-11604)*
Forever Flooring and More LLC .... G 517 745-6194
  Lowell *(G-10029)*
▲ HP Pelzer Auto Systems Inc .... E 248 280-1010
  Troy *(G-16405)*
▲ HR Technologies Inc .... C 248 284-1170
  Madison Heights *(G-10271)*
James E Sullivan & Associates .... G 616 453-0345
  Grand Rapids *(G-6551)*
Marceau Enterprises Inc .... G 586 697-8100
  Washington *(G-17307)*
Mohawk Industries Inc .... G 248 486-4075
  Wixom *(G-17858)*
▲ N A Visscher-Caravelle Inc .... G 248 851-9800
  Bloomfield Hills *(G-1786)*
▲ Plant Df .... E 734 397-0397
  Van Buren Twp *(G-16780)*
Prestwick Group LLP .... G 248 360-6113
  Commerce Township *(G-3442)*
Professional Rug Works Inc .... G 248 577-1400
  Troy *(G-16567)*
Pwv Studios Ltd .... F 616 361-5659
  Grand Rapids *(G-6798)*
▲ Scott Group Custom Carpets LLC .... C 616 954-3200
  Grand Rapids *(G-6854)*
Seelye Group Ltd .... G 517 267-2001
  Lansing *(G-9423)*
Shelter Carpet Specialties .... G 616 475-4944
  Grand Rapids *(G-6859)*
Usmats Inc .... G 810 765-4545
  Marine City *(G-10485)*
W A Thomas Company .... G 734 955-6500
  Taylor *(G-15779)*

2281 Yarn Spinning Mills
True Teknit Inc .... E 616 656-5111
  Grand Rapids *(G-6938)*
▲ Woolly & Co LLC .... G 248 480-4354
  Birmingham *(G-1709)*

2282 Yarn Texturizing, Throwing, Twisting & Winding Mills
Ophir Crafts LLC .... G 734 794-7777
  Ann Arbor *(G-584)*

2284 Thread Mills
American & Efird LLC .... F 248 399-1166
  Berkley *(G-1579)*
Notions Marketing .... B 616 243-8424
  Grand Rapids *(G-6722)*
RPC Company .... F 989 752-3618
  Saginaw *(G-14134)*

2295 Fabrics Coated Not Rubberized
APS Machine LLC .... F 906 212-5600
  Escanaba *(G-4814)*
Bentzer Enterprises .... G 269 663-2289
  Edwardsburg *(G-4758)*
▼ Duro-Last Inc .... B 800 248-0280
  Saginaw *(G-14031)*
Duro-Last Inc .... D 800 248-0280
  Saginaw *(G-14032)*
Duro-Last Inc .... D 800 248-0280
  Saginaw *(G-14033)*
Elden Industries Corporation .... F 734 946-6900
  Taylor *(G-15715)*
Haartz Corporation .... G 248 646-8200
  Bloomfield Hills *(G-1771)*
Hig Recovery Fund Inc .... G 269 435-8414
  Constantine *(G-3537)*
Mp-Tec Inc .... E 734 367-1284
  Livonia *(G-9852)*
Pioneer Plastics Inc .... E 586 262-0159
  Shelby Township *(G-14667)*
Plastatech Engineering Ltd .... D 989 754-6500
  Saginaw *(G-14123)*
Plastatech Engineering Ltd .... E 989 754-6500
  Saginaw *(G-14124)*
Shawmut Corporation .... C 810 987-2222
  Port Huron *(G-12965)*
Tpi Industries LLC .... G 810 987-2222
  Port Huron *(G-12973)*
Tri-City Vinyl Inc .... E 989 401-7992
  Saginaw *(G-14167)*
Witchcraft Tape Products Inc .... D 269 468-3399
  Coloma *(G-3368)*
Worthen Industries Inc .... E 616 742-8990
  Grand Rapids *(G-7004)*

2296 Tire Cord & Fabric
Ferro Fab LLC .... F 586 791-3561
  Clinton Township *(G-3115)*
Takata Americas .... E 336 547-1600
  Auburn Hills *(G-1012)*
Ton-Tex Corporation .... G 616 957-3200
  Greenville *(G-7158)*

2298 Cordage & Twine
▲ American Twisting Company .... E 269 637-8581
  South Haven *(G-14752)*
Bundeze LLC .... G 248 343-9179
  West Olive *(G-17532)*
Canco Inc .... G 810 664-3520
  Lapeer *(G-9449)*
Cascade Paper Converters LLC .... F 616 974-9165
  Grand Rapids *(G-6263)*
▲ Great Lakes Cordage Inc .... F 616 842-4455
  Spring Lake *(G-15148)*
Hestia Inc .... G 231 747-8157
  Norton Shores *(G-11760)*
▲ Mason Tackle Company .... E 810 631-4571
  Otisville *(G-12233)*
Nelson Rapids Co Inc .... G 616 691-8041
  Belding *(G-1427)*
Networks Enterprises Inc .... G 248 446-8590
  New Hudson *(G-11549)*
Poly-Green Foam LLC .... E 517 279-8019
  Coldwater *(G-3320)*
Quickmitt Inc .... G 517 849-2141
  Jonesville *(G-8667)*

2299 Textile Goods, NEC
3-D Designs LLC .... G 313 658-1249
  Detroit *(G-3823)*
Acoufelt LLC .... G 800 966-8557
  Clawson *(G-2969)*
Airlite Synthetics Mfg Inc .... F 248 335-8131
  Pontiac *(G-12799)*
Augustine Innovations LLC .... G 248 686-1822
  Commerce Township *(G-3392)*
Auto Tex .... G 248 340-0844
  Auburn Hills *(G-783)*
Clamp Industries Incorporated .... F 248 335-8131
  Pontiac *(G-12809)*
Gabriel North America Inc .... G 616 202-5770
  Grand Rapids *(G-6429)*
Guilford of Maine Marketing Co .... D 616 554-2250
  Grand Rapids *(G-6485)*
Martak Cultured Marble .... G 313 891-5400
  Detroit *(G-4219)*
Thomasine D Jones LLC .... G 773 726-1404
  Union Pier *(G-16739)*
Zeilinger Wool Co LLC .... E 989 652-2920
  Frankenmuth *(G-5597)*

23 APPAREL AND OTHER FINISHED PRODUCTS MADE FROM FABRICS AND SIMILAR MATERIAL

2311 Men's & Boys' Suits, Coats & Overcoats
Allie Brothers Inc .... F 248 477-4434
  Livonia *(G-9635)*
Baryames Tux Shop Inc .... G 517 349-6555
  Okemos *(G-12116)*
▲ P & D Uniforms and ACC Inc .... G 313 881-3881
  Eastpointe *(G-4708)*
Peckham Vocational Inds Inc .... A 517 316-4000
  Lansing *(G-9252)*
Peckham Vocational Inds Inc .... C 517 316-4478
  Lansing *(G-9253)*
Priority One Emergency Inc .... G 734 398-5900
  Canton *(G-2419)*
▲ SM Smith Co .... G 906 774-8258
  Kingsford *(G-9066)*

2321 Men's & Boys' Shirts
Pvh Corp .... G 989 345-7939
  West Branch *(G-17517)*
Pvh Corp .... G 989 624-5651
  Birch Run *(G-1668)*
Zemis 5 LLC .... G 317 946-7015
  Detroit *(G-4457)*

2322 Men's & Boys' Underwear & Nightwear
Harrys Meme LLC .... G 248 977-0168
  Novi *(G-11897)*

2325 Men's & Boys' Separate Trousers & Casual Slacks
◆ Carhartt Inc .... B 313 271-8460
  Dearborn *(G-3686)*
Guess Inc .... F 517 546-2933
  Howell *(G-8046)*

2326 Men's & Boys' Work Clothing
Acme Mills Company .... C 517 437-8940
  Hillsdale *(G-7513)*
◆ Carhartt Inc .... B 313 271-8460
  Dearborn *(G-3686)*

Employee Codes: A=Over 500 employees, B=251-500
C=101-250, D=51-100, E=20-50, F=10-19, G=3-9

23 APPAREL AND OTHER FINISHED PRODUCTS MADE FROM FABRICS AND SIMILAR MATERIAL

Carhartt Inc .... G 517 282-4193
  Dewitt *(G-4461)*
Gerald Froberg .... G 906 346-3311
  Gwinn *(G-7219)*
▲ P & D Uniforms and ACC Inc ..... G 313 881-3881
  Eastpointe *(G-4708)*
Peckham Vocational Inds Inc .... A 517 316-4000
  Lansing *(G-9252)*
Shoulders LLC .... G 248 843-1536
  Pontiac *(G-12865)*
Tha Shopp LLC .... G 734 231-9991
  Ypsilanti *(G-18105)*
Traverse Bay Manufacturing Inc ... D 231 264-8111
  Elk Rapids *(G-4781)*
Vega Manufacturing LLC .... G 231 668-6365
  Traverse City *(G-16136)*

2329 Men's & Boys' Clothing, NEC

Avidasports LLC .... G 313 447-5670
  Harper Woods *(G-7299)*
◆ Carhartt Inc .... B 313 271-8460
  Dearborn *(G-3686)*
▲ Cliff Keen Wrestling Pdts Inc .... E 734 975-8800
  Ann Arbor *(G-401)*
Custom Giant LLC .... G 313 799-2085
  Southfield *(G-14875)*
Graphic Gear Inc .... G 734 283-3864
  Lincoln Park *(G-9579)*
Harvard Clothing Company .... F 517 542-2986
  Litchfield *(G-9602)*
Hemp Global Products Inc .... G 616 617-6476
  Holland *(G-7661)*
◆ J America LLC .... E 517 521-2525
  Webberville *(G-17451)*
Kinder Company Inc .... G 810 240-3065
  Mount Morris *(G-11163)*
Sams Suit Fctry & Alteration .... F 248 424-8666
  Southfield *(G-15021)*
Traverse Bay Manufacturing Inc ... D 231 264-8111
  Elk Rapids *(G-4781)*
Van Boven Incorporated .... G 734 665-7228
  Ann Arbor *(G-690)*
Vega Manufacturing LLC .... G 231 668-6365
  Traverse City *(G-16136)*
Vetta LLC .... G 517 521-2525
  Webberville *(G-17455)*

2331 Women's & Misses' Blouses

Peckham Vocational Inds Inc .... A 517 316-4000
  Lansing *(G-9252)*
Peckham Vocational Inds Inc .... C 517 316-4478
  Lansing *(G-9253)*

2335 Women's & Misses' Dresses

Demmem Enterprises LLC .... F 810 564-9500
  Clio *(G-3269)*
G-III Apparel Group Ltd .... C 248 332-4922
  Auburn Hills *(G-879)*
Recollections Co .... E 989 734-0566
  Hawks *(G-7261)*
Runway Liquidation LLC .... G 989 624-4756
  Birch Run *(G-1670)*
White Dress The LLC .... G 810 588-6147
  Brighton *(G-2009)*

2337 Women's & Misses' Suits, Coats & Skirts

Motor City Sewing .... G 313 595-5275
  Detroit *(G-4257)*

2339 Women's & Misses' Outerwear, NEC

Baa Baa Zuzu .... G 231 256-7176
  Lake Leelanau *(G-9100)*
Brintley Enterprises .... G 248 991-4086
  Detroit *(G-3918)*
▲ Clean Clothes Inc .... G 734 482-4000
  Dexter *(G-4482)*
▲ Cliff Keen Wrestling Pdts Inc .... E 734 975-8800
  Ann Arbor *(G-401)*
Excellent Designs Swimwear .... E 586 977-9140
  Warren *(G-17025)*
Graphic Gear Inc .... G 734 283-3864
  Lincoln Park *(G-9579)*
Guess Inc .... F 517 546-2933
  Howell *(G-8046)*
Harvard Clothing Company .... F 517 542-2986
  Litchfield *(G-9602)*
Hemp Global Products Inc .... G 616 617-6476
  Holland *(G-7661)*

Moxies Boutique LLC .... G 269 983-4273
  Saint Joseph *(G-14329)*
Natural Attraction .... G 231 398-0787
  Manistee *(G-10432)*
▲ Otter Company .... G 248 566-3235
  Troy *(G-16539)*
Peckham Vocational Inds Inc .... A 517 316-4000
  Lansing *(G-9252)*
Pvh Corp .... E 989 624-5575
  Birch Run *(G-1667)*
Reed Sportswear Mfg Co .... G 313 963-7980
  Detroit *(G-4337)*
St John .... G 313 576-8212
  Detroit *(G-4372)*
St John .... G 313 499-4065
  Grosse Pointe Park *(G-7196)*
Tall City LLC .... G 248 854-0713
  Auburn Hills *(G-1013)*
Traverse Bay Manufacturing Inc ... D 231 264-8111
  Elk Rapids *(G-4781)*

2341 Women's, Misses' & Children's Underwear & Nightwear

▲ Minor Creations Incorporated .. F 517 347-2900
  Okemos *(G-12132)*

2342 Brassieres, Girdles & Garments

Busted Bra Shop LLC .... G 313 288-0449
  Detroit *(G-3921)*
Shefit Inc .... F 616 209-7003
  Hudsonville *(G-8182)*

2353 Hats, Caps & Millinery

Bahama Souvenirs Inc .... G 269 964-8275
  Battle Creek *(G-1149)*

2369 Girls' & Infants' Outerwear, NEC

Carters Inc .... G 616 647-9452
  Grand Rapids *(G-6257)*
Just Girls LLC .... G 248 952-1967
  Troy *(G-16441)*
▲ Mossworld Enterprises Inc ...... G 248 828-7460
  Oakland *(G-12107)*

2371 Fur Goods

Practical Solar .... G 586 864-6886
  Saint Clair Shores *(G-14267)*
Wolvering Fur .... G 313 961-0620
  Detroit *(G-4447)*

2381 Dress & Work Gloves

Kaul Glove and Mfg Co .... E 313 894-9494
  Detroit *(G-4172)*

2386 Leather & Sheep Lined Clothing

▲ Lee-Cobb Company .... G 269 553-0873
  Kalamazoo *(G-8808)*
▲ Reed Sportswear Mfg Co .... E 313 963-7980
  Detroit *(G-4336)*

2387 Apparel Belts

Vega Manufacturing LLC .... G 231 668-6365
  Traverse City *(G-16136)*

2389 Apparel & Accessories, NEC

Bioflex Inc .... G 734 327-2946
  Ann Arbor *(G-384)*
Bond Manufacturing LLC .... G 313 671-0799
  Detroit *(G-3909)*
Davis Girls .... G 586 781-6865
  Shelby Township *(G-14572)*
Excellent Designs Swimwear .... E 586 977-9140
  Warren *(G-17025)*
Fabjunky LLC .... G 323 572-4988
  Muskegon *(G-11319)*
▲ Gags and Games Inc .... E 734 591-1717
  Livonia *(G-9747)*
GLS Enterprises Inc .... G 616 243-2574
  Comstock Park *(G-3482)*
Kalamazoo Regalia Inc .... F 269 344-4299
  Kalamazoo *(G-8797)*
Lewmar Custom Designs Inc ...... G 586 677-5135
  Shelby Township *(G-14626)*
▲ Logofit LLC .... E 810 715-1980
  Flint *(G-5461)*
Mopega LLC .... G 231 631-2580
  Traverse City *(G-16044)*

Museum Apparel .... G 248 644-2303
  Bloomfield Hills *(G-1785)*
▲ Retro-A-Go-go LLC .... G 734 476-0300
  Howell *(G-8090)*
▲ Superfly Manufacturing Co ...... F 313 454-1492
  Farmington *(G-4913)*

2391 Curtains & Draperies

Barons Inc .... E 517 484-1366
  Lansing *(G-9347)*
Benton Harbor Awning & Tent ..... E 800 272-2187
  Benton Harbor *(G-1485)*
Cardinal Custom Designs Inc ...... G 586 296-2060
  Fraser *(G-5635)*
Detroit Custom Services Inc .... E 586 465-3631
  Mount Clemens *(G-11129)*
Hospital Curtain Solutions Inc ..... G 248 293-9785
  Rochester Hills *(G-13445)*
Lorne Hanley .... G 248 547-9865
  Huntington Woods *(G-8189)*
Melco Dctg & Furn Restoration ... G 989 723-3335
  Owosso *(G-12303)*
Nieddu Drapery Mfg .... G 586 977-0065
  Sterling Heights *(G-15434)*
Parkway Drapery & Uphl Co Inc .. G 734 779-1300
  Livonia *(G-9884)*
Sassy Fabrics Inc .... G 810 694-0440
  Grand Blanc *(G-5982)*
▲ Signature Designs Inc .... G 248 426-9735
  Farmington Hills *(G-5123)*
Triangle Window Fashions Inc .... E 616 538-9676
  Wyoming *(G-18036)*

2392 House furnishings: Textile

▲ Anchor Wiping Cloth Inc .... D 313 892-4000
  Detroit *(G-3870)*
▲ Arden Companies LLC .... E 248 415-8500
  Bingham Farms *(G-1648)*
Cellulose Mtl Solutions LLC .... G 616 669-2990
  Jenison *(G-8620)*
Custom Quilts .... G 517 626-6399
  Lansing *(G-9212)*
▲ Down Inc .... E 616 241-3922
  Grand Rapids *(G-6360)*
Gails Carpet Care Repair .... G 248 684-8789
  Milford *(G-10964)*
▲ Gamco Inc .... F 269 683-4280
  Niles *(G-11613)*
Grabber Inc .... E 616 940-1914
  Byron Center *(G-2193)*
Inplast Interior Tech LLC .... G 810 724-3500
  Almont *(G-258)*
Intramode LLC .... G 313 964-6990
  Detroit *(G-4146)*
Jackson Manufacturing & Distrg .. G 616 451-3030
  Grand Rapids *(G-6550)*
▲ Jacquart Fabric Products Inc .. C 906 932-1339
  Ironwood *(G-8332)*
K and J Absorbent Products LLC ... G 517 486-3110
  Blissfield *(G-1716)*
▲ Krams Enterprises Inc .... A 248 415-8500
  Bingham Farms *(G-1655)*
Preferred Products Inc .... G 248 255-0200
  Commerce Township *(G-3441)*
Spec International Inc .... E 616 248-9116
  Grand Rapids *(G-6878)*
▲ Star Textile Inc .... E 888 527-5700
  Madison Heights *(G-10361)*
Three Chairs Co .... G 734 665-2796
  Ann Arbor *(G-674)*
▲ Tuway American Group Inc .... C 248 205-9999
  Troy *(G-16658)*
Vega Manufacturing LLC .... G 231 668-6365
  Traverse City *(G-16136)*

2393 Textile Bags

Acme Mills Company .... C 517 437-8940
  Hillsdale *(G-7513)*
Birlon Group LLC .... G 313 551-5341
  Inkster *(G-8225)*
Foreward Logistics LLC .... G 877 488-9724
  Oak Park *(G-12068)*
Industrial Bag & Spc Inc .... F 248 559-5550
  Southfield *(G-14945)*
JAC Custom Pouches Inc .... E 269 782-3190
  Dowagiac *(G-4544)*
Total Packaging Solutions LLC ... G 248 519-2376
  Troy *(G-16649)*

SIC SECTION 23 APPAREL AND OTHER FINISHED PRODUCTS MADE FROM FABRICS AND SIMILAR MATERIAL

2394 Canvas Prdts

Ace Canvas & Tent Co ....F 313 842-3011
Troy (G-16166)
Acme Mills Company ....C 517 437-8940
Hillsdale (G-7513)
Advanced Inc ....G 231 938-2233
Acme (G-2)
▲ American Roll Shutter Awng Co ....E 734 422-7110
Livonia (G-9645)
Anchor Bay Canv and Upholstery ....G 810 512-4325
Algonac (G-141)
Armstrong Display Concepts ....F 231 652-1675
Newaygo (G-11563)
Battle Creek Tent & Awning Co ....G 269 964-1824
Battle Creek (G-1152)
Belle Isle Awning Co Inc ....E 586 294-6050
Warren (G-16954)
Benton Harbor Awning & Tent ....E 800 272-2187
Benton Harbor (G-1485)
Blanco Canvas Company Inc ....G 313 963-7787
Farmington Hills (G-4942)
Blue Water Sail & Canvas Inc ....G 231 941-5224
Traverse City (G-15914)
Bluewater Canvas LLC ....G 586 727-5345
Columbus (G-3377)
▲ Boat Guard Inc ....G 989 424-1490
Gladwin (G-5923)
Canco Inc ....G 810 664-3520
Lapeer (G-9449)
Canvas Concepts Inc ....G 810 794-3305
Algonac (G-142)
Canvas Kings ....G 616 846-6220
Spring Lake (G-15135)
Canvas Shop ....G 734 782-2222
Flat Rock (G-5350)
Canvas Shoppe Inc ....G 810 733-1841
Flint (G-5395)
Case-Free Inc ....G 616 245-3136
Grand Rapids (G-6265)
▲ Detroit Tarpaulin Repr Sp Inc ....E 734 955-8200
Romulus (G-13666)
Dial Tent & Awning Co ....F 989 793-0741
Saginaw (G-14027)
Dockside Canvas Co Inc ....F 586 463-1231
Harrison Township (G-7329)
Feb Inc ....F 231 759-0911
Muskegon (G-11321)
Gibraltar Canvas Inc ....G 734 675-4891
Rockwood (G-13604)
Golden Needle Awnings LLC ....G 517 404-6219
Gaines (G-5804)
Grand Traverse Canvas Works ....F 231 947-3140
Traverse City (G-15982)
Holiday Distributing Co ....E 517 782-7146
Jackson (G-8466)
▲ Holland Awning Co ....D 616 772-2052
Zeeland (G-18152)
Industrial Bag & Spc Inc ....F 248 559-5550
Southfield (G-14945)
◆ Industrial Fabric Products Inc ....G 269 932-4440
Saint Joseph (G-14318)
J & K Canvas Products ....G 810 635-7711
Flint (G-5451)
J C Goss Company ....G 313 259-3520
Romulus (G-13689)
JAC Custom Pouches Inc ....E 269 782-3190
Dowagiac (G-4544)
Jackson Canvas Company ....E 517 768-8459
Jackson (G-8475)
▲ Jacquart Fabric Products Inc ....C 906 932-1339
Ironwood (G-8332)
Kent Sail Co Inc ....G 586 791-2580
Harrison Township (G-7335)
Kts Enterprises ....G 269 624-3435
Lawton (G-9512)
Lakeside Canvas & Upholstery ....G 231 755-2514
Muskegon (G-11363)
Larrys Tarpaulin Shop LLC ....G 313 563-2292
Inkster (G-8229)
Luker Enterprises Inc ....G 231 894-9702
Montague (G-11094)
▲ Magna Car Top Systems Amer Inc ....D 248 836-4500
Auburn Hills (G-932)
Magna Car Top Systems Amer Inc ....F 248 619-8133
Troy (G-16470)
Millers Canvas Shop ....G 231 821-0771
Holton (G-7934)
Millers Custom Boat Top Inc ....G 586 468-5533
Harrison Township (G-7340)
Muskegon Awning & Mfg Co ....E 231 759-0911
Muskegon (G-11387)
National Case Corporation ....G 586 726-1710
Sterling Heights (G-15432)
North Sails Group LLC ....G 586 776-1330
Saint Clair Shores (G-14265)
Paddle King Inc ....F 989 235-6776
Carson City (G-2495)
Peerless Canvas Products Inc ....G 269 429-0600
Saint Joseph (G-14335)
Performance Sailing Inc ....F 586 790-7500
Clinton Township (G-3193)
Quality Awning Shops Inc ....G 517 882-2491
Lansing (G-9415)
Quick Draw Tarpaulin Systems ....F 313 561-0554
Inkster (G-8234)
▲ Quick Draw Tarpaulin Systems ....F 313 945-0766
Dearborn (G-3752)
Royal Oak & Birmingham Tent ....F 248 542-5552
Royal Oak (G-13967)
Shelby Auto Trim Inc ....F 586 939-9090
Sterling Heights (G-15495)
▲ Specilty Vhcl Acquisition Corp ....E 586 446-4701
Warren (G-17245)
▲ TD Industrial Coverings Inc ....D 586 731-2080
Sterling Heights (G-15521)
Traverse Bay Canvas Inc ....G 231 347-3001
Harbor Springs (G-7296)

2395 Pleating & Stitching For The Trade

1365267 Ontario Inc ....G 888 843-5245
Port Huron (G-12879)
A Design Line Embroidery LLC ....G 734 697-3545
Van Buren Twp (G-16745)
Adams Shirt Shack Inc ....G 269 964-3323
Battle Creek (G-1137)
Adlib Grafix & Apparel ....G 269 964-2810
Battle Creek (G-1139)
Advanced Printwear Inc ....G 248 585-4412
Madison Heights (G-10182)
Aisin Holdings America Inc ....G 734 453-5551
Northville (G-11676)
Alfie Embroidery Inc ....F 231 935-1488
Traverse City (G-15892)
All About Quilting and Design ....G 269 471-7359
Berrien Springs (G-1591)
AP Impressions Inc ....G 734 464-8009
Livonia (G-9650)
▲ Apparel Sales Inc ....G 616 842-5650
Jenison (G-8617)
Authority Customwear Ltd ....E 248 588-8075
Madison Heights (G-10199)
Bay Supply & Marketing Inc ....G 231 943-3249
Traverse City (G-15908)
Bd Classic Sewing ....G 231 825-2628
Mc Bain (G-10677)
Beck & Boys Custom Apparel ....G 734 458-4015
Livonia (G-9663)
C R Stitching ....G 313 538-1660
Redford (G-13151)
Celia Corporation ....D 616 887-7341
Sparta (G-15091)
Charlevoix Screen Masters Inc ....G 231 547-5111
Charlevoix (G-2612)
Classic Images Embroidery ....G 616 844-1702
Grand Haven (G-6004)
Classy Threadz ....G 989 479-9595
Harbor Beach (G-7264)
Colorful Stitches ....G 269 683-6442
Niles (G-11600)
Creative Loop ....G 231 629-8228
Paris (G-12383)
Creative Promotions ....G 734 854-2292
Lambertville (G-9181)
Custom Embroidery & Sewing ....G 586 749-7669
Ray (G-13132)
Custom Embroidery Plus LLC ....G 989 227-9432
Saint Johns (G-14282)
D & M Silkscreening ....G 517 694-4199
Holt (G-7906)
Delta Sports Service & EMB ....G 517 482-6565
Lansing (G-9215)
Design Tech LLC ....G 616 459-2885
Grand Rapids (G-6346)
Designs By Bean ....G 989 845-4371
Chesaning (G-2723)
Dun Mor Embroidery & Designs ....F 248 577-1155
Troy (G-16329)
E Q R 2 Inc ....G 586 731-3383
Sterling Heights (G-15324)
Earthbound Inc ....G 616 774-0096
Grand Rapids (G-6366)
Embroidery & Much More LLC ....F 586 771-3832
Saint Clair Shores (G-14246)
Embroidery House Inc ....G 616 669-6400
Jenison (G-8625)
Embroidery Products LLC ....G 734 483-0293
Ypsilanti (G-18071)
Embroidery Shoppe LLC ....G 734 595-7612
Westland (G-17552)
Embroidery Wearhouse ....G 906 228-5818
Marquette (G-10529)
Ensign Emblem Ltd ....D 231 946-7703
Traverse City (G-15964)
Exposure Unlimited Inc ....G 248 459-9104
Fenton (G-5205)
Grasel Graphics Inc ....G 989 652-5151
Frankenmuth (G-5589)
Heikkinen Productions Inc ....G 734 485-4020
Ypsilanti (G-18076)
I D Pro Embroidery LLC ....G 734 847-6650
Temperance (G-15832)
Ideal Wholesale Inc ....G 989 873-5850
Prescott (G-13080)
Impact Label Corporation ....D 269 381-4280
Galesburg (G-5811)
Imprint House LLC ....G 810 985-8203
Port Huron (G-12929)
Initial Artistry ....G 313 277-6300
Dearborn Heights (G-3787)
Inkpressions LLC ....E 248 461-2555
Commerce Township (G-3416)
◆ J America LLC ....E 517 521-2525
Webberville (G-17451)
▲ J2 Licensing Inc ....G 586 307-3400
Troy (G-16431)
Janet Kelly ....F 231 775-2313
Cadillac (G-2256)
Jean Smith Designs ....E 616 942-9212
Grand Rapids (G-6556)
Jene Holly Designs Inc ....G 586 954-0255
Harrison Township (G-7334)
JJ Jinkleheimer & Co Inc ....F 517 546-4345
Howell (G-8056)
Keeping You In Stitches ....G 586 421-9509
Chesterfield (G-2794)
Kountry Keepsakes ....G 586 294-4895
Fraser (G-5680)
Lansing Athletics ....G 517 327-8828
Lansing (G-9305)
Lazer Graphics ....E 269 926-1066
Benton Harbor (G-1522)
Logospot ....G 616 785-7170
Belmont (G-1467)
Mach II Enterprises Inc ....G 248 347-8822
Northville (G-11708)
Mackellar Associates Inc ....F 248 335-4440
Rochester Hills (G-13466)
Markit Products ....G 616 458-7881
Grand Rapids (G-6644)
Meridian Screen Prtg & Design ....G 517 351-2525
Okemos (G-12130)
Michigan Graphic Arts ....G 517 278-4120
Coldwater (G-3315)
Midwest Custom Embroidery Co ....G 269 381-7660
Kalamazoo (G-8827)
MJB Concepts Inc ....G 616 866-1470
Rockford (G-13580)
Monogram Etc ....G 989 743-5999
Corunna (G-3582)
Monograms & More Inc ....E 313 299-3140
Taylor (G-15746)
Nobby Inc ....E 810 984-3300
Fort Gratiot (G-5550)
Northville Stitching Post ....G 248 347-7622
Northville (G-11717)
On Green Logos ....G 616 669-1928
Hudsonville (G-8173)
P S Monograms ....G 616 698-1177
Byron Center (G-2206)
▲ Perrin Souvenir Distrs Inc ....B 616 785-9700
Comstock Park (G-3508)
Personal Graphics ....G 231 347-6347
Petoskey (G-12468)
Personalized Embroidery Co ....G 208 263-1267
Traverse City (G-16066)
Pierson Fine Art ....G 269 385-4974
Kalamazoo (G-8851)
Quilters Garden Inc ....G 810 750-8104
Fenton (G-5233)

S I C

Employee Codes: A=Over 500 employees, B=251-500
C=101-250, D=51-100, E=20-50, F=10-19, G=3-9
2020 Harris Michigan
Industrial Directory
711

23 APPAREL AND OTHER FINISHED PRODUCTS MADE FROM FABRICS AND SIMILAR MATERIAL SIC SECTION

Quilting By Cheryl G 616 669-5636 Jenison *(G-8639)*
▲ Royal Stewart Enterprises G 734 224-7994 Temperance *(G-15843)*
S & H Trophy & Sports G 616 754-0005 Greenville *(G-7151)*
Saginaw Knitting Mills Inc F 989 695-2481 Freeland *(G-5759)*
Shelly Meehof G 231 775-3065 Cadillac *(G-2276)*
Shirts n More Inc F 269 963-3266 Battle Creek *(G-1246)*
Silk Screenstuff G 517 543-7716 Charlotte *(G-2664)*
Slick Shirts Screen Printing F 517 371-3600 Lansing *(G-9424)*
Special T Custom Products G 810 654-9602 Davison *(G-3663)*
Spirit of Livingston Inc G 517 545-8831 Howell *(G-8102)*
Sporting Image Inc F 269 657-5646 Paw Paw *(G-12413)*
Sports Junction G 989 791-5900 Saginaw *(G-14156)*
Sports Junction G 989 835-9696 Midland *(G-10920)*
Sports Stop G 517 676-2199 Mason *(G-10660)*
Sportswear Specialties Inc G 734 416-9941 Canton *(G-2428)*
◆ Stahls Inc D 800 478-2457 Sterling Heights *(G-15508)*
Student Book Store Inc G 517 351-6768 East Lansing *(G-4677)*
Sylvesters G 989 348-9097 Grayling *(G-7116)*
T - Shirt Printing Plus Inc F 269 383-3666 Kalamazoo *(G-8907)*
Threadworks Ltd Inc G 517 548-9745 New Boston *(G-11513)*
Trophy Center West Michigan G 231 893-1686 Whitehall *(G-17678)*
Twin City Engraving Company G 269 983-0601 Saint Joseph *(G-14346)*
Ultra Stitch Embroidery F 586 498-5600 Roseville *(G-13886)*

2396 Automotive Trimmings, Apparel Findings, Related Prdts

1st Class Embroidery LLC G 734 282-7745 Southgate *(G-15071)*
A Game Apparel F 810 564-2600 Mount Morris *(G-11155)*
Advance Graphic Systems Inc E 248 656-8000 Rochester Hills *(G-13365)*
Advanced Composite Tech Inc G 248 709-9097 Rochester *(G-13311)*
▲ AGM Automotive LLC D 248 776-0600 Farmington Hills *(G-4923)*
American Silk Screen & EMB E 248 474-1000 Farmington Hills *(G-4930)*
▲ American Twisting Company E 269 637-8581 South Haven *(G-14752)*
AP Impressions Inc G 734 464-8009 Livonia *(G-9650)*
Applause Inc G 517 485-9880 Lansing *(G-9338)*
Applied Graphics & Fabricating F 989 662-3334 Auburn *(G-750)*
Ascott Corporation G 734 663-2023 Ann Arbor *(G-369)*
Athletic Uniform Lettering G 313 533-9071 Redford *(G-13145)*
Authority Customwear Ltd E 248 588-8075 Madison Heights *(G-10199)*
▲ Automotive Trim Technologies E 734 947-0344 Taylor *(G-15691)*
Bay Supply & Marketing Inc G 231 943-3249 Traverse City *(G-15908)*
Bivins Graphics G 616 453-2211 Grand Rapids *(G-6226)*
Bivins Graphics G 616 453-2211 Grand Rapids *(G-6227)*
Blts Wearable Art Inc G 517 669-9659 Dewitt *(G-4459)*
Britten Inc C 231 941-8200 Traverse City *(G-15920)*
C & C Enterprises Inc G 989 772-5095 Mount Pleasant *(G-11182)*
▲ Cadillac Prsentation Solutions E 248 288-9777 Troy *(G-16255)*
▲ Canadian Amrcn Rstoration Sups E 248 853-8900 Rochester Hills *(G-13384)*
Cedar Springs Sales LLC G 616 696-2111 Cedar Springs *(G-2548)*
Celia Corporation D 616 887-7341 Sparta *(G-15091)*
Chromatic Graphics Inc G 616 393-0034 Holland *(G-7590)*
▲ Cni Enterprises Inc G 248 586-3300 Madison Heights *(G-10212)*
▲ Cni-Owosso LLC G 248 586-3300 Madison Heights *(G-10213)*
Crawford Associates Inc G 248 549-9494 Royal Oak *(G-13915)*
Delux Monogramming Screen Prtg G 989 288-5321 Durand *(G-4607)*
Design Tech LLC G 616 459-2885 Grand Rapids *(G-6346)*
Designs By Bean G 989 845-4371 Chesaning *(G-2723)*
▲ Detroit Name Plate Etching Inc E 248 543-5200 Ferndale *(G-5278)*
E Q R 2 Inc G 586 731-3383 Sterling Heights *(G-15324)*
East End Sports Awards Inc G 906 293-8895 Newberry *(G-11579)*
▲ Eissmann Auto Port Huron LLC C 810 216-6300 Port Huron *(G-12916)*
Eissmann Auto Port Huron LLC E 248 829-4990 Rochester Hills *(G-13416)*
Elephant Head LLC G 734 256-4555 Romulus *(G-13670)*
Elite Active Wear Inc G 616 396-1229 Holland *(G-7621)*
Embroidery House Inc G 616 669-6400 Jenison *(G-8625)*
Ethnic Artwork Inc F 586 726-1400 Sterling Heights *(G-15333)*
Exclusive Imagery Inc G 248 436-2999 Royal Oak *(G-13927)*
Fibre Converters Inc E 269 279-1700 Constantine *(G-3535)*
Field Crafts Inc E 231 325-1122 Honor *(G-7952)*
Flaunt It Sportswear G 616 696-9084 Cedar Springs *(G-2556)*
Flint Group Packaging Inks G 513 619-2085 Livonia *(G-9738)*
Flint Group Packaging Inks G 734 781-4600 Livonia *(G-9739)*
▲ Futuris Automotive (us) Inc E 248 439-7800 Oak Park *(G-12069)*
Futuris Global Holdings LLC D 248 439-7800 Oak Park *(G-12070)*
Gottch-Ya Graphix USA G 269 979-7587 Battle Creek *(G-1193)*
Great Lakes Embroidery G 248 543-5164 Madison Heights *(G-10260)*
Gst Autoleather Inc F 248 436-2300 Rochester Hills *(G-13436)*
Hankerds Sportswear Basic TS G 989 725-2979 Owosso *(G-12294)*
Hayes-Albion Corporation F 517 629-2141 Jackson *(G-8463)*
Hexon Corporation F 248 585-7585 Farmington Hills *(G-5018)*
Hi-Lites Graphic Inc G 231 924-4540 Fremont *(G-5776)*
Imprint House LLC G 810 985-8203 Port Huron *(G-12929)*
Innovative Material Handling F 586 291-3694 Detroit *(G-4141)*
Inplast Interior Tech LLC G 810 724-3500 Almont *(G-258)*
International Automotive Compo B 810 987-8500 Port Huron *(G-12930)*
Irvin Acquisition LLC F 248 451-4100 Pontiac *(G-12837)*
▲ Irvin Automotive Products LLC C 248 451-4100 Pontiac *(G-12838)*
◆ J America LLC E 517 521-2525 Webberville *(G-17451)*
▲ J2 Licensing Inc G 586 307-3400 Troy *(G-16431)*
Jam Enterprises G 313 417-9200 Detroit *(G-4156)*
Janet Kelly F 231 775-2313 Cadillac *(G-2256)*
Jbl Enterprises G 616 530-8647 Grand Rapids *(G-6555)*
Jean Smith Designs E 616 942-9212 Grand Rapids *(G-6556)*
JS Original Silkscreens LLC G 586 779-5456 Eastpointe *(G-4705)*
Kalamazoo Regalia Inc F 269 344-4299 Kalamazoo *(G-8797)*
Kalamazoo Sportswear Inc F 269 344-4242 Kalamazoo *(G-8798)*
▲ Kay Screen Printing Inc C 248 377-4999 Lake Orion *(G-9141)*
Lacks Exterior Systems LLC B 616 949-6570 Grand Rapids *(G-6605)*
Lacks Industries Inc C 616 698-9852 Grand Rapids *(G-6609)*
Larsen Graphics Inc E 989 823-3000 Vassar *(G-16812)*
Lazer Graphics E 269 926-1066 Benton Harbor *(G-1522)*
Lear Corporation A 248 447-1500 Mason *(G-10644)*
◆ Lear Corporation B 248 447-1500 Southfield *(G-14962)*
▲ Logofit LLC E 810 715-1980 Flint *(G-5461)*
Loyalty 1977 Ink G 313 759-1006 Detroit *(G-4211)*
M & M Associates G 231 845-7034 Ludington *(G-10070)*
Mackellar Associates Inc F 248 335-4440 Rochester Hills *(G-13466)*
◆ Marketing Displays Inc C 248 553-1900 Farmington Hills *(G-5058)*
▲ Mayfair Golf Accessories F 989 732-8400 Gaylord *(G-5879)*
Michael Anderson G 231 652-5717 Newaygo *(G-11575)*
Mid-Michigan Industries Inc D 989 773-6918 Mount Pleasant *(G-11208)*
Mid-Michigan Industries Inc E 989 386-7707 Clare *(G-2877)*
Mvp Sports Store G 517 764-5165 Jackson *(G-8539)*
▲ Nalcor LLC D 248 541-1140 Ferndale *(G-5303)*
Neighborhood Artisans Inc G 313 865-5373 Detroit *(G-4265)*
Nobby Inc E 810 984-3300 Fort Gratiot *(G-5550)*
Peckham Vocational Inds Inc A 517 316-4000 Lansing *(G-9252)*
Peckham Vocational Inds Inc C 517 316-4478 Lansing *(G-9253)*
Perrin Screen Printing Inc D 616 785-9900 Comstock Park *(G-3507)*
▲ Perrin Souvenir Distrs Inc B 616 785-9700 Comstock Park *(G-3508)*
Plasti-Fab Inc E 248 543-1415 Ferndale *(G-5311)*
Player Prints LLC G 844 774-7773 Clarkston *(G-2946)*
Qmi Group Inc E 248 589-0505 Madison Heights *(G-10342)*
R H & Company Inc F 269 345-7814 Kalamazoo *(G-8867)*
Real Green Systems Inc D 888 345-2154 Commerce Township *(G-3447)*
Regents of The University Mich E 734 764-6230 Ann Arbor *(G-615)*
▲ Rj Corp F 616 396-0552 Holland *(G-7788)*
Rsls Corp G 248 726-0675 Shelby Township *(G-14683)*
Rtlf-Hope LLC E 313 538-1700 Detroit *(G-4349)*
S & H Trophy & Sports G 616 754-0005 Greenville *(G-7151)*
Saginaw Knitting Mills Inc F 989 695-2481 Freeland *(G-5759)*
Shirts n More Inc F 269 963-3266 Battle Creek *(G-1246)*
◆ Sigma International Inc E 248 230-9681 Livonia *(G-9928)*
Sign Screen Inc G 810 239-1100 Flint *(G-5499)*
Silk Screenstuff G 517 543-7716 Charlotte *(G-2664)*
Sporting Image Inc F 269 657-5646 Paw Paw *(G-12413)*

Sports Stop ... G ... 517 676-2199
Mason *(G-10660)*

Srg Global Inc ... C ... 248 509-1100
Troy *(G-16617)*

Srg Global Inc ... F ... 586 757-7800
Taylor *(G-15772)*

▲ Strattec Power Access LLC ... F ... 248 649-9742
Auburn Hills *(G-1004)*

Suite 600 T-Shirts LLC ... G ... 866 712-7749
Detroit *(G-4382)*

Sunset Sportswear Inc ... F ... 248 437-7611
Wixom *(G-17900)*

Sylvesters ... G ... 989 348-9097
Grayling *(G-7116)*

T - Shirt Printing Plus Inc ... F ... 269 383-3666
Kalamazoo *(G-8907)*

Takata Americas ... E ... 336 547-1600
Auburn Hills *(G-1012)*

Tempro Industries Inc ... F ... 734 451-5900
Plymouth *(G-12768)*

Tennant & Associates Inc ... G ... 248 643-6140
Troy *(G-16636)*

Tesca Usa Inc ... E ... 586 991-0744
Rochester Hills *(G-13524)*

Timbertech Inc ... E ... 231 348-2750
Harbor Springs *(G-7295)*

Twin City Engraving Company ... G ... 269 983-0601
Saint Joseph *(G-14346)*

▲ Universal Trim Inc ... E ... 248 586-3300
Madison Heights *(G-10374)*

▲ V&R Enterprize ... G ... 313 837-5545
Detroit *(G-4420)*

Vomela Specialty Company ... E ... 269 927-6500
Benton Harbor *(G-1562)*

Wec Group LLC ... F ... 248 260-4252
Rochester Hills *(G-13546)*

▲ Yanfeng USA Automotive Trim Sy ... D ... 586 354-2101
Harrison Township *(G-7359)*

2397 Schiffli Machine Embroideries

Chromatic Graphics Inc ... G ... 616 393-0034
Holland *(G-7590)*

Circles Way To Go Around Inc ... F ... 313 384-1193
Clinton Township *(G-3081)*

Ideal Wholesale Inc ... G ... 989 873-5850
Prescott *(G-13080)*

2399 Fabricated Textile Prdts, NEC

▲ AGM Automotive LLC ... D ... 248 776-0600
Farmington Hills *(G-4923)*

American Flag & Banner Company ... G ... 248 288-3010
Clawson *(G-2972)*

▲ Bannergalaxycom LLC ... G ... 231 941-8200
Traverse City *(G-15903)*

Bay Supply & Marketing Inc ... G ... 231 943-3249
Traverse City *(G-15908)*

Britten Inc ... C ... 231 941-8200
Traverse City *(G-15920)*

Britten Pop LLC ... G ... 800 426-9496
Traverse City *(G-15922)*

Brollytime Inc ... F ... 312 854-7606
Royal Oak *(G-13911)*

Consort Corporation ... E ... 269 388-4532
Kalamazoo *(G-8713)*

▲ Dag Ltd LLC ... F ... 586 276-9310
Sterling Heights *(G-15307)*

▲ Ed Cumings Inc ... E ... 810 736-0130
Flint *(G-5423)*

Engineering Reproduction Inc ... F ... 313 366-3390
Detroit *(G-4038)*

Faurecia North America Inc ... F ... 248 288-1000
Auburn Hills *(G-863)*

Flo-Tec Inc ... D ... 734 455-7655
Livonia *(G-9742)*

Gerry Gostenik ... G ... 313 319-0100
Dearborn *(G-3714)*

Get In Game Marketing LLC ... G ... 231 846-1976
Traverse City *(G-15979)*

Hamilton Equine Products LLC ... G ... 616 842-2406
Grand Haven *(G-6031)*

Huron Vlleys Hrse Blnket Hdqtr ... G ... 248 859-2398
Wixom *(G-17831)*

Jack Ripper & Associates Inc ... G ... 734 453-7333
Plymouth *(G-12652)*

▲ Key Safety Systems Inc ... C ... 586 726-3800
Auburn Hills *(G-926)*

◆ Key Sfety Rstraint Systems Inc ... A ... 586 726-3800
Auburn Hills *(G-927)*

Lamacs Inc ... G ... 248 643-9210
Troy *(G-16456)*

◆ McCarthy Group Incorporated ... G ... 616 977-2900
Grand Rapids *(G-6652)*

Michigan Industrial Trim Inc ... F ... 734 947-0344
Taylor *(G-15742)*

Powder It Inc ... G ... 586 949-0395
Chesterfield *(G-2820)*

Priority One Emergency Inc ... G ... 734 398-5900
Canton *(G-2419)*

▲ Randlis Manufacturing Co ... G ... 313 368-0220
Detroit *(G-4329)*

Sage Automotive Interiors Inc ... F ... 248 355-9055
Southfield *(G-15020)*

Silk Reflections ... G ... 313 292-1150
Taylor *(G-15766)*

Snoeks Automotive N Amer Inc ... G ... 586 716-9588
New Baltimore *(G-11493)*

Spartan Flag Company Inc ... F ... 231 386-5150
Northport *(G-11672)*

◆ Stahls Inc ... D ... 800 478-2457
Sterling Heights *(G-15508)*

Takata Americas ... E ... 336 547-1600
Auburn Hills *(G-1012)*

Teamtech Motorsports Safety ... G ... 989 792-4880
Saginaw *(G-14163)*

Technotrim Inc ... A ... 734 254-5243
Plymouth *(G-12767)*

Thorpe Printing Services Inc ... G ... 810 364-6222
Marysville *(G-10622)*

Tk Holdings Inc ... C ... 517 545-9535
Howell *(G-8112)*

Tk Mexico Inc ... G ... 248 373-8040
Auburn Hills *(G-1028)*

▲ Verduyn Tarps Detroit Inc ... G ... 313 270-4890
Detroit *(G-4425)*

Wooshin Safety Systems ... G ... 248 615-4946
Farmington Hills *(G-5153)*

24 LUMBER AND WOOD PRODUCTS, EXCEPT FURNITURE

2411 Logging

Abcor Partners LLC ... E ... 616 994-9577
Holland *(G-7546)*

Aj Logging ... F ... 989 725-9610
Henderson *(G-7465)*

Alexa Forest Products ... G ... 906 265-2347
Iron River *(G-8307)*

Allen Whitehouse ... G ... 231 824-3000
Manton *(G-10450)*

Anderson Logging Inc ... G ... 906 482-7505
Houghton *(G-7971)*

Antilla Logging Inc ... G ... 906 376-2374
Republic *(G-13244)*

▼ Atwood Forest Products Inc ... E ... 616 696-0081
Cedar Springs *(G-2545)*

Beacom Enterprises Inc ... G ... 906 647-3831
Pickford *(G-12481)*

Bear Creek Logging ... G ... 269 317-7475
Ceresco *(G-2601)*

Bennett Sawmill ... G ... 231 734-5733
Evart *(G-4879)*

Bixby Logging ... G ... 231 348-9794
Petoskey *(G-12442)*

Bosanic Lwrnce Sons Tmber Pdts ... G ... 906 341-5609
Manistique *(G-10439)*

Bourdo Logging ... G ... 269 623-4981
Delton *(G-3816)*

Brent Bastian Logging LLC ... G ... 906 482-6378
Hancock *(G-7249)*

▲ Bruning Forest Products ... C ... 989 733-2880
Onaway *(G-12145)*

Bryan K Sergent ... G ... 231 670-2106
Stanwood *(G-15232)*

Budd Logging LLC ... G ... 989 329-1578
Farwell *(G-5159)*

Bugay Logging ... G ... 906 428-2125
Gladstone *(G-5909)*

Bundy Logging ... G ... 231 824-6054
Manton *(G-10451)*

C D C Logging ... G ... 906 524-6369
Lanse *(G-9188)*

Cain Brothers Logging Inc ... G ... 906 345-9252
Negaunee *(G-11468)*

Cal Park Logging LLC ... G ... 231 796-4662
Big Rapids *(G-1623)*

Casselman Logging ... G ... 231 885-1040
Mesick *(G-10768)*

Cdn Loading Inc ... G ... 906 338-2630
Pelkie *(G-12421)*

Cg Logging ... G ... 906 322-1018
Brimley *(G-2014)*

Charles William Carr Sr ... G ... 231 854-3643
Hesperia *(G-7477)*

Chris Muma Forest Products ... F ... 989 426-5916
Gladwin *(G-5927)*

Chris Underhill ... G ... 231 349-5228
Big Rapids *(G-1624)*

Dale Routley Logging ... G ... 231 861-2596
Hart *(G-7370)*

Dales LLC ... G ... 734 444-4620
Lapeer *(G-9456)*

Danny K Bundy ... G ... 231 590-6924
Manton *(G-10452)*

Darrell A Curtice ... G ... 231 745-9890
Bitely *(G-1710)*

David Boyd ... G ... 517 567-2302
Waldron *(G-16857)*

David Gauss Logging ... G ... 517 851-8102
Stockbridge *(G-15588)*

David Jenks ... G ... 810 793-7340
North Branch *(G-11659)*

Davis Logging ... G ... 517 617-4550
Bronson *(G-2023)*

Dawzye Excavation Inc ... G ... 906 786-5276
Gladstone *(G-5912)*

Dees Logging ... G ... 616 796-8050
Holland *(G-7606)*

Dehaan Forest Products Inc ... F ... 906 883-3417
Mass City *(G-10661)*

Dillon Charles Logging & Cnstr ... G ... 906 376-8470
Republic *(G-13245)*

DJL Logging Inc ... G ... 231 590-2012
Manton *(G-10453)*

Donald Lll Sons Logging ... G ... 231 420-3800
Pellston *(G-12425)*

Doug Anderson Logging ... G ... 906 337-3707
Calumet *(G-2327)*

Doyle Forest Products Inc ... E ... 231 832-5586
Paris *(G-12384)*

Duane F Proehl Inc ... G ... 906 474-6630
Rapid River *(G-13112)*

Duane Young & Son Lumber ... G ... 586 727-1470
Columbus *(G-3378)*

Duberville Logging ... G ... 906 586-6267
Curtis *(G-3619)*

E H Tulgestka & Sons Inc ... F ... 989 734-2129
Rogers City *(G-13615)*

Earl St John Forest Products ... E ... 906 497-5667
Spalding *(G-15086)*

East Branch Forest Products ... G ... 906 852-3315
Kenton *(G-8995)*

Ej Timber Producers Inc ... F ... 231 544-9866
East Jordan *(G-4635)*

Erickson Logging Inc ... G ... 906 523-4049
Chassell *(G-2673)*

Fahl Forest Products Inc ... D ... 231 258-9734
Mancelona *(G-10390)*

Forest Blake Products Inc ... G ... 231 879-3913
Fife Lake *(G-5340)*

GA Dalbeck Logging LLC ... F ... 906 364-3300
Wakefield *(G-16852)*

Gendzwill Co ... G ... 906 786-9321
Escanaba *(G-4830)*

Gentz Forest Robert Products ... F ... 231 398-9194
Manistee *(G-10423)*

Giguere Logging Inc ... G ... 906 786-3975
Escanaba *(G-4832)*

Gordon Hackworth Logging ... G ... 517 589-9218
Leslie *(G-9541)*

Great Lakes Log & Firewd Co ... G ... 231 206-4073
Twin Lake *(G-16712)*

Gustafson Logging ... G ... 906 250-2482
Trout Creek *(G-16163)*

H & N Hauling ... G ... 989 640-3847
Elsie *(G-4796)*

Heidtman Logging Inc ... G ... 906 249-3914
Marquette *(G-10534)*

Heritage Forestry LLC ... G ... 231 689-5721
White Cloud *(G-17624)*

Hiawatha Log Homes Inc ... E ... 877 275-9090
Munising *(G-11244)*

Hincka Logging LLC ... G ... 989 766-8893
Posen *(G-13069)*

Holli Forest Products ... E ... 906 486-9352
Ishpeming *(G-8346)*

Hytec Equipment ... G ... 906 789-5811
Escanaba *(G-4835)*

Inman Forest Products Inc ... G ... 989 370-4473
Glennie *(G-5943)*

S I C

J & D Logging .... G 517 543-3873
Charlotte ***(G-2655)***

J Carey Logging Inc .... F 906 542-3420
Channing ***(G-2603)***

James L Miller .... G 989 539-5540
Harrison ***(G-7313)***

James Pollard Logging .... G 906 884-6744
Ontonagon ***(G-12158)***

James Spicer Inc .... G 906 265-2385
Iron River ***(G-8311)***

Jason Lutke .... E 231 824-6655
Manton ***(G-10456)***

Jeffery Lucas .... G 231 797-5152
Luther ***(G-10093)***

Jeffrey L Hackworth .... G 517 589-5884
Leslie ***(G-9543)***

Jerome Miller Lumber Co .... G 231 745-3694
Baldwin ***(G-1084)***

Jesse James Logging .... G 906 395-6819
Lanse ***(G-9193)***

Jim Detweiler .... G 269 467-7728
Sturgis ***(G-15608)***

Jns Sawmill .... G 989 352-5430
Coral ***(G-3574)***

Joe Bosanic Forest Products .... G 906 341-2037
Manistique ***(G-10441)***

John Barnes .... G 231 885-1561
Copemish ***(G-3572)***

John Sivula Logging & Cnstr .... G 906 639-2714
Daggett ***(G-3621)***

John Vuk & Son Inc .... G 906 524-6074
Lanse ***(G-9194)***

Johnson Logging Firewoo .... G 231 578-5833
Ravenna ***(G-13122)***

Joseph Lakosky Logging .... G 906 573-2783
Manistique ***(G-10442)***

Jungnitsch Bros Logging .... G 989 233-8091
Saint Charles ***(G-14193)***

K & M Industrial LLC .... G 906 420-8770
Gladstone ***(G-5914)***

Kanerva Forest Products Inc .... G 906 356-6061
Rock ***(G-13554)***

Karttunen Logging .... G 906 884-4312
Ontonagon ***(G-12161)***

Keith Falan .... G 231 834-7358
Grant ***(G-7080)***

Kells Sawmill Inc .... G 906 753-2778
Stephenson ***(G-15236)***

Kelly St Amour .... G 231 625-9789
Cheboygan ***(G-2685)***

Kenneth A Gould .... G 231 828-4705
Twin Lake ***(G-16713)***

Ketola Logging .... G 906 524-6479
Lanse ***(G-9196)***

Kk Logging .... G 906 524-6047
Lanse ***(G-9197)***

Kostamo Logging .... G 906 353-6171
Pelkie ***(G-12422)***

Lake Brothers Forest Products .... G 906 485-5639
Ishpeming ***(G-8348)***

Lake Superior Logging .... G 906 440-3567
Brimley ***(G-2016)***

Lawrence Beaudoin Logging .... G 906 296-0549
Lake Linden ***(G-9108)***

Laws & Ponies Logging Show .... G 269 838-3942
Delton ***(G-3817)***

Lee J Cummings .... G 906 932-3298
Ironwood ***(G-8334)***

Leep Logging Inc .... G 517 852-1540
Nashville ***(G-11459)***

Leonard J Hill Logging Co .... F 906 337-3435
Calumet ***(G-2329)***

Lindsay Nettell Inc .... G 906 482-3549
Atlantic Mine ***(G-737)***

Logging Long Branch .... G 231 549-3031
Boyne Falls ***(G-1840)***

Long Lake Forest Products .... G 989 239-6527
Harrison ***(G-7314)***

Low Impact Logging Inc .... G 906 250-5117
Iron River ***(G-8315)***

Lucas Logging .... G 906 246-3629
Bark River ***(G-1120)***

Lumberjack Logging LLC .... G 616 799-4657
Pierson ***(G-12484)***

M V A Enterprises Inc .... G 906 282-6288
Felch ***(G-5168)***

Manigg Enterprises Inc .... F 989 356-4986
Alpena ***(G-296)***

Mannisto Forest Products Inc .... G 906 387-3836
Munising ***(G-11245)***

Mark A Nelson .... G 989 305-5769
Lupton ***(G-10092)***

Mark Honkala Logging Inc .... G 906 485-1570
Ishpeming ***(G-8349)***

Marshall Clayton & Sons Log .... G 269 623-8898
Delton ***(G-3819)***

Marvin Nelson Forest Products .... F 906 384-6700
Cornell ***(G-3575)***

McNamara & Mcnamara .... F 906 293-5281
Newberry ***(G-11580)***

Michael Graves Logging .... G 906 387-2852
Wetmore ***(G-17615)***

Mid Michigan Logging .... F 231 229-4501
Lake City ***(G-9093)***

Mike Hughes .... G 269 377-3578
Nashville ***(G-11461)***

Miljevich Corporation .... F 906 229-5367
Wakefield ***(G-16853)***

Minerick Logging Inc .... E 906 542-3583
Sagola ***(G-14187)***

Motto Cedar Products Inc .... G 906 753-4892
Daggett ***(G-3622)***

Ndsay Nettell Logging .... G 906 482-3549
Atlantic Mine ***(G-738)***

Nickels Logging .... G 906 563-5880
Norway ***(G-11818)***

Noble Forestry Inc .... G 989 866-6495
Blanchard ***(G-1711)***

P G K Enterprises LLC .... G 248 535-4411
Southfield ***(G-14995)***

Patrick Newland Logging Ltd .... G 906 524-2255
Lanse ***(G-9199)***

Paul Marshall & Son Log LLC .... G 269 998-4440
Plainwell ***(G-12534)***

Peacocks Eco Log & Sawmill LLC .... G 231 250-3462
Morley ***(G-11117)***

Pearson Dean Excavating & Log .... G 906 932-3513
Ironwood ***(G-8337)***

Pinneys Logging Inc .... G 231 536-7730
East Jordan ***(G-4643)***

Piwarski Brothers Logging Inc .... G 906 265-2914
Iron River ***(G-8319)***

Plum Creek Timber Company Inc .... G 715 453-7952
Escanaba ***(G-4852)***

Pomeroy Forest Products Inc .... G 906 474-6780
Rapid River ***(G-13113)***

Precision Forestry .... G 989 619-1016
Onaway ***(G-12150)***

Proctor Logging Inc .... G 231 775-3820
Cadillac ***(G-2272)***

R & R Forest Products Inc .... G 989 766-8227
Posen ***(G-13071)***

Rapid River Rustic Inc .... E 906 474-6404
Rapid River ***(G-13114)***

Rex Rush Inc .... G 248 684-0221
Commerce Township ***(G-3448)***

Robert Crawford & Son Logging .... G 989 379-2712
Lachine ***(G-9078)***

Robert McIntyre Logging .... G 906 446-3158
Rapid River ***(G-13115)***

Rodney E Harter .... G 231 796-6734
Big Rapids ***(G-1644)***

Roger Bazuin & Sons Inc .... E 231 825-2889
Mc Bain ***(G-10684)***

Rosenthal Logging .... G 231 348-8168
Petoskey ***(G-12473)***

Rothig Forest Products Inc .... E 231 266-8292
Irons ***(G-8322)***

Roxbury Creek LLC .... G 989 731-2062
Gaylord ***(G-5890)***

S & S Forest Products .... G 906 892-8268
Munising ***(G-11249)***

S&M Logging LLC .... G 231 821-0588
Twin Lake ***(G-16714)***

Saninocencio Logging .... G 269 945-3567
Hastings ***(G-7426)***

Santti Brothers Inc .... G 906 355-2347
Watton ***(G-17395)***

Scott Johnson Forest Pdts Co .... G 906 482-3978
Houghton ***(G-7982)***

Shamco Inc .... G 906 265-5065
Iron River ***(G-8320)***

Shamion Brothers .... E 906 265-5065
Iron River ***(G-8321)***

Shawn Muma .... G 989 426-9505
Gladwin ***(G-5937)***

Shawn Muma Logging .... G 989 426-6852
Gladwin ***(G-5938)***

Sheski Logging .... G 906 786-1886
Escanaba ***(G-4859)***

Smith Logging LLC .... G 616 558-0729
Hopkins ***(G-7962)***

Spencer Forest Products .... G 906 341-6791
Gulliver ***(G-7213)***

Stachnik Logging LLC .... G 231 275-7641
Cedar ***(G-2542)***

Steigers Timber Operations .... G 906 667-0266
Bessemer ***(G-1607)***

Steven Crandell .... G 231 582-7445
Charlevoix ***(G-2632)***

Tarrs Tree Service Inc .... F 248 528-3313
Troy ***(G-16631)***

Thomas Logging LLC .... G 269 838-2020
Woodland ***(G-17943)***

Timberline Logging Inc .... F 989 731-2794
Gaylord ***(G-5895)***

Tom Clisch Logging Inc .... G 906 338-2900
Pelkie ***(G-12423)***

Total Chips Company Inc .... F 989 866-2610
Shepherd ***(G-14731)***

TR Timber Co .... F 989 345-5350
West Branch ***(G-17526)***

Tri-Forestry .... G 906 474-9379
Rapid River ***(G-13116)***

Triple Ddd Firewood .... G 231 734-5215
Evart ***(G-4887)***

Turpeinen Bros Inc .... F 906 338-2870
Pelkie ***(G-12424)***

Tuttle Forest Products .... G 906 283-3871
Gulliver ***(G-7214)***

Usher Logging LLC .... G 906 238-4261
Arnold ***(G-725)***

Usher Logging LLC .... G 906 238-4261
Cornell ***(G-3576)***

Utility Supply and Cnstr Co .... G 231 832-2297
Reed City ***(G-13225)***

Van Duinen Forest Products .... F 231 328-4507
Lake City ***(G-9097)***

Vic Freed Logging .... G 906 477-9933
Engadine ***(G-4799)***

Vulcan Wood Products Inc .... F 906 563-8995
Vulcan ***(G-16847)***

W J Z & Sons Harvesting Inc .... E 906 586-6360
Germfask ***(G-5902)***

Wade Logging .... G 231 463-0363
Fife Lake ***(G-5344)***

Welch Land & Timber Inc .... G 989 848-5197
Curran ***(G-3617)***

Wender Logging Inc .... G 906 779-1483
Iron Mountain ***(G-8305)***

Whittaker Timber Corporation .... G 989 872-3065
Cass City ***(G-2525)***

Wood Brothers Logging .... G 989 350-6064
Atlanta ***(G-734)***

Woodside Logging LLC .... G 906 482-0150
Hancock ***(G-7259)***

Yamaha Logging .... G 989 657-1706
Grayling ***(G-7119)***

Yates Forest Products Inc .... G 989 739-8412
Oscoda ***(G-12225)***

Yoder Forest Products L L C .... G 989 848-2437
Curran ***(G-3618)***

Younggren Farm & Forest Inc .... G 906 355-2272
Covington ***(G-3593)***

Younggren Timber Company .... G 906 355-2272
Covington ***(G-3594)***

Zellar Forest Products .... G 906 586-9817
Germfask ***(G-5903)***

2421 Saw & Planing Mills

/// 702 Cedar River Lbr Inc .... E 906 497-5365
Powers ***(G-13076)***

A J D Forest Pdts Ltd Partnr .... D 989 348-5412
Grayling ***(G-7101)***

All-Wood Inc .... G 906 353-6642
Baraga ***(G-1096)***

American Classic Homes Inc .... G 616 594-5900
Holland ***(G-7558)***

Ann Lake Hardwood Inc .... G 231 275-6406
Lake Ann ***(G-9084)***

▼ Applegate Insul Systems Inc .... E 517 521-3545
Webberville ***(G-17446)***

▼ Atwood Forest Products Inc .... E 616 696-0081
Cedar Springs ***(G-2545)***

▼ Banks Hardwoods Inc .... D 269 483-2323
White Pigeon ***(G-17645)***

Bennett Sawmill .... G 231 734-5733
Evart ***(G-4879)***

Besse Forest Products Inc .... E 906 353-7193
Baraga ***(G-1098)***

24 LUMBER AND WOOD PRODUCTS, EXCEPT FURNITURE

Biewer Forest Management LLC .... G 231 825-2855
  Mc Bain *(G-10678)*
Black Creek Timber LLC .... G 517 202-2169
  Rudyard *(G-13983)*
Blough Hardwoods Inc .... G 616 693-2174
  Clarksville *(G-2966)*
Burt Moeke & Son Hardwoods .... E 231 587-5388
  Mancelona *(G-10388)*
Buskirk Lumber Company .... E 616 765-5103
  Freeport *(G-5763)*
Caledonia Cmnty Sawmill LLC .... G 616 891-8561
  Alto *(G-324)*
Casselman Logging .... G 231 885-1040
  Mesick *(G-10768)*
Cedar Mill LLC .... G 906 297-2318
  De Tour Village *(G-3667)*
Coe Creek Portable Sawmill .... G 231 829-3035
  Tustin *(G-16710)*
Collins Brothers Sawmill Inc .... F 906 524-5511
  Lanse *(G-9190)*
Country Side Sawmill .... G 989 352-7198
  Lakeview *(G-9171)*
Creekside Lumber .... G 231 924-1934
  Newaygo *(G-11566)*
Cruse Hardwood Lumber Inc .... G 517 688-4891
  Birmingham *(G-1679)*
Cygeirts Sawmill .... G 231 821-0083
  Brunswick *(G-2107)*
Cyrus Forest Products .... G 269 751-6535
  Allegan *(G-154)*
Daniel D Slater .... G 989 833-7135
  Riverdale *(G-13284)*
▲ Decatur Wood Products Inc .... E 269 657-6041
  Decatur *(G-3802)*
Decorative Panels Intl Inc .... E 989 354-2121
  Alpena *(G-285)*
▼ Devereaux Saw Mill Inc .... D 989 593-2552
  Pewamo *(G-12478)*
Diversified Pdts & Svcs LLC .... G 616 836-6600
  Holland *(G-7608)*
Don Sawmill Inc .... G 989 733-2780
  Onaway *(G-12146)*
Dowd Brothers Forestry .... G 989 345-7459
  Alger *(G-138)*
Duane Young & Son Lumber .... G 586 727-1470
  Columbus *(G-3378)*
Dyers Sawmill Inc .... E 231 768-4438
  Leroy *(G-9531)*
E H Tulgestka & Sons Inc .... F 989 734-2129
  Rogers City *(G-13615)*
E U P Woods Shavings .... G 906 495-1141
  Kincheloe *(G-9050)*
Ecostrat USA Inc .... G 416 968-8884
  Madison Heights *(G-10239)*
Elenz Inc .... F 989 732-7233
  Gaylord *(G-5857)*
Eovations LLC .... G 616 361-7136
  Grand Rapids *(G-6382)*
Fairview Sawmill Inc .... G 989 848-5238
  Fairview *(G-4890)*
Forest Blake Products Inc .... G 231 879-3913
  Fife Lake *(G-5340)*
Forest Corullo Products Corp .... E 906 667-0275
  Bessemer *(G-1605)*
Forest Elders Products Inc .... F 616 866-9317
  Rockford *(G-13569)*
◆ Forestry Management Svcs Inc .... C 517 456-7431
  Clinton *(G-3020)*
◆ Forte Industries Mill Inc .... F 906 753-6256
  Stephenson *(G-15235)*
Gatien Farm & Forest Pdts LLC .... G 906 497-5541
  Powers *(G-13077)*
Gilchrist Premium Lumber Pdts .... F 989 826-8300
  Mio *(G-11002)*
Grand Traverse Assembly Inc .... E 231 588-2406
  Ellsworth *(G-4788)*
Great Northern Lumber Mich LLC .... E 989 736-6192
  Lincoln *(G-9562)*
Green Gables Saw Mill .... G 989 386-7846
  Clare *(G-2871)*
Gyms Sawmill .... G 989 826-8299
  Mio *(G-11003)*
Hmi Hardwoods LLC .... D 517 456-7431
  Clinton *(G-3023)*
Hochstetler Sawmill .... G 269 467-7018
  Centreville *(G-2595)*
Housler Sawmill Inc .... F 231 824-6353
  Mesick *(G-10770)*
Ida D Byler .... G 810 672-9355
  Cass City *(G-2515)*

Integrity Forest Products LLC .... G 513 871-8988
  Kenton *(G-8996)*
Jaroche Brothers Inc .... F 231 525-8100
  Wolverine *(G-17934)*
Jerome Miller Lumber Co .... G 231 745-3694
  Baldwin *(G-1083)*
Jerome Miller Lumber Co .... G 231 745-3694
  Baldwin *(G-1084)*
John A Biewer Lumber Company .... G 231 839-7646
  Lake City *(G-9089)*
John A Biewer Lumber Company .... D 231 825-2855
  Mc Bain *(G-10682)*
Kappen Saw Mill .... G 989 872-4410
  Cass City *(G-2516)*
Kells Sawmill Inc .... G 906 753-2778
  Stephenson *(G-15236)*
Lumber Jack Hardwoods Inc .... F 906 863-7090
  Menominee *(G-10742)*
Maeder Bros Inc .... E 989 644-2235
  Weidman *(G-17459)*
Maeder Bros Qlty WD Pllets Inc .... F 989 644-3500
  Weidman *(G-17460)*
Maple Ridge Hardwoods Inc .... G 989 873-5305
  Sterling *(G-15244)*
Maples Sawmill Inc .... E 906 484-3926
  Hessel *(G-7481)*
Master Woodworks .... G 269 240-3262
  Saint Joseph *(G-14328)*
Matthews Mill Inc .... F 989 257-3271
  South Branch *(G-14749)*
Mc Guire Mill & Lumber .... G 989 735-3851
  Glennie *(G-5945)*
McPhails Pallets Inc .... F 810 384-6458
  Kenockee *(G-8985)*
Meeders Lumber Co .... G 231 587-8611
  Mancelona *(G-10395)*
Met Inc .... G 231 845-1737
  Ludington *(G-10072)*
Michigan Lumber & Wood Fiber I .... E 989 848-2100
  Comins *(G-3383)*
Mlc of Wakefield Inc .... F 906 224-1120
  Wakefield *(G-16854)*
Nelsons Saw Mill Inc .... G 231 829-5220
  Tustin *(G-16711)*
Nettleton Wood Products Inc .... G 906 297-5791
  De Tour Village *(G-3668)*
▲ North American Forest Products ...... C 269 663-8500
  Edwardsburg *(G-4769)*
North American Forest Products .... G 269 663-8500
  Edwardsburg *(G-4770)*
Northern Hardwoods Oper Co LLC ...... D 860 632-3505
  South Range *(G-14818)*
Northern Industrial Wood Inc .... E 989 736-6192
  Lincoln *(G-9568)*
Northern Mich Hardwoods Inc .... F 231 347-4575
  Petoskey *(G-12460)*
Northern Michigan Sawmill .... G 231 409-1314
  Williamsburg *(G-17716)*
Northern Products of Wisconsin .... G 715 589-4417
  Iron Mountain *(G-8293)*
Northern Sawmills Inc .... G 231 547-9452
  Charlevoix *(G-2622)*
Northwest Hardwoods Inc .... E 989 786-6100
  Lewiston *(G-9554)*
Northwood Lumber .... G 989 826-1751
  Mio *(G-11007)*
Nu-Tran LLC .... G 616 350-9575
  Wyoming *(G-18023)*
Oceana Forest Products Inc .... G 231 861-6115
  Shelby *(G-14532)*
Old Sawmill Woodworking Co .... G 248 366-6245
  Commerce Township *(G-3434)*
▲ Open Air Lifestyles LLC .... F 586 716-2233
  Macomb *(G-10150)*
Ottawa Forest Products Inc .... E 906 932-9701
  Ironwood *(G-8336)*
Paris North Hardwood Lumber .... E 231 584-2500
  Elmira *(G-4792)*
Parks Sawmill Products .... G 231 229-4551
  Lake City *(G-9095)*
PDM Company .... F 231 946-4444
  Lake Leelanau *(G-9105)*
Pine Tech Inc .... E 989 426-0006
  Plymouth *(G-12716)*
Pollums Natural Resources .... G 810 245-7268
  Lapeer *(G-9481)*
Post Hardwoods Inc .... F 269 751-2221
  Hamilton *(G-7237)*
Potlatchdeltic Corporation .... C 906 346-3215
  Gwinn *(G-7222)*

◆ Precision Hrdwood Rsources Inc ..... F 734 475-0144
  Chelsea *(G-2718)*
Prells Saw Mill Inc .... E 989 734-2939
  Hawks *(G-7430)*
Pulpwood & Forestry Products .... F 231 788-3088
  Muskegon *(G-11408)*
Pure Products International In .... G 989 471-1104
  Ossineke *(G-12231)*
Quigley Lumber Inc .... G 989 257-5116
  South Branch *(G-14750)*
R & N Lumber .... G 989 848-5553
  Mio *(G-11008)*
Rapid River Rustic Inc .... E 906 474-6404
  Rapid River *(G-13114)*
Richter Sawmill .... G 231 829-3071
  Leroy *(G-9537)*
Ridgewood Stoves LLC .... G 989 488-3397
  Hersey *(G-7475)*
Riverbend Timber Framing Inc .... D 517 486-3629
  Blissfield *(G-1726)*
Sabertooth Enterprises LLC .... F 989 539-9842
  Harrison *(G-7316)*
Sagola Hardwoods Inc .... D 906 542-7200
  Sagola *(G-14188)*
Sawing Logz LLC .... G 586 883-5649
  Warren *(G-17231)*
Sawmill Estates .... G 269 792-7500
  Wayland *(G-17414)*
Schleben Forest Products Inc .... G 989 734-2858
  Rogers City *(G-13622)*
▲ Sensitile Systems LLC .... E 313 872-6314
  Ypsilanti *(G-18100)*
Silver Leaf Sawmill .... G 231 584-2003
  Elmira *(G-4793)*
Southwestern Hardwoods LLC .... G 269 795-0004
  Middleville *(G-10808)*
St Charles Hardwood Michigan .... F 989 865-9299
  Saint Charles *(G-14201)*
Superior Lumber Inc .... G 906 786-1638
  Gladstone *(G-5920)*
T Warren Sawmill .... G 989 619-0840
  Grayling *(G-7117)*
Terry Heiden .... G 906 753-6248
  Stephenson *(G-15241)*
Thorn Creek Lumber LLC .... G 231 832-1600
  Reed City *(G-13223)*
Timber Products Co Ltd Partnr .... C 906 452-6221
  Munising *(G-11250)*
Total Chips Company Inc .... F 989 866-2610
  Shepherd *(G-14731)*
Town & Country Cedar Homes .... G 231 347-4360
  Boyne Falls *(G-1842)*
Ufp Atlantic LLC .... G 616 364-6161
  Grand Rapids *(G-6945)*
◆ Ufp Eastern Division Inc .... E 616 364-6161
  Grand Rapids *(G-6946)*
Ufp Grand Rapids LLC .... F 616 464-1650
  Grand Rapids *(G-6947)*
Ufp West Central LLC .... G 616 364-6161
  Grand Rapids *(G-6949)*
▼ Universal Forest Products Inc .... C 616 364-6161
  Grand Rapids *(G-6954)*
Waltons Sawmill .... G 517 841-5241
  Jackson *(G-8604)*
Weber Bros Sawmill Inc .... E 989 644-2206
  Mount Pleasant *(G-11235)*
West Michigan Sawmill .... F 616 693-0044
  Clarksville *(G-2967)*
Weyerhaeuser Company .... G 989 348-2881
  Grayling *(G-7118)*
Wheelers Wolf Lake Sawmill .... G 231 745-7078
  Baldwin *(G-1086)*
Whitens Kiln & Lumber Inc .... F 906 498-2116
  Hermansville *(G-7469)*
William S Wixtrom .... G 906 376-8247
  Republic *(G-13247)*
Willsie Lumber Company .... F 989 695-5094
  Freeland *(G-5761)*
Yard & Home LLC .... G 844 927-3466
  Grand Rapids *(G-7007)*
Zulski Lumber Inc .... G 231 539-8909
  Pellston *(G-12427)*

2426 Hardwood Dimension & Flooring Mills

▼ Atwood Forest Products Inc .... E 616 696-0081
  Cedar Springs *(G-2545)*
B & B Heartwoods Inc .... G 734 332-9525
  Ann Arbor *(G-379)*
▼ Banks Hardwoods Inc .... D 269 483-2323
  White Pigeon *(G-17645)*

Besse Forest Products Inc....E.... 906 353-7193
Baraga *(G-1098)*
Burt Moeke & Son Hardwoods....E.... 231 587-5388
Mancelona *(G-10388)*
Component Solutions LLC....E.... 906 863-2682
Menominee *(G-10729)*
Connor Sports Flooring Corp....F.... 906 822-7311
Amasa *(G-330)*
Counterpoint By Hlf....D.... 734 699-7100
Van Buren Twp *(G-16754)*
Craftwood Industries Inc....E.... 616 796-1209
Holland *(G-7599)*
De Meester Saw Mill....G.... 616 677-3144
Coopersville *(G-3555)*
Demeester Wood Products Inc....F.... 616 677-5995
Coopersville *(G-3556)*
▼ Devereaux Saw Mill Inc....D.... 989 593-2552
Pewamo *(G-12478)*
Doltek Enterprises Inc....E.... 616 837-7828
Nunica *(G-12036)*
Duane Young & Son Lumber....G.... 586 727-1470
Columbus *(G-3378)*
Dyers Sawmill Inc....E.... 231 768-4438
Leroy *(G-9531)*
Erickson Lumber & True Value....G.... 906 524-6295
Lanse *(G-9191)*
Forest Elders Products Inc....F.... 616 866-9317
Rockford *(G-13569)*
◆ Forestry Management Svcs Inc....C.... 517 456-7431
Clinton *(G-3020)*
◆ Forte Industries Mill Inc....F.... 906 753-6256
Stephenson *(G-15235)*
Gem Wood Products Inc....G.... 616 384-3460
Coopersville *(G-3559)*
Genesis Seating Inc....G.... 616 954-1040
Grand Rapids *(G-6436)*
◆ Genesis Seating Inc....G.... 616 954-1040
Grand Rapids *(G-6437)*
Grand Rapids Carvers Inc....E.... 616 538-0022
Grand Rapids *(G-6452)*
Grants Woodshop Inc....G.... 517 543-1116
Charlotte *(G-2653)*
H & R Wood Specialties Inc....E.... 269 628-2181
Gobles *(G-5947)*
▼ Horner Flooring Company Inc....D.... 906 482-1180
Dollar Bay *(G-4521)*
IKEA Chip LLC....G.... 877 218-9931
Troy *(G-16409)*
Interntonal Hardwoods Michiana....G.... 517 278-8446
Coldwater *(G-3310)*
Jaroche Brothers Inc....F.... 231 525-8100
Wolverine *(G-17934)*
Jarvis Saw Mill Inc....G.... 231 861-2078
Shelby *(G-14526)*
John A Biewer Lumber Company....D.... 231 825-2855
Mc Bain *(G-10682)*
▲ Kentwood Manufacturing Co....E.... 616 698-6370
Grand Rapids *(G-6579)*
Lumber Jack Hardwoods Inc....F.... 906 863-7090
Menominee *(G-10742)*
Maple Ridge Hardwoods Inc....E.... 989 873-5305
Sterling *(G-15244)*
Matelski Lumber Company....E.... 231 549-2780
Boyne Falls *(G-1841)*
McLeod Wood and Christmas Pdts....G.... 989 777-4800
Bridgeport *(G-1853)*
Meeders Dim & Lbr Pdts Co....G.... 231 587-8611
Mancelona *(G-10394)*
▲ Menomnee Rver Lbr Dmnsions LLC E.... 906 863-2682
Menominee *(G-10749)*
Metter Flooring LLC....G.... 517 914-2004
Rives Junction *(G-13309)*
Motto Cedar Products Inc....G.... 906 753-4892
Daggett *(G-3622)*
Nettleton Wood Products Inc....G.... 906 297-5791
De Tour Village *(G-3668)*
North American Forest Products....G.... 269 663-8500
Edwardsburg *(G-4770)*
Northern Mich Hardwoods Inc....F.... 231 347-4575
Petoskey *(G-12460)*
Omara Sprung Floors Inc....G.... 810 743-8281
Burton *(G-2160)*
Ottawa Forest Products Inc....E.... 906 932-9701
Ironwood *(G-8336)*
Paris North Hardwood Lumber....E.... 231 584-2500
Elmira *(G-4792)*
PAW Enterprises LLC....F.... 269 329-1865
Kalamazoo *(G-8845)*
Pine Tech Inc....E.... 989 426-0006
Plymouth *(G-12716)*
Potlatchdeltic Corporation....C.... 906 346-3215
Gwinn *(G-7222)*
Quigley Lumber Inc....G.... 989 257-5116
South Branch *(G-14750)*
▲ Rare Earth Hardwoods Inc....F.... 231 946-0043
Traverse City *(G-16090)*
▲ Richwood Industries Inc....E.... 616 243-2700
Grand Rapids *(G-6824)*
Robbins Inc....G.... 513 619-5936
Negaunee *(G-11475)*
Ron Fisk Hardwoods Inc....G.... 616 887-3826
Sparta *(G-15108)*
Rt Baldwin Enterprises Inc....G.... 616 669-1626
Hudsonville *(G-8181)*
Solaire Medical Storage LLC....D.... 888 435-2256
Marne *(G-10513)*
Southeastern Equipment Co Inc....G.... 248 349-9922
Novi *(G-12002)*
Timber Pdts Mich Ltd Partnr....G.... 906 779-2000
Iron Mountain *(G-8303)*
Vocational Strategies Inc....E.... 906 482-6142
Calumet *(G-2335)*
Warner Door....G.... 989 823-8397
Vassar *(G-16817)*
Weber Bros Sawmill Inc....E.... 989 644-2206
Mount Pleasant *(G-11235)*
Whitens Kiln & Lumber Inc....F.... 906 498-2116
Hermansville *(G-7469)*
William S Wixtrom....G.... 906 376-8247
Republic *(G-13247)*
Yooper WD Wrks Restoration LLC....G.... 906 203-0056
Sault Sainte Marie *(G-14480)*
Zemis 5 LLC....G.... 317 946-7015
Detroit *(G-4457)*

2429 Special Prdt Sawmills, NEC

Biewer Sawmill Inc....E.... 231 825-2855
Mc Bain *(G-10679)*
Holmquist Feed Mill....G.... 906 446-3325
Trenary *(G-16151)*

2431 Millwork

A & L Woods....G.... 616 374-7820
Lake Odessa *(G-9110)*
▲ Air Conditioning Products Co....D.... 734 326-0050
Romulus *(G-13649)*
American Bldrs Contrs Sup Inc....G.... 906 226-9665
Marquette *(G-10517)*
Andersen Corporation....A.... 734 237-1052
Livonia *(G-9648)*
Andoor Craftmaster....G.... 989 672-2020
Caro *(G-2465)*
Architectural Design Wdwrk Inc....G.... 586 726-9050
Shelby Township *(G-14548)*
Architectural Elements Inc....F.... 616 241-6001
Grand Rapids *(G-6179)*
Architectural Planners Inc....E.... 248 674-1340
Waterford *(G-17322)*
Architectural Products Inc....G.... 248 585-8272
Royal Oak *(G-13905)*
Area Exteriors....G.... 248 544-0706
Leonard *(G-9526)*
Audia Woodworking & Fine Furn....F.... 586 296-6330
Clinton Township *(G-3058)*
B & W Woodwork Inc....G.... 616 772-4577
Holland *(G-7564)*
Bay Wood Homes Inc....E.... 989 245-4156
Fenton *(G-5187)*
Beaver Stair Company....F.... 248 628-0441
Oxford *(G-12340)*
Beechcraft Products Inc....E.... 989 288-2606
Durand *(G-4606)*
Black Creek Timber LLC....G.... 517 202-2169
Rudyard *(G-13983)*
BMC East LLC....E.... 313 963-2044
Detroit *(G-3906)*
Bohley Industries....G.... 734 455-3430
Northville *(G-11680)*
Bourne Specialties....G.... 269 663-2187
Edwardsburg *(G-4760)*
Britten Woodworks Inc....E.... 231 275-5457
Interlochen *(G-8237)*
Brunt Associates Inc....E.... 248 960-8295
Wixom *(G-17779)*
C & A Wood Products Inc....F.... 313 365-8400
Detroit *(G-3924)*
C & K Hardwoods LLC....G.... 269 231-0048
Three Oaks *(G-15848)*
C & S Millwork Inc....F.... 586 465-6470
Clinton Township *(G-3072)*
Canusa Inc....G.... 906 446-3327
Gwinn *(G-7217)*
Carson Wood Specialties Inc....G.... 269 465-6091
Stevensville *(G-15559)*
Casing Innovations LLC....G.... 248 939-0821
Clinton *(G-3016)*
Cedar Log Lbr Millersburg Inc....F.... 989 733-2676
Millersburg *(G-10991)*
Champion Window & Patio Room....E.... 616 554-1600
Grand Rapids *(G-6270)*
▼ Chippewa Development Inc....F.... 269 685-2646
Plainwell *(G-12519)*
Classic Woodworks of Michigan....G.... 248 628-3356
Oxford *(G-12343)*
Comfort Blinds....G.... 248 926-9300
Wixom *(G-17788)*
Creative Millwork Corporation....G.... 231 526-0201
Harbor Springs *(G-7280)*
Crossroads Industries Inc....D.... 989 732-1233
Gaylord *(G-5853)*
D & D Building Inc....F.... 616 248-7908
Grand Rapids *(G-6328)*
Dads Panels Inc....G.... 810 245-1871
Lapeer *(G-9455)*
Dagenham Millworks LLC....G.... 616 698-8883
Grand Rapids *(G-6332)*
Daniel D Slater....G.... 989 833-7135
Riverdale *(G-13284)*
▲ Decatur Wood Products Inc....E.... 269 657-6041
Decatur *(G-3802)*
Doltek Enterprises Inc....E.... 616 837-7828
Nunica *(G-12036)*
Double Otis Inc....E.... 616 878-3998
Grand Rapids *(G-6359)*
Dovetails Inc....F.... 248 674-8777
Waterford *(G-17337)*
Downriver Creative Woodworking....G.... 313 274-4090
Allen Park *(G-197)*
Duane Young & Son Lumber....G.... 586 727-1470
Columbus *(G-3378)*
E Leet Woodworking....G.... 269 664-5203
Plainwell *(G-12524)*
▲ E-Zee Set Wood Products Inc....G.... 248 398-0090
Oak Park *(G-12063)*
Elan Designs Inc....G.... 248 682-3000
Pontiac *(G-12820)*
Elenbaas Hardwood Incorporated....G.... 616 669-3085
Jenison *(G-8624)*
Elenbaas Hardwood Incorporated....G.... 269 343-7791
Kalamazoo *(G-8733)*
Emery Design & Woodwork LLC....G.... 734 709-1687
South Lyon *(G-14790)*
◆ Empire Company LLC....C.... 800 253-9000
Zeeland *(G-18134)*
▲ Euclid Industries Inc....C.... 989 686-8920
Bay City *(G-1310)*
▼ Fiber-Char Corporation....E.... 989 356-5501
Alpena *(G-289)*
Five Lakes Manufacturing Inc....E.... 586 463-4123
Clinton Township *(G-3120)*
Flairwood Industries Inc....E.... 231 798-8324
Norton Shores *(G-11756)*
Forsyth Millwork and Farms....G.... 810 266-4000
Byron *(G-2171)*
G F Inc....F.... 231 946-5330
Traverse City *(G-15975)*
◆ G-M Wood Products Inc....D.... 231 652-2201
Newaygo *(G-11568)*
General Hardwood Company....F.... 313 365-7733
Detroit *(G-4080)*
George Washburn....G.... 269 694-2930
Otsego *(G-12240)*
Gl Millworks Inc....F.... 734 451-1100
Plymouth *(G-12627)*
Gibouts Sash & Door....G.... 906 863-2224
Menominee *(G-10738)*
Goodrich Brothers Inc....G.... 989 224-4944
Saint Johns *(G-14283)*
Goodrich Brothers Inc....E.... 989 593-2104
Pewamo *(G-12479)*
Goodwill Inds Nthrn Mich Inc....G.... 231 779-1311
Cadillac *(G-2250)*
Goodwill Inds Nthrn Mich Inc....G.... 231 922-4890
Traverse City *(G-15981)*
Goodwill Inds Nthrn Mich Inc....G.... 231 779-1361
Cadillac *(G-2251)*
Grand Rapids Carvers Inc....E.... 616 538-0022
Grand Rapids *(G-6452)*
Grand Valley Wood Products Inc....E.... 616 475-5890
Grand Rapids *(G-6471)*

▼ **Great Lake Woods Inc** ......C 616 399-3300
Holland *(G-7651)*
Great Lakes Stair & Case Co ......G 269 465-3777
Bridgman *(G-1865)*
Great Lakes Wood Products ......G 906 228-3737
Negaunee *(G-11470)*
H & R Wood Specialties Inc ......E 269 628-2181
Gobles *(G-5947)*
▼ **Heartwood Mills LLC** ......F 888 829-5909
Boyne Falls *(G-1839)*
Iannuzzi Millwork Inc ......F 586 285-1000
Fraser *(G-5667)*
▲ **Idp Inc** ......E 248 352-0044
Southfield *(G-14944)*
Innovative Woodworking ......G 269 926-9663
Benton Harbor *(G-1513)*
Innovtive Dsplay Solutions LLC ......F 616 896-6080
Hudsonville *(G-8160)*
Interntonal Hardwoods Michiana ......G 517 278-8446
Coldwater *(G-3310)*
J J Wohlferts Custom Furniture ......F 989 593-3283
Fowler *(G-5553)*
Jeld-Wen Inc ......C 616 554-3551
Caledonia *(G-2303)*
Jeld-Wen Inc ......D 616 531-5440
Grand Rapids *(G-6558)*
Kent Door & Specialty Inc ......E 616 534-9691
Grand Rapids *(G-6576)*
Kropp Woodworking Inc ......F 586 463-2300
Mount Clemens *(G-11138)*
Kropp Woodworking Inc ......G 586 997-3000
Sterling Heights *(G-15391)*
L E Q Inc ......G 248 257-5466
Waterford *(G-17356)*
Lakeview Manufacturing ......G 231 348-2596
Petoskey *(G-12453)*
Lapeer Plating & Plastics Inc ......C 810 667-4240
Lapeer *(G-9468)*
Legendary Millwork Inc ......G 248 588-5663
Troy *(G-16460)*
Lemica Corporation ......F 313 839-2150
Detroit *(G-4198)*
Lsd Investments Inc ......G 248 333-9085
Bloomfield Hills *(G-1779)*
Macomb Stairs Inc ......F 586 226-2800
Shelby Township *(G-14631)*
Magiglide Inc ......F 906 822-7321
Crystal Falls *(G-3611)*
Masonite International Corp ......F 517 545-5811
Howell *(G-8060)*
Masters Millwork LLC ......F 248 987-4511
Farmington Hills *(G-5059)*
Maw Ventures Inc ......E 231 798-8324
Norton Shores *(G-11772)*
McCoy Craftsman LLC ......F 616 634-7455
Grand Rapids *(G-6654)*
Mendota Mantels LLC ......G 651 271-7544
Ironwood *(G-8335)*
Metrie Inc ......F 313 299-1860
Taylor *(G-15740)*
Michael Nadeau Cabinet Making ......G 989 356-0229
Alpena *(G-298)*
Michigan Overhead Door ......F 734 425-0295
Livonia *(G-9842)*
Michigan Woodwork ......G 517 204-4394
Mason *(G-10647)*
▲ **Mlc Window Co Inc** ......E 586 731-3500
Shelby Township *(G-14642)*
Mod Interiors Inc ......E 586 725-8227
Ira *(G-8261)*
Modern Millwork Inc ......F 248 347-4777
Wixom *(G-17857)*
Modern Woodsmith LLC ......G 906 387-5577
Wetmore *(G-17616)*
Monarch Millwork Inc ......G 989 348-8292
Grayling *(G-7113)*
Moore Products Inc ......G 269 782-3957
Dowagiac *(G-4553)*
North American Forest Products ......G 269 663-8500
Edwardsburg *(G-4770)*
▲ **North Amrcn Mlding Lqdtion LLC** ......E 269 663-5300
Edwardsburg *(G-4771)*
Northern Mich Hardwoods Inc ......F 231 347-4575
Petoskey *(G-12460)*
Northern Millwork Co ......F 313 365-7733
Detroit *(G-4276)*
Northern Staircase Co Inc ......F 248 836-0652
Pontiac *(G-12852)*
Northern Woods Finishing LLC ......G 231 536-9640
East Jordan *(G-4640)*
Northview Window & Door ......G 231 889-4565
Bear Lake *(G-1379)*
Novo Building Products LLC ......G 800 253-9000
Zeeland *(G-18169)*
Nowaks Window Door & Cab Co ......G 989 734-2808
Rogers City *(G-13617)*
Oak North Manufacturing Inc ......F 906 475-7992
Negaunee *(G-11472)*
▲ **Odl Incorporated** ......B 616 772-9111
Zeeland *(G-18170)*
Odl Incorporated ......B 616 772-9111
Zeeland *(G-18171)*
Owens Building Co Inc ......E 989 835-1293
Midland *(G-10901)*
Oxbowindo ......E 248 698-9400
White Lake *(G-17636)*
Parkway Drapery & Uphl Co Inc ......G 734 779-1300
Livonia *(G-9884)*
Pete Pullum Company Inc ......G 313 837-9440
Detroit *(G-4299)*
Phil Elenbaas Millwork Inc ......G 231 526-8399
Harbor Springs *(G-7291)*
Phil Elenbaas Millwork Inc ......E 616 791-1616
Grand Rapids *(G-6754)*
Pine Tech Inc ......E 989 426-0006
Plymouth *(G-12716)*
Poor Boy Woodworks Inc ......G 989 799-9440
Saginaw *(G-14125)*
Prime Wood Products Inc ......G 616 399-4700
Holland *(G-7775)*
Quality Wood Products Inc ......F 989 658-2160
Ubly *(G-16722)*
Rekmakker Millwork Inc ......G 616 546-3680
Holland *(G-7786)*
Richmond Millwork Inc ......F 586 727-6747
Lenox *(G-9524)*
Rosati Specialties LLC ......G 586 783-3866
Clinton Township *(G-3214)*
Sawmill Bill Lumber Inc ......G 231 275-3000
Interlochen *(G-8245)*
Shayn Allen Marquetry ......G 586 991-0445
Shelby Township *(G-14691)*
Snd Manufacturing LLC ......G 313 996-5088
Dearborn *(G-3761)*
Specialty Hardwood Moldings ......F 734 847-3997
Temperance *(G-15844)*
Stair Specialist Inc ......G 269 964-2351
Battle Creek *(G-1252)*
Standale Lumber and Supply Co ......D 616 530-8200
Grandville *(G-7072)*
Sterling Millwork Inc ......D 248 427-1400
Farmington Hills *(G-5131)*
Sunek Co ......F 231 421-5317
Traverse City *(G-16116)*
Superior Wood Products Inc ......F 616 453-4100
Allendale *(G-226)*
▼ **Tafcor Inc** ......F 269 471-2351
Berrien Springs *(G-1601)*
Tapco Holdings Inc ......C 248 668-6400
Wixom *(G-17905)*
Thomas and Milliken Mllwk Inc ......F 231 386-7236
Northport *(G-11673)*
Thomas Cheal ......G 906 288-3487
Toivola *(G-15885)*
Town & Country Cedar Homes ......G 231 347-4360
Boyne Falls *(G-1842)*
Trend Millwork LLC ......E 313 383-6300
Lincoln Park *(G-9586)*
Troy Millwork Inc ......G 248 852-8383
Rochester Hills *(G-13532)*
True Built Woodworking ......G 517 626-6482
Eagle *(G-4617)*
True Built Woodworking ......G 989 587-3041
Fowler *(G-5556)*
Uncle Rons Woodworking ......G 248 585-7837
Madison Heights *(G-10372)*
United Mill & Cabinet Company ......F 734 482-1981
Willis *(G-17745)*
Valley Enterprises Ubly Inc ......F 989 269-6272
Ubly *(G-16725)*
Van Beeks Custom Wood Products ......F 616 583-9002
Byron Center *(G-2214)*
Van Enk Woodcrafters LLC ......F 616 931-0090
Zeeland *(G-18191)*
Vander Roest Homes Fine Wdwkg ......G 269 353-3175
Kalamazoo *(G-8917)*
Virtuoso Custom Creations LLC ......G 313 332-1299
Detroit *(G-4431)*
Wayne-Craft Inc ......F 734 421-8800
Livonia *(G-10001)*
Weatherproof Inc ......E 517 764-1330
Jackson *(G-8606)*
▲ **Western Reflections LLC** ......E 616 772-9111
Zeeland *(G-18196)*
Wexford Wood Workings LLC ......G 231 876-9663
Cadillac *(G-2285)*
William S Wixtrom ......G 906 376-8247
Republic *(G-13247)*
▲ **Wood Smiths Inc** ......F 269 372-6432
Kalamazoo *(G-8927)*
Woodcrafters ......G 517 741-7423
Sherwood *(G-14737)*
Woodworks & Design Company ......F 517 482-6665
Lansing *(G-9434)*

2434 Wood Kitchen Cabinets

A K Services Inc ......G 313 972-1010
Detroit *(G-3827)*
AAM Wholesale Carpet Corp ......G 313 898-5101
Detroit *(G-3832)*
▼ **Albers Cabinet Company** ......G 586 727-9090
Lenox *(G-9520)*
Avon Cabinets Atkins ......G 248 237-1103
Rochester Hills *(G-13373)*
Bayshore Kitchen and Bath Inc ......G 586 725-8800
New Baltimore *(G-11481)*
Belash Inc ......G 248 379-4444
Wixom *(G-17772)*
Berrien Custom Cabinet Inc ......G 269 473-3404
Berrien Springs *(G-1593)*
Better-Bilt Cabinet Co ......G 586 469-0080
Mount Clemens *(G-11125)*
Biotec Incorporated ......D 616 772-2133
Zeeland *(G-18120)*
C&C Doors Inc ......G 586 232-4538
Macomb *(G-10113)*
Cabinet One Inc ......G 248 625-9440
Clarkston *(G-2910)*
Cabinets By Robert Inc ......F 231 947-3261
Traverse City *(G-15927)*
Carson Wood Specialties Inc ......G 269 465-6091
Stevensville *(G-15559)*
Case Systems Inc ......C 989 496-9510
Midland *(G-10822)*
CCM Modernization Co ......G 586 231-0396
Clinton Township *(G-3076)*
Charlotte Cabinets Inc ......G 517 543-1522
Charlotte *(G-2639)*
Classic Cabinets Interiors LLC ......G 517 817-5650
Jackson *(G-8410)*
Classic Cabinets Interiors LLC ......G 517 423-2600
Tecumseh *(G-15784)*
Cole Wagner Cabinetry ......G 248 642-5330
Birmingham *(G-1677)*
Cole Wagner Cabinetry ......F 248 852-2406
Rochester Hills *(G-13390)*
▲ **Crystal Lake Apartments Family** ......E 586 731-3500
Shelby Township *(G-14571)*
D & M Cabinet Shop Inc ......G 989 479-9271
Ruth *(G-13988)*
David Hirn Cabinets and Contg ......G 906 428-1935
Gladstone *(G-5911)*
Designtech Custom Interiors ......G 989 695-6306
Freeland *(G-5754)*
E & W Cabinet & Counter ......G 734 895-7497
Romulus *(G-13668)*
Edwards Building & HM Sup Inc ......G 313 368-9120
Detroit *(G-4029)*
Elan Designs Inc ......G 248 682-3000
Pontiac *(G-12820)*
Elite Woodworking LLC ......E 586 204-5882
Saint Clair Shores *(G-14245)*
Euro-Craft Interiors Inc ......F 586 254-9130
Sterling Heights *(G-15334)*
▲ **European Cabinet Mfg Co** ......E 586 445-8909
Roseville *(G-13802)*
Expo Kitchen & Bath Ltd ......G 734 741-5888
Ann Arbor *(G-451)*
Farmington Cabinet Company ......F 248 476-2666
Livonia *(G-9735)*
Flagg Distribution LLC ......F 248 926-0510
Wixom *(G-17811)*
Flairwood Industries Inc ......E 231 798-8324
Norton Shores *(G-11756)*
Fort Grtiot Cbnets Counter LLC ......F 810 364-1924
Port Huron *(G-12919)*
G & G Wood & Supply Inc ......F 586 293-0450
Roseville *(G-13805)*
Gast Cabinet Co ......E 269 422-1587
Baroda *(G-1125)*

Employee Codes: A=Over 500 employees, B=251-500
C=101-250, D=51-100, E=20-50, F=10-19, G=3-9
2020 Harris Michigan
Industrial Directory
717

George Washburn .... G 269 694-2930
Otsego *(G-12240)*
Great Lakes Fine Cabinetry .... G 906 493-5780
Sault Sainte Marie *(G-14465)*
Greenia Custom Woodworking Inc .... E 989 868-9790
Reese *(G-13230)*
Greenville Cabinet Distri .... G 616 225-2424
Greenville *(G-7133)*
Handorn Inc .... E 616 241-6181
Grand Rapids *(G-6490)*
I S Two .... G 616 396-5634
Holland *(G-7685)*
Impressive Cabinets Inc .... F 248 542-1185
Oak Park *(G-12074)*
Interior Spc of Holland .... E 616 396-5634
Holland *(G-7690)*
Janice Morse Inc .... E 248 624-7300
West Bloomfield *(G-17482)*
Jeff R Cabinets LLC .... G 989 233-0976
Gagetown *(G-5802)*
Jmc Custom Cabinetry .... G 989 345-0475
West Branch *(G-17509)*
Kaliniak Design LLC .... G 616 675-3850
Kent City *(G-8992)*
Kurtis Mfg & Distrg Corp .... E 734 522-7600
Livonia *(G-9802)*
Lafata Cabinet Shop .... E 586 247-6536
Shelby Township *(G-14620)*
Lakeshore Marble Company Inc .... E 269 429-8241
Stevensville *(G-15574)*
Lloyds Cabinet Shop Inc .... F 989 879-3015
Pinconning *(G-12509)*
M and G Laminated Products .... G 517 784-4974
Jackson *(G-8502)*
Marbelite Corp .... E 248 348-1900
Novi *(G-11934)*
Masco Cabinetry LLC .... D 517 263-0771
Ann Arbor *(G-544)*
Masco Cabinetry LLC .... B 740 286-5033
Ann Arbor *(G-545)*
◆ **Masco Cabinetry LLC** .... B 734 205-4600
Ann Arbor *(G-546)*
Masco Cabinetry LLC .... F 239 561-7266
Ann Arbor *(G-547)*
Masco Cabinetry LLC .... G 407 857-4444
Ann Arbor *(G-548)*
Masco Cabinetry LLC .... C 517 263-0771
Adrian *(G-78)*
Masco Cabinetry LLC .... D 770 447-6363
Ann Arbor *(G-549)*
◆ **Masco Corporation** .... A 313 274-7400
Livonia *(G-9826)*
Masco Services Inc .... G 313 274-7400
Livonia *(G-9827)*
Merillat Industries LLC .... G 517 263-0269
Adrian *(G-79)*
▲ **Merillat LP** .... C 517 263-0771
Adrian *(G-80)*
Michigan Counter Tops Company .... F 313 369-1511
Warren *(G-17152)*
Mid Michigan Wood Specialites .... F 989 855-3667
Lyons *(G-10094)*
Mikes Cabinet Shop Inc .... G 734 722-1800
Westland *(G-17580)*
Millennm-The Inside Sltion Inc .... E 248 645-9005
Farmington Hills *(G-5069)*
Millwork Inc .... F 586 791-2330
Fraser *(G-5692)*
Millwork Design Group LLC .... G 248 472-2178
Milford *(G-10972)*
Miltons Cabinet Shop Inc .... G 269 473-2743
Berrien Springs *(G-1599)*
Murphys Custom Craftsmen Inc .... G 989 205-7305
Coleman *(G-3349)*
New Line Inc .... G 586 228-4820
Shelby Township *(G-14652)*
North State Sales .... G 989 681-2806
Saint Louis *(G-14367)*
Nowak Cabinets Inc .... G 231 264-8603
Williamsburg *(G-17718)*
Oak North Manufacturing Inc .... F 906 475-7992
Negaunee *(G-11472)*
OBrien Harris Woodworks LLc .... E 616 248-0779
Grand Rapids *(G-6726)*
Owens Building Co Inc .... E 989 835-1293
Midland *(G-10901)*
Pazzel Inc .... G 616 291-0257
Grand Rapids *(G-6745)*
Perspectives Custom Cabinetry .... E 248 288-4100
Troy *(G-16544)*
Pinnacle Cabinet Company Inc .... E 989 772-3866
Mount Pleasant *(G-11217)*
Pioneer Cabinetry Inc .... D 810 658-2075
Davison *(G-3659)*
Prime Wood Products Inc .... G 616 399-4700
Holland *(G-7775)*
Progressive Cabinets Inc .... G 810 631-4611
Otisville *(G-12234)*
Putnam Cabinetry .... G 248 442-0118
Farmington Hills *(G-5108)*
Rohloff Builders Inc .... E 989 868-3191
Reese *(G-13232)*
Rose Corporation .... E 734 426-0005
Dexter *(G-4508)*
Ross Cabinets II Inc .... E 586 752-7750
Shelby Township *(G-14682)*
Royal Cabinets .... G 313 541-1190
Redford *(G-13188)*
Sawdust Bin Inc .... F 906 932-5518
Ironwood *(G-8340)*
Shayn Allen Marquetry .... G 586 991-0445
Shelby Township *(G-14691)*
Showcase Cabinetry Inc .... G 810 798-9966
Almont *(G-266)*
Stanisci Design and Mfg Inc .... G 586 752-3368
Oxford *(G-12373)*
Straight Line Design .... G 616 296-0920
Spring Lake *(G-15180)*
Surface Expressions LLC .... G 231 843-8282
Ludington *(G-10081)*
Tims Cabinet Inc .... G 989 846-9831
Pinconning *(G-12513)*
Van Daeles Inc .... G 734 587-7165
Monroe *(G-11082)*
Village Cabinet Shoppe Inc .... G 586 264-6464
Sterling Heights *(G-15539)*
W S Townsend Company .... G 517 393-7300
Lansing *(G-9433)*
W S Townsend Company .... C 269 781-5131
Marshall *(G-10593)*
West Michigan Cabinet Supply .... F 616 896-6990
Hudsonville *(G-8186)*
Wickey Custom Cabinets .... G 517 858-1119
Bronson *(G-2035)*
Woodways Industries LLC .... E 616 956-3070
Grand Rapids *(G-7003)*
World Wide Cabinets Inc .... F 248 683-2680
Sylvan Lake *(G-15674)*
Young Cabinetry Inc .... G 734 316-2896
Saline *(G-14422)*

2435 Hardwood Veneer & Plywood

Bay Wood Homes Inc .... E 989 245-4156
Fenton *(G-5187)*
◆ **Coldwater Veneer Inc** .... C 517 278-5676
Coldwater *(G-3297)*
▲ **Decatur Wood Products Inc** .... E 269 657-6041
Decatur *(G-3802)*
Dyers Sawmill Inc .... E 231 768-4438
Leroy *(G-9531)*
Forest Corullo Products Corp .... E 906 667-0275
Bessemer *(G-1605)*
◆ **Forte Industries Mill Inc** .... F 906 753-6256
Stephenson *(G-15235)*
J A S Veneer & Lumber Inc .... E 906 635-0710
Sault Sainte Marie *(G-14466)*
▲ **Manthei Inc** .... C 231 347-4672
Petoskey *(G-12456)*
Manthei Veneer Mill Inc .... G 231 347-4688
Petoskey *(G-12458)*
Midwest Panel Systems Inc .... E 517 486-4844
Blissfield *(G-1720)*
Northern Mich Chrstn Cunseling .... G 989 278-2590
Lachine *(G-9075)*
Northern Mich Endocrine Pllc .... G 989 281-1125
Roscommon *(G-13752)*
Northern Mich Hardwoods Inc .... F 231 347-4575
Petoskey *(G-12460)*
Northern Mich Mmrals Monuments .... G 231 290-2333
Cheboygan *(G-2688)*
Northern Mich Pain Specialist .... G 231 487-4650
Petoskey *(G-12461)*
Northern Mich Residential Svcs .... G 231 547-6144
Vanderbilt *(G-16808)*
Northern Mich Rgional Hlth Sys .... F 231 487-4094
Petoskey *(G-12462)*
Northern Mich Supportive Hsing .... G 231 929-1309
Traverse City *(G-16050)*
Northern Mich Wdding Offciants .... G 231 938-1683
Williamsburg *(G-17715)*
▲ **Northern Michigan Veneers Inc** .... D 906 428-1082
Gladstone *(G-5917)*
Ply-Forms Incorporated .... F 989 686-5681
Bay City *(G-1341)*
Precision Framing Systems Inc .... E 704 588-6680
Taylor *(G-15755)*
▼ **Programmed Products Corp** .... D 248 348-7755
Novi *(G-11983)*
Quincy Woodwrights LLC .... G 808 397-0818
Houghton *(G-7981)*
◆ **Richelieu America Ltd** .... E 586 264-1240
Sterling Heights *(G-15469)*
Rosati Specialties LLC .... G 586 783-3866
Clinton Township *(G-3214)*
Timber Pdts Mich Ltd Partnr .... G 906 779-2000
Iron Mountain *(G-8303)*
Timber Products Co Ltd Partnr .... C 906 452-6221
Munising *(G-11250)*

2436 Softwood Veneer & Plywood

Forest Corullo Products Corp .... E 906 667-0275
Bessemer *(G-1605)*
◆ **Forte Industries Mill Inc** .... F 906 753-6256
Stephenson *(G-15235)*
Ply-Forms Incorporated .... F 989 686-5681
Bay City *(G-1341)*

2439 Structural Wood Members, NEC

Allwood Building Components .... D 586 727-2731
Richmond *(G-13259)*
Bay Wood Homes Inc .... E 989 245-4156
Fenton *(G-5187)*
Better-Bilt Cabinet Co .... G 586 469-0080
Mount Clemens *(G-11125)*
Calderwood WD Pdts & Svcs LLC .... G 906 852-3232
Trout Creek *(G-16162)*
Century Truss .... G 248 486-4000
Livonia *(G-9682)*
Custom Components Truss Co .... E 810 744-0771
Burton *(G-2153)*
G & G Wood & Supply Inc .... F 586 293-0450
Roseville *(G-13805)*
Heart Truss & Engineering Corp .... D 517 372-0850
Lansing *(G-9234)*
Joseph Miller .... G 231 821-2430
Holton *(G-7933)*
Ken Luneack Construction Inc .... C 989 681-5774
Saint Louis *(G-14365)*
Laketon Truss Inc .... G 231 798-3467
Norton Shores *(G-11770)*
Letherer Truss Inc .... E 989 386-4999
Clare *(G-2876)*
▲ **Lumber & Truss Inc** .... E 810 664-7290
Lapeer *(G-9472)*
Maple Valley Truss Co .... E 989 389-4267
Prudenville *(G-13085)*
Marshall Bldg Components Corp .... F 269 781-4236
Marshall *(G-10575)*
Maverick Building Systems LLC .... F 248 366-9410
Commerce Township *(G-3428)*
Midwest Panel Systems Inc .... E 517 486-4844
Blissfield *(G-1720)*
North American Forest Products .... G 269 663-8500
Edwardsburg *(G-4770)*
Precision Framing Systems Inc .... E 704 588-6680
Taylor *(G-15755)*
Rapid River Rustic Inc .... E 906 474-6404
Rapid River *(G-13114)*
Riverbend Timber Framing Inc .... D 517 486-3629
Blissfield *(G-1726)*
Superior Country Wood Truss .... G 906 499-3354
Seney *(G-14522)*
Truss Development .... G 248 624-8100
Bloomfield Hills *(G-1808)*
Truss Technologies Inc .... E 231 788-6330
Muskegon *(G-11443)*
Trussway .... G 713 691-6900
Jenison *(G-8645)*
Wendricks Truss Inc .... F 906 635-8822
Sault Sainte Marie *(G-14479)*
Wendricks Truss Inc .... E 906 498-7709
Hermansville *(G-7468)*
Wood Tech Inc .... E 616 455-0800
Byron Center *(G-2217)*

2441 Wood Boxes

Anbren Inc .... G 269 944-5066
Benton Harbor *(G-1481)*
Auto Pallets-Boxes Inc .... F 248 559-7744
Lathrup Village *(G-9498)*

SIC SECTION

24 LUMBER AND WOOD PRODUCTS, EXCEPT FURNITURE

▲ **Bennett Wood Specialties Inc** ....F 616 772-6683
Zeeland *(G-18117)*
C & K Box Company Inc ....E 517 784-1779
Jackson *(G-8397)*
Charlies Wood Shop ....F 989 845-2632
Chesaning *(G-2722)*
Complete Packaging Inc ....E 734 241-2794
Monroe *(G-11025)*
Crossroads Industries Inc ....D 989 732-1233
Gaylord *(G-5853)*
Czuk Studio ....G 269 628-2568
Kendall *(G-8983)*
Demeester Wood Products Inc ....F 616 677-5995
Coopersville *(G-3556)*
Diversified Pdts & Svcs LLC ....G 616 836-6600
Holland *(G-7608)*
Donald Gleason ....G 269 673-6802
Allegan *(G-158)*
▲ **Export Corporation** ....D 810 227-6153
Brighton *(G-1920)*
Garcia Company ....G 248 459-0952
Holly *(G-7879)*
Grigg Box Co Inc ....E 313 273-9000
Detroit *(G-4106)*
Home Shop ....G 517 543-5325
Charlotte *(G-2654)*
▼ **Michigan Box Company** ....D 313 873-9500
Detroit *(G-4237)*
Mollewood Export Inc ....E 248 624-1885
Wixom *(G-17859)*
National Case Corporation ....G 586 726-1710
Sterling Heights *(G-15432)*
▲ **Packaging Specialties Inc** ....E 586 473-6703
Romulus *(G-13718)*
Scotts Enterprises Inc ....E 989 275-5011
Roscommon *(G-13754)*
Vaive Wood Products Co ....E 586 949-4900
Macomb *(G-10172)*

2448 Wood Pallets & Skids

AAR Manufacturing Inc ....E 231 779-8800
Cadillac *(G-2220)*
Acme Pallet Inc ....E 616 738-6452
Holland *(G-7548)*
Akers Wood Products Inc ....G 269 962-3802
Battle Creek *(G-1144)*
All American Container Corp ....F 586 949-0000
Macomb *(G-10105)*
All Size Pallets ....E 810 721-1999
Imlay City *(G-8195)*
American Pallet Company LLC ....G 231 834-5056
Grant *(G-7078)*
Anayas Pallets & Transport Inc ....E 313 843-6570
Detroit *(G-3869)*
Anbren Inc ....G 269 944-5066
Benton Harbor *(G-1481)*
Artists Pallet ....G 248 889-2440
Highland *(G-7486)*
Auto Pallets-Boxes Inc ....F 248 559-7744
Lathrup Village *(G-9498)*
Auto Pallets-Boxes Inc ....G 734 782-1110
Flat Rock *(G-5347)*
Baby Pallet ....G 248 210-3851
Waterford *(G-17324)*
Black River Pallet Company ....E 616 772-6211
Zeeland *(G-18121)*
Breiten Box & Packaging Co Inc ....G 586 469-0800
Harrison Township *(G-7324)*
Brindley Lumber & Pallet Co ....G 989 345-3497
Lupton *(G-10091)*
Bunker & Sons Sawmill LLC ....G 989 983-2715
Vanderbilt *(G-16803)*
Burnrite Pellet Corporation ....G 989 429-1067
Clare *(G-2865)*
C & J Pallets Inc ....G 517 263-7415
Adrian *(G-52)*
C & K Box Company Inc ....E 517 784-1779
Jackson *(G-8397)*
C&D Pallets Inc ....G 517 285-5228
Eagle *(G-4616)*
Cannonsburg Wood Products Inc ....E 616 866-4459
Rockford *(G-13563)*
Caveman Pallets LLC ....F 616 675-7270
Conklin *(G-3529)*
Complete Packaging Inc ....E 734 241-2794
Monroe *(G-11025)*
County Line Pallet ....G 231 834-8416
Kent City *(G-8989)*
Curtis Country Connection LLC ....F 517 368-5542
Camden *(G-2339)*
D T Fowler Mfg Co Inc ....G 810 245-9336
Lapeer *(G-9454)*
▲ **Delta Containers Inc** ....C 810 742-2730
Bay City *(G-1299)*
▲ **Delta Packaging International** ....G 517 321-6548
Lansing *(G-9214)*
Demeester Wood Products Inc ....F 616 677-5995
Coopersville *(G-3556)*
Discount Pallets ....G 616 453-5455
Grand Rapids *(G-6354)*
Diversified Pdts & Svcs LLC ....G 616 836-6600
Holland *(G-7608)*
Donald Gleason ....G 269 673-6802
Allegan *(G-158)*
DRYE Custom Pallets Inc ....D 313 381-2681
Melvindale *(G-10696)*
Envirnmntal Pllet Slutions Inc ....G 616 283-1784
Zeeland *(G-18135)*
Fair & Square Pallet & Lbr Co ....G 989 727-3949
Hubbard Lake *(G-8125)*
Fontana Forest Products ....E 313 841-8950
Detroit *(G-4066)*
Four Way Pallet Service ....F 734 782-5914
Flat Rock *(G-5354)*
General Wood Products Co ....F 248 221-0214
Big Rapids *(G-1630)*
Golden Eagle Pallets LLC ....F 616 233-0970
Wyoming *(G-18004)*
Gonzalez Jr Pallets LLC ....G 616 885-0201
Grand Rapids *(G-6446)*
Gonzalez Universal Pallets LLC ....G 616 243-5524
Grand Rapids *(G-6447)*
Grand Industries Inc ....E 616 846-7120
Grand Haven *(G-6026)*
Grand Rustic Pallet Co ....G 231 329-5035
Grand Rapids *(G-6470)*
Great Lakes Pallet Inc ....G 989 883-9220
Sebewaing *(G-14515)*
Great Northern Lumber Mich LLC ....E 989 736-6192
Lincoln *(G-9562)*
Guerreros Pallets ....G 616 808-4721
Grand Rapids *(G-6484)*
H & M Pallet LLC ....F 231 821-8800
Holton *(G-7932)*
Hills Crate Mill Inc ....G 616 761-3555
Belding *(G-1417)*
Hillsdale Pallet LLC ....G 517 254-4777
Hillsdale *(G-7527)*
Hillside Pallets ....G 231 824-3761
Manton *(G-10455)*
Holland Pallet Repair Inc ....E 616 875-8642
Holland *(G-7673)*
Hugo Brothers Pallet Mfg ....G 989 684-5564
Kawkawlin *(G-8973)*
Industrial Packaging Corp ....F 248 677-0084
Berkley *(G-1584)*
J & G Pallets Inc ....G 313 921-0222
Detroit *(G-4154)*
J & G Pallets Inc ....G 313 921-0222
Detroit *(G-4155)*
J and K Pallet ....G 517 648-5974
North Adams *(G-11655)*
Jarvis Saw Mill Inc ....G 231 861-2078
Shelby *(G-14526)*
Jerrys Pallets ....G 734 242-1577
Monroe *(G-11043)*
Just Cover It Up ....G 734 247-4729
Romulus *(G-13694)*
K&P Discount Pallets Inc ....G 616 835-1661
Belding *(G-1422)*
Kamps Inc ....E 313 381-2681
Detroit *(G-4170)*
Kamps Inc ....D 616 453-9676
Grand Rapids *(G-6569)*
Kamps Inc ....F 517 645-2800
Potterville *(G-13074)*
Kamps Inc ....E 734 281-3300
Taylor *(G-15732)*
Kamps Inc ....D 517 322-2500
Lansing *(G-9302)*
Kamps Inc ....E 269 342-8113
Kalamazoo *(G-8800)*
▲ **Karjo Trucking Inc** ....F 248 597-3700
Troy *(G-16443)*
Kerry J McNeely ....G 734 776-1928
Livonia *(G-9796)*
Krauter Forest Products LLC ....F 815 317-6561
Reed City *(G-13218)*
L & M Hardwood & Skids LLC ....G 734 281-3043
Southgate *(G-15079)*
Lakeland Pallets Inc ....E 616 949-9515
Grand Rapids *(G-6615)*
Lakeland Pallets Inc ....G 616 997-4441
Coopersville *(G-3563)*
Lanny Bensinger ....G 989 658-2590
Ubly *(G-16718)*
Lansing Pallet ....G 517 322-2500
Lansing *(G-9307)*
Las Tortugas Pallet Co ....G 313 283-3279
Lincoln Park *(G-9580)*
Lightning Technologies LLC ....F 248 977-5566
Lake Orion *(G-9146)*
Lightning Technologies LLC ....E 248 572-6700
Oxford *(G-12355)*
Lock and Load Corp ....G 800 975-9658
Marion *(G-10490)*
Luberda Wood Products Inc ....G 989 876-4334
Omer *(G-12144)*
Maple Valley Pallet Co ....F 231 228-6641
Maple City *(G-10463)*
Marion Pallet ....G 231 743-6124
Marion *(G-10491)*
Matelski Lumber Company ....E 231 549-2780
Boyne Falls *(G-1841)*
Matthews Mill Inc ....F 989 257-3271
South Branch *(G-14749)*
McPhails Pallets Inc ....F 810 384-6458
Kenockee *(G-8985)*
Metzger Sawmill ....G 269 963-3022
Battle Creek *(G-1227)*
Michael Chris Storms ....G 231 263-7516
Kingsley *(G-9072)*
Michigan Pallet Inc ....F 517 543-0606
Charlotte *(G-2660)*
Michigan Pallet Inc ....F 989 865-9915
Saint Charles *(G-14196)*
Michigan Pallet Inc ....F 269 685-8802
Plainwell *(G-12530)*
Mid West Pallet ....G 810 919-3072
Burton *(G-2158)*
Mobile Pallet Service Inc ....E 269 792-4200
Wayland *(G-17407)*
Nelson Company ....G 517 788-6117
Jackson *(G-8542)*
Northern Pallet ....G 989 386-7556
Clare *(G-2882)*
Ottawa Forest Products Inc ....E 906 932-9701
Ironwood *(G-8336)*
Pallet Man ....G 269 274-8825
Springfield *(G-15199)*
Pallet Masters ....G 313 995-1131
Livonia *(G-9882)*
Pallet Pros LLC ....G 586 864-3353
Center Line *(G-2581)*
Patchwood Products Inc ....G 989 742-2605
Hillman *(G-7509)*
Patchwood Products Inc ....F 989 742-2605
Lachine *(G-9077)*
Pink Pallet LLC ....G 586 873-2982
Grand Blanc *(G-5977)*
Prairie Wood Products Inc ....F 269 659-1163
Sturgis *(G-15630)*
Precision Pallet LLC ....G 252 943-5193
Charlevoix *(G-2627)*
▲ **Process Systems Inc** ....D 586 757-5711
Warren *(G-17198)*
Quality Pallet Inc ....G 231 788-5161
Muskegon *(G-11409)*
Quality Pallets LLC ....F 231 825-8361
Mc Bain *(G-10683)*
R Andrews Pallet Co Inc ....F 616 677-3270
Marne *(G-10512)*
Rochester Pallet ....G 248 266-1094
Rochester Hills *(G-13506)*
Rose Acres Pallets LLC ....G 989 268-3074
Vestaburg *(G-16828)*
Rose Acres Tallets ....G 989 268-3074
Vestaburg *(G-16829)*
Ross Pallet Co ....G 810 966-4945
Port Huron *(G-12963)*
Schmieding Saw Mill Inc ....G 231 861-4189
Shelby *(G-14535)*
Scotts Enterprises Inc ....E 989 275-5011
Roscommon *(G-13754)*
Sfi Acquisition Inc ....E 248 471-1500
Farmington Hills *(G-5122)*
Spartan Pallet LLC ....G 586 291-8898
Clinton Township *(G-3232)*
Stoutenburg Inc ....E 810 648-4400
Sandusky *(G-14444)*

SIC

Employee Codes: A=Over 500 employees, B=251-500
C=101-250, D=51-100, E=20-50, F=10-19, G=3-9

2020 Harris Michigan
Industrial Directory

719

Tamsco Inc ....F 586 415-1500
Fraser (G-5737)
Tk Enterprises Inc ....E 989 865-9915
Saint Charles (G-14202)
Tommy Joe Reed ....G 989 291-5768
Sheridan (G-14735)
Union Pallet & Cont Co Inc ....E 517 279-4888
Coldwater (G-3339)
Vaive Wood Products Co ....E 586 949-4900
Macomb (G-10172)
Vocational Strategies Inc ....E 906 482-6142
Calumet (G-2335)
WB Pallets Inc ....E 616 669-3000
Hudsonville (G-8185)
White Pallet Chair ....G 989 424-8771
Clare (G-2892)
World of Pallets and Trucking ....G 313 899-2000
Detroit (G-4449)

2449 Wood Containers, NEC

AAR Manufacturing Inc ....E 231 779-8800
Cadillac (G-2220)
▲ Action Wood Technologies Inc ....E 586 468-2300
Clinton Township (G-3036)
AS Property Management Inc ....F 586 427-8000
Warren (G-16941)
Black River Pallet Company ....E 616 772-6211
Zeeland (G-18121)
C & K Box Company Inc ....E 517 784-1779
Jackson (G-8397)
Classic Container Corporation ....E 734 853-3000
Livonia (G-9684)
▲ Delta Packaging International ....G 517 321-6548
Lansing (G-9214)
Demeester Wood Products Inc ....F 616 677-5995
Coopersville (G-3556)
Diversified Pdts & Svcs LLC ....G 616 836-6600
Holland (G-7608)
Industrial Wood Fab & Packg Co ....G 734 284-4808
Riverview (G-13298)
Kamps Inc ....F 517 645-2800
Potterville (G-13074)
Luberda Wood Products Inc ....G 989 876-4334
Omer (G-12144)
Millers Woodworking ....G 989 386-8110
Clare (G-2878)
Mollewood Export Inc ....E 248 624-1885
Wixom (G-17859)
Monte Package Company LLC ....E 269 849-1722
Riverside (G-13285)
Northern Packaging Mi Inc ....F 734 692-4700
Grosse Ile (G-7174)
Quinlan Lumber Co ....G 810 743-0700
Burton (G-2162)
Scotts Enterprises Inc ....E 989 275-5011
Roscommon (G-13754)
Setco Inc ....G 616 459-6311
Grand Rapids (G-6858)
Tk Enterprises Inc ....E 989 865-9915
Saint Charles (G-14202)
Union Pallet & Cont Co Inc ....E 517 279-4888
Coldwater (G-3339)

2451 Mobile Homes

Advantage Housing Inc ....G 269 792-6291
Wayland (G-17397)
Arbor Woods Mfg Home Community ....G 734 482-4305
Ypsilanti (G-18052)
CCI Arnheim Inc ....G 906 353-6330
Baraga (G-1099)
Cedar Mobile Home Service Inc ....G 616 696-1580
Cedar Springs (G-2546)
Champion Home Builders Inc ....D 248 614-8200
Troy (G-16263)
Continental Communities ....G 586 757-7412
Warren (G-16992)
Cross Country Homes ....G 517 694-0778
Potterville (G-13073)
Flex Building Systems LLC ....G 586 803-6000
Sterling Heights (G-15342)
Hometown America LLC ....G 810 686-7020
Mount Morris (G-11162)
Larkhite Development System ....G 616 457-6722
Jenison (G-8632)
Montrose Trailers Inc ....G 810 639-7431
Montrose (G-11105)
Sun Communities Inc ....C 248 208-2500
Southfield (G-15036)
Windsong Mobile Home ....G 248 758-2140
Bloomfield Hills (G-1811)

2452 Prefabricated Wood Buildings & Cmpnts

/// 702 Cedar River Lbr Inc ....E 906 497-5365
Powers (G-13076)
4d Building Inc ....F 248 799-7384
Milford (G-10952)
Ahs LLC ....F 888 355-3050
Holland (G-7552)
▲ Backyard Products LLC ....G 734 242-6900
Monroe (G-11015)
Bay Wood Homes Inc ....E 989 245-4156
Fenton (G-5187)
Beaver Log Homes Inc ....F 231 258-5020
Kalkaska (G-8938)
Classic Log Homes Incorporated ....F 989 821-6118
Higgins Lake (G-7482)
Cronkhite Farms Trucking LLC ....G 269 489-5225
Sturgis (G-15602)
Dickinson Homes Inc ....E 906 774-5800
Kingsford (G-9057)
E B I Inc ....G 810 227-8180
Brighton (G-1914)
G B Wolfgram and Sons Inc ....F 231 238-4638
Indian River (G-8217)
Harman Lumber & Supply Inc ....G 269 641-5424
Union (G-16729)
Hiawatha Log Homes Inc ....E 877 275-9090
Munising (G-11244)
Hunt Hoppough Custom Crafted ....E 616 794-3455
Belding (G-1418)
J B Log Homes Inc ....G 906 875-6581
Crystal Falls (G-3610)
Koskis Log Homes Inc ....G 906 884-4937
Ontonagon (G-12162)
Little Buildings Inc ....G 586 752-7100
Romeo (G-13632)
Lorencz Construction Co ....G 989 798-3151
Chesaning (G-2727)
Mallory Pole Buildings Inc ....F 269 668-2627
Mattawan (G-10665)
Manufactured Homes Inc ....E 269 781-2887
Marshall (G-10574)
Marshalls Crossing ....G 810 639-4740
Montrose (G-11104)
Masons Lumber & Hardware Inc ....G 989 685-3999
Rose City (G-13763)
Meyer Wood Products ....G 269 657-3450
Paw Paw (G-12409)
Michigan Dutch Barns Inc ....F 616 693-2754
Lake Odessa (G-9118)
Midwest Panel Systems Inc ....E 517 486-4844
Blissfield (G-1720)
North Arrow Log Homes Inc ....G 906 484-5524
Pickford (G-12482)
Northwoods Hot Sprng Spas Inc ....G 231 347-1134
Petoskey (G-12465)
Pageant Homes Inc ....G 517 694-0431
Holt (G-7921)
Pioneer Pole Buildings N Inc ....E 989 386-2570
Clare (G-2884)
Premier Panel Company ....E 734 427-1700
Livonia (G-9897)
Ritz-Craft Corp PA Inc ....E 517 849-7425
Jonesville (G-8668)
Riverbend Timber Framing Inc ....D 517 486-3629
Blissfield (G-1726)
Source Capital Backyard LLC ....G 734 242-6900
Monroe (G-11066)
Wolf Log Home Buildings ....G 231 757-7000
Scottville (G-14511)
Woodtech Builders Inc ....F 906 932-8055
Ironwood (G-8341)

2491 Wood Preserving

/// 702 Cedar River Lbr Inc ....E 906 497-5365
Powers (G-13076)
▲ 2nd Chance Wood Company ....G 989 472-4488
Durand (G-4604)
▲ Biewer Lumber LLC ....E 810 326-3930
Saint Clair (G-14206)
Biewer Sawmill Inc ....E 231 825-2855
Mc Bain (G-10679)
▲ Charter Inds Extrusions Inc ....G 616 245-3388
Grand Rapids (G-6272)
Hoover Treated Wood Pdts Inc ....E 313 365-4200
Detroit (G-4127)
JKL Hardwoods Inc ....F 906 265-9130
Iron River (G-8312)
John A Biewer Co of Illinois ....E 810 326-3930
Saint Clair (G-14224)
▲ John A Biewer Lumber Company ....B 810 329-4789
Saint Clair (G-14225)
John A Biewer Lumber Company ....D 231 825-2855
Mc Bain (G-10682)
Midwest Timber Inc ....E 269 663-5315
Edwardsburg (G-4767)
Paris North Hardwood Lumber ....E 231 584-2500
Elmira (G-4792)
Riverbend Woodworing ....G 231 869-4965
Pentwater (G-12431)
Straits Corporation ....F 989 684-3584
Bay City (G-1361)
Straits Corporation ....F 989 684-5088
Tawas City (G-15679)
Straits Operations Company ....G 989 684-5088
Tawas City (G-15680)
Straits Service Corporation ....F 989 684-5088
Tawas City (G-15681)
Straits Wood Treating Inc ....G 989 684-5088
Tawas City (G-15682)
Ufp Lansing LLC ....G 517 322-0025
Lansing (G-9328)
▲ United Global Sourcing Inc ....F 248 952-5700
Troy (G-16663)
Utility Supply and Cnstr Co ....G 231 832-2297
Reed City (G-13225)
West Branch Wood Treating Inc ....G 989 343-0066
West Branch (G-17528)
Yooper WD Wrks Restoration LLC ....G 906 203-0056
Sault Sainte Marie (G-14480)

2493 Reconstituted Wood Prdts

Abcor Industries LLC ....F 616 994-9577
Holland (G-7545)
Alpena Biorefinery ....G 989 340-1190
Alpena (G-274)
▼ Applegate Insul Systems Inc ....E 517 521-3545
Webberville (G-17446)
Arauco North America Inc ....C 800 261-4896
Grayling (G-7103)
Bourne Industries Inc ....E 989 743-3461
Corunna (G-3578)
Brookfield Inc ....G 616 997-9663
Coopersville (G-3550)
Dorel Home Furnishings Inc ....B 269 782-8661
Dowagiac (G-4540)
Fultz Manufacturing Inc ....G 231 947-5801
Traverse City (G-15974)
Hammond Publishing Company ....G 810 686-8879
Mount Morris (G-11161)
Holland Panel Products Inc ....E 616 392-1826
Holland (G-7674)
Norbord Panels USA Inc ....A 248 608-0387
Rochester (G-13336)
Northeastern Products Corp ....E 906 265-6241
Caspian (G-2509)
▲ Nu-Wool Co Inc ....D 800 748-0128
Jenison (G-8635)
Ox Engineered Products LLC ....F 248 289-9950
Northville (G-11720)
Ox Engineered Products LLC ....D 269 435-2425
Constantine (G-3542)
◆ Rospatch Jessco Corporation ....B 269 782-8661
Dowagiac (G-4558)
Weyerhaeuser Company ....C 989 348-2881
Grayling (G-7118)
Wood-N-Stuff Inc ....G 616 677-0177
Marne (G-10516)

2499 Wood Prdts, NEC

A&Lb Custom Framing LLC ....G 517 783-3810
Jackson (G-8370)
Aisin Holdings America Inc ....G 734 453-5551
Northville (G-11676)
▲ Anthony and Company ....F 906 786-7573
Escanaba (G-4813)
Apple Fence Co ....F 231 276-9888
Grawn (G-7097)
▼ Applegate Insul Systems Inc ....E 517 521-3545
Webberville (G-17446)
Art of Custom Framing Inc ....G 248 435-3726
Troy (G-16218)
Astro Wood Stake Inc ....G 616 875-8118
Zeeland (G-18114)
Ausable Upholstery ....G 989 366-5219
Cadillac (G-2229)
Ausable Woodworking Co Inc ....E 989 348-7086
Frederic (G-5750)
Bainbridge Manufacturing Inc ....G 616 447-7631
Grand Rapids (G-6200)

Beaver Creek Wood Products LLC ....E 920 680-9663
Menominee *(G-10725)*
Blade Industrial Products Inc ....G 248 773-7400
Wixom *(G-17774)*
Bremer Authentic Ingredients ....G 616 772-9100
Zeeland *(G-18123)*
Buck-Spica Equipment Ltd ....F 269 792-2251
Wayland *(G-17402)*
◆ Cards of Wood Inc ....G 616 887-8680
Belmont *(G-1460)*
Chainsaw Man of Michigan ....G 586 977-7856
Chesterfield *(G-2752)*
Cherry Creek Post LLC ....G 231 734-2466
Evart *(G-4880)*
Chivis Sportsman Cases ....G 231 834-1162
Grant *(G-7079)*
CHR W LLC ....E 989 755-4000
Saginaw *(G-14017)*
Contractors Fence Service ....E 313 592-1300
Detroit *(G-3947)*
Custom Door Parts ....G 616 949-5000
Byron Center *(G-2186)*
Custom Rustic Flags LLC ....G 906 203-6935
Sault Sainte Marie *(G-14463)*
Czuk Studio ....G 269 628-2568
Kendall *(G-8983)*
Derby Fabg Solutions LLC ....D 616 866-1650
Rockford *(G-13566)*
Dko Intl ....F 248 926-9115
Commerce Township *(G-3401)*
Doltek Enterprises Inc ....E 616 837-7828
Nunica *(G-12036)*
Dynamic Wood Solutions ....G 616 935-7727
Spring Lake *(G-15139)*
Enviro Industries Inc ....G 906 492-3402
Paradise *(G-12382)*
▲ Faulkner Fabricators Inc ....F 269 473-3073
Berrien Springs *(G-1596)*
Grants Woodshop Inc ....G 517 543-1116
Charlotte *(G-2653)*
▲ Hangers Plus LLC ....G 616 997-4264
Coopersville *(G-3560)*
▲ Heath Manufacturing Company ....D 616 997-8181
Coopersville *(G-3561)*
Hillside Creations LLC ....G 269 496-7041
Mendon *(G-10713)*
Holland Bowl Mill ....E 616 396-6513
Holland *(G-7669)*
▲ Home Niches Inc ....G 734 330-9189
Ann Arbor *(G-494)*
Home Style Co ....G 989 871-3654
Millington *(G-10996)*
Hydrolake Inc ....G 231 825-2233
Reed City *(G-13215)*
Hydrolake Inc ....G 231 825-2233
Mc Bain *(G-10681)*
Innovtive Dsplay Solutions LLC ....F 616 896-6080
Hudsonville *(G-8160)*
Jonathan Showalter ....G 269 496-7001
Mendon *(G-10714)*
Kamps Inc ....E 313 381-2681
Detroit *(G-4170)*
Kamps Inc ....D 616 453-9676
Grand Rapids *(G-6569)*
Kells Sawmill Inc ....G 906 753-2778
Stephenson *(G-15236)*
Klein Bros Fence & Stakes LLC ....G 248 684-6919
Milford *(G-10967)*
Koetje Wood Products Inc ....G 616 393-9191
Holland *(G-7712)*
Ladder Carolina Company Inc ....F 734 482-5946
Ypsilanti *(G-18083)*
Lakestate Industries Inc ....E 906 786-9212
Escanaba *(G-4838)*
Larson-Juhl US LLC ....G 734 416-3302
Plymouth *(G-12671)*
M C Products ....G 248 960-0590
Commerce Township *(G-3424)*
▲ Maine Ornamental LLC ....F 800 556-8449
White Pigeon *(G-17652)*
Mark Beem ....G 231 510-8122
Lake City *(G-9092)*
Martin Products Company Inc ....F 269 651-1721
Sturgis *(G-15615)*
Mbwwproducts Inc ....F 616 464-1650
Grand Rapids *(G-6651)*
Michael Nadeau Cabinet Making ....G 989 356-0229
Alpena *(G-298)*
▲ Michigan Ladder Company LLC ......F 734 482-5946
Ypsilanti *(G-18090)*
Michigan Wood Fibers Llc ....G 616 875-2241
Zeeland *(G-18164)*
Michigan Wood Fuels LLC ....F 616 355-4955
Holland *(G-7747)*
◆ Millworks Engineering Inc ....F 517 741-5511
Union City *(G-16735)*
Moonlight Tiffanies LLC ....G 517 372-2795
Lansing *(G-9402)*
Nevill Supply Incorporated ....G 989 386-4522
Clare *(G-2879)*
Newberry Wood Enterprises Inc ....F 906 293-3131
Newberry *(G-11585)*
▲ Nu-Wool Co Inc ....D 800 748-0128
Jenison *(G-8635)*
Nuwood Components ....G 616 395-1905
Holland *(G-7761)*
Oakwood Sports Inc ....G 517 321-6852
Lansing *(G-9316)*
◆ Oakwood Veneer Company ....F 248 720-0288
Troy *(G-16531)*
Paddle King Inc ....F 989 235-6776
Carson City *(G-2495)*
◆ Paddlesports Warehouse Inc ....G 231 757-9051
Scottville *(G-14510)*
Paddletek LLC ....F 269 340-5967
Niles *(G-11635)*
Pwgg ....F 989 506-9402
Weidman *(G-17461)*
Rapid River Rustic Inc ....E 906 474-6404
Rapid River *(G-13114)*
▲ Rhino Seed & Landscape Sup LLC ..E 800 482-3130
Wayland *(G-17411)*
▲ Richwood Industries Inc ....E 616 243-2700
Grand Rapids *(G-6824)*
Russell Farms Inc ....G 269 349-6120
Kalamazoo *(G-8876)*
Setco Inc ....G 616 459-6311
Grand Rapids *(G-6858)*
▲ Sheffler Manufacturing LLC ....F 248 409-0966
Clarkston *(G-2954)*
Shelfactory LLC ....G 734 709-3615
Dearborn *(G-3759)*
▲ Silver Street Incorporated ....E 231 861-2194
Shelby *(G-14536)*
Smith Manufacturing Co Inc ....F 269 925-8155
Benton Harbor *(G-1549)*
Studio of Fine Arts Inc ....G 313 280-1177
Royal Oak *(G-13974)*
◆ T&M Usa Inc ....F 517 789-9420
Jackson *(G-8580)*
Tc Moulding ....G 248 588-2333
Madison Heights *(G-10366)*
Thompson Art Glass Inc ....G 810 225-8766
Brighton *(G-1998)*
Toms World of Wood ....G 517 264-2836
Adrian *(G-98)*
Tree Tech ....G 248 543-2166
Royal Oak *(G-13976)*
Ufp Lansing LLC ....G 517 322-0025
Lansing *(G-9328)*
Unique Namecraft Inc ....G 906 863-3644
Menominee *(G-10759)*
▲ Veldheer Tulip Garden Inc ....D 616 399-1900
Holland *(G-7844)*
Whisper Creative Products Inc ....G 734 529-2734
Dundee *(G-4603)*
Wood Shop Inc ....G 231 582-9835
Boyne City *(G-1838)*

25 FURNITURE AND FIXTURES

2511 Wood Household Furniture

A K Services Inc ....G 313 972-1010
Detroit *(G-3827)*
Alo LLC ....G 313 318-9029
Detroit *(G-3860)*
Anderson Manufacturing Co Inc ....F 906 863-8223
Menominee *(G-10723)*
Audia Woodworking & Fine Furn ....F 586 296-6330
Clinton Township *(G-3058)*
▲ Backyard Products LLC ....G 734 242-6900
Monroe *(G-11015)*
Backyard Services LLC ....C 734 242-6900
Monroe *(G-11016)*
Best Self Storage ....G 810 227-7050
Brighton *(G-1889)*
Boese Associates Inc ....G 231 347-3995
Petoskey *(G-12443)*
Center of World Woodshop Inc ....G 269 469-5687
Sawyer *(G-14484)*
Charles Phipps and Sons Ltd ....F 810 359-7141
Lexington *(G-9556)*
Charlies Wood Shop ....F 989 845-2632
Chesaning *(G-2722)*
Charlotte Cabinets Inc ....G 517 543-1522
Charlotte *(G-2639)*
Compass Interiors LLC ....G 231 348-5353
Petoskey *(G-12446)*
Context Furniture L L C ....G 248 200-0724
Ferndale *(G-5267)*
Contract Furn Solutions Inc ....E 734 941-2750
Brownstown *(G-2061)*
Craftwood Industries Inc ....E 616 796-1209
Holland *(G-7599)*
Custom Interiors of Toledo ....G 419 865-3090
Ottawa Lake *(G-12261)*
Czuk Studio ....G 269 628-2568
Kendall *(G-8983)*
Deweys Lumberville Inc ....G 313 885-0960
Grosse Pointe *(G-7178)*
Distinctive Custom Furniture ....G 248 399-9175
Ferndale *(G-5279)*
Dorel Home Furnishings Inc ....B 269 782-8661
Dowagiac *(G-4540)*
Eb Enterprises LLC ....G 231 768-5072
Leroy *(G-9532)*
Ejw Contract Inc ....G 616 293-5181
Whitmore Lake *(G-17696)*
Essilor Laboratories Amer Inc ....C 616 361-6000
Grand Rapids *(G-6386)*
▲ European Cabinet Mfg Co ....E 586 445-8909
Roseville *(G-13802)*
Flairwood Industries Inc ....E 231 798-8324
Norton Shores *(G-11756)*
G&J Products & Services ....G 734 522-2984
Westland *(G-17560)*
Genesis Seating Inc ....G 616 954-1040
Grand Rapids *(G-6436)*
◆ Genesis Seating Inc ....G 616 954-1040
Grand Rapids *(G-6437)*
Grand Rapids Carvers Inc ....E 616 538-0022
Grand Rapids *(G-6452)*
▲ Grand Rapids Chair Company ....C 616 774-0561
Byron Center *(G-2194)*
Great Lakes Wood Products ....G 906 228-3737
Negaunee *(G-11470)*
H L F Furniture Incorporated ....E 734 697-3000
Van Buren Twp *(G-16762)*
▲ Hekman Furniture Company ....E 616 748-2660
Zeeland *(G-18146)*
Home Shop ....G 517 543-5325
Charlotte *(G-2654)*
▼ Industrial Woodworking Corp ....E 616 741-9663
Zeeland *(G-18158)*
J B Cutting Inc ....G 586 468-4765
Mount Clemens *(G-11135)*
▲ Jack-Post Corporation ....F 269 695-7000
Buchanan *(G-2121)*
Janice Morse Inc ....E 248 624-7300
West Bloomfield *(G-17482)*
Kaliniak Design LLC ....G 616 675-3850
Kent City *(G-8992)*
▲ Kentwood Manufacturing Co ....E 616 698-6370
Grand Rapids *(G-6579)*
▲ Kindel Furniture Company LLC ....C 616 243-3676
Grand Rapids *(G-6583)*
▲ La-Z-Boy Casegoods Inc ....E 734 242-1444
Monroe *(G-11047)*
◆ La-Z-Boy Incorporated ....A 734 242-1444
Monroe *(G-11049)*
▼ Lakeland Mills Inc ....E 989 427-5133
Edmore *(G-4752)*
Lapointe Cedar Products Inc ....F 906 753-4072
Ingalls *(G-8224)*
M C M Fixture Company Inc ....E 248 547-9280
Hazel Park *(G-7442)*
Meeders Dim & Lbr Pdts Co ....G 231 587-8611
Mancelona *(G-10394)*
▲ Mega Mania Diversions LLC ....G 888 322-9076
Commerce Township *(G-3430)*
▲ Merdel Game Manufacturing Co ....G 231 845-1263
Ludington *(G-10071)*
Meyer Wood Products ....G 269 657-3450
Paw Paw *(G-12409)*
Mid-State Distributors Inc ....G 989 793-1820
Saginaw *(G-14094)*
▲ Mien Company Inc ....F 616 818-1970
Grand Rapids *(G-6688)*
Millennm-The Inside Sltion Inc ....E 248 645-9005
Farmington Hills *(G-5069)*

S
I
C

Nu-Tran LLC ....G.... 616 350-9575
Wyoming (G-18023)
▲ Nuvar Inc....E.... 616 394-5779
Holland (G-7760)
Perspectives Custom Cabinetry....E.... 248 288-4100
Troy (G-16544)
Picwood USA LLC....G.... 844 802-1599
Kalamazoo (G-8850)
Plum Tree....G.... 269 469-5980
Union Pier (G-16738)
Prime Wood Products Inc....G.... 616 399-4700
Holland (G-7775)
▲ R-Bo Co Inc....E.... 616 748-9733
Zeeland (G-18184)
▲ Rgm New Ventures Inc....D.... 248 624-5050
Wixom (G-17885)
Rooms of Grand Rapids LLC....F.... 616 260-1452
Spring Lake (G-15173)
◆ Rospatch Jessco Corporation....B.... 269 782-8661
Dowagiac (G-4558)
Sawdust Bin Inc....F.... 906 932-5518
Ironwood (G-8340)
Shop Makarios LLC....G.... 800 479-0032
Byron Center (G-2211)
Source Capital Backyard LLC....G.... 734 242-6900
Monroe (G-11066)
▲ Stow Company....C.... 616 399-3311
Holland (G-7816)
Terry Hanover....G.... 269 426-4199
New Troy (G-11560)
Theradapt Products Inc....G.... 231 480-4008
Ludington (G-10082)
Two Feathers Enterprise LLC....G.... 231 924-3612
Fremont (G-5785)
Van Peete Enterprises....G.... 517 369-2123
Bronson (G-2034)
▲ Van Zee Acquisitions Inc....E.... 616 855-7000
Grand Rapids (G-6958)
Woodard—Cm LLC....E.... 989 725-4265
Owosso (G-12331)
Woodcraft Customs LLC....G.... 248 987-4473
Farmington Hills (G-5152)
Woodcrafters....G.... 517 741-7423
Sherwood (G-14737)
▲ Woodland Creek Furniture Inc....E.... 231 518-4084
Kalkaska (G-8968)
Woodways Industries LLC....E.... 616 956-3070
Grand Rapids (G-7003)

2512 Wood Household Furniture, Upholstered

Debbink and Sons Inc....G.... 231 845-6421
Ludington (G-10055)
Homespun Furniture Inc....F.... 734 284-6277
Riverview (G-13297)
International Seating Co....G.... 586 293-2201
Fraser (G-5672)
La-Z-Boy Global Limited....G.... 734 241-2438
Monroe (G-11048)
◆ La-Z-Boy Incorporated....A.... 734 242-1444
Monroe (G-11049)
▲ Leland International Inc....E.... 616 975-9260
Grand Rapids (G-6626)
▲ Lzb Manufacturing Inc....G.... 734 242-1444
Monroe (G-11051)
Plum Tree....G.... 269 469-5980
Union Pier (G-16738)
◆ Sherwood Studios Inc....E.... 248 855-1600
West Bloomfield (G-17495)
Singh Senior Living LLC....E.... 248 865-1600
West Bloomfield (G-17497)
Tamarack Uphl & Interiors....G.... 616 866-2922
Rockford (G-13592)

2514 Metal Household Furniture

◆ Flanders Industries Inc....C.... 906 863-4491
Menominee (G-10736)
Industrial Reflections Inc....G.... 734 782-4454
Flat Rock (G-5355)
▲ Jack-Post Corporation....F.... 269 695-7000
Buchanan (G-2121)
M C M Fixture Company Inc....E.... 248 547-9280
Hazel Park (G-7442)
Martin and Hattie Rasche Inc....D.... 616 245-1223
Grand Rapids (G-6646)
▼ MTS Burgess LLC....D.... 734 847-2937
Temperance (G-15839)
Premium Machine & Tool Inc....F.... 989 855-3326
Lyons (G-10095)
Rivmax Manufacturing Inc....F.... 517 784-2556
Jackson (G-8563)
Spec International Inc....F.... 616 248-3022
Grand Rapids (G-6879)

2515 Mattresses & Bedsprings

Artisans Cstm Mmory Mattresses....F.... 989 793-3208
Saginaw (G-13996)
Clare Bedding Mfg Co....E.... 906 789-9902
Escanaba (G-4822)
▲ Comfort Mattress Co....D.... 586 293-4000
Roseville (G-13784)
▲ Grand Rapids Bedding Co....E.... 616 459-8234
Grand Rapids (G-6451)
Helping Hearts Helping Hands....G.... 248 980-5090
Constantine (G-3536)
Indratech LLC....D.... 248 377-1877
Troy (G-16416)
Jonathan Stevens Mattress Co....G.... 616 243-4342
Grand Rapids (G-6564)
Marrs Discount Furniture....G.... 989 720-5436
Owosso (G-12300)
Mattress Wholesale....F.... 248 968-2200
Oak Park (G-12082)
Michigan Mattress Limited LLC....G.... 248 669-6345
Commerce Township (G-3432)
Midwest Quality Bedding Inc....F.... 614 504-5971
Waterford (G-17359)
◆ Recticel Foam Corporation....G.... 248 241-9100
Clarkston (G-2951)
Richards Quality Bedding Co....E.... 616 363-0070
Grand Rapids (G-6823)
▲ Serta Restokraft Mat Co Inc....C.... 734 727-9000
Romulus (G-13733)
Spine Align Inc....G.... 616 395-5407
Holland (G-7812)

2517 Wood T V, Radio, Phono & Sewing Cabinets

A & A Woodwork Studio LLC....G.... 248 691-8380
Oak Park (G-12047)
▲ European Cabinet Mfg Co....E.... 586 445-8909
Roseville (G-13802)
George Washburn....G.... 269 694-2930
Otsego (G-12240)
Millennm-The Inside Sltion Inc....E.... 248 645-9005
Farmington Hills (G-5069)
Pazzel Inc....G.... 616 291-0257
Grand Rapids (G-6745)
Ross Cabinets II Inc....E.... 586 752-7750
Shelby Township (G-14682)
Sterling Millwork Inc....D.... 248 427-1400
Farmington Hills (G-5131)

2519 Household Furniture, NEC

D & R Fabrication Inc....D.... 616 794-1130
Belding (G-1408)
Dozy Dotes LLC....G.... 866 870-1048
Grand Blanc (G-5965)
◆ Flanders Industries Inc....C.... 906 863-4491
Menominee (G-10736)
▲ Innovative Pdts Unlimited Inc....E.... 269 684-5050
Niles (G-11620)
New Line Inc....G.... 586 228-4820
Shelby Township (G-14652)
Nickels Boat Works Inc....F.... 810 767-4050
Flint (G-5472)

2521 Wood Office Furniture

Boese Associates Inc....G.... 231 347-3995
Petoskey (G-12443)
Bold Companies Inc....D.... 231 773-8026
Muskegon (G-11282)
Bourne Industries Inc....E.... 989 743-3461
Corunna (G-3578)
Case Systems Inc....C.... 989 496-9510
Midland (G-10822)
Cornerstone Furniture Inc....G.... 269 795-3379
Middleville (G-10801)
Counterpoint By Hlf....D.... 734 699-7100
Van Buren Twp (G-16754)
Craftwood Industries Inc....E.... 616 796-1209
Holland (G-7599)
Custom Components Corporation....F.... 616 523-1111
Ionia (G-8247)
Custom Crafters....G.... 269 763-9180
Bellevue (G-1453)
Cygnus Inc....E.... 231 347-5404
Petoskey (G-12447)
D & M Cabinet Shop Inc....G.... 989 479-9271
Ruth (G-13988)
Debbink and Sons Inc....G.... 231 845-6421
Ludington (G-10055)
Designtec Services Inc....G.... 734 216-6051
Howell (G-8028)
Dynamic Wood Products Inc....G.... 616 897-8114
Saranac (G-14454)
Farnell Contracting Inc....F.... 810 714-3421
Linden (G-9590)
Flairwood Industries Inc....E.... 231 798-8324
Norton Shores (G-11756)
◆ Genesis Seating Inc....G.... 616 954-1040
Grand Rapids (G-6437)
Grand Rapids Carvers Inc....E.... 616 538-0022
Grand Rapids (G-6452)
Grand Valley Wood Products Inc....E.... 616 475-5890
Grand Rapids (G-6471)
H L F Furniture Incorporated....E.... 734 697-3000
Van Buren Twp (G-16762)
◆ Haworth Inc....A.... 616 393-3000
Holland (G-7659)
Haworth Inc....B.... 231 796-1400
Big Rapids (G-1633)
◆ Haworth International Ltd....A.... 616 393-3000
Holland (G-7660)
Hekman Furniture Company....D.... 616 735-3905
Grand Rapids (G-6502)
Herman Miller....F.... 616 296-3422
Spring Lake (G-15151)
◆ Herman Miller Inc....B.... 616 654-3000
Zeeland (G-18147)
Herman Miller Inc....G.... 616 846-0280
Spring Lake (G-15152)
Herman Miller Inc....E.... 616 654-7456
Holland (G-7662)
Herman Miller Inc....G.... 616 654-3716
Van Buren Twp (G-16763)
Herman Miller Inc....E.... 616 654-8078
Holland (G-7663)
Holland Stitchcraft Inc....F.... 616 399-3868
Holland (G-7678)
Howe US Inc....D.... 616 419-2226
Grand Rapids (G-6517)
▼ Interior Concepts Corporation....E.... 616 842-5550
Spring Lake (G-15155)
▲ Izzy Plus....G.... 574 821-1200
Grand Haven (G-6038)
Jsj Corporation....C.... 616 847-7000
Spring Lake (G-15157)
▲ Jsj Furniture Corporation....E.... 616 847-6534
Grand Haven (G-6043)
Knoll Inc....C.... 616 949-1050
Grand Rapids (G-6587)
Knoll Inc....E.... 231 755-2270
Norton Shores (G-11767)
Konwinski Kabnets Inc....G.... 989 773-2906
Mount Pleasant (G-11201)
◆ Michigan Tube Swagers & Fab....B.... 734 847-3875
Temperance (G-15838)
Mooreco Inc....E.... 616 451-7800
Grand Rapids (G-6706)
▼ Nucraft Furniture Company....D.... 616 784-6016
Comstock Park (G-3503)
▲ Omt-Veyhl USA Corporation....E.... 616 738-6688
Holland (G-7764)
Paladin Ind Inc....E.... 616 698-7495
Grand Rapids (G-6740)
Pazzel Inc....G.... 616 291-0257
Grand Rapids (G-6745)
Phillip Anderson....G.... 269 687-7166
Niles (G-11639)
Primeway Inc....F.... 248 583-6922
Royal Oak (G-13958)
R J Woodworking Inc....F.... 231 766-2511
Muskegon (G-11412)
▲ R T London Company....D.... 616 364-4800
Grand Rapids (G-6804)
▲ Rj Operating Company....F.... 616 392-7101
Holland (G-7789)
Rose Corporation....E.... 734 426-0005
Dexter (G-4508)
S & J Inc....G.... 248 299-0822
Rochester Hills (G-13508)
▲ S F Gilmore Inc....C.... 616 475-5100
Grand Rapids (G-6849)
▲ Silver Street Incorporated....E.... 231 861-2194
Shelby (G-14536)
◆ Steelcase Inc....A.... 616 247-2710
Grand Rapids (G-6889)

SIC SECTION 25 FURNITURE AND FIXTURES

T F Boyer Industries Inc ....G.... 248 674-8420 Waterford *(G-17380)*
Tims Cabinet Inc ....G.... 989 846-9831 Pinconning *(G-12513)*
Tranquil Systems Intl LLC ....F.... 800 631-0212 Clare *(G-2891)*
◆ Trendway Corporation ....B.... 616 399-3900 Holland *(G-7836)*
Viable Inc ....G.... 616 774-2022 Grand Rapids *(G-6970)*
West Mich Off Interiors Inc ....G.... 269 344-0768 Kalamazoo *(G-8923)*
West Shore Services Inc ....E.... 616 895-4347 Allendale *(G-227)*
Woodard—Cm LLC ....E.... 989 725-4265 Owosso *(G-12331)*

2522 Office Furniture, Except Wood

▲ Agritek Industries Inc ....D.... 616 786-9200 Holland *(G-7551)*
▲ Altus Industries Inc ....F.... 616 233-9530 Walker *(G-16861)*
◆ American Seating Company ....B.... 616 732-6600 Grand Rapids *(G-6166)*
Amneon Acquisitions LLC ....E.... 616 895-6640 Holland *(G-7559)*
Anso Products ....G.... 248 357-2300 Southfield *(G-14839)*
▲ Autoexec Inc ....G.... 616 971-0080 Grand Rapids *(G-6193)*
▲ Avantis Inc ....G.... 616 285-8000 Grand Rapids *(G-6195)*
▼ Bostontec Inc ....F.... 989 496-9510 Midland *(G-10818)*
Cerny Industries LLC ....E.... 231 929-2140 Traverse City *(G-15935)*
Compact Engineering Corp ....F.... 231 788-5470 Muskegon *(G-11298)*
▲ Contract Source & Assembly Inc ....F.... 616 897-2185 Grand Rapids *(G-6305)*
Counterpoint By Hlf ....D.... 734 699-7100 Van Buren Twp *(G-16754)*
Craftwood Industries Inc ....E.... 616 796-1209 Holland *(G-7599)*
Custom Components Corporation ....F.... 616 523-1111 Ionia *(G-8247)*
▲ Electra-Tec Inc ....G.... 269 694-6652 Otsego *(G-12238)*
Essilor Laboratories Amer Inc ....C.... 616 361-6000 Grand Rapids *(G-6386)*
▲ Greenfield Cabinetry Inc ....F.... 586 759-3300 Warren *(G-17066)*
Haskell Office ....G.... 616 988-0880 Wyoming *(G-18008)*
◆ Haworth Inc ....A.... 616 393-3000 Holland *(G-7659)*
Haworth Inc ....B.... 231 796-1400 Big Rapids *(G-1633)*
Haworth Inc ....D.... 231 845-0607 Ludington *(G-10064)*
◆ Haworth International Ltd ....A.... 616 393-3000 Holland *(G-7660)*
◆ Herman Miller Inc ....B.... 616 654-3000 Zeeland *(G-18147)*
Hmi Liquidating Company Inc ....G.... 616 654-5055 Zeeland *(G-18151)*
▼ Interior Concepts Corporation ....E.... 616 842-5550 Spring Lake *(G-15155)*
Jem Computers Inc ....F.... 586 783-3400 Clinton Township *(G-3149)*
◆ Jsj Corporation ....E.... 616 842-6350 Grand Haven *(G-6042)*
Knoll Inc ....E.... 231 755-2270 Norton Shores *(G-11767)*
▲ Metal Arc Inc ....E.... 231 865-3111 Muskegon *(G-11375)*
▲ Metal Components LLC ....D.... 616 252-1900 Grand Rapids *(G-6660)*
Mica TEC Inc ....G.... 586 758-4404 Warren *(G-17151)*
◆ Mobile Office Vehicle Inc ....G.... 616 971-0080 Grand Rapids *(G-6693)*
Mooreco Inc ....E.... 616 451-7800 Grand Rapids *(G-6706)*
Office Design & Furn LLC ....G.... 734 217-2717 Ypsilanti *(G-18093)*
Office Updating ....G.... 248 770-4769 White Lake *(G-17635)*
Premium Machine & Tool Inc ....F.... 989 855-3326 Lyons *(G-10095)*
▲ Rj Operating Company ....F.... 616 392-7101 Holland *(G-7789)*
◆ Srg Global Coatings Inc ....C.... 248 509-1100 Troy *(G-16618)*
◆ Steelcase Inc ....A.... 616 247-2710 Grand Rapids *(G-6889)*
Steelcase Inc ....D.... 616 247-2710 Grand Rapids *(G-6890)*
Systems Design & Installation ....G.... 269 543-4204 Fennville *(G-5177)*
Total Innovative Mfg LLC ....E.... 616 399-9903 Holland *(G-7831)*
◆ Trendway Corporation ....B.... 616 399-3900 Holland *(G-7836)*
Trendway Svcs Organization LLC ....G.... 616 994-5327 Holland *(G-7837)*
Tvb Inc ....F.... 616 456-9629 Grand Rapids *(G-6942)*
Up Officeexpress LLC ....G.... 906 281-0089 Calumet *(G-2334)*
West Mich Off Interiors Inc ....G.... 269 344-0768 Kalamazoo *(G-8923)*

2531 Public Building & Related Furniture

Adient Inc ....D.... 734 254-5000 Plymouth *(G-12563)*
Alr Products Inc ....E.... 517 649-2243 Mulliken *(G-11238)*
American Athletic ....F.... 231 798-7300 Muskegon *(G-11266)*
American Metal Fab Inc ....D.... 269 279-5108 Three Rivers *(G-15854)*
◆ American Seating Company ....B.... 616 732-6600 Grand Rapids *(G-6166)*
B/E Aerospace Inc ....G.... 734 425-6200 Livonia *(G-9658)*
Baker Road Upholstery Inc ....G.... 616 794-3027 Belding *(G-1398)*
Big Bear Products Inc ....G.... 269 657-3550 Paw Paw *(G-12398)*
Bourne Industries Inc ....E.... 989 743-3461 Corunna *(G-3578)*
Bracy & Associates Ltd ....G.... 616 298-8120 Holland *(G-7574)*
Bridgewater Interiors LLC ....F.... 517 322-4800 Lansing *(G-9279)*
Bridgewater Interiors LLC ....A.... 586 582-0882 Warren *(G-16967)*
▲ Bridgewater Interiors LLC ....C.... 313 842-3300 Detroit *(G-3916)*
▲ Brill Company Inc ....E.... 231 843-2430 Ludington *(G-10050)*
Carson Wood Specialties Inc ....G.... 269 465-6091 Stevensville *(G-15559)*
Counterpoint By Hlf ....D.... 734 699-7100 Van Buren Twp *(G-16754)*
Craftwood Industries Inc ....E.... 616 796-1209 Holland *(G-7599)*
Everest Expedition LLC ....D.... 616 392-1848 Holland *(G-7627)*
Faurecia Auto Seating LLC ....B.... 248 563-9241 Highland Park *(G-7503)*
Faurecia Auto Seating LLC ....C.... 248 563-9241 Highland Park *(G-7504)*
◆ Fisher & Company Incorporated ....B.... 586 746-2000 Saint Clair Shores *(G-14249)*
Fisher & Company Incorporated ....G.... 248 280-0808 Troy *(G-16362)*
Fisher Dynamics Corporation ....E.... 586 746-2000 Saint Clair Shores *(G-14251)*
Flint Stool & Chair Co Inc ....G.... 810 235-7001 Flint *(G-5430)*
Furniture Partners LLC ....D.... 616 355-3051 Holland *(G-7638)*
Grand Rapids Carvers Inc ....E.... 616 538-0022 Grand Rapids *(G-6452)*
Greene Manufacturing Inc ....E.... 734 428-8304 Chelsea *(G-2712)*
Greenfield Holdings LLC ....F.... 734 530-5600 Brownstown *(G-2064)*
◆ Herman Miller Inc ....B.... 616 654-3000 Zeeland *(G-18147)*
▲ Hoover Universal Inc ....E.... 734 454-0994 Plymouth *(G-12642)*
Integrated Mfg & Assembly LLC ....E.... 313 267-2634 Detroit *(G-4143)*
▲ Integrated Mfg & Assembly LLC ....B.... 734 530-5600 Detroit *(G-4144)*
Interkal LLC ....G.... 989 486-1788 Midland *(G-10872)*
◆ Interkal LLC ....C.... 269 349-1521 Kalamazoo *(G-8773)*
◆ Irwin Seating Holding Company ....B.... 616 574-7400 Grand Rapids *(G-6545)*
▲ Isringhausen Inc ....C.... 269 484-5333 Galesburg *(G-5812)*
▼ ITW Dahti Seating ....E.... 616 866-1323 Rockford *(G-13573)*
Joes Tables LLC ....G.... 989 846-4970 Standish *(G-15220)*
Johnson Controls Inc ....D.... 616 283-5578 Holland *(G-7696)*
Johnson Controls Inc ....G.... 269 226-4748 Portage *(G-13003)*
Johnson Controls Inc ....G.... 866 252-3677 Grand Rapids *(G-6563)*
Johnson Controls Inc ....E.... 616 847-2766 Spring Lake *(G-15156)*
Johnson Controls Inc ....E.... 269 323-0988 Kalamazoo *(G-8781)*
Johnson Controls Inc ....B.... 734 254-5000 Plymouth *(G-12655)*
Jrt Enterprises LLC ....G.... 877 318-7661 Holland *(G-7703)*
Kawkawlin Manufacturing Co ....G.... 989 684-5470 Midland *(G-10879)*
Kawkawlin Manufacturing Co ....G.... 989 684-5470 Kawkawlin *(G-8974)*
▲ Knoedler Manufacturers Inc ....F.... 269 969-7722 Battle Creek *(G-1221)*
◆ Kotocorp (usa) Inc ....G.... 269 349-1521 Kalamazoo *(G-8802)*
▲ Lanzen Incorporated ....D.... 586 771-7070 Bruce Twp *(G-2090)*
Lear Corporation ....B.... 269 496-2215 Mendon *(G-10715)*
Lear Corporation ....A.... 248 447-1500 Mason *(G-10644)*
◆ Lear Corporation ....B.... 248 447-1500 Southfield *(G-14962)*
Lear European Operations Corp ....G.... 248 447-1500 Southfield *(G-14963)*
▲ Lear Mexican Seating Corp ....G.... 248 447-1500 Southfield *(G-14964)*
Midwest Seating Solutions Inc ....F.... 616 222-0636 Grand Rapids *(G-6687)*
Milcare Inc ....B.... 616 654-8000 Zeeland *(G-18166)*
Milsco LLC ....B.... 517 787-3650 Jackson *(G-8531)*
Multiform Studios LLC ....G.... 248 437-5964 South Lyon *(G-14803)*
▲ Promax Engineering LLC ....C.... 734 979-0888 Westland *(G-17591)*
▲ R T London Company ....D.... 616 364-4800 Grand Rapids *(G-6804)*
RCO Aerospace Products LLC ....D.... 586 774-8400 Roseville *(G-13859)*
RCO Engineering Inc ....D.... 586 620-4133 Roseville *(G-13860)*
Recaro North America Inc ....B.... 313 842-3479 Detroit *(G-4333)*
◆ Recaro North America Inc ....D.... 734 254-5000 Plymouth *(G-12733)*
Recycletech Products Inc ....E.... 517 649-2243 Mulliken *(G-11240)*
Stadium Bleachers LLC ....G.... 810 245-6258 Lapeer *(G-9488)*
Subassembly Plus Inc ....E.... 616 395-2075 Holland *(G-7819)*
▲ Syncreonus Inc ....D.... 248 377-4700 Auburn Hills *(G-1010)*
▲ Tachi-S Engineering USA Inc ....D.... 248 478-5050 Farmington Hills *(G-5139)*
TMC Furniture Inc ....G.... 734 622-0080 Ann Arbor *(G-678)*
TMC Furniture Inc ....E.... 734 622-0080 Kentwood *(G-9034)*
▲ Toyo Seat USA Corporation ....C.... 606 849-3009 Imlay City *(G-8212)*
Woodard—Cm LLC ....E.... 989 725-4265 Owosso *(G-12331)*
▲ Woodbridge Holdings Inc ....G.... 248 288-0100 Troy *(G-16697)*
Woodbridge Holdings Inc ....C.... 734 942-0458 Romulus *(G-13742)*
Worden Group LLC ....D.... 616 392-1848 Holland *(G-7861)*
Yanfeng US Automotive ....B.... 248 319-7333 Novi *(G-12027)*

SIC

Employee Codes: A=Over 500 employees, B=251-500
C=101-250, D=51-100, E=20-50, F=10-19, G=3-9
2020 Harris Michigan
Industrial Directory
723

Yanfeng US Automotive ..... D 734 289-4841
Monroe *(G-11086)*
Yanfeng US Automotive ..... E 616 394-1199
Holland *(G-7865)*
Yanfeng US Automotive ..... F 586 354-2101
Harrison Township *(G-7358)*
Yanfeng US Automotive ..... G 616 394-1523
Holland *(G-7866)*

2541 Wood, Office & Store Fixtures

AME For Auto Dealers Inc ..... G 248 720-0245
Auburn Hills *(G-768)*
Bay Wood Homes Inc ..... E 989 245-4156
Fenton *(G-5187)*
▲ Bennett Wood Specialties Inc ..... F 616 772-6683
Zeeland *(G-18117)*
Bourne Industries Inc ..... E 989 743-3461
Corunna *(G-3578)*
Cameo Countertops Inc ..... E 616 458-8745
Grand Rapids *(G-6252)*
Carpenters Cabinets ..... G 989 777-1070
Saginaw *(G-14010)*
◆ Compatico Inc ..... E 616 940-1772
Grand Rapids *(G-6291)*
Competitive Edge Wood Spc Inc ..... D 616 842-1063
Muskegon *(G-11299)*
Custom Components Corporation ..... F 616 523-1111
Ionia *(G-8247)*
Custom Counter Top Company ..... G 616 534-5894
Grand Rapids *(G-6323)*
Custom Crafters ..... G 269 763-9180
Bellevue *(G-1453)*
Dads Panels Inc ..... G 810 245-1871
Lapeer *(G-9455)*
Dallas Design Inc ..... G 810 238-4546
Flint *(G-5413)*
▲ Design Fabrications Inc ..... D 248 597-0988
Madison Heights *(G-10229)*
▲ Eagle Marble & Granite ..... G 586 421-1912
Chesterfield *(G-2770)*
▲ European Cabinet Mfg Co ..... E 586 445-8909
Roseville *(G-13802)*
Ferrante Manufacturing Co ..... E 313 571-1111
Detroit *(G-4056)*
Flairwood Industries Inc ..... E 231 798-8324
Norton Shores *(G-11756)*
G & G Wood & Supply Inc ..... F 586 293-0450
Roseville *(G-13805)*
G & W Display Fixtures Inc ..... E 517 369-7110
Bronson *(G-2026)*
Gast Cabinet Co ..... E 269 422-1587
Baroda *(G-1125)*
Grand Valley Wood Products Inc ..... E 616 475-5890
Grand Rapids *(G-6471)*
Granite Planet LLC ..... G 734 522-0190
Livonia *(G-9757)*
Great Lakes Woodworking Co Inc ..... E 313 892-8500
Detroit *(G-4101)*
▲ Greenfield Cabinetry Inc ..... F 586 759-3300
Warren *(G-17066)*
H & R Wood Specialties Inc ..... E 269 628-2181
Gobles *(G-5947)*
H L F Furniture Incorporated ..... E 734 697-3000
Van Buren Twp *(G-16762)*
◆ Harbor Industries Inc ..... D 616 842-5330
Grand Haven *(G-6032)*
Harbor Industries Inc ..... D 616 842-5330
Charlevoix *(G-2618)*
Harbor Industries Inc ..... D 616 842-5330
Grand Haven *(G-6033)*
Harbor Industries Inc ..... B 231 547-3280
Charlevoix *(G-2617)*
◆ Herman Miller Inc ..... B 616 654-3000
Zeeland *(G-18147)*
▼ Hilco Fixture Finders LLC ..... E 616 453-1300
Grand Rapids *(G-6511)*
Holsinger Manufacturing Corp ..... F 989 684-3101
Kawkawlin *(G-8972)*
Howes Custom Counter Tops ..... G 989 498-4044
Saginaw *(G-14063)*
Hudsonville Products LLC ..... G 616 836-1904
Grand Rapids *(G-6518)*
Industrial Assemblies Inc ..... F 231 865-6500
Fruitport *(G-5793)*
J & J Laminate Connection Inc ..... G 810 227-1824
Brighton *(G-1944)*
◆ Knape & Vogt Manufacturing Co ..... A 616 459-3311
Grand Rapids *(G-6585)*
Knoll Inc ..... C 616 949-1050
Grand Rapids *(G-6587)*
Korcast Products Incorporated ..... G 248 740-2340
Troy *(G-16448)*
Korcast Products Incorporated ..... G 248 740-2340
Troy *(G-16449)*
Kreations Inc ..... F 313 255-1230
Detroit *(G-4183)*
KS Liquidating LLC ..... E 248 577-8220
Madison Heights *(G-10295)*
Kurtis Mfg & Distrg Corp ..... E 734 522-7600
Livonia *(G-9802)*
Lafata Cabinet Shop ..... E 586 247-6536
Shelby Township *(G-14620)*
M and G Laminated Products ..... G 517 784-4974
Jackson *(G-8502)*
Maw Ventures Inc ..... E 231 798-8324
Norton Shores *(G-11772)*
Mica Crafters Inc ..... E 517 548-2924
Howell *(G-8063)*
Michael Nadeau Cabinet Making ..... G 989 356-0229
Alpena *(G-298)*
Millennm-The Inside Sltion Inc ..... E 248 645-9005
Farmington Hills *(G-5069)*
▲ Modular Systems Inc ..... G 231 865-3167
Fruitport *(G-5797)*
National Millwork Inc ..... F 248 307-1299
Madison Heights *(G-10314)*
Natures Edge Stone Produ ..... G 231 943-3440
Traverse City *(G-16047)*
Nieboers Pit Stop ..... G 616 997-2026
Coopersville *(G-3566)*
Nu-Tran LLC ..... G 616 350-9575
Wyoming *(G-18023)*
Owens Building Co Inc ..... E 989 835-1293
Midland *(G-10901)*
Pageant Homes Inc ..... G 517 694-0431
Holt *(G-7921)*
Panel Processing Inc ..... E 517 279-8051
Coldwater *(G-3317)*
Panel Processing Oregon Inc ..... E 989 356-9007
Alpena *(G-306)*
Paxton Products Inc ..... E 517 627-3688
Lansing *(G-9317)*
PCI Industries Inc ..... D 248 542-2570
Oak Park *(G-12090)*
▲ PDC ..... F 269 651-9975
Sturgis *(G-15627)*
Phoenix Countertops LLC ..... G 586 254-1450
Sterling Heights *(G-15444)*
Pohls Custom Counter Tops ..... G 989 593-2174
Fowler *(G-5555)*
▼ Programmed Products Corp ..... D 248 348-7755
Novi *(G-11983)*
Reis Custom Cabinets ..... G 586 791-4925
Reese *(G-13231)*
Ross Cabinets II Inc ..... E 586 752-7750
Shelby Township *(G-14682)*
Royal Cabinet Inc ..... F 517 787-2940
Jackson *(G-8565)*
Sterling Millwork Inc ..... D 248 427-1400
Farmington Hills *(G-5131)*
Top Form Inc ..... G 815 653-9616
Twin Lake *(G-16715)*
Unislat LLC ..... G 616 844-4211
Grand Haven *(G-6091)*
Van Zee Corporation ..... D 616 245-9000
Grand Rapids *(G-6959)*
Village Cabinet Shoppe Inc ..... G 586 264-6464
Sterling Heights *(G-15539)*
W S Townsend Company ..... C 269 781-5131
Marshall *(G-10593)*
Zuckero & Sons Inc ..... E 586 772-3377
Roseville *(G-13893)*

2542 Partitions & Fixtures, Except Wood

Allen Pattern of Michigan ..... F 269 963-4131
Battle Creek *(G-1145)*
Arbor Gage & Tooling Inc ..... E 616 454-8266
Grand Rapids *(G-6178)*
Arlington Display Inds Inc ..... G 313 837-1212
Detroit *(G-3877)*
Associated Rack Corporation ..... G 616 554-6004
Grand Rapids *(G-6187)*
Basc Manufacturing Inc ..... G 248 360-2272
Commerce Township *(G-3393)*
◆ Borroughs Corporation ..... D 800 748-0227
Kalamazoo *(G-8700)*
C F Plastic Fabricating Inc ..... G 586 954-1296
Harrison Township *(G-7325)*
Casper Corporation ..... F 248 442-9000
Farmington Hills *(G-4959)*
Childs Carpentry ..... G 734 425-8783
Garden City *(G-5821)*
Compact Engineering Corp ..... F 231 788-5470
Muskegon *(G-11298)*
Construction Retail Svcs Inc ..... G 586 469-2289
Clinton Township *(G-3088)*
Creative Solutions Group Inc ..... D 248 288-9700
Clawson *(G-2975)*
Creative Solutions Group Inc ..... G 734 425-2257
Redford *(G-13154)*
Dads Panels Inc ..... G 810 245-1871
Lapeer *(G-9455)*
Dee-Blast Corporation ..... F 269 428-2400
Stevensville *(G-15563)*
F & F Industries Inc ..... E 313 278-7600
Taylor *(G-15718)*
F F Industries ..... G 313 291-7600
Taylor *(G-15719)*
Ferrante Manufacturing Co ..... E 313 571-1111
Detroit *(G-4056)*
Fmmb LLC ..... E 313 372-7420
Detroit *(G-4065)*
G & W Display Fixtures Inc ..... E 517 369-7110
Bronson *(G-2026)*
◆ Glastender Inc ..... C 989 752-4275
Saginaw *(G-14045)*
Gonzalez Prod Systems Inc ..... D 313 297-6682
Detroit *(G-4097)*
Grand Valley Wood Products Inc ..... E 616 475-5890
Grand Rapids *(G-6471)*
▲ Greenfield Cabinetry Inc ..... F 586 759-3300
Warren *(G-17066)*
H G Geiger Manufacturing Co ..... F 517 369-7357
Bronson *(G-2028)*
Harbor Industries Inc ..... B 231 547-3280
Charlevoix *(G-2617)*
◆ Herman Miller Inc ..... B 616 654-3000
Zeeland *(G-18147)*
▲ Hss Industries Inc ..... E 231 946-6101
Traverse City *(G-16000)*
Impert Industries Inc ..... G 269 694-2727
Otsego *(G-12241)*
J H P Inc ..... G 248 588-0110
Madison Heights *(G-10280)*
▼ JMJ Inc ..... E 269 948-2828
Hastings *(G-7417)*
◆ Knape & Vogt Manufacturing Co ..... A 616 459-3311
Grand Rapids *(G-6585)*
▲ L & S Products LLC ..... G 517 238-4645
Coldwater *(G-3313)*
Loudon Steel Inc ..... D 989 871-9353
Millington *(G-10997)*
▲ Mega Wall Inc ..... F 616 647-4190
Comstock Park *(G-3499)*
Michalski Enterprises Inc ..... E 517 703-0777
Lansing *(G-9245)*
National Case Corporation ..... G 586 726-1710
Sterling Heights *(G-15432)*
▲ National Intgrated Systems Inc ..... F 734 927-3030
Wixom *(G-17861)*
Phoenix Fixtures LLC (az) ..... G 616 847-0895
Spring Lake *(G-15168)*
Pinnacle Cabinet Company Inc ..... E 989 772-3866
Mount Pleasant *(G-11217)*
Pipp Mobil Stora Syste Holdi C ..... C 616 735-9100
Walker *(G-16873)*
▼ Royal Design & Manufacturing ..... D 248 588-0110
Madison Heights *(G-10346)*
SC Custom Display Inc ..... G 616 940-0563
Kentwood *(G-9032)*
Sfi Acquisition Inc ..... E 248 471-1500
Farmington Hills *(G-5122)*
▲ Shaw & Slavsky Inc ..... E 313 834-3990
Detroit *(G-4359)*
Shaw & Slavsky Inc ..... E 313 834-3990
Detroit *(G-4360)*
◆ Structural Concepts Corp ..... B 231 798-8888
Norton Shores *(G-11798)*
Structural Plastics Inc ..... E 810 953-9400
Holly *(G-7898)*
T M Shea Products Inc ..... F 800 992-5233
Troy *(G-16630)*
Tarpon Industries Inc ..... C 810 364-7421
Marysville *(G-10620)*
Top Shop Inc ..... G 517 323-9085
Lansing *(G-9270)*
Vista Manufacturing Inc ..... E 616 719-5520
Walker *(G-16881)*

2591 Drapery Hardware, Window Blinds & Shades

A ME Vertical Incorporated	G	248 720-0245
Troy *(G-16164)*		
Blinds and Designs Inc	D	770 971-5524
Wixom *(G-17776)*		
Custom Verticals Unlimited	G	734 522-1615
Oak Park *(G-12057)*		
Dave Brand	G	269 651-4693
Sturgis *(G-15603)*		
Detroit Custom Services Inc	E	586 465-3631
Mount Clemens *(G-11129)*		
Elsie Inc	F	734 421-8844
Livonia *(G-9726)*		
Kyler Industries Inc	G	616 392-1042
Holland *(G-7714)*		
Lorne Hanley	G	248 547-9865
Huntington Woods *(G-8189)*		
McDonald Wholesale Distributor	G	313 273-2870
Detroit *(G-4222)*		
Melody Digiglio	F	586 754-4405
Warren *(G-17147)*		
MSC Blinds & Shades Inc	G	269 489-5188
Bronson *(G-2033)*		
Muskegon Awning & Mfg Co	E	231 759-0911
Muskegon *(G-11387)*		
Parkway Drapery & Uphl Co Inc	G	734 779-1300
Livonia *(G-9884)*		
PCI Industries Inc	D	248 542-2570
Oak Park *(G-12090)*		
Royal Crest Inc	G	248 399-2476
Oak Park *(G-12095)*		
▲ Signature Designs Inc	G	248 426-9735
Farmington Hills *(G-5123)*		
▲ Sophias Textiles & Furn Inc	F	586 759-6231
Center Line *(G-2584)*		
Sunburst Shutters	G	248 674-4600
Waterford *(G-17378)*		
Time For Blinds Inc	G	248 363-9174
White Lake *(G-17640)*		
Tri City Blinds Inc	G	989 695-5699
Freeland *(G-5760)*		
Triangle Window Fashions Inc	E	616 538-9676
Wyoming *(G-18036)*		

2599 Furniture & Fixtures, NEC

B & W Woodwork Inc	G	616 772-4577
Holland *(G-7564)*		
Banta Furniture Company	F	616 575-8180
Grand Rapids *(G-6203)*		
Benchwork Inc	G	586 464-6699
Clinton Township *(G-3065)*		
▲ Billco Acquisition LLC	E	616 928-0637
Holland *(G-7570)*		
Boars Belly	G	231 722-2627
Muskegon *(G-11281)*		
▲ Brill Company Inc	E	231 843-2430
Ludington *(G-10050)*		
Consort Corporation	E	269 388-4532
Kalamazoo *(G-8713)*		
Custom Components Corporation	F	616 523-1111
Ionia *(G-8247)*		
▲ Effizient LLC	G	616 935-3170
Grand Haven *(G-6012)*		
Firehouse Woodworks LLC	E	616 285-2300
Grand Rapids *(G-6407)*		
Frank Terlecki Company Inc	F	586 759-5770
Warren *(G-17045)*		
Harborfront Interiors Inc	F	231 777-3838
Muskegon *(G-11343)*		
Hmi Liquidating Company Inc	G	616 654-5055
Zeeland *(G-18151)*		
▲ Holland Bar Stool Company	F	616 399-5530
Holland *(G-7668)*		
Holland Stitchcraft Inc	E	616 399-3868
Holland *(G-7678)*		
Holsinger Manufacturing Corp	F	989 684-3101
Kawkawlin *(G-8972)*		
▲ Innovative Pdts Unlimited Inc	E	269 684-5050
Niles *(G-11620)*		
International Seating Co	G	586 293-2201
Fraser *(G-5672)*		
Kennedys Irish Pub Inc	G	248 681-1050
Waterford *(G-17354)*		
La Rosa Refrigeration & Eqp Co	E	313 368-6620
Detroit *(G-4187)*		
M and G Laminated Products	G	517 784-4974
Jackson *(G-8502)*		
Midtown Bar	G	989 584-6212
Carson City *(G-2493)*		
Newkirk and Associates Inc	G	616 863-9899
Rockford *(G-13582)*		
Orangebox Us Inc	G	616 988-8624
Grand Rapids *(G-6733)*		
Paladin Ind Inc	E	616 698-7495
Grand Rapids *(G-6740)*		
Perfect Dish LLC	G	313 784-3976
Taylor *(G-15753)*		
Pinetree Trading LLC	F	313 584-2700
Dearborn *(G-3748)*		
Pinnacle Cabinet Company Inc	E	989 772-3866
Mount Pleasant *(G-11217)*		
Royal Oak Millwork Company LLC	G	248 547-1210
Royal Oak *(G-13968)*		
Stan Kell Inc	G	734 283-0005
Southgate *(G-15083)*		
Stryker Corporation	E	269 385-2600
Portage *(G-13038)*		
Stryker Corporation	B	269 329-2100
Portage *(G-13040)*		
Stryker Far East Inc	E	269 385-2600
Portage *(G-13044)*		
Superior Fixture & Tooling LLC	G	616 828-1566
Grand Rapids *(G-6903)*		
▲ Symbiote Inc	E	616 772-1790
Zeeland *(G-18189)*		
West Michigan Gage Inc	F	616 735-0585
Walker *(G-16882)*		
Wm Kloeffler Industries Inc	E	810 765-4068
Marine City *(G-10487)*		
Woodard—Cm LLC	G	989 725-4265
Owosso *(G-12331)*		

26 PAPER AND ALLIED PRODUCTS

2611 Pulp Mills

Anchor Recycling Inc	G	810 984-5545
Port Huron *(G-12891)*		
Bpv LLC	E	616 281-4502
Byron Center *(G-2180)*		
Custom Crushing & Recycle Inc	G	616 249-3329
Byron Center *(G-2185)*		
Fibrek Inc	C	906 864-9125
Menominee *(G-10733)*		
◆ Fibrek Recycling US Inc	C	906 863-8137
Menominee *(G-10734)*		
Fibrek US Inc	G	906 864-9125
Menominee *(G-10735)*		
Forest Blake Products Inc	G	231 879-3913
Fife Lake *(G-5340)*		
Forest Corullo Products Corp	E	906 667-0275
Bessemer *(G-1605)*		
Friedland Industries Inc	E	517 482-3000
Lansing *(G-9232)*		
General Mill Supply Company	E	248 668-0800
Wixom *(G-17816)*		
Gfl Environmental Real Property	E	888 877-4996
Southfield *(G-14919)*		
Gfl Environmental Real Property	G	586 774-1360
Warren *(G-17057)*		
Great Lakes Paper Stock Corp	D	586 779-1310
Roseville *(G-13811)*		
Infinity Recycling LLC	F	248 939-2563
Clinton Township *(G-3140)*		
Kevin Butzin Recycling Inc	G	734 587-3710
Willis *(G-17744)*		
Long Lake Forest Products	G	989 239-6527
Harrison *(G-7314)*		
Louis Padnos Iron and Metal Co	E	616 459-4208
Grand Rapids *(G-6631)*		
Midland Cmpnding Cnsulting Inc	E	989 495-9367
Midland *(G-10888)*		
Recycling Concepts W Mich Inc	D	616 942-8888
Grand Rapids *(G-6815)*		
Recycling Rizzo Services LLC	D	248 541-4020
Royal Oak *(G-13964)*		
Ricks Custom Cycle LLP	G	734 762-2077
Garden City *(G-5836)*		
Ronald Bradley	G	989 422-5609
Houghton Lake *(G-7996)*		
Southast Berrien Cnty Landfill	F	269 695-2500
Niles *(G-11646)*		
United Fr Survl St Joseph Recy	E	269 983-3820
Saint Joseph *(G-14347)*		
Upcycle Polymers LLC	G	248 446-8750
Howell *(G-8120)*		
V & M Corporation	E	248 541-4020
Royal Oak *(G-13980)*		
Verso Paper Holding LLC	F	906 779-3200
Quinnesec *(G-13104)*		

2621 Paper Mills

▲ Ace-Tex Enterprises Inc	E	313 834-4000
Detroit *(G-3839)*		
▲ American Twisting Company	E	269 637-8581
South Haven *(G-14752)*		
Anchor Bay Manufacturing Corp	G	586 949-4040
Chesterfield *(G-2737)*		
Cadillac Products Inc	D	989 766-2294
Rogers City *(G-13613)*		
Dh2 Inc	G	616 887-2700
Comstock Park *(G-3477)*		
Domtar Industries Inc	D	810 982-0191
Port Huron *(G-12912)*		
Dunn Paper Holdings Inc	G	810 984-5521
Port Huron *(G-12914)*		
E B Eddy Paper Inc	B	810 982-0191
Port Huron *(G-12915)*		
Eagle Ridge Paper Ltd	G	248 376-9503
Romulus *(G-13669)*		
Elegus Eps LLC	G	734 224-9900
Ann Arbor *(G-440)*		
◆ French Paper Company	D	269 683-1100
Niles *(G-11612)*		
Great Lakes Tissue Company	D	231 627-0200
Cheboygan *(G-2680)*		
◆ Handy Wacks Corporation	E	616 887-8268
Sparta *(G-15096)*		
International Paper Company	G	269 273-8461
Three Rivers *(G-15866)*		
Kimberly-Clark Corporation	C	586 949-1649
Macomb *(G-10135)*		
Kimberly-Clark Corporation	C	810 985-1830
Port Huron *(G-12934)*		
Kolossos Printing Inc	G	734 741-1600
Ann Arbor *(G-518)*		
▼ Menominee Acquisition Corp	C	906 863-5595
Menominee *(G-10745)*		
Neenah Paper Inc	B	906 387-2700
Munising *(G-11246)*		
Northstar Sourcing LLC	G	313 782-4749
Troy *(G-16527)*		
Otsego Paper Inc	E	269 692-6141
Otsego *(G-12247)*		
Package Design & Mfg Inc	E	248 486-4390
Brighton *(G-1972)*		
Pure Pulp Products Inc	G	269 385-5050
Kalamazoo *(G-8863)*		
Rizzo Packaging Inc	E	269 685-5808
Plainwell *(G-12542)*		
▼ Sanitor Mfg Co	F	269 327-3001
Portage *(G-13031)*		
▲ Thetford Corporation	C	734 769-6000
Ann Arbor *(G-670)*		
Verso Corporation	A	906 786-1660
Escanaba *(G-4865)*		
Verso Corporation	B	906 779-3371
Norway *(G-11821)*		
Verso Paper Holding LLC	F	906 779-3200
Quinnesec *(G-13104)*		
Verso Quinnesec LLC	G	877 447-2737
Quinnesec *(G-13106)*		
Verso Quinnesec Rep LLC	G	906 779-3200
Quinnesec *(G-13107)*		
Vision Solutions Inc	G	810 695-9569
Grand Blanc *(G-5987)*		

2631 Paperboard Mills

Aactus Inc	G	734 425-1212
Livonia *(G-9623)*		
Anchor Bay Packaging Corp	E	586 949-1500
Chesterfield *(G-2739)*		
Artistic Carton Company	D	269 483-7601
White Pigeon *(G-17644)*		
Campbell Industrial Force LLC	E	989 427-0011
Edmore *(G-4749)*		
Cascade Paper Converters LLC	F	616 974-9165
Grand Rapids *(G-6263)*		
Classic Container Corporation	E	734 853-3000
Livonia *(G-9684)*		
Coveris	E	269 964-1130
Battle Creek *(G-1169)*		
Display Pack Disc Inc	G	616 451-3061
Cedar Springs *(G-2554)*		
Display Pack Disc Vdh Inc	G	616 451-3061
Cedar Springs *(G-2555)*		
Fibre Converters Inc	E	269 279-1700
Constantine *(G-3535)*		
Graphic Packaging Intl LLC	D	269 383-5000
Kalamazoo *(G-8754)*		

26 PAPER AND ALLIED PRODUCTS

Graphic Packaging Intl LLC .... B 269 343-6104
  Kalamazoo *(G-8755)*
Graphic Packaging Intl LLC .... C 269 963-6135
  Battle Creek *(G-1195)*
Handy Wacks Corporation .... E 616 887-8268
  Sparta *(G-15097)*
Highland Supply Inc .... F 248 714-8355
  Highland *(G-7494)*
▲ IBC North America Inc .... E 248 625-8700
  Clarkston *(G-2929)*
IBC North America Inc .... F 248 625-8700
  Clarkston *(G-2930)*
▲ Kentwood Packaging Corporation ... D 616 698-9000
  Walker *(G-16869)*
Lotis Technologies Inc .... G 248 340-6065
  Orion *(G-12182)*
Lydall Performance Mtls US Inc .... G 248 596-2800
  Northville *(G-11705)*
M & J Entp Grnd Rapids LLC .... F 616 485-9775
  Comstock Park *(G-3494)*
M-Industries LLC .... F 616 682-4642
  Ada *(G-22)*
MRC Industries Inc .... D 269 343-0747
  Kalamazoo *(G-8832)*
Ox Paperboard Michigan LLC .... D 800 345-8881
  Constantine *(G-3543)*
▲ Packaging Specialties Inc .... E 586 473-6703
  Romulus *(G-13718)*
Rizzo Packaging Inc .... E 269 685-5808
  Plainwell *(G-12542)*
Sonoco Products Company .... D 269 408-0182
  Saint Joseph *(G-14339)*
South Park Sales & Mfg Inc .... G 313 381-7579
  Dearborn *(G-3762)*
◆ Spartan Paperboard Company Inc ... F 269 381-0192
  Kalamazoo *(G-8896)*
Trim Pac Inc .... G 269 279-9498
  Three Rivers *(G-15881)*
Utility Supply and Cnstr Co .... G 231 832-2297
  Reed City *(G-13225)*

2652 Set-Up Paperboard Boxes

Chelsea Milling Company .... F 269 781-2823
  Marshall *(G-10564)*
▼ Michigan Box Company .... D 313 873-9500
  Detroit *(G-4237)*
▲ Packaging Specialties Inc .... E 586 473-6703
  Romulus *(G-13718)*

2653 Corrugated & Solid Fiber Boxes

Action Packaging LLC .... E 616 871-5200
  Caledonia *(G-2287)*
▲ Advance Packaging Acquisition .... D 616 949-6610
  Grand Rapids *(G-6146)*
Advance Packaging Corporation .... C 616 949-6610
  Grand Rapids *(G-6147)*
Advance Packaging Corporation .... D 616 949-6610
  Jackson *(G-8372)*
Aero Box Company .... G 586 415-0000
  Roseville *(G-13769)*
Aldez North America LLC .... G 810 577-3891
  Almont *(G-251)*
All Packaging Solutions Inc .... G 248 880-1548
  Madison Heights *(G-10187)*
Alma Container Corporation .... F 989 463-2106
  Alma *(G-233)*
▲ Anchor Bay Packaging Corp .... E 586 949-4040
  Chesterfield *(G-2738)*
Anchor Bay Packaging Corp .... E 586 949-1500
  Chesterfield *(G-2739)*
Armstrong Display Concepts .... F 231 652-1675
  Newaygo *(G-11563)*
▲ Arvco Container Corporation .... E 269 381-0900
  Kalamazoo *(G-8685)*
Arvco Container Corporation .... C 269 381-0900
  Kalamazoo *(G-8686)*
Arvco Container Corporation .... E 269 381-0900
  Kalamazoo *(G-8687)*
Arvco Container Corporation .... F 231 876-0935
  Cadillac *(G-2228)*
▲ Bay Corrugated Container Inc .... C 734 243-5400
  Monroe *(G-11020)*
Blossomland Container Corp .... F 269 926-8206
  Benton Harbor *(G-1487)*
▲ Bradford Company .... C 616 399-3000
  Holland *(G-7575)*
Bramco Containers Inc .... G 906 428-2855
  Gladstone *(G-5907)*
C/W South Inc .... E 810 767-2806
  Burton *(G-2148)*
Caraustar Cstm Packg Group Inc .... E 616 247-5100
  Grand Rapids *(G-6255)*
Classic Container Corporation .... E 734 853-3000
  Livonia *(G-9684)*
Coastal Container Corporation .... D 616 355-9800
  Holland *(G-7593)*
Compak Inc .... G 810 767-2806
  Burton *(G-2151)*
Compak Inc .... G 989 288-3199
  Burton *(G-2152)*
Complete Packaging Inc .... E 734 241-2794
  Monroe *(G-11025)*
Corr Pack In .... G 248 348-4188
  Northville *(G-11684)*
Corrugated Options LLC .... G 734 850-1300
  Temperance *(G-15825)*
Corrugated Pratt .... G 734 853-3030
  Livonia *(G-9690)*
D T Fowler Mfg Co Inc .... G 810 245-9336
  Lapeer *(G-9454)*
▲ Delta Containers Inc .... E 810 742-2730
  Bay City *(G-1299)*
Delta Containers Inc .... E 810 742-2730
  Bay City *(G-1300)*
Dewitt Packaging Corporation .... E 616 698-0210
  Grand Rapids *(G-6347)*
Eco Paper .... G 248 652-3601
  Rochester Hills *(G-13415)*
Flint Boxmakers Inc .... E 810 743-0400
  Burton *(G-2154)*
General Wood Products Co .... F 248 221-0214
  Big Rapids *(G-1630)*
▲ Genesee Group Inc .... E 810 235-8041
  Flint *(G-5439)*
Genesee Group Inc .... D 810 235-6120
  Flint *(G-5440)*
Georgia-Pacific LLC .... D 734 439-2441
  Milan *(G-10938)*
Georgia-Pacific LLC .... C 989 725-5191
  Owosso *(G-12293)*
Grand Traverse Reels Inc .... E 231 946-1057
  Traverse City *(G-15987)*
Great Lakes-Triad Plastic .... D 616 241-6441
  Grand Rapids *(G-6480)*
Green Bay Packaging Inc .... G 269 552-1000
  Kalamazoo *(G-8757)*
Industrial Packaging Corp .... F 248 677-0084
  Berkley *(G-1584)*
Inter-Pack Corporation .... E 734 242-7755
  Monroe *(G-11042)*
Jet Box Co Inc .... F 248 362-1260
  Troy *(G-16437)*
Jetco Packaging Solutions LLC .... G 616 588-2492
  Grand Rapids *(G-6559)*
▲ Kentwood Packaging Corporation ... D 616 698-9000
  Walker *(G-16869)*
Kraft-Wrap Inc .... F 586 755-2050
  Warren *(G-17121)*
▲ Lepages 2000 Inc .... G 416 357-0041
  Romulus *(G-13700)*
Loope Enterprises Inc .... F 269 639-1567
  South Haven *(G-14763)*
Mall City Containers Inc .... E 269 381-2706
  Kalamazoo *(G-8817)*
Mall City Containers Inc .... G 616 249-3657
  Grand Rapids *(G-6641)*
Menasha Packaging Company LLC ... F 800 253-1526
  Coloma *(G-3361)*
Michcor Container Inc .... E 616 452-7089
  Grand Rapids *(G-6666)*
Michiana Corrugated Pdts Co .... E 269 651-5225
  Sturgis *(G-15617)*
▼ Michigan Box Company .... D 313 873-9500
  Detroit *(G-4237)*
▲ Michigan Packaging Company .... D 517 676-8700
  Mason *(G-10646)*
Monte Package Company LLC .... E 269 849-1722
  Riverside *(G-13285)*
MRC Industries Inc .... D 269 343-0747
  Kalamazoo *(G-8832)*
National Packaging Corporation .... F 248 652-3600
  Rochester Hills *(G-13479)*
Packaging Corporation America .... C 616 530-5700
  Grandville *(G-7062)*
Packaging Corporation America .... D 734 453-6262
  Plymouth *(G-12706)*
Packaging Corporation America .... E 734 266-1877
  Livonia *(G-9881)*
Packaging Corporation America .... B 231 723-1442
  Filer City *(G-5345)*
Packaging Corporation America .... G 231 947-2220
  Edmore *(G-4753)*
Packaging Corporation America .... D 989 427-5129
  Edmore *(G-4754)*
▲ Packaging Specialties Inc .... E 586 473-6703
  Romulus *(G-13718)*
Patriot Solutions LLC .... G 616 240-8164
  Grand Rapids *(G-6744)*
Phoenix Packaging Corporation .... E 734 944-3916
  Saline *(G-14407)*
Pratt Industries Inc .... C 616 452-2111
  Grand Rapids *(G-6760)*
Pratt Industries Inc .... G 734 853-3000
  Livonia *(G-9895)*
Premier Corrugated Inc .... E 517 629-5700
  Albion *(G-129)*
Recycled Paperboard Pdts Corp .... G 313 579-6608
  Detroit *(G-4334)*
Roberts Movable Walls Inc .... G 269 626-0227
  Scotts *(G-14506)*
Royal Container Inc .... E 248 967-0910
  Oak Park *(G-12094)*
Russell R Peters Co LLC .... G 989 732-0660
  Gaylord *(G-5891)*
Scotts Enterprises Inc .... E 989 275-5011
  Roscommon *(G-13754)*
Shipping Container Corporation .... E 313 937-2411
  Redford *(G-13191)*
Shoreline Container Inc .... C 616 399-2088
  Holland *(G-7800)*
South Haven Packaging Inc .... F 269 639-1567
  South Haven *(G-14773)*
▲ St Clair Packaging Inc .... E 810 364-4230
  Marysville *(G-10619)*
Tecumseh Packg Solutions Inc .... E 517 423-2126
  Tecumseh *(G-15811)*
Understated Corrugated LLC .... G 248 880-5767
  Northville *(G-11733)*
Universal Container Corp .... E 248 543-2788
  Ferndale *(G-5326)*
▲ Webcor Packaging Corporation .... D 810 767-2806
  Burton *(G-2170)*
Westrock Company .... E 734 453-6700
  Plymouth *(G-12793)*
Westrock Cp LLC .... F 810 787-6503
  Flint *(G-5522)*
Westrock Rkt LLC .... C 269 963-5511
  Battle Creek *(G-1267)*
World Corrugated Container Inc .... E 517 629-9400
  Albion *(G-136)*
Wrkco Inc .... E 269 964-7181
  Battle Creek *(G-1268)*
Zoomer Display LLC .... G 616 734-0300
  Grand Rapids *(G-7014)*

2655 Fiber Cans, Tubes & Drums

Action Packaging LLC .... E 616 871-5200
  Caledonia *(G-2287)*
Caraustar Industries Inc .... E 989 793-4820
  Saginaw *(G-14009)*
Cascade Paper Converters LLC .... F 616 974-9165
  Grand Rapids *(G-6263)*
E & M Cores Inc .... G 989 386-9223
  Clare *(G-2869)*
Eteron Inc .... E 248 478-2900
  Farmington Hills *(G-4991)*
Goodpack .... G 248 458-0041
  Troy *(G-16385)*
Greif Inc .... E 586 415-0000
  Roseville *(G-13812)*
Kraft-Wrap Inc .... F 586 755-2050
  Warren *(G-17121)*
▲ Mauser .... G 248 795-2330
  Clarkston *(G-2936)*
▲ Nagel Paper Inc .... E 989 753-4405
  Swartz Creek *(G-15669)*
Plasan Us Inc .... F 616 559-0032
  Walker *(G-16876)*
Quanta Containers LLC .... G 734 282-3044
  Taylor *(G-15760)*
Rokan Corp .... G 810 735-9170
  Linden *(G-9595)*
Russell R Peters Co LLC .... G 989 732-0660
  Gaylord *(G-5891)*
Star Paper Converters Inc .... F 313 963-5200
  Detroit *(G-4375)*
Technova Corporation .... F 517 485-1402
  Okemos *(G-12138)*
Xpress Packaging Solutions LLC .... G 231 629-0463
  Shelby Township *(G-14724)*

2656 Sanitary Food Containers

Acumedia Manufacturers Inc ......E 517 372-9200
Lansing *(G-9332)*
▲ AJM Packaging Corporation ......D 248 901-0040
Bloomfield Hills *(G-1743)*
AJM Packaging Corporation ......C 313 842-7530
Detroit *(G-3851)*
▲ Dart Container Michigan LLC ......E 800 248-5960
Mason *(G-10634)*
Dart Container Michigan LLC ......E 517 694-9455
Holt *(G-7909)*
Huhtamaki Inc ......B 989 633-8900
Coleman *(G-3346)*
◆ Letica Corporation ......C 248 652-0557
Rochester Hills *(G-13460)*
▼ Scic LLC ......E 800 248-5960
Mason *(G-10655)*
◆ SF Holdings Group Inc ......D 800 248-5960
Mason *(G-10656)*
▲ Solo Cup Company LLC ......C 800 248-5960
Mason *(G-10657)*
▼ Solo Cup Operating Corporation ......D 800 248-5960
Mason *(G-10658)*

2657 Folding Paperboard Boxes

Americraft Carton Inc ......D 269 651-2365
Sturgis *(G-15596)*
Caraustar Cstm Packg Group Inc ......E 616 247-0330
Grand Rapids *(G-6255)*
Complete Packaging Inc ......E 734 241-2794
Monroe *(G-11025)*
Graphic Packaging Intl LLC ......D 269 969-7446
Battle Creek *(G-1194)*
Michigan Carton Paper Boy ......G 269 963-4004
Battle Creek *(G-1228)*
▲ Packaging Specialties Inc ......E 586 473-6703
Romulus *(G-13718)*
Rapid-Packaging Corporation ......E 616 949-0950
Grand Rapids *(G-6811)*
S & C Industries Inc ......F 269 381-6022
Kalamazoo *(G-8880)*
Steketee-Van Huis Inc ......C 616 392-2326
Holland *(G-7814)*
Wrkco Inc ......E 269 964-7181
Battle Creek *(G-1268)*
▲ Wynalda Litho Inc ......C 616 866-1561
Belmont *(G-1476)*

2671 Paper Coating & Laminating for Packaging

Advance Engineering Company ......E 989 435-3641
Beaverton *(G-1382)*
Allsales Enterprises Inc ......F 616 437-0639
Grand Rapids *(G-6164)*
Alpha Data Business Forms Inc ......G 248 540-5930
Birmingham *(G-1674)*
American Label & Tag Inc ......E 734 454-7600
Canton *(G-2347)*
Anchor Bay Packaging Corp ......E 586 949-1500
Chesterfield *(G-2739)*
Andex Industries Inc ......D 800 338-9882
Escanaba *(G-4811)*
Andex Industries Inc ......E 906 786-7588
Escanaba *(G-4812)*
Argent Tape & Label Inc ......F 734 582-9956
Plymouth *(G-12573)*
CAM Packaging LLC ......F 989 426-1200
Gladwin *(G-5925)*
Cello-Foil Products Inc ......C 229 435-4777
Battle Creek *(G-1164)*
Central Ohio Paper & Packg Inc ......G 734 955-9960
Romulus *(G-13662)*
Cherokee Industries Inc ......G 248 333-1343
Pontiac *(G-12808)*
Classic Container Corporation ......E 734 853-3000
Livonia *(G-9684)*
Creative Foam Corporation ......D 810 714-0140
Fenton *(G-5199)*
Cummins Label Company ......E 269 345-3386
Kalamazoo *(G-8721)*
▲ Delta Containers Inc ......C 810 742-2730
Bay City *(G-1299)*
◆ Dunn Paper Inc ......F 810 984-5521
Port Huron *(G-12913)*
▲ Fabricon Products Inc ......F 313 841-8200
River Rouge *(G-13276)*
Fibre Converters Inc ......E 269 279-1700
Constantine *(G-3535)*
▲ Filcon Inc ......F 989 386-2986
Clare *(G-2870)*
General Tape Label Liquidating ......D 248 437-5200
Wixom *(G-17817)*
▲ Holo-Source Corporation ......G 734 427-1530
Livonia *(G-9773)*
Impact Label Corporation ......D 269 381-4280
Galesburg *(G-5811)*
International Master Pdts Corp ......C 231 894-5651
Montague *(G-11091)*
J W Manchester Company Inc ......G 810 632-5409
Hartland *(G-7393)*
Jetco Packaging Solutions LLC ......G 616 588-2492
Grand Rapids *(G-6559)*
Loper Corporation ......G 810 620-0202
Mount Morris *(G-11164)*
Macarthur Corp ......E 810 606-1777
Grand Blanc *(G-5975)*
◆ MPS Lansing Inc ......A 517 323-9000
Lansing *(G-9248)*
▲ Noble Films Corporation ......G 616 977-3770
Ada *(G-25)*
Nyx Inc ......B 734 261-7535
Livonia *(G-9870)*
▲ Nyx LLC ......C 734 462-2385
Livonia *(G-9871)*
▲ Packaging Specialties Inc ......E 586 473-6703
Romulus *(G-13718)*
Quality Transparent Bag Inc ......F 989 893-3561
Bay City *(G-1344)*
Shawmut Corporation ......C 810 987-2222
Port Huron *(G-12965)*
Shoreline Container Inc ......C 616 399-2088
Holland *(G-7800)*
Siliconature Corporation ......E 312 987-1848
Caledonia *(G-2315)*
Smartstart Medical LLC ......G 616 227-4560
Grand Rapids *(G-6869)*
Stamp-Rite Incorporated ......E 517 487-5071
Lansing *(G-9267)*
▲ Stewart Sutherland Inc ......C 269 649-0530
Vicksburg *(G-16844)*
Svrc Industries Inc ......D 989 723-8205
Owosso *(G-12320)*
Tesa Tape Inc ......G 616 785-6970
Grand Rapids *(G-6924)*
Tesa Tape Inc ......D 616 887-3107
Sparta *(G-15116)*
Timbertech Inc ......E 231 348-2750
Harbor Springs *(G-7295)*
Tryco Inc ......F 734 953-6800
Farmington Hills *(G-5144)*
Ufp Technologies Inc ......D 616 949-8100
Grand Rapids *(G-6948)*
Unique Fabricating Inc ......E 248 853-2333
Auburn Hills *(G-1034)*
▲ Unique Fabricating Na Inc ......B 248 853-2333
Auburn Hills *(G-1035)*
Venchurs Inc ......E 517 263-1206
Adrian *(G-99)*
Venchurs Inc ......F 517 263-8937
Adrian *(G-100)*
Verso Paper Holding LLC ......F 906 779-3200
Quinnesec *(G-13104)*
Verso Paper Holding LLC ......B 906 396-2358
Quinnesec *(G-13105)*
Watson Sales ......G 517 296-4275
Montgomery *(G-11100)*
Zajac Industries Inc ......F 586 489-6746
Clinton Township *(G-3264)*

2672 Paper Coating & Laminating, Exc for Packaging

Alpha Data Business Forms Inc ......G 248 540-5930
Birmingham *(G-1674)*
American Label & Tag Inc ......E 734 454-7600
Canton *(G-2347)*
Argent Tape & Label Inc ......F 734 582-9956
Plymouth *(G-12573)*
▲ Celia Corporation ......G 616 887-7387
Sparta *(G-15090)*
Celia Corporation ......D 616 887-7341
Sparta *(G-15091)*
Cummins Label Company ......E 269 345-3386
Kalamazoo *(G-8721)*
Cytec Industries Inc ......C 269 349-6677
Kalamazoo *(G-8722)*
◆ Dunn Paper Inc ......F 810 984-5521
Port Huron *(G-12913)*
Dunn Paper Holdings Inc ......G 810 984-5521
Port Huron *(G-12914)*
▲ Elliott Tape Inc ......E 248 475-2000
Auburn Hills *(G-854)*
Fedex Office & Print Svcs Inc ......E 616 336-1900
Grand Rapids *(G-6404)*
Fedex Office & Print Svcs Inc ......F 313 359-3124
Dearborn *(G-3705)*
Flamingo Label Co ......F 586 469-9587
Clinton Township *(G-3121)*
Impact Label Corporation ......D 269 381-4280
Galesburg *(G-5811)*
Independent Die Cutting Inc ......F 616 452-3197
Grand Rapids *(G-6532)*
Intertape Polymer Corp ......C 810 364-9000
Marysville *(G-10604)*
Kent Manufacturing Company ......D 616 454-9495
Grand Rapids *(G-6577)*
▲ Laminin Medical Products Inc ......E 616 871-3390
Grand Rapids *(G-6616)*
Lawson Printers Inc ......E 269 965-0525
Battle Creek *(G-1222)*
▲ Lepages 2000 Inc ......G 416 357-0041
Romulus *(G-13700)*
Litsenberger Print Shop ......G 906 482-3903
Houghton *(G-7976)*
◆ Lowry Holding Company Inc ......C 810 229-7200
Brighton *(G-1952)*
Macarthur Corp ......E 810 606-1777
Grand Blanc *(G-5975)*
McCray Press ......E 989 792-8681
Saginaw *(G-14084)*
Mead Westvaco Paper Div ......G 906 233-2362
Escanaba *(G-4841)*
Michigan Shippers Supply Inc ......F 616 935-6680
Spring Lake *(G-15163)*
Michigan Tape Inc ......G 734 582-9800
Plymouth *(G-12692)*
▲ Oliver Packaging and Eqp Co ......D 616 356-2950
Walker *(G-16872)*
Plasti-Fab Inc ......E 248 543-1415
Ferndale *(G-5311)*
Qrp Inc ......G 989 496-2955
Midland *(G-10905)*
Ron Rowe ......G 231 652-2642
Newaygo *(G-11577)*
Shawmut Corporation ......C 810 987-2222
Port Huron *(G-12965)*
▲ Stewart Sutherland Inc ......C 269 649-0530
Vicksburg *(G-16844)*
Technology MGT & Budgt Dept ......D 517 322-1897
Lansing *(G-9430)*
Tesa Tape Inc ......G 616 785-6970
Grand Rapids *(G-6924)*
Tesa Tape Inc ......D 616 887-3107
Sparta *(G-15116)*
◆ Trimas Corporation ......E 248 631-5450
Bloomfield Hills *(G-1807)*
Witchcraft Tape Products Inc ......D 269 468-3399
Coloma *(G-3368)*
▲ Yamato International Corp ......E 734 675-6055
Woodhaven *(G-17942)*

2673 Bags: Plastics, Laminated & Coated

A-Pac Manufacturing Company ......E 616 791-7222
Grand Rapids *(G-6126)*
Bear Packaging and Supply ......G 989 772-2268
Mount Pleasant *(G-11177)*
Bioplstic Plymers Cmpsites LLC ......G 517 349-2970
Okemos *(G-12117)*
Cadillac Products Inc ......D 586 774-1700
Roseville *(G-13779)*
▲ Cadillac Products Inc ......B 248 813-8200
Troy *(G-16253)*
Cadillac Products Inc ......D 989 766-2294
Rogers City *(G-13613)*
Carroll Products Inc ......E 586 254-6300
Sterling Heights *(G-15282)*
Coveris ......E 269 964-1130
Battle Creek *(G-1169)*
D&Js Plastics LLC ......G 616 745-5798
Hudsonville *(G-8154)*
▲ Idea Mia LLC ......G 248 891-8939
Lathrup Village *(G-9500)*
Lbv Sales LLC ......G 616 874-9390
Belmont *(G-1465)*
Michigan Poly Supplies Inc ......G 734 282-5554
Taylor *(G-15743)*
Olivo LLC ......G 313 573-7202
Lincoln Park *(G-9582)*

SIC

26 PAPER AND ALLIED PRODUCTS

P-S Business Acquisition Inc ....E.... 616 887-8837
  Sparta *(G-15104)*
Packaging Personified Inc ....C.... 616 887-8837
  Sparta *(G-15105)*
▲ Plasport Inc ....G.... 231 935-1580
  Traverse City *(G-16073)*
Quality Transparent Bag Inc ....F.... 989 893-3561
  Bay City *(G-1344)*
Superior Polyolefin Films Inc ....G.... 248 334-8074
  Bloomfield Hills *(G-1800)*
Transcontinental US LLC ....D.... 269 964-7137
  Battle Creek *(G-1259)*

2674 Bags: Uncoated Paper & Multiwall

Acme Mills Company ....C.... 517 437-8940
  Hillsdale *(G-7513)*
AJM Packaging Corporation ....E.... 313 291-6500
  Taylor *(G-15685)*
▲ AJM Packaging Corporation ....D.... 248 901-0040
  Bloomfield Hills *(G-1743)*
AJM Packaging Corporation ....C.... 313 842-7530
  Detroit *(G-3851)*
Concorde Inc ....F.... 248 391-8177
  Auburn Hills *(G-817)*
Lisa Bain ....G.... 313 389-9661
  Allen Park *(G-200)*
McKenna Enterprises Inc ....E.... 248 375-3388
  Rochester Hills *(G-13470)*
Olivo LLC ....G.... 313 573-7202
  Lincoln Park *(G-9582)*
Pak-Rite Industries Inc ....D.... 313 388-6400
  Ecorse *(G-4744)*
▲ Stewart Sutherland Inc ....C.... 269 649-0530
  Vicksburg *(G-16844)*

2675 Die-Cut Paper & Board

▲ Accu-Shape Die Cutting Inc ....E.... 810 230-2445
  Flint *(G-5368)*
▲ Bradford Company ....C.... 616 399-3000
  Holland *(G-7575)*
▲ Cadillac Prsentation Solutions ......E.... 248 288-9777
  Troy *(G-16255)*
Celia Corporation ....D.... 616 887-7341
  Sparta *(G-15091)*
Classic Container Corporation ....E.... 734 853-3000
  Livonia *(G-9684)*
▲ Delta Containers Inc ....C.... 810 742-2730
  Bay City *(G-1299)*
Design Converting Inc ....F.... 616 942-7780
  Grand Rapids *(G-6344)*
Diecutting Service Inc ....F.... 734 426-0290
  Dexter *(G-4489)*
Edgewater Apartments ....G.... 517 663-8123
  Eaton Rapids *(G-4722)*
Graphic Specialties Inc ....E.... 616 247-0060
  Grand Rapids *(G-6475)*
Hamblin Company ....E.... 517 423-7491
  Tecumseh *(G-15796)*
Hexon Corporation ....F.... 248 585-7585
  Farmington Hills *(G-5018)*
Industrial Imprntng & Die Ctng ....G.... 586 778-9470
  Eastpointe *(G-4704)*
▲ Jacobsen Industries Inc ....D.... 734 591-6111
  Livonia *(G-9791)*
Macarthur Corp ....E.... 810 606-1777
  Grand Blanc *(G-5975)*
Michigan Paper Die Inc ....F.... 313 873-0404
  Detroit *(G-4242)*
Nu-Fold Inc ....F.... 313 898-4695
  Detroit *(G-4279)*
▲ Oliver Packaging and Eqp Co ......D.... 616 356-2950
  Walker *(G-16872)*
Rizzo Packaging Inc ....E.... 269 685-5808
  Plainwell *(G-12542)*
Russell R Peters Co LLC ....G.... 989 732-0660
  Gaylord *(G-5891)*
Schultz Bindery Inc ....F.... 586 771-0777
  Warren *(G-17233)*
Trim Pac Inc ....G.... 269 279-9498
  Three Rivers *(G-15881)*

2676 Sanitary Paper Prdts

AJM Packaging Corporation ....C.... 313 842-7530
  Detroit *(G-3851)*
Chambers Ottawa Inc ....G.... 231 238-2122
  Cheboygan *(G-2676)*
Gadget Locker LLC ....G.... 702 901-1440
  Detroit *(G-4075)*
Happy Bums ....G.... 616 987-3159
  Lowell *(G-10030)*

Integrated Cmnty Commerce LLC ....G.... 313 220-2253
  Detroit *(G-14142)*
Kimberly-Clark Corporation ....C.... 586 949-1649
  Macomb *(G-10135)*
Kimberly-Clark Corporation ....G.... 810 985-1830
  Port Huron *(G-12934)*
Michigan Poly Supplies Inc ....G.... 734 282-5554
  Taylor *(G-15743)*
▲ Universal Product Mktg LLC ....G.... 248 585-9959
  Grosse Pointe Park *(G-7197)*

2677 Envelopes

F M Envelope Inc ....E.... 313 899-4065
  Detroit *(G-4048)*
Husky Envelope Products Inc ....D.... 248 624-7070
  Walled Lake *(G-16895)*
Michigan Envelope Inc ....G.... 616 554-3404
  Grand Rapids *(G-6670)*
The Envelope Printery Inc ....D.... 734 398-7700
  Van Buren Twp *(G-16787)*

2678 Stationery Prdts

Edward and Cole Inc ....G.... 734 996-9074
  Ann Arbor *(G-434)*
Presscraft Papers Inc ....E.... 231 882-5505
  Benzonia *(G-1576)*
Scientific Notebook Company ....F.... 269 429-8285
  Stevensville *(G-15580)*

2679 Converted Paper Prdts, NEC

AJM Packaging Corporation ....E.... 313 291-6500
  Taylor *(G-15685)*
Allegiance Packaging LLC ....G.... 586 846-2453
  Clinton Township *(G-3042)*
Amaris International LLC ....G.... 248 427-0472
  Novi *(G-11824)*
Artex Label & Graphics Inc ....E.... 616 748-9655
  Zeeland *(G-18112)*
B & B Entps Prtg Cnvrting Inc ....G.... 313 891-9840
  Detroit *(G-3890)*
Dedicated Converting Group Inc ......F.... 269 685-8430
  Plainwell *(G-12523)*
Delta Containers Inc ....E.... 810 742-2730
  Bay City *(G-1300)*
Everest Manufacturing Inc ....F.... 313 401-2608
  Farmington Hills *(G-4993)*
Fibers of Kalamazoo Inc ....E.... 269 344-3122
  Kalamazoo *(G-8743)*
▲ Fineeye Color Solutions Inc ....G.... 616 988-6119
  Muskegon *(G-11322)*
Macarthur Corp ....E.... 810 606-1777
  Grand Blanc *(G-5975)*
Manchester Industries Inc VA ....E.... 269 496-2715
  Mendon *(G-10716)*
Middleton Printing Inc ....G.... 616 247-8742
  Grand Rapids *(G-6684)*
Pressed Paperboard Tech LLC ....D.... 248 646-6500
  Bingham Farms *(G-1658)*
Progressive Paper Corp ....G.... 269 279-6320
  Three Rivers *(G-15875)*
Richman Company Products Inc ......G.... 989 686-6251
  Bay City *(G-1350)*
◆ Shepherd Speciality Papers Inc ....G.... 269 629-8001
  Richland *(G-13255)*
▼ Sks Industries Inc ....F.... 517 546-1117
  Howell *(G-8098)*
Str Company ....E.... 517 206-6058
  Grass Lake *(G-7094)*
Trim Pac Inc ....G.... 269 279-9498
  Three Rivers *(G-15881)*
Tru Blu Industries LLC ....G.... 269 684-4989
  Niles *(G-11650)*
Venture Label Inc ....G.... 313 928-2545
  Detroit *(G-4424)*
Venture Labels USA Inc ....G.... 313 928-2545
  Lincoln Park *(G-9587)*
Walters Seed Co LLC ....F.... 616 355-7333
  Holland *(G-7852)*
Watson Sales ....G.... 517 296-4275
  Montgomery *(G-11100)*
Whisper Creative Products Inc ....G.... 734 529-2734
  Dundee *(G-4603)*

27 PRINTING, PUBLISHING, AND ALLIED INDUSTRIES

2711 Newspapers: Publishing & Printing

21st Century Newspapers Inc ....C.... 586 469-4510
  Clinton Township *(G-3026)*
21st Century Newspapers Inc ....D.... 810 664-0811
  Lapeer *(G-9439)*
21st Century Newspapers Inc ....D.... 586 469-4510
  Pontiac *(G-12797)*
A B Rusgo Inc ....G.... 586 296-7714
  Fraser *(G-5610)*
Action Ad Newspapers Inc ....G.... 734 740-6966
  Belleville *(G-1439)*
Adrian Team LLC ....G.... 517 264-6148
  Adrian *(G-47)*
Advance BCI Inc ....D.... 616 669-1366
  Grand Rapids *(G-6144)*
Advance BCI Inc ....D.... 616 669-5210
  Grand Rapids *(G-6145)*
Alcona County Review ....G.... 989 724-6384
  Harrisville *(G-7361)*
Algo Especial Variety Str Inc ....G.... 313 963-9013
  Detroit *(G-3854)*
Angler Strategies LLC ....G.... 248 439-1420
  Royal Oak *(G-13902)*
Ann Arbor Chronicle ....G.... 734 645-2633
  Ann Arbor *(G-356)*
Ann Arbor Journal ....G.... 734 429-7380
  Saline *(G-14376)*
Ann Arbor Observer Company ....E.... 734 769-3175
  Ann Arbor *(G-358)*
Anteebo Publishers Inc ....E.... 313 882-6900
  Grosse Pointe Park *(G-7190)*
Arab American News Inc ....G.... 313 582-4888
  Dearborn *(G-3678)*
Argus Press Company ....D.... 989 725-5136
  Owosso *(G-12280)*
Associated Newspapers Michigan ....G.... 734 467-1900
  Wayne *(G-17424)*
Belleville Area Independent ....G.... 734 699-9020
  Belleville *(G-1441)*
Benson Distribution Inc ....G.... 269 344-5529
  Kalamazoo *(G-8696)*
Billie Times Ltd ....G.... 248 813-9114
  Troy *(G-16240)*
Board For Student Publications ....B.... 734 418-4115
  Ann Arbor *(G-385)*
Booth Newspaper ....G.... 517 487-8888
  Lansing *(G-9348)*
Boyne City Gazette ....G.... 231 582-2799
  Boyne City *(G-1817)*
Brown City Banner Inc ....G.... 810 346-2753
  Brown City *(G-2047)*
Budget Europe Travel Service ....G.... 734 668-0529
  Ann Arbor *(G-391)*
Bulletin Moon ....G.... 734 453-9985
  Plymouth *(G-12592)*
Bulletin of Concerned Asi ....G.... 231 228-7116
  Cedar *(G-2539)*
Business News ....G.... 231 929-7919
  Traverse City *(G-15925)*
Business News Publishing ....B.... 248 362-3700
  Troy *(G-16248)*
Buyers Guide ....F.... 616 897-9261
  Lowell *(G-10025)*
C & G News Inc ....D.... 586 498-8000
  Warren *(G-16970)*
C & G Publishing Inc ....D.... 586 498-8000
  Warren *(G-16971)*
Calcomco Inc ....G.... 313 885-9228
  Kalamazoo *(G-8703)*
Calhoun Communications Inc ....F.... 517 629-0041
  Albion *(G-116)*
Campub Inc ....F.... 517 368-0365
  Camden *(G-2338)*
Cass City Chronicle Inc ....G.... 989 872-2010
  Cass City *(G-2512)*
Cedar Springs Post Inc ....G.... 616 696-3655
  Cedar Springs *(G-2547)*
Central Michigan University ....G.... 989 774-3493
  Mount Pleasant *(G-11186)*
Chaldean News LLC ....F.... 248 996-8360
  Bingham Farms *(G-1650)*
Chris Faulknor ....G.... 231 645-1970
  Boyne City *(G-1819)*
City of Greenville ....E.... 616 754-0100
  Greenville *(G-7124)*

27 PRINTING, PUBLISHING, AND ALLIED INDUSTRIES

Clare County Cleaver Inc .... G 989 539-7496
Harrison *(G-7310)*
Clare County Review .... G 989 386-4414
Clare *(G-2866)*
Cmu .... F 989 774-7143
Mount Pleasant *(G-11189)*
Community Marketing Group LLC ..... G 810 966-9982
Port Huron *(G-12909)*
Community Shoppers Guide Inc .... G 269 694-9431
Otsego *(G-12235)*
Conine Publishing Company .... G 231 832-5566
Reed City *(G-13212)*
Conine Publishing Inc .... E 231 723-3592
Manistee *(G-10418)*
Conine Publishing Inc .... G 231 352-9659
Frankfort *(G-5600)*
Coopersville Observer Inc .... G 616 997-5049
Coopersville *(G-3554)*
County Journal Inc .... F 517 543-1099
Charlotte *(G-2643)*
County Press .... G 517 531-4542
Parma *(G-12389)*
Crain Communications Inc .... B 313 446-6000
Detroit *(G-3950)*
Crain Communications Inc .... B 313 446-6000
Detroit *(G-3951)*
Crawford County Avalanche .... G 989 348-6811
Grayling *(G-7104)*
Current .... G 906 563-5212
Norway *(G-11816)*
Daily Bill .... G 989 631-2068
Midland *(G-10828)*
Daily Brews Gourmet Coffe .... G 269 792-2739
Wayland *(G-17403)*
Daily Contracts LLC .... G 734 676-0903
Grosse Ile *(G-7169)*
Daily De-Lish .... G 616 450-9562
Ada *(G-12)*
Daily Fantasy King .... G 734 238-2622
Southgate *(G-15076)*
Daily Gardener LLC .... G 734 754-6527
Ann Arbor *(G-411)*
Daily Oakland Press .... B 248 332-8181
Pontiac *(G-12813)*
Daily Recycling of Michigan .... G 734 654-9800
Carleton *(G-2453)*
Daily Reporter .... E 517 278-2318
Coldwater *(G-3300)*
Daughtry Nwspapers Investments .... F 269 683-2100
Niles *(G-11606)*
Deadline Detroit .... G 248 219-5985
Detroit *(G-3964)*
Detroit Jewish News Ltd Partnr .... D 248 354-6060
Southfield *(G-14881)*
▲ Detroit Legal News Company .... D 313 961-6000
Detroit *(G-3987)*
Detroit Legal News Pubg LLC .... E 248 577-6100
Troy *(G-16314)*
Detroit Legal News Pubg LLC .... G 734 477-0201
Ann Arbor *(G-418)*
Detroit News Inc .... B 313 222-6400
Detroit *(G-3990)*
Detroit News Inc .... B 313 222-2300
Detroit *(G-3991)*
Detroit News Inc .... G 313 223-4500
Detroit *(G-3992)*
Detroit News Inc .... G 313 222-6400
Sterling Heights *(G-15313)*
Detroit News Inc .... G 313 222-6400
Detroit *(G-3993)*
Detroit Newspaper Partnr LP .... G 989 752-3023
Saginaw *(G-14026)*
Detroit Newspaper Partnr LP .... A 586 826-7187
Sterling Heights *(G-15314)*
Detroit Newspaper Partnr LP .... A 313 222-2300
Detroit *(G-3994)*
Detroit Newspaper Partnr LP .... A 313 222-6400
Detroit *(G-3995)*
Eager Beaver Clean & Store .... G 231 448-2476
Beaver Island *(G-1381)*
Eastern Michigan University .... D 734 487-1010
Ypsilanti *(G-18068)*
El Informador LLC .... G 616 272-1092
Wyoming *(G-17998)*
El Vocero Hispano Inc .... F 616 246-6023
Grand Rapids *(G-6372)*
Eldon Publishing LLC .... G 810 648-5282
Sandusky *(G-14433)*
Evening News .... G 734 242-1100
Monroe *(G-11030)*

Express Publications Inc .... F 231 947-8787
Traverse City *(G-15967)*
Famethis Inc .... G 734 645-9100
Pinckney *(G-12497)*
Federated Publications Inc .... C 269 962-5394
Battle Creek *(G-1186)*
Fedex Office & Print Svcs Inc .... G 248 651-2679
Rochester *(G-13321)*
Fenton Chamber Commerce .... G 810 629-5447
Fenton *(G-5207)*
Fine Tool Journal LLC .... G 269 463-8255
Watervliet *(G-17392)*
Forum and Link Inc .... G 313 945-5465
Dearborn *(G-3713)*
Four Seasons Publishing Inc .... G 906 341-5200
Manistique *(G-10440)*
Fowlerville News & Views .... G 517 223-8760
Fowlerville *(G-5567)*
Gannett Co Inc .... C 269 964-7161
Battle Creek *(G-1191)*
Gannett Co Inc .... D 517 377-1000
Lansing *(G-9371)*
Gannett Co Inc .... F 517 548-2000
Howell *(G-8043)*
Gannett Stllite Info Ntwrk Inc .... C 734 229-1150
Detroit *(G-4077)*
Gatehouse Media LLC .... F 517 265-5111
Adrian *(G-66)*
Gatehouse Media LLC .... E 269 651-5407
Sturgis *(G-15604)*
Gatehouse Media Mich Holdings ...... D 585 598-0030
Coldwater *(G-3304)*
Gazelle Publishing .... G 734 529-2688
Dundee *(G-4584)*
Gazette Newspapers Inc .... G 248 524-4868
Troy *(G-16380)*
Gemini Corporation .... E 616 459-4545
Grand Rapids *(G-6434)*
General Media LLC .... G 586 541-0075
Saint Clair Shores *(G-14254)*
Genesee County Herald Inc .... F 810 686-3840
Clio *(G-3272)*
GLS Diocesan Reports .... G 989 793-7661
Saginaw *(G-14046)*
Grand Haven Publishing Corp .... E 616 842-6400
Grand Haven *(G-6024)*
Grand Rapids Legal News .... G 616 454-9293
Grand Rapids *(G-6456)*
Grand Rapids Press Inc .... F 616 459-1400
Grand Rapids *(G-6461)*
Grand Rapids Times Inc .... F 616 245-8737
Grand Rapids *(G-6466)*
Graphics Hse Spt Prmotions Inc .... E 231 739-4004
Muskegon *(G-11334)*
Great American Publishing Co .... E 616 887-9008
Sparta *(G-15095)*
Great Lakes Pilot Pubg Co .... G 906 494-2391
Grand Marais *(G-6118)*
Great Lakes Post LLC .... G 248 941-1349
Milford *(G-10965)*
Green Sheet .... G 517 548-2570
Howell *(G-8045)*
Grosse Pointe News .... G 734 674-0131
Canton *(G-2380)*
Hamp .... G 989 366-5341
Houghton Lake *(G-7991)*
Hamtramck Review Inc .... G 313 874-2100
Detroit *(G-4115)*
Harbor Beach Times .... G 989 479-3605
Harbor Beach *(G-7266)*
Harold K Schultz .... F 517 279-9764
Coldwater *(G-3308)*
Harvey Bock Co .... G 616 566-1372
Holland *(G-7658)*
Herald Newspapers Company Inc ..... C 269 345-3511
Kalamazoo *(G-8764)*
Herald Newspapers Company Inc ..... D 231 722-3161
Muskegon *(G-11344)*
Herald Newspapers Company Inc ..... G 616 222-5400
Grand Rapids *(G-6506)*
Herald Newspapers Company Inc ..... C 734 926-4510
Ann Arbor *(G-489)*
Herald Newspapers Company Inc ..... G 989 752-7171
Flint *(G-5445)*
Herald Newspapers Company Inc ..... D 810 766-6100
Flint *(G-5446)*
Herald Newspapers Company Inc ..... C 517 787-2300
Jackson *(G-8464)*
Herald Newspapers Company Inc ..... G 734 834-6376
Grand Rapids *(G-6507)*

Herald Newspapers Company Inc ..... E 989 895-8551
Flint *(G-5447)*
Herald Newspapers Company Inc ..... E 269 373-7100
Kalamazoo *(G-8765)*
Herald Newspapers Company Inc ..... D 269 388-8501
Kalamazoo *(G-8766)*
Herald Publishing Company .... E 517 423-2174
Tecumseh *(G-15797)*
Herald Publishing Company LLC ...... G 616 222-5400
Grand Rapids *(G-6508)*
Herald Publishing Company LLC ...... E 616 222-5400
Walker *(G-16867)*
Heritage Newspapers .... G 586 783-0300
Pontiac *(G-12834)*
Homer Index .... G 517 568-4646
Homer *(G-7944)*
Hometown Publishing Inc .... G 989 834-2264
Ovid *(G-12272)*
Houghton Lake Resorter Inc .... E 989 366-5341
Houghton Lake *(G-7993)*
Hudson Post Gazette .... G 517 448-2611
Hudson *(G-8132)*
Huron Publishing Company Inc .... D 989 269-6461
Bad Axe *(G-1067)*
Hydraulic Press Service .... G 586 859-7099
Shelby Township *(G-14602)*
Igan Mich Publishing LLC .... E 248 877-4649
West Bloomfield *(G-17481)*
▲ Independent Newspapers Inc .... C 586 469-4510
Mount Clemens *(G-11134)*
Indepndnt Advsor Nwsppr Group ..... E 989 723-1118
Owosso *(G-12296)*
Indiana Newspapers LLC .... E 248 680-9905
Troy *(G-16415)*
Infoguys Inc .... G 517 482-2125
Lansing *(G-9385)*
Iosco News Press Publishing Co .... G 989 739-2054
Oscoda *(G-12212)*
Iosco News Press Publishing Co .... F 989 362-3456
East Tawas *(G-4689)*
Island Sun Times Inc .... F 810 230-1735
Flint *(G-5450)*
Italian Tribune .... G 586 783-3260
Macomb *(G-10132)*
J R C Inc .... F 810 648-4000
Sandusky *(G-14436)*
J-Ad Graphics Inc .... D 800 870-7085
Hastings *(G-7416)*
J-Ad Graphics Inc .... E 269 965-3955
Battle Creek *(G-1202)*
J-Ad Graphics Inc .... G 269 945-9554
Marshall *(G-10573)*
Jams Media LLC .... G 810 664-0811
Lapeer *(G-9465)*
Journal Register Company .... D 586 790-1600
Mount Clemens *(G-11137)*
Kaechele Inc .... G 269 857-2570
Saugatuck *(G-14459)*
Kaechele Publications Inc .... E 269 673-5534
Allegan *(G-168)*
L D J Inc .... F 906 524-6194
Lanse *(G-9198)*
Lansing Labor News Inc .... G 517 484-7408
Lansing *(G-9306)*
Latino Press Inc .... G 313 361-3000
Detroit *(G-4194)*
Leader Publications LLC .... D 269 683-2100
Niles *(G-11623)*
Leelanau Enterprise Inc .... F 231 256-9827
Lake Leelanau *(G-9104)*
Livonia Observer .... G 734 525-4657
Livonia *(G-9815)*
Local Media Group Inc .... D 313 885-2612
Detroit *(G-4208)*
Ludington Daily News Inc .... D 231 845-5181
Ludington *(G-10069)*
Macdonald Publications Inc .... F 989 875-4151
Ithaca *(G-8363)*
Macomb County Republican Party .... G 586 662-3703
Sterling Heights *(G-15406)*
Macomb North Clinton Advisor .... E 586 731-1000
Shelby Township *(G-14630)*
Maquet Monthly .... G 906 226-6500
Marquette *(G-10542)*
Mark Sikorski MD .... G 586 786-1800
Macomb *(G-10139)*
McClatchy Newspapers Inc .... D 734 525-2224
Livonia *(G-9830)*
McComb County Legal News .... G 586 463-4300
Mount Clemens *(G-11141)*

Employee Codes: A=Over 500 employees, B=251-500
C=101-250, D=51-100, E=20-50, F=10-19, G=3-9

27 PRINTING, PUBLISHING, AND ALLIED INDUSTRIES SIC SECTION

Menominee Cnty Jurnl Print Sp .... F 906 753-2296
Stephenson *(G-15237)*
Metro Times Inc .... E 313 961-4060
Ferndale *(G-5301)*
MI News 26 .... G 231 577-1844
Cadillac *(G-2265)*
Michigan Bingo Bugle .... G 616 784-9344
Grand Rapids *(G-6668)*
Michigan Chronicle Pubg Co .... E 313 963-5522
Detroit *(G-4240)*
Michigan Front Page LLC .... G 313 963-5522
Detroit *(G-4241)*
Michigan Live Inc .... F 734 997-7090
Ann Arbor *(G-555)*
Michigan Maps Inc .... G 231 264-6800
Elk Rapids *(G-4779)*
Midland Publishing Company .... C 989 835-7171
Midland *(G-10891)*
Milliman Communications Inc .... G 517 327-8407
Lansing *(G-9312)*
Minden City Herald .... G 989 864-3630
Minden City *(G-11000)*
Mining Jrnl Bsness Offc-Dtrial .... E 906 228-2500
Marquette *(G-10546)*
Mlive Com .... G 517 768-4984
Jackson *(G-8533)*
Monroe Evening News .... G 734 242-1100
Monroe *(G-11055)*
Monroe Publishing Company .... D 734 242-1100
Monroe *(G-11057)*
Monroe Success Vlc .... G 734 682-3720
Monroe *(G-11058)*
Montmorency Press Inc .... G 989 785-4214
Atlanta *(G-732)*
Moormann Printing Inc .... G 269 646-2101
Marcellus *(G-10466)*
Moormann Printing Inc .... G 269 423-2411
Decatur *(G-3805)*
Morenci Observer .... G 517 458-6811
Morenci *(G-11113)*
Morning Star .... G 989 755-2660
Saginaw *(G-14099)*
Morning Star Publishing Co .... F 989 463-6071
Alma *(G-243)*
Morning Star Publishing Co .... C 989 779-6000
Alma *(G-244)*
Morning Star Publishing Co .... G 989 779-6000
Alma *(G-245)*
Morning Star Publishing Co .... F 989 732-5125
Pontiac *(G-12851)*
Morris Communications Co LLC .... E 517 437-3253
Hillsdale *(G-7532)*
Morris Communications Co LLC .... D 616 546-4200
Holland *(G-7748)*
Morris Communications Corp .... C 269 673-2141
Allegan *(G-177)*
Muslim Observer .... G 248 426-7777
Farmington Hills *(G-5074)*
Ndex .... F 248 432-9000
Farmington Hills *(G-5078)*
Neumann Enterprises Inc .... G 906 293-8122
Newberry *(G-11581)*
New Buffalo Times .... G 269 469-1100
New Buffalo *(G-11517)*
New Monitor .... G 248 439-1863
Hazel Park *(G-7447)*
Newark Morning Ledger Co .... E 517 487-8888
Lansing *(G-9406)*
Newberry News Inc .... G 906 293-8401
Newberry *(G-11583)*
News One Inc .... F 231 798-4669
Norton Shores *(G-11780)*
North Wind Student Newspaper .... E 906 227-2545
Marquette *(G-10547)*
Northern Michigan Review Inc .... E 231 547-6558
Petoskey *(G-12463)*
Northern Michigan Review Inc .... G 231 547-6558
Petoskey *(G-12464)*
Northland Publishers Inc .... F 906 265-9927
Iron River *(G-8318)*
Now Ogden News Pubg of Mich .... F 906 774-3708
Iron Mountain *(G-8295)*
Npi Wireless .... E 231 922-9273
Traverse City *(G-16053)*
Nutting Newspapers Inc .... E 906 482-1500
Houghton *(G-7979)*
Oakland Sail Inc .... E 248 370-4268
Rochester *(G-13338)*
Oceanas Herald-Journal Inc .... F 231 873-5602
Hart *(G-7378)*
Ogden Newspapers Inc .... D 906 786-2021
Escanaba *(G-4849)*
Ogden Newspapers Inc .... G 906 497-5652
Powers *(G-13078)*
Ogden Newspapers Inc .... F 906 774-2772
Iron Mountain *(G-8296)*
Ogden Newspapers Inc .... D 906 228-2500
Marquette *(G-10548)*
Ogden Newspapers Inc .... G 906 789-9122
Escanaba *(G-4850)*
Ogden Newspapers Virginia LLC .... G 906 228-8920
Marquette *(G-10549)*
Ogemaw County Herald Inc .... E 989 345-0044
West Branch *(G-17514)*
Old Mission Gazette .... G 231 590-4715
Traverse City *(G-16057)*
Onesian Enterprises Inc .... G 313 382-5875
Allen Park *(G-203)*
Ontonagon Herald Co Inc .... G 906 884-2826
Ontonagon *(G-12163)*
Otsego County Herald Times .... F 989 732-1111
Gaylord *(G-5886)*
Page One Inc .... E 810 724-0254
Imlay City *(G-8209)*
Paxton Media Group LLC .... D 269 429-2400
Saint Joseph *(G-14334)*
Peterson Publishing Inc .... G 906 387-3282
Munising *(G-11247)*
Pgi Holdings Inc .... E 231 723-3592
Manistee *(G-10435)*
Pgi Holdings Inc .... G 231 745-4635
Baldwin *(G-1085)*
Pgi Holdings Inc .... G 231 937-4740
Big Rapids *(G-1641)*
Pgi Holdings Inc .... E 231 796-4831
Big Rapids *(G-1640)*
Pinconning Journal .... G 989 879-3811
Pinconning *(G-12511)*
Plymouth-Canton Cmnty Crier .... E 734 453-6900
Plymouth *(G-12721)*
Plymouth-Canton Cmnty Crier .... E 734 453-6900
Plymouth *(G-12722)*
Polish Daily News Inc .... G 313 365-1990
Detroit *(G-4306)*
Porcupine Press Inc .... G 906 439-5111
Chatham *(G-2675)*
Presque Isle Newspapers Inc .... F 989 734-2105
Rogers City *(G-13621)*
Punkin Dsign Seds Orgnlity LLC .... G 313 347-8488
Detroit *(G-4317)*
Qp Acquisition 2 Inc .... E 248 594-7432
Southfield *(G-15006)*
Real Detroit Weekly LLC .... F 248 591-7325
Ferndale *(G-5315)*
Reminder Shopping Guide Inc .... G 269 427-7474
Bangor *(G-1094)*
Reporter Papers Inc .... F 734 429-5428
Saline *(G-14412)*
River Raisin Publications .... G 517 486-2400
Blissfield *(G-1725)*
Rockman & Sons Publishing LLC .... F 810 750-6011
Fenton *(G-5235)*
Rockman Communications Inc .... E 810 433-6800
Fenton *(G-5236)*
Royal Lux Magazine .... G 248 602-6565
Southfield *(G-15018)*
Sault Tribe News .... F 906 632-6398
Sault Sainte Marie *(G-14473)*
Schepeler Corporation .... F 517 592-6811
Brooklyn *(G-2042)*
Sherman Publications Inc .... E 248 628-4801
Oxford *(G-12372)*
Sherman Publications Inc .... G 248 625-3370
Clarkston *(G-2955)*
Sherman Publications Inc .... G 248 693-8331
Lake Orion *(G-9161)*
Sherman Publications Inc .... G 248 627-4332
Ortonville *(G-12204)*
Shoppers Fair Inc .... E 231 627-7144
Cheboygan *(G-2695)*
Silent Observer .... G 616 392-4443
Holland *(G-7805)*
Silent Observer .... G 269 966-3550
Battle Creek *(G-1248)*
South Haven Tribune .... G 269 637-1104
South Haven *(G-14774)*
Splash In Time LLC .... G 269 775-1204
Kalamazoo *(G-8898)*
Springer Publishing Co Inc .... F 586 939-6800
Warren *(G-17250)*
St Ignace News .... F 906 643-9150
Saint Ignace *(G-14279)*
Stafford Media Inc .... E 616 754-9301
Greenville *(G-7154)*
State News Inc .... C 517 295-1680
East Lansing *(G-4676)*
Straitsland Resorter .... G 231 238-7362
Indian River *(G-8223)*
Sun Daily .... G 248 842-2925
Orchard Lake *(G-12170)*
Telegram Newspaper .... G 313 928-2955
River Rouge *(G-13281)*
Three Rivers Commercial News .... E 269 279-7488
Three Rivers *(G-15880)*
Thumbprint News .... G 810 794-2300
Clay *(G-3004)*
Times Herald Company .... F 810 985-7171
Port Huron *(G-12971)*
Times Indicator Publications .... G 231 924-4400
Fremont *(G-5784)*
Traverse Cy Record- Eagle Inc .... G 231 946-2000
Traverse City *(G-16129)*
Treasure Enterprise LLC .... F 810 233-7141
Flint *(G-5513)*
Tri City Record LLC .... G 269 463-6397
Watervliet *(G-17394)*
Tuscola County Advertiser Inc .... E 989 673-3181
Caro *(G-2479)*
Univesity Michigan-Dearborn .... F 313 593-5428
Dearborn *(G-3767)*
Up Catholic Newspaper .... G 906 226-8821
Marquette *(G-10560)*
Up North Publications Inc .... G 231 587-8471
Mancelona *(G-10400)*
USA Today Advertising .... G 248 680-6530
Troy *(G-16668)*
View Newspaper .... G 734 697-8255
Belleville *(G-1452)*
Vineyard Press Inc .... F 269 657-5080
Paw Paw *(G-12416)*
Vintage Views Press .... G 616 475-7662
Grand Rapids *(G-6973)*
Voice Communications Corp .... E 586 716-8100
Clinton Township *(G-3257)*
W News .... G 231 946-4446
Traverse City *(G-16141)*
W Vbh .... G 269 927-1527
Benton Harbor *(G-1563)*
Wakefield News .... G 906 224-9561
Wakefield *(G-16856)*
Wall Street Journal Gate A 20 .... G 734 941-4139
Detroit *(G-4435)*
Washtenaw Voice .... G 734 677-5405
Ann Arbor *(G-697)*
West Michigan Medical .... G 269 673-2141
Allegan *(G-191)*
White Lake Beacon Inc .... G 231 894-5356
Whitehall *(G-17680)*
Wochen-Post .... E 248 641-9944
Warren *(G-17295)*
Yale Expositor .... G 810 387-2300
Yale *(G-18048)*
Your Custom Image .... G 989 621-2250
Mount Pleasant *(G-11236)*
Your Hometown Shopper LLC .... F 586 412-8500
Shelby Township *(G-14725)*
Z & A News .... G 231 747-6232
Muskegon *(G-11456)*

2721 Periodicals: Publishing & Printing

A & F Enterprises Inc .... F 248 714-6529
Milford *(G-10953)*
Adjunct Advocate Corporation .... G 734 930-6854
Ann Arbor *(G-344)*
Advisor Inc .... G 906 341-2424
Manistique *(G-10438)*
African American Parent Pubg .... G 248 398-3400
Ferndale *(G-5254)*
Agenda 2020 Inc .... F 616 581-6271
Grand Rapids *(G-6153)*
All Dealer Inventory LLC .... G 231 342-9823
Lake Ann *(G-9083)*
All Kids Considered Publishing .... F 248 398-3400
Ferndale *(G-5257)*
All Seasons Agency Inc .... G 586 752-6381
Bruce Twp *(G-2077)*
Ambassador Magazine .... G 313 965-6789
Detroit *(G-3864)*
American Journal Hlth Prom Inc .... G 248 682-0707
Troy *(G-16196)*

Ann Arbor Observer Company E 734 769-3175
Ann Arbor *(G-358)*
Arena Publishing Co Inc G 586 296-5369
Fraser *(G-5621)*
Auto Connection G 586 752-6371
Bruce Twp *(G-2078)*
Big Money Magazine G 810 655-0621
Swartz Creek *(G-15662)*
BNP Media Inc C 248 362-3700
Troy *(G-16242)*
Bob Allison Enterprises G 248 540-8467
Bloomfield Hills *(G-1752)*
Bowman Enterprises Inc G 269 720-1946
Portage *(G-12987)*
Caribbean Adventure LLC F 269 441-5675
Battle Creek *(G-1163)*
Castine Communications Inc G 248 477-1600
Farmington *(G-4895)*
Chas Levy Circulating Co G 231 779-8940
Cadillac *(G-2241)*
Choice Publications Inc G 989 732-8160
Gaylord *(G-5852)*
Crain Communications Inc B 313 446-6000
Detroit *(G-3950)*
Crain Communications Inc B 313 446-6000
Detroit *(G-3951)*
Crain Communications Inc B 313 446-6000
Detroit *(G-3952)*
Cte Publishing LLC G 313 338-4335
Detroit *(G-3956)*
Dale Corporation E 248 542-2400
Madison Heights *(G-10227)*
Dental Consultants Inc E 734 663-6777
Ann Arbor *(G-415)*
▲ **Detroit Legal News Company** D 313 961-6000
Detroit *(G-3987)*
Diocese of Lansing F 517 484-4449
Lansing *(G-9361)*
Double Gun Journal G 231 536-7439
East Jordan *(G-4628)*
Dynamic Color Publications G 248 553-3115
Farmington Hills *(G-4976)*
Effective Schools Products G 517 349-8841
Okemos *(G-12121)*
Elsie Publishing Institute F 517 371-5257
Lansing *(G-9365)*
Engravers Journal G 810 229-5725
Brighton *(G-1919)*
▲ **Faith Alive Christn Resources** E 800 333-8300
Grand Rapids *(G-6397)*
Faith Publishing Service E 517 853-7600
Lansing *(G-9228)*
Farago & Associates LLC F 248 546-7070
Southfield *(G-14903)*
Foreword Magazine Inc F 231 933-3699
Traverse City *(G-15972)*
G L Nelson Inc G 630 682-5958
Indian River *(G-8218)*
Gemini Corporation E 616 459-4545
Grand Rapids *(G-6434)*
Gongwer News Service Inc G 517 482-3500
Lansing *(G-9375)*
Grand Traverse Woman Mag G 231 276-5105
Interlochen *(G-8242)*
Graphics Hse Spt Prmotions Inc E 231 739-4004
Muskegon *(G-11334)*
Greater Lansing Bus Monthly G 517 203-0123
Lansing *(G-9376)*
Halloween Events G 248 332-7884
Troy *(G-16389)*
Harbor House Publishers Inc F 231 582-2814
Boyne City *(G-1821)*
Harp Column LLC G 215 564-3232
Zeeland *(G-18145)*
Hour Media LLC E 248 691-1800
Troy *(G-16403)*
Infoguys Inc G 517 482-2125
Lansing *(G-9385)*
Informa Business Media Inc E 248 357-0800
Southfield *(G-14947)*
International Smart Tan Netwrk E 517 841-4920
Jackson *(G-8472)*
K and A Publishing Co LLC G 734 743-1541
Detroit *(G-4168)*
Karle Pblctions Communications G 517 351-2791
East Lansing *(G-4667)*
Kissman Consulting LLC G 517 256-1077
Okemos *(G-12128)*
Land & Homes Inc G 616 534-5792
Grand Rapids *(G-6617)*
Laribits Keaton Publ Group G 231 537-3330
Harbor Springs *(G-7286)*
Lexicom Publishing Group G 734 994-8600
Ann Arbor *(G-529)*
Living Word International Inc E 989 832-7547
Midland *(G-10882)*
Logan Marketing Group LLC F 248 731-7650
Bloomfield Hills *(G-1778)*
Magazines In Motion Inc G 248 310-7647
Farmington Hills *(G-5048)*
Mary Pantely Associates G 248 723-8771
Rochester *(G-13333)*
Metra Inc G 248 543-3500
Hazel Park *(G-7443)*
Michigan Banker Magazine G 517 484-0775
Lansing *(G-9397)*
Michigan Movie Magazine LLC G 734 726-5299
Dexter *(G-4499)*
Michigan Oil and Gas Assn G 517 487-0480
Lansing *(G-9399)*
Michigan Vue Magazine G 248 681-2410
Waterford *(G-17357)*
Morris Communications Co LLC D 616 546-4200
Holland *(G-7748)*
Morris Communications Corp C 269 673-2141
Allegan *(G-177)*
Nationwide Network Inc E 989 793-0123
Saginaw *(G-14103)*
Opensystems Publishing LLC F 586 415-6500
Saint Clair Shores *(G-14266)*
Pathway Publishing Corporation G 269 521-3025
Bloomingdale *(G-1813)*
Pierian Press Inc G 734 434-4074
Ypsilanti *(G-18094)*
Planning & Zoning Center Inc G 517 886-0555
Lansing *(G-9258)*
Pressure Releases Corporation F 616 531-8116
Grand Rapids *(G-6770)*
Pride Source Corporation F 734 293-7200
Livonia *(G-9898)*
Prism Publications Inc E 231 941-8174
Traverse City *(G-16078)*
Profiles Magazine G 313 531-9041
Detroit *(G-4313)*
R J Michaels Inc F 517 783-2637
Jackson *(G-8560)*
Reliable Freight Fwdg Inc G 734 595-6165
Romulus *(G-13727)*
Renaissance Media LLC D 248 354-6060
Southfield *(G-15013)*
Resort + Recreation Magazine G 616 891-5747
Caledonia *(G-2313)*
Revue Holding Company G 616 608-6170
Grand Rapids *(G-6820)*
Rider Report Magazine G 248 854-8460
Auburn Hills *(G-990)*
Rockman & Sons Publishing LLC F 810 750-6011
Fenton *(G-5235)*
Roe LLC G 231 755-5043
Muskegon *(G-11415)*
Shoreline Creations Ltd E 616 393-2077
Holland *(G-7801)*
Southwest Michigan Living G 269 344-7438
Kalamazoo *(G-8894)*
Stoney Creek Collection Inc E 616 363-4858
Grand Rapids *(G-6893)*
Suburban Hockey LLC G 248 478-1600
Farmington Hills *(G-5133)*
Sway Magazine Publishing G 517 394-4295
Lansing *(G-9428)*
Timothy J Tade Inc G 248 552-8583
Troy *(G-16644)*
Toastmasters International F 810 385-5477
Burtchville *(G-2141)*
Toastmasters International E 517 651-6507
Laingsburg *(G-9081)*
Towing & Equipment Magazine G 248 601-1385
Rochester Hills *(G-13530)*
United Kennel Club Inc E 269 343-9020
Portage *(G-13052)*
Upston Associates Inc G 269 349-2782
Battle Creek *(G-1263)*
Vanguard Publications Inc G 517 336-1600
Okemos *(G-12140)*
Varsity Monthly Thumb G 810 404-5297
Caro *(G-2481)*
Verdoni Productions Inc G 989 790-0845
Saginaw *(G-14179)*
▲ **Village Shop Inc** D 231 946-3712
Traverse City *(G-16138)*
W W Thayne Advertising Cons F 269 979-1411
Battle Creek *(G-1264)*
Wallace Studios LLC G 248 917-2459
Southfield *(G-15065)*
West Michigan Printing Inc G 616 676-2190
Ada *(G-34)*
Womens Lifestyle Inc G 616 458-2121
Grand Rapids *(G-7001)*
Wright Communications Inc F 248 585-3838
Troy *(G-16700)*
Your Home Town USA Inc E 517 529-9421
Clarklake *(G-2902)*

2731 Books: Publishing & Printing

▲ **A B Publishing Inc** G 989 875-4985
Ithaca *(G-8355)*
American Soc AG Blgcal Engners E 269 429-0300
Saint Joseph *(G-14300)*
Amplified Life Network LLC G 800 453-7733
Byron Center *(G-2176)*
Avko Eductl Res Foundation F 810 686-9283
Birch Run *(G-1663)*
▲ **Baker Book House Company** C 616 676-9185
Ada *(G-10)*
Baker Book House Company E 616 957-3110
Grand Rapids *(G-6201)*
Banggameus G 734 904-1916
Ann Arbor *(G-380)*
Black Cobra Financial Svcs LLC G 248 298-9368
Bloomfield Hills *(G-1751)*
Boskage Commerce Publications G 269 673-7242
Portage *(G-12986)*
Broadblade Press G 810 635-3156
Swartz Creek *(G-15664)*
Cbm LLC F 800 487-2323
Ann Arbor *(G-396)*
Central Michigan University F 989 774-3216
Mount Pleasant *(G-11187)*
Chandler Ricchio Pubg LLC G 269 660-0840
Battle Creek *(G-1166)*
Childrens Bible Hour Inc F 616 647-4500
Grand Rapids *(G-6274)*
Christian Schools Intl E 616 957-1070
Grand Rapids *(G-6275)*
Complete Services LLC F 248 470-8247
Livonia *(G-9686)*
Conant Gardeners G 313 863-2624
Detroit *(G-3946)*
Cooper Publishing Group LLC G 231 933-9958
Traverse City *(G-15946)*
Creative Characters Inc G 231 544-6084
Central Lake *(G-2589)*
Dac Inc E 313 388-4342
Detroit *(G-3960)*
Dalton Armond Publishers Inc G 517 351-8520
Okemos *(G-12118)*
Developmental Services Inc G 313 653-1185
Detroit *(G-4006)*
Diocese of Lansing F 517 484-4449
Lansing *(G-9361)*
Dzanc Books Inc G 734 756-5701
Ann Arbor *(G-429)*
E D C O Publishing Inc G 248 690-9184
Clarkston *(G-2917)*
Elmont District Library G 810 798-3100
Almont *(G-256)*
Entertainment Publications Inc B 248 404-1000
Troy *(G-16348)*
Evia Learning Inc G 616 393-8803
Holland *(G-7628)*
▲ **Faith Alive Christn Resources** E 800 333-8300
Grand Rapids *(G-6397)*
Foreword Magazine Inc F 231 933-3699
Traverse City *(G-15972)*
Front Porch Press G 888 484-1997
Bath *(G-1134)*
Harbor House Publishers Inc F 231 582-2814
Boyne City *(G-1821)*
Harper Arrington Pubg LLC G 313 282-6751
Detroit *(G-4117)*
Harvard Square Editions G 734 668-7523
Ann Arbor *(G-483)*
Hayden - McNeil LLC E 734 455-7900
Plymouth *(G-12635)*
HSP Epi Acquisition LLC D 248 404-1520
Troy *(G-16406)*
Iris Design & Print Inc G 313 277-0505
Dearborn *(G-3727)*
▲ **Jenkins Group Inc** F 231 933-4954
Traverse City *(G-16010)*

Jkr Ventures LLC G 734 645-2320
Traverse City *(G-16013)*
K S B Promotions Inc G 616 676-0758
Ada *(G-20)*
Living Word International Inc E 989 832-7547
Midland *(G-10882)*
Master Handyman Press Inc G 248 616-0810
Troy *(G-16489)*
Mehring Books Inc G 248 967-2924
Oak Park *(G-12083)*
Mendenhall Associates Inc G 734 741-4710
Ann Arbor *(G-552)*
Michigan State Univ Press F 517 355-9543
East Lansing *(G-4671)*
Mott Media LLC F 810 714-4280
Fenton *(G-5226)*
◆ **MPS Lansing Inc** A 517 323-9000
Lansing *(G-9248)*
NA Publishing Inc E 734 302-6500
Saline *(G-14405)*
New Issues Poetry and Prose G 269 387-8185
Kalamazoo *(G-8835)*
Next Level Media Inc G 248 762-7043
Southfield *(G-14991)*
Pierian Press Inc G 734 434-4074
Ypsilanti *(G-18094)*
Pull Our Own Weight G 313 686-4685
Detroit *(G-4316)*
Quirkroberts Publishing Ltd G 248 879-2598
Troy *(G-16573)*
▲ **Rbc Ministries** C 616 942-6770
Grand Rapids *(G-6812)*
Regents of The University Mich E 734 764-6230
Ann Arbor *(G-615)*
Regents of The University Mich E 734 764-4388
Ann Arbor *(G-616)*
▲ **Remnant Publications Inc** E 517 279-1304
Coldwater *(G-3327)*
▲ **Robbie Dean Press LLC** G 734 973-9511
Ann Arbor *(G-622)*
Rockman & Sons Publishing LLC F 810 750-6011
Fenton *(G-5235)*
Roger D Rapoport G 231 755-6665
Muskegon *(G-11416)*
Sheptime Music F 586 806-9058
Warren *(G-17238)*
Stoney Creek Collection Inc E 616 363-4858
Grand Rapids *(G-6893)*
Team Breadwinner LLC G 313 460-0152
Detroit *(G-4396)*
Thomson Reuters Corporation D 734 913-3930
Ann Arbor *(G-672)*
▲ **Thunder Bay Press Inc** E 517 694-3205
Holt *(G-7930)*
Watchdog Quarterly Inc G 734 593-7039
Chelsea *(G-2721)*
▲ **William B Eerdmans Pubg Co** E 616 459-4591
Grand Rapids *(G-6994)*
Windword Press G 248 681-7905
Keego Harbor *(G-8982)*
XMCO Inc D 586 558-8510
Warren *(G-17301)*
▲ **Zondervan Corporation LLC** B 616 698-6900
Grand Rapids *(G-7013)*
Zonya Health International G 517 467-6995
Onsted *(G-12157)*

2732 Book Printing, Not Publishing

A Time To Remember G 517 263-1960
Adrian *(G-41)*
Best Binding LLC G 734 459-7785
Plymouth *(G-12586)*
Creative Graphics Inc G 517 784-0391
Jackson *(G-8424)*
Cushing-Malloy Inc E 734 663-8554
Ann Arbor *(G-409)*
Edward Brothers Malloy G 734 665-6113
Ann Arbor *(G-435)*
▲ **Edwards Brothers Inc** C 800 722-3231
Ann Arbor *(G-436)*
Edwards Brothers Malloy Inc B 734 665-6113
Ann Arbor *(G-437)*
Epi Printers Inc D 734 261-9400
Livonia *(G-9729)*
Great Lakes Photo Inc G 586 784-5446
Richmond *(G-13264)*
Imagemaster Printing LLC E 734 821-2511
Ann Arbor *(G-502)*
▼ **Imperial Clinical RES Svcs Inc** C 616 784-0100
Grand Rapids *(G-6528)*
▲ **Jenkins Group Inc** F 231 933-4954
Traverse City *(G-16010)*
Lottery Info G 734 326-0097
Wayne *(G-17437)*
Malloy Incorporated A 734 665-6113
Ann Arbor *(G-542)*
▼ **McNaughton & Gunn Inc** C 734 429-5411
Saline *(G-14399)*
Mel Printing Co Inc E 313 928-5440
Taylor *(G-15738)*
Michigan Brlle Trnscrbing Fund G 517 780-5096
Jackson *(G-8519)*
Practical Paper Inc F 616 887-1723
Cedar Springs *(G-2559)*
Printing Perspectives LLC G 810 410-8186
Flint *(G-5485)*
R W Patterson Printing Co D 269 925-2177
Benton Harbor *(G-1542)*
Rogers Printing Inc C 231 853-2244
Ravenna *(G-13128)*
Sheridan Pubg Grnd Rapids Inc D 616 957-5100
Grand Rapids *(G-6860)*
Success By Design Inc F 800 327-0057
Wyoming *(G-18033)*
Superior Text LLC F 866 482-8762
Ypsilanti *(G-18104)*
▲ **Tweddle Group Inc** C 586 307-3700
Clinton Township *(G-3252)*
▲ **William B Eerdmans Pubg Co** E 616 459-4591
Grand Rapids *(G-6994)*

2741 Misc Publishing

Adtek Graphics Inc F 517 663-2460
Eaton Rapids *(G-4715)*
Advance BCI Inc D 616 669-1366
Grand Rapids *(G-6144)*
Advertiser Publishing Co Inc G 616 642-9411
Saranac *(G-14452)*
AGS Publishing G 313 494-1000
Detroit *(G-3846)*
Ahearn Signs and Printing G 734 699-3777
Belleville *(G-1440)*
All Kids Considered Pubg Group G 248 398-3400
Ferndale *(G-5256)*
American Mathematical Society D 734 996-5250
Ann Arbor *(G-352)*
Amplified Life Network LLC G 800 453-7733
Byron Center *(G-2176)*
Automotive Info Systems Inc G 734 332-1970
Ann Arbor *(G-374)*
Avanti Press Inc E 800 228-2684
Detroit *(G-3886)*
Avery Color Studios Inc G 906 346-3908
Gwinn *(G-7216)*
Ayotte Cstm Mscal Engrvngs LLC G 734 595-1901
Westland *(G-17545)*
Ball Hard Music Group LLC G 734 636-0038
Monroe *(G-11018)*
Black Cobra Financial Svcs LLC G 248 298-9368
Bloomfield Hills *(G-1751)*
Blackberry Publications E 313 627-1520
Ecorse *(G-4742)*
Boone Express G 248 583-7080
Ortonville *(G-12196)*
Bramin Enterprises G 313 960-1528
Detroit *(G-3913)*
Buyers Guide F 616 897-9261
Lowell *(G-10025)*
Buyers Guide F 231 722-3784
Muskegon *(G-11287)*
Caffeinated Press Inc G 888 809-1686
Grand Rapids *(G-6251)*
Campub Inc F 517 368-0365
Camden *(G-2338)*
City Press Inc G 800 867-2626
Ortonville *(G-12197)*
Cobblestone Press G 989 832-0166
Midland *(G-10825)*
Complete Services LLC F 248 470-8247
Livonia *(G-9686)*
Computer Composition Corp F 248 545-4330
Madison Heights *(G-10218)*
Concordant Publishing Concern G 810 798-3563
Almont *(G-254)*
Conine Publishing Inc E 231 723-3592
Manistee *(G-10418)*
Copyright Traveler S Trunk P G 937 903-9233
Cedar Springs *(G-2550)*
Cornell Publications LLC G 810 225-3075
Brighton *(G-1903)*
Country Register of Mich Inc G 989 793-4211
Saginaw *(G-14022)*
Cs Express Inc G 248 425-1726
Rochester Hills *(G-13399)*
Curvy LLC G 917 960-3774
Northville *(G-11685)*
Deslatae G 313 820-4321
Detroit *(G-3968)*
Diggypod Inc G 734 429-3307
Tecumseh *(G-15787)*
Digital Success Network E 517 244-0771
Mason *(G-10636)*
Digitalmuni LLC G 248 237-4077
Wyandotte *(G-17955)*
Dillion Renee Entities G 989 443-0654
Lansing *(G-9360)*
Diocesan Publications E 616 878-5200
Byron Center *(G-2187)*
Diocese of Lansing F 517 484-4449
Lansing *(G-9361)*
Direct Aim Media LLC E 800 817-7101
Grand Rapids *(G-6353)*
▲ **Discovery House Publishers** E 616 942-9218
Grand Rapids *(G-6355)*
E D C O Publishing Inc G 248 690-9184
Clarkston *(G-2917)*
E D P Technical Services Inc G 734 591-9176
Livonia *(G-9718)*
◆ **Edward G Hinkelman** F 707 778-1124
Traverse City *(G-15960)*
Eiklae Products G 734 671-0752
Grosse Ile *(G-7172)*
▲ **Elm International Inc** G 517 332-4900
Okemos *(G-12122)*
Encore Publishing Group Inc G 269 383-4433
Kalamazoo *(G-8737)*
Engai G 313 605-8220
Wixom *(G-17805)*
Ethnicemedia LLC G 248 762-8904
Troy *(G-16352)*
EZ Vent LLC G 616 874-2787
Rockford *(G-13568)*
Flashes Publishers Inc C 269 673-2141
Allegan *(G-162)*
Flashes Shoppers Guide & News G 517 663-2361
Charlotte *(G-2649)*
Flipsnack LLC E 650 741-1328
Troy *(G-16367)*
Forensic Press G 734 997-0256
Ann Arbor *(G-464)*
Forsons Inc G 517 787-4562
Jackson *(G-8450)*
Fourth Seacoast Publishing Co G 586 779-5570
Saint Clair Shores *(G-14252)*
Frontlines Publishing E 616 887-6256
Grand Rapids *(G-6419)*
Fusion Design Group Ltd G 269 469-8226
New Buffalo *(G-11514)*
G L Nelson Inc G 630 682-5958
Indian River *(G-8218)*
Gemini Corporation E 616 459-4545
Grand Rapids *(G-6434)*
Graphics Hse Spt Prmotions Inc E 231 739-4004
Muskegon *(G-11334)*
Grayton Integrated Pubg LLC G 313 881-1734
Grosse Pointe *(G-7180)*
Great Lakes Publishing Inc G 517 647-4444
Portland *(G-13062)*
Great Lakes Spt Publications G 734 507-0241
Ann Arbor *(G-478)*
Great Northern Publishing Inc E 810 648-4000
Sandusky *(G-14434)*
Hammond Publishing Company G 810 686-8879
Mount Morris *(G-11161)*
Hang On Express G 231 271-0202
Suttons Bay *(G-15652)*
Health Enhancement Systems Inc F 989 839-0852
Midland *(G-10868)*
▲ **Helm Incorporated** D 734 468-3700
Plymouth *(G-12637)*
Herald Bi-County Inc G 517 448-2201
Hudson *(G-8129)*
Hi-Lites Graphic Inc E 231 924-0630
Fremont *(G-5775)*
Hmg Agency F 989 443-3819
Saginaw *(G-14059)*
House of Hero LLC G 248 260-8300
Bloomfield Hills *(G-1774)*
Human Synergistics Inc E 734 459-1030
Plymouth *(G-12644)*

Ideation Inc .... E 734 761-4360
Ann Arbor *(G-499)*
Ifca International Inc .... G 616 531-1840
Grandville *(G-7051)*
J-Ad Graphics Inc .... D 800 870-7085
Hastings *(G-7416)*
J-Ad Graphics Inc .... E 269 965-3955
Battle Creek *(G-1202)*
J-Ad Graphics Inc .... G 269 945-9554
Marshall *(G-10573)*
J-Ad Graphics Inc .... G 517 543-4041
Charlotte *(G-2656)*
Konnections Blog .... G 888 921-1114
Detroit *(G-4181)*
Leader Publications LLC .... D 269 683-2100
Niles *(G-11623)*
Little Blue Book Inc .... F 313 469-0052
Grosse Pointe Woods *(G-7206)*
Live Track Productions Inc .... G 313 704-2224
Detroit *(G-4207)*
Llomen Inc .... G 269 345-3555
Portage *(G-13011)*
Lucky Press LLC .... G 614 309-0048
Harbor Springs *(G-7288)*
Ludington Daily News Inc .... D 231 845-5181
Ludington *(G-10069)*
Macdonald Publications Inc .... F 989 875-4151
Ithaca *(G-8363)*
Manistee News Advocate .... F 231 723-3592
Manistee *(G-10427)*
Maple Press LLC .... F 248 733-9669
Madison Heights *(G-10301)*
Metro Graphic Arts Inc .... F 616 245-2271
Grand Rapids *(G-6663)*
Michigan Acedmy Fmly Physcians .... G 517 347-0098
Okemos *(G-12131)*
Michigan Legal Publishing Ltd .... G 877 525-1990
Grandville *(G-7057)*
Midwest Press and Automtn LLC .... G 586 212-1937
Clinton Township *(G-3175)*
MJL Publishing LLC .... G 734 268-6187
Pinckney *(G-12501)*
Morning Star .... G 989 755-2660
Saginaw *(G-14099)*
Morning Star Publishing Co .... F 989 463-6071
Alma *(G-243)*
Morning Star Publishing Co .... G 989 779-6000
Alma *(G-245)*
Morris Communications Corp .... C 269 673-2141
Allegan *(G-177)*
New Genesis Enterprise Inc .... F 313 220-0365
Westland *(G-17583)*
Northern Michigan Publishing .... G 231 946-7878
Traverse City *(G-16052)*
Npi Wireless .... E 231 922-9273
Traverse City *(G-16053)*
Oceanas Herald-Journal Inc .... F 231 873-5602
Hart *(G-7378)*
Paine Press LLC .... G 231 645-1970
Boyne City *(G-1832)*
Panda King Express .... G 616 796-3286
Holland *(G-7765)*
▲ Parker & Associates .... G 269 694-6709
Otsego *(G-12248)*
Paul F Hester .... F 616 302-6039
Pullman *(G-13087)*
Pgi Holdings Inc .... G 231 937-4740
Big Rapids *(G-1641)*
Pierian Press Inc .... G 734 434-4074
Ypsilanti *(G-18094)*
Presque Isle Newspapers Inc .... F 989 734-2105
Rogers City *(G-13621)*
Press On Juice .... G 231 409-9971
Traverse City *(G-16077)*
Press Play LLC .... G 248 802-3837
Auburn Hills *(G-980)*
Proquest Outdoor Solutions Inc .... G 734 761-4700
Ann Arbor *(G-606)*
Quality Guest Publishing Inc .... F 616 894-1111
Cedar Springs *(G-2561)*
R & R Harwood Inc .... G 616 669-6400
Jenison *(G-8640)*
R S C Productions .... G 586 532-9200
Shelby Township *(G-14677)*
Raymond S Ross .... G 231 922-0235
Traverse City *(G-16092)*
▲ Reflective Art Inc .... E 616 452-0712
Grand Rapids *(G-6817)*
Review Directories Inc .... F 231 347-8606
Petoskey *(G-12472)*
Roe Publishing Department .... G 517 522-3598
Jackson *(G-8564)*
S G Publications Inc .... F 517 676-5100
Mason *(G-10653)*
SAE International .... E 248 273-2455
Troy *(G-16589)*
Saginaw Valley Shopper Inc .... G 989 842-3164
Breckenridge *(G-1846)*
Salesman Inc .... F 517 563-8860
Concord *(G-3524)*
Sharedbook Inc .... E 734 302-6500
Ann Arbor *(G-629)*
Shoreline Creations Ltd .... E 616 393-2077
Holland *(G-7801)*
Source Point Press .... G 269 501-3690
Midland *(G-10918)*
Spry Publishing Llc .... G 877 722-2264
Ann Arbor *(G-643)*
Srose Publishing Company .... G 248 208-7073
Southfield *(G-15032)*
Stafford Media Inc .... E 616 754-9301
Greenville *(G-7154)*
Star Buyers Guide .... G 989 366-8341
Houghton Lake *(G-7998)*
Star Design Metro Detroit LLC .... E 734 740-0189
Livonia *(G-9944)*
Subterranean Press .... G 810 232-1489
Flint *(G-5507)*
Summit Training Source Inc .... E 800 842-0466
Grand Rapids *(G-6897)*
Synod of Great Lakes .... C 616 698-7071
Grand Rapids *(G-6910)*
Tapoos LLC .... G 619 319-4872
Taylor *(G-15776)*
Technical Illustration Corp .... F 313 982-9660
Canton *(G-2432)*
◆ Thomson-Shore Inc .... C 734 426-3939
Dexter *(G-4514)*
Thumb Blanket .... G 989 269-9918
Bad Axe *(G-1073)*
Timothy J Tade Inc .... G 248 552-8583
Troy *(G-16644)*
Total Local Acquisitions LLC .... G 517 663-2405
Eaton Rapids *(G-4735)*
Tuscola County Advertiser Inc .... F 989 823-8651
Vassar *(G-16815)*
Tuscola County Advertiser Inc .... E 989 673-3181
Caro *(G-2479)*
▲ Tweddle Group Inc .... C 586 307-3700
Clinton Township *(G-3252)*
◆ Upper Michigan Newspapers LLC .... F 989 732-5125
Gaylord *(G-5898)*
Valley Publishing .... C 989 671-1200
Bay City *(G-1369)*
Vanguard Publications Inc .... G 517 336-1600
Okemos *(G-12140)*
Verdoni Productions Inc .... G 989 790-0845
Saginaw *(G-14179)*
Village Press Inc .... G 231 946-3712
Traverse City *(G-16137)*
Vineyard Press Inc .... F 269 657-5080
Paw Paw *(G-12416)*
▲ Visible Ink Press LLC .... G 734 667-3211
Canton *(G-2439)*
Wallace Publishing LLC .... E 248 416-7259
Hazel Park *(G-7458)*
Walsworth Publishing Co Inc .... B 269 428-2054
Saint Joseph *(G-14350)*
Weyv Inc .... F 248 614-2400
Troy *(G-16690)*
Wicwas Press .... G 269 344-8027
Kalamazoo *(G-8924)*
Yeungs Lotus Express .... G 248 380-3820
Novi *(G-12029)*
Zenwolf Technologies Group .... E 517 618-2000
Howell *(G-8124)*
Zimbell House Publishing LLC .... G 248 909-0143
Waterford *(G-17388)*
Zoomer Display LLC .... G 616 734-0300
Grand Rapids *(G-7014)*

2752 Commercial Printing: Lithographic

A 1 Printing and Copy Center .... G 269 381-0093
Kalamazoo *(G-8671)*
A B C Printing Inc .... G 248 887-0010
Highland *(G-7483)*
A Koppel Color Image Company .... G 616 534-3600
Grandville *(G-7015)*
Aalpha Tinadawn Inc .... G 517 351-1200
East Lansing *(G-4649)*
Acadia Group LLC .... E 734 944-1404
Saline *(G-14371)*
Accelerated Press Inc .... G 248 524-1850
Troy *(G-16165)*
Action Printech Inc .... E 734 207-6000
Plymouth *(G-12561)*
Adair Printing Company .... E 734 426-2822
Dexter *(G-4472)*
Admore Inc .... D 586 949-8200
Macomb *(G-10102)*
Advance BCI Inc .... D 616 669-5210
Grand Rapids *(G-6145)*
Advance BCI Inc .... D 616 669-1366
Grand Rapids *(G-6144)*
Advance Graphic Systems Inc .... E 248 656-8000
Rochester Hills *(G-13365)*
Advance Print & Graphics Inc .... E 734 663-6816
Ann Arbor *(G-345)*
Ahearn Signs and Printing .... G 734 699-3777
Belleville *(G-1440)*
Aladdin Printing .... G 248 360-2842
Commerce Township *(G-3386)*
Alco Printing Services Inc .... G 248 280-1124
Royal Oak *(G-13899)*
Alcock Printing Inc .... G 586 731-4366
Shelby Township *(G-14544)*
Aldinger Inc .... E 517 394-2424
Lansing *(G-9334)*
Allagra Print and Imaging .... G 586 263-0060
Clinton Township *(G-3041)*
Allegra Network LLC .... F 248 360-1290
West Bloomfield *(G-17464)*
Allegra Print & Imaging .... G 248 354-1313
Southfield *(G-14827)*
Allegra Print and Imaging .... G 616 784-6699
Grand Rapids *(G-6160)*
Allesk Enterprises Inc .... G 231 941-5770
Traverse City *(G-15894)*
Alliance Franchise Brands LLC .... E 248 596-8600
Plymouth *(G-12568)*
Allied Mailing and Prtg Inc .... E 810 750-8291
Fenton *(G-5181)*
Allied Printing Co Inc .... E 248 541-0551
Ferndale *(G-5259)*
Allied Printing Co Inc .... E 248 514-7394
Ferndale *(G-5260)*
Alpha Data Business Forms Inc .... G 248 540-5930
Birmingham *(G-1674)*
Ameri-Print Inc .... E 734 427-2887
Livonia *(G-9642)*
America Ink Print .... G 586 790-2555
Clinton Township *(G-3045)*
American Graphics Inc .... G 586 774-8880
Saint Clair Shores *(G-14240)*
American Ink USA Prntg & Grphc .... G 586 790-2555
Clinton Township *(G-3047)*
American Speedy Printing Ctrs .... G 989 723-5196
Owosso *(G-12279)*
American Speedy Printing Ctrs .... G 313 928-5820
Taylor *(G-15686)*
Americas Finest Prtg Graphics .... G 586 296-1312
Fraser *(G-5618)*
An Corporate Center LLC .... E 248 669-1188
Plymouth *(G-12571)*
▲ Anchor Printing Company .... E 248 335-7440
Novi *(G-11827)*
Andex Industries Inc .... E 906 786-7588
Escanaba *(G-4812)*
AP Impressions Inc .... G 734 464-8009
Livonia *(G-9650)*
Apb Inc .... G 248 528-2990
Troy *(G-16204)*
Apms Incorporated .... G 248 268-1477
Madison Heights *(G-10193)*
Arbor Press LLC .... D 248 549-0150
Royal Oak *(G-13904)*
Argus Press Company .... D 989 725-5136
Owosso *(G-12280)*
Arrow Printing LLC .... G 248 738-2222
Waterford *(G-17323)*
Artcraft Printing Corporation .... G 734 455-8893
Plymouth *(G-12574)*
Artech Printing Inc .... G 248 545-0088
Madison Heights *(G-10196)*
Artigy Printing .... G 269 373-6591
Kalamazoo *(G-8684)*
Artistic Printing Inc .... G 248 356-1004
Southfield *(G-14840)*
ASAP Printing Inc .... G 517 882-3500
Lansing *(G-9341)*

SIC

ASAP Printing Inc .... E 517 882-3500
Okemos ***(G-12114)***
Associated Print & Graphics .... G 734 676-8896
Grosse Ile ***(G-7167)***
August Communications Inc .... G 313 561-8000
Dearborn Heights ***(G-3780)***
Automotive Media LLC .... C 248 537-8500
Pontiac ***(G-12806)***
▲ **Avanzado LLC** .... E 248 615-0538
Farmington Hills ***(G-4938)***
Avery Color Studios Inc .... G 906 346-3908
Gwinn ***(G-7216)***
B & M Imaging Inc .... G 269 968-2403
Battle Creek ***(G-1148)***
B-Quick Instant Printing .... G 616 243-6562
Grand Rapids ***(G-6199)***
Bagnall Enterprises Inc .... G 734 457-0500
Monroe ***(G-11017)***
Bastian Brothers & Company .... E 989 239-5107
Freeland ***(G-5752)***
▲ **Batson Printing Inc** .... D 269 926-6011
Benton Harbor ***(G-1484)***
Bayside Printing Inc .... G 231 352-4440
Frankfort ***(G-5598)***
BCI Group Inc .... E 248 925-2000
Troy ***(G-16234)***
Behrmann Printing Company Inc .... F 248 799-7771
Southfield ***(G-14851)***
Benjamin Press .... G 269 964-7562
Battle Creek ***(G-1153)***
Berci Printing Services Inc .... G 248 350-0206
Southfield ***(G-14852)***
Bizcard Xpress .... G 248 288-4800
Rochester ***(G-13315)***
Blue Water Printing Co Inc .... G 810 664-0643
Lapeer ***(G-9443)***
▲ **Book Concern Printers** .... G 906 482-1250
Hancock ***(G-7248)***
Bowman Printing Inc .... G 810 982-8202
Port Huron ***(G-12904)***
Brd Printing Inc .... E 517 372-0268
Lansing ***(G-9350)***
Breck Graphics Incorporated .... E 616 248-4110
Grand Rapids ***(G-6235)***
Bretts Printing Service .... G 517 482-2256
Lansing ***(G-9351)***
Bronco Printing Company .... G 248 544-1120
Hazel Park ***(G-7435)***
Brophy Engraving Co Inc .... E 313 871-2333
Detroit ***(G-3919)***
Bruce Inc .... G 517 371-5205
Lansing ***(G-9352)***
Business Cards Plus Inc .... D 269 327-7727
Portage ***(G-12988)***
Business Design Solutions Inc .... G 248 672-8007
Southfield ***(G-14861)***
Business Helper LLC .... G 231 271-4404
Suttons Bay ***(G-15651)***
Business Press Inc .... G 248 652-8855
Rochester ***(G-13316)***
C H M Graphics & Litho Inc .... G 586 777-4550
Saint Clair Shores ***(G-14241)***
C J Graphics Inc .... G 906 774-8636
Kingsford ***(G-9055)***
C S L Inc .... G 248 549-4434
Royal Oak ***(G-13912)***
C W Enterprises Inc .... G 810 385-9100
Fort Gratiot ***(G-5547)***
Cadillac Printing Company .... F 231 775-2488
Cadillac ***(G-2239)***
Capital City Blue Print Inc .... G 517 482-5431
Lansing ***(G-9207)***
Capital Imaging Inc .... F 517 482-2292
Lansing ***(G-9355)***
Carrigan Graphics Inc .... G 734 455-6550
Canton ***(G-2357)***
Cascade Printing and Graphics .... G 616 222-2937
Grand Rapids ***(G-6264)***
Celani Printing Co .... G 810 395-1609
Capac ***(G-2447)***
Celia Corporation .... D 616 887-7341
Sparta ***(G-15091)***
Central Michigan Rapid Print .... G 989 772-3110
Mount Pleasant ***(G-11185)***
Child Evngelism Fellowship Inc .... E 269 461-6953
Berrien Center ***(G-1590)***
Chiodini & Sons Printing .... G 248 548-0064
Hazel Park ***(G-7436)***
Christman Screenprint Inc .... F 800 962-9330
Springfield ***(G-15189)***
City Printing Co of Ypsilanti .... G 734 482-8490
Ypsilanti ***(G-18060)***
Clare Print & Pulp .... G 989 386-3497
Clare ***(G-2867)***
Clark Graphic Service Inc .... D 586 772-4900
Warren ***(G-16981)***
Clemco Printing Inc .... G 989 269-8364
Bad Axe ***(G-1059)***
Color Connection .... G 248 351-0920
Southfield ***(G-14870)***
▲ **Color House Graphics Inc** .... E 616 241-1916
Grand Rapids ***(G-6289)***
Color Source Graphics Inc .... G 248 458-2040
Troy ***(G-16272)***
Colorhub LLC .... F 616 333-4411
Grand Rapids ***(G-6290)***
Colortech Graphics Inc .... D 586 779-7800
Roseville ***(G-13783)***
Commercial Graphics Company .... G 517 278-2159
Coldwater ***(G-3299)***
Commercial Graphics Inc .... G 586 726-8150
Sterling Heights ***(G-15292)***
▲ **Commercial Graphics of Mich** .... G 810 744-2102
Burton ***(G-2150)***
Commercial Trck Transf Signs .... G 586 754-7100
Warren ***(G-16988)***
Complete Home Adv Media/Promo .... G 586 254-9555
Shelby Township ***(G-14565)***
Copies & More Inc .... G 231 865-6370
Fruitport ***(G-5791)***
Copies Plus Printing Co LLC .... G 616 696-1288
Cedar Springs ***(G-2549)***
Copilot Printing .... G 248 398-5301
Madison Heights ***(G-10220)***
Copper Island Prtg Grphic Svcs .... G 906 337-1300
Calumet ***(G-2326)***
Copy Central Inc .... G 231 941-2298
Traverse City ***(G-15947)***
Copyrite Printing Inc .... G 586 774-0006
Roseville ***(G-13787)***
Corporate Electronic Sty Inc .... D 248 583-7070
Troy ***(G-16283)***
Country Printing .... G 734 782-4044
Flat Rock ***(G-5351)***
CPM Services Group Inc .... G 248 624-5100
Wixom ***(G-17791)***
Craft Press Printing Inc .... G 269 683-9694
Niles ***(G-11602)***
Creative Characters Inc .... G 231 544-6084
Central Lake ***(G-2589)***
Creative Print Crew LLC .... G 248 629-9404
Troy ***(G-16286)***
Creative Printing & Graphics .... G 810 235-8815
Flint ***(G-5407)***
Crop Marks Printing .... G 616 356-5555
Grand Rapids ***(G-6317)***
Curtis Printing Inc .... G 810 230-6711
Flint ***(G-5410)***
Cushing-Malloy Inc .... E 734 663-8554
Ann Arbor ***(G-409)***
Custom Embroidery Plus LLC .... G 517 316-9902
Lansing ***(G-9211)***
Custom Printers Inc .... D 616 454-9224
Grand Rapids ***(G-6326)***
Custom Printing of Michigan .... F 248 585-9222
Troy ***(G-16290)***
Custom Service Printers Inc .... F 231 726-3297
Muskegon ***(G-11303)***
D & D Printing Co .... E 616 454-7710
Grand Rapids ***(G-6330)***
D J Rotunda Associates Inc .... G 586 772-3350
West Bloomfield ***(G-17472)***
Daily Oakland Press .... B 248 332-8181
Pontiac ***(G-12813)***
Daily Reporter .... E 517 278-2318
Coldwater ***(G-3300)***
Daniel Ward .... G 810 965-6535
Mount Morris ***(G-11160)***
▼ **Data Reproductions Corporation** .... D 248 371-3700
Auburn Hills ***(G-837)***
David H Bosley & Associates .... G 734 261-8390
Livonia ***(G-9698)***
De Vru Printing Co .... G 616 452-5451
Grand Rapids ***(G-6339)***
Dearborn Lithograph Inc .... E 734 464-4242
Livonia ***(G-9701)***
Dearborn Offset Printing Inc .... G 313 561-1173
Dearborn ***(G-3690)***
Decka Digital LLC .... G 231 347-1253
Harbor Springs ***(G-7281)***
Dekoff & Sons Inc .... G 269 344-5816
Kalamazoo ***(G-8724)***
Depex Print Services .... G 586 465-6820
Clinton Township ***(G-3100)***
Derk Pieter Co Inc .... G 616 554-7777
Grand Rapids ***(G-6343)***
Designotype Printers Inc .... G 906 482-2424
Laurium ***(G-9503)***
Detroit Litho Inc .... G 313 993-6186
Detroit ***(G-3988)***
Detroit News Inc .... G 313 222-6400
Sterling Heights ***(G-15313)***
Detroit Newspaper Partnr LP .... A 586 826-7187
Sterling Heights ***(G-15314)***
DGa Printing Inc .... G 586 979-2244
Troy ***(G-16315)***
Digital Imaging Group Inc .... C 269 686-8744
Allegan ***(G-157)***
Digital Printing & Graphics .... G 586 566-9499
Shelby Township ***(G-14577)***
Digital Printing Solutions LLC .... G 586 566-4910
Shelby Township ***(G-14578)***
Dla Document Services .... G 269 961-4895
Battle Creek ***(G-1175)***
Dobb Printing Inc .... E 231 722-1060
Muskegon ***(G-11306)***
Donalyn Enterprises Inc .... F 517 546-9798
Howell ***(G-8032)***
DPrinter Inc .... G 517 423-6554
Tecumseh ***(G-15791)***
E & S Graphics Inc .... G 989 875-2828
Ithaca ***(G-8359)***
E and J Advertising LLC .... G 586 977-3500
Warren ***(G-17013)***
Earle Press Inc .... E 231 773-2111
Muskegon ***(G-11312)***
Econo Print Inc .... G 734 878-5806
Pinckney ***(G-12496)***
▲ **Egt Printing Solutions LLC** .... C 248 583-2500
Madison Heights ***(G-10241)***
Elston Enterprises Inc .... F 313 561-8000
Dearborn Heights ***(G-3784)***
Embroidery House Inc .... G 616 669-6400
Jenison ***(G-8625)***
Empire Printing .... G 248 547-9223
Royal Oak ***(G-13924)***
Encore Impression LLC .... G 248 478-1221
Farmington Hills ***(G-4987)***
Enjoyment Image Publications .... G 269 782-8259
Dowagiac ***(G-4542)***
◆ **Epi Printers Inc** .... E 800 562-9733
Battle Creek ***(G-1179)***
Epi Printers Inc .... C 269 968-2221
Battle Creek ***(G-1180)***
Epi Printers Inc .... D 269 968-2221
Battle Creek ***(G-1181)***
Epi Printers Inc .... D 734 261-9400
Livonia ***(G-9729)***
Epi Printers Inc .... D 269 964-6744
Battle Creek ***(G-1183)***
Epi Printers Inc .... E 269 964-4600
Battle Creek ***(G-1182)***
Excel Graphics .... G 248 442-9390
Livonia ***(G-9731)***
Exclusive Imagery Inc .... G 248 436-2999
Royal Oak ***(G-13927)***
Extreme Screen Prints .... G 616 889-8305
Grand Rapids ***(G-6394)***
F P Horak Company .... C 989 892-6505
Bay City ***(G-1312)***
Fairfax Prints Ltd .... G 517 321-5590
Lansing ***(G-9227)***
Falcon Printing Inc .... E 616 676-3737
Ada ***(G-15)***
Faubles Prtg & Specialities .... G 231 775-4973
Cadillac ***(G-2246)***
Fedex Office & Print Svcs Inc .... F 734 522-7322
Westland ***(G-17555)***
Fedex Office & Print Svcs Inc .... F 734 374-0225
Taylor ***(G-15722)***
Fenton Printing Inc .... G 810 750-9450
Fenton ***(G-5211)***
Flashes Publishers Inc .... C 269 673-2141
Allegan ***(G-162)***
Flashes Shoppers Guide & News .... G 517 663-2361
Charlotte ***(G-2649)***
Fletcher Printing .... G 517 625-7030
Morrice ***(G-11119)***
Foltz Screen Printing .... G 989 772-3947
Mount Pleasant ***(G-11193)***

Foremost Graphics LLC ....D 616 453-4747
Grand Rapids *(G-6415)*
Forsons Inc ....G 517 787-4562
Jackson *(G-8450)*
Franklin Press Inc ....F 616 538-5320
Grand Rapids *(G-6418)*
Frye Printing Company Inc ....F 517 456-4124
Clinton *(G-3021)*
Future Reproductions Inc ....F 248 350-2060
Southfield *(G-14916)*
G G & D Inc ....G 248 623-1212
Clarkston *(G-2924)*
Gage Company ....F 269 965-4279
Springfield *(G-15191)*
Gannett Co Inc ....C 269 964-7161
Battle Creek *(G-1191)*
Gannett Co Inc ....D 517 377-1000
Lansing *(G-9371)*
Garants Office Sups & Prtg Inc ....G 989 356-3930
Alpena *(G-291)*
Gary Cork Incorporated ....G 231 946-1061
Traverse City *(G-15976)*
Gary Printing Company Inc ....G 313 383-3222
Lincoln Park *(G-9578)*
Generation Press Inc ....G 616 392-4405
Holland *(G-7642)*
Genesee County Herald Inc ....F 810 686-3840
Clio *(G-3272)*
Genesis Service Associates LLC ....G 734 994-3900
Dexter *(G-4493)*
Global Digital Printing ....G 734 244-5010
Monroe *(G-11036)*
Globe Printing & Specialties ....F 906 485-1033
Ishpeming *(G-8345)*
Goetz Craft Printers Inc ....F 734 973-7604
Brooklyn *(G-2037)*
Gombar Corp ....G 989 793-9427
Saginaw *(G-14048)*
Grahams Printing Company Inc ....G 313 925-1188
Detroit *(G-4098)*
Grand Blanc Printing Inc ....E 810 694-1155
Grand Blanc *(G-5968)*
Grand Haven Publishing Corp ....E 616 842-6400
Grand Haven *(G-6024)*
Grand Rapids Letter Service ....G 616 459-4711
Grand Rapids *(G-6457)*
Grand Traverse Continuous Inc ....E 231 941-5400
Traverse City *(G-15983)*
▼ Grandville Printing Co ....C 616 534-8647
Grandville *(G-7040)*
Graph-ADS Printing Inc ....C 989 779-6000
Mount Pleasant *(G-11195)*
Graphic Enterprises Inc ....D 248 616-4900
Madison Heights *(G-10258)*
Graphic Impressions Inc ....G 616 455-0303
Grand Rapids *(G-6474)*
Graphics & Printing Co Inc ....G 269 381-1482
Kalamazoo *(G-8756)*
Graphics 3 Inc ....F 517 278-2159
Coldwater *(G-3306)*
Graphics East Inc ....E 586 598-1500
Roseville *(G-13810)*
Graphics House Publishing ....E 231 739-4004
Muskegon *(G-11333)*
Graphics Plus Inc ....G 989 893-0651
Bay City *(G-1318)*
Graphics Unlimited Inc ....G 231 773-2696
Muskegon *(G-11336)*
Great Lakes Prtg Solutions Inc ....F 231 799-6000
Norton Shores *(G-11758)*
Greko Print & Imaging Inc ....F 734 453-0341
Plymouth *(G-12632)*
Grigg Graphic Services Inc ....F 248 356-5005
Southfield *(G-14932)*
Grondin Printing and Awards ....G 269 781-5447
Marshall *(G-10570)*
H E L P Printers Inc ....G 734 847-0554
Temperance *(G-15830)*
Hadd Enterprises ....G 586 773-4260
Eastpointe *(G-4702)*
Halsan Inc ....G 734 285-5420
Southgate *(G-15078)*
Hamblin Company ....E 517 423-7491
Tecumseh *(G-15796)*
Hanon Printing Company ....G 248 541-9099
Pleasant Ridge *(G-12555)*
Harold K Schultz ....F 517 279-9764
Coldwater *(G-3308)*
Hatteras Inc ....E 734 525-5500
Dearborn *(G-3719)*

Hawk Design Inc ....G 989 781-1152
Saginaw *(G-14055)*
Herald Bi-County Inc ....G 517 448-2201
Hudson *(G-8129)*
Herald Publishing Company ....E 517 423-2174
Tecumseh *(G-15797)*
Hess Printing ....G 734 285-4377
Wyandotte *(G-17960)*
Hi-Lites Graphic Inc ....E 231 924-0630
Fremont *(G-5775)*
HI-Lites Graphic Inc ....G 231 924-4540
Fremont *(G-5776)*
Higgins Printing Services LLC ....G 734 414-6203
Plymouth *(G-12639)*
Hodges & Irvine Inc ....F 810 329-4787
Saint Clair *(G-14222)*
Holland Litho Service Inc ....D 616 392-4644
Zeeland *(G-18153)*
Holland Printing Center Inc ....F 616 786-3101
Holland *(G-7676)*
Homestead Graphics Design Inc ....G 906 353-6741
Baraga *(G-1103)*
Horn Corporation ....E 248 583-7789
Troy *(G-16402)*
Houghton Lake Resorter Inc ....E 989 366-5341
Houghton Lake *(G-7993)*
Huron Publishing Company Inc ....D 989 269-6461
Bad Axe *(G-1067)*
I D Enterprises LLC ....G 734 513-0800
Livonia *(G-9777)*
Ideal Printing Company ....E 616 454-9224
Grand Rapids *(G-6525)*
Image Factory Inc ....G 989 732-2712
Gaylord *(G-5866)*
Image Printing Inc ....G 248 585-4080
Royal Oak *(G-13935)*
Imax Printing Co ....G 248 629-9680
Ferndale *(G-5294)*
Imperial Press Inc ....G 734 728-5430
Wayne *(G-17432)*
Inco Development Corporation ....D 517 323-8448
Lansing *(G-9297)*
Industrial Imprntng & Die Ctng ....G 586 778-9470
Eastpointe *(G-4704)*
Instant Framer ....G 231 947-8908
Traverse City *(G-16005)*
Insty-Prints West Inc ....G 517 321-7091
Lansing *(G-9299)*
Intelliform Inc ....G 248 541-4000
Berkley *(G-1586)*
International Master Pdts Corp ....C 231 894-5651
Montague *(G-11091)*
International Master Pdts Corp ....G 800 253-0439
Montague *(G-11092)*
Iris Design & Print Inc ....G 313 277-0505
Dearborn *(G-3727)*
Irwin Enterprises Inc ....E 810 732-0770
Flint *(G-5449)*
▼ J & M Reproductions Corp ....E 248 588-8100
Troy *(G-16429)*
J R C Inc ....F 810 648-4000
Sandusky *(G-14436)*
J-Ad Graphics Inc ....D 800 870-7085
Hastings *(G-7416)*
J-Ad Graphics Inc ....G 517 543-4041
Charlotte *(G-2656)*
J-Ad Graphics Inc ....E 269 965-3955
Battle Creek *(G-1202)*
Jackpine Press Incorporated ....F 231 723-8344
Manistee *(G-10425)*
Jackson Printing Company Inc ....F 517 783-2705
Jackson *(G-8480)*
Janet Kelly ....F 231 775-2313
Cadillac *(G-2256)*
Janutol Printing Co Inc ....G 313 526-6196
Detroit *(G-4157)*
Jerrys Quality Quick Print ....G 248 354-1313
Southfield *(G-14952)*
Jet Speed Printing Company ....G 989 224-6475
Saint Johns *(G-14285)*
Jiffy Print ....G 269 692-3128
Otsego *(G-12242)*
JMS Printing Svc LLC ....G 734 414-6203
Warren *(G-17115)*
Job Shop Ink Inc ....G 517 372-3900
Lansing *(G-9300)*
Johnnie On Spot Inc ....G 248 673-2233
Waterford *(G-17352)*
Johnson-Clark Printers Inc ....F 231 947-6898
Traverse City *(G-16014)*

Johnston Printing & Offset ....G 906 786-1493
Escanaba *(G-4837)*
Jomark Inc ....F 248 478-2600
Farmington Hills *(G-5033)*
Journal Disposition Corp ....G 269 428-2054
Saint Joseph *(G-14319)*
K & S Printing Centers Inc ....G 734 482-1680
Ann Arbor *(G-514)*
K Printing Public Relations Co ....G 810 648-4410
Sandusky *(G-14438)*
Kaufman Enterprises Inc ....G 269 324-0040
Portage *(G-13006)*
▲ Kay Screen Printing Inc ....C 248 377-4999
Lake Orion *(G-9141)*
Kendall & Company Inc ....G 810 733-7330
Flint *(G-5454)*
Kent Communications Inc ....D 616 957-2120
Grand Rapids *(G-6575)*
Keystone Printing Inc ....F 517 627-4078
Grand Ledge *(G-6109)*
Kimprint Inc ....E 734 459-2960
Plymouth *(G-12668)*
Kmak Inc ....G 517 784-8800
Jackson *(G-8489)*
Knapp Printing Services Inc ....G 616 754-9159
Greenville *(G-7143)*
Kolossos Printing Inc ....F 734 994-5400
Ann Arbor *(G-517)*
Kwikie Inc ....G 231 946-9942
Traverse City *(G-16019)*
L D J Inc ....F 906 524-6194
Lanse *(G-9198)*
L&L Printing Inc ....G 586 263-0060
Clinton Township *(G-3158)*
Lake Michigan Mailers Inc ....D 269 383-9333
Kalamazoo *(G-8804)*
Lake Superior Press Inc ....F 906 228-7450
Marquette *(G-10538)*
Lamour Printing Co ....G 734 241-6006
Monroe *(G-11050)*
Larsen Graphics Inc ....E 989 823-3000
Vassar *(G-16812)*
Lawson Printers Inc ....E 269 965-0525
Battle Creek *(G-1222)*
Leader Printing and Design Inc ....F 313 565-0061
Dearborn Heights *(G-3788)*
Leader Publications LLC ....D 269 683-2100
Niles *(G-11623)*
Lee Printing Company ....F 586 463-1564
Clinton Township *(G-3160)*
Lesnau Printing Company ....F 586 795-9200
Sterling Heights *(G-15396)*
Lighthouse Direct Buy LLC ....G 313 340-1850
Detroit *(G-4204)*
Lightning Litho Inc ....F 517 394-2995
Lansing *(G-9392)*
Lindy Press Inc ....G 231 937-6169
Howard City *(G-8003)*
Litho Printers Inc ....F 269 651-7309
Sturgis *(G-15613)*
Litho Printing Service Inc ....G 586 772-6067
Eastpointe *(G-4706)*
Litsenberger Print Shop ....G 906 482-3903
Houghton *(G-7976)*
Lloyd Waters & Associates ....G 734 525-2777
Livonia *(G-9817)*
Local Printers Inc ....G 586 795-1290
Sterling Heights *(G-15402)*
Logan Brothers Printing Inc ....F 517 485-3771
Dewitt *(G-4463)*
Logospot ....G 616 785-7170
Belmont *(G-1467)*
Lopez Reproductions Inc ....G 313 386-4526
Detroit *(G-4209)*
M Beshara Inc ....G 248 542-9220
Oak Park *(G-12079)*
Macdonald Publications Inc ....F 989 875-4151
Ithaca *(G-8363)*
Macomb Business Forms Inc ....F 586 790-8500
Clinton Township *(G-3162)*
Macomb Printing Inc ....E 586 463-2301
Clinton Township *(G-3163)*
Madden Enterprises Inc ....G 734 284-5330
Wyandotte *(G-17966)*
Maleports Sault Prtg Co Inc ....E 906 632-3369
Sault Sainte Marie *(G-14468)*
Malloy Incorporated ....A 734 665-6113
Ann Arbor *(G-542)*
Marketing VI Group Inc ....G 989 793-3933
Saginaw *(G-14081)*

SIC

Employee Codes: A=Over 500 employees, B=251-500
C=101-250, D=51-100, E=20-50, F=10-19, G=3-9
2020 Harris Michigan
Industrial Directory
735

Maslin Corporation G 586 777-7500
Harper Woods *(G-7302)*
Mega Printing Inc G 248 624-6065
Walled Lake *(G-16898)*
Megee Printing Inc F 269 344-3226
Kalamazoo *(G-8820)*
Mel Printing Co Inc E 313 928-5440
Taylor *(G-15738)*
Mendoza Enterprises G 248 792-9120
Bloomfield Hills *(G-1782)*
Menominee Cnty Jurnl Print Sp F 906 753-2296
Stephenson *(G-15237)*
Merritt Press Inc F 517 394-0118
Lansing *(G-9396)*
Messenger Printing & Copy Svc G 616 669-5620
Hudsonville *(G-8166)*
Messenger Printing Service E 313 381-0300
Taylor *(G-15739)*
◆ **Metro Printing Service Inc** G 248 545-4444
Troy *(G-16501)*
Metro Prints Inc F 586 979-9690
Sterling Heights *(G-15417)*
Metropolitan Indus Lithography G 269 323-9333
Portage *(G-13016)*
Mettes Printery Inc G 734 261-6262
Livonia *(G-9841)*
Michigan State Medical Society E 517 337-1351
East Lansing *(G-4670)*
Michigan Wholesale Prtg Inc G 248 350-8230
Farmington Hills *(G-5066)*
Micrgraphics Printing Inc E 231 739-6575
Norton Shores *(G-11773)*
Microforms Inc D 586 939-7900
Beverly Hills *(G-1620)*
Mid North Printing Inc G 989 732-1313
Gaylord *(G-5882)*
Mid-Michigan Screen Printing G 989 624-9827
Birch Run *(G-1666)*
Mid-State Printing Inc F 989 875-4163
Ithaca *(G-8364)*
Midland Publishing Company C 989 835-7171
Midland *(G-10891)*
Millbrook Press Works G 517 323-2111
Lansing *(G-9311)*
Millbrook Printing Co E 517 627-4078
Grand Ledge *(G-6112)*
Minden City Herald G 989 864-3630
Minden City *(G-11000)*
▲ **Mitchell Graphics Inc** E 231 347-4635
Petoskey *(G-12459)*
Mj Creative Printing LLC G 248 891-1117
Livonia *(G-9846)*
MKP Enterprises Inc G 248 809-2525
Southfield *(G-14985)*
Model Printing Service Inc F 989 356-0834
Alpena *(G-301)*
Modern Printing Services Inc G 586 792-9700
Ira *(G-8262)*
Monarch Print and Mail LLC G 734 620-8378
Westland *(G-17581)*
Monarch Print Solutions LLC G 517 522-8457
Michigan Center *(G-10788)*
Moormann Printing Inc G 269 646-2101
Marcellus *(G-10466)*
Moormann Printing Inc G 269 423-2411
Decatur *(G-3805)*
Morris Communications Co LLC D 616 546-4200
Holland *(G-7748)*
Morris Communications Corp C 269 673-2141
Allegan *(G-177)*
Motivation Ideas Inc G 989 356-1817
Alpena *(G-302)*
MPS/Ih LLC G 517 323-9001
Lansing *(G-9249)*
Msw Print and Imaging F 734 544-1626
Ypsilanti *(G-18092)*
Muhleck Enterprises Inc F 517 333-0713
Okemos *(G-12133)*
Munro Printing G 586 773-9579
Eastpointe *(G-4707)*
National Printing Services G 616 813-0758
Wyoming *(G-18022)*
National Wholesale Prtg Corp G 734 416-8400
Plymouth *(G-12699)*
Nationwide Envlope Spclsts Inc F 248 354-5500
Walled Lake *(G-16900)*
Neetz Printing Inc G 989 684-4620
Bay City *(G-1336)*
Newberry News Inc G 906 293-8401
Newberry *(G-11583)*
Nje Enterprises LLC G 313 963-3600
Detroit *(G-4273)*
North American Color Inc E 269 323-0552
Portage *(G-13019)*
North American Graphics Inc E 586 486-1110
Warren *(G-17173)*
Northamerican Reproduction F 734 421-6800
Livonia *(G-9863)*
Northern Specialty Co G 906 376-8165
Republic *(G-13246)*
Northwest Graphic Services G 248 349-9480
Rochester Hills *(G-13485)*
Npi Wireless E 231 922-9273
Traverse City *(G-16053)*
Ntvb Media Inc E 248 583-4190
Troy *(G-16528)*
Nutting Newspapers Inc E 906 482-1500
Houghton *(G-7979)*
Office Connection Inc E 248 871-2003
Farmington Hills *(G-5086)*
Office Express Inc E 248 307-1850
Troy *(G-16534)*
Ogemaw County Herald Inc E 989 345-0044
West Branch *(G-17514)*
On The Side Sign Dsign Grphics G 810 266-7446
Byron *(G-2174)*
P J Printing G 269 673-3372
Allegan *(G-179)*
Page Litho Inc E 313 885-8555
Grosse Pointe *(G-7181)*
Palmer Envelope Co E 269 965-1336
Battle Creek *(G-1235)*
Pariseaus Printing Inc G 810 653-8420
Davison *(G-3657)*
Parkside Printing Inc G 810 765-4500
Marine City *(G-10479)*
Parkside Speedy Print Inc G 810 985-8484
Port Huron *(G-12955)*
Patton Printing Inc G 313 535-9099
Redford *(G-13178)*
Paul C Doerr G 734 242-2058
Monroe *(G-11060)*
PDQ Ink Inc F 810 229-2989
Brighton *(G-1975)*
Peg-Master Business Forms Inc G 586 566-8694
Shelby Township *(G-14662)*
Pellow Printing Co G 906 475-9431
Negaunee *(G-11473)*
Perfect Impressions Inc G 248 478-2644
Farmington Hills *(G-5091)*
Performance Print and Mktg G 517 896-9682
Williamston *(G-17736)*
Perrigo Printing Inc G 616 454-6761
Grand Rapids *(G-6751)*
Personal Graphics G 231 347-6347
Petoskey *(G-12468)*
Pgi Holdings Inc E 231 796-4831
Big Rapids *(G-1640)*
Phase III Graphics Inc G 616 949-9290
Grand Rapids *(G-6753)*
Phoenix Press Incorporated E 248 435-8040
Troy *(G-16546)*
Photo Offset Inc G 906 786-5800
Escanaba *(G-4851)*
Pickle Print & Marketing LLC G 231 668-4148
Traverse City *(G-16069)*
Pioneer Press F 231 796-8072
Big Rapids *(G-1642)*
Pioneer Press Printing G 231 864-2404
Bear Lake *(G-1380)*
Pippa Custom Design Printing G 734 552-1598
Woodhaven *(G-17941)*
▲ **Pleasant Graphics Inc** F 989 773-7777
Mount Pleasant *(G-11219)*
Pointe Printing Inc G 313 821-0030
Grosse Pointe Park *(G-7195)*
Popcorn Press Inc E 248 588-4444
Madison Heights *(G-10332)*
Postal Savings Direct Mktg F 810 238-8866
Flint *(G-5480)*
Preferred Printing Inc F 269 782-5488
Dowagiac *(G-4557)*
Presscraft Papers Inc E 231 882-5505
Benzonia *(G-1576)*
Prestige Printing Inc G 616 532-5133
Grand Rapids *(G-6771)*
Presto Print Inc F 616 364-7132
Grand Rapids *(G-6772)*
Pride Printing Inc G 906 228-8182
Marquette *(G-10554)*
Print All G 586 430-4383
Richmond *(G-13268)*
Print Haus G 616 786-4030
Holland *(G-7776)*
Print House Inc F 248 473-1414
Farmington Hills *(G-5100)*
Print Masters Inc F 248 548-7100
Madison Heights *(G-10339)*
Print Metro Inc G 616 887-1723
Sparta *(G-15106)*
Print n go G 989 362-6041
East Tawas *(G-4694)*
Print Plus Inc G 586 888-8000
Saint Clair Shores *(G-14268)*
Print Shop G 231 347-2000
Petoskey *(G-12471)*
Print Tech Printing Place Inc G 989 772-6109
Mount Pleasant *(G-11221)*
Print Xpress G 313 886-6850
Grosse Pointe Woods *(G-7208)*
▲ **Print-Tech Inc** E 734 996-2345
Ann Arbor *(G-604)*
Printcomm Inc D 810 239-5763
Flint *(G-5484)*
Printed Impressions Inc G 248 473-5333
Farmington Hills *(G-5101)*
▲ **Printer Ink Warehousecom LLC** G 269 649-5492
Vicksburg *(G-16841)*
Printery Inc E 616 396-4655
Holland *(G-7777)*
Printex Printing & Graphics G 269 629-0122
Richland *(G-13253)*
Printing Buying Service G 586 907-2011
Saint Clair Shores *(G-14269)*
▲ **Printing By Marc** G 248 355-0848
Southfield *(G-15005)*
Printing Centre Inc F 517 694-2400
Holt *(G-7922)*
Printing Industries of Mich G 248 946-5895
Novi *(G-11982)*
Printing Plus Inc G 734 482-1680
Ypsilanti *(G-18096)*
Printing Productions Ink G 616 871-9292
Grand Rapids *(G-6777)*
Printing Service Inc G 586 718-4103
Clay *(G-3001)*
Printing Services G 269 321-9826
Portage *(G-13024)*
Printing Services Inc E 734 944-1404
Saline *(G-14409)*
Printing Systems Inc G 734 946-5111
Taylor *(G-15757)*
Printmill Inc G 269 382-0428
Kalamazoo *(G-8862)*
Printwand Inc G 248 738-7225
Pontiac *(G-12859)*
Prism Printing G 586 786-1250
Macomb *(G-10157)*
Professional Instant Printing G 248 335-1117
Waterford *(G-17372)*
Proforma Pltnum Prtg Prmotions G 248 341-3814
Clawson *(G-2985)*
Progress Printers Inc E 231 947-5311
Traverse City *(G-16081)*
▼ **Progressive Prtg & Graphics** G 269 965-8909
Battle Creek *(G-1238)*
Psp Office Solutions LLC F 517 817-0680
Jackson *(G-8558)*
Pummill Print Services Lc G 616 785-7960
Comstock Park *(G-3510)*
Qg LLC B 989 496-3333
Midland *(G-10904)*
Qrp Inc G 989 496-2955
Midland *(G-10905)*
Qrp Inc E 989 496-2955
Midland *(G-10906)*
Quad/Graphics Inc G 248 637-9950
Troy *(G-16572)*
Quad/Graphics Inc F 989 698-5598
Midland *(G-10907)*
Quad/Graphics Inc C 616 754-3672
Greenville *(G-7150)*
Quality Printing & Graphics G 616 949-3400
Grand Rapids *(G-6801)*
Quantum Digital Ventures LLC E 248 292-5686
Warren *(G-17212)*
Quick Printing Company Inc G 616 241-0506
Grand Rapids *(G-6802)*
Quickprint of Adrian Inc F 517 263-2290
Adrian *(G-89)*

SIC SECTION — 27 PRINTING, PUBLISHING, AND ALLIED INDUSTRIES

R & L Color Graphics Inc ....G....... 313 345-3838
 Detroit *(G-4324)*
R & R Harwood Inc ....G....... 616 669-6400
 Jenison *(G-8640)*
R N E Business Enterprises.................G....... 313 963-3600
 Detroit *(G-4326)*
R R Donnelley & Sons Company ....D....... 313 964-1330
 Detroit *(G-4327)*
R W Patterson Printing Co ....D....... 269 925-2177
 Benton Harbor *(G-1542)*
Raenell Press LLC ....G....... 616 534-8890
 Grand Rapids *(G-6806)*
Rapid Graphics Inc ....G....... 269 925-7087
 Benton Harbor *(G-1543)*
Rar Group Inc ....G....... 248 353-2266
 Southfield *(G-15010)*
Ray Printing Company Inc ....F....... 517 787-4130
 Jackson *(G-8561)*
Raze-It Printing ....G....... 248 543-3813
 Hazel Park *(G-7452)*
Real Estate One Inc ....G....... 248 851-2600
 Commerce Township *(G-3446)*
Real Love Printwear.................G....... 248 327-7181
 Southfield *(G-15011)*
Regents of The University Mich ....E....... 734 764-6230
 Ann Arbor *(G-615)*
Reimold Printing Corporation.................G....... 989 799-0784
 Saginaw *(G-14132)*
Rex Printing Company ....G....... 586 323-4002
 Sterling Heights *(G-15467)*
Richard Larabee.................G....... 248 827-7755
 Southfield *(G-15015)*
Richards Printing ....G....... 906 786-3540
 Escanaba *(G-4856)*
Rider Type & Design ....G....... 989 839-0015
 Midland *(G-10908)*
Riegle Press Inc ....E....... 810 653-9631
 Davison *(G-3661)*
Rite Way Printing ....G....... 734 721-2746
 Romulus *(G-13729)*
River Run Press Inc ....E....... 269 349-7603
 Kalamazoo *(G-8873)*
Riverside Prtg of Grnd Rapids.................G....... 616 458-8011
 Grand Rapids *(G-6828)*
Rocket Print Copy Ship Center.................G....... 248 336-3636
 Royal Oak *(G-13966)*
Rogers Printing Inc ....C....... 231 853-2244
 Ravenna *(G-13128)*
Romeo Printing Company Inc.................G....... 586 752-9003
 Romeo *(G-13637)*
Ron Rowe ....G....... 231 652-2642
 Newaygo *(G-11577)*
Rose Business Forms Company ....,E....... 734 424-5200
 Southfield *(G-15017)*
Rtr Alpha Inc.................G....... 248 377-4060
 Auburn Hills *(G-994)*
Rumler Brothers Inc ....G....... 517 437-2990
 Hillsdale *(G-7538)*
Rush Stationers Printers Inc.................F....... 989 891-9305
 Bay City *(G-1351)*
S & N Aziza Inc ....G....... 248 879-9396
 Troy *(G-16586)*
S & N Graphic Solutions LLC ....G....... 734 495-3314
 Canton *(G-2424)*
Safran Printing Company Inc.................E....... 586 939-7600
 Beverly Hills *(G-1621)*
▲ SBR Printing USA Inc ....F....... 810 388-9441
 Port Huron *(G-12964)*
Schepeler Corporation ....F....... 517 592-6811
 Brooklyn *(G-2042)*
Seifert City-Wide Printing Co ....G....... 248 477-9525
 Farmington *(G-4912)*
Shamrock Printing ....G....... 586 752-8580
 Bruce Twp *(G-2100)*
Shayleslie Corporation.................G....... 517 694-4115
 Holt *(G-7929)*
◆ Sheridan Books Inc ....C....... 734 475-9145
 Chelsea *(G-2719)*
Sinclair Graphics LLC ....G....... 269 621-3651
 Hartford *(G-7387)*
Skip Printing and Dup Co.................G....... 586 779-2640
 Roseville *(G-13870)*
Slades Printing Company Inc ....F....... 248 334-6257
 Pontiac *(G-12866)*
Sourceone Imaging LLC ....G....... 616 452-2001
 Grand Rapids *(G-6872)*
▲ Spartan Printing Inc ....E....... 517 372-6910
 Lansing *(G-9264)*
Specifications Service Company ....F....... 248 353-0244
 Bloomfield *(G-1736)*

Spectrum Printers Inc.................E....... 517 423-5735
 Tecumseh *(G-15809)*
Spectrum Printing ....G....... 248 625-5014
 Clarkston *(G-2957)*
Spinnaker Forms Systems Corp ....G....... 616 956-7677
 Grand Rapids *(G-6886)*
Sports Ink Screen Prtg EMB LLC ....G....... 231 723-5696
 Manistee *(G-10437)*
Stafford Media Inc.................E....... 616 754-9301
 Greenville *(G-7154)*
Stamp-Rite Incorporated ....E....... 517 487-5071
 Lansing *(G-9267)*
Standard Printing.................G....... 734 483-0339
 Ypsilanti *(G-18102)*
Standard Printing of Warren ....G....... 586 771-3770
 Warren *(G-17253)*
Steketee-Van Huis Inc.................C....... 616 392-2326
 Holland *(G-7814)*
Stewart Printing Company Inc.................G....... 734 283-8440
 Wyandotte *(G-17976)*
Straits Area Printing Corp ....G....... 231 627-5647
 Cheboygan *(G-2696)*
▲ Stylecraft Printing Co ....D....... 734 455-5500
 Canton *(G-2430)*
Sugar Bush Printing Inc ....G....... 248 373-8888
 Bloomfield Hills *(G-1799)*
Sullivan Reproductions Inc.................E....... 313 965-3666
 Detroit *(G-4383)*
Summit Printing & Graphics ....G....... 989 892-2267
 Bay City *(G-1362)*
Sunrise Print Cmmnications Inc.................F....... 989 345-4475
 West Branch *(G-17523)*
Superior Graphics Studios Ltd.................G....... 906 482-7891
 Houghton *(G-7985)*
Superior Imaging Services Inc ....G....... 269 382-0428
 Kalamazoo *(G-8904)*
Superior Typesetting Service ....G....... 269 382-0428
 Kalamazoo *(G-8905)*
Swift Printing Co.................F....... 616 459-4263
 Grand Rapids *(G-6908)*
Systems Duplicating Co Inc.................F....... 248 585-7590
 Troy *(G-16629)*
T J K Inc.................G....... 586 731-9639
 Sterling Heights *(G-15518)*
T-Print USA.................G....... 269 751-4603
 Hamilton *(G-7240)*
Tatum Bindery Company ....G....... 616 458-8991
 Grand Rapids *(G-6915)*
Technology MGT & Budgt Dept ....D....... 517 322-1897
 Lansing *(G-9430)*
Tee To Green Print & Promo Pro ....G....... 517 322-3088
 Lansing *(G-9325)*
Temperance Printing ....F....... 419 290-6846
 Lambertville *(G-9186)*
TGI Direct Inc.................F....... 810 239-5553
 Ann Arbor *(G-667)*
The Envelope Printery Inc.................D....... 734 398-7700
 Van Buren Twp *(G-16787)*
Thomas Kenyon Inc.................G....... 248 476-8130
 Saint Clair Shores *(G-14272)*
Thorpe Printing Services Inc ....G....... 810 364-6222
 Marysville *(G-10622)*
Tigner Printing Inc ....G....... 989 465-6916
 Coleman *(G-3351)*
Timbertech Inc ....E....... 231 348-2750
 Harbor Springs *(G-7295)*
Times Herald Company ....F....... 810 985-7171
 Port Huron *(G-12971)*
TLC Printing ....G....... 248 620-3228
 Clarkston *(G-2961)*
Total Business Systems Inc.................F....... 248 307-1076
 Madison Heights *(G-10368)*
Traverse Cy Record- Eagle Inc ....G....... 231 946-2000
 Traverse City *(G-16129)*
Triangle Printing Inc ....G....... 586 293-7530
 Roseville *(G-13881)*
Tsunami Inc ....G....... 989 497-5200
 Saginaw *(G-14168)*
Turner Business Forms Inc.................E....... 989 752-5540
 Saginaw *(G-14171)*
Turner Business Forms Inc.................G....... 810 244-6980
 Flint *(G-5515)*
Tuteur Inc ....G....... 269 983-1246
 Saint Joseph *(G-14344)*
▲ Tweddle Group Inc.................G....... 586 307-3700
 Clinton Township *(G-3252)*
Ultra Printing ....G....... 248 352-7238
 Southfield *(G-15053)*
Ultra-Tech Printing Co ....F....... 616 249-0500
 Wyoming *(G-18038)*

Unigraphics ....G....... 517 337-9316
 East Lansing *(G-4681)*
Unique-Intasco Usa Inc ....G....... 810 982-3360
 Auburn Hills *(G-1036)*
Universal Print ....G....... 989 525-5055
 Bay City *(G-1367)*
Universal Printing Company Inc.................F....... 989 671-9409
 Bay City *(G-1368)*
US Printers ....G....... 906 639-3100
 Daggett *(G-3623)*
Utley Brothers Inc ....E....... 248 585-1700
 Troy *(G-16672)*
Val Valley Inc ....G....... 248 474-7335
 Farmington Hills *(G-5145)*
Valassis International Inc ....B....... 734 591-3000
 Livonia *(G-9987)*
Ver Duins Inc ....G....... 616 842-0730
 Grand Haven *(G-6095)*
Village Graphics Inc.................G....... 231 547-4172
 Charlevoix *(G-2634)*
Village Printing & Supply Inc ....G....... 810 664-2270
 Lapeer *(G-9491)*
▲ Village Shop Inc ....D....... 231 946-3712
 Traverse City *(G-16138)*
Voila Print Inc ....G....... 866 942-1677
 Livonia *(G-9991)*
Vtec Graphics Inc.................G....... 734 953-9729
 Livonia *(G-9993)*
W B Mason Co Inc.................D....... 734 947-6370
 Taylor *(G-15780)*
▲ Walker Printery Inc.................F....... 248 548-5100
 Oak Park *(G-12104)*
Washington Street Printers LLC ....G....... 734 240-5541
 Monroe *(G-11083)*
Waterman and Sons Prtg Co Inc ....G....... 313 864-5562
 Detroit *(G-4436)*
Web Litho Inc.................G....... 586 803-9000
 Rochester Hills *(G-13542)*
Web Printing & Mktg Concepts ....G....... 269 983-4646
 Saint Joseph *(G-14351)*
Weighman Enterprises Inc ....G....... 989 755-2116
 Saginaw *(G-14181)*
West Colony Graphic Inc ....G....... 269 375-6625
 Kalamazoo *(G-8922)*
West Michigan Printing Inc.................G....... 616 676-2190
 Ada *(G-34)*
West Michigan Tag & Label Inc ....E....... 616 235-0120
 Grand Rapids *(G-6987)*
Whipple Printing Inc ....G....... 313 382-8033
 Allen Park *(G-213)*
Whisper Creative Products Inc.................G....... 734 529-2734
 Dundee *(G-4603)*
White Pines Corporation ....E....... 734 761-2670
 Ann Arbor *(G-699)*
Wholesale Ticket Co Inc ....F....... 616 642-9476
 Saranac *(G-14457)*
William C Fox Enterprises Inc ....E....... 231 775-2732
 Cadillac *(G-2286)*
Willoughby Press ....G....... 989 723-3360
 Owosso *(G-12330)*
Wolverine Printing Company LLC ....E....... 616 451-2075
 Grand Rapids *(G-6999)*
Woodhams Enterprises Inc.................G....... 269 383-0600
 Climax *(G-3014)*
Word Baron Inc ....F....... 248 471-4080
 Ann Arbor *(G-702)*
Workman Printing Inc.................G....... 231 744-5500
 Muskegon *(G-11455)*
Worten Copy Center Inc ....G....... 231 845-7030
 Ludington *(G-10089)*
▲ Wynalda Litho Inc ....C....... 616 866-1561
 Belmont *(G-1476)*
X-Treme Printing Inc.................G....... 810 232-3232
 Flint *(G-5528)*
Yale Expositor ....G....... 810 387-2300
 Yale *(G-18048)*
Yti Office Express LLC ....G....... 866 996-8952
 Troy *(G-16704)*
Zak Brothers Printing LLC ....G....... 313 831-3216
 Detroit *(G-4456)*
Zeeland Print Shop Co ....G....... 616 772-6636
 Zeeland *(G-18202)*

2754 Commercial Printing: Gravure

Advantage Label and Packg Inc ....E....... 616 656-1900
 Grand Rapids *(G-6150)*
Aip Group Inc ....G....... 248 828-4400
 Troy *(G-16173)*
Axis Digital Inc ....E....... 616 698-9890
 Grand Rapids *(G-6197)*

Capital Imaging Inc F 517 482-2292
Lansing *(G-9355)*
▼ **Eagile Incorporated** F 616 243-1200
Grand Rapids *(G-6364)*
▲ **Exone Americas LLC** G 248 740-1580
Troy *(G-16356)*
High Impact Solutions Inc G 248 473-9804
Farmington Hills *(G-5019)*
Hodges & Irvine Inc F 810 329-4787
Saint Clair *(G-14222)*
Norman Industries Inc G 248 669-6213
Wixom *(G-17867)*
Occasions G 517 694-6437
Holt *(G-7918)*
Rainbow Tape & Label Inc E 734 941-6090
Romulus *(G-13726)*
Rainbow Wrap F 586 949-3976
Chesterfield *(G-2830)*
Safran Printing Company Inc E 586 939-7600
Beverly Hills *(G-1621)*
Seeley Inc E 517 655-5631
Williamston *(G-17740)*
Taylor Communications Inc F 248 304-4800
Southfield *(G-15043)*

2759 Commercial Printing

1365267 Ontario Inc G 888 843-5245
Port Huron *(G-12879)*
A B C Printing Inc G 248 887-0010
Highland *(G-7483)*
A-1 Screenprinting LLC D 734 665-2692
Ann Arbor *(G-335)*
Adair Printing Company E 734 426-2822
Dexter *(G-4472)*
Adams Shirt Shack Inc G 269 964-3323
Battle Creek *(G-1137)*
Adlib Grafix & Apparel G 269 964-2810
Battle Creek *(G-1139)*
Adrians Screen Print G 734 994-1367
Holland *(G-7550)*
ADS Plus Printing G 810 659-7190
Flushing *(G-5530)*
Advance Graphic Systems Inc E 248 656-8000
Rochester Hills *(G-13365)*
Advanced Screenprinting G 586 979-4412
Sterling Heights *(G-15254)*
▼ **Advanced Tex Screen Printing** E 989 643-7288
Bay City *(G-1272)*
Advantage Label and Packg Inc E 616 656-1900
Grand Rapids *(G-6150)*
Al Corp F 734 475-7357
Chelsea *(G-2701)*
Aldinger Inc E 517 394-2424
Lansing *(G-9334)*
All Access Name Tags G 866 955-8247
Troy *(G-16188)*
Allesk Enterprises Inc G 231 941-5770
Traverse City *(G-15894)*
Allgraphics Corp G 248 994-7373
Farmington Hills *(G-4928)*
Alpha Data Business Forms Inc G 248 540-5930
Birmingham *(G-1674)*
Amazing Engraving G 989 652-8503
Frankenmuth *(G-5582)*
American Reprographics Co LLC E 248 299-8900
Clawson *(G-2973)*
American Thermographers E 248 398-3810
Madison Heights *(G-10190)*
Americas Finest Prtg Graphics G 586 296-1312
Fraser *(G-5618)*
Amery Tape & Label Co Inc G 586 759-3230
Warren *(G-16932)*
An Corporate Center LLC E 248 669-1188
Plymouth *(G-12571)*
▲ **Anchor Printing Company** E 248 335-7440
Novi *(G-11827)*
Ancor Information MGT LLC D 248 740-8866
Troy *(G-16201)*
AP Impressions Inc G 734 464-8009
Livonia *(G-9650)*
Apb Inc G 248 528-2990
Troy *(G-16204)*
Apparel Printers Limited G 517 882-5700
Lansing *(G-9337)*
▲ **Apparel Sales Inc** G 616 842-5650
Jenison *(G-8617)*
Applied Graphics & Fabricating F 989 662-3334
Auburn *(G-750)*
▼ **Applied Visual Concepts LLC** G 866 440-6888
Warren *(G-16937)*

Ar2 Engineering LLC E 248 735-9999
Novi *(G-11829)*
▼ **ARC Print Solutions LLC** F 248 917-7052
Beverly Hills *(G-1613)*
Arrow Printing LLC G 248 738-2222
Waterford *(G-17323)*
Art Craft Display Inc D 517 485-2221
Lansing *(G-9278)*
Artistic Printing Inc G 248 356-1004
Southfield *(G-14840)*
B C P Printing G 269 695-3877
Buchanan *(G-2109)*
Bastian Brothers & Company E 989 239-5107
Freeland *(G-5752)*
Bayside Printing Inc G 231 352-4440
Frankfort *(G-5598)*
Behrmann Printing Company Inc F 248 799-7771
Southfield *(G-14851)*
Berci Printing Services Inc G 248 350-0206
Southfield *(G-14852)*
Best Impressions G 313 389-1202
Lincoln Park *(G-9574)*
Beyond Embroidery G 616 726-7000
Grand Rapids *(G-6216)*
Bible Doctrines To Live By Inc G 616 453-0493
Comstock Park *(G-3463)*
Big Color Printing Center G 313 933-9290
Detroit *(G-3903)*
Big D LLC G 248 787-2724
Redford *(G-13149)*
Big Rapids Printing G 231 796-8588
Grand Rapids *(G-6220)*
Bivins Graphics G 616 453-2211
Grand Rapids *(G-6226)*
Bivins Graphics G 616 453-2211
Grand Rapids *(G-6227)*
Bk Mattson Enterprises Inc G 906 774-0097
Iron Mountain *(G-8278)*
Blts Wearable Art Inc G 517 669-9659
Dewitt *(G-4459)*
Blue Water Printing Co Inc G 810 664-0643
Lapeer *(G-9443)*
Bradford Printing Inc G 517 887-0044
Lansing *(G-9349)*
Brightformat Inc E 616 247-1161
Grand Rapids *(G-6236)*
Bronco Printing Company G 248 544-1120
Hazel Park *(G-7435)*
Brophy Engraving Co Inc E 313 871-2333
Detroit *(G-3919)*
C2 Imaging LLC C 248 743-2903
Troy *(G-16251)*
▲ **Cadillac Prsentation Solutions** E 248 288-9777
Troy *(G-16255)*
Cedar Springs Sales LLC G 616 696-2111
Cedar Springs *(G-2548)*
Celebrations G 906 482-4946
Hancock *(G-7250)*
▲ **Celia Corporation** G 616 887-7387
Sparta *(G-15090)*
Christian Unity Press Inc G 402 362-5133
Flint *(G-5397)*
City Printing Co of Ypsilanti G 734 482-8490
Ypsilanti *(G-18060)*
Clemco Printing Inc G 989 269-8364
Bad Axe *(G-1059)*
Cobrex Ltd G 734 429-9758
Saline *(G-14382)*
Columbia Marking Tools Inc E 586 949-8400
Chesterfield *(G-2754)*
Commercial Blueprint Inc E 517 372-8360
Lansing *(G-9357)*
Community Mental Health D 517 323-9558
Lansing *(G-9210)*
Complete Source Inc G 616 285-9110
Grand Rapids *(G-6293)*
Consoldted Dcment Slutions LLC F 586 293-8100
Fraser *(G-5638)*
Contractors Printing G 517 622-1888
Grand Ledge *(G-6103)*
Converting Systems Inc G 616 698-1882
Nunica *(G-12034)*
Corporate Colors Inc G 269 323-2000
Kalamazoo *(G-8719)*
Corporate Electronic Sty Inc D 248 583-7070
Troy *(G-16283)*
Creative Awards G 586 739-4999
Sterling Heights *(G-15303)*
Cummins Label Company E 269 345-3386
Kalamazoo *(G-8721)*

Custom Printers Inc D 616 454-9224
Grand Rapids *(G-6326)*
Custom Royaltees G 586 943-9849
Clinton Township *(G-3096)*
Custom Threads and Sports LLC G 248 391-0088
Lake Orion *(G-9133)*
D & M Silkscreening G 517 694-4199
Holt *(G-7906)*
D J Rotunda Associates Inc G 586 772-3350
West Bloomfield *(G-17472)*
Danmark Graphics LLC G 616 675-7499
Casnovia *(G-2507)*
Darson Corporation F 313 875-7781
Ferndale *(G-5269)*
Data Mail Services Inc E 248 588-2415
Madison Heights *(G-10228)*
De Vru Printing Co G 616 452-5451
Grand Rapids *(G-6339)*
Dearborn Imaging Group LLC G 313 561-1173
Dearborn *(G-3689)*
Dekoff & Sons Inc G 269 344-5816
Kalamazoo *(G-8724)*
Del Printing Inc F 586 445-3044
Saint Clair Shores *(G-14243)*
Delta Sports Service & EMB G 517 482-6565
Lansing *(G-9215)*
Designs By Bean G 989 845-4371
Chesaning *(G-2723)*
Designshirtscom Inc G 734 414-7604
Plymouth *(G-12609)*
Detroit Evrlasting Dezigns Inc G 248 790-0850
West Bloomfield *(G-17475)*
Detroit Impression Company Inc G 313 921-9077
Detroit *(G-3986)*
Digital Imaging Group Inc C 269 686-8744
Allegan *(G-157)*
Display Pack Inc C 616 451-3061
Cedar Springs *(G-2553)*
Dobb Printing Inc E 231 722-1060
Muskegon *(G-11306)*
Domart LLC G 616 285-9177
Grand Rapids *(G-6357)*
Domer Industries LLC F 269 226-4000
Kalamazoo *(G-8731)*
Donna Jeroy G 313 554-2722
River Rouge *(G-13275)*
E & S Graphics Inc G 989 875-2828
Ithaca *(G-8359)*
E X P Screen Printers G 586 772-6660
Eastpointe *(G-4700)*
Earle Press Inc E 231 773-2111
Muskegon *(G-11312)*
Earthbound Inc G 616 774-0096
Grand Rapids *(G-6366)*
Eclipse Print Emporium Inc G 248 477-8337
Livonia *(G-9720)*
Ecoprint Services LLC G 616 254-8019
Grand Rapids *(G-6369)*
Edens Political G 313 277-0700
Dearborn *(G-3699)*
Edwards Sign & Screen Printing G 989 725-2988
Owosso *(G-12290)*
Elite Business Services & Exec D 734 956-4550
Bloomfield Hills *(G-1763)*
Emerald Graphics Inc G 616 871-3020
Grand Rapids *(G-6376)*
Epi Printers Inc D 734 261-9400
Livonia *(G-9729)*
Essential Screen Printing LLC G 313 300-6411
Detroit *(G-4042)*
Extreme Fitness Gym G 989 681-8339
Saint Louis *(G-14363)*
Extreme Screenprints G 616 889-8305
Grandville *(G-7034)*
F & A Enterprises of Michigan G 906 228-3222
Marquette *(G-10531)*
F P Horak Company C 989 892-6505
Bay City *(G-1312)*
Fabulous Printing Inc G 734 422-5555
Livonia *(G-9733)*
Fams T-Shirts and Designs G 248 841-1086
Rochester *(G-13320)*
Faro Screen Process Inc F 734 207-8400
Canton *(G-2375)*
Fedex Office & Print Svcs Inc E 734 996-0050
Ann Arbor *(G-460)*
Fedex Office & Print Svcs Inc F 313 359-3124
Dearborn *(G-3705)*
Fedex Office & Print Svcs Inc F 248 932-3373
Farmington Hills *(G-4998)*

Fedex Office & Print Svcs Inc ....E 248 355-5670
Southfield ***(G-14915)***
Fedex Office & Print Svcs Inc ....F 248 680-0280
Troy ***(G-16361)***
Fedex Office & Print Svcs Inc ....F 734 374-0225
Taylor ***(G-15722)***
Field Crafts Inc ....E 231 325-1122
Honor ***(G-7952)***
First Imprssons Cstm Printwear ....F 586 783-5210
Clinton Township ***(G-3119)***
Flavored Group LLC ....G 517 775-4371
Lansing ***(G-9289)***
Fletcher Printing ....G 517 625-7030
Morrice ***(G-11119)***
Flint Group US LLC ....A 734 781-4600
Livonia ***(G-9741)***
Flint Group US LLC ....D 269 279-5161
Three Rivers ***(G-15862)***
Flying Colors Imprinting Inc ....F 734 641-1300
Melvindale ***(G-10698)***
Focus Marketing ....E 616 355-4362
Holland ***(G-7633)***
Fonts About Inc ....G 248 767-7504
Northville ***(G-11692)***
Foresight Group Inc ....E 517 485-5700
Lansing ***(G-9230)***
Fortis Sltions Group Centl LLC ....D 248 437-5200
Wixom ***(G-17812)***
Frye Printing Company Inc ....F 517 456-4124
Clinton ***(G-3021)***
FSI Label Company ....E 586 776-4110
Holland ***(G-7637)***
Fug Inc ....G 269 781-8036
Marshall ***(G-10568)***
Futuristic Artwear Inc ....E 248 680-0200
Rochester Hills ***(G-13429)***
Gary Printing Company Inc ....G 313 383-3222
Lincoln Park ***(G-9578)***
Gemini Sales Org LLC ....G 248 765-1118
Sterling Heights ***(G-15355)***
General Tape Label Liquidating ....D 248 437-5200
Wixom ***(G-17817)***
Genesee County Herald Inc ....F 810 686-3840
Clio ***(G-3272)***
Genesis Graphics Inc ....G 906 786-4913
Escanaba ***(G-4831)***
Globe Printing & Specialties ....F 906 485-1033
Ishpeming ***(G-8345)***
Gods Children In Unity Intl M ....G 313 528-8285
Detroit ***(G-4095)***
Grafaktri Inc ....G 734 665-0717
Ann Arbor ***(G-476)***
Grand Blanc Printing Inc ....E 810 694-1155
Grand Blanc ***(G-5968)***
Grand Rapids Graphix ....G 616 359-2383
Wyoming ***(G-18005)***
Grand Rapids Label Company ....D 616 459-8134
Grand Rapids ***(G-6455)***
Grand Rapids Letter Service ....G 616 459-4711
Grand Rapids ***(G-6457)***
Grand Traverse Continuous Inc ....E 231 941-5400
Traverse City ***(G-15983)***
Graphic Enterprises Inc ....D 248 616-4900
Madison Heights ***(G-10258)***
Graphic Impressions Inc ....G 616 455-0303
Grand Rapids ***(G-6474)***
Graphic Specialties Inc ....E 616 247-0060
Grand Rapids ***(G-6475)***
Graphicolor Systems Inc ....G 248 347-0271
Livonia ***(G-9758)***
Graphics & Printing LLC ....G 313 942-2022
Dearborn Heights ***(G-3786)***
Graphics Embossed Images Inc ....G 616 791-0404
Grand Rapids ***(G-6476)***
Graphix 2 Go Inc ....G 269 969-7321
Battle Creek ***(G-1196)***
Grasel Graphics Inc ....G 989 652-5151
Frankenmuth ***(G-5589)***
Great Lakes Label LLC ....E 616 647-9880
Comstock Park ***(G-3483)***
Greystone Imaging LLC ....G 616 742-3810
Grand Rapids ***(G-6482)***
Group 7500 Inc ....F 313 875-9026
Detroit ***(G-4107)***
H E L P Printers Inc ....G 734 847-0554
Temperance ***(G-15830)***
Hadd Enterprises ....G 586 773-4260
Eastpointe ***(G-4702)***
Hamblin Company ....E 517 423-7491
Tecumseh ***(G-15796)***

Handy Bindery Co Inc ....E 586 469-2240
Clinton Township ***(G-3133)***
Help-U-Sell RE Big Rapids ....F 231 796-3966
Big Rapids ***(G-1634)***
Herald Newspapers Company Inc ....E 989 895-8551
Flint ***(G-5447)***
Hilton Screeners Inc ....G 810 653-0711
Davison ***(G-3654)***
Hodges & Irvine Inc ....F 810 329-4787
Saint Clair ***(G-14222)***
Holland Screen Print Inc ....G 616 396-7630
Holland ***(G-7677)***
Homestead Graphics Design Inc ....G 906 353-6741
Baraga ***(G-1103)***
Houghton Lake Resorter Inc ....E 989 366-5341
Houghton Lake ***(G-7993)***
Husky Envelope Products Inc ....D 248 624-7070
Walled Lake ***(G-16895)***
IAC Creative LLC ....F 248 455-7000
Southfield ***(G-14940)***
▲ Imagemaster LLC ....E 734 821-2500
Ann Arbor ***(G-501)***
Impact Label Corporation ....D 269 381-4280
Galesburg ***(G-5811)***
▼ Imperial Clinical RES Svcs Inc ....C 616 784-0100
Grand Rapids ***(G-6528)***
Impression Center Co ....G 248 989-8080
Troy ***(G-16413)***
Imprint House LLC ....G 810 985-8203
Port Huron ***(G-12929)***
Industrial Imprntng & Die Ctng ....G 586 778-9470
Eastpointe ***(G-4704)***
Industrial Mtal Idntfction Inc ....G 616 847-0060
Spring Lake ***(G-15153)***
Inkorporate ....G 734 261-4657
Garden City ***(G-5827)***
Integrity Marketing Products ....G 734 522-5050
Garden City ***(G-5829)***
International Master Pdts Corp ....C 231 894-5651
Montague ***(G-11091)***
Interntonal Innovative Systems ....G 248 524-2222
Troy ***(G-16421)***
Invitations By Design ....G 269 342-8551
Kalamazoo ***(G-8775)***
Irwin Enterprises Inc ....E 810 732-0770
Flint ***(G-5449)***
IXL Graphics Inc ....G 313 350-2800
South Lyon ***(G-14796)***
J-Ad Graphics Inc ....D 800 870-7085
Hastings ***(G-7416)***
▲ J2 Licensing Inc ....G 586 307-3400
Troy ***(G-16431)***
JD Group Inc ....E 248 735-9999
Novi ***(G-11911)***
Jentees Custom Screen Prtg LLC ....F 231 929-3610
Traverse City ***(G-16011)***
Job Shop Ink Inc ....G 517 372-3900
Lansing ***(G-9300)***
Johnson-Clark Printers Inc ....F 231 947-6898
Traverse City ***(G-16014)***
Jomar Inc ....F 269 925-2222
Benton Harbor ***(G-1515)***
Jomark Inc ....F 248 478-2600
Farmington Hills ***(G-5033)***
Just Wing It Inc ....G 248 549-9338
Madison Heights ***(G-10286)***
K G S Screen Process Inc ....G 313 794-2777
Detroit ***(G-4169)***
Kenewell Group ....G 810 714-4290
Fenton ***(G-5222)***
Kennedy Acquisition Inc ....G 616 871-3020
Grand Rapids ***(G-6573)***
Kick It Around Sports ....G 810 232-4986
Flint ***(G-5455)***
Kpmf Usa Inc ....F 248 377-4999
Lake Orion ***(G-9142)***
▲ Ktr Printing Inc ....F 989 386-9740
Clare ***(G-2875)***
Label Tech Inc ....F 586 247-6444
Shelby Township ***(G-14619)***
Labor Education and Res Prj ....G 313 842-6262
Detroit ***(G-4189)***
▲ Lamon Group Inc ....E 616 710-3169
Byron Center ***(G-2196)***
Lamour Printing Co ....G 734 241-6006
Monroe ***(G-11050)***
Lansing Athletics ....G 517 327-8828
Lansing ***(G-9305)***
Larsen Graphics Inc ....E 989 823-3000
Vassar ***(G-16812)***

Lasertec Inc ....E 586 274-4500
Madison Heights ***(G-10298)***
Lawson Printers Inc ....E 269 965-0525
Battle Creek ***(G-1222)***
Lesnau Printing Company ....F 586 795-9200
Sterling Heights ***(G-15396)***
Let Love Rule ....G 734 749-7435
Rockwood ***(G-13607)***
Lithotech ....F 269 471-6027
Berrien Springs ***(G-1598)***
Livonia Trophy & Screen Prtg ....G 734 464-9191
Livonia ***(G-9816)***
Lowery Corporation ....C 616 554-5200
Grand Rapids ***(G-6633)***
M & J Graphics Enterprises Inc ....E 734 542-8800
Livonia ***(G-9820)***
M&S Printmedia Inc ....G 248 601-1200
Rochester Hills ***(G-13464)***
Macarthur Corp ....E 810 606-1777
Grand Blanc ***(G-5975)***
Mahoney & Associates Inc ....G 517 669-4300
Dewitt ***(G-4464)***
Main Street Portraits ....G 269 321-3310
Richland ***(G-13251)***
Main Street Printing ....G 517 851-3816
Stockbridge ***(G-15591)***
Malachi Printing LLC ....G 517 395-4813
Jackson ***(G-8508)***
Maleports Sault Prtg Co Inc ....E 906 632-3369
Sault Sainte Marie ***(G-14468)***
Marking Machine Co ....F 517 767-4155
Tekonsha ***(G-15820)***
Marquee Engraving Inc ....G 810 686-7550
Clio ***(G-3275)***
Materialise Usa LLC ....D 734 259-6445
Plymouth ***(G-12686)***
Mayfair Accessories Inc ....G 989 732-8400
Gaylord ***(G-5878)***
MBA Printing Inc ....G 616 243-1600
Comstock Park ***(G-3498)***
McKay Press Inc ....C 989 631-2360
Midland ***(G-10883)***
Mega Screen Corp ....G 517 849-7057
Jonesville ***(G-8663)***
Melco Engraving Inc ....G 248 656-9000
Rochester Hills ***(G-13471)***
Meta4mat LLC ....G 616 214-7418
Comstock Park ***(G-3500)***
Meteor Web Marketing Inc ....F 734 822-4999
Ann Arbor ***(G-553)***
Mettek LLC ....G 616 895-2033
Allendale ***(G-222)***
Michael Anderson ....G 231 652-5717
Newaygo ***(G-11575)***
Michael Niederpruem ....G 231 935-0241
Kalkaska ***(G-8951)***
Michigan Screen Printing ....G 810 687-5550
Clio ***(G-3276)***
Micrgraphics Printing Inc ....E 231 739-6575
Norton Shores ***(G-11773)***
Microforms Inc ....D 586 939-7900
Beverly Hills ***(G-1620)***
Mid-State Printing Inc ....F 989 875-4163
Ithaca ***(G-8364)***
Middleton Printing Inc ....G 616 247-8742
Grand Rapids ***(G-6684)***
Midwest Graphics & Awards Inc ....G 734 424-3700
Dexter ***(G-4500)***
MJB Concepts Inc ....G 616 866-1470
Rockford ***(G-13580)***
Modzel Screen Printing ....G 231 941-0911
Traverse City ***(G-16040)***
Mogul Minds LLC ....G 682 217-9506
Wayne ***(G-17438)***
Monograms & More Inc ....E 313 299-3140
Taylor ***(G-15746)***
Monroe Publishing Company ....D 734 242-1100
Monroe ***(G-11057)***
Monroe Sp Inc ....G 517 374-6544
Lansing ***(G-9313)***
Moonlight Graphics Inc ....G 616 243-3166
Grand Rapids ***(G-6704)***
Moonpeace ....G 616 456-1128
Grand Rapids ***(G-6705)***
Moormann Printing Inc ....G 269 423-2411
Decatur ***(G-3805)***
MPS Holdco Inc ....C 517 886-2526
Lansing ***(G-9246)***
MPS Hrl LLC ....F 800 748-0517
Lansing ***(G-9247)***

Employee Codes: A=Over 500 employees, B=251-500
C=101-250, D=51-100, E=20-50, F=10-19, G=3-9

2020 Harris Michigan
Industrial Directory

739

◆ **MPS Lansing Inc** A 517 323-9000
Lansing *(G-9248)*

Multi Packaging Solutions Inc E 616 355-6024
Holland *(G-7751)*

Multi Packg Solutions Intl Ltd A 517 323-9000
Lansing *(G-9250)*

Munideals LLC G 248 945-0991
Madison Heights *(G-10313)*

▲ **Mylockercom LLC** B 877 898-3366
Detroit *(G-4261)*

▲ **Nalcor LLC** D 248 541-1140
Ferndale *(G-5303)*

New Echelon Direct Mktg LLC G 248 809-2485
Brighton *(G-1967)*

New World Etching N Amer Ve G 586 296-8082
Fraser *(G-5698)*

Ninja Tees N More G 248 541-2547
Hazel Park *(G-7448)*

Nje Enterprises LLC G 313 963-3600
Detroit *(G-4273)*

North Country Publishing Corp G 231 526-2191
Harbor Springs *(G-7290)*

Northern Label Inc G 231 854-6301
Hesperia *(G-7479)*

Northern Screen Printing & EMB G 906 786-0373
Escanaba *(G-4848)*

Nu-Tech North Inc G 231 347-1992
Petoskey *(G-12466)*

Ogemaw County Herald Inc E 989 345-0044
West Branch *(G-17514)*

Ozland Enterprises Inc G 269 649-0706
Vicksburg *(G-16840)*

P D Q Press Inc G 586 725-1888
Ira *(G-8265)*

Parkside Printing Inc G 810 765-4500
Marine City *(G-10479)*

Pds Plastics Inc F 616 896-1109
Dorr *(G-4525)*

Peg-Master Business Forms Inc G 586 566-8694
Shelby Township *(G-14662)*

Pellow Printing Co G 906 475-9431
Negaunee *(G-11473)*

▲ **Perrin Souvenir Distrs Inc** B 616 785-9700
Comstock Park *(G-3508)*

Personal Graphics G 231 347-6347
Petoskey *(G-12468)*

Pilgrim Printing G 586 752-9664
Washington *(G-17309)*

Pioneer Press E 231 723-3592
Manistee *(G-10436)*

Pioneer Press Printing G 231 864-2404
Bear Lake *(G-1380)*

Pointe Printing Inc G 313 821-0030
Grosse Pointe Park *(G-7195)*

Precision Dial Co G 269 375-5601
Kalamazoo *(G-8857)*

Precision Label Inc G 616 534-9935
Grandville *(G-7066)*

▼ **Precision Label Specialist** G 248 673-5010
Waterford *(G-17371)*

Premiums Plus More G 734 485-2423
Ypsilanti *(G-18095)*

Presscraft Papers Inc E 231 882-5505
Benzonia *(G-1576)*

Prest Sales Co G 586 566-6900
Sterling Heights *(G-15451)*

Primo Crafts G 248 373-3229
Pontiac *(G-12858)*

Print Shop 4u LLC G 810 721-7500
Imlay City *(G-8211)*

Print Tech Printing Place Inc G 989 772-6109
Mount Pleasant *(G-11221)*

Printcomm Inc D 810 239-5763
Flint *(G-5484)*

Printery Inc E 616 396-4655
Holland *(G-7777)*

Printing Consolidation Co LLC G 616 233-3161
Grand Rapids *(G-6776)*

▲ **Printlink Short Run** F 269 965-1336
Battle Creek *(G-1237)*

▲ **Printwell Acquisition Co Inc** D 734 941-6300
Taylor *(G-15758)*

Printxpress Inc G 313 846-1644
Dearborn *(G-3751)*

Pro Connections LLC G 269 962-4219
Springfield *(G-15201)*

Pro Shop The/P S Graphics G 517 448-8490
Hudson *(G-8139)*

Progress Custom Screen Prtg G 248 982-4247
Ferndale *(G-5314)*

Progressive Graphics G 269 945-9249
Hastings *(G-7423)*

Prop Art Studio Inc G 313 824-2200
Detroit *(G-4314)*

Qrp Inc E 989 496-2955
Midland *(G-10906)*

Quality Engraving Service G 269 781-4822
Marshall *(G-10586)*

Quantum Graphics Inc E 586 566-5656
Shelby Township *(G-14675)*

R & J Quality Screenprinting G 989 345-8614
West Branch *(G-17518)*

R & R Harwood Inc G 616 669-6400
Jenison *(G-8640)*

R S V P Inc G 734 455-7229
Plymouth *(G-12729)*

Raenell Press LLC G 616 534-8890
Grand Rapids *(G-6806)*

Ray Printing Company Inc F 517 787-4130
Jackson *(G-8561)*

Rbd Creative G 313 259-5507
Plymouth *(G-12731)*

Regents of The University Mich E 734 764-6230
Ann Arbor *(G-615)*

Religious Communications LLC G 313 822-3361
Detroit *(G-4340)*

Reynolds Bus Solutions LLC G 616 293-6449
Grand Rapids *(G-6821)*

Riegle Press Inc E 810 653-9631
Davison *(G-3661)*

River Run Press Inc E 269 349-7603
Kalamazoo *(G-8873)*

Riverhill Publications & Prtg F 586 468-6011
Ira *(G-8268)*

Robert J Lidzan G 616 361-6446
Grand Rapids *(G-6831)*

Rodriguez Printing Services G 248 651-7774
Farmington Hills *(G-5116)*

Rods Prints & Promotions G 269 639-8814
South Haven *(G-14769)*

Rodzina Industries Inc G 810 235-2341
Flint *(G-5493)*

Rogers Printing Inc C 231 853-2244
Ravenna *(G-13128)*

Romeo Printing Company Inc G 586 752-9003
Romeo *(G-13637)*

▲ **Royal Stewart Enterprises** G 734 224-7994
Temperance *(G-15843)*

RPC Company F 989 752-3618
Saginaw *(G-14134)*

Rusas Printing Co Inc G 313 952-2977
Redford *(G-13190)*

Safran Printing Company Inc E 586 939-7600
Beverly Hills *(G-1621)*

Sage Direct Inc F 616 940-8311
Grand Rapids *(G-6850)*

Sandlot Sports F 989 391-9684
Bay City *(G-1355)*

Sandlot Sports G 989 835-9696
Saginaw *(G-14145)*

Save On Everything Inc D 248 362-9119
Troy *(G-16594)*

Screen Graphics Co Inc G 231 238-4499
Indian River *(G-8222)*

Screen Ideas Inc G 616 458-5119
Grand Rapids *(G-6855)*

Screen Print Department E 616 235-2200
Grand Rapids *(G-6856)*

Screened Image Graphic Design G 906 226-6112
Marquette *(G-10556)*

Screentek Imaging G 586 759-4850
Warren *(G-17235)*

Screenworks Cstm Scrn Printg & G 616 754-7762
Greenville *(G-7152)*

Serviscreen Inc D 616 669-1640
Jenison *(G-8643)*

Shannons Innovative Creat LLC G 313 282-2724
Harper Woods *(G-7305)*

Shirt Tails Inc G 906 774-3370
Iron Mountain *(G-8300)*

Sign Screen Inc G 810 239-1100
Flint *(G-5499)*

Signal-Return Inc G 313 567-8970
Detroit *(G-4362)*

Signs365com LLC G 800 265-8830
Shelby Township *(G-14694)*

Silk Screenstuff G 517 543-7716
Charlotte *(G-2664)*

Slick Shirts Screen Printing F 517 371-3600
Lansing *(G-9424)*

Solutionsnowbiz G 269 321-5062
Portage *(G-13033)*

Source One Digital LLC E 231 799-4040
Norton Shores *(G-11797)*

Source One Dist Svcs Inc F 248 399-5060
Madison Heights *(G-10355)*

Spartan Forms Inc G 313 278-6960
Dearborn Heights *(G-3797)*

Spectrum Graphics Inc F 248 589-2795
Troy *(G-16615)*

Sports Inc G 734 728-1313
Wayne *(G-17443)*

Sports Junction G 989 791-5900
Saginaw *(G-14156)*

Sports Junction G 989 835-9696
Midland *(G-10920)*

Stamp-Rite Incorporated E 517 487-5071
Lansing *(G-9267)*

Standard Printing G 734 483-0339
Ypsilanti *(G-18102)*

Standard Printing of Warren G 586 771-3770
Warren *(G-17253)*

Star Line Commercial Printing F 810 733-1152
Flushing *(G-5542)*

Statewide Printing LLC G 517 485-4466
Lansing *(G-9268)*

Step Into Success Inc G 734 426-1075
Pinckney *(G-12504)*

Straits Area Printing Corp G 231 627-5647
Cheboygan *(G-2696)*

Stylerite Label Corporation E 248 853-7977
Rochester Hills *(G-13519)*

Sunrise Screen Printing Inc G 734 769-3888
Ann Arbor *(G-650)*

Swift Printing Co F 616 459-4263
Grand Rapids *(G-6908)*

Sylvesters G 989 348-9097
Grayling *(G-7116)*

T J K Inc G 586 731-9639
Sterling Heights *(G-15518)*

Techno Urban 3d LLC F 313 740-8110
Detroit *(G-4398)*

Tectonics Industries LLC G 248 597-1600
Auburn Hills *(G-1015)*

▲ **TGI Direct Inc** E 810 239-5553
Flint *(G-5509)*

TGI Direct Inc F 810 239-5553
Ann Arbor *(G-667)*

The Envelope Printery Inc D 734 398-7700
Van Buren Twp *(G-16787)*

Thomas Kenyon Inc G 248 476-8130
Saint Clair Shores *(G-14272)*

Thorpe Printing Services Inc G 810 364-6222
Marysville *(G-10622)*

Threadworks Ltd Inc G 517 548-9745
New Boston *(G-11513)*

Tickets Plus Inc E 616 222-4000
Grand Rapids *(G-6931)*

Timbertech Inc E 231 348-2750
Harbor Springs *(G-7295)*

Total Lee Sports Inc G 989 772-6121
Mount Pleasant *(G-11234)*

Travel Information Services F 989 275-8042
Roscommon *(G-13755)*

Tribar Manufacturing LLC E 248 669-0077
Wixom *(G-17916)*

Trikala Inc G 517 646-8188
Dimondale *(G-4520)*

Triple Creek Shirts and More G 269 273-5154
Three Rivers *(G-15882)*

Triple Thread G 248 321-7757
Clawson *(G-2987)*

Troy Haygood G 313 478-3308
Ferndale *(G-5322)*

Turner Business Forms Inc E 989 752-5540
Saginaw *(G-14171)*

Tuscola County Advertiser Inc B 517 673-3181
Caro *(G-2480)*

▲ **Tweddle Group Inc** C 586 307-3700
Clinton Township *(G-3252)*

Ultra-Tech Printing Co F 616 249-0500
Wyoming *(G-18038)*

Unique Reproductions Inc G 248 788-2887
West Bloomfield *(G-17504)*

Utley Brothers Inc E 248 585-1700
Troy *(G-16672)*

▲ **V&R Enterprize** G 313 837-5545
Detroit *(G-4420)*

Val Valley Inc G 248 474-7335
Farmington Hills *(G-5145)*

Valassis International Inc......B...... 734 591-3000
Livonia *(G-9987)*
Van Kehrberg Vern......G...... 810 364-1066
Marysville *(G-10625)*
▲ **Vector Distribution LLC**......G...... 616 361-2021
Grand Rapids *(G-6962)*
Vgkids Inc......F...... 734 485-5128
Ypsilanti *(G-18107)*
Village Printing & Supply Inc......G...... 810 664-2270
Lapeer *(G-9491)*
Vision Designs Inc......G...... 616 994-7054
Holland *(G-7848)*
Waterman and Sons Prtg Co Inc......G...... 313 864-5562
Detroit *(G-4436)*
Weighman Enterprises Inc......G...... 989 755-2116
Saginaw *(G-14181)*
Wellard Inc......G...... 312 752-0155
West Olive *(G-17536)*
Whipple Printing Inc......G...... 313 382-8033
Allen Park *(G-213)*
Whitlam Group Inc......C...... 586 757-5100
Center Line *(G-2586)*
Whitlock Distribution Svcs LLC......D...... 248 548-1040
Madison Heights *(G-10382)*
Wholesale Ticket Co Inc......F...... 616 642-9476
Saranac *(G-14457)*
Your Home Town USA Inc......E...... 517 529-9421
Clarklake *(G-2902)*
Zak Brothers Printing LLC......G...... 313 831-3216
Detroit *(G-4456)*
Zeeland Record Co......G...... 616 772-2131
Zeeland *(G-18203)*
Zodiac Enterprises LLC......G...... 810 640-7146
Mount Morris *(G-11167)*

2761 Manifold Business Forms

Alpha Data Business Forms Inc......G...... 248 540-5930
Birmingham *(G-1674)*
BCI Group Inc......E...... 248 925-2000
Troy *(G-16234)*
Business Press Inc......G...... 248 652-8855
Rochester *(G-13316)*
Earle Press Inc......E...... 231 773-2111
Muskegon *(G-11312)*
F P Horak Company......C...... 989 892-6505
Bay City *(G-1312)*
Forms Trac Enterprises Inc......G...... 248 524-0006
Sterling Heights *(G-15345)*
Frye Printing Company Inc......F...... 517 456-4124
Clinton *(G-3021)*
Grand Traverse Continuous Inc......E...... 231 941-5400
Traverse City *(G-15983)*
Hi-Speed Business Forms Inc......G...... 269 927-3191
Benton Harbor *(G-1509)*
▼ **Imperial Clinical RES Svcs Inc**......C...... 616 784-0100
Grand Rapids *(G-6528)*
Micrgraphics Printing Inc......E...... 231 739-6575
Norton Shores *(G-11773)*
Microforms Inc......D...... 586 939-7900
Beverly Hills *(G-1620)*
◆ **MPS Lansing Inc**......A...... 517 323-9000
Lansing *(G-9248)*
Peg-Master Business Forms Inc......G...... 586 566-8694
Shelby Township *(G-14662)*
Riegle Press Inc......E...... 810 653-9631
Davison *(G-3661)*
Rotary Multiforms Inc......G...... 586 558-7960
Madison Heights *(G-10344)*
Timbertech Inc......E...... 231 348-2750
Harbor Springs *(G-7295)*
Total Business Systems Inc......F...... 248 307-1076
Madison Heights *(G-10368)*
Ultra Forms Plus Inc......F...... 269 337-6000
Kalamazoo *(G-8916)*
Whitlock Business Systems Inc......E...... 248 548-1040
Madison Heights *(G-10381)*

2771 Greeting Card Publishing

Avanti Press Inc......E...... 800 228-2684
Detroit *(G-3886)*
Avanti Press Inc......E...... 313 961-0022
Taylor *(G-15692)*
Denali Seed Co......G...... 907 344-0347
Pentwater *(G-12429)*
◆ **Design Design Inc**......C...... 866 935-2648
Grand Rapids *(G-6345)*
Katys Kards......G...... 989 793-4094
Saginaw *(G-14070)*
Notes From Man Cave LLC......G...... 586 604-1997
Detroit *(G-4278)*
Reyers Company Inc......F...... 616 414-5530
Spring Lake *(G-15172)*

2782 Blankbooks & Looseleaf Binders

Artful Scrapbooking & Rubber......G...... 586 651-1577
Washington *(G-17302)*
▲ **Cadillac Prsentation Solutions**......E...... 248 288-9777
Troy *(G-16255)*
Hexon Corporation......F...... 248 585-7585
Farmington Hills *(G-5018)*
Janelle Peterson......G...... 616 447-9070
Grand Rapids *(G-6552)*
Memories Manor......G...... 810 329-2800
Saint Clair *(G-14228)*
Microforms Inc......D...... 586 939-7900
Beverly Hills *(G-1620)*
Sab America Inc......G...... 313 363-3392
Dearborn *(G-3755)*
Scrapaloo......G...... 269 623-7310
Delton *(G-3820)*
Scrappy Chic......G...... 248 426-9020
Livonia *(G-9923)*
Superior Receipt Book Co Inc......E...... 269 467-8265
Centreville *(G-2597)*

2789 Bookbinding

A Koppel Color Image Company......G...... 616 534-3600
Grandville *(G-7015)*
Aladdin Printing......G...... 248 360-2842
Commerce Township *(G-3386)*
Allied Bindery LLC......E...... 248 588-5990
Madison Heights *(G-10188)*
American Label & Tag Inc......E...... 734 454-7600
Canton *(G-2347)*
Americas Finest Prtg Graphics......G...... 586 296-1312
Fraser *(G-5618)*
An Corporate Center LLC......E...... 248 669-1188
Plymouth *(G-12571)*
Apb Inc......G...... 248 528-2990
Troy *(G-16204)*
Arrow Printing LLC......G...... 248 738-2222
Waterford *(G-17323)*
ASAP Printing Inc......E...... 517 882-3500
Okemos *(G-12114)*
Bastian Brothers & Company......E...... 989 239-5107
Freeland *(G-5752)*
Bayside Printing Inc......G...... 231 352-4440
Frankfort *(G-5598)*
Bessenberg Bindery Corporation......G...... 734 996-9696
Ann Arbor *(G-383)*
Brd Printing Inc......E...... 517 372-0268
Lansing *(G-9350)*
Breck Graphics Incorporated......E...... 616 248-4110
Grand Rapids *(G-6235)*
Bronco Printing Company......G...... 248 544-1120
Hazel Park *(G-7435)*
Bruce Inc......G...... 517 371-5205
Lansing *(G-9352)*
Business Press Inc......G...... 248 652-8855
Rochester *(G-13316)*
Clark Graphic Service Inc......D...... 586 772-4900
Warren *(G-16981)*
Color Connection......G...... 248 351-0920
Southfield *(G-14870)*
▲ **Commercial Graphics of Mich**......G...... 810 744-2102
Burton *(G-2150)*
Copy Central Inc......G...... 231 941-2298
Traverse City *(G-15947)*
Cushing-Malloy Inc......E...... 734 663-8554
Ann Arbor *(G-409)*
Custom Printers Inc......D...... 616 454-9224
Grand Rapids *(G-6326)*
David H Bosley & Associates......G...... 734 261-8390
Livonia *(G-9698)*
De Vru Printing Co......G...... 616 452-5451
Grand Rapids *(G-6339)*
Derk Pieter Co Inc......G...... 616 554-7777
Grand Rapids *(G-6343)*
Dobb Printing Inc......E...... 231 722-1060
Muskegon *(G-11306)*
DPrinter Inc......G...... 517 423-6554
Tecumseh *(G-15791)*
E & R Bindery Service Inc......G...... 734 464-7954
Livonia *(G-9717)*
Earle Press Inc......E...... 231 773-2111
Muskegon *(G-11312)*
Econo Print Inc......G...... 734 878-5806
Pinckney *(G-12496)*
Edia Technologies Inc......G...... 517 349-0322
Okemos *(G-12120)*
▲ **Edwards Brothers Inc**......C...... 800 722-3231
Ann Arbor *(G-436)*
F P Horak Company......C...... 989 892-6505
Bay City *(G-1312)*
Fedex Office & Print Svcs Inc......E...... 248 443-2679
Lathrup Village *(G-9499)*
Fedex Office & Print Svcs Inc......E...... 616 336-1900
Grand Rapids *(G-6404)*
Fedex Office & Print Svcs Inc......F...... 734 761-4539
Ann Arbor *(G-459)*
Fedex Office & Print Svcs Inc......F...... 313 359-3124
Dearborn *(G-3705)*
Fedex Office & Print Svcs Inc......F...... 248 932-3373
Farmington Hills *(G-4998)*
Fedex Office & Print Svcs Inc......G...... 517 332-5855
East Lansing *(G-4657)*
Fedex Office & Print Svcs Inc......E...... 248 355-5670
Southfield *(G-14915)*
Fedex Office & Print Svcs Inc......E...... 269 344-7445
Portage *(G-12995)*
Fedex Office & Print Svcs Inc......F...... 734 522-7322
Westland *(G-17555)*
Fedex Office & Print Svcs Inc......F...... 313 271-8877
Dearborn *(G-3706)*
Fedex Office & Print Svcs Inc......F...... 248 680-0280
Troy *(G-16361)*
Fedex Office & Print Svcs Inc......F...... 517 347-8656
Okemos *(G-12123)*
Fedex Office & Print Svcs Inc......F...... 248 377-2222
Auburn Hills *(G-870)*
Fedex Office & Print Svcs Inc......E...... 586 296-4890
Roseville *(G-13803)*
Fedex Office & Print Svcs Inc......F...... 734 374-0225
Taylor *(G-15722)*
Foremost Graphics LLC......D...... 616 453-4747
Grand Rapids *(G-6415)*
Forsons Inc......G...... 517 787-4562
Jackson *(G-8450)*
Frye Printing Company Inc......F...... 517 456-4124
Clinton *(G-3021)*
Future Reproductions Inc......F...... 248 350-2060
Southfield *(G-14916)*
Gatherall Bindery Inc......G...... 248 669-6850
Wixom *(G-17815)*
Gombar Corp......G...... 989 793-9427
Saginaw *(G-14048)*
Grand Blanc Printing Inc......E...... 810 694-1155
Grand Blanc *(G-5968)*
Graphic Impressions Inc......G...... 616 455-0303
Grand Rapids *(G-6474)*
Graphic Specialties Inc......E...... 616 247-0060
Grand Rapids *(G-6475)*
Great Lakes Bindery Inc......F...... 616 245-5264
Grand Rapids *(G-6477)*
Halsan Inc......G...... 734 285-5420
Southgate *(G-15078)*
Hamblin Company......E...... 517 423-7491
Tecumseh *(G-15796)*
Handy Bindery Co Inc......E...... 586 469-2240
Clinton Township *(G-3133)*
Hatteras Inc......E...... 734 525-5500
Dearborn *(G-3719)*
Hi-Lites Graphic Inc......E...... 231 924-0630
Fremont *(G-5775)*
Hoag & Sons Book Bindery Inc......F...... 517 857-2033
Eaton Rapids *(G-4726)*
Hodges & Irvine Inc......F...... 810 329-4787
Saint Clair *(G-14222)*
J-Ad Graphics Inc......E...... 269 965-3955
Battle Creek *(G-1202)*
J-Ad Graphics Inc......D...... 800 870-7085
Hastings *(G-7416)*
▼ **John H Dekker & Sons Inc**......D...... 616 257-4120
Grand Rapids *(G-6562)*
Kent Communications Inc......D...... 616 957-2120
Grand Rapids *(G-6575)*
Lee Industries Inc......E...... 231 777-2537
Muskegon *(G-11365)*
Litsenberger Print Shop......G...... 906 482-3903
Houghton *(G-7976)*
Logan Brothers Printing Inc......F...... 517 485-3771
Dewitt *(G-4463)*
Macomb Printing Inc......E...... 586 463-2301
Clinton Township *(G-3163)*
Maleports Sault Prtg Co Inc......E...... 906 632-3369
Sault Sainte Marie *(G-14468)*
Malloy Incorporated......A...... 734 665-6113
Ann Arbor *(G-542)*
▼ **McNaughton & Gunn Inc**......C...... 734 429-5411
Saline *(G-14399)*

S
I
C

Mel Printing Co Inc E 313 928-5440 Taylor *(G-15738)*

Metropolitan Indus Lithography G 269 323-9333 Portage *(G-13016)*

Micrgraphics Printing Inc E 231 739-6575 Norton Shores *(G-11773)*

Mid-State Printing Inc F 989 875-4163 Ithaca *(G-8364)*

Millbrook Printing Co E 517 627-4078 Grand Ledge *(G-6112)*

▲ **Mitchell Graphics Inc** E 231 347-4635 Petoskey *(G-12459)*

Ogemaw County Herald Inc E 989 345-0044 West Branch *(G-17514)*

▲ **Owosso Graphic Arts Inc** E 989 725-7112 Owosso *(G-12309)*

Page Litho Inc E 313 885-8555 Grosse Pointe *(G-7181)*

Parkside Printing Inc G 810 765-4500 Marine City *(G-10479)*

Parkside Speedy Print Inc G 810 985-8484 Port Huron *(G-12955)*

Paul C Doerr G 734 242-2058 Monroe *(G-11060)*

Phase III Graphics Inc G 616 949-9290 Grand Rapids *(G-6753)*

▲ **Print-Tech Inc** E 734 996-2345 Ann Arbor *(G-604)*

Printcomm Inc D 810 239-5763 Flint *(G-5484)*

Printery Inc E 616 396-4655 Holland *(G-7777)*

Printing Plus Inc G 734 482-1680 Ypsilanti *(G-18096)*

▲ **Printwell Acquisition Co Inc** D 734 941-6300 Taylor *(G-15758)*

Qrp Inc E 989 496-2955 Midland *(G-10906)*

Qrp Inc G 989 496-2955 Midland *(G-10905)*

R & R Harwood Inc G 616 669-6400 Jenison *(G-8640)*

R W Patterson Printing Co D 269 925-2177 Benton Harbor *(G-1542)*

Reyers Company Inc F 616 414-5530 Spring Lake *(G-15172)*

Riegle Press Inc E 810 653-9631 Davison *(G-3661)*

River Run Press Inc E 269 349-7603 Kalamazoo *(G-8873)*

Ron Rowe G 231 652-2642 Newaygo *(G-11577)*

Schultz Bindery Inc F 586 771-0777 Warren *(G-17233)*

▲ **Spartan Printing Inc** E 517 372-6910 Lansing *(G-9264)*

Spectrum Printers Inc E 517 423-5735 Tecumseh *(G-15809)*

T J K Inc G 586 731-9639 Sterling Heights *(G-15518)*

Tatum Bindery Company G 616 458-8991 Grand Rapids *(G-6915)*

Technology MGT & Budgt Dept D 517 322-1897 Lansing *(G-9430)*

Thomas Kenyon Inc G 248 476-8130 Saint Clair Shores *(G-14272)*

Thorpe Printing Services Inc G 810 364-6222 Marysville *(G-10622)*

Trade Bindery Service Inc G 734 425-7500 Livonia *(G-9968)*

Tribar Manufacturing LLC E 248 669-0077 Wixom *(G-17916)*

Turner Business Forms Inc E 989 752-5540 Saginaw *(G-14171)*

Val Valley Inc G 248 474-7335 Farmington Hills *(G-5145)*

▲ **Village Shop Inc** D 231 946-3712 Traverse City *(G-16138)*

Wolverine Printing Company LLC E 616 451-2075 Grand Rapids *(G-6999)*

Woodhams Enterprises Inc G 269 383-0600 Climax *(G-3014)*

2791 Typesetting

A 1 Printing and Copy Center G 269 381-0093 Kalamazoo *(G-8671)*

A Koppel Color Image Company G 616 534-3600 Grandville *(G-7015)*

AAA Language Services F 248 239-1138 Bloomfield *(G-1731)*

Adgravers Inc E 313 259-3780 Detroit *(G-3842)*

Advance BCI Inc D 616 669-5210 Grand Rapids *(G-6145)*

Advance Graphic Systems Inc E 248 656-8000 Rochester Hills *(G-13365)*

Al Corp F 734 475-7357 Chelsea *(G-2701)*

Aladdin Printing G 248 360-2842 Commerce Township *(G-3386)*

Aldinger Inc E 517 394-2424 Lansing *(G-9334)*

American Reprographics Co LLC E 248 299-8900 Clawson *(G-2973)*

Americas Finest Prtg Graphics G 586 296-1312 Fraser *(G-5618)*

Anteebo Publishers Inc E 313 882-6900 Grosse Pointe Park *(G-7190)*

AP Impressions Inc G 734 464-8009 Livonia *(G-9650)*

Apb Inc G 248 528-2990 Troy *(G-16204)*

Argus Press Company D 989 725-5136 Owosso *(G-12280)*

ASAP Printing Inc E 517 882-3500 Okemos *(G-12114)*

Bastian Brothers & Company E 989 239-5107 Freeland *(G-5752)*

Beljan Ltd Inc F 734 426-3503 Dexter *(G-4476)*

Bookcomp Inc F 616 774-9700 Belmont *(G-1459)*

Breck Graphics Incorporated E 616 248-4110 Grand Rapids *(G-6235)*

Bronco Printing Company G 248 544-1120 Hazel Park *(G-7435)*

Brophy Engraving Co Inc E 313 871-2333 Detroit *(G-3919)*

Bruce Inc G 517 371-5205 Lansing *(G-9352)*

Business Press Inc G 248 652-8855 Rochester *(G-13316)*

Clark Graphic Service Inc D 586 772-4900 Warren *(G-16981)*

Color Connection G 248 351-0920 Southfield *(G-14870)*

▲ **Commercial Graphics of Mich** G 810 744-2102 Burton *(G-2150)*

Composition Unlimited Inc G 616 451-2222 Grand Rapids *(G-6295)*

Computer Composition Corp F 248 545-4330 Madison Heights *(G-10218)*

Copy Central Inc G 231 941-2298 Traverse City *(G-15947)*

Corporate Electronic Sty Inc D 248 583-7070 Troy *(G-16283)*

Daily Oakland Press B 248 332-8181 Pontiac *(G-12813)*

De Vru Printing Co G 616 452-5451 Grand Rapids *(G-6339)*

Dekoff & Sons Inc G 269 344-5816 Kalamazoo *(G-8724)*

Delmas Typesetting G 734 662-8899 Ann Arbor *(G-414)*

Derk Pieter Co Inc G 616 554-7777 Grand Rapids *(G-6343)*

Detroit Legal News Pubg LLC E 248 577-6100 Troy *(G-16314)*

Different By Design Inc E 248 588-4840 Farmington Hills *(G-4972)*

DPrinter Inc G 517 423-6554 Tecumseh *(G-15791)*

Earle Press Inc E 231 773-2111 Muskegon *(G-11312)*

Econo Print Inc G 734 878-5806 Pinckney *(G-12496)*

F P Horak Company C 989 892-6505 Bay City *(G-1312)*

Fedex Office & Print Svcs Inc E 616 336-1900 Grand Rapids *(G-6404)*

Fedex Office & Print Svcs Inc F 734 761-4539 Ann Arbor *(G-459)*

Fedex Office & Print Svcs Inc F 248 932-3373 Farmington Hills *(G-4998)*

Fedex Office & Print Svcs Inc G 517 332-5855 East Lansing *(G-4657)*

Fedex Office & Print Svcs Inc E 248 355-5670 Southfield *(G-14915)*

Fedex Office & Print Svcs Inc E 269 344-7445 Portage *(G-12995)*

Fedex Office & Print Svcs Inc F 734 522-7322 Westland *(G-17555)*

Fedex Office & Print Svcs Inc F 313 271-8877 Dearborn *(G-3706)*

Fedex Office & Print Svcs Inc E 734 996-0050 Ann Arbor *(G-460)*

Fedex Office & Print Svcs Inc F 248 680-0280 Troy *(G-16361)*

Fedex Office & Print Svcs Inc F 517 347-8656 Okemos *(G-12123)*

Fedex Office & Print Svcs Inc F 248 377-2222 Auburn Hills *(G-870)*

Fedex Office & Print Svcs Inc E 616 957-7888 Grand Rapids *(G-6405)*

Fedex Office & Print Svcs Inc E 586 296-4890 Roseville *(G-13803)*

Fedex Office & Print Svcs Inc F 734 374-0225 Taylor *(G-15722)*

Foremost Graphics LLC D 616 453-4747 Grand Rapids *(G-6415)*

Forsons Inc G 517 787-4562 Jackson *(G-8450)*

Future Reproductions Inc F 248 350-2060 Southfield *(G-14916)*

GAMS Inc G 269 926-6765 Benton Harbor *(G-1502)*

Gazette Newspapers Inc G 248 524-4868 Troy *(G-16380)*

Genesee County Herald Inc F 810 686-3840 Clio *(G-3272)*

Gombar Corp G 989 793-9427 Saginaw *(G-14048)*

Grand Blanc Printing Inc E 810 694-1155 Grand Blanc *(G-5968)*

Graphics Unlimited Inc G 231 773-2696 Muskegon *(G-11336)*

Halsan Inc G 734 285-5420 Southgate *(G-15078)*

Hatteras Inc E 734 525-5500 Dearborn *(G-3719)*

Hi-Lites Graphic Inc E 231 924-0630 Fremont *(G-5775)*

J & M International Corp G 248 588-8108 Troy *(G-16428)*

J-Ad Graphics Inc D 800 870-7085 Hastings *(G-7416)*

Jomark Inc F 248 478-2600 Farmington Hills *(G-5033)*

Jtc Inc E 517 784-0576 Jackson *(G-8486)*

Kalamazoo Photo Comp Svcs E 269 345-3706 Kalamazoo *(G-8794)*

Larsen Graphics Inc E 989 823-3000 Vassar *(G-16812)*

Lasertec Inc E 586 274-4500 Madison Heights *(G-10298)*

Litsenberger Print Shop G 906 482-3903 Houghton *(G-7976)*

Loc Industries Inc G 586 759-8412 Warren *(G-17129)*

Macomb Printing Inc E 586 463-2301 Clinton Township *(G-3163)*

Marketing VI Group Inc G 989 793-3933 Saginaw *(G-14081)*

Metropolitan Indus Lithography G 269 323-9333 Portage *(G-13016)*

Micrgraphics Printing Inc E 231 739-6575 Norton Shores *(G-11773)*

Microforms Inc D 586 939-7900 Beverly Hills *(G-1620)*

Mid-State Printing Inc F 989 875-4163 Ithaca *(G-8364)*

Millbrook Printing Co E 517 627-4078 Grand Ledge *(G-6112)*

▲ **Mitchell Graphics Inc** E 231 347-4635 Petoskey *(G-12459)*

Moormann Printing Inc G 269 423-2411 Decatur *(G-3805)*

Morris Communications Corp C 269 673-2141 Allegan *(G-177)*

North American Graphics Inc E 586 486-1110 Warren *(G-17173)*

Ogemaw County Herald Inc E 989 345-0044 West Branch *(G-17514)*

P D Q Press Inc G 586 725-1888 Ira *(G-8265)*

Parkside Printing Inc G 810 765-4500 Marine City *(G-10479)*

Parkside Speedy Print Inc G 810 985-8484 Port Huron *(G-12955)*

Paul C Doerr ....G.... 734 242-2058
Monroe (G-11060)
Peg-Master Business Forms Inc ....G.... 586 566-8694
Shelby Township (G-14662)
Phase III Graphics Inc ....G.... 616 949-9290
Grand Rapids (G-6753)
Plymouth-Canton Cmnty Crier ....E.... 734 453-6900
Plymouth (G-12722)
Poly Tech Industries Inc ....G.... 248 589-9950
Madison Heights (G-10331)
Print Masters Inc ....F.... 248 548-7100
Madison Heights (G-10339)
▲ Print-Tech Inc ....E.... 734 996-2345
Ann Arbor (G-604)
Printcomm Inc ....D.... 810 239-5763
Flint (G-5484)
Printery Inc ....E.... 616 396-4655
Holland (G-7777)
Printing Centre Inc ....F.... 517 694-2400
Holt (G-7922)
▼ Progressive Prtg & Graphics ....G.... 269 965-8909
Battle Creek (G-1238)
Qrp Inc ....E.... 989 496-2955
Midland (G-10906)
Qrp Inc ....G.... 989 496-2955
Midland (G-10905)
Quick Printing Company Inc ....G.... 616 241-0506
Grand Rapids (G-6802)
R R Donnelley & Sons Company ....D.... 313 964-1330
Detroit (G-4327)
Richard Larabee ....G.... 248 827-7755
Southfield (G-15015)
Rider Type & Design ....G.... 989 839-0015
Midland (G-10908)
River Run Press Inc ....E.... 269 349-7603
Kalamazoo (G-8873)
Safran Printing Company Inc ....E.... 586 939-7600
Beverly Hills (G-1621)
Sans Serif Inc ....G.... 734 944-1190
Saline (G-14414)
Skip Printing and Dup Co ....G.... 586 779-2640
Roseville (G-13870)
▲ Spartan Printing Inc ....E.... 517 372-6910
Lansing (G-9264)
Spectrum Printers Inc ....E.... 517 423-5735
Tecumseh (G-15809)
Stafford Media Inc ....E.... 616 754-9301
Greenville (G-7154)
Stafford Media Inc ....D.... 616 754-1178
Greenville (G-7155)
Statewide Printing LLC ....G.... 517 485-4466
Lansing (G-9268)
T J K Inc ....G.... 586 731-9639
Sterling Heights (G-15518)
Technology MGT & Budgt Dept ....D.... 517 322-1897
Lansing (G-9430)
TGI Direct Inc ....F.... 810 239-5553
Ann Arbor (G-667)
The Envelope Printery Inc ....D.... 734 398-7700
Van Buren Twp (G-16787)
Thomas Kenyon Inc ....G.... 248 476-8130
Saint Clair Shores (G-14272)
Thorpe Printing Services Inc ....G.... 810 364-6222
Marysville (G-10622)
Times Herald Company ....F.... 810 985-7171
Port Huron (G-12971)
Turner Business Forms Inc ....E.... 989 752-5540
Saginaw (G-14171)
▲ Tweddle Group Inc ....C.... 586 307-3700
Clinton Township (G-3252)
Val Valley Inc ....G.... 248 474-7335
Farmington Hills (G-5145)
▲ Village Shop Inc ....D.... 231 946-3712
Traverse City (G-16138)
We Print Everything Inc ....G.... 989 723-6499
Owosso (G-12328)
Whiteside Consulting Group LLC ....G.... 313 288-6598
Detroit (G-4440)
Wolverine Printing Company LLC ....E.... 616 451-2075
Grand Rapids (G-6999)
Woodhams Enterprises Inc ....G.... 269 383-0600
Climax (G-3014)
Worten Copy Center Inc ....G.... 231 845-7030
Ludington (G-10089)

2796 Platemaking & Related Svcs

A D Johnson Engraving Co Inc ....F.... 269 385-0044
Kalamazoo (G-8672)
A-1 Engraving & Signs Inc ....G.... 810 231-2227
Brighton (G-1875)
Adgravers Inc ....E.... 313 259-3780
Detroit (G-3842)
Al Corp ....F.... 734 475-7357
Chelsea (G-2701)
Alpha 21 LLC ....G.... 248 352-7330
Southfield (G-14828)
Art In Transit Inc ....G.... 248 585-5566
Troy (G-16217)
Behrmann Printing Company Inc ....F.... 248 799-7771
Southfield (G-14851)
Breck Graphics Incorporated ....E.... 616 248-4110
Grand Rapids (G-6235)
Britten Inc ....C.... 231 941-8200
Traverse City (G-15920)
Brophy Engraving Co Inc ....E.... 313 871-2333
Detroit (G-3919)
Celia Corporation ....D.... 616 887-7341
Sparta (G-15091)
Dearborn Lithograph Inc ....E.... 734 464-4242
Livonia (G-9701)
Diamond Graphics Inc ....G.... 269 345-1164
Kalamazoo (G-8726)
F & A Enterprises of Michigan ....G.... 906 228-3222
Marquette (G-10531)
Fortis Sltions Group Centl LLC ....D.... 248 437-5200
Wixom (G-17812)
Fusion Flexo LLC ....G.... 269 685-5827
Richland (G-13249)
Fusion Flexo LLC ....E.... 269 685-5827
Plainwell (G-12525)
Graphic Enterprises Inc ....D.... 248 616-4900
Madison Heights (G-10258)
Graphic Specialties Inc ....E.... 616 247-0060
Grand Rapids (G-6475)
Hamblin Company ....E.... 517 423-7491
Tecumseh (G-15796)
Industrial Imprntng & Die Ctng ....G.... 586 778-9470
Eastpointe (G-4704)
Kalamazoo Photo Comp Svcs ....E.... 269 345-3706
Kalamazoo (G-8794)
Mark Maker Company Inc ....E.... 616 538-6980
Grand Rapids (G-6643)
Marketing VI Group Inc ....G.... 989 793-3933
Saginaw (G-14081)
Mel Printing Co Inc ....E.... 313 928-5440
Taylor (G-15738)
Microforms Inc ....D.... 586 939-7900
Beverly Hills (G-1620)
North American Color Inc ....E.... 269 323-0552
Portage (G-13019)
North American Graphics Inc ....E.... 586 486-1110
Warren (G-17173)
▲ Owosso Graphic Arts Inc ....E.... 989 725-7112
Owosso (G-12309)
Panoplate Lithographics Inc ....G.... 269 343-4644
Kalamazoo (G-8840)
Qrp Inc ....G.... 989 496-2955
Midland (G-10905)
Rob Enterprises Inc ....F.... 269 685-5827
Plainwell (G-12543)
Rose Engraving Company ....G.... 616 243-3108
Grand Rapids (G-6837)
Safran Printing Company Inc ....E.... 586 939-7600
Beverly Hills (G-1621)
Schawk Inc ....G.... 269 381-3820
Kalamazoo (G-8884)
Sgk LLC ....D.... 269 381-3820
Battle Creek (G-1245)
Southern Lithoplate Inc ....D.... 616 957-2650
Grand Rapids (G-6873)
Stamp-Rite Incorporated ....E.... 517 487-5071
Lansing (G-9267)
Standex International Corp ....E.... 586 296-5500
Fraser (G-5735)
Trico Incorporated ....G.... 517 764-1780
Jackson (G-8592)
Twin City Engraving Company ....G.... 269 983-0601
Saint Joseph (G-14346)
Weighman Enterprises Inc ....G.... 989 755-2116
Saginaw (G-14181)

28 CHEMICALS AND ALLIED PRODUCTS

2812 Alkalies & Chlorine

Arkema Inc ....C.... 616 243-4578
Grand Rapids (G-6181)
◆ Dow Chemical Company ....B.... 989 636-1000
Midland (G-10834)
Dow Chemical Company ....D.... 989 636-5409
Midland (G-10848)
Jci Jones Chemicals Inc ....E.... 734 283-0677
Wyandotte (G-17963)
▲ Kassouni Manufacturing Inc ....E.... 616 794-0989
Belding (G-1423)
Occidental Chemical Corp ....E.... 231 845-4411
Ludington (G-10075)
Pittsburgh Glass Works LLC ....C.... 248 371-1700
Rochester Hills (G-13494)
PPG Industries Inc ....F.... 248 641-2000
Troy (G-16557)

2813 Industrial Gases

Affordable Neon Ent ....G.... 906 356-6168
Rock (G-13552)
Air Products and Chemicals Inc ....E.... 313 297-2006
Detroit (G-3847)
Airgas Usa LLC ....F.... 517 673-0997
Blissfield (G-1712)
Airserve LLC ....G.... 586 427-5349
Center Line (G-2576)
Argon Group LLC ....G.... 248 370-0003
Rochester Hills (G-13370)
Caseq Technologies Inc ....G.... 734 730-5407
Holland (G-7586)
Fremont Community Digester LLC ....F.... 248 735-6684
Novi (G-11887)
Great Lakes Neon ....G.... 517 582-7451
Grand Ledge (G-6108)
Greenville Trck Wldg Sups LLC ....F.... 616 754-6120
Greenville (G-7136)
Helium Home Base LLC ....G.... 734 895-3608
Westland (G-17568)
Hydrogen Assist Development ....G.... 734 823-4969
Dundee (G-4589)
Linde Gas LLC ....G.... 616 754-7575
Greenville (G-7144)
Linde Gas North America LLC ....G.... 630 857-6460
Southfield (G-14969)
Linde Gas North America LLC ....F.... 616 475-0203
Wyoming (G-18017)
Linde Gas North America LLC ....G.... 734 397-7373
Canton (G-2392)
Linde Inc ....G.... 517 541-2473
Charlotte (G-2658)
Matheson ....G.... 586 498-8315
Roseville (G-13831)
Matheson Tri-Gas Inc ....F.... 734 425-8870
Garden City (G-5833)
Praxair Inc ....F.... 586 751-7400
Warren (G-17191)
Praxair Inc ....E.... 269 276-0442
Kalamazoo (G-8856)
Praxair Inc ....E.... 231 796-3266
Grand Rapids (G-6761)
Praxair Inc ....E.... 269 926-8296
Benton Harbor (G-1538)
Praxair Inc ....E.... 231 722-3773
Muskegon (G-11405)
Praxair Inc ....G.... 313 319-6220
Dearborn (G-3750)
Praxair Inc ....E.... 313 849-4200
River Rouge (G-13280)
Praxair Distribution Inc ....E.... 616 451-3055
Grand Rapids (G-6762)
Praxair Distribution Inc ....E.... 313 778-7085
Detroit (G-4308)
South Park Welding Sups LLC ....F.... 810 364-6521
Marysville (G-10618)
Spectrum Neon Co ....G.... 248 246-1142
Madison Heights (G-10358)
Tite Neon Cat ....G.... 734 755-7349
Monroe (G-11076)

2816 Inorganic Pigments

Alloying Surfaces Inc ....G.... 248 524-9200
Troy (G-16191)
Douglas Corp ....F.... 517 767-4112
Tekonsha (G-15818)
▲ Ebonex Corporation ....F.... 313 388-0063
Melvindale (G-10697)
Oerlikon Metco (us) Inc ....E.... 248 288-0027
Troy (G-16533)
Sun Chemical Corporation ....C.... 231 788-2371
Muskegon (G-11432)

2819 Indl Inorganic Chemicals, NEC

Airgas Usa LLC ....F.... 517 673-0997
Blissfield (G-1712)

S I C

Albemarle Corporation ....C 269 637-8474
South Haven (G-14751)
Algoma Products Inc ....F 616 285-6440
Grand Rapids (G-6157)
Alonzo Products Inc ....F 269 445-0847
Cassopolis (G-2526)
Antonios Leather Experts ....G 734 762-5000
Livonia (G-9649)
Assay Designs Inc ....E 734 214-0923
Ann Arbor (G-370)
Axchem Inc ....G 734 641-9842
Wayne (G-17425)
Blue Cube Holding LLC ....E 989 636-1000
Midland (G-10817)
Boropharm Inc ....G 248 348-5776
Novi (G-11839)
Boropharm Inc ....G 734 585-0601
Ann Arbor (G-387)
Cabot Corporation ....E 989 495-2113
Midland (G-10821)
Cal-Chlor Corp ....E 231 843-1147
Ludington (G-10051)
Caravan Technologies Inc ....F 313 341-2551
Detroit (G-3929)
▲ Ceratizit Usa Inc ....C 586 759-2280
Warren (G-16977)
Chemico Systems Inc ....G 586 986-2343
Warren (G-16980)
Chemico Systems Inc ....E 248 723-3263
Southfield (G-14866)
Chemtrade Chemicals US LLC ....G 313 842-5222
Detroit (G-3933)
Cole King LLC ....G 248 276-1278
Orion (G-12176)
Continental Carbide Ltd Inc ....F 586 463-9577
Clinton Township (G-3090)
Cytec Industries Inc ....C 269 349-6677
Kalamazoo (G-8722)
▲ Dando Chemicals US LLC ....G 248 629-9434
Southfield (G-14878)
Diazem Corp ....G 989 832-3612
Midland (G-10832)
Drw Systems Carbide LLC ....G 810 392-3526
Riley (G-13273)
Element 80 Engraving LLC ....G 616 318-7407
Grand Rapids (G-6374)
Element Salon and Day Spa ....G 989 708-6006
Midland (G-10860)
Element Services LLC ....G 517 672-1005
Howell (G-8038)
Empirical Bioscience Inc ....G 877 479-9949
Grand Rapids (G-6377)
Freiborne Industries Inc ....E 248 333-2490
Pontiac (G-12825)
Great Lakes Chemical Services ....E 269 372-6886
Portage (G-12999)
◆ Haviland Products Company ....C 616 361-6691
Grand Rapids (G-6498)
Haviland Products Company ....G 800 456-1134
Grand Rapids (G-6499)
Henkel US Operations Corp ....C 586 759-5555
Warren (G-17080)
Henkel US Operations Corp ....B 248 588-1082
Madison Heights (G-10266)
High-Po-Chlor Inc ....G 734 942-1500
Ann Arbor (G-490)
Hydro-Zone Inc ....G 734 247-4488
Brownstown (G-2065)
I C S Corporation America Inc ....F 616 554-9300
Grand Rapids (G-6522)
▲ ICM Products Inc ....E 269 445-0847
Cassopolis (G-2531)
▲ Icmp Inc ....E 269 445-0847
Cassopolis (G-2532)
Inpore Technologies Inc ....G 517 481-2270
East Lansing (G-4663)
Jade Scientific Inc ....F 734 207-3775
Westland (G-17572)
Jci Jones Chemicals Inc ....E 734 283-0677
Wyandotte (G-17963)
Kage Group LLC ....E 734 604-5052
Van Buren Twp (G-16767)
Koppers Performance Chem Inc ....E 906 296-8271
Hubbell (G-8126)
Lily Products Michigan Inc ....G 616 245-9193
Grand Rapids (G-6628)
Liquid Dustlayer Inc ....G 231 723-3750
Manistee (G-10426)
McGean-Rohco Inc ....E 216 441-4900
Livonia (G-9832)

Metrex Research LLC ....D 734 947-6700
Romulus (G-13706)
Nanocerox Inc ....F 734 741-9522
Ann Arbor (G-569)
Nelsonite Chemical Products ....G 616 456-7098
Grand Rapids (G-6713)
Nextcat Inc ....G 248 514-6742
Birmingham (G-1695)
Nugentec Oilfield Chem LLC ....G 517 518-2712
Howell (G-8072)
Oerlikon Metco (us) Inc ....E 248 288-0027
Troy (G-16533)
▲ Pacific Industrial Dev Corp ....D 734 930-9292
Ann Arbor (G-588)
◆ Pressure Vessel Service Inc ....E 313 921-1200
Detroit (G-4310)
PVS Chemical Solutions Inc ....G 313 921-1200
Detroit (G-4318)
◆ Pvs-Nolwood Chemicals Inc ....E 313 921-1200
Detroit (G-4320)
R L Schmitt Company Inc ....E 734 525-9310
Livonia (G-9905)
Rap Products Inc ....G 989 893-5583
Bay City (G-1348)
Raven Carbide Die LLC ....G 313 228-8776
New Boston (G-11510)
Sbz Corporation ....G 248 649-1166
Troy (G-16595)
◆ Silbond Corporation ....E 517 436-3171
Weston (G-17613)
Solutia Inc ....B 734 676-4400
Trenton (G-16157)
Specialty Minerals Inc ....F 906 779-9138
Quinnesec (G-13102)
Sterling Diagnostics Inc ....F 586 979-2141
Sterling Heights (G-15511)
Sumitomo Electric Carbide Inc ....F 734 451-0200
Plymouth (G-12761)
◆ Transtar Autobody Tech LLC ....C 810 220-3000
Brighton (G-1999)
United Abrasive Inc ....F 906 563-9249
Vulcan (G-16846)
US Bio Carbon LLC ....G 616 334-9862
Caledonia (G-2320)
USA Carbide ....G 248 817-5137
Troy (G-16667)
Weiser Metal Products Inc ....G 989 736-6055
Harrisville (G-7367)
Wilkinson Chemical Corporation ....F 989 843-6163
Mayville (G-10676)
▼ Xg Sciences Inc ....G 517 703-1110
Lansing (G-9437)

2821 Plastics, Mtrls & Nonvulcanizable Elastomers

Acp Technologies LLC ....G 586 322-3511
Sterling Heights (G-15251)
Advanced Elastomers Corp ....G 734 458-4194
Livonia (G-9628)
Advanced Polymers Composites ....G 248 766-1507
Clarkston (G-2906)
▲ Alliance Polymers and Svcs LLC ....G 734 710-6700
Romulus (G-13650)
Allnex USA Inc ....D 269 385-1205
Kalamazoo (G-8675)
▲ Alumilite Corporation ....F 269 488-4000
Galesburg (G-5805)
American Compounding Spc LLC ....D 810 227-3500
Brighton (G-1884)
Amplas Compounding LLC ....F 586 795-2555
Sterling Heights (G-15260)
◆ Anderson Development Company ....C 517 263-2121
Adrian (G-49)
API Polymers Inc ....G 855 274-7659
Clinton Township (G-3055)
▼ Argonics Inc ....D 906 226-9747
Gwinn (G-7215)
▲ Arvron Inc ....E 616 530-1888
Grand Rapids (G-6186)
◆ Asahi Kasei Plas N Amer Inc ....C 517 223-2000
Fowlerville (G-5559)
▲ Asahi Kasei Plastics Amer Inc ....E 517 223-2000
Fowlerville (G-5560)
Bakelite N Sumitomo Amer Inc ....G 248 313-7000
Novi (G-11837)
BASF Corporation ....D 734 591-5560
Livonia (G-9660)
Blue Water Bioproducts LLC ....G 586 453-9219
Port Huron (G-12902)

C & D Enterprises Inc ....F 248 373-0011
Burton (G-2147)
▲ Camryn Industries LLC ....C 248 663-5850
Southfield (G-14863)
Camryn Industries LLC ....E 248 663-5900
Detroit (G-3927)
Cartex Corporation ....D 734 857-5961
Romulus (G-13660)
Cass Polymers ....E 517 543-7510
Charlotte (G-2636)
Century Plastics Inc ....G 586 566-3900
Shelby Township (G-14560)
Chase Plastic Services Inc ....G 616 246-7190
Grand Rapids (G-6273)
Chelsea-Megan Holding Inc ....F 248 307-9160
Troy (G-16265)
Cleanese Americas LLC ....G 248 377-2700
Auburn Hills (G-814)
CMC Plastyk LLC ....G 989 588-4468
Farwell (G-5160)
Cole Polymer Technologies Inc ....G 269 695-6275
Buchanan (G-2114)
Concepp Technologies ....F 734 324-6750
Wyandotte (G-17953)
Coplas Inc ....G 586 739-8940
Sterling Heights (G-15300)
Covestro LLC ....E 248 475-7700
Auburn Hills (G-828)
Csn Manufacturing Inc ....E 616 364-0027
Grand Rapids (G-6320)
Cytec Industries Inc ....C 269 349-6677
Kalamazoo (G-8722)
▲ D T M 1 Inc ....E 248 889-9210
Highland (G-7491)
◆ Dart Container Corp Kentucky ....B 517 676-3800
Mason (G-10632)
▲ Delta Polymers Co ....E 586 795-2900
Sterling Heights (G-15309)
◆ Dow Chemical Company ....B 989 636-1000
Midland (G-10834)
Dow Chemical Company ....D 231 845-4285
Ludington (G-10056)
Dow Chemical Company ....D 989 636-1000
Midland (G-10835)
Dow Chemical Company ....D 810 966-9816
Clyde (G-3282)
Dow Chemical Company ....G 989 708-6737
Midland (G-10837)
Dow Chemical Company ....G 989 636-1000
Midland (G-10838)
Dow Chemical Company ....G 989 636-8587
Midland (G-10839)
Dow Chemical Company ....G 989 636-1000
Midland (G-10840)
Dow Chemical Company ....C 989 832-1000
Midland (G-10844)
Dow Chemical Company ....D 989 636-0540
Midland (G-10845)
Dow Chemical Company ....D 989 636-6351
Midland (G-10847)
Dow Chemical Company ....D 989 636-5409
Midland (G-10848)
Dow Inc ....G 989 636-1000
Midland (G-10851)
Dow International Holdings Co ....G 989 636-1000
Midland (G-10852)
◆ Dow Silicones Corporation ....A 989 496-4000
Auburn (G-751)
Dow Silicones Corporation ....D 989 496-4137
Midland (G-10855)
◆ Durez Corporation ....C 248 313-7000
Novi (G-11874)
E I Du Pont De Nemours & Co ....E 302 999-6566
Auburn Hills (G-849)
Eagle Design & Technology Inc ....E 616 748-1022
Zeeland (G-18133)
Eastman Chemical Company ....G 734 672-7823
Trenton (G-16153)
Envisiontec Inc ....D 313 436-4300
Dearborn (G-3702)
Florida Production Engrg Inc ....F 248 588-4870
Troy (G-16368)
FM Research Management LLC ....G 906 360-5833
Trenary (G-16150)
▲ Foampartner Americas Inc ....G 248 243-3100
Rochester Hills (G-13426)
◆ Freudenberg N Amer Ltd Partnr ....G 734 354-5505
Plymouth (G-12623)
▲ Freudenberg-Nok General Partnr ....C 734 451-0020
Plymouth (G-12624)

SIC SECTION
28 CHEMICALS AND ALLIED PRODUCTS

Geomembrane Research.................G....... 231 943-2266
  Traverse City *(G-15978)*
Georgia-Pacific LLC..........................E...... 989 348-7275
  Grayling *(G-7107)*
Grand Traverse Tool Inc..................G....... 231 929-4743
  Traverse City *(G-15989)*
Harbor Green Solutions LLC...........G....... 269 352-0265
  Benton Harbor *(G-1507)*
Heritage Mfg Inc.................................G....... 586 949-7446
  Chesterfield *(G-2784)*
Huntsman Advanced Materials AM.....C...... 517 351-5900
  East Lansing *(G-4662)*
Huntsman Corporation......................D...... 248 322-8682
  Auburn Hills *(G-901)*
Huntsman-Cooper LLC.....................D...... 248 322-7300
  Auburn Hills *(G-902)*
Indelco Plastics Corporation............G....... 616 452-7077
  Grand Rapids *(G-6531)*
Innovatec LLC.....................................G....... 813 545-6818
  Berkley *(G-1585)*
◆ Innovative Polymers Inc ....F....... 989 224-9500
  Saint Johns *(G-14284)*
Interfibe Corporation.........................F....... 269 327-6141
  Schoolcraft *(G-14495)*
▲ JB Products Inc..............................G....... 248 549-1900
  Troy *(G-16434)*
Jsp International LLC......................D...... 517 748-5200
  Jackson *(G-8485)*
Kayler Mold & Engineering..............G....... 586 739-0699
  Sterling Heights *(G-15388)*
▲ Kentwood Packaging Corporation...D...... 616 698-9000
  Walker *(G-16869)*
Lakeshore Marble Company Inc.......E...... 269 429-8241
  Stevensville *(G-15574)*
Lauren Plastics LLC..........................G....... 330 339-3373
  Spring Lake *(G-15158)*
Lej Investments LLC........................G....... 616 452-3707
  Grandville *(G-7056)*
Lyondellbasell Industries Inc...........F....... 517 336-4800
  Lansing *(G-9393)*
Mac Material Acquisition Co............G....... 248 685-8393
  Highland *(G-7496)*
Marketlab Inc.....................................F....... 616 656-5359
  Caledonia *(G-2306)*
McKechnie Vhcl Cmpnnts USA Inc.....E...... 218 894-1218
  Roseville *(G-13802)*
Michigan Polymer Reclaim Inc........F....... 989 227-0497
  Saint Johns *(G-14290)*
Midwest Resin Inc.............................G....... 586 803-3417
  Roseville *(G-13838)*
Mitsubishi Chls Perf Plyrs Inc........E...... 586 755-1660
  Warren *(G-17157)*
MRM Industries Inc..........................F....... 989 723-7443
  Owosso *(G-12306)*
Nano Materials & Processes Inc......G....... 248 529-3873
  Milford *(G-10974)*
Navtech LLC.......................................G....... 248 427-1080
  Wixom *(G-17862)*
New Boston Rtm Inc..........................E...... 734 753-9956
  New Boston *(G-11505)*
Next Specialty Resins Inc................F....... 419 843-4600
  Addison *(G-37)*
Oscoda Plastics Inc..........................E...... 989 739-6900
  Oscoda *(G-12216)*
Pacific Epoxy Polymers Inc.............E...... 616 949-1634
  Grand Rapids *(G-6738)*
Package Design & Mfg Inc...............E...... 248 486-4390
  Brighton *(G-1972)*
◆ Palmer Distributors Inc.................D...... 586 772-4225
  Fraser *(G-5703)*
▲ Pier One Polymers Incorporated......F....... 810 326-1456
  Saint Clair *(G-14231)*
Pittsburgh Glass Works LLC............C...... 248 371-1700
  Rochester Hills *(G-13494)*
▲ Plascon Inc......................................E...... 231 935-1580
  Traverse City *(G-16070)*
Plascon Films Inc.............................F....... 231 935-1580
  Traverse City *(G-16071)*
Plascon Packaging LLC....................G....... 231 935-1580
  Traverse City *(G-16072)*
▲ Plasteel Corporation.......................F....... 313 562-5400
  Inkster *(G-8231)*
Plastic Flow LLC................................G....... 906 483-0691
  Hancock *(G-7255)*
Plasticos Inc......................................G....... 586 493-1908
  Clinton Township *(G-3195)*
▲ Plastics Plus Inc..............................E...... 800 975-8694
  Auburn Hills *(G-975)*
PPG Industries Inc............................F....... 248 641-2000
  Troy *(G-16557)*

▲ Pro Polymers Inc..............................G....... 734 222-8820
  Stockbridge *(G-15592)*
Quality Dairy Company.....................D...... 517 319-4302
  Lansing *(G-9416)*
▲ Quantum Composites Inc................F....... 989 922-3863
  Bay City *(G-1345)*
Recycled Polymetric Materials........G....... 313 957-6373
  Detroit *(G-4335)*
Reklein Plastics Incorporated..........G....... 586 739-8850
  Sterling Heights *(G-15463)*
Resin Services Inc............................F....... 586 254-6770
  Sterling Heights *(G-15465)*
Resinate Materials Group Inc..........F....... 800 891-2955
  Plymouth *(G-12734)*
Revstone Industries LLC..................F....... 248 351-1000
  Troy *(G-16577)*
Revstone Industries LLC..................F....... 248 351-8800
  Southfield *(G-15014)*
Rhe-Tech LLC.....................................G....... 517 223-4874
  Fowlerville *(G-5579)*
Rohm Haas Dnmark Invstmnts LLC.....G....... 989 636-1463
  Midland *(G-10909)*
▲ Rosler Metal Finishing USA LLC......D...... 269 441-3000
  Battle Creek *(G-1242)*
Rubber & Plastics Co.........................E...... 248 370-0700
  Auburn Hills *(G-995)*
Saint-Gobain Prfmce Plas Corp........D...... 989 435-9533
  Beaverton *(G-1391)*
Sekisui America Corporation............F....... 517 279-7587
  Coldwater *(G-3331)*
Sekisui Polymr Innovations LLC.......D...... 616 392-9004
  Holland *(G-7799)*
Shapeshift LLC...................................G....... 517 910-3078
  Lansing *(G-9322)*
◆ Sigma International Inc..................E...... 248 230-9681
  Livonia *(G-9928)*
▲ Sika Auto Eaton Rapids Inc............F....... 248 588-2270
  Madison Heights *(G-10352)*
Solutia Inc..B...... 734 676-4400
  Trenton *(G-16157)*
Spartan Polymers LLC......................G....... 586 255-5644
  Bruce Twp *(G-2103)*
Specialty Products Us LLC..............G....... 989 636-4341
  Midland *(G-10919)*
Stonecrafters Inc...............................F....... 517 529-4990
  Clarklake *(G-2801)*
▲ Sulfo-Technologies LLC..................G....... 248 307-9150
  Madison Heights *(G-10363)*
▲ Sumika Polymers North Amer LLC....E...... 248 284-4797
  Farmington Hills *(G-5134)*
Summit Polymers Inc........................C...... 269 649-4900
  Vicksburg *(G-16845)*
▲ Toray Resin Company.....................D...... 248 269-8800
  Troy *(G-16647)*
Total Molding Solutions Inc............E...... 517 424-5900
  Tecumseh *(G-15813)*
Trinseo..G....... 989 636-5409
  Midland *(G-10921)*
Ufp Technologies Inc........................D...... 616 949-8100
  Grand Rapids *(G-6948)*
◆ United Foam A Ufp Tech Brnd..........D...... 616 949-8100
  Grand Rapids *(G-6952)*
United Resin Inc.................................E...... 800 521-4757
  Royal Oak *(G-13978)*
▲ Universal Consumer Pdts Inc..........G....... 616 364-6161
  Grand Rapids *(G-6953)*
▲ Vi-Chem Corp....................................E...... 616 247-8501
  Grand Rapids *(G-6969)*
◆ Vibracoustic North America L P......G....... 269 637-2116
  South Haven *(G-14780)*
Vibracoustic North America LP.......G....... 248 410-5066
  Farmington Hills *(G-5148)*
Weatherproof Inc...............................E...... 517 764-1330
  Jackson *(G-8606)*
▲ Wmc LLC..E...... 616 560-4142
  Greenville *(G-7161)*
Woodbridge Sales & Engrg Inc.......E...... 248 288-0100
  Troy *(G-16698)*
Xc LLC...E...... 586 755-1660
  Warren *(G-17300)*
Xg Sciences Inc.................................F....... 517 316-2038
  Lansing *(G-9436)*
◆ Zander Colloids Lc..........................G....... 810 714-1623
  Fenton *(G-5249)*

2822 Synthetic Rubber (Vulcanizable Elastomers)

A-Line Products Corporation............F....... 313 571-8300
  Detroit *(G-3830)*

Aptargroup Inc....................................C...... 989 631-8030
  Midland *(G-10816)*
Armada Rubber Manufacturing Co....D...... 586 784-9135
  Armada *(G-716)*
Covestro LLC......................................E...... 248 475-7700
  Auburn Hills *(G-828)*
Dawson Manufacturing Company.....C...... 269 925-0100
  Benton Harbor *(G-1493)*
Dendritech Inc....................................G....... 989 496-1152
  Midland *(G-10830)*
Dow Corning Corporation.................G....... 989 839-2808
  Midland *(G-10849)*
▲ Flexfab Horizons Intl Inc..................E...... 269 945-4700
  Hastings *(G-7409)*
▲ Flexfab LLC..G....... 269 945-2433
  Hastings *(G-7410)*
Grm Corporation.................................D...... 989 453-2322
  Pigeon *(G-12489)*
▲ ICM Products Inc..............................E...... 269 445-0847
  Cassopolis *(G-2531)*
Mitsubishi Chls Perf Plyrs Inc........E...... 586 755-1660
  Warren *(G-17157)*
▲ Mykin Inc...E...... 248 667-8030
  South Lyon *(G-14804)*
Saint-Gobain Prfmce Plas Corp........D...... 989 435-9533
  Beaverton *(G-1392)*
Specialty Manufacturing Inc............E...... 989 790-9011
  Saginaw *(G-14155)*

2823 Cellulosic Man-Made Fibers

▼ Applegate Insul Systems Inc..........E...... 517 521-3545
  Webberville *(G-17446)*
▲ J Rettenmaier USA LP.....................C...... 269 679-2340
  Schoolcraft *(G-14497)*
Kraig Biocraft Labs Inc......................G....... 734 619-8066
  Ann Arbor *(G-520)*

2824 Synthetic Organic Fibers, Exc Cellulosic

ABC Nails LLC....................................G....... 616 776-6000
  Grand Rapids *(G-6129)*
Cytec Industries Inc..........................C...... 269 349-6677
  Kalamazoo *(G-8722)*
Dal-Tile Corporation..........................F....... 248 471-7150
  Farmington Hills *(G-4968)*
Protein Procurement Svcs Inc.........G....... 248 738-7970
  Bloomfield Hills *(G-1792)*
Solutia Inc..B...... 734 676-4400
  Trenton *(G-16157)*

2833 Medicinal Chemicals & Botanical Prdts

Aapharmasyn LLC..............................F....... 734 213-2123
  Ann Arbor *(G-337)*
▲ Access Business Group LLC..........B...... 616 787-6000
  Ada *(G-3)*
Alticor Global Holdings Inc..............F....... 616 787-1000
  Ada *(G-5)*
◆ Alticor Inc..C...... 616 787-1000
  Ada *(G-6)*
Aureogen Inc.......................................G....... 269 353-3805
  Kalamazoo *(G-8688)*
Darling Ingredients Inc....................D...... 313 928-7400
  Melvindale *(G-10695)*
Degrasyn Biosciences LLC...............G....... 713 582-3395
  Ann Arbor *(G-413)*
Hearing Health Science Inc.............G....... 734 476-9490
  Ann Arbor *(G-487)*
Kinder Products Unlimited LLC........G....... 586 557-3453
  Sterling Heights *(G-15389)*
▲ Little Silver Corp..............................G....... 248 642-0860
  Birmingham *(G-1688)*
Metabolic Solutions Dev Co LLC......F....... 269 343-6732
  Kalamazoo *(G-8822)*
Pharmacia & Upjohn Company LLC....D...... 908 901-8000
  Kalamazoo *(G-8849)*
Solohill Engineering Inc...................E...... 734 973-2956
  Ann Arbor *(G-640)*
Visionary Vitamin Co.........................G....... 734 788-5934
  Melvindale *(G-10708)*

2834 Pharmaceuticals

▲ Abaco Partners LLC..........................C...... 616 532-1700
  Kentwood *(G-8997)*
Abbott Laboratories...........................B...... 269 651-0600
  Sturgis *(G-15594)*
Abbott Laboratories...........................E...... 734 324-6666
  Wyandotte *(G-17944)*
Abbvie Inc..G....... 734 324-6650
  Wyandotte *(G-17945)*

28 CHEMICALS AND ALLIED PRODUCTS

Affiliated Troy Dermatologist..............F   248 267-5020
  Troy *(G-16171)*
Akorn Inc ....E   800 579-8327
  Ann Arbor *(G-350)*
Aspire Pharmacy..............................G   989 773-7849
  Mount Pleasant *(G-11171)*
Astellas Pharma Us Inc ....F   616 698-8825
  Grand Rapids *(G-6188)*
Astellas Pharma Us Inc ....G   231 947-3630
  Traverse City *(G-15897)*
Atterocor Inc ....G   734 845-9300
  Ann Arbor *(G-372)*
Avomeen LLC ....E   734 222-1090
  Ann Arbor *(G-377)*
Barclay Pharmacy.............................G   248 852-4600
  Rochester Hills *(G-13375)*
Berkley Pharmacy LLC ....F   586 573-8300
  Warren *(G-16955)*
Biolyte Laboratories LLC ....G   616 350-9055
  Grand Rapids *(G-6223)*
Biopolymer Innovations LLC ....G   517 432-3044
  East Lansing *(G-4652)*
Bristol-Myers Squibb Company ....D   248 528-2476
  Troy *(G-16247)*
▲ Caraco Pharma Inc ....G   313 871-8400
  Detroit *(G-3928)*
Cayman Chemical Company Inc ....D   734 971-3335
  Ann Arbor *(G-395)*
Central Admxture Phrm Svcs Inc ......E   734 953-6760
  Livonia *(G-9680)*
◆ Charles Bowman & Company ......F   616 786-4000
  Holland *(G-7588)*
Charles Bridenstine..........................G   269 699-5170
  Edwardsburg *(G-4762)*
Cns Inc ....G   616 242-7704
  Grand Rapids *(G-6283)*
Copagen LLC ....G   734 904-0365
  Ann Arbor *(G-405)*
Corium International Inc ....E   616 656-4563
  Grand Rapids *(G-6310)*
Diapin Therapeutics LLC ....G   734 764-9123
  Ann Arbor *(G-421)*
Diplomat Spclty Phrm Flint LLC ....B   810 768-9000
  Flint *(G-5419)*
Dow Chemical Company C   989 636-4406
  Midland *(G-10836)*
Ds Biotech LLC ....G   248 894-1474
  Bloomfield Hills *(G-1761)*
▲ DSC Laboratories LLC ....E   800 492-5988
  Muskegon *(G-11307)*
Eastside Pharmacy Inc.....................F   313 579-1755
  Detroit *(G-4024)*
▲ Elba Inc ....E   248 288-6098
  Troy *(G-16336)*
Emergent Biodef Oper Lnsng LLC ....B   517 327-1500
  Lansing *(G-9224)*
Esperion Therapeutics Inc ....D   734 887-3903
  Ann Arbor *(G-448)*
▲ Ferndale Laboratories Inc ....B   248 548-0900
  Ferndale *(G-5284)*
Ferndale Pharma Group Inc ....B   248 548-0900
  Ferndale *(G-5285)*
GE Healthcare Inc ....E   616 554-5717
  Grand Rapids *(G-6432)*
Gemphire Therapeutics Inc...............F   734 245-1700
  Livonia *(G-9750)*
Genentech Inc ....G   650 225-1000
  Lake Orion *(G-9136)*
Genoa Healthcare LLC ....G   313 989-0536
  Detroit *(G-4088)*
Glaxosmithkline LLC ....E   989 450-9859
  Frankenmuth *(G-5588)*
Glaxosmithkline LLC ....E   989 928-6535
  Oxford *(G-12347)*
Glaxosmithkline LLC ....E   989 280-1225
  Midland *(G-10866)*
Glaxosmithkline LLC ....E   248 561-3022
  Bloomfield Hills *(G-1769)*
Grand River Aseptic Mfg Inc ....F   616 464-5072
  Grand Rapids *(G-6467)*
Grass Lake Community Pharmacy....G   517 522-4100
  Grass Lake *(G-7088)*
Greenmark Biomedical Inc ....G   517 336-4665
  Lansing *(G-9378)*
H & A Pharmacy II LLC ....G   313 995-4552
  Westland *(G-17567)*
Harper Dermatology PC ....G   586 776-7546
  Grosse Pointe Shores *(G-7199)*
Healthplus Spclty Pharma.................G   734 769-1300
  Ann Arbor *(G-486)*

▲ Hello Life Inc................................F   616 808-3290
  Grand Rapids *(G-6504)*
Hello Life Inc....................................F   616 808-3290
  Grand Rapids *(G-6505)*
Housey Phrm RES Labs LLC ....G   248 663-7000
  Southfield *(G-14938)*
Innovative Pharmaceuticals...............G   248 789-0999
  Brighton *(G-1943)*
Ionxhealth Inc...................................F   616 808-3290
  Grand Rapids *(G-6544)*
Jade Pharmaceuticals Entp LLC ....G   248 716-8333
  Livonia *(G-9792)*
Jice Pharmaceuticals Co Inc ....G   616 897-5910
  Belding *(G-1420)*
▲ Kassouni Manufacturing Inc........E   616 794-0989
  Belding *(G-1423)*
King Pharmaceuticals LLC ....D   248 650-6400
  Rochester *(G-13332)*
◆ L Perrigo Company ....A   269 673-8451
  Allegan *(G-170)*
L Perrigo Company ....G   269 673-7962
  Allegan *(G-171)*
L Perrigo Company ....B   616 738-0150
  Holland *(G-7716)*
L Perrigo Company ....G   269 673-7962
  Allegan *(G-172)*
L Perrigo Company ....G   269 673-1608
  Allegan *(G-173)*
L Perrigo Company ....D   248 687-1036
  Troy *(G-16453)*
LLC Ash Stevens ....D   734 282-3370
  Riverview *(G-13300)*
Lxr Biotech LLC ....E   248 860-4246
  Auburn Hills *(G-931)*
Lymphogen Inc ....G   906 281-7372
  Houghton *(G-7977)*
McKesson Corporation ....D   734 953-2523
  Livonia *(G-9833)*
MD Hiller Corp ....G   877 751-9010
  Dearborn *(G-3737)*
Med Share Inc ....F   888 266-3567
  Dearborn *(G-3738)*
Mercury Drugs LLC ....G   248 545-3600
  Oak Park *(G-12084)*
Meridianrx LLC ....D   855 323-4580
  Detroit *(G-4226)*
Millendo Therapeutics Inc................E   734 845-9000
  Ann Arbor *(G-559)*
Millendo Transactionsub Inc.............G   734 845-9300
  Ann Arbor *(G-560)*
Mills Phrm & Apothecary LLC ....G   248 633-2872
  Birmingham *(G-1693)*
Motor City Naturals LLC ....G   313 329-4071
  Warren *(G-17161)*
N F P Inc..G   989 631-0009
  Midland *(G-10896)*
Nopras Technologies Inc ....G   248 486-6684
  South Lyon *(G-14807)*
Norman A Lewis ....G   248 219-5736
  Farmington Hills *(G-5080)*
Ocusano Inc ....G   734 730-5407
  Grand Rapids *(G-6727)*
Onl Therapeutics LLC......................G   734 998-8339
  Ann Arbor *(G-583)*
Painex Corporation...........................G   313 863-1200
  Detroit *(G-4286)*
Painexx Corporation.........................G   313 863-1200
  Detroit *(G-4287)*
Pancheck LLC ....F   989 288-6886
  Durand *(G-4611)*
Par Sterile Products LLC.................C   248 651-9081
  Rochester *(G-13344)*
Parkedale Pharmaceuticals Inc ....D   248 650-6400
  Rochester *(G-13345)*
PBM Nutritionals LLC ....F   269 673-8451
  Allegan *(G-180)*
Penrose Therapeutix LLC ....G   847 370-0303
  Plymouth *(G-12711)*
Perrigo Company ....G   269 686-1973
  Allegan *(G-181)*
◆ Perrigo Company ....A   269 673-8451
  Allegan *(G-182)*
Perrigo Company ....G   616 396-0941
  Holland *(G-7770)*
Perrigo Company ....G   269 673-7962
  Allegan *(G-183)*
Perrigo Pharmaceuticals Co ....F   269 673-8451
  Allegan *(G-184)*
Pfizer Inc..C   248 867-9067
  Clarkston *(G-2944)*

Pfizer Inc..F   248 650-6400
  Rochester *(G-13346)*
Pfizer Inc..G   734 679-7368
  Grosse Ile *(G-7175)*
Pfizer Inc..G   734 671-9315
  Trenton *(G-16156)*
Pfizer Inc..C   269 833-5143
  Kalamazoo *(G-8848)*
Pharmacia & Upjohn Company LLC ....D   908 901-8000
  Kalamazoo *(G-8849)*
Physicians Compounding Phrm........G   248 758-9100
  Bloomfield Hills *(G-1791)*
Plasma Biolife Services L P ....G   616 667-0264
  Grandville *(G-7064)*
PMI Branded Pharmaceuticals ....F   269 673-8451
  Allegan *(G-185)*
Port Huron Medical Assoc ....G   810 982-0100
  Fort Gratiot *(G-5551)*
▲ Pro Bottle LLC.............................G   248 345-9224
  Williamston *(G-17737)*
Qsv Pharma LLC..............................G   269 324-2358
  Portage *(G-13025)*
Renucell ....G   888 400-6032
  Grand Haven *(G-6071)*
▲ Safe N Simple LLC ....F   248 875-0840
  Clarkston *(G-2953)*
Soleo Health Inc ....G   248 513-8687
  Novi *(G-12000)*
Sun Pharmaceutical Inds Inc ....G   248 346-7302
  Farmington Hills *(G-5135)*
Sun Pharmaceutical Inds Inc ....E   609 495-2800
  Detroit *(G-4384)*
Supplement Group Inc ....F   248 588-2055
  Madison Heights *(G-10365)*
Tabletting Inc ....G   616 957-0281
  Grand Rapids *(G-6913)*
Team Pharma....................................G   269 344-8326
  Kalamazoo *(G-8908)*
Telocyte LLC ....G   616 570-4515
  Ada *(G-30)*
Tetra Corporation ....F   401 529-1630
  Eaton Rapids *(G-4734)*
◆ Uckele Health and Nutrition ....E   800 248-0330
  Blissfield *(G-1729)*
United State Phrm Group ....G   734 462-3685
  Livonia *(G-9981)*
Urban Specialty Apparel Inc ....F   248 395-9500
  Southfield *(G-15056)*
Vectech Pharmaceutical Cons..........F   248 478-5820
  Brighton *(G-2005)*
Velesco Phrm Svcs Inc.....................G   734 545-0696
  Wixom *(G-17924)*
Velesco Phrm Svcs Inc.....................F   734 527-9125
  Plymouth *(G-12787)*
Vortech Pharmaceutical Ltd..............G   313 584-4088
  Dearborn *(G-3770)*
Wandas Barium Cookie LLC ....G   906 281-1788
  Calumet *(G-2336)*
◆ Welchdry Inc ....F   616 399-2711
  Holland *(G-7853)*
Zoetis LLC ....E   888 963-8471
  Kalamazoo *(G-8929)*
Zomedica Pharmaceutical Inc ....G   734 369-2555
  Ann Arbor *(G-710)*
Zomedica Pharmaceuticals Corp .....F   734 369-2555
  Ann Arbor *(G-711)*

2835 Diagnostic Substances

Anatech Ltd ....F   269 964-6450
  Battle Creek *(G-1146)*
Biosan Laboratories Inc ....F   586 755-8970
  Warren *(G-16961)*
Connies Clutter ....G   517 684-7291
  Bay City *(G-1298)*
Cooper Genomics ....G   313 579-9650
  Plymouth *(G-12602)*
Everist Genomics Inc ....F   734 929-9475
  Ann Arbor *(G-450)*
Greenmark Biomedical Inc...............G   517 336-4665
  Lansing *(G-9378)*
Isensium ....G   517 580-9022
  East Lansing *(G-4666)*
Lynx Dx Inc ....G   734 274-3144
  Northville *(G-11707)*
Med Share Inc ....G   888 266-3567
  Dearborn *(G-3738)*
Nanorete Inc ....G   517 336-4680
  Lansing *(G-9404)*
Neogen Corporation ....G   800 327-5487
  Saint Joseph *(G-14331)*

SIC SECTION

28 CHEMICALS AND ALLIED PRODUCTS

▲ Neogen Corporation .... B 517 372-9200
Lansing *(G-9405)*
Ortho-Clinical Diagnostics Inc .... C 248 797-8087
Troy *(G-16538)*
Ova Science Inc .... G 617 758-8605
Ann Arbor *(G-586)*
Petnet Solutions Inc .... G 865 218-2000
Royal Oak *(G-13956)*
Plasma Biolife Services L P .... E 906 226-9080
Marquette *(G-10553)*
Plasma Biolife Services L P .... G 616 667-0264
Grandville *(G-7064)*
Retrosense Therapeutics LLC .... G 734 369-9333
Ann Arbor *(G-620)*
▲ Sigma Diagnostics Inc .... G 734 744-4846
Livonia *(G-9927)*
Swift Biosciences Inc .... G 734 330-2568
Ann Arbor *(G-652)*
Versant Medical Physics .... E 888 316-3644
Kalamazoo *(G-8918)*

2836 Biological Prdts, Exc Diagnostic Substances

Arbor Assays Inc .... F 734 677-1774
Ann Arbor *(G-362)*
Axonia Medical Inc .... G 269 615-6632
Kalamazoo *(G-8689)*
Biolife Plasma Services LP .... G 989 773-1500
Mount Pleasant *(G-11180)*
Biosan Laboratories Inc .... F 586 755-8970
Warren *(G-16961)*
Biosavita Inc .... G 734 233-3146
Plymouth *(G-12587)*
Bruce Kane Enterprises LLC .... G 410 727-0637
Farmington Hills *(G-4948)*
Emergent Biodef Oper Lnsng LLC .... B 517 327-1500
Lansing *(G-9224)*
Esperovax Inc .... G 248 667-1845
Plymouth *(G-12619)*
Immuno Concepts NA Ltd .... E 734 464-0701
Livonia *(G-9780)*
▲ Koppert Biological Systems .... E 734 641-3763
Howell *(G-8057)*
▲ Neogen Corporation .... B 517 372-9200
Lansing *(G-9405)*
Novavax Inc .... G 248 656-5336
Rochester *(G-13337)*
Octapharma Plasma Inc .... G 248 597-0314
Madison Heights *(G-10316)*
Oxford Biomedical Research Inc .... G 248 852-8815
Metamora *(G-10779)*
Plasma Pros .... G 734 354-6737
Westland *(G-17588)*
Stel Technologies LLC .... G 248 802-9457
Ann Arbor *(G-645)*
Transtechbio Inc .... G 734 994-4728
Saline *(G-14419)*
Venom Motorsports Inc .... G 616 635-2519
Grand Rapids *(G-6964)*

2841 Soap & Detergents

Amway International Dev Inc .... F 616 787-6000
Ada *(G-8)*
Aqua-Gel Corporation .... G 313 538-9240
Redford *(G-13143)*
Caravan Technologies Inc .... F 313 341-2551
Detroit *(G-3929)*
Cindys Suds LLC .... G 616 485-1983
Lowell *(G-10026)*
Continental Bldg Svs of Cinci .... F 313 336-8543
Grosse Pointe Woods *(G-7202)*
Cul-Mac Industries Inc .... E 734 728-9700
Wayne *(G-17429)*
Diversified Chemical Tech Inc .... C 313 867-5444
Detroit *(G-4011)*
▲ DSC Laboratories Inc .... E 800 492-5988
Muskegon *(G-11307)*
Ecolab Inc .... E 248 697-0202
Novi *(G-11879)*
Expert Cleaning Solutions Inc .... G 517 545-9095
Howell *(G-8039)*
Fred Carter .... G 989 799-7176
Saginaw *(G-14039)*
Gage Global Services Inc .... E 248 541-3824
Ferndale *(G-5287)*
Great Lakes Bath & Body Inc .... G 231 421-9160
Traverse City *(G-15991)*
Hydro-Chem Systems Inc .... E 616 531-6420
Caledonia *(G-2301)*

Ipax Atlantic LLC .... F 313 933-4211
Detroit *(G-4149)*
K C M Inc .... F 616 245-8599
Grand Rapids *(G-6565)*
L I S Manufacturing Inc .... F 734 525-3070
Livonia *(G-9803)*
Moon River Soap Co LLC .... G 248 930-9467
Rochester *(G-13335)*
National Soap Company Inc .... G 248 545-8180
Royal Oak *(G-13953)*
Oil Chem Inc .... E 810 235-3040
Flint *(G-5476)*
Rhema Products Inc .... G 313 561-6800
Dearborn Heights *(G-3795)*
Sanitation Strategies LLC .... F 517 268-3303
Holt *(G-7925)*
Sterling Laboratories Inc .... G 248 233-1190
Southfield *(G-15034)*
▲ Stone Soap Company Inc .... E 248 706-1000
Sylvan Lake *(G-15672)*
Trinity Seven Enterprises Inc .... G 216 906-0984
Canton *(G-2436)*
Vaughan Industries Inc .... F 313 935-2040
Detroit *(G-4423)*

2842 Spec Cleaning, Polishing & Sanitation Preparations

Able Solutions LLC .... G 810 216-6106
Port Huron *(G-12880)*
▲ Access Business Group LLC .... B 616 787-6000
Ada *(G-3)*
All-Chem Corporation .... G 313 865-3600
Detroit *(G-3857)*
◆ American Jetway Corporation .... D 734 721-5930
Wayne *(G-17423)*
▲ Anchor Wiping Cloth Inc .... D 313 892-4000
Detroit *(G-3870)*
Arrow Chemical Products Inc .... G 313 237-0277
Detroit *(G-3879)*
▲ B W Manufacturing Inc .... G 616 447-9076
Comstock Park *(G-3461)*
▼ Bio Kleen Products Inc .... G 269 567-9400
Kalamazoo *(G-8697)*
Biosolutions LLC .... F 616 846-1210
Grand Haven *(G-5997)*
Bissell Better Life LLC .... G 800 237-7691
Grand Rapids *(G-6224)*
Burge Incorporated .... G 616 791-2214
Grand Rapids *(G-6242)*
Cal Chemical Manufacturing Co .... G 586 778-7006
Saint Clair Shores *(G-14242)*
Caravan Technologies Inc .... F 313 341-2551
Detroit *(G-3929)*
Chemeisters Inc .... G 313 538-5550
Redford *(G-13152)*
Chemetall US Inc .... F 517 787-4846
Jackson *(G-8408)*
Chemical Company of America .... G 313 272-4310
Detroit *(G-3932)*
Chemloc Inc .... F 989 465-6541
Coleman *(G-3342)*
◆ Chrysan Industries Inc .... E 734 451-5411
Plymouth *(G-12597)*
Coastal Concierge .... G 269 639-1515
South Haven *(G-14757)*
▲ Colonial Chemical Corp .... F 517 789-8161
Jackson *(G-8415)*
County of Muskegon .... G 231 724-6219
Muskegon *(G-11301)*
◆ Coxen Enterprises Inc .... D 248 486-3800
Brighton *(G-1906)*
Cul-Mac Industries Inc .... E 734 728-9700
Wayne *(G-17429)*
Diversified Chemical Tech Inc .... C 313 867-5444
Detroit *(G-4011)*
Diversified Davitco LLC .... F 248 681-9197
Waterford *(G-17334)*
▲ DSC Laboratories Inc .... E 800 492-5988
Muskegon *(G-11307)*
Enviro-Brite Solutions LLC .... G 989 387-2758
Oscoda *(G-12209)*
Formax Manufacturing Corp .... E 616 456-5458
Grand Rapids *(G-6416)*
Global Wholesale & Marketing .... G 248 910-8302
Sterling Heights *(G-15361)*
Grav Co LLC .... F 269 651-5467
Sturgis *(G-15605)*
Great Lakes Laboratories Inc .... G 734 525-8300
Livonia *(G-9760)*

H & J Mfg Consulting Svcs Corp .... G 734 941-8314
Romulus *(G-13684)*
Healthcure LLC .... F 313 743-2331
Detroit *(G-4119)*
▲ Henkel Surface Technologies .... G 248 307-0240
Madison Heights *(G-10265)*
High-Po-Chlor Inc .... G 734 942-1500
Ann Arbor *(G-490)*
Hydro-Chem Systems Inc .... E 616 531-6420
Caledonia *(G-2301)*
Innovative Fluids LLC .... F 734 241-5699
Milan *(G-10941)*
Ipax Atlantic LLC .... F 313 933-4211
Detroit *(G-4149)*
▼ Ipax Cleanogel Inc .... G 313 933-4211
Detroit *(G-4150)*
▲ Kath Khemicals LLC .... F 586 275-2646
Sterling Heights *(G-15387)*
Kmi Cleaning Solutions Inc .... F 269 964-2557
Battle Creek *(G-1220)*
Labtech Corporation .... F 313 862-1737
Detroit *(G-4190)*
Liedel Power Cleaning .... F 734 848-2827
Erie *(G-4805)*
McGean-Rohco Inc .... E 216 441-4900
Livonia *(G-9832)*
Metals Preservation Group LLC .... F 586 944-2720
Saint Clair Shores *(G-14263)*
Mr Eds Sewer Cleaning Service .... G 313 565-2740
Dearborn Heights *(G-3790)*
Native Green LLC .... F 248 365-4200
Orion *(G-12186)*
Odor Gone Inc .... F 888 636-7292
Zeeland *(G-18172)*
P & F Enterprises LLC .... G 616 340-1265
Wyoming *(G-18024)*
Peerless Quality Products .... F 313 933-7525
Detroit *(G-4294)*
▲ Premiere Packaging Inc .... D 810 239-7650
Flint *(G-5483)*
▼ Progress Chemical Inc .... G 616 534-6103
Grandville *(G-7067)*
▼ Punati Chemical Corp .... F 248 276-0101
Auburn Hills *(G-983)*
Rhino Linings of Grand Rapids .... G 616 361-9786
Grand Rapids *(G-6822)*
Rooto Corporation .... F 517 546-8330
Howell *(G-8093)*
S C Johnson & Son Inc .... F 248 822-2174
Troy *(G-16587)*
S C Johnson & Son Inc .... C 989 667-0211
Bay City *(G-1354)*
SC Johnson & Son .... G 989 667-0235
Bay City *(G-1356)*
Schaffner Manufacturing Co .... G 248 735-8900
Northville *(G-11724)*
Southwin Ltd .... E 734 525-9000
Livonia *(G-9936)*
Superior Manufacturing Corp .... F 313 935-1550
Troy *(G-16627)*
▼ Tennant Commercial .... B 616 994-4000
Holland *(G-7826)*
Thetford Corporation .... D 734 769-6000
Dexter *(G-4513)*
▲ Thetford Corporation .... C 734 769-6000
Ann Arbor *(G-670)*
◆ Transtar Autobody Tech LLC .... C 810 220-3000
Brighton *(G-1999)*
Wilbur Products Inc .... F 231 755-3805
Muskegon *(G-11451)*
▼ Ziebart International Corp .... C 248 588-4100
Troy *(G-16706)*

2843 Surface Active & Finishing Agents, Sulfonated Oils

BASF Corporation .... C 734 324-6000
Wyandotte *(G-17948)*
Ipax Atlantic LLC .... F 313 933-4211
Detroit *(G-4149)*
◆ McCarthy Group Incorporated .... G 616 977-2900
Grand Rapids *(G-6652)*
▲ Metalworking Lubricants Co .... C 248 332-3500
Pontiac *(G-12849)*

2844 Perfumes, Cosmetics & Toilet Preparations

▲ Abaco Partners LLC .... C 616 532-1700
Kentwood *(G-8997)*

28 CHEMICALS AND ALLIED PRODUCTS

▲ Agrestal Hygienics LLC ....G...... 800 410-9053
Kalamazoo *(G-8674)*
Amour Your Body LLC ....G...... 586 846-3100
Clinton Township *(G-3049)*
Amway International Dev Inc ....F...... 616 787-6000
Ada *(G-8)*
Art of Shaving - FI LLC ....G...... 248 649-5872
Troy *(G-16219)*
Beard Balm LLC ....G...... 313 451-3653
Detroit *(G-3895)*
Bio Source Naturals LLC ....G...... 734 335-6798
Canton *(G-2352)*
Brun Laboratories Inc ....G...... 616 456-1114
Grand Rapids *(G-6237)*
Can You Handlebar LLC ....F...... 248 821-2171
Mount Clemens *(G-11126)*
Conquest Scents ....E...... 810 653-2759
Davison *(G-3643)*
Detroit Fine Products LLC ....F...... 877 294-5826
Ferndale *(G-5277)*
Eve Salonspa ....G...... 269 327-4811
Portage *(G-12994)*
Fragrance Outlet Inc ....G...... 517 552-9545
Howell *(G-8042)*
◆ Homedics Usa LLC ....B...... 248 863-3000
Commerce Township *(G-3414)*
Jogue Inc ....E...... 248 349-1501
Northville *(G-11703)*
◆ Jogue Inc ....E...... 734 207-0100
Plymouth *(G-12654)*
Jogue Inc ....G...... 313 921-4802
Detroit *(G-4163)*
Merchandising Productions ....E...... 616 676-6000
Ada *(G-23)*
Microcide Inc ....G...... 248 526-9663
Troy *(G-16506)*
Mineral Cosmetics Inc ....G...... 248 542-7733
Southfield *(G-14983)*
◆ Murrays Worldwide Inc ....F...... 248 691-9156
Oak Park *(G-12086)*
Northport Naturals ....G...... 231 420-9448
Cheboygan *(G-2689)*
NV Labs Inc ....F...... 248 358-9022
Southfield *(G-14993)*
▲ Platinum Skin Care Inc ....G...... 586 598-6075
Clinton Township *(G-3196)*
Pur E Clat ....G...... 313 208-5763
Farmington Hills *(G-5107)*
Ravenwood ....G...... 231 421-5682
Traverse City *(G-16091)*
Rejoice International Corp ....G...... 855 345-5575
Northville *(G-11721)*
Rodco Ltd ....G...... 517 244-0200
Holt *(G-7923)*
S C Johnson & Son Inc ....F...... 248 822-2174
Troy *(G-16587)*
▲ Sb3 LLC ....G...... 877 978-6286
Ada *(G-29)*
Scentmatchers LLC ....G...... 800 859-9878
Gaylord *(G-5892)*
▲ Smo International Inc ....F...... 248 275-1091
Warren *(G-17241)*
Smooches Blend Bar LLC ....G...... 734 756-7152
Ypsilanti *(G-18101)*
Soulfull Earth Herbals ....G...... 517 316-0547
Lansing *(G-9425)*
Stellar Scents ....G...... 989 868-3477
Reese *(G-13233)*
▲ Stone Soap Company Inc ....E...... 248 706-1000
Sylvan Lake *(G-15672)*
Viladon Corporation ....G...... 248 548-0043
Oak Park *(G-12103)*
▲ Wellington Fragrance ....G...... 734 261-5531
Livonia *(G-10005)*
Whimsical Fusions LLC ....G...... 248 956-0952
Detroit *(G-4439)*

2851 Paints, Varnishes, Lacquers, Enamels

A-Line Products Corporation ....F...... 313 571-8300
Detroit *(G-3830)*
Akzo Nobel Coatings Inc ....D...... 248 451-6231
Pontiac *(G-12800)*
Akzo Nobel Coatings Inc ....E...... 248 637-0400
Troy *(G-16177)*
Akzo Nobel Coatings Inc ....E...... 248 451-6231
Troy *(G-16178)*
Akzo Nobel Coatings Inc ....G...... 248 528-0715
Troy *(G-16179)*
Akzo Nobel Coatings Inc ....E...... 248 637-0400
Pontiac *(G-12801)*

Akzo Nobel Coatings Inc ....E...... 312 544-7000
Troy *(G-16180)*
All-Cote Coatings Company LLC ......G...... 586 427-0062
Center Line *(G-2577)*
Alloying Surfaces Inc ....G...... 248 524-9200
Troy *(G-16191)*
Axalta Coating Systems LLC ....G...... 586 846-4160
Clinton Township *(G-3061)*
Axson Tech Us Inc ....F...... 517 663-8191
Eaton Rapids *(G-4718)*
B & G Enterprises ....G...... 231 348-2705
Charlevoix *(G-2607)*
BASF Construction Chem LLC ....E...... 269 668-3371
Mattawan *(G-10662)*
Benchmark Coating Systems LLC ...G...... 517 782-4061
Ann Arbor *(G-382)*
Carboline Company ....E...... 734 525-2824
Livonia *(G-9675)*
Cass Polymers ....E...... 517 543-7510
Charlotte *(G-2636)*
Chemetall US Inc ....E...... 517 787-4846
Jackson *(G-8408)*
Coat It Inc of Detroit..........................G...... 313 869-8500
Detroit *(G-3941)*
▲ Conway-Cleveland Corp ....G...... 616 458-0056
Grand Rapids *(G-6309)*
Creative Surfaces Inc ....F...... 586 226-2950
Clinton Township *(G-3092)*
Dhake Industries Inc ....E...... 734 420-0101
Plymouth *(G-12610)*
Douglas Corp ....F...... 517 767-4112
Tekonsha *(G-15818)*
Eco Smart Coatings LLC ....G...... 574 370-5708
Cassopolis *(G-2529)*
▲ Eftec North America LLC ....D...... 248 585-2200
Taylor *(G-15713)*
Epoxy Pro Flr Ctngs Rstoration ....G...... 248 990-8890
Shelby Township *(G-14590)*
Flow Coatings LLC ....G...... 248 625-3052
Clarkston *(G-2922)*
Full Spektrem LLC ....G...... 313 910-1920
Saint Clair Shores *(G-14253)*
◆ General Chemical Corporation .....G...... 248 587-5600
Brighton *(G-1929)*
Gougeon Holding Co ....G...... 989 684-7286
Bay City *(G-1317)*
▼ Great Lake Woods Inc ....C...... 616 399-3300
Holland *(G-7651)*
Greenglow Products LLC ....G...... 248 827-1451
Southfield *(G-14931)*
HB Fuller Company ....E...... 616 453-8271
Grand Rapids *(G-6500)*
▼ Helen Inc ....F...... 616 698-8102
Caledonia *(G-2297)*
Hygratek LLC ....G...... 847 962-6180
Ann Arbor *(G-498)*
Industrial Finishing Co LLC ....G...... 616 784-5737
Comstock Park *(G-3485)*
Innovative Engineering Mich ....G...... 517 977-0460
Lansing *(G-9236)*
◆ Innovative Polymers Inc ....F...... 989 224-9500
Saint Johns *(G-14284)*
Innovative Solutions Tech Inc ....G...... 734 335-6665
Canton *(G-2387)*
◆ Instacoat Premium Products LLC ....G...... 586 770-1773
Oscoda *(G-12211)*
Kelley Laboratories Inc ....G...... 231 861-6257
Shelby *(G-14528)*
Lancast Urethane Inc ....G...... 517 485-6070
Commerce Township *(G-3419)*
Lenawee Industrial Pnt Sup Inc ....G...... 734 729-8080
Wayne *(G-17436)*
▼ Lymtal International Inc ....E...... 248 373-8100
Orion *(G-12183)*
Marshall Ryerson Co ....F...... 616 299-1751
Grand Rapids *(G-6645)*
◆ Materials Processing Inc ....D...... 734 282-1888
Riverview *(G-13301)*
Michigan Coating Products Inc ....G...... 616 456-8800
Grand Rapids *(G-6669)*
Michigan Industrial Finishes ....E...... 248 553-7014
Farmington Hills *(G-5065)*
MPS Trading Group LLC ....G...... 313 841-7588
Farmington Hills *(G-5073)*
Nb Coatings Inc ....G...... 248 365-1100
Auburn Hills *(G-954)*
▲ Ncoc Inc ....E...... 248 548-5950
Oak Park *(G-12088)*
Ncp Coatings Inc ....D...... 269 683-3377
Niles *(G-11631)*

▲ ND Industries Inc ....C...... 248 288-0000
Clawson *(G-2982)*
Nelson Paint Co of Mich Inc ....G...... 906 774-5566
Kingsford *(G-9063)*
Nelson Paint Company Ala Inc ....G...... 906 774-5566
Kingsford *(G-9064)*
Nelson Paint Company Mich Inc ......G...... 906 774-5566
Iron Mountain *(G-8291)*
North Group Inc ....G...... 517 540-0038
Howell *(G-8069)*
▼ Northern Coatings & Chem Co .....E...... 906 863-2641
Menominee *(G-10753)*
Ot Dynamics LLC ....G...... 734 984-7022
Flat Rock *(G-5358)*
Pacific Epoxy Polymers Inc ....E...... 616 949-1634
Grand Rapids *(G-6738)*
▲ Palmer Paint Products Inc ....D...... 248 588-4500
Troy *(G-16541)*
▲ Peter-Lacke Usa LLC ....G...... 248 588-9400
Troy *(G-16545)*
Pittsburgh Glass Works LLC ....C...... 248 371-1700
Rochester Hills *(G-13494)*
▲ Polymer Inc ....D...... 248 353-3035
Southfield *(G-15001)*
Port City Paints Mfg Inc ....G...... 231 726-5911
Muskegon *(G-11402)*
▲ Portland Plastics Co ....E...... 517 647-4115
Portland *(G-13065)*
PPG Coating Services ....D...... 734 421-7300
Livonia *(G-9894)*
PPG Industrial Coatings ....G...... 616 844-4391
Grand Haven *(G-6062)*
PPG Industries Inc ....E...... 248 640-4174
Macomb *(G-10153)*
PPG Industries Inc ....E...... 517 394-9093
Lansing *(G-9412)*
PPG Industries Inc ....E...... 810 767-8030
Flint *(G-5481)*
PPG Industries Inc ....E...... 616 846-4400
Grand Haven *(G-6063)*
PPG Industries Inc ....E...... 248 625-7282
Clarkston *(G-2948)*
PPG Industries Inc ....E...... 517 784-6138
Jackson *(G-8555)*
PPG Industries Inc ....E...... 248 478-1300
Novi *(G-11977)*
PPG Industries Inc ....E...... 586 566-3789
Shelby Township *(G-14670)*
PPG Industries Inc ....E...... 248 357-4817
Southfield *(G-15002)*
PPG Industries Inc ....G...... 734 287-2110
Taylor *(G-15754)*
PPG Industries Inc ....E...... 248 683-8052
Waterford *(G-17370)*
PPG Industries Inc ....E...... 517 263-7831
Adrian *(G-86)*
PPG Industries Inc ....E...... 248 641-2000
Troy *(G-16557)*
PPG Industries Inc ....E...... 586 755-2011
Warren *(G-17189)*
Pro Coatings Inc ....F...... 616 887-8808
Sparta *(G-15107)*
Quantum Chemical LLC ....G...... 734 429-0033
Livonia *(G-9901)*
Rap Products Inc ....G...... 989 893-5583
Bay City *(G-1348)*
▲ Red Spot Westland Inc ....C...... 734 729-1913
Westland *(G-17594)*
Repcolite Paints Inc ....D...... 616 396-5213
Holland *(G-7787)*
Richter Precision Inc ....E...... 586 465-0500
Fraser *(G-5718)*
Riverside Spline & Gear Inc ....E...... 810 765-9174
Marine City *(G-10481)*
▲ Rolled Alloys Inc ....D...... 800 521-0332
Temperance *(G-15842)*
Rollie Williams Paint Spot ....G...... 616 791-6100
Grand Rapids *(G-6835)*
▼ S P Kish Industries Inc ....E...... 517 543-2650
Charlotte *(G-2663)*
▲ Simiron Inc ....E...... 248 585-7500
Madison Heights *(G-10354)*
Single Source Inc ....G...... 765 825-4111
Flat Rock *(G-5365)*
▼ Specialty Coatings Inc ....F...... 586 294-8343
Fraser *(G-5729)*
Star 10 Inc ....G...... 231 830-8070
Muskegon *(G-11430)*
Statistical Processed Products ....E...... 586 792-6900
Clinton Township *(G-3235)*

2020 Harris Michigan
Industrial Directory

▲ **Sun Chemical Corporation**................F 513 681-5950
Muskegon *(G-11431)*
Supreme Media Blasting and Pow ....G....... 586 792-7705
Clinton Township *(G-3239)*
Titan Sales International LLC ....G....... 313 469-7105
Detroit *(G-4401)*
Tru Custom Blends Inc..........................G....... 810 407-6207
Flint *(G-5514)*
United Paint and Chemical Corp...........D....... 248 353-3035
Southfield *(G-15054)*
Vinyl Industrial Paints Inc.......................G....... 734 284-3536
Wyandotte *(G-17979)*
West System Inc.....................................E 989 684-7286
Bay City *(G-1370)*
▲ **Z Technologies Corporation** ....E 313 937-0710
Redford *(G-13209)*
▼ **Ziebart International Corp**.................C....... 248 588-4100
Troy *(G-16706)*

2861 Gum & Wood Chemicals

▲ **Conway-Cleveland Corp**....................G....... 616 458-0056
Grand Rapids *(G-6309)*
Country Schoolhouse Kingsford...........G....... 906 828-1971
Kingsford *(G-9056)*

2865 Cyclic-Crudes, Intermediates, Dyes & Org Pigments

Aubio Life Sciences LLC........................G....... 561 289-1888
Wixom *(G-17767)*
◆ **Chromatech Inc**.................................F 734 451-1230
Canton *(G-2361)*
Cut-Tech..G....... 269 687-9005
Niles *(G-11605)*
Diversified Chem Technologies.............C....... 313 867-5444
Detroit *(G-4010)*
◆ **Durez Corporation**.............................C....... 248 313-7000
Novi *(G-11874)*
▲ **Esco Company LLC**...........................D....... 231 726-3106
Grand Rapids *(G-6384)*
Flint CPS Inks North Amer LLC.............G....... 734 781-4600
Plymouth *(G-12621)*
◆ **Flint Group US LLC**...........................B....... 734 781-4600
Livonia *(G-9740)*
Mis Associates Inc................................G....... 844 225-8156
Pontiac *(G-12850)*
Sun Chemical Corporation.....................C....... 231 788-2371
Muskegon *(G-11432)*
▲ **Sun Chemical Corporation**................F 513 681-5950
Muskegon *(G-11431)*

2869 Industrial Organic Chemicals, NEC

Aapharmasyn LLC...................................F 734 213-2123
Ann Arbor *(G-337)*
Adrian Lva Biofuel LLC..........................F 517 920-4863
Adrian *(G-44)*
▲ **Advanced Urethanes Inc**...................G....... 313 273-5705
Detroit *(G-3844)*
Ahlusion LLC...G....... 888 277-0001
Swartz Creek *(G-15659)*
Akzo Nobel Coatings Inc........................D....... 248 451-6231
Pontiac *(G-12800)*
Albasara Fuel LLC...................................G....... 313 443-6581
Dearborn *(G-3674)*
▲ **American Chemical Tech Inc** ....E 517 223-0300
Fowlerville *(G-5557)*
American Farm Products Inc..................F 734 484-4180
Saline *(G-14374)*
Ana Fuel Inc...G....... 810 422-5659
Ann Arbor *(G-355)*
Assi Fuel Inc..G....... 586 759-4759
Warren *(G-16944)*
BASF Corporation...................................D....... 810 639-0492
Montrose *(G-11101)*
BASF Corporation...................................C....... 734 324-6963
Wyandotte *(G-17947)*
BASF Corporation...................................G....... 313 382-4250
Lincoln Park *(G-9573)*
BASF Corporation...................................C....... 734 324-6000
Wyandotte *(G-17948)*
BASF Corporation...................................A....... 734 324-6100
Wyandotte *(G-17949)*
BASF Corporation...................................D....... 734 591-5560
Livonia *(G-9660)*
BASF Corporation...................................C....... 248 827-4670
Southfield *(G-14850)*
Beebe Fuel Systems Inc.........................G....... 248 437-3322
South Lyon *(G-14786)*
Berry & Associates Inc...........................F 734 426-3787
Dexter *(G-4478)*
Bioelectrica Inc.......................................G....... 517 884-4542
East Lansing *(G-4651)*
BKM Fuels LLC.......................................G....... 269 342-9576
Kalamazoo *(G-8698)*
Boropharm Inc..E 517 455-7847
Ann Arbor *(G-386)*
BP Gas/ JB Fuel......................................G....... 517 531-3400
Parma *(G-12387)*
Burhani Labs Inc.....................................G....... 313 212-3842
Detroit *(G-3920)*
Camerons of Jackson LLC.....................G....... 517 531-3400
Parma *(G-12388)*
Caravan Technologies Inc......................F 313 341-2551
Detroit *(G-3929)*
Carbon Green Bioenergy LLC ....E 616 374-4000
Lake Odessa *(G-9112)*
▲ **Century Fuel Products**........................F 734 728-0300
Van Buren Twp *(G-16751)*
◆ **Chem-Trend Limited Partnership**......C....... 517 546-4520
Howell *(G-8022)*
Chouteau Fuels Company LLC..............G....... 734 302-4800
Ann Arbor *(G-399)*
CJ Chemicals LLC...................................F 888 274-1044
Perry *(G-12433)*
Cjg LLC..F 734 793-1400
Livonia *(G-9683)*
Clariant Plas Coatings USA LLC...........D....... 517 629-9101
Albion *(G-120)*
D M J Corp...G....... 810 239-9071
Flint *(G-5412)*
Ddp Specialty Electnc............................G....... 989 496-4400
Midland *(G-10829)*
Dow Chemical Company........................E 989 638-6571
Beaverton *(G-1384)*
Dow Chemical Company........................C....... 989 496-2246
Midland *(G-10841)*
Dow Chemical Company........................C....... 989 636-2636
Midland *(G-10842)*
Dow Chemical Company........................D....... 989 695-2584
Freeland *(G-5755)*
Dow Chemical Company........................E 989 638-6441
Midland *(G-10846)*
Dow Corning Corporation......................G....... 989 839-2808
Midland *(G-10849)*
Dow Silicones Corporation....................C....... 989 496-4400
Midland *(G-10853)*
Dow Silicones Corporation....................C....... 800 248-2481
Hemlock *(G-7462)*
Dow Silicones Corporation....................C....... 989 496-4000
Midland *(G-10854)*
Dow Silicones Corporation....................B....... 989 895-3397
Bay City *(G-1306)*
Dow Silicones Corporation....................C....... 989 496-1306
Auburn *(G-752)*
◆ **Dow Silicones Corporation** ....A....... 989 496-4000
Auburn *(G-751)*
Dow Silicones Corporation....................D....... 989 496-4137
Midland *(G-10855)*
Draths Corporation.................................E 517 349-0668
Howell *(G-8035)*
Dynamic Staffing Solutions...................F 616 399-5220
Holland *(G-7614)*
Ecology Coatings....................................G....... 248 723-2223
Bloomfield *(G-1733)*
Ecovia Renewables Inc..........................G....... 248 953-0594
Ann Arbor *(G-433)*
Elite Fuels LLC..G....... 313 871-6308
Detroit *(G-4032)*
Eq Resource Recovery Inc.....................G....... 734 727-5500
Romulus *(G-13673)*
Ether LLC...G....... 248 795-8830
Ortonville *(G-12199)*
EZ Fuel Inc...G....... 810 744-4452
Flint *(G-5428)*
Fit Fuel By Kt LLC...................................G....... 517 643-8827
East Lansing *(G-4658)*
Fk Fuel Inc...G....... 313 383-6005
Lincoln Park *(G-9577)*
Flat Iron LLC..G....... 248 268-1668
Roseville *(G-13804)*
Freal Fuel Inc..G....... 248 790-7202
Chesterfield *(G-2780)*
Frontier Rnwable Resources LLC.........G....... 906 228-7960
Marquette *(G-10533)*
Fuel Tobacco Stop..................................G....... 810 487-2040
Flushing *(G-5535)*
Fuel Woodfire Grill LLC..........................G....... 810 479-4933
Port Huron *(G-12920)*
Gage Corporation...................................F 248 541-3824
Ferndale *(G-5286)*
Gage Products Company.......................D....... 248 541-3824
Ferndale *(G-5288)*
Gb Dynamics Inc....................................E 313 400-3570
Port Huron *(G-12921)*
Georgia-Pacific LLC................................E 989 348-7275
Grayling *(G-7107)*
Green Fuels Llc.......................................G....... 734 735-6802
Carleton *(G-2455)*
Grm Corporation.....................................D....... 989 453-2322
Pigeon *(G-12489)*
Henkel US Operations Corp...................B....... 248 588-1082
Madison Heights *(G-10266)*
Hercules LLC...D....... 269 388-8676
Kalamazoo *(G-8767)*
Hydrosciences LLC.................................G....... 248 890-8116
Keego Harbor *(G-8979)*
Ibidltd-Blue Green Energy.....................G....... 909 547-5160
Dearborn *(G-3723)*
Il Adrian LLC W2fuel..............................E 517 920-4863
Adrian *(G-68)*
Inkster Fuel & Food Inc..........................G....... 313 565-8230
Inkster *(G-8228)*
J&J Freon Removal................................G....... 586 264-6379
Warren *(G-17110)*
Jade Scientific Inc..................................F 734 207-3775
Westland *(G-17572)*
K&S Fuel Ventures.................................G....... 248 360-0055
Commerce Township *(G-3418)*
Kelley Laboratories Inc..........................F 231 861-6257
Shelby *(G-14528)*
▲ **Kemai (usa) Chemical Co Ltd**...........G....... 248 924-2225
Northville *(G-11704)*
Kentwood Fuel Inc..................................G....... 616 455-2387
Kentwood *(G-9013)*
Kern Auto Sales and Svc LLC................F 734 475-2722
Chelsea *(G-2715)*
Lansing Fuel Ventures Inc.....................G....... 517 371-1198
Lansing *(G-9389)*
Lillian Fuel Inc..G....... 734 439-8505
Milan *(G-10945)*
Lin Adam Fuel Inc..................................G....... 313 733-6631
Detroit *(G-4206)*
M and A Fuels...G....... 313 397-7141
Detroit *(G-4213)*
Marks Fuel Dock.....................................G....... 586 445-8525
Saint Clair Shores *(G-14262)*
Medtest Dx Inc...D....... 866 540-2715
Canton *(G-2400)*
Metal Mates Inc.......................................G....... 248 646-9831
Beverly Hills *(G-1618)*
▲ **Metalworking Lubricants Co**.............C....... 248 332-3500
Pontiac *(G-12849)*
Michigan Agricultural Fuel......................G....... 419 490-6599
Grand Rapids *(G-6667)*
Michigan Ethanol LLC............................E 989 672-1222
Caro *(G-2471)*
Michigan Fuels..G....... 313 886-7110
Grosse Pointe Woods *(G-7207)*
Microcide Inc...G....... 248 526-9663
Troy *(G-16506)*
Mind Fuel LLC...G....... 248 414-5296
Royal Oak *(G-13952)*
Monroe Fuel Company LLC...................G....... 734 302-4824
Ann Arbor *(G-563)*
Naked Fuel Juice Bar.............................G....... 248 325-9735
West Bloomfield *(G-17489)*
Nation Wide Fuel Inc..............................G....... 734 721-7110
Dearborn *(G-3743)*
▼ **National Flavors LLC**..........................E 800 525-2431
Kalamazoo *(G-8833)*
National Fuels Inc...................................G....... 734 895-7836
Canton *(G-2411)*
Nine Mile Dequindre Fuel Stop..............G....... 586 757-7721
Warren *(G-17167)*
▼ **Northern Coatings & Chem Co**..........E 906 863-2641
Menominee *(G-10753)*
Oasis Fuel Corporation...........................G....... 906 486-4126
Ishpeming *(G-8351)*
Organicorp Inc...G....... 616 540-0295
Lowell *(G-10040)*
Paw Paw Fuel Stop.................................G....... 269 657-7357
Paw Paw *(G-12412)*
Performance Fuels Systems Inc............G....... 248 202-1789
Troy *(G-16543)*
Pira Testing LLC.....................................F 517 574-4297
Lansing *(G-9318)*
Rap Products Inc.....................................G....... 989 893-5583
Bay City *(G-1348)*
Real Flavors LLC.....................................F 855 443-9685
Bay City *(G-1349)*

S I C

28 CHEMICALS AND ALLIED PRODUCTS

Reed Fuel LLC ....G...... 574 520-3101
  Niles *(G-11642)*
S& A Fuel LLC ....G...... 313 945-6555
  Dearborn *(G-3754)*
Saad Fuels Inc ....G...... 734 425-2829
  Westland *(G-17598)*
Seven Mile and Grnd River Fuel ......G...... 313 535-3000
  Hamtramck *(G-7246)*
Sixteen Crooks BP Fuel ....G...... 248 643-7272
  Troy *(G-16605)*
Specialty Products Us LLC ....G...... 989 636-4341
  Midland *(G-10919)*
Suite Spa Manufacturing LLC ....G...... 616 560-2713
  Caledonia *(G-2318)*
Sy Fuel Inc ....G...... 313 531-5894
  Redford *(G-13198)*
Taiz Fuel Inc ....G...... 313 485-2972
  Dearborn Heights *(G-3798)*
Temperance Fuel Stop Inc ....G...... 734 206-2676
  Grosse Pointe Woods *(G-7210)*
Thumb Bioenergy LLC ....G...... 810 404-2466
  Sandusky *(G-14445)*
Tpa Inc ....G...... 248 302-9131
  Detroit *(G-4405)*
Trisco Chemical Co ....G...... 586 779-8260
  Saint Clair Shores *(G-14274)*
Twin Ash Frms Organic Proc LLC ....G...... 810 404-1943
  Snover *(G-14744)*
Tygrus LLC ....G...... 248 218-0347
  Troy *(G-16660)*
Valero Renewable Fuels Co LLC ......E...... 517 486-6190
  Blissfield *(G-1730)*
Van Dyke Fuell ....G...... 586 758-0120
  Warren *(G-17277)*
Vertellus LLC ....C...... 616 772-2193
  Zeeland *(G-18194)*
Vision Fuels LLC ....G...... 586 997-3286
  Shelby Township *(G-14720)*
◆ Wacker Chemical Corporation ......A...... 517 264-8500
  Adrian *(G-103)*
Wamu Fuel LLC ....G...... 313 386-8700
  Livonia *(G-9996)*
Warren City Fuel ....G...... 586 759-4759
  Dearborn *(G-3772)*
Wild Flavors Inc ....E...... 269 216-2603
  Kalamazoo *(G-8925)*
Working Bugs LLC ....G...... 517 203-4744
  East Lansing *(G-4683)*
Zunairah Fuels Inc ....G...... 647 405-1606
  Clinton Township *(G-3265)*

2873 Nitrogenous Fertilizers

◆ Advanced McRonutrient Pdts Inc ....E...... 989 752-2138
  Reese *(G-13228)*
Agrigenetics Inc ....G...... 317 337-3000
  Midland *(G-10812)*
Detroit Dirt LLC ....G...... 616 260-4383
  Detroit *(G-3981)*
Earthworm Cstngs Unlimited LLC ....F...... 248 882-3329
  Waterford *(G-17341)*
Gantec Inc ....G...... 989 631-9300
  Midland *(G-10864)*
Harmony Products ....G...... 906 387-5411
  Munising *(G-11243)*
Hyponex Corporation ....E...... 810 724-2875
  Imlay City *(G-8202)*
Scotts Company LLC ....D...... 586 254-6849
  Sterling Heights *(G-15487)*

2874 Phosphatic Fertilizers

Andersons Inc ....G...... 989 642-5291
  Hemlock *(G-7459)*
Cog Marketers Ltd ....E...... 989 224-4117
  Saint Johns *(G-14280)*
F C Simpson Lime Co ....G...... 810 367-3510
  Kimball *(G-9043)*

2875 Fertilizers, Mixing Only

Bay-Houston Towing Company ....E...... 810 648-2210
  Sandusky *(G-14430)*
Cog Marketers Ltd ....F...... 434 455-3209
  Ashley *(G-727)*
Cog Marketers Ltd ....F...... 989 224-4117
  Saint Johns *(G-14281)*
Great Lakes Nursery Soils Inc ....G...... 231 788-3123
  Muskegon *(G-11339)*
▲ Hydrodynamics International ....G...... 517 887-2007
  Lansing *(G-9383)*
Hyponex Corporation ....E...... 810 724-2875
  Imlay City *(G-8202)*

Indian Summer Recycling Inc ....G...... 586 725 1340
  Casco *(G-2500)*
Markham Peat Corp ....F...... 800 851-7230
  Lakeview *(G-9175)*
Michigan Grower Products Inc ....F...... 269 665-7071
  Galesburg *(G-5813)*
Morgan Composting Inc ....G...... 231 734-2451
  Sears *(G-14512)*
Morgan Composting Inc ....E...... 231 734-2790
  Sears *(G-14513)*
Natures Best Top Soil Compost ......G...... 810 657-9528
  Carsonville *(G-2497)*
Nutrien AG Solutions Inc ....G...... 989 842-1185
  Breckenridge *(G-1844)*
Spurt Industries LLC ....G...... 616 688-5575
  Zeeland *(G-18187)*
Sun Gro Horticulture Dist Inc ....D...... 517 639-3115
  Quincy *(G-13100)*
Trp Enterprises Inc ....G...... 810 329-4027
  East China *(G-4821)*
Tuthill Farms & Composting ....G...... 248 437-7354
  South Lyon *(G-14815)*

2879 Pesticides & Agricultural Chemicals, NEC

Avian Enterprises LLC ....E...... 888 366-0709
  Sylvan Lake *(G-15671)*
Bayer Cropscience LP ....D...... 231 744-4711
  Muskegon *(G-11277)*
Biobest USA Inc ....G...... 734 626-5693
  Romulus *(G-13657)*
Centen AG LLC ....G...... 989 636-1000
  Midland *(G-10823)*
Dow Agrosciences LLC ....E...... 989 636-4400
  Midland *(G-10833)*
Dow Agrosciences LLC ....G...... 989 479-3245
  Harbor Beach *(G-7265)*
Dow Chemical Company ....C...... 989 636-4406
  Midland *(G-10836)*
Dow Chemical Company ....D...... 989 636-0540
  Midland *(G-10845)*
◆ Dow Chemical Company ....B...... 989 636-1000
  Midland *(G-10834)*
Dow Chemical Company ....D...... 989 636-5409
  Midland *(G-10848)*
E I Du Pont De Nemours & Co ....B...... 248 549-4794
  Royal Oak *(G-13920)*
E I Du Pont De Nemours & Co ....B...... 586 263-0258
  Clinton Township *(G-3107)*
Envirodine Inc ....G...... 231 723-5905
  Manistee *(G-10420)*
Gantec Inc ....G...... 989 631-9300
  Midland *(G-10864)*
Hpi Products Inc ....G...... 248 773-7460
  Northville *(G-11698)*
Monsanto Company ....E...... 269 483-1300
  Constantine *(G-3540)*
Monsanto Company ....G...... 517 676-2479
  Mason *(G-10648)*
Rim Guard Inc ....G...... 616 608-7745
  Wyoming *(G-18031)*

2891 Adhesives & Sealants

A & B Display Systems Inc ....F...... 989 893-6642
  Bay City *(G-1269)*
Action Fabricators Inc ....C...... 616 957-2032
  Grand Rapids *(G-6136)*
Adco Global Inc ....B...... 517 764-0334
  Michigan Center *(G-10783)*
Adco Products LLC ....C...... 517 841-7238
  Michigan Center *(G-10784)*
▲ Adhesive Systems Inc ....E...... 313 865-4448
  Detroit *(G-3843)*
Adhesives and Processes Tech ....G...... 231 737-4418
  Norton Shores *(G-11807)*
Alco Products LLC ....E...... 313 823-7500
  Detroit *(G-3853)*
AM Tech Services LLC ....G...... 734 762-7209
  Livonia *(G-9640)*
Applied Molecules LLC ....G...... 810 355-1475
  Whitmore Lake *(G-17688)*
◆ Argent International Inc ....C...... 734 582-9800
  Plymouth *(G-12572)*
▲ Bars Products Inc ....E...... 248 634-8278
  Holly *(G-7871)*
Bear Cub Holdings Inc ....G...... 231 242-1152
  Harbor Springs *(G-7274)*
Cass Polymers ....E...... 517 543-7510
  Charlotte *(G-2636)*

Chem Link Inc ....D...... 269 679-4440
  Schoolcraft *(G-14491)*
Clair Evans-St Inc ....G...... 313 259-2266
  Detroit *(G-3938)*
Concrete Manufacturing Inc ....G...... 586 777-3320
  Roseville *(G-13785)*
▲ Conley Composites LLC ....E...... 918 299-5051
  Grand Rapids *(G-6300)*
Connells Restoration & Sealan ....G...... 269 370-0805
  Vandalia *(G-16800)*
Covalent Medical Inc ....G...... 734 604-0688
  Ann Arbor *(G-406)*
Daring Company ....G...... 248 340-0741
  Orion *(G-12179)*
Dawson Manufacturing ....G...... 269 639-4213
  Sandusky *(G-14432)*
Denarco Inc ....G...... 269 435-8404
  Constantine *(G-3533)*
Dico Manufacturing LLC ....G...... 586 731-3008
  Chesterfield *(G-2766)*
Diversified Chemical Tech Inc ....C...... 313 867-5444
  Detroit *(G-4011)*
▲ Diversitak Inc ....E...... 313 869-8500
  Detroit *(G-4012)*
Dow Chemical Company ....C...... 517 439-4400
  Hillsdale *(G-7523)*
Dyna Tech ....G...... 248 358-3962
  Southfield *(G-14891)*
▲ Eftec North America LLC ....D...... 248 585-2200
  Taylor *(G-15713)*
▲ Eternabond Inc ....G...... 847 540-0600
  Michigan Center *(G-10786)*
Fairmount Santrol Inc ....G...... 440 279-0204
  Detroit *(G-4051)*
◆ Genova Products Inc ....D...... 810 744-4500
  Davison *(G-3650)*
HB Fuller Company ....E...... 616 453-8271
  Grand Rapids *(G-6500)*
Henkel Loctite Corporation ....G...... 787 264-7534
  Madison Heights *(G-10264)*
Henniges Auto Holdings Inc ....B...... 248 340-4100
  Auburn Hills *(G-896)*
◆ Henniges Auto Sling Systems N ....C...... 248 340-4100
  Auburn Hills *(G-897)*
Highland Industrial Inc ....G...... 989 391-9992
  Bay City *(G-1320)*
Huhnseal USA Inc ....G...... 248 347-0606
  Novi *(G-11903)*
Huntler Industries Inc ....E...... 586 566-7684
  Shelby Township *(G-14601)*
▼ Huron Industries Inc ....G...... 810 984-4213
  Port Huron *(G-12928)*
Kent Manufacturing Company ....D...... 616 454-9495
  Grand Rapids *(G-6577)*
▲ Kiilunen Mfg Group Inc ....G...... 906 337-2433
  Calumet *(G-2328)*
Kleiberit Adhesives USA Inc ....G...... 248 709-9308
  Royal Oak *(G-13941)*
L & L Products Inc ....B...... 586 752-6681
  Bruce Twp *(G-2088)*
Lenderink Inc ....F...... 616 887-8257
  Belmont *(G-1466)*
Lj/Hah Holdings Corporation ....G...... 248 340-4100
  Auburn Hills *(G-929)*
▼ Lymtal International Inc ....E...... 248 373-8100
  Orion *(G-12183)*
◆ M Argueso & Co Inc ....G...... 231 759-7304
  Norton Shores *(G-11771)*
Master Mix Company ....F...... 734 487-7870
  Ypsilanti *(G-18089)*
◆ Materials Processing Inc ....D...... 734 282-1888
  Riverview *(G-13301)*
◆ Michigan Adhesive Mfg Inc ....E...... 616 850-0507
  Spring Lake *(G-15162)*
Millennium Adhesive Products ....G...... 800 248-4010
  Michigan Center *(G-10787)*
▲ Ncoc Inc ....E...... 248 548-5950
  Oak Park *(G-12088)*
▲ ND Industries Inc ....C...... 248 288-0000
  Clawson *(G-2982)*
Nyatex Chemical Company ....F...... 517 546-4046
  Howell *(G-8073)*
◆ Paramelt Usa Inc ....C...... 231 759-7304
  Norton Shores *(G-11786)*
▲ Parson Adhesives Inc ....G...... 248 299-5585
  Rochester Hills *(G-13490)*
Plasco Formulating Division ....G...... 586 281-3714
  Bruce Twp *(G-2092)*
▲ Portland Plastics Co ....E...... 517 647-4115
  Portland *(G-13065)*

SIC SECTION 28 CHEMICALS AND ALLIED PRODUCTS

PPG Industries Inc ....E 517 263-7831
Adrian *(G-86)*
Precision Packing Corporation ....E 586 756-8700
Warren *(G-17194)*
Pro Sealants ....G 616 318-6067
Grand Rapids *(G-6779)*
Royal Adhesives & Sealants LLC ....D 517 764-0334
Michigan Center *(G-10790)*
Scodeller Construction Inc ....D 248 374-1102
Wixom *(G-17890)*
Seal Support Systems Inc ....E 586 331-7251
Romeo *(G-13638)*
Sealex Inc ....G 231 348-5020
Harbor Springs *(G-7293)*
Sika Corporation ....D 248 577-0020
Madison Heights *(G-10353)*
Specilty Adhesives Coating Inc ....F 269 345-3801
Kalamazoo *(G-8897)*
◆ **Stahls Inc** ....D 800 478-2457
Sterling Heights *(G-15508)*
Sugru Inc ....G 877 990-9888
Livonia *(G-9947)*
◆ **Transtar Autobody Tech LLC** ....C 810 220-3000
Brighton *(G-1999)*
◆ **Trenton Corporation** ....E 734 424-3600
Ann Arbor *(G-680)*
◆ **Wall Colmonoy Corporation** ....E 248 585-6400
Madison Heights *(G-10380)*
West System Inc ....E 989 684-7286
Bay City *(G-1370)*
Western Adhesive Inc ....F 616 874-5869
Rockford *(G-13596)*
Wilbur Products Inc ....F 231 755-3805
Muskegon *(G-11451)*
Worthen Industries Inc ....E 616 742-8990
Grand Rapids *(G-7004)*
Wright Sealant Restoration Inc ....G 616 453-5914
Walker *(G-16883)*
▲ **Z Technologies Corporation** ....E 313 937-0710
Redford *(G-13209)*
▼ **Ziebart International Corp** ....C 248 588-4100
Troy *(G-16706)*

2892 Explosives

Austin Powder Company ....F 989 595-2400
Presque Isle *(G-13082)*
Dyno Nobel Inc ....F 906 486-4473
Ishpeming *(G-8344)*
Mission Critical Firearms LLC ....G 586 232-5185
Shelby Township *(G-14641)*
Pepin-Ireco Inc ....E 906 486-4473
Ishpeming *(G-8352)*

2893 Printing Ink

America Ink and Technology ....G 269 345-4657
Portage *(G-12981)*
▲ **Celia Corporation** ....G 616 887-7387
Sparta *(G-15090)*
D & D Business Machines Inc ....G 616 364-8446
Grand Rapids *(G-6329)*
Flint CPS Inks North Amer LLC ....G 734 781-4600
Plymouth *(G-12621)*
Flint Group LLC ....G 734 641-3062
Westland *(G-17557)*
◆ **Flint Group North America LLC** ....C 734 781-4600
Livonia *(G-9737)*
Flint Group US LLC ....G 313 538-0479
Detroit *(G-4063)*
Flint Group US LLC ....E 269 381-1955
Kalamazoo *(G-8745)*
◆ **Flint Group US LLC** ....B 734 781-4600
Livonia *(G-9740)*
Flint Ink Receivables Corp ....G 734 781-4600
Plymouth *(G-12622)*
▲ **Grand Rapids Printing Ink Co** ....F 616 241-5681
Grand Rapids *(G-6462)*
Graphics Unlimited Inc ....G 616 662-0455
Hudsonville *(G-8157)*
▲ **Great Lakes Toll Services** ....G 616 847-1868
Spring Lake *(G-15149)*
Intra Business LLC ....G 269 262-0863
Niles *(G-11621)*
Pittsburgh Glass Works LLC ....C 248 371-1700
Rochester Hills *(G-13494)*
Red Tie Group Inc ....F 734 458-2011
Livonia *(G-9906)*
Wikoff Color Corporation ....E 616 245-3930
Grand Rapids *(G-6991)*

2899 Chemical Preparations, NEC

A-Line Products Corporation ....F 313 571-8300
Detroit *(G-3830)*
Aapharmasyn LLC ....F 734 213-2123
Ann Arbor *(G-337)*
American Chem Solutions LLC ....F 231 655-5840
Muskegon *(G-11267)*
◆ **American Jetway Corporation** ....D 734 721-5930
Wayne *(G-17423)*
▲ **Antimicrobial Specialist Assoc** ....F 989 662-0377
Auburn *(G-749)*
▲ **Aurora Spclty Chemistries Corp** ....E 517 372-9121
Lansing *(G-9344)*
▲ **Bars Products Inc** ....E 248 634-8278
Holly *(G-7871)*
BASF ....G 231 719-3019
Muskegon *(G-11275)*
BASF Construction Chem LLC ....E 269 668-3371
Mattawan *(G-10662)*
BASF Corporation ....D 734 591-5560
Livonia *(G-9660)*
Bay City Fireworks Festival ....G 989 892-2264
Bay City *(G-1286)*
Bio Source Naturals LLC ....G 734 335-6798
Canton *(G-2352)*
◆ **Bohning Company Ltd** ....E 231 229-4247
Lake City *(G-9085)*
◆ **Bridge Organics Company** ....E 269 649-4200
Vicksburg *(G-16831)*
Brighton Laboratories Inc ....F 810 225-9520
Brighton *(G-1890)*
BV Technology LLC ....G 616 558-1746
Alto *(G-323)*
Cabot Corporation ....E 989 495-2113
Midland *(G-10821)*
Caravan Technologies Inc ....F 313 341-2551
Detroit *(G-3929)*
Carco Inc ....F 313 925-1053
Detroit *(G-3930)*
Cargill Incorporated ....B 810 329-2736
Saint Clair *(G-14207)*
▲ **Cau Acquisition Company LLC** ....D 989 875-8133
Ithaca *(G-8357)*
Cayman Chemical Company Inc ....D 734 971-3335
Ann Arbor *(G-395)*
Cerco Inc ....E 734 362-8664
Brownstown Twp *(G-2071)*
Chames LLC ....G 616 363-0000
Grand Rapids *(G-6269)*
◆ **Chem-Trend Holding Inc** ....G 517 545-7980
Howell *(G-8021)*
◆ **Chem-Trend Limited Partnership** ....C 517 546-4520
Howell *(G-8022)*
Chem-Trend Limited Partnership ....F 517 546-4520
Howell *(G-8023)*
Chemetall US Inc ....F 517 787-4846
Jackson *(G-8408)*
Clearwater Treatment Systems ....G 517 688-9316
Clarklake *(G-2896)*
Covaron Inc ....G 480 298-9433
Ann Arbor *(G-407)*
▲ **Cows Locomotive Mfg Co** ....E 248 583-7150
Madison Heights *(G-10221)*
CRC Industries Inc ....E 313 883-6977
Detroit *(G-3953)*
▲ **Cross Technologies Group Inc** ....F 734 895-8084
Westland *(G-17548)*
▲ **Cummings-Moore Graphite Co** ....E 313 841-1615
Detroit *(G-3957)*
Cytec Industries Inc ....C 269 349-6677
Kalamazoo *(G-8722)*
▼ **Dell Marking Systems Inc** ....G 248 547-7750
Rochester Hills *(G-13407)*
Diversified Chemical Tech Inc ....C 313 867-5444
Detroit *(G-4011)*
▲ **Doerken Corporation** ....G 517 522-4600
Grass Lake *(G-7087)*
Dow Chemical Company ....C 517 439-4400
Hillsdale *(G-7523)*
Dow Credit Corporation ....G 989 636-8949
Midland *(G-10850)*
Dsw Holdings Inc ....G 313 567-4500
Detroit *(G-4018)*
Eastern Oil Company ....E 248 333-1333
Pontiac *(G-12819)*
▲ **Eftec North America LLC** ....D 248 585-2200
Taylor *(G-15713)*
Emco Chemical Inc ....F 313 894-7650
Detroit *(G-4036)*

Enerco Corporation ....E 517 627-1669
Grand Ledge *(G-6106)*
Ernie Romanco ....E 517 531-3686
Albion *(G-123)*
◆ **General Chemical Corporation** ....G 248 587-5600
Brighton *(G-1929)*
◆ **Ginsan Liquidating Company LLC** ....D 616 791-8100
Grand Rapids *(G-6443)*
Great Lakes Treatment Corp ....G 517 566-8008
Sunfield *(G-15646)*
H M Products Inc ....G 313 875-5148
Detroit *(G-4109)*
H-O-H Water Technology Inc ....F 248 669-6667
Commerce Township *(G-3409)*
Haas Group International LLC ....G 810 236-0032
Flint *(G-5444)*
Haltermann Carless Us Inc ....G 248 422-6548
Troy *(G-16390)*
▲ **Haviland Enterprises Inc** ....C 616 361-6691
Grand Rapids *(G-6497)*
Henkel US Operations Corp ....B 248 588-1082
Madison Heights *(G-10266)*
Henkel US Operations Corp ....C 586 759-5555
Warren *(G-17080)*
Hercules LLC ....D 269 388-8676
Kalamazoo *(G-8767)*
Houghton International Inc ....F 248 641-3231
Livonia *(G-9774)*
Hydro Chem Laboratories Inc ....G 248 348-1737
Novi *(G-11904)*
Jones Chemical Inc ....G 734 283-0677
Riverview *(G-13299)*
Khi Coating ....G 248 236-2100
Oxford *(G-12353)*
▼ **Kolene Corporation** ....E 313 273-9220
Detroit *(G-4180)*
Lenderink Inc ....F 616 887-8257
Belmont *(G-1466)*
▼ **Lymtal International Inc** ....E 248 373-8100
Orion *(G-12183)*
Macdermid Incorporated ....E 248 399-3553
Ferndale *(G-5298)*
Macdermid Incorporated ....E 248 437-8161
New Hudson *(G-11547)*
▲ **Magni Group Inc** ....F 248 647-4500
Birmingham *(G-1690)*
▲ **Magni-Industries Inc** ....E 313 843-7855
Detroit *(G-4215)*
Marshall Ryerson Co ....F 616 299-1751
Grand Rapids *(G-6645)*
McGean-Rohco Inc ....E 216 441-4900
Livonia *(G-9832)*
Midland Cmpnding Cnsulting Inc ....G 989 495-9367
Midland *(G-10888)*
Morin Fireworks ....G 906 353-6650
Baraga *(G-1110)*
Morning Star Land Company LLC ....E 734 459-8022
Canton *(G-2408)*
N A Suez ....G 734 379-3855
Rockwood *(G-13609)*
Nanosynthons LLC ....G 989 317-3737
Mount Pleasant *(G-11214)*
▲ **Ncoc Inc** ....E 248 548-5950
Oak Park *(G-12088)*
Nelsonite Chemical Products ....G 616 456-7098
Grand Rapids *(G-6713)*
Nof Metal Coatings N Amer Inc ....G 810 966-9240
Port Huron *(G-12949)*
▼ **Northern Coatings & Chem Co** ....E 906 863-2641
Menominee *(G-10753)*
Patriot Pyrotechnics ....G 989 831-7788
Sheridan *(G-14733)*
Petroleum Environmental Tech ....G 231 258-0400
Rapid City *(G-13110)*
Pfb Manufacturing LLC ....E 517 486-4844
Blissfield *(G-1723)*
◆ **Photo Systems Inc** ....E 734 424-9625
Dexter *(G-4503)*
Pinecrest Industries ....G 269 545-8125
Galien *(G-5819)*
▲ **Plating Systems and Tech Inc** ....G 517 783-4776
Jackson *(G-8554)*
◆ **Pressure Vessel Service Inc** ....E 313 921-1200
Detroit *(G-4310)*
Quaker Chemical Corporation ....D 313 931-6910
Detroit *(G-4321)*
Questron Packaging LLC ....G 313 657-1630
Detroit *(G-4323)*
R J Marshall Company ....E 734 379-4044
Rockwood *(G-13611)*

28 CHEMICALS AND ALLIED PRODUCTS

R J Marshall Company .... E 734 848-5325
  Erie *(G-4810)*
Ralrube Inc .... G 734 429-0033
  Saline *(G-14411)*
Recycling Fluid Technologies .... F 269 788-0488
  Battle Creek *(G-1240)*
▲ Rolled Alloys Inc .... D 800 521-0332
  Temperance *(G-15842)*
Rooto Corporation .... F 517 546-8330
  Howell *(G-8093)*
▼ Rustop Technologies LLC .... G 517 223-5098
  Howell *(G-8094)*
Selkey Fabricators LLC .... F 906 353-7104
  Baraga *(G-1115)*
Shay Water Co Inc .... E 989 755-3221
  Saginaw *(G-14148)*
Sika Corporation .... D 248 577-0020
  Madison Heights *(G-10353)*
▼ Sks Industries Inc .... F 517 546-1117
  Howell *(G-8098)*
Smith Wa Inc .... E 313 883-6977
  Detroit *(G-4366)*
St Evans Inc .... G 269 663-6100
  Edwardsburg *(G-4772)*
Stony Creek Essential Oils .... G 989 227-5500
  Saint Johns *(G-14297)*
Surface Activation Tech LLC .... G 248 273-0037
  Troy *(G-16628)*
Svn Inc .... G 734 707-7131
  Saline *(G-14417)*
Teachout and Associates Inc .... G 269 729-4440
  Athens *(G-729)*
▲ Thetford Corporation .... C 734 769-6000
  Ann Arbor *(G-670)*
▲ Toda America Incorporated .... G 269 962-0353
  Battle Creek *(G-1258)*
Topduck Products LLC .... F 517 322-3202
  Lansing *(G-9327)*
▲ Trace Zero Inc .... F 248 289-1277
  Auburn Hills *(G-1029)*
◆ Transtar Autobody Tech LLC ..... C 810 220-3000
  Brighton *(G-1999)*
Tuocai America LLC .... G 248 346-5910
  Troy *(G-16657)*
V & V Industries Inc .... F 248 624-7943
  Wixom *(G-17923)*
Varn International Inc .... G 734 781-4600
  Plymouth *(G-12785)*
◆ Vertellus Hlth Spclty Pdts LLC ... G 616 772-2193
  Zeeland *(G-18193)*
▲ Wacker Biochem Corporation .... B 517 264-8500
  Adrian *(G-102)*
Wilbur Products Inc .... F 231 755-3805
  Muskegon *(G-11451)*
Xaerus Performance Fluids LLC ... G 989 631-7871
  Midland *(G-10926)*

29 PETROLEUM REFINING AND RELATED INDUSTRIES

2911 Petroleum Refining

Amrican Petro Inc .... G 313 520-8404
  Detroit *(G-3868)*
Avflight Corporation .... G 734 663-6466
  Ann Arbor *(G-376)*
Belding Quicklube Plus .... G 616 794-9548
  Belding *(G-1401)*
Bertoldi Oil Service Inc .... G 906 774-1707
  Iron Mountain *(G-8276)*
◆ Bva Inc .... E 248 348-4920
  New Hudson *(G-11533)*
Corrigan Enterprises Inc .... E 810 229-6323
  Brighton *(G-1904)*
▲ Fortech Products Inc .... E 248 446-9500
  Brighton *(G-1925)*
◆ Genova Products Inc .... D 810 744-4500
  Davison *(G-3650)*
Hitachi America Ltd .... E 248 477-5400
  Farmington Hills *(G-5021)*
▼ Huron Industries Inc .... G 810 984-4213
  Port Huron *(G-12928)*
Jet Fuel .... G 231 767-9566
  Muskegon *(G-11353)*
Joy-Max Inc .... G 616 847-0990
  Grand Haven *(G-6040)*
Lube Zone LLC .... G 313 543-2910
  Redford *(G-13169)*
Marysville Hydrocarbons LLC .... G 586 445-2300
  Warren *(G-17142)*
Marysville Hydrocarbons LLC .... E 586 445-2300
  Marysville *(G-10606)*
▲ Michigan Paving and Mtls Co .... E 734 397-2050
  Canton *(G-2405)*
Miller Exploration Company .... E 231 941-0004
  Traverse City *(G-16037)*
Motor City Quick Lube One Inc ..... G 734 367-6457
  Livonia *(G-9849)*
Murphy USA Inc .... F 517 541-0502
  Charlotte *(G-2661)*
Nano Materials & Processes Inc ... G 248 529-3873
  Milford *(G-10974)*
Pacific Oil Resources Inc .... E 734 397-1120
  Van Buren Twp *(G-16777)*
Stop & Go Transportation LLC ...... G 313 346-7114
  Washington *(G-17311)*
W2fuel LLC .... E 517 920-4868
  Adrian *(G-101)*

2951 Paving Mixtures & Blocks

A & M Distributors .... G 586 755-9045
  Warren *(G-16907)*
A Plus Asphalt LLC .... E 888 754-1125
  Bloomfield Hills *(G-1739)*
Ajax Materials Corporation .... E 248 244-3300
  Troy *(G-16174)*
Ajax Materials Corporation .... F 248 244-3445
  Brighton *(G-1882)*
Ajax Paving Industries Inc .... C 248 244-3300
  Troy *(G-16175)*
Alco Products LLC .... E 313 823-7500
  Detroit *(G-3853)*
Angelos Crushed Concrete Inc ..... G 586 756-1070
  Warren *(G-16934)*
Aztec Azphalt Technology Inc .... E 248 627-2120
  Goodrich *(G-5951)*
Barrett Paving Materials Inc .... C 248 362-0850
  Troy *(G-16233)*
Barrett Paving Materials Inc .... E 734 985-9480
  Ypsilanti *(G-18055)*
Bdk Group Northern Mich Inc .... E 574 875-5183
  Charlevoix *(G-2942)*
Cadillac Asphalt LLC .... E 248 215-0416
  Southfield *(G-14862)*
Cadillac Asphalt LLC .... D 734 397-2050
  Canton *(G-2356)*
Carlo John Inc .... E 586 254-3800
  Shelby Township *(G-14557)*
Celia Deboer .... F 269 279-9102
  Three Rivers *(G-15859)*
Central Asphalt Inc .... F 989 772-0720
  Mount Pleasant *(G-11183)*
Colorado Pavers & Walls Inc .... E 517 881-1704
  Flint *(G-5400)*
D O W Asphalt Paving LLC .... F 810 743-2633
  Swartz Creek *(G-15665)*
Dans Concrete LLC .... G 517 242-0754
  Grand Ledge *(G-6104)*
Delta Paving Inc .... F 810 232-0220
  Flint *(G-5417)*
Edw C Levy Co .... G 248 634-0879
  Davisburg *(G-3631)*
▲ Edw C Levy Co .... B 313 429-2200
  Dearborn *(G-3700)*
Edw C Levy Co .... E 248 349-8600
  Novi *(G-11880)*
Edw C Levy Co .... G 313 843-7200
  Detroit *(G-4028)*
Elmers Crane and Dozer Inc .... C 231 943-3443
  Traverse City *(G-15962)*
Fendt Builders Supply Inc .... E 248 474-3211
  Farmington Hills *(G-4999)*
H & T Skidmore Asphalt .... G 269 468-3530
  Benton Harbor *(G-1506)*
Hd Selcating Pav Solutions LLC ... E 248 241-6526
  Clarkston *(G-2925)*
Hess Asphalt Pav Sand Cnstr Co .. F 810 984-4466
  Clyde *(G-3283)*
Hhj Holdings Limited .... F 248 652-9716
  Troy *(G-16396)*
J L Milling Inc .... F 269 679-5769
  Schoolcraft *(G-14496)*
Lafarge North America Inc .... F 703 480-3600
  Dundee *(G-4591)*
Lakeland Asphalt Corporation .... E 269 964-1720
  Springfield *(G-15196)*
Laser Mfg Inc .... G 313 292-2299
  Romulus *(G-13699)*
Lite Load Services LLC .... F 269 751-6037
  Hamilton *(G-7236)*
Michigan Paving and Mtls Co .... E 734 485-1717
  Van Buren Twp *(G-16772)*
Michigan Paving and Mtls Co .... E 616 459-9545
  Grand Rapids *(G-6675)*
Michigan Paving and Mtls Co .... E 989 463-1323
  Alma *(G-242)*
Michigan Paving and Mtls Co .... D 517 787-4200
  Jackson *(G-8520)*
Nagle Paving Company .... E 248 553-0600
  Novi *(G-11951)*
Nagle Paving Company .... C 734 591-1484
  Livonia *(G-9856)*
North American Asphalt .... E 586 754-0014
  Warren *(G-17172)*
Oldcastle Materials Inc .... D 248 625-5891
  Clarkston *(G-2942)*
Oldcastle Materials Inc .... E 269 343-4659
  Kalamazoo *(G-8839)*
Peake Asphalt Inc .... E 586 254-4567
  Shelby Township *(G-14661)*
Pyramid Paving and Contg Co ...... E 989 895-5861
  Bay City *(G-1343)*
Rieth-Riley Cnstr Co Inc .... E 231 263-2100
  Grawn *(G-7100)*
Rieth-Riley Cnstr Co Inc .... E 616 248-0920
  Wyoming *(G-18030)*
Rite Way Asphalt Inc .... E 586 264-1020
  Sterling Heights *(G-15472)*
RWS & Associates LLC .... F 517 278-3134
  Coldwater *(G-3328)*
▲ Saginaw Asphalt Paving Co ...... D 989 755-8147
  Carrollton *(G-2487)*
Shooks Asphalt Paving Co Inc ...... F 989 236-7740
  Perrinton *(G-12432)*
Tri-City Aggregates Inc .... E 248 634-8276
  Holly *(G-7900)*
Woodland Paving Co .... E 616 784-5220
  Comstock Park *(G-3521)*

2952 Asphalt Felts & Coatings

Alco Products LLC .... E 313 823-7500
  Detroit *(G-3853)*
Arnt Asphalt Sealing Inc .... D 269 927-1532
  Benton Harbor *(G-1482)*
Curbco Inc .... G 810 232-2121
  Flint *(G-5409)*
▲ De Witt Products Co .... E 313 554-0575
  Detroit *(G-3963)*
Detroit Cornice & Slate Co Inc ...... E 248 398-7690
  Ferndale *(G-5275)*
◆ Genova Products Inc .... D 810 744-4500
  Davison *(G-3650)*
Green Link Inc .... F 269 216-9229
  Kalamazoo *(G-8758)*
Liveroof LLC .... E 616 842-1392
  Nunica *(G-12040)*
Marshall Ryerson Co .... F 616 299-1751
  Grand Rapids *(G-6645)*
McElroy Metal Mill Inc .... E 269 781-8313
  Marshall *(G-10582)*
Michigan Paving and Mtls Co .... D 517 787-4200
  Jackson *(G-8520)*
Michigan Steel and Trim Inc .... E 517 647-4555
  Portland *(G-13063)*
Over Top Steel Coating LLC .... G 616 647-9140
  Comstock Park *(G-3504)*
Pine River Inc .... F 231 758-3400
  Charlevoix *(G-2626)*
Reurink Roof Maint & Coating ...... G 269 795-2337
  Middleville *(G-10806)*

2992 Lubricating Oils & Greases

A K Oil LLC DBA Speedy Oil and .. G 616 233-9505
  Grand Rapids *(G-6125)*
▲ Amcol Corporation .... E 248 414-5700
  Hazel Park *(G-7434)*
Apollo Idemitsu Corporation .... G 248 675-4345
  Wixom *(G-17761)*
Argent Limited .... G 734 427-5533
  Livonia *(G-9652)*
Big Rays Express Lube 28th St .... G 616 447-9710
  Grand Rapids *(G-6221)*
BP Lubricants USA Inc .... E 231 689-0002
  White Cloud *(G-17620)*
▼ Cadillac Oil Company .... F 313 365-6200
  Detroit *(G-3926)*
Chemtool Incorporated .... G 734 439-7010
  Milan *(G-10934)*
Chicago Mfg & Dist Co .... G 989 665-2531
  Gagetown *(G-5801)*

SIC SECTION
30 RUBBER AND MISCELLANEOUS PLASTICS PRODUCTS

◆ Chrysan Industries Inc ....E 734 451-5411
  Plymouth *(G-12597)*
Cobb Robert 3 Rachel ....G 616 374-7420
  Lake Odessa *(G-9113)*
◆ Condat Corporation ....E 734 944-4994
  Saline *(G-14383)*
◆ Coxen Enterprises Inc ....D 248 486-3800
  Brighton *(G-1906)*
▲ Cummings-Moore Graphite Co .....E 313 841-1615
  Detroit *(G-3957)*
Diversified Chemical Tech Inc ....C 313 867-5444
  Detroit *(G-4011)*
Eastern Oil Company ....E 248 333-1333
  Pontiac *(G-12819)*
Eastpointe Lube Express ....G 586 775-3234
  Eastpointe *(G-4701)*
Edrich Products Inc ....F 586 296-3350
  Fraser *(G-5647)*
Excelda Mfg Holdg LLC ....F 517 223-8000
  Fowlerville *(G-5563)*
▲ Fortech Products Inc ....E 248 446-9500
  Brighton *(G-1925)*
Fuchs Lubricants Co ....G 708 333-8900
  Grand Rapids *(G-6423)*
Fuel Source LLC ....G 313 506-0448
  Grosse Ile *(G-7173)*
Graphtek Inc ....G 810 985-4545
  Port Huron *(G-12923)*
H and M Lube DBA Jlube ....G 231 929-1197
  Traverse City *(G-15995)*
Houghton International Inc ....D 313 273-7374
  Detroit *(G-4131)*
▼ Huron Industries Inc ....G 810 984-4213
  Port Huron *(G-12928)*
Idemitsu Lubricants Amer Corp ......F 248 355-0666
  Southfield *(G-14943)*
Khi Coating ....G 248 236-2100
  Oxford *(G-12353)*
Lord Laboratories ....G 586 447-8955
  Saint Clair Shores *(G-14260)*
▲ Lub-Tech Inc ....G 616 299-3540
  Grand Rapids *(G-6634)*
Lube-Tech Inc ....G 269 329-1269
  Portage *(G-13012)*
Lubecon Systems Inc ....G 231 689-0002
  White Cloud *(G-17625)*
Marand Products Company Inc ......G 313 369-2000
  Detroit *(G-4218)*
MB Fluid Services LLC ....F 616 392-7036
  Holland *(G-7741)*
▲ Metalworking Lubricants Co ....C 248 332-3500
  Pontiac *(G-12849)*
Mr Lube Inc ....G 313 615-6161
  Wyandotte *(G-17969)*
Oil Chem Inc ....E 810 235-3040
  Flint *(G-5476)*
▲ Permawick Company Inc ....D 248 433-3500
  Birmingham *(G-1697)*
Persons Inc ....G 989 734-3835
  Rogers City *(G-13620)*
PMS Products Inc ....G 616 355-6615
  Holland *(G-7772)*
Quality Lube Express Inc ....G 586 421-0600
  Chesterfield *(G-2828)*
Rap Products Inc ....G 989 893-5583
  Bay City *(G-1348)*
Sterling Oil & Chemical Co ....G 248 298-2973
  Royal Oak *(G-13973)*
Stt Usa Inc ....G 248 522-9655
  Wixom *(G-17898)*
TMC Group Inc ....F 248 819-6063
  Pleasant Ridge *(G-12556)*
Vaughan Industries Inc ....F 313 935-2040
  Detroit *(G-4423)*
Warner Oil Company ....F 517 278-5844
  Coldwater *(G-3341)*
Wilbur Products Inc ....F 231 755-3805
  Muskegon *(G-11451)*
Xaerus Performance Fluids LLC .....E 989 631-7871
  Midland *(G-10927)*

30 RUBBER AND MISCELLANEOUS PLASTICS PRODUCTS

3011 Tires & Inner Tubes

▲ Avon Machining LLC ....D 586 884-2200
  Shelby Township *(G-14551)*
Avon Machining Holdings Inc ....C 586 884-2200
  Shelby Township *(G-14552)*

▼ Fastube LLC ....F 734 398-0474
  Canton *(G-2376)*
Goodyear Tire & Rubber Company ..G 248 336-0135
  Royal Oak *(G-13930)*
Great Lakes Tire LLC ....D 586 939-7000
  Warren *(G-17063)*
▲ Hot Wheels City Inc ....E 248 589-8800
  Madison Heights *(G-10268)*
◆ Hutchinson Corporation ....G 616 459-4541
  Grand Rapids *(G-6520)*
Jam Tire Inc ....D 586 772-2900
  Clinton Township *(G-3147)*
Omni United (usa) Inc ....G 231 943-9804
  Interlochen *(G-8244)*
Plastic Omnium Inc ....G 248 458-0772
  Troy *(G-16550)*
Tire Wholesalers Company ....D 269 349-9401
  Kalamazoo *(G-8913)*
Universal Components LLC ....G 517 861-7064
  Howell *(G-8119)*

3021 Rubber & Plastic Footwear

Atlantic Precision Pdts Inc ....F 586 532-9420
  Shelby Township *(G-14550)*
Fernand Corporation ....G 231 882-9622
  Kalamazoo *(G-8742)*
Musical Sneakers Incorporated .....F 888 410-7050
  Grandville *(G-7061)*
Nike Retail Services Inc ....E 248 858-9291
  Auburn Hills *(G-958)*
Original Footwear Company ....B 231 796-5828
  Big Rapids *(G-1639)*
▲ Wolverine Procurement Inc ....F 616 866-5500
  Rockford *(G-13598)*

3052 Rubber & Plastic Hose & Belting

Akwel Cadillac Usa Inc ....G 231 876-1361
  Cadillac *(G-2225)*
Akwel Cadillac Usa Inc ....E 248 848-9599
  Farmington Hills *(G-4926)*
▲ Anand Nvh North America Inc ...C 810 724-2400
  Imlay City *(G-8196)*
Andronaco Inc ....G 616 554-4600
  Kentwood *(G-8998)*
Atcoflex Inc ....F 616 842-4661
  Grand Haven *(G-5994)*
▲ Continental Plastics Co ....A 586 294-4600
  Shelby Township *(G-14567)*
Dayco Products LLC ....D 248 404-6506
  Troy *(G-16298)*
Dayco Products LLC ....C 248 404-6537
  Roseville *(G-13789)*
Douglass Safety Systems LLC ......G 989 687-7600
  Sanford *(G-14449)*
Eaton-Aeroquip Llc ....B 949 452-9575
  Jackson *(G-8440)*
▲ Ena North America Corporation ..F 248 926-0011
  Wixom *(G-17803)*
Fabricated Flex & Hose Sup Inc ....G 269 342-2221
  Kalamazoo *(G-8741)*
Factory Products Inc ....G 269 668-3329
  Mattawan *(G-10664)*
Flexfab LLC ....E 269 945-3533
  Grand Rapids *(G-6412)*
▲ Flexfab Horizons Intl Inc ....E 269 945-4700
  Hastings *(G-7409)*
▲ Flexfab LLC ....G 269 945-2433
  Hastings *(G-7410)*
Gates Corporation ....D 248 260-2300
  Rochester Hills *(G-13431)*
▲ Haviland Contoured Plastics .....G 616 361-6691
  Walker *(G-16866)*
◆ Kadant Johnson LLC ....C 269 278-1715
  Three Rivers *(G-15867)*
▲ Mol Belting Systems Inc ....D 616 453-2484
  Grand Rapids *(G-6696)*
▲ Piranha Hose Products Inc ....E 231 779-4390
  Cadillac *(G-2271)*
▲ Pureflex Inc ....C 616 554-1100
  Kentwood *(G-9026)*
▲ Sejasmi Industries Inc ....C 586 725-5300
  Ira *(G-8270)*
Snook Inc ....F 231 799-3333
  Norton Shores *(G-11795)*
▲ Sparks Belting Company Inc .....D 616 949-2750
  Grand Rapids *(G-6875)*
Stephen A James ....G 269 641-5879
  Cassopolis *(G-2536)*
Thunder Technologies LLC ....F 248 844-4875
  Rochester Hills *(G-13526)*

▲ TI Automotive LLC ....C 248 494-5000
  Auburn Hills *(G-1020)*
TI Group Auto Systems LLC ....D 517 437-7462
  Hillsdale *(G-7543)*
◆ TI Group Auto Systems LLC ......B 248 296-8000
  Auburn Hills *(G-1022)*
Ton-Tex Corporation ....E 616 957-3200
  Greenville *(G-7158)*

3053 Gaskets, Packing & Sealing Devices

Action Fabricators Inc ....C 616 957-2032
  Grand Rapids *(G-6136)*
Air Supply Company Inc ....G 616 874-7751
  Rockford *(G-13556)*
Aircraft Precision Pdts Inc ....D 989 875-4186
  Ithaca *(G-8356)*
Armada Rubber Manufacturing Co .D 586 784-9135
  Armada *(G-716)*
Basic Rubber and Plastics Co ....E 248 360-7400
  Walled Lake *(G-16891)*
Blade Industrial Products Inc ....G 248 773-7400
  Wixom *(G-17774)*
C W Marsh Company ....E 231 722-3781
  Muskegon *(G-11288)*
Champion Gasket & Rubber Inc ....E 248 624-6140
  Commerce Township *(G-3394)*
Copeland-Gibson Products Corp ...F 248 740-4400
  Troy *(G-16282)*
Cpj Company Inc ....E 616 784-6355
  Comstock Park *(G-3472)*
Creative Foam Corporation ....D 810 714-0140
  Fenton *(G-5199)*
▲ Creative Foam Corporation ....C 810 629-4149
  Fenton *(G-5198)*
Crk Ltd ....G 586 779-5240
  Eastpointe *(G-4699)*
Derby Fabg Solutions LLC ....D 616 866-1650
  Rockford *(G-13566)*
Energy Manufacturing Inc ....G 248 360-0065
  Wixom *(G-17804)*
▲ Federal-Mogul Ignition LLC ....F 248 354-7700
  Southfield *(G-14907)*
▲ Federal-Mogul Piston Rings Inc ..F 248 354-7700
  Southfield *(G-14909)*
Federal-Mogul Powertrain Inc ....C 616 887-8231
  Sparta *(G-15094)*
▲ Federal-Mogul Powertrain LLC ..G 248 354-7700
  Southfield *(G-14910)*
Federal-Mogul Powertrain LLC .....E 734 930-1590
  Ann Arbor *(G-458)*
Federl-Mgul Dutch Holdings Inc ....D 248 354-7700
  Southfield *(G-14914)*
▲ Flexfab Horizons Intl Inc ....E 269 945-4700
  Hastings *(G-7409)*
Flowserve US Inc ....C 269 381-2650
  Kalamazoo *(G-8746)*
◆ Freudenberg N Amer Ltd Partnr .F 734 354-5505
  Plymouth *(G-12623)*
Freudenberg-Nok General Partnr ..C 734 451-0020
  Plymouth *(G-12625)*
▲ Freudenberg-Nok General Partnr .F 734 451-0020
  Plymouth *(G-12624)*
▲ Garco Gaskets Inc ....G 734 728-4912
  Livonia *(G-9749)*
Gasket Holdings Inc ....G 248 354-7700
  Southfield *(G-14918)*
Grand Haven Gasket Company ......F 616 842-7682
  Grand Haven *(G-6022)*
Green Polymeric Materials Inc ......E 313 933-7390
  Detroit *(G-4102)*
Grm Corporation ....G 989 453-2322
  Pigeon *(G-12490)*
◆ Henniges Auto Sling Systems N ..C 248 340-4100
  Auburn Hills *(G-897)*
▲ Henniges Automotive N America .C 248 340-4100
  Auburn Hills *(G-898)*
Industrial Converting Inc ....F 586 757-8820
  Warren *(G-17091)*
▲ Ishino Gasket North Amer LLC ..G 734 451-0020
  Plymouth *(G-12650)*
J L Schroth Co ....G 586 759-4240
  Warren *(G-17107)*
▲ Jacobsen Industries Inc ....D 734 591-6111
  Livonia *(G-9791)*
John Crane Inc ....F 989 496-9292
  Midland *(G-10876)*
◆ Kaydon Corporation ....B 734 747-7025
  Ann Arbor *(G-516)*
Kent Manufacturing Company ....D 616 454-9495
  Grand Rapids *(G-6577)*

Employee Codes: A=Over 500 employees, B=251-500
C=101-250, D=51-100, E=20-50, F=10-19, G=3-9

Ksb Dubric Inc........E....... 616 784-6355
Comstock Park (G-3492)
◆ L & L Products Inc........A....... 586 336-1600
Bruce Twp (G-2087)
L & L Products Inc........B....... 586 752-6681
Bruce Twp (G-2088)
L & L Products Inc........B....... 586 336-1600
Bruce Twp (G-2089)
Lamons........G....... 989 488-4580
Midland (G-10881)
Lydall Sealing Solutions Inc........D....... 248 596-2800
Northville (G-11706)
M-Seal Products Co LLC........G....... 313 884-6147
Grosse Pointe Shores (G-7200)
Macarthur Corp........E....... 810 606-1777
Grand Blanc (G-5975)
◆ Marshall Excelsior Co........E....... 269 789-6700
Marshall (G-10577)
▲ Martin Fluid Power Company........D....... 248 585-8170
Madison Heights (G-10302)
Memtech Inc........F....... 734 455-8550
Plymouth (G-12689)
Michael-Stephens Company........G....... 248 583-7767
Troy (G-16503)
Michigan Rbr & Gasket Co Inc........E....... 586 323-4100
Sterling Heights (G-15421)
Midwest Fbrglas Fbricators Inc........F....... 810 765-7445
Marine City (G-10478)
N-K Sealing Technologies LLC........G....... 616 248-3200
Grand Rapids (G-6711)
Nci Mfg Inc........F....... 248 380-4151
Livonia (G-9862)
Oliver Products Company........D....... 616 456-7711
Grand Rapids (G-6728)
Package Design & Mfg Inc........E....... 248 486-4390
Brighton (G-1972)
Parker-Hannifin Corporation........D....... 330 253-5239
Otsego (G-12251)
Pipeline Packaging........G....... 248 743-0248
Troy (G-16548)
▲ Plastomer Corporation........C....... 734 464-0700
Livonia (G-9889)
Precision Packing Corporation........E....... 586 756-8700
Warren (G-17194)
R & J Manufacturing Company........E....... 248 669-2460
Commerce Township (G-3445)
R H M Rubber & Manufacturing........G....... 248 624-8277
Novi (G-11984)
Rhino Strapping Products Inc........F....... 734 442-4040
Taylor (G-15763)
Rodzina Industries Inc........G....... 810 235-2341
Flint (G-5493)
Roger Zatkoff Company........E....... 586 264-3593
Warren (G-17223)
▲ Roger Zatkoff Company........E....... 248 478-2400
Farmington Hills (G-5117)
SKF USA Inc........D....... 734 414-6585
Plymouth (G-12756)
Snyder Plastics Inc........E....... 989 684-8355
Bay City (G-1358)
Speyside Real Estate LLC........F....... 248 354-7700
Southfield (G-15031)
Spray Booth Products Inc........E....... 313 766-4400
Redford (G-13193)
▲ Tri-TEC Seal LLC........E....... 810 655-3900
Fenton (G-5246)
▲ U S Graphite Inc........C....... 989 755-0441
Saginaw (G-14172)
Uniflex Inc........G....... 248 486-6000
Brighton (G-2002)
Unique Fabricating Inc........E....... 248 853-2333
Auburn Hills (G-1034)
Unique Fabricating Inc........E....... 248 853-2333
Rochester Hills (G-13535)
▲ Unique Fabricating Na Inc........B....... 248 853-2333
Auburn Hills (G-1035)
Unique Fabricating Na Inc........C....... 517 524-9010
Concord (G-3526)
Upper Peninsula Rubber Co Inc........G....... 906 786-0460
Escanaba (G-4864)
◆ Vibracoustic North America L P........E....... 269 637-2116
South Haven (G-14780)
▲ Yates Industries Inc........D....... 586 778-7680
Saint Clair Shores (G-14277)
Zephyros Inc........A....... 586 336-1600
Bruce Twp (G-2106)

3061 Molded, Extruded & Lathe-Cut Rubber Mechanical Goods

Advanced Manufacturing LLC........G....... 231 826-3859
Falmouth (G-4891)
▲ Akwel Cadillac Usa Inc........B....... 231 876-8020
Cadillac (G-2223)
Akwel Cadillac Usa Inc........C....... 231 775-6571
Cadillac (G-2224)
Akwel Usa Inc........C....... 231 775-6571
Cadillac (G-2226)
▲ Anand Nvh North America Inc........C....... 810 724-2400
Imlay City (G-8196)
Armada Rubber Manufacturing Co........D....... 586 784-9135
Armada (G-716)
Basic Rubber and Plastics Co........E....... 248 360-7400
Walled Lake (G-16891)
Black River Manufacturing Inc........E....... 810 982-9812
Port Huron (G-12900)
BRC Rubber & Plastics Inc........G....... 248 745-9200
Auburn Hills (G-806)
Contitech North America Inc........F....... 248 312-3050
Rochester Hills (G-13396)
▲ Creative Foam Corporation........C....... 810 629-4149
Fenton (G-5198)
▲ Dawson Manufacturing Company........C....... 269 925-0100
Benton Harbor (G-1492)
Dawson Manufacturing Company........C....... 269 925-0100
Benton Harbor (G-1493)
Die Stampco Inc........F....... 989 893-7790
Bay City (G-1302)
▲ Fluid Hutchinson Management........D....... 248 679-1327
Auburn Hills (G-876)
Four Star Rubber Inc........G....... 810 632-3335
Commerce Township (G-3407)
◆ Freudenberg N Amer Ltd Partnr........G....... 734 354-5505
Plymouth (G-12623)
▲ Freudenberg-Nok General Partnr........C....... 734 451-0020
Plymouth (G-12624)
▲ HP Pelzer Auto Systems Inc........E....... 248 280-1010
Troy (G-16405)
▲ Hutchinson Antivibration........B....... 616 459-4541
Grand Rapids (G-6519)
Hutchinson Antivibration........C....... 231 775-9737
Cadillac (G-2254)
Midwest Rubber Company........D....... 810 376-2085
Deckerville (G-3809)
▲ Opeo Inc........F....... 248 299-4000
Auburn Hills (G-966)
Polymer Products Group Inc........G....... 989 723-9510
Owosso (G-12311)
▲ Pullman Company........F....... 734 243-8000
Monroe (G-11064)
R & J Manufacturing Company........E....... 248 669-2460
Commerce Township (G-3445)
R H M Rubber & Manufacturing........G....... 248 624-8277
Novi (G-11984)
Reliance Rubber Industries Inc........G....... 734 641-4100
Westland (G-17596)
Rosta USA Corp........F....... 269 841-5448
Benton Harbor (G-1544)
Trelleborg Automotive USA Inc........E....... 734 254-9140
Northville (G-11731)
Uchiyama Mktg & Dev Amer LLC........F....... 248 859-3986
Novi (G-12022)
Uniflex Inc........G....... 248 486-6000
Brighton (G-2002)
◆ Vibracoustic North America L P........E....... 269 637-2116
South Haven (G-14780)
▲ Vibracoustic Usa Inc........C....... 269 637-2116
South Haven (G-14781)
Vibracoustic Usa Inc........B....... 810 648-2100
Sandusky (G-14446)
Vibracoustic Usa Inc........G....... 810 648-2100
Sandusky (G-14447)

3069 Fabricated Rubber Prdts, NEC

Advanced Rubber & Plastic........G....... 586 754-7398
Warren (G-16920)
Advanced Rubber Tech Inc........F....... 231 775-3112
Cadillac (G-2222)
Aerofab Company Inc........F....... 248 542-0051
Ferndale (G-5253)
▲ Airboss Flexible Products Co........C....... 248 852-5500
Auburn Hills (G-763)
Americo Corporation........G....... 313 565-6550
Dearborn (G-3675)
▲ Anand Nvh North America Inc........C....... 810 724-2400
Imlay City (G-8196)
▼ Apex Marine Inc........D....... 989 681-4300
Saint Louis (G-14359)
Aptargroup Inc........C....... 989 631-8030
Midland (G-10816)
Armada Rubber Manufacturing Co........D....... 586 784-9135
Armada (G-716)
Basic Rubber and Plastics Co........E....... 248 360-7400
Walled Lake (G-16891)
Blade Industrial Products Inc........G....... 248 773-7400
Wixom (G-17774)
◆ Bushings Inc........F....... 248 650-0603
Rochester Hills (G-13381)
Cartex Corporation........G....... 610 759-1650
Troy (G-16261)
Cg & D Group........G....... 248 310-9166
Farmington Hills (G-4960)
▲ Changan US RES & Dev Ctr Inc........G....... 734 259-6440
Plymouth (G-12596)
Clair Evans-St Inc........G....... 313 259-2266
Detroit (G-3938)
▲ Creative Foam Corporation........C....... 810 629-4149
Fenton (G-5198)
◆ Day International Group Inc........E....... 734 781-4600
Plymouth (G-12606)
Derby Fabg Solutions LLC........D....... 616 866-1650
Rockford (G-13566)
Ds Sales Inc........G....... 248 960-6411
Wixom (G-17796)
Dti Molded Products Inc........F....... 248 647-0400
Bingham Farms (G-1652)
▲ Ehc Inc........G....... 313 259-2266
Detroit (G-4030)
▲ Evans Industries Inc........G....... 313 259-2266
Detroit (G-4045)
Exotic Rubber & Plastics Corp........D....... 248 477-2122
Farmington Hills (G-4996)
First Class Tire Shredders Inc........F....... 810 639-5888
Clio (G-3271)
Flint Group US LLC........D....... 269 279-5161
Three Rivers (G-15862)
Flint Group US LLC........A....... 734 781-4600
Livonia (G-9741)
▲ Gaco Sourcing LLC........G....... 248 633-2656
Birmingham (G-1684)
Giv LLC........G....... 248 467-6852
Livonia (G-9752)
▲ Go Cat Feather Toys........G....... 517 543-7519
Charlotte (G-2652)
Great Lake Foam Technologies........F....... 517 563-8030
Hanover (G-7260)
Great Lakes Rubber Co........D....... 248 624-5710
Wixom (G-17819)
Green Polymeric Materials Inc........E....... 313 933-7390
Detroit (G-4102)
H A King Co Inc........G....... 248 280-0006
Royal Oak (G-13931)
Henniges Auto Holdings Inc........B....... 248 340-4100
Auburn Hills (G-896)
HI-Tech Flexible Products Inc........F....... 517 783-5911
Jackson (G-8465)
Hold-It Inc........G....... 810 984-4213
Port Huron (G-12925)
▲ Hutchinson Antivibration........B....... 616 459-4541
Grand Rapids (G-6519)
Hutchinson Antivibration........C....... 231 775-9737
Cadillac (G-2254)
◆ Hutchinson Corporation........G....... 616 459-4541
Grand Rapids (G-6520)
Hutchinson Seal Corporation........G....... 248 375-4190
Auburn Hills (G-903)
Hutchinson Sealing Syst........D....... 248 375-3721
Auburn Hills (G-904)
▲ Hutchinson Sealing Systems Inc........D....... 248 375-3720
Auburn Hills (G-905)
Inoac Interior Systems LLC........E....... 248 488-7610
Farmington Hills (G-5028)
Interdyne Inc........E....... 517 849-2281
Jonesville (G-8656)
Jedtco Corp........E....... 734 326-3010
Westland (G-17573)
Jfp Acquisition LLC........E....... 517 787-8877
Jackson (G-8483)
Kent Manufacturing Company........D....... 616 454-9495
Grand Rapids (G-6577)
Korens........G....... 248 817-5188
Rochester Hills (G-13456)
◆ Luebke & Vogt Corporation........G....... 248 449-3232
Novi (G-11930)
Marco Rollo Inc........F....... 269 279-5246
Three Rivers (G-15869)
Massee Products Ltd........G....... 269 684-8255
Niles (G-11624)

SIC SECTION

30 RUBBER AND MISCELLANEOUS PLASTICS PRODUCTS

MCS Consultants Inc .... F 810 229-4222
Brighton *(G-1958)*
Meccom Industrial Products Co ..... F 586 463-2828
Clinton Township *(G-3172)*
Michigan Roller Inc .... G 269 651-2304
Sturgis *(G-15618)*
Milsco LLC .... B 517 787-3650
Jackson *(G-8531)*
▲ Minowitz Manufacturing Co .... E 586 779-5940
Huntington Woods *(G-8190)*
Missaukee Molded Rubber Inc ..... F 231 839-5309
Lake City *(G-9094)*
▲ Mykin Inc .... F 248 667-8030
South Lyon *(G-14804)*
Nitto Inc .... F 734 729-7800
Romulus *(G-13714)*
Northern Tire Inc .... F 906 486-4463
Ishpeming *(G-8350)*
▲ Opeo Inc .... F 248 299-4000
Auburn Hills *(G-966)*
Peck Engineering Inc .... F 313 534-2950
Redford *(G-13179)*
Pegasus Tool LLC .... G 313 255-5900
Detroit *(G-4295)*
Power Seal International LLC .... E 248 537-1103
Troy *(G-16555)*
PRA Company .... D 989 846-1029
Standish *(G-15226)*
Procraft Custom Builder .... G 586 323-1605
Oxford *(G-12364)*
R H M Rubber & Manufacturing .... E 248 624-8277
Novi *(G-11984)*
◆ Rajason International Corp .... G 248 506-4456
Troy *(G-16576)*
Rehau Incorporated .... E 269 651-7845
Sturgis *(G-15632)*
Republic Roller Corporation .... E 269 273-9591
Three Rivers *(G-15876)*
Rex M Tubbs .... G 734 459-3180
Plymouth *(G-12735)*
Schroth Enterprises Inc .... E 586 759-4240
Grosse Pointe Farms *(G-7187)*
Simolex Rubber Corporation .... F 734 453-4500
Plymouth *(G-12755)*
▲ Specialty Pdts & Polymers Inc .... E 269 684-5931
Niles *(G-11648)*
Thunder Technologies LLC .... F 248 844-4875
Rochester Hills *(G-13526)*
Tillerman Jfp LLC .... E 616 443-8346
Middleville *(G-10810)*
Tissue Seal LLC .... F 734 213-5530
Ann Arbor *(G-675)*
◆ Toyoda Gosei North Amer Corp .. C 248 280-2100
Troy *(G-16650)*
◆ Trico Products Corporation .... C 248 371-1700
Rochester Hills *(G-13531)*
Trinseo LLC .... E 888 789-7661
Midland *(G-10922)*
Uniflex Inc .... E 248 486-6000
Brighton *(G-2002)*
▲ Vte Inc .... E 231 539-8000
Pellston *(G-12426)*
Wiley & Co .... G 616 361-7110
Grand Rapids *(G-6993)*
▲ Zhongding Saling Parts USA Inc . G 734 241-8870
Monroe *(G-11088)*

3081 Plastic Unsupported Sheet & Film

A-Pac Manufacturing Company .... E 616 791-7222
Grand Rapids *(G-6126)*
Berry Global Inc .... B 616 772-4635
Zeeland *(G-18118)*
Berry Global Inc .... C 269 435-2425
Constantine *(G-3532)*
▲ Cadillac Products Inc .... B 248 813-8200
Troy *(G-16253)*
Cadillac Products Inc .... D 586 774-1700
Roseville *(G-13779)*
Cadillac Products Inc .... D 989 766-2294
Rogers City *(G-13613)*
Cadillac Products Packaging Co .. C 248 879-5000
Troy *(G-16254)*
Coral Corporation .... G 616 868-6295
Alto *(G-326)*
Corotech Acquisition Co .... F 616 456-5557
Grand Rapids *(G-6312)*
Dow Chemical Company .... C 989 636-4406
Midland *(G-10836)*
◆ Dow Chemical Company .... B 989 636-1000
Midland *(G-10834)*
Dow Chemical Company .... G 989 636-1000
Midland *(G-10840)*
Dow Chemical Company .... D 989 636-0540
Midland *(G-10845)*
Dow Chemical Company .... D 989 636-5409
Midland *(G-10848)*
Dow Inc .... G 989 636-1000
Midland *(G-10851)*
▲ Durakon Industries Inc .... E 608 742-5301
Lapeer *(G-9457)*
▲ Encore Commercial Products Inc . F 248 354-4090
Farmington Hills *(G-4986)*
Environmental Protection Inc .... F 231 943-2265
Traverse City *(G-15965)*
▲ Filcon Inc .... F 989 386-2986
Clare *(G-2870)*
Great Lakes Containment Inc .... F 231 258-8800
Kalkaska *(G-8943)*
Jsp International LLC .... F 248 397-3200
Madison Heights *(G-10285)*
Jsp International LLC .... E 313 834-0612
Detroit *(G-4167)*
Kraft-Wrap Inc .... F 586 755-2050
Warren *(G-17121)*
◆ Link Tech Inc .... G 269 427-8297
Bangor *(G-1092)*
Loose Plastics Inc .... C 989 246-1880
Gladwin *(G-5933)*
▲ Mpf Acquisitions Inc .... E 269 672-5511
Martin *(G-10596)*
National Plastek Inc .... E 616 698-9559
Caledonia *(G-2310)*
◆ Petoskey Plastics Inc .... E 231 347-2602
Petoskey *(G-12469)*
Petoskey Plastics Inc .... C 231 347-2602
Petoskey *(G-12470)*
Profile Industrial Packg Corp .... C 616 245-7260
Grand Rapids *(G-6785)*
Quality Transparent Bag Inc .... F 989 893-3561
Bay City *(G-1344)*
Zenith Global LLC .... E 517 546-7402
Howell *(G-8123)*

3082 Plastic Unsupported Profile Shapes

Alloy Exchange Inc .... F 616 863-0640
Rockford *(G-13557)*
Belmont Plastics Solutions LLC .... G 616 340-3147
Belmont *(G-1458)*
Dlhbowles Inc .... F 248 569-0652
Southfield *(G-14883)*
Gazelle Prototype LLC .... G 616 844-1820
Spring Lake *(G-15145)*
Highland Plastics Inc .... E 989 828-4400
Shepherd *(G-14728)*
▲ Idemitsu Chemicals USA Corp ... E 248 355-0666
Southfield *(G-14942)*
Plastic Plaque Inc .... G 810 982-9591
Port Huron *(G-12957)*
Porex Technologies Corporation .. E 989 865-8200
Saint Charles *(G-14198)*
Spiratex Company .... D 734 289-4800
Monroe *(G-11069)*
◆ Tg Fluid Systems USA Corp .... B 810 220-6161
Brighton *(G-1997)*
◆ Trico Products Corporation .... C 248 371-1700
Rochester Hills *(G-13531)*

3083 Plastic Laminated Plate & Sheet

Advanced Drainage Systems Inc .. D 989 723-5208
Owosso *(G-12275)*
Bangor Plastics Inc .... E 269 427-7971
Bangor *(G-1088)*
Basic Rubber and Plastics Co ...... E 248 360-7400
Walled Lake *(G-16891)*
Bordener Engnred Laminates Inc . G 989 835-6881
Bay City *(G-1292)*
▼ Duo-Gard Industries Inc .... D 734 207-9700
Canton *(G-2367)*
H & R Wood Specialties Inc .... E 269 628-2181
Gobles *(G-5947)*
Hanwha Azdel Inc .... F 810 629-2496
Warren *(G-17075)*
J Kaltz & Co .... G 616 942-6070
Grand Rapids *(G-6547)*
Janice Morse Inc .... E 248 624-7300
West Bloomfield *(G-17482)*
Kent Manufacturing Company ...... D 616 454-9495
Grand Rapids *(G-6577)*
Key Plastics LLC .... G 248 449-6100
Plymouth *(G-12667)*
McKechnie Vhcl Cmpnnts USA Inc . E 218 894-1218
Roseville *(G-13832)*
Mediaform LLC .... E 248 548-0260
Royal Oak *(G-13950)*
Noron Composite Technologies ... E 231 723-9277
Manistee *(G-10433)*
Paramount Solutions Inc .... G 586 914-0708
Ray *(G-13135)*
Paul Murphy Plastics Co .... E 586 774-4880
Roseville *(G-13851)*
Plascore Inc .... D 616 772-1220
Zeeland *(G-18176)*
Polyply Composites LLC .... E 616 842-6330
Grand Haven *(G-6061)*
Rehau Incorporated .... E 269 651-7845
Sturgis *(G-15632)*
Ronald M Davis Co Inc .... G 313 864-5588
Detroit *(G-4347)*
Scooters Refuse Service Inc .... G 269 962-2201
Battle Creek *(G-1244)*
Shawmut Corporation .... C 810 987-2222
Port Huron *(G-12965)*
Spiratex Company .... D 734 289-4800
Monroe *(G-11069)*
Summit Polymers Inc .... B 269 323-1301
Portage *(G-13047)*
Summit Polymers Inc .... B 269 651-1643
Sturgis *(G-15638)*
▲ Total Plastics Resources LLC .... D 269 344-0009
Kalamazoo *(G-8914)*
Tuscarora Inc -Vs .... G 989 729-2780
Owosso *(G-12325)*
▼ Vidon Plastics Inc .... D 810 667-0634
Lapeer *(G-9490)*

3084 Plastic Pipe

Advanced Drainage Systems Inc .. G 989 761-7610
Clifford *(G-3009)*
Advanced Drainage Systems Inc .. D 989 723-5208
Owosso *(G-12275)*
▲ Conley Composites LLC .... E 918 299-5051
Grand Rapids *(G-6300)*
Creek Plastics LLC .... F 517 423-1003
Tecumseh *(G-15786)*
▲ Ethylene LLC .... E 616 554-3464
Kentwood *(G-9005)*
◆ Genova Products Inc .... D 810 744-4500
Davison *(G-3650)*
▼ Vidon Plastics Inc .... D 810 667-0634
Lapeer *(G-9490)*

3085 Plastic Bottles

◆ Alpha Packaging Michigan Inc .... D 314 427-4300
Ypsilanti *(G-18050)*
Graham Packaging Company LP . E 616 355-0479
Holland *(G-7647)*
▲ Inoac Usa Inc .... E 248 619-7031
Troy *(G-16419)*
Novares US LLC .... B 616 554-3555
Grand Rapids *(G-6723)*
◆ Plastipak Packaging Inc .... C 734 455-3600
Plymouth *(G-12719)*
Plastipak Packaging Inc .... C 734 326-6184
Westland *(G-17589)*
▲ Plastipak Packaging Inc .... F 734 467-7519
Romulus *(G-13722)*
▼ R N Fink Manufacturing Co .... E 517 655-4351
Williamston *(G-17738)*

3086 Plastic Foam Prdts

Action Fabricators Inc .... C 616 957-2032
Grand Rapids *(G-6136)*
Advance Engineering Company ... E 989 435-3641
Beaverton *(G-1382)*
Ameripak Inc .... F 248 858-9000
Pontiac *(G-12804)*
◆ Armaly Sponge Company .... E 248 669-2100
Commerce Township *(G-3391)*
▲ Aspen Technologies Inc .... D 248 446-1485
Brighton *(G-1887)*
Atlas Roofing Corporation .... C 616 878-1568
Byron Center *(G-2177)*
Barber Packaging Company .... E 269 427-7995
Bangor *(G-1089)*
Bespro Pattern Inc .... F 586 268-6970
Madison Heights *(G-10204)*
Blue Water Bioproducts LLC .... G 586 453-9219
Port Huron *(G-12902)*
Bremen Corp .... G 574 546-4238
Fenton *(G-5191)*

Employee Codes: A=Over 500 employees, B=251-500
C=101-250, D=51-100, E=20-50, F=10-19, G=3-9

30 RUBBER AND MISCELLANEOUS PLASTICS PRODUCTS SIC SECTION

Briggs Industries Inc ..... E 586 749-5191
Chesterfield *(G-2747)*
◆ Brooklyn Products Intl ..... E 517 592-2185
Brooklyn *(G-2036)*
Cantrick Kip Co ..... G 248 644-7622
Birmingham *(G-1675)*
▲ Carcoustics Usa Inc ..... D 517 548-6700
Howell *(G-8019)*
Classic Container Corporation ..... E 734 853-3000
Livonia *(G-9684)*
Creative Foam Corporation ..... C 269 782-3483
Dowagiac *(G-4537)*
▲ Creative Foam Corporation ..... C 810 629-4149
Fenton *(G-5198)*
Creative Foam Corporation ..... D 810 714-0140
Fenton *(G-5199)*
Creatv Foam Cmpsite Systms ..... E 810 629-4149
Flint *(G-5408)*
◆ Dart Container Corp Kentucky ..... B 517 676-3800
Mason *(G-10632)*
◆ Dart Container Corporation ..... A 800 248-5960
Mason *(G-10633)*
▲ Dart Container Michigan LLC ..... E 800 248-5960
Mason *(G-10634)*
Dart Container Michigan LLC ..... E 517 694-9455
Holt *(G-7909)*
Dart Container Michigan LLC ..... C 517 676-3803
Mason *(G-10635)*
Derby Fabg Solutions LLC ..... D 616 866-1650
Rockford *(G-13566)*
Dow Chemical Company ..... D 989 636-5430
Midland *(G-10843)*
Dow Chemical Company ..... C 989 636-4406
Midland *(G-10836)*
◆ Dow Chemical Company ..... B 989 636-1000
Midland *(G-10834)*
Dow Chemical Company ..... D 989 636-0540
Midland *(G-10845)*
Dow Chemical Company ..... D 989 636-5409
Midland *(G-10848)*
Dow Inc ..... G 989 636-1000
Midland *(G-10851)*
Duna USA Inc ..... G 231 425-4300
Ludington *(G-10058)*
▲ Eagle Industries Inc ..... E 248 624-4266
Wixom *(G-17797)*
Envirolite LLC ..... D 888 222-2191
Coldwater *(G-3302)*
▲ Envirolite LLC ..... F 248 792-3184
Troy *(G-16349)*
Epic Materials Inc ..... G 586 294-0300
Fraser *(G-5652)*
Everest Manufacturing Inc ..... F 313 401-2608
Farmington Hills *(G-4993)*
Fapco Inc ..... G 269 695-6889
Buchanan *(G-2115)*
◆ Floracraft Corporation ..... C 231 845-5127
Ludington *(G-10059)*
Fomcore LLC ..... D 231 366-4791
Muskegon *(G-11325)*
Fxi Inc ..... F 248 553-1039
Southfield *(G-14917)*
Fxi Novi ..... G 248 994-0630
Novi *(G-11889)*
▲ G & T Industries Inc ..... D 616 452-8611
Byron Center *(G-2192)*
Gemini Plastics Inc ..... C 989 658-8557
Ubly *(G-16716)*
Genesis Manufacturing Entps ..... G 734 243-5302
Monroe *(G-11032)*
Global Autopack LLC ..... G 248 390-2434
New Hudson *(G-11541)*
Green Polymeric Materials Inc ..... E 313 933-7390
Detroit *(G-4102)*
▲ Harbor Foam Inc ..... G 616 855-8150
Grandville *(G-7044)*
High Tech Insulators Inc ..... E 734 525-9030
Livonia *(G-9770)*
Huntington Foam LLC ..... E 661 225-9951
Greenville *(G-7139)*
Inter-Pack Corporation ..... E 734 242-7755
Monroe *(G-11042)*
Janesville LLC ..... B 248 948-1811
Southfield *(G-14950)*
Jason Incorporated ..... E 248 948-1811
Southfield *(G-14951)*
Joy Products Inc ..... G 269 683-1662
Niles *(G-11622)*
◆ Jsj Corporation ..... E 616 842-6350
Grand Haven *(G-6042)*
Kalamazoo Plastics Company ..... E 269 381-0010
Kalamazoo *(G-8795)*
Kent Manufacturing Company ..... D 616 454-9495
Grand Rapids *(G-6577)*
Kringer Industrial Corporation ..... F 519 818-3509
Warren *(G-17122)*
▲ Leon Interiors Inc ..... B 616 422-7479
Holland *(G-7721)*
Light Metal Forming Corp ..... F 248 851-3984
Bloomfield Hills *(G-1777)*
Meiki Corporation ..... G 248 680-4638
Troy *(G-16492)*
▲ Michigan Foam Products Inc ..... F 616 452-9611
Grand Rapids *(G-6671)*
N Pack Ship Center ..... G 906 863-4095
Menominee *(G-10752)*
▲ Nanosystems Inc ..... F 734 274-0020
Ann Arbor *(G-570)*
Nu-Pak Solutions Inc ..... F 231 755-1662
Norton Shores *(G-11784)*
Ortus Enterprises LLC ..... G 269 491-1447
Portage *(G-13020)*
Package Design & Mfg Inc ..... E 248 486-4390
Brighton *(G-1972)*
Packaging Engineering LLC ..... G 248 437-9444
Brighton *(G-1973)*
Pedmic Converting Inc ..... E 810 679-9600
Croswell *(G-3602)*
Plascore Inc ..... D 616 772-1220
Zeeland *(G-18176)*
▲ Plasteel Corporation ..... F 313 562-5400
Inkster *(G-8231)*
Pregis LLC ..... F 616 520-1550
Grand Rapids *(G-6767)*
Pregis LLC ..... D 810 320-3005
Marysville *(G-10611)*
Reklein Plastics Incorporated ..... G 586 739-8850
Sterling Heights *(G-15463)*
Revstone Industries LLC ..... F 248 351-1000
Troy *(G-16577)*
▲ Rogers Foam Automotive Corp ..... E 810 820-6323
Flint *(G-5494)*
Russell R Peters Co LLC ..... G 989 732-0660
Gaylord *(G-5891)*
Schmitz Foam Products LLC ..... E 517 781-6615
Coldwater *(G-3330)*
Sekisui America Corporation ..... C 517 279-7587
Coldwater *(G-3331)*
Sekisui Plastics US A Inc ..... F 248 308-3000
Wixom *(G-17892)*
Sekisui Voltek LLC ..... C 517 279-7587
Coldwater *(G-3332)*
▲ Simco Automotive Trim Inc ..... E 616 608-9818
Grand Rapids *(G-6865)*
Sonoco Prtective Solutions Inc ..... D 989 723-3720
Owosso *(G-12317)*
Southwestern Foam Tech Inc ..... E 616 726-1677
Grand Rapids *(G-6874)*
▲ Special Projects Engineering ..... G 517 676-8525
Mason *(G-10659)*
Superior Surface Protection Co ..... G 517 206-1541
Jackson *(G-8579)*
Transpak Inc ..... E 586 264-2064
Sterling Heights *(G-15528)*
Ufp Technologies Inc ..... D 616 949-8100
Grand Rapids *(G-6948)*
Unique Fabricating Inc ..... E 248 853-2333
Auburn Hills *(G-1034)*
Unique Fabricating Inc ..... E 248 853-2333
Rochester Hills *(G-13535)*
▲ Unique Fabricating Na Inc ..... B 248 853-2333
Auburn Hills *(G-1035)*
Unique Molded Foam Tech Inc ..... C 517 524-9010
Concord *(G-3527)*
◆ United Foam A Ufp Tech Brnd ..... D 616 949-8100
Grand Rapids *(G-6952)*
Westpack Inc ..... G 231 725-9200
Muskegon *(G-11448)*
Whisper Creative Products Inc ..... G 734 529-2734
Dundee *(G-4603)*
Woodbridge Holdings Inc ..... C 734 942-0458
Romulus *(G-13742)*
▲ Woodbridge Holdings Inc ..... G 248 288-0100
Troy *(G-16697)*

3087 Custom Compounding Of Purchased Plastic Resins

◆ Aci Plastics Inc ..... E 810 767-3800
Flint *(G-5369)*
Alpha Resins LLC ..... G 313 366-9300
Detroit *(G-3861)*
▲ Alumilite Corporation ..... F 269 488-4000
Galesburg *(G-5805)*
American Commodities Inc ..... E 810 767-3800
Flint *(G-5376)*
Amplas Compounding LLC ..... F 586 795-2555
Sterling Heights *(G-15260)*
▲ Azon Usa Inc ..... F 269 385-5942
Kalamazoo *(G-8690)*
Azon Usa Inc ..... E 269 385-5942
Kalamazoo *(G-8691)*
Byk USA Inc ..... E 203 265-2086
Rochester Hills *(G-13382)*
Cass Polymers ..... E 517 543-7510
Charlotte *(G-2636)*
▲ Clean Tech Inc ..... E 734 455-3600
Plymouth *(G-12598)*
Clean Tech Inc ..... E 734 529-2475
Dundee *(G-4577)*
▲ Eco Bio Plastics Midland Inc ..... F 989 496-1934
Midland *(G-10858)*
Georgia-Pacific LLC ..... E 989 348-7275
Grayling *(G-7107)*
Material Difference Tech LLC ..... F 888 818-1283
Macomb *(G-10140)*
Nano Materials & Processes Inc ..... G 248 529-3873
Milford *(G-10974)*
▲ Portland Plastics Co ..... E 517 647-4115
Portland *(G-13065)*
Rhe-Tech LLC ..... G 517 223-4874
Fowlerville *(G-5579)*
Ssb Holdings Inc ..... E 586 755-1660
Rochester Hills *(G-13517)*
Ticona Polymers Inc ..... D 248 377-6868
Auburn Hills *(G-1026)*

3088 Plastic Plumbing Fixtures

Aquatic Co ..... D 269 279-7461
Three Rivers *(G-15855)*
◆ Conway Products Corporation ..... E 616 698-2601
Grand Rapids *(G-6308)*
D and G Glass Inc ..... G 734 341-0038
Carleton *(G-2452)*
Duo-Form Acquisition Corp ..... C 269 663-8525
Edwardsburg *(G-4765)*
Lakeshore Marble Company Inc ..... E 269 429-8241
Stevensville *(G-15574)*
▼ Lyons Industries Inc ..... C 269 782-3404
Dowagiac *(G-4548)*
Lyons Industries Inc ..... G 269 782-9516
Dowagiac *(G-4549)*
◆ Masco Corporation ..... A 313 274-7400
Livonia *(G-9826)*
Masco Corporation of Indiana ..... D 810 664-8501
Lapeer *(G-9474)*
R A Townsend Company ..... G 989 498-7000
Saginaw *(G-14129)*
Rick Owen & Jason Vogel Partnr ..... G 734 417-3401
Dexter *(G-4507)*
Warm Rain Corporation ..... D 906 482-3750
Calumet *(G-2337)*
Your Shower Door ..... G 616 940-0900
Grand Rapids *(G-7010)*
Zimmer Marble Co Inc ..... F 517 787-1500
Jackson *(G-8615)*

3089 Plastic Prdts

▲ 21st Century Plastics Corp ..... D 517 645-2695
Potterville *(G-13072)*
2255srv Llv ..... E 616 678-4900
Kent City *(G-8986)*
3d Polymers Inc ..... D 248 588-5562
Orchard Lake *(G-12164)*
A M R Inc ..... G 810 329-9049
East China *(G-4619)*
A S Plus Industries Inc ..... G 586 741-0400
Clinton Township *(G-3030)*
◆ ABC Group Holdings Inc ..... G 248 352-3706
Southfield *(G-14823)*
ABC Packaging Equipment & Mtls ..... F 616 784-2330
Comstock Park *(G-3458)*
Able Solutions LLC ..... G 810 216-6106
Port Huron *(G-12880)*
Accurate Injection Molds Inc ..... F 586 954-2553
Clinton Township *(G-3033)*
▲ Acm Plastic Products Inc ..... D 269 651-7888
Sturgis *(G-15595)*
Acrylic Specialties ..... G 248 588-4390
Madison Heights *(G-10180)*

Active Plastics Inc ....F 616 813-5109
Caledonia *(G-2288)*
▲ Adac Automotive Trim Inc ....E 616 957-0311
Grand Rapids *(G-6138)*
▲ Adac Door Components Inc ....G 616 957-0311
Grand Rapids *(G-6139)*
▲ Adac Plastics Inc ....E 616 957-0311
Grand Rapids *(G-6140)*
Adac Plastics Inc ....C 231 777-2645
Muskegon *(G-11260)*
Adac Plastics Inc ....F 616 957-0311
Grand Rapids *(G-6141)*
Adac Plastics Inc ....C 616 957-0520
Muskegon *(G-11261)*
Adac Plastics Inc ....B 616 957-0311
Muskegon *(G-11262)*
Adac Plastics Inc ....E 616 957-0311
Grand Rapids *(G-6142)*
▲ Adduxi ....E 248 564-2000
Rochester Hills *(G-13364)*
Adept Plastic Finishing Inc ....F 248 863-5930
Wixom *(G-17753)*
Advance Engineering Company ....E 989 435-3641
Beaverton *(G-1382)*
▲ Advanced Auto Trends Inc ....E 248 628-6111
Oxford *(G-12333)*
Advanced Auto Trends Inc ....E 810 672-9203
Snover *(G-14741)*
Advanced Auto Trends Inc ....E 248 628-4850
Oxford *(G-12334)*
Advanced Blnding Solutions LLC ....E 920 664-1469
Wallace *(G-16885)*
Advanced Composite Tech Inc ....G 248 709-9097
Rochester *(G-13311)*
Advanced Fibermolding Inc ....E 231 768-5177
Leroy *(G-9529)*
▲ Advanced Plastic Mfg Inc ....G 269 962-9697
Battle Creek *(G-1140)*
Advanced Rubber & Plastic ....G 586 754-7398
Warren *(G-16920)*
▲ Advanced Special Tools Inc ....C 269 962-9697
Battle Creek *(G-1141)*
Aees Power Systems Ltd Partnr ....F 269 668-4429
Farmington Hills *(G-4921)*
▲ Affinity Custom Molding Inc ....E 269 496-8423
Mendon *(G-10711)*
Agape Plastics Inc ....C 616 735-4091
Grand Rapids *(G-6152)*
Aim Plastics Inc ....E 586 954-2553
Clinton Township *(G-3040)*
AIN Plastics ....F 248 356-4000
Southfield *(G-14824)*
Airpark Plastics LLC ....F 989 846-1029
Standish *(G-15215)*
Aktis Engrg Solutions Inc ....G 313 450-2420
Southfield *(G-14826)*
Akwel Cadillac Usa Inc ....E 248 848-9599
Farmington Hills *(G-4926)*
▲ Akwel Cadillac Usa Inc ....B 231 876-8020
Cadillac *(G-2223)*
Albar Industries Inc ....B 810 667-0150
Lapeer *(G-9440)*
Alco Plastics Inc ....D 586 752-4527
Romeo *(G-13623)*
Alp Lighting Ceiling Pdts Inc ....D 231 547-6584
Charlevoix *(G-2606)*
Alternative Systems Inc ....F 269 384-2008
Kalamazoo *(G-8677)*
▲ Alumilite Corporation ....F 269 488-4000
Galesburg *(G-5805)*
Aluminum Textures Inc ....E 616 538-3144
Grandville *(G-7020)*
Amcor Rigid Packaging Usa LLC ....C 734 336-3812
Manchester *(G-10401)*
◆ Amcor Rigid Packaging Usa LLC ....D 734 428-9741
Plymouth *(G-12569)*
▲ Ameri-Kart(mi) Corp ....C 269 641-5811
Cassopolis *(G-2527)*
American Standard Windows ....F 734 788-2261
Farmington Hills *(G-4931)*
Americo Corporation ....G 313 565-6550
Dearborn *(G-3675)*
AMP Innovative Tech LLC ....E 586 465-2700
Harrison Township *(G-7319)*
Amplas Compounding LLC ....F 586 795-2555
Sterling Heights *(G-15260)*
Anderton Machining LLC ....G 517 905-5155
Jackson *(G-8384)*
Ann Arbor Plastics Inc ....G 734 944-0800
Saline *(G-14377)*

Ansco Pattern & Machine Co ....G 248 625-1362
Clarkston *(G-2907)*
Antcliff Windows & Doors Inc ....F 810 742-5963
Burton *(G-2144)*
Anticipated Plastics Inc ....F 586 427-9450
Warren *(G-16935)*
Aqpe LLC ....G 810 329-9259
Saint Clair *(G-14204)*
◆ Armaly Sponge Company ....E 248 669-2100
Commerce Township *(G-3391)*
Armoured Rsstnce McHanisms Inc ....F 517 223-7618
Fowlerville *(G-5558)*
Arrow Die & Mold Repair ....G 231 689-1829
White Cloud *(G-17619)*
Astar Inc ....E 574 234-2137
Niles *(G-11595)*
Atlantic Precision Pdts Inc ....F 586 532-9420
Shelby Township *(G-14550)*
Automotive Manufacturing ....G 517 566-8174
Sunfield *(G-15645)*
Automotive Plastics Recycling ....E 810 767-3800
Flint *(G-5381)*
Avon Plastic Products Inc ....D 248 852-1000
Rochester Hills *(G-13374)*
B & H Plastic Co Inc ....F 586 727-7100
Richmond *(G-13260)*
B & N Plastics Inc ....G 586 758-0030
Warren *(G-16948)*
B C & A Co ....E 734 429-3129
Saline *(G-14379)*
Bangor Plastics Inc ....E 269 427-7971
Bangor *(G-1088)*
Batts Group Ltd ....G 616 956-3053
Grand Rapids *(G-6206)*
Beechcraft Products Inc ....E 989 288-2606
Durand *(G-4606)*
▲ Belmont Engineered Plas LLC ....D 616 785-6279
Belmont *(G-1457)*
Bentzer Incorporated ....E 269 663-3649
Edwardsburg *(G-4759)*
Bermar Associates Inc ....F 248 589-2460
Troy *(G-16238)*
Berry Global Inc ....C 269 435-2425
Constantine *(G-3532)*
Berry Global Inc ....B 616 772-4635
Zeeland *(G-18118)*
◆ Blackmore Co Inc ....D 734 483-8661
Belleville *(G-1442)*
Blade Industrial Products Inc ....G 248 773-7400
Wixom *(G-17774)*
Bloem LLC ....F 616 622-6344
Hudsonville *(G-8148)*
Blue Fire Manufacturing LLC ....E 248 714-7166
Waterford *(G-17325)*
Bomaur Quality Plastics Inc ....F 810 629-9701
Fenton *(G-5190)*
Boral Building Products Inc ....C 248 668-6400
Wixom *(G-17777)*
Bradys Fence Company Inc ....G 313 492-8804
South Rockwood *(G-14820)*
Bridgville Plastics Inc ....F 269 465-6516
Stevensville *(G-15558)*
Built Rite Tool and Engrg LLC ....G 810 966-5133
Port Huron *(G-12905)*
▼ Butler Plastics Company ....E 810 765-8811
Marine City *(G-10471)*
C E B Tooling Inc ....G 269 489-2251
Burr Oak *(G-2134)*
C M E Plastic Company ....G 517 456-7722
Clinton *(G-3015)*
C-Plastics Inc ....E 616 837-7396
Nunica *(G-12033)*
▲ Cadillac Engineered Plas Inc ....F 231 775-2900
Cadillac *(G-2237)*
Cadillac Products Inc ....D 989 766-2294
Rogers City *(G-13613)*
▲ Cadillac Products Inc ....B 248 813-8200
Troy *(G-16253)*
Camcar Plastics Inc ....F 231 726-5000
Muskegon *(G-11289)*
Capsonic Automotive Inc ....G 248 754-1100
Auburn Hills *(G-809)*
◆ Cascade Engineering Inc ....A 616 975-4800
Grand Rapids *(G-6260)*
Cascade Engineering Inc ....C 616 975-4800
Grand Rapids *(G-6261)*
Cascade Engineering Inc ....C 616 975-4923
Grand Rapids *(G-6262)*
Case-Free Inc ....G 616 245-3136
Grand Rapids *(G-6265)*

Castano Plastics Inc ....G 248 624-3724
Wolverine Lake *(G-17935)*
Castino Corporation ....E 734 941-7200
Romulus *(G-13661)*
Cel Plastics Inc ....F 231 777-3941
Muskegon *(G-11292)*
Century Plastics LLC ....G 586 697-5752
Macomb *(G-10115)*
▲ Century Plastics LLC ....C 586 566-3900
Shelby Township *(G-14559)*
Certainteed Corporation ....B 517 787-8898
Jackson *(G-8405)*
Cg Plastics Inc ....G 616 785-1900
Comstock Park *(G-3468)*
Chadko LLC ....G 616 402-9207
Grand Haven *(G-6002)*
▲ Chambers Industrial Tech Inc ....G 616 249-8190
Wyoming *(G-17991)*
Champion Plastics Inc ....F 248 373-8995
Auburn Hills *(G-812)*
▲ Clarion Technologies Inc ....C 616 698-7277
Holland *(G-7592)*
Clarion Technologies Inc ....C 616 754-1199
Greenville *(G-7125)*
▲ Classic Die Inc ....E 616 454-3760
Grand Rapids *(G-6277)*
Clearform ....G 616 656-5359
Caledonia *(G-2295)*
Cni Plastics LLC ....E 517 541-4960
Charlotte *(G-2641)*
▲ Colonial Engineering Inc ....F 269 323-2495
Portage *(G-12989)*
▲ Colonial Manufacturing LLC ....F 269 926-1000
Benton Harbor *(G-1490)*
Colonial Plastics Incorporated ....E 586 469-4944
Shelby Township *(G-14564)*
Composite Development Corporat ....G 269 694-4159
Otsego *(G-12236)*
Composite Techniques Inc ....F 616 878-9795
Byron Center *(G-2181)*
▲ Conatus Inc ....G 810 494-6210
Brighton *(G-1901)*
Concord Industrial Corporation ....G 248 646-9225
Bloomfield Hills *(G-1756)*
▲ Conley Composites LLC ....E 918 299-5051
Grand Rapids *(G-6300)*
▲ Continental Strl Plas Inc ....C 248 237-7800
Auburn Hills *(G-823)*
Continental Strl Plas Inc ....E 248 593-9500
Troy *(G-16278)*
Continntal Strl Plas Hldngs Co ....C 248 237-7800
Auburn Hills *(G-824)*
Contour Engineering Inc ....F 989 828-6526
Shepherd *(G-14727)*
Coral Corporation ....G 616 868-6295
Alto *(G-326)*
▲ Craig Assembly Inc ....C 810 326-1374
Saint Clair *(G-14212)*
Creative Foam Corporation ....D 810 714-0140
Fenton *(G-5199)*
▲ Creative Foam Corporation ....C 810 629-4149
Fenton *(G-5198)*
Creative Techniques Inc ....D 248 373-3050
Orion *(G-12178)*
Creed Development ....G 248 926-9811
Novi *(G-11857)*
Crescent Machining Inc ....G 248 541-7010
Oak Park *(G-12055)*
▲ Crw Plastics Usa Inc ....C 517 545-0900
Howell *(G-8027)*
◆ Cs Manufacturing Inc ....C 616 696-2772
Cedar Springs *(G-2551)*
CSP Holding Corp ....F 248 237-7800
Auburn Hills *(G-831)*
CSP Holding Corp ....G 248 724-4410
Auburn Hills *(G-832)*
Cup Acquisition LLC ....C 616 735-4410
Grand Rapids *(G-6322)*
Cusolar Industries Inc ....E 586 949-3880
Chesterfield *(G-2757)*
D & W Awning and Window Co ....E 810 742-0340
Davison *(G-3645)*
D B International LLC ....G 616 796-0679
Holland *(G-7603)*
▲ D Find Corporation ....G 248 641-2858
Troy *(G-16293)*
▲ D T M 1 Inc ....E 248 889-9210
Highland *(G-7491)*
D&Js Plastics LLC ....G 616 745-5798
Hudsonville *(G-8154)*

SIC

Employee Codes: A=Over 500 employees, B=251-500
C=101-250, D=51-100, E=20-50, F=10-19, G=3-9
2020 Harris Michigan
Industrial Directory
757

D&W Fine Pack LLC....G....866 296-2020
Gladwin (G-5928)
▲ Daiek Products Inc....F....248 816-1360
Troy (G-16295)
▲ Dare Products Inc....E....269 965-2307
Springfield (G-15190)
◆ Dart Container Corp Georgia....B....517 676-3800
Mason (G-10631)
Datacover Inc....G....844 875-4076
Pontiac (G-12814)
Datacover Inc....F....248 391-2163
Lake Orion (G-9134)
Davalor Mold Company LLC....C....586 598-0100
Chesterfield (G-2762)
◆ Decade Products LLC....F....616 975-4965
Grand Rapids (G-6340)
◆ Delfingen Us Inc....E....716 215-0300
Rochester Hills (G-13404)
▲ Delfingen Us- Holding Inc....G....248 519-0534
Rochester Hills (G-13405)
Delfingen Us-Central Amer Inc....G....248 230-3500
Rochester Hills (G-13406)
Delta Molded Products....G....586 731-9595
Sterling Heights (G-15308)
Deluxe Frame Company Inc....E....248 373-8811
Auburn Hills (G-840)
Denali Incorporated....G....517 574-0047
Hartland (G-7389)
Dendritic Nanotechnologies Inc....G....989 774-3096
Midland (G-10831)
Denso Manufacturing NC Inc....A....269 441-2040
Battle Creek (G-1172)
Derby Fabg Solutions LLC....D....616 866-1650
Rockford (G-13566)
Destiny Plastics Incorporated....F....810 622-0018
Deckerville (G-3807)
Die Stampco Inc....F....989 893-7790
Bay City (G-1302)
Display Pack Inc....C....616 451-3061
Cedar Springs (G-2553)
Display Pack Inc....B....616 451-3061
Grand Rapids (G-6356)
Diversified Engrg & Plas LLC....D....517 789-8118
Jackson (G-8434)
Djw Enterprises Inc....D....262 251-9500
Crystal Falls (G-3609)
Dl Engineering & Tech Inc....G....248 852-6900
Rochester Hills (G-13409)
Dlhbowles Inc....F....248 569-0652
Southfield (G-14883)
Do-All Plastic Inc....F....313 824-6565
Detroit (G-4014)
◆ Do-It Corporation....D....269 637-1121
South Haven (G-14758)
Downriver Plastics Inc....G....734 246-3031
Canton (G-2366)
Dr Schneider Auto Systems Inc....G....270 858-5400
Brighton (G-1912)
Dse Industries LLC....G....313 530-6668
Macomb (G-10118)
▲ Dunnage Engineering Inc....E....810 229-9501
Brighton (G-1913)
▼ Duo-Gard Industries Inc....D....734 207-9700
Canton (G-2367)
Dupearl Technology LLC....D....248 390-9609
Bloomfield Hills (G-1762)
▼ E & D Engineering Systems LLC....G....989 246-0770
Gladwin (G-5929)
▲ E-T-M Enterprises I Inc....C....517 627-8461
Grand Ledge (G-6105)
▲ Eagle Fasteners Inc....F....248 577-1441
Troy (G-16333)
Eagle Manufacturing Corp....F....586 323-0303
Shelby Township (G-14585)
▲ Eaton Inoac Company....E....248 226-6200
Southfield (G-14895)
Echo Engrg & Prod Sups Inc....D....734 241-9622
Monroe (G-11029)
Eclipse Mold Incorporated....C....586 792-3320
Chesterfield (G-2771)
Eco - Composites LLC....G....616 395-8902
Holland (G-7617)
▲ Ehc Inc....G....313 259-2266
Detroit (G-4030)
▲ Eimo Technologies Inc....E....269 649-0545
Vicksburg (G-16834)
Ejs Engraving....G....616 534-8104
Grandville (G-7029)
◆ Eliason Corporation....D....269 327-7003
Portage (G-12992)
Elite Plastic Products Inc....E....586 247-5800
Shelby Township (G-14587)
▲ Ell Tron Manufacturing Co....E....989 983-3181
Vanderbilt (G-16804)
Ell Tron Manufacturing Co....G....989 983-3181
Vanderbilt (G-16805)
Elmet North America Inc....F....517 664-9011
Lansing (G-9364)
Engineered Plastic Components....C....810 326-1650
Saint Clair (G-14217)
Engineered Plastic Components....C....810 326-3010
Saint Clair (G-14218)
Engineered Polymer Products....E....269 461-6955
Eau Claire (G-4738)
Enginred Plstic Components Inc....D....248 825-4508
Troy (G-16347)
Engtechnik Inc....G....734 667-4237
Canton (G-2371)
Enkon LLC....F....937 890-5678
Manchester (G-10405)
Enovapremier LLC....G....517 541-3200
Charlotte (G-2646)
Enterprise Plastics LLC....F....586 665-1030
Shelby Township (G-14588)
Epc-Columbia Inc....D....810 326-1650
Saint Clair (G-14219)
▲ Erwin Quarder Inc....D....616 575-1600
Grand Rapids (G-6383)
Ess Tec Inc....D....616 394-0230
Holland (G-7625)
▲ Ethylene LLC....E....616 554-3464
Kentwood (G-9005)
▼ Etx Holdings Inc....G....989 463-1151
Alma (G-237)
▲ Evans Industries Inc....G....313 259-2266
Detroit (G-4045)
Excel Medical Products Inc....F....810 714-4775
Wixom (G-17808)
Exo-S US LLC....G....248 614-9707
Troy (G-16355)
Exo-S US LLC....D....517 278-8567
Coldwater (G-3303)
Exotic Rubber & Plastics Corp....D....248 477-2122
Farmington Hills (G-4996)
Exsto US Inc....G....734 834-7225
Ann Arbor (G-453)
Extreme Tool and Engrg Inc....G....906 229-9100
Wakefield (G-16851)
Extrusions Division Inc....G....616 247-3611
Grand Rapids (G-6396)
Fabri-Kal Corporation....E....269 385-5050
Kalamazoo (G-8740)
Factory Products Inc....G....269 668-3329
Mattawan (G-10664)
Faith Plastics LLC....E....269 646-2294
Marcellus (G-10465)
Ferro Industries Inc....E....586 792-6001
Harrison Township (G-7330)
▲ Fido Enterprises Inc....G....586 790-8200
Clinton Township (G-3116)
▲ Filcon Inc....F....989 386-2986
Clare (G-2870)
▲ Fischer America Inc....C....248 276-1940
Auburn Hills (G-874)
Fitness Finders Inc....E....517 750-1500
Jackson (G-8449)
◆ Five Peaks Technology LLC....E....231 830-8099
Muskegon (G-11323)
Flex-N Gate Shelby LLC....C....586 759-8092
Warren (G-17035)
Flex-N-Gate Detroit LLC....B....586 759-8092
Warren (G-17038)
Flight Mold & Engineering Inc....E....810 329-2900
Saint Clair (G-14220)
◆ Formed Solutions Inc....F....616 395-5455
Holland (G-7635)
Forming Technologies LLC....D....231 777-7030
Muskegon (G-11326)
▲ Future Technologies Group LLC....G....810 733-3870
Flushing (G-5536)
Garett Tunison....G....248 330-9835
Oakland (G-12106)
Gem Plastics Inc....G....616 538-5966
Grand Rapids (G-6433)
Gemini Group Inc....F....989 269-6272
Bad Axe (G-1062)
Gemini Group Plastic Sales....G....248 435-7991
Auburn Hills (G-881)
Gemini Group Services Inc....G....248 435-7271
Bad Axe (G-1063)
Gemini Plastics De Mexico Inc....G....989 658-8557
Ubly (G-16717)
Genex Window Inc....G....586 754-2917
Warren (G-17055)
◆ Genova Products Inc....D....810 744-4500
Davison (G-3650)
▼ Genova-Minnesota Inc....D....810 744-4500
Davison (G-3651)
Ghsp Inc....F....231 873-3300
Hart (G-7371)
▲ Global Automotive Products Inc....E....734 589-6179
Romulus (G-13680)
Global Enterprise Limited....G....586 948-4100
Chesterfield (G-2782)
Global Mfg & Assembly Corp....B....517 789-8116
Jackson (G-8458)
Global Supply Integrator LLC....G....586 484-0734
Davisburg (G-3635)
Global Technology Ventures Inc....G....248 324-3707
Farmington Hills (G-5011)
Glov Enterprises LLC....D....517 423-9700
Tecumseh (G-15794)
▲ Glove Coaters Incorporated....E....517 741-8402
Union City (G-16734)
GLS Industries LLC....G....586 255-9221
Warren (G-17058)
GLS Industries LLC....E....586 255-9221
Warren (G-17059)
▲ GMI Composites Inc....D....231 755-1611
Muskegon (G-11331)
Golden Pointe Inc....G....313 581-8284
Detroit (G-4096)
Grace Production Services LLC....G....810 643-8070
Chesterfield (G-2783)
Graflex Inc....F....616 842-3654
Spring Lake (G-15146)
Graham Packaging Company LP....E....616 355-0479
Holland (G-7647)
Grand Haven Custom Molding LLC....E....616 935-3160
Grand Haven (G-6021)
▲ Great Lakes Die Cast Corp....D....231 726-4002
Muskegon (G-11337)
Green Plastics LLC....E....616 295-2718
Holland (G-7654)
Greg Linska Sales Inc....G....248 765-6354
Troy (G-16387)
Grm Corporation....D....989 453-2322
Pigeon (G-12489)
▲ Grw Technologies Inc....C....616 575-8119
Grand Rapids (G-6483)
Gt Plastics & Equipment LLC....F....616 678-7445
Kent City (G-8991)
Gt Plastics Incorporated....F....989 739-7803
Oscoda (G-12210)
◆ Gt Technologies Inc....E....734 467-8371
Westland (G-17566)
▲ Guardian Automotive Corp....D....586 757-7800
Warren (G-17070)
▲ Handley Industries Inc....F....517 787-8821
Jackson (G-8462)
▲ Hangers Plus LLC....G....616 997-4264
Coopersville (G-3560)
Hanwha Azdel Inc....F....810 629-2496
Warren (G-17075)
Harbor Green Solutions LLC....G....269 352-0265
Benton Harbor (G-1507)
▲ Harbor Isle Plastics LLC....E....269 465-6004
Stevensville (G-15570)
▲ Harman Corporation....E....248 651-4477
Rochester (G-13324)
Harry Miller Flowers Inc....G....313 581-2328
Dearborn (G-3718)
Henry Machine Shop....G....989 777-8495
Saginaw (G-14056)
Heritage Services Company Inc....G....734 282-4566
Riverview (G-13296)
Hi-Craft Engineering Inc....D....586 293-0551
Fraser (G-5663)
Hicks Plastics Company Inc....D....586 786-5640
Macomb (G-10129)
Hilco Industrial Plastics LLC....G....616 323-1330
Grand Rapids (G-6512)
Hilco Plastic Products Co....E....616 554-8833
Caledonia (G-2300)
▲ HMS Mfg Co....D....248 689-3232
Troy (G-16397)
▼ Hold It Products Corporation....G....248 624-1195
Commerce Township (G-3413)
▲ Holland Plastics Corporation....E....616 844-2505
Grand Haven (G-6037)

SIC SECTION 30 RUBBER AND MISCELLANEOUS PLASTICS PRODUCTS

Homestead Products Inc........F....... 989 465-6182
Coleman (G-3343)
Hubble Enterprises Inc........G....... 616 676-4485
Ada (G-18)
Huhtamaki Inc........C....... 989 465-9046
Coleman (G-3345)
Huhtamaki Inc........B....... 989 633-8900
Coleman (G-3346)
Humphrey Companies LLC........C....... 616 530-1717
Grandville (G-7048)
IAC Mexico Holdings Inc........G....... 248 455-7000
Southfield (G-14941)
IAC Plymouth LLC........E....... 734 207-7000
Plymouth (G-12645)
ICM Enterprises LLC........G....... 586 415-2567
Fraser (G-5668)
Icon Industries Inc........G....... 616 241-1877
Grand Rapids (G-6524)
▼ Ideal Shield LLC........E....... 866 825-8659
Detroit (G-4133)
Idrink Products Inc........G....... 734 531-6324
Ann Arbor (G-500)
▲ Iig-Dss Technologies LLC........E....... 586 725-5300
Ira (G-8258)
Illinois Tool Works Inc........D....... 248 969-4248
Oxford (G-12350)
Illinois Tool Works Inc........D....... 248 589-2500
Troy (G-16410)
Imlay City Molded Pdts Corp........E....... 810 721-9100
Imlay City (G-8204)
Impact Label Corporation........D....... 269 381-4280
Galesburg (G-5811)
Imperial Industries Inc........F....... 734 397-1400
Saline (G-14395)
▲ Ims/Chinatool Jv LLC........G....... 734 466-5151
Livonia (G-9781)
Industrial Pattern of Lansing........G....... 517 482-9835
Lansing (G-9298)
Industries Unlimited Inc........E....... 586 949-4300
Chesterfield (G-2788)
Inflatable Marine Products Inc........G....... 616 723-8140
Howard City (G-8002)
Innovative Engineering Mich........G....... 517 977-0460
Lansing (G-9236)
Innovative Packg Solutions LLC........G....... 517 213-3169
Holt (G-7914)
Inoac Interior Systems LLC........E....... 248 488-7610
Farmington Hills (G-5028)
Inplast Interior Tech LLC........G....... 810 724-3500
Almont (G-258)
Installations Inc........F....... 313 532-9000
Redford (G-13166)
▲ Instaset Plastics Company LLC........B....... 586 725-0229
Anchorville (G-331)
Integra Mold Inc........G....... 269 327-4337
Portage (G-13002)
International Automotive Compo........B....... 734 456-2800
Plymouth (G-12648)
International Automotive Compo........B....... 586 795-7800
Sterling Heights (G-15376)
◆ International Automotive Compo........A....... 248 455-7000
Southfield (G-14948)
Inteva Products LLC........B....... 517 266-8030
Adrian (G-69)
Intrepid Plastics Mfg Inc........F....... 616 901-5718
Lakeview (G-9174)
▲ Ironwood Plastics Inc........C....... 906 932-5025
Ironwood (G-8330)
◆ Jac Holding Corporation........G....... 248 874-1800
Pontiac (G-12839)
Jac Products Inc........D....... 248 874-1800
Pontiac (G-12840)
JD Plastics Inc........G....... 517 264-6858
Adrian (G-72)
Jer-Den Plastics Inc........E....... 989 681-4303
Saint Louis (G-14364)
Jgr Plastics LLC........E....... 810 990-1957
Port Huron (G-12932)
▲ Jimdi Plastics Inc........E....... 616 895-7766
Allendale (G-219)
JK Machining Inc........F....... 269 344-0870
Kalamazoo (G-8779)
Jma Tool Company Inc........E....... 586 270-6706
New Haven (G-11524)
▲ John Allen Enterprises........G....... 734 426-2507
Ann Arbor (G-512)
Johns Glass........G....... 269 468-4227
Coloma (G-3357)
Johnson Walker & Assoc LLC........G....... 810 688-1600
North Branch (G-11660)
Jolicor Manufacturing Services........F....... 586 323-5090
Shelby Township (G-14612)
◆ Jsj Corporation........E....... 616 842-6350
Grand Haven (G-6042)
Jvis - Usa LLC........F....... 586 884-5700
Shelby Township (G-14613)
Jvis Fh LLC........E....... 248 478-2900
Farmington Hills (G-5036)
▲ Jvis International LLC........D....... 586 739-9542
Shelby Township (G-14614)
▲ Kam Plastics Corp........D....... 616 355-5900
Holland (G-7705)
Kamex Molded Products LLC........G....... 616 355-5900
Holland (G-7706)
Kautex Inc........B....... 313 633-2254
Detroit (G-4173)
▲ Keiper LLC........C....... 248 655-5100
Troy (G-16445)
Keltrol Enterprises Inc........G....... 734 697-3011
Belleville (G-1447)
Kem Enterprises Inc........G....... 616 676-0213
Ada (G-21)
Kent City Plastics LLC........F....... 616 678-4900
Kent City (G-8993)
Klann........G....... 313 565-4135
Dearborn (G-3730)
Km and I........G....... 248 792-2782
Troy (G-16447)
Kreft Injection Technology LLC........G....... 248 589-9202
Madison Heights (G-10294)
Kruger Plastic Products LLC........G....... 269 465-6404
Bridgman (G-1869)
Kruger Plastics Products LLC........E....... 269 545-3311
Galien (G-5818)
▲ Kunststoff Technik Scherer........D....... 734 944-5080
Troy (G-16452)
Kurt Dubowski........G....... 231 796-0055
Big Rapids (G-1637)
Kyrie Enterprises LLC........E....... 248 549-8690
Royal Oak (G-13943)
Lacks Enterprises Inc........D....... 616 949-6570
Grand Rapids (G-6595)
Lacks Enterprises Inc........D....... 616 656-2910
Grand Rapids (G-6596)
Lacks Enterprises Inc........D....... 616 698-2030
Grand Rapids (G-6597)
Lacks Enterprises Inc........D....... 616 949-6570
Grand Rapids (G-6598)
◆ Lacks Exterior Systems LLC........A....... 616 949-6570
Grand Rapids (G-6600)
Lacks Exterior Systems LLC........E....... 616 949-6570
Grand Rapids (G-6601)
Lacks Exterior Systems LLC........F....... 248 351-0555
Novi (G-11926)
Lacks Exterior Systems LLC........C....... 616 949-6570
Grand Rapids (G-6602)
Lacks Exterior Systems LLC........F....... 616 554-7805
Kentwood (G-9015)
Lacks Exterior Systems LLC........C....... 616 949-6570
Grand Rapids (G-6603)
Lacks Exterior Systems LLC........C....... 616 949-6570
Grand Rapids (G-6604)
Lacks Industries Inc........C....... 616 698-6890
Grand Rapids (G-6606)
Lacks Industries Inc........C....... 616 698-3600
Grand Rapids (G-6607)
Lacks Industries Inc........E....... 616 554-7135
Kentwood (G-9017)
Lacks Industries Inc........D....... 616 698-6854
Grand Rapids (G-6608)
Lacks Industries Inc........D....... 616 554-7134
Grand Rapids (G-6610)
Lacks Industries Inc........D....... 616 698-2776
Grand Rapids (G-6611)
Lacks Industries Inc........D....... 616 656-2910
Grand Rapids (G-6612)
Lacks Wheel Trim Systems LLC........F....... 248 351-0555
Novi (G-11927)
Lacks Wheel Trim Systems LLC........E....... 616 949-6570
Grand Rapids (G-6613)
Lapeer Plating & Plastics Inc........C....... 810 667-4240
Lapeer (G-9468)
Latin American Industries LLC........G....... 616 301-1878
Grand Rapids (G-6622)
▼ Lawrence Plastics LLC........D....... 248 475-0186
Clarkston (G-2934)
▼ LDB Plastics Inc........G....... 586 566-9698
Shelby Township (G-14623)
◆ Lear Operations Corporation........G....... 248 447-1500
Southfield (G-14965)
Leeann Plastics Inc........F....... 269 489-5035
Burr Oak (G-2136)
▲ Leon Interiors Inc........B....... 616 422-7479
Holland (G-7721)
◆ Letica Corporation........C....... 248 652-0557
Rochester Hills (G-13460)
Lexamar Corporation........B....... 231 582-3163
Boyne City (G-1827)
Liberty Plastics Inc........G....... 616 994-7033
Holland (G-7724)
Ligon Helicopter Corporation........G....... 810 706-1885
Almont (G-261)
Lincoln Industries........G....... 989 736-6421
Lincoln (G-9565)
Lites Alternative Inc........F....... 989 685-3476
Rose City (G-13762)
Little Traverse Disposal LLC........G....... 231 487-0780
Harbor Springs (G-7287)
Loper Corporation........G....... 810 620-0202
Mount Morris (G-11164)
Luckmarr Plastics Inc........D....... 586 978-8498
Sterling Heights (G-15403)
Luttmann Precision Mold Inc........E....... 269 651-1193
Sturgis (G-15614)
M & E Plastics LLC........F....... 989 875-4191
Ithaca (G-8362)
M C Molds Inc........E....... 517 655-5481
Williamston (G-17733)
M-R Products Inc........G....... 231 378-2251
Copemish (G-3573)
Macauto U S A Inc........G....... 248 499-8208
Rochester Hills (G-13465)
Macauto Usa Inc........G....... 248 556-5256
Troy (G-16469)
Machine Tool & Gear Inc........D....... 989 743-3936
Corunna (G-3581)
Maine Plastics Incorporated........E....... 269 679-3988
Kalamazoo (G-8815)
Mann + Hummel Usa Inc........F....... 248 857-8500
Bloomfield Hills (G-1780)
Mann + Hummel Usa Inc........E....... 248 857-8501
Kalamazoo (G-8818)
▲ Mann + Hummel Usa Inc........F....... 269 329-3900
Portage (G-13014)
Mantissa Industries Inc........G....... 517 694-2260
Holt (G-7915)
Manufacturers Services Inds........G....... 906 493-6685
Drummond Island (G-4565)
Maple Valley Plastics LLC........E....... 810 346-3040
Brown City (G-2055)
▲ Marcon Technologies LLC........E....... 269 279-1701
Constantine (G-3538)
▲ Mark Schwager Inc........G....... 248 275-1978
Shelby Township (G-14633)
Martinrea Industries Inc........C....... 231 832-5504
Reed City (G-13220)
▲ Martinrea Industries Inc........E....... 734 428-2400
Manchester (G-10408)
▲ Mason Tackle Company........E....... 810 631-4571
Otisville (G-12233)
▲ Matrix Manufacturing Inc........G....... 616 532-6000
Grand Rapids (G-6649)
May-Day Window Manufacturing........G....... 989 348-2809
Grayling (G-7111)
Maya Plastics Inc........E....... 586 997-6000
Shelby Township (G-14636)
Mayco International LLC........C....... 586 803-6000
Clinton Township (G-3171)
Mayco International LLC........E....... 586 803-6000
Auburn Hills (G-944)
▲ Mayco International LLC........A....... 586 803-6000
Sterling Heights (G-15414)
▲ Mayfair Plastics Inc........D....... 989 732-2441
Gaylord (G-5880)
Mc Pherson Plastics Inc........D....... 269 694-9487
Otsego (G-12244)
McCray Press........E....... 989 792-8681
Saginaw (G-14084)
McG Plastics Inc........E....... 989 667-4349
Bay City (G-1328)
McKechnie Vhcl Cmpnnts USA Inc........E....... 218 894-1218
Roseville (G-13832)
McKechnie Vhcl Cmpnnts USA Inc........F....... 586 491-2600
Roseville (G-13833)
▲ Mecaplast Usa LLC........G....... 248 594-8082
Livonia (G-9836)
▲ Medbio Inc........D....... 616 245-0214
Grand Rapids (G-6656)
Mega Screen Corp........G....... 517 849-7057
Jonesville (G-8663)

SIC

Employee Codes: A=Over 500 employees, B=251-500
C=101-250, D=51-100, E=20-50, F=10-19, G=3-9
2020 Harris Michigan
Industrial Directory
759

30 RUBBER AND MISCELLANEOUS PLASTICS PRODUCTS

Meyers Boat Company Inc .... F 517 265-9821
  Adrian *(G-81)*
◆ MGR Molds Inc .... F 586 254-6020
  Sterling Heights *(G-15419)*
Michigan Church Supply Co Inc .... F 810 686-8877
  Mount Morris *(G-11165)*
▲ Michigan Manufactured Pdts Inc .... G 586 770-2584
  Port Huron *(G-12941)*
Micro Plastics Mfg & Sls .... G 517 320-2488
  Hillsdale *(G-7531)*
▲ Midwest Plastic Engineering .... D 269 651-5223
  Sturgis *(G-15620)*
Mig Molding LLC .... G 810 660-8435
  Almont *(G-264)*
▲ Miniature Custom Mfg LLC .... F 269 998-1277
  Vicksburg *(G-16839)*
Mmi Companies LLC .... E 248 528-1680
  Troy *(G-16510)*
▲ Mmi Engineered Solutions Inc .... D 734 429-4664
  Saline *(G-14403)*
Mmi Engineered Solutions Inc 734 429-5130
  Warren *(G-17158)*
Modern Builders Supply Inc .... G 517 787-3633
  Jackson *(G-8535)*
Mohr Engineering Inc .... E 810 227-4598
  Brighton *(G-1963)*
▲ Mold Masters Co .... C 810 245-4100
  Lapeer *(G-9475)*
Mold-Msters Injctioneering LLC .... F 905 877-0185
  Madison Heights *(G-10309)*
Mold-Rite LLC .... G 586 296-3970
  Fraser *(G-5695)*
Molded Plastic Industries Inc .... E 517 694-7434
  Holt *(G-7916)*
Molded Plastics & Tooling .... G 517 268-0849
  Holt *(G-7917)*
Moldex3d Northern America Inc .... F 248 946-4570
  Farmington Hills *(G-5072)*
Molding Concepts Inc .... E 586 264-6990
  Sterling Heights *(G-15426)*
▲ Molding Solutions Inc .... E 616 847-6822
  Grand Haven *(G-6056)*
▲ Moller Group North America Inc .... F 586 532-0860
  Shelby Township *(G-14647)*
▲ Mollertech LLC .... C 586 532-0860
  Shelby Township *(G-14648)*
Mollewood Export Inc .... E 248 624-1885
  Wixom *(G-17859)*
Monroe LLC .... B 616 942-9820
  Grand Rapids *(G-6702)*
Monroe Inc .... G 616 284-3358
  Grand Rapids *(G-6703)*
Monroe Mold LLC .... G 734 241-6898
  Monroe *(G-11056)*
Montaplast North America Inc .... F 248 353-5553
  Auburn Hills *(G-947)*
Moon Roof Corporation America .... E 586 772-8730
  Roseville *(G-13839)*
Moon Roof Corporation America .... E 586 552-1901
  Roseville *(G-13840)*
Morren Mold & Machine Inc 616 892-7474
  Allendale *(G-223)*
Morren Plastic Molding Inc .... F 616 997-7474
  Allendale *(G-224)*
Motus LLC .... G 734 266-3237
  Livonia *(G-9851)*
Mp6 LLC .... G 231 409-7530
  Traverse City *(G-16045)*
Mpi Plastics .... G 201 502-1534
  Macomb *(G-10146)*
◆ MPS Lansing Inc .... A 517 323-9000
  Lansing *(G-9248)*
▲ Msinc .... G 248 275-1978
  Shelby Township *(G-14650)*
Mubea Inc .... D 248 393-9600
  Auburn Hills *(G-950)*
Mueller Industries Inc .... D 248 446-3720
  Brighton *(G-1964)*
Multi-Form Plastics Inc .... F 586 786-4229
  Macomb *(G-10147)*
Munimula Inc .... G 517 605-5343
  Quincy *(G-13097)*
▲ N A Actuaplast Inc .... F 734 744-4010
  Livonia *(G-9855)*
▲ N-K Manufacturing Tech LLC .... E 616 248-3200
  Grand Rapids *(G-6710)*
National Case Corporation .... G 586 726-1710
  Sterling Heights *(G-15432)*
New Product Development LLC .... G 616 399-6253
  Holland *(G-7758)*

Noack Ventures LLC .... G 248 583-0311
  Troy *(G-16526)*
Noble Polymers LLC .... F 616 975-4800
  Grand Rapids *(G-6717)*
North American Assembly LLC .... E 248 335-6702
  Auburn Hills *(G-960)*
North American Mold LLC .... E 248 335-6702
  Auburn Hills *(G-961)*
Northern Logistics LLC 989 386-2389
  Clare *(G-2881)*
Northern Plastics Inc .... F 586 979-7737
  Sterling Heights *(G-15438)*
Nova Industries Inc 586 294-9182
  Fraser *(G-5700)*
Novares Corporation US Inc .... G 248 449-6100
  Livonia *(G-9865)*
Novares US Eng Components Inc .... D 248 799-8949
  Southfield *(G-14992)*
▲ Novares US LLC .... D 248 449-6100
  Livonia *(G-9866)*
Novares US LLC .... C 517 546-1900
  Howell *(G-8071)*
Novares US LLC .... B 616 554-3555
  Grand Rapids *(G-6723)*
▲ NPR of America Inc .... C 248 449-8955
  Novi *(G-11959)*
▲ Nyloncraft of Michigan Inc .... B 517 849-9911
  Jonesville *(G-8665)*
Nyx Inc .... B 734 261-7535
  Livonia *(G-9870)*
▲ Nyx LLC .... C 734 462-2385
  Livonia *(G-9871)*
Nyx LLC .... C 734 467-7200
  Westland *(G-17585)*
Nyx LLC .... C 734 421-3850
  Livonia *(G-9872)*
Oakley Industries Inc .... E 586 791-3194
  Clinton Township *(G-3187)*
Oakwood Custom Coating Inc .... C 313 561-7740
  Dearborn *(G-3745)*
▲ Oakwood Energy Management Inc .... C 734 947-7700
  Taylor *(G-15750)*
▲ Oakwood Metal Fabricating Co .... B 313 561-7740
  Dearborn *(G-3746)*
Omega Plastics Inc .... D 586 954-2100
  Clinton Township *(G-3190)*
▲ Opeo Inc .... F 248 299-4000
  Auburn Hills *(G-966)*
Orbis Corporation .... C 248 616-3232
  Troy *(G-16537)*
Osco Inc .... E 248 852-7310
  Rochester Hills *(G-13489)*
Oscoda Plastics Inc .... E 989 739-6900
  Oscoda *(G-12216)*
Oth Consultants Inc .... C 586 598-0100
  Chesterfield *(G-2813)*
Overhead Door Company Alpena .... G 989 354-8316
  Alpena *(G-305)*
P & K Technologies Inc .... G 586 336-9545
  Romeo *(G-13634)*
Pace Industries LLC .... A 231 777-3941
  Muskegon *(G-11396)*
◆ Palmer Distributors Inc .... D 586 772-4225
  Fraser *(G-5703)*
Park Molded Specialties Inc .... G 906 225-0385
  Marquette *(G-10551)*
Parousia Plastics Inc 989 832-4054
  Midland *(G-10902)*
Patton Tool and Die Inc .... F 810 359-5336
  Lexington *(G-9559)*
Paul Murphy Plastics Co .... E 586 774-4880
  Roseville *(G-13851)*
PDM Industries Inc .... E 231 943-9601
  Traverse City *(G-16063)*
Pds Plastics Inc .... F 616 896-1109
  Dorr *(G-4525)*
Pearce Plastics LLC .... G 231 519-5994
  Fremont *(G-5781)*
Pegasus Tool LLC .... C 313 255-5900
  Detroit *(G-4295)*
▲ Penguin LLC .... C 269 651-9488
  Sturgis *(G-15628)*
Penguin Molding LLC .... F 847 297-0560
  Sturgis *(G-15629)*
Peninsula Plastics Company Inc .... D 248 852-3731
  Auburn Hills *(G-971)*
Pepro Enterprises Inc 989 658-3200
  Ubly *(G-16720)*
▲ Pepro Enterprises Inc .... C 989 658-3200
  Ubly *(G-16721)*

◆ Performance Systematix Inc .... D 616 949-9090
  Grand Rapids *(G-6749)*
Petersen Products Inc .... F 248 446-0500
  Brighton *(G-1978)*
Phillips-Medisize LLC .... C 616 878-5030
  Byron Center *(G-2207)*
Phillips-Medisize LLC .... F 248 592-2144
  West Bloomfield *(G-17493)*
Phoenix Packaging Corporation .... G 734 944-3916
  Saline *(G-14407)*
Pierburg Pump Tech US LLC .... G 864 688-1322
  Auburn Hills *(G-972)*
Pinconning Metals Inc .... G 989 879-3144
  Pinconning *(G-12512)*
▲ Pioneer Molded Products Inc .... E 616 977-4172
  Grand Rapids *(G-6755)*
Pioneer Plastics Inc 586 262-0159
  Warren *(G-17187)*
▲ Plast-O-Foam LLC .... D 586 307-3790
  Clinton Township *(G-3194)*
Plastech Weld 313 963-3194
  Detroit *(G-4305)*
Plastechs LLC .... G 734 429-3129
  Saline *(G-14408)*
Plasti-Fab Inc .... E 248 543-1415
  Ferndale *(G-5311)*
Plastic Dress-Up Service Inc .... E 586 727-7878
  Port Huron *(G-12956)*
▲ Plastic Mold Technology Inc .... D 616 698-9810
  Kentwood *(G-9022)*
Plastic Mold Technology Inc 616 698-9810
  Grand Rapids *(G-6756)*
Plastic Molding Development .... G 586 739-4500
  Sterling Heights *(G-15446)*
Plastic Ominium Auto Inergy .... C 517 265-1100
  Adrian *(G-85)*
▲ Plastic Omnium Auto Exteriors .... B 248 458-0700
  Troy *(G-16551)*
Plastic Solutions LLC .... G 231 824-7350
  Traverse City *(G-16074)*
Plastic Tag & Trade Check Co .... F 989 892-7913
  Bay City *(G-1340)*
▲ Plastic Trim Inc .... B 937 429-1100
  Tawas City *(G-15676)*
Plastic Trim International Inc .... C 989 362-4419
  East Tawas *(G-4693)*
Plastico Industries Inc .... F 616 304-6289
  Carson City *(G-2496)*
▲ Plasticrafts Inc .... G 313 532-1900
  Redford *(G-13183)*
Plastics Technology Co .... G 586 421-0479
  Chesterfield *(G-2818)*
◆ Plastipak Holdings Inc .... F 734 455-3600
  Plymouth *(G-12718)*
Plastipak Packaging Inc 734 529-2475
  Dundee *(G-4597)*
Plastipak Packaging Inc .... C 734 326-6184
  Westland *(G-17589)*
Plexicase Inc .... G 616 246-6400
  Wyoming *(G-18028)*
▲ Pliant Plastics Corp .... D 616 844-0300
  Spring Lake *(G-15169)*
Pliant Plastics Corp .... F 616 844-3215
  Spring Lake *(G-15170)*
◆ Poly Flex Products Inc .... E 734 458-4194
  Farmington Hills *(G-5096)*
Polymer Process Dev LLC .... D 586 464-6400
  Shelby Township *(G-14669)*
▲ Polymerica Limited Company .... C 248 542-2000
  Huntington Woods *(G-8191)*
Polyply Composites LLC .... E 616 842-6330
  Grand Haven *(G-6061)*
▲ Polytec Foha Inc .... F 586 978-9386
  Warren *(G-17188)*
Poncraft Door Co Inc .... F 248 373-6060
  Auburn Hills *(G-976)*
Port City Group Inc .... F 231 777-3941
  Muskegon *(G-11400)*
PRA Company .... D 989 846-1029
  Standish *(G-15226)*
Precision Industries Inc .... F 810 239-5816
  Flint *(G-5482)*
Precision Masters Inc 248 648-8071
  Auburn Hills *(G-979)*
▲ Precision Mold & Engineering .... E 586 774-2421
  Warren *(G-17193)*
▲ Precision Polymer Mfg Inc .... E 269 344-2044
  Kalamazoo *(G-8860)*
Preferred Plastics Inc .... D 269 685-5873
  Plainwell *(G-12540)*

SIC SECTION 30 RUBBER AND MISCELLANEOUS PLASTICS PRODUCTS

Primera Plastics Inc D 616 748-6248
Zeeland (G-18177)
Prism Plastics Inc F 810 292-6300
Chesterfield (G-2821)
Prism Plastics Inc E 810 292-6300
Shelby Township (G-14671)
▲ Pro Slot Ltd G 616 897-6000
Hartford (G-7386)
Prompt Plastics G 586 307-8525
Warren (G-17202)
Proper Group International Inc C 586 552-5267
Warren (G-17204)
▲ Proper Group International Inc G 586 779-8787
Warren (G-17205)
Proper Polymers - Anderson LLC G 586 408-9120
Warren (G-17206)
Proper Polymers - Warren LLC E 586 552-5267
Warren (G-17207)
Proper Polymers - Warren LLC E 586 552-5267
Warren (G-17208)
Proper Polymers-Pulaski LLC D 931 371-3147
Warren (G-17209)
Proto Crafts Inc D 810 376-3665
Deckerville (G-3810)
▲ Proto Shapes Inc F 517 278-3947
Coldwater (G-3321)
Proto-TEC Inc F 616 772-9511
Zeeland (G-18181)
Protojet LLC F 810 956-8000
Fraser (G-5712)
▲ Pti Engineered Plastics Inc B 586 263-5100
Macomb (G-10159)
▼ Purforms Inc E 616 897-3000
Lowell (G-10041)
Qfd Recycling F 810 733-2335
Flint (G-5487)
Quality Assured Plastics Inc E 269 674-3888
Lawrence (G-9506)
▲ Quality Models Intl Inc G 519 727-4255
Melvindale (G-10706)
R & L Frye G 989 821-6661
Roscommon (G-13753)
▲ R B L Plastics Incorporated E 313 873-8800
Detroit (G-4325)
◆ R C Plastics Inc F 517 523-2112
Osseo (G-12228)
R L Adams Plastics Inc D 616 261-4400
Grand Rapids (G-6803)
Range Cards G 248 880-8444
Clarkston (G-2950)
Ray Scott Industries Inc G 248 535-2528
Port Huron (G-12962)
▲ Rbl Products Inc F 313 873-8806
Detroit (G-4331)
RCO Engineering Inc D 586 620-4133
Roseville (G-13860)
Realbio Technology Inc G 269 544-1088
Kalamazoo (G-8869)
▲ Reed City Group LLC D 231 832-7500
Reed City (G-13222)
Reeves Plastics LLC E 616 997-0777
Coopersville (G-3569)
Regal Finishing Co Inc D 269 849-2963
Coloma (G-3364)
Regency Plastics - Ubly Inc D 989 658-8504
Ubly (G-16723)
Rehrig Pacific Company G 517 278-9808
Coldwater (G-3326)
Reklein Plastics Incorporated G 586 739-8850
Sterling Heights (G-15463)
Reliable Reasonable Tl Svc LLC F 586 630-6016
Clinton Township (G-3209)
Retro Enterprises Inc G 269 435-8583
Constantine (G-3544)
◆ Reutter LLC G 248 621-9220
Bingham Farms (G-1659)
Revere Plastics Systems LLC C 586 415-4823
Fraser (G-5717)
▲ Revere Plastics Systems LLC B 419 547-6918
Novi (G-11986)
Riverside Plastic Co E 231 937-7333
Howard City (G-8006)
▲ Rkaa Business LLC E 231 734-5517
Evart (G-4886)
Roberts Tool Company F 517 423-6691
Tecumseh (G-15807)
▼ Robinson Industries Inc C 989 465-6111
Coleman (G-3350)
Robmar Plastics Inc G 989 386-9600
Clare (G-2885)
Robroy Industries Inc D 616 794-0700
Belding (G-1429)
Rockford Molding & Trim G 616 874-8997
Rockford (G-13588)
Rocktech Systems LLC E 586 330-9031
Chesterfield (G-2832)
▲ Romeo-Rim Inc C 586 336-5800
Bruce Twp (G-2096)
Ronningen Research and Dev Co C 269 649-0520
Vicksburg (G-16842)
Roto-Plastics Corporation D 517 263-8981
Adrian (G-92)
Royal Container Services Inc G 586 775-7600
Warren (G-17224)
Royal Plastics LLC G 616 669-3393
Hudsonville (G-8176)
Royal Technologies Corporation C 616 667-4102
Hudsonville (G-8177)
◆ Royal Technologies Corporation A 616 669-3393
Hudsonville (G-8178)
Royal Technologies Corporation C 616 667-4102
Hudsonville (G-8179)
Royal Technologies Corporation C 616 669-3393
Hudsonville (G-8180)
RPS Tool and Engineering Inc E 586 298-6590
Roseville (G-13864)
S&S Precision LLC G 248 266-4770
Wixom (G-17889)
▲ SA Automotive Ltd C 517 521-4205
Webberville (G-17453)
Sac Plastics Inc G 616 846-0820
Spring Lake (G-15174)
▲ Saginaw Bay Plastics Inc D 989 686-7860
Kawkawlin (G-8975)
Saint-Gobain Prfmce Plas Corp D 989 435-9533
Beaverton (G-1392)
Schrier Plastics Corp E 616 669-7174
Jenison (G-8642)
▲ Schwintek Inc G 269 445-9999
Cassopolis (G-2535)
▼ Scic LLC E 800 248-5960
Mason (G-10655)
Scooters Refuse Service Inc G 269 962-2201
Battle Creek (G-1244)
▲ Seabrook Plastics Inc E 231 759-8820
Norton Shores (G-11792)
Seagate Plastics Company E 517 547-8123
Addison (G-39)
Seaway Plastics Corporation E 810 765-8864
Marine City (G-10482)
▲ Sebro Plastics Inc E 248 348-4121
Wixom (G-17891)
Sequoia Molding G 586 463-4400
Grosse Pointe (G-7183)
Sgp Technologies G 810 744-1715
Burton (G-2164)
◆ Shape Corp B 616 846-8700
Grand Haven (G-6077)
Shape Corp E 616 844-3215
Grand Haven (G-6078)
Shoreline Mold & Engrg LLC G 269 926-2223
Benton Harbor (G-1546)
▼ Shuert Industries Inc C 586 254-4590
Sterling Heights (G-15497)
▲ Silikids Inc G 866 789-7454
Traverse City (G-16104)
▲ Sohner Plastics LLC F 734 222-4847
Dexter (G-4511)
▲ Solo Cup Company LLC C 800 248-5960
Mason (G-10657)
▼ Solo Cup Operating Corporation D 800 248-5960
Mason (G-10658)
Soltis Plastics Corp G 248 698-1440
White Lake (G-17639)
◆ Sonus Engineered Solutions LLC C 586 427-3838
Warren (G-17244)
Soroc Products Inc E 810 743-2660
Burton (G-2166)
Special Mold Engineering Inc E 248 652-6600
Rochester Hills (G-13516)
Special-Lite Inc C 800 821-6531
Decatur (G-3806)
▼ Speed Cinch Inc G 269 646-2016
Marcellus (G-10468)
Spencer Plastics Inc E 231 942-7100
Cadillac (G-2279)
SPI Blow Molding LLC E 269 849-3200
Coloma (G-3365)
SPI LLC E 586 566-5870
Shelby Township (G-14701)
Spiratex Company D 734 289-4800
Monroe (G-11069)
Spirit Industries Inc G 517 371-7840
Lansing (G-9266)
Sr Injection Molding Inc G 586 260-2360
Harrison Township (G-7350)
◆ Srg Global Coatings Inc C 248 509-1100
Troy (G-16618)
Ssb Holdings Inc E 586 755-1660
Rochester Hills (G-13517)
Standard Plaque Incorporated F 313 383-7233
Melvindale (G-10707)
Statistical Processed Products E 586 792-6900
Clinton Township (G-3235)
Stellar Plastics Corporation G 313 527-7337
Detroit (G-4377)
Stellar Plastics Fabg LLC G 313 527-7337
Detroit (G-4378)
Stexley-Brake LLC G 231 421-3092
Traverse City (G-16111)
▲ Stone Plastics and Mfg Inc C 616 748-9740
Zeeland (G-18188)
Sturgis Molded Products Co C 269 651-9381
Sturgis (G-15636)
Su-Dan Plastics Inc B 248 651-6035
Rochester (G-13354)
Su-Dan Plastics Inc F 248 651-6035
Rochester Hills (G-13520)
Sumitomo Chemical America Inc G 248 284-4797
Novi (G-12008)
▲ Summit Plastic Molding Inc E 586 262-4500
Shelby Township (G-14703)
Summit Plastic Molding II Inc G 586 977-8300
Sterling Heights (G-15515)
▲ Summit Plastic Molding II Inc F 586 262-4500
Shelby Township (G-14704)
▲ Summit Polymers Inc C 269 324-9330
Portage (G-13045)
Summit Polymers Inc G 269 324-9320
Portage (G-13046)
Summit Polymers Inc B 269 324-9330
Kalamazoo (G-8901)
Summit Polymers Inc B 269 323-1301
Portage (G-13047)
Summit Polymers Inc B 269 651-1643
Sturgis (G-15638)
Sunaire Window Manufacturing G 248 437-5870
Brighton (G-1993)
Supreme Industries LLC G 586 725-2500
Ira (G-8273)
Sur-Form LLC E 586 221-1950
Chesterfield (G-2844)
Svrc Industries Inc E 989 280-3038
Saginaw (G-14159)
▲ Systex Products Corporation D 269 964-8800
Battle Creek (G-1257)
Talco Industries G 989 269-6260
Bad Axe (G-1072)
Tapco Holdings Inc C 248 668-6400
Wixom (G-17905)
TAW Plastics LLC G 616 302-0954
Greenville (G-7157)
Tech Group Grand Rapids Inc B 616 643-6001
Walker (G-16879)
Techniplas LLC B 517 849-9911
Jonesville (G-8669)
▲ Tecla Company Inc E 248 624-8200
Commerce Township (G-3453)
▲ Teijin Advan Compo Ameri Inc G 248 365-6600
Auburn Hills (G-1016)
Ten X Plastics LLC G 616 813-3037
Grand Rapids (G-6920)
Tepso Gen-X Plastics LLC G 248 869-2130
Wixom (G-17908)
Tesca Usa Inc E 586 991-0744
Rochester Hills (G-13524)
◆ Tg Fluid Systems USA Corp B 810 220-6161
Brighton (G-1997)
▲ Th Plastics Inc B 269 496-8495
Mendon (G-10719)
Th Plastics Inc D 269 496-8495
Mendon (G-10720)
Thermoforms Inc F 616 974-0055
Kentwood (G-9033)
▲ Thetford Corporation C 734 769-6000
Ann Arbor (G-670)
Thomson Plastics Inc D 517 545-5026
Howell (G-8109)
▲ Three 60 Corporation F 517 545-3600
Howell (G-8110)

SIC

Employee Codes: A=Over 500 employees, B=251-500
C=101-250, D=51-100, E=20-50, F=10-19, G=3-9
2020 Harris Michigan
Industrial Directory
761

Thumb Plastics Inc ....E 989 269-9791
Bad Axe (G-1074)
Thunder Bay Pattern Works Inc ....E 586 783-1126
Clinton Township (G-3246)
TI Group Auto Systems LLC ....C 810 364-3277
Marysville (G-10623)
Tomas Plastics Inc ....F 734 455-4706
Plymouth (G-12774)
Tooling Cncepts Design Not Inc ....F 810 444-9807
Port Huron (G-12972)
Total Plastics Resources LLC ....F 248 299-9500
Rochester Hills (G-13529)
▼ Tower Tag & Label LLC ....F 269 927-1065
Benton Harbor (G-1555)
◆ Toyoda Gosei North Amer Corp ....C 248 280-2100
Troy (G-16650)
Trans Industries Plastics LLC ....E 248 310-0008
Rochester (G-13355)
Transnav Holdings Inc ....C 586 716-5600
New Baltimore (G-11494)
▲ Transnav Technologies Inc ....C 888 249-9955
New Baltimore (G-11495)
Travis Creek Tooling ....G 269 685-2000
Plainwell (G-12549)
Trellborg Sling Sltions US Inc ....G 269 639-4217
Benton Harbor (G-1556)
Trellborg Sling Sltions US Inc ....G 734 354-1250
Northville (G-11730)
Trestle Plastic Services LLC ....G 616 262-5484
Hamilton (G-7241)
Tri-Star Molding Inc ....E 269 646-0062
Marcellus (G-10469)
▲ Tri-Way Manufacturing Inc ....E 586 776-0700
Roseville (G-13880)
Tribar Manufacturing LLC ....E 248 669-0077
Wixom (G-17916)
Tribar Manufacturing LLC ....G 248 374-5870
Wixom (G-17917)
Tribar Manufacturing LLC ....B 248 516-1600
Howell (G-8115)
Tribar Technologies Inc ....B 248 516-1600
Wixom (G-17918)
Tribar Technologies Inc ....A 248 516-1600
Wixom (G-17919)
Trinseo LLC ....E 888 789-7661
Midland (G-10922)
Triple C Geothermal Inc ....G 517 282-7249
Muskegon (G-11442)
Two Mitts Inc ....G 800 888-5054
Kalamazoo (G-8915)
U S Farathane Port Huron LLC ....G 248 754-7000
Auburn Hills (G-1033)
▲ Undercar Products Group Inc ....B 616 719-4571
Wyoming (G-18039)
Uniflex Inc ....G 248 486-6000
Brighton (G-2002)
Universal Consumer Pdts Inc ....D 616 365-4201
White Pigeon (G-17656)
▲ Universal Products Inc ....E 231 937-5555
Rockford (G-13595)
University Plastics Inc ....G 734 668-8773
Ann Arbor (G-688)
Urgent Plastic Services Inc ....G 248 852-8999
Rochester Hills (G-13537)
US Farathane LLC ....E 248 754-7000
Auburn Hills (G-1037)
US Farathane Holdings Corp ....C 586 726-1200
Sterling Heights (G-15535)
◆ US Farathane Holdings Corp ....B 586 726-1200
Shelby Township (G-14714)
US Farathane Holdings Corp ....D 586 978-2800
Troy (G-16666)
US Farathane Holdings Corp ....C 248 754-7000
Port Huron (G-12974)
US Farathane Holdings Corp ....B 248 754-7000
Shelby Township (G-14715)
US Farathane Holdings Corp ....F 248 754-7000
Lake Orion (G-9168)
US Farathane Holdings Corp ....C 780 246-1034
Auburn Hills (G-1038)
US Farathane Holdings Corp ....F 248 391-6801
Auburn Hills (G-1039)
US Farathane Holdings Corp ....D 586 978-2800
Westland (G-17607)
US Farathane Holdings Corp ....E 586 685-4000
Sterling Heights (G-15537)
US Farathane Holdings Corp ....C 248 754-7000
Auburn Hills (G-1040)
US Farathane Holdings Corp ....D 248 754-7000
Orion (G-12191)
USA Summit Plas Silao 1 LLC ....G 269 324-9330
Portage (G-13053)
USF Westland LLC ....G 248 754-7000
Auburn Hills (G-1042)
Vacuum Orna Metal Company Inc ....E 734 941-9100
Romulus (G-13738)
▲ Valley Enterprises Ubly Inc ....C 989 658-3200
Ubly (G-16726)
Valtec LLC ....C 810 724-5048
Imlay City (G-8213)
Vaupell Molding & Tooling Inc ....D 269 435-8414
Constantine (G-3545)
▲ Ventra Evart LLC ....G 231 734-9000
Evart (G-4888)
Ventra Ionia Main LLC ....E 616 597-3220
Ionia (G-8252)
▲ Ventra Ionia Main LLC ....C 616 597-3220
Ionia (G-8253)
▼ Vidon Plastics Inc ....D 810 667-0634
Lapeer (G-9490)
▲ Vintech Industries Inc ....C 810 724-7400
Imlay City (G-8214)
Vintech Mexico Holdings LLC ....G 810 387-3224
Imlay City (G-8215)
Vinyl Craft Window LLC ....F 231 832-8905
Hersey (G-7476)
Vinyl Tech Window Systems Inc ....F 248 634-8900
Holly (G-7901)
▲ Vitec LLC ....B 313 633-2254
Detroit (G-4433)
Vivatar Inc ....E 616 928-0750
Holland (G-7849)
▲ W T Beresford Co ....G 248 350-2900
Southfield (G-15064)
▲ Weather King Windows Doors Inc ....D 313 933-1234
Farmington (G-4915)
Weather King Windows Doors Inc ....E 248 478-7788
Farmington (G-4916)
Weather Pane Inc ....G 810 798-8695
Almont (G-270)
Weathergard Window Company Inc ....D 248 967-8822
Oak Park (G-12105)
▲ West Michigan Molding Inc ....C 616 846-4950
Grand Haven (G-6097)
Western Diversified Plas LLC ....G 269 668-3393
Mattawan (G-10671)
▲ Western Michigan Plastics ....F 616 394-9269
Holland (G-7857)
Willco Extrusion LLC ....G 248 817-2373
Troy (G-16691)
▲ Williamston Products Inc ....D 517 655-2131
Williamston (G-17742)
Williamston Products Inc ....E 517 655-2273
Williamston (G-17743)
Williamston Products Inc ....D 989 723-0149
Owosso (G-12329)
WI Molding of Michigan LLC ....D 269 327-3075
Portage (G-13057)
World Class Prototypes Inc ....F 616 355-0200
Holland (G-7862)
Worswick Mold & Tool Inc ....F 810 765-1700
Marine City (G-10488)
Wow Plastics LLC ....G 760 827-7800
Caro (G-2482)
Wow Products USA ....G 989 672-1300
Caro (G-2483)
Wright Plastic Products Co LLC ....D 810 326-3000
Saint Clair (G-14237)
▲ Wright Plastic Products Co LLC ....D 989 291-3211
Sheridan (G-14736)
Yanfeng US Automotive ....C 734 254-5000
Plymouth (G-12796)
Yanfeng US Automotive ....C 734 289-4841
Monroe (G-11087)
Yanfeng US Automotive ....F 517 721-0179
Novi (G-12028)
Yanfeng US Automotive ....C 313 259-3226
Detroit (G-4454)
Yanfeng US Automotive ....E 734 946-0600
Romulus (G-13744)
Yapp USA Auto Systems Inc ....G 248 404-8696
Romulus (G-13745)
Zayna LLC ....G 616 452-4522
Grand Rapids (G-7011)
◆ ZF Active Safety & Elec US LLC ....C 734 855-2600
Livonia (G-10014)
ZF Passive Safety ....B 586 232-7200
Washington (G-17316)

31 LEATHER AND LEATHER PRODUCTS

3111 Leather Tanning & Finishing

▲ Afx Industries LLC ....G 810 966-4650
Port Huron (G-12881)
Afx Industries LLC ....G 517 768-8993
Jackson (G-8376)
Horn Corp ....G 248 358-8883
Brighton (G-1940)
K & K Tannery LLC ....G 517 849-9720
Jonesville (G-8659)
Larrys Taxidermy Inc ....G 517 769-6104
Pleasant Lake (G-12552)
Lear Corporation ....E 248 853-3122
Rochester Hills (G-13459)
Lynn Noyes Industries Inc ....G 313 841-3130
Ypsilanti (G-18086)
Mexico Express ....F 313 843-6717
Detroit (G-4235)
Michigan Diversfd Holdings Inc ....F 248 280-0450
Madison Heights (G-10305)
Modern Fur Dressing LLC ....G 517 589-5575
Leslie (G-9545)
National Manufacturing Inc ....G 586 755-8983
Warren (G-17166)
Russell Farms Inc ....G 269 349-6120
Kalamazoo (G-8876)
Transnav Holdings Inc ....C 586 716-5600
New Baltimore (G-11494)
◆ Wolverine World Wide Inc ....C 616 866-5500
Rockford (G-13600)

3131 Boot & Shoe Cut Stock & Findings

Bean Counter Inc ....G 906 523-5027
Calumet (G-2325)
Bond Manufacturing LLC ....G 313 671-0799
Detroit (G-3909)
Canusa LLC ....F 906 259-0800
Sault Sainte Marie (G-14462)
▲ David Epstein Inc ....F 248 542-0802
Ferndale (G-5270)
Fresh Strt Transitional Living ....G 269 757-5195
Benton Harbor (G-1499)
Midwest Cabinet Counters ....G 248 586-4260
Madison Heights (G-10306)
Paul Murphy Plastics Co ....E 586 774-4880
Roseville (G-13851)
Quarter Mania ....G 734 368-2765
Belleville (G-1450)
Quarters Vending LLC ....G 313 510-5555
Commerce Township (G-3444)
Rand L Industries Inc ....G 989 657-5175
Alpena (G-311)
Rand Worldwide Subsidiary Inc ....G 616 261-8183
Grandville (G-7069)
S A S ....G 586 725-6381
Chesterfield (G-2834)
Security Countermeasures Tech ....G 248 237-6263
Livonia (G-9924)
Wolverine Procurement Inc ....E 616 866-9521
Rockford (G-13597)
Zobl Quarter Horses ....G 810 479-9534
Clyde (G-3285)

3142 House Slippers

Wolverine Slipper Group Inc ....G 616 866-5500
Rockford (G-13599)

3143 Men's Footwear, Exc Athletic

Hush Puppies Retail LLC ....E 231 937-1004
Howard City (G-8001)
Hy-Test Inc ....G 616 866-5500
Rockford (G-13572)
Kalamazoo Orthotics & Dbtc ....F 269 349-2247
Kalamazoo (G-8793)
Millers Shoe Parlor Inc ....G 517 783-1258
Jackson (G-8530)
Original Footwear Company ....B 231 796-5828
Big Rapids (G-1639)
Orthotool LLC ....G 734 455-8103
Plymouth (G-12704)
Shoe Shop ....G 231 739-2174
Muskegon (G-11422)
▲ Veldheer Tulip Garden Inc ....D 616 399-1900
Holland (G-7844)
Wolverine Procurement Inc ....E 616 866-9521
Rockford (G-13597)

3144 Women's Footwear, Exc Athletic

Bella Sposa Bridal & Prom	G	616 364-0777
Grand Rapids (G-6209)		
Millers Shoe Parlor Inc	G	517 783-1258
Jackson (G-8530)		
Orthotool LLC	G	734 455-8103
Plymouth (G-12704)		
Wolverine Procurement Inc	E	616 866-9521
Rockford (G-13597)		
◆ Wolverine World Wide Inc	C	616 866-5500
Rockford (G-13600)		

3149 Footwear, NEC

Orthotool LLC	G	734 455-8103
Plymouth (G-12704)		
Saucony Inc	G	616 866-5500
Rockford (G-13589)		
▲ Warrior Sports Inc	D	800 968-7845
Warren (G-17289)		
◆ Wolverine World Wide Inc	C	616 866-5500
Rockford (G-13600)		

3151 Leather Gloves & Mittens

Kaul Glove and Mfg Co	E	313 894-9494
Detroit (G-4172)		

3161 Luggage

Birlon Group LLC	G	313 551-5341
Inkster (G-8225)		
Grand Trunk RR	G	248 452-4881
Pontiac (G-12830)		
Mary Boggs Baggs	G	586 731-2513
Shelby Township (G-14634)		
Rhino Products Inc	F	269 674-8309
Lawrence (G-9507)		
Shaun Jackson Design Inc	G	734 975-7500
Saline (G-14415)		
Sound Productions Entrmt	E	989 386-2221
Clare (G-2889)		
Tallulahs Satchels	G	231 775-4082
Cadillac (G-2281)		

3171 Handbags & Purses

Accessories By Gigi LLC	G	248 242-0036
Clawson (G-2968)		
Mary Boggs Baggs	G	586 731-2513
Shelby Township (G-14634)		
Nicole Acarter LLC	G	248 251-2800
Detroit (G-4270)		
Sandusky Concrete & Supply	G	810 648-2627
Sandusky (G-14442)		
Tapestry Inc	F	631 724-8066
Sterling Heights (G-15519)		
Tmb Trends Inc	G	866 445-2344
Troy (G-16646)		

3172 Personal Leather Goods

Birlon Group LLC	G	313 551-5341
Inkster (G-8225)		
C W Marsh Company	E	231 722-3781
Muskegon (G-11288)		
Charlies Wood Shop	F	989 845-2632
Chesaning (G-2722)		
Original Footwear Company	B	231 796-5828
Big Rapids (G-1639)		

3199 Leather Goods, NEC

Birlon Group LLC	G	313 551-5341
Inkster (G-8225)		
C I M Product	G	269 983-5348
Saint Joseph (G-14303)		
C W Marsh Company	E	231 722-3781
Muskegon (G-11288)		
Grozdanovski Vasilka	G	989 731-0723
Gaylord (G-5862)		
Ihicore LLC	G	800 960-0448
Lansing (G-9384)		
Leathercrafts By Bear	G	616 453-8308
Grand Rapids (G-6623)		
▲ Wolverine Procurement Inc	F	616 866-6500
Rockford (G-13598)		
◆ Wolverine World Wide Inc	C	616 866-5500
Rockford (G-13600)		
Wolverine World Wide Inc	G	616 863-3983
Rockford (G-13601)		
Wolverine World Wide Inc	G	616 866-5500
Rockford (G-13602)		
▲ Low Cost Surcing Solutions LLC	G	248 535-7721
Washington (G-17306)		
▲ Protecto Horse Equipment Inc	G	586 754-4820
Warren (G-17210)		
Sharadans Leather Goods Inc	G	586 468-0666
Mount Clemens (G-11150)		
▲ Shinola/Detroit LLC	C	888 304-2534
Detroit (G-4361)		
Tapestry Inc	F	616 538-5802
Grandville (G-7073)		

32 STONE, CLAY, GLASS, AND CONCRETE PRODUCTS

3211 Flat Glass

Astro Lite Window Company Inc	E	734 326-2455
Romulus (G-13652)		
Beechcraft Products Inc	E	989 288-2606
Durand (G-4606)		
Carlex Glass America LLC	A	248 824-8800
Troy (G-16258)		
Ford Motor Company	A	313 446-5945
Detroit (G-4067)		
Furniture City Glass Corp	E	616 784-5500
Grand Rapids (G-6425)		
Guardian Fabrication LLC	G	248 340-1800
Auburn Hills (G-892)		
Guardian Fabrication Inc	A	248 340-1800
Auburn Hills (G-893)		
Guardian Industries LLC	F	517 629-9464
Albion (G-125)		
Guardian Industries LLC	B	734 654-4285
Carleton (G-2456)		
◆ Guardian Industries LLC	B	248 340-1800
Auburn Hills (G-894)		
Guardian Industries LLC	D	734 654-1111
Carleton (G-2457)		
I2 International Dev LLC	F	616 534-8100
Grandville (G-7050)		
Johnson Glass Cleaning Inc	G	906 361-0361
Negaunee (G-11471)		
Lippert Components Mfg Inc	C	323 663-1261
Chesaning (G-2726)		
Magna International Amer Inc	G	616 786-7000
Holland (G-7733)		
Mirror Image Inc	G	248 446-8440
South Lyon (G-14802)		
Pilkington North America Inc	F	989 754-2956
Saginaw (G-14122)		
Pilkington North America Inc	F	248 542-8300
Royal Oak (G-13957)		
Pilkington North America Inc	B	269 687-2100
Niles (G-11640)		
Pittsburgh Glass Works LLC	C	248 371-1700
Rochester Hills (G-13494)		
Pollack Glass Co	F	517 349-6380
Okemos (G-12134)		
PPG Industries Inc	F	248 641-2000
Troy (G-16557)		
Saint Gobain Glass Corporation	G	248 816-0060
Troy (G-16590)		
Saint-Gobain Sekurit Usa Inc	F	586 264-1072
Sterling Heights (G-15483)		
Superior Auto Glass of Mich	G	989 366-9691
Houghton Lake (G-7999)		
Valley Glass Co Inc	G	989 790-9342
Saginaw (G-14175)		
Weatherproof Inc	E	517 764-1330
Jackson (G-8606)		

3221 Glass Containers

Owens-Brockway Glass Cont Inc	G	269 435-2535
Constantine (G-3541)		

3229 Pressed & Blown Glassware, NEC

▲ City Auto Glass Co	G	616 842-3235
Grand Haven (G-6003)		
▲ Dare Products Inc	E	269 965-2307
Springfield (G-15190)		
Essilor Laboratories Amer Inc	C	616 361-6000
Grand Rapids (G-6386)		
▲ General Scientific Corporation	E	734 996-9200
Ann Arbor (G-471)		
Glassicart Decorative Glwr	G	231 739-5956
Muskegon (G-11330)		
Great Lakes Aero Products	F	810 235-1402
Flint (G-5441)		
Guardian Industries LLC	B	734 654-4285
Carleton (G-2456)		
Hudson Industries Inc	G	800 459-1077
Warren (G-17082)		
Jordan Valley Glassworks	G	231 536-0539
East Jordan (G-4638)		
Keweenaw Bay Indian Community	F	906 524-5757
Baraga (G-1104)		
Knickerbocker R Yr Brickr Blk	G	517 531-5369
Parma (G-12390)		
Laidco Sales Inc	G	231 832-1327
Hersey (G-7473)		
Light Speed Usa LLC	A	616 308-0054
Grand Rapids (G-6627)		
▲ Lumecon LLC	G	248 505-1090
Farmington Hills (G-5047)		
Meints Glass Blowing	G	269 349-1958
Kalamazoo (G-8821)		
Optrand Inc	F	734 451-3480
Plymouth (G-12703)		
PPG Industries Inc	F	248 641-2000
Troy (G-16557)		
▲ Precision Polymer Mfg Inc	E	269 344-2044
Kalamazoo (G-8860)		
Pubsof Chicago LLC	G	312 448-8282
Traverse City (G-16083)		
▲ Rgm New Ventures Inc	D	248 624-5050
Wixom (G-17885)		
Robroy Enclosures Inc	C	616 794-0700
Belding (G-1428)		
Thompson John	G	810 225-8780
Howell (G-8108)		
Tig Entity LLC	G	810 629-9558
Fenton (G-5244)		

3231 Glass Prdts Made Of Purchased Glass

A & B Display Systems Inc	F	989 893-6642
Bay City (G-1269)		
A K Services Inc	G	313 972-1010
Detroit (G-3827)		
Alexanders Custom GL & Mirror	G	734 513-5850
Garden City (G-5820)		
Boyer Glassworks Inc	G	231 526-6359
Harbor Springs (G-7275)		
C & B Glass Inc	G	248 625-4376
Clarkston (G-2909)		
Case Island Glass LLC	G	810 252-1704
Flint (G-5396)		
▲ City Auto Glass Co	G	616 842-3235
Grand Haven (G-6003)		
Classic Glass Battle Creek Inc	F	269 968-2791
Battle Creek (G-1167)		
▼ Duo-Gard Industries Inc	D	734 207-9700
Canton (G-2367)		
Engrave A Remembrance Inc	G	586 772-7480
Warren (G-17018)		
Etched Glass Works & A Bldg Co	G	517 819-4343
Lansing (G-9367)		
▲ Exatec LLC	E	248 926-4200
Wixom (G-17807)		
Fox Fire Glass LLC	G	248 332-2442
Fenton (G-5215)		
Full Spectrum Stained GL Inc	G	269 432-2610
Colon (G-3373)		
Furniture City Glass Corp	E	616 784-5500
Grand Rapids (G-6425)		
Gentex Corporation	C	616 772-1800
Zeeland (G-18138)		
Gentex Corporation	E	616 772-1800
Zeeland (G-18139)		
Gentex Corporation	C	616 772-1800
Zeeland (G-18140)		
Gentex Corporation	C	616 772-1800
Zeeland (G-18141)		
Gentex Corporation	C	616 772-1800
Zeeland (G-18143)		
Glass Recyclers Ltd	D	313 584-3434
Dearborn (G-3715)		
Grand River Interiors Inc	E	616 454-2800
Grand Rapids (G-6468)		
Guardian Fabrication LLC	G	248 340-1800
Auburn Hills (G-892)		
Guardian Industries LLC	B	734 654-4285
Carleton (G-2456)		
▲ Hensley Mfg Inc	F	810 653-3226
Davison (G-3653)		
Heritage Glass Inc	G	248 887-1010
Highland (G-7493)		
▲ Inalfa Road System Inc	B	248 371-3060
Auburn Hills (G-908)		
Jordan Valley Glassworks	G	231 536-0539
East Jordan (G-4638)		

32 STONE, CLAY, GLASS, AND CONCRETE PRODUCTS

Keeler-Glasgow Company Inc ....E...... 269 621-2415
  Hartford (G-7384)
▲ Kentwood Manufacturing Co ....E...... 616 698-6370
  Grand Rapids (G-6579)
Knight Tonya ....G...... 313 255-3434
  Southfield (G-14956)
Lippert Components Mfg Inc ....C...... 989 845-3061
  Chesaning (G-2725)
Lippert Components Mfg Inc ....C...... 323 663-1261
  Chesaning (G-2726)
Louis Padnos Iron and Metal Co ....E...... 616 459-4208
  Grand Rapids (G-6631)
Luxottica of America Inc ....G...... 989 624-8958
  Birch Run (G-1665)
M2 Scientifics LLC ....G...... 616 379-9080
  Holland (G-7728)
Magna ....G...... 616 786-7403
  Holland (G-7732)
◆ Magna Mirrors America Inc ....E...... 616 786-5120
  Grand Rapids (G-6640)
Magna Mirrors America Inc ....E...... 616 786-7000
  Holland (G-7734)
Magna Mirrors America Inc ....D...... 616 786-7300
  Holland (G-7735)
Magna Mirrors America Inc ....C...... 616 942-0163
  Newaygo (G-11573)
Magna Mirrors America Inc ....B...... 616 738-0115
  Holland (G-7736)
Magna Mirrors America Inc ....E...... 616 786-7000
  Grand Haven (G-6052)
Magna Mirrors America Inc ....E...... 616 786-7000
  Kentwood (G-9019)
Magna Mirrors America Inc ....A...... 616 786-7772
  Holland (G-7738)
Magna Mirrors America Inc ....C...... 616 868-6122
  Alto (G-328)
Magna Mirrors America Inc ....B...... 231 652-4450
  Newaygo (G-11574)
Magna Mirrors America Inc ....C...... 616 786-7000
  Holland (G-7737)
▲ Magna Mirrors North Amer LLC ....A...... 616 868-6122
  Alto (G-329)
Narens Associates Inc ....G...... 248 304-0300
  Farmington Hills (G-5076)
Oldcastle Buildingenvelope Inc ....F...... 734 947-9670
  Taylor (G-15752)
Oldcastle Buildingenvelope Inc ....E...... 616 896-8341
  Burnips (G-2133)
On The Side Sign Dsign Grphics ....G...... 810 266-7446
  Byron (G-2174)
Paragon Tempered Glass LLC ....E...... 269 684-5060
  Niles (G-11636)
Penstone Inc ....E...... 734 379-3160
  Rockwood (G-13610)
Polymer Process Dev LLC ....D...... 586 464-6400
  Shelby Township (G-14669)
PPG Industries Inc ....F...... 248 641-2000
  Troy (G-16557)
Pristine Glass Company ....G...... 616 454-2092
  Grand Rapids (G-6778)
▲ Rgm New Ventures Inc ....D...... 248 624-5050
  Wixom (G-17885)
Schefenalker Vision Systems ....G...... 810 388-2511
  Marysville (G-10613)
Se-Kure Controls Inc ....E...... 269 651-9351
  Sturgis (G-15633)
Se-Kure Domes & Mirrors Inc ....E...... 269 651-9351
  Sturgis (G-15634)
Signature Glass Inc ....G...... 586 447-9000
  Roseville (G-13869)
▲ SMR Atmtive Mrror Intl USA Inc ......B...... 810 364-4141
  Marysville (G-10615)
SMR Automotive Systems USA Inc .....F...... 810 937-2456
  Port Huron (G-12968)
▲ SMR Automotive Systems USA Inc ..A...... 810 364-4141
  Marysville (G-10616)
▲ SMR Automotive Technology ....F...... 810 364-4141
  Marysville (G-10617)
Solutia Inc ....B...... 734 676-4400
  Trenton (G-16157)
Stained Glass and Gifts ....G...... 810 736-6766
  Flint (G-5504)
Sydeline Corporation ....G...... 734 675-9330
  Grosse Ile (G-7177)
▲ Syncreonus Inc ....D...... 248 377-4700
  Auburn Hills (G-1010)
Thompson Art Glass Inc ....G...... 810 225-8766
  Brighton (G-1998)
Valley Glass Co Inc ....G...... 989 790-9342
  Saginaw (G-14175)

Vitro Automotriz SA De CV ....F...... 734 727-5001
  Westland (G-17608)
▲ Wolverine Glass Products Inc ....E...... 616 538-0100
  Wyoming (G-18044)
Wyse Glass Specialties Inc ....G...... 989 496-3510
  Freeland (G-5762)

3241 Cement, Hydraulic

Holcim (us) Inc ....D...... 734 529-2411
  Dundee (G-4587)
Holcim (us) Inc ....C...... 734 529-4600
  Dundee (G-4588)
Holcim (us) Inc ....F...... 989 755-7515
  Saginaw (G-14060)
Joe Davis Crushing Inc ....G...... 586 757-3612
  Sterling Heights (G-15381)
Knust Masonry ....G...... 231 322-2587
  Rapid City (G-13109)
Lafarge North America Inc ....G...... 989 399-1005
  Saginaw (G-14076)
Lafarge North America Inc ....G...... 989 894-0157
  Essexville (G-4875)
Lafarge North America Inc ....C...... 989 595-3820
  Presque Isle (G-13083)
Lafarge North America Inc ....E...... 216 566-0545
  Essexville (G-4876)
Lafarge North America Inc ....F...... 703 480-3649
  Dundee (G-4592)
Lafarge North America Inc ....G...... 989 354-4171
  Alpena (G-295)
Lafarge North America Inc ....F...... 989 755-7515
  Saginaw (G-14077)
Lafarge North America Inc ....F...... 703 480-3600
  Dundee (G-4591)
Nb Cement Co ....G...... 313 278-8299
  Dearborn Heights (G-3792)
St Marys Cement Inc (us) ....G...... 616 846-8553
  Ferrysburg (G-5338)
St Marys Cement US LLC ....E...... 231 547-9971
  Charlevoix (G-2631)

3251 Brick & Structural Clay Tile

Heb Development LLC ....G...... 616 363-3825
  Grand Rapids (G-6501)
Sineramics Incorporated ....G...... 248 879-0812
  Troy (G-16604)
Tabs Wall Systems LLC ....G...... 616 554-5400
  Grand Rapids (G-6914)
Theut Products Inc ....F...... 810 364-7132
  Marysville (G-10621)

3253 Ceramic Tile

Mannino Tile & Marble Inc ....F...... 586 978-3390
  Sterling Heights (G-15411)
Motawi Tileworks Inc ....E...... 734 213-0017
  Ann Arbor (G-565)
Yoxheimer Tile Co ....F...... 517 788-7542
  Jackson (G-8614)

3255 Clay Refractories

Alco Products LLC ....E...... 313 823-7500
  Detroit (G-3853)
◆ Alpha Resources LLC ....E...... 269 465-5559
  Stevensville (G-15553)
Harbisonwalker Intl Inc ....C...... 231 689-6641
  White Cloud (G-17623)
◆ Marshall-Gruber Company LLC ....F...... 248 353-4100
  Southfield (G-14973)
▲ Mono Ceramics Inc ....E...... 269 925-0212
  Benton Harbor (G-1532)
Pewabic Society Inc ....E...... 313 626-2000
  Detroit (G-4300)
Schad Boiler Setting Company ....D...... 313 273-2235
  Detroit (G-4355)

3259 Structural Clay Prdts, NEC

Architectural Bldg Pdts Inc ....G...... 248 680-1563
  Troy (G-16216)
Precision Plumbing - T ....G...... 269 695-2402
  Buchanan (G-2125)

3261 China Plumbing Fixtures & Fittings

Americast LLC ....G...... 989 681-4800
  Saint Louis (G-14358)
York Electric Inc ....E...... 517 487-6400
  Lansing (G-9438)

3263 Earthenware, Whiteware, Table & Kitchen Articles

Mdg Commercial Kitchen LLC ....G...... 269 207-1344
  Portage (G-13015)

3264 Porcelain Electrical Splys

◆ Leco Corporation ....B...... 269 983-5531
  Saint Joseph (G-14324)
Leco Corporation ....F...... 269 982-2230
  Saint Joseph (G-14325)
My Permit Pal Inc ....G...... 248 432-2699
  West Bloomfield (G-17488)
▲ NGK Spark Plugs (usa) Inc ....C...... 248 926-6900
  Wixom (G-17865)
▲ Tengam Engineering Inc ....E...... 269 694-9466
  Otsego (G-12256)

3269 Pottery Prdts, NEC

▲ Creative Arts Studio Royal Oak ....F...... 248 544-2234
  Royal Oak (G-13916)
Karla-Von Ceramics Inc ....G...... 616 866-0563
  Rockford (G-13576)
Make It Yours ....G...... 517 990-6799
  Jackson (G-8507)
Penzo America Inc ....G...... 248 723-0802
  Bloomfield Hills (G-1789)
Reilchz Inc ....G...... 231 421-9600
  Traverse City (G-16093)
▲ Veldheer Tulip Garden Inc ....D...... 616 399-1900
  Holland (G-7844)

3271 Concrete Block & Brick

A2z Outside Services Inc ....G...... 586 430-1143
  Richmond (G-13257)
Bark River Concrete Pdts Co ....F...... 906 466-9940
  Bark River (G-1118)
Best Block Company ....E...... 586 772-7000
  Warren (G-16956)
Branch West Concrete Products ....F...... 989 345-0794
  West Branch (G-17507)
Carlesimo Products Inc ....E...... 248 474-0415
  Farmington Hills (G-4957)
Cheboygan Cement Products Inc ....E...... 231 627-5631
  Cheboygan (G-2677)
Clay & Graham Inc ....G...... 989 354-5292
  Alpena (G-283)
Consumers Concrete Corp ....E...... 616 243-3651
  Wyoming (G-17993)
Consumers Concrete Corp ....E...... 269 384-0977
  Kalamazoo (G-8714)
Consumers Concrete Corporation ....E...... 269 342-0136
  Kalamazoo (G-8715)
Consumers Concrete Corporation ....F...... 231 777-3981
  Muskegon (G-11300)
Declarks Landscaping Inc ....G...... 586 752-7200
  Bruce Twp (G-2082)
Fendt Builders Supply Inc ....F...... 734 663-4277
  Ann Arbor (G-461)
Fendt Builders Supply Inc ....G...... 248 474-3211
  Farmington Hills (G-4999)
Ferguson Block Co Inc ....F...... 810 653-2812
  Davison (G-3647)
Fraco ....F...... 906 249-1476
  Marquette (G-10532)
Grand Blanc Cement Pdts Inc ....F...... 810 694-7500
  Grand Blanc (G-5967)
Hagen Cement Products Inc ....F...... 269 483-9641
  White Pigeon (G-17651)
Hampton Block Co ....G...... 248 628-1333
  Oxford (G-12348)
Hobe Inc ....G...... 231 845-5196
  Ludington (G-10065)
Interlock Design ....F...... 616 784-5901
  Comstock Park (G-3486)
K-Tel Corporation ....F...... 517 543-6174
  Charlotte (G-2657)
Kurtz Gravel Company Inc ....E...... 810 787-6543
  Farmington Hills (G-5040)
Lafarge North America Inc ....F...... 703 480-3600
  Dundee (G-4591)
Livingston County Concrete Inc ....F...... 810 632-3030
  Brighton (G-1951)
Ludvanwall Inc ....E...... 616 842-4500
  Spring Lake (G-15159)
Maple Valley Concrete Products ....G...... 517 852-1900
  Nashville (G-11460)
Mbcd Inc ....E...... 517 484-4426
  Lansing (G-9395)

Miller Products & Supply Co F 906 774-1243
Iron Mountain *(G-8290)*
National Block Company E 734 721-4050
Westland *(G-17582)*
New Buffalo Concrete Products B 269 469-2515
New Buffalo *(G-11516)*
Port Huron Building Supply Co F 810 987-2666
Port Huron *(G-12958)*
Ruppe Manufacturing Company E 906 932-3540
Ironwood *(G-8339)*
Simply Green Outdoor Svcs LLC G 734 385-6190
Dexter *(G-4510)*
Springfield Landscape Mtls G 269 965-6748
Springfield *(G-15204)*
St Marys Cement Inc (us) G 269 679-5253
Schoolcraft *(G-14501)*
Superior Block Company Inc F 906 482-2731
Houghton *(G-7984)*
Swartzmiller Lumber Company G 989 845-6625
Chesaning *(G-2728)*
Theut Concrete Products Inc F 810 679-3376
Croswell *(G-3604)*
Waanders Concrete Co E 269 673-6352
Allegan *(G-190)*

3272 Concrete Prdts

Acme Septic Tank Co F 989 684-3852
Kawkawlin *(G-8969)*
ADL Systems Inc G 517 647-7543
Portland *(G-13060)*
Advance Concrete Products Co E 248 887-4173
Highland *(G-7484)*
Ajax Paving Industries Inc C 248 244-3300
Troy *(G-16175)*
All About Drainage LLC G 248 921-0766
Commerce Township *(G-3387)*
Arbor Stone G 517 750-1340
Spring Arbor *(G-15119)*
▲ Arnets Inc F 734 665-3650
Ann Arbor *(G-367)*
Asphalt Paving Inc F 231 733-1409
Muskegon *(G-11272)*
Atlas Cut Stone Company G 248 545-5100
Oak Park *(G-12049)*
Beck Mobile Concrete LLC G 517 655-4996
Williamston *(G-17726)*
Becker & Scrivens Con Pdts Inc E 517 437-4250
Hillsdale *(G-7517)*
Best Block Company E 586 772-7000
Warren *(G-16956)*
Bonsal American Inc F 248 338-0335
Auburn Hills *(G-794)*
Bonsal American Inc F 734 753-4413
New Boston *(G-11497)*
Bostwick Enterprises Inc F 231 946-8613
Traverse City *(G-15917)*
Brutsche Concrete Products Co E 269 963-1554
Battle Creek *(G-1159)*
Burrell Tri-County Vaults Inc F 734 483-2024
Ypsilanti *(G-18058)*
Bush Concrete Products Inc F 231 733-1904
Norton Shores *(G-11742)*
Busscher Septic Tank Service G 616 392-9653
Holland *(G-7582)*
Carlesimo Products Inc E 248 474-0415
Farmington Hills *(G-4957)*
Central Michigan Crematory E 269 963-1554
Battle Creek *(G-1165)*
Cheboygan Cement Products Inc G 989 742-4107
Hillman *(G-7508)*
Cheboygan Cement Products Inc E 231 627-5631
Cheboygan *(G-2677)*
Christy Vault Company Inc G 415 994-1378
Grand Rapids *(G-6276)*
Clancy Excavating Co G 586 294-2900
Roseville *(G-13781)*
Co-Pipe Products Inc E 734 287-1000
Taylor *(G-15702)*
Concrete Manufacturing Inc G 586 777-3320
Roseville *(G-13785)*
Concrete Pipe Northern G 616 608-6025
Wyoming *(G-17992)*
Concrete Step Co G 810 789-3061
Flint *(G-5402)*
Consumers Concrete Corp E 616 243-3651
Wyoming *(G-17993)*
Consumers Concrete Corporation F 517 784-9108
Jackson *(G-8419)*
Cosella Dorken Products Inc G 888 433-5824
Rochester *(G-13317)*
Cremation Service of Michigan G 586 465-1700
Clinton Township *(G-3093)*
Darby Ready Mix Concrete Co E 517 547-7004
Addison *(G-36)*
Daves Concrete Products Inc F 269 624-4100
Lawton *(G-9511)*
Deforest & Bloom Septic Tanks G 231 544-3599
Central Lake *(G-2590)*
Detroit Recycled Concrete Co G 248 553-0600
Novi *(G-11865)*
Detroit Wilbert Cremation Serv G 248 853-0559
Rochester Hills *(G-13408)*
Dlh World LLC G 313 915-0274
Detroit *(G-4013)*
E & M Cores Inc G 989 386-9223
Clare *(G-2869)*
Ej Ardmore Inc C 231 536-2261
East Jordan *(G-4630)*
Elastizell Corporation America G 734 426-6076
Dexter *(G-4490)*
Eppert Concrete Products Inc G 248 647-1800
Southfield *(G-14900)*
Espinoza Bros G 313 468-7775
Detroit *(G-4041)*
Everlast Concrete Tech LLC G 248 894-1900
Farmington Hills *(G-4994)*
Felicity Fountains G 517 663-1324
Eaton Rapids *(G-4723)*
Fendt Builders Supply Inc E 248 474-3211
Farmington Hills *(G-4999)*
Fenton Corporation G 810 629-2858
Fenton *(G-5209)*
Fenton Memorials & Vaults Inc F 810 629-2858
Fenton *(G-5210)*
Forbes Sanitation & Excavation F 231 723-2311
Manistee *(G-10422)*
Fraco Products Ltd G 248 667-9260
Troy *(G-16374)*
Franke Salisbury Virginia G 231 775-7014
Cadillac *(G-2248)*
Gambles Redi-Mix Inc F 989 539-6460
Harrison *(G-7312)*
Gibbs Precast Co Inc G 517 768-9100
Jackson *(G-8457)*
Gibraltar National Corporation F 248 634-8257
Holly *(G-7881)*
Grand Rpids Wilbert Burial Vlt E 616 453-9429
Grand Rapids *(G-6469)*
Great Lakes Precast Systems G 616 784-5900
Comstock Park *(G-3484)*
High Grade Materials Company E 616 754-5545
Greenville *(G-7138)*
Holcim (us) Inc C 734 529-4600
Dundee *(G-4588)*
Imlay City Concrete Inc F 810 724-3905
Imlay City *(G-8203)*
Interntnal Prcast Slutions LLC D 313 843-0073
River Rouge *(G-13278)*
Iron City Enterprises Inc G 906 863-2630
Menominee *(G-10739)*
Jarvis Concrete Products Inc G 269 463-3000
Watervliet *(G-17393)*
Jordan Valley Concrete Service F 231 536-7701
East Jordan *(G-4637)*
K-Mar Structures LLC F 231 924-3895
Fremont *(G-5777)*
Kelder LLC G 231 757-3000
Scottville *(G-14509)*
▲ Kerkstra Precast Inc C 616 457-4920
Grandville *(G-7054)*
Kurtz Gravel Company Inc E 810 787-6543
Farmington Hills *(G-5040)*
Lafarge North America Inc F 703 480-3600
Dundee *(G-4591)*
Lake Orion Concrete Orna Pdts G 248 693-8683
Lake Orion *(G-9144)*
Lakeshore Cement Products G 989 739-9341
Oscoda *(G-12213)*
Leelanau Redi-Mix Inc E 231 228-5005
Maple City *(G-10462)*
Lenox Cement Products Inc G 586 727-1488
Lenox *(G-9521)*
Lenox Inc G 586 727-1488
Lenox *(G-9522)*
Liberty Transit Mix LLC G 586 254-2212
Shelby Township *(G-14627)*
M 37 Concrete Products Inc G 231 689-1785
White Cloud *(G-17626)*
Mack Industries Michigan Inc C 248 620-7400
White Lake *(G-17634)*
Marquette Castings LLC G 248 798-8035
Royal Oak *(G-13947)*
Martin Structural Consult G 810 633-9111
Applegate *(G-712)*
Maxs Concrete Inc G 231 972-7558
Mecosta *(G-10690)*
Mbcd Inc E 517 484-4426
Lansing *(G-9395)*
McCann G 734 429-2781
Caledonia *(G-2308)*
MEGA Precast Inc F 586 477-5959
Shelby Township *(G-14637)*
Metro Cast Corporation G 734 728-0210
Westland *(G-17579)*
Milan Burial Vault Inc F 734 439-1538
Milan *(G-10946)*
National Block Company E 734 721-4050
Westland *(G-17582)*
National Concrete Products Co E 734 453-8448
Plymouth *(G-12698)*
Nears Inc G 989 756-2203
Whittemore *(G-17709)*
Newberry Redi-Mix Inc G 906 293-5178
Newberry *(G-11584)*
Northern Concrete Pipe Inc D 517 645-2777
Charlotte *(G-2662)*
Northern Concrete Pipe Inc E 989 892-3545
Bay City *(G-1338)*
Northfield Block Company G 989 777-2575
Bridgeport *(G-1854)*
Nucon Schokbeton C 269 381-1550
Kalamazoo *(G-8836)*
▲ Oaks Concrete Products Inc F 248 684-5004
Wixom *(G-17872)*
Paschal Burial Vault Svc LLC G 517 448-8868
Hudson *(G-8138)*
Paul Murphy Plastics Co E 586 774-4880
Roseville *(G-13851)*
Pearson Precast Concrete Pdts G 517 486-4060
Blissfield *(G-1722)*
Peninsula Products Inc G 906 296-9801
Lake Linden *(G-9109)*
Perfected Grave Vault Co G 616 243-3375
Grand Rapids *(G-6748)*
Polycem LLC E 231 799-1040
Norton Shores *(G-11813)*
Port Huron Building Supply Co F 810 987-2666
Port Huron *(G-12958)*
Premier Fireplace Co LLC G 586 949-4315
Macomb *(G-10156)*
Quality Precast Inc E 269 342-0539
Kalamazoo *(G-8866)*
Quality Way Products LLC F 248 634-2401
Holly *(G-7891)*
Quikrete Companies Inc E 616 784-5790
Walker *(G-16878)*
Royal Stone LLC E 248 343-6232
Williamston *(G-17739)*
Rudy Goupille & Sons Inc G 906 475-9816
Negaunee *(G-11476)*
Ruth Drain Tile Inc G 989 864-3406
Ruth *(G-13989)*
Sandusky Concrete & Supply G 810 648-2627
Sandusky *(G-14442)*
Sanglo International Inc G 248 894-1900
Oak Park *(G-12098)*
Sanilac Drain and Tile Co G 810 648-4100
Sandusky *(G-14443)*
Signature Cnstr Svcs LLC G 616 451-0549
Comstock Park *(G-3516)*
Simmons Gravel Co G 616 754-7073
Greenville *(G-7153)*
Smith Concrete Products G 989 875-4687
North Star *(G-11667)*
Stress Con Industries Inc B 269 381-1550
Kalamazoo *(G-8899)*
Superior Monuments Co G 231 728-2211
Muskegon *(G-11433)*
Superior Vault Co G 989 643-4200
Merrill *(G-10762)*
Surface Mausoleum Company Inc G 989 864-3460
Minden City *(G-11001)*
Ted Voss & Sons Inc G 616 396-8344
Holland *(G-7825)*
Terrys Precast Products Inc G 616 396-7042
Holland *(G-7828)*
▼ Total Security Solutions Inc E 517 223-7807
Fowlerville *(G-5580)*
Unit Step Company Inc G 989 684-9361
Bay City *(G-1366)*

Employee Codes: A=Over 500 employees, B=251-500
C=101-250, D=51-100, E=20-50, F=10-19, G=3-9

2020 Harris Michigan
Industrial Directory

765

Upper Peninsula Con Pipe Co ....F 906 786-0934
Escanaba ***(G-4863)***

Van Sloten Enterprises Inc ....F 906 635-5151
Sault Sainte Marie ***(G-14477)***

W L Snow Enterprises Inc ....G 989 732-9501
Gaylord ***(G-5899)***

White Lake Excavating Inc ....F 231 894-6918
Whitehall ***(G-17681)***

Wilbert Burial Vault Company ....G 231 773-6631
Muskegon ***(G-11449)***

Wilbert Burial Vault Company ....G 231 773-6631
Muskegon ***(G-11450)***

Wilbert Burial Vault Works ....G 906 786-0261
Kingsford ***(G-9068)***

Wilbert Saginaw Vault Corp ....G 989 753-3065
Saginaw ***(G-14183)***

Willbee Concrete Products Co ....F 517 782-8246
Jackson ***(G-8607)***

Wolverine Concrete Products ....G 313 931-7189
Detroit ***(G-4445)***

3273 Ready-Mixed Concrete

Aggregate Industries - Mwr Inc ....E 734 529-5876
Dundee ***(G-4574)***

Aggregate Industries - Mwr Inc ....E 269 321-3800
Kalamazoo ***(G-8673)***

Aggregate Industries - Mwr Inc ....E 269 685-5937
Plainwell ***(G-12517)***

Aggregate Industries - Mwr Inc ....G 734 475-2531
Grass Lake ***(G-7083)***

Aggregate Industries Centl Reg ....G 734 475-2531
Grass Lake ***(G-7084)***

Aggregate Industries-Wcr Inc ....G 269 963-7263
Battle Creek ***(G-1143)***

Ajax Paving Industries Inc ....C 248 244-3300
Troy ***(G-16175)***

Alma Concrete Products Company ....G 989 463-5476
Alma ***(G-232)***

American Concrete Products Inc ....G 517 546-2810
Howell ***(G-8013)***

Angelos Crushed Concrete Inc ....G 586 756-1070
Warren ***(G-16934)***

Arquette Concrete & Supply ....G 989 846-4131
Standish ***(G-15216)***

Associated Constructors LLC ....D 906 226-6505
Negaunee ***(G-11467)***

Baraga County Concrete Company ....G 906 353-6595
Baraga ***(G-1097)***

Bardon Inc ....E 734 529-5876
Dundee ***(G-4576)***

Beck Mobile Concrete LLC ....G 517 655-4996
Williamston ***(G-17726)***

Becker & Scrivens Con Pdts Inc ....E 517 437-4250
Hillsdale ***(G-7517)***

Beckman Brothers Inc ....E 231 861-2031
Shelby ***(G-14523)***

Beechbed Mix ....G 616 263-7422
Holland ***(G-7565)***

Best Concrete & Supply Inc ....G 734 283-7055
Brownstown ***(G-2059)***

Bichler Gravel & Concrete Co ....F 906 786-0343
Escanaba ***(G-4818)***

Bigos Precast ....G 517 223-5000
Fowlerville ***(G-5561)***

Bischer Ready-Mix Inc ....G 989 479-3267
Ruth ***(G-13987)***

Bogen Concrete Inc ....G 269 651-6751
Sturgis ***(G-15598)***

Bonsal American Inc ....F 734 753-4413
New Boston ***(G-11497)***

Bos Concrete Inc ....F 269 468-7267
Coloma ***(G-3354)***

Bozzer Brothers Inc ....G 989 732-9684
Gaylord ***(G-5851)***

Branch West Concrete Products ....F 989 345-0794
West Branch ***(G-17507)***

Brewers City Dock Inc ....E 616 396-6563
Holland ***(G-7578)***

Bwb LLC ....D 231 439-9200
Farmington Hills ***(G-4950)***

C F Long & Sons Inc ....F 248 624-1562
Walled Lake ***(G-16892)***

Carrollton Concrete Mix Inc ....G 989 753-7737
Saginaw ***(G-14011)***

Carrollton Paving Co ....F 989 752-7139
Saginaw ***(G-14012)***

Cemex Cement Inc ....C 231 547-9971
Charlevoix ***(G-2610)***

Central Concrete Products Inc ....F 810 659-7488
Flushing ***(G-5532)***

Cheboygan Cement Products Inc ....E 231 627-5631
Cheboygan ***(G-2677)***

Cheboygan Cement Products Inc ....G 989 742-4107
Hillman ***(G-7508)***

Coit Avenue Gravel Co Inc ....E 616 363-7777
Grand Rapids ***(G-6287)***

Concrete To Go ....G 734 455-3531
Plymouth ***(G-12600)***

Consumers Concrete Corp ....E 269 384-0977
Kalamazoo ***(G-8714)***

Consumers Concrete Corporation ....E 269 342-0136
Kalamazoo ***(G-8715)***

Consumers Concrete Corporation ....G 800 643-4235
Plainwell ***(G-12520)***

Consumers Concrete Corporation ....F 231 777-3981
Muskegon ***(G-11300)***

Consumers Concrete Corporation ....F 231 924-6131
Fremont ***(G-5768)***

Consumers Concrete Corporation ....G 616 827-0063
Byron Center ***(G-2182)***

Consumers Concrete Corporation ....F 269 342-5983
Kalamazoo ***(G-8716)***

Consumers Concrete Corporation ....G 616 392-6190
Holland ***(G-7598)***

Consumers Concrete Corporation ....G 269 684-8760
Niles ***(G-11601)***

Consumers Concrete Corporation ....F 231 894-2705
Whitehall ***(G-17664)***

Consumers Concrete Corporation ....F 517 784-9108
Jackson ***(G-8419)***

Cornillie Acquisitions LLC ....F 231 946-5600
Cadillac ***(G-2242)***

Cornillie Acquisitions LLC ....G 231 946-5600
Bear Lake ***(G-1377)***

Cornillie Concrete ....E 231 439-9200
Harbor Springs ***(G-7279)***

Crete Dry-Mix & Supply Co ....F 616 784-5790
Comstock Park ***(G-3473)***

Darby Ready Mix Concrete Co ....E 517 547-7004
Addison ***(G-36)***

Darby Ready Mix-Dundee LLC ....F 734 529-7100
Dundee ***(G-4578)***

Daves Concrete Products Inc ....F 269 624-4100
Lawton ***(G-9511)***

Dekes Concrete Inc ....E 810 686-5570
Clarkston ***(G-2916)***

Detroit Ready Mix Concrete ....F 313 931-7043
Detroit ***(G-3998)***

Dewent Redi-Mix LLC ....G 616 457-2100
Jenison ***(G-8623)***

Doan Construction Co ....F 734 971-4678
Ypsilanti ***(G-18067)***

Downriver Crushed Concrete ....G 734 283-1833
Taylor ***(G-15708)***

Drayton Iron & Metal Inc ....F 248 673-1269
Waterford ***(G-17339)***

E A Wood Inc ....F 989 739-9118
Oscoda ***(G-12208)***

Edw C Levy Co ....F 248 334-4302
Auburn Hills ***(G-851)***

Edw C Levy Co ....D 313 843-7200
Detroit ***(G-4028)***

Edward E Yates ....G 517 467-4961
Onsted ***(G-12152)***

Elmers Crane and Dozer Inc ....C 231 943-3443
Traverse City ***(G-15962)***

Fenton Concrete Inc ....G 810 629-0783
Fenton ***(G-5208)***

Ferguson Block Co Inc ....F 810 653-2812
Davison ***(G-3647)***

Fisher Redi Mix Concrete ....F 989 723-1622
Owosso ***(G-12291)***

Fisher Sand and Gravel Company ....E 989 835-7187
Midland ***(G-10861)***

Fraco ....F 906 249-1476
Marquette ***(G-10532)***

Gale Briggs Inc ....G 517 543-1320
Charlotte ***(G-2651)***

Gambles Redi-Mix Inc ....F 989 539-6460
Harrison ***(G-7312)***

Gene Brow & Sons Inc ....F 906 635-0859
Sault Sainte Marie ***(G-14464)***

Gildners Concrete ....G 989 356-5156
Alpena ***(G-292)***

Gotts Transit Mix Inc ....E 734 439-1528
Milan ***(G-10939)***

Grand Rapids Gravel Company ....F 616 538-9000
Grand Rapids ***(G-6454)***

Grand Rapids Gravel Company ....G 616 538-9000
Grandville ***(G-7038)***

Grand Rapids Gravel Company ....F 616 538-9000
Belmont ***(G-1462)***

Grand Rapids Gravel Company ....E 616 538-9000
Holland ***(G-7648)***

Grand Rapids Gravel Company ....E 231 777-2777
Muskegon ***(G-11332)***

Great Lakes Sand & Gravel LLC ....G 616 374-3169
Lake Odessa ***(G-9115)***

Guidobono Concrete Inc ....F 810 229-2666
Brighton ***(G-1935)***

Hamilton Block & Ready Mix Co ....F 269 751-5129
Hamilton ***(G-7232)***

Hardcrete Inc ....G 989 644-5543
Weidman ***(G-17457)***

Hart Concrete LLC ....G 231 873-2183
Spring Lake ***(G-15150)***

High Grade Materials Company ....E 616 554-8828
Caledonia ***(G-2299)***

High Grade Materials Company ....E 616 754-5545
Greenville ***(G-7138)***

High Grade Materials Company ....F 269 926-6900
Benton Harbor ***(G-1510)***

High Grade Materials Company ....F 269 349-8222
Kalamazoo ***(G-8769)***

High Grade Materials Company ....F 616 677-1271
Grand Rapids ***(G-6510)***

High Grade Materials Company ....F 517 374-1029
Lansing ***(G-9235)***

High Grade Materials Company ....G 989 584-6004
Carson City ***(G-2491)***

High Grade Materials Company ....F 989 365-3010
Six Lakes ***(G-14740)***

High Grade Materials Company ....E 616 696-9540
Sand Lake ***(G-14423)***

Huizenga & Sons Inc ....E 616 772-6241
Zeeland ***(G-18155)***

Hunderman & Sons Redi-Mix Inc ....G 616 453-5999
Walker ***(G-16868)***

Imlay City Concrete Inc ....F 810 724-3905
Imlay City ***(G-8203)***

Ironwood Ready Mix & Trucking ....G 906 932-4531
Ironwood ***(G-8331)***

Ishpeming Concrete Corporation ....G 906 485-5851
Ishpeming ***(G-8347)***

Jordan Valley Concrete Service ....F 231 536-7701
East Jordan ***(G-4637)***

Kens Redi Mix Inc ....F 810 687-6000
Clio ***(G-3273)***

Kens Redi Mix Inc ....G 810 238-4931
Goodrich ***(G-5955)***

Koenig Fuel & Supply Co ....G 313 368-1870
Wayne ***(G-17433)***

Kuhlman Concrete Inc ....G 517 265-2722
Adrian ***(G-74)***

Kuhlman Corporation ....G 734 241-8692
Monroe ***(G-11045)***

Kurtz Gravel Company Inc ....E 810 787-6543
Farmington Hills ***(G-5040)***

▲ L & S Transit Mix Concrete Co ....F 989 354-5363
Alpena ***(G-294)***

Lafarge North America Inc ....G 269 983-6333
Saint Joseph ***(G-14322)***

Lafarge North America Inc ....F 703 480-3600
Dundee ***(G-4591)***

Lafarge North America Inc ....G 231 726-3291
Muskegon ***(G-11362)***

Lafarge North America Inc ....G 313 842-9258
Detroit ***(G-4191)***

Lakeside Building Products ....G 248 349-3500
Detroit ***(G-4192)***

Land Star Inc ....G 313 834-2366
Detroit ***(G-4193)***

Lattimore Material ....G 972 837-2462
Dundee ***(G-4593)***

Lc Materials ....G 231 796-8685
Big Rapids ***(G-1638)***

Lc Materials ....G 989 422-4202
Houghton Lake ***(G-7995)***

Lc Materials ....G 231 825-2473
Cadillac ***(G-2260)***

Lc Materials ....G 231 775-9301
Cadillac ***(G-2261)***

Lc Materials ....F 231 258-8633
Kalkaska ***(G-8948)***

Lc Materials ....G 231 832-5460
Reed City ***(G-13219)***

Lc Materials ....G 989 344-0235
Grayling ***(G-7110)***

Leelanau Redi-Mix Inc ....E 231 228-5005
Maple City ***(G-10462)***

- **Lees Ready Mix Inc** ... G ... 989 734-7666 — Rogers City *(G-13616)*
- **Lewiston Concrete Inc** ... G ... 989 786-3722 — Lewiston *(G-9551)*
- **Little Bay Concrete Products** ... G ... 906 428-9859 — Gladstone *(G-5915)*
- **Livingston County Concrete Inc** ... F ... 810 632-3030 — Brighton *(G-1951)*
- **M 37 Concrete Products Inc** ... E ... 231 733-8247 — Muskegon *(G-11371)*
- **M 37 Concrete Products Inc** ... G ... 231 689-1785 — White Cloud *(G-17626)*
- **Manistique Rentals Inc** ... G ... 906 341-6955 — Manistique *(G-10443)*
- **Manthei Development Corp** ... G ... 231 347-6282 — Petoskey *(G-12457)*
- **Massive Mineral Mix LLC** ... G ... 517 857-4544 — Springport *(G-15212)*
- **Maxs Concrete Inc** ... G ... 231 972-7558 — Mecosta *(G-10690)*
- **McCoig Materials LLC** ... E ... 734 414-6179 — Plymouth *(G-12688)*
- **Meredith Lea Sand Gravel** ... G ... 517 930-3662 — Charlotte *(G-2659)*
- **Messina Concrete Inc** ... E ... 734 783-1020 — Flat Rock *(G-5357)*
- **Midway Group LLC** ... E ... 586 264-5380 — Sterling Heights *(G-15423)*
- **Milford Redi-Mix Company** ... E ... 248 684-1465 — Milford *(G-10971)*
- **Miller Sand & Gravel Company** ... G ... 269 672-5601 — Hopkins *(G-7959)*
- **Millers Redi-Mix Inc** ... F ... 989 587-6511 — Fowler *(G-5554)*
- **Mini-Mix Inc** ... E ... 586 792-2260 — Clinton Township *(G-3178)*
- **Mirkwood Properties Inc** ... G ... 586 727-3363 — Richmond *(G-13266)*
- **Mix Factory One LLC** ... G ... 248 799-9390 — Southfield *(G-14984)*
- **Mix Masters Inc** ... G ... 616 490-8520 — Byron Center *(G-2203)*
- **Mix Street** ... G ... 616 241-6550 — Grand Rapids *(G-6692)*
- **Mobile Mix** ... G ... 734 497-3256 — Monroe *(G-11053)*
- **Modern Industries Inc** ... E ... 810 767-3330 — Flint *(G-5469)*
- **Morse Concrete & Excavating** ... F ... 989 826-3975 — Mio *(G-11006)*
- **Mottes Materials Inc** ... E ... 906 265-9955 — Iron River *(G-8316)*
- **National Block Company** ... E ... 734 721-4050 — Westland *(G-17582)*
- **New Buffalo Concrete Products** ... B ... 269 469-2515 — New Buffalo *(G-11516)*
- **New Mix 96** ... G ... 231 941-0963 — Traverse City *(G-16048)*
- **Newberry Redi-Mix Inc** ... G ... 906 293-5178 — Newberry *(G-11584)*
- **Northfork Readi Mix Inc** ... G ... 906 341-3445 — Manistique *(G-10444)*
- **Novi Crushed Concrete LLC** ... G ... 248 305-6020 — Novi *(G-11957)*
- **Osborne Concrete Co** ... G ... 734 941-3008 — Romulus *(G-13717)*
- **Owosso Ready Mix Co** ... G ... 989 723-1295 — Owosso *(G-12310)*
- **P D P LLC** ... F ... 616 437-9618 — Wyoming *(G-18025)*
- **Paragon Ready Mix Inc** ... E ... 586 731-8000 — Shelby Township *(G-14659)*
- **Peterman Mobile Concrete Inc** ... E ... 269 324-1211 — Portage *(G-13022)*
- **Piedmont Concrete Inc** ... F ... 248 474-7740 — Farmington Hills *(G-5093)*
- **Port Huron Building Supply Co** ... F ... 810 987-2666 — Port Huron *(G-12958)*
- **Quarrystone Inc** ... E ... 906 786-0343 — Escanaba *(G-4854)*
- **R & C Redi-Mix Inc** ... G ... 616 636-5650 — Sand Lake *(G-14425)*
- **R & R Ready-Mix Inc** ... G ... 810 686-5570 — Clio *(G-3280)*
- **R & R Ready-Mix Inc** ... F ... 989 753-3862 — Saginaw *(G-14127)*
- **R & R Ready-Mix Inc** ... G ... 989 892-9313 — Bay City *(G-1346)*
- **Readysetmail** ... G ... 810 982-1924 — Saint Clair *(G-14232)*
- **Riverside Block Co Inc** ... G ... 989 865-9951 — Saint Charles *(G-14200)*
- **Rock Redi-Mix Inc** ... G ... 989 752-0795 — Carrollton *(G-2486)*
- **Roger Mix Storage** ... G ... 231 352-9762 — Frankfort *(G-5605)*
- **Rudy Goupille & Sons Inc** ... G ... 906 475-9816 — Negaunee *(G-11476)*
- **Ruppe Manufacturing Company** ... E ... 906 932-3540 — Ironwood *(G-8339)*
- **Ruth Drain Tile Inc** ... G ... 989 864-3406 — Ruth *(G-13989)*
- ◆ **Saginaw Rock Products Co** ... E ... 989 754-6589 — Saginaw *(G-14144)*
- **Scheels Concrete Inc** ... G ... 734 782-1464 — Livonia *(G-9922)*
- **Sebewaing Concrete Pdts Inc** ... F ... 989 883-3860 — Sebewaing *(G-14518)*
- **Shafer Bros Inc** ... G ... 517 629-4800 — Albion *(G-130)*
- **Shafer Redi-Mix Inc** ... D ... 517 629-4800 — Albion *(G-131)*
- **Shafer Redi-Mix Inc** ... D ... 517 764-0517 — Jackson *(G-8572)*
- **St Marys Cement Inc (us)** ... G ... 616 846-8553 — Ferrysburg *(G-5338)*
- **Stevenson Building and Sup Co** ... G ... 734 856-3931 — Lambertville *(G-9185)*
- **Summertime Concrete Inc** ... G ... 517 641-6966 — Bath *(G-1136)*
- **Superior Materials LLC** ... E ... 248 788-8000 — Farmington Hills *(G-5136)*
- **Superior Materials LLC** ... C ... 734 941-2479 — Romulus *(G-13735)*
- **Superior Materials Inc** ... F ... 888 988-4400 — Detroit *(G-4387)*
- **Superior Materials Inc** ... E ... 248 788-8000 — Farmington Hills *(G-5137)*
- **Superior Mtls Holdings LLC** ... G ... 248 788-8000 — Farmington Hills *(G-5138)*
- **Swansons Excavating Inc** ... G ... 989 873-4419 — Prescott *(G-13081)*
- **Swartzmiller Lumber Company** ... G ... 989 845-6625 — Chesaning *(G-2728)*
- **Theut Concrete Products Inc** ... F ... 810 679-3376 — Croswell *(G-3604)*
- **Theut Products Inc** ... F ... 810 765-9321 — Marine City *(G-10484)*
- **Theut Products Inc** ... E ... 586 949-1300 — Chesterfield *(G-2847)*
- **Tuckey Concrete Products** ... G ... 989 872-4779 — Cass City *(G-2523)*
- **Van Horn Bros Inc** ... E ... 248 623-4830 — Waterford *(G-17382)*
- **Van Horn Bros Inc** ... E ... 248 623-6000 — Waterford *(G-17383)*
- **Van Sloten Enterprises Inc** ... F ... 906 635-5151 — Sault Sainte Marie *(G-14477)*
- **Vhb-123 Corporation** ... G ... 248 623-4830 — Waterford *(G-17384)*
- **Vollmer Ready-Mix Inc** ... G ... 989 453-2262 — Pigeon *(G-12494)*
- **Voorheis Hausbeck Excavating** ... F ... 989 752-9666 — Reese *(G-13235)*
- **Waanders Concrete Co** ... E ... 269 673-6352 — Allegan *(G-190)*
- **Westendorff Transit Mix** ... G ... 989 593-2488 — Pewamo *(G-12480)*
- **Whats Your Mix Menchies LLC** ... G ... 248 840-1668 — Shelby Township *(G-14722)*
- **Willbee Transit-Mix Co Inc** ... E ... 517 782-9493 — Jackson *(G-8608)*
- **Williams Reddi Mix Inc** ... G ... 906 875-6952 — Crystal Falls *(G-3615)*
- **Williams Redi Mix** ... G ... 906 875-6839 — Crystal Falls *(G-3616)*

3275 Gypsum Prdts

- **New Ngc Inc** ... E ... 989 756-2741 — National City *(G-11464)*
- **United States Gypsum Company** ... C ... 269 384-6335 — Otsego *(G-12257)*
- **United States Gypsum Company** ... F ... 313 624-4232 — River Rouge *(G-13282)*
- **United States Gypsum Company** ... C ... 313 842-4455 — Detroit *(G-4415)*
- **US Gypsum Co** ... G ... 313 842-5800 — River Rouge *(G-13283)*

3281 Cut Stone Prdts

- **A E G M Inc** ... G ... 313 304-5279 — Dearborn *(G-3670)*
- **Ardo Granite LLC** ... F ... 517 253-7139 — Lansing *(G-9204)*
- **Atlas Tile & Stone LLC** ... G ... 586 264-7720 — Warren *(G-16945)*
- ▲ **Booms Stone Company** ... D ... 313 531-3000 — Redford *(G-13150)*
- ▲ **Botsg Inc** ... D ... 231 929-2121 — Traverse City *(G-15918)*
- **Cig Jan Products Ltd** ... F ... 616 698-9070 — Caledonia *(G-2294)*
- **Classic Stone Creations Inc** ... G ... 269 637-9497 — South Haven *(G-14756)*
- **Classic Stone MBL & Gran Inc** ... G ... 248 588-1599 — Troy *(G-16269)*
- **Dura Sill Corporation** ... G ... 248 348-2490 — Novi *(G-11873)*
- **Ecogranite LLC** ... G ... 248 820-9196 — Livonia *(G-9721)*
- **Eternal Image Inc** ... G ... 248 932-3333 — Farmington Hills *(G-4990)*
- **Farnese North America Inc** ... G ... 616 844-8651 — Grand Rapids *(G-6398)*
- ▲ **Genesee Cut Stone & Marble Co** ... E ... 810 743-1800 — Flint *(G-5437)*
- ▲ **Gmr Stone Products LLC** ... F ... 586 739-2700 — Sterling Heights *(G-15363)*
- **Grand River Granite Inc** ... G ... 616 399-9324 — Holland *(G-7649)*
- **Granite City Inc** ... F ... 248 478-0033 — Livonia *(G-9756)*
- **K2 Stoneworks LLC** ... G ... 989 790-3250 — Saginaw *(G-14068)*
- **Korcast Products Incorporated** ... G ... 248 740-2340 — Troy *(G-16449)*
- **Lakeshore Marble Company Inc** ... E ... 269 429-8241 — Stevensville *(G-15574)*
- **Landscape Stone Supply Inc** ... G ... 616 953-2028 — Holland *(G-7719)*
- **Leonardos Marble & Granite** ... F ... 248 468-2900 — Wixom *(G-17845)*
- **Lewiston Sand & Gravel Inc** ... G ... 989 786-2742 — Lewiston *(G-9552)*
- **Marbelite Corp** ... E ... 248 348-1900 — Novi *(G-11934)*
- **Marble Deluxe A C** ... G ... 248 668-8200 — Commerce Township *(G-3427)*
- **Marble ERA Products Inc** ... E ... 989 742-4513 — Gaylord *(G-5876)*
- **Marblecast of Michigan Inc** ... F ... 248 398-0600 — Oak Park *(G-12081)*
- **Mellemas Cut Stone** ... G ... 616 984-2493 — Sand Lake *(G-14424)*
- ▲ **Michigan Tile and Marble Co** ... E ... 313 931-1700 — Detroit *(G-4244)*
- **Mis Controls Inc** ... F ... 586 339-3900 — Rochester Hills *(G-13475)*
- **Moderne Slate Inc** ... G ... 231 584-3499 — Mancelona *(G-10397)*
- **Muskegon Monument & Stone Co** ... G ... 231 722-2730 — Muskegon *(G-11390)*
- **Parker Property Dev Inc** ... F ... 616 842-6118 — Grand Haven *(G-6060)*
- **Patten Monument Company** ... D ... 616 785-4141 — Comstock Park *(G-3506)*
- **Pearson Precast Concrete Pdts** ... G ... 517 486-4060 — Blissfield *(G-1722)*
- **Quarry Ridge Stone Inc** ... F ... 616 827-8244 — Byron Center *(G-2210)*
- **Rockwood Quarry LLC** ... C ... 734 783-7415 — South Rockwood *(G-14822)*
- **Rockwood Quarry LLC** ... G ... 734 783-7400 — Newport *(G-11590)*
- **Royal Stone LLC** ... E ... 248 343-6232 — Williamston *(G-17739)*
- **Solutions In Stone Inc** ... G ... 734 453-4444 — Plymouth *(G-12758)*
- **Steinbrecher Stone Corp** ... G ... 906 563-5852 — Norway *(G-11820)*
- **Stone Shop Inc** ... F ... 248 852-4700 — Port Huron *(G-12969)*
- ▲ **Stone Specialists Inc** ... F ... 810 744-2278 — Burton *(G-2167)*
- **Stonecrafters Inc** ... F ... 517 529-4990 — Clarklake *(G-2901)*
- **Superior Monuments Co** ... G ... 616 844-1700 — Grand Haven *(G-6087)*

S I C

32 STONE, CLAY, GLASS, AND CONCRETE PRODUCTS

Superior Monuments Co ....G....... 231 728-2211
  Muskegon (G-11433)
▲ Tile Craft Inc ....F....... 231 929-7207
  Traverse City (G-16124)
TNT Marble and Stone Inc ....G....... 248 887-8237
  Hartland (G-7394)
▲ Unilock Michigan Inc ....E....... 248 437-1380
  Brighton (G-2003)
Usm Acquisition LLC ....D....... 989 561-2293
  Remus (G-13243)
Yellowstone Products Inc ....G....... 616 299-7855
  Comstock Park (G-3522)
Zimmer Marble Co Inc ....F....... 517 787-1500
  Jackson (G-8615)

3291 Abrasive Prdts

3M Company ....E....... 313 372-4200
  Detroit (G-3824)
Abrasive Diamond Tool Company ....E....... 248 588-4800
  Madison Heights (G-10179)
◆ Abrasive Finishing Inc ....G....... 734 433-9236
  Chelsea (G-2698)
▲ Abrasive Materials LLC ....G....... 517 437-4796
  Hillsdale (G-7512)
Acme Holding Company ....E....... 586 759-3332
  Warren (G-16917)
◆ Afi Enterprises Inc ....E....... 734 475-9111
  Chelsea (G-2700)
Auto Quip Inc ....F....... 810 364-3466
  Kimball (G-9042)
Belanger Inc ....E....... 248 349-7010
  Northville (G-11678)
▲ Belanger Abrasives Inc ....D....... 248 735-8900
  Northville (G-11679)
▲ Botsg Inc ....D....... 231 929-2121
  Traverse City (G-15918)
Cdp Diamond Products Inc ....E....... 734 591-1041
  Livonia (G-9678)
▲ Cincinnati Tyrolit Inc ....C....... 513 458-8121
  Shelby Township (G-14562)
▼ Crippen Manufacturing Company ..E....... 989 681-4323
  Saint Louis (G-14361)
D R W Systems ....G....... 989 874-4663
  Filion (G-5346)
Detroit Abrasives Company ....G....... 989 725-2405
  Owosso (G-12289)
▲ Detroit Abrasives Company ....G....... 734 475-1651
  Chelsea (G-2706)
Di-Coat Corporation ....E....... 248 349-1211
  Novi (G-11868)
Diamond Tool Manufacturing Inc ....E....... 734 416-1900
  Plymouth (G-12611)
Diamondback Corp ....E....... 248 960-8260
  Commerce Township (G-3399)
Dianamic Abrasive Products ....F....... 248 280-1185
  Troy (G-16316)
Dryden Steel LLC ....G....... 586 777-7600
  Dryden (G-4569)
▲ Duramic Abrasive Products Inc ...E....... 586 755-7220
  Warren (G-17009)
▲ E C Moore Company ....D....... 313 581-7878
  Dearborn (G-3696)
E S I Industries ....F....... 231 256-9345
  Lake Leelanau (G-9102)
Enkon LLC ....F....... 937 890-5678
  Manchester (G-10405)
Ervin Industries Inc ....E....... 517 265-6118
  Adrian (G-62)
◆ Ervin Industries Inc ....E....... 734 769-4600
  Ann Arbor (G-447)
Ervin Industries Inc ....E....... 517 423-5477
  Tecumseh (G-15792)
▲ Even-Cut Abrasive Company ......D....... 216 881-9595
  Grand Rapids (G-6390)
Ferro Industries Inc ....E....... 586 792-6001
  Harrison Township (G-7330)
▲ Finishing Technologies Inc ....F....... 616 794-4001
  Belding (G-1415)
Formax Manufacturing Corp ....E....... 616 456-5458
  Grand Rapids (G-6416)
▲ GMA Industries Inc ....E....... 734 595-7300
  Romulus (G-13682)
Hammond Machinery Inc ....D....... 269 345-7151
  Kalamazoo (G-8759)
Heartland Steel Products LLC ....E....... 810 364-7421
  Marysville (G-10603)
▼ Helro Corporation ....G....... 248 650-8500
  Rochester (G-13325)
Howell Tool Service Inc ....F....... 517 548-1114
  Howell (G-8052)

▼ IGA Abrasives LLC ....E....... 616 243-5566
  Grand Rapids (G-6526)
▲ Inland Diamond Products Co ......E....... 248 585-1762
  Madison Heights (G-10276)
Internal Grinding Abrasives ....E....... 616 243-5566
  Grand Rapids (G-6540)
◆ International Abrasives Inc ....G....... 586 778-8490
  Roseville (G-13820)
Kalamazoo Company ....E....... 269 345-7151
  Kalamazoo (G-8786)
Kevin S Macaddino ....E....... 248 642-0333
  Birmingham (G-1687)
▲ Krmc LLC ....E....... 734 955-9311
  Romulus (G-13698)
▲ L R Oliver and Company Inc ......E....... 810 765-1000
  Cottrellville (G-3590)
◆ Metaltec Steel Abrasive Co ....E....... 734 459-7900
  Canton (G-2404)
Michigan Carbide Company Inc ......F....... 586 264-8780
  Troy (G-16504)
▲ Midwest Superior Abrasives ....G....... 248 202-0454
  Novi (G-11949)
Nakagawa Special Stl Amer Inc ......E....... 248 449-6050
  Novi (G-11952)
Patch Works Farms Inc ....G....... 989 430-3610
  Wheeler (G-17617)
◆ Roto-Finish Company Inc ....E....... 269 327-7071
  Kalamazoo (G-8875)
Saint-Gobain Delaware Corp ....G....... 734 941-1300
  Romulus (G-13731)
▲ Sam Brown Sales LLC ....E....... 248 358-2626
  Farmington (G-4911)
▲ Sandbox Solutions Inc ....C....... 248 349-7010
  Northville (G-11723)
Schaffner Manufacturing Co ....G....... 248 735-8900
  Northville (G-11724)
Schwab Industries Inc ....C....... 586 566-8090
  Shelby Township (G-14688)
▲ Sidley Diamond Tool Company ....E....... 734 261-7970
  Garden City (G-5841)
Stan Sax Corp ....F....... 248 683-9199
  Detroit (G-4373)
Stewart Reed Inc ....G....... 616 846-2550
  Grand Haven (G-6086)
▲ Superabrasives Inc ....E....... 248 348-7670
  Wixom (G-17901)
Superior Abrasive Products ....E....... 248 969-4090
  Oxford (G-12374)
▼ Trinity Tool Co ....E....... 586 296-5900
  Fraser (G-5741)
United Abrasive Inc ....G....... 906 563-9249
  Vulcan (G-16846)
▲ Vachon Industries Inc ....F....... 517 278-2354
  Coldwater (G-3340)
Van Industries Inc ....E....... 248 398-6990
  Ferndale (G-5329)
Warren Abrasives Inc ....F....... 586 772-0002
  Warren (G-17285)

3292 Asbestos products

Cobalt Friction Technologies ....F....... 734 274-3030
  Ann Arbor (G-402)
K-Value Insulation LLC ....E....... 248 688-5816
  Troy (G-16442)

3295 Minerals & Earths: Ground Or Treated

D J McQuestion & Sons Inc ....F....... 231 768-4403
  Leroy (G-9530)
Edw C Levy Co ....D....... 313 843-7200
  Detroit (G-4028)
▲ Edw C Levy Co ....B....... 313 429-2200
  Dearborn (G-3700)
Fritz Enterprises ....G....... 734 283-7272
  Trenton (G-16154)
Graphite Machining Inc ....E....... 810 678-2227
  Metamora (G-10775)
Imerys Perlite Usa Inc ....F....... 269 649-1352
  Vicksburg (G-16836)
Mersen USA Bay City-MI LLC ....G....... 989 894-2911
  Bay City (G-1330)
Michigan Metals and Mfg Inc ....G....... 248 910-7674
  Southfield (G-14981)
Montcalm Aggregates Inc ....G....... 989 772-7038
  Mount Pleasant (G-11209)
Novaceuticals LLC ....E....... 248 309-3402
  Auburn Hills (G-962)
▲ R J Marshall Company ....F....... 248 353-4100
  Southfield (G-15009)
R J Marshall Company ....E....... 734 848-5325
  Erie (G-4810)

R J Marshall Company ....E....... 734 379-4044
  Rockwood (G-13611)
Runyan Pottery Supply Inc ....G....... 810 687-4500
  Clio (G-3281)
Sgl Technic Inc ....G....... 248 540-9508
  Shelby Township (G-14690)
Tms International LLC ....F....... 734 241-3007
  Monroe (G-11078)

3296 Mineral Wool

Autoneum North America Inc ....D....... 248 848-0100
  Farmington Hills (G-4936)
Certainteed Gypsum Inc ....C....... 906 524-6101
  Lanse (G-9189)
Dgp Inc ....E....... 989 635-7531
  Marlette (G-10495)
▲ Eftec North America LLC ....D....... 248 585-2200
  Taylor (G-15713)
Fiberglass Concepts West Mich ......G....... 616 392-4909
  Holland (G-7630)
HP Pelzer Auto Systems Inc ....E....... 810 987-4444
  Port Huron (G-12926)
Integrated Interiors Inc ....F....... 586 756-4840
  Warren (G-17094)
Knauf Insulation Inc ....E....... 517 630-2000
  Albion (G-127)
Manta Group LLC ....E....... 248 325-8264
  Pontiac (G-12847)
Mbcd Inc ....E....... 517 484-4426
  Lansing (G-9395)
Midwest Fbrglas Fbricators Inc ......F....... 810 765-7445
  Marine City (G-10478)
Owens Corning Sales LLC ....E....... 248 668-7500
  Novi (G-11968)
Ufp Technologies Inc ....D....... 616 949-8100
  Grand Rapids (G-6948)
Unique Fabricating Inc ....E....... 248 853-2333
  Auburn Hills (G-1034)
▲ Unique Fabricating Na Inc ....B....... 248 853-2333
  Auburn Hills (G-1035)

3297 Nonclay Refractories

▲ Ajf Inc ....E....... 734 753-4410
  New Boston (G-11496)
Cerco Inc ....E....... 734 362-8664
  Brownstown Twp (G-2071)
Chase Nedrow Manufacturing Inc ..E....... 248 669-9886
  Wixom (G-17786)
Chemincon Inc ....E....... 734 439-2478
  Milan (G-10933)
Harbisonwalker Intl Inc ....C....... 231 689-6641
  White Cloud (G-17623)
Martin Mretta Magnesia Spc LLC ....E....... 231 723-2577
  Manistee (G-10429)
▲ Midwest Product Spc Inc ....G....... 231 767-9942
  Muskegon (G-11381)
Nedrow Refractories Co ....E....... 248 669-2500
  Wixom (G-17863)
Osmi Inc ....F....... 561 504-3924
  Whitmore Lake (G-17705)
Rex Materials Inc ....E....... 517 223-3787
  Howell (G-8092)
Stellar Materials Intl LLC ....E....... 561 504-3924
  Whitmore Lake (G-17707)
Taylor Controls Inc ....F....... 269 637-8521
  South Haven (G-14777)

3299 Nonmetallic Mineral Prdts, NEC

▲ HC Starck Inc ....E....... 517 279-9511
  Coldwater (G-3309)
Nano Innovations LLC ....G....... 906 231-2101
  Houghton (G-7978)
Neuvokas Corporation ....G....... 906 934-2661
  Ahmeek (G-108)
R L Hume Award Co ....G....... 269 324-3063
  Portage (G-13026)
Spare Time Studios ....G....... 810 653-2337
  Davison (G-3662)
▲ Vico Company ....G....... 734 453-3777
  Plymouth (G-12789)
Wonderland Graphics Inc ....F....... 616 452-0712
  Grand Rapids (G-7002)

33 PRIMARY METAL INDUSTRIES

3312 Blast Furnaces, Coke Ovens, Steel & Rolling Mills

A B C Roll Co ....G....... 586 465-9125
  Mount Clemens (G-11122)

A Raymond Tinnerman Auto Inc ....F 248 537-3147
Rochester Hills *(G-13360)*
ABC Coating Company Inc ....F 616 245-4626
Grand Rapids *(G-6128)*
Accutek Mold & Engineering ....F 586 978-1335
Sterling Heights *(G-15250)*
Acme Tool & Die Co ....G 231 938-1260
Acme *(G-1)*
AK Steel Corporation ....B 313 317-8900
Dearborn *(G-3672)*
AK Steel Corporation ....E 513 425-2707
Troy *(G-16176)*
AK Steel Corporation ....A 800 532-8857
Dearborn *(G-3673)*
Alan Bruce Enterprises ....G 616 262-4609
Byron Center *(G-2175)*
Alloy Resources LLC ....E 231 777-3941
Muskegon *(G-11265)*
American Axle Oxford ....E 248 361-6044
Oxford *(G-12335)*
ARC Mit ....G 248 399-4800
Ferndale *(G-5261)*
Arlington Metals Corporation ....D 269 426-3371
Sawyer *(G-14481)*
Atlantis Tech Corp ....G 989 356-6954
Alpena *(G-277)*
▲ Autocam-Pax Inc ....E 269 782-5186
Dowagiac *(G-4534)*
▲ Aweba Tool & Die Corp ....F 478 296-2002
Hastings *(G-7401)*
▲ Axle of Dearborn Inc ....C 248 543-5995
Ferndale *(G-5263)*
Bar Processing Corporation ....D 734 782-4454
Warren *(G-16952)*
Bazzi Tire & Wheels ....G 313 846-8888
Detroit *(G-3893)*
Bbg North America Ltd Partnr ....F 248 572-6550
Oxford *(G-12339)*
Benteler Automotive Corp ....B 616 247-3936
Auburn Hills *(G-791)*
Benteler Defense Corp ....G 248 377-9999
Auburn Hills *(G-793)*
Bjerke Forgings Inc ....A 313 382-2600
Taylor *(G-15696)*
Blades Enterprises LLC ....F 734 449-4479
Wixom *(G-17775)*
Bnb Welding & Fabrication Inc ....G 810 820-1508
Burton *(G-2145)*
Borneman & Peterson Inc ....F 810 744-1890
Flint *(G-5393)*
Brake Roller Co Inc ....E 269 965-2371
Battle Creek *(G-1157)*
Broaching Industries Inc ....E 586 949-3775
Chesterfield *(G-2748)*
Burnham & Northern Inc ....G 517 279-7501
Coldwater *(G-3292)*
C & M Manufacturing Corp Inc ....E 586 749-3455
Chesterfield *(G-2750)*
C P I Inc ....G 810 664-8686
Lapeer *(G-9448)*
▲ Cannon-Muskegon Corporation ....C 231 755-1681
Norton Shores *(G-11744)*
Carry Manufacturing Inc ....G 989 672-2779
Caro *(G-2467)*
◆ Central Lake Armor Express Inc ....C 231 544-6090
Central Lake *(G-2588)*
Champlain Specialty Metals Inc ....E 269 926-7241
Benton Harbor *(G-1489)*
Chrome Wheel Exchange LLC ....G 810 360-0298
Howell *(G-8024)*
Coach House Iron Inc ....G 616 785-8967
Sparta *(G-15092)*
Creform Corporation ....F 248 926-2555
Novi *(G-11858)*
▲ Crown Steel Rail Co ....G 248 593-7100
West Bloomfield *(G-17471)*
Custom Mold Tool and Die Corp ....G 810 688-3711
North Branch *(G-11658)*
De Luxe Die Set Inc ....G 810 227-2556
Brighton *(G-1910)*
Delaco Steel Corporation ....D 313 491-1200
Dearborn *(G-3692)*
Detroit Steel Group Inc ....G 248 298-2900
Royal Oak *(G-13918)*
Die Cast Press Mfg Co Inc ....E 269 657-6060
Paw Paw *(G-12403)*
Disrupttech LLC ....G 248 225-8383
Saint Clair Shores *(G-14244)*
Dpr Manufacturing & Svcs Inc ....E 586 757-1421
Warren *(G-17006)*
▲ Eaton Steel Corporation ....D 248 398-3434
Oak Park *(G-12064)*
Eaton Steel Corporation ....D 248 398-3434
Livonia *(G-9719)*
Euridium Solutions LLC ....G 248 535-7005
Troy *(G-16353)*
Fab Concepts ....G 586 466-6411
Clinton Township *(G-3111)*
Fabtronic Inc ....E 586 786-6114
Macomb *(G-10121)*
First Place Manufacturing LLC ....G 231 798-1694
Norton Shores *(G-11755)*
Fluid Routing Solutions Inc ....E 231 592-1700
Big Rapids *(G-1628)*
▲ Form G Tech Co ....D 248 583-3610
Troy *(G-16369)*
Frank W Small Met Fabrication ....G 269 422-2001
Baroda *(G-1124)*
Fritz Enterprises ....G 734 283-7272
Trenton *(G-16154)*
Fritz Enterprises Inc ....F 734 283-7272
River Rouge *(G-13277)*
G & G Steel Fabricating Co ....G 586 979-4112
Warren *(G-17048)*
Gale Tool Co Inc ....G 248 437-4610
South Lyon *(G-14792)*
General Motors LLC ....B 810 236-1970
Flint *(G-5436)*
Georgetown Steel LLC ....G 734 568-6148
Ottawa Lake *(G-12264)*
Gerdau Macsteel Inc ....B 517 764-3920
Jackson *(G-8455)*
Gerdau Macsteel Inc ....A 734 243-2446
Monroe *(G-11033)*
Gerdau Macsteel Inc ....B 734 243-2446
Monroe *(G-11034)*
◆ Gerdau Macsteel Inc ....E 517 782-0415
Jackson *(G-8456)*
▲ Gill Corporation ....B 616 453-4491
Grand Rapids *(G-6438)*
Gill Corporation ....C 616 453-4491
Grand Rapids *(G-6439)*
Gladiator Quality Sorting LLC ....G 734 578-1950
Canton *(G-2378)*
Grant Industries Incorporated ....D 586 293-9200
Fraser *(G-5657)*
Greer Industries Inc ....E 800 388-2868
Ferndale *(G-5292)*
Harrison Steel LLC ....G 586 247-1230
Shelby Township *(G-14599)*
▲ Hayes Lemmerz Intl-GA LLC ....C 734 737-5000
Novi *(G-11898)*
▲ Hot Wheels City Inc ....E 248 589-8800
Madison Heights *(G-10268)*
Hydraulic Tubes & Fittings LLC ....E 810 660-8088
Lapeer *(G-9464)*
Industrial Engineering Service ....F 616 794-1330
Belding *(G-1419)*
Industrial Marking Products ....G 517 699-2160
Holt *(G-7913)*
Iron Clad Security Inc ....G 313 837-0390
Detroit *(G-4151)*
Ivan Doverspike ....E 313 579-3000
Detroit *(G-4153)*
JIT Steel Corp ....C 313 491-3212
Dearborn *(G-3728)*
Kena Corporation ....G 586 873-4761
Chesterfield *(G-2795)*
▲ King Steel Corporation ....E 800 638-2530
Grand Blanc *(G-5972)*
Lake Michigan Wire LLC ....F 616 786-9200
Holland *(G-7717)*
▲ Major Industries Ltd ....D 810 985-9372
Port Huron *(G-12938)*
Manistee Wldg & Piping Svc Inc ....G 231 723-2551
Manistee *(G-10428)*
Marjo Plastics Company Inc ....G 734 455-4130
Plymouth *(G-12684)*
Mean Erectors Inc ....E 989 737-3285
Saginaw *(G-14085)*
Meyers Metal Fab Inc ....G 248 620-5411
Clarkston *(G-2937)*
◆ Michigan Rod Products Inc ....D 517 552-9812
Howell *(G-8065)*
Mill Steel Co ....D 616 949-6700
Grand Rapids *(G-6690)*
Mueller Industrial Realty Co ....B 810 987-7770
Port Huron *(G-12947)*
National Galvanizing LP ....A 734 243-1882
Monroe *(G-11059)*
Nelson Manufacturing Inc ....G 810 648-0065
Sandusky *(G-14440)*
Omega Steel Incorporated ....G 616 877-3782
Wayland *(G-17408)*
Paich Railworks Inc ....G 734 397-2424
Van Buren Twp *(G-16778)*
Parton & Preble Inc ....E 586 773-6000
Warren *(G-17180)*
Pat McArdle ....G 989 375-4321
Elkton *(G-4782)*
Pdf Mfg Inc ....G 517 522-8431
Grass Lake *(G-7091)*
Peerless Steel Company ....E 616 530-6695
Grandville *(G-7063)*
Percor Manufacturing Inc ....F 616 554-1668
Wyoming *(G-18026)*
Premium Air Systems Inc ....D 248 680-8800
Troy *(G-16562)*
Prime Wheel Corporation ....G 248 207-4739
Canton *(G-2418)*
▲ Primetals Technologies USA LLC ....G 269 927-3591
Benton Harbor *(G-1539)*
Proservice Machine Ltd ....E 734 317-7266
Erie *(G-4809)*
Quality Cavity Inc ....F 248 344-9995
Wixom *(G-17882)*
Ram Die Corp ....F 616 647-2855
Grand Rapids *(G-6807)*
Refab LLC ....G 616 842-9705
Grand Haven *(G-6070)*
Repair Industries Michigan Inc ....C 313 365-5300
Detroit *(G-4344)*
Resetar Equipment Inc ....G 313 291-0500
Dearborn Heights *(G-3794)*
River Valley Machine Inc ....E 269 673-8070
Allegan *(G-187)*
▼ Rod Chomper Inc ....F 616 392-9677
Holland *(G-7790)*
Rucci Forged Wheels Inc ....G 248 577-3500
Sterling Heights *(G-15481)*
S F R Precision Turning Inc ....G 517 709-3367
Holt *(G-7924)*
Sabre Manufacturing ....G 269 945-4120
Hastings *(G-7425)*
Samuel Son & Co (usa) Inc ....D 414 486-1556
Troy *(G-16592)*
Sandvik Inc ....E 269 926-7241
Benton Harbor *(G-1545)*
Service Iron Works Inc ....E 248 446-9750
South Lyon *(G-14812)*
Set Enterprises Inc ....E 586 573-3600
Sterling Heights *(G-15493)*
Shoreline Recycling & Supply ....E 231 722-6081
Muskegon *(G-11424)*
▲ SL Wheels Inc ....G 734 744-8500
Livonia *(G-9932)*
St Johns Computer Machining ....G 989 224-7664
Saint Johns *(G-14296)*
Stage Stop ....G 989 838-4039
Ithaca *(G-8367)*
Steel 21 LLC ....E 616 884-2121
Cedar Springs *(G-2562)*
◆ Steel Industries Inc ....C 313 535-8505
Redford *(G-13194)*
Steel Mill Components Inc ....F 586 920-2595
Warren *(G-17255)*
Strong Steel Products LLC ....E 313 267-3300
Detroit *(G-4381)*
Sundown Sheet Metal Inc ....G 616 846-7674
Spring Lake *(G-15181)*
Taylor Tooling Group LLC ....E 616 805-3917
Grand Rapids *(G-6917)*
The Pom Group Inc ....F 248 409-7900
Auburn Hills *(G-1018)*
▲ TI Automotive LLC ....C 248 494-5000
Auburn Hills *(G-1020)*
◆ TI Group Auto Systems LLC ....B 248 296-8000
Auburn Hills *(G-1022)*
TI Group Auto Systems LLC ....D 517 437-7462
Hillsdale *(G-7543)*
Timkensteel Corporation ....G 248 994-4422
Novi *(G-12017)*
Tms International LLC ....G 734 241-3007
Monroe *(G-11077)*
Tms International LLC ....G 517 764-5123
Jackson *(G-8590)*
Tms International LLC ....G 313 378-6502
Ecorse *(G-4746)*
United States Steel Corp ....C 313 749-2100
Ecorse *(G-4747)*

S I C

Employee Codes: A=Over 500 employees, B=251-500
C=101-250, D=51-100, E=20-50, F=10-19, G=3-9
2020 Harris Michigan
Industrial Directory
769

Universal Hdlg Eqp Owosso LLC .... E 989 720-1650
Owosso (G-12326)
W A Thomas Company .... G 734 955-6500
Taylor (G-15779)
Welk-Ko Fabricators Inc .... G 248 486-2598
New Hudson (G-11559)
Wiesen EDM Inc .... E 616 794-9870
Belding (G-1433)
WM Tube & Wire Forming Inc .... F 231 830-9393
Muskegon (G-11454)
Woodbridge Group Inc .... G 269 324-8993
Troy (G-16696)
▲ Worthington Steel of Michigan .... E 734 374-3260
Taylor (G-15783)

3313 Electrometallurgical Prdts

Alloying Surfaces Inc .... G 248 524-9200
Troy (G-16191)
◆ Alpha Resources LLC .... E 269 465-5559
Stevensville (G-15553)
▲ Cannon-Muskegon Corporation .... C 231 755-1681
Norton Shores (G-11744)
Kena Corporation .... G 586 873-4761
Chesterfield (G-2795)
▲ Miccus Inc .... F 616 604-4449
Howell (G-8064)

3315 Steel Wire Drawing & Nails & Spikes

▲ AG Manufacturing Inc .... E 989 479-9590
Harbor Beach (G-7263)
Barrette Outdoor Living Inc .... E 810 235-0400
Flint (G-5383)
Benteler Defense Corp .... G 248 377-9999
Auburn Hills (G-793)
Breasco LLC .... G 734 961-9020
Ypsilanti (G-18057)
▲ Dw-National Standard-Niles LLC .... C 269 683-8100
Niles (G-11610)
▲ Elco Enterprises Inc .... E 517 782-8040
Jackson (G-8443)
Ernest Industries Acquisition, ... E 734 595-9500
Westland (G-17554)
Flexpost Inc .... G 616 928-0829
Holland (G-7632)
▲ Hangers Plus LLC .... G 616 997-4264
Coopersville (G-3560)
Jems of Litchfield Inc .... F 517 542-5367
Litchfield (G-9605)
▼ Kendall Microtech Inc .... G 517 565-3802
Stockbridge (G-15589)
Marathon Weld Group LLC .... E 517 782-8040
Jackson (G-8509)
▲ McClure Metals Group Inc .... G 616 957-5955
Grand Rapids (G-6653)
Metter Flooring LLC .... G 517 914-2004
Rives Junction (G-13309)
Morstar Inc .... F 248 605-3291
Livonia (G-9848)
◆ National Nail Corp .... C 616 538-8000
Wyoming (G-18021)
▲ National-Standard LLC .... C 269 683-9902
Niles (G-11630)
Philips Machining Company .... F 616 997-7777
Coopersville (G-3568)
Pro-Soil Site Services Inc .... G 517 267-8767
Lansing (G-9260)
Richfield Industries Inc .... F 810 233-0440
Flint (G-5492)
Stephens Pipe & Steel LLC .... E 616 248-3433
Grand Rapids (G-6892)
◆ Straits Steel and Wire Company .... D 231 843-3416
Ludington (G-10080)
Transportation Tech Group Inc .... E 810 233-0440
Flint (G-5512)
Van Ron Steel Services LLC .... F 616 813-6907
Marne (G-10515)
◆ Ventura Manufacturing Inc .... C 616 772-7405
Zeeland (G-18192)
Wapc Holdings Inc .... F 586 939-0770
Sterling Heights (G-15543)
▲ West Michigan Wire Co .... D 231 845-1281
Ludington (G-10087)
Whisper Creative Products Inc .... G 734 529-2734
Dundee (G-4603)
WM Tube & Wire Forming Inc .... F 231 830-9393
Muskegon (G-11454)

3316 Cold Rolled Steel Sheet, Strip & Bars

Alro Steel Corporation .... E 517 371-9600
Lansing (G-9335)
Bar Processing Corporation .... D 734 782-4454
Warren (G-16952)
BR Safety Products Inc .... G 734 582-4499
Plymouth (G-12589)
Cold Heading Co .... D 586 497-7016
Warren (G-16986)
Diez Group LLC .... D 734 675-1700
Woodhaven (G-17939)
Fabtec Enterprises Inc .... F 616 878-9288
Byron Center (G-2190)
Flat Rock Metal Inc .... C 734 782-4454
Flat Rock (G-5353)
Georgetown Steel LLC .... G 734 568-6148
Ottawa Lake (G-12264)
◆ Gerdau Macsteel Inc .... E 517 782-0415
Jackson (G-8456)
Gerdau Macsteel Inc .... B 517 764-3920
Jackson (G-8455)
Gerdau Macsteel Inc .... B 734 243-2446
Monroe (G-11034)
Grant Industries Incorporated .... D 586 293-9200
Fraser (G-5657)
Greer Industries Inc .... E 800 388-2868
Ferndale (G-5292)
H & L Tool Company Inc .... D 248 585-7474
Madison Heights (G-10263)
Heidtman Steel Products Inc .... D 734 848-2115
Erie (G-4803)
Kena Corporation .... G 586 873-4761
Chesterfield (G-2795)
National Galvanizing LP .... A 734 243-1882
Monroe (G-11059)
◆ Nss Technologies Inc .... E 734 459-9500
Canton (G-2412)
Peerless Steel Company .... E 616 530-6695
Grandville (G-7063)
Samuel Son & Co (usa) Inc .... D 414 486-1556
Troy (G-16592)
Sandvik Inc .... E 269 926-7241
Benton Harbor (G-1545)
Van Emon Bruce .... G 269 467-7803
Centreville (G-2598)
Wolverine Carbide Die Company .... E 248 280-0300
Troy (G-16695)
Worthington Industries Inc .... G 734 397-6187
Canton (G-2444)
▲ Worthington Steel of Michigan .... E 734 374-3260
Taylor (G-15783)

3317 Steel Pipe & Tubes

A & B Tube Benders Inc .... E 586 773-0440
Warren (G-16905)
A S Rivard and Son Well Drlg .... G 231 331-4508
Mancelona (G-10384)
▲ Ace Consulting & MGT Inc .... E 989 821-7040
Roscommon (G-13747)
Advanced Drainage Systems Inc .... D 989 723-5208
Owosso (G-12275)
All Bending & Tubular Pdts LLC .... F 616 333-2364
Grand Rapids (G-6158)
◆ Angstrom USA LLC .... E 313 295-0100
Southfield (G-14838)
Arcelormittal USA LLC .... F 313 332-5600
Detroit (G-3874)
◆ Atlas Tube (plymouth) Inc .... D 734 738-5600
Plymouth (G-12575)
Austin Tube Products Inc .... E 231 745-2741
Baldwin (G-1082)
Benteler Automotive Corp .... A 616 245-4607
Grand Rapids (G-6212)
Benteler Automotive Corp .... B 616 247-3936
Auburn Hills (G-791)
Berkley Industries Inc .... F 989 656-2171
Bay Port (G-1372)
▼ Burgaflex North America Inc .... E 810 584-7296
Grand Blanc (G-5961)
◆ Burr Oak Tool Inc .... C 269 651-9393
Sturgis (G-15599)
Delta Tube & Fabricating Corp .... E 248 634-8267
Holly (G-7874)
Detroit Tubing Mill Inc .... E 313 491-8823
Detroit (G-4004)
Diversified Tube LLC .... F 313 790-7348
Southfield (G-14882)
Dundee Products Company .... E 734 529-2441
Dundee (G-4581)
Dwm Holdings Inc .... D 586 541-0013
Warren (G-17011)
▼ Energy Steel & Supply Co .... D 810 538-4990
Lapeer (G-9458)
Ernest Industries Acquisition, ... E 734 595-9500
Westland (G-17554)
Exceptional Product Sales LLC .... F 586 286-3240
Clinton Township (G-3110)
Forged Tubular Products Inc .... G 313 843-6720
Detroit (G-4069)
Formfab LLC .... E 248 844-3676
Rochester Hills (G-13427)
General Structures Inc .... E 586 774-6105
Warren (G-17054)
Grinding Specialists Inc .... E 734 729-1775
Westland (G-17565)
Inline Tube .... G 586 294-4093
Fraser (G-5670)
Interntonal Specialty Tube LLC .... C 313 923-2000
Livonia (G-9784)
James Steel & Tube Company .... E 248 547-4200
Madison Heights (G-10282)
M & W Manufacturing Co LLC .... G 586 741-8897
Chesterfield (G-2800)
Martinrea Industries Inc .... C 231 832-5504
Reed City (G-13220)
▲ Martinrea Industries Inc .... E 734 428-2400
Manchester (G-10408)
▲ Michigan Seamless Tube LLC .... B 248 486-0100
South Lyon (G-14801)
Midway Strl Pipe & Sup Inc .... G 517 787-1350
Jackson (G-8527)
New 11 Inc .... E 616 494-9370
Holland (G-7754)
Parma Tube Corp .... E 269 651-2351
Sturgis (G-15626)
Perforated Tubes Inc .... E 616 942-4550
Ada (G-28)
Rbc Enterprises Inc .... E 313 491-3350
Detroit (G-4330)
Rock River Fabrications Inc .... E 616 281-5769
Grand Rapids (G-6832)
▲ Rolled Alloys Inc .... D 800 521-0332
Temperance (G-15842)
Roman Engineering .... D 231 238-7644
Afton (G-106)
S & S Tube Inc .... F 989 656-7211
Bay Port (G-1375)
Seadrift Pipeline Corp .... F 989 636-6636
Midland (G-10913)
Specialty Tube Solutions .... G 989 848-0880
Mio (G-11009)
Tarpon Industries Inc .... C 810 364-7421
Marysville (G-10620)
TI Automotive LLC .... F 586 948-6036
New Haven (G-11528)
▲ TI Automotive LLC .... C 248 494-5000
Auburn Hills (G-1020)
◆ TI Group Auto Systems LLC .... B 248 296-8000
Auburn Hills (G-1022)
TI Group Auto Systems LLC .... C 859 235-5420
Auburn Hills (G-1023)
TI Group Auto Systems LLC .... B 248 475-4663
Auburn Hills (G-1025)
Trans Tube Inc .... F 248 334-5720
Pontiac (G-12871)
Transportation Tech Group Inc .... E 810 233-0440
Flint (G-5512)
◆ Usui International Corporation .... E 734 354-3626
Plymouth (G-12784)
Van Pelt Corporation .... F 313 365-6500
Detroit (G-4422)

3321 Gray Iron Foundries

American Axle & Mfg Inc .... D 248 522-4500
Southfield (G-14836)
Anstey Foundry Co Inc .... E 269 429-3229
Stevensville (G-15556)
Awcco USA Incorporated .... G 586 336-9135
Romeo (G-13624)
Berne Enterprises Inc .... F 989 453-3235
Pigeon (G-12487)
Bernier Cast Metals Inc .... G 989 754-7571
Saginaw (G-14006)
▲ Betz Industries Inc .... D 616 453-4429
Grand Rapids (G-6214)
Blue Fire Manufacturing LLC .... E 248 714-7166
Waterford (G-17325)
◆ Brillion Iron Works Inc .... C 248 727-1800
Southfield (G-14858)
Cadillac Casting Inc .... D 231 779-9600
Cadillac (G-2235)
Calhoun Foundry Company Inc .... D 517 568-4415
Homer (G-7940)

Casting Industries Inc ....F 586 776-5700
Saint Clair (G-14208)
Citation Camden Cast Ctr LLC ....C 248 727-1800
Southfield (G-14867)
Citation Michigan LLC ....E 248 522-4500
Novi (G-11848)
City of East Jordan ....G 231 536-2561
East Jordan (G-4627)
E & M Cores Inc ....G 989 386-9223
Clare (G-2869)
◆ Eagle Quest International Ltd ....F 616 850-2630
Norton Shores (G-11750)
Ej Americas LLC ....G 231 536-2261
East Jordan (G-4629)
Ej Asia-Pacific Inc ....G 231 536-2261
East Jordan (G-4631)
Ej Co ....E 231 536-4527
East Jordan (G-4632)
Ej Europe LLC ....G 231 536-2261
East Jordan (G-4633)
Ej Group Inc ....E 231 536-2261
East Jordan (G-4634)
▼ Ej Usa Inc ....B 800 874-4100
East Jordan (G-4636)
Ej Usa Inc ....E 248 546-2004
Oak Park (G-12065)
Ej Usa Inc ....F 616 538-2040
Wyoming (G-17997)
Elco Inc ....G 586 778-6858
Roseville (G-13799)
Eqi Ltd ....G 616 850-2630
Norton Shores (G-11753)
▲ Federal Group Usa Inc ....F 248 545-5000
Southfield (G-14905)
Federal-Mogul Powertrain Inc ....C 616 887-8231
Sparta (G-15094)
General Motors LLC ....B 989 757-0528
Saginaw (G-14044)
Global Technology Ventures Inc ....G 248 324-3707
Farmington Hills (G-5011)
Great Lakes Castings LLC ....C 231 843-2501
Ludington (G-10061)
Great Lakes Castings LLC ....E 616 399-9710
Holland (G-7652)
◆ Grede Foundries Inc ....C 248 440-9500
Southfield (G-14923)
Grede Holdings LLC ....E 248 440-9500
Southfield (G-14924)
▲ Grede II LLC ....E 248 727-1800
Southfield (G-14925)
Grede LLC ....B 906 774-7250
Kingsford (G-9058)
▲ Grede LLC ....B 248 440-9500
Southfield (G-14926)
▼ Grede Wscnsin Subsidiaries LLC ....B 248 727-1800
Southfield (G-14930)
Holland Alloys Inc ....E 616 396-6444
Holland (G-7667)
JP Castings Inc ....E 517 857-3660
Springport (G-15211)
Kent Foundry Company ....E 616 754-1100
Greenville (G-7142)
M & E Manufacturing Inc ....G 616 241-5509
Grand Rapids (G-6638)
Metal Technologies Inc ....C 231 853-0300
Ravenna (G-13124)
Metal Technologies Indiana Inc ....C 269 278-1765
Three Rivers (G-15870)
Michigan Poly Pipe Inc ....G 517 709-8100
Grand Ledge (G-6111)
Midland Iron Works Inc ....F 989 832-3041
Midland (G-10889)
Northland Castings Corporation ....F 231 873-4974
Hart (G-7377)
▲ Paragon Metals LLC ....G 517 639-4629
Hillsdale (G-7533)
Pioneer Foundry Company Inc ....F 517 782-9469
Jackson (G-8552)
Ravenna Casting Center Inc ....C 231 853-0300
Ravenna (G-13126)
Robert Bosch LLC ....F 269 429-3221
Saint Joseph (G-14338)
Smith Castings Inc ....E 906 774-4956
Iron Mountain (G-8301)
▲ Steeltech Ltd ....D 616 243-7920
Grand Rapids (G-6891)
Steeltech Ltd ....F 616 696-1130
Cedar Springs (G-2563)
Threaded Products Co ....E 586 727-3435
Richmond (G-13272)

▲ Triton Global Sources Inc ....G 734 668-7107
Ypsilanti (G-18106)
◆ Triumph Gear Systems - Macomb ....C 586 781-2800
Macomb (G-10170)
Vx-LLC ....G 734 854-8700
Lambertville (G-9187)

3322 Malleable Iron Foundries

Grede LLC ....B 906 774-7250
Kingsford (G-9058)
Holland Alloys Inc ....E 616 396-6444
Holland (G-7667)
International Casting Corp ....F 586 293-8220
Roseville (G-13821)
Kramer International Inc ....G 586 726-4300
Troy (G-16451)
▲ Paragon Metals LLC ....G 517 639-4629
Hillsdale (G-7533)
Peerless Steel Company ....E 616 530-6695
Grandville (G-7063)
Prompt Pattern Inc ....E 586 759-2030
Warren (G-17201)
Robert Bosch LLC ....F 269 429-3221
Saint Joseph (G-14338)
Smith Castings Inc ....E 906 774-4956
Iron Mountain (G-8301)
◆ Teksid Inc ....F 734 846-5897
Farmington (G-4914)
Tooling Technology LLC ....D 937 381-9211
Macomb (G-10169)
Wolverine Bronze Company ....D 586 776-8180
Roseville (G-13891)

3324 Steel Investment Foundries

▼ Acra Cast Inc ....E 989 893-3961
Bay City (G-1271)
Barber Steel Foundry Corp ....F 231 894-1830
Rothbury (G-13894)
Barron Industries Inc ....D 248 628-4300
Oxford (G-12338)
◆ Barron Industries Inc ....D 248 628-4300
Oxford (G-12337)
▲ Chain Industries Inc ....E 248 348-7722
Wixom (G-17783)
Douglas King Industries Inc ....E 989 642-2865
Hemlock (G-7461)
Eagle Precision Cast Parts Inc ....E 231 788-3318
Muskegon (G-11310)
Eps Industries Inc ....E 616 844-9220
Ferrysburg (G-5334)
Eutectic Engineering Co Inc ....E 313 892-2248
Bloomfield Hills (G-1765)
▲ Federal Group Usa Inc ....F 248 545-5000
Southfield (G-14905)
◆ Howmet Corporation ....E 231 894-5686
Whitehall (G-17669)
Howmet Corporation ....D 231 894-7183
Whitehall (G-17670)
Howmet Corporation ....C 231 894-7290
Whitehall (G-17671)
Howmet Corporation ....C 231 981-3269
Whitehall (G-17672)
▲ Howmet Holdings Corporation ....G 231 894-5686
Whitehall (G-17676)
Invecast Corporation ....E 586 755-4050
Warren (G-17096)
▲ Onodi Tool & Engineering Co ....E 313 386-6682
Melvindale (G-10704)
▲ Paragon Metals LLC ....G 517 639-4629
Hillsdale (G-7533)
▲ R L M Industries Inc ....D 248 628-5103
Oxford (G-12366)
▲ Triton Global Sources Inc ....G 734 668-7107
Ypsilanti (G-18106)

3325 Steel Foundries, NEC

◆ Allied Metals Corp ....E 248 680-2400
Auburn Hills (G-765)
Alloying Surfaces Inc ....G 248 524-9200
Troy (G-16191)
Arcanum Alloys Inc ....G 312 810-4479
Kentwood (G-8999)
Astech Inc ....E 989 823-7211
Vassar (G-16811)
Axis Machining Inc ....D 989 453-3943
Pigeon (G-12486)
Axly Production Machining Inc ....B 989 269-2444
Bad Axe (G-1057)
◆ Bay Cast Inc ....D 989 892-0511
Bay City (G-1283)

Berne Enterprises Inc ....F 989 453-3235
Pigeon (G-12487)
▲ Bico Michigan Inc ....E 616 453-2400
Grand Rapids (G-6218)
Detroit Materials Inc ....G 248 924-5436
Farmington (G-4897)
Federal Screw Works ....G 231 922-9500
Traverse City (G-15969)
G M Brass & Alum Fndry Inc ....F 269 926-6366
Benton Harbor (G-1500)
GAL Gage Co ....E 269 465-5750
Bridgman (G-1863)
General Motors Company ....E 989 757-1576
Saginaw (G-14043)
General Motors LLC ....B 989 757-0528
Saginaw (G-14044)
Hackett Brass Foundry Co ....E 313 331-6005
Detroit (G-4113)
Heckett Multiserve ....G 313 842-2120
Detroit (G-4120)
Holland Alloys Inc ....E 616 396-6444
Holland (G-7667)
◆ Huron Casting Inc ....B 989 453-3933
Pigeon (G-12491)
International Casting Corp ....F 586 293-8220
Roseville (G-13821)
Invecast Corporation ....E 586 755-4050
Warren (G-17096)
▲ J & M Machine Products Inc ....D 231 755-1622
Norton Shores (G-11764)
Mannix RE Holdings LLC ....G 231 972-0088
Mecosta (G-10689)
Northfield Manufacturing Inc ....E 734 729-2890
Westland (G-17584)
Pal-TEC Inc ....G 906 788-4229
Wallace (G-16887)
▲ Paragon Metals LLC ....G 517 639-4629
Hillsdale (G-7533)
Pennisular Packaging LLC ....G 313 304-4724
Plymouth (G-12710)
RCO Engineering Inc ....D 586 620-4133
Roseville (G-13860)
▼ Saarsteel Incorporated ....G 248 608-0849
Rochester Hills (G-13509)
Smith Castings Inc ....E 906 774-4956
Iron Mountain (G-8301)
▲ Steeltech Ltd ....D 616 243-7920
Grand Rapids (G-6891)
Steeltech Ltd ....F 616 696-1130
Cedar Springs (G-2563)
▲ Temperform LLC ....E 248 349-5230
Novi (G-12012)
Temperform Corp ....G 248 851-9611
Bloomfield Hills (G-1801)
▲ Torch Steel Processing LLC ....E 313 571-7000
Detroit (G-4404)
Usmfg Inc ....G 262 993-9197
South Haven (G-14779)

3331 Primary Smelting & Refining Of Copper

Center Cupcakes ....G 248 302-6503
West Bloomfield (G-17470)
Materion Brush Inc ....F 586 443-4925
Warren (G-17143)
PM Power Group Inc ....G 906 885-7100
White Pine (G-17658)
Specialty Steel Treating Inc ....E 586 293-5355
Fraser (G-5730)

3334 Primary Production Of Aluminum

Aleris International Inc ....E 517 279-9596
Coldwater (G-3287)
Arconic Inc ....F 231 981-3002
Whitehall (G-17661)
Arconic Inc ....G 231 894-5686
Whitehall (G-17662)
Constellium Automotive USA LLC ....C 734 879-9700
Van Buren Twp (G-16752)
Fritz Enterprises ....E 313 841-9460
Detroit (G-4073)
General Motors LLC ....B 989 757-0528
Saginaw (G-14044)
Kaiser Aluminum Fab Pdts LLC ....D 269 250-8400
Kalamazoo (G-8784)
▼ Kkt Inc ....E 734 425-5330
Livonia (G-9798)
Nemak Commercial Services Inc ....E 248 350-3999
Southfield (G-14989)
Real Alloy Recycling LLC ....C 517 279-9596
Coldwater (G-3325)

S I C

Employee Codes: A=Over 500 employees, B=251-500
C=101-250, D=51-100, E=20-50, F=10-19, G=3-9
2020 Harris Michigan
Industrial Directory
771

▲ United Global Sourcing Inc .... F 248 952-5700
Troy *(G-16663)*
Viking Industries Inc .... F 734 421-5416
Garden City *(G-5846)*
Wayne-Craft Inc .... F 734 421-8800
Livonia *(G-10001)*

3339 Primary Nonferrous Metals, NEC

Airtec Corporation .... G 313 892-7800
Detroit *(G-3849)*
Arco Alloys Corp .... E 313 871-2680
Detroit *(G-3876)*
▲ Cannon-Muskegon Corporation .... C 231 755-1681
Norton Shores *(G-11744)*
Eclectic Metal Arts LLC .... G 248 251-5924
Detroit *(G-4026)*
◆ Expan Inc .... E 586 725-0405
New Baltimore *(G-11484)*
Materion Brush Inc .... F 586 443-4925
Warren *(G-17143)*
Mayer Alloys Corporation .... G 248 399-2233
Ferndale *(G-5299)*
Meter of America Inc .... G 810 216-6074
Port Huron *(G-12940)*
Metropolitan Alloys Corp .... E 313 366-4443
Detroit *(G-4233)*
Resource Rcovery Solutions Inc .... G 248 454-3442
Pontiac *(G-12861)*
Snyder Plastics Inc .... E 989 684-8355
Bay City *(G-1358)*
Specialty Steel Treating Inc .... E 586 293-5355
Fraser *(G-5730)*
Usmfg Inc .... G 269 637-6392
Southfield *(G-15057)*

3341 Secondary Smelting & Refining Of Nonferrous Metals

◆ Allied Metals Corp .... E 248 680-2400
Auburn Hills *(G-765)*
Alloying Surfaces Inc .... G 248 524-9200
Troy *(G-16191)*
▲ Aluminum Blanking Co Inc .... D 248 338-4422
Pontiac *(G-12802)*
Arco Alloys Corp .... E 313 871-2680
Detroit *(G-3876)*
Astech Inc .... E 989 823-7211
Vassar *(G-16811)*
▲ Benteler Aluminium Systems .... E 616 396-6591
Holland *(G-7568)*
▲ Cannon-Muskegon Corporation .... C 231 755-1681
Norton Shores *(G-11744)*
Colfran Industrial Sales Inc .... F 734 595-8920
Romulus *(G-13663)*
Constellium Automotive USA LLC .... C 734 879-9700
Van Buren Twp *(G-16752)*
Continental Aluminum LLC .... E 248 437-1001
New Hudson *(G-11534)*
Eutectic Engineering Co Inc .... E 313 892-2248
Bloomfield Hills *(G-1765)*
▲ Fpt Schlafer .... E 313 925-8200
Detroit *(G-4071)*
Franklin Iron & Metal Co Inc .... E 269 968-6111
Battle Creek *(G-1190)*
Franklin Metal Trading Corp .... E 616 374-7171
Lake Odessa *(G-9114)*
Friedland Industries Inc .... E 517 482-3000
Lansing *(G-9232)*
Great Lakes Paper Stock Corp .... D 586 779-1310
Roseville *(G-13811)*
◆ Huron Valley Steel Corporation .... C 734 479-3500
Trenton *(G-16155)*
Intern Metals and Energy .... G 248 765-7747
Jackson *(G-8471)*
Johnson Matthey North Amer Inc .... G 734 946-9856
Taylor *(G-15731)*
▼ Lorbec Metals - Usa Ltd .... E 810 736-0961
Flint *(G-5462)*
Louis Padnos Iron and Metal Co .... E 616 459-4208
Grand Rapids *(G-6631)*
Louis Padnos Iron and Metal Co .... E 517 372-6600
Lansing *(G-9309)*
Louis Padnos Iron and Metal Co .... G 616 452-6037
Grand Rapids *(G-6632)*
Martin Bros Mill Fndry Sup Co .... E 269 927-1355
Benton Harbor *(G-1525)*
Materion Brush Inc .... F 586 443-4925
Warren *(G-17143)*
Mayer Metals Corporation .... G 248 742-0077
Ferndale *(G-5300)*
Metropolitan Alloys Corp .... E 313 366-4443
Detroit *(G-4233)*
National Galvanizing LP .... A 734 243-1882
Monroe *(G-11059)*
National Zinc Processors Inc .... F 269 926-1161
Benton Harbor *(G-1535)*
Oerlikon Metco (us) Inc .... E 248 288-0027
Troy *(G-16533)*
Real Alloy Recycling LLC .... D 517 279-9596
Coldwater *(G-3324)*
Real Alloy Recycling LLC .... C 517 279-9596
Coldwater *(G-3325)*
Revstone Industries LLC .... F 248 351-1000
Troy *(G-16577)*
▲ Rolled Alloys Inc .... D 800 521-0332
Temperance *(G-15842)*
Sandvik Inc .... G 989 345-6138
West Branch *(G-17520)*
Schneider Iron & Metal Inc .... F 906 774-0644
Iron Mountain *(G-8299)*
Shoreline Recycling & Supply .... E 231 722-6081
Muskegon *(G-11424)*
Strong Steel Products LLC .... E 313 267-3300
Detroit *(G-4381)*
Total MGT Reclamation Svcs LLC .... G 734 384-3500
Taylor *(G-15777)*
◆ Trelleborg Corporation .... G 269 639-9891
South Haven *(G-14778)*
V & M Corporation .... E 248 541-4020
Royal Oak *(G-13980)*
▲ White Pine Copper Refinery Inc .... G 906 885-7100
White Pine *(G-17659)*

3351 Rolling, Drawing & Extruding Of Copper

▲ Aluminum Blanking Co Inc .... D 248 338-4422
Pontiac *(G-12802)*
Anchor Lamina America Inc .... C 231 533-8646
Bellaire *(G-1434)*
J M L Contracting & Sales Inc .... F 586 756-4133
Warren *(G-17108)*
Materion Brush Inc .... F 586 443-4925
Warren *(G-17143)*
Midbrook Medical Dist Inc .... G 517 787-3481
Jackson *(G-8526)*
Mueller Brass Co .... D 810 987-7770
Port Huron *(G-12945)*
Mueller Industries Inc .... D 248 446-3720
Brighton *(G-1964)*
Vx-LLC .... G 734 854-8700
Lambertville *(G-9187)*

3353 Aluminum Sheet, Plate & Foil

▲ Alcoa Automotive- Indiana .... B 248 489-4900
Farmington Hills *(G-4927)*
Alcoa Howmet .... F 231 894-5686
Whitehall *(G-17660)*
▲ Aluminum Blanking Co Inc .... D 248 338-4422
Pontiac *(G-12802)*
Arconic Inc .... G 231 894-5686
Whitehall *(G-17662)*
▲ Brazeway Inc .... D 517 265-2121
Adrian *(G-51)*
Christianson Industries Inc .... E 269 663-8502
Edwardsburg *(G-4763)*
Diez Group LLC .... D 734 675-1700
Woodhaven *(G-17939)*
▲ Erbsloeh Alum Solutions Inc .... B 269 323-2565
Portage *(G-12993)*
Howmet Corporation .... C 231 894-5686
Whitehall *(G-17674)*
Howmet Corporation .... C 231 894-5686
Whitehall *(G-17675)*
J M L Contracting & Sales Inc .... F 586 756-4133
Warren *(G-17108)*
Kaiser Aluminum Fab Pdts LLC .... D 269 250-8400
Kalamazoo *(G-8784)*
Mat Tek Inc .... G 810 659-0322
Flushing *(G-5540)*
Novelis Corporation .... G 248 668-5111
Novi *(G-11956)*
On The Side Sign Dsign Grphics .... G 810 266-7446
Byron *(G-2174)*
▼ Permaloc Corporation .... F 616 399-9600
Holland *(G-7769)*
Richmond Steel Inc .... E 586 948-4700
Chesterfield *(G-2831)*
▲ Tech Forms Metal Ltd .... G 616 956-0430
Grand Rapids *(G-6918)*

3354 Aluminum Extruded Prdts

Aacoa Extrusions Inc .... C 269 697-6063
Niles *(G-11592)*
▲ Air Conditioning Products Co .... D 734 326-0050
Romulus *(G-13649)*
Aluminum Textures Inc .... E 616 538-3144
Grandville *(G-7020)*
Arconic Inc .... E 248 489-4900
Farmington Hills *(G-4932)*
Austin Tube Products Inc .... E 231 745-2741
Baldwin *(G-1082)*
▲ Benteler Aluminium Systems .... E 616 396-6591
Holland *(G-7568)*
▲ Brazeway Inc .... D 517 265-2121
Adrian *(G-51)*
C & C Manufacturing Inc .... F 586 268-3650
Sterling Heights *(G-15278)*
D & W Awning and Window Co .... E 810 742-0340
Davison *(G-3645)*
▲ Erbsloeh Alum Solutions Inc .... B 269 323-2565
Portage *(G-12993)*
Extruded Aluminum Corporation .... F 616 794-0300
Belding *(G-1413)*
▲ Extruded Metals Inc .... C 616 794-4851
Belding *(G-1414)*
Flotronics Inc .... G 248 620-1820
Clarkston *(G-2921)*
General Structures Inc .... E 586 774-6105
Warren *(G-17054)*
▲ Hancock Enterprises Inc .... D 734 287-8840
Taylor *(G-15728)*
Hydro Extrusion North Amer LLC .... B 269 349-6626
Kalamazoo *(G-8772)*
International Extrusions Inc .... C 734 427-8700
Garden City *(G-5830)*
Kaiser Aluminum Corporation .... F 269 488-0957
Kalamazoo *(G-8783)*
Kaiser Aluminum Fab Pdts LLC .... D 269 250-8400
Kalamazoo *(G-8784)*
▼ Light Metals Corporation .... B 616 538-3030
Wyoming *(G-18016)*
Lippert Components Mfg Inc .... C 989 845-3061
Chesaning *(G-2725)*
Loftis Alumi-TEC Inc .... E 616 846-1990
Grand Haven *(G-6050)*
◆ Marketing Displays Inc .... C 248 553-1900
Farmington Hills *(G-5058)*
Michigan Aluminum Extrusion .... D 517 764-5400
Jackson *(G-8518)*
Mike Manufacturing Corporation .... G 586 759-1140
Warren *(G-17156)*
Minerals Processing Corp .... E 906 753-9602
Stephenson *(G-15238)*
▼ Mueller Impacts Company Inc .... C 810 364-3700
Marysville *(G-10608)*
Petschke Manufacturing Company .... F 586 463-0841
Mount Clemens *(G-11144)*
Plascore Inc .... F 616 772-1220
Zeeland *(G-18175)*
Quality Alum Acquisition LLC .... F 734 783-0990
Flat Rock *(G-5359)*
Quality Alum Acquisition LLC .... D 800 550-1667
Hastings *(G-7424)*
Quality Model & Pattern Co .... E 616 791-1156
Grand Rapids *(G-6800)*
Sign Cabinets Inc .... G 231 725-7187
Muskegon *(G-11425)*
◆ Signcomp LLC .... E 616 784-0405
Grand Rapids *(G-6862)*
Special-Lite Inc .... C 800 821-6531
Decatur *(G-3806)*
◆ Superior Extrusion Inc .... C 906 346-7308
Gwinn *(G-7223)*
Tubelite Inc .... D 800 866-2227
Walker *(G-16880)*
Uacj Auto Whitehall Inds Inc .... C 231 845-5101
Ludington *(G-10084)*
▲ Ube Machinery Inc .... D 734 741-7000
Ann Arbor *(G-685)*

3355 Aluminum Rolling & Drawing, NEC

AAR Manufacturing Inc .... E 231 779-8800
Cadillac *(G-2220)*
▲ Alcotec Wire Corporation .... D 800 228-0750
Traverse City *(G-15891)*
▲ Brooks & Perkins Inc .... D 231 775-2229
Cadillac *(G-2234)*
CPM Acquisition Corp .... G 231 947-6400
Traverse City *(G-15950)*

SIC SECTION
33 PRIMARY METAL INDUSTRIES

Dw Aluminum LLC .... E .... 269 445-5601 Cassopolis *(G-2528)*
▲ Extrunet America Inc .... G .... 517 301-4504 Tecumseh *(G-15793)*
General Structures Inc .... E .... 586 774-6105 Warren *(G-17054)*
Madison Electric Company .... E .... 586 294-8300 Fraser *(G-5689)*
Northern Extrusion Inc .... G .... 989 386-7556 Clare *(G-2880)*
Turn Key Harness & Wire LLC .... G .... 248 236-9915 Oxford *(G-12379)*

3356 Rolling, Drawing-Extruding Of Nonferrous Metals

Anchor Lamina America Inc .... C .... 231 533-8646 Bellaire *(G-1434)*
▲ Anchor Lamina America Inc .... E .... 248 489-9122 Novi *(G-11826)*
▲ Autocam-Pax Inc .... E .... 269 782-5186 Dowagiac *(G-4534)*
Carbide Technologies Inc .... E .... 586 296-5200 Fraser *(G-5634)*
▲ Concept Alloys Inc .... G .... 734 449-9680 Whitmore Lake *(G-17692)*
David Nickels .... G .... 248 634-5420 Holly *(G-7873)*
▲ Dirksen Screw Products Co .... E .... 586 247-5400 Shelby Township *(G-14579)*
Dodge West Joe Nickel .... G .... 810 691-2133 Clio *(G-3270)*
◆ Eureka Welding Alloys Inc .... E .... 248 588-0001 Madison Heights *(G-10250)*
Fine Arts .... E .... 269 695-6263 Buchanan *(G-2116)*
Moheco Products Company .... G .... 734 855-4194 Livonia *(G-9847)*
Nanomag LLC .... G .... 734 261-2800 Livonia *(G-9858)*
▲ Ncoc Inc .... E .... 248 548-5950 Oak Park *(G-12088)*
Nolans Top Tin Inc .... G .... 586 899-3421 Warren *(G-17169)*
Norton Equipment Corporation .... F .... 517 486-2113 Blissfield *(G-1721)*
Oerlikon Metco (us) Inc .... E .... 248 288-0027 Troy *(G-16533)*
Radiolgical Fabrication Design .... G .... 810 632-6000 Howell *(G-8087)*
Red Tin Boat .... G .... 734 239-3796 Ann Arbor *(G-613)*
Scitex LLC .... G .... 517 694-7449 Holt *(G-7926)*
Scitex LLC .... E .... 517 694-7449 Holt *(G-7927)*
Scitex Trick Titanium LLC .... G .... 517 349-3736 Okemos *(G-12137)*
Titanium Building Co Inc .... G .... 586 634-8580 Macomb *(G-10168)*
Titanium Operations LLC .... G .... 616 717-0218 Ada *(G-32)*
Titanium Sports LLC .... G .... 734 818-0904 Dundee *(G-4602)*
Titanium Technologies Inc .... G .... 248 836-2100 Auburn Hills *(G-1027)*
Tom Nickels .... G .... 248 348-7974 Northville *(G-11729)*
Traverse City Products Inc .... D .... 231 946-4414 Traverse City *(G-16128)*
Weldall Corporation .... G .... 989 375-2251 Elkton *(G-4786)*

3357 Nonferrous Wire Drawing

Active Solutions Group Inc .... G .... 313 278-4522 Dearborn *(G-3671)*
▲ AGM Automotive LLC .... D .... 248 776-0600 Farmington Hills *(G-4923)*
▲ American Furukawa Inc .... E .... 734 254-0344 Plymouth *(G-12570)*
Anwc LLC .... G .... 248 759-1164 Oakland Township *(G-12110)*
Bulls-Eye Wire & Cable Inc .... G .... 810 245-8600 Lapeer *(G-9445)*
Cardell Corporation .... F .... 248 371-9700 Auburn Hills *(G-810)*
◆ Coppertec Inc .... E .... 313 278-0139 Inkster *(G-8226)*
Engineered Prfmce Mtls Co LLC .... G .... 734 904-4023 Whitmore Lake *(G-17698)*
▲ Ews Legacy LLC .... E .... 248 853-6363 Rochester Hills *(G-13421)*
Federal Screw Works .... C .... 734 941-4211 Romulus *(G-13677)*
Gemo Hopkins Usa Inc .... G .... 734 330-1271 Auburn Hills *(G-882)*
▲ Glassmaster Controls Co Inc .... E .... 269 382-2010 Kalamazoo *(G-8753)*
▲ Hi-Lex America Incorporated .... B .... 269 968-0781 Battle Creek *(G-1198)*
▲ Kurabe America Corporation .... A .... 248 939-5803 Farmington Hills *(G-5039)*
Madison Electric Company .... E .... 586 294-8300 Fraser *(G-5689)*
Matrix Engineering and Sls Inc .... G .... 734 981-7321 Canton *(G-2399)*
◆ Morrell Incorporated .... D .... 248 373-1600 Auburn Hills *(G-949)*
▲ Quad Electronics Inc .... D .... 800 969-9220 Troy *(G-16571)*
Reeling Systems LLC .... G .... 810 364-3900 Saint Clair *(G-14233)*
Sanderson Insulation .... G .... 269 496-7660 Mendon *(G-10718)*
Shikoku Cable North Amer Inc .... G .... 248 488-8620 Novi *(G-11996)*
▲ Sine Systems Corporation .... C .... 586 465-3131 Clinton Township *(G-3230)*
T R S Fieldbus Systems Inc .... G .... 586 826-9696 Birmingham *(G-1703)*
Temprel Inc .... E .... 231 582-6585 Boyne City *(G-1835)*
Tsk of America Inc .... F .... 517 542-2955 Litchfield *(G-9612)*
▼ Weather-Rite LLC .... D .... 612 338-1401 Comstock Park *(G-3520)*

3363 Aluminum Die Castings

Aludyne Inc .... F .... 269 556-9236 Stevensville *(G-15554)*
Aludyne Inc .... G .... 248 506-1692 Warren *(G-16926)*
Angstrom Aluminum Castings LLC .... E .... 616 309-1208 Grand Rapids *(G-6170)*
▲ Cascade Die Casting Group Inc .... G .... 616 281-1774 Grand Rapids *(G-6258)*
Cascade Die Casting Group Inc .... D .... 616 887-1771 Sparta *(G-15089)*
Centracore De Mexico LLC .... E .... 586 776-5700 Saint Clair *(G-14210)*
Charles Group Inc .... B .... 336 882-0186 Grand Rapids *(G-6271)*
Connell Limited Partnership .... D .... 989 875-5135 Ithaca *(G-8358)*
Cooper Foundry Inc .... F .... 269 343-2808 Kalamazoo *(G-8717)*
Elco Inc .... G .... 586 778-6858 Roseville *(G-13799)*
▲ Evans Industries Inc .... G .... 313 259-2266 Detroit *(G-4045)*
▲ Federal Group Usa Inc .... F .... 248 545-5000 Southfield *(G-14905)*
▲ Great Lakes Die Cast Corp .... D .... 231 726-4002 Muskegon *(G-11337)*
Hackett Brass Foundry Co .... E .... 313 822-1214 Detroit *(G-4112)*
Hanson International Inc .... D .... 269 429-5555 Saint Joseph *(G-14316)*
Hoffmann Die Cast LLC .... C .... 269 983-1102 Saint Joseph *(G-14317)*
Homestead Tool and Machine .... E .... 989 465-6182 Coleman *(G-3344)*
Husite Engineering Co Inc .... E .... 248 588-0337 Clinton Township *(G-3136)*
Key Casting Company Inc .... G .... 269 426-3800 Sawyer *(G-14486)*
Lakeshore Die Cast Inc .... F .... 269 422-1523 Baroda *(G-1126)*
▼ M & M Die Cast Inc .... E .... 269 465-6206 Bridgman *(G-1871)*
▲ Mag-TEC Casting Corporation .... E .... 517 789-8505 Jackson *(G-8505)*
Michigan Die Casting LLC .... D .... 269 471-7715 Dowagiac *(G-4551)*
Montague Metal Products Inc .... E .... 231 893-0547 Montague *(G-11095)*
▲ Muskegon Castings LLC .... C .... 231 777-3941 Muskegon *(G-11388)*
Mv Metal Pdts & Solutions LLC .... D .... 269 462-4010 Dowagiac *(G-4554)*
▲ North Shore Mfg Corp .... E .... 269 849-2551 Coloma *(G-3363)*
Pace Industries LLC .... D .... 231 777-3941 Muskegon *(G-11394)*
Pace Industries LLC .... E .... 231 773-4491 Muskegon *(G-11395)*
▲ Paragon Metals LLC .... G .... 517 639-4629 Hillsdale *(G-7533)*
Precision Die Cast Inc .... G .... 586 463-1800 Clinton Township *(G-3199)*
▲ Prototype Cast Mfg Inc .... G .... 586 739-0180 Shelby Township *(G-14674)*
Prototype Cast Mfg Inc .... G .... 586 615-8524 Sterling Heights *(G-15455)*
Quality Castings Co .... G .... 269 349-7449 Kalamazoo *(G-8864)*
Shiloh Industries Inc .... D .... 989 463-6166 Alma *(G-249)*
Soper Manufacturing Company .... E .... 269 429-5245 Saint Joseph *(G-14340)*
Supreme Casting Inc .... D .... 269 465-5757 Stevensville *(G-15583)*
T C H Industries Incorporated .... G .... 616 942-0505 Grand Rapids *(G-6912)*
Tooling Technology LLC .... D .... 937 381-9211 Macomb *(G-10169)*
Tri-State Aluminum LLC .... F .... 231 722-7825 Muskegon *(G-11440)*
▲ Triton Global Sources Inc .... G .... 734 668-7107 Ypsilanti *(G-18106)*
▲ Tru Die Cast Corporation .... E .... 269 426-3361 New Troy *(G-11561)*
▲ Ube Machinery Inc .... D .... 734 741-7000 Ann Arbor *(G-685)*
Wolverine Die Cast Ltd Ptnshp .... E .... 586 757-1900 Warren *(G-17296)*

3364 Nonferrous Die Castings, Exc Aluminum

▲ Cascade Die Casting Group Inc .... G .... 616 281-1774 Grand Rapids *(G-6258)*
Cascade Die Casting Group Inc .... D .... 616 887-1771 Sparta *(G-15089)*
Cascade Die Casting Group Inc .... E .... 616 455-4010 Grand Rapids *(G-6259)*
Charles Group Inc .... B .... 336 882-0186 Grand Rapids *(G-6271)*
Cobra Patterns & Models Inc .... E .... 248 588-2669 Madison Heights *(G-10215)*
Cooper Foundry Inc .... F .... 269 343-2808 Kalamazoo *(G-8717)*
▲ Evans Industries Inc .... G .... 313 259-2266 Detroit *(G-4045)*
▲ Flare Fittings Incorporated .... E .... 269 344-7600 Kalamazoo *(G-8744)*
Hackett Brass Foundry Co .... E .... 313 822-1214 Detroit *(G-4112)*
Hoffmann Die Cast LLC .... C .... 269 983-1102 Saint Joseph *(G-14317)*
Key Casting Company Inc .... G .... 269 426-3800 Sawyer *(G-14486)*
Lakeshore Die Cast Inc .... F .... 269 422-1523 Baroda *(G-1126)*
▲ Lubo Usa Inc .... G .... 810 244-5826 Madison Heights *(G-10300)*
▲ Mag-TEC Casting Corporation .... E .... 517 789-8505 Jackson *(G-8505)*
Magnesium Products America Inc .... G .... 517 663-2700 Eaton Rapids *(G-4728)*
▲ Magnesium Products America Inc .... B .... 734 416-8600 Plymouth *(G-12681)*
Mv Metal Pdts & Solutions LLC .... D .... 269 462-4010 Dowagiac *(G-4554)*
Mv Metal Pdts & Solutions LLC .... A .... 269 471-7715 Portage *(G-13017)*
▲ North Shore Mfg Corp .... E .... 269 849-2551 Coloma *(G-3363)*
Proto-Cast Inc .... E .... 313 565-5400 Inkster *(G-8233)*
Superior Non-Ferrous Inc .... G .... 586 791-7988 Clinton Township *(G-3238)*
T C H Industries Incorporated .... G .... 616 942-0505 Grand Rapids *(G-6912)*
▲ Tru Die Cast Corporation .... E .... 269 426-3361 New Troy *(G-11561)*
Wolverine Bronze Company .... D .... 586 776-8180 Roseville *(G-13891)*
Wolverine Die Cast Ltd Ptnshp .... E .... 586 757-1900 Warren *(G-17296)*

SIC

Employee Codes: A=Over 500 employees, B=251-500
C=101-250, D=51-100, E=20-50, F=10-19, G=3-9
2020 Harris Michigan
Industrial Directory
773

3365 Aluminum Foundries

▼ **Acra Cast Inc** .... E 989 893-3961
Bay City *(G-1271)*
Algonac Marine Cast LLC .... F 810 794-9391
Clay *(G-2992)*
Bernier Cast Metals Inc .... G 989 754-7571
Saginaw *(G-14006)*
Birkhold Pattern Company Inc .... G 269 467-8705
Centreville *(G-2593)*
Cascade Die Casting Group Inc .... D 616 887-1771
Sparta *(G-15089)*
Castalloy Corporation .... G 517 265-2452
Adrian *(G-54)*
Casting Industries Inc .... F 586 776-5700
Saint Clair *(G-14208)*
▲ **Centracore LLC** .... F 586 776-5700
Saint Clair *(G-14209)*
Century Foundry Inc .... E 231 733-1572
Muskegon *(G-11293)*
Cytec Industries Inc .... C 269 349-6677
Kalamazoo *(G-8722)*
▲ **Dundee Castings Company** .... D 734 529-2455
Dundee *(G-4579)*
Eagle Aluminum Cast Pdts Inc .... G 231 788-4884
Muskegon *(G-11309)*
▲ **Ehc Inc** .... G 313 259-2266
Detroit *(G-4030)*
Eps Industries Inc .... E 616 844-9220
Ferrysburg *(G-5334)*
G M Brass & Alum Fndry Inc .... F 269 926-6366
Benton Harbor *(G-1500)*
Hackett Brass Foundry Co .... E 313 331-6005
Detroit *(G-4113)*
Hoffmann Die Cast LLC .... C 269 983-1102
Saint Joseph *(G-14317)*
Holland Alloys Inc .... E 616 396-6444
Holland *(G-7667)*
IBC Precision Inc .... G 248 373-8202
Auburn Hills *(G-907)*
Infinity Tech & Arospc Inc .... G 734 480-9001
Ypsilanti *(G-18080)*
International Fenestration .... G 248 735-6880
Northville *(G-11701)*
▲ **J & M Machine Products Inc** .... D 231 755-1622
Norton Shores *(G-11764)*
Line Precision Inc .... E 248 474-5280
Farmington Hills *(G-5044)*
Mall City Aluminum Inc .... G 269 349-5088
Kalamazoo *(G-8816)*
Max Casting Company Inc .... F 269 925-8081
Benton Harbor *(G-1527)*
Milan Cast Metal Corporation .... E 734 439-0510
Milan *(G-10947)*
▼ **Non-Ferrous Cast Alloys Inc** .... D 231 799-0550
Norton Shores *(G-11782)*
▲ **Onodi Tool & Engineering Co** .... E 313 386-6682
Melvindale *(G-10704)*
Prompt Pattern Inc .... E 586 759-2030
Warren *(G-17201)*
RCO Engineering Inc .... D 586 620-4133
Roseville *(G-13860)*
◆ **Shipston Alum Tech Mich Inc** .... G 616 842-3500
Fruitport *(G-5800)*
Specialty Steel Treating Inc .... E 586 293-5355
Fraser *(G-5730)*
Sterling Metal Works LLC .... G 586 977-9577
Sterling Heights *(G-15512)*
Superior Non-Ferrous Inc .... G 586 791-7988
Clinton Township *(G-3238)*
Supreme Casting Inc .... D 269 465-5757
Stevensville *(G-15583)*
Tooling & Equipment Intl Corp .... C 734 522-1422
Livonia *(G-9957)*
Tooling Technology LLC .... D 937 381-9211
Macomb *(G-10169)*
▲ **Tower Defense & Aerospace LLC** .... C 248 675-6000
Livonia *(G-9966)*
Tri-State Cast Technologies Co .... G 231 582-0452
Boyne City *(G-1836)*
▲ **Whitehall Products LLC** .... D 231 894-2688
Whitehall *(G-17682)*
Wolverine Bronze Company .... D 586 776-8180
Roseville *(G-13891)*
Wolverine Die Cast Ltd Ptnshp .... E 586 757-1900
Warren *(G-17296)*

3366 Copper Foundries

Allusion Star Inc .... G 231 264-5858
Elk Rapids *(G-4774)*
Anchor Lamina America Inc .... C 231 533-8646
Bellaire *(G-1434)*
▲ **Anchor Lamina America Inc** .... E 248 489-9122
Novi *(G-11826)*
Axly Production Machining Inc .... B 989 269-2444
Bad Axe *(G-1057)*
◆ **Barron Industries Inc** .... D 248 628-4300
Oxford *(G-12337)*
Belwith Products LLC .... F 616 247-4000
Grandville *(G-7022)*
Bernier Cast Metals Inc .... G 989 754-7571
Saginaw *(G-14006)*
▲ **Conway Detroit Corporation** .... E 586 552-8413
Roseville *(G-13786)*
Duplicast Corporation .... G 586 756-5900
Warren *(G-17008)*
▲ **Ehc Inc** .... G 313 259-2266
Detroit *(G-4030)*
Enterprise Tool and Gear Inc .... D 989 269-9797
Bad Axe *(G-1060)*
Eps Industries Inc .... E 616 844-9220
Ferrysburg *(G-5334)*
G M Brass & Alum Fndry Inc .... F 269 926-6366
Benton Harbor *(G-1500)*
◆ **GKN Sinter Metals LLC** .... G 248 296-7832
Auburn Hills *(G-888)*
▲ **Global CNC Industries Ltd** .... E 734 464-1920
Plymouth *(G-12629)*
Hackett Brass Foundry Co .... E 313 331-6005
Detroit *(G-4113)*
Holland Alloys Inc .... E 616 396-6444
Holland *(G-7667)*
▲ **Huron Tool & Engineering Co** .... E 989 269-9927
Bad Axe *(G-1068)*
◆ **Jsj Corporation** .... E 616 842-6350
Grand Haven *(G-6042)*
L & L Pattern Inc .... G 231 733-2646
Muskegon *(G-11359)*
Lewkowicz Corporation .... F 734 941-0411
Romulus *(G-13701)*
◆ **Michigan Wheel Operations LLC** ..... E 616 452-6941
Grand Rapids *(G-6677)*
Mueller Brass Co .... D 810 987-7770
Port Huron *(G-12945)*
▼ **Non-Ferrous Cast Alloys Inc** .... D 231 799-0550
Norton Shores *(G-11782)*
Parker-Hannifin Corporation .... B 269 694-9411
Otsego *(G-12249)*
Production Tube Company Inc .... G 313 259-3990
Detroit *(G-4312)*
Prompt Pattern Inc .... E 586 759-2030
Warren *(G-17201)*
Smith Castings Inc .... E 906 774-4956
Iron Mountain *(G-8301)*
Sterling Metal Works LLC .... G 586 977-9577
Sterling Heights *(G-15512)*
Threaded Products Co .... E 586 727-3435
Richmond *(G-13272)*
White Cloud Mfg Co .... G 231 689-6087
White Cloud *(G-17627)*

3369 Nonferrous Foundries: Castings, NEC

▼ **Acra Cast Inc** .... E 989 893-3961
Bay City *(G-1271)*
Algonac Marine Cast LLC .... F 810 794-9391
Clay *(G-2992)*
Alloy Machining LLC .... G 517 204-3306
Lansing *(G-9274)*
Apollo Trick Titanium Inc .... F 517 694-7449
Troy *(G-16205)*
Ascent Integrated Platforms .... F 586 726-0500
Macomb *(G-10110)*
Astech Inc .... E 989 823-7211
Vassar *(G-16811)*
Awcco USA Incorporated .... G 586 336-9135
Romeo *(G-13624)*
◆ **Barron Industries Inc** .... D 248 628-4300
Oxford *(G-12337)*
Berne Enterprises Inc .... F 989 453-3235
Pigeon *(G-12487)*
Cascade Die Casting Group Inc .... E 616 455-4010
Grand Rapids *(G-6259)*
Computer Operated Mfg .... E 989 686-1333
Bay City *(G-1297)*
Douglas King Industries Inc .... E 989 642-2865
Hemlock *(G-7461)*
▲ **Dundee Castings Company** .... D 734 529-2455
Dundee *(G-4579)*
Elden Industries Corporation .... F 734 946-6900
Taylor *(G-15715)*
▲ **Federal Group Usa Inc** .... F 248 545-5000
Southfield *(G-14905)*
▲ **Federal-Mogul Piston Rings Inc** .... F 248 354-7700
Southfield *(G-14909)*
◆ **GKN Sinter Metals LLC** .... G 248 296-7832
Auburn Hills *(G-888)*
Gokoh Coldwater Incorporated .... F 517 279-1080
Coldwater *(G-3305)*
Grosse Tool and Machine Co .... E 586 773-6770
Warren *(G-17068)*
Hackett Brass Foundry Co .... E 313 331-6005
Detroit *(G-4113)*
High-Tech Inds of Holland .... E 616 399-5430
Holland *(G-7666)*
Hoffmann Die Cast LLC .... C 269 983-1102
Saint Joseph *(G-14317)*
Holland Alloys Inc .... E 616 396-6444
Holland *(G-7667)*
Holland Pattern Co .... E 616 396-6348
Holland *(G-7675)*
◆ **Huron Casting Inc** .... B 989 453-3933
Pigeon *(G-12491)*
Husite Engineering Co Inc .... E 248 588-0337
Clinton Township *(G-3136)*
Inland Lakes Machine Inc .... E 231 775-6543
Cadillac *(G-2255)*
Invecast Corporation .... E 586 755-4050
Warren *(G-17096)*
Kuhlman Casting Co Inc .... F 248 853-2382
Detroit *(G-4185)*
Line Precision Inc .... E 248 474-5280
Farmington Hills *(G-5044)*
▲ **Magnesium Products America Inc** ... B 734 416-8600
Plymouth *(G-12681)*
▼ **Non-Ferrous Cast Alloys Inc** .... D 231 799-0550
Norton Shores *(G-11782)*
▲ **Onodi Tool & Engineering Co** .... E 313 386-6682
Melvindale *(G-10704)*
▲ **Paragon Metals LLC** .... G 517 639-4629
Hillsdale *(G-7533)*
Premiere Tool & Die Cast .... G 269 782-3030
Kalamazoo *(G-8861)*
Prompt Pattern Inc .... E 586 759-2030
Warren *(G-17201)*
Proto-Cast Inc .... E 313 565-5400
Inkster *(G-8233)*
▲ **Rolled Alloys Inc** .... D 800 521-0332
Temperance *(G-15842)*
Shellcast Inc .... E 231 893-8245
Montague *(G-11097)*
Smith Castings Inc .... E 906 774-4956
Iron Mountain *(G-8301)*
Soper Manufacturing Company .... E 269 429-5245
Saint Joseph *(G-14340)*
Stegman Tool Co Inc .... E 248 588-4634
Troy *(G-16621)*
Superior Brass & Alum Cast Co .... F 517 351-7534
East Lansing *(G-4678)*
Trin-Mac Company Inc .... G 586 774-1900
Saint Clair Shores *(G-14273)*
▲ **Triton Global Sources Inc** .... G 734 668-7107
Ypsilanti *(G-18106)*
White Cloud Manufacturing Co .... E 231 796-8603
Big Rapids *(G-1646)*
Wil-Kast Inc .... E 616 281-2850
Grand Rapids *(G-6992)*

3398 Metal Heat Treating

Advanced Heat Treat Corp .... E 734 243-0063
Monroe *(G-11013)*
Ajax Metal Processing Inc .... F 586 497-7000
Warren *(G-16922)*
▲ **Ajax Metal Processing Inc** .... G 313 267-2100
Detroit *(G-3850)*
Al-Fe Heat Treating Inc .... E 989 752-2819
Saginaw *(G-13994)*
▲ **Ald Thermal Treatment Inc** .... C 810 357-0693
Port Huron *(G-12884)*
Alloy Steel Treating Company .... F 269 628-2154
Gobles *(G-5946)*
Almar Industries Inc .... G 248 541-5617
Hazel Park *(G-7433)*
Alpha Steel Treating Inc .... E 734 523-1035
Livonia *(G-9637)*
▲ **American Metal Processing Co** .... E 586 757-7144
Warren *(G-16931)*
American Metallurgical Svcs .... F 313 893-8328
Detroit *(G-3867)*
Anstey Foundry Co Inc .... E 269 429-3229
Stevensville *(G-15556)*

SIC SECTION — 33 PRIMARY METAL INDUSTRIES

Apollo Heat Treating Proc LLC ....E 248 398-3434
  Oak Park (G-12048)
▲ Applied Process Inc ....E 734 464-8000
  Livonia (G-9651)
Atmosphere Annealing LLC ....D 517 485-5090
  Lansing (G-9342)
Atmosphere Annealing LLC ....E 517 482-1374
  Lansing (G-9343)
Atmosphere Group Inc ....G 248 624-8191
  Wixom (G-17763)
Atmosphere Heat Treating Inc ....F 248 960-4700
  Wixom (G-17764)
Austemper Inc ....E 586 293-4554
  Wixom (G-17768)
Austemper Inc ....E 616 458-7061
  Grand Rapids (G-6189)
Authority Flame Hardening & St ....F 586 598-5887
  Chesterfield (G-2743)
▲ Autocam-Pax Inc ....E 269 782-5186
  Dowagiac (G-4534)
Bell Induction Heating Inc ....G 734 697-0133
  Van Buren Twp (G-16748)
Bellaire Log Homes Indus Hm ....G 231 533-6669
  Bellaire (G-1435)
Bellevue Proc Met Prep Inc ....E 313 921-1931
  Detroit (G-3900)
Benton Harbor LLC ....G 269 925-6581
  Benton Harbor (G-1486)
Bluewater Thermal Solutions ....G 989 753-7770
  Saginaw (G-14008)
Bodycote Thermal Proc Inc ....D 616 399-6880
  Holland (G-7573)
Bodycote Thermal Proc Inc ....D 616 245-0465
  Grand Rapids (G-6234)
Bodycote Thermal Proc Inc ....G 313 442-2387
  Romulus (G-13659)
Bodycote Thermal Proc Inc ....E 734 459-8514
  Canton (G-2353)
Bodycote Thermal Proc Inc ....E 734 451-0338
  Canton (G-2354)
Bodycote Thermal Proc Inc ....F 734 427-6814
  Livonia (G-9666)
Bodycote Thermal Proc Inc ....F 734 427-6814
  Livonia (G-9667)
Burkk Inc ....G 616 365-0354
  Grand Rapids (G-6244)
▲ Century Inc ....C 231 947-6400
  Traverse City (G-15932)
Century Inc ....D 231 941-7800
  Traverse City (G-15934)
▲ Commercial Steel Treating Corp ....D 248 588-3300
  Madison Heights (G-10217)
Curtis Metal Finishing Co ....G 248 588-3300
  Madison Heights (G-10224)
Cyprium Induction LLC ....G 586 884-4982
  Sterling Heights (G-15305)
Darby Metal Treating Inc ....F 269 204-6504
  Plainwell (G-12521)
Detroit Edge Tool Company ....G 586 776-3727
  Roseville (G-13793)
Detroit Flame Hardening Co ....G 586 484-1726
  Clinton Township (G-3101)
Detroit Steel Treating Company ....E 248 334-7436
  Pontiac (G-12816)
Die Heat Systems Inc ....G 586 749-9756
  Chesterfield (G-2767)
▲ Dynamic Mtal Treating Intl Inc ....E 734 459-8022
  Canton (G-2368)
East - Lind Heat Treat Inc ....E 248 585-1415
  Madison Heights (G-10237)
Eltro Services Inc ....G 248 628-9790
  Oxford (G-12345)
▲ Emerald Consulting Group LLC ....E 248 720-0573
  Madison Heights (G-10245)
◆ Engineered Heat Treat Inc ....E 248 588-5141
  Madison Heights (G-10248)
Federal Industrial Svcs Inc ....F 586 427-6383
  Warren (G-17032)
▲ Fire-Rite Inc ....E 313 273-3730
  Detroit (G-4060)
▲ Gerdau Macsteel Atmosphere Ann ...F 517 782-0415
  Lansing (G-9373)
Gerdau Macsteel Atmosphere Ann ....E 517 482-1374
  Lansing (G-9374)
◆ Gestamp Mason LLC ....B 517 244-8800
  Mason (G-10641)
▲ Grand Blanc Processing LLC ....D 810 694-6000
  Holly (G-7882)
Heat Treating Svcs Corp Amer ....E 248 858-2230
  Pontiac (G-12832)

Heat Treating Svcs Corp Amer ....E 248 332-1510
  Pontiac (G-12833)
Heat Treating Svcs Corp Amer ....E 248 253-9560
  Waterford (G-17350)
Hi-Tech Steel Treating Inc ....D 800 835-8294
  Saginaw (G-14058)
Hycal Corp ....F 216 671-6161
  Gibraltar (G-5904)
Induction Engineering Inc ....F 586 716-4700
  New Baltimore (G-11486)
Induction Processing Inc ....F 586 756-5101
  Warren (G-17088)
Induction Services Inc ....E 586 754-1640
  Warren (G-17089)
Industrial Steel Treating Co ....D 517 787-6312
  Jackson (G-8470)
▲ Ionbond LLC ....D 248 398-9100
  Madison Heights (G-10278)
J Hansen-Balk Stl Treating Co ....E 616 458-1414
  Grand Rapids (G-6546)
L & L Machine & Tool Inc ....E 517 784-5575
  Jackson (G-8491)
Laydon Enterprises Inc ....E 906 774-4633
  Iron Mountain (G-8288)
M P D Welding Inc ....E 248 340-0330
  Orion (G-12184)
Magnum Induction Inc ....E 586 716-4700
  New Baltimore (G-11488)
MB Aerospace Warren LLC ....C 586 772-2500
  Warren (G-17144)
Metal Improvement Company LLC ......D 734 728-8600
  Romulus (G-13705)
Metal Prep Technology Inc ....F 313 843-2890
  Dearborn (G-3739)
Metallurgical Processing LLC ....E 586 758-3100
  Warren (G-17149)
Metro Machine Works Inc ....D 734 941-4571
  Romulus (G-13707)
Mjc Industries Inc ....F 313 838-2800
  Detroit (G-4251)
Modern Metal Processing Corp ....G 517 655-4402
  Williamston (G-17735)
Mpd Welding - Grand Rapids Inc ....F 616 248-9353
  Grand Rapids (G-6708)
▲ Ncoc Inc ....E 248 548-5950
  Oak Park (G-12088)
▲ Nitrex Inc ....E 517 676-6370
  Mason (G-10649)
Nitro-Vac Heat Treat Inc ....F 586 754-4350
  Warren (G-17168)
Nor-Cote Inc ....E 586 756-1200
  Warren (G-17170)
▲ Nssc America Incorporated ....G 248 449-6050
  Novi (G-11960)
Omc Archtrim ....E 517 482-9411
  Lansing (G-9407)
Pioneer Metal Finishing LLC ....C 734 384-9000
  Monroe (G-11062)
Precision Heat Treating Co ....E 269 382-4660
  Kalamazoo (G-8858)
Production Tube Company Inc ....G 313 259-3990
  Detroit (G-4312)
Richter Precision Inc ....E 586 465-0500
  Fraser (G-5718)
Rmt Acquisition Company LLC ....G 248 353-5487
  Southfield (G-15016)
Rmt Acquisition Company LLC ....G 248 353-4229
  Plymouth (G-12740)
Savanna Inc ....E 734 254-0566
  Plymouth (G-12750)
▲ Savanna Inc ....D 248 353-8180
  Southfield (G-15022)
Schroth Enterprises Inc ....E 586 759-4240
  Grosse Pointe Farms (G-7187)
Solution Steel Treating LLC ....F 586 247-9250
  Shelby Township (G-14698)
South Haven Finishing Inc ....E 269 637-2047
  South Haven (G-14772)
Specialty Steel Treating Inc ....E 586 293-5355
  Farmington Hills (G-5127)
Specialty Steel Treating Inc ....F 586 415-8346
  Fraser (G-5731)
Specialty Steel Treating Inc ....E 586 415-8346
  Fraser (G-5732)
Specialty Steel Treating Inc ....F 586 415-8346
  Fraser (G-5733)
Specialty Steel Treating Inc ....E 586 293-5355
  Fraser (G-5730)
State Heat Treating Company ....E 616 243-0178
  Grand Rapids (G-6887)

◆ Steel Industries Inc ....C 313 535-8505
  Redford (G-13194)
Steel Processing Company Inc ....F 586 772-3310
  Warren (G-17256)
Stokes Steel Treating Company ....E 810 235-3573
  Flint (G-5506)
Sun Steel Treating Inc ....D 877 471-0844
  South Lyon (G-14813)
▲ Super Steel Treating Inc ....D 586 755-9140
  Warren (G-17258)
Superior Heat Treat LLC ....E 586 792-9500
  Clinton Township (G-3237)
Temp Rite Steel Treating Inc ....E 586 469-3071
  Harrison Township (G-7353)
Thermal One Inc ....F 734 721-8500
  Westland (G-17603)
Tri-State Flame Hardening Co ....G 586 776-0035
  Warren (G-17268)
Trojan Heat Treat Inc ....E 517 568-4403
  Homer (G-7951)
Universal Induction Inc ....G 269 925-9890
  Benton Harbor (G-1557)
Vac-Met Inc ....E 586 264-8100
  Warren (G-17276)
Walker Wire (ispat) Inc ....G 248 399-4800
  Sterling Heights (G-15542)
◆ Wall Co Incorporated ....E 248 585-6400
  Madison Heights (G-10379)
West Side Flamehardening Inc ....F 734 729-1665
  Westland (G-17611)
Western Engineered Products ....G 248 371-9259
  Lake Orion (G-9170)
Woodworth Inc ....E 810 820-6780
  Flint (G-5525)
Woodworth Inc ....E 248 481-2354
  Pontiac (G-12876)
Wyatt Services Inc ....F 586 264-8000
  Sterling Heights (G-15547)
Zion Industries Inc ....F 517 622-3409
  Grand Ledge (G-6117)

3399 Primary Metal Prdts, NEC

▲ Advantage Sintered Metals Inc ....C 269 964-1212
  Battle Creek (G-1142)
Arch Global Precision LLC ....F 734 266-6900
  Bloomfield Hills (G-1747)
▲ Century Inc ....C 231 947-6400
  Traverse City (G-15932)
Century Inc ....D 231 941-7800
  Traverse City (G-15934)
Coldwater Sintered Met Pdts Inc ....E 517 278-8750
  Coldwater (G-3298)
Cox Industries Inc ....F 586 749-6650
  Chesterfield (G-2756)
Custom Powder Coating LLC ....G 616 454-9730
  Grand Rapids (G-6325)
H & H Powdercoating Inc ....G 810 750-1800
  Fenton (G-5218)
Lakeshore Custom Powdr Coating ......G 616 296-9330
  Grand Haven (G-6046)
Lisi Automotive HI Vol Inc ....F 734 266-6958
  Livonia (G-9812)
▲ Mueller Brass Co ....E 616 794-1200
  Belding (G-1426)
▲ Nitto Seiko Co Ltd ....E 248 588-0133
  Troy (G-16525)
Nylok LLC ....G 586 786-0100
  Macomb (G-10149)
Panter Company Inc ....F 313 537-5700
  Detroit (G-4288)
Paul Tousley Inc ....F 313 841-5400
  Detroit (G-4291)
Peerless Metal Powders ....F 313 841-5400
  Detroit (G-4293)
Revwires LLC ....G 269 683-8100
  Niles (G-11643)
Tapex American Corporation ....F 810 987-4722
  Port Huron (G-12970)
◆ Wall Co Incorporated ....E 248 585-6400
  Madison Heights (G-10379)
Wes Corp ....G 231 536-2500
  East Jordan (G-4647)
Westside Powder Coat LLC ....G 734 729-1667
  Romulus (G-13739)
WS Molnar Co ....E 313 923-0400
  Detroit (G-4451)

34 FABRICATED METAL PRODUCTS, EXCEPT MACHINERY AND TRANSPORTATION EQUIPMENT

3411 Metal Cans

AAR Manufacturing Inc .... E 231 779-8800
  Cadillac *(G-2220)*
Contract Welding and Fabg Inc .... E 734 699-5561
  Van Buren Twp *(G-16753)*
Delta Tube & Fabricating Corp .... C 248 634-8267
  Holly *(G-7875)*
Mh Industries Ltd .... G 734 261-7560
  West Bloomfield *(G-17485)*
▼ Oktober LLC .... G 231 750-1998
  Muskegon *(G-11392)*
▼ Royal Design & Manufacturing .... D 248 588-0110
  Madison Heights *(G-10346)*
Tin Can Dewitt .... G 517 624-2078
  Dewitt *(G-4467)*

3412 Metal Barrels, Drums, Kegs & Pails

Actron Steel Inc .... E 231 947-3981
  Traverse City *(G-15890)*
Advance Packaging Corporation .... C 616 949-6610
  Grand Rapids *(G-6147)*
Associated Metals Inc .... G 734 369-3851
  Ann Arbor *(G-371)*
Chemtool Incorporated .... G 734 439-7010
  Milan *(G-10934)*
Delta Tube & Fabricating Corp .... C 248 634-8267
  Holly *(G-7875)*
Eagle Buckets Inc .... G 517 787-0385
  Jackson *(G-8436)*
▲ Geerpres Inc .... E 231 773-3211
  Muskegon *(G-11329)*
Georgia-Pacific LLC .... D 734 439-2441
  Milan *(G-10938)*
Georgia-Pacific LLC .... C 989 725-5191
  Owosso *(G-12293)*
Green Bay Packaging Inc .... C 269 552-1000
  Kalamazoo *(G-8757)*
▲ Mauser .... G 248 795-2330
  Clarkston *(G-2936)*
Rap Products Inc .... G 989 893-5583
  Bay City *(G-1348)*
Repair Industries Michigan Inc .... C 313 365-5300
  Detroit *(G-4344)*
Royal ARC Welding Company .... E 734 789-9099
  Flat Rock *(G-5362)*
Shamrock Fabricating Inc .... F 810 744-0677
  Burton *(G-2165)*
Zayna LLC .... G 616 452-4522
  Grand Rapids *(G-7011)*

3421 Cutlery

Art of Shaving - FI LLC .... G 248 649-5872
  Troy *(G-16219)*
▲ Crl Inc .... E 906 428-3710
  Gladstone *(G-5910)*
Edgewell Personal Care Company .... G 866 462-8669
  Taylor *(G-15712)*
Jerkies Jerky Factory .... G 231 652-8008
  Newaygo *(G-11570)*
Los Cuarto Amigos .... G 989 984-0200
  East Tawas *(G-4690)*
Meijer Inc .... F 269 556-2400
  Stevensville *(G-15577)*
Midwest Tool and Cutlery Co .... F 231 258-2341
  Kalkaska *(G-8953)*
▼ Midwest Tool and Cutlery Co .... D 269 651-2476
  Sturgis *(G-15621)*
Stewart Knives LLC .... E 906 789-1801
  Escanaba *(G-4861)*
T S M Foods LLC .... G 313 262-6556
  Detroit *(G-4393)*
Tool Sales & Engineering .... G 810 714-5000
  Fenton *(G-5245)*
Yacks Dry Dock .... G 989 689-6749
  Hope *(G-7958)*

3423 Hand & Edge Tools

▲ Affinity Tool Works LLC .... G 248 588-0395
  Troy *(G-16172)*
◆ Assembly Technologies Intl .... F 248 280-2810
  Troy *(G-16224)*
Atlas Welding Accessories Inc .... D 248 588-4666
  Troy *(G-16226)*

▲ Aven Inc .... F 734 973-0099
  Ann Arbor *(G-375)*
▲ Balance Technology Inc .... D 734 769-2100
  Whitmore Lake *(G-17689)*
Bartlett Manufacturing Co LLC .... G 989 635-8900
  Marlette *(G-10494)*
Bay-Houston Towing Company .... E 810 648-2210
  Sandusky *(G-14430)*
Boral Building Products Inc .... C 248 668-6400
  Wixom *(G-17777)*
Cobra Manufacturing .... F 248 585-1606
  Troy *(G-16271)*
▲ Cows Locomotive Mfg Co .... E 248 583-7150
  Madison Heights *(G-10221)*
Custom Sockets Inc .... G 616 355-1971
  Holland *(G-7601)*
▲ Detroit Edge Tool Company .... D 313 366-4120
  Detroit *(G-3983)*
Detroit Steel Treating Company .... E 248 334-7436
  Pontiac *(G-12816)*
▼ E M I Construction Products .... D 616 392-7207
  Holland *(G-7615)*
Eagle Tool Group LLC .... F 586 997-0800
  Sterling Heights *(G-15328)*
Ferrees Tools Inc .... E 269 965-0511
  Battle Creek *(G-1187)*
Gill Industries Inc .... C 616 559-2700
  Grand Rapids *(G-6442)*
Grace Metal Prods Inc .... G 231 264-8133
  Williamsburg *(G-17712)*
Growgeneration Michigan Corp .... G 248 473-0450
  Lansing *(G-9379)*
Hanchett Manufacturing Inc .... C 231 796-7678
  Big Rapids *(G-1632)*
Hank Thorn Co .... F 248 348-7800
  Wixom *(G-17823)*
Hansen Machine & Tool Corp .... G 616 361-2842
  Grand Rapids *(G-6494)*
◆ Hastings Fiber Glass Pdts Inc .... D 269 945-9541
  Hastings *(G-7412)*
Hgks Industrial Clay Tool Co I .... G 734 340-5500
  Canton *(G-2383)*
Lach Diamond .... E 616 698-0101
  Grand Rapids *(G-6594)*
▼ Lakeland Mills Inc .... E 989 427-5133
  Edmore *(G-4752)*
Megapro Marketing Usa Inc .... F 866 522-3652
  Niles *(G-11625)*
Mercedes-Benz Extra LLC .... E 205 747-8006
  Farmington Hills *(G-5063)*
Micro Engineering Inc .... E 616 534-9681
  Byron Center *(G-2200)*
Muskegon Tools LLC .... G 231 788-4633
  Muskegon *(G-11391)*
▲ Ontario Die Company America ..... D 810 987-5060
  Marysville *(G-10609)*
Patco Air Tool Inc .... G 248 648-8830
  Orion *(G-12188)*
Performnce Dcutting Finshg LLC ...... G 616 245-3636
  Grand Rapids *(G-6750)*
◆ Persico Usa Inc .... D 248 299-5100
  Shelby Township *(G-14664)*
Port Austin Level & TI Mfg Co .... F 989 738-5291
  Port Austin *(G-12878)*
R J S Tool & Gage Co .... E 248 642-8620
  Birmingham *(G-1700)*
▲ Rock Tool & Machine Co Inc .... C 734 455-9840
  Plymouth *(G-12743)*
Roesch Maufacturing Co LLC .... G 517 424-6300
  Tecumseh *(G-15808)*
RTS Cutting Tools Inc .... E 586 954-1900
  Clinton Township *(G-3217)*
▲ Safecutters Inc .... G 866 865-7171
  Norton Shores *(G-11791)*
▲ Saginaw Products Corporation ..... E 989 753-1411
  Saginaw *(G-14141)*
Schenck USA Corp .... E 248 377-2100
  Southfield *(G-15024)*
Schimmelmanns Tool .... G 586 795-0538
  Warren *(G-17232)*
▲ Shaws Enterprises Inc .... E 810 664-2981
  Lapeer *(G-9486)*
▲ Sourcehub LLC .... G 800 246-1844
  Troy *(G-16613)*
Specialty Steel Treating Inc .... E 586 293-5355
  Fraser *(G-5730)*
Steelcraft Tool Co Inc .... E 734 522-7130
  Livonia *(G-9945)*
Sulzer Mixpac USA Inc .... E 517 339-3330
  Haslett *(G-7400)*

Summit Tooling & Mfg Inc .... G 231 856-7037
  Morley *(G-11118)*
◆ Sure-Loc Aluminum Edging Inc .... E 616 392-3209
  Holland *(G-7822)*
Tapco Holdings Inc .... C 248 668-6400
  Wixom *(G-17905)*
◆ Tekton Inc .... D 616 243-2443
  Grand Rapids *(G-6919)*
▲ Umix Dissoultion Corp .... G 586 446-9950
  Sterling Heights *(G-15532)*
Wranosky & Sons Inc .... G 586 336-9761
  Romeo *(G-13642)*

3425 Hand Saws & Saw Blades

Martin Saw & Tool Inc .... G 906 863-6812
  Menominee *(G-10744)*
▼ Menominee Saw and Supply Co ... E 906 863-2609
  Menominee *(G-10747)*
Saw Tubergen Service Inc .... G 616 534-0701
  Grand Rapids *(G-6852)*
Schott Saw Co .... G 269 782-3203
  Dowagiac *(G-4560)*
Workblades Inc .... E 586 778-0060
  Warren *(G-17297)*

3429 Hardware, NEC

A & A Marine & Mfg Inc .... G 231 723-8308
  Manistee *(G-10413)*
A & B Tube Benders Inc .... E 586 773-0440
  Warren *(G-16905)*
◆ Aba of America Inc .... F 815 332-5170
  Auburn Hills *(G-759)*
Acme Mills Company .... C 517 437-8940
  Hillsdale *(G-7513)*
Adjustable Locking Tech LLC .... D 248 443-9664
  Bloomfield Hills *(G-1742)*
Admat Manufacturing Inc .... F 269 641-7453
  Union *(G-16727)*
▲ ADS Us Inc .... C 989 871-4550
  Millington *(G-10993)*
▲ Albion Industries LLC .... C 800 835-8911
  Albion *(G-113)*
▲ Alpha Technology Corporation ..... E 517 546-9700
  Howell *(G-8011)*
American Arrow Corp Inc .... G 248 435-6115
  Clawson *(G-2971)*
◆ Anchor Coupling Inc .... C 906 863-2672
  Menominee *(G-10722)*
Antolin Interiors Usa Inc .... A 517 548-0052
  Howell *(G-8015)*
Apex Spring & Stamping Corp .... D 616 453-5463
  Grand Rapids *(G-6171)*
◆ Attwood Corporation .... C 616 897-9241
  Lowell *(G-10023)*
B & B Electrical Inc .... G 248 391-3800
  Keego Harbor *(G-8978)*
▲ Bauer Products Inc .... E 616 245-4540
  Grand Rapids *(G-6207)*
▲ BDS Company Inc .... E 517 279-2135
  Coldwater *(G-3291)*
Belwith Products LLC .... F 616 247-4000
  Grandville *(G-7022)*
Berkley Screw Machine Pdts Inc .... E 248 853-0044
  Rochester Hills *(G-13376)*
▲ Brauer Clamps USA .... C 586 427-5304
  Warren *(G-16965)*
C & S Security Inc .... G 989 821-5759
  Roscommon *(G-13748)*
Caillau Usa Inc .... C 248 446-1900
  Brighton *(G-1896)*
Caster Concepts Inc .... C 517 629-2456
  Albion *(G-119)*
Clamptech LLC .... G 989 832-8027
  Bay City *(G-1295)*
▲ Commando Lock Company LLC ... F 248 709-7901
  Troy *(G-16274)*
Consolidated Clips Clamps Inc .... D 734 455-0880
  Plymouth *(G-12601)*
Consort Corporation .... E 269 388-4532
  Kalamazoo *(G-8713)*
Custom Fireplace Doors Inc .... F 248 673-3121
  Waterford *(G-17330)*
D A C Industries Inc .... G 616 235-0140
  Grand Rapids *(G-6331)*
▲ Detmar Corporation .... F 313 831-1155
  Detroit *(G-3969)*
▲ Detroit Auto Specialties Inc .... G 248 496-3856
  West Bloomfield *(G-17474)*
Dgh Enterprises Inc .... G 269 925-0657
  Benton Harbor *(G-1495)*

34 FABRICATED METAL PRODUCTS, EXCEPT MACHINERY AND TRANSPORTATION EQUIPMENT

Die Cast Press Mfg Co Inc ....E 269 657-6060
Paw Paw *(G-12403)*

Doctor Flue Inc ....G 517 423-2832
Tecumseh *(G-15790)*

Dolphin Manufacturing Inc ....E 734 946-6322
Taylor *(G-15707)*

Door SEC Solutions of Mich ....F 616 301-1991
Grand Rapids *(G-6358)*

Douglass Safety Systems LLC ......G 989 687-7600
Sanford *(G-14449)*

▲ Dover Energy Inc ....C 248 836-6700
Auburn Hills *(G-843)*

▲ Dowding Industries Inc ....E 517 663-5455
Eaton Rapids *(G-4720)*

Dundee Manufacturing Co Inc ....E 734 529-2540
Dundee *(G-4580)*

◆ Dura Operating LLC ....C 248 299-7500
Auburn Hills *(G-846)*

E K Hydraulics Inc ....G 800 632-7112
Petoskey *(G-12448)*

Eaton-Aeroquip Llc ....B 949 452-9575
Jackson *(G-8440)*

▲ Engineered Products Company ..E 810 767-2050
Flint *(G-5425)*

▲ Enterprise Hinge Inc ....G 269 857-2111
Douglas *(G-4531)*

Ervins Group LLC ....E 248 203-2000
Bloomfield Hills *(G-1764)*

▲ Euro-Locks Inc ....F 616 994-0490
Holland *(G-7626)*

Evans Industries Inc ....G 313 272-8200
Detroit *(G-4046)*

Fathom Drones Inc ....G 586 216-7047
Grand Rapids *(G-6402)*

Five Star Manufacturing Inc ....E 815 723-2245
Auburn Hills *(G-875)*

Flexible Steel Lacing Company .....D 616 459-3196
Grand Rapids *(G-6413)*

Flextronics Intl USA Inc ....B 616 837-9711
Coopersville *(G-3558)*

Flue Sentinel LLC ....G 586 739-4373
Shelby Township *(G-14594)*

▲ Fluid Hutchinson Management ..D 248 679-1327
Auburn Hills *(G-876)*

▼ Franklin Fastener Company ....E 313 537-8900
Redford *(G-13162)*

G T Gundrilling Inc ....G 586 992-3301
Macomb *(G-10124)*

▲ G&G Industries Inc ....E 586 726-6000
Shelby Township *(G-14595)*

GAL Gage Co ....E 269 465-5750
Bridgman *(G-1863)*

Gates Corporation ....D 248 260-2300
Rochester Hills *(G-13431)*

General Dynamics Glbl IMG Tech ..F 248 293-2929
Rochester Hills *(G-13433)*

Grand Traverse Garage Doors ......E 231 943-9897
Traverse City *(G-15985)*

Grant Industries Incorporated ......D 586 293-9200
Fraser *(G-5657)*

Great Lakes Trim Inc ....D 231 267-3000
Williamsburg *(G-17713)*

Grupo Antolin Michigan Inc ....E 989 635-5080
Warren *(G-17069)*

Guardian Automotive Corp ....C 586 757-7800
Sterling Heights *(G-15365)*

▲ H & L Advantage Inc ....E 616 532-1012
Grandville *(G-7042)*

Hearth-N-Home Inc ....G 517 625-5586
Owosso *(G-12295)*

◆ Hella Corporate Center USA Inc ..E 586 232-4788
Northville *(G-11697)*

Herman Miller Inc ....G 616 453-5995
Grand Rapids *(G-6509)*

HI TEC Stainless Inc ....E 269 543-4205
Fennville *(G-5174)*

Hurley Marine Inc ....G 906 553-6249
Escanaba *(G-4834)*

▲ Hydra-Zorb Company ....F 248 373-5151
Auburn Hills *(G-906)*

Hydro-Craft Inc ....E 248 652-8100
Rochester Hills *(G-13448)*

Incoe Corporation ....C 248 616-0220
Auburn Hills *(G-910)*

International Automotive Compo ..B 810 987-8500
Port Huron *(G-12930)*

▲ International Engrg & Mfg Inc ....D 989 689-4911
Hope *(G-7954)*

Invent Detroit R&D Collaborati .....G 313 451-2658
Detroit *(G-4147)*

▼ Jay & Kay Manufacturing LLC ....E 810 679-2333
Croswell *(G-3598)*

Jay & Kay Manufacturing LLC ......G 810 679-3079
Croswell *(G-3599)*

▲ Jay Cee Sales & Rivet Inc ....F 248 478-2150
Farmington *(G-4901)*

K & W Manufacturing Co Inc ....F 517 369-9708
Bronson *(G-2031)*

Keglove LLC ....E 616 610-7289
Holland *(G-7708)*

◆ Knape & Vogt Manufacturing Co ..A 616 459-3311
Grand Rapids *(G-6585)*

Kriewall Enterprises Inc ....E 586 336-0600
Romeo *(G-13631)*

▲ L & W Inc ....D 734 397-6300
New Boston *(G-11502)*

Lacks Industries Inc ....C 616 698-6890
Grand Rapids *(G-6606)*

Magna Mirrors America Inc ....B 231 652-4450
Newaygo *(G-11574)*

Marine Industries Inc ....E 989 635-3644
Marlette *(G-10500)*

Masco Building Products Corp .....G 313 274-7400
Livonia *(G-9825)*

◆ Masco Corporation ....A 313 274-7400
Livonia *(G-9826)*

◆ Michigan Wheel Operations LLC ..E 616 452-6941
Grand Rapids *(G-6677)*

Milan Screw Products Inc ....E 734 439-2431
Milan *(G-10949)*

Miller Industrial Products Inc ....E 517 783-2756
Jackson *(G-8528)*

Milton Manufacturing Inc ....E 313 366-2450
Detroit *(G-4250)*

Moheco Products Company ....E 734 855-4194
Livonia *(G-9847)*

◆ Motion Systems Incorporated ...F 586 774-5666
Warren *(G-17160)*

Mvc Holdings LLC ....F 586 491-2600
Roseville *(G-13843)*

▲ Myrtle Industries Inc ....F 517 784-8579
Jackson *(G-8540)*

Norma Michigan Inc ....F 248 373-4300
Lake Orion *(G-9151)*

▲ Norma Michigan Inc ....C 248 373-4300
Auburn Hills *(G-959)*

Northwest Metal Products Inc ......F 616 453-0556
Grand Rapids *(G-6720)*

OBrien Engineered Products ....F 517 447-3602
Deerfield *(G-3814)*

Options Cabinetry Inc ....F 248 669-0000
Commerce Township *(G-3436)*

Orion Manufacturing Inc ....F 616 527-5994
Ionia *(G-8250)*

Peninsular Inc ....E 586 775-7211
Roseville *(G-13853)*

Penn Automotive Inc ....D 313 299-8500
Romulus *(G-13720)*

▲ Penn Automotive Inc ....B 248 599-3700
Waterford *(G-17366)*

Penn Engineering & Mfg Corp .....B 313 299-8500
Waterford *(G-17367)*

Penstone Inc ....E 734 379-3160
Rockwood *(G-13610)*

Peterson American Corp ....D 269 279-7421
Three Rivers *(G-15872)*

▲ Polytec Foha Inc ....F 586 978-9386
Warren *(G-17188)*

▲ Precision Polymer Mfg Inc ....E 269 344-2044
Kalamazoo *(G-8860)*

Pressweld Manufacturing Co ....G 734 675-8282
Portland *(G-13066)*

Probe-TEC ....G 765 252-0257
Chesterfield *(G-2822)*

Probotic Services LLC ....G 586 524-9589
Macomb *(G-10158)*

◆ R & D Enterprises Inc ....E 248 349-7077
Plymouth *(G-12728)*

▲ R G Ray Corporation ....F 248 373-4300
Auburn Hills *(G-984)*

R M Wright Company Inc ....E 248 476-9800
Farmington Hills *(G-5111)*

R T Gordon Inc ....E 586 294-6100
Fraser *(G-5715)*

▲ R W Fernstrum & Company ......E 906 863-5553
Menominee *(G-10756)*

Rayomar Enterprises Inc ....G 313 415-9102
Warren *(G-17217)*

▲ Refrigeration Sales Inc ....G 517 784-8579
Jackson *(G-8562)*

Regency Construction Corp ....E 586 741-8000
Clinton Township *(G-3208)*

River Valley Machine Inc ....E 269 673-8070
Allegan *(G-187)*

▲ RSR Sales Inc ....E 734 668-8166
Ann Arbor *(G-625)*

Scaff-All Inc ....G 888 204-9990
Clay *(G-3002)*

Select Products Limited ....E 269 323-4433
Portage *(G-13032)*

▲ Shane Group LLC ....G 517 439-4316
Hillsdale *(G-7541)*

Shark Tool & Die Inc ....G 586 749-7400
Chesterfield *(G-2839)*

▲ Shepherd Hardware Products Inc ..D 269 756-3830
Three Oaks *(G-15850)*

Shwayder Company ....G 248 645-9511
Birmingham *(G-1702)*

Solidbody Technology Company ..E 248 709-7901
Troy *(G-16610)*

Souris Enterprises Inc ....F 810 664-2964
Lapeer *(G-9487)*

Spiral Industries Inc ....E 810 632-6300
Howell *(G-8101)*

Startech-Solutions LLC ....G 248 419-0650
Southfield *(G-15033)*

Sterling Die & Engineering Inc ....E 586 677-0707
Macomb *(G-10163)*

Strattec Security Corporation ......E 248 649-9742
Auburn Hills *(G-1005)*

▲ Stromberg-Carlson Products Inc ..F 231 947-8600
Traverse City *(G-16114)*

T & L Products ....G 989 868-4428
Reese *(G-13234)*

Teamtech Motorsports Safety ......G 989 792-4880
Saginaw *(G-14163)*

TEC-3 Prototypes Inc ....E 810 678-8909
Metamora *(G-10782)*

▲ Tecla Company Inc ....E 248 624-8200
Commerce Township *(G-3453)*

TI Group Auto Systems LLC ....C 248 494-5000
Auburn Hills *(G-1024)*

TI Group Auto Systems LLC ....C 586 948-6006
Chesterfield *(G-2848)*

Tops All Clamps Inc ....G 313 533-7500
Redford *(G-13202)*

▲ Toyo Seat USA Corporation ....C 606 849-3009
Imlay City *(G-8212)*

Tubular PDT Solutions NA LLC .....G 248 388-4664
Troy *(G-16656)*

Twb of Indiana Inc ....E 734 289-6400
Monroe *(G-11081)*

Unist Inc ....E 616 949-0853
Grand Rapids *(G-6951)*

Vacuum Orna Metal Company Inc ..E 734 941-9100
Romulus *(G-13738)*

Vogt Industries Inc ....G 616 531-4830
Grand Rapids *(G-6974)*

W-Lok Corporation ....G 616 355-4015
Holland *(G-7851)*

▲ Wartian Lock Company ....G 586 777-2244
Saint Clair Shores *(G-14276)*

Weber Security Group Inc ....G 586 582-0000
Mount Clemens *(G-11153)*

▲ Wico Metal Products Company ..C 586 755-9600
Warren *(G-17293)*

◆ Zsi-Foster Inc ....D 734 844-0055
Canton *(G-2446)*

3431 Enameled Iron & Metal Sanitary Ware

▲ Aviv Global LLC ....G 248 737-5777
Farmington Hills *(G-4939)*

▲ Hotwater Works Inc ....G 517 364-8827
Lansing *(G-9382)*

Kohler Co ....E 810 208-0032
Fenton *(G-5223)*

Lakeshore Marble Company Inc ..E 269 429-8241
Stevensville *(G-15574)*

Marbelite Corp ....E 248 348-1900
Novi *(G-11934)*

▲ Pure Liberty Manufacturing LLC ..E 734 224-0333
Ottawa Lake *(G-12269)*

Sage International Inc ....D 972 623-2004
Novi *(G-11989)*

Sloan Valve Company ....D 248 446-5300
New Hudson *(G-11555)*

Thetford Corporation ....D 734 769-6000
Dexter *(G-4513)*

▲ Thetford Corporation ....C 734 769-6000
Ann Arbor *(G-670)*

Zurn Industries LLC.....F..... 313 864-2800
Detroit (G-4458)

3432 Plumbing Fixture Fittings & Trim, Brass

▲ American Beverage Equipment Co ..E..... 586 773-0094
Roseville (G-13772)
Barbron Corporation.....E..... 586 716-3530
Kalkaska (G-8937)
▲ Brasscraft Manufacturing Co.....C..... 248 305-6000
Novi (G-11840)
▲ Decker Manufacturing Corp.....D..... 517 629-3955
Albion (G-122)
Epic Fine Arts Company Inc.....G..... 313 274-7400
Taylor (G-15716)
Etna Distributors LLC.....G..... 906 273-2331
Marquette (G-10530)
◆ Fernco Inc.....C..... 810 503-9000
Davison (G-3648)
Incoe Corporation.....C..... 248 616-0220
Auburn Hills (G-910)
Ingersoll-Rand Company.....E..... 248 398-6200
Madison Heights (G-10275)
▲ Kerkstra Precast Inc.....C..... 616 457-4920
Grandville (G-7054)
Key Gas Components Inc.....E..... 269 673-2151
Allegan (G-169)
Machine Guard & Cover Co.....G..... 616 392-8188
Holland (G-7731)
▲ Marquis Industries Inc.....F..... 616 842-2810
Spring Lake (G-15160)
◆ Masco Corporation.....A..... 313 274-7400
Livonia (G-9826)
Masco De Puerto Rico Inc.....G..... 313 274-7400
Taylor (G-15737)
Parker-Hannifin Corporation.....B..... 269 694-9411
Otsego (G-12249)
◆ Plastic Trends Inc.....D..... 586 232-4167
Shelby Township (G-14668)
SH Leggitt Company.....C..... 269 781-3901
Marshall (G-10588)
Titan Sprinkler LLC.....G..... 517 540-1851
Howell (G-8111)
Tops All Clamps Inc.....G..... 313 533-7500
Redford (G-13202)
United Brass Manufacturers Inc.....D..... 734 941-0700
Romulus (G-13736)
United Brass Manufacturers Inc.....E..... 734 942-9224
Romulus (G-13737)
Vic Bond Sales Inc.....G..... 517 548-0107
Howell (G-8121)
Village & Country Water Trtmnt.....F..... 810 632-7880
Hartland (G-7395)

3433 Heating Eqpt

Alhern-Martin Indus Frnc Co.....E..... 248 689-6363
Troy (G-16187)
▲ Armstrong Hot Water Inc.....E..... 269 278-1413
Three Rivers (G-15857)
Banner Engineering & Sales Inc.....F..... 989 755-0584
Saginaw (G-14000)
▲ Burners Inc.....G..... 248 676-9141
Milford (G-10957)
Commercial Works.....C..... 269 795-2060
Middleville (G-10800)
Crown Heating Inc.....G..... 248 352-1688
Detroit (G-3955)
D S C Services Inc.....G..... 734 241-9500
Monroe (G-11026)
Dempsey Manufacturing Co.....G..... 810 346-2273
Brown City (G-2049)
▲ Detroit Radiant Products Co.....E..... 586 756-0950
Warren (G-17000)
▲ Detroit Stoker Company.....C..... 734 241-9500
Monroe (G-11028)
Great Lakes Electric LLC.....G..... 269 408-8276
Saint Joseph (G-14313)
▲ Hamilton Engineering Inc.....E..... 734 419-0200
Livonia (G-9764)
Kampers Woodfire Company Inc.....G..... 906 478-7902
Rudyard (G-13984)
Leaders Inc.....G..... 269 372-1072
Kalamazoo (G-8807)
Marshall Excelsior Co.....G..... 269 789-6700
Marshall (G-10576)
◆ Marshall Excelsior Co.....E..... 269 789-6700
Marshall (G-10577)
Messersmith Manufacturing Inc.....G..... 906 466-9010
Bark River (G-1121)
Milair LLC.....G..... 513 576-0123
Sterling Heights (G-15425)
▲ Nu-Way Stove Inc.....G..... 989 733-8792
Onaway (G-12149)
▲ Pyrinas LLC.....G..... 810 422-7535
Traverse City (G-16084)
Refrigeration Research Inc.....D..... 810 227-1151
Brighton (G-1985)
River Valley Machine Inc.....E..... 269 673-8070
Allegan (G-187)
Rlh Industries Inc.....F..... 989 732-0493
Gaylord (G-5889)
Seelye Equipment Specialist.....G..... 231 547-9430
Charlevoix (G-2630)
Solar Control Systems.....G..... 734 671-6899
Grosse Ile (G-7176)
Solar EZ Inc.....F..... 989 773-3347
Mount Pleasant (G-11229)
▲ Solaronics Inc.....E..... 248 651-5333
Rochester (G-13352)
U S Distributing Inc.....E..... 248 646-0550
Birmingham (G-1707)
Ventura Aerospace LLC.....E..... 734 357-0114
Wixom (G-17925)
Wood Burn LLC.....G..... 810 614-4204
Millington (G-10999)

3441 Fabricated Structural Steel

A & S Industrial LLC.....G..... 906 482-8007
Hancock (G-7247)
A N M Products.....G..... 269 483-1228
White Pigeon (G-17643)
A-1 Fabrication Inc.....G..... 586 775-8392
Roseville (G-13766)
AB Custom Fabricating LLC.....E..... 269 663-8100
Edwardsburg (G-4756)
Ability Mfg & Engrg Co.....F..... 269 227-3292
Fennville (G-5169)
Ace Welding & Machine Inc.....F..... 231 941-9664
Traverse City (G-15887)
Actron Steel Inc.....E..... 231 947-3981
Traverse City (G-15890)
Admin Industries LLC.....F..... 989 685-3438
Rose City (G-13756)
Adrian Tool Corporation.....E..... 517 263-6530
Adrian (G-48)
ADW Industries Inc.....E..... 989 466-4742
Alma (G-231)
Aero Inc.....F..... 248 669-4085
Walled Lake (G-16889)
Afco Manufacturing Corp.....F..... 248 634-4415
Holly (G-7869)
Alco Products LLC.....E..... 313 823-7500
Detroit (G-3853)
Allegan Metal Fabricators Inc.....G..... 269 751-7130
Hamilton (G-7229)
▲ Allor Manufacturing Inc.....D..... 248 486-4500
Brighton (G-1883)
Alloy Construction Service Inc.....E..... 989 486-6960
Midland (G-10813)
Alro Steel Corporation.....D..... 810 695-7300
Grand Blanc (G-5958)
Ambassador Steel Corporation.....E..... 517 455-7216
Lansing (G-9336)
American Steel Fabricators.....F..... 248 476-8433
Farmington (G-4894)
American Steel Works Inc.....F..... 734 282-0300
Riverview (G-13290)
Amerikam Inc.....D..... 616 243-5833
Grand Rapids (G-6167)
Amhawk LLC.....F..... 269 468-4141
Coloma (G-3353)
Amhawk LLC.....E..... 269 468-4177
Hartford (G-7381)
◆ Amigo Mobility Intl Inc.....D..... 989 777-0910
Bridgeport (G-1848)
Austin Tube Products Inc.....E..... 231 745-2741
Baldwin (G-1082)
B & G Custom Works Inc.....E..... 269 686-9420
Allegan (G-150)
Baker Enterprises Inc.....E..... 989 354-2189
Alpena (G-280)
Bauer Sheet Metal & Fabg Inc.....E..... 231 773-3244
Muskegon (G-11276)
Bennett Steel LLC.....F..... 616 401-5271
Grand Rapids (G-6211)
Black River Manufacturing Inc.....E..... 810 982-9812
Port Huron (G-12900)
▲ Boomer Company.....E..... 313 832-5050
Detroit (G-3910)
Boones Welding & Fabricating.....G..... 517 782-7461
Jackson (G-8393)
Bridgeport Manufacturing Inc.....G..... 989 777-4314
Bridgeport (G-1850)
Bristol Steel & Conveyor Corp.....E..... 810 658-9510
Davison (G-3641)
Builders Iron Inc.....E..... 616 887-9127
Comstock Park (G-3465)
Burnham & Northern Inc.....G..... 517 279-7501
Coldwater (G-3292)
Busch Industries Inc.....G..... 616 957-3737
Grand Rapids (G-6246)
C & J Fabrication Inc.....G..... 586 791-6269
Clinton Township (G-3071)
C & M Manufacturing Inc.....E..... 517 279-0013
Coldwater (G-3293)
Cadillac Fabrication Inc.....E..... 231 775-7386
Cadillac (G-2238)
CAM Fab.....G..... 269 685-1000
Martin (G-10595)
Campbell & Shaw Steel Inc.....F..... 810 364-5100
Marysville (G-10600)
Camryn Fabrication LLC.....C..... 586 949-0818
Chesterfield (G-2751)
Capital Steel & Builders Sup.....F..... 517 694-0451
Holt (G-7905)
Cardinal Fabricating Inc.....E..... 517 655-2155
Williamston (G-17728)
Casadei Structural Steel Inc.....E..... 586 698-2898
Sterling Heights (G-15283)
Cbp Fabrication Inc.....E..... 313 653-4220
Detroit (G-3931)
Centerline Indus Fabrication.....G..... 313 977-9056
Newport (G-11587)
Cerco Inc.....E..... 734 362-8664
Brownstown Twp (G-2071)
Chicago Blow Pipe Company.....F..... 773 533-6100
Marquette (G-10522)
▼ Circle S Products Inc.....G..... 734 675-2960
Woodhaven (G-17938)
Clair Sawyer.....G..... 906 228-8242
Marquette (G-10523)
▼ Complex Steel & Wire Corp.....F..... 734 326-1600
Wayne (G-17428)
Cooper & Cooper Sales Inc.....G..... 810 327-6247
Port Huron (G-12910)
Corban Industries Inc.....D..... 248 393-2720
Orion (G-12177)
Cornerstone Fabg & Cnstr Inc.....E..... 989 642-5241
Hemlock (G-7460)
Corsair Engineering Inc.....D..... 810 234-3664
Flint (G-5404)
Cox Brothers Machining Inc.....E..... 517 796-4662
Jackson (G-8422)
Custom Architectural Products.....G..... 616 748-1905
Zeeland (G-18129)
Custom Design & Manufacturing.....F..... 989 754-9962
Carrollton (G-2484)
Custom Welding Service LLC.....F..... 616 402-6681
Grand Haven (G-6007)
Cvm Services LLC.....E..... 269 521-4811
Allegan (G-153)
David A Mohr Jr.....G..... 517 266-2694
Adrian (G-58)
Dedoes Innovative Mfg Inc.....E..... 517 223-2500
Fowlerville (G-5562)
Delducas Welding & Co Inc.....G..... 810 743-1990
Flint (G-5416)
Delta Steel Inc.....G..... 989 752-5129
Saginaw (G-14025)
Demaria Building Company Inc.....G..... 248 486-2598
New Hudson (G-11537)
▲ Demmer Corporation.....C..... 517 321-3600
Lansing (G-9217)
Diversified Fabricators Inc.....F..... 586 868-1000
Clinton Township (G-3104)
▲ Dobson Industrial Inc.....E..... 800 298-6063
Bay City (G-1304)
Douglas King Industries Inc.....E..... 989 642-2865
Hemlock (G-7461)
Douglas Steel Fabricating Corp.....D..... 517 322-2050
Lansing (G-9288)
▲ Dowding Industries Inc.....E..... 517 663-5455
Eaton Rapids (G-4720)
▲ Dunnage Engineering Inc.....E..... 810 229-9501
Brighton (G-1913)
Dunns Welding Inc.....G..... 248 356-3866
Southfield (G-14887)
Eab Fabrication Inc.....E..... 517 639-7080
Quincy (G-13094)
Eastern Michigan Industries.....E..... 586 757-4140
Warren (G-17015)

SIC SECTION — 34 FABRICATED METAL PRODUCTS, EXCEPT MACHINERY AND TRANSPORTATION EQUIPMENT

EMC Welding & Fabrication Inc .... G 231 788-4172
Muskegon *(G-11316)*

Empire Machine & Conveyors Inc .... F 989 541-2060
Durand *(G-4608)*

▲ Engineered Alum Fabricators Co ..... G 248 582-3430
Ferndale *(G-5282)*

▲ Ethylene LLC .... E 616 554-3464
Kentwood *(G-9005)*

Fab Masters Company Inc .... D 269 646-5315
Marcellus *(G-10464)*

Fab-Lite Inc .... D 231 398-8280
Manistee *(G-10421)*

Fabricated Components & Assemb .... F 269 673-7100
Allegan *(G-160)*

Ferguson Steel Inc .... F 810 984-3918
Fort Gratiot *(G-5549)*

Ferro Fab LLC .... F 586 791-3561
Clinton Township *(G-3115)*

Frankenmuth Industrial Svcs .... E 989 652-3322
Frankenmuth *(G-5587)*

Fusion Fabricating and Mfg LLC .... G 586 739-1970
Sterling Heights *(G-15351)*

Gen-Oak Fabricators Inc .... G 248 373-1515
Orion *(G-12181)*

▲ Genco Alliance LLC .... E 269 216-5500
Kalamazoo *(G-8748)*

General Motors LLC .... G 517 242-2158
Lansing *(G-9372)*

General Motors LLC .... B 989 894-7210
Bay City *(G-1315)*

Gerref Industries Inc .... E 616 794-3110
Belding *(G-1416)*

◆ Global Strgc Sup Solutions LLC ...... D 734 525-9100
Livonia *(G-9753)*

Gosen Tool & Machine Inc .... F 989 777-6493
Saginaw *(G-14049)*

Gray Brothers Mfg Inc .... E 269 483-7615
White Pigeon *(G-17650)*

Great Lakes Contracting Inc .... F 616 846-8888
Grand Haven *(G-6027)*

Great Lakes Metal Works .... G 269 789-2342
Marshall *(G-10569)*

Great Lakes Stainless Inc .... E 231 943-7648
Traverse City *(G-15993)*

▲ Great Lakes Towers LLC .... C 734 682-4000
Monroe *(G-11037)*

▲ Greene Metal Products Inc .... E 586 465-6800
Clinton Township *(G-3130)*

▲ Griptrac Inc .... F 231 853-2284
Ravenna *(G-13120)*

H & M Welding and Fabricating .... G 517 764-3630
Jackson *(G-8461)*

Hamilton Steel Fabrications .... G 269 751-8757
Hamilton *(G-7234)*

Harrington Construction Co .... G 269 543-4251
Fennville *(G-5173)*

▲ HC Starck Inc .... E 517 279-9511
Coldwater *(G-3309)*

Heys Fabrication and Mch Co .... F 616 247-0065
Wyoming *(G-18009)*

▼ Highland Engineering Inc .... E 517 548-4372
Howell *(G-8048)*

Howard Structural Steel Inc .... E 989 752-3000
Saginaw *(G-14062)*

Ideal Steel & Bldrs Sups LLC .... E 313 849-0000
Detroit *(G-4134)*

Imm Inc .... E 989 344-7662
Grayling *(G-7108)*

Industrial Fabricating Inc .... F 734 676-2710
Rockwood *(G-13605)*

Industrial Fabrication LLC .... G 269 465-5960
Bridgman *(G-1867)*

Industrial Machine & Tool .... G 231 734-2794
Evart *(G-4883)*

Innovative Iron Inc .... G 616 248-4250
Grand Rapids *(G-6538)*

Inter-Lakes Bases Inc .... E 586 294-8120
Fraser *(G-5671)*

International Extrusions Inc .... C 734 427-8700
Garden City *(G-5830)*

Iron Fetish Metalworks Inc .... F 586 776-8311
Roseville *(G-13697)*

J & B Metal Fabicators LLC .... E 616 837-6764
Nunica *(G-12037)*

J & J Burning Co .... E 586 758-7619
Warren *(G-17103)*

J & J Fabrications Inc .... G 269 673-5488
Allegan *(G-166)*

J & J United Industries LLC .... G 734 443-3737
Livonia *(G-9787)*

▲ J & M Machine Products Inc .... D 231 755-1622
Norton Shores *(G-11764)*

J & S Livonia Inc .... G 734 793-9000
Livonia *(G-9788)*

Jaimes Liquidation Inc .... F 248 356-8600
Southfield *(G-14949)*

Jay Industries Inc .... G 313 240-7535
Northville *(G-11702)*

Jr Kandler & Sons .... G 734 241-0270
Monroe *(G-11044)*

JS Welding Inc .... G 517 451-2098
Britton *(G-2018)*

K & L Sheet Metal LLC .... G 269 965-0027
Battle Creek *(G-1205)*

K & M Industrial LLC .... G 906 420-8770
Gladstone *(G-5914)*

K-R Metal Engineers Corp .... F 989 892-1901
Bay City *(G-1324)*

Kalamazoo Metal Muncher Inc .... G 269 492-0268
Plainwell *(G-12528)*

Kehrig Steel Inc .... E 586 716-9700
Ira *(G-8259)*

Ken Gorsline Welding .... G 269 649-0650
Vicksburg *(G-16837)*

Kenowa Industries Inc .... G 517 322-0311
Lansing *(G-9304)*

Kirby Metal Corporation .... E 810 743-3360
Burton *(G-2157)*

▲ Kraftube Inc .... E 231 832-5562
Reed City *(G-13217)*

Kriewall Enterprises Inc .... E 586 336-0600
Romeo *(G-13631)*

L & W Inc .... C 734 397-8085
Van Buren Twp *(G-16769)*

▲ L & W Inc .... D 734 397-6300
New Boston *(G-11502)*

Laduke Corporation .... E 248 414-6600
Oak Park *(G-12077)*

Lake Shore Services Inc .... F 734 285-7007
Wyandotte *(G-17965)*

Laser Craft LLC .... F 248 340-8922
Lake Orion *(G-9145)*

Lasers Unlimited Inc .... F 616 977-2668
Grand Rapids *(G-6621)*

Liberty Fabricators Inc .... F 810 877-7117
Flint *(G-5458)*

Lincoln Welding Company .... G 313 292-2299
Stockbridge *(G-15590)*

▲ Lna Solutions Inc .... F 734 677-2305
Ann Arbor *(G-532)*

Loudon Steel Inc .... D 989 871-9353
Millington *(G-10997)*

Madar Metal Fabricating LLC .... F 517 267-9610
Lansing *(G-9243)*

Magnum Fabricating .... G 734 484-5800
Ypsilanti *(G-18087)*

Manistee Wldg & Piping Svc Inc .... G 231 723-2551
Manistee *(G-10428)*

▲ Marsh Plating Corporation .... D 734 483-5767
Ypsilanti *(G-18088)*

Maslo Fabrication LLC .... E 616 298-7700
Holland *(G-7740)*

Matrix North Amercn Cnstr Inc .... C 734 847-4605
Temperance *(G-15836)*

Mayo Welding & Fabricating Co .... G 248 435-2730
Royal Oak *(G-13948)*

Mbm Fabricators Co Inc .... C 734 941-0100
Romulus *(G-13704)*

MCS Industries Inc .... E 517 568-4161
Homer *(G-7946)*

Meccom Corporation .... G 313 895-4900
Detroit *(G-4224)*

Mechanical Fabricators Inc .... F 810 765-8853
Marine City *(G-10477)*

Men of Steel Inc .... G 989 635-4866
Marlette *(G-10501)*

Merrill Institute Inc .... G 989 462-0330
Alma *(G-240)*

Metal Mart USA Inc .... G 586 977-5820
Warren *(G-17148)*

Metalbuilt LLC .... E 586 786-9106
Chesterfield *(G-2804)*

Metaldyne Tblar Components LLC .... E 248 727-1800
Southfield *(G-14979)*

Metalfab Inc .... G 313 381-7579
Dearborn *(G-3740)*

Metalfab Manufacturing Inc .... E 989 826-2301
Mio *(G-11004)*

Michigan Diversified Metals .... G 517 223-7930
Fowlerville *(G-5576)*

Michigan Indus Met Pdts Inc .... E 616 786-3922
Muskegon *(G-11378)*

Michigan Steel Fabricators Inc .... E 810 785-1478
Flint *(G-5466)*

Mid Michigan Pipe Inc .... G 989 772-5664
Grand Rapids *(G-6683)*

Mid-West Innovators Inc .... F 989 358-7147
Alpena *(G-300)*

Midco 2 Inc .... G 517 467-2222
Onsted *(G-12154)*

Midwest Fabricating Inc .... G 734 921-3914
Taylor *(G-15744)*

Midwest Steel Inc .... E 313 873-2220
Detroit *(G-4248)*

Mike Manufacturing Corporation .... G 586 759-1140
Warren *(G-17156)*

Milton Manufacturing Inc .... E 313 366-2450
Detroit *(G-4250)*

Mitchell Welding Co LLC .... G 517 265-8105
Adrian *(G-82)*

Mkr Fabricating Inc .... F 989 753-8100
Saginaw *(G-14098)*

Moore Flame Cutting Co .... D 586 978-1090
Bloomfield Hills *(G-1784)*

Moran Iron Works Inc .... D 989 733-2011
Onaway *(G-12148)*

Morkin and Sowards Inc .... F 734 729-4242
Wayne *(G-17439)*

Mound Steel & Supply Inc .... F 248 852-6630
Troy *(G-16513)*

Mtw Performance & Fab .... G 989 317-3301
Mount Pleasant *(G-11212)*

National Metal Sales Inc .... G 734 942-3000
Romulus *(G-13711)*

National Ordanance Auto Mfg LLC ... D 248 853-8822
Auburn Hills *(G-952)*

NBC Truck Equipment Inc .... E 586 774-4900
Roseville *(G-13845)*

Nelson Iron Works Inc .... G 313 925-5355
Detroit *(G-4266)*

Newco Industries LLC .... E 517 542-0105
Litchfield *(G-9610)*

Nisshinbo Automotive Mfg Inc .... D 586 997-1000
Sterling Heights *(G-15436)*

Northern Chain Specialties .... F 231 889-3151
Kaleva *(G-8934)*

Northern Concrete Pipe Inc .... E 989 892-3545
Bay City *(G-1338)*

Northern Machining & Repr Inc .... E 906 786-0526
Escanaba *(G-4847)*

Northwest Fabrication Inc .... G 231 536-3229
East Jordan *(G-4641)*

▲ Northwoods Manufacturing Inc ...... D 906 779-2370
Kingsford *(G-9065)*

Oakwood Custom Coating Inc .... F 313 561-7740
Dearborn *(G-3745)*

▲ Oakwood Energy Management Inc ..C 734 947-7700
Taylor *(G-15750)*

▲ Oakwood Metal Fabricating Co ..... B 313 561-7740
Dearborn *(G-3745)*

ONiel Metal Forming Inc .... G 248 960-1804
Commerce Township *(G-3435)*

P I W Corporation .... G 989 448-2501
Gaylord *(G-5887)*

Parton & Preble Inc .... E 586 773-6000
Warren *(G-17180)*

▲ Paul W Marino Gages Inc .... E 586 772-2400
Roseville *(G-13852)*

Pioneer Machine and Tech Inc .... G 248 546-4451
Madison Heights *(G-10327)*

Pk Fabricating Inc .... F 248 398-4500
Ferndale *(G-5310)*

Plutchak Fab .... G 906 864-4650
Menominee *(G-10755)*

Ponder Industrial Incorporated .... E 989 684-9841
Bay City *(G-1342)*

▼ Powell Fabrication & Mfg Inc .... E 989 681-2158
Saint Louis *(G-14369)*

Power Industries Corp .... G 586 783-3818
Harrison Township *(G-7343)*

Precision Metals Plus Inc .... G 269 342-6330
Kalamazoo *(G-8859)*

Precision Mtl Hdlg Eqp LLC .... D 313 789-8101
Inkster *(G-8232)*

Precision Mtl Hdlg Eqp LLC .... D 734 351-7350
Romulus *(G-13724)*

Premier Prototype Inc .... E 586 323-6114
Sterling Heights *(G-15450)*

▲ Production Fabricators Inc .... E 231 777-3822
Muskegon *(G-11407)*

Employee Codes: A=Over 500 employees, B=251-500
C=101-250, D=51-100, E=20-50, F=10-19, G=3-9

2020 Harris Michigan Industrial Directory

34 FABRICATED METAL PRODUCTS, EXCEPT MACHINERY AND TRANSPORTATION EQUIPMENT

▼ PSI Marine Inc .... F 989 695-2646
  Saginaw *(G-14126)*
Quality Fabg & Erection Co .... G 989 288-5210
  Durand *(G-4613)*
Quality Finishing Systems .... F 231 834-9131
  Grant *(G-7081)*
R B Machine .... G 616 928-8690
  Holland *(G-7783)*
R Betker & Associates .... G 269 927-3233
  Benton Harbor *(G-1541)*
R T C Enviro Fab Inc .... F 517 596-2987
  Munith *(G-11254)*
▲ R-Bo Co Inc .... E 616 748-9733
  Zeeland *(G-18184)*
Red Iron Strl Consulting Corp .... G 810 364-5100
  Harbor Springs *(G-7292)*
Red Laser Inc .... E 517 540-1300
  Howell *(G-8089)*
REO Fab LLC .... G 810 969-4667
  Lapeer *(G-9485)*
Richard Bennett & Associates .... G 313 831-4262
  Detroit *(G-4345)*
Richmonds Steel Inc .... F 989 453-7010
  Pigeon *(G-12492)*
Rives Manufacturing Inc .... E 517 569-3380
  Rives Junction *(G-13310)*
▲ RKP Consulting Inc .... E 616 698-0300
  Caledonia *(G-2314)*
Rohmann Iron Works Inc .... F 810 233-5611
  Flint *(G-5495)*
Royal ARC Welding Company .... E 734 789-9099
  Flat Rock *(G-5362)*
RSI Global Sourcing LLC .... F 734 604-2448
  Novi *(G-11988)*
Rt Manufacturing Inc .... F 906 233-9158
  Escanaba *(G-4858)*
Ruess Winchester Inc .... F 989 725-5809
  Owosso *(G-12312)*
S & G Erection Company .... F 517 546-9240
  Howell *(G-8095)*
S & N Machine & Fabricating .... F 231 894-2658
  Rothbury *(G-13895)*
Sales & Engineering Inc .... E 734 525-9030
  Livonia *(G-9919)*
Samuel Son & Co (usa) Inc .... D 414 486-1556
  Troy *(G-16592)*
Sanilac Steel Inc .... F 989 635-2992
  Marlette *(G-10502)*
◆ Sas Global Corporation .... C 248 414-4470
  Warren *(G-17229)*
Sas Global Corporation .... E 248 414-4470
  Warren *(G-17230)*
Savs Welding Services Inc .... G 313 841-3430
  Detroit *(G-4354)*
Schneider Fabrication Inc .... G 989 224-6937
  Saint Johns *(G-14294)*
Service Iron Works Inc .... E 248 446-9750
  South Lyon *(G-14812)*
Servotech Industries Inc .... F 734 697-5555
  Taylor *(G-15764)*
Sexton Enterprize Inc .... G 248 545-5880
  Ferndale *(G-5318)*
Sharpe Fabricating Inc .... G 586 465-4468
  Clinton Township *(G-3224)*
Sherwood Manufacturing Corp .... E 231 386-5132
  Northport *(G-11671)*
Shoreline Mtal Fabricators Inc .... G 231 722-4443
  Muskegon *(G-11423)*
Signa Group Inc .... B 231 845-5101
  Ludington *(G-10078)*
SL Holdings Inc .... G 586 949-0818
  Chesterfield *(G-2841)*
Smede-Son Steel and Sup Co Inc .... D 313 937-8300
  Redford *(G-13192)*
Smede-Son Steel and Sup Co Inc .... G 248 332-0300
  Pontiac *(G-12868)*
SMI American Inc .... G 313 438-0096
  Taylor *(G-15767)*
Sol-I-Cor Industries .... F 248 476-0670
  Livonia *(G-9935)*
South Park Sales & Mfg Inc .... G 313 381-7579
  Dearborn *(G-3762)*
Spartan Metal Fab LLC .... G 517 322-9050
  Lansing *(G-9263)*
Special Fabricators Inc .... G 248 588-6717
  Madison Heights *(G-10357)*
Special Projects Inc .... E 734 455-7130
  Plymouth *(G-12759)*
Spirit Steel Co Inc .... G 517 750-4885
  Jackson *(G-8576)*

Steel Craft Inc .... E 989 358-7196
  Alpena *(G-314)*
Steel Mill Components Inc .... E 313 386-0893
  Allen Park *(G-210)*
Steel Supply & Engineering Co .... E 616 452-3281
  Grand Rapids *(G-6888)*
Stevens Custom Fabrication .... G 989 340-1184
  Alpena *(G-315)*
Stevens Custom Fabrication .... G 989 340-1184
  Alpena *(G-316)*
Stone For You .... G 248 651-9940
  Rochester *(G-13353)*
Structural Standards Inc .... F 616 813-1798
  Sparta *(G-15115)*
Superior Suppliers Network LLC ...... F 906 284-1561
  Crystal Falls *(G-3614)*
Surplus Steel Inc .... G 248 338-0000
  Auburn Hills *(G-1007)*
Synergy Additive Mfg LLC .... G 248 719-2194
  Clinton Township *(G-3241)*
Tartan Industries Inc .... G 810 387-4255
  Yale *(G-18047)*
Tbl Fabrications Inc .... E 586 294-2087
  Roseville *(G-13877)*
Tfi Inc .... E 231 728-2310
  Muskegon *(G-11436)*
Tg Manufacturing LLC .... F 616 935-7575
  Byron Center *(G-2212)*
Tower International Inc .... G 616 802-1600
  Grand Rapids *(G-6935)*
Tri-County Fab Inc .... G 586 443-5130
  Roseville *(G-13879)*
Trimet Industries Inc .... E 231 929-9100
  Traverse City *(G-16130)*
U P Fabricating Co Inc .... F 906 475-4400
  Negaunee *(G-11478)*
U S Fabrication & Design LLC .... F 248 919-2910
  Livonia *(G-9979)*
Uacj Automotive Whitehall Inds .... C 231 845-5101
  Ludington *(G-10085)*
Unistrut International Corp .... C 734 721-4040
  Wayne *(G-17445)*
United Fabricating Company .... G 248 887-7289
  Highland *(G-7501)*
▼ Universal Manufacturing Co .... F 586 463-2560
  Clinton Township *(G-3254)*
Upnorth Design & Repair Inc .... G 231 824-6025
  Manton *(G-10458)*
Utica Steel Inc .... D 586 949-1900
  Chesterfield *(G-2853)*
Valley Steel Company .... F 989 799-2600
  Saginaw *(G-14177)*
Van Dam Iron Works Inc .... E 616 452-8627
  Grand Rapids *(G-6957)*
Van Dellen Steel Inc .... E 616 698-9950
  Caledonia *(G-2321)*
▲ Van Pelt Corporation .... G 313 365-3600
  Sterling Heights *(G-15538)*
Van Pelt Corporation .... F 313 365-6500
  Detroit *(G-4422)*
Vanco Steel Inc .... F 810 688-4333
  North Branch *(G-11666)*
Varneys Fab & Weld LLC .... G 231 865-6856
  Nunica *(G-12046)*
Vci Inc .... E 269 659-3676
  Sturgis *(G-15640)*
▲ Vci Inc .... D 269 659-3676
  Sturgis *(G-15639)*
Versatile Fabrication Co Inc .... E 231 739-7115
  Muskegon *(G-11446)*
Vertigo .... B 910 381-8925
  Quinnesec *(G-13108)*
Very Best Steel LLC .... G 734 697-8609
  Belleville *(G-1451)*
Vochaska Engineering .... G 269 637-5670
  South Haven *(G-14782)*
▲ Wagon Automotive Inc .... D 248 262-2020
  Wixom *(G-17927)*
Wahmhoff Farms LLC .... F 269 628-4308
  Gobles *(G-5950)*
▲ Webasto Roof Systems Inc .... B 248 997-5100
  Rochester Hills *(G-13543)*
Webasto Roof Systems Inc .... F 248 997-5100
  Rochester Hills *(G-13545)*
West Michigan Metals LLC .... G 269 978-7021
  Allegan *(G-192)*
Wisner Machine Works LLC .... G 989 274-7690
  Akron *(G-109)*
Wm Kloeffler Industries Inc .... F 810 765-4068
  Marine City *(G-10487)*

Wpw Inc .... F 810 785-1478
  Flint *(G-5527)*

3442 Metal Doors, Sash, Frames, Molding & Trim

1395 Jarvis LLC .... G 248 545-6800
  Ferndale *(G-5251)*
Alliance Engnred Sltons NA Ltd .... C 586 291-3694
  Detroit *(G-3858)*
Aluminum Textures Inc .... E 616 538-3144
  Grandville *(G-7020)*
▲ American Roll Shutter Awng Co ... E 734 422-7110
  Livonia *(G-9645)*
Andoor Craftmaster .... G 989 672-2020
  Caro *(G-2465)*
Architectural Glass & Mtls Inc .... F 269 375-6165
  Kalamazoo *(G-8682)*
Arnold & Sautter Co .... F 989 684-7557
  Bay City *(G-1276)*
Astro Building Products Inc .... G 231 941-0324
  Traverse City *(G-15898)*
Atlantic Shutter .... G 248 668-6408
  Wixom *(G-17762)*
Beechcraft Products Inc .... E 989 288-2606
  Durand *(G-4606)*
Behind Shutter LLC .... G 248 467-7237
  Grand Blanc *(G-5960)*
Caliber Metals Inc .... E 586 465-7650
  New Baltimore *(G-11482)*
▲ Cross Aluminum Products Inc ..... F 269 697-8340
  Niles *(G-11603)*
Curbs & Damper Products Inc .... F 586 776-7890
  Roseville *(G-13788)*
▲ Daiek Products Inc .... E 248 816-1360
  Troy *(G-16295)*
▼ Duo-Gard Industries Inc .... D 734 207-9700
  Canton *(G-2367)*
▲ E-Zee Set Wood Products Inc ...... E 248 398-0090
  Oak Park *(G-12063)*
◆ Eliason Corporation .... D 269 327-7003
  Portage *(G-12992)*
Fbh Architectural Security Inc .... E 734 332-3740
  Ann Arbor *(G-457)*
Fft Sidney LLC .... F 248 647-0400
  Sidney *(G-14739)*
Forma-Kool Manufacturing Inc .... E 586 949-4813
  Chesterfield *(G-2778)*
▲ Fox Aluminum Products Inc .... E 248 399-4288
  Hazel Park *(G-7438)*
George W Trapp Co .... E 313 531-7180
  Redford *(G-13163)*
Grand Valley Wood Products Inc ..... E 616 475-5890
  Grand Rapids *(G-6471)*
Great Lakes Trim Inc .... D 231 267-3000
  Williamsburg *(G-17713)*
Guardian Automotive Corp .... C 586 757-7800
  Sterling Heights *(G-15365)*
H S Die & Engineering Inc .... F 248 373-4048
  Rochester Hills *(G-13437)*
Hacks Key Shop Inc .... F 517 485-9488
  Lansing *(G-9380)*
Hollow Metal Services LLC .... G 248 394-0233
  Clarkston *(G-2926)*
Integrity Door LLC .... G 616 896-8077
  Dorr *(G-4524)*
International Door Inc .... E 248 547-7240
  Canton *(G-2388)*
Ken Rodenhouse Door & Window .... F 616 784-3365
  Comstock Park *(G-3488)*
La Force Inc .... G 248 588-5601
  Troy *(G-16455)*
▲ Lean Factory America LLC .... G 513 297-3086
  Buchanan *(G-2123)*
Lippert Components Mfg Inc .... C 989 845-3061
  Chesaning *(G-2725)*
Litex Inc .... E 517 439-9361
  Hillsdale *(G-7528)*
Litex Inc .... G 248 852-0661
  Rochester Hills *(G-13461)*
▲ Llink Technologies LLC .... E 586 336-9370
  Brown City *(G-2054)*
Lorenzo White .... G 313 943-3667
  Detroit *(G-4210)*
Magna .... G 616 786-7403
  Holland *(G-7732)*
▲ Magna Mirrors North Amer LLC ... A 616 868-6122
  Alto *(G-329)*
Memtech Inc .... F 734 455-8550
  Plymouth *(G-12689)*

SIC SECTION 34 FABRICATED METAL PRODUCTS, EXCEPT MACHINERY AND TRANSPORTATION EQUIPMENT

Midynaco LLC G 989 550-8552
Kingston *(G-9073)*
Mt Clemens Glass & Mirror Co F 586 465-1733
Clinton Township *(G-3182)*
◆ National Nail Corp C 616 538-8000
Wyoming *(G-18021)*
Northern Mich Hardwoods Inc F 231 347-4575
Petoskey *(G-12460)*
▲ Openings Inc E 248 623-6899
Waterford *(G-17363)*
Panel Processing Oregon Inc E 989 356-9007
Alpena *(G-306)*
Paul Murphy Plastics Co E 586 774-4880
Roseville *(G-13851)*
Proto-Form Engineering Inc B 586 727-9803
Columbus *(G-3381)*
PTL Engineering Inc F 810 664-2310
Lapeer *(G-9483)*
◆ Quality Edge Inc D 616 735-3833
Walker *(G-16877)*
Reliable Glass Company E 313 924-9750
Detroit *(G-4339)*
Rubbair LLC G 269 327-7003
Portage *(G-13028)*
Scott Iron Works Inc F 248 548-2822
Hazel Park *(G-7454)*
Seal All Aluminum Pdts Corp G 248 585-6061
Southfield *(G-15025)*
Secure Door LLC F 586 792-2402
Mount Clemens *(G-11149)*
Shure Star LLC G 248 365-4382
Dearborn *(G-3760)*
Shure Star LLC E 248 365-4382
Auburn Hills *(G-998)*
Shutterbooth G 734 680-6067
Ann Arbor *(G-630)*
Shutterbooth G 586 747-4110
West Bloomfield *(G-17496)*
Shutters Chandeliers LLC G 989 773-0929
Mount Pleasant *(G-11226)*
Special-Lite Inc C 800 821-6531
Decatur *(G-3806)*
Storm Seal Co Inc G 248 689-1900
Troy *(G-16623)*
▼ Taylor Building Products Inc D 989 345-5110
West Branch *(G-17525)*
Total Door II Inc E 866 781-2069
Waterford *(G-17381)*
Tubelite Inc D 800 866-2227
Walker *(G-16880)*
Vertex Steel Inc E 248 684-4177
Milford *(G-10990)*
Vinyl Sash of Flint Inc E 810 234-4831
Flint *(G-5521)*
Wallside Inc F 313 292-4400
Taylor *(G-15781)*
▲ Weather King Windows Doors Inc D 313 933-1234
Farmington *(G-4915)*
Weather King Windows Doors Inc E 248 478-7788
Farmington *(G-4916)*
Weatherproof Inc E 517 764-1330
Jackson *(G-8606)*
Wojan Aluminum Products Corp D 231 547-2931
Charlevoix *(G-2635)*

3443 Fabricated Plate Work

A & B Welding & Fabricating G 231 733-2661
Muskegon *(G-11255)*
A A Tanks Co G 586 427-7700
Warren *(G-16908)*
▲ Acorn Stamping Inc F 248 628-5216
Oxford *(G-12332)*
Actron Steel Inc E 231 947-3981
Traverse City *(G-15890)*
Admin Industries LLC F 989 685-3438
Rose City *(G-13756)*
Alro Riverside LLC G 517 782-8322
Jackson *(G-8382)*
Ambassador Steel Corporation E 517 455-7216
Lansing *(G-9336)*
American Dumpster Services LLC G 586 501-3600
Center Line *(G-2578)*
American Metal Fab Inc D 269 279-5108
Three Rivers *(G-15854)*
American Tank Fabrication LLC F 780 663-3552
Okemos *(G-12113)*
Amhawk LLC E 269 468-4177
Hartford *(G-7381)*
▲ Anchor Lamina America Inc E 248 489-9122
Novi *(G-11826)*
Anderson Welding & Mfg Inc F 906 523-4661
Chassell *(G-2671)*
Aqua Systems Inc G 810 346-2525
Brown City *(G-2044)*
B & G Products Inc F 616 698-9050
Grand Rapids *(G-6198)*
Baker Enterprises Inc E 989 354-2189
Alpena *(G-280)*
Berrien Metal Products Inc F 269 695-5000
Buchanan *(G-2110)*
◆ Besser Company B 989 354-4111
Alpena *(G-282)*
Best Rate Dumpster Rental Inc G 248 391-5956
Ortonville *(G-12194)*
Big Steel Rack LLC G 517 740-5428
Jackson *(G-8389)*
Bills Custom Fab Inc F 989 772-5817
Mount Pleasant *(G-11179)*
BMC Global LLC D 517 486-2121
Blissfield *(G-1714)*
Bosch Auto Svc Solutions Inc E 586 574-1820
Warren *(G-16964)*
Brian A Broomfield G 989 309-0709
Remus *(G-13238)*
◆ Burr Oak Tool Inc C 269 651-9393
Sturgis *(G-15599)*
CAM Fab G 269 685-1000
Martin *(G-10595)*
Chicago Blow Pipe Company F 773 533-6100
Marquette *(G-10522)*
Clawson Tank Company E 248 625-8700
Clarkston *(G-2914)*
Cmi-Schneible Group E 810 354-0404
Fenton *(G-5196)*
Commercial Welding Company Inc G 269 782-5252
Dowagiac *(G-4536)*
Conner Steel Products G 248 852-5110
Rochester Hills *(G-13394)*
▲ Conquest Manufacturing LLC D 586 576-7600
Warren *(G-16991)*
Constructive Sheet Metal Inc E 616 245-5306
Allendale *(G-215)*
Contech Engnered Solutions LLC G 517 676-3000
Mason *(G-10630)*
Contract Welding and Fabg Inc E 734 699-5561
Van Buren Twp *(G-16753)*
Cooper-Standard Automotive Inc D 989 362-5631
East Tawas *(G-4687)*
Cooper-Standard Automotive Inc B 248 836-9400
Auburn Hills *(G-825)*
Cooper-Standard Automotive Inc D 989 739-1423
Oscoda *(G-12206)*
Cooper-Standard Automotive Inc D 248 628-4899
Leonard *(G-9527)*
Corotech Acquisition Co F 616 456-5557
Grand Rapids *(G-6312)*
▲ Custom Biogenic Systems Inc E 586 331-2600
Bruce Twp *(G-2080)*
◆ D-M-E USA Inc E 616 754-4601
Greenville *(G-7126)*
Davco Manufacturing LLC D 734 429-5665
Saline *(G-14385)*
Delta Iron Works Inc F 313 579-1445
Detroit *(G-3967)*
Detroit Boiler Company F 313 921-7060
Detroit *(G-3972)*
Detroit Dumpster Inc G 313 466-3174
Detroit *(G-3982)*
Detroit Plate Fabricators Inc G 313 921-7020
Detroit *(G-3997)*
Die-Mold-Automation Component G 313 581-6510
Dearborn *(G-3693)*
Dino S Dumpsters LLC G 989 225-5635
Bay City *(G-1303)*
Diversfied Prcurement Svcs LLC G 248 821-1147
Ferndale *(G-5280)*
Diversified Mech Svcs Inc F 616 785-2735
Comstock Park *(G-3478)*
Diversified Tooling Group Inc F 248 837-5828
Madison Heights *(G-10232)*
Dmg Dumpsters Inc G 313 610-3476
Farmington Hills *(G-4974)*
Dolphin Dumpsters LLC G 734 272-8981
Farmington Hills *(G-4975)*
Dumpster Express LLC G 855 599-7255
Holly *(G-7877)*
E K Hydraulics Inc G 800 632-7112
Petoskey *(G-12448)*
E L Nickell Co F 269 435-2475
Constantine *(G-3534)*
Elden Cylinder Testing Inc E 734 946-6900
Taylor *(G-15714)*
Fab-Alloy Company G 517 787-4313
Jackson *(G-8447)*
Fabrication Services Inc G 517 796-8197
Jackson *(G-8448)*
Fabrications Unlimited Inc G 313 567-9616
Shelby Township *(G-14591)*
Fabrications Unlimited Inc G 313 567-9616
Detroit *(G-4049)*
Fabrilaser Mfg LLC E 269 789-9490
Marshall *(G-10567)*
Fischer Tanks LLC D 231 362-8265
Kaleva *(G-8932)*
▲ Fluid Hutchinson Management D 248 679-1327
Auburn Hills *(G-876)*
Formrite Inc G 517 521-1373
Webberville *(G-17449)*
Geomembrane Services Inc F 231 264-9030
Kewadin *(G-9038)*
Gladwin Tank Manufacturing Inc F 989 426-4768
Gladwin *(G-5932)*
Gld Holdings Inc F 616 877-4288
Moline *(G-11010)*
Glycon Corp E 517 423-8356
Tecumseh *(G-15795)*
Great Lakes Gauge Company F 989 652-6136
Bridgeport *(G-1852)*
Great Lakes Laser Dynamics Inc D 616 892-7070
Allendale *(G-218)*
▲ Greene Metal Products Inc E 586 465-6800
Clinton Township *(G-3130)*
Greens Welding & Repair Co G 734 721-5434
Westland *(G-17564)*
Grossel Tool Co D 586 294-3660
Fraser *(G-5658)*
H & M Welding and Fabricating G 517 764-3630
Jackson *(G-8461)*
Hammars Contracting LLC F 810 367-3037
Kimball *(G-9044)*
▼ Highland Engineering Inc E 517 548-4372
Howell *(G-8048)*
◆ Hines Corporation F 231 799-6240
Norton Shores *(G-11812)*
Hornet Manufacturing Inc G 517 448-8203
Hudson *(G-8131)*
Hydro-Craft Inc E 248 652-8100
Rochester Hills *(G-13448)*
Ian Davidson & Assoc Inc G 269 925-7552
Benton Harbor *(G-1512)*
Ideal Fabricators Inc E 734 422-5320
Livonia *(G-9778)*
Impert Industries Inc G 269 694-2727
Otsego *(G-12241)*
Industrial Container Inc F 313 923-8778
Detroit *(G-4138)*
Industrial Fabg Systems Inc E 248 685-7373
Milford *(G-10966)*
JB Equipment LLC E 219 285-0668
Gibraltar *(G-5905)*
Johnston Boiler Company E 616 842-5050
Ferrysburg *(G-5335)*
K & W Manufacturing Co Inc F 517 369-9708
Bronson *(G-2031)*
K and W Landfill Inc F 906 883-3504
Ontonagon *(G-12160)*
Kerr Pump and Supply Inc E 248 543-3880
Oak Park *(G-12076)*
Krista Messer G 734 459-1952
Canton *(G-2391)*
Kurrent Welding Inc G 734 753-9197
New Boston *(G-11501)*
L & W Inc B 734 397-2212
Van Buren Twp *(G-16770)*
L & W Inc C 616 394-9665
Holland *(G-7715)*
L Barge & Associates Inc F 248 582-3430
Ferndale *(G-5297)*
Larsen Service Inc G 810 374-6132
Otisville *(G-12232)*
Liberty Steel Fabricating Inc E 269 556-9792
Saint Joseph *(G-14327)*
Lochinvar LLC E 734 454-4480
Plymouth *(G-12676)*
M&D Dumpsters LLC G 616 299-0234
Hudsonville *(G-8163)*
▲ Magnetic Products Inc D 248 887-5600
Highland *(G-7497)*
Mahle Eng Components USA Inc F 248 305-8200
Farmington Hills *(G-5051)*

S I C

34 FABRICATED METAL PRODUCTS, EXCEPT MACHINERY AND TRANSPORTATION EQUIPMENT

Marix Specialty Welding Co ....E..... 586 754-9685
  Warren *(G-17140)*
Marsh Industrial Services Inc ....F..... 231 258-4870
  Kalkaska *(G-8949)*
Massie Mfg Inc ....E..... 906 353-6381
  Baraga *(G-1109)*
Matrix North Amercn Cnstr Inc ....C..... 734 847-4605
  Temperance *(G-15836)*
Mayo Welding & Fabricating Co ....G..... 248 435-2730
  Royal Oak *(G-13948)*
MB Aerospace Warren LLC ....C..... 586 772-2500
  Warren *(G-17144)*
McM Disposal LLC ....G..... 616 656-4049
  Byron Center *(G-2199)*
▲ Merrill Technologies Group Inc ....D..... 989 791-6676
  Saginaw *(G-14090)*
Merrill Technologies Group Inc ....C..... 989 462-0330
  Alma *(G-241)*
Metal Quest Inc ....D..... 989 733-2011
  Onaway *(G-12147)*
Metal Tech Products Inc ....E..... 313 533-5277
  Detroit *(G-4227)*
Michigan Metal Fabricators ....G..... 586 754-0421
  Warren *(G-17153)*
Mitchells Fabrication Co ....G..... 248 373-2199
  Auburn Hills *(G-946)*
Moore Flame Cutting Co ....D..... 586 978-1090
  Bloomfield Hills *(G-1784)*
Nelson Steel Products Inc ....D..... 616 396-1515
  Holland *(G-7753)*
▲ Nicholson Terminal & Dock Co ....C..... 313 842-4300
  River Rouge *(G-13279)*
North Central Welding Co ....E..... 989 275-8054
  Roscommon *(G-13751)*
Northern Fab & Machine LLC ....F..... 906 863-8506
  Menominee *(G-10754)*
Northern Machining & Repr Inc ....E..... 906 786-0526
  Escanaba *(G-4847)*
Northwest Fabrication Inc ....G..... 231 536-3229
  East Jordan *(G-4641)*
Old Xembedded LLC ....G..... 734 975-0577
  Ann Arbor *(G-582)*
Parton & Preble Inc ....E..... 586 773-6000
  Warren *(G-17180)*
Peninsular Inc ....E..... 586 775-7211
  Roseville *(G-13853)*
Plesh Industries Inc ....F..... 716 873-4916
  Brighton *(G-1979)*
Power Industries Corp ....G..... 586 783-3818
  Harrison Township *(G-7343)*
Power Marine LLC ....G..... 586 344-1192
  Harrison Township *(G-7344)*
Precise Finishing Systems Inc ....E..... 517 552-9200
  Howell *(G-8081)*
Printing Cylinders Inc ....G..... 586 791-5231
  Clinton Township *(G-3204)*
Priority Waste LLC ....E..... 586 228-1200
  Clinton Township *(G-3205)*
▲ Process Systems Inc ....D..... 586 757-5711
  Warren *(G-17198)*
▲ Production Fabricators Inc ....E..... 231 777-3822
  Muskegon *(G-11407)*
PSC Industrial Outsourcing LP ....D..... 313 824-5859
  Detroit *(G-4315)*
Quigley Industries Inc ....D..... 248 426-8600
  Farmington Hills *(G-5109)*
◆ R & D Enterprises Inc ....E..... 248 349-7077
  Plymouth *(G-12728)*
R and J Dumpsters LLC ....G..... 248 863-8579
  Howell *(G-8085)*
R T C Enviro Fab Inc ....F..... 517 596-2987
  Munith *(G-11254)*
▲ R W Fernstrum & Company ....E..... 906 863-5553
  Menominee *(G-10756)*
Rae Manufacturing Company ....F..... 810 987-9170
  Port Huron *(G-12960)*
RC Metal Products Inc ....G..... 616 696-1694
  Sand Lake *(G-14427)*
Refrigeration Research Inc ....D..... 810 227-1151
  Brighton *(G-1985)*
Rendon & Sons Machining Inc ....F..... 269 628-2200
  Gobles *(G-5949)*
Returnable Packaging Corp ....F..... 586 206-8050
  Clinton Township *(G-3210)*
▼ Riverside Tank & Mfg Corp ....F..... 810 329-7143
  Saint Clair *(G-14234)*
RK Wojan Inc ....E..... 231 347-1160
  Charlevoix *(G-2628)*
Rlh Industries Inc ....F..... 989 732-0493
  Gaylord *(G-5889)*

S N D Steel Fabrication Inc ....F..... 586 997-1500
  Shelby Township *(G-14684)*
Saline Manufacturing Inc ....F..... 586 294-4701
  Roseville *(G-13865)*
Saranac Tank Inc ....G..... 616 642-9481
  Saranac *(G-14455)*
Schad Boiler Setting Company ....D..... 313 273-2235
  Detroit *(G-4355)*
Seal Support Systems Inc ....E..... 586 331-7251
  Romeo *(G-13638)*
Sfi Acquisition Inc ....E..... 248 471-1500
  Farmington Hills *(G-5122)*
Sloan Valve Company ....D..... 248 446-5300
  New Hudson *(G-11555)*
Smith Dumpsters ....G..... 616 675-9399
  Kent City *(G-8994)*
Southfield Machining Inc ....G..... 313 871-8200
  Detroit *(G-4368)*
Special Mold Engineering Inc ....E..... 248 652-6600
  Rochester Hills *(G-13516)*
SPX Corporation ....C..... 586 574-2332
  Warren *(G-17251)*
SPX Corporation ....D..... 989 652-6136
  Bridgeport *(G-1857)*
SPX Corporation ....D..... 313 768-2103
  Livonia *(G-9940)*
SPX Corporation ....C..... 586 574-2332
  Warren *(G-17252)*
◆ Steel Tank & Fabricating Co ....D..... 248 625-8700
  Clarkston *(G-2959)*
Steel Tank & Fabricating Co ....E..... 231 587-8412
  Mancelona *(G-10399)*
Superior Steel Components Inc ....D..... 616 866-4759
  Grand Rapids *(G-6904)*
Taylor Controls Inc ....F..... 269 637-8521
  South Haven *(G-14777)*
▲ Tower Defense & Aerospace LLC ....C..... 248 675-6000
  Livonia *(G-9966)*
◆ Trimas Corporation ....E..... 248 631-5450
  Bloomfield Hills *(G-1807)*
True Fabrications & Machine ....F..... 248 288-0140
  Troy *(G-16653)*
Van Loon Industries Inc ....E..... 586 532-8530
  Shelby Township *(G-14716)*
Vent-Rite Valve Corp ....E..... 269 925-8812
  Benton Harbor *(G-1560)*
Vierson Boiler & Repair Co ....F..... 616 949-0500
  Grand Rapids *(G-6972)*
W Soule & Co ....C..... 269 344-0139
  Kalamazoo *(G-8920)*
Walbro LLC ....C..... 989 872-2131
  Cass City *(G-2524)*
Waltz-Holst Blow Pipe Company ....E..... 616 676-8119
  Ada *(G-33)*
Welding & Joining Tech LLC ....G..... 248 625-3045
  Clarkston *(G-2965)*
▲ Western International Inc ....E..... 866 814-2470
  Troy *(G-16689)*
▲ Wolverine Metal Stamping Inc ....D..... 269 429-6600
  Saint Joseph *(G-14354)*
Yale Steel Inc ....G..... 810 387-2567
  Brockway *(G-2021)*
Yello Dumpster ....G..... 616 915-0506
  Grand Rapids *(G-7008)*

3444 Sheet Metal Work

A & B Welding & Fabricating ....G..... 231 733-2661
  Muskegon *(G-11255)*
A-1 Awning Company ....G..... 734 421-0680
  Westland *(G-17537)*
Access Heating & Cooling Inc ....G..... 734 464-0566
  Livonia *(G-9625)*
Accuform Industries Inc ....F..... 616 363-3801
  Grand Rapids *(G-6132)*
Accuform Industries Inc ....F..... 616 363-3801
  Grand Rapids *(G-6133)*
Accurate Engineering & Mfg LLC ....F..... 616 738-1261
  Holland *(G-7547)*
Ace Welding & Machine Inc ....F..... 231 941-9664
  Traverse City *(G-15887)*
Ackerman Brothers Inc ....G..... 989 892-4122
  Bay City *(G-1270)*
Acme Carbide Die Inc ....E..... 734 722-2303
  Westland *(G-17538)*
Acme Tool & Die Co ....G..... 231 938-1260
  Acme *(G-1)*
Admin Industries LLC ....F..... 989 685-3438
  Rose City *(G-13756)*
Advanced Sheet Metal ....G..... 616 301-3828
  Grand Rapids *(G-6149)*

Advantage Laser Inc ....G..... 734 367-9936
  Livonia *(G-9629)*
▲ Air Conditioning Products Co ....D..... 734 326-0050
  Romulus *(G-13649)*
Alliance Sheet Metal Inc ....F..... 269 795-2954
  Middleville *(G-10797)*
Allied Machine Inc ....E..... 231 834-0050
  Grant *(G-7077)*
▲ Allor Manufacturing Inc ....D..... 248 486-4500
  Brighton *(G-1883)*
▲ Aluminum Blanking Co Inc ....D..... 248 338-4422
  Pontiac *(G-12802)*
▲ American Blower Supply Inc ....F..... 586 771-7337
  Warren *(G-16929)*
American Fabricated Pdts Inc ....F..... 616 607-8785
  Spring Lake *(G-15133)*
American Metal Fab Inc ....D..... 269 279-5108
  Three Rivers *(G-15854)*
▲ American Roll Shutter Awng Co ....E..... 734 422-7110
  Livonia *(G-9645)*
American Tchncal Fbrcators LLC ....E..... 989 269-6262
  Bad Axe *(G-1056)*
Amhawk LLC ....E..... 269 468-4177
  Hartford *(G-7381)*
Amjs Incorporated ....G.....
  Lawton *(G-9510)*
Anderson Welding & Mfg Inc ....F..... 906 523-4661
  Chassell *(G-2671)*
Arnold & Sautter Co ....F..... 989 684-7557
  Bay City *(G-1276)*
Attentive Industries Inc ....F..... 810 233-7077
  Flint *(G-5379)*
▲ Attentive Industries Inc ....G..... 810 233-7077
  Flint *(G-5380)*
Austin Tube Products Inc ....E..... 231 745-2741
  Baldwin *(G-1082)*
▲ B & D Thread Rolling Inc ....D..... 734 728-7070
  Taylor *(G-15693)*
B & L Industries Inc ....F..... 810 987-9121
  Port Huron *(G-12896)*
▲ Baldauf Enterprises Inc ....D..... 989 686-0350
  Bay City *(G-1279)*
Bar Processing Corporation ....D..... 734 782-4454
  Warren *(G-16952)*
Bauer Sheet Metal & Fabg Inc ....G..... 231 757-4993
  Scottville *(G-14508)*
Bauer Sheet Metal & Fabg Inc ....E..... 231 773-3244
  Muskegon *(G-11276)*
Belco Industries Inc ....C..... 616 794-0410
  Belding *(G-1399)*
▲ Belco Industries Inc ....E..... 616 794-0410
  Belding *(G-1400)*
Benteler Automotive Corp ....B..... 616 247-3936
  Auburn Hills *(G-791)*
Bestway Building Supply Co ....G..... 810 732-6280
  Flint *(G-5388)*
▲ Beswick Corporation ....F..... 248 589-0562
  Troy *(G-16239)*
▲ Bico Michigan Inc ....E..... 616 453-2400
  Grand Rapids *(G-6218)*
Blade Welding Service Inc ....G..... 734 941-4253
  Van Buren Twp *(G-16749)*
Bmc/Industrial Eductl Svcs Inc ....E..... 231 733-1206
  Muskegon *(G-11280)*
Boral Building Products Inc ....C..... 248 668-6400
  Wixom *(G-17777)*
Bristol Steel & Conveyor Corp ....E..... 810 658-9510
  Davison *(G-3641)*
Britten Inc ....C..... 231 941-8200
  Traverse City *(G-15920)*
Burnham & Northern Inc ....G..... 517 279-7501
  Coldwater *(G-3292)*
Buy Best Manufacturing LLC ....F..... 248 875-2491
  Brighton *(G-1891)*
▲ C & T Fabrication LLC ....G..... 616 678-5133
  Kent City *(G-8988)*
▲ C L Rieckhoff Company Inc ....C..... 734 946-8220
  Taylor *(G-15697)*
Carlson Metal Products Inc ....E..... 248 528-1931
  Troy *(G-16259)*
Case-Free Inc ....G..... 616 245-3136
  Grand Rapids *(G-6265)*
Cdp Environmental Inc ....E..... 586 776-7890
  Roseville *(G-13780)*
Ceeflow Inc ....G..... 231 526-5579
  Harbor Springs *(G-7276)*
Certainteed Corporation ....B..... 517 787-8898
  Jackson *(G-8405)*
Certainteed Corporation ....E..... 517 787-1737
  Jackson *(G-8406)*

34 FABRICATED METAL PRODUCTS, EXCEPT MACHINERY AND TRANSPORTATION EQUIPMENT

Chicago Blow Pipe Company ....F..... 773 533-6100
 Marquette *(G-10522)*
Cmn Fabrication Inc ....G..... 586 294-1941
 Roseville *(G-13782)*
CNC Products LLC ....E..... 269 684-5500
 Niles *(G-11599)*
Commercial Fabricating & Engrg ....F..... 248 887-1595
 Highland *(G-7488)*
Commercial Indus A Sltions LLC ....G..... 269 373-8797
 Kalamazoo *(G-8709)*
▲ Commercial Mfg & Assembly Inc ....E..... 616 847-9980
 Grand Haven *(G-6005)*
Conner Steel Products ....G..... 248 852-5110
 Rochester Hills *(G-13394)*
▲ Conquest Manufacturing LLC ....D..... 586 576-7600
 Warren *(G-16991)*
Consolidated Metal Pdts Inc ....G..... 616 538-1000
 Grand Rapids *(G-6302)*
Constructive Sheet Metal Inc ....E..... 616 245-5306
 Allendale *(G-215)*
Contractors Sheet Metal Inc ....G..... 231 348-0753
 Harbor Springs *(G-7278)*
Corlett-Turner Co ....G..... 616 772-9082
 Grand Rapids *(G-6311)*
Coxline Inc ....E..... 269 345-1132
 Kalamazoo *(G-8720)*
Cse Morse Inc ....D..... 269 962-5548
 Battle Creek *(G-1170)*
Curbs & Damper Products Inc ....F..... 586 776-7890
 Roseville *(G-13788)*
Custo Arch Shee Meta ....F..... 313 571-2277
 Detroit *(G-3958)*
Custom Design & Manufacturing ....F..... 989 754-9962
 Carrollton *(G-2484)*
Custom Fab Inc ....G..... 586 755-7260
 Warren *(G-16995)*
Custom Metal Products Corp ....G..... 734 591-2500
 Livonia *(G-9695)*
Custom Metal Works Inc ....G..... 810 420-0390
 Marine City *(G-10472)*
Custom Products Inc ....F..... 269 983-9500
 Saint Joseph *(G-14305)*
Customer Metal Fabrication Inc ....E..... 906 774-3216
 Iron Mountain *(G-8282)*
D & W Awning and Window Co ....E..... 810 742-0340
 Davison *(G-3645)*
D&M Metal Products Company ....E..... 616 784-0601
 Comstock Park *(G-3474)*
Dee Cramer Inc ....E..... 517 485-5519
 Lansing *(G-9286)*
Delducas Welding & Co Inc ....G..... 810 743-1990
 Flint *(G-5416)*
Delta Iron Works Inc ....F..... 313 579-1445
 Detroit *(G-3967)*
Delta Tube & Fabricating Corp ....C..... 248 634-8267
 Holly *(G-7875)*
Denlin Industries Inc ....E..... 586 303-5209
 Milford *(G-10960)*
Design Metal Inc ....F..... 248 547-4170
 Oak Park *(G-12059)*
Designers Sheet Metal Inc ....G..... 269 429-4133
 Saint Joseph *(G-14306)*
Detroit Cornice & Slate Co Inc ....E..... 248 398-7690
 Ferndale *(G-5275)*
Detronic Industries Inc ....D..... 586 268-6392
 Sterling Heights *(G-15315)*
▲ Dewys Manufacturing Inc ....C..... 616 677-5281
 Marne *(G-10507)*
▲ Digital Fabrication Inc ....F..... 616 794-2848
 Belding *(G-1409)*
Diversified Fabricators Inc ....E..... 586 868-1000
 Clinton Township *(G-3104)*
Diversified Metal Fabricators ....E..... 248 541-0500
 Ferndale *(G-5281)*
Dorris Company ....E..... 586 293-5260
 Fraser *(G-5644)*
Douglas King Industries Inc ....E..... 989 642-2865
 Hemlock *(G-7461)*
Douglas West Company Inc ....G..... 734 676-8882
 Grosse Ile *(G-7171)*
▲ Dowding Industries Inc ....E..... 517 663-5455
 Eaton Rapids *(G-4720)*
Dowding Tool Products LLC ....F..... 517 541-2795
 Springport *(G-15210)*
Dri-Design Inc ....E..... 616 355-2970
 Holland *(G-7612)*
Dts Enterprises Inc ....E..... 231 599-3123
 Ellsworth *(G-4787)*
Dubois Production Services Inc ....E..... 616 785-0088
 Comstock Park *(G-3480)*

▼ Duo-Gard Industries Inc ....D..... 734 207-9700
 Canton *(G-2367)*
E & S Sheet Metal ....G..... 989 871-2067
 Millington *(G-10995)*
East Muskegon Roofg Shtmtl Co ....D..... 231 744-2461
 Muskegon *(G-11313)*
East Muskegon Roofg Shtmtl Co ....F..... 616 791-6900
 Grand Rapids *(G-6367)*
Ecolo-Tech Inc ....F..... 248 541-1100
 Madison Heights *(G-10238)*
Ede Co ....G..... 586 756-7555
 Warren *(G-17016)*
Electrolabs Inc ....F..... 586 294-4150
 Fraser *(G-5650)*
Elevated Technologies Inc ....F..... 616 288-9817
 Grand Rapids *(G-6375)*
▼ EMI Construction Products ....G..... 800 603-9965
 Holland *(G-7622)*
▲ Envirodyne Technologies Inc ....E..... 269 342-1918
 Kalamazoo *(G-8739)*
▲ Envision Engineering LLC ....G..... 616 897-0599
 Lowell *(G-10027)*
▲ Erbsloeh Alum Solutions Inc ....B..... 269 323-2565
 Portage *(G-12993)*
Experi-Metal Inc ....C..... 586 977-7800
 Sterling Heights *(G-15335)*
Fab-Alloy Company ....G..... 517 787-4313
 Jackson *(G-8447)*
Fabrication Specialties Inc ....G..... 313 891-7181
 Davisburg *(G-3632)*
Fabrications Plus Inc ....G..... 269 749-3050
 Olivet *(G-12141)*
Fabrilaser Mfg LLC ....E..... 269 789-9490
 Marshall *(G-10567)*
◆ Federal Screw Works ....F..... 734 941-4211
 Romulus *(G-13676)*
Fenixx Technologies LLC ....G..... 586 254-6000
 Sterling Heights *(G-15338)*
Fhc Holding Company ....G..... 616 538-3231
 Wyoming *(G-18001)*
Flat-To-Form Metal Spc Inc ....F..... 231 924-1288
 Fremont *(G-5771)*
Flex-N-Gate Stamping LLC ....F..... 810 772-1514
 Warren *(G-17040)*
▲ Flex-N-Gate Stamping LLC ....E..... 586 759-8900
 Warren *(G-17041)*
Fortress Manufacturing Inc ....F..... 269 925-1336
 Benton Harbor *(G-1498)*
Frank W Small Met Fabrication ....G..... 269 422-2001
 Baroda *(G-1124)*
Frankenmuth Welding & Fabg ....G..... 989 754-9457
 Saginaw *(G-14038)*
Frenchys Skirting Inc ....G..... 734 721-3013
 Wayne *(G-17430)*
▲ G A Richards Company ....D..... 616 243-2800
 Grand Rapids *(G-6427)*
G A Richards Plant Two ....G..... 616 850-8528
 Spring Lake *(G-15143)*
◆ Gallagher-Kaiser Corporation ....D..... 313 368-3100
 Troy *(G-16378)*
Gee & Missler Inc ....E..... 734 284-1224
 Wyandotte *(G-17959)*
▲ Geerpres Inc ....E..... 231 773-3211
 Muskegon *(G-11329)*
General Motors LLC ....D..... 810 234-2710
 Flint *(G-5434)*
Gladwin Tank Manufacturing Inc ....F..... 989 426-4768
 Gladwin *(G-5932)*
Gokoh Coldwater Incorporated ....F..... 517 279-1080
 Coldwater *(G-3305)*
Gray Brothers Mfg Inc ....E..... 269 483-7615
 White Pigeon *(G-17650)*
Great Lakes Mechanical Corp ....C..... 313 581-1400
 Dearborn *(G-3717)*
Great Lakes Powder Coating LLC ......F..... 248 522-6222
 Walled Lake *(G-16894)*
Greene Manufacturing Inc ....E..... 734 428-8304
 Chelsea *(G-2712)*
▲ Greene Metal Products Inc ....E..... 586 465-6800
 Clinton Township *(G-3130)*
Greene Metal Products Inc ....F..... 586 465-6800
 Clinton Township *(G-3131)*
Greens Welding & Repair Co ....G..... 734 721-5434
 Westland *(G-17564)*
H & M Welding and Fabricating ....G..... 517 764-3630
 Jackson *(G-8461)*
▲ Hancock Enterprises Inc ....D..... 734 287-8840
 Taylor *(G-15728)*
Harris Sheet Metal Co ....F..... 989 496-3080
 Midland *(G-10867)*

Hart Acquisition Company LLC ....E..... 313 537-0490
 Redford *(G-13164)*
Hdn F&A Inc ....E..... 269 965-3268
 Battle Creek *(G-1197)*
Hmw Contracting LLC ....C..... 313 531-8477
 Detroit *(G-4125)*
HPS Fabrications Inc ....F..... 734 282-2285
 Wyandotte *(G-17961)*
Hutchinson Sealing Syst ....D..... 248 375-3721
 Auburn Hills *(G-904)*
Hydro Extrusion North Amer LLC ......B..... 269 349-6626
 Kalamazoo *(G-8772)*
Industrial Ducts Systems Inc ....G..... 586 498-3993
 Roseville *(G-13818)*
Industrial Mtal Fbricators LLC ....F..... 810 765-8960
 Cottrellville *(G-3588)*
Innovate Industries Inc ....G..... 586 558-8990
 Warren *(G-17092)*
Innovative Sheet Metals ....G..... 231 788-5751
 Muskegon *(G-11348)*
Integrated Industries Inc ....D..... 586 790-1550
 Clinton Township *(G-3141)*
J & J Metal Products Inc ....G..... 586 792-2680
 Clinton Township *(G-3146)*
J & L Mfg Co ....E..... 586 445-9530
 Warren *(G-17104)*
▲ J & M Machine Products Inc ....D..... 231 755-1622
 Norton Shores *(G-11764)*
J and N Fabrications Inc ....G..... 586 751-6350
 Warren *(G-17105)*
J M L Contracting & Sales Inc ....F..... 586 756-4133
 Warren *(G-17108)*
Jackson Architctural Mtl Fabri ....G..... 517 782-8884
 Jackson *(G-8474)*
Jbs Sheet Metal Inc ....G..... 231 777-2802
 Muskegon *(G-11352)*
JC Metal Fabricating Inc ....G..... 231 629-0425
 Reed City *(G-13216)*
Jensen Bridge & Supply Company .....E..... 810 648-3000
 Sandusky *(G-14437)*
Jervis B Webb Company ....D..... 231 582-6558
 Boyne City *(G-1825)*
Jones Mfg & Sup Co Inc ....E..... 616 877-4442
 Moline *(G-11011)*
K & W Manufacturing Co Inc ....F..... 517 369-9708
 Bronson *(G-2031)*
Kalamazoo Mechanical Inc ....F..... 269 343-5351
 Kalamazoo *(G-8790)*
Kimbow Inc ....F..... 616 774-4680
 Comstock Park *(G-3490)*
Kolkema Fabricating ....G..... 231 865-6380
 Fruitport *(G-5794)*
▲ Kraftube Inc ....C..... 231 832-5562
 Reed City *(G-13217)*
Kriewall Enterprises Inc ....E..... 586 336-0600
 Romeo *(G-13631)*
Krupp Industries LLC ....D..... 734 261-0410
 Livonia *(G-9801)*
Krupp Industries LLC ....E..... 616 475-5905
 Walker *(G-16870)*
Kulick Enterprises Inc ....G..... 734 283-6999
 Wyandotte *(G-17964)*
L D S Sheet Metal Inc ....G..... 313 892-2624
 Warren *(G-17124)*
Lahti Fabrication Inc ....F..... 989 343-0420
 West Branch *(G-17510)*
▲ Lanzen Incorporated ....D..... 586 771-7070
 Bruce Twp *(G-2090)*
Lanzen-Petoskey LLC ....E..... 231 881-9602
 Petoskey *(G-12454)*
Laser Fab Inc ....G..... 586 415-8090
 Fraser *(G-5683)*
Legacy Metal Fabricating LLC ....E..... 616 258-8406
 Grand Rapids *(G-6625)*
Liberty Steel Fabricating Inc ....E..... 269 556-9792
 Saint Joseph *(G-14327)*
▼ Light Metals Corporation ....B..... 616 538-3030
 Wyoming *(G-18016)*
▲ Llink Technologies LLC ....E..... 586 336-9370
 Brown City *(G-2054)*
Loftis Machine Company ....E..... 616 846-1990
 Grand Haven *(G-6051)*
Longstreet Group LLC ....F..... 517 278-4487
 Coldwater *(G-3314)*
Lv Metals Inc ....G..... 734 654-8081
 Carleton *(G-2460)*
Lyndon Fabricators Inc ....G..... 313 937-3640
 Detroit *(G-4212)*
M C M Fixture Company Inc ....E..... 248 547-9280
 Hazel Park *(G-7442)*

Employee Codes: A=Over 500 employees, B=251-500
C=101-250, D=51-100, E=20-50, F=10-19, G=3-9

M J Mechanical Inc E 989 865-9633
Saint Charles (G-14195)
Magic City Heating & Cooling G 269 467-6406
Centreville (G-2596)
▲ Magnetic Products Inc D 248 887-5600
Highland (G-7497)
Manning Enterprises Inc E 269 657-2346
Paw Paw (G-12408)
Marsh Industrial Services Inc F 231 258-4870
Kalkaska (G-8949)
▲ Material Handling Tech Inc D 586 725-5546
Ira (G-8260)
Matrix Tool Co E 586 296-6010
Clinton Township (G-3170)
Mayo Welding & Fabricating Co G 248 435-2730
Royal Oak (G-13948)
MB Aerospace Warren LLC C 586 772-2500
Warren (G-17144)
McElroy Metal Mill Inc E 269 781-8313
Marshall (G-10582)
Mechanical Sheet Metal Co F 734 284-1006
Wyandotte (G-17967)
▲ Metal Components LLC D 616 252-1900
Grand Rapids (G-6660)
Metal Components Employment D 616 252-1900
Grand Rapids (G-6661)
Metal Merchants of Michigan E 248 293-0621
Rochester Hills (G-13472)
Metal Sales Manufacturing Corp E 989 686-5879
Bay City (G-1331)
Metallist Inc G 517 437-4476
Hillsdale (G-7530)
Metalworks Inc C 231 845-5136
Ludington (G-10073)
▲ Meter Devices Company Inc A 330 455-0301
Farmington Hills (G-5064)
Metro Duct Inc E 517 783-2646
Jackson (G-8517)
Metro-Fabricating LLC D 989 667-8100
Bay City (G-1332)
Michigan Metal Fabricators G 586 754-0421
Warren (G-17153)
◆ Midbrook Inc D 800 966-9274
Jackson (G-8525)
Midwest Wall Company LLC F 517 881-3701
Dewitt (G-4465)
Mike Manufacturing Corporation G 586 759-1140
Warren (G-17156)
Milton Manufacturing Inc E 313 366-2450
Detroit (G-4250)
Mlp Mfg Inc E 616 842-8767
Spring Lake (G-15164)
Modern Metalcraft Inc F 989 835-3716
Midland (G-10895)
Modulated Metals Inc F 586 749-8400
Chesterfield (G-2807)
Monarch Metal Mfg Inc G 616 247-0412
Grand Rapids (G-6699)
Monarch Welding & Engrg Inc F 231 733-7222
Muskegon (G-11384)
MSE Fabrication LLC F 586 991-6138
Sterling Heights (G-15429)
Muskegon Awning & Mfg Co E 231 759-0911
Muskegon (G-11387)
Nankin Welding Co Inc G 734 458-3980
Livonia (G-9857)
National Ordnance Auto Mfg LLC G 248 853-8822
Auburn Hills (G-953)
National Roofg & Shtmtl Co Inc D 989 964-0557
Saginaw (G-14102)
Nelson Steel Products Inc D 616 396-1515
Holland (G-7753)
▲ Nicholson Terminal & Dock Co C 313 842-4300
River Rouge (G-13279)
North Woods Industrial G 616 784-2840
Comstock Park (G-3502)
Northern Machining & Repr Inc E 906 786-0526
Escanaba (G-4847)
Northland Corporation D 616 754-5601
Greenville (G-7147)
◆ Northland Corporation C 616 754-5601
Greenville (G-7148)
Northwest Fabrication Inc G 231 536-3229
East Jordan (G-4641)
▲ Northwoods Manufacturing Inc D 906 779-2370
Kingsford (G-9065)
Pardon Inc E 906 428-3494
Gladstone (G-5918)
Parton & Preble Inc E 586 773-6000
Warren (G-17180)

Patio Land Mfg Inc G 586 758-5660
Warren (G-17184)
Plesko Sheet Metal Inc G 989 847-3771
Ashley (G-728)
Portage Wire Systems Inc E 231 889-4215
Onekama (G-12151)
Precision Prototype & Mfg Inc F 517 663-4114
Eaton Rapids (G-4729)
▲ Production Fabricators Inc E 231 777-3822
Muskegon (G-11407)
Production Tube Company Inc G 313 259-3990
Detroit (G-4312)
Professional Fabricating Inc E 616 531-1240
Grand Rapids (G-6782)
Professional Metal Works Inc E 517 351-7411
Haslett (G-7398)
Progressive Manufacturing LLC G 231 924-9975
Fremont (G-5783)
Protofab Corporation G 248 689-3730
Troy (G-16569)
Prototech Laser Inc E 586 598-6900
Chesterfield (G-2827)
Providence Worldwide LLC E 313 586-4144
Westland (G-17592)
Quality Alum Acquisition LLC F 734 783-0990
Flat Rock (G-5359)
Quality Alum Acquisition LLC D 800 550-1667
Hastings (G-7424)
Quality Finishing Systems F 231 834-9131
Grant (G-7081)
▲ Quality Metalcraft Inc C 734 261-6700
Livonia (G-9900)
Quality Stainless Mfg Co F 248 546-4141
Madison Heights (G-10343)
R & DS Manufacturing LLC G 586 716-9900
New Baltimore (G-11490)
R B I Mechanical Inc E 231 582-2970
Boyne City (G-1834)
Rainbow Seamless Systems Inc F 231 933-8888
Traverse City (G-16089)
Reurink Sales & Service LLC G 616 522-9100
Ionia (G-8251)
Richmond Bros Fabrication LLC G 989 551-1996
Bay Port (G-1374)
Rick Wykle LLC G 734 839-6376
Livonia (G-9909)
Rochester Welding Company Inc E 248 628-0801
Oxford (G-12369)
Roth Fabricating Inc E 517 458-7541
Morenci (G-11114)
▲ Roura Acquisition Inc F 586 790-6100
Clinton Township (G-3216)
S & B Roofing Services Inc D 248 334-5372
Pontiac (G-12863)
S & N Machine & Fabricating F 231 894-2658
Rothbury (G-13895)
Sage International Inc D 972 623-2004
Novi (G-11989)
▲ Saginaw Control & Engrg Inc B 989 799-6871
Saginaw (G-14138)
Salem/Savard Industries LLC E 313 931-6880
Detroit (G-4352)
Sandvik Inc E 269 926-7241
Benton Harbor (G-1545)
Schneider Iron & Metal Inc F 906 774-0644
Iron Mountain (G-8299)
Schneider Sheet Metal Sup Inc G 517 694-7661
Lansing (G-9422)
◆ Schuler Incorporated D 734 207-7200
Canton (G-2425)
Scotten Steel Processing Inc F 313 897-8837
Detroit (G-4356)
Seal All Aluminum Pdts Corp G 248 585-6061
Southfield (G-15025)
Security Steelcraft Corp E 231 733-1101
Muskegon (G-11420)
▲ Selkirk Corporation E 616 656-8200
Grand Rapids (G-6857)
Sequoia Tool Inc D 586 463-4400
Clinton Township (G-3223)
Servotech Industries Inc F 734 697-5555
Taylor (G-15764)
Set Duct Manufacturing LLC E 313 491-4380
Detroit (G-4358)
Set Enterprises of Mi Inc C 586 573-3600
Sterling Heights (G-15494)
Sfi Acquisition Inc E 248 471-1500
Farmington Hills (G-5122)
Sheren Plumbing & Heating Inc E 231 943-7916
Traverse City (G-16101)

Shouldice Indus Mfrs Cntrs Inc D 269 962-5579
Battle Creek (G-1247)
Sintel Inc C 616 842-6960
Spring Lake (G-15178)
Sparta Sheet Metal Inc F 616 784-9035
Grand Rapids (G-6876)
Spectrum Metal Products Inc G 734 595-7600
Westland (G-17600)
Spinform Inc G 810 767-4660
Flint (G-5502)
◆ Stageright Corporation C 989 386-7393
Clare (G-2890)
Stainless Fabg & Engrg Inc G 269 329-6142
Portage (G-13034)
State Building Product Inc E 586 772-8878
Warren (G-17254)
Steel-Guard Company LLC G 586 232-3909
Macomb (G-10162)
Steinke-Fenton Fabricators F 517 782-8174
Jackson (G-8577)
Stelmatic Industries Inc F 586 949-0160
Chesterfield (G-2843)
Stewart Steel Specialties G 248 477-0680
Farmington Hills (G-5132)
Stus Welding & Fabrication G 616 392-8459
Holland (G-7818)
Sure-Weld & Plating Rack Co G 248 304-9430
Southfield (G-15040)
Tapco Holdings Inc C 248 668-6400
Wixom (G-17905)
Tara Industries Inc F 248 477-6520
Livonia (G-9953)
Target Construction Inc D 616 866-7728
Cedar Springs (G-2564)
TEC International II E 586 469-9611
Macomb (G-10166)
TEC-3 Prototypes Inc E 810 678-8909
Metamora (G-10782)
Tel-X Corporation E 734 425-2225
Garden City (G-5843)
Thermal Designs & Manufacturng E 586 773-5231
Roseville (G-13878)
▼ Thierica Equipment Corporation E 616 453-6570
Grand Rapids (G-6928)
Tigmaster Co E 800 824-4830
Baroda (G-1132)
Town & Country Cedar Homes G 231 347-4360
Boyne Falls (G-1842)
Trade Specific Solutions LLC G 734 752-7124
Southgate (G-15085)
Tri-Vision LLC F 313 526-6020
Detroit (G-4407)
Trigon Metal Products Inc G 734 513-3488
Livonia (G-9971)
◆ Triumph Gear Systems - Macomb C 586 781-2800
Macomb (G-10170)
Tru Flo Carbide Inc D 989 658-8515
Ubly (G-16724)
Tubelite Inc D 800 866-2227
Walker (G-16880)
Turnkey Fabrication LLC G 616 248-9116
Grand Rapids (G-6941)
Unifab Corporation E 269 382-2803
Portage (G-13051)
Universal Fabricators Inc E 248 399-7565
Madison Heights (G-10373)
Van Loon Industries Inc E 586 532-8530
Shelby Township (G-14716)
Vanmeer Corporation F 269 694-6090
Otsego (G-12258)
Ventcon Inc C 313 336-4000
Allen Park (G-212)
Ventilation + Plus Eqp Inc G 231 487-1156
Harbor Springs (G-7297)
Versatile Fabrication Co Inc E 231 739-7115
Muskegon (G-11446)
W Soule & Co E 616 975-6272
Grand Rapids (G-6975)
W Soule & Co D 269 324-7001
Portage (G-13054)
W Soule & Co C 269 344-0139
Kalamazoo (G-8920)
Waltz-Holst Blow Pipe Company E 616 676-8119
Ada (G-33)
Welk-Ko Fabricators Inc F 734 425-6840
Livonia (G-10004)
Welk-Ko Fabricators Inc G 810 227-7500
Brighton (G-2008)
Wendling Sheet Metal Inc E 989 753-5286
Saginaw (G-14182)

West Side Mfg Fabrication Inc..........F....... 248 380-6640
Wixom *(G-17928)*
Westco Metalcraft Inc..........F....... 734 425-0900
Livonia *(G-10008)*
Williams Business Services..........G....... 248 280-0073
Rochester Hills *(G-13547)*
Wm Kloeffler Industries Inc..........E....... 810 765-4068
Marine City *(G-10487)*
Wolfgang Moneta..........G....... 269 422-2296
Baroda *(G-1133)*
Worthington Armstrong Venture..........F....... 269 934-6200
Benton Harbor *(G-1572)*
Zinger Sheet Metal Inc..........F....... 616 532-3121
Grand Rapids *(G-7012)*

3446 Architectural & Ornamental Metal Work

A D Johnson Engraving Co Inc..........F....... 269 385-0044
Kalamazoo *(G-8672)*
▲ Alliance Interiors LLC..........D....... 517 322-0711
Lansing *(G-9273)*
Alro Steel Corporation..........F....... 989 893-9553
Bay City *(G-1274)*
Aluminum Architectural Met Co..........F....... 313 895-2555
Detroit *(G-3862)*
▲ Aluminum Blanking Co Inc..........D....... 248 338-4422
Pontiac *(G-12802)*
Aluminum Supply Company Inc..........E....... 313 491-5040
Detroit *(G-3863)*
Aquarius Recreational Products..........G....... 586 469-4600
Harrison Township *(G-7320)*
Arnold & Sautter Co..........F....... 989 684-7557
Bay City *(G-1276)*
Blacksmith Shop LLC..........G....... 616 754-4719
Greenville *(G-7123)*
Bradys Fence Company Inc..........G....... 313 492-8804
South Rockwood *(G-14820)*
Britten Inc..........C....... 231 941-8200
Traverse City *(G-15920)*
◆ Brown-Campbell Company..........F....... 586 884-2180
Shelby Township *(G-14555)*
CEi Composite Materials LLC..........E....... 734 212-3006
Manchester *(G-10403)*
Cr Forge LLC..........G....... 231 924-2033
Fremont *(G-5769)*
Creative Composites Inc..........E....... 906 474-9941
Rapid River *(G-13111)*
Davis Iron Works Inc..........E....... 248 624-5960
Commerce Township *(G-3398)*
Delta Tube & Fabricating Corp..........C....... 810 239-0154
Flint *(G-5418)*
▲ Grattan Family Enterprises LLC..........D....... 248 547-3870
Ferndale *(G-5290)*
Greenwell Machine Shop Inc..........G....... 231 347-3346
Petoskey *(G-12450)*
Guile & Son Inc..........G....... 517 376-2116
Byron *(G-2172)*
Harbor Steel and Supply Corp..........F....... 616 786-0002
Holland *(G-7657)*
Harlow Sheet Metal LLC..........G....... 734 996-1509
Ann Arbor *(G-482)*
▲ Hart & Cooley Inc..........C....... 616 656-8200
Grand Rapids *(G-6495)*
Ideal Wrought Iron..........G....... 313 581-1324
Detroit *(G-4135)*
Iron Capital of America Co..........G....... 586 771-5840
Warren *(G-17098)*
Iron Fetish Metalworks Inc..........F....... 586 776-8311
Roseville *(G-13822)*
▲ ITT Motion Tech Amer LLC..........F....... 248 863-2161
Novi *(G-11909)*
J D Russell Company..........E....... 586 254-8500
Utica *(G-16743)*
▲ Jack-Post Corporation..........F....... 269 695-7000
Buchanan *(G-2121)*
Kern-Liebers Pieron Inc..........E....... 248 427-1100
Farmington Hills *(G-5037)*
Land Enterprises Inc..........G....... 248 398-7276
Madison Heights *(G-10297)*
Marquette Fence Company Inc..........G....... 906 249-8000
Marquette *(G-10544)*
Mayo Welding & Fabricating Co..........G....... 248 435-2730
Royal Oak *(G-13948)*
Merrill Technologies Group Inc..........C....... 989 462-0330
Alma *(G-241)*
Michigan Ornamental Ir & Fabg..........F....... 616 899-2441
Conklin *(G-3530)*
Minuteman Metal Works Inc..........G....... 989 269-8342
Bad Axe *(G-1069)*
▲ Mol Belting Systems Inc..........D....... 616 453-2484
Grand Rapids *(G-6696)*
Niles Aluminum Products Inc..........F....... 269 683-1191
Niles *(G-11632)*
O I K Industries Inc..........E....... 269 382-1210
Kalamazoo *(G-8838)*
▲ Phoenix Wire Cloth Inc..........E....... 248 585-6350
Troy *(G-16547)*
R B Christian Inc..........G....... 269 963-9327
Battle Creek *(G-1239)*
▼ San Marino Iron Company..........G....... 313 526-9255
Warren *(G-17228)*
Scott Iron Works Inc..........F....... 248 548-2822
Hazel Park *(G-7454)*
▼ Soundtech Inc..........D....... 616 575-0866
Grand Rapids *(G-6871)*
Southwest Metals Incorporated..........G....... 313 842-2700
Detroit *(G-4369)*
Spartan Metal Fab LLC..........G....... 517 322-9050
Lansing *(G-9263)*
St USA Holding Corp..........D....... 517 278-7144
Coldwater *(G-3334)*
St USA Holding Corp..........C....... 800 637-3303
Coldwater *(G-3335)*
Stus Welding & Fabrication..........G....... 616 392-8459
Holland *(G-7818)*
Swing-Lo Suspended Scaffold Co..........F....... 269 764-8989
Covert *(G-3591)*
▲ Symbiote Inc..........E....... 616 772-1790
Zeeland *(G-18189)*
Syncreonus Inc..........G....... 586 754-4100
Warren *(G-17259)*
▲ Syncreonus Inc..........D....... 248 377-4700
Auburn Hills *(G-1010)*
United Lighting Standards Inc..........D....... 586 774-5650
Warren *(G-17273)*
Valley City Sign Company..........E....... 616 784-5711
Comstock Park *(G-3519)*
Vogt Industries Inc..........G....... 616 531-4830
Grand Rapids *(G-6974)*
Worthington Armstrong Venture..........F....... 269 934-6200
Benton Harbor *(G-1572)*

3448 Prefabricated Metal Buildings & Cmp-nts

4ever Aluminum Products Inc..........F....... 517 368-0000
Coldwater *(G-3286)*
All Season Enclosures..........G....... 248 650-8020
Shelby Township *(G-14545)*
Alumiramp Inc..........F....... 517 639-5103
Quincy *(G-13088)*
Berlin Holdings LLC..........G....... 517 523-2444
Pittsford *(G-12515)*
◆ Brasco International Inc..........D....... 313 393-0393
Madison Heights *(G-10206)*
Classic Car Port & Canopies..........F....... 586 759-5490
Warren *(G-16982)*
Classic Dock & Lift LLC..........G....... 231 882-4374
Beulah *(G-1609)*
Compact Engineering Corp..........F....... 231 788-5470
Muskegon *(G-11298)*
Con-De Manufacturing Inc..........G....... 269 651-3756
Sturgis *(G-15601)*
Control Dekk LLC..........G....... 616 828-4862
Wyoming *(G-17994)*
▼ Duo-Gard Industries Inc..........D....... 734 207-9700
Canton *(G-2367)*
G & C Carports..........F....... 616 678-4308
Kent City *(G-8990)*
Great Lakes Lift Inc..........G....... 989 673-2109
Caro *(G-2469)*
Huys Electrodes Inc..........G....... 215 723-4897
Romulus *(G-13686)*
I B P Inc..........E....... 248 588-4710
Clarkston *(G-2927)*
Icon Shelters Inc..........E....... 616 396-0919
Holland *(G-7686)*
Inner Box Loading Systems Inc..........G....... 616 241-4330
Grand Rapids *(G-6536)*
Innovate Industries Inc..........G....... 586 558-8990
Warren *(G-17092)*
▲ Instant Marine Inc..........G....... 248 398-1011
Clarkston *(G-2931)*
Keeler-Glasgow Company Inc..........E....... 269 621-2415
Hartford *(G-7384)*
Laser North Inc..........G....... 906 353-6090
Baraga *(G-1106)*
Little Buildings Inc..........G....... 586 752-7100
Romeo *(G-13632)*
▲ Luiten Greenhouse Tech..........G....... 269 381-4020
Kalamazoo *(G-8811)*
Marine Automated Doc System..........F....... 989 539-9010
Harrison *(G-7315)*
Mark Adler Homes..........G....... 586 850-0630
Birmingham *(G-1691)*
McElroy Metal Mill Inc..........E....... 269 781-8313
Marshall *(G-10582)*
Mobile Mini Inc..........F....... 586 759-4916
Warren *(G-17159)*
Morton Buildings Inc..........F....... 616 696-4747
Three Rivers *(G-15871)*
Mpi Products Holdings LLC..........G....... 248 237-3007
Rochester Hills *(G-13477)*
Nathan Shetler..........F....... 269 521-4554
Bloomingdale *(G-1812)*
Pioneer Pole Buildings N Inc..........E....... 989 386-2570
Clare *(G-2884)*
Porter Corp..........D....... 616 399-1963
Holland *(G-7773)*
Progressive Panel Systems..........F....... 616 748-1384
Zeeland *(G-18180)*
RB Construction Company..........E....... 586 264-9478
Mount Clemens *(G-11147)*
Ridgeview Metals Incorporated..........G....... 850 259-1808
Casnovia *(G-2508)*
Ross Sheet Metal Inc..........G....... 248 543-1170
Ferndale *(G-5316)*
Serenus Johnson Portables LLC..........F....... 989 839-2324
Midland *(G-10915)*
Shore-Mate Products LLC..........G....... 616 874-5438
Rockford *(G-13590)*
▲ Temo Inc..........C....... 800 344-8366
Clinton Township *(G-3244)*
▼ Thoreson-Mc Cosh Inc..........E....... 248 362-0960
Troy *(G-16638)*
Tj Rampit Usa Inc..........E....... 517 278-9015
Coldwater *(G-3337)*
Trigon Steel Components Inc..........G....... 616 834-0506
Holland *(G-7841)*
Twin Bay Dock and Products..........G....... 231 943-8420
Traverse City *(G-16131)*
Vets Access LLC..........G....... 810 639-2222
Flushing *(G-5544)*
Wheelock & Son Welding Shop..........G....... 231 947-6557
Traverse City *(G-16145)*
Wildcat Buildings Inc..........F....... 231 824-6406
Manton *(G-10459)*

3449 Misc Structural Metal Work

A & B Welding & Fabricating..........G....... 231 733-2661
Muskegon *(G-11255)*
Aarons Fabrication of Steel..........G....... 586 883-0652
Clinton Township *(G-3032)*
Ambassador Steel Corporation..........E....... 517 455-7216
Lansing *(G-9336)*
Bach Ornamental & Strl Stl Inc..........G....... 517 694-4311
Holt *(G-7904)*
Bowling Enterprises Inc..........G....... 231 864-2653
Kaleva *(G-8930)*
Bristol Steel & Conveyor Corp..........E....... 810 658-9510
Davison *(G-3641)*
Butler Mill Service Company..........C....... 313 429-2486
Detroit *(G-3922)*
Campbell & Shaw Steel Inc..........F....... 810 364-5100
Marysville *(G-10600)*
Challenge Mfg Company..........G....... 616 735-6500
Lansing *(G-9209)*
Concept Metal Products Inc..........D....... 231 799-3202
Spring Lake *(G-15136)*
Corson Fabricating LLC..........F....... 810 326-0532
Saint Clair *(G-14211)*
Cotson Fabricating Inc..........E....... 248 589-2758
Sterling Heights *(G-15301)*
Creform Corporation..........F....... 248 926-2555
Novi *(G-11858)*
D & D Fabrications Inc..........G....... 810 798-2491
Almont *(G-255)*
Daughtery Group Inc..........G....... 313 452-7918
Detroit *(G-3961)*
Depottey Acquisition Inc..........E....... 616 846-4150
Grand Haven *(G-6009)*
Die Stampco Inc..........F....... 989 893-7790
Bay City *(G-1302)*
Dlh Rollform LLC..........G....... 586 231-0507
New Baltimore *(G-11483)*
▲ Dowding Industries Inc..........E....... 517 663-5455
Eaton Rapids *(G-4720)*
Econ-O-Line Abrasive Products..........E....... 616 846-4150
Grand Haven *(G-6011)*
F&B Technologies..........F....... 734 856-2118
Ottawa Lake *(G-12262)*

S I C

Employee Codes: A=Over 500 employees, B=251-500
C=101-250, D=51-100, E=20-50, F=10-19, G=3-9

2020 Harris Michigan
Industrial Directory

785

34 FABRICATED METAL PRODUCTS, EXCEPT MACHINERY AND TRANSPORTATION EQUIPMENT SIC SECTION

Frankenmuth Welding & Fabg .... G 989 754-9457
Saginaw *(G-14038)*
Global Lift Corp .... F 989 269-5900
Bad Axe *(G-1066)*
Great Lakes Wire Packaging LLC .... G 269 428-7220
Stevensville *(G-15568)*
Grippe Machining and Mfg Co .... F 586 778-3150
Roseville *(G-13813)*
Howard Finishing LLC .... C 248 588-9050
Madison Heights *(G-10269)*
▼ **Ideal Shield LLC** .... E 866 825-8659
Detroit *(G-4133)*
Jcr Fabrication LLC .... G 906 235-2683
Ontonagon *(G-12159)*
JD Metalworks Inc .... D 989 386-3231
Clare *(G-2873)*
Kenowa Industries Inc .... E 616 392-7080
Holland *(G-7709)*
Kenowa Industries Inc .... G 517 322-0311
Lansing *(G-9304)*
Kustom Creations Inc .... G 586 997-4141
Sterling Heights *(G-15394)*
Laser North Inc .... G 906 353-6090
Baraga *(G-1107)*
▲ **Llink Technologies LLC** .... E 586 336-9370
Brown City *(G-2054)*
Lor Products Inc .... G 989 382-9020
Remus *(G-13240)*
M J Day Machine Tool Company .... G 313 730-1200
Allen Park *(G-201)*
Metro Rebar Inc .... G 248 851-5894
West Bloomfield *(G-17484)*
Mig Molding LLC .... G 810 724-7400
Imlay City *(G-8208)*
N & K Fulbright LLC .... E 269 695-4580
Niles *(G-11629)*
Netshape International LLC .... C 616 846-8700
Grand Haven *(G-6059)*
Northern Michigan Glass LLC .... E 231 941-0050
Traverse City *(G-16051)*
Porter Steel & Welding Company .... F 231 733-4495
Muskegon *(G-11404)*
R & S Propeller Inc .... F 616 636-8202
Sand Lake *(G-14426)*
Raq LLC .... F 313 473-7271
Pontiac *(G-12860)*
S & N Machine & Fabricating .... F 231 894-2658
Rothbury *(G-13895)*
Shape Corp .... B 616 296-6300
Grand Haven *(G-6076)*
◆ **Shape Corp** .... B 616 846-8700
Grand Haven *(G-6077)*
Shape Corp .... G 616 846-8700
Spring Lake *(G-15176)*
Shape Corp .... G 616 846-8700
Norton Shores *(G-11815)*
Shape Corp .... E 616 844-3215
Grand Haven *(G-6078)*
Shape Corp .... C 616 846-8700
Grand Haven *(G-6079)*
Shape Corp .... C 248 788-8444
Novi *(G-11995)*
Shape Corp .... D 616 842-2825
Spring Lake *(G-15177)*
Shape Corp .... C 616 846-8700
Grand Haven *(G-6080)*
Speedrack Products Group Ltd .... C 517 639-8781
Quincy *(G-13098)*
▼ **Speedrack Products Group Ltd** .... E 616 887-0002
Sparta *(G-15113)*
Standard Coating Inc .... D 248 297-6650
Madison Heights *(G-10359)*
Superior Fabricating Inc .... F 989 354-8877
Alpena *(G-318)*
Tennessee Fabricators LLC .... G 615 793-4444
Sterling Heights *(G-15522)*
Ter Molen & Hart Inc .... G 616 458-4832
Grand Rapids *(G-6922)*
Tial Products Inc .... E 989 729-8553
Owosso *(G-12322)*
Tracy Wilk .... G 231 477-5135
Brethren *(G-1847)*
Tubelite Inc .... D 800 866-2227
Walker *(G-16880)*
Tubelite Inc .... F 800 866-2227
Reed City *(G-13224)*
◆ **Walther Trowal LLC** .... F 616 455-8940
Grand Rapids *(G-6978)*
▲ **Weldaloy Products Company** .... D 586 758-5550
Warren *(G-17290)*
Welk-Ko Fabricators Inc .... G 248 486-2598
New Hudson *(G-11559)*
◆ **Witzenmann Usa LLC** .... C 248 588-6033
Troy *(G-16692)*
Worthington Armstrong Venture .... F 269 934-6200
Benton Harbor *(G-1572)*

3451 Screw Machine Prdts

AAA Industries Inc .... E 313 255-0420
Redford *(G-13140)*
Accuspec Grinding Inc .... E 269 556-1410
Stevensville *(G-15552)*
Advance Turning and Mfg Inc .... C 517 783-2713
Jackson *(G-8373)*
Air-Matic Products Company Inc .... E 248 356-4200
Southfield *(G-14825)*
Alco Manufacturing Corp .... E 734 426-3941
Dexter *(G-4474)*
▲ **Allan Tool & Machine Co Inc** .... D 248 585-2910
Troy *(G-16190)*
American Screw Products Inc .... G 248 543-0991
Madison Heights *(G-10189)*
Amerikam Inc .... D 616 243-5833
Grand Rapids *(G-6167)*
Atf Inc .... E 989 685-2468
Rose City *(G-13760)*
Atg Precision Products LLC .... E 586 247-5400
Canton *(G-2349)*
▲ **Autocam-Pax Inc** .... E 269 782-5186
Dowagiac *(G-4534)*
B M Industries Inc .... G 810 658-0052
Lapeer *(G-9442)*
Belgian Screw Machine Pdts Inc .... G 517 524-8825
Concord *(G-3523)*
Berkley Screw Machine Pdts Inc .... E 248 853-0044
Rochester Hills *(G-13376)*
Black River Manufacturing Inc .... E 810 982-9812
Port Huron *(G-12900)*
BMC Bil-Mac Corporation .... D 616 538-1930
Grandville *(G-7024)*
Borneman & Peterson Inc .... F 810 744-1890
Flint *(G-5393)*
Brown City Machine Pdts LLC .... G 810 346-3070
Brown City *(G-2048)*
▲ **Bulk AG Innovations LLC** .... F 269 925-0900
Benton Harbor *(G-1488)*
C S M Manufacturing Corp .... D 248 471-0700
Farmington Hills *(G-4952)*
▲ **C Thorrez Industries Inc** .... D 517 750-3160
Jackson *(G-8399)*
Cap Collet & Tool Co Inc .... F 734 283-4040
Wyandotte *(G-17951)*
Cardinal Group Industries Corp .... E 517 437-6000
Hillsdale *(G-7521)*
▲ **Central Screw Products Company** ... F 313 893-9100
Troy *(G-16262)*
Comtronics .... G 517 750-3160
Jackson *(G-8417)*
Condor Manufacturing Inc .... E 586 427-4715
Warren *(G-16990)*
Core Electric Company Inc .... F 313 382-7140
Melvindale *(G-10694)*
Corlett-Turner Co .... D 616 772-9082
Zeeland *(G-18127)*
▲ **CPM Acquisition Corp** .... D 231 947-6400
Traverse City *(G-15951)*
Davison-Rite Products Co .... E 734 513-0505
Livonia *(G-9699)*
Dennison Automatics LLC .... G 616 837-7063
Nunica *(G-12035)*
Denny Grice Inc .... F 269 279-6113
Three Rivers *(G-15860)*
Dexter Automatic Products Co .... C 734 426-8900
Dexter *(G-4485)*
Dimension Machine Tech LLC .... F 586 649-4747
Bloomfield Hills *(G-1759)*
▲ **Dirksen Screw Products Co** .... E 586 247-5400
Shelby Township *(G-14579)*
▲ **DPM Manufacturing LLC** .... F 248 349-6375
Livonia *(G-9715)*
Drews Manufacturing Co .... G 616 534-3482
Grand Rapids *(G-6361)*
Durant and Sons Inc .... G 248 548-8646
Oak Park *(G-12061)*
Dynamic Corporation .... D 616 399-9391
Holland *(G-7613)*
E and P Form Tool Company Inc .... F 734 261-3530
Garden City *(G-5823)*
Eagle Creek Mfg & Sales .... G 989 643-7521
Saint Charles *(G-14192)*
ECM Specialties Inc .... G 810 736-0299
Flint *(G-5422)*
Edmore Tool & Grinding Inc .... E 989 427-3790
Edmore *(G-4750)*
Elkins Machine & Tool Co Inc .... E 734 941-0266
Romulus *(G-13671)*
Elkins Machine & Tool Co Inc .... E 734 941-0266
Romulus *(G-13672)*
Embers Ballscrew Repair .... F 586 216-8444
Detroit *(G-4035)*
Extreme Precision Screw Pdts .... E 810 744-1980
Flint *(G-5427)*
F & H Manufacturing Co Inc .... E 517 783-2311
Jackson *(G-8445)*
Federal Screw Works .... E 734 941-4211
Big Rapids *(G-1626)*
Federal Screw Works .... E 810 227-7712
Brighton *(G-1922)*
Fettes Manufacturing Co .... E 586 939-8500
Sterling Heights *(G-15339)*
Fordsell Machine Products Co .... E 586 751-4700
Warren *(G-17042)*
Form All Tool Company .... F 231 894-6303
Whitehall *(G-17666)*
Fox Mfg Co .... E 586 468-1421
Harrison Township *(G-7331)*
▲ **Grace Engineering Corp** .... D 810 392-2181
Memphis *(G-10710)*
Grand Haven Steel Products Inc .... G 616 842-2740
Grand Haven *(G-6025)*
Green Industries Inc .... F 248 446-8900
South Lyon *(G-14793)*
Greendale Screw Pdts Co Inc .... E 586 759-8100
Warren *(G-17065)*
H & K Machine Company Inc .... G 269 756-7339
Three Oaks *(G-15849)*
H & L Tool Company Inc .... D 248 585-7474
Madison Heights *(G-10263)*
H G Geiger Manufacturing Co .... F 517 369-7357
Bronson *(G-2028)*
Harbor Screw Machine Products .... G 269 925-5855
Benton Harbor *(G-1508)*
Hemingway Screw Products Inc .... G 313 383-7300
Melvindale *(G-10699)*
▲ **Hibshman Screw Mch Pdts Inc** .... E 269 641-7525
Union *(G-16730)*
Hil-Man Automation LLC .... F 616 741-9099
Zeeland *(G-18149)*
Hill Screw Machine Products .... G 734 427-8237
Westland *(G-17570)*
Hollander Machine Co Inc .... G 810 742-1660
Burton *(G-2156)*
Holt Products Company .... D 517 699-2111
Holt *(G-7912)*
Hosco Inc .... F 248 912-1750
Wixom *(G-17828)*
▲ **Huron Inc** .... E 810 359-5344
Lexington *(G-9558)*
Inland Lakes Machine Inc .... E 231 775-6543
Cadillac *(G-2255)*
J & J Industries Inc .... G 517 784-3586
Jackson *(G-8473)*
J C Gibbons Mfg Inc .... E 734 266-5544
Livonia *(G-9789)*
J&J Machine Products Co Inc .... E 313 534-8024
Redford *(G-13167)*
Jamco Manufacturing Inc .... G 248 852-1988
Auburn Hills *(G-918)*
▲ **K & Y Manufacturing Inc** .... E 734 414-7000
Canton *(G-2390)*
Kalkaska Screw Products Inc .... E 231 258-2560
Kalkaska *(G-8946)*
Kerr Screw Products Co Inc .... G 248 589-2200
Madison Heights *(G-10290)*
L A Martin Company .... E 313 581-3444
Dearborn *(G-3732)*
Lakeshore Automatic Pdts Inc .... G 616 846-4005
Grand Haven *(G-6045)*
Lakeshore Fittings Inc .... D 616 846-5090
Grand Haven *(G-6047)*
Lester Detterbeck Entps Ltd .... E 906 265-5121
Iron River *(G-8314)*
Liberty Research Co Inc .... G 734 508-6237
Milan *(G-10943)*
Liberty Turned Components LLC .... F 734 508-6237
Milan *(G-10944)*
Livonia Automatic Incorporated .... G 734 591-0321
Livonia *(G-9814)*
Lyon Manufacturing Inc .... E 734 359-3000
Canton *(G-2395)*

SIC SECTION — 34 FABRICATED METAL PRODUCTS, EXCEPT MACHINERY AND TRANSPORTATION EQUIPMENT

Lyons Tool and Mfg Corp .... E 248 344-9644
  Wixom *(G-17849)*
M & N Machine LLC .... G 231 722-7085
  Muskegon *(G-11370)*
Malabar Manufacturing Inc .... F 517 448-2155
  Hudson *(G-8135)*
Master Automatic Mch Co Inc .... C 734 414-0500
  Plymouth *(G-12685)*
◆ Maynard L Maclean L C .... D 586 949-0471
  Chesterfield *(G-2802)*
McNees Manufacturing Inc .... F 616 675-7480
  Bailey *(G-1080)*
◆ Melling Tool Co .... B 517 787-8172
  Jackson *(G-8514)*
▲ Merchants Automatic Pdts Inc ..... E 734 829-0020
  Canton *(G-2401)*
▲ Mercury Manufacturing Company ... D 734 285-5150
  Wyandotte *(G-17968)*
Michigan Precision Swiss Prts .... E 810 329-2270
  Saint Clair *(G-14229)*
Micromatic Screw Products Inc ...... F 517 787-3666
  Jackson *(G-8522)*
Mid-West Screw Products Co .... F 734 591-1800
  Livonia *(G-9843)*
Milan Screw Products Inc .... E 734 439-2431
  Milan *(G-10949)*
▲ MK Chambers Company .... E 810 688-3750
  North Branch *(G-11663)*
Modern Tech Machining LLC .... G 810 531-7992
  Port Huron *(G-12944)*
Mohr Engineering Inc .... E 810 227-4598
  Brighton *(G-1963)*
Mountain Machine LLC .... F 734 480-2200
  Van Buren Twp *(G-16774)*
Nelms Technologies Inc .... D 734 955-6500
  Romulus *(G-13712)*
North Shore Machine Works Inc ..... F 616 842-8360
  Ferrysburg *(G-5336)*
Northern Precision Pdts Inc .... E 231 768-4435
  Leroy *(G-9534)*
▲ Nuko Precision LLC .... E 734 464-6856
  Livonia *(G-9868)*
Omlor Enterprises Inc .... F 616 837-6361
  Coopersville *(G-3567)*
Petschke Manufacturing Company ... F 586 463-0841
  Mount Clemens *(G-11144)*
Phillips Bros Screw Pdts Co .... G 517 882-0279
  Lansing *(G-9411)*
Pinckney Automatic & Mfg .... G 734 878-3430
  Pinckney *(G-12502)*
▲ Piper Industries Inc .... D 586 771-5100
  Roseville *(G-13855)*
Precision Machine Co S Haven .... G 269 637-2372
  South Haven *(G-14768)*
Prescott Products Inc .... G 517 787-8172
  Jackson *(G-8556)*
▲ Pro Slot Ltd .... G 616 897-6000
  Hartford *(G-7386)*
Qualtek Inc .... G 269 781-2835
  Marshall *(G-10587)*
R & D Screw Products Inc .... E 517 546-2380
  Howell *(G-8084)*
Rae Manufacturing Company .... F 810 987-9170
  Port Huron *(G-12960)*
Rempco Acquisition Inc .... E 231 775-0108
  Cadillac *(G-2274)*
Rima Manufacturing Company .... D 517 448-8921
  Hudson *(G-8141)*
Rite Machine Products Inc .... F 586 465-9393
  Clinton Township *(G-3212)*
▲ Riverside Screw Mch Pdts Inc ..... F 269 962-5449
  Battle Creek *(G-1241)*
Ryan Polishing Corporation .... F 248 548-6832
  Oak Park *(G-12096)*
Ryder Automatic & Mfg .... G 586 293-2109
  Fraser *(G-5720)*
SH Leggitt Company .... C 269 781-3901
  Marshall *(G-10588)*
Sharp Screw Products Inc .... G 586 598-0440
  Chesterfield *(G-2840)*
Sigma Machine Inc .... D 269 345-6316
  Kalamazoo *(G-8887)*
Slater Tools Inc .... E 586 465-5000
  Clinton Township *(G-3231)*
South Park Sales & Mfg Inc .... G 313 381-7579
  Dearborn *(G-3762)*
Springdale Automatics Inc .... G 517 523-2424
  Osseo *(G-12229)*
St Joe Tool Co .... E 269 426-4300
  Bridgman *(G-1874)*

Stagg Machine Products Inc .... G 231 775-2355
  Cadillac *(G-2280)*
State Screw Products Corp .... F 586 463-3892
  Clinton Township *(G-3234)*
Steadfast Engineered Pdts LLC ...... F 616 846-4747
  Grand Haven *(G-6085)*
Stockbridge Manufacturing Co .... E 517 851-7865
  Stockbridge *(G-15593)*
▲ Stonebridge Industries Inc .... A 586 323-0348
  Sterling Heights *(G-15513)*
Supreme Domestic Intl Sls Corp ..... G 616 842-6550
  Spring Lake *(G-15182)*
▲ Supreme Machined Pdts Co Inc ... C 616 842-6550
  Spring Lake *(G-15183)*
Supreme Machined Pdts Co Inc ..... E 616 842-6550
  Spring Lake *(G-15184)*
Swiss American Screw Pdts Inc ..... F 734 397-1600
  Canton *(G-2431)*
Swiss Industries Inc .... G 517 437-3682
  Hillsdale *(G-7542)*
T & D Machine Inc .... G 517 423-0778
  Tecumseh *(G-15810)*
Taylor Machine Products Inc .... C 734 287-3550
  Plymouth *(G-12765)*
Taylor Screw Products Company .... G 734 697-8018
  Van Buren Twp *(G-16786)*
Terry Tool & Die Co .... F 517 750-1771
  Jackson *(G-8587)*
◆ Tompkins Products Inc .... D 313 894-2222
  Detroit *(G-4403)*
▲ Topcraft Metal Products Inc .... E 616 669-1790
  Hudsonville *(G-8184)*
Tri-Matic Screw Products Co .... E 517 548-6414
  Howell *(G-8114)*
▲ Tribal Manufacturing Inc .... E 269 781-3901
  Marshall *(G-10591)*
Trinity Holding Inc .... E 517 787-3100
  Jackson *(G-8593)*
Tru-Line Screw Products Inc .... E 734 261-8780
  Livonia *(G-9972)*
Tru-Line Screw Products Inc .... E 734 261-8780
  Livonia *(G-9973)*
United Precision Pdts Co Inc .... E 313 292-0100
  Dearborn Heights *(G-3800)*
Victor Screw Products Co .... G 269 489-2760
  Burr Oak *(G-2138)*
W A Thomas Company .... G 734 475-8626
  Chelsea *(G-2720)*
Warren Screw Products Inc .... C 586 757-1280
  Warren *(G-17288)*
Warren Scrw Products Inc .... G 586 994-0342
  Rochester Hills *(G-13541)*
Westgood Manufacturing Co .... E 586 771-3970
  Roseville *(G-13890)*
Wolverine Machine Products Co .... E 248 634-9952
  Holly *(G-7902)*
Wsp Management LLC .... G 586 447-2750
  Warren *(G-17299)*
Yankee Screw Products Company ... F 248 634-3011
  Holly *(G-7903)*
Yarbrough Precision Screws LLC .... F 586 776-0752
  Fraser *(G-5749)*
Zimmermann Engineering Co Inc .... G 248 358-0044
  Southfield *(G-15070)*
Zygot Operations Limited .... F 810 736-2900
  Flint *(G-5529)*

3452 Bolts, Nuts, Screws, Rivets & Washers

A A Anchor Bolt Inc .... F 248 349-6565
  Northville *(G-11675)*
AAA Industries Inc .... E 313 255-0420
  Redford *(G-13140)*
Acument Global Tech Inc .... B 586 254-3900
  Sterling Heights *(G-15253)*
Acument Global Tech Inc .... C 810 953-4575
  Holly *(G-7868)*
Aero Auto Stud Specialists Inc ...... E 248 437-2171
  Whitmore Lake *(G-17685)*
▲ Aerospace Nylok Corporation ..... G 586 786-0100
  Macomb *(G-10104)*
▲ Ajax Spring and Mfg Co .... E 248 588-5700
  Madison Heights *(G-10184)*
All Tool Sales Inc .... F 231 941-4302
  Traverse City *(G-15893)*
Amanda Manufacturing LLC .... G 740 385-9380
  Livonia *(G-9641)*
Anchor Lamina America Inc .... C 231 533-8646
  Bellaire *(G-1434)*
Ankara Industries Incorporated ..... F 586 749-1190
  Chesterfield *(G-2740)*

Apex Spring & Stamping Corp .... D 616 453-5463
  Grand Rapids *(G-6171)*
▲ Applied Instruments Company .... E 810 227-5510
  Brighton *(G-1886)*
▲ B & D Thread Rolling Inc .... D 734 728-7070
  Taylor *(G-15693)*
B & S Manufacturing Inc .... G 586 939-5130
  Clinton Township *(G-3062)*
B and D Thd Rolling Fas Indus ...... G 734 728-7070
  Wayne *(G-17426)*
Basch Olovson Engineering Co ...... G 231 865-2027
  Fruitport *(G-5788)*
▲ BDS Company Inc .... E 517 279-2135
  Coldwater *(G-3291)*
◆ Beaver Aerospace & Defense Inc ... D 734 853-5003
  Livonia *(G-9662)*
Belwith Products LLC .... F 616 247-4000
  Grandville *(G-7022)*
Bollhoff Rivnut .... G 248 269-0475
  Troy *(G-16243)*
Broaching Industries Inc .... E 586 949-3775
  Chesterfield *(G-2748)*
Camcar LLC .... G 586 254-3900
  Sterling Heights *(G-15279)*
◆ Cold Heading Co .... D 586 497-7000
  Warren *(G-16985)*
Cold Heading Co .... D 586 497-7016
  Warren *(G-16986)*
▲ Connection Service Company .... F 269 926-2658
  Benton Harbor *(G-1491)*
Consolidated Metal Pdts Inc .... G 616 538-1000
  Grand Rapids *(G-6302)*
▲ Decker Manufacturing Corp ...... D 517 629-3955
  Albion *(G-122)*
Detroit Tubular Rivet Inc .... D 734 282-7979
  Wyandotte *(G-17954)*
▲ Dexter Fastener Tech Inc .... C 734 426-0311
  Dexter *(G-4486)*
Dexter Fastener Tech Inc .... E 734 426-5200
  Dexter *(G-4487)*
Die Cast Press Mfg Co Inc .... E 269 657-6060
  Paw Paw *(G-12403)*
▲ Dirksen Screw Products Co .... E 586 247-5400
  Shelby Township *(G-14579)*
▲ DPM Manufacturing LLC .... F 248 349-6375
  Livonia *(G-9715)*
Dyer Corporation .... G 231 894-4282
  Montague *(G-11090)*
E & E Manufacturing Co Inc .... F 248 616-1300
  Clawson *(G-2977)*
E J M Ball Screw LLC .... F 989 893-7674
  Bay City *(G-1307)*
E M P Manufacturing Corp .... F 586 949-8277
  Chesterfield *(G-2769)*
▲ Ecoclean Inc .... C 248 450-2000
  Southfield *(G-14897)*
▲ Fastco Industries Inc .... D 616 453-5428
  Grand Rapids *(G-6399)*
Fastco Industries Inc .... G 616 389-1390
  Grand Rapids *(G-6400)*
Fastco Industries Inc .... G 616 453-5428
  Grand Rapids *(G-6401)*
▲ Fastener Advance PDT Co Ltd ... F 734 428-8070
  Manchester *(G-10406)*
Fastentech Inc .... G 313 299-8500
  Romulus *(G-13675)*
Federal Screw Works .... C 231 796-7664
  Big Rapids *(G-1627)*
Federal Screw Works .... G 231 922-9500
  Traverse City *(G-15969)*
Federal Screw Works .... C 734 941-4211
  Romulus *(G-13677)*
◆ Federal Screw Works .... F 734 941-4211
  Romulus *(G-13676)*
Federal Screw Works .... E 734 941-4211
  Big Rapids *(G-1626)*
▼ Franklin Fastener Company .... E 313 537-8900
  Redford *(G-13162)*
Fred Oswalts Pins Unltd .... G 269 342-1387
  Portage *(G-12997)*
Gage Bilt Inc .... E 586 226-1500
  Clinton Township *(G-3128)*
General Motors LLC .... B 989 894-7210
  Bay City *(G-1315)*
Glycon Corp .... E 517 423-8356
  Tecumseh *(G-15795)*
Grant Industries Incorporated ...... D 586 293-9200
  Fraser *(G-5657)*
H & L Tool Company Inc .... D 248 585-7474
  Madison Heights *(G-10263)*

Employee Codes: A=Over 500 employees, B=251-500
C=101-250, D=51-100, E=20-50, F=10-19, G=3-9

34 FABRICATED METAL PRODUCTS, EXCEPT MACHINERY AND TRANSPORTATION EQUIPMENT SIC SECTION

◆ Henrob Corporation ....D 248 493-3800
New Hudson (G-11543)
Henry Plambeck ....G 586 463-3410
Harrison Township (G-7332)
Hexagon Enterprises Inc ....E 248 583-0550
Troy (G-16395)
▲ Huron Tool & Engineering Co ....E 989 269-9927
Bad Axe (G-1068)
◆ Kamax Inc ....B 248 879-0200
Rochester Hills (G-13454)
Lay Manufacturing Inc ....G 313 369-1627
Warren (G-17125)
Leader Tool Company - HB Inc ....D 989 479-3281
Harbor Beach (G-7269)
Mac Lean-Fogg Company ....C 248 280-0880
Royal Oak (G-13945)
◆ Maynard L Maclean L C ....D 586 949-0471
Chesterfield (G-2802)
▲ Merchants Automatic Pdts Inc ....E 734 829-0020
Canton (G-2401)
◆ Michigan Rod Products Inc ....D 517 552-9812
Howell (G-8065)
Michigan Steel Finishing Co ....F 313 838-3925
Detroit (G-4243)
Mid-States Bolt & Screw Co ....F 989 732-3265
Gaylord (G-5883)
Midwest Acorn Nut Company ....E 800 422-6887
Troy (G-16508)
▲ MNP Corporation ....A 586 254-1320
Utica (G-16744)
MNP Corporation ....E 248 585-5010
Madison Heights (G-10308)
▲ Modular Systems Inc ....G 231 865-3167
Fruitport (G-5797)
▲ ND Industries Inc ....C 248 288-0000
Clawson (G-2982)
Northern Industrial Mfg Corp ....E 586 468-2790
Harrison Township (G-7341)
◆ Nss Technologies Inc ....E 734 459-9500
Canton (G-2412)
Nss Technologies Inc ....E 734 459-9500
Canton (G-2413)
Oakland Bolt & Nut Co LLC ....G 313 659-1677
Detroit (G-4282)
Perigee Manufacturing Co Inc ....F 313 933-4420
Detroit (G-4298)
Pgm Products Inc ....F 586 757-4400
Warren (G-17185)
Phillips Service Inds Inc ....F 734 853-5000
Plymouth (G-12714)
Pinckney Automatic & Mfg ....G 734 878-3430
Pinckney (G-12502)
Pink Pin Lady LLC ....G 586 731-1532
Shelby Township (G-14666)
Prestige Stamping LLC ....C 586 773-2700
Warren (G-17196)
PSI Hydraulics ....C 734 261-4160
Plymouth (G-12725)
Rae Manufacturing Company ....F 810 987-9170
Port Huron (G-12960)
Ring Screw LLC ....C 810 629-6602
Fenton (G-5234)
Ring Screw LLC ....D 810 695-0800
Holly (G-7894)
▲ Ring Screw LLC ....D 586 997-5600
Sterling Heights (G-15470)
Rippa Products Inc ....E 906 337-0010
Calumet (G-2333)
Roy A Hutchins Company ....G 248 437-3470
New Hudson (G-11554)
Rush Machining Inc ....F 248 583-0550
Troy (G-16585)
SA Industries 2 Inc ....G 248 693-9100
Lake Orion (G-9158)
◆ Saf-Holland Inc ....B 231 773-3271
Muskegon (G-11417)
▼ Securit Metal Products Co ....E 269 782-7076
Dowagiac (G-4561)
Shannon Precision Fastener LLC ....E 248 589-9670
Auburn Hills (G-996)
▲ Shannon Precision Fastener LLC ....D 248 589-9670
Madison Heights (G-10351)
Shannon Precision Fastener LLC ....E 248 658-3015
Madison Heights (G-10350)
Shellys Pins N Needles ....G 517 861-7110
Howell (G-8096)
Smsg LLC ....G 517 787-9447
Jackson (G-8574)
Steel Master LLC ....E 810 771-4943
Grand Blanc (G-5984)
T F G Gage Components ....G 734 427-2274
Livonia (G-9952)
Taper-Line Inc ....G 586 775-5960
Clinton Township (G-3243)
Tip-Top Screw Mfg Inc ....E 989 739-5157
Oscoda (G-12222)
◆ Trimas Corporation ....E 248 631-5450
Bloomfield Hills (G-1807)
Under Pressure Pwr Washers LLC ....G 616 292-4289
Marne (G-10514)
United Precision Pdts Co Inc ....E 313 292-0100
Dearborn Heights (G-3800)
Utica Washers ....G 313 571-1568
Detroit (G-4419)
▲ Vamp Screw Products Company ....E 734 676-8020
Brownstown Twp (G-2076)
▲ Vico Products Co ....C 734 453-3777
Plymouth (G-12790)
W G Benjey Inc ....G 989 356-0027
Alpena (G-320)
Warren Screw Works Inc ....G 734 525-2920
Livonia (G-9998)
Washers Incorporated ....C 734 523-1000
Livonia (G-9999)
Washers Incorporated ....G 734 523-1000
Livonia (G-10000)
Wedin International Inc ....D 231 779-8650
Cadillac (G-2284)
Whitesell Frmed Components Inc ....D 313 299-1178
Waterford (G-17385)
▲ Wico Metal Products Company ....C 586 755-9600
Warren (G-17293)
◆ Williams Form Engineering Corp ....D 616 866-0815
Belmont (G-1474)
Wilson-Garner Company ....E 586 466-5880
Harrison Township (G-7355)

3462 Iron & Steel Forgings

▲ Allor Manufacturing Inc ....D 248 486-4500
Brighton (G-1883)
▲ Avon Machining LLC ....D 586 884-2200
Shelby Township (G-14551)
Avon Machining Holdings Inc ....C 586 884-2200
Shelby Township (G-14552)
Bjerke Forgings Inc ....A 313 382-2600
Taylor (G-15696)
Boos Products Inc ....F 734 498-2207
Gregory (G-7164)
Borgwarner Powdered Metals Inc ....E 734 261-5322
Livonia (G-9668)
▲ Buchanan Metal Forming Inc ....E 269 695-3836
Buchanan (G-2111)
Cambric Corporation ....B 801 415-7300
Novi (G-11842)
Chardam Gear Company Inc ....D 586 795-8900
Sterling Heights (G-15287)
▲ Composite Forgings Ltd Partnr ....D 313 496-1226
Detroit (G-3944)
Computer Operated Mfg ....E 989 686-1333
Bay City (G-1297)
Decker Gear Inc ....F 810 388-1500
Saint Clair (G-14216)
Delt Forge Inc ....G 989 685-2118
Rose City (G-13761)
Detail Precision Products Inc ....E 248 544-3390
Ferndale (G-5271)
Dorris Company ....E 586 293-5260
Fraser (G-5644)
Enterprise Tool and Gear Inc ....D 989 269-9797
Bad Axe (G-1060)
Equitable Engineering Co Inc ....E 248 689-9700
Troy (G-16351)
Formax Precision Gear Inc ....E 586 323-9067
Sterling Heights (G-15344)
Gage Eagle Spline Inc ....D 586 776-7240
Warren (G-17049)
Gearx LLC ....G 248 766-6903
Sterling Heights (G-15354)
Global Engine Mfg Aliance LLC ....G 734 529-9888
Dundee (G-4585)
Global Gear Inc ....E 734 979-0888
Westland (G-17562)
▲ Goertz+schiele Corporation ....C 248 393-0414
Auburn Hills (G-890)
Goodyear Horseshoe Supply Inc ....G 810 639-2591
Montrose (G-11102)
▲ Great Lakes Forge Inc ....G 231 947-4931
Traverse City (G-15992)
▲ Great Lakes Industry Inc ....E 517 784-3153
Jackson (G-8459)
Hephaestus Holdings LLC ....G 248 479-2700
Novi (G-11900)
Hhi Forging LLC ....E 248 284-2900
Royal Oak (G-13932)
▲ Hhi Form Tech LLC ....B 248 597-3800
Royal Oak (G-13933)
Hhi Formtech LLC ....E 586 415-2000
Fraser (G-5662)
▼ Hhi Formtech Industries LLC ....A 248 597-3800
Royal Oak (G-13934)
Hl Tech Gear Inc ....G 248 548-8649
Huntington Woods (G-8188)
Hutchinson Arospc & Indust Inc ....F 989 875-2052
Ithaca (G-8360)
▲ Hy Lift Johnson Inc ....G 231 722-1100
Muskegon (G-11345)
Invo Spline Inc ....E 586 757-8840
Warren (G-17097)
▲ Iwis Engine Systems LP ....G 248 247-3178
Troy (G-16427)
◆ Jervis B Webb Company ....B 248 553-1000
Novi (G-11912)
Kendor Steel Rule Die Inc ....E 586 293-7111
Fraser (G-5678)
Lansing Forge Inc ....F 517 882-2056
Lansing (G-9388)
Lansing Holding Company Inc ....G 517 882-2056
Lansing (G-9390)
Lc Manufacturing LLC ....C 231 839-7102
Lake City (G-9090)
Lc Manufacturing LLC ....E 734 753-3990
New Boston (G-11503)
▲ Letts Industries Inc ....G 313 579-1100
Detroit (G-4200)
▼ Lincoln Park Die & Tool Co ....E 734 285-1680
Brownstown (G-2067)
Linear Mold & Engineering LLC ....E 734 744-4548
Livonia (G-9809)
▲ Linear Mold & Engineering LLC ....F 734 422-6060
Livonia (G-9810)
Lisi Automotive Hl Vol Inc ....C 734 266-6900
Livonia (G-9813)
Lyons Tool & Engineering Inc ....E 586 200-3003
Warren (G-17133)
M P I International Inc ....D 608 764-5416
Rochester Hills (G-13463)
Mason Forge & Die Inc ....F 517 676-2992
Mason (G-10645)
Mat Tek Inc ....G 810 659-0322
Flushing (G-5540)
Meritor Indus Aftermarket LLC ....G 248 658-7345
Troy (G-16495)
Metal Forming & Coining Corp ....G 586 731-2003
Shelby Township (G-14638)
Michigan Forge Company LLC ....E 815 758-6400
Lansing (G-9398)
Midwest Gear & Tool Inc ....E 586 779-1300
Roseville (G-13836)
◆ Motion Systems Incorporated ....F 586 774-5666
Warren (G-17160)
▲ MSP Industries Corporation ....C 248 628-4150
Oxford (G-12362)
Plesh Industries Inc ....F 716 873-4916
Brighton (G-1979)
Power Industries Corp ....G 586 783-3818
Harrison Township (G-7343)
Quality Steel Products Inc ....E 248 684-0555
Milford (G-10981)
Rack & Pinion Inc ....G 517 563-8872
Horton (G-7970)
Ringmasters Mfg LLC ....E 734 729-6110
Wayne (G-17442)
Riverside Spline & Gear Inc ....E 810 765-8302
Marine City (G-10481)
Schwartz Precision Gear Co ....E 586 754-4600
Bloomfield Hills (G-1797)
Shadko Enterprises Inc ....G 248 816-1712
Troy (G-16598)
▲ Sinoscan Inc ....G 269 966-0932
Battle Creek (G-1249)
Somers Steel ....G 734 729-3700
Westland (G-17599)
Sonic Edm LLC ....G 248 379-2888
Roseville (G-13872)
▲ Stonebridge Industries Inc ....A 586 323-0348
Sterling Heights (G-15513)
Tech Tool Company Inc ....G 313 836-4131
Detroit (G-4397)
Tenneco Inc ....F 248 354-7700
Southfield (G-15044)

SIC SECTION 34 FABRICATED METAL PRODUCTS, EXCEPT MACHINERY AND TRANSPORTATION EQUIPMENT

TI Group Auto Systems LLC .... D 517 437-7462
Hillsdale *(G-7543)*

Titanium Industries Inc .... G 973 983-1185
Plymouth *(G-12771)*

Total MGT Reclamation Svcs LLC .... G 734 384-3500
Taylor *(G-15777)*

Trenton Forging Company .... D 734 675-1620
Trenton *(G-16159)*

◆ **Triumph Gear Systems - Macomb** .... C 586 781-2800
Macomb *(G-10170)*

Vectorall Manufacturing Inc .... E 248 486-4570
Brighton *(G-2006)*

▲ **Wartian Lock Company** .... G 586 777-2244
Saint Clair Shores *(G-14276)*

Webster Cold Forge Co .... F 313 554-4500
Northville *(G-11734)*

Wedin International Inc .... D 231 779-8650
Cadillac *(G-2284)*

▼ **Wilkie Bros Conveyors Inc** .... E 810 364-4820
Marysville *(G-10626)*

Will Lent Horseshoe Co .... G 231 861-5033
Shelby *(G-14537)*

▲ **Wkw Roof Rail Systems LLC** .... D 205 338-4242
Portage *(G-13056)*

Wyman-Gordon Forgings Inc .... E 810 229-9550
Brighton *(G-2011)*

3463 Nonferrous Forgings

AAM International Holdings Inc .... E 313 758-2000
Detroit *(G-3831)*

▲ **AGC Grand Haven LLC** .... G 616 842-1820
Grand Haven *(G-5990)*

▲ **Alliance Automation LLC** .... G 810 953-9539
Flint *(G-5375)*

Borgwarner Powdered Metals Inc .... E 734 261-5322
Livonia *(G-9668)*

D Mac Industries Inc .... F 734 536-7754
Livonia *(G-9697)*

G R Investment Group Ltd .... G 248 588-3946
Clawson *(G-2979)*

Global Fmi LLC .... D 810 964-5555
Fenton *(G-5216)*

Greenseed LLC .... G 313 295-0100
Taylor *(G-15727)*

Hephaestus Holdings LLC .... G 248 479-2700
Novi *(G-11900)*

Hhi Formtech LLC .... E 586 415-2000
Fraser *(G-5662)*

▼ **Lincoln Park Die & Tool Co** .... E 734 285-1680
Brownstown *(G-2067)*

Mat Tek Inc .... G 810 659-0322
Flushing *(G-5540)*

Mueller Brass Forging Co Inc .... D 810 987-7770
Port Huron *(G-12946)*

▼ **Mueller Impacts Company Inc** .... C 810 364-3700
Marysville *(G-10608)*

Mueller Industries Inc .... D 248 446-3720
Brighton *(G-1964)*

▲ **Resistance Welding Machne & AC** ... F 269 428-4770
Saint Joseph *(G-14337)*

United Brass Manufacturers Inc .... E 734 942-9224
Romulus *(G-13737)*

United Brass Manufacturers Inc .... D 734 941-0700
Romulus *(G-13736)*

▲ **Weldaloy Products Company** .... D 586 758-5550
Warren *(G-17290)*

Wonder Makers Environmental .... F 269 382-4154
Kalamazoo *(G-8926)*

3465 Automotive Stampings

3715-11th Street Corp .... G 734 523-1000
Livonia *(G-9615)*

A G Simpson (usa) Inc .... D 586 268-4817
Sterling Heights *(G-15245)*

A G Simpson (usa) Inc .... F 586 268-4817
Sterling Heights *(G-15246)*

A G Simpson (usa) Inc .... E 586 268-5844
Sterling Heights *(G-15247)*

A-1 Stampings Inc .... G 586 294-7790
Fraser *(G-5611)*

Aaron Incorporated .... G 586 791-0320
Clinton Township *(G-3031)*

▲ **Acemco Incorporated** .... C 231 799-8612
Norton Shores *(G-11806)*

Advance Engineering Company .... D 313 537-3500
Canton *(G-2344)*

▲ **Advanced Auto Trends Inc** .... E 248 628-6111
Oxford *(G-12333)*

Advanced Auto Trends Inc .... E 248 628-4850
Oxford *(G-12334)*

▲ **Ajax Spring and Mfg Co** .... F 248 588-5700
Madison Heights *(G-10184)*

Allied Engineering Inc .... G 616 748-7990
Zeeland *(G-18110)*

Aludyne International Inc .... G 248 728-8642
Southfield *(G-14833)*

Aludyne US LLC .... D 810 987-1112
Port Huron *(G-12889)*

Aludyne US LLC .... D 810 966-9350
Port Huron *(G-12890)*

Aludyne US LLC .... F 248 728-8642
Warren *(G-16928)*

AM Specialties Inc .... G 586 795-9000
Sterling Heights *(G-15257)*

AMI Livonia LLC .... D 734 428-3132
Livonia *(G-9646)*

Anderton Equity LLC .... G 248 430-6650
Troy *(G-16202)*

Android Indstrs-Shreveport LLC .... C 248 454-0500
Auburn Hills *(G-771)*

▲ **Anjun America Inc** .... F 248 680-8825
Auburn Hills *(G-773)*

Ankara Industries Incorporated .... F 586 749-1190
Chesterfield *(G-2740)*

Aphase II Inc .... D 586 977-0790
Sterling Heights *(G-15262)*

ARC Metal Stamping LLC .... D 517 448-8954
Hudson *(G-8127)*

ARC-Kecy LLC .... D 517 448-8954
Hudson *(G-8128)*

Arcturian LLC .... G 313 643-5326
Dearborn *(G-3679)*

Arvinmeritor Inc .... E 248 435-1000
Troy *(G-16222)*

Auto Metal Craft Inc .... E 248 398-2240
Oak Park *(G-12051)*

Automatic Spring Products Corp .... C 616 842-2284
Grand Haven *(G-5995)*

Autombili Lamborghini Amer LLC .... G 866 681-6276
Auburn Hills *(G-787)*

Autowares Inc .... G 248 473-0928
Farmington Hills *(G-4937)*

▲ **Avon Machining LLC** .... D 586 884-2200
Shelby Township *(G-14551)*

Avon Machining Holdings Inc .... C 586 884-2200
Shelby Township *(G-14552)*

▲ **Bae Industries Inc** .... C 586 754-3000
Warren *(G-16950)*

Bae Industries Inc .... F 248 475-9600
Auburn Hills *(G-790)*

Benesh Corporation .... E 734 244-4143
Monroe *(G-11023)*

Benteler Automotive Corp .... B 616 247-3936
Auburn Hills *(G-791)*

◆ **Benteler Automotive Corp** .... C 248 364-7190
Auburn Hills *(G-792)*

▲ **Bopp-Busch Manufacturing Co** .... E 989 876-7121
Au Gres *(G-744)*

Bopp-Busch Manufacturing Co .... E 989 876-7924
Au Gres *(G-745)*

Britten Metalworks LLC .... G 231 421-1615
Traverse City *(G-15921)*

▲ **Burkland Inc** .... D 810 636-2233
Goodrich *(G-5952)*

C & H Stamping Inc .... E 517 750-3600
Jackson *(G-8396)*

C & M Manufacturing Corp Inc .... E 586 749-3455
Chesterfield *(G-2750)*

▼ **Caparo Vehicle Components Inc** ...... D 734 513-2859
Livonia *(G-9674)*

Capco Automotive .... G 248 616-8888
Troy *(G-16257)*

Capital Stamping & Machine Inc .... E 248 471-0700
Farmington Hills *(G-4956)*

Cg & D Group .... G 248 310-9166
Farmington Hills *(G-4960)*

Challenge Mfg Company .... F 616 735-6530
Walker *(G-16862)*

Challenge Mfg Company .... C 616 735-6500
Grand Rapids *(G-6268)*

Challenge Mfg Company .... A 616 396-2079
Holland *(G-7587)*

Challenge Mfg Company LLC .... F 616 735-6500
Walker *(G-16863)*

▲ **Challenge Mfg Company LLC** .... B 616 735-6500
Walker *(G-16864)*

▲ **Concord Tool and Mfg Inc** .... C 586 465-6537
Mount Clemens *(G-11127)*

Cooper-Standard Automotive Inc .... G 248 630-7262
Auburn Hills *(G-826)*

Crescive Die and Tool Inc .... B 734 482-0303
Saline *(G-14384)*

▲ **D & N Bending Corp** .... E 586 752-5511
Romeo *(G-13626)*

▲ **D T M 1 Inc** .... E 248 889-9210
Highland *(G-7491)*

Dajaco Industries Inc .... D 586 949-1590
Chesterfield *(G-2760)*

Dayco Incorporated .... G 248 404-6500
Troy *(G-16297)*

Delaco Steel Corporation .... D 313 491-1200
Dearborn *(G-3692)*

▲ **Demmer Corporation** .... C 517 321-3600
Lansing *(G-9217)*

Design Metal Inc .... F 248 547-4170
Oak Park *(G-12059)*

▲ **Dexter Stamping Company LLC** .... D 517 750-3414
Jackson *(G-8432)*

▼ **Dgh Enterprises Inc** .... E 269 925-0657
Benton Harbor *(G-1494)*

Diversfied Prcurement Svcs LLC .... G 248 821-1147
Ferndale *(G-5280)*

◆ **Dongah America Inc** .... E 248 918-5810
Troy *(G-16322)*

Douglas Stamping Company .... G 248 542-3940
Madison Heights *(G-10234)*

◆ **Dst Industries Inc** .... C 734 941-0300
Romulus *(G-13667)*

Dti Molded Products Inc .... F 248 647-0400
Bingham Farms *(G-1652)*

Dunne-Rite Performance Inc .... F 616 828-0908
Warren *(G-17007)*

Dynetics Inc .... G 248 619-1681
Troy *(G-16331)*

E & E Manufacturing Co Inc .... E 734 451-7600
Plymouth *(G-12616)*

E & E Manufacturing Co Inc .... F 248 616-1300
Clawson *(G-2977)*

Elring Klinger Sealing Systems .... G 734 542-1522
Livonia *(G-9725)*

▲ **Elringklinger Auto Mfg Inc** .... E 248 727-6600
Southfield *(G-14898)*

Elringklinger Auto Mfg Inc .... G 586 445-3050
Roseville *(G-13800)*

Fab-All Manufacturing Inc .... D 248 585-6700
Troy *(G-16358)*

Faurecia Interior Systems Inc .... C 248 409-3500
Auburn Hills *(G-862)*

FCA US LLC .... A 248 512-2950
Auburn Hills *(G-867)*

FCA US LLC .... A 586 497-3630
Warren *(G-17029)*

Fisher & Company Incorporated .... C 248 280-0808
Troy *(G-16363)*

Flex-N-Gate Corporation .... C 517 223-5900
Fowlerville *(G-5564)*

Ford Global Technologies LLC .... F 313 312-3000
Bingham Farms *(G-1653)*

Forged Tubular .... G 313 843-4870
Detroit *(G-4068)*

Forward Metal Craft Inc .... F 616 459-6051
Grand Rapids *(G-6417)*

▼ **Franklin Fastener Company** .... E 313 537-8900
Redford *(G-13162)*

Gedia Michigan Inc .... E 248 392-9090
Orion *(G-12180)*

General Motors LLC .... C 517 721-2000
Lansing *(G-9291)*

General Motors LLC .... D 810 234-2710
Flint *(G-5434)*

General Motors LLC .... F 810 234-2710
Flint *(G-5435)*

General Motors LLC .... B 810 236-1970
Flint *(G-5436)*

Gestamp Alabama LLC .... C 810 245-3100
Lapeer *(G-9462)*

◆ **Gestamp Mason LLC** .... B 517 244-8800
Mason *(G-10641)*

Gestamp Washtenaw LLC .... E 248 251-3004
Chelsea *(G-2711)*

Gfm LLC .... E 586 777-4542
Roseville *(G-13807)*

▲ **Gill Corporation** .... B 616 453-4491
Grand Rapids *(G-6438)*

Gill Holding Company Inc .... E 616 559-2700
Grand Rapids *(G-6440)*

◆ **Gill Industries Inc** .... C 616 559-2700
Grand Rapids *(G-6441)*

Global Fmi LLC .... D 810 964-5555
Fenton *(G-5216)*

SIC

Employee Codes: A=Over 500 employees, B=251-500
C=101-250, D=51-100, E=20-50, F=10-19, G=3-9

2020 Harris Michigan
Industrial Directory

789

▲ **Globe Tech LLC**....E.... 734 656-2200
Plymouth *(G-12630)*
Gns North America Inc....G.... 616 796-0433
Holland *(G-7646)*
Grant Industries Incorporated....D.... 586 293-9200
Fraser *(G-5657)*
Great Lakes Trim Inc....D.... 231 267-3000
Williamsburg *(G-17713)*
Guardian Automotive Corp....C.... 586 757-7800
Sterling Heights *(G-15365)*
▲ **Guardian Automotive Corp**....D.... 586 757-7800
Warren *(G-17070)*
Guelph Tool Sales Inc....B.... 586 755-3333
Warren *(G-17071)*
▲ **Guyoung Tech Usa Inc**....E.... 248 746-4261
Southfield *(G-14934)*
Hamlin Tool & Machine Co Inc....D.... 248 651-6302
Rochester Hills *(G-13438)*
Hatch Stamping Company LLC....C.... 517 540-1021
Howell *(G-8047)*
Hatch Stamping Company LLC....C.... 734 433-1903
Chelsea *(G-2713)*
Hbpo North America Inc....C.... 248 823-7076
Troy *(G-16392)*
Hilltop Manufacturing Co Inc....G.... 248 437-2530
New Hudson *(G-11544)*
Illinois Tool Works Inc....D.... 248 589-2500
Troy *(G-16410)*
▲ **Inalfa/Ssi Roof Systems LLC**....D.... 586 758-6620
Warren *(G-17086)*
Integrated Program MGT LLC....G.... 248 241-9257
Clarkston *(G-2932)*
Invention Evolution Comp LLC....G.... 517 219-0180
Fowlerville *(G-5570)*
◆ **Iroquois Industries Inc**....D.... 586 771-5734
Warren *(G-17100)*
Iroquois Industries Inc....E.... 586 465-1023
Cottrellville *(G-3589)*
Iroquois Industries Inc....E.... 586 353-1410
Warren *(G-17102)*
J & J Spring Co Inc....F.... 586 566-7600
Shelby Township *(G-14606)*
J & L Mfg Co....E.... 586 445-9530
Warren *(G-17104)*
Jaytec LLC....F.... 734 713-4500
Milan *(G-10942)*
Jaytec LLC....F.... 734 397-6300
Chelsea *(G-2714)*
▲ **Jaytec LLC**....F.... 517 451-8272
New Boston *(G-11500)*
◆ **Jsj Corporation**....E.... 616 842-6350
Grand Haven *(G-6042)*
▲ **K & K Mfg Inc**....G.... 616 784-4286
Sparta *(G-15100)*
K & K Sales Assoc LLC....G.... 248 623-7378
Waterford *(G-17353)*
▲ **K&K Stamping Company**....E.... 586 443-7900
Saint Clair Shores *(G-14257)*
Kadest Industries....G.... 810 614-5362
Brown City *(G-2053)*
▲ **Kecy Products Inc**....D.... 517 448-8954
Hudson *(G-8134)*
Kirchhoff Auto Tecumseh Inc....F.... 517 490-9965
Tecumseh *(G-15799)*
▲ **Kirchhoff Auto Tecumseh Inc**....B.... 517 423-2400
Tecumseh *(G-15800)*
Kirchhoff Automotive USA Inc....F.... 248 247-3740
Troy *(G-16446)*
Kirmin Die & Tool Inc....E.... 734 722-9210
Romulus *(G-13697)*
L & W Inc....C.... 734 397-8085
Van Buren Twp *(G-16769)*
L & W Inc....C.... 517 486-6321
Blissfield *(G-1717)*
L & W Inc....F.... 734 529-7290
Dundee *(G-4590)*
▲ **L & W Inc**....D.... 734 397-6300
New Boston *(G-11502)*
L & W Inc....B.... 734 397-2212
Van Buren Twp *(G-16770)*
L & W Inc....C.... 616 394-9665
Holland *(G-7715)*
L Barge & Associates Inc....F.... 248 582-3430
Ferndale *(G-5297)*
Lacks Exterior Systems LLC....E.... 616 554-7180
Kentwood *(G-9016)*
Lacy Tool Company Inc....G.... 248 476-5250
Novi *(G-11928)*
Laser Cutting Co....E.... 586 468-5300
Harrison Township *(G-7337)*

Lgb USA Inc....G.... 586 777-4542
Roseville *(G-13826)*
▲ **Llink Technologies LLC**....E.... 586 336-9370
Brown City *(G-2054)*
Manufacturing Products & Svcs....F.... 734 927-1964
Plymouth *(G-12683)*
▲ **Manufcturing Assembly Intl LLC**....F.... 248 549-4700
Royal Oak *(G-13946)*
Marcus Automotive LLC....G.... 616 494-6400
Holland *(G-7739)*
Martinrea Hot Stampings Inc....E.... 859 509-3031
Warren *(G-17141)*
▲ **Martinrea Jonesville LLC**....D.... 517 849-2195
Jonesville *(G-8662)*
Martinrea Jonesville LLC....G.... 248 630-7730
Auburn Hills *(G-943)*
Matcor Automotive Michigan Inc....C.... 616 527-4050
Ionia *(G-8248)*
Means Industries Inc....D.... 989 754-3300
Saginaw *(G-14087)*
◆ **Means Industries Inc**....C.... 989 754-1433
Saginaw *(G-14086)*
Melling Products North LLC....D.... 989 588-6147
Farwell *(G-5164)*
▲ **Merit Tech Worldwide LLC**....E.... 734 927-9520
Canton *(G-2403)*
◆ **Meritor Inc**....C.... 248 435-1000
Troy *(G-16493)*
Mh Industries Ltd....G.... 734 261-7560
West Bloomfield *(G-17485)*
Michigan Vehicle Solutions LLC....G.... 734 720-7649
Southgate *(G-15081)*
Microgauge Machining Inc....C.... 248 446-3720
Brighton *(G-1961)*
Middleville Tool & Die Co Inc....D.... 269 795-3646
Middleville *(G-10805)*
Midstates Industrial Group Inc....E.... 586 307-3414
Clinton Township *(G-3174)*
▲ **Midway Products Group Inc**....C.... 734 241-7242
Monroe *(G-11052)*
▲ **Milan Metal Systems LLC**....C.... 734 439-1546
Milan *(G-10948)*
Minth North America Inc....D.... 248 259-7468
Wixom *(G-17856)*
▲ **Motor City Stampings Inc**....B.... 586 949-8420
Chesterfield *(G-2808)*
Motor City Stampings Inc....C.... 586 949-8420
Chesterfield *(G-2809)*
Motus Holdings LLC....A.... 616 422-7557
Holland *(G-7749)*
▲ **Motus LLC**....C.... 616 422-7557
Holland *(G-7750)*
Multimatic Michigan LLC....E.... 517 962-7190
Jackson *(G-8538)*
Mvc Holdings LLC....F.... 586 491-2600
Roseville *(G-13843)*
▲ **N A Sodecia Inc**....B.... 586 879-8969
Troy *(G-16518)*
North American Auto Inds Inc....G.... 734 288-3877
Riverview *(G-13302)*
Northern Industrial Mfg Corp....E.... 586 468-2790
Harrison Township *(G-7341)*
Northern Metalcraft Inc....F.... 586 997-9630
Shelby Township *(G-14656)*
Oakland Stamping LLC....G.... 313 867-3700
New Boston *(G-11506)*
Oakley Industries Inc....E.... 586 791-3194
Clinton Township *(G-3187)*
Oakley Industries Inc....E.... 586 792-1261
Clinton Township *(G-3188)*
Oakwood Metal Fabricating Co....B.... 734 947-7740
Taylor *(G-15751)*
Oblut Ltd....F.... 248 645-9130
Clarkston *(G-2941)*
Orion Manufacturing Inc....F.... 616 527-5994
Ionia *(G-8250)*
▲ **P & C Group I Inc**....E.... 248 442-6800
Farmington Hills *(G-5087)*
Pacific Engineering Corp....G.... 248 359-7823
Novi *(G-11970)*
Page Components Corporation....F.... 231 922-3600
Traverse City *(G-16062)*
Pinconning Metals Inc....G.... 989 879-3144
Pinconning *(G-12512)*
▲ **Plastic Trim International Inc**....E.... 248 259-7468
East Tawas *(G-4692)*
Precision Parts Holdings Inc....A.... 248 853-9010
Rochester Hills *(G-13498)*
Precision Stamping Co Inc....E.... 517 546-5656
Howell *(G-8082)*

Press-Way Inc....D.... 586 790-3324
Clinton Township *(G-3201)*
Prestige Advanced Inc....D.... 586 868-4000
Madison Heights *(G-10335)*
Prestige Stamping LLC....C.... 586 773-2700
Warren *(G-17196)*
▲ **Pridgeon & Clay Inc**....A.... 616 241-5675
Grand Rapids *(G-6774)*
Pt Tech Stamping Inc....E.... 586 293-1810
Fraser *(G-5713)*
Qp Acquisition 2 Inc....E.... 248 594-7432
Southfield *(G-15006)*
▲ **Quality Metalcraft Inc**....C.... 734 261-6700
Livonia *(G-9900)*
Quigley Industries Inc....D.... 248 426-8600
Farmington Hills *(G-5109)*
Quigley Manufacturing Inc....C.... 248 426-8600
Farmington Hills *(G-5110)*
R D M Enterprises Co Inc....G.... 810 985-4721
Port Huron *(G-12959)*
Radar Mexican Investments LLC....G.... 586 779-0300
Warren *(G-17215)*
Ralco Industries Inc....E.... 248 853-3200
Auburn Hills *(G-987)*
Reko International Holdings....G.... 519 737-6974
Bloomfield Hills *(G-1793)*
Reliant Industries Inc....E.... 586 275-0479
Sterling Heights *(G-15464)*
▲ **Royal Flex-N-Gate Oak LLC**....B.... 248 549-3800
Warren *(G-17225)*
S & G Prototype Inc....F.... 586 716-3600
New Baltimore *(G-11491)*
▲ **Sakaiya Company America Ltd**....E.... 517 521-5633
Webberville *(G-17454)*
Sales & Engineering Inc....E.... 734 525-9030
Livonia *(G-9919)*
Schwab Industries Inc....C.... 586 566-8090
Shelby Township *(G-14688)*
Set Enterprises Inc....E.... 586 573-3600
Sterling Heights *(G-15493)*
Shiloh Manufacturing LLC....F.... 586 873-2835
Roseville *(G-13868)*
Shiloh Manufacturing LLC....D.... 586 779-0300
Warren *(G-17239)*
Sierra Plastics Inc....E.... 989 269-6272
Bad Axe *(G-1070)*
Sodecia Auto Detroit Corp....E.... 586 759-2200
Sterling Heights *(G-15502)*
Sodecia Auto Detroit Corp....B.... 586 759-2200
Roseville *(G-13871)*
◆ **Sodecia Auto Detroit Corp**....C.... 586 759-2200
Troy *(G-16609)*
Sodecia Auto Detroit Corp....C.... 586 759-2200
Lake Orion *(G-9162)*
Sodecia Auto Detroit Corp....C.... 248 276-6647
Orion *(G-12190)*
Sodecia Auto Detroit Corp....C.... 586 759-2200
Center Line *(G-2583)*
Span America Detroit Inc....E.... 734 957-1600
Van Buren Twp *(G-16784)*
▲ **Spheros North America Inc**....G.... 734 218-7350
Canton *(G-2427)*
Spoiler Wing King....G.... 810 733-9464
Flint *(G-5503)*
◆ **Stanco Metal Products Inc**....E.... 616 842-5000
Grand Haven *(G-6082)*
Startech Services Inc....G.... 586 752-2460
Romeo *(G-13639)*
Statistical Processed Products....E.... 586 792-6900
Clinton Township *(G-3235)*
Stemco Products Inc....G.... 888 854-6474
Millington *(G-10998)*
Sterling Die & Engineering Inc....E.... 586 677-0707
Macomb *(G-10163)*
Style Craft Prototype Inc....F.... 248 619-9048
Troy *(G-16624)*
▲ **Su-Dan Company**....D.... 248 651-6035
Lake Orion *(G-9164)*
Superior Cam Inc....D.... 248 588-1100
Madison Heights *(G-10364)*
Superior Machining Inc....F.... 248 446-9451
New Hudson *(G-11556)*
▲ **Tajco North America Inc**....G.... 248 418-7550
Auburn Hills *(G-1011)*
TEC-3 Prototypes Inc....E.... 810 678-8909
Metamora *(G-10782)*
Technique Inc....D.... 517 789-8988
Jackson *(G-8585)*
Tel-X Corporation....E.... 734 425-2225
Garden City *(G-5843)*

Tesca Usa Inc .... E 586 991-0744
Rochester Hills ***(G-13524)***
Tower Acquisition Co II LLC .... G 248 675-6000
Livonia ***(G-9958)***
Tower Autmtve Oprtns USA III .... G 248 675-6000
Livonia ***(G-9959)***
▲ **Tower Auto Holdings I LLC** .... G 248 675-6000
Livonia ***(G-9960)***
Tower Auto Holdings II A LLC .... G 248 675-6000
Livonia ***(G-9961)***
Tower Auto Holdings II B LLC .... G 248 675-6000
Livonia ***(G-9962)***
▲ **Tower Auto Holdings USA LLC** .... F 248 675-6000
Livonia ***(G-9963)***
▲ **Tower Automotive Operations** .... D 248 675-6000
Livonia ***(G-9964)***
▲ **Tower Automotive Operations** .... G 248 675-6000
Livonia ***(G-9965)***
Tower Automotive Operations I .... B 989 375-2201
Elkton ***(G-4784)***
Tower Automotive Operations I .... D 616 802-1600
Grand Rapids ***(G-6934)***
Tower Automotive Operations I .... B 586 465-5158
Clinton Township ***(G-3250)***
Tower Automotive Operations I .... C 734 414-3100
Plymouth ***(G-12776)***
▲ **Tower Defense & Aerospace LLC** .... C 248 675-6000
Livonia ***(G-9966)***
Tower International Inc .... G 989 623-2174
Elkton ***(G-4785)***
▲ **Tower International Inc** .... B 248 675-6000
Livonia ***(G-9967)***
▲ **Trans-Matic Mfg Co Inc** .... C 616 820-2500
Holland ***(G-7834)***
Traverse City Products Inc .... D 231 946-4414
Traverse City ***(G-16128)***
Trianon Industries Corporation .... A 586 759-2200
Center Line ***(G-2585)***
▲ **Troy Design & Manufacturing Co** .... C 734 738-2300
Plymouth ***(G-12781)***
▲ **Tubular Metal Systems LLC** .... E 989 879-2611
Pinconning ***(G-12514)***
▲ **Twb Company LLC** .... C 734 289-6400
Monroe ***(G-11080)***
▼ **UNI Vue Inc** .... E 248 545-0810
Ferndale ***(G-5325)***
Van-Rob Inc .... C 517 657-2450
Lansing ***(G-9271)***
▲ **Variety Die & Stamping Co** .... D 734 426-4488
Dexter ***(G-4517)***
Ventra Grand Rapids 5 LLC .... B 616 222-3296
Grand Rapids ***(G-6965)***
▲ **Versatube Corporation** .... F 248 524-0299
Troy ***(G-16683)***
Visor Frames LLC .... F 586 864-6058
Sterling Heights ***(G-15541)***
Washers Incorporated .... C 734 523-1000
Livonia ***(G-9999)***
Washers Incorporated .... G 734 523-1000
Livonia ***(G-10000)***
Webster Cold Forge Co .... F 313 554-4500
Northville ***(G-11734)***
▲ **Wellington Industries Inc** .... C 734 942-1060
Van Buren Twp ***(G-16796)***
Wellington Industries Inc .... E 734 403-6112
Van Buren Twp ***(G-16797)***
Wellington-Almont LLC .... D 734 942-1060
Van Buren Twp ***(G-16798)***
▲ **Wico Metal Products Company** .... C 586 755-9600
Warren ***(G-17293)***
▼ **Wirco Manufacturing LLC** .... F 810 984-5576
Port Huron ***(G-12976)***
Wirco Products Inc .... F 810 984-5576
Port Huron ***(G-12977)***
Yarema Die & Engineering Co .... D 248 585-2830
Troy ***(G-16702)***

3466 Crowns & Closures

Adcaa LLC .... G 734 623-4236
Ann Arbor ***(G-343)***
▲ **Roll Rite Corporation** .... E 989 345-3434
Gladwin ***(G-5935)***
▲ **Roll-Rite LLC** .... E 989 345-3434
Gladwin ***(G-5936)***

3469 Metal Stampings, NEC

A & A Manufacturing Co .... G 616 846-1730
Spring Lake ***(G-15130)***
A & R Specialty Services Corp .... E 313 933-8750
Detroit ***(G-3826)***
A & S Reel & Tackle Inc .... G 313 928-1667
Ecorse ***(G-4741)***
A Raymond Corp N Amer Inc .... E 248 853-2500
Rochester Hills ***(G-13358)***
A-1 Stampings Inc .... G 586 294-7790
Fraser ***(G-5611)***
▲ **Acemco Incorporated** .... C 231 799-8612
Norton Shores ***(G-11806)***
Acme Tool & Die Co .... G 231 938-1260
Acme ***(G-1)***
▲ **Acorn Stamping Inc** .... F 248 628-5216
Oxford ***(G-12332)***
Actron Steel Inc .... E 231 947-3981
Traverse City ***(G-15890)***
Admat Manufacturing Inc .... F 269 641-7453
Union ***(G-16727)***
▼ **Adrian Steel Company** .... B 517 265-6194
Adrian ***(G-46)***
Advance Engineering Company .... D 313 537-3500
Canton ***(G-2344)***
▲ **Advanced Auto Trends Inc** .... E 248 628-6111
Oxford ***(G-12333)***
▲ **Ajax Spring and Mfg Co** .... F 248 588-5700
Madison Heights ***(G-10184)***
Allen Tool .... G 517 566-2200
Sunfield ***(G-15644)***
Alternate Number Five Inc .... D 616 842-2581
Grand Haven ***(G-5991)***
▲ **Aluminum Blanking Co Inc** .... D 248 338-4422
Pontiac ***(G-12802)***
Aluminum Textures Inc .... E 616 538-3144
Grandville ***(G-7020)***
American Engnred Cmponents Inc .... C 734 428-8301
Manchester ***(G-10402)***
American Fabricated Pdts Inc .... F 616 607-8785
Spring Lake ***(G-15133)***
American Metal Fab Inc .... D 269 279-5108
Three Rivers ***(G-15854)***
▲ **Anand Nvh North America Inc** .... C 810 724-2400
Imlay City ***(G-8196)***
Anrod Screen Cylinder Company .... E 989 872-2101
Cass City ***(G-2511)***
Apex Spring & Stamping Corp .... D 616 453-5463
Grand Rapids ***(G-6171)***
Arnold Tool & Die Co .... E 586 598-0099
Chesterfield ***(G-2741)***
Automatic Spring Products Corp .... C 616 842-2284
Grand Haven ***(G-5995)***
Automotive Prototype Stamping .... G 586 445-6792
Clinton Township ***(G-3060)***
▲ **Bae Industries Inc** .... C 586 754-3000
Warren ***(G-16950)***
Bae Industries Inc .... F 248 475-9600
Auburn Hills ***(G-790)***
Barnes Group Inc .... G 734 737-0958
Plymouth ***(G-12582)***
Barnes Group Inc .... E 734 429-2022
Plymouth ***(G-12583)***
Barnes Group Inc .... G 586 415-6677
Fraser ***(G-5627)***
Bay Manufacturing Corporation .... E 989 358-7198
Alpena ***(G-281)***
▲ **Bayloff Stmped Pdts Dtroit Inc** .... D 734 397-9116
Van Buren Twp ***(G-16747)***
Belwith Products LLC .... F 616 247-4000
Grandville ***(G-7022)***
Benteler Automotive Corp .... B 616 247-3936
Auburn Hills ***(G-791)***
Benteler Defense Corp .... G 248 377-9999
Auburn Hills ***(G-793)***
Big Rapids Products Inc .... D 231 796-3593
Big Rapids ***(G-1622)***
Blue Fire Manufacturing LLC .... E 248 714-7166
Waterford ***(G-17325)***
Bopp-Busch Manufacturing Co .... E 989 876-7924
Au Gres ***(G-745)***
Broaching Industries Inc .... E 586 949-3775
Chesterfield ***(G-2748)***
◆ **Brooks Utility Products Group** .... E 248 477-0250
Novi ***(G-11841)***
▲ **Burkland Inc** .... D 810 636-2233
Goodrich ***(G-5952)***
Burnside Acquisition LLC .... G 616 243-2800
Grand Rapids ***(G-6245)***
Burnside Acquisition LLC .... D 231 798-3394
Norton Shores ***(G-11810)***
Burnside Industries LLC .... D 231 798-3394
Norton Shores ***(G-11811)***
▲ **Cameron Tool Corporation** .... D 517 487-3671
Lansing ***(G-9353)***
Challenge Mfg Company .... C 616 735-6500
Grand Rapids ***(G-6268)***
Challenge Mfg Company .... A 616 396-2079
Holland ***(G-7587)***
Clark Perforating Company Inc .... F 734 439-1170
Milan ***(G-10935)***
Co-Dee Stamping Inc .... G 269 948-8631
Hastings ***(G-7404)***
▲ **Commercial Mfg & Assembly Inc** .... E 616 847-9980
Grand Haven ***(G-6005)***
Complete Metalcraft LLC .... G 248 990-0850
Highland ***(G-7489)***
Conner Steel Products .... G 248 852-5110
Rochester Hills ***(G-13394)***
Consolidated Clips Clamps Inc .... D 734 455-0880
Plymouth ***(G-12601)***
Consolidated Metal Pdts Inc .... G 616 538-1000
Grand Rapids ***(G-6302)***
▲ **Continental Strctrl Plstc Mch** .... D 734 428-8301
Manchester ***(G-10404)***
Contour Engineering Inc .... F 989 828-6526
Shepherd ***(G-14727)***
Contract Welding and Fabg Inc .... E 734 699-5561
Van Buren Twp ***(G-16753)***
Corban Industries Inc .... D 248 393-2720
Orion ***(G-12177)***
Covenant Cpitl Investments Inc .... F 248 477-4230
Farmington Hills ***(G-4967)***
Craft Steel Products Inc .... E 616 935-7575
Spring Lake ***(G-15137)***
D & D Driers Timber Product .... G 906 224-7251
Wakefield ***(G-16849)***
Dajaco Ind Inc .... G 586 949-1590
Chesterfield ***(G-2759)***
Dajaco Industries Inc .... D 586 949-1590
Chesterfield ***(G-2760)***
Dee-Blast Corporation .... F 269 428-2400
Stevensville ***(G-15563)***
Degele Manufacturing Inc .... E 586 949-3550
Chesterfield ***(G-2763)***
Demmer Investments Inc .... G 517 321-3600
Lansing ***(G-9221)***
▼ **Dgh Enterprises Inc** .... E 269 925-0657
Benton Harbor ***(G-1494)***
Dgh Enterprises Inc .... G 269 925-0657
Benton Harbor ***(G-1495)***
Diamond Press Solutions LLC .... G 269 945-1997
Hastings ***(G-7406)***
Die-Verse Solutions LLC .... F 616 384-3550
Coopersville ***(G-3557)***
Dietech Tool & Mfg Inc .... D 810 724-0505
Imlay City ***(G-8198)***
Diversfied Prcurement Svcs LLC .... G 248 821-1147
Ferndale ***(G-5280)***
Dorr Industries Inc .... F 616 681-9440
Dorr ***(G-4523)***
Douglas Stamping Company .... G 248 542-3940
Madison Heights ***(G-10234)***
▼ **Duggan Manufacturing LLC** .... C 586 254-7400
Shelby Township ***(G-14581)***
Duggans Limited LLC .... F 586 254-7400
Shelby Township ***(G-14582)***
Duquaine Incorporated .... G 906 228-7290
Marquette ***(G-10527)***
Dynamic Corporation .... D 616 399-9391
Holland ***(G-7613)***
▼ **E & E Manufacturing Co Inc** .... B 734 451-7600
Plymouth ***(G-12615)***
E & E Manufacturing Co Inc .... F 248 616-1300
Clawson ***(G-2977)***
Echo Quality Grinding Inc .... F 231 544-6637
Central Lake ***(G-2591)***
▲ **Edmar Manufacturing Inc** .... D 616 392-7218
Holland ***(G-7618)***
Electro Optics Mfg Inc .... F 734 283-3000
Wyandotte ***(G-17957)***
Elkins Machine & Tool Co Inc .... E 734 941-0266
Romulus ***(G-13672)***
Elmhirst Industries Inc .... E 586 731-8663
Sterling Heights ***(G-15330)***
Ernest Inds Acquisition LLC .... G 734 459-8881
Plymouth ***(G-12618)***
Ernest Industries Acquisition, ... E 734 595-9500
Westland ***(G-17554)***
Euclid Manufacturing Co Inc .... E 734 397-6300
Detroit ***(G-4043)***
▲ **European Cabinet Mfg Co** .... E 586 445-8909
Roseville ***(G-13802)***
◆ **Expan Inc** .... E 586 725-0405
New Baltimore ***(G-11484)***

34 FABRICATED METAL PRODUCTS, EXCEPT MACHINERY AND TRANSPORTATION EQUIPMENT SIC SECTION

Experi-Metal Inc .... C 586 977-7800
Sterling Heights *(G-15335)*
▼ **Falcon Stamping Inc** .... G 517 540-6197
Howell *(G-8040)*
Fisher & Company Incorporated .... D 586 746-2000
Sterling Heights *(G-15341)*
Fisher & Company Incorporated .... C 248 280-0808
Troy *(G-16363)*
Fortress Manufacturing Inc .... F 269 925-1336
Benton Harbor *(G-1498)*
Forward Metal Craft Inc .... F 616 459-6051
Grand Rapids *(G-6417)*
Four Star Tooling & Engrg Inc .... G 586 264-4090
Sterling Heights *(G-15346)*
Four Way Industries Inc .... F 248 588-5421
Clawson *(G-2978)*
▼ **Franklin Fastener Company** .... E 313 537-8900
Redford *(G-13162)*
Future Industries Inc .... E 616 844-0772
Grand Haven *(G-6017)*
Gar-V Manufacturing Inc .... G 269 279-5134
Three Rivers *(G-15863)*
▲ **Gill Corporation** .... B 616 453-4491
Grand Rapids *(G-6438)*
▲ **Global Advanced Products LLC** .... D 586 749-6800
Chesterfield *(G-2781)*
Global Automotive Systems LLC .... E 248 299-7500
Auburn Hills *(G-889)*
Global Rollforming Systems LLC .... G 586 218-5100
Roseville *(G-13808)*
▲ **Globe Tech LLC** .... E 734 656-2200
Plymouth *(G-12630)*
▲ **Globe Technologies Corporation** .... E 989 846-9591
Standish *(G-15219)*
▲ **Gns Holland Inc** .... G 616 796-0433
Holland *(G-7645)*
Gordon Metal Products Inc .... F 586 445-0960
Livonia *(G-9754)*
Grant Industries Incorporated .... D 586 293-9200
Fraser *(G-5657)*
▲ **Grattan Family Enterprises LLC** .... D 248 547-3870
Ferndale *(G-5290)*
Gray Bros Stamping & Mch Inc .... E 269 483-7615
White Pigeon *(G-17649)*
Gray Brothers Mfg Inc .... E 269 483-7615
White Pigeon *(G-17650)*
▲ **Great Lakes Metal Stamping Inc** .... E 269 465-4415
Bridgman *(G-1864)*
Greenfield Die & Mfg Corp .... C 734 454-4000
Canton *(G-2379)*
◆ **Haerter Stamping LLC** .... D 616 871-9400
Kentwood *(G-9008)*
Hatch Stamping Company LLC .... D 517 223-1293
Fowlerville *(G-5569)*
Hatch Stamping Company LLC .... C 517 540-1021
Howell *(G-8047)*
Heinzmann D Tool & Die Inc .... F 248 363-5115
Commerce Township *(G-3410)*
▲ **Hibshman Screw Mch Pdts Inc** .... E 269 641-7525
Union *(G-16730)*
◆ **High-Star Corporation** .... G 734 743-1503
Westland *(G-17569)*
▼ **Highland Engineering Inc** .... E 517 548-4372
Howell *(G-8048)*
Highwood Die & Engineering Inc .... E 248 338-1807
Pontiac *(G-12835)*
Hilite Industries Inc .... G 248 475-4580
Lake Orion *(G-9138)*
Hilltop Manufacturing Co Inc .... G 248 437-2530
New Hudson *(G-11544)*
Hope Network West Michigan .... E 231 775-3425
Cadillac *(G-2252)*
Hope Network West Michigan .... C 231 796-4801
Paris *(G-12385)*
Hti Associates LLC .... E 616 399-5430
Holland *(G-7682)*
Hz Industries Inc .... B 616 453-4491
Grand Rapids *(G-6521)*
Illinois Tool Works Inc .... B 616 772-1910
Zeeland *(G-18157)*
Illinois Tool Works Inc .... E 734 855-3709
Livonia *(G-9779)*
▲ **Inalfa/Ssi Roof Systems LLC** .... D 586 758-6620
Warren *(G-17086)*
Independent Tool and Mfg Co .... E 269 521-4811
Allegan *(G-165)*
Industrial Engineering Service .... F 616 794-1330
Belding *(G-1419)*
Industrial Exprmental Tech LLC .... E 248 371-8000
Auburn Hills *(G-912)*
Industrial Innovations Inc .... F 616 249-1525
Grandville *(G-7052)*
Industrial Machine Pdts Inc .... D 248 628-3621
Oxford *(G-12351)*
Industrial Stamping & Mfg Co .... E 586 772-8430
Roseville *(G-13819)*
▲ **Innotec Corp** .... D 616 772-5959
Zeeland *(G-18160)*
Innovation Fab Inc .... F 586 752-3092
Bruce Twp *(G-2084)*
▲ **Innovative Tool and Design Inc** .... E 248 542-1831
Oak Park *(G-12075)*
Interior Resource Supply Inc .... G 313 584-4399
Dearborn *(G-3726)*
Iroquois Industries Inc .... E 586 756-6922
Warren *(G-17101)*
J & L Mfg Co .... E 586 445-9530
Warren *(G-17104)*
Jackson Precision Inds Inc .... E 517 782-8103
Jackson *(G-8479)*
Jad Products Inc .... G 517 456-4810
Clinton *(G-3024)*
Jireh Metal Products Inc .... D 616 531-7581
Grandville *(G-7053)*
▼ **JMS of Holland Inc** .... D 616 796-2727
Holland *(G-7694)*
John Lamantia Corporation .... G 269 428-8100
Stevensville *(G-15572)*
Jordan Manufacturing Company .... E 616 794-0900
Belding *(G-1421)*
Jsj Corporation .... B 616 842-5500
Grand Haven *(G-6041)*
◆ **Jsj Corporation** .... E 616 842-6350
Grand Haven *(G-6042)*
K & K Die Inc .... E 586 268-8812
Sterling Heights *(G-15384)*
▲ **K&K Stamping Company** .... E 586 443-7900
Saint Clair Shores *(G-14257)*
Ka-Wood Gear & Machine Co .... E 248 585-8870
Madison Heights *(G-10287)*
KB Stamping Inc .... F 616 866-5917
Belmont *(G-1464)*
▲ **Kecy Corporation** .... E 517 448-8954
Hudson *(G-8133)*
▲ **Kecy Products Inc** .... D 517 448-8954
Hudson *(G-8134)*
Kendor Steel Rule Die Inc .... E 586 293-7111
Fraser *(G-5678)*
Keyes-Davis Company .... E 269 962-7505
Springfield *(G-15195)*
Kinney Tool and Die Inc .... D 616 997-0901
Coopersville *(G-3562)*
Kriewall Enterprises Inc .... E 586 336-0600
Romeo *(G-13631)*
L & W Inc .... F 517 627-7333
Grand Ledge *(G-6110)*
L & W Inc .... C 734 397-8085
Van Buren Twp *(G-16769)*
L & W Inc .... C 517 486-6321
Blissfield *(G-1717)*
L & W Inc .... F 734 529-7290
Dundee *(G-4590)*
▲ **L & W Inc** .... D 734 397-6300
New Boston *(G-11502)*
L Barge & Associates Inc .... F 248 582-3430
Ferndale *(G-5297)*
▲ **L T C Roll & Engineering Co** .... E 586 465-1023
Clinton Township *(G-3157)*
Lab Tool and Engineering Corp .... E 517 750-4131
Spring Arbor *(G-15124)*
Lacy Tool Company Inc .... G 248 476-5250
Novi *(G-11928)*
Lake Fabricators Inc .... E 269 651-1935
Sturgis *(G-15611)*
Laser Cutting Co .... E 586 468-5300
Harrison Township *(G-7337)*
▲ **Llink Technologies LLC** .... E 586 336-9370
Brown City *(G-2054)*
▲ **Low Cost Surcing Solutions LLC** .... G 248 535-7721
Washington *(G-17306)*
Luckmarr Plastics Inc .... D 586 978-8498
Sterling Heights *(G-15403)*
Lupaul Industries Inc .... F 517 783-3223
Saint Johns *(G-14286)*
▼ **M D Hubbard Spring Co Inc** .... E 248 628-2528
Oxford *(G-12358)*
M P I International Inc .... D 608 764-5416
Rochester Hills *(G-13463)*
Marshall Metal Products Inc .... G 269 781-3924
Marshall *(G-10579)*
Max2 LLC .... F 269 468-3452
Coloma *(G-3360)*
Mayville Engineering Co Inc .... B 616 878-5235
Byron Center *(G-2197)*
Means Industries Inc .... D 989 754-3300
Saginaw *(G-14087)*
▲ **Metal Flow Corporation** .... C 616 392-7976
Holland *(G-7743)*
Metal Stmping Spport Group LLC .... F 586 777-7440
Roseville *(G-13834)*
Metro Stamping & Mfg Co .... F 313 538-6464
Redford *(G-13173)*
◆ **Michigan Rod Products Inc** .... D 517 552-9812
Howell *(G-8065)*
Michigan Scientific Corp .... D 231 547-5511
Charlevoix *(G-2620)*
Mico Industries Inc .... D 616 245-6426
Grand Rapids *(G-6679)*
Mico Industries Inc .... F 616 245-6426
Grand Rapids *(G-6680)*
Mico Industries Inc .... E 616 514-1143
Grand Rapids *(G-6681)*
Mid-Tech Inc .... G 734 426-4327
Ann Arbor *(G-557)*
Middleville Tool & Die Co Inc .... D 269 795-3646
Middleville *(G-10805)*
Mittex Group .... G 616 878-4090
Byron Center *(G-2202)*
◆ **Modineer Co** .... C 269 683-2550
Niles *(G-11627)*
Modineer Co .... C 269 684-3138
Niles *(G-11628)*
▼ **Mpi Products LLC** .... E 248 237-3007
Rochester Hills *(G-13478)*
▼ **Mueller Impacts Company Inc** .... C 810 364-3700
Marysville *(G-10608)*
Munn Manufacturing Company .... E 616 765-3067
Freeport *(G-5766)*
Nelson Manufacturing Inc .... G 810 648-0065
Sandusky *(G-14440)*
Nelson Steel Products Inc .... D 616 396-1515
Holland *(G-7753)*
New 11 Inc .... E 616 494-9370
Holland *(G-7754)*
New Center Stamping Inc .... C 313 872-3500
Detroit *(G-4267)*
New Line Inc .... G 586 228-4820
Shelby Township *(G-14652)*
Nor-Dic Tool Company Inc .... F 734 326-3610
Romulus *(G-13715)*
Northern Industrial Mfg Corp .... E 586 468-2790
Harrison Township *(G-7341)*
Northern Stampings Inc .... F 586 598-6969
Rochester Hills *(G-13483)*
Northwest Pattern Company .... G 248 477-7070
Farmington Hills *(G-5082)*
▲ **Oakland Stamping LLC** .... C 734 397-6300
Detroit *(G-4283)*
Oakland Stamping LLC .... G 248 340-2520
Lake Orion *(G-9152)*
Ort Tool & Die Corporation .... D 419 242-9553
Erie *(G-4807)*
Os Holdings LLc .... G 734 397-6300
New Boston *(G-11507)*
Ovidon Manufacturing LLC .... D 517 548-4005
Howell *(G-8075)*
P-T Stamping Co Ltd .... G 517 278-5961
Coldwater *(G-3316)*
Pac-Cnc Inc .... E 616 288-3389
Grand Rapids *(G-6737)*
Page Components Corporation .... F 231 922-3600
Traverse City *(G-16062)*
Palmer Engineering Inc .... E 517 321-3600
Lansing *(G-9251)*
Paradigm Engineering Inc .... G 586 776-5910
Roseville *(G-13849)*
Patton Tool and Die Inc .... F 810 359-5336
Lexington *(G-9559)*
Paw Paw Everlast Label Company .... G 269 657-4921
Paw Paw *(G-12411)*
▲ **PEC of America Corporation** .... F 248 675-3130
Novi *(G-11972)*
Pentar Stamping Inc .... E 517 782-0700
Jackson *(G-8549)*
▼ **Permaloc Corporation** .... F 616 399-9600
Holland *(G-7769)*
Pinconning Metals Inc .... G 989 879-3144
Pinconning *(G-12512)*
▲ **Pinnacle Tool Incorporated** .... E 616 257-2700
Wyoming *(G-18027)*

SIC SECTION — 34 FABRICATED METAL PRODUCTS, EXCEPT MACHINERY AND TRANSPORTATION EQUIPMENT

Precision Parts Holdings Inc ....A...... 248 853-9010
 Rochester Hills *(G-13498)*
Precision Prototype & Mfg Inc...........F...... 517 663-4114
 Eaton Rapids *(G-4729)*
Precision Resource Inc ....G...... 248 478-3704
 Troy *(G-16561)*
Precision Stamping Co Inc ....E...... 517 546-5656
 Howell *(G-8082)*
Premier Prototype Inc.......................E...... 586 323-6114
 Sterling Heights *(G-15450)*
Press-Way Inc ....D...... 586 790-3324
 Clinton Township *(G-3201)*
Pro Stamp Plus LLC ....G...... 616 447-2988
 Grand Rapids *(G-6780)*
▲ Production Fabricators Inc ....E...... 231 777-3822
 Muskegon *(G-11407)*
Production Spring LLC......................E...... 248 583-0036
 Troy *(G-16566)*
Profile Inc...E...... 517 224-8012
 Potterville *(G-13075)*
Proos Manufacturing Inc...................D...... 616 454-5622
 Grand Rapids *(G-6791)*
Punching Concepts Inc ....F...... 989 358-7070
 Alpena *(G-309)*
▲ Quality Metalcraft Inc ....C...... 734 261-6700
 Livonia *(G-9900)*
▲ Quality Tool & Stamping Co Inc....C...... 231 733-2538
 Muskegon *(G-11410)*
Quigley Industries Inc ....D...... 248 426-8600
 Farmington Hills *(G-5109)*
Quigley Manufacturing Inc................C...... 248 426-8600
 Farmington Hills *(G-5110)*
R & L Machine Products Inc ....G...... 734 992-2574
 Romulus *(G-13725)*
R E D Industries Inc..........................F...... 248 542-2211
 Hazel Park *(G-7451)*
▲ R-Bo Co Inc ....E...... 616 748-9733
 Zeeland *(G-18184)*
Radar Mexican Investments LLC.....G...... 586 779-0300
 Warren *(G-17215)*
Ranger Tool & Die Co ....E...... 989 754-1403
 Saginaw *(G-14130)*
Rel Machine Inc ....G...... 906 337-3018
 Calumet *(G-2332)*
▲ Reliance Metal Products Inc ....G...... 734 641-3334
 Westland *(G-17595)*
Reliant Industries Inc........................E...... 586 275-0479
 Sterling Heights *(G-15464)*
Rew Industries Inc ....E...... 586 803-1150
 Shelby Township *(G-14679)*
Ridgeview Industries Inc..................B...... 616 453-8636
 Grand Rapids *(G-6825)*
Ridgeview Industries Inc..................D...... 616 414-6500
 Nunica *(G-12043)*
▲ Ridgeview Industries Inc ....C...... 616 453-8636
 Grand Rapids *(G-6826)*
Riverside Tool & Mold Inc ....G...... 989 435-9142
 Beaverton *(G-1390)*
Riverview Products Inc ....G...... 616 866-1305
 Rockford *(G-13586)*
▲ Rj Acquisition Corp ....E...... 586 268-2300
 Sterling Heights *(G-15474)*
Rose Engraving Company................G...... 616 243-3108
 Grand Rapids *(G-6837)*
Rose-A-Lee Technologies Inc..........G...... 586 799-4555
 Sterling Heights *(G-15479)*
▲ Royal Flex-N-Gate Oak LLC ....B...... 248 549-3800
 Warren *(G-17225)*
Sage International Inc......................D...... 972 623-2004
 Novi *(G-11989)*
Schaller Corporation.........................C...... 586 949-6000
 Chesterfield *(G-2837)*
Schwab Industries Inc......................C...... 586 566-8090
 Shelby Township *(G-14688)*
Seasoned Home LLC........................G...... 616 392-8350
 Holland *(G-7797)*
Selective Industries Inc ....D...... 810 765-4666
 Marine City *(G-10483)*
Set Enterprises of Mi Inc..................C...... 586 573-3600
 Sterling Heights *(G-15494)*
Shape Corp..D...... 616 842-2825
 Spring Lake *(G-15177)*
Sharp Industries Incorporated.........G...... 810 229-6305
 Brighton *(G-1989)*
Shiloh Industries Inc.........................D...... 734 454-4000
 Canton *(G-2426)*
Shiloh Manufacturing LLC ....D...... 586 779-0300
 Warren *(G-17239)*
Shiloh Manufacturing LLC ....F...... 586 873-2835
 Roseville *(G-13868)*

Silver Creek Manufacturing Inc ....F...... 231 798-3003
 Norton Shores *(G-11793)*
Sintel Inc ....C...... 616 842-6960
 Spring Lake *(G-15178)*
SOS Engineering Inc ....F...... 616 846-5767
 Grand Haven *(G-6081)*
Southtec LLC ....G...... 734 397-6300
 New Boston *(G-11511)*
▲ Southtec LLC ....C...... 734 397-6300
 New Boston *(G-11512)*
Specialty Tube LLC ....E...... 616 949-5990
 Grand Rapids *(G-6882)*
Spinform Inc......................................G...... 810 767-4660
 Flint *(G-5502)*
Spirit Industries Inc ....G...... 517 371-7840
 Lansing *(G-9266)*
◆ Stanco Metal Products Inc ....E...... 616 842-5000
 Grand Haven *(G-6082)*
Standard Die International Inc ....E...... 800 838-5464
 Livonia *(G-9941)*
Sterling Die & Engineering Inc ....E...... 586 677-0707
 Macomb *(G-10163)*
Stus Welding & Fabrication ....G...... 616 392-8459
 Holland *(G-7818)*
▲ Su-Dan Company ....D...... 248 651-6035
 Lake Orion *(G-9164)*
Sycron Technologies Inc..................G...... 810 694-4007
 Grand Blanc *(G-5985)*
Synergy Prototype Stamping LLC....E...... 586 961-6109
 Clinton Township *(G-3242)*
Ta Delaware Inc ....E...... 248 675-6000
 Novi *(G-12011)*
Technical Stamping Inc....................G...... 586 948-3285
 Chesterfield *(G-2846)*
Technique Inc....................................D...... 517 789-8988
 Jackson *(G-8585)*
Tenibac-Graphion Inc ....D...... 586 792-0150
 Clinton Township *(G-3245)*
Tenibac-Graphion Inc ....F...... 616 647-3333
 Grand Rapids *(G-6921)*
Tg Manufacturing LLC.......................E...... 616 842-1503
 Grand Rapids *(G-6925)*
Tg Manufacturing LLC.......................E...... 616 935-7575
 Byron Center *(G-2212)*
◆ Thai Summit America Corp ....D...... 517 548-4900
 Howell *(G-8107)*
▲ Thomas Industrial Rolls Inc ....F...... 313 584-9696
 Dearborn *(G-3766)*
TI Automotive LLC............................E...... 248 393-4525
 Auburn Hills *(G-1021)*
Trans-Matic Mfg Co Inc....................G...... 616 820-2541
 Holland *(G-7835)*
▲ Trans-Matic Mfg Co Inc...................C...... 616 820-2500
 Holland *(G-7834)*
Transfer Tool Systems Inc ....D...... 616 846-8510
 Grand Rapids *(G-6090)*
TRW Automotive US LLC ....E...... 248 426-3901
 Farmington Hills *(G-5143)*
Uei Inc ....E...... 616 361-6093
 Grand Rapids *(G-6944)*
Ultraform Industries Inc ....D...... 586 752-4508
 Bruce Twp *(G-2105)*
Unified Brands Inc ....E...... 989 644-3331
 Weidman *(G-17462)*
Unique Products ....G...... 616 794-3800
 Belding *(G-1430)*
United Manufacturing Inc.................E...... 616 738-8888
 Holland *(G-7842)*
Universal Stamping Inc ....E...... 269 925-5300
 Benton Harbor *(G-1558)*
Usher Tool & Die Inc.........................F...... 616 583-9160
 Byron Center *(G-2213)*
Van Loon Industries Inc ....E...... 586 532-8530
 Shelby Township *(G-14716)*
Van S Fabrications Inc.....................G...... 810 679-2115
 Croswell *(G-3605)*
Van-Dies Engineering Inc.................E...... 586 293-1430
 Fraser *(G-5745)*
▲ Variety Die & Stamping Co ....D...... 734 426-4488
 Dexter *(G-4517)*
Ventra Ionia Main LLC ....E...... 616 597-3220
 Ionia *(G-8252)*
▲ Ventra Ionia Main LLC ....C...... 616 597-3220
 Ionia *(G-8253)*
▲ Versatube Corporation....................E...... 248 524-0299
 Troy *(G-16683)*
Vinewood Metalcraft Inc...................E...... 734 946-8733
 Taylor *(G-15778)*
Vintech Mexico Holdings LLC ....G...... 810 387-3224
 Imlay City *(G-8215)*

Wallin Brothers Inc ....G...... 734 525-7750
 Livonia *(G-9995)*
Webasto Roof Systems Inc ....A...... 248 299-2000
 Rochester Hills *(G-13544)*
Webasto Roof Systems Inc ....F...... 248 997-5100
 Rochester Hills *(G-13545)*
Webasto Roof Systems Inc ....C...... 734 452-2600
 Livonia *(G-10002)*
Weber Bros & White Metal Works ...G...... 269 751-5193
 Hamilton *(G-7242)*
Webster Cold Forge Co ....F...... 313 554-4500
 Northville *(G-11734)*
West Mich Auto Stl & Engrg Inc ......E...... 616 560-8198
 Belding *(G-1431)*
Western Engineered Products.........G...... 248 371-9259
 Lake Orion *(G-9170)*
▲ Wico Metal Products Company .....C...... 586 755-9600
 Warren *(G-17293)*
▲ Wolverine Metal Stamping Inc ....D...... 269 429-6600
 Saint Joseph *(G-14354)*
Yarema Die & Engineering Co ....E...... 248 689-5777
 Troy *(G-16703)*
◆ ZF Active Safety & Elec US LLC....C...... 734 855-2600
 Livonia *(G-10014)*
ZF North America Inc.......................G...... 248 478-7210
 Farmington Hills *(G-5154)*
ZF Passive Safety ....G...... 734 855-3631
 Livonia *(G-10018)*
ZF Passive Safety ....B...... 586 232-7200
 Washington *(G-17316)*
Zygot Operations Limited ....F...... 810 736-2900
 Flint *(G-5529)*

3471 Electroplating, Plating, Polishing, Anodizing & Coloring

A-W Custom Chrome Inc..................G...... 586 775-2040
 Eastpointe *(G-4697)*
ABC Custom Chrome Inc ....G...... 248 674-4333
 Waterford *(G-17321)*
Able Welding Inc...............................G...... 989 865-9611
 Saint Charles *(G-14189)*
Abrasive Services Incorporated ......G...... 734 941-2144
 Romulus *(G-13647)*
Abrasive Solutions LLC ....G...... 517 592-2668
 Cement City *(G-2574)*
Accurate Coating Inc ....G...... 616 452-0016
 Grand Rapids *(G-6134)*
Ace Finishing Inc ....G...... 586 777-1390
 Warren *(G-16914)*
Acme Plating Inc ....G...... 313 838-3870
 Detroit *(G-3840)*
Acorn Industries Inc ....D...... 734 261-2940
 Livonia *(G-9627)*
Aft..G...... 313 320-0218
 Detroit *(G-3845)*
▲ Ajax Metal Processing Inc ....G...... 313 267-2100
 Detroit *(G-3850)*
All Chrome LLC.................................G...... 517 554-1649
 Albion *(G-115)*
▲ Allan Tool & Machine Co Inc ....D...... 248 585-2910
 Troy *(G-16190)*
Allegan Metal Finishing C ....G...... 269 673-6604
 Allegan *(G-148)*
Allied Finishing Inc ....C...... 616 698-7550
 Grand Rapids *(G-6163)*
Almond Products Inc ....D...... 616 844-1813
 Spring Lake *(G-15132)*
Alpha Metal Finishing Co ....F...... 734 426-2855
 Dexter *(G-4475)*
Aluminum Finishing Company ....G...... 269 382-4010
 Kalamazoo *(G-8678)*
◆ American Metal Restoration ....G...... 810 364-4820
 Marysville *(G-10598)*
Ano-Kal Company ....F...... 269 685-5743
 Plainwell *(G-12518)*
Apollo Plating Inc.............................C...... 586 777-0070
 Roseville *(G-13773)*
ARC Services of Macomb Inc ....E...... 586 469-1600
 Clinton Township *(G-3056)*
Arted Chrome Plating ....G...... 586 758-0050
 Warren *(G-16939)*
Arted Chrome Plating Inc..................F...... 313 871-3331
 Detroit *(G-3880)*
Asp Plating Company.......................G...... 616 842-8080
 Grand Haven *(G-5992)*
Auto Anodics Inc ....E...... 810 984-5600
 Port Huron *(G-12895)*
Automotive Tumbling Co Inc ....G...... 313 925-7450
 Detroit *(G-3885)*

Employee Codes: A=Over 500 employees, B=251-500
C=101-250, D=51-100, E=20-50, F=10-19, G=3-9

2020 Harris Michigan Industrial Directory

793

34 FABRICATED METAL PRODUCTS, EXCEPT MACHINERY AND TRANSPORTATION EQUIPMENT SIC SECTION

B & K Buffing Inc G 734 941-2144
Romulus *(G-13654)*
B & L Plating Co Inc G 586 778-9300
Warren *(G-16947)*
B and L Metal Finishing LLC G 269 767-2225
Allegan *(G-151)*
Bar Processing Corporation D 734 243-8937
Monroe *(G-11019)*
▲ Bar Processing Corporation C 734 782-4454
Flat Rock *(G-5349)*
Bar Processing Corporation D 734 782-4454
Warren *(G-16952)*
Beacon Park Finishing LLC F 248 318-4286
Roseville *(G-13777)*
Beech & Rich Inc E 269 968-8012
Springfield *(G-15188)*
Bellevue Proc Met Prep Inc E 313 921-1931
Detroit *(G-3900)*
Blough Inc D 616 897-8407
Lowell *(G-10024)*
Bopp-Busch Manufacturing Co E 989 876-7924
Au Gres *(G-745)*
Cadillac Plating Corporation D 586 771-9191
Warren *(G-16975)*
Cadon Plating & Coatings LLC D 734 282-8100
Wyandotte *(G-17950)*
Cal Grinding Inc E 906 786-8749
Escanaba *(G-4821)*
Cds Specialty Coatings LLC G 734 244-6708
Westland *(G-17547)*
▲ Cg Liquidation Incorporated E 586 575-9800
Warren *(G-16978)*
Changeover Integration LLC F 231 845-5320
Ludington *(G-10053)*
Charlotte Anodizing Pdts Inc D 517 543-1911
Charlotte *(G-2638)*
Chemical Process Inds LLC F 248 547-5200
Madison Heights *(G-10209)*
Chor Industries Inc E 248 585-3323
Troy *(G-16267)*
Classic Metal Finishing Inc E 517 990-0011
Jackson *(G-8411)*
Classic Plating Inc G 313 532-1440
Redford *(G-13153)*
Coles Polishing G 269 625-2542
Colon *(G-3371)*
Color Coat Plating Company F 248 744-0445
Madison Heights *(G-10216)*
Complete Metal Finishing Inc F 269 343-0500
Kalamazoo *(G-8711)*
Controlled Plating Tech Inc E 616 243-6622
Grand Rapids *(G-6307)*
Crown Industrial Services Inc E 734 483-7270
Ypsilanti *(G-18062)*
Crown Industrial Services Inc E 517 905-5300
Jackson *(G-8425)*
Cyclone Manufacturing Inc G 269 782-9670
Dowagiac *(G-4539)*
D & B Metal Finishing G 586 725-6056
Chesterfield *(G-2758)*
D & D Buffing & Polishing G 616 866-1015
Rockford *(G-13565)*
DC Byers Co/Grand Rapids Inc F 616 538-7300
Grand Rapids *(G-6338)*
Deburring Company F 734 542-9800
Livonia *(G-9702)*
Detroit Chrome Inc E 313 341-9478
Detroit *(G-3976)*
Detroit Metalcraft Finishing G 586 415-7760
Fraser *(G-5643)*
Detroit Steel Treating Company E 248 334-7436
Pontiac *(G-12816)*
Di-Anodic Finishing Corp E 616 454-0470
Grand Rapids *(G-6348)*
Diamond Chrome Plating Inc D 517 546-0150
Howell *(G-8030)*
Diamond Tool Manufacturing Inc E 734 416-1900
Plymouth *(G-12611)*
Dmi Automotive Inc F 517 548-1414
Howell *(G-8031)*
Dn-Lawrence Industries Inc F 269 552-4999
Kalamazoo *(G-8730)*
DNR Inc G 734 722-4000
Plymouth *(G-12613)*
DNR Inc F 734 722-4000
Westland *(G-17550)*
Downriver Deburring Inc G 313 388-2640
Taylor *(G-15709)*
Dyna Plate Inc E 616 452-6763
Grand Rapids *(G-6363)*
Dynamic Finishing LLC G 231 727-8811
Muskegon *(G-11308)*
Dynamic Finishing LLC F 231 737-8130
Fruitport *(G-5792)*
Eastern Oil Company E 248 333-1333
Pontiac *(G-12819)*
ECJ Processing G 248 540-2336
Southfield *(G-14896)*
▲ Electro Chemical Finishing Co F 616 531-0670
Grandville *(G-7031)*
Electro Chemical Finishing Co E 616 531-1250
Grand Rapids *(G-6373)*
Electro Chemical Finishing Co F 616 531-0670
Wyoming *(G-17999)*
Electro Chemical Finishing Co G 616 249-7092
Grandville *(G-7032)*
Electro-Plating Service Inc F 248 541-0035
Madison Heights *(G-10242)*
Electroplating Industries Inc F 586 469-2390
Clinton Township *(G-3109)*
Elm Plating G 517 795-1574
Jackson *(G-8444)*
Empire Hardchrome G 810 392-3122
Richmond *(G-13262)*
▲ Erbsloeh Alum Solutions Inc B 269 323-2565
Portage *(G-12993)*
Expert Coating Company Inc F 616 453-8261
Grand Rapids *(G-6393)*
Fini Finish Metal Finishing F 586 758-0050
Warren *(G-17033)*
▲ Finishing Services Inc C 734 484-1700
Ypsilanti *(G-18073)*
Finishing Touch Inc E 517 542-5581
Litchfield *(G-9601)*
▲ Fintex LLC E 734 946-3100
Romulus *(G-13678)*
▲ Fire-Rite Inc E 313 273-3730
Detroit *(G-4060)*
Fitzgerald Finishing LLC D 313 368-3630
Detroit *(G-4061)*
Flat Rock Metal Inc C 734 782-4454
Flat Rock *(G-5353)*
Flexible Controls Corporation D 313 368-3630
Detroit *(G-4062)*
Gj Prey Coml & Indus Pntg Cov G 248 250-4792
Clawson *(G-2980)*
Gladwin Metal Processing Inc G 989 426-9038
Gladwin *(G-5931)*
Gokoh Coldwater Incorporated F 517 279-1080
Coldwater *(G-3305)*
Grand Northern Products G 800 968-1811
Grand Rapids *(G-6450)*
Grand Rapids Stripping Co G 616 361-0794
Grand Rapids *(G-6464)*
Grand River Polishing Co Corp E 616 846-1420
Spring Lake *(G-15147)*
Great Lakes Finishing Inc F 231 733-9566
Muskegon *(G-11338)*
Great Lakes Metal Finshg LLC E 517 764-1335
Jackson *(G-8460)*
Hayes-Albion Corporation F 517 629-2141
Jackson *(G-8463)*
Heidtman Steel Products Inc D 734 848-2115
Erie *(G-4803)*
Hi-Tech Coatings Inc E 586 759-3559
Warren *(G-17081)*
High Prfmce Met Finshg Inc F 269 327-8897
Portage *(G-13000)*
Highpoint Finshg Solutions Inc D 616 772-4425
Zeeland *(G-18148)*
Holly Plating Co Inc E 810 714-9213
Fenton *(G-5220)*
Honhart Mid-Nite Black Co E 248 588-1515
Troy *(G-16399)*
Howard Finishing LLC D 586 777-0070
Roseville *(G-13816)*
Hpc Holdings Inc E 248 634-9361
Holly *(G-7883)*
Ihc Inc C 313 535-3210
Detroit *(G-4136)*
Industrial Finishing Co LLC G 616 784-5737
Comstock Park *(G-3485)*
International Paint Stripping F 734 942-0500
Romulus *(G-13687)*
International Paint Stripping F 734 942-0500
Romulus *(G-13688)*
J & L Products Inc G 248 544-8500
Hazel Park *(G-7439)*
Jackson Tumble Finish Corp E 517 787-0368
Jackson *(G-8481)*
▲ JD Plating Company Inc E 248 547-5200
Madison Heights *(G-10283)*
Jo-Mar Enterprises Inc G 313 365-9200
Detroit *(G-4162)*
Kalamazoo Metal Finishers Inc F 269 382-1611
Kalamazoo *(G-8791)*
Kalamazoo Stripping Derusting F 269 323-1340
Portage *(G-13005)*
◆ KC Jones Plating Co E 586 755-4900
Warren *(G-17119)*
KC Jones Plating Co E 248 399-8500
Hazel Park *(G-7440)*
▲ Keen Point International Inc E 248 340-8732
Auburn Hills *(G-925)*
Kenwal Pickling LLC E 313 739-1040
Dearborn *(G-3729)*
Kepco Inc E 269 649-5800
Vicksburg *(G-16838)*
Kevco Metal Surface Prep G 616 538-1377
Wyoming *(G-18014)*
Kriseler Welding Inc G 989 624-9266
Birch Run *(G-1664)*
Lacks Enterprises Inc D 616 698-2030
Grand Rapids *(G-6597)*
Lacks Industries Inc C 616 698-9852
Grand Rapids *(G-6609)*
Lansing Plating Company G 517 485-6915
Lansing *(G-9241)*
Lawrence Surface Tech Inc G 248 609-9001
Troy *(G-16459)*
Lee Industries Inc E 231 777-2537
Muskegon *(G-11365)*
Liberty Burnishing Co G 313 366-7878
Detroit *(G-4203)*
◆ Lorin Industries Inc D 231 722-1631
Muskegon *(G-11367)*
M&M Polishing Inc F 269 468-4407
Coloma *(G-3359)*
Mann Metal Finishing Inc D 269 621-6359
Hartford *(G-7385)*
Marble Grinding & Polishing G 586 321-0543
Ray *(G-13134)*
Margate Industries Inc G 810 387-4300
Yale *(G-18046)*
▲ Marsh Plating Corporation D 734 483-5767
Ypsilanti *(G-18088)*
Martin and Hattie Rasche Inc D 616 245-1223
Grand Rapids *(G-6646)*
Master Finish Co C 877 590-5819
Grand Rapids *(G-6648)*
▲ Material Sciences Corporation F 734 207-4444
Canton *(G-2398)*
Matthews Plating Inc E 517 784-3535
Jackson *(G-8510)*
McGean-Rohco Inc E 216 441-4900
Livonia *(G-9832)*
McNichols Polsg & Anodizing F 313 538-3470
Redford *(G-13171)*
McNichols Polsg & Anodizing G 313 538-3470
Redford *(G-13172)*
Metal Finishing Quotecom LLC G 248 890-1096
Whitmore Lake *(G-17703)*
Metal Finishing Technology G 231 733-9736
Muskegon *(G-11376)*
Metal Prep Technology Inc F 313 843-2890
Dearborn *(G-3739)*
Michigan Plating LLC G 248 544-3500
Hazel Park *(G-7444)*
Michner Plating Company D 517 789-6627
Jackson *(G-8521)*
▲ Micro Platers Sales Inc E 313 865-2293
Detroit *(G-4245)*
Mid-Michigan Industries Inc D 989 773-6918
Mount Pleasant *(G-11208)*
Mid-Michigan Industries Inc E 989 386-7707
Clare *(G-2877)*
Mid-State Plating Co Inc E 810 767-1622
Flint *(G-5467)*
Midwest II Inc C 734 856-5200
Ottawa Lake *(G-12266)*
Midwest Plating Company Inc E 616 451-2007
Grand Rapids *(G-6685)*
Muskegon Industrial Finishng G 231 733-7663
Muskegon *(G-11389)*
Mvc Holdings LLC F 586 491-2600
Roseville *(G-13843)*
National Galvanizing LP A 734 243-1882
Monroe *(G-11059)*
National Zinc Processors Inc F 269 926-1161
Benton Harbor *(G-1535)*

SIC SECTION 34 FABRICATED METAL PRODUCTS, EXCEPT MACHINERY AND TRANSPORTATION EQUIPMENT

New Lfe Cppr & Brss Maint Free ....G.... 586 725-3286
Casco *(G-2503)*
Nicro Finishing LLC ....F.... 313 924-0661
Detroit *(G-4271)*
▼ Non-Ferrous Cast Alloys Inc ....D.... 231 799-0550
Norton Shores *(G-11782)*
Nor-Cote Inc ....E.... 586 756-1200
Warren *(G-17170)*
Norbrook Plating Inc ....E.... 586 755-4110
Warren *(G-17171)*
Norbrook Plating Inc ....G.... 313 369-9304
Detroit *(G-4275)*
Northwest Fabrication Inc ....G.... 231 536-3229
East Jordan *(G-4641)*
Northwest Polishing & Buffing ....G.... 616 899-2682
Grand Rapids *(G-6721)*
Oliver Industries Inc ....E.... 586 977-7750
Sterling Heights *(G-15440)*
▲ Patmai Company Inc ....E.... 586 294-0370
Fraser *(G-5705)*
Perfection Industries Inc ....E.... 313 272-4040
Detroit *(G-4297)*
Pfg Enterprises Inc ....E.... 586 755-1053
Chesterfield *(G-2816)*
Pioneer Metal Finishing LLC ....C.... 734 384-9000
Monroe *(G-11062)*
Plating Specialties Inc ....F.... 248 547-8660
Madison Heights *(G-10330)*
Plymouth Plating Works Inc ....F.... 734 453-1560
Plymouth *(G-12720)*
Port City Industrial Finishing ....D.... 231 726-4288
Muskegon *(G-11401)*
Ppi LLC ....E.... 586 772-7736
Warren *(G-17190)*
Precision Finishing Co Inc ....E.... 616 245-2255
Grand Rapids *(G-6765)*
Premier Finishing Inc ....E.... 616 785-3070
Grand Rapids *(G-6768)*
Production Tube Company Inc ....G.... 313 259-3990
Detroit *(G-4312)*
Professional Metal Finishers ....F.... 616 365-2620
Grand Rapids *(G-6783)*
Prs Manufacturing Inc ....G.... 616 784-4409
Grand Rapids *(G-6794)*
Qmi Group Inc ....E.... 248 589-0505
Madison Heights *(G-10342)*
Quali Tone Corporation ....F.... 269 426-3664
Sawyer *(G-14487)*
Richcoat LLC ....E.... 586 978-1311
Sterling Heights *(G-15468)*
Robert & Son Black Ox Special ....G.... 586 778-7633
Roseville *(G-13862)*
Ryan Polishing Corporation ....F.... 248 548-6832
Oak Park *(G-12096)*
Schwartz Boiler Shop Inc ....G.... 231 627-2556
Cheboygan *(G-2694)*
Seaver Industrial Finishing Co ....D.... 616 842-8560
Grand Haven *(G-6074)*
Selfridge Plating Inc ....D.... 586 469-3141
Harrison Township *(G-7348)*
Shields Acquisition Co Inc ....G.... 734 782-4454
Flat Rock *(G-5364)*
▲ Siemens Vai Services LLC ....F.... 269 927-3591
Benton Harbor *(G-1548)*
◆ Sigma International Inc ....E.... 248 230-9681
Livonia *(G-9928)*
▲ SMS Modern Hard Chrome LLC ....D.... 586 445-0330
Warren *(G-17242)*
Sodus Hard Chrome Inc ....F.... 269 925-2077
Sodus *(G-14747)*
South Haven Finishing Inc ....E.... 269 637-2047
South Haven *(G-14772)*
Spec Abrasives and Finishing ....F.... 231 722-1926
Muskegon *(G-11428)*
▲ Spectrum Industries Inc ....D.... 616 451-0784
Grand Rapids *(G-6884)*
Spencer Zdanowitz Inc ....G.... 517 841-9380
Jackson *(G-8575)*
Spring Arbor Coatings LLC ....D.... 517 750-2903
Spring Arbor *(G-15128)*
Superior Mtal Finshg Rustproof ....F.... 313 893-1050
Detroit *(G-4388)*
Supreme Media Blasting and Pow ....G.... 586 792-7705
Clinton Township *(G-3239)*
Synthetic Lubricants Inc ....G.... 616 754-1050
Greenville *(G-7156)*
Tawas Plating Company ....D.... 989 362-2011
Tawas City *(G-15683)*
Technickel Inc ....F.... 269 926-8505
Benton Harbor *(G-1553)*
Thomas Frankini ....G.... 517 783-2400
Jackson *(G-8589)*
Togreencleancom ....G.... 269 428-4812
Stevensville *(G-15584)*
Tri K Cylinder Service Inc ....G.... 269 965-3981
Springfield *(G-15207)*
Tru-Coat Inc ....G.... 810 785-3331
Montrose *(G-11106)*
USA Quality Metal Finshg LLC ....F.... 269 427-9000
Lawrence *(G-9509)*
V & V Inc ....F.... 616 842-8611
Grand Haven *(G-6093)*
Vacuum Orna Metal Company Inc ....E.... 734 941-9100
Romulus *(G-13738)*
W A Thomas Company ....G.... 734 955-6500
Taylor *(G-15779)*
▲ Wandres Corporation ....F.... 734 214-9903
Ann Arbor *(G-694)*
Western Engineered Products ....G.... 248 371-9259
Lake Orion *(G-9170)*
Williams Diversified Inc ....E.... 734 421-6100
Livonia *(G-10009)*
Williams Finishing Inc ....G.... 734 421-6100
Livonia *(G-10010)*
▲ Wolverine Plating Corporation ....E.... 586 771-5000
Roseville *(G-13892)*
WSi Industrial Services Inc ....E.... 734 942-9300
Riverview *(G-13307)*
Zav-Tech Metal Finishing ....G.... 269 422-2559
Stevensville *(G-15587)*

3479 Coating & Engraving, NEC

A & K Finishing Inc ....E.... 616 949-9100
Grand Rapids *(G-6122)*
A2z Coating ....G.... 616 805-3281
Grand Rapids *(G-6127)*
Aactron Inc ....E.... 248 543-6740
Madison Heights *(G-10177)*
AB Custom Fabricating LLC ....E.... 269 663-8100
Edwardsburg *(G-4756)*
▲ Act Test Panels LLC ....E.... 517 439-1485
Hillsdale *(G-7515)*
Action Asphalt LLC ....F.... 734 449-8565
Whitmore Lake *(G-17684)*
Adrian Coatings Company ....E.... 517 438-8699
Adrian *(G-43)*
▲ Ajax Metal Processing Inc ....G.... 313 267-2100
Detroit *(G-3850)*
Albah Manufacturing Tech Corp ....E.... 519 972-7222
Troy *(G-16182)*
Almond Products Inc ....D.... 616 844-1813
Spring Lake *(G-15132)*
Alpha Coatings Inc ....E.... 734 523-9000
Livonia *(G-9636)*
American Porcelain Enamel Co ....E.... 231 744-3013
Muskegon *(G-11268)*
Anchor Bay Powder Coat LLC ....F.... 586 725-3255
New Baltimore *(G-11480)*
Applied Coatings Solutions LLC ....G.... 269 341-9757
Kalamazoo *(G-8680)*
Aristo-Cote Inc ....D.... 586 447-9049
Shelby Township *(G-14549)*
Aristo-Cote Inc ....D.... 586 447-9049
Fraser *(G-5622)*
Aristo-Cote Inc ....E.... 586 336-9421
Harrison Township *(G-7321)*
August Lighting Inc ....G.... 616 895-4951
Zeeland *(G-18115)*
B & J Enmeling Inc A Mich Corp ....F.... 313 365-6620
Detroit *(G-3892)*
Baron Acquisition LLC ....G.... 248 585-0444
Madison Heights *(G-10202)*
Beech & Rich Inc ....E.... 269 968-8012
Springfield *(G-15188)*
Bio-Vac Inc ....E.... 248 350-2150
Southfield *(G-14853)*
Bk Mattson Enterprises Inc ....G.... 906 774-0097
Iron Mountain *(G-8278)*
▲ Blackmer ....D.... 616 241-1611
Grand Rapids *(G-6229)*
Bolyea Industries ....F.... 586 293-8600
Fraser *(G-5631)*
▲ Boss Electro Static Inc ....E.... 616 575-0577
Wyoming *(G-17989)*
▲ Burkard Industries Inc ....C.... 586 791-6520
Clinton Township *(G-3070)*
C & M Coatings Inc ....F.... 616 842-1925
Grand Haven *(G-5999)*
▼ Cadillac Oil Company ....F.... 313 365-6200
Detroit *(G-3926)*
Carbide Surface Company ....G.... 586 465-6110
Clinton Township *(G-3075)*
Cast Coatings Inc ....E.... 269 545-8373
Galien *(G-5817)*
▲ Cg Liquidation Incorporated ....E.... 586 575-9800
Warren *(G-16978)*
Changeover Integration LLC ....F.... 231 845-5320
Ludington *(G-10053)*
Coatings Plus Inc ....E.... 616 451-2427
Grand Rapids *(G-6284)*
Color Factory ....G.... 810 577-2974
Flushing *(G-5534)*
▲ Commercial Steel Treating Corp ....D.... 248 588-3300
Madison Heights *(G-10217)*
Conformance Coatings Prototype ....E.... 810 364-4333
Marysville *(G-10601)*
Corlin Company ....G.... 616 842-7093
Grand Haven *(G-6006)*
Cox Brothers Machining Inc ....E.... 517 796-4662
Jackson *(G-8422)*
Crm Inc ....D.... 231 947-0304
Traverse City *(G-15952)*
Csquared Innovations Inc ....F.... 734 998-8330
Novi *(G-11860)*
Cushion Lrry Trphies Engrv LLC ....G.... 517 332-1667
Lansing *(G-9358)*
Custom Anything LLC ....G.... 231 282-1981
Stanwood *(G-15233)*
Custom Coating Technologies ....G.... 734 244-3610
Flat Rock *(G-5352)*
Custom Powder Coating LLC ....G.... 616 454-9730
Grand Rapids *(G-6325)*
▲ Dag Ltd LLC ....F.... 586 276-9310
Sterling Heights *(G-15307)*
▲ Decc Company Inc ....E.... 616 245-0431
Grand Rapids *(G-6341)*
▲ Depor Industries Inc ....G.... 248 362-3900
Troy *(G-16313)*
▲ Detroit Name Plate Etching Inc ....E.... 248 543-5200
Ferndale *(G-5278)*
Done Right Engraving Inc ....G.... 248 332-3133
Pontiac *(G-12818)*
Double Eagle Steel Coating Co ....C.... 313 203-9800
Dearborn *(G-3695)*
Douglas Corp ....F.... 517 767-4112
Tekonsha *(G-15818)*
▲ Dunnage Engineering Inc ....E.... 810 229-9501
Brighton *(G-1913)*
Eagle Powder Coating ....E.... 517 784-2556
Jackson *(G-8437)*
Eisele Connectors Inc ....G.... 616 726-7714
Grand Rapids *(G-6370)*
Ejs Engraving ....G.... 616 534-8104
Grandville *(G-7029)*
Electro Chemical Finishing Co ....F.... 616 531-0670
Wyoming *(G-17999)*
Engineered Prfmce Coatings Inc ....G.... 616 988-7927
Grand Rapids *(G-6379)*
Engrave & Graphic Inc ....G.... 616 245-8082
Grand Rapids *(G-6381)*
Evans Coatings L L C ....G.... 248 583-9890
Troy *(G-16354)*
Exclusive Imagery Inc ....G.... 248 436-2999
Royal Oak *(G-13927)*
Expert Coating Company Inc ....F.... 616 453-8261
Grand Rapids *(G-6393)*
Express Coat Corporation ....E.... 586 773-2682
Warren *(G-17026)*
Fastener Coatings Inc ....F.... 269 279-5134
Three Rivers *(G-15861)*
Finishers Unlimited Monroe Inc ....E.... 734 243-3502
Monroe *(G-11031)*
▲ Finishing Services Inc ....C.... 734 484-1700
Ypsilanti *(G-18073)*
Finishing Specialties Inc ....G.... 586 954-1338
Clinton Township *(G-3118)*
Fricia Enterprises Inc ....G.... 586 977-1900
Sterling Heights *(G-15348)*
Gannons General Contract ....F.... 734 429-5859
Saline *(G-14392)*
Gladwin Metal Processing Inc ....G.... 989 426-9038
Gladwin *(G-5931)*
Glw Finishing ....E.... 616 395-0112
Holland *(G-7644)*
Godfrey & Wing Inc ....G.... 330 562-1440
Saginaw *(G-14047)*
Grand Haven Powder Coating Inc ....E.... 616 850-8822
Grand Haven *(G-6023)*
Great Lakes Powder Coating LLC ....F.... 248 522-6222
Walled Lake *(G-16894)*

S I C

34 FABRICATED METAL PRODUCTS, EXCEPT MACHINERY AND TRANSPORTATION EQUIPMENT

Gyro Powder Coating Inc ....F 616 846-2580
  Grand Haven (G-6030)
H & J Mfg Consulting Svcs Corp ....G 734 941-8314
  Romulus (G-13684)
Hice and Summey Inc ....F 269 651-6217
  Bronson (G-2029)
Hice and Summey Inc ....F 269 651-6217
  Bronson (G-2030)
▲ Hj Manufacturing Inc ....F 906 233-1500
  Escanaba (G-4833)
Hope Network West Michigan ....C 231 796-4801
  Paris (G-12385)
Howmet Corporation ....F 231 981-3000
  Whitehall (G-17673)
◆ Howmet Corporation ....E 231 894-5686
  Whitehall (G-17669)
▲ Howmet Holdings Corporation .....G 231 894-5686
  Whitehall (G-17676)
I S P Coatings Corp ....E 586 752-5020
  Romeo (G-13630)
Imagecraft ....G 517 750-0077
  Jackson (G-8469)
Instacote Inc ....G 734 847-5260
  Erie (G-4804)
Integricoat Inc ....E 616 935-7878
  Spring Lake (G-15154)
▲ Ionbond LLC ....D 248 398-9100
  Madison Heights (G-10278)
Jackson Industrial Coating Svc ....G 517 782-8169
  Jackson (G-8477)
Jandron II ....G 906 225-9600
  Marquette (G-10536)
Jbl Enterprises ....G 616 530-8647
  Grand Rapids (G-6555)
▲ JD Plating Company Inc ....E 248 547-5200
  Madison Heights (G-10283)
Johnson Cleaning & Painting ....G 231 627-2211
  Cheboygan (G-2683)
Joseph M Hoffman Inc ....F 586 774-8500
  Roseville (G-13824)
Kalb & Associates Inc ....E 586 949-2735
  Chesterfield (G-2793)
◆ KC Jones Plating Co ....E 586 755-4900
  Warren (G-17119)
Kentwood Powder Coat Inc ....E 616 698-8181
  Grand Rapids (G-6580)
◆ Knape Industries Inc ....E 616 866-1651
  Rockford (G-13577)
Kopacz Industrial Painting ....G 734 427-6740
  Livonia (G-9799)
Lacks Exterior Systems LLC ....C 616 554-3419
  Grand Rapids (G-6599)
Lampco Manufacturing Company ......G 517 784-4393
  Jackson (G-8495)
Liberty Bell Powdr Coating LLC ....G 586 557-6328
  Lincoln Park (G-9581)
Lincoln Industries ....G 989 736-6421
  Lincoln (G-9565)
Locpac Inc ....E 734 453-2300
  Plymouth (G-12677)
Magna Extrors Intrors Amer Inc ....G 616 786-7000
  Kentwood (G-9018)
▲ Magni Group Inc ....F 248 647-4500
  Birmingham (G-1690)
Magnum Powder Coating Inc ....G 616 785-3155
  Comstock Park (G-3495)
March Coatings Inc ....D 810 229-6464
  Brighton (G-1953)
Martin Products Company Inc ....F 269 651-1721
  Sturgis (G-15615)
Master Coat LLC ....F 734 405-2340
  Westland (G-17578)
Master Mix Company ....F 734 487-7870
  Ypsilanti (G-18089)
▲ Material Sciences Corporation .....F 734 207-4444
  Canton (G-2398)
Mdm Enterprises Inc ....F 616 452-1591
  Grand Rapids (G-6655)
Metal Finishing Technology ....G 231 733-9736
  Muskegon (G-11376)
Michigan Metal Coatings Co ....D 810 966-9240
  Port Huron (G-12942)
Midland Silicon Company LLC ....F 248 674-3736
  Waterford (G-17358)
Midwest Products Finshg Co Inc .....C 734 856-5200
  Ottawa Lake (G-12267)
Mirrage Ltd ....F 734 697-6447
  Van Buren Twp (G-16773)
Modineer Coatings Division ....G 269 925-0702
  Benton Harbor (G-1531)

Monarch Powder Coating Inc ....G 231 798-1422
  Norton Shores (G-11775)
▼ Motor City Metal Fab Inc ....E 734 345-1001
  Taylor (G-15747)
MSC Pre Finish Metals Egv Inc ....G 734 207-4400
  Canton (G-2409)
N O F Metal Coatings N Amer ....G 248 228-8610
  Southfield (G-14988)
Nano Materials & Processes Inc ....G 248 529-3873
  Milford (G-10974)
ND Industries Inc ....E 248 288-0000
  Troy (G-16522)
▲ ND Industries Inc ....C 248 288-0000
  Clawson (G-2982)
Normic Industries Inc ....E 231 947-8860
  Traverse City (G-16049)
Oakwood Custom Coating Inc ....F 313 561-7740
  Dearborn (G-3745)
▲ Oakwood Energy Management Inc ..C 734 947-7700
  Taylor (G-15750)
Oerlikon Blzers Cating USA Inc ....E 248 409-5900
  Lake Orion (G-9154)
Oerlikon Blzers Cating USA Inc ....G 989 463-6268
  Alma (G-246)
Oerlikon Blzers Cating USA Inc ....E 586 465-0412
  Harrison Township (G-7342)
Oerlikon Blzers Cating USA Inc ....E 248 960-9055
  Wixom (G-17873)
Oerlikon Blzers Cating USA Inc ....G 989 362-3515
  East Tawas (G-4691)
On The Side Sign Dsign Grphics ....G 810 266-7446
  Byron (G-2174)
P C S Companies Inc ....G 616 754-2229
  Greenville (G-7149)
Paint Work Incorporated ....F 586 759-6640
  Warren (G-17179)
PDM Industries Inc ....E 231 943-9601
  Traverse City (G-16063)
Peninsula Powder Coating Inc ....F 906 353-7234
  Baraga (G-1112)
Performcoat of Michigan LLC ....F 269 282-7030
  Springfield (G-15200)
Permacoat Inc ....F 313 388-7798
  Allen Park (G-204)
Plasma-Tec Inc ....F 616 455-2593
  Wayland (G-17409)
Plasti - Paint Inc ....C 989 285-2280
  Saint Louis (G-14368)
Powco Inc ....F 269 646-5385
  Marcellus (G-10467)
▲ Powder Cote II Inc ....C 586 463-7040
  Mount Clemens (G-11145)
Powder Cote II Inc ....G 586 463-7040
  Mount Clemens (G-11146)
PPG Coating Services ....D 313 922-8433
  Detroit (G-4307)
PPG Coating Services ....F 586 575-9800
  Troy (G-16556)
PPG Coating Services ....D 734 421-7300
  Livonia (G-9894)
Precision Coatings Inc ....D 248 363-8361
  Commerce Township (G-3440)
▲ Pro - Tech Graphics Ltd ....F 586 791-6363
  Clinton Township (G-3206)
Pro-Finish Powder Coating Inc ....E 616 245-7550
  Grand Rapids (G-6781)
Protective Ctngs Epoxy Systems .....G 517 223-1192
  Fowlerville (G-5577)
Quali Tone Corporation ....F 269 426-3664
  Sawyer (G-14487)
Reliance Finishing Co ....D 616 241-4436
  Grand Rapids (G-6818)
Richcoat LLC ....E 586 978-1311
  Sterling Heights (G-15468)
Richter Precision Inc ....F 586 465-0500
  Fraser (G-5718)
Royal Oak Name Plate Company ......F 586 774-8500
  Roseville (G-13559)
◆ Sas Global Corporation ....C 248 414-4470
  Warren (G-17229)
Schmidt Grinding ....G 269 649-4604
  Vicksburg (G-16843)
Schroth Enterprises Inc ....E 586 759-4240
  Grosse Pointe Farms (G-7187)
Seaver Finishing Inc ....D 616 844-4360
  Grand Haven (G-6073)
Seaver Industrial Finishing Co ....D 616 842-8560
  Grand Haven (G-6074)
Seaver-Smith Inc ....E 616 842-8560
  Grand Haven (G-6075)

▲ Serma Coat LLC ....F 810 229-0829
  Brighton (G-1988)
Serviscreen Inc ....D 616 669-1640
  Jenison (G-8643)
Simmons & Courtright Plastic ....G 616 365-0045
  Grand Rapids (G-6866)
Spartan Steel Coating LLC ....D 734 289-5400
  Monroe (G-11067)
▲ Spectrum Industries Inc ....F 616 451-0784
  Grand Rapids (G-6884)
Specular LLC ....G 248 680-1720
  Sterling Heights (G-15505)
▲ Spraytek Inc ....F 248 546-3551
  Ferndale (G-5319)
▲ Star Cutter Co ....E 248 474-8200
  Farmington Hills (G-5129)
Stechschulte/Wegerly AG LLC ....F 586 739-0101
  Sterling Heights (G-15510)
◆ Straits Steel and Wire Company ...D 231 843-3416
  Ludington (G-10080)
Sun Plastics Coating Company ....F 734 453-0822
  Plymouth (G-12762)
Superior Collision Inc ....G 231 946-4983
  Traverse City (G-16117)
Superior Mtal Finshg Rustproof ....F 313 893-1050
  Detroit (G-4388)
Sure-Weld & Plating Rack Co ....G 248 304-9430
  Southfield (G-15040)
Tawas Powder Coating Inc ....E 989 362-2011
  Tawas City (G-15684)
TEC International II ....E 248 724-1800
  Auburn Hills (G-1014)
Techno-Coat Inc ....G 616 396-6446
  Holland (G-7824)
Teknicolors Inc ....G 734 414-9900
  Canton (G-2434)
▲ Thierica Inc ....F 616 458-1538
  Grand Rapids (G-6926)
Three Oaks Engraving & Engrg ....G 269 469-2124
  Three Oaks (G-15851)
Ti-Coating Inc ....E 586 726-1900
  Shelby Township (G-14709)
Toefco Engineering Inc ....E 269 683-0188
  Niles (G-11649)
Unicote Corporation ....F 586 296-0700
  Fraser (G-5743)
Universal Coating Inc ....D 810 785-7555
  Flint (G-5518)
Universal Coating Technology ....G 616 847-6036
  Grand Haven (G-6092)
V & S Detroit Galvanizing LLC ....F 313 535-2600
  Redford (G-13205)
Voigt & Schweitzer LLC ....E 313 535-2600
  Redford (G-13206)
Voigt Schwtzer Galvanizers Inc ....D 313 535-2600
  Redford (G-13207)
Volcor Finishing Inc ....E 616 527-5555
  Ionia (G-8254)
Wealthy Street Corporation ....C 616 451-0784
  Grand Rapids (G-6980)
West Michigan Coating LLC ....E 616 647-9509
  Grand Rapids (G-6986)
West Michigan Stamp & Seal ....G 269 323-1913
  Portage (G-13055)
Whites Industrial Service ....G 616 291-3706
  Lowell (G-10046)
WS Molnar Co ....E 313 923-0400
  Detroit (G-4451)
▲ X-Cel Industries Inc ....C 248 226-6000
  Southfield (G-15067)
Yale Tool & Engraving Inc ....G 734 459-7171
  Plymouth (G-12795)
▲ Z Technologies Corporation ....E 313 937-0710
  Redford (G-13209)

3482 Small Arms Ammunition

Bold Ammo & Guns Inc ....G 616 826-0913
  Rockford (G-13559)
General Dynamics Land ....B 586 825-4805
  Sterling Heights (G-15356)
Michigan Ammo LLC ....G 313 383-4430
  Detroit (G-4236)
Michigan Rifle and Pistol Assn ....G 269 781-1223
  Marshall (G-10583)
On The Mark Inc ....G 989 317-8033
  Mount Pleasant (G-11216)
▲ Sage Control Ordnance Inc ....F 989 739-2200
  Oscoda (G-12219)
Scorpion Reloads LLC ....G 586 214-3843
  Fraser (G-5722)

Tactical Simplicity LLC.....G..... 248 410-4523
Wixom *(G-17903)*

3484 Small Arms

AB Weapons Division Inc.....G..... 616 696-2008
Cedar Springs *(G-2544)*
Aerospace America Inc.....E..... 989 684-2121
Bay City *(G-1273)*
Combat Action LLC.....G..... 810 772-3758
Brighton *(G-1900)*
▲ Crl Inc.....E..... 906 428-3710
Gladstone *(G-5910)*
Kirtland Products LLC.....F..... 231 582-7505
Boyne City *(G-1826)*
Manly Innovations LLC.....G..... 734 548-0200
Chelsea *(G-2716)*
Marbles Gun Sights Inc.....G..... 906 428-3710
Gladstone *(G-5916)*
Olivo LLC.....G..... 313 573-7202
Lincoln Park *(G-9582)*
Pierce Engineers Inc.....G..... 517 321-5051
Lansing *(G-9255)*
Sage International Limited.....F..... 989 739-7000
Oscoda *(G-12220)*
Sbn Enterprises LLC.....G..... 586 839-4782
Bruce Twp *(G-2098)*

3489 Ordnance & Access, NEC

Autoneum North America Inc.....D..... 248 848-0100
Farmington Hills *(G-4936)*
Camdex Inc.....G..... 248 528-2300
Troy *(G-16256)*
▲ Lanzen Incorporated.....D..... 586 771-7070
Bruce Twp *(G-2090)*

3491 Industrial Valves

▲ Armstrong International Inc.....C..... 269 273-1415
Three Rivers *(G-15858)*
Asco LP.....C..... 810 648-9141
Sandusky *(G-14428)*
Asco LP.....C..... 248 596-3200
Novi *(G-11830)*
▲ Automatic Valve Corp.....E..... 248 474-6761
Novi *(G-11835)*
▲ Century Instrument Company.....E..... 734 427-0340
Livonia *(G-9681)*
Champion Charter Sls & Svc Inc.....G..... 906 779-2300
Iron Mountain *(G-8280)*
▲ Conley Composites LLC.....E..... 918 299-5051
Grand Rapids *(G-6300)*
Dss Valve Products Inc.....F..... 269 409-6080
Niles *(G-11609)*
Dutchman Mfg Co LLC.....G..... 734 922-5803
Traverse City *(G-15959)*
Ecorse McHy Sls & Rbldrs Inc.....E..... 313 383-2100
Wyandotte *(G-17956)*
Fcx Performance Inc.....E..... 734 654-2201
Carleton *(G-2454)*
Flaretite Inc.....G..... 810 750-4140
Brighton *(G-1923)*
Flowtek Inc.....F..... 231 734-3415
Evart *(G-4881)*
▲ Hills-Mccanna LLC.....D..... 616 554-9308
Kentwood *(G-9011)*
Honeywell International Inc.....D..... 248 926-4800
Wixom *(G-17827)*
◆ Hydronic Components Inc.....F..... 586 268-1640
Warren *(G-17084)*
Instrument and Valve Services.....G..... 734 459-0375
Plymouth *(G-12647)*
Jdl Enterprises Inc.....G..... 586 977-8863
Warren *(G-17113)*
Jdl Enterprises Inc.....F..... 586 977-8863
Sterling Heights *(G-15380)*
Key Gas Components Inc.....E..... 269 673-2151
Allegan *(G-169)*
Mac Valve Asia Inc.....G..... 248 624-7700
Wixom *(G-17851)*
▲ Mac Valves Inc.....A..... 248 624-7700
Wixom *(G-17852)*
Mac Valves Inc.....E..... 734 529-5099
Dundee *(G-4594)*
Marshall Gas Controls Inc.....G..... 269 781-3901
Marshall *(G-10578)*
▲ Mercury Manufacturing Company.....D..... 734 285-5150
Wyandotte *(G-17968)*
Morgold Inc.....G..... 269 445-3844
Cassopolis *(G-2534)*
Neptech Inc.....E..... 810 225-2222
Highland *(G-7498)*
▲ Nil-Cor LLC.....C..... 616 554-3100
Kentwood *(G-9021)*
Nordson Corporation.....D..... 734 459-8600
Wixom *(G-17866)*
Novi Tool & Machine Company.....D..... 313 532-0900
Redford *(G-13176)*
Primore Inc.....F..... 517 263-2220
Adrian *(G-87)*
Primore Inc.....E..... 517 263-2220
Adrian *(G-88)*
Rocon LLC.....G..... 248 542-9635
Hazel Park *(G-7453)*
▼ Sedco Inc.....E..... 517 263-2220
Adrian *(G-95)*
SH Leggitt Company.....C..... 269 781-3901
Marshall *(G-10588)*
▲ Sloan Transportation Pdts Inc.....D..... 616 395-5600
Holland *(G-7806)*
▲ Triad Process Equipment Inc.....G..... 248 685-9938
Milford *(G-10989)*

3492 Fluid Power Valves & Hose Fittings

A Raymond Corp N Amer Inc.....G..... 810 964-7994
Rochester Hills *(G-13359)*
Aircraft Precision Pdts Inc.....D..... 989 875-4186
Ithaca *(G-8356)*
Airman Inc.....E..... 248 960-1354
Brighton *(G-1880)*
▲ Airman Products LLC.....E..... 248 960-1354
Brighton *(G-1881)*
Alco Manufacturing Corp.....E..... 734 426-3941
Dexter *(G-4474)*
Austin Tube Products Inc.....E..... 231 745-2741
Baldwin *(G-1082)*
▲ Automatic Valve Corp.....E..... 248 474-6761
Novi *(G-11835)*
▲ Bucher Hydraulics Inc.....C..... 616 458-1306
Grand Rapids *(G-6238)*
Bucher Hydraulics Inc.....E..... 231 652-2773
Newaygo *(G-11564)*
Buhler Technologies LLC.....F..... 248 652-1546
Rochester Hills *(G-13379)*
▲ Burgaflex North America LLC.....E..... 810 714-3285
Fenton *(G-5192)*
Central Industrial Corporation.....G..... 616 784-9612
Grand Rapids *(G-6267)*
▲ Craig Assembly Inc.....C..... 810 326-1374
Saint Clair *(G-14212)*
◆ Dadco Inc.....D..... 734 207-1100
Plymouth *(G-12604)*
Dutchman Mfg Co LLC.....G..... 734 922-5803
Traverse City *(G-15959)*
Eaton-Aeroquip Llc.....B..... 949 452-9575
Jackson *(G-8440)*
▲ Fluid Hutchinson Management.....D..... 248 679-1327
Auburn Hills *(G-876)*
GM Components Holdings LLC.....E..... 616 246-2000
Grand Rapids *(G-6444)*
Hilite International Inc.....C..... 231 894-3200
Whitehall *(G-17668)*
Hosco Fittings LLC.....E..... 248 912-1750
Wixom *(G-17829)*
▲ Humphrey Products Company.....C..... 269 381-5500
Kalamazoo *(G-8770)*
Kord Industrial Inc.....G..... 248 374-8900
Wixom *(G-17843)*
Loryco Inc.....G..... 248 674-4673
Pontiac *(G-12845)*
Mac Valve Asia Inc.....G..... 248 624-7700
Wixom *(G-17851)*
▲ Mac Valves Inc.....A..... 248 624-7700
Wixom *(G-17852)*
McLaren Inc.....G..... 989 720-4328
Owosso *(G-12302)*
Northland Maintenance Co Inc.....G..... 906 253-9161
Sault Sainte Marie *(G-14469)*
Novi Tool & Machine Company.....D..... 313 532-0900
Redford *(G-13176)*
▲ Oilgear Company.....D..... 231 929-1660
Traverse City *(G-16055)*
Parker-Hannifin Corporation.....D..... 330 253-5239
Otsego *(G-12251)*
Parker-Hannifin Corporation.....B..... 269 629-5000
Richland *(G-13252)*
Pinckney Automatic & Mfg.....G..... 734 878-3430
Pinckney *(G-12502)*
▲ Piper Industries Inc.....D..... 586 771-5100
Roseville *(G-13855)*
Precision Packing Corporation.....E..... 586 756-8700
Warren *(G-17194)*
Quaker Chemical Corporation.....G..... 586 826-6454
Sterling Heights *(G-15458)*
▲ Sames Kremlin Inc.....C..... 734 979-0100
Plymouth *(G-12747)*
Scott Machine Inc.....E..... 517 787-6616
Jackson *(G-8571)*
Spiral Industries Inc.....E..... 810 632-6300
Howell *(G-8101)*
Stonebrdge Technical Entps Ltd.....F..... 810 750-0040
Fenton *(G-5240)*
Thomas Toys Inc.....G..... 810 629-8707
Fenton *(G-5243)*
Wmh Fluidpower Inc.....F..... 269 327-7011
Portage *(G-13058)*

3493 Steel Springs, Except Wire

A N L Spring Manufacturing.....G..... 313 837-0200
Detroit *(G-3828)*
▲ Ajax Spring and Mfg Co.....F..... 248 588-5700
Madison Heights *(G-10184)*
American MSC Inc.....D..... 248 589-7770
Troy *(G-16197)*
▲ American MSC Inc.....E..... 248 589-7770
Troy *(G-16198)*
American Ring Manufacturing.....F..... 734 402-0426
Livonia *(G-9644)*
Arvinmeritor Inc.....E..... 248 435-1000
Troy *(G-16222)*
Automatic Spring Products Corp.....C..... 616 842-2284
Grand Haven *(G-5995)*
Eaton Detroit Spring Svc Co.....F..... 313 963-3839
Detroit *(G-4025)*
▲ Gill Corporation.....B..... 616 453-4491
Grand Rapids *(G-6438)*
Gill Corporation.....C..... 616 453-4491
Grand Rapids *(G-6439)*
J & J Spring Co Inc.....F..... 586 566-7600
Shelby Township *(G-14606)*
Jade Mfg Inc.....G..... 734 942-1462
Romulus *(G-13691)*
▲ Llink Technologies LLC.....E..... 586 336-9370
Brown City *(G-2054)*
M & S Spring Company Inc.....F..... 586 296-9850
Fraser *(G-5687)*
▼ M D Hubbard Spring Co Inc.....E..... 248 628-2528
Oxford *(G-12358)*
◆ Meritor Inc.....C..... 248 435-1000
Troy *(G-16493)*
Mid-West Spring & Stamping Inc.....E..... 231 777-2707
Muskegon *(G-11380)*
Muskegon Brake & Distrg Co LLC.....E..... 231 733-0874
Norton Shores *(G-11776)*
▲ Novi Spring Inc.....F..... 248 486-4220
Brighton *(G-1971)*
P J Wallbank Springs Inc.....D..... 810 987-2992
Port Huron *(G-12953)*
Peterson American Corporation.....E..... 248 616-3380
Madison Heights *(G-10323)*
Qp Acquisition 2 Inc.....E..... 248 594-7432
Southfield *(G-15006)*
◆ Quality Spring/Togo Inc.....C..... 517 278-2391
Coldwater *(G-3323)*
Rhino Strapping Products Inc.....F..... 734 442-4040
Taylor *(G-15763)*
Weiser Metal Products Inc.....G..... 989 736-8151
Lincoln *(G-9571)*

3494 Valves & Pipe Fittings, NEC

2 Brothers Holdings LLC.....G..... 517 487-3900
Lansing *(G-9330)*
Anrod Screen Cylinder Company.....E..... 989 872-2101
Cass City *(G-2511)*
▲ Autocam-Pax Inc.....E..... 269 782-5186
Dowagiac *(G-4534)*
▲ Automatic Valve Corp.....E..... 248 474-6761
Novi *(G-11835)*
Barbron Corporation.....E..... 586 716-3530
Kalkaska *(G-8937)*
Beaden Screen Inc.....E..... 810 679-3119
Croswell *(G-3595)*
Bucher Hydraulics Inc.....E..... 231 652-2773
Newaygo *(G-11564)*
Cal Grinding Inc.....E..... 906 786-8749
Escanaba *(G-4821)*
▲ Colonial Engineering Inc.....F..... 269 323-2495
Portage *(G-12989)*
Computer Operated Mfg.....E..... 989 686-1333
Bay City *(G-1297)*
▲ Conley Composites LLC.....E..... 918 299-5051
Grand Rapids *(G-6300)*

Employee Codes: A=Over 500 employees, B=251-500
C=101-250, D=51-100, E=20-50, F=10-19, G=3-9
2020 Harris Michigan
Industrial Directory
797

34 FABRICATED METAL PRODUCTS, EXCEPT MACHINERY AND TRANSPORTATION EQUIPMENT

Creform Corporation ....F 248 926-2555
 Novi *(G-11858)*
Dart Energy Center ....G 248 203-2924
 Birmingham *(G-1680)*
▼ Dcl Inc ....C 231 547-5600
 Charlevoix *(G-2613)*
▲ Delta Machining Inc ....D 269 683-7775
 Niles *(G-11608)*
Dexter Automatic Products Co ....C 734 426-8900
 Dexter *(G-4485)*
Dover Energy Inc ....C 248 836-6750
 Auburn Hills *(G-842)*
Dutchman Mfg Co LLC ....G 734 922-5803
 Traverse City *(G-15959)*
Eaton Corporation ....C 517 787-7220
 Jackson *(G-8439)*
Eaton-Aeroquip Llc ....B 949 452-9575
 Jackson *(G-8440)*
Extrusion Punch & Tool Inc ....E 248 689-3300
 Troy *(G-16357)*
Flow-Rite Controls Ltd ....E 616 583-1700
 Byron Center *(G-2191)*
◆ Genova Products Inc ....D 810 744-4500
 Davison *(G-3650)*
Great Lakes Hydra Corporation ....F 616 949-8844
 Grand Rapids *(G-6479)*
Hill Machinery Co ....D 616 940-2800
 Grand Rapids *(G-6514)*
J D Russell Company ....E 586 254-8500
 Utica *(G-16743)*
Jdl Enterprises Inc ....F 586 977-8863
 Sterling Heights *(G-15380)*
▲ Jet Industries Inc ....E 734 641-0900
 Westland *(G-17574)*
◆ Kadant Johnson LLC ....C 269 278-1715
 Three Rivers *(G-15867)*
Key Gas Components Inc ....E 269 673-2151
 Allegan *(G-169)*
Lennon Fluid Systems LLC ....E 248 474-6624
 Farmington Hills *(G-5043)*
Loftis Alumi-TEC Inc ....E 616 846-1990
 Grand Haven *(G-6050)*
Lpm Supply Inc ....G 248 333-9440
 Pontiac *(G-12846)*
Mac Valve Asia Inc ....G 248 624-7700
 Wixom *(G-17851)*
▲ Mac Valves Inc ....A 248 624-7700
 Wixom *(G-17852)*
Mac Valves Inc ....E 734 529-5099
 Dundee *(G-4594)*
◆ Marshall Excelsior Co ....E 269 789-6700
 Marshall *(G-10577)*
▲ Maxitrol Company ....D 248 356-1400
 Southfield *(G-14974)*
Maxitrol Company ....E 517 486-2820
 Blissfield *(G-1719)*
◆ Melling Tool Co ....B 517 787-8172
 Jackson *(G-8514)*
▲ Metal Forming Technology Inc ....F 586 949-4586
 Chesterfield *(G-2803)*
Metro Piping Inc ....F 313 872-4330
 Detroit *(G-4231)*
Mueller Industries Inc ....D 248 446-3720
 Brighton *(G-1964)*
Nitz Valve Hardware Inc ....F 989 883-9500
 Sebewaing *(G-14517)*
Nordson Corporation ....D 734 459-8600
 Wixom *(G-17866)*
Novi Tool & Machine Company ....D 313 532-0900
 Redford *(G-13176)*
Npi ....G 248 478-0010
 Farmington Hills *(G-5083)*
O2/Specialty Mfg Holdings LLC ....G 248 554-4228
 Bloomfield Hills *(G-1787)*
Parker-Hannifin Corporation ....B 269 629-5000
 Richland *(G-13252)*
Parker-Hannifin Corporation ....C 517 694-0491
 Mason *(G-10651)*
Parker-Hannifin Corporation ....B 269 694-9411
 Otsego *(G-12249)*
Perfection Sprinkler Company ....G 734 761-5110
 Ann Arbor *(G-590)*
▲ Piper Industries Inc ....D 586 771-5100
 Roseville *(G-13855)*
▲ Pittsfield Products Inc ....E 734 665-3771
 Ann Arbor *(G-593)*
Power Process Engrg Co Inc ....G 248 473-8450
 Novi *(G-11975)*
Primore Inc ....E 517 263-2220
 Adrian *(G-88)*

Quality Filters Inc ....F 734 668-0211
 Ann Arbor *(G-611)*
◆ Quality Pipe Products Inc ....E 734 606-5100
 New Boston *(G-11509)*
R M Wright Company Inc ....E 248 476-9800
 Farmington Hills *(G-5111)*
River Valley Machine Inc ....E 269 673-8070
 Allegan *(G-187)*
◆ Rosedale Products Inc ....D 734 665-8201
 Ann Arbor *(G-624)*
Scott Machine Inc ....E 517 787-6616
 Jackson *(G-8571)*
▲ Set Liquidation Inc ....D 517 694-2300
 Holt *(G-7928)*
SGS Inc ....G 989 239-1726
 Birch Run *(G-1671)*
SH Leggitt Company ....C 269 781-3901
 Marshall *(G-10588)*
Sloan Valve Company ....D 248 446-5300
 New Hudson *(G-11555)*
◆ Srg Global Coatings Inc ....C 248 509-1100
 Troy *(G-16618)*
Tops All Clamps Inc ....G 313 533-7500
 Redford *(G-13202)*
▲ Tribal Manufacturing Inc ....E 269 781-3901
 Marshall *(G-10591)*
Unist Inc ....E 616 949-0853
 Grand Rapids *(G-6951)*
Ventura Aerospace LLC ....E 734 357-0114
 Wixom *(G-17925)*
▲ W L Hamilton & Co ....E 269 781-6941
 Marshall *(G-10592)*
Wayne Wire Cloth Products Inc ....C 989 742-4591
 Hillman *(G-7510)*

3495 Wire Springs

A N L Spring Manufacturing ....G 313 837-0200
 Detroit *(G-3828)*
Apex Spring & Stamping Corp ....D 616 453-5463
 Grand Rapids *(G-6171)*
Barnes Group Inc ....G 734 737-0958
 Plymouth *(G-12582)*
Barnes Group Inc ....E 734 429-2022
 Plymouth *(G-12583)*
Barnes Group Inc ....G 586 415-6677
 Fraser *(G-5627)*
▲ De-Sta-Co Cylinders Inc ....B 248 836-6700
 Auburn Hills *(G-838)*
Demlow Products Inc ....F 517 436-3529
 Clayton *(G-3006)*
Dover Energy Inc ....C 248 836-6750
 Auburn Hills *(G-842)*
Dowsett Spring Company ....G 269 782-2138
 Dowagiac *(G-4541)*
General Automatic Mch Pdts Co ....E 517 437-6000
 Hillsdale *(G-7526)*
◆ Gill Corporation ....B 616 453-4491
 Grand Rapids *(G-6438)*
Gill Corporation ....C 616 453-4491
 Grand Rapids *(G-6439)*
Hilite Industries Inc ....E 248 475-4580
 Lake Orion *(G-9138)*
Hyde Spring and Wire Company ....F 313 272-2201
 Detroit *(G-4132)*
Hz Industries Inc ....B 616 453-4491
 Grand Rapids *(G-6521)*
J & J Spring Co Inc ....F 586 566-7600
 Shelby Township *(G-14606)*
J & J Spring Enterprises LLC ....G 586 566-7600
 Shelby Township *(G-14607)*
Lakeside Spring Products Inc ....G 616 847-2706
 Muskegon *(G-11364)*
M & S Spring Company Inc ....F 586 296-9850
 Fraser *(G-5687)*
▼ M D Hubbard Spring Co Inc ....E 248 628-2528
 Oxford *(G-12358)*
Magiera Holdings Inc ....D 269 685-1768
 Plainwell *(G-12529)*
Mc Guire Spring Corporation ....E 517 546-7311
 Brighton *(G-1957)*
Michigan Spring & Stamp ....E 248 344-1459
 Novi *(G-11948)*
▲ Michigan Spring & Stamping LLC ....C 231 755-1691
 Muskegon *(G-11379)*
Michigan Steel Finishing Co ....F 313 838-3925
 Detroit *(G-4243)*
Mid-West Spring & Stamping Inc ....E 231 777-2707
 Muskegon *(G-11380)*
Motion Dynamics Corporation ....D 231 865-7400
 Fruitport *(G-5798)*

Peterson American Corp ....D 269 279-7421
 Three Rivers *(G-15872)*
Peterson American Corporation ....E 248 616-3380
 Madison Heights *(G-10323)*
▲ Peterson American Corporation ....E 248 799-5400
 Southfield *(G-14997)*
Peterson American Corporation ....G 248 799-5400
 Madison Heights *(G-10324)*
Peterson American Corporation ....F 269 279-7421
 Three Rivers *(G-15873)*
Peterson American Corporation ....G 248 799-5410
 Commerce Township *(G-3438)*
◆ Quality Spring/Togo Inc ....C 517 278-2391
 Coldwater *(G-3323)*
▲ Scherdel Sales & Tech Inc ....D 231 777-7774
 Muskegon *(G-11419)*
Serra Spring & Mfg LLC ....G 586 932-2202
 Sterling Heights *(G-15491)*
Spring Design and Mfg Inc ....E 586 566-9741
 Shelby Township *(G-14702)*
▲ Spring Dynamics Inc ....E 810 798-2622
 Almont *(G-267)*
Spring Saginaw Company ....G 989 624-9333
 Birch Run *(G-1673)*
Sterling Spring LLC ....E 517 782-2479
 Jackson *(G-8578)*
▲ Stumpp Schlele Somappa Sprng ....E 616 361-2791
 Grand Rapids *(G-6895)*
Stumpp Schuele Somappa USA Inc ....F 616 361-2791
 Grand Rapids *(G-6896)*
TEC-3 Prototypes Inc ....E 810 678-8909
 Metamora *(G-10782)*
Tokusen Hytech Inc ....C 269 685-1768
 Plainwell *(G-12547)*
Tokusen Hytech Inc ....D 269 658-1768
 Plainwell *(G-12548)*
Wolverine Coil Spring Company ....D 616 459-3504
 Grand Rapids *(G-6996)*

3496 Misc Fabricated Wire Prdts

A A A Wire Rope & Splicing Inc ....F 734 283-1765
 Riverview *(G-13288)*
AB Electrical Wires Inc ....E 231 737-9200
 Muskegon *(G-11258)*
Accra-Wire Controls Inc ....F 616 866-3434
 Rockford *(G-13555)*
Acme Wire & Iron Works LLC ....F 313 923-7555
 Detroit *(G-3841)*
▼ Adrian Steel Company ....B 517 265-6194
 Adrian *(G-46)*
▲ Ajax Spring and Mfg Co ....F 248 588-5700
 Madison Heights *(G-10184)*
Ambassador Steel Corporation ....E 517 455-7216
 Lansing *(G-9336)*
American Indus Training Inc ....G 734 752-2451
 Brownstown *(G-2058)*
Anrod Screen Cylinder Company ....E 989 872-2101
 Cass City *(G-2511)*
Apex Spring & Stamping Corp ....D 616 453-5463
 Grand Rapids *(G-6171)*
Archer Wire International Corp ....D 231 869-6911
 Pentwater *(G-12428)*
Automatic Spring Products Corp ....C 616 842-2284
 Grand Haven *(G-5995)*
Awcoa Inc ....G 313 892-4100
 Detroit *(G-3887)*
Barbron Corporation ....E 586 716-3530
 Kalkaska *(G-8937)*
Beaden Screen Inc ....E 810 679-3119
 Croswell *(G-3595)*
▲ Benmill LLC ....E 616 243-7555
 Grand Rapids *(G-6210)*
Big Foot Manufacturing Co ....F 231 775-5588
 Cadillac *(G-2231)*
Blade Welding Service Inc ....E 734 941-4253
 Van Buren Twp *(G-16749)*
Bopp-Busch Manufacturing Co ....E 989 876-7924
 Au Gres *(G-1885)*
Burnside Industries LLC ....D 231 798-3394
 Norton Shores *(G-11811)*
▼ Center Mass Inc ....G 734 207-8934
 Canton *(G-2359)*
Clark Engineering Co ....E 989 723-7930
 Owosso *(G-12282)*
▲ Clipper Belt Lacer Company ....E 616 459-3196
 Grand Rapids *(G-6281)*
Columbus McKinnon Corporation ....G 800 955-5541
 Muskegon *(G-11296)*
▼ Commercial Group Inc ....E 313 931-6100
 Taylor *(G-15704)*

SIC SECTION — 34 FABRICATED METAL PRODUCTS, EXCEPT MACHINERY AND TRANSPORTATION EQUIPMENT

Consolidated Clips Clamps Inc ....D...... 734 455-0880
Plymouth *(G-12601)*

Constructive Sheet Metal Inc ....E...... 616 245-5306
Allendale *(G-215)*

◆ Cor-Met Inc ....E...... 810 227-0004
Brighton *(G-1902)*

Corners Limited ....G...... 269 353-8311
Kalamazoo *(G-8718)*

Corsair Engineering Inc ....D...... 810 234-3664
Flint *(G-5404)*

Corsair Engineering Inc ....F...... 810 233-0440
Flint *(G-5403)*

▲ Dare Products Inc ....E...... 269 965-2307
Springfield *(G-15190)*

Delta Tube & Fabricating Corp ....E...... 248 634-8267
Holly *(G-7874)*

Demlow Products Inc ....F...... 517 436-3529
Clayton *(G-3006)*

Deshler Group Inc ....C...... 734 525-9100
Livonia *(G-9706)*

Detroit Wire Rope Splcing Corp ....F...... 248 585-1063
Madison Heights *(G-10230)*

▼ E M I Construction Products ....D...... 616 392-7207
Holland *(G-7615)*

Essex Weld USA Inc ....E...... 519 776-9153
Warren *(G-17021)*

Fab-Jet Services LLC ....G...... 586 463-9622
Clinton Township *(G-3112)*

Fabric Patch Ltd ....G...... 906 932-5260
Ironwood *(G-8328)*

Flex-N-Gate Stamping LLC ....F...... 810 772-1514
Warren *(G-17040)*

▲ Flex-N-Gate Stamping LLC ....E...... 586 759-8900
Warren *(G-17041)*

▼ Franklin Fastener Company ....E...... 313 537-8900
Redford *(G-13162)*

Gill Corporation ....C...... 616 453-4491
Grand Rapids *(G-6439)*

▲ Gill Corporation ....B...... 616 453-4491
Grand Rapids *(G-6438)*

▲ Glassmaster Controls Co Inc ....E...... 269 382-2010
Kalamazoo *(G-8753)*

Great Lakes Grilling Co ....F...... 616 791-8600
Grand Rapids *(G-6478)*

▲ Hi-Lex America Incorporated ....B...... 269 968-0781
Battle Creek *(G-1198)*

Hi-Lex America Incorporated ....G...... 517 542-2955
Litchfield *(G-9603)*

Hi-Lex America Incorporated ....D...... 248 844-0096
Rochester Hills *(G-13440)*

Industries Unlimited Inc ....E...... 586 949-4300
Chesterfield *(G-2788)*

Jaslin Assembly Inc ....G...... 248 528-3024
Troy *(G-16432)*

▲ Kentwood Packaging Corporation ...D...... 616 698-9000
Walker *(G-16869)*

▲ King Hughes Fasteners Inc ....E...... 810 721-0300
Imlay City *(G-8206)*

Law Enforcement Supply Inc ....G...... 616 895-7875
Allendale *(G-220)*

Leisure Studios Inc ....C...... 269 428-5299
Saint Joseph *(G-14326)*

Lesco Design & Mfg Co Inc ....B...... 248 596-9301
Wixom *(G-17846)*

Loudon Steel Inc ....D...... 989 871-9353
Millington *(G-10997)*

Lupaul Industries Inc ....F...... 517 783-3223
Saint Johns *(G-14286)*

▼ M D Hubbard Spring Co Inc ....E...... 248 628-2528
Oxford *(G-12358)*

▲ Maine Ornamental LLC ....F...... 800 556-8449
White Pigeon *(G-17652)*

▲ Mason Tackle Company ....E...... 810 631-4571
Otisville *(G-12233)*

Mazzella Lifting Tech Inc ....G...... 734 953-7300
Livonia *(G-9829)*

Mazzella Lifting Tech Inc ....G...... 248 585-1063
Madison Heights *(G-10303)*

Memtech Inc ....F...... 734 455-8550
Plymouth *(G-12689)*

Merchants Metals Inc ....E...... 810 227-3036
Howell *(G-8061)*

◆ Michigan Rod Products Inc ....D...... 517 552-9812
Howell *(G-8065)*

Mid-West Spring & Stamping Inc ....E...... 231 777-2707
Muskegon *(G-11380)*

▼ Mid-West Wire Products Inc ....D...... 248 548-3200
Rochester Hills *(G-13474)*

Milton Manufacturing Inc ....E...... 313 366-2450
Detroit *(G-4250)*

National Industrial Sup Co Inc ....F...... 248 588-1828
Troy *(G-16520)*

▲ National-Standard LLC ....C...... 269 683-9902
Niles *(G-11630)*

Northern Cable & Automtn LLC ....D...... 231 937-8000
Howard City *(G-8004)*

Northern Process Systems Inc ....G...... 810 714-5200
Fenton *(G-5227)*

Omni Technical Services Inc ....E...... 989 227-8900
Saint Johns *(G-14292)*

▲ Orri Corp ....F...... 248 618-1104
Waterford *(G-17364)*

▲ PA Products Inc ....G...... 734 421-1060
Livonia *(G-9880)*

Petschke Manufacturing Company ....F...... 586 463-0841
Mount Clemens *(G-11144)*

▲ Phoenix Wire Cloth Inc ....E...... 248 585-6350
Troy *(G-16547)*

▲ Pittsfield Products Inc ....E...... 734 665-3771
Ann Arbor *(G-593)*

Plastgage Cstm Fabrication LLC ....G...... 517 817-0719
Jackson *(G-8553)*

◆ Polytorx LLC ....G...... 734 322-2114
Ann Arbor *(G-594)*

▲ Precision Wire Forms Inc ....E...... 269 279-0053
Three Rivers *(G-15874)*

▲ Production Fabricators Inc ....E...... 231 777-3822
Muskegon *(G-11407)*

Quality Filters Inc ....F...... 734 668-0211
Ann Arbor *(G-611)*

Quality Manufacturing ....E...... 989 736-8121
Lincoln *(G-9570)*

Ranch Life Plastics Inc ....F...... 517 663-2350
Eaton Rapids *(G-4731)*

Rapid River Rustic Inc ....E...... 906 474-6404
Rapid River *(G-13114)*

Richfield Industries Inc ....F...... 810 233-0440
Flint *(G-5492)*

Rives Manufacturing Inc ....E...... 517 569-3380
Rives Junction *(G-13310)*

Robinson Fence Co Inc ....G...... 906 647-3301
Pickford *(G-12483)*

▼ Rod Chomper Inc ....F...... 616 392-9677
Holland *(G-7790)*

Royal Aluminum and Steel Inc ....F...... 586 421-0057
Chesterfield *(G-2833)*

Salco Engineering and Mfg Inc ....F...... 517 789-9010
Jackson *(G-8569)*

Schroth Enterprises Inc ....F...... 586 939-0770
Sterling Heights *(G-15486)*

Schroth Enterprises Inc ....E...... 586 759-4240
Grosse Pointe Farms *(G-7187)*

Ssw Holding Company LLC ....G...... 231 780-0230
Ludington *(G-10079)*

Sterling Die & Engineering Inc ....E...... 586 677-0707
Macomb *(G-10163)*

▲ Stonebridge Industries Inc ....A...... 586 323-0348
Sterling Heights *(G-15513)*

◆ Straits Steel and Wire Company ....D...... 231 843-3416
Ludington *(G-10080)*

Strema Sales Corp ....G...... 248 645-0626
Bingham Farms *(G-1660)*

TEC-3 Prototypes Inc ....E...... 810 678-8909
Metamora *(G-10782)*

Tigmaster Co ....E...... 800 824-4830
Baroda *(G-1132)*

Ton-Tex Corporation ....F...... 616 957-3200
Greenville *(G-7158)*

Ultraform Industries Inc ....D...... 586 752-4508
Bruce Twp *(G-2105)*

Unifab Corporation ....E...... 269 382-2803
Portage *(G-13051)*

Unified Screening and Crushing ....F...... 888 464-9473
Saint Johns *(G-14299)*

▲ US Wire Rope Supply Inc ....E...... 313 925-0444
Detroit *(G-4417)*

▲ Wayne Wire A Bag Cmponents Inc ...E...... 231 258-9187
Kalkaska *(G-8966)*

Wayne Wire Cloth Products Inc ....D...... 231 258-9187
Kalkaska *(G-8967)*

Wayne Wire Cloth Products Inc ....C...... 989 742-4591
Hillman *(G-7510)*

▲ Wcscarts LLC ....F...... 248 901-0965
Troy *(G-16688)*

▲ West Michigan Wire Co ....D...... 231 845-1281
Ludington *(G-10087)*

Wire Fab Inc ....F...... 313 893-8816
Detroit *(G-4443)*

Yokohama Inds Americas Inc ....C...... 248 276-0480
Auburn Hills *(G-1051)*

3497 Metal Foil & Leaf

Barbron Corporation ....E...... 586 716-3530
Kalkaska *(G-8937)*

Graphic Specialties Inc ....E...... 616 247-0060
Grand Rapids *(G-6475)*

Illinois Tool Works Inc ....D...... 231 258-5521
Kalkaska *(G-8944)*

Ungar Frozen Food Product ....G...... 248 626-3148
Bloomfield Hills *(G-1809)*

3498 Fabricated Pipe & Pipe Fittings

A & B Tube Benders Inc ....E...... 586 773-0440
Warren *(G-16906)*

A & B Tube Benders Inc ....E...... 586 773-0440
Warren *(G-16905)*

◆ Acme Tube Bending Company ....G...... 248 545-8500
Berkley *(G-1578)*

Allegan Tubular Products Inc ....D...... 269 673-6636
Allegan *(G-149)*

Almarc Tube Co Inc ....G...... 989 654-2660
Sterling *(G-15242)*

Alro Steel Corporation ....E...... 989 893-9553
Bay City *(G-1274)*

Alternative Components LLC ....E...... 586 755-9177
Warren *(G-16924)*

Angstrom Automotive Group LLC ....E...... 248 627-2871
Ortonville *(G-12193)*

Austin Tube Products Inc ....E...... 231 745-2741
Baldwin *(G-1082)*

B L Harroun and Son Inc ....E...... 269 345-8657
Kalamazoo *(G-8692)*

▲ Baldauf Enterprises Inc ....D...... 989 686-0350
Bay City *(G-1279)*

Berkley Industries Inc ....F...... 989 656-2171
Bay Port *(G-1372)*

Big Foot Manufacturing Co ....F...... 231 775-5588
Cadillac *(G-2231)*

▲ Blissfield Manufacturing Co ....B...... 517 486-2121
Blissfield *(G-1713)*

Bundy Corporation ....G...... 517 439-1132
Hillsdale *(G-7519)*

Burnham & Northern Inc ....G...... 517 279-7501
Coldwater *(G-3292)*

Cadillac Culvert Inc ....F...... 231 775-3761
Cadillac *(G-2236)*

Computer Operated Mfg ....E...... 989 686-1333
Bay City *(G-1297)*

▲ Denso Air Systems Michigan Inc ....D...... 269 962-9676
Battle Creek *(G-1171)*

Detroit Nipple Works Inc ....F...... 313 872-6370
Detroit *(G-3996)*

Detroit Tube Products LLC ....E...... 313 841-0300
Detroit *(G-4003)*

Erin Industries Inc ....E...... 248 669-2050
Walled Lake *(G-16893)*

Fabricari LLC ....G...... 734 972-2042
Dexter *(G-4492)*

Ferguson Enterprises Inc ....E...... 989 790-2220
Saginaw *(G-14037)*

◆ Fernco Inc ....C...... 810 503-9000
Davison *(G-3648)*

Fhc Holding Company ....E...... 616 538-3231
Wyoming *(G-18001)*

Flexible Metal Inc ....D...... 810 231-1300
Hamburg *(G-7225)*

Fluid Routing Solutions Inc ....E...... 231 592-1700
Big Rapids *(G-1628)*

Formfab LLC ....E...... 248 844-3676
Rochester Hills *(G-13427)*

Future Industries Inc ....E...... 616 844-0772
Grand Haven *(G-6017)*

Gonzalez Group Jonesville LLC ....E...... 517 849-9908
Jonesville *(G-8655)*

Gray Bros Stamping & Mch Inc ....E...... 269 483-7615
White Pigeon *(G-17649)*

Gray Brothers Mfg Inc ....E...... 269 483-7615
White Pigeon *(G-17650)*

Harbor Steel and Supply Corp ....F...... 616 786-0002
Holland *(G-7657)*

Hosco Inc ....E...... 248 912-1750
Wixom *(G-17828)*

▲ Huron Inc ....E...... 810 359-5344
Lexington *(G-9558)*

Invent Detroit R&D Collaborati ....G...... 313 451-2658
Detroit *(G-4147)*

▲ J & L Manufacturing Co Inc ....E...... 269 789-1507
Marshall *(G-10572)*

JCs Tool & Mfg Co Inc ....E...... 989 892-8975
Essexville *(G-4873)*

Employee Codes: A=Over 500 employees, B=251-500
C=101-250, D=51-100, E=20-50, F=10-19, G=3-9

Jems of Litchfield Inc F 517 542-5367
Litchfield (G-9605)
Jep Industries LLC G 734 844-3506
Canton (G-2389)
Key Gas Components Inc E 269 673-2151
Allegan (G-169)
L & R Machine Inc F 517 523-2978
Osseo (G-12226)
L A Burnhart Inc G 810 227-4567
Brighton (G-1948)
Lapine Metal Products Inc F 269 388-5900
Kalamazoo (G-8805)
Leggett Platt Components Inc D 616 784-7000
Sparta (G-15101)
Loftis Alumi-TEC Inc E 616 846-1990
Grand Haven (G-6050)
Macomb Tube Fabricating Co F 586 445-6770
Warren (G-17135)
Manistee Wldg & Piping Svc Inc G 231 723-2551
Manistee (G-10428)
◆ Marshall Excelsior Co E 269 789-6700
Marshall (G-10577)
Masterbilt Products Corp E 269 749-4841
Olivet (G-12142)
Mayville Engineering Co Inc C 989 748-6031
Vanderbilt (G-16806)
Mayville Engineering Co Inc D 616 877-2073
Wayland (G-17406)
Meccom Corporation G 313 895-4900
Detroit (G-4224)
Melling Products North LLC D 989 588-6147
Farwell (G-5164)
Metaldyne Tblar Components LLC C 248 727-1800
Southfield (G-14979)
▲ Midwest Tube Fabricators Inc E 586 264-9898
Sterling Heights (G-15424)
Motor City Bending & Rolling G 313 368-4400
Detroit (G-4255)
◆ Myco Enterprises Inc G 248 348-3806
Northville (G-11713)
Nelson Hardware G 269 327-3583
Portage (G-13018)
▲ Norma Michigan Inc C 248 373-4300
Auburn Hills (G-959)
Novi Tool & Machine Company D 313 532-0900
Redford (G-13176)
Oilpatch Machine Tool Inc G 989 772-0637
Mount Pleasant (G-11215)
Parma Tube Corp E 269 651-2351
Sturgis (G-15626)
Patton Welding Inc F 231 258-9925
Kalkaska (G-8957)
Paumac Tubing LLC D 810 985-9400
Marysville (G-10610)
Picko Ferrum Fabricating LLC G 810 626-7086
Hamburg (G-7227)
Pipe Fabricators Inc D 269 345-8657
Kalamazoo (G-8853)
▲ Pontiac Coil Inc C 248 922-1100
Clarkston (G-2947)
Power Process Piping Inc C 734 451-0130
Plymouth (G-12724)
Production Tube Company Inc G 313 259-3990
Detroit (G-4312)
Pyramid Tubular Tech Inc G 810 732-6335
Flint (G-5486)
Quality Manufacturing G 989 736-8121
Lincoln (G-9570)
◆ Quality Pipe Products Inc E 734 606-5100
New Boston (G-11509)
Quigley Manufacturing Inc C 248 426-8600
Farmington Hills (G-5110)
Refrigeration Concepts Inc E 616 785-7335
Comstock Park (G-3514)
Ridgid Slotting LLC F 616 847-0332
Grand Haven (G-6072)
River Valley Machine Inc E 269 673-8070
Allegan (G-187)
Rochester Tube Products Ltd E 586 726-4816
Shelby Township (G-14680)
Rock River Fabrications Inc E 616 281-5769
Grand Rapids (G-6832)
Roman Engineering D 231 238-7644
Afton (G-106)
Ryson Tube Inc F 810 227-4567
Brighton (G-1987)
S & S Tube Inc F 989 656-7211
Bay Port (G-1375)
Sales & Engineering Inc E 734 525-9030
Livonia (G-9919)
South Park Sales & Mfg Inc G 313 381-7579
Dearborn (G-3762)
Spiral Industries Inc E 810 632-6300
Howell (G-8101)
St Regis Culvert Inc F 517 543-3430
Charlotte (G-2668)
Superior Fluid Systems G 734 246-4550
Taylor (G-15773)
Tempro Industries Inc F 734 451-5900
Plymouth (G-12768)
Tg Manufacturing LLC E 616 935-7575
Byron Center (G-2212)
Tl Group Auto Systems LLC C 248 494-5000
Auburn Hills (G-1024)
Tl Group Auto Systems LLC C 859 235-5420
Auburn Hills (G-1023)
Toolcraft Machine Co Inc G 517 223-9265
Gregory (G-7166)
Troy Tube & Manufacturing Co D 586 949-8700
Chesterfield (G-2851)
Tube Fab/Roman Engrg Co Inc C 231 238-9366
Afton (G-107)
▼ Tube Forming and Machine Inc E 989 739-3323
Oscoda (G-12223)
Tube Wright Inc E 810 227-4567
Brighton (G-2000)
Tube-Co Inc G 586 775-0244
Warren (G-17272)
▲ Tubesource Manufacturing Inc F 248 543-4746
Ferndale (G-5324)
▲ Unified Industries Inc F 517 546-3220
Howell (G-8118)
▲ Universal Tube Inc C 248 853-5100
Rochester Hills (G-13536)
Universal Warranty Corpor G 248 263-6900
Southfield (G-15055)
Van Pelt Industries LLC G 616 842-1200
Grand Haven (G-6094)
Volos Tube Form Inc E 586 416-3600
Macomb (G-10174)
W Soule & Co E 616 975-6272
Grand Rapids (G-6975)
West Michigan Fab Corp G 616 794-3750
Belding (G-1432)

3499 Fabricated Metal Prdts, NEC

A & L Metal Products G 734 654-8990
Carleton (G-2451)
A & S Enterprises LLC G 906 482-9007
Laurium (G-9502)
A&G Corporate Holdings LLC G 734 513-3488
Livonia (G-9620)
A2 Energy Systems G 734 622-9800
Plymouth (G-12558)
AAA Waterjet and Machining Inc G 586 759-3736
Warren (G-16910)
◆ Ace Controls Inc C 248 476-0213
Farmington Hills (G-4919)
▲ Advanced Magnet Source Corp G 734 398-7188
Canton (G-2345)
Advanced Metal Fabricators G 616 570-4847
Lowell (G-10022)
Aquarius Recreational Products G 586 469-4600
Harrison Township (G-7320)
Arrowhead Industries Inc E 231 238-9366
Afton (G-105)
Atf Inc E 989 685-2468
Rose City (G-13760)
Avian Control Technologies LLC G 231 349-9050
Stanwood (G-15231)
Bergamot Inc G 586 372-7109
Lakeville (G-9177)
Bulman Products Inc E 616 363-4416
Grand Rapids (G-6241)
▲ Camaco LLC E 248 442-6800
Farmington Hills (G-4954)
Campbell & Shaw Steel Inc F 810 364-5100
Marysville (G-10600)
Con-De Manufacturing Inc G 269 651-3756
Sturgis (G-15601)
Contemporary Industries Inc G 248 478-8850
Farmington Hills (G-4966)
Cruux LLC G 248 515-8411
Troy (G-16288)
Dag R&D G 248 444-0575
Milford (G-10959)
Down Home Inc G 517 545-5955
Howell (G-8034)
Dts Enterprises Inc E 231 599-3123
Ellsworth (G-4787)
East End Sports Awards Inc G 906 293-8895
Newberry (G-11579)
Fab-Alloy Company G 517 787-4313
Jackson (G-8447)
Fluxtrol Inc G 248 393-2000
Auburn Hills (G-877)
Focal Point Metal Fab LLC G 616 844-7670
Spring Lake (G-15142)
Fournier Enterprises Inc G 586 323-9160
Mount Clemens (G-11131)
Friendship Industries Inc E 586 323-0033
Sterling Heights (G-15349)
▲ Gallatin Tank Works LLC G 734 856-5107
Ottawa Lake (G-12263)
◆ Gibraltar Inc E 616 748-4857
Zeeland (G-18144)
Give-Em A Brake Safety LLC E 616 531-8705
Grandville (G-7037)
Great Lakes Laser Dynamics Inc D 616 892-7070
Allendale (G-218)
Greene Manufacturing Tech LLC C 810 982-9720
Port Huron (G-12924)
Greenville Engineered & Tooled G 616 292-0701
Greenville (G-7134)
▲ Heath Manufacturing Company D 616 997-8181
Coopersville (G-3561)
Hollingsworth Container LLC G 313 768-1400
Dearborn (G-3720)
Hyper Alloys Inc E 586 772-0571
Clinton Township (G-3138)
Incoe Corporation C 248 616-0220
Auburn Hills (G-910)
▲ Industrial Magnetics Inc D 231 582-3100
Boyne City (G-1823)
J Solutions LLC G 586 477-0127
Chesterfield (G-2792)
Jershon Inc G 231 861-2900
Shelby (G-14527)
Johnson Systems Inc G 616 455-1900
Caledonia (G-2304)
▲ Jokab Safety North America Inc F 888 282-2123
Westland (G-17575)
Joyce Zahradnik G 616 874-3350
Rockford (G-13574)
Lachman Enterprises Inc G 248 948-9944
Southfield (G-14958)
Laddertech LLC F 248 437-7100
Brighton (G-1950)
Lafave Hydraulics & Metal G 989 872-2163
Cass City (G-2517)
Lock and Load Corp G 800 975-9658
Marion (G-10490)
Lsr Incorporated F 734 455-6530
Plymouth (G-12679)
M & J Manufacturing Inc G 586 778-6322
Roseville (G-13827)
▲ Magnetic Systems Intl Inc F 231 582-9600
Boyne City (G-1828)
Magnum Fabricating G 734 484-5800
Ypsilanti (G-18087)
▲ Metal Standard Corp D 616 396-6356
Holland (G-7744)
Metalbuilt Tactical LLC G 586 786-9106
Macomb (G-10141)
Metalworks Inc C 231 845-5136
Ludington (G-10073)
▲ Meter USA LLC F 810 388-9373
Marysville (G-10607)
◆ Miba Hydramechanica Corp D 586 264-3094
Sterling Heights (G-15420)
▲ Mpg Inc A 734 207-6200
Plymouth (G-12696)
National Ordnance Auto Mfg LLC G 248 853-8822
Auburn Hills (G-953)
Neucadia LLC G 989 572-0324
Carson City (G-2494)
Nortech LLC E 248 446-7575
New Hudson (G-11550)
North East Fabrication Co Inc F 517 849-8090
Jonesville (G-8664)
▲ Northwoods Manufacturing Inc D 906 779-2370
Kingsford (G-9065)
▲ Omt Veyhl G 616 738-6688
Holland (G-7763)
Oronoko Iron Works Inc G 269 326-7045
Baroda (G-1128)
Ottawa Tool & Machine LLC G 616 677-1743
Grand Rapids (G-6735)
▲ P & C Group I Inc E 248 442-6800
Farmington Hills (G-5087)

Poco Inc E 313 220-6752
Canton *(G-2416)*
Poetry Factory Ltd G 586 296-3125
Fraser *(G-5707)*
Praxair Distribution Inc F 586 598-9020
Macomb *(G-10155)*
Proper Arospc & Machining LLC G 586 779-8787
Warren *(G-17203)*
Prototech Laser Inc E 586 598-6900
Chesterfield *(G-2827)*
Prs Manufacturing Inc G 616 784-4409
Grand Rapids *(G-6794)*
Quality Metal Fabricating G 616 901-5510
Grand Rapids *(G-6799)*
Quick - Burn LLC G 616 402-4874
Holland *(G-7780)*
R L Hume Award Co G 269 324-3063
Portage *(G-13026)*
Scenario Systems Ltd G 586 532-1320
Shelby Township *(G-14686)*
Signature Wall Solutions Inc G 616 366-4242
Midland *(G-10916)*
Spartan Barricading G 313 292-2488
Romulus *(G-13734)*
Specialty Metal Fabricators G 616 698-9020
Caledonia *(G-2316)*
Spraying Systems Co F 248 473-1331
Farmington Hills *(G-5128)*
▲ Synchronous Manufacturing Inc E 517 764-6930
Michigan Center *(G-10791)*
▲ Tengam Engineering Inc E 269 694-9466
Otsego *(G-12256)*
Toughbuoy Co G 989 465-6111
Coleman *(G-3352)*
Tpi Powder Metallurgy Inc D 989 865-9921
Saint Charles *(G-14203)*
Ultimate Manufacturing Inc G 313 538-6212
Redford *(G-13203)*
▲ Unisorb Inc E 517 764-6060
Michigan Center *(G-10792)*
Universal Magnetics Inc G 231 937-5555
Howard City *(G-8007)*
Van Dyken Mechanical Inc D 616 224-7030
Grandville *(G-7075)*
◆ Viking Corporation B 269 945-9501
Hastings *(G-7428)*
▲ Viking Fabrication Svcs LLC B 269 945-9501
Hastings *(G-7429)*
Virtec Manufacturing LLC G 313 369-4858
Detroit *(G-4430)*
West Mich Auto Stl & Engrg Inc E 616 560-8198
Belding *(G-1431)*
Yarema Die & Engineering Co E 248 689-5777
Troy *(G-16703)*
Zks Sales G 810 360-0682
Brighton *(G-2012)*

35 INDUSTRIAL AND COMMERCIAL MACHINERY AND COMPUTER EQUIPMENT

3511 Steam, Gas & Hydraulic Turbines & Engines

3dfx Interactive Inc E 918 938-8967
Saginaw *(G-13990)*
Ahd LLC G 586 922-6511
Shelby Township *(G-14543)*
Altronics Energy LLC F 616 662-7401
Hudsonville *(G-8145)*
Behco Inc G 248 478-6336
Farmington Hills *(G-4940)*
▲ Dowding Machining LLC F 517 663-5455
Eaton Rapids *(G-4721)*
Dynamic Energy Tech LLC G 248 212-5904
Oak Park *(G-12062)*
Elderberry Steam Engines G 989 245-0652
Saginaw *(G-14034)*
Ener2 LLC F 248 842-2662
Brighton *(G-1918)*
Horiba Instruments Inc D 734 213-6555
Ann Arbor *(G-495)*
Kinetic Wave Power LLC G 989 839-9757
Midland *(G-10880)*
▲ Marsh Plating Corporation D 734 483-5767
Ypsilanti *(G-18088)*
Metro Machine Works Inc D 734 941-4571
Romulus *(G-13707)*
Multi-Sync Power LLC G 734 658-3384
Canton *(G-2410)*
Nu Con Corporation E 734 525-0770
Livonia *(G-9867)*
Plasma-Tec Inc E 616 455-2593
Wayland *(G-17409)*
Steel Tool & Engineering Co D 734 692-8580
Brownstown Twp *(G-2072)*
Windtronics Inc G 231 332-1200
Muskegon *(G-11453)*
Wmh Fluidpower Inc F 269 327-7011
Portage *(G-13058)*

3519 Internal Combustion Engines, NEC

Ash Industries Inc F 269 672-9630
Martin *(G-10594)*
Chandas Engineering Inc F 313 582-8666
Dearborn *(G-3687)*
▲ Combat Advanced Propulsion LLC G 231 724-2100
Muskegon *(G-11297)*
Cosworth LLC E 586 353-5403
Shelby Township *(G-14569)*
Creek Diesel Services Inc F 800 974-4600
Grand Rapids *(G-6316)*
Cummins Bridgeway Grove Cy LLC G 614 604-6000
New Hudson *(G-11535)*
Cummins Inc F 586 469-2010
Clinton Township *(G-3095)*
Cummins Inc E 616 281-2211
Grand Rapids *(G-6321)*
Cummins Inc E 313 843-6200
Dearborn *(G-3688)*
Cummins Inc E 248 573-1900
New Hudson *(G-11536)*
Cummins Inc F 989 732-5055
Gaylord *(G-5854)*
Cummins Inc E 989 752-5200
Saginaw *(G-14023)*
Cummins Npower LLC E 906 475-8800
Negaunee *(G-11469)*
D & S Engine Specialist Inc F 248 583-9240
Clawson *(G-2976)*
◆ Detroit Diesel Corporation A 313 592-5000
Detroit *(G-3980)*
Detroit Diesel Corporation F 313 592-8256
Redford *(G-13157)*
Dewitts Radiator LLC F 517 548-0600
Howell *(G-8029)*
Double H Mfg Inc E 734 729-3450
Westland *(G-17551)*
▲ Ehc Inc G 313 259-2266
Detroit *(G-4030)*
▲ Emp Racing Inc G 906 786-8404
Escanaba *(G-4825)*
Engine Guru LLC G 616 430-3114
Wyoming *(G-18000)*
◆ Engineered Machined Pdts Inc B 906 786-8404
Escanaba *(G-4826)*
Extreme Machine Inc D 810 231-0521
Whitmore Lake *(G-17699)*
Extreme Machine Inc D 810 231-0521
Whitmore Lake *(G-17700)*
Falvey Limited G 517 263-2699
Adrian *(G-64)*
FCA US LLC C 313 957-7000
Detroit *(G-4054)*
Fev Test Systems Inc G 248 373-6000
Auburn Hills *(G-872)*
▲ Geislinger Corporation F 269 441-7000
Battle Creek *(G-1192)*
Global Fmi LLC D 810 964-5555
Fenton *(G-5216)*
GM Components Holdings LLC E 616 246-2000
Grand Rapids *(G-6444)*
GM Powertrain-Romulus Engine G 734 595-5203
Romulus *(G-13681)*
Gnutti Carlo Usa Inc B 517 223-1059
Webberville *(G-17450)*
Hdp Inc G 248 674-4967
Waterford *(G-17349)*
Holbrook Racing Engines F 734 762-4315
Livonia *(G-9772)*
Impco Technologies Inc E 586 264-1200
Sterling Heights *(G-15370)*
K & S Property Inc A 248 573-1600
New Hudson *(G-11546)*
Katech Inc E 586 791-4120
Clinton Township *(G-3153)*
Logan Diesel Incorporated G 517 589-8811
Leslie *(G-9544)*
Metaldyne Pwrtrain Cmpnnts Inc C 517 542-5555
Litchfield *(G-9607)*
▲ Metaldyne Pwrtrain Cmpnnts Inc C 313 758-2000
Detroit *(G-4229)*
▲ Minowitz Manufacturing Co E 586 779-5940
Huntington Woods *(G-8190)*
▲ Mtu America Inc C 248 560-8000
Novi *(G-11950)*
Mtu America Incorporated G 734 261-0309
Livonia *(G-9854)*
Mtu America Incorporated C 734 561-2040
Brownstown Township *(G-2070)*
Navarre Inc E 313 892-7300
Detroit *(G-4264)*
Paice Technologies LLC G 248 376-1115
Orchard Lake *(G-12168)*
▲ Peaker Services Inc D 248 437-4174
Brighton *(G-1976)*
Perfit Corporation G 734 524-9208
Livonia *(G-9886)*
▲ Powertrain Integration LLC F 248 577-0010
Madison Heights *(G-10333)*
▲ PSI Holding Company D 248 437-4174
Brighton *(G-1982)*
◆ R & D Enterprises Inc E 248 349-7077
Plymouth *(G-12728)*
Shadowood Technology Inc G 810 358-2569
Metamora *(G-10780)*
Trend Performance Products E 586 792-6620
Clinton Township *(G-3251)*
W W Williams Company LLC E 313 584-6150
Dearborn *(G-3771)*
Wilson Stamping & Mfg Inc G 989 823-8521
Vassar *(G-16820)*

3523 Farm Machinery & Eqpt

▲ A & B Packing Equipment Inc C 269 539-4700
Lawrence *(G-9504)*
Advanced Drainage Systems Inc D 989 723-5208
Owosso *(G-12275)*
Advanced Farm Equipment LLC F 989 268-5711
Vestaburg *(G-16825)*
AG Harvesters LLC E 989 876-7161
Au Gres *(G-740)*
▲ Agritek Industries Inc D 616 786-9200
Holland *(G-7551)*
Andersen Oakleaf Inc G 517 546-1805
Howell *(G-8014)*
Bader & Co E 810 648-2404
Sandusky *(G-14429)*
▼ BEI International LLC E 616 204-8274
Holland *(G-7566)*
◆ Big Dutchman Inc D 616 392-5981
Holland *(G-7569)*
Big Foot Manufacturing Co F 231 775-5588
Cadillac *(G-2231)*
Boxer Equipment/Morbark Inc G 989 866-2381
Winn *(G-17746)*
Brilar LLC D 248 547-6439
Oak Park *(G-12053)*
Buddingh Weeder Co G 616 698-8613
Caledonia *(G-2293)*
Burly Oak Builders Inc G 734 368-4912
Dexter *(G-4480)*
CPM Acquisition Corp G 231 947-6400
Traverse City *(G-15950)*
▼ Crippen Manufacturing Company E 989 681-4323
Saint Louis *(G-14361)*
◆ Diamond Moba Americas Inc C 248 476-7100
Farmington Hills *(G-4971)*
Do-Mor Products G 269 651-7362
Burr Oak *(G-2135)*
Eagle Group II Ltd E 616 754-7777
Greenville *(G-7129)*
Ebels Hardware Inc F 231 826-3334
Falmouth *(G-4892)*
Express Welding Inc G 906 786-8808
Escanaba *(G-4829)*
◆ Gillisons Var Fabrication Inc E 231 882-5921
Benzonia *(G-1575)*
Glenn Knochel G 989 684-7869
Kawkawlin *(G-8971)*
▲ Griptrac Inc F 231 853-2284
Ravenna *(G-13120)*
Harrison Partners Inv Group G 419 708-8154
Milan *(G-10940)*
▲ Heath Manufacturing Company D 616 997-8181
Coopersville *(G-3561)*
Holland Transplanter Co Inc E 616 392-3579
Holland *(G-7680)*

35 INDUSTRIAL AND COMMERCIAL MACHINERY AND COMPUTER EQUIPMENT

Howey Tree Baler Corporation ....G..... 231 328-4321
 Merritt (G-10763)
Ikes Welding Shop and Mfg ....G..... 989 892-2783
 Munger (G-11242)
Keays Family Truckin ....F..... 231 838-6430
 Gaylord (G-5871)
Knoerr Farms ....G..... 989 670-2199
 Sandusky (G-14439)
Liver Transplant/Univ of Mich ....G..... 734 936-7670
 Ann Arbor (G-531)
Logan Diesel Incorporated ....G..... 517 589-8811
 Leslie (G-9544)
Mahindra Tractor Assembly Inc ....E..... 734 274-2239
 Ann Arbor (G-541)
▲ Mechanical Transplanter Co LLC ....E..... 616 396-8738
 Holland (G-7742)
Mensch Manufacturing LLC ....G..... 269 945-5300
 Hastings (G-7420)
Mensch Mfg Mar Div Inc ....E..... 269 945-5300
 Hastings (G-7421)
▲ Michigan AG Services Inc ....F..... 616 374-8803
 Lake Odessa (G-9117)
◆ Morbark LLC ....B..... 989 866-2381
 Winn (G-17747)
Nelson Farms ....F..... 989 560-1303
 Elwell (G-4797)
Overstreet Property MGT Co ....G..... 269 252-1560
 Benton Harbor (G-1537)
Packard Farms LLC ....E..... 989 386-3816
 Clare (G-2883)
▲ Phil Brown Welding Corporation ....F..... 616 784-3046
 Conklin (G-3531)
Recon Technologies LLC ....G..... 616 241-1877
 Grand Rapids (G-6814)
◆ Root-Lowell Manufacturing Co ....D..... 616 897-9211
 Lowell (G-10042)
Roto-Feeders Inc ....G..... 269 782-2456
 Dowagiac (G-4559)
S & S Mowing Inc ....G..... 906 466-9009
 Bark River (G-1122)
Schuette Farms ....G..... 989 550-0563
 Elkton (G-4783)
▲ Steiner Tractor Parts Inc ....E..... 810 621-3000
 Lennon (G-9519)
Stephens Pipe & Steel LLC ....G..... 616 248-3433
 Grand Rapids (G-6892)
Stuff A Pal ....G..... 734 646-3775
 Maybee (G-10674)
Superior Attachment Inc ....G..... 906 864-1708
 Menominee (G-10758)
Tindall Packaging Inc ....G..... 269 649-1163
 Portage (G-13050)
Triple K Farms Inc ....G..... 517 458-9741
 Morenci (G-11116)
Turkey Creek Inc ....F..... 517 451-5221
 Tecumseh (G-15814)
Ultimate Turf of Flint LLC ....G..... 810 202-0203
 Flint (G-5517)
Unist Inc ....E..... 616 949-0853
 Grand Rapids (G-6951)
Van Paemels Equipment Company ....G..... 586 784-5295
 Armada (G-724)
Venchurs Inc. ....F..... 517 263-8937
 Adrian (G-100)

3524 Garden, Lawn Tractors & Eqpt

Big Green Tomato LLC ....G..... 269 282-1593
 Battle Creek (G-1154)
Buyers Development Group LLC ....F..... 734 677-0009
 Ann Arbor (G-393)
Cjm Maintenance ....G..... 734 285-0247
 Wyandotte (G-17952)
Coffman Electrical Eqp Co ....E..... 616 452-8708
 Grand Rapids (G-6286)
◆ Contech (us) Inc ....E..... 616 459-4139
 Grand Rapids (G-6303)
▼ Dynamic Manufacturing LLC ....E..... 989 644-8109
 Weidman (G-17456)
Ebels Hardware Inc ....F..... 231 826-3334
 Falmouth (G-4892)
Grandville Tractor Svcs LLC ....F..... 616 530-2030
 Grandville (G-7041)
Harrells LLC ....G..... 248 446-8070
 New Hudson (G-11542)
Hydro Giant 4 Inc ....F..... 248 661-0034
 West Bloomfield (G-17480)
Milsco LLC ....B..... 517 787-3650
 Jackson (G-8531)
Nolans Outdoor Power Inc ....G..... 810 664-3798
 Lapeer (G-9477)

▼ Root Spring Scraper Co ....E..... 269 382-2025
 Kalamazoo (G-8874)
Superior Cedar Products Inc ....E..... 906 639-2132
 Carney (G-2464)
◆ Sure-Loc Aluminum Edging Inc ....G..... 616 392-3209
 Holland (G-7822)
UP Coin & Cultivation LLC ....G..... 906 341-4769
 Manistique (G-10447)
Wells Equipment Sales Inc ....F..... 517 542-2376
 Litchfield (G-9613)
▲ Whitehall Products LLC ....D..... 231 894-2688
 Whitehall (G-17682)

3531 Construction Machinery & Eqpt

ABI International ....G..... 248 583-7150
 Madison Heights (G-10178)
Ais Construction Eqp Svc Corp ....E..... 616 538-2400
 Grand Rapids (G-6155)
Ajax Materials Corporation ....F..... 248 244-3445
 Brighton (G-1882)
All-Lift Systems Inc ....F..... 906 779-1620
 Iron Mountain (G-8274)
Alta Construction Eqp LLC ....D..... 248 356-5200
 New Hudson (G-11530)
AME For Auto Dealers Inc ....G..... 248 720-0245
 Auburn Hills (G-768)
Amw Machine Control Inc ....G..... 616 642-9514
 Saranac (G-14453)
Arcosa Shoring Products Inc ....F..... 800 292-1225
 Lansing (G-9203)
▲ Arcosa Shoring Products Inc ....E..... 517 741-4300
 Union City (G-16731)
◆ B&P Littleford LLC ....G..... 989 757-1300
 Saginaw (G-13999)
◆ Bandit Industries Inc ....B..... 989 561-2270
 Remus (G-13237)
◆ Besser Company ....B..... 989 354-4111
 Alpena (G-282)
Big Foot Manufacturing Co ....F..... 231 775-5588
 Cadillac (G-2231)
Bme Inc ....G..... 810 937-2974
 Port Huron (G-12903)
Bob-O-Link Associates LLC ....G..... 616 891-6939
 Caledonia (G-2292)
Boral Building Products Inc ....C..... 248 668-6400
 Wixom (G-17777)
Border City Tool and Mfg Co ....E..... 586 758-5574
 Warren (G-16962)
Brawn Mixer Inc ....G..... 616 399-5600
 Holland (G-7576)
▲ C & B Machinery Company ....E..... 734 462-0600
 Brighton (G-1894)
Capital Equipment Clare LLC ....F..... 517 669-5533
 Dewitt (G-4460)
Contract Welding and Fabg Inc ....E..... 734 699-5561
 Van Buren Twp (G-16753)
CPS LLC ....F..... 517 639-1464
 Quincy (G-13093)
Creative Surfaces Inc ....F..... 586 226-2950
 Clinton Township (G-3092)
D P Equipment Co ....F..... 517 368-5266
 Camden (G-2340)
Di-Coat Corporation ....E..... 248 349-1211
 Novi (G-11868)
▲ Drag Finishing Tech LLC ....G..... 616 785-0400
 Comstock Park (G-3479)
▼ E M I Construction Products ....D..... 616 392-7207
 Holland (G-7615)
Eagle Buckets Inc ....G..... 517 787-0385
 Jackson (G-8436)
▲ Fireboy-Xintex Inc ....F..... 616 735-9380
 Grand Rapids (G-6406)
Fleming Fabrication Machining ....G..... 906 542-3573
 Sagola (G-14186)
Fw Shoring Company ....D..... 517 676-8800
 Mason (G-10639)
Gerken Materials Inc ....G..... 734 243-1851
 Monroe (G-11035)
Globe Industries Incorporated ....F..... 906 932-3540
 Ironwood (G-8329)
Great Lakes Snow & Ice Inc ....G..... 989 584-1211
 Carson City (G-2490)
Griff & Son Tree Service Inc ....G..... 989 735-5160
 Glennie (G-5942)
Harsco Corporation ....D..... 231 843-3431
 Ludington (G-10062)
Harsco Corporation ....F..... 231 843-3431
 Ludington (G-10063)
◆ Hines Corporation ....F..... 231 799-6240
 Norton Shores (G-11812)

Independent Machine Co Inc ....E..... 906 428-4524
 Escanaba (G-8836)
Jackson Pandrol Inc ....B..... 231 843-3431
 Ludington (G-10068)
JG Distributing Inc ....G..... 906 225-0882
 Marquette (G-10537)
Jolman & Jolman Enterprises ....G..... 231 744-4500
 Muskegon (G-11355)
JP Skidmore LLC ....G..... 906 424-4127
 Menominee (G-10740)
K&H Supply of Lansing Inc ....G..... 517 482-7600
 Lansing (G-9301)
K2 Engineering Inc ....G..... 906 356-6303
 Rock (G-13553)
Kaufman Custom Sheet M ....G..... 906 932-2130
 Ironwood (G-8333)
Keizer-Morris Intl Inc ....E..... 810 688-1234
 North Branch (G-11661)
▲ Lang Tool Company ....G..... 989 435-9864
 Beaverton (G-1387)
Lawrence J Julio LLC ....G..... 906 483-4781
 Houghton (G-7974)
▲ Leedy Manufacturing Co LLC ....D..... 616 245-0517
 Grand Rapids (G-6624)
Lsp Inc ....E..... 517 639-3815
 Quincy (G-13095)
Lyonnais Inc ....G..... 616 868-6625
 Lowell (G-10035)
▲ Magnum Toolscom LLC ....F..... 734 595-4600
 Romulus (G-13703)
Mid State Seawall Inc ....G..... 989 435-3887
 Beaverton (G-1389)
Midwest Vibro Inc ....G..... 616 532-7670
 Grandville (G-7058)
Milan Metal Worx LLC ....G..... 734 369-7115
 Petersburg (G-12437)
Mmgg Inc ....G..... 616 405-3807
 Midland (G-10893)
Mmgg Inc ....E..... 989 495-9332
 Midland (G-10894)
Mull-It-Over Products Inc ....G..... 616 843-6470
 Grandville (G-7059)
Nordson Corporation ....D..... 734 459-8600
 Wixom (G-17866)
Oshkosh Defense LLC ....E..... 586 576-8301
 Warren (G-17178)
Outline Industries LLC ....G..... 303 632-6782
 Boyne City (G-1831)
◆ Paladin Brands Group Inc ....F..... 319 378-3696
 Dexter (G-4502)
▲ Petter Investments Inc ....F..... 269 637-1997
 South Haven (G-14767)
Plastech Holding Corp ....E..... 313 565-5927
 Dearborn (G-3749)
▼ PSI Marine Inc ....F..... 989 695-2646
 Saginaw (G-14126)
Quality Marine Electronics LLC ....G..... 616 566-2101
 Zeeland (G-18182)
Repair Rite Machine Inc ....G..... 616 681-9711
 Dorr (G-4526)
▼ Root Spring Scraper Co ....E..... 269 382-2025
 Kalamazoo (G-8874)
◆ Ryans Equipment Inc ....E..... 989 427-2829
 Edmore (G-4755)
Shred-Pac Inc ....E..... 269 793-7978
 Hopkins (G-7961)
Simpson Industrial Svcs LLC ....E..... 810 392-2717
 Wales (G-16860)
Spaulding Mfg Inc ....E..... 989 777-4550
 Saginaw (G-14154)
Ss Services ....G..... 616 866-6453
 Rockford (G-13591)
Stoneco of Michigan Inc ....G..... 734 236-6538
 Newport (G-11591)
Stoneco of Michigan Inc ....E..... 734 241-8966
 Monroe (G-11070)
▲ Superior Fabrication Co LLC ....D..... 906 495-5634
 Kincheloe (G-9053)
Syncon Inc ....E..... 313 914-4481
 Livonia (G-9950)
Tapco Holdings Inc ....C..... 248 668-6400
 Wixom (G-17905)
Terex Corporation ....G..... 360 993-0515
 Durand (G-4614)
Thomas J Moyle Jr Incorporated ....G..... 906 482-3000
 Houghton (G-7986)
Timberland Forestry ....F..... 906 387-4350
 Munising (G-11251)
Top of Line Crane Service LLC ....G..... 231 267-5326
 Williamsburg (G-17722)

Toro Company B 888 492-6841 — Iron Mountain *(G-8304)*
Trelan Manufacturing E 989 561-2280 — Remus *(G-13242)*
U P Fabricating Co Inc E 906 475-4400 — Negaunee *(G-11478)*
W & S Development Inc F 989 724-5463 — Greenbush *(G-7121)*
Wacker Neuson Corporation F 231 799-4500 — Norton Shores *(G-11804)*
◆ **Weber Machine (usa) Inc** G 207 947-4990 — Grand Rapids *(G-6982)*
West Michigan Aerial LLc E 269 998-4455 — Lawton *(G-9517)*
White Lake Excavating Inc F 231 894-6918 — Whitehall *(G-17681)*
Wmc Sales LLC G 616 813-7237 — Ada *(G-35)*
▲ **Wmv Incorporated** G 248 333-1380 — Sylvan Lake *(G-15673)*
Zeeland Component Sales LLC G 616 399-8614 — Zeeland *(G-18200)*

3532 Mining Machinery & Eqpt

Centerpoint Tungsten LLC G 810 797-5196 — Metamora *(G-10773)*
Classfcation Flotation Systems G 810 714-5200 — Fenton *(G-5194)*
Contract Welding and Fabg Inc E 734 699-5561 — Van Buren Twp *(G-16753)*
▲ **Cows Locomotive Mfg Co** E 248 583-7150 — Madison Heights *(G-10221)*
▲ **General Machine Services** G 269 695-2244 — Buchanan *(G-2119)*
▲ **Lake Shore Systems Inc** D 906 774-1500 — Kingsford *(G-9061)*
Lake Shore Systems Inc D 906 265-5414 — Iron River *(G-8313)*
Michigan Wood Pellet LLC F 989 348-4100 — Grayling *(G-7112)*
Mq Operating Company E 906 337-1515 — Calumet *(G-2330)*
▲ **Pillar Manufacturing Inc** F 269 628-5605 — Gobles *(G-5948)*
▲ **Ring Screw LLC** D 586 997-5600 — Sterling Heights *(G-15470)*
Rock-Way LLC G 734 357-2112 — Plymouth *(G-12744)*
Thermo Vac Inc D 248 969-0300 — Oxford *(G-12375)*
U P Fabricating Co Inc E 906 475-4400 — Negaunee *(G-11478)*
Yerington Brothers Inc G 269 695-7669 — Niles *(G-11652)*

3533 Oil Field Machinery & Eqpt

▲ **Blackmer** D 616 241-1611 — Grand Rapids *(G-6229)*
Cameron International Corp D 248 646-6743 — Beverly Hills *(G-1615)*
Cameron International Corp E 231 788-7020 — Muskegon *(G-11290)*
Gds Enterprises G 989 644-3115 — Lake *(G-9082)*
▲ **General Machine Services** G 269 695-2244 — Buchanan *(G-2119)*
Merrill Technologies Group Inc C 989 462-0330 — Alma *(G-241)*
Milan Supply Company G 231 238-9200 — Indian River *(G-8221)*
Millennium Planet LLC G 248 835-2331 — Farmington Hills *(G-5068)*
◆ **Murphy Water Well Bits** G 810 658-1554 — Davison *(G-3656)*
N G S G I Natural Gas Ser G 989 786-3788 — Lewiston *(G-9553)*
Ranch Production LLC F 231 869-2050 — Pentwater *(G-12430)*
Titan Global Oil Services Inc F 248 594-5983 — Birmingham *(G-1705)*
United Metal Technology Inc F 517 787-7940 — Jackson *(G-8599)*

3534 Elevators & Moving Stairways

◆ **Automated Systems Inc** E 248 373-5600 — Auburn Hills *(G-786)*
Central Elevator Co Inc F 269 329-0705 — Vicksburg *(G-16833)*
Chelsea Grain LLC G 734 475-1386 — Chelsea *(G-2703)*
▼ **Commercial Group Inc** E 313 931-6100 — Taylor *(G-15704)*
Detroit Elevator Company E 248 591-7484 — Ferndale *(G-5276)*
Elevated Technologies Inc F 616 288-9817 — Grand Rapids *(G-6375)*
Lake Shore Systems Inc D 906 265-5414 — Iron River *(G-8313)*
Mc Nally Elevator Company F 269 381-1860 — Kalamazoo *(G-8819)*
Mitsubishi Electric Us Inc D 734 453-6200 — Northville *(G-11711)*
▲ **Nylube Products Company LLC** E 248 852-6500 — Rochester Hills *(G-13486)*
Schafers Elevator Co G 517 263-7202 — Adrian *(G-93)*
Schindler Elevator Corporation F 517 272-1234 — Lansing *(G-9421)*
Thyssenkrupp Elevator Corp F 616 942-4710 — Grand Rapids *(G-6930)*
▼ **Vertical Solutions Company** G 517 655-8164 — Williamston *(G-17741)*

3535 Conveyors & Eqpt

ADW Industries Inc E 989 466-4742 — Alma *(G-231)*
Allied Indus Solutions LLC G 810 422-5093 — Fenton *(G-5180)*
▲ **Allor Manufacturing Inc** D 248 486-4500 — Brighton *(G-1883)*
Ally Equipment LLC G 810 422-5093 — Fenton *(G-5182)*
Alternative Engineering Inc E 616 785-7200 — Belmont *(G-1455)*
Altron Automation Inc D 616 669-7711 — Hudsonville *(G-8144)*
▲ **Anchor Conveyor Products Inc** G 313 582-5045 — Dearborn *(G-3676)*
Arrowhead Systems Inc G 810 720-4770 — Flint *(G-5377)*
Ase Industries Inc D 586 754-7480 — Warren *(G-16942)*
Auto/Con Services LLC E 586 791-7474 — Fraser *(G-5624)*
◆ **Automated Systems Inc** E 248 373-5600 — Auburn Hills *(G-786)*
▲ **Automatic Handling Intl Inc** D 734 847-0633 — Erie *(G-4800)*
▲ **Automtion Mdlar Components Inc** D 248 922-4740 — Davisburg *(G-3625)*
Bay Manufacturing Corporation E 989 358-7198 — Alpena *(G-281)*
Belco Industries Inc C 616 794-0410 — Belding *(G-1399)*
▲ **Belco Industries Inc** E 616 794-0410 — Belding *(G-1400)*
Benesh Corporation E 734 244-4143 — Monroe *(G-11023)*
Best Industrial Group Inc F 586 826-8800 — Warren *(G-16957)*
▲ **Blue Water Manufacturing Inc** F 810 364-6170 — Marysville *(G-10599)*
◆ **Bos Manufacturing LLC** G 231 398-3328 — Manistee *(G-10417)*
▲ **Bradford Company** C 616 399-3000 — Holland *(G-7575)*
Bristol Steel & Conveyor Corp E 810 658-9510 — Davison *(G-3641)*
C T & G Enterprises Inc G 810 798-8661 — Almont *(G-253)*
Caliber Industries LLC F 586 774-6775 — Clinton Township *(G-3074)*
▲ **Central Conveyor Company LLC** D 248 446-0118 — Wixom *(G-17782)*
Change Parts Incorporated E 231 845-5107 — Ludington *(G-10052)*
▲ **Chip Systems International** F 269 626-8000 — Scotts *(G-14503)*
◆ **Cignys Inc** G 989 753-1411 — Saginaw *(G-14018)*
Clinton Machine Inc E 989 834-2235 — Ovid *(G-12271)*
Colombo Sales & Engrg Inc F 248 547-2820 — Davisburg *(G-3630)*
Columbus McKinnon Corporation G 800 955-5541 — Muskegon *(G-11296)*
Constructive Sheet Metal Inc E 616 245-5306 — Allendale *(G-215)*
Continental Crane & Service F 586 294-7900 — Fraser *(G-5639)*
Conveyor Concepts Michigan LLC F 616 997-5200 — Coopersville *(G-3553)*
Cornerstone Fabg & Cnstr Inc E 989 642-5241 — Hemlock *(G-7460)*
▲ **CPI Products Inc** C 231 547-6064 — Auburn Hills *(G-829)*
▼ **Crippen Manufacturing Company** E 989 681-4323 — Saint Louis *(G-14361)*
Daifuku North America Holdg Co E 248 553-1000 — Novi *(G-11862)*
▼ **Dcl Inc** C 231 547-5600 — Charlevoix *(G-2613)*
▲ **Dearborn Mid West Conveyor Co** G 313 273-2804 — Detroit *(G-3966)*
▲ **Dearborn Mid-West Company LLC** C 734 288-4400 — Taylor *(G-15706)*
Dematic G 616 395-8671 — Holland *(G-7607)*
◆ **Diamond Automation Ltd** G 734 838-7138 — Livonia *(G-9710)*
Dimension Machine Tech LLC F 586 649-4747 — Bloomfield Hills *(G-1759)*
Dunkley International Inc C 269 343-5583 — Kalamazoo *(G-8732)*
Durr Systems Inc E 586 755-7500 — Warren *(G-17010)*
Dynamic Conveyor Corporation E 231 798-0014 — Norton Shores *(G-11748)*
Eagle Buckets Inc G 517 787-0385 — Jackson *(G-8436)*
Eagle Engineering & Supply Co E 989 356-4526 — Alpena *(G-286)*
▲ **Egemin Automation Inc** C 616 393-0101 — Holland *(G-7619)*
Empire Machine & Conveyors Inc F 989 541-2060 — Durand *(G-4608)*
▼ **Endura-Veyor Inc** F 989 358-7060 — Alpena *(G-287)*
Ensign Equipment Inc G 616 738-9000 — Holland *(G-7623)*
Ermanco F 231 798-4547 — Norton Shores *(G-11754)*
Esys Automation LLC D 248 754-1900 — Auburn Hills *(G-856)*
▲ **Fata Automation Inc** D 248 724-7660 — Auburn Hills *(G-860)*
Fibro Laepple Technology Inc G 248 591-4494 — Sterling Heights *(G-15340)*
Fraser Fab and Machine Inc E 248 852-9050 — Rochester Hills *(G-13428)*
Frost Inc G 616 785-9030 — Grand Rapids *(G-6420)*
◆ **Frost Incorporated** E 616 453-7781 — Grand Rapids *(G-6421)*
▲ **Frost Links** G 616 785-9030 — Grand Rapids *(G-6422)*
GMI Packaging Co G 734 972-7389 — Ann Arbor *(G-474)*
Gonzalez Prod Systems Inc C 248 745-1200 — Pontiac *(G-12829)*
Great Lakes Tech & Mfg LLC G 810 593-0257 — Fenton *(G-5217)*
▲ **Gudel Inc** D 734 214-0000 — Ann Arbor *(G-480)*
Hapman F 269 343-1675 — Kalamazoo *(G-8760)*
▲ **Harry Major Machine & Tool Co** D 586 783-7030 — Clinton Township *(G-3134)*
Harvey S Freeman E 248 852-2222 — West Bloomfield *(G-17479)*
▲ **Herkules Equipment Corporation** E 248 960-7100 — Commerce Township *(G-3411)*
▼ **Highland Engineering Inc** E 517 548-4372 — Howell *(G-8048)*
◆ **Hines Corporation** F 231 799-6240 — Norton Shores *(G-11812)*
▲ **HMS Products Co** D 248 689-8120 — Troy *(G-16398)*
Howard Structural Steel Inc E 989 752-3000 — Saginaw *(G-14062)*
Integrated Conveyor Ltd G 231 747-6430 — Muskegon *(G-11349)*
International Material Co F 616 355-2800 — Holland *(G-7691)*
Intersrce Recovery Systems Inc E 269 375-5100 — Kalamazoo *(G-8774)*
Intralox LLC G 616 259-7471 — Grand Rapids *(G-6543)*
Jantec Incorporated E 231 941-4339 — Traverse City *(G-16009)*

Employee Codes: A=Over 500 employees, B=251-500
C=101-250, D=51-100, E=20-50, F=10-19, G=3-9
2020 Harris Michigan Industrial Directory
803

35 INDUSTRIAL AND COMMERCIAL MACHINERY AND COMPUTER EQUIPMENT

Jervis B Webb Company ....B...... 248 553-1222
  Farmington Hills *(G-5032)*
Jervis B Webb Company ....C...... 231 347-3931
  Harbor Springs *(G-7285)*
Jervis B Webb Company ....D...... 231 582-6558
  Boyne City *(G-1825)*
◆ Jervis B Webb Company ....B...... 248 553-1000
  Novi *(G-11912)*
Kalamazoo Mfg Corp Globl ....C...... 269 382-8200
  Kalamazoo *(G-8792)*
Lenawee Tool & Automation Inc ....G...... 517 458-7222
  Morenci *(G-11112)*
Livonia Magnetics LLC ....F...... 734 397-8844
  Canton *(G-2393)*
Loudon Steel Inc ....D...... 989 871-9353
  Millington *(G-10997)*
Lrh & Associates Inc ....E...... 517 784-1055
  Jackson *(G-8500)*
Magline Inc ....D...... 800 624-5463
  Standish *(G-15222)*
▲ Magnetic Products Inc ....D...... 248 887-5600
  Highland *(G-7497)*
Mark One Corporation ....D...... 989 732-2427
  Gaylord *(G-5877)*
▼ Material Control Inc ....G...... 630 892-4274
  Croswell *(G-3600)*
Material Transfer and Stor Inc ....E...... 800 836-7068
  Allegan *(G-176)*
Max Endura Inc ....E...... 989 356-1593
  Alpena *(G-297)*
McNichols Conveyor Company ....F...... 248 357-6077
  Southfield *(G-14976)*
Metzgar Conveyor Co ....E...... 616 784-0930
  Grand Rapids *(G-6664)*
Milan Metal Worx LLC ....G...... 734 369-7115
  Petersburg *(G-12437)*
▲ Mol Belting Systems Inc ....D...... 616 453-2484
  Grand Rapids *(G-6696)*
Mondrella Process Systems LLC ....G...... 616 281-9836
  Grand Rapids *(G-6700)*
▲ Motan Inc ....E...... 269 685-1050
  Plainwell *(G-12531)*
Motion Industries Inc ....G...... 989 771-0200
  Saginaw *(G-14100)*
Motion Machine Company ....F...... 810 664-9901
  Lapeer *(G-9476)*
National Element Inc ....E...... 248 486-1810
  Brighton *(G-1966)*
New Technologies Tool & Mfg ....F...... 810 694-5426
  Grand Blanc *(G-5976)*
North Woods Industrial ....G...... 616 784-2840
  Comstock Park *(G-3502)*
▲ Omni Metalcraft Corp ....E...... 989 354-4075
  Alpena *(G-304)*
Overhead Conveyor Company ....E...... 248 547-3800
  Ferndale *(G-5307)*
P & A Conveyor Sales Inc ....G...... 734 285-7970
  Riverview *(G-13303)*
Paradigm Conveyor LLC ....G...... 616 520-1926
  Marne *(G-10510)*
Paslin Company ....C...... 248 953-8419
  Shelby Township *(G-14660)*
PCI Procal Inc ....F...... 989 358-7070
  Alpena *(G-307)*
Peak Industries Co Inc ....D...... 313 846-8666
  Dearborn *(G-3747)*
Pneumatic Tube Products Co ....C...... 503 968-0200
  Oakley *(G-12111)*
Powerscreen USA LLC ....G...... 989 288-3121
  Durand *(G-4612)*
▲ Prab Inc ....C...... 269 382-8200
  Kalamazoo *(G-8854)*
Prab Inc ....D...... 269 343-1675
  Kalamazoo *(G-8855)*
◆ Pressure Vessel Service Inc ....E...... 313 921-1200
  Detroit *(G-4310)*
Production Accessories Co ....G...... 313 366-1500
  Detroit *(G-4311)*
▲ PVS Holdings Inc ....G...... 313 921-1200
  Detroit *(G-4319)*
RK Wojan Inc ....E...... 231 347-1160
  Charlevoix *(G-2628)*
Roberts Sinto Corporation ....D...... 517 371-2471
  Grand Ledge *(G-6114)*
▲ Roberts Sinto Corporation ....C...... 517 371-2460
  Lansing *(G-9323)*
▲ Saginaw Products Corporation ....E...... 989 753-1411
  Saginaw *(G-14141)*
Santanna Tool & Design LLC ....D...... 248 541-3500
  Madison Heights *(G-10348)*

Siemens Industry Inc ....C...... 616 913-7700
  Grand Rapids *(G-6861)*
Simplified Control Solutions ....G...... 248 652-1449
  Oakland *(G-12108)*
▲ Sinto America Inc ....E...... 517 371-2460
  Lansing *(G-9323)*
Sparks Belting Company Inc ....G...... 800 451-4537
  Spring Lake *(G-15179)*
▲ Sparks Belting Company Inc ....D...... 616 949-2750
  Grand Rapids *(G-6875)*
Spectrum Automation Company ....E...... 734 522-2160
  Livonia *(G-9938)*
Steel Craft Inc ....E...... 989 358-7196
  Alpena *(G-314)*
Steel Master LLC ....E...... 810 771-4943
  Grand Blanc *(G-5984)*
▲ Storch Products Company Inc ....F...... 734 591-2200
  Livonia *(G-9946)*
Straatsma Associates Inc ....E...... 810 735-6957
  Linden *(G-9597)*
Structural Equipment Co ....E...... 248 547-3800
  Ferndale *(G-5320)*
Sure Conveyors Inc ....E...... 248 926-2100
  Wixom *(G-17902)*
▲ Symbiote Inc ....E...... 616 772-1790
  Zeeland *(G-18189)*
Symorex Ltd ....F...... 734 971-6000
  Ann Arbor *(G-653)*
Systems Unlimited Inc ....E...... 517 279-8407
  Coldwater *(G-3336)*
◆ Tacs Automation LLC ....F...... 586 446-8828
  Rochester Hills *(G-13523)*
◆ Tgw Systems Inc ....C...... 231 798-4547
  Norton Shores *(G-11800)*
▼ Thoreson-Mc Cosh Inc ....E...... 248 362-0960
  Troy *(G-16638)*
Ton-Tex Corporation ....E...... 616 957-3200
  Greenville *(G-7158)*
▲ Triad Industrial Corp ....F...... 989 358-7191
  Atlanta *(G-733)*
Ultimation Industries LLC ....E...... 586 771-1881
  Roseville *(G-13885)*
▲ Uniband Usa LLC ....F...... 616 676-6011
  Grand Rapids *(G-6950)*
Unified Screening and Crushing ....F...... 888 464-9473
  Saint Johns *(G-14299)*
Versa Handling Co ....G...... 313 491-0500
  Detroit *(G-4427)*
Versa Handling Co ....G...... 313 891-1420
  Detroit *(G-4428)*
Versa-Craft Inc ....G...... 586 465-5999
  Clinton Township *(G-3255)*
Verstraete Conveyability Inc ....E...... 800 798-0410
  Grand Rapids *(G-6968)*
Via-Tech Corp ....F...... 989 358-7028
  Lachine *(G-9079)*
W Soule & Co ....C...... 269 344-0139
  Kalamazoo *(G-8920)*
Wardcraft Industries LLC ....E...... 517 750-9100
  Spring Arbor *(G-15129)*
Wedin International Inc ....D...... 231 779-8650
  Cadillac *(G-2284)*
Whites Bridge Tooling Inc ....E...... 616 897-4151
  Lowell *(G-10045)*
Whiting Corporation ....G...... 734 451-0400
  Plymouth *(G-12794)*
▼ Wilkie Bros Conveyors Inc ....E...... 810 364-4820
  Marysville *(G-10626)*

3536 Hoists, Cranes & Monorails

Ats Assembly and Test Inc ....D...... 734 266-4713
  Livonia *(G-9657)*
▲ Besser Company USA ....E...... 616 399-5215
  Zeeland *(G-18119)*
Bulmann Enterprises Inc ....E...... 231 549-5020
  Boyne City *(G-1818)*
C R B Crane & Service Co ....G...... 586 757-1222
  Warren *(G-16973)*
Crane 1 Services Inc ....E...... 586 468-0909
  Harrison Township *(G-7327)*
▲ Crane Technologies Group Inc ....E...... 248 652-8700
  Rochester Hills *(G-13397)*
Crb Crane Services Inc ....E...... 517 552-5699
  Howell *(G-8026)*
Demag Cranes & Components Corp ....D...... 586 954-1000
  Chesterfield *(G-2764)*
▲ Detroit Hoist & Crane Co L L C ....E...... 586 268-2600
  Sterling Heights *(G-15312)*
F&B Technologies ....F...... 734 856-2118
  Ottawa Lake *(G-12262)*

Frost Inc ....G...... 616 785-9030
  Grand Rapids *(G-6420)*
◆ Frost Incorporated ....E...... 616 453-7781
  Grand Rapids *(G-6421)*
Grand Traverse Crane Corp ....G...... 231 943-7787
  Traverse City *(G-15984)*
Great Lakes Lift Inc ....G...... 989 673-2109
  Caro *(G-2469)*
Harbor Master Ltd ....F...... 616 669-3170
  Hudsonville *(G-8159)*
Harsco Corporation ....D...... 231 843-3431
  Ludington *(G-10062)*
Hme Inc ....C...... 616 534-1463
  Wyoming *(G-18011)*
Interlochen Boat Shop Inc ....G...... 231 275-7112
  Interlochen *(G-8243)*
James W Liess Co Inc ....G...... 248 547-9160
  Rochester Hills *(G-13452)*
Jered LLC ....G...... 906 776-1800
  Iron Mountain *(G-8286)*
◆ Jervis B Webb Company ....B...... 248 553-1000
  Novi *(G-11912)*
K&S Consultants LLC ....G...... 269 240-7767
  Buchanan *(G-2122)*
Konecranes Inc ....E...... 248 380-2626
  Novi *(G-11917)*
L & M Mfg Inc ....G...... 989 689-4010
  Hope *(G-7955)*
▲ Leedy Manufacturing Co LLC ....D...... 616 245-0517
  Grand Rapids *(G-6624)*
North Central Welding Co ....E...... 989 275-8054
  Roscommon *(G-13751)*
Odonnells Docks ....G...... 269 244-1446
  Jones *(G-8652)*
Royal ARC Welding Company ....E...... 734 789-9099
  Flat Rock *(G-5362)*
Shore-Mate Products LLC ....G...... 616 874-5438
  Rockford *(G-13590)*
Simpson Industrial Svcs LLC ....G...... 810 392-2717
  Wales *(G-16860)*
Star Crane Hist Svc of Klmazoo ....G...... 269 321-8882
  Portage *(G-13035)*
Symorex Ltd ....F...... 734 971-6000
  Ann Arbor *(G-653)*
▲ Unified Industries Inc ....F...... 517 546-3220
  Howell *(G-8118)*
Versa Handling Co ....G...... 313 491-0500
  Detroit *(G-4427)*
Whiting Corporation ....G...... 734 451-0400
  Plymouth *(G-12794)*
▲ Wolverine Crane & Service Inc ....E...... 616 538-4870
  Grand Rapids *(G-6997)*
Wolverine Crane & Service Inc ....F...... 734 467-9066
  Romulus *(G-13741)*

3537 Indl Trucks, Tractors, Trailers & Stackers

AAR Manufacturing Inc ....E...... 231 779-8800
  Cadillac *(G-2220)*
Aimrite LLC ....G...... 248 693-8925
  Lake Orion *(G-9124)*
Air-Hydraulics Inc ....F...... 517 787-9444
  Jackson *(G-8377)*
Alta Equipment Holdings Inc ....E...... 248 449-6700
  Livonia *(G-9638)*
American Fabricated Pdts Inc ....F...... 616 607-8785
  Spring Lake *(G-15133)*
Archer Wire International Corp ....D...... 231 869-6911
  Pentwater *(G-12428)*
Automated Machine Systems Inc ....E...... 616 662-1309
  Jenison *(G-8618)*
Baker Enterprises Inc ....E...... 989 354-2189
  Alpena *(G-280)*
Bay Wood Homes Inc ....G...... 989 245-4156
  Fenton *(G-5187)*
Bell Fork Lift Inc ....F...... 313 841-1220
  Detroit *(G-3899)*
Bell Forklifts ....F...... 586 469-7979
  Clinton Township *(G-3064)*
▲ Besser Company USA ....E...... 616 399-5215
  Zeeland *(G-18119)*
Bondfire Company ....F...... 231 834-5696
  Bailey *(G-1078)*
Bristol Manufacturing Inc ....E...... 810 658-9510
  Davison *(G-3640)*
Bucher Hydraulics Inc ....E...... 231 652-2773
  Newaygo *(G-11564)*
Budd Magnetic Products Inc ....G...... 248 353-2533
  Southfield *(G-14859)*

Charles Lange ... G ... 989 777-0110
Saginaw *(G-14016)*
Circle K Service Corporation ... E ... 989 496-0511
Midland *(G-10824)*
Columbus McKinnon Corporation ... G ... 800 955-5541
Muskegon *(G-11296)*
▼ Commercial Group Inc ... E ... 313 931-6100
Taylor *(G-15704)*
Crown Equipment Corporation ... G ... 616 530-3000
Traverse City *(G-15953)*
Crown Equipment Corporation ... D ... 734 414-0160
Plymouth *(G-12603)*
Crown Equipment Corporation ... E ... 616 530-3000
Grand Rapids *(G-6319)*
Delta Tube & Fabricating Corp ... C ... 248 634-8267
Holly *(G-7875)*
Dematic ... G ... 616 395-8671
Holland *(G-7607)*
▲ Egemin Automation Inc ... C ... 616 393-0101
Holland *(G-7619)*
◆ Frost Incorporated ... E ... 616 453-7781
Grand Rapids *(G-6421)*
Great Lakes Dock & Door LLC ... E ... 313 368-6300
Detroit *(G-4100)*
Harlo Corporation ... C ... 616 538-0550
Grandville *(G-7045)*
Harlo Corporation ... E ... 616 538-0550
Grandville *(G-7046)*
▲ Harlo Products Corporation ... E ... 616 538-0550
Grandville *(G-7047)*
Hart Precision Products Inc ... E ... 313 537-0490
Redford *(G-13165)*
Harvey S Freeman ... E ... 248 852-2222
West Bloomfield *(G-17479)*
Hme Inc ... C ... 616 534-1463
Wyoming *(G-18011)*
Hobart Brothers Company ... F ... 231 933-1234
Traverse City *(G-15998)*
Humphrey Companies LLC ... C ... 616 530-1717
Grandville *(G-7048)*
Ihs Inc ... G ... 616 464-4224
Grand Rapids *(G-6527)*
Independent Machine Co Inc ... E ... 906 428-4524
Escanaba *(G-4836)*
J & J Transport LLC ... G ... 231 582-6083
Boyne City *(G-1824)*
◆ Jervis B Webb Company ... B ... 248 553-1000
Novi *(G-11912)*
Joam Inc ... G ... 989 828-5749
Shepherd *(G-14729)*
JW Pennington LLC ... G ... 989 965-2736
Roscommon *(G-13749)*
Keller Tool Ltd ... D ... 734 425-4500
Livonia *(G-9794)*
L A S Leasing Inc ... F ... 734 727-5148
Wayne *(G-17435)*
▲ Lake Shore Systems Inc ... D ... 906 774-1500
Kingsford *(G-9061)*
Lakewood Machine Products Co ... E ... 734 654-6677
Carleton *(G-2459)*
Lock and Load Corp ... G ... 800 975-9658
Marion *(G-10490)*
Logistics Insight Corp ... C ... 810 424-0511
Flint *(G-5460)*
Loudon Steel Inc ... D ... 989 871-9353
Millington *(G-10997)*
◆ Magline Inc ... C ... 800 624-5463
Standish *(G-15221)*
Magline Inc ... D ... 800 624-5463
Standish *(G-15222)*
Magline International LLC ... G ... 989 512-1000
Standish *(G-15223)*
Marsh Industrial Services Inc ... F ... 231 258-4870
Kalkaska *(G-8949)*
Metzgar Conveyor Co ... E ... 616 784-0930
Grand Rapids *(G-6664)*
Midwest National LLC ... G ... 260 894-0963
Clarkston *(G-2939)*
Midwest Tractor & Equipment Co ... F ... 231 269-4100
Buckley *(G-2130)*
Milsco LLC ... B ... 517 787-3650
Jackson *(G-8531)*
▲ Mollers North America Inc ... D ... 616 942-6504
Grand Rapids *(G-6698)*
Montrose Trailers Inc ... G ... 810 639-7431
Montrose *(G-11105)*
Nyx Inc ... B ... 734 464-0800
Livonia *(G-9869)*
O Keller Tool Engrg Co LLC ... E ... 734 425-4500
Livonia *(G-9873)*
PCI Procal Inc ... F ... 989 358-7070
Alpena *(G-307)*
Peninsular Inc ... E ... 586 775-7211
Roseville *(G-13853)*
◆ Perfecto Industries Inc ... E ... 989 732-2941
Gaylord *(G-5888)*
▲ Pettibone/Traverse Lift LLC ... E ... 906 353-4800
Baraga *(G-1113)*
Pettibone/Traverse Lift LLC ... E ... 906 353-6668
Baraga *(G-1114)*
Progressive Metal Mfg Co ... E ... 248 546-2827
Warren *(G-17200)*
Prophotonix Limited ... E ... 586 778-1100
Roseville *(G-13856)*
Roberts Sinto Corporation ... D ... 517 371-2471
Grand Ledge *(G-6114)*
Sadia Enterprises Inc ... G ... 248 854-4666
Troy *(G-16588)*
◆ Saf-Holland Inc ... B ... 231 773-3271
Muskegon *(G-11417)*
▲ Saginaw Products Corporation ... E ... 989 753-1411
Saginaw *(G-14141)*
Sfi Acquisition Inc ... E ... 248 471-1500
Farmington Hills *(G-5122)*
Steelhead Industries LLC ... F ... 989 506-7416
Mount Pleasant *(G-11231)*
▼ Sterling Truck and Wstn Star ... E ... 313 592-4200
Redford *(G-13196)*
Superior Distribution Svcs LLC ... G ... 616 453-6358
Grand Rapids *(G-6902)*
Superior Equipment & Supply Co ... G ... 906 774-1789
Iron Mountain *(G-8302)*
Systems Unlimited Inc ... E ... 517 279-8407
Coldwater *(G-3336)*
T & L Transport Inc ... F ... 313 350-1535
Plymouth *(G-12764)*
▼ Thoreson-Mc Cosh Inc ... E ... 248 362-0960
Troy *(G-16638)*
▲ Vci Inc ... D ... 269 659-3676
Sturgis *(G-15639)*
Versatile Fabrication Co Inc ... E ... 231 739-7115
Muskegon *(G-11446)*
West Michigan Forklift Inc ... G ... 616 262-4949
Wayland *(G-17420)*

3541 Machine Tools: Cutting

A & D Run Off Inc ... G ... 231 759-0950
Muskegon *(G-11256)*
AAA Industries Inc ... E ... 313 255-0420
Redford *(G-13140)*
ABC Boring Co Inc ... E ... 586 751-2580
Warren *(G-16911)*
ABC Precision Machining Inc ... G ... 269 926-6322
Benton Harbor *(G-1478)*
Abrasive Services Incorporated ... G ... 734 941-2144
Romulus *(G-13647)*
Accra Tool Inc ... G ... 248 680-9936
Lake Orion *(G-9122)*
Accubilt Automated Systems LLC ... E ... 517 787-9353
Jackson *(G-8371)*
Accurate Machined Service Inc ... G ... 734 421-4660
Livonia *(G-9626)*
◆ Acme Manufacturing Company ... D ... 248 393-7300
Auburn Hills *(G-760)*
Acme Manufacturing Company ... F ... 248 393-7300
Lake Orion *(G-9123)*
Advanced Maintenance Tech ... G ... 810 820-2554
Flint *(G-5371)*
Advanced Stage Tooling LLC ... G ... 810 444-9807
East China *(G-4620)*
◆ Allfi Robotics Inc ... G ... 586 248-1198
Wixom *(G-17757)*
Alliance Tool ... G ... 586 465-3960
Harrison Township *(G-7318)*
Alto Manufacturing Inc ... F ... 734 641-8800
Westland *(G-17540)*
◆ American Broach & Machine Co ... E ... 734 961-0300
Ypsilanti *(G-18051)*
American Gator Tool Company ... G ... 231 347-3222
Harbor Springs *(G-7272)*
American Gear & Engrg Co Inc ... E ... 734 595-6400
Westland *(G-17541)*
American Pride Machining Inc ... G ... 586 294-6404
Fraser *(G-5617)*
Amex Mfg & Distrg Co Inc ... G ... 734 439-8560
Milan *(G-10932)*
Antech Tool Inc ... F ... 734 207-3622
Canton *(G-2348)*
Apex Broaching Systems Inc ... F ... 586 758-2626
Warren *(G-16936)*
Ascent Aerospace LLC ... A ... 586 726-0500
Macomb *(G-10108)*
▲ Atlas Technologies LLC ... D ... 810 714-2128
Fenton *(G-5183)*
Aw Carbide Fabricators Inc ... F ... 586 294-1850
Fraser *(G-5626)*
Axly Production Machining Inc ... B ... 989 269-2444
Bad Axe *(G-1057)*
B & O Saws Inc ... E ... 616 794-7297
Belding *(G-1397)*
Belco Industries Inc ... C ... 616 794-0410
Belding *(G-1399)*
▲ Belco Industries Inc ... E ... 616 794-0410
Belding *(G-1400)*
Berg Tool Inc ... F ... 586 646-7100
Chesterfield *(G-2745)*
▲ Berger LLC ... G ... 734 414-0402
Plymouth *(G-12585)*
Bielomatik USA Inc ... E ... 248 446-9910
New Hudson *(G-11532)*
◆ Bmt Aerospace Usa Inc ... D ... 586 285-7700
Fraser *(G-5630)*
Bob G Machining LLC ... G ... 586 285-1400
Clinton Township *(G-3068)*
Boride Engineered Abr Inc ... F ... 231 929-2121
Traverse City *(G-15916)*
Broaching Industries Inc ... E ... 586 949-3775
Chesterfield *(G-2748)*
▲ Bulk AG Innovations LLC ... F ... 269 925-0900
Benton Harbor *(G-1488)*
▲ C & B Machinery Company ... E ... 734 462-0600
Brighton *(G-1894)*
Carb-A-Tron Tool Co ... G ... 517 782-2249
Jackson *(G-8402)*
Casalbi Company Inc ... F ... 517 782-0345
Jackson *(G-8403)*
CBS Tool Inc ... F ... 586 566-5945
Shelby Township *(G-14558)*
CDM Machine Co ... F ... 313 538-9100
Southfield *(G-14864)*
▲ Cellular Concepts Co Inc ... E ... 313 371-4800
Rochester Hills *(G-13388)*
Champion Screw Machine Svcs ... G ... 248 624-4545
Wixom *(G-17784)*
Champion Screw Mch Engrg Inc ... F ... 248 624-4545
Wixom *(G-17785)*
Changeover Integration LLC ... F ... 231 845-5320
Ludington *(G-10053)*
City Animation Co ... E ... 248 589-0600
Troy *(G-16268)*
City Animation Co ... F ... 989 743-3458
Corunna *(G-3579)*
Clas Carbide ... G ... 248 236-8353
Oxford *(G-12342)*
Clausing Industrial Inc ... E ... 269 345-7155
Kalamazoo *(G-8706)*
▲ Clausing Industrial Inc ... D ... 269 345-7155
Kalamazoo *(G-8707)*
Clear Cut Water Jet Machining ... G ... 616 534-9119
Grand Rapids *(G-6280)*
▲ Cleary Developments Inc ... E ... 248 588-7011
Madison Heights *(G-10210)*
Clm Vibetech Inc ... F ... 269 344-3878
Kalamazoo *(G-8708)*
Craft Industries Inc ... A ... 586 726-4300
Shelby Township *(G-14570)*
Crankshaft Machine Company ... E ... 517 787-3791
Jackson *(G-8423)*
Cutex Inc ... G ... 734 953-8908
Livonia *(G-9696)*
D & D Production Inc ... F ... 248 334-2112
Waterford *(G-17332)*
D W Machine Inc ... F ... 517 787-9929
Jackson *(G-8426)*
David A Mohr Jr ... G ... 517 266-2694
Adrian *(G-58)*
Davison-Rite Products Co ... E ... 734 513-0505
Livonia *(G-9699)*
Design Services Unlimited Inc ... G ... 586 463-3225
Chesterfield *(G-2765)*
Detroit Boring & Mch Co LLC ... G ... 586 604-6506
Sterling Heights *(G-15311)*
Detroit Edge Tool Company ... E ... 586 776-1598
Roseville *(G-13794)*
Dikar Tool Company Inc ... F ... 248 348-0010
Novi *(G-11869)*
Dimond Machinery Company Inc ... E ... 269 945-5908
Hastings *(G-7407)*
Diversified Precision Pdts Inc ... E ... 517 750-2310
Spring Arbor *(G-15121)*

SIC

Employee Codes: A=Over 500 employees, B=251-500
C=101-250, D=51-100, E=20-50, F=10-19, G=3-9
2020 Harris Michigan
Industrial Directory
805

35 INDUSTRIAL AND COMMERCIAL MACHINERY AND COMPUTER EQUIPMENT SIC SECTION

Donald E Rogers Associates ....G....... 248 673-9878
Waterford *(G-17335)*

DTe Hankin Inc ....F....... 734 279-1831
Petersburg *(G-12435)*

Dvs Technology America Inc ....G....... 734 656-2080
Plymouth *(G-12614)*

Dyna- Bignell Products LLC ....G....... 989 418-5050
Clare *(G-2868)*

▲ **Dynamic Robotic Solutions Inc** ....C....... 248 829-2800
Auburn Hills *(G-848)*

Ecorse McHy Sls & Rbldrs Inc ....E....... 313 383-2100
Wyandotte *(G-17956)*

Electro ARC Manufacturing Co ....E....... 734 483-4233
Dexter *(G-4491)*

Elite Tooling LLC ....G....... 269 383-9714
Kalamazoo *(G-8734)*

Elk Rapids Engineering Inc ....E....... 231 264-5661
Elk Rapids *(G-4778)*

▲ **Emag LLC** ....E....... 248 477-7440
Farmington Hills *(G-4983)*

Emcor Inc ....F....... 989 667-0652
Bay City *(G-1308)*

Emhart Teknologies LLC ....F....... 586 949-0440
Chesterfield *(G-2773)*

Emhart Teknologies LLC ....F....... 800 783-6427
Troy *(G-16343)*

Enagon LLC ....G....... 269 455-5110
Saugatuck *(G-14458)*

Enihcam Corp ....G....... 810 354-0404
Fenton *(G-5203)*

Esco Group Inc ....F....... 616 453-5458
Grand Rapids *(G-6385)*

Esr ....G....... 989 619-7160
Harrisville *(G-7363)*

Exlterra Inc ....G....... 248 268-2336
Hazel Park *(G-7437)*

Extrude Hone LLC ....F....... 616 647-9050
Grand Rapids *(G-6395)*

Fair Industries LLC ....C....... 248 740-7841
Troy *(G-16359)*

Falcon Motorsports Inc ....G....... 248 328-2222
Holly *(G-7878)*

Faro Technologies Inc ....F....... 248 669-8620
Wixom *(G-17809)*

▲ **Federal Broach & Mch Co LLC** ....C....... 989 539-7420
Harrison *(G-7311)*

Fitz-Rite Products Inc ....G....... 248 360-3730
Commerce Township *(G-3405)*

Five Star Industries Inc ....E....... 586 786-0500
Macomb *(G-10122)*

▲ **Forst-Usa Incorporated** ....G....... 586 759-9380
Warren *(G-17044)*

Fortune Tool & Machine Inc ....E....... 248 669-9119
Wixom *(G-17813)*

Fourway Machinery Sales Co ....F....... 517 782-9371
Jackson *(G-8451)*

Framon Mfg Co Inc ....G....... 989 356-6296
Alpena *(G-290)*

G & W Machine Co ....G....... 616 363-4435
Grand Rapids *(G-6426)*

Gehring Corporation ....D....... 248 478-8060
Farmington Hills *(G-5008)*

General Broach & Engrg Inc ....E....... 586 726-4300
Troy *(G-16381)*

▲ **General Broach Company** ....E....... 517 458-7555
Morenci *(G-11109)*

George Kotzian ....G....... 231 861-6520
Shelby *(G-14525)*

Gerald Harris ....G....... 985 774-0261
Detroit *(G-4089)*

▲ **Globe Tech LLC** ....E....... 734 656-2200
Plymouth *(G-12630)*

Godin Tool Inc ....G....... 231 946-2210
Traverse City *(G-15980)*

Govro-Nelson Co ....G....... 810 329-4727
Commerce Township *(G-3408)*

Graflex Inc ....F....... 616 842-3654
Spring Lake *(G-15146)*

Great Lakes Waterjet Laser LLC ....G....... 517 629-9900
Albion *(G-124)*

H & G Tool Company ....F....... 586 573-7040
Warren *(G-17073)*

▲ **Hal International Inc** ....G....... 248 488-0440
Livonia *(G-9763)*

Hammond Machinery Inc ....D....... 269 345-7151
Kalamazoo *(G-8759)*

▲ **Hegenscheidt-Mfd Corporation** ....E....... 586 274-4900
Sterling Heights *(G-15367)*

Helical Lap & Manufacturing Co ....F....... 586 307-8322
Mount Clemens *(G-11132)*

Heller Inc ....E....... 248 288-5000
Troy *(G-16394)*

◆ **High-Star Corporation** ....G....... 734 743-1503
Westland *(G-17569)*

Highland Machine Design Inc ....G....... 248 669-6150
Commerce Township *(G-3412)*

Hollander Machine Co Inc ....G....... 810 742-1660
Burton *(G-2156)*

Hot Tool Cutter Grinding Co ....E....... 586 790-4867
Fraser *(G-5666)*

◆ **Hougen Manufacturing Inc** ....C....... 810 635-7111
Swartz Creek *(G-15667)*

▲ **Huron Tool & Engineering Co** ....E....... 989 269-9927
Bad Axe *(G-1068)*

Hydro-Craft Inc ....E....... 248 652-8100
Rochester Hills *(G-13448)*

Ideal Tool Inc ....F....... 989 893-8336
Bay City *(G-1321)*

Illinois Tool Works Inc ....D....... 248 589-2500
Troy *(G-16410)*

Industrial Boring Company ....G....... 586 756-9110
Warren *(G-17090)*

Infra Corporation ....F....... 248 623-0400
Waterford *(G-17351)*

▲ **Ingersoll CM Systems LLC** ....D....... 989 495-5000
Midland *(G-10870)*

Inland Lakes Machine Inc ....E....... 231 775-6543
Cadillac *(G-2255)*

Integrity Design & Mfg LLC ....G....... 248 628-6927
Oxford *(G-12352)*

Internal Grinding Abrasives ....E....... 616 243-5566
Grand Rapids *(G-6540)*

Iron River Mfg Co Inc ....E....... 906 265-5121
Iron River *(G-8310)*

Ivan Doverspike ....E....... 313 579-3000
Detroit *(G-4153)*

J & R Tool Inc ....G....... 989 662-0026
Auburn *(G-754)*

J & W Machine Inc ....G....... 989 773-9951
Mount Pleasant *(G-11199)*

J C Manufacturing Company ....G....... 586 757-2713
Warren *(G-17106)*

J W Holdings Inc ....E....... 616 530-9889
Grand Rapids *(G-6549)*

Jdl Enterprises Inc ....G....... 586 977-8863
Warren *(G-17113)*

Jdl Enterprises Inc ....F....... 586 977-8863
Sterling Heights *(G-15380)*

JF Hubert Enterprises Inc ....F....... 586 293-8660
Fraser *(G-5675)*

JPS Mfg Inc ....G....... 586 415-8702
Fraser *(G-5676)*

Jtekt Toyoda Americas Corp ....F....... 847 506-2415
Wixom *(G-17839)*

K&S Consultants LLC ....G....... 269 240-7767
Buchanan *(G-2122)*

▲ **K-Tool Corporation Michigan** ....D....... 863 603-0777
Plymouth *(G-12661)*

▲ **Kadia Inc** ....G....... 248 446-1970
Brighton *(G-1945)*

Kalamazoo Company ....E....... 269 345-7151
Kalamazoo *(G-8786)*

▲ **Kalamazoo Machine Tool Co Inc** ....G....... 269 321-8860
Portage *(G-13004)*

▲ **Kasper Machine Co** ....F....... 248 547-3150
Madison Heights *(G-10289)*

Kbe Precision Products LLC ....G....... 586 725-4200
New Baltimore *(G-11487)*

▲ **Kelm Acubar Lc** ....F....... 269 927-3000
Benton Harbor *(G-1516)*

Koch Limited ....G....... 586 296-3103
Fraser *(G-5679)*

▲ **Krmc LLC** ....G....... 734 955-9311
Romulus *(G-13698)*

Laydon Enterprises Inc ....E....... 906 774-4633
Iron Mountain *(G-8288)*

Leader Corporation ....E....... 586 566-7114
Shelby Township *(G-14624)*

Lester Detterbeck Entps Ltd ....E....... 906 265-5121
Iron River *(G-8314)*

Liberty Steel Fabricating Inc ....E....... 269 556-9792
Saint Joseph *(G-14327)*

Liberty Tool Inc ....E....... 586 726-2449
Sterling Heights *(G-15398)*

Lincoln Precision Carbide Inc ....E....... 989 736-8113
Lincoln *(G-9566)*

Liquid Drive Corporation ....E....... 248 634-5382
Mount Clemens *(G-11139)*

Lloyd Tool & Mfg Corp ....E....... 810 694-3519
Grand Blanc *(G-5973)*

▲ **Loc Performance Products Inc** ....C....... 734 453-2300
Plymouth *(G-12674)*

Loc Performance Products Inc ....C....... 734 453-2300
Lansing *(G-9242)*

Loc Performance Products Inc ....G....... 734 453-2300
Sterling Heights *(G-15401)*

Loon Lake Precision Inc ....G....... 810 953-0732
Grand Blanc *(G-5974)*

Love Machinery Inc ....G....... 734 427-0824
Livonia *(G-9819)*

M C Carbide Tool Co ....F....... 248 486-9590
Wixom *(G-17850)*

M S Machining Systems Inc ....F....... 517 546-1170
Howell *(G-8059)*

Machine Control Technology ....G....... 517 655-3506
Williamston *(G-17734)*

Maes Tool & Die Co Inc ....F....... 517 750-3131
Jackson *(G-8504)*

▲ **Mag-Powertrain** ....F....... 586 446-7000
Sterling Heights *(G-15408)*

Manufacturing Associates Inc ....G....... 248 421-4943
Livonia *(G-9822)*

Max2 LLC ....F....... 269 468-3452
Coloma *(G-3360)*

MB Liquidating Corporation ....D....... 810 638-5388
Flushing *(G-5541)*

Mc Pherson Industrial Corp ....D....... 586 752-5555
Romeo *(G-13633)*

▼ **Menominee Saw and Supply Co** ....E....... 906 863-2609
Menominee *(G-10747)*

Metal-Line Corp ....E....... 231 723-7041
Muskegon *(G-11377)*

Methods Machine Tools Inc ....E....... 248 624-8601
Wixom *(G-17854)*

Mi-Tech Tooling Inc ....E....... 989 912-2440
Cass City *(G-2519)*

Michigan Cnc Tool Inc ....F....... 734 449-9590
Whitmore Lake *(G-17704)*

Microform Tool Company Inc ....G....... 586 776-4840
Saint Clair Shores *(G-14264)*

Microprecision Cleaning ....E....... 586 997-6960
Sterling Heights *(G-15422)*

Microtap USA Inc ....G....... 248 852-8277
Rochester Hills *(G-13473)*

Migatron Precision Products ....F....... 989 739-1439
Oscoda *(G-12214)*

Millennium Screw Machine Inc ....G....... 734 525-5235
Livonia *(G-9845)*

Miller Broach Inc ....D....... 810 395-8810
Capac *(G-2449)*

▼ **Miller Tool & Die Co** ....E....... 517 782-0347
Jackson *(G-8529)*

MNP Corporation ....F....... 810 982-8996
Port Huron *(G-12943)*

Modern Machine Tool Co ....F....... 517 788-9120
Jackson *(G-8536)*

Moore Production Tool Spc ....E....... 248 476-1200
Farmington *(G-4905)*

Morgan Machine LLC ....G....... 248 293-3277
Auburn Hills *(G-948)*

▲ **Multifinish-Usa Inc** ....G....... 248 528-1154
Troy *(G-16516)*

◆ **Nagel Precision Inc** ....C....... 734 426-5650
Ann Arbor *(G-568)*

New Dimension Laser Inc ....G....... 586 415-6041
Roseville *(G-13847)*

◆ **New Unison Corporation** ....E....... 248 544-9500
Ferndale *(G-5304)*

▼ **Neway Manufacturing Inc** ....G....... 989 743-3458
Corunna *(G-3583)*

Normac Incorporated ....F....... 248 349-2644
Northville *(G-11714)*

Novi Tool & Machine Company ....D....... 313 532-0900
Redford *(G-13176)*

Oliver of Adrian Inc ....G....... 517 263-2132
Adrian *(G-83)*

P M R Industries Inc ....F....... 810 989-5020
Port Huron *(G-12954)*

Palfam Industries Inc ....F....... 248 922-0590
Ortonville *(G-12201)*

Paragon Tool Company ....G....... 734 326-1702
Romulus *(G-13719)*

▲ **Peiseler LLC** ....G....... 616 235-8460
Grand Rapids *(G-6746)*

Pentech Industries Inc ....E....... 586 445-1070
Roseville *(G-13854)*

Performance Crankshaft Inc ....G....... 586 549-7557
Ferndale *(G-5309)*

Petty Machine & Tool Inc ....E....... 517 782-9355
Jackson *(G-8551)*

SIC SECTION
35 INDUSTRIAL AND COMMERCIAL MACHINERY AND COMPUTER EQUIPMENT

Pinnacle Engineering Co Inc ....F 734 428-7039
Manchester (G-10410)

Pioneer Broach Midwest Inc ....F 231 768-5800
Leroy (G-9535)

Plason Scraping Co Inc ....G....... 248 588-7280
Madison Heights (G-10329)

Posa-Cut Corporation ....E 248 474-5620
Farmington Hills (G-5097)

Precision Guides LLC ....G....... 517 536-7234
Michigan Center (G-10789)

Precision Honing ....G....... 586 757-0304
Warren (G-17192)

Precision Jig Grinding Inc ....G....... 989 865-7953
Saint Charles (G-14199)

Prime Industries Inc ....E 734 946-8588
Taylor (G-15756)

Pro Precision Inc ....G....... 586 247-6160
Sterling Heights (G-15452)

Production Threaded Parts Co ....F 810 688-3186
North Branch (G-11665)

Productivity Technologies ....C....... 810 714-0200
Fenton (G-5231)

Punch Tech ....E 810 364-4811
Marysville (G-10612)

◆ Quality Pipe Products Inc ....E 734 606-5100
New Boston (G-11509)

Quality Tool Company Inc ....G....... 517 869-2490
Allen (G-193)

R E Gallaher Corp ....E 586 725-3333
Ira (G-8267)

▲ R F M Incorporated ....F 810 229-4567
Brighton (G-1983)

▲ R P T Cincinnati Inc ....G....... 313 382-5880
Lincoln Park (G-9584)

Ra Prcsion Grnding Mtlwrks Inc ....F 586 783-7776
Harrison Township (G-7346)

Rae Manufacturing Company ....F 810 987-9170
Port Huron (G-12960)

Rapid Cnc Solutions ....G....... 586 850-6385
Hamtramck (G-7245)

Rapid Grinding & Machine Co ....G....... 989 753-1744
Saginaw (G-14131)

▲ Rattunde Corporation ....G....... 616 940-3340
Caledonia (G-2312)

▲ Raven Engineering Inc ....E 248 969-9450
Oxford (G-12367)

Reggie McKenzie Indus Mtls ....G....... 734 261-0844
Livonia (G-9908)

Richardson Acqstions Group Inc ....E 248 624-2272
Walled Lake (G-16902)

Riverside Cnc LLC ....G....... 616 246-6000
Wyoming (G-18032)

Riverside Spline & Gear Inc ....E 810 765-8302
Marine City (G-10481)

Riverside Tool Corp ....E 616 241-1424
Grand Rapids (G-6829)

Rnd Engineering LLC ....G....... 734 328-8277
Canton (G-2423)

Robert Bosch LLC ....E 248 921-9054
Novi (G-11987)

Robert Bosch LLC ....A 734 979-3000
Plymouth (G-12741)

▲ Rock Tool & Machine Co Inc ....E 734 455-9840
Plymouth (G-12743)

▼ Rod Chomper Inc ....F 616 392-9677
Holland (G-7790)

◆ Roto-Finish Company Inc ....E 269 327-7071
Kalamazoo (G-8875)

Roussin M & Ubelhor R Inc ....G....... 586 783-6015
Harrison Township (G-7347)

Roy A Hutchins Company ....G....... 248 437-3470
New Hudson (G-11554)

RSI Global Sourcing LLC ....F 734 604-2448
Novi (G-11988)

RTS Cutting Tools Inc ....E 586 954-1900
Clinton Township (G-3217)

Rwc Inc ....D....... 989 684-4030
Bay City (G-1352)

S & L Tool Inc ....G....... 734 464-4200
Livonia (G-9917)

S & S Machine Tool Repair LLC ....G....... 616 877-4930
Dorr (G-4527)

Sabre-TEC Inc ....F 586 949-5386
Chesterfield (G-2835)

▲ Saginaw Machine Systems Inc ....D....... 989 753-8465
Saginaw (G-14140)

Schenck USA Corp ....E 248 377-2100
Southfield (G-15024)

Schienke Products Inc ....G....... 586 752-5454
Bruce Twp (G-2099)

▲ Schutte MSA LLC ....F 517 782-3600
Jackson (G-8570)

Select Steel Fabricators Inc ....F 248 945-9582
Southfield (G-15026)

SMS Holding Co Inc ....C....... 989 753-8465
Saginaw (G-14150)

SMW Tooling Inc ....F 616 355-9822
Holland (G-7808)

Snap Jaws Manufacturing Inc ....G....... 248 588-1099
Troy (G-16608)

Snyder Corporation ....E 586 726-4300
Shelby Township (G-14697)

Soaring Concepts Aerospace LLC ....F 574 286-9670
Hastings (G-7427)

Soils and Structures Inc ....E 800 933-3959
Norton Shores (G-11796)

Solidica Inc ....F 734 222-4680
Ann Arbor (G-639)

Stanhope Tool Inc ....F 248 585-5711
Madison Heights (G-10360)

Star Cutter Co ....G....... 248 474-8200
Lewiston (G-9555)

▲ Star Cutter Co ....E 248 474-8200
Farmington Hills (G-5129)

Star Su Company LLC ....E 248 474-8200
Farmington Hills (G-5130)

Steadfast Tool & Machine Inc ....G....... 989 856-8127
Caseville (G-2506)

Stoney Crest Regrind Service ....F 989 777-7190
Bridgeport (G-1858)

Sunrise Tool Products Inc ....F 989 724-6688
Harrisville (G-7366)

▲ Superabrasives Inc ....E 248 348-7670
Wixom (G-17901)

Systems Unlimited Inc ....E 517 279-8407
Coldwater (G-3336)

T E C Boring ....G....... 586 443-5437
Roseville (G-13876)

Tank Truck Service & Sales Inc ....G....... 989 731-4887
Gaylord (G-5894)

Tank Truck Service & Sales Inc ....E 586 757-6500
Warren (G-17262)

▲ Tarus Products Inc ....D....... 586 977-1400
Sterling Heights (G-15520)

Tawas Tool Co Inc ....D....... 989 362-0414
East Tawas (G-4696)

Tech Tooling Specialties Inc ....F 517 782-8898
Jackson (G-8584)

▲ Telsonic Ultrasonics Inc ....E 586 802-0033
Shelby Township (G-14708)

▲ Thielenhaus Microfinish Corp ....E 248 349-9450
Novi (G-12015)

▲ Thyssenkrupp System Engrg ....C....... 248 340-8000
Auburn Hills (G-1019)

Transfer Tool Systems Inc ....D....... 616 846-8510
Grand Haven (G-6090)

Tri-Power Manufacturing Inc ....G....... 734 414-8084
Plymouth (G-12779)

Triangle Broach Company ....F 313 838-2150
Detroit (G-4408)

Trispec Precision Products Inc ....G....... 248 308-3231
Wixom (G-17921)

Troy Industries Inc ....F 586 739-7760
Shelby Township (G-14711)

Tru Tech Systems LLC ....D....... 586 469-2700
Mount Clemens (G-11152)

True Fabrications & Machine ....F 248 288-0140
Troy (G-16653)

▲ U S Equipment Co ....E 313 526-8300
Rochester Hills (G-13533)

U S Tool & Cutter Co ....F 248 553-7745
Novi (G-12020)

Ultra-Dex USA LLC ....G....... 810 638-5388
Flushing (G-5543)

United Mfg Netwrk Inc ....G....... 586 321-7887
Warren (G-17274)

Utica Body & Assembly Inc ....E 586 726-4330
Troy (G-16669)

▲ Utica Enterprises Inc ....C....... 586 726-4300
Troy (G-16670)

▼ Van-Mark Products Corporation ....E 248 478-1200
Farmington Hills (G-5146)

Variable Machining & Tool Inc ....G....... 586 778-8803
Warren (G-17278)

Ventra Greenwich Holdings Corp ....G....... 586 759-8900
Warren (G-17282)

Viscount Equipment Co Inc ....G....... 586 293-5900
Fraser (G-5746)

W W J Form Tool Company Inc ....G....... 313 565-0015
Inkster (G-8235)

Waber Tool & Engineering Co ....E 269 342-0765
Kalamazoo (G-8921)

Warren Broach & Machine Corp ....F 586 254-7080
Sterling Heights (G-15544)

Warren Industries Inc ....D....... 586 741-0420
Clinton Township (G-3259)

◆ Wfl Millturn Technologies Inc ....G....... 440 729-0896
Wixom (G-17930)

Wolverine Carbide Die Company ....E 248 280-0300
Troy (G-16695)

Wolverine Machine Products Co ....E 248 634-9952
Holly (G-7902)

Wright-K Technology Inc ....E 989 752-2588
Saginaw (G-14184)

3542 Machine Tools: Forming

3M Company ....E 248 926-2500
Wixom (G-17749)

◆ A W B Industries Inc ....E 989 739-1447
Oscoda (G-12205)

▲ Advance Products Corporation ....E 269 849-1000
Benton Harbor (G-1480)

Advanced Feedlines LLC ....D....... 248 583-9400
Troy (G-16169)

Air-Hydraulics Inc ....F 517 787-9444
Jackson (G-8377)

American Brake and Clutch Inc ....F 586 948-3730
Chesterfield (G-2736)

American Wldg & Press Repr Inc ....F 248 358-2050
Southfield (G-14837)

▲ Anderson-Cook Inc ....D....... 586 954-0700
Clinton Township (G-3053)

Anderson-Cook Inc ....D....... 586 293-0800
Fraser (G-5620)

Anderson-Cook Inc ....E 586 954-0700
Clinton Township (G-3054)

▲ Atlas Technologies LLC ....D....... 810 714-2128
Fenton (G-5183)

Automated Indus Motion Inc ....F 231 865-1800
Fruitport (G-5787)

B & B Holdings Groesbeck LLC ....F 586 554-7600
Sterling Heights (G-15269)

B & M Bending & Forging Inc ....G....... 586 731-3332
Shelby Township (G-14553)

◆ B&P Littleford LLC ....E 989 757-1300
Saginaw (G-13999)

Baldauf Enterprises Inc ....E 989 686-0350
Bay City (G-1280)

▼ Birdsall Tool & Gage Co ....E 248 474-5150
Farmington Hills (G-4941)

Bmax USA LLC ....E 248 794-4176
Pontiac (G-12807)

Boral Building Products Inc ....C....... 248 668-6400
Wixom (G-17777)

Brake Roller Co Inc ....E 269 965-2371
Battle Creek (G-1157)

▲ Buhlerprince Inc ....C....... 616 394-8248
Holland (G-7581)

Burton Press Co Inc ....G....... 248 853-0212
Rochester Hills (G-13380)

Buster Mathis Foundation ....G....... 616 843-4433
Wyoming (G-17990)

▲ Centerless Rebuilders Inc ....E 586 749-6529
New Haven (G-11523)

▲ Century Inc ....C....... 231 947-6400
Traverse City (G-15932)

▲ Clark Granco Inc ....D....... 616 794-2600
Belding (G-1407)

CNB International Inc ....D....... 269 948-3300
Hastings (G-7403)

▲ Cold Forming Technology Inc ....F 586 254-4600
Sterling Heights (G-15291)

Columbia Marking Tools Inc ....E 586 949-8400
Chesterfield (G-2754)

Contractors Steel Company ....E 616 531-4000
Grand Rapids (G-6306)

Davison Tool Service Inc ....G....... 810 653-6920
Davison (G-3646)

Die Cast Press Mfg Co Inc ....E 269 657-6060
Paw Paw (G-12403)

Die Cast Press Mfg Co Inc ....G....... 269 427-5408
Bangor (G-1090)

Die-Matic LLC ....E 616 531-0060
Grand Rapids (G-6349)

Digital Die Solutions Inc ....F 734 542-2222
Livonia (G-9712)

Dimond Machinery Company Inc ....E 269 945-5908
Hastings (G-7407)

Diversified Metal Products Inc ....E 989 448-7120
Gaylord (G-5856)

S I C

Employee Codes: A=Over 500 employees, B=251-500
C=101-250, D=51-100, E=20-50, F=10-19, G=3-9
2020 Harris Michigan
Industrial Directory
807

Dm Tool & Fab Inc..........D....... 586 726-8390
Sterling Heights *(G-15319)*
Eagle Machine Tool Corporation..........G....... 231 798-8473
Norton Shores *(G-11749)*
Enprotech Industrial Tech LLC..........C....... 517 372-0950
Lansing *(G-9226)*
Enprotech Industrial Tech LLC..........E....... 517 319-5306
Lansing *(G-9366)*
◆ Fanuc America Corporation..........B....... 248 377-7000
Rochester Hills *(G-13423)*
▲ Feed - Lease Corp..........E....... 248 377-0000
Auburn Hills *(G-871)*
Flagler Corporation..........E....... 586 749-6300
Chesterfield *(G-2776)*
▲ Fontijne Grotnes Inc..........E....... 269 262-4700
Niles *(G-11611)*
◆ Global Strgc Sup Solutions LLC..........D....... 734 525-9100
Livonia *(G-9753)*
▲ Globe Tech LLC..........E....... 734 656-2200
Plymouth *(G-12630)*
Green Oak Tool and Svcs Inc..........G....... 586 531-2255
Brighton *(G-1934)*
Hamilton Industrial Products..........E....... 269 751-5153
Hamilton *(G-7233)*
▲ HMS Products Co..........D....... 248 689-8120
Troy *(G-16398)*
◆ Howmet Corporation..........E....... 231 894-5686
Whitehall *(G-17669)*
▲ Howmet Holdings Corporation..........G....... 231 894-5686
Whitehall *(G-17676)*
Hti Cybernetics Inc..........E....... 586 826-8346
Sterling Heights *(G-15369)*
Impel Industries Inc..........E....... 586 254-5800
Sterling Heights *(G-15371)*
Industrial Innovations Inc..........F....... 616 249-1525
Grandville *(G-7052)*
▲ Jier North America Inc..........F....... 734 404-6683
Plymouth *(G-12653)*
▼ Kasten Machinery Inc..........G....... 269 945-1999
Hastings *(G-7419)*
Koppy Corporation..........D....... 248 373-1900
Royal Oak *(G-13942)*
Lloyd Tool & Mfg Corp..........E....... 810 694-3519
Grand Blanc *(G-5973)*
M & M Turning Co..........E....... 586 791-7188
Fraser *(G-5686)*
M C Molds Inc..........E....... 517 655-5481
Williamston *(G-17733)*
▲ Magnetool Inc..........E....... 248 588-5400
Troy *(G-16479)*
Martinrea Industries Inc..........C....... 231 832-5504
Reed City *(G-13220)*
Metal Mechanics Inc..........F....... 269 679-2525
Schoolcraft *(G-14499)*
Michigan Roll Form Inc..........E....... 248 669-3700
Commerce Township *(G-3433)*
Midwest Tool and Cutlery Co..........F....... 231 258-2341
Kalkaska *(G-8953)*
▼ Miller Tool & Die Co..........E....... 517 782-0347
Jackson *(G-8529)*
Monroe LLC..........B....... 616 942-9820
Grand Rapids *(G-6702)*
Moore Production Tool Spc..........E....... 248 476-1200
Farmington *(G-4905)*
Mor-Tech Design Inc..........E....... 586 254-7982
Sterling Heights *(G-15427)*
Mor-Tech Manufacturing Inc..........E....... 586 254-7982
Sterling Heights *(G-15428)*
◆ Oak Press Solutions Inc..........E....... 269 651-8513
Sturgis *(G-15624)*
Orbitform Group LLC..........D....... 800 957-4838
Jackson *(G-8545)*
P M R Industries Inc..........F....... 810 989-5020
Port Huron *(G-12954)*
Pace Industries LLC..........A....... 231 777-3941
Muskegon *(G-11396)*
Penka Tool Corporation..........G....... 248 543-3940
Madison Heights *(G-10322)*
Port City Group Inc..........F....... 231 777-3941
Muskegon *(G-11400)*
Press Room Eqp Sls & Svc Co..........G....... 248 334-1880
Pontiac *(G-12857)*
Product and Tooling Tech Inc..........E....... 586 293-1810
Fraser *(G-5710)*
▲ Production Fabricators Inc..........E....... 231 777-3822
Muskegon *(G-11407)*
Productivity Technologies..........C....... 810 714-0200
Fenton *(G-5231)*
Prophotonix Limited..........E....... 586 778-1100
Roseville *(G-13856)*
Pt Tech Stamping Inc..........E....... 586 293-1810
Fraser *(G-5713)*
R and T West Michigan Inc..........E....... 616 698-9931
Caledonia *(G-2311)*
RC Directional Boring Inc..........F....... 517 545-4887
Howell *(G-8088)*
Reliable Sales Co..........G....... 248 969-0943
Oxford *(G-12368)*
Rempco Acquisition Inc..........E....... 231 775-0108
Cadillac *(G-2274)*
S & L Tool Inc..........G....... 734 464-4200
Livonia *(G-9917)*
Salvo Tool & Engineering Co..........E....... 810 346-2727
Brown City *(G-2057)*
Seg Automotive North Amer LLC..........F....... 248 465-2602
Novi *(G-11991)*
Selmuro Ltd..........E....... 810 603-2117
Grand Blanc *(G-5983)*
Shannon Precision Fastener LLC..........E....... 248 658-3015
Madison Heights *(G-10350)*
Shape Dynamics Intl Inc..........G....... 231 733-2164
Muskegon *(G-11421)*
Spline Specialist Inc..........G....... 586 731-4569
Sterling Heights *(G-15506)*
Stilson Products LLC..........E....... 586 778-1100
Roseville *(G-13875)*
T & D Machine Inc..........G....... 517 423-0778
Tecumseh *(G-15810)*
Tapco Holdings Inc..........C....... 248 668-6400
Wixom *(G-17905)*
Tech Tooling Specialties Inc..........F....... 517 782-8898
Jackson *(G-8584)*
Titanium Industries Inc..........G....... 973 983-1185
Plymouth *(G-12771)*
Tox Presso Technik..........G....... 248 374-1877
Wixom *(G-17913)*
Triple Tool..........F....... 586 795-1785
Sterling Heights *(G-15530)*
U S Baird Corporation..........F....... 616 826-5013
Middleville *(G-10811)*
▲ United States Socket..........F....... 586 469-8811
Fraser *(G-5744)*
▼ Van-Mark Products Corporation..........E....... 248 478-1200
Farmington Hills *(G-5146)*
▲ West Michigan Spline Inc..........F....... 616 399-4078
Holland *(G-7856)*

3543 Industrial Patterns

Acme Casting Enterprises Inc..........G....... 586 755-0300
Warren *(G-16916)*
Advanced Technology and Design..........G....... 248 889-5658
Highland *(G-7485)*
Advantage Industries Inc..........E....... 616 669-2400
Jenison *(G-8616)*
Al-Craft Design & Engrg Inc..........G....... 248 589-3827
Troy *(G-16181)*
Allen Pattern of Michigan..........F....... 269 963-4131
Battle Creek *(G-1145)*
▲ Anderson Global Inc..........C....... 231 733-2164
Muskegon *(G-11270)*
Arbor Gage & Tooling Inc..........E....... 616 454-8266
Grand Rapids *(G-6178)*
Associate Mfg Inc..........G....... 989 345-0025
West Branch *(G-17506)*
Astro-Netics Inc..........D....... 248 585-4890
Madison Heights *(G-10197)*
Aurora Cad CAM Inc..........F....... 810 678-2128
Metamora *(G-10772)*
Azko Manufacturing Inc..........G....... 231 733-0888
Muskegon *(G-11273)*
Azko Pattern Mfg Inc..........G....... 231 733-0888
Muskegon *(G-11274)*
B & L Pattern Company..........G....... 269 982-0214
Saint Joseph *(G-14301)*
Bespro Pattern Inc..........F....... 586 268-6970
Madison Heights *(G-10204)*
▲ Big Dome Holdings Inc..........D....... 616 735-6228
Grand Rapids *(G-6219)*
Briggs Industries Inc..........E....... 586 749-5191
Chesterfield *(G-2747)*
C & D Enterprises Inc..........F....... 248 373-0011
Burton *(G-2147)*
C & D Gage Inc..........G....... 517 548-7049
Howell *(G-8018)*
Champion Charter Sls & Svc Inc..........G....... 906 779-2300
Iron Mountain *(G-8280)*
Cobra Patterns & Models Inc..........E....... 248 588-2669
Madison Heights *(G-10215)*
Complete Prototype Svcs Inc..........B....... 586 690-8897
Clinton Township *(G-3085)*
Crescent Pattern Company..........F....... 248 541-1052
Oak Park *(G-12056)*
D & K Pattern Inc..........G....... 989 865-9955
Saint Charles *(G-14191)*
Decca Pattern Co Inc..........G....... 586 775-8450
Roseville *(G-13790)*
Dhs Inc..........G....... 313 724-6566
Detroit *(G-4007)*
Elmhirst Industries Inc..........E....... 586 731-8663
Sterling Heights *(G-15330)*
Gage Pattern & Model Inc..........E....... 248 361-6609
Madison Heights *(G-10255)*
Gicmac Industrial Inc..........G....... 248 308-2743
Novi *(G-11891)*
GM Bassett Pattern Inc..........G....... 248 477-6454
Farmington Hills *(G-5012)*
Grand Rapids Carvers Inc..........E....... 616 538-0022
Grand Rapids *(G-6452)*
Harvey Pattern Works Inc..........F....... 906 774-4285
Kingsford *(G-9059)*
Holland Pattern Co..........E....... 616 396-6348
Holland *(G-7675)*
Homestead Tool and Machine..........E....... 989 465-6182
Coleman *(G-3344)*
Husite Engineering Co Inc..........E....... 248 588-0337
Clinton Township *(G-3136)*
Industrial Model Inc..........G....... 586 254-0450
Auburn Hills *(G-913)*
J J Pattern & Castings Inc..........G....... 248 543-7119
Madison Heights *(G-10281)*
Jay/Enn Corporation..........D....... 248 588-2393
Troy *(G-16433)*
L & L Pattern Inc..........G....... 231 733-2646
Muskegon *(G-11359)*
Logan Pattern & Engrg Co LLC..........G....... 810 364-9298
Saint Clair *(G-14226)*
Majestic Pattern Company Inc..........G....... 313 892-5800
Detroit *(G-4216)*
Mantissa Industries Inc..........G....... 517 694-2260
Holt *(G-7915)*
Marten Models & Molds Inc..........E....... 586 293-2260
Fraser *(G-5691)*
Metro Technologies Ltd..........D....... 248 528-9240
Troy *(G-16502)*
Michalski Enterprises Inc..........E....... 517 703-0777
Lansing *(G-9245)*
Michigan Pattern Works Inc..........E....... 616 245-9259
Grand Rapids *(G-6674)*
Model Pattern Company Inc..........E....... 616 878-9710
Byron Center *(G-2204)*
Modern Age Pattern Mfg Inc..........G....... 231 788-1222
Muskegon *(G-11383)*
▲ National Pattern Inc..........E....... 989 755-6274
Saginaw *(G-14101)*
Northern Sierra Corporation..........G....... 989 777-4784
Saginaw *(G-14116)*
Paragon Molds Corporation..........E....... 586 294-7630
Fraser *(G-5704)*
Parker Pattern Inc..........F....... 586 466-5900
Mount Clemens *(G-11143)*
Parker Tooling & Design Inc..........F....... 616 791-1080
Grand Rapids *(G-6743)*
Portenga Manufacturing Company..........G....... 616 846-2691
Ferrysburg *(G-5337)*
Pre-Cut Patterns Inc..........G....... 616 392-4415
Holland *(G-7774)*
Prompt Pattern Inc..........E....... 586 759-2030
Warren *(G-17201)*
Proto-Cast Inc..........E....... 313 565-5400
Inkster *(G-8233)*
Quality Model & Pattern Co..........E....... 616 791-1156
Grand Rapids *(G-6800)*
Ravenna Pattern & Mfg..........E....... 231 853-2264
Ravenna *(G-13127)*
Rehau Incorporated..........E....... 269 651-7845
Sturgis *(G-15632)*
Sbti Company..........D....... 586 726-5756
Shelby Township *(G-14685)*
Simpsons Enterprises Inc..........E....... 269 279-7237
Three Rivers *(G-15877)*
Tedson Industries Inc..........F....... 248 588-9230
Troy *(G-16635)*
Tri-Star Tooling LLC..........F....... 586 978-0435
Sterling Heights *(G-15529)*
Vans Pattern Corp..........E....... 616 364-9483
Grand Rapids *(G-6961)*
Wing Pattern Inc..........G....... 248 588-1121
Sterling Heights *(G-15546)*
Wolverine Products Inc..........F....... 586 792-3740
Clinton Township *(G-3261)*

3544 Dies, Tools, Jigs, Fixtures & Indl Molds

2k Tool LLC ... G ... 616 452-4927
Wyoming *(G-17983)*
3d Polymers Inc ... D ... 248 588-5562
Orchard Lake *(G-12164)*
A & A Manufacturing Co ... G ... 616 846-1730
Spring Lake *(G-15130)*
A & D Plastics Inc ... E ... 734 455-2255
Plymouth *(G-12557)*
▲ A & O Mold and Eng Inc ... E ... 269 649-0600
Vicksburg *(G-16830)*
A B M Tool & Die Inc ... G ... 734 432-6060
Livonia *(G-9619)*
A C Steel Rule Dies Inc ... G ... 248 588-5600
Madison Heights *(G-10175)*
A D Johnson Engraving Co Inc ... F ... 269 385-0044
Kalamazoo *(G-8672)*
A J Tool Co ... F ... 517 787-5755
Jackson *(G-8369)*
A S A P Tool Inc ... G ... 586 790-6550
Clinton Township *(G-3029)*
Accu Die & Mold Inc ... E ... 269 465-4020
Stevensville *(G-15551)*
▲ Accu-Shape Die Cutting Inc ... E ... 810 230-2445
Flint *(G-5368)*
Accubilt Automated Systems LLC ... E ... 517 787-9353
Jackson *(G-8371)*
Acg Services Inc ... G ... 586 232-4698
Shelby Township *(G-14540)*
Acme Carbide Die Inc ... E ... 734 722-2303
Westland *(G-17538)*
Acme Tool & Die Co ... G ... 231 938-1260
Acme *(G-1)*
Action Die & Tool Inc ... G ... 616 538-2326
Grandville *(G-7016)*
▲ Action Mold & Machining Inc ... E ... 616 452-1580
Grand Rapids *(G-6137)*
Action Tool & Machine Inc ... E ... 810 229-6300
Brighton *(G-1877)*
Ada Gage Inc ... G ... 616 676-3338
Ada *(G-4)*
Adaptive Mfg Solutions LLC ... G ... 810 743-1600
Burton *(G-2142)*
Adept Tool & Mold Inc ... G ... 269 461-3765
Eau Claire *(G-4737)*
Adrian Precision Machining LLC ... E ... 517 263-4564
Adrian *(G-45)*
Adrian Tool Corporation ... E ... 517 263-6530
Adrian *(G-48)*
Advance Tool Co ... F ... 231 587-5286
Mancelona *(G-10385)*
Advanced Auto Trends Inc ... E ... 248 628-4850
Oxford *(G-12334)*
▲ Advanced Integ Tooling Solns ... C ... 586 749-5525
Chesterfield *(G-2733)*
Advanced Mold Solutions ... G ... 586 468-6883
Clinton Township *(G-3038)*
▲ Advanced Special Tools Inc ... C ... 269 962-9697
Battle Creek *(G-1141)*
▼ Advanced Tooling Systems Inc ... F ... 616 784-7513
Comstock Park *(G-3459)*
Advantage Design & Tool Inc ... G ... 586 463-2800
Clinton Township *(G-3039)*
Advantage Design and Tool ... G ... 586 801-7413
Richmond *(G-13258)*
Advantage Industries Inc ... E ... 616 669-2400
Jenison *(G-8616)*
▼ Aero Foil International Inc ... E ... 231 773-0200
Muskegon *(G-11263)*
▲ Affinity Custom Molding Inc ... E ... 269 496-8423
Mendon *(G-10711)*
Aggressive Tool & Die Inc ... E ... 616 837-1983
Coopersville *(G-3547)*
Aggressive Tooling Inc ... E ... 616 754-1404
Greenville *(G-7122)*
Air-Hydraulics Inc ... F ... 517 787-9444
Jackson *(G-8377)*
Airmetal Corporation ... F ... 517 784-6000
Jackson *(G-8378)*
Al-Craft Design & Engrg Inc ... G ... 248 589-3827
Troy *(G-16181)*
Albion Machine and Tool LLC ... F ... 517 629-8838
Albion *(G-114)*
Alcona Tool & Machine Inc ... E ... 989 736-8151
Harrisville *(G-7362)*
Alcona Tool & Machine Inc ... G ... 989 736-8151
Lincoln *(G-9561)*
Alliance Industries Inc ... E ... 248 656-3473
Macomb *(G-10106)*
Alliance Tool and Machine Co ... F ... 586 427-6411
Saint Clair Shores *(G-14239)*
Allied Tool and Machine Co ... E ... 989 755-5384
Saginaw *(G-13995)*
Amber Manufacturing Inc ... G ... 586 218-6080
Fraser *(G-5615)*
American Assemblers Inc ... G ... 248 334-9777
Pontiac *(G-12803)*
American Die and Mold Inc ... G ... 231 269-3788
Buckley *(G-2128)*
American Die Corporation ... E ... 810 794-4080
Clay *(G-2993)*
American Hydro-Works Engrg LLC ... G ... 906 282-8890
Harrison *(G-7307)*
American Tooling Center Inc ... G ... 517 522-8411
Lansing *(G-9202)*
American Tooling Center Inc ... G ... 517 522-8411
Jackson *(G-8383)*
▲ American Tooling Center Inc ... D ... 517 522-8411
Grass Lake *(G-7085)*
American Vault Service ... G ... 989 366-8657
Prudenville *(G-13084)*
Anchor Danly Inc ... G ... 519 966-4431
Madison Heights *(G-10191)*
▲ Anchor Lamina America Inc ... E ... 248 489-9122
Novi *(G-11826)*
Anchor Lamina America Inc ... E ... 519 966-4431
Grand Rapids *(G-6169)*
Anitom Automation LLC ... E ... 517 278-6205
Coldwater *(G-3288)*
Apex Spring & Stamping Corp ... D ... 616 453-5463
Grand Rapids *(G-6171)*
Applied Mechanics Corporation ... G ... 616 677-1355
Grand Rapids *(G-6174)*
Arbor Gage & Tooling Inc ... E ... 616 454-8266
Grand Rapids *(G-6178)*
Argus Corporation ... E ... 313 937-2900
Redford *(G-13144)*
Armick Inc ... G ... 616 481-5882
Grand Rapids *(G-6182)*
Arnold Tool & Die Co ... E ... 586 598-0099
Chesterfield *(G-2741)*
Artiflex Manufacturing LLC ... C ... 616 459-8285
Grand Rapids *(G-6185)*
Ascent Aerospace LLC ... A ... 586 726-0500
Macomb *(G-10108)*
Assembly Concepts Inc ... E ... 989 685-2603
Rose City *(G-13759)*
Astar Inc ... E ... 574 234-2137
Niles *(G-11595)*
Athey Precision Inc ... G ... 989 386-4523
Clare *(G-2864)*
Atlantic Tool Inc ... G ... 586 954-9268
Clinton Township *(G-3057)*
Atra Plastics Inc ... F ... 734 237-3393
Plymouth *(G-12576)*
▲ Auto Craft Tool & Die Co ... E ... 810 794-4929
Clay *(G-2994)*
Auto Craft Tool & Die Co ... E ... 810 794-4929
Clay *(G-2995)*
Auto Metal Craft Inc ... E ... 248 398-2240
Oak Park *(G-12051)*
▲ Autodie LLC ... C ... 616 454-9361
Grand Rapids *(G-6192)*
Aw Carbide Fabricators Inc ... F ... 586 294-1850
Fraser *(G-5626)*
Axis Machine & Tool Inc ... G ... 616 738-2196
Holland *(G-7563)*
Axis Mold Works Inc ... F ... 616 866-2222
Rockford *(G-13558)*
B & B Mold & Engineering Inc ... G ... 586 773-6664
Warren *(G-16946)*
B & L Pattern Company ... G ... 269 982-0214
Saint Joseph *(G-14301)*
B & M Machine & Tool Company ... G ... 989 288-2934
Durand *(G-4605)*
B C Manufacturing Inc ... F ... 248 344-0101
Wixom *(G-17770)*
Bailey Roll Form Company Inc ... G ... 586 777-4890
Warren *(G-16951)*
▲ Baker Industries Inc ... C ... 586 286-4900
Macomb *(G-10111)*
Bauer Precision Tool Co ... G ... 586 758-7370
Warren *(G-16953)*
Baumann Tool & Die ... G ... 616 772-6768
Zeeland *(G-18116)*
Bawden Industries Inc ... F ... 734 721-6414
Romulus *(G-13655)*
Baxter Machine & Tool Co ... E ... 517 782-2808
Jackson *(G-8388)*
Bay Area Tool LLC ... G ... 231 946-3500
Traverse City *(G-15905)*
Bay Products Inc ... E ... 586 296-7130
Fraser *(G-5628)*
▲ Bekum America Corporation ... C ... 517 655-4331
Williamston *(G-17727)*
Bel-Kur Inc ... E ... 734 847-0651
Temperance *(G-15823)*
Benteler Automotive Corp ... B ... 616 247-3936
Auburn Hills *(G-791)*
Berg Tool Inc ... F ... 586 646-7100
Chesterfield *(G-2745)*
▲ Bernal LLC ... D ... 248 299-3600
Rochester Hills *(G-13377)*
Bessey Tool & Die Inc ... F ... 616 887-8820
Sparta *(G-15088)*
Best Tool & Engineering Co ... F ... 586 792-4119
Clinton Township *(G-3066)*
Betz Contracting Inc ... G ... 269 746-3320
Climax *(G-3012)*
Big 3 Precision Products Inc ... E ... 313 846-6601
Dearborn *(G-3682)*
Bilco Tool Corporation ... G ... 586 574-9300
Warren *(G-16959)*
Blackledge Tool Inc ... G ... 989 865-8393
Saint Charles *(G-14190)*
Boda Corporation ... G ... 906 353-7320
Chassell *(G-2672)*
Bold Ammo & Guns Inc ... G ... 616 826-0913
Rockford *(G-13559)*
Bolman Die Services Inc ... F ... 810 919-2262
Sterling Heights *(G-15276)*
Bonal Technologies Inc ... F ... 248 582-0900
Royal Oak *(G-13910)*
Borgia Die & Engineering Inc ... F ... 616 677-3595
Marne *(G-10505)*
Borgman Tool & Engineering LLC ... G ... 231 733-4133
Muskegon *(G-11283)*
Boyers Tool and Die Inc ... G ... 517 782-7869
Jackson *(G-8394)*
Bradford Tool & Die Company ... G ... 810 664-8653
Lapeer *(G-9444)*
Bradley-Thompson Tool Company ... E ... 248 352-1466
Southfield *(G-14855)*
Bravo Machine and Tool Inc ... F ... 586 790-3463
Clinton Township *(G-3069)*
Bridge Tool and Die LLC ... G ... 231 269-3200
Buckley *(G-2129)*
Briggs Industries Inc ... E ... 586 749-5191
Chesterfield *(G-2747)*
Briggs Mold & Die Inc ... G ... 517 784-6908
Jackson *(G-8395)*
Bry Mac Inc ... F ... 231 799-2211
Norton Shores *(G-11741)*
Btm National Holdings LLC ... F ... 616 794-0100
Belding *(G-1404)*
Btmc Holdings Inc ... G ... 616 794-0100
Belding *(G-1405)*
Buckingham Tool Corp ... F ... 734 591-2333
Livonia *(G-9671)*
Buiter Tool & Die Inc ... E ... 616 455-7410
Grand Rapids *(G-6239)*
▲ Burkland Inc ... D ... 810 636-2233
Goodrich *(G-5952)*
Byrne Tool & Die Inc ... F ... 616 866-4479
Rockford *(G-13562)*
Byrnes Manufacturing Co LLC ... G ... 810 664-3686
Lapeer *(G-9446)*
Byrnes Tool Co Inc ... G ... 810 664-3686
Lapeer *(G-9447)*
C & D Tool & Die Company Inc ... E ... 248 922-5937
Davisburg *(G-3628)*
C & H Stamping Inc ... E ... 517 750-3600
Jackson *(G-8396)*
C & M Tool LLC ... G ... 734 944-3355
Saline *(G-14380)*
C & N Manufacturing Inc ... E ... 586 293-9150
Fraser *(G-5633)*
C & R Tool Die ... G ... 231 584-3588
Alba *(G-112)*
Cad CAM Services Inc ... F ... 616 554-5222
Grand Rapids *(G-6250)*
Cadillac Tool and Die Inc ... G ... 231 775-9007
Cadillac *(G-2240)*
Cambria Tool and Machine Inc ... F ... 517 437-3500
Hillsdale *(G-7520)*
Cambron Engineering Inc ... E ... 989 684-5890
Bay City *(G-1293)*
▲ Cameron Tool Corporation ... D ... 517 487-3671
Lansing *(G-9353)*

S I C

Employee Codes: A=Over 500 employees, B=251-500
C=101-250, D=51-100, E=20-50, F=10-19, G=3-9
2020 Harris Michigan
Industrial Directory
809

Cammand Machining LLC.....F 586 752-0366
Romeo *(G-13625)*
Carlet Tool Inc.....G....... 248 435-0319
Clawson *(G-2974)*
Carroll Tool and Die Co.....E 586 949-7670
Macomb *(G-10114)*
Cascade Metal Works Inc.....F 616 868-0668
Alto *(G-325)*
Cascade Tool & Die Inc.....G....... 269 429-2210
Saint Joseph *(G-14304)*
Case Diamond Linear.....G....... 800 293-2496
Rochester Hills *(G-13387)*
Cav Tool Company.....F 248 349-7860
Novi *(G-11845)*
CBS Tool Inc.....F 586 566-5945
Shelby Township *(G-14558)*
Centennial Technologies Inc.....E 989 752-6167
Saginaw *(G-14013)*
Center Line Gage Inc.....G....... 810 387-4300
Brockway *(G-2019)*
Centerline Engineering Inc.....D....... 616 735-2506
Comstock Park *(G-3466)*
Central Industrial Mfg Inc.....F 231 347-5920
Harbor Springs *(G-7277)*
Centurn Machine & Tool Inc.....G....... 231 947-4773
Traverse City *(G-15931)*
▲ **Century Inc**.....C 231 947-6400
Traverse City *(G-15932)*
Century Inc.....G....... 231 946-7500
Traverse City *(G-15933)*
Century Inc.....D....... 231 941-7800
Traverse City *(G-15934)*
Century Tool & Gage LLC.....D....... 810 629-0784
Fenton *(G-5193)*
Certified Metal Products Inc.....F 586 598-1000
Clinton Township *(G-3077)*
CG Automation & Fixture Inc.....E 616 785-5400
Comstock Park *(G-3467)*
Champion Die Incorporated.....E 616 784-2397
Comstock Park *(G-3469)*
Charlies Wood Shop.....F 989 845-2632
Chesaning *(G-2722)*
Choice Corporation.....E 586 783-5600
Clinton Township *(G-3078)*
▲ **Choice Mold Components Inc**.....E 586 783-5600
Clinton Township *(G-3079)*
Christensen Fiberglass LLC.....E 616 738-1219
Holland *(G-7589)*
Circle C Mold & Plastics Group.....F 269 496-5515
Mendon *(G-10712)*
Circle Engineering Inc.....G....... 586 978-8120
Sterling Heights *(G-15289)*
Class A Tool & Machine LLC.....G....... 231 788-3822
Muskegon *(G-11294)*
▲ **Classic Die Inc**.....E 616 454-3760
Grand Rapids *(G-6277)*
Cleary Developments Inc.....E 248 588-6614
Madison Heights *(G-10211)*
Cole Tooling Systems Inc.....F 586 573-9450
Lake Orion *(G-9130)*
Coles Machine Service Inc.....E 810 658-5373
Davison *(G-3642)*
Colonial Mold Inc.....E 586 469-4944
Clinton Township *(G-3083)*
Columbia Marking Tools Inc.....E 586 949-8400
Chesterfield *(G-2754)*
▲ **Commercial Mfg & Assembly Inc**.....E 616 847-9980
Grand Haven *(G-6005)*
Company Products Inc.....G....... 586 757-6160
Warren *(G-16989)*
Complete Surface Technologies.....E 586 493-5800
Clinton Township *(G-3086)*
Concept Molds Inc.....E 269 679-2100
Schoolcraft *(G-14493)*
Concept Tool & Die Inc.....G....... 616 875-4600
Zeeland *(G-18125)*
Concept Tooling Systems Inc.....E 616 301-6906
Grand Rapids *(G-6298)*
▲ **Concord Tool and Mfg Inc**.....C 586 465-6537
Mount Clemens *(G-11127)*
Connell Limited Partnership.....D....... 989 875-5135
Ithaca *(G-8358)*
Contour Mold Corporation.....G....... 810 245-4070
Lapeer *(G-9451)*
Contour Tool & Engineering Inc.....G....... 616 772-6360
Zeeland *(G-18126)*
Convex Mold Inc.....G....... 586 978-0808
Sterling Heights *(G-15299)*
Corban Industries Inc.....D....... 248 393-2720
Orion *(G-12177)*

Craft Industries Inc.....A....... 586 726-4300
Shelby Township *(G-14570)*
Crash Tool Inc.....F 517 552-0250
Howell *(G-8025)*
Creative Steel Rule Dies Inc.....F 630 307-8880
Grand Rapids *(G-6315)*
Creative Techniques Inc.....D....... 248 373-3050
Orion *(G-12178)*
Cs Tool Engineering Inc.....E 616 696-0940
Cedar Springs *(G-2552)*
CTS Manufacturing Inc.....G....... 586 465-4594
Clinton Township *(G-3094)*
Custer Tool & Mfg LLC.....G....... 734 854-5943
Lambertville *(G-9182)*
Custom Design Inc.....E 269 323-8561
Portage *(G-12990)*
Custom Tool & Die Service Inc.....G....... 616 662-1068
Hudsonville *(G-8153)*
Custom Tool and Die Co.....E 269 465-9130
Stevensville *(G-15560)*
Custom Tooling Systems Inc.....D....... 616 748-9880
Zeeland *(G-18130)*
Cutting Edge Technologies Inc.....F 616 738-0800
Holland *(G-7602)*
D & F Corporation.....D....... 586 254-5300
Sterling Heights *(G-15306)*
D & F Mold LLC.....F 269 465-6633
Bridgman *(G-1862)*
D & L Tooling Inc.....G....... 517 369-5655
Bronson *(G-2022)*
D W Machine Inc.....F 517 787-9929
Jackson *(G-8426)*
◆ **D-M-E USA Inc**.....E 616 754-4601
Greenville *(G-7126)*
Danly IEM.....G....... 800 243-2659
Grand Rapids *(G-6335)*
▲ **Datum Industries LLC**.....D....... 616 977-1995
Grand Rapids *(G-6336)*
Davis Steel Rule Die.....G....... 269 492-9908
Kalamazoo *(G-8723)*
Dayton Lamina Corp.....G....... 231 533-8646
Bellaire *(G-1437)*
DD Parker Enterprises Inc.....E 734 241-6898
Monroe *(G-11027)*
De Luxe Die Set Inc.....G....... 810 227-2556
Brighton *(G-1910)*
Dehring Mold E-D-M.....G....... 269 683-5970
Niles *(G-11607)*
Deland Manufacturing Inc.....E 586 323-2350
Shelby Township *(G-14574)*
Delta Precision Inc.....G....... 586 415-9005
Fraser *(G-5641)*
▲ **Demmer Corporation**.....C 517 321-3600
Lansing *(G-9217)*
Deppe Mold & Tooling Inc.....E 616 530-1331
Grandville *(G-7027)*
Detroit Steel Treating Company.....E 248 334-7436
Pontiac *(G-12816)*
Dexter Automatic Products Co.....C 734 426-8900
Dexter *(G-4485)*
Dexter Roll Form Company.....G....... 586 573-6930
Warren *(G-17001)*
▲ **Diamond Case Holdings LLC**.....G....... 800 293-2496
Pontiac *(G-12817)*
Diamond Die and Mold Company.....F 586 791-0700
Clinton Township *(G-3102)*
Die & Slide Technologies Inc.....G....... 810 326-0986
China *(G-2859)*
Die Tech Services Inc.....E 616 363-6604
Walker *(G-16865)*
Die-Mold-Automation Component.....G....... 313 581-6510
Dearborn *(G-3693)*
Die-Namic Inc.....C 734 710-3200
Van Buren Twp *(G-16759)*
Die-Namic Tool & Design Llc.....F 517 787-4900
Jackson *(G-8433)*
Die-Namic Tool Corp.....G....... 616 954-7882
Grand Rapids *(G-6350)*
Die-Tech and Engineering Inc.....E 616 530-9030
Grand Rapids *(G-6351)*
Die-Verse Solutions LLC.....F 616 384-3550
Coopersville *(G-3557)*
Diecrafters Inc.....G....... 734 425-8000
Livonia *(G-9711)*
Dietech North America LLC.....D....... 586 771-8580
Roseville *(G-13795)*
▲ **Digital Tool & Die Inc**.....E 616 532-8020
Grandville *(G-7028)*
Diversified Tool & Engineering.....F 734 692-1260
Grosse Ile *(G-7170)*

Dixon & Ryan Corporation.....F 248 549-4000
Royal Oak *(G-13919)*
DK Tool & Machine Inc.....G....... 517 369-1401
Bronson *(G-2024)*
▲ **Dlt Industries Inc**.....G....... 616 754-2762
Greenville *(G-7128)*
Dm Tool & Fab Inc.....D....... 586 726-8390
Sterling Heights *(G-15319)*
▲ **Dme Company LLC**.....B....... 248 398-6000
Madison Heights *(G-10233)*
Do Rite Tool Inc.....G....... 734 522-7510
Garden City *(G-5822)*
Dolphin Manufacturing Inc.....E 734 946-6322
Taylor *(G-15707)*
Douglas King Industries Inc.....E 989 642-2865
Hemlock *(G-7461)*
▲ **DPM Manufacturing LLC**.....F 248 349-6375
Livonia *(G-9715)*
Dr & HI Mold & Machine In.....G....... 989 746-9290
Saginaw *(G-14029)*
Drive System Integration Inc.....G....... 248 568-7750
Beverly Hills *(G-1616)*
Ds Mold LLC.....E 616 794-1639
Belding *(G-1411)*
Du Val Industries LLC.....E 586 737-2710
Sterling Heights *(G-15321)*
Dubetsky K9 Academy LLC.....F 586 997-1717
Shelby Township *(G-14580)*
Dubois Production Services Inc.....E 616 785-0088
Comstock Park *(G-3480)*
▲ **Dura Mold Inc**.....D....... 269 465-3301
Stevensville *(G-15565)*
Dura Thread Gage Inc.....F 248 545-2890
Madison Heights *(G-10236)*
Dynamic Corporation.....D....... 616 399-9391
Holland *(G-7613)*
Dynamic Jig Grinding Corp.....E 248 589-3110
Troy *(G-16330)*
Dynamic Plastics Inc.....E 586 749-6100
Chesterfield *(G-2768)*
E D M Specialties Inc.....G....... 248 344-4080
Novi *(G-11875)*
E Z Tool Inc.....G....... 269 429-0070
Stevensville *(G-15566)*
▲ **E-T-M Enterprises I Inc**.....C 517 627-8461
Grand Ledge *(G-6105)*
Eagle Indus Group Federal LLC.....G....... 616 863-8623
Grand Rapids *(G-6365)*
Eagle Masking Fabrication Inc.....G....... 586 992-3080
Sterling Heights *(G-15326)*
East River Machine & Tool Inc.....G....... 231 767-1701
Muskegon *(G-11314)*
Eclipse Tool & Die Inc.....E 616 877-3717
Wayland *(G-17405)*
▲ **Edmar Manufacturing Inc**.....D....... 616 392-7218
Holland *(G-7618)*
Edwards Machining Inc.....E 517 782-2568
Jackson *(G-8441)*
Eifel Mold & Engineering Inc.....E 586 296-9640
Fraser *(G-5648)*
Eimo Technologies Inc.....D....... 269 649-5031
Vicksburg *(G-16835)*
▲ **Eimo Technologies Inc**.....E 269 649-0545
Vicksburg *(G-16834)*
▼ **Ekstrom Industries Inc**.....D....... 248 477-0040
Novi *(G-11881)*
Elite Mold & Engineering Inc.....E 586 873-1770
Shelby Township *(G-14586)*
Ellis Machine & Tool Co Inc.....G....... 734 847-4113
Temperance *(G-15827)*
Emcor Inc.....F 989 667-0652
Bay City *(G-1308)*
EMD Wire Tek.....G....... 810 235-5344
Flint *(G-5424)*
Emmie Die and Engineering Corp.....G....... 810 346-2914
Brown City *(G-2050)*
Empire Machine Company.....F 269 684-3713
Saint Joseph *(G-14309)*
▲ **Engineered Tooling Systems Inc**.....F 616 647-5063
Grand Rapids *(G-6380)*
Enkon LLC.....F 937 890-5678
Manchester *(G-10405)*
Enmark Tool Company.....E 586 293-2797
Fraser *(G-5651)*
Enterprise Tool & Die LLC.....D....... 616 538-0920
Grandville *(G-7033)*
Enterprise Tool and Gear Inc.....D....... 989 269-9797
Bad Axe *(G-1060)*
Envisiontec Inc.....D....... 313 436-4300
Dearborn *(G-3702)*

SIC SECTION 35 INDUSTRIAL AND COMMERCIAL MACHINERY AND COMPUTER EQUIPMENT

Epic Machine Inc E 810 629-9400
Fenton *(G-5204)*
ERA Tool & Engineering Co F 810 227-3509
Livonia *(G-9730)*
▲ **Erwin Quarder Inc** D 616 575-1600
Grand Rapids *(G-6383)*
Everson Tool & Machine Ltd F 906 932-3440
Ironwood *(G-8327)*
Evolution Tool Inc G 810 664-5500
Lapeer *(G-9460)*
Excell Machine & Tool Co LLC G 231 728-1210
Muskegon *(G-11318)*
▲ **Exco Extrusion Dies Inc** C 586 749-5400
Chesterfield *(G-2774)*
Experi-Metal Inc C 586 977-7800
Sterling Heights *(G-15335)*
Experienced Concepts Inc F 586 752-4200
Armada *(G-719)*
Expert Machine & Tool Inc G 810 984-2323
Port Huron *(G-12917)*
Express Machine & Tool Co G 586 758-5080
Warren *(G-17027)*
▲ **Extreme Tool and Engrg Inc** D 906 229-9100
Wakefield *(G-16850)*
Extreme Wire EDM Service Inc G 616 249-3901
Grandville *(G-7035)*
Extrusion Punch & Tool Inc E 248 689-3300
Troy *(G-16357)*
F & F Mold Inc G 517 287-5866
North Adams *(G-11654)*
F J Lucido & Associates E 586 574-3577
Warren *(G-17028)*
Fair Industries LLC C 248 740-7841
Troy *(G-16359)*
Fairlane Co E 586 294-6100
Fraser *(G-5653)*
Falcon Corporation E 616 842-7071
Spring Lake *(G-15141)*
Falcon Industry Inc F 586 468-7010
Clinton Township *(G-3113)*
Falcon Lakeside Mfg Inc E 269 429-6193
Stevensville *(G-15567)*
FCA US LLC A 313 369-7312
Detroit *(G-4053)*
Federal Screw Works E 810 227-7712
Brighton *(G-1922)*
Feg Gage Inc F 248 616-3631
Madison Heights *(G-10252)*
Fega Tool & Gage Company F 586 469-4400
Clinton Township *(G-3114)*
▲ **Fischer Tool & Die Corp** D 734 847-4788
Temperance *(G-15828)*
◆ **Fisher Kellering Co** G 586 749-6616
Chesterfield *(G-2775)*
Fitz-Rite Products Inc E 248 528-8440
Troy *(G-16366)*
Five Star Industries Inc E 586 786-0500
Macomb *(G-10122)*
▲ **Fixtureworks LLC** G 586 294-6100
Fraser *(G-5654)*
Flagler Corporation E 586 749-6300
Chesterfield *(G-2776)*
Flannery Machine & Tool Inc E 231 587-5076
Mancelona *(G-10391)*
Florance Turning Company Inc G 248 347-0068
Northville *(G-11691)*
Forge Die & Tool Corp E 248 477-0020
Farmington Hills *(G-5004)*
Formfab LLC E 248 844-3676
Rochester Hills *(G-13427)*
Forrest Company G 269 384-6120
Kalamazoo *(G-8747)*
Fortune Tool & Machine Inc E 248 669-9119
Wixom *(G-17813)*
Four Star Tooling & Engrg Inc G 586 264-4090
Sterling Heights *(G-15346)*
Four-Way Tool and Die Inc E 248 585-8255
Troy *(G-16372)*
Four-Way Tool and Die Inc E 248 585-8255
Troy *(G-16373)*
Foust Electro Mold Inc G 517 439-1062
Hillsdale *(G-7524)*
Fowlerville Machine Tool Inc G 517 223-8871
Fowlerville *(G-5566)*
Franchino Mold & Engrg Co D 517 321-5609
Lansing *(G-9231)*
Frankfort Manufacturing Inc E 231 352-7551
Frankfort *(G-5601)*
Freedom Tool & Mfg Co G 231 788-2898
Muskegon *(G-11327)*
▲ **Freer Tool & Die Inc** E 586 463-3200
Clinton Township *(G-3124)*
Freer Tool & Die Inc G 586 741-5274
Clinton Township *(G-3125)*
▲ **Frimo Inc** C 248 668-3160
Wixom *(G-17814)*
Fulgham Machine & Tool Company G 517 937-8316
Jackson *(G-8453)*
Futuramic Tool & Engrg Co C 586 758-2200
Warren *(G-17046)*
Future Mold Corporation D 989 588-9948
Farwell *(G-5161)*
G & F Tool Products E 517 663-3646
Eaton Rapids *(G-4724)*
▲ **G & G Die and Engineering Inc** E 586 716-8099
Ira *(G-8256)*
G & L Tool Inc F 734 728-1990
Westland *(G-17559)*
G A Machine Company Inc G 313 836-5646
Detroit *(G-4074)*
G F Proto-Type Plaster Inc E 586 296-2750
Fraser *(G-5656)*
Gage Eagle Spline Inc D 586 776-7240
Warren *(G-17049)*
Gage Pattern & Model Inc E 248 361-6609
Madison Heights *(G-10255)*
Garden City Products Inc F 269 684-6264
Niles *(G-11614)*
Gemini Precision Machining Inc C 989 269-9702
Bad Axe *(G-1064)*
Gemini Precision Machining Inc D 989 269-9702
Bad Axe *(G-1065)*
General Die & Engineering Inc E 616 698-6961
Grand Rapids *(G-6435)*
General Motors LLC B 810 236-1970
Flint *(G-5436)*
Generation Tool Inc G 734 641-6937
Westland *(G-17561)*
Gill Holding Company Inc E 616 559-2700
Grand Rapids *(G-6440)*
◆ **Gill Industries Inc** C 616 559-2700
Grand Rapids *(G-6441)*
Gladwin Machine Inc G 989 426-8753
Gladwin *(G-5930)*
Gleason Holbrook Mfg Co F 586 749-5519
Ray *(G-13133)*
Global Engineering Inc E 586 566-0423
Shelby Township *(G-14596)*
▲ **Globe Tech LLC** E 734 656-2200
Plymouth *(G-12630)*
Glycon Corp E 517 423-8356
Tecumseh *(G-15795)*
Gollnick Tool Co G 586 755-0100
Warren *(G-17061)*
Gonzalez Prod Systems Inc G 248 209-1836
Oak Park *(G-12071)*
Grandville Industries Inc D 616 538-0920
Grandville *(G-7039)*
Granite Precision Tool Corp G 248 299-8317
Rochester Hills *(G-13435)*
Gray Bros Stamping & Mch Inc E 269 483-7615
White Pigeon *(G-17649)*
Great Lakes Jig & Fixture G 269 795-4349
Middleville *(G-10803)*
Greenfield Die & Mfg Corp C 734 454-4000
Canton *(G-2379)*
▲ **Greenville Tool & Die Co** C 616 754-5693
Greenville *(G-7135)*
Griffin Tool Inc E 269 429-4077
Stevensville *(G-15569)*
Grosse Tool and Machine Co E 586 773-6770
Warren *(G-17068)*
Group B Industries Inc G 734 941-6640
Romulus *(G-13683)*
▲ **Grw Technologies Inc** C 616 575-8119
Grand Rapids *(G-6483)*
H & M Machining Inc F 586 778-5028
Roseville *(G-13814)*
H & S Mold Inc F 989 732-3566
Gaylord *(G-5864)*
H B D M Inc G 269 273-1976
Three Rivers *(G-15864)*
H B D M Inc F 269 273-1976
Three Rivers *(G-15865)*
▼ **H S Die & Engineering Inc** C 616 453-5451
Grand Rapids *(G-6488)*
Hacker Machine Inc F 517 569-3348
Rives Junction *(G-13308)*
Hallmark Tool and Gage Co Inc E 248 669-4010
Wixom *(G-17821)*
Hanson International Inc G 269 429-5555
Saint Joseph *(G-14315)*
Hanson International Inc D 269 429-5555
Saint Joseph *(G-14316)*
Harbrook Tool Inc F 248 477-8040
Novi *(G-11895)*
Hard Milling Solutions Inc G 586 286-2300
Bruce Twp *(G-2083)*
Hardy-Reed Tool & Die Co Inc F 517 547-7107
Manitou Beach *(G-10448)*
Harper Machine Tool Inc G 586 756-0140
Warren *(G-17077)*
Harris Tooling G 269 465-5870
Stevensville *(G-15571)*
Hatch Stamping Company LLC C 517 540-1021
Howell *(G-8047)*
Havercroft Tool & Die Inc G 989 724-5913
Greenbush *(G-7120)*
HB Carbide Company D 989 786-4223
Lewiston *(G-9550)*
Heinzmann D Tool & Die Inc F 248 363-5115
Commerce Township *(G-3410)*
Hercules Machine Tl & Die LLC E 586 778-4120
Fraser *(G-5661)*
Hhi Formtech LLC E 586 415-2000
Fraser *(G-5662)*
Hi-Craft Engineering Inc D 586 293-0551
Fraser *(G-5663)*
Hi-Tech Mold & Engineering Inc E 248 844-0722
Rochester Hills *(G-13441)*
Hi-Tech Mold & Engineering Inc F 248 844-9159
Rochester Hills *(G-13442)*
▲ **Hi-Tech Mold & Engineering Inc** E 248 852-6600
Rochester Hills *(G-13443)*
▼ **Highland Engineering Inc** E 517 548-4372
Howell *(G-8048)*
Highwood Die & Engineering Inc E 248 338-1807
Pontiac *(G-12835)*
Hill Machinery Co D 616 940-2800
Grand Rapids *(G-6514)*
Hillman Extrusion Tool Inc G 989 736-8010
Lincoln *(G-9563)*
Hite Tool Co Inc G 734 422-1777
Garden City *(G-5826)*
Hogle Sales & Mfg LLC G 517 592-1980
Brooklyn *(G-2038)*
▲ **Holland Plastics Corporation** E 616 844-2505
Grand Haven *(G-6037)*
Holland Tool & Die LLC G 269 751-5862
Holland *(G-7679)*
Homestead Tool and Machine E 989 465-6182
Coleman *(G-3344)*
HQT Inc G 248 589-7960
Madison Heights *(G-10270)*
Hti Cybernetics Inc E 586 826-8346
Sterling Heights *(G-15369)*
Hub Tool and Machine Inc G 586 772-7866
Chesterfield *(G-2785)*
▲ **Huron Tool & Engineering Co** E 989 269-9927
Bad Axe *(G-1068)*
Huron Tool & Gage Co Inc G 313 381-1900
Wixom *(G-17830)*
I & G Tool Co Inc E 586 777-7690
New Baltimore *(G-11485)*
I E & E Industries Inc F 248 544-8181
Madison Heights *(G-10272)*
I M F Inc G 269 948-2345
Hastings *(G-7415)*
Idel LLC G 231 929-3195
Traverse City *(G-16001)*
Illinois Tool Works Inc D 248 589-2500
Troy *(G-16410)*
Imperial Engineering Inc G 248 588-2022
Troy *(G-16412)*
▲ **Inalfa/Ssi Roof Systems LLC** D 586 758-6620
Warren *(G-17086)*
Incoe Corporation C 248 616-0220
Auburn Hills *(G-910)*
Incoe International Inc G 248 616-0220
Auburn Hills *(G-911)*
Independent Die Association G 586 773-9000
Warren *(G-17087)*
Independent Tool and Mfg Co E 269 521-4811
Allegan *(G-165)*
Industrial Converting Inc F 586 757-8820
Warren *(G-17091)*
▲ **Industrial Tooling Tech Inc** F 231 766-2155
Muskegon *(G-11347)*
▲ **Inglass Usa Inc** F 616 228-6900
Byron Center *(G-2195)*

S I C

Employee Codes: A=Over 500 employees, B=251-500
C=101-250, D=51-100, E=20-50, F=10-19, G=3-9
2020 Harris Michigan
Industrial Directory
811

35 INDUSTRIAL AND COMMERCIAL MACHINERY AND COMPUTER EQUIPMENT SIC SECTION

Innovative Mold Inc.................................E....... 586 752-2996
Washington (G-17305)
Integrity Fab & Machine Inc ....F....... 989 481-3200
Breckenridge (G-1843)
International Mech Design ....E....... 248 546-5740
Royal Oak (G-13936)
International Mold Corporation ....G....... 586 801-2314
Clinton Township (G-3142)
▲ International Mold Corporation ....D....... 586 783-6890
Clinton Township (G-3143)
Invo Spline Inc..E....... 586 757-8840
Warren (G-17097)
Iq Manufacturing LLC............................G....... 586 634-7185
Auburn Hills (G-915)
Iron Tool & Die Inc ....G....... 586 791-1389
Clinton Township (G-3145)
ITT Gage Inc ....G....... 231 766-2155
Muskegon (G-11350)
J & C Industries Inc ....G....... 248 549-4866
Royal Oak (G-13937)
J C Manufacturing Company ....G....... 586 757-2713
Warren (G-17106)
J M Kusch Inc..E....... 989 684-8820
Bay City (G-1323)
J M Mold Technologies Inc ....F....... 586 773-6664
Warren (G-17109)
▲ Jacobsen Industries Inc...................D....... 734 591-6111
Livonia (G-9791)
Jamesway Tool and Die Inc ....E....... 616 396-3731
Holland (G-7693)
Jay/Enn Corporation...............................D....... 248 588-2393
Troy (G-16433)
Jbl Systems Inc.......................................G....... 586 802-6700
Shelby Township (G-14609)
JCs Tool & Mfg Co Inc...........................E....... 989 892-8975
Essexville (G-4873)
Jeffery Tool & Mfg Co.............................F....... 586 307-8846
Clinton Township (G-3148)
▲ Jemar Tool Inc...................................E....... 586 726-6960
Shelby Township (G-14610)
Jems of Litchfield Inc ....F....... 517 542-5367
Litchfield (G-9605)
Jerrys Tool & Die.....................................G....... 989 732-4689
Gaylord (G-5868)
Jet Gage & Tool Inc.................................G....... 586 294-3770
Fraser (G-5674)
▲ Jimdi Plastics Inc................................E....... 616 895-7766
Allendale (G-219)
Jirgens Modern Tool Corp ....F....... 269 381-5588
Kalamazoo (G-8778)
Jo-Ad Industries Inc ....E....... 248 588-4810
Madison Heights (G-10284)
▼ Jo-Mar Industries Inc.........................F....... 248 588-9625
Troy (G-16439)
Joggle Tool & Die Co Inc........................G....... 586 792-7477
Clinton Township (G-3150)
John Lamantia Corporation....................G....... 269 428-8100
Stevensville (G-15572)
Johnson Precision Mold & Engrg ....G....... 269 651-2553
Sturgis (G-15609)
Jolico/J-B Tool Inc ....E....... 586 739-5555
Shelby Township (G-14611)
Jordan Manufacturing Company...........E....... 616 794-0900
Belding (G-1421)
Jordan Tool Corporation ....E....... 586 755-6700
Warren (G-17117)
K & K Precision Tool LLC.......................G....... 586 294-1030
Sterling Heights (G-15385)
K & T Tool and Die Inc ....F....... 616 884-5900
Rockford (G-13575)
K and K Machine Tools Inc ....G....... 586 463-1177
Clinton Township (G-3152)
▲ K&K Stamping Company ....E....... 586 443-7900
Saint Clair Shores (G-14257)
K-B Tool Corporation..............................G....... 586 795-9003
Sterling Heights (G-15386)
▲ K-Tool Corporation Michigan............D....... 863 603-0777
Plymouth (G-12661)
Kapex Manufacturing LLC ....G....... 989 928-4993
Saginaw (G-14069)
Karr Unlimited Inc...................................G....... 231 652-9045
Newaygo (G-11571)
Katai Machine Shop................................F....... 269 465-6051
Bridgman (G-1868)
KDI Technologies Inc..............................D....... 616 667-1600
Jenison (G-8631)
Keenan Enterprises Inc..........................G....... 231 943-0516
Traverse City (G-16016)
Keller Tool Ltd ....D....... 734 425-4500
Livonia (G-9794)
Kemco Inc..G....... 517 543-2888
Eaton Rapids (G-4727)
Kendor Steel Rule Die Inc ....E....... 586 293-7111
Fraser (G-5678)
Kent Tool and Die Inc ....F....... 586 949-6600
Chesterfield (G-2796)
Kentwater Tool & Mfg Co ....G....... 616 784-7171
Comstock Park (G-3489)
Kenyon Specialties Inc...........................G....... 810 686-3190
Clio (G-3274)
Kern Industries Inc ....E....... 248 349-4866
Novi (G-11914)
Ketchum Machine Corporated...............F....... 616 765-5101
Freeport (G-5765)
Key Casting Company Inc......................G....... 269 426-3800
Sawyer (G-14486)
Kidder Machine Company......................G....... 231 775-9271
Cadillac (G-2258)
Kimastle Corporation ....D....... 586 949-2355
Chesterfield (G-2797)
Kinney Tool and Die Inc ....D....... 616 997-0901
Coopersville (G-3562)
Kirmin Die & Tool Inc..............................E....... 734 722-9210
Romulus (G-13697)
Koch Limited ....G....... 586 296-3103
Fraser (G-5679)
Komarnicki Tool & Die Company ....E....... 586 776-9300
Roseville (G-13825)
Koppy Corporation ....D....... 248 373-1900
Royal Oak (G-13942)
▲ Kraftube Inc..C....... 231 832-5562
Reed City (G-13217)
Kremin Inc ....E....... 989 790-5147
Frankenmuth (G-5592)
Krieger Craftsmen Inc ....E....... 616 735-9200
Grand Rapids (G-6591)
Kriseler Welding Inc ....G....... 989 624-9266
Birch Run (G-1664)
Krt Precision Tool & Mfg Co ....G....... 517 783-5715
Jackson (G-8490)
Kurek Tool Inc ....F....... 989 777-5300
Saginaw (G-14075)
Kwik Tech Inc..E....... 586 268-6201
Shelby Township (G-14617)
Kwk Industries Inc...................................G....... 269 423-6213
Decatur (G-3804)
L & L Machine & Tool Inc........................G....... 517 784-5575
Jackson (G-8491)
L & M Tool Co Inc....................................F....... 586 677-4700
Macomb (G-10136)
L S Machining Inc ....G....... 248 583-7277
Troy (G-16454)
Lab Tool and Engineering Corp.............E....... 517 750-4131
Spring Arbor (G-15124)
Labor Aiding Systems Corp...................E....... 517 768-7478
Jackson (G-8493)
Laingsburg Screw Inc.............................G....... 517 651-2757
Laingsburg (G-9080)
Lake Design and Mfg Co ....G....... 616 794-0290
Belding (G-1424)
Lakeshore Mold and Die LLC.................G....... 269 429-6764
Stevensville (G-15575)
Lakeside Manufacturing Co...................E....... 269 429-6193
Stevensville (G-15576)
Lakeview Quality Tool Inc ....G....... 989 732-6417
Gaylord (G-5873)
Lambert Industries Inc ....F....... 734 668-6864
Ann Arbor (G-525)
Lane Tool and Mfg Corp ....G....... 248 528-1606
Troy (G-16457)
▲ Lapeer Industries Inc.........................C....... 810 664-1816
Lapeer (G-9467)
Laser North Inc..G....... 906 353-6090
Baraga (G-1107)
Lasercutting Services Inc ....F....... 616 975-2000
Grand Rapids (G-6619)
Latin American Industries LLC..............G....... 616 301-1878
Grand Rapids (G-6622)
Lavalier Corp...E....... 248 616-8880
Troy (G-16458)
Lc Manufacturing LLC ....C....... 231 839-7102
Lake City (G-9090)
Lca Mold & Engineering Inc...................G....... 269 651-1193
Sturgis (G-15612)
Leader Tool Company - HB Inc.............D....... 989 479-3281
Harbor Beach (G-7269)
Leeward Tool Inc.....................................G....... 586 754-7200
Warren (G-17126)
Legacy Precision Molds Inc...................G....... 616 532-6536
Grandville (G-7055)
Lenway Machine Company Inc..............G....... 269 751-5183
Hamilton (G-7235)
Leonard Machine Tool Systems ....E....... 586 757-8040
Warren (G-17127)
▲ Leroy Tool & Die Inc ....D....... 231 768-4336
Leroy (G-9533)
Lester Detterbeck Entps Ltd..................E....... 906 265-5121
Iron River (G-8314)
Levannes Inc ....F....... 269 327-4484
Portage (G-13007)
▲ Liberty Manufacturing Company......E....... 269 327-0997
Portage (G-13008)
Liberty Tool Inc ....E....... 586 726-2449
Sterling Heights (G-15398)
▼ Lincoln Park Die & Tool Co...............E....... 734 285-1680
Brownstown (G-2067)
Lincoln Tool Co Inc.................................G....... 989 736-8711
Harrisville (G-7364)
Line Precision Inc...................................E....... 248 474-5280
Farmington Hills (G-5044)
Link Tool & Mfg Co LLC ....D....... 734 710-0010
Westland (G-17577)
Lloyd Tool & Mfg Corp............................E....... 810 694-3519
Grand Blanc (G-5973)
Lomar Machine & Tool Co......................E....... 517 563-8136
Horton (G-7966)
Lonero Engineering Co Inc....................E....... 248 689-9120
Troy (G-16465)
Lotus Corporation...................................G....... 616 494-0112
Holland (G-7727)
▲ Louca Mold Arspc Machining Inc.....C....... 248 391-1616
Auburn Hills (G-930)
LP Products...F....... 989 465-0287
Coleman (G-3347)
LP Products...G....... 989 465-1485
Coleman (G-3348)
Lrs Inc ....G....... 734 416-5050
Plymouth (G-12678)
Ls Precision Tool & Die Inc....................G....... 269 963-9910
Battle Creek (G-1224)
Luckmarr Plastics Inc............................D....... 586 978-8498
Sterling Heights (G-15403)
Lupaul Industries Inc..............................F....... 517 783-3223
Saint Johns (G-14286)
Lutco Inc..G....... 231 972-5566
Mecosta (G-10688)
Lyons Tool & Engineering Inc................E....... 586 200-3003
Warren (G-17133)
M & F Machine & Tool Inc......................E....... 734 847-0571
Erie (G-4806)
M & M Services Inc ....G....... 248 619-9861
Troy (G-16467)
M C Molds Inc..E....... 517 655-5481
Williamston (G-17733)
M C Ward Inc ....E....... 810 982-9720
Port Huron (G-12936)
M Curry Corporation...............................E....... 989 777-7950
Saginaw (G-14080)
M P D Welding Inc...................................E....... 248 340-0330
Orion (G-12184)
Mac-Mold Base Inc..................................E....... 586 752-1956
Bruce Twp (G-2091)
Mach Mold Incorporated ....E....... 269 925-2044
Benton Harbor (G-1524)
Maco Tool & Engineering Inc.................E....... 989 224-6723
Saint Johns (G-14287)
Maddox Industries Inc.............................E....... 517 369-8665
Bronson (G-2032)
Madison Machine Company...................G....... 517 265-8532
Adrian (G-76)
Maes Tool & Die Co Inc ....F....... 517 750-3131
Jackson (G-8504)
◆ Magna Exteriors America Inc ....A....... 248 631-1100
Troy (G-16472)
Magna Exteriors America Inc................B....... 248 409-1817
Auburn Hills (G-936)
▲ Majestic Industries Inc ....D....... 586 786-9100
Macomb (G-10138)
Malmac Tool and Fixture Inc..................G....... 517 448-8244
Hudson (G-8136)
Manufax Inc ....G....... 231 929-3226
Traverse City (G-16031)
Manufctring Solutions Tech LLC...........G....... 734 744-5050
Commerce Township (G-3426)
Mark Carbide Co ....G....... 248 545-0606
Troy (G-16487)
Mark Four CAM Inc ....G....... 586 204-5906
Saint Clair Shores (G-14261)
Mark Maker Company Inc.......................E....... 616 538-6980
Grand Rapids (G-6643)

35 INDUSTRIAL AND COMMERCIAL MACHINERY AND COMPUTER EQUIPMENT

Mark Mold and Engineering ....F 989 687-9786
  Sanford *(G-14451)*
Marten Models & Molds Inc ....E 586 293-2260
  Fraser *(G-5691)*
Martin Tool & Machine Inc ....G 586 775-1800
  Roseville *(G-13830)*
Martinrea Industries Inc ....C 231 832-5504
  Reed City *(G-13220)*
▲ Martinrea Industries Inc ....E 734 428-2400
  Manchester *(G-10408)*
Marton Tool & Die Co Inc ....G 616 361-7337
  Grand Rapids *(G-6647)*
Marvel Tool & Machine Company ......G 810 329-2781
  Saint Clair *(G-14227)*
Master Craft Extrusion Tls Inc ....F 231 386-5149
  Northport *(G-11670)*
Master Jig Grinding & Gage Co ....G 248 380-8515
  Novi *(G-11935)*
Master Machine & Tool Co Inc ....G 586 469-4243
  Clinton Township *(G-3169)*
Master Model & Fixture Inc ....F 586 532-1153
  Shelby Township *(G-14635)*
◆ Master Precision Products Inc ....E 616 754-5483
  Greenville *(G-7145)*
Master Precision Tool Corp ....F 586 739-3240
  Sterling Heights *(G-15412)*
Masters Tool & Die Inc ....G 989 777-2450
  Saginaw *(G-14083)*
Matrix Engineering Inc ....G 810 231-0212
  Brighton *(G-1955)*
Matrix Tool Co ....E 586 296-6010
  Clinton Township *(G-3170)*
Mattson Tool & Die Corp ....G 616 447-9012
  Grand Rapids *(G-6650)*
Max 3 LLC ....E 269 925-2044
  Benton Harbor *(G-1526)*
Maya Jig Grinding & Gage Co ....F 248 471-0820
  Farmington Hills *(G-5060)*
Mayco Tool ....G 616 785-7350
  Comstock Park *(G-3497)*
▲ Mayer Tool & Engineering Inc ....E 269 651-1428
  Sturgis *(G-15616)*
McKechnie Vhcl Cmpnnts USA Inc ....E 218 894-1218
  Roseville *(G-13832)*
Merriman Products Inc ....G 517 787-1825
  Jackson *(G-8515)*
Mesick Mold Co ....E 231 885-1304
  Mesick *(G-10771)*
Met-L-Tec LLC ....E 734 847-7004
  Temperance *(G-15837)*
Metal Punch Corporation ....E 231 775-8391
  Cadillac *(G-2264)*
Metalcraft Impression Die Co ....G 734 513-8058
  Livonia *(G-9839)*
Metalfab Tool & Machine Inc ....G 989 826-6044
  Mio *(G-11005)*
Metalform Industries LLC ....E 248 462-0056
  Shelby Township *(G-14639)*
Metalform LLC ....G 517 569-3313
  Jackson *(G-8516)*
Metalmite Corporation ....F 248 651-9415
  Rochester *(G-13334)*
Metro Technologies Ltd ....D 248 528-9240
  Troy *(G-16502)*
◆ MGR Molds Inc ....F 586 254-6020
  Sterling Heights *(G-15419)*
Michalski Enterprises Inc ....E 517 703-0777
  Lansing *(G-9245)*
Michigan Auto Bending Corp ....E 248 528-1150
  Madison Heights *(G-10304)*
▲ Michigan Drill Corporation ....F 248 689-5050
  Troy *(G-16505)*
▲ Michigan Manufactured Pdts Inc ....G 586 770-2584
  Port Huron *(G-12941)*
Michigan Metal Tech Inc ....E 586 598-7800
  Chesterfield *(G-2806)*
Michigan Mold Inc ....E 269 468-3346
  Coloma *(G-3362)*
Michigan Precision TI & Engrg ....E 269 783-1300
  Dowagiac *(G-4552)*
Michigan Tool & Engineering ....G 586 786-0540
  Macomb *(G-10143)*
Michigan Tool & Gauge Inc ....E 517 548-4604
  Howell *(G-8066)*
Micro Engineering Inc ....E 616 534-9681
  Byron Center *(G-2200)*
Micro Precision Molds Inc ....D 269 344-2044
  Kalamazoo *(G-8825)*
Mid Michigan Pipe Inc ....G 989 772-5664
  Grand Rapids *(G-6683)*

Mid-Tech Inc ....G 734 426-4327
  Ann Arbor *(G-557)*
Middleville Tool & Die Co Inc ....D 269 795-3646
  Middleville *(G-10805)*
Midland Mold & Machining Inc ....G 989 832-9534
  Midland *(G-10890)*
Midwest Die Corp ....F 269 422-2171
  Baroda *(G-1127)*
Midwest Machining Inc ....E 616 837-0165
  Coopersville *(G-3565)*
▲ Midwest Mold Services Inc ....E 586 888-8800
  Roseville *(G-13837)*
▲ Midwest Plastic Engineering ....D 269 651-5223
  Sturgis *(G-15620)*
Millennium Mold & Tool Inc ....G 586 791-1711
  Clinton Township *(G-3177)*
Miller Mold Co ....E 989 793-8881
  Frankenmuth *(G-5594)*
▼ Miller Tool & Die Co ....E 517 782-0347
  Jackson *(G-8529)*
Mistequay Group Ltd ....F 989 752-7700
  Saginaw *(G-14096)*
▲ Mistequay Group Ltd ....F 989 752-7700
  Saginaw *(G-14097)*
Misumi Investment USA Corp ....F 989 875-5400
  Ithaca *(G-8365)*
MNP Corporation ....F 810 982-8996
  Port Huron *(G-12943)*
Model-Matic Inc ....F 248 528-1680
  Troy *(G-16511)*
Models & Tools Inc ....C 586 580-6900
  Shelby Township *(G-14644)*
Modified Technologies Inc ....D 586 725-0448
  Ira *(G-8263)*
◆ Modineer Co ....E 269 683-2550
  Niles *(G-11627)*
Modineer Co ....C 269 684-3138
  Niles *(G-11628)*
Mol-Son Inc ....D 269 668-3377
  Mattawan *(G-10666)*
Mold Matter ....G 231 933-6653
  Traverse City *(G-16041)*
Mold Specialties Inc ....G 586 247-4660
  Shelby Township *(G-14646)*
Mold Tooling Systems Inc ....F 616 735-6653
  Grand Rapids *(G-6697)*
Momentum Industries Inc ....E 989 681-5735
  Saint Louis *(G-14366)*
Monroe LLC ....B 616 942-9820
  Grand Rapids *(G-6702)*
▲ Motor City Stampings Inc ....B 586 949-8420
  Chesterfield *(G-2808)*
Motor City Stampings Inc ....C 586 949-8420
  Chesterfield *(G-2809)*
▲ Mpp Corp ....E 810 364-2939
  Kimball *(G-9045)*
Msx International Inc ....D 248 585-6654
  Madison Heights *(G-10312)*
MTI Precision Machining Inc ....F 989 865-9880
  Saint Charles *(G-14197)*
Multi-Precision Detail Inc ....E 248 373-3330
  Auburn Hills *(G-951)*
Nankin Welding Co Inc ....E 734 458-3980
  Livonia *(G-9857)*
Nesco Tool & Fixture LLC ....G 517 618-7052
  Howell *(G-8068)*
Next Tool LLC ....E 734 405-7079
  Belleville *(G-1449)*
Northern Machine Tool Company ....E 231 755-1603
  Norton Shores *(G-11783)*
Northern Precision Inc ....E 989 736-6322
  Lincoln *(G-9569)*
Northland Tool & Die Inc ....E 616 866-4451
  Rockford *(G-13721)*
Northwest Tool & Machine Inc ....E 517 750-1332
  Jackson *(G-8544)*
▲ Novi Precision Products Inc ....E 810 227-1024
  Brighton *(G-1970)*
O Keller Tool Engrg Co LLC ....E 734 425-4500
  Livonia *(G-9873)*
Oakwood Custom Coating Inc ....F 313 561-7740
  Dearborn *(G-3745)*
▲ Oakwood Energy Management Inc ..C 734 947-7700
  Taylor *(G-15750)*
Oceans Sands Scuba ....G 616 396-0068
  Holland *(G-7762)*
Odyssey Tool LLC ....F 586 468-6696
  Clinton Township *(G-3189)*
Olive Engineering Company ....G 616 399-1756
  West Olive *(G-17533)*

Olivet Machine Tool Engrg Co ....F 269 749-2671
  Olivet *(G-12143)*
Olympian Tool LLC ....E 989 224-4817
  Saint Johns *(G-14291)*
Omega Plastics Inc ....D 586 954-2100
  Clinton Township *(G-3190)*
One-Way Tool & Die Inc ....G 248 477-2964
  Livonia *(G-9875)*
▲ Ontario Die Company America ....D 810 987-5060
  Marysville *(G-10609)*
Opus Mach LLC ....G 586 270-5170
  Warren *(G-17177)*
Ort Tool & Die Corporation ....D 419 242-9553
  Erie *(G-4807)*
Ovidon Manufacturing LLC ....D 517 548-4005
  Howell *(G-8075)*
▲ Owosso Graphic Arts Inc ....E 989 725-7112
  Owosso *(G-12309)*
Oxbow Machine Products Inc ....E 734 422-7730
  Livonia *(G-9878)*
P X Tool Co ....G 248 585-9330
  Madison Heights *(G-10319)*
Pace Industries LLC ....F 231 777-5615
  Muskegon *(G-11397)*
Pacific Tool & Engineering Ltd ....G 586 737-2710
  Sterling Heights *(G-15441)*
Par Molds Inc ....F 616 396-5249
  Holland *(G-7766)*
▲ Paragon Die & Engineering Co ....C 616 949-2220
  Grand Rapids *(G-6741)*
Paragon Molds Corporation ....E 586 294-7630
  Fraser *(G-5704)*
Paramount Tool and Die Inc ....F 616 677-0000
  Marne *(G-10511)*
Paravis Industries Inc ....E 248 393-2300
  Auburn Hills *(G-970)*
Park Street Machine Inc ....E 231 739-9165
  Muskegon *(G-11399)*
Parker Tooling & Design Inc ....F 616 791-1080
  Grand Rapids *(G-6743)*
Parkway Tool Die ....G 248 889-3490
  Highland *(G-7499)*
Parry Precision Inc ....F 248 585-1234
  Madison Heights *(G-10321)*
▲ Paslin Company ....A 586 758-0200
  Warren *(G-17182)*
Paslin Company ....C 248 953-8419
  Shelby Township *(G-14660)*
Paterek Mold & Engineering ....G 586 784-8030
  Armada *(G-722)*
Patrick Carbide Die LLC ....G 517 546-5646
  Howell *(G-8076)*
Patriot Tool & Die Inc ....E 269 687-9024
  Niles *(G-11637)*
Patton Tool and Die Inc ....F 810 359-5336
  Lexington *(G-9559)*
▲ PCS Company ....D 586 294-7780
  Fraser *(G-5706)*
Pdf Mfg Inc ....E 517 522-8431
  Grass Lake *(G-7091)*
Peak Industries Co Inc ....D 313 846-8666
  Dearborn *(G-3747)*
Pedri Mold Inc ....G 586 598-0882
  Chesterfield *(G-2815)*
Pegasus Industries Inc ....F 313 937-0770
  Redford *(G-13180)*
Pegasus Mold & Die Inc ....E 517 423-2009
  Tecumseh *(G-15804)*
Peloton Inc ....G 269 694-9702
  Otsego *(G-12252)*
Pentagon Mold Co ....G 269 496-7072
  Mendon *(G-10717)*
Pentel Tool & Die Inc ....G 734 782-9500
  Romulus *(G-13721)*
Peterson Jig & Fixture Inc ....E 616 866-8296
  Rockford *(G-13585)*
Philips Machining Company ....F 616 997-7777
  Coopersville *(G-3568)*
Pinnacle Engineering Co Inc ....F 734 428-7039
  Manchester *(G-10410)*
Pinnacle Mold & Machine Inc ....G 616 892-9018
  West Olive *(G-17534)*
Pioneer Steel Corporation ....E 616 878-5800
  Byron Center *(G-2208)*
Pioneer Steel Corporation ....E 313 933-9400
  Detroit *(G-4303)*
Plas-TEC Inc ....G 248 853-7777
  Rochester Hills *(G-13495)*
▲ Plas-Tech Mold and Design Inc ....G 269 225-1223
  Plainwell *(G-12538)*

35 INDUSTRIAL AND COMMERCIAL MACHINERY AND COMPUTER EQUIPMENT SIC SECTION

▲ **Plastic Engrg Tchncal Svcs Inc**........E....... 248 373-0800
Auburn Hills *(G-974)*
Plastic Mold Technology Inc.................G....... 616 698-9810
Grand Rapids *(G-6756)*
Plastic-Plate Inc..F....... 616 698-2030
Grand Rapids *(G-6758)*
▲ **Pollington Machine Tool Inc**............E....... 231 743-2003
Marion *(G-10493)*
Poseidon Industries Inc........................G....... 586 949-3550
Chesterfield *(G-2819)*
Positive Tool & Engineering Co.............G....... 313 532-1674
Redford *(G-13184)*
Praet Tool & Engineering Inc...............E....... 586 677-3800
Macomb *(G-10154)*
▲ **Pratt & Whitney Autoair Inc**.............B....... 517 393-4040
Lansing *(G-9413)*
Precision Gage Inc..................................D....... 517 439-1690
Hillsdale *(G-7534)*
Precision Jig & Fixture Inc....................E....... 616 696-2595
Cedar Springs *(G-2560)*
Precision Machining................................G....... 269 925-5321
Sodus *(G-14746)*
Precision Masking Inc...........................E....... 734 848-4200
Erie *(G-4808)*
▲ **Precision Masters Inc**.........................E....... 248 853-0308
Rochester Hills *(G-13497)*
▲ **Precision Mold & Engineering**..........E....... 586 774-2421
Warren *(G-17193)*
Precision Parts Holdings Inc.................A....... 248 853-9010
Rochester Hills *(G-13498)*
Precision Tool & Mold LLC...................F....... 906 932-3440
Ironwood *(G-8338)*
Precision Tool Company Inc.................E....... 231 733-0811
Muskegon *(G-11406)*
▲ **Preferred Industries Inc**....................E....... 810 364-4090
Kimball *(G-9048)*
▲ **Preferred Tool & Die Co Inc**..............E....... 616 784-6789
Comstock Park *(G-3509)*
Prima Technologies Inc..........................F....... 586 759-0250
Center Line *(G-2582)*
Prime Industries Inc...............................E....... 734 946-8588
Taylor *(G-15756)*
Prime Mold LLC.......................................F....... 586 221-2512
Clinton Township *(G-3203)*
Pro Tool LLC...G....... 616 850-0556
Grand Haven *(G-6066)*
Pro-Tech Machine Inc.............................E....... 810 743-1854
Burton *(G-2161)*
Product and Tooling Tech Inc................E....... 586 293-1810
Fraser *(G-5710)*
Proficient Products Inc..........................G....... 586 977-8630
Sterling Heights *(G-15453)*
Project Die and Mold Inc.......................G....... 616 862-8689
Grand Rapids *(G-6788)*
Prophotonix Limited..............................E....... 586 778-1100
Roseville *(G-13856)*
Prosper-Tech Machine & Tl LLC............F....... 586 727-8800
Richmond *(G-13269)*
Proto Gage Inc..D....... 586 978-2783
Sterling Heights *(G-15454)*
Proto-TEC Inc..F....... 616 772-9511
Zeeland *(G-18181)*
Proto-Tek Manufacturing Inc.................E....... 586 772-2663
Roseville *(G-13857)*
▲ **Pti Engineered Plastics Inc**...............B....... 586 263-5100
Macomb *(G-10159)*
Punch Tech...E....... 810 364-4811
Marysville *(G-10612)*
▲ **Punchcraft McHning Tooling LLC**....E....... 586 573-4840
Warren *(G-17211)*
▼ **Q M E Inc**..E....... 269 422-2137
Baroda *(G-1129)*
Qc Tech LLC..D....... 248 597-3984
Madison Heights *(G-10341)*
Quad Precision Tool Co Inc....................F....... 248 608-2400
Rochester Hills *(G-13499)*
▲ **Quality Metalcraft Inc**.........................C....... 734 261-6700
Livonia *(G-9900)*
Quality Model & Pattern Co...................E....... 616 791-1156
Grand Rapids *(G-6800)*
Quantum Mold & Engineering LLC.......F....... 586 276-0100
Sterling Heights *(G-15460)*
Quasar Industries Inc.............................C....... 248 844-7190
Rochester Hills *(G-13501)*
Quasar Industries Inc.............................C....... 248 852-0300
Rochester Hills *(G-13502)*
Qwik Tool & Mfg Inc...............................G....... 231 739-8849
Muskegon *(G-11411)*
▲ **R & A Tool & Engineering Co**............E....... 734 981-2000
Westland *(G-17593)*

◆ **R & B Plastics Machinery LLC**...........E....... 734 429-9421
Saline *(G-14410)*
R & D Machine and Tool Inc...................G....... 231 798-8500
Norton Shores *(G-11789)*
R & S Tool & Die Inc................................G....... 989 673-8511
Caro *(G-2476)*
R C M Inc..G....... 586 336-1237
Bruce Twp *(G-2093)*
R D M Enterprises Co Inc.......................G....... 810 985-4721
Port Huron *(G-12959)*
▲ **R E B Tool Inc**...C....... 734 397-9116
Van Buren Twp *(G-16781)*
R S L Tool LLC..G....... 616 786-2880
Holland *(G-7784)*
R T Gordon Inc...E....... 586 294-6100
Fraser *(G-5715)*
Radar Tool & Manufacturing Co...........G....... 586 759-2800
Warren *(G-17216)*
Ralco Industries Inc.................................D....... 248 853-3200
Auburn Hills *(G-985)*
Ralco Industries Inc.................................E....... 248 853-3200
Auburn Hills *(G-986)*
Ran-Mark Co..F....... 231 873-5103
Hart *(G-7379)*
Ranger Tool & Die Co..............................E....... 989 754-1403
Saginaw *(G-14130)*
Rapids Tool & Engineering....................G....... 517 663-8721
Eaton Rapids *(G-4732)*
Rare Tool Inc...F....... 517 423-5000
Tecumseh *(G-15806)*
Ravenna Pattern & Mfg..........................E....... 231 853-2264
Ravenna *(G-13127)*
Rdc Machine Inc.......................................G....... 810 695-5587
Grand Blanc *(G-5980)*
Ready Molds Inc.......................................E....... 248 474-4007
Farmington Hills *(G-5113)*
Reagan Testing Tools..............................G....... 248 894-3423
Rochester Hills *(G-13505)*
Reef Tool & Gage Co...............................F....... 586 468-3000
Clinton Township *(G-3207)*
Reeves Plastics LLC................................E....... 616 997-0777
Coopersville *(G-3569)*
Reger Manufacturing Company............G....... 586 293-5096
Fraser *(G-5716)*
Reid Industries Inc..................................G....... 586 776-2070
Roseville *(G-13861)*
Reliance Spray Mask Co Inc..................F....... 616 784-3664
Grand Rapids *(G-6819)*
Reliance Tool Company Inc...................G....... 734 946-9130
Romulus *(G-13728)*
Rens LLC...F....... 586 756-6777
Warren *(G-17220)*
Republic Die & Tool Co...........................E....... 734 699-3400
Van Buren Twp *(G-16782)*
Research Tool Corporation....................E....... 989 834-2246
Ovid *(G-12274)*
▲ **Resistance Welding Machne & AC**...F....... 269 428-4770
Saint Joseph *(G-14337)*
▲ **Richard Tool & Die Corporation**........D....... 248 486-0900
New Hudson *(G-11553)*
Rivercity Rollform Inc............................F....... 231 799-9550
Norton Shores *(G-11790)*
Riverside Tool & Mold Inc......................G....... 989 435-9142
Beaverton *(G-1390)*
Rk Boring Inc..G....... 734 542-7920
Livonia *(G-9910)*
RK Tool Inc..G....... 586 731-5640
Sterling Heights *(G-15475)*
▲ **Rkaa Business LLC**...............................E....... 231 734-5517
Evart *(G-4886)*
Rm Machine & Mold.................................G....... 734 721-8800
Romulus *(G-13730)*
Robb Machine Tool Co.............................G....... 616 532-6642
Grand Rapids *(G-6830)*
Roll Tech Inc...E....... 517 283-3811
Reading *(G-13137)*
Rolleigh Inc..F....... 517 283-3811
Reading *(G-13138)*
Romeo Mold Technologies Inc..............F....... 586 336-1245
Bruce Twp *(G-2094)*
Romeo Technologies Inc.........................D....... 586 336-5015
Bruce Twp *(G-2095)*
Ronald R Wellington................................F....... 586 488-3087
Bruce Twp *(G-2097)*
Ronningen Research and Dev Co.........C....... 269 649-0520
Vicksburg *(G-16842)*
Ross Design & Engineering Inc.............E....... 517 547-6033
Cement City *(G-2575)*
Roth-Williams Industries Inc.................F....... 586 792-0090
Clinton Township *(G-3215)*

Rowland Mold & Machine Inc................G....... 616 875-5400
Zeeland *(G-18185)*
Royal ARC Inc...G....... 586 758-0718
Madison Heights *(G-10345)*
Ruelle Industries Inc...............................G....... 248 618-0333
Waterford *(G-17373)*
S & K Tool & Die Company Inc..............F....... 269 345-2174
Portage *(G-13029)*
S & S Die Co...E....... 517 272-1100
Lansing *(G-9420)*
S F R Precision Turning Inc...................G....... 517 709-3367
Holt *(G-7924)*
Sampson Tool Incorporated..................G....... 248 651-3313
Rochester *(G-13351)*
Sbti Company..D....... 586 726-5756
Shelby Township *(G-14685)*
Schaenzle Tool and Die Inc...................G....... 248 656-0596
Rochester Hills *(G-13511)*
Schaller Tool & Die Co............................E....... 586 949-5500
Chesterfield *(G-2838)*
Schmald Tool & Die Inc..........................F....... 810 743-1600
Burton *(G-2163)*
Schuler Tool & Die Company.................G....... 269 489-2900
Burr Oak *(G-2137)*
Schwab Industries Inc............................C....... 586 566-8090
Shelby Township *(G-14688)*
Select Tool and Die Inc...........................G....... 269 422-2812
Baroda *(G-1131)*
Service Extrusion Die Co Inc.................G....... 616 784-6933
Comstock Park *(G-3515)*
Set Enterprises Inc...................................E....... 586 573-3600
Sterling Heights *(G-15493)*
Set Enterprises of Mi Inc.......................C....... 586 573-3600
Sterling Heights *(G-15494)*
Sfi Acquisition Inc...................................E....... 248 471-1500
Farmington Hills *(G-5122)*
Shark Tool & Die Inc................................G....... 586 749-7400
Chesterfield *(G-2839)*
Sharp Die & Mold Co...............................F....... 586 293-8660
Fraser *(G-5724)*
Sharp Model Co...D....... 586 752-3099
Bruce Twp *(G-2101)*
Shiloh Manufacturing LLC.....................F....... 586 873-2835
Roseville *(G-13868)*
Shoreline Mold & Engrg LLC.................G....... 269 926-2223
Benton Harbor *(G-1546)*
Shores Engineering Co Inc....................F....... 586 792-2748
Clinton Township *(G-3226)*
Sigma Tool Mfg Inc..................................G....... 586 792-3300
Clinton Township *(G-3227)*
Simpsons Enterprises Inc.....................E....... 269 279-7237
Three Rivers *(G-15877)*
Sink Rite Die Company............................F....... 586 268-0000
Sterling Heights *(G-15499)*
Skylark Machine Inc................................G....... 616 931-1010
Zeeland *(G-18186)*
Slater Tools Inc...E....... 586 465-5000
Clinton Township *(G-3231)*
Smeko Inc...E....... 586 254-5310
Sterling Heights *(G-15501)*
Smith Brothers Tool Company..............D....... 586 726-5756
Shelby Township *(G-14695)*
Sollman & Son Mold & Tool....................G....... 269 236-6700
Grand Junction *(G-6098)*
Soper Manufacturing Company............E....... 269 429-5245
Saint Joseph *(G-14340)*
Spare Die Inc...G....... 734 522-2508
Livonia *(G-9937)*
Special Mold Engineering Inc...............E....... 248 652-6600
Rochester Hills *(G-13516)*
Special Tool & Engineering Inc.............D....... 586 285-5900
Fraser *(G-5728)*
Specialty Tool & Mold Inc.......................G....... 616 531-3870
Grand Rapids *(G-6880)*
Spray Metal Mold Technology...............G....... 269 781-7151
Marshall *(G-10589)*
Ssrm Machine Shop Inc..........................G....... 989 379-4075
Herron *(G-7470)*
Stampede Die Corp...................................D....... 616 877-0100
Wayland *(G-17417)*
▼ **Standard Components LLC**..............D....... 586 323-9700
Sterling Heights *(G-15509)*
Standard Die International Inc...............E....... 800 838-5464
Livonia *(G-9941)*
▲ **Standard Tool & Die Inc**......................D....... 269 465-6004
Stevensville *(G-15582)*
Stanhope Tool Inc....................................F....... 248 585-5711
Madison Heights *(G-10360)*
Steenson Enterprises...............................G....... 248 628-0036
Leonard *(G-9528)*

Steeplechase Tool & Die Inc ....E 989 352-5544
Lakeview (G-9176)
▲ Stellar Forge Products Inc ....F 313 535-7631
Redford (G-13195)
Sterling Die & Engineering Inc ....E 586 677-0707
Macomb (G-10163)
Stm Mfg Inc................D 616 392-4656
Holland (G-7815)
Sturgis Molded Products Co................C 269 651-9381
Sturgis (G-15636)
Sturgis Tool and Die Inc ....E 269 651-5435
Sturgis (G-15637)
Su-Dan Plastics Inc................B 248 651-6035
Rochester (G-13354)
Su-Dan Plastics Inc................F 248 651-6035
Rochester Hills (G-13520)
Suburban Industries Inc................F 734 676-6141
Brownstown Twp (G-2073)
Summit Services Inc................E 586 977-8300
Shelby Township (G-14705)
Superior Mold Services Inc................F 586 264-9570
Sterling Heights (G-15516)
Superior Products Mfg Inc................G 810 679-4479
Croswell (G-3603)
Supreme Tool & Machine Inc................F 248 673-8408
Waterford (G-17379)
Sweeney Metalworking LLC................F 989 401-6531
Saginaw (G-14160)
T & C Tool & Sales Inc................F 586 677-8390
Washington (G-17312)
T & W Tool & Die Corporation................E 248 548-5400
Oak Park (G-12101)
Tadey Frank R Radian Tool Co ....G 586 754-7422
Warren (G-17260)
Talent Industries Inc................F 313 531-4700
Redford (G-13200)
Talon LLC................D 313 392-1000
Detroit (G-4395)
Tamara Tool Inc................F 269 273-1463
Three Rivers (G-15878)
Target Mold Corporation ....F 231 798-3535
Norton Shores (G-11799)
Tartan Industries Inc................G 810 387-4255
Yale (G-18047)
Taylor Turning Inc................E 248 960-7920
Wixom (G-17906)
Tech Tooling Specialties Inc ....F 517 782-8898
Jackson (G-8584)
▲ Telco Tools................F 616 296-0253
Spring Lake (G-15185)
Tenants Tolerance Tooling................G 269 349-6907
Portage (G-13048)
Terry Tool & Die Co................F 517 750-1771
Jackson (G-8587)
▲ Thumb Tool & Engineering Co................C 989 269-9731
Bad Axe (G-1075)
Tijer Inc ....G 586 741-0308
Clinton Township (G-3247)
Tiller Tool and Die Inc................F 517 458-6602
Morenci (G-11115)
Titan Tool & Die Inc................G 231 799-8680
Norton Shores (G-11803)
◆ Tk Mold & Engineering Inc ....E 586 752-5840
Romeo (G-13640)
Tnr Machine Inc................E 269 623-2827
Dowling (G-4564)
TNT-Edm Inc................E 734 459-1700
Plymouth (G-12772)
Tolerance Tool & Engineering ....E 313 592-4011
Detroit (G-4402)
Tony S Die Machine Company................F 586 773-7379
Warren (G-17266)
Tool & Die Futures Initiative................G 586 336-1237
Bruce Twp (G-2104)
Tool & Die Systems Inc ....G 248 446-1499
Wixom (G-17911)
Tool Company Inc................G 586 598-1519
Chesterfield (G-2849)
Tool North Inc................E 231 941-1150
Traverse City (G-16125)
Toolco Inc ....E 734 453-9911
Plymouth (G-12775)
▲ Tooling Systems Group Inc ....F 616 863-8623
Grand Rapids (G-6933)
Tooling Technology LLC ....D 937 381-9211
Macomb (G-10169)
Top Craft Tool Inc................E 586 461-4600
Clinton Township (G-3248)
Tops All Clamps Inc................G 313 533-7500
Redford (G-13202)
Trademark Die & Engineering................E 616 863-6660
Belmont (G-1473)
Trainer Metal Forming Co Inc ....E 616 844-9982
Grand Haven (G-6089)
▲ Tranor Industries LLC................F 313 733-4888
Detroit (G-4406)
Tregets Tool & Engineering Co................G 517 782-0044
Jackson (G-8591)
▲ Tri Tech Tooling Inc................F 616 396-6000
Holland (G-7838)
Tri-M-Mold Inc................D 269 465-3301
Stevensville (G-15585)
Tri-Star Tool & Machine Co ....F 734 729-5700
Westland (G-17605)
Tri-Star Tooling LLC................F 586 978-0435
Sterling Heights (G-15529)
▲ Tri-Way Manufacturing Inc ....E 586 776-0700
Roseville (G-13880)
Triangle Broach Company ....F 313 838-2150
Detroit (G-4408)
Trianon Industries Corporation ....A 586 759-2200
Center Line (G-2585)
Tric Tool Ltd................E 616 395-1530
Holland (G-7840)
Trispec Precision Products Inc ....G 248 308-3231
Wixom (G-17921)
Tru Flo Carbide Inc ....D 989 658-8515
Ubly (G-16724)
Tru Point Corporation................G 313 897-9100
Detroit (G-4409)
▲ True Industrial Corporation................D 586 771-3500
Roseville (G-13882)
▼ Trutron Corporation................E 248 583-9166
Troy (G-16655)
Turbine Tool & Gage Inc................F 734 427-2270
Livonia (G-9978)
Twin Mold and Engineering LLC ....E 586 532-8558
Shelby Township (G-14713)
U K Edm Ltd ....G 248 437-9500
Brighton (G-2001)
Uei Inc ....E 616 361-6093
Grand Rapids (G-6944)
Ultra-Sonic Extrusion Dies Inc ....E 586 791-8550
Clinton Township (G-3253)
Unified Tool and Die Inc ....G 517 768-8070
Jackson (G-8597)
Unique Products ....G 616 794-3800
Belding (G-1430)
Unique Tool & Mfg Co Inc ....F 734 850-1050
Temperance (G-15846)
Unytrex Inc ....F 810 796-9074
Dryden (G-4572)
US Boring Inc................G 586 756-7511
Warren (G-17275)
◆ USF Delta Tooling LLC................C 248 391-6800
Auburn Hills (G-1041)
Usher Tool & Die Inc................F 616 583-9160
Byron Center (G-2213)
▲ Utica Enterprises Inc ....C 586 726-4300
Troy (G-16670)
Utica International Inc ....C 586 726-4330
Troy (G-16671)
Van Emon Bruce ....G 269 467-7803
Centreville (G-2598)
Vanex Mold Inc................G 616 662-4100
Jenison (G-8647)
Veit Tool & Gage Inc ....F 810 658-4949
Davison (G-3665)
▲ Velocity Manufacturing LLC................G 517 630-0408
Albion (G-134)
Venture Manufacturing Inc................G 269 429-6337
Saint Joseph (G-14349)
Vertical Technologies LLC ....E 586 619-0141
Warren (G-17283)
▲ Vicount Industries Inc ....D 248 471-5071
Farmington Hills (G-5149)
◆ Viking Tool & Engineering Inc................E 231 893-0031
Whitehall (G-17679)
Vinco Tool Inc................G 586 465-1961
Clinton Township (G-3256)
Vision Global Industries................G 248 390-5805
Macomb (G-10173)
▲ Visioneering Inc ....B 248 622-5600
Auburn Hills (G-1045)
Vogel Tooling & Machine LLC................G 517 414-7635
Jackson (G-8601)
Vortec................G 616 292-2401
Zeeland (G-18195)
W & W Tool and Die Inc................G 989 835-5522
Midland (G-10923)
Waber Tool & Engineering Co................E 269 342-0765
Kalamazoo (G-8921)
◆ Walker Tool & Die Inc ....D 616 453-5471
Grand Rapids (G-6977)
Wallin Brothers Inc ....G 734 525-7750
Livonia (G-9995)
Wardcraft Industries LLC ....E 517 750-9100
Spring Arbor (G-15129)
Wartrom Machine Systems................E 586 469-1915
Clinton Township (G-3260)
Waterman Tool & Machine Corp................F 989 823-8181
Vassar (G-16818)
Wayne Allen Lambert................G 269 467-4624
Centreville (G-2600)
Wefa Cedar Inc................F 616 696-0873
Cedar Springs (G-2565)
Weldmet Industries Inc................G 586 773-0533
Warren (G-17291)
West Michigan Tool & Die Co ....E 269 925-0900
Benton Harbor (G-1564)
Westgood Manufacturing Co................E 586 771-3970
Roseville (G-13890)
▲ Westool Corporation ....E 734 847-2520
Temperance (G-15847)
Wetzel Tool & Engineering Inc................F 248 960-0430
Wixom (G-17929)
White Automation & Tool Co................F 734 947-9822
Romulus (G-13740)
White Engineering Inc ....G 269 695-0825
Niles (G-11651)
White River Knife and Tool ....G 616 997-0026
Fremont (G-5786)
Whitesell Frmed Components Inc................D 313 299-1178
Waterford (G-17385)
Wico Metal Products Company ....F 586 755-9600
Center Line (G-2587)
Widell Industries Inc................E 989 742-4528
Hillman (G-7511)
Wieske Tool Inc................G 989 288-2648
Durand (G-4615)
Williams Tooling & Mfg................F 616 681-2093
Dorr (G-4529)
Wire Dynamics Inc................G 586 879-0321
Fraser (G-5748)
Withers Corporation ....E 586 758-2750
Warren (G-17294)
Wolverine Carbide & Tool Inc ....D 248 247-3888
Troy (G-16694)
Wolverine Carbide Die Company ....E 248 280-0300
Troy (G-16695)
Wolverine Products Inc................F 586 792-3740
Clinton Township (G-3261)
Wolverine Tool & Engrg Co................E 616 785-9796
Belmont (G-1475)
Wolverine Tool Co................F 810 664-2964
Lapeer (G-9492)
Woodpecker Industries LLC ....G 231 347-0970
Harbor Springs (G-7298)
Worswick Mold & Tool Inc................F 810 765-1700
Marine City (G-10488)
Wright Plastic Products Co LLC................D 810 326-3000
Saint Clair (G-14237)
Wyke Die & Engineering Inc ....G 616 871-1175
Grand Rapids (G-7005)
X L T Engineering Inc ....F 989 684-4344
Kawkawlin (G-8977)
▲ X-L Machine Co Inc................E 269 279-5128
Three Rivers (G-15883)
Xcentric Mold & Engrg Inc ....F 586 598-4636
Clinton Township (G-3262)
Yarema Die & Engineering Co ....D 248 585-2830
Troy (G-16702)
Z Mold & Engineering Inc................G 586 948-5000
Chesterfield (G-2857)

3545 Machine Tool Access

A & D Run Off Inc................G 231 759-0950
Muskegon (G-11256)
A A Anchor Bolt Inc ....F 248 349-6565
Northville (G-11675)
Abrasive Diamond Tool Company................E 248 588-4800
Madison Heights (G-10179)
Accell Technologies Inc................G 248 360-3762
Commerce Township (G-3384)
▲ Accu Products International ....G 734 429-9571
Saline (G-14372)
Accurate Carbide Tool Co Inc................F 989 755-0429
Saginaw (G-13991)
Ace Drill Corporation................G 517 265-5184
Adrian (G-42)

S I C

35 INDUSTRIAL AND COMMERCIAL MACHINERY AND COMPUTER EQUIPMENT SIC SECTION

Acg Services Inc ....G 586 232-4698
Shelby Township *(G-14540)*
Acme Carbide Die Inc ....E 734 722-2303
Westland *(G-17538)*
Acme Grooving Tool Co ....F 800 633-8828
Clarkston *(G-2903)*
Action Tool & Machine Inc ....E 810 229-6300
Brighton *(G-1877)*
Active Tooling LLC ....F 616 875-8111
Zeeland *(G-18109)*
Adaptable Tool Supply LLC ....F 248 439-0866
Clawson *(G-2970)*
▲ Admiral Broach Company Inc ....E 586 468-8411
Clinton Township *(G-3037)*
▲ Advance Products Corporation ....E 269 849-1000
Benton Harbor *(G-1480)*
Advanced Feedlines LLC ....D 248 583-9400
Troy *(G-16169)*
Advantage Design and Tool ....G 586 801-7413
Richmond *(G-13258)*
AG Davis Gage & Engrg Co ....E 586 977-9000
Sterling Heights *(G-15256)*
Alberts Machine Tool Inc ....G 231 743-2457
Marion *(G-10489)*
◆ American Broach & Machine Co ....E 734 961-0300
Ypsilanti *(G-18051)*
American Gator Tool Company ....G 231 347-3222
Harbor Springs *(G-7272)*
American Gear & Engrg Co Inc ....E 734 595-6400
Westland *(G-17541)*
American Industrial Gauge Inc ....G 248 280-0048
Royal Oak *(G-13901)*
American Lap Company ....G 231 526-7121
Harbor Springs *(G-7273)*
Anbo Tool & Manufacturing Inc ....G 586 465-7610
Clinton Township *(G-3052)*
Anchor Lamina America Inc ....C 231 533-8646
Bellaire *(G-1434)*
▲ Anderson-Cook Inc ....D 586 954-0700
Clinton Township *(G-3053)*
Anderson-Cook Inc ....D 586 293-0800
Fraser *(G-5620)*
Apex Broaching Systems Inc ....F 586 758-2626
Warren *(G-16936)*
Apollo Broach Inc ....G 734 467-5750
Westland *(G-17542)*
Apollo Tool & Engineering Inc ....F 616 735-4934
Grand Rapids *(G-6172)*
Arm Tooling Systems Inc ....F 586 759-5677
Warren *(G-16938)*
Art Laser Inc ....F 248 391-6600
Auburn Hills *(G-780)*
Artcraft Pattern Works Inc ....F 734 729-0022
Westland *(G-17543)*
Associated Broach Corporation ....E 810 798-9112
Almont *(G-252)*
Atlas Thread Gage Inc ....G 248 477-3230
Farmington Hills *(G-4935)*
▲ Avon Broach & Prod Co LLC ....E 248 650-8080
Rochester Hills *(G-13372)*
Aw Carbide Fabricators Inc ....F 586 294-1850
Fraser *(G-5626)*
Award Cutter Company Inc ....F 616 531-0430
Grand Rapids *(G-6196)*
B C I Collet Inc ....E 734 326-1222
Westland *(G-17546)*
Baxter Machine & Tool Co ....E 517 782-2808
Jackson *(G-8388)*
Benny Gage Inc ....E 734 455-3080
Wixom *(G-17773)*
Bilco Tool Corporation ....G 586 574-9300
Warren *(G-16959)*
Bitner Tooling Technologies ....F 586 803-1100
Sterling Heights *(G-15275)*
Bob G Machining LLC ....G 586 285-1400
Clinton Township *(G-3068)*
Borite Manufacturing Corp ....G 248 588-7260
Madison Heights *(G-10205)*
Bower Tool & Manufacturing Inc ....G 734 522-0444
Livonia *(G-9669)*
Breckers ABC Tool Company Inc ....F 586 779-1122
Roseville *(G-13778)*
▼ Breesport Holdings Inc ....C 248 685-9500
Milford *(G-10956)*
Briggs Industries Inc ....E 586 749-5191
Chesterfield *(G-2747)*
Broaching Industries Inc ....E 586 949-3775
Chesterfield *(G-2748)*
Buddy Tda Inc ....G 269 349-8105
Kalamazoo *(G-8702)*
Bullion Tool Technology LLC ....G 313 881-1404
Harper Woods *(G-7300)*
Buster Mathis Foundation ....G 616 843-4433
Wyoming *(G-17990)*
Cap Collet & Tool Co Inc ....F 734 283-4040
Wyandotte *(G-17951)*
Capitol Tool Grinding Co ....G 517 321-8230
Lansing *(G-9280)*
Carbide Form Master Inc ....G 248 625-9373
Davisburg *(G-3629)*
Carbide Surface Company ....G 586 465-6110
Clinton Township *(G-3075)*
Carbide Technologies Inc ....E 586 296-5200
Fraser *(G-5634)*
Cardinal Machine Co ....E 810 686-1190
Clio *(G-3267)*
Caro Carbide Corporation ....E 248 588-4252
Troy *(G-16260)*
Cdp Diamond Products Inc ....E 734 591-1041
Livonia *(G-9678)*
Center Line Gage Inc ....G 810 387-4300
Brockway *(G-2019)*
Century Inc ....G 231 946-7500
Traverse City *(G-15933)*
▲ Ceratizit Usa Inc ....C 586 759-2280
Warren *(G-16977)*
Champagne Grinding & Mfg Co ....F 734 459-1759
Canton *(G-2360)*
Champion Tool Company ....G 248 474-6200
Farmington Hills *(G-4961)*
Clymer Manufacturing Company ....G 248 853-5555
Rochester Hills *(G-13389)*
Cogsdill Tool Products Inc ....G 734 744-4500
Livonia *(G-9685)*
Cole Carbide Industries Inc ....F 248 276-1278
Lake Orion *(G-9129)*
Cole Carbide Industries Inc ....D 989 872-4348
Cass City *(G-2513)*
Coles Machine Service Inc ....E 810 658-5373
Davison *(G-3642)*
Colonial Bushings Inc ....F 586 954-3880
Clinton Township *(G-3082)*
▲ Colonial Tool Sales & Svc LLC ....F 734 946-2733
Taylor *(G-15703)*
◆ Comau LLC ....B 248 353-8888
Southfield *(G-14871)*
Complete Cutting Tl & Mfg Inc ....G 248 662-9811
Wixom *(G-17789)*
Complex Tool & Machine Inc ....G 248 625-0664
Clarkston *(G-2915)*
Component Engrg Solutions LLC ....F 616 514-1343
Grand Rapids *(G-6294)*
Conical Cutting Tools Inc ....E 616 531-8500
Grand Rapids *(G-6299)*
Contour Tool and Machine Inc ....G 517 787-6806
Jackson *(G-8420)*
▲ Control Gaging Inc ....E 734 668-6750
Ann Arbor *(G-404)*
◆ Costello Machine LLC ....E 586 749-0136
Chesterfield *(G-2755)*
Cougar Cutting Tools Inc ....F 586 469-1310
Clinton Township *(G-3091)*
▲ Cows Locomotive Mfg Co ....E 248 583-7150
Madison Heights *(G-10221)*
Coyne Machine & Tool LLC ....G 231 944-8755
Kewadin *(G-9037)*
Cross Paths Corp ....G 616 248-5371
Grand Rapids *(G-6318)*
Crystal Cut Tool Inc ....G 734 494-5076
Romulus *(G-13665)*
Cz Industries Inc ....G 248 475-4415
Auburn Hills *(G-834)*
D & F Corporation ....D 586 254-5300
Sterling Heights *(G-15306)*
Davison-Rite Products Co ....E 734 513-0505
Livonia *(G-9699)*
Dependable Gage & Tool Co ....F 248 545-2100
Oak Park *(G-12058)*
Detail Precision Products Inc ....E 248 544-3390
Ferndale *(G-5271)*
Detroit Edge Tool Company ....E 586 776-1598
Roseville *(G-13794)*
▲ Detroit Edge Tool Company ....D 313 366-4120
Detroit *(G-3983)*
Di-Coat Corporation ....E 248 349-1211
Novi *(G-11868)*
Diamond Broach Company ....G 586 757-5131
Warren *(G-17002)*
Diamond Tool Manufacturing Inc ....E 734 416-1900
Plymouth *(G-12611)*
Dianamic Abrasive Products ....F 248 280-1185
Troy *(G-16316)*
▲ Die Services International LLC ....D 734 699-3400
Van Buren Twp *(G-16758)*
▲ Dijet Incorporated ....G 734 454-9100
Plymouth *(G-12612)*
Dixon & Ryan Corporation ....F 248 549-4000
Royal Oak *(G-13919)*
▲ Dme Company LLC ....B 248 398-6000
Madison Heights *(G-10233)*
Dobday Manufacturing Co Inc ....E 586 254-6777
Sterling Heights *(G-15320)*
Douglas Gage Inc ....F 586 727-2089
Richmond *(G-13261)*
▲ Dowding Machining LLC ....F 517 663-5455
Eaton Rapids *(G-4721)*
Drill Technology ....G 616 676-1287
Ada *(G-14)*
Dumbarton Tool Inc ....F 231 775-4342
Cadillac *(G-2245)*
Dura Thread Gage Inc ....F 248 545-2890
Madison Heights *(G-10236)*
Dynamic Jig Grinding Corp ....E 248 589-3110
Troy *(G-16330)*
E & E Special Products LLC ....F 586 978-3377
Warren *(G-17012)*
Ecco Tool Co Inc ....G 248 349-0840
Novi *(G-11878)*
Elk Lake Tool Co ....E 231 264-5616
Elk Rapids *(G-4777)*
Ellsworth Cutting Tools LLC ....F 586 598-6040
Chesterfield *(G-2772)*
Elmhirst Industries Inc ....E 586 731-8663
Sterling Heights *(G-15330)*
Emtron Corporation Inc ....F 248 347-3333
New Hudson *(G-11539)*
Engineered Tools Corp ....D 989 673-8733
Caro *(G-2468)*
Enmark Tool Company ....E 586 293-2797
Fraser *(G-5651)*
Enterprise Tool and Gear Inc ....D 989 269-9797
Bad Axe *(G-1060)*
Equitable Engineering Co Inc ....E 248 689-9700
Troy *(G-16351)*
Erdman Machine Co ....E 231 894-1010
Whitehall *(G-17665)*
Est Tools America Inc ....G 810 824-3323
Ira *(G-8255)*
▲ Etcs Inc ....F 586 268-4870
Warren *(G-17022)*
Evans Tool & Engineering Inc ....F 616 791-6333
Grand Rapids *(G-6389)*
Excel Screw Machine Tools ....G 313 383-4200
Taylor *(G-15717)*
Express Machine & Tool Co ....G 586 758-5080
Warren *(G-17027)*
F & S Tool & Gauge Co Inc ....G 517 787-2661
Jackson *(G-8446)*
Fab-Jet Services LLC ....G 586 463-9622
Clinton Township *(G-3112)*
Falcon Motorsports Inc ....G 248 328-2222
Holly *(G-7878)*
▲ Federal Broach & Mch Co LLC ....C 989 539-7420
Harrison *(G-7311)*
▲ Feed - Lease Corp ....E 248 377-0000
Auburn Hills *(G-871)*
Fega Tool & Gage Company ....F 586 469-4400
Clinton Township *(G-3114)*
Fisk Precision Tech LLC ....G 616 514-1415
Wyoming *(G-18002)*
Fitz Manufacturing Inc ....F 248 589-1780
Troy *(G-16365)*
Fitz-Rite Products Inc ....E 248 528-8440
Troy *(G-16366)*
Five Star Industries Inc ....E 586 786-0500
Macomb *(G-10122)*
FL Tool Holders LLC ....E 734 591-0134
Livonia *(G-9736)*
Flex Manufacturing Inc ....F 586 469-1076
Clinton Township *(G-3122)*
▲ Fontijne Grotnes Inc ....E 269 262-4700
Niles *(G-11611)*
Forkardt Inc ....E 231 995-8300
Traverse City *(G-15973)*
Formula One Tool & Engineering ....G 810 794-3617
Algonac *(G-144)*
▲ Fraser Tool & Gauge LLC ....G 313 882-9192
Grosse Pointe Park *(G-7193)*
Fsp Inc ....F 248 585-0760
Troy *(G-16375)*

SIC SECTION
35 INDUSTRIAL AND COMMERCIAL MACHINERY AND COMPUTER EQUIPMENT

Fulgham Machine & Tool Company ...... G 517 937-8316
Jackson *(G-8453)*
Fullerton Tool Company Inc ...... C 989 799-4550
Saginaw *(G-14041)*
G A Machine Company Inc ...... G 313 836-5646
Detroit *(G-4074)*
▲ **G&G Industries Inc** ...... E 586 726-6000
Shelby Township *(G-14595)*
Gage Eagle Spline Inc ...... D 586 776-7240
Warren *(G-17049)*
Gage Numerical Inc ...... G 231 328-4426
Lake City *(G-9087)*
Gage Rite Products Inc ...... F 248 588-7796
Troy *(G-16377)*
GAL Gage Co ...... E 269 465-5750
Bridgman *(G-1863)*
Gemini Precision Machining Inc ...... D 989 269-9702
Bad Axe *(G-1065)*
General Broach & Engrg Inc ...... E 586 726-4300
Troy *(G-16381)*
▲ **General Broach Company** ...... E 517 458-7555
Morenci *(G-11109)*
General Broach Company ...... E 517 458-7555
Morenci *(G-11110)*
▲ **Global CNC Industries Ltd** ...... E 734 464-1920
Plymouth *(G-12629)*
Global Engineering Inc ...... E 586 566-0423
Shelby Township *(G-14596)*
Global Retool Group Amer LLC ...... F 248 289-5820
Wixom *(G-17818)*
▼ **Global Tooling Systems LLC** ...... E 586 726-0500
Macomb *(G-10127)*
Gr Innovations LLC ...... G 248 618-3813
Waterford *(G-17347)*
Grand Rapids Metaltek Inc ...... E 616 791-2373
Grand Rapids *(G-6460)*
Great Lakes Tool LLC ...... F 586 759-5253
Warren *(G-17064)*
Green Manufacturing Inc ...... G 517 458-1500
Morenci *(G-11111)*
Green Oak Tool and Svcs Inc ...... G 586 531-2255
Brighton *(G-1934)*
Grind-All Precision Tool Co ...... F 586 954-3430
Clinton Township *(G-3132)*
Groholski Mfg Solutions LLC ...... E 517 278-9339
Coldwater *(G-3307)*
◆ **Gt Technologies Inc** ...... E 734 467-8371
Westland *(G-17566)*
Guardian Manufacturing Corp ...... E 734 591-1454
Livonia *(G-9761)*
Guhring Inc ...... E 262 784-6730
Novi *(G-11892)*
H & G Tool Company ...... F 586 573-7040
Warren *(G-17073)*
H E Morse Co ...... D 616 396-4604
Holland *(G-7656)*
Haller International Tech Inc ...... G 313 821-0809
Detroit *(G-4114)*
Hanchett Manufacturing Inc ...... C 231 796-7678
Big Rapids *(G-1632)*
Hank Thorn Co ...... F 248 348-7800
Wixom *(G-17823)*
Hanlo Gauges & Engineering Co ...... G 734 422-4224
Livonia *(G-9766)*
Hardy-Reed Tool & Die Co Inc ...... F 517 547-7107
Manitou Beach *(G-10448)*
▲ **Harroun Enterprises Inc** ...... G 810 629-9885
Fenton *(G-5219)*
▲ **Hope Focus Companies Inc** ...... E 313 494-5500
Detroit *(G-4130)*
◆ **Hougen Manufacturing Inc** ...... C 810 635-7111
Swartz Creek *(G-15667)*
Howell Tool Service Inc ...... F 517 548-1114
Howell *(G-8052)*
▲ **Htc Sales Corporation** ...... E 800 624-2027
Ira *(G-8257)*
Hti Cybernetics Inc ...... E 586 826-8346
Sterling Heights *(G-15369)*
▲ **Huron Tool & Engineering Co** ...... E 989 269-9927
Bad Axe *(G-1068)*
Huron Tool & Gage Co Inc ...... G 313 381-1900
Wixom *(G-17830)*
Hydra-Lock Corporation ...... E 586 783-5007
Mount Clemens *(G-11133)*
Hydro-Craft Inc ...... E 248 652-8100
Rochester Hills *(G-13448)*
I & G Tool Co Inc ...... E 586 777-7690
New Baltimore *(G-11485)*
Ideal Heated Knives Inc ...... G 248 437-1510
New Hudson *(G-11545)*
Illinois Tool Works Inc ...... D 231 947-5755
Traverse City *(G-16002)*
Illinois Tool Works Inc ...... G 231 947-5755
Traverse City *(G-16003)*
Image Machine & Tool Inc ...... G 586 466-3400
Fraser *(G-5669)*
Indepndnce Tling Solutions LLC ...... E 586 274-2300
Troy *(G-16414)*
Indexable Cutter Engineering ...... G 586 598-1540
Chesterfield *(G-2787)*
International Mech Design ...... E 248 546-5740
Royal Oak *(G-13936)*
Invo Spline Inc ...... E 586 757-8840
Warren *(G-17097)*
J & B Precision Inc ...... G 313 565-3431
Taylor *(G-15729)*
J & L Turning Inc ...... F 810 765-5755
East China *(G-4623)*
J E Wood Co ...... F 248 585-5711
Madison Heights *(G-10279)*
Jade Tool Inc ...... E 231 946-7710
Traverse City *(G-16008)*
Johan Van De Weerd Co Inc ...... G 517 542-3817
Litchfield *(G-9606)*
Joint Production Tech Inc ...... E 586 786-0080
Macomb *(G-10133)*
Jt Manufacturing Inc ...... E 517 849-2923
Jonesville *(G-8658)*
▲ **K-Tool Corporation Michigan** ...... D 863 603-0777
Plymouth *(G-12661)*
Kalamazoo Chuck Mfg Svc Ctr Co ...... F 269 679-2325
Schoolcraft *(G-14498)*
Karr Spring Company ...... E 616 394-1277
Holland *(G-7707)*
▲ **Kasper Machine Co** ...... F 248 547-3150
Madison Heights *(G-10289)*
Kel Tool Inc ...... G 517 750-4515
Spring Arbor *(G-15123)*
Keller Tool Ltd ...... D 734 425-4500
Livonia *(G-9794)*
Kennametal Inc ...... D 231 946-2100
Traverse City *(G-16018)*
Kenrie Inc ...... F 616 494-3200
Holland *(G-7710)*
Keo Cutters Inc ...... E 586 771-2050
Warren *(G-17120)*
Khalsa Metal Products Inc ...... G 616 791-4794
Kentwood *(G-9014)*
Kingsford Broach & Tool Inc ...... E 906 774-4917
Kingsford *(G-9060)*
Knight Carbide Inc ...... E 586 598-4888
Chesterfield *(G-2798)*
Kooiker Tool & Die Inc ...... F 616 554-3630
Caledonia *(G-2305)*
Krebs Tool Inc ...... G 734 697-8611
Van Buren Twp *(G-16768)*
▲ **Krmc LLC** ...... G 734 955-9311
Romulus *(G-13698)*
Kurek Tool Inc ...... F 989 777-5300
Saginaw *(G-14075)*
Kwik Tech Inc ...... E 586 268-6201
Shelby Township *(G-14617)*
▲ **Kyocera Unimerco Tooling Inc** ...... E 734 944-4433
Saline *(G-14397)*
L & M Tool Co Inc ...... F 586 677-4700
Macomb *(G-10136)*
▲ **L E Jones Company** ...... B 906 863-1043
Menominee *(G-10741)*
Lab Tool and Engineering Corp ...... E 517 750-4131
Spring Arbor *(G-15124)*
Lamina Inc ...... C 248 489-9122
Farmington Hills *(G-5042)*
Lance Industries LLC ...... G 248 549-1968
Madison Heights *(G-10296)*
Lancer Tool Co ...... F 248 380-8830
Wixom *(G-17844)*
Lavalier Corp ...... E 248 616-8880
Troy *(G-16458)*
Laydon Enterprises Inc ...... E 906 774-4633
Iron Mountain *(G-8288)*
▼ **Lead Screws International Inc** ...... E 262 786-1500
Traverse City *(G-16022)*
Leader Corporation ...... E 586 566-7114
Shelby Township *(G-14624)*
Legacy Tool LLC ...... G 231 335-8983
Newaygo *(G-11572)*
Lester Detterbeck Entps Ltd ...... E 906 265-5121
Iron River *(G-8314)*
Lightning Machine Holland LLC ...... F 616 786-9280
Holland *(G-7725)*
Linamar Holding Nevada Inc ...... F 248 477-6240
Livonia *(G-9807)*
Lincoln Precision Carbide Inc ...... E 989 736-8113
Lincoln *(G-9566)*
Line Precision Inc ...... E 248 474-5280
Farmington Hills *(G-5044)*
Link Manufacturing Inc ...... E 231 238-8741
Indian River *(G-8219)*
Lumco Manufacturing Company ...... F 810 724-0582
Lum *(G-10090)*
Lyons Tool & Engineering Inc ...... E 586 200-3003
Warren *(G-17133)*
M & M Thread & Assembly Inc ...... G 248 583-9696
Sterling Heights *(G-15405)*
M C Carbide Tool Co ...... F 248 486-9590
Wixom *(G-17850)*
M Curry Corporation ...... E 989 777-7950
Saginaw *(G-14080)*
Mac-Tech Tooling Corporation ...... G 248 743-1400
Troy *(G-16468)*
Machining & Fabricating Inc ...... E 586 773-9288
Roseville *(G-13828)*
Machining Technologies LLC ...... G 248 379-4201
Clarkston *(G-2935)*
Maes Tool & Die Co Inc ...... F 517 750-3131
Jackson *(G-8504)*
Magnetic Chuck Services Co Inc ...... G 586 822-9441
Casco *(G-2502)*
Majeske Machine Inc ...... F 319 273-8905
Plymouth *(G-12682)*
Malmac Tool and Fixture Inc ...... G 517 448-8244
Hudson *(G-8136)*
◆ **Mapal Inc** ...... D 810 364-8020
Port Huron *(G-12939)*
Maro Precision Tool Company ...... F 734 261-3100
West Bloomfield *(G-17483)*
◆ **Marshall-Gruber Company LLC** ...... F 248 353-4100
Southfield *(G-14973)*
Martel Tool Corporation ...... F 313 278-2420
Allen Park *(G-202)*
Master Jig Grinding & Gage Co ...... G 248 380-8515
Novi *(G-11935)*
Master Machine & Tool Co Inc ...... G 586 469-4243
Clinton Township *(G-3169)*
MB Liquidating Corporation ...... D 810 638-5388
Flushing *(G-5541)*
Mc Pherson Industrial Corp ...... D 586 752-5555
Romeo *(G-13633)*
Measuring Tool Services ...... G 734 261-1107
Livonia *(G-9835)*
Merrifield McHy Solutions Inc ...... E 248 494-7335
Pontiac *(G-12848)*
Metal Punch Corporation ...... E 231 775-8391
Cadillac *(G-2264)*
Metro Machine Works Inc ...... D 734 941-4571
Romulus *(G-13707)*
▲ **Michigan Drill Corporation** ...... F 248 689-5050
Troy *(G-16505)*
Micro Form Inc ...... G 517 750-3660
Spring Arbor *(G-15126)*
▼ **Midwest Tool and Cutlery Co** ...... D 269 651-2476
Sturgis *(G-15621)*
Millennium Technology II Inc ...... F 734 479-4440
Romulus *(G-13709)*
Miller Broach Inc ...... D 810 395-8810
Capac *(G-2449)*
▼ **Miller Tool & Die Co** ...... E 517 782-0347
Jackson *(G-8529)*
Milo Boring & Machining Inc ...... G 586 293-8611
Fraser *(G-5693)*
▲ **Mistequay Group Ltd** ...... F 989 752-7700
Saginaw *(G-14097)*
Mjc Tool & Machine Co Inc ...... G 586 790-4766
Clinton Township *(G-3179)*
MNP Corporation ...... F 810 982-8996
Port Huron *(G-12943)*
Modern CAM and Tool Co ...... G 734 946-9800
Taylor *(G-15745)*
Moehrle Inc ...... F 734 761-2000
Ann Arbor *(G-562)*
Montague Tool and Mfg Co ...... E 810 686-0000
Clio *(G-3279)*
Motor Tool Manufacturing Co ...... G 734 425-3300
Livonia *(G-9850)*
Mp Tool & Engineering Company ...... E 586 772-7730
Roseville *(G-13841)*
◆ **Nagel Precision Inc** ...... C 734 426-5650
Ann Arbor *(G-568)*
Nexteer Automotive Corporation ...... B 989 757-5000
Saginaw *(G-14104)*

SIC

Employee Codes: A=Over 500 employees, B=251-500
C=101-250, D=51-100, E=20-50, F=10-19, G=3-9
2020 Harris Michigan
Industrial Directory
817

North-East Gage Inc ..... G 586 792-6790
Clinton Township **(G-3186)**
Northern Precision Inc ..... E 989 736-6322
Lincoln **(G-9569)**
O Keller Tool Engrg Co LLC ..... E 734 425-4500
Livonia **(G-9873)**
Olivet Machine Tool Engrg Co ..... F 269 749-2671
Olivet **(G-12143)**
Olympian Tool LLC ..... E 989 224-4817
Saint Johns **(G-14291)**
Oneida Tool Corporation ..... E 313 537-0770
Redford **(G-13177)**
◆ **Ossineke Industries Inc** ..... D 989 471-2197
Ossineke **(G-12230)**
Owosso Automation Inc ..... G 989 725-8804
Owosso **(G-12307)**
P & P Manufacturing Co Inc ..... E 810 667-2712
Lapeer **(G-9479)**
P L Schmitt Crbide Tooling LLC ..... G 313 706-5756
Grass Lake **(G-7090)**
P T M Corporation ..... D 586 725-2211
Ira **(G-8266)**
P&L Development & Mfg LLC ..... D 989 739-5203
Oscoda **(G-12217)**
Pace Grinding Inc ..... G 231 861-0448
Shelby **(G-14533)**
Paslin Company ..... E 586 755-1693
Warren **(G-17181)**
▲ **Paslin Company** ..... A 586 758-0200
Warren **(G-17182)**
Patriot Manufacturing LLC ..... G 734 259-2059
Plymouth **(G-12709)**
Peak Industries Co Inc ..... D 313 846-8666
Dearborn **(G-3747)**
Perry Tool Company Inc ..... G 734 283-7393
Riverview **(G-13304)**
Philips Machining Company ..... F 616 997-7777
Coopersville **(G-3568)**
Pioneer Broach Midwest Inc ..... F 231 768-5800
Leroy **(G-9535)**
Pioneer Michigan Broach Co ..... F 231 768-5800
Leroy **(G-9536)**
PL Schmitt Crbide Toling LLC ..... G 517 522-6891
Grass Lake **(G-7092)**
Posa-Cut Corporation ..... E 248 474-5620
Farmington Hills **(G-5097)**
Precise Cnc Routing Inc ..... E 616 538-8608
Grand Rapids **(G-6763)**
Precision Components ..... F 248 588-5650
Troy **(G-16559)**
Precision Devices Inc ..... E 734 439-2462
Milan **(G-10950)**
Precision Gage Inc ..... D 517 439-1690
Hillsdale **(G-7534)**
▲ **Precision Threading Corp** ..... G 231 627-3133
Cheboygan **(G-2691)**
Precision Tool Company Inc ..... E 231 733-0811
Muskegon **(G-11406)**
Primary Tool & Cutter Grinding ..... F 248 588-1530
Madison Heights **(G-10337)**
Prime Industries Inc ..... E 734 946-8588
Taylor **(G-15756)**
Principal Diamond Works ..... G 248 589-1111
Madison Heights **(G-10338)**
Productivity Technologies ..... C 810 714-0200
Fenton **(G-5231)**
Proto Design & Manufacturing ..... G 419 346-8416
Fraser **(G-5711)**
Proto Tool & Gage Inc ..... G 734 487-0830
Ypsilanti **(G-18097)**
Puritan Automation LLC ..... F 248 668-1114
Wixom **(G-17881)**
Pyramid Tool Company Inc ..... G 248 549-0602
Royal Oak **(G-13960)**
▲ **Qc American LLC** ..... G 734 961-0300
Ypsilanti **(G-18098)**
▲ **R & A Tool & Engineering Co** ..... E 734 981-2000
Westland **(G-17593)**
▼ **R & B Industries Inc** ..... E 734 462-9478
Livonia **(G-9903)**
R & S Tool & Die Inc ..... G 989 673-8511
Caro **(G-2476)**
R J S Tool & Gage Co ..... E 248 642-8620
Birmingham **(G-1700)**
R L Schmitt Company Inc ..... E 734 525-9310
Livonia **(G-9905)**
R T Gordon Inc ..... E 586 294-6100
Fraser **(G-5715)**
Raal Industries Inc ..... G 734 782-6216
Flat Rock **(G-5361)**
Rayco Manufacturing Inc ..... F 586 795-2884
Sterling Heights **(G-15462)**
Reef Tool & Gage Co ..... F 586 468-3000
Clinton Township **(G-3207)**
Reid Industries Inc ..... G 586 776-2070
Roseville **(G-13861)**
Reif Carbide Tool Co Inc ..... F 586 754-1890
Warren **(G-17219)**
Rhinevault Olsen Machine & Tl ..... G 989 753-4363
Saginaw **(G-14133)**
Riverside Spline & Gear Inc ..... E 810 765-8302
Marine City **(G-10481)**
Riviera Industries Inc ..... G 313 381-5500
Allen Park **(G-206)**
Rodan Tool & Mold LLC ..... G 248 926-9200
Commerce Township **(G-3450)**
Roesch Maufacturing Co LLC ..... G 517 424-6300
Tecumseh **(G-15808)**
Rose Tool & Die Inc ..... E 989 343-1015
West Branch **(G-17519)**
Roth-Williams Industries Inc ..... F 586 792-0090
Clinton Township **(G-3215)**
▼ **Royal Design & Manufacturing** ..... D 248 588-0110
Madison Heights **(G-10346)**
RTS Cutting Tools Inc ..... E 586 954-1900
Clinton Township **(G-3217)**
S F S Carbide Tool ..... G 989 777-3890
Saginaw **(G-14135)**
Salerno Tool Works Inc ..... G 586 755-5000
Warren **(G-17227)**
SB Investments LLC ..... E 734 462-9478
Livonia **(G-9921)**
Sbti Company ..... D 586 726-5756
Shelby Township **(G-14685)**
Schaller Tool & Die Co ..... E 586 949-5500
Chesterfield **(G-2838)**
Schenck USA Corp ..... E 248 377-2100
Southfield **(G-15024)**
▲ **Seco Holding Co Inc** ..... A 248 528-5200
Troy **(G-16596)**
Select Steel Fabricators Inc ..... F 248 945-9582
Southfield **(G-15026)**
Selector Spline Products Co ..... F 586 254-4020
Sterling Heights **(G-15488)**
Selmuro Ltd ..... E 810 603-2117
Grand Blanc **(G-5983)**
Service Diamond Tool Company ..... G 248 669-3100
Novi **(G-11993)**
Sesco Products Group Inc ..... D 586 979-4400
Sterling Heights **(G-15492)**
Setco Sales Company ..... F 248 888-8989
Novi **(G-11994)**
Severance Tool Industries Inc ..... E 989 777-5500
Saginaw **(G-14146)**
Severance Tool Industries Inc ..... G 989 777-5500
Saginaw **(G-14147)**
Shape Dynamics Intl Inc ..... G 231 733-2164
Muskegon **(G-11421)**
Shouse Tool Inc ..... F 810 629-0391
Fenton **(G-5238)**
Shwayder Company ..... G 248 645-9511
Birmingham **(G-1702)**
▲ **Sidley Diamond Tool Company** ..... E 734 261-7970
Garden City **(G-5841)**
Simonds International LLC ..... D 231 527-2322
Big Rapids **(G-1645)**
Skill-Craft Company Inc ..... F 586 716-4300
Ira **(G-8271)**
Sme Holdings LLC ..... E 586 254-5310
Sterling Heights **(G-15500)**
Smeko Inc ..... E 586 254-5310
Sterling Heights **(G-15501)**
Snap Jaws Manufacturing Inc ..... G 248 588-1099
Troy **(G-16608)**
Southwest Broach ..... G 714 356-2967
Cadillac **(G-2277)**
Spartan Carbide Inc ..... E 586 285-9786
Fraser **(G-5727)**
Spartan Tool Sales Inc ..... F 586 268-1556
Sterling Heights **(G-15504)**
Special Drill and Reamer Corp ..... F 248 588-5333
Madison Heights **(G-10356)**
Spence Industries Inc ..... G 586 758-3800
Warren **(G-17246)**
Stanhope Tool Inc ..... F 248 585-5711
Madison Heights **(G-10360)**
Stapels Manufacturing LLC ..... F 248 577-5570
Troy **(G-16619)**
▲ **Star Cutter Co** ..... E 248 474-8200
Farmington Hills **(G-5129)**
Star Ringmaster ..... G 734 641-7147
Canton **(G-2429)**
Steel Craft Technologies Inc ..... C 616 866-4400
Belmont **(G-1471)**
Steelcraft Tool Co Inc ..... E 734 522-7130
Livonia **(G-9945)**
Sterling Edge Inc ..... G 248 438-6034
Wixom **(G-17897)**
Stoney Crest Regrind Service ..... F 989 777-7190
Bridgeport **(G-1858)**
Superior Controls Inc ..... C 734 454-0500
Plymouth **(G-12763)**
Superior Design & Mfg ..... F 810 678-3950
Metamora **(G-10781)**
T M Smith Tool Intl Corp ..... E 586 468-1465
Mount Clemens **(G-11151)**
Target Mold Corporation ..... F 231 798-3535
Norton Shores **(G-11799)**
▲ **Tawas Tool Co Inc** ..... D 989 362-6121
East Tawas **(G-4695)**
Tawas Tool Co Inc ..... D 989 362-0414
East Tawas **(G-4696)**
Taylor Turning Inc ..... E 248 960-7920
Wixom **(G-17906)**
Tazz Broach and Machine Inc ..... G 586 296-7755
Harrison Township **(G-7352)**
TEC Industries Inc ..... G 248 446-9560
New Hudson **(G-11558)**
Techni CAM and Manufacturing ..... F 734 261-6477
Livonia **(G-9954)**
Technical Rotary Services Inc ..... G 586 772-6755
Warren **(G-17264)**
Teknikut Corporation ..... G 586 778-7150
Canton **(G-2435)**
Tenants Tolerance Tooling ..... G 269 349-6907
Portage **(G-13048)**
▲ **Thielenhaus Microfinish Corp** ..... E 248 349-9450
Novi **(G-12015)**
▲ **Thread-Craft Inc** ..... D 586 323-1116
Sterling Heights **(G-15524)**
Three-Dimensional Services Inc ..... C 248 852-1333
Rochester Hills **(G-13525)**
Tolerance Tool & Engineering ..... E 313 592-4011
Detroit **(G-4402)**
Tool Service Company Inc ..... G 586 296-2500
Fraser **(G-5738)**
Tool-Craft Industries Inc ..... F 248 549-0077
Sterling Heights **(G-15525)**
Tooltech Machinery Inc ..... G 248 628-1813
Oxford **(G-12376)**
Total Tooling Concepts Inc ..... G 616 785-8402
Comstock Park **(G-3518)**
Triangle Broach Company ..... F 313 838-2150
Detroit **(G-4408)**
Trig Tool Inc ..... G 248 543-2550
Madison Heights **(G-10370)**
◆ **Trimas Corporation** ..... E 248 631-5450
Bloomfield Hills **(G-1807)**
Tru Flo Carbide Inc ..... D 989 658-8515
Ubly **(G-16724)**
Tru Point Corporation ..... G 313 897-9100
Detroit **(G-4409)**
Truing Systems Inc ..... F 248 588-9060
Troy **(G-16654)**
Trusted Tool Mfg Inc ..... G 810 750-6000
Fenton **(G-5247)**
TS Carbide Inc ..... G 248 486-8330
Commerce Township **(G-3455)**
Turbine Tool & Gage Inc ..... F 734 427-2270
Livonia **(G-9978)**
Universal / Devlieg Inc ..... F 989 752-3077
Saginaw **(G-14173)**
▼ **Universal Tool Inc** ..... G 248 733-9800
Troy **(G-16665)**
▲ **Universal/Devlieg LLC** ..... F 989 752-7700
Saginaw **(G-14174)**
▲ **Utica Enterprises Inc** ..... C 586 726-4300
Troy **(G-16670)**
V J Industries Inc ..... F 810 364-6470
Marine City **(G-10486)**
Van Emon Bruce ..... G 269 467-7803
Centreville **(G-2598)**
Vigel North America Inc ..... G 734 947-9900
Madison Heights **(G-10376)**
Wachtel Tool & Broach Inc ..... G 586 758-0110
Saint Clair **(G-14236)**
Warren Broach & Machine Corp ..... F 586 254-7080
Sterling Heights **(G-15544)**
Weber Precision Grinding Inc ..... G 616 842-1634
Spring Lake **(G-15186)**

SIC SECTION
35 INDUSTRIAL AND COMMERCIAL MACHINERY AND COMPUTER EQUIPMENT

Wedin International Inc	D	231 779-8650
Cadillac *(G-2284)*		
West Michigan Gage Inc	F	616 735-0585
Walker *(G-16882)*		
Westech Inc	E	231 766-3914
Muskegon *(G-11447)*		
Western Pegasus Inc	G	616 393-9580
Holland *(G-7858)*		
Westside Tool & Gage LLC	G	734 728-9520
Westland *(G-17612)*		
Widell Industries Inc	E	989 742-4528
Hillman *(G-7511)*		
Wilco Tooling & Mfg LLC	F	517 901-0147
Reading *(G-13139)*		
Wire Fab Inc	F	313 893-8816
Detroit *(G-4443)*		
Wit-Son Carbide Tool Inc	E	231 536-2247
East Jordan *(G-4648)*		
Witco Inc	D	810 387-4231
Greenwood *(G-7163)*		
Wolverine Broach Co Inc	E	586 468-4445
Harrison Township *(G-7356)*		
Wolverine Production & Engrg	F	586 468-2890
Harrison Township *(G-7357)*		
Wolverine Special Tool Inc	E	616 791-1027
Grand Rapids *(G-7000)*		
Wolverine Tool Co	F	810 664-2964
Lapeer *(G-9492)*		
Wood-Cutters Tooling Inc	G	616 257-7930
Grandville *(G-7076)*		
Workblades Inc	E	586 778-0060
Warren *(G-17297)*		
Wyandotte Collet and Tool Inc	F	734 283-8055
Wyandotte *(G-17982)*		
Wyser Innovative Products LLC	G	616 583-9225
Byron Center *(G-2218)*		
▲ Yost Vises LLC	G	616 396-2063
Holland *(G-7867)*		
Zakron USA Inc	F	313 582-0462
Dearborn *(G-3776)*		
▲ Zcc USA Inc	F	734 997-3811
Ann Arbor *(G-706)*		
Zimmermann Engineering Co Inc	G	248 358-0044
Southfield *(G-15070)*		

3546 Power Hand Tools

◆ A W B Industries Inc	E	989 739-1447
Oscoda *(G-12205)*		
Ace Drill Corporation	G	517 265-5184
Adrian *(G-42)*		
▲ Anchor Lamina America Inc	E	248 489-9122
Novi *(G-11826)*		
Anchor Lamina America Inc	C	231 533-8646
Bellaire *(G-1434)*		
Area Cycle Inc	G	989 777-0850
Bridgeport *(G-1849)*		
Avalon Tools Inc	E	248 269-0001
Troy *(G-16230)*		
Black & Decker (us) Inc	G	410 716-3900
Grand Rapids *(G-6228)*		
Black & Decker (us) Inc	G	616 261-0425
Grandville *(G-7023)*		
Carbide Technologies Inc	E	586 296-5200
Fraser *(G-5634)*		
Clausing Industrial Inc	E	269 345-7155
Kalamazoo *(G-8706)*		
▲ Clausing Industrial Inc	D	269 345-7155
Kalamazoo *(G-8707)*		
▲ Conway-Cleveland Corp	G	616 458-0056
Grand Rapids *(G-6309)*		
Coxline Inc	E	269 345-1132
Kalamazoo *(G-8720)*		
D & D Production Inc	F	248 334-2112
Waterford *(G-17332)*		
Ebels Hardware Inc	F	231 826-3334
Falmouth *(G-4892)*		
Elmo Manufacturing Co Inc	G	734 995-5966
Ann Arbor *(G-441)*		
▲ Gch Tool Group Inc	E	586 777-6250
Warren *(G-17050)*		
Hank Thorn Co	F	248 348-7800
Wixom *(G-17823)*		
▲ Heck Industries Incorporated	F	810 632-5400
Hartland *(G-7390)*		
Hme Inc	C	616 534-1463
Wyoming *(G-18011)*		
◆ Hougen Manufacturing Inc	C	810 635-7111
Swartz Creek *(G-15667)*		
Jemms-Cascade Inc	F	248 526-8100
Troy *(G-16436)*		
Jones & Hollands Inc	G	810 364-6400
Marysville *(G-10605)*		
K M S Company	G	616 994-7000
Holland *(G-7704)*		
Lamina Inc	C	248 489-9122
Farmington Hills *(G-5042)*		
Lumberjack Shack Inc	G	810 724-7230
Imlay City *(G-8207)*		
Lutco Inc	G	231 972-5566
Mecosta *(G-10688)*		
▼ Menominee Saw and Supply Co	E	906 863-2609
Menominee *(G-10747)*		
Michigan Deburring Tool LLC	G	810 227-1000
Brighton *(G-1959)*		
Pitchford Bertie	G	517 627-1151
Grand Ledge *(G-6113)*		
Plum Brothers LLC	G	734 947-8100
Romulus *(G-13723)*		
Roesch Manufacturing Co LLC	G	517 424-6300
Tecumseh *(G-15808)*		
RTS Cutting Tools Inc	E	586 954-1900
Clinton Township *(G-3217)*		
▲ Star Cutter Co	E	248 474-8200
Farmington Hills *(G-5129)*		
Striker Tools LLC	G	248 990-7767
Manitou Beach *(G-10449)*		
▲ Telco Tools	F	616 296-0253
Spring Lake *(G-15185)*		
Waber Tool & Engineering Co	E	269 342-0765
Kalamazoo *(G-8921)*		

3547 Rolling Mill Machinery & Eqpt

D-N-S Industries Inc	F	586 465-2444
Clinton Township *(G-3098)*		
▲ Dalton Industries LLC	E	248 673-0755
Waterford *(G-17333)*		
Delta Tube & Fabricating Corp	C	248 634-8267
Holly *(G-7875)*		
Dexter Roll Form Company	G	586 573-6930
Warren *(G-17001)*		
▲ Feed - Lease Corp	E	248 377-0000
Auburn Hills *(G-871)*		
▲ Fontijne Grotnes Inc	E	269 262-4700
Niles *(G-11611)*		
Mikes Garage	G	734 779-7383
Belleville *(G-1448)*		
Mill Assist Services Inc	F	269 692-3211
Otsego *(G-12245)*		
Novi Tool & Machine Company	D	313 532-0900
Redford *(G-13176)*		
◆ Perfecto Industries Inc	E	989 732-2941
Gaylord *(G-5888)*		
▼ Rod Chomper Inc	F	616 392-9677
Holland *(G-7790)*		
▼ Tube Forming and Machine Inc	E	989 739-3323
Oscoda *(G-12223)*		

3548 Welding Apparatus

1271 Associates Inc	D	586 948-4300
Chesterfield *(G-2730)*		
Airgas Usa LLC	E	248 545-9353
Ferndale *(G-5255)*		
▲ Alcotec Wire Corporation	D	800 228-0750
Traverse City *(G-15891)*		
▲ All-Fab Corporation	G	269 673-6572
Allegan *(G-147)*		
Amada Miyachi America Inc	G	248 313-3078
Wixom *(G-17759)*		
Anroid Industries Inc	E	248 732-0000
Auburn Hills *(G-774)*		
▲ Aro Welding Technologies Inc	D	586 949-9353
Chesterfield *(G-2742)*		
Arplas USA LLC	G	888 527-5553
Detroit *(G-3878)*		
Atlas Welding Accessories Inc	D	248 588-4666
Troy *(G-16226)*		
▲ Bielomatik Inc	E	248 446-9910
New Hudson *(G-11531)*		
Cobra Truck & Fabrication	G	734 854-5663
Ottawa Lake *(G-12260)*		
◆ Comau LLC	B	248 353-8888
Southfield *(G-14871)*		
Comau LLC	C	248 305-9662
Novi *(G-11851)*		
◆ Cor-Met Inc	E	810 227-0000
Brighton *(G-1902)*		
Craft Industries Inc	A	586 726-4300
Shelby Township *(G-14570)*		
D J and G Enterprise Inc	G	231 258-9925
Kalkaska *(G-8941)*		
Delfab Inc	E	906 428-9570
Gladstone *(G-5913)*		
Dytron Corporation	E	586 296-9600
Fraser *(G-5645)*		
Emabond Solutions LLC	E	201 767-7400
Auburn Hills *(G-855)*		
◆ Eureka Welding Alloys Inc	E	248 588-0001
Madison Heights *(G-10250)*		
Fair Industries LLC	C	248 740-7841
Troy *(G-16359)*		
◆ Fanuc America Corporation	B	248 377-7000
Rochester Hills *(G-13423)*		
GAL Gage Co	E	269 465-5750
Bridgman *(G-1863)*		
Great Lakes Laser Services	G	248 584-1828
Madison Heights *(G-10262)*		
Grossel Tool Co	D	586 294-3660
Fraser *(G-5658)*		
Hilltop Manufacturing Co Inc	G	248 437-2530
New Hudson *(G-11544)*		
Hmr Fabrication Unlimited Inc	F	586 569-4288
Fraser *(G-5664)*		
Hobart Brothers Company	F	231 933-1234
Traverse City *(G-15998)*		
Hti Cybernetics Inc	E	586 826-8346
Sterling Heights *(G-15369)*		
Huebner E W & Son Mfg Co Inc	G	734 427-2600
Livonia *(G-9775)*		
J W Holdings Inc	E	616 530-9889
Grand Rapids *(G-6549)*		
K&S Consultants LLC	G	269 240-7767
Buchanan *(G-2122)*		
KIWOTO Inc	G	269 944-1552
Benton Harbor *(G-1520)*		
Knight Kraft Inc	F	586 726-6821
Sterling Heights *(G-15390)*		
Lakeland Elec Mtr Svcs Inc	E	616 647-0331
Comstock Park *(G-3493)*		
Lloyd Tool & Mfg Corp	E	810 694-3519
Grand Blanc *(G-5973)*		
Mc REA Corporation	G	734 420-2116
Plymouth *(G-12687)*		
Mid Michigan Repair Service	G	989 835-6014
Midland *(G-10886)*		
MST Steel Corp	F	586 359-2648
Roseville *(G-13842)*		
▲ Nadex of America Corporation	E	248 477-3900
Farmington Hills *(G-5075)*		
▲ Northwoods Manufacturing Inc	D	906 779-2370
Kingsford *(G-9065)*		
▲ Nortronic Company	G	313 893-3730
Detroit *(G-4277)*		
▲ Obara Corporation USA	G	586 755-1250
Novi *(G-11962)*		
Owosso Automation Inc	G	989 725-8804
Owosso *(G-12307)*		
▲ Paslin Company	A	586 758-0200
Warren *(G-17182)*		
Paslin Company	C	248 953-8419
Shelby Township *(G-14660)*		
Paslin Company	E	586 755-3606
Warren *(G-17183)*		
Peak Industries Co Inc	D	313 846-8666
Dearborn *(G-3747)*		
Purity Cylinder Gases Inc	G	517 321-9555
Lansing *(G-9262)*		
▲ Resistance Welding Machne & AC	F	269 428-4770
Saint Joseph *(G-14337)*		
RSI Global Sourcing LLC	F	734 604-2448
Novi *(G-11988)*		
▲ Saginaw Machine Systems Inc	D	989 753-8465
Saginaw *(G-14140)*		
Santanna Tool & Design LLC	D	248 541-3500
Madison Heights *(G-10348)*		
▲ Sanyo Machine America Corp	D	248 651-5911
Rochester Hills *(G-13510)*		
Sas Global Corporation	E	248 414-4470
Warren *(G-17230)*		
▲ Thyssenkrupp System Engrg	C	248 340-8000
Auburn Hills *(G-1019)*		
▲ Tipaloy Inc	F	313 875-5145
Detroit *(G-4400)*		
Tupes of Saginaw Inc	F	989 799-1550
Saginaw *(G-14169)*		
▲ Utica Enterprises Inc	C	586 726-4300
Troy *(G-16670)*		
Utica International Inc	C	586 726-4330
Troy *(G-16671)*		
◆ Welding Technology Corp	F	248 477-3900
Farmington Hills *(G-5151)*		

Employee Codes: A=Over 500 employees, B=251-500
C=101-250, D=51-100, E=20-50, F=10-19, G=3-9

Welform Electrodes Inc D 586 755-1184
Warren *(G-17292)*
Wolverine Hydraulics & Mfg Co G 248 543-5261
Madison Heights *(G-10383)*

3549 Metalworking Machinery, NEC

Accu-Rite Industries LLC E 586 247-0060
Shelby Township *(G-14538)*
Advanced Feedlines LLC D 248 583-9400
Troy *(G-16169)*
Ais Automation Systems Inc F 734 365-2384
Rockwood *(G-13603)*
Allied Tool and Machine Co E 989 755-5384
Saginaw *(G-13995)*
Aludyne US LLC D 810 987-1112
Port Huron *(G-12889)*
▲ Anderson-Cook Inc D 586 954-0700
Clinton Township *(G-3053)*
Anderson-Cook Inc D 586 293-0800
Fraser *(G-5620)*
Apollo Seiko Ltd F 269 465-3400
Bridgman *(G-1859)*
▲ Atlas Technologies LLC D 810 714-2128
Fenton *(G-5183)*
Ats Assembly and Test Inc D 734 266-4713
Livonia *(G-9657)*
Auto/Con Corp D 586 791-7474
Fraser *(G-5623)*
Automation Specialists Inc F 616 738-8288
Holland *(G-7562)*
Basis Machining LLC G 517 542-3818
Litchfield *(G-9600)*
Bay Plastics Machinery Co LLC E 989 671-9630
Bay City *(G-1288)*
Bel-Kur Inc E 734 847-0651
Temperance *(G-15823)*
Boxer Equipment/Morbark Inc G 989 866-2381
Winn *(G-17746)*
◆ Burke E Porter Machinery Co C 616 234-1200
Grand Rapids *(G-6243)*
▲ Burton Industries Inc E 906 932-5970
Ironwood *(G-8323)*
Burton Press Co Inc G 248 853-0212
Rochester Hills *(G-13380)*
Cardinal Machine Co E 810 686-1190
Clio *(G-3267)*
▲ Carter Products Company Inc F 616 647-3380
Grand Rapids *(G-6256)*
▲ Coleman Machine Inc E 906 863-1113
Menominee *(G-10728)*
Columbia Marking Tools Inc E 586 949-8400
Chesterfield *(G-2754)*
▲ Creative Automation Inc E 734 780-3175
Whitmore Lake *(G-17694)*
D K Products Inc G 517 263-3025
Adrian *(G-56)*
▲ Dake Corporation D 616 842-7110
Grand Haven *(G-6008)*
▲ Dane Systems LLC D 269 465-3263
Stevensville *(G-15562)*
Das Group Inc G 248 670-2718
Royal Oak *(G-13917)*
Demmer Investments Inc G 517 321-3600
Lansing *(G-9221)*
◆ Diamond Automation Ltd G 734 838-7138
Livonia *(G-9710)*
Dnl Fabrication LLC F 586 872-2656
Roseville *(G-13796)*
◆ Dominion Tech Group Inc C 586 773-3303
Roseville *(G-13797)*
Duo Robotic Solutions Inc F 586 883-7559
Sterling Heights *(G-15322)*
▲ Edgewater Automation LLC D 269 983-1300
Saint Joseph *(G-14308)*
Esys Automation LLC D 248 754-1900
Auburn Hills *(G-856)*
Experienced Concepts Inc F 586 752-4200
Armada *(G-719)*
▲ Feed - Lease Corp E 248 377-0000
Auburn Hills *(G-871)*
Fives Cinetic Corp D 248 477-0800
Farmington Hills *(G-5002)*
Flagler Corporation E 586 749-6300
Chesterfield *(G-2776)*
Fluid Innovations Inc G 810 241-0990
Sterling Heights *(G-15343)*
▲ Fontijne Grotnes Inc E 269 262-4700
Niles *(G-11611)*
Friendship Industries Inc E 586 323-0033
Sterling Heights *(G-15349)*
Friendship Industries Inc F 586 997-1325
Sterling Heights *(G-15350)*
Gatco Incorporated F 734 453-2295
Plymouth *(G-12626)*
Hak Inc G 231 587-5322
Mancelona *(G-10392)*
Hanson International Inc D 269 429-5555
Saint Joseph *(G-14316)*
▲ Hanwha Techm Usa LLC G 248 588-1242
Rochester Hills *(G-13439)*
Harvey S Freeman E 248 852-2222
West Bloomfield *(G-17479)*
Heidtman Steel Products Inc D 734 848-2115
Erie *(G-4803)*
▲ HMS Products Co D 248 689-8120
Troy *(G-16398)*
Hti Cybernetics Inc E 586 826-8346
Sterling Heights *(G-15369)*
I Machine LLC G 616 532-8020
Grandville *(G-7049)*
Ideal Tool Inc F 989 893-8336
Bay City *(G-1321)*
Impres Engineering Svcs LLC G 616 283-4112
Holland *(G-7689)*
◆ Industrial Automation LLC D 248 598-5900
Rochester Hills *(G-13449)*
▲ J W Froehlich Inc G 586 580-0025
Sterling Heights *(G-15379)*
J W Holdings Inc E 616 530-9889
Grand Rapids *(G-6549)*
▲ JR Automation Tech LLC C 616 399-2168
Holland *(G-7698)*
JR Automation Tech LLC G 616 399-2168
Holland *(G-7699)*
JR Automation Tech LLC G 616 399-2168
Holland *(G-7700)*
JR Automation Tech LLC G 616 399-2168
Holland *(G-7701)*
Jr Technology Group LLC C 616 399-2168
Holland *(G-7702)*
Kailing Machine Shop G 616 677-3629
Marne *(G-10509)*
Kapex Manufacturing LLC G 989 928-4993
Saginaw *(G-14069)*
▲ Kuka Assembly and Test Corp C 989 220-3088
Saginaw *(G-14074)*
Kuka Robotics Corporation E 586 795-2000
Shelby Township *(G-14615)*
▲ Kuka Systems North America LLC B 586 795-2000
Sterling Heights *(G-15392)*
Kuka Systems North America LLC G 586 726-4300
Shelby Township *(G-14616)*
▲ Kuka US Holding Company LLC F 586 795-2000
Sterling Heights *(G-15393)*
L & H Diversified Mfg USA LLC G 586 615-4873
Shelby Township *(G-14618)*
Lab Tool and Engineering Corp E 517 750-4131
Spring Arbor *(G-15124)*
Leonard Machine Tool Systems E 586 757-8040
Warren *(G-17127)*
◆ Letnan Industries Inc E 586 726-1155
Sterling Heights *(G-15397)*
Lomar Machine & Tool Co E 517 563-8136
Horton *(G-7966)*
M & F Machine & Tool Inc E 734 847-0571
Erie *(G-4806)*
Manufacturers / Mch Bldrs Svcs G 734 748-3706
Livonia *(G-9821)*
Manufctring Solutions Tech LLC G 734 744-5050
Commerce Township *(G-3426)*
Mark 7 Machine Inc G 989 922-7335
Bay City *(G-1327)*
Mark One Corporation D 989 732-2427
Gaylord *(G-5877)*
Marking Machine Co F 517 767-4155
Tekonsha *(G-15820)*
Mega Screen Corp G 517 849-7057
Jonesville *(G-8663)*
Metal Stmping Spport Group LLC F 586 777-7440
Roseville *(G-13834)*
Milacron LLC E 517 424-8981
Tecumseh *(G-15802)*
Modern Tool and Tapping Inc G 586 777-5144
Fraser *(G-5694)*
◆ Morbark LLC B 989 866-2381
Winn *(G-17747)*
Motion Machine Company F 810 664-9901
Lapeer *(G-9476)*
Naams LLC F 586 285-5684
Warren *(G-17165)*
National Advanced Mobility G 734 995-3098
Ann Arbor *(G-571)*
ND Industries Inc E 248 288-0000
Troy *(G-16521)*
◆ New Unison Corporation E 248 544-9500
Ferndale *(G-5304)*
▲ Norgren Automtn Solutions LLC C 734 429-4989
Saline *(G-14406)*
Norgren Automtn Solutions LLC C 586 463-3000
Rochester Hills *(G-13481)*
Northwest Tool & Machine Inc E 517 750-1332
Jackson *(G-8544)*
▲ Novi Precision Products Inc E 810 227-1024
Brighton *(G-1970)*
On The Mark Inc G 989 317-8033
Mount Pleasant *(G-11216)*
◆ Perfecto Industries Inc E 989 732-2941
Gaylord *(G-5888)*
Precision Plus F 906 553-7900
Escanaba *(G-4853)*
Priority Tool Inc G 616 847-1337
Grand Haven *(G-6064)*
Pro-Tech Machine Inc E 810 743-1854
Burton *(G-2161)*
Prosys Industries Inc E 734 207-3710
Canton *(G-2421)*
R & S Tool & Die Inc G 989 673-8511
Caro *(G-2476)*
Reger Manufacturing Company G 586 293-5096
Fraser *(G-5716)*
▲ Rock Tool & Machine Co Inc E 734 455-9840
Plymouth *(G-12743)*
▼ Rod Chomper Inc F 616 392-9677
Holland *(G-7790)*
Roma Tool Inc F 248 218-1889
Lake Orion *(G-9156)*
Savard Corporation F 313 931-6880
Detroit *(G-4353)*
SB Investments LLC E 734 462-9478
Livonia *(G-9921)*
Schenck USA Corp E 248 377-2100
Southfield *(G-15024)*
Sharp Die & Mold Co F 586 293-8660
Fraser *(G-5724)*
Signet Machine Inc G 616 261-2939
Grandville *(G-7071)*
Smartcoast LLC G 231 571-2020
Grand Rapids *(G-6868)*
Spen-Tech Machine Engrg Corp D 810 275-6800
Flint *(G-5501)*
TA Systems Inc D 248 656-5150
Rochester Hills *(G-13522)*
▲ Tannewitz Inc E 616 457-5999
Jenison *(G-8644)*
Tarpon Automation & Design Co E 586 774-8020
Warren *(G-17263)*
▲ Thielenhaus Microfinish Corp E 248 349-9450
Novi *(G-12015)*
Toman Industries Inc G 734 289-1393
Monroe *(G-11079)*
Tri-Mation Industries Inc F 269 668-4333
Mattawan *(G-10670)*
▼ Trinity Tool Co E 586 296-5900
Fraser *(G-5741)*
Utica Body & Assembly Inc E 586 726-4330
Troy *(G-16669)*
▲ Utica Enterprises Inc C 586 726-4300
Troy *(G-16670)*
Utica International Inc C 586 726-4330
Troy *(G-16671)*
▼ Van-Mark Products Corporation E 248 478-1200
Farmington Hills *(G-5146)*
Veet Industries Inc F 586 776-3000
Warren *(G-17281)*
▲ Weber Electric Mfg Co E 586 323-9000
Shelby Township *(G-14721)*
Wright-K Technology Inc E 989 752-2588
Saginaw *(G-14184)*
Yaskawa America Inc F 248 668-8800
Rochester Hills *(G-13549)*

3552 Textile Machinery

All American Embroidery Inc F 734 421-9292
Livonia *(G-9634)*
B&P Littleford Day LLC D 989 757-1300
Saginaw *(G-13998)*
Becmar Corp G 616 675-7479
Bailey *(G-1077)*
Bpg International Fin Co LLC G 616 855-1480
Ada *(G-11)*

Carry-All Products Inc............F....... 616 399-8080
Holland (G-7585)
Craft Press Printing Inc............G....... 269 683-9694
Niles (G-11602)
▲ Fabri-Tech Inc............E....... 616 662-0150
Jenison (G-8626)
Groholski Mfg Solutions LLC............E....... 517 278-9339
Coldwater (G-3307)
Howa USA Holdings Inc............G....... 248 715-4000
Novi (G-11902)
Needles N Pins Inc............G....... 734 459-0625
Plymouth (G-12700)
Oji Intertech Inc............G....... 248 373-7733
Auburn Hills (G-964)
▲ Orri Corp............F....... 248 618-1104
Waterford (G-17364)
Precision Spindle Service Co............F....... 248 544-0100
Ferndale (G-5313)
Star Shade Cutter Co............G....... 269 983-2403
Saint Joseph (G-14341)
Superior Threading Inc............F....... 989 729-1160
Owosso (G-12319)
Tri-State Technical Services............G....... 517 563-8743
Hanover (G-7262)

3553 Woodworking Machinery

▲ Alexander Dodds Company............G....... 616 784-6000
Grand Rapids (G-6156)
Automated Precision Eqp LLC............G....... 517 481-2414
Eaton Rapids (G-4717)
Bespro Pattern Inc............F....... 586 268-6970
Madison Heights (G-10204)
Boxer Equipment/Morbark Inc............G....... 989 866-2381
Winn (G-17746)
▲ Carter Products Company Inc............F....... 616 647-3380
Grand Rapids (G-6256)
▲ Conway-Cleveland Corp............G....... 616 458-0056
Grand Rapids (G-6309)
Coxline Inc............E....... 269 345-1132
Kalamazoo (G-8720)
Gudho USA Inc............F....... 616 682-7814
Ada (G-17)
▲ Homag Machinery North Amer Inc...F....... 616 254-8181
Grand Rapids (G-6515)
International Fenestration............G....... 248 735-6880
Northville (G-11701)
Macali Inc............G....... 616 447-1202
Grand Rapids (G-6639)
Moda Manufacturing LLC............G....... 586 204-5120
Farmington Hills (G-5071)
◆ Morbark LLC............B....... 989 866-2381
Winn (G-17747)
Northern Woodcrafters............G....... 989 348-2553
Grayling (G-7114)
Northwest Pattern Company............G....... 248 477-7070
Farmington Hills (G-5082)
Parma Manufacturing Co Inc............G....... 517 531-4111
Parma (G-12392)
R J Flood Professional Co............G....... 269 930-3608
Stevensville (G-15579)
Saginaw Industries LLC............F....... 989 752-5514
Saginaw (G-14139)
Straitoplane Inc............G....... 616 997-2211
Coopersville (G-3570)
▲ Tannewitz Inc............E....... 616 457-5999
Jenison (G-8644)
Wing Pattern Inc............G....... 248 588-1121
Sterling Heights (G-15546)

3554 Paper Inds Machinery

A S R C Inc............G....... 517 545-7430
Howell (G-8008)
▲ Accu-Shape Die Cutting Inc............E....... 810 230-2445
Flint (G-5368)
B&P Littleford Day LLC............D....... 989 757-1300
Saginaw (G-13998)
Bell Packaging Corp............D....... 616 452-2111
Grand Rapids (G-6208)
▲ Bernal LLC............D....... 248 299-3600
Rochester Hills (G-13377)
▲ Challenge Machinery Company............E....... 231 799-8484
Norton Shores (G-11745)
Euclid Coating Systems Inc............F....... 989 922-4789
Bay City (G-1309)
Graphic Art Service & Supply............G....... 810 229-4700
Brighton (G-1933)
▲ Graphic Arts Service & Sup Inc............F....... 616 698-9300
Grand Rapids (G-6473)
Hycorr LLC............F....... 269 381-6349
Kalamazoo (G-8771)
Paper Machine Service Inds............F....... 989 695-2646
Saginaw (G-14119)
S & W Holdings Ltd............G....... 248 723-2870
Birmingham (G-1701)

3555 Printing Trades Machinery & Eqpt

A C Steel Rule Dies Inc............G....... 248 588-5600
Madison Heights (G-10175)
Alpine Sign and Prtg Sup Inc............F....... 517 487-1400
Lansing (G-9275)
Benmar Communications LLC............F....... 313 593-0690
Dearborn (G-3681)
◆ Brown LLC............C....... 989 435-7741
Beaverton (G-1383)
▲ Conrad Machine Company............F....... 231 893-7455
Whitehall (G-17663)
▲ Douthitt Corporation............E....... 313 259-1565
Detroit (G-4016)
Eagle Press Repairs & Ser............F....... 419 539-7206
Adrian (G-60)
Elk Lake Tool Co............E....... 231 264-5616
Elk Rapids (G-4777)
▲ F P Rosback Co............E....... 269 983-2582
Saint Joseph (G-14310)
Haynie and Hess Realty Co LLC............F....... 586 296-2750
Fraser (G-5659)
▲ Innovative Machines Inc............G....... 616 669-1649
Jenison (G-8630)
M & M Typewriter Service Inc............G....... 734 995-4033
Ann Arbor (G-536)
Maple Leaf Press Inc............G....... 616 846-8844
Grand Haven (G-6054)
Qmi Group Inc............E....... 248 589-0505
Madison Heights (G-10342)
Sgk LLC............D....... 269 381-3820
Battle Creek (G-1245)
▲ Sunraise Inc............F....... 810 359-7301
Lexington (G-9560)
Thermoforming Tech Group LLC............G....... 989 435-7741
Beaverton (G-1395)
Unique-Intasco Usa Inc............G....... 810 982-3360
Auburn Hills (G-1036)
Varn International Inc............G....... 734 781-4600
Plymouth (G-12785)
▲ Voxeljet America Inc............F....... 734 709-8237
Canton (G-2442)

3556 Food Prdts Machinery

APV Baker............G....... 616 784-3111
Grand Rapids (G-6177)
▼ Automated Process Equipment............E....... 616 374-1000
Lake Odessa (G-9111)
B&P Littleford Day LLC............D....... 989 757-1300
Saginaw (G-13998)
◆ Baker Perkins Inc............D....... 616 784-3111
Grand Rapids (G-6202)
Banner Engineering & Sales Inc............F....... 989 755-0584
Saginaw (G-14000)
Blackmer Dover Resources Inc............G....... 616 475-9285
Grand Rapids (G-6230)
Carb-A-Tron Tool Co............G....... 517 782-2249
Jackson (G-8402)
D C Norris North America LLC............G....... 231 935-1519
Traverse City (G-15955)
Dawn Equipment Company Inc............C....... 517 789-4500
Jackson (G-8427)
◆ Dawn Food Products Inc............C....... 517 789-4400
Jackson (G-8429)
◆ Dawn Foods Inc............C....... 517 789-4400
Jackson (G-8430)
▲ Duke De Jong LLC............G....... 734 403-1708
Taylor (G-15710)
Dunkley International Inc............C....... 269 343-5583
Kalamazoo (G-8732)
Foodtools Inc............E....... 269 637-9969
South Haven (G-14759)
▲ Frontier Technology Inc............F....... 269 673-9464
Allegan (G-163)
Indian Summer Cooperative Inc............E....... 231 873-7504
Hart (G-7374)
Infusco Coffee Roasters LLC............G....... 269 213-5282
Sawyer (G-14485)
▲ J J Steel Inc............E....... 269 964-0474
Battle Creek (G-1201)
Kitchenaid............G....... 800 541-6390
Benton Harbor (G-1519)
◆ Lematic Inc............D....... 517 787-3301
Jackson (G-8497)
Lowry Joanellen............G....... 231 873-2323
Hesperia (G-7478)
◆ Marshall Middleby Holding LLC............F....... 906 863-4401
Menominee (G-10743)
Middleby Corporation............C....... 906 863-4401
Menominee (G-10750)
▲ Oliver Packaging and Eqp Co............D....... 616 356-2950
Walker (G-16872)
Pappas Cutlery-Grinding Inc............G....... 800 521-0888
Detroit (G-4289)
Peanut Shop Inc............G....... 517 374-0008
Lansing (G-9409)
▲ Pisces Fish Machinery Inc............E....... 906 789-1636
Gladstone (G-5919)
Precision Extraction Corp............G....... 855 420-0020
Troy (G-16560)
Process Partners Inc............G....... 616 875-2156
Hudsonville (G-8174)
Rustic Cking Dsigns Strlng Hts............G....... 586 795-4897
Sterling Heights (G-15482)
Saa Tech Inc............G....... 313 933-4960
Detroit (G-4351)
Schallips Inc............G....... 906 635-0941
Barbeau (G-1117)
Spiral-Matic Inc............G....... 248 486-5080
Brighton (G-1992)
Spotted Cow............E....... 517 265-6188
Adrian (G-97)
Taylor Freezer Michigan Inc............F....... 616 453-0531
Grand Rapids (G-6916)
Twin Beginnings LLC............G....... 248 542-6250
Huntington Woods (G-8192)
▲ Vendco LLC............G....... 800 764-8245
Shelby Township (G-14718)

3559 Special Ind Machinery, NEC

◆ Ace Controls Inc............C....... 248 476-0213
Farmington Hills (G-4919)
▲ AGC Grand Haven LLC............G....... 616 842-1820
Grand Haven (G-5990)
Air Tight Solutions LLC............G....... 248 629-0461
Detroit (G-3848)
Air-Hydraulics Inc............F....... 517 787-9444
Jackson (G-8377)
◆ Aisin Technical Ctr Amer Inc............D....... 734 453-5551
Northville (G-11677)
▲ Alliance Automation LLC............G....... 810 953-9539
Flint (G-5375)
AME For Auto Dealers Inc............G....... 248 720-0245
Auburn Hills (G-768)
Amerivet Engineering LLC............G....... 269 751-9092
Hamilton (G-7230)
▲ AMI Industries Inc............D....... 989 786-3755
Lewiston (G-9547)
AMI Industries Inc............F....... 989 872-8823
Cass City (G-2510)
Anwar Atwa Prism Autobody............F....... 313 655-0000
Detroit (G-3872)
▲ Applied Instruments Company............E....... 810 227-5510
Brighton (G-1886)
Arcon Vernova Inc............G....... 734 904-1895
Saline (G-14378)
Art Glass Inc............G....... 586 731-8627
Sterling Heights (G-15264)
Automotive Component Mfg............G....... 705 549-7406
Sterling Heights (G-15267)
Automotive Technology LLC............C....... 586 446-7000
Sterling Heights (G-15268)
B & J Tool Services Inc............G....... 810 629-8577
Fenton (G-5185)
B K Corporation............G....... 989 777-2111
Saginaw (G-13997)
B&P Littleford Day LLC............D....... 989 757-1300
Saginaw (G-13998)
◆ B&P Littleford LLC............E....... 989 757-1300
Saginaw (G-13999)
▲ Bekum America Corporation............C....... 517 655-4331
Williamston (G-17727)
Berghof Group North Amer Inc............F....... 313 720-6884
Troy (G-16237)
◆ Besser Company............B....... 989 354-4111
Alpena (G-282)
Best Mfg Tooling Solutions Ltd............G....... 616 877-0504
Wayland (G-17400)
Black Creek Timber LLC............G....... 517 202-2169
Rudyard (G-13983)
Blockmatic Inc............G....... 269 683-1655
Niles (G-11597)
▲ Brothers Industrials Inc............G....... 248 794-5080
Farmington Hills (G-4947)
◆ Brown LLC............C....... 989 435-7741
Beaverton (G-1383)

S
I
C

Employee Codes: A=Over 500 employees, B=251-500
C=101-250, D=51-100, E=20-50, F=10-19, G=3-9
2020 Harris Michigan
Industrial Directory
821

35 INDUSTRIAL AND COMMERCIAL MACHINERY AND COMPUTER EQUIPMENT SIC SECTION

◆ **Burke E Porter Machinery Co** .... C 616 234-1200
Grand Rapids ***(G-6243)***
▲ **Burton Industries Inc** .... E 906 932-5970
Ironwood ***(G-8323)***
▲ **Busche Southfield Inc** .... C 248 357-5180
Southfield ***(G-14860)***
C M E Plastic Company .... G 517 456-7722
Clinton ***(G-3015)***
▲ **CCS Design LLC** .... G 248 313-9178
Wixom ***(G-17781)***
Centennial Technologies Inc .... E 989 752-6167
Saginaw ***(G-14013)***
▲ **Centracore LLC** .... F 586 776-5700
Saint Clair ***(G-14209)***
▲ **Century Inc** .... C 231 947-6400
Traverse City ***(G-15932)***
Cincinnati Time Systems Inc .... F 248 615-8300
Farmington Hills ***(G-4963)***
Compac Specialties Inc .... F 616 786-9100
Holland ***(G-7595)***
Considine Sales & Marketing .... G 248 889-7887
Highland ***(G-7490)***
Corr-Fac Corporation .... G 989 358-7050
Alpena ***(G-284)***
Corvac Composites LLC .... E 812 256-2287
Grand Rapids ***(G-6313)***
Corvac Composites LLC .... C 616 281-2430
Grand Rapids ***(G-6314)***
◆ **Corvac Composites LLC** .... E 616 281-4026
Byron Center ***(G-2184)***
Creative Performance Racg LLC .... G 248 250-6187
Troy ***(G-16285)***
Ctmf Inc .... E 734 482-3086
Ypsilanti ***(G-18063)***
D & F Corporation .... D 586 254-5300
Sterling Heights ***(G-15306)***
D Marsh Company Inc .... G 616 677-5276
Marne ***(G-10506)***
DAS Technologies Inc .... G 269 657-0541
Paw Paw ***(G-12401)***
Dayco Products LLC .... C 989 775-0689
Mount Pleasant ***(G-11191)***
Dayco Products LLC .... E 517 439-0689
Hillsdale ***(G-7522)***
Detroit Tech Innovation LLC .... G 734 259-4168
Redford ***(G-13158)***
▲ **Dipsol of America Inc** .... E 734 367-0530
Livonia ***(G-9713)***
▲ **Drew Technologies Inc** .... G 734 222-5228
Ann Arbor ***(G-425)***
▲ **Durr Inc** .... G 734 459-6800
Southfield ***(G-14888)***
◆ **Durr Systems Inc** .... B 248 450-2000
Southfield ***(G-14889)***
Durr Systems Inc .... C 248 745-8500
Southfield ***(G-14890)***
Eaton Aerospace LLC .... B 616 949-1090
Grand Rapids ***(G-6368)***
Eberspaecher North America Inc .... C 810 225-4582
Brighton ***(G-1915)***
Energy Suppliers LLC .... F 269 342-9482
Kalamazoo ***(G-8738)***
Environ Manufacturing Inc .... G 616 644-6846
Battle Creek ***(G-1178)***
Environmental Products Corp .... G 248 471-4770
Livonia ***(G-9728)***
Ep Magnets & Components LLC .... G 734 398-7188
Canton ***(G-2372)***
Erae AMS Usa LLC .... F 419 386-8876
Farmington Hills ***(G-4989)***
Erae AMS USA Manufacturing LLC .... F 248 770-6969
Pontiac ***(G-12824)***
Esoc Inc .... F 248 624-7992
Wixom ***(G-17806)***
Ess Tec Inc .... D 616 394-0230
Holland ***(G-7625)***
Euclid Coating Systems Inc .... F 989 922-4789
Bay City ***(G-1309)***
◆ **Extol Inc** .... D 616 741-0231
Zeeland ***(G-18136)***
◆ **Fanuc America Corporation** .... B 248 377-7000
Rochester Hills ***(G-13423)***
▲ **Fata Aluminum LLC** .... F 248 724-7669
Auburn Hills ***(G-859)***
▲ **Fbe Corp** .... G 517 333-2605
East Lansing ***(G-4656)***
Federal-Mogul Powertrain LLC .... G 616 754-1272
Greenville ***(G-7131)***
▲ **Firstronic LLC** .... B 616 456-9220
Grand Rapids ***(G-6408)***

▲ **Frontier Technology Inc** .... F 269 673-9464
Allegan ***(G-163)***
Gd Enterprises LLC .... G 248 486-9800
Brighton ***(G-1928)***
▲ **Geep USA Inc** .... E 313 937-5350
Auburn Hills ***(G-880)***
Generation Tool Inc .... G 734 641-6937
Westland ***(G-17561)***
Genix LLC .... C 248 761-3030
West Bloomfield ***(G-17478)***
Genix LLC .... F 248 419-0231
Sterling Heights ***(G-15360)***
▲ **Giffin Inc** .... D 248 494-9600
Auburn Hills ***(G-884)***
◆ **Global Strgc Sup Solutions LLC** .... D 734 525-9100
Livonia ***(G-9753)***
▲ **Gluco Inc** .... G 616 457-1212
Jenison ***(G-8627)***
Glycon Corp .... E 517 423-8356
Tecumseh ***(G-15795)***
Gokoh Coldwater Incorporated .... F 517 279-1080
Coldwater ***(G-3305)***
Graminex LLC .... G 989 797-5502
Saginaw ***(G-14051)***
Grav Co LLC .... F 269 651-5467
Sturgis ***(G-15605)***
Gravel Flow Inc .... G 269 651-5467
Sturgis ***(G-15606)***
◆ **Great Lakes Allied LLC** .... G 231 924-5794
White Cloud ***(G-17622)***
Greene Manufacturing Tech LLC .... C 810 982-9720
Port Huron ***(G-12924)***
H A Eckhart & Associates Inc .... E 517 321-7700
Lansing ***(G-9233)***
HP Pelzer Auto Systems Inc .... E 810 987-4444
Port Huron ***(G-12926)***
Hti Cybernetics Inc .... E 586 826-8346
Sterling Heights ***(G-15369)***
◆ **Huron Valley Steel Corporation** .... C 734 479-3500
Trenton ***(G-16155)***
Ied Inc .... G 231 728-9154
Muskegon ***(G-11346)***
▲ **Il Enterprises Inc** .... F 734 285-6030
Wyandotte ***(G-17962)***
Imperial Industries Inc .... F 734 397-1400
Saline ***(G-14395)***
▲ **Ims/Chinatool Jv LLC** .... G 734 466-5151
Livonia ***(G-9781)***
◆ **Innovative Cleaning Eqp Inc** .... E 616 656-9225
Grand Rapids ***(G-6537)***
Innovative Engineering Mich .... G 517 977-0460
Lansing ***(G-9236)***
▼ **International Wheel & Tire Inc** .... E 248 298-0207
Farmington Hills ***(G-5029)***
Iroquois Assembly Systems Inc .... F 586 771-5734
Warren ***(G-17099)***
J H P Inc .... G 248 588-0110
Madison Heights ***(G-10280)***
Jcu International Inc .... G 248 313-6630
Wixom ***(G-17837)***
Jvis - Usa LLC .... B 586 803-6056
Clinton Township ***(G-3151)***
K & K Technology Inc .... G 989 399-9910
Flushing ***(G-5538)***
Kansmackers Manufacturing Co .... F 248 249-6666
Lansing ***(G-9239)***
Kapex Manufacturing LLC .... G 989 928-4993
Saginaw ***(G-14069)***
Karamon Sales Company .... G 810 984-1750
Port Huron ***(G-12933)***
Kiln Kreations .... G 989 435-3296
Beaverton ***(G-1386)***
Kimastle Corporation .... D 586 949-2355
Chesterfield ***(G-2797)***
Kmj Boring Co Inc .... G 586 465-8771
Clinton Township ***(G-3155)***
Knight Industries Inc .... G 248 377-4950
Auburn Hills ***(G-928)***
▲ **Koins Corp** .... G 248 548-3038
Madison Heights ***(G-10293)***
Kolco Industries Inc .... G 248 486-1690
South Lyon ***(G-14799)***
Liberty Fabricators Inc .... F 810 877-7117
Flint ***(G-5458)***
Libra Industries Inc Michigan .... G 517 787-5675
Jackson ***(G-8499)***
◆ **Loadmaster Corporation** .... E 906 563-9226
Norway ***(G-11817)***
Lumbee Custom Painting LLC .... G 586 296-5083
Fraser ***(G-5685)***

Lumbertown Portable Sawmill .... G 231 206-4600
Muskegon ***(G-11369)***
Lumen North America Inc .... G 248 289-6100
Rochester Hills ***(G-13462)***
▲ **Lyle Industries** .... D 989 435-7717
Beaverton ***(G-1388)***
Mag Automotive LLC .... D 586 446-7000
Sterling Heights ***(G-15407)***
Mag Automotive LLC .... G 586 446-7000
Port Huron ***(G-12937)***
▲ **Magnetic Products Inc** .... D 248 887-5600
Highland ***(G-7497)***
▲ **Mann + Hummel Inc** .... G 269 329-3900
Portage ***(G-13013)***
Martinrea Metal Industries Inc .... D 517 849-2195
North Adams ***(G-11656)***
Master Automatic Mch Co Inc .... E 734 414-0500
Livonia ***(G-9828)***
Met-L-Tec LLC .... E 734 847-7004
Temperance ***(G-15837)***
Michigan Roll Form Inc .... E 248 669-3700
Commerce Township ***(G-3433)***
◆ **Midbrook Inc** .... D 800 966-9274
Jackson ***(G-8525)***
Miller Mold Co .... E 989 793-8881
Frankenmuth ***(G-5594)***
Minland Machine Inc .... G 269 641-7998
Edwardsburg ***(G-4768)***
Modern Diversified Products .... G 989 736-3430
Lincoln ***(G-9567)***
◆ **Morrell Incorporated** .... D 248 373-1600
Auburn Hills ***(G-949)***
Mountain Machine LLC .... F 734 480-2200
Van Buren Twp ***(G-16774)***
Mp Tool & Engineering Company .... E 586 772-7730
Roseville ***(G-13841)***
▼ **Myron Zucker Inc** .... G 586 979-9955
Sterling Heights ***(G-15430)***
New-Matic Industries Inc .... G 586 415-9801
Fraser ***(G-5699)***
Northwoods Prperty Holdings LLC .... G 231 334-3000
Glen Arbor ***(G-5941)***
Nyx Inc .... B 734 464-0800
Livonia ***(G-9869)***
Oakley Industries Sub Assembly .... D 586 754-5555
Warren ***(G-17176)***
Omega Industries Michigan LLC .... G 616 460-0500
Grand Rapids ***(G-6729)***
Oneiric Systems Inc .... G 248 554-3090
Madison Heights ***(G-10317)***
Online Engineering Inc .... F 906 341-0090
Manistique ***(G-10445)***
Operations Research Tech LLC .... G 248 626-8960
West Bloomfield ***(G-17492)***
Ovshinsky Technologies LLC .... G 248 390-3564
Pontiac ***(G-12854)***
Oxmaster Inc .... G 810 987-7600
Port Huron ***(G-12952)***
Palm Industries LLC .... G 248 444-7922
South Lyon ***(G-14808)***
Peloton Inc .... G 269 694-9702
Otsego ***(G-12252)***
Perfected Grave Vault Co .... G 616 243-3375
Grand Rapids ***(G-6748)***
Pine Needle People LLC .... G 517 242-4752
Lansing ***(G-9256)***
▲ **Pioneer Metal Finishing LLC** .... G 877 721-1100
Warren ***(G-17186)***
▼ **Powell Fabrication & Mfg Inc** .... E 989 681-2158
Saint Louis ***(G-14369)***
Protege Concepts Corp .... G 248 419-5330
Farmington Hills ***(G-5104)***
Puritan Magnetics Inc .... F 248 628-3808
Oxford ***(G-12365)***
Quantum Mold & Engineering LLC .... F 586 276-0100
Sterling Heights ***(G-15460)***
◆ **R & B Plastics Machinery LLC** .... E 734 429-9421
Saline ***(G-14410)***
R & S Tool & Die Inc .... G 989 673-8511
Caro ***(G-2476)***
R B Machine .... G 616 928-8690
Holland ***(G-7783)***
Race Ramps LLC .... G 866 464-2788
Escanaba ***(G-4855)***
RB Oil Enterprises LLC .... G 734 354-0700
Plymouth ***(G-12730)***
Rnj Services Inc .... F 906 786-0585
Escanaba ***(G-4857)***
▲ **Roberts Sinto Corporation** .... C 517 371-2460
Lansing ***(G-9320)***

35 INDUSTRIAL AND COMMERCIAL MACHINERY AND COMPUTER EQUIPMENT

▲ Rosler Metal Finishing USA LLC .... D 269 441-3000
  Battle Creek *(G-1242)*
▼ Royal Design & Manufacturing .... D 248 588-0110
  Madison Heights *(G-10346)*
Safety-Kleen Systems Inc .... E 989 753-3261
  Saginaw *(G-14136)*
Sarns Industries Inc .... F 586 463-5829
  Harrison Twp *(G-7360)*
Schneider National Inc .... F 810 636-2220
  Goodrich *(G-5957)*
Senstronic Inc .... C 586 466-4108
  Clinton Township *(G-3222)*
SGC Industries Inc .... E 586 293-5260
  Fraser *(G-5723)*
▲ Sinto America Inc .... E 517 371-2460
  Lansing *(G-9323)*
Size Reduction Specialists .... G 517 333-2605
  East Lansing *(G-4675)*
◆ Somero Enterprises Inc .... D 906 482-7252
  Houghton *(G-7983)*
Spartan Automation Inc .... G 586 206-7231
  Shelby Township *(G-14699)*
Spirit Industries Inc .... G 517 371-7840
  Lansing *(G-9266)*
Stec Usa Inc .... F 248 307-1440
  Madison Heights *(G-10362)*
Sungwoo Hitech Co Ltd .... G 248 509-0445
  Troy *(G-16626)*
▲ Superior Automotive Eqp Inc .... G 231 829-9902
  Leroy *(G-9538)*
▲ Sure Solutions Corporation .... G 248 674-7210
  Auburn Hills *(G-1006)*
Surface Blasting Systems LLC .... G 616 384-3351
  Coopersville *(G-3571)*
Syncreon Acquisition Corp .... F 248 377-4700
  Auburn Hills *(G-1009)*
▲ Technology & Manufacturing Inc .... G 248 755-1444
  Milford *(G-10988)*
Tenneco Inc .... F 248 354-7700
  Southfield *(G-15044)*
Thermfrmer Parts Suppliers LLC .... G 989 435-3800
  Beaverton *(G-1394)*
Thermoforming Tech Group LLC .... G 989 435-7741
  Beaverton *(G-1395)*
Thomas-Ward Systems LLC .... G 734 929-0644
  Ann Arbor *(G-671)*
▼ Thoreson-Mc Cosh Inc .... E 248 362-0960
  Troy *(G-16638)*
Ti-Coating Inc .... F 586 726-1900
  Shelby Township *(G-14709)*
▲ Tks Industrial Company .... E 248 786-5000
  Troy *(G-16645)*
Toyota Industries Elctc Sys N .... G 248 489-7700
  Novi *(G-12018)*
Traffic Sfety Ctrl Systems Inc .... E 248 348-0570
  Wixom *(G-17914)*
◆ Tzamco Inc .... E 248 624-7710
  Walled Lake *(G-16904)*
▲ Ube Machinery Inc .... D 734 741-7000
  Ann Arbor *(G-685)*
Uniloy Inc .... D 514 424-8900
  Tecumseh *(G-15815)*
Universal Magnetics Inc .... G 231 937-5555
  Howard City *(G-8007)*
Universal Tire Recycling Inc .... F 313 429-1212
  Detroit *(G-4416)*
Upton Industries Inc .... E 586 771-1200
  Roseville *(G-13887)*
Usher Enterprises Inc .... E 313 834-7055
  Detroit *(G-4418)*
Valley Gear and Machine Inc .... F 989 269-8177
  Bad Axe *(G-1076)*
Van-Rob USA Holdings .... E 517 423-2400
  Tecumseh *(G-15816)*
Vanova Technologies LLC .... G 734 476-7204
  Superior Township *(G-15648)*
Velesco Phrm Svcs Inc .... G 734 545-0696
  Wixom *(G-17924)*
Velesco Phrm Svcs Inc .... F 734 527-9125
  Plymouth *(G-12787)*
W G Benjey Inc .... F 989 356-0016
  Alpena *(G-319)*
Webasto Convertibles USA Inc .... G 734 582-5900
  Plymouth *(G-12792)*
◆ Williams Form Engineering Corp .... G 616 866-0815
  Belmont *(G-1474)*
▲ Wirtz Manufacturing Co Inc .... D 810 987-7600
  Port Huron *(G-12978)*
▲ Wolverine Advanced Mtls LLC .... E 313 749-6100
  Dearborn *(G-3774)*

Z-Brite Metal Finishing Inc .... F 269 422-2191
  Stevensville *(G-15586)*

3561 Pumps & Pumping Eqpt

AA Anderson & Co Inc .... G 734 432-9800
  Livonia *(G-9622)*
Backos Engineering Co .... G 734 513-0020
  Livonia *(G-9659)*
▲ Becktold Enterprises Inc .... G 269 349-3656
  Kalamazoo *(G-8694)*
▲ Benecor Inc .... F 248 437-4437
  Fenton *(G-5188)*
Clyde Union (holdings) Inc .... B 269 966-4600
  Battle Creek *(G-1168)*
Cpj Company Inc .... E 616 784-6355
  Comstock Park *(G-3472)*
Emp Advanced Development LLC .... D 906 789-7497
  Escanaba *(G-4824)*
Engineered Machined Pdts Inc .... E 906 789-7497
  Escanaba *(G-4827)*
◆ Engineered Machined Pdts Inc .... B 906 786-8404
  Escanaba *(G-4826)*
Flowserve US Inc .... G 989 496-3897
  Midland *(G-10862)*
Fluid Systems Engineering Inc .... E 586 790-8880
  Clinton Township *(G-3123)*
Ford Motor Company .... A 734 484-8000
  Ypsilanti *(G-18074)*
◆ Gast Manufacturing Inc .... B 269 926-6171
  Benton Harbor *(G-1503)*
General Motors LLC .... B 989 894-7210
  Bay City *(G-1315)*
◆ Global Pump Company LLC .... G 810 653-4828
  Davison *(G-3652)*
H & R Industries Inc .... F 616 247-1165
  Grand Rapids *(G-6487)*
Hydra-Tech Inc .... G 586 232-4479
  Macomb *(G-10130)*
Independent Mfg Solutions Corp .... E 248 960-3550
  Wixom *(G-17833)*
Ingersoll-Rand Company .... E 734 525-6030
  Livonia *(G-9783)*
Jacksons Industrial Mfg .... F 616 531-1820
  Wyoming *(G-18012)*
◆ Jetech Inc .... E 269 965-6311
  Battle Creek *(G-1204)*
K & M Industrial LLC .... G 906 420-8770
  Gladstone *(G-5914)*
K and K Machine Tools Inc .... G 586 463-1177
  Clinton Township *(G-3152)*
Kerr Pump and Supply Inc .... E 248 543-3880
  Oak Park *(G-12076)*
▲ Kristus Inc .... F 269 321-3330
  Scotts *(G-14505)*
Ksb Dubric Inc .... E 616 784-6355
  Comstock Park *(G-3492)*
▲ M P Pumps Inc .... D 586 293-8240
  Fraser *(G-5688)*
◆ Melling Tool Co .... B 517 787-8172
  Jackson *(G-8514)*
▲ Neptune Chemical Pump Company .C 215 699-8700
  Grand Rapids *(G-6714)*
Nortek Air Solutions LLC .... D 616 738-7148
  Holland *(G-7759)*
North America Fuel Systems R .... C 616 541-1100
  Grand Rapids *(G-6719)*
Pinnacle Technology Group .... D 734 568-6600
  Ottawa Lake *(G-12268)*
Plasma-Tec Inc .... E 616 455-2593
  Wayland *(G-17409)*
▲ Process Systems Inc .... D 586 757-5711
  Warren *(G-17198)*
Pump Solutions Group .... E 616 241-1611
  Grand Rapids *(G-6797)*
Pump Solutions Group .... B 616 241-1611
  Grand Rapids *(G-6796)*
▲ QEd Envmtl Systems Inc .... D 734 995-2547
  Dexter *(G-4506)*
Ramparts LLC .... C 616 656-2250
  Kentwood *(G-9028)*
◆ Sales Driven Ltd Liability Co .... E 269 254-8497
  Kalamazoo *(G-8881)*
▲ Sales Driven Services LLC .... G 586 854-9494
  Rochester *(G-13350)*
Sames Kremlin Inc .... F 734 979-0100
  Plymouth *(G-12748)*
Shellback Manufacturing Co .... G 248 544-4600
  Hazel Park *(G-7455)*
▲ Sloan Transportation Pdts Inc .... D 616 395-5600
  Holland *(G-7806)*

Standfast Industries Inc .... E 248 380-3223
  Livonia *(G-9942)*
Thin Line Pump .... G 231 258-2692
  Kalkaska *(G-8963)*
▲ Tramec Sloan LLC .... G 616 395-5600
  Holland *(G-7833)*
Vent-Rite Valve Corp .... E 269 925-8812
  Benton Harbor *(G-1560)*
Vogel Engineering Inc .... G 231 821-2125
  Holton *(G-7935)*
Walbro LLC .... C 989 872-2131
  Cass City *(G-2524)*
Water Department .... E 313 943-2307
  Dearborn *(G-3773)*
Water Master Inc .... G 313 255-3930
  Canton *(G-2443)*
Yoe Industries Inc .... G 586 791-7660
  Clinton Township *(G-3263)*

3562 Ball & Roller Bearings

▲ ABC Acquisition Company LLC .... E 734 335-4083
  Livonia *(G-9624)*
Carter Manufacturing Co Inc .... D 616 842-8760
  Grand Haven *(G-6001)*
Cw Manufacturing LLC .... E 734 781-4000
  Northville *(G-11686)*
Evans Industries Inc .... E 313 272-8200
  Detroit *(G-4046)*
Federal-Mogul Powertrain LLC .... E 734 930-1551
  Ann Arbor *(G-458)*
◆ Frost Incorporated .... E 616 453-7781
  Grand Rapids *(G-6421)*
Independent Mfg Solutions Corp .... E 248 960-3550
  Wixom *(G-17833)*
Jtekt North America Corp .... E 734 454-1500
  Plymouth *(G-12660)*
◆ Kaydon Corporation .... B 734 747-7025
  Ann Arbor *(G-516)*
Kaydon Corporation .... C 231 755-3741
  Norton Shores *(G-11766)*
Maureen I Martin Caster .... G 810 233-0484
  Flint *(G-5464)*
▲ Saginaw Products Corporation .... E 989 753-1411
  Saginaw *(G-14141)*
Schaeffler Group USA Inc .... B 810 360-0294
  Milford *(G-10984)*
Shepherd Caster Corp .... G 269 668-4800
  Mattawan *(G-10669)*
SKF Motion Technologies LLC .... E 586 752-0060
  Armada *(G-723)*
SKF USA Inc .... D 734 414-6585
  Plymouth *(G-12756)*
Stearns & Stafford Inc .... F 269 624-4541
  Lawton *(G-9515)*
▲ Sunhill America LLC .... G 616 249-3600
  Grand Rapids *(G-6898)*
TN Michigan LLC .... D 906 632-7310
  Sault Sainte Marie *(G-14476)*

3563 Air & Gas Compressors

Belco Industries Inc .... C 616 794-0410
  Belding *(G-1399)*
▲ Blissfield Manufacturing Co .... B 517 486-2121
  Blissfield *(G-1713)*
Can-AM Engineered Products .... G 734 427-2020
  Livonia *(G-9673)*
Correct Compression Inc .... G 231 864-2101
  Bear Lake *(G-1378)*
Engineering Interests Inc .... G 248 461-6706
  Waterford *(G-17342)*
Flame Spray Technologies Inc .... G 616 988-2622
  Grand Rapids *(G-6410)*
◆ Gast Manufacturing Inc .... B 269 926-6171
  Benton Harbor *(G-1503)*
Gast Manufacturing Inc .... B 269 926-6171
  Benton Harbor *(G-1504)*
Gast Manufacturing Inc .... B 269 926-6171
  Benton Harbor *(G-1505)*
Harvey S Freeman .... E 248 852-2222
  West Bloomfield *(G-17479)*
Metallurgical High Vacuum Corp .... F 269 543-4291
  Fennville *(G-5175)*
◆ Michigan Auto Comprsr Inc .... B 517 796-3200
  Parma *(G-12391)*
Millennium Planet LLC .... G 248 835-2331
  Farmington Hills *(G-5068)*
Natural Gas Compress .... E 231 941-0107
  Traverse City *(G-16046)*
Nordson Corporation .... D 734 459-8600
  Wixom *(G-17866)*

Employee Codes: A=Over 500 employees, B=251-500
C=101-250, D=51-100, E=20-50, F=10-19, G=3-9

35 INDUSTRIAL AND COMMERCIAL MACHINERY AND COMPUTER EQUIPMENT

▲ Okuno International Corp ....G 248 536-2727
  Novi *(G-11963)*
Parker Engineering Amer Co Ltd ....F 734 326-7630
  Westland *(G-17586)*
Pr39 Industries LLC ....G 248 481-8512
  Auburn Hills *(G-977)*
Precision Masking Inc ....E 734 848-4200
  Erie *(G-4808)*
Primore Inc ....F 517 263-2220
  Adrian *(G-87)*
Reeling Systems LLC ....G 810 364-3900
  Saint Clair *(G-14233)*
▲ Saylor-Beall Manufacturing Co........B 989 224-2371
  Saint Johns *(G-14293)*
Spray Foam Fabrication LLC ....G 517 745-7885
  Parma *(G-12394)*
Stop & Go No 10 Inc ....G 734 281-7500
  Southgate *(G-15084)*
▼ Thierica Equipment Corporation ....E 616 453-6570
  Grand Rapids *(G-6928)*
Unist Inc ....E 616 949-0853
  Grand Rapids *(G-6951)*

3564 Blowers & Fans

AC Covers Inc ....F 313 541-7770
  Redford *(G-13141)*
▲ Advance Products Corporation ....E 269 849-1000
  Benton Harbor *(G-1480)*
▲ Advanced Air Technologies Inc........G 989 743-5544
  Corunna *(G-3577)*
Aero Filter Inc ....E 248 837-4100
  Madison Heights *(G-10183)*
▲ Air and Liquid Systems Inc ....E 248 656-3610
  Rochester Hills *(G-13367)*
Air Filter & Equipment Inc ....G 734 261-1860
  Livonia *(G-9632)*
Airhug LLC ....G 734 262-0431
  Canton *(G-2346)*
▲ Airmaster Fan Company ....D 517 764-2300
  Clarklake *(G-2894)*
▼ American Cooling Systems LLC ......E 616 954-0280
  Grand Rapids *(G-6165)*
Anrod Screen Cylinder Company.........E 989 872-2101
  Cass City *(G-2511)*
▲ Avl Test Systems Inc ....C 734 414-9600
  Plymouth *(G-12580)*
Baker Enterprises Inc ....E 989 354-2189
  Alpena *(G-280)*
Beckert & Hiester Inc ....G 989 793-2420
  Saginaw *(G-14003)*
◆ Besser Company ....B 989 354-4111
  Alpena *(G-282)*
Borgwarner Thermal Systems Inc........E 231 779-7500
  Cadillac *(G-2233)*
◆ Cdgjl Inc ....E 517 787-2100
  Jackson *(G-8404)*
Chicago Blow Pipe Company ....F 773 533-6100
  Marquette *(G-10522)*
Clarkson Controls & Eqp Co..............G 248 380-9915
  Novi *(G-11850)*
Clean Air Technology Inc ....E 734 459-6320
  Canton *(G-2362)*
Clean Rooms International Inc ....E 616 452-8700
  Grand Rapids *(G-6278)*
◆ Combustion Research Corp ....E 248 852-3611
  Rochester Hills *(G-13391)*
▲ Complete Filtration Inc ....E 248 693-0500
  Lake Orion *(G-9132)*
Compressor Technologies Inc............F 616 949-7000
  Grand Rapids *(G-6296)*
Constructive Sheet Metal Inc ....E 616 245-5306
  Allendale *(G-215)*
Control Manufacturing Corp ....E 734 283-4300
  Riverview *(G-13292)*
Custom Service & Design Inc............E 248 340-9005
  Auburn Hills *(G-833)*
D-Mark Inc ....E 586 949-3610
  Mount Clemens *(G-11128)*
▼ Dcl Inc ....C 231 547-5600
  Charlevoix *(G-2613)*
Depierre Industries Inc ....E 517 263-5781
  Adrian *(G-59)*
Dexter Automatic Products Co..........C 734 426-8900
  Dexter *(G-4485)*
Entrepreneurial Pursuits ....E 248 829-6903
  Rochester Hills *(G-13418)*
Expert Air Cleaner Maint ....G 248 889-3760
  Highland *(G-7492)*
Forma-Kool Manufacturing Inc ....E 586 949-4813
  Chesterfield *(G-2778)*

Forrest Brothers Inc ....C 989 356-4011
  Gaylord *(G-5859)*
◆ Gallagher-Kaiser Corporation ....D 313 368-3100
  Troy *(G-16378)*
▲ Gelman Sciences Inc ....A 734 665-0651
  Ann Arbor *(G-469)*
▲ General Filters Inc ....E 248 476-5100
  Novi *(G-11890)*
Hammond Machinery Inc ....D 269 345-7151
  Kalamazoo *(G-8759)*
Howden North America Inc ....G 313 931-4000
  Dearborn *(G-3721)*
Key Gas Components Inc ....E 269 673-2151
  Allegan *(G-169)*
Madison Street Holdings LLC............E 517 252-2031
  Adrian *(G-77)*
Met-Pro Technologies LLC ....D 989 725-8184
  Lennon *(G-9518)*
▼ Midwest Air Products Co Inc ....E 231 941-5865
  Traverse City *(G-16035)*
▼ Midwest Intl Std Pdts Inc ....G 231 547-4073
  Charlevoix *(G-2621)*
MKI Products ....E 517 748-5075
  Jackson *(G-8532)*
Murtech Energy Services LLC...........G 810 653-5681
  Port Huron *(G-12948)*
New Way Air Solution Company.........G 248 676-9418
  Milford *(G-10976)*
Nortek Air Solutions LLC ....D 616 738-7148
  Holland *(G-7759)*
Parker-Hannifin Corporation ....B 269 629-5000
  Richland *(G-13252)*
Paul Horn and Associates ....G 248 682-8490
  Waterford *(G-17365)*
▲ Pittsfield Products Inc ....E 734 665-3771
  Ann Arbor *(G-593)*
▲ Process Systems Inc ....D 586 757-5711
  Warren *(G-17198)*
Quality Filters Inc ....F 734 668-0211
  Ann Arbor *(G-611)*
◆ Robovent Products Group Inc ....E 586 698-1800
  Sterling Heights *(G-15476)*
Ron Pair Enterprises Inc ....E 231 547-4000
  Charlevoix *(G-2629)*
Ronal Industries Inc ....F 248 616-9691
  Sterling Heights *(G-15478)*
◆ Rosedale Products Inc ....D 734 665-8201
  Ann Arbor *(G-624)*
Salem/Savard Industries LLC ....E 313 931-6880
  Detroit *(G-4352)*
▲ SER Inc ....E 586 725-0192
  New Baltimore *(G-11492)*
Skyblade Fan Company ....G 586 806-5107
  Warren *(G-17240)*
Tanis Technologies LLC ....G 616 796-2712
  Holland *(G-7823)*
Technical Air Products LLC ....F 616 863-9115
  Belmont *(G-1472)*
Thermo Vac Inc ....D 248 969-0300
  Oxford *(G-12375)*
Tri-Dim Filter Corporation ....F 734 229-0877
  Van Buren Twp *(G-16788)*
◆ Viron International Corp ....D 254 773-9292
  Owosso *(G-12327)*
Waltz-Holst Blow Pipe Company.........E 616 676-8119
  Ada *(G-33)*
Wayne Wire Cloth Products Inc.........C 989 742-4591
  Hillman *(G-7510)*
West Mich Auto Stl & Engrg Inc ......E 616 560-8198
  Belding *(G-1431)*

3565 Packaging Machinery

A & B Packing Equipment Inc............G 616 294-3539
  Holland *(G-7544)*
A-OK Precision Prototype Inc............F 586 758-3430
  Ray *(G-13131)*
Ameri-Serv Group ....F 734 426-9700
  Troy *(G-16195)*
▲ Anchor Bay Packaging Corp ....E 586 949-4040
  Chesterfield *(G-2738)*
B & G Products Inc ....F 616 698-9050
  Grand Rapids *(G-6198)*
BP Pack Inc ....G 612 594-0839
  Bellaire *(G-1436)*
▲ British Cnvrtng Sltns Nrth AME .....E 281 764-6651
  Kalamazoo *(G-8701)*
Butcher Engineering Entps................D 734 246-7700
  Brownstown *(G-2060)*
▲ Camaco LLC ....E 248 442-6800
  Farmington Hills *(G-4954)*

Change Parts Incorporated ....E 231 845-5107
  Ludington *(G-10052)*
Coleman Bowman & Associates ....G 248 642-8221
  Bloomfield Hills *(G-1755)*
Converting Systems Inc ....G 616 698-1882
  Nunica *(G-12034)*
▲ D J S Systems Inc ....E 517 568-4444
  Homer *(G-7941)*
▲ Dura-Pack Inc ....E 313 299-9600
  Taylor *(G-15711)*
▲ Elopak Inc ....C 248 486-4600
  Wixom *(G-17801)*
◆ Elopak-Americas Inc ....C 248 486-4600
  Wixom *(G-17802)*
◆ Filler Specialties Inc ....E 616 772-9235
  Zeeland *(G-18137)*
Gentile Packaging Machinery Co........G 734 429-1177
  Saline *(G-14393)*
▲ Highlight Industries Inc ....D 616 531-2464
  Wyoming *(G-18010)*
▼ Hot Melt Technologies Inc............E 248 853-2011
  Rochester Hills *(G-13446)*
Industrial Model Inc ....G 586 254-0450
  Auburn Hills *(G-913)*
Kalamazoo Packaging Systems ....G 616 534-2600
  Grand Rapids *(G-6568)*
Kalamazoo Packg Systems LLC........F 616 534-2600
  Wyoming *(G-18013)*
◆ Korten Quality Inc ....C 586 752-6255
  Bruce Twp *(G-2086)*
▲ Meca-Systeme Usa Inc ....G 616 843-5566
  Grand Haven *(G-6055)*
Nyx Inc ....B 734 261-7535
  Livonia *(G-9870)*
▲ Nyx LLC ....C 734 462-2385
  Livonia *(G-9871)*
RED Stamp Inc ....E 616 878-7771
  Grand Rapids *(G-6816)*
Robert Bosch LLC ....D 616 466-4063
  Bridgman *(G-1873)*
Robert Bosch LLC ....G 616 302-2000
  Ann Arbor *(G-623)*
Robert Bosch LLC ....E 248 921-9054
  Novi *(G-11987)*
Robert Bosch LLC ....A 734 979-3000
  Plymouth *(G-12741)*
Rollstock Inc ....G 616 803-5370
  Grand Rapids *(G-6836)*
Take-A-Label Inc ....F 616 698-1882
  Nunica *(G-12044)*
Tekkra Systems Inc ....E 517 568-4121
  Homer *(G-7950)*
Tetra Pak Inc ....G 517 629-2163
  Albion *(G-133)*
Tindall Packaging Inc ....G 269 649-1163
  Portage *(G-13050)*
XI Engineering LLC ....G 616 656-0324
  Caledonia *(G-2323)*

3566 Speed Changers, Drives & Gears

Alma Products Company ....G 989 463-1151
  Alma *(G-234)*
American Gear & Engrg Co Inc ....E 734 595-6400
  Westland *(G-17541)*
Arthur R Sommers ....G 586 469-1280
  Harrison Township *(G-7322)*
▲ Atlas Gear Company ....F 248 583-2964
  Madison Heights *(G-10198)*
Broaching Diamond Service LLC ....G 586 757-5131
  Warren *(G-16968)*
Certified Reducer Rbldrs Inc ....F 248 585-0883
  Sterling Heights *(G-15285)*
◆ Cone Drive Operations Inc ....C 231 946-8410
  Traverse City *(G-15945)*
Cone Drive Operations Inc ....E 231 843-3393
  Ludington *(G-10054)*
Custom Gears Inc ....G 616 243-2723
  Grand Rapids *(G-6324)*
Dama Tool & Gauge Company..........F 616 842-9631
  Norton Shores *(G-11747)*
Decker Gear Inc ....F 810 388-1500
  Saint Clair *(G-14216)*
Dorris Company ....E 586 293-5260
  Fraser *(G-5644)*
Eaton Corporation ....A 248 226-6347
  Southfield *(G-14893)*
Fairlane Gear Inc ....G 734 459-2440
  Canton *(G-2374)*
◆ Gast Manufacturing Inc ....B 269 926-6171
  Benton Harbor *(G-1503)*

Gear Gear Inc ....G....... 517 861-7757
Ypsilanti *(G-18075)*
Geartec Inc ....G....... 810 987-4700
Port Huron *(G-12922)*
Great Lakes Hydra Corporation..........F....... 616 949-8844
Grand Rapids *(G-6479)*
Invo Spline Inc..................E....... 586 757-8840
Warren *(G-17097)*
▲ J G Kern Enterprises Inc..........D....... 586 531-9472
Sterling Heights *(G-15378)*
▲ Porite USA Co Ltd..................G....... 248 597-9988
Troy *(G-16554)*
Quantum Machining Inc..................G....... 810 796-2035
Dryden *(G-4571)*
Spindel Corp Specialized..................F....... 616 554-2200
Grand Rapids *(G-6885)*
▲ Tri-TEC Seal LLC..................E....... 810 655-3900
Fenton *(G-5246)*
Truemner Enterprises Inc..................G....... 586 756-6470
Warren *(G-17270)*
Valley Gear and Machine Inc..........F....... 989 269-8177
Bad Axe *(G-1076)*
▼ Wilkie Bros Conveyors Inc..........E....... 810 364-4820
Marysville *(G-10626)*

3567 Indl Process Furnaces & Ovens

Able Htng Clng & Plmbng..................G....... 231 779-5430
Cadillac *(G-2221)*
▲ Afc-Holcroft LLC..................D....... 248 624-8191
Wixom *(G-17754)*
▲ Aichelin Heat Treatment Syst..........G....... 734 459-9850
Wixom *(G-17756)*
Ajax Tocco Magnethermic Corp..........E....... 248 589-2524
Madison Heights *(G-10185)*
Ajax Tocco Magnethermic Corp..........F....... 248 585-1140
Madison Heights *(G-10186)*
Alhern-Martin Indus Frnc Co..........E....... 248 689-6363
Troy *(G-16187)*
Allegan Tubular Products Inc..........D....... 269 673-6636
Allegan *(G-149)*
Atmosphere Group Inc..................G....... 248 624-8191
Wixom *(G-17763)*
Belco Industries Inc..................C....... 616 794-0410
Belding *(G-1399)*
▲ Belco Industries Inc..................E....... 616 794-0410
Belding *(G-1400)*
▼ Capital Induction Inc..................F....... 586 322-1444
Sterling Heights *(G-15280)*
▲ Ce II Holdings Inc..................F....... 248 305-7700
Brighton *(G-1899)*
▲ Clark Granco Inc..................D....... 616 794-2600
Belding *(G-1407)*
▲ Complete Filtration Inc..................F....... 248 693-0500
Lake Orion *(G-9132)*
Custom Electric Mfg LLC..................E....... 248 305-7700
Wixom *(G-17793)*
Cyprium Induction LLC..................G....... 586 884-4982
Sterling Heights *(G-15305)*
D K Enterprises Inc..................G....... 586 756-7350
Warren *(G-16997)*
▲ Ddr Heating Inc..................E....... 269 673-2145
Allegan *(G-155)*
Ddr Heating Inc..................G....... 269 673-2145
Allegan *(G-156)*
Detroit Steel Treating Company..........E....... 248 334-7436
Pontiac *(G-12816)*
Dfc Inc..................G....... 734 285-6749
Riverview *(G-13293)*
▲ Durr Inc..................G....... 734 459-6800
Southfield *(G-14888)*
◆ Durr Systems Inc..................B....... 248 450-2000
Southfield *(G-14889)*
▲ E H Inc..................E....... 269 673-6456
Allegan *(G-159)*
▲ Efd Induction Inc..................F....... 248 658-0700
Madison Heights *(G-10240)*
Eldec LLC..................F....... 248 364-4750
Auburn Hills *(G-852)*
Electroheat Technologies LLC..........E....... 810 798-2400
Auburn Hills *(G-853)*
Evenheat Kiln Inc..................F....... 989 856-2281
Caseville *(G-2505)*
Florheat Company..................G....... 517 272-4441
Lansing *(G-9368)*
▲ Fluid Hutchinson Management..........D....... 248 679-1327
Auburn Hills *(G-876)*
Fluidtherm Corp Michigan..................G....... 989 344-1500
Frederic *(G-5751)*
Fritz Enterprises..................E....... 313 841-9460
Detroit *(G-4073)*
◆ Gallagher-Kaiser Corporation..........D....... 313 368-3100
Troy *(G-16378)*
Gemini Precision Machining Inc..........D....... 989 269-9702
Bad Axe *(G-1065)*
Gerref Industries Inc..................E....... 616 794-3110
Belding *(G-1416)*
Great Lkes Indus Frnc Svcs Inc..........F....... 586 323-9200
Sterling Heights *(G-15364)*
Heating Induction Services Inc..........G....... 586 791-3160
Clinton Township *(G-3135)*
▲ Hi-Tech Furnace Systems Inc..........F....... 586 566-0600
Shelby Township *(G-14600)*
Industrial Frnc Interiors Inc..................G....... 586 977-9600
Sterling Heights *(G-15373)*
Industrial Temperature Control..........G....... 734 451-8740
Canton *(G-2384)*
▲ Inter-Power Corporation..................E....... 810 798-7050
Almont *(G-259)*
Interpower Induction Svcs Inc..........G....... 586 296-7697
Fraser *(G-5673)*
J L Becker Acquisition LLC..........E....... 734 656-2000
Plymouth *(G-12651)*
Jackson Oven Supply Inc..................F....... 517 784-9660
Jackson *(G-8478)*
Jensen Industries Inc...................F....... 810 224-5005
Fenton *(G-5221)*
Kernel Burner..................G....... 989 792-2808
Saginaw *(G-14071)*
▼ Kolene Corporation..................E....... 313 273-9220
Detroit *(G-4180)*
▲ Macair Inc..................G....... 248 242-6860
Commerce Township *(G-3425)*
▲ National Appliance Parts Co..........F....... 269 639-1469
South Haven *(G-14766)*
National Element Inc..................E....... 248 486-1810
Brighton *(G-1966)*
▲ Nexthermal Corporation..................D....... 269 964-0271
Battle Creek *(G-1233)*
Nortek Air Solutions LLC..................D....... 616 738-7148
Holland *(G-7759)*
North Woods Industrial..................G....... 616 784-2840
Comstock Park *(G-3502)*
Perceptive Industries Inc..................E....... 269 204-6768
Plainwell *(G-12536)*
Phoenix Induction Corporation..........F....... 248 486-7377
South Lyon *(G-14809)*
Pillar Induction..................G....... 586 254-8470
Madison Heights *(G-10326)*
Pulverdryer Usa LLC..................E....... 269 552-5290
Springfield *(G-15202)*
R J Manufacturing Incorporated..........G....... 906 779-9151
Crystal Falls *(G-3613)*
▲ Rapid Engineering LLC..................D....... 616 784-0500
Comstock Park *(G-3513)*
Salem/Savard Industries LLC..........E....... 313 931-6880
Detroit *(G-4352)*
Sheler Corporation..................F....... 586 979-8560
Sterling Heights *(G-15496)*
SMS Elotherm North America LLC........G....... 586 469-8324
Shelby Township *(G-14696)*
▲ Solaronics Inc..................E....... 248 651-5333
Rochester *(G-13352)*
▲ Strik-Wstfen-Dynarad Frnc Corp.....G....... 616 355-2327
Holland *(G-7817)*
Thermal Designs & Manufacturng.........E....... 586 773-5231
Roseville *(G-13878)*
Thermal Designs & Mfg..................E....... 248 476-2978
Novi *(G-12014)*
Thermalfab Products Inc..................F....... 517 486-2073
Blissfield *(G-1728)*
▼ Thoreson-Mc Cosh Inc..................E....... 248 362-0960
Troy *(G-16638)*
Tomtek Hvac Inc..................G....... 517 546-0357
Howell *(G-8113)*
Tps LLC..................D....... 269 849-2700
Riverside *(G-13287)*
Ultra-Temp Corporation..................G....... 810 794-4709
Clay *(G-3005)*
Upton Industries Inc..................E....... 586 771-1200
Roseville *(G-13887)*
Vconverter Corporation..................D....... 248 388-0549
Whitmore Lake *(G-17708)*

3568 Mechanical Power Transmission Eqpt, NEC

Accurate Gauge & Mfg Inc..................D....... 248 853-2400
Rochester Hills *(G-13362)*
▲ Allor Manufacturing Inc..................D....... 248 486-4500
Brighton *(G-1883)*
Altra Industrial Motion Corp..........D....... 586 758-5000
Warren *(G-16925)*
Arthur R Sommers..................G....... 586 469-1280
Harrison Township *(G-7322)*
Auburn Hills Manufacturing Inc..........C....... 313 758-2000
Auburn Hills *(G-782)*
Baker Inc..................E....... 517 339-3835
Haslett *(G-7396)*
Barnes Industries Inc..................E....... 248 541-2333
Madison Heights *(G-10201)*
▲ BDS Company Inc..................E....... 517 279-2135
Coldwater *(G-3291)*
Borgwarner Powdered Metals Inc..........E....... 734 261-5322
Livonia *(G-9668)*
Borgwarner Thermal Systems Inc..........E....... 231 779-7500
Cadillac *(G-2233)*
Colonial Bushings Inc..................F....... 586 954-3880
Clinton Township *(G-3082)*
Con-Vel Inc..................G....... 864 281-2228
Lansing *(G-9284)*
Craft Steel Products Inc..................E....... 616 935-7575
Spring Lake *(G-15137)*
Dayco LLC..................G....... 248 404-6500
Troy *(G-16296)*
Dayco Products LLC..................B....... 248 404-6500
Troy *(G-16299)*
◆ Engineered Machined Pdts Inc..........B....... 906 786-8404
Escanaba *(G-4826)*
Equitable Engineering Co Inc..........E....... 248 689-9700
Troy *(G-16351)*
Evans Industries Inc..................G....... 313 272-8200
Detroit *(G-4046)*
Federal-Mogul Powertrain LLC..........B....... 616 754-5681
Greenville *(G-7132)*
Ford Motor Company..................E....... 313 805-5938
Dearborn *(G-3712)*
▲ Formsprag LLC..................C....... 586 758-5000
Warren *(G-17043)*
Friction Control LLC..................G....... 586 741-8493
Clinton Township *(G-3127)*
Gates Corporation..................D....... 248 260-2300
Rochester Hills *(G-13431)*
Gateway Engineering Inc..................E....... 616 284-1425
Grand Rapids *(G-6430)*
▲ Geislinger Corporation..................F....... 269 441-7000
Battle Creek *(G-1192)*
◆ GKN Sinter Metals LLC..................G....... 248 296-7832
Auburn Hills *(G-888)*
▲ Great Lakes Industry Inc..................E....... 517 784-3153
Jackson *(G-8459)*
▲ Hayes Manufacturing Inc..................E....... 231 879-3372
Fife Lake *(G-5342)*
Hole Industries Incorporated..........G....... 517 548-4229
Howell *(G-8050)*
Idc Industries Inc..................E....... 586 427-4321
Clinton Township *(G-3139)*
◆ Jatco Usa Inc..................D....... 248 306-9390
Farmington Hills *(G-5031)*
JD Norman Industries Inc..................D....... 517 589-8241
Leslie *(G-9542)*
Kaydon Corporation..................C....... 231 755-3741
Norton Shores *(G-11766)*
▲ Leedy Manufacturing Co LLC..........D....... 616 245-0517
Grand Rapids *(G-6624)*
Liquid Drive Corporation..................E....... 248 634-5382
Mount Clemens *(G-11139)*
Lovejoy Inc..................D....... 269 637-3017
South Haven *(G-14764)*
Lovejoy Curtis LLC..................G....... 269 637-5132
South Haven *(G-14765)*
M C Carbide Tool Co..................F....... 248 486-9590
Wixom *(G-17850)*
Masterline Design & Mfg..................E....... 586 463-5888
Harrison Township *(G-7339)*
◆ Melling Tool Co..................B....... 517 787-8172
Jackson *(G-8514)*
◆ Michigan Auto Comprsr Inc..........B....... 517 796-3200
Parma *(G-12391)*
Milan Screw Products Inc..................E....... 734 439-2431
Milan *(G-10949)*
Mq Operating Company..................E....... 906 337-1515
Calumet *(G-2330)*
Murray Equipment Company Inc..........F....... 313 869-4444
Warren *(G-17163)*
National Element Inc..................E....... 248 486-1810
Brighton *(G-1966)*
◆ Neapco Holdings LLC..................C....... 248 699-6500
Farmington Hills *(G-5079)*
O TP Industrial Solutions..................G....... 248 745-5503
Pontiac *(G-12853)*

Employee Codes: A=Over 500 employees, B=251-500
C=101-250, D=51-100, E=20-50, F=10-19, G=3-9
2020 Harris Michigan
Industrial Directory
825

35 INDUSTRIAL AND COMMERCIAL MACHINERY AND COMPUTER EQUIPMENT

Orlandi Gear Company Inc ....E..... 586 285-9900
Fraser *(G-5701)*
PCI Procal Inc ....F..... 989 358-7070
Alpena *(G-307)*
▲ Powertrain Integration LLC ....F..... 248 577-0010
Madison Heights *(G-10333)*
▲ Precision Torque Control Inc .....F..... 989 495-9330
Midland *(G-10903)*
Production Industries II Inc ....F..... 231 352-7500
Traverse City *(G-16080)*
Quality Steel Products Inc ....E..... 248 684-0555
Milford *(G-10981)*
Riverside Spline & Gear Inc ....E..... 810 765-8302
Marine City *(G-10481)*
S R P Inc ....D..... 517 784-3153
Jackson *(G-8568)*
◆ Saf-Holland Inc ....B..... 231 773-3271
Muskegon *(G-11417)*
Saginaw Bearing Company ....F..... 989 752-3169
Saginaw *(G-14137)*
Supreme Gear Co ....E..... 586 775-6325
Fraser *(G-5736)*
▲ System Components Inc ....E..... 269 637-2191
South Haven *(G-14776)*
Ton-Tex Corporation ....E..... 616 957-3200
Greenville *(G-7158)*
Ton-Tex Corporation ....G..... 616 957-3200
Grand Rapids *(G-6932)*
Tractech Inc ....E..... 248 226-6800
Southfield *(G-15048)*
▲ U S Graphite Inc ....C..... 989 755-0441
Saginaw *(G-14172)*
▼ Wilkie Bros Conveyors Inc ....E..... 810 364-4820
Marysville *(G-10626)*
Wolverine Machine Products Co ....E..... 248 634-9952
Holly *(G-7902)*

3569 Indl Machinery & Eqpt, NEC

◆ +vantage Corporation ....E..... 734 432-5055
Livonia *(G-9614)*
AA Anderson & Co Inc ....E..... 248 476-7782
Plymouth *(G-12559)*
Acme Mills Company ....E..... 517 437-8940
Hillsdale *(G-7514)*
Acme Mills Company ....G..... 800 521-8585
Bloomfield Hills *(G-1741)*
Acumen Technologies Inc ....F..... 586 566-8600
Shelby Township *(G-14541)*
▲ Advance Products Corporation ..E..... 269 849-1000
Benton Harbor *(G-1480)*
Advanced Recovery Tech Corp .....F..... 231 788-2911
Nunica *(G-12031)*
Airtificial Intelligent Robots ....G..... 989 799-6669
Saginaw *(G-13993)*
Alberts Machine Tool Inc ....G..... 231 743-2457
Marion *(G-10489)*
◆ Allfi Robotics Inc ....G..... 586 248-1198
Wixom *(G-17757)*
◆ Amcol Corporation ....E..... 248 414-5700
Hazel Park *(G-7434)*
Aoa Productions LLC ....G..... 517 256-0820
Williamston *(G-17725)*
Applied & Integrated Mfg Inc ....G..... 248 370-8950
Rochester *(G-13313)*
Arbor International Inc ....G..... 734 761-5200
Ann Arbor *(G-363)*
Asw Amerca Inc ....G..... 248 957-9638
Farmington Hills *(G-4934)*
Ats Assembly and Test Inc ....B..... 937 222-3030
Wixom *(G-17766)*
Auto/Con Services LLC ....E..... 586 791-7474
Fraser *(G-5624)*
Avl North Amer Corp Svcs Inc ....A..... 734 414-9600
Plymouth *(G-12579)*
Baird Investments LLC ....G..... 586 665-0154
Orion *(G-12174)*
Baird Investments LLC ....G..... 586 665-0154
Sterling Heights *(G-15271)*
Barbron Corporation ....E..... 586 716-3530
Kalkaska *(G-8937)*
Becker Robotic Equipment Corp ...G..... 470 249-7880
Orion *(G-12175)*
▲ Beswick Corporation ....F..... 248 589-0562
Troy *(G-16239)*
Bme Inc ....G..... 810 937-2974
Port Huron *(G-12903)*
Bobier Tool Supply Inc ....F..... 810 732-4030
Flint *(G-5392)*
Borneman & Peterson Inc ....F..... 810 744-1890
Flint *(G-5393)*

Boulding Filtration Co LLC ....G..... 313 300-2388
Detroit *(G-3911)*
▲ Bratten Enterprises Inc ....D..... 248 427-9090
Farmington Hills *(G-4946)*
Buhler Technologies LLC ....G..... 248 652-1546
Rochester Hills *(G-13379)*
Bulldog Fabricating Corp ....G..... 734 761-3111
Ann Arbor *(G-392)*
Centrum Force Fabrication LLC ....G..... 517 857-4774
Ann Arbor *(G-398)*
Change Parts Incorporated ....E..... 231 845-5107
Ludington *(G-10052)*
▲ Chip Systems International ....F..... 269 626-8000
Scotts *(G-14503)*
Classic Systems LLC ....C..... 248 588-2738
Troy *(G-16270)*
Conair North America ....E..... 814 437-6861
Pinconning *(G-12507)*
Craft Industries Inc ....A..... 586 726-4300
Shelby Township *(G-14570)*
D B Tool Company Inc ....G..... 989 453-2429
Pigeon *(G-12488)*
Dee-Blast Corporation ....F..... 269 428-2400
Stevensville *(G-15563)*
Dispense Technologies LLC ....G..... 248 486-6244
Brighton *(G-1911)*
▲ Duperon Corporation ....D..... 800 383-8479
Saginaw *(G-14030)*
E Power Remote Ltd ....G..... 231 689-5448
White Cloud *(G-17621)*
Engineered Automation Systems ..G..... 616 897-0920
Belding *(G-1412)*
Esirpal Inc ....G..... 586 337-7848
Macomb *(G-10120)*
▲ Essex Brass Corporation ....F..... 586 757-8200
Warren *(G-17020)*
Everest Energy Fund L L C ....G..... 586 445-2300
Warren *(G-17023)*
Fabrication Concepts LLC ....F..... 517 750-4742
Spring Arbor *(G-15122)*
◆ Fanuc America Corporation ....B..... 248 377-7000
Rochester Hills *(G-13423)*
▲ Fec Inc ....E..... 586 580-2622
Shelby Township *(G-14592)*
Fergin & Associates Inc ....G..... 906 477-0040
Engadine *(G-4798)*
Filtra-Systems Company LLC ....F..... 248 427-9090
Farmington Hills *(G-5001)*
First Due Fire Supply Company .....G..... 517 969-3065
Mason *(G-10638)*
Flodraulic Group Incorporated ......D..... 734 326-5400
Westland *(G-17558)*
Flow Ezy Filters Inc ....F..... 734 665-8777
Ann Arbor *(G-463)*
Front Line Services Inc ....F..... 989 695-6633
Freeland *(G-5757)*
G P Reeves Inc ....E..... 616 399-8893
Holland *(G-7639)*
Gallagher Fire Equipment Co ....E..... 248 477-1540
Livonia *(G-9748)*
▲ Gelman Sciences Inc ....A..... 734 665-0651
Ann Arbor *(G-469)*
General Electric Company ....F..... 616 676-0870
Ada *(G-16)*
Geofabrica Inc ....G..... 810 728-2468
Bloomfield Hills *(G-1767)*
Global Electronics Limited ....E..... 248 353-0100
Bloomfield Hills *(G-1770)*
Global Hoses & Fittings LLC ....G..... 248 219-9581
Farmington Hills *(G-5010)*
▼ Global Tooling Systems LLC ......E..... 586 726-0500
Macomb *(G-10127)*
▲ Hanson Systems LLC ....C..... 269 465-6986
Bridgman *(G-1866)*
Haosen Automation N Amer Inc ....G..... 248 556-6398
Auburn Hills *(G-895)*
Harloff Manufacturing Co LLC ....G..... 269 655-1097
Paw Paw *(G-12405)*
Harvey S Freeman ....E..... 248 852-2222
West Bloomfield *(G-17479)*
▲ Haven Innovation Inc ....F..... 616 935-1040
Grand Haven *(G-6034)*
◆ Hirotec America Inc ....B..... 248 836-5100
Auburn Hills *(G-899)*
Hoff Engineering Co Inc ....G..... 248 969-8272
Oxford *(G-12349)*
▲ Hoffmann Filter Corporation ......F..... 248 486-8430
Brighton *(G-1939)*
▼ Hot Melt Technologies Inc ....E..... 248 853-2011
Rochester Hills *(G-13446)*

Hydraulic Systems Inc ....E..... 517 787-7818
Jackson *(G-8467)*
Independent Mfg Solutions Corp ..E..... 248 960-3550
Wixom *(G-17833)*
Industrial Atomated Design LLC ...G..... 810 648-9200
Sandusky *(G-14435)*
Industrial Service Tech Inc ....F..... 616 288-3352
Grand Rapids *(G-6533)*
Infra Corporation ....G..... 248 623-0400
Waterford *(G-17351)*
Inovatech Automation Inc ....F..... 586 210-9010
Macomb *(G-10131)*
Intellichem LLC ....F..... 810 765-4075
Marine City *(G-10474)*
Intersrce Recovery Systems Inc ....E..... 269 375-5100
Kalamazoo *(G-8774)*
Jack Weaver Corp ....G..... 517 263-6500
Adrian *(G-71)*
Jax Services LLC ....G..... 586 703-3212
Warren *(G-17112)*
Jomesa North America Inc ....G..... 248 457-0023
Troy *(G-16440)*
K and J Absorbent Products LLC ..G..... 517 486-3110
Blissfield *(G-1716)*
◆ Kaydon Corporation ....B..... 734 747-7025
Ann Arbor *(G-516)*
Kdf Fluid Treatment Inc ....F..... 269 273-3300
Three Rivers *(G-15868)*
Keane Saunders & Associates ......G..... 616 954-7088
Grand Rapids *(G-6571)*
Krush Industries Inc ....G..... 248 238-2296
Taylor *(G-15733)*
Lampco Industries Inc ....G..... 517 783-3414
Jackson *(G-8494)*
Light Robotics Automation Inc .....G..... 586 254-6655
Sterling Heights *(G-15399)*
◆ Lube - Power Inc ....D..... 586 247-6500
Shelby Township *(G-14628)*
M-B-M Manufacturing Inc ....G..... 231 924-9614
Fremont *(G-5778)*
Mahle Powertrain ....E..... 248 473-6511
Farmington Hills *(G-5055)*
Mark One Corporation ....D..... 989 732-2427
Gaylord *(G-5877)*
Master Robotics LLC ....E..... 586 484-7710
Almont *(G-262)*
Metalform Industries LLC ....G..... 248 462-0056
Shelby Township *(G-14639)*
Mhr Inc ....F..... 616 394-0191
Holland *(G-7746)*
Microphoto Incorporated ....E..... 586 772-1999
Roseville *(G-13835)*
Millennium Planet LLC ....G..... 248 835-2331
Farmington Hills *(G-5068)*
Motion Industries Inc ....G..... 269 926-7216
Benton Harbor *(G-1533)*
Muskegon Heights Water Filter ....G..... 231 780-3415
Norton Shores *(G-11777)*
New 9 Inc ....E..... 616 459-8274
Grand Rapids *(G-6715)*
◆ New Cnc Routercom Inc ....G..... 616 994-8844
Holland *(G-7755)*
Norman Township ....E..... 231 848-4495
Wellston *(G-17463)*
Northern Processes & Sales LLC ..G..... 248 669-3918
Wixom *(G-17869)*
▲ Ntz Micro Filtration LLC ....F..... 248 449-8700
Wixom *(G-17870)*
Nu-ERA Holdings Inc ....E..... 810 794-4935
Clay *(G-3000)*
Nu-Ice Age Inc ....F..... 517 990-0665
Clarklake *(G-2897)*
Ohio Transmission Corporation ....E..... 616 784-3228
Belmont *(G-1469)*
Onyx Manufacturing Inc ....G..... 248 687-8611
Rochester Hills *(G-13487)*
▼ Opco Lubrication Systems Inc ...G..... 231 924-6160
Fremont *(G-5780)*
▲ Orsco Inc ....G..... 314 679-4200
Armada *(G-721)*
Pan-Teck Corporation ....G..... 989 792-2422
Saginaw *(G-14118)*
Parker-Hannifin Corporation ....D..... 330 253-5239
Otsego *(G-12251)*
▲ Permawick Company Inc ....E..... 248 433-3500
Birmingham *(G-1697)*
▲ Petter Investments Inc ....F..... 269 637-1997
South Haven *(G-14767)*
▲ Pittsfield Products Inc ....E..... 734 665-3771
Ann Arbor *(G-593)*

Plamondon Oil Co Inc ... G ... 231 256-9261 — Lake Leelanau *(G-9106)*
Polk Gas Producer LLC ... G ... 734 913-2970 — Ann Arbor *(G-594)*
Positech Inc ... G ... 616 949-4024 — Grand Rapids *(G-6759)*
▼ **Progressive Surface Inc** ... D ... 616 957-0871 — Grand Rapids *(G-6786)*
Progressive Surface Inc ... E ... 616 957-0871 — Grand Rapids *(G-6787)*
Puritan Automation LLC ... F ... 248 668-1114 — Wixom *(G-17881)*
Quality Filters Inc ... F ... 734 668-0211 — Ann Arbor *(G-611)*
R Concepts Incorporated ... G ... 810 632-4857 — Howell *(G-8086)*
REB Research & Consulting Co ... G ... 248 545-0155 — Oak Park *(G-12092)*
REB Research & Consulting Co ... G ... 248 547-7942 — Detroit *(G-3821)*
Recco Products Inc ... E ... 269 792-2243 — Wayland *(G-17410)*
Recognition Robotics Inc ... G ... 440 590-0499 — Wixom *(G-17884)*
◆ **Rosedale Products Inc** ... D ... 734 665-8201 — Ann Arbor *(G-624)*
▲ **Sanyo Machine America Corp** ... D ... 248 651-5911 — Rochester Hills *(G-13510)*
Schap Specialty Machine Inc ... E ... 616 846-6530 — Spring Lake *(G-15175)*
▲ **Service Tectonics Inc** ... F ... 517 263-0758 — Adrian *(G-96)*
Sk Enterprises Inc ... F ... 616 785-1070 — Grand Rapids *(G-6867)*
Smart Diet Scale LLC ... G ... 586 383-6734 — Bruce Twp *(G-2102)*
SMS Group Inc ... D ... 734 246-8230 — Taylor *(G-15768)*
SMS Technical Services ... G ... 586 445-0330 — Warren *(G-17243)*
Smullen Fire App Sales & Svcs ... G ... 517 546-8898 — Howell *(G-8100)*
Solutions 4 Automation Inc ... F ... 989 790-2778 — Saginaw *(G-14151)*
Superior Design & Mfg ... F ... 810 678-3950 — Metamora *(G-10781)*
Surclean Inc ... G ... 248 791-2226 — Brighton *(G-1994)*
Terrell Manufacturing Svcs Inc ... F ... 231 788-2000 — Muskegon *(G-11435)*
▲ **Thyssenkrupp System Engrg** ... C ... 248 340-8000 — Auburn Hills *(G-1019)*
Tool North Inc ... E ... 231 941-1150 — Traverse City *(G-16125)*
▼ **Trinity Tool Co** ... E ... 586 296-5900 — Fraser *(G-5741)*
United Fbrcnts Strainrite Corp ... E ... 800 487-3136 — Pontiac *(G-12873)*
Universal Tl Eqp & Contrls Inc ... D ... 586 268-4380 — Sterling Heights *(G-15534)*
US Jack Company ... G ... 269 925-7777 — Benton Harbor *(G-1559)*
Venturedyne Ltd ... E ... 616 392-1491 — Holland *(G-7846)*
Viking Group Inc ... G ... 616 432-6800 — Caledonia *(G-2322)*
Volos Tube Form Inc ... E ... 586 416-3600 — Macomb *(G-10174)*
Wal Fuel Systems (usa) Inc ... G ... 248 579-4147 — Livonia *(G-9994)*
Wartrom Machine Systems ... E ... 586 469-1915 — Clinton Township *(G-3260)*
Wayne Wire Cloth Products Inc ... C ... 989 742-4591 — Hillman *(G-7510)*
▲ **Weiss Technik North Amer Inc** ... D ... 616 554-5020 — Grand Rapids *(G-6983)*
West Mich Flcking Assembly LLC ... D ... 269 639-1634 — Covert *(G-3592)*
Whites Bridge Tooling Inc ... E ... 616 897-4151 — Lowell *(G-10045)*
William Shaw Inc ... F ... 231 536-3569 — Traverse City *(G-16146)*
Wolverine Water Works Inc ... G ... 248 673-4310 — Waterford *(G-17387)*
Yaskawa America Inc ... G ... 248 668-8800 — Rochester Hills *(G-13550)*
Youngtronics LLC ... F ... 248 896-5790 — Wixom *(G-17933)*

3571 Electronic Computers

3dfx Interactive Inc ... E ... 918 938-8967 — Saginaw *(G-13990)*
Advanced Integrated Mfg ... F ... 586 439-0300 — Fraser *(G-5613)*
Artemis Technologies Inc ... E ... 517 336-9915 — East Lansing *(G-4650)*
Bk Computing ... G ... 231 865-3558 — Fruitport *(G-5789)*
Bull Hn Info Systems Inc ... F ... 616 942-7126 — Grand Rapids *(G-6240)*
Christopher S Campion ... G ... 517 414-6796 — Jackson *(G-8409)*
Compudyne Inc ... F ... 906 360-9081 — Marquette *(G-10525)*
▲ **Cypress Computer Systems Inc** ... F ... 810 245-2300 — Lapeer *(G-9453)*
Disrupttech LLC ... G ... 248 225-8383 — Saint Clair Shores *(G-14244)*
Dynamic Software Group LLC ... F ... 734 716-0925 — Livonia *(G-9716)*
Eaton Aerospace LLC ... B ... 616 949-1090 — Grand Rapids *(G-6368)*
Enovate It ... F ... 248 721-8104 — Ferndale *(G-5283)*
Entron Computer Systems Inc ... G ... 248 349-8898 — Northville *(G-11690)*
▲ **Ews Legacy LLC** ... E ... 248 853-6363 — Rochester Hills *(G-13421)*
Exaconnect Corp ... G ... 810 232-1400 — Flint *(G-5426)*
HP Inc ... G ... 650 857-1501 — Lansing *(G-9293)*
HP Inc ... G ... 248 614-6600 — Troy *(G-16404)*
I S My Department Inc ... G ... 248 622-0622 — Clarkston *(G-2928)*
Indocomp Systems Inc ... F ... 810 678-3990 — Metamora *(G-10776)*
Innovation Unlimited LLC ... G ... 574 635-1064 — Bay City *(G-1322)*
▲ **Innovtive Design Solutions Inc** ... C ... 248 583-1010 — Sterling Heights *(G-15374)*
Intellibee Inc ... G ... 313 586-4122 — Detroit *(G-4145)*
International Bus Mchs Corp ... E ... 989 832-6000 — Midland *(G-10873)*
International Bus Mchs Corp ... B ... 517 391-5248 — East Lansing *(G-4665)*
Kismet Strategic Sourcing Part ... G ... 269 932-4990 — Saint Joseph *(G-14321)*
Lga Retail Inc ... G ... 248 910-1918 — South Lyon *(G-14800)*
Opto Solutions Inc ... G ... 269 254-9716 — Plainwell *(G-12532)*
PC Techs On Wheels ... G ... 734 262-4424 — Canton *(G-2414)*
PCI Procal Inc ... F ... 989 358-7070 — Alpena *(G-307)*
Plymouth Computer & ... G ... 734 744-9563 — Livonia *(G-9890)*
▲ **Pro-Face America LLC** ... E ... 734 477-0600 — Ann Arbor *(G-605)*
▼ **Protxs Inc** ... C ... 989 255-3836 — Jenison *(G-8638)*
Rave Computer Association Inc ... E ... 586 939-8230 — Sterling Heights *(G-15461)*
Reply Inc ... F ... 248 686-2481 — Auburn Hills *(G-989)*
S T A Inc ... E ... 248 328-5000 — Holly *(G-7896)*
Secord Solutions LLC ... G ... 734 363-8887 — Ecorse *(G-4745)*
Speedway Ordering Systems Inc ... G ... 734 420-0482 — Livonia *(G-9939)*
Stellar Computer Services LLC ... G ... 989 732-7153 — Gaylord *(G-5893)*
Stratos Technologies Inc ... G ... 248 808-2117 — Ann Arbor *(G-649)*
Third Vault Inc ... G ... 248 353-5555 — Bloomfield Hills *(G-1803)*
William Penn Systems Inc ... G ... 313 383-8299 — Lincoln Park *(G-9588)*
▲ **Zareason Inc** ... F ... 510 868-5000 — Lapeer *(G-9493)*

3572 Computer Storage Devices

▲ **American Furukawa Inc** ... E ... 734 254-0344 — Plymouth *(G-12570)*
Aperion Information Tech Inc ... F ... 248 969-9791 — Oxford *(G-12336)*
▲ **Autocam Corporation** ... B ... 616 698-0707 — Kentwood *(G-9000)*
Digilink Technology Inc ... F ... 517 381-8888 — Okemos *(G-12119)*
EMC Corporation ... C ... 248 957-5800 — Farmington Hills *(G-4984)*
International Bus Mchs Corp ... B ... 517 391-5248 — East Lansing *(G-4665)*
Magnetic Systems International ... G ... 231 582-9600 — Petoskey *(G-12455)*
Piolax Corporation ... F ... 734 668-6005 — Plymouth *(G-12717)*
Quantam Solutions LLC ... G ... 248 395-2200 — Southfield *(G-15007)*
Quantum Innovations LLC ... G ... 734 576-2000 — Livonia *(G-9902)*
Quantum Labs LLC ... G ... 248 262-7731 — Southfield *(G-15008)*
Quantum Ventures LLC ... G ... 248 325-8380 — Holly *(G-7892)*
Rave Computer Association Inc ... E ... 586 939-8230 — Sterling Heights *(G-15461)*
Virtual Technology Inc ... F ... 248 528-6565 — Troy *(G-16686)*

3575 Computer Terminals

Dynics Inc ... D ... 734 677-6100 — Ann Arbor *(G-428)*
Freedom Technologies Corp ... E ... 810 227-3737 — Brighton *(G-1926)*
Geeks of Detroit LLC ... G ... 734 576-2363 — Detroit *(G-4079)*
Mmp Molded Magnesium Pdts LLC ... G ... 517 789-8505 — Jackson *(G-8534)*
Mobile Knowlege Group Services ... G ... 248 625-3327 — Clarkston *(G-2940)*
▲ **Photodon LLC** ... G ... 847 377-1185 — Traverse City *(G-16068)*
▲ **Pro-Face America LLC** ... E ... 734 477-0600 — Ann Arbor *(G-605)*
Union Built PC Inc ... G ... 248 910-3955 — Jackson *(G-8598)*

3577 Computer Peripheral Eqpt, NEC

Acromag Incorporated ... D ... 248 624-1541 — Wixom *(G-17751)*
Advanced Integrated Mfg ... F ... 586 439-0300 — Fraser *(G-5613)*
Ampm Inc ... F ... 989 837-8800 — Midland *(G-10814)*
Appliction Spclist Kompany Inc ... F ... 517 676-6633 — Lansing *(G-9339)*
Artic Technologies Intl ... G ... 248 689-9884 — Troy *(G-16220)*
Bbcm Inc ... G ... 248 410-2528 — Bloomfield Hills *(G-1750)*
Bcc Distribution Inc ... F ... 734 737-9300 — Canton *(G-2350)*
Berkshire & Associates Inc ... F ... 734 719-1822 — Canton *(G-2351)*
Black Box Corporation ... G ... 248 743-1320 — Troy *(G-16241)*
Black Box Corporation ... F ... 616 246-1320 — Caledonia *(G-2290)*
Bull Hn Info Systems Inc ... F ... 616 942-7126 — Grand Rapids *(G-6240)*
Cisco Systems Inc ... A ... 800 553-6387 — Detroit *(G-3937)*
Comptek Inc ... F ... 248 477-5215 — Farmington Hills *(G-4965)*
Compunetics Systems Inc ... G ... 248 531-0015 — Rochester Hills *(G-13393)*
Computers Edge ... G ... 989 659-3179 — Munger *(G-11241)*
◆ **Daco Hand Controllers Inc** ... F ... 248 982-3266 — Novi *(G-11861)*
Electronics For Imaging Inc ... D ... 734 641-3062 — Ypsilanti *(G-18069)*
Elite Engineering Inc ... F ... 517 304-3254 — Rochester Hills *(G-13417)*
▲ **Ensure Technologies Inc** ... F ... 734 668-8800 — Ypsilanti *(G-18072)*
Envisiontec Inc ... D ... 313 436-4300 — Dearborn *(G-3702)*
▲ **Graphic Resource Group Inc** ... E ... 248 588-6100 — Troy *(G-16386)*
Innovative Support Svcs Inc ... E ... 248 585-3600 — Troy *(G-16418)*

SIC

35 INDUSTRIAL AND COMMERCIAL MACHINERY AND COMPUTER EQUIPMENT

Interface Associates Inc .... G.... 734 327-9500
  Ann Arbor (G-507)
Jant Group LLC .... G.... 616 863-6600
  Belmont (G-1463)
Jem Computers Inc .... F.... 586 783-3400
  Clinton Township (G-3149)
▲ Jo-Dan International Inc .... G.... 248 340-0300
  Auburn Hills (G-919)
Kace Logistics LLC .... D.... 734 946-8600
  Carleton (G-2458)
Kingdom Cartridge Inc .... G.... 734 564-1590
  Plymouth (G-12669)
▲ Law Enforcement Development Co .. D.... 734 656-4100
  Plymouth (G-12672)
Lexmark International Inc .... F.... 248 352-0616
  Southfield (G-14967)
LMI Technologies Inc .... G.... 248 298-2839
  Royal Oak (G-13944)
Mirror Image .... G.... 231 775-2939
  Cadillac (G-2267)
Printek Inc .... C.... 269 925-3200
  Saint Joseph (G-14336)
▲ Pro-Face America LLC .... E.... 734 477-0600
  Ann Arbor (G-605)
Quartech Corporation .... G.... 586 781-0373
  Macomb (G-10160)
Sakor Technologies Inc .... F.... 989 720-2700
  Owosso (G-12315)
Scs Embedded Tech LLC .... G.... 248 615-2244
  Novi (G-11990)
Startech-Solutions LLC .... G.... 248 419-0650
  Southfield (G-15033)
Toshiba Amer Bus Solutions Inc .... F.... 248 427-8100
  Southfield (G-15046)
◆ Triangle Product Distributors .... F.... 970 609-9001
  Holland (G-7839)
Visionit Supplies and Svcs Inc .... A.... 313 664-5650
  Detroit (G-4432)
Winstanley Associates LLC .... G.... 231 946-3552
  Traverse City (G-16147)
▲ Yakel Enterprises LLC .... G.... 586 943-5885
  Washington Township (G-17320)

3578 Calculating & Accounting Eqpt

Atm International Services LLC ..... F.... 734 524-9771
  Westland (G-17544)
Cornelius Systems Inc .... E.... 248 545-5558
  Berkley (G-1582)
Family Fare LLC .... G.... 269 965-5631
  Battle Creek (G-1184)
Great Lakes Atm .... G.... 248 542-2613
  Ferndale (G-5291)
▲ Marketing Communications Inc .. G.... 616 784-4488
  Comstock Park (G-3496)
PC Complete Inc .... G.... 248 545-4211
  Ferndale (G-5308)

3579 Office Machines, NEC

A A A Mailing & Packg Sups LLC .. G.... 616 481-9120
  Grand Rapids (G-6123)
Central Michigan Engravers .... G.... 517 485-5865
  Lansing (G-9208)
▲ Digital Finishing Corp .... G.... 586 427-6003
  Shelby Township (G-14576)
Pitney Bowes Inc .... D.... 248 625-1666
  Davisburg (G-3637)
Pitney Bowes Inc .... D.... 203 356-5000
  South Lyon (G-14810)
Pitney Bowes Inc .... F.... 248 591-2800
  Madison Heights (G-10328)

3581 Automatic Vending Machines

Gail Parker .... G.... 734 261-3842
  Garden City (G-5825)
◆ Maytag Corporation .... C.... 269 923-5000
  Benton Harbor (G-1529)
Quarters LLC .... G.... 313 510-5555
  Plymouth (G-12727)

3582 Commercial Laundry, Dry Clean & Pressing Mchs

AEC Systems Usa Inc .... E.... 616 257-9502
  Grandville (G-7018)
▲ Kah .... G.... 734 727-0478
  Westland (G-17576)
Pressing Point .... G.... 810 387-3441
  Brockway (G-2020)

3585 Air Conditioning & Heating Eqpt

Acme Tool & Die Co .... G.... 231 938-1260
  Acme (G-1)
▲ Air International (us) Inc .... D.... 248 391-7970
  Auburn Hills (G-762)
Auction Masters .... G.... 586 576-7777
  Oak Park (G-12050)
▲ Blissfield Manufacturing Co .... B.... 517 486-2121
  Blissfield (G-1713)
Bolhouse LLC .... G.... 616 209-7543
  Jenison (G-8619)
◆ Cdgjl Inc .... E.... 517 787-2100
  Jackson (G-8404)
▲ Check Technology Solutions LLC .. E.... 248 680-2323
  Troy (G-16264)
Chrysler & Koppin Company .... F.... 313 491-7100
  Detroit (G-3936)
Clear Advantage Mechanical .... G.... 616 520-5884
  Grand Rapids (G-6279)
◆ Combustion Research Corp .... E.... 248 852-3611
  Rochester Hills (G-13391)
Compressor Industries LLC .... F.... 313 389-2800
  Melvindale (G-10693)
Crown Heating Inc .... G.... 248 352-1688
  Detroit (G-3955)
D & B Heat Transfer Pdts Inc .... F.... 616 827-0028
  Grand Rapids (G-6327)
▲ Dimplex Thermal Solutions Inc ... C.... 269 349-6800
  Kalamazoo (G-8728)
Espar Inc .... E.... 248 994-7010
  Novi (G-11885)
▼ Etx Holdings Inc .... G.... 989 463-1151
  Alma (G-237)
Evans Tempcon Delaware LLC .... G.... 616 361-2681
  Grand Rapids (G-6388)
▲ Fluid Chillers Inc .... E.... 517 484-9190
  Lansing (G-9369)
Forma-Kool Manufacturing Inc ...... E.... 586 949-4813
  Chesterfield (G-2778)
Forzza Corporation .... F.... 616 884-6121
  Middleville (G-10802)
▲ General Filters Inc .... E.... 248 476-5100
  Novi (G-11890)
◆ Glastender Inc .... C.... 989 752-4275
  Saginaw (G-14045)
Grand Traverse Mech Contg LLC .. G.... 231 943-7400
  Interlochen (G-8241)
▲ Great Lakes Air Products Inc ..... E.... 734 326-7080
  Westland (G-17563)
Hanon Systems Usa LLC .... B.... 248 907-8000
  Novi (G-11893)
◆ Hella Corporate Center USA Inc .. E.... 586 232-4788
  Northville (G-11697)
Hussmann Corporation .... D.... 248 668-0790
  Wixom (G-17832)
Johnson Controls Inc .... C.... 313 842-3479
  Van Buren Twp (G-16766)
Kelley Brothers Lc .... F.... 734 462-6266
  Livonia (G-9795)
▲ Kraftube Inc .... C.... 231 832-5562
  Reed City (G-13217)
La Rosa Refrigeration & Eqp Co ... E.... 313 368-6620
  Detroit (G-4187)
▲ Mahle Behr Industy America Lp .. D.... 616 647-3490
  Belmont (G-1468)
▲ Mahle Behr Troy Inc .... C.... 248 743-3700
  Troy (G-16481)
▲ Mann + Hummel Inc .... G.... 269 329-3900
  Portage (G-13013)
Marelli North America Inc .... C.... 248 848-4800
  Farmington Hills (G-5057)
Mechanical Air System Inc .... G.... 248 346-7995
  Commerce Township (G-3429)
◆ Michigan Auto Comprsr Inc .... B.... 517 796-3200
  Parma (G-12391)
Microtemp Fluid Systems LLC ...... C.... 248 703-5056
  Farmington Hills (G-5067)
Milair LLC .... G.... 513 576-0123
  Sterling Heights (G-15425)
Murtech Energy Services LLC ...... C.... 810 653-5681
  Port Huron (G-12948)
National Aircraft Service Inc .... F.... 517 423-7589
  Tecumseh (G-15803)
Nortek Inc .... G.... 616 719-5588
  Grand Rapids (G-6718)
Nortek Air Solutions LLC .... D.... 616 738-7148
  Holland (G-7759)
▲ Northstar Wholesale .... G.... 517 545-2379
  Howell (G-8070)

Opti Temp Inc .... E.... 231 946-2931
  Traverse City (G-16060)
Ostrander Company Inc .... G.... 248 646-6680
  Madison Heights (G-10318)
▲ Rapid Engineering LLC .... D.... 616 784-0500
  Comstock Park (G-3513)
Refrigeration Research Inc .... G.... 989 773-7540
  Mount Pleasant (G-11223)
Refrigeration Research Inc .... D.... 810 227-1151
  Brighton (G-1985)
Remacon Compressors Inc .... G.... 313 842-8219
  Detroit (G-4341)
▲ Riedel USA Inc .... G.... 734 595-9820
  Kalamazoo (G-8871)
Rush Air Inc .... F.... 810 694-5763
  Holly (G-7895)
Scientemp Corp .... F.... 517 263-6020
  Adrian (G-94)
▲ Snow Machines Incorporated .... E.... 989 631-6091
  Midland (G-10917)
Snow Technologies Incorporated .. G.... 734 425-3600
  Livonia (G-9934)
◆ Stahls Inc .... D.... 800 478-2457
  Sterling Heights (G-15508)
Su-Tec Inc .... F.... 248 852-4711
  Rochester Hills (G-13521)
Tecumseh Compressor Co LLC .... A.... 662 566-2231
  Ann Arbor (G-657)
▲ Tecumseh Compressor Company .. G.... 734 585-9500
  Ann Arbor (G-658)
Tecumseh Products Company ...... F.... 734 973-1359
  Ann Arbor (G-659)
Tecumseh Products Company ...... C.... 734 769-0650
  Ann Arbor (G-660)
◆ Tecumseh Products Company LLC .. A.... 734 585-9500
  Ann Arbor (G-661)
Tecumseh Products Company LLC .. G.... 734 585-9500
  Ann Arbor (G-662)
Tecumseh Products Holdings LLC .. F.... 734 585-9500
  Ann Arbor (G-663)
▲ TI Automotive LLC .... C.... 248 494-5000
  Auburn Hills (G-1020)
◆ TI Group Auto Systems LLC .... B.... 248 296-8000
  Auburn Hills (G-1022)
TMI Climate Solutions Inc .... C.... 810 603-3300
  Holly (G-7899)
Trane US Inc .... E.... 800 245-3964
  Flint (G-5511)
Trane US Inc .... G.... 734 367-0700
  Livonia (G-9969)
Trane US Inc .... D.... 734 452-2000
  Livonia (G-9970)
U S Distributing Inc .... E.... 248 646-0550
  Birmingham (G-1707)
Universal Heating and Cooling ...... G.... 734 216-5826
  South Lyon (G-14816)
▼ Weather-Rite LLC .... D.... 612 338-1401
  Comstock Park (G-3520)
Whirlpool Corporation .... B.... 269 923-5000
  Benton Harbor (G-1570)
▼ Whirlpool Corporation .... A.... 269 923-5000
  Benton Harbor (G-1565)
Whirlpool Corporation .... G.... 269 923-5000
  Benton Harbor (G-1566)
Whirlpool Corporation .... C.... 269 849-0907
  Coloma (G-3367)
Whirlpool Corporation .... C.... 269 923-3009
  Benton Harbor (G-1571)
Wilson Stamping & Mfg Inc .... G.... 989 823-8521
  Vassar (G-16820)
▲ Young Supply Company .... E.... 313 875-3280
  Detroit (G-4455)

3586 Measuring & Dispensing Pumps

Accurate Gauge & Mfg Inc .... D.... 248 853-2400
  Rochester Hills (G-13362)
▲ Atlas Copco Ias LLC .... D.... 248 377-9722
  Auburn Hills (G-781)
Bennett Commercial Pump Co ...... D.... 231 798-1310
  Norton Shores (G-11808)
Bpc Acquisition Company .... D.... 231 798-1310
  Norton Shores (G-11809)
Dispense Technologies LLC .... G.... 248 486-6244
  Brighton (G-1911)
▲ Neptune Chemical Pump Company .C.... 215 699-8700
  Grand Rapids (G-6714)
Nordson Corporation .... D.... 734 459-8600
  Wixom (G-17866)

3589 Service Ind Machines, NEC

Admiral G 989 356-6419
Alpena *(G-271)*
Aerospace America Inc E 989 684-2121
Bay City *(G-1273)*
Amos Mfg Inc E 989 358-7187
Alpena *(G-276)*
Bauer Soft Water Co G 269 695-7900
Niles *(G-11596)*
Birks Works Environmental LLC G 313 891-1310
Detroit *(G-3904)*
Bissell Better Life LLC G 800 237-7691
Grand Rapids *(G-6224)*
Business Connect L3c G 616 443-8070
Grandville *(G-7025)*
Cascade Equipment Company G 734 697-7870
Van Buren Twp *(G-16750)*
Central Lenawee Sewage Plant G 517 263-0955
Adrian *(G-55)*
▲ **Chip Systems International** F 269 626-8000
Scotts *(G-14503)*
City of Port Huron E 810 984-9775
Port Huron *(G-12908)*
▲ **Creative Products Intl** F 616 335-3333
Holland *(G-7600)*
Custom Service & Design Inc E 248 340-9005
Auburn Hills *(G-833)*
▲ **D & L Water Control Inc** F 734 455-6982
Canton *(G-2363)*
Dancorp Inc F 269 663-5566
Edwardsburg *(G-4764)*
▲ **Delfield Company LLC** A 989 773-7981
Mount Pleasant *(G-11192)*
Digested Organics LLC G 844 934-4378
Farmington Hills *(G-4973)*
Dihydro Services Inc E 586 978-0900
Sterling Heights *(G-15317)*
Douglas Water Conditioning E 248 363-8383
Waterford *(G-17336)*
Doulton & Co G 248 258-6977
Southfield *(G-14886)*
Easy Scrub LLC G 586 565-1777
Roseville *(G-13798)*
Ener-TEC Inc F 517 741-5015
Union City *(G-16733)*
Environmental Resources G 248 446-9639
New Hudson *(G-11540)*
Evoqua Water Technologies LLC D 616 772-9011
Holland *(G-7629)*
Garbage Man LLC G 810 225-3001
Brighton *(G-1927)*
GCI Water Solutions LLC G 312 928-9992
Midland *(G-10865)*
▲ **Geerpres Inc** E 231 773-3211
Muskegon *(G-11329)*
▲ **Getecha Inc** G 269 373-8896
Kalamazoo *(G-8752)*
◆ **Ginsan Liquidating Company LLC** D 616 791-8100
Grand Rapids *(G-6443)*
◆ **Glastender Inc** C 989 752-4275
Saginaw *(G-14045)*
Great Lakes Ncw LLC G 616 355-2626
Holland *(G-7653)*
Great Lakes Service & Supplies G 734 854-8542
Petersburg *(G-12436)*
H & R Electrical Contrs LLC G 517 669-2102
Dewitt *(G-4462)*
H-O-H Water Technology Inc F 248 669-6667
Commerce Township *(G-3409)*
◆ **Hines Corporation** F 231 799-6240
Norton Shores *(G-11812)*
Hollis Sewer & Plumbing Svc G 517 263-8151
Adrian *(G-67)*
Horizon Bros Painting Corp G 810 632-3362
Howell *(G-8051)*
Hydrochem LLC C 313 841-5800
Monroe *(G-11040)*
Hygratek LLC G 847 962-6180
Ann Arbor *(G-498)*
▼ **Inland Management Inc** G 313 899-3014
Detroit *(G-4140)*
◆ **Interclean Equipment LLC** E 734 961-3300
Ypsilanti *(G-18082)*
J Mark Systems Inc G 616 784-6005
Grand Rapids *(G-6548)*
Lampco Industries Inc G 517 783-3414
Jackson *(G-8494)*
Lane Soft Water G 269 673-3272
Allegan *(G-175)*
▲ **Lincoln-Remi Group LLC** G 248 255-0200
Commerce Township *(G-3421)*
Mar Cor Purification Inc F 248 373-7844
Lake Orion *(G-9148)*
Max Endura Inc E 989 356-1593
Alpena *(G-297)*
McIntyre Softwater Service E 810 735-5778
Linden *(G-9593)*
Menominee City of Michigan G 906 863-3050
Menominee *(G-10746)*
Michigan Soft Water of Centr D 517 339-0722
East Lansing *(G-4669)*
Midwest Stainless Fabricating G 248 476-4502
Livonia *(G-9844)*
◆ **Monroe Environmental Corp** E 734 242-2420
Monroe *(G-11054)*
▲ **Motor City Wash Works Inc** E 248 313-0272
Wixom *(G-17860)*
MRM Ida Products Co Inc G 313 834-0200
Detroit *(G-4259)*
North American Aqua Envmtl LLC F 269 476-2092
Vandalia *(G-16802)*
▲ **Pacific Stamex Clg Systems Inc** E 231 773-1330
Muskegon *(G-11398)*
▲ **Plymouth Technology Inc** F 248 537-0081
Rochester Hills *(G-13496)*
Power-Brite of Michigan Inc F 734 591-7911
Livonia *(G-9891)*
Prime Solution Inc F 269 694-6666
Otsego *(G-12253)*
Products Engineered Daley G 616 748-0162
Zeeland *(G-18179)*
▲ **Reynolds Water Conditioning Co** F 248 888-5000
Farmington Hills *(G-5114)*
▲ **Royal Accoutrements Inc** G 517 347-7983
Okemos *(G-12136)*
Royce Rolls Ringer Company E 616 361-9266
Grand Rapids *(G-6847)*
▲ **Sandbox Solutions Inc** C 248 349-7010
Northville *(G-11723)*
Sebright Products Inc E 269 793-7183
Hopkins *(G-7960)*
Sebright Products Inc E 269 792-6229
Wayland *(G-17415)*
Seymour Dehaan G 269 672-7377
Martin *(G-10597)*
Shred-Pac Inc E 269 793-7978
Hopkins *(G-7961)*
Sludgehammer Group Ltd G 231 348-5866
Petoskey *(G-12476)*
▲ **Solaronics Inc** E 248 651-5333
Rochester *(G-13352)*
Sparta Wash & Storage LLC G 616 887-1034
Sparta *(G-15111)*
▲ **Spartan Tool LLC** E 815 539-7411
Niles *(G-11647)*
▼ **Sweepster Attachments LLC** A 734 996-9116
Dexter *(G-4512)*
Telespector Corporation F 248 373-5400
Auburn Hills *(G-1017)*
▼ **Tennant Commercial** B 616 994-4000
Holland *(G-7826)*
Tennant Company G 616 994-4000
Holland *(G-7827)*
Vaclovers Inc E 616 246-1700
Grand Rapids *(G-6956)*
Vanaire Inc D 906 428-4656
Gladstone *(G-5921)*
Vans Car Wash Inc F 231 744-4831
Muskegon *(G-11445)*
Vital Technologies G 231 352-9364
Frankfort *(G-5607)*
Wayne County Laboratory G 734 285-5215
Wyandotte *(G-17981)*
William Cosgriff Electrc G 313 832-6958
Detroit *(G-4442)*
Wonder Makers Environmental F 269 382-4154
Kalamazoo *(G-8926)*

3592 Carburetors, Pistons, Rings & Valves

Air Brake Systems Inc G 989 775-8880
Mount Pleasant *(G-11168)*
Aircraft Precision Pdts Inc D 989 875-4186
Ithaca *(G-8356)*
▲ **Autocam-Pax Inc** E 269 782-5186
Dowagiac *(G-4534)*
Bucher Hydraulics Inc E 231 652-2773
Newaygo *(G-11564)*
Cal Grinding Inc E 906 786-8749
Escanaba *(G-4821)*
Dexter Automatic Products Co C 734 426-8900
Dexter *(G-4485)*
◆ **Federal Screw Works** F 734 941-4211
Romulus *(G-13676)*
Federal Screw Works E 734 941-4211
Big Rapids *(G-1626)*
▲ **Federal-Mogul Piston Rings Inc** F 248 354-7700
Southfield *(G-14909)*
Federal-Mogul Powertrain Inc C 616 887-8231
Sparta *(G-15094)*
Federal-Mogul Powertrain LLC E 734 930-1590
Ann Arbor *(G-458)*
Federal-Mogul Valve Train Inte E 248 354-7700
Southfield *(G-14912)*
Flowcor LLC G 616 554-1100
Kentwood *(G-9006)*
General Motors LLC B 989 894-7210
Bay City *(G-1315)*
▲ **Hastings Manufacturing Company** D 269 945-2491
Hastings *(G-7413)*
◆ **Kaydon Corporation** B 734 747-7025
Ann Arbor *(G-516)*
▲ **L E Jones Company** B 906 863-1043
Menominee *(G-10741)*
Mahle Eng Components USA Inc F 248 305-8200
Farmington Hills *(G-5051)*
▲ **Minowitz Manufacturing Co** E 586 779-5940
Huntington Woods *(G-8190)*
Nelms Technologies Inc D 734 955-6500
Romulus *(G-13712)*
▲ **Polyvalve LLC** G 616 656-2264
Kentwood *(G-9025)*
Trend Performance Products E 586 792-6620
Clinton Township *(G-3251)*
Tyde Group Worldwide LLC G 248 879-7656
Troy *(G-16659)*
Walbro LLC C 989 872-2131
Cass City *(G-2524)*

3593 Fluid Power Cylinders & Actuators

◆ **Ace Controls Inc** C 248 476-0213
Farmington Hills *(G-4919)*
Air Devices Co G 989 354-5740
Alpena *(G-272)*
▲ **Airman Products LLC** E 248 960-1354
Brighton *(G-1881)*
◆ **Beaver Aerospace & Defense Inc** D 734 853-5003
Livonia *(G-9662)*
Behco Inc F 586 755-0200
Madison Heights *(G-10203)*
▲ **Best Metal Products Co Inc** C 616 942-7141
Grand Rapids *(G-6213)*
Bucher Hydraulics Inc E 231 652-2773
Newaygo *(G-11564)*
Cpj Company Inc E 616 784-6355
Comstock Park *(G-3472)*
Crankshaft Machine Company E 517 787-3791
Jackson *(G-8423)*
◆ **Dadco Inc** D 734 207-1100
Plymouth *(G-12604)*
Dadco Inc G 616 785-2888
Comstock Park *(G-3475)*
▲ **De-Sta-Co Cylinders Inc** B 248 836-6700
Auburn Hills *(G-838)*
E J M Ball Screw LLC F 989 893-7674
Bay City *(G-1307)*
E K Hydraulics Inc G 800 632-7112
Petoskey *(G-12448)*
Eaton Corporation C 517 787-7220
Jackson *(G-8439)*
Hilite International Inc C 231 894-3200
Whitehall *(G-17668)*
Ksb Dubric Inc E 616 784-6355
Comstock Park *(G-3492)*
Lor Manufacturing Co Inc G 866 644-8622
Weidman *(G-17458)*
Npi G 248 478-0010
Farmington Hills *(G-5083)*
Nu-ERA Holdings Inc F 248 477-2288
Farmington Hills *(G-5084)*
Pacora River Defense LLC G 248 546-1142
Hazel Park *(G-7450)*
Parker-Hannifin Corporation D 330 253-5239
Otsego *(G-12251)*
Parker-Hannifin Corporation B 269 629-5000
Richland *(G-13252)*
Parker-Hannifin Corporation B 269 384-3459
Kalamazoo *(G-8843)*
Peninsular Inc E 586 775-7211
Roseville *(G-13853)*

S
I
C

Employee Codes: A=Over 500 employees, B=251-500
C=101-250, D=51-100, E=20-50, F=10-19, G=3-9
2020 Harris Michigan
Industrial Directory
829

35 INDUSTRIAL AND COMMERCIAL MACHINERY AND COMPUTER EQUIPMENT

Quality Cylinder Service ....G..... 269 345-0699
Kalamazoo *(G-8865)*
R M Wright Company Inc ....E..... 248 476-9800
Farmington Hills *(G-5111)*
Superior Tool & Fabg LLC ....G..... 906 353-7588
Keeweenaw Bay *(G-9041)*
▲ Suspa Incorporated ....C..... 616 241-4200
Grand Rapids *(G-6906)*
Total Flow Products Inc ....G..... 248 588-4490
Troy *(G-16648)*
Tri-Tech Engineering Inc ....E..... 734 283-3700
Wyandotte *(G-17978)*
▲ Yates Industries Inc ....D..... 586 778-7680
Saint Clair Shores *(G-14277)*

3594 Fluid Power Pumps & Motors

◆ Ace Controls Inc ....C..... 248 476-0213
Farmington Hills *(G-4919)*
▲ Armstrong Fluid Handling Inc ....C..... 269 279-3600
Three Rivers *(G-15856)*
▲ Bucher Hydraulics Inc ....C..... 616 458-1306
Grand Rapids *(G-6238)*
Bucher Hydraulics Inc ....E..... 231 652-2773
Newaygo *(G-11564)*
Dare Auto Inc ....E..... 734 228-6243
Plymouth *(G-12605)*
▲ Ddks Industries LLC ....C..... 586 323-5909
Shelby Township *(G-14573)*
Eaton Aerospace LLC ....B..... 616 949-1090
Grand Rapids *(G-6368)*
Eaton Corporation ....C..... 517 787-7220
Jackson *(G-8439)*
Eaton-Aeroquip Llc ....B..... 949 452-9575
Jackson *(G-8440)*
◆ Flint Hydrostatics Inc ....F..... 901 794-2462
Chesterfield *(G-2777)*
Flow-Rite Controls Ltd ....E..... 616 583-1700
Byron Center *(G-2191)*
◆ Gast Manufacturing Inc ....B..... 269 926-6171
Benton Harbor *(G-1503)*
Gds Enterprises ....G..... 989 644-3115
Lake *(G-9082)*
GM Components Holdings LLC ....E..... 616 246-2000
Grand Rapids *(G-6444)*
Great Lakes Hydra Corporation ....F..... 616 949-8844
Grand Rapids *(G-6479)*
Hilite International Inc ....C..... 231 894-3200
Whitehall *(G-17668)*
Hydraulex Intl Holdings Inc ....A..... 914 682-2700
Chesterfield *(G-2786)*
Hydraulic Systems Inc ....E..... 517 787-7818
Jackson *(G-8467)*
Hydro-Craft Inc ....E..... 248 652-8100
Rochester Hills *(G-13448)*
▲ J H Bennett and Company Inc ....E..... 248 596-5100
Novi *(G-11910)*
Jamco Manufacturing Inc ....G..... 248 852-1988
Auburn Hills *(G-918)*
▲ Kawasaki Prcision McHy USA Inc ...E..... 616 975-3100
Grand Rapids *(G-6570)*
Kennedy Industries Inc ....D..... 248 684-1200
Wixom *(G-17840)*
Limo-Reid Inc ....G..... 517 447-4164
Deerfield *(G-3812)*
Loftis Alumi-TEC Inc ....E..... 616 846-1990
Grand Haven *(G-6050)*
▲ M P Pumps Inc ....D..... 586 293-8240
Fraser *(G-5688)*
Matt and Dave LLC ....G..... 734 439-1988
Dundee *(G-4595)*
Med-Kas Hydraulics Inc ....F..... 248 585-3220
Troy *(G-16491)*
Metaris Hydraulics ....G..... 586 949-4240
Chesterfield *(G-2805)*
Mfp Automation Engineering Inc ....D..... 616 538-5700
Hudsonville *(G-8167)*
Npi ....G..... 248 478-0010
Farmington Hills *(G-5083)*
▲ Oilgear Company ....D..... 231 929-1660
Traverse City *(G-16055)*
Parker HSD ....F..... 269 384-3915
Kalamazoo *(G-8842)*
Parker-Hannifin Corporation ....D..... 734 455-1700
Plymouth *(G-12708)*
Parker-Hannifin Corporation ....C..... 269 692-6254
Otsego *(G-12250)*
Parker-Hannifin Corporation ....A..... 269 384-3400
Kalamazoo *(G-8844)*
Parker-Hannifin Corporation ....B..... 269 384-3459
Kalamazoo *(G-8843)*

▲ Piper Industries Inc ....D..... 586 771-5100
Roseville *(G-13100)*
Prophotonix Limited ....E..... 586 778-1100
Roseville *(G-13856)*
Pump Solutions Group ....B..... 616 241-1611
Grand Rapids *(G-6796)*
REO Hydraulic & Mfg Inc ....E..... 313 891-2244
Detroit *(G-4342)*
Robert Bosch LLC ....F..... 269 429-3221
Saint Joseph *(G-14338)*
Truform Machine Inc ....E..... 517 782-8523
Jackson *(G-8594)*
Usi Inc ....F..... 248 583-9337
Madison Heights *(G-10375)*
Wmh Fluidpower Inc ....F..... 269 327-7011
Portage *(G-13058)*
Wolverine Water Works Inc ....E..... 248 673-4310
Waterford *(G-17387)*
▲ Yates Industries Inc ....D..... 586 778-7680
Saint Clair Shores *(G-14277)*

3596 Scales & Balances, Exc Laboratory

Hanchett Manufacturing Inc ....C..... 231 796-7678
Big Rapids *(G-1632)*
Heco Inc ....D..... 269 381-7200
Kalamazoo *(G-8762)*
Kanawha Scales & Systems Inc ....F..... 734 947-4030
Romulus *(G-13695)*
M2 Scientifics LLC ....G..... 616 379-9080
Holland *(G-7728)*
Standard Scale & Supply Co ....G..... 313 255-6700
Detroit *(G-4374)*
Sterling Scale Company ....G..... 248 358-0590
Southfield *(G-15035)*
▼ Trucksforsalecom ....G..... 989 883-3382
Sebewaing *(G-14520)*
Universal Impex Inc ....G..... 734 306-6684
Canton *(G-2437)*

3599 Machinery & Eqpt, Indl & Commercial, NEC

2 E Fabricating ....G..... 616 498-7036
Marne *(G-10503)*
4-M Industries Incorporated ....F..... 734 762-7200
Livonia *(G-9616)*
4-M Industries Incorporated ....D..... 734 762-7200
Livonia *(G-9617)*
A & M Industries Inc ....E..... 586 791-5610
Clinton Township *(G-3027)*
A C Machining LLC ....G..... 616 455-3870
Grand Rapids *(G-6124)*
▲ A M Grinding ....G..... 616 847-8373
Ferrysburg *(G-5332)*
A M Manufacturing LLC ....G..... 231 437-3377
Charlevoix *(G-2604)*
A S A P Machine Company ....F..... 734 459-2447
Canton *(G-2343)*
A S K Machining Services ....G..... 810 650-0019
Allenton *(G-228)*
A&E Machine & Fabrication Inc ....E..... 740 820-4701
Whitmore Lake *(G-17683)*
A&T Machining Co Inc ....G..... 734 761-6006
Ann Arbor *(G-334)*
A-OK Grinding Co ....G..... 248 589-3070
Madison Heights *(G-10176)*
AA EDM Corporation ....G..... 734 253-2784
Dexter *(G-4470)*
ABC Grinding Inc ....G..... 313 295-1060
Dearborn Heights *(G-3777)*
ABC Machining & Fabricating ....F..... 586 758-0680
Warren *(G-16912)*
Ability Mfg & Engrg Co ....F..... 269 227-3292
Fennville *(G-5169)*
Able Manufacturing Inc ....F..... 616 235-3322
Grand Rapids *(G-6130)*
Abrasive Diamond Tool Company ......E..... 248 588-4800
Madison Heights *(G-10179)*
Acal Universal Grinding Co ....F..... 586 296-3900
Roseville *(G-13767)*
Accelerated Tooling LLC ....F..... 616 293-9612
Grand Rapids *(G-6131)*
Accu-Tech Manufacturing Inc ....E..... 586 532-4000
Shelby Township *(G-14539)*
Accurate Boring Company Inc ....F..... 586 294-7555
Fraser *(G-5612)*
Accurate Gauge & Mfg Inc ....D..... 248 853-2400
Rochester Hills *(G-13362)*
Accurate Machine & TI USA Ltd ....F..... 269 205-2610
Middleville *(G-10796)*

Accurate Machining & Fabg Inc ....G..... 989 426-5400
Gladwin *(G-5922)*
Accutronic Incorporated ....G..... 586 756-2510
Warren *(G-16913)*
Accuworx LLC ....E..... 734 847-6115
Temperance *(G-15822)*
Ace Tool & Engineering Inc ....G..... 616 361-4800
Belding *(G-1396)*
Acme Gear Company Inc ....F..... 586 465-7740
Clinton Township *(G-3035)*
Acro-Tech Manufacturing Inc ....F..... 269 629-4300
Plainwell *(G-12516)*
Action Tool & Machine Inc ....E..... 810 229-6300
Brighton *(G-1877)*
▲ Active Manufacturing Corp ....E..... 616 842-0800
Spring Lake *(G-15131)*
Acubar Inc ....G..... 269 927-3000
Benton Harbor *(G-1479)*
Adept Broaching Co ....G..... 734 427-9221
Plymouth *(G-12562)*
Advance Cnc Machine Inc ....E..... 269 751-7005
Hamilton *(G-7228)*
Advance Machine Corp ....G..... 989 362-9192
Tawas City *(G-15675)*
Advance Precision Grinding Co ....G..... 586 773-1330
Roseville *(G-13768)*
Advance Scraping Company ....G..... 810 796-2676
Dryden *(G-4567)*
Advance Turning and Mfg Inc ....E..... 517 750-3580
Jackson *(G-8374)*
Advance Turning and Mfg Inc ....E..... 517 783-2713
Jackson *(G-8373)*
Advanced Automotive Group LLC ......F..... 586 206-2478
Clay *(G-2991)*
Advanced Boring and Tool Co ....D..... 586 598-9300
Chesterfield *(G-2732)*
Advanced Cnc Machining LLC ....G..... 616 226-6706
Grandville *(G-7017)*
Advanced Electric ....G..... 517 529-9050
Clarklake *(G-2893)*
Advanced Industries Inc ....E..... 734 433-1800
Chelsea *(G-2699)*
Advanced Machining Ltd ....E..... 586 465-2220
Chesterfield *(G-2735)*
▲ Ae Group LLC ....C..... 734 942-0615
Romulus *(G-13648)*
Aero Grinding Inc ....G..... 586 774-6450
Roseville *(G-13771)*
Aero Grinding Inc ....G..... 586 774-6450
Roseville *(G-13770)*
Aero Marine Inc ....G..... 734 721-6241
Westland *(G-17539)*
Aertech Machining & Mfg Inc ....E..... 517 782-4644
Jackson *(G-8375)*
◆ Air Way Automation Inc ....E..... 989 348-1802
Grayling *(G-7102)*
Airmetal Corporation ....F..... 517 784-6000
Jackson *(G-8378)*
Albright Precision Inc ....G..... 517 545-7642
Howell *(G-8010)*
Alcona Tool & Machine Inc ....E..... 989 736-8151
Harrisville *(G-7362)*
All Metal Designs Inc ....G..... 616 392-3696
Holland *(G-7554)*
All-Tech Inc ....E..... 616 406-0681
Wyoming *(G-17985)*
Allen Pattern of Michigan ....E..... 269 963-4131
Battle Creek *(G-1145)*
Alliance Cnc LLC ....F..... 616 971-4700
Grand Rapids *(G-6161)*
Allied Chucker and Engrg Co ....E..... 517 787-1370
Jackson *(G-8380)*
Allied Chucker and Engrg Co ....C..... 517 787-1370
Jackson *(G-8381)*
Allied Machine & Tool Inc ....F..... 269 623-7295
Delton *(G-3815)*
Allied Machine Inc ....E..... 231 834-0050
Grant *(G-7077)*
Allmet Industries Inc ....G..... 248 280-4600
Royal Oak *(G-13900)*
Alloy Industries Corporation ....G..... 734 433-1112
Chelsea *(G-2702)*
Allynn Corp ....G..... 269 383-1199
Kalamazoo *(G-8676)*
Alro Riverside LLC ....G..... 517 782-8322
Jackson *(G-8382)*
Alton Boring Co Inc ....G..... 734 522-9595
Livonia *(G-9639)*
American Axle & Mfg Inc ....D..... 248 522-4500
Southfield *(G-14836)*

American Grinding Machining Co ... F ... 313 388-0440
Lincoln Park *(G-9572)*
American Mfg Innovators Inc ... F ... 248 669-5990
Commerce Township *(G-3389)*
▲ Amphenol Borisch Tech Inc ... C ... 616 554-9820
Grand Rapids *(G-6168)*
Anderson Welding & Mfg Inc ... F ... 906 523-4661
Chassell *(G-2671)*
▲ Anderson-Cook Inc ... D ... 586 954-0700
Clinton Township *(G-3053)*
Anderson-Cook Inc ... D ... 586 293-0800
Fraser *(G-5620)*
Antrim Machine Products Inc ... E ... 231 587-9114
Mancelona *(G-10386)*
Aqua Tool LLC ... E ... 248 307-1984
Madison Heights *(G-10194)*
Arnold Tool & Die Co ... E ... 586 598-0099
Chesterfield *(G-2741)*
Art Laser Inc ... F ... 248 391-6600
Auburn Hills *(G-780)*
Ase Industries Inc ... D ... 586 754-7480
Warren *(G-16942)*
Assembly Concepts Inc ... E ... 989 685-2603
Rose City *(G-13759)*
Astraeus Wind Energy Inc ... G ... 517 663-5455
Eaton Rapids *(G-4716)*
Atd Engineering and Mch LLC ... E ... 989 876-7161
Au Gres *(G-741)*
▲ Ats Assembly and Test Inc ... B ... 937 222-3030
Wixom *(G-17765)*
Austin Machine & Tool LLC ... G ... 517 278-1717
Coldwater *(G-3290)*
Auto Builders Inc ... E ... 586 948-3780
Chesterfield *(G-2744)*
Automated Indus Motion Inc ... F ... 231 865-1800
Fruitport *(G-5787)*
Automated Prod Assemblies ... F ... 586 293-3990
Fraser *(G-5625)*
Automated Techniques LLC ... G ... 810 346-4670
Brown City *(G-2045)*
Autosport Development LLC ... G ... 734 675-1620
Trenton *(G-16152)*
Avid Industries Inc ... G ... 810 672-9100
Argyle *(G-713)*
▲ Avon Broach & Prod Co LLC ... E ... 248 650-8080
Rochester Hills *(G-13372)*
Awd Associates Inc ... F ... 248 922-9898
Davisburg *(G-3626)*
▲ Azon Usa Inc ... F ... 269 385-5942
Kalamazoo *(G-8690)*
Azon Usa Inc ... E ... 269 385-5942
Kalamazoo *(G-8691)*
B & B Custom and Prod Wldg ... F ... 517 524-7121
Spring Arbor *(G-15120)*
B & B Production LLC ... G ... 586 822-9960
Detroit *(G-3891)*
B & J Tool Co ... F ... 810 629-8577
Fenton *(G-5184)*
B & K Machine Products Inc ... E ... 269 637-3001
South Haven *(G-14755)*
B & M Machine & Tool Company ... G ... 989 288-2934
Durand *(G-4605)*
B & R Gear Company Inc ... F ... 517 787-8381
Jackson *(G-8386)*
B & W Tool Co ... G ... 734 485-2540
Ypsilanti *(G-18054)*
B G Industries Inc ... F ... 313 292-5355
Taylor *(G-15694)*
B-J Industries Inc ... G ... 586 778-7200
Warren *(G-16949)*
Baade Fabricating & Engrg ... G ... 517 639-4536
Quincy *(G-13089)*
Back Machine Shop LLC ... G ... 269 963-7061
Springfield *(G-15187)*
Bairds Machine Shop ... G ... 269 795-9524
Middleville *(G-10798)*
Basis Machining LLC ... G ... 517 542-3818
Litchfield *(G-9600)*
Baxter Machine & Tool Co ... E ... 517 782-2808
Jackson *(G-8388)*
▼ Bay Cast Technologies Inc ... E ... 989 892-9500
Bay City *(G-1284)*
Bay City Crane Inc ... G ... 989 867-4292
Turner *(G-16708)*
Bay Machine Inc ... G ... 906 250-0458
Calumet *(G-2324)*
Bay Machine Tool Co Inc ... E ... 989 894-2863
Essexville *(G-4870)*
Bay Machining and Sales Inc ... F ... 989 316-1801
Bay City *(G-1287)*
Bay Tool Inc ... G ... 989 894-2863
Essexville *(G-4871)*
BCT-2017 Inc ... E ... 231 832-3114
Reed City *(G-13210)*
BCT-2017 Inc ... E ... 231 832-3114
Reed City *(G-13211)*
Beck Industries Inc ... G ... 586 790-4060
Clinton Township *(G-3063)*
Beckan Industries Inc ... E ... 269 381-6984
Kalamazoo *(G-8693)*
Bedford Machinery Inc ... G ... 734 848-4980
Erie *(G-4801)*
Belding Tool Acquisition LLC ... F ... 586 816-4450
Belding *(G-1402)*
Belding Tool Acquisition LLC ... G ... 616 794-0100
Belding *(G-1403)*
Bell Engineering Inc ... E ... 989 753-3127
Saginaw *(G-14004)*
Bell Engineering LLC ... F ... 989 753-3127
Saginaw *(G-14005)*
Benzie Manufacturing LLC ... G ... 231 631-0498
Frankfort *(G-5599)*
Bergen R C Helicopters LLC ... G ... 269 445-2060
Vandalia *(G-16799)*
▼ Bermont Gage & Automation Inc ... F ... 586 296-1103
Fraser *(G-5629)*
▲ Best Metal Products Co Inc ... C ... 616 942-7141
Grand Rapids *(G-6213)*
Bischoff Enterprises LLC ... G ... 734 856-8490
Ottawa Lake *(G-12259)*
Blackledge Tool Inc ... G ... 989 865-8393
Saint Charles *(G-14190)*
Blain Machining Inc ... G ... 616 877-0426
Wayland *(G-17401)*
Blevins Screw Products Inc ... E ... 810 744-1820
Flint *(G-5391)*
▲ Blissfield Manufacturing Co ... B ... 517 486-2121
Blissfield *(G-1713)*
Blue Water Boring LLC ... G ... 586 421-2100
Macomb *(G-10112)*
Boburka Custom Mold ... F ... 906 864-9930
Menominee *(G-10726)*
Bond Bailey and Smith Company ... G ... 313 496-0177
Detroit *(G-3908)*
Boos Products Inc ... F ... 734 498-2207
Gregory *(G-7164)*
Borneman & Peterson Inc ... F ... 810 744-1890
Flint *(G-5393)*
BOS Field Machining Inc ... G ... 517 204-1688
Houghton Lake *(G-7987)*
Boxer Equipment/Morbark Inc ... G ... 989 866-2381
Winn *(G-17746)*
Breco LLC ... G ... 517 317-2211
Quincy *(G-13090)*
▼ Breesport Holdings Inc ... C ... 248 685-9500
Milford *(G-10956)*
Brembo North America Inc ... E ... 517 568-3301
Homer *(G-7938)*
Brembo North America Homer Inc ... E ... 517 568-4398
Homer *(G-7939)*
Bridgeport Manufacturing Inc ... G ... 989 777-4314
Bridgeport *(G-1850)*
Bron Machine Inc ... F ... 616 392-5320
Holland *(G-7579)*
Brown Jig Grinding Co ... F ... 248 349-7744
Wixom *(G-17778)*
Buck-N-Ham Machines Inc ... G ... 231 587-5322
Mancelona *(G-10387)*
Buffoli North America Corp ... G ... 616 610-4362
Holland *(G-7580)*
Burmeister Engineering ... G ... 989 654-2537
Sterling *(G-15243)*
▼ Burrow Industries Inc ... F ... 734 847-1842
Temperance *(G-15824)*
Byrne Tool & Die Inc ... F ... 616 866-4479
Rockford *(G-13562)*
C & C Grinding Corp ... G ... 248 689-1979
Troy *(G-16249)*
C & C Machine Tool Inc ... G ... 248 693-3347
Lake Orion *(G-9127)*
C & N Manufacturing Inc ... E ... 586 293-9150
Fraser *(G-5633)*
C & S Machine Products Inc ... E ... 269 695-6859
Niles *(G-11598)*
C & S Machine Products Inc ... E ... 269 695-6859
Buchanan *(G-2112)*
C D Tool and Gage ... G ... 616 682-1111
Grand Rapids *(G-6248)*
C E S Industries Inc ... E ... 734 425-0522
Livonia *(G-9672)*
C L Design Inc ... G ... 248 474-4220
Farmington Hills *(G-4951)*
C S M Manufacturing Corp ... D ... 248 471-0700
Farmington Hills *(G-4952)*
C T Machining Inc ... G ... 586 772-0320
Warren *(G-16974)*
Cambria Tool and Machine Inc ... F ... 517 437-3500
Hillsdale *(G-7520)*
Cannon Machine Inc ... G ... 616 363-4014
Grand Rapids *(G-6254)*
Carbon Tool & Manufacturing ... F ... 734 422-0380
Livonia *(G-9676)*
▼ Casemer Tool & Machine Inc ... E ... 248 628-4807
Oxford *(G-12341)*
CDK Enterprises LLC ... E ... 586 296-9300
Fraser *(G-5636)*
Celano Precision Mfg Inc ... G ... 734 748-1744
Livonia *(G-9679)*
Centech Inc ... F ... 517 546-9185
Howell *(G-8020)*
Center Machine & Tool LLC ... G ... 517 748-2500
Michigan Center *(G-10785)*
Centerless Rebuilders Inc ... F ... 517 596-3233
Munith *(G-11252)*
Central Gear Inc ... F ... 800 589-1602
Madison Heights *(G-10208)*
Chalker Tool & Gauge Inc ... F ... 586 977-8660
Sterling Heights *(G-15286)*
Champion Fortune Corporation ... F ... 989 422-6130
Houghton Lake *(G-7988)*
Charlevoix Machine Products ... G ... 231 547-2697
Charlevoix *(G-2611)*
Chelsea Grinding Company ... E ... 517 796-0343
Royal Oak *(G-13914)*
Chelsea Tool Inc ... G ... 734 475-9679
Chelsea *(G-2705)*
Cherry Bend Tool & Die ... G ... 231 947-3046
Cedar *(G-2540)*
Chesterfield Engines Inc ... G ... 586 949-5777
Chesterfield *(G-2753)*
Chief EDM ... G ... 586 752-5078
Bruce Twp *(G-2079)*
Clair Sawyer ... G ... 906 228-8242
Marquette *(G-10523)*
Clark Manufacturing Company ... D ... 231 946-5110
Traverse City *(G-15942)*
Clarklake Machine Incorporated ... E ... 517 529-9454
Clarklake *(G-2895)*
Clarkston Carbide Tool & Mch ... G ... 248 625-3182
Ortonville *(G-12198)*
Classic Metal Finishing Inc ... E ... 517 990-0011
Jackson *(G-8411)*
Classic Precision Inc ... E ... 248 349-8811
Wixom *(G-17787)*
Classic Tool & Boring Inc ... G ... 586 795-8967
Sterling Heights *(G-15290)*
Classic Turning Inc ... D ... 517 764-1335
Jackson *(G-8412)*
Cleary Developments Inc ... E ... 248 588-6614
Madison Heights *(G-10211)*
▲ Cleary Developments Inc ... E ... 248 588-7011
Madison Heights *(G-10210)*
Clinton Machine Tool Inc ... F ... 517 456-4810
Clinton *(G-3017)*
▲ Clipper Belt Lacer Company ... D ... 616 459-3196
Grand Rapids *(G-6281)*
Cobra Enterprises Inc ... F ... 248 588-2669
Madison Heights *(G-10214)*
Cochran Corporation ... F ... 517 857-2211
Springport *(G-15209)*
Codo Machine & Tool Inc ... G ... 517 789-5113
Jackson *(G-8414)*
▲ Coleman Machine Inc ... E ... 906 863-1113
Menominee *(G-10728)*
Coles Machine Service Inc ... E ... 810 658-5373
Davison *(G-3642)*
Colt - 7 Corporation ... F ... 586 792-9050
Clinton Township *(G-3084)*
▲ Commercial Tool & Die Inc ... C ... 616 785-8100
Comstock Park *(G-3470)*
Competitive Edge Designs Inc ... G ... 616 257-0565
Grand Rapids *(G-6292)*
Competitive Machining Inc ... F ... 989 846-6069
Standish *(G-15217)*
Complex Tool & Machine Inc ... G ... 248 625-0664
Clarkston *(G-2915)*
Computer Operated Mfg ... E ... 989 686-1333
Bay City *(G-1297)*
Concentric Industries Inc ... E ... 734 848-5133
Erie *(G-4802)*

Employee Codes: A=Over 500 employees, B=251-500
C=101-250, D=51-100, E=20-50, F=10-19, G=3-9
2020 Harris Michigan
Industrial Directory
831

Concept Metal Machining LLC..............E....... 616 647-9200
Comstock Park *(G-3471)*
Conner Engineering LLC.......................E....... 586 465-9590
Clinton Township *(G-3087)*
Consolidated Metal Pdts Inc.................G....... 616 538-1000
Grand Rapids *(G-6302)*
Contour Machining Inc...........................F....... 734 525-4877
Livonia *(G-9687)*
Contour Tool and Machine Inc...............G....... 517 787-6806
Jackson *(G-8420)*
Controlled Turning Inc...........................G....... 517 782-0517
Jackson *(G-8421)*
Cook Industries Inc................................G....... 586 754-4070
Warren *(G-16993)*
Cortz Industries.......................................G....... 734 856-5091
Temperance *(G-15826)*
Cousins Manufacturing Inc....................G....... 586 323-6033
Sterling Heights *(G-15302)*
Cox Machine LLC....................................G....... 269 953-5446
Traverse City *(G-15949)*
Craft Precision Inc..................................E....... 269 679-5121
Schoolcraft *(G-14494)*
Crandall Precision Inc............................G....... 231 775-7101
Cadillac *(G-2243)*
Crankshaft Craftsman Inc......................G....... 313 366-0140
Commerce Township *(G-3396)*
Creative Machine Company...................E....... 248 669-4230
Wixom *(G-17792)*
Cross Paths Corp....................................G....... 616 248-5371
Grand Rapids *(G-6318)*
Custom Design Components Inc.........F....... 231 937-6166
Howard City *(G-8000)*
Custom Machining By Farley.................G....... 616 896-8469
Hudsonville *(G-8152)*
Customer Metal Fabrication Inc............E....... 906 774-3216
Iron Mountain *(G-8282)*
Cut All Water Jet Cutting Inc.................G....... 734 946-7880
Taylor *(G-15705)*
Cut-Tech..G....... 269 687-9005
Niles *(G-11605)*
D & D Tool Inc..G....... 616 772-2416
Zeeland *(G-18131)*
D & J Mfg & Machining...........................G....... 231 830-9522
Muskegon *(G-11304)*
D B Mattson Co..G....... 734 697-8056
Van Buren Twp *(G-16755)*
D G Grinding Inc......................................G....... 248 624-7280
Commerce Township *(G-3397)*
D L R Manufacturing Inc.........................G....... 734 394-0690
Van Buren Twp *(G-16756)*
▲ D M C International Inc.....................G....... 586 465-1112
Harrison Township *(G-7328)*
D Michael Services..................................G....... 810 794-2407
Clay *(G-2996)*
D W Hines Manufacturing Corp.............G....... 586 775-1200
Warren *(G-16998)*
D-N-S Industries Inc................................F....... 586 465-2444
Clinton Township *(G-3098)*
▲ Dalton Industries LLC.........................E....... 248 673-0755
Waterford *(G-17333)*
Damar Machinery Co...............................F....... 616 453-4655
Grand Rapids *(G-6334)*
Damick Enterprises..................................F....... 248 652-7500
Rochester Hills *(G-13401)*
Damm Company Inc.................................G....... 248 427-9060
Farmington Hills *(G-4969)*
Daniel Pruitoff...G....... 616 392-1371
Holland *(G-7605)*
Darrell R Hanson......................................G....... 810 364-7892
Marysville *(G-10602)*
▲ Dart Machinery Ltd..............................D....... 248 362-1188
Warren *(G-16999)*
Das Group Inc...G....... 248 670-2718
Royal Oak *(G-13917)*
Datum Precision Machine Inc................G....... 586 790-1120
Clinton Township *(G-3099)*
David A Mohr Jr..G....... 517 266-2694
Adrian *(G-58)*
DD Parker Enterprises Inc.....................E....... 734 241-6898
Monroe *(G-11027)*
▲ Ddks Industries LLC...........................G....... 586 323-5909
Shelby Township *(G-14573)*
Decker Gear Inc..F....... 810 388-1500
Saint Clair *(G-14216)*
Deco Engineering Inc..............................C....... 989 761-7521
Clifford *(G-3010)*
Decockers Inc..G....... 517 447-3635
Deerfield *(G-3811)*
Defense Components America LLC......G....... 248 789-1578
Farmington Hills *(G-4970)*

Deland Manufacturing Inc......................E....... 586 323-2350
Shelby Township *(G-14574)*
▲ Delta Gear Inc......................................E....... 734 525-8000
Livonia *(G-9704)*
▲ Delta Machining Inc............................D....... 269 683-7775
Niles *(G-11608)*
Demmak Industries LLC.........................G....... 586 884-6441
Sterling Heights *(G-15310)*
Demmer Corporation...............................D....... 517 703-3116
Lansing *(G-9216)*
Demmer Corporation...............................D....... 517 703-3163
Lansing *(G-9218)*
Demmer Corporation...............................D....... 517 703-3131
Lansing *(G-9219)*
Demmer Corporation...............................E....... 517 321-3600
Lansing *(G-9287)*
Deshler Group Inc....................................C....... 734 525-9100
Livonia *(G-9706)*
Desrochers Brothers Inc.........................F....... 906 353-6346
Baraga *(G-1101)*
Detail Technologies LLC........................E....... 616 261-1313
Wyoming *(G-17996)*
Detroit Diameters Inc..............................G....... 248 669-2330
Novi *(G-11864)*
▲ Detroit Edge Tool Company................D....... 313 366-4120
Detroit *(G-3983)*
Detroit Edge Tool Company...................E....... 586 776-1598
Roseville *(G-13794)*
Dexter Manufacturing Inc.......................G....... 734 475-8046
Chelsea *(G-2708)*
Diamond Racing Products Inc...............F....... 586 792-6620
Clinton Township *(G-3103)*
Die Therm Engineering LLC...................G....... 616 915-6975
Ada *(G-13)*
Digitrace Machine Works Ltd................E....... 616 877-4818
Wayland *(G-17404)*
Dimension Machine Tech LLC...............F....... 586 649-4747
Bloomfield Hills *(G-1759)*
Directional Regulated Systems.............G....... 734 451-1416
Canton *(G-2365)*
Distinctive Machine Corp.......................E....... 616 433-4111
Rockford *(G-13567)*
Diversified E D M Inc..............................G....... 248 547-2320
Madison Heights *(G-10231)*
Diversified Tool & Engineering..............F....... 734 692-1260
Grosse Ile *(G-7170)*
DMS Electric Apparatus Service...........E....... 269 349-7000
Kalamazoo *(G-8729)*
Dobday Manufacturing Co Inc...............E....... 586 254-6777
Sterling Heights *(G-15320)*
Dorr Industries Inc...................................F....... 616 681-9440
Dorr *(G-4523)*
Double Eagle Defense LLC....................G....... 313 562-5550
Dearborn *(G-3694)*
Douglas King Industries Inc..................E....... 989 642-2865
Hemlock *(G-7461)*
▲ Dowding Industries Inc......................E....... 517 663-5455
Eaton Rapids *(G-4720)*
▼ Draco Mfg Inc.......................................G....... 248 585-0320
Troy *(G-16327)*
Dubois Production Services Inc............E....... 616 785-0088
Comstock Park *(G-3480)*
▲ Dun-Rite Machine Co..........................G....... 616 688-5266
Zeeland *(G-18132)*
Dura Hog Inc..G....... 586 825-0066
Sterling Heights *(G-15323)*
Dusevoir Acquisitions LLC....................F....... 313 562-5550
Howell *(G-8036)*
Dyna Sales & Service LLC.....................G....... 231 734-4433
Millington *(G-10994)*
Dynamic Custom Machining LLC..........G....... 231 853-8648
Ravenna *(G-13119)*
Dynamic Jig Grinding Corp....................E....... 248 589-3110
Troy *(G-16330)*
Dynamite Machining Inc.........................G....... 586 247-8230
Shelby Township *(G-14583)*
E & C Manufacturing LLC.......................F....... 248 330-0400
Troy *(G-16332)*
▼ E & D Engineering Systems LLC......G....... 989 246-0770
Gladwin *(G-5929)*
E & D Machine Company Inc..................F....... 248 473-0255
Farmington *(G-4898)*
E D M Cut-Rite Inc...................................F....... 586 566-0100
Shelby Township *(G-14584)*
E D M Shuttle Inc.....................................G....... 586 468-9880
Clinton Township *(G-3106)*
E R Tool Company Inc.............................G....... 586 757-1159
Warren *(G-17014)*
Eagle Machine Products Company........G....... 586 268-2460
Sterling Heights *(G-15325)*

Eagle T M C Technologies.......................F....... 231 766-3914
Muskegon *(G-11311)*
East Central Machine Inc........................G....... 313 579-2315
Detroit *(G-4023)*
Echo Quality Grinding Inc.......................F....... 231 544-6637
Central Lake *(G-2591)*
Edmore Tool & Grinding Inc...................E....... 989 427-3790
Edmore *(G-4750)*
Efesto LLC..G....... 734 913-0428
Superior Township *(G-15647)*
Eidemller Prcsion McHining Inc............E....... 248 669-2660
Milford *(G-10962)*
Eiler Brothers Inc......................................F....... 517 784-0970
Jackson *(G-8442)*
Elco Inc...G....... 586 778-6858
Roseville *(G-13799)*
Electro-Way Co..G....... 586 771-9450
Fraser *(G-5649)*
Elite Machining...G....... 586 598-9008
Macomb *(G-10119)*
Elkins Machine & Tool Co Inc................E....... 734 941-0266
Romulus *(G-13671)*
Elkins Machine & Tool Co Inc................E....... 734 941-0266
Romulus *(G-13672)*
EMD Wire Tek...G....... 810 235-5344
Flint *(G-5424)*
Emerald Tool Inc..G....... 231 799-9193
Norton Shores *(G-11752)*
Emma Sogoian Inc....................................E....... 248 549-8690
Royal Oak *(G-13923)*
Engineered Concepts Inc........................F....... 574 333-9110
Cassopolis *(G-2530)*
◆ Engineered Machined Pdts Inc..........B....... 906 786-8404
Escanaba *(G-4826)*
Engineered Resources Inc......................G....... 248 399-5500
Oak Park *(G-12066)*
Enkon LLC..F....... 937 890-5678
Manchester *(G-10405)*
Epic Equipment & Engrg Inc..................D....... 586 314-0020
Shelby Township *(G-14589)*
Epic Machine Inc.......................................E....... 810 629-9400
Fenton *(G-5204)*
Eptech Inc...G....... 586 254-2722
Rochester Hills *(G-13420)*
Equip Consumable Group........................G....... 248 588-9981
Madison Heights *(G-10249)*
Equivalent Base Co..................................F....... 586 759-2030
Warren *(G-17019)*
Ervott Tool Co LLC...................................G....... 616 842-3688
Grand Haven *(G-6016)*
Esco Group Inc..F....... 616 453-5458
Grand Rapids *(G-6385)*
▲ Essex Brass Corporation....................F....... 586 757-8200
Warren *(G-17020)*
Esys Automation LLC..............................D....... 248 754-1900
Auburn Hills *(G-856)*
▲ Euclid Industries Inc............................C....... 989 686-8920
Bay City *(G-1310)*
Euclid Machine & Mfg Co........................F....... 734 941-1080
Romulus *(G-13674)*
Experienced Concepts Inc.......................F....... 586 752-4200
Armada *(G-719)*
Expernced Prcsion McHining Inc..........G....... 989 635-2299
Marlette *(G-10496)*
Express Cnc & Fabrication LLC.............G....... 517 937-8760
Jonesville *(G-8654)*
Express Machine & Tool Co.....................G....... 586 758-5080
Warren *(G-17027)*
Extreme Machine Inc................................D....... 810 231-0521
Whitmore Lake *(G-17699)*
Extreme Machine Inc................................D....... 810 231-0521
Whitmore Lake *(G-17700)*
Extreme Precision Screw Pdts...............E....... 810 744-1980
Flint *(G-5427)*
Extrusion Punch & Tool Inc....................E....... 248 689-3300
Troy *(G-16357)*
F & G Tool Company.................................G....... 734 261-0022
Livonia *(G-9732)*
F & S Enterprises Inc..............................G....... 269 672-7145
Otsego *(G-12239)*
F J Manufacturing Co..............................F....... 248 583-4777
Madison Heights *(G-10251)*
Fabx Industries Inc...................................E....... 616 225-1724
Greenville *(G-7130)*
Falcon Consulting Services LLC............G....... 989 262-9325
Alpena *(G-288)*
Family Machinists....................................G....... 734 340-1848
Redford *(G-13160)*
Far Associates Inc....................................G....... 734 282-1881
Riverview *(G-13294)*

SIC SECTION
35 INDUSTRIAL AND COMMERCIAL MACHINERY AND COMPUTER EQUIPMENT

Fega Tool & Gage Company ....F 586 469-4400
Clinton Township *(G-3114)*
Fenton Radiator & Garage Inc ....G 810 629-0923
Fenton *(G-5212)*
Finazzo Manufacturing Co Inc ....G 586 757-3955
Clinton Township *(G-3117)*
Fischell Machinery LLC ....G 517 445-2828
Clayton *(G-3007)*
Fleetwood Tool & Gage Inc ....F 734 326-6737
Westland *(G-17556)*
Flex Slotter Inc ....G 586 756-6444
Warren *(G-17034)*
▲ **Flexfab Horizons Intl Inc** ....E 269 945-4700
Hastings *(G-7409)*
Forge Precision Company ....E 248 477-0020
Farmington Hills *(G-5005)*
Frame Products Inc ....G 269 695-5884
Buchanan *(G-2117)*
Fran Technology LLC ....G 586 336-4085
Romeo *(G-13628)*
Fraser Fab and Machine Inc ....E 248 852-9050
Rochester Hills *(G-13428)*
Fraser Grinding Co ....F 586 293-6060
Fraser *(G-5655)*
Friction Coating Corporation ....E 586 731-0990
Clinton Township *(G-3126)*
Fusion Mfg Solutions LLC ....G 734 224-7216
Temperance *(G-15829)*
Future Mill Inc ....G 586 754-8088
Warren *(G-17047)*
Future Tool and Machine Inc ....E 734 946-2100
Romulus *(G-13679)*
G & G Metal Products Inc ....G 248 625-8099
Clarkston *(G-2923)*
G P Manufacturing Inc ....G 269 695-1202
Buchanan *(G-2118)*
Gaastra Welding & Supply Inc ....G 906 265-4288
Iron River *(G-8309)*
Gaishin Manufacturing Inc ....E 269 934-9340
Benton Harbor *(G-1501)*
Garden City Products Inc ....F 269 684-6264
Niles *(G-11614)*
Gaylord Mch & Fabrication LLC ....F 989 732-0817
Gaylord *(G-5860)*
Geiger EDM Inc ....F 517 369-9752
Bronson *(G-2027)*
Genco Tool ....G 989 785-5588
Atlanta *(G-731)*
General Broach & Engrg Inc ....E 586 726-4300
Troy *(G-16381)*
General Machine & Boring Inc ....G 810 220-1203
Brighton *(G-1930)*
General Machine Service Inc ....E 989 752-5161
Saginaw *(G-14042)*
▲ **General Machine Services** ....G 269 695-2244
Buchanan *(G-2119)*
General Parts Inc ....E 989 686-3114
Bay City *(G-1316)*
General Processing Systems Inc ....F 630 554-7804
Holland *(G-7640)*
General Technology Inc ....F 269 751-7516
Holland *(G-7641)*
Generl-Lctrical-Mechanical Inc ....G 248 698-1110
White Lake *(G-17633)*
Genix LLC ....F 248 419-0231
Sterling Heights *(G-15360)*
Gentle Machine Tool & Die ....G 734 699-2013
Van Buren Twp *(G-16761)*
Geolean USA LLC ....F 313 859-9780
Livonia *(G-9751)*
◆ **Gil-Mar Manufacturing Co** ....D 248 640-4303
Canton *(G-2377)*
◆ **Gillisons Var Fabrication Inc** ....E 231 882-5921
Benzonia *(G-1575)*
Gladwin Machine Inc ....G 989 426-8753
Gladwin *(G-5930)*
Gosen Tool & Machine Inc ....F 989 777-6493
Saginaw *(G-14049)*
Grand Rapids Machine Repair ....E 616 248-4760
Grand Rapids *(G-6458)*
Grand Rapids Metaltek Inc ....E 616 791-2373
Grand Rapids *(G-6460)*
Grand Traverse Machine Co ....D 231 946-8006
Traverse City *(G-15986)*
Graphite Electrodes Ltd ....F 989 893-3635
Bay City *(G-1319)*
Graphite Machining Inc ....F 810 678-2227
Metamora *(G-10775)*
▲ **Graphite Products Corp** ....G 248 548-7800
Madison Heights *(G-10259)*

Great Lakes Laser Services ....G 248 584-1828
Madison Heights *(G-10262)*
Great Lakes Precision Machine ....F 269 695-4580
Niles *(G-11615)*
Green Age Products & Svcs LLC ....F 586 207-5724
Washington *(G-17304)*
Greens Welding & Repair Co ....G 734 721-5434
Westland *(G-17564)*
Greenwell Machine Shop Inc ....G 231 347-3346
Petoskey *(G-12450)*
Gregory M Boese ....F 989 754-2990
Saginaw *(G-14052)*
Grind-All Precision Tool Co ....F 586 954-3430
Clinton Township *(G-3132)*
Grinding Products Company Inc ....F 586 757-2118
Warren *(G-17067)*
Grinding Specialists Inc ....E 734 729-1775
Westland *(G-17565)*
Gross Machine Shop ....G 989 587-4021
Westphalia *(G-17614)*
GSe McHining Fabrication Inc ....F 517 663-9500
Eaton Rapids *(G-4725)*
Guerne Precision Machining ....G 231 834-7417
Bailey *(G-1079)*
H & L Tool & Engineering Inc ....G 586 755-2806
Warren *(G-17074)*
H G Geiger Manufacturing Co ....F 517 369-7357
Bronson *(G-2028)*
Hallmark Tool and Gage Co Inc ....E 248 669-4010
Wixom *(G-17821)*
Hallstrom Company ....G 906 439-5439
Eben Junction *(G-4740)*
Hamilton Industrial Products ....E 269 751-5153
Hamilton *(G-7233)*
Hamtech Inc ....G 231 796-3917
Big Rapids *(G-1631)*
Harbor Tool and Machine ....F 989 479-6708
Harbor Beach *(G-7267)*
Hardy-Reed Tool & Die Co Inc ....F 517 547-7107
Manitou Beach *(G-10448)*
Harmon Sign Inc ....G 248 348-8150
Wixom *(G-17824)*
Harrington Construction Co ....G 269 543-4251
Fennville *(G-5173)*
Hart Industries LLC ....F 313 588-1837
Sterling Heights *(G-15366)*
Haven Manufacturing Company ....F 616 842-1260
Grand Haven *(G-6035)*
Hawk Tool and Machine Inc ....F 248 349-0121
Wixom *(G-17825)*
Hawkins Industries Inc ....G 734 663-9889
Ann Arbor *(G-484)*
Hemingway Screw Products Inc ....G 313 383-7300
Melvindale *(G-10699)*
Hensley Precision Carbide Inc ....F 734 727-0810
Livonia *(G-9768)*
Heritage Hone & Gage Inc ....G 248 926-8449
Wolverine Lake *(G-17936)*
Heritage Mfg Inc ....G 586 949-7446
Chesterfield *(G-2784)*
HI Tech Mechanical Svcs LLC ....G 734 847-1831
Temperance *(G-15831)*
▼ **Highland Engineering Inc** ....E 517 548-4372
Howell *(G-8048)*
Highland Manufacturing Inc ....F 248 585-8040
Madison Heights *(G-10267)*
Holder Corporation ....G 517 484-5453
Lansing *(G-9292)*
Holloway Equipment Co Inc ....F 810 748-9577
Harsens Island *(G-7369)*
Hosco Inc ....F 248 912-1750
Wixom *(G-17828)*
Hosford & Co Inc ....G 734 769-5660
Ann Arbor *(G-496)*
Howell Machine Products Inc ....F 517 546-0580
Brighton *(G-1941)*
Hudson Industries Inc ....G 800 459-1077
Warren *(G-17082)*
Huff Machine & Tool Co Inc ....F 231 734-3291
Evart *(G-4882)*
Hurless Machine Shop Inc ....G 269 945-9362
Hastings *(G-7414)*
Huron Quality Mfg Inc ....G 989 736-8121
Lincoln *(G-9564)*
Husky LLC ....F 586 774-6148
Roseville *(G-13817)*
Hutsons Machine & Tool Inc ....G 517 688-3674
Horton *(G-7964)*
Hylite Tool & Machine Inc ....G 586 465-7878
Clinton Township *(G-3137)*

I M F Inc ....G 269 948-2345
Hastings *(G-7415)*
IBC Precision Inc ....G 248 373-8202
Auburn Hills *(G-907)*
ID Engnring Atmted Systems Inc ....F 616 656-0182
Kentwood *(G-9012)*
Ideal Tool Inc ....F 989 893-8336
Bay City *(G-1321)*
Impact Fab Inc ....F 616 399-9970
Holland *(G-7688)*
Imperial Metal Products Co ....E 616 452-1700
Grand Rapids *(G-6530)*
Independent Machine Co Inc ....E 906 428-4524
Escanaba *(G-4836)*
Industrial Exprmental Tech LLC ....E 248 948-1100
Southfield *(G-14946)*
Industrial Machine Tech LLC ....G 269 683-4689
Niles *(G-11617)*
Ingham Tool LLC ....G 734 929-2390
Ann Arbor *(G-505)*
Inland Lakes Machine Inc ....E 231 775-6543
Cadillac *(G-2255)*
Innovation Machining Corp ....F 269 683-3343
Niles *(G-11619)*
Innovative Fab Inc ....G 269 782-9154
Dowagiac *(G-4543)*
Innovative Machine Technology ....F 248 348-1630
Northville *(G-11700)*
Innovative Tool Inc ....E 586 329-4922
Chesterfield *(G-2789)*
▼ **Innovative Works Inc** ....G 586 231-1960
Chesterfield *(G-2790)*
Integrity Machine Services ....G 989 386-0216
Clare *(G-2872)*
▲ **Intelligent Mch Solutions Inc** ....F 616 607-9751
Norton Shores *(G-11762)*
Interlochen Boat Shop Inc ....G 231 275-7112
Interlochen *(G-8243)*
International Machining Svc ....G 248 486-3600
South Lyon *(G-14795)*
International Mch Tl Svcs LLC ....G 734 667-2233
Hartland *(G-7392)*
Intricate Grinding Mch Spc Inc ....E 231 798-2154
Norton Shores *(G-11763)*
Invo Spline Inc ....E 586 757-8840
Warren *(G-17097)*
Iq Manufacturing LLC ....G 586 634-7185
Auburn Hills *(G-915)*
Island Machine and Engrg LLC ....G 810 765-8228
Marine City *(G-10475)*
IXL Machine Shop Inc ....D 616 392-9803
Holland *(G-7692)*
J & E Manufacturing Company ....G 586 777-5614
Roseville *(G-13823)*
J & J Engineering and Machine ....G 616 554-3302
Caledonia *(G-2302)*
J & J Machine Ltd ....F 231 773-4100
Muskegon *(G-11351)*
J & L Turning Inc ....F 810 765-5755
East China *(G-4623)*
▲ **J & M Machine Products Inc** ....D 231 755-1622
Norton Shores *(G-11764)*
J & T Machining Inc ....G 616 897-6744
Lowell *(G-10032)*
J B Lunds & Sons Inc ....G 231 627-9070
Cheboygan *(G-2682)*
J C Manufacturing Company ....G 586 757-2713
Warren *(G-17106)*
J E Enterprises ....G 586 463-5129
Harrison Township *(G-7333)*
J I B Properties LLC ....G 313 382-3234
Melvindale *(G-10701)*
J W Harris Co Inc ....G 248 634-0737
Davisburg *(G-3636)*
J&S Technologies Inc ....G 616 837-7080
Nunica *(G-12038)*
Jackson Grinding Co Inc ....F 517 782-8080
Jackson *(G-8476)*
Jamison Industries Inc ....F 734 946-3088
Taylor *(G-15730)*
Jansen Industries Inc ....D 517 788-6800
Jackson *(G-8482)*
Jbj Products and Machinery ....G 517 655-4734
Williamston *(G-17732)*
Jds Small Machine Repair ....G 517 323-7236
Lansing *(G-9238)*
Jedi Machining Corp ....G 313 272-9500
Detroit *(G-4160)*
Jefferson Iron Works Inc ....G 248 542-3554
Ferndale *(G-5295)*

SIC

Employee Codes: A=Over 500 employees, B=251-500
C=101-250, D=51-100, E=20-50, F=10-19, G=3-9
2020 Harris Michigan
Industrial Directory
833

35 INDUSTRIAL AND COMMERCIAL MACHINERY AND COMPUTER EQUIPMENT SIC SECTION

Jeffrey Alan Mfg & Engrg LLC .... G 810 325-1119
Wales (G-16859)
Jem Jig Grinding Inc .... G 248 486-7006
Wixom (G-17838)
Jems of Litchfield Inc .... F 517 542-5367
Litchfield (G-9605)
Jerz Machine Tool Corporation .... G 269 782-3535
Dowagiac (G-4545)
Jess Enterprises LLC .... G 517 546-5818
Howell (G-8055)
◆ Jetech Inc .... E 269 965-6311
Battle Creek (G-1204)
Jex Manufacturing Inc .... G 586 463-4274
Mount Clemens (G-11136)
Jhs Grinding LLC .... E 586 427-6006
Warren (G-17114)
▲ JNB Machining Company Inc .... E 517 223-0725
Fowlerville (G-5573)
▲ Jobs Inc .... G 810 714-0522
Allen Park (G-199)
John Sams Tool Co .... G 586 776-3560
Warren (G-17116)
Johnson & Berry Mfg Inc .... G 906 524-6433
Lanse (G-9195)
Johnson Precision Mold & Engrg .... G 269 651-2553
Sturgis (G-15609)
Jolico/J-B Tool Inc .... E 586 739-5555
Shelby Township (G-14611)
Jones Precision Jig Grinding .... G 248 549-4866
Royal Oak (G-13939)
Jorgensen Stl Mch & Fab Inc .... F 517 767-4600
Tekonsha (G-15819)
Jsk Specialties .... G 616 218-2416
Zeeland (G-18161)
Jt Manufacturing Inc .... E 517 849-2923
Jonesville (G-8658)
▲ K & M Machine-Fabricating Inc .... C 269 445-2495
Cassopolis (G-2533)
K & W Manufacturing Co Inc .... F 517 369-9708
Bronson (G-2031)
K&A Machine and Tool Inc .... D 517 750-9244
Jackson (G-8487)
K&W Tool and Machine Inc .... F 616 754-7540
Greenville (G-7141)
Kasper Industries Inc .... E 989 705-1177
Gaylord (G-5870)
Kelley Machining Inc .... G 231 861-0951
Shelby (G-14529)
Kelly Industrial Service Corp .... G 989 865-6111
Saint Charles (G-14194)
Kelm Acubar Lc .... G 269 925-2007
Benton Harbor (G-1517)
Kentwater Tool & Mfg Co .... G 616 784-7171
Comstock Park (G-3489)
Ketchum Machine Corporated .... F 616 765-5101
Freeport (G-5765)
▲ King Tool & Die Inc .... F 517 265-2741
Adrian (G-73)
Kiser Industrial Mfg Co .... F 269 934-9220
Benton Harbor (G-1518)
Kksp Precision Machining LLC .... E 810 329-4731
East China (G-4624)
Kmk Machining .... F 231 629-8068
Big Rapids (G-1636)
Knapp Manufacturing Inc .... F 517 279-9538
Coldwater (G-3311)
Kodiak Manufacturing Co Inc .... G 248 335-5552
Pontiac (G-12844)
Koehler Industries Inc .... G 269 934-9670
Benton Harbor (G-1521)
Koppel Tool & Engineering LLC .... G 616 638-2611
Norton Shores (G-11768)
Koski Welding Inc .... G 906 353-7588
Baraga (G-1105)
Kotzian Tool Inc .... F 231 861-5377
Shelby (G-14530)
Kremin Inc .... E 989 790-5147
Frankenmuth (G-5592)
Kriewall Enterprises Inc .... E 586 336-0600
Romeo (G-13631)
Kriseler Welding Inc .... G 989 624-9266
Birch Run (G-1664)
Krontz General Machine & Tool .... G 269 651-5882
Sturgis (G-15610)
Krt Precision Tool & Mfg Co .... G 517 783-5715
Jackson (G-8490)
Kurt Machine Tool Co Inc .... F 586 296-5070
Fraser (G-5681)
Kuzimski Enterprises Inc .... G 989 422-5377
Houghton Lake (G-7994)

L & L Pattern Inc .... G 231 733-2646
Muskegon (G-11359)
L & M Machining & Mfg Inc .... G 586 498-7110
Warren (G-17123)
L & M Tool Co Inc .... F 586 677-4700
Macomb (G-10136)
L A Burnhart Inc .... G 810 227-4567
Brighton (G-1948)
L F M Enterprises Inc .... E 586 792-7220
Clinton Township (G-3156)
L S Machining Inc .... G 248 583-7277
Troy (G-16454)
Lagos Farms & Machining .... G 989 872-4895
Cass City (G-2518)
Lakeside Boring Inc .... G 586 286-8883
Clinton Township (G-3159)
Lakeside Manufacturing Co .... E 269 429-6193
Stevensville (G-15576)
Lakeview Quality Tool Inc .... G 989 732-6417
Gaylord (G-5873)
Lam Industries .... G 734 266-1404
Livonia (G-9804)
Lambert Industries Inc .... F 734 668-6864
Ann Arbor (G-525)
Langenberg Machine Products .... G 517 485-9450
Lansing (G-9387)
Lanphear Tool Works Inc .... F 269 674-8877
Lawrence (G-9505)
Lanzen Fabricating North Inc .... E 231 587-8200
Mancelona (G-10393)
Laser Cutting Co .... E 586 468-5300
Harrison Township (G-7337)
Lawson Manufacturing Inc .... F 248 624-1818
Walled Lake (G-16896)
Laydon Enterprises Inc .... E 906 774-4633
Iron Mountain (G-8288)
LE Warren Inc .... F 517 784-8701
Jackson (G-8496)
Le-Q Fabricators Ltd .... G 906 246-3402
Felch (G-5167)
Leading Edge Engineering Inc .... F 586 786-0382
Shelby Township (G-14625)
Leading Edge Fabricating Inc .... G 231 893-2605
Montague (G-11093)
Lee Manufacturing Inc .... F 231 865-3359
Fruitport (G-5795)
Leelanau Industries Inc .... E 231 947-0372
Traverse City (G-16024)
Lenco Boring Inc .... G 734 483-8880
Ypsilanti (G-18085)
Lenway Machine Company Inc .... G 269 751-5183
Hamilton (G-7235)
Leonard Machine & Tooling Inc .... G 517 782-8140
Jackson (G-8498)
Letty Manufacturing Inc .... G 248 461-6604
Commerce Township (G-3420)
Levy Machining LLC .... G 517 563-2013
Hanover (G-7261)
Lewkowicz Corporation .... F 734 941-0411
Romulus (G-13701)
Liberty Tool Inc .... E 586 726-2449
Sterling Heights (G-15398)
Libra Precision Machining Inc .... F 517 423-1365
Tecumseh (G-15801)
Lightning Machine Holland LLC .... F 616 786-9280
Holland (G-7725)
▲ Lincoln Park Boring Co .... E 734 946-8300
Romulus (G-13702)
Lindemann Machining & Welding .... G 906 353-6424
Baraga (G-1108)
Line Precision Inc .... E 248 474-5280
Farmington Hills (G-5044)
Linear Measurement Instrs Corp .... E 810 714-5811
Fenton (G-5225)
Link Mechanical Solutions LLC .... F 734 744-5616
Livonia (G-9811)
Livingston Machine Inc .... E 517 546-4253
Howell (G-8058)
Lmm Group Inc .... G 269 276-9909
Kalamazoo (G-8810)
Loftis Machine Company .... E 616 846-1990
Grand Haven (G-6051)
Logan Tool and Engineering .... G 586 755-3555
Warren (G-17130)
Lomar Machine & Tool Co .... E 517 563-8136
Horton (G-7965)
Lomar Machine & Tool Co .... F 517 750-4089
Spring Arbor (G-15125)
Lomar Machine & Tool Co .... G 517 563-8136
Horton (G-7967)

Lomar Machine & Tool Co .... E 517 563-8800
Horton (G-7968)
Lorenz Propellers & Engrg Co .... G 231 728-3245
Muskegon (G-11366)
Louis Padnos Iron and Metal Co .... F 231 722-6081
Muskegon (G-11368)
Louis Padnos Iron and Metal Co .... F 616 301-7900
Wyoming (G-18018)
Lowing Products LLC .... G 616 530-7440
Wyoming (G-18019)
Ltek Industries Inc .... G 734 747-6105
Ann Arbor (G-535)
M & A Machining Inc .... F 269 342-0026
Kalamazoo (G-8812)
M & F Machine & Tool Inc .... E 734 847-0571
Erie (G-4806)
M & M Automatic Products Inc .... F 517 782-0577
Jackson (G-8501)
M & M Machining Inc .... G 586 997-9910
Sterling Heights (G-15404)
M & M Services Inc .... G 248 619-9861
Troy (G-16467)
M & R Machine Company .... G 313 277-1570
Dearborn Heights (G-3789)
M R D Industries .... G 269 623-8452
Delton (G-3818)
M&I Machine Inc .... F 269 849-3624
Coloma (G-3358)
M-A Metals Inc .... G 989 268-5080
Vestaburg (G-16826)
Machine Tool & Gear Inc .... G 989 723-5486
Owosso (G-12299)
Machined Solutions .... G 517 759-4075
Adrian (G-75)
Machining Specialists Inc Mich .... G 517 881-2863
Flint (G-5463)
Magiera Holdings Inc .... D 269 685-1768
Plainwell (G-12529)
Magnesium Alum Machining LLC .... E 616 309-1202
Lowell (G-10036)
Magnum Machine and Tool Inc .... G 616 844-1940
Grand Haven (G-6053)
◆ Magnumm Corporation .... F 586 427-9420
Warren (G-17138)
Magnus Precision Tool LLC .... G 586 285-2500
Fraser (G-5690)
Mahnke Machine Inc .... G 231 775-0581
Cadillac (G-2262)
Main & Company .... F 517 789-7183
Jackson (G-8506)
Man U TEC Inc .... G 586 262-4085
Sterling Heights (G-15410)
Manor Industries Inc .... F 586 463-4604
Clinton Township (G-3166)
Manus Tool Inc .... E 989 724-7171
Harrisville (G-7365)
▼ Marine Machining and Mfg .... G 586 791-8800
Clinton Township (G-3168)
Marked Tool Inc .... G 616 669-3201
Hudsonville (G-8164)
◆ Marshall Excelsior Co .... E 269 789-6700
Marshall (G-10577)
Marshall Tool Service Inc .... G 989 777-3137
Saginaw (G-14082)
Martin Saw & Tool Inc .... G 906 863-6812
Menominee (G-10744)
Mason Tool and Gage Inc .... G 248 344-0412
Wixom (G-17853)
Master Machining Inc .... F 248 454-9890
Troy (G-16490)
Master Mfg Inc .... E 248 628-9400
Oxford (G-12359)
Mathew Parmelee .... G 248 894-5955
Rochester Hills (G-13468)
Matteson Manufacturing Inc .... G 231 779-2898
Cadillac (G-2263)
Maverick Machine Tool .... E 269 789-1617
Marshall (G-10581)
▲ Maximum Mold Inc .... G 269 468-6291
Benton Harbor (G-1528)
Maxum LLC .... G 248 726-7110
Rochester Hills (G-13469)
▲ MB Aerospace Sterling Hts Inc .... D 586 977-9200
Sterling Heights (G-15415)
McDonald Acquisitions LLC .... E 616 878-7800
Byron Center (G-2198)
McDonald Enterprises Inc .... F 734 464-4664
Livonia (G-9831)
Melling Industries Inc .... E 517 787-8172
Jackson (G-8512)

Melling Manufacturing Inc E 517 750-3580 Jackson *(G-8513)*
▲ **Merchants Automatic Pdts Inc** E 734 829-0020 Canton *(G-2401)*
Merchants Industries Inc G 734 397-3031 Canton *(G-2402)*
Meritt Tool & Die G 517 726-1452 Vermontville *(G-16822)*
Merrill Technologies Group Inc C 989 643-7981 Merrill *(G-10760)*
▲ **Merrill Technologies Group Inc** D 989 791-6676 Saginaw *(G-14090)*
▲ **Metal Arc Inc** E 231 865-3111 Muskegon *(G-11375)*
Metal Mechanics Inc F 269 679-2525 Schoolcraft *(G-14499)*
Metal-Line Corp E 231 723-7041 Muskegon *(G-11377)*
Metallurgical High Vacuum Corp F 269 543-4291 Fennville *(G-5175)*
Metalmite Corporation F 248 651-9415 Rochester *(G-13334)*
Metalution Tool Die F 616 355-9700 Holland *(G-7745)*
Metric Manufacturing Co Inc C 616 897-5959 Lowell *(G-10037)*
Metric Tool Company Inc F 313 369-9610 Detroit *(G-4230)*
Metro Broach Inc F 586 758-2340 Warren *(G-17150)*
Metro Turn Inc G 313 937-1904 Redford *(G-13174)*
Michigan Custom Machines Inc E 248 347-7900 Novi *(G-11946)*
Michigan General Grinding LLC G 616 454-5089 Grand Rapids *(G-6672)*
Michigan Machining Inc G 810 686-6655 Mount Morris *(G-11166)*
▲ **Michigan Prod Machining Inc** C 586 228-9700 Macomb *(G-10142)*
▼ **Michigan Rebuild & Automtn Inc** F 517 542-6000 Litchfield *(G-9609)*
Michigan Slotting Company Inc G 586 772-1270 Warren *(G-17154)*
Michigan Tool Works LLC E 269 651-5139 Sturgis *(G-15619)*
◆ **Michigan Wheel Operations LLC** E 616 452-6941 Grand Rapids *(G-6677)*
Michigan Wire EDM Services G 616 742-0940 Grand Rapids *(G-6678)*
Micro EDM Co LLC G 989 872-4306 Cass City *(G-2520)*
Micro Engineering Inc E 616 534-9681 Byron Center *(G-2200)*
Micro Gauge Inc C 248 446-3720 Brighton *(G-1960)*
Micro Grind Co Inc G 248 398-9770 Hazel Park *(G-7446)*
Micro Machine Company LLC D 269 388-2440 Kalamazoo *(G-8824)*
Micro Manufacturing Inc E 616 554-9200 Caledonia *(G-2309)*
Micron Mfg Company E 616 453-5486 Grand Rapids *(G-6682)*
Micron Precision Machining Inc E 989 759-1030 Saginaw *(G-14092)*
Micron Precision Machining Inc G 989 790-2425 Saginaw *(G-14093)*
Microtech Gaging LLC G 517 750-2169 Jackson *(G-8523)*
Microtech Machine Company G 517 750-4422 Jackson *(G-8524)*
Mid-America Machining Inc D 517 592-4945 Brooklyn *(G-2040)*
Mid-Tech Inc G 734 426-4327 Ann Arbor *(G-557)*
Midway Machine Tech Inc E 616 772-0808 Zeeland *(G-18165)*
Mika Tool & Die Inc G 989 662-6979 Auburn *(G-757)*
Millennium Machine Inc G 810 687-0671 Clio *(G-3277)*
Miller Machine Inc G 734 455-5333 Plymouth *(G-12693)*
Miller Prod & Machining Inc E 810 395-8810 Capac *(G-2450)*
Millplex Machine Products Inc G 734 497-0763 Rockwood *(G-13608)*
Minland Machine Inc G 269 641-7998 Edwardsburg *(G-4768)*

Model Shop Inc G 734 645-8290 Ann Arbor *(G-561)*
Modern Machine Co E 989 895-8563 Bay City *(G-1334)*
Modern Machining Inc G 269 964-4415 Battle Creek *(G-1229)*
Modern Metalcraft Inc F 989 835-3716 Midland *(G-10895)*
Modified Gear and Spline Inc F 313 893-3511 Detroit *(G-4253)*
◆ **Modineer Co** C 269 683-2550 Niles *(G-11627)*
Modineer Co C 269 684-3138 Niles *(G-11628)*
Mogultech LLC G 734 944-5053 Saline *(G-14404)*
Momentum Industries Inc E 989 681-5735 Saint Louis *(G-14366)*
Montague Tool and Mfg Co E 810 686-0000 Clio *(G-3279)*
Montina Manufacturing Inc G 616 846-1080 Grand Haven *(G-6057)*
◆ **Morbark LLC** B 989 866-2381 Winn *(G-17747)*
Morren Mold & Machine Inc G 616 892-7474 Allendale *(G-223)*
Motion Machine Company F 810 664-9901 Lapeer *(G-9476)*
Motor City Bending & Rolling G 313 368-4400 Detroit *(G-4255)*
Mountain Machine LLC F 734 480-2200 Van Buren Twp *(G-16774)*
MSI Machine Tool Parts Inc F 248 589-0515 Madison Heights *(G-10311)*
Mtm Machine Inc G 586 443-5703 Fraser *(G-5696)*
Multi Grinding Inc E 586 268-7388 Warren *(G-17162)*
Multi McHning Capabilities Inc G 734 955-5592 Romulus *(G-13710)*
Multi Tech Precision Inc G 616 514-1415 Grand Rapids *(G-6709)*
Munn Manufacturing Company E 616 765-3067 Freeport *(G-5766)*
▲ **Murray Grinding Inc** F 313 295-6030 Dearborn Heights *(G-3791)*
▲ **N C Brighton Machine Corp** C 810 227-6190 Brighton *(G-1965)*
N-P Grinding Inc G 586 756-6262 Warren *(G-17164)*
N/C Production & Grinding Inc G 586 731-2150 Sterling Heights *(G-15431)*
◆ **National Bulk Equipment Inc** C 616 399-2220 Holland *(G-7752)*
Nephew Fabrication Inc G 616 875-2121 Zeeland *(G-18168)*
New Concept Products Inc G 269 679-5970 Schoolcraft *(G-14500)*
New Technologies Tool & Mfg F 810 694-5426 Grand Blanc *(G-5976)*
Nikolic Industries Inc E 586 254-4810 Sterling Heights *(G-15435)*
Niles Machine & Tool Company G 269 684-2594 Niles *(G-11633)*
Nims Precision Machining Inc G 248 446-1053 South Lyon *(G-14805)*
Nitro EDM and Machining Inc G 586 247-8035 Shelby Township *(G-14653)*
Nmp Inc E 231 798-8851 Norton Shores *(G-11781)*
Norbert Industries Inc G 586 977-9200 Sterling Heights *(G-15437)*
North American Mch & Engrg Co G 586 726-6700 Shelby Township *(G-14655)*
North American Tool Inc G 586 463-1746 Clinton Township *(G-3185)*
North Branch Machining & Engrg G 989 795-2324 Fostoria *(G-5552)*
North Shore Machine Works Inc F 616 842-8360 Ferrysburg *(G-5336)*
Northern Fab & Machine LLC F 906 863-8506 Menominee *(G-10754)*
Northern Machining & Repr Inc E 906 786-0526 Escanaba *(G-4847)*
Northwest Tool & Machine Inc E 517 750-1332 Jackson *(G-8544)*
▲ **Nu-Core Inc** G 231 547-2600 Charlevoix *(G-2623)*
O & S Tool and Machine Inc G 248 926-8045 Wixom *(G-17871)*

Oakland Automation LLC F 810 874-3061 Novi *(G-11961)*
Oakland Machine Company F 248 674-2201 Waterford *(G-17361)*
Ohler Machine G 517 852-1900 Nashville *(G-11463)*
Oneida Tool Corporation E 313 537-0770 Redford *(G-13177)*
Orion Machine Inc G 231 728-1229 Muskegon *(G-11393)*
Orvis Machine Tool Inc G 517 548-7638 Howell *(G-8074)*
Oxid Corporation E 248 474-9817 Novi *(G-11969)*
P & G Technologies Inc G 248 399-3135 Hazel Park *(G-7449)*
P & M Industries Inc F 517 223-1000 Gregory *(G-7165)*
P D E Systems Inc E 586 725-3330 Chesterfield *(G-2814)*
P M R Industries Inc F 810 989-5020 Port Huron *(G-12954)*
P2r Metal Fabrication Inc G 888 727-5587 Macomb *(G-10151)*
Pace Machine Tool Inc E 248 960-9903 Commerce Township *(G-3437)*
Padnos Leitelt Inc F 616 363-3817 Grand Rapids *(G-6739)*
Panter Master Controls Inc F 810 687-5600 Flint *(G-5478)*
Paragon Manufacturing Corp F 810 629-4100 Fenton *(G-5228)*
Paragon Model and Tool Inc G 248 960-1223 Wixom *(G-17875)*
Paragon Model Shop Inc G 616 693-3224 Freeport *(G-5767)*
Paramont Machine Co LLC G 330 339-3489 Kalamazoo *(G-8841)*
Paravis Industries Inc E 248 393-2300 Auburn Hills *(G-970)*
Park Street Machine Inc E 231 739-9165 Muskegon *(G-11399)*
Parker Machine & Engineering G 734 692-4600 Woodhaven *(G-17940)*
Patch Works Farms Inc G 989 430-3610 Wheeler *(G-17617)*
Patriot Tool Inc G 313 299-1400 Dearborn Heights *(G-3793)*
Patterson Precision Mfg Inc F 231 733-1913 Norton Shores *(G-11787)*
Paul Jeffrey Kenny G 989 828-6109 Shepherd *(G-14730)*
Pdf Mfg Inc G 517 522-8431 Grass Lake *(G-7091)*
Pentier Group Inc F 810 664-7997 Lapeer *(G-9480)*
Perceptive Machining Inc G 248 577-0380 Troy *(G-16542)*
◆ **Perfecto Industries Inc** E 989 732-2941 Gaylord *(G-5888)*
Performance Cnc Inc G 269 624-3206 Lawton *(G-9514)*
Performance Machining Inc G 269 683-4370 Niles *(G-11638)*
Performance Tool Inc G 231 943-9338 Traverse City *(G-16065)*
Perman Industries LLC F 586 991-5600 Shelby Township *(G-14663)*
Pezco Industries Inc G 248 589-1140 Madison Heights *(G-10325)*
Photographic Support Inc G 586 264-9957 Sterling Heights *(G-15445)*
Pl Optima Inc F 616 772-2138 Zeeland *(G-18173)*
Pioneer Machine and Tech Inc G 248 546-4451 Madison Heights *(G-10327)*
Plasma-Tec Inc E 616 455-2593 Wayland *(G-17409)*
Platt Mounts - Usa Inc G 586 202-2920 Lake Orion *(G-9155)*
Plesh Industries Inc F 716 873-4916 Brighton *(G-1979)*
Polaris Engineering Inc F 586 296-1603 Fraser *(G-5708)*
▲ **Pollington Machine Tool Inc** E 231 743-2003 Marion *(G-10493)*
Post Production Solutions LLC F 734 428-7000 Manchester *(G-10411)*
Power Precision Industries Inc G 586 997-0600 Sterling Heights *(G-15448)*

S I C

Employee Codes: A=Over 500 employees, B=251-500 C=101-250, D=51-100, E=20-50, F=10-19, G=3-9

2020 Harris Michigan Industrial Directory

835

Praet Tool & Engineering Inc ....E.... 586 677-3800
Macomb *(G-10154)*
Precise Machining Inc ....G.... 231 937-7957
Howard City *(G-8005)*
Precise Metal Components Inc ....G.... 734 769-0790
Ann Arbor *(G-598)*
Precise Tool & Cutter Inc ....G.... 248 684-8480
Wixom *(G-17879)*
Precision Aerospace Corp ....C.... 616 243-8112
Grand Rapids *(G-6764)*
Precision Automotive Mch Sp ....G.... 616 534-6946
Wyoming *(G-18029)*
Precision Boring and Machine ....G.... 248 371-9140
Auburn Hills *(G-978)*
▲ **Precision Boring Company** ....E.... 586 463-3900
Clinton Township *(G-3198)*
Precision Gage Inc ....D.... 517 439-1690
Hillsdale *(G-7534)*
Precision Hone & Tool Inc ....G.... 313 493-9760
Detroit *(G-4309)*
Precision Machining ....E.... 248 669-2660
Milford *(G-10980)*
Precision Machining Company ....E.... 810 688-8674
North Branch *(G-11664)*
Precision Manufacturing Svcs ....G.... 734 995-3505
Ann Arbor *(G-600)*
Precision Tool Inc ....E.... 517 726-1060
Vermontville *(G-16823)*
Precision Tool & Machine Inc ....G.... 989 291-3365
Sheridan *(G-14734)*
Precision Wire EDM Service ....F.... 616 453-4360
Grand Rapids *(G-6766)*
Precisioncraft Co ....F.... 586 954-9510
Clinton Township *(G-3200)*
Preferred Machine LLC ....E.... 616 272-6334
Jenison *(G-8637)*
Preferred Tool & Machine Ltd ....G.... 248 399-6919
Madison Heights *(G-10334)*
Prestige Engrg Rsrces Tech Inc ....F.... 586 573-3070
Clinton Township *(G-3202)*
Prestige Engrg Rsrces Tech Inc ....E.... 586 573-3070
Madison Heights *(G-10336)*
Primo Tool & Manufacturing ....G.... 231 592-5262
Big Rapids *(G-1643)*
Pro Source Manufacturing Inc ....G.... 616 607-2990
Grand Haven *(G-6065)*
Pro-CAM Services LLC ....G.... 616 748-4200
Zeeland *(G-18178)*
Production Dev Systems LLC ....F.... 810 648-2111
Sandusky *(G-14441)*
Production Honing Company Inc ....G.... 586 757-1800
Warren *(G-17199)*
▲ **Production Machining of Alma** ....E.... 989 463-1495
Alma *(G-247)*
Production Saw & Machine Co ....D.... 517 529-4014
Clarklake *(G-2898)*
Production Tooling Inc ....G.... 269 668-6789
Mattawan *(G-10667)*
Proficient Machining Inc ....F.... 616 453-9496
Grand Rapids *(G-6784)*
▲ **Profile Gear Inc** ....G.... 810 324-2731
North Street *(G-11668)*
Progress Machine & Tool Inc ....E.... 231 798-3410
Norton Shores *(G-11814)*
Progressive Cutter Grinding Co ....G.... 586 580-2367
Shelby Township *(G-14672)*
Progressive Finishing Inc ....E.... 586 949-6961
Chesterfield *(G-2825)*
Prosper-Tech Machine & Tl LLC ....F.... 586 727-8800
Richmond *(G-13269)*
Proto Tool & Gage Inc ....G.... 734 487-0830
Ypsilanti *(G-18097)*
Proto Tool Company ....G.... 248 471-0577
Farmington Hills *(G-5105)*
Proto-CAM Inc ....F.... 616 454-9810
Grand Rapids *(G-6793)*
Proto-Tek Manufacturing Inc ....E.... 586 772-2663
Roseville *(G-13857)*
Prototech Laser Inc ....E.... 586 598-6900
Chesterfield *(G-2827)*
▲ **Prototype Cast Mfg Inc** ....G.... 586 739-0180
Shelby Township *(G-14674)*
PT&t Precise Machining LLC ....G.... 517 748-9325
Jackson *(G-8559)*
Pushman Manufacturing Co Inc ....E.... 810 629-9688
Fenton *(G-5232)*
Putnam Machine Products Inc ....E.... 517 278-2364
Coldwater *(G-3322)*
▲ **Pyxis Technologies LLC** ....E.... 734 414-0261
Plymouth *(G-12726)*
Quality Bending Threading Inc ....F.... 313 898-5100
Detroit *(G-4322)*
Quality Cavity Inc ....F.... 248 344-9995
Wixom *(G-17882)*
Quality Eqp Installations ....G.... 616 249-3649
Grandville *(G-7068)*
Quality Grinding Inc ....G.... 586 293-3780
Fraser *(G-5714)*
Quality Machine & Automation ....F.... 616 399-4415
Holland *(G-7779)*
Quality Steel ....G.... 989 823-1524
Vassar *(G-16814)*
Quality Tool & Gear Inc ....E.... 734 266-1500
Redford *(G-13186)*
Quantum Machining Inc ....G.... 810 796-2035
Dryden *(G-4571)*
Quasar Industries Inc ....C.... 248 852-0300
Rochester Hills *(G-13502)*
Quasar Industries Inc ....C.... 248 844-7190
Rochester Hills *(G-13501)*
Quest Industries Inc ....E.... 810 245-4535
Lapeer *(G-9484)*
Quick Built ....G.... 586 286-2900
Shelby Township *(G-14676)*
R & B Grinding Service Inc ....G.... 231 824-6798
Manton *(G-10457)*
▼ **R & B Industries Inc** ....E.... 734 462-9478
Livonia *(G-9903)*
R & D Cnc Machining Inc ....F.... 269 751-4171
Hamilton *(G-7239)*
R & D Machine and Tool Inc ....G.... 231 798-8500
Norton Shores *(G-11789)*
R & I Repair Shop ....G.... 906 283-6000
Gulliver *(G-7212)*
R & M Machine Inc ....F.... 586 754-8447
Warren *(G-17213)*
R & M Machine Tool Inc ....E.... 989 695-6601
Freeland *(G-5758)*
R & M Manufacturing Company ....F.... 269 683-9550
Niles *(G-11641)*
R & R Broach Inc ....G.... 586 779-2227
Roseville *(G-13858)*
R & R Tool Inc ....G.... 616 394-4200
Holland *(G-7782)*
R & S Cutter Grind Inc ....G.... 989 791-3100
Saginaw *(G-14128)*
R & S Tool & Die Inc ....G.... 989 673-8511
Caro *(G-2476)*
R B Machine ....G.... 616 928-8690
Holland *(G-7783)*
R C Grinding and Tool Company ....G.... 586 949-4373
Chesterfield *(G-2829)*
▲ **R F M Incorporated** ....F.... 810 229-4567
Brighton *(G-1983)*
R K C Corporation ....G.... 231 627-9131
Cheboygan *(G-2692)*
R M N Machining & Fabricating ....G.... 616 772-4111
Zeeland *(G-18183)*
R N B Machine & Tool Inc ....G.... 616 784-6868
Comstock Park *(G-3512)*
R+r Mfg/Eng Inc ....G.... 586 758-4420
Warren *(G-17214)*
Rae Precision Products Inc ....G.... 810 987-9170
Port Huron *(G-12961)*
Ramtec Corp ....F.... 586 752-9270
Romeo *(G-13636)*
Randall Tool & Mfg LLC ....G.... 616 669-1260
Jenison *(G-8641)*
Rapid EDM Service Inc ....G.... 616 243-5781
Grand Rapids *(G-6810)*
Rapid Grinding & Machine Co ....G.... 989 753-1744
Saginaw *(G-14131)*
▲ **Rassey Industries Inc** ....E.... 586 803-9500
Shelby Township *(G-14678)*
Ratio Machining Inc ....G.... 313 531-5155
Redford *(G-13187)*
Rdc Machine Inc ....G.... 810 695-5587
Grand Blanc *(G-5980)*
RE-Source Industries Inc ....E.... 231 728-1155
Muskegon *(G-11413)*
Reau Manufacturing Co ....G.... 734 823-5603
Dundee *(G-4598)*
Rebecca Eiben ....G.... 586 231-0548
Mount Clemens *(G-11148)*
Reemco Incorporated ....G.... 734 522-8988
Livonia *(G-9907)*
▲ **Rehmann Industries Inc** ....F.... 810 748-7793
Warren *(G-17218)*
Rel Machine Inc ....G.... 906 337-3018
Calumet *(G-2332)*
Rendon & Sons Machining Inc ....F.... 269 628-2200
Gobles *(G-5949)*
▲ **REO Hydro-Pierce Inc** ....E.... 313 891-2244
Detroit *(G-4343)*
Resetar Equipment Inc ....G.... 313 291-0500
Dearborn Heights *(G-3794)*
Revak Precision Grinding Inc ....G.... 313 388-2626
Taylor *(G-15762)*
Rex Materials Inc ....E.... 517 223-3787
Howell *(G-8092)*
Richland Machine & Pump Co ....G.... 269 629-4344
Richland *(G-13254)*
Rima Manufacturing Company ....D.... 517 448-8921
Hudson *(G-8141)*
Rise Machine Company Inc ....G.... 989 772-2151
Mount Pleasant *(G-11225)*
Rite Mark Stamp Company ....E.... 248 391-7600
Auburn Hills *(G-992)*
Rite Tool Company Inc ....G.... 586 264-1900
Sterling Heights *(G-15471)*
Ritsema Prcision Machining Inc ....G.... 269 344-8882
Kalamazoo *(G-8872)*
Robertson Tool & Engineering ....G.... 248 624-3838
Commerce Township *(G-3449)*
Robmar Precision Mfg Inc ....E.... 734 326-2664
Westland *(G-17597)*
Rocar Precision Inc ....G.... 586 226-2711
Warren *(G-17222)*
Ronal Industries Inc ....F.... 248 616-9691
Sterling Heights *(G-15478)*
Roush Industries Inc ....C.... 734 779-7000
Livonia *(G-9914)*
Royal Oak Industries Inc ....D.... 248 628-2830
Oxford *(G-12370)*
Rsb North America LLC ....G.... 517 568-4171
Homer *(G-7948)*
▲ **Rsb Transmissions Na Inc** ....F.... 517 568-4171
Homer *(G-7949)*
RTD Manufacturing Inc ....E.... 517 783-1550
Jackson *(G-8567)*
Rvm Company of Toledo ....E.... 734 654-2201
Carleton *(G-2462)*
S & C Tool & Manufacturing ....G.... 313 378-1003
Livonia *(G-9916)*
S & L Machine Products Inc ....F.... 248 543-6633
Madison Heights *(G-10347)*
S & M Machining Company ....G.... 248 348-0310
Wixom *(G-17887)*
S & S Tool Inc ....G.... 616 458-3219
Grand Rapids *(G-6848)*
S P Jig Grinding ....G.... 734 525-6335
Livonia *(G-9918)*
S-3 Engineering Inc ....F.... 734 996-2303
Ann Arbor *(G-626)*
Saber Tool Company Inc ....F.... 231 779-4340
Cadillac *(G-2275)*
Saginaw Products Corporation ....D.... 989 753-1411
Saginaw *(G-14142)*
Saginaw Products Corporation ....D.... 989 753-1411
Saginaw *(G-14143)*
▲ **Saginaw Products Corporation** ....E.... 989 753-1411
Saginaw *(G-14141)*
Salem Tool Company ....G.... 248 349-2632
Northville *(G-11722)*
Sappington Henry Machine & Tl ....E.... 989 345-0711
West Branch *(G-17522)*
Sattler Inc ....F.... 586 725-1140
Ira *(G-8269)*
▲ **Schaefer Screw Products Co** ....E.... 734 522-0020
Garden City *(G-5838)*
Schaller Tool & Die Co ....E.... 586 949-5500
Chesterfield *(G-2838)*
◆ **Schuler Incorporated** ....D.... 734 207-7200
Canton *(G-2425)*
Schuler Tool & Die Company ....G.... 269 489-2900
Burr Oak *(G-2137)*
Schwartz Machine Co ....E.... 586 756-2300
Warren *(G-17234)*
Scott & ITOH Machine Company ....E.... 248 585-5385
Madison Heights *(G-10349)*
Scranton Machine Inc ....F.... 517 437-6000
Hillsdale *(G-7539)*
◆ **Sebewaing Tool and Engrg Co** ....E.... 989 883-2000
Sebewaing *(G-14519)*
Sebright Machining Inc ....F.... 616 399-0445
Holland *(G-7798)*
Servotech Industries Inc ....F.... 734 697-5555
Taylor *(G-15764)*
Sfs LLC ....G.... 734 947-4377
Taylor *(G-15765)*

SGI Manufacturing Inc .... F 734 425-2680
Garden City *(G-5839)*

Sherwood Prototype Inc .... F 313 883-3880
Highland Park *(G-7507)*

Shively Corp .... F 269 683-9503
Niles *(G-11645)*

Shomo Tool Company Inc .... G 734 422-5588
Garden City *(G-5840)*

Signet Machine Inc .... G 616 261-2939
Grandville *(G-7071)*

Siler Precision Machine Inc .... G 989 643-7793
Merrill *(G-10761)*

Simmys Edm LLC .... G 989 802-2516
Beaverton *(G-1393)*

Skylark Machine Inc .... G 616 931-1010
Zeeland *(G-18186)*

◆ **Skyway Precision Inc** .... C 734 454-3550
Plymouth *(G-12757)*

Slaco Tool and Manufacturing .... G 248 449-9911
Novi *(G-11999)*

Slotting Ingram & Machine .... F 248 478-2430
Livonia *(G-9933)*

Smith Metal LLC .... G 269 731-5211
Augusta *(G-1054)*

Smith Metal Turning Inc .... G 269 731-5211
Augusta *(G-1055)*

◆ **Smiths Machine & Grinding Inc** .... E 269 665-4231
Galesburg *(G-5814)*

Smoracy LLC .... G 989 561-2270
Remus *(G-13241)*

▲ **SMS Modern Hard Chrome LLC** .... D 586 445-0330
Warren *(G-17242)*

Smw Mfg Inc .... D 517 596-3300
Van Buren Twp *(G-16783)*

Smw Mfg Inc .... E 517 596-3300
Taylor *(G-15769)*

Solid Manufacturing Inc .... E 517 522-5895
Grass Lake *(G-7093)*

SOO Welding Inc .... F 906 632-8241
Sault Sainte Marie *(G-14474)*

South Shore Tool & Die Inc .... E 269 925-9660
Benton Harbor *(G-1550)*

Southfield Machining Inc .... G 313 871-8200
Detroit *(G-4368)*

Spartan Grinding Inc .... F 586 774-1970
Roseville *(G-13873)*

Spaulding Machine Co Inc .... E 989 777-0694
Saginaw *(G-14153)*

Spec Technologies Inc .... D 586 726-0000
Shelby Township *(G-14700)*

Spec Tool Company .... D 888 887-1717
Sparta *(G-15112)*

Specialty Tooling Systems Inc .... E 616 784-2353
Grand Rapids *(G-6881)*

Spen-Tech Machine Engrg Corp .... D 810 275-6800
Flint *(G-5501)*

Spirit Industries Inc .... G 517 371-7840
Lansing *(G-9266)*

Spm Industries Inc .... D 586 758-1100
Warren *(G-17249)*

Springfield Machine and Tl Inc .... G 269 968-8223
Springfield *(G-15205)*

Squires Industries Inc .... E 248 449-6092
Wixom *(G-17895)*

SRS Manufacturing Inc .... F 586 792-5693
Clinton Township *(G-3233)*

St Joe Valley Grinding Inc .... G 269 925-0709
Benton Harbor *(G-1551)*

St Johns Computer Machining .... G 989 224-7664
Saint Johns *(G-14296)*

St Pierre Inc .... G 248 620-2755
Clarkston *(G-2958)*

Stanhope Tool Inc .... F 248 585-5711
Madison Heights *(G-10360)*

Starbuck Machining Inc .... F 616 399-9720
Holland *(G-7813)*

State Wide Grinding Co .... G 586 778-5700
Roseville *(G-13874)*

Statewide Boring and Mch Inc .... E 734 397-5950
Van Buren Twp *(G-16785)*

Steel-Fab Wilson & Machine .... G 989 773-6046
Mount Pleasant *(G-11230)*

Sterling Prod Machining LLC .... G 586 493-0633
Harrison Township *(G-7351)*

Stevens Custom Fabrication .... G 989 340-1184
Alpena *(G-315)*

Stirnemann Tool & Mch Co Inc .... G 248 435-4040
Clawson *(G-2986)*

Stoney Crest Regrind Service .... F 989 777-7190
Bridgeport *(G-1858)*

Strauss Tool Inc .... G 989 743-4741
Corunna *(G-3585)*

Sturdy Grinding Machining Inc .... F 586 463-8880
New Haven *(G-11526)*

Stus Welding & Fabrication .... G 616 392-8459
Holland *(G-7818)*

Sun Tool Company .... G 313 837-2442
Detroit *(G-4385)*

Superb Machine Repair Inc .... F 586 749-8800
New Haven *(G-11527)*

Superior Cutter Grinding Inc .... G 586 781-2365
Shelby Township *(G-14706)*

Superior Cutting Service Inc .... F 616 796-0114
Holland *(G-7821)*

Superior Design & Mfg .... F 810 678-3950
Metamora *(G-10781)*

Superior Gun Drilling .... G 810 744-1112
Flint *(G-5508)*

Superior Products Mfg Inc .... G 810 679-4479
Croswell *(G-3603)*

Superior Roll LLC .... F 734 279-1831
Petersburg *(G-12438)*

Supreme Tool & Machine Inc .... F 248 673-8408
Waterford *(G-17379)*

Swiss Precision Machining Inc .... F 586 677-7558
Macomb *(G-10165)*

Sws - Trimac Inc .... E 989 791-4595
Saginaw *(G-14162)*

Symonds Machine Co Inc .... G 269 782-8051
Dowagiac *(G-4563)*

Systrand Prsta Eng Systems LLC .... F 734 479-8100
Brownstown Twp *(G-2075)*

T S Manufacturing & Design .... G 517 543-5368
Charlotte *(G-2669)*

TAC Industrial Group LLC .... G 517 917-8976
Jackson *(G-8581)*

Tait Grinding Service Inc .... G 248 437-5100
New Hudson *(G-11557)*

Tdrn Inc .... G 906 497-5510
Spalding *(G-15087)*

▲ **Tec-Option Inc** .... F 517 486-6055
Blissfield *(G-1727)*

Tech Tooling Specialties Inc .... F 517 782-8898
Jackson *(G-8584)*

Techni CAM and Manufacturing .... F 734 261-6477
Livonia *(G-9954)*

Ted Senk Tooling Inc .... G 989 725-6067
Owosso *(G-12321)*

Tenants Tolerance Tooling .... G 269 349-6907
Portage *(G-13048)*

Thermfrmer Parts Suppliers LLC .... G 989 435-3800
Beaverton *(G-1394)*

Thermotron Industries Inc .... E 616 928-9044
Holland *(G-7829)*

▼ **Thierica Equipment Corporation** .... E 616 453-6570
Grand Rapids *(G-6928)*

Thoman Tool Inc .... G 517 768-0114
Jackson *(G-8588)*

Thomas A Despres Inc .... F 313 633-9648
Williamsburg *(G-17721)*

▲ **Thomas L Snarey & Assoc Inc** .... F 734 241-8474
Monroe *(G-11075)*

Thor Tool and Machine LLC .... G 248 628-3185
Lakeville *(G-9180)*

Thread Grinding Service Inc .... G 248 474-5350
Farmington Hills *(G-5140)*

▲ **Thread-Craft Inc** .... D 586 323-1116
Sterling Heights *(G-15524)*

Three M Tool & Machine Inc .... E 248 363-0982
Commerce Township *(G-3454)*

Thunder Technologies LLC .... F 248 844-4875
Rochester Hills *(G-13526)*

▲ **TI Automotive LLC** .... C 248 494-5000
Auburn Hills *(G-1020)*

◆ **TI Group Auto Systems LLC** .... B 248 296-8000
Auburn Hills *(G-1022)*

Tmd Machining Inc .... E 269 685-3091
Plainwell *(G-12546)*

Tomco Fabricating & Engrg Inc .... F 248 669-2900
Wixom *(G-17910)*

Top Craft Tool Inc .... E 586 461-4600
Clinton Township *(G-3248)*

Total Quality Machining Inc .... F 231 767-1825
Muskegon *(G-11439)*

Tramm Tech Inc .... G 989 723-2944
Owosso *(G-12323)*

Treib Inc .... F 989 752-4821
Saginaw *(G-14166)*

Trend Performance Products .... E 586 792-6620
Clinton Township *(G-3251)*

Tri County Precision Grinding .... F 586 776-6600
Warren *(G-17267)*

Tri Matics Mfg Inc .... G 586 469-3150
Harrison Township *(G-7354)*

Tri-City Repair Company .... G 989 835-4784
Hope *(G-7957)*

Tri-Star Tool & Machine Co .... F 734 729-5700
Westland *(G-17605)*

Tri-State Cast Technologies Co .... G 231 582-0452
Boyne City *(G-1836)*

Tri-Tool Boring Machine Co .... F 586 598-0036
Chesterfield *(G-2850)*

▲ **Tri-Way Manufacturing Inc** .... E 586 776-0700
Roseville *(G-13880)*

Triad Manufacturing Co Inc .... F 248 583-9636
Madison Heights *(G-10369)*

Triangle Grinding Company Inc .... E 586 749-6540
New Haven *(G-11529)*

▲ **Tribal Manufacturing Inc** .... E 269 781-3901
Marshall *(G-10591)*

Tric Tool Ltd .... E 616 395-1530
Holland *(G-7840)*

Trinity Industries Inc .... D 517 741-4300
Union City *(G-16736)*

Triple E LLC .... E 517 531-4481
Parma *(G-12395)*

Trison Tool and Machine Inc .... G 248 628-8770
Oxford *(G-12377)*

◆ **Triumph Gear Systems - Macomb** .... C 586 781-2800
Macomb *(G-10170)*

Trolley Rebuilders Inc .... G 810 364-4820
Marysville *(G-10624)*

Tru-Bore Machine Tool Co Inc .... G 734 729-9590
Westland *(G-17606)*

Tru-Thread Co Inc .... G 248 399-0255
Ferndale *(G-5323)*

True Tool Cnc Regrinding & Mfg .... G 616 677-1751
Grand Rapids *(G-6939)*

Truform Machine Inc .... E 517 782-8523
Jackson *(G-8594)*

Trusted Tool Mfg Inc .... G 810 750-6000
Fenton *(G-5247)*

▲ **Tsm Corporation** .... D 248 276-4700
Auburn Hills *(G-1032)*

▲ **Tuff Automation Inc** .... E 616 735-3939
Grand Rapids *(G-6940)*

Turbo-Spray Midwest Inc .... F 517 548-9096
Howell *(G-8116)*

Turn Tech Inc .... E 586 415-8090
Fraser *(G-5742)*

Tyler Crockett Marine Engines .... G 810 324-2720
North Street *(G-11669)*

Tyrone Tool Company Inc .... G 810 742-4762
Burton *(G-2168)*

U P Fabricating Co Inc .... G 906 341-2868
Manistique *(G-10446)*

U P Machine & Engineering Co .... E 906 497-5278
Powers *(G-13079)*

▼ **U S Group Inc** .... G 313 372-7900
Rochester Hills *(G-13534)*

Ultra Fab & Machine Inc .... G 248 628-7065
Oxford *(G-12380)*

United Engineered Tooling .... E 231 947-3650
Traverse City *(G-16134)*

United Systems .... G 248 583-9670
Troy *(G-16664)*

Urgent Design and Mfg Inc .... E 810 245-1300
Lapeer *(G-9489)*

Valade Precision Machining Inc .... G 586 771-7705
Eastpointe *(G-4710)*

Van Machine Co .... G 269 729-9540
East Leroy *(G-4685)*

Van S Fabrications Inc .... G 810 679-2115
Croswell *(G-3605)*

Vassar Welding & Machine Co .... G 989 823-8266
Vassar *(G-16816)*

Vectorall Manufacturing Inc .... E 248 486-4570
Brighton *(G-2006)*

Veet Axelson Liberty Industry .... F 586 776-3000
Warren *(G-17280)*

Veit Tool & Gage Inc .... F 810 658-4949
Davison *(G-3665)*

Venture Tool & Metalizing .... G 989 883-9121
Sebewaing *(G-14521)*

▲ **Versatube Corporation** .... F 248 524-0299
Troy *(G-16683)*

Versi-Tech Incorporated .... F 586 944-2230
Roseville *(G-13888)*

Verstar Group Inc .... F 586 465-5033
Chesterfield *(G-2854)*

Employee Codes: A=Over 500 employees, B=251-500
C=101-250, D=51-100, E=20-50, F=10-19, G=3-9

2020 Harris Michigan
Industrial Directory

837

35 INDUSTRIAL AND COMMERCIAL MACHINERY AND COMPUTER EQUIPMENT

Vickers Engineering Inc ....C 269 426-8545
New Troy *(G-11562)*
▲ Vicount Industries Inc ....D 248 471-5071
Farmington Hills *(G-5149)*
Viking Oil LLC ....G 989 366-4772
Prudenville *(G-13086)*
Village Automatics Inc ....F 269 663-8521
Edwardsburg *(G-4773)*
Vince Krstevski ....G 586 739-7600
Sterling Heights *(G-15540)*
Vinnies Machining Tool Die ....G 231 546-3290
Elmira *(G-4794)*
W T & M Inc ....G 313 533-7888
Redford *(G-13208)*
Waber Tool & Engineering Co ....E 269 342-0765
Kalamazoo *(G-8921)*
Walter Sappington ....G 989 345-1052
West Branch *(G-17527)*
Warren Manufacturing ....G 269 483-0603
White Pigeon *(G-17657)*
Webb Partners Inc ....E 734 727-0560
Westland *(G-17610)*
Weber Steel Inc ....F 989 868-4162
Vassar *(G-16819)*
Webo Detroit Corp ....F 586 268-8900
Sterling Heights *(G-15545)*
Wells Helicopter Service Inc ....G 616 874-6255
Greenville *(G-7160)*
Welz Tool Mch & Boring Co Inc .....E 734 425-3920
Livonia *(G-10006)*
Werkema Machine Company Inc ...F 616 455-7650
Grand Rapids *(G-6984)*
West Mich Prcsion McHining Inc ...F 616 791-1970
Grand Rapids *(G-6985)*
West Michigan Grinding Svc Inc ....F 231 739-4245
Norton Shores *(G-11805)*
Westech Corp ....E 231 766-3914
Muskegon *(G-11447)*
▲ Whitehall Products LLC ....D 231 894-2688
Whitehall *(G-17682)*
▲ Willenborg Associates Inc ....F 810 724-5678
Imlay City *(G-8216)*
Wiretech Wire EDM Service Inc ....G 810 966-9912
Kimball *(G-9049)*
Witson Quality Tools LLC ....G 989 471-2317
Spruce *(G-15214)*
Wmt Properties Inc ....F 248 486-6400
Brighton *(G-2010)*
Wolverine Carbide Die Company ...E 248 280-0300
Troy *(G-16695)*
Wolverine Grinding Inc ....G 734 769-4499
Ann Arbor *(G-700)*
Wolverine Tool Co ....F 810 664-2964
Lapeer *(G-9492)*
Woodie Manufacturing Inc ....G 517 782-7663
Jackson *(G-8613)*
Woodville Heights Enterprises ....F 231 629-7750
Big Rapids *(G-1647)*
World Class Equipment Company ..F 586 331-2121
Shelby Township *(G-14723)*
Worldtek Industries LLC ....G 734 494-5204
Romulus *(G-13743)*
Wyandotte Collet and Tool Inc ....F 734 283-8055
Wyandotte *(G-17982)*
X L T Engineering Inc ....F 989 684-4344
Kawkawlin *(G-8977)*
Yale Tool & Engraving Inc ....G 734 459-7171
Plymouth *(G-12795)*
Yen Group LLC ....F 810 201-6457
Port Huron *(G-12979)*
Yorkshire Edm Inc ....G 248 349-3017
Novi *(G-12030)*
Z & R Electric Service Inc ....F 906 774-0468
Iron Mountain *(G-8306)*
Zellco Precision Inc ....G 269 684-1720
Niles *(G-11653)*

36 ELECTRONIC AND OTHER ELECTRICAL EQUIPMENT AND COMPONENTS, EXCEPT COMPUTER

3612 Power, Distribution & Specialty Transformers

Advance Cylinder Products LLC ....G 586 991-2445
Shelby Township *(G-14542)*
Ajax Tocco Magnethermic Corp .....E 248 589-2524
Madison Heights *(G-10185)*
Ajax Tocco Magnethermic Corp .....F 248 585-1140
Madison Heights *(G-10186)*
▼ Aprotech Powertrain LLC ....E 248 649-9200
Troy *(G-16206)*
Controlled Magnetics Inc ....F 734 449-7225
Whitmore Lake *(G-17693)*
▼ Controlled Power Company ....C 248 528-3700
Troy *(G-16281)*
D & W Square LLC ....G 313 493-4970
Detroit *(G-3959)*
Detroit Renewable Energy LLC .....C 313 972-5700
Detroit *(G-3999)*
Eastern Power and Lighting ....G 248 739-0908
Dearborn Heights *(G-3783)*
▲ Ebw Electronics Inc ....E 616 786-0575
Holland *(G-7616)*
Gti Liquidating Inc ....D 616 842-5430
Grand Haven *(G-6028)*
Gti Power Acquisition LLC ....D 616 842-5430
Grand Haven *(G-6029)*
Heyboer Transformers Inc ....E 616 842-5830
Grand Haven *(G-6036)*
▼ Houseart LLC ....G 248 651-8124
Rochester *(G-13327)*
Marcie Electric Inc ....G 248 486-1200
Brighton *(G-1954)*
▲ Maxitrol Company ....D 248 356-1400
Southfield *(G-14974)*
▲ Meiden America Inc ....F 734 459-1781
Northville *(G-11709)*
▲ Nextek Power Systems Inc ....E 313 887-1321
Detroit *(G-4269)*
Osborne Transformer Corp ....F 586 218-6900
Fraser *(G-5702)*
Parker-Hannifin Corporation ....B 269 629-5000
Richland *(G-13252)*
Power Control Systems Inc ....E 517 339-1442
Okemos *(G-12135)*
Rizk National Industries Inc ....E 586 757-4700
Warren *(G-17221)*
Rtg Products Inc ....F 734 323-8916
Redford *(G-13189)*
Sandcastle For Kids Inc ....F 616 396-5955
Holland *(G-7796)*
SH Leggitt Company ....C 269 781-3901
Marshall *(G-10588)*
Syndevco Inc ....F 248 356-2839
Southfield *(G-15042)*
Tara Industries Inc ....F 248 477-6520
Livonia *(G-9953)*
US Green Energy Solutions LLC ...G 810 955-2992
Livonia *(G-9983)*

3613 Switchgear & Switchboard Apparatus

A & L Metal Products ....G 734 654-8990
Carleton *(G-2451)*
AB Electrical Wires Inc ....E 231 737-9200
Muskegon *(G-11258)*
Alpha Tran Engineering Co ....E 616 837-7341
Nunica *(G-12032)*
Benesh Corporation ....E 734 244-4143
Monroe *(G-11023)*
C L Design Inc ....G 248 474-4220
Farmington Hills *(G-4951)*
Clarkston Control Products ....G 248 394-1430
Clarkston *(G-2912)*
▲ Classic Accents Inc ....G 734 284-7661
Southgate *(G-15075)*
▲ Command Electronics Inc ....E 269 679-4011
Schoolcraft *(G-14492)*
Conductive Bolton Systems LLC ...D 248 669-7080
Novi *(G-11852)*
Continental Electrical Pdts ....G 248 589-2758
Sterling Heights *(G-15296)*
Control Technique Incorporated .....D 586 997-3200
Sterling Heights *(G-15298)*
Danlyn Controls Inc ....G 586 773-6797
Chesterfield *(G-2761)*
Die Heat Systems Inc ....G 586 749-9756
Chesterfield *(G-2767)*
Eagle Engineering & Supply Co ....E 989 356-4526
Alpena *(G-286)*
Electrical Design and Ctrl Co ....E 248 743-2400
Troy *(G-16338)*
▲ Ews Legacy LLC ....E 248 853-6363
Rochester Hills *(G-13421)*
Fairchilds Daughters & Son LLC ...G 906 239-6061
Iron Mountain *(G-8283)*
Generl-Lctrical-Mechanical Inc ......G 248 698-1110
White Lake *(G-17633)*
H H Barnum Co ....G 248 486-5982
Brighton *(G-1937)*
Harlo Corporation ....C 616 538-0550
Grandville *(G-7045)*
Harlo Corporation ....C 616 538-0550
Grandville *(G-7046)*
Hear Clear Inc ....G 734 525-8467
Saline *(G-14394)*
Henshaw Inc ....E 586 752-0700
Romeo *(G-13629)*
Hydro-Logic Inc ....E 586 757-7477
Warren *(G-17083)*
Indicon Corporation ....C 586 274-0505
Sterling Heights *(G-15372)*
Infra Corporation ....F 248 623-0400
Waterford *(G-17351)*
Intec Automated Controls Inc ....E 586 532-8881
Sterling Heights *(G-15375)*
International Door Inc ....E 248 547-7240
Canton *(G-2388)*
Java Manufacturing Inc ....G 616 784-3873
Comstock Park *(G-3487)*
◆ Jervis B Webb Company ....B 248 553-1000
Novi *(G-11912)*
Kirk Enterprises Inc ....G 248 357-5070
Southfield *(G-14955)*
▲ Kostal of America Inc ....C 248 284-6500
Troy *(G-16450)*
M & N Controls Inc ....G 734 850-2127
Temperance *(G-15835)*
M P Jackson LLC ....E 517 782-0391
Jackson *(G-8503)*
▲ Magnetech Corporation ....G 248 426-8840
Novi *(G-11933)*
Memcon North America LLC ....F 269 281-0478
Stevensville *(G-15578)*
Metro-Fabricating LLC ....D 989 667-8100
Bay City *(G-1332)*
Motor City Electric Tech Inc ....D 313 921-5300
Detroit *(G-4256)*
▲ Mp Hollywood LLC ....E 517 782-0391
Jackson *(G-8537)*
Parker-Hannifin Corporation ....B 269 629-5000
Richland *(G-13252)*
Patriot Sensors & Contrls Corp .....D 810 378-5511
Peck *(G-12420)*
◆ Patriot Sensors & Contrls Corp ...D 248 435-0700
Clawson *(G-2983)*
▲ PEC of America Corporation ......F 248 675-3130
Novi *(G-11972)*
Power Controllers LLC ....G 248 888-9896
Farmington Hills *(G-5098)*
S Main Company LLC ....E 248 960-1540
Wixom *(G-17888)*
Schneider Electric Usa Inc ....G 810 733-9400
Flint *(G-5497)*
Solarbos ....G 616 588-7270
Grand Rapids *(G-6870)*
Spec Corporation ....E 517 529-4105
Clarklake *(G-2900)*
▲ Ssi Electronics Inc ....E 616 866-8880
Belmont *(G-1470)*
Superior Controls Inc ....C 734 454-0500
Plymouth *(G-12763)*
Tara Industries Inc ....F 248 477-6520
Livonia *(G-9953)*
Thierica Controls Inc ....F 616 956-5500
Grand Rapids *(G-6927)*
US Energia LLC ....D 248 669-1462
Rochester *(G-13356)*
▲ West Michigan Technical Supply ...G 616 735-0991
Grand Rapids *(G-6988)*
X-Bar Automation Inc ....E 248 616-9890
Troy *(G-16701)*
▲ X-Rite Incorporated ....C 616 803-2100
Grand Rapids *(G-7006)*

3621 Motors & Generators

3dfx Interactive Inc ....E 918 938-8967
Saginaw *(G-13990)*
ABB Motors and Mechanical Inc ...F 586 978-9800
Sterling Heights *(G-15248)*
Acat Global LLC ....F 231 437-5000
White Cloud *(G-17618)*
▲ Ainsworth Electric Inc ....E 810 984-5768
Port Huron *(G-12883)*
Allied Motion Technologies Inc ......C 989 725-5151
Owosso *(G-12278)*
Altagas Rnwable Enrgy Colo LLC ...G 810 987-2200
Port Huron *(G-12887)*

American Mitsuba Corporation ....C....... 989 773-0377
Mount Pleasant *(G-11169)*
Ametek Inc ....F....... 248 435-7540
Peck *(G-12418)*
▲ **Ballard Power Systems Corp** ....A....... 313 583-5980
Dearborn *(G-3680)*
Bay Motor Products Inc ....E....... 231 941-0411
Traverse City *(G-15907)*
Car Audio Outlet LLC ....G....... 810 686-3300
Clio *(G-3266)*
Celerity Systems N Amer Inc ....G....... 248 994-7696
Novi *(G-11846)*
Continental Auto Systems Inc ....B....... 248 209-4000
Auburn Hills *(G-820)*
Continental Auto Systems Inc ....E....... 248 267-9408
Troy *(G-16277)*
Controlled Power Tech Inc ....D....... 248 825-0100
Southfield *(G-14873)*
Denso Manufacturing NC Inc ....A....... 269 441-2040
Battle Creek *(G-1172)*
▲ **Detroit Coil Co** ....E....... 248 658-1543
Ferndale *(G-5274)*
Diamond Electric Mfg Corp ....F....... 734 995-5525
Ann Arbor *(G-420)*
DMS Electric Apparatus Service ....E....... 269 349-7000
Kalamazoo *(G-8729)*
Edwards Industrial Sales Inc ....G....... 517 887-6100
Lansing *(G-9363)*
▲ **Ehc Inc** ....G....... 313 259-2266
Detroit *(G-4030)*
Electric Apparatus Company ....E....... 248 682-7992
Howell *(G-8037)*
Elite Industrial Mfg LLC ....G....... 616 895-1873
Allendale *(G-216)*
Eltek Inc ....G....... 616 363-6397
Belmont *(G-1461)*
Energy Products Inc ....G....... 248 866-5622
Troy *(G-16345)*
▼ **Etx Holdings Inc** ....G....... 989 463-1151
Alma *(G-237)*
Ev Anywhere LLC ....G....... 313 653-9870
Detroit *(G-4044)*
▲ **Feed - Lease Corp** ....E....... 248 377-0000
Auburn Hills *(G-871)*
◆ **Flint Hydrostatics Inc** ....F....... 901 794-2462
Chesterfield *(G-2777)*
Ford Motor Company ....A....... 734 484-8000
Ypsilanti *(G-18074)*
Fortis Energy Services Inc ....E....... 231 258-4596
Bloomfield Hills *(G-1766)*
Fortis Energy Services Inc ....D....... 248 283-7100
Troy *(G-16370)*
◆ **Gast Manufacturing Inc** ....B....... 269 926-6171
Benton Harbor *(G-1503)*
▲ **Genco Alliance LLC** ....E....... 269 216-5500
Kalamazoo *(G-8748)*
▼ **Global Fleet Sales LLC** ....G....... 248 327-6483
Southfield *(G-14920)*
H W Jencks Incorporated ....E....... 231 352-4422
Frankfort *(G-5603)*
Heco Inc ....D....... 269 381-7200
Kalamazoo *(G-8762)*
Hydraulex Intl Holdings Inc ....E....... 914 682-2700
Chesterfield *(G-2786)*
Independent Mfg Solutions Corp ....E....... 248 960-3550
Wixom *(G-17833)*
Induction Engineering Inc ....F....... 586 716-4700
New Baltimore *(G-11486)*
Industrial Computer & Controls ....F....... 734 697-4152
Van Buren Twp *(G-16765)*
Jlm Elec ....G....... 989 486-3788
Midland *(G-10875)*
◆ **Kaydon Corporation** ....B....... 734 747-7025
Ann Arbor *(G-516)*
Kraft Power Corporation ....F....... 989 748-4040
Gaylord *(G-5872)*
Mackinaw Power LLC ....G....... 906 264-5025
Marquette *(G-10541)*
Magna E-Car USA LLC ....C....... 248 606-0600
Holly *(G-7885)*
Magna E-Car USA LLC ....G....... 248 606-0600
Holly *(G-7886)*
▲ **Magnetech Corporation** ....G....... 248 426-8840
Novi *(G-11933)*
Maxitrol Company ....E....... 517 486-2820
Blissfield *(G-1719)*
Milair LLC ....G....... 513 576-0123
Sterling Heights *(G-15425)*
▲ **Minowitz Manufacturing Co** ....E....... 586 779-5940
Huntington Woods *(G-8190)*
Monarch Electric Service Co ....E....... 313 388-7800
Melvindale *(G-10702)*
◆ **Morrell Incorporated** ....D....... 248 373-1600
Auburn Hills *(G-949)*
▲ **Motor Products Corporation** ....C....... 989 725-5151
Owosso *(G-12305)*
Mtu Onsite Energy Corporation ....G....... 805 879-3499
Walled Lake *(G-16899)*
Nidec Motors & Actuators (usa) ....E....... 248 340-9977
Auburn Hills *(G-957)*
◆ **Patriot Sensors & Contrls Corp** ....D....... 248 435-0700
Clawson *(G-2983)*
▲ **Pontiac Coil Inc** ....C....... 248 922-1100
Clarkston *(G-2947)*
Power Controllers LLC ....G....... 248 888-9896
Farmington Hills *(G-5098)*
Powerthru Inc ....G....... 734 583-5004
Livonia *(G-9892)*
Powerthru Inc ....F....... 734 853-5004
Livonia *(G-9893)*
Precision Power Inc ....G....... 517 371-4274
Lansing *(G-9414)*
▲ **Prestolite Electric LLC** ....G....... 248 313-3807
Novi *(G-11978)*
Prestolite Electric Holding ....A....... 248 313-3807
Novi *(G-11979)*
▲ **Prestolite Electric Inc** ....F....... 866 463-7078
Novi *(G-11980)*
▲ **Pro Slot Ltd** ....G....... 616 897-6000
Hartford *(G-7386)*
Reuland Electric Co ....D....... 517 546-4400
Howell *(G-8091)*
Revealed Engineering LLC ....G....... 734 642-5551
Carleton *(G-2461)*
▲ **Satori E-Technology Inc** ....G....... 408 517-9130
Farmington Hills *(G-5120)*
▲ **Southern Auto Wholesalers Inc** ....F....... 248 335-5555
Pontiac *(G-12869)*
Spina Wind LLC ....G....... 586 771-8080
Warren *(G-17248)*
Standby Power USA LLC ....G....... 586 716-9610
Ira *(G-8272)*
Twm Technology LLC ....F....... 989 684-7050
Bay City *(G-1365)*
Vandervest Electric Mtr & Fabg ....G....... 231 843-6196
Ludington *(G-10086)*
Z & R Electric Service Inc ....F....... 906 774-0468
Iron Mountain *(G-8306)*

3624 Carbon & Graphite Prdts

Acp Technologies LLC ....G....... 586 322-3511
Sterling Heights *(G-15251)*
American Graphite Corporation ....G....... 586 757-3540
Warren *(G-16930)*
Astech Inc ....E....... 989 823-7211
Vassar *(G-16811)*
Bay Carbon Inc ....E....... 989 686-8090
Bay City *(G-1282)*
▲ **Bay Composites Inc** ....F....... 989 891-9159
Essexville *(G-4869)*
Carbone of America ....F....... 989 894-2911
Bay City *(G-1294)*
Composite Builders LLC ....G....... 616 377-7767
Holland *(G-7596)*
▲ **Cummings-Moore Graphite Co** ....E....... 313 841-1615
Detroit *(G-3957)*
Fortress Stblztion Systems LLC ....G....... 616 355-1421
Holland *(G-7636)*
Graphite Electrodes Ltd ....F....... 989 893-3635
Bay City *(G-1319)*
Graphite Machining Inc ....F....... 810 678-2227
Metamora *(G-10775)*
Mersen ....F....... 989 894-2911
Bay City *(G-1329)*
▲ **Mersen USA Greenville-Mi Corp** ....C....... 616 754-5671
Greenville *(G-7146)*
National Carbon Tech LLC ....E....... 651 330-4063
Gwinn *(G-7220)*
Sankuer Composite Tech Inc ....F....... 586 264-1880
Sterling Heights *(G-15484)*
▲ **U S Graphite Inc** ....C....... 989 755-0441
Saginaw *(G-14172)*
Wahoo Composites LLC ....F....... 734 424-0966
Dexter *(G-4518)*

3625 Relays & Indl Controls

AB Electrical Wires Inc ....E....... 231 737-9200
Muskegon *(G-11258)*
Acculift Inc ....G....... 313 382-5121
Melvindale *(G-10692)*
Acromag Incorporated ....D....... 248 624-1541
Wixom *(G-17751)*
▲ **Advanced Automation Group LLC** ....G....... 248 299-8100
Rochester Hills *(G-13366)*
AEL/Span LLC ....E....... 734 957-1600
Van Buren Twp *(G-16746)*
Affordable Mobile Devices LLC ....G....... 313 433-9242
Lathrup Village *(G-9497)*
AG Davis Gage & Engrg Co ....E....... 586 977-9000
Sterling Heights *(G-15256)*
Altair Systems Inc ....F....... 248 668-0116
Wixom *(G-17758)*
American Brake and Clutch Inc ....F....... 586 948-3730
Chesterfield *(G-2736)*
Amtex Inc ....G....... 586 792-7888
Clinton Township *(G-3051)*
Amx Corp ....G....... 469 624-8000
Sterling Heights *(G-15261)*
▲ **Apollo America Inc** ....D....... 248 332-3900
Auburn Hills *(G-776)*
Arvinmeritor Inc ....E....... 248 435-1000
Troy *(G-16222)*
Automated Control Systems Inc ....G....... 248 476-9490
Novi *(G-11834)*
Balogh Tag Inc ....G....... 248 486-7343
Brighton *(G-1888)*
Bay Electronics Inc ....E....... 586 296-0900
Roseville *(G-13776)*
Borgwarner Thermal Systems Inc ....E....... 231 779-7500
Cadillac *(G-2233)*
▲ **Burners Inc** ....G....... 248 676-9141
Milford *(G-10957)*
Burr Engineering & Dev Co ....G....... 269 965-2371
Battle Creek *(G-1160)*
Complete Dsign Automtn Systems ....G....... 734 424-2789
Dexter *(G-4483)*
Comptek Inc ....F....... 248 477-5215
Farmington Hills *(G-4965)*
Concentric Labs Inc ....G....... 517 969-3038
Mason *(G-10629)*
Control One Inc ....G....... 586 979-6106
Sterling Heights *(G-15297)*
Controls For Industries Inc ....F....... 517 468-3385
Webberville *(G-17448)*
▲ **Ctc Acquisition Company LLC** ....C....... 616 884-7100
Rockford *(G-13564)*
Cusolar Industries Inc ....E....... 586 949-3880
Chesterfield *(G-2757)*
Custom Engineering & Design ....G....... 248 680-1435
Troy *(G-16289)*
Dare Auto Inc ....E....... 734 228-6243
Plymouth *(G-12605)*
Data Acquisition Ctrl Systems ....F....... 248 437-6096
Brighton *(G-1909)*
Denso International Amer Inc ....G....... 248 359-4177
Van Buren Twp *(G-16757)*
▲ **Detroit Coil Co** ....E....... 248 658-1543
Ferndale *(G-5274)*
Dura Operating LLC ....B....... 231 924-0930
Fremont *(G-5770)*
Eaton Aerospace LLC ....B....... 616 949-1090
Grand Rapids *(G-6368)*
Eaton Corporation ....C....... 586 228-2029
Clinton Township *(G-3108)*
Edon Controls Inc ....G....... 248 280-0420
Troy *(G-16335)*
Electrocraft Michigan Inc ....F....... 603 516-1297
Saline *(G-14387)*
▲ **Electrojet Inc** ....G....... 734 272-4709
Wixom *(G-17800)*
Electromech Service Corp ....G....... 989 362-6066
East Tawas *(G-4688)*
▲ **Emergency Technology Inc** ....D....... 616 896-7100
Hudsonville *(G-8155)*
Energy Products Inc ....G....... 248 866-5622
Troy *(G-16345)*
▲ **Energy Products Inc** ....D....... 248 545-7700
Madison Heights *(G-10247)*
▲ **Eto Magnetic Corp** ....D....... 616 957-2570
Grand Rapids *(G-6387)*
Fenton Systems Inc ....G....... 810 636-6318
Goodrich *(G-5953)*
▲ **Fidia Co** ....F....... 248 680-0700
Rochester Hills *(G-13424)*
Fitz-Rite Products Inc ....E....... 248 528-8440
Troy *(G-16366)*
▲ **Flextronics Automotive USA Inc** ....D....... 248 853-5724
Rochester Hills *(G-13425)*
Flextronics Intl USA Inc ....B....... 616 837-9711
Coopersville *(G-3558)*

S I C

Ford Motor Company A 734 484-8000
Ypsilanti *(G-18074)*
Fortis Energy Services Inc E 231 258-4596
Bloomfield Hills *(G-1766)*
Fortis Energy Services Inc D 248 283-7100
Troy *(G-16370)*
Galco Industrial Elec Inc G 248 542-9090
Madison Heights *(G-10256)*
Ghsp Inc D 248 588-5095
Grand Haven *(G-6019)*
▲ Glassmaster Controls Co Inc E 269 382-2010
Kalamazoo *(G-8753)*
Great Lakes Electric LLC G 269 408-8276
Saint Joseph *(G-14313)*
H&H Automation Controls G 616 457-5994
Jenison *(G-8628)*
◆ Hella Corporate Center USA Inc E 586 232-4788
Northville *(G-11697)*
▲ Hella Lighting Corporation E 734 414-0900
Plymouth *(G-12636)*
Hewtech Electronics G 810 765-0820
China *(G-2860)*
HI-Lex Controls Incorporated C 517 448-2752
Hudson *(G-8130)*
Hydraulic Systems Technology G 248 656-5810
Rochester Hills *(G-13447)*
Hydro-Logic Inc E 586 757-7477
Warren *(G-17083)*
Incoe Corporation C 248 616-0220
Auburn Hills *(G-910)*
Indicon Corporation C 586 274-0505
Sterling Heights *(G-15372)*
Industrial Computer & Controls F 734 697-4152
Van Buren Twp *(G-16765)*
Industrial Temperature Control G 734 451-8740
Canton *(G-2384)*
Inertia Cycleworks G 269 684-2000
Niles *(G-11618)*
Infinity Controls & Engrg Inc G 248 397-8267
Lake Orion *(G-9139)*
Innovative Support Svcs Inc E 248 585-3600
Troy *(G-16418)*
▲ ITT Motion Tech Amer LLC F 248 863-2161
Novi *(G-11909)*
Jenda Controls Inc E 248 656-0090
Rochester *(G-13331)*
Jered LLC G 906 776-1800
Iron Mountain *(G-8286)*
▲ Johnson Electric N Amer Inc D 734 392-5300
Plymouth *(G-12658)*
Lor Manufacturing Co Inc G 866 644-8622
Weidman *(G-17458)*
M P Jackson LLC E 517 782-0391
Jackson *(G-8503)*
▲ Magnetech Corporation G 248 426-8840
Novi *(G-11933)*
Mahle Powertrain LLC D 248 305-8200
Farmington Hills *(G-5056)*
Manufacturing Ctrl Systems Inc G 248 853-7400
Rochester Hills *(G-13467)*
▲ Maxitrol Company D 248 356-1400
Southfield *(G-14974)*
Maxitrol Company C 269 432-3291
Colon *(G-3374)*
Maxitrol Company E 517 486-2820
Blissfield *(G-1719)*
◆ Melling Tool Co B 517 787-8172
Jackson *(G-8514)*
▲ Mercury Displacement Inds Inc D 269 663-8574
Edwardsburg *(G-4766)*
◆ Meritor Inc C 248 435-1000
Troy *(G-16493)*
▲ Meter Devices Company Inc A 330 455-0301
Farmington Hills *(G-5064)*
Motor Control Incorporated G 313 389-4000
Melvindale *(G-10703)*
Murray Equipment Company Inc F 313 869-4444
Warren *(G-17163)*
Nabco Inc G 231 832-2001
Reed City *(G-13221)*
▲ Nadex of America Corporation E 248 477-3900
Farmington Hills *(G-5075)*
National Control Systems Inc G 810 231-2901
Hamburg *(G-7226)*
National Crane & Hoist Service G 248 789-4535
Lakeville *(G-9179)*
Noelco Inc G 586 846-4955
Clinton Township *(G-3183)*
Noisemeters Inc G 248 840-6559
Berkley *(G-1588)*

Parker-Hannifin Corporation B 269 384-3459
Kalamazoo *(G-8843)*
Patriot Sensors & Contrls Corp D 810 378-5511
Peck *(G-12420)*
◆ Patriot Sensors & Contrls Corp D 248 435-0700
Clawson *(G-2983)*
Peak Industries Co Inc D 313 846-8666
Dearborn *(G-3747)*
▲ Peaker Services Inc D 248 437-4174
Brighton *(G-1976)*
Precise Power Systems LLC G 248 709-4750
Whitmore Lake *(G-17706)*
▲ Precision Controls Company E 734 663-3104
Ann Arbor *(G-599)*
▲ Prestolite Electric LLC G 248 313-3807
Novi *(G-11978)*
Radam Motors LLC G 269 365-4982
Otsego *(G-12254)*
Radius LLC G 248 685-0773
Milford *(G-10982)*
Rick Wykle LLC G 734 839-6376
Livonia *(G-9909)*
Rjg Technologies Inc C 231 947-3111
Traverse City *(G-16096)*
Rockwell Automation Inc D 248 696-1200
Troy *(G-16582)*
Rockwell Automation Inc D 269 792-9137
Wayland *(G-17412)*
▲ Ross Decco Company E 248 764-1845
Troy *(G-16584)*
▲ Safari Circuits Inc C 269 694-9471
Otsego *(G-12255)*
▲ Saginaw Products Corporation E 989 753-1411
Saginaw *(G-14141)*
Seelye Equipment Specialist G 231 547-9430
Charlevoix *(G-2630)*
▲ Serapid Inc F 586 274-0774
Sterling Heights *(G-15490)*
▲ Sine Systems Corporation C 586 465-3131
Clinton Township *(G-3230)*
▲ Sloan Transportation Pdts Inc D 616 395-5600
Holland *(G-7806)*
Solutions For Industry Inc G 517 448-8608
Hudson *(G-8142)*
▲ Southern Auto Wholesalers Inc F 248 335-5555
Pontiac *(G-12869)*
Ssi Technology Inc D 248 582-0600
Sterling Heights *(G-15507)*
▲ Static Controls Corp E 248 926-4400
Wixom *(G-17896)*
Stegner Controls LLC E 248 904-0400
Auburn Hills *(G-1003)*
Stonebrdge Technical Entps Ltd F 810 750-0040
Fenton *(G-5240)*
◆ Stoneridge Inc G 248 489-9300
Novi *(G-12004)*
Stoneridge Control Devices Inc G 248 489-9300
Novi *(G-12005)*
Superior Controls Inc C 734 454-0500
Plymouth *(G-12763)*
Sycron Technologies Inc G 810 694-4007
Grand Blanc *(G-5985)*
Symorex Ltd F 734 971-6000
Ann Arbor *(G-653)*
▲ Synchronous Manufacturing Inc E 517 764-6930
Michigan Center *(G-10791)*
▲ TAC Manufacturing Inc B 517 789-7000
Jackson *(G-8582)*
Tachyon Corporation E 586 598-4320
Chesterfield *(G-2845)*
Temcor Systems Inc G 810 229-0006
Brighton *(G-1996)*
▲ Tramec Sloan LLC D 616 395-5600
Holland *(G-7833)*
Valeo North America Inc C 248 619-8300
Troy *(G-16676)*
Valley Group of Companies F 989 799-9669
Saginaw *(G-14176)*
Valmec Inc G 810 629-8750
Fenton *(G-5248)*
Venus Controls Inc F 248 477-0448
Livonia *(G-9988)*
Versatile Systems LLC F 734 397-3957
Canton *(G-2438)*
▲ Vibracoustic Usa Inc C 269 637-2116
South Haven *(G-14781)*
▲ Von Weise LLC F 517 618-9763
Eaton Rapids *(G-4736)*
Warner Instruments G 616 843-5342
Grand Haven *(G-6096)*

Winford Engineering LLC G 989 671-9721
Auburn *(G-758)*
Wired Technologies LLC G 313 800-1611
Livonia *(G-10011)*
Woodward Inc G 970 482-5811
Ann Arbor *(G-701)*

3629 Electrical Indl Apparatus, NEC

Adam Electronics Incorporated E 248 583-2000
Madison Heights *(G-10181)*
▲ Blissfield Manufacturing Co B 517 486-2121
Blissfield *(G-1713)*
▼ Controlled Power Company C 248 528-3700
Troy *(G-16281)*
Equipment Material Sales LLC G 734 284-8711
Wyandotte *(G-17958)*
Exide Technologies F 248 853-5000
Auburn Hills *(G-858)*
Gei Global Energy Corp G 810 610-2816
Flint *(G-5433)*
Jem Computers Inc F 586 783-3400
Clinton Township *(G-3149)*
Optimystic Enterprises Inc G 269 695-7741
Buchanan *(G-2124)*
Redeem Power Services G 248 679-5277
Novi *(G-11985)*
Sparta Outlets G 616 887-6010
Sparta *(G-15110)*
Ssi Technology Inc D 248 582-0600
Sterling Heights *(G-15507)*
Winford Engineering LLC G 989 671-9721
Auburn *(G-758)*
Xalt Energy LLC G 816 525-1153
Midland *(G-10929)*

3631 Household Cooking Eqpt

American Household Inc G 601 296-5000
Livonia *(G-9643)*
Delorean Associates Inc G 248 646-1930
Bloomfield Hills *(G-1757)*
Lockett Enterprises LLC G 810 407-6644
Flint *(G-5459)*
M & D Distribution Inc G 313 592-1467
Redford *(G-13770)*
◆ Maytag Corporation C 269 923-5000
Benton Harbor *(G-1529)*
Richmond Meat Packers Inc G 586 727-1450
Richmond *(G-13270)*
Trenton Hearthside Shop Inc G 734 558-5860
Trenton *(G-16160)*
Whirlpool Corporation B 269 923-5000
Benton Harbor *(G-1570)*

3632 Household Refrigerators & Freezers

Flow Gas Misture Solutions Inc G 810 216-9004
Port Huron *(G-12918)*
Forma-Kool Manufacturing Inc E 586 949-4813
Chesterfield *(G-2778)*
◆ Maytag Corporation C 269 923-5000
Benton Harbor *(G-1529)*
Norcold Inc G 734 769-6000
Ann Arbor *(G-575)*
◆ Northland Corporation C 616 754-5601
Greenville *(G-7148)*
Scientemp Corp E 517 263-6020
Adrian *(G-94)*
▲ Thetford Corporation C 734 769-6000
Ann Arbor *(G-670)*
Whirlpool Corporation C 269 923-7400
Benton Harbor *(G-1567)*
Whirlpool Corporation B 269 923-5000
Benton Harbor *(G-1570)*
▼ Whirlpool Corporation A 269 923-5000
Benton Harbor *(G-1565)*
Whirlpool Corporation G 269 923-5000
Benton Harbor *(G-1566)*
Whirlpool Corporation C 269 849-0907
Coloma *(G-3367)*
Whirlpool Corporation C 269 923-3009
Benton Harbor *(G-1571)*

3633 Household Laundry Eqpt

◆ Maytag Corporation C 269 923-5000
Benton Harbor *(G-1529)*
▼ Whirlpool Corporation A 269 923-5000
Benton Harbor *(G-1565)*
Whirlpool Corporation C 269 923-7441
Saint Joseph *(G-14352)*

SIC SECTION 36 ELECTRONIC AND OTHER ELECTRICAL EQUIPMENT AND COMPONENTS, EXCEPT COMPUTER

Whirlpool Corporation ....G.... 269 923-5000
Benton Harbor *(G-1566)*
Whirlpool Corporation ....C.... 269 923-7400
Benton Harbor *(G-1567)*
Whirlpool Corporation ....C.... 269 849-0907
Coloma *(G-3367)*
Whirlpool Corporation ....D.... 269 923-5000
Benton Harbor *(G-1568)*
Whirlpool Corporation ....C.... 269 923-6057
Saint Joseph *(G-14353)*
Whirlpool Corporation ....B.... 269 923-6486
Benton Harbor *(G-1569)*
Whirlpool Corporation ....C.... 269 923-3009
Benton Harbor *(G-1571)*
Whirlpool Corporation ....B.... 269 923-5000
Benton Harbor *(G-1570)*

3634 Electric Household Appliances

▲ Advanced Blnding Solutions LLC ....F.... 906 914-4180
Menominee *(G-10721)*
◆ Cdgjl Inc ....E.... 517 787-2100
Jackson *(G-8404)*
Detroit Buyers Club LLC ....G.... 248 871-7827
Detroit *(G-3973)*
▲ Distinctive Appliances Distrg ....F.... 248 380-2007
Wixom *(G-17795)*
▲ E H Inc ....E.... 269 673-6456
Allegan *(G-159)*
Eesco Inc ....G.... 517 265-5148
Adrian *(G-61)*
◆ Fka Distributing Co LLC ....B.... 248 863-3000
Commerce Township *(G-3406)*
National Element Inc ....E.... 248 486-1810
Brighton *(G-1966)*
Neptech Inc ....E.... 810 225-2222
Highland *(G-7498)*
New Century Heaters Ltd ....G.... 989 671-1994
Bay City *(G-1337)*
Nippa Sauna Stoves LLC ....G.... 231 882-7707
Beulah *(G-1611)*
Ogilvie Manufacturing Company ....G.... 810 793-6598
Lapeer *(G-9478)*
Sampling Bag Technologies LLC ....G.... 734 525-8600
Livonia *(G-9920)*
▲ Therm Technology Corp ....G.... 616 530-6540
Grandville *(G-7074)*
▼ Thoreson-Mc Cosh Inc ....E.... 248 362-0960
Troy *(G-16638)*
▲ Weco International Inc ....G.... 810 686-7221
Flushing *(G-5545)*

3635 Household Vacuum Cleaners

Bissell Better Life LLC ....G.... 800 237-7691
Grand Rapids *(G-6224)*
◆ Bissell Homecare Inc ....C.... 616 453-4451
Grand Rapids *(G-6225)*
Electrolux Professional Inc ....G.... 248 338-4320
Pontiac *(G-12821)*
◆ Maytag Corporation ....C.... 269 923-5000
Benton Harbor *(G-1529)*
◆ Rexair Holdings Inc ....G.... 248 643-7222
Troy *(G-16578)*
◆ Rexair LLC ....G.... 248 643-7222
Troy *(G-16579)*
Wal-Vac Inc ....G.... 616 241-6717
Wyoming *(G-18042)*
▼ Whirlpool Corporation ....A.... 269 923-5000
Benton Harbor *(G-1565)*
Whirlpool Corporation ....G.... 269 923-5000
Benton Harbor *(G-1566)*
Whirlpool Corporation ....B.... 269 923-5000
Benton Harbor *(G-1570)*

3639 Household Appliances, NEC

Bradford-White Corporation ....A.... 269 795-3364
Middleville *(G-10799)*
Company Products Inc ....G.... 586 757-6160
Warren *(G-16989)*
J & E Appliance Company Inc ....G.... 248 642-9191
Beverly Hills *(G-1617)*
Masco Building Products Corp ....G.... 313 274-7400
Livonia *(G-9825)*
◆ Maytag Corporation ....C.... 269 923-5000
Benton Harbor *(G-1529)*
Nikis Food Co Inc ....G.... 313 925-0876
Detroit *(G-4272)*
Three D Precision Tool ....G.... 810 765-9418
China *(G-2862)*
Whirlpool Corporation ....B.... 269 923-5000
Benton Harbor *(G-1570)*
Whirlpool Corporation ....C.... 269 923-3009
Benton Harbor *(G-1571)*

3641 Electric Lamps

▲ Chicl LLC ....A.... 859 294-5590
Troy *(G-16266)*
Earthtronics Inc ....E.... 231 332-1188
Norton Shores *(G-11751)*
Elumigen LLC ....G.... 855 912-0477
Troy *(G-16341)*
Emitted Energy Inc ....F.... 855 752-3347
Sterling Heights *(G-15332)*
Energy Efficient Ltg LLC Eel ....G.... 586 214-5557
West Bloomfield *(G-17476)*
▲ Ews Legacy LLC ....E.... 248 853-6363
Rochester Hills *(G-13421)*
G & L Powerup Inc ....G.... 586 200-2169
Roseville *(G-13806)*
High Q Lighting Inc ....E.... 616 396-3591
Holland *(G-7665)*
▲ Ilumisys Inc ....G.... 844 864-4533
Troy *(G-16411)*
Inland Vapor of Michigan LLC ....G.... 734 738-6312
Canton *(G-2385)*
Inland Vapor of Michigan LLC ....F.... 734 237-4389
Garden City *(G-5828)*
Johnico LLC ....E.... 248 895-7820
Detroit *(G-4164)*
Optic Edge Corporation ....G.... 231 547-6090
Charlevoix *(G-2624)*
Philips North America LLC ....E.... 248 553-9080
Farmington Hills *(G-5092)*
▲ Trident Lighting LLC ....C.... 616 957-9500
Grand Rapids *(G-6937)*
Wickedglow Industries Inc ....G.... 586 776-4132
Mount Clemens *(G-11154)*

3643 Current-Carrying Wiring Devices

Aees Power Systems Ltd Partnr ....F.... 269 668-4429
Farmington Hills *(G-4921)*
▲ American Pwr Cnnection Systems ....F.... 989 686-6302
Bay City *(G-1275)*
Armada Rubber Manufacturing Co ....D.... 586 784-9135
Armada *(G-716)*
Astra Associates Inc ....E.... 586 254-6500
Sterling Heights *(G-15266)*
Break-A-Beam ....F.... 586 758-7790
Warren *(G-16966)*
◆ Brooks Utility Products Group ....E.... 248 477-0250
Novi *(G-11841)*
Cardell Corporation ....F.... 248 371-9700
Auburn Hills *(G-810)*
◆ Coppertec Inc ....E.... 313 278-0139
Inkster *(G-8226)*
Dollars Sense ....G.... 231 369-3610
Fife Lake *(G-5339)*
▼ Ekstrom Industries Inc ....D.... 248 477-0040
Novi *(G-11881)*
Electrical Concepts Inc ....E.... 616 847-0293
Grand Haven *(G-6013)*
Electrical Product Sales Inc ....F.... 248 583-6100
Troy *(G-16339)*
Electrocom Midwest Sales Inc ....G.... 248 449-2643
Madison Heights *(G-10243)*
Emm Inc ....G.... 248 478-1182
Farmington Hills *(G-4985)*
▲ Ews Legacy LLC ....E.... 248 853-6363
Rochester Hills *(G-13421)*
▲ Flextronics Automotive USA Inc ....D.... 248 853-5724
Rochester Hills *(G-13425)*
Flextronics Intl USA Inc ....B.... 616 837-9711
Coopersville *(G-3558)*
Four-Way Tool and Die Inc ....E.... 248 585-8255
Troy *(G-16372)*
▲ Frank Condon Inc ....E.... 517 849-2505
Hillsdale *(G-7525)*
Gary L Melchi Inc ....G.... 810 231-0262
Whitmore Lake *(G-17701)*
H W Jencks Incorporated ....E.... 231 352-4422
Frankfort *(G-5603)*
▲ Harman Corporation ....E.... 248 651-4477
Rochester *(G-13324)*
Hi-Lex America Incorporated ....D.... 248 844-0096
Rochester Hills *(G-13440)*
Hug-A-Plug Inc ....G.... 810 626-1224
Brighton *(G-1942)*
Imperial Industries Inc ....F.... 734 397-1400
Saline *(G-14395)*
▲ JST Sales America Inc ....E.... 248 324-1957
Farmington Hills *(G-5034)*
▲ Kostal of America Inc ....C.... 248 284-6500
Troy *(G-16450)*
◆ Lear Corporation ....B.... 248 447-1500
Southfield *(G-14962)*
▲ Mercury Displacement Inds Inc ....D.... 269 663-8574
Edwardsburg *(G-4766)*
▲ Meter Devices Company Inc ....A.... 330 455-0301
Farmington Hills *(G-5064)*
Metropolitan Alloys Corp ....E.... 313 366-4443
Detroit *(G-4233)*
Mike Degrow ....G.... 734 353-4752
Lansing *(G-9401)*
◆ Morrell Incorporated ....D.... 248 373-1600
Auburn Hills *(G-949)*
National Zinc Processors Inc ....F.... 269 926-1161
Benton Harbor *(G-1535)*
▲ NGK Spark Plugs (usa) Inc ....C.... 248 926-6900
Wixom *(G-17865)*
Nyx Inc ....B.... 734 464-0800
Livonia *(G-9869)*
▲ Owosso Graphic Arts Inc ....E.... 989 725-7112
Owosso *(G-12309)*
Panel Pro LLC ....G.... 734 427-1691
Livonia *(G-9883)*
Patriot Sensors & Contrls Corp ....D.... 810 378-5511
Peck *(G-12420)*
◆ Patriot Sensors & Contrls Corp ....D.... 248 435-0700
Clawson *(G-2983)*
▲ Prestolite Electric LLC ....G.... 248 313-3807
Novi *(G-11978)*
Prime Assemblies Inc ....F.... 906 875-6420
Crystal Falls *(G-3612)*
▲ Semtron Inc ....F.... 810 732-9080
Flint *(G-5498)*
▲ Sine Systems Corporation ....C.... 586 465-3131
Clinton Township *(G-3230)*
▲ Southern Auto Wholesalers Inc ....F.... 248 335-5555
Pontiac *(G-12869)*
▲ Ssi Electronics Inc ....E.... 616 866-8880
Belmont *(G-1470)*
State Tool & Manufacturing Co ....D.... 269 927-3153
Benton Harbor *(G-1552)*
Syndevco Inc ....F.... 248 356-2839
Southfield *(G-15042)*
Teradyne Inc ....C.... 313 425-3900
Allen Park *(G-211)*
Testron Incorporated ....F.... 734 513-6820
Livonia *(G-9955)*
TI Group Auto Systems LLC ....C.... 586 948-6006
Chesterfield *(G-2848)*
▲ Tram Inc ....C.... 734 254-8500
Plymouth *(G-12778)*
▲ Trmi Inc ....A.... 269 966-0800
Battle Creek *(G-1261)*
◆ Yazaki International Corp ....G.... 734 983-1000
Canton *(G-2445)*

3644 Noncurrent-Carrying Wiring Devices

Adnic Products Co ....G.... 810 789-0321
Mount Morris *(G-11156)*
Allied Tube & Conduit Corp ....C.... 734 721-4040
Wayne *(G-17422)*
Apw ....G.... 231 922-1863
Traverse City *(G-15895)*
Austin Company ....F.... 269 329-1181
Portage *(G-12982)*
▲ Dare Products Inc ....E.... 269 965-2307
Springfield *(G-15190)*
▲ Ews Legacy LLC ....E.... 248 853-6363
Rochester Hills *(G-13421)*
Masco Building Products Corp ....G.... 313 274-7400
Livonia *(G-9825)*
Merritt Raceway LLC ....G.... 231 590-4431
Mancelona *(G-10396)*
▲ Meter Devices Company Inc ....A.... 330 455-0301
Farmington Hills *(G-5064)*
Monoco Inc ....G.... 616 459-9800
Grand Rapids *(G-6701)*
Riley Enterprises LLC ....G.... 517 263-9115
Adrian *(G-90)*
Tesa Tape Inc ....G.... 616 785-6970
Grand Rapids *(G-6924)*
Tesa Tape Inc ....D.... 616 887-3107
Sparta *(G-15116)*
Zygot Operations Limited ....F.... 810 736-2900
Flint *(G-5529)*

3645 Residential Lighting Fixtures

A & D Lighting ....G.... 269 327-1126
Kalamazoo *(G-8670)*

SIC

Employee Codes: A=Over 500 employees, B=251-500
C=101-250, D=51-100, E=20-50, F=10-19, G=3-9
2020 Harris Michigan
Industrial Directory
841

36 ELECTRONIC AND OTHER ELECTRICAL EQUIPMENT AND COMPONENTS, EXCEPT COMPUTER SIC SECTION

Baylume Inc .... G 877 881-3641
Beverly Hills *(G-1614)*
Casual Ptio Furn Rfnishing Inc .... G 586 254-1900
Canton *(G-2358)*
▲ Full Spectrum Solutions Inc .... E 517 783-3800
Jackson *(G-8454)*
H U R Enterprises Inc .... G 906 774-0833
Iron Mountain *(G-8284)*
▲ Lighting Enterprises Inc .... G 313 693-9504
Detroit *(G-4205)*
▲ R-Bo Co Inc .... E 616 748-9733
Zeeland *(G-18184)*
Sunshine Systems Inc .... G 616 363-9272
Grand Rapids *(G-6901)*

3646 Commercial, Indl & Institutional Lighting Fixtures

Alumalight LLC .... E 248 457-9302
Troy *(G-16193)*
Burst Led .... G 248 321-6262
Farmington Hills *(G-4949)*
▲ Command Electronics Inc .... E 269 679-4011
Schoolcraft *(G-14492)*
E-Light LLC .... G 734 427-0600
Commerce Township *(G-3402)*
Energy Design Svc Systems LLC .... F 810 227-3377
Whitmore Lake *(G-17697)*
Global Green Corporation .... F 734 560-1743
Ann Arbor *(G-473)*
GT Solutions LLC .... G 616 259-0700
Holland *(G-7655)*
Haworth Inc .... D 231 845-0607
Ludington *(G-10064)*
Hazloc Industries LLC .... E 810 679-2551
Croswell *(G-3597)*
High Q Lighting Inc .... E 616 396-3591
Holland *(G-7665)*
Johnico LLC .... E 248 895-7820
Detroit *(G-4164)*
Landmark Energy Development Co .... G 586 457-0200
Sterling Heights *(G-15395)*
▲ Leif Distribution LLC .... E 517 481-2122
Lansing *(G-9308)*
▲ Light Corp Inc .... C 616 842-5100
Grand Haven *(G-6049)*
◆ Lumificient Corporation .... F 763 424-3702
Oxford *(G-12356)*
Lyte Poles Incorporated .... D 586 771-4610
Warren *(G-17134)*
▲ Nylube Products Company LLC .... E 248 852-6500
Rochester Hills *(G-13486)*
▼ Pro Lighting Group Inc .... G 810 229-5600
Brighton *(G-1980)*
▲ R-Bo Co Inc .... E 616 748-9733
Zeeland *(G-18184)*
Robogistics LLC .... F 409 234-1033
Adrian *(G-91)*
Skyworks LLC .... F 972 284-9093
Northville *(G-11726)*
Smart Vision Lights LLC .... F 231 722-1199
Norton Shores *(G-11794)*
Sound Productions Entrmt .... E 989 386-2221
Clare *(G-2889)*
Suntech Industrials LLC .... G 734 678-5922
Ann Arbor *(G-651)*
Woodward Energy Solutions LLC .... F 888 967-4533
Detroit *(G-4448)*

3647 Vehicular Lighting Eqpt

A S Auto Lights Inc .... G 734 941-1164
Romulus *(G-13644)*
Automotive Lighting LLC .... G 248 418-3000
Clarkston *(G-2908)*
◆ Automotive Lighting LLC .... E 248 418-3000
Auburn Hills *(G-789)*
Autosystems America Inc .... B 734 582-2300
Plymouth *(G-12577)*
B/E Aerospace Inc .... G 734 425-6200
Livonia *(G-9658)*
▲ Emergency Technology Inc .... D 616 896-7100
Hudsonville *(G-8155)*
▲ Eto Magnetic Corp .... D 616 957-2570
Grand Rapids *(G-6387)*
▲ F M T Products Inc .... G 517 568-3373
Homer *(G-7942)*
▲ Fisher-Baker Corporation .... G 810 765-3548
Marine City *(G-10473)*
Gyb LLC .... F 586 218-3222
Warren *(G-17072)*
HA Automotive Systems Inc .... F 248 781-0001
Troy *(G-16388)*
▲ Il Stanley Co Inc .... A 269 660-7777
Battle Creek *(G-1199)*
International Automotive Compo .... D 231 734-9000
Evart *(G-4884)*
◆ Magna Mirrors America Inc .... E 616 786-5120
Grand Rapids *(G-6640)*
Magna Mirrors America Inc .... G 616 786-7000
Holland *(G-7734)*
Magna Mirrors America Inc .... D 616 786-7300
Holland *(G-7735)*
Magna Mirrors America Inc .... C 616 942-0163
Newaygo *(G-11573)*
Mid American AEL LLC .... G 810 229-5483
Brighton *(G-1962)*
MLS Automotive Incorporated .... F 844 453-3669
Farmington Hills *(G-5070)*
North American Lighting Inc .... D 248 553-6408
Farmington Hills *(G-5081)*
▲ Penske Company LLC .... G 248 648-2000
Bloomfield Hills *(G-1788)*
▲ Progressive Dynamics Inc .... D 269 781-4241
Marshall *(G-10585)*
Rebo Lighting & Elec LLC .... F 734 213-4159
Ann Arbor *(G-612)*
▲ Tecniq Inc .... E 269 629-4440
Galesburg *(G-5816)*
▲ Trident Lighting LLC .... C 616 957-9500
Grand Rapids *(G-6937)*
Zkw Lighting Systems Usa Inc .... G 248 525-4600
Troy *(G-16707)*

3648 Lighting Eqpt, NEC

Affordable OEM Autolighting .... G 989 400-6106
Stanton *(G-15227)*
Ci Lighting LLC .... G 248 997-4415
Auburn Hills *(G-813)*
Coreled Systems LLC .... G 734 516-2060
Livonia *(G-9689)*
D & G Equipment Inc .... C 517 655-4606
Williamston *(G-17729)*
Dakkota Lighting Tech LLC .... E 517 993-7700
Holt *(G-7908)*
▲ Emergency Technology Inc .... D 616 896-7100
Hudsonville *(G-8155)*
Energy Design Svc Systems LLC .... F 810 227-3377
Whitmore Lake *(G-17697)*
Gadget Factory LLC .... G 517 449-1444
Lansing *(G-9370)*
General Structures Inc .... E 586 774-6105
Warren *(G-17054)*
Global Green Corporation .... F 734 560-1743
Ann Arbor *(G-473)*
GT Solutions LLC .... G 616 259-0700
Holland *(G-7655)*
High Q Lighting Inc .... E 616 396-3591
Holland *(G-7665)*
▲ I Parth Inc .... G 248 548-9722
Ferndale *(G-5293)*
Infection Prevention Tech LLC .... G 248 340-8800
Grand Blanc *(G-5970)*
▼ J & B Products Ltd .... F 989 792-6119
Saginaw *(G-14065)*
J & M Products and Service LLC .... G 517 263-3082
Adrian *(G-70)*
Johnico LLC .... E 248 895-7820
Detroit *(G-4164)*
▲ Leif Distribution LLC .... E 517 481-2122
Lansing *(G-9308)*
▲ Lumasmart Technology Intl Inc .... C 586 232-4125
Macomb *(G-10137)*
▼ Lumerica Corporation .... F 248 543-8085
Warren *(G-17132)*
Michigan Lightning Protection .... G 616 453-1174
Grand Rapids *(G-6673)*
Off Grid LLC .... G 734 780-4434
Ann Arbor *(G-580)*
▼ Phoenix Imaging Inc .... G 248 476-4200
Livonia *(G-9888)*
▲ Qualite Inc .... E 517 439-4316
Hillsdale *(G-7535)*
Randy L Palmer .... G 586 298-7629
Clarkston *(G-2949)*
Solar Tonic LLC .... G 734 368-0215
Ann Arbor *(G-638)*
Sonrize LLC .... G 586 329-3225
Chesterfield *(G-2842)*
Sound Productions Entrmt .... E 989 386-2221
Clare *(G-2889)*
Spectrum Illumination Co Inc .... G 231 894-4590
Montague *(G-11098)*
◆ Steelcase Inc .... A 616 247-2710
Grand Rapids *(G-6889)*
Tanfaster Inc .... G 248 669-3312
Wixom *(G-17904)*
Tls Productions Inc .... E 810 220-8577
Ann Arbor *(G-677)*
▼ Universal Manufacturing Co .... F 586 463-2560
Clinton Township *(G-3254)*
Wayne Novick .... G 269 685-9818
Plainwell *(G-12551)*

3651 Household Audio & Video Eqpt

◆ Alpine Electronics America Inc .... C 248 409-9444
Auburn Hills *(G-766)*
American Mus Environments Inc .... F 248 646-2020
Bloomfield Hills *(G-1744)*
Audio Technologies Inc .... G 586 323-3890
Troy *(G-16229)*
◆ B Company Inc .... F 734 283-7080
Riverview *(G-13291)*
BBC Communications Inc .... G 616 399-0432
West Olive *(G-17531)*
Bluewater Tech Group Inc .... C 248 356-4399
Southfield *(G-14854)*
Bluewater Tech Group Inc .... G 231 885-2600
Mesick *(G-10767)*
Bluewater Tech Group Inc .... F 616 656-9380
Grand Rapids *(G-6233)*
Bluewater Tech Group Inc .... G 248 356-4399
Farmington Hills *(G-4943)*
Cartalign Research Co .... G 248 681-6689
West Bloomfield *(G-17468)*
Cco Holdings LLC .... G 517 583-4125
Tekonsha *(G-15817)*
Cco Holdings LLC .... G 616 244-2071
Belding *(G-1406)*
Cco Holdings LLC .... G 616 384-2060
Coopersville *(G-3551)*
Cco Holdings LLC .... G 517 639-1060
Quincy *(G-13091)*
Cco Holdings LLC .... G 734 244-8028
Monroe *(G-11024)*
Cco Holdings LLC .... G 734 868-5044
Ida *(G-8193)*
Cco Holdings LLC .... G 810 270-1002
North Branch *(G-11657)*
Cco Holdings LLC .... G 810 375-7020
Dryden *(G-4568)*
Cco Holdings LLC .... G 810 545-4020
Columbiaville *(G-3376)*
Cco Holdings LLC .... G 906 285-6497
Ironwood *(G-8325)*
Cco Holdings LLC .... G 906 239-3763
Iron Mountain *(G-8279)*
Cco Holdings LLC .... G 906 346-1000
Gwinn *(G-7218)*
Cco Holdings LLC .... G 231 720-0688
Muskegon *(G-11291)*
Cco Holdings LLC .... G 248 494-4550
Auburn Hills *(G-811)*
Cco Holdings LLC .... G 269 202-3286
Coloma *(G-3355)*
Cco Holdings LLC .... G 269 216-6680
Kalamazoo *(G-8704)*
Cco Holdings LLC .... G 269 432-0052
Colon *(G-3370)*
Cco Holdings LLC .... G 269 464-3454
White Pigeon *(G-17646)*
Cco Holdings LLC .... G 989 328-4187
Sidney *(G-14738)*
Cco Holdings LLC .... G 989 567-0151
Shepherd *(G-14726)*
Cco Holdings LLC .... G 989 863-4023
Reese *(G-13229)*
Cco Holdings LLC .... G 989 853-2008
Muir *(G-11237)*
Clarion Corporation America .... E 248 991-3100
Farmington *(G-4896)*
Corporate AV Services LLC .... G 248 939-0900
Commerce Township *(G-3395)*
Digital Systems Adio Video LLC .... G 248 454-0387
Bloomfield Hills *(G-1758)*
▲ Driven Designs Inc .... G 616 794-9977
Belding *(G-1410)*
Earbyte Inc .... G 734 418-8661
Southfield *(G-14892)*
Fast Cash .... G 269 966-0079
Battle Creek *(G-1185)*

36 ELECTRONIC AND OTHER ELECTRICAL EQUIPMENT AND COMPONENTS, EXCEPT COMPUTER

Harman Becker Auto Systems Inc ....D....... 248 848-0393
  Farmington Hills *(G-5016)*
Intaglio LLC ....F....... 616 243-3300
  Grand Rapids *(G-6539)*
Intellitech Systems Inc ....G....... 586 219-3737
  Troy *(G-16420)*
▲ Leon Speakers Inc ....E....... 734 213-2151
  Ann Arbor *(G-528)*
Lg Electronics USA Inc ....C....... 248 268-5100
  Troy *(G-16463)*
Logical Digital Audio Video ....G....... 734 572-0022
  Ann Arbor *(G-534)*
◆ Lotus International Company ....A....... 734 245-0140
  Canton *(G-2394)*
M A S Information Age Tech ....G....... 248 352-0162
  Southfield *(G-14971)*
Mitsubishi Elc Auto Amer Inc ....D....... 734 453-2617
  Northville *(G-11710)*
Moss Audio Corporation ....D....... 616 451-9933
  Grand Rapids *(G-6707)*
Pioneer North America Inc ....E....... 248 449-6799
  Farmington Hills *(G-5094)*
▲ Pro-Vision Solutions LLC ....E....... 616 583-1520
  Byron Center *(G-2209)*
▲ Salk Communications Inc ....G....... 248 342-7109
  Pontiac *(G-12864)*
▲ Shinola/Detroit LLC ....C....... 888 304-2534
  Detroit *(G-4361)*
Startech-Solutions LLC ....G....... 248 419-0650
  Southfield *(G-15033)*
Stedman Corp ....G....... 269 629-5930
  Richland *(G-13256)*

3652 Phonograph Records & Magnetic Tape

Archer Record Pressing Co ....G....... 313 365-9545
  Detroit *(G-3875)*
▲ Brilliance Publishing Inc ....C....... 616 846-5256
  Grand Haven *(G-5998)*
River City Studios Ltd ....G....... 616 456-1404
  Grand Rapids *(G-6827)*
Summit Training Source Inc ....E....... 800 842-0466
  Grand Rapids *(G-6897)*
Super Video Service Center ....G....... 248 358-4794
  Southfield *(G-15037)*

3661 Telephone & Telegraph Apparatus

Balogh ....G....... 734 283-3972
  Taylor *(G-15695)*
Central On Line Data Systems ....G....... 586 939-7000
  Sterling Heights *(G-15284)*
Clarity Comm Advisors Inc ....E....... 248 327-4390
  Southfield *(G-14869)*
▲ Code Blue Corporation ....E....... 616 392-8296
  Holland *(G-7594)*
DB Communications Inc ....F....... 800 692-8200
  Livonia *(G-9700)*
Fox Charlevoix Ford Modem ....G....... 231 547-4401
  Charlevoix *(G-2614)*
Huron Valley Telecom ....G....... 734 995-9780
  Ann Arbor *(G-497)*
Lol Telcom Inc ....B....... 616 888-6171
  Hudsonville *(G-8162)*
Multiax International Inc ....G....... 616 534-4530
  Grandville *(G-7060)*
Nuwave Technology Partners LLC ....F....... 616 942-7520
  Grand Rapids *(G-6725)*
Nuwave Technology Partners LLC ....G....... 269 342-4400
  Saint Joseph *(G-14333)*
Nuwave Technology Partners LLC ....F....... 517 336-9915
  East Lansing *(G-4672)*
Nuwave Technology Partners LLC ....F....... 517 322-2200
  Lansing *(G-9315)*
Nuwave Technology Partners LLC ....F....... 269 342-4400
  Kalamazoo *(G-8837)*
Omnilink Communications Corp ....E....... 517 336-1800
  Lansing *(G-9408)*
Phone Guy LLC ....G....... 248 361-0132
  Oxford *(G-12363)*
▲ Rti Products LLC ....F....... 269 684-9960
  Niles *(G-11644)*
▲ Safari Circuits Inc ....C....... 269 694-9471
  Otsego *(G-12255)*
▲ Semtron Inc ....F....... 810 732-9080
  Flint *(G-5498)*
Spectra Link ....G....... 313 417-3723
  Grosse Pointe Woods *(G-7209)*
Wireless 4 Less Inc ....G....... 313 653-3345
  Detroit *(G-4444)*

3663 Radio & T V Communications, Systs & Eqpt, Broadcast/Studio

Amphenol T&M Antennas Inc ....G....... 847 478-5600
  Brighton *(G-1885)*
▲ Antenna Technologies Inc ....G....... 586 697-5626
  Shelby Township *(G-14547)*
Bob Allison Enterprises ....G....... 248 540-8467
  Bloomfield Hills *(G-1752)*
C & A Wholesale Inc ....G....... 248 302-3555
  Detroit *(G-3923)*
C & V Services Inc ....G....... 810 632-9677
  Hartland *(G-7388)*
Cco Holdings LLC ....G....... 517 583-4125
  Tekonsha *(G-15817)*
Cco Holdings LLC ....G....... 616 244-2071
  Belding *(G-1406)*
Cco Holdings LLC ....G....... 616 384-2060
  Coopersville *(G-3551)*
Cco Holdings LLC ....G....... 517 639-1060
  Quincy *(G-13091)*
Cco Holdings LLC ....G....... 734 244-8028
  Monroe *(G-11024)*
Cco Holdings LLC ....G....... 734 868-5044
  Ida *(G-8193)*
Cco Holdings LLC ....G....... 810 270-1002
  North Branch *(G-11657)*
Cco Holdings LLC ....G....... 810 375-7020
  Dryden *(G-4568)*
Cco Holdings LLC ....G....... 810 545-4020
  Columbiaville *(G-3376)*
Cco Holdings LLC ....G....... 906 285-6497
  Ironwood *(G-8325)*
Cco Holdings LLC ....G....... 906 239-3763
  Iron Mountain *(G-8279)*
Cco Holdings LLC ....G....... 906 346-1000
  Gwinn *(G-7218)*
Cco Holdings LLC ....G....... 231 720-0688
  Muskegon *(G-11291)*
Cco Holdings LLC ....G....... 248 494-4550
  Auburn Hills *(G-811)*
Cco Holdings LLC ....G....... 269 202-3286
  Coloma *(G-3355)*
Cco Holdings LLC ....G....... 269 216-6680
  Kalamazoo *(G-8704)*
Cco Holdings LLC ....G....... 269 432-0052
  Colon *(G-3370)*
Cco Holdings LLC ....G....... 269 464-3454
  White Pigeon *(G-17646)*
Cco Holdings LLC ....G....... 989 328-4187
  Sidney *(G-14738)*
Cco Holdings LLC ....G....... 989 567-0151
  Shepherd *(G-14726)*
Cco Holdings LLC ....G....... 989 863-4023
  Reese *(G-13229)*
Cco Holdings LLC ....G....... 989 853-2008
  Muir *(G-11237)*
Change Healthcare Tech LLC ....G....... 810 985-0029
  Port Huron *(G-12906)*
Community Access Center ....F....... 269 343-2211
  Kalamazoo *(G-8710)*
Emag Technologies Inc ....F....... 734 996-3624
  Ann Arbor *(G-442)*
▲ Harada Industry America Inc ....D....... 248 374-2587
  Novi *(G-11894)*
Information Stn Specialists ....F....... 616 772-2300
  Zeeland *(G-18159)*
L3 Technologies Inc ....A....... 231 724-2151
  Muskegon *(G-11361)*
L3 Technologies Inc ....C....... 734 741-8868
  Ann Arbor *(G-523)*
Livbig LLC ....G....... 888 519-8290
  Portage *(G-13010)*
Livespace LLC ....F....... 616 929-0191
  Grand Rapids *(G-6629)*
Lor Manufacturing Co Inc ....G....... 866 644-8622
  Weidman *(G-17458)*
Michigan Satellite ....E....... 989 792-6666
  Saginaw *(G-14091)*
Mobimogul Inc ....G....... 313 575-2795
  Southfield *(G-14986)*
Moody Bible Inst of Chicago ....G....... 616 772-7300
  Zeeland *(G-18167)*
Nht Sales Inc ....G....... 248 623-6114
  Auburn Hills *(G-956)*
Plymouth Computer & ....G....... 734 744-9563
  Livonia *(G-9890)*
R A Miller Industries Inc ....C....... 888 845-9450
  Grand Haven *(G-6067)*
Satellite Tracking Systems ....G....... 248 627-3334
  Ortonville *(G-12202)*
▼ Signal Group LLC ....E....... 248 479-1517
  Novi *(G-11997)*
Sound Productions Entrmt ....E....... 989 386-2221
  Clare *(G-2889)*
Spectrum Wireless (usa) Inc ....G....... 586 693-7525
  Saint Clair Shores *(G-14270)*
Stanecki Inc ....D....... 734 432-9900
  West Bloomfield *(G-17498)*
Startech-Solutions LLC ....G....... 248 419-0650
  West Bloomfield *(G-17499)*
Thalner Electronic Labs Inc ....E....... 734 761-4506
  Ann Arbor *(G-668)*
Washtenaw Communications Inc ....G....... 734 662-7138
  Ann Arbor *(G-696)*

3669 Communications Eqpt, NEC

Aaccess Entertainment ....G....... 734 260-1002
  Brighton *(G-1876)*
Ademco Inc ....G....... 586 759-1455
  Warren *(G-16918)*
Ademco Inc ....E....... 248 926-5510
  Wixom *(G-17752)*
Advanced-Cable LLC ....F....... 586 491-3073
  Troy *(G-16170)*
Aero Systems ....F....... 253 269-3000
  Livonia *(G-9630)*
▲ Apollo America Inc ....D....... 248 332-3900
  Auburn Hills *(G-776)*
Axis Tms Corp ....E....... 248 509-2440
  Troy *(G-16231)*
Blackbox Visual Design Inc ....G....... 734 459-1307
  Plymouth *(G-12588)*
Bluewater Tech Group Inc ....G....... 248 356-4399
  Farmington Hills *(G-4943)*
Causey Consulting LLC ....E....... 248 671-4979
  West Bloomfield *(G-17469)*
City of Saginaw ....F....... 989 759-1670
  Saginaw *(G-14019)*
▲ Code Blue Corporation ....E....... 616 392-8296
  Holland *(G-7594)*
Controller Systems Corporation ....E....... 586 772-6100
  Eastpointe *(G-4698)*
Curbell Plastics Inc ....G....... 734 513-0531
  Livonia *(G-9694)*
Em A Give Break Safety ....F....... 231 263-6625
  Kingsley *(G-9071)*
▲ Emergency Technology Inc ....D....... 616 896-7100
  Hudsonville *(G-8155)*
Engineered Control Systems Inc ....E....... 509 483-6215
  Washington *(G-17303)*
Gentex Corporation ....C....... 616 392-7195
  Zeeland *(G-18142)*
Gentex Corporation ....C....... 616 772-1800
  Zeeland *(G-18140)*
Gentex Corporation ....C....... 616 772-1800
  Zeeland *(G-18138)*
Give-Em A Brake Safety LLC ....E....... 616 531-8705
  Grandville *(G-7037)*
Monitec Services Incorporated ....G....... 231 943-2227
  Traverse City *(G-16042)*
National Sign & Signal Co ....E....... 269 963-2817
  Battle Creek *(G-1231)*
National Time and Signal Corp ....E....... 248 291-5867
  Oak Park *(G-12087)*
Nationwide Communications LLC ....G....... 517 990-1223
  Jackson *(G-8541)*
R A Miller Industries Inc ....C....... 888 845-9450
  Grand Haven *(G-6067)*
▲ R H K Technology Inc ....E....... 248 577-5426
  Troy *(G-16574)*
▲ Safety Technology Intl Inc ....E....... 248 673-9898
  Waterford *(G-17374)*
Safety Technology Intl Inc ....E....... 248 673-9898
  Waterford *(G-17375)*
▲ Select Fire LLC ....G....... 586 924-1974
  Lenox *(G-9525)*
Techncal Audio Video Solutions ....G....... 810 899-5546
  Howell *(G-8105)*
Tecumseh Signals LLC ....G....... 517 301-2064
  Tecumseh *(G-15812)*
▲ Tpk America LLC ....F....... 616 786-5300
  Holland *(G-7832)*
◆ Vidatak LLC ....G....... 877 392-6273
  Ann Arbor *(G-692)*
West Shore Services Inc ....E....... 616 895-4347
  Allendale *(G-227)*

3671 Radio & T V Receiving Electron Tubes

Puff Baby LLC ....G....... 734 620-9991
  Garden City *(G-5835)*

36 ELECTRONIC AND OTHER ELECTRICAL EQUIPMENT AND COMPONENTS, EXCEPT COMPUTER

3672 Printed Circuit Boards

3dxtech LLC .... G 616 717-3811
  Grand Rapids *(G-6121)*
A and D Design Electronics .... G 989 493-1884
  Auburn *(G-748)*
Acromag Incorporated .... D 248 624-1541
  Wixom *(G-17751)*
Aero Embedded Technologies Inc ...... G 586 251-2980
  Sterling Heights *(G-15255)*
Amtech Electrocircuits Inc .... G 248 583-1801
  Troy *(G-16200)*
Assem-Tech Inc .... E 616 846-3410
  Grand Haven *(G-5993)*
Assembly Alternatives Inc .... G 248 362-1616
  Rochester Hills *(G-13371)*
Boyd Manufacturing LLC .... G 734 649-9765
  Muskegon *(G-11284)*
Bralyn Inc .... F 231 865-3186
  Fruitport *(G-5790)*
Burton Industries Inc .... E 906 932-5970
  Ironwood *(G-8324)*
Ci Lighting LLC .... G 248 997-4415
  Auburn Hills *(G-813)*
Cusolar Industries Inc .... E 586 949-3880
  Chesterfield *(G-2757)*
Debron Industrial Elec Inc .... E 248 588-7220
  Troy *(G-16300)*
Diversified Mfg & Assembly LLC .... G 313 758-4797
  Sterling Hts *(G-15549)*
Dse Industries LLC .... G 313 530-6668
  Macomb *(G-10118)*
Dupearl Technology LLC .... D 248 390-9609
  Bloomfield Hills *(G-1762)*
Excel Circuits LLC .... F 248 373-0700
  Auburn Hills *(G-857)*
Flextronics Intl USA Inc .... B 616 837-9711
  Coopersville *(G-3558)*
◆ Ghi Electronics LLC .... F 248 397-8856
  Madison Heights *(G-10257)*
▲ Glassmaster Controls Co Inc .... E 269 382-2010
  Kalamazoo *(G-8753)*
Hewtech Electronics .... G 810 765-0820
  China *(G-2860)*
Hgc Westshore LLC .... D 616 796-1218
  Holland *(G-7664)*
Hughes Electronics Pdts Corp .... E 734 427-8310
  Livonia *(G-9776)*
▲ I Parth Inc .... G 248 548-9722
  Ferndale *(G-5293)*
Ips Assembly Corp .... F 734 391-0080
  Livonia *(G-9786)*
Jabil Circuit Inc .... A 248 292-6000
  Auburn Hills *(G-916)*
Jabil Circuit Michigan Inc .... E 248 292-6000
  Auburn Hills *(G-917)*
K & F Electronic Inc .... E 586 294-8720
  Fraser *(G-5677)*
Keska LLC .... G 616 283-7056
  Holland *(G-7711)*
M T S Chenault LLC .... G 269 861-0053
  Benton Harbor *(G-1523)*
▲ Magna Electronics Inc .... C 248 729-2643
  Auburn Hills *(G-933)*
Micro Logic .... G 248 432-7209
  West Bloomfield *(G-17486)*
▲ N S International Ltd .... C 248 251-1600
  Troy *(G-16519)*
Northville Circuits Inc .... G 248 853-3232
  Rochester Hills *(G-13484)*
Nu Tek Sales .... F 616 258-0631
  Grand Rapids *(G-6724)*
▲ Obertron Electronic Mfg Inc .... F 734 428-0722
  Manchester *(G-10409)*
▲ Odyssey Electronics Inc .... D 734 421-8340
  Livonia *(G-9874)*
P M Z Technology Inc .... G 248 471-0447
  Livonia *(G-9879)*
Petra Electronic Mfg Inc .... F 616 877-1991
  Holland *(G-7771)*
Pgf Technology Group Inc .... G 248 852-2800
  Rochester Hills *(G-13492)*
Plymouth Computer & .... G 734 744-9563
  Livonia *(G-9890)*
Protodesign Inc .... E 586 739-4340
  Shelby Township *(G-14673)*
Ram Electronics Inc .... F 231 865-3186
  Fruitport *(G-5799)*
Rockstar Digital Inc .... F 888 808-5868
  Sterling Heights *(G-15477)*
▲ Saline Lectronics Inc .... C 734 944-1972
  Saline *(G-14413)*
▲ Saturn Electronics Corp .... C 734 941-8100
  Romulus *(G-13732)*
Semicndctor Hybrid Assmbly Inc .... F 248 668-9050
  Wixom *(G-17893)*
Xilinx Inc .... G 248 344-0786
  Wixom *(G-17932)*

3674 Semiconductors

ABB Enterprise Software Inc .... G 313 863-1909
  Detroit *(G-3836)*
Advanced Photonix Inc .... G 734 864-5647
  Ann Arbor *(G-346)*
AG Precision Gage Inc .... G 248 374-0063
  Wixom *(G-17755)*
Allegro Microsystems LLC .... G 248 242-5044
  Auburn Hills *(G-764)*
Alsentis LLC .... G 616 395-8254
  Holland *(G-7555)*
Altronics Energy LLC .... F 616 662-7401
  Hudsonville *(G-8145)*
American Wind & Solar LLC .... G 734 904-8490
  Woodhaven *(G-17937)*
AMF-Nano Corporation .... G 734 726-0148
  Ann Arbor *(G-353)*
API Technologies Corp .... G 301 846-9222
  Ann Arbor *(G-361)*
Bay Carbon Inc .... E 989 686-8090
  Bay City *(G-1282)*
▼ Birdsall Tool & Gage Co .... E 248 474-5150
  Farmington Hills *(G-4941)*
Compucom Computers Inc .... G 989 837-1895
  Midland *(G-10826)*
Compunetics Incorporated .... G 248 524-6376
  Troy *(G-16276)*
Edward D Jones & Co LP .... G 616 583-0387
  Byron Center *(G-2188)*
▲ Electro-Matic Ventures Inc .... D 248 478-1182
  Farmington Hills *(G-4981)*
Evjump Solar Inc .... G 734 277-5075
  Saline *(G-14388)*
Fuel Cell System Mfg LLC .... G 313 319-5571
  Brownstown Township *(G-2069)*
Gan Systems Corp .... G 248 609-7643
  Ann Arbor *(G-468)*
Helios Solar LLC .... G 269 343-5581
  Kalamazoo *(G-8763)*
▲ Hemlock Smcndctor Oprtions LLC .. B 989 642-5201
  Hemlock *(G-7463)*
Hewtech Electronics .... G 810 765-0820
  China *(G-2860)*
Infineon Tech Americas Corp .... D 734 464-0891
  Livonia *(G-9782)*
Instrumented Sensor Tech Inc .... G 517 349-8487
  Okemos *(G-12126)*
International Bus Mchs Corp .... B 517 391-5248
  East Lansing *(G-4665)*
▲ Johnson Electric N Amer Inc .... D 734 392-5300
  Plymouth *(G-12658)*
▲ Kimberly Lighting LLC .... E 888 480-0070
  Clarkston *(G-2933)*
Lexatronics LLC .... G 734 878-6237
  Pinckney *(G-12499)*
Maxim Integrated Products Inc .... G 408 601-1000
  Brighton *(G-1956)*
Moog Inc .... E 734 738-5862
  Plymouth *(G-12695)*
Nihil Ultra Corporation .... G 413 723-3218
  Troy *(G-16524)*
▲ Nuvosun Inc .... D 408 514-6200
  Midland *(G-10897)*
Optimems Technology Inc .... G 248 660-0380
  Novi *(G-11966)*
Ovshinsky Technologies LLC .... G 248 390-3564
  Pontiac *(G-12854)*
Pacific Insight Elec Corp .... E 248 344-2569
  Southfield *(G-14996)*
▲ Patriot Solar Group LLC .... E 517 629-9292
  Albion *(G-128)*
Piezonix LLC .... G 517 231-9586
  East Lansing *(G-4674)*
Powerlase Photonics Inc .... G 248 305-2963
  Novi *(G-11976)*
Precision Gage Inc .... D 517 439-1690
  Hillsdale *(G-7534)*
Prochimir Inc .... G 248 457-4538
  Troy *(G-16564)*
Promethient Inc .... G 231 525-0500
  Traverse City *(G-16082)*
Qualcomm Incorporated .... B 248 853-2017
  Rochester Hills *(G-13500)*
Regener-Eyes LLC .... G 248 207-4641
  Ann Arbor *(G-614)*
Riverside Cnc LLC .... G 616 246-6000
  Wyoming *(G-18032)*
Sand Traxx .... G 616 460-5137
  Wayland *(G-17413)*
Seelye Equipment Specialist .... G 231 547-9430
  Charlevoix *(G-2630)*
Siemens AG .... G 248 307-3400
  Troy *(G-16599)*
▲ Sigma Luminous LLC .... G 800 482-1327
  Livonia *(G-9929)*
Sonima Corp .... G 302 450-6452
  Lake Orion *(G-9163)*
Star Board Multi Media Inc .... G 616 296-0823
  Grand Haven *(G-6084)*
Suematek .... G 517 614-2235
  Ypsilanti *(G-18103)*
◆ T E Technology Inc .... E 231 929-3966
  Traverse City *(G-16118)*
Tenneco Inc .... F 248 354-7700
  Southfield *(G-15044)*
Teradyne Inc .... C 313 425-3900
  Allen Park *(G-211)*
Terametrix LLC .... G 540 769-8430
  Ann Arbor *(G-664)*
Teslir LLC .... G 248 644-5500
  Bloomfield Hills *(G-1802)*
Tetradyn Ltd .... G 202 415-7295
  Traverse City *(G-16120)*
Texas Instruments Incorporated .... F 248 305-5718
  Novi *(G-12013)*
Toshiba America Electronic .... G 248 347-2608
  Wixom *(G-17912)*
US Trade LLC .... G 800 676-0208
  Garden City *(G-5845)*
▲ Uusi LLC .... E 231 832-5513
  Reed City *(G-13226)*
Veoneer Us Inc .... C 248 223-8074
  Southfield *(G-15059)*
▼ Viking Technologies Inc .... G 586 914-0819
  Madison Heights *(G-10377)*
White River .... G 231 894-9216
  Montague *(G-11099)*
Xilinx Inc .... G 248 344-0786
  Wixom *(G-17932)*
Ziel Optics Inc .... G 734 994-9803
  Ann Arbor *(G-707)*

3676 Electronic Resistors

Touchstone Systems & Svcs Inc .... G 616 532-0060
  Wyoming *(G-18035)*

3677 Electronic Coils & Transformers

▼ Controlled Power Company .... C 248 528-3700
  Troy *(G-16281)*
Cusolar Industries Inc .... E 586 949-3880
  Chesterfield *(G-2757)*
▲ Ecoclean Inc .... C 248 450-2000
  Southfield *(G-14897)*
Ford Motor Company .... A 734 484-8000
  Ypsilanti *(G-18074)*
H W Jencks Incorporated .... E 231 352-4422
  Frankfort *(G-5603)*
Heco Inc .... D 269 381-7200
  Kalamazoo *(G-8762)*
Induction Engineering Inc .... F 586 716-4700
  New Baltimore *(G-11486)*
▲ Innovative Air Management LLC .... G 586 201-3513
  Highland *(G-7495)*
◆ La Solucion Corp .... G 313 893-9760
  Detroit *(G-4188)*
Ntf Manufacturing Usa LLC .... F 989 739-8560
  Oscoda *(G-12215)*
Osborne Transformer Corp .... F 586 218-6900
  Fraser *(G-5702)*
Performance Induction .... G 734 658-1676
  Howell *(G-8080)*
▲ Pontiac Coil Inc .... C 248 922-1100
  Clarkston *(G-2947)*
Powertran Corporation .... E 248 399-4300
  Ferndale *(G-5312)*
Prosys Industries Inc .... E 734 207-3710
  Canton *(G-2421)*
South Haven Coil Inc .... E 269 637-5201
  South Haven *(G-14771)*
Techna Systems Inc .... G 248 681-1717
  Orchard Lake *(G-12171)*

SIC SECTION 36 ELECTRONIC AND OTHER ELECTRICAL EQUIPMENT AND COMPONENTS, EXCEPT COMPUTER

Trucent Inc....G.... 734 426-9015
Dexter (G-4515)
Trucent Separation Tech LLC....D.... 734 426-9015
Dexter (G-4516)

3678 Electronic Connectors

Aees Power Systems Ltd Partnr....F.... 269 668-4429
Farmington Hills (G-4921)
Amphenol Corporation....G.... 256 417-4338
Novi (G-11825)
Amphenol Corporation....B.... 586 465-3131
Clinton Township (G-3050)
Cardell Corporation....F.... 248 371-9700
Auburn Hills (G-810)
Harsco Corporation....D.... 231 843-3431
Ludington (G-10062)
Hirschmann Auto N Amer LLC....G.... 248 495-2677
Rochester Hills (G-13444)
▲ Iriso USA Inc....E.... 248 324-9780
Farmington Hills (G-5030)
▲ Kostal Kontakt Systeme Inc....C.... 248 284-7600
Rochester Hills (G-13457)
Mac Lean-Fogg Company....C.... 248 280-0880
Royal Oak (G-13945)
Midwest Sales Associates Inc....G.... 248 348-9600
Wixom (G-17855)
Norma Group Craig Assembly....G.... 810 326-1374
Saint Clair (G-14230)
Nvent Thermal LLC....D.... 248 273-3359
Troy (G-16530)
Rapp & Son Inc....C.... 734 283-1000
Wyandotte (G-17971)
▲ Sine Systems Corporation....C.... 586 465-3131
Clinton Township (G-3230)
Te Connectivity Corporation....C.... 248 273-3344
Troy (G-16633)
Teradyne Inc....C.... 313 425-3900
Allen Park (G-211)
Winford Engineering LLC....G.... 989 671-9721
Auburn (G-758)

3679 Electronic Components, NEC

A B Electrical Inc....E.... 231 737-9200
Muskegon (G-11257)
AB Electrical Wires Inc....E.... 231 737-9200
Muskegon (G-11258)
Accessories Wholesale Inc....F.... 248 755-7465
Pontiac (G-12798)
Ace Electronics LLC Michigan....G.... 443 327-6100
Troy (G-16167)
▲ Adco Circuits Inc....C.... 248 853-6620
Rochester Hills (G-13363)
Aees Inc....B.... 248 489-4700
Farmington Hills (G-4920)
Affinity Electronics Inc....G.... 586 477-4920
Fraser (G-5614)
Aktv8 LLC....G.... 517 775-1270
South Lyon (G-14785)
◆ Alpine Electronics America Inc....C.... 248 409-9444
Auburn Hills (G-766)
▲ Amphenol Borisch Tech Inc....C.... 616 554-9820
Grand Rapids (G-6168)
▲ Amptech Inc....G.... 231 464-5492
Manistee (G-10415)
▲ Asimco International Inc....G.... 248 213-5200
Southfield (G-14841)
Assem-Tech Inc....E.... 616 846-3410
Grand Haven (G-5993)
Automotive Electronic Spc....E.... 248 335-3229
Bloomfield Hills (G-1748)
Aztecnology LLC....G.... 734 857-2045
Southgate (G-15074)
Bay Electronics Inc....E.... 586 296-0900
Roseville (G-13776)
▲ Byrne Elec Specialists Inc....C.... 616 866-3461
Rockford (G-13560)
Byrne Elec Specialists Inc....G.... 616 866-3461
Rockford (G-13561)
Cardell Corporation....F.... 248 371-9700
Auburn Hills (G-810)
Chrouch Communications Inc....G.... 231 972-0339
Mecosta (G-10687)
Circuits of Sound....G.... 313 886-5599
Grosse Pointe Woods (G-7201)
Cobham McRlctrnic Slutions Inc....G.... 734 426-1230
Ann Arbor (G-403)
Code Systems Inc....E.... 248 307-3884
Auburn Hills (G-816)
Connect With Us LLC....E.... 586 262-4359
Shelby Township (G-14566)
Contract People Corporation....F.... 248 304-9900
Southfield (G-14872)
Control Electronics....E.... 734 941-5008
Romulus (G-13664)
▲ Ctc Acquisition Company LLC....C.... 616 884-7100
Rockford (G-13564)
Debron Industrial Elec Inc....E.... 248 588-7220
Troy (G-16300)
Detectir Inc....G.... 724 681-0975
East Lansing (G-4655)
Direct Connect Systems LLC....E.... 248 694-0130
Commerce Township (G-3400)
Diversfied Tchncal Systems Inc....E.... 248 513-6050
Novi (G-11870)
Dupearl Technology LLC....D.... 248 390-9609
Bloomfield Hills (G-1762)
Dynamic Supply Solutions Inc....G.... 248 987-2205
Grosse Pointe Shores (G-7198)
▲ Ebw Electronics Inc....E.... 616 786-0575
Holland (G-7616)
Electro Panel Inc....G.... 989 832-2110
Midland (G-10859)
▲ Electro-Matic Integrated Inc....G.... 248 478-1182
Farmington Hills (G-4979)
Enertech Corporation....F.... 231 832-5587
Hersey (G-7472)
▲ Etcs Inc....F.... 586 268-4870
Warren (G-17022)
▲ Eto Magnetic Corp....D.... 616 957-2570
Grand Rapids (G-6387)
Fema Corporation of Michigan....C.... 269 323-1369
Portage (G-12996)
Five-Way Switch Music....G.... 269 425-2843
Battle Creek (G-1188)
◆ Fka Distributing Co LLC....B.... 248 863-3000
Commerce Township (G-3406)
Gadget Locker LLC....G.... 702 901-1440
Detroit (G-4075)
General Motors LLC....F.... 931 486-1914
Warren (G-17052)
◆ Ghs Corporation....B.... 269 968-3351
Springfield (G-15192)
H and H Electronics....G.... 586 725-5412
Clay (G-2997)
High Effcncy Pwr Solutions Inc....G.... 800 833-7094
Whitmore Lake (G-17702)
▲ Hirschmann Car Comm Inc....F.... 248 373-7150
Auburn Hills (G-900)
▲ House of Marley LLC....G.... 248 863-3000
Commerce Township (G-3415)
▲ Innotec Corp....D.... 616 772-5959
Zeeland (G-18160)
Intuitive Circuits LLC....G.... 248 588-4400
Troy (G-16426)
◆ Kaydon Corporation....B.... 734 747-7025
Ann Arbor (G-516)
Kyocera International Inc....F.... 734 416-8500
Plymouth (G-12670)
Lappans of Gaylord Inc....G.... 989 732-3274
Gaylord (G-5874)
Lectronix Inc....D.... 517 492-1900
Lansing (G-9391)
Leoni Wiring Systems Inc....F.... 586 782-4444
Warren (G-17128)
Liberty Circuits Corporation....G.... 269 226-8743
Kalamazoo (G-8809)
Madison Electric Company....D.... 586 825-0200
Warren (G-17136)
Magna Electronics Inc....E.... 248 606-0606
Auburn Hills (G-934)
▲ Magna Electronics Inc....C.... 248 729-2643
Auburn Hills (G-933)
▲ Magnetech Corporation....G.... 248 426-8840
Novi (G-11933)
MAKS INCORPORATED....E.... 248 733-9771
Troy (G-16484)
Mark Griessel....G.... 810 378-6060
Melvin (G-10691)
▲ Memtron Technologies Co....D.... 989 652-2656
Frankenmuth (G-5593)
Mitech Electronics Corporation....C.... 269 694-9471
Otsego (G-12246)
Mobile Knowlege Group Services....G.... 248 625-3327
Clarkston (G-2940)
Movellus Circuits Inc....G.... 877 321-7667
Ann Arbor (G-566)
▲ Nass Corporation....F.... 586 725-6610
New Baltimore (G-11489)
Nelson Specialties Company....F.... 269 983-1878
Saint Joseph (G-14330)
Netcon Enterprises Inc....E.... 248 673-7855
Waterford (G-17360)
No Limit Wireless-Michigan Inc....G.... 313 285-8402
Detroit (G-4274)
Nova-Tron Controls Corp....G.... 989 358-6126
Alpena (G-303)
Omtron Inc....G.... 248 673-3896
Waterford (G-17362)
▲ Onegene America Inc....G.... 734 855-4460
Livonia (G-9876)
Parkway Elc Communications LLC....D.... 616 392-2788
Holland (G-7767)
Pcb Piezotronics Inc....F.... 888 684-0014
Novi (G-11971)
Phoenix Sound Systems....G.... 734 662-6405
Ann Arbor (G-592)
Photo-Tron Corp....G.... 248 852-5200
Rochester Hills (G-13493)
Pkc Group USA Inc....F.... 248 489-4700
Farmington Hills (G-5095)
Practical Power....G.... 866 385-2961
Rochester (G-13347)
Pribusin Inc....G.... 734 677-0459
Ann Arbor (G-603)
▲ Progressive Dynamics Inc....D.... 269 781-4241
Marshall (G-10585)
Renewable World Energies LLC....F.... 906 828-0808
Norway (G-11819)
Rockford Contract Mfg....G.... 616 304-3837
Rockford (G-13587)
▲ Safari Circuits Inc....C.... 269 694-9471
Otsego (G-12255)
Sage Acoustics LLC....G.... 269 861-5593
Bangor (G-1095)
Saldet Sales and Services Inc....E.... 586 469-4312
Clinton Township (G-3220)
Sensata Technologies Inc....G.... 805 523-2000
Northville (G-11725)
Sensor Manufacturing Company....F.... 248 474-7300
Novi (G-11992)
▲ Ssi Electronics Inc....E.... 616 866-8880
Belmont (G-1470)
◆ Stoneridge Inc....G.... 248 489-9300
Novi (G-12004)
◆ Tecumseh Products Company LLC....A.... 734 585-9500
Ann Arbor (G-661)
Tecumseh Products Holdings LLC....F.... 734 585-9500
Ann Arbor (G-663)
TMC Group Inc....F.... 248 819-6063
Pleasant Ridge (G-12556)
Touchstone Systems & Svcs Inc....G.... 616 532-0060
Wyoming (G-18035)
Turn Key Harness & Wire LLC....G.... 248 236-9915
Oxford (G-12379)
Venntis Technologies LLC....F.... 616 395-8254
Holland (G-7845)
Wh Manufacturing Inc....E.... 616 534-7560
Grand Rapids (G-6990)
▲ Wmc Lievense Company....E.... 231 946-3800
Traverse City (G-16148)
◆ ZF Active Safety & Elec US LLC....C.... 734 855-2600
Livonia (G-10014)
ZF Passive Safety....B.... 586 232-7200
Washington (G-17316)

3691 Storage Batteries

A123 Systems LLC....C.... 734 466-6521
Livonia (G-9621)
A123 Systems LLC....C.... 734 772-0600
Romulus (G-13646)
▼ A123 Systems LLC....B.... 248 412-9249
Novi (G-11822)
Adana Voltaics LLC....G.... 734 622-0193
Ann Arbor (G-342)
▲ Advanced Battery Concepts LLC....E.... 989 424-6645
Clare (G-2863)
Arotech Corporation....E.... 800 281-0356
Ann Arbor (G-368)
Auto Clinic....G.... 906 774-5780
Iron Mountain (G-8275)
Batteries Shack....G.... 586 580-2893
Sterling Heights (G-15273)
Contemporary Amperex Corp....G.... 248 289-6200
Rochester Hills (G-13395)
East Penn Manufacturing Co....F.... 586 979-5300
Sterling Heights (G-15329)
Ematrix Energy Systems Inc....G.... 248 797-2149
Royal Oak (G-13921)
Ematrix Energy Systems Inc....G.... 248 629-9111
Royal Oak (G-13922)

S I C

Employee Codes: A=Over 500 employees, B=251-500
C=101-250, D=51-100, E=20-50, F=10-19, G=3-9
2020 Harris Michigan
Industrial Directory
845

Energy Powercell LLC .... E 248 585-1000
Pontiac *(G-12822)*

Exide Technologies .... F 248 853-5000
Auburn Hills *(G-858)*

G & L Powerup Inc .... G 586 200-2169
Roseville *(G-13806)*

▲ Harding Energy Inc .... E 231 798-7033
Norton Shores *(G-11759)*

Httm LLC .... F 616 820-2500
Holland *(G-7683)*

Innovative Weld Solutions LLC .... G 937 545-7695
Rochester *(G-13329)*

Johnson Controls Inc .... G 734 995-3016
Ann Arbor *(G-513)*

Lg Chem Michigan Inc .... G 248 291-2385
Troy *(G-16461)*

Lg Chem Michigan Inc .... G 248 307-1800
Troy *(G-16462)*

◆ Lg Chem Michigan Inc .... C 616 494-7100
Holland *(G-7722)*

M & M Irish Enterprises Inc .... G 248 644-0666
Birmingham *(G-1689)*

▲ Navitas Systems LLC .... F 630 755-7920
Ann Arbor *(G-572)*

Redeem Power Services .... G 248 679-5277
Novi *(G-11985)*

▲ Robert Bosch Btry Systems LLC .... D 248 620-5700
Orion *(G-12189)*

▲ Seeo Inc .... F 510 782-7336
Lake Orion *(G-9159)*

TMC Group Inc .... F 248 819-6063
Pleasant Ridge *(G-12556)*

Xalt Energy LLC .... G 248 409-5419
Pontiac *(G-12877)*

▲ Xalt Energy LLC .... F 989 486-8501
Midland *(G-10928)*

◆ Xalt Energy Mi LLC .... D 989 486-8501
Midland *(G-10930)*

3692 Primary Batteries: Dry & Wet

Bargain Business Supplies Inc .... G 810 750-0999
Fenton *(G-5186)*

G & L Powerup Inc .... G 586 200-2169
Roseville *(G-13806)*

▲ Mophie LLC .... D 269 743-1340
Kalamazoo *(G-8831)*

▲ Robert Bosch Btry Systems LLC .... D 248 620-5700
Orion *(G-12189)*

3694 Electrical Eqpt For Internal Combustion Engines

◆ 3con Corporation .... E 248 859-5440
Wixom *(G-17748)*

▲ Aees Power Systems Ltd Partnr .... D 248 489-4900
Allen Park *(G-194)*

Aees Power Systems Ltd Partnr .... F 269 668-4429
Farmington Hills *(G-4921)*

◆ Aptiv Services 2 Us Inc .... E 248 813-2000
Troy *(G-16211)*

Arotech Corporation .... E 800 281-0356
Ann Arbor *(G-368)*

▲ Auto Electric International .... F 248 354-2082
Southfield *(G-14846)*

Blade Welding Service Inc .... G 734 941-4253
Van Buren Twp *(G-16749)*

▲ Bontaz Centre Usa Inc .... F 248 588-8113
Troy *(G-16244)*

▲ Borgwrner Emssions Systems LLC .... G 248 754-9600
Auburn Hills *(G-805)*

Brose New Boston Inc .... G 248 339-4000
Auburn Hills *(G-807)*

◆ Brose New Boston Inc .... C 248 339-4021
New Boston *(G-11498)*

Calsonickansei North Amer Inc .... G 248 848-4727
West Bloomfield *(G-17467)*

Cignet LLC .... E 586 307-3790
Clinton Township *(G-3080)*

Continental Auto Systems Inc .... B 248 253-2969
Auburn Hills *(G-818)*

Continental Auto Systems Inc .... A 248 874-2597
Auburn Hills *(G-821)*

▲ Crosscon Industries LLC .... F 248 852-5888
Rochester Hills *(G-13398)*

Cusolar Industries Inc .... E 586 949-3880
Chesterfield *(G-2757)*

Daewon America Inc .... G 334 364-1630
Troy *(G-16294)*

Daimay North America Auto Inc .... G 313 533-9860
Redford *(G-13155)*

Denso International Amer Inc .... G 248 359-4177
Van Buren Twp *(G-16757)*

Diamond Electric Mfg Corp .... F 734 995-5525
Ann Arbor *(G-420)*

Digital Dimensions Inc .... G 419 630-4343
Camden *(G-2341)*

▲ Don Duff Rebuilding .... G 734 522-7700
Livonia *(G-9714)*

Eldor Automotive N Amer Inc .... G 248 878-9193
Troy *(G-16337)*

Electra Cable & Communication .... G 586 754-3479
Warren *(G-17017)*

Electrical Concepts Inc .... E 616 847-0293
Grand Haven *(G-6013)*

Electro-Matic Products Inc .... G 248 478-1182
Farmington Hills *(G-4980)*

▲ Electrodynamics Inc .... G 734 422-5420
Livonia *(G-9723)*

▲ Emp Racing Inc .... G 906 786-8404
Escanaba *(G-4825)*

Ford Motor Company .... A 734 484-8000
Ypsilanti *(G-18074)*

H & L Manufacturing Co .... C 269 795-5000
Middleville *(G-10804)*

Kathrein Automotive N Amer Inc .... G 248 230-2951
Rochester Hills *(G-13455)*

Kessler USA Inc .... F 734 404-0152
Plymouth *(G-12666)*

Keystone Cable Corporation .... G 313 924-9720
Detroit *(G-4177)*

▲ Kirks Automotive Incorporated .... E 313 933-7030
Detroit *(G-4179)*

Lg Electronics Vehicle Compone .... C 248 268-5851
Hazel Park *(G-7441)*

Lg Electronics Vehicle Compone .... C 248 268-5851
Troy *(G-16464)*

Magnecor Australia Limited .... F 248 471-9505
Farmington Hills *(G-5049)*

Meritor Indus Intl Hldings LLC .... G 248 658-7345
Troy *(G-16496)*

Midwest International Dist LLC .... G 616 901-4621
Ionia *(G-8249)*

▲ Minowitz Manufacturing Co .... E 586 779-5940
Huntington Woods *(G-8190)*

Nabco Inc .... G 231 832-2001
Reed City *(G-13221)*

Omron Automotive Electronics .... E 248 893-0200
Novi *(G-11964)*

Omron Automotive Electronics .... E 248 893-0200
Novi *(G-11965)*

Overseas Auto Parts Inc .... E 734 427-4840
Livonia *(G-9877)*

Portable Factory .... F 586 883-6843
Sterling Heights *(G-15447)*

Portage Wire Systems Inc .... E 231 889-4215
Onekama *(G-12151)*

Precision Power Inc .... G 517 371-4274
Lansing *(G-9414)*

▲ Prestolite Electric LLC .... G 248 313-3807
Novi *(G-11978)*

Prestolite Electric Holding .... A 248 313-3807
Novi *(G-11979)*

▲ Prestolite Electric Inc .... F 866 463-7078
Novi *(G-11980)*

▲ Prestolite Wire LLC .... E 248 355-4422
Southfield *(G-15004)*

Protean Electric Inc .... D 248 504-4940
Auburn Hills *(G-981)*

Protean Holdings Corp .... G 248 504-4940
Auburn Hills *(G-982)*

Rizk National Industries Inc .... E 586 757-4700
Warren *(G-17221)*

Robert Bosch LLC .... E 248 921-9054
Novi *(G-11987)*

Robert Bosch LLC .... A 734 979-3000
Plymouth *(G-12741)*

Seg Automotive North Amer LLC .... F 248 465-2602
Novi *(G-11991)*

▲ Southern Auto Wholesalers Inc .... F 248 335-5555
Pontiac *(G-12869)*

Starlight Technologies Inc .... G 248 250-9607
Troy *(G-16620)*

▲ USA Switch Inc .... F 248 960-8500
Wixom *(G-17922)*

Veoneer Inc .... A 248 223-0600
Southfield *(G-15058)*

Veoneer Us Inc .... C 248 223-8074
Southfield *(G-15059)*

Veoneer Us Inc .... B 248 223-0600
Southfield *(G-15060)*

▲ Vte Inc .... E 231 539-8000
Pellston *(G-12426)*

Walbro LLC .... C 989 872-2131
Cass City *(G-2524)*

◆ Walther Trowal LLC .... F 616 455-8940
Grand Rapids *(G-6978)*

◆ Wiric Corporation .... E 248 598-5297
Rochester Hills *(G-13548)*

▲ Wolverine Advanced Mtls LLC .... E 313 749-6100
Dearborn *(G-3774)*

Xytek Industries Inc .... F 313 838-6961
Detroit *(G-4453)*

3695 Recording Media

Ade Inc .... G 248 625-7200
Clarkston *(G-2904)*

▲ Applied Automation Tech Inc .... E 248 656-4930
Rochester Hills *(G-13369)*

Naneva Inc .... G 248 561-6425
West Bloomfield *(G-17490)*

Rutherford & Associates Inc .... E 616 392-5000
Holland *(G-7792)*

Stans Affordable Videography .... G 734 671-2975
Trenton *(G-16158)*

▲ Storch Products Company Inc .... F 734 591-2200
Livonia *(G-9946)*

Transit Solutions LLC .... G 989 893-3230
Bay City *(G-1363)*

3699 Electrical Machinery, Eqpt & Splys, NEC

◆ Ace Filtration Inc .... G 248 624-6300
Commerce Township *(G-3385)*

Advanced Avionics Inc .... G 734 259-5300
Plymouth *(G-12567)*

Advanced Research Company .... F 248 475-4770
Orion *(G-12173)*

Aerobee Electric Inc .... G 248 549-2044
Ferndale *(G-5252)*

AMS Co Ltd .... G 248 712-4435
Troy *(G-16199)*

Andex Laser Inc .... G 734 947-9840
Taylor *(G-15688)*

Arin Inc .... F 586 779-3410
Roseville *(G-13774)*

Arkin Automotive Inc .... G 248 542-1192
Ferndale *(G-5262)*

Asco Power Technologies LP .... G 248 957-9050
Farmington Hills *(G-4933)*

Assa Abloy Entrance Systems US .... E 734 462-2348
Livonia *(G-9654)*

B & M Sonics and Machine LLC .... G 810 793-1236
Lapeer *(G-9441)*

Band-Ayd Systems Intl Inc .... F 586 294-8851
Madison Heights *(G-10200)*

Boyd Manufacturing LLC .... G 734 649-9765
Muskegon *(G-11284)*

Branson Ultrasonics Corp .... F 586 276-0150
Sterling Heights *(G-15277)*

◆ Bronner Display Sign Advg Inc .... C 989 652-9931
Frankenmuth *(G-5584)*

BT Engineering LLC .... G 734 417-2218
Spring Lake *(G-15134)*

Challenger Communications LLC .... F 517 680-0125
Springport *(G-15208)*

Changer & Dresser Inc .... G 256 832-4392
Novi *(G-11847)*

Combat Action LLC .... G 810 772-3758
Brighton *(G-1900)*

Comptek Inc .... F 248 477-5215
Farmington Hills *(G-4965)*

▲ Computerized SEC Systems Inc .... C 248 837-3700
Madison Heights *(G-10219)*

Connolly .... G 248 683-7985
Waterford *(G-17329)*

Cortar Laser and Fab LLC .... G 248 446-1110
Brighton *(G-1905)*

Csh Incorporated .... F 989 723-8985
Owosso *(G-12286)*

▲ Cypress Computer Systems Inc .... F 810 245-2300
Lapeer *(G-9453)*

▲ Dare Products Inc .... E 269 965-2307
Springfield *(G-15190)*

Dataspeed Inc .... F 248 879-0528
Rochester Hills *(G-13402)*

Diamond Electric .... G 734 995-5525
Ann Arbor *(G-419)*

Dice Corporation .... E 989 891-2800
Bay City *(G-1301)*

Dm3d Technology LLC .... F 248 409-7900
Auburn Hills *(G-841)*

37 TRANSPORTATION EQUIPMENT

Eesco Inc ....G...... 517 265-5148
Adrian *(G-61)*
Electric Eye Cafe ....G...... 734 369-6904
Ann Arbor *(G-439)*
Electro-Matic Visual Inc ....G...... 248 478-1182
Farmington Hills *(G-4982)*
Electronic Design & Packg Co...........F...... 734 591-9176
Livonia *(G-9724)*
Elite Electro Coaters Inc....................G...... 517 886-1020
Lansing *(G-9223)*
▲ Emergency Technology Inc ....D...... 616 896-7100
Hudsonville *(G-8155)*
Faac Incorporated ....G...... 734 761-5836
Ann Arbor *(G-455)*
Fabrilaser Mfg LLC ....E...... 269 789-9490
Marshall *(G-10567)*
Farr & Faron Associates Inc ....G...... 810 229-7730
Brighton *(G-1921)*
Fire Equipment Company ....E...... 313 891-3164
Detroit *(G-4059)*
Fusion Laser Services........................G...... 586 739-7716
Sterling Heights *(G-15352)*
▲ Gelman Sciences Inc ....A...... 734 665-0651
Ann Arbor *(G-469)*
General Electric Company ....D...... 734 728-1472
Wayne *(G-17431)*
George Jensen ....G...... 269 329-1543
Portage *(G-12998)*
Gnutti Carlo Usa Inc ....B...... 517 223-1059
Webberville *(G-17450)*
Grt Avionics Inc..................................G...... 616 245-7700
Wyoming *(G-18006)*
▲ Gvn Group Corp ....E...... 248 340-0342
Pontiac *(G-12831)*
H & R Industries Inc..........................F...... 616 247-1165
Grand Rapids *(G-6487)*
Hanon Systems Usa LLC ....B...... 248 907-8000
Novi *(G-11893)*
Harold G Schaevitz Inds LLC ....G...... 248 636-1515
Bloomfield Hills *(G-1772)*
Heco Inc ....D...... 269 381-7200
Kalamazoo *(G-8762)*
Hirose Electric USA Inc ....D...... 734 542-9963
Livonia *(G-9771)*
▼ Iaec Corporation ....D...... 586 354-5996
Armada *(G-720)*
Identify Inc ....F...... 313 802-2015
Madison Heights *(G-10273)*
Imperial Laser Inc ....G...... 616 735-9315
Grand Rapids *(G-6529)*
Imra America Inc ....E...... 734 669-7377
Ann Arbor *(G-503)*
Insulation Wholesale Supply ....G...... 269 968-9746
Battle Creek *(G-1200)*
▼ Integrated Security Corp ....F...... 248 624-0700
Novi *(G-11906)*
Ipg Photonics Corporation ....F...... 248 863-5001
Novi *(G-11908)*
J N B Machinery LLC ....G...... 517 223-0711
Fowlerville *(G-5572)*
Jervis B Webb Company ....D...... 231 582-6558
Boyne City *(G-1825)*
▲ Kore Inc ....E...... 616 785-5900
Comstock Park *(G-3491)*
Lakepoint Elec ....G...... 586 983-2510
Shelby Township *(G-14621)*
Laser Access Inc................................C...... 616 459-5496
Grand Rapids *(G-6618)*
Laser Fab Inc......................................G...... 586 415-8090
Fraser *(G-5683)*
▲ Laser Marking Technologies LLC....F...... 989 673-6690
Caro *(G-2470)*
Laser Mechanisms Inc.......................D...... 248 474-9480
Novi *(G-11929)*
Laser Product Development LLC ....G...... 800 765-4424
Center Line *(G-2580)*
Lastek Industries LLC ....G...... 586 739-6666
Shelby Township *(G-14622)*
Lighthouse Elec Protection LLC ....G...... 586 932-2690
Sterling Heights *(G-15400)*
Macomb Sheet Metal Inc ....E...... 586 790-4600
Clinton Township *(G-3164)*
Magna Electronics Inc ....E...... 810 606-0444
Troy *(G-16471)*
Magna Mirrors America Inc ....B...... 231 652-4450
Newaygo *(G-11574)*
Metropoulos Amplification Inc ....G...... 810 614-3905
Holly *(G-7888)*
Midwest Sales Associates Inc ....G...... 248 348-9600
Wixom *(G-17855)*

Montronix Inc ....G...... 734 213-6500
Ann Arbor *(G-564)*
Morstar Inc..F...... 248 605-3291
Livonia *(G-9848)*
▲ Ms Plastic Welders LLC ....E...... 517 223-1059
Webberville *(G-17452)*
Oleco Inc ....E...... 616 842-6790
Spring Lake *(G-15167)*
▲ Operator Specialty Company Inc ....D...... 616 675-5050
Grand Rapids *(G-6732)*
Parker Engineering and Mfg Co ....G...... 616 784-6500
Grand Rapids *(G-6742)*
Pct Security Inc ....G...... 888 567-3287
Clinton Township *(G-3192)*
Peak Edm Inc.....................................G...... 248 380-0871
Wixom *(G-17876)*
▼ Picpatch LLC ....G...... 248 670-2681
Milford *(G-10979)*
Power Cleaning Systems Inc ....G...... 248 347-7727
Wixom *(G-17878)*
Quad City Innovations LLC................G...... 513 200-6980
Ann Arbor *(G-610)*
Quality Door & More Inc ....G...... 989 317-8314
Mount Pleasant *(G-11222)*
Ram Electronics Inc ....F...... 231 865-3186
Fruitport *(G-5799)*
Realm ....G...... 313 706-4401
Wayne *(G-17441)*
Reau Manufacturing Co ....G...... 734 823-5603
Dundee *(G-4598)*
Robroy Industries Inc ....D...... 616 794-0700
Belding *(G-1429)*
Rofin-Sinar Technologies LLC...........F...... 734 416-0206
Plymouth *(G-12745)*
Rydin and Associates Inc ....F...... 586 783-9772
Clinton Township *(G-3219)*
▲ Saginaw Control & Engrg Inc ....B...... 989 799-6871
Saginaw *(G-14138)*
Se-Kure Controls Inc ....E...... 269 651-9351
Sturgis *(G-15633)*
Secure Crossing RES & Dev Inc......F...... 248 535-3800
Dearborn *(G-3756)*
Securecom Inc ....G...... 989 837-4005
Midland *(G-10914)*
Semmler Electric LLC ....G...... 517 869-2211
Hillsdale *(G-7540)*
Sensigma LLC....................................G...... 734 998-8328
Ann Arbor *(G-628)*
▲ Silent Call Corporation ....F...... 248 673-7353
Waterford *(G-17377)*
SLM Solutions Na Inc ....E...... 248 243-5400
Wixom *(G-17894)*
Tandis LLC..G...... 248 345-3448
West Bloomfield *(G-17500)*
Tech Electric Co LLC ....G...... 586 697-5095
Macomb *(G-10167)*
Tech-Source International Inc............E...... 231 652-9100
Newaygo *(G-11578)*
▲ Telsonic Ultrasonics Inc ....E...... 586 802-0033
Shelby Township *(G-14708)*
Tenneco Automotive Oper Co Inc ....E...... 734 243-8000
Lansing *(G-9269)*
▲ Testek LLC ....D...... 248 573-4980
Wixom *(G-17909)*
Troy Laser & Fab LLC ....G...... 586 510-4570
Warren *(G-17269)*
Trumpf Inc. ....E...... 734 354-9770
Plymouth *(G-12783)*
Visotek Inc ....F...... 734 427-4800
Livonia *(G-9990)*
Volkswagen Group America Inc ....D...... 248 754-5000
Auburn Hills *(G-1048)*
Walker Telecommunications...............G...... 989 274-7384
Saginaw *(G-14180)*
Weber Security Group Inc ....G...... 586 582-0000
Mount Clemens *(G-11153)*
▲ Weber Ultrasonics America LLC ....G...... 248 620-5142
Clarkston *(G-2964)*
Welform Electrodes Inc ....D...... 586 755-1184
Warren *(G-17292)*
Welk-Ko Fabricators Inc ....F...... 734 425-6840
Livonia *(G-10004)*
Yakkertech Limited ....G...... 734 568-6162
Ottawa Lake *(G-12270)*

37 TRANSPORTATION EQUIPMENT

3711 Motor Vehicles & Car Bodies

A & A Manufacturing Co....................G...... 616 846-1730
Spring Lake *(G-15130)*
Aapico Detroit LLC ....G...... 313 652-5254
Detroit *(G-3833)*
Aapico Detroit LLC ....B...... 313 551-6001
Detroit *(G-3834)*
▲ Adac Door Components Inc..........G...... 616 957-0311
Grand Rapids *(G-6139)*
Advance Vehicle Assembly Inc ....F...... 989 823-3800
Vassar *(G-16810)*
Advanced Def Vhcl Systems Corp ....E...... 248 391-3200
Clarkston *(G-2905)*
Aftershock Motorsports ....G...... 586 273-1333
Casco *(G-2498)*
Ai-Genesee LLC ....D...... 810 720-4848
Flint *(G-5373)*
American Axle Mfg Holdings Inc ......C...... 313 758-2000
Detroit *(G-3866)*
American Fabricated Pdts Inc ....F...... 616 607-8785
Spring Lake *(G-15133)*
Android Industries-Sterling ....E...... 586 486-5616
Warren *(G-16933)*
Aom Engineering Solutions LLC ....G...... 313 406-8130
Dearborn Heights *(G-3778)*
Armartis Manufacturing Inc ....E...... 248 308-9622
Roseville *(G-13775)*
◆ Armored Group LLC ....E...... 602 840-2271
Dearborn Heights *(G-3779)*
Asp Grede Acquisitionco LLC ....G...... 248 727-1800
Southfield *(G-14842)*
Asp Grede Intrmdate Hldngs LLC ....A...... 313 758-2000
Detroit *(G-3882)*
Asp Hhi Acquisition Co Inc ....G...... 313 758-2000
Detroit *(G-3883)*
Asp Hhi Intermediate Holdings..........G...... 248 727-1800
Southfield *(G-14843)*
Asp Hhi Intrmdate Holdings Inc ....G...... 248 727-1800
Southfield *(G-14844)*
◆ Autoalliance Management Co ....A...... 734 782-7800
Flat Rock *(G-5348)*
Autoform Development Inc ....F...... 616 392-4909
Holland *(G-7561)*
Axle of Dearborn Inc.........................G...... 313 581-3300
Detroit *(G-3888)*
▲ BDS Company Inc ....E...... 517 279-2135
Coldwater *(G-3291)*
Bearing Holdings LLC ....G...... 313 758-2000
Detroit *(G-3896)*
Bennett Funeral Coaches Inc ....G...... 616 538-8100
Byron Center *(G-2179)*
Bordrin Motor Corporation Inc ....G...... 877 507-3267
Oak Park *(G-12052)*
CATI Armor LLC ....G...... 269 788-4322
Charlotte *(G-2637)*
▲ Champion Bus Inc ....B...... 810 724-1753
Imlay City *(G-8197)*
Chrysler Group LLC...........................D...... 586 977-4900
Sterling Heights *(G-15288)*
Citation Lost Foam Pttrns LLC ....E...... 248 727-1800
Southfield *(G-14868)*
Cloyes Gear Holdings LLC ....G...... 313 758-2000
Detroit *(G-3940)*
▲ Comstar Automotive USA LLC .....F...... 517 266-2445
Tecumseh *(G-15785)*
Creative Automation Solutions ....G...... 313 790-4848
Livonia *(G-9692)*
▲ Dakkota Integrated Systems LLC....B...... 517 694-6500
Brighton *(G-1908)*
Dakkota Integrated Systems LLC.....D...... 517 321-3064
Lansing *(G-9213)*
Dakkota Integrated Systems LLC.....E...... 517 694-6500
Holt *(G-7907)*
Demmer Corporation ....D...... 517 323-4504
Lansing *(G-9220)*
▲ Detroit Chassis LLC ....G...... 313 571-2100
Detroit *(G-3974)*
Detroit Custom Chassis LLC ....C...... 313 571-2100
Detroit *(G-3978)*
Detroit Mfg Systems LLC ....D...... 313 243-0700
Detroit *(G-3989)*
Dynamic Corporation ....F...... 248 338-1100
Auburn Hills *(G-847)*
Eagle Assemblies Inc ....G...... 586 296-4836
Fraser *(G-5646)*
▲ Famek Inc ....G...... 734 895-6794
Southfield *(G-14902)*
FCA North America Holdings LLC ....E...... 248 512-2950
Auburn Hills *(G-866)*
FCA US LLC ....C...... 586 468-2891
Mount Clemens *(G-11130)*
FCA US LLC ....D...... 313 956-6460
Detroit *(G-4055)*

FCA US LLC....B....248 576-5741
Warren (G-17031)
FCA US LLC....A....586 497-3630
Warren (G-17029)
FCA US LLC....A....800 247-9753
Auburn Hills (G-868)
FCA US LLC....D....586 978-0067
Sterling Heights (G-15337)
◆ FCA US LLC....C....248 576-5741
Auburn Hills (G-869)
Federal-Mogul Chassis LLC....F....248 354-7700
Southfield (G-14906)
Federal-Mogul Motorparts LLC....C....248 354-7700
Southfield (G-14908)
▲ Ficosa North America Corp....E....248 307-2230
Madison Heights (G-10253)
Finish Line Fabricating LLC....G....269 686-8400
Allegan (G-161)
Ford Global Treasury Inc....G....313 322-3000
Dearborn (G-3708)
Ford Motor Company....B....313 322-3000
Dearborn (G-3709)
Ford Motor Company....A....313 322-7715
Dearborn (G-3711)
Forging Holdings LLC....G....313 758-2000
Detroit (G-4070)
Frank Industries Inc....E....810 346-3234
Brown City (G-2051)
G Tech Sales LLC....G....586 803-9393
Sterling Heights (G-15353)
Gearing Holdings LLC....G....313 758-2000
Detroit (G-4078)
General Coach America Inc....G....810 724-6474
Imlay City (G-8200)
General Motors Company....B....313 667-1500
Detroit (G-4082)
General Motors LLC....A....313 972-6000
Detroit (G-4084)
General Motors LLC....C....248 874-1737
Pontiac (G-12826)
General Motors LLC....A....313 972-6000
Detroit (G-4086)
General Motors LLC....A....313 556-5000
Detroit (G-4087)
General Motors LLC....A....248 857-3500
Pontiac (G-12828)
◆ Gestamp Mason LLC....B....517 244-8800
Mason (G-10641)
▲ Gibbs Sports Amphibians Inc....D....248 572-6670
Oxford (G-12346)
Global Impact Group LLC....G....248 895-9900
Grand Blanc (G-5966)
▲ GM Gdls Defense Group LLC....G....586 825-4000
Sterling Heights (G-15362)
GM Laam Holdings LLC....G....313 556-5000
Detroit (G-4093)
GM Orion Assembly....G....248 377-5260
Lake Orion (G-9137)
Grede Machining LLC....E....248 727-1800
Southfield (G-14927)
Grede Omaha LLC....E....248 727-1800
Southfield (G-14928)
Grede Radford LLC....E....248 727-1800
Southfield (G-14929)
GSC Riii - Grede LLC....G....248 727-1800
Southfield (G-14933)
Hayes-Albion Corporation....F....517 629-2141
Jackson (G-8463)
Hhi Formtech LLC....B....313 758-2000
Detroit (G-4121)
Hhi Formtech Holdings LLC....G....313 758-2000
Detroit (G-4122)
Hhi Funding II LLC....C....313 758-2000
Detroit (G-4123)
Hhi Holdings LLC....G....313 758-2000
Detroit (G-4124)
Hme Inc....C....616 534-1463
Wyoming (G-18011)
Holbrook Racing Engines....F....734 762-4315
Livonia (G-9772)
Horizon Global Corporation....C....248 593-8820
Troy (G-16401)
Horstman Inc....E....586 737-2100
Sterling Heights (G-15368)
▲ HP Pelzer Automotive Systems....E....810 987-0725
Port Huron (G-12927)
Illinois Tool Works Inc....D....248 589-2500
Troy (G-16410)
Impact Forge Holdings LLC....G....313 758-2000
Detroit (G-4137)
Inventev LLC....G....248 535-0477
Detroit (G-4148)
Jasco International LLC....F....313 841-5000
Detroit (G-4159)
Jeff Schaller Transport Inc....G....810 724-7640
Imlay City (G-8205)
Jernberg Holdings LLC....G....313 758-2000
Detroit (G-4161)
Junk Man LLC....G....248 459-7359
Pontiac (G-12843)
KYB Americas Corporation....G....248 374-0100
Novi (G-11923)
Kyklos Holdings Inc....G....313 758-2000
Detroit (G-4186)
▲ Magna Steyr LLC....C....248 740-0214
Troy (G-16478)
Mahindra North American....C....248 268-6600
Auburn Hills (G-940)
Mahindra Vehicle Mfrs Ltd....C....248 268-6600
Auburn Hills (G-941)
Manufacturing Products & Svcs....F....734 927-1964
Plymouth (G-12683)
▲ Marrel Corporation....G....616 863-9155
Rockford (G-13578)
Maven Drive LLC....D....313 667-1541
Detroit (G-4220)
May Mobility Inc....F....312 869-2711
Ann Arbor (G-550)
▲ Meritor Heavy Vhcl Systems LLC....C....248 435-1000
Troy (G-16494)
Meyers John....G....989 236-5400
Middleton (G-10793)
Mico Industries Inc....D....616 245-6426
Grand Rapids (G-6679)
Mid-West Truck Accessories....G....313 592-1788
Detroit (G-4247)
Midstates Industrial Group Inc....E....586 307-3414
Clinton Township (G-3174)
Mobility Innovations LLC....G....586 843-3816
Shelby Township (G-14643)
Morris Associates Inc....E....248 355-9055
Southfield (G-14987)
Moser Racing Inc....F....248 348-6502
Northville (G-11712)
Nationwide Design Inc....F....586 254-5493
Sterling Heights (G-15433)
Nexteer Automotive Corporation....B....989 757-5000
Saginaw (G-14104)
Omaha Automation Inc....G....313 557-3565
Detroit (G-4284)
▲ Onodi Tool & Engineering Co....E....313 386-6682
Melvindale (G-10704)
Onyx Manufacturing Inc....G....248 687-8611
Rochester Hills (G-13487)
Osbern Racing....G....313 538-8933
Detroit (G-4285)
Oshkosh Defense LLC....E....586 576-8301
Warren (G-17178)
P2r Metal Fabrication Inc....G....888 727-5587
Macomb (G-10151)
Pcm US Steering Holding LLC....G....313 556-5000
Detroit (G-4292)
Pims Co....G....313 665-8837
Detroit (G-4301)
Quality First Fire Alarm....G....810 736-4911
Flint (G-5488)
Quality Inspections Inc....G....586 323-6135
Sterling Heights (G-15459)
R V Wolverine....F....989 426-9241
Gladwin (G-5934)
Racers Inc....G....586 727-4069
Columbus (G-3382)
Ralyas Auto Body Incorporated....G....517 694-6512
Mason (G-10652)
Redline Fabrications....G....810 984-5621
Clyde (G-3284)
Rivian Automotive Inc....D....734 855-4350
Plymouth (G-12737)
Rivian Automotive Inc....G....408 483-1987
Plymouth (G-12738)
◆ Rivian Automotive LLC....D....734 855-4350
Plymouth (G-12739)
Roush Enterprises Inc....E....313 294-8200
Allen Park (G-207)
Ruhlman Race Cars....G....517 529-4661
Clarklake (G-2899)
▲ Saleen Special Vehicles Inc....B....909 978-6700
Troy (G-16591)
▲ Sas Automotive Usa Inc....E....248 606-1152
Sterling Heights (G-15485)
SGC Industries Inc....E....586 293-5260
Fraser (G-5723)
Shop IV Sbusid Inv Grede LLC....B....248 727-1800
Southfield (G-15027)
Skinny Kid Race Cars....G....248 668-1040
Commerce Township (G-3452)
▲ Smart Automation Systems Inc....G....248 651-5911
Rochester Hills (G-13514)
◆ Spartan Motors Inc....A....517 543-6400
Charlotte (G-2665)
▼ Spartan Motors Chassis Inc....A....517 543-6400
Charlotte (G-2666)
◆ Spartan Motors Usa Inc....D....517 543-6400
Charlotte (G-2667)
Special Projects Inc....E....734 455-7130
Plymouth (G-12759)
Spectra Lmp LLC....C....313 571-2100
Detroit (G-4370)
Spencer Manufacturing Inc....F....269 637-9459
South Haven (G-14775)
Supreme Gear Co....E....586 775-6325
Fraser (G-5736)
Tecstar LP....D....734 604-8962
Grand Blanc (G-5986)
Tesla Inc....G....248 205-3206
Troy (G-16637)
Think North America Inc....E....313 565-6781
Dearborn (G-3765)
Township of Saline....F....734 429-4440
Saline (G-14418)
Trailer Tech Repair Inc....G....734 354-6680
Plymouth (G-12777)
Transglobal Design & Mfg LLC....D....734 525-2651
Auburn Hills (G-1030)
▲ Trynex International LLC....F....248 586-3500
Madison Heights (G-10371)
▲ Tunkers Inc....E....734 744-5990
Sterling Heights (G-15531)
Turn Key Automotive LLC....E....248 628-5556
Oxford (G-12378)
United Collision....G....269 792-7274
Wayland (G-17418)
UPF Inc....D....810 768-0001
Flint (G-5519)
Valley Truck Parts Inc....D....616 241-5431
Wyoming (G-18040)
Veigel North America LLC....F....586 843-3816
Shelby Township (G-14717)
Visteon Intl Holdings Inc....F....734 710-2000
Van Buren Twp (G-16794)
▲ Visteon Systems LLC....C....313 755-9500
Dearborn (G-3768)
▲ Wgs Global Services LC....D....810 239-4947
Flint (G-5523)
Wgs Global Services LC....D....810 694-3843
Grand Blanc (G-5989)
◆ ZF TRW Auto Holdings Corp....A....734 855-2600
Livonia (G-10021)

3713 Truck & Bus Bodies

Advanced C & T Manufacturers....G....517 882-2444
Lansing (G-9333)
Aerofficient LLC....G....847 784-8100
Livonia (G-9631)
AM General LLC....B....734 523-8098
Auburn Hills (G-767)
Armada Rubber Manufacturing Co....D....586 784-9135
Armada (G-716)
Automotive Service Co....F....517 784-6131
Jackson (G-8385)
▲ BDS Company Inc....E....517 279-2135
Coldwater (G-3291)
Borgwarner Thermal Systems Inc....E....231 779-7500
Cadillac (G-2233)
Bucks Cement Inc....G....810 233-4141
Burton (G-2146)
Cameron Kirk Forest Pdts Inc....G....989 426-3439
Gladwin (G-5926)
Carter Industries Inc....E....510 324-6700
Adrian (G-53)
Central Mich Knwrth Lnsing LLC....G....517 394-7000
Lansing (G-9356)
Central Mich Knwrth Sginaw LLC....G....989 754-4500
Saginaw (G-14014)
Csi Emergency Apparatus LLC....F....989 348-2877
Grayling (G-7105)
D & W Management Company Inc....E....586 758-2284
Warren (G-16996)
▲ Durakon Industries Inc....G....608 742-5301
Lapeer (G-9457)

▲ **E-T-M Enterprises I Inc** ....C....... 517 627-8461 Grand Ledge *(G-6105)*
Eleven Mile Trck Frme & Ax ....D....... 248 399-7536 Madison Heights *(G-10244)*
Ford Motor Company ....B....... 313 322-3000 Dearborn *(G-3709)*
Ford Motor Company ....A....... 313 322-7715 Dearborn *(G-3711)*
Ford Motor Company ....E....... 910 381-7998 Taylor *(G-15723)*
Ford Motor Company ....A....... 734 523-3000 Livonia *(G-9744)*
Ford Motor Company ....A....... 734 942-6248 Brownstown *(G-2062)*
▲ **Gac** ....E....... 269 639-3010 South Haven *(G-14760)*
Hme Inc ....C....... 616 534-1463 Wyoming *(G-18011)*
Hovertechnics LLC ....G....... 269 461-3934 Benton Harbor *(G-1511)*
Hulet Body Co Inc ....E....... 313 931-6000 Northville *(G-11699)*
Johnson Controls Inc ....B....... 734 254-5000 Plymouth *(G-12655)*
◆ **Loadmaster Corporation** ....E....... 906 563-9226 Norway *(G-11817)*
◆ **Lodal Inc** ....D....... 906 779-1700 Kingsford *(G-9062)*
Mahindra North American ....C....... 248 268-6600 Auburn Hills *(G-940)*
Mahindra Vehicle Mfrs Ltd ....C....... 248 268-6600 Auburn Hills *(G-941)*
Marsh Industrial Services Inc ....F....... 231 258-4870 Kalkaska *(G-8949)*
▲ **Midwest Bus Corporation** ....D....... 989 723-5241 Owosso *(G-12304)*
Mobile Haulaway LLC ....G....... 616 402-7878 Muskegon *(G-11382)*
Mobility Trnsp Svcs Inc ....E....... 734 453-6452 Canton *(G-2406)*
Mobilitytrans LLC ....E....... 734 453-6452 Canton *(G-2407)*
Monroe Truck Equipment Inc ....E....... 810 238-4603 Flint *(G-5470)*
◆ **Morgan Olson LLC** ....A....... 269 659-0200 Sturgis *(G-15622)*
NBC Truck Equipment Inc ....E....... 586 774-4900 Roseville *(G-13845)*
▲ **Norma Michigan Inc** ....C....... 248 373-4300 Auburn Hills *(G-959)*
Norma Michigan Inc ....F....... 248 373-4300 Lake Orion *(G-9151)*
Novi Manufacturing Co ....D....... 248 476-4350 Novi *(G-11958)*
O E M Parts Supply Inc ....G....... 313 729-4283 Detroit *(G-4281)*
▲ **Off Site Mfg Tech Inc** ....D....... 586 598-3110 Chesterfield *(G-2810)*
Perspective Enterprises Inc ....G....... 269 327-0869 Portage *(G-13021)*
Precision Laser & Mfg LLC ....G....... 519 733-8422 Sterling Heights *(G-15449)*
Ralyas Auto Body Incorporated ....G....... 517 694-6512 Mason *(G-10652)*
Saf-Holland Inc ....F....... 616 396-6501 Holland *(G-7794)*
▼ **Steffens Enterprises Inc** ....E....... 616 656-6886 Caledonia *(G-2317)*
Tectum Holdings Inc ....E....... 734 677-0444 Ann Arbor *(G-655)*
Tractech Inc ....E....... 248 226-6800 Southfield *(G-15048)*
Transit Bus Rebuilders Inc ....E....... 989 277-3645 Owosso *(G-12324)*
Velcro USA Inc ....G....... 248 583-6060 Troy *(G-16682)*
Weiderman Motorsports ....G....... 269 689-0264 Sturgis *(G-15641)*
Wolverine Trailers Inc ....F....... 517 782-4950 Jackson *(G-8612)*
◆ **Worldwide Marketing Services** ....E....... 269 556-2000 Saint Joseph *(G-14355)*

3714 Motor Vehicle Parts & Access

1st Quality LLC ....G....... 313 908-4864 Dearborn *(G-3669)*
3d Polymers Inc ....D....... 248 588-5562 Orchard Lake *(G-12164)*
A I Flint LLC ....A....... 810 732-8760 Flint *(G-5367)*
A&M Assembly and Machining LLC ....E....... 313 369-9475 Detroit *(G-3829)*
AA Gear LLC ....F....... 517 552-3100 Howell *(G-8009)*
AAM Pwder Metal Components Inc ....F....... 248 597-3800 Royal Oak *(G-13898)*
Aapico Detroit LLC ....D....... 313 551-6001 Detroit *(G-3835)*
ABC Precision Machining Inc ....G....... 269 926-6322 Benton Harbor *(G-1478)*
Acat Global LLC ....F....... 231 330-2553 Charlevoix *(G-2605)*
Accel Performance Group LLC ....F....... 248 380-2780 Wixom *(G-17750)*
Access Works Inc ....G....... 231 777-2537 Muskegon *(G-11259)*
◆ **Ace Controls Inc** ....C....... 248 476-0213 Farmington Hills *(G-4919)*
Adac Plastics Inc ....C....... 616 957-0520 Muskegon *(G-11261)*
Adac Plastics Inc ....B....... 616 957-0311 Muskegon *(G-11262)*
◆ **Adient US LLC** ....A....... 734 254-5000 Plymouth *(G-12564)*
Adient US LLC ....B....... 734 414-9215 Plymouth *(G-12565)*
Adient US LLC ....G....... 734 414-9215 Plymouth *(G-12566)*
Adient US LLC ....C....... 616 394-8510 Holland *(G-7549)*
Adient US LLC ....B....... 269 968-3000 Battle Creek *(G-1138)*
▲ **ADS Us Inc** ....C....... 989 871-4550 Millington *(G-10993)*
Advance Motor Rebuilders Inc ....G....... 586 222-9583 Warren *(G-16919)*
▲ **Advanced Assembly Products Inc** ....G....... 248 543-2427 Hazel Park *(G-7432)*
Advanced Auto Trends Inc ....E....... 248 628-4850 Oxford *(G-12334)*
▲ **Advanced Auto Trends Inc** ....E....... 248 628-6111 Oxford *(G-12333)*
▼ **Advantage Truck ACC Inc** ....E....... 800 773-3110 Ann Arbor *(G-347)*
ADW Industries Inc ....E....... 989 466-4742 Alma *(G-231)*
Aer ....G....... 517 345-7272 Grand Ledge *(G-6099)*
Aerospace America Inc ....E....... 989 684-2121 Bay City *(G-1273)*
Affinia Group Inc ....E....... 734 827-5400 Ann Arbor *(G-348)*
Aftech Inc ....G....... 616 866-1650 Grand Rapids *(G-6151)*
AGM Automotive Mexico LLC ....G....... 248 925-4152 Farmington Hills *(G-4924)*
▲ **Agritek Industries Inc** ....D....... 616 786-9200 Holland *(G-7551)*
◆ **Air Lift Company** ....E....... 517 322-2144 Lansing *(G-9272)*
▲ **Airboss Flexible Products Co** ....C....... 248 852-5500 Auburn Hills *(G-763)*
◆ **Akebono Brake Corporation** ....C....... 248 489-7400 Farmington Hills *(G-4925)*
Albion Automotive Limited ....B....... 313 758-2000 Detroit *(G-3852)*
Alfmeier Friedrichs & Rath LLC ....G....... 248 526-1650 Troy *(G-16186)*
Allegan Tubular Products Inc ....D....... 269 673-6636 Allegan *(G-149)*
◆ **Alma Products I LLC** ....C....... 989 463-0290 Alma *(G-235)*
▲ **Alpha Technology Corporation** ....E....... 517 546-9700 Howell *(G-8011)*
Alternative Fuel Tech LLC ....G....... 313 417-9212 Grosse Pointe Park *(G-7189)*
Aludyne Inc ....C....... 248 728-8642 Southfield *(G-14831)*
▲ **Aludyne Columbus LLC** ....B....... 248 728-8642 Southfield *(G-14832)*
▲ **Aludyne East Michigan LLC** ....D....... 810 987-7633 Port Huron *(G-12888)*
▲ **Aludyne Montague LLC** ....A....... 248 479-6455 Southfield *(G-14834)*
▲ **Aludyne North America Inc** ....G....... 248 728-8642 Southfield *(G-14835)*
Aludyne North America Inc ....C....... 248 728-8642 Howell *(G-8012)*
▲ **Aludyne US LLC** ....C....... 586 782-0200 Warren *(G-16927)*
Aludyne US LLC ....D....... 810 987-1112 Port Huron *(G-12889)*
▲ **Aludyne West Michigan LLC** ....F....... 248 728-8642 Stevensville *(G-15555)*
AM Specialties Inc ....F....... 586 795-9000 Sterling Heights *(G-15258)*
Amalgamated Uaw ....G....... 231 734-9286 Evart *(G-4878)*
American Axle & Mfg Inc ....G....... 586 415-2000 Fraser *(G-5616)*
▲ **American Axle & Mfg Inc** ....B....... 313 758-3600 Detroit *(G-3865)*
American Axle & Mfg Inc ....A....... 269 278-0211 Three Rivers *(G-15853)*
American Axle & Mfg Inc ....E....... 248 299-2900 Rochester Hills *(G-13368)*
American Axle & Mfg Inc ....F....... 248 276-2328 Auburn Hills *(G-769)*
American Axle Mfg Holdings Inc ....C....... 313 758-2000 Detroit *(G-3866)*
◆ **American Mitsuba Corporation** ....B....... 989 779-4962 Mount Pleasant *(G-11170)*
Ameristeel Inc ....F....... 586 585-5250 Fraser *(G-5619)*
▲ **Anand Nvh North America Inc** ....C....... 810 724-2400 Imlay City *(G-8196)*
▲ **Anderson-Cook Inc** ....D....... 586 954-0700 Clinton Township *(G-3053)*
Anderson-Cook Inc ....D....... 586 293-0800 Fraser *(G-5620)*
Anderson-Cook Inc ....E....... 586 954-0700 Clinton Township *(G-3054)*
▲ **Android Industries-Delta Towns** ....C....... 517 322-0657 Lansing *(G-9277)*
Android Industries-Wixom LLC ....F....... 248 255-5434 Shelby Township *(G-14546)*
▲ **Android Industries-Wixom LLC** ....E....... 248 732-0000 Auburn Hills *(G-772)*
Angstrom Automotive Group LLC ....G....... 313 295-0100 Taylor *(G-15689)*
Angstrom Automotive Group LLC ....E....... 248 627-2871 Ortonville *(G-12193)*
▲ **Anjun America Inc** ....F....... 248 680-8825 Auburn Hills *(G-773)*
Anrod Screen Cylinder Company ....E....... 989 872-2101 Cass City *(G-2511)*
▲ **Antolin Interiors Usa Inc** ....B....... 248 373-1749 Auburn Hills *(G-775)*
Antolin Interiors Usa Inc ....A....... 517 548-0052 Howell *(G-8015)*
Antolin Interiors Usa Inc ....G....... 248 567-4000 Troy *(G-16203)*
Antolin Interiors Usa Inc ....A....... 810 329-1045 China *(G-2858)*
Applied Technology Group ....G....... 586 286-6442 Sterling Heights *(G-15263)*
Aptiv Corporation ....G....... 248 724-5900 Auburn Hills *(G-777)*
Aptiv Corporation ....A....... 248 813-2000 Troy *(G-16207)*
Aptiv Holdings (us) LLC ....E....... 248 813-2000 Troy *(G-16208)*
Aptiv Mexican Holdings US LLC ....G....... 248 813-2000 Troy *(G-16209)*
Aptiv PLC ....G....... 248 813-2000 Troy *(G-16210)*
◆ **Aptiv Services 3 (us) LLC** ....G....... 248 813-2000 Troy *(G-16212)*
Aptiv Services Us LLC ....F....... 616 246-2471 Grand Rapids *(G-6176)*
Aptiv Services Us LLC ....G....... 313 322-6845 Dearborn *(G-3677)*
Aptiv Services Us LLC ....G....... 810 459-8809 Auburn Hills *(G-778)*
Aptiv Services Us LLC ....D....... 248 724-5900 Auburn Hills *(G-779)*
Aptiv Services Us LLC ....G....... 248 813-2000 Hudsonville *(G-8146)*
Aptiv Services Us LLC ....D....... 248 813-2000 Troy *(G-16213)*
◆ **Aptiv Services Us LLC** ....B....... 248 813-2000 Troy *(G-16214)*
Aptiv Trade MGT Svcs US LLC ....G....... 248 813-2000 Troy *(G-16215)*
Aqueous Orbital Systems LLC ....G....... 269 501-7461 Kalamazoo *(G-8681)*
Arete Industries Inc ....F....... 231 582-4470 Boyne City *(G-1815)*
Argent Tape & Label Inc ....F....... 734 582-9956 Plymouth *(G-12573)*

37 TRANSPORTATION EQUIPMENT

Artisans Cstm Mmory Mattresses ....F 989 793-3208
 Saginaw *(G-13996)*
▲ Arvin Intl Holdings LLC ....G........ 248 435-1000
 Troy *(G-16221)*
Arvinmeritor Inc ....E 248 435-1000
 Troy *(G-16222)*
▲ Arvinmeritor Oe LLC ....G........ 248 435-1000
 Troy *(G-16223)*
▲ Asama Coldwater Mfg Inc ....B 517 279-1090
 Coldwater *(G-3289)*
▲ Asmo Detroit Inc ....G........ 248 359-4440
 Novi *(G-11831)*
Asp Grede Acquisitionco LLC ....G........ 248 727-1800
 Southfield *(G-14842)*
Asp Grede Intrmdate Hldngs LLC .....A 313 758-2000
 Detroit *(G-3882)*
Asp Hhi Acquisition Co Inc ....G........ 313 758-2000
 Detroit *(G-3883)*
Asp Hhi Holdings Inc ....F 248 597-3800
 Royal Oak *(G-13906)*
Asp Hhi Intermediate Holdings ....G........ 248 727-1800
 Southfield *(G-14843)*
Asp Hhi Intrmdate Holdings Inc ....G........ 248 727-1800
 Southfield *(G-14844)*
▲ Aspra World Inc ....D........ 248 872-7030
 Warren *(G-16943)*
Atf Inc ....E 989 685-2468
 Rose City *(G-13760)*
Atlantic Boat Brokers ....G........ 231 941-8050
 Traverse City *(G-15899)*
▲ Atlas Gear Company ....F 248 583-2964
 Madison Heights *(G-10198)*
Auria Solutions USA Inc ....F 734 456-2800
 Southfield *(G-14845)*
Auria St Clair LLC ....E 810 329-8400
 Saint Clair *(G-14205)*
Auto-Tech Plastics Inc ....G........ 586 783-0103
 Mount Clemens *(G-11124)*
Autocam Corporation ....D........ 269 789-4000
 Marshall *(G-10562)*
Autocam Corporation ....C 269 782-5186
 Dowagiac *(G-4533)*
Autocam Corporation ....C 616 698-0707
 Kentwood *(G-9001)*
▲ Autocam Corporation ....B 616 698-0707
 Kentwood *(G-9000)*
Autoform Development Inc ....F 616 392-4909
 Holland *(G-7561)*
Autoliv Asp Inc ....C 248 761-0081
 Pontiac *(G-12805)*
Autoliv Asp Inc ....B 248 475-9000
 Auburn Hills *(G-784)*
Autoliv Holding Inc ....D........ 248 475-9000
 Auburn Hills *(G-785)*
◆ Automotive LLC ....C 248 712-1175
 Southfield *(G-14847)*
Automotive Exteriors LLC ....G........ 248 458-0702
 Auburn Hills *(G-788)*
▲ Autoneum North America Inc ....D........ 248 848-0100
 Novi *(G-11836)*
Avon Plastic Products Inc ....D........ 248 852-1000
 Rochester Hills *(G-13374)*
▲ Aw Transmission Engrg USA Inc ...D........ 734 454-1710
 Plymouth *(G-12581)*
Axletech Intl Holdings LLC ....D........ 248 658-7200
 Troy *(G-16232)*
▲ Aztec Manufacturing Corp ....C 734 942-7433
 Romulus *(G-13653)*
Baldwin Precision Inc ....E 231 237-4515
 Charlevoix *(G-2608)*
Barker Manufacturing Co ....E 269 965-2371
 Battle Creek *(G-1150)*
Barker Manufacturing Co ....E 269 965-2371
 Battle Creek *(G-1151)*
Bay Alphi Manufacturing Inc ....E 517 849-9945
 Jonesville *(G-8653)*
Bcs Automotive Interface Solut ....G........ 734 855-3297
 Livonia *(G-9661)*
▲ BDS Company Inc ....E 517 279-2135
 Coldwater *(G-3291)*
Bearing Holdings LLC ....G........ 313 758-2000
 Detroit *(G-3896)*
Benteler Aluminium Systems ....G........ 616 396-6591
 Holland *(G-7567)*
Benteler Automotive Corp ....A 616 245-4607
 Grand Rapids *(G-6212)*
◆ Benteler Automotive Corp ....C 248 364-7190
 Auburn Hills *(G-792)*
Benteler Automotive Corp ....B 269 665-4261
 Galesburg *(G-5807)*

Bentler Industries Inc ....G........ 269 665-4261
 Galesburg *(G-5808)*
Best Products Inc ....E 313 538-7414
 Redford *(G-13148)*
Black River Manufacturing Inc ....E 810 982-9812
 Port Huron *(G-12900)*
Black River Manufacturing Inc ....D........ 810 982-9812
 Port Huron *(G-12901)*
Bleistahl N Amer Ltd Partnr ....E 269 719-8585
 Battle Creek *(G-1155)*
Borg Warner Automotive ....E 248 754-9200
 Auburn Hills *(G-795)*
▲ Borgwarner Emissions ....D........ 248 754-9600
 Auburn Hills *(G-796)*
Borgwarner Inc ....G........ 248 371-0040
 Auburn Hills *(G-797)*
Borgwarner Inc ....E 231 779-7500
 Cadillac *(G-2232)*
Borgwarner Inc ....G........ 248 754-9600
 Auburn Hills *(G-798)*
Borgwarner Inc ....B 248 754-9200
 Auburn Hills *(G-799)*
Borgwarner Inc ....E 248 754-9600
 Auburn Hills *(G-800)*
Borgwarner Inc ....E 248 754-9200
 Auburn Hills *(G-801)*
Borgwarner Inv Holdg Inc ....E 248 754-9200
 Auburn Hills *(G-802)*
▲ Borgwarner Pds (usa) Inc ....B 248 754-9600
 Auburn Hills *(G-803)*
Borgwarner Pds Anderson LLC ....E 248 641-3045
 Troy *(G-16245)*
Borgwarner Powdered Metals Inc .....E 734 261-5322
 Livonia *(G-9668)*
▲ Borgwarner Thermal Systems Inc ....C 269 781-1228
 Marshall *(G-10563)*
▲ Borgwarner Transm Systems Inc ....B 248 754-9200
 Auburn Hills *(G-804)*
▲ Bos Automotive Products Inc ....E 248 289-6072
 Rochester Hills *(G-13378)*
◆ Bosal Industries-Georgia Inc ....E 734 547-7022
 Ypsilanti *(G-18056)*
▲ Bosch Auto Svc Solutions Inc ......C 586 574-2332
 Warren *(G-16963)*
Bpi Holdings International Inc ....G........ 815 363-9000
 Ann Arbor *(G-389)*
Braetec Inc ....G........ 269 968-4711
 Battle Creek *(G-1156)*
Brembo North America Inc ....E 517 568-4398
 Homer *(G-7937)*
◆ Brembo North America Inc ....D........ 734 416-1275
 Plymouth *(G-12590)*
▲ Brose North America Inc ....C 248 339-4000
 Auburn Hills *(G-808)*
▲ Brugola Oeb Indstriale USA Inc .....F 734 468-0009
 Plymouth *(G-12591)*
▲ Bullseye Power ....G........ 231 788-5209
 Muskegon *(G-11286)*
Burr Engineering & Dev Co ....G........ 269 965-2371
 Battle Creek *(G-1160)*
◆ Bushings Inc ....F 248 650-0603
 Rochester Hills *(G-13381)*
Bwi Chassis Dynamics NA Inc ....G........ 937 455-5308
 Brighton *(G-1892)*
Bwi North America Inc ....C 810 494-4584
 Brighton *(G-1893)*
C W A Manufacturing Co Inc ....E 810 686-3030
 Mount Morris *(G-11159)*
▲ Cadillac Products Inc ....B 248 813-8200
 Troy *(G-16253)*
Cadillac Products Inc ....D........ 586 774-1700
 Roseville *(G-13779)*
Cadillac Products Inc ....D........ 989 766-2294
 Rogers City *(G-13613)*
Cambria Tool and Machine Inc ....F 517 437-3500
 Hillsdale *(G-7520)*
Cambridge Sharpe Inc ....D........ 248 613-5562
 South Lyon *(G-14788)*
Cambro Products Inc ....E 586 468-8847
 Harrison Township *(G-7326)*
Camshaft Acquisition Inc ....E 517 787-2040
 Jackson *(G-8400)*
Camshaft Machine Company LLC ....E 517 787-2040
 Jackson *(G-8401)*
Carter Fuel Systems LLC ....E 248 371-8392
 Rochester Hills *(G-13386)*
Carter Industries Inc ....E 510 324-6700
 Adrian *(G-53)*
Casco Products Corporation ....F 248 957-0400
 Novi *(G-11844)*

◆ CC Industries LLC ....D........ 269 426-3342
 Sawyer *(G-14483)*
CCI Driveline LLC ....G........ 586 716-1160
 Casco *(G-2499)*
Cequent Uk Ltd ....G........ 734 656-3000
 Plymouth *(G-12595)*
Champion Laboratories Inc ....D........ 586 247-9044
 Shelby Township *(G-14561)*
Chassis Brakes Intl USA ....G........ 248 957-9997
 Farmington Hills *(G-4962)*
Chassix Blackstone Operat ....G........ 586 782-7311
 Warren *(G-16979)*
▲ Check Technology Solutions LLC ....E 248 680-2323
 Troy *(G-16264)*
Chicago Blow Pipe Company ....F 773 533-6100
 Marquette *(G-10522)*
Cinnabar Engineering Inc ....F 810 648-2444
 Sandusky *(G-14431)*
▲ Cipa Usa Inc ....E 810 982-3555
 Port Huron *(G-12907)*
▲ Circuit Controls Corporation ....C 231 347-0760
 Petoskey *(G-12444)*
Citation Lost Foam Pttrns LLC ....E 248 727-1800
 Southfield *(G-14868)*
▼ Classic Design Concepts LLC ....F 248 504-5202
 Milford *(G-10958)*
Cloyes Gear Holdings LLC ....G........ 313 758-2000
 Detroit *(G-3940)*
Clutch Masters Inc ....G........ 586 759-1300
 Warren *(G-16984)*
Complete Prototype Svcs Inc ....B 586 690-8897
 Clinton Township *(G-3085)*
Con-Vel Inc ....G........ 864 281-2228
 Lansing *(G-9284)*
▲ Concent Grinding Inc ....E 517 787-8172
 Jackson *(G-8418)*
Concorde Inc ....F 248 391-8177
 Auburn Hills *(G-817)*
◆ Continental Auto Systems Inc ....A 248 393-5300
 Auburn Hills *(G-819)*
Continental Auto Systems Inc ....B 248 209-4000
 Auburn Hills *(G-820)*
Continental Auto Systems Inc ....F 906 248-6700
 Brimley *(G-2015)*
Continental Auto Systems Inc ....B 248 874-1801
 Auburn Hills *(G-822)*
Continental Auto Systems Inc ....E 248 267-9408
 Troy *(G-16277)*
Cooper-Standard Auto OH LLC ....G........ 248 596-5900
 Novi *(G-11853)*
▲ Cooper-Standard Automotive Inc ....B 248 596-5900
 Novi *(G-11854)*
Cooper-Standard Automotive Inc .....D........ 734 542-6300
 Livonia *(G-9688)*
Cooper-Standard Automotive Inc .....C 248 754-2000
 Auburn Hills *(G-827)*
Cooper-Standard Automotive Inc .....C 989 848-2272
 Fairview *(G-4889)*
▲ Cooper-Standard Fhs LLC ....G........ 248 596-5900
 Novi *(G-11855)*
Cooper-Standard Holdings Inc ....G........ 248 596-5900
 Novi *(G-11856)*
Corvac Composites LLC ....C 616 281-4059
 Kentwood *(G-9004)*
▲ Cosma International Amer Inc ....B 248 631-1100
 Troy *(G-16284)*
▲ Creative Controls Inc ....E 248 577-9800
 Madison Heights *(G-10222)*
Creative Performance Racg LLC ......G........ 248 250-6187
 Troy *(G-16285)*
Crowne Group LLC ....G........ 734 855-4512
 Livonia *(G-9693)*
Csa Services Inc ....G........ 248 596-6184
 Novi *(G-11859)*
▲ CTA Acoustics Inc ....E 248 544-2580
 Madison Heights *(G-10223)*
Cummins Inc ....C 906 774-2424
 Iron Mountain *(G-8281)*
Cusolar Industries Inc ....E 586 949-3880
 Chesterfield *(G-2757)*
Cutversion Technologies Corp ....G........ 586 634-1339
 Sterling Heights *(G-15304)*
D & M Truck Top Co Inc ....G........ 248 792-7972
 Troy *(G-16292)*
D M P E ....G........ 269 428-5070
 Stevensville *(G-15561)*
▲ D2t America Inc ....F 248 680-9001
 Rochester Hills *(G-13400)*
Daimay North America Auto Inc ......E 313 533-9680
 Redford *(G-13156)*

SIC SECTION
37 TRANSPORTATION EQUIPMENT

Dakkota Integrated Systems LLC ....E 517 694-6500
Holt *(G-7907)*
Dana Driveshaft Mfg LLC ....C 248 623-2185
Auburn Hills *(G-835)*
Dana Limited ....D 810 329-2500
Saint Clair *(G-14213)*
Dana Off-Hghway Components LLC ....E 586 467-1600
Flint *(G-5414)*
Dana Thermal Products LLC ....D 810 329-2500
Saint Clair *(G-14214)*
Dana Thermal Products LLC ....C 810 329-2500
Saint Clair *(G-14215)*
Davco Manufacturing LLC ....D 734 429-5665
Saline *(G-14385)*
◆ Davco Technology LLC ....D 734 429-5665
Saline *(G-14386)*
Dawson Manufacturing Company ....C 269 925-0100
Benton Harbor *(G-1493)*
Dayco Products LLC ....C 989 775-0689
Mount Pleasant *(G-11191)*
Dayco Products LLC ....E 517 439-0689
Hillsdale *(G-7522)*
Dearborn Total Auto Svc Ctr ....F 313 291-6300
Dearborn Heights *(G-3781)*
Debron Industrial Elec Inc ....E 248 588-7220
Troy *(G-16300)*
Delco Elec Overseas Corp ....G 248 813-2000
Troy *(G-16301)*
Delphi ....G 248 813-2000
Troy *(G-16302)*
Delphi Automotive Systems ....G 248 813-2000
Troy *(G-16303)*
Delphi Powertrain Corporation ....G 248 813-2000
Troy *(G-16304)*
Delphi Powertrain Systems LLC ....F 248 280-8340
Troy *(G-16305)*
Delphi Powertrain Systems LLC ....G 248 813-2000
Troy *(G-16306)*
Delphi Powertrain Systems LLC ....E 248 813-1549
Troy *(G-16307)*
Delphi Powertrain Systems LLC ....C 248 813-2000
Auburn Hills *(G-839)*
Delphi Powertrain Systems LLC ....C 248 813-2000
Troy *(G-16308)*
Delphi Powertrain Systems LLC ....D 248 280-8319
Troy *(G-16309)*
Delphi Powertrain Systems LLC ....E 800 521-4784
Troy *(G-16310)*
Delphi Pwertrain Intl Svcs LLC ....G 248 813-2000
Troy *(G-16311)*
Delphi Pwrtrain Tech Gen Prtnr ....G 248 813-2000
Troy *(G-16312)*
▲ Delta Research Corporation ....E 734 261-6400
Livonia *(G-9705)*
▲ Denso Air Systems Michigan Inc ....D 269 962-9676
Battle Creek *(G-1171)*
◆ Denso International Amer Inc ....A 248 350-7500
Southfield *(G-14879)*
▼ Denso Sales Michigan Inc ....E 269 965-3322
Battle Creek *(G-1173)*
Design Converting Inc ....F 616 942-7780
Grand Rapids *(G-6344)*
Design Usa Inc ....G 734 233-8677
Livonia *(G-9707)*
Detail Production Company Inc ....F 248 544-3390
Ferndale *(G-5272)*
◆ Detroit Diesel Corporation ....A 313 592-5000
Detroit *(G-3980)*
Detroit Diesel Corporation ....F 313 592-8256
Redford *(G-13157)*
Detroit Technologies Inc ....F 248 647-0400
Macomb *(G-10117)*
▲ Detroit Technologies Inc ....F 248 647-0400
Bingham Farms *(G-1651)*
▼ Dgh Enterprises Inc ....E 269 925-0657
Benton Harbor *(G-1494)*
Dicastal North America Inc ....B 616 303-0306
Greenville *(G-7127)*
Dieomatic Incorporated ....F 269 966-4900
Battle Creek *(G-1174)*
Dieomatic Incorporated ....D 319 668-2031
Troy *(G-16319)*
Diesel Performance Products ....G 586 726-7478
Shelby Township *(G-14575)*
Diversified Mfg & Assembly LLC ....F 586 272-2431
Sterling Heights *(G-15318)*
Dmi Edon LLC ....G 586 782-7311
Warren *(G-17003)*
▲ Dmi Edon LLC ....G 248 728-8642
Southfield *(G-14884)*

Dolphin Manufacturing Inc ....E 734 946-6322
Taylor *(G-15707)*
▲ Donnelly Corp ....F 231 652-8425
Newaygo *(G-11567)*
Dontech Solutions LLC ....E 248 789-3086
Howell *(G-8033)*
◆ Douglas Autotech Corporation ....E 517 369-2315
Bronson *(G-2025)*
◆ Dph LLC ....A 248 813-2000
Troy *(G-16323)*
◆ Dph Holdings Corp ....C 248 813-2000
Troy *(G-16324)*
▲ Dph-Das Global (holdings) LLC ....A 248 813-2000
Troy *(G-16325)*
◆ Dph-Das LLC ....A 248 813-2000
Troy *(G-16326)*
▲ Drake Enterprises Inc ....E 586 783-3009
Clinton Township *(G-3105)*
Dreal Inc ....G 248 813-2000
Troy *(G-16328)*
Dse Industries LLC ....G 313 530-6668
Macomb *(G-10118)*
Dst Industries Inc ....F 734 941-0300
Clinton *(G-3018)*
Dura Auto Systems Cble Oprtons ....G 248 299-7500
Auburn Hills *(G-844)*
◆ Dura Automotive Systems LLC ....C 248 299-7500
Auburn Hills *(G-845)*
Dura Brake Systems LLC ....G 248 299-7500
Rochester Hills *(G-13410)*
Dura Cables North LLC ....G 248 299-7500
Rochester Hills *(G-13411)*
Dura Cables South LLC ....G 248 299-7500
Rochester Hills *(G-13412)*
Dura Global Technologies Inc ....G 248 299-7500
Rochester Hills *(G-13413)*
◆ Dura Operating LLC ....C 248 299-7500
Auburn Hills *(G-846)*
Dura Shifter LLC ....G 248 299-7500
Rochester Hills *(G-13414)*
▲ Durakon Industries Inc ....G 608 742-5301
Lapeer *(G-9457)*
E & E Manufacturing Co Inc ....F 248 616-1300
Clawson *(G-2977)*
▲ E-T-M Enterprises I Inc ....C 517 627-8461
Grand Ledge *(G-6105)*
Eagle Assemblies Inc ....G 586 296-4836
Fraser *(G-5646)*
Eagle Thread Verifier LLC ....G 586 764-8218
Sterling Heights *(G-15327)*
Eaton Aerospace LLC ....B 616 949-1090
Grand Rapids *(G-6368)*
Eaton Corporation ....B 269 342-3000
Galesburg *(G-5809)*
Eaton Corporation ....C 269 342-3000
Galesburg *(G-5810)*
Eaton Corporation ....E 248 226-6200
Southfield *(G-14894)*
Eberspaecher North America Inc ....E 248 778-5231
Novi *(G-11876)*
◆ Eberspaecher North America Inc ....E 248 994-7010
Novi *(G-11877)*
Eberspaecher North America Inc ....E 517 303-1775
Wixom *(G-17798)*
Eberspecher Contrls N Amer Inc ....G 248 994-7010
Brighton *(G-1916)*
Ecotrons LLC ....G 248 891-6965
Wixom *(G-17799)*
Egr Incorporated ....G 248 848-1411
Farmington Hills *(G-4978)*
Elite Plastic Products Inc ....E 586 247-5800
Shelby Township *(G-14587)*
Elmwood Manufacturing Company ....G 313 571-1777
Detroit *(G-4034)*
Emergency Services LLC ....G 231 727-7400
Muskegon *(G-11317)*
Emergency Vehicle Products ....G 269 342-0973
Kalamazoo *(G-8736)*
Emma Sogoian Inc ....E 248 549-8690
Royal Oak *(G-13923)*
Enertrols Inc ....E 734 595-4500
Farmington Hills *(G-4988)*
▲ Engine Power Components Inc ....B 616 846-0110
Grand Haven *(G-6015)*
◆ Engineered Machined Pdts Inc ....B 906 786-8404
Escanaba *(G-4826)*
Engineered Machined Pdts Inc ....E 906 789-7497
Escanaba *(G-4827)*
Engineering Service of America ....D 248 357-3800
Southfield *(G-14899)*

Enovapremier LLC ....G 517 541-3200
Charlotte *(G-2646)*
Environmental Catalysts LLC ....G 248 813-2000
Troy *(G-16350)*
Erae AMS America Corp ....F 419 386-8876
Pontiac *(G-12823)*
Ervins Group LLC ....G 248 203-2000
Bloomfield Hills *(G-1764)*
▲ Erwin Quarder Inc ....D 616 575-1600
Grand Rapids *(G-6383)*
▲ Ese LLc ....G 810 538-1000
Lapeer *(G-9459)*
▼ Etx Holdings Inc ....G 989 463-1151
Alma *(G-237)*
▲ Euclid Industries Inc ....C 989 686-8920
Bay City *(G-1310)*
Everblades Inc ....G 906 483-0174
Atlantic Mine *(G-735)*
Excellence Manufacturing Inc ....D 616 456-9928
Grand Rapids *(G-6391)*
Exedy-Dynax America Corp ....F 734 397-6556
Van Buren Twp *(G-16760)*
Expernced Prcsion McHining Inc ....G 989 635-2299
Marlette *(G-10496)*
▲ Extang Corporation ....D 734 677-0444
Ann Arbor *(G-454)*
Extreme Machine Inc ....D 810 231-0521
Whitmore Lake *(G-17699)*
Extreme Machine Inc ....D 810 231-0521
Whitmore Lake *(G-17700)*
Fabulous Operating Pdts LLC ....G 810 245-5759
Lapeer *(G-9461)*
Fastime Racing Engines & Parts ....G 734 947-1600
Taylor *(G-15720)*
▲ Faurecia ....G 248 917-1702
Southfield *(G-14904)*
Faurecia Emissions Contl Tech ....B 734 947-1688
Taylor *(G-15721)*
Faurecia Interior Systems Inc ....E 734 429-0030
Saline *(G-14389)*
▲ Faurecia USA Holdings Inc ....G 248 724-5100
Auburn Hills *(G-864)*
◆ FCA Intrntional Operations LLC ....E 800 334-9200
Auburn Hills *(G-865)*
FCA North America Holdings LLC ....E 248 512-2950
Auburn Hills *(G-866)*
FCA US LLC ....B 734 478-5658
Dundee *(G-4582)*
FCA US LLC ....A 586 497-2500
Warren *(G-17030)*
Fcaus Dundee Engine Plant ....A 734 529-9256
Dundee *(G-4583)*
Federal Screw Works ....C 231 796-7664
Big Rapids *(G-1627)*
Federal-Mogul Powertrain Inc ....C 616 887-8231
Sparta *(G-15094)*
Federal-Mogul Powertrain LLC ....C 734 254-0100
Plymouth *(G-12620)*
Federal-Mogul Powertrain LLC ....B 616 754-5681
Greenville *(G-7132)*
▲ Federal-Mogul Products US LLC ....A 248 354-7700
Southfield *(G-14911)*
Federal-Mogul World Wide LLC ....G 248 354-7700
Southfield *(G-14913)*
Fft Sidney LLC ....F 248 647-0400
Sidney *(G-14739)*
Fiamm Technologies LLC ....F 231 775-2900
Cadillac *(G-2247)*
◆ Fiamm Technologies LLC ....C 248 427-3200
Farmington Hills *(G-5000)*
Fisher & Company Incorporated ....E 586 746-2280
Saint Clair Shores *(G-14250)*
Fisher & Company Incorporated ....D 586 746-2101
Troy *(G-16364)*
▲ Fleet Engineers Inc ....C 231 777-2537
Muskegon *(G-11324)*
▲ Flex-N-Gate LLC ....C 800 398-1496
Warren *(G-17036)*
▲ Flex-N-Gate Battle Creek LLC ....C 269 962-2982
Battle Creek *(G-1189)*
Flex-N-Gate Corporation ....B 616 222-3296
Grand Rapids *(G-6411)*
Flex-N-Gate Corporation ....E 586 773-0800
Warren *(G-17037)*
▲ Flex-N-Gate Michigan LLC ....E 586 759-8900
Warren *(G-17039)*
▲ Flextronics Automotive USA Inc ....D 248 853-5724
Rochester Hills *(G-13425)*
Flextronics Intl USA Inc ....B 616 837-9711
Coopersville *(G-3558)*

S I C

Employee Codes: A=Over 500 employees, B=251-500
C=101-250, D=51-100, E=20-50, F=10-19, G=3-9

2020 Harris Michigan
Industrial Directory

851

37 TRANSPORTATION EQUIPMENT

▲ Fluid Hutchinson Management......D   248 679-1327
   Auburn Hills (G-876)
Fluid Routing Solutions Inc ....E   231 796-4489
   Big Rapids (G-1629)
Fluid Routing Solutions Inc ....E   231 592-1700
   Big Rapids (G-1628)
▲ Fontijne Grotnes Inc ....E   269 262-4700
   Niles (G-11611)
Ford Motor Company..............................A   313 594-0050
   Dearborn (G-3710)
Ford Motor Company..............................A   734 377-4954
   Livonia (G-9743)
Ford Motor Company..............................A   313 594-4090
   Allen Park (G-198)
Ford Motor Company..............................B   313 322-3000
   Dearborn (G-3709)
Ford Motor Company..............................A   734 523-3000
   Livonia (G-9744)
Ford Motor Company..............................A   734 942-6248
   Brownstown (G-2062)
Forging Holdings LLC ....G   313 758-2000
   Detroit (G-4070)
Formfab LLC...E   248 844-3676
   Rochester Hills (G-13427)
Formtech Inds Holdings LLC................G   248 597-3800
   Royal Oak (G-13928)
Frank Industries Inc................................E   810 346-3234
   Brown City (G-2051)
▲ Fremont L Dura L C ....G   248 299-7500
   Auburn Hills (G-878)
◆ Freudenberg N Amer Ltd Partnr......G   734 354-5505
   Plymouth (G-12623)
▲ Freudenberg-Nok General Partnr....C   734 451-0020
   Plymouth (G-12624)
◆ Fte Automotive USA Inc....................C   248 209-8239
   Highland Park (G-7505)
▲ Fujikura Automotive Amer LLC ....E   248 957-0130
   Farmington Hills (G-5006)
G P Dura..G   248 299-7500
   Rochester Hills (G-13430)
Gabriel Ride Control LLC......................D   248 247-7600
   Farmington Hills (G-5007)
Gage Pattern & Model Inc ....E   248 361-6609
   Madison Heights (G-10255)
Garrisons Hitch Center Inc...................G   810 239-5728
   Flint (G-5432)
Gates Corporation ....D   248 260-2300
   Rochester Hills (G-13431)
Gearing Holdings LLC ....G   313 758-2000
   Detroit (G-4078)
General Motors China Inc ....D   313 556-5000
   Detroit (G-4081)
General Motors Company ....F   248 249-6347
   Brownstown (G-2063)
General Motors Company ....B   586 218-9240
   Warren (G-17051)
General Motors Company ....B   313 667-1500
   Detroit (G-4082)
▲ General Motors Holdings LLC ....E   313 556-5000
   Detroit (G-4083)
General Motors LLC................................B   989 894-7210
   Bay City (G-1315)
General Motors LLC................................F   586 731-2743
   Sterling Heights (G-15358)
General Motors LLC................................A   517 885-6669
   Lansing (G-9290)
General Motors LLC................................A   313 972-6000
   Detroit (G-4084)
General Motors LLC................................F   931 486-5049
   Warren (G-17053)
General Motors LLC................................C   248 874-1737
   Pontiac (G-12826)
▼ General Motors LLC...........................C   313 410-2704
   Detroit (G-4085)
General Motors LLC................................E   248 456-5000
   Pontiac (G-12827)
General Motors LLC................................A   313 556-5000
   Detroit (G-4087)
Gentex Corporation.................................C   616 772-1800
   Zeeland (G-18138)
▲ Gentherm Incorporated....................B   248 504-0500
   Northville (G-11694)
◆ Gestamp Mason LLC.......................B   517 244-8800
   Mason (G-10641)
▲ Gestamp North America Inc..........C   248 743-3400
   Troy (G-16382)
Getrag Transmissions Corp..................C   586 620-1300
   Troy (G-16383)
▲ Ghsp Inc..B   616 842-5500
   Grand Haven (G-6018)

Ghsp Inc...D   248 588-5095
   Grand Haven (G-6019)
Ghsp Inc...D   248 581-0890
   Troy (G-16384)
Ghsp Inc..F   231 873-3300
   Hart (G-7371)
◆ GKN Driveline North Amer Inc........B   248 296-7000
   Auburn Hills (G-885)
GKN North America Inc..........................A   248 296-7200
   Auburn Hills (G-886)
GKN North America Services Inc ....F   248 377-1200
   Auburn Hills (G-887)
◆ GKN Sinter Metals LLC...................G   248 296-7832
   Auburn Hills (G-888)
▲ Glassmaster Controls Co Inc...........E   269 382-2010
   Kalamazoo (G-8753)
Gleason Works...F   248 522-0305
   Farmington Hills (G-5009)
Global Fmi LLC ....D   810 964-5555
   Fenton (G-5216)
GM Components Holdings LLC............E   616 246-2000
   Grand Rapids (G-6444)
▲ GM Components Holdings LLC.....C   313 665-4707
   Detroit (G-4092)
GM Laam Holdings LLC ....G   313 556-5000
   Detroit (G-4093)
Grakon LLC...G   734 462-1201
   Livonia (G-9755)
Grand Traverse Stamping Co ....F   231 929-4215
   Traverse City (G-15988)
▲ Grattan Family Enterprises LLC ....D   248 547-3870
   Ferndale (G-5290)
Grede Machining LLC.............................E   248 727-1800
   Southfield (G-14927)
Grede Omaha LLC...................................E   248 727-1800
   Southfield (G-14928)
Grede Radford LLC..................................E   248 727-1800
   Southfield (G-14929)
Ground Effects LLC.................................C   810 250-5560
   Flint (G-5443)
▲ Grupo Antolin Michigan Inc C   989 635-5055
   Marlette (G-10497)
Grupo Antolin Michigan Inc ....E   989 635-5080
   Warren (G-17069)
▲ Grupo Antolin North Amer Inc C   248 373-1749
   Auburn Hills (G-891)
▲ Grupo Antolin Primera Auto Sys ....D   734 495-9180
   Canton (G-2381)
GSC Riii - Grede LLC ....G   248 727-1800
   Southfield (G-14933)
◆ Gt Technologies Inc ....E   734 467-8371
   Westland (G-17566)
H & L Manufacturing Co C   269 795-5000
   Middleville (G-10804)
H R P Motor Sports Inc..........................G   616 874-6338
   Rockford (G-13570)
Hacker Machine Inc ....F   517 569-3348
   Rives Junction (G-13308)
◆ Hadley Products Corporation..........C   616 530-1717
   Grandville (G-7043)
Haldex Brake Products Corp C   616 827-9641
   Wyoming (G-18007)
Hamaton Inc..D   248 308-3856
   Wixom (G-17822)
Hamlin Tool & Machine Co Inc.............D   248 651-6302
   Rochester Hills (G-13438)
Hanho America Co Ltd ....G   248 422-6921
   Troy (G-16391)
Hanon Systems Usa LLC ....B   248 907-8000
   Novi (G-11893)
Hanwha Advanced Mtls Amer LLC ......E   810 629-2496
   Monroe (G-11038)
Harrys Steering Gear Repair.................G   586 677-5580
   Macomb (G-10128)
Harvey S Freeman ....E   248 852-2222
   West Bloomfield (G-17479)
▲ Havis Inc..E   734 414-0699
   Plymouth (G-12634)
▲ Hayes Lemmerz Intl-GA LLC C   734 737-5000
   Novi (G-11898)
Hayes-Albion Corporation ....F   517 629-2141
   Jackson (G-8463)
Hdt Automotive Solutions LLC..............G   810 359-5344
   Livonia (G-9767)
▲ Heatex Warehouse LLC ....E   586 773-0770
   Roseville (G-13815)
Heavy Duty Radiator LLC ....E   800 525-0011
   Riverview (G-13295)
Hemco Machine Co Inc..........................G   586 264-8911
   Warren (G-17079)

Hengst of North America Inc ....G   586 757-2995
   Novi (G-11899)
Henniges Auto Holdings Inc ....B   248 340-4100
   Auburn Hills (G-896)
◆ Henniges Auto Sling Systems N ...C   248 340-4100
   Auburn Hills (G-897)
Hhi Formtech LLC ....B   313 758-2000
   Detroit (G-4121)
Hhi Formtech LLC ....E   586 415-2000
   Fraser (G-5662)
Hhi Formtech Holdings LLC ....G   313 758-2000
   Detroit (G-4122)
Hhi Funding II LLC C   313 758-2000
   Detroit (G-4123)
Hhi Holdings LLC ....G   313 758-2000
   Detroit (G-4124)
Hi-Lex America Incorporated................D   248 844-0096
   Rochester Hills (G-13440)
HI-Lex Controls Incorporated................C   517 448-2752
   Hudson (G-8130)
▲ Hi-Lex Controls Incorporated ....F   517 542-2955
   Litchfield (G-9604)
Highland Manufacturing Inc..................E   248 585-8040
   Madison Heights (G-10267)
Hitachi America Ltd ....E   248 477-5400
   Farmington Hills (G-5021)
Hoff Engineering Co Inc ....G   248 969-8272
   Oxford (G-12349)
Honeywell International Inc ....G   248 827-6460
   Southfield (G-14937)
Hope Focus ....E   313 494-4500
   Detroit (G-4128)
Hope Focus C   313 494-5500
   Detroit (G-4129)
Hope Network West Michigan...............C   231 796-4801
   Paris (G-12385)
◆ Horizon Global Americas Inc..........C   734 656-3000
   Plymouth (G-12643)
Horizon Global Corporation...................C   248 593-8820
   Troy (G-16401)
Horizon Intl Group LLC ....D   734 341-9336
   Birmingham (G-1686)
Horstman Inc ....E   586 737-2100
   Sterling Heights (G-15368)
Howe Racing Enterprises Inc ....F   989 435-7080
   Beaverton (G-1385)
Howell Engine Developments Inc.........F   810 765-5100
   Cottrellville (G-3587)
HP Pelzer Auto Systems Inc ....E   810 987-4444
   Port Huron (G-12926)
Hudson Industries Inc ....G   800 459-1077
   Warren (G-17082)
Huf North America Automoti.................E   248 213-4605
   Farmington Hills (G-5022)
Humphrey Companies LLC....................C   616 530-1717
   Grandville (G-7048)
Hutchinson Sealing Syst ....D   248 375-3721
   Auburn Hills (G-904)
Hydro-Craft Inc ....E   248 652-8100
   Rochester Hills (G-13448)
Ididit Inc ....E   517 424-0577
   Tecumseh (G-15798)
▲ Ilmor Engineering Inc ....D   734 456-3600
   Plymouth (G-12646)
Impact Forge Holdings LLC ....G   313 758-2000
   Detroit (G-4137)
Impco Technologies Inc ....E   586 264-1200
   Sterling Heights (G-15370)
▲ In Line Tube Inc...................................F   586 532-1338
   Shelby Township (G-14604)
▲ Inalfa Road System Inc....................B   248 371-3060
   Auburn Hills (G-908)
◆ Inalfa Roof Systems Inc ....B   248 371-3060
   Auburn Hills (G-909)
Inalfa Roof Systems Inc C   586 758-6620
   Warren (G-17085)
▲ Inoac Usa Inc......................................E   248 619-7031
   Troy (G-16419)
Integrated Program MGT LLC................G   248 241-9257
   Clarkston (G-2932)
International Automotive Compo ....B   989 620-7649
   Alma (G-238)
International Automotive Compo ....B   810 987-8500
   Port Huron (G-12930)
▲ Interntional Catalyst Tech Inc ....G   248 340-1040
   Auburn Hills (G-914)
Interstate Power Systems Inc ....F   952 854-2044
   Iron Mountain (G-8285)
▲ Intertec Systems LLC ....D   734 254-3268
   Plymouth (G-12649)

37 TRANSPORTATION EQUIPMENT

Inteva Products LLC ....F 248 655-8886
Troy *(G-16422)*
Inteva Products LLC ....F 248 655-8886
Troy *(G-16423)*
◆ Inteva Products LLC ....B 248 655-8886
Troy *(G-16424)*
Inteva Products Usa LLC ....G 248 655-8886
Troy *(G-16425)*
▲ Inzi Controls Detroit LLC ....G 334 282-4237
Rochester Hills *(G-13451)*
Iochpe Holdings LLC ....D 734 737-5000
Novi *(G-11907)*
J & J Industries Inc ....G 517 784-3586
Jackson *(G-8473)*
J Drummond Service Inc ....G 248 624-0190
Livonia *(G-9790)*
▲ J G Kern Enterprises Inc ....D 586 531-9472
Sterling Heights *(G-15378)*
J L International Inc ....C 734 941-0300
Romulus *(G-13690)*
Jac Products Inc ....G 586 254-1534
Shelby Township *(G-14608)*
Jac Products Inc ....D 248 874-1800
Pontiac *(G-12840)*
▲ Jasper Weller LLC ....C 616 724-2000
Grand Rapids *(G-6554)*
▼ Jay & Kay Manufacturing LLC ....E 810 679-2333
Croswell *(G-3598)*
Jay & Kay Manufacturing LLC ....G 810 679-3079
Croswell *(G-3599)*
Jernberg Holdings LLC ....G 313 758-2000
Detroit *(G-4161)*
▲ Jet Industries Inc ....E 734 641-0900
Westland *(G-17574)*
Johnson Controls Inc ....C 313 842-3300
Detroit *(G-4165)*
Johnson Controls Inc ....C 734 254-5000
Plymouth *(G-12656)*
Johnson Controls Inc ....E 734 254-7200
Plymouth *(G-12657)*
Johnson Controls Inc ....B 616 392-5151
Holland *(G-7697)*
Johnson Controls Inc ....C 586 826-8845
Sterling Heights *(G-15382)*
Joint Clutch & Gear Svc Inc ....E 734 641-7575
Romulus *(G-13693)*
Jomar Performance Products LLC ....G 248 322-3080
Pontiac *(G-12841)*
Jorgensen Stl Mch & Fab Inc ....F 517 767-4600
Tekonsha *(G-15819)*
◆ Jost International Corp ....C 616 846-7700
Grand Haven *(G-6039)*
Joyson Safety Systems ....G 248 364-6023
Auburn Hills *(G-921)*
◆ Joyson Sfety Systems Acqstion ....F 248 373-8040
Auburn Hills *(G-923)*
Jtekt Automotive N Amer Inc ....A 734 454-1500
Plymouth *(G-12659)*
Kar-Bones Inc......................................G 313 582-5551
Detroit *(G-4171)*
▲ Katcon Usa Inc ....D 248 499-1500
Auburn Hills *(G-924)*
Kautex Inc..B 231 739-2704
Muskegon *(G-11357)*
▲ Kautex Inc..A 248 616-5100
Troy *(G-16444)*
Kay Manufacturing Company ....E 269 408-8344
Saint Joseph *(G-14320)*
Kearsley Lake Terrace LLC ....G 810 736-7000
Flint *(G-5453)*
▲ Keihin Michigan Mfg LLC ....C 317 462-3015
Mussey *(G-11457)*
Kellogg Crankshaft Co ....D 517 788-9200
Jackson *(G-8488)*
Kenona Industries LLC........................C 616 735-6226
Grand Rapids *(G-6574)*
Kerkstra Mechanical LLC ....G 616 532-6100
Grand Rapids *(G-6581)*
▲ Key Safety Systems Inc ....C 586 726-3800
Auburn Hills *(G-926)*
◆ Key Sfety Rstraint Systems Inc ....A 586 726-3800
Auburn Hills *(G-927)*
Kiekert Usa Inc ....D 248 960-4100
Wixom *(G-17841)*
▲ Kiekert Usa Inc ....C 248 960-4100
Wixom *(G-17842)*
▲ Knoedler Manufacturers Inc ....F 269 969-7722
Battle Creek *(G-1221)*
▲ Kongsberg Automotive Inc ....D 248 468-1300
Novi *(G-11918)*

Kongsberg Holding I Inc ....G 248 468-1300
Novi *(G-11919)*
Kongsberg Holding III Inc ....E 248 468-1300
Novi *(G-11920)*
▲ Kongsberg Intr Systems I Inc ....F 956 465-4541
Novi *(G-11921)*
▲ Kostal of America Inc ....C 248 284-6500
Troy *(G-16450)*
▲ Kurabe America Corporation ....A 248 939-5803
Farmington Hills *(G-5039)*
Kyklos Holdings Inc............................G 313 758-2000
Detroit *(G-4186)*
Kysor Industrial Corporation ....C 231 779-7500
Cadillac *(G-2259)*
L & C Hanwha ....G 734 457-5600
Monroe *(G-11046)*
L T C Roll & Engineering Co ....F 586 465-1023
Fraser *(G-5682)*
Lab Tool and Engineering Corp..........E 517 750-4131
Spring Arbor *(G-15124)*
Lacks Industries Inc ....C 616 698-6890
Grand Rapids *(G-6606)*
Lacks Industries Inc ....D 616 656-2910
Grand Rapids *(G-6612)*
Lakeland Finishing Corporation ....D 616 949-8001
Grand Rapids *(G-6614)*
Laurmark Enterprises Inc ....E 818 365-9000
Ann Arbor *(G-526)*
Lear Automotive Mfg LLC ....F 248 447-1603
Detroit *(G-4196)*
Lear Automotive Mfg LLC ....F 248 447-1603
Detroit *(G-4197)*
▼ Lear Corp Eeds and Interiors ....F 248 447-1500
Southfield *(G-14960)*
Lear Corporation ....A 313 852-7800
Southfield *(G-14961)*
Lear Corporation ....B 989 588-6181
Farwell *(G-5163)*
Lear Corporation ....B 248 299-7100
Rochester Hills *(G-13458)*
Lear Corporation ....C 989 275-5794
Roscommon *(G-13750)*
◆ Lear Corporation ....B 248 447-1500
Southfield *(G-14962)*
Lear Corporation ....C 231 947-0160
Traverse City *(G-16023)*
Lear Corporation ....C 734 946-1600
Taylor *(G-15734)*
Lear Corporation ....A 313 731-0833
Flint *(G-5457)*
Lear Corporation ....B 269 496-2215
Mendon *(G-10715)*
Lear European Operations Corp ....G 248 447-1500
Southfield *(G-14963)*
Lear Trim LP ....G 248 447-1500
Southfield *(G-14966)*
Lee Industries Inc ....E 231 777-2537
Muskegon *(G-11365)*
▲ Leedy Manufacturing Co LLC ....D 616 245-0517
Grand Rapids *(G-6624)*
▲ Leon Interiors Inc ....B 616 422-7479
Holland *(G-7721)*
▲ Letts Industries Inc ....G 313 579-1100
Detroit *(G-4200)*
▼ Libertys High Prfmce Pdts Inc ....F 586 469-1140
Harrison Township *(G-7338)*
Line X of Westbranch ....G 989 345-7800
West Branch *(G-17512)*
Lippert Components Mfg Inc ....C 989 845-3061
Chesaning *(G-2725)*
Litebrake Tech LLC ....G 906 523-2007
Houghton *(G-7975)*
Lj/Hah Holdings Corporation ....G 248 340-4100
Auburn Hills *(G-929)*
M P I International Inc ....D 608 764-5416
Rochester Hills *(G-13463)*
M S Manufacturing Inc ....F 586 463-2788
Clinton Township *(G-3161)*
M&M Mfg Inc ....G 248 356-6543
Southfield *(G-14972)*
M-Tek Inc..F 248 553-1581
Novi *(G-11931)*
Mac Lean-Fogg Company ....C 248 280-0880
Royal Oak *(G-13945)*
Machine Tool & Gear Inc ....D 989 743-3936
Corunna *(G-3581)*
Machinery Prts Specialists LLC ....G 989 662-7810
Auburn *(G-756)*
▲ Magna Electronics Tech Inc ....E 810 606-0145
Holly *(G-7887)*

Magna Exteriors America Inc..............G 248 844-5446
Auburn Hills *(G-935)*
◆ Magna Exteriors America Inc ....A 248 631-1100
Troy *(G-16472)*
Magna Exteriors America Inc..............B 248 409-1817
Auburn Hills *(G-936)*
Magna Extrors Intrors Amer Inc ....C 248 729-2400
Troy *(G-16473)*
Magna International Amer Inc............C 248 729-2400
Troy *(G-16474)*
Magna International Amer Inc............B 313 422-6000
Detroit *(G-4214)*
Magna International Inc.....................F 248 617-3200
New Hudson *(G-11548)*
Magna Modular Systems LLC ....C 586 279-2000
Warren *(G-17137)*
Magna Powertrain America Inc..........G 517 316-1013
Lansing *(G-9394)*
▲ Magna Powertrain America Inc .....C 248 597-7811
Troy *(G-16475)*
Magna Powertrain Usa Inc ....C 586 264-8180
Sterling Heights *(G-15409)*
▲ Magna Powertrain Usa Inc ....D 248 680-4900
Troy *(G-16476)*
Magna Powertrain Usa Inc ....B 248 524-1397
Troy *(G-16477)*
Magna Seating America Inc ....C 248 243-7158
Auburn Hills *(G-937)*
▲ Magna Seating America Inc ....B 248 567-4000
Novi *(G-11932)*
Magna Seating America Inc ....G 586 816-1400
Shelby Township *(G-14632)*
▲ Magnesium Products America Inc ..B 734 416-8600
Plymouth *(G-12681)*
Magneti Marelli Holdg USA LLC ....E 248 418-3000
Auburn Hills *(G-938)*
▲ Magneti Marelli North Amer Inc ....G 248 418-3000
Auburn Hills *(G-939)*
◆ Magnumm Corporation ....F 586 427-9420
Warren *(G-17138)*
Mahle Inc...E 248 305-8200
Farmington Hills *(G-5050)*
▲ Mahle Aftermarket Inc.....................C 248 347-9700
Farmington *(G-4904)*
Mahle Behr Mfg MGT Inc ....A 248 735-3623
Troy *(G-16480)*
Mahle Behr Troy Inc ....D 248 735-3623
Troy *(G-16482)*
▲ Mahle Behr Troy Inc ....C 248 743-3700
Troy *(G-16481)*
▲ Mahle Behr USA Inc ....B 248 743-3700
Troy *(G-16483)*
Mahle Industries Incorporated............C 989 224-5423
Saint Johns *(G-14288)*
Mahle Industries Incorporated............E 248 305-8200
Farmington Hills *(G-5052)*
▲ Mahle Industries Incorporated........G 248 305-8200
Farmington Hills *(G-5053)*
Mahle Industries Incorporated............C 231 722-1300
Muskegon *(G-11372)*
Mahle Manufacturing MGT Inc ....G 248 735-3623
Farmington Hills *(G-5054)*
Mall Tooling & Engineering ....F 586 463-6520
Mount Clemens *(G-11140)*
Mann + Hummel Usa Inc ....F 248 857-8500
Bloomfield Hills *(G-1780)*
Mann + Hummel Usa Inc ....E 248 857-8501
Kalamazoo *(G-8818)*
▲ Mann + Hummel Usa Inc ....F 269 329-3900
Portage *(G-13014)*
Marelli Tennessee USA LLC................G 248 418-3000
Auburn Hills *(G-942)*
Marelli Tennessee USA LLC................A 248 680-8872
Troy *(G-16485)*
◆ Mariah Industries Inc ....E 248 237-0404
Troy *(G-16486)*
▲ Marimba Auto LLC ....D 734 398-9000
Canton *(G-2397)*
Marley Precision Inc ....E 269 963-7374
Battle Creek *(G-1226)*
▲ Martinrea Industries Inc ....F 734 428-2400
Manchester *(G-10408)*
Martinrea Industries Inc ....F 517 849-2195
Jonesville *(G-8661)*
Mason Forge & Die Inc ....F 517 676-2992
Mason *(G-10645)*
Master Mfg Inc....................................E 248 628-9400
Oxford *(G-12359)*
▲ Maxable Inc..E 517 592-5638
Brooklyn *(G-2039)*

Employee Codes: A=Over 500 employees, B=251-500
C=101-250, D=51-100, E=20-50, F=10-19, G=3-9

37 TRANSPORTATION EQUIPMENT SIC SECTION

Maxion Fumagalli Auto USA D 734 737-5000
Novi *(G-11938)*

▲ **Maxion Import LLC** F 734 737-5000
Novi *(G-11939)*

◆ **Maxion Wheels** D 734 737-5000
Novi *(G-11940)*

Maxion Wheels Akron LLC G 734 737-5000
Novi *(G-11941)*

Maxion Wheels USA LLC D 734 737-5000
Novi *(G-11942)*

Mayser Usa Inc D 734 858-1290
Van Buren Twp *(G-16771)*

Mayville Engineering Co Inc E 989 983-3911
Vanderbilt *(G-16807)*

◆ **Means Industries Inc** C 989 754-1433
Saginaw *(G-14086)*

Med-Kas Hydraulics Inc F 248 585-3220
Troy *(G-16491)*

▲ **Medallion Instrumentation** C 616 847-3700
Spring Lake *(G-15161)*

Melling Products North LLC D 989 588-6147
Farwell *(G-5164)*

◆ **Melling Tool Co** B 517 787-8172
Jackson *(G-8514)*

◆ **Meritor Inc** C 248 435-1000
Troy *(G-16493)*

Meritor Indus Aftermarket LLC G 248 658-7345
Troy *(G-16495)*

▲ **Meritor Industrial Pdts LLC** F 248 658-7200
Troy *(G-16497)*

Meritor Intl Holdings LLC G 248 435-1000
Troy *(G-16498)*

Meritor Specialty Products LLC G 248 435-1000
Livonia *(G-9838)*

Meritor Specialty Products LLC D 517 545-5800
Howell *(G-8062)*

Metaldyne LLC C 734 207-6200
Detroit *(G-4228)*

Metaldyne Prfmce Group Inc E 248 727-1800
Southfield *(G-14978)*

Metaldyne Pwrtrain Cmpnnts Inc F 517 542-5555
Litchfield *(G-9608)*

Metaldyne Pwrtrain Cmpnnts Inc C 517 542-5555
Litchfield *(G-9607)*

Metaldyne Sintered Components F 734 207-6200
Plymouth *(G-12691)*

Metaldyne Tblar Components LLC C 248 727-1800
Southfield *(G-14979)*

Metalsa Structural Pdts Inc G 248 669-3704
Sterling Heights *(G-15416)*

▲ **Metalsa Structural Pdts Inc** D 248 669-3704
Novi *(G-11945)*

◆ **Metavation LLC** E 248 351-1000
Troy *(G-16499)*

Metcalf Machine Inc G 616 837-8128
Ravenna *(G-13125)*

◆ **Michigan Auto Comprsr Inc** B 517 796-3200
Parma *(G-12391)*

▲ **Micro Rim Corporation** F 313 865-1090
Detroit *(G-4246)*

Micron Holdings Inc A 616 698-0707
Kentwood *(G-9020)*

Midwest Brake Bond Co E 586 775-3000
Warren *(G-17155)*

▲ **Millennium Steering LLC** D 989 872-8823
Cass City *(G-2521)*

Miller Industrial Products Inc E 517 783-2756
Jackson *(G-8528)*

▲ **Minowitz Manufacturing Co** E 586 779-5940
Huntington Woods *(G-8190)*

▲ **Mint Steel Forge Inc** F 248 276-9000
Lake Orion *(G-9149)*

▼ **Misc Products** D 586 263-3300
Macomb *(G-10144)*

▲ **Mistequay Group Ltd** F 989 752-7700
Saginaw *(G-14097)*

Mistequay Group Ltd D 989 846-1000
Standish *(G-15224)*

Mitsubishi Steel Mfg Co Ltd E 248 502-8000
Troy *(G-16509)*

Mj Mfg Co G 810 744-3840
Burton *(G-2159)*

MNP Corporation E 248 585-5010
Madison Heights *(G-10308)*

▲ **MNP Corporation** A 586 254-1320
Utica *(G-16744)*

Model-Matic Inc F 248 528-1680
Troy *(G-16511)*

Moldex Crank Shaft Inc G 313 561-7676
Redford *(G-13175)*

Montaplast North America Inc F 248 353-5553
Auburn Hills *(G-947)*

Motor Parts Inc of Michigan E 248 852-1522
Rochester Hills *(G-13476)*

Mpt Driveline Systems G 248 680-3786
Troy *(G-16514)*

◆ **Mpt Lansing LLC** C 517 316-1013
Lansing *(G-9403)*

Mr Axle F 231 788-4624
Muskegon *(G-11386)*

▲ **Mssc Inc** E 248 502-8000
Troy *(G-16515)*

▲ **Musashi Auto Parts Mich Inc** B 269 965-0057
Battle Creek *(G-1230)*

Mvc Holdings LLC F 586 491-2600
Roseville *(G-13843)*

▲ **National Fleet Service LLC** E 313 923-1799
Detroit *(G-4263)*

National Ordnance Auto Mfg LLC G 248 853-8822
Auburn Hills *(G-953)*

Nationwide Design Inc F 586 254-5493
Sterling Heights *(G-15433)*

Navarre Inc E 313 892-7300
Detroit *(G-4264)*

Nbhx Trim USA Corporation F 616 785-9400
Walker *(G-16871)*

▲ **Nbhx Trim USA Corporation** C 616 785-9400
Comstock Park *(G-3501)*

Neapco Drivelines LLC B 734 447-1316
Van Buren Twp *(G-16775)*

▲ **Neapco Drivelines LLC** C 734 447-1300
Van Buren Twp *(G-16776)*

◆ **Neapco Holdings LLC** C 248 699-6500
Farmington Hills *(G-5079)*

Newcor Inc C 248 537-0014
Corunna *(G-3584)*

Newtech 3 Inc E 248 912-0807
Wixom *(G-17864)*

Nexteer Automotive Corporation B 989 754-1920
Saginaw *(G-14105)*

Nexteer Automotive Corporation A 989 757-5000
Saginaw *(G-14106)*

Nexteer Automotive Corporation B 989 757-5000
Saginaw *(G-14107)*

Nexteer Automotive Corporation A 989 757-5000
Saginaw *(G-14108)*

Nexteer Automotive Corporation A 989 757-5000
Saginaw *(G-14109)*

Nexteer Automotive Corporation A 989 757-5000
Saginaw *(G-14110)*

Nexteer Automotive Corporation D 989 757-5000
Saginaw *(G-14111)*

Nexteer Automotive Corporation E 989 757-5000
Saginaw *(G-14112)*

Nexteer Automotive Corporation C 989 757-5000
Saginaw *(G-14113)*

Nexteer Automotive Corporation B 989 757-5000
Saginaw *(G-14114)*

◆ **Nexteer Automotive Corporation** A 248 340-8200
Auburn Hills *(G-955)*

Nexteer Automotive Corporation B 989 757-5000
Saginaw *(G-14104)*

Nexteer Automotive Group Ltd A 989 757-5000
Saginaw *(G-14115)*

Nisshinbo Automotive Mfg Inc D 586 997-1000
Sterling Heights *(G-15436)*

▲ **Nitrex Inc** E 517 676-6370
Mason *(G-10649)*

Nitto Inc G 732 276-1039
Romulus *(G-13713)*

Nodel-Co F 248 543-1325
Ferndale *(G-5306)*

Norma Michigan Inc F 248 373-4300
Lake Orion *(G-9151)*

▲ **Norma Michigan Inc** C 248 373-4300
Auburn Hills *(G-959)*

Norplas Industries Inc D 517 999-1400
Lansing *(G-9314)*

Northern Classics Trucks Inc G 586 254-2835
Rochester Hills *(G-13482)*

Northrop Grmmn Spce & Mssn Sys A 734 266-2600
Livonia *(G-9864)*

▼ **Nostrum Energy LLC** F 734 548-8677
Ann Arbor *(G-576)*

Novares US LLC B 616 554-3555
Grand Rapids *(G-6723)*

▲ **NSK Americas Inc** C 734 913-7500
Ann Arbor *(G-577)*

▲ **NSK Steering Systems Amer Inc** C 734 913-7500
Ann Arbor *(G-578)*

Nu Con Corporation E 734 525-0770
Livonia *(G-9867)*

Nyx Inc B 734 261-7535
Livonia *(G-9870)*

▲ **Nyx LLC** C 734 462-2385
Livonia *(G-9871)*

Oakley Industries Sub Assembly D 586 754-5555
Warren *(G-17176)*

Oakley Industries Sub Assembly E 810 720-4444
Flint *(G-5473)*

Oakley Sub Assembly Inc E 810 720-4444
Flint *(G-5474)*

Oakley Sub Assembly Intl Inc G 810 720-4444
Flint *(G-5475)*

▲ **Oakwood Metal Fabricating Co** B 313 561-7740
Dearborn *(G-3746)*

Offsite Manufacturing Inc G 586 598-8850
Chesterfield *(G-2811)*

▲ **Ogura Corporation** C 586 749-1900
Chesterfield *(G-2812)*

Oiles America Corporation D 734 414-7400
Plymouth *(G-12702)*

▲ **Old Dura Inc** G 248 299-7500
Auburn Hills *(G-965)*

▲ **Opeo Inc** F 248 299-4000
Auburn Hills *(G-966)*

▲ **Orotex Corporation** C 248 773-8630
Novi *(G-11967)*

Oscar W Larson Company G 248 575-0320
Clarkston *(G-2943)*

▼ **Owens Products Inc** E 269 651-2300
Sturgis *(G-15625)*

P G S Inc C 248 526-3800
Troy *(G-16540)*

P T M Corporation D 586 725-2211
Ira *(G-8266)*

P3 Product Solutions Inc F 248 703-7724
Madison Heights *(G-10320)*

▲ **Panagon Systems Inc** E 586 786-3920
Macomb *(G-10152)*

Pardon Inc E 906 428-3494
Gladstone *(G-5918)*

Patent Lcnsing Clringhouse LLC G 248 299-7500
Rochester Hills *(G-13491)*

PCI Procal Inc F 989 358-7070
Alpena *(G-307)*

Pcm US Steering Holding LLC G 313 556-5000
Detroit *(G-4292)*

Peckham Vocational Inds Inc C 517 316-4478
Lansing *(G-9253)*

Performance Engrg Racg Engs G 616 669-5800
Jenison *(G-8636)*

Performance Springs Inc F 248 486-3372
New Hudson *(G-11551)*

▲ **Performnce Assmbly Sltions LLC** E 734 466-6380
Livonia *(G-9887)*

Pgf Technology Group Inc E 248 852-2800
Rochester Hills *(G-13492)*

Pierburg Us LLC F 864 688-1322
Auburn Hills *(G-973)*

Pims Co G 313 665-8837
Detroit *(G-4301)*

◆ **Piston Automotive LLC** B 313 541-8674
Redford *(G-13182)*

Piston Automotive LLC D 313 541-8789
Van Buren Twp *(G-16779)*

Piston Automotive LLC E 313 541-8789
Detroit *(G-4304)*

Piston Group LLC G 248 226-3976
Southfield *(G-14999)*

▲ **Plasan Carbon Composites Inc** C 616 965-9450
Walker *(G-16874)*

Plastic Ominium Auto Inergy B 734 753-1350
New Boston *(G-11508)*

Plastic Ominium Auto Inergy C 517 265-1100
Adrian *(G-85)*

Plastic Omnium Auto Inergy LLC E 248 743-5700
Troy *(G-16552)*

▲ **Plastic Omnium Auto Inergy LLC** B 248 743-5700
Troy *(G-16553)*

Plastic Plate LLC E 616 455-5240
Grand Rapids *(G-6757)*

Plastic Plate LLC C 616 698-3678
Kentwood *(G-9023)*

Plastic Plate LLC D 616 949-6570
Kentwood *(G-9024)*

▲ **Pontiac Coil Inc** C 248 922-1100
Clarkston *(G-2947)*

Powergrid Inc G 586 484-7185
Farmington Hills *(G-5099)*

SIC SECTION 37 TRANSPORTATION EQUIPMENT

Precision Gage Inc D 517 439-1690 Hillsdale *(G-7534)*

Precision Race Services Inc G 248 634-4010 Davisburg *(G-3638)*

▲ **Precision Torque Control Inc** F 989 495-9330 Midland *(G-10903)*

Prestige Engrg Rsrces Tech Inc F 586 573-3070 Clinton Township *(G-3202)*

Prestige Engrg Rsrces Tech Inc E 586 573-3070 Madison Heights *(G-10336)*

▲ **Prestige Warehouse & Assembly** E 586 777-1820 Warren *(G-17197)*

▲ **Pridgeon & Clay Inc** A 616 241-5675 Grand Rapids *(G-6774)*

◆ **Pritech Corporation** G 248 488-9120 Canton *(G-2420)*

Product Assembly Group LLC G 586 549-8601 Troy *(G-16565)*

Profile Mfg Inc E 586 598-0007 Chesterfield *(G-2824)*

Propride Inc G 810 695-1127 Grand Blanc *(G-5978)*

Prototech Laser Inc F 586 948-3032 Chesterfield *(G-2826)*

Prototypes Plus Inc G 269 751-7141 Hamilton *(G-7238)*

▲ **Pullman Company** F 734 243-8000 Monroe *(G-11064)*

Qp Acquisition 2 Inc E 248 594-7432 Southfield *(G-15006)*

Quality Clutches Inc G 734 782-0783 Flat Rock *(G-5360)*

▲ **Quality Engineering Company** F 248 351-9000 Wixom *(G-17883)*

◆ **Quality Spring/Togo Inc** C 517 278-2391 Coldwater *(G-3323)*

Quality Steel Products Inc E 248 684-0555 Milford *(G-10981)*

Quigley Co E 989 983-3911 Vanderbilt *(G-16809)*

▲ **R Cushman & Associates Inc** E 248 477-9900 Livonia *(G-9904)*

Rack & Pinion Inc G 517 563-8872 Horton *(G-7970)*

Ralco Industries Inc D 248 853-3200 Auburn Hills *(G-985)*

Ralco Industries Inc E 248 853-3200 Auburn Hills *(G-986)*

Rapp & Son Inc C 734 283-1000 Wyandotte *(G-17971)*

▲ **Rassey Industries Inc** E 586 803-9500 Shelby Township *(G-14678)*

Rassini Brakes LLC G 810 780-4600 Flint *(G-5490)*

▲ **Raval USA Inc** F 248 260-4050 Rochester Hills *(G-13503)*

Ravenna Casting Center Inc C 231 853-0300 Ravenna *(G-13126)*

RCO Engineering Inc D 586 620-4133 Roseville *(G-13860)*

Regency Plastics - Ubly Inc D 989 658-8504 Ubly *(G-16723)*

◆ **Ride Control LLC** D 248 247-7600 Farmington Hills *(G-5115)*

Ridge & Kramer Motor Supply Co G 269 685-5838 Plainwell *(G-12541)*

Rieke-Arminak Corp G 248 631-5450 Bloomfield Hills *(G-1795)*

▲ **Rivas Inc** D 586 566-0326 Sterling Heights *(G-15473)*

▼ **Riverside Tank & Mfg Corp** E 810 329-7143 Saint Clair *(G-14234)*

◆ **Rivian Automotive LLC** D 734 855-4350 Plymouth *(G-12739)*

Robert Bosch Fuel Systems LLC C 616 554-6500 Kentwood *(G-9030)*

Robert Bosch LLC E 248 921-9054 Novi *(G-11987)*

Robert Bosch LLC A 734 979-3000 Plymouth *(G-12741)*

Robert Bosch LLC B 734 979-3412 Plymouth *(G-12742)*

Robert Bosch LLC F 269 429-3221 Saint Joseph *(G-14338)*

Robertson-Stewart Inc F 810 227-4500 Brighton *(G-1986)*

Rochester Gear Inc D 989 659-2899 Clifford *(G-3011)*

Rose-A-Lee Technologies Inc G 586 799-4555 Sterling Heights *(G-15479)*

Roush Enterprises Inc A 734 779-7006 Livonia *(G-9911)*

Roush Enterprises Inc E 313 294-8200 Allen Park *(G-207)*

Roush Enterprises Inc C 734 805-4400 Farmington *(G-4909)*

Roush Industries Inc E 734 779-7016 Livonia *(G-9912)*

Roush Industries Inc E 734 779-7013 Livonia *(G-9913)*

Roush Manufacturing Inc D 734 805-4400 Farmington *(G-4910)*

▲ **Roush Manufacturing Inc** C 734 779-7006 Livonia *(G-9915)*

Royce Corporation G 586 758-1500 Warren *(G-17226)*

◆ **Rugged Liner Inc** E 989 725-8354 Owosso *(G-12313)*

Ryder Integrated Logistics Inc A 517 492-4446 Lansing *(G-9321)*

S & S Tube Inc F 989 656-7211 Bay Port *(G-1375)*

S & W Holdings Ltd G 248 723-2870 Birmingham *(G-1701)*

SA Automotive Ltd LLC F 989 723-0425 Owosso *(G-12314)*

Saf-Holland Inc F 616 396-6501 Holland *(G-7794)*

Saf-Holland Inc C 616 396-6501 Holland *(G-7795)*

◆ **Saf-Holland Inc** B 231 773-3271 Muskegon *(G-11417)*

▲ **Sam Brown Sales LLC** E 248 358-2626 Farmington *(G-4911)*

Sas Automotive Usa Inc G 248 606-1152 Fraser *(G-5721)*

▲ **Sas Automotive Usa Inc** E 248 606-1152 Sterling Heights *(G-15485)*

Schwab Industries Inc F 586 566-8090 Shelby Township *(G-14687)*

Seaman Industries Inc G 586 776-9620 Roseville *(G-13867)*

Seg Automotive North Amer LLC F 248 465-2602 Novi *(G-11991)*

Servotech Industries Inc F 734 697-5555 Taylor *(G-15764)*

SH Leggitt Company C 269 781-3901 Marshall *(G-10588)*

Shaftmasters G 313 383-6347 Lincoln Park *(G-9585)*

Sharp Model Co D 586 752-3099 Bruce Twp *(G-2101)*

Shelby Antolin Inc F 734 395-0328 Shelby Township *(G-14692)*

Shiloh Industries Inc D 989 463-6166 Alma *(G-249)*

Shop IV Sbsid Inv Grede LLC B 248 727-1800 Southfield *(G-15027)*

Skg International Inc F 248 620-4139 Clarkston *(G-2956)*

▲ **Skilled Manufacturing Inc** C 231 941-0290 Traverse City *(G-16105)*

Skilled Manufacturing Inc E 231 941-0032 Traverse City *(G-16106)*

Skokie Castings LLC D 248 727-1800 Southfield *(G-15030)*

SL America Corporation E 586 731-8511 Auburn Hills *(G-1000)*

Sliding Systems Inc E 517 339-1455 Haslett *(G-7399)*

▲ **Sloan Transportation Pdts Inc** D 616 395-5600 Holland *(G-7806)*

◆ **Slw Automotive Inc** C 248 464-6200 Rochester Hills *(G-13513)*

Sort-Tek Insptn Systems Inc F 248 273-5200 Troy *(G-16612)*

◆ **Spartan Motors Inc** A 517 543-6400 Charlotte *(G-2665)*

▲ **Specialty Eng Components LLC** D 734 955-6500 Taylor *(G-15770)*

▲ **Spectrum Cubic Inc** D 616 459-8751 Grand Rapids *(G-6883)*

Sports Resorts International D 989 725-8354 Owosso *(G-12318)*

Stackpole Pwrtrn Intl USA LLC G 248 481-4600 Auburn Hills *(G-1001)*

Stant USA Corp E 765 827-8104 Rochester Hills *(G-13518)*

◆ **Steering Solutions Corporation** E 989 757-5000 Saginaw *(G-14158)*

▲ **Steinbauer Performance LLC** G 704 587-0856 Dowagiac *(G-4562)*

Stemco Products Inc G 888 854-6474 Millington *(G-10998)*

▲ **Sterling Performance Inc** E 248 685-7811 Milford *(G-10987)*

Stewart Industries LLC D 269 660-9290 Battle Creek *(G-1253)*

◆ **Stoneridge Inc** G 248 489-9300 Novi *(G-12004)*

Strattec Security Corporation E 248 649-9742 Auburn Hills *(G-1005)*

▲ **Stromberg-Carlson Products Inc** F 231 947-8600 Traverse City *(G-16114)*

Su-Dan Plastics Inc F 248 651-6035 Lake Orion *(G-9165)*

▲ **Superior Industries Intl Inc** C 248 352-7300 Southfield *(G-15038)*

▲ **Superior Industries N Amer LLC** E 248 352-7300 Southfield *(G-15039)*

Supply Line International LLC F 248 242-7140 Novi *(G-12010)*

Sweet Manufacturing Inc E 269 344-2086 Kalamazoo *(G-8906)*

Swiss American Screw Pdts Inc F 734 397-1600 Canton *(G-2431)*

▲ **Swoboda Inc** C 616 554-6161 Grand Rapids *(G-6909)*

Sycron Technologies Inc G 810 694-4007 Grand Blanc *(G-5985)*

▲ **Synchronous Manufacturing Inc** E 517 764-6930 Michigan Center *(G-10791)*

▲ **Syncreonus Inc** D 248 377-4700 Auburn Hills *(G-1010)*

▲ **Systrand Manufacturing Corp** C 734 479-8100 Brownstown Twp *(G-2074)*

▲ **TAC Manufacturing Inc** B 517 789-7000 Jackson *(G-8582)*

Takata Americas E 336 547-1600 Auburn Hills *(G-1012)*

Tata Autocomp Systems Limited G 248 680-4608 Troy *(G-16632)*

Teamtech Motorsports Safety G 989 792-4880 Saginaw *(G-14163)*

Technique Inc D 517 789-8988 Jackson *(G-8585)*

Tectum Holdings Inc D 734 926-2362 Ann Arbor *(G-656)*

◆ **Teksid Inc** F 734 846-5897 Farmington *(G-4914)*

Telmar Manufacturing Company G 810 577-7050 Fenton *(G-5241)*

Tenneco Automotive Oper Co B 248 849-1258 Northville *(G-11728)*

Tenneco Automotive Oper Co Inc C 517 522-5520 Grass Lake *(G-7095)*

Tenneco Automotive Oper Co Inc E 734 243-8000 Lansing *(G-9269)*

Tenneco Automotive Oper Co Inc G 734 243-8039 Monroe *(G-11072)*

Tenneco Automotive Oper Co Inc C 269 781-1350 Marshall *(G-10590)*

Tenneco Automotive Oper Co Inc C 517 542-5511 Litchfield *(G-9611)*

Tenneco Automotive Oper Co Inc D 517 522-5525 Jackson *(G-8586)*

Tenneco Automotive Oper Co Inc F 734 243-4615 Monroe *(G-11073)*

Tenneco Automotive Oper Co Inc B 734 243-8000 Monroe *(G-11074)*

Tenneco Clean Air US Inc G 734 384-7867 Lansing *(G-9432)*

Tenneco Inc G 734 254-1122 Plymouth *(G-12769)*

Tenneco Inc G 248 354-7700 Southfield *(G-15045)*

Tesca Usa Inc E 586 991-0744 Rochester Hills *(G-13524)*

Th Plastics Inc D 269 496-8495 Mendon *(G-10720)*

Therma-Tech Engineering Inc E 313 537-5330 Redford *(G-13201)*

Thermal Solutions Mfg G 734 655-7145 Livonia *(G-9956)*

Thk Rhythm Auto Mich Corp C 517 647-4121 Portland *(G-13068)*

Thyssenkrupp Automotive Sales F 248 530-2991 Troy *(G-16639)*

◆ **Thyssenkrupp Automotive Sales** E 248 530-2902 Troy *(G-16640)*

Employee Codes: A=Over 500 employees, B=251-500 C=101-250, D=51-100, E=20-50, F=10-19, G=3-9

2020 Harris Michigan Industrial Directory

855

Thyssenkrupp Bilstein Amer Inc ... F ... 248 530-2900
Troy ***(G-16641)***

▲ **TI Automotive LLC** ... C ... 248 494-5000
Auburn Hills ***(G-1020)***

TI Group Auto Systems LLC ... B ... 989 672-1200
Caro ***(G-2477)***

TI Group Auto Systems LLC ... D ... 989 673-7727
Caro ***(G-2478)***

TI Group Auto Systems LLC ... E ... 248 494-5000
Troy ***(G-16642)***

TI Group Auto Systems LLC ... C ... 810 364-3277
Marysville ***(G-10623)***

TI Group Auto Systems LLC ... C ... 586 948-6006
Chesterfield ***(G-2848)***

TI Group Auto Systems LLC ... C ... 859 235-5420
Auburn Hills ***(G-1023)***

TI Group Auto Systems LLC ... B ... 248 475-4663
Auburn Hills ***(G-1025)***

TI Group Auto Systems LLC ... D ... 517 437-7462
Hillsdale ***(G-7543)***

◆ **TI Group Auto Systems LLC** ... B ... 248 296-8000
Auburn Hills ***(G-1022)***

▲ **Tianhai Electric N Amer Inc** ... D ... 248 987-2100
Pontiac ***(G-12870)***

Torsion Control Products Inc ... F ... 248 537-1900
Rochester Hills ***(G-13528)***

▲ **Toyo Seat USA Corporation** ... C ... 606 849-3009
Imlay City ***(G-8212)***

Tractech Inc ... E ... 248 226-6800
Southfield ***(G-15048)***

▲ **Tram Inc** ... C ... 734 254-8500
Plymouth ***(G-12778)***

▲ **Tramec Sloan LLC** ... D ... 616 395-5600
Holland ***(G-7833)***

Trans Parts Plus Inc ... G ... 734 427-6844
Garden City ***(G-5844)***

Transform Automotive LLC ... D ... 586 826-8500
Shelby Township ***(G-14710)***

▲ **Transform Automotive LLC** ... C ... 586 826-8500
Sterling Heights ***(G-15527)***

Transpak Inc ... E ... 586 264-2064
Sterling Heights ***(G-15528)***

Trend Performance Products ... E ... 586 792-6620
Clinton Township ***(G-3251)***

◆ **Trico Products Corporation** ... C ... 248 371-1700
Rochester Hills ***(G-13531)***

▲ **Trident Lighting LLC** ... C ... 616 957-9500
Grand Rapids ***(G-6937)***

◆ **Trimas Corporation** ... E ... 248 631-5450
Bloomfield Hills ***(G-1807)***

Trin Inc ... G ... 260 587-9282
Plymouth ***(G-12780)***

Tristone Flowtech USA Inc ... G ... 248 560-1724
Southfield ***(G-15049)***

▲ **Trmi Inc** ... A ... 269 966-0800
Battle Creek ***(G-1261)***

▲ **Truck Trailer Transit Inc** ... E ... 313 516-7151
Troy ***(G-16652)***

Truck Acquisition Inc ... G ... 877 875-4376
Ann Arbor ***(G-681)***

Truck Hero Inc ... D ... 877 875-4376
Ann Arbor ***(G-682)***

Truck Holdings Inc ... G ... 877 875-4376
Ann Arbor ***(G-683)***

TRW Auto Holdings Inc ... G ... 734 855-2600
Livonia ***(G-9974)***

TRW Automotive JV LLC ... G ... 734 855-2787
Livonia ***(G-9975)***

TRW East Inc ... G ... 734 855-2600
Livonia ***(G-9976)***

TRW Odyssey Mexico LLC ... G ... 734 855-2600
Livonia ***(G-9977)***

Turn One Inc ... G ... 989 652-2778
Saginaw ***(G-14170)***

▲ **U-Shin America Inc** ... G ... 248 449-3155
Novi ***(G-12021)***

Uc Holdings Inc ... D ... 248 728-8642
Southfield ***(G-15052)***

Ufi Filters Usa Inc ... G ... 248 376-0441
Troy ***(G-16661)***

▲ **Ufi Filters Usa Inc** ... F ... 248 376-0441
Troy ***(G-16662)***

Ufp Technologies Inc ... D ... 616 949-8100
Grand Rapids ***(G-6948)***

Uncle Eds Oil Shoppes Inc ... G ... 248 288-4738
Clawson ***(G-2988)***

Unifilter Inc ... E ... 248 476-5100
Novi ***(G-12023)***

Unique Fabricating Inc ... E ... 248 853-2333
Auburn Hills ***(G-1034)***

◆ **United Foam A Ufp Tech Brnd** ... D ... 616 949-8100
Grand Rapids ***(G-6952)***

▲ **United Machining Inc** ... C ... 586 323-4300
Sterling Heights ***(G-15533)***

United Machining Inc ... G ... 586 323-4300
Macomb ***(G-10171)***

United Metal Technology Inc ... F ... 517 787-7940
Jackson ***(G-8599)***

United Systems Group LLC ... G ... 810 227-4567
Brighton ***(G-2004)***

US Farathane Holdings Corp ... E ... 586 991-6922
Sterling Heights ***(G-15536)***

◆ **Usui International Corporation** ... E ... 734 354-3626
Plymouth ***(G-12784)***

▲ **Valeo Friction Materials Inc** ... G ... 248 619-8300
Troy ***(G-16675)***

Valeo North America Inc ... C ... 248 209-8253
Auburn Hills ***(G-1043)***

◆ **Valeo North America Inc** ... D ... 248 619-8300
Troy ***(G-16677)***

Valeo North America Inc ... C ... 313 883-8850
Detroit ***(G-4421)***

Valeo Radar Systems Inc ... F ... 248 619-8300
Troy ***(G-16678)***

▲ **Valeo Switches & Dete** ... E ... 248 619-8300
Troy ***(G-16679)***

Valley Truck Parts Inc ... G ... 269 429-9953
Saint Joseph ***(G-14348)***

Veet Industries Inc ... F ... 586 776-3000
Warren ***(G-17281)***

◆ **Vehma International Amer Inc** ... D ... 248 631-2800
Troy ***(G-16681)***

Vehma International Amer Inc ... C ... 248 585-4800
Troy ***(G-16680)***

Venchurs Inc ... E ... 517 263-1206
Adrian ***(G-99)***

Venchurs Inc ... F ... 517 263-8937
Adrian ***(G-100)***

Veoneer Inc ... A ... 248 223-0600
Southfield ***(G-15058)***

Veritas USA Corporation ... G ... 248 374-5019
Novi ***(G-12026)***

◆ **Vibracoustic North America L P** ... E ... 269 637-2116
South Haven ***(G-14780)***

▲ **Victora Usa Inc** ... G ... 810 798-0253
Almont ***(G-269)***

Vihi LLC ... G ... 734 710-2277
Van Buren Twp ***(G-16789)***

Visions Car & Truck Acc ... G ... 269 342-2962
Kalamazoo ***(G-8919)***

Visteon Corporation ... D ... 734 718-8927
Canton ***(G-2440)***

Visteon Corporation ... B ... 800 847-8366
Van Buren Twp ***(G-16790)***

Visteon Electronics Corp ... G ... 800 847-8366
Van Buren Twp ***(G-16791)***

Visteon Global Electronics Inc ... G ... 800 847-8366
Van Buren Twp ***(G-16792)***

Visteon Global Electronics Inc ... G ... 734 710-5000
Van Buren Twp ***(G-16793)***

Visteon Systems LLC ... E ... 800 847-8366
Van Buren Twp ***(G-16795)***

Vitesco Technologies ... C ... 313 583-5980
Dearborn ***(G-3769)***

Vitesco Technologies ... G ... 248 393-5880
Detroit ***(G-4434)***

Vitesco Technologies ... G ... 704 442-8000
Auburn Hills ***(G-1046)***

Vitesco Technologies Usa LLC ... F ... 248 209-4000
Auburn Hills ***(G-1047)***

▲ **Von Weise LLC** ... F ... 517 618-9763
Eaton Rapids ***(G-4736)***

Vortek ... G ... 248 767-2992
Pinckney ***(G-12505)***

▲ **Wabco Holdings Inc** ... C ... 248 270-9300
Auburn Hills ***(G-1049)***

Walbro LLC ... C ... 989 872-2131
Cass City ***(G-2524)***

Waldrons Antique Exhaust ... G ... 269 467-7185
Centreville ***(G-2599)***

Walter Sappington ... G ... 989 345-1052
West Branch ***(G-17527)***

▲ **Walther Trowal GMBH & Co KG** ... G ... 616 871-0031
Grand Rapids ***(G-6979)***

Warn Industries Inc ... G ... 734 953-9870
Livonia ***(G-9997)***

Warren Chassix ... G ... 248 728-8700
Warren ***(G-17286)***

Warren Screw Products Inc ... C ... 586 757-1280
Warren ***(G-17288)***

▲ **Webasto Convertibles USA Inc** ... C ... 734 582-5900
Plymouth ***(G-12791)***

Webasto Roof Systems Inc ... C ... 734 452-2600
Livonia ***(G-10002)***

▲ **Webasto Roof Systems Inc** ... B ... 248 997-5100
Rochester Hills ***(G-13543)***

Webasto Roof Systems Inc ... F ... 248 997-5100
Rochester Hills ***(G-13545)***

▲ **Weber Automotive Corporation** ... C ... 248 393-5520
Auburn Hills ***(G-1050)***

West Mich Auto Stl & Engrg Inc ... E ... 616 560-8198
Belding ***(G-1431)***

West Michigan Gage Inc ... F ... 616 735-0585
Walker ***(G-16882)***

West/Win Ltd ... G ... 734 525-9000
Livonia ***(G-10007)***

Windsor Mch & Stamping 2009 ... D ... 734 941-7320
Taylor ***(G-15782)***

Wiper Shaker LLC ... G ... 231 668-2418
Williamsburg ***(G-17724)***

◆ **Wiric Corporation** ... E ... 248 598-5297
Rochester Hills ***(G-13548)***

Wkw Erbsloeh N Amer Holdg Inc ... D ... 205 338-4242
Troy ***(G-16693)***

Wolfgang Moneta ... G ... 269 422-2296
Baroda ***(G-1133)***

Yanfeng US Automotive ... E ... 616 392-5151
Holland ***(G-7863)***

Yanfeng US Automotive ... D ... 616 392-5151
Holland ***(G-7864)***

Yapp USA Auto Systems Inc ... G ... 248 404-8696
Romulus ***(G-13745)***

Young Diversified Industries ... G ... 248 353-1867
Southfield ***(G-15069)***

ZF Active Safety & Elec US LLC ... A ... 586 843-2100
Livonia ***(G-10013)***

ZF Active Safety US Inc ... G ... 906 248-3882
Brimley ***(G-2017)***

▲ **ZF Active Safety US Inc** ... B ... 734 855-2542
Livonia ***(G-10015)***

ZF Active Safety US Inc ... C ... 517 223-8330
Fowlerville ***(G-5581)***

◆ **ZF Active Safety US Inc** ... F ... 734 812-6979
Livonia ***(G-10016)***

ZF Active Safety US Inc ... C ... 810 750-1036
Fenton ***(G-5250)***

ZF Active Safety US Inc ... A ... 586 232-7200
Washington ***(G-17315)***

ZF Active Safety US Inc ... C ... 586 899-2807
Sterling Heights ***(G-15548)***

ZF Active Safety US Inc ... E ... 734 855-2470
Livonia ***(G-10017)***

ZF Active Safety US Inc ... C ... 248 863-2412
Saginaw ***(G-14185)***

▲ **ZF Axle Drives Marysville LLC** ... B ... 810 989-8702
Marysville ***(G-10627)***

◆ **ZF Chassis Components LLC** ... C ... 810 245-2000
Lapeer ***(G-9494)***

ZF Chassis Components LLC ... B ... 810 245-2000
Lapeer ***(G-9495)***

ZF Lemforder Corp ... F ... 810 245-7136
Lapeer ***(G-9496)***

◆ **ZF North America Inc** ... B ... 734 416-6200
Northville ***(G-11735)***

ZF North America Inc ... G ... 734 416-6200
Northville ***(G-11736)***

ZF Passive Safety ... B ... 248 478-7210
Farmington Hills ***(G-5155)***

ZF Passive Safety Systems US ... E ... 586 752-1409
Romeo ***(G-13643)***

ZF Passive Safety Systems US ... B ... 586 781-5511
Washington ***(G-17317)***

▲ **ZF Passive Safety US Inc** ... F ... 734 855-2600
Livonia ***(G-10019)***

ZF Passive Safety US Inc ... G ... 586 232-7200
Washington ***(G-17318)***

▲ **ZF Passive Sfety Systems US In** ... A ... 586 232-7200
Washington ***(G-17319)***

▲ **ZF String Active Safety US Inc** ... G ... 734 855-2600
Livonia ***(G-10020)***

◆ **ZF TRW Auto Holdings Corp** ... A ... 734 855-2600
Livonia ***(G-10021)***

▲ **Zhongli North America Inc** ... D ... 248 733-9300
Troy ***(G-16705)***

▲ **Zynp International Corp** ... E ... 734 947-1000
Romulus ***(G-13746)***

3715 Truck Trailers

Ajax Trailers Inc ... F ... 586 757-7676
Warren ***(G-16923)***

37 TRANSPORTATION EQUIPMENT

Anderson Welding & Mfg Inc .... F 906 523-4661
  Chassell (G-2671)
Arboc Ltd .... G 248 684-2895
  Commerce Township (G-3390)
Automotive Service Co .... F 517 784-6131
  Jackson (G-8385)
Benlee Inc .... E 586 791-1830
  Romulus (G-13656)
Bobbys Mobile Service LLC .... G 517 206-6026
  Jackson (G-8392)
Clydes Frame & Wheel Service .... F 248 338-0323
  Pontiac (G-12810)
Eddies Quick Stop Inc .... G 313 712-1818
  Dearborn (G-3698)
Executive Operations LLC .... E 313 312-0653
  Canton (G-2474)
Express Welding Inc .... G 906 786-8808
  Escanaba (G-4829)
Hulet Body Co Inc .... E 313 931-6000
  Northville (G-11699)
Intermodal Technologies Inc .... G 989 775-3799
  Mount Pleasant (G-11198)
Jbs Transport LLC .... G 248 636-5546
  Troy (G-16435)
Joes Trailer Manufacturing .... G 734 261-0050
  Livonia (G-9793)
Leonard & Randy Inc .... G 734 287-9500
  Taylor (G-15735)
Lupa R A and Sons Repair .... G 810 346-3579
  Marlette (G-10498)
Merhow Acquisition LLC .... D 269 483-0010
  White Pigeon (G-17653)
Montrose Trailers Inc .... G 810 639-7431
  Montrose (G-11105)
Mtm Transport .... G 989 709-0475
  Alger (G-139)
Neo Manufacturing Inc .... F 269 503-7630
  Sturgis (G-15623)
Oshkosh Defense LLC .... E 586 576-8301
  Warren (G-17178)
▲ Pratt Industries Inc .... D 269 465-7676
  Bridgman (G-1872)
▲ Pullman Company .... F 734 243-8000
  Monroe (G-11064)
◆ Saf-Holland Inc .... B 231 773-3271
  Muskegon (G-11417)
Saf-Holland Inc .... C 616 396-6501
  Holland (G-7795)
Scott Enterprises .... G 734 279-2078
  Dundee (G-4600)
Superior Synchronized Sys .... D 906 863-7824
  Wallace (G-16888)
Technology Plus Trailers Inc .... F 734 928-0001
  Canton (G-2433)
Thumb Truck and Trailer Co .... G 989 453-3133
  Pigeon (G-12493)
Tow-Line Trailers .... G 989 752-0055
  Saginaw (G-14165)
◆ Trailer Tech Holdings LLC .... E 248 960-9700
  Wixom (G-17915)
Transport Trailers Co .... G 269 543-4405
  Fennville (G-5178)
Trimas Company LLC .... F 248 631-5450
  Bloomfield Hills (G-1806)
Wolverine Trailers Inc .... G 517 782-4950
  Jackson (G-8610)
Wolverine Trailers Inc .... G 517 782-4950
  Jackson (G-8611)
Woodland Industries .... G 989 686-6176
  Kawkawlin (G-8976)
Xpo Cnw Inc .... C 734 757-1444
  Ann Arbor (G-705)

3716 Motor Homes

Auto-Masters Inc .... E 616 455-4510
  Grand Rapids (G-6190)
Frank Industries Inc .... E 810 346-3234
  Brown City (G-2051)
Riverside Vans Inc .... F 269 432-3212
  Colon (G-3375)

3721 Aircraft

Aero Inspection & Tool LLC .... G 517 525-7373
  Leslie (G-9540)
Aerostatica Inc .... F 734 426-4525
  Dexter (G-4473)
Ascent Aerospace Holdings LLC .... G 212 916-8142
  Macomb (G-10109)
Boeing Company 248 258-7191
  Bloomfield Hills (G-1753)

C H Industries Inc .... F 586 997-1717
  Shelby Township (G-14556)
Eaton Aerospace LLC .... F 517 787-8121
  Jackson (G-8438)
◆ Enstrom Helicopter Corporation ..... C 906 863-1200
  Menominee (G-10731)
G-Force Tooling LLC .... G 517 541-2747
  Charlotte (G-2650)
G-Force Tooling LLC .... G 517 712-8177
  Grand Ledge (G-6107)
Great Lakes Aviaiton Svcs LLC .... G 586 770-3450
  Clinton Township (G-3129)
Manufacturing & Indus Tech Inc .... E 248 814-8544
  Lake Orion (G-9147)
Midwest Build Center LLC .... G 989 672-1388
  Caro (G-2474)
Mohyi Labs LLC .... G 248 973-7321
  West Bloomfield (G-17487)
Mustang Aeronautics Inc .... G 248 649-6818
  Troy (G-16517)
P2r Metal Fabrication Inc .... G 888 727-5587
  Macomb (G-10151)
Sika Corporation .... D 248 577-0020
  Madison Heights (G-10353)
Soaring Concepts Aerospace LLC .... F 574 286-9670
  Hastings (G-7427)
Textron Inc .... G 248 545-2035
  Madison Heights (G-10367)
Traverse City Helicopters LLC .... G 231 668-6000
  Traverse City (G-16126)
Waco Classic Aircraft Corp .... E 269 565-1000
  Battle Creek (G-1265)

3724 Aircraft Engines & Engine Parts

AAR Corp .... F 231 779-4859
  Cadillac (G-2219)
Advance Turning and Mfg Inc .... C 517 783-2713
  Jackson (G-8373)
Aerovision Aircraft Svcs LLC .... E 231 799-9000
  Norton Shores (G-11737)
Aerovision International LLC .... E 231 799-9000
  Norton Shores (G-11738)
Aircraft Precision Pdts Inc .... D 989 875-4186
  Ithaca (G-8356)
Approved Aircraft Accessories .... G 734 946-9000
  Romulus (G-13651)
AVI Inventory Services LLC .... E 231 799-9000
  Norton Shores (G-11740)
Barnes Group Inc .... A 517 393-5110
  Lansing (G-9346)
Dorris Company .... E 586 293-5260
  Fraser (G-5644)
◆ Dry Coolers Inc .... E 248 969-3400
  Oxford (G-12344)
Eaton Corporation .... B 269 781-0200
  Marshall (G-10566)
Expernced Prcsion McHining Inc .... G 989 635-2299
  Marlette (G-10496)
Filtration Machine .... G 810 845-0536
  Davison (G-3649)
GE Aviation Muskegon .... F 231 777-2685
  Norton Shores (G-11757)
Honeywell International Inc .... E 989 792-8707
  Saginaw (G-14061)
Honeywell International Inc .... A 586 777-7870
  Fraser (G-5665)
Honeywell International Inc .... E 734 392-5501
  Plymouth (G-12641)
▲ Johnson Technology Inc .... B 231 777-2685
  Muskegon (G-11354)
LAY Precision Machine Inc .... G 989 726-5022
  West Branch (G-17511)
Manufacturing & Indus Tech Inc .... E 248 814-8544
  Lake Orion (G-9147)
MB Aerospace Warren LLC .... C 586 772-2500
  Warren (G-17144)
Merrill Technologies Group .... E 989 921-1490
  Saginaw (G-14089)
▲ Merrill Technologies Group Inc ...... D 989 791-6676
  Saginaw (G-14090)
Metro Machine Works Inc .... D 734 941-4571
  Romulus (G-13707)
Moeller Aerospace Tech Inc .... C 231 347-9575
  Harbor Springs (G-7289)
Moeller Mfg Company LLC .... G 616 285-5012
  Grand Rapids (G-6695)
Niles Precision Company .... C 269 683-0585
  Niles (G-11634)
Nu Con Corporation .... E 734 525-0770
  Livonia (G-9867)

▲ Pratt & Whitney Autoair Inc .... B 517 393-4040
  Lansing (G-9413)
Rapp & Son Inc .... C 734 283-1000
  Wyandotte (G-17971)
SGC Industries Inc .... E 586 293-5260
  Fraser (G-5723)
Steel Tool & Engineering Co .... D 734 692-8580
  Brownstown Twp (G-2072)
Steven J Devlin .... G 734 439-1325
  Milan (G-10951)
Stm Power Inc .... F 734 214-1448
  Ann Arbor (G-647)
Supreme Gear Co .... E 586 775-6325
  Fraser (G-5736)
T Q Machining Inc .... E 231 726-5914
  Muskegon (G-11434)
Tidy Mro Enterprises LLC .... G 734 649-1122
  Manchester (G-10412)
Turbine Conversions Ltd .... G 616 837-9428
  Nunica (G-12045)
United Precision Pdts Co Inc .... E 313 292-0100
  Dearborn Heights (G-3800)
▲ Williams International Co LLC .... B 248 624-5200
  Pontiac (G-12875)
Williams International Co LLC .... C 248 762-8713
  Waterford (G-17386)
Woodward Fst Inc .... C 616 772-9171
  Zeeland (G-18198)

3728 Aircraft Parts & Eqpt, NEC

360 Group Au Pty Ltd .... G 586 219-2005
  Rochester Hills (G-13357)
Advance Turning and Mfg Inc .... C 517 783-2713
  Jackson (G-8373)
Advanced Integration Tech LP .... E 586 749-5525
  Chesterfield (G-2734)
Aero Train Corp .... G 810 230-8096
  Flint (G-5372)
Aerostatica Inc .... F 734 426-5525
  Dexter (G-4473)
Aerovision Aircraft Svcs LLC .... E 231 799-9000
  Norton Shores (G-11737)
Aerovision International LLC .... E 231 799-9000
  Norton Shores (G-11738)
Air Craft Industries Inc .... G 269 663-8544
  Edwardsburg (G-4757)
Aircraft Precision Pdts Inc .... D 989 875-4186
  Ithaca (G-8356)
Aj Aircraft .... G 734 244-4015
  Monroe (G-11014)
American Aircraft Parts Mfg Co .... E 586 294-3300
  Clinton Township (G-3046)
AVI Inventory Services LLC .... E 231 799-9000
  Norton Shores (G-11740)
B/E Aerospace Inc .... G 734 425-6200
  Livonia (G-9658)
◆ Beaver Aerospace & Defense Inc ... D 734 853-5003
  Livonia (G-9662)
Bgt Aerospace LLC .... G 989 225-5812
  Bay City (G-1290)
◆ Bmt Aerospace Usa Inc .... D 586 285-7700
  Fraser (G-5630)
Bradley-Thompson Tool Company ...... E 248 352-1466
  Southfield (G-14855)
Chardam Gear Company Inc .... D 586 795-8900
  Sterling Heights (G-15287)
Detail Precision Products Inc .... E 248 544-3390
  Ferndale (G-5271)
▲ Detroit Coil Co .... E 248 658-1543
  Ferndale (G-5274)
Dolphin Manufacturing Inc .... G 734 946-6322
  Taylor (G-15707)
Dorris Company .... E 586 293-5260
  Fraser (G-5644)
Eagle Industrial Group Inc .... E 616 647-9904
  Comstock Park (G-3481)
Eaton-Aeroquip Llc .... B 949 452-9575
  Jackson (G-8440)
Extreme Precision Screw Pdts .... E 810 744-1980
  Flint (G-5427)
Fema Corporation of Michigan .... C 269 323-1369
  Portage (G-12996)
Flow-Rite Controls Ltd .... E 616 583-1700
  Byron Center (G-2191)
Gear Master Inc .... F 810 798-9254
  Almont (G-257)
General Dynamics Glbl IMG Tech .... F 248 293-2929
  Rochester Hills (G-13433)
Grand Rapids Technologies Inc .... G 616 245-7700
  Grand Rapids (G-6465)

Employee Codes: A=Over 500 employees, B=251-500
C=101-250, D=51-100, E=20-50, F=10-19, G=3-9

Hart Precision Products Inc........E....... 313 537-0490
Redford *(G-13165)*
Honeywell International Inc........C....... 231 582-5686
Boyne City *(G-1822)*
Hytrol Manufacturing Inc........E....... 734 261-8030
Jackson *(G-8468)*
Intergrted Dspnse Slutions LLC........F....... 586 554-7404
Shelby Township *(G-14605)*
Jedco Inc........C....... 616 459-5161
Grand Rapids *(G-6557)*
▲ **Lapeer Industries Inc**........C....... 810 664-1816
Lapeer *(G-9467)*
Liberty Tool Inc........E....... 586 726-2449
Sterling Heights *(G-15398)*
▲ **Liebherr Aerospace Saline Inc**........C....... 734 429-7225
Saline *(G-14398)*
▲ **Linear Motion LLC**........C....... 989 759-8300
Saginaw *(G-14078)*
Manufacturing & Indus Tech Inc........E....... 248 814-8544
Lake Orion *(G-9147)*
Mas Inc........G....... 231 894-0409
Whitehall *(G-17677)*
Masterbilt Products Corp........E....... 269 749-4841
Olivet *(G-12142)*
Melling Manufacturing Inc........E....... 517 750-3580
Jackson *(G-8513)*
Merrill Technologies Group........E....... 989 921-1490
Saginaw *(G-14089)*
Military & Veterans Affairs........D....... 231 775-7222
Cadillac *(G-2266)*
Moose Mfg & Machining LLC........G....... 586 765-4686
Detroit *(G-4254)*
Motor City Aerospace........E....... 616 916-5473
Rockford *(G-13581)*
National Aircraft Service Inc........F....... 517 423-7589
Tecumseh *(G-15803)*
Niles Precision Company........C....... 269 683-0585
Niles *(G-11634)*
◆ **Northern Wings Repair Inc**........E....... 906 477-6176
Newberry *(G-11586)*
Nu Con Corporation........E....... 734 525-0770
Livonia *(G-9867)*
Odyssey Industries LLC........C....... 248 814-8800
Lake Orion *(G-9153)*
Parker-Hannifin Corporation........B....... 269 384-3459
Kalamazoo *(G-8843)*
▲ **Phoenix Cmposite Solutions LLC**........C....... 989 739-7108
Oscoda *(G-12218)*
Pifers Airmotive Inc........G....... 248 674-0909
Waterford *(G-17369)*
Pontoon Rentals........G....... 906 387-2685
Munising *(G-11248)*
Prime Products Inc........E....... 616 531-8970
Grand Rapids *(G-6775)*
R & B Electronics Inc........D....... 906 632-1542
Sault Sainte Marie *(G-14471)*
Saf-Air Products Inc........G....... 734 522-8360
Garden City *(G-5837)*
Scott Machine Inc........E....... 517 787-6616
Jackson *(G-8571)*
SGC Industries Inc........E....... 586 293-5260
Fraser *(G-5723)*
Teamtech Motorsports Safety........G....... 989 792-4880
Saginaw *(G-14163)*
◆ **Triumph Gear Systems - Macomb**........C....... 586 781-2800
Macomb *(G-10170)*
United Precision Pdts Co Inc........E....... 313 292-0100
Dearborn Heights *(G-3800)*
Veet Industries Inc........F....... 586 776-3000
Warren *(G-17281)*
Ventura Aerospace LLC........E....... 734 357-0114
Wixom *(G-17925)*
Ventura Industries Inc........E....... 734 357-0114
Plymouth *(G-12788)*
Visioneering Inc........E....... 248 622-5600
Fraser *(G-5747)*
Waller Machine Co Inc........G....... 517 789-7707
Jackson *(G-8603)*
Wmh Fluidpower Inc........F....... 269 327-7011
Portage *(G-13058)*

3731 Shipbuilding & Repairing

▲ **Arcosa Shoring Products Inc**........E....... 517 741-4300
Union City *(G-16731)*
Beardslee Investments Inc........F....... 810 748-9951
Harsens Island *(G-7368)*
▲ **FD Lake Company**........F....... 616 241-5639
Grand Rapids *(G-6403)*
Floatation Docking Inc........E....... 906 484-3422
Cedarville *(G-2567)*
General Dynamics Corporation........E....... 586 825-8228
Macomb *(G-10125)*
Jag Industrial Services Inc........G....... 678 592-6860
Jonesville *(G-8657)*
LA East Inc........D....... 269 476-7170
Vandalia *(G-16801)*
Lake Shore Systems Inc........D....... 906 265-5414
Iron River *(G-8313)*
▲ **Lake Shore Systems Inc**........D....... 906 774-1500
Kingsford *(G-9061)*
Merchant Holdings Inc........G....... 906 786-7120
Escanaba *(G-4844)*
▲ **Nicholson Terminal & Dock Co**........C....... 313 842-4300
River Rouge *(G-13279)*
Nk Dockside Service & Repair........G....... 906 420-0777
Escanaba *(G-4846)*

3732 Boat Building & Repairing

A & B Tube Benders Inc........E....... 586 773-0440
Warren *(G-16905)*
Abrahamson Marine Inc........G....... 231 843-2142
Ludington *(G-10047)*
Advanced Fiberglass Services........G....... 810 785-7541
Flint *(G-5370)*
American Pleasure Products Inc........G....... 989 685-8484
Rose City *(G-13758)*
◆ **Ameriform Acquisition Co LLC**........B....... 231 733-2725
Muskegon *(G-11269)*
Andersen Boat Works........G....... 616 836-2502
South Haven *(G-14753)*
Artisans Cstm Mmory Mattresses........F....... 989 793-3208
Saginaw *(G-13996)*
Avalon & Tahoe Mfg Inc........C....... 989 463-2112
Alma *(G-236)*
Bay City Fiberglass Inc........G....... 989 751-9622
Bay City *(G-1285)*
Beacon Marine Sales & Service........G....... 586 465-2539
Harrison Township *(G-7323)*
Beardslee Investments Inc........F....... 810 748-9951
Harsens Island *(G-7368)*
Bingham Boat Works Ltd........G....... 906 225-0050
Marquette *(G-10519)*
C & C Sports Inc........E....... 810 227-7068
Brighton *(G-1895)*
Crest Marine LLC........E....... 989 725-5188
Owosso *(G-12285)*
D B A Richards Boatworks Mar........G....... 906 789-4168
Escanaba *(G-4823)*
▼ **Douglas Marine Corporation**........E....... 269 857-1764
Douglas *(G-4530)*
Eldean Company........E....... 616 335-5843
Macatawa *(G-10096)*
Eldean Yacht Basin Ltd........E....... 616 786-2205
Holland *(G-7620)*
▼ **Glastron LLC**........B....... 800 354-3141
Cadillac *(G-2249)*
Invision Boatworks LLC........G....... 989 754-3341
Saginaw *(G-14064)*
Irish Boat Shop Inc........E....... 231 547-9967
Charlevoix *(G-2619)*
Jans Sport Shop Inc........F....... 810 636-2241
Goodrich *(G-5954)*
Marsh Brothers Inc........F....... 517 869-2653
Quincy *(G-13096)*
▲ **Maurell Products Inc**........C....... 989 725-5188
Owosso *(G-12301)*
Max Manufacturing........F....... 517 990-9180
Jackson *(G-8511)*
Meyers Boat Company Inc........F....... 517 265-9821
Adrian *(G-81)*
Mid-Tech Inc........G....... 734 426-4327
Ann Arbor *(G-557)*
Midwest Aquatics Group Inc........G....... 734 426-4155
Pinckney *(G-12500)*
Morin Boats........G....... 989 686-7353
Bay City *(G-1335)*
Murleys Marine........G....... 586 725-7446
Ira *(G-8264)*
N D R Enterprises Inc........G....... 269 857-4556
Saugatuck *(G-14460)*
Nauticraft Corporation........G....... 231 798-8440
Norton Shores *(G-11779)*
Northshore Pontoon........G....... 517 547-8877
Hudson *(G-8137)*
Ocean Express Powerboats Inc........G....... 810 794-5551
Algonac *(G-145)*
Paddle King Inc........F....... 989 235-6776
Carson City *(G-2495)*
Powell & Crisp Plankters LLC........G....... 231 271-6769
Suttons Bay *(G-15654)*
Powersports Dales LLC........G....... 248 682-4200
Keego Harbor *(G-8981)*
▼ **Quantum Sails Design Group LLC**........F....... 231 941-1222
Traverse City *(G-16087)*
◆ **Rec Boat Holdings LLC**........D....... 231 775-1351
Cadillac *(G-2273)*
Reed Yacht Sales LLC........G....... 419 304-4405
La Salle *(G-9074)*
Reed Yacht Sales LLC........F....... 616 842-8899
Grand Haven *(G-6069)*
Ricks Cove Inc........G....... 734 283-7505
Wyandotte *(G-17972)*
Rubber Rope Products Company........G....... 906 358-4133
Watersmeet *(G-17389)*
▼ **S 2 Yachts Inc**........A....... 616 392-7163
Holland *(G-7793)*
Spicers Boat Cy of Houghton Lk........E....... 989 366-8384
Houghton Lake *(G-7997)*
▲ **Sterling Performance Inc**........E....... 248 685-7811
Milford *(G-10987)*
Sunsation Products Inc........E....... 810 794-4888
Clay *(G-3003)*
▲ **Swivl - Eze Marine**........E....... 616 897-9241
Lowell *(G-10044)*
T D Vinette Company........G....... 906 786-1884
Escanaba *(G-4862)*
Tassier Boat Works Inc........G....... 906 484-2573
Cedarville *(G-2572)*
Unlimited Marine Inc........G....... 248 249-0222
White Lake *(G-17641)*
▲ **Van Dam Marine Co**........F....... 231 582-2323
Boyne City *(G-1837)*
Viking Boat Harbor Inc........F....... 906 484-3303
Cedarville *(G-2573)*
Wooden Runabout Co........G....... 616 396-7248
Holland *(G-7860)*

3743 Railroad Eqpt

Amsted Rail Company Inc........G....... 517 568-4161
Homer *(G-7936)*
▲ **Arcosa Shoring Products Inc**........E....... 517 741-4300
Union City *(G-16731)*
Braetec Inc........G....... 269 968-4711
Battle Creek *(G-1156)*
Delta Tube & Fabricating Corp........E....... 248 634-8267
Holly *(G-7874)*
First Choice of Elkhart Inc........G....... 269 483-2010
White Pigeon *(G-17648)*
Floss Automotive Group........G....... 734 773-2524
Inkster *(G-8227)*
Gorang Industries Inc........G....... 248 651-9010
Rochester *(G-13322)*
Harsco Corporation........D....... 231 843-3431
Ludington *(G-10062)*
▲ **Hj Manufacturing Inc**........F....... 906 233-1500
Escanaba *(G-4833)*
▼ **Mitchell Equipment Corporation**........E....... 734 529-3400
Dundee *(G-4596)*
▲ **Peaker Services Inc**........D....... 248 437-4174
Brighton *(G-1976)*
Rescar Inc........G....... 517 486-3130
Blissfield *(G-1724)*
▲ **S & S Parts LLC**........G....... 517 467-6511
Onsted *(G-12156)*
▲ **Trinity Equipment Co**........G....... 231 719-1813
Muskegon *(G-11441)*
Trinity Industries Inc........G....... 586 285-1692
Fraser *(G-5740)*

3751 Motorcycles, Bicycles & Parts

Aerospoke Incorporated........G....... 248 685-9009
Brighton *(G-1878)*
Alter Cycles Ltd........G....... 313 737-1196
Grandville *(G-7019)*
Assenmacher Lightweight Cycles........G....... 810 635-7844
Swartz Creek *(G-15661)*
Blueshift Motorcycles LLC........G....... 231 946-8772
Traverse City *(G-15915)*
Detriot Choppers Inc........G....... 586 498-8909
Roseville *(G-13792)*
▲ **Detroit Bikes LLC**........G....... 313 646-4109
Detroit *(G-3971)*
Gift Bikes 4 Kids........G....... 313 573-5619
Detroit *(G-4090)*
▲ **ITT Motion Tech Amer LLC**........F....... 248 863-2161
Novi *(G-11909)*
▲ **Marlin Corporation**........G....... 248 683-1536
Orchard Lake *(G-12167)*
◆ **Pritech Corporation**........G....... 248 488-9120
Canton *(G-2420)*

Ron Watkins ....G.... 517 439-5451
Hillsdale *(G-7537)*
▲ **Shinola/Detroit LLC** ....C.... 888 304-2534
Detroit *(G-4361)*
Technique Inc ....D.... 517 789-8988
Jackson *(G-8585)*
▲ **Varroc Lighting Systems Inc** ....D.... 734 446-4400
Plymouth *(G-12786)*
▲ **Velocity Worldwide Inc** ....F.... 616 243-3400
Grand Rapids *(G-6963)*
▲ **Wiz Wheelz Inc** ....F.... 616 455-5988
Grand Rapids *(G-6995)*

3761 Guided Missiles & Space Vehicles

Bear Creek Ballistics Co ....G.... 269 806-2020
East Leroy *(G-4684)*
Telic Corporation ....G.... 219 406-2164
Saint Joseph *(G-14343)*

3764 Guided Missile/Space Vehicle Propulsion Units & parts

Federal-Mogul Powertrain LLC ....E.... 734 930-1590
Ann Arbor *(G-458)*
Hytrol Manufacturing Inc ....E.... 734 261-8030
Jackson *(G-8468)*
Northrop Grumman Innovation ....D.... 313 424-9411
Shelby Township *(G-14657)*
▲ **Williams International Co LLC** ....B.... 248 624-5200
Pontiac *(G-12875)*
Williams International Co LLC ....C.... 248 762-8713
Waterford *(G-17386)*

3769 Guided Missile/Space Vehicle Parts & Eqpt, NEC

Advance Turning and Mfg Inc ....C.... 517 783-2713
Jackson *(G-8373)*
Dorris Company ....E.... 586 293-5260
Fraser *(G-5644)*
MB Aerospace Warren LLC ....C.... 586 772-2500
Warren *(G-17144)*
Mistequay Group Ltd ....D.... 989 846-1000
Standish *(G-15224)*
Parker-Hannifin Corporation ....B.... 269 384-3459
Kalamazoo *(G-8843)*
Rapp & Son Inc ....C.... 734 283-1000
Wyandotte *(G-17971)*
SGC Industries Inc ....E.... 586 293-5260
Fraser *(G-5723)*
Swiss American Screw Pdts Inc ....F.... 734 397-1600
Canton *(G-2431)*
Truform Machine Inc ....E.... 517 782-8523
Jackson *(G-8594)*

3792 Travel Trailers & Campers

Ajax Trailers Inc ....F.... 586 757-7676
Warren *(G-16923)*
Bnm Trailers Sales Inc ....E.... 989 862-5252
Elsie *(G-4795)*
County of Muskegon ....F.... 231 744-3580
Muskegon *(G-11302)*
D & W Management Company Inc ....E.... 586 758-2284
Warren *(G-16996)*
Forest River Inc ....D.... 269 471-6321
Centreville *(G-2594)*
Frank Industries Inc ....E.... 810 346-3234
Brown City *(G-2051)*
Gibbys Transport LLC ....G.... 269 838-2794
Hastings *(G-7411)*
Michigan East Side Sales LLC ....G.... 989 354-6867
Alpena *(G-299)*
Monroes Custom Campers Inc ....G.... 231 773-0005
Muskegon *(G-11385)*
Montrose Trailers Inc ....G.... 810 639-7431
Montrose *(G-11105)*
Mvm7 LLC ....E.... 989 317-3901
Mount Pleasant *(G-11213)*
Northland ....G.... 231 775-3101
Cadillac *(G-2268)*
R V Wolverine ....F.... 989 426-9241
Gladwin *(G-5934)*
▼ **Steffens Enterprises Inc** ....E.... 616 656-6886
Caledonia *(G-2317)*
Technology Plus Trailers Inc ....F.... 734 928-0001
Canton *(G-2433)*
Van Kam Inc ....F.... 231 744-2658
Muskegon *(G-11444)*

3795 Tanks & Tank Components

American Rhnmtall Vehicles LLC ....G.... 703 221-9288
Sterling Heights *(G-15259)*
Bae Systems Land Armaments LP ....F.... 586 596-4123
Sterling Heights *(G-15270)*
Benteler Defense Corp ....G.... 248 377-9999
Auburn Hills *(G-793)*
Burch Tank & Truck Inc ....G.... 989 495-0342
Midland *(G-10820)*
Burch Tank & Truck Inc ....D.... 989 772-6266
Mount Pleasant *(G-11181)*
Demmer Corporation ....D.... 517 703-3116
Lansing *(G-9216)*
▲ **Demmer Corporation** ....C.... 517 321-3600
Lansing *(G-9217)*
Demmer Corporation ....D.... 517 703-3163
Lansing *(G-9218)*
Demmer Corporation ....D.... 517 703-3131
Lansing *(G-9219)*
Demmer Corporation ....E.... 517 321-3600
Lansing *(G-9287)*
Demmer Corporation ....D.... 517 323-4504
Lansing *(G-9220)*
General Dynamics Land ....G.... 586 825-8400
Sterling Heights *(G-15357)*
Generaleral Dynamics ....G.... 601 877-6436
Sterling Heights *(G-15359)*
Horstman Inc ....E.... 586 737-2100
Sterling Heights *(G-15368)*
Odt Systems Inc ....F.... 248 953-9512
Rochester *(G-13339)*
◆ **Plasan North America Inc** ....D.... 616 559-0032
Walker *(G-16875)*
◆ **Reutter LLC** ....G.... 248 621-9220
Bingham Farms *(G-1659)*
Ronal Industries Inc ....F.... 248 616-9691
Sterling Heights *(G-15478)*
Supreme Gear Co ....E.... 586 775-6325
Fraser *(G-5736)*
Tank Truck Service & Sales Inc ....E.... 586 757-6500
Warren *(G-17262)*

3799 Transportation Eqpt, NEC

Bedford Machinery Inc ....G.... 734 848-4980
Erie *(G-4801)*
Boat Customs Trailers LLC ....G.... 517 712-3512
Caledonia *(G-2291)*
Chassis Shop Prfmce Pdts Inc ....G.... 231 873-3640
Mears *(G-10686)*
Christmas Sports Enterprise ....G.... 616 895-6238
Hudsonville *(G-8150)*
▼ **Composite Sign Products Inc** ....G.... 616 252-9110
Jenison *(G-8621)*
Detroit Wrecker Sales Llc ....G.... 313 835-8700
Detroit *(G-4005)*
Dexko Global Inc ....G.... 248 533-0029
Novi *(G-11867)*
Dragon Acquisition Intermediat ....G.... 248 692-4367
Novi *(G-11871)*
Dragon Acquisition Parent Inc ....G.... 248 692-4367
Novi *(G-11872)*
Ds Automotion LLC ....G.... 248 370-8950
Rochester *(G-13319)*
Great Lakes Lift Inc ....G.... 989 673-2109
Caro *(G-2469)*
Guiding Our Destiny Ministry ....G.... 313 212-9063
Detroit *(G-4108)*
H W Motor Homes Inc ....G.... 734 394-2000
Canton *(G-2382)*
▲ **Hensley Mfg Inc** ....F.... 810 653-3226
Davison *(G-3653)*
◆ **Horizon Global Americas Inc** ....C.... 734 656-3000
Plymouth *(G-12643)*
Hydro King Incorporated ....F.... 313 835-8700
Southfield *(G-14939)*
Jrm Industries Inc ....F.... 616 837-9758
Nunica *(G-12039)*
▼ **Justin Carriage Works LLC** ....G.... 517 852-9743
Nashville *(G-11458)*
K & J Enterprises Inc ....G.... 231 548-5222
Alanson *(G-111)*
K & K Racing LLC ....F.... 906 322-1276
Sault Sainte Marie *(G-14467)*
▲ **Liberty Products Inc** ....F.... 231 853-2323
Ravenna *(G-13123)*
Midwest Direct Transport Inc ....F.... 616 698-8900
Byron Center *(G-2201)*
Montrose Trailers Inc ....G.... 810 639-7431
Montrose *(G-11105)*

Nash Car Trailer Corporation ....F.... 269 673-5776
Allegan *(G-178)*
P2r Metal Fabrication Inc ....G.... 888 727-5587
Macomb *(G-10151)*
Phoenix Trailer & Body Company ....F.... 248 360-7184
Commerce Township *(G-3439)*
Phoenix Trailers LLC ....G.... 231 536-9760
East Jordan *(G-4642)*
Power Sports Ann Arbor LLC ....F.... 734 585-3300
Ann Arbor *(G-597)*
Precision Concepts Inc ....G.... 989 673-8555
Caro *(G-2475)*
Pro-Powersports ....G.... 734 457-0829
Monroe *(G-11063)*
Quadra Manufacturing Inc ....E.... 269 483-9633
White Pigeon *(G-17655)*
▼ **Rapidtek LLC** ....G.... 616 662-0954
Hudsonville *(G-8175)*
Rdz Racing Incorporated ....G.... 517 468-3254
Fowlerville *(G-5578)*
Rieke-Arminak Corp ....G.... 248 631-5450
Bloomfield Hills *(G-1795)*
Rocky Mountain Rv ....G.... 435 713-4242
Grand Rapids *(G-6833)*
▲ **RSM & Associates Co** ....F.... 517 750-9330
Jackson *(G-8566)*
Sled Shed Enterprises LLC ....G.... 517 783-5136
Jackson *(G-8573)*
◆ **Trimas Corporation** ....E.... 248 631-5450
Bloomfield Hills *(G-1807)*
US 223 Inland Marine LLC ....G.... 517 547-2628
Addison *(G-40)*
▲ **Viking Sales Inc** ....F.... 810 227-2222
Brighton *(G-2007)*
Windsor Mold USA Inc ....E.... 734 944-5080
Saline *(G-14421)*
Xpo Nlm ....G.... 866 251-3651
Southfield *(G-15068)*
Yanfeng US Automotive ....C.... 616 975-4000
Kentwood *(G-9035)*

38 MEASURING, ANALYZING AND CONTROLLING INSTRUMENTS; PHOTOGRAPHIC, MEDICAL AN

3812 Search, Detection, Navigation & Guidance Systs & Instrs

A2 Motus LLC ....G.... 734 780-7334
Ann Arbor *(G-336)*
Adept Defense LLC ....G.... 231 758-2792
Petoskey *(G-12439)*
Aerospace Mfg Svcs Inc ....G.... 269 697-4800
Buchanan *(G-2108)*
Aertech Machining & Mfg Inc ....E.... 517 782-4644
Jackson *(G-8375)*
AMF Defense ....G.... 586 684-3365
New Baltimore *(G-11479)*
Antrim Machine Products Inc ....E.... 231 587-9114
Mancelona *(G-10386)*
Applied Analytics Inc ....F.... 616 285-7810
Grand Rapids *(G-6173)*
◆ **Beaver Aerospace & Defense Inc** ....D.... 734 853-5003
Livonia *(G-9662)*
Bg Defense Co LLC ....F.... 616 710-0609
Grand Rapids *(G-6217)*
▼ **Burtek Enterprises Inc** ....C.... 586 421-8000
Chesterfield *(G-2749)*
Cammenga Company LLC ....G.... 313 914-7160
Dearborn *(G-3685)*
Charles Walton ....G.... 517 332-1842
East Lansing *(G-4654)*
Cheboygan Housing Commission ....G.... 231 627-7189
Cheboygan *(G-2679)*
Consoldted Rsource Imaging LLC ....E.... 616 735-2080
Grand Rapids *(G-6301)*
Defense Company of America ....G.... 248 763-6509
Rochester Hills *(G-13403)*
Defense Material Recapitalizat ....G.... 248 698-9333
White Lake *(G-17632)*
▲ **Demmer Corporation** ....C.... 517 321-3600
Lansing *(G-9217)*
Eaton Corporation ....F.... 517 787-8121
Ann Arbor *(G-430)*
Electronic Design & Packg Co ....F.... 734 591-9176
Livonia *(G-9724)*
Elite Tooling LLC ....G.... 269 383-9714
Kalamazoo *(G-8734)*

S I C

Employee Codes: A=Over 500 employees, B=251-500
C=101-250, D=51-100, E=20-50, F=10-19, G=3-9
2020 Harris Michigan
Industrial Directory
859

Envisics LLC G 248 802-4461
Rochester Hills *(G-13419)*

Equitable Engineering Co Inc E 248 689-9700
Troy *(G-16351)*

Flight Management Corporation G 517 327-0400
Lansing *(G-9229)*

G Defense Company B G 616 202-4500
Grand Rapids *(G-6428)*

GE Aviation Systems LLC E 616 224-6480
Grand Rapids *(G-6431)*

General Dynamics Corporation E 615 427-5768
Taylor *(G-15725)*

▲ Glassmaster Controls Co Inc E 269 382-2010
Kalamazoo *(G-8753)*

Grand Rapids Machine Repr Inc E 616 245-9102
Grand Rapids *(G-6459)*

Green Bridge Tech Intl Inc G 810 410-8177
Linden *(G-9591)*

◆ Harman Becker Auto Systems Inc B 248 785-2361
Novi *(G-11896)*

Herrmann Aerospace G 810 695-1758
Grand Blanc *(G-5969)*

His & Her Self Defense G 248 767-9085
Bloomfield Hills *(G-1773)*

Honeywell International Inc C 231 582-5686
Boyne City *(G-1822)*

Hytrol Manufacturing Inc E 734 261-8030
Jackson *(G-8468)*

Instrumented Sensor Tech Inc G 517 349-8487
Okemos *(G-12126)*

Interactive Aerial Inc G 231 715-1422
Traverse City *(G-16007)*

Kba Defense G 586 552-9268
Lakeville *(G-9178)*

Kings Self Defense LLC G 910 890-4322
Grand Rapids *(G-6584)*

Kva Engineering Inc G 616 745-7483
Grand Rapids *(G-6592)*

L3 Aviation Products Inc B 616 949-6600
Grand Rapids *(G-6593)*

L3harris Technologies Inc G 517 780-0695
Jackson *(G-8492)*

Leviathan Defense Group G 419 575-7792
Newport *(G-11589)*

Mercy Health Partners D 231 728-4032
Muskegon *(G-11373)*

Micromet Corp G 231 885-1047
Bloomfield Hills *(G-1783)*

▲ Mistequay Group Ltd F 989 752-7700
Saginaw *(G-14097)*

▲ N S International Ltd C 248 251-1600
Troy *(G-16519)*

Navistar Defense LLC G 248 680-7505
Madison Heights *(G-10315)*

Niles Precision Company C 269 683-0585
Niles *(G-11634)*

Novatron Corporation C 609 815-2100
Warren *(G-17174)*

Parker-Hannifin Corporation B 269 384-3459
Kalamazoo *(G-8843)*

Personal & Home Defense LLC G 517 596-3027
Munith *(G-11253)*

Ppi LLC G 248 841-7721
Troy *(G-16558)*

Preferred Avionics Instrs LLC F 800 521-5130
Howell *(G-8083)*

Quanenergy Systems Inc G 248 859-5587
Commerce Township *(G-3443)*

R A Miller Industries Inc C 888 845-9450
Grand Haven *(G-6067)*

Rapp & Son Inc C 734 283-1000
Wyandotte *(G-17971)*

Riverside Defense Training LLC G 231 825-2895
Lake City *(G-9096)*

Rs Defense Tactics G 248 693-2337
Lake Orion *(G-9157)*

Second Nature Self Defense G 734 775-6257
Flat Rock *(G-5363)*

Senscomp Inc E 734 953-4783
Livonia *(G-9925)*

Sierra 3 Defense LLC G 248 343-1066
Auburn Hills *(G-999)*

Slip Defense Inc G 248 366-4423
White Lake *(G-17638)*

Small Scale Defense G 616 238-2671
Holland *(G-7807)*

Sniffer Robotics LLC G 855 476-4333
Ann Arbor *(G-637)*

Split Second Defense LLC G 586 709-1385
Fraser *(G-5734)*

Star Lite International LLC G 248 546-4489
Oak Park *(G-12100)*

▲ Superior Fabrication Co LLC D 906 495-5634
Kincheloe *(G-9053)*

Swiss Precision Machining Inc F 586 677-7558
Macomb *(G-10165)*

Talkin Tackle LLC G 517 474-6241
Jackson *(G-8583)*

Teslir LLC G 248 644-5500
Bloomfield Hills *(G-1802)*

Tetradyn Ltd G 202 415-7295
Traverse City *(G-16120)*

▲ Thierica Inc D 616 458-1538
Grand Rapids *(G-6926)*

Truform Machine Inc E 517 782-8523
Jackson *(G-8594)*

Tyght Defense G 616 427-3760
Wyoming *(G-18037)*

Universal Magnetics Inc G 231 937-5555
Howard City *(G-8007)*

Utica Aerospace Inc F 586 598-9300
Chesterfield *(G-2852)*

Valeo Radar Systems Inc E 248 340-3126
Auburn Hills *(G-1044)*

Woodward Inc B 616 772-9171
Zeeland *(G-18197)*

3821 Laboratory Apparatus & Furniture

Absolute Nano LLC G 617 319-9617
Ann Arbor *(G-339)*

Accuri Cytometers Inc E 734 994-8000
Ann Arbor *(G-340)*

AG Davis Gage & Engrg Co E 586 977-9000
Sterling Heights *(G-15256)*

Air Master Systems Corp E 231 798-1111
Norton Shores *(G-11739)*

◆ Alpha Resources LLC E 269 465-5559
Stevensville *(G-15553)*

▲ Balance Technology Inc D 734 769-2100
Whitmore Lake *(G-17689)*

Bmc/Industrial Eductl Svcs Inc E 231 733-1206
Muskegon *(G-11280)*

Boyd Manufacturing LLC G 734 649-9765
Muskegon *(G-11284)*

Case Systems Inc C 989 496-9510
Midland *(G-10822)*

▲ Cmg America Inc G 810 686-3064
Clio *(G-3268)*

▲ Counter Reaction LLC G 248 624-7900
Wixom *(G-17790)*

▼ Coy Laboratory Products Inc E 734 433-9296
Grass Lake *(G-7086)*

Eberbach Corporation E 734 665-8877
Belleville *(G-1444)*

▲ Gelman Sciences Inc A 734 665-0651
Ann Arbor *(G-469)*

Gross Ventures Inc G 231 767-1301
Muskegon *(G-11341)*

Holland Community Hosp Aux Inc E 616 355-3926
Holland *(G-7670)*

ID Systems Inc F 231 799-8760
Norton Shores *(G-11761)*

Impert Industries Inc G 269 694-2727
Otsego *(G-12241)*

Jade Scientific Inc F 734 207-3775
Westland *(G-17572)*

◆ Leco Corporation B 269 983-5531
Saint Joseph *(G-14324)*

Leco Corporation F 269 982-2230
Saint Joseph *(G-14325)*

M2 Scientifics LLC G 616 379-9080
Holland *(G-7728)*

Marketlab Inc D 866 237-3722
Caledonia *(G-2307)*

▲ Metal Arc Inc E 231 865-3111
Muskegon *(G-11375)*

Multi-Lab LLC F 616 846-6990
Spring Lake *(G-15165)*

Peerless Waste Solutions LLC G 616 355-2800
Holland *(G-7768)*

▲ Plas-Labs Incorporated E 517 372-7178
Lansing *(G-9259)*

▼ Rankin Biomedical Corporation F 248 625-4104
Holly *(G-7893)*

Security Steelcraft Corp E 231 733-1101
Muskegon *(G-11420)*

Sleep Diagnosis Northern Mich G 231 935-9275
Traverse City *(G-16107)*

▲ Snow Machines Incorporated E 989 631-6091
Midland *(G-10917)*

Southwest Mich Innovation Ctr G 269 353-1823
Kalamazoo *(G-8893)*

▲ Symbiote Inc E 616 772-1790
Zeeland *(G-18189)*

Teclab Inc E 269 372-6000
Kalamazoo *(G-8909)*

Total Toxicology Labs LLC G 248 352-7171
Southfield *(G-15047)*

3822 Automatic Temperature Controls

Ademco Inc G 586 759-1455
Warren *(G-16918)*

Ademco Inc E 248 926-5510
Wixom *(G-17752)*

AMF-Nano Corporation G 734 726-0148
Ann Arbor *(G-353)*

Astra Associates Inc E 586 254-6500
Sterling Heights *(G-15266)*

▲ Century Instrument Company E 734 427-0340
Livonia *(G-9681)*

Commonwealth Associates Inc C 517 788-3000
Jackson *(G-8416)*

Control Solutions Inc D 616 247-9422
Byron Center *(G-2183)*

Control Systems & Service G 616 887-2738
Sparta *(G-15093)*

Crewbotiq LLC E 248 939-4229
Troy *(G-16287)*

Easi LLC E 248 712-2750
Troy *(G-16334)*

Eaton Corporation A 248 226-6347
Southfield *(G-14893)*

Edmore Tool & Grinding Inc E 989 427-3790
Edmore *(G-4750)*

Energy Control Solutions Inc G 810 735-2800
Fenton *(G-5202)*

Energy Development Assoc LLC G 313 354-2644
Dearborn *(G-3701)*

Enertemp Inc E 616 243-2752
Grand Rapids *(G-6378)*

▲ Hart & Cooley Inc C 616 656-8200
Grand Rapids *(G-6495)*

◆ Hella Corporate Center USA Inc E 586 232-4788
Northville *(G-11697)*

Hydronix Ltd G 231 439-5000
Harbor Springs *(G-7284)*

Industrial Temperature Control G 734 451-8740
Canton *(G-2384)*

Inland Vapor of Michigan LLC F 734 237-4389
Garden City *(G-5828)*

Integrated Building Solutions F 616 889-3070
Chesaning *(G-2724)*

James G Gallagher G 989 832-3458
Midland *(G-10874)*

Johnson Controls Inc D 248 276-6000
Auburn Hills *(G-920)*

Kanawha Scales & Systems Inc F 734 947-4030
Romulus *(G-13695)*

Lyman Thornton G 248 762-8433
Wixom *(G-17847)*

Maxitrol Company C 269 432-3291
Colon *(G-3374)*

▲ Maxitrol Company D 248 356-1400
Southfield *(G-14974)*

▲ Mercury Displacement Inds Inc D 269 663-8574
Edwardsburg *(G-4766)*

Peak Industries Co Inc D 313 846-8666
Dearborn *(G-3747)*

▲ Precision Speed Equipment Inc C 269 651-4303
Sturgis *(G-15631)*

▲ Pyro Service Company G 248 547-2552
Madison Heights *(G-10340)*

Refrigerant Services LLC G 248 586-6988
New Hudson *(G-11552)*

Releaf Michigan Inc G 734 662-6350
Ann Arbor *(G-619)*

Rhombus Energy Solutions Inc G 313 406-3292
Dearborn *(G-3753)*

Seelye Equipment Specialist G 231 547-9430
Charlevoix *(G-2630)*

Siemens Industry Inc D 269 927-3591
Benton Harbor *(G-1547)*

Softaire Diffusers Inc G 810 730-1668
Linden *(G-9596)*

Solidica Inc F 734 222-4680
Ann Arbor *(G-639)*

Swat Environmental Inc E 517 322-2999
Lansing *(G-9427)*

System Controls Inc E 734 427-0440
Livonia *(G-9951)*

SIC SECTION
38 MEASURING, ANALYZING AND CONTROLLING INSTRUMENTS; PHOTOGRAPHIC, MEDICAL AN

◆ T E Technology Inc ....E 231 929-3966
  Traverse City *(G-16118)*
Taylor Controls Inc ....F 269 637-8521
  South Haven *(G-14777)*
Vibration Controls Tech LLC ....G 248 822-8010
  Troy *(G-16684)*
Warner Instruments ....G 616 843-5342
  Grand Haven *(G-6096)*

3823 Indl Instruments For Meas, Display & Control

▲ A&D Technology Inc ....D 734 973-1111
  Ann Arbor *(G-333)*
ABB Enterprise Software Inc ....D 248 471-0888
  Farmington Hills *(G-4917)*
ABB Enterprise Software Inc ....D 313 965-8900
  Detroit *(G-3837)*
Acromag Incorporated ....D 248 624-1541
  Wixom *(G-17751)*
ADS LLC ....G 248 740-9593
  Troy *(G-16168)*
Advance Engineering Company ....D 313 537-3500
  Canton *(G-2344)*
Advanced Integrated Mfg ....F 586 439-0300
  Fraser *(G-5613)*
AG Davis Gage & Engrg Co ....E 586 977-9000
  Sterling Heights *(G-15256)*
Air Pump Valve Corporation ....G 810 655-6444
  Swartz Creek *(G-15660)*
Airflow Sciences Equipment LLC ......F 734 525-0300
  Livonia *(G-9633)*
Allrout Inc ....G 616 748-7696
  Zeeland *(G-18111)*
Altair Systems Inc ....F 248 668-0116
  Wixom *(G-17758)*
Astra Associates Inc ....E 586 254-6500
  Sterling Heights *(G-15266)*
Ateq Tpms Tools Lc ....F 734 838-3104
  Livonia *(G-9656)*
Atmo-Seal Inc ....G 248 528-9640
  Troy *(G-16227)*
Auric Enterprises Inc ....G 231 882-7251
  Beulah *(G-1608)*
Avl Michigan Holding Corp ....E 734 414-9600
  Plymouth *(G-12578)*
▲ Avl Test Systems Inc ....C 734 414-9600
  Plymouth *(G-12580)*
▲ Balance Technology Inc ....D 734 769-2100
  Whitmore Lake *(G-17689)*
Banner Engineering & Sales Inc ....F 989 755-0584
  Saginaw *(G-14000)*
Beet LLC ....F 248 432-0052
  Plymouth *(G-12584)*
Benny Gage Inc ....E 734 455-3080
  Wixom *(G-17773)*
Binsfeld Engineering Inc ....F 231 334-4383
  Maple City *(G-10460)*
Bisbee Infrared Services Inc ....G 517 787-4620
  Jackson *(G-8391)*
Broadteq Incorporated ....G 248 794-9323
  Waterford *(G-17327)*
◆ Burke E Porter Machinery Co ......C 616 234-1200
  Grand Rapids *(G-6243)*
◆ C E C Controls Company Inc ......D 586 779-0222
  Warren *(G-16972)*
C E C Controls Company Inc ....G 248 926-5701
  Wixom *(G-17780)*
Clarkson Controls & Eqp Co ....G 248 380-9915
  Novi *(G-11850)*
Complete Auto-Mation Inc ....D 248 693-0500
  Lake Orion *(G-9131)*
◆ Custom Valve Concepts Inc ....E 248 597-8999
  Madison Heights *(G-10225)*
D & C Investment Group Inc ....F 734 994-0591
  Ann Arbor *(G-410)*
▲ D2t America Inc ....F 248 680-9001
  Rochester Hills *(G-13400)*
Debron Industrial Elec Inc ....E 248 588-7220
  Troy *(G-16300)*
Dexter Research Center Inc ....D 734 426-3921
  Dexter *(G-4488)*
Digital Performance Tech ....F 877 983-4230
  Troy *(G-16320)*
Dura Thread Gage Inc ....F 248 545-2890
  Madison Heights *(G-10236)*
Eagle Engineering & Supply Co ....E 989 356-4526
  Alpena *(G-286)*
◆ Electronic Apps Speclsts Inc ......G 248 491-4988
  Milford *(G-10963)*

Emerson Electric Co ....E 616 846-3950
  Grand Haven *(G-6014)*
Emerson Electric Co ....E 586 268-3104
  Sterling Heights *(G-15331)*
Emerson Electric Co ....G 734 420-0832
  Plymouth *(G-12617)*
Emerson Process Management ....C 313 874-0860
  Detroit *(G-4037)*
Emitted Energy Inc ....F 855 752-3347
  Sterling Heights *(G-15332)*
Endlich Studios LLC ....G 248 524-9671
  Troy *(G-16344)*
Engineered Combustn Systems LLC .G 248 549-1703
  Royal Oak *(G-13925)*
▲ Fannon Products LLC ....F 810 794-2000
  Algonac *(G-143)*
Flow-Rite Controls Ltd ....E 616 583-1700
  Byron Center *(G-2191)*
Forefront Control Systems LLC ....G 616 796-3495
  Holland *(G-7634)*
Forrest Brothers Inc ....C 989 356-4011
  Gaylord *(G-5859)*
Geotech Environmental Eqp Inc ....G 517 655-5616
  Williamston *(G-17730)*
Gic LLC ....F 231 237-7000
  Charlevoix *(G-2616)*
Gordinier Electronics Corp ....E 586 778-0426
  Roseville *(G-13809)*
▲ H O Trerice Co Inc ....E 248 399-8000
  Oak Park *(G-12072)*
Harvest Energy Inc ....F 269 838-4595
  Grand Rapids *(G-6496)*
Henkel US Operations Corp ....B 248 588-1082
  Madison Heights *(G-10266)*
Henshaw Inc ....F 586 752-0700
  Romeo *(G-13629)*
Hexagon Metrology Inc ....D 248 662-1740
  Wixom *(G-17826)*
◆ Hines Corporation ....F 231 799-6240
  Norton Shores *(G-11812)*
◆ Hines Industries Inc ....E 734 769-2300
  Ann Arbor *(G-492)*
Hitec Sensor Developments Inc ....E 313 506-2460
  Plymouth *(G-12640)*
Honeywell International Inc ....C 231 582-5686
  Boyne City *(G-1822)*
Horiba Instruments Inc ....D 734 213-6555
  Ann Arbor *(G-495)*
Horiba Instruments Inc ....D 248 689-9000
  Troy *(G-16400)*
▲ Howard Miller Company ....B 616 772-9131
  Zeeland *(G-18154)*
IMC Dataworks LLC ....G 248 356-4311
  Novi *(G-11905)*
Incoe Corporation ....C 248 616-0220
  Auburn Hills *(G-910)*
Industrial Temperature Control ....F 734 451-8740
  Canton *(G-2384)*
Infrared Telemetrics Inc ....F 906 482-0012
  Hancock *(G-7252)*
Innovative Support Svcs Inc ....E 248 585-3600
  Troy *(G-16418)*
▲ Integral Vision Inc ....G 248 668-9230
  Wixom *(G-17835)*
Integrated Marketing Svcs LLC ....F 248 625-7444
  Pontiac *(G-12836)*
▼ Integrated Security Corp ....F 248 624-0700
  Novi *(G-11906)*
International Temperature Ctrl ....G 989 876-8075
  Au Gres *(G-746)*
Jay/Enn Corporation ....D 248 588-2393
  Troy *(G-16433)*
◆ Jcp LLC ....E 989 754-7496
  Saginaw *(G-14066)*
Jdl Enterprises Inc ....F 586 977-8863
  Sterling Heights *(G-15380)*
K-TEC Systems Inc ....F 248 414-4100
  Ferndale *(G-5296)*
▼ Kaltec Scientific Inc ....G 248 349-8100
  Novi *(G-11913)*
Kubica Corp ....F 248 344-7750
  Novi *(G-11922)*
Labortrio Elttrofisico USA Inc ....G 248 340-7040
  Lake Orion *(G-9143)*
Leader Corporation ....E 586 566-7114
  Shelby Township *(G-14624)*
◆ Leco Corporation ....B 269 983-5531
  Saint Joseph *(G-14324)*
Leco Corporation ....F 269 982-2230
  Saint Joseph *(G-14325)*

Maes Tool & Die Co Inc ....F 517 750-3131
  Jackson *(G-8504)*
Mahle Powertrain LLC ....D 248 305-8200
  Farmington Hills *(G-5056)*
Martel Tool Corporation ....F 313 278-2420
  Allen Park *(G-202)*
Maxitrol Company ....E 517 486-2820
  Blissfield *(G-1719)*
▲ Maxitrol Company ....D 248 356-1400
  Southfield *(G-14974)*
Metric Hydraulic Components LLC ...F 586 786-6990
  Shelby Township *(G-14640)*
▲ Midwest Timer Service Inc ....D 269 849-2800
  Benton Harbor *(G-1530)*
▲ Montague Latch Company ....F 810 687-4242
  Clio *(G-3278)*
Mycrona Inc ....F 734 453-9348
  Plymouth *(G-12697)*
Norcross Viscosity Controls ....G 586 336-0700
  Washington *(G-17308)*
Nordson Corporation ....D 734 459-8600
  Wixom *(G-17866)*
Oden Machinery Inc ....G 716 874-3000
  Ludington *(G-10076)*
Oflow-Rite Controls Ltd ....D 616 583-1700
  Byron Center *(G-2205)*
Online Engineering Inc ....F 906 341-0090
  Manistique *(G-10445)*
Parjana Distribution LLC ....G 313 915-5406
  Detroit *(G-4290)*
◆ Patriot Sensors & Contrls Corp ...D 248 435-0700
  Clawson *(G-2983)*
Patriot Sensors & Contrls Corp ....D 810 378-5511
  Peck *(G-12420)*
▲ Peaker Services Inc ....D 248 437-4174
  Brighton *(G-1976)*
◆ Peaktronics Inc ....G 248 542-5640
  Clawson *(G-2984)*
Perceptive Controls Inc ....E 269 685-3040
  Plainwell *(G-12535)*
Perpetual Measurement Inc ....D 248 343-2952
  Waterford *(G-17368)*
Pierburg Instruments ....C 734 414-9600
  Plymouth *(G-12715)*
Piping Components Inc ....G 313 382-6400
  Melvindale *(G-10705)*
Precise Finishing Systems Inc ....E 517 552-9200
  Howell *(G-8081)*
Ptspower LLC ....F 734 268-6076
  Pinckney *(G-12503)*
▲ Pyro Service Company ....G 248 547-2552
  Madison Heights *(G-10340)*
▲ QEd Envmtl Systems Inc ....D 734 995-2547
  Dexter *(G-4506)*
R Concepts Incorporated ....G 810 632-4857
  Howell *(G-8086)*
Rjg Technologies Inc ....C 231 947-3111
  Traverse City *(G-16096)*
Service & Technical Assoc LLC ....F 248 233-3761
  Troy *(G-16597)*
▲ Sinto America Inc ....E 517 371-2460
  Lansing *(G-9323)*
Smarteye Incorporated ....F 248 853-4495
  Rochester Hills *(G-13515)*
Ssi Technology Inc ....D 248 582-0600
  Sterling Heights *(G-15507)*
Stewart Metrology LLC ....G 269 660-9290
  Battle Creek *(G-1254)*
Superior Controls Inc ....C 734 454-0500
  Plymouth *(G-12763)*
Taylor Controls Inc ....F 269 637-8521
  South Haven *(G-14777)*
Tech Tool Supply LLC ....G 734 207-7700
  Plymouth *(G-12766)*
Temprel Inc ....E 231 582-6585
  Boyne City *(G-1835)*
Terametrix LLC ....A 540 769-8430
  Ann Arbor *(G-664)*
Testron Incorporated ....F 734 513-6820
  Livonia *(G-9955)*
Therm-O-Disc Incorporated ....B 231 799-4100
  Norton Shores *(G-11801)*
Therm-O-Disc Midwest Inc ....F 231 799-4100
  Norton Shores *(G-11802)*
Thermo Arl US Inc ....F 313 336-3901
  Dearborn *(G-3764)*
Toledo Molding & Die Inc ....G 734 233-6338
  Plymouth *(G-12773)*
Transology Associates ....G 517 694-8645
  East Lansing *(G-4680)*

Employee Codes: A=Over 500 employees, B=251-500
C=101-250, D=51-100, E=20-50, F=10-19, G=3-9

38 MEASURING, ANALYZING AND CONTROLLING INSTRUMENTS; PHOTOGRAPHIC, MEDICAL AN

Turbine Tool & Gage Inc ....F 734 427-2270
Livonia (G-9978)
Universal Flow Monitors Inc ....E 248 542-9635
Hazel Park (G-7457)
Warner Instruments ....G 616 843-5342
Grand Haven (G-6096)
◆ Welding Technology Corp ....F 248 477-3900
Farmington Hills (G-5151)
Welform Electrodes Inc ....D 586 755-1184
Warren (G-17292)
▲ X-Rite Incorporated ....C 616 803-2100
Grand Rapids (G-7006)

3824 Fluid Meters & Counters

Advance Tech Solutions LLC ....G 989 928-1806
Saginaw (G-13992)
Advanced Integrated Mfg ....F 586 439-0300
Fraser (G-5613)
▲ Carlon Meter Company Inc ....G 616 842-0420
Grand Haven (G-6000)
▲ Clark Brothers Instrument Co ....F 586 781-7000
Shelby Township (G-14563)
Dearborn Collision Service Inc ....G 734 455-3299
Northville (G-11687)
Ernest Industries Acquisition, ...E 734 595-9500
Westland (G-17554)
▲ Essex Brass Corporation ....F 586 757-8200
Warren (G-17020)
L Thompson Co LLC ....F 616 844-1135
Grand Haven (G-6044)
▲ Medallion Instrumentation ....C 616 847-3700
Spring Lake (G-15161)
Micro-Systems Inc ....G 616 481-1601
Norton Shores (G-11774)
Modular Data Systems Inc ....F 586 739-5870
Shelby Township (G-14645)
▲ New Vintage Usa LLC ....G 248 259-4964
Oak Park (G-12089)
Northville Circuits Inc ....G 248 853-3232
Rochester Hills (G-13484)
Pierburg Instruments ....C 734 414-9600
Plymouth (G-12715)
▲ Prestolite Electric LLC ....G 248 313-3807
Novi (G-11978)
Rap Electronics & Machines ....F 616 846-1437
Grand Haven (G-6068)
Re-Sol LLC ....F 248 270-7777
Auburn Hills (G-988)
▼ Royal Design & Manufacturing ....D 248 588-0110
Madison Heights (G-10346)
SLC Meter LLC ....F 248 625-0667
Pontiac (G-12867)
▲ Southern Auto Wholesalers Inc ....F 248 335-5555
Pontiac (G-12869)
▲ U S Speedo Inc ....F 810 244-0909
Flint (G-5516)
Woodward Inc ....B 616 772-9171
Zeeland (G-18197)

3825 Instrs For Measuring & Testing Electricity

▲ A&D Technology Inc ....D 734 973-1111
Ann Arbor (G-333)
Abtech Installation & Svc Inc ....E 800 548-2381
Southgate (G-15073)
Accurate Technologies Inc ....D 248 848-9200
Novi (G-11823)
Advanced Systems & Contrls Inc ....E 586 992-9684
Macomb (G-10103)
Aerospace America Inc ....E 989 684-2121
Bay City (G-1273)
AG Davis Gage & Engrg Co ....E 586 977-9000
Sterling Heights (G-15256)
API / Inmet Inc ....C 734 426-5553
Ann Arbor (G-360)
Ats Assembly and Test Inc ....B 937 222-3030
Wixom (G-17766)
Auric Enterprises Inc ....G 231 882-7251
Beulah (G-1608)
▲ Balance Technology Inc ....D 734 769-2100
Whitmore Lake (G-17689)
Benesh Corporation ....E 734 244-4143
Monroe (G-11023)
Brothers Mead 3 LLC ....G 269 883-6241
Battle Creek (G-1158)
◆ Burke E Porter Machinery Co ....C 616 234-1200
Grand Rapids (G-6243)
▲ Classic Instruments Inc ....G 231 582-0461
Boyne City (G-1820)
Cobham McRlctrnic Slutions Inc ....G 734 426-1230
Ann Arbor (G-403)
Concept Technology Inc ....E 248 765-0100
Birmingham (G-1678)
CPR III Inc ....F 248 652-2900
Rochester (G-13318)
Creative Power Systems Inc ....E 313 961-2460
Detroit (G-3954)
CSM Products Inc ....F 248 836-4995
Auburn Hills (G-830)
▲ D2t America Inc ....F 248 680-9001
Rochester Hills (G-13400)
Debron Industrial Elec Inc ....F 248 588-7220
Troy (G-16300)
Design & Test Technology Inc ....G 734 665-4111
Dexter (G-4484)
Design & Test Technology Inc ....F 734 665-4316
Ann Arbor (G-416)
Diagnostic Systems Association ....F 269 544-9000
Kalamazoo (G-8725)
Dynamic Auto Test Engineering ....G 269 342-1334
Portage (G-12991)
▼ Eagile Incorporated ....F 616 243-1200
Grand Rapids (G-6364)
▲ Electrodynamics Inc ....G 734 422-5420
Livonia (G-9723)
◆ Electronic Apps Speclsts Inc ....C 248 491-4988
Milford (G-10963)
Elmet LLC ....G 248 473-2924
Novi (G-11882)
Esirpal Inc ....G 586 337-7848
Macomb (G-10120)
Ezm LLC ....G 248 438-6570
Novi (G-11886)
Global Electronics Limited ....E 248 353-0100
Bloomfield Hills (G-1770)
▲ Greening Associates Inc ....E 313 366-7160
Detroit (G-4105)
Hale Manufacturing Inc ....G 231 529-6271
Alanson (G-110)
Hole Industries Incorporated ....G 517 548-4229
Howell (G-8050)
Honeywell International Inc ....C 231 582-5686
Boyne City (G-1822)
Horiba Instruments Inc ....D 734 213-6555
Ann Arbor (G-495)
Ideal Gas Inc ....G 734 365-7192
Melvindale (G-10700)
Industrial Optical Measurement ....G 734 975-0436
Ann Arbor (G-504)
Infrared Telemetrics Inc ....F 906 482-0012
Hancock (G-7252)
Instrumented Sensor Tech Inc ....G 517 349-8487
Okemos (G-12126)
Ix Innovations LLC ....G
Ann Arbor (G-508)
Jodon Engineering Assoc Inc ....F 734 761-4044
Ann Arbor (G-511)
◆ Leco Corporation ....B 269 983-5531
Saint Joseph (G-14324)
Leco Corporation ....F 269 982-2230
Saint Joseph (G-14325)
Mahle Powertrain Inc ....D 248 305-8200
Farmington Hills (G-5056)
Medical Infrmtics Slutions LLC ....G 248 851-3124
Bloomfield Hills (G-1781)
▲ Meiden America Inc ....F 734 459-1781
Northville (G-11709)
Merc-O-Tronic Instruments Corp ....F 586 894-9529
Almont (G-263)
Michigan Scientific Corp ....D 231 547-5511
Charlevoix (G-2620)
▲ Nadex of America Corporation ....E 248 477-3900
Farmington Hills (G-5075)
Nanorete Inc ....G 517 336-4680
Lansing (G-9404)
Netwave ....F 586 263-4469
Macomb (G-10148)
Network Machinery Inc ....G 586 992-2459
Shelby Township (G-14651)
Opteos Inc ....G 734 929-3333
Ann Arbor (G-585)
▲ Orion Test Systems Inc ....D 248 373-9097
Auburn Hills (G-967)
▲ Ptm-Electronics Inc ....F 248 987-4446
Farmington Hills (G-5106)
Racelogic USA Corporation ....F 248 994-9050
Farmington Hills (G-5112)
Ram Meter Inc ....F 248 362-0990
Royal Oak (G-13962)
S and S Enterprise LLC ....G 989 894-7002
Bay City (G-1353)
Sciemetric Inc ....F 248 509-2209
Rochester Hills (G-13512)
Seneca Enterprises LLC ....G 231 943-1171
Traverse City (G-16100)
Servo Innovations LLC ....G 269 792-9279
Wayland (G-17416)
Smart Label Solutions LLC ....G 800 996-7343
Howell (G-8099)
◆ Srg Global Coatings Inc ....C 248 509-1100
Troy (G-16618)
Standard Electric Company ....G 906 774-4455
Kingsford (G-9067)
Swain Meter Company ....G 989 773-3700
Farwell (G-5166)
▲ Tengam Engineering Inc ....G 269 694-9466
Otsego (G-12256)
Teradyne Inc ....C 313 425-3900
Allen Park (G-211)
Test Products Incorporated ....E 586 997-9600
Sterling Heights (G-15523)
Testron Incorporated ....F 734 513-6820
Livonia (G-9955)
Volta Power Systems LLC ....G 616 226-4224
Holland (G-7850)
VSR Technologies Inc ....F 734 425-7172
Livonia (G-9992)

3826 Analytical Instruments

Alliance Hni LLC ....D 989 729-2804
Owosso (G-12277)
Auric Enterprises Inc ....G 231 882-7251
Beulah (G-1608)
Authentic 3d ....G 248 469-8809
Bingham Farms (G-1649)
Best Products Inc ....E 313 538-7414
Redford (G-13148)
◆ Burke E Porter Machinery Co ....C 616 234-1200
Grand Rapids (G-6243)
Carl Zeiss Microscopy LLC ....F 248 486-7600
Brighton (G-1898)
Celsee Diagnostics Inc ....E 866 748-1448
Ann Arbor (G-397)
Clark-Mxr Inc ....E 734 426-2803
Dexter (G-4481)
Espec Corp ....E 616 896-6100
Hudsonville (G-8156)
Essen Instruments Inc ....D 734 769-1600
Ann Arbor (G-449)
▲ Hanse Environmental Inc ....F 269 673-8638
Allegan (G-164)
Hiden Analytical Inc ....E 734 542-6666
Livonia (G-9769)
Horiba Instruments Inc ....D 734 213-6555
Ann Arbor (G-495)
▲ Hti Usa Inc ....E 248 358-5533
Farmington (G-4900)
Jade Scientific Inc ....F 734 207-3775
Westland (G-17572)
Jodon Engineering Assoc Inc ....F 734 761-4044
Ann Arbor (G-511)
Kuka Assembly and Test Corp ....D 810 593-0350
Fenton (G-5224)
Lake Erie Med Surgical Sup Inc ....E 734 847-3847
Temperance (G-15833)
◆ Leco Corporation ....B 269 983-5531
Saint Joseph (G-14324)
Leco Corporation ....F 269 982-2230
Saint Joseph (G-14325)
Lumigen Inc ....E 248 351-5600
Southfield (G-14970)
Marshall Ryerson Co ....F 616 299-1751
Grand Rapids (G-6645)
▲ Mectron Engineering Co Inc ....E 734 944-8777
Saline (G-14400)
Neptech Inc ....E 810 225-2222
Highland (G-7498)
Pioneer Technologies Corp ....E 702 806-3152
Fremont (G-5782)
Proto Manufacturing Inc ....E 734 946-0974
Taylor (G-15759)
◆ Q-Photonics LLC ....G 734 477-0133
Ann Arbor (G-608)
▲ QEd Envmtl Systems Inc ....D 734 995-2547
Dexter (G-4506)
▲ R H K Technology Inc ....E 248 577-5426
Troy (G-16574)
◆ Richard-Allan Scientific Co ....E 269 544-5600
Kalamazoo (G-8870)

Rigaku Innovative Tech Inc....C.... 248 232-6400
Auburn Hills (G-991)
◆ Srg Global Coatings Inc....C.... 248 509-1100
Troy (G-16618)
Thermo Arl US Inc....F.... 313 336-3901
Dearborn (G-3764)
Thermo Fisher Scientific Inc....G.... 231 932-0242
Traverse City (G-16121)
Thermo Fisher Scientific Inc....F.... 800 346-4364
Portage (G-13049)
Thermo Fisher Scientific Inc....B.... 269 544-5600
Kalamazoo (G-8911)
Thermo Fisher Scientific Inc....F.... 734 662-4117
Ann Arbor (G-669)
Thermo Shandon Inc....G.... 269 544-7500
Kalamazoo (G-8912)
▲ TS Enterprise Associates Inc....F.... 248 348-2963
Northville (G-11732)
Venturedyne Ltd....B.... 616 392-6550
Holland (G-7847)
Venturedyne Ltd....E.... 616 392-1491
Holland (G-7846)
X-Ray and Specialty Instrs....G.... 734 485-6300
Ypsilanti (G-18108)
▲ X-Rite Incorporated....C.... 616 803-2100
Grand Rapids (G-7006)

3827 Optical Instruments

Berner Scientific Inc....G.... 248 253-0077
Dexter (G-4477)
Browe Inc....G.... 248 877-3800
Madison Heights (G-10207)
Carl Zeiss Indus Metrology LLC....E.... 248 486-2670
Brighton (G-1897)
Clark-Mxr Inc....E.... 734 426-2803
Dexter (G-4481)
Contour Metrological & Mfg Inc....F.... 248 273-1111
Troy (G-16279)
▲ Crl Inc....E.... 906 428-3710
Gladstone (G-5910)
Data Optics Inc....G.... 734 483-8228
Ypsilanti (G-18064)
Diagnostic Instruments Inc....E.... 586 731-6000
Sterling Heights (G-15316)
▲ Electro-Optics Technology Inc....D.... 231 935-4044
Traverse City (G-15961)
Eotech Inc....G.... 734 741-8868
Ann Arbor (G-446)
Eyewear Detroit Company....G.... 248 396-2214
Clarkston (G-2920)
First Optometry Lab....G.... 248 546-1300
Madison Heights (G-10254)
▲ General Dynamics Glbl IMG Tech....A.... 248 293-2929
Rochester Hills (G-13432)
General Dynamics Mission....A.... 530 271-2500
Rochester Hills (G-13434)
▲ General Scientific Corporation....E.... 734 996-9200
Ann Arbor (G-471)
Genx Corporation....G.... 269 341-4242
Kalamazoo (G-8751)
▲ Integral Vision Inc....G.... 248 668-9230
Wixom (G-17835)
◆ Jenoptik Automotive N Amer LLC....C.... 248 853-5888
Rochester Hills (G-13453)
▲ Kaiser Optical Systems Inc....D.... 734 665-8083
Ann Arbor (G-515)
Kwik-Site Corporation....F.... 734 326-1500
Wayne (G-17434)
L-3 Communications Eotech Inc....C.... 734 741-8868
Ann Arbor (G-522)
◆ Leapers Inc....E.... 734 542-1500
Livonia (G-9805)
Lumenflow Corp....G.... 269 795-9007
Grand Rapids (G-6636)
◆ Magna Mirrors America Inc....E.... 616 786-5120
Grand Rapids (G-6640)
Magna Mirrors America Inc....G.... 616 786-7000
Holland (G-7734)
Magna Mirrors America Inc....D.... 616 786-7300
Holland (G-7735)
Magna Mirrors America Inc....C.... 616 942-0163
Newaygo (G-11573)
Meridian Mechatronics LLC....G.... 517 447-4587
Deerfield (G-3813)
Michigan Development Corp....C.... 734 302-4600
Ann Arbor (G-554)
Optec Inc....F.... 616 897-9351
Lowell (G-10039)
▲ Perceptron Inc....C.... 734 414-6100
Plymouth (G-12712)
Perform3-D LLC....G.... 734 604-4100
Ann Arbor (G-591)
Phoenix Imaging Inc....G.... 248 476-4578
Farmington (G-4907)
▼ Phoenix Imaging Inc....G.... 248 476-4200
Livonia (G-9888)
Planewave Instruments Inc....G.... 310 639-1662
Adrian (G-84)
Seneca Enterprises LLC....G.... 231 943-1171
Traverse City (G-16100)
Trijicon Inc....C.... 248 960-7700
Wixom (G-17920)
Visioncraft....G.... 586 949-6540
Chesterfield (G-2855)
Visotek Inc....F.... 734 427-4800
Livonia (G-9990)
Visual Precision Inc....G.... 248 546-7984
Madison Heights (G-10378)
▼ Williams Gun Sight Company....D.... 800 530-9028
Davison (G-3666)
▲ X-Rite Incorporated....C.... 616 803-2100
Grand Rapids (G-7006)

3829 Measuring & Controlling Devices, NEC

2 Brothers Holdings LLC....G.... 517 487-3900
Lansing (G-9330)
A S I Instruments Inc....G.... 586 756-1222
Warren (G-16909)
▲ A&D Technology Inc....D.... 734 973-1111
Ann Arbor (G-333)
Abletech Industries LLC....G.... 734 677-2420
Dexter (G-4471)
Acromag Incorporated....D.... 248 624-1541
Wixom (G-17751)
Adcole Corporation....G.... 508 485-9100
Orion (G-12172)
Advanced Systems & Contrls Inc....E.... 586 992-9684
Macomb (G-10103)
Ambiance LLC....G.... 269 657-6027
Paw Paw (G-12396)
Analytical Process Systems Inc....E.... 248 393-0700
Auburn Hills (G-770)
▲ Apollo America Inc....D.... 248 332-3900
Auburn Hills (G-776)
Assay Designs Inc....E.... 734 214-0923
Ann Arbor (G-370)
Astra Associates Inc....E.... 586 254-6500
Sterling Heights (G-15266)
▲ Ateq Corporation....F.... 734 838-3100
Livonia (G-9655)
Ats Assembly and Test Inc....D.... 734 266-4713
Livonia (G-9657)
Auric Enterprises Inc....G.... 231 882-7251
Beulah (G-1608)
Avidhrt Inc....G.... 517 214-9041
Okemos (G-12115)
▲ Avl Test Systems Inc....C.... 734 414-9600
Plymouth (G-12580)
▲ Balance Technology Inc....D.... 734 769-2100
Whitmore Lake (G-17689)
Beet LLC....F.... 248 432-0052
Plymouth (G-12584)
Benesh Corporation....E.... 734 244-4143
Monroe (G-11023)
Biosan Laboratories Inc....F.... 586 755-8970
Warren (G-16961)
Bonal International Inc....F.... 248 582-0900
Royal Oak (G-13909)
Bonal Technologies Inc....F.... 248 582-0900
Royal Oak (G-13910)
Bti Measurement Tstg Svcs LLC....G.... 734 769-2100
Whitmore Lake (G-17691)
Bti Measurement Tstg Svcs LLC....G.... 734 769-2100
Dexter (G-4479)
Calhoun County Med Care Fcilty....E.... 269 962-5458
Battle Creek (G-1162)
Cammenga & Associates LLC....E.... 313 914-7160
Dearborn (G-3684)
Clark Instrument Inc....F.... 248 669-3100
Novi (G-11849)
◆ Comau LLC....B.... 248 353-8888
Southfield (G-14871)
Control Power-Reliance LLC....G.... 248 583-1020
Troy (G-16280)
▲ Conway-Cleveland Corp....G.... 616 458-0056
Grand Rapids (G-6309)
Creative Engineering Inc....G.... 734 996-5900
Ann Arbor (G-408)
▼ Crippen Manufacturing Company....E.... 989 681-4323
Saint Louis (G-14361)
D & N Gage Inc....F.... 586 336-2110
Romeo (G-13627)
▲ D2t America Inc....F.... 248 680-9001
Rochester Hills (G-13400)
Data Optics Inc....G.... 734 483-8228
Ypsilanti (G-18064)
Demmer Investments Inc....G.... 517 321-3600
Lansing (G-9221)
Detroit Testing Machine Co....G.... 248 669-3100
Novi (G-11866)
Dietert Foundry Testing Eqp....G.... 313 491-4680
Detroit (G-4008)
Dimension Products Corporation....F.... 616 842-6050
Grand Haven (G-6010)
Electro ARC Manufacturing Co....E.... 734 483-4233
Dexter (G-4491)
◆ Electronic Apps Speclsts Inc....G.... 248 491-4988
Milford (G-10963)
Endecra LLC....G.... 734 476-9381
Ann Arbor (G-444)
Equitable Engineering Co Inc....E.... 248 689-9700
Troy (G-16351)
Exquise Inc....G.... 248 220-9048
Detroit (G-4047)
Ezm LLC....F.... 248 438-6570
Novi (G-11886)
F I D Corporation....F.... 248 373-7005
Rochester Hills (G-13422)
Family Safety Products Inc....G.... 616 530-6540
Grandville (G-7036)
Fatigue Dynamics Inc....G.... 248 641-9487
Troy (G-16360)
Force Dynamics Inc....G.... 248 673-9878
Waterford (G-17344)
◆ Froude Inc....G.... 248 579-4295
Novi (G-11888)
Gage Eagle Spline Inc....D.... 586 776-7240
Warren (G-17049)
General Inspection LLC....F.... 248 625-0529
Davisburg (G-3634)
Gfg Instrumentation Inc....E.... 734 769-0573
Ann Arbor (G-472)
Gic LLC....F.... 231 237-7000
Charlevoix (G-2616)
Gravikor Inc....G.... 734 302-3200
Ann Arbor (G-477)
▲ Greening Incorporated....G.... 313 366-7160
Detroit (G-4104)
▲ Greening Associates Inc....E.... 313 366-7160
Detroit (G-4105)
◆ Hines Industries Inc....E.... 734 769-2300
Ann Arbor (G-492)
Horiba Instruments Inc....D.... 734 213-6555
Ann Arbor (G-495)
▲ Howard Miller Company....B.... 616 772-9131
Zeeland (G-18154)
◆ Humantics Innvtive Sltions Inc....C.... 734 451-7878
Farmington Hills (G-5023)
Ibg Nbt Systems Corp....G.... 248 478-9490
Farmington Hills (G-5024)
Infrared Telemetrics Inc....F.... 906 482-0012
Hancock (G-7252)
Innkeeper LLC....G.... 734 743-1707
Canton (G-2386)
Inora Technologies Inc....F.... 734 302-7488
Ann Arbor (G-506)
Instrumented Sensor Tech Inc....G.... 517 349-8487
Okemos (G-12126)
Integrated Sensing Systems Inc....E.... 734 547-9896
Ypsilanti (G-18081)
Intelligent Dynamics LLC....F.... 313 727-9920
Dearborn (G-3725)
Intelligent Vision Systems LLC....G.... 734 426-3921
Dexter (G-4494)
▲ International Met Systems Inc....F.... 616 971-1005
Grand Rapids (G-6541)
▲ Intra Corporation....C.... 734 326-7030
Westland (G-17571)
Inventron Inc....G.... 248 473-9250
Livonia (G-9785)
Invertech Inc....F.... 734 944-4400
Saline (G-14396)
Invo Spline Inc....E.... 586 757-8840
Warren (G-17097)
J E Myles Inc....E.... 248 583-1020
Troy (G-16430)
Jgs Machining LLC....G.... 810 329-4210
Saint Clair (G-14223)
Jomat Industries Ltd....F.... 586 336-1801
Bruce Twp (G-2085)

S I C

Employee Codes: A=Over 500 employees, B=251-500
C=101-250, D=51-100, E=20-50, F=10-19, G=3-9
2020 Harris Michigan
Industrial Directory
863

K-Space Associates Inc ....E 734 426-7977
Dexter (G-4497)
Kemkraft Engineering Inc ....F 734 414-6500
Plymouth (G-12664)
▲ Kistler Instrument Corporation........D 248 668-6900
Novi (G-11916)
KLC Enterprises Inc........F 989 753-0496
Saginaw (G-14072)
▲ Kuka Assembly and Test Corp ....C 989 220-3088
Saginaw (G-14074)
Labortrio Elttrofisico USA Inc........G 248 340-7040
Lake Orion (G-9143)
Landis Precision Inc........G 248 685-8032
Milford (G-10968)
▲ Link Manufacturing Inc........C 734 453-0800
Plymouth (G-12673)
Link Manufacturing Inc........F 734 387-1001
Ottawa Lake (G-12265)
M Antonik........G 248 236-0333
Oxford (G-12357)
M&B Holdings LLC ....G 734 677-0454
Ann Arbor (G-538)
Martel Tool Corporation ....F 313 278-2420
Allen Park (G-202)
Michael Engineering Ltd ....E 989 772-4073
Mount Pleasant (G-11204)
◆ Michigan Scientific Corp ....E 248 685-3939
Milford (G-10969)
Michigan Scientific Corp........D 231 547-5511
Charlevoix (G-2620)
Michigan Spline Gage Co Inc........F 248 544-7303
Hazel Park (G-7445)
Midwest Flex Systems Inc........F 810 424-0060
Flint (G-5468)
▲ Miljoco Corp ....D 586 777-4280
Mount Clemens (G-11142)
Montronix Inc ....G 734 213-6500
Ann Arbor (G-564)
Mri Consultants LLC........G 248 619-9771
Madison Heights (G-10310)
Neptech Inc........E 810 225-2222
Highland (G-7498)
◆ Nikon Metrology Inc ....C 810 220-4360
Brighton (G-1968)
Nikon Metrology Inc........G 810 220-4347
Brighton (G-1969)
▼ North American Controls Inc ....E 586 532-7140
Shelby Township (G-14654)
North Amrcn Masurement Systems......G 734 646-3458
Plymouth (G-12701)
Novatron Corporation........C 609 815-2100
Warren (G-17174)
▲ Og Technologies Inc........F 734 973-7500
Ann Arbor (G-581)
Oxford Instruments America Inc ....F 734 821-3003
Ann Arbor (G-587)
Parker-Hannifin Corporation........D 330 253-5239
Otsego (G-12251)
◆ Patriot Sensors & Contrls Corp ....D 248 435-0700
Clawson (G-2983)
Pcb Load & Torque Inc........E 248 471-0065
Farmington Hills (G-5089)
Pcb Piezotronics Inc........F 888 684-0014
Novi (G-11971)
Pcb Piezotronics Inc........G 716 684-0001
Farmington Hills (G-5090)
▲ Perceptron Inc........C 734 414-6100
Plymouth (G-12712)
Pierburg Instruments........C 734 414-9600
Plymouth (G-12715)
Pinto Products Inc........G 269 383-0015
Kalamazoo (G-8852)
Port Austin Level & Tl Mfg Co ....F 989 738-5291
Port Austin (G-12878)
Precision Devices Inc........E 734 439-2462
Milan (G-10950)
Precision Measurement Co........E 734 995-0041
Ann Arbor (G-601)
Promess Inc........C 810 229-9334
Brighton (G-1981)
◆ Quality First Systems Inc ....F 248 922-4780
Davisburg (G-3639)
Quigley Manufacturing Inc........C 248 426-8600
Farmington Hills (G-5110)
R & J Manufacturing Company........E 248 669-2460
Commerce Township (G-3445)
R M Young Company ....E 231 946-3980
Traverse City (G-16088)
Ram Meter Inc ....F 248 362-0990
Royal Oak (G-13962)
Ramer Products Inc........G 269 409-8583
Buchanan (G-2126)
Rayco Manufacturing Inc ....F 586 795-2884
Sterling Heights (G-15462)
Richmond Instrs & Systems Inc........F 586 954-3770
Clinton Township (G-3211)
Rs Technologies Ltd........E 248 888-8260
Farmington Hills (G-5118)
Russells Technical Pdts Inc........E 616 392-3161
Holland (G-7791)
Safety Technology Holdings Inc........G 415 983-2706
Farmington Hills (G-5119)
▲ Saginaw Machine Systems Inc ....D 989 753-8465
Saginaw (G-14140)
Schap Specialty Machine Inc........E 616 846-6530
Spring Lake (G-15175)
Schenck USA Corp ....E 248 377-2100
Southfield (G-15024)
Sensordata Technologies Inc ....F 586 739-4254
Shelby Township (G-14689)
Service Diamond Tool Company ....G 248 669-3100
Novi (G-11993)
Shield Material Handling Inc ....F 248 418-0986
Auburn Hills (G-997)
▲ Siko Products Inc........G 734 426-3476
Dexter (G-4509)
◆ Solar Street Lights Usa LLC ....G 616 399-6166
Holland (G-7809)
Ssi Technology Inc ....D 248 582-0600
Sterling Heights (G-15507)
▲ Storage Control Systems Inc ....E 616 887-7994
Sparta (G-15114)
▲ Sun-Tec Corp........G 248 669-3100
Novi (G-12009)
Superior Controls Inc ....C 734 454-0500
Plymouth (G-12763)
◆ T E Technology Inc........E 231 929-3966
Traverse City (G-16118)
T-Mach Industries LLC ....G 734 673-6964
Taylor (G-15775)
Tecat Performance Systems LLC ....F 248 615-9862
Ann Arbor (G-654)
Temprel Inc........E 231 582-6585
Boyne City (G-1835)
Teradyne Inc........C 313 425-3900
Allen Park (G-211)
Tessonics Corp ....G 248 885-8335
Birmingham (G-1704)
▲ Testek LLC........D 248 573-4980
Wixom (G-17909)
Testron Incorporated ....F 734 513-6820
Livonia (G-9955)
Thermal Wave Imaging Inc........F 248 414-3730
Ferndale (G-5321)
▼ Thermotron Industries Inc ....B 616 392-1491
Holland (G-7830)
▲ Thielenhaus Microfinish Corp ....E 248 349-9450
Novi (G-12015)
▲ Thierica Inc........D 616 458-1538
Grand Rapids (G-6926)
Triangle Broach Company ....F 313 838-2150
Detroit (G-4408)
United Abrasive Inc ....F 906 563-9249
Vulcan (G-16846)
Verimation Technology Inc ....F 248 471-0000
Farmington Hills (G-5147)
Versicor LLC........F 734 306-9137
Royal Oak (G-13981)
Vgage LLC ....D 248 589-7455
Oak Park (G-12102)
Vibration Research Corporation........E 616 669-3028
Jenison (G-8648)
Waber Tool & Engineering Co........E 269 342-0765
Kalamazoo (G-8921)
▲ Wellsense USA Inc........G 888 335-0995
Birmingham (G-1708)
▲ Wmc Lievense Company........E 231 946-3800
Traverse City (G-16148)

3841 Surgical & Medical Instrs & Apparatus

Aees Power Systems Ltd Partnr........F 269 668-4429
Farmington Hills (G-4921)
▲ Alliant Enterprises LLC ....E 269 629-0300
Grand Rapids (G-6162)
American Laser Centers LLC........A 248 426-8250
Farmington Hills (G-4929)
Animal Medical Ctr of Lapeer ....F 989 631-3350
Midland (G-10815)
▼ Artisan Medical Displays LLC........E 616 748-8950
Zeeland (G-18113)
Assuramed Inc ....G 616 419-2020
Wyoming (G-17987)
▲ Autocam Corporation ....B 616 698-0707
Kentwood (G-9000)
Autocam Med DVC Holdings LLC ....G 616 541-8080
Kentwood (G-9002)
Autocam Medical Devices LLC ....E 877 633-8080
Grand Rapids (G-6191)
Barron Precision Instruments ....E 810 695-2080
Grand Blanc (G-5959)
Bd Diagnostic Systems........E 313 442-8800
Detroit (G-3894)
Becton Dickinson and Company........E 313 442-8700
Detroit (G-3898)
Berchtold Corporation........G 269 329-2001
Portage (G-12984)
Bio-Vac Inc........E 248 350-2150
Southfield (G-14853)
Bonwrx Ltd ....G 517 481-2924
Lansing (G-9206)
Brio Device LLC........G 734 945-5728
Ann Arbor (G-390)
C2dx Inc........F 269 409-0068
Schoolcraft (G-14489)
Capnesity Inc........G 317 401-6766
Lapeer (G-9450)
Cardiac Assist Holdings LLC........G 781 727-1391
Plymouth (G-12593)
Cardinal Health Inc ....C 248 685-9655
Highland (G-7487)
Clear Image Devices LLC........G 734 645-6459
Ann Arbor (G-400)
Cnd Products LLC ....G 616 361-1000
Grand Rapids (G-6282)
Complete Health System........G 810 720-3891
Flint (G-5401)
▼ Crippen Manufacturing Company ....E 989 681-4323
Saint Louis (G-14361)
▲ David Epstein Inc........F 248 542-0802
Ferndale (G-5270)
Delphinus Medical Technologies ....E 248 522-9600
Novi (G-11863)
Deuwave LLC ....G 888 238-9283
Northville (G-11688)
DForte Inc........F 269 657-6996
Paw Paw (G-12402)
Di-Coat Corporation........E 248 349-1211
Novi (G-11868)
Domico Med-Device LLC........D 810 750-5300
Fenton (G-5200)
Ferndale Pharma Group Inc........B 248 548-0900
Ferndale (G-5285)
Filter Plus Inc ....F 734 475-7403
Chelsea (G-2710)
Flexdex Inc ....F 810 522-9009
Brighton (G-1924)
▲ Gelman Sciences Inc........A 734 665-0651
Ann Arbor (G-469)
Genesis Innovation Group LLC........G 616 294-1026
Holland (G-7643)
▲ Grace Engineering Corp........D 810 392-2181
Memphis (G-10710)
Hanna Instruments Inc ....G 734 971-8160
Ann Arbor (G-481)
Hart Enterprises USA Inc ....D 616 887-0400
Sparta (G-15098)
Healthcare Dme LLC........G 734 975-6668
Ann Arbor (G-485)
▲ Healthmark Industries Co Inc ....C 586 774-7600
Fraser (G-5660)
Helix Devices LLC........G 724 681-0975
East Lansing (G-4660)
Imagen Orthopedics LLC ....G 616 294-1026
Holland (G-7687)
Infusystem Holdings Inc ....D 248 291-1210
Madison Heights (G-10274)
Isensium ....G 517 580-9022
East Lansing (G-4666)
J Sterling Industries LLC ....F 269 492-6922
Kalamazoo (G-8776)
Jodon Engineering Assoc Inc ....F 734 761-4044
Ann Arbor (G-511)
▲ Keystone Manufacturing LLC ....F 269 343-4108
Kalamazoo (G-8801)
Krasitys Med Surgical Sup Inc ....F 313 274-2210
Dearborn (G-3731)
Lake Erie Med Surgical Sup Inc........E 734 847-3847
Temperance (G-15833)
Lake Lansing ASC Partners LLC ....F 517 708-3333
Lansing (G-9386)

SIC SECTION 38 MEASURING, ANALYZING AND CONTROLLING INSTRUMENTS; PHOTOGRAPHIC, MEDICAL AN

Link Technology Inc F 269 324-8212
Portage *(G-13009)*
▲ **Mar-Med Inc** G 616 454-3000
Grand Rapids *(G-6642)*
Marketlab Inc D 866 237-3722
Caledonia *(G-2307)*
Medical Engineering & Dev G 517 563-2352
Horton *(G-7969)*
▲ **Medical Laser Resources LLC** G 248 628-8120
Oxford *(G-12360)*
Medisurge LLC F 888 307-1144
Grand Rapids *(G-6657)*
Medtronic Inc G 248 349-6987
Novi *(G-11943)*
Medtronic Inc G 616 643-5200
Grand Rapids *(G-6658)*
Medtronic Inc F 616 643-5200
Grand Rapids *(G-6659)*
Medtronic Usa Inc G 248 449-5027
Novi *(G-11944)*
Melling Manufacturing Inc E 517 750-3580
Jackson *(G-8513)*
Metro Wbe Associates Inc G 248 504-7563
Detroit *(G-4232)*
Michigan Med Innovations LLC G 616 682-4848
Ada *(G-24)*
Mitovation Inc G 734 395-1635
Saline *(G-14402)*
Morrison & Barnett Anesth G 248 814-0609
Lake Orion *(G-9150)*
Myco Industries Inc G 248 685-2496
Milford *(G-10973)*
▲ **Neogen Corporation** B 517 372-9200
Lansing *(G-9405)*
Omega Surgical Instruments G 810 695-9800
Flint *(G-5477)*
Operations Research Tech LLC G 248 626-8960
West Bloomfield *(G-17492)*
Orchid Orthpd Sltons Organ Inc D 203 877-3341
Holt *(G-7919)*
Orchid Orthpd Solutions LLC F 989 746-0780
Bridgeport *(G-1855)*
Orchid Orthpd Solutions LLC C 517 694-2300
Holt *(G-7920)*
▲ **Oxus America Inc** G 248 475-0925
Auburn Hills *(G-968)*
Oxygenplus LLC G 586 221-9112
Clinton Township *(G-3191)*
◆ **Performance Systematix Inc** D 616 949-9090
Grand Rapids *(G-6749)*
Perspective Enterprises Inc G 269 327-0869
Portage *(G-13021)*
Pinnacle Technology Group D 734 568-6600
Ottawa Lake *(G-12268)*
Pioneer Surgical Tech Inc C 906 226-9909
Marquette *(G-10552)*
Plasma Biolife Services L P G 616 667-0264
Grandville *(G-7064)*
▲ **Pointe Scientific Inc** E 734 487-8300
Canton *(G-2417)*
Precision Edge Srgcal Pdts LLC C 231 459-4304
Boyne City *(G-1833)*
Precision Edge Srgcal Pdts LLC D 906 632-5600
Sault Sainte Marie *(G-14470)*
Predxion Bio Inc G 734 353-0191
Dexter *(G-4504)*
Premier Imaging Center G 248 594-3201
Franklin *(G-5608)*
▲ **Progressive Dynamics Inc** D 269 781-4241
Marshall *(G-10585)*
Protomatic Inc E 734 426-3655
Dexter *(G-4505)*
R H Cross Enterprises Inc G 269 488-4009
Kalamazoo *(G-8868)*
RJL Sciences Inc F 800 528-4513
Clinton Township *(G-3213)*
Rls Interventional Inc F 616 301-7800
Kentwood *(G-9029)*
Robert A Nelson G 231 597-9225
Cheboygan *(G-2693)*
Rose Technologies Company E 616 233-3000
Grand Rapids *(G-6838)*
Saint-Gobain Prfmce Plas Corp F 231 264-0101
Williamsburg *(G-17720)*
SGC Industries Inc E 586 293-5260
Fraser *(G-5723)*
Shoulder Innovations Inc G 616 294-1029
Holland *(G-7803)*
Slaughter Instrument Company F 269 428-7471
Stevensville *(G-15581)*
Sonetics Ultrasound Inc G 734 260-4800
Ann Arbor *(G-641)*
Steele Supply Co G 269 983-0920
Saint Joseph *(G-14342)*
Stryker Australia LLC G 269 385-2600
Portage *(G-13036)*
Stryker Corporation E 269 385-2600
Portage *(G-13038)*
Stryker Corporation C 269 324-5346
Portage *(G-13039)*
Stryker Corporation G 248 374-6352
Novi *(G-12006)*
Stryker Corporation B 269 329-2100
Portage *(G-13040)*
Stryker Corporation C 269 389-2300
Portage *(G-13041)*
Stryker Corporation E 269 389-3741
Portage *(G-13037)*
Stryker Corporation E 269 323-1027
Portage *(G-13042)*
Stryker Far East Inc E 269 385-2600
Portage *(G-13044)*
▲ **Sunmed LLC** D 616 259-8400
Grand Rapids *(G-6899)*
Sunmed Holdings LLC F 616 259-8400
Grand Rapids *(G-6900)*
Supreme Gear Co E 586 775-6325
Fraser *(G-5736)*
Surgitech Surgical Svcs Inc E 248 593-0797
Highland *(G-7500)*
Symmetry Medical Inc F 517 887-3424
Lansing *(G-9429)*
Tambra Investments Inc G 866 662-7897
Warren *(G-17261)*
Tecomet Inc B 517 882-4311
Lansing *(G-9431)*
Terumo Americas Holding Inc B 734 663-4145
Ann Arbor *(G-665)*
▲ **Terumo Crdvscular Systems Corp** C 734 663-4145
Ann Arbor *(G-666)*
Tesma Instruments LLC G 517 940-1362
Howell *(G-8106)*
Thompson Surgical Instrs Inc E 231 922-0177
Traverse City *(G-16122)*
Thompson Surgical Instrs Inc G 231 922-5169
Traverse City *(G-16123)*
Thoratec Corporation C 734 827-7422
Ann Arbor *(G-673)*
Tiger Neuroscience LLC G 872 903-1904
Muskegon *(G-11437)*
Tilco Inc G 248 644-0901
Troy *(G-16643)*
TMJ Manufacturing LLC E 248 987-7857
Farmington Hills *(G-5142)*
Truform Machine Inc E 517 782-8523
Jackson *(G-8594)*
Viant Medical Inc D 616 643-5200
Grand Rapids *(G-6971)*
Virotech Biomaterials Inc G 313 421-1648
Warren *(G-17284)*
Warmilu LLC G 855 927-6458
Ann Arbor *(G-695)*
Wright & Filippis Inc E 248 336-8460
Detroit *(G-3822)*
Wright & Filippis Inc E 313 386-3330
Lincoln Park *(G-9589)*
Wysong Medical Corporation E 989 631-0009
Midland *(G-10925)*

3842 Orthopedic, Prosthetic & Surgical Appliances/Splys

3dm Source Inc F 616 647-9513
Grand Rapids *(G-6120)*
A and J Industries G 616 877-4845
Wayland *(G-17396)*
Aactus Inc G 734 425-1212
Livonia *(G-9623)*
Active Brace and Limb LLC F 231 932-8702
Traverse City *(G-15889)*
Agelessmage Fcial Asthtics LLC G 269 998-5547
Farmington Hills *(G-4922)*
Air Supply Inc G 586 773-6600
Warren *(G-16921)*
American Prosthetic Institute G 517 349-3130
Okemos *(G-12112)*
◆ **Amigo Mobility Intl Inc** D 989 777-0910
Bridgeport *(G-1848)*
Anew Lf Prsthtics Orthtics LLC G 313 870-9610
Detroit *(G-3871)*
Assistive Technology Mich Inc G 248 348-7161
Novi *(G-11832)*
Audionet America Inc G 586 944-0043
Clinton Township *(G-3059)*
Auric Enterprises Inc G 231 882-7251
Beulah *(G-1608)*
Auto Engineering Lab E 734 764-4254
Ann Arbor *(G-373)*
Autocam Med DVC Holdings LLC G 616 541-8080
Kentwood *(G-9002)*
Autocam Medical Devices LLC E 877 633-8080
Grand Rapids *(G-6191)*
Avasure Holdings Inc E 616 301-0129
Belmont *(G-1456)*
◆ **Avon Protection Systems Inc** C 231 779-6200
Cadillac *(G-2230)*
Axiobionics G 734 327-2946
Ann Arbor *(G-378)*
Becker Oregon Inc E 248 588-7480
Troy *(G-16235)*
▲ **Becker Orthopedic Appliance Co** D 248 588-7480
Troy *(G-16236)*
Beltone Skoric Hearng Aid Cntr G 906 379-0606
Sault Sainte Marie *(G-14461)*
Beltone Skoric Hearng Aid Cntr G 906 553-4660
Escanaba *(G-4817)*
Berchtold Corporation G 269 329-2001
Portage *(G-12984)*
Binson-Becker Inc F 888 246-7667
Center Line *(G-2579)*
Biocorrect Orthotics Lab G 616 356-5030
Kentwood *(G-9003)*
Biomedical Designs G 517 784-6617
Jackson *(G-8390)*
Biopro Inc E 810 982-7777
Port Huron *(G-12899)*
Bms Great Lakes LLC G 248 390-1598
Lake Orion *(G-9126)*
Bold Fusion Fabg & Customs LLC G 269 345-0681
Kalamazoo *(G-8699)*
Brand Orthopedic & Shoe Svcs G 248 352-0000
Southfield *(G-14856)*
Bremer Prosthetic Design Inc G 810 733-3375
Flint *(G-5394)*
Brenner Orthtic Prsthetic Labs G 248 615-0600
Livonia *(G-9670)*
Carlson Technology Inc G 248 476-0013
Livonia *(G-9677)*
◆ **Central Lake Armor Express Inc** C 231 544-6090
Central Lake *(G-2588)*
Clinton River Medical Pdts LLC G 248 289-1825
Auburn Hills *(G-815)*
College Park Industries Inc E 586 294-7950
Warren *(G-16987)*
Cooper Glove and Safety LLC G 706 512-0486
Bridgeport *(G-1851)*
Crescent Corporation G 810 982-2784
Fort Gratiot *(G-5548)*
Curbell Plastics Inc G 734 513-0531
Livonia *(G-9694)*
Dabir Surfaces Inc G 248 796-0802
Southfield *(G-14877)*
Danmar Products Inc E 734 761-1990
Ann Arbor *(G-412)*
▲ **David Epstein Inc** F 248 542-0802
Ferndale *(G-5270)*
Davis Dental Laboratory G 616 261-9191
Wyoming *(G-17995)*
Davismade Inc F 810 743-5262
Flint *(G-5415)*
Douglass Safety Systems LLC G 989 687-7600
Sanford *(G-14449)*
Ever-Flex Inc E 313 389-2060
Lincoln Park *(G-9576)*
First Response Med Sups LLC F 313 731-2554
Dearborn *(G-3707)*
Georgia Walker & Assoc Inc G 248 594-6447
Bloomfield Hills *(G-1768)*
Gipson Fabrications G 616 245-7331
Wyoming *(G-18003)*
Going Out On A Limb G 231 347-4631
Petoskey *(G-12449)*
Greater Lansing Orthotic Clini G 517 337-0856
Lansing *(G-9377)*
Gresham Driving Aids Inc E 248 624-1533
Wixom *(G-17820)*
Hackley Health Ventures Inc G 231 728-5720
Muskegon *(G-11342)*
Hanger Inc F 616 949-0075
Grand Rapids *(G-6491)*

S I C

38 MEASURING, ANALYZING AND CONTROLLING INSTRUMENTS; PHOTOGRAPHIC, MEDICAL AN

Hanger Inc ..... E 616 458-8080
Grand Rapids *(G-6492)*
Hanger Inc ..... E 248 615-0601
Livonia *(G-9765)*
Hanger Inc ..... D 616 940-0878
Grand Rapids *(G-6493)*
Hanger Prsthetcs & Ortho Inc ..... F 517 394-5850
Lansing *(G-9381)*
Hanger Prsthetcs & Ortho Inc ..... G 248 683-5070
Waterford *(G-17348)*
Hellner & Associates Inc ..... G 810 220-3472
Brighton *(G-1938)*
Hi-Tech Optical Inc ..... E 989 799-9390
Saginaw *(G-14057)*
Hi-Trac Industries Inc ..... G 810 625-7193
Linden *(G-9592)*
Howmedica Osteonics Corp ..... G 269 389-8959
Portage *(G-13001)*
Innovative Cargo Systems LLC ..... G 734 568-6084
Lambertville *(G-9183)*
Instep Pedorthics LLC ..... G 810 285-9109
Traverse City *(G-16006)*
▲ Jacquart Fabric Products Inc ..... C 906 932-1339
Ironwood *(G-8332)*
James Glove & Supply ..... F 810 733-5780
Flint *(G-5452)*
Joyson Safety Systems ..... B 248 373-8040
Auburn Hills *(G-922)*
Landra Prsthtics Orthotics Inc ..... G 586 294-7188
Saint Clair Shores *(G-14259)*
Landra Prsthtics Orthotics Inc ..... G 734 281-8144
Southgate *(G-15080)*
Lift Aid Inc ..... G 248 345-5110
Farmington *(G-4903)*
Luma Laser and Medi Spa ..... G 248 817-5499
Troy *(G-16466)*
Magnetic Ventures LLC ..... G 313 670-3036
Dearborn *(G-3736)*
▲ McKeon Products Inc ..... E 586 427-7560
Warren *(G-17146)*
Medical Cmfort Specialists LLC ..... F 810 229-4222
Fowlerville *(G-5575)*
Medtronic Inc ..... G 616 643-5200
Grand Rapids *(G-6658)*
Mercy Health Partners ..... G 231 672-4886
Muskegon *(G-11374)*
Metro Medical Eqp Mfg Inc ..... D 734 522-8400
Livonia *(G-9840)*
Micro Engineering Inc ..... E 616 534-9681
Byron Center *(G-2200)*
MII Disposition Inc ..... E 616 554-9696
Grand Rapids *(G-6689)*
▲ Miller Technical Services Inc ..... F 734 207-3159
Plymouth *(G-12694)*
Mobile Prosthetics ..... G 989 875-7000
Ithaca *(G-8366)*
Mount Clemens Orthopedic Appls ..... G 586 463-3600
Clinton Township *(G-3181)*
Noir Medical Technologies LLC ..... F 248 486-3760
South Lyon *(G-14806)*
Northern Orthotics Prosthetics ..... G 906 353-7161
Baraga *(G-1111)*
Northwest Orthotics-Prosthetic ..... G 248 477-1443
Novi *(G-11955)*
O and P Sparton ..... G 517 220-4960
East Lansing *(G-4673)*
Oakland Orthopedic Appls Inc ..... D 989 893-7544
Bay City *(G-1339)*
Oakland Orthopedic Appls Inc ..... G 989 839-9241
Midland *(G-10898)*
Orthopaedic Associates Mich ..... D 616 459-7101
Grand Rapids *(G-6734)*
Orthotic Insoles LLC ..... G 517 641-4166
Bath *(G-1135)*
Orthotic Shop Inc ..... G 800 309-0412
Shelby Township *(G-14658)*
P & O Services Inc ..... G 248 809-3072
Southfield *(G-14994)*
Paul W Reed DDS ..... F 231 347-4145
Petoskey *(G-12467)*
Plasma Biolife Services L P ..... G 616 667-0264
Grandville *(G-7064)*
Porex Technologies Corporation ..... E 989 865-8200
Saint Charles *(G-14198)*
Precision Gage Inc ..... D 517 439-1690
Hillsdale *(G-7534)*
Preferred Products Inc ..... E 248 255-0200
Commerce Township *(G-3441)*
Pros-Tech Inc ..... F 248 680-2800
Troy *(G-16568)*

Prosthetic & Implant Dentistry ..... G 248 254-3945
Farmington Hills *(G-5103)*
Prosthetic Center Inc ..... G 517 372-7007
Dimondale *(G-4519)*
Radiolgical Fabrication Design ..... G 810 632-6000
Howell *(G-8087)*
Reflection Medical Inc ..... G 734 850-0777
Temperance *(G-15841)*
Regents of The University Mich ..... E 734 973-2400
Ann Arbor *(G-618)*
Ropp Orthopedic Clinic LLC ..... G 248 669-9222
Commerce Township *(G-3451)*
▲ Rpb Safety LLC ..... E 866 494-4599
Royal Oak *(G-13969)*
SC Industries Inc ..... F 312 366-3899
Southfield *(G-15023)*
Se-Kure Controls Inc ..... E 269 651-9351
Sturgis *(G-15633)*
▲ Set Liquidation Inc ..... D 517 694-2300
Holt *(G-7928)*
Shock-Tek LLC ..... E 313 886-0530
Grosse Pointe Farms *(G-7188)*
Signal Medical Corporation ..... F 810 364-7070
Marysville *(G-10614)*
Sigvaris Inc ..... E 616 741-4281
Holland *(G-7804)*
Skyline Window Cleaning Inc ..... G 616 813-0536
West Olive *(G-17535)*
Solus Innovations LLC ..... G 231 744-9832
Muskegon *(G-11427)*
Springer Prsthtic Orthtic Svcs ..... F 517 337-0300
Lansing *(G-9426)*
Standing Company ..... F 989 746-9100
Saginaw *(G-14157)*
Steele Supply Co ..... G 269 983-0920
Saint Joseph *(G-14342)*
Strive Orthtics Prsthetics LLC ..... G 586 803-4325
Sterling Heights *(G-15514)*
Stryker Australia LLC ..... G 269 385-2600
Portage *(G-13036)*
Stryker Corporation ..... E 269 389-3741
Portage *(G-13037)*
Stryker Corporation ..... E 269 323-1027
Portage *(G-13042)*
Stryker Corporation ..... E 269 385-2600
Portage *(G-13038)*
Stryker Corporation ..... B 269 329-2100
Portage *(G-13040)*
Stryker Customs Brokers LLC ..... F 269 389-2300
Portage *(G-13043)*
Stryker Far East Inc ..... E 269 385-2600
Portage *(G-13044)*
Studio One Midwest Inc ..... F 269 962-3475
Battle Creek *(G-1255)*
Sure-Fit Glove & Safety ..... G 734 729-4960
Westland *(G-17601)*
Swanson Orthtic Prsthetics Ctr ..... G 734 241-4397
Monroe *(G-11071)*
Tesa Tape Inc ..... G 616 785-6970
Grand Rapids *(G-6924)*
Tesa Tape Inc ..... D 616 887-3107
Sparta *(G-15116)*
Teter Orthotics & Prosthetics ..... G 231 779-8022
Cadillac *(G-2282)*
▼ Thierica Equipment Corporation ..... E 616 453-6570
Grand Rapids *(G-6928)*
Total Health Colon Care ..... G 586 268-5444
Sterling Heights *(G-15526)*
Troy Orthopedic Associates PLC ..... G 248 244-9426
Troy *(G-16651)*
Trulife ..... E 800 492-1088
Jackson *(G-8595)*
▲ Trulife Inc ..... E 517 787-1600
Jackson *(G-8596)*
Tulip US Holdings Inc ..... E 517 694-2300
Holt *(G-7931)*
Twin Cities Orthotic & Prosthe ..... G 269 428-2910
Saint Joseph *(G-14345)*
Ultralight Prosthetics Inc ..... G 313 538-8500
Redford *(G-13204)*
Um Orthotics Pros Cntr ..... G 734 764-3100
Ann Arbor *(G-687)*
Warwick Mas & Equipment Co ..... G 810 966-3431
Port Huron *(G-12975)*
Wolverine Orthotics Inc ..... G 248 360-3736
Commerce Township *(G-3457)*
Wright & Filippis Inc ..... F 517 484-2624
Lansing *(G-9435)*
Wright & Filippis Inc ..... F 586 756-4020
Warren *(G-17298)*

Wright & Filippis Inc ..... G 313 832-5020
Detroit *(G-4450)*
Wright & Filippis Inc ..... E 248 336-8460
Detroit *(G-3822)*
Wright & Filippis Inc ..... E 313 386-3330
Lincoln Park *(G-9589)*
Wright Brace & Limb Inc ..... G 989 343-0300
West Branch *(G-17530)*
XYZ McHine TI Fabrications Inc ..... E 517 482-3668
Lansing *(G-9329)*

3843 Dental Eqpt & Splys

▲ Air Force Inc ..... G 616 399-8511
Holland *(G-7553)*
Akervall Technologies Inc ..... F 800 444-0570
Saline *(G-14373)*
Aluwax Dental Products Co Inc ..... G 616 895-4385
Allendale *(G-214)*
Andrew J Reisterer D D S Pllc ..... G 231 845-8989
Ludington *(G-10049)*
Axsys Inc ..... E 248 926-8810
Wixom *(G-17769)*
Biotec Incorporated ..... D 616 772-2133
Zeeland *(G-18120)*
Dental Art Laboratories Inc ..... D 517 485-2200
Lansing *(G-9222)*
Dental Impressions ..... G 231 719-0033
Muskegon *(G-11305)*
E C Moore Company ..... E 313 581-7878
Dearborn *(G-3697)*
▲ E C Moore Company ..... D 313 581-7878
Dearborn *(G-3696)*
End Product Results LLC ..... F 586 585-1210
Roseville *(G-13801)*
Garrison Dental Solutions LLC ..... E 616 842-2035
Spring Lake *(G-15144)*
Ghost Mfg LLC ..... G 269 281-0489
Saint Joseph *(G-14312)*
Kalamazoo Dental Supply ..... G 269 345-0260
Kalamazoo *(G-8787)*
Kerr Corporation ..... C 734 946-7800
Romulus *(G-13696)*
Ktr Dental Lab & Pdts LLC ..... F 248 224-9158
Southfield *(G-14957)*
Liquid Otc LLC ..... G 248 214-7771
Commerce Township *(G-3422)*
Microdental Laboratories Inc ..... G 877 711-8778
Troy *(G-16507)*
New Image Dental P C ..... G 586 727-1100
Richmond *(G-13267)*
Patrick Wyman ..... G 810 227-2199
Brighton *(G-1974)*
Phoenix Dental Inc ..... G 810 750-2328
Fenton *(G-5230)*
▲ Ranir LLC ..... B 616 698-8880
Grand Rapids *(G-6808)*
Ranir Global Holdings LLC ..... A 616 698-8880
Grand Rapids *(G-6809)*
Select Dental Groupcom ..... G 734 459-3200
Plymouth *(G-12751)*
Stanford Dental Pllc ..... G 248 476-4500
Livonia *(G-9943)*
Tokusen Hytech Inc ..... C 269 685-1768
Plainwell *(G-12547)*
Visual Chimera ..... F 586 585-1210
Eastpointe *(G-4711)*

3844 X-ray Apparatus & Tubes

I D Medical Systems Inc ..... G 616 698-0535
Grand Rapids *(G-6523)*
Kgf Enterprise Inc ..... G 586 430-4182
Columbus *(G-3380)*

3845 Electromedical & Electrotherapeutic Apparatus

Accutherm Systems Inc ..... G 734 930-0461
Ann Arbor *(G-341)*
American Lazer Centers ..... G 248 798-6552
Clinton Township *(G-3048)*
Benesh Corporation ..... E 734 244-4143
Monroe *(G-11023)*
Bieri Hearing Instruments Inc ..... F 989 793-2701
Saginaw *(G-14007)*
Cerephex Corporation ..... G 517 719-0414
Bancroft *(G-1087)*
E3 Diagnostics Inc ..... G 734 981-3655
Canton *(G-2369)*
Eaton Industries Inc ..... G 734 428-0000
Ann Arbor *(G-431)*

Endoscopic Solutions .... G 248 625-4055
Clarkston *(G-2918)*

Endra Life Sciences Inc .... G 734 255-0242
Ann Arbor *(G-445)*

▲ **Gelman Sciences Inc** .... A 734 665-0651
Ann Arbor *(G-469)*

Healthcare Dme LLC .... G 734 975-6668
Ann Arbor *(G-485)*

Heart Sync Inc .... F 734 213-5530
Ann Arbor *(G-488)*

Helping Hands Therapy .... G 313 492-6007
Southfield *(G-14936)*

Histosonics Inc .... G 734 926-4630
Ann Arbor *(G-493)*

Iha Vsclar Endvsclar Spcalists .... G 734 712-8150
Ypsilanti *(G-18078)*

Innovtive Srgcal Solutions LLC .... F 248 595-0420
Wixom *(G-17834)*

Isensium .... G 517 580-9022
East Lansing *(G-4666)*

Medtronic Inc .... G 616 643-5200
Grand Rapids *(G-6658)*

▲ **Merlin Simulation Inc** .... F 703 560-7203
Dexter *(G-4498)*

Metrex Research LLC .... D 734 947-6700
Romulus *(G-13706)*

Mll Disposition Inc .... E 616 554-9696
Grand Rapids *(G-6689)*

Oncofusion Therapeutics Inc .... G 248 361-3341
Northville *(G-11719)*

Physicians Technology LLC .... F 734 241-5060
Monroe *(G-11061)*

Rockwell Medical Inc .... C 248 960-9009
Wixom *(G-17886)*

Rofin-Sinar Technologies LLC .... F 734 416-0206
Plymouth *(G-12745)*

Sobaks Pharmacy Inc .... F 989 725-2785
Owosso *(G-12316)*

Somanetics .... F 248 689-3050
Troy *(G-16611)*

▲ **Terumo Crdvscular Systems Corp** ... C 734 663-4145
Ann Arbor *(G-666)*

Thoratec Corporation .... C 734 827-7422
Ann Arbor *(G-673)*

Uv Partners Inc .... G 616 204-5416
Livonia *(G-9984)*

Xoran Holdings LLC .... G 734 418-5108
Ann Arbor *(G-703)*

Xoran Technologies LLC .... D 734 663-7194
Ann Arbor *(G-704)*

3851 Ophthalmic Goods

Art Optical Contact Lens Inc .... C 616 453-1888
Grand Rapids *(G-6183)*

Bad Axe Family Vision Center .... G 989 269-5393
Bad Axe *(G-1058)*

Cooperative Optical Services .... D 313 366-5100
Detroit *(G-3948)*

Dennis OBryan Od .... G 231 348-1255
Harbor Springs *(G-7282)*

Diagnostic Instruments Inc .... E 586 731-6000
Sterling Heights *(G-15316)*

Essilor Laboratories Amer Inc .... C 616 361-6000
Grand Rapids *(G-6386)*

Essilor Laboratories Amer Inc .... E 231 922-0344
Traverse City *(G-15966)*

Fairway Optical Inc .... G 231 744-6168
Muskegon *(G-11320)*

Flint Optical Company Inc .... G 810 235-4607
Flint *(G-5429)*

▲ **General Scientific Corporation** .... E 734 996-9200
Ann Arbor *(G-471)*

Hi-Tech Optical Inc .... E 989 799-9390
Saginaw *(G-14057)*

▲ **Inland Diamond Products Co** .... E 248 585-1762
Madison Heights *(G-10276)*

Luxottica of America Inc .... E 517 349-0784
Okemos *(G-12129)*

▲ **McKeon Products Inc** .... E 586 427-7560
Warren *(G-17146)*

Noir Laser Company LLC .... E 800 521-9746
Milford *(G-10977)*

Noir Medical Technologies LLC .... E 734 769-5565
Milford *(G-10978)*

Noir Medical Technologies LLC .... F 248 486-3760
South Lyon *(G-14806)*

Rx Optical Laboratories Inc .... G 269 349-7627
Kalamazoo *(G-8879)*

Rx Optical Laboratories Inc .... G 269 965-5106
Battle Creek *(G-1243)*

Rx Optical Laboratories Inc .... D 269 342-5958
Kalamazoo *(G-8878)*

Rx-Rite Optical Co .... E 586 294-8500
Fraser *(G-5719)*

Tri State Optical Inc .... G 517 279-2701
Coldwater *(G-3338)*

Vision-Craft Inc .... E 248 669-1130
Commerce Township *(G-3456)*

3861 Photographic Eqpt & Splys

Accuform Prtg & Graphics Inc .... F 313 271-5600
Detroit *(G-3838)*

Arts Crafts Hardware .... F 586 231-5344
Mount Clemens *(G-11123)*

Cognisys Inc .... G 231 943-2425
Traverse City *(G-15944)*

Compatible Laser Products Inc .... F 810 629-0459
Fenton *(G-5197)*

▲ **Douthitt Corporation** .... E 313 259-1565
Detroit *(G-4016)*

Douthitt Corporation .... F 313 259-1565
Detroit *(G-4017)*

Envirodrone Inc .... G 226 344-5614
Detroit *(G-4039)*

▲ **General Dynamics Glbl IMG Tech** .... A 248 293-2929
Rochester Hills *(G-13432)*

General Dynamics Mission .... A 530 271-2500
Rochester Hills *(G-13434)*

Just Rite Bracket .... G 248 477-0592
Farmington Hills *(G-5035)*

Laser Connection LLC .... E 989 662-4022
Auburn *(G-755)*

Lasers Resource Inc .... E 616 554-5555
Grand Rapids *(G-6620)*

Nationwide Laser Technologies .... G 248 488-0155
Farmington Hills *(G-5077)*

Northern Michig .... F 989 340-1272
Lachine *(G-9076)*

▲ **Orion Test Systems Inc** .... D 248 373-9097
Auburn Hills *(G-967)*

Precision Printer Services Inc .... F 269 384-5725
Portage *(G-13023)*

Skypersonic LLC .... G 248 648-4822
Troy *(G-16607)*

▲ **X-Rite Incorporated** .... C 616 803-2100
Grand Rapids *(G-7006)*

3873 Watch & Clock Devices & Parts

Ausable Woodworking Co Inc .... E 989 348-7086
Frederic *(G-5750)*

Czuk Studio .... G 269 628-2568
Kendall *(G-8983)*

▼ **Ernst Benz Company LLC** .... G 248 203-2323
Birmingham *(G-1683)*

▲ **Howard Miller Company** .... B 616 772-9131
Zeeland *(G-18154)*

▼ **Lumichron Inc** .... G 616 245-8888
Grand Rapids *(G-6637)*

National Time and Signal Corp .... E 248 291-5867
Oak Park *(G-12087)*

Quality Time Components .... F 231 947-1071
Traverse City *(G-16086)*

▲ **Shinola/Detroit LLC** .... C 888 304-2534
Detroit *(G-4361)*

Visual Identification Products .... G 231 941-7272
Traverse City *(G-16139)*

39 MISCELLANEOUS MANUFACTURING INDUSTRIES

3911 Jewelry: Precious Metal

Abracadabra Jewelry .... G 734 994-4848
Ann Arbor *(G-338)*

Alex and Ani LLC .... G 248 649-7348
Troy *(G-16183)*

Alexander J Bongiorno Inc .... G 248 689-7766
Troy *(G-16185)*

Amalgamations Ltd .... G 248 879-7345
Troy *(G-16194)*

Aurum Design Inc .... G 248 651-9040
Rochester *(G-13314)*

Bauble Patch Inc .... G 616 785-1100
Comstock Park *(G-3462)*

Bednarsh Mrris Jwly Design Mfg .... F 248 671-0087
Bloomfield *(G-1732)*

Birmingham Jewelry Inc .... G 586 939-5100
Sterling Heights *(G-15274)*

C I I Ltd .... G 248 585-9905
Troy *(G-16250)*

C T & T Inc .... F 248 623-9422
Waterford *(G-17328)*

▲ **Combine International Inc** .... C 248 585-9900
Troy *(G-16273)*

Daves Diamond Inc .... F 248 693-2482
Lake Orion *(G-9135)*

David Wachler & Sons Inc .... F 248 540-4622
Birmingham *(G-1681)*

Diamond Setters Inc .... G 734 439-8655
Milan *(G-10936)*

Discount Jewelry Center Inc .... G 734 266-8200
Westland *(G-17549)*

George Koueiter Jewelers .... G 313 882-1110
Grosse Pointe Woods *(G-7203)*

Glitterbug USA .... G 586 247-7569
Macomb *(G-10126)*

Herff Jones LLC .... G 810 632-6500
Hartland *(G-7391)*

HL Manufacturing Inc .... F 586 731-2800
Utica *(G-16742)*

Jewelers Workshop .... G 616 791-6500
Grand Rapids *(G-6560)*

Joseph A Dimaggio .... G 313 881-5353
Grosse Pointe Woods *(G-7205)*

Just Jewelers .... G 248 476-9011
Farmington *(G-4902)*

Kayayan Hayk Jewelry Mfg Co .... E 248 626-3060
Bloomfield *(G-1734)*

La Gold Mine Inc .... G 517 540-1050
Brighton *(G-1949)*

LLC Stahl Cross .... G 810 688-2505
Lapeer *(G-9471)*

Marquis Jewelers Ltd .... G 586 725-3990
Chesterfield *(G-2801)*

▲ **Michels Inc** .... G 313 441-3620
Dearborn *(G-3741)*

Milford Jewelers Inc .... G 248 676-0721
Milford *(G-10970)*

Mount-N-Repair .... G 248 647-8670
Birmingham *(G-1694)*

Newell Brands Inc .... G 734 284-2528
Taylor *(G-15749)*

Novus Corporation .... E 248 545-8600
Warren *(G-17175)*

Orin Jewelers Inc .... F 734 422-7030
Garden City *(G-5834)*

Otters Oasis .... G 269 788-9987
Battle Creek *(G-1234)*

▲ **Pure & Simple Solutions LLC** .... E 248 398-4600
Troy *(G-16570)*

Rebel Nell L3c .... G 716 640-4267
Detroit *(G-4332)*

Rolfs Jewelers Ltd .... G 586 739-3906
Shelby Township *(G-14681)*

Seoul International Inc .... G 586 275-2494
Sterling Heights *(G-15489)*

◆ **Terryberry Company LLC** .... C 616 458-1391
Grand Rapids *(G-6923)*

▲ **Touchstone Distributing Inc** .... G 517 669-8200
Dewitt *(G-4468)*

Tva Kane Inc .... G 248 946-4670
Novi *(G-12019)*

Wattsson & Wattsson Jewelers .... F 906 228-5775
Marquette *(G-10561)*

Weyhing Bros Manufacturing Co .... F 313 567-0600
Detroit *(G-4438)*

3914 Silverware, Plated & Stainless Steel Ware

American Awards & Engrv LLC .... G 810 229-5911
Milford *(G-10954)*

Carry Manufacturing Inc .... G 989 672-2779
Caro *(G-2467)*

Fun Promotion LLC .... G 616 453-4245
Grand Rapids *(G-6424)*

H M Products Inc .... G 313 875-5148
Detroit *(G-4109)*

Infra Corporation .... F 248 623-0400
Waterford *(G-17351)*

Isby Industry LLC .... G 313 269-4213
Sterling Heights *(G-15377)*

M P C Awards .... G 586 254-4660
Shelby Township *(G-14629)*

McCallum Fabricating LLC .... F 586 784-5555
Allenton *(G-229)*

▲ **Michigan Plaques & Awards Inc** .... E 248 398-6400
Berkley *(G-1587)*

Pneumatic Innovations LLC .... G 989 734-3435
Millersburg *(G-10992)*

S
I
C

Employee Codes: A=Over 500 employees, B=251-500
C=101-250, D=51-100, E=20-50, F=10-19, G=3-9

▼ Quicktrophy LLC F 906 228-2604
Marquette (G-10555)

Rivore Metals LLC D 800 248-1250
Troy (G-16581)

Rivore Metals LLC E 248 397-8724
Detroit (G-4346)

Rivore Metals LLC E 248 397-8724
Pontiac (G-12862)

Samco Industries LLC F 586 447-3900
Roseville (G-13866)

3915 Jewelers Findings & Lapidary Work

Alex and Ani LLC G 248 649-7348
Troy (G-16183)

Au Enterprises Inc F 248 544-9700
Berkley (G-1580)

Finger Fit Co G 734 522-2935
Saint Clair Shores (G-14248)

Jostens Inc G 734 308-3879
Ada (G-19)

Kevin Wheat & Assoc Ltd G 517 349-0101
Okemos (G-12127)

L N T Inc G 248 347-6006
Novi (G-11925)

Trenton Jewelers Ltd G 734 676-0188
Trenton (G-16161)

3931 Musical Instruments

Adams Jerroll Organ Builder G 734 439-7203
Milan (G-10931)

Alf Enterprises Inc G 734 665-2012
Ann Arbor (G-351)

▲ Black Swamp Percussion LLC G 800 557-0988
Zeeland (G-18122)

Brian M Fowler Pipe Organs G 517 485-3748
Eaton Rapids (G-4719)

Farmer Musical Instruments G 206 412-5379
Cedar (G-2541)

Ferrees Tools Inc E 269 965-0511
Battle Creek (G-1187)

Fred Kelly Picks LLC G 989 348-2938
Grayling (G-7106)

◆ Ghs Corporation B 269 968-3351
Springfield (G-15192)

GHS Corporation E 800 388-4447
Springfield (G-15193)

Grip Studios G 248 757-0796
Plymouth (G-12633)

Guarneri House LLC G 616 451-4960
Hudsonville (G-8158)

Gundry Media Inc G 616 734-8977
Grand Rapids (G-6486)

◆ Harman Becker Auto Systems Inc B 248 785-2361
Novi (G-11896)

Heritage Guitar Inc F 269 385-5721
Kalamazoo (G-8768)

▲ Klingler Consulting & Mfg F 810 765-3700
Marine City (G-10476)

Kyoei Electronics America Inc F 248 773-3690
Novi (G-11924)

Lauck Pipe Organ Co G 269 694-4500
Otsego (G-12243)

Rebeats F 989 463-4757
Alma (G-248)

Rt Swanson Inc G 517 627-4955
Grand Ledge (G-6115)

Wigton Pipe Organs Inc G 810 796-3311
Dryden (G-4573)

3942 Dolls & Stuffed Toys

▲ Bear Factory LLC F 248 437-4930
Wixom (G-17771)

Dolls By Maurice Inc G 586 739-5147
Utica (G-16741)

Marshal E Hyman and Associates G 248 643-0642
Troy (G-16488)

3944 Games, Toys & Children's Vehicles

Abbotts Magic Manufacturing Co G 269 432-3235
Colon (G-3369)

▲ American Models G 248 437-6800
Whitmore Lake (G-17687)

◆ American Plastic Toys Inc B 248 624-4881
Walled Lake (G-16890)

American Plastic Toys Inc D 989 685-2455
Rose City (G-13757)

Ann Williams Group LLC G 248 731-8588
Bloomfield Hills (G-1746)

▲ Au Gres Sheep Factory F 989 876-8787
Au Gres (G-742)

Charlies Wood Shop F 989 845-2632
Chesaning (G-2722)

Claybanks Kids LLC G 231 893-4071
Montague (G-11089)

Dog Might LLC F 734 679-0646
Ann Arbor (G-423)

Eca Educational Services Inc E 248 669-7170
Commerce Township (G-3403)

Fourth Ave Birkenstock G 734 663-1644
Ann Arbor (G-466)

Hallwell Games LLC G 586 879-3404
Southfield (G-14935)

Hampton Company Inc G 517 765-2222
Burlington (G-2132)

Houseparty G 616 422-1226
Holland (G-7681)

Kid By Kid Inc G 586 781-2345
Macomb (G-10134)

Lost Horizons Inc G 248 366-6858
Commerce Township (G-3423)

▲ Mac Enterprises Inc F 313 846-4567
Manchester (G-10407)

▲ Merdel Game Manufacturing Co G 231 845-1263
Ludington (G-10071)

Meteor Web Marketing Inc F 734 822-4999
Ann Arbor (G-553)

National Ambucs Inc E 231 798-4244
Norton Shores (G-11778)

Pannell S-Erynn G 248 692-3192
Farmington (G-4906)

Poof-Slinky LLC E 734 454-9552
Plymouth (G-12723)

Proto Spec G 269 934-8615
Benton Harbor (G-1540)

Sassy 14 LLC E 616 243-0767
Kentwood (G-9031)

◆ Shelti Inc E 989 893-1739
Bay City (G-1357)

Spark Games LLC G 269 303-7201
Kalamazoo (G-8895)

▲ Talicor Inc E 269 685-2345
Plainwell (G-12545)

3949 Sporting & Athletic Goods, NEC

Accessories & Specialties Inc G 989 235-3331
Crystal (G-3607)

Aerospace America Inc E 989 684-2121
Bay City (G-1273)

Arrowmat LLC G 800 920-6035
Howell (G-8016)

Assenmacher Lightweight Cycles G 810 232-2994
Flint (G-5378)

Assra F 906 225-1828
Marquette (G-10518)

B4 Sports Inc G 248 454-9700
Bloomfield Hills (G-1749)

Baum Sports Inc G 231 922-2125
Traverse City (G-15904)

Bay De Noc Lure Company F 906 428-1133
Gladstone (G-5906)

Bbp Investment Holdings LLC F 231 725-4966
Muskegon (G-11278)

Bill Eldridge Associates G 248 698-3705
White Lake (G-17630)

Bitzenburger Machine & Tool G 517 627-8433
Grand Ledge (G-6102)

BJ Sports Inc F 269 342-2415
Portage (G-12985)

◆ Bohning Company Ltd E 231 229-4247
Lake City (G-9085)

Bohning Company Ltd E 231 229-4247
Lake City (G-9086)

Bronco Connection Inc G 616 997-2263
Coopersville (G-3549)

◆ Brunswick Bowling Products LLC B 231 725-3300
Muskegon (G-11285)

Buck Stop Lure Company Inc G 989 762-5091
Stanton (G-15228)

Bucks Sports Products Inc G 763 229-1331
Gladstone (G-5908)

Carbon Impact Inc E 231 929-8152
Traverse City (G-15930)

Cheboygan Golf and Country CLB E 231 627-4264
Cheboygan (G-2678)

Chiipss G 248 345-6112
Detroit (G-3935)

Consumer Advntage Rference Svc G 586 783-1806
Clinton Township (G-3089)

Container Specialties Inc E 989 728-4231
Hale (G-7224)

◆ Conway Products Corporation E 616 698-2601
Grand Rapids (G-6308)

Craig C Askins G 810 231-4340
Brighton (G-1907)

▲ Crl Inc E 906 428-3710
Gladstone (G-5910)

Delta 6 LLC G 248 778-6414
Livonia (G-9703)

▲ Discraft Inc E 248 624-2250
Wixom (G-17794)

Double Six Sports Complex F 989 762-5342
Stanton (G-15229)

▲ Dreamweaver Lure Company Inc F 231 843-3652
Ludington (G-10057)

Dunhams Athleisure Corporation F 248 658-1382
Madison Heights (G-10235)

▲ Ed Cumings Inc E 810 736-0130
Flint (G-5423)

▲ Edens Technologies LLC F 517 304-1324
Northville (G-11689)

Elite Arms Inc F 734 424-9955
Chelsea (G-2709)

Eppinger Mfg Co F 313 582-3205
Dearborn (G-3703)

Family Trdtons Tree Stands LLC G 517 543-3926
Charlotte (G-2647)

Fish On Sports Inc G 231 342-5231
Interlochen (G-8240)

▲ G5 Outdoors LLC G 866 456-8836
Memphis (G-10709)

Golf Store G 517 347-8733
Okemos (G-12125)

Grapentin Specialties Inc G 810 724-0636
Imlay City (G-8201)

Great Lakes Fish Decoy Collect G 734 427-7768
Livonia (G-9759)

▲ Guys Timing Inc G 517 404-3746
Brighton (G-1936)

Hl Outdoors G 989 422-3264
Houghton Lake (G-7992)

J C Walker & Sons Corp G 248 752-8165
Swartz Creek (G-15668)

James D Frisbie F 616 868-0092
Alto (G-327)

K & E Tackle Inc F 269 945-4496
Hastings (G-7418)

Kennedy Sales Inc G 586 228-9390
Clinton Township (G-3154)

Killer Paint Ball G 248 491-0088
South Lyon (G-14798)

▲ King Par, LLC D 810 732-2470
Flushing (G-5539)

Kokaly Sports G 989 671-7412
Bay City (G-1325)

Liebner Enterprises LLC G 231 331-3076
Cheboygan (G-2686)

Lone Wolf Custom Bows G 989 735-3358
Glennie (G-5944)

M B B M Inc G 269 344-6361
Kalamazoo (G-8813)

M-22 Challenge G 231 392-2212
Traverse City (G-16029)

M-B-M Manufacturing Inc G 231 924-9614
Fremont (G-5778)

Marhar Snowboards LLC G 616 432-3104
Fruitport (G-5796)

▲ Mason Tackle Company E 810 631-4571
Otisville (G-12233)

McClure Tables Inc G 616 662-5974
Hudsonville (G-8165)

McClure Tables Inc G 616 662-5974
Jenison (G-8633)

▲ McKeon Products Inc E 586 427-7560
Warren (G-17146)

▲ Mike Vaughn Custom Sports Inc E 248 969-8956
Oxford (G-12361)

Mitchell Coates D 231 582-5878
Boyne City (G-1829)

Mmp Molded Magnesium Pdts LLC G 517 789-8505
Jackson (G-8534)

My-Can LLC G 989 288-7779
Durand (G-4610)

National Credit Corporation F 734 459-8100
West Bloomfield (G-17491)

Nelson Technologies Inc D 906 774-5566
Iron Mountain (G-8292)

Nipguards LLC G 734 544-4490
Ann Arbor (G-574)

39 MISCELLANEOUS MANUFACTURING INDUSTRIES

North Post Inc ....G..... 906 482-5210
 Hancock (G-7254)
Northern Trading Group LLC ....G..... 248 885-8750
 Birmingham (G-1696)
Northport Manufacturing Inc ....G..... 616 874-6455
 Rockford (G-13584)
▲ Nustep LLC ....D..... 734 769-3939
 Ann Arbor (G-579)
Overkill Research & Dev Labs ....G..... 517 768-8155
 Jackson (G-8546)
Owosso Country Club Pro Shop ....G..... 989 723-1470
 Owosso (G-12308)
Penchura LLC ....F..... 810 229-6245
 Brighton (G-1977)
Perfect Expressions ....G..... 248 640-1287
 Bloomfield Hills (G-1790)
Plastisnow LLC ....G..... 414 397-1233
 Plainwell (G-12539)
Pluskate Boarding Company ....G..... 248 426-0899
 Farmington (G-4908)
Powerplus Mouthguard ....G..... 231 357-2167
 Traverse City (G-16075)
Pressweld Manufacturing Co ....G..... 734 675-8282
 Portland (G-13066)
▲ Pro Release Inc ....G..... 810 512-4120
 Marine City (G-10480)
Proos Manufacturing Inc ....D..... 616 454-5622
 Grand Rapids (G-6791)
▲ Pull-Buoy Inc ....G..... 586 997-0900
 Sterling Heights (G-15456)
Qsr Outdoor Products Inc.................G..... 989 354-0777
 Alpena (G-310)
Quality Industries Inc ....E..... 517 439-1591
 Hillsdale (G-7536)
R and T Sporting Clays Inc ....G..... 586 215-9861
 Harrison Township (G-7345)
▲ Randlis Manufacturing Co ....G..... 313 368-0220
 Detroit (G-4329)
Ripper Ventures LLC ....G..... 248 808-2325
 Plymouth (G-12736)
Riverfront Cycle Inc ....G..... 517 482-8585
 Lansing (G-9418)
Rochester Sports LLC ....F..... 248 608-6000
 Rochester Hills (G-13507)
Rogers Athletic ....G..... 989 386-7393
 Clare (G-2887)
Rogers Athletic Company Inc ....F..... 989 386-2950
 Farwell (G-5165)
Rolston Hockey Academy LLC ....G..... 248 450-5300
 Oak Park (G-12093)
Ryan Reynolds Golf Shop LLC ....G..... 269 629-9311
 Rochester (G-13349)
▲ Shane Group LLC ....G..... 517 439-4316
 Hillsdale (G-7541)
Soupcan Inc ....F..... 269 381-2101
 Galesburg (G-5815)
Spieth Anderson USA Lc ....F..... 817 536-3366
 Lansing (G-9265)
Superior Hockey ....G..... 906 225-9008
 Marquette (G-10559)
Superior Marine Products LLC ....G..... 906 370-9908
 Hancock (G-7257)
Supertramp Custom Trampoline ....F..... 616 634-2010
 Grand Rapids (G-6905)
▲ T L V Inc ....F..... 989 773-4362
 Mount Pleasant (G-11232)
Thomson Plastics Inc ....D..... 517 545-5026
 Howell (G-8109)
Thunderdome Media LLC ....G..... 800 978-0206
 Plymouth (G-12770)
Total Tennis LLC ....G..... 248 594-1749
 Bloomfield Hills (G-1805)
Trainingmask LLC ....F..... 888 407-7555
 Cadillac (G-2283)
Turkey Creek Inc ....F..... 517 451-5221
 Tecumseh (G-15814)
U S Target Inc ....G..... 586 445-3131
 Roseville (G-13884)
▲ United Shield Intl LLC ....E..... 231 933-1179
 Traverse City (G-16135)
▲ Warrior Sports Inc ....D..... 800 968-7845
 Warren (G-17289)
Wellmans Sport Center ....G..... 989 739-2869
 Oscoda (G-12224)
Winn Archery Equipment Co ....G..... 269 637-2658
 South Haven (G-14784)
Witchcraft Tape Products Inc ....D..... 269 468-3399
 Coloma (G-3368)
▲ Xenith LLC ....E..... 866 888-2322
 Detroit (G-4452)

Y M C A Family Center ....G..... 269 428-9622
 Saint Joseph (G-14356)

3951 Pens & Mechanical Pencils

Carco Inc...F..... 313 925-1053
 Detroit (G-3930)

3952 Lead Pencils, Crayons & Artist's Mtrls

J Cilluffo Son Studio ....G..... 810 794-2911
 Clay (G-2998)
▲ Mac Enterprises Inc ....F..... 313 846-4567
 Manchester (G-10407)
▲ Markerboard People Inc ....E..... 517 372-1666
 Lansing (G-9244)
Panoplate Lithographics Inc ....G..... 269 343-4644
 Kalamazoo (G-8840)
Pro Search ....G..... 248 553-7700
 Farmington Hills (G-5102)

3953 Marking Devices

All American Embroidery Inc ....F..... 734 421-9292
 Livonia (G-9634)
▲ Argon Tool Inc ....F..... 248 583-1605
 Madison Heights (G-10195)
Borries Mkg Systems Partnr ....G..... 734 761-9549
 Ann Arbor (G-388)
Carco Inc...F..... 313 925-1053
 Detroit (G-3930)
Carcone Co ....G..... 248 348-2677
 Novi (G-11843)
Collier Enterprise III ....G..... 269 503-3402
 Sturgis (G-15600)
Columbia Marking Tools Inc ....E..... 586 949-8400
 Chesterfield (G-2754)
Detroit Marking Products Corp..........F..... 313 838-9760
 Canton (G-2364)
F & A Enterprises of Michigan ....G..... 906 228-3222
 Marquette (G-10531)
JL Geisler Sign Company ....F..... 586 574-1800
 Troy (G-16438)
Lakeside Property Services ....G..... 863 455-9038
 Holland (G-7718)
Mark Maker Company Inc.................E..... 616 538-6980
 Grand Rapids (G-6643)
Mark-Pack Inc ....E..... 616 837-5400
 Coopersville (G-3564)
Michigan Shippers Supply Inc ....F..... 616 935-6680
 Spring Lake (G-15163)
Mlh Services LLC ....G..... 313 768-4403
 Detroit (G-4252)
Nelson Paint Co of Mich Inc..............G..... 906 774-5566
 Kingsford (G-9063)
▼ New Method Steel Stamps Inc ....G..... 586 293-0200
 Fraser (G-5697)
Rite Mark Stamp Company ....E..... 248 391-7600
 Auburn Hills (G-992)
Rodzina Industries Inc ....G..... 810 235-2341
 Flint (G-5493)
Rubber Stamps Unlimited Inc............F..... 734 451-7300
 Plymouth (G-12746)
Stamp-Rite Incorporated ....E..... 517 487-5071
 Lansing (G-9267)
Stamping Grounds Inc ....G..... 248 851-6764
 Bloomfield Hills (G-1798)
Volk Corporation ....G..... 616 940-9900
 Farmington Hills (G-5150)
West Michigan Stamp & Seal ....G..... 269 323-1913
 Portage (G-13055)

3955 Carbon Paper & Inked Ribbons

▲ Cau Acquisition Company LLC ....D..... 989 875-8133
 Ithaca (G-8357)
Compatible Laser Products Inc ....F..... 810 629-0459
 Fenton (G-5197)
Lps-2 Inc ....G..... 313 538-0181
 Redford (G-13168)
Mikan Corporation ....F..... 734 944-9447
 Saline (G-14401)
Visionit Supplies and Svcs Inc ....A..... 313 664-5650
 Detroit (G-4432)

3961 Costume Jewelry & Novelties

Amalgamations Ltd ....G..... 248 879-7345
 Troy (G-16194)
Bead Gallery ....F..... 734 663-6800
 Ann Arbor (G-381)
HL Manufacturing Inc ....F..... 586 731-2800
 Utica (G-16742)

Preusser Jewelers ....G..... 616 458-1425
 Grand Rapids (G-6773)
Rosary Workshop ....G..... 906 788-4846
 Stephenson (G-15239)
Swarovski North America Ltd ....E..... 248 874-0753
 Auburn Hills (G-1008)
Swarovski North America Ltd ....G..... 616 977-5008
 Grand Rapids (G-6907)

3965 Fasteners, Buttons, Needles & Pins

A Raymond Tinnerman Mexico..........G..... 248 537-3404
 Rochester Hills (G-13361)
▲ Acument Global Tech Inc ....E..... 586 254-3900
 Sterling Heights (G-15252)
Axis Enterprises Inc ....D..... 616 677-5281
 Marne (G-10504)
▲ Baker Fastening Systems Inc ....G..... 616 669-7400
 Hudsonville (G-8147)
Decoties Inc ....G..... 906 285-1286
 Bessemer (G-1604)
◆ Ebinger Manufacturing Company ..F..... 248 486-8880
 Brighton (G-1917)
Elkay Industries Inc ....G..... 269 381-4266
 Kalamazoo (G-8735)
Fas N Nedschroef Amer Inc ....G..... 586 795-1220
 Sterling Heights (G-15336)
Fourslides Inc....................................F..... 313 564-5600
 Chesterfield (G-2779)
▲ Michigan ATF Holdings LLC ......D..... 734 941-2220
 Romulus (G-13708)
Ortus Enterprises LLC ....G..... 269 491-1447
 Portage (G-13020)
▲ Penn Automotive Inc ....B..... 248 599-3700
 Waterford (G-17366)
Penn Engineering & Mfg Corp ....B..... 313 299-8500
 Waterford (G-17367)
Punch Tech ....E..... 810 364-4811
 Marysville (G-10612)
Rayomar Enterprises Inc ....G..... 313 415-9102
 Warren (G-17217)
Rhino Strapping Products Inc ....F..... 734 442-4040
 Taylor (G-15763)
Rodenhouse Inc.................................G..... 616 454-3100
 Grand Rapids (G-6834)
Schafer Products Co ....G..... 517 238-2266
 Coldwater (G-3329)
Scs Fasteners LLC ....G..... 586 563-0865
 Eastpointe (G-4709)
Transfer Tool Systems Inc ....D..... 616 846-8510
 Grand Haven (G-6090)
Universal Components LLC ....G..... 517 861-7064
 Howell (G-8119)

3991 Brooms & Brushes

Brollytime Inc ....F..... 312 854-7606
 Royal Oak (G-13911)
City of Taylor ....E..... 734 374-1372
 Taylor (G-15700)
Custom Built Brush Company ....F..... 269 463-3171
 Watervliet (G-17390)
▲ Detroit Qulty Brush Mfg Co Inc ...D..... 734 525-5660
 Livonia (G-9708)
Duff Brush LLC ....G..... 906 863-3319
 Menominee (G-10730)
Eco Brushes and Fibers ....G..... 231 683-9202
 Muskegon (G-11315)
Even Weight Brush LLC ....G..... 906 863-3319
 Menominee (G-10732)
Halonen Mfg Group Inc ....G..... 906 483-4077
 Atlantic Mine (G-736)
▲ Laco Inc.......................................E..... 231 929-3300
 Traverse City (G-16020)
Mack Andrew & Son Brush Co ....G..... 517 849-9272
 Jonesville (G-8660)
Michigan Brush Mfg Co.....................E..... 313 834-1070
 Detroit (G-4238)
R J Manufacturing Incorporated ....G..... 906 779-9151
 Crystal Falls (G-3613)
▲ Ranir LLC ....B..... 616 698-8880
 Grand Rapids (G-6808)
Rbt Mfg LLC ....G..... 800 691-8204
 Plymouth (G-12732)
Shais Ldscpg Snow Plowing LLC .....G..... 248 234-3663
 Walled Lake (G-16903)
Superior Equipment LLC ....G..... 269 388-2871
 Kalamazoo (G-8903)
▼ Sweepster Attachments LLC .....A..... 734 996-9116
 Dexter (G-4512)
▼ Thierica Equipment Corporation ..E..... 616 453-6570
 Grand Rapids (G-6928)

Employee Codes: A=Over 500 employees, B=251-500
C=101-250, D=51-100, E=20-50, F=10-19, G=3-9

39 MISCELLANEOUS MANUFACTURING INDUSTRIES SIC SECTION

3993 Signs & Advertising Displays

▲ 3 D & A Display LLC .... G 616 827-3323
Grand Rapids *(G-6119)*
5 Pyn Inc .... G 906 228-2828
Negaunee *(G-11466)*
A D Johnson Engraving Co Inc .... F 269 385-0044
Kalamazoo *(G-8672)*
A-1 Engraving & Signs Inc .... G 810 231-2227
Brighton *(G-1875)*
A-1 Signs .... G 269 488-9411
Portage *(G-12980)*
Adams Outdoor Advg Ltd Partnr .... E 517 321-2121
Lansing *(G-9201)*
Advance Graphic Systems Inc .... E 248 656-8000
Rochester Hills *(G-13365)*
Advanced Signs Incorporated .... F 616 846-4667
Ferrysburg *(G-5333)*
▲ Advantage Sign Supply Inc .... E 877 237-4464
Hudsonville *(G-8143)*
Advertsing Ntwrk Solutions Inc .... G 248 475-7881
Rochester *(G-13312)*
Agnew Grphics Signs Promotions .... G 989 723-4621
Owosso *(G-12276)*
Alex Delvecchio Entps Inc .... E 248 619-9600
Troy *(G-16184)*
All American Embroidery Inc .... F 734 421-9292
Livonia *(G-9634)*
Allen Pattern of Michigan .... F 269 963-4131
Battle Creek *(G-1145)*
Allied Signs Inc .... F 586 791-7900
Clinton Township *(G-3043)*
Allstate Sign Company Inc .... G 989 386-4045
Farwell *(G-5157)*
Alternative Heating & Fuel .... G 231 745-6110
Baldwin *(G-1081)*
American Label & Tag Inc .... E 734 454-7600
Canton *(G-2347)*
Amor Sign Studios Inc .... F 231 723-8361
Manistee *(G-10414)*
Ar2 Engineering LLC .... E 248 735-9999
Novi *(G-11829)*
Archer Wire International Corp .... D 231 869-6911
Pentwater *(G-12428)*
Arlington Display Inds Inc .... G 313 837-1212
Detroit *(G-3877)*
Armstrong Display Concepts .... F 231 652-1675
Newaygo *(G-11563)*
▲ Arnets Inc .... F 734 665-3650
Ann Arbor *(G-367)*
Art & Image .... G 800 566-4162
Benton Harbor *(G-1483)*
Art/Fx Sign Co .... G 269 465-5706
Bridgman *(G-1860)*
Attitude & Experience Inc .... F 231 946-7446
Traverse City *(G-15900)*
Ausable Woodworking Co Inc .... E 989 348-7086
Frederic *(G-5750)*
Auto Trim Northwest Ohio In .... G 517 265-3202
Adrian *(G-50)*
Auxier & Associates LLC .... G 231 486-0641
Traverse City *(G-15901)*
Auxier & Associates LLC .... G 231 933-7446
Traverse City *(G-15902)*
Banacom Instant Signs .... G 810 230-0233
Flint *(G-5382)*
Barrett Signs .... F 989 792-7446
Saginaw *(G-14001)*
Barrys Sign Company .... G 810 234-9919
Flint *(G-5384)*
Bauman Engraving & Signs Inc .... G 906 774-9460
Kingsford *(G-9054)*
Bayview Sign & Design .... G 231 922-7759
Traverse City *(G-15910)*
Bcs Creative LLC .... G 248 917-1660
Davisburg *(G-3627)*
Berline Group Inc .... E 248 203-0492
Royal Oak *(G-13907)*
Bigsignscom .... E 800 790-7611
Grand Haven *(G-5996)*
Bill Carr Signs Inc .... F 810 232-1569
Flint *(G-5389)*
Bill Daup Signs Inc .... G 810 235-4080
Swartz Creek *(G-15663)*
Blue De-Signs LLC .... G 248 808-2583
Royal Oak *(G-13908)*
Bright Star Sign Inc .... G 313 933-4460
Detroit *(G-3917)*
Britten Inc .... C 231 941-8200
Traverse City *(G-15920)*
Broadmoor Motor Sales Inc .... G 269 320-6304
Hastings *(G-7402)*
Bronco Printing Company .... G 248 544-1120
Hazel Park *(G-7435)*
Brownie Signs LLC .... G 248 437-0800
South Lyon *(G-14787)*
Burkett Signs Corp .... F 269 746-4285
Climax *(G-3013)*
C G Witvoet & Sons Company .... E 616 534-6677
Grand Rapids *(G-6249)*
C M S Sales Company Inc .... G 248 853-7446
Rochester Hills *(G-13383)*
C T L Enterprises Inc .... F 616 392-1159
Holland *(G-7583)*
Carrier & Gable Inc .... E 248 477-8700
Farmington Hills *(G-4958)*
Castleton Village Center Inc .... G 616 247-8100
Grand Rapids *(G-6266)*
Charlies Wood Shop .... F 989 845-2632
Chesaning *(G-2722)*
City Animation Co .... E 248 589-0600
Troy *(G-16268)*
City Animation Co .... F 989 743-3458
Corunna *(G-3579)*
Classic Stamp & Signs .... G 231 737-0200
Norton Shores *(G-11746)*
Clips Coupons of Ann Arbo .... G 248 437-9294
South Lyon *(G-14789)*
Cobrex Ltd .... G 734 429-9758
Saline *(G-14382)*
Colonial Sign Co .... G 616 534-1400
Newaygo *(G-11565)*
▲ Commercial Graphics of Mich .... G 810 744-2102
Burton *(G-2150)*
Company B Graphic Design Inc .... G 906 228-5887
Marquette *(G-10524)*
Consort Corporation .... E 269 388-4532
Kalamazoo *(G-8713)*
Cook Sign Plus .... G 586 254-7000
Shelby Township *(G-14568)*
Copy Central Inc .... G 231 941-2298
Traverse City *(G-15947)*
Cotton Concepts Printing LLC .... G 313 444-3857
Detroit *(G-3949)*
Craigs Signs .... G 810 667-7446
Lapeer *(G-9452)*
Creative Designs & Signs Inc .... G 248 334-5580
Pontiac *(G-12811)*
Creative Promotions .... G 734 854-2292
Lambertville *(G-9181)*
Creative Vinyl .... G 269 782-2833
Dowagiac *(G-4538)*
Cronen Signs LLC .... G 269 692-2159
Otsego *(G-12237)*
Custom Vinyl Signs & Designs .... G 989 261-7446
Sheridan *(G-14732)*
D & D Signs Inc .... G 231 941-0340
Traverse City *(G-15954)*
D & G Signs LLC .... G 810 230-6445
Flint *(G-5411)*
D Sign LLC .... G 616 392-3841
Holland *(G-7604)*
D T R Sign Co LLC .... G 616 889-8927
Hastings *(G-7405)*
Dearborn Signs & Awnings .... G 313 584-8828
Dearborn *(G-3691)*
Decor Group International Inc .... F 248 307-2430
Orchard Lake *(G-12165)*
Delux Monogramming Screen Prtg .... G 989 288-5321
Durand *(G-4607)*
▲ Design Fabrications Inc .... D 248 597-0988
Madison Heights *(G-10229)*
Detroit Art Collection LLC .... G 313 373-7689
Detroit *(G-3970)*
Detroit Marking Products Corp .... F 313 838-9760
Canton *(G-2364)*
▲ Detroit Name Plate Etching Inc .... E 248 543-5200
Ferndale *(G-5278)*
Dicks Signs .... G 810 987-9002
Port Huron *(G-12911)*
Digital Impact Design Inc .... G 269 337-4200
Kalamazoo *(G-8727)*
Digital Information Svcs LLC .... G 313 365-7299
Detroit *(G-4009)*
Dimension Graphics Inc .... G 616 245-1447
Grand Rapids *(G-6352)*
Display Structures Inc .... F 810 991-0801
Troy *(G-16321)*
Dmp Sign Company .... G 248 996-9281
Southfield *(G-14885)*
Donald Francis Strzynski .... G 231 929-7443
Cadillac *(G-2244)*
Dornbos Sign Inc .... F 517 543-4000
Charlotte *(G-2645)*
Douglas E Fulk .... G 517 482-2090
Lansing *(G-9362)*
E and J Advertising LLC .... G 586 977-3500
Warren *(G-17013)*
Eagle Graphics and Design .... G 248 618-0000
Waterford *(G-17340)*
Earl Daup Signs .... F 810 767-2020
Flint *(G-5420)*
Eberhard and Father Signworks .... G 989 892-5566
Essexville *(G-4872)*
Eco Sign Solutions LLC .... G 734 276-8585
Ann Arbor *(G-432)*
Edwards Outdoor Science .... G 906 353-7375
Baraga *(G-1102)*
Engineering Reproduction Inc .... F 313 366-3390
Detroit *(G-4038)*
Epi Printers Inc .... D 734 261-9400
Livonia *(G-9729)*
Epic Fine Arts Company Inc .... G 313 274-7400
Taylor *(G-15716)*
Erie Marking Inc .... F 989 754-8360
Saginaw *(G-14035)*
Euko Design-Signs Inc .... G 248 478-1330
Farmington Hills *(G-4992)*
Expressign Design .... G 734 747-7444
Ann Arbor *(G-452)*
▲ Fairfield Investment Co .... G 734 427-4141
Livonia *(G-9734)*
Fairmont Sign Company .... E 313 368-4000
Detroit *(G-4050)*
Fantastic Images Signs .... G 248 683-5556
Waterford *(G-17343)*
Fastsigns .... G 248 488-9010
Farmington Hills *(G-4997)*
Fastsigns International Inc .... G 231 941-0300
Traverse City *(G-15968)*
Fedex Office & Print Svcs Inc .... F 313 359-3124
Dearborn *(G-3705)*
Fedex Office & Print Svcs Inc .... E 734 996-0050
Ann Arbor *(G-460)*
Fire Safety Displays Co .... G 313 274-7888
Dearborn Heights *(G-3785)*
▲ Firebolt Group Inc .... F 248 624-8880
Wixom *(G-17810)*
Flairwood Industries Inc .... E 231 798-8324
Norton Shores *(G-11756)*
Fosters Ventures LLC .... F 248 519-7446
Troy *(G-16371)*
Freshwater Dgtal Mdia Prtnrs .... F 616 446-1771
Kentwood *(G-9007)*
Fug Inc .... G 269 781-8036
Marshall *(G-10568)*
G & W Display Fixtures Inc .... E 517 369-7110
Bronson *(G-2026)*
Gardner Signs Inc .... F 248 689-9100
Troy *(G-16379)*
General Scoreboard Services .... G 734 753-5652
Belleville *(G-1445)*
Genesee County Herald Inc .... F 810 686-3840
Clio *(G-3272)*
▲ George P Johnson Company .... D 248 475-2500
Auburn Hills *(G-883)*
Golden Pointe Inc .... G 313 581-8284
Detroit *(G-4096)*
Grafaktri Inc .... G 734 665-0717
Ann Arbor *(G-476)*
Graph-X Signs .... G 734 420-0906
Plymouth *(G-12631)*
Graphic Cmmnctions Design Svcs .... G 586 566-5200
Shelby Township *(G-14597)*
Graphic Visions Inc .... F 248 347-3355
Farmington Hills *(G-5013)*
Graphics Hse Spt Prmotions Inc .... E 231 733-1877
Muskegon *(G-11335)*
Graphicus Signs & Designs .... G 231 652-9160
Newaygo *(G-11569)*
Graphix Signs & Embroidery .... G 616 396-0009
Holland *(G-7650)*
Grasshopper Signs Graphics LLC .... F 248 946-8475
Farmington Hills *(G-5014)*
▼ Griffon Inc .... F 231 788-4630
Muskegon *(G-11340)*
H M Day Signs Inc .... G 231 946-7132
Traverse City *(G-15996)*
Handicap Sign Inc .... G 616 454-9416
Grand Rapids *(G-6489)*

SIC SECTION | 39 MISCELLANEOUS MANUFACTURING INDUSTRIES

Harbor Industries Inc .... B 231 547-3280
Charlevoix *(G-2617)*

◆ **Harbor Industries Inc** .... D 616 842-5330
Grand Haven *(G-6032)*

Hardy & Sons Sign Service Inc .... G 586 779-8018
Saint Clair Shores *(G-14256)*

Harmon Sign Inc .... G 248 348-8150
Wixom *(G-17824)*

HB Stubbs Company LLC .... F 586 574-9700
Warren *(G-17078)*

Heileman Sons Signs & Ltg Svcs .... G 810 364-2900
Saint Clair *(G-14221)*

Hexon Corporation .... F 248 585-7585
Farmington Hills *(G-5018)*

HI-Lites Graphic Inc .... G 231 924-4540
Fremont *(G-5776)*

Higgins Electric Sign Co .... G 517 351-5255
East Lansing *(G-4661)*

Highlander Graphics LLC .... G 734 449-9733
Ann Arbor *(G-491)*

Huron Advertising Company Inc .... E 734 483-2000
Ypsilanti *(G-18077)*

Icon Sign & Design Inc .... G 517 372-1104
Lansing *(G-9294)*

Identicom Sign Solutions LLC .... G 248 344-9590
Farmington Hills *(G-5026)*

Illusion Signs & Graphics Inc .... G 313 581-4376
Dearborn *(G-3724)*

Imagepro Inc .... G 231 723-7906
Manistee *(G-10424)*

Images Unlimited LLC .... G 248 608-8685
Rochester *(G-13328)*

Infonorm Inc .... G 248 276-9027
Lake Orion *(G-9140)*

Inter City Neon Inc .... G 586 754-6020
Warren *(G-17095)*

Jacobs Signs .... G 810 659-2149
Flushing *(G-5537)*

James D Frisbie .... F 616 868-0092
Alto *(G-327)*

Janet Kelly .... F 231 775-2313
Cadillac *(G-2256)*

Japhil Inc .... G 616 455-0260
Grand Rapids *(G-6553)*

JD Group Inc .... E 248 735-9999
Novi *(G-11911)*

JD Hemp Inc .... G 248 549-0095
Royal Oak *(G-13938)*

Jetco Signs .... G 269 420-0202
Battle Creek *(G-1203)*

JL Geisler Sign Company .... F 586 574-1800
Troy *(G-16438)*

Johnson Sign Company Inc .... F 517 784-3720
Jackson *(G-8484)*

Johnson Sign Mint Cnslting LLC .... F 231 796-8880
Paris *(G-12386)*

Jordan Advertising Inc .... F 989 792-7446
Saginaw *(G-14067)*

Jvrf Unified Inc .... G 248 973-2006
Sterling Heights *(G-15383)*

K-Bur Enterprises Inc .... G 616 447-7446
Grand Rapids *(G-6566)*

Kore Group Inc .... G 248 449-6500
Livonia *(G-9800)*

Kore Group Inc .... G 734 677-1500
Ann Arbor *(G-519)*

Kurth Bayard Co .... F 586 771-5174
Saint Clair Shores *(G-14258)*

Landers Drafting Inc .... G 906 228-8690
Marquette *(G-10539)*

Laughabits LLC .... G 248 990-3011
Detroit *(G-4195)*

Lavanway Sign Co Inc .... G 248 356-1600
Southfield *(G-14959)*

Lettering Inc of Michigan .... F 248 223-9700
Livonia *(G-9806)*

Lobo Signs Inc .... E 231 941-7739
Traverse City *(G-16027)*

Mackellar Associates Inc .... F 248 335-4440
Rochester Hills *(G-13466)*

Majik Graphics Inc .... G 586 792-8055
Clinton Township *(G-3165)*

◆ **Marketing Displays Inc** .... C 248 553-1900
Farmington Hills *(G-5058)*

Marketplace Signs .... G 248 393-1609
Orion *(G-12185)*

Marygrove Awnings .... F 734 422-7110
Livonia *(G-9824)*

Maw Ventures Inc .... E 231 798-8324
Norton Shores *(G-11772)*

▲ **Mayfair Golf Accessories** .... F 989 732-8400
Gaylord *(G-5879)*

Media Solutions Inc .... G 313 831-3152
Detroit *(G-4225)*

Media Swing LLC .... G 313 885-2525
Grosse Pointe Farms *(G-7186)*

Meiers Signs Inc .... G 906 786-3424
Escanaba *(G-4843)*

Metro Sign Fabricators Inc .... G 586 493-0502
Clinton Township *(G-3173)*

MHR Investments Inc .... F 989 832-5395
Midland *(G-10884)*

MI Custom Signs LLC .... F 734 946-7446
Taylor *(G-15741)*

Michigan Graphic Arts .... G 517 278-4120
Coldwater *(G-3315)*

Michigan Graphics & Signs .... G 989 224-1936
Saint Johns *(G-14289)*

Michigan Highway Signs Inc .... G 810 695-7529
Flint *(G-5465)*

▲ **Michigan Plaques & Awards Inc** .... E 248 398-6400
Berkley *(G-1587)*

Michigan Signs Inc .... G 734 662-1503
Ann Arbor *(G-556)*

Midwest Safety Products Inc .... E 616 554-5155
Grand Rapids *(G-6686)*

Miller Designworks LLC .... G 313 562-4000
Dearborn *(G-3742)*

Mitchart Inc .... G 989 835-3964
Midland *(G-10892)*

MLS Signs Inc .... F 586 948-0200
Macomb *(G-10145)*

Mod Signs Inc .... F 616 455-0260
Grand Rapids *(G-6694)*

Modern Neon Sign Co Inc .... F 269 349-8636
Kalamazoo *(G-8830)*

Moody Sign Co .... G 517 626-6404
Portland *(G-13064)*

Moore Signs Investments Inc .... E 586 783-9339
Shelby Township *(G-14649)*

Motor City Manufacturing Ltd .... G 586 731-1086
Ferndale *(G-5302)*

Motor City Wraps LLC .... G 734 812-4580
Howell *(G-8067)*

Mrj Sign Company LLC .... G 248 521-2431
Ortonville *(G-12200)*

▲ **Nalcor LLC** .... D 248 541-1140
Ferndale *(G-5303)*

National Sign & Signal Co .... E 269 963-2817
Battle Creek *(G-1231)*

New Rules Marketing Inc .... E 800 962-3119
Spring Lake *(G-15166)*

Nicolet Sign & Design .... G 906 265-5220
Iron River *(G-8317)*

Normic Industries Inc .... E 231 947-8860
Traverse City *(G-16049)*

Norris Graphics Inc .... G 586 447-0646
Clinton Township *(G-3184)*

Northwood Signs Inc .... G 231 843-3956
Ludington *(G-10074)*

On The Side Sign Dsign Grphics .... G 810 266-7446
Byron *(G-2174)*

Outfront Media LLC .... F 616 452-3171
Grand Rapids *(G-6736)*

P D Q Signs Inc .... G 248 669-8600
White Lake *(G-17637)*

Pappys Pad LLC .... G 231 894-0888
Montague *(G-11096)*

Perfect Impressions Inc .... G 248 478-2644
Farmington Hills *(G-5091)*

Perfect Signs .... G 231 233-3721
Manistee *(G-10434)*

Phillips Enterprises Inc .... E 586 615-6208
Shelby Township *(G-14665)*

▲ **Plasticrafts Inc** .... G 313 532-1900
Redford *(G-13183)*

Poco Inc .... E 313 220-6752
Canton *(G-2416)*

▲ **Port Cy Archtctral Signage LLC** .... G 231 739-3463
Muskegon *(G-11403)*

Praise Sign Company .... G 616 439-0315
Grandville *(G-7065)*

Printastic LLC .... F 248 761-5697
Novi *(G-11981)*

Pro Image Design .... G 231 322-8052
Traverse City *(G-16079)*

▲ **Pro-Motion Tech Group LLC** .... D 248 668-3100
Wixom *(G-17880)*

▼ **Programmed Products Corp** .... D 248 348 7755
Novi *(G-11983)*

Qmi Group Inc .... E 248 589-0505
Madison Heights *(G-10342)*

▼ **Quicktrophy LLC** .... F 906 228-2604
Marquette *(G-10555)*

R & R Harwood Inc .... G 616 669-6400
Jenison *(G-8640)*

R J Designers Inc .... G 517 750-1990
Spring Arbor *(G-15127)*

R L Hume Award Co .... G 269 324-3063
Portage *(G-13026)*

Radiant Electric Sign Corp .... G 313 835-1400
Detroit *(G-4328)*

Rathco Safety Supply Inc .... E 269 323-0153
Portage *(G-13027)*

Revolutions Signs Designs LLC .... G 248 439-0727
Royal Oak *(G-13965)*

Richman Company Products Inc .... G 989 686-6251
Bay City *(G-1350)*

Rockstar Digital Inc .... F 888 808-5868
Sterling Heights *(G-15477)*

Rodzina Industries Inc .... G 810 235-2341
Flint *(G-5493)*

Route One .... G 616 455-4883
Grand Rapids *(G-6845)*

Royal Oak Name Plate Company .... F 586 774-8500
Roseville *(G-13863)*

Rsls Corp .... G 248 726-0675
Shelby Township *(G-14683)*

Rwl Sign Co LLC .... G 269 372-3629
Kalamazoo *(G-8877)*

S S Graphics Inc .... G 734 246-4420
Wyandotte *(G-17974)*

Scott Roberts .... G 269 668-5355
Kalamazoo *(G-8885)*

Scotts Signs .... G 616 532-2034
Grandville *(G-7070)*

Sgo Corporate Center LLC .... F 248 596-8626
Plymouth *(G-12752)*

▲ **Shaw & Slavsky Inc** .... E 313 834-3990
Detroit *(G-4359)*

Shelby Signarama Township .... G 586 843-3702
Shelby Township *(G-14693)*

Shields & Shields Enterprises .... G 269 345-7744
Kalamazoo *(G-8886)*

Shop Makarios LLC .... G 800 479-0032
Byron Center *(G-2211)*

Shorecrest Enterprises Inc .... G 586 948-9226
Clinton Township *(G-3225)*

Sign & Art Inc .... G 734 522-0520
Livonia *(G-9930)*

Sign & Graphics Operations LLC .... E 248 596-8626
Plymouth *(G-12753)*

Sign A Rama Canton .... G 734 844-9068
Riverview *(G-13305)*

Sign A Rama Inc .... G 810 494-7446
Brighton *(G-1990)*

Sign and Design .... G 231 348-9256
Petoskey *(G-12475)*

Sign Art Inc .... E 269 381-3012
Kalamazoo *(G-8888)*

Sign Center of Kalamazoo Inc .... G 269 381-6869
Kalamazoo *(G-8889)*

Sign City Inc .... G 269 375-1385
Kalamazoo *(G-8890)*

Sign Concepts Corporation .... F 248 680-8970
Troy *(G-16600)*

Sign Fabricators Inc .... G 586 468-7360
Harrison Township *(G-7349)*

Sign Image Inc .... F 989 781-5229
Saginaw *(G-14149)*

Sign Impressions Inc .... G 269 382-5152
Kalamazoo *(G-8891)*

Sign On Inc .... G 269 381-6869
Kalamazoo *(G-8892)*

Sign Screen Inc .... G 810 239-1100
Flint *(G-5499)*

Sign Specialties Co Inc .... G 313 928-4230
Allen Park *(G-209)*

Sign Stuff Inc .... G 734 458-1055
Livonia *(G-9931)*

Sign Up Inc .... G 906 789-7446
Escanaba *(G-4860)*

Sign Works Inc .... G 517 546-3620
Howell *(G-8097)*

Sign-A-Rama .... G 586 792-7446
Clinton Township *(G-3228)*

Sign-A-Rama Inc .... G 734 522-6661
Garden City *(G-5842)*

Signarama Ann Arbor .... G 734 221-5141
Ann Arbor *(G-632)*

Employee Codes: A=Over 500 employees, B=251-500
C=101-250, D=51-100, E=20-50, F=10-19, G=3-9
2020 Harris Michigan
Industrial Directory
871

39 MISCELLANEOUS MANUFACTURING INDUSTRIES

Signature Signs Inc ..... G 989 777-8701
Bridgeport *(G-1856)*
Signcrafters Inc ..... G 231 773-3343
Muskegon *(G-11426)*
Signmakers Ltd ..... G 616 455-4220
Grand Rapids *(G-6863)*
Signplicity Sign Systems Inc ..... G 231 943-3800
Traverse City *(G-16103)*
Signproco Inc ..... F 248 585-6880
Troy *(G-16601)*
Signs & Designs Inc ..... G 248 549-4850
Royal Oak *(G-13970)*
Signs & Designs Inc ..... G 269 968-8909
Springfield *(G-15203)*
Signs & Laser Engraving ..... G 248 577-6191
Troy *(G-16602)*
Signs By Crannie Inc ..... E 810 487-0000
Flint *(G-5500)*
Signs By Tomorrow ..... G 810 225-7446
Brighton *(G-1991)*
Signs By Tomorrow ..... G 734 822-0537
Ann Arbor *(G-633)*
Signs Etc ..... G 734 941-6991
Wyandotte *(G-17975)*
Signs Letters & Graphics Inc ..... G 231 536-7929
East Jordan *(G-4644)*
Signs Now ..... G 248 623-4966
Waterford *(G-17376)*
Signs Plus ..... F 810 987-7446
Port Huron *(G-12966)*
Signs Unlimited ..... G 906 226-7446
Marquette *(G-10557)*
Signs365com LLC ..... G 800 265-8830
Shelby Township *(G-14694)*
Signtext Incorporated ..... E 248 442-9080
Farmington Hills *(G-5124)*
Signworks of Michigan Inc ..... G 616 954-2554
Grand Rapids *(G-6864)*
Signz LLC ..... G 586 940-9891
Sterling Heights *(G-15498)*
Sky Promotions ..... F 248 613-1637
Ann Arbor *(G-635)*
Spectrum Neon Company ..... G 313 366-7333
Detroit *(G-4371)*
Sporting Image Inc ..... F 269 657-5646
Paw Paw *(G-12413)*
Spry Sign & Graphics Co LLC ..... G 517 524-7685
Concord *(G-3525)*
Stamp-Rite Incorporated ..... E 517 487-5071
Lansing *(G-9267)*
Star Design Metro Detroit LLC ..... E 734 740-0189
Livonia *(G-9944)*
Steel Skinz LLC ..... G 517 545-9955
Howell *(G-8103)*
Steves Custom Signs Inc ..... F 734 662-5964
Ann Arbor *(G-646)*
Sun Ray Sign Group Inc ..... G 616 392-2824
Holland *(G-7820)*
Sunset Enterprises Inc ..... F 269 373-6440
Kalamazoo *(G-8902)*
Superior Graphics Studios Ltd ..... G 906 482-7891
Houghton *(G-7985)*
Supersine Company ..... E 313 892-6200
Lathrup Village *(G-9501)*
Sylvesters ..... G 989 348-9097
Grayling *(G-7116)*
▼ System 2/90 Inc ..... D 616 656-4310
Grand Rapids *(G-6911)*
T M Shea Products Inc ..... F 800 992-5233
Troy *(G-16630)*
▲ Tecart Industries Inc ..... E 248 624-8880
Wixom *(G-17907)*
Terrell Assoc Signs & Disp ..... G 517 726-0455
Vermontville *(G-16824)*
Tile By Bill & Sondra ..... G 616 554-5413
Caledonia *(G-2319)*
Tischco Signs ..... G 231 755-5529
Muskegon *(G-11438)*
Toms Sign Service ..... G 248 852-3550
Rochester Hills *(G-13527)*
▲ Top Deck Systems Inc ..... G 586 263-1550
Clinton Township *(G-3249)*
Traffic Displays LLC ..... G 616 225-8865
Greenville *(G-7159)*
Traffic Signs Inc ..... G 269 964-7511
Springfield *(G-15206)*
Transign LLC ..... G 248 623-6400
Auburn Hills *(G-1031)*
▲ TSS Inc ..... E 586 427-0070
Warren *(G-17271)*

Tyes Inc ..... F 888 219-6301
Ludington *(G-10083)*
Ucb Advertising ..... G 269 808-2411
Plainwell *(G-12550)*
Universal Sign Inc ..... E 616 554-9999
Grand Rapids *(G-6955)*
Upper Level Graphics Inc ..... G 734 525-7111
Livonia *(G-9982)*
USA Sign Frame & Stake Inc ..... G 616 662-9100
Jenison *(G-8646)*
Valassis International Inc ..... B 734 591-3000
Livonia *(G-9987)*
Valley City Sign Company ..... E 616 784-5711
Comstock Park *(G-3519)*
Van Kehrberg Vern ..... G 810 364-1066
Marysville *(G-10625)*
Venture Grafix LLC ..... G 248 449-1330
Wixom *(G-17926)*
Versatility Inc ..... G 616 957-5555
Grand Rapids *(G-6967)*
Vinyl Express ..... G 269 469-5165
New Buffalo *(G-11518)*
Vinyl Graphix Inc ..... G 586 774-1188
Saint Clair Shores *(G-14275)*
Visual Productions Inc ..... E 248 356-4399
Southfield *(G-15061)*
▲ Visual Workplace LLC ..... F 616 583-9400
Byron Center *(G-2215)*
Vital Signs Inc ..... G 313 491-2010
Canton *(G-2441)*
Vital Signs Michigan Inc ..... G 906 632-7602
Sault Sainte Marie *(G-14478)*
Vocational Strategies Inc ..... E 906 482-6142
Calumet *(G-2335)*
Wenz & Gibbens Enterprises ..... G 248 333-7938
Pontiac *(G-12874)*
West Shore Signs Inc ..... G 734 324-7076
Riverview *(G-13306)*
▲ Westcott Displays Inc ..... E 313 872-1200
Detroit *(G-4437)*
Wheelhouse Graphix LLC ..... F 800 732-0815
Bloomfield Hills *(G-1810)*
Whitcomb and Sons Sign Co Inc ..... G 586 752-3576
Romeo *(G-13641)*
▲ Whitehall Products LLC ..... D 231 894-2688
Whitehall *(G-17682)*
Wilde Signs ..... F 231 727-1200
Muskegon *(G-11452)*
Wilfred Swartz & Swartz G ..... G 989 652-6322
Reese *(G-13236)*
Wooden Moon Studio ..... G 269 329-3229
Portage *(G-13059)*
Woods Graphics ..... F 616 691-8025
Greenville *(G-7162)*
Zk Enterprises Inc ..... G 989 728-4439
Alger *(G-140)*

3995 Burial Caskets

Eternal Image Inc ..... G 248 932-3333
Farmington Hills *(G-4990)*
◆ Genesis International LLC ..... E 317 777-6700
Mason *(G-10640)*
Superior Casket Co ..... E 313 592-3190
Redford *(G-13197)*
▲ Universal Casket Co ..... E 269 476-2163
Cassopolis *(G-2537)*

3996 Linoleum & Hard Surface Floor Coverings, NEC

Floorcovering Engineers LLC ..... G 616 299-1007
Grand Rapids *(G-6414)*
Flor TEC Inc ..... G 616 897-3122
Lowell *(G-10028)*
Innovative Surface Works ..... F 734 261-3010
Farmington Hills *(G-5027)*
Pro Floor Service ..... G 517 663-5012
Eaton Rapids *(G-4730)*

3999 Manufacturing Industries, NEC

826 Michigan ..... G 734 761-3463
Ann Arbor *(G-332)*
A & B Display Systems Inc ..... F 989 893-6642
Bay City *(G-1269)*
Abbotts Magic Manufacturing Co ..... G 269 432-3235
Colon *(G-3369)*
Abletech Industries LLC ..... G 734 677-2420
Dexter *(G-4471)*
▲ Access Manufacturing Techn ..... F 224 610-0171
Niles *(G-11593)*

Accurate Mfg Solutions LLC ..... G 248 553-2225
Farmington Hills *(G-4918)*
Achieve Industries LLC ..... G 586 493-9780
Clinton Township *(G-3034)*
Active Plastics Inc ..... F 616 813-5109
Caledonia *(G-2288)*
Actuator Services LLC ..... G 734 242-5456
Monroe *(G-11012)*
Adapt ..... G 989 343-9755
West Branch *(G-17505)*
Admin Industries LLC ..... F 989 685-3438
Rose City *(G-13756)*
Aftermarket Industries LLC ..... G 810 229-3200
Brighton *(G-1879)*
Airman Inc ..... E 248 960-1354
Brighton *(G-1880)*
Allied Support Systems ..... G 734 721-4040
Wayne *(G-17421)*
Alta Distribution LLC ..... F 313 363-1682
Southfield *(G-14829)*
◆ Altus Brands LLC ..... F 231 421-3810
Grawn *(G-7096)*
Ambrosia Inc ..... G 734 529-7174
Dundee *(G-4575)*
AME International LLC ..... E 586 532-8981
Clinton Township *(G-3044)*
American Battery Solutions Inc ..... G 248 462-6364
Lake Orion *(G-9125)*
American Laser Centers LLC ..... A 248 426-8250
Farmington Hills *(G-4929)*
American Marine Shore Control ..... F 248 887-7855
White Lake *(G-17628)*
▲ American MSC Inc ..... E 248 589-7770
Troy *(G-16198)*
AMI Entertainment Network Inc ..... G 877 762-6765
Wyoming *(G-17986)*
▲ Android Industries LLC ..... G 517 322-0141
Lansing *(G-9276)*
Arbor Kitchen LLC ..... G 248 921-4602
Ann Arbor *(G-364)*
Aurora Preserved Flowers ..... G 989 498-0290
Bay City *(G-1278)*
B T I Industries ..... F 586 532-8411
Shelby Township *(G-14554)*
Bach Mobilities Inc ..... G 906 789-9490
Escanaba *(G-4815)*
Bay Archery Sales Co ..... G 989 894-5800
Essexville *(G-4868)*
Bay Home Medical and Rehab Inc ..... E 231 933-1200
Grandville *(G-7021)*
BEAM Industries Inc ..... G 989 799-4044
Saginaw *(G-14002)*
Bee Dazzled Candle Works ..... G 231 882-7765
Benzonia *(G-1573)*
◆ Benteler Automotive Corp ..... C 248 364-7190
Auburn Hills *(G-792)*
Bentley Industries ..... G 810 625-0400
Flint *(G-5387)*
Berlin Holdings LLC ..... G 517 523-2444
Pittsford *(G-12515)*
Best Buy Bones Inc ..... G 810 631-6971
Mount Morris *(G-11158)*
Bloom Industries LLC ..... G 616 890-8029
Traverse City *(G-15913)*
Bloom Industries LLC ..... G 616 453-2946
Grand Rapids *(G-6232)*
Body Contour Ventures LLC ..... G 248 579-6772
Farmington Hills *(G-4945)*
Bolden Industries Inc ..... F 248 387-9489
Detroit *(G-3907)*
Brollytime Inc ..... F 312 854-7606
Royal Oak *(G-13911)*
Brumley Tools Inc ..... G 586 260-8326
Warren *(G-16969)*
◆ Burr Oak Tool Inc ..... C 269 651-9393
Sturgis *(G-15599)*
Burtrum Furs ..... G 810 771-4563
Grand Blanc *(G-5962)*
Busch Machine Tool Supply LLC ..... G 989 798-4794
Freeland *(G-5753)*
Caflor Industries LLC ..... G 734 604-1168
Ypsilanti *(G-18059)*
Candela Products Inc ..... G 248 541-2547
Warren *(G-16976)*
Candle Factory Grand Traverse ..... F 231 946-2280
Traverse City *(G-15929)*
Candle Wick ..... G 248 547-2987
Ferndale *(G-5266)*
Capler Mfg ..... G 586 264-7851
Sterling Heights *(G-15281)*

◆ **Charter House Holdings LLC** ... C ... 616 399-6000
Zeeland *(G-18124)*
Clarity Cbd LLC ... G ... 248 251-6991
Detroit *(G-3939)*
Classic Sea Scapes ... G ... 517 323-7775
Lansing *(G-9282)*
Cmb Mfg LLC ... G ... 920 915-2079
Menominee *(G-10727)*
Collective Industries Corp ... G ... 313 879-1080
Allen Park *(G-195)*
Connely Company ... G ... 586 977-0700
Sterling Heights *(G-15295)*
◆ **Conway Products Corporation** ... E ... 616 698-2601
Grand Rapids *(G-6308)*
Coventry Creations Inc ... G ... 248 547-2987
Ferndale *(G-5268)*
Coventry Industries LLC ... G ... 248 761-8462
Holly *(G-7872)*
Crescent Manufacturing Company ... E ... 517 486-2670
Blissfield *(G-1715)*
Cultivation Stn - Detroit Inc ... G ... 313 383-1766
Allen Park *(G-196)*
D & F Corporation ... D ... 586 254-5300
Sterling Heights *(G-15306)*
Danif Industries Inc ... G ... 248 539-0295
West Bloomfield *(G-17473)*
Dealer Aid Enterprises ... G ... 313 331-5800
Detroit *(G-3965)*
Deans Hobby Stop ... G ... 989 720-2137
Owosso *(G-12288)*
Deluxe Technologies LLC ... E ... 586 294-2340
Fraser *(G-5642)*
Denton Atd Inc ... D ... 734 451-7878
Plymouth *(G-12608)*
Design Manufacturing LLC ... E ... 616 647-2229
Comstock Park *(G-3476)*
Dewsbury Manufacturing Company ... G ... 734 839-6376
Livonia *(G-9709)*
▼ **Dgh Enterprises Inc** ... E ... 269 925-0657
Benton Harbor *(G-1494)*
Diverse Manufacturing Soltion ... G ... 517 423-6691
Tecumseh *(G-15788)*
DMS Manufacturing Solutions ... G ... 517 423-6691
Tecumseh *(G-15789)*
Dog Brown Manufacturing LLC ... G ... 313 255-1400
Redford *(G-13159)*
▲ **Dorden & Company Inc** ... G ... 313 834-7910
Detroit *(G-4015)*
▲ **Dover Metals Inc** ... G ... 269 849-1411
Hartford *(G-7383)*
Eagleburgmann Industries LP ... G ... 989 486-1571
Midland *(G-10857)*
◆ **Ebinger Manufacturing Company** ... F ... 248 486-8880
Brighton *(G-1917)*
ECM Manufacturing Inc ... G ... 810 736-0299
Flint *(G-5421)*
Eileen Smeltzer ... G ... 269 629-8056
Richland *(G-13248)*
▲ **Emag LLC** ... E ... 248 477-7440
Farmington Hills *(G-4983)*
Emerald Mfg ... G ... 269 483-2676
White Pigeon *(G-17647)*
◆ **Emhart Teknologies LLC** ... D ... 248 677-9693
Troy *(G-16342)*
▲ **Endless Possibilities Inc** ... G ... 248 262-7443
Madison Heights *(G-10246)*
Engineering Graphics Inc ... G ... 517 485-5828
Lansing *(G-9225)*
Esl Supplies LLC ... G ... 517 525-7877
Mason *(G-10637)*
Esyntrk Industries LLC ... G ... 248 730-0640
Orchard Lake *(G-12166)*
Exquise Inc ... G ... 248 220-9048
Detroit *(G-4047)*
▲ **Faurecia Interior Systems Inc** ... B ... 248 724-5100
Auburn Hills *(G-861)*
Fieldturf Usa Inc ... G ... 706 625-6533
Auburn Hills *(G-873)*
◆ **Flexi Display Marketing Inc** ... G ... 800 875-1725
Farmington Hills *(G-5003)*
Flowers By Kevin ... G ... 810 376-4600
Deckerville *(G-3808)*
Fowlerville Feed & Pet Sups ... G ... 517 223-9115
Fowlerville *(G-5565)*
Fruit Haven Nursery Inc ... G ... 231 889-9973
Kaleva *(G-8933)*
Fun Learning Company LLC ... F ... 269 362-0651
Macomb *(G-10123)*
Fusion Strategies LLC ... G ... 734 776-1734
Livonia *(G-9745)*

G & L Mfg Inc ... G ... 810 724-4101
Imlay City *(G-8199)*
G & R Machine Tool Inc ... G ... 734 641-6560
Taylor *(G-15724)*
Ganas LLC ... F ... 734 748-0434
Detroit *(G-4076)*
Gearx LLC ... G ... 248 766-6903
Sterling Heights *(G-15354)*
Gr X Manufacturing ... G ... 616 541-7420
Caledonia *(G-2296)*
Grany Greenthumbs LLC ... G ... 517 223-1302
Fowlerville *(G-5568)*
Grh Inc ... G ... 888 344-6639
Lapeer *(G-9463)*
H & H Wildlife Desgn & Furng I ... F ... 231 832-7002
Reed City *(G-13214)*
Haven Sports Manufacturing LLC ... G ... 269 639-8782
South Haven *(G-14762)*
Havers Heritage ... G ... 517 423-3455
Clinton *(G-3022)*
Head Over Heels ... G ... 248 435-2954
Troy *(G-16393)*
Helsels Tree Service Inc ... G ... 231 879-3666
Manton *(G-10454)*
Heritage ... G ... 734 414-0343
Plymouth *(G-12638)*
Hgks Industrial Clay Tool Co I ... G ... 734 340-5500
Canton *(G-2383)*
Hilljack Industries LLC ... G ... 517 552-3874
Howell *(G-8049)*
Hills Manufacturing LLC ... G ... 248 536-3307
Farmington Hills *(G-5020)*
Holland House Candles Inc ... F ... 800 238-8467
Holland *(G-7672)*
Holloway Fur Dressing ... G ... 231 258-5200
Lake City *(G-9088)*
Hoosier Tank and Manufacturing ... G ... 269 683-2550
Niles *(G-11616)*
Imagillation Inc ... G ... 734 481-0140
Ypsilanti *(G-18079)*
Industrial Mtal Idntfction Inc ... G ... 616 847-0060
Spring Lake *(G-15153)*
Industrial Pattern of Lansing ... G ... 517 482-9835
Lansing *(G-9298)*
Industrial Services Group ... E ... 269 945-5291
Lowell *(G-10031)*
Inglis Farms Inc ... G ... 989 727-8727
Alpena *(G-293)*
Innovative Fabrication LLC ... E ... 734 789-9099
Flat Rock *(G-5356)*
Innovative Thermal Systems LLC ... G ... 586 920-2900
Warren *(G-17093)*
International Wood Inds Inc ... G ... 800 598-9663
Grand Rapids *(G-6542)*
Intuitive Technology Inc ... G ... 602 249-5750
Dexter *(G-4495)*
Irene Industries LLC ... G ... 757 696-3969
Commerce Township *(G-3417)*
▲ **J F McCaughin Co** ... E ... 231 759-7304
Norton Shores *(G-11765)*
J&D Industries LLC ... G ... 734 430-6582
Newport *(G-11588)*
Jamieson Fabrication Unlimited ... G ... 269 760-1473
Richland *(G-13250)*
Jennco Industries LLC ... G ... 269 290-3145
Allegan *(G-167)*
Jeremy Jelinek ... G ... 231 313-7124
Traverse City *(G-16012)*
Jk Manufacturing Co ... F ... 231 258-2638
Kalkaska *(G-8945)*
Joshs Frogs ... G ... 517 648-0260
Byron *(G-2173)*
Jupiter Manufacturing ... G ... 989 551-0519
Harbor Beach *(G-7268)*
K12 Inc ... C ... 616 309-1600
Grand Rapids *(G-6567)*
Kalamazoo Candle Company ... F ... 269 532-9816
Kalamazoo *(G-8785)*
Kalamazoo Promise ... G ... 269 337-0037
Kalamazoo *(G-8796)*
Karmann Manufacturing LLC ... E ... 734 582-5900
Plymouth *(G-12662)*
Kenny G Mfg & Sls LLC ... G ... 313 218-6297
Brownstown *(G-2066)*
Kenyon Tj & Associates Inc ... E ... 231 544-1144
Bellaire *(G-1438)*
Kevin Larkin Inc ... G ... 248 736-8203
Waterford *(G-17355)*
Keyes-Davis Company ... E ... 269 962-7505
Springfield *(G-15195)*

Keystone Products LLC ... G ... 248 363-5552
Southfield *(G-14954)*
Kidde Safety ... G ... 800 880-6788
Novi *(G-11915)*
Kims Mart Inc ... G ... 313 592-4929
Detroit *(G-4178)*
Kitty Condo LLC ... E ... 419 690-9063
Livonia *(G-9797)*
Knapp Manufacturing LLC ... G ... 517 279-9538
Coldwater *(G-3312)*
Kopach Filter LLC ... G ... 906 863-8611
Wallace *(G-16886)*
Kriewall Enterprises Inc ... E ... 586 336-0600
Romeo *(G-13631)*
Larrys Button Box ... G ... 734 425-4239
Garden City *(G-5832)*
Lee Beauty & Gen Mechandise ... G ... 586 294-4400
Fraser *(G-5684)*
Liberty Automotive Tech LLC ... G ... 269 487-8114
Holland *(G-7723)*
Loonar Stn Two The 2 or 2nd ... G ... 419 720-1222
Temperance *(G-15834)*
M P C Awards ... G ... 586 254-4660
Shelby Township *(G-14629)*
Mannetron ... E ... 269 962-3475
Battle Creek *(G-1225)*
Manufctring Partners Group LLC ... G ... 517 749-4050
Lapeer *(G-9473)*
Maple Ridge Companies Inc ... E ... 989 356-4807
Posen *(G-13070)*
Marrone Michigan Manufactoring ... G ... 269 427-0300
Bangor *(G-1093)*
McLeod Wood and Christmas Pdts ... G ... 989 777-4800
Bridgeport *(G-1853)*
Metro Engrg of Grnd Rapids ... F ... 616 458-2823
Grand Rapids *(G-6662)*
Mettle Craft Manufacturing LLC ... G ... 586 306-8962
Sterling Heights *(G-15418)*
Midwest Defense Corp ... G ... 231 590-6857
Traverse City *(G-16036)*
Modern Fur Dressing LLC ... G ... 517 589-5575
Leslie *(G-9545)*
Mote Industries Inc ... F ... 248 613-3413
New Haven *(G-11525)*
Mount Mfg LLC ... G ... 231 487-2118
Boyne City *(G-1830)*
Mr McGooz Products Inc ... G ... 313 693-4003
Detroit *(G-4258)*
Msmac Designs LLC ... G ... 313 521-6289
Detroit *(G-4260)*
Nathan Slagter ... G ... 616 648-7423
Lowell *(G-10038)*
New Boston Candle Company ... F ... 734 782-5809
New Boston *(G-11504)*
Next Level Manufacturing LLC ... E ... 269 397-1220
Jenison *(G-8634)*
Niemela ... G ... 906 523-4362
Chassell *(G-2674)*
Nodel-Co ... F ... 248 543-1325
Ferndale *(G-5306)*
North Coast Studios Inc ... F ... 586 359-6630
Roseville *(G-13848)*
▲ **Northwoods Manufacturing Inc** ... D ... 906 779-2370
Kingsford *(G-9065)*
Northwoods Wreathing Company ... G ... 906 202-2888
Gwinn *(G-7221)*
Oak Mountain Industries ... G ... 734 941-7000
Romulus *(G-13716)*
Odin Defense Industries Inc ... G ... 248 434-5072
Troy *(G-16532)*
Palm Industries LLC ... G ... 248 444-7922
South Lyon *(G-14808)*
Palm Industries LLC ... G ... 248 444-7921
Plymouth *(G-12707)*
Palo Alto Manufacturing LLC ... G ... 248 266-3669
Auburn Hills *(G-969)*
Paragon Molds Corporation ... E ... 586 294-7630
Fraser *(G-5704)*
Patricia Huellmantel Pubg ... G ... 248 634-9894
Holly *(G-7890)*
Patriot Manufacturing LLC ... G ... 734 259-2059
Plymouth *(G-12709)*
Perfection Industries Inc ... G ... 231 779-5325
Cadillac *(G-2270)*
Pet Supplies Plus ... F ... 616 554-3600
Grand Rapids *(G-6752)*
Pl Optima Manufacturing LLC ... F ... 616 931-9750
Zeeland *(G-18174)*
Pingree Mfg L3c ... G ... 313 444-8428
Detroit *(G-4302)*

Employee Codes: A=Over 500 employees, B=251-500
C=101-250, D=51-100, E=20-50, F=10-19, G=3-9
2020 Harris Michigan
Industrial Directory
873

Potteryland Inc........G....... 586 781-4425
Washington *(G-17310)*
Precious Furs Llc........G....... 734 262-6262
Livonia *(G-9896)*
Precision Engrg & Mfg Inc........G....... 616 837-6764
Nunica *(G-12041)*
Precision Mfg Group Inc........F....... 616 837-6764
Nunica *(G-12042)*
Preeminence Inc........G....... 313 737-7920
Redford *(G-13185)*
Pro-Built Mfg........G....... 989 354-1321
Alpena *(G-308)*
Probus Technical Services Inc........F....... 876 226-5692
Troy *(G-16563)*
Product Resource Company........G....... 517 484-8400
Lansing *(G-9261)*
Production & Prototype Svc LLC........G....... 586 924-7479
Lenox *(G-9523)*
Profile EDM LLC........G....... 586 949-4586
Chesterfield *(G-2823)*
Protojet LLC........F....... 810 956-8000
Fraser *(G-5712)*
PSI Labs........G....... 734 369-6273
Ann Arbor *(G-607)*
Qsdg Manufacturing LLC........F....... 231 941-1222
Traverse City *(G-16085)*
R J Manufacturing........G....... 810 610-0205
Davison *(G-3660)*
▲ **Rayconnect Inc**........D....... 248 265-4000
Rochester Hills *(G-13504)*
Real Steel Manufacturing LLC........G....... 231 457-4673
Muskegon *(G-11414)*
Recycledlps Com........G....... 810 623-4498
Brighton *(G-1984)*
Red Rock Industries Inc........G....... 734 992-3522
Allen Park *(G-205)*
Redbud Roots Lab I LLC........G....... 312 656-3823
Buchanan *(G-2127)*
Rena DRane Enterprises Inc........G....... 248 796-2765
Southfield *(G-15012)*
Rilas & Rogers LLC........F....... 937 901-4228
Canton *(G-2422)*
River Raisin Models........G....... 248 366-9621
West Bloomfield *(G-17494)*
Rmcs Wings Enterprise........G....... 269 426-3559
Sawyer *(G-14488)*
Rodco Ltd........G....... 517 244-0200
Holt *(G-7923)*
Rodzina Industries Inc........G....... 810 235-2341
Flint *(G-5493)*
Roses Susies Feather........G....... 989 689-6570
Hope *(G-7956)*
Rottman Manufacturing Group........G....... 586 693-5676
Sterling Heights *(G-15480)*
Rpd Manufacturing LLC........G....... 248 760-4796
Milford *(G-10983)*
Ruff Life LLC........G....... 231 347-1214
Petoskey *(G-12474)*
Sampo Company LLC........G....... 734 664-9761
Plymouth *(G-12749)*
Sashabaw Bead Co........G....... 248 969-1353
Oxford *(G-12371)*
Seewald Industries........G....... 586 322-1042
Almont *(G-265)*
Select Distributors LLC........F....... 586 510-4647
Warren *(G-17237)*
Services To Enhance Potential........G....... 313 278-3040
Dearborn *(G-3757)*
Sheba Professional Nail Pdts........G....... 313 291-8010
Dearborn Heights *(G-3796)*
Sheri Boston........G....... 248 627-9576
Ortonville *(G-12203)*
Shoreline Manufacturing LLC........G....... 616 834-1503
Holland *(G-7802)*
▲ **Sika Auto Eaton Rapids Inc**........F....... 248 588-2270
Madison Heights *(G-10352)*
Sizmek Dsp Inc........G....... 313 516-4482
Troy *(G-16606)*
Sk Enterprises Inc........F....... 616 785-1070
Grand Rapids *(G-6867)*
Skin Bar VII LLC........G....... 313 701-7958
Detroit *(G-4364)*
Smart Swatter LLC........G....... 989 763-2626
Harbor Springs *(G-7294)*
Sparks Exhbits Envrnments Corp........G....... 248 291-0007
Royal Oak *(G-13972)*
Spec International Inc........F....... 616 248-3022
Grand Rapids *(G-6879)*
Speed Industry LLC........G....... 248 458-1335
Troy *(G-16616)*
Spike Bros Natures Treasures........G....... 989 833-5443
Sumner *(G-15643)*
SPX Corporation........G....... 704 752-4400
Muskegon *(G-11429)*
◆ **Stageright Corporation**........C....... 989 386-7393
Clare *(G-2890)*
Stansley Industries Inc........G....... 810 515-1919
Flint *(G-5505)*
Steadfast Lab........G....... 248 242-2291
Hazel Park *(G-7456)*
▲ **Stewart Manufacturing LLC**........D....... 906 498-7600
Hermansville *(G-7466)*
Studio One Midwest Inc........F....... 269 962-3475
Battle Creek *(G-1255)*
Studtmans Stuff........G....... 269 673-3126
Allegan *(G-189)*
Summit Cutting Tools and Mfg........G....... 248 859-2625
Wixom *(G-17899)*
Sustainable Industries LLC........G....... 248 213-6599
Detroit *(G-4390)*
Tallman Industries Inc........G....... 231 879-4755
Fife Lake *(G-5343)*
Technacraft Corp........G....... 810 227-8281
Brighton *(G-1995)*
▲ **Tecla Company Inc**........E....... 248 624-8200
Commerce Township *(G-3453)*
The Spott........G....... 269 459-6462
Kalamazoo *(G-8910)*
Tide Rings LLC........G....... 586 206-3142
Allenton *(G-230)*
Tip Top Screw Manufacturi........G....... 989 739-5157
Saginaw *(G-14164)*
Tjb Industries........G....... 248 690-9608
Oakland *(G-12109)*
◆ **Top Shelf Barber Supplies LLC**........G....... 586 453-6809
Lansing *(G-9326)*
Total Repair Express MI LLC........F....... 248 690-9410
Lake Orion *(G-9166)*
Triunfar Industries Inc........G....... 313 790-5592
South Lyon *(G-14814)*
Tru-Fit International Inc........G....... 248 855-8845
West Bloomfield *(G-17502)*
Uis Industries LLC........G....... 734 443-3737
Livonia *(G-9980)*
Ultramouse Ltd........G....... 734 761-1144
Ann Arbor *(G-686)*
United Mfg Netwrk Inc........G....... 586 321-7887
Warren *(G-17274)*
US Energy Systems Inc........G....... 248 765-7995
Rochester Hills *(G-13538)*
▲ **US Salon Supply LLC**........G....... 616 365-5790
Paw Paw *(G-12415)*
◆ **USF Delta Tooling LLC**........C....... 248 391-6800
Auburn Hills *(G-1041)*
Vanity Fur........G....... 810 744-3000
Burton *(G-2169)*
Vb Chesaning LLC........G....... 989 323-2333
Chesaning *(G-2729)*
Venture Technology Groups Inc........F....... 248 473-8450
Novi *(G-12025)*
▼ **Viking Spas Inc**........F....... 616 248-7800
Wyoming *(G-18041)*
Viladon Corporation........G....... 248 548-0043
Oak Park *(G-12103)*
Vision Global Industries........G....... 248 390-5805
Macomb *(G-10173)*
W M Enterprises........G....... 810 694-4384
Grand Blanc *(G-5988)*
West Mich Flcking Assembly LLC........D....... 269 639-1634
Covert *(G-3592)*
Wholesale Weave Inc........F....... 800 762-2037
Detroit *(G-4441)*
Williams Diversified Inc........E....... 734 421-6100
Livonia *(G-10009)*
Willies Wicks........G....... 810 730-4176
Flushing *(G-5546)*
Willow Mfg Inc........G....... 231 275-1026
Interlochen *(G-8246)*
Winsol Electronics LLC........G....... 810 767-2987
Flint *(G-5524)*
Wooley Industries Inc........G....... 810 341-8823
Flint *(G-5526)*
World Class Steel & Proc Inc........G....... 586 585-1734
Troy *(G-16699)*
World Industries Inc........G....... 248 288-0000
Clawson *(G-2990)*
Wreaths By Heather RE Nee........G....... 810 874-3119
Swartz Creek *(G-15670)*
Wright & Filippis Inc........F....... 517 484-2624
Lansing *(G-9435)*
Young Manufacturing Inc........G....... 906 483-3851
Dollar Bay *(G-4522)*
Yukon Manufacturing........F....... 989 358-6248
Alpena *(G-321)*
Zoe Health........G....... 616 485-1909
Kentwood *(G-9036)*
Zoyes East Inc........G....... 248 584-3300
Ferndale *(G-5331)*

73 BUSINESS SERVICES

7372 Prepackaged Software

21st Century Graphic Tech LLC........G....... 586 463-9599
Utica *(G-16740)*
313 Certified LLC........G....... 248 915-8419
Bloomfield Hills *(G-1738)*
360ofme Inc........G....... 844 360-6363
Royal Oak *(G-13897)*
3dfx Interactive Inc........E....... 918 938-8967
Saginaw *(G-13990)*
3r Info LLC........F....... 201 221-6133
Canton *(G-2342)*
4d Systems LLC........E....... 800 380-9165
Flint *(G-5366)*
Accessible Information LLC........G....... 248 338-4928
Bloomfield Hills *(G-1740)*
AK Rewards LLC........G....... 734 272-7078
Ann Arbor *(G-349)*
Akamai Technologies Inc........G....... 734 424-1142
Pinckney *(G-12495)*
Alta Vista Technology LLC........F....... 248 733-4504
Southfield *(G-14830)*
Altair Engineering Inc........C....... 248 614-2400
Troy *(G-16192)*
Amicus Software........G....... 313 417-9550
White Lake *(G-17629)*
Amt Software LLC........G....... 248 458-0359
Bloomfield Hills *(G-1745)*
Ansys Inc........G....... 248 613-2677
Ann Arbor *(G-359)*
Apis North America LLC........G....... 800 470-8970
Royal Oak *(G-13903)*
Applied Computer Technologies........F....... 248 388-0211
West Bloomfield *(G-17465)*
Appropos LLC........E....... 844 462-7776
Grand Rapids *(G-6175)*
Arbormetrix Inc........F....... 734 661-7944
Ann Arbor *(G-366)*
Arctuition LLC........G....... 616 635-9959
Ada *(G-9)*
Argus Technologies LLC........E....... 616 538-9895
Grand Rapids *(G-6180)*
Asset Health Inc........E....... 248 822-2870
Troy *(G-16225)*
Atos Syntel Inc........C....... 248 619-2800
Troy *(G-16228)*
Autodesk Inc........D....... 248 347-9650
Novi *(G-11833)*
Automated Bookkeeping Inc........G....... 866 617-3122
Detroit *(G-3884)*
Automated Media Inc........D....... 313 662-0185
Redford *(G-13146)*
Auvesy Inc........G....... 616 888-3770
Grand Rapids *(G-6194)*
Avocadough LLC........G....... 908 596-1437
Byron Center *(G-2178)*
Bell and Howell LLC........G....... 734 421-1727
Livonia *(G-9664)*
Biscayne and Associates Inc........E....... 248 304-0600
Milford *(G-10955)*
Black Ski Weekend LLC........G....... 313 879-7150
West Bloomfield *(G-17466)*
Blue Pony LLC........G....... 616 291-5554
Hudsonville *(G-8149)*
Blujay Solutions Co........G....... 616 738-6400
Holland *(G-7571)*
BMC Software Inc........F....... 248 888-4600
Farmington Hills *(G-4944)*
Bokhara Pet Care Centers........F....... 231 264-6667
Elk Rapids *(G-4775)*
Braiq Inc........G....... 858 729-4116
Detroit *(G-3912)*
Brinston Acquisition LLC........E....... 248 269-1000
Troy *(G-16246)*
Broadsword Solutions Corp........F....... 248 341-3367
Waterford *(G-17326)*
C R T & Associates Inc........G....... 231 946-1680
Traverse City *(G-15926)*
C S Systems Inc........G....... 269 962-8434
Battle Creek *(G-1161)*

Cadfem Americas Inc ....G.... 248 919-8410
Farmington Hills *(G-4953)*
Capital Billing Systems Inc ....G.... 248 478-7298
Farmington Hills *(G-4955)*
Capital Software Inc Michigan ....G.... 517 324-9100
East Lansing *(G-4653)*
Catalina Software ....G.... 734 429-3550
Saline *(G-14381)*
Chain-Sys Corporation ....F.... 517 627-1173
Lansing *(G-9281)*
Chalq LLC ....G.... 269 330-1514
Kalamazoo *(G-8705)*
Change Dynamix Inc ....G.... 248 671-6700
Royal Oak *(G-13913)*
Click Care LLC ....G.... 989 792-1544
Saginaw *(G-14020)*
Coeus LLC ....F.... 248 564-1958
Bloomfield Hills *(G-1754)*
Collagecom LLC ....G.... 248 971-0538
White Lake *(G-17631)*
Comet Information Systems LLC ....F.... 248 686-2600
Grand Blanc *(G-5963)*
Competitive Cmpt Info Tech Inc ....E.... 732 829-9699
Northville *(G-11683)*
Complete Data Products Inc ....G.... 248 651-8602
Troy *(G-16275)*
Compucare ....G.... 616 245-5371
Grand Rapids *(G-6297)*
Computer Mail Services Inc ....F.... 248 352-6700
Sterling Heights *(G-15293)*
Computer Sciences Corporation ....C.... 586 825-5043
Sterling Heights *(G-15294)*
▲ Compuware Corporation ....C.... 313 227-7300
Detroit *(G-3945)*
Consistacom Inc ....G.... 906 482-7653
Houghton *(G-7972)*
Core Technology Corporation ....F.... 517 627-1521
Lansing *(G-9285)*
Covisint Corporation ....D.... 248 483-2000
Southfield *(G-14874)*
Cq Simple LLC ....G.... 989 492-7068
Midland *(G-10827)*
Cyberlogic Technologies Inc ....E.... 248 631-2200
Troy *(G-16291)*
Cygnet Financial Planning Inc ....G.... 248 673-2900
Waterford *(G-17331)*
Dassault Systemes Americas ....C.... 248 267-9696
Auburn Hills *(G-836)*
Datamatic Processing Inc ....E.... 517 882-4401
Lansing *(G-9359)*
Design Safety Engineering Inc ....G.... 734 483-2033
Ypsilanti *(G-18065)*
Detroit Art Collection LLC ....G.... 313 373-7689
Detroit *(G-3970)*
Dna Software Inc ....F.... 734 222-9080
Ann Arbor *(G-422)*
DRae LLC ....G.... 313 923-7230
Oak Park *(G-12060)*
Driven-4 LLC ....G.... 269 281-7567
Saint Joseph *(G-14307)*
Duo Security Inc ....C.... 734 330-2673
Ann Arbor *(G-427)*
Dynatrace LLC ....D.... 313 227-7300
Detroit *(G-4022)*
E Z Logic Data Systems Inc ....E.... 248 817-8800
Farmington Hills *(G-4977)*
E-Con LLC ....E.... 248 766-9000
Birmingham *(G-1682)*
E-Procurement Services LLC ....E.... 248 630-7200
Auburn Hills *(G-850)*
Eca Educational Services Inc ....E.... 248 669-7170
Commerce Township *(G-3403)*
Edi Experts LLC ....G.... 734 844-7016
Canton *(G-2370)*
Ejustice Solutions LLC ....E.... 248 232-0509
Ann Arbor *(G-438)*
EMC Corporation ....G.... 248 374-5009
Novi *(G-11883)*
EMC Corporation ....C.... 248 957-5800
Farmington Hills *(G-4984)*
Empower Financials Inc ....F.... 734 747-9393
Ann Arbor *(G-443)*
Engineering Tech Assoc Inc ....D.... 248 729-3010
Troy *(G-16346)*
Enterprise Services LLC ....F.... 734 523-6525
Livonia *(G-9727)*
Epath Logic Inc ....G.... 313 375-5375
Royal Oak *(G-13926)*
Epic 4d LLC ....G.... 800 470-8948
Detroit *(G-4040)*

Eview 360 Corp ....E.... 248 306-5191
Farmington Hills *(G-4995)*
Expectancy Learning LLC ....G.... 866 829-9533
Grand Rapids *(G-6392)*
Export Service International ....G.... 248 620-7100
Clarkston *(G-2919)*
Faac Incorporated ....C.... 734 761-5836
Ann Arbor *(G-456)*
Fbe Associates Inc ....G.... 989 894-2785
Bay City *(G-1314)*
Flashplays Live LLC ....G.... 978 888-3935
Ann Arbor *(G-462)*
Foresee Session Replay Inc ....G.... 800 621-2850
Ann Arbor *(G-465)*
Freedom Imaging Systems ....E.... 734 327-5600
Ann Arbor *(G-467)*
Gene Codes Forensics Inc ....F.... 734 769-7249
Ann Arbor *(G-470)*
Genesee Free Net ....G.... 810 720-2880
Flint *(G-5438)*
Gentry Services of Alabama ....G.... 248 321-6368
Warren *(G-17056)*
Ginkgotree Inc ....G.... 734 707-7191
Detroit *(G-4091)*
Global Information Systems ....D.... 248 223-9800
Southfield *(G-14921)*
Gnu Software Development Inc ....G.... 586 778-9182
Warren *(G-17060)*
Great Lakes Infotronics Inc ....E.... 248 476-2500
Northville *(G-11695)*
Greenback Inc ....G.... 313 443-4272
Birmingham *(G-1685)*
Greenview Data Inc ....E.... 734 426-7500
Ann Arbor *(G-479)*
Grit Obstacle Training LLP ....G.... 248 829-0414
Rochester *(G-13323)*
Harbor Software Intl Inc ....G.... 231 347-8866
Petoskey *(G-12451)*
Harper Arrington Pubg LLC ....G.... 313 282-6751
Detroit *(G-4117)*
Herfert Software ....G.... 586 776-2880
Eastpointe *(G-4703)*
High Touch Healthcare LLC ....G.... 248 513-2425
Novi *(G-11901)*
Hilgraeve Inc ....G.... 734 243-0576
Monroe *(G-11039)*
Ht Computing Services ....G.... 313 563-0087
Dearborn *(G-3722)*
Hypertek Corporation ....G.... 248 619-0395
Troy *(G-16407)*
I-9 Advantage ....G.... 800 724-8546
Troy *(G-16408)*
Ideation International Inc ....F.... 248 737-8854
Farmington Hills *(G-5025)*
Idv Solutions LLC ....E.... 517 853-3755
Lansing *(G-9295)*
Infor (us) Inc ....C.... 616 258-3311
Grand Rapids *(G-6534)*
Information Builders Inc ....E.... 248 641-8820
Troy *(G-16417)*
Infotech Imaging Inc ....F.... 616 458-8686
Grand Rapids *(G-6535)*
Innovative Programming Systems ....G.... 810 695-9332
Grand Blanc *(G-5971)*
Inora Technologies Inc ....F.... 734 302-7488
Ann Arbor *(G-506)*
Inovision Inc ....E.... 248 299-1915
Rochester Hills *(G-13450)*
Inovision Sftwr Solutions Inc ....G.... 586 598-8750
Chesterfield *(G-2791)*
Integrated Practice Service ....G.... 248 646-7009
South Lyon *(G-14794)*
Integrted Database Systems Inc ....F.... 989 546-4512
Mount Pleasant *(G-11197)*
Intellibee Inc ....G.... 313 586-4122
Detroit *(G-4145)*
Interact Websites Inc ....F.... 800 515-9672
Midland *(G-10871)*
Interpro Technology Inc ....F.... 248 650-8695
Rochester *(G-13330)*
Intrinsic4d LLC ....F.... 248 469-8811
Bingham Farms *(G-1654)*
J H P Inc ....G.... 248 588-0110
Madison Heights *(G-10280)*
Jam-Live LLC ....G.... 517 282-5410
Howell *(G-8054)*
Jda Software Group Inc ....G.... 734 741-4205
Ann Arbor *(G-510)*
Jrop LLC ....F.... 800 404-9494
Royal Oak *(G-13940)*

Kemari LLC ....G.... 248 348-7407
South Lyon *(G-14797)*
Kingston Educational Software ....G.... 248 895-4803
Farmington Hills *(G-5038)*
Kumanu Inc ....F.... 734 822-6673
Ann Arbor *(G-521)*
Lakeside Software Inc ....F.... 248 686-1700
Ann Arbor *(G-524)*
Lakeside Software Inc ....E.... 248 686-1700
Bloomfield Hills *(G-1776)*
Laydon Technology Inc ....G.... 906 774-5780
Iron Mountain *(G-8289)*
Level Eleven LLC ....E.... 313 662-2000
Detroit *(G-4201)*
Life Is Digital LLC ....G.... 734 252-6449
Southfield *(G-14968)*
Linked Live Inc ....G.... 248 345-5993
Madison Heights *(G-10299)*
Lintech Global Inc ....D.... 248 553-8033
Farmington Hills *(G-5045)*
Local Mobile Services LLC ....G.... 313 963-1917
Plymouth *(G-12675)*
Logic Solutions Inc ....G.... 734 930-0009
Ann Arbor *(G-533)*
Lokol LLC ....G.... 586 615-1727
Walled Lake *(G-16897)*
Lspedia LLC ....G.... 248 320-1909
Farmington Hills *(G-5046)*
Luhu LLC ....G.... 320 469-3162
East Lansing *(G-4668)*
Magnetic Michigan ....D.... 734 922-7068
Ann Arbor *(G-540)*
Magnus Software Inc ....G.... 517 294-0315
Fowlerville *(G-5574)*
Marc Schreiber & Company LLC ....F.... 734 222-9930
Ann Arbor *(G-543)*
Marketplus Software Inc ....F.... 269 968-4240
Springfield *(G-15198)*
Marykay Software Inc ....G.... 989 463-4385
Alma *(G-239)*
Master Data Center Inc ....D.... 248 352-5810
Bingham Farms *(G-1656)*
Mastery Technologies Inc ....F.... 248 888-8420
Novi *(G-11936)*
Mathworks Inc ....F.... 248 596-7920
Novi *(G-11937)*
Matthews Software Inc ....G.... 248 593-6999
Birmingham *(G-1692)*
Mc Donald Computer Corporation ....F.... 248 350-9290
Southfield *(G-14975)*
McKesson Pharmacy Systems LLC ....A.... 800 521-1758
Livonia *(G-9834)*
Medical Systems Resource Group ....G.... 248 476-5400
Farmington Hills *(G-5061)*
Medimage Inc ....G.... 734 665-5400
Ann Arbor *(G-551)*
Mejenta Systems Inc ....E.... 248 434-2583
Southfield *(G-14977)*
Melange Computer Services Inc ....E.... 517 321-8434
Lansing *(G-9310)*
Menu Pulse Inc ....G.... 989 708-1207
Saginaw *(G-14088)*
Method Technology Service LLC ....E.... 312 622-7697
Troy *(G-16500)*
Michigan Interactive LLC ....G.... 517 241-4341
Bingham Farms *(G-1657)*
Micro Focus Software Inc ....A.... 248 353-8010
Southfield *(G-14982)*
Mighty Co ....E.... 616 822-1013
Hudsonville *(G-8170)*
Mighty Legal LLC ....G.... 800 870-4605
Ann Arbor *(G-558)*
Mscsoftware Corporation ....C.... 734 994-3800
Ann Arbor *(G-567)*
National Instruments Corp ....B.... 734 464-2310
Livonia *(G-9860)*
Nemo Capital Partners LLC ....F.... 248 213-9899
Southfield *(G-14990)*
Neurable LLC ....G.... 206 696-4469
Ann Arbor *(G-573)*
New Concepts Software Inc ....G.... 586 776-2855
Roseville *(G-13846)*
Nexiq Technologies Inc ....F.... 248 293-8200
Rochester Hills *(G-13480)*
Nits Solutions Inc ....F.... 248 231-2267
Novi *(G-11953)*
Novation Analytics LLC ....G.... 313 910-3280
Auburn Hills *(G-963)*
Nuance Communications Inc ....G.... 248 919-7700
Farmington Hills *(G-5085)*

SIC

73 BUSINESS SERVICES

Onestream Software Corp .... G 248 841-1356
  Rochester *(G-13341)*
Onestream Software LLC .... F 248 342-1541
  Rochester *(G-13342)*
Opio LLc .... F 313 433-1098
  Wayne *(G-17440)*
◆ Ops Solutions LLC .... E 248 374-8000
  Wixom *(G-17874)*
Optimizerx Corporation .... G 248 651-6568
  Rochester *(G-13343)*
Oracle America Inc .... E 989 495-0465
  Midland *(G-10900)*
Oracle America Inc .... G 248 273-1934
  Troy *(G-16535)*
Oracle Corporation .... B 248 393-2498
  Orion *(G-12187)*
Oracle Systems Corporation .... B 248 614-5139
  Rochester Hills *(G-13488)*
Oracle Systems Corporation .... C 248 816-8050
  Troy *(G-16536)*
Orbit Technology Inc .... G 906 776-7248
  Iron Mountain *(G-8297)*
Orion Bus Accnting Sltions LLC .... G 248 893-1060
  Wyandotte *(G-17970)*
Orthoview LLC .... G 800 318-0923
  Plymouth *(G-12705)*
Pace Software Systems Inc .... F 586 727-3189
  Casco *(G-2504)*
Parameter Driven Software Inc .... F 248 553-6410
  Farmington Hills *(G-5088)*
Paramount Technologies Inc .... E 248 960-0909
  Walled Lake *(G-16901)*
PC Solutions .... F 517 787-9934
  Jackson *(G-8548)*
Peninsular Technologies LLC .... F 616 676-9811
  Ada *(G-27)*
Perception Anlytics Rbtics LLC .... G 734 846-5650
  Ann Arbor *(G-589)*
Perennial Software .... F 734 414-0760
  Canton *(G-2415)*
Phoenix Data Incorporated .... F 248 281-0054
  Southfield *(G-14998)*
Pitss America LLC .... E 248 740-0935
  Troy *(G-16549)*
Platform Computing Inc .... G 248 359-7825
  Southfield *(G-15000)*
Platformsh Inc .... F 734 707-9124
  Brooklyn *(G-2041)*
Polyhedron LLC .... G 313 318-4807
  Grosse Pointe *(G-7182)*
Polyworks USA Training Center ...... G 216 226-1617
  Novi *(G-11974)*
Possibilities For Change LLC .... G 810 333-1347
  Ann Arbor *(G-596)*
Prehab Technologies LLC .... G 734 368-9983
  Ann Arbor *(G-602)*
Premier Software Inc .... G 616 940-8601
  Grand Rapids *(G-6769)*
Professional Sftwr Assoc Inc .... G 727 724-0000
  Lapeer *(G-9482)*
Pure Virtual Studios LLC .... G 248 250-4070
  Oak Park *(G-12091)*
Qe Tools LLC .... G 734 330-4707
  Ann Arbor *(G-609)*
Quantum Compliance Systems .... D 734 930-0009
  Ypsilanti *(G-18099)*
Quest - IV Incorporated .... F 734 847-5487
  Lambertville *(G-9184)*
Radley Corporation .... E 616 554-9060
  Grand Rapids *(G-6805)*
Rane Innovation LLC .... G 419 577-2126
  Bay City *(G-1347)*
Rearden Development Corp .... G 616 464-4434
  Grand Rapids *(G-6813)*
Redtail Software .... G 231 587-0720
  Mancelona *(G-10398)*
Regents of The University Mich ...... F 734 936-0435
  Ann Arbor *(G-617)*
Reilly & Associates Inc .... F 248 605-9393
  Clarkston *(G-2952)*
Relative Path LLC .... G 217 840-6376
  Mount Pleasant *(G-11224)*
Rezoop LLC .... G 248 952-8070
  Bloomfield *(G-1735)*
Ringmaster Software Corp .... F 802 383-1050
  Troy *(G-16580)*
Ripple Science Corporation .... G 919 451-0241
  Ann Arbor *(G-621)*
Riverside Internet Services .... G 231 652-2562
  Newaygo *(G-11576)*

Rose Mobile Computer Repr LLC ... F 248 653-0865
  Troy *(G-16583)*
Rutherford & Associates Inc .... E 616 392-5000
  Holland *(G-7792)*
S2 Games LLC .... D 269 344-8020
  Portage *(G-13030)*
Saagara LLC .... F 734 658-4693
  Ann Arbor *(G-627)*
Saba Software Inc .... G 248 228-7300
  Southfield *(G-15019)*
Sales Page Technologies Inc .... G 269 567-7401
  Kalamazoo *(G-8882)*
Salespage Technologies LLC .... D 269 567-7400
  Kalamazoo *(G-8883)*
Sbsi Software Inc .... G 248 567-3044
  Farmington Hills *(G-5121)*
Securitysnares Inc .... G 734 308-5106
  Maybee *(G-10672)*
Selfies 2 Helpease Inc .... G 517 769-6900
  Pleasant Lake *(G-12554)*
Siemens Product Life Mgmt Sftw .... E 313 317-6100
  Allen Park *(G-208)*
Siemens Product Life Mgmt Sftw ... D 734 953-2700
  Livonia *(G-9926)*
Siemens Product Life Mgmt Sftw ... D 734 994-7300
  Ann Arbor *(G-631)*
Signalx Technologies LLC .... F 248 935-4237
  Plymouth *(G-12754)*
Signmeupcom Inc .... G 312 343-1263
  Monroe *(G-11065)*
Silkroute Global Inc .... E 248 854-3409
  Troy *(G-16603)*
Simerics Inc .... G 248 513-3200
  Novi *(G-11998)*
Simna Solutions LLC .... G 313 442-7305
  Farmington Hills *(G-5125)*
Sims Software II Inc .... G 586 491-0058
  Clinton Township *(G-3229)*
Sizzl LLC .... F 201 454-1938
  Ann Arbor *(G-634)*
Skysync Inc .... G 734 822-6858
  Ann Arbor *(G-636)*
Sodius Corporation .... G 720 507-7078
  Royal Oak *(G-13971)*
Software Advantage Consulting ...... G 586 264-5632
  Sterling Heights *(G-15503)*
Software Finesse LLC .... G 248 737-8990
  Farmington Hills *(G-5126)*
Solid Logic LLC .... F 616 738-8922
  Holland *(G-7810)*
Spiders Software Solutions LLC ...... E 248 305-3225
  Northville *(G-11727)*
Spindance Inc .... G 616 355-7000
  Holland *(G-7811)*
Star Board Multi Media Inc .... G 616 296-0823
  Grand Haven *(G-6084)*
Stardock Systems Inc .... E 734 927-0677
  Plymouth *(G-12760)*
Startech Software Systems Inc .... G 248 344-2266
  Novi *(G-12003)*
Sterling Software Inc .... G 248 528-6500
  Troy *(G-16622)*
Strategic Computer Solutions .... G 248 888-0666
  Ann Arbor *(G-648)*
Strider Software Inc .... G 906 863-7798
  Menominee *(G-10757)*
Stunt3 Multimedia LLC .... G 313 417-0909
  Grosse Pointe *(G-7184)*
Sunera Technologies Inc .... E 248 524-0222
  Troy *(G-16625)*
Superior Information Tech LLC .... F 734 666-9963
  Livonia *(G-9948)*
Supported Intelligence LLC .... G 517 908-4420
  East Lansing *(G-4679)*
Suse LLC .... F 248 353-8010
  Southfield *(G-15041)*
Talbot & Associates Inc .... F 248 723-9700
  Franklin *(G-5609)*
Taxtime USA Inc .... G 248 642-7070
  Bingham Farms *(G-1661)*
Tebis America Inc .... E 248 524-0430
  Troy *(G-16634)*
Technology Network Svcs Inc .... F 586 294-7771
  Saint Clair Shores *(G-14271)*
Tecra Systems Inc .... E 248 888-1116
  Westland *(G-17602)*
Thangbom LLC .... G 517 862-0144
  Flint *(G-5510)*
Therapyline Technologies Inc .... E 734 407-9626
  Brownstown *(G-2068)*

Third Wave Computing .... G 616 855-5501
  Grand Rapids *(G-6929)*
Thunderhead Enterprises LLC .... G 248 210-1146
  Novi *(G-12016)*
Titania Software LLC .... G 734 786-8225
  Ann Arbor *(G-676)*
Torenzo Inc .... F 313 732-7874
  Bloomfield Hills *(G-1804)*
Totle Inc .... G 248 645-1111
  Birmingham *(G-1706)*
Towerline Software LLC .... G 517 669-8112
  Dewitt *(G-4469)*
Tru-Syzygy Inc .... G 248 622-7211
  Lake Orion *(G-9167)*
Truarx Inc .... F 248 538-7809
  Southfield *(G-15050)*
True Analytics Mfg Slutions LLC ..... G 517 902-9700
  Ida *(G-8194)*
TST Tooling Software Tech LLC ...... G 248 922-9293
  Clarkston *(G-2962)*
Tweddle Group Inc .... E 586 840-3275
  Detroit *(G-4410)*
Tyler Technologies Inc .... F 734 677-0550
  Ann Arbor *(G-684)*
Ultimate Software Group Inc .... E 517 540-9718
  Howell *(G-8117)*
Umakanth Consultants Inc .... F 517 347-7500
  Okemos *(G-12139)*
Universal Sftwr Solutions Inc .... F 810 653-5000
  Davison *(G-3664)*
Urefer Inc .... G 734 585-5684
  Ann Arbor *(G-689)*
V E S T Inc .... G 248 649-9550
  Troy *(G-16673)*
▲ Valassis Communications Inc .... C 734 591-3000
  Livonia *(G-9985)*
Valassis Communications Inc .... C 734 432-8000
  Livonia *(G-9986)*
Vanroth LLC .... F 734 929-5268
  Ann Arbor *(G-691)*
Varatech Inc .... F 616 393-6408
  Holland *(G-7843)*
Vector North America Inc .... D 248 449-9290
  Novi *(G-12024)*
Ventuor LLC .... G 248 790-8700
  Flint *(G-5520)*
Vertigee Corporation .... G 313 999-1020
  Saline *(G-14420)*
Virtual Advantage LLc .... G 877 772-6886
  Troy *(G-16685)*
Virtual Emergency Services LLC ..... F 734 324-2299
  Wyandotte *(G-17980)*
Visiun Inc .... G 734 741-0356
  Ann Arbor *(G-693)*
Visual Components N Amer Corp ... G 855 823-3746
  Orion *(G-12192)*
Vivian Enterprises LLC .... E 248 792-9925
  Southfield *(G-15063)*
Weaver Instructional Systems .... G 616 942-2891
  Grand Rapids *(G-6981)*
Wilson Technologies Inc .... G 248 655-0005
  Clawson *(G-2989)*
Workforce Payhub Inc .... G 517 759-4026
  Adrian *(G-104)*
Workforce Software LLC .... C 734 542-4100
  Livonia *(G-10012)*
World of Cd-Rom .... F 269 382-3766
  Kalamazoo *(G-8928)*
Wowza ME LLC .... G 734 636-4460
  Monroe *(G-11085)*
Xilinx Inc .... G 248 344-0786
  Wixom *(G-17932)*
Zferral Inc .... G 248 792-3472
  Royal Oak *(G-13982)*
Zume It Inc .... G 248 522-6868
  Farmington Hills *(G-5156)*

76 MISCELLANEOUS REPAIR SERVICES

7692 Welding Repair

A & B Welding & Fabricating .... G 231 733-2661
  Muskegon *(G-11255)*
A M T Welding Inc .... G 586 463-7030
  Clinton Township *(G-3028)*
A R C Welding & Repair .... G 517 628-2475
  Mason *(G-10628)*
Ability Mfg & Engrg Co .... F 269 227-3292
  Fennville *(G-5169)*

Able Welding Inc G 989 865-9611
Saint Charles *(G-14189)*
Absolute Lser Wldg Sltions LLC F 586 932-2597
Sterling Heights *(G-15249)*
Ace Welding & Machine Inc F 231 941-9664
Traverse City *(G-15887)*
Achs Metal Products Inc G 586 772-2734
Warren *(G-16915)*
Ackerman Brothers Inc G 989 892-4122
Bay City *(G-1270)*
▲ **Advanced Special Tools Inc** C 269 962-9697
Battle Creek *(G-1141)*
Aegis Welding Supply G 248 475-9860
Auburn Hills *(G-761)*
Aggressive Tooling Inc E 616 754-1404
Greenville *(G-7122)*
Airway Welding Inc F 517 789-6125
Jackson *(G-8379)*
All Phase Welding Service Inc G 616 235-6100
Grand Rapids *(G-6159)*
All Welding and Fabg Co Inc F 248 689-0986
Troy *(G-16189)*
Allegan Metal Fabricators Inc G 269 751-7130
Hamilton *(G-7229)*
Allied Machine Inc E 231 834-0050
Grant *(G-7077)*
Allied Welding Incorporated G 248 360-1122
Commerce Township *(G-3388)*
Allynn Corp G 269 383-1199
Kalamazoo *(G-8676)*
American Welding Inc G 734 279-1625
Petersburg *(G-12434)*
American Wldg & Press Repr Inc F 248 358-2050
Southfield *(G-14837)*
◆ **Amtrade Systems Inc** G 734 522-9500
Livonia *(G-9647)*
Anderson Brazing Co Inc G 248 399-5155
Madison Heights *(G-10192)*
Andritz Metals Inc G 248 305-2969
Novi *(G-11828)*
Angstrom Automotive Group LLC G 313 295-0100
Taylor *(G-15689)*
Anywhere Welding G 906 250-7217
Trenary *(G-16149)*
Arcelormittal Tailored Blanks B 313 332-5300
Detroit *(G-3873)*
Austin Engineering G 269 659-6335
Sturgis *(G-15597)*
Autorack Technologies Inc E 517 437-4800
Hillsdale *(G-7516)*
B & G Custom Works Inc E 269 686-9420
Allegan *(G-150)*
Bach Ornamental & Strl Stl Inc G 517 694-4311
Holt *(G-7904)*
Bairds Machine Shop G 269 795-9524
Middleville *(G-10798)*
Bakker Welding & Mechanics LLC G 616 828-8664
Coopersville *(G-3548)*
Bannasch Welding Inc F 517 482-2916
Lansing *(G-9205)*
Beattie Spring & Welding Svc G 810 239-9151
Flint *(G-5386)*
Beishlag Welding LLC G 231 881-5023
Elmira *(G-4790)*
Bel-Kur Inc E 734 847-0651
Temperance *(G-15823)*
Blade Welding Service Inc G 734 941-4253
Van Buren Twp *(G-16749)*
Bnb Welding & Fabrication Inc G 810 820-1508
Burton *(G-2145)*
Bobs Welding & Fabricating F 810 324-2592
Kenockee *(G-8984)*
Bond Bailey and Smith Company G 313 496-0177
Detroit *(G-3908)*
Bopp-Busch Manufacturing Co E 989 876-7924
Au Gres *(G-745)*
Boyne Area Wldg & Fabrication F 231 582-6078
Boyne City *(G-1816)*
Brico Welding & Fab Inc E 586 948-8881
Chesterfield *(G-2746)*
Britten Metalworks LLC G 231 421-1615
Traverse City *(G-15921)*
Buckeys Contracting & Service G 989 835-9512
Midland *(G-10819)*
Buiter Tool & Die Inc E 616 455-7410
Grand Rapids *(G-6239)*
C & R Tool Die G 231 584-3588
Alba *(G-112)*
C C Welding G 517 783-2305
Jackson *(G-8398)*

Cal Manufacturing Company Inc G 269 649-2942
Vicksburg *(G-16832)*
Cal Tolliver G 586 790-1610
Clinton Township *(G-3073)*
▲ **Campbell Inc Press Repair** E 517 371-1034
Lansing *(G-9354)*
Case Welding & Fabrication Inc G 517 278-2729
Coldwater *(G-3294)*
Century Tool Welding Inc G 586 758-3330
Fraser *(G-5637)*
Clair Sawyer G 906 228-8242
Marquette *(G-10523)*
Classic Welding Inc F 586 758-2400
Warren *(G-16983)*
Cobra Torches Inc G 248 499-8122
Lake Orion *(G-9128)*
Cobra Truck & Fabrication G 734 854-5663
Ottawa Lake *(G-12260)*
Colberg Radiator & Welding G 810 742-0028
Burton *(G-2149)*
▲ **Commercial Mfg & Assembly Inc** E 616 847-9980
Grand Haven *(G-6005)*
Consolidated Metal Pdts Inc G 616 538-1000
Grand Rapids *(G-6302)*
Contract Welding and Fabg Inc E 734 699-5561
Van Buren Twp *(G-16753)*
Cooks Blacksmith Welding Inc G 231 796-6819
Big Rapids *(G-1625)*
◆ **Coppertec Inc** E 313 278-0139
Inkster *(G-8226)*
Corban Industries Inc D 248 393-2720
Orion *(G-12177)*
Cramblits Welding LLC G 906 932-1908
Ironwood *(G-8326)*
Custom Design & Manufacturing F 989 754-9962
Carrollton *(G-2484)*
Customer Metal Fabrication Inc E 906 774-3216
Iron Mountain *(G-8282)*
Cw Champion Welding Alloys LLC G 906 296-9633
Lake Linden *(G-9107)*
Cw Creative Welding Inc G 586 294-1050
Fraser *(G-5640)*
D K Enterprises Inc G 586 756-7350
Warren *(G-16997)*
David A Mohr Jr G 517 266-2694
Adrian *(G-58)*
Delducas Welding & Co Inc G 810 743-1990
Flint *(G-5416)*
Deltaic Welding Inc G 734 207-1080
Plymouth *(G-12607)*
Dickaren Inc G 517 283-2444
Reading *(G-13136)*
Diversified Welding & Fabg G 616 738-0400
Holland *(G-7609)*
Dons Welding G 989 792-0287
Saginaw *(G-14028)*
Dubois Production Services Inc E 616 785-0088
Comstock Park *(G-3480)*
Dunns Welding Inc G 248 356-3866
Southfield *(G-14887)*
Dutchmans Welding & Repair G 989 584-6861
Carson City *(G-2488)*
Eagle Welding LLC G 810 750-0772
Fenton *(G-5201)*
Elden Industries Corporation F 734 946-6900
Taylor *(G-15715)*
Envision Machine and Mfg LLC G 616 953-8580
Holland *(G-7624)*
▲ **Erwin Quarder Inc** D 616 575-1600
Grand Rapids *(G-6383)*
Escanaba and Lk Superior RR Co G 906 786-9399
Escanaba *(G-4828)*
Express Machine & Tool Co G 586 758-5080
Warren *(G-17027)*
Express Welding Inc G 906 786-8808
Escanaba *(G-4829)*
Fab-N-Weld Sheetmetal G 269 471-7453
Berrien Springs *(G-1594)*
Figlan Welding G 586 739-6837
Shelby Township *(G-14593)*
Frankenmuth Industrial Svcs E 989 652-3322
Frankenmuth *(G-5587)*
Frankenmuth Welding & Fabg G 989 754-9457
Saginaw *(G-14038)*
Fraser Fab and Machine Inc E 248 852-9050
Rochester Hills *(G-13428)*
Gaastra Welding & Supply Inc G 906 265-4288
Iron River *(G-8309)*
Garden City Products Inc F 269 684-6264
Niles *(G-11614)*

Gonzalez Welding G 248 469-3016
Waterford *(G-17346)*
Grand Rapids Metaltek Inc E 616 791-2373
Grand Rapids *(G-6460)*
Great Lakes Weld LLC G 231 943-4180
Traverse City *(G-15994)*
Greens Welding & Repair Co G 734 721-5434
Westland *(G-17564)*
▲ **Griptrac Inc** F 231 853-2284
Ravenna *(G-13120)*
Gustos Quality Systems G 231 409-0219
Fife Lake *(G-5341)*
H & H Welding & Repair LLC D 517 676-1800
Mason *(G-10642)*
H & M Machining Inc F 586 778-5028
Roseville *(G-13814)*
H & M Welding and Fabricating G 517 764-3630
Jackson *(G-8461)*
Hanks Welding Service Inc G 517 568-3804
Homer *(G-7943)*
Hel Inc F 616 774-9032
Grand Rapids *(G-6503)*
Ianna Fab Inc G 586 739-2410
Shelby Township *(G-14603)*
Innovated Portable Weldin G 586 322-4442
Casco *(G-2501)*
Integrity Fab & Machine Inc F 989 481-3200
Breckenridge *(G-1843)*
Iron Fetish Metalworks Inc F 586 776-8311
Roseville *(G-13822)*
Iron Mikes WELding& Fabg G 810 234-2996
Flint *(G-5448)*
Ithaca Manufacturing Corp G 989 875-4949
Ithaca *(G-8361)*
J G Welding & Maintenance Inc G 586 758-0150
China *(G-2861)*
Jerrys Welding Inc G 231 853-6494
Ravenna *(G-13121)*
Jerz Machine Tool Corporation G 269 782-3535
Dowagiac *(G-4545)*
Jlore Welding G 989 402-7201
Sparta *(G-15099)*
Joy Industries Inc F 248 334-4062
Pontiac *(G-12842)*
JS Welding Inc G 517 451-2098
Britton *(G-2018)*
K & S Welding G 517 629-7842
Albion *(G-126)*
K-C Welding Supply Inc F 989 893-6509
Essexville *(G-4874)*
Kardux Welding & Fabricating G 231 873-4648
Hart *(G-7375)*
KC Jones Brazing Inc G 586 755-4900
Warren *(G-17118)*
Kenowa Industries Inc E 616 392-7080
Holland *(G-7709)*
Kent Welding Inc G 616 363-4414
Grand Rapids *(G-6578)*
Kinross Fab & Machine Inc E 906 495-1900
Kincheloe *(G-9052)*
Kk Welding Services Inc G 810 664-5564
North Branch *(G-11662)*
Koski Welding Inc G 906 353-7588
Baraga *(G-1105)*
Krause Welding Inc F 231 773-4443
Muskegon *(G-11358)*
Kriseler Welding Inc G 989 624-9266
Birch Run *(G-1664)*
Kurrent Welding Inc G 734 753-9197
New Boston *(G-11501)*
Lake Shore Services Inc F 734 285-7007
Wyandotte *(G-17965)*
Lakeside Mechanical Contrs E 616 786-0211
Allegan *(G-174)*
Laser Access Inc C 616 459-5496
Grand Rapids *(G-6618)*
Laylin Welding Inc G 269 782-2910
Dowagiac *(G-4547)*
Le Forges Pipe & Fab Inc G 734 482-2100
Ypsilanti *(G-18084)*
Lewis Welding Inc E 616 452-9226
Wyoming *(G-18015)*
Lincolns Welding G 269 964-1858
Springfield *(G-15197)*
Loneys Welding & Excvtg Inc G 231 328-4408
Merritt *(G-10764)*
Luans Welding LLC G 248 787-5735
Oak Park *(G-12078)*
M & B Welding Inc G 989 635-8017
Marlette *(G-10499)*

SIC

Employee Codes: A=Over 500 employees, B=251-500
C=101-250, D=51-100, E=20-50, F=10-19, G=3-9

2020 Harris Michigan
Industrial Directory

877

M P D Welding Inc................E....... 248 340-0330
Orion *(G-12184)*
Manistee Wldg & Piping Svc Inc..........G....... 231 723-2551
Manistee *(G-10428)*
Manning Enterprises Inc..........E....... 269 657-2346
Paw Paw *(G-12408)*
Marsh Industrial Services Inc..........F....... 231 258-4870
Kalkaska *(G-8949)*
Marshall Welding & Fabrication..........G....... 269 781-4010
Marshall *(G-10580)*
▲ **Material Handling Tech Inc**..........D....... 586 725-5546
Ira *(G-8260)*
Matteson Manufacturing Inc..........G....... 231 779-2898
Cadillac *(G-2263)*
Matuschek Welding Products Inc..........G....... 586 991-2434
Sterling Heights *(G-15413)*
▲ **Maxable Inc**..........E....... 517 592-5638
Brooklyn *(G-2039)*
Mayo Welding & Fabricating Co..........G....... 248 435-2730
Royal Oak *(G-13948)*
McCullys Wldg Fabrication LLC..........G....... 231 499-3842
East Jordan *(G-4639)*
Meccom Corporation..........G....... 313 895-4900
Detroit *(G-4224)*
Mechanical Supply A Division..........E....... 906 789-0355
Escanaba *(G-4842)*
Menominee Saw and Supply Co..........G....... 906 863-8998
Menominee *(G-10748)*
Metal Worxs Inc..........G....... 586 484-9355
Clay *(G-2999)*
Metal-Line Corp..........E....... 231 723-7041
Muskegon *(G-11377)*
Metro Machine Works Inc..........D....... 734 941-4571
Romulus *(G-13707)*
Mico Industries Inc..........D....... 616 245-6426
Grand Rapids *(G-6679)*
Mid Michigan Repair Service..........G....... 989 835-6014
Midland *(G-10886)*
Midwest Fabricating Inc..........G....... 734 921-3914
Taylor *(G-15744)*
Mj-Hick Inc..........G....... 989 345-7610
West Branch *(G-17513)*
Monarch Welding & Engrg Inc..........F....... 231 733-7222
Muskegon *(G-11384)*
Morgans Welding..........G....... 517 523-3666
Osseo *(G-12227)*
Mpd Welding - Grand Rapids Inc..........E....... 616 248-9353
Grand Rapids *(G-6708)*
Nash Services..........G....... 269 782-2016
Dowagiac *(G-4555)*
National Tool & Die Welding..........F....... 734 522-0072
Livonia *(G-9861)*
Nelson Steel Products Inc..........D....... 616 396-1515
Holland *(G-7753)*
▲ **Nicholson Terminal & Dock Co**..........C....... 313 842-4300
River Rouge *(G-13279)*
Northern Design Services Inc..........E....... 231 258-9900
Kalkaska *(G-8956)*
Northern Machining & Repr Inc..........E....... 906 786-0526
Escanaba *(G-4847)*
O E M Company Inc..........E....... 810 985-9070
Port Huron *(G-12951)*
Oilpatch Machine Tool Inc..........G....... 989 772-0637
Mount Pleasant *(G-11215)*
Olivet Machine Tool Engrg Co..........F....... 269 749-2671
Olivet *(G-12143)*
Parker Tooling & Design Inc..........F....... 616 791-1080
Grand Rapids *(G-6743)*
Parma Tube Corp..........E....... 269 651-2351
Sturgis *(G-15626)*
▲ **Phil Brown Welding Corporation**..........F....... 616 784-3046
Conklin *(G-3531)*
Pin Point Welding Inc..........G....... 586 598-7382
Chesterfield *(G-2817)*
Pinnacle Engineering Co Inc..........F....... 734 428-7039
Manchester *(G-10410)*
Pipe Fabricators Inc..........D....... 269 345-8657
Kalamazoo *(G-8853)*
Plymouth Brazing Inc..........D....... 734 453-6274
Westland *(G-17590)*
Porter Steel & Welding Company..........F....... 231 733-4495
Muskegon *(G-11404)*
▲ **Precision Polymer Mfg Inc**..........E....... 269 344-2044
Kalamazoo *(G-8860)*
Prima Welding & Experimental..........G....... 586 415-8873
Fraser *(G-5709)*
Proto Tool & Gage Inc..........G....... 734 487-0830
Ypsilanti *(G-18097)*
Pushard Welding LLC..........G....... 269 760-9611
Mattawan *(G-10668)*
Pushman Manufacturing Co Inc..........E....... 810 629-9688
Fenton *(G-5232)*
Rak Welding..........G....... 231 651-0732
Honor *(G-7953)*
Ranger Tool & Die Co..........E....... 989 754-1403
Saginaw *(G-14130)*
Rays Welding Co Inc..........G....... 269 473-1140
Berrien Springs *(G-1600)*
Response Welding Inc..........G....... 586 795-8090
Sterling Heights *(G-15466)*
▲ **Ridgeview Industries Inc**..........C....... 616 453-8636
Grand Rapids *(G-6826)*
Ripley Products Company Inc..........G....... 906 482-1380
Hancock *(G-7256)*
Rise Machine Company Inc..........G....... 989 772-2151
Mount Pleasant *(G-11225)*
▲ **Robotic Welded Parts Inc**..........E....... 989 386-5376
Clare *(G-2886)*
Ryson Tube Inc..........F....... 810 227-4567
Brighton *(G-1987)*
Salenbien Welding Service Inc..........F....... 734 529-3280
Dundee *(G-4599)*
Savs Welding Services Inc..........G....... 313 841-3430
Detroit *(G-4354)*
Senneker Enterprises Inc..........G....... 616 877-4440
Dorr *(G-4528)*
Set Enterprises of Mi Inc..........C....... 586 573-3600
Sterling Heights *(G-15494)*
Sexton Enterprize Inc..........G....... 248 545-5880
Ferndale *(G-5318)*
Sharpco Wldg & Fabrication LLC..........G....... 989 915-0556
Clare *(G-2888)*
Sherwood Manufacturing Corp..........E....... 231 386-5132
Northport *(G-11671)*
Smith Welding and Repair LLC..........G....... 616 374-1445
Lake Odessa *(G-9119)*
SOO Welding Inc..........F....... 906 632-8241
Sault Sainte Marie *(G-14474)*
Soutec Div of Andritz Bricmont..........G....... 248 305-2955
Novi *(G-12001)*
Spaulding Machine Co Inc..........E....... 989 777-0694
Saginaw *(G-14153)*
Specialty Welding..........G....... 517 627-5566
Grand Ledge *(G-6116)*
Starlite Tool & Die Welding..........G....... 313 533-3462
Detroit *(G-4376)*
Stus Welding & Fabrication..........G....... 616 392-8459
Holland *(G-7818)*
◆ **Superior Welding & Mfg Inc**..........E....... 906 498-7616
Hermansville *(G-7467)*
Supreme Welding Inc..........G....... 586 791-8860
Clinton Township *(G-3240)*
Sws - Trimac Inc..........E....... 989 791-4595
Saginaw *(G-14162)*
Systems Unlimited Inc..........E....... 517 279-8407
Coldwater *(G-3336)*
▲ **Tec-Option Inc**..........F....... 517 486-6055
Blissfield *(G-1727)*
Technique Inc..........D....... 517 789-8988
Jackson *(G-8585)*
▼ **Texas Metal Industries Inc**..........G....... 586 261-0090
Warren *(G-17265)*
Thermal Designs & Manufacturng..........E....... 586 773-5231
Roseville *(G-13878)*
Tigmaster Co..........E....... 800 824-4830
Baroda *(G-1132)*
Titanium Products Corp..........G....... 810 326-4325
Saint Clair *(G-14235)*
Titus Welding Company..........F....... 248 476-9366
Farmington Hills *(G-5141)*
Todds Welding Service Inc..........F....... 231 587-9969
Kalkaska *(G-8964)*
Troy Tube & Manufacturing Co..........D....... 586 949-8700
Chesterfield *(G-2851)*
Tumblweed Weld/Fab..........G....... 313 277-6860
Dearborn Heights *(G-3799)*
Tupes of Saginaw Inc..........F....... 989 799-1550
Saginaw *(G-14169)*
◆ **UP Truck Center Inc**..........E....... 906 774-0098
Quinnesec *(G-13103)*
▲ **V S America Inc**..........G....... 248 585-6715
Troy *(G-16674)*
Valiant Specialties Inc..........G....... 248 656-1001
Rochester Hills *(G-13539)*
Van Straten Brothers Inc..........E....... 906 353-6490
Baraga *(G-1116)*
Virtec Manufacturing LLC..........F....... 313 590-2367
Roseville *(G-13889)*
Vochaska Engineering..........G....... 269 637-5670
South Haven *(G-14782)*
Vs Products..........G....... 989 831-4861
Stanton *(G-15230)*
Vulcanmasters Welding Inc..........F....... 313 843-5043
White Lake *(G-17642)*
Walter Sappington..........G....... 989 345-1052
West Branch *(G-17527)*
Warren Industrial Welding Co..........F....... 586 756-0230
Warren *(G-17287)*
Warren Industrial Welding Co..........G....... 586 463-6600
Clinton Township *(G-3258)*
Weld Tech Unlimited Inc..........G....... 231 627-7531
Cheboygan *(G-2697)*
Weldcraft Inc..........G....... 734 779-1303
Livonia *(G-10003)*
Welders & Presses Inc..........G....... 586 948-4300
Chesterfield *(G-2856)*
Welding & Joining Tech LLC..........G....... 248 625-3045
Clarkston *(G-2965)*
Welding Fabricating Inc..........G....... 616 877-4345
Wayland *(G-17419)*
Wellington Industries Inc..........E....... 734 403-6112
Van Buren Twp *(G-16797)*
West Side Mfg Fabrication Inc..........F....... 248 380-6640
Wixom *(G-17928)*
Wheelock & Son Welding Shop..........G....... 231 947-6557
Traverse City *(G-16145)*
Whites Bridge Tooling Inc..........E....... 616 897-4151
Lowell *(G-10045)*
Williams Welding and Repair..........G....... 517 783-3977
Jackson *(G-8609)*
Wm Kloeffler Industries Inc..........E....... 810 765-4068
Marine City *(G-10487)*
Yonker Welding Service Inc..........G....... 616 534-2774
Grand Rapids *(G-7009)*

7694 Armature Rewinding Shops

A & C Electric Company..........E....... 586 773-2746
Harrison Township *(G-7317)*
All City Electric Motor Repair..........G....... 734 284-2268
Riverview *(G-13289)*
Alpena Electric Motor Service..........G....... 989 354-8780
Alpena *(G-275)*
American Electric Motor Corp..........F....... 810 743-6080
Burton *(G-2143)*
Arrow Motor & Pump Inc..........E....... 734 285-7860
Wyandotte *(G-17946)*
Barry Electric-Rovill Co..........G....... 810 985-8960
Port Huron *(G-12898)*
Bay United Motors Inc..........F....... 989 684-3972
Bay City *(G-1289)*
Birclar Electric and Elec LLC..........F....... 734 941-7400
Romulus *(G-13658)*
Commercial Electric Co..........G....... 269 731-3350
Augusta *(G-1052)*
Commonwealth Service Sls Corp..........G....... 313 581-8050
Rochester Hills *(G-13392)*
Complete Electric..........G....... 517 629-9267
Albion *(G-121)*
Core Electric Company Inc..........F....... 313 382-7140
Melvindale *(G-10694)*
DMS Electric Apparatus Service..........E....... 269 349-7000
Kalamazoo *(G-8729)*
Electric Equipment Company..........G....... 269 925-3266
Benton Harbor *(G-1496)*
Electric Motor & Contg Co..........F....... 313 871-3775
Detroit *(G-4031)*
Electric Motor Service..........G....... 269 945-5113
Hastings *(G-7408)*
Electric Motor Service Ctr Inc..........G....... 616 532-6007
Grandville *(G-7030)*
Fife Pearce Electric Company..........F....... 313 369-2560
Detroit *(G-4058)*
Fixall Electric Motor Service..........G....... 616 454-6863
Grand Rapids *(G-6409)*
Franklin Electric Corporation..........F....... 248 442-8000
Garden City *(G-5824)*
Gower Corporation..........G....... 989 249-5938
Saginaw *(G-14050)*
Grand Rapids Elc Mtr Svc LLC..........G....... 616 243-8866
Grand Rapids *(G-6453)*
Gustos Quality Systems..........G....... 231 409-0219
Fife Lake *(G-5341)*
Hamilton Electric Co..........F....... 989 799-6291
Saginaw *(G-14053)*
Heco Inc..........D....... 269 381-7200
Kalamazoo *(G-8762)*
Holland Electric Motor Co..........G....... 616 392-1115
Holland *(G-7671)*
Industrial Elc Co Detroit Inc..........D....... 313 872-1133
Detroit *(G-4139)*

76 MISCELLANEOUS REPAIR SERVICES

John V Gedda Jr ..... G 906 482-5037
  Hancock *(G-7253)*
Jones Electric Company ..... F 231 726-5001
  Muskegon *(G-11356)*
Kalamazoo Electric Motor Inc ..... G 269 345-7802
  Kalamazoo *(G-8788)*
Lincoln Service LLC ..... G 734 793-0083
  Livonia *(G-9808)*
Lorna Icr LLC ..... G 586 582-1500
  Warren *(G-17131)*
Martin Electric Mtrs Sls & Svc ..... G 989 584-3850
  Carson City *(G-2492)*
Master Mfg Inc ..... E 248 628-9400
  Oxford *(G-12359)*
Medsker Electric Inc ..... E 248 855-3383
  Farmington Hills *(G-5062)*
Metal-Line Corp ..... E 231 723-7041
  Muskegon *(G-11377)*
Midw Inc ..... G 269 343-7090
  Kalamazoo *(G-8826)*
Monarch Electric Service Co ..... E 313 388-7800
  Melvindale *(G-10702)*
Moore Brothers Electrical Co ..... G 810 232-2148
  Flint *(G-5471)*

Motown Harley-Davidson Inc ..... D 734 947-4647
  Taylor *(G-15748)*
Nieboer Electric Inc ..... F 231 924-0960
  Fremont *(G-5779)*
North End Electric Company ..... G 248 398-8187
  Royal Oak *(G-13954)*
Phillips Service Inds Inc ..... F 734 853-5000
  Plymouth *(G-12714)*
Pontiac Electric Motor Works ..... G 248 332-4622
  Pontiac *(G-12856)*
PSI Repair Services Inc ..... C 734 853-5000
  Livonia *(G-9899)*
Rapa Electric Inc ..... E 269 673-3157
  Allegan *(G-186)*
Reliance Electric Machine Co ..... F 810 232-3355
  Flint *(G-5491)*
Riverside Electric Service Inc ..... G 269 849-1222
  Riverside *(G-13286)*
Setco Sales Company ..... F 248 888-8989
  Novi *(G-11994)*
Spina Electric Company ..... E 586 771-8080
  Warren *(G-17247)*
Sturgis Electric Motor Service ..... G 269 651-2955
  Sturgis *(G-15635)*

Superior Elc Mtr Sls & Svc Inc ..... G 906 226-9051
  Marquette *(G-10558)*
Timco Engine Center Inc ..... D 989 739-2194
  Oscoda *(G-12221)*
Valley Truck Parts Inc ..... D 616 241-5431
  Wyoming *(G-18040)*
Waddell Electric Company ..... G 616 791-4860
  Grand Rapids *(G-6976)*
Warfield Electric Company Inc ..... G 734 722-4044
  Westland *(G-17609)*
Werner Electric Co ..... G 313 561-0854
  Dearborn Heights *(G-3801)*
▼ Winans Inc ..... G 810 744-1240
  Corunna *(G-3586)*
York Electric Inc ..... D 989 684-7460
  Bay City *(G-1371)*
York Electric Inc ..... E 517 487-6400
  Lansing *(G-9438)*
Z & R Electric Service Inc ..... F 906 774-0468
  Iron Mountain *(G-8306)*

ALPHABETIC SECTION

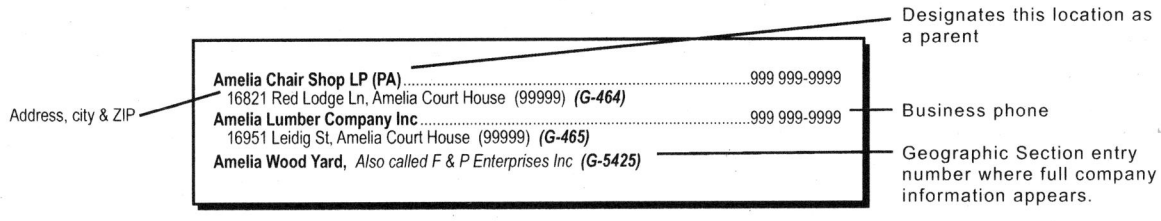

- Designates this location as a parent
- Address, city & ZIP
- **Amelia Chair Shop LP (PA)**..999 999-9999
  - 16821 Red Lodge Ln, Amelia Court House (99999) *(G-464)*
- **Amelia Lumber Company Inc**..999 999-9999
  - 16951 Leidig St, Amelia Court House (99999) *(G-465)*
- **Amelia Wood Yard**, *Also called F & P Enterprises Inc (G-5425)*
- Business phone
- Geographic Section entry number where full company information appears.

See footnotes for symbols and codes identification.
* Companies listed alphabetically.
* Complete physical or mailing address.

+vantage Corporation..734 432-5055
 12651 Newburgh Rd Livonia (48150) *(G-9614)*
/// 702 Cedar River Lbr Inc..906 497-5365
 W4249 Us Hwy 2 Powers (49874) *(G-13076)*
127 Brewing..517 258-1346
 3090 Shirley Dr Jackson (49201) *(G-8368)*
1271 Associates Inc (PA)...586 948-4300
 27295 Luckino Dr Chesterfield (48047) *(G-2730)*
1365267 Ontario Inc..888 843-5245
 2014 Holland Ave Port Huron (48060) *(G-12879)*
1395 Jarvis LLC..248 545-6800
 1395 Jarvis St Ferndale (48220) *(G-5251)*
18th Street Deli Inc..313 921-7710
 8800 Conant St Hamtramck (48211) *(G-7243)*
1st Choice Trckg & Rentl Inc.......................................231 258-0417
 1256 Thomas Rd Kalkaska (49646) *(G-8935)*
1st Class Embroidery LLC..734 282-7745
 11205 Morningview Southgate (48195) *(G-15071)*
1st Quality LLC...313 908-4864
 6700 Wyoming St Ste A Dearborn (48126) *(G-3669)*
2 Brothers Holdings LLC..517 487-3900
 1115 S Penn Ave Ste B Lansing (48912) *(G-9330)*
2 E Fabricating...616 498-7036
 1202 Comstock St Marne (49435) *(G-10503)*
2/90 Sign Systems, Grand Rapids *Also called System 2/90 Inc (G-6911)*
21st Century Graphic Tech LLC..................................586 463-9599
 8344 Hall Rd Ste 210 Utica (48317) *(G-16740)*
21st Century Newspapers Inc (HQ)............................586 469-4510
 19176 Hall Rd Ste 200 Clinton Township (48038) *(G-3026)*
21st Century Newspapers Inc....................................810 664-0811
 1521 Imlay City Rd Lapeer (48446) *(G-9439)*
21st Century Newspapers Inc....................................586 469-4510
 28 W Huron St Pontiac (48342) *(G-12797)*
21st Century Plastics Corp (PA).................................517 645-2695
 300 Wright Pkwy Potterville (48876) *(G-13072)*
2255srv Llv..616 678-4900
 2825 17 Mile Rd Ste A Kent City (49330) *(G-8986)*
2k Tool LLC...616 452-4927
 3025 Madison Ave Se Wyoming (49548) *(G-17983)*
2nd Chance Wood Company......................................989 472-4488
 7505 E M 71 Ste B Durand (48429) *(G-4604)*
2v Industries, Wixom *Also called V & V Industries Inc (G-17923)*
3 D & A Display LLC..616 827-3323
 7377 Expressway Dr Sw Grand Rapids (49548) *(G-6119)*
3 Dimensional Services, Lapeer *Also called Urgent Design and Mfg Inc (G-9489)*
3-D Designs LLC..313 658-1249
 5566 Radnor St Detroit (48224) *(G-3823)*
3-Dimensional Service, Rochester Hills *Also called Three-Dimensional Services Inc (G-13525)*
313 Certified LLC..248 915-8419
 6379 Muirfield Dr Bloomfield Hills (48301) *(G-1738)*
313certified, Bloomfield Hills *Also called 313 Certified LLC (G-1738)*
360 Group Au Pty Ltd..586 219-2005
 2990 Technology Dr Rochester Hills (48309) *(G-13357)*
360ofme Inc..844 360-6363
 225 S Main St Ste 200 Royal Oak (48067) *(G-13897)*
3715-11th Street Corp...734 523-1000
 32711 Glendale St Livonia (48150) *(G-9615)*
3con Corporation..248 859-5440
 47295 Cartier Dr Wixom (48393) *(G-17748)*
3d Polymers Inc...248 588-5562
 4084 Commerce Rd Orchard Lake (48324) *(G-12164)*
3dfx Interactive Inc...918 938-8967
 1813 Mackinaw St Saginaw (48602) *(G-13990)*
3dm Source Inc...616 647-9513
 555 Plymouth Ave Ne Grand Rapids (49505) *(G-6120)*
3dx Tech, Byron Center *Also called Lamon Group Inc (G-2196)*
3dxtech LLC..616 717-3811
 904 36th St Se Ste B Grand Rapids (49508) *(G-6121)*
3M Company...313 372-4200
 11900 E 8 Mile Rd Detroit (48205) *(G-3824)*
3M Company...248 926-2500
 30975 Century Dr Wixom (48393) *(G-17749)*
3r Info LLC..201 221-6133
 5840 N Canton Center Rd # 295 Canton (48187) *(G-2342)*
4 Mile Graphics, Newberry *Also called East End Sports Awards Inc (G-11579)*
4-M Industries Incorporated.....................................734 762-7200
 33855 Capitol St Livonia (48150) *(G-9616)*
4-M Industries Incorporated (PA)............................734 762-7200
 35300 Glendale St Livonia (48150) *(G-9617)*
45 North Vineyard & Winery....................................231 271-1188
 8580 E Horn Rd Lake Leelanau (49653) *(G-9098)*
45th Parallel, Traverse City *Also called Bowers Harbor Vinyrd & Winery (G-15919)*
4d Building Inc...248 799-7384
 54500 Pontiac Trl Milford (48381) *(G-10952)*
4d Systems LLC...800 380-9165
 4130 Market Pl Flint (48507) *(G-5366)*
4ever Aluminum Products Inc..................................517 368-0000
 628 Pebblestone Dr Coldwater (49036) *(G-3286)*
5 By 5 LLC...855 369-6757
 333 W Grandview Pkwy Traverse City (49684) *(G-15886)*
5 Mile Brewing Company LLC (PA)..........................313 348-1628
 2515 Riopelle St Detroit (48207) *(G-3825)*
5 Pyn Inc..906 228-2828
 363 Us Highway 41 E Ste 1 Negaunee (49866) *(G-11466)*
5 Star Drctional Drlg Svcs Ind..................................231 263-2050
 8553 Blackman Rd Kingsley (49649) *(G-9069)*
5 Water Socks LLC..248 735-1730
 17679 Stonebrook Dr Northville (48168) *(G-11674)*
51 North Brewing..248 690-7367
 51 N Broadway St Lake Orion (48362) *(G-9121)*
7 Up Bottling Co, Cadillac *Also called American Bottling Company (G-2227)*
7 Up Holland, Holland *Also called American Bottling Company (G-7557)*
7 Up Lansing, Grand Ledge *Also called American Bottling Company (G-6100)*
7-Up Flint, Mount Morris *Also called American Bottling Company (G-11157)*
7-Up of Gaylord, Gaylord *Also called American Bottling Company (G-5848)*
734 Brewing Company Inc......................................734 649-6453
 15 E Cross St Ypsilanti (48198) *(G-18049)*
826 Michigan..734 761-3463
 115 E Liberty St Ann Arbor (48104) *(G-332)*
917 Chittock Street LLC..866 945-0269
 114 Bank St Lansing (48910) *(G-9331)*
A & A Manufacturing Co...616 846-1730
 19033 174th Ave Spring Lake (49456) *(G-15130)*
A & A Marine & Mfg Inc..231 723-8308
 270 3rd St Manistee (49660) *(G-10413)*
A & A Woodwork Studio LLC..................................248 691-8380
 8575 Capital St Oak Park (48237) *(G-12047)*
A & B Display Systems Inc.....................................989 893-6642
 1111 S Henry St Bay City (48706) *(G-1269)*
A & B Packing Equipment Inc (PA).........................269 539-4700
 732 W Saint Joseph St Lawrence (49064) *(G-9504)*
A & B Packing Equipment Inc.................................616 294-3539
 414 E 40th St Holland (49423) *(G-7544)*
A & B Tube Benders Inc (PA).................................586 773-0440
 13465 E 9 Mile Rd Warren (48089) *(G-16905)*
A & B Tube Benders Inc...586 773-0440
 23133 Schoenherr Rd Warren (48089) *(G-16906)*
A & B Welding & Fabricating..................................231 733-2661
 2532 S Getty St Muskegon (49444) *(G-11255)*
A & C Electric Company...586 773-2746
 41225 Irwin Dr Harrison Township (48045) *(G-7317)*
A & C Electric Motor Sls & Svc, Harrison Township *Also called A & C Electric Company (G-7317)*

(PA)=Parent Co (HQ)=Headquarters (DH)=Div Headquarters

A & D Lighting — ALPHABETIC SECTION

A & D Lighting 269 327-1126
  3711 New Farm St Kalamazoo (49048) *(G-8670)*
A & D Plastics Inc 734 455-2255
  1255 S Mill St Plymouth (48170) *(G-12557)*
A & D Run Off Inc 231 759-0950
  701 W Clay Ave Muskegon (49440) *(G-11256)*
A & E Agg Inc 248 547-4711
  3500 11 Mile Rd Ste D Berkley (48072) *(G-1577)*
A & E Sign, Traverse City Also called Attitude & Experience Inc *(G-15900)*
A & F Enterprises Inc 248 714-6529
  1203 N Milford Rd Milford (48381) *(G-10953)*
A & F Wood Products, Howell Also called Masonite International Corp *(G-8060)*
A & J Pallets, Sheridan Also called Tommy Joe Reed *(G-14735)*
A & K Finishing Inc 616 949-9100
  4175 Danvers Ct Se Grand Rapids (49512) *(G-6122)*
A & L Metal Products 734 654-8990
  11984 Telegraph Rd Carleton (48117) *(G-2451)*
A & L Woods 616 374-7820
  5670 Brown Rd Lake Odessa (48849) *(G-9110)*
A & M Distributors 586 755-9045
  31239 Mound Rd Warren (48092) *(G-16907)*
A & M Industries Inc 586 791-5610
  35590 Groesbeck Hwy Clinton Township (48035) *(G-3027)*
A & M Label, Wixom Also called General Tape Label Liquidating *(G-17817)*
A & M Label, Wixom Also called Fortis Sltions Group Centl LLC *(G-17812)*
A & O Mold and Eng Inc 269 649-0600
  301 N 4th St Vicksburg (49097) *(G-16830)*
A & R Packing Co Inc 734 422-2060
  34165 Autry St Livonia (48150) *(G-9618)*
A & R Specialty Services Corp 313 933-8750
  8101 Lyndon St Detroit (48238) *(G-3826)*
A & S Enterprises LLC 906 482-9007
  175 Woodland Ave Laurium (49913) *(G-9502)*
A & S Industrial LLC 906 482-8007
  19273 Kiiskila Rd Hancock (49930) *(G-7247)*
A & S Reel & Tackle Inc 313 928-1667
  4420 High St Ecorse (48229) *(G-4741)*
A & S Silver Brazing Co, Warren Also called D K Enterprises Inc *(G-16997)*
A 1 Printing and Copy Center 269 381-0093
  129 E Michigan Ave 131 Kalamazoo (49007) *(G-8671)*
A A A Machine, Centreville Also called Van Emon Bruce *(G-2598)*
A A A Mailing & Packg Sups LLC 616 481-9120
  3148 Plainfield Ave Ne # 258 Grand Rapids (49525) *(G-6123)*
A A A Wire Rope & Splicing Inc 734 283-1765
  12650 Sibley Rd Riverview (48193) *(G-13288)*
A A Anchor Bolt Inc 248 349-6565
  7390 Salem Rd Northville (48168) *(G-11675)*
A A P, Hazel Park Also called Advanced Assembly Products Inc *(G-7432)*
A A Tanks Co 586 427-7700
  25110 Thomas Dr Warren (48091) *(G-16908)*
A and D Design Electronics 989 493-1884
  301 W Midland Rd Auburn (48611) *(G-748)*
A and J Industries 616 877-4845
  4066 Division Rd Ste C Wayland (49348) *(G-17396)*
A B C Printing Inc 248 887-0010
  2983 E Highland Rd Highland (48356) *(G-7483)*
A B C Roll Co 586 465-9125
  301 Church St Mount Clemens (48043) *(G-11122)*
A B Electrical Inc 231 737-9200
  2246 Olthoff St Muskegon (49444) *(G-11257)*
A B M Tool & Die Inc 734 432-6060
  38281 Schoolcraft Rd D Livonia (48150) *(G-9619)*
A B Publishing Inc 989 875-4985
  3039 S Bagley Rd Ithaca (48847) *(G-8355)*
A B Rusgo Inc (PA) 586 296-7714
  32064 Utica Rd Fraser (48026) *(G-5610)*
A C I Plastics, Flint Also called Aci Plastics Inc *(G-5369)*
A C Machining LLC 616 455-3870
  7490 Division Ave S Grand Rapids (49548) *(G-6124)*
A C Steel Rule Dies Inc 248 588-5600
  324 E Mandoline Ave Madison Heights (48071) *(G-10175)*
A D Johnson Engraving Co Inc 269 385-0044
  2129 Portage St Kalamazoo (49001) *(G-8672)*
A D S Environmental Srvs, Troy Also called ADS LLC *(G-16168)*
A Dependable Property MGT, Lansing Also called 917 Chittock Street LLC *(G-9331)*
A Design Line Embroidery LLC 734 697-3545
  10669 Belleville Rd Van Buren Twp (48111) *(G-16745)*
A E G M Inc 313 304-5279
  335 S Telegraph Rd Dearborn (48124) *(G-3670)*
A F I, Plymouth Also called American Furukawa Inc *(G-12570)*
A G, Rochester Hills Also called Accurate Gauge & Mfg Inc *(G-13362)*
A G Simpson (usa) Inc 586 268-4817
  6700 18 1/2 M Sterling Heights (48314) *(G-15245)*
A G Simpson (usa) Inc 586 268-4817
  6700 18 1/2 Sterling Heights (48314) *(G-15246)*
A G Simpson (usa) Inc (HQ) 586 268-5844
  6640 Sterling Dr S Sterling Heights (48312) *(G-15247)*

A Game Apparel 810 564-2600
  4330 W Mount Morris Rd # 1 Mount Morris (48458) *(G-11155)*
A H Webster, Saginaw Also called RPC Company *(G-14134)*
A I Flint LLC 810 732-8760
  4444 W Maple Ave Flint (48507) *(G-5367)*
A I M I, Clinton Township Also called Accurate Injection Molds Inc *(G-3033)*
A J D Forest Pdts Ltd Partnr 989 348-5412
  4440 W 4 Mile Rd Grayling (49738) *(G-7101)*
A J M, Bloomfield Hills Also called AJM Packaging Corporation *(G-1743)*
A J Tool Co 517 787-5755
  3525 Scheele Dr Ste A Jackson (49202) *(G-8369)*
A K Oil LLC DBA Speedy Oil and 616 233-9505
  925 Leonard St Nw Grand Rapids (49504) *(G-6125)*
A K Services Inc 313 972-1010
  1604 Clay St Ste 137 Detroit (48211) *(G-3827)*
A Koppel Color Image Company 616 534-3600
  4025 Chicago Dr Sw Grandville (49418) *(G-7015)*
A La Don Seasonings 734 532-7862
  16201 Allen Rd Apt 145 Southgate (48195) *(G-15072)*
A Lindberg & Sons Inc (PA) 906 485-5705
  599 Washington St Ishpeming (49849) *(G-8342)*
A M D, Holland Also called All Metal Designs Inc *(G-7554)*
A M F, Three Rivers Also called American Metal Fab Inc *(G-15854)*
A M Grinding 616 847-8373
  303 S 2nd St Ferrysburg (49409) *(G-5332)*
A M I, Commerce Township Also called American Mfg Innovators Inc *(G-3389)*
A M Manufacturing LLC 231 437-3377
  6300 Us Highway 31 S Charlevoix (49720) *(G-2604)*
A M P, Reese Also called Advanced McRonutrient Pdts Inc *(G-13228)*
A M R Inc 810 329-9049
  671 Hathaway St East China (48054) *(G-4619)*
A M T Welding Inc 586 463-7030
  21446 Carlo Dr Clinton Township (48038) *(G-3028)*
A ME Vertical Incorporated 248 720-0245
  675 E Big Beaver Rd Troy (48083) *(G-16164)*
A N L Spring Manufacturing 313 837-0200
  18307 Weaver St Detroit (48228) *(G-3828)*
A N M Products 269 483-1228
  10645 Silver Creek Rd White Pigeon (49099) *(G-17643)*
A P Engineering, Holly Also called Falcon Motorsports Inc *(G-7878)*
A P S, Auburn Hills Also called Analytical Process Systems Inc *(G-770)*
A Plus Asphalt LLC 888 754-1125
  41000 Woodward Ave Bloomfield Hills (48304) *(G-1739)*
A R C Welding & Repair 517 628-2475
  5261 Bunker Rd Mason (48854) *(G-10628)*
A Raymond Corp N Amer Inc (HQ) 248 853-2500
  2350 Austin Ave Ste 200 Rochester Hills (48309) *(G-13358)*
A Raymond Corp N Amer Inc 810 964-7994
  2350 Austin Ave Ste 100 Rochester Hills (48309) *(G-13359)*
A Raymond Tinnerman Auto Inc 248 537-3147
  2900 Technology Dr Rochester Hills (48309) *(G-13360)*
A Raymond Tinnerman Mexico 248 537-3404
  3091 Research Dr Rochester Hills (48309) *(G-13361)*
A S A P Machine Company 734 459-2447
  8575 Ronda Dr Canton (48187) *(G-2343)*
A S A P Tool Inc 586 790-6550
  35660 Groesbeck Hwy Clinton Township (48035) *(G-3029)*
A S Auto Lights Inc 734 941-1164
  15326 Oakwood Dr Romulus (48174) *(G-13644)*
A S I, Warren Also called Air Supply Inc *(G-16921)*
A S I Instruments Inc 586 756-1222
  12900 E 10 Mile Rd Warren (48089) *(G-16909)*
A S K Machining Services 810 650-0019
  14919 Hough Rd Allenton (48002) *(G-228)*
A S P, Saline Also called American Soy Products Inc *(G-14375)*
A S Plus Industries Inc 586 741-0400
  34728 Centaur Dr Clinton Township (48035) *(G-3030)*
A S R C Inc 517 545-7430
  4285 Westhill Dr Howell (48843) *(G-8008)*
A S Rivard and Son Well Drlg 231 331-4508
  2085 Twin Lake Rd Ne Mancelona (49659) *(G-10384)*
A Time To Remember 517 263-1960
  4450 W Carleton Rd Adrian (49221) *(G-41)*
A W B Industries Inc 989 739-1447
  1000 Ausable Rd Oscoda (48750) *(G-12205)*
A W C, Rockford Also called Accra-Wire Controls Inc *(G-13555)*
A Y Sand and Gravel 313 779-4825
  27416 Ecorse Rd Romulus (48174) *(G-13645)*
A&B Welding, Muskegon Also called A & B Welding & Fabricating *(G-11255)*
A&D Technology Inc 734 973-1111
  4622 Runway Blvd Ann Arbor (48108) *(G-333)*
A&E Machine & Fabrication Inc 740 820-4701
  7540 Wheeler Rd Whitmore Lake (48189) *(G-17683)*
A&G Corporate Holdings LLC 734 513-3488
  12725 Inkster Rd Livonia (48150) *(G-9620)*
A&Lb Custom Framing LLC 517 783-3810
  866 N Wisner St Jackson (49202) *(G-8370)*

ALPHABETIC SECTION

A&M Assembly and Machining LLC 313 369-9475
6400 E Hildale St Detroit (48234) *(G-3829)*
A&T Machining Co Inc 734 761-6006
240 Parkland Plz Ann Arbor (48103) *(G-334)*
A-1 Awning Company 734 421-0680
27618 Warren Rd Westland (48185) *(G-17537)*
A-1 Engraving & Signs Inc 810 231-2227
397 Washington St Ste A Brighton (48116) *(G-1875)*
A-1 Fabrication Inc 586 775-8392
16601 Eastland St Roseville (48066) *(G-13766)*
A-1 Screenprinting LLC (PA) 734 665-2692
260 Metty Dr Ste G Ann Arbor (48103) *(G-335)*
A-1 Signs 269 488-9411
2318 Winters Dr Portage (49002) *(G-12980)*
A-1 Stampings Inc 586 294-7790
33381 Kelly Rd Fraser (48026) *(G-5611)*
A-Day Badge Co, Detroit Also called Dealer Aid Enterprises *(G-3965)*
A-Line Products Corporation 313 571-8300
2955 Bellevue St Detroit (48207) *(G-3830)*
A-OK Grinding Co 248 589-3070
32466 Townley St Madison Heights (48071) *(G-10176)*
A-OK Precision Prototype Inc 586 758-3430
59539 Romeo Plank Rd Ray (48096) *(G-13131)*
A-Pac Manufacturing Company 616 791-7222
2719 Courier Dr Nw Grand Rapids (49534) *(G-6126)*
A-W Custom Chrome Inc 586 775-2040
17726 E 9 Mile Rd Eastpointe (48021) *(G-4697)*
A. R. Lintern Division, Redford Also called Therma-Tech Engineering Inc *(G-13201)*
A.M. Todd, Kalamazoo Also called Wild Flavors Inc *(G-8925)*
A/C Covers, Redford Also called AC Covers Inc *(G-13141)*
A1 Utility Contractor Inc 989 324-8581
8399 Evergreen Rd Evart (49631) *(G-4877)*
A123 Systems LLC (HQ) 248 412-9249
27101 Cabaret Dr Novi (48377) *(G-11822)*
A123 Systems LLC 734 466-6521
28200 Plymouth Rd Livonia (48150) *(G-9621)*
A123 Systems LLC 734 772-0600
38100 Ecorse Rd Romulus (48174) *(G-13646)*
A123 Systems Rmulus Operations, Romulus Also called A123 Systems LLC *(G-13646)*
A2 Energy Systems 734 622-9800
45209 Helm St Plymouth (48170) *(G-12558)*
A2 Motus LLC 734 780-7334
3575 Stanton Ct Ann Arbor (48105) *(G-336)*
A2z Coating 616 805-3281
200 Garden St Se Grand Rapids (49507) *(G-6127)*
A2z Outside Services Inc 586 430-1143
33922 Armada Ridge Rd Richmond (48062) *(G-13257)*
AA Anderson & Co Inc 248 476-7782
41304 Concept Dr Plymouth (48170) *(G-12559)*
AA Anderson & Co Inc 734 432-9800
35569 Industrial Rd Livonia (48150) *(G-9622)*
AA EDM Corporation 734 253-2784
7455 Newman Blvd Dexter (48130) *(G-4470)*
AA Gear LLC 517 552-3100
1045 Durant Dr Howell (48843) *(G-8009)*
Aa Gear & Manufacturing, Howell Also called Meritor Specialty Products LLC *(G-8062)*
AAA Industries Inc 313 255-0420
24500 Capitol Redford (48239) *(G-13140)*
AAA Language Services 248 239-1138
1573 S Telegraph Rd Bloomfield (48302) *(G-1731)*
AAA Waterjet and Machining Inc 586 759-3736
23720 Hoover Rd Warren (48089) *(G-16910)*
Aaccess Entertainment 734 260-1002
11552 Eagle Way Brighton (48114) *(G-1876)*
Aacoa Extrusions Inc 269 697-6063
2005 Mayflower Rd Niles (49120) *(G-11592)*
Aactron Inc 248 543-6740
29306 Stephenson Hwy Madison Heights (48071) *(G-10177)*
Aactus Inc 734 425-1212
12671 Richfield Ct Livonia (48150) *(G-9623)*
Aadvanced Truck Caps Mfrs, Lansing Also called Advanced C & T Manufacturers *(G-9333)*
Aalpha Tinadawn Inc 517 351-1200
974 Trowbridge Rd East Lansing (48823) *(G-4649)*
AAM, Detroit Also called American Axle Mfg Holdings Inc *(G-3866)*
AAM Fraser Mfg Fcilty, Fraser Also called American Axle & Mfg Inc *(G-5616)*
AAM International Holdings Inc (HQ) 313 758-2000
1 Dauch Dr Detroit (48211) *(G-3831)*
AAM Pwder Metal Components Inc 248 597-3800
2727 W 14 Mile Rd Royal Oak (48073) *(G-13898)*
AAM Southfield, Southfield Also called American Axle & Mfg Inc *(G-14836)*
AAM Technical Center, Rochester Hills Also called American Axle & Mfg Inc *(G-13368)*
AAM Wholesale Carpet Corp (PA) 313 898-5101
9504 Whittier St Detroit (48224) *(G-3832)*
AAMCO Transmissions, Detroit Also called American Axle & Mfg Inc *(G-3865)*
Aapharmasyn LLC 734 213-2123
3985 Res Pk Dr Ste 500 Ann Arbor (48108) *(G-337)*
Aapico Detroit LLC (PA) 313 652-5254
6401 W Fort St Detroit (48209) *(G-3833)*

Aapico Detroit LLC 313 551-6001
6401 W Fort St Bldg 2 Detroit (48209) *(G-3834)*
Aapico Detroit LLC 313 551-6001
100 American Way St Detroit (48209) *(G-3835)*
AAR Corp 231 779-4859
10732 Pine Shore Dr Cadillac (49601) *(G-2219)*
AAR Manufacturing Inc 231 779-8800
201 Haynes St Cadillac (49601) *(G-2220)*
AAR Mobility Systems, Cadillac Also called AAR Manufacturing Inc *(G-2220)*
Aaron Incorporated 586 791-0320
33674 Kelly Rd Clinton Township (48035) *(G-3031)*
Aarons Fabrication of Steel 586 883-0652
21427 Carlo Dr Clinton Township (48038) *(G-3032)*
Aati, Oxford Also called Advanced Auto Trends Inc *(G-12334)*
AB Custom Fabricating LLC 269 663-8100
27531 May St Edwardsburg (49112) *(G-4756)*
AB Electrical Wires Inc 231 737-9200
2240 Glade St Muskegon (49444) *(G-11258)*
AB Weapons Division Inc 616 696-2008
25 S Main 2 Cedar Springs (49319) *(G-2544)*
Aba of America Inc (HQ) 815 332-5170
2430 E Walton Blvd Auburn Hills (48326) *(G-759)*
Abaco Partners LLC 616 532-1700
4560 Danvers Dr Se Kentwood (49512) *(G-8997)*
ABB Enterprise Software Inc 248 471-0888
23629 Industrial Park Dr Farmington Hills (48335) *(G-4917)*
ABB Enterprise Software Inc 313 863-1909
16503 Manor St Detroit (48221) *(G-3836)*
ABB Enterprise Software Inc 313 965-8900
65 Cadillac Sq Detroit (48226) *(G-3837)*
ABB Motors and Mechanical Inc 586 978-9800
5993 Progress Dr Sterling Heights (48312) *(G-15248)*
Abbott Laboratories 269 651-0600
901 N Centerville Rd Sturgis (49091) *(G-15594)*
Abbott Laboratories 734 324-6666
1609 Biddle Ave Wyandotte (48192) *(G-17944)*
Abbott Magic, Colon Also called Abbotts Magic Manufacturing Co *(G-3369)*
Abbotts Magic Manufacturing Co 269 432-3235
124 S Saint Joseph St Colon (49040) *(G-3369)*
Abbvie Inc 734 324-6650
1609 Biddle Ave Wyandotte (48192) *(G-17945)*
Abby's Printing, Grand Rapids Also called Quality Printing & Graphics *(G-6801)*
ABC Acquisition Company LLC 734 335-4083
31778 Enterprise Dr Livonia (48150) *(G-9624)*
ABC Boring Co Inc 586 751-2580
30600 Ryan Rd Warren (48092) *(G-16911)*
ABC Coating Company Inc 616 245-4626
1503 Burlingame Ave Sw Grand Rapids (49509) *(G-6128)*
ABC Coating Company Michigan, Grand Rapids Also called ABC Coating Company Inc *(G-6128)*
ABC Custom Chrome Inc 248 674-4333
3370 Warren Dr Waterford (48329) *(G-17321)*
ABC Grinding Inc 313 295-1060
26950 Van Born Rd Dearborn Heights (48125) *(G-3777)*
ABC Group Holdings Inc (HQ) 248 352-3706
24133 Northwestern Hwy Southfield (48075) *(G-14823)*
ABC Group Sale & Marketing, Southfield Also called ABC Group Holdings Inc *(G-14823)*
ABC Industrial Supply, Troy Also called Superior Manufacturing Corp *(G-16627)*
ABC Machining & Fabricating 586 758-0680
6737 E 8 Mile Rd Warren (48091) *(G-16912)*
ABC Nails LLC 616 776-6000
20 Monroe Center St Ne # 110 Grand Rapids (49503) *(G-6129)*
ABC Packaging Equipment & Mtls 616 784-2330
544 7 Mile Rd Nw Comstock Park (49321) *(G-3458)*
ABC Precision Machining Inc 269 926-6322
2077 Yore Ave Benton Harbor (49022) *(G-1478)*
ABC Supply 693, Marquette Also called American Bldrs Contrs Sup Inc *(G-10517)*
Abco, Pontiac Also called Aluminum Blanking Co Inc *(G-12802)*
Abcor Industries LLC 616 994-9577
4690 128th Ave Holland (49424) *(G-7545)*
Abcor Partners LLC 616 994-9577
4690 128th Ave Holland (49424) *(G-7546)*
ABI International 248 583-7150
32052 Edward Ave Madison Heights (48071) *(G-10178)*
Ability Mfg & Engrg Co 269 227-3292
1585 68th St Fennville (49408) *(G-5169)*
Abl Enterprises, Grand Rapids Also called Jbl Enterprises *(G-6555)*
Able Htng Clng & Plmbng 231 779-5430
9542 Peterson Dr Cadillac (49601) *(G-2221)*
Able Manufacturing Inc 616 235-3322
601 Crosby St Nw Grand Rapids (49504) *(G-6130)*
Able Solutions LLC 810 216-6106
2030 10th St Port Huron (48060) *(G-12880)*
Able Welding Inc 989 865-9611
5265 S Graham Rd Saint Charles (48655) *(G-14189)*
Abletech Industries LLC 734 677-2420
8383 Millview Ct Dexter (48130) *(G-4471)*
Abracadabra Jewelry 734 994-4848
205 E Liberty St Ann Arbor (48104) *(G-338)*

Abrahamson Marine Inc....231 843-2142
820 1st St Ludington (49431) *(G-10047)*
Abrasive Diamond Tool Company (PA)....248 588-4800
30231 Stephenson Hwy Madison Heights (48071) *(G-10179)*
Abrasive Finishing Inc....734 433-9236
11770 Dexter Chelsea Rd Chelsea (48118) *(G-2698)*
Abrasive Materials LLC....517 437-4796
90 W Fayette St Hillsdale (49242) *(G-7512)*
Abrasive Services Incorporated....734 941-2144
29040 Northline Rd Romulus (48174) *(G-13647)*
Abrasive Solutions LLC....517 592-2668
12875 Mack Ave Cement City (49233) *(G-2574)*
ABS, Menominee *Also called Advanced Blnding Solutions LLC (G-10721)*
Absolute Lser Wldg Sltions LLC....586 932-2597
6545 19 Mile Rd Sterling Heights (48314) *(G-15249)*
Absolute Nano LLC....617 319-9617
303 S Main St Apt 304 Ann Arbor (48104) *(G-339)*
Absopure Water Company LLC....734 459-8000
8835 General Dr Plymouth (48170) *(G-12560)*
Abtech Installation & Svc Inc....800 548-2381
11900 Reeck Rd Ste 100 Southgate (48195) *(G-15073)*
Abz Steel Systems, Clinton Township *Also called Ferro Fab LLC (G-3115)*
AC Covers Inc....313 541-7770
25544 5 Mile Rd Redford (48239) *(G-13141)*
Academicpub Xanedu, Ann Arbor *Also called Sharedbook Inc (G-629)*
Acadia Group LLC....734 944-1404
1283 Industrial Dr Saline (48176) *(G-14371)*
Acal Precision Products, Roseville *Also called Acal Universal Grinding Co (G-13767)*
Acal Universal Grinding Co....586 296-3900
20200 Cornillie Dr Roseville (48066) *(G-13767)*
Acat Global LLC (PA)....231 330-2553
5339 M 66 N Charlevoix (49720) *(G-2605)*
Acat Global LLC....231 437-5000
66 N North St White Cloud (49349) *(G-17618)*
Accel DFI, Wixom *Also called Accel Performance Group LLC (G-17750)*
Accel Performance Group LLC....248 380-2780
29387 Lorie Ln Wixom (48393) *(G-17750)*
Accelerated Press Inc....248 524-1850
1337 Piedmont Dr Troy (48083) *(G-16165)*
Accelerated Tooling LLC....616 293-9612
2909 Buchanan Ave Sw Grand Rapids (49548) *(G-6131)*
Accell Technologies Inc....248 360-3762
4143 Pioneer Dr Commerce Township (48390) *(G-3384)*
Accents Custom Printwear Plus, Lincoln Park *Also called Graphic Gear Inc (G-9579)*
Access Business Group LLC (HQ)....616 787-6000
7575 Fulton St E Ada (49355) *(G-3)*
Access Heating & Cooling Inc....734 464-0566
39001 Ann Arbor Trl Livonia (48150) *(G-9625)*
Access Manufacturing Techn....224 610-0171
1530 W River Rd Niles (49120) *(G-11593)*
Access Works Inc....231 777-2537
1800 E Keating Ave Muskegon (49442) *(G-11259)*
Accessible Information LLC....248 338-4928
124 N Berkshire Rd Bloomfield Hills (48302) *(G-1740)*
Accessories & Specialties Inc....989 235-3331
121 E Park St Crystal (48818) *(G-3607)*
Accessories By Gigi LLC....248 242-0036
452 E Elmwood Ave Apt 103 Clawson (48017) *(G-2968)*
Accessories R US, Pontiac *Also called Accessories Wholesale Inc (G-12798)*
Accessories Wholesale Inc....248 755-7465
555 Friendly St Pontiac (48341) *(G-12798)*
Accord Paper and Packaging, Coopersville *Also called Mark-Pack Inc (G-3564)*
Accra Tool Inc....248 680-9936
1218 Cottonwood St Lake Orion (48360) *(G-9122)*
Accra-Wire Controls Inc (PA)....616 866-3434
10891 Northland Dr Ne Rockford (49341) *(G-13555)*
Accu Die & Mold Inc....269 465-4020
7473 Red Arrow Hwy Stevensville (49127) *(G-15551)*
Accu Products International....734 429-9571
7836 Bethel Church Rd Saline (48176) *(G-14372)*
Accu-Form Metal Products, Grand Rapids *Also called Accuform Industries Inc (G-6133)*
Accu-Rite Industries LLC (PA)....586 247-0060
51047 Oro Dr Shelby Township (48315) *(G-14538)*
Accu-Shape Die Cutting Inc....810 230-2445
4050 Market Pl Flint (48507) *(G-5368)*
Accu-Tech Manufacturing Inc....586 532-4000
51559 Oro Dr Shelby Township (48315) *(G-14539)*
Accubilt Automated Systems LLC....517 787-9353
2365 Research Dr Jackson (49203) *(G-8371)*
Accucam/Pmc, Coopersville *Also called Omlor Enterprises Inc (G-3567)*
Accuform Industries Inc (PA)....616 363-3801
1701 Broadway Ave Nw Grand Rapids (49504) *(G-6132)*
Accuform Industries Inc....616 363-3801
1701 Broadway Ave Nw Grand Rapids (49504) *(G-6133)*
Accuform Prtg & Graphics Inc....313 271-5600
7231 Southfield Fwy Detroit (48228) *(G-3838)*
Acculift Inc....313 382-5121
17516 Dix Rd Melvindale (48122) *(G-10692)*

Accurate Boring Company Inc....586 294-7555
17420 Malyn Blvd Fraser (48026) *(G-5612)*
Accurate Carbide Tool Co Inc....989 755-0429
5655 N Westervelt Rd Saginaw (48604) *(G-13991)*
Accurate Coating Inc....616 452-0016
955 Godfrey Ave Sw Grand Rapids (49503) *(G-6134)*
Accurate Engineering & Mfg LLC....616 738-1261
13569 New Holland St Holland (49424) *(G-7547)*
Accurate Gauge & Mfg Inc (PA)....248 853-2400
2943 Technology Dr Rochester Hills (48309) *(G-13362)*
Accurate Injection Molds Inc....586 954-2553
22264 Starks Dr Clinton Township (48036) *(G-3033)*
Accurate Machine & Tl USA Ltd....269 205-2610
987 Grand Rapids St Middleville (49333) *(G-10796)*
Accurate Machine Service, Livonia *Also called Accurate Machined Service Inc (G-9626)*
Accurate Machined Service Inc....734 421-4660
30948 Industrial Rd Livonia (48150) *(G-9626)*
Accurate Machining & Fabg Inc....989 426-5400
1650 S M 30 Gladwin (48624) *(G-5922)*
Accurate Mfg Solutions LLC....248 553-2225
28232 Schroeder St Farmington Hills (48331) *(G-4918)*
Accurate Technologies Inc (PA)....248 848-9200
26999 Meadowbrook Rd Novi (48377) *(G-11823)*
Accurate Welding, Chesterfield *Also called Verstar Group Inc (G-2854)*
Accuri Cytometers Inc....734 994-8000
173 Parkland Plz Ann Arbor (48103) *(G-340)*
Accuspec Grinding Inc (PA)....269 556-1410
2660 Lawrence St Stevensville (49127) *(G-15552)*
Accutek Mold & Engineering....586 978-1335
35815 Stanley Dr Sterling Heights (48312) *(G-15250)*
Accutherm Systems Inc....734 930-0461
41 Enterprise Dr Ann Arbor (48103) *(G-341)*
Accutronic Incorporated....586 756-2510
11281 E 9 Mile Rd Warren (48089) *(G-16913)*
Accuworx LLC (PA)....734 847-6115
7156 Sulier Dr Temperance (48182) *(G-15822)*
Ace Asphalt Products Company, Dearborn *Also called Edw C Levy Co (G-3700)*
Ace Canvas & Tent Co....313 842-3011
465 Stephenson Hwy Troy (48083) *(G-16166)*
Ace Consulting & MGT Inc....989 821-7040
10386 S Leline Rd Roscommon (48653) *(G-13747)*
Ace Controls Inc (HQ)....248 476-0213
23435 Industrial Park Dr Farmington Hills (48335) *(G-4919)*
Ace Drill Corporation....517 265-5184
2600 E Maumee St Adrian (49221) *(G-42)*
Ace Electronics LLC Michigan....443 327-6100
401 Minnesota Dr Troy (48083) *(G-16167)*
Ace Filtration Inc....248 624-6300
4123 Pioneer Dr Commerce Township (48390) *(G-3385)*
Ace Finishing Inc....586 777-1390
13195 E 8 Mile Rd Warren (48089) *(G-16914)*
Ace Purification, Commerce Township *Also called Ace Filtration Inc (G-3385)*
Ace Tool & Engineering Inc....616 361-4800
500 Reed St Belding (48809) *(G-1396)*
Ace Tooling, Norton Shores *Also called Patterson Precision Mfg Inc (G-11787)*
Ace Vending Service Inc....616 243-7983
3417 R B Chaffee Memrl Grand Rapids (49548) *(G-6135)*
Ace Welding & Machine Inc....231 941-9664
1505 Premier St Traverse City (49686) *(G-15887)*
Ace Wiping Cloth, Detroit *Also called Ace-Tex Enterprises Inc (G-3839)*
Ace-Tex Enterprises Inc (PA)....313 834-4000
7601 Central St Detroit (48210) *(G-3839)*
Acecd, Jackson *Also called Allied Chucker and Engrg Co (G-8380)*
Acemco Automotive, Norton Shores *Also called Acemco Incorporated (G-11806)*
Acemco Incorporated....231 799-8612
7297 Enterprise Dr Norton Shores (49456) *(G-11806)*
Acg Services Inc....586 232-4698
51512 Schoenherr Rd Shelby Township (48315) *(G-14540)*
Achatzs Hand Made Pie Co (PA)....586 749-2882
30301 Commerce Blvd Chesterfield (48051) *(G-2731)*
Achieve Industries LLC....586 493-9780
44421 N Groesbeck Hwy Clinton Township (48036) *(G-3034)*
Achs Metal Products Inc....586 772-2734
22238 Schoenherr Rd Warren (48089) *(G-16915)*
Aci, Rose City *Also called Assembly Concepts Inc (G-13759)*
Aci Plastics Inc (PA)....810 767-3800
2945 Davison Rd Flint (48506) *(G-5369)*
Ackerman Brothers Inc....989 892-4122
200 S Linn St Bay City (48706) *(G-1270)*
Acm, Coldwater *Also called Asama Coldwater Mfg Inc (G-3289)*
Acm, Sterling Heights *Also called Automotive Component Mfg (G-15267)*
Acm Plastic Products Inc....269 651-7888
507 Saint Joseph St Sturgis (49091) *(G-15595)*
Acme Abrasive Co., Warren *Also called Acme Holding Company (G-16917)*
Acme Bedding Company, Grand Rapids *Also called Jonathan Stevens Mattress Co (G-6564)*
Acme Carbide Die Inc (PA)....734 722-2303
6202 E Executive Dr Westland (48185) *(G-17538)*

ALPHABETIC SECTION — Adept Defense LLC

Acme Casting Enterprises Inc 586 755-0300
2565 John B Ave Warren (48091) *(G-16916)*

Acme Gear Company Inc 586 465-7740
23402 Reynolds Ct Clinton Township (48036) *(G-3035)*

Acme Grooving Tool Co 800 633-8828
7409 S Village Dr Clarkston (48346) *(G-2903)*

Acme Holding Company 586 759-3332
24200 Marmon Ave Warren (48089) *(G-16917)*

Acme Manufacturing Company (PA) 248 393-7300
4240 N Atlantic Blvd Auburn Hills (48326) *(G-760)*

Acme Manufacturing Company 248 393-7300
101 Premier Dr Lake Orion (48359) *(G-9123)*

Acme Mills Company 517 437-8940
301 Arch Ave Hillsdale (49242) *(G-7513)*

Acme Mills Company 517 437-8940
301 Arch Ave Hillsdale (49242) *(G-7514)*

Acme Mills Company 800 521-8585
33 Bloomfield Hills Pkwy Bloomfield Hills (48304) *(G-1741)*

Acme Pallet Inc 616 738-6452
13450 New Holland St Holland (49424) *(G-7548)*

Acme Plating Inc 313 838-3870
18636 Fitzpatrick St Detroit (48228) *(G-3840)*

Acme Septic Tank Co 989 684-3852
2888 S Huron Rd Kawkawlin (48631) *(G-8969)*

Acme Tool & Die Co 231 938-1260
5181 S Lautner Rd Acme (49610) *(G-1)*

Acme Tube Bending Company 248 545-8500
3180 W 11 Mile Rd Berkley (48072) *(G-1578)*

Acme Wire & Iron Works LLC 313 923-7555
3527 E Canfield St Detroit (48207) *(G-3841)*

Acorn Industries Inc (PA) 734 261-2940
11844 Brookfield St Livonia (48150) *(G-9627)*

Acorn Stamping Inc 248 628-5216
600 S Glaspie St Oxford (48371) *(G-12332)*

Acoufelt LLC 800 966-8557
1238 Anderson Rd Fl 2 Clawson (48017) *(G-2969)*

Acoustic Tap Room 231 714-5028
119 N Maple St Traverse City (49684) *(G-15888)*

Acp Technologies LLC 586 322-3511
7205 Sterling Ponds Ct Sterling Heights (48312) *(G-15251)*

Acra Cast Inc 989 893-3961
1837 1st St Bay City (48708) *(G-1271)*

Acro-Feed Industries, Detroit *Also called Haller International Tech Inc* *(G-4114)*

Acro-Tech Manufacturing Inc 269 629-4300
12229 M 89 Plainwell (49080) *(G-12516)*

Acromag Incorporated (PA) 248 624-1541
30765 S Wixom Rd Wixom (48393) *(G-17751)*

Acrylic Specialties, Detroit *Also called Ronald M Davis Co Inc* *(G-4347)*

Acrylic Specialties 248 588-4390
32336 Edward Ave Madison Heights (48071) *(G-10180)*

ACS, Fraser *Also called Auto/Con Services LLC* *(G-5624)*

ACS, Brighton *Also called American Compounding Spc LLC* *(G-1884)*

Act Test Panels LLC 517 439-1485
273 Industrial Dr Hillsdale (49242) *(G-7515)*

Action Ad Newspapers Inc 734 740-6966
45223 Wear Rd Belleville (48111) *(G-1439)*

Action Asphalt LLC 734 449-8565
11224 Lemen Rd Ste A Whitmore Lake (48189) *(G-17684)*

Action Die & Tool Inc 616 538-2326
4621 Spartan Indus Dr Sw Grandville (49418) *(G-7016)*

Action Fabricators Inc 616 957-2032
3760 East Paris Ave Se Grand Rapids (49512) *(G-6136)*

Action Mold & Machining Inc 616 452-1580
3120 Ken O Sha Ind Park S Grand Rapids (49508) *(G-6137)*

Action Packaging LLC 616 871-5200
6995 Southbelt Dr Se Caledonia (49316) *(G-2287)*

Action Printech Inc 734 207-6000
41079 Concept Dr Plymouth (48170) *(G-12561)*

Action Shopper, Marquette *Also called Ogden Newspapers Virginia LLC* *(G-10549)*

Action Tool & Machine Inc 810 229-6300
5976 Ford Ct Brighton (48116) *(G-1877)*

Action Wood 360, Clinton Township *Also called Action Wood Technologies Inc* *(G-3036)*

Action Wood Technologies Inc 586 468-2300
44500 Reynolds Dr Clinton Township (48036) *(G-3036)*

Active and Passive Safety, Livonia *Also called ZF Active Safety & Elec US LLC* *(G-10014)*

Active Brace and Limb LLC (PA) 231 932-8702
5123 N Royal Dr Traverse City (49684) *(G-15889)*

Active Feed Company (PA) 989 453-2472
7564 Pigeon Rd Pigeon (48755) *(G-12485)*

Active Manufacturing Corp 616 842-0800
17127 Hickory St Spring Lake (49456) *(G-15131)*

Active Plastics Inc 616 813-5109
125 Mill Ave Se Caledonia (49316) *(G-2288)*

Active Solutions Group Inc 313 278-4522
4 Parklane Blvd Ste 170 Dearborn (48126) *(G-3671)*

Active Tooling LLC 616 875-8111
6017 Chicago Dr Zeeland (49464) *(G-18109)*

Actron Steel Inc 231 947-3981
2341 Molon Dr Traverse City (49684) *(G-15890)*

Actuator Services LLC 734 242-5456
1620 Rose St Monroe (48162) *(G-11012)*

Actuator Specialties, Monroe *Also called Actuator Services LLC* *(G-11012)*

Acubar Inc (PA) 269 927-3000
1055 N Shore Dr Benton Harbor (49022) *(G-1479)*

Acumedia Manufacturers Inc 517 372-9200
620 Lesher Pl Lansing (48912) *(G-9332)*

Acumen Technologies Inc 586 566-8600
51445 Celeste Shelby Township (48315) *(G-14541)*

Acument Global Tech Inc (HQ) 586 254-3900
6125 18 Mile Rd Sterling Heights (48314) *(G-15252)*

Acument Global Tech Inc 586 254-3900
6125 18 Mile Rd Sterling Heights (48314) *(G-15253)*

Acument Global Tech Inc 810 953-4575
4160 Baldwin Rd Holly (48442) *(G-7868)*

Acutex Division, Whitehall *Also called Hilite International Inc* *(G-17668)*

Acutus Gladwin Industries, Taylor *Also called SMS Group Inc* *(G-15768)*

Ad-Mission, Battle Creek *Also called Shirts n More Inc* *(G-1246)*

Ad-Tech Plastics Systems, Charlotte *Also called Cass Polymers* *(G-2636)*

Ada Gage Inc 616 676-3338
9450 Grand River Dr Se Ada (49301) *(G-4)*

Adac Automotive, Grand Rapids *Also called Adac Plastics Inc* *(G-6140)*

Adac Automotive, Grand Rapids *Also called Adac Door Components Inc* *(G-6139)*

Adac Automotive, Grand Rapids *Also called Adac Plastics Inc* *(G-6141)*

Adac Automotive, Muskegon *Also called Adac Plastics Inc* *(G-11262)*

Adac Automotive Trim Inc (HQ) 616 957-0311
5920 Tahoe Dr Se Grand Rapids (49546) *(G-6138)*

Adac Door Components Inc 616 957-0311
5920 Tahoe Dr Se Grand Rapids (49546) *(G-6139)*

Adac Plastics Inc (PA) 616 957-0311
5920 Tahoe Dr Se Grand Rapids (49546) *(G-6140)*

Adac Plastics Inc 231 777-2645
2653 Olthoff St Muskegon (49444) *(G-11260)*

Adac Plastics Inc 616 957-0311
2929 32nd St Se Grand Rapids (49512) *(G-6141)*

Adac Plastics Inc 616 957-0520
2050 Port City Blvd Muskegon (49442) *(G-11261)*

Adac Plastics Inc 616 957-0311
1801 E Keating Ave Muskegon (49442) *(G-11262)*

Adac Plastics Inc 616 957-0311
5670 Eagle Dr Se Grand Rapids (49512) *(G-6142)*

Adair Printing Company (PA) 734 426-2822
7850 2nd St Dexter (48130) *(G-4472)*

Adam Electronics Incorporated 248 583-2000
32020 Edward Ave Madison Heights (48071) *(G-10181)*

Adams Jerroll Organ Builder 734 439-7203
226 E Main St Ste 228 Milan (48160) *(G-10931)*

Adams Outdoor Advg Ltd Partnr 517 321-2121
3801 Capitol City Blvd Lansing (48906) *(G-9201)*

Adams Shirt Shack Inc 269 964-3323
100 Beadle Lake Rd Battle Creek (49014) *(G-1137)*

Adana Voltaics LLC 734 622-0193
5776 Cedar Ridge Dr Ann Arbor (48103) *(G-342)*

Adapt 989 343-9755
105 W Houghton Ave West Branch (48661) *(G-17505)*

Adaptable Tool Supply LLC 248 439-0866
309 N Chocolay Ave Clawson (48017) *(G-2970)*

Adaptive Mfg Solutions LLC 810 743-1600
4206 S Saginaw St Burton (48529) *(G-2142)*

ADC, Adrian *Also called Anderson Development Company* *(G-49)*

Adcaa LLC 734 623-4236
3110 W Liberty Rd Ste B Ann Arbor (48103) *(G-343)*

Adco Circuits Inc (PA) 248 853-6620
2868 Bond St Rochester Hills (48309) *(G-13363)*

Adco Global Inc 517 764-0334
4401 Page Ave Michigan Center (49254) *(G-10783)*

Adco Products, Michigan Center *Also called Adco Global Inc* *(G-10783)*

Adco Products LLC 517 841-7238
4401 Page Ave Michigan Center (49254) *(G-10784)*

Adco Products, Inc., Michigan Center *Also called Adco Products LLC* *(G-10784)*

Adco Specialties Inc 616 452-6882
4331 E Beltline Ave Ne Grand Rapids (49525) *(G-6143)*

Adcole Corporation 508 485-9100
40 Engelwood Dr Ste G Orion (48359) *(G-12172)*

Adcr, Fenton *Also called Zander Colloids Lc* *(G-5249)*

Addison Awning Co, Jackson *Also called Holiday Distributing Co* *(G-8466)*

Adduxi 248 564-2000
2791 Research Dr Rochester Hills (48309) *(G-13364)*

Ade Inc 248 625-7200
8949 Dixie Hwy Clarkston (48348) *(G-2904)*

Ademco Inc 586 759-1455
24749 Forterra Dr Warren (48089) *(G-16918)*

Ademco Inc 248 926-5510
47247 Cartier Dr Wixom (48393) *(G-17752)*

Adept Broaching Co 734 427-9221
6253 Barbara Ln Plymouth (48170) *(G-12562)*

Adept Defense LLC 231 758-2792
1307 Howard St Petoskey (49770) *(G-12439)*

Adept Plastic Finishing, Wixom *Also called Tribar Manufacturing LLC* ***(G-17917)***
Adept Plastic Finishing Inc......248 863-5930
30540 Beck Rd Wixom (48393) ***(G-17753)***
Adept Tool & Mold Inc......269 461-3765
6892 E Main St Eau Claire (49111) ***(G-4737)***
Adgravers Inc......313 259-3780
269 Walker St Detroit (48207) ***(G-3842)***
Adhesive Systems Inc......313 865-4448
15477 Woodrow Wilson St Detroit (48238) ***(G-3843)***
Adhesives and Processes Tech......231 737-4418
1202 E Pontaluna Rd Ste B Norton Shores (49456) ***(G-11807)***
ADI Global Distribution, Warren *Also called Ademco Inc* ***(G-16918)***
ADI Global Distribution, Wixom *Also called Ademco Inc* ***(G-17752)***
Adient Inc (HQ)......734 254-5000
49200 Halyard Dr Plymouth (48170) ***(G-12563)***
Adient US LLC (HQ)......734 254-5000
49200 Halyard Dr Plymouth (48170) ***(G-12564)***
Adient US LLC......734 414-9215
47700 Halyard Dr Plymouth (48170) ***(G-12565)***
Adient US LLC......734 414-9215
45000 Helm St Plymouth (48170) ***(G-12566)***
Adient US LLC......616 394-8510
205 Douglas Ave Holland (49424) ***(G-7549)***
Adient US LLC......269 968-3000
76 Armstrong Rd Battle Creek (49037) ***(G-1138)***
Adjunct Advocate Corporation......734 930-6854
817 Brookside Dr Ann Arbor (48105) ***(G-344)***
Adjustable Locking Tech LLC......248 443-9664
6632 Telegraph Rd Ste 298 Bloomfield Hills (48301) ***(G-1742)***
ADL Systems Inc......517 647-7543
5596 E Grand River Ave Portland (48875) ***(G-13060)***
Adler Pelzer Group, Troy *Also called HP Pelzer Auto Systems Inc* ***(G-16405)***
Adlib Grafix & Apparel......269 964-2810
10 Van Armon Ave Battle Creek (49017) ***(G-1139)***
ADM, Battle Creek *Also called Archer-Daniels-Midland Company* ***(G-1147)***
ADM, Snover *Also called Archer-Daniels-Midland Company* ***(G-14743)***
ADM, Grand Ledge *Also called Archer-Daniels-Midland Company* ***(G-6101)***
ADM, Portland *Also called Archer-Daniels-Midland Company* ***(G-13061)***
Admat Manufacturing Inc......269 641-7453
16744 Us Highway 12 Union (49130) ***(G-16727)***
Admin Industries LLC......989 685-3438
3049 Beechwood Rd Rose City (48654) ***(G-13756)***
Admiral......989 356-6419
2520 Us Highway 23 S Alpena (49707) ***(G-271)***
Admiral Box Company, Warren *Also called AS Property Management Inc* ***(G-16941)***
Admiral Broach Company Inc......586 468-8411
21391 Carlo Dr Clinton Township (48038) ***(G-3037)***
Admore Inc......586 949-8200
24707 Wood Ct Macomb (48042) ***(G-10102)***
Adnic Products Co......810 789-0321
6261 N Saginaw St Mount Morris (48458) ***(G-11156)***
Adrian Coatings Company......517 438-8699
3202 Northmor Dr W Adrian (49221) ***(G-43)***
Adrian Lva Biofuel LLC......517 920-4863
1571 W Beecher Rd Adrian (49221) ***(G-44)***
Adrian Precision Machining LLC......517 263-4564
605 Industrial Dr Adrian (49221) ***(G-45)***
Adrian Sand & Stone, Clinton *Also called Stansley Mineral Resources Inc* ***(G-3025)***
Adrian Steel Company (PA)......517 265-6194
906 James St Adrian (49221) ***(G-46)***
Adrian Team LLC......517 264-6148
795 Richlyn Dr Adrian (49221) ***(G-47)***
Adrian Tool Corporation......517 263-6530
1441 Enterprise Ave Adrian (49221) ***(G-48)***
Adrian's T-Shirt Printery, Holland *Also called Adrians Screen Print* ***(G-7550)***
Adrians Screen Print......734 994-1367
3735 Hollywood St Holland (49424) ***(G-7550)***
ADS LLC......248 740-9593
1100 Owendale Dr Ste K Troy (48083) ***(G-16168)***
ADS Plus Printing......810 659-7190
767 E Main St Flushing (48433) ***(G-5530)***
ADS Us Inc (PA)......989 871-4550
4705 Industrial Dr Millington (48746) ***(G-10993)***
Adtco, Madison Heights *Also called Abrasive Diamond Tool Company* ***(G-10179)***
Adtek Graphics Inc......517 663-2460
228 1/2 S Main St Eaton Rapids (48827) ***(G-4715)***
Advance, Rogers City *Also called Presque Isle Newspapers Inc* ***(G-13621)***
Advance BCI Inc (PA)......616 669-1366
3102 Walker Ridge Dr Nw Grand Rapids (49544) ***(G-6144)***
Advance BCI Inc......616 669-5210
3102 Walker Ridge Dr Nw Grand Rapids (49544) ***(G-6145)***
Advance Central Services Mich, Walker *Also called Herald Publishing Company LLC* ***(G-16867)***
Advance Cnc Machine Inc......269 751-7005
3051 Lincoln Rd Hamilton (49419) ***(G-7228)***
Advance Concrete Products Co......248 887-4173
975 N Milford Rd Highland (48357) ***(G-7484)***
Advance Cylinder Products LLC......586 991-2445
50300 Rizzo Dr Shelby Township (48315) ***(G-14542)***
Advance Engineering Co Mich, Canton *Also called Advance Engineering Company* ***(G-2344)***
Advance Engineering Company (PA)......313 537-3500
7505 Baron Dr Canton (48187) ***(G-2344)***
Advance Engineering Company......989 435-3641
3982 Terry Dianne St Beaverton (48612) ***(G-1382)***
Advance Graphic Systems Inc......248 656-8000
1806 Rochester Indl Dr Rochester Hills (48309) ***(G-13365)***
Advance Machine Corp......989 362-9192
612 9th Ave Tawas City (48763) ***(G-15675)***
Advance Motor Rebuilders Inc......586 222-9583
22850 Groesbeck Hwy Warren (48089) ***(G-16919)***
Advance Newspapers, Grand Rapids *Also called Advance BCI Inc* ***(G-6144)***
Advance Packaging Acquisition (HQ)......616 949-6610
4450 36th St Se Grand Rapids (49512) ***(G-6146)***
Advance Packaging Corporation (PA)......616 949-6610
4459 40th St Se Grand Rapids (49512) ***(G-6147)***
Advance Packaging Corporation......616 949-6610
2400 E High St Jackson (49203) ***(G-8372)***
Advance Precision Grinding Co......586 773-1330
29739 Groesbeck Hwy Roseville (48066) ***(G-13768)***
Advance Print & Graphics Inc......734 663-6816
4553 Concourse Dr Ann Arbor (48108) ***(G-345)***
Advance Products Corporation......269 849-1000
2527 N M 63 Benton Harbor (49022) ***(G-1480)***
Advance Publishing & Printing, Blissfield *Also called River Raisin Publications* ***(G-1725)***
Advance Scraping Company......810 796-2676
5063 Hollow Corners Rd Dryden (48428) ***(G-4567)***
Advance Specialties, Ann Arbor *Also called Advance Print & Graphics Inc* ***(G-345)***
Advance Tech Solutions LLC......989 928-1806
1348 Delta Dr Saginaw (48638) ***(G-13992)***
Advance Tool Co......231 587-5286
407 Rose St Mancelona (49659) ***(G-10385)***
Advance Turning and Mfg Inc (PA)......517 783-2713
4005 Morrill Rd Jackson (49201) ***(G-8373)***
Advance Turning and Mfg Inc......517 750-3580
4901 James Mcdevitt St Jackson (49201) ***(G-8374)***
Advance Vehicle Assembly Inc......989 823-3800
555 E Huron Ave Vassar (48768) ***(G-16810)***
Advanced Air Technologies Inc......989 743-5544
300 Sleeseman Dr Corunna (48817) ***(G-3577)***
Advanced Altrntive Sltions LLC......616 607-6956
2600 De Laat Ave Sw Wyoming (49519) ***(G-17984)***
Advanced Assembly Products Inc (PA)......248 543-2427
1300 E 9 Mile Rd Hazel Park (48030) ***(G-7432)***
Advanced Auto Trends Inc (PA)......248 628-6111
2230 Metamora Rd Oxford (48371) ***(G-12333)***
Advanced Auto Trends Inc......810 672-9203
3279 Washington St Snover (48472) ***(G-14741)***
Advanced Auto Trends Inc......248 628-4850
3485 Metamora Rd Oxford (48371) ***(G-12334)***
Advanced Automation Group LLC......248 299-8100
1685 W Hamlin Rd Rochester Hills (48309) ***(G-13366)***
Advanced Automotive Group LLC......586 206-2478
8784 Folkert Rd Clay (48001) ***(G-2991)***
Advanced Avionics Inc......734 259-5300
6118 Gotfredson Rd Plymouth (48170) ***(G-12567)***
Advanced Battery Concepts LLC......989 424-6645
8 Consumes Energy Pkwy Clare (48617) ***(G-2863)***
Advanced Blnding Solutions LLC......920 664-1469
W5649 County Road 342 Wallace (49893) ***(G-16885)***
Advanced Blnding Solutions LLC......906 914-4180
949 1st St Menominee (49858) ***(G-10721)***
Advanced Boring and Tool Co......586 598-9300
26950 23 Mile Rd Lowr Chesterfield (48051) ***(G-2732)***
Advanced C & T Manufacturers......517 882-2444
3315 S Cedar St Lansing (48910) ***(G-9333)***
Advanced Cnc Machining LLC......616 226-6706
3086 Dixie Ave Sw Ste E Grandville (49418) ***(G-7017)***
Advanced Composite Tech Inc......248 709-9097
417 E 2nd St Rochester (48307) ***(G-13311)***
Advanced Conveyor Systems, Allegan *Also called B & G Custom Works Inc* ***(G-150)***
Advanced Cutting Tool Systems, Taylor *Also called Colonial Tool Sales & Svc LLC* ***(G-15703)***
Advanced Decorative Systems, Millington *Also called ADS Us Inc* ***(G-10993)***
Advanced Def Vhcl Systems Corp......248 391-3200
6716 Ridgeview Dr Clarkston (48346) ***(G-2905)***
Advanced Drainage Systems Inc......989 761-7610
4800 Marlette Rd Clifford (48727) ***(G-3009)***
Advanced Drainage Systems Inc......989 723-5208
770 S Chestnut St Owosso (48867) ***(G-12275)***
Advanced Elastomers Corp......734 458-4194
34481 Industrial Rd Livonia (48150) ***(G-9628)***
Advanced Electric......517 529-9050
10300 Hayes Dr Clarklake (49234) ***(G-2893)***
Advanced Energy Services LLC......231 369-2602
5894 Puffer Rd Sw South Boardman (49680) ***(G-14748)***
Advanced Energy Svc, South Boardman *Also called Advanced Energy Services LLC* ***(G-14748)***

Advanced Farm Equipment LLC 989 268-5711
5773 N Crystal Rd Vestaburg (48891) *(G-16825)*
Advanced Feedlines LLC 248 583-9400
103 Park Dr Troy (48083) *(G-16169)*
Advanced Fiberglass Services 810 785-7541
3612 Circle Dr Flint (48507) *(G-5370)*
Advanced Fibermolding Inc 231 768-5177
23095 14 Mile Rd Leroy (49655) *(G-9529)*
Advanced Finishing Tech, Comstock Park *Also called Drag Finishing Tech LLC (G-3479)*
Advanced Food Technologies Inc 616 574-4144
1140 Butterworth St Sw Grand Rapids (49504) *(G-6148)*
Advanced Heat Treat Corp 734 243-0063
1625 Rose St Monroe (48162) *(G-11013)*
Advanced Inc 231 938-2233
5474 Em 72 Acme (49610) *(G-2)*
Advanced Industries Inc 734 433-1800
3955 S Fletcher Rd Chelsea (48118) *(G-2699)*
Advanced Integ Tooling Solns 586 749-5525
29700 Commerce Blvd Chesterfield (48051) *(G-2733)*
Advanced Integrated Mfg 586 439-0300
34673 Bennett Fraser (48026) *(G-5613)*
Advanced Integration Tech LP 586 749-5525
29700 Commerce Blvd Chesterfield (48051) *(G-2734)*
Advanced Integration Tech Mich, Chesterfield *Also called Advanced Integ Tooling Solns (G-2733)*
Advanced Machining Ltd 586 465-2220
25425 Terra Industrial Dr Chesterfield (48051) *(G-2735)*
Advanced Magnet Source Corp 734 398-7188
5033 Belleville Rd Canton (48188) *(G-2345)*
Advanced Maintenance Tech 810 820-2554
3118 S Dye Rd Flint (48507) *(G-5371)*
Advanced Manufacturing LLC 231 826-3859
311 E Prosper Rd Falmouth (49632) *(G-4891)*
Advanced Material Process, Romulus *Also called Metal Improvement Company LLC (G-13705)*
Advanced McRonutrient Pdts Inc 989 752-2138
2405 W Vassar Rd Reese (48757) *(G-13228)*
Advanced Metal Fabricators 616 570-4847
12958 Christopher Dr Lowell (49331) *(G-10022)*
Advanced Mold Solutions 586 468-6883
43682 N Gratiot Ave Clinton Township (48036) *(G-3038)*
Advanced Molding Solutions, Grand Haven *Also called Molding Solutions Inc (G-6056)*
Advanced Photonix Inc (PA) 734 864-5647
2925 Boardwalk St Ann Arbor (48104) *(G-346)*
Advanced Plastic Mfg Inc 269 962-9697
5501 Wayne Rd Battle Creek (49037) *(G-1140)*
Advanced Polymers Composites 248 766-1507
7111 Dixie Hwy 110 Clarkston (48346) *(G-2906)*
Advanced Printing & Graphics, Muskegon *Also called Workman Printing Inc (G-11455)*
Advanced Printwear Inc 248 585-4412
31171 Stephenson Hwy Madison Heights (48071) *(G-10182)*
Advanced Recovery Tech Corp 231 788-2911
16684 130th Ave Nunica (49448) *(G-12031)*
Advanced Research Company 248 475-4770
4140 S Lapeer Rd Orion (48359) *(G-12173)*
Advanced Rubber & Plastic (PA) 586 754-7398
3035 Otis Ave Warren (48091) *(G-16920)*
Advanced Rubber Tech Inc 231 775-3112
10640 W Cadillac Rd Cadillac (49601) *(G-2222)*
Advanced Screenprinting 586 979-4412
35957 Mound Rd Ste 2 Sterling Heights (48310) *(G-15254)*
Advanced Sheet Metal 616 301-3828
320 Marion Ave Sw Grand Rapids (49504) *(G-6149)*
Advanced Signs Incorporated 616 846-4667
401 2nd St Ferrysburg (49409) *(G-5333)*
Advanced Special Tools Inc 269 962-9697
320 Clark Rd Battle Creek (49037) *(G-1141)*
Advanced Stage Tooling LLC 810 444-9807
4317 River Rd East China (48054) *(G-4620)*
Advanced Systems & Contrls Inc 586 992-9684
15773 Leone Dr Macomb (48042) *(G-10103)*
Advanced Technologies Cons, Northville *Also called TS Enterprise Associates Inc (G-11732)*
Advanced Technology and Design 248 889-5658
1458 Energy Way Highland (48357) *(G-7485)*
Advanced Tex Screen Printing 989 643-7288
4177 3 Mile Rd Bay City (48706) *(G-1272)*
Advanced Tex Screenprinting, Bay City *Also called Advanced Tex Screen Printing (G-1272)*
Advanced Tooling Systems Inc (HQ) 616 784-7513
1166 7 Mile Rd Nw Comstock Park (49321) *(G-3459)*
Advanced Urethanes Inc 313 273-5705
12727 Westwood St Detroit (48223) *(G-3844)*
Advanced-Cable LLC 586 491-3073
1179 Chicago Rd Troy (48083) *(G-16170)*
Advantage Design & Tool Inc 586 463-2800
22760 Macomb Indus Dr Clinton Township (48036) *(G-3039)*
Advantage Design and Tool 586 801-7413
35800 Big Hand Rd Richmond (48062) *(G-13258)*
Advantage Housing Inc 269 792-6291
3555 12th St Wayland (49348) *(G-17397)*
Advantage Industries Inc 616 669-2400
2196 Port Sheldon St Jenison (49428) *(G-8616)*
Advantage Label & Packg Pdts, Grand Rapids *Also called Advantage Label and Packg Inc (G-6150)*
Advantage Label and Packg Inc 616 656-1900
5575 Executive Pkwy Se Grand Rapids (49512) *(G-6150)*
Advantage Laser Inc 734 367-9936
35684 Veronica St Livonia (48150) *(G-9629)*
Advantage Millwork, Grand Rapids *Also called D & D Building Inc (G-6328)*
Advantage Sign Grphic Slutions, Hudsonville *Also called Advantage Sign Supply Inc (G-8143)*
Advantage Sign Supply Inc (PA) 877 237-4464
4182 Royal Ct Hudsonville (49426) *(G-8143)*
Advantage Sintered Metals Inc 269 964-1212
60 Clark Rd Battle Creek (49037) *(G-1142)*
Advantage Truck ACC Inc 800 773-3110
5400 S State Rd Ann Arbor (48108) *(G-347)*
Advertiser Publishing Co Inc 616 642-9411
13 N Bridge St Saranac (48881) *(G-14452)*
Advertiser, The, Iron Mountain *Also called Now Ogden News Pubg of Mich (G-8295)*
Advertiser, The, Warren *Also called C & G Publishing Inc (G-16971)*
Advertising Accents Inc 313 937-3890
18845 Denby Redford (48240) *(G-13142)*
Advertising Age Magazine, Detroit *Also called Crain Communications Inc (G-3952)*
Advertsing Ntwrk Solutions Inc (PA) 248 475-7881
530 Pine St Ste F Rochester (48307) *(G-13312)*
Advisor Inc 906 341-2424
311 Oak St Manistique (49854) *(G-10438)*
Advisor The, Shelby Township *Also called Macomb North Clinton Advisor (G-14630)*
Advs, Clarkston *Also called Advanced Def Vhcl Systems Corp (G-2905)*
ADW Industries Inc 989 466-4742
130 Woodworth Ave Alma (48801) *(G-231)*
Ae Group LLC 734 942-0615
28275 Northline Rd Romulus (48174) *(G-13648)*
AEC Systems Usa Inc 616 257-9502
3665 Iris Dr Sw Grandville (49418) *(G-7018)*
Aees Inc (HQ) 248 489-4700
36555 Corp Dr Ste 300 Farmington Hills (48331) *(G-4920)*
Aees Power Systems Ltd Partnr 269 668-4429
36555 Corp Dr Ste 300 Farmington Hills (48331) *(G-4921)*
Aees Power Systems Ltd Partnr (HQ) 248 489-4900
999 Republic Dr Allen Park (48101) *(G-194)*
Aegis Welding Supply 248 475-9860
1080 Centre Rd Auburn Hills (48326) *(G-761)*
AEL/Span LLC (PA) 734 957-1600
41775 Ecorse Rd Ste 100 Van Buren Twp (48111) *(G-16746)*
Aer 517 345-7272
16574 S Bauer Rd Grand Ledge (48837) *(G-6099)*
Aero Inc 248 669-4085
1010 W West Maple Rd Walled Lake (48390) *(G-16889)*
Aero Auto Stud Specialists Inc 248 437-2171
10769 Plaza Dr Whitmore Lake (48189) *(G-17685)*
Aero Box Company 586 415-0000
20101 Cornillie Dr Roseville (48066) *(G-13769)*
Aero Embedded Technologies Inc 586 251-2980
6580 Cotter Ave Sterling Heights (48314) *(G-15255)*
Aero Filter Inc 248 837-4100
1604 E Avis Dr Madison Heights (48071) *(G-10183)*
Aero Foil International Inc 231 773-0200
1920 Port City Blvd Muskegon (49442) *(G-11263)*
Aero Grinding Inc (PA) 586 774-6450
28300 Groesbeck Hwy Roseville (48066) *(G-13770)*
Aero Grinding Inc 586 774-6450
28240 Groesbeck Hwy Roseville (48066) *(G-13771)*
Aero Inspection & Tool LLC 517 525-7373
856 Ewers Rd Leslie (49251) *(G-9540)*
Aero Marine Inc 734 721-6241
1517 N Wayne Rd Westland (48185) *(G-17539)*
Aero Systems 253 269-3000
13475 Wayne Rd Livonia (48150) *(G-9630)*
Aero Test, Romulus *Also called Approved Aircraft Accessories (G-13651)*
Aero Train Corp 810 230-8096
5083 Miller Rd Flint (48507) *(G-5372)*
Aerobee Electric Inc 248 549-2044
3030 Hilton Rd Ferndale (48220) *(G-5252)*
Aerofab Company Inc 248 542-0051
2335 Goodrich St Ferndale (48220) *(G-5253)*
Aerofficient LLC 847 784-8100
12001 Farmington Rd Livonia (48150) *(G-9631)*
Aerospace America Inc 989 684-2121
900 Harry S Truman Pkwy Bay City (48706) *(G-1273)*
Aerospace Group, Jackson *Also called Eaton-Aeroquip Llc (G-8440)*
Aerospace Mfg Svcs Inc 269 697-4800
206 Main St Ste 2 Buchanan (49107) *(G-2108)*
Aerospace Nylok Corporation (PA) 586 786-0100
15260 Hallmark Ct Macomb (48042) *(G-10104)*
Aerospoke Incorporated 248 685-9009
5034 Walnut Hills Dr Brighton (48116) *(G-1878)*

ALPHABETIC

Aerostar Manufacturing, Romulus *Also called Ae Group LLC* ***(G-13648)***

Aerostatica Inc 734 426-5525
7399 Newman Blvd Dexter (48130) ***(G-4473)***

Aerotech Caps, Jenison *Also called Composite Sign Products Inc* ***(G-8621)***

Aerovision Aircraft Svcs LLC 231 799-9000
620 E Ellis Rd Norton Shores (49441) ***(G-11737)***

Aerovision International LLC 231 799-9000
620 E Ellis Rd Norton Shores (49441) ***(G-11738)***

Aertech Machining & Mfg Inc 517 782-4644
2020 Micor Dr Jackson (49203) ***(G-8375)***

Aerus Electrolux, Pontiac *Also called Electrolux Professional Inc* ***(G-12821)***

Aesi, Bloomfield Hills *Also called Automotive Electronic Spc* ***(G-1748)***

Aetna Bearing Company, Livonia *Also called ABC Acquisition Company LLC* ***(G-9624)***

Aetna Engineering, Grand Rapids *Also called Fireboy-Xintex Inc* ***(G-6406)***

Afc-Holcroft LLC (HQ) 248 624-8191
49630 Pontiac Trl Wixom (48393) ***(G-17754)***

Afco Manufacturing Corp 248 634-4415
428 Cogshall St Holly (48442) ***(G-7869)***

Affiliated Troy Dermatologist 248 267-5020
4600 Investment Dr Troy (48098) ***(G-16171)***

Affinia Group Inc 734 827-5400
1101 Technology Dr Ann Arbor (48108) ***(G-348)***

Affinity Custom Molding Inc 269 496-8423
21198 M 60 Mendon (49072) ***(G-10711)***

Affinity Electronics Inc 586 477-4920
33710 Doreka Fraser (48026) ***(G-5614)***

Affinity Solutions, Zeeland *Also called Extol Inc* ***(G-18136)***

Affinity Tool Works LLC 248 588-0395
1161 Rankin Dr Troy (48083) ***(G-16172)***

Affordable Mobile Devices LLC 313 433-9242
28211 Southfield Rd # 760092 Lathrup Village (48076) ***(G-9497)***

Affordable Neon Ent 906 356-6168
17498 State Highway M35 Rock (49880) ***(G-13552)***

Affordable OEM Autolighting 989 400-6106
3068 W Klees Rd Stanton (48888) ***(G-15227)***

Afgco Sand & Gravel Co Inc 810 798-3293
5171 Sandhill Rd Almont (48003) ***(G-250)***

Afi, Muskegon *Also called Aero Foil International Inc* ***(G-11263)***

Afi Enterprises Inc 734 475-9111
11770 Dexter Chelsea Rd Chelsea (48118) ***(G-2700)***

African American Parent Pubg 248 398-3400
22041 Woodward Ave Ferndale (48220) ***(G-5254)***

Aft 313 320-0218
16555 Shaftsbury Ave Detroit (48219) ***(G-3845)***

Aftech, Rockford *Also called Derby Fabg Solutions LLC* ***(G-13566)***

Aftech Inc 616 866-1650
3056 Walker Ridge Dr Nw A Grand Rapids (49544) ***(G-6151)***

Aftermarket Industries LLC 810 229-3200
315 E Main St Brighton (48116) ***(G-1879)***

Aftershock Motorsports 586 273-1333
5831 Church Rd Casco (48064) ***(G-2498)***

Afx Industries LLC (HQ) 810 966-4650
1411 3rd St Ste G Port Huron (48060) ***(G-12881)***

Afx Industries LLC 517 768-8993
4111 County Farm Rd Jackson (49201) ***(G-8376)***

Afx/Trim, Port Huron *Also called Afx Industries LLC* ***(G-12881)***

AG Davis, Sterling Heights *Also called AG Davis Gage & Engrg Co* ***(G-15256)***

AG Davis Gage & Engrg Co (PA) 586 977-9000
6533 Sims Dr Sterling Heights (48313) ***(G-15256)***

AG Harvesters LLC 989 876-7161
533 N Court St Au Gres (48703) ***(G-740)***

AG Manufacturing Inc 989 479-9590
319 Industrial Dr Harbor Beach (48441) ***(G-7263)***

AG Precision Gage Inc 248 374-0063
28317 Beck Rd Ste E6 Wixom (48393) ***(G-17755)***

Ag-Pro, Grand Rapids *Also called Allsales Enterprises Inc* ***(G-6164)***

Agape Plastics Inc 616 735-4091
11474 1st Ave Nw Grand Rapids (49534) ***(G-6152)***

AGC Grand Haven LLC 616 842-1820
16750 Comstock St Grand Haven (49417) ***(G-5990)***

Agelessmage Fcial Asthtics LLC 269 998-5547
28499 Orchard Lake Rd Farmington Hills (48334) ***(G-4922)***

Agenda 2020 Inc 616 581-6271
555 Cascade West Pkwy Se Grand Rapids (49546) ***(G-6153)***

Aget Manufacturing Company, Adrian *Also called Madison Street Holdings LLC* ***(G-77)***

Aget Manufacturing Company, Adrian *Also called Depierre Industries Inc* ***(G-59)***

Aggregate, Cedarville *Also called O-N Minerals Michigan Company* ***(G-2570)***

Aggregate and Developing LLC 269 217-5492
1108 Lincoln Rd Allegan (49010) ***(G-146)***

Aggregate Industries, Dundee *Also called Bardon Inc* ***(G-4576)***

Aggregate Industries - Mwr Inc 734 529-5876
6211 N Ann Arbor Rd Dundee (48131) ***(G-4574)***

Aggregate Industries - Mwr Inc 269 321-3800
822 Schuster Ave Kalamazoo (49001) ***(G-8673)***

Aggregate Industries - Mwr Inc 269 685-5937
475 12th St Plainwell (49080) ***(G-12517)***

Aggregate Industries - Mwr Inc 734 475-2531
4950 Loveland Rd Grass Lake (49240) ***(G-7083)***

Aggregate Industries Centl Reg 734 475-2531
4950 Loveland Rd Grass Lake (49240) ***(G-7084)***

Aggregate Industries-Wcr Inc 269 963-7263
18646 12 Mile Rd Battle Creek (49014) ***(G-1143)***

Aggregtes Excvtg Logistics LLC 231 737-4949
951 E Barney Ave Ste B Muskegon (49444) ***(G-11264)***

Aggressive Mfg Innovations, Lewiston *Also called AMI Industries Inc* ***(G-9547)***

Aggressive Tool & Die Inc 616 837-1983
728 Main St Coopersville (49404) ***(G-3547)***

Aggressive Tooling Inc 616 754-1404
608 Industrial Park Dr Greenville (48838) ***(G-7122)***

Agi Ccaa Inc 715 355-0856
1755 Yeager St Port Huron (48060) ***(G-12882)***

Agio Imaging, Kalamazoo *Also called Domer Industries LLC* ***(G-8731)***

AGM Automotive LLC (HQ) 248 776-0600
27755 Stansbury Blvd # 300 Farmington Hills (48334) ***(G-4923)***

AGM Automotive Mexico LLC (HQ) 248 925-4152
27755 Stansbury Blvd # 300 Farmington Hills (48334) ***(G-4924)***

Agnew Grphics Signs Promotions 989 723-4621
1905 W M 21 A Owosso (48867) ***(G-12276)***

Agrestal Hygienics LLC 800 410-9053
10463 W H Ave Kalamazoo (49009) ***(G-8674)***

Agriculture Liqiud Fertilizers, Saint Johns *Also called Cog Marketers Ltd* ***(G-14280)***

Agrigenetics Inc 317 337-3000
2030 Dow Ctr Midland (48674) ***(G-10812)***

Agritek Industries Inc 616 786-9200
4211 Hallacy Dr Holland (49424) ***(G-7551)***

Agritemp, Livonia *Also called Hamilton Engineering Inc* ***(G-9764)***

Agro-Clture Liquid Fertilizers, Ashley *Also called Cog Marketers Ltd* ***(G-727)***

Agropur Inc 616 538-3822
5252 Clay Ave Sw Grand Rapids (49548) ***(G-6154)***

AGS Publishing 313 494-1000
7312 2nd Ave Detroit (48202) ***(G-3846)***

Ahd LLC 586 922-6511
50649 Central Indus Dr Shelby Township (48315) ***(G-14543)***

Ahearn Signs and Printing 734 699-3777
290 Industrial Park Dr Belleville (48111) ***(G-1440)***

Ahh Publishing, Jackson *Also called Superior Surface Protection Co* ***(G-8579)***

Ahlusion LLC 888 277-0001
8048 Miller Rd Swartz Creek (48473) ***(G-15659)***

Ahs LLC (HQ) 888 355-3050
25 W 8th St Ste 200 Holland (49423) ***(G-7552)***

Ai Warren, Warren *Also called Android Industries-Sterling* ***(G-16933)***

Ai-Delta Township, Lansing *Also called Android Industries-Delta Towns* ***(G-9277)***

Ai-Genesee LLC 810 720-4848
4400 Matthew Flint (48507) ***(G-5373)***

Aichelin Heat Treatment Syst 734 459-9850
49630 Pontiac Trl Wixom (48393) ***(G-17756)***

Aim, Rochester *Also called Applied & Integrated Mfg Inc* ***(G-13313)***

Aim Mail Centers, Fruitport *Also called Automated Indus Motion Inc* ***(G-5787)***

Aim Plastics Inc 586 954-2553
22264 Starks Dr Clinton Township (48036) ***(G-3040)***

Aim Systems Warren, Warren *Also called Magna Modular Systems LLC* ***(G-17137)***

Aim-Rite Hauling, Lake Orion *Also called Aimrite LLC* ***(G-9124)***

Aimrite LLC 248 693-8925
941 Hinford Ave Lake Orion (48362) ***(G-9124)***

AIN Plastics 248 356-4000
23235 Telegraph Rd Southfield (48033) ***(G-14824)***

Ainsworth Electric Inc 810 984-5768
3200 Dove Rd Ste A Port Huron (48060) ***(G-12883)***

Aip Aerospace, Macomb *Also called Ascent Aerospace Holdings LLC* ***(G-10109)***

Aip Aerospace, Macomb *Also called Ascent Integrated Platforms* ***(G-10110)***

Aip Group Inc 248 828-4400
2041 E Square Lake Rd # 100 Troy (48085) ***(G-16173)***

Air and Liquid Systems Inc 248 656-3610
1680 S Livernois Rd Rochester Hills (48307) ***(G-13367)***

Air Brake Systems Inc 989 775-8880
4356 E Valley Rd Mount Pleasant (48858) ***(G-11168)***

Air Conditioning Products Co (PA) 734 326-0050
30350 Ecorse Rd Romulus (48174) ***(G-13649)***

Air Craft Industries Inc 269 663-8544
27328 May St Edwardsburg (49112) ***(G-4757)***

Air Devices Co 989 354-5740
2723 Pearl Rd Alpena (49707) ***(G-272)***

Air Feeds/Roll Feeds, Roseville *Also called Metal Stmping Spport Group LLC* ***(G-13834)***

Air Filter & Equipment Inc 734 261-1860
37007 Industrial Rd Livonia (48150) ***(G-9632)***

Air Filter Sales & Service, Madison Heights *Also called Aero Filter Inc* ***(G-10183)***

Air Force Inc 616 399-8511
933 Butternut Dr Holland (49424) ***(G-7553)***

Air International (us) Inc (HQ) 248 391-7970
750 Standard Pkwy Auburn Hills (48326) ***(G-762)***

Air Intrntonal Thermal Systems, Auburn Hills *Also called Air International (us) Inc* ***(G-762)***

Air Lift Company (PA) 517 322-2144
2727 Snow Rd Lansing (48917) ***(G-9272)***

Air Master Systems Corp 231 798-1111
6480 Norton Center Dr Norton Shores (49441) ***(G-11739)***

Air Products and Chemicals Inc 313 297-2006
1025 Oakwood Blvd Detroit (48217) ***(G-3847)***

Air Products and Controls, Auburn Hills *Also called Apollo America Inc* ***(G-776)***

Air Pump Valve Corporation 810 655-6444
6503 Linden Rd Swartz Creek (48473) ***(G-15660)***

Air Source, Stevensville *Also called Dee-Blast Corporation* ***(G-15563)***

Air Supply Inc 586 773-6600
21300 Groesbeck Hwy Warren (48089) ***(G-16921)***

Air Supply Company Inc 616 874-7751
7459 9 Mile Rd Ne Rockford (49341) ***(G-13556)***

Air Tight Solutions LLC 248 629-0461
18677 Robson St Detroit (48235) ***(G-3848)***

Air Way Automation Inc 989 348-1802
2268 Industrial Dr Grayling (49738) ***(G-7102)***

Air-Hydraulics Inc 517 787-9444
545 Hupp Ave Jackson (49203) ***(G-8377)***

Air-Matic Products Company Inc (PA) 248 356-4200
22218 Telegraph Rd Southfield (48033) ***(G-14825)***

Airboss Flexible Products Co 248 852-5500
2600 Auburn Ct Auburn Hills (48326) ***(G-763)***

Aircraft Precision Pdts Inc 989 875-4186
185 Industrial Pkwy Ithaca (48847) ***(G-8356)***

Aircraft Tool Supply, Oscoda *Also called A W B Industries Inc* ***(G-12205)***

Airflow Sciences Equipment LLC 734 525-0300
12190 Hubbard St Livonia (48150) ***(G-9633)***

Airgas Usa LLC 517 673-0997
7031 Silberhorn Hwy Blissfield (49228) ***(G-1712)***

Airgas Usa LLC 248 545-9353
1200 Farrow St Ferndale (48220) ***(G-5255)***

Airhug LLC 734 262-0431
47960 Red Run Dr Canton (48187) ***(G-2346)***

Airlite Synthetics Mfg Inc 248 335-8131
342 Irwin Ave Pontiac (48341) ***(G-12799)***

Airman Inc 248 960-1354
6150 Whitmore Lake Rd Brighton (48116) ***(G-1880)***

Airman Products LLC 248 960-1354
6150 Whitmore Lake Rd Brighton (48116) ***(G-1881)***

Airmaster Fan Company 517 764-2300
9229 S Meridian Rd Clarklake (49234) ***(G-2894)***

Airmetal Corporation 517 784-6000
1309 Bagley Ave Jackson (49203) ***(G-8378)***

Airpark Plastics LLC 989 846-1029
1415 W Cedar St Standish (48658) ***(G-15215)***

Airpower America, Scotts *Also called Kristus Inc* ***(G-14505)***

Airserve LLC 586 427-5349
26770 Liberal Center Line (48015) ***(G-2576)***

Airtec Corporation 313 892-7800
17565 Walter P Chrysler Detroit (48203) ***(G-3849)***

Airtificial Intelligent Robots 989 799-6669
3175 Christy Way S Ste 5 Saginaw (48603) ***(G-13993)***

Airway Welding Inc 517 789-6125
2415 E High St Jackson (49203) ***(G-8379)***

Airwest Engineering, Grand Rapids *Also called Lacks Industries Inc* ***(G-6611)***

Ais Automation Systems Inc 734 365-2384
20950 Woodruff Rd Rockwood (48173) ***(G-13603)***

Ais Construction Eqp Svc Corp 616 538-2400
4781 Clay Ave Sw Grand Rapids (49548) ***(G-6155)***

Aisin Holdings America Inc 734 453-5551
15300 Centennial Dr Northville (48168) ***(G-11676)***

Aisin Technical Ctr Amer Inc 734 453-5551
15300 Centennial Dr Northville (48168) ***(G-11677)***

Ait Tooling, Chesterfield *Also called Advanced Integration Tech LP* ***(G-2734)***

Aj Aircraft 734 244-4015
2410 N Monroe St Monroe (48162) ***(G-11014)***

Aj Logging 989 725-9610
8203 N M 52 Henderson (48841) ***(G-7465)***

Ajax Materials Corporation (HQ) 248 244-3300
1957 Crooks Rd A Troy (48084) ***(G-16174)***

Ajax Materials Corporation 248 244-3445
7329 Kensington Rd Brighton (48116) ***(G-1882)***

Ajax Metal Processing Inc (PA) 313 267-2100
4651 Bellevue St Detroit (48207) ***(G-3850)***

Ajax Metal Processing Inc 586 497-7000
22105 Hoover Rd Warren (48089) ***(G-16922)***

Ajax Paving Industries, Brighton *Also called Ajax Materials Corporation* ***(G-1882)***

Ajax Paving Industries Inc (HQ) 248 244-3300
1957 Crooks Rd A Troy (48084) ***(G-16175)***

Ajax Spring and Mfg Co 248 588-5700
700 Ajax Dr Madison Heights (48071) ***(G-10184)***

Ajax Tocco Magnethermic Corp 248 589-2524
30100 Stephenson Hwy Madison Heights (48071) ***(G-10185)***

Ajax Tocco Magnethermic Corp 248 585-1140
32350 Howard Ave Madison Heights (48071) ***(G-10186)***

Ajax Trailers Inc (PA) 586 757-7676
2089 E 10 Mile Rd Warren (48091) ***(G-16923)***

Ajf Inc 734 753-4410
37015 Pennsylvania Rd New Boston (48164) ***(G-11496)***

AJM Packaging Corporation (PA) 248 901-0040
E-4111 Andover Rd Bloomfield Hills (48302) ***(G-1743)***

AJM Packaging Corporation 313 842-7530
6910 Dix St Detroit (48209) ***(G-3851)***

AJM Packaging Corporation 313 291-6500
21130 Trolley Indus Dr Taylor (48180) ***(G-15685)***

AK Rewards LLC 734 272-7078
2723 S State St Ste 150 Ann Arbor (48104) ***(G-349)***

AK Steel Corporation 313 317-8900
14661 Rotunda Dr Dearborn (48120) ***(G-3672)***

AK Steel Corporation 513 425-2707
5440 Corporate Dr Ste 125 Troy (48098) ***(G-16176)***

AK Steel Corporation 800 532-8857
4001 Miller Rd Dearborn (48120) ***(G-3673)***

Akamai Technologies Inc 734 424-1142
9394 Anne St Pinckney (48169) ***(G-12495)***

Akebono Brake Corporation (HQ) 248 489-7400
34385 W 12 Mile Rd Farmington Hills (48331) ***(G-4925)***

Akers Wood Products Inc (PA) 269 962-3802
1124 River Rd W Battle Creek (49037) ***(G-1144)***

Akervall Technologies Inc (PA) 800 444-0570
1512 Woodland Dr Saline (48176) ***(G-14373)***

Akki Products, Saline *Also called Mikan Corporation* ***(G-14401)***

Akorn Inc 800 579-8327
2929 Plymouth Rd Ann Arbor (48105) ***(G-350)***

Akorn Consumer Health, Ann Arbor *Also called Akorn Inc* ***(G-350)***

Akston Hughes Intl LLC 989 448-2322
1865 Orourke Blvd Ste A Gaylord (49735) ***(G-5847)***

Aktis Engrg Solutions Inc 313 450-2420
17340 W 12 Mile Rd Ste 20 Southfield (48076) ***(G-14826)***

Aktv8 LLC 517 775-1270
10056 Colonial Indus Dr South Lyon (48178) ***(G-14785)***

Akwel Cadillac Usa Inc (HQ) 231 876-8020
603 7th St Cadillac (49601) ***(G-2223)***

Akwel Cadillac Usa Inc 231 775-6571
603 7th St Cadillac (49601) ***(G-2224)***

Akwel Cadillac Usa Inc 248 848-9599
39205 Country Clb Ste C16 Farmington Hills (48331) ***(G-4926)***

Akwel Cadillac Usa Inc 231 876-1361
603 7th St Cadillac (49601) ***(G-2225)***

Akwel Usa Inc 231 775-6571
603 7th St Cadillac (49601) ***(G-2226)***

Akzo Nobel Coatings Inc 248 451-6231
120 Franklin Rd Pontiac (48341) ***(G-12800)***

Akzo Nobel Coatings Inc 248 637-0400
1845 Maxwell Dr Ste 100 Troy (48084) ***(G-16177)***

Akzo Nobel Coatings Inc 248 451-6231
27 Brush St Troy (48084) ***(G-16178)***

Akzo Nobel Coatings Inc 248 528-0715
2373 John R Rd Ste A Troy (48083) ***(G-16179)***

Akzo Nobel Coatings Inc 248 637-0400
117 Brush St Pontiac (48341) ***(G-12801)***

Akzo Nobel Coatings Inc 312 544-7000
1696 Maxwell Dr Troy (48084) ***(G-16180)***

Al Corp 734 475-7357
525 Glazier Rd Chelsea (48118) ***(G-2701)***

Al Dente Inc 734 449-8522
9815 Main St Whitmore Lake (48189) ***(G-17686)***

Al's Cabinet Shop, Monroe *Also called Van Daeles Inc* ***(G-11082)***

Al-Craft Design & Engrg Inc (PA) 248 589-3827
710 Minnesota Dr Troy (48083) ***(G-16181)***

Al-Craft Industries, Troy *Also called Al-Craft Design & Engrg Inc* ***(G-16181)***

Al-Fe Heat Treating Inc 989 752-2819
1300 Leon Scott Ct Saginaw (48601) ***(G-13994)***

Aladdin Printing 248 360-2842
1546 Union Lake Rd Commerce Township (48382) ***(G-3386)***

Alan Bruce Enterprises 616 262-4609
4590 28th St Sw Byron Center (49315) ***(G-2175)***

Alba Plastics, Troy *Also called Noack Ventures LLC* ***(G-16526)***

Albah Manufacturing Tech Corp 519 972-7222
1985 Ring Dr Troy (48083) ***(G-16182)***

Albar Industries Inc 810 667-0150
780 Whitney Dr Lapeer (48446) ***(G-9440)***

Albasara Fuel LLC 313 443-6581
10419 Ford Rd Dearborn (48126) ***(G-3674)***

Albemarle Corporation 269 637-8474
1421 Kalamazoo St South Haven (49090) ***(G-14751)***

Albers Cabinet Company 586 727-9090
65151 Gratiot Ave Lenox (48050) ***(G-9520)***

Albert Sand & Gravel, Holt *Also called Delhi Leasing Inc* ***(G-7910)***

Alberts Machine Tool Inc 231 743-2457
16971 10th Ave Marion (49665) ***(G-10489)***

Albion Automotive Limited 313 758-2000
1 Dauch Dr Detroit (48211) ***(G-3852)***

Albion Industries LLC (PA) 800 835-8911
800 N Clark St Albion (49224) ***(G-113)***

Albion Machine and Tool LLC 517 629-8838
1001 Industrial Blvd Albion (49224) ***(G-114)***

Albion Recorder, Albion *Also called Calhoun Communications Inc* ***(G-116)***

Albrecht Sand & Gravel Co 810 672-9272
3790 W Sanilac Rd Snover (48472) ***(G-14742)***

Albright Precision Inc 517 545-7642
4921 W Grand River Ave Howell (48855) **(G-8010)**
Alco Manufacturing Corp 734 426-3941
8763 Dexter Chelsea Rd Dexter (48130) **(G-4474)**
Alco Plastics Inc (PA) 586 752-4527
160 E Pond Dr Romeo (48065) **(G-13623)**
Alco Printing Services Inc 248 280-1124
4921 Delemere Ave Royal Oak (48073) **(G-13899)**
Alco Products LLC 313 823-7500
580 Saint Jean St Detroit (48214) **(G-3853)**
Alcoa, Farmington Hills *Also called Arconic Inc* **(G-4932)**
Alcoa Automotive- Indiana (HQ) 248 489-4900
37000 W 12 Mile Rd # 115 Farmington Hills (48331) **(G-4927)**
Alcoa Howmet 231 894-5686
1 Misco Dr Whitehall (49461) **(G-17660)**
Alcoa Howmet, Thermatech, Whitehall *Also called Howmet Corporation* **(G-17674)**
Alcoa Howmet, Wthl, Casting Op, Whitehall *Also called Howmet Corporation* **(G-17675)**
Alcoa Power & Propulsion, Whitehall *Also called Howmet Corporation* **(G-17669)**
Alcock Printing Inc 586 731-4366
46723 Van Dyke Ave Shelby Township (48317) **(G-14544)**
Alcona County Review 989 724-6384
111 N Lake St Harrisville (48740) **(G-7361)**
Alcona Tool & Machine Inc (PA) 989 736-8151
3040 E Carbide Dr Harrisville (48740) **(G-7362)**
Alcona Tool & Machine Inc 989 736-8151
325 N Lake St Lincoln (48742) **(G-9561)**
Alcotec Wire Corporation (HQ) 800 228-0750
2750 Aero Park Dr Traverse City (49686) **(G-15891)**
Ald Thermal Treatment Inc 810 357-0693
2656 24th St Port Huron (48060) **(G-12884)**
Aldez North America LLC 810 577-3891
4260 Van Dyke Rd Ste 109 Almont (48003) **(G-251)**
Aldinger Inc 517 394-2424
1669 E Jolly Rd Lansing (48910) **(G-9334)**
Aldoa Company, Detroit *Also called Advanced Urethanes Inc* **(G-3844)**
Aldos Bakery Inc 810 744-9123
G5131 S Saginaw St Flint (48507) **(G-5374)**
Aldridge Trucking, Holly *Also called South Flint Gravel Inc* **(G-7897)**
Aleris, Coldwater *Also called Real Alloy Recycling LLC* **(G-3325)**
Aleris International Inc 517 279-9596
368 W Garfield Ave Coldwater (49036) **(G-3287)**
Alex and Ani LLC 248 649-7348
2800 W Big Beaver Rd Troy (48084) **(G-16183)**
Alex Brands, Plymouth *Also called Poof-Slinky LLC* **(G-12723)**
Alex Delvecchio Entps Inc 248 619-9600
1343 Piedmont Dr Troy (48083) **(G-16184)**
Alexa Forest Products 906 265-2347
137 Dirkman Rd Iron River (49935) **(G-8307)**
Alexander and Hornung Inc 586 771-9880
20643 Stephens St Saint Clair Shores (48080) **(G-14238)**
Alexander Directional Boring 989 362-9506
2395 Robinet Dr East Tawas (48730) **(G-4686)**
Alexander Dodds Company 616 784-6000
3000 Walkent Dr Nw Grand Rapids (49544) **(G-6156)**
Alexander J Bongiorno Inc 248 689-7766
101 W Big Beavr Rd # 135 Troy (48084) **(G-16185)**
Alexanders Custom GL & Mirror 734 513-5850
29455 James St Garden City (48135) **(G-5820)**
Alexis Manufacturing Div, Grand Rapids *Also called Hekman Furniture Company* **(G-6502)**
Alf Enterprises Inc 734 665-2012
1342 N Main St Ste 11a Ann Arbor (48104) **(G-351)**
Alf Studios, Ann Arbor *Also called Alf Enterprises Inc* **(G-351)**
Alfie Embroidery Inc 231 935-1488
2425 Switch Dr Ste A Traverse City (49684) **(G-15892)**
Alfmeier Friedrichs & Rath LLC 248 526-1650
340 E Big Beaver Rd # 135 Troy (48083) **(G-16186)**
Algal Scientific, Plymouth *Also called Kemin Industries Inc* **(G-12663)**
Algen County Shopper, Munising *Also called Peterson Publishing Inc* **(G-11247)**
Algo Especial Variety Str Inc 313 963-9013
2628 Bagley St Detroit (48216) **(G-3854)**
Algoma Products Inc 616 285-6440
4201 Brockton Dr Se Grand Rapids (49512) **(G-6157)**
Algonac Marine Cast LLC 810 794-9391
9300 Stone Rd Clay (48001) **(G-2992)**
Alhern-Martin Indus Frnc Co 248 689-6363
2155 Austin Dr Troy (48083) **(G-16187)**
Alien Resources, Lansing *Also called Pine Needle People LLC* **(G-9256)**
Alinosi French Ice Cream Co 313 527-3195
12748 E Mcnichols Rd Detroit (48205) **(G-3855)**
Alinosi Ice Cream Co., Detroit *Also called Alinosi French Ice Cream Co* **(G-3855)**
All About Drainage LLC 248 921-0766
1940 Alton Cir Commerce Township (48390) **(G-3387)**
All About Quilting and Design 269 471-7359
4683 E Hillcrest Dr Berrien Springs (49103) **(G-1591)**
All Access Name Tags 866 955-8247
1435 Rochester Rd Troy (48083) **(G-16188)**
All American Container Corp 586 949-0000
24600 Wood Ct Macomb (48042) **(G-10105)**
All American Embroidery Inc 734 421-9292
31600 Plymouth Rd Livonia (48150) **(G-9634)**
All American Essentials, Livonia *Also called All American Embroidery Inc* **(G-9634)**
All American Whse & Cold Stor 313 865-3870
14401 Dexter Ave Detroit (48238) **(G-3856)**
All Bending & Tubular Pdts LLC 616 333-2364
430 Cummings Ave Nw Ste G Grand Rapids (49534) **(G-6158)**
All Chrome LLC 517 554-1649
512 N Clark St Albion (49224) **(G-115)**
All City Electric Motor Repair 734 284-2268
18750 Fort St Apt 15 Riverview (48193) **(G-13289)**
All Dealer Inventory LLC 231 342-9823
8148 Maple City Hwy Lake Ann (49650) **(G-9083)**
All Integrated Solutions, Traverse City *Also called All Tool Sales Inc* **(G-15893)**
All Kids Considered Pubg Group 248 398-3400
22041 Woodward Ave Ferndale (48220) **(G-5256)**
All Kids Considered Publishing 248 398-3400
22041 Woodward Ave Ferndale (48220) **(G-5257)**
All Metal Designs Inc 616 392-3696
13131 Reflections Dr Holland (49424) **(G-7554)**
All Metal Finishing, Casco *Also called New Lfe Cppr & Brss Maint Free* **(G-2503)**
All Overhead Door Operator Co, Detroit *Also called General Hardwood Company* **(G-4080)**
All Packaging Solutions Inc 248 880-1548
29380 John R Rd Madison Heights (48071) **(G-10187)**
All Phase Welding Service Inc 616 235-6100
711 Ionia Ave Nw Grand Rapids (49503) **(G-6159)**
All Season Enclosures 248 650-8020
2760 Marissa Way Shelby Township (48316) **(G-14545)**
All Seasons Agency Inc 586 752-6381
5455 34 Mile Rd Bruce Twp (48065) **(G-2077)**
All Seasons Communications, Bruce Twp *Also called All Seasons Agency Inc* **(G-2077)**
All Size Pallets 810 721-1999
4005 N Van Dyke Rd Imlay City (48444) **(G-8195)**
All Things Made In America, Ann Arbor *Also called Ideation Inc* **(G-499)**
All Tool Sales Inc 231 941-4302
812 Hughes Dr Traverse City (49696) **(G-15893)**
All Type Truck and Trlr Repr, Warren *Also called D & W Management Company Inc* **(G-16996)**
All Welding and Fabg Co Inc 248 689-0986
1882 Woodslee Dr Troy (48083) **(G-16189)**
All Wood Log Splitters, Petersburg *Also called Milan Metal Worx LLC* **(G-12437)**
All-Chem Corporation 313 865-3600
15120 3rd St Detroit (48203) **(G-3857)**
All-Cote Coatings Company LLC 586 427-0062
23896 Sherwood Center Line (48015) **(G-2577)**
All-Fab Corporation 269 673-6572
1235 Lincoln Rd Unit 1235 # 1235 Allegan (49010) **(G-147)**
All-Lift Systems Inc 906 779-1620
1400 Cedar Ave Iron Mountain (49801) **(G-8274)**
All-Tech Inc (PA) 616 406-0681
1030 58th St Sw Wyoming (49509) **(G-17985)**
All-Tech Engineering, Wyoming *Also called All-Tech Inc* **(G-17985)**
All-Wood Inc 906 353-6642
101 Us Highway 41 S Baraga (49908) **(G-1096)**
Allagra Print and Imaging 586 263-0060
42120 Garfield Rd Clinton Township (48038) **(G-3041)**
Allan Tool & Machine Co Inc (PA) 248 585-2910
1822 E Maple Rd Troy (48083) **(G-16190)**
Allegan Flashes, Allegan *Also called Flashes Publishers Inc* **(G-162)**
Allegan Metal Fabricators Inc 269 751-7130
3280 Lincoln Rd Hamilton (49419) **(G-7229)**
Allegan Metal Finishing C 269 673-6604
1274 Lincoln Rd Allegan (49010) **(G-148)**
Allegan News & Gazette, Allegan *Also called Kaechele Publications Inc* **(G-168)**
Allegan Tubular Products Inc 269 673-6636
1276 Lincoln Rd Allegan (49010) **(G-149)**
Allegiance Packaging LLC 586 846-2453
23361 Quinn Rd Clinton Township (48035) **(G-3042)**
Allegra Alpena, Alpena *Also called Model Printing Service Inc* **(G-301)**
Allegra Battle Creek, Battle Creek *Also called B & M Imaging Inc* **(G-1148)**
Allegra DH API 382, Dearborn Heights *Also called August Communications Inc* **(G-3780)**
Allegra Marketing Print Signs, Auburn Hills *Also called Rtr Alpha Inc* **(G-994)**
Allegra Network LLC 248 360-1290
7015 Cooley Lake Rd West Bloomfield (48324) **(G-17464)**
Allegra Print & Imaging, Saline *Also called Acadia Group LLC* **(G-14371)**
Allegra Print & Imaging, Grand Rapids *Also called Breck Graphics Incorporated* **(G-6235)**
Allegra Print & Imaging, Troy *Also called Apb Inc* **(G-16204)**
Allegra Print & Imaging, Holland *Also called Holland Printing Center Inc* **(G-7676)**
Allegra Print & Imaging, Okemos *Also called Muhleck Enterprises Inc* **(G-12133)**
Allegra Print & Imaging 248 354-1313
28810 Northwestern Hwy Southfield (48034) **(G-14827)**
Allegra Print & Imaging No 38, Portage *Also called Kaufman Enterprises Inc* **(G-13006)**
Allegra Print and Imaging 616 784-6699
929 Alpine Commerce Park Grand Rapids (49544) **(G-6160)**
Allegra Print Imaging Detroit, Detroit *Also called Nje Enterprises LLC* **(G-4273)**
Allegra Print Imaging-Lansing, Lansing *Also called Lightning Litho Inc* **(G-9392)**

Allegra Print Imging Port Hron, Fort Gratiot *Also called C W Enterprises Inc* ***(G-5547)***
Allegra Printing, Traverse City *Also called Allesk Enterprises Inc* ***(G-15894)***
Allegra Printing & Imaging, Saline *Also called Printing Services Inc* ***(G-14409)***
Allegro Microsystems LLC 248 242-5044
691 N Squirrel Rd Ste 107 Auburn Hills (48326) ***(G-764)***
Allen Pattern of Michigan 269 963-4131
202 Mcgrath Pl Battle Creek (49014) ***(G-1145)***
Allen Tool 517 566-2200
110 Jackson St Sunfield (48890) ***(G-15644)***
Allen Whitehouse 231 824-3000
1270 E 16 1/2 Rd Manton (49663) ***(G-10450)***
Allender & Company 248 398-5776
615 Livernois St Ferndale (48220) ***(G-5258)***
Allesk Enterprises Inc (PA) 231 941-5770
1224 Centre St Traverse City (49686) ***(G-15894)***
Allfi Robotics Inc 586 248-1198
48829 West Rd Wixom (48393) ***(G-17757)***
Allgraphics Corp 248 994-7373
28960 E King William Dr Farmington Hills (48331) ***(G-4928)***
Alliance Automation LLC 810 953-9539
4072 Market Pl Flint (48507) ***(G-5375)***
Alliance Broach and Tool, East China *Also called J & L Turning Inc* ***(G-4623)***
Alliance Cnc LLC 616 971-4700
3987 Brockton Dr Se Ste A Grand Rapids (49512) ***(G-6161)***
Alliance Cnc Ctter Grnding Svc, Grand Rapids *Also called Alliance Cnc LLC* ***(G-6161)***
Alliance Engnred Sltons NA Ltd 586 291-3694
18615 Sherwood St Detroit (48234) ***(G-3858)***
Alliance Franchise Brands LLC (PA) 248 596-8600
47585 Galleon Dr Plymouth (48170) ***(G-12568)***
Alliance Hni LLC 989 729-2804
525 S Gould St Owosso (48867) ***(G-12277)***
Alliance Industries Inc 248 656-3473
51820 Regency Center Dr Macomb (48042) ***(G-10106)***
Alliance Interiors LLC 517 322-0711
4521 W Mount Hope Hwy Lansing (48917) ***(G-9273)***
Alliance Polymers and Svcs LLC 734 710-6700
30735 Cypress Rd Ste 400 Romulus (48174) ***(G-13650)***
Alliance Sheet Metal Inc 269 795-2954
6262 N Moe Rd Middleville (49333) ***(G-10797)***
Alliance Tool 586 465-3960
41239 Irwin Dr Harrison Township (48045) ***(G-7318)***
Alliance Tool and Machine Co 586 427-6411
21418 Timberidge St Saint Clair Shores (48082) ***(G-14239)***
Alliant Enterprises LLC 269 629-0300
333 Bridge St Nw Ste 1125 Grand Rapids (49504) ***(G-6162)***
Alliant Healthcare Products, Grand Rapids *Also called Alliant Enterprises LLC* ***(G-6162)***
Allie Brothers Inc 248 477-4434
20295 Middlebelt Rd Livonia (48152) ***(G-9635)***
Allie Brothers Men's Wear, Livonia *Also called Allie Brothers Inc* ***(G-9635)***
Allied Baltic Rubber, Monroe *Also called Zhongding Saling Parts USA Inc* ***(G-11088)***
Allied Bindery LLC 248 588-5990
32501 Dequindre Rd Madison Heights (48071) ***(G-10188)***
Allied Chucker and Engrg Co (PA) 517 787-1370
3529 Scheele Dr Jackson (49202) ***(G-8380)***
Allied Chucker and Engrg Co 517 787-1370
3525 Scheele Dr Jackson (49202) ***(G-8381)***
Allied Concrete Products, Midland *Also called Fisher Sand and Gravel Company* ***(G-10861)***
Allied Distribution, Ferndale *Also called Allied Printing Co Inc* ***(G-5259)***
Allied Engineering Inc 616 748-7990
3424 88th Ave Ste 6 Zeeland (49464) ***(G-18110)***
Allied Finishing Inc 616 698-7550
4100 Broadmoor Ave Se Grand Rapids (49512) ***(G-6163)***
Allied Indus Solutions LLC 810 422-5093
3061 W Thompson Rd Ste 1 Fenton (48430) ***(G-5180)***
Allied Kelite, New Hudson *Also called Macdermid Incorporated* ***(G-11547)***
Allied Machine & Tool Inc 269 623-7295
3590 Hope Industry Dr Delton (49046) ***(G-3815)***
Allied Machine Inc 231 834-0050
11171 Spruce Ave Grant (49327) ***(G-7077)***
Allied Mailing and Prtg Inc 810 750-8291
240 N Fenway Dr Fenton (48430) ***(G-5181)***
Allied Media.net, Fenton *Also called Allied Mailing and Prtg Inc* ***(G-5181)***
Allied Metals Corp 248 680-2400
2668 Lapeer Rd Auburn Hills (48326) ***(G-765)***
Allied Motion Technologies Inc 989 725-5151
201 S Delaney Rd Owosso (48867) ***(G-12278)***
Allied Printing Co Inc (PA) 248 541-0551
2035 Hilton Rd Ferndale (48220) ***(G-5259)***
Allied Printing Co Inc 248 514-7394
965 Wanda St Ferndale (48220) ***(G-5260)***
Allied Signs Inc 586 791-7900
33650 Giftos Dr Clinton Township (48035) ***(G-3043)***
Allied Support Systems 734 721-4040
4205 Elizabeth St Wayne (48184) ***(G-17421)***
Allied Tool and Machine Co 989 755-5384
3545 Janes Ave Saginaw (48601) ***(G-13995)***
Allied Tube & Conduit Corp 734 721-4040
4205 Elizabeth St Wayne (48184) ***(G-17422)***
Allied Welding Incorporated 248 360-1122
8240 Goldie St Commerce Township (48390) ***(G-3388)***
Allmet Industries Inc 248 280-4600
5030 Leafdale Blvd Royal Oak (48073) ***(G-13900)***
Allnex USA Inc 269 385-1205
2715 Miller Rd Kalamazoo (49001) ***(G-8675)***
Allor Manufacturing Inc 248 486-4500
12534 Emerson Dr Brighton (48116) ***(G-1883)***
Alloy Construction Service Inc (PA) 989 486-6960
3500 Contractors Dr Midland (48642) ***(G-10813)***
Alloy Exchange Inc (PA) 616 863-0640
300 Rockford Park Dr Ne Rockford (49341) ***(G-13557)***
Alloy Industries Corporation 734 433-1112
13500 Luick Dr Chelsea (48118) ***(G-2702)***
Alloy Machining LLC 517 204-3306
437 N Rosemary St Lansing (48917) ***(G-9274)***
Alloy Resources Corp., Muskegon *Also called Alloy Resources LLC* ***(G-11265)***
Alloy Resources LLC 231 777-3941
1985 E Laketon Ave Muskegon (49442) ***(G-11265)***
Alloy Steel Treating Company 269 628-2154
22138 M 40 Gobles (49055) ***(G-5946)***
Alloying Surfaces Inc 248 524-9200
1346 Wheaton Dr Troy (48083) ***(G-16191)***
Allpacks, Madison Heights *Also called All Packaging Solutions Inc* ***(G-10187)***
Allpro Vector Group, Northville *Also called Hpi Products Inc* ***(G-11698)***
Allrout Inc 616 748-7696
3382 Production Ct Zeeland (49464) ***(G-18111)***
Allsales Enterprises Inc 616 437-0639
1013 Country Gdns Nw Grand Rapids (49534) ***(G-6164)***
Allstate, Detroit *Also called Amrican Petro Inc* ***(G-3868)***
Allstate Sign Company Inc 989 386-4045
1291 E Surrey Rd Farwell (48622) ***(G-5157)***
Allusion Star Inc 231 264-5858
11672 S Us Hwy 31 Elk Rapids (49629) ***(G-4774)***
Allwood Building Components 586 727-2731
35377 Division Rd Richmond (48062) ***(G-13259)***
Ally Equipment LLC 810 422-5093
3061 W Thompson Rd Fenton (48430) ***(G-5182)***
Ally Equipment Solutions, Fenton *Also called Allied Indus Solutions LLC* ***(G-5180)***
Ally Servicing LLC (HQ) 248 948-7702
500 Woodward Ave Fl 1 Detroit (48226) ***(G-3859)***
Allynn Corp 269 383-1199
7868 Douglas Ave Kalamazoo (49009) ***(G-8676)***
Alma Concrete Products Company (PA) 989 463-5476
1277 Bridge Rd Alma (48801) ***(G-232)***
Alma Container Corporation 989 463-2106
1000 Charles Ave Alma (48801) ***(G-233)***
Alma Products Company 989 463-1151
150 N Court Ave Alma (48801) ***(G-234)***
Alma Products I LLC (HQ) 989 463-0290
2000 Michigan Ave Alma (48801) ***(G-235)***
Alma Reminder, Alma *Also called Morning Star Publishing Co* ***(G-243)***
Almar Industries Inc 248 541-5617
21005 Dequindre Rd Hazel Park (48030) ***(G-7433)***
Almar Orchards LLC 810 659-6568
1431 Duffield Rd Flushing (48433) ***(G-5531)***
Almarc Tube Co Inc 989 654-2660
129 Main St Sterling (48659) ***(G-15242)***
Almond Products Inc 616 844-1813
17150 148th Ave Spring Lake (49456) ***(G-15132)***
Alnco, Constantine *Also called E L Nickell Co* ***(G-3534)***
Alo LLC 313 318-9029
3011 W Grand Blvd Ste 105 Detroit (48202) ***(G-3860)***
Alonzo Products Inc 269 445-0847
805 Wolfe Ave Cassopolis (49031) ***(G-2526)***
Alp Lighting Ceiling Pdts Inc 231 547-6584
10163 Us Highway 31 N Charlevoix (49720) ***(G-2606)***
Alpena Aggregate Inc 989 595-2511
7590 Weiss Rd Alpena (49707) ***(G-273)***
Alpena Biorefinery 989 340-1190
412 Ford Ave Alpena (49707) ***(G-274)***
Alpena Electric Motor Service 989 354-8780
1581 M 32 W Alpena (49707) ***(G-275)***
Alpena Print Master, Alpena *Also called Motivation Ideas Inc* ***(G-302)***
Alpha 21 LLC 248 352-7330
22400 Telegraph Rd Ste A Southfield (48033) ***(G-14828)***
Alpha Coatings Inc 734 523-9000
32711 Glendale St Livonia (48150) ***(G-9636)***
Alpha Data Business Forms Inc 248 540-5930
757 S Eton St Ste D Birmingham (48009) ***(G-1674)***
Alpha Directional Boring 586 405-0171
11910 Scott Rd Davisburg (48350) ***(G-3624)***
Alpha Engineered Refrigeration, Rochester Hills *Also called Su-Tec Inc* ***(G-13521)***
Alpha Group, Livonia *Also called Alpha Coatings Inc* ***(G-9636)***
Alpha Group of Companies, The, Livonia *Also called 3715-11th Street Corp* ***(G-9615)***
Alpha Metal Finishing Co 734 426-2855
8155 Huron St Dexter (48130) ***(G-4475)***
Alpha Packaging Michigan Inc 314 427-4300
1236 Watson St Ypsilanti (48198) ***(G-18050)***

ALPHABETIC

(PA)=Parent Co (HQ)=Headquarters (DH)=Div Headquarters
2020 Harris Michigan Industrial Directory
891

Alpha Resins LLC...313 366-9300
17350 Ryan Rd Detroit (48212) ***(G-3861)***
Alpha Resources LLC...269 465-5559
3090 Johnson Rd Stevensville (49127) ***(G-15553)***
Alpha Steel Treating Inc...734 523-1035
32969 Glendale St Livonia (48150) ***(G-9637)***
Alpha Technology Corporation...517 546-9700
1450 Mcpherson Park Dr Howell (48843) ***(G-8011)***
Alpha Tran Engineering Co...616 837-7341
12575 Cleveland St Nunica (49448) ***(G-12032)***
AlphaGraphics 336, Canton *Also called Carrigan Graphics Inc* ***(G-2357)***
Alphausa, Livonia *Also called Washers Incorporated* ***(G-9999)***
Alpine Electronics America Inc (HQ)...248 409-9444
1500 Atlantic Blvd Auburn Hills (48326) ***(G-766)***
Alpine Sign and Prtg Sup Inc...517 487-1400
3105 Sanders Rd Lansing (48917) ***(G-9275)***
Alr Products Inc...517 649-2243
12 Charlotte St Mulliken (48861) ***(G-11238)***
Alro Riverside LLC...517 782-8322
829 Belden Rd Jackson (49203) ***(G-8382)***
Alro Steel Corporation...989 893-9553
3125 N Water St Bay City (48708) ***(G-1274)***
Alro Steel Corporation...810 695-7300
3000 Tri Park Dr Grand Blanc (48439) ***(G-5958)***
Alro Steel Corporation...517 371-9600
1800 W Willow St Lansing (48915) ***(G-9335)***
Alsentis LLC...616 395-8254
1261 S Waverly Rd Holland (49423) ***(G-7555)***
Alt, Bloomfield Hills *Also called Adjustable Locking Tech LLC* ***(G-1742)***
Alta Construction Eqp LLC...248 356-5200
56195 Pontiac Trl New Hudson (48165) ***(G-11530)***
Alta Distribution LLC...313 363-1682
21650 W 11 Mile Rd Southfield (48076) ***(G-14829)***
Alta Equipment Holdings Inc (PA)...248 449-6700
13211 Merriman Rd Livonia (48150) ***(G-9638)***
Alta Vista Technology LLC...248 733-4504
24700 Northwestern Hwy Southfield (48075) ***(G-14830)***
Altagas Marketing (us) Inc...810 887-4105
1411 3rd St Ste A Port Huron (48060) ***(G-12885)***
Altagas Power Holdings US Inc (HQ)...810 887-4105
1411 3rd St Ste A Port Huron (48060) ***(G-12886)***
Altagas Rnwable Enrgy Colo LLC...810 987-2200
1411 3rd St Ste A Port Huron (48060) ***(G-12887)***
Altair Engineering Inc (PA)...248 614-2400
1820 E Big Beaver Rd Troy (48083) ***(G-16192)***
Altair Systems Inc...248 668-0116
30553 S Wixom Rd Ste 400 Wixom (48393) ***(G-17758)***
Altec, Howell *Also called Alpha Technology Corporation* ***(G-8011)***
Altec Financial, Rockford *Also called Joyce Zahradnik* ***(G-13574)***
Alter Cycles Ltd...313 737-1196
2910 Quarter Ct Sw Grandville (49418) ***(G-7019)***
Alternate Number Five Inc (PA)...616 842-2581
11095 W Olive Rd Grand Haven (49417) ***(G-5991)***
Alternative Components LLC (PA)...586 755-9177
24055 Mound Rd Warren (48091) ***(G-16924)***
Alternative Engineering Inc...616 785-7200
5670 West River Dr Ne Belmont (49306) ***(G-1455)***
Alternative Fuel Tech LLC...313 417-9212
1350 Buckingham Rd Grosse Pointe Park (48230) ***(G-7189)***
Alternative Heating & Fuel...231 745-6110
910 N M 37 Baldwin (49304) ***(G-1081)***
Alternative Systems Inc...269 384-2008
5519 E Cork St Ste A Kalamazoo (49048) ***(G-8677)***
Alternatives In Advertising, Southfield *Also called MKP Enterprises Inc* ***(G-14985)***
Alticor Global Holdings Inc (PA)...616 787-1000
7575 Fulton St E Ada (49301) ***(G-5)***
Alticor Inc (HQ)...616 787-1000
7575 Fulton St E Ada (49355) ***(G-6)***
Alto Manufacturing Inc...734 641-8800
38338 Abruzzi Dr Westland (48185) ***(G-17540)***
Alto Meat Processing...616 868-6080
12605 60th St Se Alto (49302) ***(G-322)***
Alton Boring Co Inc...734 522-9595
30950 Industrial Rd Ste A Livonia (48150) ***(G-9639)***
Altra Industrial Motion Corp...586 758-5000
23601 Hoover Rd Warren (48089) ***(G-16925)***
Altron Automation Inc...616 669-7711
3523 Highland Dr Hudsonville (49426) ***(G-8144)***
Altronics Energy LLC...616 662-7401
3523 Highland Dr Hudsonville (49426) ***(G-8145)***
Altus Brands LLC (PA)...231 421-3810
6893 Sullivan Rd Grawn (49637) ***(G-7096)***
Altus Industries Inc...616 233-9530
3731 Northridge Dr Nw # 1 Walker (49544) ***(G-16861)***
Aludyne Inc...269 556-9236
2800 Yasdick Dr Stevensville (49127) ***(G-15554)***
Aludyne Inc...248 506-1692
24155 Wahl St Warren (48089) ***(G-16926)***
Aludyne Inc (HQ)...248 728-8642
300 Galleria Ofcntr Ste 5 Southfield (48034) ***(G-14831)***
Aludyne Columbus LLC (HQ)...248 728-8642
300 Galleria Ofcntr Ste 5 Southfield (48034) ***(G-14832)***
Aludyne East Michigan LLC...810 987-7633
2223 Dove St Port Huron (48060) ***(G-12888)***
Aludyne International Inc (HQ)...248 728-8642
300 Galleria Ofcntr Ste 5 Southfield (48034) ***(G-14833)***
Aludyne Montague LLC (HQ)...248 479-6455
300 Galleria Ofcntr Ste 5 Southfield (48034) ***(G-14834)***
Aludyne North America Inc (HQ)...248 728-8642
300 Galleria Ofcntr Ste 5 Southfield (48034) ***(G-14835)***
Aludyne North America Inc...248 728-8642
2280 W Grand River Ave Howell (48843) ***(G-8012)***
Aludyne US LLC...810 987-1112
3150 Dove St Port Huron (48060) ***(G-12889)***
Aludyne US LLC...810 966-9350
2347 Dove St Port Huron (48060) ***(G-12890)***
Aludyne US LLC (HQ)...586 782-0200
12700 Stephens Rd Warren (48089) ***(G-16927)***
Aludyne US LLC...248 728-8642
23300 Blackstone Ave Warren (48089) ***(G-16928)***
Aludyne West Michigan LLC...248 728-8642
2800 Yasdick Dr Stevensville (49127) ***(G-15555)***
Alufix Services Inspection, Roseville *Also called Paul W Marino Gages Inc* ***(G-13852)***
Alumalight LLC...248 457-9302
1307 E Maple Rd Ste E Troy (48083) ***(G-16193)***
Alumi Span, Pittsford *Also called Berlin Holdings LLC* ***(G-12515)***
Alumilite Corporation...269 488-4000
1458 S 35th St Galesburg (49053) ***(G-5805)***
Aluminum Architectural Met Co...313 895-2555
8711 Epworth St Detroit (48204) ***(G-3862)***
Aluminum Blanking Co Inc...248 338-4422
360 W Sheffield Ave Pontiac (48340) ***(G-12802)***
Aluminum Finishing Company...269 382-4010
615 W Ransom St Kalamazoo (49007) ***(G-8678)***
Aluminum Supply Company Inc...313 491-5040
14359 Meyers Rd Detroit (48227) ***(G-3863)***
Aluminum Textures Inc...616 538-3144
2925 Remico St Sw Ste A Grandville (49418) ***(G-7020)***
Alumiramp Inc...517 639-5103
855 E Chicago Rd Quincy (49082) ***(G-13088)***
Alure International, Bloomfield Hills *Also called Elite Business Services & Exec* ***(G-1763)***
Aluwax Dental Products Co Inc...616 895-4385
5260 Edgewater Dr Allendale (49401) ***(G-214)***
AM General LLC...734 523-8098
1399 Pacific Dr Auburn Hills (48326) ***(G-767)***
AM Industries, Cass City *Also called AMI Industries Inc* ***(G-2510)***
AM Specialties Inc...586 795-9000
5985 Wall St Sterling Heights (48312) ***(G-15257)***
AM Specialties Inc...586 795-9000
5985 Wall St Sterling Heights (48312) ***(G-15258)***
AM Tech Services LLC...734 762-7209
29647 Oakley St Livonia (48154) ***(G-9640)***
AM Twist, South Haven *Also called American Twisting Company* ***(G-14752)***
Amada Miyachi America Inc...248 313-3078
50384 Dennis Ct Wixom (48393) ***(G-17759)***
Amalgamated Uaw...231 734-9286
601 W 7th St Evart (49631) ***(G-4878)***
Amalgamated Uaw Local 2270, Evart *Also called Amalgamated Uaw* ***(G-4878)***
Amalgamations Ltd...248 879-7345
6181 Elmoor Dr Troy (48098) ***(G-16194)***
Amanda Manufacturing LLC...740 385-9380
34450 Industrial Rd Livonia (48150) ***(G-9641)***
Amaris International LLC...248 427-0472
23481 Haggerty Rd Novi (48375) ***(G-11824)***
Amazing Engraving...989 652-8503
9720 Junction Rd Ste B Frankenmuth (48734) ***(G-5582)***
Ambassador Magazine...313 965-6789
151 W Congress St 306 Detroit (48226) ***(G-3864)***
Ambassador Software, Royal Oak *Also called Zferral Inc* ***(G-13982)***
Ambassador Steel Corporation...517 455-7216
1501 E Jolly Rd Lansing (48910) ***(G-9336)***
Amber Manufacturing Inc...586 218-6080
18320 Malyn Blvd Fraser (48026) ***(G-5615)***
Ambiance LLC...269 657-6027
42839 W Red Arrow Hwy Paw Paw (49079) ***(G-12396)***
Ambrosia Inc...734 529-7174
129 Riley St Dundee (48131) ***(G-4575)***
Ambucs Muskegon Chapter, Norton Shores *Also called National Ambucs Inc* ***(G-11778)***
AMC, Davisburg *Also called Automtion Mdlar Components Inc* ***(G-3625)***
Amcane Sugar, Taylor *Also called Americane Sugar Refining LLC* ***(G-15687)***
Amcol Corporation...248 414-5700
21435 Dequindre Rd Hazel Park (48030) ***(G-7434)***
Amcor, Grand Rapids *Also called Applied Mechanics Corporation* ***(G-6174)***
Amcor Rigid Packaging Usa LLC...734 336-3812
10521 S M 52 Manchester (48158) ***(G-10401)***
Amcor Rigid Packaging Usa LLC (HQ)...734 428-9741
40600 Ann Arbor Rd E # 201 Plymouth (48170) ***(G-12569)***

ALPHABETIC SECTION American Mitsuba Corporation

Amcor Rigid Plas - Manchester, Plymouth *Also called Amcor Rigid Packaging Usa LLC* ***(G-12569)***
AME For Auto Dealers Inc....248 720-0245
1000 N Opdyke Rd Ste J Auburn Hills (48326) ***(G-768)***
AME International LLC....586 532-8981
21481 Carlo Dr Clinton Township (48038) ***(G-3044)***
Ameco, Fennville *Also called Ability Mfg & Engrg Co* ***(G-5169)***
Amelectro, Troy *Also called Amtech Electrocircuits Inc* ***(G-16200)***
Ameri-Kart(mi) Corp....269 641-5811
19300 Grange St Cassopolis (49031) ***(G-2527)***
Ameri-Print Inc....734 427-2887
35175 Plymouth Rd Livonia (48150) ***(G-9642)***
Ameri-Serv Group....734 426-9700
2855 Coolidge Hwy Ste 112 Troy (48084) ***(G-16195)***
America Ink and Technology....269 345-4657
8975 Shaver Rd Portage (49024) ***(G-12981)***
America Ink Print....586 790-2555
33812 Groesbeck Hwy Clinton Township (48035) ***(G-3045)***
America's Green Line, Detroit *Also called Johnico LLC* ***(G-4164)***
America's Master Handyman, Troy *Also called Master Handyman Press Inc* ***(G-16489)***
Americam Solutions, Plymouth *Also called Patriot Manufacturing LLC* ***(G-12709)***
American & Efird LLC....248 399-1166
1919 Coolidge Hwy Berkley (48072) ***(G-1579)***
American Aggregate Inc....269 683-6160
2041 M 140 Niles (49120) ***(G-11594)***
American Aggregates Mich Inc (HQ)....248 348-8511
51445 W 12 Mile Rd Wixom (48393) ***(G-17760)***
American Aircraft Parts Mfg Co....586 294-3300
44801 Centre Ct E Clinton Township (48038) ***(G-3046)***
American Arrow Corp Inc....248 435-6115
105 Kinross Ave Clawson (48017) ***(G-2971)***
American Assemblers Inc....248 334-9777
40 W Howard St Ste 222 Pontiac (48342) ***(G-12803)***
American Athletic....231 798-7300
418 W Hackley Ave Muskegon (49444) ***(G-11266)***
American Awards & Engrv LLC....810 229-5911
1240 S Garner Rd Milford (48380) ***(G-10954)***
American Axle & Mfg Inc....586 415-2000
18450 15 Mile Rd Fraser (48026) ***(G-5616)***
American Axle & Mfg Inc (HQ)....313 758-3600
1 Dauch Dr Detroit (48211) ***(G-3865)***
American Axle & Mfg Inc....269 278-0211
1 Manufacturing Dr Three Rivers (49093) ***(G-15853)***
American Axle & Mfg Inc....248 299-2900
2965 Technology Dr Rochester Hills (48309) ***(G-13368)***
American Axle & Mfg Inc....248 522-4500
4000 Town Ctr Ste 500 Southfield (48075) ***(G-14836)***
American Axle & Mfg Inc....248 276-2328
2007 Taylor Rd Auburn Hills (48326) ***(G-769)***
American Axle Mfg Holdings Inc (PA)....313 758-2000
1 Dauch Dr Detroit (48211) ***(G-3866)***
American Axle Oxford....248 361-6044
2300 Xcelsior Dr Ste 230 Oxford (48371) ***(G-12335)***
American Battery Solutions Inc....248 462-6364
3768 S Lapeer Rd Lake Orion (48359) ***(G-9125)***
American Beauty Tools, Troy *Also called Assembly Technologies Intl* ***(G-16224)***
American Beverage Equipment Co....586 773-0094
27560 Groesbeck Hwy Roseville (48066) ***(G-13772)***
American Bldrs Contrs Sup Inc....906 226-9665
908 W Baraga Ave Marquette (49855) ***(G-10517)***
American Blower Supply Inc....586 771-7337
14219 E 10 Mile Rd Warren (48089) ***(G-16929)***
American Bottling Company....810 564-1432
7300 Enterprise Pkwy Mount Morris (48458) ***(G-11157)***
American Bottling Company....616 396-1281
545 E 32nd St Holland (49423) ***(G-7556)***
American Bottling Company....616 392-2124
900 Brooks Ave Ste 1 Holland (49423) ***(G-7557)***
American Bottling Company....989 731-5392
1923 Orourke Blvd Gaylord (49735) ***(G-5848)***
American Bottling Company....231 775-7393
1481 Potthoff St Cadillac (49601) ***(G-2227)***
American Bottling Company....517 622-8605
1145 Comet Ln Grand Ledge (48837) ***(G-6100)***
American Brake and Clutch Inc....586 948-3730
50631 E Russell Schmidt Chesterfield (48051) ***(G-2736)***
American Broach & Machine Co....734 961-0300
575 S Mansfield St Ypsilanti (48197) ***(G-18051)***
American Charcoal, Hazel Park *Also called Amcol Corporation* ***(G-7434)***
American Chem Solutions LLC....231 655-5840
2406 Roberts St Muskegon (49444) ***(G-11267)***
American Chemical Tech Inc (PA)....517 223-0300
485 E Van Riper Rd Fowlerville (48836) ***(G-5557)***
American Classic Homes Inc....616 594-5900
13352 Van Buren St Holland (49424) ***(G-7558)***
American Classics Corp....231 843-0523
3750 W Hansen Rd Ludington (49431) ***(G-10048)***
American Cmmnities Media Group, Southfield *Also called Business Design Solutions Inc* ***(G-14861)***
American Commodities, Flint *Also called Automotive Plastics Recycling* ***(G-5381)***
American Commodities Inc....810 767-3800
2945 Davison Rd Flint (48506) ***(G-5376)***
American Compounding Spc LLC....810 227-3500
9984 Borderline Dr Brighton (48116) ***(G-1884)***
American Concrete Products Inc....517 546-2810
4944 Mason Rd Howell (48843) ***(G-8013)***
American Cooling Systems LLC....616 954-0280
3099 Wilson Dr Nw Grand Rapids (49534) ***(G-6165)***
American Die and Mold Inc....231 269-3788
141 S Industrial Dr Buckley (49620) ***(G-2128)***
American Die Corporation....810 794-4080
6860 Holland Rd Clay (48001) ***(G-2993)***
American Dowel & Fastener, Harrison Township *Also called Henry Plambeck* ***(G-7332)***
American Dumpster Services LLC....586 501-3600
6490 E 10 Mile Rd Center Line (48015) ***(G-2578)***
American Eagle Systems, Commerce Township *Also called Michigan Roll Form Inc* ***(G-3433)***
American Electric Motor Corp (PA)....810 743-6080
4102 Davison Rd Burton (48509) ***(G-2143)***
American Engnred Cmponents Inc (PA)....734 428-8301
17951 W Austin Rd Manchester (48158) ***(G-10402)***
American Fabricated Pdts Inc....616 607-8785
16910 148th Ave Spring Lake (49456) ***(G-15133)***
American Fan & Blower, Warren *Also called American Blower Supply Inc* ***(G-16929)***
American Farm Products Inc....734 484-4180
1382 Industrial Dr Ste 4 Saline (48176) ***(G-14374)***
American Flag & Banner Company....248 288-3010
28 S Main St Clawson (48017) ***(G-2972)***
American Furukawa Inc (HQ)....734 254-0344
47677 Galleon Dr Plymouth (48170) ***(G-12570)***
American Gator Tool Company....231 347-3222
1225 W Conway Rd Unit C Harbor Springs (49740) ***(G-7272)***
American Gear & Engrg Co Inc....734 595-6400
38200 Abruzzi Dr Westland (48185) ***(G-17541)***
American Gear Tools, Ypsilanti *Also called American Broach & Machine Co* ***(G-18051)***
American Gourmet Snacks LLC....989 892-4856
1211 Woodside Ave Essexville (48732) ***(G-4867)***
American Graphics Inc....586 774-8880
27413 Harper Ave Saint Clair Shores (48081) ***(G-14240)***
American Graphics Printing, Clinton Township *Also called Macomb Business Forms Inc* ***(G-3162)***
American Graphite Corporation....586 757-3540
21756 Dequindre Rd Warren (48091) ***(G-16930)***
American Grinding Machining Co....313 388-0440
1415 Dix Hwy Lincoln Park (48146) ***(G-9572)***
American Grow Rack, Marne *Also called Dewys Manufacturing Inc* ***(G-10507)***
American Household Inc....601 296-5000
33067 Industrial Rd Livonia (48150) ***(G-9643)***
American Hydro-Works Engrg LLC....906 282-8890
6817 Swallow Dr Harrison (48625) ***(G-7307)***
American Indus Training Inc....734 752-2451
32715 Groat Blvd Brownstown (48173) ***(G-2058)***
American Industrial Door, Canton *Also called International Door Inc* ***(G-2388)***
American Industrial Gauge Inc....248 280-0048
4839 Leafdale Blvd Royal Oak (48073) ***(G-13901)***
American Ink USA Prntg & Grphc....586 790-2555
33812 Groesbeck Hwy Clinton Township (48035) ***(G-3047)***
American Jetway Corporation....734 721-5930
34136 Myrtle St Wayne (48184) ***(G-17423)***
American Journal Hlth Prom Inc....248 682-0707
55 E Long Lake Rd 466 Troy (48085) ***(G-16196)***
American Label & Tag Inc....734 454-7600
41878 Koppernick Rd Canton (48187) ***(G-2347)***
American Lap Company....231 526-7121
220 Franklin Park Harbor Springs (49740) ***(G-7273)***
American Laser Centers LLC....248 426-8250
24555 Hallwood Ct Farmington Hills (48335) ***(G-4929)***
American Lazer Centers....248 798-6552
16010 19 Mile Rd Ste 100 Clinton Township (48038) ***(G-3048)***
American Made Tubcraft Plus, Baraga *Also called Keweenaw Bay Indian Community* ***(G-1104)***
American Marine SC, White Lake *Also called American Marine Shore Control* ***(G-17628)***
American Marine Shore Control....248 887-7855
6777 Highland Rd White Lake (48383) ***(G-17628)***
American Mathematical Society....734 996-5250
416 4th St Ann Arbor (48103) ***(G-352)***
American Metal Fab Inc....269 279-5108
55515 Franklin Dr Three Rivers (49093) ***(G-15854)***
American Metal Processing Co....586 757-7144
22720 Nagel St Warren (48089) ***(G-16931)***
American Metal Restoration....810 364-4820
1765 Michigan Ave Ste 2 Marysville (48040) ***(G-10598)***
American Metallurgical Svcs....313 893-8328
2731 Jerome St Detroit (48212) ***(G-3867)***
American Mfg Innovators Inc....248 669-5990
1840 W West Maple Rd Commerce Township (48390) ***(G-3389)***
American Mitsuba Corporation....989 773-0377
2945 Three Leaves Dr Mount Pleasant (48858) ***(G-11169)***

ALPHABETIC

American Mitsuba Corporation (HQ) 989 779-4962
2945 Three Leaves Dr Mount Pleasant (48858) *(G-11170)*
American Models 248 437-6800
11770 Green Oak Indus Dr Whitmore Lake (48189) *(G-17687)*
American MSC Inc 248 589-7770
2451 Elliott Dr Troy (48083) *(G-16197)*
American MSC Inc (HQ) 248 589-7770
2401 Elliott Dr Troy (48083) *(G-16198)*
American Mus Environments Inc 248 646-2020
1133 W Long Lake Rd # 200 Bloomfield Hills (48302) *(G-1744)*
American Newspaper Solutions, Rochester *Also called Advertsing Ntwrk Solutions Inc (G-13312)*
American Pallet Company LLC 231 834-5056
11421 S Peach Ave Grant (49327) *(G-7078)*
American Panel, Norton Shores *Also called Hestia Inc (G-11760)*
American Plastic Toys Inc (PA) 248 624-4881
799 Ladd Rd Walled Lake (48390) *(G-16890)*
American Plastic Toys Inc 989 685-2455
3059 Beechwood Rd Rose City (48654) *(G-13757)*
American Pleasure Products Inc 989 685-8484
2823 E Industrial Dr Rose City (48654) *(G-13758)*
American Porcelain Enamel Co 231 744-3013
1709 Ruddiman Dr Muskegon (49445) *(G-11268)*
American Pride Machining Inc 586 294-6404
34062 James J Pompo Dr Fraser (48026) *(G-5617)*
American Prosthetic Institute 517 349-3130
2145 University Park Dr # 100 Okemos (48864) *(G-12112)*
American Pwr Cnnection Systems 989 686-6302
2460 Midland Rd Bay City (48706) *(G-1275)*
American Reprographics Co LLC 248 299-8900
1009 W Maple Rd Clawson (48017) *(G-2973)*
American Resources Group, Spring Arbor *Also called American Sales Co (G-15118)*
American Rhnmtall Vehicles LLC 703 221-9288
7205 Sterling Sterling Heights (48312) *(G-15259)*
American Ring Manufacturing 734 402-0426
35955 Veronica St Livonia (48150) *(G-9644)*
American Rod Consumers, Grand Blanc *Also called King Steel Corporation (G-5972)*
American Roll Manufacturing, Clinton Township *Also called D-N-S Industries Inc (G-3098)*
American Roll Shutter Awng Co 734 422-7110
12700 Merriman Rd Livonia (48150) *(G-9645)*
American Sales Co 517 750-4070
3215 Chapel Rd Spring Arbor (49283) *(G-15118)*
American Screw Products Inc 248 543-0991
29866 John R Rd Madison Heights (48071) *(G-10189)*
American Seating Company (PA) 616 732-6600
801 Broadway Ave Nw # 200 Grand Rapids (49504) *(G-6166)*
American Shortening and Oil Co, Livonia *Also called Asao LLC (G-9653)*
American Silk Screen & EMB 248 474-1000
24601 Hallwood Ct Farmington Hills (48335) *(G-4930)*
American Soc AG Blgcal Engners 269 429-0300
2950 Niles Rd Saint Joseph (49085) *(G-14300)*
American Soft Trim Inc 989 681-0037
300 Woodside Dr Saint Louis (48880) *(G-14357)*
American Soy Products Inc 734 429-2310
1474 Woodland Dr Saline (48176) *(G-14375)*
American Speedy Printing, Saint Clair Shores *Also called American Graphics Inc (G-14240)*
American Speedy Printing, Rochester *Also called Business Press Inc (G-13316)*
American Speedy Printing, Wyandotte *Also called Madden Enterprises Inc (G-17966)*
American Speedy Printing, Shelby Township *Also called Alcock Printing Inc (G-14544)*
American Speedy Printing, Plymouth *Also called An Corporate Center LLC (G-12571)*
American Speedy Printing, Detroit *Also called R N E Business Enterprises (G-4326)*
American Speedy Printing, Clinton Township *Also called Allagra Print and Imaging (G-3041)*
American Speedy Printing, Southfield *Also called Jerrys Quality Quick Print (G-14952)*
American Speedy Printing, Clinton Township *Also called L&L Printing Inc (G-3158)*
American Speedy Printing, Jackson *Also called Kmak Inc (G-8489)*
American Speedy Printing, Monroe *Also called Bagnall Enterprises Inc (G-11017)*
American Speedy Printing Ctrs 989 723-5196
111 S Washington St Owosso (48867) *(G-12279)*
American Speedy Printing Ctrs 313 928-5820
20320 Ecorse Rd Taylor (48180) *(G-15686)*
American Spoon Foods Inc (PA) 231 347-9030
1668 Clarion Ave Petoskey (49770) *(G-12440)*
American Standard Windows 734 788-2261
30281 Pipers Ln Farmington Hills (48334) *(G-4931)*
American Steel Fabricators 248 476-8433
34150 W 9 Mile Rd Farmington (48335) *(G-4894)*
American Steel Works Inc 734 282-0300
12615 Nixon Ave Riverview (48193) *(G-13290)*
American Tank Fabrication LLC 780 663-3552
2222 W Grand Okemos (48864) *(G-12113)*
American Tchncal Fbrcators LLC 989 269-6262
414 E Soper Rd Bad Axe (48413) *(G-1056)*
American Thermographers 248 398-3810
291 E 12 Mile Rd Madison Heights (48071) *(G-10190)*
American Tooling Center Inc 517 522-8411
705 E Oakland Ave Lansing (48906) *(G-9202)*
American Tooling Center Inc 517 522-8411
11505 Elm St Jackson (49202) *(G-8383)*
American Tooling Center Inc (PA) 517 522-8411
4111 Mount Hope Rd Grass Lake (49240) *(G-7085)*
American Trading International, Grand Rapids *Also called Sunhill America LLC (G-6898)*
American Twisting Company (PA) 269 637-8581
1675 Stieve Dr South Haven (49090) *(G-14752)*
American Vault Service (PA) 989 366-8657
2063 Norway Ln Prudenville (48651) *(G-13084)*
American Welding Inc 734 279-1625
16057 Ida West Rd Petersburg (49270) *(G-12434)*
American Wind & Solar LLC 734 904-8490
18638 Van Horn Rd Apt 11 Woodhaven (48183) *(G-17937)*
American Wldg & Press Repr Inc 248 358-2050
26500 W 8 Mile Rd Southfield (48033) *(G-14837)*
Americane Sugar Refining LLC (PA) 313 299-1300
21010 Trolley Indus Dr Taylor (48180) *(G-15687)*
Americas Finest Prtg Graphics (PA) 586 296-1312
17060 Masonic Ste 101 Fraser (48026) *(G-5618)*
Americast LLC 989 681-4800
107 Enterprize Dr Saint Louis (48880) *(G-14358)*
Americo Corporation 313 565-6550
25120 Trowbridge St Dearborn (48124) *(G-3675)*
Americraft Carton Inc 269 651-2365
305 W South St Sturgis (49091) *(G-15596)*
Ameriform Acquisition Co LLC 231 733-2725
700 Terrace Point Dr # 200 Muskegon (49440) *(G-11269)*
Amerikam Inc 616 243-5833
1337 Judd Ave Sw Grand Rapids (49509) *(G-6167)*
Ameripak Inc 248 858-9000
591 Bradford St Pontiac (48341) *(G-12804)*
Ameriplastic Imprinting Co, Flint *Also called Rodzina Industries Inc (G-5493)*
Ameristeel Inc 586 585-5250
33900 Doreka Fraser (48026) *(G-5619)*
Amerivet Engineering LLC 269 751-9092
3146 53rd St Hamilton (49419) *(G-7230)*
Ameriwood Furniture, Dowagiac *Also called Rospatch Jessco Corporation (G-4558)*
Amery Tape & Label Co Inc 586 759-3230
4145 E 10 Mile Rd Warren (48091) *(G-16932)*
Ametek Inc 248 435-7540
6380 Brockway Rd Peck (48466) *(G-12418)*
Ametek Automtn & Process Tech, Peck *Also called Ametek Inc (G-12418)*
Ametek Patriot Sensors, Peck *Also called Patriot Sensors & Contrls Corp (G-12420)*
Ametek-APT, Clawson *Also called Patriot Sensors & Contrls Corp (G-2983)*
Amex Mfg & Distrg Co Inc 734 439-8560
640 Ash St Milan (48160) *(G-10932)*
AMF Defense 586 684-3365
51528 Industrial Dr New Baltimore (48047) *(G-11479)*
AMF-Nano Corporation 734 726-0148
320 Miller Ave Ste 140 Ann Arbor (48103) *(G-353)*
Amhawk LLC 269 468-4141
236 N West St Coloma (49038) *(G-3353)*
Amhawk LLC (PA) 269 468-4177
200 Dunbar St Hartford (49057) *(G-7381)*
AMI Entertainment Network Inc 877 762-6765
4147 Estm Ave Se Ste 200 Wyoming (49508) *(G-17986)*
AMI Industries Inc (PA) 989 786-3755
5093 N Red Oak Rd Lewiston (49756) *(G-9547)*
AMI Industries Inc 989 872-8823
6285 Garfield Ave Cass City (48726) *(G-2510)*
AMI Livonia LLC 734 428-3132
36930 Industrial Rd Livonia (48150) *(G-9646)*
Amicus Software 313 417-9550
11231 Sugden Lake Rd White Lake (48386) *(G-17629)*
Amigo Mobility Intl Inc (PA) 989 777-0910
6693 Dixie Hwy Bridgeport (48722) *(G-1848)*
Amish Country Cheese, Linwood *Also called Williams Cheese Co (G-9599)*
Amjs Incorporated ....
828 S Main St Lawton (49065) *(G-9510)*
Ammex Plastics, Monroe *Also called Echo Engrg & Prod Sups Inc (G-11029)*
Amneon Acquisitions LLC 616 895-6640
199 E 17th St Holland (49423) *(G-7559)*
Among Friends LLC 734 997-9720
191 Orchard Hills Ct Ann Arbor (48104) *(G-354)*
Among Friends Baking Mixes, Ann Arbor *Also called Among Friends LLC (G-354)*
Amor Imagepro, Manistee *Also called Amor Sign Studios Inc (G-10414)*
Amor Sign Studios Inc 231 723-8361
443 Water St Manistee (49660) *(G-10414)*
Amos Mfg Inc 989 358-7187
3490 Us Highway 23 N Alpena (49707) *(G-276)*
Amour Your Body LLC 586 846-3100
16518 Festian Dr Clinton Township (48035) *(G-3049)*
AMP Innovative Tech LLC 586 465-2700
42050 Executive Dr Harrison Township (48045) *(G-7319)*
Amphenol Borisch Tech Inc (HQ) 616 554-9820
4511 East Paris Ave Se Grand Rapids (49512) *(G-6168)*
Amphenol Corporation 256 417-4338
41180 Bridge St Novi (48375) *(G-11825)*

ALPHABETIC SECTION
Animal Medical Ctr of Lapeer

Amphenol Corporation 586 465-3131
44724 Morley Dr Clinton Township (48036) *(G-3050)*
Amphenol Saa, Brighton *Also called Amphenol T&M Antennas Inc (G-1885)*
Amphenol Sine Systems, Clinton Township *Also called Amphenol Corporation (G-3050)*
Amphenol T&M Antennas Inc 847 478-5600
7117 Fieldcrest Dr Brighton (48116) *(G-1885)*
Amplas Compounding LLC 586 795-2555
6675 Sterling Dr N Sterling Heights (48312) *(G-15260)*
Amplified Life Network LLC 800 453-7733
7791 Byron Center Ave Sw Byron Center (49315) *(G-2176)*
Amplifinity, Ann Arbor *Also called Urefer Inc (G-689)*
Ampm Inc 989 837-8800
7403 W Wackerly St Midland (48642) *(G-10814)*
Amptech Inc (HQ) 231 464-5492
201 Glocheski Dr Manistee (49660) *(G-10415)*
Amrican Petro Inc 313 520-8404
9210 Freeland St Detroit (48228) *(G-3868)*
AMS, Buchanan *Also called Aerospace Mfg Svcs Inc (G-2108)*
AMS America, Troy *Also called AMS Co Ltd (G-16199)*
AMS Co Ltd 248 712-4435
3221 W Big Beaver Rd # 117 Troy (48084) *(G-16199)*
Amsa, Auburn *Also called Antimicrobial Specialist Assoc (G-749)*
Amsted Rail Company Inc 517 568-4161
124 W Platt St Homer (49245) *(G-7936)*
Amt Software LLC 248 458-0359
21 E Long Lake Rd Ste 225 Bloomfield Hills (48304) *(G-1745)*
Amtech Electrocircuits Inc 248 583-1801
701 Minnesota Dr Troy (48083) *(G-16200)*
Amtex Inc 586 792-7888
34680 Nova Dr Clinton Township (48035) *(G-3051)*
Amtrade Systems Inc 734 522-9500
12885 Wayne Rd Livonia (48150) *(G-9647)*
Amw Machine Control Inc 616 642-9514
6963 Cherrywood Ln Saranac (48881) *(G-14453)*
Amway, Ada *Also called Alticor Inc (G-6)*
Amway International Inc (HQ) 616 787-1000
7575 Fulton St E Ada (49355) *(G-7)*
Amway International Dev Inc (HQ) 616 787-6000
7575 Fulton St E Ada (49301) *(G-8)*
Amx Corp 469 624-8000
38780 Hartwell Dr Sterling Heights (48312) *(G-15261)*
An Andronaco Industries Co, Grand Rapids *Also called Conley Composites LLC (G-6300)*
An Andronaco Industries Co, Kentwood *Also called Polyvalve LLC (G-9025)*
An Corporate Center LLC 248 669-1188
47585 Galleon Dr Plymouth (48170) *(G-12571)*
Ana Fuel Inc 810 422-5659
2759 Seminole Rd Ann Arbor (48108) *(G-355)*
Analytical Process Systems Inc 248 393-0700
1771 Harmon Rd Ste 100 Auburn Hills (48326) *(G-770)*
Anand Nvh North America Inc 810 724-2400
2083 Reek Rd Imlay City (48444) *(G-8196)*
Anantics, Livonia *Also called Superior Information Tech LLC (G-9948)*
Anatech Ltd 269 964-6450
1020 Harts Lake Rd Battle Creek (49037) *(G-1146)*
Anayas Pallets & Transport Inc 313 843-6570
163 Morrell St Detroit (48209) *(G-3869)*
Anbo Tool & Manufacturing Inc 586 465-7610
22785 Macomb Indus Dr Clinton Township (48036) *(G-3052)*
Anbren Inc 269 944-5066
1025 Point O Woods Dr Benton Harbor (49022) *(G-1481)*
Anchor Bay Canv and Upholstery 810 512-4325
2001 Pointe Tremble Rd Algonac (48001) *(G-141)*
Anchor Bay Manufacturing Corp (PA) 586 949-4040
30905 23 Mile Rd Chesterfield (48047) *(G-2737)*
Anchor Bay Packaging Corp (PA) 586 949-4040
30905 23 Mile Rd Chesterfield (48047) *(G-2738)*
Anchor Bay Packaging Corp 586 949-1500
30871 23 Mile Rd Chesterfield (48047) *(G-2739)*
Anchor Bay Powder Coat LLC 586 725-3255
51469 Birch St New Baltimore (48047) *(G-11480)*
Anchor Conveyor Products Inc 313 582-5045
6830 Kingsley St Dearborn (48126) *(G-3676)*
Anchor Coupling Inc (HQ) 906 863-2672
5520 13th St Menominee (49858) *(G-10722)*
Anchor Danly, Farmington Hills *Also called Lamina Inc (G-5042)*
Anchor Danly Inc 519 966-4431
95 E 10 Mile Rd Madison Heights (48071) *(G-10191)*
Anchor Die Supply, Novi *Also called Anchor Lamina America Inc (G-11826)*
Anchor Flexible Packg & Label, Novi *Also called Anchor Printing Company (G-11827)*
Anchor Lamina America Inc 231 533-8646
3650 S Derenzy Rd Bellaire (49615) *(G-1434)*
Anchor Lamina America Inc (HQ) 248 489-9122
39830 Grand River Ave B-2 Novi (48375) *(G-11826)*
Anchor Lamina America Inc 519 966-4431
4300 40th St Se Grand Rapids (49512) *(G-6169)*
Anchor Printing Company 248 335-7440
22790 Heslip Dr Novi (48375) *(G-11827)*
Anchor Recycling Inc 810 984-5545
2829 Goulden St Port Huron (48060) *(G-12891)*
Anchor Wiping Cloth Inc 313 892-4000
3855 E Outer Dr Detroit (48234) *(G-3870)*
Ancor Information MGT LLC (PA) 248 740-8866
1911 Woodslee Dr Troy (48083) *(G-16201)*
Anders University Lithotech, Berrien Springs *Also called Lithotech (G-1598)*
Andersen Boat Works 616 836-2502
815 Wells St South Haven (49090) *(G-14753)*
Andersen Corporation 734 237-1052
37720 Amrhein Rd Livonia (48150) *(G-9648)*
Andersen Oakleaf Inc 517 546-1805
4330 Jewell Rd Howell (48843) *(G-8014)*
Anderson Brazing Co Inc 248 399-5155
1544 E 11 Mile Rd Madison Heights (48071) *(G-10192)*
Anderson Cook Machine Tool, Fraser *Also called Anderson-Cook Inc (G-5620)*
Anderson Development Company 517 263-2121
1415 E Michigan St Adrian (49221) *(G-49)*
Anderson Global Inc 231 733-2164
500 W Sherman Blvd Muskegon (49444) *(G-11270)*
Anderson Logging Inc 906 482-7505
50433 Canal Rd Houghton (49931) *(G-7971)*
Anderson Manufacturing Co Inc (PA) 906 863-8223
5300 13th St Menominee (49858) *(G-10723)*
Anderson Process, Plymouth *Also called AA Anderson & Co Inc (G-12559)*
Anderson Screen Printing, Newaygo *Also called Michael Anderson (G-11575)*
Anderson Technologies, Inc., Grand Haven *Also called Holland Plastics Corporation (G-6037)*
Anderson Welding & Mfg Inc 906 523-4661
41315 Us 41 Chassell (49916) *(G-2671)*
Anderson-Cook Inc (PA) 586 954-0700
44785 Macomb Indus Dr Clinton Township (48036) *(G-3053)*
Anderson-Cook Inc 586 293-0800
17650 15 Mile Rd Fraser (48026) *(G-5620)*
Anderson-Cook Inc 586 954-0700
44785 Macomb Indus Dr Clinton Township (48036) *(G-3054)*
Andersons Inc 989 642-5291
485 S Hemlock Rd Hemlock (48626) *(G-7459)*
Anderton Equity LLC (PA) 248 430-6650
3001 W Big Beaver Rd # 310 Troy (48084) *(G-16202)*
Anderton Machining LLC 517 905-5155
2400 Enterprise St 1 Jackson (49203) *(G-8384)*
Andex Industries Inc (PA) 800 338-9882
1911 4th Ave N Escanaba (49829) *(G-4811)*
Andex Industries Inc 906 786-7588
2300 20th Ave N Escanaba (49829) *(G-4812)*
Andex Laser Inc 734 947-9840
12222 Universal Dr Taylor (48180) *(G-15688)*
Andex Printing Division, Escanaba *Also called Andex Industries Inc (G-4812)*
Andoor Craftmaster 989 672-2020
3521 Lobdell Rd Caro (48723) *(G-2465)*
Andretta & Associates Inc 586 557-6226
48945 Austrian Pine Dr Macomb (48044) *(G-10107)*
Andrew J Reisterer D D S Pllc 231 845-8989
902 E Ludington Ave Ludington (49431) *(G-10049)*
Andritz Metals Inc 248 305-2969
26800 Meadowbrook Rd Novi (48377) *(G-11828)*
Android Indstrs-Shreveport LLC 248 454-0500
2155 Executive Hills Dr Auburn Hills (48326) *(G-771)*
Android Industries LLC 517 322-0141
8175 Millett Hwy Lansing (48917) *(G-9276)*
Android Industries-Delta Towns 517 322-0657
2051 S Canal Rd Lansing (48917) *(G-9277)*
Android Industries-Sterling (HQ) 586 486-5616
27767 George Merrelli Dr Warren (48092) *(G-16933)*
Android Industries-Wixom LLC 248 255-5434
50150 Ryan Rd Shelby Township (48317) *(G-14546)*
Android Industries-Wixom LLC (HQ) 248 732-0000
4444 W Maple Dr Auburn Hills (48326) *(G-772)*
Andronaco Inc (PA) 616 554-4600
4855 Broadmoor Ave Se Kentwood (49512) *(G-8998)*
Anew Lf Prsthtics Orthtics LLC 313 870-9610
6438 Woodward Ave Detroit (48202) *(G-3871)*
Angela's Book Shelf, Ithaca *Also called A B Publishing Inc (G-8355)*
Angelos Crushed Concrete Inc (PA) 586 756-1070
26300 Sherwood Ave Warren (48091) *(G-16934)*
Angler Strategies LLC 248 439-1420
2815 Benjamin Ave Royal Oak (48073) *(G-13902)*
Angstrom Aluminum Castings LLC 616 309-1208
3559 Kraft Ave Se Grand Rapids (49512) *(G-6170)*
Angstrom Automotive Group LLC 248 627-2871
85 Myron St Ortonville (48462) *(G-12193)*
Angstrom Automotive Group LLC (PA) 313 295-0100
26980 Trolley Indus Dr Taylor (48180) *(G-15689)*
Angstrom USA LLC (HQ) 313 295-0100
2000 Town Ctr Ste 1100 Southfield (48075) *(G-14838)*
Animal Medical Ctr of Lapeer 989 631-3350
4925 Jefferson Ave Midland (48640) *(G-10815)*

ALPHABETIC

Anitom Automation LLC 517 278-6205
349 S Clay St Coldwater (49036) **(G-3288)**
Anjun America Inc 248 680-8825
2735 Paldan Dr Auburn Hills (48326) **(G-773)**
Ankara Industries Incorporated 586 749-1190
56359 N Bay Dr Chesterfield (48051) **(G-2740)**
Ann Arbor Chronicle 734 645-2633
330 Mulholland Ave Ann Arbor (48103) **(G-356)**
Ann Arbor Distilling Co 734 769-6075
220 Felch St Ann Arbor (48103) **(G-357)**
Ann Arbor Gear, Howell *Also called AA Gear LLC* **(G-8009)**
Ann Arbor Journal 734 429-7380
106 W Michigan Ave Saline (48176) **(G-14376)**
Ann Arbor News, Grand Rapids *Also called Herald Newspapers Company Inc* **(G-6507)**
Ann Arbor News, The, Ann Arbor *Also called Herald Newspapers Company Inc* **(G-489)**
Ann Arbor Observer Company 734 769-3175
2390 Winewood Ave Ann Arbor (48103) **(G-358)**
Ann Arbor Optical Company, Ypsilanti *Also called Data Optics Inc* **(G-18064)**
Ann Arbor Plastics Inc 734 944-0800
815 Woodland Dr Saline (48176) **(G-14377)**
Ann Lake Hardwood Inc 231 275-6406
17437 Almira Rd Lake Ann (49650) **(G-9084)**
Ann Williams Group LLC 248 731-8588
784 Industrial Ct Bloomfield Hills (48302) **(G-1746)**
Ano-Kal Company 269 685-5743
734 Jersey St Plainwell (49080) **(G-12518)**
Anrod Screen Cylinder Company 989 872-2101
6160 Garfield Ave Cass City (48726) **(G-2511)**
Anroid Industries Inc 248 732-0000
2155 Executive Hills Dr Auburn Hills (48326) **(G-774)**
Ansco Pattern & Machine Co 248 625-1362
7945 Perry Lake Rd Clarkston (48348) **(G-2907)**
Anso Products 248 357-2300
21380 Telegraph Rd Southfield (48033) **(G-14839)**
Anstey Foundry Co Inc 269 429-3229
2788 Lawrence St Stevensville (49127) **(G-15556)**
Ansys Inc 248 613-2677
2805 S Industrial Hwy # 100 Ann Arbor (48104) **(G-359)**
Antcliff Windows & Doors Inc 810 742-5963
2417 E Judd Rd Burton (48529) **(G-2144)**
Antech Tool Inc 734 207-3622
7553 Baron Dr Canton (48187) **(G-2348)**
Anteebo Publishers Inc 313 882-6900
16980 Kercheval Pl Grosse Pointe Park (48230) **(G-7190)**
Antelope Audio, Southfield *Also called Earbyte Inc* **(G-14892)**
Antenna Technologies Inc 586 697-5626
56716 Mound Rd Shelby Township (48316) **(G-14547)**
Anterior Quest, Jenison *Also called Fabri-Tech Inc* **(G-8626)**
Anthony and Company 906 786-7573
1503 N 23rd St Escanaba (49829) **(G-4813)**
Anticipated Plastics Inc 586 427-9450
24392 Gibson Dr Warren (48089) **(G-16935)**
Antilla Logging Inc 906 376-2374
7794 State Highway M95 Republic (49879) **(G-13244)**
Antimicrobial Specialist Assoc 989 662-0377
4714 Garfield Rd Auburn (48611) **(G-749)**
Antolin Interiors Usa Inc (HQ) 248 373-1749
1700 Atlantic Blvd Auburn Hills (48326) **(G-775)**
Antolin Interiors Usa Inc 517 548-0052
3705 W Grand River Ave Howell (48855) **(G-8015)**
Antolin Interiors Usa Inc 248 567-4000
600 Wilshire Dr Troy (48084) **(G-16203)**
Antolin Interiors Usa Inc 810 329-1045
4662 Puttygut Rd China (48054) **(G-2858)**
Antonios Leather Experts 734 762-5000
12409 Stark Rd Livonia (48150) **(G-9649)**
Antrim County News, Mancelona *Also called Up North Publications Inc* **(G-10400)**
Antrim Machine Products Inc 231 587-9114
9142 Johnson Rd Mancelona (49659) **(G-10386)**
Anwar Atwa Prism Autobody 313 655-0000
15800 Tireman St Detroit (48228) **(G-3872)**
Anwc LLC 248 759-1164
4236 Calumet Dr Oakland Township (48306) **(G-12110)**
Anywhere Welding 906 250-7217
N3550 Et Rd Trenary (49891) **(G-16149)**
Aoa Productions LLC 517 256-0820
2447 N Williamston Rd Williamston (48895) **(G-17725)**
Aom Engineering Solutions LLC (PA) 313 406-8130
26300 Ford Rd Ste 315 Dearborn Heights (48127) **(G-3778)**
AP Impressions Inc (PA) 734 464-8009
17360 N Laurel Park Dr Livonia (48152) **(G-9650)**
AP Southridge, Livonia *Also called Applied Process Inc* **(G-9651)**
Apb Inc 248 528-2990
3334 Rochester Rd Troy (48083) **(G-16204)**
Apec, Lake Odessa *Also called Automated Process Equipment* **(G-9111)**
Aperion Information Tech Inc (PA) 248 969-9791
144 S Washington St Oxford (48371) **(G-12336)**
Apex Broaching Systems Inc 586 758-2626
22862 Hoover Rd Warren (48089) **(G-16936)**
Apex Dental Milling, Ann Arbor *Also called Adcaa LLC* **(G-343)**
Apex Marine Inc 989 681-4300
300 Woodside Dr Saint Louis (48880) **(G-14359)**
Apex Spring & Stamping Corp 616 453-5463
11420 1st Ave Nw Grand Rapids (49534) **(G-6171)**
Apg - Spclty Vlve McHined Pdts, Wyandotte *Also called Mercury Manufacturing Company* **(G-17968)**
Aphase II Inc (PA) 586 977-0790
6120 Center Dr Sterling Heights (48312) **(G-15262)**
API / Inmet Inc 734 426-5553
300 Dino Dr Ann Arbor (48103) **(G-360)**
API Plan Design Build, Waterford *Also called Architectural Planners Inc* **(G-17322)**
API Polymers Inc 855 274-7659
34654 Nova Dr Clinton Township (48035) **(G-3055)**
API Promotional Products, Armada *Also called Armada Printwear Inc* **(G-715)**
API Technologies Corp 301 846-9222
300 Dino Dr Ann Arbor (48103) **(G-361)**
Apis North America LLC 800 470-8970
938 N Washington Ave Royal Oak (48067) **(G-13903)**
Apms Incorporated 248 268-1477
31211 Stvnson Hwy Ste 100 Madison Heights (48071) **(G-10193)**
Apogee Technologies Inc 269 639-1616
170 Veterans Blvd 3 South Haven (49090) **(G-14754)**
Apollo America Inc 248 332-3900
25 Corporate Dr Auburn Hills (48326) **(G-776)**
Apollo Broach Inc 734 467-5750
39001 Webb Ct Westland (48185) **(G-17542)**
Apollo E.D.M. Company, Fraser *Also called CDK Enterprises LLC* **(G-5636)**
Apollo Heat Treating Proc LLC 248 398-3434
10400 Capital St Oak Park (48237) **(G-12048)**
Apollo Idemitsu Corporation 248 675-4345
48325 Alpha Dr Ste 200 Wixom (48393) **(G-17761)**
Apollo Plating Inc 586 777-0070
15765 Sturgeon St Roseville (48066) **(G-13773)**
Apollo Seiko Ltd 269 465-3400
3969 Lemon Creek Rd Bridgman (49106) **(G-1859)**
Apollo Tool & Engineering Inc 616 735-4934
3020 Wilson Dr Nw Grand Rapids (49534) **(G-6172)**
Apollo Trick Titanium Inc 517 694-7449
321 Elmwood Dr Troy (48083) **(G-16205)**
Apparel Printers Limited 517 882-5700
3505 S Cedar St Ste A Lansing (48910) **(G-9337)**
Apparel Printers, The, Lansing *Also called Apparel Printers Limited* **(G-9337)**
Apparel Sales Inc 616 842-5650
2712 Edward St Ste A Jenison (49428) **(G-8617)**
Apparelmaster-Muskegon Inc 231 728-5406
341 E Apple Ave Muskegon (49442) **(G-11271)**
Applause Inc 517 485-9880
2519 S Cedar St Lansing (48910) **(G-9338)**
Apple Blossom Winery LLC 269 668-3724
6970 Texas Dr Kalamazoo (49009) **(G-8679)**
Apple Fence Co 231 276-9888
1893 Pine Tree Grawn (49637) **(G-7097)**
Apple Quest Inc 616 299-4834
1380 Coolidge St Conklin (49403) **(G-3528)**
Apple Valley Natural Foods (PA) 269 471-3234
9067 Us Highway 31 Ofc A Berrien Springs (49103) **(G-1592)**
Applegate Insul Systems Inc (PA) 517 521-3545
1000 Highview Dr Webberville (48892) **(G-17446)**
Application Specialists Co, Lansing *Also called Appliction Spclist Kompany Inc* **(G-9339)**
Appliction Spclist Kompany Inc 517 676-6633
316 Moores River Dr Lansing (48910) **(G-9339)**
Applied & Integrated Mfg Inc 248 370-8950
280 Mill St Ste 8 Rochester (48307) **(G-13313)**
Applied Analytics Inc 616 285-7810
4767 Broadmoor Ave Se # 7 Grand Rapids (49512) **(G-6173)**
Applied Automation Tech Inc 248 656-4930
1688 Star Batt Dr Rochester Hills (48309) **(G-13369)**
Applied Ballistics Weapons Div, Cedar Springs *Also called AB Weapons Division Inc* **(G-2544)**
Applied Coatings Solutions LLC 269 341-9757
1830 Reed Ave Kalamazoo (49001) **(G-8680)**
Applied Computer Technologies 248 388-0211
4301 Orchard Lake Rd # 160 West Bloomfield (48323) **(G-17465)**
Applied Graphics & Fabricating 989 662-3334
1994 W Midland Rd Auburn (48611) **(G-750)**
Applied Imaging, Grand Rapids *Also called Lowery Corporation* **(G-6633)**
Applied Instruments Company 810 227-5510
37 Summit St Brighton (48116) **(G-1886)**
Applied Mechanics Corporation 616 677-1355
14122 Ironwood Dr Nw Grand Rapids (49534) **(G-6174)**
Applied Molecules LLC 810 355-1475
11042 Hi Tech Dr Whitmore Lake (48189) **(G-17688)**
Applied Process Inc (HQ) 734 464-8000
12202 Newburgh Rd Livonia (48150) **(G-9651)**
Applied Tech Industries, Chesterfield *Also called Kalb & Associates Inc* **(G-2793)**
Applied Technology Group 586 286-6442
7205 Sterling Ponds Ct Sterling Heights (48312) **(G-15263)**

Applied Visual Concepts LLC 866 440-6888
24680 Mound Rd Warren (48091) *(G-16937)*
Appropos Digital, Grand Rapids *Also called Appropos LLC (G-6175)*
Appropos LLC 844 462-7776
678 Front Ave Nw Ste 100 Grand Rapids (49504) *(G-6175)*
Approved Aircraft Accessories 734 946-9000
29300 Goddard Rd Romulus (48174) *(G-13651)*
Aprotech Powertrain LLC (PA) 248 649-9200
2150 Butterfield Dr Troy (48084) *(G-16206)*
APS Elastomers, Romulus *Also called Alliance Polymers and Svcs LLC (G-13650)*
APS Machine LLC 906 212-5600
2501 Danforth Rd Escanaba (49829) *(G-4814)*
APT Division, Southfield *Also called Durr Systems Inc (G-14890)*
Aptargroup Inc 989 631-8030
2202 Ridgewood Dr Midland (48642) *(G-10816)*
Aptec, Norton Shores *Also called Adhesives and Processes Tech (G-11807)*
Aptiv Corporation 248 724-5900
2611 Superior Ct Auburn Hills (48326) *(G-777)*
Aptiv Corporation (HQ) 248 813-2000
5820 Innovation Dr Troy (48098) *(G-16207)*
Aptiv Holdings (us) LLC (HQ) 248 813-2000
5820 Innovation Dr Troy (48098) *(G-16208)*
Aptiv Mexican Holdings US LLC (HQ) 248 813-2000
5820 Innovation Dr Troy (48098) *(G-16209)*
Aptiv PLC 248 813-2000
5725 Innovation Dr Troy (48098) *(G-16210)*
Aptiv Services 2 Us Inc (HQ) 248 813-2000
5820 Innovation Dr Troy (48098) *(G-16211)*
Aptiv Services 3 (us) LLC 248 813-2000
5725 Innovation Dr Troy (48098) *(G-16212)*
Aptiv Services Us LLC 616 246-2471
2100 Burlingame Ave Sw Grand Rapids (49509) *(G-6176)*
Aptiv Services Us LLC 313 322-6845
15021 S Commerce Dr # 100 Dearborn (48120) *(G-3677)*
Aptiv Services Us LLC 810 459-8809
3000 University Dr Auburn Hills (48326) *(G-778)*
Aptiv Services Us LLC 248 724-5900
2611 Superior Ct Auburn Hills (48326) *(G-779)*
Aptiv Services Us LLC 248 813-2000
4254 Oak Meadow Dr Hudsonville (49426) *(G-8146)*
Aptiv Services Us LLC 248 813-2000
5725 Innovation Dr Troy (48098) *(G-16213)*
Aptiv Services Us LLC (HQ) 248 813-2000
5725 Innovation Dr Troy (48098) *(G-16214)*
Aptiv Trade MGT Svcs US LLC 248 813-2000
5820 Innovation Dr Troy (48098) *(G-16215)*
APV Baker 616 784-3111
3223 Kraft Ave Se Grand Rapids (49512) *(G-6177)*
Apw 231 922-1863
1801 Garfield Rd N Traverse City (49696) *(G-15895)*
Aqpe LLC 810 329-9259
561 N Riverside Ave Saint Clair (48079) *(G-14204)*
Aqua Fine Inc 616 392-7843
1120 Washington Ave Ste A Holland (49423) *(G-7560)*
Aqua Systems Inc 810 346-2525
7070 Enterprise Dr Brown City (48416) *(G-2044)*
Aqua Tool LLC 248 307-1984
32360 Edward Ave Ste 100 Madison Heights (48071) *(G-10194)*
Aqua Water System of Holland, Holland *Also called Aqua Fine Inc (G-7560)*
Aqua-Gel Corporation 313 538-9240
12700 Marion Redford (48239) *(G-13143)*
Aquarich Water Treatment Pdts, Fraser *Also called Edrich Products Inc (G-5647)*
Aquarius Recreational Products 586 469-4600
41201 Production Dr Harrison Township (48045) *(G-7320)*
Aquatic Co 269 279-7461
888 W Broadway St Three Rivers (49093) *(G-15855)*
Aqueous Orbital Systems LLC 269 501-7461
301 N 26th St Kalamazoo (49048) *(G-8681)*
Aquest Machining & Assembly, Greenville *Also called Fabx Industries Inc (G-7130)*
Aquila Resources Inc (PA) 906 352-4024
414 10th Ave Ste 1 Menominee (49858) *(G-10724)*
Ar2 Engineering LLC (PA) 248 735-9999
26600 Heyn Dr Novi (48374) *(G-11829)*
Arab American News Inc 313 582-4888
5706 Chase Rd Dearborn (48126) *(G-3678)*
Arauco North America Inc 800 261-4896
5851 Arauco Rd Grayling (49738) *(G-7103)*
Arboc Ltd (PA) 248 684-2895
3504 Car Dr Commerce Township (48382) *(G-3390)*
Arbor Assays Inc 734 677-1774
1514 Eisenhower Pl Ann Arbor (48108) *(G-362)*
Arbor Gage & Tooling Inc 616 454-8266
2031 Calvin Ave Se Grand Rapids (49507) *(G-6178)*
Arbor International Inc 734 761-5200
143 Enterprise Dr Ann Arbor (48103) *(G-363)*
Arbor Kitchen LLC 248 921-4602
124 W Summit St Ste B Ann Arbor (48103) *(G-364)*
Arbor Operating LLC 231 941-2237
333 W Grandview Pkwy # 4 Traverse City (49684) *(G-15896)*
Arbor Press LLC 248 549-0150
4303 Normandy Ct Royal Oak (48073) *(G-13904)*
Arbor Springs Water Company (PA) 734 668-8270
1440 Plymouth Rd Ann Arbor (48105) *(G-365)*
Arbor Stone 517 750-1340
6718 Spring Arbor Rd Spring Arbor (49283) *(G-15119)*
Arbor Woods Mfg Home Community 734 482-4305
1993 Arbor Woods Blvd Ypsilanti (48198) *(G-18052)*
Arbormetrix Inc 734 661-7944
339 E Liberty St Ste 210 Ann Arbor (48104) *(G-366)*
Arboroakland Group, Royal Oak *Also called Arbor Press LLC (G-13904)*
Arbre Farms Corporation 231 873-3337
6362 N 192nd Ave Walkerville (49459) *(G-16884)*
ARC Metal Stamping LLC 517 448-8954
4111 Munson Hwy Hudson (49247) *(G-8127)*
ARC Mit 248 399-4800
660 E 10 Mile Rd Ferndale (48220) *(G-5261)*
ARC Print Solutions LLC 248 917-7052
19101 Saxon Dr Beverly Hills (48025) *(G-1613)*
ARC Services of Macomb Inc 586 469-1600
44050 N Gratiot Ave Clinton Township (48036) *(G-3056)*
ARC-Kecy LLC 517 448-8954
4111 Munson Hwy Hudson (49247) *(G-8128)*
Arcanum Alloys Inc 312 810-4479
4460 44th St Se Ste F Kentwood (49512) *(G-8999)*
Arcelormittal Tailored Blanks 313 332-5300
8650 Mount Elliott St Detroit (48211) *(G-3873)*
Arcelormittal USA LLC 313 332-5600
8650 Mount Elliott St Detroit (48211) *(G-3874)*
Arch Global Precision LLC (HQ) 734 266-6900
2600 S Telg Rd Ste 180 Bloomfield Hills (48302) *(G-1747)*
Archangel's Jewelry, Warren *Also called Novus Corporation (G-17175)*
Archer Record Pressing Co 313 365-9545
7401 E Davison St Detroit (48212) *(G-3875)*
Archer Wire International Corp 231 869-6911
474 S Carroll St Pentwater (49449) *(G-12428)*
Archer-Daniels-Midland Company 269 968-2900
436 Porter St Unit F2 Battle Creek (49014) *(G-1147)*
Archer-Daniels-Midland Company 810 672-9221
1337 W Elevator St Snover (48472) *(G-14743)*
Archer-Daniels-Midland Company 517 627-4017
16994 Wright Rd Grand Ledge (48837) *(G-6101)*
Archer-Daniels-Midland Company 517 647-4155
401 E Grand River Ave Portland (48875) *(G-13061)*
Architectural Bldg Pdts Inc 248 680-1563
1441 E Maple Rd Ste 360 Troy (48083) *(G-16216)*
Architectural Design Wdwrk Inc 586 726-9050
52976 Van Dyke Ave Shelby Township (48316) *(G-14548)*
Architectural Elements Inc 616 241-6001
4707 40th St Se Grand Rapids (49512) *(G-6179)*
Architectural Glass & Mtls Inc (PA) 269 375-6165
604 S 8th St Kalamazoo (49009) *(G-8682)*
Architectural Model Studios, Ferndale *Also called Zoyes East Inc (G-5331)*
Architectural Planners Inc 248 674-1340
5101 Williams Lake Rd Waterford (48329) *(G-17322)*
Architectural Products Inc 248 585-8272
4850 Coolidge Hwy B Royal Oak (48073) *(G-13905)*
Architrave Woodworking, Waterford *Also called L E Q Inc (G-17356)*
Arco Alloys Corp 313 871-2680
1891 Trombly St Detroit (48211) *(G-3876)*
Arcon Vernova Inc 734 904-1895
271 Old Creek Dr Saline (48176) *(G-14378)*
Arconic Howmet 10 Plant, Whitehall *Also called Arconic Inc (G-17661)*
Arconic Inc 231 981-3002
3850 White Lake Dr Whitehall (49461) *(G-17661)*
Arconic Inc 231 894-5686
1 Misco Dr Whitehall (49461) *(G-17662)*
Arconic Inc 248 489-4900
37000 W 12 Mile Rd # 115 Farmington Hills (48331) *(G-4932)*
Arconic Power & Propulsion RES, Whitehall *Also called Howmet Corporation (G-17671)*
Arcosa Shoring Products Inc (HQ) 517 741-4300
8530 M 60 Union City (49094) *(G-16731)*
Arcosa Shoring Products Inc 800 292-1225
4837 W Grand River Ave Lansing (48906) *(G-9203)*
Arctic Glacier, Port Huron *Also called Agi Ccaa Inc (G-12882)*
Arctic Glacier Grayling Inc 810 987-7100
1755 Yeager St Port Huron (48060) *(G-12892)*
Arctic Glacier Inc 734 485-0430
1755 Yeager St Port Huron (48060) *(G-12893)*
Arctic Glacier PA Inc 610 494-8200
1755 Yeager St Port Huron (48060) *(G-12894)*
Arctic Glacier Texas Inc 517 999-3500
5635 Commerce St Ste B Lansing (48911) *(G-9340)*
Arctuition LLC 616 635-9959
8011 Thornapple Clb Dr Se Ada (49301) *(G-9)*
Arcturian LLC 313 643-5326
3319 Greenfield Rd 423 Dearborn (48120) *(G-3679)*
Arden Companies LLC (PA) 248 415-8500
30400 Telg Rd Ste 200 Bingham Farms (48025) *(G-1648)*

ALPHABETIC

Arden-Benhar Mills, Bingham Farms *Also called Krams Enterprises Inc* ***(G-1655)***
Ardo Granite LLC.....517 253-7139
919 Filley St Ste B Lansing (48906) ***(G-9204)***
Area Cycle Inc.....989 777-0850
7482 Dixie Hwy Bridgeport (48722) ***(G-1849)***
Area Exteriors.....248 544-0706
4075 Forest St Leonard (48367) ***(G-9526)***
Arena Publishing Co Inc.....586 296-5369
15767 Kingston Dr Fraser (48026) ***(G-5621)***
Arete Industries Inc.....231 582-4470
1 Altair Dr Boyne City (49712) ***(G-1815)***
Argent Automotive Systems, Plymouth *Also called Argent International Inc* ***(G-12572)***
Argent International Inc.....734 582-9800
41016 Concept Dr Plymouth (48170) ***(G-12572)***
Argent Limited.....734 427-5533
11966 Brookfield St Livonia (48150) ***(G-9652)***
Argent Tape & Label Inc (PA).....734 582-9956
41016 Concept Dr Ste A Plymouth (48170) ***(G-12573)***
Argo Liquid, Saint Johns *Also called Cog Marketers Ltd* ***(G-14281)***
Argo Systems, Holland *Also called FSI Label Company* ***(G-7637)***
Argon & Tool Manufacturing Co, Madison Heights *Also called Argon Tool Inc* ***(G-10195)***
Argon Group LLC.....248 370-0003
1021 Olympia Dr Rochester Hills (48306) ***(G-13370)***
Argon Tool Inc.....248 583-1605
32309 Milton Ave Madison Heights (48071) ***(G-10195)***
Argonics Inc (PA).....906 226-9747
520 9th St Gwinn (49841) ***(G-7215)***
Argus Corporation (PA).....313 937-2900
12540 Beech Daly Rd Redford (48239) ***(G-13144)***
Argus Press Company.....989 725-5136
201 E Exchange St Owosso (48867) ***(G-12280)***
Argus Technologies LLC.....616 538-9895
560 5th St Nw Ste 100 Grand Rapids (49504) ***(G-6180)***
Argyle Socks LLC.....269 615-0097
3800 Winding Way Kalamazoo (49004) ***(G-8683)***
Arhouzz, Kalkaska *Also called Woodland Creek Furniture Inc* ***(G-8968)***
Aria Furniture, Rochester Hills *Also called S & J Inc* ***(G-13508)***
Arin Inc.....586 779-3410
29139 Calahan Rd Roseville (48066) ***(G-13774)***
Aristo Industries, Fraser *Also called Aristo-Cote Inc* ***(G-5622)***
Aristo Industries, Harrison Township *Also called Aristo-Cote Inc* ***(G-7321)***
Aristo-Cote Inc.....586 447-9049
11655 Park Ct Shelby Township (48315) ***(G-14549)***
Aristo-Cote Inc.....586 447-9049
32100 Groesbeck Hwy Fraser (48026) ***(G-5622)***
Aristo-Cote Inc (PA).....586 336-9421
24951 Henry B Joy Blvd Harrison Township (48045) ***(G-7321)***
Ark Industrial, Benton Harbor *Also called West Michigan Tool & Die Co* ***(G-1564)***
Arkema Coating Resins, Grand Rapids *Also called Arkema Inc* ***(G-6181)***
Arkema Inc.....616 243-4578
1415 Steele Ave Sw Grand Rapids (49507) ***(G-6181)***
Arkin Automotive Inc.....248 542-1192
2600 Wolcott St Ferndale (48220) ***(G-5262)***
Arlington Display Inds Inc.....313 837-1212
19303 W Davison St Detroit (48223) ***(G-3877)***
Arlington Metals Corporation.....269 426-3371
13100 Arlington Dr Sawyer (49125) ***(G-14481)***
Arm Fulfillment, Battle Creek *Also called Epi Printers Inc* ***(G-1182)***
Arm Tooling Systems Inc.....586 759-5677
2453 John B Ave Warren (48091) ***(G-16938)***
Armada Grain Co (PA).....586 784-5911
73180 Fulton St Armada (48005) ***(G-714)***
Armada Printwear Inc.....586 784-5553
74135 Church St Armada (48005) ***(G-715)***
Armada Rubber Manufacturing Co.....586 784-9135
24586 Armada Ridge Rd Armada (48005) ***(G-716)***
Armaly Brands, Commerce Township *Also called Armaly Sponge Company* ***(G-3391)***
Armaly Sponge Company (PA).....248 669-2100
1900 Easy St Commerce Township (48390) ***(G-3391)***
Armartis Manufacturing Inc.....248 308-9622
20815 Kraft Blvd Roseville (48066) ***(G-13775)***
Armi, Fowlerville *Also called Armoured Rsstnce McHanisms Inc* ***(G-5558)***
Armick Inc (PA).....616 481-5882
1516 Blaine Ave Se Grand Rapids (49507) ***(G-6182)***
Armor Protective Packaging, Howell *Also called Sks Industries Inc* ***(G-8098)***
Armored Group LLC.....602 840-2271
2727 S Beech Daly St Dearborn Heights (48125) ***(G-3779)***
Armoured Rsstnce McHanisms Inc.....517 223-7618
345 W Frank St Fowlerville (48836) ***(G-5558)***
Armstrong Display Concepts.....231 652-1675
480 S Park St Newaygo (49337) ***(G-11563)***
Armstrong Fluid Handling Inc.....269 279-3600
221 Armstrong Blvd Three Rivers (49093) ***(G-15856)***
Armstrong Graphics, Milford *Also called A & F Enterprises Inc* ***(G-10953)***
Armstrong Hot Water Inc (HQ).....269 278-1413
221 Armstrong Blvd Three Rivers (49093) ***(G-15857)***
Armstrong International Inc (PA).....269 273-1415
816 Maple St Three Rivers (49093) ***(G-15858)***
Arnet's Memorials, Ann Arbor *Also called Arnets Inc* ***(G-367)***
Arnets Inc (PA).....734 665-3650
5060 Jackson Rd Ste H Ann Arbor (48103) ***(G-367)***
Arnold & Sautter Co (PA).....989 684-7557
408 N Euclid Ave Bay City (48706) ***(G-1276)***
Arnold Tool & Die Co (PA).....586 598-0099
48800 Structural Dr Chesterfield (48051) ***(G-2741)***
Arnt Asphalt Sealing Inc (PA).....269 927-1532
1240 S Crystal Ave Benton Harbor (49022) ***(G-1482)***
Aro Welding Technologies Inc.....586 949-9353
48500 Structural Dr Chesterfield (48051) ***(G-2742)***
Arotech Corporation (PA).....800 281-0356
1229 Oak Valley Dr Ann Arbor (48108) ***(G-368)***
Arplas USA LLC.....888 527-5553
1928 Marston St Detroit (48211) ***(G-3878)***
Arquette Concrete & Supply (PA).....989 846-4131
4374 Airpark Dr Standish (48658) ***(G-15216)***
Arrow Chemical Products Inc.....313 237-0277
2067 Sainte Anne St Detroit (48216) ***(G-3879)***
Arrow Die & Mold Repair.....231 689-1829
8527 E Wilderness Trl White Cloud (49349) ***(G-17619)***
Arrow Drilling Services LLC.....231 258-4596
4030 Columbus Dr Ne Kalkaska (49646) ***(G-8936)***
Arrow Material & Handling, Paw Paw *Also called Big Bear Products Inc* ***(G-12398)***
Arrow Motor & Pump Inc.....734 285-7860
629 Cent St Wyandotte (48192) ***(G-17946)***
Arrow Printing LLC.....248 738-2222
5457 Elizabeth Lake Rd Waterford (48327) ***(G-17323)***
Arrow Swift Printing, Hillsdale *Also called Rumler Brothers Inc* ***(G-7538)***
Arrow Swift Prtg & Copy Ctr, Greenville *Also called Knapp Printing Services Inc* ***(G-7143)***
Arrowhead Industries Inc.....231 238-9366
1715 E M 68 Hwy Afton (49705) ***(G-105)***
Arrowhead Systems Inc.....810 720-4770
3018 S Dye Rd Flint (48507) ***(G-5377)***
Arrowmat LLC.....800 920-6035
6540 Munsell Rd Howell (48843) ***(G-8016)***
Art & Image.....800 566-4162
582 E Napier Ave Benton Harbor (49022) ***(G-1483)***
Art Craft Display Inc (PA).....517 485-2221
500 Business Centre Dr Lansing (48917) ***(G-9278)***
Art Glass Inc.....586 731-8627
44045 Donley Dr Sterling Heights (48314) ***(G-15264)***
Art In Transit Inc.....248 585-5566
1260 Rankin Dr Ste F Troy (48083) ***(G-16217)***
Art Laser Inc.....248 391-6600
4141 N Atlantic Blvd Auburn Hills (48326) ***(G-780)***
Art of Custom Framing Inc.....248 435-3726
3863 Rochester Rd Troy (48083) ***(G-16218)***
Art of Shaving - Fl LLC.....248 649-5872
2800 W Big Beavr Rd Fl 2 Troy (48084) ***(G-16219)***
Art Optical Contact Lens Inc.....616 453-1888
3175 3 Mile Rd Nw Grand Rapids (49534) ***(G-6183)***
Art/Fx Sign Co.....269 465-5706
9751 Red Arrow Hwy Bridgman (49106) ***(G-1860)***
Artco Mfg, Livonia *Also called American Ring Manufacturing* ***(G-9644)***
Artcraft Pattern Works Inc.....734 729-0022
6430 Commerce Dr Westland (48185) ***(G-17543)***
Artcraft Printing Corporation.....734 455-8893
14919 Maplewood Ln Plymouth (48170) ***(G-12574)***
Artech Printing Inc.....248 545-0088
26346 John R Rd Madison Heights (48071) ***(G-10196)***
Arted Chrome Plating.....586 758-0050
24657 Mound Rd Warren (48091) ***(G-16939)***
Arted Chrome Plating Inc.....313 871-3331
38 Piquette St Detroit (48202) ***(G-3880)***
Artemis Technologies Inc.....517 336-9915
2501 Coolidge Rd Ste 503 East Lansing (48823) ***(G-4650)***
Artesian Distillers.....616 252-1700
955 Ken O Sha Ind Park Grand Rapids (49508) ***(G-6184)***
Artex Label & Graphics Inc.....616 748-9655
740 Case Karsten Dr Zeeland (49464) ***(G-18112)***
Artful Scrapbooking & Rubber.....586 651-1577
7220 Smale St Washington (48094) ***(G-17302)***
Arthur R Sommers.....586 469-1280
41700 Conger Bay Dr Harrison Township (48045) ***(G-7322)***
Artic Technologies Intl.....248 689-9884
3456 Rochester Rd Troy (48083) ***(G-16220)***
Artificial Sky, Northville *Also called Skyworks LLC* ***(G-11726)***
Artiflex Manufacturing LLC.....616 459-8285
731 Broadway Ave Nw Grand Rapids (49504) ***(G-6185)***
Artigy Printing.....269 373-6591
5285 E Fg Ave Kalamazoo (49004) ***(G-8684)***
Artisan Bread Co LLC.....586 756-0100
25000 Guenther Warren (48091) ***(G-16940)***
Artisan Medical Displays LLC.....616 748-8950
219 N Church St Zeeland (49464) ***(G-18113)***
Artisans Cstm Mmory Mattresses.....989 793-3208
2200 S Hamilton St Ste 3 Saginaw (48602) ***(G-13996)***
Artisans Mattresses, Saginaw *Also called Artisans Cstm Mmory Mattresses* ***(G-13996)***

Artistic, Troy *Also called Combine International Inc* ***(G-16273)***
Artistic Carton Company....269 483-7601
15781 River St White Pigeon (49099) ***(G-17644)***
Artistic European Granich MBL, Dearborn *Also called A E G M Inc* ***(G-3670)***
Artistic Printing Inc....248 356-1004
26040 W 12 Mile Rd Southfield (48034) ***(G-14840)***
Artists Pallet....248 889-2440
203 S Milford Rd Highland (48357) ***(G-7486)***
Artjen Complexus Usa LLC....519 919-0814
440 Burroughs St Ste 250 Detroit (48202) ***(G-3881)***
Arts Crafts Hardware....586 231-5344
169 Smith St Mount Clemens (48043) ***(G-11123)***
Arvan Specialty Products, Kalamazoo *Also called Arvco Container Corporation* ***(G-8686)***
Arvco Container Corporation (PA)....269 381-0900
845 Gibson St Kalamazoo (49001) ***(G-8685)***
Arvco Container Corporation....269 381-0900
845 Gibson St Kalamazoo (49001) ***(G-8686)***
Arvco Container Corporation....269 381-0900
351 Rochester Ave Kalamazoo (49007) ***(G-8687)***
Arvco Container Corporation....231 876-0935
1355 Marty Paul St Cadillac (49601) ***(G-2228)***
Arvco Speciality Packaging, Kalamazoo *Also called Arvco Container Corporation* ***(G-8685)***
Arvin Intl Holdings LLC (HQ)....248 435-1000
2135 W Maple Rd Troy (48084) ***(G-16221)***
Arvinmeritor Inc....248 435-1000
2135 W Maple Rd Troy (48084) ***(G-16222)***
Arvinmeritor Oe LLC (HQ)....248 435-1000
2135 W Maple Rd Troy (48084) ***(G-16223)***
Arvron Inc....616 530-1888
4720 Clay Ave Sw Grand Rapids (49548) ***(G-6186)***
As, Grand Rapids *Also called Design Design Inc* ***(G-6345)***
AS Property Management Inc....586 427-8000
25133 Thomas Dr Warren (48091) ***(G-16941)***
Asahi Kasei Plas N Amer Inc (HQ)....517 223-2000
1 Thermofil Way Fowlerville (48836) ***(G-5559)***
Asahi Kasei Plastics Amer Inc....517 223-2000
1 Thermofil Way Fowlerville (48836) ***(G-5560)***
Asama Coldwater Mfg Inc....517 279-1090
180 Asama Pkwy Coldwater (49036) ***(G-3289)***
Asao LLC....734 522-6333
34115 Industrial Rd Livonia (48150) ***(G-9653)***
ASAP Printing Inc....517 882-3500
1110 Keystone Ave Lansing (48911) ***(G-9341)***
ASAP Printing Inc (PA)....517 882-3500
2323 Jolly Rd Okemos (48864) ***(G-12114)***
ASAP Source, Ann Arbor *Also called Ltek Industries Inc* ***(G-535)***
ASC, Warren *Also called Specilty Vhcl Acquisition Corp* ***(G-17245)***
Ascent Aerospace LLC (HQ)....586 726-0500
16445 23 Mile Rd Macomb (48042) ***(G-10108)***
Ascent Aerospace Holdings LLC (PA)....212 916-8142
16445 23 Mile Rd Macomb (48042) ***(G-10109)***
Ascent Integrated Platforms....586 726-0500
16445 23 Mile Rd Macomb (48042) ***(G-10110)***
Asco LP....810 648-9141
360 Thelma St Sandusky (48471) ***(G-14428)***
Asco LP....248 596-3200
46280 Dylan Dr Ste 100 Novi (48377) ***(G-11830)***
Asco Power Technologies LP....248 957-9050
27280 Haggerty Rd C-16 Farmington Hills (48331) ***(G-4933)***
Ascott Corporation....734 663-2023
1202 N Main St Ann Arbor (48104) ***(G-369)***
Ase Industries Inc....586 754-7480
23850 Pinewood St Warren (48091) ***(G-16942)***
Aseltine Cider Company Inc....616 784-7676
533 Lamoreaux Dr Nw Comstock Park (49321) ***(G-3460)***
Ash Industries Inc....269 672-9630
362 116th Ave Martin (49070) ***(G-10594)***
Ashland Slag Company, Dearborn *Also called Levy Indiana Slag Co* ***(G-3733)***
Asi Signage Innovation, Troy *Also called Sign Concepts Corporation* ***(G-16600)***
Asian Noodle LLC....989 316-2380
200 Center Ave Bay City (48708) ***(G-1277)***
Asimco International Inc....248 213-5200
1000 Town Ctr Ste 1050 Southfield (48075) ***(G-14841)***
Ask Your Neighbor, Bloomfield Hills *Also called Bob Allison Enterprises* ***(G-1752)***
Asmo Detroit Inc....248 359-4440
39575 Lewis Dr Ste 800 Novi (48377) ***(G-11831)***
Asmus Seasoning Inc....586 939-4505
36625 Metro Ct Ste A Sterling Heights (48312) ***(G-15265)***
Asp Grede Acquisitionco LLC (HQ)....248 727-1800
1 Towne Sq Ste 550 Southfield (48076) ***(G-14842)***
Asp Grede Intrmdate Hldngs LLC (HQ)....313 758-2000
1 Dauch Dr Detroit (48211) ***(G-3882)***
Asp Hhi Acquisition Co Inc (HQ)....313 758-2000
1 Dauch Dr Detroit (48211) ***(G-3883)***
Asp Hhi Holdings Inc (HQ)....248 597-3800
2727 W 14 Mile Rd Royal Oak (48073) ***(G-13906)***
Asp Hhi Intermediate Holdings (HQ)....248 727-1800
1 Towne Sq Ste 550 Southfield (48076) ***(G-14843)***
Asp Hhi Intrmdate Holdings Inc (HQ)....248 727-1800
1 Towne Sq Ste 550 Southfield (48076) ***(G-14844)***
Asp Plating Company....616 842-8080
211 N Griffin St Grand Haven (49417) ***(G-5992)***
Aspen Technologies Inc (PA)....248 446-1485
7963 Lochlin Dr Brighton (48116) ***(G-1887)***
Asphalt Paving Inc....231 733-1409
1000 E Sherman Blvd Muskegon (49444) ***(G-11272)***
Aspire Pharmacy....989 773-7849
121 E Broadway St D Mount Pleasant (48858) ***(G-11171)***
Aspra World Inc....248 872-7030
25160 Easy St Warren (48089) ***(G-16943)***
Assa Abloy Entrance Systems US....734 462-2348
38291 Schoolcraft Rd # 103 Livonia (48150) ***(G-9654)***
Assay Designs Inc....734 214-0923
5777 Hines Dr Ann Arbor (48108) ***(G-370)***
Assem-Tech Inc....616 846-3410
1600 Kooiman St Grand Haven (49417) ***(G-5993)***
Assemacher's Cycling Center, Flint *Also called Assenmacher Lightweight Cycles* ***(G-5378)***
Assembly Alternatives Inc....248 362-1616
501 Longford Dr Rochester Hills (48309) ***(G-13371)***
Assembly Concepts Inc....989 685-2603
2651 S M 33 Rose City (48654) ***(G-13759)***
Assembly Technologies Intl....248 280-2810
1937 Barrett Dr Troy (48084) ***(G-16224)***
Assenmacher Lightweight Cycles (PA)....810 635-7844
8053 Miller Rd Swartz Creek (48473) ***(G-15661)***
Assenmacher Lightweight Cycles....810 232-2994
1272 W Hill Rd Flint (48507) ***(G-5378)***
Assenmachers Hill Road Cyclery, Swartz Creek *Also called Assenmacher Lightweight Cycles* ***(G-15661)***
Asset Health Inc....248 822-2870
2250 Butterfield Dr # 100 Troy (48084) ***(G-16225)***
Assi Fuel Inc....586 759-4759
8309 E 8 Mile Rd Warren (48089) ***(G-16944)***
Assistive Technology Cal, Novi *Also called Assistive Technology Mich Inc* ***(G-11832)***
Assistive Technology Mich Inc....248 348-7161
43000 W 9 Mile Rd Ste 113 Novi (48375) ***(G-11832)***
Associate Mfg Inc....989 345-0025
3977 S M 30 West Branch (48661) ***(G-17506)***
Associated Broach Corporation....810 798-9112
7481 Research Dr Almont (48003) ***(G-252)***
Associated Constructors LLC....906 226-6505
14 Industrial Park Dr Negaunee (49866) ***(G-11467)***
Associated Metals Inc....734 369-3851
6235 Jackson Rd Ste B Ann Arbor (48103) ***(G-371)***
Associated Newspapers Michigan....734 467-1900
35128 W Michigan Ave Wayne (48184) ***(G-17424)***
Associated Print & Graphics....734 676-8896
9617 Island Dr Grosse Ile (48138) ***(G-7167)***
Associated Print & Marketing, Madison Heights *Also called Apms Incorporated* ***(G-10193)***
Associated Rack Corporation....616 554-6004
4910 Kraft Ave Se Grand Rapids (49512) ***(G-6187)***
Associated Redi Mix and Block, Negaunee *Also called Associated Constructors LLC* ***(G-11467)***
Associated Spring, Plymouth *Also called Barnes Group Inc* ***(G-12583)***
Associated Spring- Nat Sls, Plymouth *Also called Barnes Group Inc* ***(G-12582)***
Assra....906 225-1828
625 Pine St Marquette (49855) ***(G-10518)***
Assuramed Inc....616 419-2020
3576 R B Chaffee Mem Se Wyoming (49548) ***(G-17987)***
Astar Inc....574 234-2137
71135 Fir Rd Niles (49120) ***(G-11595)***
Astech Inc....989 823-7211
5512 Scotch Rd Vassar (48768) ***(G-16811)***
Astellas Pharma Us Inc....616 698-8825
5905 Kraft Ave Se Grand Rapids (49512) ***(G-6188)***
Astellas Pharma Us Inc....231 947-3630
807 Airport Access Rd # 209 Traverse City (49686) ***(G-15897)***
Astra Associates Inc....586 254-6500
6500 Dobry Dr Sterling Heights (48314) ***(G-15266)***
Astraeus Wind Energy Inc....517 663-5455
503 Marilin Ave Eaton Rapids (48827) ***(G-4716)***
Astral Projections Stage Ltg, Plainwell *Also called Wayne Novick* ***(G-12551)***
Astro Building Products Inc (HQ)....231 941-0324
221 W South Airport Rd Traverse City (49686) ***(G-15898)***
Astro Lite Window Co Factory, Romulus *Also called Astro Lite Window Company Inc* ***(G-13652)***
Astro Lite Window Company Inc....734 326-2455
28615 Beverly Rd Romulus (48174) ***(G-13652)***
Astro Wood Stake Inc....616 875-8118
6017 Chicago Dr Zeeland (49464) ***(G-18114)***
Astro-Netics Inc....248 585-4890
1780 E 14 Mile Rd Madison Heights (48071) ***(G-10197)***
Asw Amerca Inc....248 957-9638
24762 Crestview Ct Farmington Hills (48335) ***(G-4934)***
Atco Rubber Products, Grand Haven *Also called Atcoflex Inc* ***(G-5994)***

A L P H A B E T I C

Atcoflex Inc 616 842-4661
14261 172nd Ave Grand Haven (49417) *(G-5994)*
Atd Engineering and Mch LLC 989 876-7161
533 N Court St Au Gres (48703) *(G-741)*
Ateq Corporation (HQ) 734 838-3100
35980 Industrial Rd Livonia (48150) *(G-9655)*
Ateq Leak Detecting Service, Livonia *Also called Ateq Corporation (G-9655)*
Ateq Tpms Tools Lc 734 838-3104
35990 Industrial Rd Livonia (48150) *(G-9656)*
Atf Inc 989 685-2468
285 Casemaster Dr Rose City (48654) *(G-13760)*
Atg Precision Products LLC 586 247-5400
7545 N Haggerty Rd Canton (48187) *(G-2349)*
Athena Foods, Southfield *Also called Charidimos Inc (G-14865)*
Athey Precision Inc 989 386-4523
2021 S Athey Ave Clare (48617) *(G-2864)*
Athletic Uniform Lettering 313 533-9071
26114 W 6 Mile Rd Redford (48240) *(G-13145)*
ATI, Novi *Also called Accurate Technologies Inc (G-11823)*
Atk Lc, Shelby Township *Also called Northrop Grumman Innovation (G-14657)*
Atlantic Boat Brokers 231 941-8050
801 S Garfield Ave Traverse City (49686) *(G-15899)*
Atlantic Precision Pdts Inc 586 532-9420
51234 Filomena Dr Shelby Township (48315) *(G-14550)*
Atlantic Shutter 248 668-6408
29797 Beck Rd Wixom (48393) *(G-17762)*
Atlantic Tool Inc 586 954-9268
22826 Patmore Dr Clinton Township (48036) *(G-3057)*
Atlantis Tech Corp 989 356-6954
706 Island View Dr Alpena (49707) *(G-277)*
Atlas Copco Ias LLC 248 377-9722
3301 Cross Creek Pkwy Auburn Hills (48326) *(G-781)*
Atlas Cut Stone Company 248 545-5100
12920 Northend Ave Oak Park (48237) *(G-12049)*
Atlas Gear Company 248 583-2964
32801 Edward Ave Madison Heights (48071) *(G-10198)*
Atlas Oil Transportation Inc 800 878-2000
24501 Ecorse Rd Taylor (48180) *(G-15690)*
Atlas Roofing Corporation 616 878-1568
8240 Byron Center Ave Sw Byron Center (49315) *(G-2177)*
Atlas Technologies LLC 810 714-2128
3100 Copper Ave Fenton (48430) *(G-5183)*
Atlas Thread Gage Inc 248 477-3230
30990 W 8 Mile Rd Farmington Hills (48336) *(G-4935)*
Atlas Tile & Stone LLC 586 264-7720
31134 Dequindre Rd Warren (48092) *(G-16945)*
Atlas Tube (plymouth) Inc 734 738-5600
13101 Eckles Rd Plymouth (48170) *(G-12575)*
Atlas Welding Accessories Inc 248 588-4666
501 Stephenson Hwy Troy (48083) *(G-16226)*
Atm International Services LLC 734 524-9771
8351 N Wayne Rd Westland (48185) *(G-17544)*
Atmo-Seal Enginering, Troy *Also called Atmo-Seal Inc (G-16227)*
Atmo-Seal Inc 248 528-9640
1091 Wheaton Dr Troy (48083) *(G-16227)*
Atmosphere Annealing LLC (HQ) 517 485-5090
209 W Mount Hope Ave # 2 Lansing (48910) *(G-9342)*
Atmosphere Annealing LLC 517 482-1374
1801 Bassett St Lansing (48915) *(G-9343)*
Atmosphere Group Inc (PA) 248 624-8191
49630 Pontiac Trl Wixom (48393) *(G-17763)*
Atmosphere Heat Treating Inc 248 960-4700
30760 Century Dr Wixom (48393) *(G-17764)*
Atos Syntel Inc (HQ) 248 619-2800
525 E Big Beaver Rd # 300 Troy (48083) *(G-16228)*
Atra Plastics Inc (PA) 734 237-3393
43938 Plymouth Oaks Blvd Plymouth (48170) *(G-12576)*
Atreum, Auburn Hills *Also called Antolin Interiors Usa Inc (G-775)*
Ats Assembly and Test Inc 734 266-4713
12841 Stark Rd Livonia (48150) *(G-9657)*
Ats Assembly and Test Inc (HQ) 937 222-3030
1 Ats Dr Wixom (48393) *(G-17765)*
Ats Assembly and Test Inc 937 222-3030
1 Ats Dr Wixom (48393) *(G-17766)*
Attentive Industries Inc 810 233-7077
1301 Alabama Ave Flint (48505) *(G-5379)*
Attentive Industries Inc (PA) 810 233-7077
502 Kelso St Flint (48506) *(G-5380)*
Attercor Inc 734 845-9300
301 N Main St Ste 100 Ann Arbor (48104) *(G-372)*
Attitude & Experience Inc 231 946-7446
1230 S M 37 Traverse City (49685) *(G-15900)*
Attwood Corporation (HQ) 616 897-9241
1016 N Monroe St Lowell (49331) *(G-10023)*
Atwater Brewery, Detroit *Also called Detroit Rivertwn Brewing Co LL (G-4000)*
Atwater In Park 313 344-5104
1175 Lakepointe St Grosse Pointe Park (48230) *(G-7191)*
Atwood Forest Products Inc 616 696-0081
1177 17 Mile Rd Ne Cedar Springs (49319) *(G-2545)*

Au Enterprises Inc 248 544-9700
3916 11 Mile Rd Berkley (48072) *(G-1580)*
Au Gres Sheep Factory 989 876-8787
211 N Huron Rd Au Gres (48703) *(G-742)*
Aubio Life Sciences LLC 561 289-1888
50164 Pontiac Trl Unit 7 Wixom (48393) *(G-17767)*
Auburn Hills Manufacturing Inc 313 758-2000
1987 Taylor Rd Auburn Hills (48326) *(G-782)*
Auction Masters 586 576-7777
8700 Capital St Oak Park (48237) *(G-12050)*
Audia Woodworking & Fine Furn 586 296-6330
16627 Millar Rd Clinton Township (48036) *(G-3058)*
Audio Technologies Inc 586 323-3890
1713 Larchwood Dr Ste B Troy (48083) *(G-16229)*
Audionet America Inc 586 944-0043
33900 Harper Ave Ste 101 Clinton Township (48035) *(G-3059)*
Audiospace, Grand Rapids *Also called Livespace LLC (G-6629)*
August Communications Inc 313 561-8000
22250 Ford Rd Dearborn Heights (48127) *(G-3780)*
August Lighting Inc 616 895-4951
10030 Stanton St Zeeland (49464) *(G-18115)*
Augustine Innovations LLC 248 686-1822
2900 Union Lake Rd # 214 Commerce Township (48382) *(G-3392)*
Aunt Millie's Bakeries, Cadillac *Also called Perfection Bakeries Inc (G-2269)*
Aunt Millies Bakeries 989 356-6688
3450 Us Highway 23 S Alpena (49707) *(G-278)*
Aunt Millies Bakeries Inc (HQ) 734 528-1475
5331 W Michigan Ave Ypsilanti (48197) *(G-18053)*
Auntie Anne's, Lansing *Also called Karemor Inc (G-9303)*
Auntie Anne's, Southfield *Also called B & B Pretzels Inc (G-14848)*
Aureogen Inc 269 353-3805
4717 Campus Dr Ste 2300 Kalamazoo (49008) *(G-8688)*
Aureogen Biosciences, Kalamazoo *Also called Aureogen Inc (G-8688)*
Auria Solutions USA Inc (HQ) 734 456-2800
26999 Central Park Blvd # 300 Southfield (48076) *(G-14845)*
Auria St Clair LLC 810 329-8400
2001 Christian B Haas Dr Saint Clair (48079) *(G-14205)*
Auric Enterprises Inc 231 882-7251
7755 Narrow Gauge Rd Beulah (49617) *(G-1608)*
Aurora Cad CAM Inc 810 678-2128
1643 E Brocker Rd Metamora (48455) *(G-10772)*
Aurora Cellars 2015 LLC 231 994-3188
7788 E Horn Rd Lake Leelanau (49653) *(G-9099)*
Aurora Preserved Flowers 989 498-0290
7201 Westside Saginaw Rd # 5 Bay City (48706) *(G-1278)*
Aurora Spclty Chemistries Corp 517 372-9121
1520 Lake Lansing Rd Lansing (48912) *(G-9344)*
Aurum Design Inc 248 651-9040
400 S Main St Rochester (48307) *(G-13314)*
Aurum Design Jewelry, Rochester *Also called Aurum Design Inc (G-13314)*
Ausable Upholstery 989 366-5219
131 1/2 Evart St Cadillac (49601) *(G-2229)*
Ausable Woodworking Co Inc 989 348-7086
6677 Frederic St Frederic (49733) *(G-5750)*
Austemper Inc (HQ) 586 293-4554
30760 Century Dr Wixom (48393) *(G-17768)*
Austemper Inc 616 458-7061
341 Grant St Sw Grand Rapids (49503) *(G-6189)*
Austin Brothers Beer Co LLC 909 213-4194
821 W Miller St Alpena (49707) *(G-279)*
Austin Company 269 329-1181
9764 Portage Rd Portage (49002) *(G-12982)*
Austin Engineering 269 659-6335
1221 N Clay St Sturgis (49091) *(G-15597)*
Austin Machine & Tool LLC 517 278-1717
237 N Angola Rd Coldwater (49036) *(G-3290)*
Austin Powder Company 989 595-2400
11351 E Grand Lake Rd Presque Isle (49777) *(G-13082)*
Austin Tube Products Inc 231 745-2741
5629 S Forman Rd Baldwin (49304) *(G-1082)*
Authentic 3d 248 469-8809
30800 Telg Rd Ste 4775 Bingham Farms (48025) *(G-1649)*
Authority Customwear Ltd 248 588-8075
32046 Edward Ave Madison Heights (48071) *(G-10199)*
Authority Flame Hardening & St 586 598-5887
49803 Leona Dr Chesterfield (48051) *(G-2743)*
Auto & Truck Components, Co., Port Huron *Also called Cipa Usa Inc (G-12907)*
Auto Anodics Inc 810 984-5600
2407 16th St Port Huron (48060) *(G-12895)*
Auto Builders Inc 586 948-3780
46571 Continental Dr Chesterfield (48047) *(G-2744)*
Auto Chem Craft, Oak Park *Also called Auto Metal Craft Inc (G-12051)*
Auto Clinic 906 774-5780
411 Carpenter Ave Iron Mountain (49801) *(G-8275)*
Auto Connection 586 752-6371
75903 Peters Dr Bruce Twp (48065) *(G-2078)*
Auto Craft Tool & Die Co 810 794-4929
1800 Fruit St Clay (48001) *(G-2994)*

Auto Craft Tool & Die Co 810 794-4929
1800 Fruit St Clay (48001) *(G-2995)*
Auto Electric International 248 354-2082
22211 Telegraph Rd Southfield (48033) *(G-14846)*
Auto Engineering Lab 734 764-4254
1231 Beal Ave Ann Arbor (48109) *(G-373)*
Auto Metal Craft Inc 248 398-2240
12741 Capital St Oak Park (48237) *(G-12051)*
Auto Pallets-Boxes Inc (PA) 248 559-7744
28000 Southfield Rd Fl 2 Lathrup Village (48076) *(G-9498)*
Auto Pallets-Boxes Inc 734 782-1110
27945 Cooke St Flat Rock (48134) *(G-5347)*
Auto Quip Inc 810 364-3366
70 Airport Dr Kimball (48074) *(G-9042)*
Auto Tex 248 340-0844
3686 S Shimmons Cir C Auburn Hills (48326) *(G-783)*
Auto Trim Northwest Ohio In 517 265-3202
2294 Porter Hwy Adrian (49221) *(G-50)*
Auto-Air Composites, Lansing *Also called Pratt & Whitney Autoair Inc (G-9413)*
Auto-Masters Inc 616 455-4510
6521 Division Ave S Grand Rapids (49548) *(G-6190)*
Auto-Tech Plastics Inc 586 783-0103
164 Grand Ave Mount Clemens (48043) *(G-11124)*
Auto/Con Corp 586 791-7474
33842 James J Pompo Dr Fraser (48026) *(G-5623)*
Auto/Con Services LLC 586 791-7474
33661 James J Pompo Dr Fraser (48026) *(G-5624)*
Autoalliance Management Co 734 782-7800
1 International Dr Flat Rock (48134) *(G-5348)*
Autocam Corporation 269 789-4000
1511 George Brown Dr Marshall (49068) *(G-10562)*
Autocam Corporation 269 782-5186
201 Percy St Dowagiac (49047) *(G-4533)*
Autocam Corporation (HQ) 616 698-0707
4180 40th St Se Kentwood (49512) *(G-9000)*
Autocam Corporation 616 698-0707
4070 East Paris Ave Se Kentwood (49512) *(G-9001)*
Autocam Med DVC Holdings LLC (PA) 616 541-8080
4152 East Paris Ave Se Kentwood (49512) *(G-9002)*
Autocam Medical Devices LLC (HQ) 877 633-8080
4152 East Paris Ave Se Grand Rapids (49512) *(G-6191)*
Autocam Prcsion Cmpnents Group, Kentwood *Also called Autocam Corporation (G-9000)*
Autocam-Pax, Dowagiac *Also called Autocam Corporation (G-4533)*
Autocam-Pax Inc 269 782-5186
201 Percy St Dowagiac (49047) *(G-4534)*
Autodesk Inc 248 347-9650
26200 Town Center Dr # 300 Novi (48375) *(G-11833)*
Autodie LLC 616 454-9361
44 Coldbrook St Nw Grand Rapids (49503) *(G-6192)*
Autoexec Inc 616 971-0080
4477 East Paris Ave Se Grand Rapids (49512) *(G-6193)*
Autoform Development Inc 616 392-4909
257 E 32nd St Ste 2 Holland (49423) *(G-7561)*
Autoliv Asp Inc 248 761-0081
856 Featherstone St Pontiac (48342) *(G-12805)*
Autoliv Asp Inc 248 475-9000
1320 Pacific Dr Auburn Hills (48326) *(G-784)*
Autoliv Holding Inc 248 475-9000
1320 Pacific Dr Auburn Hills (48326) *(G-785)*
Autoliv N Amer Technical Cntr, Auburn Hills *Also called Autoliv Asp Inc (G-784)*
Autoliv Technical Center-W, Pontiac *Also called Autoliv Asp Inc (G-12805)*
Automated Bookkeeping Inc 866 617-3122
1555 Broadway St Detroit (48226) *(G-3884)*
Automated Control Systems Inc 248 476-9490
25168 Seeley Rd Novi (48375) *(G-11834)*
Automated Indus Motion Inc 231 865-1800
5627 Airline Rd Fruitport (49415) *(G-5787)*
Automated Machine Systems Inc 616 662-1309
6651 Pine Ridge Ct Sw Jenison (49428) *(G-8618)*
Automated Media Inc 313 662-0185
12171 Beech Daly Rd Redford (48239) *(G-13146)*
Automated Precision Eqp LLC 517 481-2414
770 Jackson St Ste A Eaton Rapids (48827) *(G-4717)*
Automated Process Equipment (PA) 616 374-1000
1201 4th Ave Lake Odessa (48849) *(G-9111)*
Automated Prod Assemblies 586 293-3990
33957 Doreka Fraser (48026) *(G-5625)*
Automated Systems Inc 248 373-5600
2400 Commercial Dr Auburn Hills (48326) *(G-786)*
Automated Techniques LLC 810 346-4670
7105 Enterprise Dr Brown City (48416) *(G-2045)*
Automatic Handling Intl Inc 734 847-0633
360 La Voy Rd Erie (48133) *(G-4800)*
Automatic Spring Products Corp (PA) 616 842-2284
803 Taylor Ave Grand Haven (49417) *(G-5995)*
Automatic Valve Corp 248 474-6761
22550 Heslip Dr Novi (48375) *(G-11835)*
Automatic Valve Nuclear, Novi *Also called Automatic Valve Corp (G-11835)*
AUTOMATION SERVICE EQUIPMENT, Warren *Also called Ase Industries Inc (G-16942)*
Automation Specialists Inc 616 738-8288
12555 Superior Ct Holland (49424) *(G-7562)*
Automatrics, Grand Rapids *Also called Thierica Controls Inc (G-6927)*
Autombili Lamborghini Amer LLC 866 681-6276
3800 Hamlin Rd Auburn Hills (48326) *(G-787)*
Automotive LLC 248 712-1175
300 Galleria Office Ctr Southfield (48034) *(G-14847)*
Automotive Component Mfg (PA) 705 549-7406
36155 Mound Rd Sterling Heights (48310) *(G-15267)*
Automotive Electronic Spc 248 335-3229
2930 Turtle Pond Ct Bloomfield Hills (48302) *(G-1748)*
Automotive Exteriors LLC (HQ) 248 458-0702
2800 High Meadow Cir Auburn Hills (48326) *(G-788)*
Automotive Info Systems Inc 734 332-1970
315 E Eisenhower Pkwy # 211 Ann Arbor (48108) *(G-374)*
Automotive Lighting LLC (HQ) 248 418-3000
3900 Automation Ave Auburn Hills (48326) *(G-789)*
Automotive Lighting LLC 248 418-3000
5600 Bow Pointe Dr Clarkston (48346) *(G-2908)*
Automotive Lighting North Amer, Auburn Hills *Also called Automotive Lighting LLC (G-789)*
Automotive Manufacturing 517 566-8174
101 Main St Sunfield (48890) *(G-15645)*
Automotive Media LLC 248 537-8500
2020 Ring Rd Pontiac (48341) *(G-12806)*
Automotive Moulding, Sterling Heights *Also called Guardian Automotive Corp (G-15365)*
Automotive Operations, Auburn Hills *Also called Henniges Automotive N America (G-898)*
Automotive Plastics Recycling 810 767-3800
2945 Davison Rd Flint (48506) *(G-5381)*
Automotive Prototype Stamping 586 445-6792
17207 Millar Rd Clinton Township (48036) *(G-3060)*
Automotive Service Co 517 784-6131
603 E Washington Ave Jackson (49203) *(G-8385)*
Automotive Technology LLC 586 446-7000
6015 Center Dr Sterling Heights (48312) *(G-15268)*
Automotive Trim Technologies 734 947-0344
12400 Universal Dr Taylor (48180) *(G-15691)*
Automotive Tumbling Co Inc 313 925-7450
3125 Meldrum St Detroit (48207) *(G-3885)*
Automtion Mdlar Components Inc (PA) 248 922-4740
10301 Enterprise Dr Davisburg (48350) *(G-3625)*
Autoneum North America Inc (HQ) 248 848-0100
29293 Haggerty Rd Novi (48377) *(G-11836)*
Autoneum North America Inc 248 848-0100
38555 Hills Tech Dr Farmington Hills (48331) *(G-4936)*
Autorack Technologies Inc 517 437-4800
20 Superior St Hillsdale (49242) *(G-7516)*
Autosport Development LLC 734 675-1620
2331 Toledo St Trenton (48183) *(G-16152)*
Autosystems America Inc 734 582-2300
46600 Port St Plymouth (48170) *(G-12577)*
Autotech, Novi *Also called Comau LLC (G-11851)*
Autowares Inc 248 473-0928
23240 Industrial Park Dr Farmington Hills (48335) *(G-4937)*
Autumaire Fan Co., Clarklake *Also called Airmaster Fan Company (G-2894)*
Auvesy Inc 616 888-3770
146 Monroe Center St Nw # 1210 Grand Rapids (49503) *(G-6194)*
Auxier & Associates LLC 231 486-0641
1702 Barlow St Ste A Traverse City (49686) *(G-15901)*
Auxier & Associates LLC 231 933-7446
741 Woodmere Ave Traverse City (49686) *(G-15902)*
Avalon & Tahoe Mfg Inc 989 463-2112
903 Michigan Ave Alma (48801) *(G-236)*
Avalon Tools Inc 248 269-0001
1910 Barrett Dr Troy (48084) *(G-16230)*
Avanti Greeting Cards, Detroit *Also called Avanti Press Inc (G-3886)*
Avanti Press Inc (PA) 800 228-2684
155 W Congress St Ste 200 Detroit (48226) *(G-3886)*
Avanti Press Inc 313 961-0022
22701 Trolley Industrial Taylor (48180) *(G-15692)*
Avantis Inc 616 285-8000
5441 36th St Se Grand Rapids (49512) *(G-6195)*
Avanzado LLC 248 615-0538
25330 Interchange Ct Farmington Hills (48335) *(G-4938)*
Avasure Holdings Inc (PA) 616 301-0129
5801 Safety Dr Ne Belmont (49306) *(G-1456)*
Aven Inc 734 973-0099
4330 Varsity Dr Ann Arbor (48108) *(G-375)*
Aven Tools, Ann Arbor *Also called Aven Inc (G-375)*
Avery Color Studios Inc 906 346-3908
511 Avenue D Gwinn (49841) *(G-7216)*
Avflight Corporation (HQ) 734 663-6466
47 W Ellsworth Rd Ann Arbor (48108) *(G-376)*
AVI Inventory Services LLC (PA) 231 799-9000
620 E Ellis Rd Norton Shores (49441) *(G-11740)*
Avian Control, Sylvan Lake *Also called Avian Enterprises LLC (G-15671)*
Avian Control Technologies LLC 231 349-9050
6800 Mayfair Dr Stanwood (49346) *(G-15231)*
Avian Enterprises LLC (PA) 888 366-0709
2000 Pontiac Dr Sylvan Lake (48320) *(G-15671)*

A L P H A B E T I C

Avid Industries Inc 810 672-9100
4887 Ubly Rd Argyle (48410) *(G-713)*
Avidasports LLC 313 447-5670
20844 Harper Ave Harper Woods (48225) *(G-7299)*
Avidhrt Inc 517 214-9041
2721 Sophiea Pkwy Okemos (48864) *(G-12115)*
Aviv Global LLC 248 737-5777
32430 Northwestern Hwy Farmington Hills (48334) *(G-4939)*
Avko Eductl Res Foundation 810 686-9283
3084 Willard Rd Birch Run (48415) *(G-1663)*
Avl Michigan Holding Corp (HQ) 734 414-9600
47519 Halyard Dr Plymouth (48170) *(G-12578)*
Avl North Amer Corp Svcs Inc 734 414-9600
47603 Halyard Dr Plymouth (48170) *(G-12579)*
Avl Test Systems Inc 734 414-9600
47603 Halyard Dr Plymouth (48170) *(G-12580)*
Avocadough LLC 908 596-1437
494 Oldfield Dr Se Byron Center (49315) *(G-2178)*
Avomeen LLC 734 222-1090
4840 Venture Dr Ann Arbor (48108) *(G-377)*
Avomeen Analytical Services, Ann Arbor *Also called Avomeen LLC (G-377)*
Avon Automotive, Cadillac *Also called Akwel Usa Inc (G-2226)*
Avon Automotive Holdings, Cadillac *Also called Akwel Cadillac Usa Inc (G-2225)*
Avon Automotive Orizaba, Cadillac *Also called Akwel Cadillac Usa Inc (G-2224)*
Avon Automotive-Orizaba, Cadillac *Also called Akwel Cadillac Usa Inc (G-2223)*
Avon Broach & Prod Co LLC 248 650-8080
1089 John R Rd Rochester Hills (48307) *(G-13372)*
Avon Cabinets Atkins 248 237-1103
2596 Hessel Ave Rochester Hills (48307) *(G-13373)*
Avon Gear, Shelby Township *Also called Avon Machining LLC (G-14551)*
Avon Machining LLC 586 884-2200
11968 Investment Dr Shelby Township (48315) *(G-14551)*
Avon Machining Holdings Inc 586 884-2200
11968 Investment Dr Shelby Township (48315) *(G-14552)*
Avon Plastic Products Inc 248 852-1000
2890 Technology Dr Rochester Hills (48309) *(G-13374)*
Avon Protection Systems Inc (HQ) 231 779-6200
503 8th St Cadillac (49601) *(G-2230)*
Aw Carbide Fabricators Inc 586 294-1850
33891 Doreka Fraser (48026) *(G-5626)*
Aw Transmission Engrg USA Inc (HQ) 734 454-1710
14920 Keel St Plymouth (48170) *(G-12581)*
Award Cutter Company Inc 616 531-0430
5577 Crippen Ave Sw Grand Rapids (49548) *(G-6196)*
Awarenessideas.com, Farmington Hills *Also called Flexi Display Marketing Inc (G-5003)*
Awcco USA Incorporated 586 336-9135
171 Shafer Dr Romeo (48065) *(G-13624)*
Awcoa Inc 313 892-4100
17210 Gable St Detroit (48212) *(G-3887)*
Awd Associates Inc 248 922-9898
10560 Enterprise Dr Ste A Davisburg (48350) *(G-3626)*
Aweba Tool & Die Corp 478 296-2002
1004 E State St Hastings (49058) *(G-7401)*
Awrey Bakeries, Livonia *Also called Marie Minnie Bakers Inc (G-9823)*
Awtech USA, Plymouth *Also called Aw Transmission Engrg USA Inc (G-12581)*
Axalta Coating Systems LLC 586 846-4160
45000 River Ridge Dr # 200 Clinton Township (48038) *(G-3061)*
Axchem Inc 734 641-9842
38070 Van Born Rd Wayne (48184) *(G-17425)*
Axelson-Veet-Liberty Inds, Warren *Also called Veet Industries Inc (G-17281)*
Axiobionics 734 327-2946
6111 Jackson Rd Ste 200 Ann Arbor (48103) *(G-378)*
Axiom Business Book Awards, Traverse City *Also called Jenkins Group Inc (G-16010)*
Axis Digital Inc 616 698-9890
6532 Clay Ave Sw Grand Rapids (49548) *(G-6197)*
Axis Engineering Div, Dundee *Also called L & W Inc (G-4590)*
Axis Enterprises Inc 616 677-5281
15300 8th Ave Marne (49435) *(G-10504)*
Axis Machine & Tool Inc 616 738-2196
7217 W Olive Rd Holland (49424) *(G-7563)*
Axis Machining Inc 989 453-3943
7061 Hartley St Pigeon (48755) *(G-12486)*
Axis Mold Works Inc 616 866-2222
8005 Childsdale Ave Ne Rockford (49341) *(G-13558)*
Axis Tms Corp 248 509-2440
780 W Maple Rd Ste A Troy (48084) *(G-16231)*
Axle of Dearborn Inc (PA) 248 543-5995
2000 W 8 Mile Rd Ferndale (48220) *(G-5263)*
Axle of Dearborn Inc 313 581-3300
20446 W Warren Ave Detroit (48228) *(G-3888)*
Axletech Distribution Center, Troy *Also called Meritor Indus Intl Hldings LLC (G-16496)*
Axletech Intl Holdings Inc 248 658-7200
1400 Rochester Rd Troy (48083) *(G-16232)*
Axletech, LLC, Troy *Also called Meritor Indus Aftermarket LLC (G-16495)*
Axly Production Machining, Bad Axe *Also called Gemini Precision Machining Inc (G-1064)*
Axly Production Machining Inc 989 269-2444
700 E Soper Rd Bad Axe (48413) *(G-1057)*
Axly-Briney Sales, Bad Axe *Also called Axly Production Machining Inc (G-1057)*
Axonia Medical Inc 269 615-6632
4321 Roxbury Ln Kalamazoo (49008) *(G-8689)*
Axson Tech Us Inc 517 663-8191
1611 Hults Dr Eaton Rapids (48827) *(G-4718)*
Axsys Inc 248 926-8810
29627 West Tech Dr Wixom (48393) *(G-17769)*
Ayb, Clinton Township *Also called Amour Your Body LLC (G-3049)*
Ayotte Cstm Mscal Engrvngs LLC 734 595-1901
36688 Rolf St Westland (48186) *(G-17545)*
AZ Automotive, Roseville *Also called Sodecia Auto Detroit Corp (G-13871)*
AZ Automotive, Orion *Also called Sodecia Auto Detroit Corp (G-12190)*
Azko Manufacturing Inc 231 733-0888
560 E Broadway Ave Muskegon (49444) *(G-11273)*
Azko Pattern Mfg Inc 231 733-0888
560 E Broadway Ave Muskegon (49444) *(G-11274)*
Azon Elite Summaries, Southfield *Also called Next Level Media Inc (G-14991)*
Azon Usa Inc (PA) 269 385-5942
643 W Crosstown Pkwy Kalamazoo (49008) *(G-8690)*
Azon Usa Inc 269 385-5942
2204 Ravine Rd Kalamazoo (49004) *(G-8691)*
Aztec Azphalt Technology Inc 248 627-2120
12447 Kipp Rd Goodrich (48438) *(G-5951)*
Aztec Manufacturing Corp 734 942-7433
15378 Oakwood Dr Romulus (48174) *(G-13653)*
Aztec Producing Co Inc 269 792-0505
3312 12th St Wayland (49348) *(G-17398)*
Aztecnology LLC 734 857-2045
15677 Noecker Way Ste 100 Southgate (48195) *(G-15074)*
Azz On Fire LLC 248 470-3742
6055 Southfield Fwy Apt 2 Detroit (48228) *(G-3889)*
Azz On Fire Salsas and Spices, Detroit *Also called Azz On Fire LLC (G-3889)*
B & B Custom and Prod Wldg 517 524-7121
10391 Spring Arbor Rd Spring Arbor (49283) *(G-15120)*
B & B Electrical Inc 248 391-3800
2804 Orchard Lake Rd # 203 Keego Harbor (48320) *(G-8978)*
B & B Entps Prtg Cnvrting Inc 313 891-9840
17800 Filer St Detroit (48212) *(G-3890)*
B & B Heartwoods Inc 734 332-9525
5444 Whitmore Lake Rd Ann Arbor (48105) *(G-379)*
B & B Holdings Groesbeck LLC 586 554-7600
42450 R Mancini Dr Sterling Heights (48314) *(G-15269)*
B & B Mold & Engineering Inc 586 773-6664
25185 Easy St Warren (48089) *(G-16946)*
B & B Pretzels Inc 248 358-1655
19155 Addison Dr Southfield (48075) *(G-14848)*
B & B Production LLC 586 822-9960
10103 Kercheval St Detroit (48214) *(G-3891)*
B & D Cold Heading, Taylor *Also called B & D Thread Rolling Inc (G-15693)*
B & D Sales and Service, Plymouth *Also called Skyway Precision Inc (G-12757)*
B & D Thread Rolling Inc 734 728-7070
25000 Brest Taylor (48180) *(G-15693)*
B & G Custom Works Inc 269 686-9420
2830 113th Ave Allegan (49010) *(G-150)*
B & G Enterprises 231 348-2705
10400 Burnett Rd Charlevoix (49720) *(G-2607)*
B & G Products Inc 616 698-9050
3631 44th St Se Ste E Grand Rapids (49512) *(G-6198)*
B & H Cementing Services Inc 989 773-5975
5580 Venture Way Mount Pleasant (48858) *(G-11172)*
B & H Machine Sales, Detroit *Also called Forged Tubular Products Inc (G-4069)*
B & H Plastic Co Inc 586 727-7100
66725 S Forest Ave Richmond (48062) *(G-13260)*
B & H Tractor & Truck Inc 989 773-5975
5580 Venture Way Mount Pleasant (48858) *(G-11173)*
B & J Enmeling Inc A Mich Corp 313 365-6620
6827 E Davison St Detroit (48212) *(G-3892)*
B & J Tool Co 810 629-8577
11289 Quality Dr Fenton (48430) *(G-5184)*
B & J Tool Services Inc 810 629-8577
11289 Quality Way Dr Fenton (48430) *(G-5185)*
B & K Buffing Inc 734 941-2144
29040 Northline Rd Romulus (48174) *(G-13654)*
B & K Machine Products Inc 269 637-3001
100 Aylworth Ave South Haven (49090) *(G-14755)*
B & L Industries Inc 810 987-9121
2121 16th St Port Huron (48060) *(G-12896)*
B & L Pattern Company 269 982-0214
191 Hawthorne Ave Apt B Saint Joseph (49085) *(G-14301)*
B & L Plating Co Inc 586 778-9300
21353 Edom Ave Warren (48089) *(G-16947)*
B & M Bending & Forging Inc 586 731-3332
47601 Shelby Rd Shelby Township (48317) *(G-14553)*
B & M Imaging Inc 269 968-2403
1514 Columbia Ave W Battle Creek (49015) *(G-1148)*
B & M Machine & Tool Company 989 288-2934
7665 E M 71 Durand (48429) *(G-4605)*
B & M Sonics and Machine LLC 810 793-1236
4301 N Lapeer Rd Lapeer (48446) *(G-9441)*

ALPHABETIC SECTION

B & N Plastics Inc 586 758-0030
  8100 E 9 Mile Rd Warren (48089) *(G-16948)*
B & O Saws Inc 616 794-7297
  825 Reed St Belding (48809) *(G-1397)*
B & P Manufacturing, Cadillac *Also called Brooks & Perkins Inc* *(G-2234)*
B & R Gear Company Inc 517 787-8381
  2102 River St Jackson (49202) *(G-8386)*
B & R Manufacturing Division, Grandville *Also called Hadley Products Corporation* *(G-7043)*
B & S Manufacturing Inc 586 939-5130
  39159 Cadborough Dr Clinton Township (48038) *(G-3062)*
B & W Tool Co 734 485-2540
  1160 Watson St Ypsilanti (48198) *(G-18054)*
B & W Woodwork Inc 616 772-4577
  11362 James St Holland (49424) *(G-7564)*
B and D Thd Rolling Fas Indus 734 728-7070
  36820 Van Born Rd Wayne (48184) *(G-17426)*
B and L Metal Finishing LLC 269 767-2225
  755 Airway Dr Allegan (49010) *(G-151)*
B C & A Co 734 429-3129
  1270 Barnes Ct Saline (48176) *(G-14379)*
B C I Collet Inc 734 326-1222
  6125 E Executive Dr Westland (48185) *(G-17546)*
B C Manufacturing Inc 248 344-0101
  29431 Lorie Ln Wixom (48393) *(G-17770)*
B C P Printing 269 695-3877
  206 Days Ave Buchanan (49107) *(G-2109)*
B Company Inc 734 283-7080
  14773 Parkview St Riverview (48193) *(G-13291)*
B Erickson Manufacturing Ltd 810 765-1144
  6317 King Rd Marine City (48039) *(G-10470)*
B G Industries Inc 313 292-5355
  6835 Monroe Blvd Taylor (48180) *(G-15694)*
B H Awning & Tent, Benton Harbor *Also called Benton Harbor Awning & Tent* *(G-1485)*
B K Corporation 989 777-2111
  5675 Dixie Hwy Saginaw (48601) *(G-13997)*
B L Harroun and Son Inc (PA) 269 345-8657
  1018 Staples Ave Kalamazoo (49007) *(G-8692)*
B M F, Buchanan *Also called Buchanan Metal Forming Inc* *(G-2111)*
B M Industries Inc 810 658-0052
  130 Harsen Rd Lapeer (48446) *(G-9442)*
B Nektar LLC 313 999-5157
  1505b Jarvis St Ferndale (48220) *(G-5264)*
B Nektar Meadery, Ferndale *Also called B Nektar LLC* *(G-5264)*
B T I Industries 586 532-8411
  49820 Oakland Dr Shelby Township (48315) *(G-14554)*
B W and F Excavating, Kenockee *Also called Bobs Welding & Fabricating* *(G-8984)*
B W Manufacturing Inc 616 447-9076
  3706 Mill Creek Dr Ne Comstock Park (49321) *(G-3461)*
B&B Dumpsters, Remus *Also called Brian A Broomfield* *(G-13238)*
B&B T-Shirt Factory, Detroit *Also called V&R Enterprize* *(G-4420)*
B&P Littleford Day LLC 989 757-1300
  1000 Hess Ave Saginaw (48601) *(G-13998)*
B&P Littleford LLC (PA) 989 757-1300
  1000 Hess Ave Saginaw (48601) *(G-13999)*
B&P Process Eqp & Systems, Saginaw *Also called B&P Littleford LLC* *(G-13999)*
B-J Industries Inc 586 778-7200
  14440 Barber Ave Warren (48088) *(G-16949)*
B-Quick Instant Printing 616 243-6562
  3120 Division Ave S Grand Rapids (49548) *(G-6199)*
B.K. Vending, Saginaw *Also called Klopp Group LLC* *(G-14073)*
B/E Aerospace Inc 734 425-6200
  34073 Schoolcraft Rd Livonia (48150) *(G-9658)*
B4 Sports Inc 248 454-9700
  2055 Franklin Rd Bloomfield Hills (48302) *(G-1749)*
Baa Baa Zuzu 231 256-7176
  1006 S Sawmill Rd Lake Leelanau (49653) *(G-9100)*
Baade Fabricating & Engrg 517 639-4536
  210 S Ray Quincy Rd Quincy (49082) *(G-13089)*
Baby Pallet 248 210-3851
  1367 Forest Bay Dr Waterford (48328) *(G-17324)*
Bach Mobilities Inc 906 789-9490
  1617 N 28th St Escanaba (49829) *(G-4815)*
Bach Ornamental & Strl Stl Inc 517 694-4311
  4140 Keller Rd Holt (48842) *(G-7904)*
Bach Services & Mfg Co LLC 231 263-2777
  2777 Lynx Ln Kingsley (49649) *(G-9070)*
Back Machine Shop LLC 269 963-7061
  685 20th St N Springfield (49037) *(G-15187)*
Backdraft Brewing Company 734 722-7639
  35122 W Michigan Ave Wayne (48184) *(G-17427)*
Backos Engineering Co 734 513-0020
  17310 Farmington Rd Livonia (48152) *(G-9659)*
Backyard Products LLC (PA) 734 242-6900
  1000 Ternes Dr Monroe (48162) *(G-11015)*
Backyard Services LLC 734 242-6900
  1000 Ternes Dr Monroe (48162) *(G-11016)*
Bad Axe Family Vision Center 989 269-5393
  1266 Sand Beach Rd Bad Axe (48413) *(G-1058)*

Bader & Co 810 648-2404
  989 W Sanilac Rd Sandusky (48471) *(G-14429)*
Badger Pipe & Piling LLC 989 965-0126
  2090 E Mannsiding Rd Harrison (48625) *(G-7308)*
Bae Industries Inc (HQ) 586 754-3000
  26020 Sherwood Ave Warren (48091) *(G-16950)*
Bae Industries Inc 248 475-9600
  1426 Pacific Dr Auburn Hills (48326) *(G-790)*
Bae Systems Land Armaments LP 586 596-4123
  34201 Van Dyke Ave Sterling Heights (48312) *(G-15270)*
Bagel Brothers Cafe, Southfield *Also called Vivian Enterprises LLC* *(G-15063)*
Bagnall Enterprises Inc 734 457-0500
  1110 N Telegraph Rd Ste 8 Monroe (48162) *(G-11017)*
Bahama Souvenirs Inc (PA) 269 964-8275
  20260 North Ave Battle Creek (49017) *(G-1149)*
Bailer and De Shaw 989 684-3610
  204 S Old Kawkawlin Rd Kawkawlin (48631) *(G-8970)*
Bailey Roll Form Company Inc 586 777-4890
  13446 E 9 Mile Rd Warren (48089) *(G-16951)*
Bailey Sand & Gravel Co 517 750-4889
  6505 W Michigan Ave Jackson (49201) *(G-8387)*
Bainbridge Manufacturing Inc 616 447-7631
  1931 Will Ave Nw Ste 1 Grand Rapids (49504) *(G-6200)*
Baird Investments LLC 586 665-0154
  4140 S Lapeer Rd Orion (48359) *(G-12174)*
Baird Investments LLC (PA) 586 665-0154
  43333 Westview Dr Sterling Heights (48313) *(G-15271)*
Bairds Machine Shop 269 795-9524
  8300 W Garbow Rd Middleville (49333) *(G-10798)*
Bak Industries, Ann Arbor *Also called Laurmark Enterprises Inc* *(G-526)*
Bake N Cakes LP 517 337-2253
  3003 E Kalamazoo St Lansing (48912) *(G-9345)*
Bake Station Bakeries Mich Inc 248 352-9000
  26000 W 8 Mile Rd Southfield (48033) *(G-14849)*
Bakelite N Sumitomo Amer Inc (HQ) 248 313-7000
  46820 Magellan Dr Ste C Novi (48377) *(G-11837)*
Baker Inc 517 339-3835
  9804 Old M 78 Haslett (48840) *(G-7396)*
Baker & Baker 810 982-2763
  2835 W Water St Port Huron (48060) *(G-12897)*
Baker Atlas, Mount Pleasant *Also called Baker Hghes Olfld Oprtions LLC* *(G-11175)*
Baker Book House Company (PA) 616 676-9185
  6030 Fulton St E Ada (49301) *(G-10)*
Baker Book House Company 616 957-3110
  2768 East Paris Ave Se Grand Rapids (49546) *(G-6201)*
Baker Drive Train, Haslett *Also called Baker Inc* *(G-7396)*
Baker Enterprises Inc (HQ) 989 354-2189
  801 Johnson St Alpena (49707) *(G-280)*
Baker Fastening Systems Inc 616 669-7400
  5030 40th Ave Hudsonville (49426) *(G-8147)*
Baker Hghes Olfld Oprtions LLC 989 772-1600
  1950 Commercial Dr Mount Pleasant (48858) *(G-11174)*
Baker Hghes Olfld Oprtions LLC 989 773-7992
  2222 Enterprise Dr Mount Pleasant (48858) *(G-11175)*
Baker Hughes A GE Company LLC 989 506-2167
  2222 Enterprise Dr Mount Pleasant (48858) *(G-11176)*
Baker Hughes A GE Company LLC 989 732-2082
  526 Barnyard Gaylord (49735) *(G-5849)*
Baker Hughes Incorporat..., Mount Pleasant *Also called Baker Hughes A GE Company LLC* *(G-11176)*
Baker Industries Inc (HQ) 586 286-4900
  16936 Enterprise Dr Macomb (48044) *(G-10111)*
Baker Oil Tools, Mount Pleasant *Also called Baker Hghes Olfld Oprtions LLC* *(G-11174)*
Baker Perkins Inc 616 784-3111
  3223 Kraft Ave Se Grand Rapids (49512) *(G-6202)*
Baker Publishing Group, Ada *Also called Baker Book House Company* *(G-10)*
Baker Rd Seating & Restoration, Belding *Also called Baker Road Upholstery Inc* *(G-1398)*
Baker Road Upholstery Inc 616 794-3027
  1122 S Bridge St Belding (48809) *(G-1398)*
Bakers Rhapsody 269 767-1368
  144 S Front St Dowagiac (49047) *(G-4535)*
Bakery Equipment/Design, Wayland *Also called Buck-Spica Equipment Ltd* *(G-17402)*
Bakery Ingredient Mfg, Fenton *Also called Ezbake Technologies LLC* *(G-5206)*
Bakewell Company 269 459-8030
  2725 E Milham Ave Portage (49002) *(G-12983)*
BAKKER METAL FABRICATION, Coopersville *Also called Bakker Welding & Mechanics LLC* *(G-3548)*
Bakker Welding & Mechanics LLC (PA) 616 828-8664
  15031 84th Ave Coopersville (49404) *(G-3548)*
Balance Technology Inc (PA) 734 769-2100
  7035 Jomar Dr Whitmore Lake (48189) *(G-17689)*
Baldauf Enterprises Inc (PA) 989 686-0350
  1321 S Valley Center Dr Bay City (48706) *(G-1279)*
Baldauf Enterprises Inc 989 686-0350
  910 Harry S Truman Pkwy Bay City (48706) *(G-1280)*
Baldor Electric Motors, Sterling Heights *Also called ABB Motors and Mechanical Inc* *(G-15248)*

Baldwin Precision Inc 231 237-4515
5339 M 66 N Charlevoix (49720) ***(G-2608)***
Ball Hard Music Group LLC (PA) 734 636-0038
330 E Elm Ave Monroe (48162) ***(G-11018)***
Ballard Power Systems Corp 313 583-5980
15001 N Commerce Dr Dearborn (48120) ***(G-3680)***
Balogh 734 283-3972
14102 Jackson St Taylor (48180) ***(G-15695)***
Balogh Tag Inc 248 486-7343
3637 S Old Us Highway 23 Brighton (48114) ***(G-1888)***
Banacom Instant Signs 810 230-0233
4463 Miller Rd Flint (48507) ***(G-5382)***
Band-Ayd Systems Intl Inc 586 294-8851
355 E Whitcomb Ave Madison Heights (48071) ***(G-10200)***
Bandit Industries Inc 989 561-2270
6750 W Millbrook Rd Remus (49340) ***(G-13237)***
Banggameus 734 904-1916
2590 Cook Creek Dr Ann Arbor (48103) ***(G-380)***
Bangor Plastics Inc 269 427-7971
809 Washington St Bangor (49013) ***(G-1088)***
Banks Hardwoods Inc (PA) 269 483-2323
69937 M 103 White Pigeon (49099) ***(G-17645)***
Banks Hardwoods Florida, White Pigeon *Also called Banks Hardwoods Inc* ***(G-17645)***
Bannasch Welding Inc 517 482-2916
807 Lake Lansing Rd Ste 1 Lansing (48906) ***(G-9205)***
Banner Engineering & Sales Inc 989 755-0584
1840 N Michigan Ave Ste 1 Saginaw (48602) ***(G-14000)***
Banner Sign Specialties, Shelby Township *Also called Phillips Enterprises Inc* ***(G-14665)***
Banner The, Brown City *Also called Brown City Banner Inc* ***(G-2047)***
Bannergalaxycom LLC 231 941-8200
2322 Cass Rd Traverse City (49684) ***(G-15903)***
Banta Furniture Company 616 575-8180
3390 Broadmoor Ave Se A Grand Rapids (49512) ***(G-6203)***
Banta Management Resources, Grand Rapids *Also called Banta Furniture Company* ***(G-6203)***
Bar Processing Corporation 734 243-8937
550 Ternes Dr Monroe (48162) ***(G-11019)***
Bar Processing Corporation (HQ) 734 782-4454
26601 W Huron River Dr Flat Rock (48134) ***(G-5349)***
Bar Processing Corporation 734 782-4454
22534 Groesbeck Hwy Warren (48089) ***(G-16952)***
Baracoa Dips 616 643-3204
435 Ionia Ave Sw Grand Rapids (49503) ***(G-6204)***
Baraga County Concrete Company 906 353-6595
468 N Superior Ave Baraga (49908) ***(G-1097)***
Baraga Lumber Division, Baraga *Also called Besse Forest Products Inc* ***(G-1098)***
Barber Creek Sand & Gravel 616 675-7619
15666 Barber Creek Ave Kent City (49330) ***(G-8987)***
Barber Packaging Company 269 427-7995
300 Industrial Park Rd Bangor (49013) ***(G-1089)***
Barber Steel Foundry Corp 231 894-1830
2625 W Winston Rd Rothbury (49452) ***(G-13894)***
Barbron Corporation 586 716-3530
200 E Dresden St Kalkaska (49646) ***(G-8937)***
Barclay Pharmacy 248 852-4600
75 Barclay Cir Ste 114 Rochester Hills (48307) ***(G-13375)***
Bardon Inc 734 529-5876
6211 N Ann Arbor Rd Dundee (48131) ***(G-4576)***
Bargain Business Supplies Inc 810 750-0999
1542 N Leroy St Ste 5 Fenton (48430) ***(G-5186)***
Bargain Hunter, Sandusky *Also called J R C Inc* ***(G-14436)***
Bark River Concrete Pdts Co (PA) 906 466-9940
1397 Us Highway 2 41 Bark River (49807) ***(G-1118)***
Barker Manufacturing Co (PA) 269 965-2371
1125 Watkins Rd Battle Creek (49015) ***(G-1150)***
Barker Manufacturing Co 269 965-2371
781 Watkins Rd Battle Creek (49015) ***(G-1151)***
Barlows Gourmet Products Inc 248 245-0393
1815 Parker Rd Holly (48442) ***(G-7870)***
Barnes and Sons Logging, Copemish *Also called John Barnes* ***(G-3572)***
Barnes Group Inc 734 737-0958
15150 Cleat St Plymouth (48170) ***(G-12582)***
Barnes Group Inc 517 393-5110
5300 Aurelius Rd Lansing (48911) ***(G-9346)***
Barnes Group Inc 734 429-2022
44330 Plymouth Oaks Blvd Plymouth (48170) ***(G-12583)***
Barnes Group Inc 586 415-6677
33280 Groesbeck Hwy Fraser (48026) ***(G-5627)***
Barnes Industries Inc 248 541-2333
1161 E 11 Mile Rd Madison Heights (48071) ***(G-10201)***
Barnes International 586 978-2880
40848 Brightside Ct Sterling Heights (48310) ***(G-15272)***
Barneys Bakery 989 895-5466
421 S Van Buren St Bay City (48708) ***(G-1281)***
Baron Acquisition LLC (PA) 248 585-0444
999 E Mandoline Ave Madison Heights (48071) ***(G-10202)***
Baron Industries, Madison Heights *Also called Baron Acquisition LLC* ***(G-10202)***
Baron's Window Coverings, Lansing *Also called Barons Inc* ***(G-9347)***
Barons Inc 517 484-1366
325 S Washington Sq Lansing (48933) ***(G-9347)***
Barracuda Mfg, Wixom *Also called Rgm New Ventures Inc* ***(G-17885)***
Barrels of Yum, Whitehall *Also called Fretty Media LLC* ***(G-17667)***
Barrett Advertising, Saginaw *Also called Jordan Advertising Inc* ***(G-14067)***
Barrett Paving Materials Inc 248 362-0850
2040 Barrett Dr Troy (48084) ***(G-16233)***
Barrett Paving Materials Inc 734 985-9480
5800 Cherry Hill Rd Ypsilanti (48198) ***(G-18055)***
Barrett Signs 989 792-7446
321 Lyon St Saginaw (48602) ***(G-14001)***
Barrette Outdoor Living Inc 810 235-0400
3200 Rbert T Longway Blvd Flint (48506) ***(G-5383)***
Barron Cast, Oxford *Also called Barron Industries Inc* ***(G-12337)***
Barron Industries Inc (PA) 248 628-4300
215 Plexus Dr Oxford (48371) ***(G-12337)***
Barron Industries Inc 248 628-4300
215 Plexus Dr Oxford (48371) ***(G-12338)***
Barron Precision Instruments 810 695-2080
8170 Embury Rd Grand Blanc (48439) ***(G-5959)***
Barry Electric-Rovill Co 810 985-8960
1431 White St Port Huron (48060) ***(G-12898)***
Barrys Sign Company 810 234-9919
3501 Blackington Ave Flint (48503) ***(G-5384)***
Bars Products Inc (PA) 248 634-8278
10386 N Holly Rd Holly (48442) ***(G-7871)***
Bartlett Arborist Sup & Mfrs, Marlette *Also called Bartlett Manufacturing Co LLC* ***(G-10494)***
Bartlett Manufacturing Co LLC 989 635-8900
7876 S Van Dyke Rd Ste 10 Marlette (48453) ***(G-10494)***
Baryames Tux Shop Inc 517 349-6555
2421 W Grand River Ave Okemos (48864) ***(G-12116)***
Basc Manufacturing Inc 248 360-2272
4325 Martin Rd Commerce Township (48390) ***(G-3393)***
Basch Olovson Engineering Co 231 865-2027
3438 E Mount Garfield Rd Fruitport (49415) ***(G-5788)***
BASF 231 719-3019
1740 Whitehall Rd Muskegon (49445) ***(G-11275)***
BASF Construction Chem LLC 269 668-3371
23930 Concord Ave Mattawan (49071) ***(G-10662)***
BASF Corporation 810 639-0492
10406 Farrand Rd Montrose (48457) ***(G-11101)***
BASF Corporation 734 324-6963
40 James Desana Dr Wyandotte (48192) ***(G-17947)***
BASF Corporation 313 382-4250
1512 John A Papalas Dr Lincoln Park (48146) ***(G-9573)***
BASF Corporation 734 324-6000
1609 Biddle Ave Wyandotte (48192) ***(G-17948)***
BASF Corporation 734 324-6100
1609 Biddle Ave Wyandotte (48192) ***(G-17949)***
BASF Corporation 734 591-5560
13000 Levan Rd Livonia (48150) ***(G-9660)***
BASF Corporation 248 827-4670
26701 Telegraph Rd Southfield (48033) ***(G-14850)***
Basic Rubber and Plastics Co (PA) 248 360-7400
8700 Boulder Ct Walled Lake (48390) ***(G-16891)***
Basin Material Handling, Sturgis *Also called Vci Inc* ***(G-15639)***
Basis Machining LLC 517 542-3818
8998 Anderson Rd Litchfield (49252) ***(G-9600)***
Bastian Brothers & Company 989 239-5107
10240 Thor Dr Ste 1 Freeland (48623) ***(G-5752)***
Batson Printing Inc 269 926-6011
195 Michigan St Benton Harbor (49022) ***(G-1484)***
Batteries Plus, Birmingham *Also called M & M Irish Enterprises Inc* ***(G-1689)***
Batteries Plus, Roseville *Also called G & L Powerup Inc* ***(G-13806)***
Batteries Shack 586 580-2893
44478 Mound Rd Sterling Heights (48314) ***(G-15273)***
Battjes Boring Inc 616 363-1969
3999 3 Mile Rd Ne Grand Rapids (49525) ***(G-6205)***
Battle Creek Chamber Commerce, Battle Creek *Also called Silent Observer* ***(G-1248)***
Battle Creek Enquirer, Battle Creek *Also called Gannett Co Inc* ***(G-1191)***
Battle Creek Tent & Awning Co 269 964-1824
110 Taylor Ave Battle Creek (49037) ***(G-1152)***
Batts Group Ltd (PA) 616 956-3053
3855 Sparks Dr Se Ste 222 Grand Rapids (49546) ***(G-6206)***
Bauble Patch Inc 616 785-1100
5228 Alpine Ave Nw Ste A Comstock Park (49321) ***(G-3462)***
Bauer Precision Tool Co 586 758-7370
8670 E 9 Mile Rd Warren (48089) ***(G-16953)***
Bauer Products Inc 616 245-4540
702 Evergreen St Se Grand Rapids (49507) ***(G-6207)***
Bauer Sheet Metal & Fabg Inc (PA) 231 773-3244
1550 Evanston Ave Muskegon (49442) ***(G-11276)***
Bauer Sheet Metal & Fabg Inc 231 757-4993
703 W 1st St Scottville (49454) ***(G-14508)***
Bauer Soft Water Co 269 695-7900
1760 Mayflower Rd Niles (49120) ***(G-11596)***
Baum Sports Inc 231 922-2125
360 Knollwood Dr Traverse City (49686) ***(G-15904)***

Bauman Engraving & Signs Inc 906 774-9460
808 John Mcneil Dr Kingsford (49802) *(G-9054)*

Baumann Tool & Die 616 772-6768
232 E Roosevelt Ave Zeeland (49464) *(G-18116)*

Baumans Running & Walking Shop, Flint *Also called Baumans Running Center Inc* *(G-5385)*

Baumans Running Center Inc 810 238-5981
1473 W Hill Rd Flint (48507) *(G-5385)*

Bawden Industries Inc 734 721-6414
29909 Beverly Rd Romulus (48174) *(G-13655)*

Baxter Machine & Tool Co 517 782-2808
103 N Horton St Jackson (49202) *(G-8388)*

Bay Alphi Manufacturing Inc 517 849-9945
576 Beck St Jonesville (49250) *(G-8653)*

Bay Archery Sales Co 989 894-5800
2713 Center Ave Essexville (48732) *(G-4868)*

Bay Area Tool LLC 231 946-3500
466 Hughes Dr Traverse City (49696) *(G-15905)*

Bay Bread Co 231 922-8022
601 Randolph St Traverse City (49684) *(G-15906)*

Bay Carbon Inc 989 686-8090
800 Marquette St Ste 2 Bay City (48706) *(G-1282)*

Bay Cast Inc 989 892-0511
2611 Center Ave Bay City (48708) *(G-1283)*

Bay Cast Technologies Inc 989 892-9500
2611 Center Ave Bay City (48708) *(G-1284)*

Bay City Crane Inc 989 867-4292
3951 Allen Rd Turner (48765) *(G-16708)*

Bay City Div, Bay City *Also called Straits Corporation* *(G-1361)*

Bay City Division, Corunna *Also called Newcor Inc* *(G-3584)*

Bay City Fiberglass Inc 989 751-9622
1809 S Water St Bay City (48708) *(G-1285)*

Bay City Fiberglass Repair, Bay City *Also called Bay City Fiberglass Inc* *(G-1285)*

Bay City Fireworks Festival 989 892-2264
3296 E Fisher Rd Bay City (48706) *(G-1286)*

Bay City Times, Flint *Also called Herald Newspapers Company Inc* *(G-5447)*

Bay Composites Inc 989 891-9159
1801 Jarman Rd Essexville (48732) *(G-4869)*

Bay Corrugated Container Inc 734 243-5400
1655 W 7th St Monroe (48161) *(G-11020)*

Bay De Noc Lure Company 906 428-1133
810 Railway Ave Gladstone (49837) *(G-5906)*

Bay Electronics Inc 586 296-0900
20805 Kraft Blvd Roseville (48066) *(G-13776)*

Bay Geophysical, Inc., Traverse City *Also called Baygeo Inc* *(G-15909)*

Bay Home Medical and Rehab Inc (PA) 231 933-1200
5752 Stonebridge Dr Sw Grandville (49418) *(G-7021)*

Bay Machine Inc 906 250-0458
53167 Golf Course Rd Calumet (49913) *(G-2324)*

Bay Machine Tool Co Inc 989 894-2863
110 Woodside Ave Essexville (48732) *(G-4870)*

Bay Machining and Sales Inc 989 316-1801
4421 Ace Commercial Ct Bay City (48706) *(G-1287)*

Bay Manufacturing Corporation 989 358-7198
3750 Us Highway 23 N Alpena (49707) *(G-281)*

Bay Motor Products Inc 231 941-0411
3100 Cass Rd Ste 1 Traverse City (49684) *(G-15907)*

Bay Plastics Machinery Co LLC 989 671-9630
3494 N Euclid Ave Bay City (48706) *(G-1288)*

Bay Products Inc 586 296-7130
17800 15 Mile Rd Fraser (48026) *(G-5628)*

Bay Supply & Marketing Inc 231 943-3249
520 Us Highway 31 S Traverse City (49685) *(G-15908)*

Bay Tool Inc 989 894-2863
110 Woodside Ave Essexville (48732) *(G-4871)*

Bay United Motors Inc 989 684-3972
4353 Wilder Rd Bay City (48706) *(G-1289)*

Bay Valley Foods LLC 269 792-2277
652 W Elm Rd Wayland (49348) *(G-17399)*

Bay Wood Homes Inc 989 245-4156
1393 Eden Gardens Dr Fenton (48430) *(G-5187)*

Bay-Houston Towing Company 810 648-2210
875 E Sanilac Rd Sandusky (48471) *(G-14430)*

Bayer Cropscience LP 231 744-4711
1740 Whitehall Rd Muskegon (49445) *(G-11277)*

Baygeo Inc 231 941-7660
528 Hughes Dr Traverse City (49696) *(G-15909)*

Bayloff Stmped Pdts Dtroit Inc (PA) 734 397-9116
5910 Belleville Rd Van Buren Twp (48111) *(G-16747)*

Baylume Inc 877 881-3641
31255 Downing Pl Beverly Hills (48025) *(G-1614)*

Bayshore Kitchen and Bath Inc 586 725-8800
51180 Washington St New Baltimore (48047) *(G-11481)*

Bayside Printing Inc 231 352-4440
515 Main St Frankfort (49635) *(G-5598)*

Bayview Sign & Design 231 922-7759
618 W Eighth St Traverse City (49684) *(G-15910)*

Bazzi Tire & Wheels 313 846-8888
8001 Schaefer Hwy Detroit (48228) *(G-3893)*

BBC Communications Inc 616 399-0432
6463 Lakeshore Dr West Olive (49460) *(G-17531)*

Bbcm Inc 248 410-2528
1015 Golf Dr Bloomfield Hills (48302) *(G-1750)*

Bbg North America Ltd Partnr 248 572-6550
2371 Xcelsior Dr Oxford (48371) *(G-12339)*

Bbi Group, Lake Orion *Also called Complete Auto-Mation Inc* *(G-9131)*

Bbp Investment Holdings LLC (PA) 231 725-4966
525 W Laketon Ave Muskegon (49441) *(G-11278)*

Bcc Distribution Inc 734 737-9300
7529 Baron Dr Canton (48187) *(G-2350)*

BCI Group Inc 248 925-2000
1717 Stutz Dr Troy (48084) *(G-16234)*

Bcs Automotive Interface Solut 734 855-3297
12000 Tech Center Dr Livonia (48150) *(G-9661)*

Bcs Creative LLC 248 917-1660
10012 Old Farm Trl Davisburg (48350) *(G-3627)*

BCT-2017 Inc 231 832-3114
710 E Church Ave Reed City (49677) *(G-13210)*

BCT-2017 Inc (PA) 231 832-3114
710 E Church Ave Reed City (49677) *(G-13211)*

Bd Classic Sewing 231 825-2628
1890 E Stoney Corners Rd Mc Bain (49657) *(G-10677)*

Bd Diagnostic Systems 313 442-8800
920 Henry St Detroit (48201) *(G-3894)*

Bdk Group Northern Mich Inc 574 875-5183
6795 Us Highway 31 N Charlevoix (49720) *(G-2609)*

BDS Company Inc 517 279-2135
491 W Garfield Ave Coldwater (49036) *(G-3291)*

Beacom Enterprises Inc 906 647-3831
6671 E Rockview Rd Pickford (49774) *(G-12481)*

Beacom's Chipping & Logging, Pickford *Also called Beacom Enterprises Inc* *(G-12481)*

Beacon Marine Sales & Service 586 465-2539
36400 Jefferson Ave Harrison Township (48045) *(G-7323)*

Beacon Park Finishing LLC 248 318-4286
15765 Sturgeon St Roseville (48066) *(G-13777)*

Bead Gallery 734 663-6800
311 E Liberty St Ann Arbor (48104) *(G-381)*

Beaden Screen Inc 810 679-3119
305 Melvin St Croswell (48422) *(G-3595)*

BEAM Industries Inc 989 799-4044
3521 State St Saginaw (48602) *(G-14002)*

Bean Counter Inc 906 523-5027
25963 Cedar St Calumet (49913) *(G-2325)*

Beano's On Site Machining, Houghton Lake *Also called BOS Field Machining Inc* *(G-7987)*

Bear Creek Ballistics Co 269 806-2020
4199 D Dr S East Leroy (49051) *(G-4684)*

Bear Creek Logging 269 317-7475
123 Court St Ceresco (49033) *(G-2601)*

Bear Cub Holdings Inc 231 242-1152
8761 M 119 Harbor Springs (49740) *(G-7274)*

Bear Factory LLC 248 437-4930
46968 Liberty Dr Wixom (48393) *(G-17771)*

Bear Packaging and Supply 989 772-2268
4265 Corporate Dr Mount Pleasant (48858) *(G-11177)*

Bear Truss & Components, Saint Louis *Also called Ken Luneack Construction Inc* *(G-14365)*

Bearcub Outfitters LLC 231 439-9500
321 E Lake St Unit 1 Petoskey (49770) *(G-12441)*

Beard Balm LLC 313 451-3653
1951 Temple St Detroit (48216) *(G-3895)*

Beardslee Investments Inc 810 748-9951
2256 N Channel Dr Harsens Island (48028) *(G-7368)*

Bearing Division, Plymouth *Also called Jtekt North America Corp* *(G-12660)*

Bearing Holdings LLC (HQ) 313 758-2000
1 Dauch Dr Detroit (48211) *(G-3896)*

Beattie Spring & Welding Svc 810 239-9151
2840 Rbert T Longway Blvd Flint (48506) *(G-5386)*

Beauty Spot, Detroit *Also called Kims Mart Inc* *(G-4178)*

Beaver Aerospace & Defense Inc (HQ) 734 853-5003
11850 Mayfield St Livonia (48150) *(G-9662)*

Beaver Creek Wood Products LLC 920 680-9663
993 26th St Menominee (49858) *(G-10725)*

Beaver Log Homes Inc 231 258-5020
850 S Cedar St Kalkaska (49646) *(G-8938)*

Beaver Stair Company 248 628-0441
549 E Lakeville Rd Oxford (48371) *(G-12340)*

Becharas Bros Coffee Co 313 869-4700
14501 Hamilton Ave Detroit (48203) *(G-3897)*

Bechtel Sand & Gravel 810 346-2041
5278 Churchill Rd Brown City (48416) *(G-2046)*

Beck & Boys Custom Apparel 734 458-4015
33650 5 Mile Rd Livonia (48154) *(G-9663)*

Beck Industries Inc 586 790-4060
24454 Sorrentino Ct Clinton Township (48035) *(G-3063)*

Beck Mobile Concrete LLC 517 655-4996
2303 E Grand River Rd Williamston (48895) *(G-17726)*

Beckan Industries Inc 269 381-6984
2700 N Pitcher St Kalamazoo (49004) *(G-8693)*

Becker & Scrivens Con Pdts Inc 517 437-4250
3340 Beck Rd Hillsdale (49242) *(G-7517)*

Becker Oregon Inc 248 588-7480
635 Executive Dr Troy (48083) *(G-16235)*

Becker Orthopedic Appliance Co (PA) 248 588-7480
635 Executive Dr Troy (48083) ***(G-16236)***
Becker Robotic Equipment Corp 470 249-7880
260 Engelwood Dr Ste E Orion (48359) ***(G-12175)***
Beckert & Hiester Inc (PA) 989 793-2420
2025 Carman Dr Saginaw (48602) ***(G-14003)***
Beckman Brothers Inc 231 861-2031
3455 W Baker Rd Shelby (49455) ***(G-14523)***
Beckman Production Svcs Inc (HQ) 231 258-9524
3786 Beebe Rd Kalkaska (49646) ***(G-8939)***
Beckman Production Svcs Inc 989 539-7126
4400 N Clare Ave Harrison (48625) ***(G-7309)***
Beckman Production Svcs Inc 231 885-1665
23862 13 Mile Rd Mesick (49668) ***(G-10766)***
Beckman Production Svcs Inc 989 732-9341
M 32 E Gaylord (49735) ***(G-5850)***
Becktold Enterprises Inc 269 349-3656
2101 Palmer Ave Kalamazoo (49001) ***(G-8694)***
Becmar Corp 616 675-7479
585 Canada Rd Bailey (49303) ***(G-1077)***
Becton Dickinson and Company 313 442-8700
920 Henry St Detroit (48201) ***(G-3898)***
Becton Dcknson Dagnstc Systems, Detroit *Also called Becton Dickinson and Company* ***(G-3898)***
Bedford Machinery Inc 734 848-4980
9899 Telegraph Rd Erie (48133) ***(G-4801)***
Bedford Press, Lambertville *Also called Temperance Printing* ***(G-9186)***
Bednarsh Mrris Jwly Design Mfg 248 671-0087
6600 Telegraph Rd Bloomfield (48301) ***(G-1732)***
Bee Dazzled Candle Works 231 882-7765
6289 River Rd Benzonia (49616) ***(G-1573)***
Bee Line Apiaries & Woodenware, Mendon *Also called Jonathan Showalter* ***(G-10714)***
Beebe Fuel Systems Inc 248 437-3322
6351 Wilderness Dr South Lyon (48178) ***(G-14786)***
Beech & Rich Inc 269 968-8012
525 20th St N Springfield (49037) ***(G-15188)***
Beechbed Mix 616 263-7422
120 James St Holland (49424) ***(G-7565)***
Beechcraft Products Inc 989 288-2606
1100 N Saginaw St Durand (48429) ***(G-4606)***
Beechem Labs, Shelby *Also called Kelley Laboratories Inc* ***(G-14528)***
Beef Jerky Unlimited, Dundee *Also called Heinzerling Enterprises Inc* ***(G-4586)***
Beem Fence, Lake City *Also called Mark Beem* ***(G-9092)***
Beet LLC 248 432-0052
45207 Helm St Plymouth (48170) ***(G-12584)***
Behavioral Health, Holland *Also called Holland Community Hosp Aux Inc* ***(G-7670)***
Behco Inc 586 755-0200
1666 E Lincoln Ave Madison Heights (48071) ***(G-10203)***
Behco Inc 248 478-6336
32613 Folsom Rd Farmington Hills (48336) ***(G-4940)***
Behind Shutter LLC 248 467-7237
7070 Anna St Grand Blanc (48439) ***(G-5960)***
Behr Climate Systems, Troy *Also called Mahle Behr Troy Inc* ***(G-16481)***
Behrmann Printing Company Inc 248 799-7771
21063 Bridge St Southfield (48033) ***(G-14851)***
BEI International LLC 616 204-8274
10753 Macatawa Dr Holland (49424) ***(G-7566)***
Beirut Bakery Inc 313 533-4422
25706 Schoolcraft Redford (48239) ***(G-13147)***
Beishlag Welding LLC 231 881-5023
3935 Buell Rd Elmira (49730) ***(G-4790)***
Bektrom Foods Inc 734 241-3796
15610 S Telegraph Rd Monroe (48161) ***(G-11021)***
Bektrom Foods Inc 734 241-3711
1010 Detroit Ave Monroe (48162) ***(G-11022)***
Bekum America Corporation 517 655-4331
1140 W Grand River Ave Williamston (48895) ***(G-17727)***
Bel Lago, Cedar *Also called Weathervane Vinyards Inc* ***(G-2543)***
Bel-Kur Inc 734 847-0651
7297 Express Rd Temperance (48182) ***(G-15823)***
Belanger Inc 248 349-7010
1001 Doheny Dr Northville (48167) ***(G-11678)***
Belanger Abrasives Inc 248 735-8900
19414 Gerald St Northville (48167) ***(G-11679)***
Belanger Industrial Products, Northville *Also called Belanger Abrasives Inc* ***(G-11679)***
Belash Inc 248 379-4444
2111 N Wixom Rd Wixom (48393) ***(G-17772)***
Belco Industries Inc 616 794-0410
9138 W Belding Rd Belding (48809) ***(G-1399)***
Belco Industries Inc (PA) 616 794-0410
9138 W Belding Rd Belding (48809) ***(G-1400)***
Belding Quicklube Plus 616 794-9548
9299 W Belding Rd Belding (48809) ***(G-1401)***
Belding Tank Technologies, Belding *Also called D & R Fabrication Inc* ***(G-1408)***
Belding Tool Acquisition LLC (PA) 586 816-4450
1114 S Bridge St Belding (48809) ***(G-1402)***
Belding Tool Acquisition LLC 616 794-0100
1114 S Bridge St Belding (48809) ***(G-1403)***
Belding Tool and Machine, Belding *Also called Belding Tool Acquisition LLC* ***(G-1402)***
Belding Tool and Machine, Belding *Also called Belding Tool Acquisition LLC* ***(G-1403)***
Belding Tool and Machine, Belding *Also called Btm National Holdings LLC* ***(G-1404)***
Belgian Screw Machine Pdts Inc 517 524-8825
600 Homer Rd Concord (49237) ***(G-3523)***
Beljan Ltd Inc 734 426-3503
4635 Mcguiness Rd Dexter (48130) ***(G-4476)***
Bell and Howell LLC 734 421-1727
12794 Currie Ct Livonia (48150) ***(G-9664)***
Bell Engineering Inc 989 753-3127
735 S Outer Dr Saginaw (48601) ***(G-14004)***
Bell Engineering LLC 989 753-3127
735 S Outer Dr Saginaw (48601) ***(G-14005)***
Bell Fork Lift Inc 313 841-1220
13700 Mellon St Detroit (48217) ***(G-3899)***
Bell Forklifts 586 469-7979
4660 Centaur Ave Clinton Township (48035) ***(G-3064)***
Bell Induction Heating Inc 734 697-0133
41241 Edison Lake Rd Van Buren Twp (48111) ***(G-16748)***
Bell Packaging Corp 616 452-2111
2000 Beverly Ave Sw Grand Rapids (49519) ***(G-6208)***
Bella Sposa Bridal & Prom 616 364-0777
4972 Plainfield Ave Ne Grand Rapids (49525) ***(G-6209)***
Bellaire Log Homes Indus Hm 231 533-6669
6633 Bellaire Hwy Bellaire (49615) ***(G-1435)***
Belle Feeds 269 628-1231
34026 M 40 Paw Paw (49079) ***(G-12397)***
Belle Isle Awning Co Inc 586 294-6050
13701 E 9 Mile Rd Warren (48089) ***(G-16954)***
Belleville Area Independent 734 699-9020
152 Main St Ste 9 Belleville (48111) ***(G-1441)***
Bellevue Proc Met Prep Inc 313 921-1931
5143 Bellevue St Detroit (48211) ***(G-3900)***
Bellevue Processing, Chesterfield *Also called Pfg Enterprises Inc* ***(G-2816)***
Bellinger Packing 989 838-2274
1557 E Wilson Rd Ashley (48806) ***(G-726)***
Bells Brewery Inc 269 382-1402
355 E Kalamazoo Ave Kalamazoo (49007) ***(G-8695)***
Bells Brewery Inc (PA) 269 382-2338
8690 Krum Ave Galesburg (49053) ***(G-5806)***
Bells Brewery Inc 906 233-5000
3525 Airport Rd Escanaba (49829) ***(G-4816)***
Belmont Engineered Plas LLC 616 785-6279
5801 Safety Dr Ne Belmont (49306) ***(G-1457)***
Belmont Equipment Company, Madison Heights *Also called Cleary Developments Inc* ***(G-10210)***
Belmont Plastics Solutions LLC 616 340-3147
8211 Graphic Dr Ne Belmont (49306) ***(G-1458)***
Beltone Skoric Hearng Aid Cntr 906 379-0606
240 W Portage Ave Sault Sainte Marie (49783) ***(G-14461)***
Beltone Skoric Hearng Aid Cntr 906 553-4660
3600 Ludington St Escanaba (49829) ***(G-4817)***
Belts & Ties By Mary Boggs, Shelby Township *Also called Mary Boggs Baggs* ***(G-14634)***
Belwith Products LLC 616 247-4000
3100 Broadway Ave Sw Grandville (49418) ***(G-7022)***
Ben Tek, Reed City *Also called BCT-2017 Inc* ***(G-13210)***
Bench Works, Clinton Township *Also called Benchwork Inc* ***(G-3065)***
Benchmark Coating Systems LLC 517 782-4061
2075 W Stadium Blvd Ann Arbor (48106) ***(G-382)***
Benchwork Inc 586 464-6699
34100 Kelly Rd Clinton Township (48035) ***(G-3065)***
Benco Manufacturing, Troy *Also called Dieomatic Incorporated* ***(G-16319)***
Benecor Inc 248 437-4437
400 S Fenway Dr Fenton (48430) ***(G-5188)***
Benesh Corporation (PA) 734 244-4143
1910 N Telegraph Rd Monroe (48162) ***(G-11023)***
Benjamin Franklin Plumbing, Buchanan *Also called Precision Plumbing - T* ***(G-2125)***
Benjamin Moore Authorized Ret, Muskegon *Also called Port City Paints Mfg Inc* ***(G-11402)***
Benjamin Press 269 964-7562
380 Van Buren St W Battle Creek (49037) ***(G-1153)***
Benlee Inc (PA) 586 791-1830
30383 Ecorse Rd Romulus (48174) ***(G-13656)***
Benmar Communications LLC 313 593-0690
1 Parklane Blvd Ste 1105e Dearborn (48126) ***(G-3681)***
Benmark Advertising, Flint *Also called Barrys Sign Company* ***(G-5384)***
Benmill LLC 616 243-7555
3522 Lousma Dr Se Grand Rapids (49548) ***(G-6210)***
Bennett Commercial Pump Co 231 798-1310
1218 E Pontaluna Rd Ste A Norton Shores (49456) ***(G-11808)***
Bennett Funeral Coaches Inc 616 538-8100
584 76th St Sw B Byron Center (49315) ***(G-2179)***
Bennett Pump Company, Norton Shores *Also called Bpc Acquisition Company* ***(G-11809)***
Bennett Sawmill 231 734-5733
4161 90th Ave Evart (49631) ***(G-4879)***
Bennett Steel LLC 616 401-5271
1239 Randolph Ave Sw Grand Rapids (49507) ***(G-6211)***
Bennett Wood Specialties Inc 616 772-6683
109 N Carlton St Zeeland (49464) ***(G-18117)***

Benny Gage Inc 734 455-3080
4875 Product Dr Ste A Wixom (48393) *(G-17773)*
Benson Distribution Inc 269 344-5529
5792 Stoney Brook Rd Kalamazoo (49009) *(G-8696)*
Bentek, Reed City *Also called BCT-2017 Inc (G-13211)*
Benteler Aluminium Systems 616 396-6591
533 Ottawa Ave Holland (49423) *(G-7567)*
Benteler Aluminium Systems (HQ) 616 396-6591
533 Ottawa Ave Holland (49423) *(G-7568)*
Benteler Automotive Corp 616 247-3936
2650 N Opdyke Rd Ste B Auburn Hills (48326) *(G-791)*
Benteler Automotive Corp 616 245-4607
3721 Hagen Dr Se Grand Rapids (49548) *(G-6212)*
Benteler Automotive Corp (HQ) 248 364-7190
2650 N Opdyke Rd Ste B Auburn Hills (48326) *(G-792)*
Benteler Automotive Corp 269 665-4261
9000 E Michigan Ave Galesburg (49053) *(G-5807)*
Benteler Defense Corp 248 377-9999
2650 N Opdyke Rd Ste B Auburn Hills (48326) *(G-793)*
Benteler Steel & Tube, Auburn Hills *Also called Benteler Automotive Corp (G-791)*
Bentler Industries Inc 269 665-4261
9000 E Michigan Ave Galesburg (49053) *(G-5808)*
Bentley Industries 810 625-0400
1105 University Ave Flint (48504) *(G-5387)*
Bently Sand & Gravel 810 629-6172
9220 Bennett Lake Rd Fenton (48430) *(G-5189)*
Benton Harbor Awning & Tent 800 272-2187
2275 M 139 Benton Harbor (49022) *(G-1485)*
Benton Harbor Heat Treating, Benton Harbor *Also called Benton Harbor LLC (G-1486)*
Benton Harbor LLC 269 925-6581
800 S Fair Ave Benton Harbor (49022) *(G-1486)*
Bentzer Enterprises 269 663-2289
26601 May St Edwardsburg (49112) *(G-4758)*
Bentzer Incorporated 269 663-3649
69953 Section St Edwardsburg (49112) *(G-4759)*
Benzie County Record-Patriot, Frankfort *Also called Conine Publishing Inc (G-5600)*
Benzie Manufacturing LLC 231 631-0498
401 Parkview Ln Frankfort (49635) *(G-5599)*
Berchtold Corporation 269 329-2001
1651 W Centre Ave Portage (49024) *(G-12984)*
Berci Printing Services Inc 248 350-0206
22400 Telegraph Rd Ste B Southfield (48033) *(G-14852)*
Berg Tool Inc 586 646-7100
56253 Precision Dr Chesterfield (48051) *(G-2745)*
Bergamot Inc 586 372-7109
110 Lena Hill Dr Lakeville (48367) *(G-9177)*
Bergen R C Helicopters LLC 269 445-2060
16672 M 60 Vandalia (49095) *(G-16799)*
Berger LLC 734 414-0402
44160 Plymouth Oaks Blvd Plymouth (48170) *(G-12585)*
Berghof Group North Amer Inc 313 720-6884
1500 W Big Beavr Rd 2nd Troy (48084) *(G-16237)*
Berkley Frosty Freeze Inc 248 336-2634
2415 Coolidge Hwy Berkley (48072) *(G-1581)*
Berkley Industries Inc (PA) 989 656-2171
9938 Pigeon Rd Bay Port (48720) *(G-1372)*
Berkley Pharmacy LLC 586 573-8300
28577 Schoenherr Rd Warren (48088) *(G-16955)*
Berkley Screw Machine Pdts Inc 248 853-0044
2100 Royce Haley Dr Rochester Hills (48309) *(G-13376)*
Berkshire & Associates Inc 734 719-1822
5840 N Canton Center Rd Canton (48187) *(G-2351)*
Berlin Holdings LLC 517 523-2444
4445 S Pittsford Rd Pittsford (49271) *(G-12515)*
Berline Group Inc 248 203-0492
423 N Main St Ste 300 Royal Oak (48067) *(G-13907)*
Bermar Associates Inc 248 589-2460
433 Minnesota Dr Troy (48083) *(G-16238)*
Bermont Gage & Automation Inc 586 296-1103
34500 Klein Rd Fraser (48026) *(G-5629)*
Bermont Technologies, Fraser *Also called Bermont Gage & Automation Inc (G-5629)*
Bernal LLC 248 299-3600
2960 Technology Dr Rochester Hills (48309) *(G-13377)*
Bernal Products, Bruce Twp *Also called Ronald R Wellington (G-2097)*
Berne Enterprises Inc 989 453-3235
7190 Berne Rd Pigeon (48755) *(G-12487)*
Berner Scientific Inc 248 253-0077
7275 Joy Rd Ste C Dexter (48130) *(G-4477)*
Bernier Cast Metals Inc 989 754-7571
2626 Hess Ave Saginaw (48601) *(G-14006)*
Bernthal Packing Inc 989 652-2648
9378 Junction Rd Frankenmuth (48734) *(G-5583)*
Berrien County Printing, Buchanan *Also called B C P Printing (G-2109)*
Berrien Custom Cab & Design, Berrien Springs *Also called Berrien Custom Cabinet Inc (G-1593)*
Berrien Custom Cabinet Inc 269 473-3404
4231 E Snow Rd Berrien Springs (49103) *(G-1593)*
Berrien Metal Products Inc 269 695-5000
460 Post Rd Ste A Buchanan (49107) *(G-2110)*
Berry & Associates Inc 734 426-3787
2434 Bishop Cir E Dexter (48130) *(G-4478)*
Berry & Sons-Rababeh 313 259-6925
2496 Orleans St Detroit (48207) *(G-3901)*
Berry Global Inc 269 435-2425
700 Centreville St Constantine (49042) *(G-3532)*
Berry Global Inc 616 772-4635
200 N Franklin St Zeeland (49464) *(G-18118)*
Bert Hazekamp & Son Inc 231 773-8302
3933 S Brooks Rd Muskegon (49444) *(G-11279)*
Berthiaume Slaughter House 989 879-4921
719 Jane St Pinconning (48650) *(G-12506)*
Bertoldi Oil Service Inc 906 774-1707
N2395 Cemetary Ln Iron Mountain (49801) *(G-8276)*
Bespro Pattern Inc 586 268-6970
31301 Mally Dr Madison Heights (48071) *(G-10204)*
Besse Forest Products Inc 906 353-7193
16522 Westland Dr Baraga (49908) *(G-1098)*
Bessenberg Bindery Corporation 734 996-9696
215 N 5th Ave Ann Arbor (48104) *(G-383)*
Besser Company (PA) 989 354-4111
801 Johnson St Alpena (49707) *(G-282)*
Besser Company USA 616 399-5215
201 W Washington Ave # 202 Zeeland (49464) *(G-18119)*
Besser Lithibar, Zeeland *Also called Besser Company USA (G-18119)*
Bessey Tool & Die Inc 616 887-8820
617 10 Mile Rd Nw Sparta (49345) *(G-15088)*
Bessinger Pickle Co Inc 989 876-8008
537 N Court St Au Gres (48703) *(G-743)*
Best Alloys, Warren *Also called Best Block Company (G-16956)*
Best Binding LLC 734 459-7785
41230 Joy Rd Plymouth (48170) *(G-12586)*
Best Block Company (PA) 586 772-7000
22001 Groesbeck Hwy Warren (48089) *(G-16956)*
Best Buy Bones Inc 810 631-6971
7426 N Dort Hwy Mount Morris (48458) *(G-11158)*
Best Concrete & Supply Inc 734 283-7055
17200 Dix Toledo Hwy Brownstown (48193) *(G-2059)*
Best Impressions 313 389-1202
1412 Dix Hwy Lincoln Park (48146) *(G-9574)*
Best Industrial Group Inc 586 826-8800
7256 Murthum Ave Warren (48092) *(G-16957)*
Best Metal Products Co Inc 616 942-7141
3570 Raleigh Dr Se Grand Rapids (49512) *(G-6213)*
Best Mfg Tooling Solutions Ltd 616 877-0504
1158 Morren Ct Wayland (49348) *(G-17400)*
Best Products Inc 313 538-7414
14208 Sarasota Redford (48239) *(G-13148)*
Best Rate Dumpster Rental Inc 248 391-5956
256 Marrin Ortonville (48462) *(G-12194)*
Best Self Storage 810 227-7050
7286 Grand River Rd Brighton (48114) *(G-1889)*
Best Tackle Manufacturing Co, Rockford *Also called Northport Manufacturing Inc (G-13584)*
Best Tool & Engineering Co 586 792-4119
34730 Nova Dr Clinton Township (48035) *(G-3066)*
Bestway Building Supply Co 810 732-6280
3021 S Dye Rd Flint (48507) *(G-5388)*
Beswick Corporation 248 589-0562
2591 Elliott Dr Troy (48083) *(G-16239)*
Better Life Cleaning Products, Grand Rapids *Also called Bissell Better Life LLC (G-6224)*
Better Made Potato Chips, Detroit *Also called Better Made Snack Foods Inc (G-3902)*
Better Made Snack Foods Inc 313 925-4774
10148 Gratiot Ave Detroit (48213) *(G-3902)*
Better-Bilt Cabinet Co 586 469-0080
99 Cass Ave Mount Clemens (48043) *(G-11125)*
Better-Form, Ferndale *Also called David Epstein Inc (G-5270)*
Between The Lines, Livonia *Also called Pride Source Corporation (G-9898)*
Betz Castings, Grand Rapids *Also called Betz Industries Inc (G-6214)*
Betz Contracting and Machining, Climax *Also called Betz Contracting Inc (G-3012)*
Betz Contracting Inc 269 746-3320
320 N Main St Climax (49034) *(G-3012)*
Betz Industries Inc 616 453-4429
2121 Bristol Ave Nw Grand Rapids (49504) *(G-6214)*
Beverage Solution Technolgies 616 252-1700
955 Ken O Sha Ind Pk Dr S Grand Rapids (49508) *(G-6215)*
Beverlin Manufacturing, Grand Rapids *Also called Specialty Tube LLC (G-6882)*
Beyond Embroidery 616 726-7000
2013 E Wyndham Hill Dr Ne # 102 Grand Rapids (49505) *(G-6216)*
Bg Defense Co LLC 616 710-0609
2291 Oak Industrial Dr Ne Grand Rapids (49505) *(G-6217)*
Bgt Aerospace LLC 989 225-5812
4412 Ace Commercial Ct Bay City (48706) *(G-1290)*
Bh Polymers, Saint Clair *Also called Pier One Polymers Incorporated (G-14231)*
Bible Doctrines Publications, Comstock Park *Also called Bible Doctrines To Live By Inc (G-3463)*
Bible Doctrines To Live By Inc 616 453-0493
895 W River Center Dr Ne Comstock Park (49321) *(G-3463)*

A L P H A B E T I C

(PA)=Parent Co (HQ)=Headquarters (DH)=Div Headquarters
2020 Harris Michigan Industrial Directory
907

Bichler Gravel & Concrete Co 906 786-0343
6851 County 426 M.5 Rd Escanaba (49829) ***(G-4818)***
Bico Michigan Inc (HQ) 616 453-2400
99 Steele St Nw Grand Rapids (49534) ***(G-6218)***
Bico Steel Service Centers, Grand Rapids *Also called Bico Michigan Inc* ***(G-6218)***
Bielomatik Inc 248 446-9910
55397 Lyon Industrial Dr New Hudson (48165) ***(G-11531)***
Bielomatik USA Inc 248 446-9910
55397 Lyon Industrial Dr New Hudson (48165) ***(G-11532)***
Bier Barrel Distillery LLC 616 633-8601
5295 West River Dr Ne # 200 Comstock Park (49321) ***(G-3464)***
Biere De Mac Brew Works LLC 616 862-8018
14277 N Mackinaw Hwy Mackinaw City (49701) ***(G-10098)***
Bieri Digital Hearing Center, Saginaw *Also called Bieri Hearing Instruments Inc* ***(G-14007)***
Bieri Hearing Instruments Inc (PA) 989 793-2701
2650 Mccarty Rd Saginaw (48603) ***(G-14007)***
Biewer Forest Management LLC 231 825-2855
6400 W Gerwoude Dr Mc Bain (49657) ***(G-10678)***
Biewer Lumber LLC (PA) 810 326-3930
812 S Riverside Ave Saint Clair (48079) ***(G-14206)***
Biewer Sawmill, Mc Bain *Also called John A Biewer Lumber Company* ***(G-10682)***
Biewer Sawmill Inc 231 825-2855
6251 W Gerwoude Dr Mc Bain (49657) ***(G-10679)***
Big 3 Precision Products Inc 313 846-6601
10611 Haggerty St Dearborn (48126) ***(G-3682)***
Big Bear Products Inc 269 657-3550
32053 E Red Arrow Hwy Paw Paw (49079) ***(G-12398)***
Big Boy Restaurant Management, Warren *Also called Big Boy Restaurants Intl LLC* ***(G-16958)***
Big Boy Restaurants Intl LLC (PA) 586 759-6000
4199 Marcy St Warren (48091) ***(G-16958)***
Big Boy Restaurants Intl LLC 586 263-6220
16880 Hall Rd Clinton Township (48038) ***(G-3067)***
Big Color Printing Center 313 933-9290
20400 Freeland St Detroit (48235) ***(G-3903)***
Big D LLC 248 787-2724
26038 Grand River Ave Redford (48240) ***(G-13149)***
Big Dipper Dough Co Inc 231 883-6035
2819 Cass Rd Ste E4 Traverse City (49684) ***(G-15911)***
Big Dome Holdings Inc 616 735-6228
3044 Wilson Dr Nw Grand Rapids (49534) ***(G-6219)***
Big Dutchman Inc (HQ) 616 392-5981
3900 John F Donnelly Dr Holland (49424) ***(G-7569)***
Big Foot, White Pigeon *Also called Quadra Manufacturing Inc* ***(G-17655)***
Big Foot Manufacturing Co 231 775-5588
1480 Potthoff St Cadillac (49601) ***(G-2231)***
Big Green Tomato LLC 269 282-1593
478 Main St Battle Creek (49014) ***(G-1154)***
Big Jon Sports Inc 231 275-1010
11455 Us Highway 31 Interlochen (49643) ***(G-8236)***
Big Money Magazine 810 655-0621
5490 Wyndemere Sq Swartz Creek (48473) ***(G-15662)***
Big O Smokehouse 616 891-5555
9740 Cherry Valley Ave Se Caledonia (49316) ***(G-2289)***
Big PDQ, Brighton *Also called PDQ Ink Inc* ***(G-1975)***
Big Rapids Box Company, Big Rapids *Also called General Wood Products Co* ***(G-1630)***
Big Rapids Components, Big Rapids *Also called Haworth Inc* ***(G-1633)***
Big Rapids Printing 231 796-8588
2801 Oak Industrial Dr Ne Grand Rapids (49505) ***(G-6220)***
Big Rapids Products Inc (PA) 231 796-3593
1313 Maple St Big Rapids (49307) ***(G-1622)***
Big Rapids Tool & Engineering, Big Rapids *Also called Big Rapids Products Inc* ***(G-1622)***
Big Rays Express Lube 28th St 616 447-9710
2241 Alpine Ave Nw Grand Rapids (49544) ***(G-6221)***
Big Red Resources, Zeeland *Also called Holland Awning Co* ***(G-18152)***
Big Ridge Forest Products, Onaway *Also called Bruning Forest Products* ***(G-12145)***
Big Steel Rack LLC 517 740-5428
2427 Research Dr Jackson (49203) ***(G-8389)***
Bigard & Huggard Drilling Inc 989 775-6608
5580 Venture Way Mount Pleasant (48858) ***(G-11178)***
Bigdaddybeauty.com, Warren *Also called Smo International Inc* ***(G-17241)***
Bigos Precast 517 223-5000
555 E Van Riper Rd Fowlerville (48836) ***(G-5561)***
Bigsignscom 800 790-7611
22 S Harbor Dr Unit 101 Grand Haven (49417) ***(G-5996)***
Biker Bobs Hrly-Dvidson Motown, Taylor *Also called Motown Harley-Davidson Inc* ***(G-15748)***
Bilco Tool Corporation 586 574-9300
30076 Dequindre Rd Warren (48092) ***(G-16959)***
Bill Carr Signs Inc 810 232-1569
719 W 12th St Flint (48503) ***(G-5389)***
Bill Daup Signs Inc 810 235-4080
7389 Ponderosa Dr Swartz Creek (48473) ***(G-15663)***
Bill Eldridge Associates 248 698-3705
331 Rosario Ln White Lake (48386) ***(G-17630)***
Billco Acquisition LLC 616 928-0637
1373 Lincoln Ave Holland (49423) ***(G-7570)***
Billco Products, Holland *Also called Billco Acquisition LLC* ***(G-7570)***
Billie Times Ltd 248 813-9114
1008 Alameda Blvd Troy (48085) ***(G-16240)***
Bills Custom Fab Inc 989 772-5817
1836 Gover Pkwy Mount Pleasant (48858) ***(G-11179)***
Billsby Lumber Company, Harrison *Also called Sabertooth Enterprises LLC* ***(G-7316)***
Bimac, Milan *Also called Chemincon Inc* ***(G-10933)***
Bimbo Bakeries Usa Inc 734 953-5741
13280 Newburgh Rd Livonia (48150) ***(G-9665)***
Bimbo Bakeries Usa Inc 906 786-4042
1924 Ludington St Escanaba (49829) ***(G-4819)***
Bimbo Bakeries Usa Inc 989 667-0551
3801 Wilder Rd Bay City (48706) ***(G-1291)***
Bimbo Bakeries Usa Inc 586 772-0055
26800 Schoenherr Rd Warren (48089) ***(G-16960)***
Bimbo Bakeries Usa Inc 616 252-2709
210 28th St Se Grand Rapids (49548) ***(G-6222)***
Bimbo Bakeries Usa Inc 810 239-8070
1356 W Hill Rd Flint (48507) ***(G-5390)***
Bimbo Bakeries Usa Inc 231 922-3296
1668 Northern Star Dr Traverse City (49696) ***(G-15912)***
Bingham Boat Works Ltd 906 225-0050
58 Middle Island Point Rd Marquette (49855) ***(G-10519)***
Binks Coca-Cola Bottling Co (PA) 906 786-4144
3001 Danforth Rd Escanaba (49829) ***(G-4820)***
Binks Coca-Cola Bottling Co 906 774-3202
617 Industrial Dr Iron Mountain (49801) ***(G-8277)***
Binsfeld Engineering Inc 231 334-4383
4571 Mcfarlane Rd Maple City (49664) ***(G-10460)***
Binson-Becker Inc 888 246-7667
26834 Lawrence Center Line (48015) ***(G-2579)***
Binsons Orthtic Prsthtics Svcs, Center Line *Also called Binson-Becker Inc* ***(G-2579)***
Bio Kleen Products Inc 269 567-9400
810 Lake St Kalamazoo (49001) ***(G-8697)***
Bio Source Naturals LLC 734 335-6798
47887 Michigan Ave # 203 Canton (48188) ***(G-2352)***
Bio-Vac Inc 248 350-2150
21316 Bridge St Southfield (48033) ***(G-14853)***
Biobest USA Inc 734 626-5693
11700 Metro Airport Ste Romulus (48174) ***(G-13657)***
Biocorrect Orthotics Lab 616 356-5030
5147 East Paris Ave Se # 21 Kentwood (49512) ***(G-9003)***
Bioelectrica Inc 517 884-4542
325 E Grand River Ave East Lansing (48823) ***(G-4651)***
Bioflex Inc 734 327-2946
6111 Jackson Rd Ste 200 Ann Arbor (48103) ***(G-384)***
Biolife Plasma Services LP 989 773-1500
4279 E Blue Grass Rd Mount Pleasant (48858) ***(G-11180)***
Biolyte Laboratories LLC 616 350-9055
310 Northern Dr Nw Grand Rapids (49534) ***(G-6223)***
Biolyte Labs, Grand Rapids *Also called Biolyte Laboratories LLC* ***(G-6223)***
Biomedical Designs 517 784-6617
306 W Washington Ave # 105 Jackson (49201) ***(G-8390)***
Bioplstic Plymers Cmpsites LLC 517 349-2970
4275 Conifer Cir Okemos (48864) ***(G-12117)***
Biopolymer Innovations LLC 517 432-3044
16647 Chandler Rd East Lansing (48823) ***(G-4652)***
Biopro Inc 810 982-7777
2929 Lapeer Rd Port Huron (48060) ***(G-12899)***
Biosan Laboratories Inc 586 755-8970
1950 Tobsal Ct Warren (48091) ***(G-16961)***
Biosavita Inc 734 233-3146
46701 Commerce Center Dr Plymouth (48170) ***(G-12587)***
Biosolutions LLC 616 846-1210
1800 Industrial Dr Ste F Grand Haven (49417) ***(G-5997)***
Biotec Incorporated 616 772-2133
652 E Main Ave Zeeland (49464) ***(G-18120)***
Bipco, Pontiac *Also called Eastern Oil Company* ***(G-12819)***
Birclar Electric and Elec LLC 734 941-7400
12060 Wayne Rd Romulus (48174) ***(G-13658)***
Birds Eye Foods Inc 269 561-8211
100 Sherman Rd Fennville (49408) ***(G-5170)***
Birdsall Tool & Gage Co 248 474-5150
24735 Crestview Ct Farmington Hills (48335) ***(G-4941)***
Birkhold Pattern Company Inc 269 467-8705
22921 S River Rd Centreville (49032) ***(G-2593)***
Birks Works Environmental LLC 313 891-1310
19719 Mount Elliott St Detroit (48234) ***(G-3904)***
Birlon Group LLC 313 551-5341
3801 Inkster Rd Ste 2 Inkster (48141) ***(G-8225)***
Birlon Sacs, Inkster *Also called Birlon Group LLC* ***(G-8225)***
Birmingham Jewelry Inc 586 939-5100
34756 Dequindre Rd Sterling Heights (48310) ***(G-15274)***
Birmingham Royal Oak Tent Awng, Royal Oak *Also called Royal Oak & Birmingham Tent* ***(G-13967)***
Bisbee Infrared Services Inc 517 787-4620
569 Wildwood Ave Unit 2 Jackson (49201) ***(G-8391)***
Biscayne and Associates Inc 248 304-0600
2515 Charms Rd Milford (48381) ***(G-10955)***

ALPHABETIC SECTION
Bluewater Tech Group Inc

Bischer Ready-Mix Inc (PA) ... 989 479-3267
6121 Purdy Rd Ruth (48470) ***(G-13987)***

Bischoff Enterprises LLC ... 734 856-8490
5732 St Anthony Rd Ottawa Lake (49267) ***(G-12259)***

Bissell Better Life LLC ... 800 237-7691
2345 Walker Ave Nw Grand Rapids (49544) ***(G-6224)***

Bissell Homecare Inc (HQ) ... 616 453-4451
2345 Walker Ave Nw Grand Rapids (49544) ***(G-6225)***

Bitner Tooling Technologies ... 586 803-1100
6650 Burroughs Ave Sterling Heights (48314) ***(G-15275)***

Bitzenburger Machine & Tool ... 517 627-8433
13060 Lawson Rd Grand Ledge (48837) ***(G-6102)***

Bivins Graphics ... 616 453-2211
808 Carpenter Ave Nw Grand Rapids (49504) ***(G-6226)***

Bivins Graphics (PA) ... 616 453-2211
1614 Vinecroft St Nw Grand Rapids (49544) ***(G-6227)***

Bixby Logging ... 231 348-9794
5056 Maxwell Rd Petoskey (49770) ***(G-12442)***

Bizcard Xpress ... 248 288-4800
229 N Alice Ave Rochester (48307) ***(G-13315)***

BJ Sports Inc ... 269 342-2415
453 W Kilgore Rd Portage (49002) ***(G-12985)***

Bjerke Forgings Inc ... 313 382-2600
20257 Ecorse Rd Taylor (48180) ***(G-15696)***

Bjg, Wixom *Also called Brown Jig Grinding Co* ***(G-17778)***

Bk Computing ... 231 865-3558
5210 E Mount Garfield Rd Fruitport (49415) ***(G-5789)***

Bk Enterprises, Iron Mountain *Also called Bk Mattson Enterprises Inc* ***(G-8278)***

Bk Mattson Enterprises Inc ... 906 774-0097
410 S Stephenson Ave Iron Mountain (49801) ***(G-8278)***

BKM Fuels LLC ... 269 342-9576
5566 Gull Rd Kalamazoo (49048) ***(G-8698)***

Blac Detroit Magazine, Ferndale *Also called African American Parent Pubg* ***(G-5254)***

Black & Decker (us) Inc ... 410 716-3900
3040 28th St Se Grand Rapids (49512) ***(G-6228)***

Black & Decker (us) Inc ... 616 261-0425
2982 28th St Sw Grandville (49418) ***(G-7023)***

Black & Red Inc ... 231 271-8888
5046 S West Bay Shore Dr 4a Suttons Bay (49682) ***(G-15649)***

Black Bottom Brewing Co Inc ... 313 205-5493
1055 Trumbull St Detroit (48216) ***(G-3905)***

Black Box Corporation ... 248 743-1320
1287 Rankin Dr Troy (48083) ***(G-16241)***

Black Box Corporation ... 616 246-1320
8180 Broadmoor Ave Se A Caledonia (49316) ***(G-2290)***

Black Cobra Financial Svcs LLC ... 248 298-9368
41000 Woodward Ave # 350 Bloomfield Hills (48304) ***(G-1751)***

Black Creek Timber LLC ... 517 202-2169
18026 S Sullivan Creek Rd Rudyard (49780) ***(G-13983)***

Black Dragon LLC ... 269 277-4874
4024 Niles Rd Saint Joseph (49085) ***(G-14302)***

Black Ops Gunsmithing, Bruce Twp *Also called Sbn Enterprises LLC* ***(G-2098)***

Black River Manufacturing Inc (PA) ... 810 982-9812
2625 20th St Port Huron (48060) ***(G-12900)***

Black River Manufacturing Inc ... 810 982-9812
2401 20th St Port Huron (48060) ***(G-12901)***

Black River Oil Corp ... 231 723-6502
65 Maple St Manistee (49660) ***(G-10416)***

Black River Pallet Company ... 616 772-6211
410 E Roosevelt Ave Zeeland (49464) ***(G-18121)***

Black Ski Weekend LLC ... 313 879-7150
7650 Cooley Lk Rd Ste 955 West Bloomfield (48324) ***(G-17466)***

Black Star Farms LLC (PA) ... 231 271-4970
10844 E Revold Rd Suttons Bay (49682) ***(G-15650)***

Black Swamp Percussion LLC ... 800 557-0988
11114 James St Zeeland (49464) ***(G-18122)***

Blackberry Publications ... 313 627-1520
3915 11th St Ecorse (48229) ***(G-4742)***

Blackbox Visual Design Inc ... 734 459-1307
265 Ann St Plymouth (48170) ***(G-12588)***

Blackledge Tool Inc ... 989 865-8393
305 Entrepreneur Dr Saint Charles (48655) ***(G-14190)***

Blackmer ... 616 241-1611
1809 Century Ave Sw Grand Rapids (49503) ***(G-6229)***

Blackmer Dover Resources Inc ... 616 475-9285
2662 Prairie St Sw Grand Rapids (49519) ***(G-6230)***

Blackmer System One, Grand Rapids *Also called Pump Solutions Group* ***(G-6797)***

Blackmore Co Inc ... 734 483-8661
10800 Blackmore Ave Belleville (48111) ***(G-1442)***

Blackrocks Brewery LLC ... 906 273-1333
950 W Washington St Marquette (49855) ***(G-10520)***

Blackrocks Brewery LLC (PA) ... 906 273-1333
424 N 3rd St Marquette (49855) ***(G-10521)***

Blacksmith Shop LLC ... 616 754-4719
809 Callaghan St Greenville (48838) ***(G-7123)***

Blade Industrial Products Inc ... 248 773-7400
29289 Lorie Ln Wixom (48393) ***(G-17774)***

Blade Welding Service Inc ... 734 941-4253
10910 Hannan Rd Van Buren Twp (48111) ***(G-16749)***

Blades Enterprises LLC ... 734 449-4479
47570 Avante Dr Wixom (48393) ***(G-17775)***

Blain Machining Inc ... 616 877-0426
1115 142nd Ave Ste 1 Wayland (49348) ***(G-17401)***

Blake's Orchard & Cider Mill, Armada *Also called Blakes Orchard Inc* ***(G-717)***

Blakes Orchard Inc (PA) ... 586 784-5343
17985 Armada Center Rd Armada (48005) ***(G-717)***

Blanco Canvas Company Inc ... 313 963-7787
23857 Industrial Park Dr Farmington Hills (48335) ***(G-4942)***

Blank Slate Creamery LLC ... 734 218-3242
4090 Lori Lynn Ln Whitmore Lake (48189) ***(G-17690)***

Blarney Castle Inc (PA) ... 231 864-3111
12218 West St Bear Lake (49614) ***(G-1376)***

Blarney Castle Oil, Bear Lake *Also called Blarney Castle Inc* ***(G-1376)***

Blast-All Sandblasting, Hart *Also called Kardux Welding & Fabricating* ***(G-7375)***

Ble Book Publishing, Grosse Pointe Woods *Also called Little Blue Book Inc* ***(G-7206)***

Bleistahl N Amer Ltd Partnr ... 269 719-8585
190 Clark Rd Battle Creek (49037) ***(G-1155)***

Blendco LLC ... 269 350-2914
5000 Advance Way Stevensville (49127) ***(G-15557)***

Blevins Screw Products Inc ... 810 744-1820
1838 Remell St Flint (48503) ***(G-5391)***

Blind Xpress, Livonia *Also called Elsie Inc* ***(G-9726)***

Blinds and Designs Inc ... 770 971-5524
29988 Anthony Dr Wixom (48393) ***(G-17776)***

Bliss & Vinegar LLC ... 616 970-0732
888 Forest Hill Ave Se Grand Rapids (49546) ***(G-6231)***

Blissfield, Blissfield *Also called BMC Global LLC* ***(G-1714)***

Blissfield Div, Blissfield *Also called Maxitrol Company* ***(G-1719)***

Blissfield Manufacturing Co (PA) ... 517 486-2121
626 Depot St Blissfield (49228) ***(G-1713)***

Blockmatic Company, Niles *Also called Blockmatic Inc* ***(G-11597)***

Blockmatic Inc ... 269 683-1655
2519 S 17th St Niles (49120) ***(G-11597)***

Bloem LLC (PA) ... 616 622-6344
3301 Hudson Trail Dr Hudsonville (49426) ***(G-8148)***

Bloem Living, Hudsonville *Also called Bloem LLC* ***(G-8148)***

Bloom Industries LLC ... 616 890-8029
726 Hastings St Ste A Traverse City (49686) ***(G-15913)***

Bloom Industries LLC (PA) ... 616 453-2946
2218 Ashcreek Ct Nw Grand Rapids (49534) ***(G-6232)***

Bloomberry ... 586 212-9510
6189 Pleasant St East China (48054) ***(G-4621)***

Blossom Berry ... 517 775-6978
44325 W 12 Mile Rd H-172 Novi (48377) ***(G-11838)***

Blossomland Container Corp ... 269 926-8206
1652 E Empire Ave Benton Harbor (49022) ***(G-1487)***

Blough Hardwoods Inc ... 616 693-2174
9975 W Clarksville Rd Clarksville (48815) ***(G-2966)***

Blough Inc ... 616 897-8407
9885 Centerline Rd Lowell (49331) ***(G-10024)***

Blts Wearable Art Inc ... 517 669-9659
1541 W Round Lake Rd Dewitt (48820) ***(G-4459)***

Blubridge, Howell *Also called Miccus Inc* ***(G-8064)***

Blue Cube Holding LLC (HQ) ... 989 636-1000
2030 Dow Ctr Midland (48674) ***(G-10817)***

Blue De-Signs LLC ... 248 808-2583
4605 Briarwood Ave Royal Oak (48073) ***(G-13908)***

Blue Diamond, South Lyon *Also called Michigan Seamless Tube LLC* ***(G-14801)***

Blue Fire Manufacturing LLC ... 248 714-7166
5405 Perry Dr Waterford (48329) ***(G-17325)***

Blue Flash Supply Co, Grosse Pointe Woods *Also called Continental Bldg Svs of Cinci* ***(G-7202)***

Blue Granite & Marble, Lansing *Also called Ardo Granite LLC* ***(G-9204)***

Blue Grill Foods, Milford *Also called Dimitri Mansour* ***(G-10961)***

Blue Lion Fitness, Ann Arbor *Also called Vanroth LLC* ***(G-691)***

Blue Pony LLC ... 616 291-5554
3479 8th Ave Hudsonville (49426) ***(G-8149)***

Blue Ribbon Linen and Mat Svcs, Muskegon *Also called Apparelmaster-Muskegon Inc* ***(G-11271)***

Blue Water Bioproducts LLC ... 586 453-9219
3735 Dove Rd Port Huron (48060) ***(G-12902)***

Blue Water Boring LLC ... 586 421-2100
46522 Erb Dr Macomb (48042) ***(G-10112)***

Blue Water Manufacturing Inc ... 810 364-6170
1765 Michigan Ave Marysville (48040) ***(G-10599)***

Blue Water Printing Co Inc ... 810 664-0643
655 Mccormick Dr Ste B Lapeer (48446) ***(G-9443)***

Blue Water Sail & Canvas Inc ... 231 941-5224
10531 E Carter Rd Traverse City (49684) ***(G-15914)***

Blueshift Motorcycles LLC ... 231 946-8772
13919 S West Bay Shore Dr G01 Traverse City (49684) ***(G-15915)***

Bluewater Canvas LLC ... 586 727-5345
2022 Bauman Rd Columbus (48063) ***(G-3377)***

Bluewater Tech Group Inc ... 248 356-4399
37900 Interchange Dr Farmington Hills (48335) ***(G-4943)***

ALPHABETIC

Bluewater Tech Group Inc (PA)...................................248 356-4399
24050 Northwestern Hwy Southfield (48075) *(G-14854)*
Bluewater Tech Group Inc..................................231 885-2600
6305 W 115 Mesick (49668) *(G-10767)*
Bluewater Tech Group Inc..................................616 656-9380
4245 44th St Se Ste 1 Grand Rapids (49512) *(G-6233)*
Bluewater Thermal Solutions..................................989 753-7770
2240 Veterans Mem Pkwy Saginaw (48601) *(G-14008)*
Bluewater Visual Services, Southfield *Also called Bluewater Tech Group Inc (G-14854)*
Blujay Solutions Co..................................616 738-6400
915 E 32nd St Ste B Holland (49423) *(G-7571)*
Blustone Partners LLC..................................231 256-0146
780 N Sylt Rd Lake Leelanau (49653) *(G-9101)*
Blustone Vineyards, Lake Leelanau *Also called Blustone Partners LLC (G-9101)*
Blusys, Troy *Also called Axis Tms Corp (G-16231)*
Bmax USA LLC..................................248 794-4176
777 Enterprise Dr Ste 100 Pontiac (48341) *(G-12807)*
BMC Bil-Mac Company, Grandville *Also called BMC Bil-Mac Corporation (G-7024)*
BMC Bil-Mac Corporation..................................616 538-1930
2995 44th St Sw Grandville (49418) *(G-7024)*
BMC East LLC..................................313 963-2044
1401 Rosa Parks Blvd Detroit (48216) *(G-3906)*
BMC Global LLC..................................517 486-2121
626 Depot St Blissfield (49228) *(G-1714)*
BMC Laboratory Casework, Muskegon *Also called Bmc/Industrial Eductl Svcs Inc (G-11280)*
BMC Software Inc..................................248 888-4600
27555 Executive Dr # 155 Farmington Hills (48331) *(G-4944)*
Bmc/Industrial Eductl Svcs Inc..................................231 733-1206
2831 Maffett St Muskegon (49444) *(G-11280)*
Bme Inc..................................810 937-2974
3763 Lapeer Rd Ste E Port Huron (48060) *(G-12903)*
Bms Great Lakes LLC..................................248 390-1598
4577 S Lapeer Rd Ste G Lake Orion (48359) *(G-9126)*
Bmt Aerospace Usa Inc..................................586 285-7700
18559 Malyn Blvd Fraser (48026) *(G-5630)*
Bnb Welding & Fabrication Inc..................................810 820-1508
3162 E Hemphill Rd Burton (48529) *(G-2145)*
Bnm Trailers Sales Inc..................................989 862-5252
7577 N Hollister Rd Elsie (48831) *(G-4795)*
BNP Media Inc (PA)..................................248 362-3700
2401 W Big Beaver Rd # 700 Troy (48084) *(G-16242)*
Board For Student Publications..................................734 418-4115
420 Maynard St Ann Arbor (48109) *(G-385)*
Boars Belly..................................231 722-2627
333 W Western Ave Muskegon (49440) *(G-11281)*
Boars Head Provisions Co Inc..................................941 955-0994
284 Roost Ave Holland (49424) *(G-7572)*
Boat Customs Trailers LLC..................................517 712-3512
3678 68th St Se Caledonia (49316) *(G-2291)*
Boat Guard Inc..................................989 424-1490
3577 N West Branch Dr Gladwin (48624) *(G-5923)*
Bob Allison Enterprises..................................248 540-8467
6560 Red Maple Ln Bloomfield Hills (48301) *(G-1752)*
Bob Evans Farms Inc..................................517 437-3349
200 N Wolcott St Hillsdale (49242) *(G-7518)*
Bob Fleming Well Drilling..................................248 627-3511
445 N Ortonville Rd Ortonville (48462) *(G-12195)*
Bob G Machining LLC..................................586 285-1400
44345 N Groesbeck Hwy Clinton Township (48036) *(G-3068)*
Bob-O-Link Associates Inc (PA)..................................616 891-6939
4668 2nd St Caledonia (49316) *(G-2292)*
Bobbys Mobile Service LLC..................................517 206-6026
1188 Herbert J Ave Jackson (49202) *(G-8392)*
Bobcat Oil & Gas Inc (PA)..................................989 426-4375
901 E Cedar Ave Gladwin (48624) *(G-5924)*
Bobier Tool Supply Inc..................................810 732-4030
G4163 Corunna Rd Flint (48532) *(G-5392)*
Bobs Welding & Fabricating..................................810 324-2592
5375 Kilgore Rd Kenockee (48006) *(G-8984)*
Boburka Custom Mold..................................906 864-9930
805 6th St Menominee (49858) *(G-10726)*
Boda Corporation..................................906 353-7320
Us 41 Chassell (49916) *(G-2672)*
Body Contour Ventures LLC..................................248 579-6772
34405 W 12 Mile Rd # 200 Farmington Hills (48331) *(G-4945)*
Body Faders, Mount Clemens *Also called Wickedglow Industries Inc (G-11154)*
Bodycote Thermal Proc Inc..................................616 399-6880
3270 John F Donnelly Dr Holland (49424) *(G-7573)*
Bodycote Thermal Proc Inc..................................616 245-0465
3700 Eastern Ave Se Grand Rapids (49508) *(G-6234)*
Bodycote Thermal Proc Inc..................................313 442-2387
38100 Jay Kay Dr Romulus (48174) *(G-13659)*
Bodycote Thermal Proc Inc..................................734 459-8514
8468 Ronda Dr Canton (48187) *(G-2353)*
Bodycote Thermal Proc Inc..................................734 451-0338
8580 N Haggerty Rd Canton (48187) *(G-2354)*
Bodycote Thermal Proc Inc..................................734 427-6814
31888 Glendale St Livonia (48150) *(G-9666)*
Bodycote Thermal Proc Inc..................................734 427-6814
31888 Glendale St Livonia (48150) *(G-9667)*

Boeing Company..................................248 258-7191
6001 N Adams Rd Ste 105 Bloomfield Hills (48304) *(G-1753)*
Boese Associates Inc..................................231 347-3995
2395 Williams Rd Petoskey (49770) *(G-12443)*
Boese Equipment Co, Saginaw *Also called Gregory M Boese (G-14052)*
Boeshield, Holland *Also called PMS Products Inc (G-7772)*
Bogen Concrete Inc..................................269 651-6751
26959 Bogen Rd Sturgis (49091) *(G-15598)*
Bohley Industries..................................734 455-3430
9595 5 Mile Rd Northville (48168) *(G-11680)*
Bohning Company Ltd (PA)..................................231 229-4247
7361 N 7 Mile Rd Lake City (49651) *(G-9085)*
Bohning Company Ltd..................................231 229-4247
7650 N 7 Mile Rd Lake City (49651) *(G-9086)*
Bokhara Pet Care Centers (PA)..................................231 264-6667
11535 S Elk Lake Rd Elk Rapids (49629) *(G-4775)*
Bokhara's Grooming, Elk Rapids *Also called Bokhara Pet Care Centers (G-4775)*
Bold Ammo & Guns Inc..................................616 826-0913
5083 Natchez Ct Ne Rockford (49341) *(G-13559)*
Bold Companies Inc..................................231 773-8026
2291 Olthoff St Muskegon (49444) *(G-11282)*
Bold Endeavors LLC..................................616 389-3902
5752 Barcroft Cir Sw Wyoming (49418) *(G-17988)*
Bold Furniture, Muskegon *Also called Bold Companies Inc (G-11282)*
Bold Fusion Fabg & Customs LLC..................................269 345-0681
5383 E Cd Ave Kalamazoo (49004) *(G-8699)*
Bold Services, Rockford *Also called Bold Ammo & Guns Inc (G-13559)*
Bolden Industries Inc..................................248 387-9489
19231 Bretton Dr Detroit (48223) *(G-3907)*
Boldsocks, Wyoming *Also called Bold Endeavors LLC (G-17988)*
Bolhouse Inc..................................616 209-7543
2704 Edward St Jenison (49428) *(G-8619)*
Bollhoff Rivnut..................................248 269-0475
800 Kirts Blvd Ste 500 Troy (48084) *(G-16243)*
Bolman Die Services Inc..................................810 919-2262
7515 19 Mile Rd Sterling Heights (48314) *(G-15276)*
Bolyea Industries..................................586 293-8600
33847 Doreka Fraser (48026) *(G-5631)*
Bomaur Quality Plastics Inc..................................810 629-9701
10388 Jayne Valley Ln Fenton (48430) *(G-5190)*
Bonal International Inc (PA)..................................248 582-0900
1300 N Campbell Rd Ste A Royal Oak (48067) *(G-13909)*
Bonal Technologies Inc..................................248 582-0900
1300 N Campbell Rd Royal Oak (48067) *(G-13910)*
Bond Bailey and Smith Company..................................313 496-0177
2707 W Fort St Detroit (48216) *(G-3908)*
Bond Manufacturing LLC..................................313 671-0799
17910 Van Dyke St Detroit (48234) *(G-3909)*
Bond, Bailey & Smith Machining, Detroit *Also called Bond Bailey and Smith Company (G-3908)*
Bondfire Company..................................231 834-5696
1373 Newaygo Rd Bailey (49303) *(G-1078)*
Bonsal American Inc..................................248 338-0335
2280 Auburn Rd Auburn Hills (48326) *(G-794)*
Bonsal American Inc..................................734 753-4413
36506 Sibley Rd New Boston (48164) *(G-11497)*
Bonsan American, New Boston *Also called Bonsal American Inc (G-11497)*
Bontaz Centre Usa Inc..................................248 588-8113
1099 Chicago Rd Troy (48083) *(G-16244)*
Bonwrx Ltd..................................517 481-2924
924 Terminal Rd Lansing (48906) *(G-9206)*
Book Concern Printers..................................906 482-1250
129 E Franklin St Hancock (49930) *(G-7248)*
Bookcomp Inc..................................616 774-9700
6124 Belmont Ave Ne Belmont (49306) *(G-1459)*
Bookwear, Honor *Also called Field Crafts Inc (G-7952)*
Boomer Company (PA)..................................313 832-5050
1940 E Forest Ave Detroit (48207) *(G-3910)*
Boomer Construction Materials, Detroit *Also called Boomer Company (G-3910)*
Booms Stone Company..................................313 531-3000
12275 Dixie Redford (48239) *(G-13150)*
Boone Express..................................248 583-7080
3920 S Hadley Rd Ortonville (48462) *(G-12196)*
Boone, Eugene, Grand Rapids *Also called Compucare (G-6297)*
Boones Welding & Fabricating..................................517 782-7461
1309 Westlane St Jackson (49203) *(G-8393)*
Boos Products Inc..................................734 498-2207
20416 Kaiser Rd Gregory (48137) *(G-7164)*
Booth Newspaper..................................517 487-8888
108 S Washington Sq Ste 1 Lansing (48933) *(G-9348)*
Bopp-Busch Manufacturing Co (PA)..................................989 876-7121
545 E Huron Rd Au Gres (48703) *(G-744)*
Bopp-Busch Manufacturing Co...................................989 876-7924
205 N Mackinaw St Au Gres (48703) *(G-745)*
Bopp-Busch Plant 2, Au Gres *Also called Bopp-Busch Manufacturing Co (G-745)*
Boral Building Products Inc (HQ)..................................248 668-6400
29797 Beck Rd Wixom (48393) *(G-17777)*

ALPHABETIC SECTION Bradford-White Corporation

Bordener Engineereed Surfaces, Bay City *Also called Bordener Engnred Laminates Inc* ***(G-1292)***
Bordener Engnred Laminates Inc.....989 835-6881
106 S Walnut St Ste 1 Bay City (48706) ***(G-1292)***
Border City Tool and Mfg Co.....586 758-5574
23325 Blackstone Ave Warren (48089) ***(G-16962)***
Bordrin Motor Corporation Inc.....877 507-3267
14925 W 11 Mile Rd Oak Park (48237) ***(G-12052)***
Boretti Div, Farmington Hills *Also called Enertrols Inc* ***(G-4988)***
Borg Warner Automotive, Cadillac *Also called Borgwarner Thermal Systems Inc* ***(G-2233)***
Borg Warner Automotive.....248 754-9200
3850 Hamlin Rd Auburn Hills (48326) ***(G-795)***
Borgia Die & Engineering Inc.....616 677-3595
14750 Raymer Cir Marne (49435) ***(G-10505)***
Borgman Tool & Engineering LLC.....231 733-4133
2912 Hamilton Rd Muskegon (49445) ***(G-11283)***
Borgwarner Automotive, Marshall *Also called Borgwarner Thermal Systems Inc* ***(G-10563)***
Borgwarner Emissions (HQ).....248 754-9600
3800 Automation Ave # 200 Auburn Hills (48326) ***(G-796)***
Borgwarner Inc.....248 371-0040
3800 Automation Ave # 100 Auburn Hills (48326) ***(G-797)***
Borgwarner Inc.....231 779-7500
1100 Wright St Cadillac (49601) ***(G-2232)***
Borgwarner Inc.....248 754-9600
3800 Automation Ave # 100 Auburn Hills (48326) ***(G-798)***
Borgwarner Inc (PA).....248 754-9200
3850 Hamlin Rd Auburn Hills (48326) ***(G-799)***
Borgwarner Inc.....248 754-9600
3800 Automation Ave Auburn Hills (48326) ***(G-800)***
Borgwarner Inc.....248 754-9200
3850 Hamlin Rd Auburn Hills (48326) ***(G-801)***
Borgwarner Inv Holdg Inc (HQ).....248 754-9200
3850 Hamlin Rd Auburn Hills (48326) ***(G-802)***
Borgwarner Pds (usa) Inc (HQ).....248 754-9600
3850 Hamlin Rd Auburn Hills (48326) ***(G-803)***
Borgwarner Pds Anderson LLC.....248 641-3045
5455 Corporate Dr Ste 116 Troy (48098) ***(G-16245)***
Borgwarner Powdered Metals Inc (HQ).....734 261-5322
32059 Schoolcraft Rd Livonia (48150) ***(G-9668)***
Borgwarner Thermal Systems Inc (HQ).....269 781-1228
1507 S Kalamazoo Ave Marshall (49068) ***(G-10563)***
Borgwarner Thermal Systems Inc.....231 779-7500
1100 Wright St Cadillac (49601) ***(G-2233)***
Borgwarner Transm Systems Inc (HQ).....248 754-9200
3800 Automation Ave # 500 Auburn Hills (48326) ***(G-804)***
Borgwrner Emssions Systems LLC (HQ).....248 754-9600
3800 Automation Ave # 200 Auburn Hills (48326) ***(G-805)***
Borgwrner Trbo Emssion Systems, Auburn Hills *Also called Borgwarner Emissions* ***(G-796)***
Boride Engineered Abr Inc.....231 929-2121
2615 Aero Park Dr Traverse City (49686) ***(G-15916)***
Boride Engineered Abrasives, Traverse City *Also called Botsg Inc* ***(G-15918)***
Borisch Mfg, Grand Rapids *Also called Amphenol Borisch Tech Inc* ***(G-6168)***
Borite Manufacturing Corp.....248 588-7260
31711 Sherman Ave Madison Heights (48071) ***(G-10205)***
Borneman & Peterson Inc.....810 744-1890
1810 Remell St Flint (48503) ***(G-5393)***
Boropharm Inc (PA).....248 348-5776
39555 Orchard Hill Pl # 600 Novi (48375) ***(G-11839)***
Boropharm Inc.....517 455-7847
2800 Plymouth Rd Bldg 40 Ann Arbor (48109) ***(G-386)***
Boropharm Inc.....734 585-0601
600 S Wagner Rd Ann Arbor (48103) ***(G-387)***
Borries Mkg Systems Partnr.....734 761-9549
3744 Plaza Dr Ste 1c Ann Arbor (48108) ***(G-388)***
Borroughs Corporation (PA).....800 748-0227
3002 N Burdick St Kalamazoo (49004) ***(G-8700)***
Bos Automotive Products Inc (HQ).....248 289-6072
2956 Waterview Dr Rochester Hills (48309) ***(G-13378)***
Bos Concrete Inc.....269 468-7267
6902 Paw Paw Lake Rd Coloma (49038) ***(G-3354)***
BOS Field Machining Inc.....517 204-1688
1750 Maywood Rd Houghton Lake (48629) ***(G-7987)***
Bos Manufacturing LLC (PA).....231 398-3328
100 Glocheski Dr Manistee (49660) ***(G-10417)***
Bosal Industries-Georgia Inc (HQ).....734 547-7022
1476 Seaver Way Ypsilanti (48197) ***(G-18056)***
Bosal International North Amer, Ypsilanti *Also called Bosal Industries-Georgia Inc* ***(G-18056)***
Bosanic Lwrnce Sons Tmber Pdts.....906 341-5609
1840n W Kendall Rd Manistique (49854) ***(G-10439)***
Bosch, Ira *Also called Sejasmi Industries Inc* ***(G-8270)***
Bosch Auto Svc Solutions Inc (HQ).....586 574-2332
28635 Mound Rd Warren (48092) ***(G-16963)***
Bosch Auto Svc Solutions Inc.....586 574-1820
5775 Enterprise Ct Warren (48092) ***(G-16964)***
Bosch Chassis St Joseph Plant, Saint Joseph *Also called Robert Bosch LLC* ***(G-14338)***
Bosco's Pizza Co., Warren *Also called Artisan Bread Co LLC* ***(G-16940)***
Boskage Commerce Publications.....269 673-7242
510 E Milham Ave Portage (49002) ***(G-12986)***
Boss Electro Static Inc.....616 575-0577
3974 Linden Ave Se Wyoming (49548) ***(G-17989)***
Boss Snowplow, Iron Mountain *Also called Toro Company* ***(G-8304)***
Bostontec Inc (PA).....989 496-9510
2700 James Savage Rd Midland (48642) ***(G-10818)***
Bostwick Enterprises Inc (PA).....231 946-8613
3575 Veterans Dr Traverse City (49684) ***(G-15917)***
Botsg Inc.....231 929-2121
2615 Aero Park Dr Traverse City (49686) ***(G-15918)***
Bottling Group Inc.....517 545-2624
755 Mcpherson Park Dr Howell (48843) ***(G-8017)***
Bouchey and Sons Inc.....989 588-4118
750 Kapplinger Dr Farwell (48622) ***(G-5158)***
Boulding Filtration Co LLC.....313 300-2388
11900 E Mcnichols Rd Detroit (48205) ***(G-3911)***
Bourdo Logging.....269 623-4981
5794 Mullen Ridge Dr Delton (49046) ***(G-3816)***
Bourne Industries Inc.....989 743-3461
491 S Comstock St Corunna (48817) ***(G-3578)***
Bourne Specialties.....269 663-2187
68989 Cass St Edwardsburg (49112) ***(G-4760)***
Bourque H James & Assoc Inc.....906 635-9191
3060 W M 28 Brimley (49715) ***(G-2013)***
Bowditch, Lawrence *Also called Rhino Products Inc* ***(G-9507)***
Bower Tool & Manufacturing Inc.....734 522-0444
27481 Schoolcraft Rd Livonia (48150) ***(G-9669)***
Bowers Harbor Vinyrd & Winery.....231 223-7615
2896 Bowers Harbor Rd Traverse City (49686) ***(G-15919)***
Bowling Enterprises Inc.....231 864-2653
9091 Chief Rd Kaleva (49645) ***(G-8930)***
Bowling Hydroseeding, Kaleva *Also called Bowling Enterprises Inc* ***(G-8930)***
Bowman Enterprises Inc.....269 720-1946
1905 Lakeview Dr Portage (49002) ***(G-12987)***
Bowman Printing Inc.....810 982-8202
600 Huron Ave Port Huron (48060) ***(G-12904)***
Bowne Financial Print, Detroit *Also called R R Donnelley & Sons Company* ***(G-4327)***
Boxer Equipment/Morbark Inc.....989 866-2381
8507 S Winn Rd Winn (48896) ***(G-17746)***
Boxer Tactical, Traverse City *Also called Vega Manufacturing LLC* ***(G-16136)***
Boyd, Grand Rapids *Also called Action Fabricators Inc* ***(G-6136)***
Boyd and Son Logging, Waldron *Also called David Boyd* ***(G-16857)***
Boyd Manufacturing LLC.....734 649-9765
1838 Ruddiman Dr Muskegon (49445) ***(G-11284)***
Boyer Glassworks Inc.....231 526-6359
207 State St Harbor Springs (49740) ***(G-7275)***
Boyers Meat Processing Inc.....734 495-1342
4125 Barr Rd Canton (48188) ***(G-2355)***
Boyers Tool and Die Inc.....517 782-7869
1729 W Ganson St Jackson (49202) ***(G-8394)***
Boyne Area Wldg & Fabrication.....231 582-6078
1095 Dam Rd Boyne City (49712) ***(G-1816)***
Boyne City Division, Big Rapids *Also called Federal Screw Works* ***(G-1626)***
Boyne City Gazette.....231 582-2799
5 W Main St Unit 7 Boyne City (49712) ***(G-1817)***
Bozzer Brothers Inc.....989 732-9684
1252 Krys Rd Gaylord (49735) ***(G-5851)***
BP, Hamtramck *Also called Seven Mile and Grnd River Fuel* ***(G-7246)***
BP Gas/ JB Fuel.....517 531-3400
107 W Main St Parma (49269) ***(G-12387)***
BP Lubricants USA Inc.....231 689-0002
201 N Webster St White Cloud (49349) ***(G-17620)***
BP Pack Inc.....612 594-0839
5332 Alpenhorn Ct Bellaire (49615) ***(G-1436)***
Bpb/Celotex, Lanse *Also called Certainteed Gypsum Inc* ***(G-9189)***
Bpc Acquisition Company.....231 798-1310
1218 E Pontaluna Rd Norton Shores (49456) ***(G-11809)***
Bpg International Fin Co LLC (PA).....616 855-1480
4760 Fulton St E Ste 201 Ada (49301) ***(G-11)***
Bpi Holdings International Inc.....815 363-9000
1101 Technology Dr Ann Arbor (48108) ***(G-389)***
Bpv Environmental, Byron Center *Also called Bpv LLC* ***(G-2180)***
Bpv LLC.....616 281-4502
511 76th St Sw Byron Center (49315) ***(G-2180)***
BR Safety Products Inc.....734 582-4499
1255 S Mill St Plymouth (48170) ***(G-12589)***
Bracy & Associates Ltd.....616 298-8120
965 N Baywood Dr Holland (49424) ***(G-7574)***
Bradford Company (PA).....616 399-3000
13500 Quincy St Holland (49424) ***(G-7575)***
Bradford Packaging, Holland *Also called Bradford Company* ***(G-7575)***
Bradford Printing Inc.....517 887-0044
1020 E Jolly Rd Lansing (48910) ***(G-9349)***
Bradford Tool & Die Company.....810 664-8653
1130 Clark Rd Lapeer (48446) ***(G-9444)***
Bradford-White Corporation.....269 795-3364
200 Lafayette St Middleville (49333) ***(G-10799)***

ALPHABETIC

Bradley-Thompson Tool Company 248 352-1466
22108 W 8 Mile Rd Southfield (48033) *(G-14855)*
Bradys Fence Company Inc 313 492-8804
11093 Armstrong Rd South Rockwood (48179) *(G-14820)*
Braetec Inc 269 968-4711
346 E Michigan Ave Battle Creek (49014) *(G-1156)*
Braiq Inc 858 729-4116
2000 Brush St Ste 201 Detroit (48226) *(G-3912)*
Brake Roller Co Inc 269 965-2371
1125 Watkins Rd Battle Creek (49015) *(G-1157)*
Bralyn Inc 231 865-3186
259 N 3rd Ave Fruitport (49415) *(G-5790)*
Bramco Containers Inc 906 428-2855
824 Clark Dr Gladstone (49837) *(G-5907)*
Bramin Enterprises 313 960-1528
2218 Ford St Detroit (48238) *(G-3913)*
Branch Office, Pontiac *Also called Erae AMS USA Manufacturing LLC (G-12824)*
Branch West Concrete Products 989 345-0794
3350 Rau Rd West Branch (48661) *(G-17507)*
Brand Orthopedic & Shoe Svcs 248 352-0000
21701 W 11 Mile Rd Ste 2 Southfield (48076) *(G-14856)*
Brandenburg, Sterling Heights *Also called Detroit Hoist & Crane Co L L C (G-15312)*
Branson Ultrasonics Corp 586 276-0150
6590 Sims Dr Sterling Heights (48313) *(G-15277)*
Brasco International Inc 313 393-0393
32400 Industrial Dr Madison Heights (48071) *(G-10206)*
Brass Craft Mfg Co, Novi *Also called Brasscraft Manufacturing Co (G-11840)*
Brasscraft Manufacturing Co (HQ) 248 305-6000
39600 Orchard Hill Pl Novi (48375) *(G-11840)*
Bratten Enterprises Inc (PA) 248 427-9090
23900 Haggerty Rd Farmington Hills (48335) *(G-4946)*
Brauer Clamps USA 586 427-5304
25269 Mound Rd Warren (48091) *(G-16965)*
Braund Manufacturing Co, Battle Creek *Also called Barker Manufacturing Co (G-1150)*
Bravo Machine and Tool Inc 586 790-3463
16453 Chatham Dr Clinton Township (48035) *(G-3069)*
Brawn Mixer Inc 616 399-5600
12838 Stainless Dr Holland (49424) *(G-7576)*
Brazeway Inc (PA) 517 265-2121
2711 E Maumee St Adrian (49221) *(G-51)*
BRC, Battle Creek *Also called Brake Roller Co Inc (G-1157)*
BRC Automotive Engrg & Sls Off, Auburn Hills *Also called BRC Rubber & Plastics Inc (G-806)*
BRC Rubber & Plastics Inc 248 745-9200
1091 Centre Rd Ste 210 Auburn Hills (48326) *(G-806)*
Brd Printing Inc 517 372-0268
912 W Saint Joseph St Lansing (48915) *(G-9350)*
Bread of Life Bakery & Cafe 906 663-4005
105 N Sophie St Bessemer (49911) *(G-1603)*
Break-A-Beam 586 758-7790
25257 Mound Rd Warren (48091) *(G-16966)*
Breasco LLC 734 961-9020
3840 Carpenter Rd Ypsilanti (48197) *(G-18057)*
Breck Graphics Incorporated (PA) 616 248-4110
3983 Linden Ave Se Grand Rapids (49548) *(G-6235)*
Breckenridge Paper & Packaging, Romulus *Also called Central Ohio Paper & Packg Inc (G-13662)*
Breckers ABC Tool Company Inc 586 779-1122
15919 E 12 Mile Rd Roseville (48066) *(G-13778)*
Breco LLC 517 317-2211
57 Cole St Quincy (49082) *(G-13090)*
Brede Inc 313 273-1079
19000 Glendale St Detroit (48223) *(G-3914)*
Breesport Holdings Inc 248 685-9500
1235 Holden Ave Milford (48381) *(G-10956)*
Breiten Box & Packaging Co Inc 586 469-0800
42828 Executive Dr Harrison Township (48045) *(G-7324)*
Breiten Lumber, Sandusky *Also called Stoutenburg Inc (G-14444)*
Brembo North America Inc 517 568-4398
5851 30 Mile Rd Homer (49245) *(G-7937)*
Brembo North America Inc (HQ) 734 416-1275
47765 Halyard Dr Plymouth (48170) *(G-12590)*
Brembo North America Inc 517 568-3301
29991 E M 60 Homer (49245) *(G-7938)*
Brembo North America Homer Inc 517 568-4398
29991 E M 60 Homer (49245) *(G-7939)*
Brembo Racing, Plymouth *Also called Brembo North America Inc (G-12590)*
Bremen Corp 574 546-4238
300 N Alloy Dr Fenton (48430) *(G-5191)*
Bremer Authentic Ingredients 616 772-9100
420 100th Ave Zeeland (49464) *(G-18123)*
Bremer Prosthetic Design Inc (PA) 810 733-3375
3487 S Linden Rd Ste U Flint (48507) *(G-5394)*
Brenner Orthtic Prsthetic Labs 248 615-0600
32975 8 Mile Rd Livonia (48152) *(G-9670)*
Brent Bastian Logging LLC 906 482-6378
54215 Salo Rd Hancock (49930) *(G-7249)*
Bretts Printing Service 517 482-2256
2435 S Rundle Ave 39 Lansing (48910) *(G-9351)*

Brew Detroit LLC 313 974-7366
1401 Abbott St Detroit (48216) *(G-3915)*
Brewer Sand & Gravel Inc 616 393-8990
877 Chicago Dr Holland (49423) *(G-7577)*
Brewers City Dock Inc 616 396-6563
24 Pine Ave Holland (49423) *(G-7578)*
Brewery Vivant, Grand Rapids *Also called One Beer At A Time LLC (G-6730)*
Brewing Company, Midland *Also called Midland Brewing Co LLC (G-10887)*
Brian A Broomfield 989 309-0709
14776 10th Ave Remus (49340) *(G-13238)*
Brian M Fowler Pipe Organs 517 485-3748
215 Dexter Rd Eaton Rapids (48827) *(G-4719)*
Brians Foods LLC 248 739-5280
21444 Bridge St Southfield (48033) *(G-14857)*
Brico Welding & Fab Inc 586 948-8881
27057 Morelli Dr Chesterfield (48051) *(G-2746)*
Bridal Nook, Clio *Also called Genesee County Herald Inc (G-3272)*
Bridge Organics Company 269 649-4200
311 W Washington St Vicksburg (49097) *(G-16831)*
Bridge Street Design & Mktg, Southfield *Also called Grigg Graphic Services Inc (G-14932)*
Bridge Tool and Die LLC 231 269-3200
125 S Industrial Dr Buckley (49620) *(G-2129)*
Bridgeport Manufacturing Inc 989 777-4314
6689 Dixie Hwy Bridgeport (48722) *(G-1850)*
Bridgewater Interiors LLC 517 322-4800
2369 S Canal Rd Lansing (48917) *(G-9279)*
Bridgewater Interiors LLC (HQ) 313 842-3300
4617 W Fort St Detroit (48209) *(G-3916)*
Bridgewater Interiors LLC 586 582-0882
7500 Tank Ave Warren (48092) *(G-16967)*
Bridgville Plastics Inc 269 465-6516
7380 Jericho Rd Stevensville (49127) *(G-15558)*
Briggs Contracting 989 687-7331
62 E Saginaw Rd Sanford (48657) *(G-14448)*
Briggs Industries Inc 586 749-5191
54145 Bates Rd Chesterfield (48051) *(G-2747)*
Briggs Mold & Die Inc 517 784-6908
414 N Jackson St 97-12 Jackson (49201) *(G-8395)*
Bright Star Sign Inc 313 933-4460
13300 Foley St Detroit (48227) *(G-3917)*
Bright Technologies, Wayland *Also called Sebright Products Inc (G-17415)*
Brightformat Inc 616 247-1161
5300 Corporate Grove Dr S Grand Rapids (49512) *(G-6236)*
Brighton Argus, The, Howell *Also called Gannett Co Inc (G-8043)*
Brighton Laboratories Inc 810 225-9520
11871 Grand River Rd Brighton (48116) *(G-1890)*
Brighton Technical Center, Brighton *Also called Bwi North America Inc (G-1893)*
Brilar LLC 248 547-6439
13200 Northend Ave Oak Park (48237) *(G-12053)*
Brill Company Inc 231 843-2430
715 S James St Ludington (49431) *(G-10050)*
Brilliance Audio, Grand Haven *Also called Brilliance Publishing Inc (G-5998)*
Brilliance Publishing Inc 616 846-5256
1704 Eaton Dr Grand Haven (49417) *(G-5998)*
Brillion Iron Works Inc (HQ) 248 727-1800
1 Towne Sq Ste 550 Southfield (48076) *(G-14858)*
Brindley Lumber & Pallet Co 989 345-3497
1971 State Rd Lupton (48635) *(G-10091)*
Brindley Pallets, Lupton *Also called Brindley Lumber & Pallet Co (G-10091)*
Brine, Warren *Also called Warrior Sports Inc (G-17289)*
Briney Tooling Systems, Bad Axe *Also called Gemini Precision Machining Inc (G-1065)*
Brinks Family Creamery LLC 231 826-0099
3560 E Mulder Rd Mc Bain (49657) *(G-10680)*
Brinston Acquisition LLC 248 269-1000
840 W Long Lake Rd Troy (48098) *(G-16246)*
Brintley Enterprises 248 991-4086
8660 Rosemont Ave Detroit (48228) *(G-3918)*
Brio Device LLC 734 945-5728
2104 Georgetown Blvd Ann Arbor (48105) *(G-390)*
Bristol Manufacturing Inc 810 658-9510
4416 N State Rd Davison (48423) *(G-3640)*
Bristol Steel & Conveyor Corp 810 658-9510
4416 N State Rd Davison (48423) *(G-3641)*
Bristol-Myers Squibb Company 248 528-2476
2460 Waltham Dr Troy (48085) *(G-16247)*
Brite Products, Detroit *Also called Smith Wa Inc (G-4366)*
British Cnvrtng Sltns Nrth AME 281 764-6651
259 E Michigan Ave # 305 Kalamazoo (49007) *(G-8701)*
Britten Inc 231 941-8200
2322 Cass Rd Traverse City (49684) *(G-15920)*
Britten Metalworks LLC 231 421-1615
1661 Northern Star Dr Traverse City (49696) *(G-15921)*
Britten Pop LLC 800 426-9496
2322 Cass Rd Traverse City (49684) *(G-15922)*
Britten Woodworks Inc 231 275-5457
1954 Betsie River Rd Interlochen (49643) *(G-8237)*
Broaching Diamond Service LLC 586 757-5131
3560 E 10 Mile Rd Warren (48091) *(G-16968)*

Broaching Industries Inc 586 949-3775
25755 Dhondt Ct Chesterfield (48051) *(G-2748)*
Broadblade Press 810 635-3156
11314 Miller Rd Swartz Creek (48473) *(G-15664)*
Broadmoor Motor Sales Inc 269 320-6304
1420 S Hanover St Hastings (49058) *(G-7402)*
Broadsword Solutions Corp 248 341-3367
3795 Dorothy Ln Waterford (48329) *(G-17326)*
Broadteq Incorporated 248 794-9323
5119 Highland Rd Ste 386 Waterford (48327) *(G-17327)*
Broadway, Manchester *Also called Enkon LLC (G-10405)*
Brokenbolt, Jackson *Also called Fulgham Machine & Tool Company (G-8453)*
Brollytime Inc 312 854-7606
306 S Washington Ave # 400 Royal Oak (48067) *(G-13911)*
Bron Machine Inc 616 392-5320
821 Productions Pl Holland (49423) *(G-7579)*
Bronco Connection Inc 616 997-2263
305 Main St Coopersville (49404) *(G-3549)*
Bronco Printing Company 248 544-1120
21841 Dequindre Rd Hazel Park (48030) *(G-7435)*
Bronner Christmas Decorations, Frankenmuth *Also called Bronner Display Sign Advg Inc (G-5584)*
Bronner Display Sign Advg Inc 989 652-9931
25 Christmas Ln Frankenmuth (48734) *(G-5584)*
Brookfield Inc 616 997-9663
8041 Leonard St Coopersville (49404) *(G-3550)*
Brooklyn Products Intl 517 592-2185
171 Wamplers Lake Rd Brooklyn (49230) *(G-2036)*
Brooks & Perkins Inc 231 775-2229
8051 E 34 Rd Cadillac (49601) *(G-2234)*
Brooks Meter Devices, Novi *Also called Brooks Utility Products Group (G-11841)*
Brooks Utility Products Group, Novi *Also called Ekstrom Industries Inc (G-11881)*
Brooks Utility Products Group (PA) 248 477-0250
43045 W 9 Mile Rd Novi (48375) *(G-11841)*
BROOKSIDE FOODS, Saint Clair Shores *Also called Alexander and Hornung Inc (G-14238)*
Brophy Engraving Co Inc 313 871-2333
626 Harper Ave Detroit (48202) *(G-3919)*
Brose New Boston Inc 248 339-4000
3933 Automation Ave Auburn Hills (48326) *(G-807)*
Brose New Boston Inc (HQ) 248 339-4021
23400 Bell Rd New Boston (48164) *(G-11498)*
Brose North America Inc (HQ) 248 339-4000
3933 Automation Ave Auburn Hills (48326) *(G-808)*
Brothers Baking, Jackson *Also called Dawn Food Products Inc (G-8428)*
Brothers Baking Company 269 663-8591
27260 Max St Edwardsburg (49112) *(G-4761)*
Brothers Industrials Inc 248 794-5080
38844 Steeple Chase # 27101 Farmington Hills (48331) *(G-4947)*
Brothers Mead 3 LLC 269 883-6241
19915 Capital Ave Ne # 208 Battle Creek (49017) *(G-1158)*
Browe Inc 248 877-3800
30870 Stephenson Hwy C Madison Heights (48071) *(G-10207)*
Brown & Sharpe Precision Ctr, Wixom *Also called Hexagon Metrology Inc (G-17826)*
Brown Auction Services, Watervliet *Also called Fine Tool Journal LLC (G-17392)*
Brown City Banner Inc 810 346-2753
4241 Main St Brown City (48416) *(G-2047)*
Brown City Machine Pdts LLC (PA) 810 346-3070
3989 Burnsline Rd Brown City (48416) *(G-2048)*
Brown Jig Grinding Co 248 349-7744
28005 Oakland Oaks Ct Wixom (48393) *(G-17778)*
Brown LLC (HQ) 989 435-7741
330 N Ross St Beaverton (48612) *(G-1383)*
Brown-Campbell Company (PA) 586 884-2180
11800 Investment Dr Shelby Township (48315) *(G-14555)*
Brown-Campbell Steel, Shelby Township *Also called Brown-Campbell Company (G-14555)*
Browndog Creamery LLC 248 361-3759
118 E Main St Northville (48167) *(G-11681)*
Brownie Signs LLC 248 437-0800
8791 Earhart Rd South Lyon (48178) *(G-14787)*
Brownwood Acres Foods Inc 231 599-3101
4819 Us 31 Eastport (49627) *(G-4714)*
Bruce Inc 517 371-5205
209 S Washington Sq Lansing (48933) *(G-9352)*
Bruce Kane Enterprises LLC (PA) 410 727-0637
28200 Orchard Lake Rd # 107 Farmington Hills (48334) *(G-4948)*
Brugola Oeb Indstriale USA Inc 734 468-0009
45555 Port St Plymouth (48170) *(G-12591)*
Brumley Tools Inc 586 260-8326
26520 Burg Rd Warren (48089) *(G-16969)*
Brun Laboratories Inc 616 456-1114
1120 Monroe Ave Nw # 180 Grand Rapids (49503) *(G-6237)*
Bruning Forest Products 989 733-2880
16854 5 Mile Hwy Onaway (49765) *(G-12145)*
Bruno Wojcik 989 785-5555
12270 E Shore Atlanta (49709) *(G-730)*
Brunswick Bowling Products, Muskegon *Also called Bbp Investment Holdings LLC (G-11278)*
Brunswick Bowling Products LLC (HQ) 231 725-3300
525 W Laketon Ave Muskegon (49441) *(G-11285)*
Brunt Associates Inc 248 960-8295
47689 Avante Dr Wixom (48393) *(G-17779)*
Brute Industries, Escanaba *Also called Race Ramps LLC (G-4855)*
Brutsche Concrete Products Co (PA) 269 963-1554
15150 6 1/2 Mile Rd Battle Creek (49014) *(G-1159)*
Bry Mac Inc 231 799-2211
865 E Porter Rd Norton Shores (49441) *(G-11741)*
Bryan K Sergent 231 670-2106
19383 10 Mile Rd Stanwood (49346) *(G-15232)*
Brys Estate Vineyard & Winery 231 223-9303
3309 Blue Water Rd Traverse City (49686) *(G-15923)*
BT Engineering LLC 734 417-2218
223 River St Spring Lake (49456) *(G-15134)*
Bti Measurement Tstg Svcs LLC (PA) 734 769-2100
7035 Jomar Dr Whitmore Lake (48189) *(G-17691)*
Bti Measurement Tstg Svcs LLC 734 769-2100
2800 Zeeb Rd Dockk Dexter (48130) *(G-4479)*
Bti Precision Measurement Tstg, Whitmore Lake *Also called Balance Technology Inc (G-17689)*
Btm National Holdings LLC 616 794-0100
1114 S Bridge St Belding (48809) *(G-1404)*
Btmc Holdings Inc (PA) 616 794-0100
1114 S Bridge St Belding (48809) *(G-1405)*
Buchanan Metal Forming Inc (PA) 269 695-3836
103 W Smith St Buchanan (49107) *(G-2111)*
Bucher Hydraulics Inc (HQ) 616 458-1306
1363 Michigan St Ne Grand Rapids (49503) *(G-6238)*
Bucher Hydraulics Inc 231 652-2773
201 Cooperative Center Dr Newaygo (49337) *(G-11564)*
Buck Pole Archery Deerranch, Marion *Also called Pollington Machine Tool Inc (G-10493)*
Buck Stop Lure Company Inc 989 762-5091
3600 N Grow Rd Stanton (48888) *(G-15228)*
Buck-N-Ham Machines Inc (HQ) 231 587-5322
413 Dale Ave Mancelona (49659) *(G-10387)*
Buck-Spica Equipment Ltd 269 792-2251
631 W Cherry St Wayland (49348) *(G-17402)*
Buckeys Contracting & Service 989 835-9512
707 Jefferson Ave Midland (48640) *(G-10819)*
Buckingham Tool Corp 734 591-2333
11915 Market St Livonia (48150) *(G-9671)*
Bucks Cement Inc 810 233-4141
4299 Fenton Rd Burton (48529) *(G-2146)*
Bucks Sports Products Inc 763 229-1331
7721 Lake Bluff 19.4 Rd Gladstone (49837) *(G-5908)*
Budd Logging LLC 989 329-1578
3595 W Maple Grove Rd Farwell (48622) *(G-5159)*
Budd Magnetic Products Inc 248 353-2533
22525 Telegraph Rd Southfield (48033) *(G-14859)*
Buddies Foods LLC 586 776-4036
17445 Malyn Blvd Fraser (48026) *(G-5632)*
Buddingh Weeder Co 616 698-8613
7015 Hammond Ave Se Caledonia (49316) *(G-2293)*
Buddy Tda Inc 269 349-8105
383 E D Ave Ste B Kalamazoo (49009) *(G-8702)*
Budget Europe Travel Service 734 668-0529
2557 Meade Ct Ann Arbor (48105) *(G-391)*
Budget Print Center, Grand Rapids *Also called Cascade Printing and Graphics (G-6264)*
Budget Printing Center, East Lansing *Also called Aalpha Tinadawn Inc (G-4649)*
Budgit Hoists, Muskegon *Also called Columbus McKinnon Corporation (G-11296)*
Buffoli North America Corp 616 610-4362
4508 128th Ave Holland (49424) *(G-7580)*
Bugay Logging 906 428-2125
8409 N P.11 Dr Gladstone (49837) *(G-5909)*
Buhler Technologies LLC 248 652-1546
1030 W Hamlin Rd Rochester Hills (48309) *(G-13379)*
Buhlerprince Inc (HQ) 616 394-8248
670 Windcrest Dr Holland (49423) *(G-7581)*
Builders Iron Inc 616 887-9127
5900 Comstock Park Dr Nw Comstock Park (49321) *(G-3465)*
Built Rite Tool and Engrg LLC 810 966-5133
1605 Beard St Port Huron (48060) *(G-12905)*
Buiter Tool & Die Inc 616 455-7410
8187 Division Ave S Grand Rapids (49548) *(G-6239)*
Bulk AG Innovations LLC 269 925-0900
1007 Nickerson Ave Benton Harbor (49022) *(G-1488)*
Bull Hn Info Systems Inc 616 942-7126
2620 Horizon Dr Se D1 Grand Rapids (49546) *(G-6240)*
Bulldog Fabricating Corp 734 761-3111
50 Enterprise Dr Ann Arbor (48103) *(G-392)*
Bulldog Factory Service, Madison Heights *Also called Santanna Tool & Design LLC (G-10348)*
Bulletin Moon 734 453-9985
44315 Plymouth Oaks Blvd Plymouth (48170) *(G-12592)*
Bulletin of Concerned Asi 231 228-7116
3693 S Bay Bluffs Dr Cedar (49621) *(G-2539)*
Bullion Tool Technology LLC 313 881-1404
20044 E 8 Mile Rd Harper Woods (48225) *(G-7300)*

ALPHABETIC

(PA)=Parent Co (HQ)=Headquarters (DH)=Div Headquarters
2020 Harris Michigan Industrial Directory
913

Bulls-Eye Wire & Cable Inc 810 245-8600
1498 N Saginaw St Ste 4 Lapeer (48446) *(G-9445)*
Bullseye Power 231 788-5209
2134 Northwoods Ave Muskegon (49442) *(G-11286)*
Bulman Products Inc 616 363-4416
1650 Mcreynolds Ave Nw Grand Rapids (49504) *(G-6241)*
Bulmann Dock & Lift, Boyne City *Also called Bulmann Enterprises Inc* *(G-1818)*
Bulmann Enterprises Inc 231 549-5020
175 Magnet Dr Boyne City (49712) *(G-1818)*
Bundeze LLC 248 343-9179
9717 Cottontail St West Olive (49460) *(G-17532)*
Bundy Corporation 517 439-1132
200 Arch Ave Hillsdale (49242) *(G-7519)*
Bundy Logging 231 824-6054
4114 E 16 Rd Manton (49663) *(G-10451)*
Bundy Tubing Division, Auburn Hills *Also called TI Group Auto Systems LLC* *(G-1023)*
Bundy, Bundy, Manton *Also called Bundy Logging* *(G-10451)*
Bunker & Sons Sawmill LLC 989 983-2715
119 Alexander Rd Vanderbilt (49795) *(G-16803)*
Bunting Sand & Gravel Products 989 345-2373
3247 Cook Rd West Branch (48661) *(G-17508)*
Burch Tank & Truck Inc 989 495-0342
4200 James Savage Rd Midland (48642) *(G-10820)*
Burch Tank & Truck Inc (PA) 989 772-6266
2253 Enterprise Dr Mount Pleasant (48858) *(G-11181)*
Burch Truck and Trailer Parts, Midland *Also called Burch Tank & Truck Inc* *(G-10820)*
Burch Truck and Trailer Parts, Mount Pleasant *Also called Burch Tank & Truck Inc* *(G-11181)*
Burgaflex North America LLC 810 714-3285
1085 Grant St Fenton (48430) *(G-5192)*
Burgaflex North America Inc 810 584-7296
8186 Industrial Park Dr Grand Blanc (48439) *(G-5961)*
Burge Chemical Products, Grand Rapids *Also called Burge Incorporated* *(G-6242)*
Burge Incorporated 616 791-2214
2751 Westbrook Dr Nw Grand Rapids (49504) *(G-6242)*
Burhani Labs Inc 313 212-3842
18254 Livernois Ave Detroit (48221) *(G-3920)*
Burkard Industries Inc 586 791-6520
35300 Kelly Rd Clinton Township (48035) *(G-3070)*
Burke E Porter Machinery Co (HQ) 616 234-1200
730 Plymouth Ave Ne Grand Rapids (49505) *(G-6243)*
Burke Porter Group, Ada *Also called Bpg International Fin Co LLC* *(G-11)*
Burke Porter Machinery Co, Grand Rapids *Also called Burke E Porter Machinery Co* *(G-6243)*
Burkett Signs Corp 269 746-4285
15886 E Michigan Ave Climax (49034) *(G-3013)*
Burkholder Excavating Inc 269 426-4227
4898 Weechik Rd Sawyer (49125) *(G-14482)*
Burkk Inc 616 365-0354
4455 Airwest Dr Se Grand Rapids (49512) *(G-6244)*
Burkland Inc (PA) 810 636-2233
6520 S State Rd Goodrich (48438) *(G-5952)*
Burly Oak Builders Inc 734 368-4912
9980 Dexter Chelsea Rd Dexter (48130) *(G-4480)*
Burmeister Engineering 989 654-2537
230 Fritz Rd Sterling (48659) *(G-15243)*
Burners Inc 248 676-9141
4901 Mccarthy Dr Milford (48381) *(G-10957)*
Burnette Foods Inc (PA) 231 264-8116
701 S Us Highway 31 Elk Rapids (49629) *(G-4776)*
Burnette Foods Inc 269 621-3181
87171 County Road 687 Hartford (49057) *(G-7382)*
Burnette Foods Inc 231 536-2284
200 State St East Jordan (49727) *(G-4626)*
Burnette Foods Inc 231 861-2151
4856 1st St New ERA (49446) *(G-11519)*
Burnette Foods Inc 231 223-4282
2955 Kroupa Rd Traverse City (49686) *(G-15924)*
Burnham & Northern Inc 517 279-7501
169 Industrial Ave Coldwater (49036) *(G-3292)*
Burnrite Pellet Corporation 989 429-1067
2495 E Rock Rd Clare (48617) *(G-2865)*
Burnside Acquisition LLC (PA) 616 243-2800
1060 Kenosha Indus Dr Se Grand Rapids (49508) *(G-6245)*
Burnside Acquisition LLC 231 798-3394
6830 Grand Haven Rd Norton Shores (49456) *(G-11810)*
Burnside Industries LLC 231 798-3394
6830 Grand Haven Rd Norton Shores (49456) *(G-11811)*
Burr Bench, Chelsea *Also called Abrasive Finishing Inc* *(G-2698)*
Burr Engineering & Dev Co (PA) 269 965-2371
730 Michigan Ave E Battle Creek (49014) *(G-1160)*
Burr Oak Tool, Sturgis *Also called Burr Oak Tool Inc* *(G-15599)*
Burr Oak Tool Inc (PA) 269 651-9393
405 W South St Sturgis (49091) *(G-15599)*
Burrell Tri-County Vaults Inc 734 483-2024
1106 E Michigan Ave Ypsilanti (48198) *(G-18058)*
Burro Graphics, Rochester Hills *Also called Mackellar Associates Inc* *(G-13466)*
Burrow Industries Inc 734 847-1842
7380 Express Rd Temperance (48182) *(G-15824)*
Burst Led 248 321-6262
29412 Windmill Ct Farmington Hills (48334) *(G-4949)*
Burt Moeke & Son Hardwoods 231 587-5388
2509 Valley Rd Mancelona (49659) *(G-10388)*
Burtek Enterprises Inc 586 421-8000
50325 Patricia St Chesterfield (48051) *(G-2749)*
Burton Industries Inc 906 932-5970
1260 Wall St Ironwood (49938) *(G-8323)*
Burton Industries Inc 906 932-5970
1260 Wall St Ironwood (49938) *(G-8324)*
Burton Press Co Inc 248 853-0212
2156 Avon Industrial Dr Rochester Hills (48309) *(G-13380)*
Burton Street Recycling, Grand Rapids *Also called Louis Padnos Iron and Metal Co* *(G-6632)*
Burtrum Furs 810 771-4563
321 E Grand Blanc Rd Grand Blanc (48439) *(G-5962)*
Busch Industries Inc 616 957-3737
900 East Paris Ave Se # 304 Grand Rapids (49546) *(G-6246)*
Busch Machine Tool Supply LLC 989 798-4794
7251 Midland Rd Freeland (48623) *(G-5753)*
Busche Aluminum Technologies, Fruitport *Also called Shipston Alum Tech Mich Inc* *(G-5800)*
Busche Performance Group, Southfield *Also called Busche Southfield Inc* *(G-14860)*
Busche Southfield Inc 248 357-5180
26290 W 8 Mile Rd Southfield (48033) *(G-14860)*
Bush Concrete Products Inc 231 733-1904
3584 Airline Rd Norton Shores (49444) *(G-11742)*
Bushings Inc 248 650-0603
1967 Rochester Indus Dr Rochester Hills (48309) *(G-13381)*
Business Cards Plus Inc 269 327-7727
8785 Portage Indus Dr Portage (49024) *(G-12988)*
Business Connect L3c 616 443-8070
3888 16th Ave Sw Grandville (49418) *(G-7025)*
Business Design Solutions Inc (PA) 248 672-8007
17360 W 12 Mile Rd # 201 Southfield (48076) *(G-14861)*
Business Helper LLC 231 271-4404
117 W Broadway Suttons Bay (49682) *(G-15651)*
Business News 231 929-7919
129 E Front St 200 Traverse City (49684) *(G-15925)*
Business News Publishing 248 362-3700
2401 W Big Beaver Rd # 700 Troy (48084) *(G-16248)*
Business Press Inc 248 652-8855
917 N Main St Rochester (48307) *(G-13316)*
Business Software Services, Jenison *Also called Nu-Wool Co Inc* *(G-8635)*
Buskirk Lumber Company 616 765-5103
319 Oak St Freeport (49325) *(G-5763)*
Busscher Septic Tank Company, Holland *Also called Busscher Septic Tank Service* *(G-7582)*
Busscher Septic Tank Service 616 392-9653
11305 E Lakewood Blvd Holland (49424) *(G-7582)*
Busted Bra Shop LLC 313 288-0449
15 E Kirby St Ste A Detroit (48202) *(G-3921)*
Buster Mathis Foundation 616 843-4433
4409 Carol Ave Sw Wyoming (49519) *(G-17990)*
Butcher Engineering Entps 734 246-7700
20501 Pennsylvania Rd # 150 Brownstown (48193) *(G-2060)*
Butler Mill Service Company 313 429-2486
8800 Dix St Detroit (48209) *(G-3922)*
Butler Plastics Company 810 765-8811
766 Degurse Ave Marine City (48039) *(G-10471)*
Butterball Farms Inc 616 243-0105
1435 Buchanan Ave Sw Grand Rapids (49507) *(G-6247)*
Buy Best Manufacturing LLC 248 875-2491
988 Rickett Rd Ste B Brighton (48116) *(G-1891)*
Buyers Development Group LLC (PA) 734 677-0009
4095 Stone School Rd Ann Arbor (48108) *(G-393)*
Buyers Guide, Sandusky *Also called Great Northern Publishing Inc* *(G-14434)*
Buyers Guide 616 897-9261
105 N Broadway St Lowell (49331) *(G-10025)*
Buyers Guide 231 722-3784
1781 5th St Ste 1 Muskegon (49441) *(G-11287)*
BV Technology LLC 616 558-1746
7855 Sandy Hollow Dr Se Alto (49302) *(G-323)*
Bva Inc 248 348-4920
29222 Trident Indus Blvd New Hudson (48165) *(G-11533)*
BVA OILS, New Hudson *Also called Bva Inc* *(G-11533)*
Bwb LLC 231 439-9200
33469 W 14 Mile Rd Farmington Hills (48331) *(G-4950)*
Bwi Chassis Dynamics NA Inc (HQ) 937 455-5308
12501 Grand River Rd Brighton (48116) *(G-1892)*
Bwi North America Inc 810 494-4584
12501 Grand River Rd Brighton (48116) *(G-1893)*
Byers Manufacturing, Lawton *Also called Amjs Incorporated* *(G-9510)*
Byers, D C Company, Grand Rapids *Also called DC Byers Co/Grand Rapids Inc* *(G-6338)*
Byk USA Inc 203 265-2086
2932 Waterview Dr Rochester Hills (48309) *(G-13382)*
Byrne Elec Specialists Inc (PA) 616 866-3461
320 Byrne Industrial Dr Rockford (49341) *(G-13560)*

Byrne Elec Specialists Inc 616 866-3461
725 Byrne Industrial Dr Rockford (49341) *(G-13561)*
Byrne Tool & Die Inc 616 866-4479
316 Byrne Industrial Dr Rockford (49341) *(G-13562)*
Byrnes Manufacturing Co LLC 810 664-3686
870 Whitney Dr Lapeer (48446) *(G-9446)*
Byrnes Tool Co Inc 810 664-3686
870 Whitney Dr Lapeer (48446) *(G-9447)*
Byron Manufacturing, Flint *Also called Engineered Products Company (G-5425)*
C & A Wholesale Inc 248 302-3555
18942 Hayes St Detroit (48205) *(G-3923)*
C & A Wood Products Inc 313 365-8400
17434 Cliff St Detroit (48212) *(G-3924)*
C & B Glass Inc 248 625-4376
3960 S Ortonville Rd Clarkston (48348) *(G-2909)*
C & B Machinery Company 734 462-0600
7771 Lochlin Dr Brighton (48116) *(G-1894)*
C & C Enterprises Inc 989 772-5095
1106 Packard Rd Mount Pleasant (48858) *(G-11182)*
C & C Grinding Corp 248 689-1979
1685 Austin Dr Troy (48083) *(G-16249)*
C & C Machine Tool Inc 248 693-3347
1584 Oneida Trl Lake Orion (48362) *(G-9127)*
C & C Manufacturing Inc 586 268-3650
35455 Stanley Dr Sterling Heights (48312) *(G-15278)*
C & C Sports Inc 810 227-7068
8090 Grand River Rd Brighton (48114) *(G-1895)*
C & D Enterprises Inc 248 373-0011
G4349 S Dort Hwy Burton (48529) *(G-2147)*
C & D Gage Inc 517 548-7049
8736 Glen Haven Dr Howell (48843) *(G-8018)*
C & D Tool & Die Company Inc 248 922-5937
12395 Shaffer Rd Davisburg (48350) *(G-3628)*
C & G News Inc 586 498-8000
13650 E 11 Mile Rd Warren (48089) *(G-16970)*
C & G Publishing Inc 586 498-8000
13650 E 11 Mile Rd Warren (48089) *(G-16971)*
C & H Stamping Inc 517 750-3600
205 Obrien Rd Jackson (49201) *(G-8396)*
C & J Fabrication Inc 586 791-6269
34885 Groesbeck Hwy Clinton Township (48035) *(G-3071)*
C & J Pallets Inc 517 263-7415
2368 E Us Highway 223 Adrian (49221) *(G-52)*
C & J Steel Processing, Detroit *Also called Scotten Steel Processing Inc (G-4356)*
C & K Box Company Inc 517 784-1779
423 Barrett Ave Jackson (49202) *(G-8397)*
C & K Hardwoods LLC 269 231-0048
7325 Elm Valley Rd Three Oaks (49128) *(G-15848)*
C & L Concrete 231 829-3386
20994 200th Ave Tustin (49688) *(G-16709)*
C & M Coatings Inc 616 842-1925
1730 Airpark Dr Ste C Grand Haven (49417) *(G-5999)*
C & M Manufacturing Corp Inc 586 749-3455
30207 Commerce Blvd Chesterfield (48051) *(G-2750)*
C & M Manufacturing Inc 517 279-0013
129 Industrial Ave Coldwater (49036) *(G-3293)*
C & M Tool LLC 734 944-3355
1235 Industrial Dr Ste 7 Saline (48176) *(G-14380)*
C & N Manufacturing Inc 586 293-9150
33722 James J Pompo Dr Fraser (48026) *(G-5633)*
C & R Tool Die 231 584-3588
4643 Alba Hwy Alba (49611) *(G-112)*
C & S Machine Products Inc (PA) 269 695-6859
2929 Saratore Dr Niles (49120) *(G-11598)*
C & S Machine Products Inc 269 695-6859
248 Post Rd Buchanan (49107) *(G-2112)*
C & S Millwork Inc 586 465-6470
44163 N Groesbeck Hwy Clinton Township (48036) *(G-3072)*
C & S Security Inc 989 821-5759
138 Argus Ct Roscommon (48653) *(G-13748)*
C & T Fabrication LLC 616 678-5133
90 Spring St Kent City (49330) *(G-8988)*
C & V Services Inc 810 632-9677
2755 Ore Valley Dr Hartland (48353) *(G-7388)*
C A P S, Livonia *Also called Central Admxture Phrm Svcs Inc (G-9680)*
C B S, Bruce Twp *Also called Custom Biogenic Systems Inc (G-2080)*
C C Welding 517 783-2305
429 Hill St Jackson (49202) *(G-8398)*
C D C Logging 906 524-6369
17311 Kent St Lanse (49946) *(G-9188)*
C D Tool and Gage 616 682-1111
3223 3 Mile Rd Nw Grand Rapids (49534) *(G-6248)*
C E B Tooling Inc 269 489-2251
335 S 2nd St Burr Oak (49030) *(G-2134)*
C E C Controls Company Inc (HQ) 586 779-0222
14555 Barber Ave Warren (48088) *(G-16972)*
C E C Controls Company Inc 248 926-5701
50208 Pontiac Trl Wixom (48393) *(G-17780)*
C E S Industries Inc 734 425-0522
12751 Inkster Rd Livonia (48150) *(G-9672)*
C F Burger Creamery Co 313 584-4040
8101 Greenfield Rd Detroit (48228) *(G-3925)*
C F Long & Sons Inc 248 624-1562
1555 E West Maple Rd Walled Lake (48390) *(G-16892)*
C F Plastic Fabricating Inc 586 954-1296
41590 Production Dr Harrison Township (48045) *(G-7325)*
C F S, Fenton *Also called Classfcation Flotation Systems (G-5194)*
C G Witvoet & Sons Company 616 534-6677
356 Crown St Sw Grand Rapids (49548) *(G-6249)*
C H Industries Inc 586 997-1717
50699 Central Indus Dr Shelby Township (48315) *(G-14556)*
C H M Graphics & Litho Inc 586 777-4550
20220 Stephens St Saint Clair Shores (48080) *(G-14241)*
C I F, Edmore *Also called Campbell Industrial Force LLC (G-4749)*
C I I Ltd 248 585-9905
354 Indusco Ct Troy (48083) *(G-16250)*
C I M Product 269 983-5348
822 Highland Ave Saint Joseph (49085) *(G-14303)*
C J Graphics Inc 906 774-8636
121 S Carpenter Ave Kingsford (49802) *(G-9055)*
C L Design Inc 248 474-4220
20739 Sunnydale St Farmington Hills (48336) *(G-4951)*
C L Rieckhoff Company Inc (PA) 734 946-8220
26265 Northline Rd Taylor (48180) *(G-15697)*
C M E Plastic Company 517 456-7722
3820 E Michigan Ave Clinton (49236) *(G-3015)*
C M I, Fenton *Also called Cmi-Schneible Group (G-5196)*
C M M, Troy *Also called Contour Metrological & Mfg Inc (G-16279)*
C M S Sales Company Inc 248 853-7446
2700 Frankson Ave Rochester Hills (48307) *(G-13383)*
C P I Inc 810 664-8686
1449 Bowers Rd Lapeer (48446) *(G-9448)*
C P R, Troy *Also called Control Power-Reliance LLC (G-16280)*
C P S, Clinton Township *Also called Complete Prototype Svcs Inc (G-3085)*
C R B Crane & Service Co (PA) 586 757-1222
3751 E 10 Mile Rd Warren (48091) *(G-16973)*
C R I, New Haven *Also called Centerless Rebuilders Inc (G-11523)*
C R Stitching 313 538-1660
26150 5 Mile Rd 1c Redford (48239) *(G-13151)*
C R T & Associates Inc 231 946-1680
806 Hastings St Ste H Traverse City (49686) *(G-15926)*
C Roy Inc 810 387-3975
444 Roy Dr Yale (48097) *(G-18045)*
C S A, Grand Rapids *Also called Contract Source & Assembly Inc (G-6305)*
C S L Inc 248 549-4434
1323 E 11 Mile Rd Royal Oak (48067) *(G-13912)*
C S M, Allendale *Also called Constructive Sheet Metal Inc (G-215)*
C S M Manufacturing Corp (PA) 248 471-0700
24650 N Industrial Dr Farmington Hills (48335) *(G-4952)*
C S Systems Inc 269 962-8434
1405 Michigan Ave W Battle Creek (49037) *(G-1161)*
C T & G Enterprises Inc (PA) 810 798-8661
79415 Scottish Hills Dr Almont (48003) *(G-253)*
C T & T Inc 248 623-9422
5619 Dixie Hwy Waterford (48329) *(G-17328)*
C T I, Sterling Heights *Also called Control Technique Incorporated (G-15298)*
C T L Enterprises Inc 616 392-1159
832 Productions Pl Holland (49423) *(G-7583)*
C T Machining Inc 586 772-0320
23031 Roseberry Ave Warren (48089) *(G-16974)*
C Thorrez Industries Inc (PA) 517 750-3160
4909 W Michigan Ave Jackson (49201) *(G-8399)*
C W A Manufacturing Co Inc 810 686-3030
7406 N Dort Hwy Mount Morris (48458) *(G-11159)*
C W Enterprises Inc 810 385-9100
4137 24th Ave Fort Gratiot (48059) *(G-5547)*
C W Marsh Company (PA) 231 722-3781
1385 Hudson St Muskegon (49441) *(G-11288)*
C&C Doors Inc 586 232-4538
51805 Milano Dr Macomb (48042) *(G-10113)*
C&D Pallets Inc 517 285-5228
13777 S Jones Rd Eagle (48822) *(G-4616)*
C-Plastics Inc 616 837-7396
12463 Cleveland St Nunica (49448) *(G-12033)*
C.A.R.S., Rochester Hills *Also called Canadian Amrcn Rstoration Sups (G-13384)*
C.H. Industries, Shelby Township *Also called C H Industries Inc (G-14556)*
C.P., Flat Rock *Also called Single Source Inc (G-5365)*
C/W South Inc 810 767-2806
1220 N Center Rd Burton (48509) *(G-2148)*
C2 Group The, Grand Rapids *Also called Argus Technologies LLC (G-6180)*
C2 Imaging LLC 248 743-2903
1725 John R Rd Troy (48083) *(G-16251)*
C2dx Inc 269 409-0068
555 E Eliza St Ste A Schoolcraft (49087) *(G-14489)*
Cabinet One Inc 248 625-9440
4571 White Lake Ct Clarkston (48346) *(G-2910)*
Cabinets By Robert Inc 231 947-3261
2774 Garfield Rd N Ste C Traverse City (49686) *(G-15927)*

ALPHABETIC

Cablcon, Troy *Also called Quad Electronics Inc* ***(G-16571)***
Cabot Corporation....989 495-2113
3603 S Saginaw Rd Midland (48640) ***(G-10821)***
Cad CAM, Metamora *Also called Aurora Cad CAM Inc* ***(G-10772)***
Cad CAM Services Inc....616 554-5222
4017 Brockton Dr Se Grand Rapids (49512) ***(G-6250)***
Cadfem Americas Inc....248 919-8410
27600 Farmington Rd # 209 Farmington Hills (48334) ***(G-4953)***
Cadillac Asphalt LLC....248 215-0416
21521 Hilltop Ste 23 Southfield (48033) ***(G-14862)***
Cadillac Asphalt LLC (PA)....734 397-2050
2575 S Haggerty Rd # 100 Canton (48188) ***(G-2356)***
Cadillac Casting Inc (PA)....231 779-9600
1500 4th Ave Cadillac (49601) ***(G-2235)***
Cadillac Coffee Company....800 438-6900
194 E Maple Rd Troy (48083) ***(G-16252)***
Cadillac Culvert Inc....231 775-3761
5305 M 115 Cadillac (49601) ***(G-2236)***
Cadillac Engineered Plas Inc....231 775-2900
1550 Leeson Ave Cadillac (49601) ***(G-2237)***
Cadillac Fabrication Inc (PA)....231 775-7386
1340 Marty Paul St Cadillac (49601) ***(G-2238)***
Cadillac Oil Company....313 365-6200
13650 Helen St Detroit (48212) ***(G-3926)***
Cadillac Plating Corporation....586 771-9191
23849 Groesbeck Hwy Warren (48089) ***(G-16975)***
Cadillac Printing Company....231 775-2488
214 S Mitchell St Cadillac (49601) ***(G-2239)***
Cadillac Products Inc (PA)....248 813-8200
5800 Crooks Rd Ste 100 Troy (48098) ***(G-16253)***
Cadillac Products Inc....989 766-2294
4858 Williams Rd Rogers City (49779) ***(G-13613)***
Cadillac Products Inc....586 774-1700
29784 Little Mack Ave Roseville (48066) ***(G-13779)***
Cadillac Products Auto Co, Roseville *Also called Cadillac Products Inc* ***(G-13779)***
Cadillac Products Packaging Co (PA)....248 879-5000
5800 Crooks Rd Troy (48098) ***(G-16254)***
Cadillac Prsentation Solutions....248 288-9777
1195 Equity Dr Troy (48084) ***(G-16255)***
Cadillac Tool and Die Inc....231 775-9007
1011 6th St Cadillac (49601) ***(G-2240)***
Cadillac Winery, Bay City *Also called Evergreen Winery LLC* ***(G-1311)***
Cadon Plating & Coatings LLC....734 282-8100
3715 11th St Wyandotte (48192) ***(G-17950)***
Caffeinated Press Inc....888 809-1686
3167 Kalamazoo Ave Se # 104 Grand Rapids (49508) ***(G-6251)***
Caffina Coffee Co....313 584-3584
7520 Greenfield Rd Dearborn (48126) ***(G-3683)***
Caflor Industries LLC....734 604-1168
2375 Parkwood Ypsilanti (48198) ***(G-18059)***
Caillau Usa Inc....248 446-1900
7000 Kensington Rd Brighton (48116) ***(G-1896)***
Cain Brothers Logging Inc....906 345-9252
1001 County Road 510 Negaunee (49866) ***(G-11468)***
Cake Connection Tc LLC....231 943-3531
5730 Cherry Blossom Dr Traverse City (49685) ***(G-15928)***
Cake Flour....231 571-3054
1811 W Norton Ave Norton Shores (49441) ***(G-11743)***
Cal Chemical Manufacturing Co....586 778-7006
605 Shore Club Dr Saint Clair Shores (48080) ***(G-14242)***
Cal Grinding Inc (PA)....906 786-8749
1401 N 26th St Stop 16 Escanaba (49829) ***(G-4821)***
Cal Manufacturing Company Inc....269 649-2942
5500 E V Ave Vicksburg (49097) ***(G-16832)***
Cal Park Logging LLC....231 796-4662
17130 15 Mile Rd Big Rapids (49307) ***(G-1623)***
Cal Tolliver....586 790-1610
36429 Groesbeck Hwy Clinton Township (48035) ***(G-3073)***
Cal-Chlor Corp....231 843-1147
5379 W 6th St Ludington (49431) ***(G-10051)***
Calcomco Inc (PA)....313 885-9228
5544 S Red Pine Cir Kalamazoo (49009) ***(G-8703)***
Calder Bros Dairy Inc....313 381-8858
1020 Southfield Rd Lincoln Park (48146) ***(G-9575)***
Calderwood WD Pdts & Svcs LLC....906 852-3232
9968 Calderwood Rd Trout Creek (49967) ***(G-16162)***
Caldwell Gasket Company, Grand Rapids *Also called N-K Sealing Technologies LLC* ***(G-6711)***
Caledonia Cmnty Sawmill LLC....616 891-8561
8298 96th St Se Alto (49302) ***(G-324)***
Calhoun Communications Inc (PA)....517 629-0041
125 E Cass St Albion (49224) ***(G-116)***
Calhoun County Med Care Fcilty....269 962-5458
1150 Michigan Ave E Battle Creek (49014) ***(G-1162)***
Calhoun Foundry Company Inc....517 568-4415
506 S Clay St Homer (49245) ***(G-7940)***
Caliber Industries LLC....586 774-6775
19000 15 Mile Rd Clinton Township (48035) ***(G-3074)***
Caliber Metals Inc....586 465-7650
36870 Green St New Baltimore (48047) ***(G-11482)***
Cals Welding Co, Clinton Township *Also called Cal Tolliver* ***(G-3073)***
Calsonickansei North Amer Inc....248 848-4727
7460 Honeysuckle Rd West Bloomfield (48324) ***(G-17467)***
Calumet Machine, Calumet *Also called Mq Operating Company* ***(G-2330)***
Calvin Lutz Farm, Kaleva *Also called Fruit Haven Nursery Inc* ***(G-8933)***
CAM Fab....269 685-1000
643 112th Ave Martin (49070) ***(G-10595)***
CAM Packaging LLC....989 426-1200
705 Weaver Ct Gladwin (48624) ***(G-5925)***
Camaco LLC (HQ)....248 442-6800
37000 W 12 Mile Rd # 105 Farmington Hills (48331) ***(G-4954)***
Cambria Tool and Machine Inc....517 437-3500
121 Mechanic Rd Hillsdale (49242) ***(G-7520)***
Cambric Corporation....801 415-7300
41050 W 11 Mile Rd Novi (48375) ***(G-11842)***
Cambridge Foods LLC....248 348-3800
47765 Bellagio Dr Northville (48167) ***(G-11682)***
Cambridge Sharpe Inc....248 613-5562
8325 N Rushton Rd South Lyon (48178) ***(G-14788)***
Cambro Products Inc....586 468-8847
41135 Irwin Dr Harrison Township (48045) ***(G-7326)***
Cambron Engineering Inc....989 684-5890
3800 Wilder Rd Bay City (48706) ***(G-1293)***
Camcar LLC (HQ)....586 254-3900
6125 18 Mile Rd Sterling Heights (48314) ***(G-15279)***
Camcar Plastics Inc....231 726-5000
1732 Glade St Muskegon (49441) ***(G-11289)***
Camden Publications, Camden *Also called Campub Inc* ***(G-2338)***
Camdex Inc....248 528-2300
2330 Alger Dr Troy (48083) ***(G-16256)***
Cameo Countertops Inc....616 458-8745
3550 3 Mile Rd Nw Grand Rapids (49534) ***(G-6252)***
Cameron Balloons - U.S., Dexter *Also called Aerostatica Inc* ***(G-4473)***
Cameron International Corp....248 646-6743
32440 Evergreen Rd Beverly Hills (48025) ***(G-1615)***
Cameron International Corp....231 788-7020
2076 Northwoods Ave Muskegon (49442) ***(G-11290)***
Cameron Kirk Forest Pdts Inc....989 426-3439
1467 S Shearer Rd Gladwin (48624) ***(G-5926)***
Cameron Tool Corporation....517 487-3671
1800 Bassett St Lansing (48915) ***(G-9353)***
Cameron/Schlumberger, Muskegon *Also called Cameron International Corp* ***(G-11290)***
Camerons of Jackson LLC....517 531-3400
107 W Main St Parma (49269) ***(G-12388)***
Cammand Machining LLC....586 752-0366
101 Shafer Dr Romeo (48065) ***(G-13625)***
Cammenga & Associates LLC....313 914-7160
2011 Bailey St Dearborn (48124) ***(G-3684)***
Cammenga Company LLC....313 914-7160
2011 Bailey St Dearborn (48124) ***(G-3685)***
Campaign-Stickers.com, Grand Rapids *Also called Middleton Printing Inc* ***(G-6684)***
Campbell & Shaw Steel Inc....810 364-5100
1705 Michigan Ave Marysville (48040) ***(G-10600)***
Campbell Inc Press Repair....517 371-1034
925 River St Lansing (48912) ***(G-9354)***
Campbell Industrial Force LLC....989 427-0011
1380 Industrial Park Dr Edmore (48829) ***(G-4749)***
Campbell Soup Company....313 295-6884
21740 Trlley Indus Dr D Taylor (48180) ***(G-15698)***
Campbell Soup Company....248 336-8486
1220 E 9 Mile Rd Ferndale (48220) ***(G-5265)***
Campub Inc (HQ)....517 368-0365
331 E Bell St Camden (49232) ***(G-2338)***
Camryn Fabrication LLC....586 949-0818
50625 Richard W Blvd Chesterfield (48051) ***(G-2751)***
Camryn Industries LLC (HQ)....248 663-5850
21624 Melrose Ave Southfield (48075) ***(G-14863)***
Camryn Industries LLC....248 663-5900
1401 Abbott St Detroit (48216) ***(G-3927)***
Camshaft Acquisition Inc....517 787-2040
717 Woodworth Rd Jackson (49202) ***(G-8400)***
Camshaft Machine Company, Jackson *Also called Camshaft Acquisition Inc* ***(G-8400)***
Camshaft Machine Company LLC (PA)....517 787-2040
717 Woodworth Rd Jackson (49202) ***(G-8401)***
Can You Handlebar LLC....248 821-2171
239 Church St Mount Clemens (48043) ***(G-11126)***
Can-AM Engineered Products....734 427-2020
30850 Industrial Rd Livonia (48150) ***(G-9673)***
Can-AM Metallurgical, Detroit *Also called American Metallurgical Svcs* ***(G-3867)***
Canadian Amrcn Rstoration Sups (PA)....248 853-8900
2600 Bond St Rochester Hills (48309) ***(G-13384)***
Canadian Harvest LP (HQ)....952 835-6429
16369 Us Highway 131 S Schoolcraft (49087) ***(G-14490)***
Canal Street Brewing Co LLC....616 776-1195
235 Grandville Ave Sw Grand Rapids (49503) ***(G-6253)***
Canco Inc....810 664-3520
1404 Imlay City Rd Lapeer (48446) ***(G-9449)***
Candela Products Inc....248 541-2547
24760 Romano St Warren (48091) ***(G-16976)***

Candle Factory Grand Traverse 231 946-2280
301 W Grandview Pkwy Traverse City (49684) *(G-15929)*
Candle Wick 248 547-2987
175 W 9 Mile Rd Ferndale (48220) *(G-5266)*
Cannon Machine Inc 616 363-4014
1641 Davis Ave Nw Grand Rapids (49504) *(G-6254)*
Cannon Vibrator Div, Edmore *Also called Edmore Tool & Grinding Inc (G-4750)*
Cannon-Muskegon Corporation 231 755-1681
2875 Lincoln St Norton Shores (49441) *(G-11744)*
Cannonsburg Wood Products Inc 616 866-4459
10251 Northland Dr Ne Rockford (49341) *(G-13563)*
Canton Manufacturing, Canton *Also called Greenfield Die & Mfg Corp (G-2379)*
Canton Manufacturing, Canton *Also called Shiloh Industries Inc (G-2426)*
Cantrick Kip Co 248 644-7622
999 S Adams Rd Birmingham (48009) *(G-1675)*
Canusa LLC 906 259-0800
2510 Ashmun St Sault Sainte Marie (49783) *(G-14462)*
Canusa Inc 906 446-3327
502 2nd St Gwinn (49841) *(G-7217)*
Canusa Wood Products, Gwinn *Also called Canusa Inc (G-7217)*
Canvas Co Inc 231 276-3083
5962 Penn Lock Colony Rd Interlochen (49643) *(G-8238)*
Canvas Concepts Inc 810 794-3305
2001 Pointe Tremble Rd Algonac (48001) *(G-142)*
Canvas Innovations LLC 616 393-4400
11276 E Lakewood Blvd Holland (49424) *(G-7584)*
Canvas Kings 616 846-6220
16506 144th Ave Spring Lake (49456) *(G-15135)*
Canvas Shop 734 782-2222
25188 Telegraph Rd Flat Rock (48134) *(G-5350)*
Canvas Shoppe Inc 810 733-1841
3198 One Half S Dye Rd Flint (48507) *(G-5395)*
Cap Collet & Tool Co Inc 734 283-4040
4082 6th St Wyandotte (48192) *(G-17951)*
Caparo Vehicle Components Inc (PA) 734 513-2859
13060 Merriman Rd Livonia (48150) *(G-9674)*
Capco Automovite 248 616-8888
82 Park Dr Troy (48083) *(G-16257)*
Capital Billing Systems Inc 248 478-7298
33533 W 12 Mile Rd # 131 Farmington Hills (48331) *(G-4955)*
Capital City Blue Print Inc 517 482-5431
1110 Center St Lansing (48906) *(G-9207)*
Capital City Reprographics, Lansing *Also called Capital City Blue Print Inc (G-9207)*
Capital Equipment Clare LLC (PA) 517 669-5533
12263 S Us Highway 27 Dewitt (48820) *(G-4460)*
Capital Imaging Inc 517 482-2292
2521 E Michigan Ave Lansing (48912) *(G-9355)*
Capital Induction Inc 586 322-1444
6505 Diplomat Dr Sterling Heights (48314) *(G-15280)*
Capital Software Inc Michigan 517 324-9100
4660 S Hagadorn Rd # 115 East Lansing (48823) *(G-4653)*
Capital Stamping & Machine Inc (PA) 248 471-0700
24650 N Industrial Dr Farmington Hills (48335) *(G-4956)*
Capital Steel & Builders Sup 517 694-0451
3897 Holt Rd Holt (48842) *(G-7905)*
Capitol Tool Grinding Co 517 321-8230
437 N Rosemary St Lansing (48917) *(G-9280)*
Capler Mfg 586 264-7851
6664 Sterling Dr N Sterling Heights (48312) *(G-15281)*
Capnesity Inc 317 401-6766
1778 Imlay City Rd Lapeer (48446) *(G-9450)*
Capsonic Automotive Inc 248 754-1100
3121 University Dr # 120 Auburn Hills (48326) *(G-809)*
Car Audio Outlet LLC 810 686-3300
11581 N Saginaw Rd Clio (48420) *(G-3266)*
Car Shop, Escanaba *Also called Escanaba and Lk Superior RR Co (G-4828)*
Car-Min-Vu Farm 517 749-9112
2965 E Howell Rd Webberville (48892) *(G-17447)*
Caraco Pharma Inc 313 871-8400
1150 Elijah Mccoy Dr Detroit (48202) *(G-3928)*
Caraustar Cstm Packg Group Inc 616 247-0330
1957 Beverly Ave Sw Grand Rapids (49519) *(G-6255)*
Caraustar Industries Inc 989 793-4820
3265 Commerce Centre Dr Saginaw (48601) *(G-14009)*
Caraustar Saginaw Plant, Saginaw *Also called Caraustar Industries Inc (G-14009)*
Caravan Technologies Inc 313 341-2551
3033 Bourke St Detroit (48238) *(G-3929)*
Carb-A-Tron Tool Co 517 782-2249
4615 S Jackson Rd Jackson (49201) *(G-8402)*
Carbide Form Master Inc 248 625-9373
10565 Dixie Hwy Davisburg (48350) *(G-3629)*
Carbide Specialties, Grand Rapids *Also called Riverside Tool Corp (G-6829)*
Carbide Surface Company (PA) 586 465-6110
44336 Reynolds Dr Clinton Township (48036) *(G-3075)*
Carbide Technologies Inc 586 296-5200
18101 Malyn Blvd Fraser (48026) *(G-5634)*
Carboline Company 734 525-2824
32820 Capitol St Livonia (48150) *(G-9675)*
Carboloy, Troy *Also called Seco Holding Co Inc (G-16596)*
Carbon Green Bioenergy LLC 616 374-4000
7795 Saddlebag Lake Rd Lake Odessa (48849) *(G-9112)*
Carbon Impact Inc 231 929-8152
2628 Garfield Rd N Ste 38 Traverse City (49686) *(G-15930)*
Carbon Tool & Manufacturing 734 422-0380
12735 Inkster Rd Livonia (48150) *(G-9676)*
Carbone of America 989 894-2911
900 Harrison St Bay City (48708) *(G-1294)*
Carco Inc 313 925-1053
10333 Shoemaker St Detroit (48213) *(G-3930)*
Carcone Co 248 348-2677
43422 W Oaks Dr Novi (48377) *(G-11843)*
Carcoustics Usa Inc 517 548-6700
1400 Durant Dr Howell (48843) *(G-8019)*
Cardell Automotive, Auburn Hills *Also called Cardell Corporation (G-810)*
Cardell Corporation 248 371-9700
2025 Taylor Rd Auburn Hills (48326) *(G-810)*
Cardiac Assist Holdings LLC 781 727-1391
46701 Commerce Center Dr Plymouth (48170) *(G-12593)*
Cardinal Custom Designs Inc 586 296-2060
31469 Utica Rd Fraser (48026) *(G-5635)*
Cardinal Fabricating Inc 517 655-2155
3394 Corwin Rd Williamston (48895) *(G-17728)*
Cardinal Group Industries Corp 517 437-6000
266 Industrial Dr Hillsdale (49242) *(G-7521)*
Cardinal Health Inc 248 685-9655
2675 S Milford Rd Ste B Highland (48357) *(G-7487)*
Cardinal Machine Co 810 686-1190
860 Tacoma Ct Clio (48420) *(G-3267)*
Cards of Wood Inc 616 887-8680
7754 Pine Island Ct Ne Belmont (49306) *(G-1460)*
Care2share Baking Company 810 280-0307
5512 Attica Rd Attica (48412) *(G-739)*
Carefluence, Grand Blanc *Also called Comet Information Systems LLC (G-5963)*
Cargill Incorporated 810 989-7242
1395 135th Ave Hersey (49639) *(G-7471)*
Cargill Incorporated 608 868-5150
1510 Hathaway St Owosso (48867) *(G-12281)*
Cargill Incorporated 810 329-2736
916 S Riverside Ave Saint Clair (48079) *(G-14207)*
Cargill Americas Inc 810 989-7689
31029 Comcast Dr Ste 100 New Haven (48048) *(G-11522)*
Carhartt Inc (PA) 313 271-8460
5750 Mercury Dr Dearborn (48126) *(G-3686)*
Carhartt Inc 517 282-4193
128 Spring Meadows Ln Dewitt (48820) *(G-4461)*
Caribbean Adventure LLC 269 441-5675
5420 Beckley Rd Ste 244 Battle Creek (49015) *(G-1163)*
Carl Zeiss Indus Metrology LLC 248 486-2670
6826 Kensington Rd Brighton (48116) *(G-1897)*
Carl Zeiss Microscopy LLC 248 486-7600
6826 Kensington Rd Brighton (48116) *(G-1898)*
Carlesimo Products Inc 248 474-0415
29800 W 8 Mile Rd Farmington Hills (48336) *(G-4957)*
Carlet Tool Inc 248 435-0319
926 W 14 Mile Rd Clawson (48017) *(G-2974)*
Carlex Glass America LLC 248 824-8800
1209 E Big Beaver Rd Troy (48083) *(G-16258)*
Carlo John Inc 586 254-3800
12345 23 Mile Rd Shelby Township (48315) *(G-14557)*
Carlon Meter Company Inc 616 842-0420
1710 Eaton Dr Grand Haven (49417) *(G-6000)*
Carlson Enterprises Inc 248 656-1442
922 S Rochester Rd Rochester Hills (48307) *(G-13385)*
Carlson Metal Products Inc 248 528-1931
2335 Alger Dr Troy (48083) *(G-16259)*
Carlson Technology Inc 248 476-0013
30945 8 Mile Rd Livonia (48152) *(G-9677)*
Carlton, Robert Hanger Company, Zeeland *Also called Bennett Wood Specialties Inc (G-18117)*
Carmeuse Lime Inc 906 484-2201
5093 E M 134 Cedarville (49719) *(G-2566)*
Carmeuse Lime Inc 313 849-9268
25 Marion Ave River Rouge (48218) *(G-13274)*
Carmeuse Lime & Stone, River Rouge *Also called Carmeuse Lime Inc (G-13274)*
Carmeuse Lime & Stone, Rogers City *Also called O-N Minerals Michigan Company (G-13618)*
Carmeuse Lime & Stone, Cedarville *Also called O-N Minerals Michigan Company (G-2571)*
Carmeuse Lime & Stone Inc 989 734-2131
1035 Calcite Rd Rogers City (49779) *(G-13614)*
Carmeuse Lime & Stone Inc 906 283-3456
15 W County Rd 432 Gulliver (49840) *(G-7211)*
Caro Carbide Corporation 248 588-4252
553 Robbins Dr Troy (48083) *(G-16260)*
Caro Test Center, Caro *Also called TI Group Auto Systems LLC (G-2477)*
Carol Packing House 989 673-2688
1131 Weeden Rd Caro (48723) *(G-2466)*
Carpenters Cabinets 989 777-1070
5066 Dixie Hwy Saginaw (48601) *(G-14010)*

ALPHABETIC

Carpet Crafters, Grand Rapids *Also called James E Sullivan & Associates* ***(G-6551)***
Carquest Auto Parts, Bay City *Also called General Parts Inc* ***(G-1316)***
Carr Brothers and Sons Inc....517 629-3549
14555 Elm Row Rd Albion (49224) ***(G-117)***
Carr Brothers and Sons Inc (PA)....517 531-3358
13613 E Erie Rd Albion (49224) ***(G-118)***
Carr Logging, Hesperia *Also called Charles William Carr Sr* ***(G-7477)***
Carrier & Gable Inc (PA)....248 477-8700
24110 Research Dr Farmington Hills (48335) ***(G-4958)***
Carrigan Graphics Inc....734 455-6550
7994 N Lilley Rd Canton (48187) ***(G-2357)***
Carroll Products Inc....586 254-6300
44056 Phoenix Dr Sterling Heights (48314) ***(G-15282)***
Carroll Tool and Die Co....586 949-7670
46650 Erb Dr Macomb (48042) ***(G-10114)***
Carrollton Concrete Mix Inc....989 753-7737
2924 Carrollton Rd Saginaw (48604) ***(G-14011)***
Carrollton Paving Co....989 752-7139
2924 Carrollton Rd Saginaw (48604) ***(G-14012)***
Carrom Company, Ludington *Also called Merdel Game Manufacturing Co* ***(G-10071)***
Carry Manufacturing Inc....989 672-2779
1360 Prospect Ave Caro (48723) ***(G-2467)***
Carry Pump Co., Caro *Also called Carry Manufacturing Inc* ***(G-2467)***
Carry-All Products Inc....616 399-8080
4498 128th Ave Holland (49424) ***(G-7585)***
Carson Wood Specialties Inc....269 465-6091
7526 Jericho Rd Stevensville (49127) ***(G-15559)***
Cartalign Research Co....248 681-6689
2667 Birch Harbor Ln West Bloomfield (48324) ***(G-17468)***
Carter Fuel Systems LLC....248 371-8392
3255 W Hamlin Rd Rochester Hills (48309) ***(G-13386)***
Carter Industries Inc....510 324-6700
906 James St Adrian (49221) ***(G-53)***
Carter Manufacturing Co Inc....616 842-8760
1725 Airpark Dr Grand Haven (49417) ***(G-6001)***
Carter Products Company Inc....616 647-3380
2871 Northridge Dr Nw Grand Rapids (49544) ***(G-6256)***
Carter's Children's Store, Grand Rapids *Also called Carters Inc* ***(G-6257)***
Carters Inc....616 647-9452
3390 Alpine Ave Nw Grand Rapids (49544) ***(G-6257)***
Cartex Corporation (HQ)....610 759-1650
1515 Equity Dr 100 Troy (48084) ***(G-16261)***
Cartex Corporation....734 857-5961
15573 Oakwood Dr Romulus (48174) ***(G-13660)***
Cartridges Are US, Ithaca *Also called Cau Acquisition Company LLC* ***(G-8357)***
Casa D'Oro, Troy *Also called Pure & Simple Solutions LLC* ***(G-16570)***
Casadei Steel, Sterling Heights *Also called Casadei Structural Steel Inc* ***(G-15283)***
Casadei Structural Steel Inc....586 698-2898
40675 Mound Rd Sterling Heights (48310) ***(G-15283)***
Casalbi Company Inc....517 782-0345
540 Wayne St Jackson (49202) ***(G-8403)***
CASCADE CART SOLUTIONS, Grand Rapids *Also called Cascade Engineering Inc* ***(G-6260)***
Cascade Die Casting Group Inc (HQ)....616 281-1774
7441 Division Ave S A1 Grand Rapids (49548) ***(G-6258)***
Cascade Die Casting Group Inc....616 887-1771
9983 Sparta Ave Nw Sparta (49345) ***(G-15089)***
Cascade Die Casting Group Inc....616 455-4010
7750 Division Ave S Grand Rapids (49548) ***(G-6259)***
Cascade Die Casting/Mid-State, Grand Rapids *Also called Cascade Die Casting Group Inc* ***(G-6259)***
Cascade Engineering Inc (PA)....616 975-4800
3400 Innovation Ct Se Grand Rapids (49512) ***(G-6260)***
Cascade Engineering Inc....616 975-4800
5050 33rd St Se Grand Rapids (49512) ***(G-6261)***
Cascade Engineering Inc....616 975-4923
5055 36th St Se Grand Rapids (49512) ***(G-6262)***
Cascade Equipment Company....734 697-7870
43412 N Interstate 94 Ser Van Buren Twp (48111) ***(G-16750)***
Cascade Manufacturing, Grand Haven *Also called Lakeshore Fittings Inc* ***(G-6047)***
Cascade Metal Works Inc....616 868-0668
6098 Alden Nash Ave Se Alto (49302) ***(G-325)***
Cascade Paper Converters LLC....616 974-9165
4935 Starr St Se Grand Rapids (49546) ***(G-6263)***
Cascade Printing and Graphics....616 222-2937
6504 28th St Se Ste A Grand Rapids (49546) ***(G-6264)***
Cascade Rental Centers, Grand Rapids *Also called Decc Company Inc* ***(G-6341)***
Cascade Tool & Die Inc....269 429-2210
4035 Lincoln Ave Saint Joseph (49085) ***(G-14304)***
Casco Products Corporation....248 957-0400
25921 Meadowbrook Rd Novi (48375) ***(G-11844)***
Case Diamond Linear....800 293-2496
1809 Rochester Indus Ct Rochester Hills (48309) ***(G-13387)***
Case Island Glass LLC....810 252-1704
1120 Beach St Flint (48502) ***(G-5396)***
Case Systems Inc....989 496-9510
2700 James Savage Rd Midland (48642) ***(G-10822)***
Case Welding & Fabrication Inc....517 278-2729
235 N Angola Rd Coldwater (49036) ***(G-3294)***
Case-Free Inc....616 245-3136
240 32nd St Se Grand Rapids (49548) ***(G-6265)***
Casemer Tool & Machine Inc....248 628-4807
2765 Metamora Rd Oxford (48371) ***(G-12341)***
Caseq Technologies Inc....734 730-5407
657 Commerce Ct Ste 40 Holland (49424) ***(G-7586)***
Caseway Industrial Products, Bay City *Also called Highland Industrial Inc* ***(G-1320)***
Casing Innovations LLC....248 939-0821
19739 15 Mill Rd Clinton (49236) ***(G-3016)***
Casper Corporation....248 442-9000
24081 Research Dr Farmington Hills (48335) ***(G-4959)***
Cass, Detroit *Also called Custo Arch Shee Meta* ***(G-3958)***
Cass City Chronicle Inc....989 872-2010
6550 Main St Cass City (48726) ***(G-2512)***
Cass Polymers (HQ)....517 543-7510
815 W Shepherd St Ste 2 Charlotte (48813) ***(G-2636)***
Cass River Trader East, Vassar *Also called Tuscola County Advertiser Inc* ***(G-16815)***
Casselman Logging....231 885-1040
23400 13 Mile Rd Mesick (49668) ***(G-10768)***
Cast Coatings Inc (PA)....269 545-8373
203 W Southeastern St Galien (49113) ***(G-5817)***
Castalloy Corporation....517 265-2452
414 Addison St Adrian (49221) ***(G-54)***
Castano Plastics Inc....248 624-3724
2337 Solano Dr Wolverine Lake (48390) ***(G-17935)***
Castel Leasing, Three Rivers *Also called Progressive Paper Corp* ***(G-15875)***
Caster Concepts Inc....517 629-2456
214 E Michigan Ave Albion (49224) ***(G-119)***
Castine Communications Inc....248 477-1600
22658 Brookdale St Farmington (48336) ***(G-4895)***
Casting Industries Inc....586 776-5700
315 Whiting St Saint Clair (48079) ***(G-14208)***
Castino Corporation (PA)....734 941-7200
16777 Wahrman St Romulus (48174) ***(G-13661)***
Castle Remedies Inc....734 973-8990
2345 S Huron Pkwy Ste 1 Ann Arbor (48104) ***(G-394)***
Castleton Village Center Inc....616 247-8100
3580 Rgr B Chaffee Mem Dr Grand Rapids (49548) ***(G-6266)***
Casual Ptio Furn Rfnishing Inc....586 254-1900
7851 Haverhill Ct N Canton (48187) ***(G-2358)***
Catalina Software....734 429-3550
3103 Overlook Ct Saline (48176) ***(G-14381)***
Catapult Business Services, Holland *Also called Trendway Svcs Organization LLC* ***(G-7837)***
Catem North America, Novi *Also called Eberspaecher North America Inc* ***(G-11877)***
Catholic Weekly, Saginaw *Also called GLS Diocesan Reports* ***(G-14046)***
CATI Armor LLC....269 788-4322
435 Packard Hwy Ste C Charlotte (48813) ***(G-2637)***
Catl USA, Rochester Hills *Also called Contemporary Amperex Corp* ***(G-13395)***
Cattlemans Fresh Mt & Fish Mkt, Taylor *Also called Cattlemans Meat Company* ***(G-15699)***
Cattlemans Meat Company....734 287-8260
11400 Telegraph Rd Taylor (48180) ***(G-15699)***
Cau Acquisition Company LLC (PA)....989 875-8133
100 Raycraft Dr Ithaca (48847) ***(G-8357)***
Causey Consulting LLC....248 671-4979
6689 Orchard Lake Rd # 242 West Bloomfield (48322) ***(G-17469)***
Cav Tool Company....248 349-7860
22605 Heslip Dr Novi (48375) ***(G-11845)***
Caveman Pallets LLC....616 675-7270
2382 Van Dyke St Conklin (49403) ***(G-3529)***
Cayman Chemical Company Inc (PA)....734 971-3335
1180 E Ellsworth Rd Ann Arbor (48108) ***(G-395)***
Cbm LLC....800 487-2323
2395 S Huron Pkwy Ste 200 Ann Arbor (48104) ***(G-396)***
Cbp Fabrication Inc....313 653-4220
12700 Mansfield St Detroit (48227) ***(G-3931)***
Cbr Industries, Traverse City *Also called Cabinets By Robert Inc* ***(G-15927)***
CBS Tool Inc....586 566-5945
51601 Oro Dr Shelby Township (48315) ***(G-14558)***
CC Industries LLC....269 426-3342
13550 Three Oaks Rd Sawyer (49125) ***(G-14483)***
Ccd Holdings, Holland *Also called Eco - Composites LLC* ***(G-7617)***
CCI, Mecosta *Also called Chrouch Communications Inc* ***(G-10687)***
CCI Arnheim Inc....906 353-6330
14935 Arnheim Baraga (49908) ***(G-1099)***
CCI Companies, Farmington Hills *Also called Covenant Cpitl Investments Inc* ***(G-4967)***
CCI Driveline LLC....586 716-1160
9568 Marine City Hwy Casco (48064) ***(G-2499)***
CCM Modernization Co....586 231-0396
41580 Janet Cir Clinton Township (48038) ***(G-3076)***
Cco Holdings LLC....517 583-4125
114 N Main St Tekonsha (49092) ***(G-15817)***
Cco Holdings LLC....616 244-2071
301 W Main St Belding (48809) ***(G-1406)***
Cco Holdings LLC....616 384-2060
327 Main St Coopersville (49404) ***(G-3551)***
Cco Holdings LLC....517 639-1060
1 W Chicago St Quincy (49082) ***(G-13091)***

Cco Holdings LLC 734 244-8028
2101 Mall Rd Monroe (48162) ***(G-11024)***
Cco Holdings LLC 734 868-5044
3245 Lewis Ave Ida (48140) ***(G-8193)***
Cco Holdings LLC 810 270-1002
3989 Huron St North Branch (48461) ***(G-11657)***
Cco Holdings LLC 810 375-7020
5121 Dryden Rd Dryden (48428) ***(G-4568)***
Cco Holdings LLC 810 545-4020
4680 Water St Columbiaville (48421) ***(G-3376)***
Cco Holdings LLC 906 285-6497
121 E Aurora St Ironwood (49938) ***(G-8325)***
Cco Holdings LLC 906 239-3763
104 N Stephenson Ave Iron Mountain (49801) ***(G-8279)***
Cco Holdings LLC 906 346-1000
105 W State Highway M35 Gwinn (49841) ***(G-7218)***
Cco Holdings LLC 231 720-0688
1595 Lakeshore Dr Muskegon (49441) ***(G-11291)***
Cco Holdings LLC 248 494-4550
4000 Baldwin Rd Auburn Hills (48326) ***(G-811)***
Cco Holdings LLC 269 202-3286
1850 Friday Rd Coloma (49038) ***(G-3355)***
Cco Holdings LLC 269 216-6680
2103 Parkview Ave Kalamazoo (49008) ***(G-8704)***
Cco Holdings LLC 269 432-0052
643 E State St Colon (49040) ***(G-3370)***
Cco Holdings LLC 269 464-3454
350 W Chicago Rd White Pigeon (49099) ***(G-17646)***
Cco Holdings LLC 989 328-4187
2894 W Sidney Rd Sidney (48885) ***(G-14738)***
Cco Holdings LLC 989 567-0151
257 W Wright Ave Shepherd (48883) ***(G-14726)***
Cco Holdings LLC 989 863-4023
9989 Saginaw St Reese (48757) ***(G-13229)***
Cco Holdings LLC 989 853-2008
156 Superior St Muir (48860) ***(G-11237)***
CCS Design LLC 248 313-9178
49620 Martin Dr Wixom (48393) ***(G-17781)***
Cdgjl Inc (PA) 517 787-2100
1900 Wellworth Jackson (49203) ***(G-8404)***
CDK Enterprises LLC 586 296-9300
16601 E 13 Mile Rd Fraser (48026) ***(G-5636)***
CDM Machine Co 313 538-9100
23009 Lake Ravines Dr Southfield (48033) ***(G-14864)***
Cdn Loading Inc 906 338-2630
13470 State Highway M38 Pelkie (49958) ***(G-12421)***
Cdp Diamond Products Inc 734 591-1041
11919 Globe St Livonia (48150) ***(G-9678)***
Cdp Environmental Inc 586 776-7890
16517 Eastland St Roseville (48066) ***(G-13780)***
Cdr Pigments & Dispersions, Livonia *Also called Flint Group US LLC* ***(G-9740)***
Cds Specialty Coatings LLC 734 244-6708
1667 Rose Ln Westland (48186) ***(G-17547)***
Ce Il Holdings Inc 248 305-7700
12866 Sutherland Rd Brighton (48116) ***(G-1899)***
Cedar Log Lbr Millersburg Inc 989 733-2676
6019 Millersburg Rd Millersburg (49759) ***(G-10991)***
Cedar Mill LLC 906 297-2318
1501 S Caribou Lake Rd De Tour Village (49725) ***(G-3667)***
Cedar Mobile Home Service Inc 616 696-1580
4720 Russell St Cedar Springs (49319) ***(G-2546)***
Cedar Springs Castings, Cedar Springs *Also called Steeltech Ltd* ***(G-2563)***
Cedar Springs Post Inc 616 696-3655
36 E Maple Cedar Springs (49319) ***(G-2547)***
Cedar Springs Post Newspaper, Cedar Springs *Also called Cedar Springs Post Inc* ***(G-2547)***
Cedar Springs Sales & Graphix, Cedar Springs *Also called Cedar Springs Sales LLC* ***(G-2548)***
Cedar Springs Sales LLC 616 696-2111
2571 20 Mile Rd Ne Cedar Springs (49319) ***(G-2548)***
CEDARVILLE MARINE, Cedarville *Also called Floatation Docking Inc* ***(G-2567)***
Ceeflow Inc 231 526-5579
5334 S Lake Shore Dr Harbor Springs (49740) ***(G-7276)***
Cei, Manchester *Also called CEi Composite Materials LLC* ***(G-10403)***
CEi Composite Materials LLC 734 212-3006
800 E Duncan St Manchester (48158) ***(G-10403)***
Ceiling Scenes, Warren *Also called Applied Visual Concepts LLC* ***(G-16937)***
Cel Plastics Inc 231 777-3941
1985 E Laketon Ave Muskegon (49442) ***(G-11292)***
Celani Printing Co 810 395-1609
126 N Main St Capac (48014) ***(G-2447)***
Celano Precision Mfg Inc 734 748-1744
30016 Richland St Livonia (48150) ***(G-9679)***
Celebrations 906 482-4946
110 E Quincy St Hancock (49930) ***(G-7250)***
Celebrations Bridal & Formal, Hancock *Also called Celebrations* ***(G-7250)***
Celerity Systems N Amer Inc 248 994-7696
28175 Haggerty Rd Novi (48377) ***(G-11846)***
Celia Corporation (PA) 616 887-7387
309 S Union St Sparta (49345) ***(G-15090)***
Celia Corporation 616 887-7341
140 E Averill St Sparta (49345) ***(G-15091)***
Celia Deboer 269 279-9102
14791 Hoffman Rd Three Rivers (49093) ***(G-15859)***
Cell-Con, Rochester Hills *Also called Cellular Concepts Co Inc* ***(G-13388)***
Cellar 849 Winery 734 254-0275
849 Penniman Ave Ste 101 Plymouth (48170) ***(G-12594)***
Cello-Foil Products Inc (HQ) 229 435-4777
155 Brook St Battle Creek (49037) ***(G-1164)***
Cellular Concepts Co Inc 313 371-4800
3667 Merriweather Ln Rochester Hills (48306) ***(G-13388)***
Cellulose Mtl Solutions LLC 616 669-2990
2472 Port Sheldon St Jenison (49428) ***(G-8620)***
Celsee Diagnostics Inc (PA) 866 748-1448
100 Phoenix Dr Ste 321 Ann Arbor (48108) ***(G-397)***
Cemex Cement Inc 231 547-9971
1600 Bells Bay Rd Charlevoix (49720) ***(G-2610)***
Centech Inc 517 546-9185
1325 Grand Oaks Dr Howell (48843) ***(G-8020)***
Centen AG Inc, Midland *Also called Centen AG LLC* ***(G-10823)***
Centen AG LLC (HQ) 989 636-1000
2030 Dow Ctr Midland (48674) ***(G-10823)***
Centennial Technologies Inc 989 752-6167
1335 Agricola Dr Saginaw (48604) ***(G-14013)***
Center Cupcakes 248 302-6503
6271 Bromley Ct West Bloomfield (48322) ***(G-17470)***
Center Line Gage Inc 810 387-4300
110 Commerce Dr Brockway (48097) ***(G-2019)***
Center Machine & Tool LLC 517 748-2500
150 Factory Rd Michigan Center (49254) ***(G-10785)***
Center Mass Inc 734 207-8934
6845 Woonsocket St Canton (48187) ***(G-2359)***
Center of The World Woodshop, New Troy *Also called Terry Hanover* ***(G-11560)***
Center of World Woodshop Inc 269 469-5687
13400 Red Arrow Hwy Sawyer (49125) ***(G-14484)***
Centerless Grinder Repair Div, Roseville *Also called Aero Grinding Inc* ***(G-13770)***
Centerless Rebuilders Inc 517 596-3233
9053 Plum Orchard Rd Munith (49259) ***(G-11252)***
Centerless Rebuilders Inc (PA) 586 749-6529
57877 Main St New Haven (48048) ***(G-11523)***
CENTERLINE DIE & ENGINEERING, Roseville *Also called True Industrial Corporation* ***(G-13882)***
Centerline Engineering Inc 616 735-2506
940 7 Mile Rd Nw Comstock Park (49321) ***(G-3466)***
Centerline Indus Fabrication 313 977-9056
7397 Mentel Rd Newport (48166) ***(G-11587)***
Centerpoint Tungsten LLC 810 797-5196
4427 Snook Rd Metamora (48455) ***(G-10773)***
Centracore LLC (PA) 586 776-5700
315 Whiting St Saint Clair (48079) ***(G-14209)***
Centracore De Mexico LLC 586 776-5700
315 Whiting St Saint Clair (48079) ***(G-14210)***
Central Admxture Phrm Svcs Inc 734 953-6760
37497 Schoolcraft Rd Livonia (48150) ***(G-9680)***
Central Asphalt Inc 989 772-0720
900 S Bradley St Mount Pleasant (48858) ***(G-11183)***
Central Concrete Products Inc 810 659-7488
4067 Commerce Dr Flushing (48433) ***(G-5532)***
Central Conveyor Company LLC (HQ) 248 446-0118
52800 Pontiac Trl Wixom (48393) ***(G-17782)***
Central Elevator Co Inc (PA) 269 329-0705
18 Baur Ln Vicksburg (49097) ***(G-16833)***
Central Gear Inc 800 589-1602
540 Ajax Dr Madison Heights (48071) ***(G-10208)***
Central Industrial Corporation 616 784-9612
2916 Walkent Dr Nw Grand Rapids (49544) ***(G-6267)***
Central Industrial Mfg Inc 231 347-5920
1211 W Conway Rd Harbor Springs (49740) ***(G-7277)***
Central Industrial Packaging, Grand Rapids *Also called Central Industrial Corporation* ***(G-6267)***
Central Lake Armor Express Inc 231 544-6090
7915 Cameron St Central Lake (49622) ***(G-2588)***
Central Lenawee Sewage Plant 517 263-0955
4350 Deerfield Rd Adrian (49221) ***(G-55)***
Central Metalizing & Machine, Saginaw *Also called Treib Inc* ***(G-14166)***
Central Mich Cmenting Svcs LLC 989 775-0940
1961 Commercial Dr Mount Pleasant (48858) ***(G-11184)***
Central Mich Knwrth Lnsing LLC 517 394-7000
2556 Alamo Dr Lansing (48911) ***(G-9356)***
Central Mich Knwrth Sginaw LLC 989 754-4500
3046 Commerce Centre Dr Saginaw (48601) ***(G-14014)***
Central Michigan Crematory 269 963-1554
151506 One Half Mile Rd Battle Creek (49014) ***(G-1165)***
Central Michigan Engravers 517 485-5865
412 W Gier St Lansing (48906) ***(G-9208)***
Central Michigan Rapid Print 989 772-3110
1206 N Fancher Ave Mount Pleasant (48858) ***(G-11185)***
Central Michigan Tank Rental 989 681-5963
9701 Gruett Rd Saint Louis (48880) ***(G-14360)***

ALPHABETIC

Central Michigan University 989 774-3493
436 Moore Hall Mount Pleasant (48859) *(G-11186)*

Central Michigan University 989 774-3216
160 Combined Svcs Bldg Mount Pleasant (48859) *(G-11187)*

Central Ohio Paper & Packg Inc 734 955-9960
9675 Harrison Ste 100-101 Romulus (48174) *(G-13662)*

Central On Line Data Systems 586 939-7000
34200 Mound Rd Sterling Heights (48310) *(G-15284)*

Central Screw Products Company 313 893-9100
1070 Maplelawn Dr Troy (48084) *(G-16262)*

Central Vac International, Dollar Bay Also called Young Manufacturing Inc *(G-4522)*

Centro Division, Detroit Also called Hackett Brass Foundry Co *(G-4113)*

Centrum Force Fabrication LLC 517 857-4774
3425 Stone School Rd Ann Arbor (48108) *(G-398)*

Centurn Machine & Tool Inc 231 947-4773
6185 E Traverse Hwy Traverse City (49684) *(G-15931)*

Century Inc (PA) 231 947-6400
2410 W Aero Park Ct Traverse City (49686) *(G-15932)*

Century Inc 231 946-7500
2410 W Aero Park Ct Traverse City (49686) *(G-15933)*

Century Inc 231 941-7800
2411 W Aero Park Ct Traverse City (49686) *(G-15934)*

Century Foundry Inc 231 733-1572
339 W Hovey Ave Muskegon (49444) *(G-11293)*

Century Fuel Products 734 728-0300
51225 Martz Rd Van Buren Twp (48111) *(G-16751)*

Century Instrument Company 734 427-0340
11865 Mayfield St Livonia (48150) *(G-9681)*

Century Plastics LLC 586 697-5752
51102 Quadrate Dr Macomb (48042) *(G-10115)*

Century Plastics LLC (HQ) 586 566-3900
15030 23 Mile Rd Shelby Township (48315) *(G-14559)*

Century Plastics Inc 586 566-3900
15030 23 Mile Rd Shelby Township (48315) *(G-14560)*

Century Tool & Gage LLC 810 629-0784
200 S Alloy Dr Fenton (48430) *(G-5193)*

Century Tool Welding Inc 586 758-3330
32873 Groesbeck Hwy Fraser (48026) *(G-5637)*

Century Truss 248 486-4000
17199 N Laurel Park Dr # 402 Livonia (48152) *(G-9682)*

Century-Sun Metal Treating, Traverse City Also called Century Inc *(G-15932)*

Century-Sun Metal Treating, Traverse City Also called Century Inc *(G-15934)*

Cequent Performance Group, Plymouth Also called Horizon Global Americas Inc *(G-12643)*

Cequent Uk Ltd 734 656-3000
47912 Halyard Dr Ste 100 Plymouth (48170) *(G-12595)*

Ceratizit Usa Inc 586 759-2280
11355 Stephens Rd Warren (48089) *(G-16977)*

Cerco Inc (PA) 734 362-8664
27301 Fort St Brownstown Twp (48183) *(G-2071)*

Cerephex Corporation 517 719-0414
3001 Miller Rd Bancroft (48414) *(G-1087)*

Cerny Industries LLC 231 929-2140
1645 Park Dr Traverse City (49686) *(G-15935)*

Certainteed Corporation 517 787-8898
701 E Washington Ave Jackson (49203) *(G-8405)*

Certainteed Corporation 517 787-1737
803 Belden Rd Jackson (49203) *(G-8406)*

Certainteed Gypsum Inc 906 524-6101
200 S Main St Lanse (49946) *(G-9189)*

Certified Metal Products Inc 586 598-1000
22802 Morelli Dr Clinton Township (48036) *(G-3077)*

Certified Reducer Rbldrs Inc 248 585-0883
6480 Sims Dr Sterling Heights (48313) *(G-15285)*

CERTIFIED SHEET METAL, Muskegon Also called East Muskegon Roofg Shtmtl Co *(G-11313)*

Certified Sheet Metal, Grand Rapids Also called East Muskegon Roofg Shtmtl Co *(G-6367)*

Cerutti Bernal, Rochester Hills Also called Bernal LLC *(G-13377)*

Cesere Enterprises Inc 989 799-3350
2614 State St Saginaw (48602) *(G-14015)*

CFC, Grand Rapids Also called Contract Flavors Inc *(G-6304)*

Cft Company, Milford Also called Breesport Holdings Inc *(G-10956)*

Cg & D Group 248 310-9166
23700 Paddock Dr Farmington Hills (48336) *(G-4960)*

CG Automation & Fixture Inc 616 785-5400
5352 Rusche Dr Nw Comstock Park (49321) *(G-3467)*

Cg Liquidation Incorporated (HQ) 586 575-9800
2111 Walter P Reuther Dr Warren (48091) *(G-16978)*

Cg Logging 906 322-1018
11375 W Irish Line Rd Brimley (49715) *(G-2014)*

Cg Plastics Inc 616 785-1900
5349 Rusche Dr Nw Comstock Park (49321) *(G-3468)*

CG&d Consulting, Farmington Hills Also called Cg & D Group *(G-4960)*

Chadko LLC 616 402-9207
725 Taylor Ave Ste B Grand Haven (49417) *(G-6002)*

Chain Industries Inc (PA) 248 348-7722
51035 Grand River Ave Wixom (48393) *(G-17783)*

Chain-Sys Corporation (PA) 517 627-1173
8530 Ember Glen Pass Lansing (48917) *(G-9281)*

Chainsaw Man of Michigan 586 977-7856
28312 Katie Rd Chesterfield (48047) *(G-2752)*

Chair City Supply, Sterling Heights Also called Richelieu America Ltd *(G-15469)*

Chaldean News LLC 248 996-8360
30850 Telg Rd Ste 220 Bingham Farms (48025) *(G-1650)*

Chalker Tool & Gauge Inc 586 977-8660
35425 Beattie Dr Sterling Heights (48312) *(G-15286)*

Challenge Machinery Company (PA) 231 799-8484
6125 Norton Center Dr Norton Shores (49441) *(G-11745)*

Challenge Mfg Company 616 735-6500
6375 W Grand River Ave Lansing (48906) *(G-9209)*

Challenge Mfg Company 616 735-6530
3200 Fruit Ridge Ave Nw Walker (49544) *(G-16862)*

Challenge Mfg Company 616 735-6500
3200 Fruit Ridge Ave Nw Grand Rapids (49544) *(G-6268)*

Challenge Mfg Company 616 396-2079
1401 Washington Ave Holland (49423) *(G-7587)*

Challenge Mfg Company LLC 616 735-6500
2969 3 Mile Rd Nw Walker (49534) *(G-16863)*

Challenge Mfg Company LLC (PA) 616 735-6500
3200 Fruit Ridge Ave Nw Walker (49544) *(G-16864)*

Challenge Packaging Division, Dearborn Also called E C Moore Company *(G-3696)*

Challenger Communications LLC 517 680-0125
7241 Monroe Rd Springport (49284) *(G-15208)*

Chalq LLC 269 330-1514
5200 Croyden Ave Kalamazoo (49009) *(G-8705)*

Chambers Industrial Tech Inc 616 249-8190
2220 Byron Center Ave Sw Wyoming (49519) *(G-17991)*

Chambers Ottawa Inc 231 238-2122
2064 Campbell Rd Cheboygan (49721) *(G-2676)*

Chames LLC 616 363-0000
163 Ann St Ne Ste 1 Grand Rapids (49505) *(G-6269)*

Champagne Grinding & Mfg Co 734 459-1759
8600 Ronda Dr Canton (48187) *(G-2360)*

Champion Alloys, Lake Odessa Also called Franklin Metal Trading Corp *(G-9114)*

Champion Bus Inc 810 724-1753
331 Graham Rd Imlay City (48444) *(G-8197)*

Champion Charter Sls & Svc Inc 906 779-2300
180 Traders Mine Rd Iron Mountain (49801) *(G-8280)*

Champion Die Incorporated 616 784-2397
5510 West River Dr Ne Comstock Park (49321) *(G-3469)*

Champion Foods LLC 734 753-3663
23900 Bell Rd New Boston (48164) *(G-11499)*

Champion Fortune Corporation 989 422-6130
387 S Harrison Rd Houghton Lake (48629) *(G-7988)*

Champion Gasket & Rubber Inc 248 624-6140
3225 Haggerty Hwy Commerce Township (48390) *(G-3394)*

Champion Home Builders Inc (HQ) 248 614-8200
755 W Big Beaver Rd # 1000 Troy (48084) *(G-16263)*

Champion Laboratories Inc 586 247-9044
51180 Celeste Shelby Township (48315) *(G-14561)*

Champion Plastics Inc 248 373-8995
1892 Taylor Rd Auburn Hills (48326) *(G-812)*

Champion Screw Machine Engrg, Wixom Also called Champion Screw Machine Svcs *(G-17784)*

Champion Screw Machine Svcs 248 624-4545
30419 Beck Rd Wixom (48393) *(G-17784)*

Champion Screw Mch Engrg Inc (PA) 248 624-4545
30419 Beck Rd Wixom (48393) *(G-17785)*

Champion Tool Company 248 474-6200
24060 Orchard Lake Rd Farmington Hills (48336) *(G-4961)*

Champion Window & Patio Room 616 554-1600
4717 Broadmoor Ave Se J Grand Rapids (49512) *(G-6270)*

Champlain Specialty Metals Inc 269 926-7241
2235 Dewey Ave Benton Harbor (49022) *(G-1489)*

Chandas Engineering Inc 313 582-8666
4800 Curtis St Dearborn (48126) *(G-3687)*

Chandler Ricchio Pubg LLC 269 660-0840
890 Wattles Rd N Battle Creek (49014) *(G-1166)*

Changan US R&D Center, Plymouth Also called Changan US RES & Dev Ctr Inc *(G-12596)*

Changan US RES & Dev Ctr Inc 734 259-6440
47799 Halyard Dr Ste 77 Plymouth (48170) *(G-12596)*

Change Dynamix Inc 248 671-6700
4327 Delemere Ct Royal Oak (48073) *(G-13913)*

Change Healthcare Tech LLC 810 985-0029
1530 Pine Grove Ave Ste 7 Port Huron (48060) *(G-12906)*

Change Parts Incorporated 231 845-5107
185 S Jebavy Dr Ludington (49431) *(G-10052)*

Changeover Integration LLC 231 845-5320
787 S Pere Marquette Hwy Ludington (49431) *(G-10053)*

Changer & Dresser Inc 256 832-4392
40000 Grand River Ave # 106 Novi (48375) *(G-11847)*

Chardam Gear Company Inc 586 795-8900
40805 Mound Rd Sterling Heights (48310) *(G-15287)*

Charidimos Inc 248 827-7733
23100 Telegraph Rd Southfield (48033) *(G-14865)*

Charles Bowman & Company 616 786-4000
3328 John F Donnelly Dr Holland (49424) *(G-7588)*

Charles Bridenstine 269 699-5170
21716 Channel Pkwy Edwardsburg (49112) *(G-4762)*

Charles Group Inc (PA)....336 882-0186
7441 Div Ave S Ste A1 Grand Rapids (49548) *(G-6271)*
Charles Lange....989 777-0110
5763 Dixie Hwy Saginaw (48601) *(G-14016)*
Charles Levy Circulating, Cadillac *Also called Chas Levy Circulating Co (G-2241)*
Charles Phipps and Sons Ltd....810 359-7141
6951 Lakeshore Rd Lexington (48450) *(G-9556)*
Charles Walton....517 332-1842
810 Roxburgh Ave East Lansing (48823) *(G-4654)*
Charles William Carr Sr....231 854-3643
6379 S Maple Island Rd Hesperia (49421) *(G-7477)*
Charlevoix Courier, The, Petoskey *Also called Northern Michigan Review Inc (G-12464)*
Charlevoix Machine Products....231 547-2697
15164 Ferry Rd Charlevoix (49720) *(G-2611)*
Charlevoix Screen Masters Inc....231 547-5111
12512 Taylor Rd Charlevoix (49720) *(G-2612)*
Charlies Wood Shop....989 845-2632
603 S Main St Chesaning (48616) *(G-2722)*
Charlotte Anodizing Pdts Inc....517 543-1911
591 Packard Hwy Charlotte (48813) *(G-2638)*
Charlotte Cabinets Inc....517 543-1522
629 W Seminary St Charlotte (48813) *(G-2639)*
Charlotte Lithograph, Charlotte *Also called J-Ad Graphics Inc (G-2656)*
Charter House Holdings LLC....616 399-6000
200 N Franklin St Ste B Zeeland (49464) *(G-18124)*
Charter Inds Extrusions Inc (PA)....616 245-3388
3900 S Greenbrooke Dr Se Grand Rapids (49512) *(G-6272)*
Chas Levy Circulating Co....231 779-8940
1125 1st Ave Cadillac (49601) *(G-2241)*
Chase Nedrow Manufacturing Inc....248 669-9886
150 Landrow Dr Wixom (48393) *(G-17786)*
Chase Plastic Services Inc....616 246-7190
1115 Cadillac Dr Se Grand Rapids (49506) *(G-6273)*
Chasix, Port Huron *Also called Aludyne US LLC (G-12890)*
Chassis Brakes Intl USA (PA)....248 957-9997
27260 Haggerty Rd Ste A8 Farmington Hills (48331) *(G-4962)*
Chassis Co. of Michigan, LLC, Port Huron *Also called Aludyne East Michigan LLC (G-12888)*
Chassis Shop Prfmce Pdts Inc....231 873-3640
1931 N 24th Ave Mears (49436) *(G-10686)*
Chassix - Dmi Montague, Southfield *Also called Aludyne Montague LLC (G-14834)*
Chassix Blackstone Operat....586 782-7311
23300 Blackstone Ave Warren (48089) *(G-16979)*
Chateau Aronautique Winery LLC....517 569-2132
101 Chief Dr Jackson (49201) *(G-8407)*
Chateau Chantal, Traverse City *Also called Chateau Operations Ltd (G-15937)*
Chateau De Leelanau Vineyard, Suttons Bay *Also called Black & Red Inc (G-15649)*
Chateau Grand Travers Ltd....231 223-7355
12239 Center Rd Traverse City (49686) *(G-15936)*
Chateau Grand Traverse, Traverse City *Also called OKeefe Centre Ltd (G-16056)*
Chateau Operations Ltd....231 223-4110
15900 Rue De Vin Traverse City (49686) *(G-15937)*
Chaubrei Gardens, Richland *Also called Eileen Smeltzer (G-13248)*
Cheal Woodworking, Toivola *Also called Thomas Cheal (G-15885)*
Cheboygan Cement Products Inc (PA)....231 627-5631
702 Lafayette Ave Cheboygan (49721) *(G-2677)*
Cheboygan Cement Products Inc....989 742-4107
800 E Progress St Hillman (49746) *(G-7508)*
Cheboygan Golf and Country CLB....231 627-4264
1431 Old Mackinaw Rd Cheboygan (49721) *(G-2678)*
Cheboygan Golf Club Pro Shop, Cheboygan *Also called Cheboygan Golf and Country CLB (G-2678)*
Cheboygan Harbor Marine, Cheboygan *Also called J B Lunds & Sons Inc (G-2682)*
Cheboygan Housing Commission....231 627-7189
659 Cuyler St Cheboygan (49721) *(G-2679)*
Cheboygan Tribune, Cheboygan *Also called Shoppers Fair Inc (G-2695)*
Check Technology Solutions LLC....248 680-2323
1800 Stephenson Hwy Troy (48083) *(G-16264)*
Cheers Embroidery, Grayling *Also called Sylvesters (G-7116)*
Cheese Lady The, Traverse City *Also called Reilchz Inc (G-16093)*
Cheeze Kurls, Grand Rapids *Also called Dedinas & Franzak Entps Inc (G-6342)*
Chefshell Catering, Port Huron *Also called Jabars Complements LLC (G-12931)*
Chelsea Grain LLC....734 475-1386
11800 Dexter Chelsea Rd Chelsea (48118) *(G-2703)*
Chelsea Grinding Company....517 796-0343
2417 Vinsetta Blvd Royal Oak (48073) *(G-13914)*
Chelsea Milling Company (PA)....734 475-1361
201 W North St Chelsea (48118) *(G-2704)*
Chelsea Milling Company....269 781-2823
310 W Oliver Dr Marshall (49068) *(G-10564)*
Chelsea Tool Inc....734 475-9679
20401 W Old Us Highway 12 # 4 Chelsea (48118) *(G-2705)*
Chelsea-Megan Holding Inc....248 307-9160
1121 Rochester Rd Troy (48083) *(G-16265)*
Chem Link Inc....269 679-4440
353 E Lyons St Schoolcraft (49087) *(G-14491)*
Chem-Trend Holding Inc....517 545-7980
1445 Mcpherson Park Dr Howell (48843) *(G-8021)*
Chem-Trend Limited Partnership (HQ)....517 546-4520
1445 Mcpherson Park Dr Howell (48843) *(G-8022)*
Chem-Trend Limited Partnership....517 546-4520
3205 E Grand River Ave Howell (48843) *(G-8023)*
Chemcast, Troy *Also called US Farathane Holdings Corp (G-16666)*
Chemcoa, Detroit *Also called Chemical Company of America (G-3932)*
Chemeisters Inc....313 538-5550
26202 W 7 Mile Rd Redford (48240) *(G-13152)*
Chemetall Americas, Jackson *Also called Chemetall US Inc (G-8408)*
Chemetall US Inc....517 787-4846
1100 Technology Dr Jackson (49201) *(G-8408)*
Chemical, Farmington Hills *Also called P & C Group I Inc (G-5087)*
Chemical Company of America....313 272-4310
8951 Freeland St Detroit (48228) *(G-3932)*
Chemical Process Inds LLC....248 547-5200
25428 John R Rd Madison Heights (48071) *(G-10209)*
Chemical Specialties, Caledonia *Also called Helen Inc (G-2297)*
Chemico Mays, Southfield *Also called Chemico Systems Inc (G-14866)*
Chemico Systems Inc (PA)....248 723-3263
25200 Telg Rd Ste 120 Southfield (48034) *(G-14866)*
Chemico Systems Inc....586 986-2343
6250 Chicago Rd Warren (48092) *(G-16980)*
Chemincon Inc....734 439-2478
345 E Main St Milan (48160) *(G-10933)*
Chemloc Inc....989 465-6541
4996 N Dickenson Rd Coleman (48618) *(G-3342)*
Chemsol, Livonia *Also called Quantum Chemical LLC (G-9901)*
Chemtool Incorporated....734 439-7010
415 Squires Dr Milan (48160) *(G-10934)*
Chemtrade Chemicals US LLC....313 842-5222
800 Marion Ave Detroit (48218) *(G-3933)*
Cherokee Industries Inc....248 333-1343
28 N Saginaw St Ste 911 Pontiac (48342) *(G-12808)*
Cherry Bend Tool & Die....231 947-3046
Hoxie Rd Cedar (49621) *(G-2540)*
Cherry Blossom....231 342-3635
8365 Park Rd Williamsburg (49690) *(G-17710)*
Cherry Central Cooperative Inc (PA)....231 946-1860
1771 N Us 31 S Traverse City (49685) *(G-15938)*
Cherry Central Cooperative Inc....231 861-2141
168 Lincoln St Shelby (49455) *(G-14524)*
Cherry Cone LLC....231 944-1036
240 E Front St Traverse City (49684) *(G-15939)*
Cherry Creek Post Co, Evart *Also called Cherry Creek Post LLC (G-4880)*
Cherry Creek Post LLC....231 734-2466
5882 7 Mile Rd Evart (49631) *(G-4880)*
Cherry Growers Inc (PA)....231 276-9241
401 S Old Woodward Ave # 340 Birmingham (48009) *(G-1676)*
Cherry Growers Inc....231 947-2502
9440 S Center Hwy Traverse City (49684) *(G-15940)*
Cherry Growers Plant 2, Traverse City *Also called Cherry Growers Inc (G-15940)*
Cherry Hut Products LLC (PA)....231 882-4431
1046 Michigan Ave Benzonia (49616) *(G-1574)*
Cherry Republic Inc (PA)....231 334-3150
6026 S Lake St Glen Arbor (49636) *(G-5940)*
Chesterfield Engines Inc....586 949-5777
52420 Gratiot Ave Chesterfield (48051) *(G-2753)*
Chesterfield Engines Nic, Chesterfield *Also called Chesterfield Engines Inc (G-2753)*
Chewys Gourmet Kitchen LLC....313 757-2595
2939 Russell St Detroit (48207) *(G-3934)*
CHI Co/Tabor Hill Winery (PA)....269 422-1161
185 Mount Tabor Rd Buchanan (49107) *(G-2113)*
CHI Co/Tabor Hill Winery....269 465-6566
10243 Red Arrow Hwy Bridgman (49106) *(G-1861)*
Chicago Blow Pipe Company....773 533-6100
405 Lakewood Ln Marquette (49855) *(G-10522)*
Chicago Mfg & Dist Co....989 665-2531
6592 Lincoln St Gagetown (48735) *(G-5801)*
Chicago Miniature Optoelectron, Troy *Also called Chicl LLC (G-16266)*
Chicl LLC....859 294-5590
1708 Northwood Dr Troy (48084) *(G-16266)*
Chief EDM....586 752-5078
9703 Cranbrook Ct Bruce Twp (48065) *(G-2079)*
Chiipss....248 345-6112
10229 Joseph Campau St Detroit (48212) *(G-3935)*
Child Evngelism Fellowship Inc....269 461-6953
7463 Elm St Berrien Center (49102) *(G-1590)*
Childrens Bible Hour Inc (PA)....616 647-4500
2060 43rd St Se Grand Rapids (49508) *(G-6274)*
Childs Carpentry....734 425-8783
31585 Birchlawn St Garden City (48135) *(G-5821)*
Chiodini & Sons Printing....248 548-0064
21721 Dequindre Rd Hazel Park (48030) *(G-7436)*
Chip Systems International....269 626-8000
10953 Norscott St Scotts (49088) *(G-14503)*
Chippewa Development Inc....269 685-2646
960 Industrial Pkwy Plainwell (49080) *(G-12519)*
Chippewa Farm Supply LLC....989 471-5523
6701 N Us Highway 23 Spruce (48762) *(G-15213)*

A L P H A B E T I C

Chippewa Plastics, Evart *Also called Rkaa Business LLC* ***(G-4886)***
Chippewa Stone & Gravel Inc.....231 867-5757
15240 110th Ave Rodney (49342) ***(G-13612)***
Chivis Sportsman Cases.....231 834-1162
1192 E 112th St Grant (49327) ***(G-7079)***
Chocolate Vault Llc.....517 688-3388
8475 Chicago Rd Horton (49246) ***(G-7963)***
Choctaw-Kaul Distribution Co, Detroit *Also called Kaul Glove and Mfg Co* ***(G-4172)***
Choice Corporation.....586 783-5600
44383 Reynolds Dr Clinton Township (48036) ***(G-3078)***
Choice Mold Components, Clinton Township *Also called Choice Corporation* ***(G-3078)***
Choice Mold Components Inc.....586 783-5600
44383 Reynolds Dr Clinton Township (48036) ***(G-3079)***
Choice Publications Inc.....989 732-8160
112 E 6th St Gaylord (49735) ***(G-5852)***
Chor Industries Inc.....248 585-3323
500 Robbins Dr Troy (48083) ***(G-16267)***
Chouteau Fuels Company LLC.....734 302-4800
414 S Main St Ste 600 Ann Arbor (48104) ***(G-399)***
CHR W LLC.....989 755-4000
2795 Harrison St Saginaw (48604) ***(G-14017)***
Chris Faulknor.....231 645-1970
5 W Main St Unit 7 Boyne City (49712) ***(G-1819)***
Chris Muma Forest Products.....989 426-5916
1154 W 1st St Gladwin (48624) ***(G-5927)***
Chris Underhill.....231 349-5228
22772 18 Mile Rd Big Rapids (49307) ***(G-1624)***
Christensen Fiberglass LLC.....616 738-1219
126 Aniline Ave N Holland (49424) ***(G-7589)***
Christian Oil Company.....269 673-2218
2589 30th St Allegan (49010) ***(G-152)***
Christian Pages, Troy *Also called Interntonal Innovative Systems* ***(G-16421)***
Christian Schools Intl.....616 957-1070
3350 East Paris Ave Se Grand Rapids (49512) ***(G-6275)***
Christian Unity Press Inc.....402 362-5133
5195 Exchange Dr Ste A Flint (48507) ***(G-5397)***
Christianson Industries Inc.....269 663-8502
27328 May St Edwardsburg (49112) ***(G-4763)***
Christman Screenprint Inc.....800 962-9330
2822 Wilbur St Springfield (49037) ***(G-15189)***
Christmas Sports Enterprise.....616 895-6238
7490 Taylor St Hudsonville (49426) ***(G-8150)***
Christopher S Campion.....517 414-6796
258 Ackerson Lake Dr Jackson (49201) ***(G-8409)***
Christy Vault Company Inc.....415 994-1378
3669 Bridgehampton Dr Ne Grand Rapids (49546) ***(G-6276)***
Chromatech Inc (PA).....734 451-1230
7723 Market Dr Canton (48187) ***(G-2361)***
Chromatic Graphics Inc.....616 393-0034
654 E Lakewood Blvd Holland (49424) ***(G-7590)***
Chrome Wheel Exchange LLC.....810 360-0298
4337 E Grand River Ave Howell (48843) ***(G-8024)***
Chrouch Communications Inc.....231 972-0339
6644 9 Mile Rd Mecosta (49332) ***(G-10687)***
Chrysan Industries Inc (PA).....734 451-5411
14707 Keel St Plymouth (48170) ***(G-12597)***
Chrysler, Auburn Hills *Also called FCA US LLC* ***(G-868)***
Chrysler & Koppin Company.....313 491-7100
7000 Intervale St Detroit (48238) ***(G-3936)***
Chrysler Engine Plant 2, Detroit *Also called FCA US LLC* ***(G-4054)***
Chrysler Group LLC.....586 977-4900
7150 Metropolitan Pkwy Sterling Heights (48312) ***(G-15288)***
Chrysler International Sales, Sterling Heights *Also called FCA US LLC* ***(G-15337)***
Chrysler Sterling Test Center, Sterling Heights *Also called Chrysler Group LLC* ***(G-15288)***
Chrysler Twinsburg Stamping, Auburn Hills *Also called FCA US LLC* ***(G-867)***
Chuck and Dave's Salsa, Fraser *Also called Buddies Foods LLC* ***(G-5632)***
Ci Lighting LLC.....248 997-4415
2083 Pontiac Rd Auburn Hills (48326) ***(G-813)***
Cie USA, Shelby Township *Also called Century Plastics LLC* ***(G-14559)***
Cig Jan Products Ltd.....616 698-9070
3300 Hanna Lk Indus Dr Se Caledonia (49316) ***(G-2294)***
Cignet LLC (PA).....586 307-3790
24601 Capital Blvd Clinton Township (48036) ***(G-3080)***
Cignys, Saginaw *Also called Saginaw Products Corporation* ***(G-14141)***
Cignys, Saginaw *Also called Saginaw Products Corporation* ***(G-14143)***
Cignys Bridgeport, Saginaw *Also called Charles Lange* ***(G-14016)***
Cignys Inc.....989 753-1411
68 Williamson St Saginaw (48601) ***(G-14018)***
Cilluffo Son Studio & Gallery, Clay *Also called J Cilluffo Son Studio* ***(G-2998)***
Cima Energy LP.....231 941-0633
125 S Park St Ste 450 Traverse City (49684) ***(G-15941)***
Cincinnati Time Systems Inc.....248 615-8300
23399 Commerce Dr Ste B3 Farmington Hills (48335) ***(G-4963)***
Cincinnati Tyrolit Inc.....513 458-8121
4636 Regency Dr Shelby Township (48316) ***(G-14562)***
Cindys Suds LLC.....616 485-1983
12415 Downes St Ne Lowell (49331) ***(G-10026)***
Cinnabar Engineering Inc.....810 648-2444
116 Orval St Sandusky (48471) ***(G-14431)***
Cipa Usa Inc (PA).....810 982-3555
3350 Griswold Rd Port Huron (48060) ***(G-12907)***
Circle C Mold & Plastics Group.....269 496-5515
55664 Parkville Rd Mendon (49072) ***(G-10712)***
Circle Engineering Inc.....586 978-8120
5495 Gatewood Dr Sterling Heights (48310) ***(G-15289)***
Circle K Service Corporation.....989 496-0511
4300 James Savage Rd Midland (48642) ***(G-10824)***
Circle S Products Inc (PA).....734 675-2960
16415 Carter Rd Woodhaven (48183) ***(G-17938)***
Circles Way To Go Around Inc.....313 384-1193
43508 Rivergate Dr Clinton Township (48038) ***(G-3081)***
Circuit Controls Corporation.....231 347-0760
2277 M 119 Petoskey (49770) ***(G-12444)***
Circuits of Sound.....313 886-5599
840 Shoreham Rd Grosse Pointe Woods (48236) ***(G-7201)***
Circular Motion LLC.....989 779-9040
4265 Corporate Dr Mount Pleasant (48858) ***(G-11188)***
Circus Procession LLC.....616 834-8048
622 Graafschap Rd Holland (49423) ***(G-7591)***
Cisco Systems Inc.....800 553-6387
200 Renaissance Ctr Detroit (48243) ***(G-3937)***
Citation Berlin, Southfield *Also called Grede Wscnsin Subsidiaries LLC* ***(G-14930)***
Citation Camden Cast Ctr LLC.....248 727-1800
1 Towne Sq Ste 550 Southfield (48076) ***(G-14867)***
Citation Lost Foam Pttrns LLC.....248 727-1800
1 Towne Sq Ste 550 Southfield (48076) ***(G-14868)***
Citation Michigan LLC.....248 522-4500
27275 Haggerty Rd Ste 420 Novi (48377) ***(G-11848)***
Citizen Newspaper, The, Ortonville *Also called Sherman Publications Inc* ***(G-12204)***
Citizens LLC.....517 541-1449
421 N Cochran Ave Charlotte (48813) ***(G-2640)***
City Animation Co (PA).....248 589-0600
57 Park Dr Troy (48083) ***(G-16268)***
City Animation Co.....989 743-3458
1013 N Shiawassee St Corunna (48817) ***(G-3579)***
City Auto Glass Co.....616 842-3235
295 N Beechtree St Grand Haven (49417) ***(G-6003)***
City of East Jordan.....231 536-2561
218 N Lake St East Jordan (49727) ***(G-4627)***
City of Greenville.....616 754-0100
415 S Lafayette St Greenville (48838) ***(G-7124)***
City of Port Huron.....810 984-9775
100 Merchant St Port Huron (48060) ***(G-12908)***
City of Saginaw.....989 759-1670
1741 S Jefferson Ave Saginaw (48601) ***(G-14019)***
City of Taylor.....734 374-1372
25605 Northline Rd Taylor (48180) ***(G-15700)***
City Press Inc.....800 867-2626
30 Rissman Ln Ortonville (48462) ***(G-12197)***
City Printing Co of Ypsilanti.....734 482-8490
411 W Cross St Ypsilanti (48197) ***(G-18060)***
City Sign Company, Pontiac *Also called Wenz & Gibbens Enterprises* ***(G-12874)***
CJ Chemicals LLC.....888 274-1044
1410 Milton Rd Perry (48872) ***(G-12433)***
Cj's Smoked Spc Dom Game Proc, Hesperia *Also called Lowry Joanellen* ***(G-7478)***
Cjg LLC.....734 793-1400
31800 Industrial Rd Livonia (48150) ***(G-9683)***
Cjm Maintenance.....734 285-0247
18322 Koester St Wyandotte (48193) ***(G-17952)***
Clair Evans-St Inc.....313 259-2266
200 Rnmiance Ctr Ste 3150 Detroit (48243) ***(G-3938)***
Clair Sawyer.....906 228-8242
1225 W Washington St Marquette (49855) ***(G-10523)***
Clamp Industries Incorporated.....248 335-8131
342 Irwin Ave Pontiac (48341) ***(G-12809)***
Clamptech LLC.....989 832-8027
106 S Walnut St Ste 1 Bay City (48706) ***(G-1295)***
Clancy Crushed Concrete, Roseville *Also called Clancy Excavating Co* ***(G-13781)***
Clancy Excavating Co.....586 294-2900
29950 Little Mack Ave Roseville (48066) ***(G-13781)***
Clare Bedding Mfg Co.....906 789-9902
433 Stephenson Ave Escanaba (49829) ***(G-4822)***
Clare County Cleaver Inc.....989 539-7496
183 W Main St Harrison (48625) ***(G-7310)***
Clare County Review.....989 386-4414
105 W 4th St Ste 1 Clare (48617) ***(G-2866)***
Clare Print & Pulp.....989 386-3497
409 N Mcewan St Clare (48617) ***(G-2867)***
Clarence McNamara Logging, Newberry *Also called McNamara & Mcnamara* ***(G-11580)***
Clariant Plas Coatings USA LLC.....517 629-9101
926 Elliott St Albion (49224) ***(G-120)***
Clarion Corporation America.....248 991-3100
34500 Grand River Ave Farmington (48335) ***(G-4896)***
Clarion Group, Farmington *Also called Clarion Corporation America* ***(G-4896)***
Clarion Technologies Inc (PA).....616 698-7277
170 College Ave Ste 300 Holland (49423) ***(G-7592)***

Clarion Technologies Inc 616 754-1199
501 S Cedar St Greenville (48838) *(G-7125)*
Clarity Cbd LLC 248 251-6991
1401 W Fort St Detroit (48232) *(G-3939)*
Clarity Comm Advisors Inc 248 327-4390
2 Corporate Dr Ste 250 Southfield (48076) *(G-14869)*
Clarity Voice, Southfield *Also called Clarity Comm Advisors Inc (G-14869)*
Clark Brothers Instrument Co 586 781-7000
56680 Mound Rd Shelby Township (48316) *(G-14563)*
Clark Engineering Co (PA) 989 723-7930
1470 Mcmillan Rd Owosso (48867) *(G-12282)*
Clark Granco Inc 616 794-2600
7298 Storey Rd Belding (48809) *(G-1407)*
Clark Graphic Service Inc 586 772-4900
21914 Schmeman Ave Warren (48089) *(G-16981)*
Clark Graphics, Warren *Also called Clark Graphic Service Inc (G-16981)*
Clark Instrument Inc 248 669-3100
46590 Ryan Ct Novi (48377) *(G-11849)*
Clark Manufacturing Company 231 946-5110
2485 Aero Park Dr Traverse City (49686) *(G-15942)*
Clark Perforating Company Inc 734 439-1170
15875 Allen Rd Milan (48160) *(G-10935)*
Clark-Mxr Inc 734 426-2803
7300 Huron River Dr Ste 1 Dexter (48130) *(G-4481)*
Clarklake Machine Incorporated 517 529-9454
9451 S Meridian Rd Clarklake (49234) *(G-2895)*
Clarkson Controls & Eqp Co 248 380-9915
42572 Cherry Hill Rd Novi (48375) *(G-11850)*
Clarkson Smoothie Inc 248 620-8005
7150 Sashabaw Rd Clarkston (48348) *(G-2911)*
Clarkston Carbide Tool & Mch (PA) 248 625-3182
1959 Viola Dr Ortonville (48462) *(G-12198)*
Clarkston Control Products 248 394-1430
4809 Crestview Dr Clarkston (48348) *(G-2912)*
Clarkston Courts LLC 248 383-8444
6110 Dixie Hwy Clarkston (48346) *(G-2913)*
Clarkston News, Clarkston *Also called Sherman Publications Inc (G-2955)*
Clas Carbide 248 236-8353
957 S Glaspie St Oxford (48371) *(G-12342)*
Class A Tool & Machine LLC 231 788-3822
770 S Maple Island Rd Muskegon (49442) *(G-11294)*
Classfcation Flotation Systems 810 714-5200
235 Industrial Way Fenton (48430) *(G-5194)*
Classic Accents Inc 734 284-7661
13631 Brest St Southgate (48195) *(G-15075)*
Classic Cabinets Interiors LLC 517 817-5650
807 S Brown St Jackson (49203) *(G-8410)*
Classic Cabinets Interiors LLC (PA) 517 423-2600
118 W Chicago Blvd Tecumseh (49286) *(G-15784)*
Classic Car Port & Canopies 586 759-5490
11800 E 9 Mile Rd Warren (48089) *(G-16982)*
Classic Container Corporation 734 853-3000
32432 Capitol St Livonia (48150) *(G-9684)*
Classic Design, Troy *Also called Classic Systems LLC (G-16270)*
Classic Design Concepts LLC 248 504-5202
53194 Pontiac Trl Milford (48381) *(G-10958)*
Classic Designs Cstm Area Rugs 616 530-0740
4370 Chicago Dr Sw # 220 Grandville (49418) *(G-7026)*
Classic Die Inc 616 454-3760
610 Plymouth Ave Ne Grand Rapids (49505) *(G-6277)*
Classic Dock & Lift LLC 231 882-4374
8862 Us Highway 31 Beulah (49617) *(G-1609)*
Classic Glass Battle Creek Inc 269 968-2791
21472 Bedford Rd N Battle Creek (49017) *(G-1167)*
Classic Images Embroidery 616 844-1702
15774 Ronny Rd Grand Haven (49417) *(G-6004)*
Classic Instruments Inc 231 582-0461
826 Moll Dr Boyne City (49712) *(G-1820)*
Classic Jerky Company 313 357-9904
21655 Trolley Indus Dr Taylor (48180) *(G-15701)*
Classic Log Homes Incorporated 989 821-6118
7340 Hillcrest Rd Higgins Lake (48627) *(G-7482)*
Classic Metal Finishing Inc 517 990-0011
2500 W Argyle St Jackson (49202) *(G-8411)*
Classic Plating Inc 313 532-1440
12600 Farley Redford (48239) *(G-13153)*
Classic Precision Inc 248 349-8811
28016 Oakland Oaks Ct Wixom (48393) *(G-17787)*
Classic Printing & Graphics, River Rouge *Also called Donna Jeroy (G-13275)*
Classic Sea Scapes 517 323-7775
7232 Glen Terra Dr Lansing (48917) *(G-9282)*
Classic Stamp & Signs 231 737-0200
772 W Broadway Ave Norton Shores (49441) *(G-11746)*
Classic Stone Creations Inc 269 637-9497
1301 M 43 Ste 3 South Haven (49090) *(G-14756)*
Classic Stone MBL & Gran Inc 248 588-1599
2340 Alger Dr Troy (48083) *(G-16269)*
Classic Systems LLC 248 588-2738
1100 Piedmont Dr Troy (48083) *(G-16270)*
Classic Tool & Boring Inc 586 795-8967
5970 Wall St Sterling Heights (48312) *(G-15290)*
Classic Turning Inc (PA) 517 764-1335
3000 E South St Jackson (49201) *(G-8412)*
Classic Welding Inc 586 758-2400
21500 Ryan Rd Warren (48091) *(G-16983)*
Classic Woodworks of Michigan 248 628-3356
3275 Metamora Rd Ste A Oxford (48371) *(G-12343)*
Classroom Farming Ltd 810 247-8410
708 Fletcher St Owosso (48867) *(G-12283)*
Classy Threadz 989 479-9595
310 State St Harbor Beach (48441) *(G-7264)*
Clausing Industrial Inc 269 345-7155
3963 Emerald Dr Kalamazoo (49001) *(G-8706)*
Clausing Industrial Inc (PA) 269 345-7155
3963 Emerald Dr Kalamazoo (49001) *(G-8707)*
Clausing Industrial Svc Ctr, Kalamazoo *Also called Clausing Industrial Inc (G-8706)*
Clawson Tank, Clarkston *Also called Steel Tank & Fabricating Co (G-2959)*
Clawson Tank Company (PA) 248 625-8700
4701 White Lake Rd Clarkston (48346) *(G-2914)*
Clay & Graham Inc 989 354-5292
4770 Werth Rd Alpena (49707) *(G-283)*
Claybanks Kids LLC 231 893-4071
7473 W Skeels Rd Montague (49437) *(G-11089)*
Claytec, East Lansing *Also called Inpore Technologies Inc (G-4663)*
Clean Air Technology Inc 734 459-6320
41105 Capital Dr Canton (48187) *(G-2362)*
Clean Clothes Inc 734 482-4000
7852 2nd St Dexter (48130) *(G-4482)*
Clean Cut Divison, Auburn Hills *Also called Rite Mark Stamp Company (G-992)*
Clean Planet Foods, Taylor *Also called Great Fresh Foods Co LLC (G-15726)*
Clean Rooms International Inc 616 452-8700
4939 Starr St Se Grand Rapids (49546) *(G-6278)*
Clean Tech Inc 734 529-2475
500 Dunham St Dundee (48131) *(G-4577)*
Clean Tech Inc (HQ) 734 455-3600
41605 Ann Arbor Rd E Plymouth (48170) *(G-12598)*
Cleanese Americas LLC 248 377-2700
1195 Centre Rd Auburn Hills (48326) *(G-814)*
Clear Advantage Mechanical 616 520-5884
1620 Acacia Dr Nw Grand Rapids (49504) *(G-6279)*
Clear Cut Water Jet Machining 616 534-9119
4515 Patterson Ave Se Grand Rapids (49512) *(G-6280)*
Clear Image Devices LLC 734 645-6459
3930 N Michael Rd Ann Arbor (48103) *(G-400)*
Clearform 616 656-5359
5220 68th St Se Ste 8 Caledonia (49316) *(G-2295)*
Clearwater Paper - Menominee, Menominee *Also called Menominee Acquisition Corp (G-10745)*
Clearwater Treatment Systems 517 688-9316
4700 Industrial Dr Clarklake (49234) *(G-2896)*
Cleary Developments Inc (PA) 248 588-7011
32055 Edward Ave Madison Heights (48071) *(G-10210)*
Cleary Developments Inc 248 588-6614
32033 Edward Ave Madison Heights (48071) *(G-10211)*
Clemco Printing Inc 989 269-8364
116 Scott St Bad Axe (48413) *(G-1059)*
Clemens Food Group LLC 517 278-2500
572 Newton Rd Coldwater (49036) *(G-3295)*
Clemens Welcome Center 517 278-2500
285 N Michigan Ave Coldwater (49036) *(G-3296)*
Cleo, Grand Rapids *Also called Viable Inc (G-6970)*
Cleveland Tramrail Systems, Detroit *Also called Versa Handling Co (G-4427)*
Cleveland-Cliffs Inc 906 475-3547
101 Tilden Mine Rd Ishpeming (49849) *(G-8343)*
Click Care LLC 989 792-1544
2650 Mcleod Dr N Saginaw (48604) *(G-14020)*
Cliff Keen Athletic, Ann Arbor *Also called Cliff Keen Wrestling Pdts Inc (G-401)*
Cliff Keen Wrestling Pdts Inc 734 975-8800
4480 Varsity Dr Ste B Ann Arbor (48108) *(G-401)*
Cliffs Sand & Gravel Inc 989 422-3463
1128 Federal Ave Houghton Lake (48629) *(G-7989)*
Clinton Machine Inc 989 834-2235
1300 S Main St Ovid (48866) *(G-12271)*
Clinton Machine Tool Inc 517 456-4810
4003 W Us Highway 12 Clinton (49236) *(G-3017)*
Clinton River Medical Pdts LLC 248 289-1825
1025 Doris Rd Auburn Hills (48326) *(G-815)*
Clio Smoothie LLC 810 691-9620
1028 N Leroy St Fenton (48430) *(G-5195)*
Clipper Belt Lacer Company 616 459-3196
1995 Oak Industrial Dr Ne Grand Rapids (49505) *(G-6281)*
Clips & Clamps Industries, Plymouth *Also called Consolidated Clips Clamps Inc (G-12601)*
Clips Coupons of Ann Arbo 248 437-9294
9477 Silverside South Lyon (48178) *(G-14789)*
Clm Vibetech Inc 269 344-3878
7025 E K Ave Kalamazoo (49048) *(G-8708)*
Cloyes Gear Holdings LLC (HQ) 313 758-2000
1 Dauch Dr Detroit (48211) *(G-3940)*

ALPHABETIC

(PA)=Parent Co (HQ)=Headquarters (DH)=Div Headquarters
2020 Harris Michigan Industrial Directory
923

Cloyes-Renold, Royal Oak *Also called AAM Pwder Metal Components Inc* ***(G-13898)***
Clutch Masters Inc....586 759-1300
7065 E 8 Mile Rd Warren (48091) ***(G-16984)***
Clyde Union (holdings) Inc....269 966-4600
4625 Beckley Rd Battle Creek (49015) ***(G-1168)***
Clydes Frame & Wheel Service....248 338-0323
725 Cesar E Chavez Ave Pontiac (48340) ***(G-12810)***
Clymer Manufacturing Company....248 853-5555
1605 W Hamlin Rd Rochester Hills (48309) ***(G-13389)***
CM Book, Ann Arbor *Also called Cushing-Malloy Inc* ***(G-409)***
Cmb Mfg LLC....920 915-2079
630 7th St Menominee (49858) ***(G-10727)***
CMC, Niles *Also called Custom Marine Carpet* ***(G-11604)***
CMC Plastyk LLC....989 588-4468
176 E Ludington Dr Farwell (48622) ***(G-5160)***
Cmg America Inc....810 686-3064
11424 N Saginaw Rd Clio (48420) ***(G-3268)***
Cmi-Schneible Group (HQ)....810 354-0404
3061 W Thompson Rd Ste 1 Fenton (48430) ***(G-5196)***
Cmn Fabrication Inc....586 294-1941
32580 Kelly Rd Roseville (48066) ***(G-13782)***
CMS, Grand Rapids *Also called Frost Incorporated* ***(G-6421)***
CMS, Jenison *Also called Cellulose Mtl Solutions LLC* ***(G-8620)***
CMS Enterprises Company (HQ)....517 788-0550
1 Energy Plaza Dr Jackson (49201) ***(G-8413)***
Cmu....989 774-7143
802 Industrial Dr Mount Pleasant (48858) ***(G-11189)***
Cmu University Press, Mount Pleasant *Also called Central Michigan University* ***(G-11187)***
CNB International Inc....269 948-3300
1004 S East St Hastings (49058) ***(G-7403)***
Cnc, Jackson *Also called Classic Turning Inc* ***(G-8412)***
CNC Products LLC....269 684-5500
2126 S 11th St Niles (49120) ***(G-11599)***
Cnd Products LLC....616 361-1000
1642 Broadway Ave Nw 3n Grand Rapids (49504) ***(G-6282)***
Cni Enterprises Inc (HQ)....248 586-3300
1451 E Lincoln Ave Madison Heights (48071) ***(G-10212)***
Cni Plastics LLC....517 541-4960
400 Parkland Dr Charlotte (48813) ***(G-2641)***
Cni-Owosso LLC....248 586-3300
1451 E Lincoln Ave Madison Heights (48071) ***(G-10213)***
Cns Inc....616 242-7704
1621 Leonard St Ne Ofc 11 Grand Rapids (49505) ***(G-6283)***
Co Optical Service, Detroit *Also called Cooperative Optical Services* ***(G-3948)***
Co-Dee Stamping Inc....269 948-8631
1657 Star School Rd Hastings (49058) ***(G-7404)***
Co-Op Machine & Tool, Durand *Also called B & M Machine & Tool Company* ***(G-4605)***
Co-Pipe Products Inc....734 287-1000
20501 Goddard Rd Taylor (48180) ***(G-15702)***
Co2 Central, Albion *Also called Ernie Romanco* ***(G-123)***
Coach House Iron Inc....616 785-8967
1005 9 Mile Rd Nw Ste 1 Sparta (49345) ***(G-15092)***
Coastal Concierge....269 639-1515
1210 Phoenix St Ste 9 South Haven (49090) ***(G-14757)***
Coastal Container Corporation....616 355-9800
1201 Indl Ave Holland (49423) ***(G-7593)***
Coastal Energy, Holland *Also called Coastal Container Corporation* ***(G-7593)***
Coat It Inc of Detroit....313 869-8500
15400 Woodrow Wilson St Detroit (48238) ***(G-3941)***
Coatings & Refinish Division, Southfield *Also called BASF Corporation* ***(G-14850)***
Coatings & Resins Division, Adrian *Also called PPG Industries Inc* ***(G-86)***
Coatings Plus Inc....616 451-2427
675 Chestnut St Sw Grand Rapids (49503) ***(G-6284)***
Cobalt Friction Technologies....734 274-3030
4595 Platt Rd Ann Arbor (48108) ***(G-402)***
Cobb Robert 3 Rachel....616 374-7420
2237 W Musgrove Hwy Lake Odessa (48849) ***(G-9113)***
Cobblestone Press....989 832-0166
4516 Washington St Midland (48642) ***(G-10825)***
Cobham McRlctrnic Slutions Inc (HQ)....734 426-1230
310 Dino Dr Ann Arbor (48103) ***(G-403)***
Cobra Enterprises, Madison Heights *Also called Cobra Patterns & Models Inc* ***(G-10215)***
Cobra Enterprises Inc....248 588-2669
32303 Howard Ave Madison Heights (48071) ***(G-10214)***
Cobra Maufacturing....248 585-1606
1147 Rankin Dr Troy (48083) ***(G-16271)***
Cobra Patterns & Models Inc....248 588-2669
32303 Howard Ave Madison Heights (48071) ***(G-10215)***
Cobra Torches Inc....248 499-8122
180 Engelwood Dr Ste J Lake Orion (48359) ***(G-9128)***
Cobra Truck & Fabrication....734 854-5663
6248 Sterns Rd Ottawa Lake (49267) ***(G-12260)***
Cobrex Ltd....734 429-9758
5880 Braun Rd Saline (48176) ***(G-14382)***
Coca-Cola, Hancock *Also called Hancock Bottling Co Inc* ***(G-7251)***
Coca-Cola Bottling Co....313 868-2167
12225 Oakland Pkwy Highland Park (48203) ***(G-7502)***
Coca-Cola Company....269 657-3171
38279 W Red Arrow Hwy Paw Paw (49079) ***(G-12399)***
Coca-Cola Company....734 397-2700
100 Coca Cola Dr Belleville (48111) ***(G-1443)***
Coca-Cola Refreshments USA Inc....989 895-8537
2500 Broadway St Bay City (48708) ***(G-1296)***
Coca-Cola Refreshments USA Inc....231 947-4150
1031 Hastings St Traverse City (49686) ***(G-15943)***
Coca-Cola Refreshments USA Inc....616 458-4536
1440 Butterworth St Sw Grand Rapids (49504) ***(G-6285)***
Coca-Cola Refreshments USA Inc....231 347-3242
1884 M 119 Petoskey (49770) ***(G-12445)***
Coca-Cola Refreshments USA Inc....269 657-8538
38279 W Red Arrow Hwy Paw Paw (49079) ***(G-12400)***
Coca-Cola Refreshments USA Inc....810 237-4000
2603 Lapeer Rd Flint (48503) ***(G-5398)***
Coca-Cola Refreshments USA Inc....313 897-2176
5981 W Warren Ave Detroit (48210) ***(G-3942)***
Coca-Cola Refreshments USA Inc....517 322-2349
3300 S Creyts Rd Lansing (48917) ***(G-9283)***
Coca-Cola Refreshments USA Inc....313 897-5000
26777 Halsted Rd Farmington Hills (48331) ***(G-4964)***
Cochran Corporation....517 857-2211
120 Mill St Springport (49284) ***(G-15209)***
Code Blue Corporation....616 392-8296
259 Hedcor St Ste 1 Holland (49423) ***(G-7594)***
Code Systems Inc....248 307-3884
2365 Pontiac Rd Frnt Auburn Hills (48326) ***(G-816)***
Codo Machine & Tool Inc....517 789-5113
1418 Lewis St Jackson (49203) ***(G-8414)***
Cody Kresta Vineyard & Winery....269 668-3800
45727 27th St Mattawan (49071) ***(G-10663)***
Coe Creek Portable Sawmill....231 829-3035
22033 230th Ave Tustin (49688) ***(G-16710)***
Coeus LLC....248 564-1958
1605 S Telegraph Rd Bloomfield Hills (48302) ***(G-1754)***
Coffee Beanery Ltd (HQ)....810 733-1020
3429 Pierson Pl Flushing (48433) ***(G-5533)***
Coffee Express Co....734 459-4900
47722 Clipper St Plymouth (48170) ***(G-12599)***
Coffman Electrical Eqp Co....616 452-8708
3300 Jefferson Ave Se Grand Rapids (49548) ***(G-6286)***
Cog Marketers Ltd....989 224-4117
3026 W M 21 Saint Johns (48879) ***(G-14280)***
Cog Marketers Ltd....434 455-3209
302 W Sectionline Rd Ashley (48806) ***(G-727)***
Cog Marketers Ltd....989 224-4117
3055 W M 21 Saint Johns (48879) ***(G-14281)***
Cognisys Inc....231 943-2425
459 Hughes Dr Traverse City (49696) ***(G-15944)***
Cogsdill Tool Products Inc....734 744-4500
11757 Globe St Livonia (48150) ***(G-9685)***
Coil Anodizing, Muskegon *Also called Lorin Industries Inc* ***(G-11367)***
Coil Drilling Technologies Inc....989 773-6504
2362 Northway Dr Mount Pleasant (48858) ***(G-11190)***
Coit Avenue Gravel Co Inc....616 363-7777
4772 Coit Ave Ne Grand Rapids (49525) ***(G-6287)***
Coke Bottle....810 424-3352
2515 Lapeer Rd Flint (48503) ***(G-5399)***
Colberg Radiator & Welding....810 742-0028
4114 Davison Rd Burton (48509) ***(G-2149)***
Cold Forming Technology Inc....586 254-4600
44476 Phoenix Dr Sterling Heights (48314) ***(G-15291)***
Cold Heading Co (HQ)....586 497-7000
21777 Hoover Rd Warren (48089) ***(G-16985)***
Cold Heading Co....586 497-7016
22155 Hoover Rd Warren (48089) ***(G-16986)***
Cold Saw Precision, Williamsburg *Also called Thomas A Despres Inc* ***(G-17721)***
Cold Stone Creamery, Washington *Also called WG Sweis Investments LLC* ***(G-17314)***
Cold Stone Creamery....313 886-4020
16823 Kercheval Ave Grosse Pointe Park (48230) ***(G-7192)***
Coldwater Bakery, Coldwater *Also called Perfection Bakeries Inc* ***(G-3319)***
Coldwater Plant, Coldwater *Also called Exo-S US LLC* ***(G-3303)***
Coldwater Veneer Inc (PA)....517 278-5676
548 Race St Coldwater (49036) ***(G-3297)***
Coldwter Sintered Met Pdts Inc....517 278-8750
300 Race St Coldwater (49036) ***(G-3298)***
Cole Carbide Industries Inc (PA)....248 276-1278
4930 S Lapeer Rd Lake Orion (48359) ***(G-9129)***
Cole Carbide Industries Inc....989 872-4348
6880 Cass City Rd Cass City (48726) ***(G-2513)***
Cole Carter Inc....269 626-8891
8713 38th St S Scotts (49088) ***(G-14504)***
Cole King Foods....313 872-0220
40 Clairmount St Detroit (48202) ***(G-3943)***
Cole King LLC....248 276-1278
4930 S Lapeer Rd Orion (48359) ***(G-12176)***
Cole Polymer Technologies Inc....269 695-6275
15512 Walton Rd Buchanan (49107) ***(G-2114)***

Cole Tooling Systems Inc 586 573-9450
4930 S Lapeer Rd Lake Orion (48359) *(G-9130)*
Cole Wagner Cabinetry 248 642-5330
735 Forest Ave Birmingham (48009) *(G-1677)*
Cole Wagner Cabinetry 248 852-2406
2511 Leach Rd Rochester Hills (48309) *(G-13390)*
Coleman Bowman & Associates 248 642-8221
3535 Wooddale Ct Bloomfield Hills (48301) *(G-1755)*
Coleman Machine Inc (PA) 906 863-1113
N1597 Us Highway 41 Menominee (49858) *(G-10728)*
Coleman Racing Products, Menominee *Also called Coleman Machine Inc (G-10728)*
Coleman Specialty Products, Bloomfield Hills *Also called Coleman Bowman & Associates (G-1755)*
Coles Machine Service Inc 810 658-5373
201 W Rising St Davison (48423) *(G-3642)*
Coles Polishing 269 625-2542
33230 Oak Leaf Trl Colon (49040) *(G-3371)*
Coles Quality Foods Inc 231 722-1651
1188 Lakeshore Dr Muskegon (49441) *(G-11295)*
Coles Quality Foods Inc (PA) 231 722-1651
38 Commerce Ave Sw # 400 Grand Rapids (49503) *(G-6288)*
Colfran Industrial Sales Inc 734 595-8920
38127 Ecorse Rd Romulus (48174) *(G-13663)*
Collagecom LLC 248 971-0538
1471 Lynwood Ln White Lake (48383) *(G-17631)*
Collective Industries Corp 313 879-1080
14835 Mclain Ave Allen Park (48101) *(G-195)*
Collective Industries Group, Allen Park *Also called Collective Industries Corp (G-195)*
College Park Industries Inc 586 294-7950
27955 College Park Dr Warren (48088) *(G-16987)*
Collier Enterprise III 269 503-3402
1510 Sunnyfield Rd Sturgis (49091) *(G-15600)*
Collins Brothers Sawmill Inc 906 524-5511
17579 Watters St Lanse (49946) *(G-9190)*
Collins Caviar Company 269 469-4576
9595 Union Pier Rd Union Pier (49129) *(G-16737)*
Coloma Frozen Foods Inc (PA) 269 849-0500
4145 Coloma Rd Coloma (49038) *(G-3356)*
Colombo Beverage Chase Systems, Davisburg *Also called Colombo Sales & Engrg Inc (G-3630)*
Colombo Sales & Engrg Inc 248 547-2820
10421 Enterprise Dr Ste A Davisburg (48350) *(G-3630)*
Colonial Bushings Inc 586 954-3880
44336 Reynolds Dr Clinton Township (48036) *(G-3082)*
Colonial Chemical Corp 517 789-8161
720 E Mansion St Jackson (49203) *(G-8415)*
Colonial Engineering Inc (PA) 269 323-2495
6400 Corporate Ave Portage (49002) *(G-12989)*
Colonial Group, Clinton Township *Also called Colonial Mold Inc (G-3083)*
Colonial Group, Shelby Township *Also called Colonial Plastics Incorporated (G-14564)*
Colonial Manufacturing LLC 269 926-1000
1246 E Empire Ave Benton Harbor (49022) *(G-1490)*
Colonial Mold Inc 586 469-4944
44479 Reynolds Dr Clinton Township (48036) *(G-3083)*
Colonial Neon Sign Co, Newaygo *Also called Colonial Sign Co (G-11565)*
Colonial Packaging, Grand Rapids *Also called Advance Packaging Acquisition (G-6146)*
Colonial Plastics Incorporated 586 469-4944
51734 Filomena Dr Shelby Township (48315) *(G-14564)*
Colonial Sign Co 616 534-1400
1170 230th Ave Newaygo (49337) *(G-11565)*
Colonial Tool Sales & Svc LLC 734 946-2733
12344 Delta St Taylor (48180) *(G-15703)*
Color Coat Plating Company 248 744-0445
355 W Girard Ave Madison Heights (48071) *(G-10216)*
Color Connection 248 351-0920
29487 Northwestern Hwy Southfield (48034) *(G-14870)*
Color Factory 810 577-2974
8034 N Mckinley Rd Flushing (48433) *(G-5534)*
Color House Graphics Inc 616 241-1916
3505 Eastern Ave Se Grand Rapids (49508) *(G-6289)*
Color Source Graphics Inc 248 458-2040
1925 W Maple Rd Ste A Troy (48084) *(G-16272)*
Colorado Pavers & Walls Inc 517 881-1704
3328 Torrey Rd Flint (48507) *(G-5400)*
Colorful Stitches 269 683-6442
225 E Main St Niles (49120) *(G-11600)*
Colorhub LLC 616 333-4411
4950 Kraft Ave Se Grand Rapids (49512) *(G-6290)*
Colorized Prints, Mount Morris *Also called Daniel Ward (G-11160)*
Colorpoint Print.com, Troy *Also called Corporate Electronic Sty Inc (G-16283)*
Colortech Graphics Inc 586 779-7800
28700 Hayes Rd Roseville (48066) *(G-13783)*
Colorworx, Macomb *Also called Admore Inc (G-10102)*
Colt - 7 Corporation 586 792-9050
34859 Groesbeck Hwy Clinton Township (48035) *(G-3084)*
Columbia Marking Tools Inc 586 949-8400
27430 Luckino Dr Chesterfield (48047) *(G-2754)*
Columbus McKinnon Corporation 800 955-5541
414 W Broadway Ave Muskegon (49444) *(G-11296)*
Columbus Oil & Gas LLC 810 385-9140
6436 Lakeshore Rd Burtchville (48059) *(G-2140)*
Columbus Tree The, Ithaca *Also called Stage Stop (G-8367)*
Comau LLC (HQ) 248 353-8888
21000 Telegraph Rd Southfield (48033) *(G-14871)*
Comau LLC 248 305-9662
43900 Grand River Ave Novi (48375) *(G-11851)*
Comau Pico, Southfield *Also called Comau LLC (G-14871)*
Combat Action LLC 810 772-3758
4124 Deeside Dr Brighton (48116) *(G-1900)*
Combat Advanced Propulsion LLC 231 724-2100
76 S Getty St Muskegon (49442) *(G-11297)*
Combine International Inc (PA) 248 585-9900
354 Indusco Ct Troy (48083) *(G-16273)*
Combustion Research Corp 248 852-3611
2516 Leach Rd Rochester Hills (48309) *(G-13391)*
Comet Information Systems LLC 248 686-2600
8359 Office Park Dr Grand Blanc (48439) *(G-5963)*
Comfoot Shoes, Kalamazoo *Also called Fernand Corporation (G-8742)*
Comfort Blinds 248 926-9300
1081 Yorick Path Wixom (48393) *(G-17788)*
Comfort Mattress Co 586 293-4000
30450 Little Mack Ave Roseville (48066) *(G-13784)*
Comfort-Aire, Jackson *Also called Cdgjl Inc (G-8404)*
Comma, Plymouth *Also called Plymouth-Canton Cmnty Crier (G-12721)*
Comma, Plymouth *Also called Plymouth-Canton Cmnty Crier (G-12722)*
Command Electronics Inc 269 679-4011
15670 Morris Indus Dr Schoolcraft (49087) *(G-14492)*
Commando Lock Company, Troy *Also called Solidbody Technology Company (G-16610)*
Commando Lock Company LLC 248 709-7901
395 Elmwood Dr Troy (48083) *(G-16274)*
Commercial Blueprint Inc 517 372-8360
3125 Pinetree Rd Ste 3b Lansing (48911) *(G-9357)*
Commercial Electric Co 269 731-3350
7255 Pin Oak Cir Augusta (49012) *(G-1052)*
Commercial Fabricating & Engrg (PA) 248 887-1595
1395 Energy Way Highland (48357) *(G-7488)*
Commercial Graphics Company 517 278-2159
205 W Garfield Ave Coldwater (49036) *(G-3299)*
Commercial Graphics Inc 586 726-8150
42704 Mound Rd Sterling Heights (48314) *(G-15292)*
Commercial Graphics of Mich 810 744-2102
1453 Walli Strasse Dr Burton (48509) *(G-2150)*
Commercial Group Inc (PA) 313 931-6100
12801 Universal Dr Taylor (48180) *(G-15704)*
Commercial Group Lifting Pdts, Taylor *Also called Commercial Group Inc (G-15704)*
Commercial Indus A Sltions LLC 269 373-8797
6830 E Michigan Ave Kalamazoo (49048) *(G-8709)*
Commercial Mfg & Assembly Inc 616 847-9980
17087 Hayes St Grand Haven (49417) *(G-6005)*
Commercial Painting Services, Quincy *Also called CPS LLC (G-13093)*
Commercial Record/Resorter, Saugatuck *Also called Kaechele Inc (G-14459)*
Commercial Steel Treating Corp (PA) 248 588-3300
31440 Stephenson Hwy Madison Heights (48071) *(G-10217)*
Commercial Tool & Die Inc 616 785-8100
5351 Rusche Dr Nw Comstock Park (49321) *(G-3470)*
Commercial Tool Group, Comstock Park *Also called Commercial Tool & Die Inc (G-3470)*
Commercial Trck Transf Signs 586 754-7100
4133 E 10 Mile Rd Warren (48091) *(G-16988)*
Commercial Welding Company Inc 269 782-5252
316 Cass Ave Dowagiac (49047) *(G-4536)*
Commercial Works 269 795-2060
200 Lafayette St Middleville (49333) *(G-10800)*
Commonwealth Associates Inc (PA) 517 788-3000
2700 W Argyle St Jackson (49202) *(G-8416)*
Commonwealth Service Sls Corp 313 581-8050
1715 W Hamlin Rd Rochester Hills (48309) *(G-13392)*
Communications Dept, Sault Sainte Marie *Also called Sault Tribe News (G-14473)*
Community Access Center 269 343-2211
359 S Kalamazoo Mall # 300 Kalamazoo (49007) *(G-8710)*
Community Marketing Group LLC 810 966-9982
1419 15th St Port Huron (48060) *(G-12909)*
Community Mental Health 517 323-9558
3200 Remy Dr Lansing (48906) *(G-9210)*
Community Shoppers Guide Inc 269 694-9431
117 N Farmer St Otsego (49078) *(G-12235)*
Compac, Burton *Also called Compak Inc (G-2152)*
Compac Specialties Inc 616 786-9100
13444 Barry St Holland (49424) *(G-7595)*
Compact Engineering Corp 231 788-5470
4512 Iris Ct Muskegon (49442) *(G-11298)*
Compact PCI Systems, Saint Clair Shores *Also called Opensystems Publishing LLC (G-14266)*
Compak Inc (PA) 810 767-2806
1220 N Center Rd Burton (48509) *(G-2151)*

A L P H A B E T I C

Compak Inc 989 288-3199
1220 N Center Rd Burton (48509) *(G-2152)*
Companions' Cuisine, Saginaw Also called *Mkr Fabricating Inc (G-14098)*
Company B Graphic Design Inc 906 228-5887
1200 Wright St Ste 4 Marquette (49855) *(G-10524)*
Company Folders, Pontiac Also called *Printwand Inc (G-12859)*
Company Products Inc 586 757-6160
11800 Commerce St Warren (48089) *(G-16989)*
Compass Graphix, Warren Also called *E and J Advertising LLC (G-17013)*
Compass Interiors LLC 231 348-5353
2666 Charlevoix Rd Petoskey (49770) *(G-12446)*
Compassionate Soils, Sears Also called *Morgan Composting Inc (G-14512)*
Compatible Laser Products Inc 810 629-0459
1045 Grant St Fenton (48430) *(G-5197)*
Compatico Inc 616 940-1772
5005 Kraft Ave Se Ste A Grand Rapids (49512) *(G-6291)*
Competitive Cmpt Info Tech Inc 732 829-9699
100 Maincentre Ste 1 Northville (48167) *(G-11683)*
Competitive Edge Designs Inc 616 257-0565
4506 R B Chaffee Mem Dr S Grand Rapids (49548) *(G-6292)*
Competitive Edge Wood Spc Inc 616 842-1063
711 E Savidge Spring Mi 4 Muskegon (49441) *(G-11299)*
Competitive Machining Inc 989 846-6069
4245 Airpark Dr Standish (48658) *(G-15217)*
Complete Auto-Mation Inc 248 693-0500
1776d W Clarkston Rd Lake Orion (48362) *(G-9131)*
Complete Companies, Lake Orion Also called *Complete Filtration Inc (G-9132)*
Complete Cutting Tl & Mfg Inc 248 662-9811
47577 Avante Dr Wixom (48393) *(G-17789)*
Complete Data Products Inc (PA) 248 651-8602
5755 New King Dr Troy (48098) *(G-16275)*
Complete Dsign Automtn Systems (PA) 734 424-2789
2117 Bishop Cir E Dexter (48130) *(G-4483)*
Complete Electric 517 629-9267
1670 E Michigan Ave Albion (49224) *(G-121)*
Complete Filtration Inc 248 693-0500
1776d W Clarkston Rd Lake Orion (48362) *(G-9132)*
Complete Health System 810 720-3891
5084 Vlla Lnde Pkwy Ste 7 Flint (48532) *(G-5401)*
Complete Home Adv Media/Promo 586 254-9555
15018 Technology Dr Shelby Township (48315) *(G-14565)*
Complete Metal Finishing Inc 269 343-0500
4301 Manchester Rd Ste A Kalamazoo (49001) *(G-8711)*
Complete Metalcraft LLC 248 990-0850
184 W Wardlow Rd Highland (48357) *(G-7489)*
Complete Packaging Inc 734 241-2794
633 Detroit Ave Monroe (48162) *(G-11025)*
Complete Prototype Svcs Inc (PA) 586 690-8897
44783 Morley Dr Clinton Township (48036) *(G-3085)*
Complete Services LLC 248 470-8247
32401 8 Mile Rd Livonia (48152) *(G-9686)*
Complete Source Inc 616 285-9110
4455 44th St Se Grand Rapids (49512) *(G-6293)*
Complete Surface Technologies 586 493-5800
21338 Carlo Dr Clinton Township (48038) *(G-3086)*
Complex Steel & Wire Corp 734 326-1600
36254 Annapolis St Wayne (48184) *(G-17428)*
Complex Tool & Machine Inc 248 625-0664
6460 Sashabaw Rd Clarkston (48346) *(G-2915)*
Component Engrg Solutions LLC 616 514-1343
1740 Chicago Dr Sw Grand Rapids (49519) *(G-6294)*
Component Solutions LLC 906 863-2682
2219 10th Ave Menominee (49858) *(G-10729)*
Composite Builders LLC 616 377-7767
430 W 18th St Holland (49423) *(G-7596)*
Composite Development Corporat 269 694-4159
1669 Oak St Otsego (49078) *(G-12236)*
Composite Forgings Ltd Partnr 313 496-1226
2300 W Jefferson Ave Detroit (48216) *(G-3944)*
Composite Sign Products Inc 616 252-9110
2148 Center Industrial Ct Jenison (49428) *(G-8621)*
Composite Techniques Inc 616 878-9795
7850 Clyde Park Ave Sw Byron Center (49315) *(G-2181)*
Composition Unlimited Inc 616 451-2222
1375 Monroe Ave Nw Grand Rapids (49505) *(G-6295)*
Compound Technology, Troy Also called *Chelsea-Megan Holding Inc (G-16265)*
Compressor Industries LLC 313 389-2800
17162 Francis St Melvindale (48122) *(G-10693)*
Compressor Technologies Inc 616 949-7000
4420 40th St Se Grand Rapids (49512) *(G-6296)*
Comptek Inc 248 477-5215
37450 Enterprise Ct Farmington Hills (48331) *(G-4965)*
Compucare 616 245-5371
3247 Brooklyn Ave Se Grand Rapids (49508) *(G-6297)*
Compucom Computers Inc 989 837-1895
28 Ashman Cir Midland (48640) *(G-10826)*
Compudyne Inc 906 360-9081
925 W Washington St # 104 Marquette (49855) *(G-10525)*
Compunetics Incorporated 248 524-6376
2500 Rochester Ct Troy (48083) *(G-16276)*
Compunetics Systems Inc 248 531-0015
3235 Fulham Dr Rochester Hills (48309) *(G-13393)*
Computer Assistanc, Grand Blanc Also called *Innovative Programming Systems (G-5971)*
Computer Composition Corp 248 545-4330
1401 W Girard Ave Madison Heights (48071) *(G-10218)*
Computer Mail Services Inc (PA) 248 352-6700
44648 Mound Rd Sterling Heights (48314) *(G-15293)*
Computer Operated Mfg 989 686-1333
1710 Lewis St Bay City (48706) *(G-1297)*
Computer Sciences Corporation 586 825-5043
6000 17 Mile Rd Sterling Heights (48313) *(G-15294)*
Computerized SEC Systems Inc (HQ) 248 837-3700
31750 Sherman Ave Madison Heights (48071) *(G-10219)*
Computers Edge 989 659-3179
230 W Brown Rd Munger (48747) *(G-11241)*
Compuware Corporation (HQ) 313 227-7300
1 Campus Martius Fl 4 Detroit (48226) *(G-3945)*
Comstar Automotive USA LLC 517 266-2445
900 Industrial Dr Tecumseh (49286) *(G-15785)*
Comstock Creamery LLC 269 929-7693
6086 E Michigan Ave Kalamazoo (49048) *(G-8712)*
Comtrex, Rochester Hills Also called *Ssb Holdings Inc (G-13517)*
Comtronics 517 750-3160
4909 W Michigan Ave Jackson (49201) *(G-8417)*
Con-De Manufacturing Inc 269 651-3756
26436 Us Highway 12 Sturgis (49091) *(G-15601)*
Con-Vel Inc 864 281-2228
7020 Old River Trl Lansing (48917) *(G-9284)*
Conagra Brands Inc 402 240-8210
4551 Squires Rd Quincy (49082) *(G-13092)*
Conagra Foods 616 392-2359
147 E 6th St Holland (49423) *(G-7597)*
Conair North America 814 437-6681
503 S Mercer St Pinconning (48650) *(G-12507)*
Conant Gardeners 313 863-2624
18621 San Juan Dr Detroit (48221) *(G-3946)*
Conatus Inc 810 494-6210
9933 Weber St Ste B Brighton (48116) *(G-1901)*
Concent Grinding Inc (HQ) 517 787-8172
2620 Saradan Dr Jackson (49202) *(G-8418)*
Concentric Industries Inc 734 848-5133
720 La Voy Rd Erie (48133) *(G-4802)*
Concentric Labs Inc 517 969-3038
715 Hall Blvd Mason (48854) *(G-10629)*
Concepp Technologies 734 324-6750
1609 Biddle Ave Wyandotte (48192) *(G-17953)*
Concept Alloys Inc 734 449-9680
11234 Lemen Rd Whitmore Lake (48189) *(G-17692)*
Concept Metal Machining LLC 616 647-9200
5320 6 Mile Ct Nw Comstock Park (49321) *(G-3471)*
Concept Metal Products Inc (PA) 231 799-3202
16928 148th Ave Spring Lake (49456) *(G-15136)*
Concept Metals Group, Spring Lake Also called *Concept Metal Products Inc (G-15136)*
Concept Molds Inc 269 679-2100
12273 N Us Highway 131 Schoolcraft (49087) *(G-14493)*
Concept Technology Inc (PA) 248 765-0100
144 Wimbleton Dr Birmingham (48009) *(G-1678)*
Concept Tool & Die Inc 616 875-4600
9371 Henry Ct Zeeland (49464) *(G-18125)*
Concept Tooling Systems Inc 616 301-6906
555 Plymouth Ave Ne Grand Rapids (49505) *(G-6298)*
Concord Industrial Corporation 248 646-9225
36400 Woodward Ave # 110 Bloomfield Hills (48304) *(G-1756)*
Concord International, Inc., Southfield Also called *Aludyne International Inc (G-14833)*
Concord Tool and Mfg Inc 586 465-6537
118 N Groesbeck Hwy Ste E Mount Clemens (48043) *(G-11127)*
Concordant Publishing Concern 810 798-3563
6800 Hough Rd Almont (48003) *(G-254)*
Concorde Inc 248 391-8177
4200 N Atlantic Blvd Auburn Hills (48326) *(G-817)*
Concrete Lifters Inc 616 669-0400
7520 Main St Ste 6 Jenison (49428) *(G-8622)*
Concrete Manufacturing Inc 586 777-3320
29100 Groesbeck Hwy Roseville (48066) *(G-13785)*
Concrete Pipe Northern 616 608-6025
2701 Chicago Dr Sw Wyoming (49519) *(G-17992)*
Concrete Step Co 810 789-3061
G5491 Clio Rd Flint (48504) *(G-5402)*
Concrete To Go 734 455-3531
702 Ann St Plymouth (48170) *(G-12600)*
Condat Corporation 734 944-4994
250 S Industrial Dr Saline (48176) *(G-14383)*
Condor Manufacturing Inc 586 427-4715
11800 E 9 Mile Rd Warren (48089) *(G-16990)*
Conductive Bolton Systems LLC 248 669-7080
28001 Cabot Dr Ste 100 Novi (48377) *(G-11852)*
Cone Drive Gearing Solutions, Traverse City Also called *Cone Drive Operations Inc (G-15945)*
Cone Drive Operations Inc (HQ) 231 946-8410
240 E Twelfth St Traverse City (49684) *(G-15945)*

Cone Drive Operations Inc 231 843-3393
5115 Progress Dr Ludington (49431) ***(G-10054)***
Cone Drive Textron, Ludington *Also called Cone Drive Operations Inc* ***(G-10054)***
Conform Automotive, Bingham Farms *Also called Dti Molded Products Inc* ***(G-1652)***
Conform Automotive, Sidney *Also called Fft Sidney LLC* ***(G-14739)***
Conform Group, Bingham Farms *Also called Detroit Technologies Inc* ***(G-1651)***
Conformance Coatings Prototype 810 364-4333
2321 Busha Hwy Marysville (48040) ***(G-10601)***
Conical Cutting Tools Inc 616 531-8500
3890 Buchanan Ave Sw Grand Rapids (49548) ***(G-6299)***
Conical Tool Company, Grand Rapids *Also called Conical Cutting Tools Inc* ***(G-6299)***
Conine Publishing Company 231 832-5566
211 W Upton Ave Ste B Reed City (49677) ***(G-13212)***
Conine Publishing Inc (HQ) 231 723-3592
75 Maple St Manistee (49660) ***(G-10418)***
Conine Publishing Inc 231 352-9659
417 Main St Frankfort (49635) ***(G-5600)***
Conley Composites LLC 918 299-5051
4855 Broadmoor Ave Se Grand Rapids (49512) ***(G-6300)***
Connect With Us LLC 586 262-4359
4311 Kingmont Dr Shelby Township (48317) ***(G-14566)***
Connected Prfmce Cmpt Cnslting, Jackson *Also called Christopher S Campion* ***(G-8409)***
Connection Service Company 269 926-2658
1377 M 139 Benton Harbor (49022) ***(G-1491)***
Connell Limited Partnership 989 875-5135
255 Industrial Pkwy Ithaca (48847) ***(G-8358)***
Connells Restoration & Sealan 269 370-0805
16011 Hoffman St Vandalia (49095) ***(G-16800)***
Connely Company 586 977-0700
36155 Mound Rd Sterling Heights (48310) ***(G-15295)***
Conner Engineering LLC 586 465-9590
21200 Carlo Dr Clinton Township (48038) ***(G-3087)***
Conner Steel Products (PA) 248 852-5110
2295 Star Ct Rochester Hills (48309) ***(G-13394)***
Connies Clutter 517 684-7291
3361 Fairway Dr Bay City (48706) ***(G-1298)***
Connolly 248 683-7985
5805 Pontiac Lake Rd Waterford (48327) ***(G-17329)***
Connor Sports Flooring Corp 906 822-7311
251 Industrial Park Rd Amasa (49903) ***(G-330)***
Conquest Manufacturing LLC 586 576-7600
28408 Lorna Ave Warren (48092) ***(G-16991)***
Conquest Scents 810 653-2759
8399 E Bristol Rd Davison (48423) ***(G-3643)***
Conrad Machine Company 231 893-7455
1525 Warner St Whitehall (49461) ***(G-17663)***
Conros, Romulus *Also called Lepages 2000 Inc* ***(G-13700)***
Considine Sales & Marketing 248 889-7887
611 S Milford Rd Highland (48357) ***(G-7490)***
Consistacom Inc 906 482-7653
47420 State Highway M26 # 27 Houghton (49931) ***(G-7972)***
Consoldted Dcment Slutions LLC 586 293-8100
17601 Malyn Blvd Fraser (48026) ***(G-5638)***
Consoldted Rsource Imaging LLC 616 735-2080
2943 S Wilson Ct Nw Grand Rapids (49534) ***(G-6301)***
Consolidated Clips Clamps Inc 734 455-0880
15050 Keel St Plymouth (48170) ***(G-12601)***
Consolidated Metal Pdts Inc 616 538-1000
3831 Clay Ave Sw Grand Rapids (49548) ***(G-6302)***
Consort Corporation (PA) 269 388-4532
2129 Portage St Kalamazoo (49001) ***(G-8713)***
Consort Display Group, Kalamazoo *Also called Consort Corporation* ***(G-8713)***
Constellium Automotive USA LLC (HQ) 734 879-9700
6331 Schooner St Van Buren Twp (48111) ***(G-16752)***
Constine Inc 989 723-6043
2625 W M 21 Owosso (48867) ***(G-12284)***
Construction Diamond Products, Livonia *Also called Cdp Diamond Products Inc* ***(G-9678)***
Construction Retail Svcs Inc 586 469-2289
38555 Moravian Dr Clinton Township (48036) ***(G-3088)***
Constructive Sheet Metal Inc 616 245-5306
11670 46th Ave Allendale (49401) ***(G-215)***
Consumer Advntage Rference Svc 586 783-1806
43830 N Groesbeck Hwy Clinton Township (48036) ***(G-3089)***
Consumers Concrete Corp 616 243-3651
1505 Burlingame Ave Sw Wyoming (49509) ***(G-17993)***
Consumers Concrete Corp 269 384-0977
3809 E Michigan Ave Kalamazoo (49048) ***(G-8714)***
Consumers Concrete Corporation (PA) 269 342-0136
3508 S Sprinkle Rd Kalamazoo (49001) ***(G-8715)***
Consumers Concrete Corporation 800 643-4235
465 12th St Plainwell (49080) ***(G-12520)***
Consumers Concrete Corporation 231 777-3981
4450 Evanston Ave Muskegon (49442) ***(G-11300)***
Consumers Concrete Corporation 231 924-6131
4550 W 72nd St Fremont (49412) ***(G-5768)***
Consumers Concrete Corporation 517 784-9108
3342 Page Ave Jackson (49203) ***(G-8419)***
Consumers Concrete Corporation 616 827-0063
8257 S Division Ave Byron Center (49315) ***(G-2182)***
Consumers Concrete Corporation 269 342-5983
700 Nazareth Rd Kalamazoo (49048) ***(G-8716)***
Consumers Concrete Corporation 616 392-6190
4312 M 40 Holland (49423) ***(G-7598)***
Consumers Concrete Corporation 269 684-8760
1523 Lake St Niles (49120) ***(G-11601)***
Consumers Concrete Corporation 231 894-2705
2259 Holton Whitehall Rd Whitehall (49461) ***(G-17664)***
Consumers Sand & Gravel Co, Kalamazoo *Also called Consumers Concrete Corporation* ***(G-8715)***
Container Specialties Inc 989 728-4231
3540 Darton Rd Hale (48739) ***(G-7224)***
Contamination Control, Livonia *Also called Acorn Industries Inc* ***(G-9627)***
Contech (us) Inc 616 459-4139
314 Straight Ave Sw Grand Rapids (49504) ***(G-6303)***
Contech Engnered Solutions LLC 517 676-3000
661 Jerico Dr Mason (48854) ***(G-10630)***
Contemporary Amperex Corp 248 289-6200
2114 Austin Ave Rochester Hills (48309) ***(G-13395)***
Contemporary Bride, Shelby Township *Also called R S C Productions* ***(G-14677)***
Contemporary Industries Inc (PA) 248 478-8850
24025 Research Dr Farmington Hills (48335) ***(G-4966)***
Context Furniture L L C 248 200-0724
1054 W Lewiston Ave Ferndale (48220) ***(G-5267)***
Continental Aluminum LLC 248 437-1001
29201 Milford Rd New Hudson (48165) ***(G-11534)***
Continental Auto Systems Inc 248 253-2969
2400 Executive Hills Dr Auburn Hills (48326) ***(G-818)***
Continental Auto Systems Inc (HQ) 248 393-5300
1 Continental Dr Auburn Hills (48326) ***(G-819)***
Continental Auto Systems Inc 248 209-4000
2400 Executive Hills Dr Auburn Hills (48326) ***(G-820)***
Continental Auto Systems Inc 248 874-2597
2400 Executive Hills Dr Auburn Hills (48326) ***(G-821)***
Continental Auto Systems Inc 906 248-6700
9301 S M 221 Brimley (49715) ***(G-2015)***
Continental Auto Systems Inc 248 874-1801
2400 Executive Hills Dr Auburn Hills (48326) ***(G-822)***
Continental Auto Systems Inc 248 267-9408
4685 Investment Dr Troy (48098) ***(G-16277)***
Continental Bldg Svs of Cinci 313 336-8543
580 Cook Rd Grosse Pointe Woods (48236) ***(G-7202)***
Continental Carbide Ltd Inc 586 463-9577
23545 Reynolds Ct Clinton Township (48036) ***(G-3090)***
Continental Communities 586 757-7412
3127 Maple St Warren (48091) ***(G-16992)***
Continental Crane & Service 586 294-7900
33681 Groesbeck Hwy Fraser (48026) ***(G-5639)***
Continental Dar Facilities LLC 616 837-7641
999 W Randall St Coopersville (49404) ***(G-3552)***
Continental Diamond, Brighton *Also called La Gold Mine Inc* ***(G-1949)***
Continental Electrical Pdts 248 589-2758
5971 Product Dr Sterling Heights (48312) ***(G-15296)***
Continental Ideification Pdts, Sparta *Also called Celia Corporation* ***(G-15091)***
Continental Plastics Co 586 294-4600
50900 Birch Rd Shelby Township (48315) ***(G-14567)***
Continental Strctrl Plstc Mch 734 428-8301
17951 W Austin Rd Manchester (48158) ***(G-10404)***
Continental Strl Plas Inc (HQ) 248 237-7800
255 Rex Blvd Auburn Hills (48326) ***(G-823)***
Continental Strl Plas Inc 248 593-9500
1805 Larchwood Dr Troy (48083) ***(G-16278)***
Continntal Strl Plas Hldngs Co (HQ) 248 237-7800
255 Rex Blvd Auburn Hills (48326) ***(G-824)***
Contitech North America Inc 248 312-3050
2044 Austin Ave Rochester Hills (48309) ***(G-13396)***
Contour Engineering Inc 989 828-6526
2305 E Coe Rd Shepherd (48883) ***(G-14727)***
Contour Machining Inc 734 525-4877
11837 Brookfield St Livonia (48150) ***(G-9687)***
Contour Metrological & Mfg Inc 248 273-1111
488 Oliver Dr Troy (48084) ***(G-16279)***
Contour Mold Corporation 810 245-4070
1830 N Lapeer Rd Lapeer (48446) ***(G-9451)***
Contour Tool & Engineering Inc 616 772-6360
2425 104th Ave Zeeland (49464) ***(G-18126)***
Contour Tool and Machine Inc 517 787-6806
2393 Research Dr Jackson (49203) ***(G-8420)***
Contract Flavors Inc 616 454-5950
3855 Linden Ave Se Grand Rapids (49548) ***(G-6304)***
Contract Furn Solutions Inc 734 941-2750
25069 Pine Ridge Dr Brownstown (48134) ***(G-2061)***
Contract People Corporation 248 304-9900
29444 Northwestern Hwy Southfield (48034) ***(G-14872)***
Contract Source & Assembly Inc 616 897-2185
5230 33rd St Se Grand Rapids (49512) ***(G-6305)***
Contract Welding and Fabg Inc 734 699-5561
385 Sumpter Rd Van Buren Twp (48111) ***(G-16753)***
Contractors Fence Service 313 592-1300
14900 Telegraph Rd Detroit (48239) ***(G-3947)***

ALPHABETIC

(PA)=Parent Co (HQ)=Headquarters (DH)=Div Headquarters
2020 Harris Michigan Industrial Directory
927

Contractors Printing   **ALPHABETIC SECTION**

Contractors Printing 517 622-1888
10236 W Grand River Hwy Grand Ledge (48837) *(G-6103)*

Contractors Sheet Metal Inc 231 348-0753
974 W Conway Rd Ste 15 Harbor Springs (49740) *(G-7278)*

Contractors Steel Company 616 531-4000
2768 Dormax St Sw Grand Rapids (49519) *(G-6306)*

Control Dekk LLC 616 828-4862
4035 Oak Valley Ct Sw Wyoming (49519) *(G-17994)*

Control Electronics 734 941-5008
29231 Northline Rd Romulus (48174) *(G-13664)*

Control Gaging Inc 734 668-6750
847 Avis Dr Ann Arbor (48108) *(G-404)*

Control Manufacturing Corp 734 283-4300
18601 Krause St Riverview (48193) *(G-13292)*

Control One Inc 586 979-6106
6460 Sims Dr Ste A Sterling Heights (48313) *(G-15297)*

Control Pak International, Fenton *Also called Energy Control Solutions Inc* *(G-5202)*

Control Panel Div, Grandville *Also called Harlo Corporation* *(G-7046)*

Control Power-Reliance LLC (HQ) 248 583-1020
310 Executive Dr 314 Troy (48083) *(G-16280)*

Control Solutions Inc 616 247-9422
8535 Byron Commerce Dr Sw A Byron Center (49315) *(G-2183)*

Control Systems & Service 616 887-2738
392 E Division St Ste A Sparta (49345) *(G-15093)*

Control Technique Incorporated 586 997-3200
41200 Technology Park Dr Sterling Heights (48314) *(G-15298)*

Controlled Magnetics Inc 734 449-7225
10766 Plaza Dr Whitmore Lake (48189) *(G-17693)*

Controlled Plating Tech Inc 616 243-6622
1100 Godfrey Ave Sw Grand Rapids (49503) *(G-6307)*

Controlled Power Company (PA) 248 528-3700
1955 Stephenson Hwy Ste G Troy (48083) *(G-16281)*

Controlled Power Tech Inc 248 825-0100
2000 Town Ctr Ste 1800 Southfield (48075) *(G-14873)*

Controlled Turning Inc 517 782-0517
1607 S Gorham St Jackson (49203) *(G-8421)*

Controller Security Systems, Eastpointe *Also called Controller Systems Corporation* *(G-4698)*

Controller Systems Corporation 586 772-6100
21363 Gratiot Ave Eastpointe (48021) *(G-4698)*

Controls For Industries Inc 517 468-3385
5279 Royce Rd Webberville (48892) *(G-17448)*

Convergence Technologies, Grand Haven *Also called Ghsp Inc* *(G-6018)*

Converting Systems Inc 616 698-1882
16900 Power Dr Nunica (49448) *(G-12034)*

Convex Mold Inc 586 978-0808
35360 Beattie Dr Sterling Heights (48312) *(G-15299)*

Conveyability, Inc., Grand Rapids *Also called Verstraete Conveyability Inc* *(G-6968)*

Conveyor Components Co Div, Croswell *Also called Material Control Inc* *(G-3600)*

Conveyor Concepts Michigan LLC 616 997-5200
743 Main St Coopersville (49404) *(G-3553)*

Conway Detroit Corporation 586 552-8413
28070 Hayes Rd Roseville (48066) *(G-13786)*

Conway Products Corporation 616 698-2601
4150 East Paris Ave Se # 1 Grand Rapids (49512) *(G-6308)*

Conway-Cleveland Corp (PA) 616 458-0056
2320 Oak Industrial Dr Ne Grand Rapids (49505) *(G-6309)*

Cook Industries Inc 586 754-4070
23515 Pinewood St Warren (48091) *(G-16993)*

Cook Sign Plus 586 254-7000
48534 Van Dyke Ave Shelby Township (48317) *(G-14568)*

Cookie Bouquet, Rochester Hills *Also called Carlson Enterprises Inc* *(G-13385)*

Cookies Cubed, Barbeau *Also called Schallips Inc* *(G-1117)*

Cooks Blacksmith Welding Inc 231 796-6819
402 Bjornson St Big Rapids (49307) *(G-1625)*

Cool Artesian Water, Crystal Falls *Also called Crystal Falls Springs Inc* *(G-3608)*

Cool Products Division, Ann Arbor *Also called Tecumseh Products Company LLC* *(G-662)*

Coolant Chillers, Lansing *Also called Fluid Chillers Inc* *(G-9369)*

Cooper & Cooper Sales Inc 810 327-6247
851 W Pointe Port Huron (48060) *(G-12910)*

Cooper Foundry Inc 269 343-2808
8216 Douglas Ave Kalamazoo (49009) *(G-8717)*

Cooper Genomics 313 579-9650
705 S Main St Plymouth (48170) *(G-12602)*

Cooper Glove and Safety LLC 706 512-0486
6100 Onyx Rd Bridgeport (48722) *(G-1851)*

Cooper Publishing Group LLC 231 933-9958
251 Knollwood Dr Traverse City (49686) *(G-15946)*

Cooper Standard, Novi *Also called Cooper-Standard Holdings Inc* *(G-11856)*

Cooper-Standard Auto OH LLC 248 596-5900
39550 Orchard Hill Pl Novi (48375) *(G-11853)*

Cooper-Standard Automotive Inc (HQ) 248 596-5900
39550 Orchard Hill Pl Novi (48375) *(G-11854)*

Cooper-Standard Automotive Inc 734 542-6300
11820 Globe St Livonia (48150) *(G-9688)*

Cooper-Standard Automotive Inc 989 362-5631
645 Aulerich Rd East Tawas (48730) *(G-4687)*

Cooper-Standard Automotive Inc 248 836-9400
2110 Executive Hills Dr Auburn Hills (48326) *(G-825)*

Cooper-Standard Automotive Inc 989 739-1423
4700 Industrial Row Oscoda (48750) *(G-12206)*

Cooper-Standard Automotive Inc 248 630-7262
2545 N Opdyke Rd Ste 102 Auburn Hills (48326) *(G-826)*

Cooper-Standard Automotive Inc 248 628-4899
180 E Elmwood Leonard (48367) *(G-9527)*

Cooper-Standard Automotive Inc 248 754-2000
2650 N Opdyke Rd Ste A Auburn Hills (48326) *(G-827)*

Cooper-Standard Automotive Inc 989 848-2272
2799 E Miller Rd Fairview (48621) *(G-4889)*

Cooper-Standard Fhs LLC (HQ) 248 596-5900
39550 Orchard Hill Pl Novi (48375) *(G-11855)*

Cooper-Standard Holdings Inc (PA) 248 596-5900
39550 Orchard Hill Pl Novi (48375) *(G-11856)*

Cooperative Optical Services (PA) 313 366-5100
2424 E 8 Mile Rd Detroit (48234) *(G-3948)*

Coopersville Observer Inc 616 997-5049
1374 W Randall St Coopersville (49404) *(G-3554)*

Copagen LLC 734 904-0365
5528 Gallery Park Dr Ann Arbor (48103) *(G-405)*

Copeland-Gibson Products Corp 248 740-4400
1025 E Maple Rd Troy (48083) *(G-16282)*

Copies & More Inc 231 865-6370
4491 Pontaluna Rd Fruitport (49415) *(G-5791)*

Copies Plus Printing Co LLC 616 696-1288
111 S Main Cedar Springs (49319) *(G-2549)*

Copilot Printing 248 398-5301
285 E 12 Mile Rd Madison Heights (48071) *(G-10220)*

Coplas Inc 586 739-8940
6700 18 1/2 Mile Rd Sterling Heights (48314) *(G-15300)*

Coplas-Tiercon, Sterling Heights *Also called Coplas Inc* *(G-15300)*

Copper Island Prtg Grphc Svcs 906 337-1300
423 Pine St Calumet (49913) *(G-2326)*

Copperforhealthcare, Jackson *Also called Midbrook Medical Dist Inc* *(G-8526)*

Coppertec Inc 313 278-0139
2424 Beech Daly Rd Inkster (48141) *(G-8226)*

Copperwood Resources Inc 906 229-3115
310 E Us Highway 2 Wakefield (49968) *(G-16848)*

Copy Cat Sign & Print, Marysville *Also called Van Kehrberg Vern* *(G-10625)*

Copy Central Inc 231 941-2298
314 E Eighth St Traverse City (49684) *(G-15947)*

Copy Shop of Newaygo, Newaygo *Also called Ron Rowe* *(G-11577)*

Copyright Traveler S Trunk P 937 903-9233
15071 Hanna Ave Ne Cedar Springs (49319) *(G-2550)*

Copyrite Printing Inc 586 774-0006
30503 Gratiot Ave Roseville (48066) *(G-13787)*

Cor Health, Flushing *Also called Vets Access LLC* *(G-5544)*

Cor-Met Inc 810 227-0004
12500 Grand River Rd Brighton (48116) *(G-1902)*

Coral Corporation 616 868-6295
8358 68th St Se Alto (49302) *(G-326)*

Corban Industries Inc 248 393-2720
4590 Joslyn Rd Orion (48359) *(G-12177)*

Core Electric Company Inc 313 382-7140
25125 Outer Dr Melvindale (48122) *(G-10694)*

Core Energy LLC 231 946-2419
1011 Noteware Dr Traverse City (49686) *(G-15948)*

Core Technology Corporation 517 627-1521
5859 W Saginaw Hwy 217 Lansing (48917) *(G-9285)*

Coreled Systems LLC 734 516-2060
31478 Industrial Rd # 400 Livonia (48150) *(G-9689)*

Corey's Bootery, Kalamazoo *Also called Kalamazoo Orthotics & Dbtc* *(G-8793)*

Corian By Solicor Industries, Livonia *Also called Sol-I-Cor Industries* *(G-9935)*

Corium International Inc 616 656-4563
4558 50th St Se Grand Rapids (49512) *(G-6310)*

Corky's Bar and Restaurant, Taylor *Also called Hancock Enterprises Inc* *(G-15728)*

Corlett-Turner Co 616 772-9082
2500 104th Ave Zeeland (49464) *(G-18127)*

Corlett-Turner Co 616 772-9082
1060 Kn O Sha Indus Dr Se Grand Rapids (49508) *(G-6311)*

Corlin Company 616 842-7093
1640 Marion Ave Grand Haven (49417) *(G-6006)*

Cornbelt Beef Corporation 313 237-0087
14150 Ludlow Pl Oak Park (48237) *(G-12054)*

Cornelius Systems Inc (PA) 248 545-5558
3966 11 Mile Rd Berkley (48072) *(G-1582)*

Cornell Publications LLC 810 225-3075
11075 Shadywood Dr Brighton (48114) *(G-1903)*

Corner Brewery LLC 734 480-2739
720 Norris St Ypsilanti (48198) *(G-18061)*

Corner Cone 810 412-4433
5515 N Irish Rd Davison (48423) *(G-3644)*

Corners Limited (PA) 269 353-8311
628 S 8th St Kalamazoo (49009) *(G-8718)*

Cornerstone Fabg & Cnstr Inc (PA) 989 642-5241
667 Watson Rd Hemlock (48626) *(G-7460)*

Cornerstone Furniture Inc 269 795-3379
915 Grand Rapids St Middleville (49333) ***(G-10801)***
Cornillie Acquisitions LLC (PA) 231 946-5600
805 W 13th St Cadillac (49601) ***(G-2242)***
Cornillie Acquisitions LLC 231 946-5600
17443 Pleasanton Hwy Bear Lake (49614) ***(G-1377)***
Cornillie Concrete, Cadillac *Also called Cornillie Acquisitions LLC* ***(G-2242)***
Cornillie Concrete, Farmington Hills *Also called Bwb LLC* ***(G-4950)***
Cornillie Concrete 231 439-9200
710 W Conway Rd Harbor Springs (49740) ***(G-7279)***
Corotech Acquisition Co 616 456-5557
1222 Burton St Se Grand Rapids (49507) ***(G-6312)***
Corotech Masonry, Grand Rapids *Also called Corotech Acquisition Co* ***(G-6312)***
Corporate, Northville *Also called Spiders Software Solutions LLC* ***(G-11727)***
Corporate AV Services LLC 248 939-0900
8508 Buffalo Dr Ste B Commerce Township (48382) ***(G-3395)***
Corporate Colors Inc 269 323-2000
3638 Miller Rd Ste A Kalamazoo (49001) ***(G-8719)***
Corporate Electronic Sty Inc 248 583-7070
2708 American Dr Troy (48083) ***(G-16283)***
Corr Pack In 248 348-4188
9833 5 Mile Rd Northville (48168) ***(G-11684)***
Corr-Fac Corporation 989 358-7050
4040 Us Highway 23 N Alpena (49707) ***(G-284)***
Correct Compression Inc 231 864-2101
11903 Chippewa Hwy Bear Lake (49614) ***(G-1378)***
Corrigan Enterprises Inc 810 229-6323
775 N 2nd St Brighton (48116) ***(G-1904)***
Corrugated Options LLC 734 850-1300
2163 Briar Ln Temperance (48182) ***(G-15825)***
Corrugated Pratt 734 853-3030
32432 Capitol St Livonia (48150) ***(G-9690)***
Corrugating Division, Grand Rapids *Also called Pratt Industries Inc* ***(G-6760)***
Corsair Engineering Inc (PA) 810 233-0440
3020 Airpark Dr S Flint (48507) ***(G-5403)***
Corsair Engineering Inc 810 234-3664
2702 N Dort Hwy Flint (48506) ***(G-5404)***
Corson Fabricating LLC 810 326-0532
1701 Sinclair St Ste B Saint Clair (48079) ***(G-14211)***
Cortar Laser and Fab LLC 248 446-1110
12828 Emerson Dr Brighton (48116) ***(G-1905)***
Cortz Industries 734 856-5091
9411 Summerfield Rd Temperance (48182) ***(G-15826)***
Corunna Mills Feed LLC 989 743-3110
417 S Shiawassee St Corunna (48817) ***(G-3580)***
Corvac Composites LLC 812 256-2287
4450 36th St Se Grand Rapids (49512) ***(G-6313)***
Corvac Composites LLC 616 281-4059
4450 36th St Se Kentwood (49512) ***(G-9004)***
Corvac Composites LLC 616 281-2430
4450 36th St Se Grand Rapids (49512) ***(G-6314)***
Corvac Composites LLC (HQ) 616 281-4026
104 84th St Sw Byron Center (49315) ***(G-2184)***
Corvette Central, Sawyer *Also called CC Industries LLC* ***(G-14483)***
Cosella Dorken Products Inc 888 433-5824
1795 Chase Dr Rochester (48307) ***(G-13317)***
Cosma Body Assembly Michigan, New Hudson *Also called Magna International Inc* ***(G-11548)***
Cosma Casting Michigan, Battle Creek *Also called Dieomatic Incorporated* ***(G-1174)***
Cosma Engineering, Troy *Also called Cosma International Amer Inc* ***(G-16284)***
Cosma Engineering, Troy *Also called Vehma International Amer Inc* ***(G-16681)***
Cosma International Amer Inc (HQ) 248 631-1100
750 Tower Dr Troy (48098) ***(G-16284)***
Costello Machine LLC 586 749-0136
56358 Precision Dr Chesterfield (48051) ***(G-2755)***
Cosworth LLC 586 353-5403
52685 Shelby Pkwy Shelby Township (48315) ***(G-14569)***
Cotson Fabricating Inc 248 589-2758
5971 Product Dr Sterling Heights (48312) ***(G-15301)***
Cottage Bakery 989 790-8135
4940 Hepburn Rd Saginaw (48603) ***(G-14021)***
Cotton Concepts Printing LLC 313 444-3857
1220 Longfellow St Detroit (48202) ***(G-3949)***
Cougar Cutting Tools Inc 586 469-1310
23529 Reynolds Ct Clinton Township (48036) ***(G-3091)***
Counter Point Furniture Pdts, Spring Lake *Also called Jsj Corporation* ***(G-15157)***
Counter Reaction LLC 248 624-7900
46915 Liberty Dr Wixom (48393) ***(G-17790)***
Counterpoint By Hlf 734 699-7100
44001 Van Born Rd Van Buren Twp (48111) ***(G-16754)***
Country Dairy Inc (PA) 231 861-4636
3476 S 80th Ave New ERA (49446) ***(G-11520)***
Country Fresh LLC 734 261-7980
31770 Enterprise Dr Livonia (48150) ***(G-9691)***
Country Home Creations Inc 810 244-7348
5132 Richfield Rd Flint (48506) ***(G-5405)***
Country Mill Farms LLC 517 543-1019
4648 Otto Rd Charlotte (48813) ***(G-2642)***
Country Printing 734 782-4044
14850 Telegraph Rd Flat Rock (48134) ***(G-5351)***
Country Register of Mich Inc 989 793-4211
3790 Manistee St Saginaw (48603) ***(G-14022)***
Country Schoolhouse Kingsford 906 828-1971
600 East Blvd Kingsford (49802) ***(G-9056)***
Country Side Sawmill 989 352-7198
7682 N Greenville Rd Lakeview (48850) ***(G-9171)***
Countryside Foods LLC (HQ) 586 447-3500
26661 Bunert Rd Warren (48089) ***(G-16994)***
Countryside Quality Meats LLC 517 741-4275
1184 Adolph Rd Union City (49094) ***(G-16732)***
County Journal Inc 517 543-1099
241 S Cochran Ave Ste 1 Charlotte (48813) ***(G-2643)***
County Line Pallet 231 834-8416
2031 22 Mile Rd Kent City (49330) ***(G-8989)***
County of Muskegon 231 724-6219
141 E Apple Ave Muskegon (49442) ***(G-11301)***
County of Muskegon 231 744-3580
1563 Scenic Dr Muskegon (49445) ***(G-11302)***
County Press 517 531-4542
123 W Main St Parma (49269) ***(G-12389)***
Cousins Manufacturing Inc 586 323-6033
43734 Merrill Rd Sterling Heights (48314) ***(G-15302)***
Covalent Medical Inc 734 604-0688
4750 S State Rd Ann Arbor (48108) ***(G-406)***
Covaron Inc 480 298-9433
4401 Varsity Dr Ste A Ann Arbor (48108) ***(G-407)***
Covenant Cpitl Investments Inc 248 477-4230
24772 Crestview Ct Farmington Hills (48335) ***(G-4967)***
Coventry Creations Inc (PA) 248 547-2987
195 W 9 Mile Rd Ferndale (48220) ***(G-5268)***
Coventry Industries LLC 248 761-8462
313 E Sherman St Holly (48442) ***(G-7872)***
Coveris 269 964-1130
155 Brook St Battle Creek (49037) ***(G-1169)***
Covestro LLC 248 475-7700
2401 E Walton Blvd Auburn Hills (48326) ***(G-828)***
Covisint Corporation (HQ) 248 483-2000
26533 Evergreen Rd # 500 Southfield (48076) ***(G-14874)***
Cowens & Sons, Livonia *Also called Alton Boring Co Inc* ***(G-9639)***
Cows Locomotive Mfg Co (PA) 248 583-7150
32052 Edward Ave Madison Heights (48071) ***(G-10221)***
Cox Brothers Machining Inc 517 796-4662
2300 E Ganson St Jackson (49202) ***(G-8422)***
Cox Industries Inc (PA) 586 749-6650
30800 26 Mile Rd Chesterfield (48051) ***(G-2756)***
Cox Machine LLC 269 953-5446
2823 Cass Rd Ste F1 Traverse City (49684) ***(G-15949)***
Cox North America, Inc., Haslett *Also called Sulzer Mixpac USA Inc* ***(G-7400)***
Coxen Enterprises Inc 248 486-3800
12785 Emerson Dr Brighton (48116) ***(G-1906)***
Coxline Inc 269 345-1132
2829 N Burdick St Kalamazoo (49004) ***(G-8720)***
Coy Laboratory Products Inc 734 433-9296
14500 Coy Dr Grass Lake (49240) ***(G-7086)***
Coye's Canvas & Awnings, Grand Rapids *Also called Case-Free Inc* ***(G-6265)***
Coyne Machine & Tool LLC 231 944-8755
13275 Winters Rd Kewadin (49648) ***(G-9037)***
Cozart Producers 810 736-1046
3130 Mcclure Ave Flint (48506) ***(G-5406)***
Cozy Cup Coffee Company Llc 989 984-7619
4083 Denise Ct Oscoda (48750) ***(G-12207)***
CPI Creative Products, Holland *Also called Creative Products Intl* ***(G-7600)***
CPI Products Inc (HQ) 231 547-6064
15 Corporate Dr Auburn Hills (48326) ***(G-829)***
Cpj Company Inc 616 784-6355
3739 Laramie Dr Ne Comstock Park (49321) ***(G-3472)***
CPM Acquisition Corp 231 947-6400
2412 W Aero Park Ct Traverse City (49686) ***(G-15950)***
CPM Acquisition Corp 231 947-6400
2412 W Aero Park Ct Traverse City (49686) ***(G-15951)***
CPM Century Extrusion, Traverse City *Also called CPM Acquisition Corp* ***(G-15951)***
CPM Services Group Inc 248 624-5100
47924 West Rd Wixom (48393) ***(G-17791)***
CPR III Inc 248 652-2900
380 South St Rochester (48307) ***(G-13318)***
Cpr Racing, Troy *Also called Creative Performance Racg LLC* ***(G-16285)***
CPS LLC 517 639-1464
11 E Chicago St Quincy (49082) ***(G-13093)***
Cq Simple LLC 989 492-7068
5103 Eastman Ave Ste 125 Midland (48640) ***(G-10827)***
Cr Forge LLC 231 924-2033
1914 S Comstock Ave Fremont (49412) ***(G-5769)***
Craft Industries Inc 586 726-4300
13231 23 Mile Rd Shelby Township (48315) ***(G-14570)***
Craft Precision Inc 269 679-5121
610 E Eliza St Schoolcraft (49087) ***(G-14494)***
Craft Press Printing Inc 269 683-9694
312 Bell Rd Niles (49120) ***(G-11602)***

ALPHABETIC

Craft Room, Union City ALPHABETIC SECTION

Craft Room, Union City *Also called Millworks Engineering Inc* ***(G-16735)***
Craft Steel Products Inc..........616 935-7575
16885 148th Ave Spring Lake (49456) ***(G-15137)***
Craftwood Industries Inc..........616 796-1209
2530 Kamar Dr Holland (49424) ***(G-7599)***
Craig Assembly Inc..........810 326-1374
1111 Fred W Moore Hwy Saint Clair (48079) ***(G-14212)***
Craig C Askins..........810 231-4340
6172 Winans Dr Brighton (48116) ***(G-1907)***
Craig EDM, Farmington Hills *Also called C L Design Inc* ***(G-4951)***
Craigs Signs..........810 667-7446
1498 N Saginaw St Ste 2 Lapeer (48446) ***(G-9452)***
Crain Communications Inc (PA)..........313 446-6000
1155 Gratiot Ave Detroit (48207) ***(G-3950)***
Crain Communications Inc..........313 446-6000
1155 Gratiot Ave Detroit (48207) ***(G-3951)***
Crain Communications Inc..........313 446-6000
1155 Gratiot Ave Detroit (48207) ***(G-3952)***
Crain's Chicago Business, Detroit *Also called Crain Communications Inc* ***(G-3951)***
Cramblits Welding LLC..........906 932-1908
1215 Wall St Ironwood (49938) ***(G-8326)***
Crandall Precision Inc..........231 775-7101
460 5th St Cadillac (49601) ***(G-2243)***
Crandell Bros Trucking Co..........517 543-2930
800 Island Hwy Charlotte (48813) ***(G-2644)***
Crane 1 Services Inc..........586 468-0909
42827 Irwin Dr Harrison Township (48045) ***(G-7327)***
Crane Pro Services, Novi *Also called Konecranes Inc* ***(G-11917)***
Crane Technologies Group Inc..........248 652-8700
1954 Rochester Indus Dr Rochester Hills (48309) ***(G-13397)***
Crankshaft Craftsman Inc..........313 366-0140
1960 W West Maple Rd Commerce Township (48390) ***(G-3396)***
Crankshaft Machine Company (HQ)..........517 787-3791
314 N Jackson St Jackson (49201) ***(G-8423)***
Crash Tool Inc..........517 552-0250
1225 Fendt Dr Howell (48843) ***(G-8025)***
Crawford Associates Inc..........248 549-9494
4526 Fernlee Ave Royal Oak (48073) ***(G-13915)***
Crawford County Avalanche..........989 348-6811
108 E Michigan Ave Grayling (49738) ***(G-7104)***
Crazy Joes Enterprises LLC..........906 395-1522
13751 State Highway M38 Baraga (49908) ***(G-1100)***
Crb Crane Services Inc (PA)..........517 552-5699
1194 Austin Ct Howell (48843) ***(G-8026)***
CRC Industries Inc..........313 883-6977
14650 Dequindre St Detroit (48212) ***(G-3953)***
Cream Cup Dairy..........231 889-4158
7377 Feldhak Rd Kaleva (49645) ***(G-8931)***
Creative Arts Studio Royal Oak..........248 544-2234
114 W 4th St Royal Oak (48067) ***(G-13916)***
Creative Automation Inc..........734 780-3175
1175 E N Territorial Rd Whitmore Lake (48189) ***(G-17694)***
Creative Automation Solutions..........313 790-4848
34552 Dover Ave Livonia (48150) ***(G-9692)***
Creative Awards..........586 739-4999
42830 Mound Rd Sterling Heights (48314) ***(G-15303)***
Creative Characters Inc..........231 544-6084
7924 Cameron St Central Lake (49622) ***(G-2589)***
Creative Composites Inc..........906 474-9941
7637 Us Highway 2 Rapid River (49878) ***(G-13111)***
Creative Controls Inc..........248 577-9800
32217 Stephenson Hwy Madison Heights (48071) ***(G-10222)***
Creative Controls Handicapped, Madison Heights *Also called Creative Controls Inc* ***(G-10222)***
Creative Designs & Signs Inc..........248 334-5580
146 Cesar E Chavez Ave Pontiac (48342) ***(G-12811)***
Creative Embroidery, Cadillac *Also called Shelly Meehof* ***(G-2276)***
Creative Engineering Inc..........734 996-5900
7621 E Joy Rd Ann Arbor (48105) ***(G-408)***
Creative Foam Corporation (PA)..........810 629-4149
300 N Alloy Dr Fenton (48430) ***(G-5198)***
Creative Foam Corporation..........269 782-3483
55210 Rudy Rd Dowagiac (49047) ***(G-4537)***
Creative Foam Corporation..........810 714-0140
555 N Fenway Dr Fenton (48430) ***(G-5199)***
Creative Graphic Concepts, Royal Oak *Also called Crawford Associates Inc* ***(G-13915)***
Creative Graphics Inc..........517 784-0391
430 N Mechanic St Jackson (49201) ***(G-8424)***
Creative Health Products, Ann Arbor *Also called Creative Engineering Inc* ***(G-408)***
Creative Kids Publication, Shelby Township *Also called Your Hometown Shopper LLC* ***(G-14725)***
Creative Loop..........231 629-8228
21241 Northland Dr Paris (49338) ***(G-12383)***
Creative Machine Company..........248 669-4230
50140 Pontiac Trl Wixom (48393) ***(G-17792)***
Creative Millwork Corporation..........231 526-0201
385 Franklin Park Harbor Springs (49740) ***(G-7280)***
Creative Performance Racg LLC..........248 250-6187
120 Birchwood Dr Troy (48083) ***(G-16285)***
Creative Power Systems Inc..........313 961-2460
1921 10th St Detroit (48216) ***(G-3954)***
Creative Print Crew LLC..........248 629-9404
1119 Rochester Rd Troy (48083) ***(G-16286)***
Creative Printing & Graphics..........810 235-8815
430 S Dort Hwy Flint (48503) ***(G-5407)***
Creative Products Intl..........616 335-3333
A-4699 61st St Unit H Holland (49423) ***(G-7600)***
Creative Promotions..........734 854-2292
3325 W Temperance Rd Lambertville (48144) ***(G-9181)***
Creative Solutions Group Inc (PA)..........248 288-9700
1250 N Crooks Rd Clawson (48017) ***(G-2975)***
Creative Solutions Group Inc..........734 425-2257
12285 Dixie Redford (48239) ***(G-13154)***
Creative Steel Rule Dies Inc..........630 307-8880
4157 Stafford Ave Sw Grand Rapids (49548) ***(G-6315)***
Creative Store Fixtures, Warren *Also called Frank Terlecki Company Inc* ***(G-17045)***
Creative Surfaces Inc..........586 226-2950
20500 Hall Rd Clinton Township (48038) ***(G-3092)***
Creative Techniques Inc..........248 373-3050
200 Northpointe Dr Orion (48359) ***(G-12178)***
Creative Vinyl..........269 782-2833
54950 M 51 N Dowagiac (49047) ***(G-4538)***
Creative Vinyl Sign, Dowagiac *Also called Creative Vinyl* ***(G-4538)***
Creatv Foam Cmpsite Systms..........810 629-4149
6401 Taylor Dr Flint (48507) ***(G-5408)***
Creed Development..........248 926-9811
22635 Venture Dr Novi (48375) ***(G-11857)***
Creek Diesel Services Inc..........800 974-4600
3748 Water Leaf Ct Ne Grand Rapids (49525) ***(G-6316)***
Creek Plastics LLC..........517 423-1003
508 Mohawk St Tecumseh (49286) ***(G-15786)***
Creekside Lumber..........231 924-1934
3810 W 72nd St Newaygo (49337) ***(G-11566)***
Creform Corporation..........248 926-2555
29795 Hudson Dr Novi (48377) ***(G-11858)***
Cremation Service of Michigan..........586 465-1700
44481 N Groesbeck Hwy Clinton Township (48036) ***(G-3093)***
Creme Curls Bakery Inc..........616 669-6230
5292 Lawndale Ave Hudsonville (49426) ***(G-8151)***
Crescent Corporation..........810 982-2784
3720 Pine Grove Ave Fort Gratiot (48059) ***(G-5548)***
Crescent Div Key Gas Cmponents, Allegan *Also called Key Gas Components Inc* ***(G-169)***
Crescent Machining Inc..........248 541-7010
8720 Northend Ave Oak Park (48237) ***(G-12055)***
Crescent Manufacturing Company..........517 486-2670
368 Sherman St Blissfield (49228) ***(G-1715)***
Crescent Pattern Company..........248 541-1052
8720 Northend Ave Oak Park (48237) ***(G-12056)***
Crescive Die and Tool Inc..........734 482-0303
905 Woodland Dr Saline (48176) ***(G-14384)***
Crest Boats, Owosso *Also called Maurell Products Inc* ***(G-12301)***
Crest Marine LLC..........989 725-5188
2710 S M 52 Owosso (48867) ***(G-12285)***
Crete Dry-Mix & Supply Co..........616 784-5790
20 N Park St Comstock Park (49321) ***(G-3473)***
Crewbotiq LLC..........248 939-4229
755 W Big Beaver Rd # 2020 Troy (48084) ***(G-16287)***
Crg Directories, Eaton Rapids *Also called Total Local Acquisitions LLC* ***(G-4735)***
Crg Directories, Eaton Rapids *Also called Adtek Graphics Inc* ***(G-4715)***
Crippen Manufacturing Company..........989 681-4323
400 Woodside Dr Saint Louis (48880) ***(G-14361)***
Crk Ltd..........586 779-5240
23205 Gratiot Ave Eastpointe (48021) ***(G-4699)***
Crl Inc..........906 428-3710
623 Rains Dr Gladstone (49837) ***(G-5910)***
Crm Inc..........231 947-0304
495 W South Airport Rd Traverse City (49686) ***(G-15952)***
Crockett, Tyler Marine Engines, North Street *Also called Tyler Crockett Marine Engines* ***(G-11669)***
Cronen Signs LLC..........269 692-2159
515 E Allegan St Otsego (49078) ***(G-12237)***
Cronkhite Farms Trucking LLC..........269 489-5225
33135 Deer Park Rd Sturgis (49091) ***(G-15602)***
Crop Marks Printing..........616 356-5555
128 Coldbrook St Ne Grand Rapids (49503) ***(G-6317)***
Cross Aluminum Products Inc..........269 697-8340
1770 Mayflower Rd Niles (49120) ***(G-11603)***
Cross Chemical Company, Westland *Also called Cross Technologies Group Inc* ***(G-17548)***
Cross Country Homes..........517 694-0778
5117 Windsor Hwy Potterville (48876) ***(G-13073)***
Cross Country Oilfld Svcs Inc..........337 366-3840
4833 Linda Ln Metamora (48455) ***(G-10774)***
Cross Country Ski Headquarters, Roscommon *Also called R & L Frye* ***(G-13753)***
Cross Paths Corp..........616 248-5371
955 Ken O Sha Ind Park Dr Grand Rapids (49508) ***(G-6318)***
Cross Technologies Group Inc..........734 895-8084
1210 Manufacturers Dr Westland (48186) ***(G-17548)***

Crosscon Industries LLC 248 852-5888
2889 Bond St Rochester Hills (48309) ***(G-13398)***
Crossroads Industries Inc 989 732-1233
2464 Silver Fox Trl Gaylord (49735) ***(G-5853)***
Crown Equipment Corporation 616 530-3000
903 Lynch Dr Ste 103 Traverse City (49686) ***(G-15953)***
Crown Equipment Corporation 734 414-0160
43896 Plymouth Oaks Blvd Plymouth (48170) ***(G-12603)***
Crown Equipment Corporation 616 530-3000
4131 Roger Chaffee Mem Se Grand Rapids (49548) ***(G-6319)***
Crown Group Co., The, Troy *Also called PPG Coating Services* ***(G-16556)***
Crown Group Detroit Plant, Detroit *Also called PPG Coating Services* ***(G-4307)***
Crown Group Livonia Plant, The, Livonia *Also called PPG Coating Services* ***(G-9894)***
Crown Heating Inc 248 352-1688
24521 W Mcnichols Rd Detroit (48219) ***(G-3955)***
Crown Industrial Services Inc (PA) 734 483-7270
2480 Airport Dr Ypsilanti (48198) ***(G-18062)***
Crown Industrial Services Inc 517 905-5300
2080 Brooklyn Rd Jackson (49203) ***(G-8425)***
Crown Lift Trucks, Traverse City *Also called Crown Equipment Corporation* ***(G-15953)***
Crown Lift Trucks, Plymouth *Also called Crown Equipment Corporation* ***(G-12603)***
Crown Lift Trucks, Grand Rapids *Also called Crown Equipment Corporation* ***(G-6319)***
Crown Steel Rail Co (PA) 248 593-7100
6347 Northfield Rd West Bloomfield (48322) ***(G-17471)***
Crown Tumbling, Ypsilanti *Also called Crown Industrial Services Inc* ***(G-18062)***
Crowne Group LLC 734 855-4512
17199 N Laurel Park Dr # 322 Livonia (48152) ***(G-9693)***
Cruse Hardwood Lumber Inc 517 688-4891
2499 Cole St Birmingham (48009) ***(G-1679)***
Cruux LLC 248 515-8411
4897 River Bank Ct Troy (48085) ***(G-16288)***
Crw Plastics Usa Inc 517 545-0900
5775 Brighton Pines Ct Howell (48843) ***(G-8027)***
Crystal Cut Tool Inc 734 494-5076
10360 Harrison Romulus (48174) ***(G-13665)***
Crystal Falls Springs Inc 906 875-3191
346 Rock Crusher Rd Crystal Falls (49920) ***(G-3608)***
Crystal Flash Inc 269 781-8221
1021 E Michigan Ave Marshall (49068) ***(G-10565)***
Crystal Lake Apartments Family (PA) 586 731-3500
2001 Crystal Lake Dr Shelby Township (48316) ***(G-14571)***
Crystal Pure Water Inc 989 681-3547
1211 Michigan Ave Saint Louis (48880) ***(G-14362)***
Cs Express Inc 248 425-1726
2181 Siboney Ct Rochester Hills (48309) ***(G-13399)***
Cs Manufacturing Inc 616 696-2772
299 W Cherry St Cedar Springs (49319) ***(G-2551)***
Cs Tool Engineering Inc 616 696-0940
251 W Cherry St Cedar Springs (49319) ***(G-2552)***
Csa Services Inc 248 596-6184
39550 Orchard Hill Pl Novi (48375) ***(G-11859)***
Cse Morse Inc 269 962-5548
17 Race Ct Battle Creek (49017) ***(G-1170)***
Cse Print, Kalamazoo *Also called Splash In Time LLC* ***(G-8898)***
Csg Storage Facility, Redford *Also called Creative Solutions Group Inc* ***(G-13154)***
Csh Incorporated 989 723-8985
2151 W M 21 Ste A Owosso (48867) ***(G-12286)***
Csi Emergency Apparatus LLC 989 348-2877
2332 Dupont St Grayling (49738) ***(G-7105)***
CSM Cold Heading, Farmington Hills *Also called C S M Manufacturing Corp* ***(G-4952)***
CSM Products Inc 248 836-4995
1920 Opdyke Ct Ste 200 Auburn Hills (48326) ***(G-830)***
Csn Manufacturing Inc 616 364-0027
1750 Elizabeth Ave Nw Grand Rapids (49504) ***(G-6320)***
CSP Holding Corp (HQ) 248 237-7800
255 Rex Blvd Auburn Hills (48326) ***(G-831)***
CSP Holding Corp 248 724-4410
1200 Harmon Rd Auburn Hills (48326) ***(G-832)***
CSP Stamping, Manchester *Also called Continental Strctrl Plstc Mch* ***(G-10404)***
CSP Truck, Troy *Also called Central Screw Products Company* ***(G-16262)***
Csquared Innovations Inc 734 998-8330
45145 W 12 Mile Rd Novi (48377) ***(G-11860)***
CST, Zeeland *Also called Spurt Industries LLC* ***(G-18187)***
CT Automotive, Livonia *Also called Ims/Chinatool Jv LLC* ***(G-9781)***
CTA Acoustics Inc (PA) 248 544-2580
25211 Dequindre Rd Madison Heights (48071) ***(G-10223)***
Ctc Acquisition Company LLC (HQ) 616 884-7100
825 Northland Dr Ne Rockford (49341) ***(G-13564)***
Cte Publishing LLC 313 338-4335
18451 Rosemont Ave Detroit (48219) ***(G-3956)***
CTI, Grand Rapids *Also called Compressor Technologies Inc* ***(G-6296)***
Ctmf Inc 734 482-3086
924 Minion St Ypsilanti (48198) ***(G-18063)***
CTS Manufacturing Inc 586 465-4594
44760 Trinity Dr Clinton Township (48038) ***(G-3094)***
Cuadvantage Mktg Solutions, Saginaw *Also called Reimold Printing Corporation* ***(G-14132)***
Cul-Mac Industries Inc 734 728-9700
3720 Venoy Rd Wayne (48184) ***(G-17429)***
Cultivation Stn - Detroit Inc 313 383-1766
6540 Allen Rd Allen Park (48101) ***(G-196)***
Cultured Love LLC 703 362-5991
2752 Meadow Dr Zeeland (49464) ***(G-18128)***
Cummings-Moore Graphite Co 313 841-1615
1646 N Green St Detroit (48209) ***(G-3957)***
Cummins Bridgeway, New Hudson *Also called K & S Property Inc* ***(G-11546)***
Cummins Bridgeway Grove Cy LLC 614 604-6000
21810 Clessie Ct New Hudson (48165) ***(G-11535)***
Cummins Inc 586 469-2010
43575 N Gratiot Ave Clinton Township (48036) ***(G-3095)***
Cummins Inc 616 281-2211
3715 Clay Ave Sw Grand Rapids (49548) ***(G-6321)***
Cummins Inc 989 732-5055
977 N Center Ave Gaylord (49735) ***(G-5854)***
Cummins Inc 989 752-5200
722 N Outer Dr Saginaw (48601) ***(G-14023)***
Cummins Inc 313 843-6200
3760 Wyoming St Dearborn (48120) ***(G-3688)***
Cummins Inc 248 573-1900
54250 Grand River Ave New Hudson (48165) ***(G-11536)***
Cummins Inc 906 774-2424
1901 N Stephenson Ave Iron Mountain (49801) ***(G-8281)***
Cummins Label Company 269 345-3386
2230 Glendenning Rd Kalamazoo (49001) ***(G-8721)***
Cummins Npower LLC 906 475-8800
75 Us Hwy 41 N Negaunee (49866) ***(G-11469)***
Cup Acquisition LLC (PA) 616 735-4410
2535 Waldorf Ct Nw Grand Rapids (49544) ***(G-6322)***
Cupcake Station 248 334-7927
47 Peggy Ave Pontiac (48341) ***(G-12812)***
Curbco Inc 810 232-2121
3145 S Dye Rd Flint (48507) ***(G-5409)***
Curbell Plastics Inc 734 513-0531
28455 Schoolcraft Rd # 5 Livonia (48150) ***(G-9694)***
Curbs & Damper Products Inc 586 776-7890
16525 Eastland St Roseville (48066) ***(G-13788)***
Curbs and Dampers, Roseville *Also called Cdp Environmental Inc* ***(G-13780)***
Current 906 563-5212
605 Saginaw St Norway (49870) ***(G-11816)***
Curtis Country Connection LLC 517 368-5542
338 E Bell St Camden (49232) ***(G-2339)***
Curtis Metal Finishing Co 248 588-3300
31440 Stephenson Hwy Madison Heights (48071) ***(G-10224)***
Curtis Printing Inc 810 230-6711
2171 Lodge Rd Flint (48532) ***(G-5410)***
Curvy LLC (PA) 917 960-3774
2959 Charing Cross Northville (48167) ***(G-11685)***
Cushing-Malloy Inc 734 663-8554
1350 N Main St Ann Arbor (48104) ***(G-409)***
Cushion Lrry Trphies Engrv LLC 517 332-1667
300 N Clippert St Ste 14 Lansing (48912) ***(G-9358)***
Cusolar Industries Inc 586 949-3880
28161 Kehrig St Chesterfield (48047) ***(G-2757)***
Custard Corner Inc 734 771-4396
2972 W Jefferson Ave Grosse Ile (48138) ***(G-7168)***
Custer Tool & Mfg LLC 734 854-5943
7714 Secor Rd Lambertville (48144) ***(G-9182)***
Custo Arch Shee Meta 313 571-2277
5641 Conner St Detroit (48213) ***(G-3958)***
Custom Anything LLC 231 282-1981
7547 River Ridge Rd Stanwood (49346) ***(G-15233)***
Custom Architectural Products 616 748-1905
430 100th Ave Zeeland (49464) ***(G-18129)***
Custom Biogenic Systems Inc 586 331-2600
74100 Van Dyke Rd Bruce Twp (48065) ***(G-2080)***
Custom Blend Feeds Inc 810 798-3265
77500 Brown Rd Bruce Twp (48065) ***(G-2081)***
Custom Built Brush Company 269 463-3171
7390 Dan Smith Rd Watervliet (49098) ***(G-17390)***
Custom Coating Technologies 734 244-3610
26601 W Huron River Dr Flat Rock (48134) ***(G-5352)***
Custom Components Corporation 616 523-1111
1111 E Main St Ionia Ionia (48846) ***(G-8247)***
Custom Components Truss Co 810 744-0771
3109 E Bristol Rd Burton (48529) ***(G-2153)***
Custom Counter Top Company 616 534-5894
4444 Division Ave S Grand Rapids (49548) ***(G-6323)***
Custom Counters By Handorn, Grand Rapids *Also called Handorn Inc* ***(G-6490)***
Custom Crafters 269 763-9180
7889 S Ionia Rd Bellevue (49021) ***(G-1453)***
Custom Crushing & Recycle Inc 616 249-3329
978 64th St Sw Byron Center (49315) ***(G-2185)***
Custom Design Inc 269 323-8561
4481 Commercial Ave Portage (49002) ***(G-12990)***
Custom Design & Manufacturing 989 754-9962
3673 Carrollton Rd Carrollton (48724) ***(G-2484)***
Custom Design Components Inc 231 937-6166
19569 W Edgar Rd Howard City (49329) ***(G-8000)***

ALPHABETIC

Custom Door Parts — ALPHABETIC SECTION

Custom Door Parts 616 949-5000
8177 Clyde Park Ave Sw Byron Center (49315) *(G-2186)*

Custom Electric Mfg LLC 248 305-7700
48941 West Rd Wixom (48393) *(G-17793)*

Custom Embroidery & Sewing 586 749-7669
63289 North Ave Ray (48096) *(G-13132)*

Custom Embroidery Plus LLC 517 316-9902
420 E Saginaw St Ste 112 Lansing (48906) *(G-9211)*

Custom Embroidery Plus LLC (PA) 989 227-9432
304 N Lansing St Saint Johns (48879) *(G-14282)*

Custom Engineering & Design 248 680-1435
3448 Rowland Ct Troy (48083) *(G-16289)*

Custom Fab Inc 586 755-7260
24440 Gibson Dr Warren (48089) *(G-16995)*

Custom Fireplace Doors Inc 248 673-3121
3809 Lakewood Dr Waterford (48329) *(G-17330)*

Custom Foods Inc 989 249-8061
634 Kendrick St Saginaw (48602) *(G-14024)*

Custom Frame Coatings, Zeeland *Also called August Lighting Inc (G-18115)*

Custom Gears Inc 616 243-2723
3761 Linden Ave Se Ste B Grand Rapids (49548) *(G-6324)*

Custom Giant LLC 313 799-2085
16216 Lamplighter Ct # 1025 Southfield (48075) *(G-14875)*

Custom Interiors of Toledo 419 865-3090
7979 Whiteford Rd Ottawa Lake (49267) *(G-12261)*

Custom Lining and Molding, Kalamazoo *Also called Clm Vibetech Inc (G-8708)*

Custom Machining By Farley 616 896-8469
2792 24th Ave Hudsonville (49426) *(G-8152)*

Custom Marine Carpet 269 684-1922
423 N 9th St Niles (49120) *(G-11604)*

Custom Metal Products Corp 734 591-2500
12283 Levan Rd Livonia (48150) *(G-9695)*

Custom Metal Works Inc 810 420-0390
316 S Belle River Ave # 11 Marine City (48039) *(G-10472)*

Custom Mold Tool and Die Corp 810 688-3711
6779 Lincoln St North Branch (48461) *(G-11658)*

Custom Powder Coating LLC 616 454-9730
1601 Madison Ave Se Ste 1 Grand Rapids (49507) *(G-6325)*

Custom Printers Inc 616 454-9224
2801 Oak Industrial Dr Ne Grand Rapids (49505) *(G-6326)*

Custom Printing of Michigan 248 585-9222
1659 Rochester Rd Troy (48083) *(G-16290)*

Custom Products Inc 269 983-9500
180 Kerth St Saint Joseph (49085) *(G-14305)*

Custom Profile, Grand Rapids *Also called Cup Acquisition LLC (G-6322)*

Custom Quilts 517 626-6399
14667 S Lowell Rd Lansing (48906) *(G-9212)*

Custom Royaltees 586 943-9849
37537 Brynford Dr Clinton Township (48036) *(G-3096)*

Custom Rustic Flags LLC 906 203-6935
1018 Bingham Ave Sault Sainte Marie (49783) *(G-14463)*

Custom Service & Design Inc (PA) 248 340-9005
1259 Doris Rd Ste B Auburn Hills (48326) *(G-833)*

Custom Service Printers Inc 231 726-3297
916 E Keating Ave Muskegon (49442) *(G-11303)*

Custom Sockets Inc 616 355-1971
1896 Russel Ct Holland (49423) *(G-7601)*

Custom Threads and Sports LLC 248 391-0088
260 Engelwood Dr Ste A Lake Orion (48359) *(G-9133)*

Custom Tool & Die Service Inc 616 662-1068
5090 40th Ave Ste A Hudsonville (49426) *(G-8153)*

Custom Tool and Die Co 269 465-9130
7059 Red Arrow Hwy Stevensville (49127) *(G-15560)*

Custom Tooling Systems Inc 616 748-9880
3331 80th Ave Zeeland (49464) *(G-18130)*

Custom Valve Concepts Inc 248 597-8999
31651 Research Park Dr Madison Heights (48071) *(G-10225)*

Custom Verticals Unlimited 734 522-1615
14621 Ludlow St Oak Park (48237) *(G-12057)*

Custom Vinyl Signs & Designs 989 261-7446
3018 Log Cabin Trl Sheridan (48884) *(G-14732)*

Custom Welding Service LLC 616 402-6681
1700 Robbins Rd Lot 470 Grand Haven (49417) *(G-6007)*

Custom Wood Products, Burton *Also called Custom Components Truss Co (G-2153)*

Custom Workroom, Huntington Woods *Also called Lorne Hanley (G-8189)*

Custombilt of Toledo, Ottawa Lake *Also called Custom Interiors of Toledo (G-12261)*

Customcat, Detroit *Also called Mylockercom LLC (G-4261)*

Customer Metal Fabrication Inc (PA) 906 774-3216
W8762 Lakeview Dr Iron Mountain (49801) *(G-8282)*

Custometal Products, Saint Joseph *Also called Custom Products Inc (G-14305)*

Cut Above Wood Designs, Niles *Also called Phillip Anderson (G-11639)*

Cut All Water Jet Cutting Inc 734 946-7880
25944 Northline Rd Taylor (48180) *(G-15705)*

Cut-Tech 269 687-9005
1951 Industrial Dr Niles (49120) *(G-11605)*

Cutex Inc 734 953-8908
12496 Globe St Livonia (48150) *(G-9696)*

Cutting Edge Technologies Inc 616 738-0800
13305 New Holland St B Holland (49424) *(G-7602)*

Cutversion Technologies Corp 586 634-1339
13335 15 Mile Rd Ste 313 Sterling Heights (48312) *(G-15304)*

Cvm Services LLC 269 521-4811
665 44th St Allegan (49010) *(G-153)*

Cw Bearing, Northville *Also called Cw Manufacturing LLC (G-11686)*

Cw Champion Welding Alloys LLC 906 296-9633
52705 State Highway M26 Lake Linden (49945) *(G-9107)*

Cw Creative Welding Inc 586 294-1050
33360 Groesbeck Hwy Fraser (48026) *(G-5640)*

Cw Manufacturing LLC 734 781-4000
15200 Technology Dr Northville (48168) *(G-11686)*

Cyberlogic Technologies Inc 248 631-2200
755 W Big Beaver Rd # 2020 Troy (48084) *(G-16291)*

Cyclone International, Holland *Also called Big Dutchman Inc (G-7569)*

Cyclone Manufacturing Inc 269 782-9670
56850 Woodhouse Dr Dowagiac (49047) *(G-4539)*

Cygeirts Sawmill 231 821-0083
6875 Marvin Rd Brunswick (49425) *(G-2107)*

Cygnet Financial Freedom House, Waterford *Also called Cygnet Financial Planning Inc (G-17331)*

Cygnet Financial Planning Inc 248 673-2900
4139 W Walton Blvd Ste D Waterford (48329) *(G-17331)*

Cygnus Inc 231 347-5404
829 Charlevoix Ave Petoskey (49770) *(G-12447)*

Cypress Computer Systems Inc 810 245-2300
1778 Imlay City Rd Lapeer (48446) *(G-9453)*

Cyprium Induction LLC 586 884-4982
42770 Mound Rd Sterling Heights (48314) *(G-15305)*

Cyrus Forest Products 269 751-6535
4234 127th Ave Allegan (49010) *(G-154)*

Cytec Industries Inc 269 349-6677
3115 Miller Rd Kalamazoo (49001) *(G-8722)*

Cz Industries Inc 248 475-4415
1929-1939 N Auburn Hills (48326) *(G-834)*

Czuk Studio 269 628-2568
26922 County Road 388 Kendall (49062) *(G-8983)*

D Mac Industries Inc 734 536-7754
31492 Glendale St Livonia (48150) *(G-9697)*

D & B Heat Transfer Pdts Inc 616 827-0028
8031 Division Ave S Ste C Grand Rapids (49548) *(G-6327)*

D & B Metal Finishing 586 725-6056
34537 Shorewood St Chesterfield (48047) *(G-2758)*

D & C Investment Group Inc (PA) 734 994-0591
5840 Interface Dr Ann Arbor (48103) *(G-410)*

D & D Buffing & Polishing 616 866-1015
6270 12 Mile Rd Ne Rockford (49341) *(G-13565)*

D & D Building Inc 616 248-7908
3959 Linden Ave Se Grand Rapids (49548) *(G-6328)*

D & D Business Machines Inc 616 364-8446
3545 Brandau Dr Ne Grand Rapids (49525) *(G-6329)*

D & D Driers Timber Product 906 224-7251
115 E Old Us 2 Wakefield (49968) *(G-16849)*

D & D Fabrications Inc 810 798-2491
8005 Tiffany Dr Almont (48003) *(G-255)*

D & D Investments Equipment, Fenton *Also called Burgaflex North America LLC (G-5192)*

D & D Printing, Kalamazoo *Also called Dekoff & Sons Inc (G-8724)*

D & D Printing Co 616 454-7710
342 Market Ave Sw Unit 1 Grand Rapids (49503) *(G-6330)*

D & D Production Inc 248 334-2112
2500 Williams Dr Waterford (48328) *(G-17332)*

D & D Signs Inc 231 941-0340
2694 Garfield Rd N Ste 25 Traverse City (49686) *(G-15954)*

D & D Tool Inc 616 772-2416
218 E Harrison Ave Zeeland (49464) *(G-18131)*

D & F Corporation 586 254-5300
42455 Merrill Rd Sterling Heights (48314) *(G-15306)*

D & F Mold LLC 269 465-6633
8088 Jericho Rd Bridgman (49106) *(G-1862)*

D & G Equipment Inc (PA) 517 655-4606
2 Industrial Park Dr Williamston (48895) *(G-17729)*

D & G Signs LLC 810 230-6445
4297 Miller Rd Flint (48507) *(G-5411)*

D & J Mfg & Machining 231 830-9522
507 W Hovey Ave Muskegon (49444) *(G-11304)*

D & K Pattern Inc 989 865-9955
12021 Beaver Rd Saint Charles (48655) *(G-14191)*

D & L Tooling Inc 517 369-5655
502 N Matteson St Bronson (49028) *(G-2022)*

D & L Water Control Inc 734 455-6982
7534 Baron Dr Canton (48187) *(G-2363)*

D & M Cabinet Shop Inc 989 479-9271
5230 Purdy Rd Ruth (48470) *(G-13988)*

D & M Silkscreening 517 694-4199
4202 Charlar Dr Ste 3 Holt (48842) *(G-7906)*

D & M Truck Top Co Inc 248 792-7972
2354 Dorchester Dr N # 108 Troy (48084) *(G-16292)*

D & N Bending Corp (PA) 586 752-5511
150 Shafer Dr Romeo (48065) *(G-13626)*

D & N Casting, Romeo *Also called D & N Bending Corp (G-13626)*

ALPHABETIC SECTION
Dake Corporation

D & N Gage Inc....586 336-2110
161 E Pond Dr Romeo (48065) ***(G-13627)***
D & R Fabrication Inc....616 794-1130
200 Gooding St Belding (48809) ***(G-1408)***
D & S Engine Specialist Inc....248 583-9240
875 N Rochester Rd Clawson (48017) ***(G-2976)***
D & T Smoke LLC....586 263-6888
41964 Hayes Rd Clinton Township (48038) ***(G-3097)***
D & W Awning and Window Co....810 742-0340
8068 E Court St Davison (48423) ***(G-3645)***
D & W Flow Testing Inc (PA)....231 258-4926
1770 M 72 Se Kalkaska (49646) ***(G-8940)***
D & W Management Company Inc....586 758-2284
23660 Sherwood Ave Warren (48091) ***(G-16996)***
D & W Square LLC....313 493-4970
8932 Coyle St Detroit (48228) ***(G-3959)***
D A C Industries Inc....616 235-0140
600 11th St Nw Grand Rapids (49504) ***(G-6331)***
D A U P Corp....906 477-1148
Us 2 Naubinway (49762) ***(G-11465)***
D and G Glass Inc....734 341-0038
3355 Carleton Rockwood Rd Carleton (48117) ***(G-2452)***
D B A Richards Boatworks Mar....906 789-4168
4085 15th Rd Escanaba (49829) ***(G-4823)***
D B International LLC....616 796-0679
650 Riley St Ste C Holland (49424) ***(G-7603)***
D B Mattson Co....734 697-8056
44505 Harmony Ln Van Buren Twp (48111) ***(G-16755)***
D B Tool Company Inc....989 453-2429
6443 Dunn Rd Pigeon (48755) ***(G-12488)***
D C Norris North America LLC....231 935-1519
2375 Traversefield Dr Traverse City (49686) ***(G-15955)***
D E Rogers & Assoc., Waterford *Also called Donald E Rogers Associates* ***(G-17335)***
D E S Group, Sterling Heights *Also called Applied Technology Group* ***(G-15263)***
D Fab, Madison Heights *Also called Design Fabrications Inc* ***(G-10229)***
D Find Corporation....248 641-2858
1955 Rolling Woods Dr Troy (48098) ***(G-16293)***
D G Grinding Inc....248 624-7280
1711 Traditional Dr Commerce Township (48390) ***(G-3397)***
D H S, Chesterfield *Also called Die Heat Systems Inc* ***(G-2767)***
D H Tool & Die, Commerce Township *Also called Heinzmann D Tool & Die Inc* ***(G-3410)***
D J and G Enterprise Inc....231 258-9925
402 E Dresden St Kalkaska (49646) ***(G-8941)***
D J McQuestion & Sons Inc....231 768-4403
17708 18 Mile Rd Leroy (49655) ***(G-9530)***
D J Rotunda Associates Inc....586 772-3350
2634 Peterboro Ct West Bloomfield (48323) ***(G-17472)***
D J S Systems Inc....517 568-4444
801 S Hillsdale St Homer (49245) ***(G-7941)***
D K Enterprises Inc....586 756-7350
21942 Dequindre Rd Warren (48091) ***(G-16997)***
D K Products Inc....517 263-3025
2370 E Us Highway 223 Adrian (49221) ***(G-56)***
D L R Manufacturing Inc....734 394-0690
44205 Yost Rd Van Buren Twp (48111) ***(G-16756)***
D M C International Inc....586 465-1112
42470 Executive Dr Harrison Township (48045) ***(G-7328)***
D M J Corp....810 239-9071
3910 Fenton Rd Ste 15 Flint (48507) ***(G-5412)***
D M P E....269 428-5070
5790 Saint Joseph Ave Stevensville (49127) ***(G-15561)***
D Marsh Company Inc....616 677-5276
3186 Leonard St Marne (49435) ***(G-10506)***
D Michael Services....810 794-2407
8855 Stone Rd Clay (48001) ***(G-2996)***
D N D Business Machines, Grand Rapids *Also called A A A Mailing & Packg Sups LLC* ***(G-6123)***
D O W Asphalt Paving LLC....810 743-2633
10421 Calkins Rd Swartz Creek (48473) ***(G-15665)***
D P Equipment Co....517 368-5266
10700 S Edon Rd Camden (49232) ***(G-2340)***
D R W Systems....989 874-4663
4484 N Van Dyke Rd Filion (48432) ***(G-5346)***
D S C Services Inc (PA)....734 241-9500
1510 E 1st St Monroe (48161) ***(G-11026)***
D S N Satellites, Mason *Also called Digital Success Network* ***(G-10636)***
D Sign LLC....616 392-3841
511 Chicago Dr Holland (49423) ***(G-7604)***
D T Fowler Mfg Co Inc (PA)....810 245-9336
101 N Mapleleaf Rd Lapeer (48446) ***(G-9454)***
D T M 1 Inc....248 889-9210
1450 N Milford Rd Ste 101 Highland (48357) ***(G-7491)***
D T R Sign Co LLC....616 889-8927
6315 Thornapple Valley Dr Hastings (49058) ***(G-7405)***
D T S, Davison *Also called Davison Tool Service Inc* ***(G-3646)***
D W Hines Manufacturing Corp....586 775-1200
21887 Schoenherr Rd Warren (48089) ***(G-16998)***
D W Machine Inc....517 787-9929
2501 Precision St Jackson (49202) ***(G-8426)***
D&E Incorporated....313 673-3284
20542 Oldham Rd Southfield (48076) ***(G-14876)***
D&Js Plastics LLC....616 745-5798
2322 Edson Dr Hudsonville (49426) ***(G-8154)***
D&M Metal Products Company....616 784-0601
4994 West River Dr Ne Comstock Park (49321) ***(G-3474)***
D&W Fine Pack LLC....866 296-2020
1191 Wolfson Ct Gladwin (48624) ***(G-5928)***
D' Printer Inc-Shop, Tecumseh *Also called DPrinter Inc* ***(G-15791)***
D'Angelico Strings, Springfield *Also called GHS Corporation* ***(G-15193)***
D-Licious Foods, Owosso *Also called Jt Foods Inc* ***(G-12297)***
D-M-E USA Inc....616 754-4601
1117 E Fairplains St Greenville (48838) ***(G-7126)***
D-Mark Inc....586 949-3610
130 N Groesbeck Hwy Mount Clemens (48043) ***(G-11128)***
D-N-S Industries Inc....586 465-2444
44805 Trinity Dr Clinton Township (48038) ***(G-3098)***
D-Sign, Holland *Also called D Sign LLC* ***(G-7604)***
D.A. Stuart Company, Detroit *Also called Houghton International Inc* ***(G-4131)***
D2t America Inc....248 680-9001
2870 Technology Dr Rochester Hills (48309) ***(G-13400)***
Dabir Surfaces Inc....248 796-0802
24585 Evergreen Rd Southfield (48075) ***(G-14877)***
Dablon Vineyards LLC....269 422-2846
111 W Shawnee Rd Baroda (49101) ***(G-1123)***
Dac Inc....313 388-4342
2930 S Dartmouth St Detroit (48217) ***(G-3960)***
DACA DIV, Romulus *Also called United Brass Manufacturers Inc* ***(G-13736)***
Daco Hand Controllers Inc....248 982-3266
24404 Catherine Industria Novi (48375) ***(G-11861)***
Dadco Inc (PA)....734 207-1100
43850 Plymouth Oaks Blvd Plymouth (48170) ***(G-12604)***
Dadco Inc....616 785-2888
848 W River Center Dr Ne C Comstock Park (49321) ***(G-3475)***
Dads Panels Inc....810 245-1871
2142 Imlay City Rd Lapeer (48446) ***(G-9455)***
Daewon America Inc....334 364-1630
1450 W Long Lake Rd # 175 Troy (48098) ***(G-16294)***
Dag Ltd LLC....586 276-9310
34400 Mound Rd Sterling Heights (48310) ***(G-15307)***
Dag R&D....248 444-0575
1677 Melody Ln Milford (48380) ***(G-10959)***
Dagenham Millworks LLC....616 698-8883
4525 Airwest Dr Se Grand Rapids (49512) ***(G-6332)***
Dager Systems, Chesterfield *Also called Kimastle Corporation* ***(G-2797)***
Daiek Door Sytem, Troy *Also called Daiek Products Inc* ***(G-16295)***
Daiek Products Inc....248 816-1360
1725 Blaney Dr Troy (48084) ***(G-16295)***
Daifuku North America Holdg Co (HQ)....248 553-1000
30100 Cabot Dr Novi (48377) ***(G-11862)***
Daily Bill....989 631-2068
610 W Saint Andrews Rd Midland (48640) ***(G-10828)***
Daily Brews Gourmet Coffe....269 792-2739
128 S Main St Wayland (49348) ***(G-17403)***
Daily Contracts LLC....734 676-0903
7779 Grays Dr Grosse Ile (48138) ***(G-7169)***
Daily De-Lish....616 450-9562
1235 Thrnpple River Dr Se Ada (49301) ***(G-12)***
Daily Fantasy King....734 238-2622
15425 Glenhurst Southgate (48195) ***(G-15076)***
Daily Gardener LLC....734 754-6527
5211 Pontiac Trl Ann Arbor (48105) ***(G-411)***
Daily Mining Gazette, Houghton *Also called Nutting Newspapers Inc* ***(G-7979)***
Daily News, The, Iron Mountain *Also called Ogden Newspapers Inc* ***(G-8296)***
Daily Oakland Press (HQ)....248 332-8181
48 W Huron St Pontiac (48342) ***(G-12813)***
Daily Press, Escanaba *Also called Ogden Newspapers Inc* ***(G-4849)***
Daily Recycling of Michigan....734 654-9800
201 Matlin Rd Carleton (48117) ***(G-2453)***
Daily Reporter....517 278-2318
15 W Pearl St Coldwater (49036) ***(G-3300)***
Daily Telegram, The, Adrian *Also called Gatehouse Media LLC* ***(G-66)***
Daimay North America Auto Inc....313 533-9860
24450 Plymouth Rd Redford (48239) ***(G-13155)***
Daimay North America Auto Inc (HQ)....313 533-9680
24400 Plymouth Rd Redford (48239) ***(G-13156)***
Dairy Farmers America Inc....517 265-5045
1336 E Maumee St Adrian (49221) ***(G-57)***
Dairy Freezzz Too LLC....248 629-6666
621 E 11 Mile Rd Madison Heights (48071) ***(G-10226)***
Dairy Queen....616 235-0102
956 Fulton St W Grand Rapids (49504) ***(G-6333)***
Dajaco Ind Inc....586 949-1590
49715 Leona Dr Chesterfield (48051) ***(G-2759)***
Dajaco Industries Inc....586 949-1590
49715 Leona Dr Chesterfield (48051) ***(G-2760)***
Dake Corporation....616 842-7110
724 Robbins Rd Grand Haven (49417) ***(G-6008)***

A
L
P
H
A
B
E
T
I
C

(PA)=Parent Co (HQ)=Headquarters (DH)=Div Headquarters
2020 Harris Michigan Industrial Directory
933

Dakkota Integrated Systems LLC (PA)......517 694-6500
123 Brighton Lake Rd # 202 Brighton (48116) ***(G-1908)***
Dakkota Integrated Systems LLC......517 321-3064
16130 Grove Rd Lansing (48906) ***(G-9213)***
Dakkota Integrated Systems LLC......517 694-6500
4147 Keller Rd Holt (48842) ***(G-7907)***
Dakkota Lighting Tech LLC (HQ)......517 993-7700
4147 Keller Rd Holt (48842) ***(G-7908)***
Dakota Cupcake Factory......810 694-7198
10529 Village Ct Grand Blanc (48439) ***(G-5964)***
Dal-Tile Corporation......248 471-7150
24640 Drake Rd Farmington Hills (48335) ***(G-4968)***
Dale Corporation......248 542-2400
28091 Dequindre Rd # 301 Madison Heights (48071) ***(G-10227)***
Dale Prentice, Oak Park *Also called Engineered Resources Inc* ***(G-12066)***
Dale Routley Logging......231 861-2596
1870 N 100th Ave Hart (49420) ***(G-7370)***
Dales LLC......734 444-4620
348 Cty Center St Lapeer (48446) ***(G-9456)***
Dallas Design Inc......810 238-4546
3432 S Saginaw St Flint (48503) ***(G-5413)***
Dallas Industries, Troy *Also called Advanced Feedlines LLC* ***(G-16169)***
Dalton Armond Publishers Inc......517 351-8520
2867 Jolly Rd Okemos (48864) ***(G-12118)***
Dalton Industries LLC......248 673-0755
2800 Alliance Ste B Waterford (48328) ***(G-17333)***
Dama Tool & Gauge Company......616 842-9631
6175 Norton Center Dr Norton Shores (49441) ***(G-11747)***
Damar Machinery Co......616 453-4655
3389 3 Mile Rd Nw Grand Rapids (49534) ***(G-6334)***
Damar Tool Manufacturing, Romulus *Also called Millennium Technology II Inc* ***(G-13709)***
Damick Enterprises......248 652-7500
1801 Rochester Indus Ct Rochester Hills (48309) ***(G-13401)***
Damm Company Inc......248 427-9060
24061 Research Dr Farmington Hills (48335) ***(G-4969)***
Dan Drummond......231 853-6200
1830 S Slocum Rd Ravenna (49451) ***(G-13118)***
Dana Driveshaft Mfg LLC......248 623-2185
4440 N Atlantic Blvd Auburn Hills (48326) ***(G-835)***
Dana Limited......810 329-2500
2020 Christian B Haas Dr Saint Clair (48079) ***(G-14213)***
Dana Off-Hghway Components LLC......586 467-1600
3040 S Dye Rd Flint (48507) ***(G-5414)***
Dana Thermal Products LLC......810 329-2500
2020 Christian B Haas Dr Saint Clair (48079) ***(G-14214)***
Dana Thermal Products LLC......810 329-2500
2020 Christian B Haas Dr Saint Clair (48079) ***(G-14215)***
Dana Trading, Grand Rapids *Also called Foremost Graphics LLC* ***(G-6415)***
Dancorp Inc......269 663-5566
27496 Max St Edwardsburg (49112) ***(G-4764)***
Dando Chemicals US LLC......248 629-9434
28560 Sutherland St Southfield (48076) ***(G-14878)***
Dane Systems LLC......269 465-3263
7275 Red Arrow Hwy Stevensville (49127) ***(G-15562)***
Daneks Goodtime Ice Co Inc......989 725-5920
210 N Gould St Owosso (48867) ***(G-12287)***
Daniel D Slater......989 833-7135
10361 W Van Buren Rd Riverdale (48877) ***(G-13284)***
Daniel Olson......269 816-1838
12646 Born St Jones (49061) ***(G-8651)***
Daniel Pruitoff......616 392-1371
271 E 26th St Holland (49423) ***(G-7605)***
Daniel Ward......810 965-6535
7352 N Tort Hi W Y Ste 2 Mount Morris (48458) ***(G-11160)***
Danif Industries Inc......248 539-0295
4289 Stoddard Rd West Bloomfield (48323) ***(G-17473)***
Danly IEM......800 243-2659
4300 40th St Se Grand Rapids (49512) ***(G-6335)***
Danlyn Controls Inc......586 773-6797
25090 Terra Industrial Dr Chesterfield (48051) ***(G-2761)***
Danmar Products Inc (PA)......734 761-1990
221 Jackson Industrial Dr Ann Arbor (48103) ***(G-412)***
Danmark Graphics LLC......616 675-7499
153 N Main St Casnovia (49318) ***(G-2507)***
Danny K Bundy......231 590-6924
2630 E 16 1/2 Rd Manton (49663) ***(G-10452)***
Dans Concrete LLC......517 242-0754
9202 Riverside Dr Grand Ledge (48837) ***(G-6104)***
Dapco Industries, Dexter *Also called Dexter Automatic Products Co* ***(G-4485)***
Darby Metal Treating Inc......269 204-6504
892 Wakefield Plainwell (49080) ***(G-12521)***
Darby Ready Mix Concrete Co......517 547-7004
U.S 12 & Herold Hwy Addison (49220) ***(G-36)***
Darby Ready Mix-Dundee LLC......734 529-7100
7801 N Ann Arbor Rd Dundee (48131) ***(G-4578)***
Darbyreadymix.com, Addison *Also called Darby Ready Mix Concrete Co* ***(G-36)***
Dare Auto Inc......734 228-6243
47548 Halyard Dr Ste B Plymouth (48170) ***(G-12605)***
Dare Products Inc......269 965-2307
860 Betterly Rd Springfield (49037) ***(G-15190)***
Daring Company......248 340-0741
180 Engelwood Dr Ste B Orion (48359) ***(G-12179)***
Darkhorse Brewing Company, The, Marshall *Also called Mor-Dall Enterprises Inc* ***(G-10584)***
Darling Ingredients Inc......313 928-7400
3350 Greenfield Rd Melvindale (48122) ***(G-10695)***
Darling Ingredients Inc......989 752-4340
340 Tyler St Carrollton (48724) ***(G-2485)***
Darling Ingredients Inc......517 279-9731
600 Jay St Coldwater (49036) ***(G-3301)***
Darling Ingredients Inc......269 751-0560
5900 Old Allegan Rd Hamilton (49419) ***(G-7231)***
Darrell A Curtice......231 745-9890
669 E Roosevelt Rd Bitely (49309) ***(G-1710)***
Darrell R Hanson......810 364-7892
579 Michigan Ave Marysville (48040) ***(G-10602)***
Darson Corporation......313 875-7781
10610 Galaxie Ave Ferndale (48220) ***(G-5269)***
Dart Container Corp Georgia (PA)......517 676-3800
500 Hogsback Rd Mason (48854) ***(G-10631)***
Dart Container Corp Kentucky (PA)......517 676-3800
500 Hogsback Rd Mason (48854) ***(G-10632)***
Dart Container Corporation (PA)......800 248-5960
500 Hogsback Rd Mason (48854) ***(G-10633)***
Dart Container Michigan LLC (HQ)......800 248-5960
500 Hogsback Rd Mason (48854) ***(G-10634)***
Dart Container Michigan LLC......517 694-9455
2148 Depot St Holt (48842) ***(G-7909)***
Dart Container Michigan LLC......517 676-3803
432 Hogsback Rd Mason (48854) ***(G-10635)***
Dart Energy Center......248 203-2924
260 E Brown St Ste 200 Birmingham (48009) ***(G-1680)***
Dart Energy Corporation......231 885-1665
23862 13 Mile Rd Mesick (49668) ***(G-10769)***
Dart Machinery Ltd......248 362-1188
2097 Bart Ave Warren (48091) ***(G-16999)***
Dart Polymers, Mason *Also called Dart Container Corp Kentucky* ***(G-10632)***
Darwin Sneller......989 977-3718
8677 Kilmanagh Rd Sebewaing (48759) ***(G-14514)***
Daryls Use Truck Sales, Pigeon *Also called Thumb Truck and Trailer Co* ***(G-12493)***
Das Group Inc (PA)......248 670-2718
2417 Vinsetta Blvd Royal Oak (48073) ***(G-13917)***
DAS Technologies Inc......269 657-0541
138 Ampey Rd Paw Paw (49079) ***(G-12401)***
Dassault Systemes Americas......248 267-9696
900 N Squirrel Rd Ste 100 Auburn Hills (48326) ***(G-836)***
Data Acquisition Ctrl Systems......248 437-6096
7965 Kensington Ct Ste A2 Brighton (48116) ***(G-1909)***
Data Center, Dearborn *Also called Active Solutions Group Inc* ***(G-3671)***
Data Cover .com, Pontiac *Also called Mis Associates Inc* ***(G-12850)***
Data Mail Services Inc......248 588-2415
747 E Whitcomb Ave Madison Heights (48071) ***(G-10228)***
Data Optics Inc......734 483-8228
115 Holmes Rd Ypsilanti (48198) ***(G-18064)***
Data Reproductions Corporation......248 371-3700
4545 Glenmeade Ln Auburn Hills (48326) ***(G-837)***
Datacover Inc......844 875-4076
1735 Highwood W Pontiac (48340) ***(G-12814)***
Datacover Inc......248 391-2163
1070 W Silverbell Rd Lake Orion (48359) ***(G-9134)***
Datamatic Processing Inc (PA)......517 882-4401
5545 Enterprise Dr Lansing (48911) ***(G-9359)***
Dataspeed Inc (PA)......248 879-0528
2736 Research Dr Rochester Hills (48309) ***(G-13402)***
Datec, Portage *Also called Dynamic Auto Test Engineering* ***(G-12991)***
Datum Industries LLC......616 977-1995
4740 44th St Se Grand Rapids (49512) ***(G-6336)***
Datum Precision Machine Inc......586 790-1120
35235 Automation Dr Clinton Township (48035) ***(G-3099)***
Daughtery Group Inc......313 452-7918
16892 Parkside St Detroit (48221) ***(G-3961)***
Daughtry Nwspapers Investments......269 683-2100
217 N 4th St Niles (49120) ***(G-11606)***
Davalor Mold, Chesterfield *Also called Oth Consultants Inc* ***(G-2813)***
Davalor Mold Company LLC......586 598-0100
46480 Continental Dr Chesterfield (48047) ***(G-2762)***
Davco Manufacturing LLC......734 429-5665
1600 Woodland Dr Saline (48176) ***(G-14385)***
Davco Technology LLC......734 429-5665
1600 Woodland Dr Saline (48176) ***(G-14386)***
Dave Brand......269 651-4693
26541 Us 12 Sturgis (49091) ***(G-15603)***
Dave Manson Precision Reamers, Grand Blanc *Also called Loon Lake Precision Inc* ***(G-5974)***
Daves Concrete Products Inc......269 624-4100
79811 M 40 Lawton (49065) ***(G-9511)***
Daves Diamond Inc......248 693-2482
416 S Broadway St Lake Orion (48362) ***(G-9135)***
David A Mohr Jr......517 266-2694
4153 Carson Hwy Adrian (49221) ***(G-58)***

David Boyd 517 567-2302
8800 Camden Rd Waldron (49288) ***(G-16857)***
David Epstein Inc 248 542-0802
1135 E 9 Mile Rd Ferndale (48220) ***(G-5270)***
David Gauss Logging 517 851-8102
4635 Cooper Rd Stockbridge (49285) ***(G-15588)***
David H Bosley & Associates 734 261-8390
16329 Middlebelt Rd Livonia (48154) ***(G-9698)***
David Hirn Cabinets and Contg 906 428-1935
1319 Delta Ave Gladstone (49837) ***(G-5911)***
David Jenks 810 793-7340
5955 Chapman Rd North Branch (48461) ***(G-11659)***
David Nickels 248 634-5420
6455 Lahring Rd Holly (48442) ***(G-7873)***
David Wachler & Sons Inc 248 540-4622
112 S Old Woodward Ave Birmingham (48009) ***(G-1681)***
Davis Dental Laboratory 616 261-9191
5830 Crossroads Cmmrce Wyoming (49519) ***(G-17995)***
Davis Girls 586 781-6865
54421 Iroquois Ln Shelby Township (48315) ***(G-14572)***
Davis Iron Works Inc 248 624-5960
1166 Benstein Rd Commerce Township (48390) ***(G-3398)***
Davis Logging 517 617-4550
857 Herl Rd Bronson (49028) ***(G-2023)***
Davis Steel Rule Die 269 492-9908
2222 Glendenning Rd 9b Kalamazoo (49001) ***(G-8723)***
Davismade Inc 810 743-5262
4400 S Saginaw St # 1470 Flint (48507) ***(G-5415)***
Davison Tool Service Inc 810 653-6920
236 Mill St Davison (48423) ***(G-3646)***
Davison-Rite Products Co 734 513-0505
12921 Stark Rd Livonia (48150) ***(G-9699)***
Dawn Equipment Company Inc 517 789-4500
2021 Micor Dr Jackson (49203) ***(G-8427)***
Dawn Food Products, Jackson *Also called Dawn Equipment Company Inc* ***(G-8427)***
Dawn Food Products Inc 517 789-4400
3333 Sargent Rd Jackson (49201) ***(G-8428)***
Dawn Food Products Inc 800 654-4843
2885 Clydon Ave Sw Grand Rapids (49519) ***(G-6337)***
Dawn Food Products Inc (HQ) 517 789-4400
3333 Sargent Rd Jackson (49201) ***(G-8429)***
Dawn Foods Inc (PA) 517 789-4400
3333 Sargent Rd Jackson (49201) ***(G-8430)***
Dawn Foods International Corp 517 789-4400
3333 Sargent Rd Jackson (49201) ***(G-8431)***
Dawson Grinding, Grand Haven *Also called Grand Haven Steel Products Inc* ***(G-6025)***
Dawson Manufacturing 269 639-4213
180 Dawson St Sandusky (48471) ***(G-14432)***
Dawson Manufacturing Company (PA) 269 925-0100
1042 N Crystal Ave Benton Harbor (49022) ***(G-1492)***
Dawson Manufacturing Company 269 925-0100
1042 N Crystal Ave Benton Harbor (49022) ***(G-1493)***
Dawzye Excavation Inc 906 786-5276
7575 Rays M.7 Cir 7m Gladstone (49837) ***(G-5912)***
Day International Group Inc (HQ) 734 781-4600
14909 N Beck Rd Plymouth (48170) ***(G-12606)***
Dayco LLC (PA) 248 404-6500
1650 Research Dr Ste 200 Troy (48083) ***(G-16296)***
Dayco Incorporated (HQ) 248 404-6500
1650 Research Dr Ste 200 Troy (48083) ***(G-16297)***
Dayco Products LLC 989 775-0689
1799 Gover Pkwy Mount Pleasant (48858) ***(G-11191)***
Dayco Products LLC 248 404-6506
1650 Research Dr Ste 200 Troy (48083) ***(G-16298)***
Dayco Products LLC 517 439-0689
215 Industrial Dr Hillsdale (49242) ***(G-7522)***
Dayco Products LLC (HQ) 248 404-6500
1650 Research Dr Ste 200 Troy (48083) ***(G-16299)***
Dayco Products LLC 248 404-6537
16000 Common Rd Roseville (48066) ***(G-13789)***
Dayton Lamina Corp 231 533-8646
3650 S Derenzy Rd Bellaire (49615) ***(G-1437)***
Dayton Precision Services, Carleton *Also called Rvm Company of Toledo* ***(G-2462)***
DB Communications Inc 800 692-8200
32922 Brookside Cir Livonia (48152) ***(G-9700)***
DC Byers Co/Grand Rapids Inc (PA) 616 538-7300
5946 Clay Ave Sw Grand Rapids (49548) ***(G-6338)***
DCI Aerotech, Detroit *Also called Detroit Chrome Inc* ***(G-3976)***
Dcl Inc (PA) 231 547-5600
8660 Ance Rd Charlevoix (49720) ***(G-2613)***
Dcr Services & Cnstr Inc (PA) 313 297-6544
828 S Dix St Detroit (48217) ***(G-3962)***
DD Parker Enterprises Inc 734 241-6898
1402 W 7th St Monroe (48161) ***(G-11027)***
Ddks Industries LLC 586 323-5909
14954 Technology Dr Shelby Township (48315) ***(G-14573)***
DDM, Clinton Township *Also called Diamond Die and Mold Company* ***(G-3102)***
Ddp Specialty Electnc (HQ) 989 496-4400
2200 W Salzburg Rd Midland (48686) ***(G-10829)***
Ddr Heating Inc (PA) 269 673-2145
700 Grand St Allegan (49010) ***(G-155)***
Ddr Heating Inc 269 673-2145
2870 116th Ave Allegan (49010) ***(G-156)***
De Antigua, Holland *Also called Prime Wood Products Inc* ***(G-7775)***
De Klomp Wden Shoe Delft Fctry, Holland *Also called Veldheer Tulip Garden Inc* ***(G-7844)***
De Lux Sportswear, Durand *Also called Delux Monogramming Screen Prtg* ***(G-4607)***
De Luxe Die Set Inc 810 227-2556
5939 Ford Ct Brighton (48116) ***(G-1910)***
De Meester Saw Mill 616 677-3144
15519 32nd Ave Coopersville (49404) ***(G-3555)***
De Vru Printing Co 616 452-5451
1446 Eastern Ave Se Grand Rapids (49507) ***(G-6339)***
De Witt Products Co 313 554-0575
5860 Plumer St Detroit (48209) ***(G-3963)***
De-Sta-Co, Auburn Hills *Also called Dover Energy Inc* ***(G-843)***
De-Sta-Co Automotive Group, Auburn Hills *Also called CPI Products Inc* ***(G-829)***
De-Sta-Co Cylinders Inc 248 836-6700
15 Corporate Dr Auburn Hills (48326) ***(G-838)***
Deadline Detroit 248 219-5985
66 Winder St Apt 443 Detroit (48201) ***(G-3964)***
Dealer Aid Enterprises 313 331-5800
8200 E Jefferson Ave # 604 Detroit (48214) ***(G-3965)***
Deans Hobby Stop 989 720-2137
116 N Washington St Owosso (48867) ***(G-12288)***
Deans Ice Cream Inc 269 685-6641
307 N Sherwood Ave Plainwell (49080) ***(G-12522)***
Dearborn Collision Service Inc 734 455-3299
39407 Jasmine Cir Northville (48168) ***(G-11687)***
Dearborn Imaging Group LLC 313 561-1173
1946 Monroe St Dearborn (48124) ***(G-3689)***
Dearborn Lithograph Inc 734 464-4242
12380 Globe St Livonia (48150) ***(G-9701)***
Dearborn Mid West Conveyor Co 313 273-2804
19440 Glendale St Detroit (48223) ***(G-3966)***
Dearborn Mid-West Company LLC (PA) 734 288-4400
20334 Superior Rd Taylor (48180) ***(G-15706)***
Dearborn Offset Printing Inc 313 561-1173
1946 Monroe St Dearborn (48124) ***(G-3690)***
Dearborn Signs & Awnings 313 584-8828
8700 Brandt St Dearborn (48126) ***(G-3691)***
Dearborn Total Auto Svc Ctr 313 291-6300
23416 Van Born Rd Dearborn Heights (48125) ***(G-3781)***
Dearborn Water Department, Dearborn *Also called Water Department* ***(G-3773)***
Dearborn Works, Dearborn *Also called AK Steel Corporation* ***(G-3672)***
Debbink and Sons Inc 231 845-6421
1010 Conrad Industrial Dr Ludington (49431) ***(G-10055)***
Debron Indus Elctronicschitran, Troy *Also called Debron Industrial Elec Inc* ***(G-16300)***
Debron Industrial Elec Inc 248 588-7220
591 Executive Dr Troy (48083) ***(G-16300)***
Deburring Company 734 542-9800
12690 Newburgh Rd Livonia (48150) ***(G-9702)***
Decade Products LLC (PA) 616 975-4965
3400 Innovation Ct Se Grand Rapids (49512) ***(G-6340)***
Decatur Republican, Decatur *Also called Moormann Printing Inc* ***(G-3805)***
Decatur Wood Products Inc 269 657-6041
79201 M 51 Decatur (49045) ***(G-3802)***
Decc Company Inc 616 245-0431
1266 Wallen Ave Sw Grand Rapids (49507) ***(G-6341)***
Decca Pattern Co Inc 586 775-8450
29778 Little Mack Ave Roseville (48066) ***(G-13790)***
Decka Digital LLC 231 347-1253
1227 W Conway Rd Harbor Springs (49740) ***(G-7281)***
Decker Gear Inc (PA) 810 388-1500
1500 Glendale St Saint Clair (48079) ***(G-14216)***
Decker Manufacturing Corp (PA) 517 629-3955
703 N Clark St Albion (49224) ***(G-122)***
Deckorators, White Pigeon *Also called Maine Ornamental LLC* ***(G-17652)***
Declarks Landscaping Inc 586 752-7200
13800 33 Mile Rd Bruce Twp (48065) ***(G-2082)***
Deco Engineering Inc 989 761-7521
9900 Main St Clifford (48727) ***(G-3010)***
Deco Finishes, Pontiac *Also called Akzo Nobel Coatings Inc* ***(G-12801)***
Decockers Inc 517 447-3635
1502 Bucholtz Hwy Deerfield (49238) ***(G-3811)***
Decoma Admark, Troy *Also called Magna Exteriors America Inc* ***(G-16472)***
Decor Group International Inc 248 307-2430
3748 Sunset Blvd Orchard Lake (48324) ***(G-12165)***
Decorative Panels Intl Inc 989 354-2121
416 Ford Ave Alpena (49707) ***(G-285)***
Decoties Inc 906 285-1286
807 Spring St Bessemer (49911) ***(G-1604)***
Dedicated Converting Group Inc 269 685-8430
155 10th St Plainwell (49080) ***(G-12523)***
Dedinas & Franzak Entps Inc 616 784-6095
2915 Walkent Dr Nw Grand Rapids (49544) ***(G-6342)***
Dedoes Innovative Mfg Inc 517 223-2500
925 Garden Ln Fowlerville (48836) ***(G-5562)***

ALPHABETIC

Dee Cramer Inc ... 517 485-5519
2623 W Saint Joseph St Lansing (48917) ***(G-9286)***

Dee-Blast Corporation (PA) ... 269 428-2400
5992 Oelke Park St Stevensville (49127) ***(G-15563)***

Deerings Jerky Co LLC ... 231 590-5687
2015 Sandy Dr Interlochen (49643) ***(G-8239)***

Dees Logging ... 616 796-8050
1907 W 32nd St Holland (49423) ***(G-7606)***

Defense Company of America ... 248 763-6509
324 Fordcroft Dr Rochester Hills (48309) ***(G-13403)***

Defense Components America LLC ... 248 789-1578
30955 Northwestern Hwy Farmington Hills (48334) ***(G-4970)***

Defense Material Recapitalizat ... 248 698-9333
9164 Elizabeth Lake Rd White Lake (48386) ***(G-17632)***

Defiance Group, The, Westland *Also called Gt Technologies Inc* ***(G-17566)***

Deforest & Bloom Septic Tanks ... 231 544-3599
7994 Houghton Rd Central Lake (49622) ***(G-2590)***

Degele Manufacturing Inc ... 586 949-3550
25700 Dhondt Ct Chesterfield (48051) ***(G-2763)***

Degrasyn Biosciences LLC ... 713 582-3395
4476 Boulder Pond Dr Ann Arbor (48108) ***(G-413)***

Dehaan Forest Products Inc ... 906 883-3417
25367 Mud Creek Rd Mass City (49948) ***(G-10661)***

Dehring Mold E-D-M ... 269 683-5970
1450 Jerome St Niles (49120) ***(G-11607)***

Deka Batteries & Cables, Sterling Heights *Also called East Penn Manufacturing Co* ***(G-15329)***

Dekes Concrete Inc ... 810 686-5570
6653 Andersonville Rd Clarkston (48346) ***(G-2916)***

Dekker Bookbinding, Grand Rapids *Also called John H Dekker & Sons Inc* ***(G-6562)***

Dekoff & Sons Inc ... 269 344-5816
2531 Azo Dr Kalamazoo (49048) ***(G-8724)***

Del Printing Inc ... 586 445-3044
19724 E 9 Mile Rd Saint Clair Shores (48080) ***(G-14243)***

Del Pueblo Tortillas ... 248 858-9835
511 N Perry St Pontiac (48342) ***(G-12815)***

Delaco Steel Corporation (PA) ... 313 491-1200
8111 Tireman Ave Ste 1 Dearborn (48126) ***(G-3692)***

Deland Manufacturing Inc ... 586 323-2350
50674 Central Indus Dr Shelby Township (48315) ***(G-14574)***

Delco Elec Overseas Corp (HQ) ... 248 813-2000
5820 Innovation Dr Troy (48098) ***(G-16301)***

Delduca Welding & Service, Flint *Also called Delducas Welding & Co Inc* ***(G-5416)***

Delducas Welding & Co Inc ... 810 743-1990
4420 S Dort Hwy Flint (48507) ***(G-5416)***

Delfab Inc ... 906 428-9570
103 N 12th St Gladstone (49837) ***(G-5913)***

Delfield Company LLC ... 989 773-7981
980 S Isabella Rd Mount Pleasant (48858) ***(G-11192)***

Delfingen Industry, Rochester Hills *Also called Delfingen Us- Holding Inc* ***(G-13405)***

Delfingen Us Inc (HQ) ... 716 215-0300
3985 W Hamlin Rd Rochester Hills (48309) ***(G-13404)***

Delfingen Us- Holding Inc (HQ) ... 248 519-0534
3985 W Hamlin Rd Rochester Hills (48309) ***(G-13405)***

Delfingen Us-Central Amer Inc ... 248 230-3500
3985 W Hamlin Rd Rochester Hills (48309) ***(G-13406)***

Delhi Leasing Inc (PA) ... 517 694-8578
1185 N Eifert Rd Holt (48842) ***(G-7910)***

Dell Marking Systems Inc ... 248 547-7750
6841 N Rochester Rd 250c Rochester Hills (48306) ***(G-13407)***

Delmas Typesetting ... 734 662-8899
461 Hilldale Dr Ann Arbor (48105) ***(G-414)***

Delorean Associates Inc ... 248 646-1930
2779 Amberly Rd Bloomfield Hills (48301) ***(G-1757)***

Delphi, Troy *Also called Dph Holdings Corp* ***(G-16324)***

Delphi, Grand Rapids *Also called Aptiv Services Us LLC* ***(G-6176)***

Delphi, Dearborn *Also called Aptiv Services Us LLC* ***(G-3677)***

Delphi, Auburn Hills *Also called Aptiv Services Us LLC* ***(G-778)***

Delphi, Troy *Also called Aptiv Services 3 (us) LLC* ***(G-16212)***

Delphi, Auburn Hills *Also called Aptiv Corporation* ***(G-777)***

Delphi, Troy *Also called Dph LLC* ***(G-16323)***

Delphi, Troy *Also called Aptiv Corporation* ***(G-16207)***

Delphi ... 248 813-2000
5725 Innovation Dr Troy (48098) ***(G-16302)***

Delphi Automotive Systems ... 248 813-2000
5820 Innovation Dr Troy (48098) ***(G-16303)***

Delphi Powertrain Corporation ... 248 813-2000
5820 Innovation Dr Troy (48098) ***(G-16304)***

Delphi Powertrain Systems LLC ... 248 280-8340
1624 Meijer Dr Troy (48084) ***(G-16305)***

Delphi Powertrain Systems LLC (HQ) ... 248 813-2000
5825 Innovation Dr Troy (48098) ***(G-16306)***

Delphi Powertrain Systems LLC ... 248 813-1549
5820 Innovation Dr Troy (48098) ***(G-16307)***

Delphi Powertrain Systems LLC ... 248 813-2000
3000 University Dr Auburn Hills (48326) ***(G-839)***

Delphi Powertrain Systems LLC ... 248 813-2000
5725 Innovation Dr Troy (48098) ***(G-16308)***

Delphi Powertrain Systems LLC ... 248 280-8319
1624 Meijer Dr Troy (48084) ***(G-16309)***

Delphi Powertrain Systems LLC ... 800 521-4784
1624 Meijer Dr Troy (48084) ***(G-16310)***

Delphi Product & Svc Solutions, Troy *Also called Aptiv Services Us LLC* ***(G-16214)***

Delphi Pwertrain Intl Svcs LLC ... 248 813-2000
5820 Innovation Dr Troy (48098) ***(G-16311)***

Delphi Pwrtrain Tech Gen Prtnr ... 248 813-2000
5820 Innovation Dr Troy (48098) ***(G-16312)***

Delphinus Medical Technologies ... 248 522-9600
45525 Grand River Ave Novi (48374) ***(G-11863)***

Delt Forge Inc ... 989 685-2118
2816 E Industrial Dr Rose City (48654) ***(G-13761)***

Delta 6 LLC ... 248 778-6414
20341 Parker St Livonia (48152) ***(G-9703)***

Delta Containers Inc (PA) ... 810 742-2730
1400 Eddy St Bay City (48708) ***(G-1299)***

Delta Containers Inc ... 810 742-2730
1400 Eddy St Bay City (48708) ***(G-1300)***

Delta Gear Inc ... 734 525-8000
36251 Schoolcraft Rd Livonia (48150) ***(G-9704)***

Delta Iron Works Inc ... 313 579-1445
1801 Meldrum St Detroit (48207) ***(G-3967)***

Delta Machining Inc ... 269 683-7775
2361 Reum Rd Niles (49120) ***(G-11608)***

Delta Manufacturing, Escanaba *Also called Hj Manufacturing Inc* ***(G-4833)***

Delta Molded Products ... 586 731-9595
42754 Mound Rd Sterling Heights (48314) ***(G-15308)***

Delta Packaging International ... 517 321-6548
3463 Millwood Rd Lansing (48906) ***(G-9214)***

Delta Paving Inc ... 810 232-0220
4186 Holiday Dr Flint (48507) ***(G-5417)***

Delta Polymers Co (PA) ... 586 795-2900
6685 Sterling Dr N Sterling Heights (48312) ***(G-15309)***

Delta Precision Inc ... 586 415-9005
33214 Janet Fraser (48026) ***(G-5641)***

Delta Rail Division, Holly *Also called Delta Tube & Fabricating Corp* ***(G-7875)***

Delta Research Corporation ... 734 261-6400
32971 Capitol St Livonia (48150) ***(G-9705)***

Delta Six, Livonia *Also called Delta 6 LLC* ***(G-9703)***

Delta Sports Service & EMB ... 517 482-6565
1611 N Grand River Ave Lansing (48906) ***(G-9215)***

Delta Stamping Div, Lansing *Also called Demmer Corporation* ***(G-9287)***

Delta Steel Inc ... 989 752-5129
1410 Webber St Saginaw (48601) ***(G-14025)***

Delta Tooling Co., Auburn Hills *Also called USF Delta Tooling LLC* ***(G-1041)***

Delta Trading Co, Sterling Heights *Also called Delta Molded Products* ***(G-15308)***

Delta Tube & Fabricating Corp ... 810 239-0154
2610 N Dort Hwy Flint (48506) ***(G-5418)***

Delta Tube & Fabricating Corp (PA) ... 248 634-8267
4149 Grange Hall Rd Holly (48442) ***(G-7874)***

Delta Tube & Fabricating Corp ... 248 634-8267
4149 Grange Hall Rd Holly (48442) ***(G-7875)***

Deltaic Welding Inc ... 734 207-1080
11803 Turkey Run Plymouth (48170) ***(G-12607)***

Delux Monogramming Screen Prtg ... 989 288-5321
9070 E Lansing Rd Durand (48429) ***(G-4607)***

Deluxe Data Printers, Madison Heights *Also called Total Business Systems Inc* ***(G-10368)***

Deluxe Frame Company Inc ... 248 373-8811
2275 N Opdyke Rd Ste D Auburn Hills (48326) ***(G-840)***

Deluxe Technologies LLC ... 586 294-2340
34537 Bennett Fraser (48026) ***(G-5642)***

Delve Communications, Davison *Also called Genova Products Inc* ***(G-3650)***

Demag Cranes & Components Corp ... 586 954-1000
46545 Continental Dr Chesterfield (48047) ***(G-2764)***

Demaria Building Company Inc ... 248 486-2598
53655 Grand River Ave New Hudson (48165) ***(G-11537)***

Dematic ... 616 395-8671
11818 James St Holland (49424) ***(G-7607)***

Demeester Wood Products Inc ... 616 677-5995
15527 32nd Ave Coopersville (49404) ***(G-3556)***

Demlow Products Inc ... 517 436-3529
7404 Tomer Rd Clayton (49235) ***(G-3006)***

Demmak Industries LLC ... 586 884-6441
43714 Utica Rd Sterling Heights (48314) ***(G-15310)***

Demmem Enterprises LLC ... 810 564-9500
4268 W Vienna Rd Clio (48420) ***(G-3269)***

Demmer - Porter St., Lansing *Also called Demmer Corporation* ***(G-9216)***

Demmer Corporation ... 517 703-3116
728 Porter St Lansing (48906) ***(G-9216)***

Demmer Corporation (HQ) ... 517 321-3600
4520 N Grand River Ave Lansing (48906) ***(G-9217)***

Demmer Corporation ... 517 703-3163
705 E Oakland Ave Lansing (48906) ***(G-9218)***

Demmer Corporation ... 517 703-3131
720 Porter St Lansing (48906) ***(G-9219)***

Demmer Corporation ... 517 321-3600
2904 Snow Rd Lansing (48917) ***(G-9287)***

ALPHABETIC SECTION

Detroit Diesel USA, Detroit

Demmer Corporation 517 323-4504
16325 Felton Rd Lansing (48906) *(G-9220)*

Demmer Investments Inc (PA) 517 321-3600
4520 N Grand River Ave Lansing (48906) *(G-9221)*

Dempsey Manufacturing Co 810 346-2273
4835 Van Dyke Rd Brown City (48416) *(G-2049)*

Denali Incorporated 517 574-0047
11600 Maxfield Blvd Hartland (48353) *(G-7389)*

Denali Seed Co 907 344-0347
6237 S Pere Marquette Hwy Pentwater (49449) *(G-12429)*

Denarco Inc 269 435-8404
301 Industrial Park Dr Constantine (49042) *(G-3533)*

Dendritech Inc 989 496-1152
3110 Schuette Rd Midland (48642) *(G-10830)*

Dendritic Nanotechnologies Inc 989 774-3096
1515 Commerce Dr Ste C Midland (48642) *(G-10831)*

Denesczuk Firebrick Company, Riverview Also called Dfc Inc *(G-13293)*

Denim Baby LLC 313 539-5309
30606 Sandhurst Ct # 207 Roseville (48066) *(G-13791)*

Denlin Industries Inc 586 303-5209
371 Mill Pond Ln Milford (48381) *(G-10960)*

Dennis OBryan Od 231 348-1255
8422 M 119 Harbor Springs (49740) *(G-7282)*

Dennison Automatics LLC 616 837-7063
16962 Woodlane Ste B Nunica (49448) *(G-12035)*

Denny Grice Inc 269 279-6113
702 Webber Ave Three Rivers (49093) *(G-15860)*

Denova, Ann Arbor Also called Masco Cabinetry LLC *(G-546)*

Denso Air Systems Michigan Inc (HQ) 269 962-9676
300 Fritz Keiper Blvd Battle Creek (49037) *(G-1171)*

Denso International Amer Inc 248 359-4177
8652 Haggerty Rd Ste 220 Van Buren Twp (48111) *(G-16757)*

Denso International Amer Inc (HQ) 248 350-7500
24777 Denso Dr Southfield (48033) *(G-14879)*

Denso Manufacturing NC Inc 269 441-2040
500 Fritz Keiper Blvd Battle Creek (49037) *(G-1172)*

Denso Sales Michigan Inc 269 965-3322
1 Denso Rd Battle Creek (49037) *(G-1173)*

Dental Art Laboratories Inc 517 485-2200
1721 N Grand River Ave # 1 Lansing (48906) *(G-9222)*

Dental Consultants Inc 734 663-6777
3100 W Liberty Rd Ann Arbor (48103) *(G-415)*

Dental Impressions 231 719-0033
1915 Holton Rd Muskegon (49445) *(G-11305)*

Denton Atd Inc 734 451-7878
47460 Galleon Dr Plymouth (48170) *(G-12608)*

Dependable Gage & Tool Co 248 545-2100
15321 W 11 Mile Rd Oak Park (48237) *(G-12058)*

Depex Print Services 586 465-6820
19751 15 Mile Rd Clinton Township (48035) *(G-3100)*

Depierre Industries Inc 517 263-5781
1408 E Church St Adrian (49221) *(G-59)*

Depor Industries Inc (HQ) 248 362-3900
1902 Northwood Dr Troy (48084) *(G-16313)*

Depottey Acquisition Inc 616 846-4150
401 N Griffin St Grand Haven (49417) *(G-6009)*

Deppe Mold & Tooling Inc 616 530-1331
2814 Franklin Ave Sw Grandville (49418) *(G-7027)*

Derby Fabg Solutions LLC 616 866-1650
687 Byrne Industrial Dr Rockford (49341) *(G-13566)*

Derk Pieter Co Inc 616 554-7777
4513 Broadmoor Ave Se A Grand Rapids (49512) *(G-6343)*

Deshler Group Inc (PA) 734 525-9100
34450 Industrial Rd Livonia (48150) *(G-9706)*

Design & Test Technology Inc 734 665-4111
2430 Scio Rd Dexter (48130) *(G-4484)*

Design & Test Technology Inc (PA) 734 665-4316
3744 Plaza Dr Ste 2 Ann Arbor (48108) *(G-416)*

Design Converting Inc 616 942-7780
3470 Raleigh Dr Se Grand Rapids (49512) *(G-6344)*

Design Design Inc 866 935-2648
19 La Grave Ave Se Grand Rapids (49503) *(G-6345)*

Design Fabrications Inc 248 597-0988
1100 E Mandoline Ave A Madison Heights (48071) *(G-10229)*

Design Manufacturing LLC 616 647-2229
950 Vitality Dr Nw Ste B Comstock Park (49321) *(G-3476)*

Design Metal Inc 248 547-4170
10841 Capital St Oak Park (48237) *(G-12059)*

Design Safety Engineering Inc 734 483-2033
305 Elm St Ypsilanti (48197) *(G-18065)*

Design Services Unlimited Inc 586 463-3225
25754 Dhondt Ct Chesterfield (48051) *(G-2765)*

Design Tech LLC 616 459-2885
2192 Trillium Ln Nw Grand Rapids (49534) *(G-6346)*

Design Usa Inc 734 233-8677
36117 Schoolcraft Rd Livonia (48150) *(G-9707)*

Designers Sheet Metal Inc 269 429-4133
205 Palladium Dr Saint Joseph (49085) *(G-14306)*

Designotype Printers Inc 906 482-2424
22950 Airpark Blvd Laurium (49913) *(G-9503)*

Designs By Bean 989 845-4371
233 W Broad St Chesaning (48616) *(G-2723)*

Designs In Stones, Muskegon Also called Muskegon Monument & Stone Co *(G-11390)*

Designs Unlimited, West Bloomfield Also called Janice Morse Inc *(G-17482)*

Designshirtscom Inc 734 414-7604
14777 Keel St Plymouth (48170) *(G-12609)*

Designtec Services Inc 734 216-6051
3050 Centennial Ct Howell (48843) *(G-8028)*

Designtech, Grand Rapids Also called Design Tech LLC *(G-6346)*

Designtech Custom Interiors 989 695-6306
8570 Carter Rd Freeland (48623) *(G-5754)*

Deslatae 313 820-4321
5522 Bluehill St Detroit (48224) *(G-3968)*

Desrochers Brothers Inc 906 353-6346
107 3rd St Baraga (49908) *(G-1101)*

Destaco Industries, Auburn Hills Also called Dover Energy Inc *(G-842)*

Destiny Plastics Incorporated 810 622-0018
2121 Stoutenburg Deckerville (48427) *(G-3807)*

Destiny River, Wyoming Also called Viking Spas Inc *(G-18041)*

Detail Precision Products Inc 248 544-3390
1480 E 9 Mile Rd Ferndale (48220) *(G-5271)*

Detail Production Company Inc 248 544-3390
1480 E 9 Mile Rd Ferndale (48220) *(G-5272)*

Detail Standard Company, Roseville Also called Paradigm Engineering Inc *(G-13849)*

Detail Technologies LLC 616 261-1313
5900 Crssrds Cmmrce Pkwy Wyoming (49519) *(G-17996)*

Detectir Inc 724 681-0975
325 E Grand River Ave # 355 East Lansing (48823) *(G-4655)*

Detmar Corporation 313 831-1155
2001 W Alexandrine St Detroit (48208) *(G-3969)*

Detroit Choppers Inc 586 498-8909
29455 Gratiot Ave Roseville (48066) *(G-13792)*

Detroit Abrasives Company 989 725-2405
1500 W Oliver St Owosso (48867) *(G-12289)*

Detroit Abrasives Company (PA) 734 475-1651
11910 Dexter Chelsea Rd Chelsea (48118) *(G-2706)*

Detroit Art Collection LLC 313 373-7689
1074 Woodward Ave Detroit (48226) *(G-3970)*

Detroit Asphalt Paving Company, Troy Also called Ajax Materials Corporation *(G-16174)*

Detroit Auto Specialties Inc 248 496-3856
6960 Orchard Lake Rd # 301 West Bloomfield (48322) *(G-17474)*

Detroit Axle, Ferndale Also called Axle of Dearborn Inc *(G-5263)*

Detroit Bikes LLC (PA) 313 646-4109
13639 Elmira St Detroit (48227) *(G-3971)*

Detroit Boiler Company (PA) 313 921-7060
2931 Beaufait St Detroit (48207) *(G-3972)*

Detroit Boring & Mch Co LLC 586 604-6506
42818 Mound Rd Sterling Heights (48314) *(G-15311)*

Detroit Brew Factory, Harper Woods Also called Harville Associates Inc *(G-7301)*

Detroit Bubble Tea Company 248 239-1131
22821 Woodward Ave Ferndale (48220) *(G-5273)*

Detroit Bullet Works, Wixom Also called Tactical Simplicity LLC *(G-17903)*

Detroit Buyers Club LLC 248 871-7827
18914 Stoepel St Detroit (48221) *(G-3973)*

Detroit Chassis LLC 313 571-2100
6501 Lynch Rd Detroit (48234) *(G-3974)*

Detroit Chili Co Inc (PA) 248 440-5933
21400 Telegraph Rd Southfield (48033) *(G-14880)*

Detroit Chili Co Inc 313 521-6323
11575 Harper Ave Detroit (48213) *(G-3975)*

Detroit Chrome Inc 313 341-9478
7515 Lyndon St Detroit (48238) *(G-3976)*

Detroit City Distillery LLC 313 338-3760
2462 Riopelle St Detroit (48207) *(G-3977)*

Detroit City Distillery LLC 734 904-3073
15295 Concord Dr Spring Lake (49456) *(G-15138)*

Detroit Coil, Troy Also called Ross Decco Company *(G-16584)*

Detroit Coil Co 248 658-1543
2435 Hilton Rd Ferndale (48220) *(G-5274)*

Detroit Cornice & Slate Co Inc 248 398-7690
1315 Academy St Ferndale (48220) *(G-5275)*

Detroit Cover, Romulus Also called John Johnson Company *(G-13692)*

Detroit Custom Chassis LLC 313 571-2100
6501 Lynch Rd Detroit (48234) *(G-3978)*

Detroit Custom Services Inc (PA) 586 465-3631
150 N Groesbeck Hwy Mount Clemens (48043) *(G-11129)*

Detroit Cycle Pub LLC 231 286-5257
16089 Diamante Dr Macomb (48044) *(G-10116)*

Detroit Denim LLC 313 626-9216
1401 Vermont St Ste 164 Detroit (48216) *(G-3979)*

Detroit Diameters Inc 248 669-2330
45380 W Park Dr Novi (48377) *(G-11864)*

Detroit Diesel Corporation (HQ) 313 592-5000
13400 W Outer Dr Detroit (48239) *(G-3980)*

Detroit Diesel Corporation 313 592-8256
12200 Telegraph Rd Redford (48239) *(G-13157)*

Detroit Diesel USA, Detroit Also called Detroit Diesel Corporation *(G-3980)*

(PA)=Parent Co (HQ)=Headquarters (DH)=Div Headquarters

Detroit Dirt LLC ... 616 260-4383
2503 22nd St Detroit (48216) ***(G-3981)***
Detroit Dumpster Inc ... 313 466-3174
8701 Grinnell St Detroit (48213) ***(G-3982)***
Detroit Edge Tool Company (PA) ... 313 366-4120
6570 E Nevada St Detroit (48234) ***(G-3983)***
Detroit Edge Tool Company ... 586 776-3727
28370 Groesbeck Hwy Roseville (48066) ***(G-13793)***
Detroit Edge Tool Company ... 586 776-1598
28370 Groesbeck Hwy Roseville (48066) ***(G-13794)***
Detroit Elevator Company ... 248 591-7484
2121 Burdette St Ste A Ferndale (48220) ***(G-5276)***
Detroit Evrlasting Dezigns Inc ... 248 790-0850
3648 Valleyview Ln West Bloomfield (48323) ***(G-17475)***
Detroit Fd Entrprnrship Acdemy ... 248 894-8941
4444 2nd Ave Detroit (48201) ***(G-3984)***
Detroit Fine Products LLC ... 877 294-5826
2615 Wolcott St Ste E Ferndale (48220) ***(G-5277)***
Detroit Flame Hardening Co ... 586 484-1726
43554 Riverbend Blvd Clinton Township (48038) ***(G-3101)***
DETROIT FOOD ACADEMY, Detroit *Also called Detroit Fd Entrprnrship Acdemy* ***(G-3984)***
Detroit Free Press, Saginaw *Also called Detroit Newspaper Partnr LP* ***(G-14026)***
Detroit Frnds Potato Chips LLC ... 313 924-0085
8230 E Forest Ave Detroit (48214) ***(G-3985)***
Detroit Fudge Company Inc ... 734 369-8573
2251 W Liberty St Ann Arbor (48103) ***(G-417)***
Detroit Grooming Company LLC, Ferndale *Also called Detroit Fine Products LLC* ***(G-5277)***
Detroit Hoist & Crane Co L L C ... 586 268-2600
6650 Sterling Dr N Sterling Heights (48312) ***(G-15312)***
Detroit Impression Company Inc ... 313 921-9077
1111 Bellevue St Unit 100 Detroit (48207) ***(G-3986)***
Detroit Jewish New, Southfield *Also called Renaissance Media LLC* ***(G-15013)***
Detroit Jewish News Ltd Partnr (PA) ... 248 354-6060
29200 Northwestern Hwy # 110 Southfield (48034) ***(G-14881)***
Detroit Legal News Company (PA) ... 313 961-6000
2001 W Lafayette Blvd Detroit (48216) ***(G-3987)***
Detroit Legal News Pubg LLC ... 248 577-6100
1409 Allen Dr Ste B Troy (48083) ***(G-16314)***
Detroit Legal News Pubg LLC ... 734 477-0201
2301 Platt Rd Ste 300 Ann Arbor (48104) ***(G-418)***
Detroit Litho Inc ... 313 993-6186
8200 W Outer Dr Detroit (48219) ***(G-3988)***
Detroit Marking Products Corp ... 313 838-9760
8201 Ronda Dr Canton (48187) ***(G-2364)***
Detroit Materials Inc ... 248 924-5436
33225 Grand River Ave Farmington (48336) ***(G-4897)***
Detroit Media Partnership, Detroit *Also called Detroit Newspaper Partnr LP* ***(G-3994)***
Detroit Metalcraft Finishing ... 586 415-7760
34277 Doreka Fraser (48026) ***(G-5643)***
Detroit Mfg Systems LLC (PA) ... 313 243-0700
12701 Suthfield Rd Bldg A Detroit (48223) ***(G-3989)***
Detroit Mini Safe Co, Carleton *Also called A & L Metal Products* ***(G-2451)***
Detroit Name Plate Etching Inc ... 248 543-5200
10610 Galaxie Ave Ferndale (48220) ***(G-5278)***
Detroit News Inc ... 313 222-6400
600 W Fort St Detroit (48226) ***(G-3990)***
Detroit News Inc (HQ) ... 313 222-2300
160 W Fort St Detroit (48226) ***(G-3991)***
Detroit News Inc ... 313 223-4500
3801 W Jefferson Ave Detroit (48216) ***(G-3992)***
Detroit News Inc ... 313 222-6400
6200 Metropolitan Pkwy Sterling Heights (48312) ***(G-15313)***
Detroit News Inc ... 313 222-6400
615 W Lafayette Blvd Detroit (48226) ***(G-3993)***
Detroit News, The, Detroit *Also called Detroit News Inc* ***(G-3990)***
Detroit News, The, Detroit *Also called Detroit News Inc* ***(G-3991)***
Detroit News, The, Detroit *Also called Detroit News Inc* ***(G-3992)***
Detroit News, The, Sterling Heights *Also called Detroit News Inc* ***(G-15313)***
Detroit News, The, Detroit *Also called Detroit News Inc* ***(G-3993)***
Detroit Newspaper Partnr LP ... 989 752-3023
2654 N Outer Dr Ste 4 Saginaw (48601) ***(G-14026)***
Detroit Newspaper Partnr LP ... 586 826-7187
6200 Metropolitan Pkwy Sterling Heights (48312) ***(G-15314)***
Detroit Newspaper Partnr LP (HQ) ... 313 222-2300
160 W Fort St Detroit (48226) ***(G-3994)***
Detroit Newspaper Partnr LP ... 313 222-6400
600 W Fort St Detroit (48226) ***(G-3995)***
Detroit Nipple Works Inc (PA) ... 313 872-6370
6530 Beaubien St Detroit (48202) ***(G-3996)***
Detroit Office & Warehouse, Detroit *Also called FCA US LLC* ***(G-4055)***
Detroit Plate Fabricators Inc ... 313 921-7020
2931 Beaufait St Detroit (48207) ***(G-3997)***
Detroit Popcorn Company, Redford *Also called Farber Concessions Inc* ***(G-13161)***
Detroit Qulty Brush Mfg Co Inc ... 734 525-5660
32165 Schoolcraft Rd Livonia (48150) ***(G-9708)***
Detroit Radiant Products Co ... 586 756-0950
21400 Hoover Rd Warren (48089) ***(G-17000)***
Detroit Radiator, Riverview *Also called Heavy Duty Radiator LLC* ***(G-13295)***
Detroit Ready Mix Concrete ... 313 931-7043
9189 Central St Detroit (48204) ***(G-3998)***
Detroit Recker Sales, Southfield *Also called Hydro King Incorporated* ***(G-14939)***
Detroit Recycled Concrete Co (PA) ... 248 553-0600
39525 W 13 Mile Rd # 300 Novi (48377) ***(G-11865)***
Detroit Renewable Energy LLC ... 313 972-5700
5700 Russell St Detroit (48211) ***(G-3999)***
Detroit Rivertwn Brewing Co LL ... 313 877-9205
237 Joseph Campau St Detroit (48207) ***(G-4000)***
Detroit Sales Office, West Bloomfield *Also called Phillips-Medisize LLC* ***(G-17493)***
Detroit Salt Company LC (HQ) ... 313 554-0456
12841 Sanders St Detroit (48217) ***(G-4001)***
Detroit Sausage Co Inc ... 313 259-0555
2715 Saint Aubin St Detroit (48207) ***(G-4002)***
Detroit Sls & Engrg Ctr Div of, Farmington Hills *Also called Akwel Cadillac Usa Inc* ***(G-4926)***
Detroit Smoke House LLC ... 313 622-9714
355 Visger Rd Ecorse (48229) ***(G-4743)***
Detroit Steel Group Inc ... 248 298-2900
916 S Washington Ave Royal Oak (48067) ***(G-13918)***
Detroit Steel Treating Company ... 248 334-7436
1631 Highwood E Pontiac (48340) ***(G-12816)***
Detroit Stoker Company ... 734 241-9500
1510 E 1st St Monroe (48161) ***(G-11028)***
Detroit Tarpaulin Repr Sp Inc ... 734 955-8200
6760 Metro Plex Dr Romulus (48174) ***(G-13666)***
Detroit Tech Innovation LLC ... 734 259-4168
25036 W 6 Mile Rd Redford (48240) ***(G-13158)***
Detroit Technologies Inc ... 248 647-0400
51258 Quadrate Dr Macomb (48042) ***(G-10117)***
Detroit Technologies Inc (PA) ... 248 647-0400
32500 Telg Rd Ste 207 Bingham Farms (48025) ***(G-1651)***
Detroit Testing Machine Co ... 248 669-3100
46590 Ryan Ct Novi (48377) ***(G-11866)***
Detroit Torch Company, Lake Orion *Also called Cobra Torches Inc* ***(G-9128)***
Detroit Tube Products LLC ... 313 841-0300
300 S Junction St Detroit (48209) ***(G-4003)***
Detroit Tubing Mill Inc ... 313 491-8823
12301 Hubbell St Detroit (48227) ***(G-4004)***
Detroit Tubular Rivet Inc (PA) ... 734 282-7979
1213 Grove St Wyandotte (48192) ***(G-17954)***
Detroit Washer & Specials, West Bloomfield *Also called Mh Industries Ltd* ***(G-17485)***
Detroit Wilbert Cremation Serv ... 248 853-0559
3658 Samuel Ave Rochester Hills (48309) ***(G-13408)***
Detroit Wire Rope Splcing Corp ... 248 585-1063
31623 Stephenson Hwy Madison Heights (48071) ***(G-10230)***
Detroit Woodworking, Saint Clair Shores *Also called Elite Woodworking LLC* ***(G-14245)***
Detroit Wrecker Sales Llc ... 313 835-8700
19303 W Davison St Detroit (48223) ***(G-4005)***
Detronic Industries Inc (PA) ... 586 268-6392
35800 Beattie Dr Sterling Heights (48312) ***(G-15315)***
Deuwave LLC ... 888 238-9283
200 S Wing St Northville (48167) ***(G-11688)***
Development Office, Plymouth *Also called Toledo Molding & Die Inc* ***(G-12773)***
Developmental Services Inc ... 313 653-1185
13621 Park Grove St Detroit (48205) ***(G-4006)***
Devereaux Saw Mill Inc ... 989 593-2552
2872 N Hubbardston Rd Pewamo (48873) ***(G-12478)***
Devonian Energy Inc ... 989 732-9400
132 N Otsego Ave Gaylord (49735) ***(G-5855)***
Dewalt Industrial Tool, Grandville *Also called Black & Decker (us) Inc* ***(G-7023)***
Dewent Redi-Mix LLC ... 616 457-2100
1601 Chicago Dr Jenison (49428) ***(G-8623)***
Deweys Lumberville Inc ... 313 885-0960
757 Notre Dame St Grosse Pointe (48230) ***(G-7178)***
Dewitt Packaging Corporation ... 616 698-0210
5080 Kraft Ave Se Grand Rapids (49512) ***(G-6347)***
Dewitts Radiator LLC ... 517 548-0600
1275 Grand Oaks Dr Howell (48843) ***(G-8029)***
Dewsbury Manufactruing Company, Livonia *Also called Rick Wykle LLC* ***(G-9909)***
Dewsbury Manufacturing Company ... 734 839-6376
12502 Globe St Livonia (48150) ***(G-9709)***
Dewys Manufacturing Inc ... 616 677-5281
15300 8th Ave Marne (49435) ***(G-10507)***
Dexko Global Inc (HQ) ... 248 533-0029
39555 Orchard Hill Pl Novi (48375) ***(G-11867)***
Dexsys, Lansing *Also called Norplas Industries Inc* ***(G-9314)***
Dextech, Dexter *Also called Dexter Fastener Tech Inc* ***(G-4486)***
Dexter Automatic Products Co ... 734 426-8900
2500 Bishop Cir E Dexter (48130) ***(G-4485)***
Dexter Cider Mill Inc ... 734 475-6419
4885 Kalmbach Rd Chelsea (48118) ***(G-2707)***
Dexter Fastener Tech Inc (PA) ... 734 426-0311
2110 Bishop Cir E Dexter (48130) ***(G-4486)***
Dexter Fastener Tech Inc ... 734 426-5200
2103 Bishop Cir W Dexter (48130) ***(G-4487)***
Dexter Manufacturing Inc ... 734 475-8046
20401 W Old Us Highway 12 # 1 Chelsea (48118) ***(G-2708)***
Dexter Research Center Inc ... 734 426-3921
7300 Huron River Dr Ste 2 Dexter (48130) ***(G-4488)***

Dexter Roll Form Company 586 573-6930
30150 Ryan Rd Warren (48092) ***(G-17001)***

Dexter Stamping Company LLC 517 750-3414
1013 Thorrez Rd Jackson (49201) ***(G-8432)***

Dfc Inc 734 285-6749
17651 Yorkshire Dr Riverview (48193) ***(G-13293)***

DFI, Clinton Township *Also called Diversified Fabricators Inc* ***(G-3104)***

DForte Inc 269 657-6996
57440 County Road 671 Paw Paw (49079) ***(G-12402)***

DGa Printing Inc 586 979-2244
567 Robbins Dr Troy (48083) ***(G-16315)***

Dgh Enterprises Inc (PA) 269 925-0657
1225 Milton St Benton Harbor (49022) ***(G-1494)***

Dgh Enterprises Inc 269 925-0657
1225 Milton St Benton Harbor (49022) ***(G-1495)***

Dgp Inc 989 635-7531
3260 Fenner St Marlette (48453) ***(G-10495)***

Dh2 Inc 616 887-2700
87 10 Mile Rd Ne Comstock Park (49321) ***(G-3477)***

Dhake Industries Inc 734 420-0101
15169 Northville Rd Plymouth (48170) ***(G-12610)***

Dhs Inc 313 724-6566
1925 Elsmere St Detroit (48209) ***(G-4007)***

Di-Anodic Finishing Corp 616 454-0470
736 Ottawa Ave Nw 38 Grand Rapids (49503) ***(G-6348)***

Di-Coat Corporation 248 349-1211
42900 W 9 Mile Rd Novi (48375) ***(G-11868)***

Diack, Beulah *Also called Auric Enterprises Inc* ***(G-1608)***

Diagnostic Instruments Inc 586 731-6000
6540 Burroughs Ave Sterling Heights (48314) ***(G-15316)***

Diagnostic Systems Association 269 544-9000
6190 Technology Ave Kalamazoo (49009) ***(G-8725)***

Dial Tent & Awning Co 989 793-0741
5330 Davis Rd Saginaw (48604) ***(G-14027)***

Dialogue, Grand Rapids *Also called Intaglio LLC* ***(G-6539)***

Diamond Automation Ltd 734 838-7138
32235 Industrial Rd Livonia (48150) ***(G-9710)***

Diamond Broach Company 586 757-5131
3560 E 10 Mile Rd Warren (48091) ***(G-17002)***

Diamond Case Holdings LLC 800 293-2496
1590 Highwood E Ste A Pontiac (48340) ***(G-12817)***

Diamond Chrome Plating Inc 517 546-0150
604 S Michigan Ave Howell (48843) ***(G-8030)***

Diamond Die and Mold Company 586 791-0700
35401 Groesbeck Hwy Clinton Township (48035) ***(G-3102)***

Diamond Electric 734 995-5525
455 E Eisenhower Pkwy # 200 Ann Arbor (48108) ***(G-419)***

Diamond Electric Mfg Corp 734 995-5525
455 E Eisenhower Pkwy # 200 Ann Arbor (48108) ***(G-420)***

Diamond Graphics Inc 269 345-1164
2328 Lake St Kalamazoo (49048) ***(G-8726)***

Diamond Moba Americas Inc 248 476-7100
23400 Haggerty Rd Farmington Hills (48335) ***(G-4971)***

Diamond Press Solutions LLC 269 945-1997
1611 S Hanover St Hastings (49058) ***(G-7406)***

Diamond Racing Products Co, Clinton Township *Also called Trend Performance Products* ***(G-3251)***

Diamond Racing Products Inc 586 792-6620
23003 Diamond Dr Clinton Township (48035) ***(G-3103)***

Diamond Setters Inc 734 439-8655
13 W Main St Milan (48160) ***(G-10936)***

Diamond Systems, Farmington Hills *Also called Diamond Moba Americas Inc* ***(G-4971)***

Diamond Tool Manufacturing Inc 734 416-1900
14540 Jib St Plymouth (48170) ***(G-12611)***

Diamondback Abrasive Co, Commerce Township *Also called Diamondback Corp* ***(G-3399)***

Diamondback Corp 248 960-8260
3141 Old Farm Ln Commerce Township (48390) ***(G-3399)***

Diamondbck-Drectional Drlg LLC 231 943-3000
2122 S M 37 Traverse City (49685) ***(G-15956)***

Dianamic Abrasive Products 248 280-1185
2566 Industrial Row Dr Troy (48084) ***(G-16316)***

Diapin Therapeutics LLC 734 764-9123
1600 Huron Pkwy B520 Ann Arbor (48109) ***(G-421)***

Diazem Corp 989 832-3612
1406 E Pine St Midland (48640) ***(G-10832)***

Dicastal North America Inc 616 303-0306
1 Dicastal Dr Greenville (48838) ***(G-7127)***

Dice Corporation 989 891-2800
1410 S Valley Center Dr Bay City (48706) ***(G-1301)***

Dick and Jane Baking Co LLC 248 519-2418
755 W Big Beaver Rd # 2020 Troy (48084) ***(G-16317)***

Dickaren Inc 517 283-2444
6491 Reading Rd Reading (49274) ***(G-13136)***

Dickinson Homes Inc (PA) 906 774-5800
1500 W Breitung Ave Kingsford (49802) ***(G-9057)***

Dicks Signs 810 987-9002
2560 40th St Port Huron (48060) ***(G-12911)***

Dicks Sporting Goods Inc 248 581-8028
750 W 14 Mile Rd Troy (48083) ***(G-16318)***

Dico Manufacturing LLC 586 731-3008
48605 Structural Dr Chesterfield (48051) ***(G-2766)***

Die & Slide Technologies Inc 810 326-0986
6630 Belle River Rd China (48054) ***(G-2859)***

Die Cast Press Mfg Co Inc (PA) 269 657-6060
56480 Kasper Dr Paw Paw (49079) ***(G-12403)***

Die Cast Press Mfg Co Inc 269 427-5408
46652 Sycamore Dr Bangor (49013) ***(G-1090)***

Die Heat Systems Inc 586 749-9756
54145 Bates Rd Chesterfield (48051) ***(G-2767)***

Die Services International LLC 734 699-3400
45000 Van Born Rd Van Buren Twp (48111) ***(G-16758)***

Die Stampco Inc 989 893-7790
1301 N Lincoln St Bay City (48708) ***(G-1302)***

Die Tech Services Inc 616 363-6604
2457 Waldorf Ct Nw Walker (49544) ***(G-16865)***

Die Therm Engineering LLC 616 915-6975
5387 Hartfield Ct Se Ada (49301) ***(G-13)***

Die-Matic LLC 616 531-0060
4309 Aldrich Ave Sw Grand Rapids (49509) ***(G-6349)***

Die-Mold-Automation Component 313 581-6510
14300 Henn St Ste A Dearborn (48126) ***(G-3693)***

Die-Namic Inc 734 710-3200
7565 Haggerty Rd Van Buren Twp (48111) ***(G-16759)***

Die-Namic Tool & Design Llc 517 787-4900
147 Hobart St Jackson (49202) ***(G-8433)***

Die-Namic Tool Corp 616 954-7882
4541 Patterson Ave Se Grand Rapids (49512) ***(G-6350)***

Die-Tech and Engineering Inc 616 530-9030
4620 Herman Ave Sw Grand Rapids (49509) ***(G-6351)***

Die-Verse Solutions LLC 616 384-3550
15630 68th Ave Coopersville (49404) ***(G-3557)***

Diebotics, Comstock Park *Also called Preferred Tool & Die Co Inc* ***(G-3509)***

Diecrafters Inc 734 425-8000
27487 Schoolcraft Rd Livonia (48150) ***(G-9711)***

Diecutting Service Inc 734 426-0290
2415 Bishop Cir W Dexter (48130) ***(G-4489)***

Diehls Orchard & Cider Mill 248 634-8981
1479 Ranch Rd Holly (48442) ***(G-7876)***

Dienetics, Jenison *Also called KDI Technologies Inc* ***(G-8631)***

Dieomatic Incorporated 269 966-4900
10 Clark Rd Battle Creek (49037) ***(G-1174)***

Dieomatic Incorporated (HQ) 319 668-2031
750 Tower Dr Mail 7000 Mail Code Troy (48098) ***(G-16319)***

Diesel Performance Products 586 726-7478
7459 Flickinger Dr Shelby Township (48317) ***(G-14575)***

Dietech, Norton Shores *Also called Bry Mac Inc* ***(G-11741)***

Dietech NA, Roseville *Also called Dietech North America LLC* ***(G-13795)***

Dietech North America LLC 586 771-8580
16630 Eastland St Roseville (48066) ***(G-13795)***

Dietech Tool & Mfg Inc 810 724-0505
385 Industrial Dr Imlay City (48444) ***(G-8198)***

Dietert Foundry Testing Eqp (PA) 313 491-4680
9190 Roselawn St Detroit (48204) ***(G-4008)***

Diez Group LLC (PA) 734 675-1700
25325 Hall Rd Woodhaven (48183) ***(G-17939)***

Different By Design Inc 248 588-4840
38611 Cedarbrook Ct Farmington Hills (48331) ***(G-4972)***

Digested Organics LLC 844 934-4378
23745 Research Dr Farmington Hills (48335) ***(G-4973)***

Diggypod Inc 734 429-3307
301 Industrial Dr Tecumseh (49286) ***(G-15787)***

DIGILIANT, Okemos *Also called Digilink Technology Inc* ***(G-12119)***

Digilink Technology Inc 517 381-8888
5100 Marsh Rd Ste E3 Okemos (48864) ***(G-12119)***

Digital Die Solutions Inc 734 542-2222
13281 Merriman Rd Livonia (48150) ***(G-9712)***

Digital Dimensions Inc 419 630-4343
4300 E Territorial Rd Camden (49232) ***(G-2341)***

Digital Fabrication Inc 616 794-2848
7251 Whites Bridge Rd Belding (48809) ***(G-1409)***

Digital Finishing Corp 586 427-6003
14050 Simone Dr Shelby Township (48315) ***(G-14576)***

Digital Imaging Group Inc 269 686-8744
504 Eastern Ave Allegan (49010) ***(G-157)***

Digital Impact Design Inc 269 337-4200
403 Balch St Kalamazoo (49001) ***(G-8727)***

Digital Information Svcs LLC 313 365-7299
19954 Conant St Ste B Detroit (48234) ***(G-4009)***

Digital Media Solutions, Bloomfield Hills *Also called Sugar Bush Printing Inc* ***(G-1799)***

Digital Performance Tech 877 983-4230
3221 W Big Beaver Rd Troy (48084) ***(G-16320)***

Digital Printing & Graphics 586 566-9499
50711 Wing Dr Shelby Township (48315) ***(G-14577)***

Digital Printing Solutions LLC 586 566-4910
48688 Eagle Butte Ct Shelby Township (48315) ***(G-14578)***

Digital Success Network 517 244-0771
205 S Cedar St Mason (48854) ***(G-10636)***

Digital Systems Adio Video LLC 248 454-0387
1668 S Telg Rd Ste L130 Bloomfield Hills (48302) ***(G-1758)***

ALPHABETIC SECTION

Digital Tool & Die Inc 616 532-8020
2606 Sanford Ave Sw Grandville (49418) *(G-7028)*

Digitalmuni LLC 248 237-4077
2245 Eureka Rd Wyandotte (48192) *(G-17955)*

Digitrace Limited, Wayland Also called Digitrace Machine Works Ltd *(G-17404)*

Digitrace Machine Works Ltd 616 877-4818
1158 Morren Ct Wayland (49348) *(G-17404)*

Dihydro Services Inc 586 978-0900
40833 Brentwood Dr Sterling Heights (48310) *(G-15317)*

Dijet Incorporated (HQ) 734 454-9100
45807 Helm St Plymouth (48170) *(G-12612)*

Dikar Tool Company Inc 248 348-0010
22635 Heslip Dr Novi (48375) *(G-11869)*

Dillion Renee Entities 989 443-0654
600 Baker St Lansing (48910) *(G-9360)*

Dillon Charles Logging & Cnstr 906 376-8470
2666 State Highway M95 Republic (49879) *(G-13245)*

Dillon Forest Products, Republic Also called Dillon Charles Logging & Cnstr *(G-13245)*

Dimaggio Jseph A Mstr Gldsmith, Grosse Pointe Woods Also called Joseph A Dimaggio *(G-7205)*

Dimension Graphics Inc 616 245-1447
800 Burton St Se Grand Rapids (49507) *(G-6352)*

Dimension Machine Tech LLC 586 649-4747
18815 Kelly Ct Bloomfield Hills (48304) *(G-1759)*

Dimension Products Corporation 616 842-6050
13746 172nd Ave Grand Haven (49417) *(G-6010)*

Dimitri Mansour 248 684-4545
426 N Main St Milford (48381) *(G-10961)*

Dimond Machinery Company Inc 269 945-5908
922 N M 37 Hwy Hastings (49058) *(G-7407)*

Dimplex Thermal Solutions Inc (HQ) 269 349-6800
2625 Emerald Dr Kalamazoo (49001) *(G-8728)*

Dina Mia Kitchens Inc 906 265-9082
751 N 4th Ave Iron River (49935) *(G-8308)*

Dino S Dumpsters LLC 989 225-5635
900 Harry S Truman Pkwy Bay City (48706) *(G-1303)*

Diocesan Publications (PA) 616 878-5200
1050 74th St Sw Byron Center (49315) *(G-2187)*

Diocese of Lansing 517 484-4449
1500 W Saginaw St Ste 2 Lansing (48915) *(G-9361)*

Diplomat Spclty Phrm Flint LLC 810 768-9000
4100 S Saginaw St Flint (48507) *(G-5419)*

Dipsol Chemicals, Livonia Also called Dipsol of America Inc *(G-9713)*

Dipsol of America Inc 734 367-0530
34005 Schoolcraft Rd Livonia (48150) *(G-9713)*

Direct Aim Media LLC 800 817-7101
1778 Grand Ct Ne Grand Rapids (49525) *(G-6353)*

Direct Connect Systems LLC 248 694-0130
8246 Goldie St Commerce Township (48390) *(G-3400)*

Directional Drilling Contrs, Traverse City Also called Diamondbck-Drectional Drlg LLC *(G-15956)*

Directional Regulated Systems 734 451-1416
8491 Ronda Dr Canton (48187) *(G-2365)*

Dirkes Industries, Saint Clair Also called Reeling Systems LLC *(G-14233)*

Dirksen Screw Products Co (PA) 586 247-5400
14490 23 Mile Rd Shelby Township (48315) *(G-14579)*

Discount Jewelry Center Inc 734 266-8200
8339 N Wayne Rd Westland (48185) *(G-17549)*

Discount Pallets 616 453-5455
4580 Airwest Dr Se Grand Rapids (49512) *(G-6354)*

Discount Vitamin Store, Jackson Also called Trulife Inc *(G-8596)*

Discovery Gold Corp 269 429-7002
4472 Winding Ln Stevensville (49127) *(G-15564)*

Discovery House Publishers 616 942-9218
3000 Kraft Ave Se Grand Rapids (49512) *(G-6355)*

Discraft Inc 248 624-2250
51000 Grand River Ave Wixom (48393) *(G-17794)*

Dispense Technologies LLC 248 486-6244
7036 Kensington Rd Brighton (48116) *(G-1911)*

Display Pack Inc (PA) 616 451-3061
650 West St Cedar Springs (49319) *(G-2553)*

Display Pack Inc 616 451-3061
1600 Monroe Ave Nw Grand Rapids (49505) *(G-6356)*

Display Pack Disc Inc 616 451-3061
650 West St Cedar Springs (49319) *(G-2554)*

Display Pack Disc Vdh Inc 616 451-3061
650 West St Cedar Springs (49319) *(G-2555)*

Display Structures Inc 810 991-0801
288 Robbins Dr Troy (48083) *(G-16321)*

Disruptive Eating LLC 734 262-0560
2874 Washtenaw Rd Ypsilanti (48197) *(G-18066)*

Disrupttech LLC 248 225-8383
22631 Bayview Dr Saint Clair Shores (48081) *(G-14244)*

Distillery 9 LLC 517 990-2929
8040 Apple Creek Ct Whitmore Lake (48189) *(G-17695)*

Distinctive Appliances Distrg 248 380-2007
51155 Grand River Ave Wixom (48393) *(G-17795)*

Distinctive Custom Furniture 248 399-9175
2425 Burdette St Ferndale (48220) *(G-5279)*

Distinctive Machine Corp 616 433-4111
300 Byrne Industrial Dr B Rockford (49341) *(G-13567)*

Div Edw C Levy Co, Wixom Also called Lyon Sand & Gravel Co *(G-17848)*

Diverse Manufacturing Soltion 517 423-6691
805 S Maumee St Tecumseh (49286) *(G-15788)*

Diversfied Prcurement Svcs LLC 248 821-1147
1530 Farrow St Ferndale (48220) *(G-5280)*

Diversfied Tchncal Systems Inc 248 513-6050
25881 Meadowbrook Rd Novi (48375) *(G-11870)*

Diversified Chem Technologies 313 867-5444
15477 Woodrow Wilson St Detroit (48238) *(G-4010)*

Diversified Chemical Tech Inc (PA) 313 867-5444
15477 Woodrow Wilson St Detroit (48238) *(G-4011)*

Diversified Davitco LLC 248 681-9197
2569 Dixie Hwy Waterford (48328) *(G-17334)*

Diversified E D M Inc 248 547-2320
1019 E 10 Mile Rd Madison Heights (48071) *(G-10231)*

Diversified Engrg & Plas LLC 517 789-8118
1801 Wildwood Ave Jackson (49202) *(G-8434)*

Diversified Fabricators Inc 586 868-1000
21482 Carlo Dr Clinton Township (48038) *(G-3104)*

Diversified Mech Svcs Inc 616 785-2735
844 W River Center Dr Ne Comstock Park (49321) *(G-3478)*

Diversified Metal Fabricators 248 541-0500
2351 Hilton Rd Ferndale (48220) *(G-5281)*

Diversified Metal Products Inc 989 448-7120
1489 Oorouk Blvd Gaylord (49735) *(G-5856)*

Diversified Mfg & Assembly LLC 313 758-4797
5545 Bridgewood Dr Sterling Hts (48310) *(G-15549)*

Diversified Mfg & Assembly LLC (PA) 586 272-2431
5545 Bridgewood Dr Sterling Heights (48310) *(G-15318)*

Diversified Pdts & Svcs LLC 616 836-6600
500 E 8th St Holland (49423) *(G-7608)*

Diversified Precision Pdts Inc 517 750-2310
6999 Spring Arbor Rd Spring Arbor (49283) *(G-15121)*

Diversified Services Tech, Romulus Also called Dst Industries Inc *(G-13667)*

Diversified Tool & Engineering 734 692-1260
10340 Ruthmere Ave Grosse Ile (48138) *(G-7170)*

Diversified Tooling Group Inc 248 837-5828
31240 Stephenson Hwy Madison Heights (48071) *(G-10232)*

Diversified Tube LLC 313 790-7348
21056 Bridge St Southfield (48033) *(G-14882)*

Diversified Welding & Fabg 616 738-0400
12813 Riley St Holland (49424) *(G-7609)*

Diversitak Inc 313 869-8500
15477 Woodrow Wilson St Detroit (48238) *(G-4012)*

Divine Dessert 313 278-3322
25930 Ford Rd Dearborn Heights (48127) *(G-3782)*

Division Oglebay Norton Co, Rogers City Also called O-N Minerals Michigan Company *(G-13619)*

Division P, Marysville Also called ZF Axle Drives Marysville LLC *(G-10627)*

Division Z, Northville Also called ZF North America Inc *(G-11735)*

Dixon & Ryan Corporation 248 549-4000
4343 Normandy Ct Ste A Royal Oak (48073) *(G-13919)*

DJL Logging Inc 231 590-2012
5905 N Brown Rd Manton (49663) *(G-10453)*

Djw Enterprises Inc 262 251-9500
324 N Light Lake Rd Crystal Falls (49920) *(G-3609)*

DK Tool & Machine Inc 517 369-1401
703 Gilead Shores Dr Bronson (49028) *(G-2024)*

Dki, Hemlock Also called Douglas King Industries Inc *(G-7461)*

Dkny, Auburn Hills Also called G-III Apparel Group Ltd *(G-879)*

Dko Intl 248 926-9115
39500 W 14 Mile Rd Commerce Township (48390) *(G-3401)*

Dl Engineering & Tech Inc 248 852-6900
1749 W Hamlin Rd Rochester Hills (48309) *(G-13409)*

Dla Document Services 269 961-4895
74 Washington Ave N 2a12 Battle Creek (49037) *(G-1175)*

Dlh Rollform LLC 586 231-0507
51751 County Line Rd New Baltimore (48047) *(G-11483)*

Dlh World LLC 313 915-0274
2517 Hazelwood St Detroit (48206) *(G-4013)*

Dlhbowles Inc 248 569-0652
20755 Greenfield Rd # 806 Southfield (48075) *(G-14883)*

Dlt Industries Inc 616 754-2762
1760 Callaghan St Greenville (48838) *(G-7128)*

Dm Tool & Fab Inc 586 726-8390
6101 18 1/2 Mile Rd Sterling Heights (48314) *(G-15319)*

Dm3d Technology LLC 248 409-7900
2350 Pontiac Rd Auburn Hills (48326) *(G-841)*

Dma, Sterling Heights Also called Diversified Mfg & Assembly LLC *(G-15318)*

Dme Company LLC (HQ) 248 398-6000
29111 Stephenson Hwy Madison Heights (48071) *(G-10233)*

Dmg Dumpsters Inc 313 610-3476
21339 Orchard Lake Rd Farmington Hills (48336) *(G-4974)*

Dmi Automotive Inc 517 548-1414
1200 Durant Dr Howell (48843) *(G-8031)*

Dmi Columbus, LLC, Southfield Also called Aludyne Columbus LLC *(G-14832)*

ALPHABETIC SECTION — Douglas Corp

Dmi Edon LLC 586 782-7311
12700 Stephens Rd Warren (48089) *(G-17003)*

Dmi Edon LLC (HQ) 248 728-8642
300 Gllria Ofc Ctr Ste 50 Southfield (48034) *(G-14884)*

Dmp Sign Company 248 996-9281
20732 Negaunee St Southfield (48033) *(G-14885)*

DMS Electric Apparatus Service 269 349-7000
630 Gibson St Kalamazoo (49007) *(G-8729)*

DMS Manufacturing Solutions 517 423-6691
800 S Maumee St Tecumseh (49286) *(G-15789)*

Dn-Lawrence Industries Inc 269 552-4999
423 Walbridge St Kalamazoo (49007) *(G-8730)*

Dna Software Inc 734 222-9080
334 E Washington St Ann Arbor (48104) *(G-422)*

Dnl Fabrication LLC 586 872-2656
28514 Hayes Rd Roseville (48066) *(G-13796)*

DNR Inc 734 722-4000
45759 Helm St Plymouth (48170) *(G-12613)*

DNR Inc (PA) 734 722-4000
38475 Webb Dr Westland (48185) *(G-17550)*

Do It Best, Port Huron Also called Port Huron Building Supply Co *(G-12958)*

Do It Best, Portage Also called Nelson Hardware *(G-13018)*

Do It Best, Rose City Also called Masons Lumber & Hardware Inc *(G-13763)*

Do Rite Tool Inc 734 522-7510
32647 Parklane St Garden City (48135) *(G-5822)*

Do-All Plastic Inc 313 824-6565
1265 Terminal St Detroit (48214) *(G-4014)*

Do-It Corporation 269 637-1121
1201 Blue Star Mem Hwy South Haven (49090) *(G-14758)*

Do-Mor Products 269 651-7362
29435 Hackman Rd Burr Oak (49030) *(G-2135)*

Doan Companies, Ypsilanti Also called Doan Construction Co *(G-18067)*

Doan Construction Co (PA) 734 971-4678
3670 Carpenter Rd Ypsilanti (48197) *(G-18067)*

Dobb Printing Inc 231 722-1060
2431 Harvey St Muskegon (49442) *(G-11306)*

Dobday Manufacturing Co Inc 586 254-6777
42750 Merrill Rd Sterling Heights (48314) *(G-15320)*

Dobson Heavy Haul Inc Division, Bay City Also called Dobson Industrial Inc *(G-1304)*

Dobson Industrial Inc (PA) 800 298-6063
3660 N Euclid Ave Bay City (48706) *(G-1304)*

Dockside Canvas Co Inc 586 463-1231
29939 S River Rd Harrison Township (48045) *(G-7329)*

Dockside Imports, Marquette Also called Wattsson & Wattsson Jewelers *(G-10561)*

Doctor Flue Inc 517 423-2832
1610 Dinius Rd Tecumseh (49286) *(G-15790)*

Doctor Prager Sensible Foods, Bloomfield Hills Also called Ungar Frozen Food Product *(G-1809)*

Dodge West Joe Nickel 810 691-2133
2219 E Farrand Rd Clio (48420) *(G-3270)*

Doerken Corporation 517 522-4600
11200 Cedar Knoll Dr Grass Lake (49240) *(G-7087)*

Dog Brown Manufacturing LLC 313 255-1400
24800 Plymouth Rd Redford (48239) *(G-13159)*

Dog Might LLC 734 679-0646
303 Metty Dr Ann Arbor (48103) *(G-423)*

Dolav, Grand Rapids Also called Decade Products LLC *(G-6340)*

Dole Packaged Food Company, Decatur Also called Dole Packaged Foods LLC *(G-3803)*

Dole Packaged Foods LLC 269 423-6375
101 W Bronson St Decatur (49045) *(G-3803)*

Doll Face Chef LLC 248 495-8280
41000 Woodward Ave # 350 Bloomfield Hills (48304) *(G-1760)*

Dollars Sense 231 369-3610
7850 Scotch Blf Sw Fife Lake (49633) *(G-5339)*

Dolls By Maurice Inc 586 739-5147
45207 Cass Ave Utica (48317) *(G-16741)*

Dolphin Dumpsters LLC 734 272-8981
30650 River Gln Farmington Hills (48336) *(G-4975)*

Dolphin Manufacturing Inc 734 946-6322
12650 Universal Dr Taylor (48180) *(G-15707)*

Doltek Enterprises Inc 616 837-7828
11335 Apple Dr Nunica (49448) *(G-12036)*

Domart LLC 616 285-9177
3923 28th St Se Grand Rapids (49512) *(G-6357)*

Domer Industries LLC 269 226-4000
3434 S Burdick St Kalamazoo (49001) *(G-8731)*

Domico Med-Device LLC 810 750-5300
14241 N Fenton Rd Fenton (48430) *(G-5200)*

Dominion Tech Group Inc 586 773-3303
15736 Sturgeon St Roseville (48066) *(G-13797)*

Dominos Pizza LLC (HQ) 734 930-3030
30 Frank Lloyd Wright Dr Ann Arbor (48105) *(G-424)*

Domnmar Manufacturing Group, Detroit Also called Gerald Harris *(G-4089)*

Domtar Eddy Specialty Papers, Port Huron Also called E B Eddy Paper Inc *(G-12915)*

Domtar Gypsum, Port Huron Also called Domtar Industries Inc *(G-12912)*

Domtar Industries Inc 810 982-0191
1700 Washington Ave Port Huron (48060) *(G-12912)*

Don Duff Rebuilding 734 522-7700
31130 Industrial Rd Livonia (48150) *(G-9714)*

Don Marcos Tortillas, Southfield Also called Mexican Food Specialties Inc *(G-14980)*

Don Sawmill Inc 989 733-2780
17131 Twin School Hwy Onaway (49765) *(G-12146)*

Don Yohe Enterprises Inc 586 784-5556
74054 Church St Armada (48005) *(G-718)*

Don-Lors Electronics, West Bloomfield Also called Stanecki Inc *(G-17498)*

Donald E Rogers Associates 248 673-9878
2627 Williams Dr Waterford (48328) *(G-17335)*

Donald Francis Strzynski 231 929-7443
1010 1st Ave Cadillac (49601) *(G-2244)*

Donald Gleason 269 673-6802
3480 125th Ave Allegan (49010) *(G-158)*

Donald LII Sons Logging 231 420-3800
260 Townline Rd Pellston (49769) *(G-12425)*

Donalyn Enterprises Inc 517 546-9798
907 Fowler St Howell (48843) *(G-8032)*

Donckers Candies & Gifts 906 226-6110
137 W Washington St Marquette (49855) *(G-10526)*

Done Right Engraving Inc 248 332-3133
119 N Saginaw St Pontiac (48342) *(G-12818)*

Done Right Enterprises, Pontiac Also called Done Right Engraving Inc *(G-12818)*

Dongah America Inc 248 918-5810
1807 E Maple Rd Troy (48083) *(G-16322)*

Donna Jeroy 313 554-2722
10460 W Jefferson Ave River Rouge (48218) *(G-13275)*

Donnelly, Holland Also called Magna Mirrors America Inc *(G-7734)*

Donnelly Corp 231 652-8425
700 Park St Newaygo (49337) *(G-11567)*

Dons Welding 989 792-0287
2461 Bellevue St Saginaw (48601) *(G-14028)*

Dontech Solutions LLC 248 789-3086
4755 Treasure Lake Dr Howell (48843) *(G-8033)*

Donutville 616 396-1160
676 Michigan Ave Ste 1 Holland (49423) *(G-7610)*

Door County White Fish, Stephenson Also called Ruleau Brothers Inc *(G-15240)*

Door SEC Solutions of Mich 616 301-1991
6757 Cascade Rd Se 304 Grand Rapids (49546) *(G-6358)*

Doors & Drawers, Dexter Also called Rose Corporation *(G-4508)*

Doors4, Portage Also called Eliason Corporation *(G-12992)*

Dorden & Company Inc 313 834-7910
7446 Central St Detroit (48210) *(G-4015)*

Dorden Squeegees, Detroit Also called Dorden & Company Inc *(G-4015)*

Dorel Home Furnishings Inc 269 782-8661
202 Spaulding St Dowagiac (49047) *(G-4540)*

Dornbos Printing Impressions, Saginaw Also called Weighman Enterprises Inc *(G-14181)*

Dornbos Sign Inc 517 543-4000
619 W Harris St Charlotte (48813) *(G-2645)*

Dorothy Dawson Food Products 517 788-9830
251 W Euclid Ave Jackson (49203) *(G-8435)*

Dorr Industries, Byron Center Also called Tg Manufacturing LLC *(G-2212)*

Dorr Industries Inc 616 681-9440
1840 142nd Ave Dorr (49323) *(G-4523)*

Dorris Company 586 293-5260
17430 Malyn Blvd Fraser (48026) *(G-5644)*

Dotmine Day Planners, Ann Arbor Also called Edward and Cole Inc *(G-434)*

Double B'S Steel and Mfg, Wheeler Also called Patch Works Farms Inc *(G-17617)*

Double Check Tools Service 231 947-1632
6937 M 72 E Williamsburg (49690) *(G-17711)*

Double Eagle Defense LLC (PA) 313 562-5550
25205 Trowbridge St Dearborn (48124) *(G-3694)*

Double Eagle Steel Coating Co 313 203-9800
3000 Miller Rd Dearborn (48120) *(G-3695)*

Double Gun Journal 231 536-7439
5014 Rockery School Rd East Jordan (49727) *(G-4628)*

Double H Mfg Inc 734 729-3450
6171 Commerce Dr Westland (48185) *(G-17551)*

Double Otis Inc 616 878-3998
1415 Division Ave S Grand Rapids (49507) *(G-6359)*

Double Six Sports Complex 989 762-5342
4860 N Sheridan Rd Stanton (48888) *(G-15229)*

DOUBLEO O SUPPLY & CRAFTSMEN, Grand Rapids Also called Double Otis Inc *(G-6359)*

Doug Anderson Logging 906 337-3707
54586 Oikarinen Rd Calumet (49913) *(G-2327)*

Doug Murdicks Fudge Inc 231 938-2330
4500 N Us Highway 31 N Traverse City (49686) *(G-15957)*

Doug Wirt Enterprises Inc 989 684-5777
400 Martin St Bay City (48706) *(G-1305)*

Dough & Spice Inc 586 756-6100
2150 E 10 Mile Rd Warren (48091) *(G-17004)*

Dough Masters 248 585-0600
23412 Dequindre Rd Warren (48091) *(G-17005)*

Doughnut World, Grand Rapids Also called Roskam Baking Company *(G-6842)*

Douglas Autotech Corporation (HQ) 517 369-2315
300 Albers Rd Bronson (49028) *(G-2025)*

Douglas Corp 517 767-4112
103 S Main St Tekonsha (49092) *(G-15818)*

Douglas E Fulk...517 482-2090
1800 S Cedar St Lansing (48910) ***(G-9362)***
Douglas Gage Inc...586 727-2089
69681 Lowe Plank Rd Richmond (48062) ***(G-13261)***
Douglas King Industries Inc...989 642-2865
16425 Northern Pintail Dr Hemlock (48626) ***(G-7461)***
Douglas Marine Corporation...269 857-1764
6780 Enterprise Dr Douglas (49406) ***(G-4530)***
Douglas Sign Company, Lansing *Also called Douglas E Fulk* ***(G-9362)***
Douglas Stamping Company...248 542-3940
25531 Dequindre Rd Madison Heights (48071) ***(G-10234)***
Douglas Steel Fabricating Corp...517 322-2050
1312 S Waverly Rd Lansing (48917) ***(G-9288)***
Douglas Water Conditioning (PA)...248 363-8383
7234 Cooley Lake Rd Waterford (48327) ***(G-17336)***
Douglas West Company Inc...734 676-8882
9177 Groh Rd Bldg 43 Grosse Ile (48138) ***(G-7171)***
Douglass Safety Systems LLC...989 687-7600
2655 N Meridian Rd Ste 6 Sanford (48657) ***(G-14449)***
Doulton & Co...248 258-6977
19541 Cherry Hill St Southfield (48076) ***(G-14886)***
Douthitt Corporation (PA)...313 259-1565
245 Adair St Detroit (48207) ***(G-4016)***
Douthitt Corporation...313 259-1565
277 Adair St Detroit (48207) ***(G-4017)***
Dover Energy Inc...248 836-6750
15 Corporate Dr Auburn Hills (48326) ***(G-842)***
Dover Energy Inc (HQ)...248 836-6700
691 N Squirrel Rd Ste 250 Auburn Hills (48326) ***(G-843)***
Dover Metals Inc...269 849-1411
117 Paras Hill Dr Hartford (49057) ***(G-7383)***
Dovetails Inc...248 674-8777
5600 Williams Lake Rd B Waterford (48329) ***(G-17337)***
Dow Agrosciences LLC...989 636-4400
433 Bldg Midland (48674) ***(G-10833)***
Dow Agrosciences LLC...989 479-3245
305 N Huron Ave Harbor Beach (48441) ***(G-7265)***
Dow Chemical Company (HQ)...989 636-1000
2211 H H Dow Way Midland (48642) ***(G-10834)***
Dow Chemical Company...231 845-4285
1600 S Madison St Ludington (49431) ***(G-10056)***
Dow Chemical Company...989 636-1000
2511 S Saginaw Rd Midland (48640) ***(G-10835)***
Dow Chemical Company...989 636-4406
1801 Larkin Center Dr Midland (48642) ***(G-10836)***
Dow Chemical Company...989 638-6571
2922 Mcculloch Rd Beaverton (48612) ***(G-1384)***
Dow Chemical Company...517 439-4400
195 Uran St Hillsdale (49242) ***(G-7523)***
Dow Chemical Company...810 966-9816
3381 Woodview Clyde (48049) ***(G-3282)***
Dow Chemical Company...989 708-6737
3800 S Saginaw Rd Gate17 Midland (48640) ***(G-10837)***
Dow Chemical Company...989 636-1000
2511 E Patrick Rd Midland (48642) ***(G-10838)***
Dow Chemical Company...989 636-8587
2030 Dow Ctr 263 Midland (48674) ***(G-10839)***
Dow Chemical Company...989 636-1000
S Saginaw Bldg 304 Midland (48667) ***(G-10840)***
Dow Chemical Company...989 496-2246
2007 Austin St Midland (48642) ***(G-10841)***
Dow Chemical Company...989 636-2636
100 Larkin Ctr Midland (48674) ***(G-10842)***
Dow Chemical Company...989 636-5430
2050 Abbott Rd Midland (48674) ***(G-10843)***
Dow Chemical Company...989 695-2584
M B S Intl Hngr 5 Freeland (48623) ***(G-5755)***
Dow Chemical Company...989 832-1000
2040 Dow Ctr Midland (48674) ***(G-10844)***
Dow Chemical Company...989 636-0540
1320 Waldo Ave Ste 300 Midland (48642) ***(G-10845)***
Dow Chemical Company...989 638-6441
Gpc Building Midland (48667) ***(G-10846)***
Dow Chemical Company...989 636-6351
Bldg 1710 Midland (48674) ***(G-10847)***
Dow Chemical Company...989 636-5409
3700 James Savage Rd Midland (48642) ***(G-10848)***
Dow Corning, Auburn *Also called Dow Silicones Corporation* ***(G-751)***
Dow Corning Corporation...989 839-2808
1404 Peppermill Cir Midland (48642) ***(G-10849)***
Dow Credit Corporation...989 636-8949
2030 Dow Ctr Unit E228 Midland (48674) ***(G-10850)***
Dow Inc (PA)...989 636-1000
2211 H H Dow Way Midland (48642) ***(G-10851)***
Dow International Holdings Co (HQ)...989 636-1000
2030 Dow Ctr Midland (48674) ***(G-10852)***
Dow Silicones Corporation...989 496-4400
3901 S Saginaw Rd Midland (48640) ***(G-10853)***
Dow Silicones Corporation (HQ)...989 496-4000
2200 W Salzburg Rd Auburn (48611) ***(G-751)***
Dow Silicones Corporation...800 248-2481
1635 N Gleaner Rd Hemlock (48626) ***(G-7462)***
Dow Silicones Corporation...989 496-4000
2651 Salzburg St Midland (48640) ***(G-10854)***
Dow Silicones Corporation...989 895-3397
1 E Main St Bay City (48708) ***(G-1306)***
Dow Silicones Corporation...989 496-1306
5300 11 Mile Rd Auburn (48611) ***(G-752)***
Dow Silicones Corporation...989 496-4137
2651 Salzburg St Midland (48640) ***(G-10855)***
Dowagiac Daily News, Niles *Also called Daughtry Nwspapers Investments* ***(G-11606)***
Dowd Brothers Forest Products, Alger *Also called Dowd Brothers Forestry* ***(G-138)***
Dowd Brothers Forestry...989 345-7459
2718 School Rd Alger (48610) ***(G-138)***
Dowding Industries Inc (PA)...517 663-5455
449 Marilin Ave Eaton Rapids (48827) ***(G-4720)***
Dowding Machining LLC...517 663-5455
503 Marilin Ave Eaton Rapids (48827) ***(G-4721)***
Dowding Tool Products LLC...517 541-2795
8950 Narrow Lake Rd Springport (49284) ***(G-15210)***
Down & Associates, Howell *Also called Down Home Inc* ***(G-8034)***
Down Home Inc (PA)...517 545-5955
110 W Grand River Ave Howell (48843) ***(G-8034)***
Down Inc...616 241-3922
635 Evergreen St Se Grand Rapids (49507) ***(G-6360)***
Downey's & Design, Waterford *Also called Downeys Potato Chips-Waterford* ***(G-17338)***
Downeys Potato Chips-Waterford...248 673-3636
4709 Highland Rd Waterford (48328) ***(G-17338)***
Downriver Creative Woodworking...313 274-4090
4631 Parkside Blvd Allen Park (48101) ***(G-197)***
Downriver Crushed Concrete...734 283-1833
20538 Pennsylvania Rd Taylor (48180) ***(G-15708)***
Downriver Deburring Inc...313 388-2640
20248 Lorne St Taylor (48180) ***(G-15709)***
Downriver Plastics Inc...734 246-3031
8349 Ronda Dr Canton (48187) ***(G-2366)***
Dowsett Spring Company...269 782-2138
27071 Marcellus Hwy Dowagiac (49047) ***(G-4541)***
Doxxpress, Calumet *Also called Up Officeexpress LLC* ***(G-2334)***
Doyle Forest Products Inc...231 832-5586
21364 Meceola Rd Paris (49338) ***(G-12384)***
Doyle Sailmakers, Traverse City *Also called Blue Water Sail & Canvas Inc* ***(G-15914)***
Dozy Dotes LLC...866 870-1048
4493 Crimson Ct Ste 200 Grand Blanc (48439) ***(G-5965)***
Dph LLC...248 813-2000
5820 Innovation Dr Troy (48098) ***(G-16323)***
Dph Holdings Corp (HQ)...248 813-2000
5725 Innovation Dr Troy (48098) ***(G-16324)***
Dph-Das Global (holdings) LLC...248 813-2000
5820 Innovation Dr Troy (48098) ***(G-16325)***
Dph-Das LLC...248 813-2000
5820 Innovation Dr Troy (48098) ***(G-16326)***
DPM Manufacturing LLC...248 349-6375
35451 Schoolcraft Rd Livonia (48150) ***(G-9715)***
Dpr Manufacturing & Svcs Inc...586 757-1421
23675 Mound Rd Warren (48091) ***(G-17006)***
DPrinter Inc...517 423-6554
6197 N Adrian Hwy Tecumseh (49286) ***(G-15791)***
Dqb Industries, Livonia *Also called Detroit Qulty Brush Mfg Co Inc* ***(G-9708)***
Dr & Hl Mold & Machine In...989 746-9290
4506 S Washington Rd Saginaw (48601) ***(G-14029)***
Dr Pepper Snapple Group, Cadillac *Also called Keurig Dr Pepper Inc* ***(G-2257)***
Dr Pepper Snapple Group...616 393-5800
777 Brooks Ave Holland (49423) ***(G-7611)***
Dr Schneider Auto Systems Inc...270 858-5400
716 Advance St Ste A Brighton (48116) ***(G-1912)***
Dr. John's Candies, Comstock Park *Also called Sugar Free Specialties LLC* ***(G-3517)***
Draco Mfg Inc...248 585-0320
629 Minnesota Dr Troy (48083) ***(G-16327)***
DRae LLC...313 923-7230
24221 Scotia Rd Oak Park (48237) ***(G-12060)***
Drag Finishing Tech LLC (PA)...616 785-0400
835 W River Center Dr Ne # 2 Comstock Park (49321) ***(G-3479)***
Dragon Acqstion Intrmdate Hldc, Novi *Also called Dexko Global Inc* ***(G-11867)***
Dragon Acquisition Intermediat (HQ)...248 692-4367
39555 Orchard Hill Pl # 52 Novi (48375) ***(G-11871)***
Dragon Acquisition Parent Inc (PA)...248 692-4367
39555 Orchard Hill Pl # 52 Novi (48375) ***(G-11872)***
Dragon Bleu USA, Bloomfield Hills *Also called RGI Brands LLC* ***(G-1794)***
Drain Commissioner, Muskegon *Also called County of Muskegon* ***(G-11301)***
Drake Enterprises Inc...586 783-3009
24800 Capital Blvd Clinton Township (48036) ***(G-3105)***
Dramatic Graphics, Warren *Also called Candela Products Inc* ***(G-16976)***
Drapery Workroom...269 463-5633
5864 N County Line Rd Watervliet (49098) ***(G-17391)***
Draths Corporation...517 349-0668
236 Crystal Ct Howell (48843) ***(G-8035)***

Draught Horse Group LLC 231 631-5218
57721 Grand River Ave New Hudson (48165) *(G-11538)*
Drayton Iron & Metal Inc (PA) 248 673-1269
5229 Williams Lake Rd Waterford (48329) *(G-17339)*
Drayton Plains Tool Company, Saline *Also called Mmi Engineered Solutions Inc (G-14403)*
Dreal Inc 248 813-2000
5820 Innovation Dr Troy (48098) *(G-16328)*
Dreamweaver Lure Company Inc 231 843-3652
5712 Brookwood Pl Ludington (49431) *(G-10057)*
Drew Technologies Inc 734 222-5228
3915 Res Pk Dr Ste A10 Ann Arbor (48108) *(G-425)*
Drews Manufacturing Co 616 534-3482
5753 Division Ave S Grand Rapids (49548) *(G-6361)*
Dri-Design Inc 616 355-2970
12480 Superior Ct Ste 1 Holland (49424) *(G-7612)*
Drill Technology 616 676-1287
399 Greentree Ln Ne Ada (49301) *(G-14)*
Drive System Integration Inc 248 568-7750
32600 Westlady Dr Beverly Hills (48025) *(G-1616)*
Driven Designs Inc 616 794-9977
1135 S Bridge St Belding (48809) *(G-1410)*
Driven-4 LLC 269 281-7567
2900 S State St Ste 2w Saint Joseph (49085) *(G-14307)*
Drought, Royal Oak *Also called Panther James LLC (G-13955)*
Drummond Dolemite, Drummond Island *Also called Osborne Materials Company (G-4566)*
Drummond Meat Processing, Ravenna *Also called Dan Drummond (G-13118)*
Drw Systems Carbide LLC 810 392-3526
12618 Masters Rd Riley (48041) *(G-13273)*
Dry Coolers Inc 248 969-3400
575 S Glaspie St Oxford (48371) *(G-12344)*
Dryden Steel LLC 586 777-7600
5585 North St Bldg D Dryden (48428) *(G-4569)*
DRYE Custom Pallets Inc 313 381-2681
19400 Allen Rd Melvindale (48122) *(G-10696)*
Ds Automction LLC 248 370-8950
280 Mill St Ste C Rochester (48307) *(G-13319)*
Ds Biotech LLC 248 894-1474
1665 Dell Rose Dr Bloomfield Hills (48302) *(G-1761)*
Ds Mold LLC 616 794-1639
807 Edna St Belding (48809) *(G-1411)*
Ds Sales Inc 248 960-6411
46903 West Rd Wixom (48393) *(G-17796)*
DSC Laboratories Inc 800 492-5988
1979 Latimer Dr Muskegon (49442) *(G-11307)*
Dse Industries LLC 313 530-6668
51315 Regency Center Dr Macomb (48042) *(G-10118)*
Dss Valve Products Inc 269 409-6080
1760 Mayflower Rd Niles (49120) *(G-11609)*
Dst Industries Inc (HQ) 734 941-0300
34364 Goddard Rd Romulus (48174) *(G-13667)*
Dst Industries Inc 734 941-0300
11900 Tecumseh Clinton Rd Clinton (49236) *(G-3018)*
DSU, Chesterfield *Also called Design Services Unlimited Inc (G-2765)*
Dsw Holdings Inc (PA) 313 567-4500
400 Renaissance Ctr Lbby Detroit (48243) *(G-4018)*
DTE Energy Co 616 632-2663
444 Wealthy St Sw Grand Rapids (49503) *(G-6362)*
DTE Energy Company (PA) 313 235-4000
1 Energy Plz Detroit (48226) *(G-4019)*
DTE Energy Resources Inc 313 297-4203
1400 Zug Island Rd Detroit (48209) *(G-4020)*
DTE Energy Resources Inc (HQ) 734 302-4800
414 S Main St Ste 600 Ann Arbor (48104) *(G-426)*
DTE Energy Trust II 313 235-8822
2000 2nd Ave Detroit (48226) *(G-4021)*
DTE Gas & Oil Company 231 995-4000
10691 E Carter Rd Ste 201 Traverse City (49684) *(G-15958)*
DTe Hankin Inc 734 279-1831
399 E Center St Petersburg (49270) *(G-12435)*
Dti, Redford *Also called Detroit Tech Innovation LLC (G-13158)*
Dti Molded Products Inc (HQ) 248 647-0400
32500 Telg Rd Ste 207 Bingham Farms (48025) *(G-1652)*
Dti Plastic Products, Macomb *Also called Detroit Technologies Inc (G-10117)*
DTR Logistics, Troy *Also called Dongah America Inc (G-16322)*
Dts Enterprises Inc 231 599-3123
9910 N Us Highway 31 Ellsworth (49729) *(G-4787)*
Du Val Industries LLC 586 737-2710
6410 19 Mile Rd Sterling Heights (48314) *(G-15321)*
Duane F Proehl Inc 906 474-6630
11064 T.65 Rd Rapid River (49878) *(G-13112)*
Duane Young & Son Lumber 586 727-1470
8760 Big Hand Rd Columbus (48063) *(G-3378)*
Duberville Logging 906 586-6267
W16683 Sandtown Rd Curtis (49820) *(G-3619)*
Dubetsky K9 Academy LLC 586 997-1717
50699 Central Indus Dr Shelby Township (48315) *(G-14580)*
Dubois Production Services Inc 616 785-0088
30 N Park St Ne Comstock Park (49321) *(G-3480)*
Duff Brush LLC 906 863-3319
630 7th St Menominee (49858) *(G-10730)*
Duggan Manufacturing LLC 586 254-7400
50150 Ryan Rd Shelby Township (48317) *(G-14581)*
Duggans Limited LLC 586 254-7400
50150 Ryan Rd Ste 15 Shelby Township (48317) *(G-14582)*
Duke De Jong LLC 734 403-1708
12680 Delta St Taylor (48180) *(G-15710)*
Dumbarton Tool Inc 231 775-4342
151 Clay Dr Cadillac (49601) *(G-2245)*
Dumpster Express LLC 855 599-7255
11177 Horton Rd Holly (48442) *(G-7877)*
Dun Mor Design, Troy *Also called Dun Mor Embroidery & Designs (G-16329)*
Dun Mor Embroidery & Designs 248 577-1155
360 E Maple Rd Ste O Troy (48083) *(G-16329)*
Dun-Rite Machine Co 616 688-5266
4526 Adams St Zeeland (49464) *(G-18132)*
Duna USA Inc 231 425-4300
5900 6th St Ludington (49431) *(G-10058)*
Dundee Castings Company 734 529-2455
500 Ypsilanti St Dundee (48131) *(G-4579)*
Dundee Manufacturing Co Inc 734 529-2540
107 Fairchild Dr Dundee (48131) *(G-4580)*
Dundee Plant, Dundee *Also called Holcim (us) Inc (G-4588)*
Dundee Products Company 734 529-2441
14490 Stowell Rd Dundee (48131) *(G-4581)*
Dunhams Athleisure Corporation 248 658-1382
32101 John R Rd Madison Heights (48071) *(G-10235)*
Dunkin Donuts & Baskin-Robbins 989 835-8412
5000 Foxcroft Dr Midland (48642) *(G-10856)*
Dunkley International Inc 269 343-5583
1910 Lake St Kalamazoo (49001) *(G-8732)*
Dunn Beverage Intl LLC 269 420-1547
95 Minges Rd N Battle Creek (49015) *(G-1176)*
Dunn Paper Inc (HQ) 810 984-5521
218 Riverview St Port Huron (48060) *(G-12913)*
Dunn Paper Holdings Inc (PA) 810 984-5521
218 Riverview St Port Huron (48060) *(G-12914)*
Dunnage Engineering Inc (PA) 810 229-9501
721 Advance St Brighton (48116) *(G-1913)*
Dunne-Rite Performance Inc 616 828-0908
26063 Newport Ave Warren (48089) *(G-17007)*
Dunns Welding Inc 248 356-3866
22930 Lahser Rd Southfield (48033) *(G-14887)*
Duo Robotic Solutions Inc 586 883-7559
36715 Metro Ct Sterling Heights (48312) *(G-15322)*
Duo Security Inc (HQ) 734 330-2673
123 N Ashley St Ste 200 Ann Arbor (48104) *(G-427)*
Duo-Form Acquisition Corp 269 663-8525
69836 Kraus Rd Edwardsburg (49112) *(G-4765)*
Duo-Form Plastics, Edwardsburg *Also called Duo-Form Acquisition Corp (G-4765)*
Duo-Gard Industries Inc 734 207-9700
40442 Koppernick Rd Canton (48187) *(G-2367)*
Dupearl Technology LLC 248 390-9609
120 Hadsell Dr Bloomfield Hills (48302) *(G-1762)*
Duperon Corporation 800 383-8479
1200 Leon Scott Ct Saginaw (48601) *(G-14030)*
Duplicast Corporation 586 756-5900
24583 Gibson Dr Warren (48089) *(G-17008)*
Dupont Performance Materials, Auburn Hills *Also called E I Du Pont De Nemours & Co (G-849)*
Duquaine Incorporated 906 228-7290
1744 Presque Isle Ave Marquette (49855) *(G-10527)*
Dura Auto Systems Cble Oprtons 248 299-7500
1780 Pond Run Auburn Hills (48326) *(G-844)*
Dura Automotive - Global Fwdg, Auburn Hills *Also called Global Automotive Systems LLC (G-889)*
Dura Automotive Systems, Auburn Hills *Also called Dura Operating LLC (G-846)*
Dura Automotive Systems, Fremont *Also called Dura Operating LLC (G-5770)*
Dura Automotive Systems LLC (HQ) 248 299-7500
1780 Pond Run Auburn Hills (48326) *(G-845)*
Dura Brake Systems LLC 248 299-7500
2791 Research Dr Rochester Hills (48309) *(G-13410)*
Dura Cables North LLC 248 299-7500
2791 Research Dr Rochester Hills (48309) *(G-13411)*
Dura Cables South LLC 248 299-7500
2791 Research Dr Rochester Hills (48309) *(G-13412)*
Dura Global Technologies Inc 248 299-7500
2791 Research Dr Rochester Hills (48309) *(G-13413)*
Dura Hog Inc 586 825-0066
33637 Sterling Ponds Blvd Sterling Heights (48312) *(G-15323)*
Dura Mold Inc 269 465-3301
3390 W Linco Rd Stevensville (49127) *(G-15565)*
Dura Operating LLC (HQ) 248 299-7500
1780 Pond Run Auburn Hills (48326) *(G-846)*
Dura Operating LLC 231 924-0930
502 Connie Ave Fremont (49412) *(G-5770)*
Dura Pack, Taylor *Also called Dura-Pack Inc (G-15711)*

Dura Shifter LLC 248 299-7500
2791 Research Dr Rochester Hills (48309) ***(G-13414)***
Dura Sill Corporation 248 348-2490
22500 Heslip Dr Novi (48375) ***(G-11873)***
Dura Thread Gage Inc 248 545-2890
971 E 10 Mile Rd Madison Heights (48071) ***(G-10236)***
Dura-Kentwood, Auburn Hills *Also called Dura Auto Systems Cble Oprtons* ***(G-844)***
Dura-Pack Inc 313 299-9600
7641 Holland Rd Taylor (48180) ***(G-15711)***
Durakon Industries Inc (HQ) 608 742-5301
2101 N Lapeer Rd Lapeer (48446) ***(G-9457)***
Duramic Abrasive Products Inc 586 755-7220
24135 Gibson Dr Warren (48089) ***(G-17009)***
Durant and Sons Inc 248 548-8646
21850 Wyoming Pl Oak Park (48237) ***(G-12061)***
Duratran Company, The, Spring Lake *Also called New Rules Marketing Inc* ***(G-15166)***
Durez Corporation (HQ) 248 313-7000
46820 Magellan Dr Ste C Novi (48377) ***(G-11874)***
Duro-Last Inc (PA) 800 248-0280
525 E Morley Dr Saginaw (48601) ***(G-14031)***
Duro-Last Inc 800 248-0280
525 W Morley Dr Saginaw (48601) ***(G-14032)***
Duro-Last Inc 800 248-0280
525 W Morley Dr Saginaw (48601) ***(G-14033)***
Duro-Last Roofing, Saginaw *Also called Duro-Last Inc* ***(G-14031)***
Durr Inc (HQ) 734 459-6800
26801 Northwestern Hwy Southfield (48033) ***(G-14888)***
Durr Systems Inc (HQ) 248 450-2000
26801 Northwestern Hwy Southfield (48033) ***(G-14889)***
Durr Systems Inc 248 745-8500
26801 Northwestern Hwy Southfield (48033) ***(G-14890)***
Durr Systems Inc 586 755-7500
12755 E 9 Mile Rd Warren (48089) ***(G-17010)***
Durr Systems Fap, Warren *Also called Durr Systems Inc* ***(G-17010)***
Dusevoir Acquisitions LLC 313 562-5550
1609 White Blossom Ln Howell (48843) ***(G-8036)***
Dusevoir Metal Products, Howell *Also called Dusevoir Acquisitions LLC* ***(G-8036)***
Dust Control & Loading Systems, Charlevoix *Also called Dcl Inc* ***(G-2613)***
Dutchman Mfg Co LLC 734 922-5803
6185 E Traverse Hwy Ste B Traverse City (49684) ***(G-15959)***
Dutchmans Welding & Repair 989 584-6861
6161 County Line Rd Carson City (48811) ***(G-2488)***
Dvs Technology America Inc 734 656-2080
44099 Plymouth Oaks Blvd Plymouth (48170) ***(G-12614)***
Dw Aluminum LLC 269 445-5601
201 N Edwards St Cassopolis (49031) ***(G-2528)***
Dw-National Standard-Niles LLC 269 683-8100
1631 Lake St Niles (49120) ***(G-11610)***
Dwm Holdings Inc 586 541-0013
24874 Groesbeck Hwy Warren (48089) ***(G-17011)***
Dyer Corporation 231 894-4282
6200 W Old Channel Trl Montague (49437) ***(G-11090)***
Dyers Sawmill Inc 231 768-4438
17688 15 Mile Rd Leroy (49655) ***(G-9531)***
Dyna Plate Inc 616 452-6763
344 Mart St Sw Grand Rapids (49548) ***(G-6363)***
Dyna Sales & Service LLC 231 734-4433
8440 State Rd Millington (48746) ***(G-10994)***
Dyna Tech 248 358-3962
27050 W 8 Mile Rd Southfield (48033) ***(G-14891)***
Dyna- Bignell Products LLC 989 418-5050
201 W 3rd St Clare (48617) ***(G-2868)***
Dyna-Con, Norton Shores *Also called Dynamic Conveyor Corporation* ***(G-11748)***
Dynaflex, Romulus *Also called Cartex Corporation* ***(G-13660)***
Dynamic Auto Test Engineering 269 342-1334
1017 W Kilgore Rd Portage (49024) ***(G-12991)***
Dynamic Color Publications 248 553-3115
32905 W 12 Mile Rd # 210 Farmington Hills (48334) ***(G-4976)***
Dynamic Conveyor Corporation 231 798-0014
5980 Grand Haven Rd Norton Shores (49441) ***(G-11748)***
Dynamic Corporation 248 338-1100
2193 Executive Hills Dr Auburn Hills (48326) ***(G-847)***
Dynamic Corporation (PA) 616 399-9391
2565 Van Ommen Dr Holland (49424) ***(G-7613)***
Dynamic Custom Machining LLC 231 853-8648
12745 Neil Rd Ravenna (49451) ***(G-13119)***
Dynamic Development Inc 231 723-8318
314 W Parkdale Ave Manistee (49660) ***(G-10419)***
Dynamic Energy Tech LLC 248 212-5904
22181 Morton St Oak Park (48237) ***(G-12062)***
Dynamic Finishing LLC 231 727-8811
823 W Western Ave Ste B Muskegon (49441) ***(G-11308)***
Dynamic Finishing LLC (PA) 231 737-8130
69 S 2nd Ave Fruitport (49415) ***(G-5792)***
Dynamic Jig Grinding Corp 248 589-3110
985 Troy Ct Troy (48083) ***(G-16330)***
Dynamic Manufacturing LLC 989 644-8109
5059 W Weidman Rd Weidman (48893) ***(G-17456)***
Dynamic Metal Treating, Canton *Also called Morning Star Land Company LLC* ***(G-2408)***
Dynamic Metrology Services, Holland *Also called Dynamic Corporation* ***(G-7613)***
Dynamic Mtal Treating Intl Inc 734 459-8022
7784 Ronda Dr Canton (48187) ***(G-2368)***
Dynamic Plastics Inc 586 749-6100
29831 Commerce Blvd Chesterfield (48051) ***(G-2768)***
Dynamic Precision Tool & Mfg, Troy *Also called Dynamic Jig Grinding Corp* ***(G-16330)***
Dynamic Prototype Operations, Auburn Hills *Also called Dynamic Corporation* ***(G-847)***
Dynamic Robotic Solutions Inc 248 829-2800
1255 Harmon Rd Auburn Hills (48326) ***(G-848)***
Dynamic Software Group LLC 734 716-0925
33006 7 Mile Rd Livonia (48152) ***(G-9716)***
Dynamic Staffing Solutions (PA) 616 399-5220
2565 Van Ommen Dr Holland (49424) ***(G-7614)***
Dynamic Supply Solutions Inc 248 987-2205
56 Sunningdale Dr Grosse Pointe Shores (48236) ***(G-7198)***
Dynamic Surface Technologies, Canton *Also called Dynamic Mtal Treating Intl Inc* ***(G-2368)***
Dynamlc Wood Products Inc 616 897-8114
9385 Potters Rd Saranac (48881) ***(G-14454)***
Dynamic Wood Solutions 616 935-7727
18518 Trimble Ct Spring Lake (49456) ***(G-15139)***
Dynamite Machining Inc 586 247-8230
51149 Filomena Dr Shelby Township (48315) ***(G-14583)***
Dynapath Systems Inc., Livonia *Also called Hal International Inc* ***(G-9763)***
Dynas Products, Millington *Also called Dyna Sales & Service LLC* ***(G-10994)***
Dynatrace LLC 313 227-7300
2000 Brush St Ste 501 Detroit (48226) ***(G-4022)***
Dynetics Inc 248 619-1681
1100 Owendale Dr Troy (48083) ***(G-16331)***
Dynics Inc 734 677-6100
620 Technology Dr Ann Arbor (48108) ***(G-428)***
Dyno Nobel Inc 906 486-4473
9045 County Road 476 Ishpeming (49849) ***(G-8344)***
Dyno Nobel Midwest, Ishpeming *Also called Dyno Nobel Inc* ***(G-8344)***
Dytron Corporation 586 296-9600
17000 Masonic Fraser (48026) ***(G-5645)***
Dzanc Books Inc 734 756-5701
2702 Lillian Rd Ann Arbor (48104) ***(G-429)***
E & B Machine Co, Otsego *Also called Vanmeer Corporation* ***(G-12258)***
E & C Manufacturing LLC 248 330-0400
2125 Butterfield Dr # 200 Troy (48084) ***(G-16332)***
E & D Engineering Systems LLC 989 246-0770
890 Industrial Dr Gladwin (48624) ***(G-5929)***
E & D Machine Company Inc 248 473-0255
32777 Chesley Dr Farmington (48336) ***(G-4898)***
E & E Manufacturing Co Inc (PA) 734 451-7600
300 400 Indus Drv Plymuth Plymouth (48170) ***(G-12615)***
E & E Manufacturing Co Inc 734 451-7600
200 Industrial Dr Plymouth (48170) ***(G-12616)***
E & E Manufacturing Co Inc 248 616-1300
701 S Main St Clawson (48017) ***(G-2977)***
E & E Special Products LLC 586 978-3377
7200 Miller Dr Warren (48092) ***(G-17012)***
E & M Cores Inc 989 386-9223
9805 S Athey Ave Clare (48617) ***(G-2869)***
E & R Bindery Service Inc 734 464-7954
37477 Schoolcraft Rd Livonia (48150) ***(G-9717)***
E & S Graphics Inc 989 875-2828
300 Industrial Pkwy Ithaca (48847) ***(G-8359)***
E & S Sheet Metal 989 871-2067
9450 Belsay Rd Millington (48746) ***(G-10995)***
E & W Cabinet & Counter 734 895-7497
8925 Hannan Rd Romulus (48174) ***(G-13668)***
E A S I, Milford *Also called Electronic Apps Speclsts Inc* ***(G-10963)***
E A Wood Inc (PA) 989 739-9118
6718 Loud Dr Oscoda (48750) ***(G-12208)***
E and J Advertising LLC 586 977-3500
32806 Ryan Rd Warren (48092) ***(G-17013)***
E and M Cores, Clare *Also called E & M Cores Inc* ***(G-2869)***
E and P Form Tool Company Inc 734 261-3530
31759 Block St Ste A Garden City (48135) ***(G-5823)***
E B Eddy Paper Inc 810 982-0191
1700 Washington Ave Port Huron (48060) ***(G-12915)***
E B I Inc 810 227-8180
10454 Grand River Rd Brighton (48116) ***(G-1914)***
E C Moore Company (PA) 313 581-7878
13325 Leonard St Dearborn (48126) ***(G-3696)***
E C Moore Company 313 581-7878
13249 Leonard St Dearborn (48126) ***(G-3697)***
E C S, Washington *Also called Engineered Control Systems Inc* ***(G-17303)***
E Coat Division, Grand Haven *Also called Seaver Finishing Inc* ***(G-6073)***
E D C O Publishing Inc 248 690-9184
990 S Baldwin Rd Clarkston (48348) ***(G-2917)***
E D M Cut-Rite Inc 586 566-0100
51445 Oro Dr Shelby Township (48315) ***(G-14584)***
E D M Shuttle Inc 586 468-9880
44695 Enterprise Dr Clinton Township (48038) ***(G-3106)***
E D M Specialties Inc 248 344-4080
26111 Lannys Rd Novi (48375) ***(G-11875)***

E D P Technical Services Inc ... 734 591-9176
36704 Commerce St Livonia (48150) *(G-9718)*
E F D, Madison Heights *Also called Efd Induction Inc (G-10240)*
E H Inc ... 269 673-6456
2870 116th Ave Allegan (49010) *(G-159)*
E H Tulgestka & Sons Inc ... 989 734-2129
1160 Hwy F 21 S Rogers City (49779) *(G-13615)*
E I Du Pont De Nemours & Co ... 248 549-4794
1412 W Windemere Ave Royal Oak (48073) *(G-13920)*
E I Du Pont De Nemours & Co ... 302 999-6566
1250 Harmon Rd Auburn Hills (48326) *(G-849)*
E I Du Pont De Nemours & Co ... 586 263-0258
15350 Renshaw Dr Clinton Township (48038) *(G-3107)*
E J I W, Oak Park *Also called Ej Usa Inc (G-12065)*
E J M Ball Screw LLC ... 989 893-7674
209 Morton St Bay City (48706) *(G-1307)*
E K Hydraulics Inc ... 800 632-7112
1458 Tracy Ln Petoskey (49770) *(G-12448)*
E L Nickell Co ... 269 435-2475
385 Centreville St Constantine (49042) *(G-3534)*
E Leet Woodworking ... 269 664-5203
10175 3 Mile Rd Plainwell (49080) *(G-12524)*
E M I Construction Products ... 616 392-7207
526 E 64th St Holland (49423) *(G-7615)*
E M P, Escanaba *Also called Engineered Machined Pdts Inc (G-4826)*
E M P Manufacturing Corp ... 586 949-8277
28190 23 Mile Rd Chesterfield (48051) *(G-2769)*
E P I, Clinton Township *Also called Electroplating Industries Inc (G-3109)*
E Power Remote Ltd ... 231 689-5448
223 N Webster St White Cloud (49349) *(G-17621)*
E Q R 2 Inc ... 586 731-3383
44479 Phoenix Dr Sterling Heights (48314) *(G-15324)*
E R Tool Company Inc ... 586 757-1159
3720 E 10 Mile Rd Ste A Warren (48091) *(G-17014)*
E S I Industries ... 231 256-9345
10 S Highland Dr Lake Leelanau (49653) *(G-9102)*
E T A, Troy *Also called Engineering Tech Assoc Inc (G-16346)*
E U P Woods Shavings ... 906 495-1141
16816 S Hugginin St Kincheloe (49788) *(G-9050)*
E X P Screen Printers ... 586 772-6660
18228 E 9 Mile Rd Eastpointe (48021) *(G-4700)*
E Z Logic Data Systems Inc ... 248 817-8800
31455 Northwestern Hwy Farmington Hills (48334) *(G-4977)*
E Z Tool Inc ... 269 429-0070
4796 Roosevelt Rd Stevensville (49127) *(G-15566)*
E-Con LLC ... 248 766-9000
320 Martin St Ste 60 Birmingham (48009) *(G-1682)*
E-Course Machinery, Detroit *Also called Ivan Doverspike (G-4153)*
E-Light LLC ... 734 427-0600
3144 Martin Rd Commerce Township (48390) *(G-3402)*
E-Procurement Services LLC ... 248 630-7200
691 N Squirrel Rd Ste 220 Auburn Hills (48326) *(G-850)*
E-T-M Enterprises I Inc (PA) ... 517 627-8461
920 N Clinton St Grand Ledge (48837) *(G-6105)*
E-Z Burr Tool, Livonia *Also called Cogsdill Tool Products Inc (G-9685)*
E-Zee Set Wood Products Inc ... 248 398-0090
21650 Coolidge Hwy Oak Park (48237) *(G-12063)*
E.a Graphics, Sterling Heights *Also called Ethnic Artwork Inc (G-15333)*
E3 Diagnostics Inc ... 734 981-3655
5918 N Lilley Rd Ste 3 Canton (48187) *(G-2369)*
E3 Gordon Stowe, Canton *Also called E3 Diagnostics Inc (G-2369)*
Eab Fabrication Inc ... 517 639-7080
64 Cole St Quincy (49082) *(G-13094)*
Eager Beaver Clean & Store ... 231 448-2476
27220 Barneys Lake Rd N Beaver Island (49782) *(G-1381)*
Eagile Incorporated ... 616 243-1200
1880 Turner Ave Nw Ste A Grand Rapids (49504) *(G-6364)*
Eagle Aluminum Cast Pdts Inc ... 231 788-4884
664 W Clay Ave Muskegon (49440) *(G-11309)*
Eagle Assemblies Inc ... 586 296-4836
33275 Groesbeck Hwy Fraser (48026) *(G-5646)*
Eagle Buckets Inc ... 517 787-0385
703 S Cooper St Jackson (49203) *(G-8436)*
Eagle Cnc Technology, Muskegon *Also called Eagle T M C Technologies (G-11311)*
Eagle Creek Mfg & Sales ... 989 643-7521
6753 S Steel Rd Saint Charles (48655) *(G-14192)*
Eagle Design & Technology Inc ... 616 748-1022
55 E Roosevelt Ave Zeeland (49464) *(G-18133)*
Eagle Engineering & Supply Co ... 989 356-4526
101 N Industrial Hwy Alpena (49707) *(G-286)*
Eagle Fasteners Inc ... 248 577-1441
185 Park Dr Troy (48083) *(G-16333)*
Eagle Graphics and Design ... 248 618-0000
2040 Airport Rd Waterford (48327) *(G-17340)*
Eagle Group II Ltd ... 616 754-7777
8384 Peck Rd Greenville (48838) *(G-7129)*
Eagle Indus Group Federal LLC ... 616 863-8623
555 Plymouth Ave Ne Grand Rapids (49505) *(G-6365)*
Eagle Industrial Group Inc ... 616 647-9904
847 W River Center Dr Ne Comstock Park (49321) *(G-3481)*
Eagle Industries Inc (PA) ... 248 624-4266
30926 Century Dr Wixom (48393) *(G-17797)*
Eagle Machine Products Company ... 586 268-2460
35440 Stanley Dr Sterling Heights (48312) *(G-15325)*
Eagle Machine Tool Corporation ... 231 798-8473
6060 Grand Haven Rd Norton Shores (49441) *(G-11749)*
Eagle Manufacturing Corp ... 586 323-0303
52113 Shelby Pkwy Shelby Township (48315) *(G-14585)*
Eagle Marble & Granite ... 586 421-1912
49763 Leona Dr Chesterfield (48051) *(G-2770)*
Eagle Masking Fabrication Inc ... 586 992-3080
6633 Diplomat Dr Sterling Heights (48314) *(G-15326)*
Eagle Mine LLC ... 906 339-7000
4547 County Road 601 Champion (49814) *(G-2602)*
Eagle Powder Coating ... 517 784-2556
2218 E High St Ste C Jackson (49203) *(G-8437)*
Eagle Precision Cast Parts Inc ... 231 788-3318
5112 Evanston Ave Muskegon (49442) *(G-11310)*
Eagle Press Repairs & Ser ... 419 539-7206
2025 E Gier Rd Adrian (49221) *(G-60)*
Eagle Quest International Ltd ... 616 850-2630
5797 Harvey St Ste D Norton Shores (49444) *(G-11750)*
Eagle Ridge Paper Ltd ... 248 376-9503
15355 Oakwood Dr Romulus (48174) *(G-13669)*
Eagle T M C Technologies ... 231 766-3914
2357 Whitehall Rd Muskegon (49445) *(G-11311)*
EAGLE TECHNOLOGIES GROUP, Bridgman *Also called Hanson Systems LLC (G-1866)*
Eagle Thread Verifier LLC ... 586 764-8218
40631 Firesteel Dr Sterling Heights (48313) *(G-15327)*
Eagle Tool, Iron Mountain *Also called Laydon Enterprises Inc (G-8288)*
Eagle Tool Group LLC ... 586 997-0800
42724 Mound Rd Sterling Heights (48314) *(G-15328)*
Eagle Welding LLC ... 810 750-0772
11413 Nora Dr Fenton (48430) *(G-5201)*
Eagleburgmann Industries LP ... 989 486-1571
1821 Austin St Midland (48642) *(G-10857)*
Eaglematic, Shelby Township *Also called Eagle Manufacturing Corp (G-14585)*
Earbyte Inc ... 734 418-8661
19785 W 12 Mile Rd 61 Southfield (48076) *(G-14892)*
Earl Daup Signs ... 810 767-2020
6060 Birch Rd Flint (48507) *(G-5420)*
Earl St John Forest Products ... 906 497-5667
N16226 Birch St Spalding (49886) *(G-15086)*
Earle Press Inc ... 231 773-2111
2140 Latimer Dr Muskegon (49442) *(G-11312)*
Earle Press Printing, Muskegon *Also called Earle Press Inc (G-11312)*
Earthbound Inc ... 616 774-0096
1116 Plnfeld Ave Ne Ste 2 Grand Rapids (49503) *(G-6366)*
Earthtronics Inc ... 231 332-1188
800 E Ellis Rd Ste 574 Norton Shores (49441) *(G-11751)*
Earthworm Cstngs Unlimited LLC ... 248 882-3329
1179 Sylvertis Dr Waterford (48328) *(G-17341)*
Easco-Sparcatron, Mount Clemens *Also called Liquid Drive Corporation (G-11139)*
Easi LLC ... 248 712-2750
340 E Big Beaver Rd Troy (48083) *(G-16334)*
East - Lind Heat Treat Inc ... 248 585-1415
32045 Dequindre Rd Madison Heights (48071) *(G-10237)*
East Branch Forest Products ... 906 852-3315
5160 E Hwy 28 Kenton (49967) *(G-8995)*
East Central Machine Inc ... 313 579-2315
5718 Saint Jean St Detroit (48213) *(G-4023)*
East End Sports Awards Inc ... 906 293-8895
13367 State Highway M123 Newberry (49868) *(G-11579)*
East Jordan Sandblasting, East Jordan *Also called Northwest Fabrication Inc (G-4641)*
East Kingsford Iron & Metal Co, Iron Mountain *Also called Schneider Iron & Metal Inc (G-8299)*
East Michigan Lumber, Sterling *Also called Maple Ridge Hardwoods Inc (G-15244)*
East Muskegon Roofg Shtmtl Co (PA) ... 231 744-2461
1665 Holton Rd Muskegon (49445) *(G-11313)*
East Muskegon Roofg Shtmtl Co ... 616 791-6900
2458 Waldorf Ct Nw Grand Rapids (49544) *(G-6367)*
East Penn Manufacturing Co ... 586 979-5300
6023 Progress Dr Sterling Heights (48312) *(G-15329)*
East River Machine & Tool Inc ... 231 767-1701
1701 Wierengo Dr Muskegon (49442) *(G-11314)*
East Side Gear, Warren *Also called Bauer Precision Tool Co (G-16953)*
East Side Locksmith, Mount Clemens *Also called Weber Security Group Inc (G-11153)*
Eastern Echo School Newspaper, Ypsilanti *Also called Eastern Michigan University (G-18068)*
Eastern Graphics & Printing, Troy *Also called S & N Aziza Inc (G-16586)*
Eastern Market Brewing, Detroit *Also called 5 Mile Brewing Company LLC (G-3825)*
Eastern Michigan Industries ... 586 757-4140
23850 Ryan Rd Warren (48091) *(G-17015)*
Eastern Michigan University ... 734 487-1010
18b Goddard Hall Ypsilanti (48197) *(G-18068)*

A L P H A B E T I C

Eastern Oil Company (PA)....248 333-1333
590 S Paddock St Pontiac (48341) ***(G-12819)***
Eastern Power and Lighting....248 739-0908
5758 Hubbell St Dearborn Heights (48127) ***(G-3783)***
Eastman Chemical Company....734 672-7823
5100 W Jefferson Ave Trenton (48183) ***(G-16153)***
Eastpointe Lube Express....586 775-3234
17375 E 8 Mile Rd Eastpointe (48021) ***(G-4701)***
Eastport Group Inc....989 732-0030
9301 M 32 E Johannesburg (49751) ***(G-8649)***
Eastside Pharmacy Inc....313 579-1755
4673 Conner St Detroit (48215) ***(G-4024)***
Eastside Spot Inc....906 226-9431
129 E Hewitt Ave Marquette (49855) ***(G-10528)***
Easy Printing Center, Saginaw *Also called Tsunami Inc* ***(G-14168)***
Easy Scrub LLC....586 565-1777
16629 Bettmar St Roseville (48066) ***(G-13798)***
Eaton Aerospace LLC....517 787-8121
300 S East Ave Jackson (49203) ***(G-8438)***
Eaton Aerospace LLC....616 949-1090
3675 Patterson Ave Se Grand Rapids (49512) ***(G-6368)***
Eaton Corporation....269 781-0200
19218 B Dr S Marshall (49068) ***(G-10566)***
Eaton Corporation....248 226-6347
26201 Northwestern Hwy Southfield (48076) ***(G-14893)***
Eaton Corporation....586 228-2029
19700 Hall Rd Ste B Clinton Township (48038) ***(G-3108)***
Eaton Corporation....269 342-3000
13100 E Michigan Ave Galesburg (49053) ***(G-5809)***
Eaton Corporation....517 787-7220
2425 W Michigan Ave Jackson (49202) ***(G-8439)***
Eaton Corporation....517 787-8121
4743 Venture Dr Ann Arbor (48108) ***(G-430)***
Eaton Corporation....269 342-3000
13100 E Michigan Ave Galesburg (49053) ***(G-5810)***
Eaton Corporation....248 226-6200
26101 Northwestern Hwy Southfield (48076) ***(G-14894)***
Eaton Detroit Spring Svc Co....313 963-3839
1555 Michigan Ave Detroit (48216) ***(G-4025)***
Eaton Fuller Reman Center, Galesburg *Also called Eaton Corporation* ***(G-5810)***
Eaton Industries Inc (PA)....734 428-0000
254 S Wagner Rd Ann Arbor (48103) ***(G-431)***
Eaton Inoac Company (HQ)....248 226-6200
26101 Northwestern Hwy Southfield (48076) ***(G-14895)***
Eaton Steel Bar Company, Oak Park *Also called Eaton Steel Corporation* ***(G-12064)***
Eaton Steel Corporation (PA)....248 398-3434
10221 Capital St Oak Park (48237) ***(G-12064)***
Eaton Steel Corporation....248 398-3434
38901 Amrhein Rd Livonia (48150) ***(G-9719)***
Eaton-Aeroquip Llc....949 452-9575
300 S East Ave Jackson (49203) ***(G-8440)***
Eb Enterprises LLC....231 768-5072
17747 Leroy Rd Leroy (49655) ***(G-9532)***
Ebels Hardware Inc....231 826-3334
490 E Prosper Rd Falmouth (49632) ***(G-4892)***
Eberbach Corporation....734 665-8877
5900 Schooner St Belleville (48111) ***(G-1444)***
Eberhard and Father Signworks....989 892-5566
108 Woodside Ave Essexville (48732) ***(G-4872)***
Eberspaecher North America Inc....248 778-5231
43700 Gen Mar Novi (48375) ***(G-11876)***
Eberspaecher North America Inc (HQ)....248 994-7010
29101 Haggerty Rd Novi (48377) ***(G-11877)***
Eberspaecher North America Inc....810 225-4582
2035 Orndorf Dr Brighton (48116) ***(G-1915)***
Eberspaecher North America Inc....517 303-1775
30220 Oak Creek Dr Wixom (48393) ***(G-17798)***
Eberspecher Contrls N Amer Inc....248 994-7010
2035 Charles Orndorf Dr Brighton (48116) ***(G-1916)***
Ebinger Manufacturing Company....248 486-8880
7869 Kensington Rd Brighton (48116) ***(G-1917)***
Ebonex Corporation (PA)....313 388-0063
18400 Rialto St Melvindale (48122) ***(G-10697)***
Ebw Electronics Inc....616 786-0575
13110 Ransom St Holland (49424) ***(G-7616)***
Ebwe, Holland *Also called Ebw Electronics Inc* ***(G-7616)***
Eca Educational Services Div, Commerce Township *Also called Eca Educational Services Inc* ***(G-3403)***
Eca Educational Services Inc....248 669-7170
1981 Dallavo Dr Commerce Township (48390) ***(G-3403)***
Ecco Tool Co Inc....248 349-0840
42525 W 11 Mile Rd Novi (48375) ***(G-11878)***
Echo Engrg & Prod Sups Inc....734 241-9622
725 Ternes Dr Monroe (48162) ***(G-11029)***
Echo Etching, Grand Rapids *Also called Grand River Interiors Inc* ***(G-6468)***
Echo Quality Grinding Inc....231 544-6637
3166 Muckle Rd Central Lake (49622) ***(G-2591)***
Echopix, Pleasant Lake *Also called Selfies 2 Helpease Inc* ***(G-12554)***
Eci, Grand Haven *Also called Electrical Concepts Inc* ***(G-6013)***
ECJ Processing....248 540-2336
17379 Park Ln Southfield (48076) ***(G-14896)***
Eckhart USA, Clay *Also called Auto Craft Tool & Die Co* ***(G-2994)***
Eclectic Metal Arts LLC....248 251-5924
20225 Livernois Ave Detroit (48221) ***(G-4026)***
Eclipse Mold Incorporated....586 792-3320
50320 Patricia St Chesterfield (48051) ***(G-2771)***
Eclipse Print Emporium Inc....248 477-8337
32753 8 Mile Rd Livonia (48152) ***(G-9720)***
Eclipse Tanning, Brighton *Also called Horn Corp* ***(G-1940)***
Eclipse Tanning, Troy *Also called Horn Corporation* ***(G-16402)***
Eclipse Tool & Die Inc....616 877-3717
4713 Circuit Ct Ste A Wayland (49348) ***(G-17405)***
ECM Manufacturing Inc....810 736-0299
4301 Western Rd Flint (48506) ***(G-5421)***
ECM Specialties Inc....810 736-0299
4301 Western Rd Flint (48506) ***(G-5422)***
Eco - Composites LLC....616 395-8902
845 Allen Dr Holland (49423) ***(G-7617)***
Eco Bio Plastics Midland Inc....989 496-1934
4037 S Saginaw Rd Midland (48640) ***(G-10858)***
Eco Brushes and Fibers....231 683-9202
2658 Heights Ravenna Rd Muskegon (49444) ***(G-11315)***
Eco Brushes and Fibers S.A.s, Muskegon *Also called Eco Brushes and Fibers* ***(G-11315)***
Eco Paper....248 652-3601
1150 W Hamlin Rd Rochester Hills (48309) ***(G-13415)***
Eco Sign Solutions LLC....734 276-8585
37 Enterprise Dr Ann Arbor (48103) ***(G-432)***
Eco Smart Coatings LLC....574 370-5708
67178 Lamb Rd Cassopolis (49031) ***(G-2529)***
Ecoclean Inc (HQ)....248 450-2000
26801 Northwestern Hwy Southfield (48033) ***(G-14897)***
Ecogranite LLC....248 820-9196
20495 Melvin St Livonia (48152) ***(G-9721)***
Ecolab Inc....248 697-0202
28550 Cabot Dr Ste 100 Novi (48377) ***(G-11879)***
Ecolo-Tech Inc....248 541-1100
1743 E 10 Mile Rd Madison Heights (48071) ***(G-10238)***
Ecology Coatings....248 723-2223
35980 Woodward Ave # 200 Bloomfield (48304) ***(G-1733)***
Econ Global Services, Birmingham *Also called E-Con LLC* ***(G-1682)***
Econ-O-Line Abrasive Products....616 846-4150
401 N Griffin St Grand Haven (49417) ***(G-6011)***
Econaway Abrasive Co, Grand Haven *Also called Stewart Reed Inc* ***(G-6086)***
Econo Print Inc....734 878-5806
10312 Dexter Pinckney Rd Pinckney (48169) ***(G-12496)***
Econoline Abrasive Products, Grand Haven *Also called Depottey Acquisition Inc* ***(G-6009)***
Economy Printing, Kalamazoo *Also called River Run Press Inc* ***(G-8873)***
Ecoprint Services LLC....616 254-8019
549 Ottawa Ave Nw Ste 103 Grand Rapids (49503) ***(G-6369)***
Ecorse McHy Sls & Rbldrs Inc....313 383-2100
4621 13th St Wyandotte (48192) ***(G-17956)***
Ecorse Precision Products, Wyandotte *Also called Ecorse McHy Sls & Rbldrs Inc* ***(G-17956)***
Ecorse Telegram Newspaper, River Rouge *Also called Telegram Newspaper* ***(G-13281)***
Ecostrat USA Inc....416 968-8884
201 W 13 Mile Rd Madison Heights (48071) ***(G-10239)***
Ecotrons LLC....248 891-6965
28287 Beck Rd Ste D5 Wixom (48393) ***(G-17799)***
Ecovia Renewables Inc....248 953-0594
600 Suth Wagner Rd Ste 15 Ann Arbor (48103) ***(G-433)***
Ecs Production, Howell *Also called Expert Cleaning Solutions Inc* ***(G-8039)***
Ed Cumings Inc....810 736-0130
2305 Branch Rd Flint (48506) ***(G-5423)***
Edco Media, Clarkston *Also called E D C O Publishing Inc* ***(G-2917)***
Eddies Quick Stop Inc....313 712-1818
5517 Middlesex St Dearborn (48126) ***(G-3698)***
Ede Co....586 756-7555
26969 Ryan Rd Warren (48091) ***(G-17016)***
Eden Foods Inc (PA)....517 456-7424
701 Tecumseh Rd Clinton (49236) ***(G-3019)***
Eden Foods Inc....313 921-2053
9104 Culver St Detroit (48213) ***(G-4027)***
Eden Organic Pasta Company, Detroit *Also called Eden Foods Inc* ***(G-4027)***
Edens Political....313 277-0700
360 Devonshire St Dearborn (48124) ***(G-3699)***
Edens Technologies LLC....517 304-1324
115 N Center St Ste 202 Northville (48167) ***(G-11689)***
Edgepark Medical Supplies, Wyoming *Also called Assuramed Inc* ***(G-17987)***
Edgewater Apartments....517 663-8123
223 N Main St Eaton Rapids (48827) ***(G-4722)***
Edgewater Automation LLC....269 983-1300
481 Renaissance Dr Saint Joseph (49085) ***(G-14308)***
Edgewell Personal Care Company....866 462-8669
12103 Delta St Taylor (48180) ***(G-15712)***
Edi Experts LLC....734 844-7016
700 Pinehurst Dr Canton (48188) ***(G-2370)***
Edia Technologies Inc....517 349-0322
1907 Penobscot Dr Okemos (48864) ***(G-12120)***

Edmar Manufacturing Inc 616 392-7218
526 E 64th St Holland (49423) ***(G-7618)***
Edmore Tool & Grinding Inc 989 427-3790
4255 E Hward Cy Edmore Rd Edmore (48829) ***(G-4750)***
Edon Controls Inc 248 280-0420
2891 Industrial Row Dr Troy (48084) ***(G-16335)***
EDP Company, Livonia *Also called Electronic Design & Packg Co* ***(G-9724)***
Edrich Products Inc 586 296-3350
33672 Doreka Fraser (48026) ***(G-5647)***
EDS Enterprises, Flint *Also called Earl Daup Signs* ***(G-5420)***
Edw C Levy Co (PA) 313 429-2200
9300 Dix Dearborn (48120) ***(G-3700)***
Edw C Levy Co 248 334-4302
2470 Auburn Rd Auburn Hills (48326) ***(G-851)***
Edw C Levy Co 248 349-8600
27575 Wixom Rd Novi (48374) ***(G-11880)***
Edw C Levy Co 313 843-7200
8800 Dix St Detroit (48209) ***(G-4028)***
Edw C Levy Co 248 634-0879
16255 Tindall Rd Davisburg (48350) ***(G-3631)***
Edward and Cole Inc 734 996-9074
5540 Tanglewood Dr Ann Arbor (48105) ***(G-434)***
Edward Brothers Malloy 734 665-6113
5949 Jackson Rd Ann Arbor (48103) ***(G-435)***
Edward D Jones & Co LP 616 583-0387
2465 Byron Station Dr Sw E Byron Center (49315) ***(G-2188)***
Edward E Yates 517 467-4961
8573 M 50 Onsted (49265) ***(G-12152)***
Edward G Hinkelman 707 778-1124
616 E Eighth St Ste 7 Traverse City (49686) ***(G-15960)***
Edward's Kitchen & Bath, Detroit *Also called Edwards Building & HM Sup Inc* ***(G-4029)***
Edwards Brothers Inc (HQ) 800 722-3231
5411 Jackson Rd Ann Arbor (48103) ***(G-436)***
Edwards Brothers Malloy, Ann Arbor *Also called Edwards Brothers Inc* ***(G-436)***
Edwards Brothers Malloy, Ann Arbor *Also called Malloy Incorporated* ***(G-542)***
Edwards Brothers Malloy Inc (PA) 734 665-6113
5411 Jackson Rd Ann Arbor (48103) ***(G-437)***
Edwards Building & HM Sup Inc 313 368-9120
30 E 8 Mile Rd Detroit (48203) ***(G-4029)***
Edwards Industrial Sales Inc 517 887-6100
5646 Commerce St Ste D Lansing (48911) ***(G-9363)***
Edwards Machine & Tool Co, Jackson *Also called Edwards Machining Inc* ***(G-8441)***
Edwards Machining Inc 517 782-2568
2335 Research Dr Jackson (49203) ***(G-8441)***
Edwards Outdoor Advertising, Baraga *Also called Edwards Outdoor Science* ***(G-1102)***
Edwards Outdoor Science 906 353-7375
419 N Superior Ave Baraga (49908) ***(G-1102)***
Edwards Sign & Screen Printing 989 725-2988
1585 S M 52 Owosso (48867) ***(G-12290)***
Ees Coke Battery, Detroit *Also called DTE Energy Resources Inc* ***(G-4020)***
Eesco Inc 517 265-5148
125 N Tecumseh St Adrian (49221) ***(G-61)***
Efd Induction Inc 248 658-0700
31511 Dequindre Rd Madison Heights (48071) ***(G-10240)***
Efesto LLC 734 913-0428
3400 Woodhill Cir Superior Township (48198) ***(G-15647)***
Effective Schools Products 517 349-8841
2199 Jolly Rd Ste 160 Okemos (48864) ***(G-12121)***
Efficiency Shoring and Supply, Mason *Also called Fw Shoring Company* ***(G-10639)***
Effizient LLC 616 935-3170
1500 S Beechtree St Grand Haven (49417) ***(G-6012)***
Efi Custom Injection Molding, Troy *Also called Eagle Fasteners Inc* ***(G-16333)***
Eflex Sytems, Rochester Hills *Also called Elite Engineering Inc* ***(G-13417)***
Eftec North America LLC (PA) 248 585-2200
20219 Northline Rd Taylor (48180) ***(G-15713)***
Egeler Industrial Services, Livonia *Also called Eis Inc* ***(G-9722)***
Egemin Automation Inc 616 393-0101
11818 James St Holland (49424) ***(G-7619)***
Egemin Group, Inc., Holland *Also called Egemin Automation Inc* ***(G-7619)***
Eggers Excavating LLC 989 695-5205
7832 Kochville Rd Ste 1 Freeland (48623) ***(G-5756)***
Egr Incorporated 248 848-1411
27280 Haggerty Rd C-18 Farmington Hills (48331) ***(G-4978)***
Egt Printing Solutions LLC 248 583-2500
32031 Townley St Madison Heights (48071) ***(G-10241)***
Ehc Inc (PA) 313 259-2266
200 Renaissance Ctr # 3150 Detroit (48243) ***(G-4030)***
Eidemller Prcsion McHining Inc 248 669-2660
4998 Mccarthy Dr Milford (48381) ***(G-10962)***
Eifel Mold & Engineering Inc 586 296-9640
31071 Fraser Dr Fraser (48026) ***(G-5648)***
Eiklae Products 734 671-0752
10286 Boucher Rd Grosse Ile (48138) ***(G-7172)***
Eileen Smeltzer 269 629-8056
8227 N 30th St Richland (49083) ***(G-13248)***
Eiler Brothers Inc 517 784-0970
2201 Brooklyn Rd Jackson (49203) ***(G-8442)***
Eimo Americas, Vicksburg *Also called Eimo Technologies Inc* ***(G-16834)***
Eimo Technologies Inc (HQ) 269 649-0545
14320 Portage Rd Vicksburg (49097) ***(G-16834)***
Eimo Technologies Inc 269 649-5031
14300 Portage Rd Vicksburg (49097) ***(G-16835)***
Eis Inc 734 266-6500
31478 Industrial Rd # 100 Livonia (48150) ***(G-9722)***
Eisele Connectors Inc 616 726-7714
99 Monroe Ave Nw Ste 200 Grand Rapids (49503) ***(G-6370)***
Eissmann Auto Port Huron LLC (HQ) 810 216-6300
2440 20th St Port Huron (48060) ***(G-12916)***
Eissmann Auto Port Huron LLC 248 829-4990
2655 Product Dr Rochester Hills (48309) ***(G-13416)***
Ej Americas LLC (HQ) 231 536-2261
301 Spring St East Jordan (49727) ***(G-4629)***
Ej Ardmore Inc 231 536-2261
301 Spring St East Jordan (49727) ***(G-4630)***
Ej Asia-Pacific Inc 231 536-2261
301 Spring St East Jordan (49727) ***(G-4631)***
Ej Co 231 536-4527
5000 Airport Rd East Jordan (49727) ***(G-4632)***
Ej Europe LLC (HQ) 231 536-2261
301 Spring St East Jordan (49727) ***(G-4633)***
Ej Group Inc (PA) 231 536-2261
301 Spring St East Jordan (49727) ***(G-4634)***
Ej Timber Producers Inc 231 544-9866
972 Toby Rd East Jordan (49727) ***(G-4635)***
Ej Usa Inc (HQ) 800 874-4100
301 Spring St East Jordan (49727) ***(G-4636)***
Ej Usa Inc 248 546-2004
13001 Northend Ave Oak Park (48237) ***(G-12065)***
Ej Usa Inc 616 538-2040
5075 Clyde Park Ave Sw Wyoming (49509) ***(G-17997)***
Ejs Engraving 616 534-8104
4450 Blackfoot Dr Sw Grandville (49418) ***(G-7029)***
Ejustice Solutions LLC 248 232-0509
3600 Green Ct Ste 780 Ann Arbor (48105) ***(G-438)***
Ejw Contract Inc 616 293-5181
7930 Forest Creek Ct Whitmore Lake (48189) ***(G-17696)***
Ekstrom Industries Inc 248 477-0040
43045 W 9 Mile Rd Novi (48375) ***(G-11881)***
El Acapulco Tamales, Burt *Also called Villanuevo Soledad* ***(G-2139)***
El Informador LLC 616 272-1092
2000 28th St Sw Ste 4 Wyoming (49519) ***(G-17998)***
El Milagro of Michigan 616 452-6625
1846 Clyde Park Ave Sw Grand Rapids (49509) ***(G-6371)***
El Paso LLC 231 587-0704
8616 Anr Storage Rd Ne Mancelona (49659) ***(G-10389)***
El Vocero Hispano Inc 616 246-6023
2818 Vineland Ave Se Grand Rapids (49508) ***(G-6372)***
Elan Designs Inc 248 682-3000
238 S Telegraph Rd Pontiac (48341) ***(G-12820)***
Elastizell Corporation America 734 426-6076
7900 2nd St Dexter (48130) ***(G-4490)***
Elba Inc 248 288-6098
1925 W Maple Rd Ste B Troy (48084) ***(G-16336)***
Elba Laboratories, Troy *Also called Elba Inc* ***(G-16336)***
Elco Enterprises Inc 517 782-8040
5750 Marathon Dr Ste B Jackson (49201) ***(G-8443)***
Elco Inc 586 778-6858
30660 Edison Dr Roseville (48066) ***(G-13799)***
Eldean Company 616 335-5843
2223 S Shore Dr Macatawa (49434) ***(G-10096)***
Eldean Shipyard & Yacht Sales, Macatawa *Also called Eldean Company* ***(G-10096)***
Eldean Yacht Basin Ltd (PA) 616 786-2205
1862 Ottawa Beach Rd Holland (49424) ***(G-7620)***
Eldec LLC 248 364-4750
3355 Bald Mountain Rd # 30 Auburn Hills (48326) ***(G-852)***
Elden Cylinder Testing Inc 734 946-6900
9465 Inkster Rd Taylor (48180) ***(G-15714)***
Elden Industries Corporation 734 946-6900
9465 Inkster Rd Taylor (48180) ***(G-15715)***
Elderberry Steam Engines 989 245-0652
5215 Pheasant Run Dr # 5 Saginaw (48638) ***(G-14034)***
Eldon Publishing LLC 810 648-5282
43 S Elk St Sandusky (48471) ***(G-14433)***
Eldor Automotive N Amer Inc 248 878-9193
100 W Big Beavr Rd # 200 Troy (48084) ***(G-16337)***
Electra Cable & Communication 586 754-3479
24846 Forterra Dr Warren (48089) ***(G-17017)***
Electra-Tec Inc 269 694-6652
567 W M 89 Hwy Otsego (49078) ***(G-12238)***
Electric Apparatus Company 248 682-7992
409 Roosevelt St Ste 100 Howell (48843) ***(G-8037)***
Electric Equipment Company 269 925-3266
401 Klock Rd Benton Harbor (49022) ***(G-1496)***
Electric Eye Cafe 734 369-6904
811 N Main St Ann Arbor (48104) ***(G-439)***
Electric Motor & Contg Co 313 871-3775
1133 W Baltimore St Detroit (48202) ***(G-4031)***

ALPHABETIC

Electric Motor Service — ALPHABETIC SECTION

Electric Motor Service 269 945-5113
  1569 S M 37 Hwy Hastings (49058) *(G-7408)*
Electric Motor Service Ctr Inc 616 532-6007
  3565 Viaduct St Sw Grandville (49418) *(G-7030)*
Electric Steam Generator, Buchanan *Also called Optimystic Enterprises Inc (G-2124)*
Electrical Concepts Inc 616 847-0293
  12999 Wilderness Trl Grand Haven (49417) *(G-6013)*
Electrical Design and Ctrl Co 248 743-2400
  2200 Stephenson Hwy Troy (48083) *(G-16338)*
Electrical Product Sales Inc 248 583-6100
  2611 Elliott Dr Troy (48083) *(G-16339)*
Electro ARC Manufacturing Co 734 483-4233
  2055 N Lima Center Rd A Dexter (48130) *(G-4491)*
Electro Chemical Finishing Co 616 531-0670
  2973 Dormax St Sw Grandville (49418) *(G-7031)*
Electro Chemical Finishing Co 616 531-1250
  379 44th St Sw Grand Rapids (49548) *(G-6373)*
Electro Chemical Finishing Co (PA) 616 531-0670
  2610 Remico St Sw Wyoming (49519) *(G-17999)*
Electro Chemical Finishing Co 616 249-7092
  2949 Remico St Sw Grandville (49418) *(G-7032)*
Electro Diamond Tools, Oxford *Also called Superior Abrasive Products (G-12374)*
Electro Optics Mfg Inc 734 283-3000
  4459 13th St Wyandotte (48192) *(G-17957)*
Electro Panel Inc 989 832-2110
  4501 Forestview Dr Midland (48642) *(G-10859)*
Electro Tech, Otsego *Also called Impert Industries Inc (G-12241)*
Electro-Heat, Allegan *Also called Ddr Heating Inc (G-155)*
Electro-Matic Company, Farmington Hills *Also called Electro-Matic Products Inc (G-4980)*
Electro-Matic Integrated Inc 248 478-1182
  23410 Industrial Park Ct Farmington Hills (48335) *(G-4979)*
Electro-Matic Products Inc (HQ) 248 478-1182
  23409 Industrial Park Ct Farmington Hills (48335) *(G-4980)*
Electro-Matic Ventures Inc (PA) 248 478-1182
  23409 Industrial Park Ct Farmington Hills (48335) *(G-4981)*
Electro-Matic Visual Inc 248 478-1182
  23409 Industrial Park Ct Farmington Hills (48335) *(G-4982)*
Electro-Matic, Inc., Farmington Hills *Also called Electro-Matic Ventures Inc (G-4981)*
Electro-Optics Technology Inc (PA) 231 935-4044
  3340 Parkland Ct Traverse City (49686) *(G-15961)*
Electro-Plating Service Inc 248 541-0035
  945 E 10 Mile Rd Madison Heights (48071) *(G-10242)*
Electro-Way Co 586 771-9450
  17505 Helro Fraser (48026) *(G-5649)*
Electrocom Midwest Sales Inc (PA) 248 449-2643
  32500 Concord Dr Ste 298 Madison Heights (48071) *(G-10243)*
Electrocraft Michigan Inc 603 516-1297
  1705 Woodland Dr Ste 101 Saline (48176) *(G-14387)*
Electrodynamics Inc 734 422-5420
  31091 Schoolcraft Rd Livonia (48150) *(G-9723)*
Electroheat Technologies LLC 810 798-2400
  691 N Squirrel Rd Ste 247 Auburn Hills (48326) *(G-853)*
Electrojet Inc 734 272-4709
  50164 Pontiac Trl Unit 5 Wixom (48393) *(G-17800)*
Electrolabs Inc 586 294-4150
  18503 E 14 Mile Rd Fraser (48026) *(G-5650)*
Electrolux Professional Inc 248 338-4320
  214 S Telegraph Rd Pontiac (48341) *(G-12821)*
Electromech Service Corp 989 362-6066
  1111 E Washington St East Tawas (48730) *(G-4688)*
Electronic Apps Speclsts Inc 248 491-4988
  1250 Holden Ave Milford (48381) *(G-10963)*
Electronic Design & Packg Co 734 591-9176
  36704 Commerce St Livonia (48150) *(G-9724)*
Electronics For Imaging Inc 734 641-3062
  1260 James L Hart Pkwy Ypsilanti (48197) *(G-18069)*
Electronics Tech Center, Troy *Also called Ghsp Inc (G-16384)*
Electroplating Industries Inc 586 469-2390
  21410 Carlo Dr Clinton Township (48038) *(G-3109)*
Eleetus, Ottawa Lake *Also called Yakkertech Limited (G-12270)*
Elegance of Season 616 296-1059
  209 N Buchanan St Spring Lake (49456) *(G-15140)*
Elegant Invitations, Plymouth *Also called Artcraft Printing Corporation (G-12574)*
Elegus Eps LLC 734 224-9900
  1600 Huron Pkwy Rm 2345 Ann Arbor (48109) *(G-440)*
Element 80 Engraving LLC 616 318-7407
  519 Macomb Ave Nw Grand Rapids (49534) *(G-6374)*
Element Salon and Day Spa 989 708-6006
  3917 E Patrick Rd Midland (48642) *(G-10860)*
Element Services LLC 517 672-1005
  3650 Norton Rd Howell (48843) *(G-8038)*
Elenbaas Hardwood Incorporated (PA) 616 669-3085
  2363 Port Sheldon Ct Jenison (49428) *(G-8624)*
Elenbaas Hardwood Incorporated 269 343-7791
  3751 Alvan Rd Kalamazoo (49001) *(G-8733)*
Elenz Inc 989 732-7233
  1455 Dickerson Rd Gaylord (49735) *(G-5857)*
Elephant Head LLC 734 256-4555
  35465 Goddard Rd Romulus (48174) *(G-13670)*

Elevated Technologies Inc 616 288-9817
  15 Ionia Ave Sw Ste 310 Grand Rapids (49503) *(G-6375)*
Eleven Mile Trck Frme & Ax 248 399-7536
  1750 E 11 Mile Rd Madison Heights (48071) *(G-10244)*
Eleven Mile Truck Collision Co, Madison Heights *Also called Eleven Mile Trck Frme & Ax (G-10244)*
Eliason Corporation (HQ) 269 327-7003
  9229 Shaver Rd Portage (49024) *(G-12992)*
Elite Active Wear Inc 616 396-1229
  701 Washington Ave Holland (49423) *(G-7621)*
Elite Arms Inc 734 424-9955
  18600 W Old Us Highway 12 Chelsea (48118) *(G-2709)*
Elite Business Services & Exec 734 956-4550
  2510 S Telg Rd Ste L280 Bloomfield Hills (48302) *(G-1763)*
Elite Defense, Chelsea *Also called Elite Arms Inc (G-2709)*
Elite Electro Coaters Inc 517 886-1020
  16261 Grove Rd Lansing (48906) *(G-9223)*
Elite Engineering Inc 517 304-3254
  210 W Tienken Rd Rochester Hills (48306) *(G-13417)*
Elite Fuels LLC 313 871-6308
  1140 Clay St Detroit (48211) *(G-4032)*
Elite Industrial Mfg LLC 616 895-1873
  9967 68th Ave Allendale (49401) *(G-216)*
Elite Machining 586 598-9008
  46516 Erb Dr Macomb (48042) *(G-10119)*
Elite Medical Molding, Shelby Township *Also called Elite Mold & Engineering Inc (G-14586)*
Elite Mold & Engineering Inc 586 873-1770
  51548 Filomena Dr Shelby Township (48315) *(G-14586)*
Elite Plastic Products Inc 586 247-5800
  51354 Filomena Dr Shelby Township (48315) *(G-14587)*
Elite Tooling Aerospace, Kalamazoo *Also called Elite Tooling LLC (G-8734)*
Elite Tooling LLC 269 383-9714
  3816 Miller Rd Kalamazoo (49001) *(G-8734)*
Elite Woodworking LLC 586 204-5882
  22960 W Industrial Dr B Saint Clair Shores (48080) *(G-14245)*
Elizabeth Jeans Pie Kits, Northville *Also called Cambridge Foods LLC (G-11682)*
Elk Lake Tool Co 231 264-5616
  203 Ec Loomis Dr Elk Rapids (49629) *(G-4777)*
Elk Rapids Engineering Inc 231 264-5661
  210 Industrial Park Dr Elk Rapids (49629) *(G-4778)*
Elkay Fastening Systems, Kalamazoo *Also called Elkay Industries Inc (G-8735)*
Elkay Industries Inc 269 381-4266
  1804 Reed Ave Kalamazoo (49001) *(G-8735)*
Elkins Machine & Tool Co Inc 734 941-0266
  27482 Northline Rd Romulus (48174) *(G-13671)*
Elkins Machine & Tool Co Inc (PA) 734 941-0266
  27510 Northline Rd Romulus (48174) *(G-13672)*
Ell Tron Manufacturing Co (PA) 989 983-3181
  11893 Old 27 Hwy N Vanderbilt (49795) *(G-16804)*
Ell Tron Manufacturing Co 989 983-3181
  10957 Old 27 Hwy N Vanderbilt (49795) *(G-16805)*
Ellenbaum Truck Sales, Sebewaing *Also called Trucksforsalecom (G-14520)*
Elliott Group International, Auburn Hills *Also called Elliott Tape Inc (G-854)*
Elliott Tape Inc (PA) 248 475-2000
  1882 Pond Run Auburn Hills (48326) *(G-854)*
Ellis Infinity LLC 313 570-0840
  1545 Clay St Unit 6 Detroit (48211) *(G-4033)*
Ellis Machine & Tool Co Inc 734 847-4113
  7168 Sulier Dr Temperance (48182) *(G-15827)*
Ellsworth Cutting Tools LLC 586 598-6040
  25190 Terra Industrial Dr Chesterfield (48051) *(G-2772)*
Ellsworth, Belinda, Pinckney *Also called Step Into Success Inc (G-12504)*
Elm International Inc (PA) 517 332-4900
  4360 Hagadorn Rd Okemos (48864) *(G-12122)*
Elm Plating 517 795-1574
  533 Hupp Ave Jackson (49203) *(G-8444)*
Elmer's, White Cloud *Also called M 37 Concrete Products Inc (G-17626)*
Elmers Construction Engrg, Traverse City *Also called Elmers Crane and Dozer Inc (G-15962)*
Elmers Crane and Dozer Inc (PA) 231 943-3443
  3600 Rennie School Rd Traverse City (49685) *(G-15962)*
Elmet LLC 248 473-2924
  40028 Grand River Ave # 400 Novi (48375) *(G-11882)*
Elmet North America Inc 517 664-9011
  4103 Grand Oak Dr B102 Lansing (48911) *(G-9364)*
Elmhirst Industries Inc 586 731-8663
  7630 19 Mile Rd Sterling Heights (48314) *(G-15330)*
Elmo Manufacturing Co Inc 734 995-5966
  98 Valhalla Dr 950 Ann Arbor (48103) *(G-441)*
Elmont District Library 810 798-3100
  213 W Saint Clair St Almont (48003) *(G-256)*
Elmwood Manufacturing Company 313 571-1777
  3925 Beaufait St Detroit (48207) *(G-4034)*
Elopak Inc 248 486-4600
  46962 Liberty Dr Wixom (48393) *(G-17801)*
Elopak-Americas Inc (HQ) 248 486-4600
  46962 Liberty Dr Wixom (48393) *(G-17802)*

ALPHABETIC SECTION

Elring Klinger Sealing Systems 734 542-1522
35955 Veronica St Livonia (48150) *(G-9725)*

Elringklinger Auto Mfg Inc (HQ) 248 727-6600
23300 Northwestern Hwy Southfield (48075) *(G-14898)*

Elringklinger Auto Mfg Inc 586 445-3050
30233 Groesbeck Hwy Roseville (48066) *(G-13800)*

Elringklinger North Amer Inc, Southfield *Also called Elringklinger Auto Mfg Inc (G-14898)*

Elsa Enterprises Inc 248 816-1454
2800 W Big Beaver Rd # 124 Troy (48084) *(G-16340)*

Elsie Inc 734 421-8844
12752 Stark Rd Ste 1 Livonia (48150) *(G-9726)*

Elsie Publishing Institute (PA) 517 371-5257
500 W Ionia St Lansing (48933) *(G-9365)*

Elston Enterprises Inc 313 561-8000
22250 Ford Rd Dearborn Heights (48127) *(G-3784)*

Eltek Inc 616 363-6397
6688 Wildwood Creek Dr Ne Belmont (49306) *(G-1461)*

Eltro Services Inc 248 628-9790
3570 Thomas Rd Oxford (48371) *(G-12345)*

Eltropuls-Usa, Oxford *Also called Eltro Services Inc (G-12345)*

Elumigen LLC 855 912-0477
820 Kirts Blvd Ste 300 Troy (48084) *(G-16341)*

Em A Give Break Safety 231 263-6625
6502 M 37 Kingsley (49649) *(G-9071)*

Emabond Solutions LLC 201 767-7400
1797 Atlantic Blvd Auburn Hills (48326) *(G-855)*

Emag LLC (HQ) 248 477-7440
38800 Grand River Ave Farmington Hills (48335) *(G-4983)*

Emag Technologies Inc 734 996-3624
775 Technology Dr Ste 300 Ann Arbor (48108) *(G-442)*

Ematrix Energy Systems Inc 248 797-2149
4706 Delemere Blvd Royal Oak (48073) *(G-13921)*

Ematrix Energy Systems Inc 248 629-9111
4425 Fernlee Ave Royal Oak (48073) *(G-13922)*

Embassy Bakery, Commerce Township *Also called Embassy Distributing Company (G-3404)*

Embassy Distributing Company 248 926-0590
39560 W 14 Mile Rd Commerce Township (48390) *(G-3404)*

Embers Ballscrew Repair 586 216-8444
10200 Grinnell St Detroit (48213) *(G-4035)*

Embest, Livonia *Also called Country Fresh LLC (G-9691)*

Embrace Premium Vodka LLC 616 617-5602
515 Ferris St Ypsilanti (48197) *(G-18070)*

Embroidery & Much More LLC 586 771-3832
27419 Harper Ave Saint Clair Shores (48081) *(G-14246)*

Embroidery House Inc 616 669-6400
2688 Edward St Jenison (49428) *(G-8625)*

Embroidery Products LLC 734 483-0293
12 S Huron St Ypsilanti (48197) *(G-18071)*

Embroidery Shoppe LLC 734 595-7612
39017 Cherry Hill Rd Westland (48186) *(G-17552)*

Embroidery Wearhouse 906 228-5818
2112 Us Highway 41 W # 3 Marquette (49855) *(G-10529)*

EMC Corporation 248 374-5009
39555 Orchard Hill Pl # 138 Novi (48375) *(G-11883)*

EMC Corporation 248 957-5800
36555 Corporate Dr # 200 Farmington Hills (48331) *(G-4984)*

EMC Welding & Fabrication Inc 231 788-4172
4966 Evanston Ave Muskegon (49442) *(G-11316)*

Emco Chemical Inc 313 894-7650
4470 Lawton St Detroit (48208) *(G-4036)*

Emcor Inc 989 667-0652
5154 Alliance Dr Bay City (48706) *(G-1308)*

EMD Wire Tek 810 235-5344
4155 Holiday Dr Flint (48507) *(G-5424)*

Emerald Consulting Group LLC 248 720-0573
31650 Stephenson Hwy Madison Heights (48071) *(G-10245)*

Emerald Graphics, Grand Rapids *Also called Kennedy Acquisition Inc (G-6573)*

Emerald Graphics Inc 616 871-3020
4949 W Greenbrooke Dr Se Grand Rapids (49512) *(G-6376)*

Emerald Mfg 269 483-2676
69223 S Kalamazoo St White Pigeon (49099) *(G-17647)*

Emerald Spa, Grand Rapids *Also called Conway Products Corporation (G-6308)*

Emerald Tool Inc 231 799-9193
6305 Norton Center Dr Norton Shores (49441) *(G-11752)*

Emergency Services LLC 231 727-7400
1660 Dodson Dr Muskegon (49442) *(G-11317)*

Emergency Technology Inc 616 896-7100
3900 Central Pkwy Hudsonville (49426) *(G-8155)*

Emergency Vehicle Products 269 342-0973
2975 Interstate Pkwy Kalamazoo (49048) *(G-8736)*

Emergent Biodef Oper Lnsng LLC 517 327-1500
3500 N Martin Luther King Lansing (48906) *(G-9224)*

Emergent Technologies Co, Vicksburg *Also called Ronningen Research and Dev Co (G-16842)*

Emerson Electric Co 616 846-3950
15399 Hofma Dr Grand Haven (49417) *(G-6014)*

Emerson Electric Co 586 268-3104
6590 Sims Dr Sterling Heights (48313) *(G-15371)*

Emerson Electric Co 734 420-0832
15024 Robinwood Dr Plymouth (48170) *(G-12617)*

Emerson Geophysical LLC 231 943-1400
3819 4 Mile Rd N Traverse City (49686) *(G-15963)*

Emerson Process Management 313 874-0860
3031 W Grand Blvd Ste 423 Detroit (48202) *(G-4037)*

Emery Design & Woodwork LLC 734 709-1687
8277 Tower Rd South Lyon (48178) *(G-14790)*

Emhart Industries, Chesterfield *Also called Emhart Teknologies LLC (G-2773)*

Emhart Teknologies LLC 586 949-0440
50501 E Russell Schmidt B Chesterfield (48051) *(G-2773)*

Emhart Teknologies LLC 248 677-9693
2500 Meijer Dr Troy (48084) *(G-16342)*

Emhart Teknologies LLC 800 783-6427
2400 Meijer Dr Bldg 2 Troy (48084) *(G-16343)*

EMI Construction Products, Holland *Also called Edmar Manufacturing Inc (G-7618)*

EMI Construction Products 800 603-9965
455 E 64th St Holland (49423) *(G-7622)*

Emitted Energy Inc (PA) 855 752-3347
6559 Diplomat Dr Sterling Heights (48314) *(G-15332)*

Emm Inc 248 478-1182
23409 Industrial Park Ct Farmington Hills (48335) *(G-4985)*

Emma Sogoian Inc 248 549-8690
4336 Normandy Ct Royal Oak (48073) *(G-13923)*

Emmie Die and Engineering Corp 810 346-2914
7254 Maple Valley Rd Brown City (48416) *(G-2050)*

Emp Advanced Development LLC 906 789-7497
2701 N 30th St Escanaba (49829) *(G-4824)*

Emp Racing Inc 906 786-8404
2701 N 30th St Escanaba (49829) *(G-4825)*

Empire Company LLC (HQ) 800 253-9000
8181 Logistics Dr Zeeland (49464) *(G-18134)*

Empire Forest Products Company, Plainwell *Also called Chippewa Development Inc (G-12519)*

Empire Hardchrome 810 392-3122
33450 Bordman Rd Richmond (48062) *(G-13262)*

Empire Iron Mining Partnership 906 475-3600
Empire Mine Rd Palmer (49871) *(G-12381)*

Empire Machine & Conveyors Inc 989 541-2060
5111 S Durand Rd Durand (48429) *(G-4608)*

Empire Machine Company 269 684-3713
350 Palladium Dr Saint Joseph (49085) *(G-14309)*

Empire Molded Plastics, Benton Harbor *Also called Colonial Manufacturing LLC (G-1490)*

Empire Printing 248 547-9223
400 E Lincoln Ave Ste A Royal Oak (48067) *(G-13924)*

Empirical Bioscience Inc 877 479-9949
2007 Eastcastle Dr Se Grand Rapids (49508) *(G-6377)*

Empower Financials Inc 734 747-9393
4343 Concourse Dr Ste 140 Ann Arbor (48108) *(G-443)*

Ems Equipment Management Svcs, Southgate *Also called Abtech Installation & Svc Inc (G-15073)*

Emtron Corporation Inc 248 347-3333
57401 Travis Rd New Hudson (48165) *(G-11539)*

Emtron Gauge, New Hudson *Also called Emtron Corporation Inc (G-11539)*

Ena North America Corporation 248 926-0011
51150 Century Ct Wixom (48393) *(G-17803)*

Enagon LLC 269 455-5110
3381 Blue Star Hwy Saugatuck (49453) *(G-14458)*

Enamelite Industries, Grand Rapids *Also called Mdm Enterprises Inc (G-6655)*

Encore Commercial Products Inc 248 354-4090
37525 Interchange Dr Farmington Hills (48335) *(G-4986)*

Encore Impression LLC 248 478-1221
20774 Orchard Lake Rd Farmington Hills (48336) *(G-4987)*

Encore Magazine, Kalamazoo *Also called Encore Publishing Group Inc (G-8737)*

Encore Publishing Group Inc 269 383-4433
350 S Kalamazoo Mall # 214 Kalamazoo (49007) *(G-8737)*

End of Road Winery LLC 906 450-1541
6917 Burns Rd Unit 1 Germfask (49836) *(G-5901)*

End Product Results LLC 586 585-1210
27115 Gratiot Ave Ste B Roseville (48066) *(G-13801)*

Endectra LLC 734 476-9381
1600 Huron Pkwy Bldg 520 Ann Arbor (48109) *(G-444)*

Endless Possibilities Inc 248 262-7443
672 Ajax Dr Madison Heights (48071) *(G-10246)*

Endlich Studios LLC 248 524-9671
2950 Bywater Dr Troy (48085) *(G-16344)*

Endoscopic Solutions 248 625-4055
5701 Bow Pointe Dr # 370 Clarkston (48346) *(G-2918)*

Endra Life Sciences Inc 734 255-0242
3600 Green Ct Ste 350 Ann Arbor (48105) *(G-445)*

Endres Processing LLC 616 878-4230
8557 Piedmont Ind Dr Sw Byron Center (49315) *(G-2189)*

Endres Processing Michigan LLC 269 965-0427
170 Angell St Battle Creek (49037) *(G-1177)*

Endura Coatings, Sterling Heights *Also called Stechschulte/Wegerly AG LLC (G-15510)*

Endura-Veyor, Alpena *Also called Max Endura Inc (G-297)*

Endura-Veyor Inc 989 358-7060
3490 Us Highway 23 N Alpena (49707) *(G-287)*

Endurance Carbide, Saginaw *Also called M Curry Corporation* ***(G-14080)***
Ener-TEC Inc........517 741-5015
306 Railroad St Union City (49094) ***(G-16733)***
Ener2 LLC........248 842-2662
7685 Athlone Dr Brighton (48116) ***(G-1918)***
Enerco Corporation (PA)........517 627-1669
317 N Bridge St Grand Ledge (48837) ***(G-6106)***
Energy Acquisition Corp........517 339-0249
2385 Delhi Commerce Dr # 5 Holt (48842) ***(G-7911)***
Energy Control Solutions Inc........810 735-2800
11494 Delmar Dr Ste 100 Fenton (48430) ***(G-5202)***
Energy Design Svc Systems LLC........810 227-3377
7050 Jomar Dr Whitmore Lake (48189) ***(G-17697)***
Energy Development Assoc LLC........313 354-2644
15201 Century Dr Dearborn (48120) ***(G-3701)***
Energy Efficient Ltg LLC Eel........586 214-5557
3297 Wdview Lk Rd Ste 200 West Bloomfield (48323) ***(G-17476)***
Energy Exploration........248 579-6531
40411 Oakwood Dr Novi (48375) ***(G-11884)***
Energy Manufacturing Inc........248 360-0065
47654 West Rd Wixom (48393) ***(G-17804)***
Energy Powercell LLC........248 585-1000
750 South Blvd E Pontiac (48341) ***(G-12822)***
Energy Products Inc........248 866-5622
315 Indusco Ct Troy (48083) ***(G-16345)***
Energy Products Inc (PA)........248 545-7700
1551 E Lincoln Ave # 101 Madison Heights (48071) ***(G-10247)***
Energy Products & Services, Rochester *Also called US Energia LLC* ***(G-13356)***
Energy Products Service Dept, Troy *Also called Energy Products Inc* ***(G-16345)***
Energy Steel & Supply Co........810 538-4990
3123 John Conley Dr Lapeer (48446) ***(G-9458)***
Energy Suppliers LLC........269 342-9482
2813 W Main St Kalamazoo (49006) ***(G-8738)***
Enertech Corporation........231 832-5587
210 S Division St Hersey (49639) ***(G-7472)***
Enertemp Inc........616 243-2752
3961 Eastern Ave Se Grand Rapids (49508) ***(G-6378)***
Enertrols Inc........734 595-4500
23435 Industrial Park Dr Farmington Hills (48335) ***(G-4988)***
Eng Advance Technology Dev Ctr, Auburn Hills *Also called American Axle & Mfg Inc* ***(G-769)***
Engai........313 605-8220
27056 Pinewood Dr Apt 203 Wixom (48393) ***(G-17805)***
Engel Printing Company, Minden City *Also called Minden City Herald* ***(G-11000)***
Engine Guru LLC........616 430-3114
6709 18th Ave Wyoming (49509) ***(G-18000)***
Engine Parts Grinding, Grand Haven *Also called Engine Power Components Inc* ***(G-6015)***
Engine Power Components Inc........616 846-0110
1333 Fulton Ave Grand Haven (49417) ***(G-6015)***
Engineered Alum Fabricators, Ferndale *Also called Engineered Alum Fabricators Co* ***(G-5282)***
Engineered Alum Fabricators Co........248 582-3430
1530 Farrow St Ferndale (48220) ***(G-5282)***
Engineered Automation Systems........616 897-0920
95 Whites Bridge Rd Belding (48809) ***(G-1412)***
Engineered Concepts Inc........574 333-9110
67990 Milmc Ln Cassopolis (49031) ***(G-2530)***
Engineered Control Systems Inc........509 483-6215
12700 31 Mile Rd Washington (48095) ***(G-17303)***
Engineered Heat Treat Inc........248 588-5141
31271 Stephenson Hwy Madison Heights (48071) ***(G-10248)***
Engineered Machined Pdts Inc (PA)........906 786-8404
3111 N 28th St Escanaba (49829) ***(G-4826)***
Engineered Machined Pdts Inc........906 789-7497
2701 N 30th St Escanaba (49829) ***(G-4827)***
Engineered Plastic Components, Farmington Hills *Also called Aees Power Systems Ltd Partnr* ***(G-4921)***
Engineered Plastic Components, Allen Park *Also called Aees Power Systems Ltd Partnr* ***(G-194)***
Engineered Plastic Components........810 326-1650
2000 Christian B Haas Dr Saint Clair (48079) ***(G-14217)***
Engineered Plastic Components........810 326-3010
2015 S Range Rd Saint Clair (48079) ***(G-14218)***
Engineered Polymer Products........269 461-6955
7988 W Eureka Rd Eau Claire (49111) ***(G-4738)***
Engineered Prfmce Coatings Inc........616 988-7927
4881 Kendrick St Se Grand Rapids (49512) ***(G-6379)***
Engineered Prfmce Mtls Co LLC........734 904-4023
11228 Lemen Rd Ste A Whitmore Lake (48189) ***(G-17698)***
Engineered Products Company (PA)........810 767-2050
601 Kelso St Flint (48506) ***(G-5425)***
Engineered Resources Inc........248 399-5500
26511 Harding St Oak Park (48237) ***(G-12066)***
Engineered Tooling Systems Inc........616 647-5063
2780 Courier Dr Nw Grand Rapids (49534) ***(G-6380)***
Engineered Tools Corp........989 673-8733
2710 W Caro Rd Caro (48723) ***(G-2468)***
Engineering and Mfg Svcs, Westland *Also called High-Star Corporation* ***(G-17569)***
Engineering Center, Kentwood *Also called Magna Mirrors America Inc* ***(G-9019)***
Engineering Graphics Inc........517 485-5828
16333 S Us Highway 27 Lansing (48906) ***(G-9225)***
Engineering Interests Inc........248 461-6706
5600 Williams Lake Rd F Waterford (48329) ***(G-17342)***
Engineering Reproduction Inc (PA)........313 366-3390
13550 Conant St Detroit (48212) ***(G-4038)***
Engineering Service of America........248 357-3800
21556 Telegraph Rd Southfield (48033) ***(G-14899)***
Engineering Systems Intl, Southfield *Also called Engineering Service of America* ***(G-14899)***
Engineering Tech Assoc Inc (PA)........248 729-3010
1133 E Maple Rd Ste 200 Troy (48083) ***(G-16346)***
Enginered Combustn Systems LLC........248 549-1703
4240 Delemere Ct Royal Oak (48073) ***(G-13925)***
Enginred Plstic Components Inc........248 825-4508
100 W Big Beavr Rd # 200 Troy (48084) ***(G-16347)***
Engrave & Graphic Inc........616 245-8082
1605 Eastern Ave Se Grand Rapids (49507) ***(G-6381)***
Engrave & Graphic Inc Fax, Grand Rapids *Also called Engrave & Graphic Inc* ***(G-6381)***
Engrave A Remembrance Inc........586 772-7480
28555 Flanders Ave Warren (48088) ***(G-17018)***
Engravers Journal........810 229-5725
10087 Spencer Rd Brighton (48114) ***(G-1919)***
Engraving Connection, Plymouth *Also called Rex M Tubbs* ***(G-12735)***
Engtechnik Inc (PA)........734 667-4237
40615 Koppernick Rd # 2 Canton (48187) ***(G-2371)***
Enhanced MSC, Madison Heights *Also called Martin Fluid Power Company* ***(G-10302)***
Enihcam Corp........810 354-0404
3061 W Thompson Rd Ste 1 Fenton (48430) ***(G-5203)***
Enjoyment Image Publications........269 782-8259
111 W Prairie Ronde St Dowagiac (49047) ***(G-4542)***
Enkon LLC........937 890-5678
10521 Mi State Road 52 Manchester (48158) ***(G-10405)***
Enmark Tool Company........586 293-2797
18100 Cross Fraser (48026) ***(G-5651)***
Enovapremier LLC........517 541-3200
403 Parkland Dr Charlotte (48813) ***(G-2646)***
Enovate It........248 721-8104
1250 Woodward Hts Ferndale (48220) ***(G-5283)***
Enprotech Industrial Tech LLC........517 372-0950
16740 16800 Indus Pkwy Lansing (48906) ***(G-9226)***
Enprotech Industrial Tech LLC........517 319-5306
2200 Olds Ave Lansing (48915) ***(G-9366)***
Enrinity Supplements Inc........734 322-4966
6480 Commerce Dr Westland (48185) ***(G-17553)***
Ensign Emblem Ltd (PA)........231 946-7703
1746 Keane Dr Traverse City (49696) ***(G-15964)***
Ensign Equipment Inc........616 738-9000
12523 Superior Ct Holland (49424) ***(G-7623)***
Ensign Technical Services, Traverse City *Also called Ensign Emblem Ltd* ***(G-15964)***
Ensley Sand & Gravel, Sand Lake *Also called R & C Redi-Mix Inc* ***(G-14425)***
Enstrom Helicopter Corporation........906 863-1200
2209 22nd St Menominee (49858) ***(G-10731)***
Ensure Technologies Inc........734 668-8800
135 S Prospect St Ste 100 Ypsilanti (48198) ***(G-18072)***
Enterprise Hinge Inc........269 857-2111
6779 Enterprise Dr Douglas (49406) ***(G-4531)***
Enterprise Plastics LLC........586 665-1030
51354 Filomena Dr Shelby Township (48315) ***(G-14588)***
Enterprise Services LLC........734 523-6525
12200 Middlebelt Rd Livonia (48150) ***(G-9727)***
Enterprise Tool & Die LLC........616 538-0920
4270 White St Sw Grandville (49418) ***(G-7033)***
Enterprise Tool and Gear Inc (PA)........989 269-9797
635 Liberty St Bad Axe (48413) ***(G-1060)***
Entertainment, Troy *Also called HSP Epi Acquisition LLC* ***(G-16406)***
Entertainment Publications Inc........248 404-1000
1401 Crooks Rd Ste 150 Troy (48084) ***(G-16348)***
Entire Rprdction Imging Sltion, Clawson *Also called American Reprographics Co LLC* ***(G-2973)***
Entrepreneurial Pursuits........248 829-6903
2727 Product Dr Rochester Hills (48309) ***(G-13418)***
Entron Computer Systems Inc........248 349-8898
44554 Chedworth Ct Northville (48167) ***(G-11690)***
Envirnmntal Pllet Slutions Inc........616 283-1784
9500 Henry Ct Ste 350 Zeeland (49464) ***(G-18135)***
Enviro Industries Inc........906 492-3402
11874 N Whitefish Pt Rd Paradise (49768) ***(G-12382)***
Enviro-Brite Solutions LLC........989 387-2758
4150 Arrow St Oscoda (48750) ***(G-12209)***
Envirodine Inc........231 723-5905
317 Washington St Manistee (49660) ***(G-10420)***
Envirodrone Inc........226 344-5614
440 Burroughs St Detroit (48202) ***(G-4039)***
Envirodyne Technologies Inc (HQ)........269 342-1918
7574 E Michigan Ave Kalamazoo (49048) ***(G-8739)***
Envirolite LLC (PA)........248 792-3184
1700 W Big Beaver Rd # 150 Troy (48084) ***(G-16349)***
Envirolite LLC........888 222-2191
421 Race St Coldwater (49036) ***(G-3302)***

Environ Manufacturing Inc 616 644-6846
972 Graham Lake Ter Battle Creek (49014) ***(G-1178)***
Environmental Catalysts LLC 248 813-2000
5820 Innovation Dr Troy (48098) ***(G-16350)***
Environmental Products Corp 248 471-4770
30421 8 Mile Rd Livonia (48152) ***(G-9728)***
Environmental Protection Inc 231 943-2265
1567 W South Airport Rd # 1 Traverse City (49686) ***(G-15965)***
Environmental Resources 248 446-9639
56901 Grand River Ave New Hudson (48165) ***(G-11540)***
Environmental Safe Oil Change, Wixom *Also called Esoc Inc* ***(G-17806)***
Envirotronics, Grand Rapids *Also called Weiss Technik North Amer Inc* ***(G-6983)***
Envisics LLC (PA) 248 802-4461
2021 Austin Ave Rochester Hills (48309) ***(G-13419)***
Envision Engineering LLC 616 897-0599
12650 Envision Dr Se Lowell (49331) ***(G-10027)***
Envision Machine & Mfg, Holland *Also called Envision Machine and Mfg LLC* ***(G-7624)***
Envision Machine and Mfg LLC 616 953-8580
741 Waverly Ct Holland (49423) ***(G-7624)***
Envisiontec Inc 313 436-4300
15162 S Commerce Dr Dearborn (48120) ***(G-3702)***
Eot, Traverse City *Also called Electro-Optics Technology Inc* ***(G-15961)***
Eotech Inc 734 741-8868
1201 E Ellsworth Rd Ann Arbor (48108) ***(G-446)***
Eovations LLC 616 361-7136
2801 E Beltline Ave Ne Grand Rapids (49525) ***(G-6382)***
Ep Magnets & Components LLC 734 398-7188
5055 Belleville Rd Canton (48188) ***(G-2372)***
Epath Logic Inc 313 375-5375
418 N Main St 200 Royal Oak (48067) ***(G-13926)***
Epc-Columbia Inc 810 326-1650
2000 Christian B Haas Dr Saint Clair (48079) ***(G-14219)***
Epcon, Rochester Hills *Also called F I D Corporation* ***(G-13422)***
Epi Market, Battle Creek *Also called Epi Printers Inc* ***(G-1181)***
Epi Marketing Services, Battle Creek *Also called Epi Printers Inc* ***(G-1179)***
Epi Marketing Services, Battle Creek *Also called Epi Printers Inc* ***(G-1183)***
Epi Printers Inc (PA) 800 562-9733
5404 Wayne Rd Battle Creek (49037) ***(G-1179)***
Epi Printers Inc 269 968-2221
61 Clark Rd Battle Creek (49037) ***(G-1180)***
Epi Printers Inc 269 968-2221
5350 W Dickman Rd Battle Creek (49037) ***(G-1181)***
Epi Printers Inc 269 964-4600
4956 Wayne Rd Battle Creek (49037) ***(G-1182)***
Epi Printers Inc 734 261-9400
13305 Wayne Rd Livonia (48150) ***(G-9729)***
Epi Printers Inc 269 964-6744
65 Clark Rd Battle Creek (49037) ***(G-1183)***
Epic 4d LLC 800 470-8948
98 Hague St Detroit (48202) ***(G-4040)***
Epic Equipment & Engrg Inc 586 314-0020
52301 Shelby Pkwy Shelby Township (48315) ***(G-14589)***
Epic Fine Arts Company Inc (HQ) 313 274-7400
21001 Van Born Rd Taylor (48180) ***(G-15716)***
Epic Machine Inc 810 629-9400
201 Industrial Way Ste A Fenton (48430) ***(G-5204)***
Epic Materials Inc 586 294-0300
33741 Groesbeck Hwy Fraser (48026) ***(G-5652)***
Epicure By Mills, The, Birmingham *Also called Mills Phrm & Apothecary LLC* ***(G-1693)***
EPM, Whitmore Lake *Also called Engineered Prfmce Mtls Co LLC* ***(G-17698)***
Epoxi-Pro, Madison Heights *Also called Simiron Inc* ***(G-10354)***
Epoxy Pro Flr Ctngs Rstoration 248 990-8890
51947 Filomena Dr Shelby Township (48315) ***(G-14590)***
Eppert Concrete Products Inc 248 647-1800
30725 Longcrest St Southfield (48076) ***(G-14900)***
Eppinger Mfg Co 313 582-3205
6340 Schaefer Rd Dearborn (48126) ***(G-3703)***
Epredia, Kalamazoo *Also called Thermo Fisher Scientific Inc* ***(G-8911)***
Eps Industries Inc 616 844-9220
585 Second St Ferrysburg (49409) ***(G-5334)***
Eptech Inc 586 254-2722
541 Oakhill Ct Rochester Hills (48309) ***(G-13420)***
Eq Resource Recovery Inc (HQ) 734 727-5500
36345 Van Born Rd Romulus (48174) ***(G-13673)***
Eqi Ltd 616 850-2630
5797 Harvey St Norton Shores (49444) ***(G-11753)***
Eqi, Ltd., Norton Shores *Also called Eagle Quest International Ltd* ***(G-11750)***
Equip Consumable Group 248 588-9981
32035 Edward Ave Madison Heights (48071) ***(G-10249)***
Equipment Material Sales LLC 734 284-8711
671 Grove St Wyandotte (48192) ***(G-17958)***
Equistar Chemicals, LP, Lansing *Also called Lyondellbasell Industries Inc* ***(G-9393)***
Equitable Engineering Co Inc 248 689-9700
1840 Austin Dr Troy (48083) ***(G-16351)***
Equivalent Base Co 586 759-2030
4175 E 10 Mile Rd Warren (48091) ***(G-17019)***
Er Simons, Auburn *Also called Ittner Bean & Grain Inc* ***(G-753)***
ERA Tool & Engineering Co 810 227-3509
35551 Schoolcraft Rd Livonia (48150) ***(G-9730)***
Erae AMS America Corp 419 386-8876
2011 Centerpoint Pkwy Pontiac (48341) ***(G-12823)***
Erae AMS Usa LLC 419 386-8876
27150 Hills Tech Ct Farmington Hills (48331) ***(G-4989)***
Erae AMS USA Manufacturing LLC 248 770-6969
2011 Centerpoint Pkwy Pontiac (48341) ***(G-12824)***
Erbsloeh Alum Solutions Inc 269 323-2565
6565 S Sprinkle Rd Portage (49002) ***(G-12993)***
Erdman Machine Co 231 894-1010
8529 Silver Creek Rd Whitehall (49461) ***(G-17665)***
Erickson Logging Inc 906 523-4049
40734 Lower Pike Rd Chassell (49916) ***(G-2673)***
Erickson Lumber & True Value 906 524-6295
17752 Us Hwy 41 Lanse (49946) ***(G-9191)***
Erie Custom Signs, Saginaw *Also called Erie Marking Inc* ***(G-14035)***
Erie Marking Inc 989 754-8360
1017 S Wheeler St Saginaw (48602) ***(G-14035)***
Erie Technologies, Ottawa Lake *Also called F&B Technologies* ***(G-12262)***
Erin Industries Inc (PA) 248 669-2050
902 N Pontiac Trl Walled Lake (48390) ***(G-16893)***
Erla's Food Center, Cass City *Also called Erlas Inc* ***(G-2514)***
Erlas Inc 989 872-2191
6233 Church St Cass City (48726) ***(G-2514)***
Ermanco 231 798-4547
1300 E Mount Garfield Rd Norton Shores (49441) ***(G-11754)***
Ernest Inds Acquisition LLC 734 459-8881
14601 Keel St Plymouth (48170) ***(G-12618)***
Ernest Industries Acquisition, (PA) 734 595-9500
39133 Webb Dr Westland (48185) ***(G-17554)***
Ernest Industries Company, Westland *Also called Ernest Industries Acquisition,* ***(G-17554)***
Ernest Industries Company, Plymouth *Also called Ernest Inds Acquisition LLC* ***(G-12618)***
Ernie Romanco 517 531-3686
661 N Concord Rd Albion (49224) ***(G-123)***
Ernst Benz Company LLC 248 203-2323
177 S Old Woodward Ave Birmingham (48009) ***(G-1683)***
Ervin Amasteel, Ann Arbor *Also called Ervin Industries Inc* ***(G-447)***
Ervin Development Center, Tecumseh *Also called Ervin Industries Inc* ***(G-15792)***
Ervin Industries Inc 517 265-6118
915 Tabor St Adrian (49221) ***(G-62)***
Ervin Industries Inc (PA) 734 769-4600
3893 Research Park Dr Ann Arbor (48108) ***(G-447)***
Ervin Industries Inc 517 423-5477
200 Industrial Dr Tecumseh (49286) ***(G-15792)***
Ervins Group LLC (PA) 248 203-2000
550 Hulet Dr Ste 103 Bloomfield Hills (48302) ***(G-1764)***
Ervott Tool Co LLC 616 842-3688
13951 132nd Ave Grand Haven (49417) ***(G-6016)***
Erwin Quarder Inc 616 575-1600
5101 Kraft Ave Se Ste B Grand Rapids (49512) ***(G-6383)***
Escanaba and Lk Superior RR Co 906 786-9399
1401 N 26th St Bldg 20 Escanaba (49829) ***(G-4828)***
Escanaba Paper Company, Escanaba *Also called Verso Corporation* ***(G-4865)***
Esco Company LLC 231 726-3106
2330 East Paris Ave Se Grand Rapids (49546) ***(G-6384)***
Esco Group Inc (PA) 616 453-5458
2887 3 Mile Rd Nw Grand Rapids (49534) ***(G-6385)***
Ese LLc 810 538-1000
3344 John Conley Dr Lapeer (48446) ***(G-9459)***
Esgar Products, Van Buren Twp *Also called Kage Group LLC* ***(G-16767)***
Esirpal Inc 586 337-7848
55549 Danube Ave Macomb (48042) ***(G-10120)***
Esl Supplies LLC 517 525-7877
600 N College Rd Mason (48854) ***(G-10637)***
Esoc Inc 248 624-7992
48553 West Rd Wixom (48393) ***(G-17806)***
ESP, Detroit *Also called Essential Screen Printing LLC* ***(G-4042)***
Espar Inc 248 994-7010
43700 Gen Mar 3 Novi (48375) ***(G-11885)***
Espec Corp 616 896-6100
4141 Central Pkwy Hudsonville (49426) ***(G-8156)***
Esperion Therapeutics Inc 734 887-3903
3891 Ranchero Dr Ste 150 Ann Arbor (48108) ***(G-448)***
Esperovax Inc 248 667-1845
46701 Commerce Center Dr Plymouth (48170) ***(G-12619)***
Espinoza Bros 313 468-7775
2397 Stair St Detroit (48209) ***(G-4041)***
Esr 989 619-7160
2225 E Tait Rd Harrisville (48740) ***(G-7363)***
Ess Tec Inc 616 394-0230
3347 128th Ave Holland (49424) ***(G-7625)***
Essen Bioscience, Ann Arbor *Also called Essen Instruments Inc* ***(G-449)***
Essen Instruments Inc (HQ) 734 769-1600
300 W Morgan Rd Ann Arbor (48108) ***(G-449)***
Essential Screen Printing LLC 313 300-6411
2630 Orleans St Detroit (48207) ***(G-4042)***
Essex Brass Corporation 586 757-8200
23500 Pinewood St Warren (48091) ***(G-17020)***

ALPHABETIC

Essex Weld USA Inc 519 776-9153
24445 Forterra Dr Warren (48089) *(G-17021)*
Essilor Laboratories Amer Inc 231 922-0344
2323 W Aero Park Ct Traverse City (49686) *(G-15966)*
Essilor Laboratories Amer Inc 616 361-6000
1526 Plainfield Ave Ne Grand Rapids (49505) *(G-6386)*
Est Tools America Inc 810 824-3323
10138 Radiance Dr Ira (48023) *(G-8255)*
Esterline Mmtron Input Cmpnnts, Frankenmuth *Also called Memtron Technologies Co* *(G-5593)*
Esto Connectors, Kalamazoo *Also called Corners Limited* *(G-8718)*
Esyntrk Industries LLC 248 730-0640
4250 Pine Ln Orchard Lake (48323) *(G-12166)*
Esys Automation LLC (HQ) 248 754-1900
1000 Brown Rd Auburn Hills (48326) *(G-856)*
Etched Glass Works & A Bldg Co 517 819-4343
300 Hill St Lansing (48912) *(G-9367)*
Etcs Inc 586 268-4870
21275 Mullin Ave Warren (48089) *(G-17022)*
Eternabond Inc 847 540-0600
4401 Page Ave Michigan Center (49254) *(G-10786)*
Eternal Image Inc 248 932-3333
28800 Orchard Lake Rd Farmington Hills (48334) *(G-4990)*
Eteron Inc 248 478-2900
23944 Freeway Park Dr Farmington Hills (48335) *(G-4991)*
Ethel's Baking Co., Saint Clair Shores *Also called Ethels Edibles LLC* *(G-14247)*
Ethels Edibles LLC 586 552-5110
22314 Harper Ave Saint Clair Shores (48080) *(G-14247)*
Ether LLC 248 795-8830
4950 Hummer Lake Rd Ortonville (48462) *(G-12199)*
Ethnic Artwork Inc 586 726-1400
42111 Van Ave Sterling Heights (48314) *(G-15333)*
Ethnicemedia LLC 248 762-8904
338 Thistle Ln Troy (48098) *(G-16352)*
Ethnicemeida, Troy *Also called Ethnicemedia LLC* *(G-16352)*
Ethylene LLC 616 554-3464
4855 Broadmoor Ave Se Kentwood (49512) *(G-9005)*
Etna Distributors LLC 906 273-2331
1922 Enterprise St Marquette (49855) *(G-10530)*
Eto Magnetic Corp (HQ) 616 957-2570
5925 Patterson Ave Se Grand Rapids (49512) *(G-6387)*
Ets Exco Tooling Solutions, Chesterfield *Also called Exco Extrusion Dies Inc* *(G-2774)*
Etx Holdings Inc (HQ) 989 463-1151
2000 Michigan Ave Alma (48801) *(G-237)*
Euclid Coating Systems Inc 989 922-4789
3494 N Euclid Ave Bay City (48706) *(G-1309)*
Euclid Industries Inc (PA) 989 686-8920
1655 Tech Dr Bay City (48706) *(G-1310)*
Euclid Machine & Mfg Co 734 941-1080
29030 Northline Rd Romulus (48174) *(G-13674)*
Euclid Manufacturing Co Inc 734 397-6300
1500 E Euclid St Detroit (48211) *(G-4043)*
Euko Design-Signs Inc 248 478-1330
24849 Hathaway St Farmington Hills (48335) *(G-4992)*
Euko Signs, Farmington Hills *Also called Euko Design-Signs Inc* *(G-4992)*
Eureka Welding Alloys Inc 248 588-0001
2000 E Avis Dr Madison Heights (48071) *(G-10250)*
Euridium Solutions LLC 248 535-7005
55 E Long Lake Rd Ste 243 Troy (48085) *(G-16353)*
Euro-Craft Interiors Inc 586 254-9130
6611 Diplomat Dr Sterling Heights (48314) *(G-15334)*
Euro-Locks Inc 616 994-0490
124 James St Holland (49424) *(G-7626)*
European Cabinet Mfg Co 586 445-8909
30665 Groesbeck Hwy Roseville (48066) *(G-13802)*
European Skin Care & Cosmetics, Southfield *Also called Mineral Cosmetics Inc* *(G-14983)*
Eutectic Engineering Co Inc 313 892-2248
817 Rock Spring Rd Bloomfield Hills (48304) *(G-1765)*
Ev Anywhere LLC 313 653-9870
3011 W Grand Blvd # 1800 Detroit (48202) *(G-4044)*
Evan's Industries, Detroit *Also called Clair Evans-St Inc* *(G-3938)*
Evans Coatings L L C 248 583-9890
1330 Souter Dr Troy (48083) *(G-16354)*
Evans Holding Company, Detroit *Also called Ehc Inc* *(G-4030)*
Evans Industries Inc (HQ) 313 259-2266
200 Renaissance Ctr # 3150 Detroit (48243) *(G-4045)*
Evans Industries Inc 313 272-8200
12402 Hubbell St Detroit (48227) *(G-4046)*
Evans Tempcon Delaware LLC 616 361-2681
3260 Eagle Park Dr Ne Ne100 Grand Rapids (49525) *(G-6388)*
Evans Tool & Engineering Inc 616 791-6333
4287 3 Mile Rd Nw Grand Rapids (49534) *(G-6389)*
Eve Salonspa 269 327-4811
7117 S Westnedge Ave 3b Portage (49002) *(G-12994)*
Evelyn Robertson Lett 248 569-8746
27125 Everett St Southfield (48076) *(G-14901)*
Evelyn's Bakery and Catering, Southfield *Also called Evelyn Robertson Lett* *(G-14901)*
Even Weight Brush LLC 906 863-3319
603 6th St Menominee (49858) *(G-10732)*
Even-Cut Abrasive Company 216 881-9595
3890 Buchanan Ave Sw Grand Rapids (49548) *(G-6390)*
Evenheat Kiln Inc 989 856-2281
6949 Legion Rd Caseville (48725) *(G-2505)*
Evening News 734 242-1100
20 W 1st St Monroe (48161) *(G-11030)*
Evening News The, Coldwater *Also called Gatehouse Media Mich Holdings* *(G-3304)*
Ever-Flex Inc 313 389-2060
1490 John A Papalas Dr Lincoln Park (48146) *(G-9576)*
Everblades Inc 906 483-0174
46104 State Highway M26 Atlantic Mine (49905) *(G-735)*
Everest Energy Fund L L C 586 445-2300
30078 Schoenherr Rd # 150 Warren (48088) *(G-17023)*
Everest Expedition LLC 616 392-1848
199 E 17th St Holland (49423) *(G-7627)*
Everest Manufacturing Inc 313 401-2608
23800 Research Dr Farmington Hills (48335) *(G-4993)*
Everfresh Beverages Inc 586 755-9500
6600 E 9 Mile Rd Warren (48091) *(G-17024)*
Evergreen Grease Service Inc 517 264-9913
4382 3rd St Adrian (49221) *(G-63)*
Evergreen Lane Farm LLC 269 543-9900
1824 66th St Fennville (49408) *(G-5171)*
Evergreen Winery LLC 989 392-2044
3835 Huszan Dr Bay City (48706) *(G-1311)*
Everist Genomics Inc (PA) 734 929-9475
455 E Eisenhower Pkwy # 200 Ann Arbor (48108) *(G-450)*
Everlast Concrete Tech LLC 248 894-1900
31876 Northwestern Hwy Farmington Hills (48334) *(G-4994)*
Everson Tool & Machine Ltd 906 932-3440
620 Easy St Ironwood (49938) *(G-8327)*
Evia Learning Inc 616 393-8803
720 E 8th St Ste 4 Holland (49423) *(G-7628)*
Eview 360 Corp 248 306-5191
39255 Country Club Dr B1 Farmington Hills (48331) *(G-4995)*
Evjump Solar Inc 734 277-5075
149 Sheffield Saline (48176) *(G-14388)*
Evolution Tool Inc 810 664-5500
587 Mccormick Dr Lapeer (48446) *(G-9460)*
Evoqua Water Technologies LLC 616 772-9011
2155 112th Ave Holland (49424) *(G-7629)*
Ews Legacy LLC (PA) 248 853-6363
2119 Austin Ave Rochester Hills (48309) *(G-13421)*
Exaconnect Corp 810 232-1400
5141 Gateway Ctr Ste 400 Flint (48507) *(G-5426)*
Exatec LLC 248 926-4200
31220 Oak Creek Dr Wixom (48393) *(G-17807)*
Excavation, Manistique *Also called Joseph Lakosky Logging* *(G-10442)*
Excel Circuits LLC 248 373-0700
2601 Lapeer Rd Auburn Hills (48326) *(G-857)*
Excel Graphics 248 442-9390
31647 8 Mile Rd Livonia (48152) *(G-9731)*
Excel Medical Products Inc 810 714-4775
28011 Grand Oaks Ct Wixom (48393) *(G-17808)*
Excel Screw Machine Tools 313 383-4200
20300 Lorne St Taylor (48180) *(G-15717)*
Excelda Mfg Holdg LLC 517 223-8000
900 Garden Ln Fowlerville (48836) *(G-5563)*
Excell Machine & Tool Co LLC 231 728-1210
1084 E Hackley Ave Muskegon (49444) *(G-11318)*
Excell Paving Plus, Coldwater *Also called RWS & Associates LLC* *(G-3328)*
Excellence Manufacturing Inc 616 456-9928
629 Ionia Ave Sw Grand Rapids (49503) *(G-6391)*
Excellent Designs Swimwear 586 977-9140
5751 E 13 Mile Rd Warren (48092) *(G-17025)*
Exceptional Product Sales LLC 586 286-3240
16010 19 Mile Rd Ste 103 Clinton Township (48038) *(G-3110)*
Exclusive Imagery Inc 248 436-2999
1505 E 11 Mile Rd Royal Oak (48067) *(G-13927)*
Exco Extrusion Dies Inc 586 749-5400
56617 N Bay Dr Chesterfield (48051) *(G-2774)*
Excrution Painting, Garden City *Also called International Extrusions Inc* *(G-5830)*
Executive Operations LLC 313 312-0653
2340 Leigh Ct Canton (48188) *(G-2373)*
Exedy-Dynax America Corp 734 397-6556
8601 Haggerty Rd Van Buren Twp (48111) *(G-16760)*
Exel Industries Group, Plymouth *Also called Sames Kremlin Inc* *(G-12747)*
Exfil, Livonia *Also called Air Filter & Equipment Inc* *(G-9632)*
Exide Technologies 248 853-5000
2750 Auburn Rd Auburn Hills (48326) *(G-858)*
Exlterra Inc 248 268-2336
618 E 10 Mile Rd Hazel Park (48030) *(G-7437)*
Exo-S US LLC 248 614-9707
1500 W Big Beaver Rd 101c Troy (48084) *(G-16355)*
Exo-S US LLC 517 278-8567
25 Concept Dr Coldwater (49036) *(G-3303)*
Exodus Pressure Control 231 258-8001
110 W Park Dr Kalkaska (49646) *(G-8942)*
Exone Americas LLC (HQ) 248 740-1580
2341 Alger Dr Troy (48083) *(G-16356)*

ALPHABETIC SECTION Fabrication Concepts LLC

Exotic Automation & Supply, Farmington Hills *Also called Exotic Rubber & Plastics Corp* ***(G-4996)***

Exotic Rubber & Plastics Corp (PA) 248 477-2122
34700 Grand River Ave Farmington Hills (48335) ***(G-4996)***

Expan Inc (PA) 586 725-0405
51513 Industrial Dr New Baltimore (48047) ***(G-11484)***

Expectancy Learning LLC 866 829-9533
3152 Peregrine Dr Ne # 110 Grand Rapids (49525) ***(G-6392)***

Experi-Metal Inc 586 977-7800
6385 Wall St Sterling Heights (48312) ***(G-15335)***

Experienced Concepts Inc 586 752-4200
15400 Chets Way St Armada (48005) ***(G-719)***

Expernced Prcsion McHining Inc 989 635-2299
2720 Lamotte St Marlette (48453) ***(G-10496)***

Expert Air Cleaner Maint 248 889-3760
359 Meribah Highland (48356) ***(G-7492)***

Expert Cleaning Solutions Inc 517 545-9095
2440 W Highland Rd Howell (48843) ***(G-8039)***

Expert Coating Company Inc 616 453-8261
2855 Marlin Ct Nw Grand Rapids (49534) ***(G-6393)***

Expert Machine & Tool Inc 810 984-2323
2424 Lapeer Rd Port Huron (48060) ***(G-12917)***

Expo Kitchen & Bath Ltd 734 741-5888
2459 W Stadium Blvd Ann Arbor (48103) ***(G-451)***

Exponent, The, Brooklyn *Also called Schepeler Corporation* ***(G-2042)***

Export Corporation 810 227-6153
6060 Whitmore Lake Rd Brighton (48116) ***(G-1920)***

Export Service International 248 620-7100
8098 Caribou Lake Ln Clarkston (48346) ***(G-2919)***

Exposure Unlimited Inc 248 459-9104
4708 Brookside Rd Fenton (48430) ***(G-5205)***

Express Care of South Lyon 248 437-6919
501 S Lafayette St South Lyon (48178) ***(G-14791)***

Express Cnc & Fabrication LLC 517 937-8760
3041 North Adams Rd Jonesville (49250) ***(G-8654)***

Express Coat Corporation 586 773-2682
27350 Gloede Dr Warren (48088) ***(G-17026)***

Express Machine & Tool Co 586 758-5080
2204 E 9 Mile Rd Warren (48091) ***(G-17027)***

Express Printer, Eastpointe *Also called Hadd Enterprises* ***(G-4702)***

Express Publications Inc 231 947-8787
129 E Front St 200 Traverse City (49684) ***(G-15967)***

Express Welding Inc 906 786-8808
2525 14th Ave N Escanaba (49829) ***(G-4829)***

Expressign Design 734 747-7444
2239 W Liberty St Ann Arbor (48103) ***(G-452)***

Exquise Inc 248 220-9048
2512 W Grand Blvd Detroit (48208) ***(G-4047)***

Exsto US Inc 734 834-7225
2723 S State St Ste 150 Ann Arbor (48104) ***(G-453)***

Extang Corporation 734 677-0444
5400 S State Rd Ann Arbor (48108) ***(G-454)***

Extol Inc (PA) 616 741-0231
651 Case Karsten Dr Zeeland (49464) ***(G-18136)***

Extreem Laser Dynamics, Traverse City *Also called Rare Earth Hardwoods Inc* ***(G-16090)***

Extreme Fitness Gym 989 681-8339
116 N Mill St Saint Louis (48880) ***(G-14363)***

Extreme Machine Inc 810 231-0521
10068 Industrial Dr Whitmore Lake (48189) ***(G-17699)***

Extreme Machine Inc (PA) 810 231-0521
10034 Industrial Dr Whitmore Lake (48189) ***(G-17700)***

Extreme Precision Screw Pdts 810 744-1980
1838 Remell St Flint (48503) ***(G-5427)***

Extreme Screen Prints 616 889-8305
3723 Burlingame Ave Sw Grand Rapids (49509) ***(G-6394)***

Extreme Screenprints 616 889-8305
3030 Sangra Ave Sw Grandville (49418) ***(G-7034)***

Extreme Tool and Engrg Inc (PA) 906 229-9100
999 Production Dr Wakefield (49968) ***(G-16850)***

Extreme Tool and Engrg Inc 906 229-9100
703 Chippawa Dr Wakefield (49968) ***(G-16851)***

Extreme Wire EDM Service Inc 616 249-3901
3636 Busch Dr Sw Grandville (49418) ***(G-7035)***

Extrude Hone LLC 616 647-9050
2882 Northridge Dr Nw Grand Rapids (49544) ***(G-6395)***

Extruded Aluminum Corporation 616 794-0300
7200 Industrial Dr Belding (48809) ***(G-1413)***

Extruded Metals Inc 616 794-4851
302 Ashfield St Belding (48809) ***(G-1414)***

Extrunet America Inc 517 301-4504
903 Industrial Dr Tecumseh (49286) ***(G-15793)***

Extrusion Punch & Tool Inc 248 689-3300
2326 Alger Dr Troy (48083) ***(G-16357)***

Extrusions Division Inc (PA) 616 247-3611
201 Cottage Grove St Se Grand Rapids (49507) ***(G-6396)***

Eyes Media, Traverse City *Also called Business News* ***(G-15925)***

Eyewear Detroit Company 248 396-2214
6466 Shappie Rd Clarkston (48348) ***(G-2920)***

EZ Fuel Inc 810 744-4452
1330 E Atherton Rd Flint (48507) ***(G-5428)***

EZ Logic, Farmington Hills *Also called E Z Logic Data Systems Inc* ***(G-4977)***

EZ Vent LLC 616 874-2787
8235 Belding Rd Ne Rockford (49341) ***(G-13568)***

Ezbake Technologies LLC 817 430-1621
7244 Driftwood Dr Fenton (48430) ***(G-5206)***

Ezm LLC 248 438-6570
39555 Orchard Hill Pl # 600 Novi (48375) ***(G-11886)***

F & A Enterprises of Michigan 906 228-3222
519 N Lakeshore Blvd Marquette (49855) ***(G-10531)***

F & A Fabricating, Battle Creek *Also called Hdn F&A Inc* ***(G-1197)***

F & F Industries Inc 313 278-7600
7620 Telegraph Rd Taylor (48180) ***(G-15718)***

F & F Mold Inc 517 287-5866
5931 Knowles Rd North Adams (49262) ***(G-11654)***

F & G Tool Company 734 261-0022
11863 Brookfield St Livonia (48150) ***(G-9732)***

F & H Manufacturing Co Inc 517 783-2311
149 W Porter St Jackson (49202) ***(G-8445)***

F & S Enterprises Inc 269 672-7145
1473 14th St Otsego (49078) ***(G-12239)***

F & S Tool & Gauge Co Inc 517 787-2661
1027 E South St Jackson (49203) ***(G-8446)***

F & T Fur Harvesters Trdg Post, Alpena *Also called Inglis Farms Inc* ***(G-293)***

F A A, Farmington Hills *Also called Fujikura Automotive Amer LLC* ***(G-5006)***

F C & A, Allegan *Also called Fabricated Components & Assemb* ***(G-160)***

F C Simpson Lime Co 810 367-3510
1293 Wadhams Rd Kimball (48074) ***(G-9043)***

F F Industries 313 291-7600
7620 Telegraph Rd Taylor (48180) ***(G-15719)***

F G Cheney Limestone Co 269 763-9541
9400 Sand Rd Bellevue (49021) ***(G-1454)***

F H C, Wyoming *Also called Fhc Holding Company* ***(G-18001)***

F I D Corporation 248 373-7005
3424 Charlwood Dr Rochester Hills (48306) ***(G-13422)***

F J Lucido & Associates (PA) 586 574-3577
29400 Van Dyke Ave Warren (48093) ***(G-17028)***

F J Manufacturing Co 248 583-4777
32329 Milton Ave Madison Heights (48071) ***(G-10251)***

F L M, Clinton Township *Also called Five Lakes Manufacturing Inc* ***(G-3120)***

F M Envelope Inc 313 899-4065
5938 Linsdale St Detroit (48204) ***(G-4048)***

F M T Products Inc 517 568-3373
140 W Main St Homer (49245) ***(G-7942)***

F P Horak Company (PA) 989 892-6505
1311 Straits Dr Bay City (48706) ***(G-1312)***

F P Rosback Co 269 983-2582
125 Hawthorne Ave Saint Joseph (49085) ***(G-14310)***

F T I, Litchfield *Also called Finishing Touch Inc* ***(G-9601)***

F&B Technologies 734 856-2118
6875 Memorial Hwy Ottawa Lake (49267) ***(G-12262)***

Faac Incorporated 734 761-5836
1195 Oak Valley Dr Ann Arbor (48108) ***(G-455)***

Faac Incorporated (HQ) 734 761-5836
1229 Oak Valley Dr Ann Arbor (48108) ***(G-456)***

Fab Concepts 586 466-6411
22791 Macomb Indus Dr Clinton Township (48036) ***(G-3111)***

Fab Masters Company Inc 269 646-5315
51787 M 40 Marcellus (49067) ***(G-10464)***

Fab-All Manufacturing Inc 248 585-6700
645 Executive Dr Troy (48083) ***(G-16358)***

Fab-Alloy Company 517 787-4313
1163 E Morrell St Jackson (49203) ***(G-8447)***

Fab-Jet Services LLC 586 463-9622
44335 Macomb Indus Dr Clinton Township (48036) ***(G-3112)***

Fab-Lite Inc 231 398-8280
330 Washington St Manistee (49660) ***(G-10421)***

Fab-N-Weld Sheetmetal 269 471-7453
4445 E Shawnee Rd Berrien Springs (49103) ***(G-1594)***

Fabco Automotive, Livonia *Also called R Cushman & Associates Inc* ***(G-9904)***

Fabco Holdings Inc., Livonia *Also called Meritor Specialty Products LLC* ***(G-9838)***

Fabiano Bros Dev - Wscnsin LLC 989 509-0200
1885 Bevanda Ct Bay City (48706) ***(G-1313)***

Fabjunky LLC 323 572-4988
1908 Euro Dr Muskegon (49444) ***(G-11319)***

Fabri-Kal Corporation 269 385-5050
4141 Manchester Rd Kalamazoo (49001) ***(G-8740)***

Fabri-Tech Inc (PA) 616 662-0150
6719 Pine Ridge Ct Sw Jenison (49428) ***(G-8626)***

Fabric Patch Ltd 906 932-5260
100 W Mcleod Ave Ironwood (49938) ***(G-8328)***

Fabricari LLC 734 972-2042
7100 Huron River Dr Dexter (48130) ***(G-4492)***

Fabricated Components & Assemb 269 673-7100
603 N Eastern Ave Allegan (49010) ***(G-160)***

Fabricated Flex & Hose Sup Inc 269 342-2221
2037 Palmer Ave Kalamazoo (49001) ***(G-8741)***

Fabrication Concepts LLC 517 750-4742
347 E Main St Spring Arbor (49283) ***(G-15122)***

ALPHABETIC

Fabrication Services Inc ALPHABETIC SECTION

Fabrication Services Inc 517 796-8197
1505 E High St Jackson (49203) ***(G-8448)***
Fabrication Specialties Inc 313 891-7181
9600 Melissa Ln Davisburg (48350) ***(G-3632)***
Fabrications Plus Inc 269 749-3050
7898 Marshall Rd Olivet (49076) ***(G-12141)***
Fabrications Unlimited Inc (PA) 313 567-9616
45757 Cornwall St Shelby Township (48317) ***(G-14591)***
Fabrications Unlimited Inc 313 567-9616
4651 Beaufait St Detroit (48207) ***(G-4049)***
Fabricon Products Inc (PA) 313 841-8200
1721 W Pleasant St River Rouge (48218) ***(G-13276)***
Fabrilaser Mfg LLC 269 789-9490
1308 S Kalamazoo Ave Marshall (49068) ***(G-10567)***
Fabristeel Romulus Div, Romulus *Also called Fastentech Inc* ***(G-13675)***
Fabtec Enterprises Inc 616 878-9288
8538 Centre Indus Dr Sw Byron Center (49315) ***(G-2190)***
Fabtronic Inc 586 786-6114
51685 Industrial Dr Macomb (48042) ***(G-10121)***
Fabulous Operating Pdts LLC 810 245-5759
401 Mccormick Dr Lapeer (48446) ***(G-9461)***
Fabulous Printing Inc 734 422-5555
15076 Middlebelt Rd Livonia (48154) ***(G-9733)***
Fabx Industries Inc 616 225-1724
715 Callaghan St Greenville (48838) ***(G-7130)***
Facements, Walker *Also called Vista Manufacturing Inc* ***(G-16881)***
Factory Products Inc 269 668-3329
26375 60th Ave Mattawan (49071) ***(G-10664)***
Fahl Forest Products Inc 231 258-9734
2509 Valley Rd Mancelona (49659) ***(G-10390)***
Fair & Square Pallet & Lbr Co 989 727-3949
5700 Ratz Rd Hubbard Lake (49747) ***(G-8125)***
Fair Industries LLC 248 740-7841
3260 Talbot Dr Troy (48083) ***(G-16359)***
Fairchilds Daughters & Son LLC 906 239-6061
617 N Stephenson Ave Iron Mountain (49801) ***(G-8283)***
Fairfax Prints Ltd 517 321-5590
4918 Delta River Dr Lansing (48906) ***(G-9227)***
Fairfield Investment Co 734 427-4141
32738 Barkley St Livonia (48154) ***(G-9734)***
Fairlane Co 586 294-6100
33792 Doreka Fraser (48026) ***(G-5653)***
Fairlane Gear Inc 734 459-2440
8182 N Canton Center Rd Canton (48187) ***(G-2374)***
Fairmont Sign Company (PA) 313 368-4000
3750 E Outer Dr Detroit (48234) ***(G-4050)***
Fairmount Santrol Inc 440 279-0204
17350 Ryan Rd Detroit (48212) ***(G-4051)***
Fairmount Santrol Inc 800 255-7263
400 Riverview Dr Ste 302 Benton Harbor (49022) ***(G-1497)***
Fairview Farms 269 449-0500
6735 S Scottdale Rd Berrien Springs (49103) ***(G-1595)***
Fairview Sawmill Inc 989 848-5238
1901 Kneeland Rd Fairview (48621) ***(G-4890)***
Fairway Optical Inc 231 744-6168
4490 W Giles Rd Muskegon (49445) ***(G-11320)***
Fairway Products Division, Hillsdale *Also called Acme Mills Company* ***(G-7513)***
Faith Alive Christn Resources (PA) 800 333-8300
1700 28th St Se Grand Rapids (49508) ***(G-6397)***
Faith Plastics LLC 269 646-2294
239 E Main St Marcellus (49067) ***(G-10465)***
Faith Publishing Service 517 853-7600
1500 E Saginaw St Ofc C Lansing (48906) ***(G-9228)***
Falcon Consulting Services LLC 989 262-9325
112 1/2 W Chisholm St A Alpena (49707) ***(G-288)***
Falcon Corporation 616 842-7071
14510 Cleveland St Spring Lake (49456) ***(G-15141)***
Falcon Industry Inc 586 468-7010
44660 Macomb Indus Dr Clinton Township (48036) ***(G-3113)***
Falcon Lakeside Mfg Inc 269 429-6193
4999 Advance Way Stevensville (49127) ***(G-15567)***
Falcon Motorsports Inc 248 328-2222
255 Elm St Holly (48442) ***(G-7878)***
Falcon Printing Inc 616 676-3737
6360 Fulton St E Ada (49301) ***(G-15)***
Falcon Promotional Tools, Ada *Also called Falcon Printing Inc* ***(G-15)***
Falcon Rme, Midland *Also called Mmgg Inc* ***(G-10894)***
Falcon Stamping Inc 517 540-6197
1125 Grand Oaks Dr Howell (48843) ***(G-8040)***
Falcon Tool & Die, Spring Lake *Also called Falcon Corporation* ***(G-15141)***
Falcon Trucking Company (PA) 313 843-7200
9300 Dix Dearborn (48120) ***(G-3704)***
Falcon Trucking Company 989 656-2831
8785 Ribble Rd Bay Port (48720) ***(G-1373)***
Falcon Trucking Company 248 634-9471
16240 Tindall Rd Davisburg (48350) ***(G-3633)***
Falvey Limited 517 263-2699
3456 N Adrian Hwy Adrian (49221) ***(G-64)***
Famek Inc 734 895-6794
2000 Town Ctr Ste 1830 Southfield (48075) ***(G-14902)***
Famethis Inc 734 645-9100
10829 Wynns Rd Pinckney (48169) ***(G-12497)***
Family Fare LLC 269 965-5631
294 Highland Ave Battle Creek (49015) ***(G-1184)***
Family Machinists 734 340-1848
20456 Lexington Redford (48240) ***(G-13160)***
Family Safety Products Inc 616 530-6540
2879 Remico St Sw Grandville (49418) ***(G-7036)***
Family Trdtons Tree Stands LLC 517 543-3926
202 Morrell St Charlotte (48813) ***(G-2647)***
Fams T-Shirts and Designs 248 841-1086
120 E University Dr Rochester (48307) ***(G-13320)***
Fannon Products LLC (PA) 810 794-2000
5318 Pointe Tremble Rd Algonac (48001) ***(G-143)***
Fantastic Images Signs 248 683-5556
1032 W Huron St Waterford (48328) ***(G-17343)***
Fanuc America Corporation (HQ) 248 377-7000
3900 W Hamlin Rd Rochester Hills (48309) ***(G-13423)***
Fapco Inc 269 695-6889
926 Terre Coupe St Buchanan (49107) ***(G-2115)***
Far Associates Inc 734 282-1881
11801 Longsdorf St Riverview (48193) ***(G-13294)***
Farago & Associates LLC 248 546-7070
29200 Northwestern Hwy # 114 Southfield (48034) ***(G-14903)***
Farber Concessions Inc 313 387-1600
14950 Telegraph Rd Redford (48239) ***(G-13161)***
Farm Country Cheese House 989 352-7779
7263 Kendalville Rd Lakeview (48850) ***(G-9172)***
Farm Country Frz Custard & Kit 989 687-6700
2890 N Meridian Rd Sanford (48657) ***(G-14450)***
Farm Crest Foods, Pigeon *Also called Active Feed Company* ***(G-12485)***
Farmer Bros Co 989 791-7985
3691 Fashion Square Blvd # 6 Saginaw (48603) ***(G-14036)***
Farmer Musical Instruments 206 412-5379
8568 E Lincoln Rd Cedar (49621) ***(G-2541)***
Farmers Egg Cooperative 517 649-8957
1300 W Mount Hope Hwy Charlotte (48813) ***(G-2648)***
Farmington Bakery 248 442-2360
33250 Grand River Ave Farmington (48336) ***(G-4899)***
Farmington Cabinet Company 248 476-2666
30795 8 Mile Rd Livonia (48152) ***(G-9735)***
Farnell Contracting Inc 810 714-3421
3355 Lahring Rd Linden (48451) ***(G-9590)***
Farnese North America Inc 616 844-8651
4095 Embassy Dr Se Grand Rapids (49546) ***(G-6398)***
Faro Screen Process Inc 734 207-8400
41805 Koppernick Rd Canton (48187) ***(G-2375)***
Faro Technologies Inc 248 669-8620
46998 Magellan Ste 100 Wixom (48393) ***(G-17809)***
Farr & Faron Associates Inc 810 229-7730
136 E Grand River Ave 3 Brighton (48116) ***(G-1921)***
Fas N Nedschroef Amer Inc 586 795-1220
6635 19 Mile Rd Sterling Heights (48314) ***(G-15336)***
Fast Cash 269 966-0079
641 Capital Ave Sw Battle Creek (49015) ***(G-1185)***
Fastco Industries Inc (PA) 616 453-5428
2685 Mullins Ct Nw Grand Rapids (49534) ***(G-6399)***
Fastco Industries Inc 616 389-1390
2700 Courier Dr Nw Grand Rapids (49534) ***(G-6400)***
Fastco Industries Inc 616 453-5428
2759 Mullins Ave Grand Rapids (49534) ***(G-6401)***
Fastener Advance PDT Co Ltd 734 428-8070
750 Hogan Rd Manchester (48158) ***(G-10406)***
Fastener Coatings Inc 269 279-5134
1111 River St Three Rivers (49093) ***(G-15861)***
Fastentech Inc 313 299-8500
7845 Middlebelt Rd # 200 Romulus (48174) ***(G-13675)***
Fastime Racing Engines & Parts 734 947-1600
12254 Universal Dr Taylor (48180) ***(G-15720)***
Fastsigns, Livonia *Also called Kore Group Inc* ***(G-9800)***
Fastsigns, Kalamazoo *Also called Digital Impact Design Inc* ***(G-8727)***
Fastsigns, Ann Arbor *Also called Kore Group Inc* ***(G-519)***
Fastsigns 248 488-9010
27853 Orchard Lake Rd Farmington Hills (48334) ***(G-4997)***
Fastsigns International Inc 231 941-0300
1420 Trade Center Dr Traverse City (49696) ***(G-15968)***
Fastube LLC 734 398-0474
41714 Haggerty Cir S Canton (48188) ***(G-2376)***
Fata Aluminum LLC (PA) 248 724-7669
2333 E Walton Blvd Auburn Hills (48326) ***(G-859)***
Fata Automation Inc (PA) 248 724-7660
2333 E Walton Blvd Auburn Hills (48326) ***(G-860)***
Fathom Drones Inc 586 216-7047
401 Hall St Sw Ste 213 Grand Rapids (49503) ***(G-6402)***
Fatigue Dynamics Inc 248 641-9487
5250 Cardinal Dr Troy (48098) ***(G-16360)***
Faubles Prtg & Specialities 231 775-4973
611 Seneca Pl Cadillac (49601) ***(G-2246)***
Faulkner Fabricators Inc 269 473-3073
10106 N Tudor Rd Berrien Springs (49103) ***(G-1596)***

ALPHABETIC SECTION Fema Corporation of Michigan

Faurecia...248 917-1702
26555 Evergreen Rd # 1700 Southfield (48076) ***(G-14904)***
Faurecia Auto Seating LLC...248 563-9241
13000 Oakland Park Blvd Highland Park (48203) ***(G-7503)***
Faurecia Auto Seating LLC...248 563-9241
12900 Oakland Park Blvd Highland Park (48203) ***(G-7504)***
Faurecia Emissions Contl Tech...734 947-1688
24850 Northline Rd Taylor (48180) ***(G-15721)***
Faurecia Interior Systems Inc (HQ)...248 724-5100
2500 Executive Hills Dr Auburn Hills (48326) ***(G-861)***
Faurecia Interior Systems Inc...248 409-3500
2500 Executive Hills Dr Auburn Hills (48326) ***(G-862)***
Faurecia Interior Systems Inc...734 429-0030
7700 E Michigan Ave Saline (48176) ***(G-14389)***
Faurecia Intr Systems Saline, Saline *Also called Faurecia Interior Systems Inc* ***(G-14389)***
Faurecia North America, Auburn Hills *Also called Faurecia Interior Systems Inc* ***(G-861)***
Faurecia North America Inc...248 288-1000
2800 High Meadow Cir Auburn Hills (48326) ***(G-863)***
Faurecia USA Holdings Inc (HQ)...248 724-5100
2800 High Meadow Cir Auburn Hills (48326) ***(G-864)***
Favi Entertainment, Washington Township *Also called Yakel Enterprises LLC* ***(G-17320)***
Faygo Beverages Inc (HQ)...313 925-1600
3579 Gratiot Ave Detroit (48207) ***(G-4052)***
Fbe Associates Inc...989 894-2785
513 N Madison Ave Ste 101 Bay City (48708) ***(G-1314)***
Fbe Corp...517 333-2605
3510 West Rd East Lansing (48823) ***(G-4656)***
Fbh Architectural Security Inc...734 332-3740
1080 Rosewood St Ann Arbor (48104) ***(G-457)***
FCA Intrntional Operations LLC...800 334-9200
1000 Chrysler Dr Auburn Hills (48326) ***(G-865)***
FCA North America Holdings LLC (HQ)...248 512-2950
1000 Chrysler Dr Auburn Hills (48326) ***(G-866)***
FCA US LLC...248 512-2950
1000 Chrysler Dr Auburn Hills (48326) ***(G-867)***
FCA US LLC...586 497-3630
22800 Mound Rd Warren (48091) ***(G-17029)***
FCA US LLC...800 247-9753
800 Chrysler Dr Auburn Hills (48326) ***(G-868)***
FCA US LLC...586 468-2891
151 Lafayette St Mount Clemens (48043) ***(G-11130)***
FCA US LLC...313 369-7312
3675 E Outer Dr Detroit (48234) ***(G-4053)***
FCA US LLC...734 478-5658
5800 N Ann Arbor Rd Dundee (48131) ***(G-4582)***
FCA US LLC...313 957-7000
4500 Saint Jean St Detroit (48214) ***(G-4054)***
FCA US LLC...586 978-0067
38111 Van Dyke Ave Sterling Heights (48312) ***(G-15337)***
FCA US LLC...586 497-2500
21500 Mound Rd Warren (48091) ***(G-17030)***
FCA US LLC...313 956-6460
12501 Chrysler Dr Detroit (48203) ***(G-4055)***
FCA US LLC (HQ)...248 576-5741
1000 Chrysler Dr Auburn Hills (48326) ***(G-869)***
FCA US LLC...248 576-5741
6565 E 8 Mile Rd Warren (48091) ***(G-17031)***
Fcaus Dundee Engine Plant...734 529-9256
5800 N Ann Arbor Rd Dundee (48131) ***(G-4583)***
Fcx Performance Inc (PA)...734 654-2201
845 Monroe St Carleton (48117) ***(G-2454)***
FD Lake Company...616 241-5639
3313 Lousma Dr Se Grand Rapids (49548) ***(G-6403)***
Fdi Group, Novi *Also called Startech Software Systems Inc* ***(G-12003)***
FDS Engineering, Iron Mountain *Also called Fairchilds Daughters & Son LLC* ***(G-8283)***
Fear Finder, The, Troy *Also called Halloween Events* ***(G-16389)***
Feb Inc...231 759-0911
2333 Henry St Muskegon (49441) ***(G-11321)***
Fec Inc...586 580-2622
51341 Celeste Shelby Township (48315) ***(G-14592)***
FEC Automation Systems, Shelby Township *Also called Fec Inc* ***(G-14592)***
Federal Broach & Mch Co LLC...989 539-7420
1961 Sullivan Dr Harrison (48625) ***(G-7311)***
Federal Group Usa Inc...248 545-5000
21126 Bridge St Southfield (48033) ***(G-14905)***
Federal Group, The, Southfield *Also called Federal Group Usa Inc* ***(G-14905)***
Federal Industrial Svcs Inc (PA)...586 427-6383
11223 E 8 Mile Rd Warren (48089) ***(G-17032)***
Federal Screw Works (PA)...734 941-4211
34846 Goddard Rd Romulus (48174) ***(G-13676)***
Federal Screw Works...734 941-4211
34846 Goddard Rd Romulus (48174) ***(G-13677)***
Federal Screw Works...734 941-4211
400 N Dekraft Ave Big Rapids (49307) ***(G-1626)***
Federal Screw Works...231 796-7664
400 N Dekraft Ave Big Rapids (49307) ***(G-1627)***
Federal Screw Works...231 922-9500
2270 Traversefield Dr Traverse City (49686) ***(G-15969)***
Federal Screw Works...810 227-7712
77 Advance St Brighton (48116) ***(G-1922)***
Federal-Mogul, Southfield *Also called Tenneco Inc* ***(G-15044)***
Federal-Mogul Chassis LLC (HQ)...248 354-7700
27300 W 11 Mile Rd Southfield (48034) ***(G-14906)***
Federal-Mogul Ignition LLC (HQ)...248 354-7700
26555 Northwestern Hwy Southfield (48033) ***(G-14907)***
Federal-Mogul Motorparts, Southfield *Also called Federal-Mogul Chassis LLC* ***(G-14906)***
Federal-Mogul Motorparts LLC (HQ)...248 354-7700
27300 W 11 Mile Rd Southfield (48034) ***(G-14908)***
Federal-Mogul Piston Rings Inc (HQ)...248 354-7700
26555 Northwestern Hwy Southfield (48033) ***(G-14909)***
Federal-Mogul Powertrain Inc...616 887-8231
200 Maple St Sparta (49345) ***(G-15094)***
Federal-Mogul Powertrain LLC...734 254-0100
47001 Port St Plymouth (48170) ***(G-12620)***
Federal-Mogul Powertrain LLC...734 930-1590
560 Avis Dr Ann Arbor (48108) ***(G-458)***
Federal-Mogul Powertrain LLC...616 754-1272
409 E Cass St Greenville (48838) ***(G-7131)***
Federal-Mogul Powertrain LLC...616 754-5681
510 E Grove St Greenville (48838) ***(G-7132)***
Federal-Mogul Powertrain LLC (HQ)...248 354-7700
27300 W 11 Mile Rd Southfield (48034) ***(G-14910)***
Federal-Mogul Products US LLC (HQ)...248 354-7700
26555 Northwestern Hwy Southfield (48033) ***(G-14911)***
Federal-Mogul Valve Train Inte (HQ)...248 354-7700
27300 W 11 Mile Rd Southfield (48034) ***(G-14912)***
Federal-Mogul World Wide LLC (HQ)...248 354-7700
26555 Northwestern Hwy Southfield (48033) ***(G-14913)***
Federated Oil & Gas Prpts Inc...231 929-4466
12719 S West Bay Shore Dr # 5 Traverse City (49684) ***(G-15970)***
Federated Publications Inc (HQ)...269 962-5394
155 Van Buren St W Battle Creek (49017) ***(G-1186)***
Federl-Mgul Dutch Holdings Inc...248 354-7700
26555 Northwestern Hwy Southfield (48033) ***(G-14914)***
Fedex Office & Print Svcs Inc...517 347-8656
4950 Marsh Rd 17 Okemos (48864) ***(G-12123)***
Fedex Office & Print Svcs Inc...616 336-1900
233 Fulton St W Grand Rapids (49503) ***(G-6404)***
Fedex Office & Print Svcs Inc...734 761-4539
505 E Liberty St Ste 400 Ann Arbor (48104) ***(G-459)***
Fedex Office & Print Svcs Inc...313 359-3124
23400 Michigan Ave # 145 Dearborn (48124) ***(G-3705)***
Fedex Office & Print Svcs Inc...248 932-3373
29306 Orchard Lake Rd Farmington Hills (48334) ***(G-4998)***
Fedex Office & Print Svcs Inc...517 332-5855
626 Michigan Ave East Lansing (48823) ***(G-4657)***
Fedex Office & Print Svcs Inc...248 377-2222
2785 University Dr Auburn Hills (48326) ***(G-870)***
Fedex Office & Print Svcs Inc...616 957-7888
3614 28th St Se Grand Rapids (49512) ***(G-6405)***
Fedex Office & Print Svcs Inc...248 355-5670
28844 Northwestern Hwy Southfield (48034) ***(G-14915)***
Fedex Office & Print Svcs Inc...269 344-7445
5730 S Westnedge Ave Portage (49002) ***(G-12995)***
Fedex Office & Print Svcs Inc...586 296-4890
31980 Gratiot Ave Roseville (48066) ***(G-13803)***
Fedex Office & Print Svcs Inc...248 443-2679
27661 Southfield Rd Lathrup Village (48076) ***(G-9499)***
Fedex Office & Print Svcs Inc...734 522-7322
7677 N Wayne Rd Westland (48185) ***(G-17555)***
Fedex Office & Print Svcs Inc...313 271-8877
15851 Ford Rd Dearborn (48126) ***(G-3706)***
Fedex Office & Print Svcs Inc...734 996-0050
2609 Plymouth Rd Ste 7 Ann Arbor (48105) ***(G-460)***
Fedex Office & Print Svcs Inc...248 680-0280
4050 Rochester Rd Troy (48085) ***(G-16361)***
Fedex Office & Print Svcs Inc...734 374-0225
23077 Eureka Rd Taylor (48180) ***(G-15722)***
Fedex Office & Print Svcs Inc...248 651-2679
133 S Main St Rochester (48307) ***(G-13321)***
Fedex Office Print & Ship Ctr, Grand Rapids *Also called Fedex Office & Print Svcs Inc* ***(G-6404)***
Fedex Office Print & Ship Ctr, Roseville *Also called Fedex Office & Print Svcs Inc* ***(G-13803)***
Feed - Lease Corp...248 377-0000
2750 Paldan Dr Auburn Hills (48326) ***(G-871)***
Feg Gage Inc...248 616-3631
32329 Milton Ave Madison Heights (48071) ***(G-10252)***
Feg Gage & Engineering, Madison Heights *Also called Feg Gage Inc* ***(G-10252)***
Fega Tool & Gage Company...586 469-4400
44837 Macomb Indus Dr Clinton Township (48036) ***(G-3114)***
Felicity Fountains...517 663-1324
411 S River St Eaton Rapids (48827) ***(G-4723)***
Felpausch Food Center 1955, Coldwater *Also called Spartannash Company* ***(G-3333)***
Felpausch Food Center 1992, Albion *Also called Spartannash Company* ***(G-132)***
Fema Corporation of Michigan...269 323-1369
1716 Vanderbilt Ave Portage (49024) ***(G-12996)***

ALPHABETIC

Fendt Builders Supply Inc (PA)....248 474-3211
22005 Gill Rd Farmington Hills (48335) ***(G-4999)***
Fendt Builders Supply Inc....734 663-4277
3285 W Liberty Rd Ann Arbor (48103) ***(G-461)***
Fenixx Technologies LLC....586 254-6000
6633 Diplomat Dr Sterling Heights (48314) ***(G-15338)***
Fenton Chamber Commerce....810 629-5447
104 S Adelaide St Fenton (48430) ***(G-5207)***
Fenton Concrete Inc....810 629-0783
10513 Old Us 23 Fenton (48430) ***(G-5208)***
Fenton Corporation (PA)....810 629-2858
3236 Owen Rd Fenton (48430) ***(G-5209)***
Fenton Memorials & Vaults Inc....810 629-2858
3236 Owen Rd Fenton (48430) ***(G-5210)***
Fenton Printing Inc....810 750-9450
14312 N Fenton Rd Fenton (48430) ***(G-5211)***
Fenton Radiator & Garage Inc....810 629-0923
1542 N Leroy St Ste 4 Fenton (48430) ***(G-5212)***
Fenton Sand & Gravel Inc....810 750-4293
11129 Delphinium Dr Fenton (48430) ***(G-5213)***
Fenton Systems Inc....810 636-6318
7160 S State Rd Ste B Goodrich (48438) ***(G-5953)***
Fenton Winery Brewery....810 373-4194
1545 N Leroy St Ste B Fenton (48430) ***(G-5214)***
Fenway Business Unit, Fenton *Also called Creative Foam Corporation* ***(G-5199)***
Fergin & Associates Inc....906 477-0040
Pk N9263 Kraus Rd Engadine (49827) ***(G-4798)***
Ferguson Block Co Inc....810 653-2812
5430 N State Rd Davison (48423) ***(G-3647)***
Ferguson Enterprises Inc....989 790-2220
3944 Fortune Blvd Saginaw (48603) ***(G-14037)***
Ferguson Landscaping....248 761-1005
22020 Westhampton St Oak Park (48237) ***(G-12067)***
Ferguson Steel Inc....810 984-3918
3755 N River Rd Fort Gratiot (48059) ***(G-5549)***
Fernand Corporation....231 882-9622
326 W Kalamazoo Ave # 105 Kalamazoo (49007) ***(G-8742)***
Fernco Inc (PA)....810 503-9000
300 S Dayton St Davison (48423) ***(G-3648)***
Fernco Joint Sealer Company, Davison *Also called Fernco Inc* ***(G-3648)***
Ferndale Contract Mfg, Ferndale *Also called Ferndale Laboratories Inc* ***(G-5284)***
Ferndale Laboratories Inc (HQ)....248 548-0900
780 W 8 Mile Rd Ferndale (48220) ***(G-5284)***
Ferndale Pharma Group Inc (PA)....248 548-0900
780 W 8 Mile Rd Ferndale (48220) ***(G-5285)***
Ferrante Manufacturing Co....313 571-1111
6626 Gratiot Ave Detroit (48207) ***(G-4056)***
Ferrees Tools Inc....269 965-0511
1477 Michigan Ave E Battle Creek (49014) ***(G-1187)***
Ferro Fab LLC....586 791-3561
23309 Quinn Rd Clinton Township (48035) ***(G-3115)***
Ferro Industries Inc....586 792-6001
35200 Union Lake Rd Harrison Township (48045) ***(G-7330)***
Ferrous Cal Co., Gibraltar *Also called Hycal Corp* ***(G-5904)***
Festida Foods, Grand Rapids *Also called Great Lkes Fstida Holdings Inc* ***(G-6481)***
Fettes Manufacturing Co....586 939-8500
35855 Stanley Dr Sterling Heights (48312) ***(G-15339)***
Fev Test Systems Inc....248 373-6000
4554 Glenmeade Ln Auburn Hills (48326) ***(G-872)***
Fft Sidney LLC....248 647-0400
1630 Ferguson Ct Sidney (48025) ***(G-14739)***
Fgm Solutions, Port Huron *Also called Flow Gas Misture Solutions Inc* ***(G-12918)***
Fhc Holding Company (PA)....616 538-3231
2509 29th St Sw Wyoming (49519) ***(G-18001)***
Fhi Family of Companies, Hastings *Also called Flexfab Horizons Intl Inc* ***(G-7409)***
Fl, Lansing *Also called Friedland Industries Inc* ***(G-9232)***
Fiamm Technologies, Cadillac *Also called Cadillac Engineered Plas Inc* ***(G-2237)***
Fiamm Technologies LLC....231 775-2900
1550 Leeson Ave Cadillac (49601) ***(G-2247)***
Fiamm Technologies LLC (HQ)....248 427-3200
23880 Industrial Park Dr Farmington Hills (48335) ***(G-5000)***
Fiat Chrysler Automobiles, Auburn Hills *Also called FCA US LLC* ***(G-869)***
Fiber-Char Corporation....989 356-5501
3336 Piper Rd Alpena (49707) ***(G-289)***
Fiberglass Concepts West Mich....616 392-4909
257 E 32nd St Ste 2 Holland (49423) ***(G-7630)***
Fiberglass Specialists, Flint *Also called Advanced Fiberglass Services* ***(G-5370)***
Fibers of Kalamazoo Inc....269 344-3122
436 W Willard St Ste A Kalamazoo (49007) ***(G-8743)***
Fibre Converters Inc (PA)....269 279-1700
1 Industrial Park Dr Constantine (49042) ***(G-3535)***
Fibrek Inc....906 864-9125
701 4th Ave Menominee (49858) ***(G-10733)***
Fibrek Recycling US Inc....906 863-8137
701 4th Ave Menominee (49858) ***(G-10734)***
Fibrek US Inc....906 864-9125
701 4th Ave Menominee (49858) ***(G-10735)***
Fibro Laepple Technology Inc....248 591-4494
33286 Sterling Ponds Blvd Sterling Heights (48312) ***(G-15340)***
Ficosa North America Corp (HQ)....248 307-2230
30870 Stephenson Hwy Madison Heights (48071) ***(G-10253)***
Fidelis Contracting LLC....313 361-1000
5640 Saint Jean St Detroit (48213) ***(G-4057)***
Fidia Co....248 680-0700
3098 Research Dr Rochester Hills (48309) ***(G-13424)***
Fido Enterprises Inc....586 790-8200
34692 Nova Dr Clinton Township (48035) ***(G-3116)***
Field Crafts Inc (PA)....231 325-1122
9930 Honor Hwy Honor (49640) ***(G-7952)***
Field House, Southgate *Also called Stan Kell Inc* ***(G-15083)***
Field Office, Stephenson *Also called Minerals Processing Corp* ***(G-15238)***
Field Tech Services Inc....989 786-7046
3860 County Road 491 Lewiston (49756) ***(G-9548)***
Fieldturf Usa Inc....706 625-6533
903 N Opdyke Rd Ste A1 Auburn Hills (48326) ***(G-873)***
Fife Pearce Electric Company....313 369-2560
20201 Sherwood St Detroit (48234) ***(G-4058)***
Figlan Welding....586 739-6837
7548 22 Mile Rd Shelby Township (48317) ***(G-14593)***
Filcon Inc....989 386-2986
528 Pioneer Pkwy Clare (48617) ***(G-2870)***
Filler Specialties Inc....616 772-9235
440 100th Ave Zeeland (49464) ***(G-18137)***
Fillmore Beef Company Inc....616 396-6693
5812 142nd Ave Holland (49423) ***(G-7631)***
Filter and Coating, Belmont *Also called Ohio Transmission Corporation* ***(G-1469)***
Filter Plus Inc....734 475-7403
2442 Mckinley Rd Chelsea (48118) ***(G-2710)***
Filtra-Systems Company LLC (PA)....248 427-9090
23900 Haggerty Rd Farmington Hills (48335) ***(G-5001)***
Filtration Machine....810 845-0536
10049 N Hunt Ct Davison (48423) ***(G-3649)***
Filtrona Porous Technologies, Saint Charles *Also called Porex Technologies Corporation* ***(G-14198)***
Finazzo Manufacturing Co Inc....586 757-3955
34654 Nova Dr Clinton Township (48035) ***(G-3117)***
Finch Sand & Gravel LLC....734 439-1044
10980 N Platt Rd Milan (48160) ***(G-10937)***
Fine Art Metalwork, Ironwood *Also called Cramblits Welding LLC* ***(G-8326)***
Fine Arts....269 695-6263
108 W Roe St Buchanan (49107) ***(G-2116)***
Fine Manufacturing & Tool Co, Oscoda *Also called Migatron Precision Products* ***(G-12214)***
Fine Tool Journal LLC....269 463-8255
9325 Dwight Boyer Rd Watervliet (49098) ***(G-17392)***
Fineeye Color Solutions Inc....616 988-6119
1218 Tall Tree Ln Muskegon (49445) ***(G-11322)***
Finger Fit Co....734 522-2935
24410 Harper Ave Saint Clair Shores (48080) ***(G-14248)***
Fini Finish Metal Finishing....586 758-0050
24657 Mound Rd Warren (48091) ***(G-17033)***
Finish Line Fabricating LLC....269 686-8400
779 38th St Allegan (49010) ***(G-161)***
Finishers Unlimited Monroe Inc....734 243-3502
757 S Telegraph Rd Monroe (48161) ***(G-11031)***
Finishing Services Inc....734 484-1700
877 Ann St Ypsilanti (48197) ***(G-18073)***
Finishing Specialties Inc....586 954-1338
44100 N Groesbeck Hwy Clinton Township (48036) ***(G-3118)***
Finishing Technologies Inc....616 794-4001
7125 Whites Bridge Rd Belding (48809) ***(G-1415)***
Finishing Touch Inc....517 542-5581
191 Simpson Dr Litchfield (49252) ***(G-9601)***
Finkbeiner L & D Feed & Farm....734 429-9777
114 W Michigan Ave Saline (48176) ***(G-14390)***
Finkl Steel- Composite, Detroit *Also called Composite Forgings Ltd Partnr* ***(G-3944)***
Fintech, Belding *Also called Finishing Technologies Inc* ***(G-1415)***
Fintex LLC....734 946-3100
8900 Inkster Rd Romulus (48174) ***(G-13678)***
Fiore Construction....517 404-0000
936 Pingree Rd Howell (48843) ***(G-8041)***
Fire Acadamy, Wayne *Also called Backdraft Brewing Company* ***(G-17427)***
Fire and Safety, Detroit *Also called Exquise Inc* ***(G-4047)***
Fire Equipment Company....313 891-3164
20100 John R St Detroit (48203) ***(G-4059)***
Fire Fabrication & Supply, Spring Arbor *Also called Fabrication Concepts LLC* ***(G-15122)***
Fire Safety Displays Co....313 274-7888
20422 Van Born Rd Dearborn Heights (48125) ***(G-3785)***
Fire-Kote, Grand Rapids *Also called Mpd Welding - Grand Rapids Inc* ***(G-6708)***
Fire-Pit Pellets, Kingsley *Also called Michael Chris Storms* ***(G-9072)***
Fire-Rite Inc....313 273-3730
13801 Lyndon St Detroit (48227) ***(G-4060)***
Firebolt Group Inc (PA)....248 624-8880
28059 Center Oaks Ct Wixom (48393) ***(G-17810)***
Firebolt Igniting Brand Prfmce, Wixom *Also called Firebolt Group Inc* ***(G-17810)***
Fireboy-Xintex Inc (HQ)....616 735-9380
O-379 Lake Michigan Dr Nw Grand Rapids (49534) ***(G-6406)***

Firehouse Woodworks LLC...616 285-2300
1945 Kalamazoo Ave Se Grand Rapids (49507) *(G-6407)*
Fireright Controls, Grand Haven *Also called Warner Instruments (G-6096)*
Fireside Coffee Company Inc...810 635-9196
3239 S Elms Rd Swartz Creek (48473) *(G-15666)*
First Choice of Elkhart Inc...269 483-2010
10888 Us Highway 12 White Pigeon (49099) *(G-17648)*
First Class Silkscreening EMB, Southgate *Also called 1st Class Embroidery LLC (G-15071)*
First Class Tire Shredders Inc...810 639-5888
7302 W Vienna Rd Clio (48420) *(G-3271)*
First Due Fire Supply Company...517 969-3065
207 E Kipp Rd Mason (48854) *(G-10638)*
First Impression Prtg Howell, Howell *Also called Donalyn Enterprises Inc (G-8032)*
First Imprssons Cstm Printwear...586 783-5210
44432 Reynolds Dr Clinton Township (48036) *(G-3119)*
First Optometry Lab...248 546-1300
195 Ajax Dr Madison Heights (48071) *(G-10254)*
First Place Manufacturing LLC...231 798-1694
6234 Norton Center Dr Norton Shores (49441) *(G-11755)*
First Response Med Sups LLC...313 731-2554
2020 N Lafayette St Dearborn (48128) *(G-3707)*
First Technology Safety System, Farmington Hills *Also called Humantics Innvtive Sltions Inc (G-5023)*
Firstronic LLC...616 456-9220
1655 Michigan St Ne Grand Rapids (49503) *(G-6408)*
Fischell Machinery LLC...517 445-2828
6122 Whaley Hwy Clayton (49235) *(G-3007)*
Fischer America Inc...248 276-1940
1084 Doris Rd Auburn Hills (48326) *(G-874)*
Fischer Automotive Systems, Auburn Hills *Also called Fischer America Inc (G-874)*
Fischer Tanks LLC...231 362-8265
13884 Rengo Ave Kaleva (49645) *(G-8932)*
Fischer Tool & Die Corp (PA)...734 847-4788
7155 Industrial Dr Ste A Temperance (48182) *(G-15828)*
Fish On Sports Inc...231 342-5231
11838 Us Highway 31 Interlochen (49643) *(G-8240)*
Fisher & Company Incorporated (PA)...586 746-2000
33300 Fisher Dr Saint Clair Shores (48082) *(G-14249)*
Fisher & Company Incorporated...248 280-0808
1625 W Maple Rd Troy (48084) *(G-16362)*
Fisher & Company Incorporated...248 280-0808
1625 W Maple Rd Troy (48084) *(G-16363)*
Fisher & Company Incorporated...586 746-2280
33200 Fisher Dr Saint Clair Shores (48082) *(G-14250)*
Fisher & Company Incorporated...586 746-2000
6550 Progress Dr Sterling Heights (48312) *(G-15341)*
Fisher & Company Incorporated...586 746-2101
1625 W Marble Rd Troy (48084) *(G-16364)*
Fisher Dynamics, Saint Clair Shores *Also called Fisher & Company Incorporated (G-14249)*
Fisher Dynamics Corporation...586 746-2000
33180 Fisher Dr Saint Clair Shores (48082) *(G-14251)*
Fisher Dynamics Metal Forming, Sterling Heights *Also called Fisher & Company Incorporated (G-15341)*
Fisher Kellering Co...586 749-6616
30500 Commerce Blvd Chesterfield (48051) *(G-2775)*
Fisher Redi Mix Concrete...989 723-1622
599 Oakwood Ave Owosso (48867) *(G-12291)*
Fisher Safety Structures, Saint Clair Shores *Also called Fisher & Company Incorporated (G-14250)*
Fisher Sand and Gravel Company...989 835-7187
921 Jefferson Ave Midland (48640) *(G-10861)*
Fisher-Baker Corporation...810 765-3548
420 S Water St Marine City (48039) *(G-10473)*
Fisk Precision Tech LLC...616 514-1415
3403 Lousma Dr Se Wyoming (49548) *(G-18002)*
Fisk Wood Products, Kent City *Also called County Line Pallet (G-8989)*
Fit Fuel By Kt LLC...517 643-8827
16400 Upton Rd Lot 227 East Lansing (48823) *(G-4658)*
Fitness Finders Inc...517 750-1500
1007 Hurst Rd Jackson (49201) *(G-8449)*
Fitz Manufacturing Inc...248 589-1780
324 Robbins Dr Troy (48083) *(G-16365)*
Fitz-Rite Products Inc...248 528-8440
1122 Naughton Dr Troy (48083) *(G-16366)*
Fitz-Rite Products Inc...248 360-3730
4228 Pioneer Dr Commerce Township (48390) *(G-3405)*
Fitzgerald Finishing, Detroit *Also called Flexible Controls Corporation (G-4062)*
Fitzgerald Finishing LLC...313 368-3630
17450 Filer St Detroit (48212) *(G-4061)*
Fitzpatrick Manufacturing, Sterling Heights *Also called Dura Hog Inc (G-15323)*
Five Lakes Manufacturing Inc...586 463-4123
24400 Capital Blvd Clinton Township (48036) *(G-3120)*
Five Peaks Technology LLC...231 830-8099
700 Terrace Point Dr # 200 Muskegon (49440) *(G-11323)*
Five Star Industries Inc...586 786-0500
51550 Hayes Rd Macomb (48042) *(G-10122)*
Five Star Manufacturing Inc...815 723-2245
2430 E Walton Blvd Auburn Hills (48326) *(G-875)*
Five Star Products, Troy *Also called Fsp Inc (G-16375)*
Five Star Window Coatings, Grand Rapids *Also called Chames LLC (G-6269)*
Five-Way Switch Music...269 425-2843
9478 Huntington Rd Battle Creek (49017) *(G-1188)*
Fives Cinetic Corp (HQ)...248 477-0800
23400 Halsted Rd Farmington Hills (48335) *(G-5002)*
Fixall Electric Motor Service...616 454-6863
737 Butterworth St Sw Grand Rapids (49504) *(G-6409)*
Fixtureworks LLC...586 294-6100
33792 Doreka Fraser (48026) *(G-5654)*
Fk Fuel Inc...313 383-6005
1312 Fort St Lincoln Park (48146) *(G-9577)*
Fka Distributing Co LLC (PA)...248 863-3000
3000 N Pontiac Trl Commerce Township (48390) *(G-3406)*
FL Tool Holders LLC...734 591-0134
36010 Industrial Rd Livonia (48150) *(G-9736)*
Flagg Distribution LLC...248 926-0510
48155 West Rd Ste 6 Wixom (48393) *(G-17811)*
Flagler Corporation...586 749-6300
56513 Precision Dr Chesterfield (48051) *(G-2776)*
Flairwood Industries Inc...231 798-8324
6230 Norton Center Dr Norton Shores (49441) *(G-11756)*
Flame Spray, Otsego *Also called F & S Enterprises Inc (G-12239)*
Flame Spray Technologies Inc...616 988-2622
4881 Kendrick St Se Grand Rapids (49512) *(G-6410)*
Flamingo Label Co...586 469-9587
21428 Carlo Dr Clinton Township (48038) *(G-3121)*
Flamm Pickle and Packaging Co...269 461-6916
4502 Hipps Hollow Rd Eau Claire (49111) *(G-4739)*
Flanders Industries Inc...906 863-4491
3010 10th St Menominee (49858) *(G-10736)*
Flannery Machine & Tool Inc...231 587-5076
8420 S Us Highway 131 Mancelona (49659) *(G-10391)*
Flare Fittings Incorporated...269 344-7600
2980 Interstate Pkwy Kalamazoo (49048) *(G-8744)*
Flaretite Inc...810 750-4140
7723 Kensington Ct Brighton (48116) *(G-1923)*
Flashes Advertising & News, Charlotte *Also called County Journal Inc (G-2643)*
Flashes Publishers Inc...269 673-2141
595 Jenner Dr Allegan (49010) *(G-162)*
Flashes Shoppers Guide & News...517 663-2361
241 S Cochran Ave Ste 1 Charlotte (48813) *(G-2649)*
Flashplays Live LLC...978 888-3935
412 Hamilton Pl Ann Arbor (48104) *(G-462)*
Flat Iron LLC...248 268-1668
27251 Gratiot Ave Roseville (48066) *(G-13804)*
Flat Rock, Flat Rock *Also called Bar Processing Corporation (G-5349)*
Flat Rock Metal Inc...734 782-4454
26601 W Huron River Dr Flat Rock (48134) *(G-5353)*
Flat-To-Form Metal Spc Inc...231 924-1288
9577 W 40th St Fremont (49412) *(G-5771)*
Flatout Inc...734 944-5445
1422 Woodland Dr Saline (48176) *(G-14391)*
Flatout Bakery, Saline *Also called Flatout Inc (G-14391)*
Flatrock Metal Bar and Proc, Flat Rock *Also called Flat Rock Metal Inc (G-5353)*
Flaunt It Sportswear...616 696-9084
34 N Main Ste B Cedar Springs (49319) *(G-2556)*
Flavored Group LLC...517 775-4371
437 Lentz Ct Lansing (48917) *(G-9289)*
Flavors & Fragrances, Northville *Also called Northville Laboratories Inc (G-11716)*
Fleet Engineers, Muskegon *Also called Access Works Inc (G-11259)*
Fleet Engineers Inc (PA)...231 777-2537
1800 E Keating Ave Muskegon (49442) *(G-11324)*
Fleet Truck Service, Roseville *Also called NBC Truck Equipment Inc (G-13845)*
Fleetwood Tool & Gage Inc...734 326-6737
39050 Webb Ct Westland (48185) *(G-17556)*
Fleming Fabrication Machining...906 542-3573
W9295 Bice Creek Ln Sagola (49881) *(G-14186)*
Fleming's Processing, Croswell *Also called Flemings Meat Processing (G-3596)*
Flemings Meat Processing...810 679-3668
4200 Old M 51 Croswell (48422) *(G-3596)*
Fletcher Printing...517 625-7030
9517 S Morrice Rd Morrice (48857) *(G-11119)*
Flex Building Systems LLC...586 803-6000
42400 Merrill Rd Sterling Heights (48314) *(G-15342)*
Flex Cable, Howard City *Also called Northern Cable & Automtn LLC (G-8004)*
Flex Manufacturing Inc...586 469-1076
44805 Trinity Dr Clinton Township (48038) *(G-3122)*
Flex Slotter Inc...586 756-6444
3462 E 10 Mile Rd Warren (48091) *(G-17034)*
Flex-N Gate Shelby LLC...586 759-8092
5663 E 9 Mile Rd Warren (48091) *(G-17035)*
Flex-N-Gate LLC...800 398-1496
5663 E 9 Mile Rd Warren (48091) *(G-17036)*
Flex-N-Gate Battle Creek LLC...269 962-2982
10250 F Dr N Battle Creek (49014) *(G-1189)*
Flex-N-Gate Corporation...616 222-3296
3075 Breton Rd Se Grand Rapids (49512) *(G-6411)*

A
L
P
H
A
B
E
T
I
C

Flex-N-Gate Corporation ... 517 223-5900
 8887 W Grand River Rd Fowlerville (48836) *(G-5564)*
Flex-N-Gate Corporation ... 586 773-0800
 26269 Groesbeck Hwy Warren (48089) *(G-17037)*
Flex-N-Gate Detroit LLC ... 586 759-8092
 5663 E 9 Mile Rd Warren (48091) *(G-17038)*
Flex-N-Gate Forming Tech, Warren Also called Flex-N-Gate Corporation *(G-17037)*
Flex-N-Gate Michigan LLC ... 586 759-8900
 5663 E 9 Mile Rd Warren (48091) *(G-17039)*
Flex-N-Gate Stamping LLC ... 810 772-1514
 27027 Groesbeck Hwy Warren (48089) *(G-17040)*
Flex-N-Gate Stamping LLC (HQ) ... 586 759-8900
 5663 E 9 Mile Rd Warren (48091) *(G-17041)*
Flexco, Grand Rapids Also called Flexible Steel Lacing Company *(G-6413)*
Flexdex Inc ... 810 522-9009
 10421 Citation Dr Ste 900 Brighton (48116) *(G-1924)*
Flexfab LLC ... 269 945-3533
 5333 33rd St Se Grand Rapids (49512) *(G-6412)*
Flexfab De Mexico, Hastings Also called Flexfab LLC *(G-7410)*
Flexfab Horizons Intl Inc (PA) ... 269 945-4700
 102 Cook Rd Hastings (49058) *(G-7409)*
Flexfab LLC (HQ) ... 269 945-2433
 1699 W M 43 Hwy Hastings (49058) *(G-7410)*
Flexi Display Marketing Inc ... 800 875-1725
 34119 W 12 Mile Rd # 203 Farmington Hills (48331) *(G-5003)*
Flexible Controls Corporation ... 313 368-3630
 17450 Filer St Detroit (48212) *(G-4062)*
Flexible Metal Inc ... 810 231-1300
 7495 E M 36 Hamburg (48139) *(G-7225)*
Flexible Steel Lacing Company ... 616 459-3196
 1995 Oak Industrial Dr Ne Grand Rapids (49505) *(G-6413)*
Flexpost Inc ... 616 928-0829
 2236 112th Ave Ste 80 Holland (49424) *(G-7632)*
Flextronics Automotive USA Inc (HQ) ... 248 853-5724
 2120 Austin Ave Rochester Hills (48309) *(G-13425)*
Flextronics Intl USA Inc ... 616 837-9711
 323 Skeels St Coopersville (49404) *(G-3558)*
Flight Department, Waterford Also called Williams International Co LLC *(G-17386)*
Flight Management Corporation ... 517 327-0400
 16637 Corporate Avi Dr Lansing (48906) *(G-9229)*
Flight Mold & Engineering Inc ... 810 329-2900
 1940 Fred W Moore Hwy Saint Clair (48079) *(G-14220)*
Flint Boxmakers Inc ... 810 743-0400
 G 2490 E Bristol Rd Burton (48529) *(G-2154)*
Flint CPS Inks North Amer LLC (PA) ... 734 781-4600
 14909 N Beck Rd Plymouth (48170) *(G-12621)*
Flint Group LLC ... 734 641-3062
 6380 Commerce Dr Westland (48185) *(G-17557)*
Flint Group North America LLC ... 734 781-4600
 17177 N Laurel Park Dr # 300 Livonia (48152) *(G-9737)*
Flint Group Packaging Inks ... 513 619-2085
 17177 N Laurel Park Dr # 300 Livonia (48152) *(G-9738)*
Flint Group Packaging Inks (PA) ... 734 781-4600
 17177 N Laurel Park Dr # 300 Livonia (48152) *(G-9739)*
Flint Group Print Media N Amer, Livonia Also called Flint Group US LLC *(G-9741)*
Flint Group US LLC (HQ) ... 734 781-4600
 17177 N Laurel Park Dr # 300 Livonia (48152) *(G-9740)*
Flint Group US LLC ... 269 279-5161
 111 Day Dr Three Rivers (49093) *(G-15862)*
Flint Group US LLC ... 313 538-0479
 25111 Glendale Detroit (48239) *(G-4063)*
Flint Group US LLC ... 269 381-1955
 2309 N Burdick St Kalamazoo (49007) *(G-8745)*
Flint Group US LLC ... 734 781-4600
 17177 N Laurel Park Dr # 300 Livonia (48152) *(G-9741)*
Flint Hydrostatics Inc (HQ) ... 901 794-2462
 48175 Gratiot Ave Chesterfield (48051) *(G-2777)*
Flint Ink North America Div, Detroit Also called Flint Group US LLC *(G-4063)*
Flint Ink North America Div, Kalamazoo Also called Flint Group US LLC *(G-8745)*
Flint Ink Receivables Corp ... 734 781-4600
 14909 N Beck Rd Plymouth (48170) *(G-12622)*
Flint Journal, The, Flint Also called Herald Newspapers Company Inc *(G-5446)*
Flint Lime Industries Inc ... 313 843-6050
 327 S Fordson St Detroit (48217) *(G-4064)*
Flint Optical Company Inc ... 810 235-4607
 518 S Saginaw St Flint (48502) *(G-5429)*
Flint Packaging Systems Div, Bay City Also called Delta Containers Inc *(G-1299)*
Flint Stool & Chair Co Inc ... 810 235-7001
 1517 N Dort Hwy Flint (48506) *(G-5430)*
Flipsnack LLC ... 650 741-1328
 2701 Troy Center Dr # 255 Troy (48084) *(G-16367)*
Flo-Tec Inc ... 734 455-7655
 13033 Fairlane St Livonia (48150) *(G-9742)*
Floatation Docking Inc (PA) ... 906 484-3422
 160 Hodeck St Cedarville (49719) *(G-2567)*
Flodraulic Group Incorporated ... 734 326-5400
 375 Manufacturers Dr Westland (48186) *(G-17558)*
Floorcovering Engineers LLC ... 616 299-1007
 2489 Maplevalley Dr Se Grand Rapids (49512) *(G-6414)*

Flor TEC Inc ... 616 897-3122
 4475 Causeway Dr Ne Lowell (49331) *(G-10028)*
Floracraft Cares, Ludington Also called Floracraft Corporation *(G-10059)*
Floracraft Corporation (PA) ... 231 845-5127
 1 Longfellow Pl Ludington (49431) *(G-10059)*
Florance Turning Company Inc ... 248 347-0068
 44862 Aspen Ridge Dr Northville (48168) *(G-11691)*
Florheat Company ... 517 272-4441
 3130 Sovereign Dr Lansing (48911) *(G-9368)*
Florida Coca-Cola Bottling Co ... 906 495-2261
 4760 W Curtis St Kincheloe (49788) *(G-9051)*
Florida Production Engrg Inc ... 248 588-4870
 550 Stephenson Hwy # 360 Troy (48083) *(G-16368)*
Floss Automotive Group ... 734 773-2524
 1742 Lexington Pkwy Inkster (48141) *(G-8227)*
Flotronics Inc ... 248 620-1820
 7214 Gateway Park Dr Clarkston (48346) *(G-2921)*
Flour Shop Bakery & Pizza, The, Stevensville Also called Klaus Nixdorf *(G-15573)*
Flow Coatings LLC ... 248 625-3052
 4866 White Lake Rd Clarkston (48346) *(G-2922)*
Flow Ezy Filters Inc ... 734 665-8777
 147 Enterprise Dr Ann Arbor (48103) *(G-463)*
Flow Gas Misture Solutions Inc ... 810 216-9004
 901 Huron Ave Ste 4 Port Huron (48060) *(G-12918)*
Flow-Rite Controls Ltd ... 616 583-1700
 960 74th St Sw Byron Center (49315) *(G-2191)*
Flowcor LLC (PA) ... 616 554-1100
 4855 Broadmoor Ave Se Kentwood (49512) *(G-9006)*
Flowers By Kevin ... 810 376-4600
 2486 Black River St Deckerville (48427) *(G-3808)*
Flowserve US Inc ... 269 381-2650
 2100 Factory St Kalamazoo (49001) *(G-8746)*
Flowserve US Inc ... 989 496-3897
 2420 Schuette Rd Midland (48642) *(G-10862)*
Flowtek Inc ... 231 734-3415
 8586 9 Mile Rd Evart (49631) *(G-4881)*
Flue Sentinel LLC ... 586 739-4373
 8123 Janis St Shelby Township (48317) *(G-14594)*
Fluid Chillers Inc ... 517 484-9190
 2730 Alpha Access St Lansing (48910) *(G-9369)*
Fluid Hutchinson Management (HQ) ... 248 679-1327
 3201 Cross Creek Pkwy Auburn Hills (48326) *(G-876)*
Fluid Innovations Inc ... 810 241-0990
 43730 Merrill Rd Sterling Heights (48314) *(G-15343)*
Fluid Routing Solutions Inc ... 231 592-1700
 600 N Dekraft Ave Big Rapids (49307) *(G-1628)*
Fluid Routing Solutions Inc ... 231 796-4489
 123 N Dekraft Ave Big Rapids (49307) *(G-1629)*
Fluid Systems Division, Marysville Also called TI Group Auto Systems LLC *(G-10623)*
Fluid Systems Engineering Inc ... 586 790-8880
 18855 E 14 Mile Rd Clinton Township (48035) *(G-3123)*
Fluidtherm Corp Michigan ... 989 344-1500
 7730 Old 27 N Frederic (49733) *(G-5751)*
Flushing Sand and Gravel ... 810 577-8260
 3502 W Mott Ave Flint (48504) *(G-5431)*
Fluxtrol Inc ... 248 393-2000
 1388 Atlantic Blvd Auburn Hills (48326) *(G-877)*
Flying Colors Imprinting Inc ... 734 641-1300
 19500 Allen Rd Melvindale (48122) *(G-10698)*
Flying Otter Winery LLC ... 517 424-7107
 3402 Chase Rd Adrian (49221) *(G-65)*
FM Research Management LLC ... 906 360-5833
 1958 Eben Trenary Rd Trenary (49891) *(G-16150)*
Fmmb LLC ... 313 372-7420
 4786 Bellevue St Detroit (48207) *(G-4065)*
Foam-It, Grand Rapids Also called Innovative Cleaning Eqp Inc *(G-6537)*
Foamex, Southfield Also called Fxi Inc *(G-14917)*
Foampartner Americas Inc ... 248 243-3100
 2923 Technology Dr Rochester Hills (48309) *(G-13426)*
Focal Point Metal Fab LLC ... 616 844-7670
 17354 Teunis Dr Spring Lake (49456) *(G-15142)*
Focus 1, Dearborn Also called Hatteras Inc *(G-3719)*
Focus Hope Logistics, Detroit Also called Hope Focus Companies Inc *(G-4130)*
Focus Hope Mfg, Detroit Also called Hope Focus *(G-4128)*
Focus Marketing ... 616 355-4362
 2495 112th Ave Ste 8 Holland (49424) *(G-7633)*
Fold A Cover, Caledonia Also called Steffens Enterprises Inc *(G-2317)*
Foltz Screen Printing ... 989 772-3947
 2094 S Isabella Rd Mount Pleasant (48858) *(G-11193)*
Fomcore LLC ... 231 366-4791
 1360 E Laketon Ave Muskegon (49442) *(G-11325)*
Fontaine Chateau ... 231 256-0000
 2290 S French Rd Lake Leelanau (49653) *(G-9103)*
Fontana Forest Products, Detroit Also called Michigan Box Company *(G-4237)*
Fontana Forest Products ... 313 841-8950
 1910 Trombly St Detroit (48211) *(G-4066)*
Fontijne Grotnes Inc ... 269 262-4700
 30257 Redfield St Niles (49120) *(G-11611)*

ALPHABETIC SECTION

Fonts About Inc 248 767-7504
  143 Cadycentre 130 Northville (48167) *(G-11692)*
Food For Thought Inc 231 326-5444
  7738 N Long Lake Rd Traverse City (49685) *(G-15971)*
Foodtools Inc 269 637-9969
  190 Veterans Blvd South Haven (49090) *(G-14759)*
For The Love of Cupcakes 906 399-3004
  5835 F Rd Bark River (49807) *(G-1119)*
Forbes Sanitation & Excavation 231 723-2311
  1878 E Parkdale Ave Manistee (49660) *(G-10422)*
Force Dynamics Inc 248 673-9878
  2627 Williams Dr Waterford (48328) *(G-17344)*
Force Energy Inc 989 732-0724
  1680 Calkins Dr Gaylord (49735) *(G-5858)*
Ford Global Technologies LLC (HQ) 313 312-3000
  30600 Telg Rd Ste 2345 Bingham Farms (48025) *(G-1653)*
Ford Global Treasury Inc 313 322-3000
  1 American Rd Dearborn (48126) *(G-3708)*
Ford Motor Company (PA) 313 322-3000
  1 American Rd Dearborn (48126) *(G-3709)*
Ford Motor Company 313 446-5945
  300 Renaissance Ctr Detroit (48243) *(G-4067)*
Ford Motor Company 734 484-8000
  10300 Textile Rd Ypsilanti (48197) *(G-18074)*
Ford Motor Company 313 594-0050
  3001 Miller Rd Dearborn (48120) *(G-3710)*
Ford Motor Company 313 322-7715
  21175 Oakwood Blvd Dearborn (48124) *(G-3711)*
Ford Motor Company 734 377-4954
  36200 Plymouth Rd Livonia (48150) *(G-9743)*
Ford Motor Company 313 594-4090
  1555 Fairlane Dr Ste 100 Allen Park (48101) *(G-198)*
Ford Motor Company 910 381-7998
  21001 Van Born Rd Taylor (48180) *(G-15723)*
Ford Motor Company 734 523-3000
  11871 Middlebelt Rd Livonia (48150) *(G-9744)*
Ford Motor Company 313 805-5938
  20100 Rotunda Dr Dearborn (48124) *(G-3712)*
Ford Motor Company 734 942-6248
  24999 Pennsylvania Rd Brownstown (48174) *(G-2062)*
Fordsell Machine Products Co 586 751-4700
  30400 Ryan Rd Warren (48092) *(G-17042)*
Fordson Health Care, Lincoln Park Also called Wright & Filippis Inc *(G-9589)*
Forefront Control Systems LLC 616 796-3495
  4314 136th Ave Ste 200 Holland (49424) *(G-7634)*
Foremost Graphics LLC 616 453-4747
  2921 Wilson Dr Nw Grand Rapids (49534) *(G-6415)*
Forensic Press 734 997-0256
  2980 Provincial Dr Ann Arbor (48104) *(G-464)*
Foresee Session Replay Inc 800 621-2850
  2500 Green Rd Ste 400 Ann Arbor (48105) *(G-465)*
Foresight Group Inc (PA) 517 485-5700
  2822 N Martin Luther Lansing (48906) *(G-9230)*
Forest Blake Products Inc 231 879-3913
  10723 Shippy Rd Sw Fife Lake (49633) *(G-5340)*
Forest Corullo Products Corp 906 667-0275
  300 S Massie Ave Bessemer (49911) *(G-1605)*
Forest Elders Products Inc 616 866-9317
  10367 Northland Dr Ne Rockford (49341) *(G-13569)*
Forest River Inc 269 471-6321
  580 W Burr Oak St Centreville (49032) *(G-2594)*
Forestry Management Svcs Inc 517 456-7431
  430 Division St Clinton (49236) *(G-3020)*
Forever Flooring and More LLC 517 745-6194
  10880 Woodbushe Dr Se Lowell (49331) *(G-10029)*
Foreward Logistics LLC 877 488-9724
  25900 Grnfeld Rd Ste 326 Oak Park (48237) *(G-12068)*
Foreword Magazine Inc 231 933-3699
  425 Boardman Ave Traverse City (49684) *(G-15972)*
Forge Die & Tool Corp 248 477-0020
  31800 W 8 Mile Rd Farmington Hills (48336) *(G-5004)*
Forge Div Midwest Tl & Cutly, Kalkaska Also called Midwest Tool and Cutlery Co *(G-8953)*
Forge Precision Company 248 477-0020
  31800 W 8 Mile Rd Farmington Hills (48336) *(G-5005)*
Forged Tubular 313 843-4870
  9339 W Fort St Detroit (48209) *(G-4068)*
Forged Tubular Products Inc (PA) 313 843-6720
  9339 W Fort St Detroit (48209) *(G-4069)*
Forgetek, Sterling Heights Also called Rucci Forged Wheels Inc *(G-15481)*
Forging Holdings LLC (HQ) 313 758-2000
  1 Dauch Dr Detroit (48211) *(G-4070)*
Forkardt Inc 231 995-8300
  2155 Traversefield Dr Traverse City (49686) *(G-15973)*
Forkardt North America, Traverse City Also called Forkardt Inc *(G-15973)*
Form All Tool Company 231 894-6303
  803 S Mears Ave Whitehall (49461) *(G-17666)*
Form G Tech Co 248 583-3610
  1291 Rochester Rd Troy (48083) *(G-16369)*
Forma-Kool Manufacturing Inc 586 949-4813
  46880 Continental Dr Chesterfield (48047) *(G-2778)*

Formax Manufacturing Corp 616 456-5458
  168 Wealthy St Sw Grand Rapids (49503) *(G-6416)*
Formax Precision Gear Inc 586 323-9067
  6047 18 Mile Rd Sterling Heights (48314) *(G-15344)*
Formed Solutions Inc 616 395-5455
  1900 Lamar Ct Holland (49423) *(G-7635)*
Formex International Div, Port Huron Also called Tapex American Corporation *(G-12970)*
Formfab LLC 248 844-3676
  3044 Research Dr Rochester Hills (48309) *(G-13427)*
Forming Technologies LLC 231 777-7030
  1885 E Laketon Ave Muskegon (49442) *(G-11326)*
Formrite Inc 517 521-1373
  2060 Elm Rd Webberville (48892) *(G-17449)*
Forms Trac Enterprises Inc 248 524-0006
  37827 Brookwood Dr Sterling Heights (48312) *(G-15345)*
Formsprag LLC 586 758-5000
  23601 Hoover Rd Warren (48089) *(G-17043)*
Formtech Inds Holdings LLC 248 597-3800
  2727 W 14 Mile Rd Royal Oak (48073) *(G-13928)*
Formula One Tool & Engineering 810 794-3617
  6052 Pointe Tremble Rd Algonac (48001) *(G-144)*
Forrest Brothers Inc (PA) 989 356-4011
  1272 Millbocker Rd Gaylord (49735) *(G-5859)*
Forrest Company 269 384-6120
  7877 N 12th St Kalamazoo (49009) *(G-8747)*
Forsons Inc 517 787-4562
  139 S Mechanic St Jackson (49201) *(G-8450)*
Forsports, Fort Gratiot Also called Nobby Inc *(G-5550)*
Forst-Usa Incorporated 586 759-9380
  23640 Hoover Rd Warren (48089) *(G-17044)*
Forsters and Sons Oil Change 248 618-6860
  4773 Dixie Hwy Waterford (48329) *(G-17345)*
Forsyth Millwork and Farms 810 266-4000
  15315 Duffield Rd Byron (48418) *(G-2171)*
Fort Grtiot Cbnets Counter LLC 810 364-1924
  3390 Ravenswood Rd Port Huron (48060) *(G-12919)*
Forte Industries Mill Inc 906 753-6256
  N8076 Us Highway 41 Stephenson (49887) *(G-15235)*
Fortech Products Inc 248 446-9500
  7600 Kensington Ct Brighton (48116) *(G-1925)*
Fortis Energy Services Inc 231 258-4596
  36700 Woodward Ave # 107 Bloomfield Hills (48304) *(G-1766)*
Fortis Energy Services Inc (PA) 248 283-7100
  3001 W Big Beaver Rd # 525 Troy (48084) *(G-16370)*
Fortis Sltions Group Centl LLC (PA) 248 437-5200
  28505 Automation Blvd Wixom (48393) *(G-17812)*
Fortress Manufacturing Inc 269 925-1336
  2255 Pipestone Rd Benton Harbor (49022) *(G-1498)*
Fortress Stblztion Systems LLC 616 355-1421
  184 W 64th St Holland (49423) *(G-7636)*
Fortune Tool & Machine Inc 248 669-9119
  29650 Beck Rd Wixom (48393) *(G-17813)*
Forum and Link Inc 313 945-5465
  12740 W Wrren Ave Ste 100 Dearborn (48126) *(G-3713)*
Forward Distributing Inc 989 846-4501
  219 N Front St Standish (48658) *(G-15218)*
Forward Metal Craft Inc 616 459-6051
  329 Summer Ave Nw Grand Rapids (49504) *(G-6417)*
Forzza Corporation 616 884-6121
  915 Grand Rapids St Middleville (49333) *(G-10802)*
Fosters Ventures LLC 248 519-7446
  1371 Souter Dr Troy (48083) *(G-16371)*
Founders Ale House, Grand Rapids Also called Canal Street Brewing Co LLC *(G-6253)*
Four Leaf Brewing, Farwell Also called James Joy LLC *(G-5162)*
Four Seasons Publishing Inc 906 341-5200
  212 Walnut St Manistique (49854) *(G-10440)*
Four Star Rubber Inc 810 632-3335
  3185 Old Farm Ln Commerce Township (48390) *(G-3407)*
Four Star Tooling & Engrg Inc 586 264-4090
  40550 Brentwood Dr Sterling Heights (48310) *(G-15346)*
Four Way Industries Inc 248 588-5421
  855 N Rochester Rd Clawson (48017) *(G-2978)*
Four Way Pallet Service 734 782-5914
  3988 Will Carleton Rd Flat Rock (48134) *(G-5354)*
Four-Way Tool and Die Inc (PA) 248 585-8255
  239 Indusco Ct Troy (48083) *(G-16372)*
Four-Way Tool and Die Inc 248 585-8255
  217 Indusco Ct Troy (48083) *(G-16373)*
Fournier Enterprises Inc 586 323-9160
  17 N Rose St Ste A Mount Clemens (48043) *(G-11131)*
Fourslides Inc 313 564-5600
  50801 E Russell Schmidt Chesterfield (48051) *(G-2779)*
Fourth Ave Birkenstock 734 663-1644
  209 N 4th Ave Ann Arbor (48104) *(G-466)*
Fourth Seacoast Publishing Co 586 779-5570
  25300 Little Mack Ave Saint Clair Shores (48081) *(G-14252)*
Fourway Machinery Sales Co 517 782-9371
  3215 Gregory Rd Jackson (49202) *(G-8451)*
Foust Electro Mold Inc 517 439-1062
  277 Industrial Dr Hillsdale (49242) *(G-7524)*

Fowler Organ Co, Eaton Rapids *Also called Brian M Fowler Pipe Organs* ***(G-4719)***
Fowlerville Feed & Pet Sups....517 223-9115
120 Hale St Fowlerville (48836) ***(G-5565)***
Fowlerville Machine Tool Inc....517 223-8871
5010 W Grand River Rd Fowlerville (48836) ***(G-5566)***
Fowlerville News & Views....517 223-8760
731 S Grand Ave Fowlerville (48836) ***(G-5567)***
Fox Aluminum Products Inc....248 399-4288
1355 E Woodward Hts Blvd Hazel Park (48030) ***(G-7438)***
Fox Charlevoix Ford Modem....231 547-4401
6725 Us Highway 31 S Charlevoix (49720) ***(G-2614)***
Fox Fire Glass LLC....248 332-2442
3071 W Thompson Rd Fenton (48430) ***(G-5215)***
Fox Mfg Co....586 468-1421
32535 S River Rd Harrison Township (48045) ***(G-7331)***
Fpe, Troy *Also called Florida Production Engrg Inc* ***(G-16368)***
Fpt Schlafer....313 925-8200
1950 Medbury St Detroit (48211) ***(G-4071)***
Fraco....906 249-1476
200 Cherry Creek Rd Marquette (49855) ***(G-10532)***
Fraco Products Ltd....248 667-9260
5225 Renshaw Dr Troy (48085) ***(G-16374)***
Fragrance Outlet Inc....517 552-9545
1475 N Burkhart Rd E115 Howell (48855) ***(G-8042)***
Framar, Clinton Township *Also called SRS Manufacturing Inc* ***(G-3233)***
Frame Products Inc....269 695-5884
206 Main St Ste B Buchanan (49107) ***(G-2117)***
Framon Mfg Co Inc (PA)....989 356-6296
1201 W Chisholm St Alpena (49707) ***(G-290)***
Fran Technology LLC....586 336-4085
132 Shafer Dr Romeo (48065) ***(G-13628)***
Franchino Mold & Engrg Co....517 321-5609
5867 W Grand River Ave Lansing (48906) ***(G-9231)***
Frandale Sub Shop....616 446-6311
11250 Kistler Dr Unit 5 Allendale (49401) ***(G-217)***
Frank Condon Inc....517 849-2505
250 Industrial Dr Hillsdale (49242) ***(G-7525)***
Frank Industries Inc....810 346-3234
4467 Vine St Brown City (48416) ***(G-2051)***
Frank Smith....313 443-8882
13021 Harper Ave Detroit (48213) ***(G-4072)***
Frank Terlecki Company Inc....586 759-5770
4129 Kendall Rd Warren (48091) ***(G-17045)***
Frank W Small Met Fabrication....269 422-2001
8961 First St Baroda (49101) ***(G-1124)***
Frank's Oil King, Detroit *Also called Frank Smith* ***(G-4072)***
Franke Salisbury Virginia....231 775-7014
11894 S Mackinaw Trl Cadillac (49601) ***(G-2248)***
Franke Septic Tank Service, Cadillac *Also called Franke Salisbury Virginia* ***(G-2248)***
Frankenmuth Brewery, Frankenmuth *Also called Frankenmuth Brewing Company* ***(G-5586)***
Frankenmuth Brewery LLC....989 262-8300
425 S Main St Frankenmuth (48734) ***(G-5585)***
Frankenmuth Brewing Company....989 262-8300
425 S Main St Frankenmuth (48734) ***(G-5586)***
Frankenmuth Industrial Svcs....989 652-3322
310 List St Frankenmuth (48734) ***(G-5587)***
Frankenmuth Printing, Davison *Also called Riegle Press Inc* ***(G-3661)***
Frankenmuth Sausage Company, Frankenmuth *Also called Kgdh LLC* ***(G-5591)***
Frankenmuth Welding & Fabg....989 754-9457
4765 E Holland Rd Saginaw (48601) ***(G-14038)***
Frankfort Manufacturing Inc....231 352-7551
1105 Main St Frankfort (49635) ***(G-5601)***
Franklin AEL, Muskegon *Also called Aggregtes Excvtg Logistics LLC* ***(G-11264)***
Franklin Electric Corporation....248 442-8000
32606 Industrial Rd Garden City (48135) ***(G-5824)***
Franklin Fastener Company....313 537-8900
12701 Beech Daly Rd Redford (48239) ***(G-13162)***
Franklin Iron & Metal Co Inc (PA)....269 968-6111
120 South Ave Battle Creek (49014) ***(G-1190)***
Franklin Metal Trading Corp....616 374-7171
609 Tupper Lake St Lake Odessa (48849) ***(G-9114)***
Franklin Plastics, Battle Creek *Also called Franklin Iron & Metal Co Inc* ***(G-1190)***
Franklin Press Inc....616 538-5320
2426 28th St Sw Grand Rapids (49519) ***(G-6418)***
Fraser Fab and Machine Inc....248 852-9050
1696 Star Batt Dr Rochester Hills (48309) ***(G-13428)***
Fraser Grinding Co (PA)....586 293-6060
34235 Riviera Fraser (48026) ***(G-5655)***
Fraser Mfg Facility, Fraser *Also called Hhi Formtech LLC* ***(G-5662)***
Fraser Tool & Gauge LLC....313 882-9192
1352 Harvard Rd Grosse Pointe Park (48230) ***(G-7193)***
Frazeli Prints, Lansing *Also called Fairfax Prints Ltd* ***(G-9227)***
Freal Fuel Inc....248 790-7202
28230 23 Mile Rd Chesterfield (48051) ***(G-2780)***
Fred Carter....989 799-7176
6 Benton Rd Saginaw (48602) ***(G-14039)***
Fred Kelly Picks LLC....989 348-2938
4333 W N Down River Rd Grayling (49738) ***(G-7106)***
Fred Oswalts Pins Unltd....269 342-1387
2610 Hill An Brook Dr Portage (49024) ***(G-12997)***
Fred's Rubber Stamp Shop, Marquette *Also called F & A Enterprises of Michigan* ***(G-10531)***
Free Rnge Ntrals Dog Trats Inc....586 737-0797
44648 Mound Rd Sterling Heights (48314) ***(G-15347)***
Freedom Dental, Brighton *Also called Patrick Wyman* ***(G-1974)***
Freedom Imaging Systems....734 327-5600
3600 Green Ct Ann Arbor (48105) ***(G-467)***
Freedom Technologies Corp (PA)....810 227-3737
10559 Citation Dr Ste 205 Brighton (48116) ***(G-1926)***
Freedom Tool & Mfg Co....231 788-2898
1741 S Wolf Lake Rd Muskegon (49442) ***(G-11327)***
Freeport Milling....616 765-8421
223 Division St Freeport (49325) ***(G-5764)***
Freer Tool & Die Inc....586 463-3200
44675 Morley Dr Clinton Township (48036) ***(G-3124)***
Freer Tool & Die Inc....586 741-5274
44675 Morley Dr Clinton Township (48036) ***(G-3125)***
Freer Tool & Supply, Clinton Township *Also called Freer Tool & Die Inc* ***(G-3125)***
Freer Tool and Supply, Clinton Township *Also called Freer Tool & Die Inc* ***(G-3124)***
Freeway, Hart *Also called Oceanas Herald-Journal Inc* ***(G-7378)***
Freiborne Industries Inc....248 333-2490
15 W Silverdome Indus Par Pontiac (48342) ***(G-12825)***
Fremont Community Digester LLC....248 735-6684
23955 Novi Rd Novi (48375) ***(G-11887)***
Fremont L Dura L C....248 299-7500
1780 Pond Run Auburn Hills (48326) ***(G-878)***
French Paper Company....269 683-1100
100 French St Niles (49120) ***(G-11612)***
Frenchys Skirting Inc....734 721-3013
34111 Michigan Ave Wayne (48184) ***(G-17430)***
Fresh Strt Transitional Living....269 757-5195
400 S Fair Ave Benton Harbor (49022) ***(G-1499)***
Fresh Tracks, Lansing *Also called Seelye Group Ltd* ***(G-9423)***
Freshwater Communications, Battle Creek *Also called Caribbean Adventure LLC* ***(G-1163)***
Freshwater Dgtal Mdia Prtnrs....616 446-1771
4585 40th St Se Kentwood (49512) ***(G-9007)***
Fretty Media LLC....231 894-8055
201 W Obell St Whitehall (49461) ***(G-17667)***
Freudenberg N Amer Ltd Partnr (HQ)....734 354-5505
47774 W Anchor Ct Plymouth (48170) ***(G-12623)***
Freudenberg-Nok, Plymouth *Also called Ishino Gasket North Amer LLC* ***(G-12650)***
Freudenberg-Nok General Partnr (HQ)....734 451-0020
47774 W Anchor Ct Plymouth (48170) ***(G-12624)***
Freudenberg-Nok General Partnr....734 451-0020
47805 Galleon Dr Plymouth (48170) ***(G-12625)***
Freudenberg-Nok Sealing Tech, Plymouth *Also called Freudenberg-Nok General Partnr* ***(G-12624)***
Fricia Enterprises Inc....586 977-1900
6070 18 Mile Rd Sterling Heights (48314) ***(G-15348)***
Friction Coating Corporation....586 731-0990
44833 Centre Ct Clinton Township (48038) ***(G-3126)***
Friction Control LLC....586 741-8493
35360 Forton Ct Clinton Township (48035) ***(G-3127)***
Friedland Industries Inc....517 482-3000
405 E Maple St Lansing (48906) ***(G-9232)***
Friendship Industries Inc (PA)....586 323-0033
6520 Arrow Dr Sterling Heights (48314) ***(G-15349)***
Friendship Industries Inc....586 997-1325
6521 Arrow Dr Sterling Heights (48314) ***(G-15350)***
Frimo Inc (HQ)....248 668-3160
50685 Century Ct Wixom (48393) ***(G-17814)***
Fris-T, Alto *Also called James D Frisbie* ***(G-327)***
Frisbie Sand & Gravel....269 432-3379
644 E State St Colon (49040) ***(G-3372)***
Frito-Lay North America Inc....989 754-0435
100 S Outer Dr Saginaw (48601) ***(G-14040)***
Fritz Advertising Company, Spring Arbor *Also called R J Designers Inc* ***(G-15127)***
Fritz Enterprises....313 841-9460
255 Marion Ave Detroit (48218) ***(G-4073)***
Fritz Enterprises (HQ)....734 283-7272
1650 W Jefferson Ave Trenton (48183) ***(G-16154)***
Fritz Enterprises Inc....734 283-7272
23550 Pennsylvania Rd River Rouge (48218) ***(G-13277)***
Fritz Products, Detroit *Also called Fritz Enterprises* ***(G-4073)***
Fritz Products Inc, Trenton *Also called Fritz Enterprises* ***(G-16154)***
Froberg's Clothing Store, Gwinn *Also called Gerald Froberg* ***(G-7219)***
Front Line Services Inc....989 695-6633
8588 Carter Rd Freeland (48623) ***(G-5757)***
Front Porch Press....888 484-1997
4733 Hawk Hollow Dr E Bath (48808) ***(G-1134)***
Frontier Rnwable Resources LLC (PA)....906 228-7960
210 N Front St Ste 1 Marquette (49855) ***(G-10533)***
Frontier Technology Inc....269 673-9464
2489 118th Ave Allegan (49010) ***(G-163)***
Frontlines Publishing....616 887-6256
72 Ransom Ave Ne Ofc Grand Rapids (49503) ***(G-6419)***
Frost Division, Fraser *Also called Hi-Craft Engineering Inc* ***(G-5663)***

ALPHABETIC SECTION

Frost Inc (PA) 616 785-9030
  2900 Northridge Dr Nw Grand Rapids (49544) *(G-6420)*
Frost Incorporated (HQ) 616 453-7781
  2900 Northridge Dr Nw Grand Rapids (49544) *(G-6421)*
Frost Links (PA) 616 785-9030
  2900 Northridge Dr Nw Grand Rapids (49544) *(G-6422)*
Frosty Cove 231 343-6643
  2133 Lakeshore Dr Muskegon (49441) *(G-11328)*
Froude 248 579-4295
  41123 Jo Dr Ste A Novi (48375) *(G-11888)*
Froyo Pinckney LLC 248 310-4465
  3282 Swarthout Rd Pinckney (48169) *(G-12498)*
Fruit Fro Yo 517 580-3967
  5100 Marsh Rd Okemos (48864) *(G-12124)*
Fruit Haven Nursery Inc 231 889-9973
  8576 Chief Rd Kaleva (49645) *(G-8933)*
Fry Krisp Company, The, Jackson *Also called Fry Krisp Food Products Inc (G-8452)*
Fry Krisp Food Products Inc 517 784-8531
  3514 Wayland Dr Jackson (49202) *(G-8452)*
Frye Printing Company Inc (PA) 517 456-4124
  11801 Tecumseh Clinton Rd Clinton (49236) *(G-3021)*
FSI, Jackson *Also called Fabrication Services Inc (G-8448)*
FSI Label Company 586 776-4110
  6227 136th Ave Holland (49424) *(G-7637)*
Fsp Inc 248 585-0760
  1270 Rankin Dr Ste B Troy (48083) *(G-16375)*
Fte Automotive USA Inc 248 209-8239
  12700 Oakland Park Blvd Highland Park (48203) *(G-7505)*
Fuchs Lubricants Co 708 333-8900
  3535 R B Chaffee Mem Dr Grand Rapids (49548) *(G-6423)*
Fuel Cell System Mfg LLC 313 319-5571
  20001 Brownstown Ctr Dr Brownstown Township (48183) *(G-2069)*
Fuel of Parma, Parma *Also called Camerons of Jackson LLC (G-12388)*
Fuel Source LLC 313 506-0448
  29112 E River Rd Grosse Ile (48138) *(G-7173)*
Fuel Systems, Troy *Also called TI Group Auto Systems LLC (G-16642)*
Fuel Tobacco Stop 810 487-2040
  226 E Main St Flushing (48433) *(G-5535)*
Fuel Woodfire Grill LLC 810 479-4933
  213 Huron Ave Port Huron (48060) *(G-12920)*
Fug Inc 269 781-8036
  315 Woolley Dr Marshall (49068) *(G-10568)*
Fujikura Automotive Amer LLC (HQ) 248 957-0130
  27555 Executive Dr # 150 Farmington Hills (48331) *(G-5006)*
Fulcrum Composites Inc 989 636-1025
  110 E Main St Apt 301 Midland (48640) *(G-10863)*
Fulgham Machine & Tool Company 517 937-8316
  2347 W High St Jackson (49203) *(G-8453)*
Full Spectrum Solutions Inc (PA) 517 783-3800
  2021 Wellworth Jackson (49203) *(G-8454)*
Full Spectrum Stained GL Inc 269 432-2610
  31323 W Colon Rd Colon (49040) *(G-3373)*
Full Spektrem LLC 313 910-1920
  21925 Harper Ave Saint Clair Shores (48080) *(G-14253)*
Fullerton Tool Company Inc 989 799-4550
  121 Perry St Saginaw (48602) *(G-14041)*
Fultz Manufacturing Inc 231 947-5801
  1631 Park Dr Ste A Traverse City (49686) *(G-15974)*
Fun Foods, Muskegon *Also called L & P LLC (G-11360)*
Fun Learning Company LLC 269 362-0651
  21341 Fairfield Dr Macomb (48044) *(G-10123)*
Fun Promotion LLC 616 453-4245
  2225 Lake Michigan Dr Nw Grand Rapids (49504) *(G-6424)*
Fun Promotion Services, Grand Rapids *Also called Fun Promotion LLC (G-6424)*
Functional Hand Strength, Plymouth *Also called Thunderdome Media LLC (G-12770)*
Fuoss Bros, Owosso *Also called Fuoss Gravel Company (G-12292)*
Fuoss Gravel Company 989 725-2084
  777 Busha Rd Owosso (48867) *(G-12292)*
Furniture City Glass Corp 616 784-5500
  1012 Ken O Sha Ind Park Grand Rapids (49508) *(G-6425)*
Furniture Partners LLC 616 355-3051
  199 E 17th St Holland (49423) *(G-7638)*
Fusion Design Group Ltd 269 469-8226
  30 N Brton St New Bffalo New Buffalo (49117) *(G-11514)*
Fusion Fabricating and Mfg LLC 586 739-1970
  42380 Mound Rd Sterling Heights (48314) *(G-15351)*
Fusion Flexo LLC (PA) 269 685-5827
  6330 Canterwood Dr Richland (49083) *(G-13249)*
Fusion Flexo LLC 269 685-5827
  156 10th St Plainwell (49080) *(G-12525)*
Fusion Laser Services 586 739-7716
  42412 Mound Rd Sterling Heights (48314) *(G-15352)*
Fusion Mfg Solutions LLC 734 224-7216
  7193 Sulier Dr Temperance (48182) *(G-15829)*
Fusion Strategies LLC 734 776-1734
  15658 Brookfield St Livonia (48154) *(G-9745)*
Futura Custom Kitchen, Warren *Also called Michigan Counter Tops Company (G-17152)*
Futuramic Tool & Engrg Co (PA) 586 758-2200
  24680 Gibson D Warren (48089) *(G-17046)*

Future Industries Inc 616 844-0772
  1729 Airpark Dr Grand Haven (49417) *(G-6017)*
Future Mill Inc 586 754-8088
  25450 Ryan Rd Warren (48091) *(G-17047)*
Future Mold Corporation 989 588-9948
  215 S Webber St Farwell (48622) *(G-5161)*
Future Reproductions Inc 248 350-2060
  21477 Bridge St Ste L Southfield (48033) *(G-14916)*
Future Technologies Group LLC 810 733-3870
  6122 W Pierson Rd 10a Flushing (48433) *(G-5536)*
Future Tool and Machine Inc 734 946-2100
  28900 Goddard Rd Romulus (48174) *(G-13679)*
Future Vision, Saginaw *Also called Michigan Satellite (G-14091)*
Futuris Automotive, Oak Park *Also called Futuris Global Holdings LLC (G-12070)*
Futuris Automotive, Madison Heights *Also called Cni Enterprises Inc (G-10212)*
Futuris Automotive, Madison Heights *Also called Cni-Owosso LLC (G-10213)*
Futuris Automotive, Charlotte *Also called Cni Plastics LLC (G-2641)*
Futuris Automotive (us) Inc (HQ) 248 439-7800
  14925 W 11 Mile Rd Oak Park (48237) *(G-12069)*
Futuris Global Holdings LLC (HQ) 248 439-7800
  14925 W 11 Mile Rd Oak Park (48237) *(G-12070)*
Futuristic Artwear Inc 248 680-0200
  787 Majestic Rochester Hills (48306) *(G-13429)*
Futuristic Furnishings, Farmington Hills *Also called Millennm-The Inside Sltion Inc (G-5069)*
Fuzzybutz 269 983-9663
  306 State St Ste A Saint Joseph (49085) *(G-14311)*
Fw Shoring Company (PA) 517 676-8800
  685 Hull Rd Mason (48854) *(G-10639)*
Fxi Inc 248 553-1039
  26777 Centrl Pk Blvd # 100 Southfield (48076) *(G-14917)*
Fxi Novi 248 994-0630
  28700 Cabot Dr Novi (48377) *(G-11889)*
Fyke Washed Sand Gravel 248 547-4714
  3500 11 Mile Rd Ste D Berkley (48072) *(G-1583)*
Fzb Technology, Plymouth *Also called Dare Auto Inc (G-12605)*
G & C Carports 616 678-4308
  1324 17 Mile Rd Kent City (49330) *(G-8990)*
G & F Prototype Plaster, Fraser *Also called G F Proto-Type Plaster Inc (G-5656)*
G & F Tool Products 517 663-3646
  7127 E 5 Point Hwy Eaton Rapids (48827) *(G-4724)*
G & G Die and Engineering Inc 586 716-8099
  6091 Corporate Dr Ira (48023) *(G-8256)*
G & G Metal Products Inc 248 625-8099
  9575 Rattalee Lake Rd Clarkston (48348) *(G-2923)*
G & G Steel Fabricating Co 586 979-4112
  31154 Dequindre Rd Warren (48092) *(G-17048)*
G & G Wood & Supply Inc 586 293-0450
  29920 Little Mack Ave Roseville (48066) *(G-13805)*
G & H Producers, Midland *Also called Oil City Venture Inc (G-10899)*
G & L Mfg Inc 810 724-4101
  2 Mountain Dr Imlay City (48444) *(G-8199)*
G & L Powerup Inc 586 200-2169
  31044 Gratiot Ave Roseville (48066) *(G-13806)*
G & L Tool Inc 734 728-1990
  5874 E Executive Dr Westland (48185) *(G-17559)*
G & L Tool & Die, Westland *Also called G & L Tool Inc (G-17559)*
G & R Machine Tool Inc 734 641-6560
  20410 Superior Rd Taylor (48180) *(G-15724)*
G & T Industries Inc (PA) 616 452-8611
  1001 76th St Sw Byron Center (49315) *(G-2192)*
G & W Display Fixtures Inc 517 369-7110
  300 Mill St Bronson (49028) *(G-2026)*
G & W Machine Co 616 363-4435
  2107 Merlin St Ne Grand Rapids (49525) *(G-6426)*
G A Machine Company Inc 313 836-5646
  8851 Mark Twain St Detroit (48228) *(G-4074)*
G A Richards Company (PA) 616 243-2800
  1060 Ken O Sha Ind Grand Rapids (49508) *(G-6427)*
G A Richards Plant Two 616 850-8528
  701 E Savidge St Spring Lake (49456) *(G-15143)*
G B Wolfgram and Sons Inc 231 238-4638
  6083 River St Indian River (49749) *(G-8217)*
G Defense Company B 616 202-4500
  823 Ottawa Ave Nw Grand Rapids (49503) *(G-6428)*
G F Inc 231 946-5330
  1032 Woodmere Ave Ste B Traverse City (49686) *(G-15975)*
G F Proto-Type Plaster Inc 586 296-2750
  33670 Riviera Fraser (48026) *(G-5656)*
G G & D Inc 248 623-1212
  5911 Dixie Hwy Clarkston (48346) *(G-2924)*
G I, Jackson *Also called Great Lakes Industry Inc (G-8459)*
G L Nelson Inc 630 682-5958
  290 Patrick Dr Indian River (49749) *(G-8218)*
G M Brass & Alum Fndry Inc 269 926-6366
  200 W Wall St Benton Harbor (49022) *(G-1500)*
G M Paris Bakery Inc 734 425-2060
  28418 Joy Rd Livonia (48150) *(G-9746)*
G M S, Coldwater *Also called Groholski Mfg Solutions LLC (G-3307)*

G P Dura 248 299-7500
  2791 Research Dr Rochester Hills (48309) *(G-13430)*
G P Manufacturing Inc 269 695-1202
  16689 Bakertown Rd Buchanan (49107) *(G-2118)*
G P Reeves Inc 616 399-8893
  4551 Holland Ave Holland (49424) *(G-7639)*
G P Technologies, Sterling Heights Also called Genix LLC *(G-15360)*
G R Investment Group Ltd 248 588-3946
  839 N Rochester Rd Clawson (48017) *(G-2979)*
G S I, Grand Rapids Also called Graphic Specialties Inc *(G-6475)*
G T Gundrilling Inc 586 992-3301
  51195 Regency Center Dr Macomb (48042) *(G-10124)*
G T Jerseys LLC 248 588-3231
  997 Rochester Rd Ste C Troy (48083) *(G-16376)*
G Tech Sales LLC 586 803-9393
  6601 Burroughs Ave Sterling Heights (48314) *(G-15353)*
G W I Engineering Division, Grand Rapids Also called New 9 Inc *(G-6715)*
G&G Industries Inc 586 726-6000
  50665 Corporate Dr Shelby Township (48315) *(G-14595)*
G&J Products & Services 734 522-2984
  8219 Roselawn St Westland (48185) *(G-17560)*
G-E-M, White Lake Also called Generl-Lctrical-Mechanical Inc *(G-17633)*
G-Force Tooling LLC (PA) 517 541-2747
  1325 Island Hwy Charlotte (48813) *(G-2650)*
G-Force Tooling LLC 517 712-8177
  425 Spring St Grand Ledge (48837) *(G-6107)*
G-III Apparel Group Ltd 248 332-4922
  4192 Baldwin Rd Auburn Hills (48326) *(G-879)*
G-M Graphics, Newaygo Also called G-M Wood Products Inc *(G-11568)*
G-M Wood Products Inc (PA) 231 652-2201
  531 S Clay St Newaygo (49337) *(G-11568)*
G-Town Techs, Hudsonville Also called Lol Telcom Inc *(G-8162)*
G. A. Rchards - Corlett Turner, Grand Rapids Also called Corlett-Turner Co *(G-6311)*
G.A. Rchrds Indstrial Oprtions, Norton Shores Also called Burnside Industries LLC *(G-11811)*
G5 Outdoors LLC (PA) 866 456-8836
  34775 Potter St Memphis (48041) *(G-10709)*
GA Dalbeck Logging LLC 906 364-3300
  205 N County Road 519 Wakefield (49968) *(G-16852)*
Gaastra John's, Iron River Also called Gaastra Welding & Supply Inc *(G-8309)*
Gaastra Welding & Supply Inc 906 265-4288
  928 Selden Rd Iron River (49935) *(G-8309)*
Gabriel North America Inc 616 202-5770
  560 5th St Nw Ste 210 Grand Rapids (49504) *(G-6429)*
Gabriel Ride Control, Farmington Hills Also called Ride Control LLC *(G-5115)*
Gabriel Ride Control LLC 248 247-7600
  39300 Country Club Dr Farmington Hills (48331) *(G-5007)*
Gac 269 639-3010
  1301 M 43 South Haven (49090) *(G-14760)*
Gaco Sourcing LLC 248 633-2656
  2254 Cole St Birmingham (48009) *(G-1684)*
Gadget Factory LLC 517 449-1444
  5157 Aurelius Rd Lansing (48911) *(G-9370)*
Gadget Locker LLC 702 901-1440
  11260 Somerset Ave Detroit (48224) *(G-4075)*
Gaffey & Associates, Holt Also called Shayleslie Corporation *(G-7929)*
Gage Bilt Inc 586 226-1500
  44766 Centre Ct Clinton Township (48038) *(G-3128)*
Gage Company 269 965-4279
  4550 Wayne Rd Springfield (49037) *(G-15191)*
Gage Corporation (PA) 248 541-3824
  821 Wanda St Ste 1 Ferndale (48220) *(G-5286)*
Gage Eagle Spline Inc 586 776-7240
  2357 E 9 Mile Rd Warren (48091) *(G-17049)*
Gage Global Services Inc (PA) 248 541-3824
  821 Wanda St Ste 2 Ferndale (48220) *(G-5287)*
Gage Numerical Inc 231 328-4426
  900 S 7 Mile Rd Lake City (49651) *(G-9087)*
Gage Pattern & Model Inc 248 361-6609
  32070 Townley St Madison Heights (48071) *(G-10255)*
Gage Printing, Springfield Also called Gage Company *(G-15191)*
Gage Products Company, Ferndale Also called Gage Global Services Inc *(G-5287)*
Gage Products Company 248 541-3824
  625 Wanda St Ferndale (48220) *(G-5288)*
Gage Rite Products Inc 248 588-7796
  356 Executive Dr Troy (48083) *(G-16377)*
Gage Well Drilling Inc 989 389-4372
  9609 Artesia Beach Rd Saint Helen (48656) *(G-14278)*
Gaging Solutions & Services, Ann Arbor Also called M&B Holdings LLC *(G-538)*
Gags and Games Inc (HQ) 734 591-1717
  35901 Veronica St Livonia (48150) *(G-9747)*
Gail Parker 734 261-3842
  847 W Rose Ave Garden City (48135) *(G-5825)*
Gails Carpet Care Repair 248 684-8789
  3110 Beach Lake Dr E Milford (48380) *(G-10964)*
Gainors Meat Packing Inc 989 269-8161
  317 N Port Crescent St Bad Axe (48413) *(G-1061)*

Gaishin Manufacturing Inc 269 934-9340
  240 Urbandale Ave Benton Harbor (49022) *(G-1501)*
GAL Gage Co 269 465-5750
  2953 Hinchman Rd Bridgman (49106) *(G-1863)*
Galco Industrial Elec Inc 248 542-9090
  1001 Lincoln St Madison Heights (48071) *(G-10256)*
Gale Briggs Inc (PA) 517 543-1320
  311 State St Charlotte (48813) *(G-2651)*
Gale Tool Co Inc 248 437-4610
  10801 N Rushton Rd South Lyon (48178) *(G-14792)*
Gallagher Fire Equipment Co 248 477-1540
  30895 8 Mile Rd Livonia (48152) *(G-9748)*
Gallagher-Kaiser Corporation (PA) 313 368-3100
  777 Chicago Rd Ste 1 Troy (48083) *(G-16378)*
Gallatin Tank Works LLC 734 856-5107
  6872 Memorial Hwy Ottawa Lake (49267) *(G-12263)*
Gambles Redi-Mix Inc 989 539-6460
  1415 N Clare Ave Harrison (48625) *(G-7312)*
Gamco Inc 269 683-4280
  3001 S 11th St Niles (49120) *(G-11613)*
Gampco, Hillsdale Also called General Automatic Mch Pdts Co *(G-7526)*
GAMS Inc 269 926-6765
  549 Nickerson Ave Benton Harbor (49022) *(G-1502)*
Gan Systems Corp 248 609-7643
  2723 S State St Ste 150 Ann Arbor (48104) *(G-468)*
Ganas LLC 734 748-0434
  7511 Intervale St Detroit (48238) *(G-4076)*
Gannett Co Inc 269 964-7161
  34 Jackson St W Ste 3b Battle Creek (49017) *(G-1191)*
Gannett Co Inc 517 377-1000
  300 S Wash Sq Ste 300 # 300 Lansing (48933) *(G-9371)*
Gannett Co Inc 517 548-2000
  323 E Grand River Ave Howell (48843) *(G-8043)*
Gannett National Newspaper Sls, Troy Also called Indiana Newspapers LLC *(G-16415)*
Gannett Stllite Info Ntwrk Inc 734 229-1150
  601 Rogell Dr Detroit (48242) *(G-4077)*
Gannons General Contract 734 429-5859
  9216 Yorkshire Dr Saline (48176) *(G-14392)*
Gantec Inc 989 631-9300
  777 E Isabella Rd Midland (48640) *(G-10864)*
Gap, Romulus Also called Global Automotive Products Inc *(G-13680)*
Gar-Ber, Novi Also called General Filters Inc *(G-11890)*
Gar-V Manufacturing Inc 269 279-5134
  1111 River St Three Rivers (49093) *(G-15863)*
Garants Office Sups & Prtg Inc 989 356-3930
  117 W Washington Ave Alpena (49707) *(G-291)*
Garbage Man LLC 810 225-3001
  5441 Ethel St Brighton (48116) *(G-1927)*
Garcia Company 248 459-0952
  10255 Fish Lake Rd Holly (48442) *(G-7879)*
Garco Gaskets Inc 734 728-4912
  11865 Globe St Livonia (48150) *(G-9749)*
Garden Bay Winery LLC (PA) 906 361-0318
  11858 Hwy Us 2 Cooks (49817) *(G-3546)*
Garden Bay Winery LLC 906 361-6136
  817 48th Ave Menominee (49858) *(G-10737)*
Garden City Products Inc 269 684-6264
  833 Carberry Rd Niles (49120) *(G-11614)*
Garden Fresh Gourmet LLC (HQ) 866 725-7239
  1220 E 9 Mile Rd Ferndale (48220) *(G-5289)*
Gardner Signs Inc 248 689-9100
  1087 Naughton Dr Troy (48083) *(G-16379)*
Garett Tunison 248 330-9835
  1829 Orion Rd Oakland (48363) *(G-12106)*
Garrison Dental Solutions LLC (PA) 616 842-2035
  150 Dewitt Ln Spring Lake (49456) *(G-15144)*
Garrisons Hitch Center Inc 810 239-5728
  1050 Meida St Flint (48532) *(G-5432)*
Gary Cork Incorporated (PA) 231 946-1061
  806 S Garfield Ave Ste B Traverse City (49686) *(G-15976)*
Gary L Melchi Inc 810 231-0262
  11275 Merrill Rd Whitmore Lake (48189) *(G-17701)*
Gary Printing Company Inc 313 383-3222
  3330 Fort St Lincoln Park (48146) *(G-9578)*
Gary's Custom Meat Processing, Union Also called Garys Custom Meats *(G-16728)*
Garys Custom Meats 269 641-5683
  16237 Mason St Union (49130) *(G-16728)*
Gas Control Systems, Sparta Also called Storage Control Systems Inc *(G-15114)*
Gas Recovery Systems LLC 248 305-7774
  10611 5 Mile Rd Northville (48168) *(G-11693)*
Gasket Holdings Inc 248 354-7700
  26555 Northwestern Hwy Southfield (48033) *(G-14918)*
Gast Cabinet Co 269 422-1587
  8836 Stevensville Baroda Baroda (49101) *(G-1125)*
Gast Manufacturing Inc (HQ) 269 926-6171
  2300 M 139 Benton Harbor (49022) *(G-1503)*
Gast Manufacturing Inc 269 926-6171
  775 Nickerson Ave Benton Harbor (49022) *(G-1504)*
Gast Manufacturing Inc 269 926-6171
  2550 Meadowbrook Rd Benton Harbor (49022) *(G-1505)*

Gatco Incorporated 734 453-2295
42330 Ann Arbor Rd E Plymouth (48170) *(G-12626)*
Gatehouse Media LLC 517 265-5111
133 N Winter St Adrian (49221) *(G-66)*
Gatehouse Media LLC 269 651-5407
209 John St Sturgis (49091) *(G-15604)*
Gatehouse Media Mich Holdings 585 598-0030
15 W Pearl St Coldwater (49036) *(G-3304)*
Gatehouse Publishing, Coldwater *Also called Daily Reporter (G-3300)*
Gates Corporation 248 260-2300
2975 Waterview Dr Rochester Hills (48309) *(G-13431)*
Gateway Engineering Inc 616 284-1425
6534 Clay Ave Sw Grand Rapids (49548) *(G-6430)*
Gatherall Bindery Inc 248 669-6850
46980 Liberty Dr Wixom (48393) *(G-17815)*
Gatien Farm & Forest Pdts LLC 906 497-5541
N16323 River Road J.5 Powers (49874) *(G-13077)*
Gayles Chocolates Limited 248 398-0001
417 S Washington Ave Royal Oak (48067) *(G-13929)*
Gaylord Herald Times, Gaylord *Also called Otsego County Herald Times (G-5886)*
Gaylord Mch & Fabrication LLC 989 732-0817
2758 Dickerson Rd Gaylord (49735) *(G-5860)*
Gazelle Prototype LLC 616 844-1820
18683 Trimble Ct Spring Lake (49456) *(G-15145)*
Gazelle Publishing 734 529-2688
112 Park Pl Ste 3 Dundee (48131) *(G-4584)*
Gazette Newspapers Inc 248 524-4868
6966 Crooks Rd Ste 22 Troy (48098) *(G-16380)*
Gb Dynamics Inc 313 400-3570
1620 Kearney St Port Huron (48060) *(G-12921)*
Gch Tool Group Inc 586 777-6250
13265 E 8 Mile Rd Warren (48089) *(G-17050)*
GCI, Coldwater *Also called Gokoh Coldwater Incorporated (G-3305)*
GCI Water Solutions LLC 312 928-9992
5202 Dale St Midland (48642) *(G-10865)*
Gd Enterprises LLC 248 486-9800
7974 Lochlin Dr Ste B4 Brighton (48116) *(G-1928)*
Gds Enterprises 989 644-3115
6500 N Brinton Rd Lake (48632) *(G-9082)*
GE Aviation Muskegon, Muskegon *Also called Johnson Technology Inc (G-11354)*
GE Aviation Muskegon 231 777-2685
6060 Norton Center Dr Norton Shores (49441) *(G-11757)*
GE Aviation Systems LLC 616 224-6480
3290 Patterson Ave Se Grand Rapids (49512) *(G-6431)*
GE Healthcare Inc 616 554-5717
4380 Brockton Dr Se Ste 3 Grand Rapids (49512) *(G-6432)*
Gear Gear Inc 517 861-7757
129 Bell St Ypsilanti (48197) *(G-18075)*
Gear Master Inc 810 798-9254
7481 Research Dr Almont (48003) *(G-257)*
Gearing Holdings LLC (HQ) 313 758-2000
1 Dauch Dr Detroit (48211) *(G-4078)*
Geartec Inc 810 987-4700
1105 24th St Port Huron (48060) *(G-12922)*
Gearx LLC 248 766-6903
35502 Mound Rd Sterling Heights (48310) *(G-15354)*
Gedda's Electrical Repair, Hancock *Also called John V Gedda Jr (G-7253)*
Gedia Michigan Inc 248 392-9090
269 Kay Industrial Dr Orion (48359) *(G-12180)*
Gee & Missler Inc 734 284-1224
744 Vinewood St Wyandotte (48192) *(G-17959)*
Geeks Gmes Brains Stem Fun Ctr, Farmington *Also called Pannell S-Erynn (G-4906)*
Geeks of Detroit LLC 734 576-2363
282 Newport St Ste 1a Detroit (48215) *(G-4079)*
Geep Global, Auburn Hills *Also called Geep USA Inc (G-880)*
Geep USA Inc 313 937-5350
20 Corporate Dr Auburn Hills (48326) *(G-880)*
Geerpres Inc 231 773-3211
1780 Harvey St Muskegon (49442) *(G-11329)*
Gehring Corporation 248 478-8060
24800 Drake Rd Farmington Hills (48335) *(G-5008)*
Gei Global Energy Corp (PA) 810 610-2816
4225 Miller Rd 269 Flint (48507) *(G-5433)*
Geiger EDM Inc 517 369-9752
898 W Chicago Rd Bronson (49028) *(G-2027)*
Geislinger Corporation 269 441-7000
200 Geislinger Dr Battle Creek (49037) *(G-1192)*
Gelman Sciences Inc 734 665-0651
674 S Wagner Rd Ann Arbor (48103) *(G-469)*
Gem Gallery, Ann Arbor *Also called Abracadabra Jewelry (G-338)*
Gem Plastics Inc 616 538-5966
2533 Thornwood St Sw Grand Rapids (49519) *(G-6433)*
Gem Wood Products Inc 616 384-3460
350 Skeels St Ste A Coopersville (49404) *(G-3559)*
Gema, Dundee *Also called Global Engine Mfg Aliance LLC (G-4585)*
Gemini Corporation 616 459-4545
401 Hall St Sw Ste 331a Grand Rapids (49503) *(G-6434)*
Gemini Group Inc (PA) 989 269-6272
175 Thompson Rd Ste A Bad Axe (48413) *(G-1062)*
Gemini Group Plastic Sales 248 435-7991
3250 University Dr # 110 Auburn Hills (48326) *(G-881)*
Gemini Group Services Inc 248 435-7271
175 Thompson Rd Ste A Bad Axe (48413) *(G-1063)*
Gemini Plastics, Ubly *Also called Pepro Enterprises Inc (G-16721)*
Gemini Plastics Inc 989 658-8557
4385 Garfield St Ubly (48475) *(G-16716)*
Gemini Plastics De Mexico Inc 989 658-8557
4385 Garfield St Ubly (48475) *(G-16717)*
Gemini Precision Machining Inc (HQ) 989 269-9702
700 E Soper Rd Bad Axe (48413) *(G-1064)*
Gemini Precision Machining Inc 989 269-9702
700 E Soper Rd Bad Axe (48413) *(G-1065)*
Gemini Publications, Grand Rapids *Also called Gemini Corporation (G-6434)*
Gemini Sales Org LLC 248 765-1118
2156 Keystone Dr Sterling Heights (48310) *(G-15355)*
Gemo Hopkins Usa Inc 734 330-1271
2900 Auburn Ct Auburn Hills (48326) *(G-882)*
Gemphire Therapeutics Inc 734 245-1700
17199 N Laurel Park Dr # 401 Livonia (48152) *(G-9750)*
Gen-Oak Fabricators Inc 248 373-1515
2501 Brown Rd Orion (48359) *(G-12181)*
Genco Alliance LLC 269 216-5500
630 Gibson St Kalamazoo (49007) *(G-8748)*
Genco Tool 989 785-5588
12510 Park St Atlanta (49709) *(G-731)*
Gendzwill Co 906 786-9321
1600 16th Ave S Escanaba (49829) *(G-4830)*
Gene Brow & Sons Inc 906 635-0859
2754 W 20th St Sault Sainte Marie (49783) *(G-14464)*
Gene Codes Forensics Inc 734 769-7249
525 Avis Dr Ste 8 Ann Arbor (48108) *(G-470)*
Genentech Inc 650 225-1000
362 Kirksway Ln Lake Orion (48362) *(G-9136)*
General Automatic Mch Pdts Co 517 437-6000
266 Industrial Dr Hillsdale (49242) *(G-7526)*
General Broach & Engrg Inc 586 726-4300
5750 New King Dr Ste 200 Troy (48098) *(G-16381)*
General Broach Company (HQ) 517 458-7555
307 Salisbury St Morenci (49256) *(G-11109)*
General Broach Company 517 458-7555
555 W Main St Ste C Morenci (49256) *(G-11110)*
General Chemical Corporation 248 587-5600
12336 Emerson Dr Brighton (48116) *(G-1929)*
General Coach America Inc (HQ) 810 724-6474
275 Graham Rd Imlay City (48444) *(G-8200)*
General Die & Engineering Inc (PA) 616 698-6961
6500 Clay Ave Sw Grand Rapids (49548) *(G-6435)*
General Dynamics Corporation 615 427-5768
25435 Brest Taylor (48180) *(G-15725)*
General Dynamics Corporation 586 825-8228
55518 Belle Ln Macomb (48042) *(G-10125)*
General Dynamics Glbl IMG Tech (HQ) 248 293-2929
2909 Waterview Dr Rochester Hills (48309) *(G-13432)*
General Dynamics Glbl IMG Tech 248 293-2929
2909 Waterview Dr Rochester Hills (48309) *(G-13433)*
General Dynamics Land 586 825-4805
6000 17 Mile Rd Sterling Heights (48313) *(G-15356)*
General Dynamics Land 586 825-8400
38500 Mound Rd Sterling Heights (48310) *(G-15357)*
General Dynamics Mission 530 271-2500
2909 Waterview Dr Rochester Hills (48309) *(G-13434)*
General Electric Company 734 728-1472
38303 Michigan Ave Wayne (48184) *(G-17431)*
General Electric Company 616 676-0870
7575 Fulton St E 74-1a Ada (49355) *(G-16)*
General Filters Inc (PA) 248 476-5100
43800 Grand River Ave Novi (48375) *(G-11890)*
General Formulations, Sparta *Also called Celia Corporation (G-15090)*
GENERAL GRAPHITES, Bay City *Also called Graphite Electrodes Ltd (G-1319)*
General Hardwood Co, Detroit *Also called Northern Millwork Co (G-4276)*
General Hardwood Company (PA) 313 365-7733
7201 E Mcnichols Rd Detroit (48212) *(G-4080)*
General Inspection LLC 248 625-0529
10585 Enterprise Dr Davisburg (48350) *(G-3634)*
General Machine & Boring Inc 810 220-1203
5983 Ford Ct Brighton (48116) *(G-1930)*
General Machine Service Inc 989 752-5161
494 E Morley Dr Saginaw (48601) *(G-14042)*
General Machine Services 269 695-2244
807 W 4th St Buchanan (49107) *(G-2119)*
General Media LLC 586 541-0075
24114 Harper Ave Saint Clair Shores (48080) *(G-14254)*
General Mill Supply Company 248 668-0800
50690 General Mill Dr Wixom (48393) *(G-17816)*
General Mills Inc 231 832-3285
128 E Slosson Ave Reed City (49677) *(G-13213)*
General Mills Inc 763 764-7600
6805 Beatrice Dr Kalamazoo (49009) *(G-8749)*

A L P H A B E T I C

General Mills Inc 269 337-0288
3800 Midlink Dr Kalamazoo (49048) *(G-8750)*
General Motors China Inc (HQ) 313 556-5000
300 Renaissance Ctr L1 Detroit (48243) *(G-4081)*
General Motors Company 248 249-6347
20001 Brownstown Ctr Dr Brownstown (48183) *(G-2063)*
General Motors Company 989 757-1576
1629 N Washington Ave Saginaw (48601) *(G-14043)*
General Motors Company 586 218-9240
7015 Edward Cole Blvd Warren (48093) *(G-17051)*
General Motors Company (PA) 313 667-1500
300 Renaissance Ctr L1 Detroit (48243) *(G-4082)*
General Motors Holdings LLC (HQ) 313 556-5000
300 Renaissance Ctr L1 Detroit (48243) *(G-4083)*
General Motors LLC 810 234-2710
G-2238 W Bristol Rd Flint (48553) *(G-5434)*
General Motors LLC 989 894-7210
1001 Woodside Ave Bay City (48708) *(G-1315)*
General Motors LLC 989 757-0528
3900 N Towerline Rd Saginaw (48601) *(G-14044)*
General Motors LLC 810 234-2710
2238 W Bristol Rd Flint (48529) *(G-5435)*
General Motors LLC 586 731-2743
6200 19 Mile Rd Sterling Heights (48314) *(G-15358)*
General Motors LLC 517 885-6669
4400 W Mount Hope Hwy Lansing (48917) *(G-9290)*
General Motors LLC 517 242-2158
920 Townsend St Lansing (48933) *(G-9372)*
General Motors LLC 313 972-6000
2500 E Grand Blvd Detroit (48211) *(G-4084)*
General Motors LLC 931 486-1914
7111 E 11 Mile Rd Warren (48092) *(G-17052)*
General Motors LLC 931 486-5049
7111 E 11 Mile Rd Warren (48092) *(G-17053)*
General Motors LLC 517 721-2000
8175 Millett Hwy Lansing (48917) *(G-9291)*
General Motors LLC 810 236-1970
425 S Stevenson St Flint (48503) *(G-5436)*
General Motors LLC 248 874-1737
895 Joslyn Ave Pontiac (48340) *(G-12826)*
General Motors LLC (HQ) 313 410-2704
300 Renaissance Ctr L1 Detroit (48243) *(G-4085)*
General Motors LLC 248 456-5000
2000 Centerpoint Pkwy Pontiac (48341) *(G-12827)*
General Motors LLC 313 972-6000
2500 E Grand Blvd Detroit (48211) *(G-4086)*
General Motors LLC 248 857-3500
1251 Joslyn Ave Pontiac (48340) *(G-12828)*
General Motors LLC 313 556-5000
2500 E Grand Motors Blvd Detroit (48211) *(G-4087)*
General Mtrs Cmpnents Holdings, Detroit *Also called GM Components Holdings LLC (G-4092)*
General Parts Inc 989 686-3114
3616 Wilder Rd Bay City (48706) *(G-1316)*
General Processing Systems Inc 630 554-7804
12838 Stainless Dr Holland (49424) *(G-7640)*
General Roofing Services, Pontiac *Also called S & B Roofing Services Inc (G-12863)*
General Scientific Corporation 734 996-9200
77 Enterprise Dr Ann Arbor (48103) *(G-471)*
General Scoreboard Services 734 753-5652
21099 Clark Rd Belleville (48111) *(G-1445)*
General Structures Inc 586 774-6105
23171 Groesbeck Hwy Warren (48089) *(G-17054)*
General Tape Label Liquidating 248 437-5200
28505 Automation Blvd Wixom (48393) *(G-17817)*
General Technology Inc 269 751-7516
4521 48th St Holland (49423) *(G-7641)*
General Wood Products Co 248 221-0214
403 Bjornson St Ste 403 # 403 Big Rapids (49307) *(G-1630)*
Generaleral Dynamics 601 877-6436
8235 San Marco Blvd Sterling Heights (48313) *(G-15359)*
Generation Press Inc 616 392-4405
10861 Paw Paw Dr Holland (49424) *(G-7642)*
Generation Tool Inc 734 641-6937
307 Manufacturers Dr Westland (48186) *(G-17561)*
Generl-Lctrical-Mechanical Inc 248 698-1110
10415 Highland Rd White Lake (48386) *(G-17633)*
Genesee County Herald Inc 810 686-3840
10098 N Dort Hwy Clio (48420) *(G-3272)*
Genesee Cut Stone & Marble Co (PA) 810 743-1800
5276 S Saginaw Rd Flint (48507) *(G-5437)*
Genesee Free Net 810 720-2880
1158 W Bristol Rd Flint (48507) *(G-5438)*
Genesee Group Inc (PA) 810 235-8041
2022 North St Flint (48505) *(G-5439)*
Genesee Group Inc 810 235-6120
1102 N Averill Flint (48506) *(G-5440)*
Genesee Packaging, Flint *Also called Genesee Group Inc (G-5439)*
Genesee Packaging, Flint *Also called Genesee Group Inc (G-5440)*
Genesee Valley Petroleum 231 946-8630
523 Cottage Arbor Ln # 5 Traverse City (49684) *(G-15977)*
Genesis Casket Company, Mason *Also called Genesis International LLC (G-10640)*
Genesis Graphics Inc 906 786-4913
1823 7th Ave N Escanaba (49829) *(G-4831)*
Genesis Innovation Group LLC 616 294-1026
13827 Port Sheldon St Holland (49424) *(G-7643)*
Genesis International LLC 317 777-6700
200 E Kipp Rd Mason (48854) *(G-10640)*
Genesis Manufacturing Entps 734 243-5302
348 Ruff Dr Monroe (48162) *(G-11032)*
Genesis Sand and Gravel Inc 313 587-8530
6689 Orchard Lake Rd # 219 West Bloomfield (48322) *(G-17477)*
Genesis Seating Inc 616 954-1040
3445 East Paris Ave Se Grand Rapids (49512) *(G-6436)*
Genesis Seating Inc (HQ) 616 954-1040
3445 East Paris Ave Se Grand Rapids (49512) *(G-6437)*
Genesis Seating 0519, Grand Rapids *Also called Genesis Seating Inc (G-6436)*
Genesis Seating 0519, Grand Rapids *Also called Genesis Seating Inc (G-6437)*
Genesis Service Associates LLC 734 994-3900
3255 Central St Apt 1 Dexter (48130) *(G-4493)*
Genex Window Inc 586 754-2917
23110 Sherwood Ave Warren (48091) *(G-17055)*
Genix LLC 248 761-3030
3151 Walnut Lake Rd West Bloomfield (48323) *(G-17478)*
Genix LLC (PA) 248 419-0231
43665 Utica Rd Sterling Heights (48314) *(G-15360)*
Genoa Healthcare LLC 313 989-0536
5716 Michigan Ave Detroit (48210) *(G-4088)*
Genoak Materials Inc 810 742-0050
3251 E Bristol Rd Burton (48529) *(G-2155)*
Genoak Materials Inc (PA) 248 634-8276
14300 Shields Rd Holly (48442) *(G-7880)*
Genomeweb, Detroit *Also called Crain Communications Inc (G-3950)*
Genova Products Inc (PA) 810 744-4500
7034 E Court St Davison (48423) *(G-3650)*
Genova-Minnesota Inc 810 744-4500
7034 E Court St Davison (48423) *(G-3651)*
Gentex Corporation (PA) 616 772-1800
600 N Centennial St Zeeland (49464) *(G-18138)*
Gentex Corporation 616 772-1800
9001 Riley St Zeeland (49464) *(G-18139)*
Gentex Corporation 616 772-1800
58 E Riley St Zeeland (49464) *(G-18140)*
Gentex Corporation 616 772-1800
675 N State St Zeeland (49464) *(G-18141)*
Gentex Corporation 616 392-7195
10985 Chicago Dr Zeeland (49464) *(G-18142)*
Gentex Corporation 616 772-1800
310 E Riley St Zeeland (49464) *(G-18143)*
Gentherm Incorporated (PA) 248 504-0500
21680 Haggerty Rd Ste 101 Northville (48167) *(G-11694)*
Gentile Packaging Machinery Co 734 429-1177
8300 Boettner Rd Saline (48176) *(G-14393)*
Gentle Machine Tool & Die 734 699-2013
13600 Martinsville Rd Van Buren Twp (48111) *(G-16761)*
Gentry Services of Alabama 248 321-6368
31943 Red Run Dr Warren (48093) *(G-17056)*
Gentz Aero, Warren *Also called MB Aerospace Warren LLC (G-17144)*
Gentz Forest Robert Products (PA) 231 398-9194
9644 Guenthardt Rd Manistee (49660) *(G-10423)*
Genx Corporation 269 341-4242
2911 Emerald Dr Kalamazoo (49001) *(G-8751)*
Geofabrica Inc 810 728-2468
1490 Lakewood Rd Bloomfield Hills (48302) *(G-1767)*
Geolean USA LLC 313 859-9780
11998 Merriman Rd Livonia (48150) *(G-9751)*
Geomembrane Research 231 943-2266
1567 W South Airport Rd Traverse City (49686) *(G-15978)*
Geomembrane Services Inc 231 264-9030
6516 Birch Lake Rd Kewadin (49648) *(G-9038)*
George Jensen 269 329-1543
2228 Beethoven Ave Portage (49024) *(G-12998)*
George Kotzian 231 861-6520
1461 S 44th Ave Shelby (49455) *(G-14525)*
George Koueiter Jewelers 313 882-1110
19815 Mack Ave Grosse Pointe Woods (48236) *(G-7203)*
George P Johnson Company (HQ) 248 475-2500
3600 Giddings Rd Auburn Hills (48326) *(G-883)*
George W Trapp Co (PA) 313 531-7180
15000 Fox Redford (48239) *(G-13163)*
George Washburn 269 694-2930
515 S Wilmott St Otsego (49078) *(G-12240)*
Georgetown Steel LLC 734 568-6148
8000 Yankee Rd Ste 440 Ottawa Lake (49267) *(G-12264)*
Georgia Walker & Assoc Inc 248 594-6447
2306 Eastways Rd Bloomfield Hills (48304) *(G-1768)*
Georgia-Pacific LLC 734 439-2441
951 County St Milan (48160) *(G-10938)*

ALPHABETIC SECTION

Georgia-Pacific LLC 989 725-5191
   465 S Delaney Rd Owosso (48867) *(G-12293)*
Georgia-Pacific LLC 989 348-7275
   4113 W 4 Mile Rd Grayling (49738) *(G-7107)*
Geostar Corporation (PA) 989 773-7050
   2480 W Campus Dr Ste C Mount Pleasant (48858) *(G-11194)*
Geotech Environmental Eqp Inc 517 655-5616
   1099 W Grnd Riv 6 Williamston (48895) *(G-17730)*
Gerald Froberg 906 346-3311
   25 E Stephenson Ave Gwinn (49841) *(G-7219)*
Gerald Harris 985 774-0261
   14846 Dexter Ave Detroit (48238) *(G-4089)*
Gerber Products Company 231 928-2076
   405 State St Fremont (49412) *(G-5772)*
Gerber Products Company 231 928-2000
   445 State St Fremont (49413) *(G-5773)*
Gerbers Home Made Sweets 231 348-3743
   8218 Pincherry Rd Charlevoix (49720) *(G-2615)*
Gerdau Macsteel Inc 517 764-3920
   3100 Brooklyn Rd Jackson (49203) *(G-8455)*
Gerdau Macsteel Inc 734 243-2446
   3000 E Front St Monroe (48161) *(G-11033)*
Gerdau Macsteel Inc 734 243-2446
   3000 E Front St Monroe (48161) *(G-11034)*
Gerdau Macsteel Inc (HQ) 517 782-0415
   5591 Morrill Rd Jackson (49201) *(G-8456)*
Gerdau Macsteel Atmosphere Ann (HQ) 517 782-0415
   209 W Mount Hope Ave # 1 Lansing (48910) *(G-9373)*
Gerdau Macsteel Atmosphere Ann 517 482-1374
   1801 Bassett St Lansing (48915) *(G-9374)*
Gerdau Special Steel N Amer, Monroe Also called Gerdau Macsteel Inc *(G-11033)*
Gerken Materials Inc 517 567-4406
   11671 Tripp Rd Waldron (49288) *(G-16858)*
Gerken Materials Inc 734 243-1851
   15205 S Telegraph Rd Monroe (48161) *(G-11035)*
Germack Nut Co, Detroit Also called Nutco Inc *(G-4280)*
German/American Newspaper Age, Warren Also called Wochen-Post *(G-17295)*
Gerref Industries Inc 616 794-3110
   206 N York St Belding (48809) *(G-1416)*
Gerry Gostenik 313 319-0100
   2745 Academy St Dearborn (48124) *(G-3714)*
Gestamp Alabama LLC 810 245-3100
   100 E Fair St Lapeer (48446) *(G-9462)*
Gestamp Mason LLC 517 244-8800
   200 E Kipp Rd Mason (48854) *(G-10641)*
Gestamp North America Inc (HQ) 248 743-3400
   2701 Troy Center Dr # 150 Troy (48084) *(G-16382)*
Gestamp Washtenaw LLC 248 251-3004
   5800 Sibley Rd Chelsea (48118) *(G-2711)*
Get In Game Marketing LLC 231 846-1976
   2322 Cass Rd Traverse City (49684) *(G-15979)*
Getecha Inc 269 373-8896
   2914 Business One Dr Kalamazoo (49048) *(G-8752)*
Getrag Transmissions Corp 586 620-1300
   1235 E Big Beaver Rd Troy (48083) *(G-16383)*
Gfg Dynamation, Ann Arbor Also called Gfg Instrumentation Inc *(G-472)*
Gfg Instrumentation Inc 734 769-0573
   1194 Oak Valley Dr Ste 20 Ann Arbor (48108) *(G-472)*
Gfl Envronmental Real Property (PA) 888 877-4996
   26999 Central Park Blvd # 200 Southfield (48076) *(G-14919)*
Gfl Envronmental Real Property 586 774-1360
   25601 Flanders Ave Warren (48089) *(G-17057)*
Gfm LLC (HQ) 586 777-4542
   29685 Calahan Rd Roseville (48066) *(G-13807)*
Gfm Corp., Roseville Also called Gfm LLC *(G-13807)*
Gh Imaging, Muskegon Also called Graphics Hse Spt Prmotions Inc *(G-11334)*
Ghi Electronics LLC 248 397-8856
   501 E Whitcomb Ave Madison Heights (48071) *(G-10257)*
Ghost Island Brewery 219 242-4800
   17656 Us Highway 12 New Buffalo (49117) *(G-11515)*
Ghost Mfg LLC (PA) 269 281-0489
   480 Ansley Dr Saint Joseph (49085) *(G-14312)*
Ghpc, Grand Haven Also called Grand Haven Powder Coating Inc *(G-6023)*
Ghs Corporation 269 968-3351
   2813 Wilbur St Springfield (49037) *(G-15192)*
GHS Corporation (PA) 800 388-4447
   2813 Wilbur St Springfield (49037) *(G-15193)*
Ghs Strings, Springfield Also called Ghs Corporation *(G-15192)*
Ghsp, Grand Haven Also called Jsj Corporation *(G-6041)*
Ghsp Inc (HQ) 616 842-5500
   1250 S Beechtree St Grand Haven (49417) *(G-6018)*
Ghsp Inc 248 588-5095
   1250 S Beechtree St Grand Haven (49417) *(G-6019)*
Ghsp Inc 231 873-3300
   1500 Industrial Park Dr Hart (49420) *(G-7371)*
Ghsp Inc 248 581-0890
   560 Kirts Blvd Ste 111 Troy (48084) *(G-16384)*
Ghsp Hart Plant, Hart Also called Ghsp Inc *(G-7371)*

GI Millworks Inc 734 451-1100
   14970 Cleat St Plymouth (48170) *(G-12627)*
Gibbies Deer Processing 231 924-6042
   215 Jerrette Ave Fremont (49412) *(G-5774)*
Gibbs Precast Co Inc 517 768-9100
   2412 Lansing Ave Jackson (49202) *(G-8457)*
Gibbs Sports Amphibians Inc 248 572-6670
   465 S Glaspie St Ste E Oxford (48371) *(G-12346)*
Gibbys Transport LLC 269 838-2794
   719 E Woodlawn Ave Hastings (49058) *(G-7411)*
Gibouts Sash & Door 906 863-2224
   2208 10th Ave Menominee (49858) *(G-10738)*
Gibraltar Canvas Inc 734 675-4891
   28599 N Gibraltar Rd Rockwood (48173) *(G-13604)*
Gibraltar Inc 616 748-4857
   421 N Centennial St Zeeland (49464) *(G-18144)*
Gibraltar National Corporation 248 634-8257
   14311 Cmi Dr Holly (48442) *(G-7881)*
Gic LLC 231 237-7000
   12575 Us Highway 31 N Charlevoix (49720) *(G-2616)*
Gic Thermo Dynamics, Charlevoix Also called Gic LLC *(G-2616)*
Gicmac Industrial Inc 248 308-2743
   43155 Main St Novi (48375) *(G-11891)*
Gielow Pickles Inc (PA) 810 359-7680
   5260 Main St Lexington (48450) *(G-9557)*
Giffin Inc 248 494-9600
   1900 Brown Rd Auburn Hills (48326) *(G-884)*
Giffin, Inc. and Affiliates, Auburn Hills Also called Giffin Inc *(G-884)*
Gift Bikes 4 Kids 313 573-5619
   3166 S Bassett St Detroit (48217) *(G-4090)*
Giguere Logging Inc 906 786-3975
   3200 5th Ave S Escanaba (49829) *(G-4832)*
Gil-Mar Manufacturing Co (PA) 248 640-4303
   7925 Ronda Dr Canton (48187) *(G-2377)*
Gilbert & Riplo Company, Ravenna Also called Griptrac Inc *(G-13120)*
Gilbert's Chocolates, Jackson Also called W2 Inc *(G-8602)*
Gilchrist Premium Lumber Pdts (PA) 989 826-8300
   1284 Mapes Rd Mio (48647) *(G-11002)*
Gildner's Concrete Products, Alpena Also called Gildners Concrete *(G-292)*
Gildners Concrete 989 356-5156
   400 Commerce Dr Alpena (49707) *(G-292)*
Gill Corporation (HQ) 616 453-4491
   706 Bond Ave Nw Grand Rapids (49503) *(G-6438)*
Gill Corporation 616 453-4491
   706 Bond Ave Nw Grand Rapids (49503) *(G-6439)*
Gill Holding Company Inc (PA) 616 559-2700
   5271 Plainfield Ave Ne Grand Rapids (49525) *(G-6440)*
Gill Industries Inc (HQ) 616 559-2700
   5271 Plainfield Ave Ne Grand Rapids (49525) *(G-6441)*
Gill Industries Inc 616 559-2700
   5271 Plainfield Ave Nw Grand Rapids (49525) *(G-6442)*
Gill Manufacturing, Grand Rapids Also called Gill Industries Inc *(G-6442)*
Gill Manufacturing Co., Grand Rapids Also called Gill Industries Inc *(G-6441)*
Gillisons Var Fabrication Inc (PA) 231 882-5921
   3033 Benzie Hwy Benzonia (49616) *(G-1575)*
Gilners Concrete, Hillman Also called Cheboygan Cement Products Inc *(G-7508)*
Ginkgotree Inc 734 707-7191
   1555 Broadway St Ste 300 Detroit (48226) *(G-4091)*
Ginsan Liquidating Company LLC 616 791-8100
   3611 3 Mile Rd Nw Grand Rapids (49534) *(G-6443)*
Giovannis Apptzing Fd Pdts Inc 586 727-9355
   37775 32 Mile Rd Richmond (48062) *(G-13263)*
Gipson Fabrications 616 245-7331
   2151 Chicago Dr Sw Wyoming (49519) *(G-18003)*
Giv LLC 248 467-6852
   38705 7 Mile Rd Ste 405 Livonia (48152) *(G-9752)*
Give-Em A Brake Safety LLC 616 531-8705
   2610 Sanford Ave Sw Grandville (49418) *(G-7037)*
Gj Prey Coml & Indus Pntg Cov 248 250-4792
   710 N Crooks Rd Clawson (48017) *(G-2980)*
Gki Foods LLC 248 486-0055
   7926 Lochlin Dr Brighton (48116) *(G-1931)*
GKN Automotive, Auburn Hills Also called GKN Driveline North Amer Inc *(G-885)*
GKN Driveline North Amer Inc (HQ) 248 296-7000
   2200 N Opdyke Rd Auburn Hills (48326) *(G-885)*
GKN North America Inc 248 296-7200
   2200 N Opdyke Rd Auburn Hills (48326) *(G-886)*
GKN North America Services Inc 248 377-1200
   3300 University Dr Auburn Hills (48326) *(G-887)*
GKN Sinter Metals LLC (HQ) 248 296-7832
   1670 Opdyke Ct Auburn Hills (48326) *(G-888)*
Gladiator Quality Sorting LLC 734 578-1950
   43220 Oakbrook Ct Canton (48187) *(G-2378)*
Gladstone Metals, Gladstone Also called Vanaire Inc *(G-5921)*
Gladstone Printing, Lansing Also called Millbrook Press Works *(G-9311)*
Gladwin Machine Inc 989 426-8753
   535 S M 18 Gladwin (48624) *(G-5930)*
Gladwin Metal Processing Inc 989 426-9038
   795 E Maple St Gladwin (48624) *(G-5931)*

Gladwin Tank Manufacturing Inc 989 426-4768
207 Industrial Park Ave Gladwin (48624) *(G-5932)*
Glas, Clinton Township *Also called Great Lakes Aviaiton Svcs LLC (G-3129)*
Glass Recyclers Ltd 313 584-3434
6465 Wyoming St Dearborn (48126) *(G-3715)*
Glassicart Decorative Glwr 231 739-5956
3128 7th St Muskegon (49444) *(G-11330)*
Glassline Incorporated 734 453-2728
199 W Ann Arbor Trl Plymouth (48170) *(G-12628)*
Glassmaster Controls Co Inc 269 382-2010
831 Cobb Ave Kalamazoo (49007) *(G-8753)*
Glassource, Grand Haven *Also called City Auto Glass Co (G-6003)*
Glastender Inc (PA) 989 752-4275
5400 N Michigan Rd Saginaw (48604) *(G-14045)*
Glastron LLC 800 354-3141
925 Frisbie St Cadillac (49601) *(G-2249)*
Glaxosmithkline LLC 989 450-9859
1331 S Dehmel Rd Frankenmuth (48734) *(G-5588)*
Glaxosmithkline LLC 989 928-6535
875 Island Lake Dr Oxford (48371) *(G-12347)*
Glaxosmithkline LLC 989 280-1225
2518 Abbott Rd Apt V11 Midland (48642) *(G-10866)*
Glaxosmithkline LLC 248 561-3022
721 Parkman Dr Bloomfield Hills (48304) *(G-1769)*
Glcc Co 269 657-3167
39149 W Red Arrow Hwy Paw Paw (49079) *(G-12404)*
Glcc Tech Center, Van Buren Twp *Also called Visteon Global Electronics Inc (G-16793)*
Gld Holdings Inc 616 877-4288
4560 Division Moline (49335) *(G-11010)*
Gle Solar Energy, Saint Joseph *Also called Great Lakes Electric LLC (G-14313)*
Gleason Holbrook Mfg Co 586 749-5519
22401 28 Mile Rd Ray (48096) *(G-13133)*
Gleason Works 248 522-0305
39255 Country Club Dr B8 Farmington Hills (48331) *(G-5009)*
Gleason's Plating, Allegan *Also called Donald Gleason (G-158)*
Glenn Knochel 989 684-7869
2152 E Beaver Rd Kawkawlin (48631) *(G-8971)*
Glitterbug USA 586 247-7569
47587 Goldridge Ln Macomb (48044) *(G-10126)*
Glm Products, Grand Rapids *Also called Great Lakes Hydra Corporation (G-6479)*
Global Advanced Products LLC 586 749-6800
30707 Commerce Blvd Chesterfield (48051) *(G-2781)*
Global Auditing Solutions, Farmington Hills *Also called Norman A Lewis (G-5080)*
Global Automotive Products Inc 734 589-6179
38100 Jay Kay Dr Romulus (48174) *(G-13680)*
Global Automotive Systems, Roseville *Also called Global Rollforming Systems LLC (G-13808)*
Global Automotive Systems LLC (HQ) 248 299-7500
1780 Pond Run Auburn Hills (48326) *(G-889)*
Global Autopack LLC 248 390-2434
30428 Milford Rd Ste 2000 New Hudson (48165) *(G-11541)*
Global Builder Supply, Ottawa Lake *Also called Pure Liberty Manufacturing LLC (G-12269)*
Global Chesterfield, Chesterfield *Also called Global Enterprise Limited (G-2782)*
Global CNC Industries Ltd 734 464-1920
15150 Cleat St Plymouth (48170) *(G-12629)*
Global Digital Printing 734 244-5010
20 W 1st St Monroe (48161) *(G-11036)*
Global Electronics Limited 248 353-0100
2075 Franklin Rd Bloomfield Hills (48302) *(G-1770)*
Global Engine Mfg Aliance LLC 734 529-9888
5800 N Ann Arbor Rd Dundee (48131) *(G-4585)*
Global Engineering Inc 586 566-0423
50685 Rizzo Dr Shelby Township (48315) *(G-14596)*
Global Enterprise Limited 586 948-4100
50450 E Rssell Schmidt Bl Chesterfield (48051) *(G-2782)*
Global Enterprises, Huntington Woods *Also called Polymerica Limited Company (G-8191)*
Global Fleet Sales LLC 248 327-6483
24725 W 12 Mile Rd # 114 Southfield (48034) *(G-14920)*
Global Fmi LLC 810 964-5555
17195 Silver Pkwy Ste 111 Fenton (48430) *(G-5216)*
Global Gear Inc 734 979-0888
6049 E Executive Dr Westland (48185) *(G-17562)*
Global Green Corporation 734 560-1743
5068 Plymouth Rd Ann Arbor (48105) *(G-473)*
Global Hoses & Fittings LLC (PA) 248 219-9581
30370 Fox Club Dr Farmington Hills (48331) *(G-5010)*
Global Impact Group LLC 248 895-9900
9082 S Saginaw Rd Grand Blanc (48439) *(G-5966)*
Global Imported Fittings, Farmington Hills *Also called Global Hoses & Fittings LLC (G-5010)*
Global Information Systems 248 223-9800
29777 Telg Rd Ste 2450 Southfield (48034) *(G-14921)*
Global Lift Corp 989 269-5900
684 N Port Crescent St C Bad Axe (48413) *(G-1066)*
Global Logistics Services, Warren *Also called GLS Industries LLC (G-17058)*
Global Mfg & Assembly Corp 517 789-8116
1801 Wildwood Ave Jackson (49202) *(G-8458)*
Global Plastic Systems, Chesterfield *Also called Grace Production Services LLC (G-2783)*
Global Pump Company LLC (PA) 810 653-4828
10162 E Coldwater Rd Davison (48423) *(G-3652)*
Global Quality Ingredients Inc 651 337-2028
10464 Bryan Hwy Onsted (49265) *(G-12153)*
Global Restaurant Group Inc 313 271-2777
13250 Rotunda Dr Dearborn (48120) *(G-3716)*
Global Retool Group Amer LLC 248 289-5820
50660 Century Ct Wixom (48393) *(G-17818)*
Global Rollforming Systems LLC 586 218-5100
15500 E 12 Mile Rd Roseville (48066) *(G-13808)*
Global Silks Gifts N Crafts, Ortonville *Also called Sheri Boston (G-12203)*
Global Strapping LLC 517 545-4900
895 Grand Oaks Dr Howell (48843) *(G-8044)*
Global Strgc Sup Solutions LLC 734 525-9100
34450 Industrial Rd Livonia (48150) *(G-9753)*
Global Supply Integrator LLC 586 484-0734
10145 Creekwood Trl Davisburg (48350) *(G-3635)*
Global Technologies, Spring Lake *Also called Oleco Inc (G-15167)*
Global Technology Ventures Inc 248 324-3707
37408 Hills Tech Dr Farmington Hills (48331) *(G-5011)*
Global Tooling Systems LLC 586 726-0500
16445 23 Mile Rd Macomb (48042) *(G-10127)*
Global Vehicle Works, Grand Blanc *Also called Global Impact Group LLC (G-5966)*
Global Wholesale & Marketing 248 910-8302
6566 Burroughs Ave Sterling Heights (48314) *(G-15361)*
Globaltech Ventures, Farmington Hills *Also called Global Technology Ventures Inc (G-5011)*
Globe Construction, Kalamazoo *Also called Oldcastle Materials Inc (G-8839)*
Globe Industries Incorporated 906 932-3540
121 Mill St Ironwood (49938) *(G-8329)*
Globe Printing & Specialties 906 485-1033
200 W Division St Ishpeming (49849) *(G-8345)*
Globe Sand & Gravel, Ironwood *Also called Globe Industries Incorporated (G-8329)*
Globe Tech LLC 734 656-2200
40300 Plymouth Rd Plymouth (48170) *(G-12630)*
Globe Tech Manufactured Pdts, Plymouth *Also called Globe Tech LLC (G-12630)*
Globe Technologies Corporation 989 846-9591
1109 W Cedar St Standish (48658) *(G-15219)*
Globe Tumbling Barrel Eqp, Jackson *Also called Casalbi Company Inc (G-8403)*
Gloria C Williams 313 220-2735
17310 Westland Ave Southfield (48075) *(G-14922)*
Glov Enterprises LLC 517 423-9700
412 S Maumee St Tecumseh (49286) *(G-15794)*
Glove Coaters Incorporated 517 741-8402
8380 M 60 Union City (49094) *(G-16734)*
Glr, Roseville *Also called Great Lakes Paper Stock Corp (G-13811)*
GLS Diocesan Reports (PA) 989 793-7661
1520 Court St Saginaw (48602) *(G-14046)*
GLS Enterprises Inc 616 243-2574
960 W River Center Dr Ne G Comstock Park (49321) *(G-3482)*
GLS Industries LLC (PA) 586 255-9221
7111 E 11 Mile Rd Warren (48092) *(G-17058)*
GLS Industries LLC 586 255-9221
8333 E 11 Mile Rd Warren (48093) *(G-17059)*
GLS Promotional Specialties, Comstock Park *Also called GLS Enterprises Inc (G-3482)*
Glt Packaging, Grand Rapids *Also called Great Lakes-Triad Plastic (G-6480)*
Gluco Inc 616 457-1212
794 Chicago Dr Jenison (49428) *(G-8627)*
Glw Finishing 616 395-0112
741 Waverly Ct Holland (49423) *(G-7644)*
Glycon Corp 517 423-8356
912 Industrial Dr Tecumseh (49286) *(G-15795)*
Glynn, Mark, Builder, Traverse City *Also called G F Inc (G-15975)*
GM, Canton *Also called Gil-Mar Manufacturing Co (G-2377)*
GM Bassett Pattern Inc 248 477-6454
31162 W 8 Mile Rd Farmington Hills (48336) *(G-5012)*
GM Components Holdings LLC 616 246-2000
2100 Burlingame Ave Sw Grand Rapids (49509) *(G-6444)*
GM Components Holdings LLC (HQ) 313 665-4707
300 Renaissance Ctr Detroit (48243) *(G-4092)*
GM Division Plant, Mason *Also called Lear Corporation (G-10644)*
GM Gdls Defense Group LLC (HQ) 586 825-4000
38500 Mound Rd Sterling Heights (48310) *(G-15362)*
GM Laam Holdings LLC (HQ) 313 556-5000
300 Renaissance Ctr Detroit (48243) *(G-4093)*
GM Orion Assembly 248 377-5260
4555 Giddings Rd Lake Orion (48359) *(G-9137)*
GM Powertrain-Romulus Engine 734 595-5203
36880 Ecorse Rd Romulus (48174) *(G-13681)*
GMA Industries Inc 734 595-7300
38127 Ecorse Rd Romulus (48174) *(G-13682)*
GME, Union City *Also called Trinity Industries Inc (G-16736)*
GMI, Chelsea *Also called Greene Manufacturing Inc (G-2712)*
GMI Composites Inc 231 755-1611
1355 W Sherman Blvd Muskegon (49441) *(G-11331)*
GMi Packaging Co (PA) 734 972-7389
1371 Centennial Ln Ann Arbor (48103) *(G-474)*
Gmr Quality Stone, Sterling Heights *Also called Gmr Stone Products LLC (G-15363)*

ALPHABETIC SECTION

Gmr Stone Products LLC..586 739-2700
36955 Metro Ct Sterling Heights (48312) *(G-15363)*
Gms Industries, Buchanan *Also called General Machine Services (G-2119)*
Gns America Co., Holland *Also called Gns Holland Inc (G-7645)*
Gns Holland Inc..616 796-0433
13341 Quincy St Holland (49424) *(G-7645)*
Gns North America Inc (PA)..616 796-0433
13341 Quincy St Holland (49424) *(G-7646)*
Gnu Software Development Inc..586 778-9182
14156 E 11 Mile Rd Warren (48089) *(G-17060)*
Gnutti Carlo Usa Inc..517 223-1059
1101 Highview Dr Webberville (48892) *(G-17450)*
Go Beyond Healthy LLC..407 255-0314
2290 Christine Ct Se Grand Rapids (49546) *(G-6445)*
Go Cat Feather Toys..517 543-7519
605 W Lovett St Charlotte (48813) *(G-2652)*
Go Frac LLC..817 731-0301
7000 Calmont Ave Ste 310 Detroit (48207) *(G-4094)*
Go Office.com, Grand Rapids *Also called Mobile Office Vehicle Inc (G-6693)*
Go Power Systems, Novi *Also called Froude Inc (G-11888)*
Godfrey & Wing Inc...330 562-1440
2240 Veterans Mem Pkwy Saginaw (48601) *(G-14047)*
Godin Tool Inc...231 946-2210
466 Hughes Dr Traverse City (49696) *(G-15980)*
Gods Children In Unity Intl M..313 528-8285
19325 Barlow St Detroit (48205) *(G-4095)*
Goertz+schiele Corporation..248 393-0414
1750 Summit Dr Auburn Hills (48326) *(G-890)*
Goetz Craft Printers Inc..734 973-7604
121 Paula Dr Brooklyn (49230) *(G-2037)*
Gofrac, Detroit *Also called Go Frac LLC (G-4094)*
Gogosqueez, Grawn *Also called Materne North America Corp (G-7099)*
Going Out On A Limb..231 347-4631
4588 Greenwood Rd Petoskey (49770) *(G-12449)*
Gokoh Coldwater Incorporated..517 279-1080
100 Concept Dr Coldwater (49036) *(G-3305)*
Gold Bond, National City *Also called New Ngc Inc (G-11464)*
Gold Coast Ice Makers LLC...231 845-2745
3785 W Us Highway 10 Ludington (49431) *(G-10060)*
Gold Coast Icemakers, Ludington *Also called Gold Coast Ice Makers LLC (G-10060)*
Golden Dental Solutions, Eastpointe *Also called Visual Chimera (G-4711)*
Golden Dental Solutions, Roseville *Also called End Product Results LLC (G-13801)*
Golden Eagle Pallets LLC..616 233-0970
1701 Clyde Park Ave Sw Wyoming (49509) *(G-18004)*
Golden Needle Awnings LLC (PA).....................................517 404-6219
8674 S County Line Rd Gaines (48436) *(G-5804)*
Golden Pointe Awning & Sign Co, Detroit *Also called Golden Pointe Inc (G-4096)*
Golden Pointe Inc..313 581-8284
16050 W Warren Ave Detroit (48228) *(G-4096)*
Golden Refrigerant, Livonia *Also called Cjg LLC (G-9683)*
Golf Store...517 347-8733
1492 W Grand River Ave Okemos (48864) *(G-12125)*
Gollnick Tool Co...586 755-0100
24300 Marmon Ave Warren (48089) *(G-17061)*
Gombar Corp...989 793-9427
5645 State St Ste B Saginaw (48603) *(G-14048)*
Gongwer News Service Inc...517 482-3500
101 S Wash Sq Ste 540 Lansing (48933) *(G-9375)*
Gonzalez Group Jonesville LLC...517 849-9908
3980 Beck Rd Jonesville (49250) *(G-8655)*
Gonzalez Jr Pallets LLC...616 885-0201
1601 Madison St Sw Grand Rapids (49507) *(G-6446)*
Gonzalez Prod Systems Inc...248 209-1836
13200 W 8 Mile Rd Oak Park (48237) *(G-12071)*
Gonzalez Prod Systems Inc...248 745-1200
1670 Highwood E Pontiac (48340) *(G-12829)*
Gonzalez Prod Systems Inc...313 297-6682
2555 Clark St Detroit (48209) *(G-4097)*
Gonzalez Universal Pallets LLC..616 243-5524
955 Godfrey Ave Sw Grand Rapids (49503) *(G-6447)*
Gonzalez Welding...248 469-3016
1385 Hira St Waterford (48328) *(G-17346)*
Good Juice, Detroit *Also called Super Fluids LLC (G-4386)*
Good Sense Coffee Inc..810 355-2349
7931 State St Brighton (48116) *(G-1932)*
Good-Rich Honey, Lapeer *Also called Grh Inc (G-9463)*
Goodale Enterprises LLC (PA)...616 453-7690
21 Fennessey St Sw Grand Rapids (49534) *(G-6448)*
Goodpack..248 458-0041
2820 W Maple Rd Ste 128 Troy (48084) *(G-16385)*
Goodrich Brothers Inc (PA)..989 593-2104
11409 E Blwter Hwy Pewamo Pewamo (48873) *(G-12479)*
Goodrich Brothers Inc..989 224-4944
3060 County Farm Rd Saint Johns (48879) *(G-14283)*
Goodwill Cadillac Transition H, Cadillac *Also called Goodwill Inds Nthrn Mich Inc (G-2250)*
Goodwill Inds Nthrn Mich Inc..231 779-1311
901 N Mitchell St Ste 15 Cadillac (49601) *(G-2250)*

Goodwill Inds Nthrn Mich Inc..231 779-1361
610 S Mitchell St Cadillac (49601) *(G-2251)*
Goodwill Inds Nthrn Mich Inc..231 922-4890
1329 S Division St Traverse City (49684) *(G-15981)*
Goodwill Inn, Traverse City *Also called Goodwill Inds Nthrn Mich Inc (G-15981)*
Goodwill Resale Store, Cadillac *Also called Goodwill Inds Nthrn Mich Inc (G-2251)*
Goodyear Horseshoe Supply Inc......................................810 639-2591
9372 Seymour Rd Montrose (48457) *(G-11102)*
Goodyear Supply, Montrose *Also called Goodyear Horseshoe Supply Inc (G-11102)*
Goodyear Tire & Rubber Company...................................248 336-0135
29444 Woodward Ave Royal Oak (48073) *(G-13930)*
Gorang Industries Inc...248 651-9010
305 South St Rochester (48307) *(G-13322)*
Gordinier Electronics Corp..586 778-0426
16380 E 13 Mile Rd Roseville (48066) *(G-13809)*
Gordon Hackworth Logging..517 589-9218
3751 Meridian Rd Leslie (49251) *(G-9541)*
Gordon Metal Products Inc...586 445-0960
31373 Industrial Rd Livonia (48150) *(G-9754)*
Gosen Tool & Machine Inc..989 777-6493
2054 Brettrager Dr Saginaw (48601) *(G-14049)*
Gottch-Ya Graphix USA...269 979-7587
5875 B Dr S Battle Creek (49014) *(G-1193)*
Gotts Transit Mix Inc..734 439-1528
605 S Platt Rd Milan (48160) *(G-10939)*
Gougeon Holding Co (PA)..989 684-7286
100 Patterson Ave Bay City (48706) *(G-1317)*
Gourmet Holdings LLC...313 432-2121
37519 Harper Ave Grosse Pointe (48230) *(G-7179)*
Gourmet Kitchen Qiuyang LLC..517 332-8866
2843 E Grand River Ave # 180 East Lansing (48823) *(G-4659)*
Govro-Nelson Co..810 329-4727
1132 Ladd Rd Commerce Township (48390) *(G-3408)*
Gower Corporation..989 249-5938
2840 Universal Dr Saginaw (48603) *(G-14050)*
GP Strategies C/O Transpak, Sterling Heights *Also called Transpak Inc (G-15528)*
Gpbc Inc..734 741-7325
120 W Washington St Ste 1 Ann Arbor (48104) *(G-475)*
Gqi, Onsted *Also called Global Quality Ingredients Inc (G-12153)*
Gr Baking Company...616 245-3446
900 Division Ave S Grand Rapids (49507) *(G-6449)*
Gr Innovations LLC..248 618-3813
6650 Highland Rd Waterford (48327) *(G-17347)*
Gr X Manufacturing...616 541-7420
7000 Dtton Indus Pk Dr Se Caledonia (49316) *(G-2296)*
Grabber Inc..616 940-1914
365 84th St Sw Ste 4 Byron Center (49315) *(G-2193)*
Grace Contracting Services LLC.......................................906 630-4680
25688 County Road 98 Mc Millan (49853) *(G-10685)*
Grace Engineering Corp..810 392-2181
34775 Potter St Memphis (48041) *(G-10710)*
Grace Extended...616 502-2078
714 Columbus Ave Grand Haven (49417) *(G-6020)*
Grace Metal Prods Inc..231 264-8133
6322 Yuba Rd Williamsburg (49690) *(G-17712)*
Grace Production Services LLC.......................................810 643-8070
52100 Sierra Dr Chesterfield (48047) *(G-2783)*
Graceland Fruit Inc...231 352-7181
1123 Main St Frankfort (49635) *(G-5602)*
Grafaktri Inc..734 665-0717
1200 N Main St Ann Arbor (48104) *(G-476)*
Graflex Inc..616 842-3654
15276 Oak Point Dr Spring Lake (49456) *(G-15146)*
Graham Packaging Company LP.....................................616 355-0479
926 S Waverly Rd Holland (49423) *(G-7647)*
Grahams Printing Company Inc.......................................313 925-1188
8620 Gratiot Ave Detroit (48213) *(G-4098)*
Grain and Cattle Farm, Morenci *Also called Triple K Farms Inc (G-11116)*
Grakon LLC..734 462-1201
19500 Victor Pkwy Ste 325 Livonia (48152) *(G-9755)*
Grakon Michigan, Livonia *Also called Grakon LLC (G-9755)*
Gram, Grand Rapids *Also called Grand River Aseptic Mfg Inc (G-6467)*
Graminex LLC (PA)...989 797-5502
95 Midland Rd Saginaw (48638) *(G-14051)*
Grand Blanc Cement Pdts Inc (PA)...................................810 694-7500
10709 Center Rd Grand Blanc (48439) *(G-5967)*
Grand Blanc Printing Inc..810 694-1155
9449 Holly Rd Grand Blanc (48439) *(G-5968)*
Grand Blanc Processing LLC..810 694-6000
10151 Gainey Rd Holly (48442) *(G-7882)*
Grand Haven Custom Molding LLC...................................616 935-3160
1500 S Beechtree St Grand Haven (49417) *(G-6021)*
Grand Haven Gasket Company.......................................616 842-7682
1701 Eaton Dr Grand Haven (49417) *(G-6022)*
Grand Haven Nursery Products, Grand Haven *Also called West Michigan Molding Inc (G-6097)*
Grand Haven Powder Coating Inc....................................616 850-8822
1710 Airpark Dr Grand Haven (49417) *(G-6023)*

Grand Haven Publishing Corp 616 842-6400
101 N 3rd St Grand Haven (49417) **(G-6024)**
Grand Haven Steel Products Inc 616 842-2740
1627 Marion Ave Grand Haven (49417) **(G-6025)**
Grand Haven Tribune, Grand Haven *Also called Grand Haven Publishing Corp* **(G-6024)**
Grand Industries Inc 616 846-7120
1700 Airpark Dr Grand Haven (49417) **(G-6026)**
Grand Northern Products 800 968-1811
400 Mart St Sw Grand Rapids (49548) **(G-6450)**
Grand Power Systems, Grand Haven *Also called Gti Power Acquisition LLC* **(G-6029)**
Grand Rapids Bedding Co (PA) 616 459-8234
630 Myrtle St Nw Grand Rapids (49504) **(G-6451)**
Grand Rapids Carvers Inc 616 538-0022
4465 Roger B Chaffee Se Grand Rapids (49548) **(G-6452)**
Grand Rapids Chair Company 616 774-0561
1250 84th St Sw Byron Center (49315) **(G-2194)**
Grand Rapids Controls Company, Rockford *Also called Ctc Acquisition Company LLC* **(G-13564)**
Grand Rapids Elc Mtr Svc LLC 616 243-8866
1057 Cottage Grove St Se Grand Rapids (49507) **(G-6453)**
Grand Rapids Graphix 616 359-2383
3853 Llewellyn Ct Sw Wyoming (49519) **(G-18005)**
Grand Rapids Gravel Company (PA) 616 538-9000
2700 28th St Sw Grand Rapids (49519) **(G-6454)**
Grand Rapids Gravel Company 616 538-9000
3706 Busch Grandville (49418) **(G-7038)**
Grand Rapids Gravel Company 616 538-9000
3800 7 Mile Rd Ne Belmont (49306) **(G-1462)**
Grand Rapids Gravel Company 616 538-9000
13180 Quincy St Holland (49424) **(G-7648)**
Grand Rapids Gravel Company 231 777-2777
1780 S Sheridan Dr Muskegon (49442) **(G-11332)**
Grand Rapids Label Company 616 459-8134
2351 Oak Industrial Dr Ne Grand Rapids (49505) **(G-6455)**
Grand Rapids Legal News, Ada *Also called West Michigan Printing Inc* **(G-34)**
Grand Rapids Legal News 616 454-9293
1430 Monroe Ave Nw # 140 Grand Rapids (49505) **(G-6456)**
Grand Rapids Letter Service 616 459-4711
315 Fuller Ave Ne Grand Rapids (49503) **(G-6457)**
Grand Rapids Machine Repair 616 248-4760
3710 Linden Ave Se Grand Rapids (49548) **(G-6458)**
Grand Rapids Machine Repr Inc 616 245-9102
4000 Eastern Ave Se Grand Rapids (49508) **(G-6459)**
Grand Rapids Metaltek Inc 616 791-2373
2860 Marlin Ct Nw Grand Rapids (49534) **(G-6460)**
Grand Rapids Press Inc 616 459-1400
3102 Walker Ridge Dr Nw Grand Rapids (49544) **(G-6461)**
Grand Rapids Printing Ink Co (PA) 616 241-5681
4920 Starr St Se Grand Rapids (49546) **(G-6462)**
Grand Rapids Salsa 616 780-1801
1301 Benjamin Ave Se Grand Rapids (49506) **(G-6463)**
Grand Rapids Stripping Co 616 361-0794
1933 Will Ave Nw Grand Rapids (49504) **(G-6464)**
Grand Rapids Technologies Inc 616 245-7700
3133 Madison Ave Se Ste B Grand Rapids (49548) **(G-6465)**
Grand Rapids Times Inc 616 245-8737
2016 Eastern Ave Se Grand Rapids (49507) **(G-6466)**
Grand River Aseptic Mfg Inc (PA) 616 464-5072
140 Front Ave Sw Ste 3 Grand Rapids (49504) **(G-6467)**
Grand River Brewery, Jackson *Also called Veritas Vineyard LLC* **(G-8600)**
Grand River Fabricating, Livonia *Also called Caparo Vehicle Components Inc* **(G-9674)**
Grand River Granite Inc 616 399-9324
13688 Port Sheldon St Holland (49424) **(G-7649)**
Grand River Interiors Inc 616 454-2800
974 Front Ave Nw Ste 2 Grand Rapids (49504) **(G-6468)**
Grand River Polishing Co Corp 616 846-1420
19191 174th Ave Spring Lake (49456) **(G-15147)**
Grand Rpids Wilbert Burial Vlt 616 453-9429
2500 3 Mile Rd Nw Grand Rapids (49534) **(G-6469)**
Grand Rustic Pallet Co 231 329-5035
1105 Aberdeen St Ne Grand Rapids (49505) **(G-6470)**
Grand Strategy LLC 269 637-8330
15038 73rd St South Haven (49090) **(G-14761)**
Grand Traverse Assembly Inc 231 588-2406
7161 Essex Rd Ellsworth (49729) **(G-4788)**
Grand Traverse Canvas Works 231 947-3140
3975 3 Mile Rd N Traverse City (49686) **(G-15982)**
Grand Traverse Container, Traverse City *Also called Grand Traverse Reels Inc* **(G-15987)**
Grand Traverse Continuous Inc 231 941-5400
1661 Park Dr Traverse City (49686) **(G-15983)**
Grand Traverse Crane Corp 231 943-7787
3876 Blair Townhall Rd Traverse City (49685) **(G-15984)**
Grand Traverse Forging & Steel, Traverse City *Also called Great Lakes Forge Inc* **(G-15992)**
Grand Traverse Garage Doors 231 943-9897
823 W Commerce Dr Traverse City (49685) **(G-15985)**
Grand Traverse Machine Co 231 946-8006
1247 Boon St Traverse City (49686) **(G-15986)**
Grand Traverse Mech Contg LLC 231 943-7400
1500 Melody Ln Interlochen (49643) **(G-8241)**
Grand Traverse Pallet, Ellsworth *Also called Grand Traverse Assembly Inc* **(G-4788)**
Grand Traverse Reels Inc 231 946-1057
1050 Business Park Dr Traverse City (49686) **(G-15987)**
Grand Traverse Stamping Co 231 929-4215
1677 Park Dr Traverse City (49686) **(G-15988)**
Grand Traverse Tool Inc 231 929-4743
396 Hughes Dr Traverse City (49696) **(G-15989)**
Grand Traverse Vineyards, Traverse City *Also called Chateau Grand Travers Ltd* **(G-15936)**
Grand Traverse Woman Mag 231 276-5105
Interlochen State Park Interlochen (49643) **(G-8242)**
Grand Trunk RR 248 452-4881
777 Cesar E Chavez Ave Pontiac (48340) **(G-12830)**
Grand Trvrse Culinary Oils LLC 231 590-2180
2780 Cass Rd Traverse City (49684) **(G-15990)**
Grand Valley Wood Products Inc 616 475-5890
3113 Hillcroft Ave Sw Grand Rapids (49548) **(G-6471)**
Grandads Sweet Tea LLC 313 320-4446
26532 Joe Dr Warren (48091) **(G-17062)**
Grandpa Hanks Maple Syrup LLC 231 826-4494
2431 E Workman Rd Falmouth (49632) **(G-4893)**
Grandpapas Inc 313 891-6830
6500 E Davison St Detroit (48212) **(G-4099)**
Grandview Foot & Ankle 989 584-3916
423 E Main St Ste C Carson City (48811) **(G-2489)**
Grandville Industries Inc 616 538-0920
4270 White St Sw Grandville (49418) **(G-7039)**
Grandville Printing Co 616 534-8647
4719 Ivanrest Ave Sw Grandville (49418) **(G-7040)**
Grandville Tractor Svcs LLC 616 530-2030
3408 Busch Dr Sw Ste E Grandville (49418) **(G-7041)**
Granite City Inc 248 478-0033
31693 8 Mile Rd Livonia (48152) **(G-9756)**
Granite Planet LLC 734 522-0190
30411 Schoolcraft Rd Livonia (48150) **(G-9757)**
Granite Precision Tool Corp 248 299-8317
2257 Star Ct Rochester Hills (48309) **(G-13435)**
Graniteonecom Inc 616 452-8372
639 Hoyt St Se Grand Rapids (49507) **(G-6472)**
Granola Kitchens, Brighton *Also called Gki Foods LLC* **(G-1931)**
Grant Industries Incorporated (PA) 586 293-9200
33415 Groesbeck Hwy Fraser (48026) **(G-5657)**
Grants Woodshop Inc 517 543-1116
3802 N Chester Rd Charlotte (48813) **(G-2653)**
Grany Greenthumbs LLC 517 223-1302
108 W Grand River Ave Fowlerville (48836) **(G-5568)**
Grapentin Specialties Inc 810 724-0636
5599 Bowers Rd Imlay City (48444) **(G-8201)**
Graph-ADS Printing Inc 989 779-6000
711 W Pickard St Ste I Mount Pleasant (48858) **(G-11195)**
Graph-X Signs 734 420-0906
45650 Mast St Plymouth (48170) **(G-12631)**
Graphic Art Service & Supply 810 229-4700
1343 Rickett Rd Brighton (48116) **(G-1933)**
Graphic Arts Service & Sup Inc (PA) 616 698-9300
3933 S Greenbrooke Dr Se Grand Rapids (49512) **(G-6473)**
Graphic Cmmnctions Design Svcs 586 566-5200
50671 Wing Dr Shelby Township (48315) **(G-14597)**
Graphic Communications, Shelby Township *Also called Graphic Cmmnctions Design Svcs* **(G-14597)**
Graphic Enterprises Inc 248 616-4900
1200 E Avis Dr Madison Heights (48071) **(G-10258)**
Graphic Gear Inc 734 283-3864
3018 Fort St Lincoln Park (48146) **(G-9579)**
Graphic Impressions Inc 616 455-0303
6621 Division Ave S Grand Rapids (49548) **(G-6474)**
Graphic Packaging Intl LLC 269 969-7446
70 Michigan Ave W Ste 500 Battle Creek (49017) **(G-1194)**
Graphic Packaging Intl LLC 269 383-5000
1500 N Pitcher St Kalamazoo (49007) **(G-8754)**
Graphic Packaging Intl LLC 269 343-6104
1421 N Pitcher St Kalamazoo (49007) **(G-8755)**
Graphic Packaging Intl LLC 269 963-6135
79 Fountain St E Battle Creek (49017) **(G-1195)**
Graphic Resource Group Inc 248 588-6100
528 Robbins Dr Troy (48083) **(G-16386)**
Graphic Services Co, Benton Harbor *Also called GAMS Inc* **(G-1502)**
Graphic Specialties Inc (PA) 616 247-0060
2350 Brton Indus Pk Dr Se Grand Rapids (49508) **(G-6475)**
Graphic Visions Inc 248 347-3355
23936 Industrial Park Dr Farmington Hills (48335) **(G-5013)**
Graphicolor Exhibits, Livonia *Also called Graphicolor Systems Inc* **(G-9758)**
Graphicolor Systems Inc 248 347-0271
12788 Currie Ct Livonia (48150) **(G-9758)**
Graphics & Printing LLC 313 942-2022
7208 Hillside Dr Dearborn Heights (48127) **(G-3786)**
Graphics & Printing Co Inc 269 381-1482
5356 N Riverview Dr Kalamazoo (49004) **(G-8756)**
Graphics 3 Inc 517 278-2159
205 W Garfield Ave Coldwater (49036) **(G-3306)**

Graphics Arts Service & Supply, Brighton *Also called Graphic Art Service & Supply* ***(G-1933)***
Graphics East Inc 586 598-1500
16005 Sturgeon St Roseville (48066) ***(G-13810)***
Graphics Embossed Images Inc 616 791-0404
1975 Waldorf St Nw Ste A Grand Rapids (49544) ***(G-6476)***
Graphics House Printing, Muskegon *Also called Graphics House Publishing* ***(G-11333)***
Graphics House Publishing 231 739-4004
2632 Peck St Muskegon (49444) ***(G-11333)***
Graphics Hse Spt Prmotions Inc (PA) 231 739-4004
444 Irwin Ave Muskegon (49442) ***(G-11334)***
Graphics Hse Spt Prmotions Inc 231 733-1877
444 Irwin Ave Muskegon (49442) ***(G-11335)***
Graphics Plus Inc 989 893-0651
2011 Columbus Ave Bay City (48708) ***(G-1318)***
Graphics Unlimited Inc 231 773-2696
2304 Olthoff St Muskegon (49444) ***(G-11336)***
Graphics Unlimited Inc 616 662-0455
2340 Chicago Dr Hudsonville (49426) ***(G-8157)***
Graphicus Signs & Designs 231 652-9160
477 S Park St Newaygo (49337) ***(G-11569)***
Graphite Electrodes Ltd 989 893-3635
1311 N Sherman St Bay City (48708) ***(G-1319)***
Graphite Machining Inc 810 678-2227
4141 S Oak St Metamora (48455) ***(G-10775)***
Graphite Products Corp 248 548-7800
1797 E 10 Mile Rd Madison Heights (48071) ***(G-10259)***
Graphix 2 Go Inc 269 969-7321
7200 Tower Rd Battle Creek (49014) ***(G-1196)***
Graphix Signs & Embroidery 616 396-0009
11223 E Lakewood Blvd Holland (49424) ***(G-7650)***
Graphtek Inc 810 985-4545
2301 16th St Port Huron (48060) ***(G-12923)***
Grasel Graphics Inc 989 652-5151
9710 Junction Rd Frankenmuth (48734) ***(G-5589)***
Grass Lake Community Pharmacy 517 522-4100
116 E Michigan Ave Grass Lake (49240) ***(G-7088)***
Grasshopper Signs Graphics LLC 248 946-8475
24655 Halsted Rd Farmington Hills (48335) ***(G-5014)***
Gratiot County Herald, Ithaca *Also called Macdonald Publications Inc* ***(G-8363)***
Grattan Family Enterprises LLC 248 547-3870
1350 Jarvis St Ferndale (48220) ***(G-5290)***
Grav Co LLC 269 651-5467
400 Norwood St Sturgis (49091) ***(G-15605)***
Gravel Flow Inc (PA) 269 651-5467
400 Norwood St Sturgis (49091) ***(G-15606)***
Gravikor Inc 734 302-3200
401 W Morgan Rd Ann Arbor (48108) ***(G-477)***
Gray & Company (HQ) 231 873-5628
3325 W Polk Rd Hart (49420) ***(G-7372)***
Gray Bros Stamping & Mch Inc 269 483-7615
424 W Chicago Rd White Pigeon (49099) ***(G-17649)***
Gray Brothers Mfg Inc 269 483-7615
424 W Chicago Rd White Pigeon (49099) ***(G-17650)***
Grayton Integrated Pubg LLC 313 881-1734
886 Washington Rd Grosse Pointe (48230) ***(G-7180)***
Graywolf Printing, Birmingham *Also called Alpha Data Business Forms Inc* ***(G-1674)***
Grazing Fields, Charlotte *Also called Farmers Egg Cooperative* ***(G-2648)***
Great American Publishing Co 616 887-9008
75 Applewood Dr Ste A Sparta (49345) ***(G-15095)***
Great Deals Magazine, Portage *Also called Bowman Enterprises Inc* ***(G-12987)***
Great Fresh Foods Co LLC 586 846-3521
21740 Trolley Industrial Taylor (48180) ***(G-15726)***
Great Harvest Bread Co 586 566-9500
48923 Hayes Rd Shelby Township (48315) ***(G-14598)***
Great Lake Foam Technologies 517 563-8030
104 W Main St Hanover (49241) ***(G-7260)***
Great Lake Woods Inc 616 399-3300
3303 John F Donnelly Dr Holland (49424) ***(G-7651)***
Great Lakes Aero Products 810 235-1402
915 Kearsley Park Blvd Flint (48503) ***(G-5441)***
Great Lakes Aggregates LLC (PA) 734 379-0311
5699 Ready Rd South Rockwood (48179) ***(G-14821)***
Great Lakes Air Products Inc 734 326-7080
1515 S Nwburgh Rd Ste 100 Westland (48186) ***(G-17563)***
Great Lakes Allied LLC 231 924-5794
87 N Benson St White Cloud (49349) ***(G-17622)***
Great Lakes American, Spring Lake *Also called Great Lakes Cordage Inc* ***(G-15148)***
Great Lakes Atm 248 542-2613
701 Woodward Hts Ferndale (48220) ***(G-5291)***
Great Lakes Aviaiton Svcs LLC 586 770-3450
41358 Lore Dr Clinton Township (48038) ***(G-3129)***
Great Lakes Bath & Body Inc 231 421-9160
110 E Front St Traverse City (49684) ***(G-15991)***
Great Lakes Bindery Inc 616 245-5264
3741 Linden Ave Se Grand Rapids (49548) ***(G-6477)***
Great Lakes Canvas Co 954 439-3090
2296 58th St Fennville (49408) ***(G-5172)***
Great Lakes Castings LLC (HQ) 231 843-2501
800 N Washington Ave Ludington (49431) ***(G-10061)***
Great Lakes Castings LLC 616 399-9710
12970 Ransom St Holland (49424) ***(G-7652)***
Great Lakes Chemical Services 269 372-6886
616 W Centre Ave Portage (49024) ***(G-12999)***
Great Lakes Coach, Muskegon *Also called Emergency Services LLC* ***(G-11317)***
Great Lakes Coating, Benton Harbor *Also called Arnt Asphalt Sealing Inc* ***(G-1482)***
Great Lakes Compression Inc 989 786-3788
3690 County Road 491 Lewiston (49756) ***(G-9549)***
Great Lakes Containment Inc 231 258-8800
731 S Cedar St Kalkaska (49646) ***(G-8943)***
Great Lakes Contracting Inc 616 846-8888
14370 172nd Ave Grand Haven (49417) ***(G-6027)***
Great Lakes Cordage Inc 616 842-4455
17045 148th Ave Spring Lake (49456) ***(G-15148)***
Great Lakes Die Cast Corp (PA) 231 726-4002
701 W Laketon Ave Muskegon (49441) ***(G-11337)***
Great Lakes Dock & Door LLC 313 368-6300
19345 John R St Detroit (48203) ***(G-4100)***
Great Lakes Draperies, Holland *Also called Window Designs Inc* ***(G-7859)***
Great Lakes Electric LLC 269 408-8276
1776 Hilltop Rd Saint Joseph (49085) ***(G-14313)***
Great Lakes Embroidery 248 543-5164
1191 E 10 Mile Rd Madison Heights (48071) ***(G-10260)***
Great Lakes Feedscrews, Tecumseh *Also called Glycon Corp* ***(G-15795)***
Great Lakes Filter, Bloomfield Hills *Also called Acme Mills Company* ***(G-1741)***
Great Lakes Fine Cabinetry 906 493-5780
844 E 3 Mile Rd Sault Sainte Marie (49783) ***(G-14465)***
Great Lakes Finishing Inc 231 733-9566
510 W Hackley Ave Muskegon (49444) ***(G-11338)***
Great Lakes Fish Decoy Collect 734 427-7768
35824 W Chicago St Livonia (48150) ***(G-9759)***
Great Lakes Food Center LLC 248 397-8166
32102 Howard Ave Madison Heights (48071) ***(G-10261)***
Great Lakes Forge Inc 231 947-4931
2465 N Aero Park Ct Traverse City (49686) ***(G-15992)***
Great Lakes Gauge Company 989 652-6136
6950 Junction Rd Bridgeport (48722) ***(G-1852)***
Great Lakes Grilling Co 616 791-8600
2685 Northridge Dr Nw C Grand Rapids (49544) ***(G-6478)***
Great Lakes Heating, Coolng, Dearborn *Also called Great Lakes Mechanical Corp* ***(G-3717)***
Great Lakes Hydra Corporation 616 949-8844
4170 36th St Se Grand Rapids (49512) ***(G-6479)***
Great Lakes Industry Inc 517 784-3153
1927 Wildwood Ave Jackson (49202) ***(G-8459)***
Great Lakes Infotronics Inc (PA) 248 476-2500
22300 Haggerty Rd 100 Northville (48167) ***(G-11695)***
Great Lakes Insulspan, Blissfield *Also called Midwest Panel Systems Inc* ***(G-1720)***
Great Lakes Jig & Fixture 269 795-4349
11610 Bowens Mill Rd Middleville (49333) ***(G-10803)***
Great Lakes Label LLC 616 647-9880
910 Metzgar Dr Nw Comstock Park (49321) ***(G-3483)***
Great Lakes Laboratories Inc 734 525-8300
27537 Schoolcraft Rd Livonia (48150) ***(G-9760)***
Great Lakes Laser Dynamics Inc 616 892-7070
4881 Allen Park Dr Allendale (49401) ***(G-218)***
Great Lakes Laser Services 248 584-1828
147 E 10 Mile Rd Madison Heights (48071) ***(G-10262)***
Great Lakes Lift Inc 989 673-2109
1382 E Caro Rd Caro (48723) ***(G-2469)***
Great Lakes Log & Firewd Co 231 206-4073
11405 Russell Rd Twin Lake (49457) ***(G-16712)***
Great Lakes Lube-Tech, Portage *Also called Lube-Tech Inc* ***(G-13012)***
Great Lakes Mechanical Corp (PA) 313 581-1400
3800 Maple St Dearborn (48126) ***(G-3717)***
Great Lakes Metal Fabricating, Niles *Also called Great Lakes Precision Machine* ***(G-11615)***
Great Lakes Metal Finshg Inc, Jackson *Also called Spencer Zdanowitz Inc* ***(G-8575)***
Great Lakes Metal Finshg LLC 517 764-1335
3000 E South St Jackson (49201) ***(G-8460)***
Great Lakes Metal Stamping Inc 269 465-4415
4607 Rambo Rd Bridgman (49106) ***(G-1864)***
Great Lakes Metal Works 269 789-2342
819 Industrial Rd Marshall (49068) ***(G-10569)***
Great Lakes Ncw LLC 616 355-2626
386 Bay Park Dr Ste 10 Holland (49424) ***(G-7653)***
Great Lakes Neon 517 582-7451
9861 W Grand River Hwy Grand Ledge (48837) ***(G-6108)***
Great Lakes Nursery Soils Inc 231 788-3123
680 S Maple Island Rd Muskegon (49442) ***(G-11339)***
Great Lakes Packing Co 231 264-5561
6556 Quarterline Rd Kewadin (49648) ***(G-9039)***
Great Lakes Pallet Inc 989 883-9220
714 N Beck St Sebewaing (48759) ***(G-14515)***
Great Lakes Paper Stock Corp 586 779-1310
30835 Groesbeck Hwy Roseville (48066) ***(G-13811)***
Great Lakes Photo Inc 586 784-5446
29080 Armada Ridge Rd Richmond (48062) ***(G-13264)***
Great Lakes Pilot Pubg Co 906 494-2391
E22029 Everett Ave Grand Marais (49839) ***(G-6118)***
Great Lakes Plastics Division, Detroit *Also called Evans Industries Inc* ***(G-4045)***

A L P H A B E T I C

Great Lakes Post LLC ... 248 941-1349
12466 Scenic View Ct Milford (48380) *(G-10965)*
Great Lakes Powder Coating LLC ... 248 522-6222
1020 Decker Rd Walled Lake (48390) *(G-16894)*
Great Lakes Precast Products, Comstock Park *Also called Great Lakes Precast Systems (G-3484)*
Great Lakes Precast Systems ... 616 784-5900
5830 Comstock Park Dr Nw Comstock Park (49321) *(G-3484)*
Great Lakes Precision Machine ... 269 695-4580
1760 Foundation Dr Niles (49120) *(G-11615)*
Great Lakes Prtg Solutions Inc ... 231 799-6000
5163 Robert Hunter Dr Norton Shores (49441) *(G-11758)*
Great Lakes Publishing Inc ... 517 647-4444
212 Kent St Ste 6 Portland (48875) *(G-13062)*
Great Lakes Pulp & Fibre, Menominee *Also called Fibrek Recycling US Inc (G-10734)*
Great Lakes Rubber Co ... 248 624-5710
30573 Anderson Ct Wixom (48393) *(G-17819)*
Great Lakes Sand & Gravel LLC ... 616 374-3169
7940 Woodland Rd Lake Odessa (48849) *(G-9115)*
Great Lakes Service & Supplies ... 734 854-8542
5520 School Rd Petersburg (49270) *(G-12436)*
Great Lakes Snow & Ice Inc ... 989 584-1211
7123 S Garlock Rd Carson City (48811) *(G-2490)*
Great Lakes Spt Publications ... 734 507-0241
3588 Plymouth Rd Ann Arbor (48105) *(G-478)*
Great Lakes Stainless Inc ... 231 943-7648
1305 Stepke Ct Traverse City (49685) *(G-15993)*
Great Lakes Stair & Case Co ... 269 465-3777
9155 Gast Rd Bridgman (49106) *(G-1865)*
Great Lakes Tech & Mfg LLC ... 810 593-0257
201 S Alloy Dr Ste C Fenton (48430) *(G-5217)*
Great Lakes Tire LLC ... 586 939-7000
12225 Stephens Rd Warren (48089) *(G-17063)*
Great Lakes Tissue Company ... 231 627-0200
437 S Main St Cheboygan (49721) *(G-2680)*
Great Lakes Toll Services ... 616 847-1868
17354 Teunis Dr Ste D Spring Lake (49456) *(G-15149)*
Great Lakes Tool LLC ... 586 759-5253
24027 Ryan Rd Warren (48091) *(G-17064)*
Great Lakes Towers LLC ... 734 682-4000
111 Borchert Park Dr Monroe (48161) *(G-11037)*
Great Lakes Treatment Corp ... 517 566-8008
5630 E Eaton Hwy Sunfield (48890) *(G-15646)*
Great Lakes Trim Inc ... 231 267-3000
6183 S Railway Cmn Williamsburg (49690) *(G-17713)*
Great Lakes Waterjet Laser LLC ... 517 629-9900
1101 Industrial Blvd Albion (49224) *(G-124)*
Great Lakes Weld LLC ... 231 943-4180
889 S East Silver Lake Rd Traverse City (49685) *(G-15994)*
Great Lakes Wellhead Inc (PA) ... 231 943-9100
4243 S M 37 Grawn (49637) *(G-7098)*
Great Lakes Wine & Spirits LLC (PA) ... 313 278-5400
373 Victor St Highland Park (48203) *(G-7506)*
Great Lakes Wire Packaging LLC ... 269 428-7220
4232 N Roosevelt Rd Stevensville (49127) *(G-15568)*
Great Lakes Wood Products ... 906 228-3737
434 Us Highway 41 E Negaunee (49866) *(G-11470)*
Great Lakes Woodworking Co Inc ... 313 892-8500
11345 Mound Rd Detroit (48212) *(G-4101)*
Great Lakes X-Cel, Niles *Also called N & K Fulbright LLC (G-11629)*
Great Lakes-Triad Plastic (PA) ... 616 241-6441
3939 36th St Se Grand Rapids (49512) *(G-6480)*
Great Lkes Fstida Holdings Inc ... 616 241-0400
219 Canton St Sw Ste A Grand Rapids (49507) *(G-6481)*
Great Lkes Indus Frnc Svcs Inc ... 586 323-9200
6780 19 1/2 Mile Rd Sterling Heights (48314) *(G-15364)*
Great Lkes Tex Restoration LLC ... 989 448-8600
651 Expressway Ct Gaylord (49735) *(G-5861)*
Great Meadhall Brewing Co LLC ... 269 427-0827
215 W Monroe St Bangor (49013) *(G-1091)*
Great Northern Lumber Mich LLC ... 989 736-6192
507 W Traverse Bay Rd Lincoln (48742) *(G-9562)*
Great Northern Publishing Inc ... 810 648-4000
356 E Sanilac Rd Sandusky (48471) *(G-14434)*
Great Openings, Ludington *Also called Metalworks Inc (G-10073)*
Great Products, Greenville *Also called Greenville Engineered & Tooled (G-7134)*
Great Put On Inc ... 810 733-8021
3240 W Pasadena Ave Flint (48504) *(G-5442)*
Greater Lansing Bus Monthly ... 517 203-0123
221 W Saginaw St Lansing (48933) *(G-9376)*
Greater Lansing Orthotic Clini ... 517 337-0856
200 N Homer St Ste A Lansing (48912) *(G-9377)*
Grede Foundries Inc (PA) ... 248 440-9500
4000 Town Ctr Ste 500 Southfield (48075) *(G-14923)*
Grede Holdings LLC (HQ) ... 248 440-9500
20750 Civic Center Dr # 100 Southfield (48076) *(G-14924)*
Grede II LLC (HQ) ... 248 727-1800
20750 Civic Center Dr # 100 Southfield (48076) *(G-14925)*
Grede LLC ... 906 774-7250
801 S Carpenter Ave Kingsford (49802) *(G-9058)*
Grede LLC (HQ) ... 248 440-9500
20750 Civic Center Dr # 100 Southfield (48076) *(G-14926)*
Grede Machining LLC ... 248 727-1800
1 Towne Sq Ste 550 Southfield (48076) *(G-14927)*
Grede Omaha LLC ... 248 727-1800
1 Towne Sq Ste 550 Southfield (48076) *(G-14928)*
Grede Radford LLC ... 248 727-1800
1 Towne Sq Ste 550 Southfield (48076) *(G-14929)*
Grede Wscnsin Subsidiaries LLC ... 248 727-1800
20750 Civic Center Dr # 100 Southfield (48076) *(G-14930)*
Green Age Organics, Washington *Also called Green Age Products & Svcs LLC (G-17304)*
Green Age Products & Svcs LLC ... 586 207-5724
64155 Van Dyke Rd Ste 238 Washington (48095) *(G-17304)*
Green Bay Packaging Inc ... 269 552-1000
5350 E N Ave Kalamazoo (49048) *(G-8757)*
Green Bridge Tech Intl Inc (PA) ... 810 410-8177
15091 Poberezny Ct Linden (48451) *(G-9591)*
Green Fuels Llc ... 734 735-6802
715 Indian Trail Rd Carleton (48117) *(G-2455)*
Green Gables Saw Mill ... 989 386-7846
5605 E Surrey Rd Clare (48617) *(G-2871)*
Green Industries Inc ... 248 446-8900
515 N Mill St South Lyon (48178) *(G-14793)*
Green Link Inc ... 269 216-9229
5519 E Cork St Ste A Kalamazoo (49048) *(G-8758)*
Green Manufacturing Inc ... 517 458-1500
9650 Packard Rd Morenci (49256) *(G-11111)*
Green Oak Tool and Svcs Inc ... 586 531-2255
9449 Maltby Rd Brighton (48116) *(G-1934)*
Green Plastics LLC ... 616 295-2718
13370 Barry St Ste A Holland (49424) *(G-7654)*
Green Polymeric Materials Inc ... 313 933-7390
6031 Joy Rd Detroit (48204) *(G-4102)*
Green Room Michigan LLC ... 248 289-3288
32000 Northwestern Hwy Farmington Hills (48334) *(G-5015)*
Green Screen, Manistee *Also called Envirodine Inc (G-10420)*
Green Sheet ... 517 548-2570
323 E Grand River Ave Howell (48843) *(G-8045)*
Green Zebra Foods Incorporated ... 248 291-7339
620 Middlesex Rd Grosse Pointe Park (48230) *(G-7194)*
Greenback Inc ... 313 443-4272
600 Suffield Ave Birmingham (48009) *(G-1685)*
Greenback.com, Birmingham *Also called Greenback Inc (G-1685)*
Greendale Screw Pdts Co Inc ... 586 759-8100
11500 Hupp Ave Warren (48089) *(G-17065)*
Greene Group Industries, Port Huron *Also called Greene Manufacturing Tech LLC (G-12924)*
Greene Manufacturing Inc ... 734 428-8304
3985 S Fletcher Rd Chelsea (48118) *(G-2712)*
Greene Manufacturing Tech LLC ... 810 982-9720
2600 20th St Port Huron (48060) *(G-12924)*
Greene Metal Products Inc (PA) ... 586 465-6800
24500 Capital Blvd Clinton Township (48036) *(G-3130)*
Greene Metal Products Inc ... 586 465-6800
24500 Capital Blvd Clinton Township (48036) *(G-3131)*
Greenfeld Homemade Egg Noodles, Detroit *Also called Greenfield Noodle Specialty Co (G-4103)*
Greenfield Cabinetry Inc ... 586 759-3300
23811 Ryan Rd Warren (48091) *(G-17066)*
Greenfield Die & Mfg Corp ... 734 454-4000
7295 N Haggerty Rd Rf Canton (48187) *(G-2379)*
Greenfield Holdings LLC (PA) ... 734 530-5600
19881 Brownstown Ctr Dr Brownstown (48183) *(G-2064)*
Greenfield Noodle Specialty Co ... 313 873-2212
600 Custer St Detroit (48202) *(G-4103)*
Greenglow Products LLC ... 248 827-1451
21170 Bridge St Southfield (48033) *(G-14931)*
Greenia Custom Woodworking Inc ... 989 868-9790
2380 W Vassar Rd Reese (48757) *(G-13230)*
Greening Incorporated (PA) ... 313 366-7160
19465 Mount Elliott St Detroit (48234) *(G-4104)*
Greening Associates Inc ... 313 366-7160
19465 Mount Elliott St Detroit (48234) *(G-4105)*
Greening Testing Laboratories, Detroit *Also called Greening Associates Inc (G-4105)*
Greenlee Printing Company, Calumet *Also called Copper Island Prtg Grphic Svcs (G-2326)*
Greenlight Home Inspection Svc ... 313 885-5616
23340 Westbury St Saint Clair Shores (48080) *(G-14255)*
Greenman's Printing & Imaging, Farmington Hills *Also called Jomark Inc (G-5033)*
Greenmark Biomedical Inc ... 517 336-4665
3815 Tech Blvd Ste 1055 Lansing (48910) *(G-9378)*
Greens Welding & Repair Co ... 734 721-5434
1507 S Wayne Rd Westland (48186) *(G-17564)*
Greenseed LLC ... 313 295-0100
26980 Trolley Indus Dr Taylor (48180) *(G-15727)*
Greenview Data Inc ... 734 426-7500
8178 Jackson Rd Ste A Ann Arbor (48103) *(G-479)*
Greenville Cabinet Distri ... 616 225-2424
425 E Fairplains St Greenville (48838) *(G-7133)*
Greenville Engineered & Tooled ... 616 292-0701
12525 Sassafras Rd Ne Greenville (48838) *(G-7134)*

Greenville Tool & Die Co......616 754-5693
1215 S Lafayette St Greenville (48838) *(G-7135)*
Greenville Trck Wldg Sups LLC (PA)......616 754-6120
201 W Greenville West Dr Greenville (48838) *(G-7136)*
Greenville Truck and Welding, Greenville *Also called Greenville Trck Wldg Sups LLC (G-7136)*
Greenville Ventr Partners LLC......616 303-2400
6501 Fitzner Rd Greenville (48838) *(G-7137)*
Greenwell Machine Shop Inc......231 347-3346
1048 Emmet St Petoskey (49770) *(G-12450)*
Greer Industries Inc......800 388-2868
1520 E 9 Mile Rd Ferndale (48220) *(G-5292)*
Greer Steel Co, Ferndale *Also called Greer Industries Inc (G-5292)*
Greg Linska Sales Inc......248 765-6354
2987 Hill Dr Troy (48085) *(G-16387)*
Gregory M Boese......989 754-2990
2929 River St Saginaw (48601) *(G-14052)*
Gregory's Canvass, Lapeer *Also called Canco Inc (G-9449)*
Greif Inc......586 415-0000
20101 Cornillie Dr Roseville (48066) *(G-13812)*
Greko Print & Imaging Inc......734 453-0341
260 Ann Arbor Rd W Plymouth (48170) *(G-12632)*
Gresham Driving Aids Inc (PA)......248 624-1533
30800 S Wixom Rd Wixom (48393) *(G-17820)*
Grey Hub Trolley Wheel Company, Detroit *Also called Versa Handling Co (G-4428)*
Greystone Imaging LLC......616 742-3810
5510 33rd St Se Ste 1 Grand Rapids (49512) *(G-6482)*
Grg, Troy *Also called Graphic Resource Group Inc (G-16386)*
Grh Inc......888 344-6639
3409 W Sutton Rd Lapeer (48446) *(G-9463)*
Grifco Inc......989 352-7965
10451 Orchard Ln Lakeview (48850) *(G-9173)*
Griff & Son Tree Service Inc......989 735-5160
2921 Lakeshore Dr Glennie (48737) *(G-5942)*
Griffin Tool Inc......269 429-4077
2951 Johnson Rd Stevensville (49127) *(G-15569)*
Griffon Inc......231 788-4630
820 S Broton Rd Muskegon (49442) *(G-11340)*
Grigg Box Co Inc......313 273-9000
18900 Fitzpatrick St Detroit (48228) *(G-4106)*
Grigg Graphic Services Inc......248 356-5005
20982 Bridge St Southfield (48033) *(G-14932)*
Grills To Go At Bannasch Wldg, Lansing *Also called Bannasch Welding Inc (G-9205)*
Grimbac Division, Ann Arbor *Also called TGI Direct Inc (G-667)*
Grind Repair, Roseville *Also called Aero Grinding Inc (G-13771)*
Grind-All Precision Tool Co......586 954-3430
21300 Carlo Dr Clinton Township (48038) *(G-3132)*
Grinding Products Company Inc......586 757-2118
11084 E 9 Mile Rd Warren (48089) *(G-17067)*
Grinding Specialists Inc......734 729-1775
38310 Abruzzi Dr Westland (48185) *(G-17565)*
Grip Studios......248 757-0796
743 Wing St Rear Bldg Plymouth (48170) *(G-12633)*
Grippe Machining and Mfg Co......586 778-3150
15642 Common Rd Roseville (48066) *(G-13813)*
Griptrac Inc......231 853-2284
4865 S Ravenna Rd Ravenna (49451) *(G-13120)*
Grit Obstacle Training LLP......248 829-0414
1389 Kentfield Dr Rochester (48307) *(G-13323)*
Grizzly Peak Brewing Company, Ann Arbor *Also called Gpbc Inc (G-475)*
Grm Corporation (PA)......989 453-2322
39 N Caseville Rd Pigeon (48755) *(G-12489)*
Grm Corporation......989 453-2322
7375 Crescent Beach Rd Pigeon (48755) *(G-12490)*
Groholski Mfg Solutions LLC......517 278-9339
127 Industrial Ave Coldwater (49036) *(G-3307)*
Grondin & Associates, Marshall *Also called Grondin Printing and Awards (G-10570)*
Grondin Printing and Awards......269 781-5447
13492 W Michigan Ave Marshall (49068) *(G-10570)*
Gross Machine Shop......989 587-4021
319 E Main St Westphalia (48894) *(G-17614)*
Gross Ventures Inc......231 767-1301
2176 E Laketon Ave Muskegon (49442) *(G-11341)*
Grosse Pointe News, Grosse Pointe Park *Also called Anteebo Publishers Inc (G-7190)*
Grosse Pointe News......734 674-0131
1167 Longfellow Dr Canton (48187) *(G-2380)*
Grosse Tool and Machine Co......586 773-6770
23080 Groesbeck Hwy Warren (48089) *(G-17068)*
Grossel Tool Co......586 294-3660
34190 Doreka Fraser (48026) *(G-5658)*
Ground Effects LLC (HQ)......810 250-5560
3302 Kent St Flint (48503) *(G-5443)*
Group 7500 Inc......313 875-9026
7500 Oakland St Detroit (48211) *(G-4107)*
Group B Industries Inc......734 941-6640
15399 Oakwood Dr Romulus (48174) *(G-13683)*
Group Tour Magazines, Holland *Also called Shoreline Creations Ltd (G-7801)*
Groupe Stahl, Sterling Heights *Also called Stahls Inc (G-15508)*

Grow Show, The, Ann Arbor *Also called Buyers Development Group LLC (G-393)*
Growgeneration Michigan Corp (HQ)......248 473-0450
5711 Enterprise Dr Lansing (48911) *(G-9379)*
Grozdanovski Vasilka......989 731-0723
4015 Hayes Tower Rd Gaylord (49735) *(G-5862)*
GRS&s, Grand Rapids *Also called Gill Corporation (G-6438)*
Grt Avionics Inc......616 245-7700
3133 Madison Ave Se Ste B Wyoming (49548) *(G-18006)*
Gruber Supplies & Accessories, Southfield *Also called Marshall-Gruber Company LLC (G-14973)*
Grupo Antolin Michigan Inc (HQ)......989 635-5055
6300 Euclid St Marlette (48453) *(G-10497)*
Grupo Antolin Michigan Inc......989 635-5080
25800 Sherwood Ave Warren (48091) *(G-17069)*
Grupo Antolin North Amer Inc (HQ)......248 373-1749
1700 Atlantic Blvd Auburn Hills (48326) *(G-891)*
Grupo Antolin Primera Auto Sys (HQ)......734 495-9180
47440 Mi Ave Ste 150 Canton (48188) *(G-2381)*
Grupo Antolin Wayne, Canton *Also called Grupo Antolin Primera Auto Sys (G-2381)*
Grw Technologies Inc......616 575-8119
4460 44th St Se Ste B Grand Rapids (49512) *(G-6483)*
Gs3, Livonia *Also called Global Strgc Sup Solutions LLC (G-9753)*
GSC Riii - Grede LLC......248 727-1800
1 Towne Sq Ste 550 Southfield (48076) *(G-14933)*
GSe McHining Fabrication Inc......517 663-9500
330 Hamman Dr Eaton Rapids (48827) *(G-4725)*
Gst Autoleather Inc (PA)......248 436-2300
2920 Waterview Dr Rochester Hills (48309) *(G-13436)*
Gt Foods Inc......734 934-2729
13467 Pullman St Southgate (48195) *(G-15077)*
Gt Plastics & Equipment LLC......616 678-7445
13425 Peach Ridge Ave Kent City (49330) *(G-8991)*
Gt Plastics Incorporated......989 739-7803
4681 Industrial Row Oscoda (48750) *(G-12210)*
GT Solutions LLC......616 259-0700
31 E 8th St Ste 310 Holland (49423) *(G-7655)*
Gt Technologies Inc (PA)......734 467-8371
5859 E Executive Dr Westland (48185) *(G-17566)*
Gti Liquidating Inc (PA)......616 842-5430
1500 Marion Ave Grand Haven (49417) *(G-6028)*
Gti Power Acquisition LLC (PA)......616 842-5430
1500 Marion Ave Grand Haven (49417) *(G-6029)*
GTM Steamer Service Inc......989 732-7678
647 Poplar Dr Gaylord (49735) *(G-5863)*
Guardian Automotive Corp (HQ)......586 757-7800
23751 Amber Ave Warren (48089) *(G-17070)*
Guardian Automotive Corp......586 757-7800
35555 Mound Rd Sterling Heights (48310) *(G-15365)*
Guardian Automotive Trim, Warren *Also called Guardian Automotive Corp (G-17070)*
Guardian Fabrication LLC (PA)......248 340-1800
2300 Harmon Rd Auburn Hills (48326) *(G-892)*
Guardian Fabrication Inc......248 340-1800
2300 Harmon Rd Auburn Hills (48326) *(G-893)*
Guardian Fiberglass, Albion *Also called Knauf Insulation Inc (G-127)*
Guardian Industries LLC......517 629-9464
1000 E North St Albion (49224) *(G-125)*
Guardian Industries LLC......734 654-4285
14600 Romine Rd Carleton (48117) *(G-2456)*
Guardian Industries LLC (HQ)......248 340-1800
2300 Harmon Rd Auburn Hills (48326) *(G-894)*
Guardian Industries LLC......734 654-1111
14511 Romine Rd Carleton (48117) *(G-2457)*
Guardian Manufacturing Corp......734 591-1454
12193 Levan Rd Livonia (48150) *(G-9761)*
Guardian Science & Tech Ctr, Carleton *Also called Guardian Industries LLC (G-2457)*
Guarneri House LLC......616 451-4960
5645 Balsam Dr Ste 800 Hudsonville (49426) *(G-8158)*
Gudel Inc......734 214-0000
4881 Runway Blvd Ann Arbor (48108) *(G-480)*
Gudho USA Inc......616 682-7814
138 Deer Run Dr Ne Ada (49301) *(G-17)*
Guelph Tool Sales Inc......586 755-3333
24150 Gibson Dr Warren (48089) *(G-17071)*
Guerne Precision Machining......231 834-7417
13761 Bailey Rd Bailey (49303) *(G-1079)*
Guernsey Dairy Stores Inc......248 349-1466
21300 Novi Rd Northville (48167) *(G-11696)*
Guernsey Farms Dairy, Northville *Also called Guernsey Dairy Stores Inc (G-11696)*
Guerreros Pallets......616 808-4721
1601 Madison Ave Se Grand Rapids (49507) *(G-6484)*
Guess Inc......517 546-2933
1475 N Burkhart Rd B100 Howell (48855) *(G-8046)*
Guess Factory Store 185, Howell *Also called Guess Inc (G-8046)*
Guhring Inc......262 784-6730
24975 Trans X Rd Novi (48375) *(G-11892)*
Guhring-Michigan, Novi *Also called Guhring Inc (G-11892)*
Guided Per Bus & Prof Svcs LLC......248 567-2121
17361 Deering St Livonia (48152) *(G-9762)*

ALPHABETIC

Guiding Our Destiny Ministry...313 212-9063
14811 Greenfield Rd A4 Detroit (48227) ***(G-4108)***
Guidobono Concrete Inc...810 229-2666
7474 Whitmore Lake Rd Brighton (48116) ***(G-1935)***
Guile & Son Inc...517 376-2116
11951 Rathbon Rd Byron (48418) ***(G-2172)***
Guilford of Maine Marketing Co...616 554-2250
5300 Corporate Grove Dr S Grand Rapids (49512) ***(G-6485)***
Gundry Media Inc...616 734-8977
800 Monroe Ave Nw Ste 220 Grand Rapids (49503) ***(G-6486)***
Gustafson Logging...906 250-2482
10857 N Agate Rd Trout Creek (49967) ***(G-16163)***
Gustafson Smoked Fish...906 292-5424
W4467 Us 2 Moran (49760) ***(G-11107)***
Gustos Quality Systems...231 409-0219
11655 Gusto Dr Fife Lake (49633) ***(G-5341)***
Guyoung Tech Usa Inc (HQ)...248 746-4261
26555 Evergreen Rd # 1515 Southfield (48076) ***(G-14934)***
Guys Timing Inc...517 404-3746
7044 Winding Trl Brighton (48116) ***(G-1936)***
Gvn Group Corp (PA)...248 340-0342
486 S Opdyke Rd Pontiac (48341) ***(G-12831)***
Gwen Frostic Prints, Benzonia *Also called Presscraft Papers Inc* ***(G-1576)***
Gyb LLC...586 218-3222
31065 Ryan Rd Warren (48092) ***(G-17072)***
Gyms Sawmill...989 826-8299
931 W Kittle Rd Mio (48647) ***(G-11003)***
Gyro Enterprises, Adrian *Also called David A Mohr Jr* ***(G-58)***
Gyro Powder Coating Inc...616 846-2580
1624 Marion Ave Grand Haven (49417) ***(G-6030)***
H & A Pharmacy II LLC...313 995-4552
2379 S Venoy Rd Westland (48186) ***(G-17567)***
H & G Tool Company...586 573-7040
30700 Ryan Rd Warren (48092) ***(G-17073)***
H & H Powdercoating Inc...810 750-1800
300 S Fenway Dr Fenton (48430) ***(G-5218)***
H & H Publications, Fowlerville *Also called Fowlerville News & Views* ***(G-5567)***
H & H Welding & Repair LLC...517 676-1800
700 Acme Dr Mason (48854) ***(G-10642)***
H & H Wildlife Desgn & Furng I (PA)...231 832-7002
5704 220th Ave Reed City (49677) ***(G-13214)***
H & J Mfg Consulting Svcs Corp...734 941-8314
15771 S Huron River Dr Romulus (48174) ***(G-13684)***
H & K Machine Company Inc...269 756-7339
7451 Us Highway 12 Three Oaks (49128) ***(G-15849)***
H & L Advantage Inc...616 532-1012
3500 Busch Dr Sw Grandville (49418) ***(G-7042)***
H & L Manufacturing Co...269 795-5000
900 E Mn St Middleville (49333) ***(G-10804)***
H & L Tool & Engineering Inc...586 755-2806
23701 Blackstone Ave Warren (48089) ***(G-17074)***
H & L Tool Company Inc...248 585-7474
32701 Dequindre Rd Madison Heights (48071) ***(G-10263)***
H & M Machining Inc...586 778-5028
29625 Parkway Roseville (48066) ***(G-13814)***
H & M Pallet LLC...231 821-8800
9148 S 200th Ave Holton (49425) ***(G-7932)***
H & M Vibro, Grandville *Also called Midwest Vibro Inc* ***(G-7058)***
H & M Welding and Fabricating...517 764-3630
3600 Page Ave Jackson (49203) ***(G-8461)***
H & N Hauling...989 640-3847
7662 E S Gratiot Line Rd Elsie (48831) ***(G-4796)***
H & R Electrical Contrs LLC...517 669-2102
10588 S Us Highway 27 Dewitt (48820) ***(G-4462)***
H & R Enterprises, Hillsdale *Also called Ron Watkins* ***(G-7537)***
H & R Industries Inc (PA)...616 247-1165
3020 Stafford Ave Sw Grand Rapids (49548) ***(G-6487)***
H & R Wood Specialties Inc...269 628-2181
20783 County Road 653 Gobles (49055) ***(G-5947)***
H & S Mold Inc...989 732-3566
1640 Orourke Blvd Gaylord (49735) ***(G-5864)***
H & T Asphalt, Benton Harbor *Also called H & T Skidmore Asphalt* ***(G-1506)***
H & T Skidmore Asphalt...269 468-3530
720 S Bainbridge Ctr Rd Benton Harbor (49022) ***(G-1506)***
H A Eckhart & Associates Inc...517 321-7700
16185 National Pkwy Lansing (48906) ***(G-9233)***
H A King Co Inc (PA)...248 280-0006
5038 Leafdale Blvd Royal Oak (48073) ***(G-13931)***
H and H Electronics...586 725-5412
7357 Bealane Rd Clay (48001) ***(G-2997)***
H and M Lube DBA Jlube...231 929-1197
529 W Fourteenth St Traverse City (49684) ***(G-15995)***
H B D M Inc (PA)...269 273-1976
207 Portage Ave Three Rivers (49093) ***(G-15864)***
H B D M Inc...269 273-1976
1149 Millard St Three Rivers (49093) ***(G-15865)***
H C I, Pigeon *Also called Huron Casting Inc* ***(G-12491)***
H E L P Printers Inc...734 847-0554
9673 Lewis Ave Temperance (48182) ***(G-15830)***
H E Morse Co...616 396-4604
455 Douglas Ave Holland (49424) ***(G-7656)***
H G Geiger Manufacturing Co...517 369-7357
416 Mill St Bronson (49028) ***(G-2028)***
H H Barnum Co...248 486-5982
12865 Silver Lake Rd Brighton (48116) ***(G-1937)***
H L F Furniture Incorporated...734 697-3000
44001 Van Born Rd Van Buren Twp (48111) ***(G-16762)***
H M Day Signs Inc...231 946-7132
233 E Twelfth St Traverse City (49684) ***(G-15996)***
H M Products Inc...313 875-5148
1435 E Milwaukee St Detroit (48211) ***(G-4109)***
H M T, Rochester Hills *Also called Hot Melt Technologies Inc* ***(G-13446)***
H M White, Detroit *Also called Hmw Contracting LLC* ***(G-4125)***
H O Trerice Co Inc...248 399-8000
12950 W 8 Mile Rd Oak Park (48237) ***(G-12072)***
H R P Motor Sports Inc...616 874-6338
8775 Belding Rd Ne Rockford (49341) ***(G-13570)***
H S Die & Engineering Inc (PA)...616 453-5451
O-215 Lake Michigan Dr Nw Grand Rapids (49534) ***(G-6488)***
H S Die & Engineering Inc...248 373-4048
1720 Star Batt Dr Rochester Hills (48309) ***(G-13437)***
H S Express, Rochester Hills *Also called H S Die & Engineering Inc* ***(G-13437)***
H U R Enterprises Inc...906 774-0833
717 W Hughitt St Iron Mountain (49801) ***(G-8284)***
H W Jencks Incorporated...231 352-4422
1339 Elm St Frankfort (49635) ***(G-5603)***
H W Motor Homes Inc...734 394-2000
5390 Belleville Rd Canton (48188) ***(G-2382)***
H&H Automation Controls...616 457-5994
7633 Bluebird Dr Jenison (49428) ***(G-8628)***
H-O-H Water Technology Inc...248 669-6667
1013 Rig St Commerce Township (48390) ***(G-3409)***
H.C. Starck Group, Coldwater *Also called HC Starck Inc* ***(G-3309)***
H1 Plant, Kentwood *Also called Hearthside Food Solutions LLC* ***(G-9010)***
H4 Plant, Kentwood *Also called Hearthside Food Solutions LLC* ***(G-9009)***
HA Automotive Systems Inc (PA)...248 781-0001
1300 Coolidge Hwy Troy (48084) ***(G-16388)***
Haartz Corporation...248 646-8200
40950 Woodward Ave # 150 Bloomfield Hills (48304) ***(G-1771)***
Haas Food Services, Negaunee *Also called Stephen Haas* ***(G-11477)***
Haas Group International LLC...810 236-0032
G3100 Van Slyke Rd Flint (48551) ***(G-5444)***
Hacht Sales, Southfield *Also called Prestige Pet Products Inc* ***(G-15003)***
Hacienda Mexican Foods LLC (PA)...313 895-8823
6100 Buchanan St Detroit (48210) ***(G-4110)***
Hacienda Mexican Foods LLC...313 843-7007
6016 W Vernor Hwy Detroit (48209) ***(G-4111)***
Hacker Machine Inc...517 569-3348
11200 Broughwell Rd Rives Junction (49277) ***(G-13308)***
Hackett Brass Foundry Co (PA)...313 822-1214
1200 Lillibridge St Detroit (48214) ***(G-4112)***
Hackett Brass Foundry Co...313 331-6005
45 Saint Jean St Detroit (48214) ***(G-4113)***
Hackley Health Ventures Inc (HQ)...231 728-5720
1675 Leahy St Ste 101 Muskegon (49442) ***(G-11342)***
Hackley Hearing Center, Muskegon *Also called Hackley Health Ventures Inc* ***(G-11342)***
Hacks Key Shop Inc...517 485-9488
1109 River St Lansing (48912) ***(G-9380)***
Hadd Enterprises...586 773-4260
15026 E 9 Mile Rd Eastpointe (48021) ***(G-4702)***
Hadley Products Corporation (HQ)...616 530-1717
2851 Prairie St Sw Ste A Grandville (49418) ***(G-7043)***
Haeco Americas Engine Services, Oscoda *Also called Timco Engine Center Inc* ***(G-12221)***
Haerter Stamping LLC...616 871-9400
3840 Model Ct Se Kentwood (49512) ***(G-9008)***
Hagen Cement Products Inc...269 483-9641
17149 Us Highway 12 White Pigeon (49099) ***(G-17651)***
Haighs Maple Syrup & Sups LLC...517 202-6975
11756 Scipio Hwy Vermontville (49096) ***(G-16821)***
Hajjar Plating, Detroit *Also called Micro Platers Sales Inc* ***(G-4245)***
Hak Inc (PA)...231 587-5322
413 Dale Ave Mancelona (49659) ***(G-10392)***
Hal International Inc...248 488-0440
34155 Industrial Rd Livonia (48150) ***(G-9763)***
Haldex Brake Products Corp...616 827-9641
5801 Weller Ct Sw Ste D Wyoming (49509) ***(G-18007)***
Hale Manufacturing Inc...231 529-6271
6235 Cupp Rd Alanson (49706) ***(G-110)***
Hall Mat, Gladwin *Also called William R Hall Kimberly* ***(G-5939)***
Haller International Tech Inc...313 821-0809
609 Old St Jean Detroit (48214) ***(G-4114)***
Halliday Sand & Gravel Inc...989 422-3463
1128 Federal Ave Houghton Lake (48629) ***(G-7990)***
Hallmark Tool and Gage Co Inc...248 669-4010
51200 Pontiac Trl Wixom (48393) ***(G-17821)***
Halloween Events...248 332-7884
36393 Dequindre Rd Troy (48083) ***(G-16389)***

ALPHABETIC SECTION

Hallstrom Company 906 439-5439
  M-94 W Eben Junction (49825) *(G-4740)*
Hallwell Games LLC 586 879-3404
  18444 W 10 Mile Rd Southfield (48075) *(G-14935)*
Halonen Mfg Group Inc 906 483-4077
  46104 State Highway M26 Atlantic Mine (49905) *(G-736)*
Halsan Inc 734 285-5420
  15315 Dix Toledo Rd Southgate (48195) *(G-15078)*
Haltermann Carless Us Inc 248 422-6548
  901 Wilshire Dr Ste 570 Troy (48084) *(G-16390)*
Hamaton Inc 248 308-3856
  47815 West Rd Ste D-109 Wixom (48393) *(G-17822)*
Hamblin Company 517 423-7491
  109 E Logan St Tecumseh (49286) *(G-15796)*
Hamilton Block & Ready Mix Co 269 751-5129
  4510 132nd Ave Hamilton (49419) *(G-7232)*
Hamilton Electric Co 989 799-6291
  3175 Pierce Rd Saginaw (48604) *(G-14053)*
Hamilton Engineering Inc 734 419-0200
  34000 Autry St Livonia (48150) *(G-9764)*
Hamilton Equine Products LLC 616 842-2406
  14057 108th Ave Grand Haven (49417) *(G-6031)*
Hamilton Industrial Products 269 751-5153
  4555 134th Ave Hamilton (49419) *(G-7233)*
Hamilton Steel Fabrications 269 751-8757
  3290 Lincoln Rd Hamilton (49419) *(G-7234)*
Hamlin Tool & Machine Co Inc 248 651-6302
  1671 E Hamlin Rd Rochester Hills (48307) *(G-13438)*
Hammar's Welding, Kimball Also called Hammars Contracting LLC *(G-9044)*
Hammars Contracting LLC 810 367-3037
  1177 Wadhams Rd Kimball (48074) *(G-9044)*
Hammond Machinery, Kalamazoo Also called Roto-Finish Company Inc *(G-8875)*
Hammond Machinery Inc 269 345-7151
  1600 Douglas Ave Kalamazoo (49007) *(G-8759)*
Hammond Publishing Company 810 686-8879
  G7166 N Saginaw St Mount Morris (48458) *(G-11161)*
Hammound Roto-Finish, Kalamazoo Also called Kalamazoo Company *(G-8786)*
Hamp 989 366-5341
  126 Winding Dr Houghton Lake (48629) *(G-7991)*
Hampton Block & Supply, Oxford Also called Hampton Block Co *(G-12348)*
Hampton Block Co 248 628-1333
  465 Tanview Dr Oxford (48371) *(G-12348)*
Hampton Company Inc 517 765-2222
  12709 M 60 E Burlington (49029) *(G-2132)*
Hamtech Inc 231 796-3917
  1916 Industrial Dr N Big Rapids (49307) *(G-1631)*
Hamtramck Review Inc 313 874-2100
  3020 Caniff St Detroit (48212) *(G-4115)*
Hanchett Manufacturing Inc 231 796-7678
  20000 19 Mile Rd Big Rapids (49307) *(G-1632)*
Hancock Bottling Co Inc 906 482-3701
  1800 Birch St Hancock (49930) *(G-7251)*
Hancock Enterprises Inc 734 287-8840
  20655 Northline Rd Taylor (48180) *(G-15728)*
Handicap Sign Inc 616 454-9416
  1142 Wealthy St Se Grand Rapids (49506) *(G-6489)*
Handley Industries Inc 517 787-8821
  2101 Brooklyn Rd Jackson (49203) *(G-8462)*
Handorn Inc 616 241-6181
  636 Crofton St Se Grand Rapids (49507) *(G-6490)*
Handy Bindery Co Inc 586 469-2240
  23170 Giacoma Ct Clinton Township (48036) *(G-3133)*
Handy Home, Monroe Also called Backyard Products LLC *(G-11015)*
Handy Wacks Corporation (PA) 616 887-8268
  100 E Averill St Sparta (49345) *(G-15096)*
Handy Wacks Corporation 616 887-8268
  100 E Averill St Sparta (49345) *(G-15097)*
Hang On Express 231 271-0202
  316 N Saint Joseph St Suttons Bay (49682) *(G-15652)*
Hanger Inc 616 949-0075
  5005 Cascade Rd Se Ste C Grand Rapids (49546) *(G-6491)*
Hanger Inc 616 458-8080
  230 Michigan St Ne Ste 200 Grand Rapids (49503) *(G-6492)*
Hanger Inc 248 615-0601
  32975 8 Mile Rd Livonia (48152) *(G-9765)*
Hanger Inc 616 940-0878
  5005 Cascade Rd Se Ste C Grand Rapids (49546) *(G-6493)*
Hanger Prsthetcs & Ortho Inc 517 394-5850
  4424 S Pennsylvania Ave Lansing (48910) *(G-9381)*
Hanger Prsthetcs & Ortho Inc 248 683-5070
  4000 Highland Rd Ste 108 Waterford (48328) *(G-17348)*
Hangers Plus LLC 616 997-4264
  411 64th Ave N Ste B Coopersville (49404) *(G-3560)*
Hanho America Co Ltd 248 422-6921
  100 E Big Beaver Rd # 845 Troy (48083) *(G-16391)*
Hank Thorn Co 248 348-7800
  29164 Wall St Wixom (48393) *(G-17823)*
Hankerds Sportswear Basic TS 989 725-2979
  116 W Exchange St Owosso (48867) *(G-12294)*
Hankins & Assoc, Petersburg Also called DTe Hankin Inc *(G-12435)*
Hanks Welding Service Inc 517 568-3804
  2379 29 Mile Rd Homer (49245) *(G-7943)*
Hanlo Gauges & Engineering Co 734 422-4224
  34403 Glendale St Livonia (48150) *(G-9766)*
Hanna Instruments Inc 734 971-8160
  3820 Packard St Ste 120 Ann Arbor (48108) *(G-481)*
Hanon Printing Company 248 541-9099
  34 Cambridge Blvd Pleasant Ridge (48069) *(G-12555)*
Hanon Systems Usa LLC (HQ) 248 907-8000
  39600 Lewis Dr Novi (48377) *(G-11893)*
Hanse Environmental Inc (PA) 269 673-8638
  235 Hubbard St Allegan (49010) *(G-164)*
Hansen Machine & Tool Corp 616 361-2842
  457 Clover Ct Nw Grand Rapids (49504) *(G-6494)*
Hanson Cold Storage Co (PA) 269 982-1390
  2900 S State St Ste 4e Saint Joseph (49085) *(G-14314)*
Hanson International Inc (PA) 269 429-5555
  3500 Hollywood Rd Saint Joseph (49085) *(G-14315)*
Hanson International Inc 269 429-5555
  3500 Hollywood Rd Saint Joseph (49085) *(G-14316)*
Hanson Logistics, Saint Joseph Also called Hanson Cold Storage Co *(G-14314)*
Hanson Mold Division, Saint Joseph Also called Hanson International Inc *(G-14315)*
Hanson Systems LLC 269 465-6986
  9850 Red Arrow Hwy Bridgman (49106) *(G-1866)*
Hanwha Advanced Mtls Amer LLC 810 629-2496
  1530 E Front St Monroe (48161) *(G-11038)*
Hanwha Azdel Inc 810 629-2496
  2200 Centerwood Dr Warren (48091) *(G-17075)*
Hanwha L&C Alabama, Monroe Also called Hanwha Advanced Mtls Amer LLC *(G-11038)*
Hanwha Techm Usa LLC 248 588-1242
  1857 Enterprise Dr Rochester Hills (48309) *(G-13439)*
Haosen Automation N Amer Inc 248 556-6398
  691 N Squirrel Rd Ste 288 Auburn Hills (48326) *(G-895)*
Hapman 269 343-1675
  6002 E N Ave Kalamazoo (49048) *(G-8760)*
Happy Bums 616 987-3159
  201 Montcalm Ave Se Lowell (49331) *(G-10030)*
Happy Candy 248 629-9819
  2325 John B Ave Warren (48091) *(G-17076)*
Happy Howies Inc 313 537-7200
  15510 Dale St Detroit (48223) *(G-4116)*
Harada Industry America Inc (HQ) 248 374-2587
  22925 Venture Dr Novi (48375) *(G-11894)*
Harbisonwalker Intl Inc 231 689-6641
  1301 E 8th St White Cloud (49349) *(G-17623)*
Harbor Beach Times 989 479-3605
  123 N 1st St Harbor Beach (48441) *(G-7266)*
Harbor Deburring & Finshg Co, Grand Haven Also called V & V Inc *(G-6093)*
Harbor Foam Inc 616 855-8150
  2950 Pririe St Sw Ste 300 Grandville (49418) *(G-7044)*
Harbor Graphics, Benton Harbor Also called Vomela Specialty Company *(G-1562)*
Harbor Green Solutions LLC 269 352-0265
  900 Davis Dr Benton Harbor (49022) *(G-1507)*
Harbor House Publishers Inc 231 582-2814
  221 Water St Boyne City (49712) *(G-1821)*
Harbor Industries Inc (PA) 616 842-5330
  14130 172nd Ave Grand Haven (49417) *(G-6032)*
Harbor Industries Inc 231 547-3280
  100 Harbor View Ln Charlevoix (49720) *(G-2617)*
Harbor Industries Inc 616 842-5330
  107 Airport Dr Charlevoix (49720) *(G-2618)*
Harbor Industries Inc 616 842-5330
  14170 172nd Ave Grand Haven (49417) *(G-6033)*
Harbor Isle Plastics LLC 269 465-6004
  2337 W Marquette Woods Rd Stevensville (49127) *(G-15570)*
Harbor Light Newspaper, Harbor Springs Also called North Country Publishing Corp *(G-7290)*
Harbor Master Ltd 616 669-3170
  3127 Highland Blvd Hudsonville (49426) *(G-8159)*
Harbor Packaging, Benton Harbor Also called Jomar Inc *(G-1515)*
Harbor Sales, Potterville Also called Cross Country Homes *(G-13073)*
Harbor Screw Machine Products 269 925-5855
  430 Cass St Benton Harbor (49022) *(G-1508)*
Harbor Software Intl Inc 231 347-8866
  231 State St Ste 5 Petoskey (49770) *(G-12451)*
Harbor Sprng Vnyrds Winery LLC 231 242-4062
  5699 S Lake Shore Dr Harbor Springs (49740) *(G-7283)*
Harbor Steel and Supply Corp 616 786-0002
  2385 112th Ave Holland (49424) *(G-7657)*
Harbor Tool and Machine 989 479-6708
  225 Hunter Industrial Dr Harbor Beach (48441) *(G-7267)*
Harborfront Interiors Inc 231 777-3838
  2300 Black Creek Rd Muskegon (49444) *(G-11343)*
Harborlite, Vicksburg Also called Imerys Perlite Usa Inc *(G-16836)*
Harbrook Tool Inc 248 477-8040
  40391 Grand River Ave Novi (48375) *(G-11895)*
Hard Milling Solutions Inc 586 286-2300
  107 Peyerk Ct Bruce Twp (48065) *(G-2083)*

Hardcrete Inc 989 644-5543
3610 N Rolland Rd Weidman (48893) *(G-17457)*
Harding Energy Inc 231 798-7033
509 E Ellis Rd Norton Shores (49441) *(G-11759)*
Hardwood Solutions Inc, Chelsea Also called Precision Hrdwood Rsources Inc *(G-2718)*
Hardwoods of Michigan, Clinton Also called Forestry Management Svcs Inc *(G-3020)*
Hardwoods Prtg & Advg Servic, Jenison Also called R & R Harwood Inc *(G-8640)*
Hardy & Sons Sign Service Inc 586 779-8018
22340 Harper Ave Saint Clair Shores (48080) *(G-14256)*
Hardy-Reed Tool & Die Co Inc 517 547-7107
16269 Manitou Beach Rd Manitou Beach (49253) *(G-10448)*
Harley Attachments, Dexter Also called Sweepster Attachments LLC *(G-4512)*
Harlo Corporation (PA) 616 538-0550
4210 Ferry St Sw Grandville (49418) *(G-7045)*
Harlo Corporation 616 538-0550
4210 Ferry St Sw Grandville (49418) *(G-7046)*
Harlo Products Corporation (HQ) 616 538-0550
4210 Ferry St Sw Grandville (49418) *(G-7047)*
Harloff Manufacturing Co LLC 269 655-1097
828 Duo Tang Rd Unit A Paw Paw (49079) *(G-12405)*
Harlow Sheet Metal LLC 734 996-1509
5140 Park Rd Ann Arbor (48103) *(G-482)*
Harman Becker Auto Systems Inc (HQ) 248 785-2361
30001 Cabot Dr Novi (48377) *(G-11896)*
Harman Becker Auto Systems Inc 248 848-0393
26500 Haggerty Rd Farmington Hills (48331) *(G-5016)*
Harman Builders, Union Also called Harman Lumber & Supply Inc *(G-16729)*
Harman Consumer Group, Novi Also called Harman Becker Auto Systems Inc *(G-11896)*
Harman Corporation (PA) 248 651-4477
360 South St Rochester (48307) *(G-13324)*
Harman Lumber & Supply Inc 269 641-5424
15479 Us Highway 12 Ste 7 Union (49130) *(G-16729)*
Harmon Sign Inc (PA) 248 348-8150
28054 Center Oaks Ct A Wixom (48393) *(G-17824)*
Harmonie International LLC 248 737-9933
30201 Orchard Lake Rd Farmington Hills (48334) *(G-5017)*
Harmony Products 906 387-5411
118 E Superior St Munising (49862) *(G-11243)*
Harnel Company, Grand Rapids Also called Zayna LLC *(G-7011)*
Harold G Schaevitz Inds LLC 248 636-1515
42690 Woodward Ave # 200 Bloomfield Hills (48304) *(G-1772)*
Harold K Schultz 517 279-9764
57 S Monroe St Coldwater (49036) *(G-3308)*
Harp Column LLC 215 564-3232
304 E Central Ave Zeeland (49464) *(G-18145)*
Harper Arrington Pubg LLC 313 282-6751
18701 Grand River Ave # 105 Detroit (48223) *(G-4117)*
Harper Dermatology PC 586 776-7546
21 Stillmeadow Ln Grosse Pointe Shores (48236) *(G-7199)*
Harper Machine Tool Inc 586 756-0140
21410 Ryan Rd Warren (48091) *(G-17077)*
Harrells LLC 248 446-8070
53410 Grand River Ave New Hudson (48165) *(G-11542)*
Harrington Construction Co 269 543-4251
6720 124th Ave Fennville (49408) *(G-5173)*
Harris Rebar, Lansing Also called Ambassador Steel Corporation *(G-9336)*
Harris Sheet Metal Co 989 496-3080
3313 S Saginaw Rd Midland (48640) *(G-10867)*
Harris Tooling 269 465-5870
6230 Jericho Rd Stevensville (49127) *(G-15571)*
Harrison Packing Co Inc (PA) 269 381-3837
3420 Stadium Pkwy Kalamazoo (49009) *(G-8761)*
Harrison Packing Co Inc 989 427-4535
394 E Deaner Rd Edmore (48829) *(G-4751)*
Harrison Partners Inv Group 419 708-8154
33 E Main St Milan (48160) *(G-10940)*
Harrison Steel LLC 586 247-1230
50390 Utica Dr Shelby Township (48315) *(G-14599)*
Harroun Enterprises Inc 810 629-9885
1111 Fenway Cir Fenton (48430) *(G-5219)*
Harry Major Machine & Tool Co (PA) 586 783-7030
24801 Capital Blvd Clinton Township (48036) *(G-3134)*
Harry Miller Flowers Inc 313 581-2328
1832 Grindley Park St Dearborn (48124) *(G-3718)*
Harrys Meme LLC 248 977-0168
41679 Magnolia Ct Novi (48377) *(G-11897)*
Harrys Steering Gear Repair 586 677-5580
52197 Sawmill Creek Dr Macomb (48042) *(G-10128)*
Harsco Corporation 231 843-3431
200 S Jackson Rd Ludington (49431) *(G-10062)*
Harsco Corporation 231 843-3431
200 S Jackson Rd Ludington (49431) *(G-10063)*
Harsco Rail, Ludington Also called Harsco Corporation *(G-10062)*
Hart & Cooley Inc (HQ) 616 656-8200
5030 Corp Exch Blvd Se Grand Rapids (49512) *(G-6495)*
Hart Acquisition Company LLC 313 537-0490
12700 Marion Redford (48239) *(G-13164)*
Hart Concrete LLC 231 873-2183
540 Maple St Spring Lake (49456) *(G-15150)*

Hart Enterprises USA Inc 616 887-0400
400 Apple Jack Ct Sparta (49345) *(G-15098)*
Hart Freeze Pack LlC 231 873-2175
835 S Griswold St Hart (49420) *(G-7373)*
Hart Industries LLC 313 588-1837
43718 Utica Rd Sterling Heights (48314) *(G-15366)*
Hart Precision Products Inc 313 537-0490
12700 Marion Redford (48239) *(G-13165)*
Harvard Clothing Company 517 542-2986
411 Marshall St Litchfield (49252) *(G-9602)*
Harvard Square Editions 734 668-7523
2112 Brockman Blvd Ann Arbor (48104) *(G-483)*
Harvest Energy Inc 269 838-4595
2820 Division Ave S Grand Rapids (49548) *(G-6496)*
Harvest Tax Services, Lincoln Park Also called William Penn Systems Inc *(G-9588)*
Harvey Bock Co 616 566-1372
141 Central Ave Ste 120 Holland (49423) *(G-7658)*
Harvey Pattern Works Inc 906 774-4285
410 North Blvd Kingsford (49802) *(G-9059)*
Harvey Richard John 269 781-5801
19611 16 Mile Rd Marshall (49068) *(G-10571)*
Harvey S Freeman 248 852-2222
4159 Ladysmith St West Bloomfield (48323) *(G-17479)*
Harville Associates Inc 313 839-5712
19666 Old Homestead Dr Harper Woods (48225) *(G-7301)*
Harwood Hritg Gold Maple Syrup, Charlevoix Also called Parsons Centennial Farm LLC *(G-2625)*
Haskell Office 616 988-0880
3770 Hagen Dr Se Wyoming (49548) *(G-18008)*
Hastings Equipment, Grand Rapids Also called Hel Inc *(G-6503)*
Hastings Fiber Glass Pdts Inc 269 945-9541
1301 W Green St Hastings (49058) *(G-7412)*
Hastings Manufacturing Company 269 945-2491
325 N Hanover St Hastings (49058) *(G-7413)*
Hatch Stamping Company LLC 517 223-1293
901 Garden Ln Fowlerville (48836) *(G-5569)*
Hatch Stamping Company LLC 517 540-1021
1051 Austin Ct Howell (48843) *(G-8047)*
Hatch Stamping Company LLC 734 433-1903
570 Cleveland St Chelsea (48118) *(G-2713)*
Hatfield Electric Industrial, Kalamazoo Also called Heco Inc *(G-8762)*
Hatfield Enterprises 616 677-5215
15627 24th Ave Marne (49435) *(G-10508)*
Hatteras Inc 734 525-5500
12801 Prospect St Dearborn (48126) *(G-3719)*
Hattiegirl Ice Cream Foods LLC 877 444-3738
16159 Wyoming St Detroit (48221) *(G-4118)*
Hausbeck Pickle Company (PA) 989 754-4721
1626 Hess Ave Saginaw (48601) *(G-14054)*
Haven Innovation Inc 616 935-1040
1705 Eaton Dr Grand Haven (49417) *(G-6034)*
Haven Manufacturing Company 616 842-1260
13720 172nd Ave Grand Haven (49417) *(G-6035)*
Haven Sports Manufacturing LLC 269 639-8782
67294 Becky Ln South Haven (49090) *(G-14762)*
Havercroft Tool & Die Inc 989 724-5913
5002 Main St Greenbush (48738) *(G-7120)*
Havers Heritage 517 423-3455
7500 Clinton Macon Rd Clinton (49236) *(G-3022)*
Haviland Contoured Plastics 616 361-6691
2168 Avastar Pkwy Nw Walker (49544) *(G-16866)*
Haviland Enterprises Inc (PA) 616 361-6691
421 Ann St Nw Grand Rapids (49504) *(G-6497)*
Haviland Products Company (HQ) 616 361-6691
421 Ann St Nw Grand Rapids (49504) *(G-6498)*
Haviland Products Company 800 456-1134
521 Ann St Nw Grand Rapids (49504) *(G-6499)*
Havis Inc 734 414-0699
47099 Five Mile Rd Plymouth (48170) *(G-12634)*
Hawk Design Inc 989 781-1152
7760 Gratiot Rd Saginaw (48609) *(G-14055)*
Hawk Tool and Machine Inc 248 349-0121
29183 Lorie Ln Wixom (48393) *(G-17825)*
Hawkins Industries Inc 734 663-9889
3660 Plaza Dr Ste 1b Ann Arbor (48108) *(G-484)*
Haworth Inc (HQ) 616 393-3000
1 Haworth Ctr Holland (49423) *(G-7659)*
Haworth Inc 231 796-1400
300 N Bronson Ave Big Rapids (49307) *(G-1633)*
Haworth Inc 231 845-0607
5170 Progress Dr Ludington (49431) *(G-10064)*
Haworth International Ltd (PA) 616 393-3000
1 Haworth Ctr Holland (49423) *(G-7660)*
Hayden - McNeil LLC 734 455-7900
14903 Pilot Dr Plymouth (48170) *(G-12635)*
Hayes Lemmerz International, Novi Also called Maxion Wheels *(G-11940)*
Hayes Lemmerz Intl-GA LLC 734 737-5000
39500 Orchard Hill Pl Novi (48375) *(G-11898)*
Hayes Manufacturing Inc 231 879-3372
6875 Us Highway 131 Fife Lake (49633) *(G-5342)*

ALPHABETIC SECTION Henkel US Operations Corp

Hayes, Lorrie, Marquette *Also called Screened Image Graphic Design* ***(G-10556)***
Hayes-Albion Corporation 517 629-2141
1999 Wildwood Ave Jackson (49202) ***(G-8463)***
Haynie and Hess Realty Co LLC 586 296-2750
33670 Riviera Fraser (48026) ***(G-5659)***
Hazekamps Wholesale Meat Co, Muskegon *Also called Bert Hazekamp & Son Inc* ***(G-11279)***
Hazloc Industries LLC 810 679-2551
304 N Howard Ave Croswell (48422) ***(G-3597)***
HB Carbide Company 989 786-4223
4210 Doyle Lewiston (49756) ***(G-9550)***
HB Fuller Company 616 453-8271
2727 Kinney Ave Nw Grand Rapids (49534) ***(G-6500)***
HB Stubbs Company LLC 586 574-9700
27027 Mound Rd Warren (48092) ***(G-17078)***
Hbeat Medical, Plymouth *Also called Cardiac Assist Holdings LLC* ***(G-12593)***
Hbpo North America Inc 248 823-7076
700 Tower Dr Troy (48098) ***(G-16392)***
HC Starck Inc 517 279-9511
460 Jay St Coldwater (49036) ***(G-3309)***
Hci, Warren *Also called Hydronic Components Inc* ***(G-17084)***
Hd Selcating Pav Solutions LLC 248 241-6526
8205 Valleyview Dr Clarkston (48348) ***(G-2925)***
Hdn F&A Inc 269 965-3268
104 Arbor St Battle Creek (49015) ***(G-1197)***
Hdp Inc 248 674-4967
4670 Hatchery Rd Ste C Waterford (48329) ***(G-17349)***
Hdt Automotive Solutions LLC (HQ) 810 359-5344
38701 7 Mile Rd Livonia (48152) ***(G-9767)***
Head Over Heels 248 435-2954
164 E Maple Rd Ste G Troy (48083) ***(G-16393)***
Headen Plant, Dowagiac *Also called Lyons Industries Inc* ***(G-4549)***
Header Products, Rose City *Also called Atf Inc* ***(G-13760)***
Header Products, Romulus *Also called Michigan ATF Holdings LLC* ***(G-13708)***
Health Enhancement Systems Inc (PA) 989 839-0852
800 Cambridge St Ste 101 Midland (48642) ***(G-10868)***
Health Mart, Detroit *Also called Eastside Pharmacy Inc* ***(G-4024)***
Healthcare Dme LLC 734 975-6668
2911 Carpenter Rd Ann Arbor (48108) ***(G-485)***
Healthcare Inds Mtls Site, Hemlock *Also called Dow Silicones Corporation* ***(G-7462)***
Healthcare Medical Supply, Ann Arbor *Also called Healthcare Dme LLC* ***(G-485)***
Healthcure LLC 313 743-2331
6501 Lynch Rd Detroit (48234) ***(G-4119)***
Healthmark Industries Co Inc 586 774-7600
18600 Malyn Blvd Fraser (48026) ***(G-5660)***
Healthplus Spclty Pharma 734 769-1300
4350 Jackson Rd Ste 250 Ann Arbor (48103) ***(G-486)***
Hear Clear Inc 734 525-8467
311 Castlebury Dr Saline (48176) ***(G-14394)***
Hearing Health Science Inc 734 476-9490
2723 S State St Ste 150 Ann Arbor (48104) ***(G-487)***
Heart of The Vnyrd Wnry/Bd/Brk, Baroda *Also called R C M S Inc* ***(G-1130)***
Heart Sync Inc 734 213-5530
4401 Varsity Dr Ste D Ann Arbor (48108) ***(G-488)***
Heart Truss & Engineering Corp 517 372-0850
1830 N Grand River Ave Lansing (48906) ***(G-9234)***
Heart-N-Home, Owosso *Also called Hearth-N-Home Inc* ***(G-12295)***
Hearth-N-Home Inc (PA) 517 625-5586
6990 W M 21 Owosso (48867) ***(G-12295)***
Hearthside Fireplace & Bbq Sp, Trenton *Also called Trenton Hearthside Shop Inc* ***(G-16160)***
Hearthside Food Solutions LLC 616 871-6240
4185 44th St Se Kentwood (49512) ***(G-9009)***
Hearthside Food Solutions LLC 616 574-2000
3061 Shaffer Ave Se Kentwood (49512) ***(G-9010)***
Heartland Steel Products LLC 810 364-7421
2420 Wills St Marysville (48040) ***(G-10603)***
Heartwood Mills LLC 888 829-5909
4740 Skop Rd Ste A Boyne Falls (49713) ***(G-1839)***
Heat Treating Svcs Corp Amer (PA) 248 858-2230
217 Central Ave Pontiac (48341) ***(G-12832)***
Heat Treating Svcs Corp Amer 248 332-1510
915 Cesar E Chavez Ave Pontiac (48340) ***(G-12833)***
Heat Treating Svcs Corp Amer 248 253-9560
2501 Williams Dr Waterford (48328) ***(G-17350)***
Heatex Warehouse LLC (PA) 586 773-0770
16174 Common Rd Roseville (48066) ***(G-13815)***
Heath Manufacturing Company (HQ) 616 997-8181
140 Mill St Ste A Coopersville (49404) ***(G-3561)***
Heath Ultra Products, Coopersville *Also called Heath Manufacturing Company* ***(G-3561)***
Heather N Holly 989 832-6460
228 E Main St Midland (48640) ***(G-10869)***
Heating Induction Services Inc 586 791-3160
24483 Sorrentino Ct Clinton Township (48035) ***(G-3135)***
Heating Treating Services, Waterford *Also called Heat Treating Svcs Corp Amer* ***(G-17350)***
Heaven Is My Home, Cedar Springs *Also called Quality Guest Publishing Inc* ***(G-2561)***
Heaven Saunas, Holland *Also called Ahs LLC* ***(G-7552)***
Heavy Duty Radiator LLC 800 525-0011
18235 Krause St Riverview (48193) ***(G-13295)***
Heb Development LLC (PA) 616 363-3825
1946 Turner Ave Nw Grand Rapids (49504) ***(G-6501)***
Heck Industries Incorporated 810 632-5400
1498 Old Us 23 Hwy Hartland (48353) ***(G-7390)***
Heckett Multiserve 313 842-2120
7819 W Jefferson Ave Detroit (48209) ***(G-4120)***
Heco Inc 269 381-7200
3509 S Burdick St Kalamazoo (49001) ***(G-8762)***
Hegenscheidt-Mfd Corporation 586 274-4900
6255 Center Dr Sterling Heights (48312) ***(G-15367)***
Hehr Michigan Division, Chesaning *Also called Lippert Components Mfg Inc* ***(G-2725)***
HEI, Howell *Also called Highland Engineering Inc* ***(G-8048)***
Heiden Lumber & Fencing, Stephenson *Also called Terry Heiden* ***(G-15241)***
Heidtman Logging Inc 906 249-3914
748 County Road 550 Marquette (49855) ***(G-10534)***
Heidtman Steel Products Inc 734 848-2115
640 La Voy Rd Erie (48133) ***(G-4803)***
Heikkinen Productions Inc 734 485-4020
1410 W Michigan Ave Ypsilanti (48197) ***(G-18076)***
Heileman Sons Signs & Ltg Ser, Saint Clair *Also called Heileman Sons Signs & Ltg Svcs* ***(G-14221)***
Heileman Sons Signs & Ltg Svcs 810 364-2900
4797 Gratiot Ave Saint Clair (48079) ***(G-14221)***
Heinzerling Enterprises Inc 734 529-9100
438 Tecumseh St Dundee (48131) ***(G-4586)***
Heinzmann D Tool & Die Inc 248 363-5115
4335 Pineview Dr Commerce Township (48390) ***(G-3410)***
Hekman Contract Division, Zeeland *Also called Hekman Furniture Company* ***(G-18146)***
Hekman Furniture Company 616 735-3905
3188 Wilson Dr Nw Grand Rapids (49534) ***(G-6502)***
Hekman Furniture Company (HQ) 616 748-2660
860 E Main Ave Zeeland (49464) ***(G-18146)***
Hel Inc 616 774-9032
450 Market Ave Sw Grand Rapids (49503) ***(G-6503)***
Helen Inc 616 698-8102
6450 Hanna Lake Ave Se Caledonia (49316) ***(G-2297)***
Helical Lap & Manufacturing Co (HQ) 586 307-8322
121 Madison Ave Mount Clemens (48043) ***(G-11132)***
Helios Solar LLC 269 343-5581
248 W Michigan Ave Kalamazoo (49007) ***(G-8763)***
Helium Home Base LLC 734 895-3608
2600 Nichols Ct Westland (48186) ***(G-17568)***
Helix Devices LLC 724 681-0975
325 E Grand River Ave East Lansing (48823) ***(G-4660)***
Helix Steel, Ann Arbor *Also called Polytorx LLC* ***(G-595)***
Hella Corporate Center USA Inc (HQ) 586 232-4788
15951 Technology Dr Northville (48168) ***(G-11697)***
Hella Lighting Corporation (HQ) 734 414-0900
43811 Plymouth Oaks Blvd Plymouth (48170) ***(G-12636)***
Hella North America, Inc., Northville *Also called Hella Corporate Center USA Inc* ***(G-11697)***
Heller Inc 248 288-5000
1225 Equity Dr Troy (48084) ***(G-16394)***
Hellner & Associates Inc 810 220-3472
2233 Euler Rd Brighton (48114) ***(G-1938)***
Hello Life Inc (PA) 616 808-3290
4635 40th St Se Grand Rapids (49512) ***(G-6504)***
Hello Life Inc 616 808-3290
4460 44th St Se Ste C600 Grand Rapids (49512) ***(G-6505)***
Helm Incorporated (HQ) 734 468-3700
47911 Halyard Dr Plymouth (48170) ***(G-12637)***
Help-U-Sell RE Big Rapids 231 796-3966
412 S State St Ofc A Big Rapids (49307) ***(G-1634)***
Helping Hands Therapy 313 492-6007
23999 Northwestern Hwy Southfield (48075) ***(G-14936)***
Helping Hearts Helping Hands 248 980-5090
285 Mill St Constantine (49042) ***(G-3536)***
Helro Corporation 248 650-8500
326 Albertson St Rochester (48307) ***(G-13325)***
Helsels Tree Service Inc 231 879-3666
320 Rose St Manton (49663) ***(G-10454)***
Hemco Machine Co Inc 586 264-8911
6785 Chicago Rd Warren (48092) ***(G-17079)***
Hemingway Screw Products Inc 313 383-7300
17840 Dix Rd Melvindale (48122) ***(G-10699)***
Hemisphere Design Works, Muskegon *Also called Ameriform Acquisition Co LLC* ***(G-11269)***
Hemlock Smcndctor Oprtions LLC 989 642-5201
12334 Geddes Rd Hemlock (48626) ***(G-7463)***
Hemp Global Products Inc 616 617-6476
503 Essenburg Dr Holland (49424) ***(G-7661)***
Hengst of North America Inc 586 757-2995
29770 Hudson Dr Novi (48377) ***(G-11899)***
Henkel Loctite Corporation 787 264-7534
32100 Stephenson Hwy Madison Heights (48071) ***(G-10264)***
Henkel Surface Technologies, Madison Heights *Also called Henkel US Operations Corp* ***(G-10266)***
Henkel Surface Technologies 248 307-0240
31200 Stephenson Hwy Madison Heights (48071) ***(G-10265)***
Henkel US Operations Corp 586 759-5555
23343 Sherwood Ave Warren (48091) ***(G-17080)***

ALPHABETIC

Henkel US Operations Corp 248 588-1082
32100 Stephenson Hwy Madison Heights (48071) **(G-10266)**
Henniges Auto Holdings Inc (HQ) 248 340-4100
2750 High Meadow Cir Auburn Hills (48326) **(G-896)**
Henniges Auto Sling Systems N (HQ) 248 340-4100
2750 High Meadow Cir Auburn Hills (48326) **(G-897)**
Henniges Automotive N America (HQ) 248 340-4100
2750 High Meadow Cir Auburn Hills (48326) **(G-898)**
Hennigs Automobiles, Auburn Hills *Also called Henniges Auto Holdings Inc* **(G-896)**
Henrob Corporation (HQ) 248 493-3800
30000 S Hill Rd New Hudson (48165) **(G-11543)**
Henry Machine Shop 989 777-8495
1553 E Moore Rd Saginaw (48601) **(G-14056)**
Henry Plambeck 586 463-3410
40962 Production Dr Harrison Township (48045) **(G-7332)**
Henry Stephens Memorial Lib, Almont *Also called Elmont District Library* **(G-256)**
Henshaw Inc 586 752-0700
100 Shafer Dr Romeo (48065) **(G-13629)**
Hensley Mfg Inc 810 653-3226
1097 S State Rd Ste 3 Davison (48423) **(G-3653)**
Hensley Precision Carbide Inc 734 727-0810
8825 Nevada St Livonia (48150) **(G-9768)**
Hephaestus Holdings LLC (HQ) 248 479-2700
39475 W 13 Mile Rd # 105 Novi (48377) **(G-11900)**
Herald Bi-County Inc 517 448-2201
115 S Church St Hudson (49247) **(G-8129)**
Herald Newspapers Company Inc 269 345-3511
6825 Beatrice Dr Ste C Kalamazoo (49009) **(G-8764)**
Herald Newspapers Company Inc 231 722-3161
379 W Western Ave Ste 100 Muskegon (49440) **(G-11344)**
Herald Newspapers Company Inc 616 222-5400
3102 Walker Ridge Dr Nw Grand Rapids (49544) **(G-6506)**
Herald Newspapers Company Inc 734 926-4510
704 Airport Blvd Ste 6 Ann Arbor (48108) **(G-489)**
Herald Newspapers Company Inc 989 752-7171
540 S Saginaw St Apt 403 Flint (48502) **(G-5445)**
Herald Newspapers Company Inc 810 766-6100
540 S Saginaw St Ste 101 Flint (48502) **(G-5446)**
Herald Newspapers Company Inc 517 787-2300
1750 S Cooper St Jackson (49203) **(G-8464)**
Herald Newspapers Company Inc 734 834-6376
3102 Walker Ridge Dr Nw Grand Rapids (49544) **(G-6507)**
Herald Newspapers Company Inc 989 895-8551
540 S Saginaw St Ste 101 Flint (48502) **(G-5447)**
Herald Newspapers Company Inc 269 373-7100
423 S Burdick St Kalamazoo (49007) **(G-8765)**
Herald Newspapers Company Inc 269 388-8501
401 S Burdick St Kalamazoo (49007) **(G-8766)**
Herald Palladium, The, Saint Joseph *Also called Paxton Media Group LLC* **(G-14334)**
Herald Publishing Company 517 423-2174
110 E Logan St Tecumseh (49286) **(G-15797)**
Herald Publishing Company LLC 616 222-5400
169 Monroe Ave Nw Grand Rapids (49503) **(G-6508)**
Herald Publishing Company LLC (HQ) 616 222-5400
3102 Walker Ridge Dr Nw Walker (49544) **(G-16867)**
Hercules Drawn Steel Div, Livonia *Also called Eaton Steel Corporation* **(G-9719)**
Hercules LLC 269 388-8676
5325 Autumn Glen St Kalamazoo (49009) **(G-8767)**
Hercules Machine Tl & Die LLC 586 778-4120
33901 James J Pompo Dr Fraser (48026) **(G-5661)**
Hercules Welding Products, Novi *Also called Obara Corporation USA* **(G-11962)**
Herfert Chiropractic Software, Eastpointe *Also called Herfert Software* **(G-4703)**
Herfert Software 586 776-2880
15700 E 9 Mile Rd Eastpointe (48021) **(G-4703)**
Herff Jones LLC 810 632-6500
3556 Avon St Hartland (48353) **(G-7391)**
Heritage 734 414-0343
1405 Gold Smith Plymouth (48170) **(G-12638)**
Heritage Business Cards, Troy *Also called Utley Brothers Inc* **(G-16672)**
Heritage Forestry LLC 231 689-5721
3729 N Evergreen Dr White Cloud (49349) **(G-17624)**
Heritage Glass Inc 248 887-1010
672 N Milford Rd Ste 140 Highland (48357) **(G-7493)**
Heritage Guitar Inc 269 385-5721
225 Parsons St Ste 286 Kalamazoo (49007) **(G-8768)**
Heritage Hone & Gage Inc 248 926-8449
1155 Ladd Rd Wolverine Lake (48390) **(G-17936)**
Heritage Mfg Inc 586 949-7446
49787 Leona Dr Chesterfield (48051) **(G-2784)**
Heritage Newspaper, Belleville *Also called View Newspaper* **(G-1452)**
Heritage Newspapers 586 783-0300
28 W Huron St Pontiac (48342) **(G-12834)**
Heritage Press, Caro *Also called Tuscola County Advertiser Inc* **(G-2480)**
Heritage Resources Inc 616 554-9888
6490 68th St Se Caledonia (49316) **(G-2298)**
Heritage Services Company Inc 734 282-4566
18582 Jefferson Riverview (48193) **(G-13296)**
Herkules Equipment Corporation 248 960-7100
2760 Ridgeway Ct Commerce Township (48390) **(G-3411)**
Herman Hillbillies Farm LLC 906 201-0760
18194 Lahti Rd Lanse (49946) **(G-9192)**
Herman Hills Sugar Bush, Lanse *Also called Herman Hillbillies Farm LLC* **(G-9192)**
Herman Miller 616 296-3422
17170 Hickory St Spring Lake (49456) **(G-15151)**
Herman Miller Inc (PA) 616 654-3000
855 E Main Ave Zeeland (49464) **(G-18147)**
Herman Miller Inc 616 453-5995
2915 Stonewood St Nw Grand Rapids (49504) **(G-6509)**
Herman Miller Inc 616 846-0280
18558 171st Ave Spring Lake (49456) **(G-15152)**
Herman Miller Inc 616 654-7456
10201 Adams St Holland (49424) **(G-7662)**
Herman Miller Inc 616 654-3716
9000 Haggerty Rd Van Buren Twp (48111) **(G-16763)**
Herman Miller Inc 616 654-8078
10001 Adams St Holland (49424) **(G-7663)**
Hermans Boy 616 866-2900
220 Northland Dr Ne Rockford (49341) **(G-13571)**
Herrmann Aerospace 810 695-1758
5202 Moceri Ln Grand Blanc (48439) **(G-5969)**
Hess Asphalt Pav Sand Cnstr Co 810 984-4466
6330 Lapeer Rd Clyde (48049) **(G-3283)**
Hess Printing 734 285-4377
201 Elm St Apt A Wyandotte (48192) **(G-17960)**
Hestia Inc 231 747-8157
650 Airport Pl Norton Shores (49441) **(G-11760)**
Hewtech Electronics 810 765-0820
5691 Starville Rd China (48054) **(G-2860)**
Hexagon Enterprises Inc 248 583-0550
256 Minnesota Dr Troy (48083) **(G-16395)**
Hexagon Metrology Inc 248 662-1740
48443 Alpha Dr Ste 100 Wixom (48393) **(G-17826)**
Hexon Corporation 248 585-7585
26050 Orchard Lake Rd # 100 Farmington Hills (48334) **(G-5018)**
Heyboer Transformers Inc (PA) 616 842-5830
17382 Hayes St Grand Haven (49417) **(G-6036)**
Heys Fabrication and Mch Co 616 247-0065
3059 Hillcroft Ave Sw Wyoming (49548) **(G-18009)**
Hf, Madison Heights *Also called Howard Finishing LLC* **(G-10269)**
Hgc Westshore LLC 616 796-1218
3440 Windquest Dr Holland (49424) **(G-7664)**
Hgks Industrial Clay Tool Co I 734 340-5500
1911 Scenic Dr Canton (48188) **(G-2383)**
Hha, Troy *Also called Hanho America Co Ltd* **(G-16391)**
Hhi Forging LLC (HQ) 248 284-2900
2727 W 14 Mile Rd Royal Oak (48073) **(G-13932)**
Hhi Form Tech LLC 248 597-3800
2727 W 14 Mile Rd Royal Oak (48073) **(G-13933)**
Hhi Formtech LLC (HQ) 313 758-2000
1 Dauch Dr Detroit (48211) **(G-4121)**
Hhi Formtech LLC 586 415-2000
18450 15 Mile Rd Fraser (48026) **(G-5662)**
Hhi Formtech Holdings LLC (HQ) 313 758-2000
1 Dauch Dr Detroit (48211) **(G-4122)**
Hhi Formtech Industries LLC 248 597-3800
2727 W 14 Mile Rd Royal Oak (48073) **(G-13934)**
Hhi Funding II LLC 313 758-2000
1 Dauch Dr Detroit (48211) **(G-4123)**
Hhi Holdings LLC (HQ) 313 758-2000
1 Dauch Dr Detroit (48211) **(G-4124)**
Hhj Holdings Limited (PA) 248 652-9716
1957 Crooks Rd A Troy (48084) **(G-16396)**
Hhsi, Ann Arbor *Also called Hearing Health Science Inc* **(G-487)**
HI TEC Stainless Inc 269 543-4205
6790 124th Ave Fennville (49408) **(G-5174)**
HI Tech Gear Inc 248 548-8649
26020 Allor Ave Huntington Woods (48070) **(G-8188)**
HI Tech Mechanical Svcs LLC 734 847-1831
7070 Crabb Rd Temperance (48182) **(G-15831)**
Hi-Craft Engineering Inc 586 293-0551
33105 Kelly Rd Ste B Fraser (48026) **(G-5663)**
Hi-Lex, Litchfield *Also called Tsk of America Inc* **(G-9612)**
Hi-Lex America Incorporated (HQ) 269 968-0781
5200 Wayne Rd Battle Creek (49037) **(G-1198)**
Hi-Lex America Incorporated 248 844-0096
2911 Research Dr Rochester Hills (48309) **(G-13440)**
Hi-Lex America Incorporated 517 542-2955
152 Simpson Dr Litchfield (49252) **(G-9603)**
Hi-Lex Automotive Centre, Rochester Hills *Also called Hi-Lex America Incorporated* **(G-13440)**
HI-Lex Controls Incorporated 517 448-2752
15780 Steger Indus Dr Hudson (49247) **(G-8130)**
Hi-Lex Controls Incorporated (HQ) 517 542-2955
152 Simpson Dr Litchfield (49252) **(G-9604)**
Hi-Lites Graphic Inc (PA) 231 924-0630
1212 Locust St Fremont (49412) **(G-5775)**
HI-Lites Graphic Inc 231 924-4540
1003 W Main St Fremont (49412) **(G-5776)**

Hi-Lites Shoppers Guide, Fremont *Also called Hi-Lites Graphic Inc* ***(G-5775)***
Hi-Speed Business Forms Inc....269 927-3191
1586 Paw Paw Ave Benton Harbor (49022) ***(G-1509)***
Hi-Tech Coatings Inc (HQ)....586 759-3559
24600 Industrial Hwy Warren (48089) ***(G-17081)***
HI-Tech Flexible Products Inc....517 783-5911
2000 Townley St Jackson (49203) ***(G-8465)***
Hi-Tech Furnace Systems Inc....586 566-0600
13179 W Star Dr Shelby Township (48315) ***(G-14600)***
Hi-Tech Industries, Farmington *Also called Sam Brown Sales LLC* ***(G-4911)***
Hi-Tech Industries, Inc., Farmington *Also called Hti Usa Inc* ***(G-4900)***
Hi-Tech Mold & Engineering Inc....248 844-0722
1758 Northfield Dr Rochester Hills (48309) ***(G-13441)***
Hi-Tech Mold & Engineering Inc....248 844-9159
1744 Northfield Dr Rochester Hills (48309) ***(G-13442)***
Hi-Tech Mold & Engineering Inc (PA)....248 852-6600
2775 Commerce Dr Rochester Hills (48309) ***(G-13443)***
Hi-Tech Optical Inc....989 799-9390
3139 Christy Way S Saginaw (48603) ***(G-14057)***
Hi-Tech Plastics, Hudsonville *Also called Royal Technologies Corporation* ***(G-8178)***
Hi-Tech Steel Treating Inc....800 835-8294
2720 Roberts St Saginaw (48601) ***(G-14058)***
Hi-Trac Industries Inc....810 625-7193
5161 Harp Dr Linden (48451) ***(G-9592)***
Hiawatha Log Homes Inc....877 275-9090
M-28 East Munising (49862) ***(G-11244)***
Hibshman Screw Mch Pdts Inc....269 641-7525
69351 Union Rd S Union (49130) ***(G-16730)***
Hice and Summey Inc (PA)....269 651-6217
404 Union St Bronson (49028) ***(G-2029)***
Hice and Summey Inc....269 651-6217
404 Union St Bronson (49028) ***(G-2030)***
Hickory Creek Winery LLC....269 422-1100
750 Browntown Rd Buchanan (49107) ***(G-2120)***
Hicks Plastics Company Inc....586 786-5640
51308 Industrial Dr Macomb (48042) ***(G-10129)***
Hiden Analytical Inc....734 542-6666
37699 Schoolcraft Rd Livonia (48150) ***(G-9769)***
Hideout Brewing Company, The, Rockford *Also called MI Brew LLC* ***(G-13579)***
Hig Recovery Fund Inc....269 435-8414
485 Florence Rd Constantine (49042) ***(G-3537)***
Higgins Electric Sign Co....517 351-5255
4100 Hunsaker Dr Ste A East Lansing (48823) ***(G-4661)***
Higgins Printing Services LLC....734 414-6203
1058 S Main St Plymouth (48170) ***(G-12639)***
High Effcncy Pwr Solutions Inc....800 833-7094
11060 Hi Tech Dr Whitmore Lake (48189) ***(G-17702)***
High Grade Concrete Pdts Co, Muskegon *Also called M 37 Concrete Products Inc* ***(G-11371)***
High Grade Materials Company....616 554-8828
6869 E Paris Ave Se Caledonia (49316) ***(G-2299)***
High Grade Materials Company (PA)....616 754-5545
9266 Snows Lake Rd Greenville (48838) ***(G-7138)***
High Grade Materials Company....269 926-6900
1915 Yore Ave Benton Harbor (49022) ***(G-1510)***
High Grade Materials Company....269 349-8222
2700 E Cork St Kalamazoo (49001) ***(G-8769)***
High Grade Materials Company....616 677-1271
10561 Linden Dr Nw Grand Rapids (49534) ***(G-6510)***
High Grade Materials Company....517 374-1029
1800 Turner St Lansing (48906) ***(G-9235)***
High Grade Materials Company....989 584-6004
10101 E Carson City Rd Carson City (48811) ***(G-2491)***
High Grade Materials Company....989 365-3010
3261 W Fleck Rd Six Lakes (48886) ***(G-14740)***
High Grade Materials Company....616 696-9540
16180 Northland Dr Sand Lake (49343) ***(G-14423)***
High Impact Solutions Inc....248 473-9804
20793 Farmington Rd # 13 Farmington Hills (48336) ***(G-5019)***
High Prfmce Met Finshg Inc....269 327-8897
1821 Vanderbilt Ave Portage (49024) ***(G-13000)***
High Q Lighting Inc....616 396-3591
11439 E Lakewood Blvd Holland (49424) ***(G-7665)***
High Tech Insulators Inc....734 525-9030
34483 Glendale St Livonia (48150) ***(G-9770)***
High Touch Healthcare LLC....248 513-2425
29307 Douglas Dr Novi (48377) ***(G-11901)***
High-Po-Chlor Inc....734 942-1500
1181 Freesia Ct Ann Arbor (48105) ***(G-490)***
High-Star Corporation....734 743-1503
6171 Commerce Dr Westland (48185) ***(G-17569)***
High-Tech Inds of Holland....616 399-5430
3269 John F Donnelly Dr Holland (49424) ***(G-7666)***
High-Tech Industries, Holland *Also called Hti Associates LLC* ***(G-7682)***
Higher Ground, Saline *Also called Shaun Jackson Design Inc* ***(G-14415)***
Highland Engineering Inc....517 548-4372
1153 Grand Oaks Dr Howell (48843) ***(G-8048)***
Highland Industrial Inc....989 391-9992
3487 Highland Dr Bay City (48706) ***(G-1320)***
Highland Machine Design Inc....248 669-6150
3125 Old Farm Ln Commerce Township (48390) ***(G-3412)***
Highland Manufacturing Inc....248 585-8040
339 E Whitcomb Ave Madison Heights (48071) ***(G-10267)***
Highland Plastics Inc....989 828-4400
525 N 2nd St Shepherd (48883) ***(G-14728)***
Highland Supply Inc....248 714-8355
294 W Wardlow Rd Highland (48357) ***(G-7494)***
Highlander Graphics LLC....734 449-9733
75 Aprill Dr Ann Arbor (48103) ***(G-491)***
Highlight Industries Inc....616 531-2464
2694 Prairie St Sw Wyoming (49519) ***(G-18010)***
Highpoint Finshg Solutions Inc....616 772-4425
541 E Roosevelt Ave Zeeland (49464) ***(G-18148)***
Hightech Signs, Grand Rapids *Also called Castleton Village Center Inc* ***(G-6266)***
Highwood Die & Engineering Inc....248 338-1807
1353 Highwood Blvd Pontiac (48340) ***(G-12835)***
Hikking Production Embroidery, Ypsilanti *Also called Imagillation Inc* ***(G-18079)***
Hil-Man Automation LLC....616 741-9099
260 E Roosevelt Ave Zeeland (49464) ***(G-18149)***
Hilco Fixture Finders LLC....616 453-1300
1345 Monroe Ave Nw # 321 Grand Rapids (49505) ***(G-6511)***
Hilco Industrial Plastics LLC....616 323-1330
4999 36th St Se Grand Rapids (49512) ***(G-6512)***
Hilco Plastic Products Co....616 554-8833
3260 Hanna Lake Ind Park Caledonia (49316) ***(G-2300)***
Hilgraeve Inc....734 243-0576
115 E Elm Ave Monroe (48162) ***(G-11039)***
Hilite Industries Inc....248 475-4580
250 Kay Industrial Dr Lake Orion (48359) ***(G-9138)***
Hilite International Inc....231 894-3200
2001 Peach St Whitehall (49461) ***(G-17668)***
Hill Bros Orchards, Grand Rapids *Also called Hill Brothers* ***(G-6513)***
Hill Brothers....616 784-2767
6159 Peach Ridge Ave Nw Grand Rapids (49544) ***(G-6513)***
Hill Machinery Co....616 940-2800
4585 Danvers Dr Se Grand Rapids (49512) ***(G-6514)***
Hill Screw Machine Products....734 427-8237
8463 Hugh St Westland (48185) ***(G-17570)***
Hilljack Industries LLC....517 552-3874
3146 New Holland Dr Howell (48843) ***(G-8049)***
Hillman Extrusion Tool Inc....989 736-8010
425 W Traverse Bay Rd Lincoln (48742) ***(G-9563)***
Hills Crate Mill Inc....616 761-3555
3851 Hoyt Rd Belding (48809) ***(G-1417)***
Hills Manufacturing LLC....248 536-3307
26700 Haggerty Rd Farmington Hills (48331) ***(G-5020)***
Hills-Mccanna LLC....616 554-9308
4855 Broadmoor Ave Se Kentwood (49512) ***(G-9011)***
Hillsdale Daily News, Hillsdale *Also called Morris Communications Co LLC* ***(G-7532)***
Hillsdale Pallet LLC....517 254-4777
1242 E Montgomery Rd Hillsdale (49242) ***(G-7527)***
Hillsdale Sand and Gravel, Waldron *Also called Gerken Materials Inc* ***(G-16858)***
Hillsdale Terminal, Hillsdale *Also called Frank Condon Inc* ***(G-7525)***
Hillshire Brands Company....616 875-8131
8300 96th Ave Zeeland (49464) ***(G-18150)***
Hillshire Brands Company....231 947-2100
2314 Sybrant Rd Traverse City (49684) ***(G-15997)***
Hillside Creations LLC....269 496-7041
58267 Walterspaugh Rd Mendon (49072) ***(G-10713)***
Hillside Finsihing, Belding *Also called West Mich Auto Stl & Engrg Inc* ***(G-1431)***
Hillside Pallets....231 824-3761
4093 N 35 Rd Manton (49663) ***(G-10455)***
Hilltop Manufacturing Co Inc....248 437-2530
56849 Rice St New Hudson (48165) ***(G-11544)***
Hilton Screeners Inc....810 653-0711
210 N Main St Davison (48423) ***(G-3654)***
Hincka Logging LLC....989 766-8893
6464 Lake Augusta Hwy Posen (49776) ***(G-13069)***
Hines Corporation (PA)....231 799-6240
1218 E Pontaluna Rd Ste B Norton Shores (49456) ***(G-11812)***
Hines Industries Inc (PA)....734 769-2300
240 Metty Dr Ste A Ann Arbor (48103) ***(G-492)***
Hirose Electric USA Inc....734 542-9963
37727 Prof Ctr Dr 100c Livonia (48154) ***(G-9771)***
Hirotec America Inc (HQ)....248 836-5100
3000 High Meadow Cir Auburn Hills (48326) ***(G-899)***
Hirschmann Auto N Amer LLC....248 495-2677
2927 Waterview Dr Rochester Hills (48309) ***(G-13444)***
Hirschmann Car Comm Inc....248 373-7150
1183 Centre Rd Auburn Hills (48326) ***(G-900)***
Hirschmann Electronics, Auburn Hills *Also called Hirschmann Car Comm Inc* ***(G-900)***
His & Her Self Defense....248 767-9085
1945 Lone Pine Rd Bloomfield Hills (48302) ***(G-1773)***
His Stamping Division, Manchester *Also called American Engnred Cmponents Inc* ***(G-10402)***
Hispanic Visions, Saginaw *Also called Verdoni Productions Inc* ***(G-14179)***
Histosonics Inc....734 926-4630
3526 W Liberty Rd Ste 100 Ann Arbor (48103) ***(G-493)***

ALPHABETIC

Hitachi America Ltd ... 248 477-5400
34500 Grand River Ave Farmington Hills (48335) *(G-5021)*
Hite Tool Co Inc ... 734 422-1777
32127 Block St Ste 200 Garden City (48135) *(G-5826)*
Hitec Sensor Developments Inc ... 313 506-2460
47460 Galleon Dr Plymouth (48170) *(G-12640)*
Hj Manufacturing Inc ... 906 233-1500
3707 19th Ave N Escanaba (49829) *(G-4833)*
HL Manufacturing Inc ... 586 731-2800
45399 Utica Park Blvd Utica (48315) *(G-16742)*
Hl Outdoors ... 989 422-3264
308 Huron St Houghton Lake (48629) *(G-7992)*
Hme Inc ... 616 534-1463
1950 Byron Center Ave Sw Wyoming (49519) *(G-18011)*
Hme Silverfox, Wyoming Also called Hme Inc *(G-18011)*
Hmg Agency ... 989 443-3819
4352 Bay Rd Ste 131 Saginaw (48603) *(G-14059)*
Hmi, Rives Junction Also called Hacker Machine Inc *(G-13308)*
Hmi Hardwoods LLC ... 517 456-7431
430 Division St Clinton (49236) *(G-3023)*
Hmi Liquidating Company Inc ... 616 654-5055
855 E Main Ave Zeeland (49464) *(G-18151)*
Hmr Fabrication Unlimited Inc ... 586 569-4288
33830 Riviera Fraser (48026) *(G-5664)*
HMS Mfg Co (PA) ... 248 689-3232
1230 E Big Beaver Rd Troy (48083) *(G-16397)*
HMS Products Co ... 248 689-8120
1200 E Big Beaver Rd Troy (48083) *(G-16398)*
Hmw Contracting LLC ... 313 531-8477
12855 Burt Rd Detroit (48223) *(G-4125)*
Hoag & Sons Book Bindery Inc ... 517 857-2033
145 N Main St Eaton Rapids (48827) *(G-4726)*
Hobart Brothers Company ... 231 933-1234
1631 International Dr Traverse City (49686) *(G-15998)*
Hobe Inc ... 231 845-5196
605 S Pere Marquette Hwy Ludington (49431) *(G-10065)*
Hoby's Sewer Cleaning, Bentley Also called Hobys Contracting *(G-1477)*
Hobys Contracting ... 989 631-4263
2463 Whitefeather Rd Bentley (48613) *(G-1477)*
Hochstetler Sawmill ... 269 467-7018
24700 Walters Rd Centreville (49032) *(G-2595)*
Hockey Weekly, Farmington Also called Castine Communications Inc *(G-4895)*
Hodges & Irvine Inc ... 810 329-4787
1900 Sinclair St Saint Clair (48079) *(G-14222)*
Hodgkiss & Douma, Charlevoix Also called Bdk Group Northern Mich Inc *(G-2609)*
Hoechst Celanese Corp, Auburn Hills Also called Cleanese Americas LLC *(G-814)*
Hoff Engineering Co Inc (PA) ... 248 969-8272
475 S Glaspie St Oxford (48371) *(G-12349)*
Hoffmann Die Cast LLC ... 269 983-1102
229 Kerth St Saint Joseph (49085) *(G-14317)*
Hoffmann Filter Corporation (PA) ... 248 486-8430
7627 Kensington Ct Brighton (48116) *(G-1939)*
Hogle Sales & Mfg LLC ... 517 592-1980
208 Irwin St Brooklyn (49230) *(G-2038)*
Holbrook Racing Engines ... 734 762-4315
31831 Schoolcraft Rd Livonia (48150) *(G-9772)*
Holcim (us) Inc ... 734 529-2411
6211 N Ann Arbor Rd Dundee (48131) *(G-4587)*
Holcim (us) Inc ... 734 529-4600
15215 Day Rd Dundee (48131) *(G-4588)*
Holcim (us) Inc ... 989 755-7515
900 N Adams St Saginaw (48604) *(G-14060)*
Hold It Products Corporation ... 248 624-1195
1900 Easy St Commerce Township (48390) *(G-3413)*
Hold-It Inc ... 810 984-4213
2301 16th St Port Huron (48060) *(G-12925)*
Holder Corporation ... 517 484-5453
2538 W Main St Lansing (48917) *(G-9292)*
Hole Chief, Schoolcraft Also called New Concept Products Inc *(G-14500)*
Hole Industries Incorporated ... 517 548-4229
600 Chukker Cv Howell (48843) *(G-8050)*
Holiday Distributing Co ... 517 782-7146
3990 Francis St Jackson (49203) *(G-8466)*
Holland Alloys Inc ... 616 396-6444
534 Chicago Dr Holland (49423) *(G-7667)*
Holland Automotive Machine, Holland Also called Daniel Pruitoff *(G-7605)*
Holland Awning Co (PA) ... 616 772-2052
10875 Chicago Dr Zeeland (49464) *(G-18152)*
Holland Bar Stool Company ... 616 399-5530
12839 Corporate Circle Pl Holland (49424) *(G-7668)*
Holland Bedding, Holland Also called Spine Align Inc *(G-7812)*
Holland Bowl Mill ... 616 396-6513
120 James St Holland (49424) *(G-7669)*
Holland Community Hosp Aux Inc ... 616 355-3926
854 Wshington Ave Ste 330 Holland (49423) *(G-7670)*
Holland Electric Motor Co ... 616 392-1115
11598 E Lakewood Blvd B Holland (49424) *(G-7671)*
Holland Honey Cake Co., Holland Also called Holland Bar Stool Company *(G-7668)*

Holland House Candles Inc (PA) ... 800 238-8467
16656 Riley St Holland (49424) *(G-7672)*
Holland Litho Printing Service, Zeeland Also called Holland Litho Service Inc *(G-18153)*
Holland Litho Service Inc ... 616 392-4644
10972 Chicago Dr Zeeland (49464) *(G-18153)*
Holland Pallet Repair Inc ... 616 875-8642
13370 Barry St Ste A Holland (49424) *(G-7673)*
Holland Panel Products Inc ... 616 392-1826
615 E 40th St Holland (49423) *(G-7674)*
Holland Pattern Co (PA) ... 616 396-6348
534 Chicago Dr Holland (49423) *(G-7675)*
Holland Plastics Corporation (PA) ... 616 844-2505
14000 172nd Ave Grand Haven (49417) *(G-6037)*
Holland Pmsc, Holland Also called Yanfeng US Automotive *(G-7863)*
Holland Printing Center Inc (PA) ... 616 786-3101
4314 136th Ave Ste 100 Holland (49424) *(G-7676)*
Holland Screen Print Inc ... 616 396-7630
4665 44th St Holland (49423) *(G-7677)*
Holland Sentinel, Holland Also called Morris Communications Co LLC *(G-7748)*
Holland Stitchcraft Inc ... 616 399-3868
13163 Reflections Dr Holland (49424) *(G-7678)*
Holland Tool & Die LLC ... 269 751-5862
4472 48th St Holland (49423) *(G-7679)*
Holland Transplanter Co Inc ... 616 392-3579
510 E 16th St Holland (49423) *(G-7680)*
Hollander Machine Co Inc ... 810 742-1660
G3333 S Dort Hwy Burton (48529) *(G-2156)*
Holli Forest Products ... 906 486-9352
900 Cooper Lake Rd Ishpeming (49849) *(G-8346)*
Hollingsworth Container LLC ... 313 768-1400
14225 W Warren Ave Dearborn (48126) *(G-3720)*
Hollis Sewer & Plumbing Svc ... 517 263-8151
311 E Hunt St Adrian (49221) *(G-67)*
Hollow Metal Services LLC ... 248 394-0233
5311 Whipple Lake Rd Clarkston (48348) *(G-2926)*
Holloway Equipment Co Inc ... 810 748-9577
4856 Middle Channel Dr Harsens Island (48028) *(G-7369)*
Holloway Fur Dressing ... 231 258-5200
3590 W Sanborn Rd Lake City (49651) *(G-9088)*
Holly Plating Co Inc ... 810 714-9213
1101 Copper Ave Fenton (48430) *(G-5220)*
Holly Sand & Gravel, Davisburg Also called Falcon Trucking Company *(G-3633)*
Holmquist Feed Mill ... 906 446-3325
232 N Main St Trenary (49891) *(G-16151)*
Holo-Source Corporation ... 734 427-1530
12280 Hubbard St Livonia (48150) *(G-9773)*
Holsinger Manufacturing Corp ... 989 684-3101
2922 S Huron Rd Kawkawlin (48631) *(G-8972)*
Holt Products Company ... 517 699-2111
4200 Legion Dr Holt (48842) *(G-7912)*
Homag Machinery North Amer Inc ... 616 254-8181
4577 Patterson Ave Se Grand Rapids (49512) *(G-6515)*
Home & Garden Concepts, Bloomfield Hills Also called Delorean Associates Inc *(G-1757)*
Home Bakery ... 248 651-4830
300 S Main St Rochester (48307) *(G-13326)*
Home City Ice Company ... 269 926-2490
2875 S Pipestone Rd Sodus (49126) *(G-14745)*
Home City Ice Company ... 734 955-9094
15475 Oakwood Dr Romulus (48174) *(G-13685)*
Home Elements, Traverse City Also called Candle Factory Grand Traverse *(G-15929)*
Home Niches Inc ... 734 330-9189
2777 Mystic Dr Ann Arbor (48103) *(G-494)*
Home Shop ... 517 543-5325
406 E Broadway Hwy Charlotte (48813) *(G-2654)*
Home Style Co ... 989 871-3654
8400 Caine Rd Millington (48746) *(G-10996)*
Home Style Foods Inc ... 313 874-3250
5163 Edwin St Detroit (48212) *(G-4126)*
Homedics, Commerce Township Also called Fka Distributing Co LLC *(G-3406)*
Homedics Group Canada, Commerce Township Also called Homedics Usa LLC *(G-3414)*
Homedics Usa LLC (HQ) ... 248 863-3000
3000 N Pontiac Trl Commerce Township (48390) *(G-3414)*
Homer Concrete Products, Imlay City Also called Imlay City Concrete Inc *(G-8203)*
Homer Index ... 517 568-4646
122 E Main St Homer (49245) *(G-7944)*
Homes For Sale, Pontiac Also called 21st Century Newspapers Inc *(G-12797)*
Homespun Furniture Inc ... 734 284-6277
18540 Fort St Riverview (48193) *(G-13297)*
Homestead Foundry, Coleman Also called Homestead Tool and Machine *(G-3344)*
Homestead Graphics Design Inc ... 906 353-6741
516 S Superior Ave Baraga (49908) *(G-1103)*
Homestead Products Inc ... 989 465-6182
2618 Coolidge Rd Coleman (48618) *(G-3343)*
Homestead Tool and Machine ... 989 465-6182
2618 Coolidge Rd Coleman (48618) *(G-3344)*
Hometown America LLC ... 810 686-7020
2197 E Mount Morris Rd Mount Morris (48458) *(G-11162)*
Hometown Publishing Inc ... 989 834-2264
200 S Main St Ovid (48866) *(G-12272)*

Hommel Movomatic, Rochester Hills *Also called Jenoptik Automotive N Amer LLC* ***(G-13453)***
Honee Bear Canning Co, Lawton *Also called Packers Canning Co Inc* ***(G-9513)***
Honey Tree..........734 697-1000
9624 Belleville Rd Van Buren Twp (48111) ***(G-16764)***
Honeywell Authorized Dealer, Marquette *Also called Duquaine Incorporated* ***(G-10527)***
Honeywell Authorized Dealer, Battle Creek *Also called Cse Morse Inc* ***(G-1170)***
Honeywell Authorized Dealer, Temperance *Also called HI Tech Mechanical Svcs LLC* ***(G-15831)***
Honeywell Authorized Dealer, Kalamazoo *Also called Kalamazoo Mechanical Inc* ***(G-8790)***
Honeywell Authorized Dealer, Livonia *Also called Kelley Brothers Lc* ***(G-9795)***
Honeywell Authorized Dealer, Grand Rapids *Also called Clear Advantage Mechanical* ***(G-6279)***
Honeywell Authorized Dealer, Howell *Also called Tomtek Hvac Inc* ***(G-8113)***
Honeywell International Inc..........248 926-4800
49116 Wixom Tech Dr Wixom (48393) ***(G-17827)***
Honeywell International Inc..........989 792-8707
5153 Hampton Pl Saginaw (48604) ***(G-14061)***
Honeywell International Inc..........231 582-5686
375 N Lake St Boyne City (49712) ***(G-1822)***
Honeywell International Inc..........586 777-7870
31807 Utica Rd Fraser (48026) ***(G-5665)***
Honeywell International Inc..........248 827-6460
20500 Ste 4004 Southfield (48076) ***(G-14937)***
Honeywell International Inc..........734 392-5501
47548 Halyard Dr Plymouth (48170) ***(G-12641)***
Honhart Mid-Nite Black Co..........248 588-1515
501 Stephenson Hwy Troy (48083) ***(G-16399)***
Hoosier Tank and Manufacturing..........269 683-2550
2190 Industrial Dr Niles (49120) ***(G-11616)***
Hoover Precision Products, Sault Sainte Marie *Also called TN Michigan LLC* ***(G-14476)***
Hoover Treated Wood Pdts Inc..........313 365-4200
7500 E Davison St Detroit (48212) ***(G-4127)***
Hoover Universal Inc (HQ)..........734 454-0994
49200 Halyard Dr Plymouth (48170) ***(G-12642)***
Hope Focus..........313 494-4500
1200 Oakman Blvd Detroit (48238) ***(G-4128)***
Hope Focus (PA)..........313 494-5500
1355 Oakman Blvd Detroit (48238) ***(G-4129)***
Hope Focus Companies Inc (HQ)..........313 494-5500
1200 Oakman Blvd Detroit (48238) ***(G-4130)***
Hope Global of Detroit, Detroit *Also called Rtlf-Hope LLC* ***(G-4349)***
Hope Network West Michigan..........231 775-3425
1610 Corwin St Cadillac (49601) ***(G-2252)***
Hope Network West Michigan..........231 796-4801
21685 Northland Dr Paris (49338) ***(G-12385)***
Hopeful Harvest Foods Inc..........248 967-1500
21800 Greenfield Rd Oak Park (48237) ***(G-12073)***
Horak Company, The, Bay City *Also called F P Horak Company* ***(G-1312)***
Horiba Instruments Inc..........734 213-6555
5900 Hines Dr Ann Arbor (48108) ***(G-495)***
Horiba Instruments Inc..........248 689-9000
2890 John R Rd Troy (48083) ***(G-16400)***
Horizon Bros Painting Corp..........810 632-3362
1053 Kendra Ln Howell (48843) ***(G-8051)***
Horizon Global Americas, Plymouth *Also called Cequent Uk Ltd* ***(G-12595)***
Horizon Global Americas Inc (HQ)..........734 656-3000
47912 Halyard Dr Ste 100 Plymouth (48170) ***(G-12643)***
Horizon Global Corporation (PA)..........248 593-8820
2600 W Big Beaver Rd # 555 Troy (48084) ***(G-16401)***
Horizon Intl Group LLC..........734 341-9336
1411 Westboro Birmingham (48009) ***(G-1686)***
Hormel Foods Corporation..........616 454-0418
801 Broadway Ave Nw Grand Rapids (49504) ***(G-6516)***
Horn Corp..........248 358-8883
2169 Corlett Rd Brighton (48114) ***(G-1940)***
Horn Corporation..........248 583-7789
1263 Rochester Rd Troy (48083) ***(G-16402)***
Horner Flooring Company Inc..........906 482-1180
23400 Hellman Ave Dollar Bay (49922) ***(G-4521)***
Hornet Manufacturing Inc..........517 448-8203
14587 Day Rd Hudson (49247) ***(G-8131)***
Horstman Inc..........586 737-2100
44215 Phoenix Dr Sterling Heights (48314) ***(G-15368)***
Hosco Inc (PA)..........248 912-1750
28026 Oakland Oaks Ct Wixom (48393) ***(G-17828)***
Hosco Fittings LLC..........248 912-1750
28026 Oakland Oaks Ct Wixom (48393) ***(G-17829)***
Hose Products Division, Mason *Also called Parker-Hannifin Corporation* ***(G-10651)***
Hosford & Co Inc..........734 769-5660
1204 N Main St Ann Arbor (48104) ***(G-496)***
Hospital Curtain Solutions Inc..........248 293-9785
2285 Star Ct Rochester Hills (48309) ***(G-13445)***
Hostess Cake ITT Contntl Bkg..........231 775-4629
838 N Mitchell St Cadillac (49601) ***(G-2253)***
Hot Melt Technologies Inc..........248 853-2011
1723 W Hamlin Rd Rochester Hills (48309) ***(G-13446)***
Hot Powder Coating, Saint Charles *Also called Kelly Industrial Service Corp* ***(G-14194)***
Hot Tool Cutter Grinding Co..........586 790-4867
33545 Groesbeck Hwy Fraser (48026) ***(G-5666)***
Hot Tubs, Lansing *Also called Hotwater Works Inc* ***(G-9382)***
Hot Wheels City Inc (PA)..........248 589-8800
32451 Dequindre Rd Madison Heights (48071) ***(G-10268)***
Hotwater Works Inc (PA)..........517 364-8827
2116 E Michigan Ave Lansing (48912) ***(G-9382)***
Hougen Manufacturing Inc..........810 635-7111
3001 Hougen Dr Swartz Creek (48473) ***(G-15667)***
Houghton International Inc..........313 273-7374
9100 Freeland St Detroit (48228) ***(G-4131)***
Houghton International Inc..........248 641-3231
17177 N Laurel Park Dr # 212 Livonia (48152) ***(G-9774)***
Houghton Lake Resorter Inc..........989 366-5341
4049 W Houghton Lake Dr Houghton Lake (48629) ***(G-7993)***
Hour Detroit Magazine, Troy *Also called Hour Media LLC* ***(G-16403)***
Hour Media LLC (PA)..........248 691-1800
5750 New King Dr Ste 100 Troy (48098) ***(G-16403)***
House of Flavors Inc (HQ)..........231 845-7369
110 N William St Ludington (49431) ***(G-10066)***
House of Hero LLC..........248 260-8300
7335 Deep Run Apt 513 Bloomfield Hills (48301) ***(G-1774)***
House of Marley LLC..........248 863-3000
3000 N Pontiac Trl Commerce Township (48390) ***(G-3415)***
House of Marley Canada, Commerce Township *Also called House of Marley LLC* ***(G-3415)***
Houseart LLC..........248 651-8124
386 South St Rochester (48307) ***(G-13327)***
Houseparty..........616 422-1226
6 Bellwood Dr Holland (49423) ***(G-7681)***
Housey Phrm RES Labs LLC..........248 663-7000
16800 W 12 Mile Rd Southfield (48076) ***(G-14938)***
Housler Sawmill Inc..........231 824-6353
222 E 16 Rd Mesick (49668) ***(G-10770)***
Hovertechnics LLC..........269 461-3934
1520 Townline Rd Bldg A Benton Harbor (49022) ***(G-1511)***
Howa USA Holdings Inc (HQ)..........248 715-4000
40220 Grand River Ave Novi (48375) ***(G-11902)***
Howard Energy Co Inc (PA)..........231 995-7850
125 S Park St Ste 250 Traverse City (49684) ***(G-15999)***
Howard Finishing LLC..........586 777-0070
15765 Sturgeon St Roseville (48066) ***(G-13816)***
Howard Finishing LLC (PA)..........248 588-9050
32565 Dequindre Rd Madison Heights (48071) ***(G-10269)***
Howard Miller Clock Company, Zeeland *Also called Howard Miller Company* ***(G-18154)***
Howard Miller Company (PA)..........616 772-9131
860 E Main Ave Zeeland (49464) ***(G-18154)***
Howard Structural Steel Inc..........989 752-3000
807 Veterans Mem Pkwy Saginaw (48601) ***(G-14062)***
Howden North America Inc..........313 931-4000
8111 Tireman Ave Dearborn (48126) ***(G-3721)***
Howe Racing Enterprises Inc..........989 435-7080
3195 Lyle Rd Beaverton (48612) ***(G-1385)***
Howe US Inc..........616 419-2226
401 Hall St Sw Ste 230 Grand Rapids (49503) ***(G-6517)***
Howell Engine Developments Inc..........810 765-5100
6201 Industrial Way Cottrellville (48039) ***(G-3587)***
Howell Machine Products Inc..........517 546-0580
6265 Grand River Rd # 100 Brighton (48114) ***(G-1941)***
Howell Tool Service Inc..........517 548-1114
5818 Sterling Dr Howell (48843) ***(G-8052)***
Howells Mainstreet Winery..........517 545-9463
201 W Grand River Ave Howell (48843) ***(G-8053)***
Howes Custom Counter Tops..........989 498-4044
3270 Bay Rd Saginaw (48603) ***(G-14063)***
Howey Tree Baler Corporation..........231 328-4321
6069 E Gaukel Rd Merritt (49667) ***(G-10763)***
Howmedica Osteonics Corp..........269 389-8959
1901 Romence Road Pkwy Portage (49002) ***(G-13001)***
Howmet Corporation (HQ)..........231 894-5686
1 Misco Dr Whitehall (49461) ***(G-17669)***
Howmet Corporation..........231 894-7183
555 Benston Rd Whitehall (49461) ***(G-17670)***
Howmet Corporation..........231 894-7290
1500 Warner St Whitehall (49461) ***(G-17671)***
Howmet Corporation..........231 981-3269
1600 Warner St Whitehall (49461) ***(G-17672)***
Howmet Corporation..........231 981-3000
3850 White Lake Dr Whitehall (49461) ***(G-17673)***
Howmet Corporation..........231 894-5686
555 Benston Rd Whitehall (49461) ***(G-17674)***
Howmet Corporation..........231 894-5686
1 Misco Dr Whitehall (49461) ***(G-17675)***
Howmet Holdings Corporation (HQ)..........231 894-5686
1 Misco Dr Whitehall (49461) ***(G-17676)***
HP Inc..........650 857-1501
7335 Westshire Dr Ste 101 Lansing (48917) ***(G-9293)***
HP Inc..........248 614-6600
560 Kirts Blvd Ste 120 Troy (48084) ***(G-16404)***
HP Pelzer Auto Systems Inc (HQ)..........248 280-1010
1175 Crooks Rd Troy (48084) ***(G-16405)***

ALPHABETIC

HP Pelzer Auto Systems Inc …………………………………………… 810 987-4444
　2415 Dove St　Port Huron　(48060)　*(G-12926)*
HP Pelzer Automotive Systems …………………………………… 810 987-0725
　2630 Dove St　Port Huron　(48060)　*(G-12927)*
Hpc Holdings Inc (PA) ………………………………………………… 248 634-9361
　111 Rosette St　Holly　(48442)　*(G-7883)*
Hpi Products Inc ………………………………………………………… 248 773-7460
　640 Griswold St Ste 200　Northville　(48167)　*(G-11698)*
HPS Fabrications Inc …………………………………………………… 734 282-2285
　4410 13th St　Wyandotte　(48192)　*(G-17961)*
HQT Inc …………………………………………………………………… 248 589-7960
　324 E Mandoline Ave　Madison Heights　(48071)　*(G-10270)*
HR Technologies Inc …………………………………………………… 248 284-1170
　32500 N Avis Dr　Madison Heights　(48071)　*(G-10271)*
HRF Exploration & Prod LLC ………………………………………… 989 732-6950
　990 S Wisconsin Ave　Gaylord　(49735)　*(G-5865)*
Hrsflow, Byron Center *Also called Inglass Usa Inc (G-2195)*
HSP Epi Acquisition LLC (PA) ……………………………………… 248 404-1520
　1401 Crooks Rd Ste 150　Troy　(48084)　*(G-16406)*
Hss Industries Inc ……………………………………………………… 231 946-6101
　2464 Cass Rd　Traverse City　(49684)　*(G-16000)*
Ht Computing Services ……………………………………………… 313 563-0087
　23253 Edward St　Dearborn　(48128)　*(G-3722)*
Htc Products, Ira *Also called Htc Sales Corporation (G-8257)*
Htc Sales Corporation ………………………………………………… 800 624-2027
　6560 Bethuy Rd　Ira　(48023)　*(G-8257)*
Htc Tops All Clamps, Redford *Also called Tops All Clamps Inc (G-13202)*
Hti Associates LLC ……………………………………………………… 616 399-5430
　3269 John F Donnelly Dr　Holland　(49424)　*(G-7682)*
Hti Cybernetics Inc (PA) ……………………………………………… 586 826-8346
　6701 Center Dr　Sterling Heights　(48312)　*(G-15369)*
Hti Usa Inc ……………………………………………………………… 248 358-5533
　33106 W 8 Mile Rd　Farmington　(48336)　*(G-4900)*
Httm LLC ………………………………………………………………… 616 820-2500
　300 E 48th St　Holland　(49423)　*(G-7683)*
Hub Tool and Machine Inc …………………………………………… 586 772-7866
　53770 Hubs Ln　Chesterfield　(48051)　*(G-2785)*
Hubble Enterprises Inc ……………………………………………… 616 676-4485
　7807 Ashwood Dr Se　Ada　(49301)　*(G-18)*
Hubert Group, Fraser *Also called Sharp Die & Mold Co (G-5724)*
Hubscher & Son Inc (PA) ……………………………………………… 989 773-5369
　1101 N Franklin Ave　Mount Pleasant　(48858)　*(G-11196)*
Hubscher & Son Inc …………………………………………………… 989 875-2151
　8189 W Washington Rd　Sumner　(48889)　*(G-15642)*
Hudson Industries Inc ………………………………………………… 800 459-1077
　24623 Ryan Rd　Warren　(48091)　*(G-17082)*
Hudson Post Gazette ………………………………………………… 517 448-2611
　113 S Market St　Hudson　(49247)　*(G-8132)*
Hudsonville Products LLC …………………………………………… 616 836-1904
　1735 Elizabeth Ave Nw　Grand Rapids　(49504)　*(G-6518)*
Hudsonvlle Crmry Ice Cream LLC …………………………………… 616 546-4005
　345 E 48th St Ste 200　Holland　(49423)　*(G-7684)*
Huebner E W & Son Mfg Co Inc …………………………………… 734 427-2600
　12871 Farmington Rd　Livonia　(48150)　*(G-9775)*
Huf North America Automoti ………………………………………… 248 213-4605
　24860 Hathaway St　Farmington Hills　(48335)　*(G-5022)*
Huff Machine & Tool Co Inc ………………………………………… 231 734-3291
　5469 85th Ave　Evart　(49631)　*(G-4882)*
Hug-A-Plug Inc ………………………………………………………… 810 626-1224
　2332 Pine Hollow Trl　Brighton　(48114)　*(G-1942)*
Hughes Electronics Pdts Corp (PA) ………………………………… 734 427-8310
　34467 Industrial Rd　Livonia　(48150)　*(G-9776)*
Hugo Brothers Pallet Mfg …………………………………………… 989 684-5564
　2474 River Rd　Kawkawlin　(48631)　*(G-8973)*
Huhnseal USA Inc ……………………………………………………… 248 347-0606
　41650 Gardenbrook Rd　Novi　(48375)　*(G-11903)*
Huhtamaki Inc …………………………………………………………… 989 465-9046
　5700 W Shaffer Rd　Coleman　(48618)　*(G-3345)*
Huhtamaki Inc …………………………………………………………… 989 633-8900
　5760 W Shaffer Rd　Coleman　(48618)　*(G-3346)*
Huhtamaki Plastics, Coleman *Also called Huhtamaki Inc (G-3346)*
Huizenga & Sons Inc …………………………………………………… 616 772-6241
　10075 Gordon St　Zeeland　(49464)　*(G-18155)*
Huizenga Gravel Company Inc (PA) ……………………………… 616 772-6241
　10075 Gordon St　Zeeland　(49464)　*(G-18156)*
Huizenga Gravel Company Inc ……………………………………… 616 457-1030
　1861 Filmore St　Jenison　(49428)　*(G-8629)*
Huizenga Redi-Mix, Zeeland *Also called Huizenga & Sons Inc (G-18155)*
Hulet Body Co Inc ……………………………………………………… 313 931-6000
　19700 Meadowbrook Rd　Northville　(48167)　*(G-11699)*
Human Synergistics Inc ……………………………………………… 734 459-1030
　39819 Plymouth Rd　Plymouth　(48170)　*(G-12644)*
Humantics Innvtive Sltions Inc (PA) ………………………………… 734 451-7878
　23300 Haggerty Rd　Farmington Hills　(48335)　*(G-5023)*
Humphrey Companies LLC (PA) …………………………………… 616 530-1717
　2851 Prairie St Sw　Grandville　(49418)　*(G-7048)*
Humphrey Products Company (PA) ………………………………… 269 381-5500
　5070 E N Ave　Kalamazoo　(49048)　*(G-8770)*
Hunderman & Sons Redi-Mix Inc …………………………………… 616 453-5999
　1050 Maynard Ave Sw　Walker　(49534)　*(G-16868)*

Hunt Hoppough Custom Crafted …………………………………… 616 794-3455
　700 Reed St　Belding　(48809)　*(G-1418)*
Huntington Foam LLC ………………………………………………… 661 225-9951
　1323 Moore St　Greenville　(48838)　*(G-7139)*
Huntler Industries Inc ………………………………………………… 586 566-7684
　51532 Schoenherr Rd　Shelby Township　(48315)　*(G-14601)*
Huntsman Advanced Materials AM ………………………………… 517 351-5900
　4917 Dawn Ave　East Lansing　(48823)　*(G-4662)*
Huntsman Corporation ………………………………………………… 248 322-8682
　2190 Exec Dr Blvd　Auburn Hills　(48326)　*(G-901)*
Huntsman Polyurethanes, Auburn Hills *Also called Huntsman-Cooper LLC (G-902)*
Huntsman-Cooper LLC ………………………………………………… 248 322-7300
　2190 Executive Hills Dr　Auburn Hills　(48326)　*(G-902)*
Hurless Machine Shop Inc …………………………………………… 269 945-9362
　2450 Lower Lake Rd　Hastings　(49058)　*(G-7414)*
Hurley Marine Inc ……………………………………………………… 906 553-6249
　2717 N Lincoln Rd　Escanaba　(49829)　*(G-4834)*
Huron Advertising Company Inc …………………………………… 734 483-2000
　663 S Mansfield St　Ypsilanti　(48197)　*(G-18077)*
Huron Casting Inc (PA) ………………………………………………… 989 453-3933
　7050 Hartley St　Pigeon　(48755)　*(G-12491)*
Huron Daily Tribune, The, Bad Axe *Also called Huron Publishing Company Inc (G-1067)*
Huron Inc (HQ) …………………………………………………………… 810 359-5344
　6554 Lakeshore Rd　Lexington　(48450)　*(G-9558)*
Huron Industries Inc …………………………………………………… 810 984-4213
　2301 16th St　Port Huron　(48060)　*(G-12928)*
Huron Publishing Company Inc (HQ) ……………………………… 989 269-6461
　211 N Heisterman St　Bad Axe　(48413)　*(G-1067)*
Huron Quality Mfg Inc ………………………………………………… 989 736-8121
　481 State St　Lincoln　(48742)　*(G-9564)*
Huron Sign Co, Ypsilanti *Also called Huron Advertising Company Inc (G-18077)*
Huron Tool & Engineering Co (HQ) ………………………………… 989 269-9927
　635 Liberty St　Bad Axe　(48413)　*(G-1068)*
Huron Tool & Gage Co Inc …………………………………………… 313 381-1900
　28005 Oakland Oaks Ct　Wixom　(48393)　*(G-17830)*
Huron Township Plant, New Boston *Also called Plastic Ominium Auto Inergy (G-11508)*
Huron Valley Steel Corporation (PA) ……………………………… 734 479-3500
　1650 W Jefferson Ave　Trenton　(48183)　*(G-16155)*
Huron Valley Telecom ………………………………………………… 734 995-9780
　605 Argo Dr　Ann Arbor　(48105)　*(G-497)*
Huron Vlleys Hrse Blnket Hdqtr …………………………………… 248 859-2398
　28525 Beck Rd Unit 102　Wixom　(48393)　*(G-17831)*
Hush Puppies Retail LLC ……………………………………………… 231 937-1004
　214 Washburn St　Howard City　(49329)　*(G-8001)*
Husite Engineering Co Inc …………………………………………… 248 588-0337
　44831 N Groesbeck Hwy　Clinton Township　(48036)　*(G-3136)*
Husky Envelope Products Inc (PA) ………………………………… 248 624-7070
　1225 E West Maple Rd　Walled Lake　(48390)　*(G-16895)*
Husky LLC ………………………………………………………………… 586 774-6148
　28100 Hayes Rd　Roseville　(48066)　*(G-13817)*
Husky Precision, Roseville *Also called Husky LLC (G-13817)*
Hussmann Corporation ………………………………………………… 248 668-0790
　46974 Liberty Dr　Wixom　(48393)　*(G-17832)*
Hutchinson Antivibration (HQ) ……………………………………… 616 459-4541
　460 Fuller Ave Ne　Grand Rapids　(49503)　*(G-6519)*
Hutchinson Antivibration ……………………………………………… 231 775-9737
　600 7th St　Cadillac　(49601)　*(G-2254)*
Hutchinson Arospc & Indust Inc …………………………………… 989 875-2052
　1300 S County Farm Rd　Ithaca　(48847)　*(G-8360)*
Hutchinson Automotive, Grand Rapids *Also called Hutchinson Antivibration (G-6519)*
Hutchinson Corporation (HQ) ……………………………………… 616 459-4541
　460 Fuller Ave Ne　Grand Rapids　(49503)　*(G-6520)*
Hutchinson Fts, Inc., Auburn Hills *Also called Fluid Hutchinson Management (G-876)*
Hutchinson Sales, Auburn Hills *Also called Hutchinson Sealing Systems Inc (G-905)*
Hutchinson Seal Corporation ……………………………………… 248 375-4190
　3201 Cross Creek Pkwy　Auburn Hills　(48326)　*(G-903)*
Hutchinson Seal De Mexico, Auburn Hills *Also called Hutchinson Seal Corporation (G-903)*
Hutchinson Sealing Syst ……………………………………………… 248 375-3721
　3201 Cross Creek Pkwy　Auburn Hills　(48326)　*(G-904)*
Hutchinson Sealing Systems Inc (HQ) …………………………… 248 375-3720
　3201 Cross Creek Pkwy　Auburn Hills　(48326)　*(G-905)*
Hutsons Machine & Tool Inc ………………………………………… 517 688-3674
　408 Maitland Dr　Horton　(49246)　*(G-7964)*
Huys Electrodes Inc …………………………………………………… 215 723-4897
　6810 Metro Plex Dr # 200　Romulus　(48174)　*(G-13686)*
Hvac Group, Auburn Hills *Also called TI Group Auto Systems LLC (G-1024)*
Hy Lift Johnson Inc …………………………………………………… 231 722-1100
　1185 E Keating Ave　Muskegon　(49442)　*(G-11345)*
Hy-Test Inc ……………………………………………………………… 616 866-5500
　9341 Courtland Dr Ne　Rockford　(49351)　*(G-13572)*
Hy-Vac Technologies, Detroit *Also called Mjc Industries Inc (G-4251)*
Hycal Corp ……………………………………………………………… 216 671-6161
　27800 W Jefferson Ave　Gibraltar　(48173)　*(G-5904)*
Hycorr LLC ……………………………………………………………… 269 381-6349
　3654 Midlink Dr　Kalamazoo　(49048)　*(G-8771)*
Hyde Spring and Wire Company …………………………………… 313 272-2201
　14341 Schaefer Hwy　Detroit　(48227)　*(G-4132)*
Hydra-Lock Corporation ……………………………………………… 586 783-5007
　25000 Joy Blvd　Mount Clemens　(48043)　*(G-11133)*

Hydra-Tech Inc......586 232-4479
1483 Quadrate Dr Ste C Macomb (48042) *(G-10130)*
Hydra-Zorb Company......248 373-5151
1751 Summit Dr Auburn Hills (48326) *(G-906)*
Hydraulex Global, Chesterfield *Also called Hydraulex Intl Holdings Inc (G-2786)*
Hydraulex Intl Holdings Inc (PA)......914 682-2700
48175 Gratiot Ave Chesterfield (48051) *(G-2786)*
Hydraulic Press Service......586 859-7099
4175 22 Mile Rd Shelby Township (48317) *(G-14602)*
Hydraulic Pump Division, Otsego *Also called Parker-Hannifin Corporation (G-12250)*
Hydraulic Systems Inc......517 787-7818
1505 E High St Jackson (49203) *(G-8467)*
Hydraulic Systems Technology......248 656-5810
1156 Whispering Knoll Ln Rochester Hills (48306) *(G-13447)*
Hydraulic Tubes & Fittings LLC......810 660-8088
434 Mccormick Dr Lapeer (48446) *(G-9464)*
Hydro Chem Laboratories Inc......248 348-1737
22859 Heslip Dr Novi (48375) *(G-11904)*
Hydro Extrusion North Amer LLC......269 349-6626
5575 N Riverview Dr Kalamazoo (49004) *(G-8772)*
Hydro Giant 4 Inc......248 661-0034
7480 Haggerty Rd West Bloomfield (48322) *(G-17480)*
Hydro King Incorporated......313 835-8700
21384 Mcclung Ave Southfield (48075) *(G-14939)*
Hydro-Chem Systems Inc......616 531-6420
6605 Broadmoor Ave Se Caledonia (49316) *(G-2301)*
Hydro-Craft Inc......248 652-8100
1821 Rochster Indus Dr Rochester Hills (48309) *(G-13448)*
Hydro-Logic Inc......586 757-7477
24832 Romano St Warren (48091) *(G-17083)*
Hydro-Zone Inc......734 247-4488
17800 Telegraph Rd Brownstown (48174) *(G-2065)*
Hydrochem LLC......313 841-5800
987 W Hurd Rd Monroe (48162) *(G-11040)*
Hydrochempsc, Monroe *Also called Hydrochem LLC (G-11040)*
Hydrochempsc, Detroit *Also called PSC Industrial Outsourcing LP (G-4315)*
Hydrodynamics International......517 887-2007
5711 Enterprise Dr Lansing (48911) *(G-9383)*
Hydrogen Assist Development......734 823-4969
669 Strawberry St Dundee (48131) *(G-4589)*
Hydrolake Inc......231 825-2233
420 S Roth St Ste A Reed City (49677) *(G-13215)*
Hydrolake Inc (HQ)......231 825-2233
6151 W Gerwoude Dr Mc Bain (49657) *(G-10681)*
Hydromation Company, Farmington Hills *Also called Bratten Enterprises Inc (G-4946)*
Hydronic Components Inc......586 268-1640
7243 Miller Dr Ste 200 Warren (48092) *(G-17084)*
Hydronix Americas, Harbor Springs *Also called Hydronix Ltd (G-7284)*
Hydronix Ltd......231 439-5000
692 W Conway Rd 24 Harbor Springs (49740) *(G-7284)*
Hydrosciences LLC......248 890-8116
3477 Orchard Lake Rd Keego Harbor (48320) *(G-8979)*
Hygratek LLC......847 962-6180
1600 Huron Pkwy Fl 2 Ann Arbor (48109) *(G-498)*
Hylite Tool & Machine Inc......586 465-7878
44685 Macomb Indus Dr Clinton Township (48036) *(G-3137)*
Hyper Alloys Inc......586 772-0571
17001 19 Mile Rd Ste 1 Clinton Township (48038) *(G-3138)*
Hypertek Corporation......248 619-0395
575 E Big Beaver Rd # 170 Troy (48083) *(G-16407)*
Hypo-Systems, Ann Arbor *Also called High-Po-Chlor Inc (G-490)*
Hyponex Corporation......810 724-2875
332 Graham Rd Imlay City (48444) *(G-8202)*
Hytec Equipment......906 789-5811
6614 N.75 Dr Escanaba (49829) *(G-4835)*
Hytech Spring and Machine, Plainwell *Also called Tokusen Hytech Inc (G-12548)*
Hytech Spring and Machine Co, Plainwell *Also called Magiera Holdings Inc (G-12529)*
Hytech Spring and Machine Co., Plainwell *Also called Tokusen Hytech Inc (G-12547)*
Hytrol Manufacturing Inc......734 261-8030
4005 Morrill Rd Jackson (49201) *(G-8468)*
Hz Industries Inc......616 453-4491
706 Bond Ave Nw Grand Rapids (49503) *(G-6521)*
I & G Tool Co Inc......586 777-7690
51528 Industrial Dr New Baltimore (48047) *(G-11485)*
I & K Distributors, Warren *Also called Countryside Foods LLC (G-16994)*
I B P Inc......248 588-4710
9295 Allen Rd Clarkston (48348) *(G-2927)*
I C R, Warren *Also called Lorna Icr LLC (G-17131)*
I C S Corporation America Inc......616 554-9300
4675 Talon Ct Se Grand Rapids (49512) *(G-6522)*
I D Enterprises LLC......734 513-0800
32788 5 Mile Rd Ste 2 Livonia (48154) *(G-9777)*
I D Medical Systems Inc......616 698-0535
3954 44th St Se Grand Rapids (49512) *(G-6523)*
I D Pro Embroidery LLC......734 847-6650
1287 W Sterns Rd Temperance (48182) *(G-15832)*
I E & E Industries Inc (PA)......248 544-8181
111 E 10 Mile Rd Madison Heights (48071) *(G-10272)*

I E T, Auburn Hills *Also called Industrial Exprmental Tech LLC (G-912)*
I F I, Sterling Heights *Also called Industrial Frnc Interiors Inc (G-15373)*
I Jams LLC......248 756-1380
1497 Beachland Blvd Keego Harbor (48320) *(G-8980)*
I M A, Detroit *Also called Integrated Mfg & Assembly LLC (G-4144)*
I M D, Royal Oak *Also called International Mech Design (G-13936)*
I M F, Cottrellville *Also called Industrial Mtal Fbricators LLC (G-3588)*
I M F Inc......269 948-2345
437 E Walnut St Hastings (49058) *(G-7415)*
I M I, Spring Lake *Also called Industrial Mtal Idntfction Inc (G-15153)*
I M I, Washington *Also called Innovative Mold Inc (G-17305)*
I M P, Oxford *Also called Industrial Machine Pdts Inc (G-12351)*
I Machine LLC......616 532-8020
2606 Sanford Ave Sw Grandville (49418) *(G-7049)*
I Parth Inc......248 548-9722
2206 Burdette St Ferndale (48220) *(G-5293)*
I S My Department Inc......248 622-0622
711 Dixie Hwy 366 Clarkston (48346) *(G-2928)*
I S P Coatings Corp......586 752-5020
130 E Pond Dr Romeo (48065) *(G-13630)*
I S Two......616 396-5634
262 E 26th St Holland (49423) *(G-7685)*
I T W Workholding, Traverse City *Also called Illinois Tool Works Inc (G-16002)*
I Way Software, Troy *Also called Information Builders Inc (G-16417)*
I'Ve Been Framed, Jackson *Also called A&Lb Custom Framing LLC (G-8370)*
I-9 Advantage......800 724-8546
101 W Big Beaver Rd 14 Troy (48084) *(G-16408)*
I.D.A., Warren *Also called Independent Die Association (G-17087)*
I.E. Communications, Detroit *Also called Industrial Elc Co Detroit Inc (G-4139)*
I.M. Branded, Pontiac *Also called Automotive Media LLC (G-12806)*
I.S.I. Automation Products, Saline *Also called Norgren Automtn Solutions LLC (G-14406)*
I.S.T., Okemos *Also called Instrumented Sensor Tech Inc (G-12126)*
I.V.C. Industrial, Grand Haven *Also called PPG Industries Inc (G-6063)*
I2 International Dev LLC......616 534-8100
2905 Wilson Ave Sw # 200 Grandville (49418) *(G-7050)*
IAC Creative LLC......248 455-7000
28333 Telegraph Rd Southfield (48034) *(G-14940)*
IAC Group, Southfield *Also called International Automotive Compo (G-14948)*
IAC Mexico Holdings Inc (HQ)......248 455-7000
28333 Telegraph Rd Southfield (48034) *(G-14941)*
IAC Plymouth LLC......734 207-7000
47785 W Anchor Ct Plymouth (48170) *(G-12645)*
Iaec Corporation......586 354-5996
21641 34 Mile Rd Armada (48005) *(G-720)*
Ian Davidson & Assoc Inc......269 925-7552
240 W Britain Ave Benton Harbor (49022) *(G-1512)*
Ianna Fab Inc......586 739-2410
5575 22 Mile Rd Shelby Township (48317) *(G-14603)*
Iannuzzi Millwork Inc......586 285-1000
33877 Doreka Fraser (48026) *(G-5667)*
IBC North America Inc (HQ)......248 625-8700
4545 Clawson Tank Dr Clarkston (48346) *(G-2929)*
IBC North America Inc......248 625-8700
4750 Clawson Tank Dr Clarkston (48346) *(G-2930)*
IBC Precision Inc......248 373-8202
2715 Paldan Dr Auburn Hills (48326) *(G-907)*
Ibg Nbt Systems Corp......248 478-9490
20793 Farmington Rd Ste 8 Farmington Hills (48336) *(G-5024)*
Ibidltd-Blue Green Energy (PA)......909 547-5160
6659 Schaefer Rd Ste 110 Dearborn (48126) *(G-3723)*
IBM, East Lansing *Also called International Bus Mchs Corp (G-4665)*
IBM, Midland *Also called International Bus Mchs Corp (G-10873)*
Ice Makers, Port Huron *Also called Northern Pure Ice Co L L C (G-12950)*
Ice Tools, Chesterfield *Also called Indexable Cutter Engineering (G-2787)*
ICM Arizona, Cassopolis *Also called Alonzo Products Inc (G-2526)*
ICM Enterprises LLC......586 415-2567
33451 James J Pompo Dr Fraser (48026) *(G-5668)*
ICM Products Inc (HQ)......269 445-0847
805 Wolfe Ave Cassopolis (49031) *(G-2531)*
Icmp Inc......269 445-0847
805 Wolfe Ave Cassopolis (49031) *(G-2532)*
Icon Industries Inc......616 241-1877
1522 Madison Ave Se Grand Rapids (49507) *(G-6524)*
Icon Shelter Systems, Holland *Also called Icon Shelters Inc (G-7686)*
Icon Shelters Inc......616 396-0919
1455 Lincoln Ave Holland (49423) *(G-7686)*
Icon Sign & Design Inc......517 372-1104
3308 W Saint Joseph St Lansing (48917) *(G-9294)*
Ics Filtration Products, Grand Rapids *Also called I C S Corporation America Inc (G-6522)*
ID Engnring Atmted Systems Inc......616 656-0182
3650 44th St Se Kentwood (49512) *(G-9012)*
ID Systems Inc......231 799-8760
676 E Ellis Rd Norton Shores (49441) *(G-11761)*
Ida D Byler......810 672-9355
4169 Moore Rd Cass City (48726) *(G-2515)*
Idadee Enterprises, Livonia *Also called I D Enterprises LLC (G-9777)*

A L P H A B E T I C

Idc Industries Inc...586 427-4321
18901 15 Mile Rd Clinton Township (48035) ***(G-3139)***
Idea Mia LLC...248 891-8939
18513 San Quentin Dr Lathrup Village (48076) ***(G-9500)***
Ideal Fabricators Inc...734 422-5320
30579 Schoolcraft Rd Livonia (48150) ***(G-9778)***
Ideal Gas Inc...734 365-7192
2750 Oakwood Blvd Melvindale (48122) ***(G-10700)***
Ideal Heated Knives Inc...248 437-1510
57007 Pontiac Trl New Hudson (48165) ***(G-11545)***
Ideal Printing Company (PA)...616 454-9224
2801 Oak Industrial Dr Ne Grand Rapids (49505) ***(G-6525)***
Ideal Shield LLC...866 825-8659
2525 Clark St Detroit (48209) ***(G-4133)***
Ideal Steel & Bldrs Sups LLC...313 849-0000
2525 Clark St Detroit (48209) ***(G-4134)***
Ideal Tool Inc...989 893-8336
1707 Marquette St Bay City (48706) ***(G-1321)***
Ideal Wholesale Inc...989 873-5850
3430 Henderson Lake Rd Prescott (48756) ***(G-13080)***
Ideal Wrought Iron...313 581-1324
7839 Greenfield Rd Detroit (48228) ***(G-4135)***
Ideation Inc...734 761-4360
3389 Breckland Ct Ann Arbor (48108) ***(G-499)***
Ideation International Inc...248 737-8854
32000 Northwestern Hwy # 145 Farmington Hills (48334) ***(G-5025)***
Idel LLC...231 929-3195
1315 Woodmere Ave Traverse City (49686) ***(G-16001)***
Idemitsu Chemicals USA Corp...248 355-0666
3000 Town Ctr Ste 2820 Southfield (48075) ***(G-14942)***
Idemitsu Lubricants Amer Corp...248 355-0666
3000 Town Ctr Ste 2820 Southfield (48075) ***(G-14943)***
Identicom, Farmington Hills *Also called Grasshopper Signs Graphics LLC* ***(G-5014)***
Identicom Sign Solutions LLC...248 344-9590
24657 Halsted Rd Farmington Hills (48335) ***(G-5026)***
Identify Inc...313 802-2015
25163 Dequindre Rd Madison Heights (48071) ***(G-10273)***
Ididit Inc...517 424-0577
610 S Maumee St Tecumseh (49286) ***(G-15798)***
Idp Inc...248 352-0044
21300 W 8 Mile Rd Southfield (48075) ***(G-14944)***
Idrink Products Inc...734 531-6324
6109 Jackson Rd Ann Arbor (48103) ***(G-500)***
IDS, Hudsonville *Also called Innovtive Dsplay Solutions LLC* ***(G-8160)***
IDS, Shelby Township *Also called Intergrted Dspnse Slutions LLC* ***(G-14605)***
IDS, Roseville *Also called Industrial Ducts Systems Inc* ***(G-13818)***
IDS, Sterling Heights *Also called Innovtive Design Solutions Inc* ***(G-15374)***
Idv Solutions LLC (HQ)...517 853-3755
6000 W St Joe Hwy Ste 100 Lansing (48917) ***(G-9295)***
IEC N.A., Fowlerville *Also called Invention Evolution Comp LLC* ***(G-5570)***
Ied Inc...231 728-9154
1938 Sanford St Muskegon (49441) ***(G-11346)***
IEM, Hope *Also called International Engrg & Mfg Inc* ***(G-7954)***
Ies Inter/Realtime Tech, Ann Arbor *Also called Faac Incorporated* ***(G-456)***
Iet, Southfield *Also called Industrial Exprmental Tech LLC* ***(G-14946)***
If Walls Could Talk Prof Svcs, Detroit *Also called Jr Larry Dudley* ***(G-4166)***
Ifc, Northville *Also called International Fenestration* ***(G-11701)***
Ifca International Inc (PA)...616 531-1840
3520 Fairlanes Ave Sw Grandville (49418) ***(G-7051)***
Ifm, Roseville *Also called Iron Fetish Metalworks Inc* ***(G-13822)***
IGA Abrasives LLC...616 243-5566
3011 Hillcroft Ave Sw Grand Rapids (49548) ***(G-6526)***
Igan Mich Publishing LLC...248 877-4649
7025 Dandison Blvd West Bloomfield (48324) ***(G-17481)***
Iha Vsclar Endvsclar Spcalists...734 712-8150
5325 Elliott Dr Ste 104 Ypsilanti (48197) ***(G-18078)***
Ihc Inc...313 535-3210
12400 Burt Rd Detroit (48228) ***(G-4136)***
Ihicore LLC...800 960-0448
1305 S Cedar St Lansing (48910) ***(G-9384)***
Ihs Inc...616 464-4224
2851 Charlevoix Dr Se # 314 Grand Rapids (49546) ***(G-6527)***
Il Adrian LLC W2fuel...517 920-4863
1571 W Beecher Rd Adrian (49221) ***(G-68)***
Il Enterprises Inc...734 285-6030
555 Grove St Wyandotte (48192) ***(G-17962)***
Il Stanley Co Inc...269 660-7777
1500 Hill Brady Rd Battle Creek (49037) ***(G-1199)***
Iig-Dss Technologies LLC...586 725-5300
6100 Bethuy Rd Ira (48023) ***(G-8258)***
IKEA Chip LLC...877 218-9931
2609 Crooks Rd Ste 235 Troy (48084) ***(G-16409)***
Ikes Welding Shop and Mfg...989 892-2783
50 N Finn Rd Munger (48747) ***(G-11242)***
Illinois Tool Works Inc...231 258-5521
111 W Park Dr Kalkaska (49646) ***(G-8944)***
Illinois Tool Works Inc...231 947-5755
2155 Traversefield Dr Traverse City (49686) ***(G-16002)***
Illinois Tool Works Inc...616 772-1910
500 N Fairview Rd Zeeland (49464) ***(G-18157)***
Illinois Tool Works Inc...231 947-5755
2155 Traversefield Dr Traverse City (49686) ***(G-16003)***
Illinois Tool Works Inc...248 969-4248
2425 N Lapeer Rd Oxford (48371) ***(G-12350)***
Illinois Tool Works Inc...248 589-2500
2002 Stephenson Hwy Troy (48083) ***(G-16410)***
Illinois Tool Works Inc...734 855-3709
12200 Tech Center Dr Livonia (48150) ***(G-9779)***
Illusion Signs & Graphics Inc...313 581-4376
14241 Michigan Ave Dearborn (48126) ***(G-3724)***
Ilmor Engineering Inc (PA)...734 456-3600
43939 Plymouth Oaks Blvd Plymouth (48170) ***(G-12646)***
Ilmor High Performance Marine, Plymouth *Also called Ilmor Engineering Inc* ***(G-12646)***
Ilowski Sausage Company Inc...810 329-9117
6650 Saint Clair Hwy East China (48054) ***(G-4622)***
Ilumisys Inc...844 864-4533
164 Indusco Ct Troy (48083) ***(G-16411)***
Im A Beer Hound...517 331-0528
602 N Grace St Lansing (48917) ***(G-9296)***
Ima Service Center - Detroit, Detroit *Also called Integrated Mfg & Assembly LLC* ***(G-4143)***
Imagamerica, Sterling Heights *Also called E Q R 2 Inc* ***(G-15324)***
Image Encore, Bloomfield Hills *Also called Stamping Grounds Inc* ***(G-1798)***
Image Factory Inc...989 732-2712
870 N Center Ave Gaylord (49735) ***(G-5866)***
Image Machine & Tool Inc...586 466-3400
34501 Bennett Fraser (48026) ***(G-5669)***
Image Printing Inc...248 585-4080
1902 Crooks Rd Royal Oak (48073) ***(G-13935)***
Image360-Plymouth, Plymouth *Also called Sgo Corporate Center LLC* ***(G-12752)***
Imagecraft...517 750-0077
100 Robinson Rd Jackson (49203) ***(G-8469)***
Imagemaster LLC (PA)...734 821-2500
1182 Oak Valley Dr Ann Arbor (48108) ***(G-501)***
Imagemaster Printing, Ann Arbor *Also called Imagemaster LLC* ***(G-501)***
Imagemaster Printing LLC...734 821-2511
1182 Oak Valley Dr Ann Arbor (48108) ***(G-502)***
Imagen Orthopedics LLC...616 294-1026
13827 Port Sheldon St Holland (49424) ***(G-7687)***
Imagepro Inc...231 723-7906
443 Water St Manistee (49660) ***(G-10424)***
Images Unlimited LLC...248 608-8685
361 South St Ste A Rochester (48307) ***(G-13328)***
Imagillation Inc...734 481-0140
133 W Michigan Ave Ste 2 Ypsilanti (48197) ***(G-18079)***
Imax Printing Co...248 629-9680
756 Livernois St Ferndale (48220) ***(G-5294)***
IMC, Escanaba *Also called Independent Machine Co Inc* ***(G-4836)***
IMC Dataworks LLC...248 356-4311
39555 Orchard Hill Pl # 225 Novi (48375) ***(G-11905)***
Imcs, Holland *Also called International Material Co* ***(G-7691)***
Imerys Perlite Usa Inc...269 649-1352
1950 E W Ave Vicksburg (49097) ***(G-16836)***
Imet, Jackson *Also called Intern Metals and Energy* ***(G-8471)***
IMI, Auburn Hills *Also called Industrial Model Inc* ***(G-913)***
Imlay City Concrete Inc (PA)...810 724-3905
205 S Cedar St Imlay City (48444) ***(G-8203)***
Imlay City High Pressure...810 395-7459
113 S Glassford St Capac (48014) ***(G-2448)***
Imlay City Molded Pdts Corp...810 721-9100
593 S Cedar St Imlay City (48444) ***(G-8204)***
Imm Inc...989 344-7662
758 Isenhauer Rd Grayling (49738) ***(G-7108)***
Immaculate Enterprises, Southfield *Also called Gloria C Williams* ***(G-14922)***
Immuno Concepts NA Ltd...734 464-0701
17199 N Laurel Park Dr # 320 Livonia (48152) ***(G-9780)***
Immunospec, Livonia *Also called Sigma Diagnostics Inc* ***(G-9927)***
Impact Fab Inc...616 399-9970
3440 John F Donnelly Dr Holland (49424) ***(G-7688)***
Impact Forge Holdings LLC (HQ)...313 758-2000
1 Dauch Dr Detroit (48211) ***(G-4137)***
Impact Label Corporation (PA)...269 381-4280
8875 Krum Ave Galesburg (49053) ***(G-5811)***
Impco Industrial Eng Systems, Sterling Heights *Also called Impco Technologies Inc* ***(G-15370)***
Impco Technologies Inc...586 264-1200
7100 15 Mile Rd Sterling Heights (48312) ***(G-15370)***
Impel Industries Inc...586 254-5800
44494 Phoenix Dr Sterling Heights (48314) ***(G-15371)***
Imperial Clinical RES Svcs Inc...616 784-0100
3100 Walkent Dr Nw Grand Rapids (49544) ***(G-6528)***
Imperial Engineering Inc...248 588-2022
1173 Combermere Dr Troy (48083) ***(G-16412)***
Imperial Graphics, Grand Rapids *Also called Imperial Clinical RES Svcs Inc* ***(G-6528)***
Imperial Industries Inc...734 397-1400
815 Woodland Dr Saline (48176) ***(G-14395)***

ALPHABETIC SECTION

Imperial Laser Inc 616 735-9315
  11473 1st Ave Nw Grand Rapids (49534) *(G-6529)*
Imperial Metal Products Co 616 452-1700
  835 Hall St Sw Grand Rapids (49503) *(G-6530)*
Imperial Plastics Mfg, North Branch Also called Johnson Walker & Assoc LLC *(G-11660)*
Imperial Press Inc 734 728-5430
  36024 W Michigan Ave Wayne (48184) *(G-17432)*
Impert Industries Inc 269 694-2727
  557 Lincoln Rd Otsego (49078) *(G-12241)*
Impres Engineering Svcs LLC 616 283-4112
  147 Douglas Ave Holland (49424) *(G-7689)*
Impression Center Co 248 989-8080
  224 Minnesota Dr Troy (48083) *(G-16413)*
Impressions Specialty Advg, Taylor Also called Monograms & More Inc *(G-15746)*
Impressive Cabinets Inc 248 542-1185
  8575 Capital St Oak Park (48237) *(G-12074)*
Impressive Design, Oak Park Also called Impressive Cabinets Inc *(G-12074)*
Imprint House LLC 810 985-8203
  1113 Military St Port Huron (48060) *(G-12929)*
Imra America Inc (HQ) 734 669-7377
  1044 Woodridge Ave Ann Arbor (48105) *(G-503)*
IMS, Pontiac Also called Integrated Marketing Svcs LLC *(G-12836)*
IMS, Norton Shores Also called Intelligent Mch Solutions Inc *(G-11762)*
IMS, Clare Also called Integrity Machine Services *(G-2872)*
Ims/Chinatool Jv LLC (PA) 734 466-5151
  17199 N Laurel Park Dr # 412 Livonia (48152) *(G-9781)*
Imservice, South Lyon Also called International Machining Svc *(G-14795)*
IMT, Northville Also called Innovative Machine Technology *(G-11700)*
In Line Tube Inc 586 532-1338
  15066 Technology Dr Shelby Township (48315) *(G-14604)*
In-Tronics, Sterling Heights Also called Aero Embedded Technologies Inc *(G-15255)*
Inalfa Road System Inc 248 371-3060
  1370 Pacific Dr Auburn Hills (48326) *(G-908)*
Inalfa Roof Systems Inc (HQ) 248 371-3060
  1370 Pacific Dr Auburn Hills (48326) *(G-909)*
Inalfa Roof Systems Inc 586 758-6620
  12500 E 9 Mile Rd Warren (48089) *(G-17085)*
Inalfa-Hollandia, Auburn Hills Also called Inalfa Roof Systems Inc *(G-909)*
Inalfa/Ssi Roof Systems LLC 586 758-6620
  12500 E 9 Mile Rd Warren (48089) *(G-17086)*
Inco Development Corporation 517 323-8448
  1628 Alan Ln Lansing (48917) *(G-9297)*
Inco Graphics, Lansing Also called Inco Development Corporation *(G-9297)*
Incoe Corporation (PA) 248 616-0220
  2850 High Meadow Cir Auburn Hills (48326) *(G-910)*
Incoe International Inc (HQ) 248 616-0220
  2850 High Meadow Cir Auburn Hills (48326) *(G-911)*
Indelco Plastics Corporation 616 452-7077
  3322 Lousma Dr Se Grand Rapids (49548) *(G-6531)*
Independent Dairy Inc (PA) 734 241-6016
  126 N Telegraph Rd Monroe (48162) *(G-11041)*
Independent Die Association 586 773-9000
  14689 E 11 Mile Rd Warren (48088) *(G-17087)*
Independent Die Cutting Inc 616 452-3197
  1265 Godfrey Ave Sw Grand Rapids (49503) *(G-6532)*
Independent Engineering Co, West Bloomfield Also called Harvey S Freeman *(G-17479)*
Independent Machine Co Inc 906 428-4524
  2501 Danforth Rd Escanaba (49829) *(G-4836)*
Independent Mfg Solutions Corp 248 960-3550
  46918 Liberty Dr Wixom (48393) *(G-17833)*
Independent Newspapers Inc (HQ) 586 469-4510
  100 Macomb Daily Dr Mount Clemens (48043) *(G-11134)*
Independent Newspapers, The, Dundee Also called Gazelle Publishing *(G-4584)*
Independent Tool and Mfg, Allegan Also called Cvm Services LLC *(G-153)*
Independent Tool and Mfg Co 269 521-4811
  661 44th St Allegan (49010) *(G-165)*
Independent Water Service, Martin Also called Seymour Dehaan *(G-10597)*
Indepndent Advsor Nwsppr Group 989 723-1118
  1907 W M 21 Owosso (48867) *(G-12296)*
Indepndnce Tling Solutions LLC 586 274-2300
  1200 Rochester Rd Troy (48083) *(G-16414)*
Indexable Cutter Engineering 586 598-1540
  50525 Metzen Dr Chesterfield (48051) *(G-2787)*
Indian River Custom Log Homes, Indian River Also called G B Wolfgram and Sons Inc *(G-8217)*
Indian Summer, Belding Also called Mizkan America Inc *(G-1425)*
Indian Summer Cooperative Inc 231 873-7504
  409 Wood St Hart (49420) *(G-7374)*
Indian Summer Cooperative Inc (PA) 231 845-6248
  3958 W Chauvez Rd Ste 1 Ludington (49431) *(G-10067)*
Indian Summer Recycling Inc 586 725-1340
  5877 Bethuy Rd Casco (48064) *(G-2500)*
Indiana Newspapers LLC 248 680-9905
  340 E Big Beaver Rd Ste 1 Troy (48083) *(G-16415)*
Indicon Corporation (PA) 586 274-0505
  6125 Center Dr Sterling Heights (48312) *(G-15372)*
Indispensable Health, Grass Lake Also called Grass Lake Community Pharmacy *(G-7088)*

Indocomp Systems Inc 810 678-3990
  3383 S Lapeer Rd Metamora (48455) *(G-10776)*
Indratech LLC (PA) 248 377-1877
  1212 E Maple Rd Troy (48083) *(G-16416)*
Indril, Kalkaska Also called Beckman Production Svcs Inc *(G-8939)*
Induction Engineering Inc 586 716-4700
  51517 Industrial Dr New Baltimore (48047) *(G-11486)*
Induction Processing Inc 586 756-5101
  24872 Gibson Dr Warren (48089) *(G-17088)*
Induction Services Inc 586 754-1640
  24800 Mound Rd Warren (48091) *(G-17089)*
Industrial Assemblies Inc 231 865-6500
  3130 Farr Rd Fruitport (49415) *(G-5793)*
Industrial Atomated Design LLC 810 648-9200
  245 S Stoutenburg Rd Sandusky (48471) *(G-14435)*
Industrial Automation LLC (PA) 248 598-5900
  2968 Waterview Dr Rochester Hills (48309) *(G-13449)*
Industrial Bag & Spc Inc 248 559-5550
  17800 Northland Park Ct # 107 Southfield (48075) *(G-14945)*
Industrial Boring Company 586 756-9110
  23175 Blackstone Ave Warren (48089) *(G-17090)*
Industrial Building Panels, Clarkston Also called I B P Inc *(G-2927)*
Industrial Computer & Controls 734 697-4152
  43774 Bemis Rd Van Buren Twp (48111) *(G-16765)*
Industrial Container Inc 313 923-8778
  6671 French Rd Detroit (48213) *(G-4138)*
Industrial Control Systems LLC 269 689-3241
  70380 M 66 Sturgis (49091) *(G-15607)*
Industrial Converting Inc 586 757-8820
  21650 Hoover Rd Warren (48089) *(G-17091)*
Industrial Dsign Innvtions Div, Dearborn Also called Big 3 Precision Products Inc *(G-3682)*
Industrial Ducts Systems Inc 586 498-3993
  30015 Groesbeck Hwy Roseville (48066) *(G-13818)*
Industrial Elc Co Detroit Inc 313 872-1133
  275 E Milwaukee St Detroit (48202) *(G-4139)*
Industrial Engineering Service 616 794-1330
  215 E High St Belding (48809) *(G-1419)*
Industrial Engnrng Service, Belding Also called Industrial Engineering Service *(G-1419)*
Industrial Exprmental Tech LLC 248 371-8000
  3199 Lapeer Rd Auburn Hills (48326) *(G-912)*
Industrial Exprmental Tech LLC 248 948-1100
  21556 Telegraph Rd Southfield (48033) *(G-14946)*
Industrial Extrusion Belting, Cassopolis Also called Stephen A James *(G-2536)*
Industrial Fabg Systems Inc 248 685-7373
  4965 Technical Dr Milford (48381) *(G-10966)*
Industrial Fabric Products Inc 269 932-4440
  4133 M 139 Saint Joseph (49085) *(G-14318)*
Industrial Fabricating Inc 734 676-2710
  28233 W Fort St Rockwood (48173) *(G-13605)*
Industrial Fabrication LLC 269 465-5960
  9550 Mathieu St Bridgman (49106) *(G-1867)*
Industrial Finishing Co LLC 616 784-5737
  3620 Mill Creek Dr Ne Comstock Park (49321) *(G-3485)*
Industrial Frnc Interiors Inc 586 977-9600
  35160 Stanley Dr Sterling Heights (48312) *(G-15373)*
Industrial Imprntng & Die Ctng 586 778-9470
  15291 E 10 Mile Rd Eastpointe (48021) *(G-4704)*
Industrial Innovations Inc 616 249-1525
  2936 Dormax St Sw Grandville (49418) *(G-7052)*
Industrial Machine & Tool 231 734-2794
  743 W 7th St Evart (49631) *(G-4883)*
Industrial Machine Pdts Inc 248 628-3621
  32 Louck St Oxford (48371) *(G-12351)*
Industrial Machine Tech LLC 269 683-4689
  32736 Bertrand St Niles (49120) *(G-11617)*
Industrial Machining Services, Zeeland Also called PI Optima Inc *(G-18173)*
Industrial Magnetics Inc (PA) 231 582-3100
  1385 S M 75 Boyne City (49712) *(G-1823)*
Industrial Marking Products 517 699-2160
  1415 Grovenburg Rd Holt (48842) *(G-7913)*
Industrial Metal Coating Co, Sterling Heights Also called Fricia Enterprises Inc *(G-15348)*
Industrial Metal Finishing Co, Sterling Heights Also called Oliver Industries Inc *(G-15440)*
Industrial Model Inc 586 254-0450
  2170 Pontiac Rd Auburn Hills (48326) *(G-913)*
Industrial Mtal Fbricators LLC 810 765-8960
  2700 Plank Rd Cottrellville (48039) *(G-3588)*
Industrial Mtal Idntfction Inc 616 847-0060
  17796 North Shore Dr Spring Lake (49456) *(G-15153)*
Industrial Optical Measurement 734 975-0436
  1349 King George Blvd Ann Arbor (48108) *(G-504)*
Industrial Packaging Corp (PA) 248 677-0084
  3060 11 Mile Rd Berkley (48072) *(G-1584)*
Industrial Pattern of Lansing 517 482-9835
  5901 W Willow Hwy Lansing (48917) *(G-9298)*
Industrial Powder Coating, Caledonia Also called RKP Consulting Inc *(G-2314)*
Industrial Reflections Inc 734 782-4454
  26601 W Huron River Dr Flat Rock (48134) *(G-5355)*
Industrial Service Tech Inc 616 288-3352
  3286 Kentland Ct Se Grand Rapids (49548) *(G-6533)*

Industrial Services Group ... 269 945-5291
683 Lincoln Lake Ave Se Lowell (49331) ***(G-10031)***
Industrial Stamping & Mfg Co ... 586 772-8430
16590 E 13 Mile Rd Roseville (48066) ***(G-13819)***
Industrial Steel Treating Co ... 517 787-6312
613 Carroll Ave Jackson (49202) ***(G-8470)***
Industrial System Services, Casco *Also called Magnetic Chuck Services Co Inc* ***(G-2502)***
Industrial Temperature Control (PA) ... 734 451-8740
7282 N Haggerty Rd Canton (48187) ***(G-2384)***
Industrial Tooling Tech Inc ... 231 766-2155
3253 Whitehall Rd Muskegon (49445) ***(G-11347)***
Industrial Wood Fab & Packg Co (PA) ... 734 284-4808
18620 Fort St Riverview (48193) ***(G-13298)***
Industrial Woodworking Corp ... 616 741-9663
9380 Pentatech Dr Zeeland (49464) ***(G-18158)***
Industries Unlimited Inc ... 586 949-4300
49739 Leona Dr Chesterfield (48051) ***(G-2788)***
Inertia Cycleworks ... 269 684-2000
211 E Main St Niles (49120) ***(G-11618)***
Infection Prevention Tech LLC ... 248 340-8800
1245 E Grand Blanc Rd Grand Blanc (48439) ***(G-5970)***
Infineon Tech Americas Corp ... 734 464-0891
19401 Victor Pkwy Livonia (48152) ***(G-9782)***
Infinity Controls & Engrg Inc ... 248 397-8267
3039 Cedar Key Dr Lake Orion (48360) ***(G-9139)***
Infinity Recycling LLC ... 248 939-2563
44057 N Groesbeck Hwy Clinton Township (48036) ***(G-3140)***
Infinity Tech & Arospc Inc ... 734 480-9001
2901 Tyler Rd Ypsilanti (48198) ***(G-18080)***
Infinity Transportation, Clinton Township *Also called Infinity Recycling LLC* ***(G-3140)***
Inflatable Marine Products Inc ... 616 723-8140
9485 N Reed Rd Ste C Howard City (49329) ***(G-8002)***
Infoguys Inc ... 517 482-2125
910 W Ottawa St Lansing (48915) ***(G-9385)***
Infonorm Inc ... 248 276-9027
4820 Joslyn Rd Lake Orion (48359) ***(G-9140)***
Infor (us) Inc ... 616 258-3311
3040 Charlevoix Dr Se # 200 Grand Rapids (49546) ***(G-6534)***
Informa Business Media Inc ... 248 357-0800
3000 Town Ctr Ste 2750 Southfield (48075) ***(G-14947)***
Information Builders Inc ... 248 641-8820
1301 W Long Lake Rd # 150 Troy (48098) ***(G-16417)***
Information Stn Specialists ... 616 772-2300
3368 88th Ave Zeeland (49464) ***(G-18159)***
Infotech Imaging Inc ... 616 458-8686
1843 Oak Industrial Dr Ne Grand Rapids (49505) ***(G-6535)***
Infra Corporation ... 248 623-0400
5454 Dixie Hwy Waterford (48329) ***(G-17351)***
Infrared Telemetrics Inc ... 906 482-0012
1780 Birch St Hancock (49930) ***(G-7252)***
Infusco Coffee Roasters LLC ... 269 213-5282
5846 Sawyer Rd Sawyer (49125) ***(G-14485)***
Infusystem Holdings Inc (PA) ... 248 291-1210
31700 Research Park Dr Madison Heights (48071) ***(G-10274)***
Ingersoll CM Systems LLC ... 989 495-5000
3505 Centennial Dr Midland (48642) ***(G-10870)***
Ingersoll-Rand Company ... 734 525-6030
13551 Merriman Rd Livonia (48150) ***(G-9783)***
Ingersoll-Rand Company ... 248 398-6200
29555 Stephenson Hwy Madison Heights (48071) ***(G-10275)***
Ingham Tool LLC ... 734 929-2390
6155 Jackson Rd Ste B Ann Arbor (48103) ***(G-505)***
Inglass Usa Inc ... 616 228-6900
920 74th St Sw Byron Center (49315) ***(G-2195)***
Inglis Farms Inc ... 989 727-8727
10681 Bushey Rd Alpena (49707) ***(G-293)***
Initial Artistry ... 313 277-6300
25450 Ford Rd Dearborn Heights (48127) ***(G-3787)***
Ink On Paper Printing, Livonia *Also called E & R Bindery Service Inc* ***(G-9717)***
Ink-Refills-Ink.com, Vicksburg *Also called Printer Ink Warehousecom LLC* ***(G-16841)***
Inkorporate ... 734 261-4657
6841 Middlebelt Rd Garden City (48135) ***(G-5827)***
Inkpressions LLC ... 248 461-2555
3175 Martin Rd Commerce Township (48390) ***(G-3416)***
Inkster Fuel & Food Inc ... 313 565-8230
1021 Inkster Rd Inkster (48141) ***(G-8228)***
Inland Craft Products, Madison Heights *Also called ABI International* ***(G-10178)***
Inland Diamond Products Co ... 248 585-1762
32051 Howard Ave Madison Heights (48071) ***(G-10276)***
Inland Lakes Machine Inc ... 231 775-6543
314 Haynes St Cadillac (49601) ***(G-2255)***
Inland Management Inc (HQ) ... 313 899-3014
4086 Michigan Ave Detroit (48210) ***(G-4140)***
Inland Press, Detroit *Also called Detroit Legal News Company* ***(G-3987)***
Inland Vapor of Michigan LLC (PA) ... 734 237-4389
33447 Ford Rd Garden City (48135) ***(G-5828)***
Inland Vapor of Michigan LLC ... 734 738-6312
125 N Haggerty Rd Canton (48187) ***(G-2385)***
Inline Tube, Shelby Township *Also called In Line Tube Inc* ***(G-14604)***
Inline Tube ... 586 294-4093
33783 Groesbeck Hwy Fraser (48026) ***(G-5670)***
Inman Forest Products Inc ... 989 370-4473
4171 Fraser Rd Glennie (48737) ***(G-5943)***
Inner Box Loading Systems Inc ... 616 241-4330
3058 Eastern Ave Se Grand Rapids (49508) ***(G-6536)***
Innkeeper LLC ... 734 743-1707
4902 Dewitt Rd Ste 104 Canton (48188) ***(G-2386)***
Innotec Corp (PA) ... 616 772-5959
441 E Roosevelt Ave Zeeland (49464) ***(G-18160)***
Innotec Automation, Zeeland *Also called Innotec Corp* ***(G-18160)***
Innova Exploration Inc ... 231 929-3985
333 W Grandview Pkwy # 502 Traverse City (49684) ***(G-16004)***
Innovate Industries Inc ... 586 558-8990
5600 Enterprise Ct Warren (48092) ***(G-17092)***
Innovatec LLC ... 813 545-6818
3972 Thomas Ave Berkley (48072) ***(G-1585)***
Innovated Portable Weldin ... 586 322-4442
5221 Lois Ct Casco (48064) ***(G-2501)***
Innovation Fab Inc ... 586 752-3092
77909 Pearl Dr Bruce Twp (48065) ***(G-2084)***
Innovation Machining Corp ... 269 683-3343
1461 S 3rd St Niles (49120) ***(G-11619)***
Innovation Unlimited LLC ... 574 635-1064
1409 4th St Bay City (48708) ***(G-1322)***
Innovative Air Management LLC ... 586 201-3513
1255 S Milford Rd Highland (48357) ***(G-7495)***
Innovative Cargo Systems LLC ... 734 568-6084
7325 Douglas Rd Lambertville (48144) ***(G-9183)***
Innovative Cleaning Eqp Inc ... 616 656-9225
3833 Soundtech Ct Se Grand Rapids (49512) ***(G-6537)***
Innovative Engineering Mich ... 517 977-0460
712 Terminal Rd Lansing (48906) ***(G-9236)***
Innovative Fab Inc ... 269 782-9154
29160 Middle Crossing Rd Dowagiac (49047) ***(G-4543)***
Innovative Fabrication LLC ... 734 789-9099
23851 Vreeland Rd Flat Rock (48134) ***(G-5356)***
Innovative Fluids LLC ... 734 241-5699
415 Squires Dr Milan (48160) ***(G-10941)***
Innovative Iron Inc ... 616 248-4250
3370 Jefferson Ave Se Grand Rapids (49548) ***(G-6538)***
Innovative Machine Technology ... 248 348-1630
7591 Chubb Rd Northville (48168) ***(G-11700)***
Innovative Machines Inc ... 616 669-1649
1811 Chicago Dr Jenison (49428) ***(G-8630)***
Innovative Material Handling ... 586 291-3694
18820 Woodward Ave Detroit (48203) ***(G-4141)***
Innovative Mold Inc ... 586 752-2996
12500 31 Mile Rd Washington (48095) ***(G-17305)***
Innovative Packg Solutions LLC ... 517 213-3169
2075 Dean Ave Ste 2 Holt (48842) ***(G-7914)***
Innovative Pdts Unlimited Inc ... 269 684-5050
2120 Industrial Dr Niles (49120) ***(G-11620)***
Innovative Pharmaceuticals ... 248 789-0999
2250 Genoa Business Park Brighton (48114) ***(G-1943)***
Innovative Polymers Inc ... 989 224-9500
208 Kuntz St Saint Johns (48879) ***(G-14284)***
Innovative Programming Systems ... 810 695-9332
8210 S Saginaw St Ste 1 Grand Blanc (48439) ***(G-5971)***
Innovative Sheet Metals ... 231 788-5751
1681 S Wolf Lake Rd Muskegon (49442) ***(G-11348)***
Innovative Solutions Tech Inc ... 734 335-6665
41158 Koppernick Rd Canton (48187) ***(G-2387)***
Innovative Support Svcs Inc ... 248 585-3600
1270 Souter Dr Troy (48083) ***(G-16418)***
Innovative Surface Works ... 734 261-3010
23206 Commerce Dr Farmington Hills (48335) ***(G-5027)***
Innovative Thermal Systems LLC ... 586 920-2900
21400 Hoover Rd Warren (48089) ***(G-17093)***
Innovative Tool Inc ... 586 329-4922
28195 Kehrig St Chesterfield (48047) ***(G-2789)***
Innovative Tool and Design Inc ... 248 542-1831
10725 Capital St Oak Park (48237) ***(G-12075)***
Innovative Weld Solutions LLC ... 937 545-7695
1022 Miners Run Rochester (48306) ***(G-13329)***
Innovative Woodworking ... 269 926-9663
2227 Plaza Dr Benton Harbor (49022) ***(G-1513)***
Innovative Works Inc ... 586 231-1960
28323 Anchor Dr Chesterfield (48047) ***(G-2790)***
Innovtive Design Solutions Inc ... 248 583-1010
6801 15 Mile Rd Sterling Heights (48312) ***(G-15374)***
Innovtive Dsplay Solutions LLC ... 616 896-6080
4256 Corp Exch Dr Ste A Hudsonville (49426) ***(G-8160)***
Innovtive Polymers Rampf Group, Saint Johns *Also called Innovative Polymers Inc* ***(G-14284)***
Innovtive Srgcal Solutions LLC ... 248 595-0420
50461 Pontiac Trl Wixom (48393) ***(G-17834)***
Inoac Automotive, Farmington Hills *Also called Inoac Interior Systems LLC* ***(G-5028)***
Inoac Interior Systems LLC ... 248 488-7610
22670 Haggerty Rd Ste 150 Farmington Hills (48335) ***(G-5028)***

ALPHABETIC SECTION

Inoac Usa Inc (PA) 248 619-7031
1515 Equity Dr Ste 200 Troy (48084) *(G-16419)*

Inora Technologies Inc (PA) 734 302-7488
333 Jackson Plz 1000 Ann Arbor (48103) *(G-506)*

Inovatech Automation Inc 586 210-9010
16105 Leone Dr Macomb (48042) *(G-10131)*

Inovision Inc 248 299-1915
2610 Bond St Rochester Hills (48309) *(G-13450)*

Inovision Sftwr Solutions Inc (PA) 586 598-8750
50561 Chesterfield Rd Chesterfield (48051) *(G-2791)*

Inplast Interior Tech LLC 810 724-3500
3863 Van Dyke Rd Almont (48003) *(G-258)*

Inpore Technologies Inc 517 481-2270
5901 E Sleepy Hollow Ln East Lansing (48823) *(G-4663)*

Inrad, Kentwood Also called Rls Interventional Inc *(G-9029)*

Insealator, Holly Also called Bars Products Inc *(G-7871)*

Inspection Control Company, Lake City Also called Gage Numerical Inc *(G-9087)*

Instacoat Premium Products LLC (PA) 586 770-1773
5920 N Huron Ave Oscoda (48750) *(G-12211)*

Instacote Inc 734 847-5260
160 La Voy Rd Ste C Erie (48133) *(G-4804)*

Installations Inc 313 532-9000
25257 W 8 Mile Rd Redford (48240) *(G-13166)*

Instant Copy Center, Flint Also called Irwin Enterprises Inc *(G-5449)*

Instant Framer 231 947-8908
322 S Union St Traverse City (49684) *(G-16005)*

Instant Marine Inc 248 398-1011
5020 White Lake Rd Clarkston (48346) *(G-2931)*

Instaset Plastics Company LLC 586 725-0229
10101 Marine City Hwy Anchorville (48004) *(G-331)*

Instep Pedorthics LLC 810 285-9109
4338 Manhattan E Traverse City (49685) *(G-16006)*

Institute Adv of Prosthetics, Lansing Also called Hanger Prsthetcs & Ortho Inc *(G-9381)*

Instrument and Valve Services 734 459-0375
14789 Keel St Plymouth (48170) *(G-12647)*

Instrumented Sensor Tech Inc 517 349-8487
4704 Moore St Okemos (48864) *(G-12126)*

Insty-Prints, Livonia Also called David H Bosley & Associates *(G-9698)*

Insty-Prints, Jackson Also called Forsons Inc *(G-8450)*

Insty-Prints, Lansing Also called Bruce Inc *(G-9352)*

Insty-Prints West Inc 517 321-7091
3121 W Saginaw St Ste A Lansing (48917) *(G-9299)*

Insulation Wholesale Supply 269 968-9746
11280 Michigan Ave E Battle Creek (49014) *(G-1200)*

Insulspan, Blissfield Also called Pfb Manufacturing LLC *(G-1723)*

Intaglio LLC 616 243-3300
3106 3 Mile Rd Nw Grand Rapids (49534) *(G-6539)*

Intaglio Associates In Design, Auburn Hills Also called George P Johnson Company *(G-883)*

Intec Automated Controls Inc 586 532-8881
44440 Phoenix Dr Sterling Heights (48314) *(G-15375)*

Integra Mold Inc 269 327-4337
10746 S Westnedge Ave Portage (49002) *(G-13002)*

Integral Vision Inc (PA) 248 668-9230
49113 Wixom Tech Dr Wixom (48393) *(G-17835)*

Integral Vision-Aid, Wixom Also called Integral Vision Inc *(G-17835)*

Integrated Building Solutions 616 889-3070
13609 Larner Rd Chesaning (48616) *(G-2724)*

Integrated Cmnty Commerce LLC 313 220-2253
200 Mount Elliott St # 105 Detroit (48207) *(G-4142)*

Integrated Conveyor Ltd 231 747-6430
301 W Laketon Ave Muskegon (49441) *(G-11349)*

Integrated Industries Inc 586 790-1550
33670 Lipke St Clinton Township (48035) *(G-3141)*

Integrated Interiors Inc 586 756-4840
21221 Hoover Rd Warren (48089) *(G-17094)*

Integrated Marketing Svcs LLC 248 625-7444
125 E Columbia Ave Pontiac (48340) *(G-12836)*

Integrated Mfg & Assembly LLC 313 267-2634
12601 Southfield Fwy C Detroit (48223) *(G-4143)*

Integrated Mfg & Assembly LLC (PA) 734 530-5600
6501 E Nevada St Detroit (48234) *(G-4144)*

Integrated Practice Service 248 646-7009
111 S Lafayette St # 609 South Lyon (48178) *(G-14794)*

Integrated Program MGT LLC 248 241-9257
5904 Warbler Dr Clarkston (48346) *(G-2932)*

Integrated Security Corp 248 624-0700
46755 Magellan Dr Novi (48377) *(G-11906)*

Integrated Sensing Systems Inc (PA) 734 547-9896
391 Airport Industrial Dr Ypsilanti (48198) *(G-18081)*

Integrated Terminals, Woodhaven Also called Diez Group LLC *(G-17939)*

Integricoat Inc 616 935-7878
16928 148th Ave Spring Lake (49456) *(G-15154)*

Integrity Beverage Inc 248 348-1010
28004 Center Oaks Ct # 102 Wixom (48393) *(G-17836)*

Integrity Design & Mfg LLC 248 628-6927
3285 Metamora Rd Ste A Oxford (48371) *(G-12352)*

Integrity Door LLC 616 896-8077
3010 143rd Ave Dorr (49323) *(G-4524)*

Integrity Fab & Machine Inc 989 481-3200
150 Enterprise Dr Breckenridge (48615) *(G-1843)*

Integrity Force Products, Negaunee Also called Robbins Inc *(G-11475)*

Integrity Forest Products LLC 513 871-8988
844 Hwy M28 Kenton (49967) *(G-8996)*

Integrity Machine Services 989 386-0216
5615 S Clare Ave Clare (48617) *(G-2872)*

Integrity Marketing Products 734 522-5050
5905 Middlebelt Rd Garden City (48135) *(G-5829)*

Integrity Printing, Clare Also called Ktr Printing Inc *(G-2875)*

Integrity Sltons Feld Svcs Inc 303 263-9522
411 W Lake Lansing Rd East Lansing (48823) *(G-4664)*

Integrity Trailers, Nunica Also called Jrm Industries Inc *(G-12039)*

Integrted Database Systems Inc 989 546-4512
2625 Denison Dr A Mount Pleasant (48858) *(G-11197)*

Integrted Systems Group Div of, Sparta Also called Speedrack Products Group Ltd *(G-15113)*

Intellibee Inc 313 586-4122
400 Renaissance Ctr # 2600 Detroit (48243) *(G-4145)*

Intellichem LLC 810 765-4075
887 Chartier Marine City (48039) *(G-10474)*

Intelliform Inc 248 541-4000
3918 12 Mile Rd Berkley (48072) *(G-1586)*

Intelligent Document Solutions, Madison Heights Also called Data Mail Services Inc *(G-10228)*

Intelligent Document Solutions, Madison Heights Also called Lasertec Inc *(G-10298)*

Intelligent Dynamics LLC 313 727-9920
456 Berkley St Dearborn (48124) *(G-3725)*

Intelligent Mch Solutions Inc 616 607-9751
1269 E Mt Grfeld Rd Ste D Norton Shores (49441) *(G-11762)*

Intelligent Vision Systems LLC 734 426-3921
7300 Huron River Dr Ste 4 Dexter (48130) *(G-4494)*

Intellitech Systems Inc 586 219-3737
303 Evaline Dr Troy (48085) *(G-16420)*

Inter City Neon Inc 586 754-6020
23920 Amber Ave Warren (48089) *(G-17095)*

Inter Dyne Systems, Norton Shores Also called ID Systems Inc *(G-11761)*

Inter State Foods Inc (PA) 517 372-5500
5133 W Grand River Ave Lansing (48906) *(G-9237)*

Inter-Lakes Bases Inc 586 294-8120
17480 Malyn Blvd Fraser (48026) *(G-5671)*

Inter-Pack Corporation (PA) 734 242-7755
399 Detroit Ave Monroe (48162) *(G-11042)*

Inter-Power Corporation (PA) 810 798-7050
3578 Van Dyke Rd Almont (48003) *(G-259)*

Interact Websites Inc 800 515-9672
3526 E Curtis Rd Midland (48642) *(G-10871)*

Interactive Aerial Inc 231 715-1422
1135 Woodmere Ave Ste A Traverse City (49686) *(G-16007)*

Interactrv, Midland Also called Interact Websites Inc *(G-10871)*

Interclean Equipment LLC 734 961-3300
709 James L Hart Pkwy Ypsilanti (48197) *(G-18082)*

Interdyne Inc 517 849-2281
530 Industrial Pkwy Jonesville (49250) *(G-8656)*

Interface Associates Inc 734 327-9500
1070 Rosewood St Ann Arbor (48104) *(G-507)*

Interfibe Corporation (PA) 269 327-6141
16369 Us Highway 131 S Schoolcraft (49087) *(G-14495)*

Intergrted Dspnse Slutions LLC 586 554-7404
14310 Industrial Ctr Dr Shelby Township (48315) *(G-14605)*

Interior Concepts Corporation 616 842-5550
18525 Trimble Ct Spring Lake (49456) *(G-15155)*

Interior Resource Supply Inc 313 584-4399
9335 Saint Stephens St Dearborn (48126) *(G-3726)*

Interior Spc of Holland 616 396-5634
262 E 26th St Holland (49423) *(G-7690)*

Interkal LLC 989 486-1788
2701 Highbrook Dr Midland (48642) *(G-10872)*

Interkal LLC (HQ) 269 349-1521
5981 E Cork St Kalamazoo (49048) *(G-8773)*

Interlochen Boat Shop Inc 231 275-7112
11512 Us Highway 31 Interlochen (49643) *(G-8243)*

Interlock Design 616 784-5901
5830 Comstock Park Dr Nw Comstock Park (49321) *(G-3486)*

Intermet Systems, Grand Rapids Also called International Met Systems Inc *(G-6541)*

Intermodal Technologies Inc 989 775-3799
915 S Deer Run Mount Pleasant (48858) *(G-11198)*

Intern Metals and Energy (PA) 248 765-7747
522 Hupp Ave Jackson (49203) *(G-8471)*

Internal Grinding Abrasives 616 243-5566
3011 Hillcroft Ave Sw Grand Rapids (49548) *(G-6540)*

International Abrasives Inc 586 778-8490
27980 Groesbeck Hwy Roseville (48066) *(G-13820)*

International Autmtv Compnents, Southfield Also called IAC Creative LLC *(G-14940)*

International Automotive Compo 989 620-7649
1965 Williams Rd Alma (48801) *(G-238)*

International Automotive Compo 734 456-2800
47785 W Anchor Ct Plymouth (48170) *(G-12648)*

ALPHABETIC SECTION

International Automotive Compo 586 795-7800
  6600 15 Mile Rd Sterling Heights (48312) *(G-15376)*
International Automotive Compo 810 987-8500
  1905 Beard St Port Huron (48060) *(G-12930)*
International Automotive Compo 231 734-9000
  601 W 7th St Evart (49631) *(G-4884)*
International Automotive Compo (HQ) 248 455-7000
  28333 Telegraph Rd Southfield (48034) *(G-14948)*
International Brands Inc 248 644-2701
  3371 W Maple Rd Bloomfield Hills (48301) *(G-1775)*
International Bus Mchs Corp 517 391-5248
  196 Crescent Rd East Lansing (48823) *(G-4665)*
International Bus Mchs Corp 989 832-6000
  2125 Ridgewood Dr Midland (48642) *(G-10873)*
International Casting Corp 586 293-8220
  28178 Hayes Rd Roseville (48066) *(G-13821)*
International Door Inc 248 547-7240
  8001 Ronda Dr Canton (48187) *(G-2388)*
International Engrg & Mfg Inc 989 689-4911
  6054 N Meridian Rd Hope (48628) *(G-7954)*
International Extrusions Inc (PA) 734 427-8700
  5800 Venoy Rd Garden City (48135) *(G-5830)*
International Fenestration (PA) 248 735-6880
  917 Pond Island Ct Northville (48167) *(G-11701)*
International Hardcoat, Detroit Also called Ihc Inc *(G-4136)*
International Machining Svc 248 486-3600
  12622 10 Mile Rd South Lyon (48178) *(G-14795)*
International Master Pdts Corp (PA) 231 894-5651
  9751 Us Hhwy 31 Montague (49437) *(G-11091)*
International Master Pdts Corp 800 253-0439
  9751 Us Highway 31 Montague (49437) *(G-11092)*
International Material Co 616 355-2800
  510 E 40th St Holland (49423) *(G-7691)*
International Mch Tl Svcs LLC 734 667-2233
  4028 Hartland Rd Hartland (48353) *(G-7392)*
International Mech Design 248 546-5740
  2015 Bellaire Ave Royal Oak (48067) *(G-13936)*
International Met Systems Inc 616 971-1005
  4767 Broadmoor Ave Se # 7 Grand Rapids (49512) *(G-6541)*
International Mfg & Assembly, Royal Oak Also called Manufcturing Assembly Intl LLC *(G-13946)*
International Minute Press, Farmington Hills Also called Val Valley Inc *(G-5145)*
International Minute Press, Climax Also called Woodhams Enterprises Inc *(G-3014)*
International Minute Press, Southgate Also called Halsan LLC *(G-15078)*
International Minute Press, Warren Also called JMS Printing Svc LLC *(G-17115)*
International Mold Corporation 586 801-2314
  44370 N Groesbeck Hwy Clinton Township (48036) *(G-3142)*
International Mold Corporation (PA) 586 783-6890
  23224 Giacoma Ct Clinton Township (48036) *(G-3143)*
International Noodle Co Inc 248 583-2479
  32811 Groveland St Madison Heights (48071) *(G-10277)*
International Paint Stripping (PA) 734 942-0500
  15300 Oakwood Dr Romulus (48174) *(G-13687)*
International Paint Stripping 734 942-0500
  15326 Oakwood Dr Romulus (48174) *(G-13688)*
International Paper Company 269 273-8461
  1321 3rd St Three Rivers (49093) *(G-15866)*
International Seating Co 586 293-2201
  31047 Fraser Dr Fraser (48026) *(G-5672)*
International Smart Tan Netwrk 517 841-4920
  3101 Page Ave Jackson (49203) *(G-8472)*
International Sports Timing, Grand Rapids Also called Industrial Service Tech Inc *(G-6533)*
International Temperature Ctrl 989 876-8075
  2415 E Huron Rd Au Gres (48703) *(G-746)*
International Wheel & Tire Inc (PA) 248 298-0207
  23255 Commerce Dr Farmington Hills (48335) *(G-5029)*
International Wood Inds Inc 800 598-9663
  2801 E Beltline Ave Ne Grand Rapids (49525) *(G-6542)*
Interntional Catalyst Tech Inc (PA) 248 340-1040
  2347 Commercial Dr Auburn Hills (48326) *(G-914)*
Interntnal Prcast Slutions LLC 313 843-0073
  60 Haltiner St River Rouge (48218) *(G-13278)*
Interntonal Hardwoods Michiana 517 278-8446
  600 1/2 W Chicago Rd Coldwater (49036) *(G-3310)*
Interntonal Innovative Systems 248 524-2222
  36551 Dequindre Rd Troy (48083) *(G-16421)*
Interntonal Specialty Tube LLC 313 923-2000
  17199 N Laurl Prk Dr # 322 Livonia (48152) *(G-9784)*
Interpower Induction Svcs Inc 586 296-7697
  34197 Doreka Fraser (48026) *(G-5673)*
Interpro Technology Inc 248 650-8695
  722 W University Dr Rochester (48307) *(G-13330)*
Intersrce Recovery Systems Inc (PA) 269 375-5100
  1470 S 8th St Kalamazoo (49009) *(G-8774)*
Interstate Power Systems Inc 952 854-2044
  600 Industrial Park Dr Iron Mountain (49801) *(G-8285)*
Interstate Powersystems, Iron Mountain Also called Interstate Power Systems Inc *(G-8285)*
Intertape Polymer Corp 810 364-9000
  317 Kendall St Marysville (48040) *(G-10604)*
Intertec Systems LLC (HQ) 734 254-3268
  45000 Helm St Ste 200 Plymouth (48170) *(G-12649)*
Inteva - Troy Engineering Ctr, Troy Also called Inteva Products LLC *(G-16423)*
Inteva Adrian, Adrian Also called Inteva Products LLC *(G-69)*
Inteva Products LLC 248 655-8886
  1401 Crooks Rd Troy (48084) *(G-16422)*
Inteva Products LLC 517 266-8030
  1450 E Beecher St Adrian (49221) *(G-69)*
Inteva Products LLC 248 655-8886
  2305 Crooks Rd Troy (48084) *(G-16423)*
Inteva Products LLC (HQ) 248 655-8886
  1401 Crooks Rd Troy (48084) *(G-16424)*
Inteva Products Usa LLC 248 655-8886
  1401 Crooks Rd Troy (48084) *(G-16425)*
Intier Automotive Seating, Novi Also called Magna Seating America Inc *(G-11932)*
Intl Giuseppes Oils & Vinegars 586 698-2754
  38033 Opatik Ct Sterling Hts (48312) *(G-15550)*
Intl Giuseppes Oils & Vinegars 586 263-4200
  17330 Hall Rd Clinton Township (48038) *(G-3144)*
Intra Business LLC 269 262-0863
  70600 Batchelor Dr Niles (49120) *(G-11621)*
Intra Corporation (PA) 734 326-7030
  885 Manufacturers Dr Westland (48186) *(G-17571)*
Intralox LLC 616 259-7471
  1430 Monroe Ave Nw # 180 Grand Rapids (49505) *(G-6543)*
Intramode LLC 313 964-6990
  1420 Brdwy St Detroit (48226) *(G-4146)*
Intrepid Plastics Mfg Inc 616 901-5718
  7675 Howard Cy Edmore Rd Lakeview (48850) *(G-9174)*
Intricate Grinding Mch Spc Inc 231 798-2154
  1081 S Gateway Blvd Norton Shores (49441) *(G-11763)*
Intrinsic4d LLC (PA) 248 469-8811
  30800 Telg Rd Ste 4775 Bingham Farms (48025) *(G-1654)*
Intuitive Circuits LLC 248 588-4400
  3928 Wardlow Ct Troy (48083) *(G-16426)*
Intuitive Technology Inc 602 249-5750
  3223 Boulder Ct Dexter (48130) *(G-4495)*
Invecast Corporation 586 755-4050
  25737 Sherwood Ave Warren (48091) *(G-17096)*
Invent Detroit R&D Collaborati 313 451-2658
  440 Burroughs St Detroit (48202) *(G-4147)*
Inventev LLC 248 535-0477
  440 Burroughs St Ste 661 Detroit (48202) *(G-4148)*
Invention Evolution Comp LLC 517 219-0180
  144 National Park Dr Fowlerville (48836) *(G-5570)*
Inventors Industries, Lowell Also called Nathan Slagter *(G-10038)*
Inventron Inc 248 473-9250
  30927 Schoolcraft Rd Livonia (48150) *(G-9785)*
Inverness Dairy Inc 231 627-4655
  1631 Woiderski Rd Cheboygan (49721) *(G-2681)*
Invertech Inc 734 944-4400
  1404 Industrial Dr Ste 1 Saline (48176) *(G-14396)*
Invision Boatworks LLC 989 754-3341
  5700 Becker Rd Saginaw (48601) *(G-14064)*
Invitations By Design 269 342-8551
  223 S Kalamazoo Mall Kalamazoo (49007) *(G-8775)*
Invo Spline Inc (PA) 586 757-8840
  2357 E 9 Mile Rd Warren (48091) *(G-17097)*
Inzi Controls Detroit LLC 334 282-4237
  2950 Technology Dr Rochester Hills (48309) *(G-13451)*
Iochpe Holdings LLC (HQ) 734 737-5000
  39500 Orchard Hill Pl # 500 Novi (48375) *(G-11907)*
Ionbond LLC (HQ) 248 398-9100
  1823 E Whitcomb Ave Madison Heights (48071) *(G-10278)*
Ionia County Shoppers Guide, Saranac Also called Advertiser Publishing Co Inc *(G-14452)*
Ionxhealth Inc 616 808-3290
  4635 40th St Se Grand Rapids (49512) *(G-6544)*
Iosco News County Herald, East Tawas Also called Iosco News Press Publishing Co *(G-4689)*
Iosco News Press Publishing Co (HQ) 989 739-2054
  311 S State St Oscoda (48750) *(G-12212)*
Iosco News Press Publishing Co 989 362-3456
  110 W State St East Tawas (48730) *(G-4689)*
Ipax Atlantic LLC 313 933-4211
  8301 Lyndon St Detroit (48238) *(G-4149)*
Ipax Cleanogel Inc 313 933-4211
  8301 Lyndon St Detroit (48238) *(G-4150)*
IPC Communication Services, Saint Joseph Also called Journal Disposition Corp *(G-14319)*
Ipg Photonics Corporation 248 863-5001
  46695 Magellan Dr Novi (48377) *(G-11908)*
Ipg Phtnics - Mdwest Oprations, Novi Also called Ipg Photonics Corporation *(G-11908)*
Ipr Automation Sohner Plastic, Dexter Also called Sohner Plastics LLC *(G-4511)*
Ips Assembly Corp 734 391-0080
  12077 Merriman Rd Livonia (48150) *(G-9786)*
Iq Manufacturing LLC 586 634-7185
  1180 Centre Rd Auburn Hills (48326) *(G-915)*
Ir Telemetrics, Hancock Also called Infrared Telemetrics Inc *(G-7252)*
Irene Industries LLC 757 696-3969
  866 Grandview Dr Commerce Township (48390) *(G-3417)*

Iridium Manufacturing, Sterling Heights *Also called Demmak Industries LLC* ***(G-15310)***
Iris Design & Print Inc 313 277-0505
24730 Michigan Ave Dearborn (48124) ***(G-3727)***
Irish Boat Shop Inc 231 547-9967
13000 Stover Rd Charlevoix (49720) ***(G-2619)***
Iriso USA Inc (HQ) 248 324-9780
34405 W 12 Mile Rd # 237 Farmington Hills (48331) ***(G-5030)***
Iron Capital of America Co 586 771-5840
21550 Groesbeck Hwy Warren (48089) ***(G-17098)***
Iron City Enterprises Inc 906 863-2630
N2404 Us Highway 41 Menominee (49858) ***(G-10739)***
Iron Clad Security Inc 313 837-0390
15047 Schaefer Hwy Detroit (48227) ***(G-4151)***
Iron Clad Security Products, Detroit *Also called Iron Clad Security Inc* ***(G-4151)***
Iron Fetish Metalworks Inc 586 776-8311
30233 Groesbeck Hwy Roseville (48066) ***(G-13822)***
Iron Mikes WELding& Fabg 810 234-2996
1535 N Dort Hwy Flint (48506) ***(G-5448)***
Iron River Mfg Co Inc 906 265-5121
3390 Us Highway 2 Iron River (49935) ***(G-8310)***
Iron Tool & Die Inc 586 791-1389
35531 Groesbeck Hwy Clinton Township (48035) ***(G-3145)***
Ironwood Plastics Inc (PA) 906 932-5025
1235 Wall St Ironwood (49938) ***(G-8330)***
Ironwood Ready Mix & Trucking 906 932-4531
500 Bonnie Rd Ironwood (49938) ***(G-8331)***
Ironwood Testing & Design Div, Ironwood *Also called Ruppe Manufacturing Company* ***(G-8339)***
Iroquois Assembly Systems Inc 586 771-5734
23220 Pinewood St Warren (48091) ***(G-17099)***
Iroquois Hoods, Muskegon *Also called Gross Ventures Inc* ***(G-11341)***
Iroquois Industries Inc (PA) 586 771-5734
24400 Hoover Rd Warren (48089) ***(G-17100)***
Iroquois Industries Inc 586 756-6922
25101 Groesbeck Hwy Warren (48089) ***(G-17101)***
Iroquois Industries Inc 586 465-1023
7177 Marine City Hwy Cottrellville (48039) ***(G-3589)***
Iroquois Industries Inc 586 353-1410
23750 Regency Park Dr Warren (48089) ***(G-17102)***
Irvin Acquisition LLC (HQ) 248 451-4100
2600 Centerpoint Pkwy Pontiac (48341) ***(G-12837)***
Irvin Automotive Products LLC (HQ) 248 451-4100
2600 Centerpoint Pkwy Pontiac (48341) ***(G-12838)***
Irwin Enterprises Inc 810 732-0770
3030 W Pasadena Ave Flint (48504) ***(G-5449)***
Irwin Seating Holding Company (PA) 616 574-7400
3251 Fruit Ridge Ave Nw Grand Rapids (49544) ***(G-6545)***
Is Field Services, East Lansing *Also called Integrity Sltons Feld Svcs Inc* ***(G-4664)***
Isby Industry LLC 313 269-4213
14534 Redford Dr Sterling Heights (48312) ***(G-15377)***
Isensium 517 580-9022
325 E Grand River Ave East Lansing (48823) ***(G-4666)***
Ishino Gasket North Amer LLC 734 451-0020
47690 E Anchor Ct Plymouth (48170) ***(G-12650)***
Ishpeming Concrete Corporation 906 485-5851
400 Stone St Ishpeming (49849) ***(G-8347)***
Island Machine and Engrg LLC 810 765-8228
847 Degurse Ave Marine City (48039) ***(G-10475)***
Island Sun Times Inc 810 230-1735
5152 Commerce Rd Flint (48507) ***(G-5450)***
Isringhausen Inc 269 484-5333
1458 S 35th St Galesburg (49053) ***(G-5812)***
ISS, Zeeland *Also called Information Stn Specialists* ***(G-18159)***
ISS, Troy *Also called Innovative Support Svcs Inc* ***(G-16418)***
Issys, Ypsilanti *Also called Integrated Sensing Systems Inc* ***(G-18081)***
Ist, Jackson *Also called Industrial Steel Treating Co* ***(G-8470)***
Ist, Livonia *Also called Interntonal Specialty Tube LLC* ***(G-9784)***
Italian BTR Bread Sticks Bky 313 893-4945
4241 E Mcnichols Rd Detroit (48212) ***(G-4152)***
Italian Tribune 586 783-3260
21852 23 Mile Rd Macomb (48042) ***(G-10132)***
Iteg, Pinconning *Also called Conair North America* ***(G-12507)***
Iterotext, Bloomfield *Also called AAA Language Services* ***(G-1731)***
Ithaca Manufacturing Corp 989 875-4949
1210 Avenue A Ithaca (48847) ***(G-8361)***
ITM, Warren *Also called FCA US LLC* ***(G-17031)***
ITT Gage Inc 231 766-2155
3253 Whitehall Rd Muskegon (49445) ***(G-11350)***
ITT Koni America, LLC, Novi *Also called ITT Motion Tech Amer LLC* ***(G-11909)***
ITT Motion Tech Amer LLC 248 863-2161
46785 Magellan Dr Novi (48377) ***(G-11909)***
Ittner Bean & Grain Inc (PA) 989 662-4461
301 Park Ave Auburn (48611) ***(G-753)***
ITW Dahti Seating 616 866-1323
206 Byrne Industrial Dr Rockford (49341) ***(G-13573)***
Ivan Doverspike 313 579-3000
9501 Conner St Detroit (48213) ***(G-4153)***
Iwis Engine Systems LP 248 247-3178
340 E Big Beaver Rd # 155 Troy (48083) ***(G-16427)***
Ix Innovations LLC ......
4488 Jackson Rd Ste 6 Ann Arbor (48103) ***(G-508)***
IXL Graphics Inc 313 350-2800
23265 Country Club Dr South Lyon (48178) ***(G-14796)***
IXL Machine Shop Inc 616 392-9803
117 W 7th St Holland (49423) ***(G-7692)***
Iza Design and Manufacturing, Sterling Heights *Also called Precision Laser & Mfg LLC* ***(G-15449)***
Izzy, Grand Haven *Also called Jsj Furniture Corporation* ***(G-6043)***
Izzy Better Together, Grand Haven *Also called Izzy Plus* ***(G-6038)***
Izzy Plus 574 821-1200
700 Robbins Rd Grand Haven (49417) ***(G-6038)***
J & B Metal Fabicators LLC 616 837-6764
16913 Power Dr Nunica (49448) ***(G-12037)***
J & B Precision Inc 313 565-3431
5886 Pelham Rd Taylor (48180) ***(G-15729)***
J & B Products Ltd 989 792-6119
2201 S Michigan Ave Saginaw (48602) ***(G-14065)***
J & C Industries Inc 248 549-4866
4520 Fernlee Ave Royal Oak (48073) ***(G-13937)***
J & D Logging 517 543-3873
1212 N Chester Rd Charlotte (48813) ***(G-2655)***
J & E Appliance Company Inc 248 642-9191
30170 Stellamar St Beverly Hills (48025) ***(G-1617)***
J & E Manufacturing Company 586 777-5614
16470 E 13 Mile Rd Roseville (48066) ***(G-13823)***
J & G Pallets Inc 313 921-0222
2971 Bellevue St Detroit (48207) ***(G-4154)***
J & G Pallets Inc (PA) 313 921-0222
2971 Bellevue St Detroit (48207) ***(G-4155)***
J & J Burning and Fabg Co, Warren *Also called J & J Burning Co* ***(G-17103)***
J & J Burning Co 586 758-7619
24622 Mound Rd Warren (48091) ***(G-17103)***
J & J Engineering and Machine 616 554-3302
3265 68th St Se Caledonia (49316) ***(G-2302)***
J & J Fabrications Inc 269 673-5488
611 N Eastern Ave Allegan (49010) ***(G-166)***
J & J Industries Inc 517 784-3586
260 W Euclid Ave Jackson (49203) ***(G-8473)***
J & J Laminate Connection Inc 810 227-1824
10603 Grand River Rd Brighton (48116) ***(G-1944)***
J & J Machine Ltd 231 773-4100
3011 S Milliron Rd Muskegon (49444) ***(G-11351)***
J & J Metal Products Inc 586 792-2680
34145 Groesbeck Hwy Clinton Township (48035) ***(G-3146)***
J & J Sheet Metal, Clinton Township *Also called J & J Metal Products Inc* ***(G-3146)***
J & J Spring Co Inc 586 566-7600
14100 23 Mile Rd Shelby Township (48315) ***(G-14606)***
J & J Spring Enterprises LLC 586 566-7600
14100 23 Mile Rd Shelby Township (48315) ***(G-14607)***
J & J Transport LLC 231 582-6083
4556 Lakeshore Rd Boyne City (49712) ***(G-1824)***
J & J United Industries LLC 734 443-3737
39111 6 Mile Rd Livonia (48152) ***(G-9787)***
J & K Canvas Products 810 635-7711
8058 Corunna Rd Flint (48532) ***(G-5451)***
J & L Manufacturing Co Inc (PA) 269 789-1507
1507 George Brown Dr Marshall (49068) ***(G-10572)***
J & L Mfg Co (PA) 586 445-9530
23334 Schoenherr Rd Warren (48089) ***(G-17104)***
J & L Plating & Sand Blasting, Hazel Park *Also called J & L Products Inc* ***(G-7439)***
J & L Products Inc 248 544-8500
21733 Dequindre Rd Hazel Park (48030) ***(G-7439)***
J & L Turning Inc 810 765-5755
5664 River Rd East China (48054) ***(G-4623)***
J & M International Corp 248 588-8108
1200 Rochester Rd Troy (48083) ***(G-16428)***
J & M Machine Products Inc 231 755-1622
1821 Manor Dr Norton Shores (49441) ***(G-11764)***
J & M Products and Service LLC 517 263-3082
615 N Scott St Adrian (49221) ***(G-70)***
J & M Reproductions Corp 248 588-8100
1200 Rochester Rd Troy (48083) ***(G-16429)***
J & R Tool Inc 989 662-0026
4575 Garfield Rd Auburn (48611) ***(G-754)***
J & S Livonia Inc 734 793-9000
12658 Richfield Ct Livonia (48150) ***(G-9788)***
J & T Machining Inc 616 897-6744
681 Lincoln Lake Ave Se Lowell (49331) ***(G-10032)***
J & W Machine & Tool, Mount Pleasant *Also called J & W Machine Inc* ***(G-11199)***
J & W Machine Inc 989 773-9951
315 E Pickard St Mount Pleasant (48858) ***(G-11199)***
J A S Veneer & Lumber Inc 906 635-0710
1300 W 12th St Sault Sainte Marie (49783) ***(G-14466)***
J America, Fowlerville *Also called J America Licensed Pdts Inc* ***(G-5571)***
J America LLC (HQ) 517 521-2525
1200 Mason Ct Webberville (48892) ***(G-17451)***

ALPHABETIC

J America Licensed Pdts Inc (PA)...517 655-8800
445 E Van Riper Rd Fowlerville (48836) ***(G-5571)***
J and K Pallet...517 648-5974
10990 N Adams Rd North Adams (49262) ***(G-11655)***
J and N Fabrications Inc...586 751-6350
30130 Ryan Rd Warren (48092) ***(G-17105)***
J B Cutting Inc...586 468-4765
171 Grand Ave Mount Clemens (48043) ***(G-11135)***
J B Dough Co...269 944-4160
5600 E Napier Ave Benton Harbor (49022) ***(G-1514)***
J B Log Homes Inc...906 875-6581
207 Fisher Rd Crystal Falls (49920) ***(G-3610)***
J B Lunds & Sons Inc...231 627-9070
707 Cleveland Ave Cheboygan (49721) ***(G-2682)***
J C Gibbons Mfg Inc...734 266-5544
35055 Glendale St Livonia (48150) ***(G-9789)***
J C Goss Company...313 259-3520
15500 Oakwood Dr Romulus (48174) ***(G-13689)***
J C Manufacturing Company...586 757-2713
23900 Ryan Rd Warren (48091) ***(G-17106)***
J C S, Essexville *Also called JCs Tool & Mfg Co Inc* ***(G-4873)***
J C Walker & Sons Corp...248 752-8165
3115 S Elms Rd Swartz Creek (48473) ***(G-15668)***
J Carey Logging Inc...906 542-3420
Sawyer Lake Rd Channing (49815) ***(G-2603)***
J Cilluffo Son Studio...810 794-2911
8397 Starville Rd Clay (48001) ***(G-2998)***
J D Russell Company...586 254-8500
44865 Utica Rd Utica (48317) ***(G-16743)***
J Drummond Service Inc...248 624-0190
31758 Enterprise Dr Livonia (48150) ***(G-9790)***
J E Enterprises...586 463-5129
38154 Willowmere St Harrison Township (48045) ***(G-7333)***
J E Myles Inc (PA)...248 583-1020
310 Executive Dr Troy (48083) ***(G-16430)***
J E Wood Co...248 585-5711
395 W Girard Ave Madison Heights (48071) ***(G-10279)***
J E Wood Comp, Madison Heights *Also called Stanhope Tool Inc* ***(G-10360)***
J F McCaughin Co (HQ)...231 759-7304
2817 Mccracken St Norton Shores (49441) ***(G-11765)***
J G Kern Enterprises Inc...586 531-9472
44044 Merrill Rd Sterling Heights (48314) ***(G-15378)***
J G Welding & Maintenance Inc...586 758-0150
7059 Lindsey Rd China (48054) ***(G-2861)***
J H Bennett and Company Inc (PA)...248 596-5100
22975 Venture Dr Novi (48375) ***(G-11910)***
J H P Inc (PA)...248 588-0110
32401 Stephenson Hwy Madison Heights (48071) ***(G-10280)***
J Hansen-Balk Stl Treating Co...616 458-1414
1230 Monroe Ave Nw Grand Rapids (49505) ***(G-6546)***
J House LLC...313 220-4449
71 Lake Shore Rd Grosse Pointe Farms (48236) ***(G-7185)***
J I B Properties LLC...313 382-3234
17100 Francis St Melvindale (48122) ***(G-10701)***
J J Pattern & Castings Inc (PA)...248 543-7119
1780 E 11 Mile Rd Madison Heights (48071) ***(G-10281)***
J J Steel Inc...269 964-0474
2000 Ottawa Trl Battle Creek (49037) ***(G-1201)***
J J Wohlferts Custom Furniture...989 593-3283
10691 W M 21 Fowler (48835) ***(G-5553)***
J Kaltz & Co...616 942-6070
3987 Brockton Dr Se Ste C Grand Rapids (49512) ***(G-6547)***
J L Becker Acquisition LLC...734 656-2000
41150 Joy Rd Plymouth (48170) ***(G-12651)***
J L International Inc (PA)...734 941-0300
34364 Goddard Rd Romulus (48174) ***(G-13690)***
J L Milling Inc...269 679-5769
15262 Industrial Dr Schoolcraft (49087) ***(G-14496)***
J L Schroth Co...586 759-4240
24074 Gibson Dr Warren (48089) ***(G-17107)***
J M Kusch Inc...989 684-8820
3530 Wheeler Rd Bay City (48706) ***(G-1323)***
J M L Contracting & Sales Inc...586 756-4133
5649 E 8 Mile Rd Warren (48091) ***(G-17108)***
J M Longyear Heirs Inc (PA)...906 228-7960
210 N Front St Ste 1 Marquette (49855) ***(G-10535)***
J M Mold Technologies Inc...586 773-6664
25185 Easy St Warren (48089) ***(G-17109)***
J Mark Systems Inc...616 784-6005
3696 Northridge Dr Nw # 10 Grand Rapids (49544) ***(G-6548)***
J N B Machinery LLC...517 223-0711
175 National Park Dr Fowlerville (48836) ***(G-5572)***
J O Well Service, Mount Pleasant *Also called JO Well Service and Tstg Inc* ***(G-11200)***
J R C Inc (PA)...810 648-4000
356 E Sanilac Rd Sandusky (48471) ***(G-14436)***
J R Productions Inc...989 732-2905
1522 Big Lake Rd Gaylord (49735) ***(G-5867)***
J Rettenmaier USA LP (HQ)...269 679-2340
16369 Us Highway 131 S Schoolcraft (49087) ***(G-14497)***

J Solutions LLC...586 477-0127
25215 Terra Industrial Dr Chesterfield (48051) ***(G-2792)***
J Sterling Industries LLC...269 492-6922
6825 Beatrice Dr Ste A Kalamazoo (49009) ***(G-8776)***
J T Express Ltd...810 724-6471
4200 Van Dyke Rd Brown City (48416) ***(G-2052)***
J T Products, Burton *Also called Tyrone Tool Company Inc* ***(G-2168)***
J W Briney Products, Clarkston *Also called Complex Tool & Machine Inc* ***(G-2915)***
J W Froehlich Inc...586 580-0025
7305 19 Mile Rd Sterling Heights (48314) ***(G-15379)***
J W Harris Co Inc...248 634-0737
6774 Country Lane Dr Davisburg (48350) ***(G-3636)***
J W Holdings Inc...616 530-9889
2530 Thornwood St Sw B Grand Rapids (49519) ***(G-6549)***
J W Manchester Company Inc...810 632-5409
3552 Hartland Rd Ste 201 Hartland (48353) ***(G-7393)***
J&D Industries LLC...734 430-6582
4611 Pointe Aux Peaux Newport (48166) ***(G-11588)***
J&J Freon Removal...586 264-6379
32344 Newcastle Dr Warren (48093) ***(G-17110)***
J&J Machine Products Co Inc...313 534-8024
12734 Inkster Rd Redford (48239) ***(G-13167)***
J&S Technologies Inc...616 837-7080
16952 Woodlane Nunica (49448) ***(G-12038)***
J-Ad Graphics Inc (PA)...800 870-7085
1351 N M 43 Hwy Hastings (49058) ***(G-7416)***
J-Ad Graphics Inc...269 965-3955
1001 Columbia Ave E Battle Creek (49014) ***(G-1202)***
J-Ad Graphics Inc...269 945-9554
514 S Kalamazoo Ave Marshall (49068) ***(G-10573)***
J-Ad Graphics Inc...517 543-4041
144 S Cochran Ave Charlotte (48813) ***(G-2656)***
J. America Retail Products, Webberville *Also called J America LLC* ***(G-17451)***
J. L. Becker Co., Plymouth *Also called J L Becker Acquisition LLC* ***(G-12651)***
J. Lewis Cooper Co., Highland Park *Also called Great Lakes Wine & Spirits LLC* ***(G-7506)***
J.L. McHael Hayk Kyyan Jwelers, Bloomfield *Also called Kayayan Hayk Jewelry Mfg Co* ***(G-1734)***
J2 Licensing Inc (PA)...586 307-3400
351 Executive Dr Troy (48083) ***(G-16431)***
Jaan Technolgies, Sterling Heights *Also called Baird Investments LLC* ***(G-15271)***
Jaan Technologies, Orion *Also called Baird Investments LLC* ***(G-12174)***
Jabars Complements LLC...810 966-8371
2639 24th St Port Huron (48060) ***(G-12931)***
Jabil Circuit Inc...248 292-6000
3800 Giddings Rd Auburn Hills (48326) ***(G-916)***
Jabil Circuit Michigan Inc...248 292-6000
3800 Giddings Rd Auburn Hills (48326) ***(G-917)***
JAC Custom Pouches Inc...269 782-3190
56525 Woodhouse Dr Dowagiac (49047) ***(G-4544)***
Jac Holding Corporation (HQ)...248 874-1800
3937 Campus Dr Pontiac (48341) ***(G-12839)***
Jac Products Inc...248 874-1800
3937 Campus Dr Pontiac (48341) ***(G-12840)***
Jac Products Inc...586 254-1534
12000 Shelby Tech Dr Shelby Township (48315) ***(G-14608)***
Jack Millikin Inc...989 348-8411
4680 W N Down River Rd Grayling (49738) ***(G-7109)***
Jack Ripper & Associates Inc...734 453-7333
14708 Keel St Plymouth (48170) ***(G-12652)***
Jack Weaver Corp...517 263-6500
343 Lawrence Ave Adrian (49221) ***(G-71)***
Jack-Post Corporation...269 695-7000
800 E 3rd St Buchanan (49107) ***(G-2121)***
Jackhill Oil Company...734 994-6599
305 E Eisenhower Pkwy # 300 Ann Arbor (48108) ***(G-509)***
Jackpine Business Center, Manistee *Also called Jackpine Press Incorporated* ***(G-10425)***
Jackpine Press Incorporated (PA)...231 723-8344
76 Filer St Manistee (49660) ***(G-10425)***
Jackson 043, Jackson *Also called Perfection Bakeries Inc* ***(G-8550)***
Jackson Architctural Mtl Fabri...517 782-8884
1421 S Cooper St Jackson (49203) ***(G-8474)***
Jackson Canvas Company...517 768-8459
2100 Brooklyn Rd Jackson (49203) ***(G-8475)***
Jackson Citizen Patriot, Jackson *Also called Herald Newspapers Company Inc* ***(G-8464)***
Jackson Flexible Products, Jackson *Also called Jfp Acquisition LLC* ***(G-8483)***
Jackson Grinding Co Inc...517 782-8080
1300 Bagley Ave Jackson (49203) ***(G-8476)***
Jackson Industrial Coating Svc...517 782-8169
3600 Scheele Dr Ste A Jackson (49202) ***(G-8477)***
Jackson Manufacturing & Distrg...616 451-3030
470 Market Ave Sw Unit 34 Grand Rapids (49503) ***(G-6550)***
Jackson Oven Supply Inc...517 784-9660
3507 Wayland Dr Jackson (49202) ***(G-8478)***
Jackson Pandrol Inc...231 843-3431
200 S Jackson Rd Ludington (49431) ***(G-10068)***
Jackson Precision Inds Inc...517 782-8103
1900 Cooper St Jackson (49202) ***(G-8479)***

Jackson Printing Company Inc ... 517 783-2705
3136 Francis St Ste 69 Jackson (49203) *(G-8480)*
Jackson Tumble Finish Corp ... 517 787-0368
1801 Mitchell St Jackson (49203) *(G-8481)*
Jackson Typesetting Company, Jackson *Also called Jtc Inc (G-8486)*
Jacksons Industrial Mfg ... 616 531-1820
2662 Prairie St Sw Wyoming (49519) *(G-18012)*
Jacobs Signs ... 810 659-2149
4182 Dillon Rd Flushing (48433) *(G-5537)*
Jacobsen Industries Inc ... 734 591-6111
12173 Market St Livonia (48150) *(G-9791)*
Jacquart Fabric Products Inc ... 906 932-1339
1238 Wall St Ironwood (49938) *(G-8332)*
Jad Products Inc ... 517 456-4810
4003 W Us Highway 12 Clinton (49236) *(G-3024)*
Jade Mfg Inc ... 734 942-1462
36535 Grant St Romulus (48174) *(G-13691)*
Jade Pharmaceuticals Entp LLC ... 248 716-8333
32229 Schoolcraft Rd Livonia (48150) *(G-9792)*
Jade Scientific Inc (PA) ... 734 207-3775
39103 Warren Rd Westland (48185) *(G-17572)*
Jade Tool Inc ... 231 946-7710
891 Duell Rd Traverse City (49686) *(G-16008)*
Jag Industrial Services Inc ... 678 592-6860
225 E Chicago St Jonesville (49250) *(G-8657)*
Jailbird Designs, Port Huron *Also called 1365267 Ontario Inc (G-12879)*
Jaimes Cupcake Haven ... 586 596-6809
26142 Fairfield Ave Warren (48089) *(G-17111)*
Jaimes Industries, Livonia *Also called J & S Livonia Inc (G-9788)*
Jaimes Liquidation Inc ... 248 356-8600
19270 W 8 Mile Rd Southfield (48075) *(G-14949)*
Jakes Cakes Inc ... 734 522-2103
418 Farmington Rd Garden City (48135) *(G-5831)*
Jam Enterprises ... 313 417-9200
16349 E Warren Ave Detroit (48224) *(G-4156)*
Jam Tire Inc ... 586 772-2900
36031 Groesbeck Hwy Clinton Township (48035) *(G-3147)*
Jam-Live LLC ... 517 282-5410
2677 Brewer Rd Howell (48855) *(G-8054)*
Jamco Manufacturing Inc ... 248 852-1988
2960 Auburn Ct Auburn Hills (48326) *(G-918)*
James Ave Catering ... 517 655-4532
1311 James Ave Williamston (48895) *(G-17731)*
James D Frisbie ... 616 868-0092
8989 66th St Se Alto (49302) *(G-327)*
James E Sullivan & Associates ... 616 453-0345
4617 Sundial Dr Ne Grand Rapids (49525) *(G-6551)*
James G Gallagher ... 989 832-3458
5609 Summerset Dr Midland (48640) *(G-10874)*
James Glove & Supply ... 810 733-5780
3422 W Pasadena Ave Flint (48504) *(G-5452)*
James Joy LLC ... 989 317-6629
412 N Mcewan St Farwell (48622) *(G-5162)*
James L Miller ... 989 539-5540
2500 Major Mountain Rd Harrison (48625) *(G-7313)*
James Pollard Logging ... 906 884-6744
37294 Tikka Rd Ontonagon (49953) *(G-12158)*
James Spicer Inc ... 906 265-2385
1571 W Adams St Iron River (49935) *(G-8311)*
James Steel & Tube Company (HQ) ... 248 547-4200
29774 Stephenson Hwy Madison Heights (48071) *(G-10282)*
James W Liess Co Inc ... 248 547-9160
3410 Baroque Ct Rochester Hills (48306) *(G-13452)*
Jamesway Tool and Die Inc ... 616 396-3731
401 120th Ave Holland (49424) *(G-7693)*
Jamieson Fabrication Unlimited ... 269 760-1473
8530 M 89 Richland (49083) *(G-13250)*
Jamison Industries Inc ... 734 946-3088
12669 Delta St Taylor (48180) *(G-15730)*
Jampot, Eagle Harbor *Also called Society of Saint John Inc (G-4618)*
Jams Media LLC ... 810 664-0811
1521 Imlay City Rd Lapeer (48446) *(G-9465)*
Jan Fan, Rochester Hills *Also called Entrepreneurial Pursuits (G-13418)*
Jandron II ... 906 225-9600
605 Couty Rd Hq Marquette (49855) *(G-10536)*
Janelle Peterson ... 616 447-9070
5274 Plainfield Ave Ne Grand Rapids (49525) *(G-6552)*
Janesville LLC ... 248 948-1811
29200 Northwestern Hwy # 400 Southfield (48034) *(G-14950)*
Janesville Acoustics, Southfield *Also called Janesville LLC (G-14950)*
Janet Kelly ... 231 775-2313
110 W River St Cadillac (49601) *(G-2256)*
Janice Morse Inc ... 248 624-7300
3160 Haggerty Rd Ste N West Bloomfield (48323) *(G-17482)*
Janitorial, Flint *Also called Lockett Enterprises LLC (G-5459)*
Jans Sport Shop Inc ... 810 636-2241
7285 S State Rd Goodrich (48438) *(G-5954)*
Jansen Industries Inc ... 517 788-6800
2400 Enterprise St Jackson (49203) *(G-8482)*
Jant Group LLC ... 616 863-6600
8111 Belmont Ave Ne Belmont (49306) *(G-1463)*
Jantec Incorporated ... 231 941-4339
1777 Northern Star Dr Traverse City (49696) *(G-16009)*
Janutol Printing Co Inc ... 313 526-6196
9920 Conner St Detroit (48213) *(G-4157)*
Japhil Inc ... 616 455-0260
7475 Division Ave S Grand Rapids (49548) *(G-6553)*
Jar-ME LLC ... 313 319-7765
16801 Grand River Ave # 2 Detroit (48227) *(G-4158)*
Jaroche Brothers Inc ... 231 525-8100
4250 Secord Rd Wolverine (49799) *(G-17934)*
Jarvis Concrete Products Inc ... 269 463-3000
7584 Red Arrow Hwy Watervliet (49098) *(G-17393)*
Jarvis Saw Mill Inc ... 231 861-2078
1570 S 112th Ave Shelby (49455) *(G-14526)*
Jarvis Sawmill, Shelby *Also called Jarvis Saw Mill Inc (G-14526)*
Jasco International LLC (PA) ... 313 841-5000
7140 W Fort St Detroit (48209) *(G-4159)*
Jaslin Assembly Inc ... 248 528-3024
4537 Harold Dr Troy (48085) *(G-16432)*
Jason Incorporated ... 248 948-1811
29200 Northwestern Hwy Southfield (48034) *(G-14951)*
Jason Lutke ... 231 824-6655
615 Rw Harris Dr Manton (49663) *(G-10456)*
Jasper Weller LLC (HQ) ... 616 724-2000
1500 Gezon Pkwy Sw Grand Rapids (49509) *(G-6554)*
Jaspers Sugar Bush LLC ... 906 639-2588
W1867 County Road 374 Carney (49812) *(G-2463)*
Jatco Usa Inc ... 248 306-9390
38700 Country Club Dr # 100 Farmington Hills (48331) *(G-5031)*
Java Manufacturing Inc ... 616 784-3873
4760 West River Dr Ne Comstock Park (49321) *(G-3487)*
Jax Services LLC ... 586 703-3212
25343 Masch Ave Warren (48091) *(G-17112)*
Jay & Kay Manufacturing LLC (PA) ... 810 679-2333
72 Louise St Croswell (48422) *(G-3598)*
Jay & Kay Manufacturing LLC ... 810 679-3079
141 E Sanborn Ave Croswell (48422) *(G-3599)*
Jay Cee Sales & Rivet Inc ... 248 478-2150
32861 Chesley Dr Farmington (48336) *(G-4901)*
Jay Enn, Troy *Also called Jay/Enn Corporation (G-16433)*
Jay Industries Inc ... 313 240-7535
7455 Fox Hill Ln Northville (48168) *(G-11702)*
Jay/Enn Corporation ... 248 588-2393
33943 Dequindre Rd Troy (48083) *(G-16433)*
Jayco Manufacturing, Novi *Also called Sage International Inc (G-11989)*
Jaytec LLC ... 734 713-4500
620 S Platt Rd Milan (48160) *(G-10942)*
Jaytec LLC ... 734 397-6300
5800 Sibley Rd Chelsea (48118) *(G-2714)*
Jaytec LLC (HQ) ... 517 451-8272
17757 Woodland Dr New Boston (48164) *(G-11500)*
JB Equipment LLC ... 219 285-0668
20200 Woodruff Rd Gibraltar (48173) *(G-5905)*
JB Products Inc ... 248 549-1900
143 Indusco Ct Troy (48083) *(G-16434)*
Jbj Products and Machinery ... 517 655-4734
125 Industrial Park Dr Williamston (48895) *(G-17732)*
Jbl Enterprises ... 616 530-8647
3535 Wentworth Dr Sw Grand Rapids (49519) *(G-6555)*
Jbl Systems Inc ... 586 802-6700
51935 Filomena Dr Shelby Township (48315) *(G-14609)*
Jbs Packerland Inc ... 269 685-6886
11 11th St Plainwell (49080) *(G-12526)*
Jbs Plainwell Inc ... 269 685-6886
11 11th St Plainwell (49080) *(G-12527)*
Jbs Sheet Metal Inc ... 231 777-2802
2226 S Getty St Muskegon (49444) *(G-11352)*
Jbs Transport LLC ... 248 636-5546
1834 Kirkton Dr Troy (48083) *(G-16435)*
Jbt Bottling LLC ... 269 377-4905
8322 Waterwood Dr Kalamazoo (49048) *(G-8777)*
JC Metal Fabricating Inc ... 231 629-0425
21831 9 Mile Rd Reed City (49677) *(G-13216)*
Jci Jones Chemicals Inc ... 734 283-0677
18000 Payne Ave Wyandotte (48192) *(G-17963)*
Jcp LLC ... 989 754-7496
1422 S 25th St Saginaw (48601) *(G-14066)*
Jcr Fabrication LLC ... 906 235-2683
23642 W State Highway M64 Ontonagon (49953) *(G-12159)*
JCs Tool & Mfg Co Inc ... 989 892-8975
193 N Powell Rd Essexville (48732) *(G-4873)*
Jcu International Inc ... 248 313-6630
51004 Century Ct Wixom (48393) *(G-17837)*
JD Group Inc ... 248 735-9999
26600 Heyn Dr Novi (48374) *(G-11911)*
JD Hemp Inc ... 248 549-0095
31930 Woodward Ave Royal Oak (48073) *(G-13938)*

A L P H A B E T I C

JD Metalworks Inc ALPHABETIC SECTION

JD Metalworks Inc 989 386-3231
635 Industrial Dr Clare (48617) ***(G-2873)***
JD Norman Industries Inc 517 589-8241
815 Rice St Leslie (49251) ***(G-9542)***
JD Plastics Inc 517 264-6858
1305 Railroad Ave Adrian (49221) ***(G-72)***
JD Plating Company Inc (PA) 248 547-5200
25428 John R Rd Madison Heights (48071) ***(G-10283)***
Jda Software Group Inc 734 741-4205
900 Victors Way Ste 360 Ann Arbor (48108) ***(G-510)***
JDG Service, Midland *Also called James G Gallagher* ***(G-10874)***
Jdi Technologies, Auburn Hills *Also called Jo-Dan International Inc* ***(G-919)***
Jdl Enterprises Inc 586 977-8863
7200 Miller Dr Warren (48092) ***(G-17113)***
Jdl Enterprises Inc (PA) 586 977-8863
36425 Maas Dr Sterling Heights (48312) ***(G-15380)***
Jds Small Machine Repair 517 323-7236
1515 Biltmore Blvd Lansing (48906) ***(G-9238)***
Jdti, Holland *Also called Amneon Acquisitions LLC* ***(G-7559)***
Jean Smith Designs 616 942-9212
2704 Boston St Se Grand Rapids (49506) ***(G-6556)***
Jedco Inc (PA) 616 459-5161
1615 Broadway Ave Nw Grand Rapids (49504) ***(G-6557)***
Jedi Machining Corp 313 272-9500
18564 Fitzpatrick St Detroit (48228) ***(G-4160)***
Jedtco Corp 734 326-3010
5899 E Executive Dr Westland (48185) ***(G-17573)***
Jeff Brown Sand & Gravel 517 445-2700
6894 Morey Hwy Clayton (49235) ***(G-3008)***
Jeff R Cabinets LLC 989 233-0976
4490 Elkton Rd Gagetown (48735) ***(G-5802)***
Jeff Schaller Transport Inc 810 724-7640
2835 N Van Dyke Rd Imlay City (48444) ***(G-8205)***
Jefferson Iron Works Inc 248 542-3554
2441 Wolcott St Ferndale (48220) ***(G-5295)***
Jeffery Lucas 231 797-5152
10975 E Old M 63 Luther (49656) ***(G-10093)***
Jeffery Tool & Mfg Co 586 307-8846
44371 Macomb Indus Dr Clinton Township (48036) ***(G-3148)***
Jeffrey Alan Mfg & Engrg LLC 810 325-1119
8625 Lapeer Rd Wales (48027) ***(G-16859)***
Jeffrey L Hackworth 517 589-5884
1162 W Fitchburg Rd Leslie (49251) ***(G-9543)***
Jeld-Wen Inc 616 554-3551
4100 Korona Ct Se Caledonia (49316) ***(G-2303)***
Jeld-Wen Inc 616 531-5440
4200 Roger B Chaffee Se Grand Rapids (49548) ***(G-6558)***
Jem Computers Inc 586 783-3400
23537 Lakepointe Dr Clinton Township (48036) ***(G-3149)***
Jem Jig Grinding Inc 248 486-7006
29450 Haas Rd Wixom (48393) ***(G-17838)***
Jem Tech Group, Clinton Township *Also called Jem Computers Inc* ***(G-3149)***
Jemar Tool Inc 586 726-6960
51268 Fischer Park Dr Shelby Township (48316) ***(G-14610)***
Jemms-Cascade Inc 248 526-8100
238 Executive Dr Troy (48083) ***(G-16436)***
Jems of Litchfield Inc 517 542-5367
174 Simpson Dr Litchfield (49252) ***(G-9605)***
Jenda Controls Inc 248 656-0090
363 South St Apt B Rochester (48307) ***(G-13331)***
Jene Holly Designs Inc 586 954-0255
39876 Shoreline Dr Harrison Township (48045) ***(G-7334)***
Jenison Printing, Grand Rapids *Also called Advance BCI Inc* ***(G-6145)***
Jenkins Group Inc 231 933-4954
1129 Woodmere Ave Ste B Traverse City (49686) ***(G-16010)***
Jennco Industries LLC 269 290-3145
3145 Babylon Rd Allegan (49010) ***(G-167)***
Jenoptik Automotive N Amer LLC 248 853-5888
1500 W Hamlin Rd Rochester Hills (48309) ***(G-13453)***
Jensen Bridge & Supply Company (PA) 810 648-3000
400 Stoney Creek Dr Sandusky (48471) ***(G-14437)***
Jensen Industries Inc. (PA) 810 224-5005
3061 W Thompson Rd Ste 1 Fenton (48430) ***(G-5221)***
Jensen Security Systems, Portage *Also called George Jensen* ***(G-12998)***
Jentees Custom Logo Gear, Traverse City *Also called Jentees Custom Screen Prtg LLC* ***(G-16011)***
Jentees Custom Screen Prtg LLC 231 929-3610
515 Wellington St Traverse City (49686) ***(G-16011)***
Jep Industries LLC 734 844-3506
1965 Oakview Dr Canton (48187) ***(G-2389)***
Jer-Den Plastics Inc (PA) 989 681-4303
750 Woodside Dr Saint Louis (48880) ***(G-14364)***
Jered LLC 906 776-1800
821 East Blvd Iron Mountain (49802) ***(G-8286)***
Jeremy Jelinek (PA) 231 313-7124
8389 E Lakeview Hills Rd Traverse City (49684) ***(G-16012)***
Jerkies Jerky Factory 231 652-8008
48 W State Rd Newaygo (49337) ***(G-11570)***
Jernberg Holdings LLC (HQ) 313 758-2000
1 Dauch Dr Detroit (48211) ***(G-4161)***
Jerome Miller Lumber Co (PA) 231 745-3694
7027 S James Rd Baldwin (49304) ***(G-1083)***
Jerome Miller Lumber Co 231 745-3694
Baldwin Rd Baldwin (49304) ***(G-1084)***
Jerrys Pallets 734 242-1577
232 E Hurd Rd Monroe (48162) ***(G-11043)***
Jerrys Quality Quick Print 248 354-1313
28810 Northwestern Hwy Southfield (48034) ***(G-14952)***
Jerrys Tool & Die 989 732-4689
5130 Alba Rd Gaylord (49735) ***(G-5868)***
Jerrys Welding Inc 231 853-6494
11210 Ellis Rd Ravenna (49451) ***(G-13121)***
Jershon Inc 231 861-2900
980 Industrial Park Dr Shelby (49455) ***(G-14527)***
Jervis B Webb Company 248 553-1222
34375 W 12 Mile Rd Farmington Hills (48331) ***(G-5032)***
Jervis B Webb Company (HQ) 248 553-1000
30100 Cabot Dr Novi (48377) ***(G-11912)***
Jervis B Webb Company 231 582-6558
1254 Boyne Ave Boyne City (49712) ***(G-1825)***
Jervis B Webb Company 231 347-3931
8212 M 119 Harbor Springs (49740) ***(G-7285)***
Jerz Machine Tool Corporation 269 782-3535
415 E Prairie Ronde St Dowagiac (49047) ***(G-4545)***
Jess Enterprises LLC 517 546-5818
5776 E Grand River Ave Howell (48843) ***(G-8055)***
Jesse James Logging 906 395-6819
16938 Dynamite Hill Rd Lanse (49946) ***(G-9193)***
Jet Box Co Inc 248 362-1260
1822 Thunderbird Troy (48084) ***(G-16437)***
Jet Fuel 231 767-9566
2177 S Mill Iron Rd Muskegon (49442) ***(G-11353)***
Jet Gage & Tool Inc 586 294-3770
31265 Kendall Fraser (48026) ***(G-5674)***
Jet Industries Inc 734 641-0900
38379 Abruzzi Dr Westland (48185) ***(G-17574)***
Jet Speed Printing Company 989 224-6475
313 N Clinton Ave Saint Johns (48879) ***(G-14285)***
Jet Subsurface Rod Pumps Corp 989 732-7513
450 Sides Dr Gaylord (49735) ***(G-5869)***
Jetco Federal Supply, Grand Rapids *Also called Jetco Packaging Solutions LLC* ***(G-6559)***
Jetco Packaging Solutions LLC 616 588-2492
525 Ottawa Ave Nw Lev Grand Rapids (49503) ***(G-6559)***
Jetco Signs 269 420-0202
302 Capital Ave Sw Battle Creek (49037) ***(G-1203)***
Jetech Inc 269 965-6311
555 Industrial Park Dr Battle Creek (49037) ***(G-1204)***
Jets Glove Manufacturing, Brighton *Also called Ebinger Manufacturing Company* ***(G-1917)***
Jewelers Workshop 616 791-6500
1624 Leonard St Nw Grand Rapids (49504) ***(G-6560)***
Jewish News, The, Southfield *Also called Detroit Jewish News Ltd Partnr* ***(G-14881)***
Jex Manufacturing Inc 586 463-4274
41 Eldredge St Mount Clemens (48043) ***(G-11136)***
JF Hubert Enterprises Inc (PA) 586 293-8660
34480 Commerce Fraser (48026) ***(G-5675)***
Jfd North, Holland *Also called Magna Mirrors America Inc* ***(G-7736)***
Jfp Acquisition LLC 517 787-8877
7765 Clinton Rd Jackson (49201) ***(G-8483)***
JG Distributing Inc 906 225-0882
120 Morgan Meadows Rd Marquette (49855) ***(G-10537)***
Jgr Plastics LLC 810 990-1957
2040 International Way Port Huron (48060) ***(G-12932)***
Jgs Machining LLC 810 329-4210
4455 Davis Rd Saint Clair (48079) ***(G-14223)***
Jh Packaging, Allegan *Also called Digital Imaging Group Inc* ***(G-157)***
Jhs Grinding LLC 586 427-6006
24700 Mound Rd Warren (48091) ***(G-17114)***
Jice Pharmaceuticals Co Inc 616 897-5910
6895 Belding Rd Belding (48809) ***(G-1420)***
Jier North America Inc 734 404-6683
14975 Cleat St Plymouth (48170) ***(G-12653)***
Jiffy Print 269 692-3128
381 W Allegan St Ste C Otsego (49078) ***(G-12242)***
Jim Detweiler 269 467-7728
64177 Rommel Rd Sturgis (49091) ***(G-15608)***
Jim Schnabelt, Dexter *Also called Siko Products Inc* ***(G-4509)***
Jimdi Plastics Inc 616 895-7766
5375 Edgeway Dr Allendale (49401) ***(G-219)***
Jireh Metal Products Inc 616 531-7581
3635 Nardin St Sw Grandville (49418) ***(G-7053)***
Jirgens Modern Tool Corp 269 381-5588
3536 Gembrit Cir Kalamazoo (49001) ***(G-8778)***
JIT Steel Corp 313 491-3212
8111 Tireman Ave Ste 1 Dearborn (48126) ***(G-3728)***
JJ Jinkleheimer & Co Inc 517 546-4345
2705 E Grand River Ave # 1 Howell (48843) ***(G-8056)***
JK Machining Inc 269 344-0870
5955 W D Ave Kalamazoo (49009) ***(G-8779)***

Jk Manufacturing Co 231 258-2638
520 E Dresden St Kalkaska (49646) **(G-8945)**
JKL Hardwoods Inc 906 265-9130
1101 Homer Rd Iron River (49935) **(G-8312)**
Jkr Ventures LLC 734 645-2320
1129 Woodmere Ave Ste B Traverse City (49686) **(G-16013)**
JL Geisler Sign Company 586 574-1800
1017 Naughton Dr Troy (48083) **(G-16438)**
Jlm Elec 989 486-3788
1854 Smith Ct Midland (48640) **(G-10875)**
Jlore Welding 989 402-7201
8810 W Sunset Pnes Sparta (49345) **(G-15099)**
Jma Manufacturing, New Haven *Also called Jma Tool Company Inc* **(G-11524)**
Jma Tool Company Inc 586 270-6706
58233 Gratiot Ave New Haven (48048) **(G-11524)**
Jmc Custom Cabinetry 989 345-0475
960 W Houghton Ave West Branch (48661) **(G-17509)**
JMJ Inc 269 948-2828
1029 Enterprise Dr Hastings (49058) **(G-7417)**
JMS of Holland Inc 616 796-2727
1010 Productions Ct Holland (49423) **(G-7694)**
JMS Printing Svc LLC 734 414-6203
14147 Edison Dr Warren (48088) **(G-17115)**
Jn Newman Construction LLC 269 968-1290
2869 W Dickman Rd Springfield (49037) **(G-15194)**
JNB Machining Company Inc (PA) 517 223-0725
9119 W Grand River Rd Fowlerville (48836) **(G-5573)**
Jns Sawmill 989 352-5430
4991 N Satterlee Rd Coral (49322) **(G-3574)**
JO Well Service and Tstg Inc 989 772-4221
6825 Lea Pick Dr Mount Pleasant (48858) **(G-11200)**
Jo-Ad Industries Inc 248 588-4810
31465 Stephenson Hwy Madison Heights (48071) **(G-10284)**
Jo-Dan International Inc (PA) 248 340-0300
2704 Paldan Dr Auburn Hills (48326) **(G-919)**
Jo-Mar Enterprises Inc 313 365-9200
7489 E Davison St Detroit (48212) **(G-4162)**
Jo-Mar Industries Inc 248 588-9625
2876 Elliott Dr Troy (48083) **(G-16439)**
Joam Inc 989 828-5749
9495 S Green Rd Shepherd (48883) **(G-14729)**
Joan Arnoudse 616 364-9075
2499 Omega Dr Ne Grand Rapids (49525) **(G-6561)**
Job Shop Ink Inc 517 372-3900
2321 W Main St Lansing (48917) **(G-9300)**
Jobs Inc 810 714-0522
14829 Philomene Blvd Allen Park (48101) **(G-199)**
Jodon Engineering Assoc Inc 734 761-4044
62 Enterprise Dr Ann Arbor (48103) **(G-511)**
Joe Bosanic Forest Products 906 341-2037
1808 Nw Kendall Rd Manistique (49854) **(G-10441)**
Joe Davis Crushing Inc 586 757-3612
42101 Bobjean St Sterling Heights (48314) **(G-15381)**
Joes Tables LLC 989 846-4970
2700 W Huron Rd Standish (48658) **(G-15220)**
Joes Trailer Manufacturing 734 261-0050
13374 Farmington Rd Ste A Livonia (48150) **(G-9793)**
Joggle Tool & Die Co Inc 586 792-7477
24424 Kolleen Ln Clinton Township (48035) **(G-3150)**
Jogue Inc 248 349-1501
100 Rural Hill St Northville (48167) **(G-11703)**
Jogue Inc (PA) 734 207-0100
14731 Helm Ct Plymouth (48170) **(G-12654)**
Jogue Inc 313 921-4802
6349 E Palmer St Detroit (48211) **(G-4163)**
Johan Van De Weerd Co Inc 517 542-3817
916 Anderson Rd Litchfield (49252) **(G-9606)**
John A Biewer Co of Illinois 810 326-3930
812 S Riverside Ave Saint Clair (48079) **(G-14224)**
John A Biewer Lumber Company 231 839-7646
1560 W Houghton Lake Rd Lake City (49651) **(G-9089)**
John A Biewer Lumber Company (PA) 810 329-4789
812 S Riverside Ave Saint Clair (48079) **(G-14225)**
John A Biewer Lumber Company 231 825-2855
6251 W Gerwoude Dr Mc Bain (49657) **(G-10682)**
John A Van Den Bosch Co (PA) 616 848-2000
4511 Holland Ave Holland (49424) **(G-7695)**
John Allen Enterprises 734 426-2507
4281 Climbing Way Ann Arbor (48103) **(G-512)**
John Barnes 231 885-1561
11783 W 8 Rd Copemish (49625) **(G-3572)**
John Crane Inc 989 496-9292
3300 Centennial Dr Midland (48642) **(G-10876)**
John Deere Authorized Dealer, Gaylord *Also called Lappans of Gaylord Inc* **(G-5874)**
John Deere Authorized Dealer, Williamston *Also called D & G Equipment Inc* **(G-17729)**
John H Dekker & Sons Inc 616 257-4120
2941 Clydon Ave Sw Grand Rapids (49519) **(G-6562)**
John Henry, Lansing *Also called MPS Hrl LLC* **(G-9247)**
John Johnson Company 313 496-0600
15500 Oakwood Dr Romulus (48174) **(G-13692)**
John L Hinkle Holding Co Inc 269 344-3640
1206 E Crosstown Pkwy Kalamazoo (49001) **(G-8780)**
John Lamantia Corporation 269 428-8100
4825 Roosevelt Rd Stevensville (49127) **(G-15572)**
John Ostrander Company, Madison Heights *Also called Ostrander Company Inc* **(G-10318)**
John R Sand & Gravel Co Inc 810 678-3715
1717 E Dryden Rd Metamora (48455) **(G-10777)**
John Sams Tool Co 586 776-3560
14478 E 9 Mile Rd Warren (48089) **(G-17116)**
John Sivula Logging & Cnstr 906 639-2714
N13300 Sivula Lane T 1 Daggett (49821) **(G-3621)**
John T Stoliker Enterprises 586 727-1402
9353 Gratiot Ave Columbus (48063) **(G-3379)**
John V Gedda Jr 906 482-5037
715 Pine St Hancock (49930) **(G-7253)**
John Vuk & Son Inc 906 524-6074
Vuk Rd Lanse (49946) **(G-9194)**
John Zellar Jr Forest Products, Germfask *Also called Zellar Forest Products* **(G-5903)**
John's Glass & Windows, Coloma *Also called Johns Glass* **(G-3357)**
Johnico LLC 248 895-7820
400 Monroe St Ste 480 Detroit (48226) **(G-4164)**
Johnnie On Spot Inc 248 673-2233
2149 Deer Run Trl Waterford (48329) **(G-17352)**
Johnnie On Spot Printing Co, Waterford *Also called Johnnie On Spot Inc* **(G-17352)**
Johnny Meyers Trucking, Middleton *Also called Meyers John* **(G-10793)**
Johns Glass 269 468-4227
271 N Paw Paw St Coloma (49038) **(G-3357)**
Johnson & Berry Mfg Inc 906 524-6433
15442 Roth Rd Lanse (49946) **(G-9195)**
Johnson Carbide Products, Saginaw *Also called Jcp LLC* **(G-14066)**
Johnson Cleaning & Painting 231 627-2211
425 Dresser St Cheboygan (49721) **(G-2683)**
Johnson Cntrls-Bttle Creek Vnt, Plymouth *Also called Hoover Universal Inc* **(G-12642)**
Johnson Contrls Authorized Dlr, Saginaw *Also called Ferguson Enterprises Inc* **(G-14037)**
Johnson Contrls Authorized Dlr, Detroit *Also called Young Supply Company* **(G-4455)**
Johnson Controls, Monroe *Also called Yanfeng US Automotive* **(G-11086)**
Johnson Controls, Lansing *Also called Bridgewater Interiors LLC* **(G-9279)**
Johnson Controls Inc 248 276-6000
2875 High Meadow Cir Auburn Hills (48326) **(G-920)**
Johnson Controls Inc 734 254-5000
49200 Halyard Dr Plymouth (48170) **(G-12655)**
Johnson Controls Inc 616 283-5578
921 E 32nd St Holland (49423) **(G-7696)**
Johnson Controls Inc 269 226-4748
5164 S Sprinkle Rd Portage (49002) **(G-13003)**
Johnson Controls Inc 866 252-3677
3312 Lousma Dr Se Grand Rapids (49548) **(G-6563)**
Johnson Controls Inc 313 842-3300
4617 W Fort St Detroit (48209) **(G-4165)**
Johnson Controls Inc 734 254-5000
49200 Halyard Dr Plymouth (48170) **(G-12656)**
Johnson Controls Inc 734 254-7200
47700 Halyard Dr Plymouth (48170) **(G-12657)**
Johnson Controls Inc 616 847-2766
15115 Leonard Rd Spring Lake (49456) **(G-15156)**
Johnson Controls Inc 269 323-0988
7684 N Sprinkle Rd Kalamazoo (49004) **(G-8781)**
Johnson Controls Inc 313 842-3479
41873 Ecorse Rd Van Buren Twp (48111) **(G-16766)**
Johnson Controls Inc 734 995-3016
1935 S Industrial Hwy Ann Arbor (48104) **(G-513)**
Johnson Controls Inc 616 392-5151
1 Prince Ctr Holland (49423) **(G-7697)**
Johnson Controls Inc 586 826-8845
6111 Sterling Dr N Sterling Heights (48312) **(G-15382)**
Johnson Electric N Amer Inc (HQ) 734 392-5300
47660 Halyard Dr Plymouth (48170) **(G-12658)**
Johnson Glass Cleaning Inc 906 361-0361
5 Pond Rd Negaunee (49866) **(G-11471)**
Johnson Home Decorating Ctr, Cheboygan *Also called Johnson Cleaning & Painting* **(G-2683)**
Johnson Logging Firewoo 231 578-5833
8473 Apple Ave Ravenna (49451) **(G-13122)**
Johnson Matthey North Amer Inc 734 946-9856
12600 Universal Dr Taylor (48180) **(G-15731)**
Johnson Precision Mold & Engrg 269 651-2553
1001 Haines Blvd Sturgis (49091) **(G-15609)**
Johnson Sign Company Inc 517 784-3720
2240 Lansing Ave Jackson (49202) **(G-8484)**
Johnson Sign Mint Cnslting LLC 231 796-8880
5555 E 13 Mile Rd Paris (49338) **(G-12386)**
Johnson Systems Inc 616 455-1900
7835 100th St Se Caledonia (49316) **(G-2304)**
Johnson Technology Inc (HQ) 231 777-2685
2034 Latimer Dr Muskegon (49442) **(G-11354)**
Johnson Walker & Assoc LLC 810 688-1600
4337 Mill St North Branch (48461) **(G-11660)**

ALPHABETIC

Johnson-Clark Printers Inc....231 947-6898
1224 Centre St Traverse City (49686) ***(G-16014)***
Johnston Boiler Company....616 842-5050
300 Pine St Ferrysburg (49409) ***(G-5335)***
Johnston Meat Processing....810 378-5455
4470 Sandusky Rd Peck (48466) ***(G-12419)***
Johnston Printing & Offset....906 786-1493
711 Ludington St Escanaba (49829) ***(G-4837)***
Joint Clutch & Gear Svc Inc (PA)....734 641-7575
30200 Cypress Rd Romulus (48174) ***(G-13693)***
Joint Production Tech Inc (PA)....586 786-0080
15381 Hallmark Ct Macomb (48042) ***(G-10133)***
Jokab Safety North America Inc (PA)....888 282-2123
6471 Commerce Dr Westland (48185) ***(G-17575)***
Joleado, Hudsonville *Also called Blue Pony LLC* ***(G-8149)***
Jolico/J-B Tool Inc....586 739-5555
4325 22 Mile Rd Shelby Township (48317) ***(G-14611)***
Jolicor Manufacturing Services....586 323-5090
13357 W Star Dr Shelby Township (48315) ***(G-14612)***
Jolly Pumpkin Artisan Ales LLC (PA)....734 426-4962
3115 Broad St Ste A Dexter (48130) ***(G-4496)***
Jolman & Jolman Enterprises....231 744-4500
1384 Linden Dr Muskegon (49445) ***(G-11355)***
Jomar Inc....269 925-2222
1090 S Crystal Ave Benton Harbor (49022) ***(G-1515)***
Jomar Performance Products LLC....248 322-3080
211 N Cass Ave Pontiac (48342) ***(G-12841)***
Jomark Inc....248 478-2600
30650 W 8 Mile Rd Farmington Hills (48336) ***(G-5033)***
Jomat Industries Ltd....586 336-1801
131 Mclean Bruce Twp (48065) ***(G-2085)***
Jomesa North America Inc....248 457-0023
2095 E Big Beaver Rd Troy (48083) ***(G-16440)***
Jon F Canty, Warren *Also called Mica TEC Inc* ***(G-17151)***
Jonathan Showalter....269 496-7001
20960 M 60 Mendon (49072) ***(G-10714)***
Jonathan Stevens Mattress Co (PA)....616 243-4342
3800 Division Ave S Grand Rapids (49548) ***(G-6564)***
Jones & Hollands Inc....810 364-6400
1777 Busha Hwy Marysville (48040) ***(G-10605)***
Jones Chemical Inc....734 283-0677
18000 Payne St Riverview (48193) ***(G-13299)***
Jones Electric Company....231 726-5001
1965 Sanford St Muskegon (49441) ***(G-11356)***
Jones Equipment Rental, Marysville *Also called Jones & Hollands Inc* ***(G-10605)***
Jones Mfg & Sup Co Inc....616 877-4442
1177 Electric Ave Moline (49335) ***(G-11011)***
Jones Precision Jig Grinding....248 549-4866
4520 Fernlee Ave Royal Oak (48073) ***(G-13939)***
Jones Ray Well Servicing Inc....989 832-8071
172 N 11 Mile Rd Midland (48640) ***(G-10877)***
Jonesville Tool and Mfg, Jonesville *Also called Jt Manufacturing Inc* ***(G-8658)***
Jonny Almond Nut Company, Flint *Also called R & J Almonds Inc* ***(G-5489)***
Jordan Advertising Inc....989 792-7446
321 Lyon St Saginaw (48602) ***(G-14067)***
Jordan Exploration Co LLC....231 935-4220
1503 Garfield Rd N Traverse City (49696) ***(G-16015)***
Jordan Manufacturing Company....616 794-0900
308 Reed St Belding (48809) ***(G-1421)***
Jordan Tool Corporation....586 755-6700
11801 Commerce St Warren (48089) ***(G-17117)***
Jordan Valley Concrete Service....231 536-7701
126 Garner Rd East Jordan (49727) ***(G-4637)***
Jordan Valley Glassworks....231 536-0539
209 State St East Jordan (49727) ***(G-4638)***
Jorgensen Stl Mch & Fab Inc....517 767-4600
166 Spires Pkwy Tekonsha (49092) ***(G-15819)***
Jorgensen's Supermarket, Greenville *Also called Jorgensens Inc* ***(G-7140)***
Jorgensens Inc....989 831-8338
1325 W Washington St Greenville (48838) ***(G-7140)***
Josefs French Pastry Shop Co....313 881-5710
21150 Mack Ave Grosse Pointe Woods (48236) ***(G-7204)***
Joseph A Dimaggio....313 881-5353
19876 Mack Ave Grosse Pointe Woods (48236) ***(G-7205)***
Joseph Lakosky Logging....906 573-2783
10502w Government Rd Manistique (49854) ***(G-10442)***
Joseph M Hoffman Inc (PA)....586 774-8500
16560 Industrial St Roseville (48066) ***(G-13824)***
Joseph M. Day Company, Saginaw *Also called Banner Engineering & Sales Inc* ***(G-14000)***
Joseph Miller....231 821-2430
7781 Brickyard Rd Holton (49425) ***(G-7933)***
Joshs Frogs....517 648-0260
11629 Glen Mary Dr Byron (48418) ***(G-2173)***
Jost International Corp (HQ)....616 846-7700
1770 Hayes St Grand Haven (49417) ***(G-6039)***
Jostens Inc....734 308-3879
4670 Fulton St E Ste 202 Ada (49301) ***(G-19)***
Journal Disposition Corp....269 428-2054
2180 Maiden Ln Saint Joseph (49085) ***(G-14319)***
Journal Register Company....586 790-1600
100 Macomb Daily Dr Mount Clemens (48043) ***(G-11137)***
Joy Industries Inc....248 334-4062
117 Turk St Pontiac (48341) ***(G-12842)***
Joy Products Inc....269 683-1662
1930 S 3rd St Niles (49120) ***(G-11622)***
Joy-Max Inc....616 847-0990
718 Elliott Ave Grand Haven (49417) ***(G-6040)***
Joyce Zahradnik....616 874-3350
8321 Kreuter Rd Ne Rockford (49341) ***(G-13574)***
Joyson Safety Systems....248 364-6023
2025 Harmon Rd Auburn Hills (48326) ***(G-921)***
Joyson Safety Systems....248 373-8040
2500 Innovation Dr Auburn Hills (48326) ***(G-922)***
Joyson Sfety Systems Acqstion (HQ)....248 373-8040
2500 Innovation Dr Auburn Hills (48326) ***(G-923)***
JP Castings Inc....517 857-3660
211 Mill St Springport (49284) ***(G-15211)***
JP Skidmore LLC....906 424-4127
W5634 Evergreen Road No 3 Menominee (49858) ***(G-10740)***
Jpg Resources Food Mfg, Battle Creek *Also called Snackwerks of Michigan LLC* ***(G-1251)***
JPS Mfg Inc....586 415-8702
17640 15 Mile Rd Fraser (48026) ***(G-5676)***
Jpt, Macomb *Also called Joint Production Tech Inc* ***(G-10133)***
Jr Automation, Holland *Also called JR Automation Tech LLC* ***(G-7698)***
JR Automation Tech LLC (HQ)....616 399-2168
13365 Tyler St Holland (49424) ***(G-7698)***
JR Automation Tech LLC....616 399-2168
4433 Holland Ave Holland (49424) ***(G-7699)***
JR Automation Tech LLC....616 399-2168
4412 136th Ave Holland (49424) ***(G-7700)***
JR Automation Tech LLC....616 399-2168
100 Aniline Ave N Holland (49424) ***(G-7701)***
Jr Automation Technologies, Holland *Also called Jr Technology Group LLC* ***(G-7702)***
Jr Automation Technologies, Stevensville *Also called Dane Systems LLC* ***(G-15562)***
Jr Kandler & Sons....734 241-0270
13657 Laplaisance Rd Monroe (48161) ***(G-11044)***
Jr Larry Dudley....313 721-3600
7701 Forrer St Detroit (48228) ***(G-4166)***
Jr Technology Group LLC (PA)....616 399-2168
13365 Tyler St Holland (49424) ***(G-7702)***
Jrb Enterprises, Oscoda *Also called Oscoda Plastics Inc* ***(G-12216)***
Jrj Energy Services LLC....231 823-2171
7302 Northland Dr Stanwood (49346) ***(G-15234)***
Jrm Industries Inc....616 837-9758
12409 Cleveland St Nunica (49448) ***(G-12039)***
Jrop LLC....800 404-9494
404 E 4th St Ste 110 Royal Oak (48067) ***(G-13940)***
Jrt Enterprises LLC....877 318-7661
199 E 17th St Holland (49423) ***(G-7703)***
JS Original Silkscreens LLC....586 779-5456
18132 E 10 Mile Rd Eastpointe (48021) ***(G-4705)***
JS Welding Inc....517 451-2098
8400 Shaw Hwy Britton (49229) ***(G-2018)***
Jsj Corporation....616 842-5500
1250 S Beechtree St Grand Haven (49417) ***(G-6041)***
Jsj Corporation (PA)....616 842-6350
700 Robbins Rd Grand Haven (49417) ***(G-6042)***
Jsj Corporation....616 847-7000
17237 Van Wagoner Rd Spring Lake (49456) ***(G-15157)***
Jsj Furniture Corporation (HQ)....616 847-6534
700 Robbins Rd Grand Haven (49417) ***(G-6043)***
Jsk Specialties....616 218-2416
11007 Chicago Dr Ste 34 Zeeland (49464) ***(G-18161)***
Jsp International LLC....517 748-5200
4335 County Farm Rd Jackson (49201) ***(G-8485)***
Jsp International LLC....248 397-3200
1443 E 12 Mile Rd Madison Heights (48071) ***(G-10285)***
Jsp International LLC....313 834-0612
13889 W Chicago St Detroit (48228) ***(G-4167)***
JST Sales America Inc....248 324-1957
37879 Interchange Dr Farmington Hills (48335) ***(G-5034)***
Jt Bakers....989 424-5102
127 W 4th St Ste 2 Clare (48617) ***(G-2874)***
Jt Foods Inc....810 772-9035
220 N Park St Owosso (48867) ***(G-12297)***
Jt Manufacturing Inc....517 849-2923
540 Industrial Pkwy Jonesville (49250) ***(G-8658)***
Jtc Inc....517 784-0576
1820 W Ganson St Jackson (49202) ***(G-8486)***
Jtekt Automotive N Amer Inc....734 454-1500
47771 Halyard Dr Plymouth (48170) ***(G-12659)***
Jtekt North America Corp....734 454-1500
47771 Halyard Dr Plymouth (48170) ***(G-12660)***
Jtekt Toyoda Americas Corp....847 506-2415
51300 Pontiac Trl Wixom (48393) ***(G-17839)***
Judy's Famous Pies, Linwood *Also called Linwood Bakery* ***(G-9598)***
Julian Brothers Inc....248 588-0280
540 S Rochester Rd Clawson (48017) ***(G-2981)***

Julie Opticians, Flint *Also called Flint Optical Company Inc* ***(G-5429)***
Jumpin Johnnys Inc 989 832-0160
1309 W Reardon St Apt 2 Midland (48640) ***(G-10878)***
Jungnitsch Bros Logging 989 233-8091
15250 W Townline Rd Saint Charles (48655) ***(G-14193)***
Junk Man LLC 248 459-7359
111 Vernon Dr Pontiac (48342) ***(G-12843)***
Junkless Foods Inc 616 560-7895
5782 Hyde Park Ave Kalamazoo (49009) ***(G-8782)***
Jupiter Manufacturing 989 551-0519
8661 Sand Beach Rd Harbor Beach (48441) ***(G-7268)***
Just Cover It Up 734 247-4729
34754 Lynn Dr Romulus (48174) ***(G-13694)***
Just Girls LLC 248 952-1967
6907 Orchard Lake Rd Troy (48098) ***(G-16441)***
Just Jewelers 248 476-9011
23105 Power Rd Farmington (48336) ***(G-4902)***
Just Rite Bracket 248 477-0592
21565 Verdun St Farmington Hills (48336) ***(G-5035)***
Just Wing It Inc 248 549-9338
31681 Dequindre Rd Madison Heights (48071) ***(G-10286)***
Justgirls Boutique, Troy *Also called Just Girls LLC* ***(G-16441)***
Justin Carriage Works LLC 517 852-9743
7615 S M 66 Hwy Nashville (49073) ***(G-11458)***
Juvenex Inc 248 436-2866
26222 Telegraph Rd Southfield (48033) ***(G-14953)***
Jvdw, Litchfield *Also called Johan Van De Weerd Co Inc* ***(G-9606)***
Jvis - USA, Shelby Township *Also called Jvis International LLC* ***(G-14614)***
Jvis - Usa LLC (PA) 586 884-5700
52048 Shelby Pkwy Shelby Township (48315) ***(G-14613)***
Jvis - Usa LLC 586 803-6056
34501 Harper Ave Clinton Township (48035) ***(G-3151)***
Jvis Fh LLC 248 478-2900
23944 Freeway Park Dr Farmington Hills (48335) ***(G-5036)***
Jvis International LLC (HQ) 586 739-9542
52048 Shelby Pkwy Shelby Township (48315) ***(G-14614)***
Jvis USA LLC - Harper, Clinton Township *Also called Jvis - Usa LLC* ***(G-3151)***
Jvrf Unified Inc 248 973-2006
13854 Lakeside Cir 503-O Sterling Heights (48313) ***(G-15383)***
JW Pennington, Roscommon *Also called JW Pennington LLC* ***(G-13749)***
JW Pennington LLC 989 965-2736
5503 W Higgins Lake Dr Roscommon (48653) ***(G-13749)***
K & D Wholesale & Embroidery, Prescott *Also called Ideal Wholesale Inc* ***(G-13080)***
K & E Tackle Inc 269 945-4496
2530 Barber Rd Hastings (49058) ***(G-7418)***
K & F Electronic Inc 586 294-8720
33041 Groesbeck Hwy Fraser (48026) ***(G-5677)***
K & J Enterprises Inc 231 548-5222
7566 S Us Highway 31 Alanson (49706) ***(G-111)***
K & K Die Inc 586 268-8812
40700 Enterprise Dr Sterling Heights (48314) ***(G-15384)***
K & K Mfg Inc 616 784-4286
951 9 Mile Rd Nw Sparta (49345) ***(G-15100)***
K & K Motorsports, Sault Sainte Marie *Also called K & K Racing LLC* ***(G-14467)***
K & K Precision Tool LLC 586 294-1030
43765 Trillium Dr Sterling Heights (48314) ***(G-15385)***
K & K Racing LLC 906 322-1276
1877 Timber Wolf Ln Sault Sainte Marie (49783) ***(G-14467)***
K & K Sales Assoc LLC 248 623-7378
3661 Dorothy Ln Waterford (48329) ***(G-17353)***
K & K Tannery LLC 517 849-9720
561 Industrial Pkwy Jonesville (49250) ***(G-8659)***
K & K Technology Inc (PA) 989 399-9910
3500 Woodridge Ct Flushing (48433) ***(G-5538)***
K & K Tool & Die, Fraser *Also called Koch Limited* ***(G-5679)***
K & L Sheet Metal LLC 269 965-0027
131 Grand Trunk Ave C Battle Creek (49037) ***(G-1205)***
K & M Industrial LLC 906 420-8770
80 Delta Ave Gladstone (49837) ***(G-5914)***
K & M Machine-Fabricating Inc 269 445-2495
20745 M 60 Cassopolis (49031) ***(G-2533)***
K & S Printing Centers Inc 734 482-1680
4860 Greenway Ct Ann Arbor (48103) ***(G-514)***
K & S Property Inc (PA) 248 573-1600
21810 Clessie Ct New Hudson (48165) ***(G-11546)***
K & S Welding 517 629-7842
17200 24 Mile Rd Albion (49224) ***(G-126)***
K & T Tool and Die Inc 616 884-5900
7805 Childsdale Ave Ne Rockford (49341) ***(G-13575)***
K & W Manufacturing Co Inc 517 369-9708
555 W Chicago Rd Bronson (49028) ***(G-2031)***
K & Y Manufacturing Inc 734 414-7000
41880 Koppernick Rd Canton (48187) ***(G-2390)***
K A L Enterprises, Shelby Township *Also called Diesel Performance Products* ***(G-14575)***
K and A Publishing Co LLC 734 743-1541
18085 Forrer St Detroit (48235) ***(G-4168)***
K and J Absorbent Products LLC 517 486-3110
10009 E Us Highway 223 Blissfield (49228) ***(G-1716)***
K and K Machine Tools Inc 586 463-1177
22393 Starks Dr Clinton Township (48036) ***(G-3152)***
K and W Landfill Inc 906 883-3504
11877 State Highway M38 Ontonagon (49953) ***(G-12160)***
K C M Inc 616 245-8599
1010 Chicago Dr Sw Grand Rapids (49509) ***(G-6565)***
K G S Screen Process Inc 313 794-2777
12650 Burt Rd Detroit (48223) ***(G-4169)***
K M I, Battle Creek *Also called Kmi Cleaning Solutions Inc* ***(G-1220)***
K M S Company 616 994-7000
5072 Lakeshore Dr Holland (49424) ***(G-7704)***
K P, Flushing *Also called King Par, LLC* ***(G-5539)***
K Printing Public Relations Co 810 648-4410
42 Austin St Sandusky (48471) ***(G-14438)***
K S B Promotions Inc 616 676-0758
55 Honey Creek Ave Ne Ada (49301) ***(G-20)***
K S S, Auburn Hills *Also called Key Sfety Rstraint Systems Inc* ***(G-927)***
K S S, Auburn Hills *Also called Key Safety Systems Inc* ***(G-926)***
K&A Machine and Tool Inc 517 750-9244
4821 W Michigan Ave Jackson (49201) ***(G-8487)***
K&F Electronics, Fraser *Also called K & F Electronic Inc* ***(G-5677)***
K&H Supply of Lansing Inc (PA) 517 482-7600
3503 W Saint Joseph St Lansing (48917) ***(G-9301)***
K&K Stamping Company 586 443-7900
23015 W Industrial Dr Saint Clair Shores (48080) ***(G-14257)***
K&P Discount Pallets Inc 616 835-1661
7165 Whites Bridge Rd Belding (48809) ***(G-1422)***
K&S Consultants LLC 269 240-7767
404 River St Buchanan (49107) ***(G-2122)***
K&S Fuel Ventures 248 360-0055
519 W Commerce Rd Commerce Township (48382) ***(G-3418)***
K&S Welding & Fabricating, Albion *Also called K & S Welding* ***(G-126)***
K&W Tool and Machine Inc 616 754-7540
1216 Shearer Rd Ste A Greenville (48838) ***(G-7141)***
K-B Tool Corporation 586 795-9003
5985 Wall St Sterling Heights (48312) ***(G-15386)***
K-Bur Enterprises Inc 616 447-7446
5120 Plainfield Ave Ne Grand Rapids (49525) ***(G-6566)***
K-C Welding Supply Inc 989 893-6509
1309 Main St Essexville (48732) ***(G-4874)***
K-Mar Structures LLC 231 924-3895
7960 Meinert Rd Fremont (49412) ***(G-5777)***
K-O Products Company, Benton Harbor *Also called Dgh Enterprises Inc* ***(G-1494)***
K-R Metal Engineers Corp 989 892-1901
815 S Henry St Bay City (48706) ***(G-1324)***
K-Space Associates Inc 734 426-7977
2182 Bishop Cir E Dexter (48130) ***(G-4497)***
K-TEC Systems Inc (PA) 248 414-4100
2615 Wolcott St Ferndale (48220) ***(G-5296)***
K-Tel Corporation 517 543-6174
518 W Lovett St Ste 1 Charlotte (48813) ***(G-2657)***
K-Tool Corporation Michigan (PA) 863 603-0777
45225 Five Mile Rd Plymouth (48170) ***(G-12661)***
K-Tool International, Plymouth *Also called K-Tool Corporation Michigan* ***(G-12661)***
K-Two Inc 269 961-2000
1 Kellogg Sq Battle Creek (49017) ***(G-1206)***
K-Value Insulation LLC 248 688-5816
4956 Butler Dr Troy (48085) ***(G-16442)***
K.I.S.M., Wixom *Also called Kennedy Industries Inc* ***(G-17840)***
K12 Inc 616 309-1600
678 Front Ave Nw Grand Rapids (49504) ***(G-6567)***
K2 Engineering Inc 906 356-6303
14444 State Highway M35 Rock (49880) ***(G-13553)***
K2 Stoneworks LLC 989 790-3250
5195 Dixie Hwy Saginaw (48601) ***(G-14068)***
Ka-Wood Gear & Machine Co 248 585-8870
32500 Industrial Dr Madison Heights (48071) ***(G-10287)***
Kace Logistics LLC (PA) 734 946-8600
862 Will Carleton Rd Carleton (48117) ***(G-2458)***
Kadant Johnson Inc., Three Rivers *Also called Kadant Johnson LLC* ***(G-15867)***
Kadant Johnson LLC (HQ) 269 278-1715
805 Wood St Three Rivers (49093) ***(G-15867)***
Kadest Industries 810 614-5362
4300 Churchill Rd Brown City (48416) ***(G-2053)***
Kadia Inc 248 446-1970
8020 Kensington Ct Brighton (48116) ***(G-1945)***
Kaechele Inc 269 857-2570
3217 Blue Star Hwy Saugatuck (49453) ***(G-14459)***
Kaechele Publications Inc 269 673-5534
241 Hubbard St Allegan (49010) ***(G-168)***
Kage Group LLC 734 604-5052
13835 Basswood Cir Van Buren Twp (48111) ***(G-16767)***
Kah 734 727-0478
38700 Webb Dr Westland (48185) ***(G-17576)***
Kailing Machine Shop 616 677-3629
14464 16th Ave Marne (49435) ***(G-10509)***
Kaines West Michigan Co, Ludington *Also called West Michigan Wire Co* ***(G-10087)***
Kaiser Aluminum Corporation 269 488-0957
5205 Midlink Dr Kalamazoo (49048) ***(G-8783)***

ALPHABETIC

Kaiser Aluminum Fab Pdts LLC 269 250-8400
5205 Kaiser Dr Kalamazoo (49048) ***(G-8784)***
Kaiser Foods Inc 989 879-2087
1474 W Cody Estey Rd Pinconning (48650) ***(G-12508)***
Kaiser Optical Systems Inc (HQ) 734 665-8083
371 Parkland Plz Ann Arbor (48103) ***(G-515)***
Kaiser Pickles, Pinconning *Also called Kaiser Foods Inc* ***(G-12508)***
Kalamazoo Candle Company 269 532-9816
5111 E Ml Ave Ste A15 Kalamazoo (49048) ***(G-8785)***
Kalamazoo Chuck Mfg Svc Ctr Co 269 679-2325
11825 S Shaver Rd Schoolcraft (49087) ***(G-14498)***
Kalamazoo Company (PA) 269 345-7151
1600 Douglas Ave Kalamazoo (49007) ***(G-8786)***
Kalamazoo Dental Supply 269 345-0260
710 Gibson St Kalamazoo (49007) ***(G-8787)***
Kalamazoo Electric Motor Inc 269 345-7802
414 Mills St Kalamazoo (49001) ***(G-8788)***
Kalamazoo Electropolishing Co, Vicksburg *Also called Kepco Inc* ***(G-16838)***
Kalamazoo Express, Allegan *Also called Morris Communications Corp* ***(G-177)***
Kalamazoo Fabricating, Kalamazoo *Also called Envirodyne Technologies Inc* ***(G-8739)***
Kalamazoo Gazette, Kalamazoo *Also called Herald Newspapers Company Inc* ***(G-8764)***
Kalamazoo Gazette, Kalamazoo *Also called Herald Newspapers Company Inc* ***(G-8766)***
Kalamazoo Holdings Inc (PA) 269 349-9711
3713 W Main St Kalamazoo (49006) ***(G-8789)***
Kalamazoo Machine Tool Co Inc 269 321-8860
6700 Quality Way Portage (49002) ***(G-13004)***
Kalamazoo Mechanical Inc 269 343-5351
5507 E Cork St Kalamazoo (49048) ***(G-8790)***
Kalamazoo Metal Finishers Inc 269 382-1611
2019 Glendenning Rd Kalamazoo (49001) ***(G-8791)***
Kalamazoo Metal Muncher Inc 269 492-0268
3428 E B Ave Plainwell (49080) ***(G-12528)***
Kalamazoo Mfg Corp Globl (PA) 269 382-8200
5944 E N Ave Kalamazoo (49048) ***(G-8792)***
Kalamazoo Orthotics & Dbtc 269 349-2247
1016 E Cork St Kalamazoo (49001) ***(G-8793)***
Kalamazoo Packaging Systems 616 534-2600
900 47th St Sw Ste I Grand Rapids (49509) ***(G-6568)***
Kalamazoo Packg Systems LLC 616 534-2600
900 47th St Sw Ste J Wyoming (49509) ***(G-18013)***
Kalamazoo Photo Comp Svcs 269 345-3706
701 Commerce Ln Kalamazoo (49004) ***(G-8794)***
Kalamazoo Plastics Company 269 381-0010
3723 Songbird Ln Kalamazoo (49008) ***(G-8795)***
Kalamazoo Promise 269 337-0037
125 W Exchange Pl Kalamazoo (49007) ***(G-8796)***
Kalamazoo Regalia Inc 269 344-4299
728 W Michigan Ave Kalamazoo (49007) ***(G-8797)***
Kalamazoo Sportswear Inc 269 344-4242
728 W Michigan Ave Kalamazoo (49007) ***(G-8798)***
Kalamazoo Stripping Derusting 269 323-1340
3921 E Centre Ave Portage (49002) ***(G-13005)***
Kalamazoo Technical Furniture, Kalamazoo *Also called Teclab Inc* ***(G-8909)***
Kalazack, Kalamazoo *Also called Kalamazoo Holdings Inc* ***(G-8789)***
Kalb & Associates Inc 586 949-2735
50271 E Russell Schm Chesterfield (48051) ***(G-2793)***
Kaliniak Design LLC 616 675-3850
13984 Eagle Ridge Dr Kent City (49330) ***(G-8992)***
Kalkaska Screw Products Inc 231 258-2560
775 Rabourn Rd Ne Kalkaska (49646) ***(G-8946)***
Kaller Gas Springs, Fraser *Also called Barnes Group Inc* ***(G-5627)***
Kalsec Inc (HQ) 269 349-9711
3713 W Main St Kalamazoo (49006) ***(G-8799)***
Kaltec Scientific Inc 248 349-8100
22425 Heslip Dr Novi (48375) ***(G-11913)***
Kam Plastics Corp (PA) 616 355-5900
611 Ottawa Ave Holland (49423) ***(G-7705)***
Kamax Inc (HQ) 248 879-0200
1606 Star Batt Dr Rochester Hills (48309) ***(G-13454)***
Kamax L.P., Rochester Hills *Also called Kamax Inc* ***(G-13454)***
Kamex Molded Products LLC 616 355-5900
611 Ottawa Ave Holland (49423) ***(G-7706)***
Kampers Woodfire Company Inc 906 478-7902
14696 S Tilson Rd Rudyard (49780) ***(G-13984)***
Kamps Inc 313 381-2681
19001 Glendale St Detroit (48223) ***(G-4170)***
Kamps Inc (PA) 616 453-9676
2900 Peach Ridge Ave Nw Grand Rapids (49534) ***(G-6569)***
Kamps Inc 517 645-2800
4400 Shance Hwy Potterville (48876) ***(G-13074)***
Kamps Inc 734 281-3300
20310 Pennsylvania Rd Taylor (48180) ***(G-15732)***
Kamps Inc 517 322-2500
4201 S Creyts Rd Lansing (48917) ***(G-9302)***
Kamps Inc 269 342-8113
1122 E Crosstown Pkwy Kalamazoo (49001) ***(G-8800)***
Kamps Pallets, Detroit *Also called Kamps Inc* ***(G-4170)***
Kamps Wood Resources, Grand Rapids *Also called Kamps Inc* ***(G-6569)***

Kanawha Scales & Systems Inc 734 947-4030
28500 Eureka Rd Romulus (48174) ***(G-13695)***
Kanerva Forest Products Inc 906 356-6061
15096 Autumn Ln Rock (49880) ***(G-13554)***
Kansmackers Manufacturing Co 248 249-6666
312 W Willow St Lansing (48906) ***(G-9239)***
Kapex Manufacturing LLC 989 928-4993
3130 Christy Way N Ste 3 Saginaw (48603) ***(G-14069)***
Kappen Saw Mill 989 872-4410
4518 Hurds Corner Rd Cass City (48726) ***(G-2516)***
Kar Enterprises, Brighton *Also called Welk-Ko Fabricators Inc* ***(G-2008)***
Kar Nut Products Company LLC 248 588-1903
1200 E 14 Mile Rd Ste A Madison Heights (48071) ***(G-10288)***
Kar's Nuts, Madison Heights *Also called Kar Nut Products Company LLC* ***(G-10288)***
Kar-Bones Inc 313 582-5551
8350 John Kronk St Detroit (48210) ***(G-4171)***
Karamon Sales Company 810 984-1750
1816 N Woodland Dr Port Huron (48060) ***(G-12933)***
Kardux Welding & Fabricating 231 873-4648
1827 E Minke Rd Hart (49420) ***(G-7375)***
Karemor Inc 517 323-3042
5242 W Saginaw Hwy Lansing (48917) ***(G-9303)***
Karges Furniture Co, Grand Rapids *Also called Kindel Furniture Company LLC* ***(G-6583)***
Karjo Trucking Inc 248 597-3700
1890 E Maple Rd Troy (48083) ***(G-16443)***
Karl Lyn Systems, Jackson *Also called Lrh & Associates Inc* ***(G-8500)***
Karla-Von Ceramics Inc 616 866-0563
10580 Northland Dr Ne Rockford (49341) ***(G-13576)***
Karlavon Ceramics, Rockford *Also called Karla-Von Ceramics Inc* ***(G-13576)***
Karle Pblctions Communications 517 351-2791
1500 Kendale Blvd Ste 207 East Lansing (48823) ***(G-4667)***
Karmann Manufacturing LLC 734 582-5900
14967 Pilot Dr Plymouth (48170) ***(G-12662)***
Karms LLC 810 229-0829
1279 Rickett Rd Brighton (48116) ***(G-1946)***
Karona, Caledonia *Also called Jeld-Wen Inc* ***(G-2303)***
Karr Spring Company 616 394-1277
966 Brooks Ave Holland (49423) ***(G-7707)***
Karr Unlimited Inc 231 652-9045
515 S Division St Newaygo (49337) ***(G-11571)***
Karttunen Logging 906 884-4312
29015 W State Highway M64 Ontonagon (49953) ***(G-12161)***
Kasper Industries Inc 989 705-1177
356 Expressway Ct Gaylord (49735) ***(G-5870)***
Kasper Machine Co (HQ) 248 547-3150
29275 Stephenson Hwy Madison Heights (48071) ***(G-10289)***
Kasson Sand & Gravel Co Inc 231 228-5455
10282 S Pierce Rd Maple City (49664) ***(G-10461)***
Kassouni Manufacturing Inc 616 794-0989
815 S Front St Belding (48809) ***(G-1423)***
Kasten Machinery Inc 269 945-1999
1611 S Hanover St Ste 107 Hastings (49058) ***(G-7419)***
Katai Machine Shop 269 465-6051
8632 Jericho Rd Bridgman (49106) ***(G-1868)***
Katcon Usa Inc 248 499-1500
2965 Lapeer Rd Auburn Hills (48326) ***(G-924)***
Katech Inc 586 791-4120
24324 Sorrentino Ct Clinton Township (48035) ***(G-3153)***
Katech Performance, Clinton Township *Also called Katech Inc* ***(G-3153)***
Kath Khemicals LLC 586 275-2646
6050 19 Mile Rd Sterling Heights (48314) ***(G-15387)***
Kathrein Automotive N Amer Inc 248 230-2951
3967 W Hamlin Rd Rochester Hills (48309) ***(G-13455)***
Kathrein Automotive USA, Rochester Hills *Also called Kathrein Automotive N Amer Inc* ***(G-13455)***
Katys Kards 989 793-4094
1200 Court St Saginaw (48602) ***(G-14070)***
Kaufman Custom Sheet M 906 932-2130
400 W Aurora St Ironwood (49938) ***(G-8333)***
Kaufman Enterprises Inc (PA) 269 324-0040
6054 Lovers Ln Portage (49002) ***(G-13006)***
Kaul Glove and Mfg Co (PA) 313 894-9494
3540 Vinewood St Detroit (48208) ***(G-4172)***
Kautex Detroit, Detroit *Also called Kautex Inc* ***(G-4173)***
Kautex Inc 231 739-2704
1085 W Sherman Blvd Muskegon (49441) ***(G-11357)***
Kautex Inc 313 633-2254
2627 Clark St Detroit (48210) ***(G-4173)***
Kautex Inc (HQ) 248 616-5100
750 Stephenson Hwy # 200 Troy (48083) ***(G-16444)***
Kawasaki Prcision McHy USA Inc 616 975-3100
3838 Broadmoor Ave Se Grand Rapids (49512) ***(G-6570)***
Kawkawlin Church Furn Mfg Co, Midland *Also called Kawkawlin Manufacturing Co* ***(G-10879)***
Kawkawlin Church Furniture, Kawkawlin *Also called Kawkawlin Manufacturing Co* ***(G-8974)***
Kawkawlin Manufacturing Co (PA) 989 684-5470
2707 Highbrook Dr Midland (48642) ***(G-10879)***

Kawkawlin Manufacturing Co.....989 684-5470
300 Spring St Kawkawlin (48631) ***(G-8974)***
Kay Automotive Graphics, Lake Orion *Also called Kay Screen Printing Inc* ***(G-9141)***
Kay Manufacturing Company.....269 408-8344
3491 S Lakeshore Dr Saint Joseph (49085) ***(G-14320)***
Kay Screen Printing Inc (HQ).....248 377-4999
57 Kay Industrial Dr Lake Orion (48359) ***(G-9141)***
Kayayan Hayk Jewelry Mfg Co (PA).....248 626-3060
869 W Long Lake Rd Bloomfield (48302) ***(G-1734)***
Kaydon Corporation (HQ).....734 747-7025
2723 S State St Ste 300 Ann Arbor (48104) ***(G-516)***
Kaydon Corporation.....231 755-3741
2860 Mccracken St Norton Shores (49441) ***(G-11766)***
Kayler Mold & Engineering.....586 739-0699
7370 19 Mile Rd Sterling Heights (48314) ***(G-15388)***
KB Stamping Inc.....616 866-5917
8110 Graphic Dr Ne Belmont (49306) ***(G-1464)***
Kba Defense.....586 552-9268
409 Race St Lakeville (48367) ***(G-9178)***
Kbd Properties, Manitou Beach *Also called Hardy-Reed Tool & Die Co Inc* ***(G-10448)***
Kbe Hoist, New Baltimore *Also called Kbe Precision Products LLC* ***(G-11487)***
Kbe Precision Products LLC.....586 725-4200
51537 Industrial Dr New Baltimore (48047) ***(G-11487)***
KC Jones Brazing Inc.....586 755-4900
2845 E 10 Mile Rd Warren (48091) ***(G-17118)***
KC Jones Plating Co (PA).....586 755-4900
2845 E 10 Mile Rd Warren (48091) ***(G-17119)***
KC Jones Plating Co.....248 399-8500
321 W 10 Mile Rd Hazel Park (48030) ***(G-7440)***
Kci Printsource, Grand Rapids *Also called Kent Communications Inc* ***(G-6575)***
Kdf Fluid Treatment Inc.....269 273-3300
1500 Kdf Dr Three Rivers (49093) ***(G-15868)***
KDI Technologies Inc.....616 667-1600
2206 Pine Ridge Dr Sw Jenison (49428) ***(G-8631)***
Kdk Downhole Tooling LLC.....231 590-3137
6671 M 72 E Williamsburg (49690) ***(G-17714)***
Kds Controls, Grand Haven *Also called Ghsp Inc* ***(G-6019)***
Keane Saunders & Associates.....616 954-7088
6350 Cascade Pointe Dr Se Grand Rapids (49546) ***(G-6571)***
Kearsley Lake Terrace LLC.....810 736-7000
3400 Benmark Pl Ofc Flint (48506) ***(G-5453)***
Keays Family Truckin.....231 838-6430
1658 Ashley Ln Gaylord (49735) ***(G-5871)***
Kecy Corporation.....517 448-8954
4111 Munson Hwy Hudson (49247) ***(G-8133)***
Kecy Metal Technologies, Hudson *Also called ARC Metal Stamping LLC* ***(G-8127)***
Kecy Products Inc.....517 448-8954
4111 Munson Hwy Hudson (49247) ***(G-8134)***
Keebler Company (HQ).....269 961-2000
1 Kellogg Sq Battle Creek (49017) ***(G-1207)***
Keebler Company.....231 445-0335
10364 Neuman Rd Cheboygan (49721) ***(G-2684)***
Keeler-Glasgow Company Inc.....269 621-2415
80444 County Road 687 Hartford (49057) ***(G-7384)***
Keen Point International Inc.....248 340-8732
1377 Atlantic Blvd Auburn Hills (48326) ***(G-925)***
Keenan Enterprises Inc.....231 943-0516
3866 Jupiter Cresent Dr Traverse City (49685) ***(G-16016)***
Keeping You In Stitches.....586 421-9509
46545 Continental Dr Chesterfield (48047) ***(G-2794)***
Keglove LLC.....616 610-7289
6403 Sand Castle Vw Holland (49423) ***(G-7708)***
Kehrig Steel Inc.....586 716-9700
9279 Marine City Hwy Ira (48023) ***(G-8259)***
Keihin Michigan Mfg LLC.....317 462-3015
14898 Koehn Rd Mussey (48014) ***(G-11457)***
Keiper LLC.....248 655-5100
2600 Bellingham Dr # 100 Troy (48083) ***(G-16445)***
Keith Falan.....231 834-7358
14097 S Mason Dr Grant (49327) ***(G-7080)***
Keizer-Morris Intl Inc.....810 688-1234
6561 Bernie Kohler Dr North Branch (48461) ***(G-11661)***
Kel Graphics, Cadillac *Also called Janet Kelly* ***(G-2256)***
Kel Tool Inc.....517 750-4515
6999 Spring Arbor Rd Spring Arbor (49283) ***(G-15123)***
Kelder LLC.....231 757-3000
979 W 1st St Scottville (49454) ***(G-14509)***
Keller Tool Ltd (PA).....734 425-4500
12701 Inkster Rd Livonia (48150) ***(G-9794)***
Kellers Farm Bakery.....734 753-4360
23888 Haggerty Rd Belleville (48111) ***(G-1446)***
Kelley Brothers Lc.....734 462-6266
37100 Amrhein Rd Livonia (48150) ***(G-9795)***
Kelley Laboratories Inc.....231 861-6257
617 Industrial Park Dr Shelby (49455) ***(G-14528)***
Kelley Machining Inc.....231 861-0951
647 Industrial Park Dr Shelby (49455) ***(G-14529)***
Kellogg (thailand) Limited.....269 969-8937
1 Kellogg Sq Battle Creek (49017) ***(G-1208)***
Kellogg Chile Inc.....269 961-2000
1 Kellogg Sq Battle Creek (49017) ***(G-1209)***
Kellogg Company.....269 961-2000
2 Hamblin Ave E Battle Creek (49017) ***(G-1210)***
Kellogg Company.....810 653-5625
2166 Oak Shade Dr Davison (48423) ***(G-3655)***
Kellogg Company (PA).....269 961-2000
1 Kellogg Sq Battle Creek (49017) ***(G-1211)***
Kellogg Company.....269 961-9387
235 Potter St Mulliken (48861) ***(G-11239)***
Kellogg Company.....269 964-8525
70 Michigan Ave W Ste 750 Battle Creek (49017) ***(G-1212)***
Kellogg Company.....269 969-8107
235 Porter St Battle Creek (49014) ***(G-1213)***
Kellogg Company.....901 373-6115
1 Kellogg Sq Battle Creek (49017) ***(G-1214)***
Kellogg Company.....269 961-2000
2 E Hammond Ave Battle Creek (49014) ***(G-1215)***
Kellogg Company.....269 961-6693
Financial Service Ctr Battle Creek (49014) ***(G-1216)***
Kellogg Company.....269 961-2000
425 Porter St Battle Creek (49014) ***(G-1217)***
Kellogg Crankshaft Co.....517 788-9200
3524 Wayland Dr Jackson (49202) ***(G-8488)***
Kellogg North America Company.....269 961-2000
1 Kellogg Sq Battle Creek (49017) ***(G-1218)***
Kellogg USA Inc (HQ).....269 961-2000
1 Kellogg Sq Battle Creek (49017) ***(G-1219)***
Kelloggs Corporation.....616 219-6100
5300 Patterson Ave Se Grand Rapids (49512) ***(G-6572)***
Kells Sawmill Inc.....906 753-2778
N8780 County Road 577 Stephenson (49887) ***(G-15236)***
Kelly Bros Inc.....989 723-4543
2615 W Garrison Rd Owosso (48867) ***(G-12298)***
Kelly Industrial Service Corp.....989 865-6111
11975 Beaver Rd Saint Charles (48655) ***(G-14194)***
Kelly Oil & Gas Inc.....231 929-0591
303 S Union St Ofc C Traverse City (49684) ***(G-16017)***
Kelly St Amour.....231 625-9789
2834 Olson Rd Cheboygan (49721) ***(G-2685)***
Kellys Catering.....231 796-5414
19077 12 Mile Rd Big Rapids (49307) ***(G-1635)***
Kellys Catering and Deer Proc, Big Rapids *Also called Kellys Catering* ***(G-1635)***
Kellys Recycling Service Inc.....313 389-7870
14800 Castleton St Detroit (48227) ***(G-4174)***
Kelm Acubar, Benton Harbor *Also called Acubar Inc* ***(G-1479)***
Kelm Acubar Company, Benton Harbor *Also called Kelm Acubar Lc* ***(G-1516)***
Kelm Acubar Lc (PA).....269 927-3000
1055 N Shore Dr Benton Harbor (49022) ***(G-1516)***
Kelm Acubar Lc.....269 925-2007
1055 N Shore Dr Benton Harbor (49022) ***(G-1517)***
Keltrol Enterprises Inc.....734 697-3011
35 Main St Ste 102 Belleville (48111) ***(G-1447)***
Kem Enterprises Inc.....616 676-0213
579 Roundtree Dr Ne Ada (49301) ***(G-21)***
Kemai (usa) Chemical Co Ltd.....248 924-2225
48948 Freestone Dr Northville (48168) ***(G-11704)***
Kemari LLC.....248 348-7407
11986 Ruth St South Lyon (48178) ***(G-14797)***
Kemco Inc.....517 543-2888
5820 W Plains Rd Eaton Rapids (48827) ***(G-4727)***
Kemin Industries Inc.....248 869-3080
14925 Galleon Ct Plymouth (48170) ***(G-12663)***
Kemkraft Engineering Inc.....734 414-6500
47650 Clipper St Plymouth (48170) ***(G-12664)***
Kemnitz Fine Candies.....734 453-0480
896 W Ann Arbor Trl Plymouth (48170) ***(G-12665)***
Kemnitz Fine Candies & Gifts, Plymouth *Also called Kemnitz Fine Candies* ***(G-12665)***
Ken Gorsline Welding (PA).....269 649-0650
2210 E Vw Ave Vicksburg (49097) ***(G-16837)***
Ken Luneack Construction Inc (PA).....989 681-5774
721 E Washington St Saint Louis (48880) ***(G-14365)***
Ken Measel Supply Inc.....810 798-3293
6343 Hayfield Ln Almont (48003) ***(G-260)***
Ken Rodenhouse Door & Window.....616 784-3365
5120 West River Dr Ne Comstock Park (49321) ***(G-3488)***
Ken's Tarp & Canvas Shop, Lawton *Also called Kts Enterprises* ***(G-9512)***
Kena Corporation.....586 873-4761
45832 Edgewater St Chesterfield (48047) ***(G-2795)***
Kendall & Company Inc.....810 733-7330
1624 Lambden Rd Flint (48532) ***(G-5454)***
Kendall Microtech Inc.....517 565-3802
3436 Parman Rd Stockbridge (49285) ***(G-15589)***
Kendall Printing, Flint *Also called Kendall & Company Inc* ***(G-5454)***
Kendor Steel Rule Die Inc.....586 293-7111
31275 Fraser Dr Fraser (48026) ***(G-5678)***
Kenewell Group.....810 714-4290
3031 W Thompson Rd Fenton (48430) ***(G-5222)***
Kennametal Inc.....231 946-2100
2879 Aero Park Dr Traverse City (49686) ***(G-16018)***

ALPHABETIC

Kennedy Acquisition Inc (PA) — 616 871-3020
4949 W Greenbrooke Dr Se Grand Rapids (49512) *(G-6573)*

Kennedy Industries Inc — 248 684-1200
4925 Holtz Dr Wixom (48393) *(G-17840)*

Kennedy Sales Inc — 586 228-9390
19683 Tanglewood Cir Clinton Township (48038) *(G-3154)*

Kennedys Irish Pub Inc — 248 681-1050
1055 W Huron St Waterford (48328) *(G-17354)*

Kenneth A Gould — 231 828-4705
2790 W Raymond Rd Twin Lake (49457) *(G-16713)*

Kenny G Mfg & Sls LLC — 313 218-6297
27275 Ritter Blvd Brownstown (48134) *(G-2066)*

Kenny Machining, Shepherd Also called Paul Jeffrey Kenny *(G-14730)*

Kenona Industries LLC — 616 735-6228
3044 Wilson Dr Nw Grand Rapids (49534) *(G-6574)*

Kenowa Industries Inc (PA) — 616 392-7080
11405 E Lakewood Blvd Holland (49424) *(G-7709)*

Kenowa Industries Inc — 517 322-0311
2924 Sanders Rd Lansing (48917) *(G-9304)*

Kenrie Inc — 616 494-3200
500 E 8th St Ste 1100 Holland (49423) *(G-7710)*

Kens Redi Mix Inc — 810 687-6000
14406 N Saginaw Rd Clio (48420) *(G-3273)*

Kens Redi Mix Inc (PA) — 810 238-4931
8016 S State Rd Goodrich (48438) *(G-5955)*

Kent City Plastics LLC — 616 678-4900
90 Spring St Ste B Kent City (49330) *(G-8993)*

Kent Commerce Center, Grand Rapids Also called Ace Vending Service Inc *(G-6135)*

Kent Communications Inc — 616 957-2120
3901 East Paris Ave Se Grand Rapids (49512) *(G-6575)*

Kent Design & Manufacturing, Grand Rapids Also called Benmill LLC *(G-6210)*

Kent Door & Specialty Inc — 616 534-9691
2535 28th St Sw Grand Rapids (49519) *(G-6576)*

Kent Door Supply, Grand Rapids Also called Kent Door & Specialty Inc *(G-6576)*

Kent Foundry Company — 616 754-1100
1413 Callaghan St Greenville (48838) *(G-7142)*

Kent Manufacturing Company — 616 454-9495
2200 Oak Industrial Dr Ne Grand Rapids (49505) *(G-6577)*

Kent Nutrition Group Inc — 517 676-9544
725 Hull Rd Mason (48854) *(G-10643)*

Kent Quality Foods Inc — 616 459-4595
3426 Quincy St Hudsonville (49426) *(G-8161)*

Kent Sail Co Inc — 586 791-2580
35942 Jefferson Ave Harrison Township (48045) *(G-7335)*

Kent Tool and Die Inc — 586 949-6600
50605 Richard W Blvd Chesterfield (48051) *(G-2796)*

Kent Welding Inc — 616 363-4414
1915 Sterling Ave Nw Grand Rapids (49504) *(G-6578)*

Kentucky Trailer Technologies, Wixom Also called Trailer Tech Holdings LLC *(G-17915)*

Kentwater Tool & Mfg Co — 616 784-7171
5516 West River Dr Ne Comstock Park (49321) *(G-3489)*

Kentwood Fuel Inc — 616 455-2387
1980 44th St Se Kentwood (49508) *(G-9013)*

Kentwood Manufacturing Co — 616 698-6370
103 76th St Sw Ste C Grand Rapids (49548) *(G-6579)*

Kentwood Packaging Corporation — 616 698-9000
2102 Avastar Pkwy Nw Walker (49544) *(G-16869)*

Kentwood Powder Coat Inc — 616 698-8181
3900 Swank Dr Se Grand Rapids (49512) *(G-6580)*

Kenwal Pickling LLC — 313 739-1040
8223 W Warren Ave Dearborn (48126) *(G-3729)*

Kenyon Specialties Inc — 810 686-3190
1153 Liberty St Clio (48420) *(G-3274)*

Kenyon Tj & Associates Inc — 231 544-1144
902 Green Acres St Bellaire (49615) *(G-1438)*

Keo Cutters Inc — 586 771-2050
25040 Easy St Warren (48089) *(G-17120)*

Kepco Inc — 269 649-5800
145 N Leja Dr Vicksburg (49097) *(G-16838)*

Kerkau Manufacturing, Bay City Also called Baldauf Enterprises Inc *(G-1280)*

Kerkau Manufacturing Company, Bay City Also called Baldauf Enterprises Inc *(G-1279)*

Kerkstra Mechanical LLC — 616 532-6100
4345 44th St Se Ste C Grand Rapids (49512) *(G-6581)*

Kerkstra Precast Inc — 616 457-4920
3373 Busch Dr Sw Grandville (49418) *(G-7054)*

Kern Auto Sales and Svc LLC — 734 475-2722
1630 S Main St Chelsea (48118) *(G-2715)*

Kern Industries Inc — 248 349-4866
43000 W 10 Mile Rd Frnt Novi (48375) *(G-11914)*

Kern-Liebers Pieron Inc — 248 427-1100
24505 Indoplex Cir Farmington Hills (48335) *(G-5037)*

Kernel Burner — 989 792-2808
6171 Tittabawassee Rd Saginaw (48603) *(G-14071)*

Kerns Sausages Inc — 989 652-2684
110 W Jefferson St Frankenmuth (48734) *(G-5590)*

Kerr Corporation — 734 946-7800
28200 Wick Rd Romulus (48174) *(G-13696)*

Kerr Manufacturing, Romulus Also called Kerr Corporation *(G-13696)*

Kerr Pump and Supply Inc — 248 543-3880
12880 Cloverdale St Oak Park (48237) *(G-12076)*

Kerr Screw Products Co Inc — 248 589-2200
32069 Milton Ave Madison Heights (48071) *(G-10290)*

Kerry Foods — 616 871-9940
4444 52nd St Se Grand Rapids (49512) *(G-6582)*

Kerry Inc — 616 871-9940
4444 52nd St Detroit (48210) *(G-4175)*

Kerry J McNeely — 734 776-1928
15810 Harrison St Livonia (48154) *(G-9796)*

Kerry's Pallets, Livonia Also called Kerry J McNeely *(G-9796)*

Keska LLC — 616 283-7056
87 Chriscraft Ln Holland (49424) *(G-7711)*

Kessler USA Inc — 734 404-0152
44099 Plymouth Oaks Blvd # 104 Plymouth (48170) *(G-12666)*

Ketchum Machine Corporated — 616 765-5101
219 Oak St Freeport (49325) *(G-5765)*

Ketola Logging — 906 524-6479
16369 Bayshore Rd Lanse (49946) *(G-9196)*

Keur Industries Acquisition Co, Spring Lake Also called Multi-Lab LLC *(G-15165)*

Keurig Dr Pepper Inc — 231 775-7393
1481 Potthoff St Cadillac (49601) *(G-2257)*

Keurig Dr Pepper Inc — 313 937-3500
12201 Beech Daly Rd Detroit (48239) *(G-4176)*

Kevco Metal Surface Prep — 616 538-1377
138 39th St Sw Wyoming (49548) *(G-18014)*

Kevin Butzin Recycling Inc — 734 587-3710
9292 Oakville Waltz Rd Willis (48191) *(G-17744)*

Kevin Larkin Inc — 248 736-8203
2611 Woodbourne Dr Waterford (48329) *(G-17355)*

Kevin S Macaddino — 248 642-0333
380 N Old Woodward Ave # 300 Birmingham (48009) *(G-1687)*

Kevin Wheat & Assoc Inc — 517 349-0101
4990 Marsh Rd Okemos (48864) *(G-12127)*

Keweenaw Bay Indian Community — 906 524-5757
16429 Bear Town Rd Baraga (49908) *(G-1104)*

Keweenaw Brewing Company LLC (PA) — 906 482-5596
408 Shelden Ave Houghton (49931) *(G-7973)*

Keweenaw Brewing Company LLC — 906 482-1937
10 4th St South Range (49963) *(G-14817)*

Key Casting Company Inc (PA) — 269 426-3800
13145 Red Arrow Hwy Sawyer (49125) *(G-14486)*

Key Energy Services Inc — 231 258-9637
4030 Columbus Dr Ne Kalkaska (49646) *(G-8947)*

Key Gas Components Inc — 269 673-2151
1303 Lincoln Rd Allegan (49010) *(G-169)*

Key Plastics, Grand Rapids Also called Novares US LLC *(G-6723)*

Key Plastics LLC — 248 449-6100
44191 Plymouth Oaks Blvd Plymouth (48170) *(G-12667)*

Key Safety Systems Inc (HQ) — 586 726-3800
2025 Harmon Rd Auburn Hills (48326) *(G-926)*

Key Sfety Rstraint Systems Inc (HQ) — 586 726-3800
2025 Harmon Rd Auburn Hills (48326) *(G-927)*

Keyes-Davis Company — 269 962-7505
74 14th St N Springfield (49037) *(G-15195)*

Keykert, Wixom Also called Kiekert Usa Inc *(G-17842)*

Keys For Kids Ministries, Grand Rapids Also called Childrens Bible Hour Inc *(G-6274)*

Keystone Cable Corporation — 313 924-9720
8200 Lynch Rd Detroit (48234) *(G-4177)*

Keystone Manufacturing LLC — 269 343-4108
6387 Technology Ave Ste B Kalamazoo (49009) *(G-8801)*

Keystone Millbrook, Grand Ledge Also called Millbrook Printing Co *(G-6112)*

Keystone Printing Inc — 517 627-4078
3540 Jefferson Hwy Grand Ledge (48837) *(G-6109)*

Keystone Products LLC — 248 363-5552
24445 Northwestern Hwy # 101 Southfield (48075) *(G-14954)*

Keystone Universal, Melvindale Also called Ebonex Corporation *(G-10697)*

Kft, Gaylord Also called Keays Family Truckin *(G-5871)*

Kgdh LLC — 989 652-9041
316 S Main St Frankenmuth (48734) *(G-5591)*

Kgf Enterprise Inc — 586 430-4182
2141 Werner Rd Columbus (48063) *(G-3380)*

Khalsa Metal Products Inc — 616 791-4794
3142 Broadmoor Ave Se Kentwood (49512) *(G-9014)*

Khi Coating — 248 236-2100
275 S Glaspie St Ste B Oxford (48371) *(G-12353)*

Kick It Around Sports — 810 232-4986
3618 Fenton Rd Flint (48507) *(G-5455)*

Kid By Kid Inc — 586 781-2345
54249 Myrica Dr Macomb (48042) *(G-10134)*

Kidde Safety — 800 880-6788
39550 W 13 Mile Rd # 101 Novi (48377) *(G-11915)*

Kidder Machine Company — 231 775-9271
702 8th St Cadillac (49601) *(G-2258)*

Kiekert Usa Inc — 248 960-4100
50695 Varsity Ct Wixom (48393) *(G-17841)*

Kiekert Usa Inc (HQ) — 248 960-4100
46941 Liberty Dr Wixom (48393) *(G-17842)*

Kiilunen Mfg Group Inc 906 337-2433
25280 Renaissance Rd Calumet (49913) ***(G-2328)***
Kilgore Industries, Buchanan *Also called K&S Consultants LLC* ***(G-2122)***
Killer Paint Ball 248 491-0088
509 S Lafayette St South Lyon (48178) ***(G-14798)***
Kiln Kreations 989 435-3296
5366 M 18 Beaverton (48612) ***(G-1386)***
Kilwins Chocolate Kitchen, Petoskey *Also called Kilwins Qulty Confections Inc* ***(G-12452)***
Kilwins Qulty Confections Inc (PA) 231 347-3800
1050 Bay View Rd Petoskey (49770) ***(G-12452)***
Kimastle Corporation 586 949-2355
28291 Kehrig St Chesterfield (48047) ***(G-2797)***
Kimberly Led Lighting, Clarkston *Also called Kimberly Lighting LLC* ***(G-2933)***
Kimberly Lighting LLC 888 480-0070
5827 Terex Clarkston (48346) ***(G-2933)***
Kimberly-Clark Corporation 586 949-1649
21346 Summerfield Dr Macomb (48044) ***(G-10135)***
Kimberly-Clark Corporation 810 985-1830
2609 Electric Ave Ste C Port Huron (48060) ***(G-12934)***
Kimbow Inc 616 774-4680
901 Metzgar Dr Nw Comstock Park (49321) ***(G-3490)***
Kimprint Inc 734 459-2960
14875 Galleon Ct Plymouth (48170) ***(G-12668)***
Kims Mart Inc 313 592-4929
20240 W 7 Mile Rd Detroit (48219) ***(G-4178)***
Kindel Furniture Company LLC (PA) 616 243-3676
4047 Eastern Ave Se Grand Rapids (49508) ***(G-6583)***
Kinder Company Inc 810 240-3065
7070 N Saginaw Rd Mount Morris (48458) ***(G-11163)***
Kinder Products Unlimited LLC 586 557-3453
6471 Metro Pkwy Sterling Heights (48312) ***(G-15389)***
Kinetic Wave Power LLC 989 839-9757
2861 N Tupelo Dr Midland (48642) ***(G-10880)***
King Coil, Roseville *Also called Comfort Mattress Co* ***(G-13784)***
King Hughes Fasteners Inc 810 721-0300
550 W 4th St Imlay City (48444) ***(G-8206)***
King Koal Barbecue Equipment, Richmond *Also called Richmond Meat Packers Inc* ***(G-13270)***
King Milling Company 616 897-9264
115 S Broadway St Lowell (49331) ***(G-10033)***
King Par, LLC 810 732-2470
5140 Flushing Rd Flushing (48433) ***(G-5539)***
King Pharmaceuticals LLC 248 650-6400
1200 Parkdale Rd Rochester (48307) ***(G-13332)***
King Products, Baroda *Also called Wolfgang Moneta* ***(G-1133)***
King Steel Corporation (PA) 800 638-2530
5225 E Cook Rd Ste K Grand Blanc (48439) ***(G-5972)***
King Tool & Die Inc 517 265-2741
971 Division St Adrian (49221) ***(G-73)***
King-Hughes Fasteners, Imlay City *Also called King Hughes Fasteners Inc* ***(G-8206)***
Kingdom Cartridge Inc 734 564-1590
11704 Morgan Ave Plymouth (48170) ***(G-12669)***
Kings Self Defense LLC 910 890-4322
6769 Bent Grass Dr Se Grand Rapids (49508) ***(G-6584)***
Kingsford Broach & Tool Inc 906 774-4917
2200 Maule Dr Kingsford (49802) ***(G-9060)***
Kingston Educational Software 248 895-4803
38452 Lynwood Ct Farmington Hills (48331) ***(G-5038)***
Kinney Tool and Die Inc 616 997-0901
1300 W Randall St Coopersville (49404) ***(G-3562)***
Kinross Fab & Machine Inc 906 495-1900
17422 S Dolan St Kincheloe (49788) ***(G-9052)***
Kiosks By Winstanley, Traverse City *Also called Winstanley Associates LLC* ***(G-16147)***
Kirby Grinding, Roseville *Also called Detroit Edge Tool Company* ***(G-13794)***
Kirby Metal Corporation 810 743-3360
4072 Flint Asphalt Dr Burton (48529) ***(G-2157)***
Kirby Steel, Burton *Also called Kirby Metal Corporation* ***(G-2157)***
Kirchhoff Auto Tecumseh Inc 517 490-9965
5550 Occidental Hwy Tecumseh (49286) ***(G-15799)***
Kirchhoff Auto Tecumseh Inc (HQ) 517 423-2400
1200 E Chicago Blvd Tecumseh (49286) ***(G-15800)***
Kirchhoff Automotive Companies, Tecumseh *Also called Van-Rob USA Holdings* ***(G-15816)***
Kirchhoff Automotive USA Inc 248 247-3740
2600 Bellingham Dr # 400 Troy (48083) ***(G-16446)***
Kirk Enterprises Inc 248 357-5070
20905 Telegraph Rd Southfield (48033) ***(G-14955)***
Kirks Automotive Incorporated (PA) 313 933-7030
9330 Roselawn St Detroit (48204) ***(G-4179)***
Kirmin Die & Tool Inc 734 722-9210
36360 Ecorse Rd Romulus (48174) ***(G-13697)***
Kirtland Products LLC 231 582-7505
1 Altair Dr Boyne City (49712) ***(G-1826)***
Kiser Industrial Mfg Co 269 934-9220
1860 Yore Ave Benton Harbor (49022) ***(G-1518)***
Kismet Strategic Sourcing Part 269 932-4990
717 Sint Jseph Dr Ste 270 Saint Joseph (49085) ***(G-14321)***
Kissco Publishing, Okemos *Also called Kissman Consulting LLC* ***(G-12128)***
Kissman Consulting LLC 517 256-1077
2109 Hamilton Rd Ste 113 Okemos (48864) ***(G-12128)***
Kistler Instrument Corporation (HQ) 248 668-6900
30280 Hudson Dr Novi (48377) ***(G-11916)***
Kitchen Supply Co, Jackson *Also called Royal Cabinet Inc* ***(G-8565)***
Kitchenaid 800 541-6390
553 Benson Rd Benton Harbor (49022) ***(G-1519)***
Kitty Condo LLC 419 690-9063
17197 N Laurel Park Dr # 402 Livonia (48152) ***(G-9797)***
KIWOTO Inc 269 944-1552
1130 E Empire Ave Benton Harbor (49022) ***(G-1520)***
Kk Logging 906 524-6047
16234 Skanee Rd Lanse (49946) ***(G-9197)***
Kk Welding Services Inc 810 664-5564
3903 Five Lakes Rd North Branch (48461) ***(G-11662)***
Kksp Precision Machining LLC 810 329-4731
650 Hathaway St East China (48054) ***(G-4624)***
Kkt Inc 734 425-5330
31251 Industrial Rd Livonia (48150) ***(G-9798)***
Klann 313 565-4135
1439 S Telegraph Rd Dearborn (48124) ***(G-3730)***
Klassic Tool Crib, Romulus *Also called Plum Brothers LLC* ***(G-13723)***
Klaus Nixdorf 269 429-3259
1727 W John Beers Rd Stevensville (49127) ***(G-15573)***
KLC Enterprises Inc 989 753-0496
4765 E Holland Rd Saginaw (48601) ***(G-14072)***
Kleiberit Adhesives USA Inc 248 709-9308
4305 Beverly Ct Royal Oak (48073) ***(G-13941)***
Klein Bros Fence & Stakes LLC 248 684-6919
2400 E Buno Rd Milford (48381) ***(G-10967)***
Klingler Consulting & Mfg 810 765-3700
837 Degurse Ave Marine City (48039) ***(G-10476)***
Kloeffler, Wm Industries, Marine City *Also called Wm Kloeffler Industries Inc* ***(G-10487)***
Klopp Group LLC 877 256-4528
3535 Bay Rd Ste 3 Saginaw (48603) ***(G-14073)***
Km and I 248 792-2782
3155 W Big Beaver Rd # 111 Troy (48084) ***(G-16447)***
Km International, North Branch *Also called Keizer-Morris Intl Inc* ***(G-11661)***
Kmak Inc 517 784-8800
1232 S West Ave Jackson (49203) ***(G-8489)***
Kmg Prestige, Wayland *Also called Sawmill Estates* ***(G-17414)***
Kmi, Belding *Also called Kassouni Manufacturing Inc* ***(G-1423)***
Kmi Cleaning Solutions Inc 269 964-2557
157 Beadle Lake Rd Battle Creek (49014) ***(G-1220)***
Kmj Boring Co Inc 586 465-8771
42965 Biland Dr Clinton Township (48038) ***(G-3155)***
Kmk Machining 231 629-8068
10842 Northland Dr Big Rapids (49307) ***(G-1636)***
Knape & Vogt Manufacturing Co (HQ) 616 459-3311
2700 Oak Industrial Dr Ne Grand Rapids (49505) ***(G-6585)***
Knape Industries Inc 616 866-1651
10701 Northland Dr Ne Rockford (49341) ***(G-13577)***
Knapp Manufacturing Inc 517 279-9538
555 Hillside Dr Coldwater (49036) ***(G-3311)***
Knapp Manufacturing LLC 517 279-9538
555 Hillside Dr Coldwater (49036) ***(G-3312)***
Knapp Printing Services Inc 616 754-9159
6540 S Greenville Rd Greenville (48838) ***(G-7143)***
Knappen Milling Company 269 731-4141
110 S Water St Augusta (49012) ***(G-1053)***
Knauf Insulation Inc 517 630-2000
1000 E North St Albion (49224) ***(G-127)***
Knickerbocker 616 345-5642
417 Bridge St Nw Grand Rapids (49504) ***(G-6586)***
Knickerbocker Baking Inc 248 541-2110
26040 Pinehurst Dr Madison Heights (48071) ***(G-10291)***
Knickerbocker R Yr Brickr Blk 517 531-5369
8997 Mccain Rd Parma (49269) ***(G-12390)***
Knight Tonya 313 255-3434
17390 W 8 Mile Rd Southfield (48075) ***(G-14956)***
Knight Carbide Inc 586 598-4888
48665 Structural Dr Chesterfield (48051) ***(G-2798)***
Knight Global, Auburn Hills *Also called Knight Industries Inc* ***(G-928)***
Knight Industries Inc 248 377-4950
2705 Commerce Pkwy Auburn Hills (48326) ***(G-928)***
Knight Kraft Inc 586 726-6821
44476 Phoenix Dr Sterling Heights (48314) ***(G-15390)***
Knights Glass Block Windows, Southfield *Also called Knight Tonya* ***(G-14956)***
Knoedler Manufacturers Inc 269 969-7722
7185 Tower Rd Battle Creek (49014) ***(G-1221)***
Knoerr Farms 989 670-2199
1700 E Custer Rd Sandusky (48471) ***(G-14439)***
Knoll Inc 616 949-1050
4300 36th St Se Grand Rapids (49512) ***(G-6587)***
Knoll Inc 231 755-2270
2800 Estes St Norton Shores (49441) ***(G-11767)***
Knoll Group, Grand Rapids *Also called Knoll Inc* ***(G-6587)***
Knouse Foods Cooperative Inc 269 657-5524
815 S Kalamazoo St Paw Paw (49079) ***(G-12406)***

A L P H A B E T I C

Knowlton Enterprises Inc (PA) 810 987-7100
1755 Yeager St Port Huron (48060) ***(G-12935)***
Knpc Holdco LLC (PA) 248 588-1903
1200 E 14 Mile Rd Madison Heights (48071) ***(G-10292)***
Knust Masonry 231 322-2587
6092 Aarwood Rd Nw Rapid City (49676) ***(G-13109)***
Ko Products, Benton Harbor *Also called Dgh Enterprises Inc* ***(G-1495)***
Koch Limited 586 296-3103
34230 Riviera Fraser (48026) ***(G-5679)***
Kodiak Manufacturing Co Inc 248 335-5552
318 Irwin Ave Pontiac (48341) ***(G-12844)***
Koegel Meats Inc (PA) 810 238-3685
3400 W Bristol Rd Flint (48507) ***(G-5456)***
Koehler Industries Inc 269 934-9670
1520 Townline Rd Benton Harbor (49022) ***(G-1521)***
Koenig Fuel & Supply Co 313 368-1870
5501 Cogswell Rd Wayne (48184) ***(G-17433)***
Koenig Sand & Gravel LLC 248 628-2711
1955 E Lakeville Rd Oxford (48371) ***(G-12354)***
Koetje Wood Products Inc 616 393-9191
11743 Greenway Dr Holland (49424) ***(G-7712)***
Koeze Company (PA) 616 724-2601
2555 Burlingame Ave Sw Grand Rapids (49509) ***(G-6588)***
Koeze Direct, Grand Rapids *Also called Koeze Company* ***(G-6588)***
Kohler Co 810 208-0032
720 Grant St Fenton (48430) ***(G-5223)***
Koins Corp 248 548-3038
25169 Dequindre Rd Madison Heights (48071) ***(G-10293)***
Kokaly Sports 989 671-7412
509 N Johnson St Bay City (48708) ***(G-1325)***
Kolco Industries Inc 248 486-1690
10078 Colonial Indus Dr South Lyon (48178) ***(G-14799)***
Kolene Corporation 313 273-9220
12890 Westwood St Detroit (48223) ***(G-4180)***
Kolkema Fabricating 231 865-6380
6439 S Walker Rd Fruitport (49415) ***(G-5794)***
Kolossos Printing Inc (PA) 734 994-5400
2055 W Stadium Blvd Ann Arbor (48103) ***(G-517)***
Kolossos Printing Inc 734 741-1600
301 E Liberty St Ann Arbor (48104) ***(G-518)***
Koltec Div, Coldwater *Also called Vachon Industries Inc* ***(G-3340)***
Komarnicki Tool & Die Company 586 776-9300
29650 Parkway Roseville (48066) ***(G-13825)***
Konecranes Inc 248 380-2626
42970 W 10 Mile Rd Novi (48375) ***(G-11917)***
Kongsberg Automotive, Novi *Also called Kongsberg Holding III Inc* ***(G-11920)***
Kongsberg Automotive Inc (HQ) 248 468-1300
27275 Haggerty Rd Ste 610 Novi (48377) ***(G-11918)***
Kongsberg Holding I Inc (PA) 248 468-1300
27275 Haggerty Rd Ste 610 Novi (48377) ***(G-11919)***
Kongsberg Holding III Inc (HQ) 248 468-1300
27275 Haggerty Rd Ste 610 Novi (48377) ***(G-11920)***
Kongsberg Intr Systems I Inc (HQ) 956 465-4541
27275 Haggerty Rd Ste 610 Novi (48377) ***(G-11921)***
KONIAG DEVELOPMENT COMPANY LLC, Warren *Also called XMCO Inc* ***(G-17301)***
Konnections Blog 888 921-1114
400 Renaissance Ctr # 26001425 Detroit (48243) ***(G-4181)***
Konwinski Kabnets Inc 989 773-2906
1900 Gover Pkwy Mount Pleasant (48858) ***(G-11201)***
Kooiker Tool & Die Inc 616 554-3630
3259 68th St Se Caledonia (49316) ***(G-2305)***
Koolblast, Chelsea *Also called Advanced Industries Inc* ***(G-2699)***
Kopach Filter LLC 906 863-8611
N3840 R 2 Ln Wallace (49893) ***(G-16886)***
Kopacz Industrial Painting 734 427-6740
12225 Merriman Rd Livonia (48150) ***(G-9799)***
Koppel A Color Image, Grandville *Also called A Koppel Color Image Company* ***(G-7015)***
Koppel Tool & Engineering LLC 616 638-2611
1099 N Gateway Blvd Norton Shores (49441) ***(G-11768)***
Koppers Performance Chem Inc 906 296-8271
52430 Duncan Ave Hubbell (49934) ***(G-8126)***
Koppert Biological Systems 734 641-3763
1502 N Old Us 23 Howell (48843) ***(G-8057)***
Koppy Corporation (PA) 248 373-1900
415 S West St Ste 200 Royal Oak (48067) ***(G-13942)***
Kor-Cast Products, Troy *Also called Korcast Products Incorporated* ***(G-16448)***
Korcast Products Incorporated (PA) 248 740-2340
1725 Larchwood Dr Troy (48083) ***(G-16448)***
Korcast Products Incorporated 248 740-2340
1725 Larchwood Dr Troy (48083) ***(G-16449)***
Kord Industrial Inc 248 374-8900
47845 Anna Ct Wixom (48393) ***(G-17843)***
Kore Inc 616 785-5900
5263 6 Mile Ct Nw Comstock Park (49321) ***(G-3491)***
Kore Group Inc 248 449-6500
37148 6 Mile Rd Livonia (48152) ***(G-9800)***
Kore Group Inc (PA) 734 677-1500
3500 Washtenaw Ave Ann Arbor (48104) ***(G-519)***
Korens 248 817-5188
1685 W Hamlin Rd Rochester Hills (48309) ***(G-13456)***
Korstone, Madison Heights *Also called KS Liquidating LLC* ***(G-10295)***
Korten Quality Inc 586 752-6255
69069 Powell Rd Bruce Twp (48065) ***(G-2086)***
Koski Log Homes, Ontonagon *Also called Koskis Log Homes Inc* ***(G-12162)***
Koski Welding Inc 906 353-7588
13529 Old 41 Rd Baraga (49908) ***(G-1105)***
Koskis Log Homes Inc 906 884-4937
35993 Us Highway 45 Ontonagon (49953) ***(G-12162)***
Kostal Group, Rochester Hills *Also called Kostal Kontakt Systeme Inc* ***(G-13457)***
Kostal Kontakt Systeme Inc 248 284-7600
1350 W Hamlin Rd Rochester Hills (48309) ***(G-13457)***
Kostal North America, Troy *Also called Kostal of America Inc* ***(G-16450)***
Kostal of America Inc 248 284-6500
350 Stephenson Hwy Troy (48083) ***(G-16450)***
Kostamo Logging 906 353-6171
10408 Kostamo Rd Pelkie (49958) ***(G-12422)***
Kotocorp (usa) Inc (HQ) 269 349-1521
5981 E Cork St Kalamazoo (49048) ***(G-8802)***
Kotzian Ironworks, Shelby *Also called George Kotzian* ***(G-14525)***
Kotzian Tool Inc 231 861-5377
6971 W Shelby Rd Shelby (49455) ***(G-14530)***
Kountry Keepsakes 586 294-4895
31772 Forrest Fraser (48026) ***(G-5680)***
Kowalski Companies Inc (PA) 313 873-8200
2270 Holbrook St Detroit (48212) ***(G-4182)***
Kowloon Noodle Company, Battle Creek *Also called New Moon Noodle Incorporated* ***(G-1232)***
Kp Sogoian, Royal Oak *Also called Kyrie Enterprises LLC* ***(G-13943)***
Kpc Graphics, Kalamazoo *Also called Kalamazoo Photo Comp Svcs* ***(G-8794)***
Kpmf Usa Inc 248 377-4999
67 Kay Industrial Dr Lake Orion (48359) ***(G-9142)***
Kraft Foods, Grand Rapids *Also called Kraft Heinz Foods Company* ***(G-6590)***
Kraft Heinz 616 940-2260
3950 Sparks Dr Se Grand Rapids (49546) ***(G-6589)***
Kraft Heinz Foods Company 616 396-6557
431 W 16th St Holland (49423) ***(G-7713)***
Kraft Heinz Foods Company 616 447-0481
3950 Sparks Dr Se Grand Rapids (49546) ***(G-6590)***
Kraft Power Corporation 989 748-4040
2852 D And M Dr Gaylord (49735) ***(G-5872)***
Kraft-Wrap Inc 586 755-2050
21650 Hoover Rd Warren (48089) ***(G-17121)***
Kraftbrau Brewery Inc 269 384-0288
402 E Kalamazoo Ave Kalamazoo (49007) ***(G-8803)***
Krafts & Thingz 810 689-2457
51382 Village Edge N Chesterfield (48047) ***(G-2799)***
Kraftube Inc 231 832-5562
925 E Church Ave Reed City (49677) ***(G-13217)***
Kraig Biocraft Labs Inc 734 619-8066
2723 S State St Ste 150 Ann Arbor (48104) ***(G-520)***
Kramer International Inc 586 726-4300
5750 New King Dr Ste 200 Troy (48098) ***(G-16451)***
Krams Enterprises Inc 248 415-8500
30400 Telg Rd Ste 200 Bingham Farms (48025) ***(G-1655)***
Krane, Menominee *Also called Plutchak Fab* ***(G-10755)***
Krasitys Med Surgical Sup Inc 313 274-2210
1825 Bailey St Dearborn (48124) ***(G-3731)***
Kraus & Co, Monroe *Also called Paul C Doerr* ***(G-11060)***
Krause Welding Inc 231 773-4443
4350 Evanston Ave Muskegon (49442) ***(G-11358)***
Krauter Forest Products LLC 815 317-6561
21224 Sylvan Rd Reed City (49677) ***(G-13218)***
Kreations Inc 313 255-1230
15340 Dale St Detroit (48223) ***(G-4183)***
Krebs Tool Inc 734 697-8611
611 Savage Rd Van Buren Twp (48111) ***(G-16768)***
Kreft Injection Technology LLC 248 589-9202
799 E Mandoline Ave Madison Heights (48071) ***(G-10294)***
Kremin Inc 989 790-5147
235 Keystone Way Frankenmuth (48734) ***(G-5592)***
Krh Industries, LLC, Sterling Heights *Also called B & B Holdings Groesbeck LLC* ***(G-15269)***
Krieger Craftsmen Inc 616 735-9200
2758 3 Mile Rd Nw Grand Rapids (49534) ***(G-6591)***
Kriewall Enterprises Inc 586 336-0600
140 Shafer Dr Romeo (48065) ***(G-13631)***
Kring Pizza Inc 586 792-0049
35415 Jefferson Ave Harrison Township (48045) ***(G-7336)***
Kringer Industrial Corporation 519 818-3509
24435 Forterra Dr Warren (48089) ***(G-17122)***
Kriseler Welding Inc 989 624-9266
11877 Maple Rd Birch Run (48415) ***(G-1664)***
Krista Messer 734 459-1952
50619 Colchester Ct Canton (48187) ***(G-2391)***
Kristus Inc 269 321-3330
8370 Greenfield Shores Dr Scotts (49088) ***(G-14505)***

ALPHABETIC SECTION — L & W Engineering Co, Holland

Krmc LLC 734 955-9311
27456 Northline Rd Romulus (48174) *(G-13698)*

Kroger Co 586 727-4946
66900 Gratiot Ave Richmond (48062) *(G-13265)*

Krontz General Machine & Tool 269 651-5882
412 W Congress St Sturgis (49091) *(G-15610)*

Kropp Woodworking Inc 586 463-2300
154 S Rose St Mount Clemens (48043) *(G-11138)*

Kropp Woodworking Inc 586 997-3000
6812 19 1/2 Mile Rd Sterling Heights (48314) *(G-15391)*

Krt Precision Tool & Mfg Co 517 783-5715
1300 Mitchell St Jackson (49203) *(G-8490)*

Kruger Plastic Products LLC (PA) 269 465-6404
4015 Lemon Creek Rd Bridgman (49106) *(G-1869)*

Kruger Plastics Products LLC 269 545-3311
117 S Grant St Galien (49113) *(G-5818)*

Krumbsnatcher Cookies, Detroit Also called Krumbsnatcher Enterprises LLC *(G-4184)*

Krumbsnatcher Enterprises LLC 313 408-6802
11000 W Mcnic Detroit (48235) *(G-4184)*

Krupp Industries LLC 734 261-0410
37050 Plymouth Rd Livonia (48150) *(G-9801)*

Krupp Industries LLC (PA) 616 475-5905
2735 West River Dr Nw Walker (49544) *(G-16870)*

Krush Industries Inc 248 238-2296
12729 Universal Dr Taylor (48180) *(G-15733)*

Krzysiak Family Restaurant 989 894-5531
1605 Michigan Ave Bay City (48708) *(G-1326)*

Krzysiak's House, Bay City Also called Krzysiak Family Restaurant *(G-1326)*

KS Liquidating LLC 248 577-8220
32031 Howard Ave Madison Heights (48071) *(G-10295)*

Ksb Dubric Inc 616 784-6355
3737 Laramie Dr Ne Comstock Park (49321) *(G-3492)*

Ktr Dental Lab & Pdts LLC 248 224-9158
17040 W 12 Mile Rd # 150 Southfield (48076) *(G-14957)*

Ktr Printing Inc 989 386-9740
801 Industrial Dr Clare (48617) *(G-2875)*

Kts Enterprises 269 624-3435
121 W 2nd St Lawton (49065) *(G-9512)*

Kubica Corp 248 344-7750
22575 Heslip Dr Novi (48375) *(G-11922)*

Kubinec Strapping Solutions, Howell Also called Global Strapping LLC *(G-8044)*

Kubisch Sausage, Auburn Hills Also called Mello Meats Inc *(G-945)*

Kuhlman Casting Co Inc 248 853-2382
20415 Woodingham Dr Detroit (48221) *(G-4185)*

Kuhlman Concrete, Monroe Also called Kuhlman Corporation *(G-11045)*

Kuhlman Concrete Inc 517 265-2722
240 W Maple Ave Adrian (49221) *(G-74)*

Kuhlman Corporation 734 241-8692
15370 S Dixie Hwy Monroe (48161) *(G-11045)*

Kuka Aerospace, Sterling Heights Also called Kuka Systems North America LLC *(G-15392)*

Kuka Assembly and Test Corp (HQ) 989 220-3088
5675 Dixie Hwy Saginaw (48601) *(G-14074)*

Kuka Assembly and Test Corp 810 593-0350
255 S Fenway Dr Fenton (48430) *(G-5224)*

Kuka Omnimove, Shelby Township Also called Kuka Robotics Corporation *(G-14615)*

Kuka Robotics, Sterling Heights Also called Kuka US Holding Company LLC *(G-15393)*

Kuka Robotics Corporation 586 795-2000
51870 Shelby Pkwy Shelby Township (48315) *(G-14615)*

Kuka Systems North America LLC (HQ) ... 586 795-2000
6600 Center Dr Sterling Heights (48312) *(G-15392)*

Kuka Systems North America LLC 586 726-4300
13231 23 Mile Rd Shelby Township (48315) *(G-14616)*

Kuka US Holding Company LLC (HQ) ... 586 795-2000
6600 Center Dr Sterling Heights (48312) *(G-15393)*

Kulick Enterprises Inc 734 283-6999
4082 Biddle Ave Wyandotte (48192) *(G-17964)*

Kumanu Inc 734 822-6673
535 W William St Ste 4n Ann Arbor (48103) *(G-521)*

Kunststoff Technik Scherer 734 944-5080
3150 Livernois Rd Ste 275 Troy (48083) *(G-16452)*

Kuntz Tool & Die, Grand Blanc Also called Rdc Machine Inc *(G-5980)*

Kurabe America Corporation 248 939-5803
37735 Interchange Dr Farmington Hills (48335) *(G-5039)*

Kurek Tool Inc 989 777-5300
4735 Dixie Hwy Saginaw (48601) *(G-14075)*

Kurrent Welding Inc 734 753-9197
18488 Wahrman Rd New Boston (48164) *(G-11501)*

Kurt Dubowski 231 796-0055
14472 Mckinley Rd Big Rapids (49307) *(G-1637)*

Kurt Machine Tool Co Inc 586 296-5070
33910 Riviera Dr Fraser (48026) *(G-5681)*

Kurth Bayard Co 586 771-5174
20628 Alger St Saint Clair Shores (48080) *(G-14258)*

Kurtis Kitchen & Bath Centers, Livonia Also called Kurtis Mfg & Distrg Corp *(G-9802)*

Kurtis Mfg & Distrg Corp (PA) 734 522-7600
12500 Merriman Rd Livonia (48150) *(G-9802)*

Kurtz Gravel Company Inc (HQ) 810 787-6543
33469 W 14 Mile Rd # 100 Farmington Hills (48331) *(G-5040)*

Kustom Creations Inc 586 997-4141
6665 Burroughs Ave Sterling Heights (48314) *(G-15394)*

Kustom Kaps, Temperance Also called Royal Stewart Enterprises *(G-15843)*

Kut-Rite Manufacturing Company, Romulus Also called Krmc LLC *(G-13698)*

Kuzimski Enterprises Inc 989 422-5377
9100 Knapp Rd Houghton Lake (48629) *(G-7994)*

Kva Engineering Inc 616 745-7483
1248 Plymouth Ave Ne Grand Rapids (49505) *(G-6592)*

Kwik Kopy Printing Canada, Plymouth Also called Alliance Franchise Brands LLC *(G-12568)*

Kwik Paint Products, Detroit Also called R B L Plastics Incorporated *(G-4325)*

Kwik Print Plus, Ludington Also called Worten Copy Center Inc *(G-10089)*

Kwik Tech Inc 586 268-6201
9068 Lone Pine Ct Shelby Township (48317) *(G-14617)*

Kwik-Site Corporation 734 326-1500
5555 Treadwell St Wayne (48184) *(G-17434)*

Kwikie Duplicating Center, Charlevoix Also called Village Graphics Inc *(G-2634)*

Kwikie Inc 231 946-9942
700 Boon St Traverse City (49686) *(G-16019)*

Kwk Industries Inc 269 423-6213
56040 Territorial Rd Decatur (49045) *(G-3804)*

KY Holdings, Rochester Also called Trans Industries Plastics LLC *(G-13355)*

KYB Americas Corporation 248 374-0100
26800 Meadowbrook Rd # 115 Novi (48377) *(G-11923)*

Kyklos Holdings Inc (HQ) 313 758-2000
1 Dauch Dr Detroit (48211) *(G-4186)*

Kyler Industries Inc 616 392-1042
192 E 48th St Holland (49423) *(G-7714)*

Kyocera International Inc 734 416-8500
46723 Five Mile Rd Plymouth (48170) *(G-12670)*

Kyocera Unimerco Tooling Inc 734 944-4433
6620 State Rd Saline (48176) *(G-14397)*

Kyoei Electronics America Inc 248 773-3690
39555 Orchard Hill Pl Novi (48375) *(G-11924)*

Kyrie Enterprises LLC 248 549-8690
4336 Normandy Ct Royal Oak (48073) *(G-13943)*

Kysor Industrial Corporation 231 779-7500
1100 Wright St Cadillac (49601) *(G-2259)*

L & C Hanwha 734 457-5600
1530 E Front St Monroe (48161) *(G-11046)*

L & H Diversified Mfg USA LLC 586 615-4873
51559 Oro Dr Shelby Township (48315) *(G-14618)*

L & J Enterprises Inc 586 995-4153
3181 Wynns Mill Ct Metamora (48455) *(G-10778)*

L & J Meat Packaging, Dowagiac Also called L&J Packaging *(G-4546)*

L & J Products K Huntington 810 919-3550
9954 Weber St Brighton (48116) *(G-1947)*

L & L Machine & Tool Inc 517 784-5575
415 Condad Ave Jackson (49202) *(G-8491)*

L & L Pattern Inc 231 733-2646
2401 Park St Muskegon (49444) *(G-11359)*

L & L Products Inc (HQ) 586 336-1600
160 Mclean Bruce Twp (48065) *(G-2087)*

L & L Products Inc 586 752-6681
160 Mclean Bruce Twp (48065) *(G-2088)*

L & L Products Inc 586 336-1600
159 Mclean Bruce Twp (48065) *(G-2089)*

L & M Hardwood & Skids LLC 734 281-3043
15361 Goddard Rd Southgate (48195) *(G-15079)*

L & M Machining & Mfg Inc 586 498-7110
14200 E 10 Mile Rd Warren (48089) *(G-17123)*

L & M Mfg Inc 989 689-4010
6016 N Meridian Rd Hope (48628) *(G-7955)*

L & M Tool Co Inc 586 677-4700
51261 Milano Dr Macomb (48042) *(G-10136)*

L & P LLC 231 733-1415
2376 Dels Dr Muskegon (49444) *(G-11360)*

L & R Grinding, Canton Also called Merchants Industries Inc *(G-2402)*

L & R Machine Inc 517 523-2978
6671 Hudson Rd Osseo (49266) *(G-12226)*

L & S Products LLC 517 238-4645
294 Block Rd Coldwater (49036) *(G-3313)*

L & S Transit Mix Concrete Co 989 354-5363
500 Tuttle St Alpena (49707) *(G-294)*

L & W Inc 734 397-8085
6771 Haggerty Rd Van Buren Twp (48111) *(G-16769)*

L & W Inc 517 486-6321
11505 E Us Highway 223 Blissfield (49228) *(G-1717)*

L & W Inc 734 529-7290
5461 Circle Seven Dr Dundee (48131) *(G-4590)*

L & W Inc (HQ) 734 397-6300
17757 Woodland Dr New Boston (48164) *(G-11502)*

L & W Inc 734 397-2212
6201 Haggerty Rd Van Buren Twp (48111) *(G-16770)*

L & W Inc 616 394-9665
808 E 32nd St Holland (49423) *(G-7715)*

L & W Inc 517 627-7333
13112 Oneida Rd Grand Ledge (48837) *(G-6110)*

L & W Engineering, New Boston Also called L & W Inc *(G-11502)*

L & W Engineering Co, Holland Also called L & W Inc *(G-7715)*

L & W Engineering Co Plant 2, Van Buren Twp *Also called L & W Inc* ***(G-16770)***
L & W, Engineering, Grand Ledge *Also called L & W Inc* ***(G-6110)***
L A Burnhart Inc (PA).......810 227-4567
2095 Euler Rd Brighton (48114) ***(G-1948)***
L A Martin Company.......313 581-3444
14400 Henn St Dearborn (48126) ***(G-3732)***
L A S Leasing Inc.......734 727-5148
36253 Michigan Ave Wayne (48184) ***(G-17435)***
L Barge & Associates Inc.......248 582-3430
1530 Farrow St Ferndale (48220) ***(G-5297)***
L C Redi Mix, Kalkaska *Also called Lc Materials* ***(G-8948)***
L D J Inc.......906 524-6194
202 N Main St Lanse (49946) ***(G-9198)***
L D S Sheet Metal Inc.......313 892-2624
21831 Schoenherr Rd Warren (48089) ***(G-17124)***
L E Jones Company.......906 863-1043
1200 34th Ave Menominee (49858) ***(G-10741)***
L E Q Inc.......248 257-5466
5600 Williams Lake Rd B Waterford (48329) ***(G-17356)***
L F M Enterprises Inc.......586 792-7220
33256 Kelly Rd Clinton Township (48035) ***(G-3156)***
L I S Manufacturing Inc.......734 525-3070
15223 Farmington Rd Ste 8 Livonia (48154) ***(G-9803)***
L L C, Midland *Also called S and P Drctnal Boring Svc LLC* ***(G-10910)***
L M Gear Company Division, Clinton Township *Also called Anderson-Cook Inc* ***(G-3053)***
L M Group, Sterling Heights *Also called Luckmarr Plastics Inc* ***(G-15403)***
L M I, Fenton *Also called Linear Measurement Instrs Corp* ***(G-5225)***
L Mawby LLC.......231 271-3522
4519 S Elm Valley Rd Suttons Bay (49682) ***(G-15653)***
L N T Inc.......248 347-6006
24300 Catherne Ind Dr # 405 Novi (48375) ***(G-11925)***
L Perrigo Company (HQ).......269 673-8451
515 Eastern Ave Allegan (49010) ***(G-170)***
L Perrigo Company.......269 673-7962
300 Water St Allegan (49010) ***(G-171)***
L Perrigo Company.......616 738-0150
13295 Reflections Dr Holland (49424) ***(G-7716)***
L Perrigo Company.......269 673-7962
809 Airway Dr Allegan (49010) ***(G-172)***
L Perrigo Company.......269 673-1608
500 Eastern Ave Allegan (49010) ***(G-173)***
L Perrigo Company.......248 687-1036
101 W Big Beaver Rd Troy (48084) ***(G-16453)***
L R Oliver and Company Inc.......810 765-1000
7445 Mayer Rd Cottrellville (48039) ***(G-3590)***
L S I, Traverse City *Also called Land Services Incorporated* ***(G-16021)***
L S Machining Inc.......248 583-7277
1250 Rankin Dr Ste E Troy (48083) ***(G-16454)***
L T C Roll & Engineering Co (PA).......586 465-1023
23500 John Gorsuch Dr Clinton Township (48036) ***(G-3157)***
L T C Roll & Engineering Co.......586 465-1023
31140 Kendall Fraser (48026) ***(G-5682)***
L T W, Lawrence *Also called Lanphear Tool Works Inc* ***(G-9505)***
L Thompson Co LLC.......616 844-1135
126 Lafayette Ave Grand Haven (49417) ***(G-6044)***
L& L Products, Bruce Twp *Also called Zephyros Inc* ***(G-2106)***
L&J Packaging.......269 782-2628
30838 Middle Crossing Rd Dowagiac (49047) ***(G-4546)***
L&L Printing Inc.......586 263-0060
42120 Garfield Rd Clinton Township (48038) ***(G-3158)***
L&W Engineering Co Plant 1, Van Buren Twp *Also called L & W Inc* ***(G-16769)***
L'Anse Sentinel, Lanse *Also called L D J Inc* ***(G-9198)***
L-3 Combat Propulsion Systems, Muskegon *Also called L3 Technologies Inc* ***(G-11361)***
L-3 Communications Eotech Inc.......734 741-8868
1201 E Ellsworth Rd Ann Arbor (48108) ***(G-522)***
L. T. C Roll & Engineering Co, Clinton Township *Also called L T C Roll & Engineering Co* ***(G-3157)***
L3 Aviation Products Inc (HQ).......616 949-6600
5353 52nd St Se Grand Rapids (49512) ***(G-6593)***
L3 Commnctons Avionics Systems, Grand Rapids *Also called L3 Aviation Products Inc* ***(G-6593)***
L3 Technologies Inc.......231 724-2151
76 S Getty St Muskegon (49442) ***(G-11361)***
L3 Technologies Inc.......734 741-8868
1201 E Ellsworth Rd Ann Arbor (48108) ***(G-523)***
L3harris Technologies Inc.......517 780-0695
3516 Wayland Dr Jackson (49202) ***(G-8492)***
La Colombe Torrefaction.......231 798-9853
1269 E Mount Garfield Rd Norton Shores (49441) ***(G-11769)***
LA East Inc.......269 476-7170
62702 Woodland Dr Vandalia (49095) ***(G-16801)***
La Familia Stop 'n' Shop, Grand Rapids *Also called Agenda 2020 Inc* ***(G-6153)***
La Fata Cabinets, Shelby Township *Also called Lafata Cabinet Shop* ***(G-14620)***
La Force Inc.......248 588-5601
289 Robbins Dr Troy (48083) ***(G-16455)***
La Gold Mine Inc.......517 540-1050
425 W Main St Brighton (48116) ***(G-1949)***
La Jalisciense Inc (PA).......313 237-0008
31048 Applewood Ln Farmington Hills (48331) ***(G-5041)***
La Rosa Refrigeration & Eqp Co.......313 368-6620
19191 Filer St Detroit (48234) ***(G-4187)***
La Rozinas Inc.......906 779-2181
921 Eagle Dr Iron Mountain (49802) ***(G-8287)***
La Solucion Corp.......313 893-9760
19930 Conner St Detroit (48234) ***(G-4188)***
La-Z-Boy, Monroe *Also called Lzb Manufacturing Inc* ***(G-11051)***
La-Z-Boy Casegoods Inc (HQ).......734 242-1444
1 Lazboy Dr Monroe (48162) ***(G-11047)***
La-Z-Boy Global Limited.......734 241-2438
1 Lazboy Dr Monroe (48162) ***(G-11048)***
La-Z-Boy Greensboro, Inc., Monroe *Also called La-Z-Boy Casegoods Inc* ***(G-11047)***
La-Z-Boy Incorporated (PA).......734 242-1444
1 Lazboy Dr Monroe (48162) ***(G-11049)***
Lab Tool and Engineering Corp.......517 750-4131
7755 King Rd Spring Arbor (49283) ***(G-15124)***
Label Tech Inc.......586 247-6444
51322 Oro Dr Shelby Township (48315) ***(G-14619)***
Labor Aiding Systems Corp.......517 768-7478
3101 Hart Rd Jackson (49201) ***(G-8493)***
Labor Education and Res Prj.......313 842-6262
7435 Michigan Ave Detroit (48210) ***(G-4189)***
Labor Notes, Detroit *Also called Labor Education and Res Prj* ***(G-4189)***
Labor World, Fraser *Also called A B Rusgo Inc* ***(G-5610)***
Labortrio Elttrofisico USA Inc.......248 340-7040
40 Engelwood Dr Ste H Lake Orion (48359) ***(G-9143)***
Labtech Corporation.......313 862-1737
7707 Lyndon St Detroit (48238) ***(G-4190)***
Lach Diamond.......616 698-0101
4350 Airwest Dr Se Ofc A Grand Rapids (49512) ***(G-6594)***
Lachman & Company, Southfield *Also called Lachman Enterprises Inc* ***(G-14958)***
Lachman Enterprises Inc.......248 948-9944
20955 Telegraph Rd Southfield (48033) ***(G-14958)***
Lacks Enterprises, Grand Rapids *Also called Lacks Exterior Systems LLC* ***(G-6599)***
Lacks Enterprises Inc.......616 949-6570
4221 Airlane Dr Se Grand Rapids (49512) ***(G-6595)***
Lacks Enterprises Inc.......616 656-2910
4365 52nd St Se Grand Rapids (49512) ***(G-6596)***
Lacks Enterprises Inc.......616 698-2030
4251 Brockton Ct Se Grand Rapids (49512) ***(G-6597)***
Lacks Enterprises Inc (PA).......616 949-6570
5460 Cascade Rd Se Grand Rapids (49546) ***(G-6598)***
Lacks Exterior Systems LLC.......616 554-3419
4245 52nd St Se Grand Rapids (49512) ***(G-6599)***
Lacks Exterior Systems LLC (HQ).......616 949-6570
5460 Cascade Rd Se Grand Rapids (49546) ***(G-6600)***
Lacks Exterior Systems LLC.......616 949-6570
5010 52nd St Se Grand Rapids (49512) ***(G-6601)***
Lacks Exterior Systems LLC.......248 351-0555
39500 Mackenzie Dr # 500 Novi (48377) ***(G-11926)***
Lacks Exterior Systems LLC.......616 949-6570
5711 Kraft Ave Se Grand Rapids (49512) ***(G-6602)***
Lacks Exterior Systems LLC.......616 554-7805
4655 Patterson Ave Se Kentwood (49512) ***(G-9015)***
Lacks Exterior Systems LLC.......616 949-6570
5801 Kraft Ave Se Grand Rapids (49512) ***(G-6603)***
Lacks Exterior Systems LLC.......616 949-6570
4315 52nd St Se Grand Rapids (49512) ***(G-6604)***
Lacks Exterior Systems LLC.......616 949-6570
3703 Patterson Sw Grand Rapids (49512) ***(G-6605)***
Lacks Exterior Systems LLC.......616 554-7180
3703 Patterson Ave Se Kentwood (49512) ***(G-9016)***
Lacks Industries Inc.......616 698-6890
4260 Airwest Dr Se Grand Rapids (49512) ***(G-6606)***
Lacks Industries Inc.......616 698-3600
4375 52nd St Se Grand Rapids (49512) ***(G-6607)***
Lacks Industries Inc.......616 554-7135
4655 Patterson Ave Se D Kentwood (49512) ***(G-9017)***
Lacks Industries Inc.......616 698-6854
4090 Barden Dr Grand Rapids (49512) ***(G-6608)***
Lacks Industries Inc.......616 698-9852
4260 Airlane Dr Se Grand Rapids (49512) ***(G-6609)***
Lacks Industries Inc.......616 554-7134
3505 Kraft Ave Se Grand Rapids (49512) ***(G-6610)***
Lacks Industries Inc.......616 698-2776
4275 Airwest Dr Se Grand Rapids (49512) ***(G-6611)***
Lacks Industries Inc.......616 656-2910
4365 52nd St Se Grand Rapids (49512) ***(G-6612)***
Lacks Trim Systems, Grand Rapids *Also called Lacks Exterior Systems LLC* ***(G-6600)***
Lacks Trim Systems, Grand Rapids *Also called Lacks Industries Inc* ***(G-6608)***
Lacks Trim Systems, Kentwood *Also called Lacks Exterior Systems LLC* ***(G-9016)***
Lacks Wheel Trim Systems, Kentwood *Also called Lacks Industries Inc* ***(G-9017)***
Lacks Wheel Trim Systems, Grand Rapids *Also called Lacks Industries Inc* ***(G-6610)***
Lacks Wheel Trim Systems LLC.......248 351-0555
39500 Mackenzie Dr # 500 Novi (48377) ***(G-11927)***
Lacks Wheel Trim Systems LLC (PA).......616 949-6570
5460 Cascade Rd Se Grand Rapids (49546) ***(G-6613)***

Laco Inc 231 929-3300
1561 Laitner Dr Traverse City (49696) ***(G-16020)***
Lacy Tool Company Inc 248 476-5250
40375 Grand River Ave Novi (48375) ***(G-11928)***
Ladder Carolina Company Inc 734 482-5946
12 E Forest Ave Ypsilanti (48198) ***(G-18083)***
Laddertech LLC 248 437-7100
7081 Dan Mcguire Dr Brighton (48116) ***(G-1950)***
Ladlas Prince, Pontiac *Also called Lpm Supply Inc* ***(G-12846)***
Laduke Corporation 248 414-6600
10311 Capital St Oak Park (48237) ***(G-12077)***
Laduke Roofing, Oak Park *Also called Laduke Corporation* ***(G-12077)***
Lady Jane Gourmet Seed Co., Metamora *Also called L & J Enterprises Inc* ***(G-10778)***
Lafarge North America Inc 989 399-1005
1701 N 1st St Saginaw (48601) ***(G-14076)***
Lafarge North America Inc 989 894-0157
1500 Main St Essexville (48732) ***(G-4875)***
Lafarge North America Inc 989 595-3820
11351 E Grand Lake Rd Presque Isle (49777) ***(G-13083)***
Lafarge North America Inc 269 983-6333
200 Upton Dr Saint Joseph (49085) ***(G-14322)***
Lafarge North America Inc 216 566-0545
1500 Main St Essexville (48732) ***(G-4876)***
Lafarge North America Inc 703 480-3600
6211 N Ann Arbor Rd Dundee (48131) ***(G-4591)***
Lafarge North America Inc 703 480-3649
6211 N Ann Arbor Rd Dundee (48131) ***(G-4592)***
Lafarge North America Inc 231 726-3291
1047 7th St Muskegon (49441) ***(G-11362)***
Lafarge North America Inc 989 354-4171
1435 Ford Ave Alpena (49707) ***(G-295)***
Lafarge North America Inc 313 842-9258
1301 Springwells Ct Detroit (48209) ***(G-4191)***
Lafarge North America Inc 989 755-7515
900 N Adams St Saginaw (48604) ***(G-14077)***
Lafargeholcim, Essexville *Also called Lafarge North America Inc* ***(G-4875)***
Lafata Cabinet Shop (PA) 586 247-6536
50905 Hayes Rd Shelby Township (48315) ***(G-14620)***
Lafave Hydraulics & Metal 989 872-2163
8260 Van Dyke Rd Cass City (48726) ***(G-2517)***
Lafave Hydrlics Met Fbrication, Cass City *Also called Lafave Hydraulics & Metal* ***(G-2517)***
Lafrontera Tortillas Inc 734 231-1701
32845 Cleveland St Rockwood (48173) ***(G-13606)***
Lagos Farms & Machining 989 872-4895
1040 Plain Rd Cass City (48726) ***(G-2518)***
Lahti Fabrication Inc 989 343-0420
651 Columbus Ave West Branch (48661) ***(G-17510)***
Laidco Sales Inc 231 832-1327
4753 175th Ave Hersey (49639) ***(G-7473)***
Laingsburg Screw Inc 517 651-2757
9805 Round Lake Rd Laingsburg (48848) ***(G-9080)***
Lake Brothers Forest Products 906 485-5639
3039 County Road 496 Ishpeming (49849) ***(G-8348)***
Lake City Forge, Lake City *Also called Lc Manufacturing LLC* ***(G-9090)***
Lake Design and Mfg Co 616 794-0290
7280 Storey Rd Belding (48809) ***(G-1424)***
Lake Erie Med Surgical Sup Inc (PA) 734 847-3847
7560 Lewis Ave Temperance (48182) ***(G-15833)***
Lake Fabricators Inc 269 651-1935
1000 N Clay St Sturgis (49091) ***(G-15611)***
Lake Lansing ASC Partners LLC 517 708-3333
1707 Lake Lansing Rd Lansing (48912) ***(G-9386)***
Lake Michigan Mailers Inc (PA) 269 383-9333
3777 Sky King Blvd Kalamazoo (49009) ***(G-8804)***
Lake Michigan Wire LLC 616 786-9200
4211 Hallacy Dr Holland (49424) ***(G-7717)***
Lake Odessa Meat Processing 616 374-8392
1423 Clark St Lake Odessa (48849) ***(G-9116)***
Lake Orion Concrete Orna Pdts 248 693-8683
62 W Scripps Rd Lake Orion (48360) ***(G-9144)***
Lake Orion Review, The, Lake Orion *Also called Sherman Publications Inc* ***(G-9161)***
Lake Shore Services Inc 734 285-7007
4354 Biddle Ave Wyandotte (48192) ***(G-17965)***
Lake Shore Systems Inc (PA) 906 774-1500
2141 Woodward Ave Kingsford (49802) ***(G-9061)***
Lake Shore Systems Inc 906 265-5414
1520 W Adams St Iron River (49935) ***(G-8313)***
Lake Superior Logging 906 440-3567
8453 Old Brimley Grade Rd Brimley (49715) ***(G-2016)***
Lake Superior Press Inc 906 228-7450
802 S Lake St Marquette (49855) ***(G-10538)***
Lake Superior Soap Co, Waterford *Also called Kevin Larkin Inc* ***(G-17355)***
Lakeland Asphalt Corporation 269 964-1720
548 Avenue A Springfield (49037) ***(G-15196)***
Lakeland Elec Mtr Svcs Inc 616 647-0331
3810 Mill Creek Dr Ne Comstock Park (49321) ***(G-3493)***
Lakeland Finishing Corporation 616 949-8001
5400 36th St Se Grand Rapids (49512) ***(G-6614)***
Lakeland Mills Inc 989 427-5133
1 Lakeland Pl Edmore (48829) ***(G-4752)***
Lakeland Pallets Inc (PA) 616 949-9515
3801 Kraft Ave Se Grand Rapids (49512) ***(G-6615)***
Lakeland Pallets Inc 616 997-4441
50 64th Ave S Coopersville (49404) ***(G-3563)***
Lakepoint Elec 586 983-2510
56812 Mound Rd Shelby Township (48316) ***(G-14621)***
Lakeshore Automatic Pdts Inc 616 846-4005
1810 Industrial Dr Ste D Grand Haven (49417) ***(G-6045)***
Lakeshore Cement Products 989 739-9341
5251 N Us Highway 23 Oscoda (48750) ***(G-12213)***
Lakeshore Custom Powdr Coating 616 296-9330
411 N Griffin St Grand Haven (49417) ***(G-6046)***
Lakeshore Die Cast Inc 269 422-1523
8829 Stvnsville Baroda Rd Baroda (49101) ***(G-1126)***
Lakeshore Fittings Inc 616 846-5090
1865 Industrial Park Dr Grand Haven (49417) ***(G-6047)***
Lakeshore Global Corporation, Detroit *Also called Lgc Global Inc* ***(G-4202)***
Lakeshore Marble Company Inc 269 429-8241
4410 N Roosevelt Rd Stevensville (49127) ***(G-15574)***
Lakeshore Mold and Die LLC 269 429-6764
2355 W Marquette Woods Rd Stevensville (49127) ***(G-15575)***
Lakeside Boring Inc 586 286-8883
16627 Terra Bella St Clinton Township (48038) ***(G-3159)***
Lakeside Building Products 248 349-3500
9189 Central St Detroit (48204) ***(G-4192)***
Lakeside Canvas, Fennville *Also called Great Lakes Canvas Co* ***(G-5172)***
Lakeside Canvas & Upholstery 231 755-2514
3200 Lakeshore Dr Muskegon (49441) ***(G-11363)***
Lakeside Manufacturing Co 269 429-6193
4999 Advance Way Stevensville (49127) ***(G-15576)***
Lakeside Mechanical Contrs 616 786-0211
1741 Forest Cove Trl Allegan (49010) ***(G-174)***
Lakeside Property Services 863 455-9038
14250 Ottawa Creek Ln Holland (49424) ***(G-7718)***
Lakeside Software Inc 248 686-1700
201 S Main St Ste 200 Ann Arbor (48104) ***(G-524)***
Lakeside Software Inc (PA) 248 686-1700
40950 Woodward Ave # 200 Bloomfield Hills (48304) ***(G-1776)***
Lakeside Spring Products Inc 616 847-2706
2615 Temple St Muskegon (49444) ***(G-11364)***
Lakestate Industries Inc 906 786-9212
1831 N 21st St Escanaba (49829) ***(G-4838)***
Laketon Truss Inc 231 798-3467
1527 Scranton Dr Norton Shores (49441) ***(G-11770)***
Lakeview Manufacturing 231 348-2596
1480 Mcdougal Rd Petoskey (49770) ***(G-12453)***
Lakeview Quality Tool Inc 989 732-6417
696 Alpine Rd Gaylord (49735) ***(G-5873)***
Lakeview Sand & Gravel, Lakeview *Also called Grifco Inc* ***(G-9173)***
Lakewood Machine Products Co 734 654-6677
12429 Maxwell Rd Carleton (48117) ***(G-2459)***
Lam Industries 734 266-1404
12985 Wayne Rd Livonia (48150) ***(G-9804)***
Lamacs Inc 248 643-9210
360 E Maple Rd Ste I Troy (48083) ***(G-16456)***
Lamantia Machine Company, Stevensville *Also called John Lamantia Corporation* ***(G-15572)***
Lambert Industries, Centreville *Also called Wayne Allen Lambert* ***(G-2600)***
Lambert Industries Inc 734 668-6864
69 Enterprise Dr Ann Arbor (48103) ***(G-525)***
Lamina Inc 248 489-9122
38505 Country Club Dr # 100 Farmington Hills (48331) ***(G-5042)***
Laminin Medical Products Inc 616 871-3390
3760 East Paris Ave Se Grand Rapids (49512) ***(G-6616)***
Lamon Group Inc 616 710-3169
889 76th St Sw Unit 1 Byron Center (49315) ***(G-2196)***
Lamons 989 488-4580
807 Pershing St Midland (48640) ***(G-10881)***
Lamour Printing Co 734 241-6006
123 E Front St Monroe (48161) ***(G-11050)***
Lampco Industries Inc 517 783-3414
1635 Losey Ave Jackson (49203) ***(G-8494)***
Lampco Manufacturing Company 517 784-4393
1635 Losey Ave Jackson (49203) ***(G-8495)***
Lancast Urethane Inc 517 485-6070
1132 Ladd Rd Commerce Township (48390) ***(G-3419)***
Lance Industries LLC 248 549-1968
1260 Kempar Ave Madison Heights (48071) ***(G-10296)***
Lancer Tool Co 248 380-8830
29289 Lorie Ln Wixom (48393) ***(G-17844)***
Land & Homes Inc 616 534-5792
1701 Porter St Sw Ste 6 Grand Rapids (49519) ***(G-6617)***
Land and Sea Group, Northville *Also called Competitive Cmpt Info Tech Inc* ***(G-11683)***
Land Enterprises Inc 248 398-7276
26641 Townley St Madison Heights (48071) ***(G-10297)***
Land Quilts, Crystal Falls *Also called Magiglide Inc* ***(G-3611)***
Land Services Incorporated 231 947-9400
401 W Front St Ste 7 Traverse City (49684) ***(G-16021)***

ALPHABETIC

Land Star Inc 313 834-2366
  14284 Meyers Rd Detroit (48227) *(G-4193)*
Landaal Packaging Systems, Bay City Also called Delta Containers Inc *(G-1300)*
Landahl Packaging Systems, Burton Also called Flint Boxmakers Inc *(G-2154)*
Landers Drafting Inc 906 228-8690
  105 Garfield Ave Marquette (49855) *(G-10539)*
Landis Machine Shop, Romulus Also called Lewkowicz Corporation *(G-13701)*
Landis Precision Inc (PA) 248 685-8032
  937 S Main St Milford (48381) *(G-10968)*
Landmark Energy Development Co 586 457-0200
  14738 Rice Dr Sterling Heights (48313) *(G-15395)*
Landra Prsthtics Orthotics Inc 586 294-7188
  29840 Harper Ave Saint Clair Shores (48082) *(G-14259)*
Landra Prsthtics Orthotics Inc (PA) 734 281-8144
  14725 Northline Rd Southgate (48195) *(G-15080)*
Landscape Stone Supply Inc 616 953-2028
  5960 136th Ave Holland (49424) *(G-7719)*
Landsculpt, Canton Also called Directional Regulated Systems *(G-2365)*
Lane Gainer Sports Co, Brighton Also called Craig C Askins *(G-1907)*
Lane Soft Water 269 673-3272
  132 Grand St Allegan (49010) *(G-175)*
Lane Tool and Mfg Corp 248 528-1606
  1830 Brinston Dr Troy (48083) *(G-16457)*
Lang Tool Company 989 435-9864
  2520 Glidden Rd Beaverton (48612) *(G-1387)*
Langenberg Machine Products 517 485-9450
  1234 S Holmes St Lansing (48912) *(G-9387)*
Langerak Upholstery, Rockford Also called Tamarack Uphl & Interiors *(G-13592)*
Langs Inc 248 634-6048
  5469 Jacobs Dr Holly (48442) *(G-7884)*
Lannis Fence Systems, Jackson Also called Midway Strl Pipe & Sup Inc *(G-8527)*
Lanny Bensinger 989 658-2590
  1491 E Morrison Rd Ubly (48475) *(G-16718)*
Lanphear Tool Works Inc 269 674-8877
  311 S Paw Paw St Lawrence (49064) *(G-9505)*
Lansing Athletics 517 327-8828
  5572 W Saginaw Hwy Lansing (48917) *(G-9305)*
Lansing Forge Inc (HQ) 517 882-2056
  5232 Aurelius Rd Lansing (48911) *(G-9388)*
Lansing Fuel Ventures Inc 517 371-1198
  601 W Saginaw St Lansing (48933) *(G-9389)*
Lansing Holding Company Inc (PA) 517 882-2056
  5232 Aurelius Rd Lansing (48911) *(G-9390)*
Lansing Ice and Fuel Company (PA) 517 372-3850
  911 Center St Lansing (48906) *(G-9240)*
Lansing Labor News Inc 517 484-7408
  210 Clare St Ste A Lansing (48917) *(G-9306)*
Lansing Pallet 517 322-2500
  4201 S Creyts Rd Lansing (48917) *(G-9307)*
Lansing Plating Company 517 485-6915
  1303 Case St Lansing (48906) *(G-9241)*
Lansing State Journal, Battle Creek Also called Federated Publications Inc *(G-1186)*
Lansing State Journal, Lansing Also called Gannett Co Inc *(G-9371)*
Lanzen Incorporated (PA) 586 771-7070
  100 Peyerk Ct Bruce Twp (48065) *(G-2090)*
Lanzen Fabricating, Bruce Twp Also called Lanzen Incorporated *(G-2090)*
Lanzen Fabricating North Inc 231 587-8200
  611 N East Limits St Mancelona (49659) *(G-10393)*
Lanzen-Petoskey LLC 231 881-9602
  126 Fulton St Petoskey (49770) *(G-12454)*
Lapeer Fuel Ventures Inc 810 664-8770
  252 S Main St Lapeer (48446) *(G-9466)*
Lapeer Industries Inc (PA) 810 664-1816
  400 Mccormick Dr Lapeer (48446) *(G-9467)*
Lapeer Manufacturing Company, Lapeer Also called Souris Enterprises Inc *(G-9487)*
Lapeer Plating & Plastics Inc 810 667-4240
  395 Demille Rd Lapeer (48446) *(G-9468)*
Lapine Metal Products Inc 269 388-5900
  5232 Azo Ct Kalamazoo (49048) *(G-8805)*
Lapointe Cedar Products Inc 906 753-4072
  N7247 17.75 Ln Ingalls (49848) *(G-8224)*
Laporte Industries, Clinton Township Also called L F M Enterprises Inc *(G-3156)*
Lappans of Gaylord Inc 989 732-3274
  4085 Old Us Highway 27 S Gaylord (49735) *(G-5874)*
Laribits Keaton Publ Group 231 537-3330
  8959 Sturgeon Bay Dr Harbor Springs (49740) *(G-7286)*
Larkhite Development System 616 457-6722
  1501 Port Sheldon St Jenison (49428) *(G-8632)*
Larry's Taxidermy Studio, Pleasant Lake Also called Larrys Taxidermy Inc *(G-12552)*
Larrys Button Box 734 425-4239
  32641 Pierce St Garden City (48135) *(G-5832)*
Larrys Tarpaulin Shop Inc 313 563-2292
  3452 Beech Daly Rd Inkster (48141) *(G-8229)*
Larrys Taxidermy Inc 517 769-6104
  8640 N Meridian Rd Pleasant Lake (49272) *(G-12552)*
Larsen Graphics Inc 989 823-3000
  1065 E Huron Ave Vassar (48768) *(G-16812)*

Larsen Service Inc 810 374-6132
  11018 Clar Eve Dr Otisville (48463) *(G-12232)*
Larson-Juhl US LLC 734 416-3302
  47584 Galleon Dr Plymouth (48170) *(G-12671)*
Las Brazas Tortillas 616 886-0737
  3416 Crystal Valley Ct Holland (49424) *(G-7720)*
Las Tortugas Pallet Co 313 283-3279
  1583 Austin Ave Lincoln Park (48146) *(G-9580)*
Laser Access Inc 616 459-5496
  3691 Northridge Dr Nw # 10 Grand Rapids (49544) *(G-6618)*
Laser Blast, Plymouth Also called Advanced Avionics Inc *(G-12567)*
Laser Connection LLC 989 662-4022
  947 W Midland Rd Auburn (48611) *(G-755)*
Laser Craft LLC 248 340-8922
  151 Premier Dr Lake Orion (48359) *(G-9145)*
Laser Cutting Co 586 468-5300
  42300 Executive Dr Harrison Township (48045) *(G-7337)*
Laser Dynamics, Auburn Hills Also called Art Laser Inc *(G-780)*
Laser Fab Inc 586 415-8090
  33901 Riviera Fraser (48026) *(G-5683)*
Laser Marking Technologies LLC 989 673-6690
  1101 W Sanilac Rd Caro (48723) *(G-2470)*
Laser Mechanisms Inc (PA) 248 474-9480
  25325 Regency Dr Novi (48375) *(G-11929)*
Laser Mfg Inc 313 292-2299
  27989 Van Born Rd Romulus (48174) *(G-13699)*
Laser North Inc 906 353-6090
  455 N Superior Ave Baraga (49908) *(G-1106)*
Laser North Inc 906 353-6090
  442 N Superior Ave Baraga (49908) *(G-1107)*
Laser Product Development LLC 800 765-4424
  24340 Sherwood Center Line (48015) *(G-2580)*
Laser Shield, Milford Also called Noir Laser Company LLC *(G-10977)*
Laser-Dynamics, Allendale Also called Great Lakes Laser Dynamics Inc *(G-218)*
Lasercutting Services Inc 616 975-2000
  4101 40th St Se Ste 7 Grand Rapids (49512) *(G-6619)*
Lasers Resource Inc 616 554-5555
  4775 40th St Se Grand Rapids (49512) *(G-6620)*
Lasers Unlimited Inc 616 977-2668
  4600 36th St Se Grand Rapids (49512) *(G-6621)*
Lasertec Inc 586 274-4500
  747 E Whitcomb Ave Madison Heights (48071) *(G-10298)*
Lastek Industries LLC 586 739-6666
  50515 Corporate Dr Shelby Township (48315) *(G-14622)*
Latin American Industries LLC 616 301-1878
  3120 Kn O Sha Indus Ct Se Grand Rapids (49508) *(G-6622)*
Latino Press Inc 313 361-3000
  6301 Michigan Ave Detroit (48210) *(G-4194)*
Lattimore Material 972 837-2462
  6211 N Ann Arbor Rd Dundee (48131) *(G-4593)*
Lauck Pipe Organ Co 269 694-4500
  92 24th St Otsego (49078) *(G-12243)*
Laughabits LLC 248 990-3011
  9301 Dwight St Detroit (48214) *(G-4195)*
Lauren Plastics LLC 330 339-3373
  17155 Van Wagoner Rd Spring Lake (49456) *(G-15158)*
Laurmark Enterprises Inc 818 365-9000
  5400 Data Ct Ann Arbor (48108) *(G-526)*
Lavalier Corp 248 616-8880
  900 Rochester Rd Troy (48083) *(G-16458)*
Lavanway Sign Co Inc 248 356-1600
  22124 Telegraph Rd Southfield (48033) *(G-14959)*
Law Enforcement Development Co 734 656-4100
  47801 W Anchor Ct Plymouth (48170) *(G-12672)*
Law Enforcement Supply Inc 616 895-7875
  10920 64th Ave Allendale (49401) *(G-220)*
Lawrence Beaudoin Logging 906 296-0549
  52972 Sawmill Rd Lake Linden (49945) *(G-9108)*
Lawrence Co, Houghton Also called Lawrence J Julio LLC *(G-7974)*
Lawrence J Julio LLC 906 483-4781
  47212 Main St Houghton (49931) *(G-7974)*
Lawrence Plastics LLC (PA) 248 475-0186
  6338 Sashabaw Rd Clarkston (48346) *(G-2934)*
Lawrence Surface Tech Inc 248 609-9001
  1895 Crooks Rd Troy (48084) *(G-16459)*
Laws & Ponies Logging Show 269 838-3942
  6805 Pine Lake Rd Delton (49046) *(G-3817)*
Lawson Manufacturing Inc 248 624-1818
  920 Ladd Rd Walled Lake (48390) *(G-16896)*
Lawson Printers Inc 269 965-0525
  685 Columbia Ave W Battle Creek (49015) *(G-1222)*
Lawton Plant, Lawton Also called Welch Foods Inc A Cooperative *(G-9516)*
Lawton Ridge Winery LLC 269 372-9463
  8456 Stadium Dr Kalamazoo (49009) *(G-8806)*
Lay Manufacturing Inc 313 369-1627
  31614 Iroquois Dr Warren (48088) *(G-17125)*
LAY Precision Machine Inc 989 726-5022
  620 Parkway Dr West Branch (48661) *(G-17511)*
Laydon Enterprises Inc (PA) 906 774-4633
  101 Woodward Ave Iron Mountain (49802) *(G-8288)*

ALPHABETIC SECTION
Lematic Inc

Laydon Technology Inc 906 774-5780
1005 Pinewood Ct Iron Mountain (49801) ***(G-8289)***
Laylin Welding Inc 269 782-2910
501 E Prairie Ronde St Dowagiac (49047) ***(G-4547)***
Lazer Graphics 269 926-1066
1101 Pipestone Rd Benton Harbor (49022) ***(G-1522)***
Lazer Images, Livonia *Also called Fairfield Investment Co* ***(G-9734)***
Lazy Ballerina Winery LLC (PA) 269 363-6218
315 State St Saint Joseph (49085) ***(G-14323)***
Lazy Ballerina Winery LLC 269 759-8486
4209 Lake St Bridgman (49106) ***(G-1870)***
Lbv Sales LLC 616 874-9390
5669 Rolling Highlands Dr Belmont (49306) ***(G-1465)***
Lc Manufacturing LLC (PA) 231 839-7102
4150 N Wolcott Rd Lake City (49651) ***(G-9090)***
Lc Manufacturing LLC 734 753-3990
36485 S Huron Rd New Boston (48164) ***(G-11503)***
Lc Materials 231 796-8685
15151 Old Millpond Rd Big Rapids (49307) ***(G-1638)***
Lc Materials 989 422-4202
9142 Knapp Rd Houghton Lake (48629) ***(G-7995)***
Lc Materials (PA) 231 825-2473
805 W 13th St Cadillac (49601) ***(G-2260)***
Lc Materials 231 839-4319
1317 E Sanborn Rd Lake City (49651) ***(G-9091)***
Lc Materials 231 775-9301
8183 E 34 Rd Cadillac (49601) ***(G-2261)***
Lc Materials 231 258-8633
500 M 72 Kalkaska (49646) ***(G-8948)***
Lc Materials 231 832-5460
955 E Church Ave Reed City (49677) ***(G-13219)***
Lc Materials 989 344-0235
3881 W 4 Mile Rd Grayling (49738) ***(G-7110)***
Lc Ready Mix, Cadillac *Also called Lc Materials* ***(G-2260)***
Lc Redi Mix, Reed City *Also called Lc Materials* ***(G-13219)***
Lca Mold & Engineering Inc 269 651-1193
1200 W Lafayette St Sturgis (49091) ***(G-15612)***
Lcss Worldwide, Washington *Also called Low Cost Surcing Solutions LLC* ***(G-17306)***
LDB Plastics Inc 586 566-9698
50845 Rizzo Dr Shelby Township (48315) ***(G-14623)***
Le Forges Pipe & Fab Inc 734 482-2100
64 Wiard Rd Ypsilanti (48198) ***(G-18084)***
Le USA Walker Scientific, Lake Orion *Also called Labortrio Elttrofisico USA Inc* ***(G-9143)***
LE Warren Inc 517 784-8701
1600 S Jackson St Jackson (49203) ***(G-8496)***
Le-Q Fabricators Ltd 906 246-3402
W4106 M 69 Felch (49831) ***(G-5167)***
Lead Screws International Inc 262 786-1500
2101 Precision Dr Traverse City (49686) ***(G-16022)***
Leader Corporation (PA) 586 566-7114
51644 Filomena Dr Shelby Township (48315) ***(G-14624)***
Leader Printing and Design Inc 313 565-0061
25034 W Warren St Dearborn Heights (48127) ***(G-3788)***
Leader Publications LLC (PA) 269 683-2100
217 N 4th St Niles (49120) ***(G-11623)***
Leader Tool Company - HB Inc 989 479-3281
630 N Huron Ave Harbor Beach (48441) ***(G-7269)***
Leaders Inc 269 372-1072
8500 W Main St Kalamazoo (49009) ***(G-8807)***
Leaders RPM, Kalamazoo *Also called Leaders Inc* ***(G-8807)***
Leading Edge Engineering Inc 586 786-0382
14498 Oakwood Dr Shelby Township (48315) ***(G-14625)***
Leading Edge Fabricating Inc 231 893-2605
5315 Industrial Park Rd Montague (49437) ***(G-11093)***
Lean Factory America LLC 513 297-3086
816 E 3rd St Buchanan (49107) ***(G-2123)***
Leapers Inc (PA) 734 542-1500
32700 Capitol St Livonia (48150) ***(G-9805)***
Lear Automotive Mfg LLC 248 447-1603
6555 E Davison St Detroit (48212) ***(G-4196)***
Lear Automotive Mfg LLC 248 447-1603
6555 E Davidson St Detroit (48212) ***(G-4197)***
Lear Corp Eeds and Interiors (HQ) 248 447-1500
21557 Telegraph Rd Southfield (48033) ***(G-14960)***
Lear Corporation 313 852-7800
21557 Telg Rd Ste 300 Southfield (48033) ***(G-14961)***
Lear Corporation 989 588-6181
505 Hoover St Farwell (48622) ***(G-5163)***
Lear Corporation 248 447-1500
454 North St Mason (48854) ***(G-10644)***
Lear Corporation 248 299-7100
3000 Research Dr Rochester Hills (48309) ***(G-13458)***
Lear Corporation 989 275-5794
10161 N Roscommon Rd Roscommon (48653) ***(G-13750)***
Lear Corporation (PA) 248 447-1500
21557 Telegraph Rd Southfield (48033) ***(G-14962)***
Lear Corporation 231 947-0160
710 Carver St Traverse City (49686) ***(G-16023)***
Lear Corporation 734 946-1600
26575 Northline Rd Taylor (48180) ***(G-15734)***
Lear Corporation 248 853-3122
2930 W Auburn Rd Rochester Hills (48309) ***(G-13459)***
Lear Corporation 269 496-2215
236 Clark St Mendon (49072) ***(G-10715)***
Lear Corporation 313 731-0833
902 E Hamilton Ave Flint (48550) ***(G-5457)***
Lear European Operations Corp 248 447-1500
21557 Telegraph Rd Southfield (48033) ***(G-14963)***
Lear Mexican Seating Corp (HQ) 248 447-1500
21557 Telegraph Rd Southfield (48033) ***(G-14964)***
Lear Operations Corporation (HQ) 248 447-1500
21557 Telegraph Rd Southfield (48033) ***(G-14965)***
Lear Trim LP (PA) 248 447-1500
21557 Telegraph Rd Southfield (48033) ***(G-14966)***
Lease Management Inc (PA) 989 773-5948
503 Industrial Dr Mount Pleasant (48858) ***(G-11202)***
Leather Unlimited, Detroit *Also called Reed Sportswear Mfg Co* ***(G-4337)***
Leathercrafts By Bear 616 453-8308
751 Brownwood Ave Nw Grand Rapids (49504) ***(G-6623)***
Lebanon Baking Company, Detroit *Also called Sophias Bakery Inc* ***(G-4367)***
Leblond Lathe Service, Imlay City *Also called Willenborg Associates Inc* ***(G-8216)***
Leco Corporation (PA) 269 983-5531
3000 Lakeview Ave Saint Joseph (49085) ***(G-14324)***
Leco Corporation 269 982-2230
3000 Lakeview Ave Saint Joseph (49085) ***(G-14325)***
Lectra Tool Company, Howell *Also called Jess Enterprises LLC* ***(G-8055)***
Lectronix Inc (PA) 517 492-1900
5858 Enterprise Dr Lansing (48911) ***(G-9391)***
Ledco-Chargeguard, Plymouth *Also called Law Enforcement Development Co* ***(G-12672)***
Ledgestone, Wixom *Also called Northern Mich Aggregates LLC* ***(G-17868)***
Lee Beauty & Gen Mechandise 586 294-4400
16724 15 Mile Rd Fraser (48026) ***(G-5684)***
Lee Industries Inc 231 777-2537
1800 E Keating Ave Muskegon (49442) ***(G-11365)***
Lee J Cummings 906 932-3298
N11689 Lake Rd Ironwood (49938) ***(G-8334)***
Lee Manufacturing Inc 231 865-3359
6406 Airline Rd Fruitport (49415) ***(G-5795)***
Lee Printing & Graphics, Norton Shores *Also called Micrgraphics Printing Inc* ***(G-11773)***
Lee Printing Company 586 463-1564
21222 Cass Ave Clinton Township (48036) ***(G-3160)***
Lee-Cobb Company 269 553-0873
415 W Maple St Kalamazoo (49001) ***(G-8808)***
Leeann Plastics Inc 269 489-5035
300 Halfway Rd Burr Oak (49030) ***(G-2136)***
Leedy Manufacturing Co LLC 616 245-0517
210 Hall St Sw Grand Rapids (49507) ***(G-6624)***
Leelanau Enterprise Inc 231 256-9827
7200 E Duck Lake Rd Lake Leelanau (49653) ***(G-9104)***
Leelanau Industries Inc 231 947-0372
6052 E Traverse Hwy Traverse City (49684) ***(G-16024)***
Leelanau Redi-Mix Inc 231 228-5005
12488 S Newman Rd Maple City (49664) ***(G-10462)***
Leelanau Redi-Mix & Gravel, Maple City *Also called Leelanau Redi-Mix Inc* ***(G-10462)***
Leelanau Wine Cellars Ltd 231 386-5201
35 Research Dr Ste 300 Ann Arbor (48103) ***(G-527)***
Leep Logging Inc 517 852-1540
8445 Guy Rd Nashville (49073) ***(G-11459)***
Lees Ready Mix Inc 989 734-7666
3232 Birchwood Dr Rogers City (49779) ***(G-13616)***
Leeward Tool Inc 586 754-7200
23781 Blackstone Ave Warren (48089) ***(G-17126)***
Left Foot Charley 231 995-0500
806 Reads Run Traverse City (49685) ***(G-16025)***
Legacy Metal Fabricating LLC 616 258-8406
21 N Park St Nw Grand Rapids (49544) ***(G-6625)***
Legacy Precision Molds Inc 616 532-6536
4668 Spartan Indus Dr Sw Grandville (49418) ***(G-7055)***
Legacy Tool LLC 231 335-8983
9023 S Baldwin Ave Newaygo (49337) ***(G-11572)***
Legal Art Works, Bingham Farms *Also called Intrinsic4d LLC* ***(G-1654)***
Legendary Millwork Inc 248 588-5663
2655 Elliott Dr Troy (48083) ***(G-16460)***
Leggett Platt Components Inc 616 784-7000
7701 Venture Ave Nw Sparta (49345) ***(G-15101)***
Leif Distribution LLC 517 481-2122
7704 Lanac St Lansing (48917) ***(G-9308)***
Leif Led, Lansing *Also called Leif Distribution LLC* ***(G-9308)***
Leighs Garden Winery Inc 906 553-7799
209 S 12th St Escanaba (49829) ***(G-4839)***
Leisure Studios Inc 269 428-5299
3909 Stonegate Park Saint Joseph (49085) ***(G-14326)***
Leitelt Iron Works, Grand Rapids *Also called Padnos Leitelt Inc* ***(G-6739)***
Lej Investments LLC 616 452-3707
2950 Pririe St Sw Ste 900 Grandville (49418) ***(G-7056)***
Leland International Inc (PA) 616 975-9260
5695 Eagle Dr Se Grand Rapids (49512) ***(G-6626)***
Lematic Inc 517 787-3301
2410 W Main St Jackson (49203) ***(G-8497)***

ALPHABETIC

Lemica Corporation 313 839-2150
11201 Manning St Detroit (48234) *(G-4198)*
Lemon Creek Farm, Berrien Springs *Also called Lemon Creek Winery Ltd (G-1597)*
Lemon Creek Winery Ltd 616 844-1709
327 N Beacon Blvd Grand Haven (49417) *(G-6048)*
Lemon Creek Winery Ltd (PA) 269 471-1321
533 E Lemon Creek Rd Berrien Springs (49103) *(G-1597)*
Len-Way Machine & Tool, Hamilton *Also called Lenway Machine Company Inc (G-7235)*
Lenawee Industrial Pnt Sup Inc (PA) 734 729-8080
5645 Cogswell Rd Wayne (48184) *(G-17436)*
Lenawee Tool & Automation Inc 517 458-7222
235 Salisbury St Morenci (49256) *(G-11112)*
Lenco Boring Inc 734 483-8880
1620 Beverly Ave Ypsilanti (48198) *(G-18085)*
Lenderink Inc 616 887-8257
1267 House St Ne Belmont (49306) *(G-1466)*
Lenderink Family Tree Farms, Belmont *Also called Lenderink Inc (G-1466)*
Lennon Fluid Systems LLC 248 474-6624
23920 Freeway Park Dr Farmington Hills (48335) *(G-5043)*
Lenox Cement Products Inc 586 727-1488
65601 Gratiot Ave Lenox (48050) *(G-9521)*
Lenox Inc 586 727-1488
65601 Gratiot Ave Lenox (48050) *(G-9522)*
Lenox Septic Tanks, Lenox *Also called Lenox Inc (G-9522)*
Lenscrafters, Okemos *Also called Luxottica of America Inc (G-12129)*
Lenway Machine Company Inc 269 751-5183
3165 60th St Hamilton (49419) *(G-7235)*
Leon Automotive Interiors, Holland *Also called Leon Interiors Inc (G-7721)*
Leon Interiors Inc (HQ) 616 422-7479
88 E 48th St Holland (49423) *(G-7721)*
Leon Speakers Inc (PA) 734 213-2151
715 W Ellsworth Rd Ste A Ann Arbor (48108) *(G-528)*
Leonard & Randy Inc 734 287-9500
20555 Northline Rd Taylor (48180) *(G-15735)*
Leonard Fountain Spc Inc 313 891-4141
4601 Nancy St Detroit (48212) *(G-4199)*
Leonard J Hill Logging Co 906 337-3435
30980 Woodbush Rd Calumet (49913) *(G-2329)*
Leonard Machine & Tooling Inc 517 782-8140
508 Condad Ave Jackson (49202) *(G-8498)*
Leonard Machine Tool Systems 586 757-8040
22800 Hoover Rd Warren (48089) *(G-17127)*
Leonard's Syrups, Detroit *Also called Leonard Fountain Spc Inc (G-4199)*
Leonardos Marble & Granite 248 468-2900
29000 S Wixom Rd Wixom (48393) *(G-17845)*
Leoni Wiring Systems Inc 586 782-4444
30500 Van Dyke Ave # 300 Warren (48093) *(G-17128)*
Lepages 2000 Inc 416 357-0041
12900 S Huron River Dr Romulus (48174) *(G-13700)*
Leprino Foods Company 989 967-3635
311 N Sheridan Ave Remus (49340) *(G-13239)*
Leprino Foods Company 616 895-5800
4700 Rich St Allendale (49401) *(G-221)*
Leroy Tool & Die Inc 231 768-4336
17951 180th Ave Leroy (49655) *(G-9533)*
Leroy Worden 231 325-3837
1944 N Marshall Rd Beulah (49617) *(G-1610)*
Les Cheneaux Distillers Inc 906 748-0505
508 E Grove St Cedarville (49719) *(G-2568)*
Lesco Design & Mfg Co Inc 248 596-9301
28243 Beck Rd Ste B1 Wixom (48393) *(G-17846)*
Lesley Elizabeth Inc 810 667-0706
449 Mccormick Dr Lapeer (48446) *(G-9469)*
Lesley Elizabeth Inc (PA) 810 667-0706
877 Whitney Dr Lapeer (48446) *(G-9470)*
Lesnau Printing Company 586 795-9200
6025 Wall St Sterling Heights (48312) *(G-15396)*
Lester Detterbeck Enterprises, Iron River *Also called Iron River Mfg Co Inc (G-8310)*
Lester Detterbeck Entps Ltd (PA) 906 265-5121
3390 Us Highway 2 Iron River (49935) *(G-8314)*
Let Love Rule 734 749-7435
21391 Russell St Rockwood (48173) *(G-13607)*
Letherer Truss Inc (PA) 989 386-4999
851 Industrial Dr Clare (48617) *(G-2876)*
Letica Corporation (HQ) 248 652-0557
52585 Dequindre Rd Rochester Hills (48307) *(G-13460)*
Letnan Industries Inc 586 726-1155
6520 Arrow Dr Sterling Heights (48314) *(G-15397)*
Lettering Inc of Michigan 248 223-9700
13324 Farmington Rd Livonia (48150) *(G-9806)*
Letts Industries Inc (PA) 313 579-1100
1111 Bellevue St Detroit (48207) *(G-4200)*
Letty Manufacturing Inc 248 461-6604
4576 Driftwood Dr Commerce Township (48382) *(G-3420)*
Levannes Inc 269 327-4484
8840 Portage Indus Dr Portage (49024) *(G-13007)*
Level Eleven LLC 313 662-2000
1520 Woodward Ave Fl 3 Detroit (48226) *(G-4201)*
Levi Ohman Micah 612 251-1293
320 W College Ave Apt 1 Marquette (49855) *(G-10540)*
Leviathan Defense Group 419 575-7792
7720 N Dixie Hwy Newport (48166) *(G-11589)*
Levy Indiana Slag Co (PA) 313 843-7200
9300 Dix Dearborn (48120) *(G-3733)*
Levy Machining LLC 517 563-2013
11901 Strait Rd Hanover (49241) *(G-7261)*
Lewis Welding Inc 616 452-9226
274 Mart St Sw Wyoming (49548) *(G-18015)*
Lewiston Concrete Inc 989 786-3722
6234 County Road 612 Lewiston (49756) *(G-9551)*
Lewiston Forest Products, Saint Charles *Also called Michigan Pallet Inc (G-14196)*
Lewiston Sand & Gravel Inc 989 786-2742
5122 County Road 612 Lewiston (49756) *(G-9552)*
Lewkowicz Corporation 734 941-0411
36425 Grant St Romulus (48174) *(G-13701)*
Lewmar Custom Designs Inc 586 677-5135
56588 Scotland Blvd Shelby Township (48316) *(G-14626)*
Lexalite, Charlevoix *Also called Alp Lighting Ceiling Pdts Inc (G-2606)*
Lexamar Corporation 231 582-3163
100 Lexamar Dr Boyne City (49712) *(G-1827)*
Lexatronics LLC 734 878-6237
9768 Cedar Lake Rd Pinckney (48169) *(G-12499)*
Lexicom Publishing Group 734 994-8600
1945 Pauline Blvd Ste 18 Ann Arbor (48103) *(G-529)*
Lexmark International Inc 248 352-0616
2 Towne Sq Ste 150 Southfield (48076) *(G-14967)*
Lg Chem Michigan Inc 248 291-2385
3221 W Big Beaver Rd Troy (48084) *(G-16461)*
Lg Chem Michigan Inc 248 307-1800
1857 Technology Dr Troy (48083) *(G-16462)*
Lg Chem Michigan Inc (HQ) 616 494-7100
1 Lg Way Holland (49423) *(G-7722)*
Lg Chem Michigan Inc Tech Ctr, Troy *Also called Lg Chem Michigan Inc (G-16462)*
Lg Electronics USA Inc 248 268-5100
1835 Technology Dr Troy (48083) *(G-16463)*
Lg Electronics Vehicle Compone (HQ) 248 268-5851
1400 E 10 Mile Rd Ste 100 Hazel Park (48030) *(G-7441)*
Lg Electronics Vehicle Compone 248 268-5851
1835 Technology Dr Bldg E Troy (48083) *(G-16464)*
Lga Retail Inc 248 910-1918
22770 Spy Glass Hill Dr South Lyon (48178) *(G-14800)*
Lgb USA Inc (HQ) 586 777-4542
15585 Sturgeon St Roseville (48066) *(G-13826)*
Lgc Global Inc 313 989-4141
7310 Woodward Ave 500a Detroit (48202) *(G-4202)*
Lgcmi, Holland *Also called Lg Chem Michigan Inc (G-7722)*
Liberty 3d Technologies, Saint Joseph *Also called Liberty Steel Fabricating Inc (G-14327)*
Liberty Automotive Tech LLC 269 487-8114
4554 128th Ave Holland (49424) *(G-7723)*
Liberty Bell Powdr Coating LLC 586 557-6328
1468 John A Papalas Dr Lincoln Park (48146) *(G-9581)*
Liberty Burnishing Co 313 366-7878
18401 Sherwood St Detroit (48234) *(G-4203)*
Liberty Cast Products, Sterling Heights *Also called Sterling Metal Works LLC (G-15512)*
Liberty Circuits Corporation 269 226-8743
630 E Walnut St Ste 1 Kalamazoo (49007) *(G-8809)*
Liberty Dairy Company 800 632-5552
302 N River St Evart (49631) *(G-4885)*
Liberty Fabricators Inc 810 877-7117
2229 W Hill Rd Flint (48507) *(G-5458)*
Liberty Manufacturing Company 269 327-0997
8631 Portage Indus Dr Portage (49024) *(G-13008)*
Liberty Molds, Portage *Also called Liberty Manufacturing Company (G-13008)*
Liberty Plastics Inc 616 994-7033
13170 Ransom St Holland (49424) *(G-7724)*
Liberty Powder Coating, Lincoln Park *Also called Liberty Bell Powdr Coating LLC (G-9581)*
Liberty Products Inc 231 853-2323
3073 Mortimer St Ravenna (49451) *(G-13123)*
Liberty Research Co Inc 734 508-6237
291 Squires Dr Milan (48160) *(G-10943)*
Liberty Steel Fabricating Inc 269 556-9792
350 Palladium Dr Saint Joseph (49085) *(G-14327)*
Liberty Tool Inc 586 726-2449
44404 Phoenix Dr Sterling Heights (48314) *(G-15398)*
Liberty Transit Mix LLC 586 254-2212
7520 23 Mile Rd Shelby Township (48316) *(G-14627)*
Liberty Turned Components LLC (PA) 734 508-6237
291 Squires Dr Milan (48160) *(G-10944)*
Libertys High Prfmce Pdts Inc 586 469-1140
41775 Production Dr Harrison Township (48045) *(G-7338)*
Libra Industries Inc Michigan (PA) 517 787-5675
1435 N Blackstone St Jackson (49202) *(G-8499)*
Libra Manufacturing, Tecumseh *Also called Libra Precision Machining Inc (G-15801)*
Libra Precision Machining Inc 517 423-1365
5353 N Rogers Hwy Tecumseh (49286) *(G-15801)*
Libstack, Grosse Pointe *Also called Polyhedron LLC (G-7182)*

ALPHABETIC SECTION

Liebherr Aerospace Saline Inc 734 429-7225
1465 Woodland Dr Saline (48176) *(G-14398)*
Liebner Enterprises LLC 231 331-3076
1160 E State St Unit C Cheboygan (49721) *(G-2686)*
Liedel Power Cleaning 734 848-2827
2850 Luna Pier Rd Erie (48133) *(G-4805)*
Life Is Digital LLC 734 252-6449
17180 Revere St Southfield (48076) *(G-14968)*
Lifegas, Wyoming Also called Linde Gas North America LLC *(G-18017)*
Lift Aid Inc 248 345-5110
33962 Moore Dr Farmington (48335) *(G-4903)*
Light Corp Inc (PA) 616 842-5100
14800 172nd Ave Grand Haven (49417) *(G-6049)*
Light Metal Forming Corp 248 851-3984
4397 Stony River Dr Bloomfield Hills (48301) *(G-1777)*
Light Metals Corporation 616 538-3030
2740 Prairie St Sw Wyoming (49519) *(G-18016)*
Light Robotics Automation Inc 586 254-6655
43252 Merrill Rd Sterling Heights (48314) *(G-15399)*
Light Speed Usa LLC 616 308-0054
1971 E Beltlin Ave Ne 106-130 Grand Rapids (49525) *(G-6627)*
Light-Rx, Farmington Hills Also called Body Contour Ventures LLC *(G-4945)*
Lighthouse Cards and Gifts, Detroit Also called Lighthouse Direct Buy LLC *(G-4204)*
Lighthouse Direct Buy LLC 313 340-1850
16143 Wyoming St Detroit (48221) *(G-4204)*
Lighthouse Elec Protection LLC 586 932-2690
7314 19 Mile Rd Sterling Heights (48314) *(G-15400)*
Lighthouse, The, Iron Mountain Also called H U R Enterprises Inc *(G-8284)*
Lighting Enterprises Inc 313 693-9504
16706 Telegraph Rd Detroit (48219) *(G-4205)*
Lightning Litho Inc 517 394-2995
5731 Enterprise Dr Lansing (48911) *(G-9392)*
Lightning Machine Holland LLC 616 786-9280
128 Manufacturers Dr Holland (49424) *(G-7725)*
Lightning Technologies LLC 248 977-5566
315 W Silverbell Rd Lake Orion (48359) *(G-9146)*
Lightning Technologies LLC (PA) 248 572-6700
2171 Xcelsior Dr Oxford (48371) *(G-12355)*
Ligon Helicopter Corporation 810 706-1885
3776 Van Dyke Rd Almont (48003) *(G-261)*
Lillian Fuel Inc 734 439-8505
1200 Dexter St Milan (48160) *(G-10945)*
Lily Products Michigan Inc 616 245-9193
2070 Calvin Ave Se Grand Rapids (49507) *(G-6628)*
Limo-Reid Inc 517 447-4164
420 Carey St Deerfield (49238) *(G-3812)*
Lin Adam Fuel Inc 313 733-6631
13330 Linwood St Detroit (48238) *(G-4206)*
Linamar Holding Nevada Inc (HQ) 248 477-6240
32233 8 Mile Rd Livonia (48152) *(G-9807)*
Lincoln Forge, Brownstown Also called Lincoln Park Die & Tool Co *(G-2067)*
Lincoln Industries (PA) 989 736-6421
202 S Second St Lincoln (48742) *(G-9565)*
Lincoln Park Boring Co 734 946-8300
28089 Wick Rd Romulus (48174) *(G-13702)*
Lincoln Park Die & Tool Co 734 285-1680
18325 Dix Toledo Hwy Brownstown (48193) *(G-2067)*
Lincoln Park Fuel, Lincoln Park Also called Fk Fuel Inc *(G-9577)*
Lincoln Precision Carbide Inc 989 736-8113
600 S 2nd St Lincoln (48742) *(G-9566)*
Lincoln Service LLC (PA) 734 793-0083
11862 Brookfield St Livonia (48150) *(G-9808)*
Lincoln Tool Co Inc 989 736-8711
3140 E M 72 Harrisville (48740) *(G-7364)*
Lincoln Welding Company 313 292-2299
4445 Brogan Rd Stockbridge (49285) *(G-15590)*
Lincoln-Remi Group LLC 248 255-0200
1200 Benstein Rd Commerce Township (48390) *(G-3421)*
Lincolns Welding 269 964-1858
256 30th St N Springfield (49037) *(G-15197)*
Lindberg Fluid Power Division, Jackson Also called Crankshaft Machine Company *(G-8423)*
Lindberg/Mph, Riverside Also called Tps LLC *(G-13287)*
Linde Gas LLC 616 754-7575
510 E Grove St Greenville (48838) *(G-7144)*
Linde Gas North America LLC 630 857-6460
21421 Hilltop St Ste 1 Southfield (48033) *(G-14969)*
Linde Gas North America LLC 616 475-0203
3535 R B Chaffee Mem Dr Wyoming (49548) *(G-18017)*
Linde Gas North America LLC 734 397-7373
5001 Dewitt Rd Canton (48188) *(G-2392)*
Linde Inc 517 541-2473
500 Packard Hwy Charlotte (48813) *(G-2658)*
Lindemann Machining & Welding 906 353-6424
14265 Lindemann Rd Baraga (49908) *(G-1108)*
Lindsay Nettell Inc 906 482-3549
47301 Janovosky Rd Atlantic Mine (49905) *(G-737)*
Lindy Press Inc 231 937-6169
9794 Locust Ave Howard City (49329) *(G-8003)*

Line Precision Inc 248 474-5280
31666 W 8 Mile Rd Farmington Hills (48336) *(G-5044)*
Line X of Westbranch 989 345-7800
155 N 4th St West Branch (48661) *(G-17512)*
Linear AMS, Livonia Also called Linear Mold & Engineering LLC *(G-9810)*
Linear Measurement Instrs Corp 810 714-5811
101 N Alloy Dr Ste B Fenton (48430) *(G-5225)*
Linear Mold & Engineering LLC 734 744-4548
34435 Glendale St Livonia (48150) *(G-9809)*
Linear Mold & Engineering LLC (PA) 734 422-6060
12163 Globe St Livonia (48150) *(G-9810)*
Linear Motion LLC 989 759-8300
628 N Hamilton St Saginaw (48602) *(G-14078)*
Link Engineering Company, Plymouth Also called Link Manufacturing Inc *(G-12673)*
Link Engineering Company, Ottawa Lake Also called Link Manufacturing Inc *(G-12265)*
Link Industries, Indian River Also called Link Manufacturing Inc *(G-8219)*
Link Manufacturing Inc (HQ) 734 453-0800
43855 Plymouth Oaks Blvd Plymouth (48170) *(G-12673)*
Link Manufacturing Inc 231 238-8741
2208 S Straits Hwy Indian River (49749) *(G-8219)*
Link Manufacturing Inc 734 387-1001
8000 Yankee Rd Ste 105 Ottawa Lake (49267) *(G-12265)*
Link Mechanical Solutions LLC 734 744-5616
11970 Mayfield St Livonia (48150) *(G-9811)*
Link Tech Inc 269 427-8297
59648 M 43 Bangor (49013) *(G-1092)*
Link Technology Inc 269 324-8212
4100 E Milham Ave Portage (49002) *(G-13009)*
Link Tool & Mfg Co LLC 734 710-0010
39115 Warren Rd Westland (48185) *(G-17577)*
Linked Live Inc 248 345-5993
30550 Brush St Madison Heights (48071) *(G-10299)*
Linktool Group, Westland Also called Link Tool & Mfg Co LLC *(G-17577)*
Linn Energy Inc 231 922-7302
226 E Sixteenth St Ste A Traverse City (49684) *(G-16026)*
Lintech Global Inc 248 553-8033
34119 W 12 Mile Rd # 200 Farmington Hills (48331) *(G-5045)*
Linwood Bakery 989 697-4430
11 S Huron Rd Linwood (48634) *(G-9598)*
Lippert Components Mfg Inc 989 845-3061
1103 Pearl St Chesaning (48616) *(G-2725)*
Lippert Components Mfg Inc 323 663-1261
200 S 1st St Chesaning (48616) *(G-2726)*
Liquid Drive Corporation 248 634-5382
18 1st St Mount Clemens (48043) *(G-11139)*
Liquid Dustlayer Inc 231 723-3750
3320 Grant Hwy Manistee (49660) *(G-10426)*
Liquid Manufacturing LLC 810 220-2802
305 Westwood Ave Ann Arbor (48103) *(G-530)*
Liquid Otc LLC 248 214-7771
3250 Old Farm Ln Ste 1 Commerce Township (48390) *(G-3422)*
Lisa Bain 313 389-9661
9636 Chatham Ave Allen Park (48101) *(G-200)*
Lisi Automotive HI Vol Inc 734 266-6958
11813 Hubbard St Livonia (48150) *(G-9812)*
Lisi Automotive HI Vol Inc (HQ) 734 266-6900
12955 Inkster Rd Livonia (48150) *(G-9813)*
Litchfield Mfg Facility, Litchfield Also called Metaldyne Pwrtrain Cmpnnts Inc *(G-9607)*
Litchfield Mfg Facility, Litchfield Also called Metaldyne Pwrtrain Cmpnnts Inc *(G-9608)*
Lite Load Services LLC 269 751-6037
3866 40th St Hamilton (49419) *(G-7236)*
Litebrake Tech LLC 906 523-2007
406 2nd St Houghton Houghton (49931) *(G-7975)*
Litehouse Inc 616 897-5911
1400 Foreman St Lowell (49331) *(G-10034)*
Lites Alternative Inc 989 685-3476
2643 S M 33 Rose City (48654) *(G-13762)*
Litesalternative, Rose City Also called Lites Alternative Inc *(G-13762)*
Litetek, Plymouth Also called Autosystems America Inc *(G-12577)*
Litex Inc 517 439-9361
400 Arch Ave Hillsdale (49242) *(G-7528)*
Litex Inc (PA) 248 852-0661
2774 Product Dr Rochester Hills (48309) *(G-13461)*
Litho Printers Inc 269 651-7309
620 N Centerville Rd Sturgis (49091) *(G-15613)*
Litho Printing Service Inc 586 772-6067
21541 Gratiot Ave Eastpointe (48021) *(G-4706)*
Lithotech 269 471-6027
212 Harrigan Hall Berrien Springs (49104) *(G-1598)*
Litsenberger Print Shop 906 482-3903
224 Shelden Ave Houghton (49931) *(G-7976)*
Little Bay Concrete Products 906 428-9859
119 N 9th St Gladstone (49837) *(G-5915)*
Little Blue Book Inc 313 469-0052
19803 Mack Ave Grosse Pointe Woods (48236) *(G-7206)*
Little Buildings Inc 586 752-7100
161 Shafer Dr Romeo (48065) *(G-13632)*
Little Man Winery LLC 616 292-3983
1666 Pinta Dr Holland (49424) *(G-7726)*

Little Silver Corp 248 642-0860
725 S Adams Rd Ste 250 Birmingham (48009) ***(G-1688)***
Little Traverse Disposal LLC 231 487-0780
1128 Mcbride Park Dr Harbor Springs (49740) ***(G-7287)***
Liturgical Commission, Lansing *Also called Diocese of Lansing* ***(G-9361)***
Livbig LLC 888 519-8290
1821 Vanderbilt Ave Ste A Portage (49024) ***(G-13010)***
Live Track Productions Inc 313 704-2224
848 Manistique St Detroit (48215) ***(G-4207)***
Liver Transplant/Univ of Mich 734 936-7670
1500 E Medical Center Dr Ann Arbor (48109) ***(G-531)***
Liveroof LLC 616 842-1392
14109 Cleveland St Nunica (49448) ***(G-12040)***
Livespace LLC 616 929-0191
4995 Starr St Se Grand Rapids (49546) ***(G-6629)***
Living Hope Books & More, Fenton *Also called Mott Media LLC* ***(G-5226)***
Living Word International Inc 989 832-7547
2010 N Stark Rd Midland (48642) ***(G-10882)***
Livingston County Concrete Inc 810 632-3030
550 N Old Us Highway 23 Brighton (48114) ***(G-1951)***
Livingston Machine Inc 517 546-4253
7445 Schrepfer Rd Howell (48855) ***(G-8058)***
Livonia Automatic Incorporated 734 591-0321
12650 Newburgh Rd Livonia (48150) ***(G-9814)***
Livonia Magnetics LLC 734 397-8844
44005 Michigan Ave Canton (48188) ***(G-2393)***
Livonia Observer 734 525-4657
8928 Virginia St Livonia (48150) ***(G-9815)***
Livonia Trophy & Screen Prtg 734 464-9191
38065 Ann Arbor Rd Livonia (48150) ***(G-9816)***
Lj/Hah Holdings Corporation (PA) 248 340-4100
2750 High Meadow Cir Auburn Hills (48326) ***(G-929)***
LLC Ash Stevens (HQ) 734 282-3370
18655 Krause St Riverview (48193) ***(G-13300)***
LLC Stahl Cross 810 688-2505
110 N Saginaw St Lapeer (48446) ***(G-9471)***
Llink Technologies LLC 586 336-9370
3953 Burnsline Rd Brown City (48416) ***(G-2054)***
Llomen Inc 269 345-3555
5346 Ivanhoe Ct Portage (49002) ***(G-13011)***
Llowds Retail Construction, Clinton Township *Also called Construction Retail Svcs Inc* ***(G-3088)***
Lloyd Flanders Industries, Menominee *Also called Flanders Industries Inc* ***(G-10736)***
Lloyd Johnson Livestock Inc 906 786-4878
3697 18th Rd Escanaba (49829) ***(G-4840)***
Lloyd Tool & Mfg Corp 810 694-3519
5505 Chatham Ln Grand Blanc (48439) ***(G-5973)***
Lloyd Waters & Associates (PA) 734 525-2777
33180 Industrial Rd Ste A Livonia (48150) ***(G-9817)***
Lloyds Cabinet Shop Inc 989 879-3015
1947 N Huron Rd Pinconning (48650) ***(G-12509)***
LMC, Wyoming *Also called Light Metals Corporation* ***(G-18016)***
LMI Technologies Inc 248 298-2839
29488 Woodward Ave # 331 Royal Oak (48073) ***(G-13944)***
Lmm Group Inc 269 276-9909
443 E D Ave Kalamazoo (49009) ***(G-8810)***
LMS, Midland *Also called Aptargroup Inc* ***(G-10816)***
Lna Solutions Inc 734 677-2305
3924a Varsity Dr Ste A Ann Arbor (48108) ***(G-532)***
Load All, Grand Rapids *Also called Inner Box Loading Systems Inc* ***(G-6536)***
Loadmaster Corporation 906 563-9226
100 E 9th Ave Norway (49870) ***(G-11817)***
Lobo Signs Inc 231 941-7739
322 E Welch Ct Traverse City (49686) ***(G-16027)***
Loc Industries Inc 586 759-8412
13001 Stephens Rd Warren (48089) ***(G-17129)***
Loc Performance Products Inc (PA) 734 453-2300
13505 N Haggerty Rd Plymouth (48170) ***(G-12674)***
Loc Performance Products Inc 734 453-2300
1600 N Larch St Lansing (48906) ***(G-9242)***
Loc Performance Products Inc 734 453-2300
33852 Sterling Ponds Blvd Sterling Heights (48312) ***(G-15401)***
Local Media Group Inc 313 885-2612
9 Alger Pl Detroit (48230) ***(G-4208)***
Local Mobile Services LLC 313 963-1917
40500 Ann Arbor Rd E Plymouth (48170) ***(G-12675)***
Local Printers Inc 586 795-1290
40594 Brentwood Dr Sterling Heights (48310) ***(G-15402)***
Lochinvar LLC 734 454-4480
45900 Port St Plymouth (48170) ***(G-12676)***
Lock and Load Corp 800 975-9658
3390 16 Mile Rd Marion (49665) ***(G-10490)***
Lockett Enterprises LLC 810 407-6644
607 E 2nd Ave Ste 30 Flint (48502) ***(G-5459)***
Lockwood Manufacturing Company, Livonia *Also called Kkt Inc* ***(G-9798)***
Locpac Inc 734 453-2300
13505 N Haggerty Rd Plymouth (48170) ***(G-12677)***
Lodal Inc 906 779-1700
620 N Hooper St Kingsford (49802) ***(G-9062)***
Loftis Alumi-TEC Inc 616 846-1990
13888 172nd Ave Grand Haven (49417) ***(G-6050)***
Loftis Machine Company 616 846-1990
13888 172nd Ave Grand Haven (49417) ***(G-6051)***
Log Cabin Lumber, Riverdale *Also called Daniel D Slater* ***(G-13284)***
Logan Brothers Printing Inc 517 485-3771
13544 Blackwood Dr Dewitt (48820) ***(G-4463)***
Logan Diesel Incorporated 517 589-8811
4567 Churchill Rd Leslie (49251) ***(G-9544)***
Logan Marketing Group LLC 248 731-7650
44 E Long Lake Rd Ste 400 Bloomfield Hills (48304) ***(G-1778)***
Logan Pattern & Engrg Co LLC 810 364-9298
5149 Bowman Rd Saint Clair (48079) ***(G-14226)***
Logan Tool and Engineering 586 755-3555
23919 Blackstone Ave Warren (48089) ***(G-17130)***
Loggers Brewing Co 989 401-3085
1215 S River Rd Saginaw (48609) ***(G-14079)***
Logging Long Branch 231 549-3031
377 Swaybury Ln Boyne Falls (49713) ***(G-1840)***
Logic Solutions Inc 734 930-0009
2929 Plymouth Rd Ste 207b Ann Arbor (48105) ***(G-533)***
Logical Digital Audio Video 734 572-0022
4602 Central Blvd Ann Arbor (48108) ***(G-534)***
Logistics Insight Corp 810 424-0511
3311 Torrey Rd Flint (48507) ***(G-5460)***
Logodance, Inc., West Olive *Also called Wellard Inc* ***(G-17536)***
Logofit LLC 810 715-1980
3202 Lapeer Rd Flint (48503) ***(G-5461)***
Logospot 616 785-7170
8200 Graphic Dr Ne Belmont (49306) ***(G-1467)***
Lokol LLC 586 615-1727
1011 Decker Rd Walled Lake (48390) ***(G-16897)***
Lol, Commerce Township *Also called Liquid Otc LLC* ***(G-3422)***
Lol Telcom Inc 616 888-6171
6897 Springfield Ave Hudsonville (49426) ***(G-8162)***
Lomar Machine & Tool Co 517 563-8136
5931 Coats Rd Horton (49246) ***(G-7965)***
Lomar Machine & Tool Co 517 750-4089
7755 King Rd Spring Arbor (49283) ***(G-15125)***
Lomar Machine & Tool Co (PA) 517 563-8136
135 Main St Horton (49246) ***(G-7966)***
Lomar Machine & Tool Co 517 563-8136
7595 Moscow Rd Horton (49246) ***(G-7967)***
Lomar Machine & Tool Co 517 563-8800
7595 Moscow Rd Horton (49246) ***(G-7968)***
Lone Wolf Archery, Glennie *Also called Lone Wolf Custom Bows* ***(G-5944)***
Lone Wolf Custom Bows 989 735-3358
3893 Gray St Glennie (48737) ***(G-5944)***
Lonero Engineering Co Inc 248 689-9120
2050 Stephenson Hwy Troy (48083) ***(G-16465)***
Loneys Welding & Excvtg Inc 231 328-4408
6735 E Houghton Lake Rd Merritt (49667) ***(G-10764)***
Long Lake Forest Products 989 239-6527
2330 E Haskell Lake Rd Harrison (48625) ***(G-7314)***
Long Manufacturing, Saint Clair *Also called Dana Thermal Products LLC* ***(G-14215)***
Long Road Distillers LLC 616 356-1770
537 Leonard St Nw Grand Rapids (49504) ***(G-6630)***
Longshot Golf, Clinton Township *Also called Consumer Advntage Rference Svc* ***(G-3089)***
Longstreet Group LLC 517 278-4487
720 E Chicago Rd Coldwater (49036) ***(G-3314)***
LONGSTREET LIVING, Coldwater *Also called Longstreet Group LLC* ***(G-3314)***
Lookingbus, Saline *Also called Svn Inc* ***(G-14417)***
Looksharp Marketing, Paw Paw *Also called Sporting Image Inc* ***(G-12413)***
Loon Lake Precision Inc 810 953-0732
8200 Embury Rd Ste 4 Grand Blanc (48439) ***(G-5974)***
Loonar Stn Two The 2 or 2nd 419 720-1222
6656 Lewis Ave Ste 5 Temperance (48182) ***(G-15834)***
Looney Baker of Livonia Inc 734 425-8569
13931 Farmington Rd Livonia (48154) ***(G-9818)***
Loope Enterprises Inc 269 639-1567
73475 8th Ave South Haven (49090) ***(G-14763)***
Loose Plastics Inc 989 246-1880
1016 E 1st St Gladwin (48624) ***(G-5933)***
Loper Corporation 810 620-0202
6031 N Clio Rd Mount Morris (48458) ***(G-11164)***
Lopez Reproductions Inc 313 386-4526
645 Griswold St Ste 27 Detroit (48226) ***(G-4209)***
Lor Manufacturing Co Inc 866 644-8622
7131 W Drew Rd Weidman (48893) ***(G-17458)***
Lor Products Inc 989 382-9020
2962 16 Mile Rd Remus (49340) ***(G-13240)***
Lorbec Metals - Usa Ltd 810 736-0961
3415 Western Rd Flint (48506) ***(G-5462)***
Lord Laboratories 586 447-8955
20416 Sunnydale St Saint Clair Shores (48081) ***(G-14260)***
Lorencz Construction Co 989 798-3151
812 E Liberty St Chesaning (48616) ***(G-2727)***
Lorenz Propellers & Engrg Co 231 728-3245
600 W Southern Ave Muskegon (49441) ***(G-11366)***

ALPHABETIC SECTION

Lorenzo White 313 943-3667
20029 Cooley St Detroit (48219) *(G-4210)*
Lorin Industries Inc (PA) 231 722-1631
1960 Roberts St Muskegon (49442) *(G-11367)*
Lorna Icr LLC 586 582-1500
28601 Lorna Ave Warren (48092) *(G-17131)*
Lorne Hanley 248 547-9865
10085 Lincoln Dr Huntington Woods (48070) *(G-8189)*
Loryco Inc 248 674-4673
51920 Woodward Ave Ste B Pontiac (48342) *(G-12845)*
Los Cuarto Amigos 989 984-0200
1626 E Us 23 East Tawas (48730) *(G-4690)*
Loshaw Bros Inc 989 732-7263
231 Meecher Rd Gaylord (49735) *(G-5875)*
Lost Horizons Inc 248 366-6858
232 Oriole St Commerce Township (48382) *(G-3423)*
Lotis Technologies Inc 248 340-6065
100 Engelwood Dr Ste F Orion (48359) *(G-12182)*
Lotte U S A, Battle Creek Also called Lotte USA Incorporated *(G-1223)*
Lotte USA Incorporated 269 963-6664
5243 Wayne Rd Battle Creek (49037) *(G-1223)*
Lottery Info 734 326-0097
8432 Hannan Rd Wayne (48184) *(G-17437)*
Lotus Corporation 616 494-0112
100 Aniline Ave N Ste 180 Holland (49424) *(G-7727)*
Lotus International Company 734 245-0140
6880 Commerce Blvd Canton (48187) *(G-2394)*
Lotus Spa & Salon, Allegan Also called Jennco Industries LLC *(G-167)*
Louca Mold & Arospc Machining, Auburn Hills Also called Louca Mold Arspc Machining Inc *(G-930)*
Louca Mold Arspc Machining Inc (PA) 248 391-1616
1925 Taylor Rd Auburn Hills (48326) *(G-930)*
Loudon Steel Inc 989 871-9353
8208 Ellis Rd Millington (48746) *(G-10997)*
Louies Meats Inc 231 946-4811
2040 Cass Rd Traverse City (49684) *(G-16028)*
Louis J Wickings 989 823-8765
4650 Waltan Rd Vassar (48768) *(G-16813)*
Louis Padnos Iron and Metal Co 616 459-4208
601 Lettellier St Sw Grand Rapids (49504) *(G-6631)*
Louis Padnos Iron and Metal Co 517 372-6600
1900 W Willow St Lansing (48917) *(G-9309)*
Louis Padnos Iron and Metal Co 231 722-6081
259 Ottawa St Muskegon (49442) *(G-11368)*
Louis Padnos Iron and Metal Co 616 452-6037
719 Burton St Sw Grand Rapids (49503) *(G-6632)*
Louis Padnos Iron and Metal Co 616 301-7900
500 44th St Sw Wyoming (49548) *(G-18018)*
Love Machinery Inc 734 427-0824
36232 Lawrence Dr Livonia (48150) *(G-9819)*
Lovejoy Inc 269 637-3017
200 Lovejoy Ave South Haven (49090) *(G-14764)*
Lovejoy Curtis LLC (HQ) 269 637-5132
200 Lovejoy Ave South Haven (49090) *(G-14765)*
Loven Spoonful 517 522-3953
119 E Main St Grass Lake (49240) *(G-7089)*
Low Cost Surcing Solutions LLC 248 535-7721
57253 Willow Way Ct Washington (48094) *(G-17306)*
Low Impact Logging Inc 906 250-5117
3172 Us Highway 2 Iron River (49935) *(G-8315)*
Low Mar, Horton Also called Lomar Machine & Tool Co *(G-7968)*
Lowell Engineering, Alto Also called Magna Mirrors North Amer LLC *(G-329)*
Lowell Litho, Lowell Also called Buyers Guide *(G-10025)*
Lowery Corporation (PA) 616 554-5200
5555 Glnwood Hlls Pkwy Se Grand Rapids (49512) *(G-6633)*
Lowing Products LLC 616 530-7440
1500 Whiting St Sw Wyoming (49509) *(G-18019)*
Lowry Joanellen 231 873-2323
7833 Lincoln St Hesperia (49421) *(G-7478)*
Lowry Holding Company Inc (PA) 810 229-7200
9420 Maltby Rd Brighton (48116) *(G-1952)*
Lowry Solutions, Brighton Also called Lowry Holding Company Inc *(G-1952)*
Loyalty 1977 Ink 313 759-1006
18528 Margareta St Detroit (48219) *(G-4211)*
LP Products (PA) 989 465-0287
6680 M 18 Coleman (48618) *(G-3347)*
LP Products 989 465-1485
4363 Us 10 Coleman (48618) *(G-3348)*
Lpm Supply Inc 248 333-9440
28 N Saginaw St Ste 801 Pontiac (48342) *(G-12846)*
Lps-2 Inc 313 538-0181
24755 5 Mile Rd Ste 100 Redford (48239) *(G-13168)*
Lrh & Associates Inc 517 784-1055
111 Randolph St Jackson (49203) *(G-8500)*
Lrs Inc 734 416-5050
9448 Northern Ave Plymouth (48170) *(G-12678)*
Ls Precision Tool & Die Inc 269 963-9910
140 Jacaranda Dr Battle Creek (49015) *(G-1224)*

Lsd Investments Inc 248 333-9085
2350 Franklin Rd Ste 115 Bloomfield Hills (48302) *(G-1779)*
Lsp Dock Systems, Quincy Also called Lsp Inc *(G-13095)*
Lsp Inc 517 639-3815
855 E Chicago Rd Quincy (49082) *(G-13095)*
Lspedia LLC 248 320-1909
30201 Orchard Lake Rd # 108 Farmington Hills (48334) *(G-5046)*
Lsr Incorporated 734 455-6530
11050 N Beck Rd Plymouth (48170) *(G-12679)*
Lst Lighting, Macomb Also called Lumasmart Technology Intl Inc *(G-10137)*
Lt Global, Grand Rapids Also called Lub-Tech Inc *(G-6634)*
Ltc, Milan Also called Liberty Turned Components LLC *(G-10944)*
Ltek Industries Inc 734 747-6105
2298 S Industrial Hwy Ann Arbor (48104) *(G-535)*
Luans Welding LLC 248 787-5735
14120 Balfour St Oak Park (48237) *(G-12078)*
Lub-Tech Inc 616 299-3540
470 Market Ave Sw Unit 13 Grand Rapids (49503) *(G-6634)*
Lube - Power Inc 586 247-6500
50146 Utica Dr Shelby Township (48315) *(G-14628)*
Lube Zone LLC 313 543-2910
9977 Telegraph Rd Redford (48239) *(G-13169)*
Lube-Tech Inc 269 329-1269
3960 Arbutus Trl Portage (49024) *(G-13012)*
Lubecon Systems Inc 231 689-0002
201 N Webster St White Cloud (49349) *(G-17625)*
Luberda Wood Products Inc 989 876-4334
1188 E Huron Rd Omer (48749) *(G-12144)*
Lubetronics, White Cloud Also called Lubecon Systems Inc *(G-17625)*
Lubo Usa Inc 810 244-5826
32250 Howard Ave Madison Heights (48071) *(G-10300)*
Lucas Logging 906 246-3629
W1564 State Highway M69 Bark River (49807) *(G-1120)*
Lucido, F J & Associates, Warren Also called F J Lucido & Associates *(G-17028)*
Luckmarr Plastics Inc 586 978-8498
35735 Stanley Dr Sterling Heights (48312) *(G-15403)*
Lucky Girl Brwing - Cross Rads 630 723-4285
34016 M 43 Paw Paw (49079) *(G-12407)*
Lucky Press LLC 614 309-0048
4929 Turfway Trl Harbor Springs (49740) *(G-7288)*
Ludington Components, Ludington Also called Haworth Inc *(G-10064)*
Ludington Concrete Products, Ludington Also called Hobe Inc *(G-10065)*
Ludington Daily News Inc 231 845-5181
202 N Rath Ave Ludington (49431) *(G-10069)*
Ludvanwall Inc 616 842-4500
19156 174th Ave Spring Lake (49456) *(G-15159)*
Ludwick's Sour Cream Donuts, Grand Rapids Also called Ludwicks Frozen Donuts Inc *(G-6635)*
Ludwicks Frozen Donuts Inc 616 453-6880
3217 3 Mile Rd Nw Grand Rapids (49534) *(G-6635)*
Luebke & Vogt Corporation 248 449-3232
25889 Meadowbrook Rd Novi (48375) *(G-11930)*
Luhu LLC 320 469-3162
540 Glenmoor Rd East Lansing (48823) *(G-4668)*
Luiten Greenhouse Tech 269 381-4020
1316 Howland Ave Kalamazoo (49001) *(G-8811)*
Luker Custom Canvas, Montague Also called Luker Enterprises Inc *(G-11094)*
Luker Enterprises Inc 231 894-9702
4530 Dowling St Montague (49437) *(G-11094)*
Luma Laser and Medi Spa 248 817-5499
700 E Big Beaver Rd Ste C Troy (48083) *(G-16466)*
Lumasmart Technology Intl Inc 586 232-4125
15809 Claire Ct Macomb (48042) *(G-10137)*
Lumbee Custom Painting LLC 586 296-5083
31725 Fraser Dr Fraser (48026) *(G-5685)*
Lumber & Truss Inc 810 664-7290
162 S Saginaw St Lapeer (48446) *(G-9472)*
Lumber Jack Hardwoods Inc (PA) 906 863-7090
N2509 O1 Dr Menominee (49858) *(G-10742)*
Lumberjack Logging LLC 616 799-4657
4778 Whitefish Woods Dr Pierson (49339) *(G-12484)*
Lumberjack Shack Inc 810 724-7230
7230 Webster Rd Imlay City (48444) *(G-8207)*
Lumbertown, Holt Also called Pageant Homes Inc *(G-7921)*
Lumbertown Portable Sawmill 231 206-4600
1650 Madison St Muskegon (49442) *(G-11369)*
Lumco Manufacturing Company 810 724-0582
2027 Mitchell Lake Rd Lum (48412) *(G-10090)*
Lumecon LLC 248 505-1090
23107 Commerce Dr Farmington Hills (48335) *(G-5047)*
Lumen North America Inc 248 289-6100
2850 Commerce Dr Rochester Hills (48309) *(G-13462)*
Lumenflow Corp 269 795-9007
3685 Hagen Dr Se Grand Rapids (49548) *(G-6636)*
Lumerica Corporation 248 543-8085
21400 Hoover Rd Warren (48089) *(G-17132)*
Lumichron Inc 616 245-8888
2215 29th St Se Ste B4 Grand Rapids (49508) *(G-6637)*

(PA)=Parent Co (HQ)=Headquarters (DH)=Div Headquarters

Lumificient Corporation....763 424-3702
1795 N Lapeer Rd Oxford (48371) ***(G-12356)***
Lumigen Inc....248 351-5600
22900 W 8 Mile Rd Southfield (48033) ***(G-14970)***
Lunar Industries, Clinton Township *Also called Roth-Williams Industries Inc* ***(G-3215)***
Lupa R A and Sons Repair....810 346-3579
3580 Willis Rd Marlette (48453) ***(G-10498)***
Lupaul Industries Inc (PA)....517 783-3223
310 E Steel St Saint Johns (48879) ***(G-14286)***
Lutco Inc....231 972-5566
8800 Midstate Dr Mecosta (49332) ***(G-10688)***
Lutke Forest Products, Manton *Also called Jason Lutke* ***(G-10456)***
Luttmann Precision Mold Inc....269 651-1193
1200 W Lafayette St Sturgis (49091) ***(G-15614)***
Luxottica of America Inc....517 349-0784
1982 W Grand River Ave # 815 Okemos (48864) ***(G-12129)***
Luxottica of America Inc....989 624-8958
8825 Market Place Dr # 340 Birch Run (48415) ***(G-1665)***
Lv Metals Inc....734 654-8081
2094 Ready Rd Carleton (48117) ***(G-2460)***
Lws - Design Center Detroit, Warren *Also called Leoni Wiring Systems Inc* ***(G-17128)***
Lxr Biotech LLC....248 860-4246
4225 N Atlantic Blvd Auburn Hills (48326) ***(G-931)***
Lydall Performance Mtls US Inc....248 596-2800
22260 Haggerty Rd Ste 200 Northville (48167) ***(G-11705)***
Lydall Sealing Solutions Inc....248 596-2800
22260 Haggerty Rd Ste 200 Northville (48167) ***(G-11706)***
Lyle Industries....989 435-7717
4144 Lyle Rd Beaverton (48612) ***(G-1388)***
Lyman Thornton....248 762-8433
2317 Gage St Wixom (48393) ***(G-17847)***
Lymphogen Inc....906 281-7372
1914 Middle Pointe Ln Houghton (49931) ***(G-7977)***
Lymtal International Inc (PA)....248 373-8100
4150 S Lapeer Rd Orion (48359) ***(G-12183)***
Lyndon Fabricators Inc....313 937-3640
12478 Beech Daly Rd Detroit (48239) ***(G-4212)***
Lynn Noyes Industries Inc....313 841-3130
2714 Ambassador Dr Ypsilanti (48198) ***(G-18086)***
Lynx Dx Inc....734 274-3144
120 W Main St Ste 300 Northville (48167) ***(G-11707)***
Lyon Manufacturing Inc....734 359-3000
7121 N Haggerty Rd Canton (48187) ***(G-2395)***
Lyon Sand & Gravel Co (PA)....313 843-7200
9300 Dix Dearborn (48120) ***(G-3734)***
Lyon Sand & Gravel Co....248 348-8511
51455 W 12 Mile Rd Wixom (48393) ***(G-17848)***
Lyondellbasell Industries Inc....517 336-4800
3610 Forest Rd Ste A Lansing (48910) ***(G-9393)***
Lyonnais Inc....616 868-6625
3760 Snow Ave Se Lowell (49331) ***(G-10035)***
Lyons Industries Inc (PA)....269 782-3404
30000 M 62 W Dowagiac (49047) ***(G-4548)***
Lyons Industries Inc....269 782-9516
414 West St Dowagiac (49047) ***(G-4549)***
Lyons Tool & Engineering Inc....586 200-3003
13720 E 9 Mile Rd Warren (48089) ***(G-17133)***
Lyons Tool and Mfg Corp....248 344-9644
47840 Anna Ct Wixom (48393) ***(G-17849)***
Lyte Poles Incorporated....586 771-4610
24874 Groesbeck Hwy Warren (48089) ***(G-17134)***
Lzb Manufacturing Inc (HQ)....734 242-1444
1 Lazboy Dr Monroe (48162) ***(G-11051)***
M & A Machining Inc....269 342-0026
1523 N Burdick St Kalamazoo (49007) ***(G-8812)***
M & B Associates, Kalamazoo *Also called M B B M Inc* ***(G-8813)***
M & B Welding Inc....989 635-8017
6411 Euclid St Marlette (48453) ***(G-10499)***
M & D Distribution Inc....313 592-1467
25550 Grand River Ave Redford (48240) ***(G-13170)***
M & E Manufacturing Inc....616 241-5509
530 32nd St Se Grand Rapids (49548) ***(G-6638)***
M & E Plastics LLC....989 875-4191
205 Industrial Pkwy Ithaca (48847) ***(G-8362)***
M & F Machine & Tool Inc....734 847-0571
6555 S Dixie Hwy Erie (48133) ***(G-4806)***
M & J Entp Grnd Rapids LLC....616 485-9775
5304 Alpine Ave Nw Comstock Park (49321) ***(G-3494)***
M & J Forest Products, Wolverine *Also called Jaroche Brothers Inc* ***(G-17934)***
M & J Graphics Enterprises Inc....734 542-8800
36060 Industrial Rd Livonia (48150) ***(G-9820)***
M & J Manufacturing Inc....586 778-6322
28184 Groesbeck Hwy Roseville (48066) ***(G-13827)***
M & M Associates (PA)....231 845-7034
4010 S Pere Marquette Hwy Ludington (49431) ***(G-10070)***
M & M Automatic Products Inc....517 782-0577
420 Ingham St Jackson (49201) ***(G-8501)***
M & M Die Cast Inc....269 465-6206
8556 Gast Rd Bridgman (49106) ***(G-1871)***
M & M Irish Enterprises Inc....248 644-0666
34164 Woodward Ave Birmingham (48009) ***(G-1689)***
M & M Machining Inc....586 997-9910
42876 Mound Rd Sterling Heights (48314) ***(G-15404)***
M & M Services Inc....248 619-9861
1844 Woodslee Dr Troy (48083) ***(G-16467)***
M & M Thread & Assembly Inc....248 583-9696
42716 Mound Rd Sterling Heights (48314) ***(G-15405)***
M & M Turning Co....586 791-7188
34480 Commerce Fraser (48026) ***(G-5686)***
M & M Typewriter Service Inc....734 995-4033
251 Collingwood St Ann Arbor (48103) ***(G-536)***
M & N Controls Inc....734 850-2127
7180 Sulier Dr Temperance (48182) ***(G-15835)***
M & N Machine LLC....231 722-7085
755 Access Hwy Muskegon (49442) ***(G-11370)***
M & R Machine Company....313 277-1570
5900 N Telegraph Rd Dearborn Heights (48127) ***(G-3789)***
M & S Extrusions, Imlay City *Also called Vintech Industries Inc* ***(G-8214)***
M & S Spring Company Inc....586 296-9850
34137 Doreka Fraser (48026) ***(G-5687)***
M & W Manufacturing Co LLC....586 741-8897
46409 Continental Dr Chesterfield (48047) ***(G-2800)***
M & W Tubing, Chesterfield *Also called M & W Manufacturing Co LLC* ***(G-2800)***
M 37 Concrete Products Inc (PA)....231 733-8247
767 E Sherman Blvd Muskegon (49444) ***(G-11371)***
M 37 Concrete Products Inc....231 689-1785
1231 E 16th St M White Cloud (49349) ***(G-17626)***
M A C, Wixom *Also called Mac Valves Inc* ***(G-17852)***
M A S Information Age Tech....248 352-0162
23132 Lake Ravines Dr Southfield (48033) ***(G-14971)***
M A T, Clarkston *Also called Flotronics Inc* ***(G-2921)***
M and A Fuels....313 397-7141
13601 Plymouth Rd Detroit (48227) ***(G-4213)***
M and G Laminated Products....517 784-4974
507 W Michigan Ave Jackson (49201) ***(G-8502)***
M Antonik....248 236-0333
690 Golf Villa Dr Oxford (48371) ***(G-12357)***
M Argueso & Co Inc....231 759-7304
2817 Mccracken St Norton Shores (49441) ***(G-11771)***
M B A Printing, Comstock Park *Also called MBA Printing Inc* ***(G-3498)***
M B B M Inc....269 344-6361
6967 E Mn Ave Kalamazoo (49048) ***(G-8813)***
M B Jewelry Design & Mfg, Bloomfield *Also called Bednarsh Mrris Jwly Design Mfg* ***(G-1732)***
M Beshara Inc....248 542-9220
10020 Capital St Oak Park (48237) ***(G-12079)***
M C, Grand Rapids *Also called Metal Components LLC* ***(G-6660)***
M C Carbide Tool Co....248 486-9590
28565 Automation Blvd Wixom (48393) ***(G-17850)***
M C M Fixture Company Inc....248 547-9280
21306 John R Rd Hazel Park (48030) ***(G-7442)***
M C M Stainless Fabricating, Hazel Park *Also called M C M Fixture Company Inc* ***(G-7442)***
M C Molds Inc....517 655-5481
125 Industrial Park Dr Williamston (48895) ***(G-17733)***
M C Products....248 960-0590
3105 Old Farm Ln Commerce Township (48390) ***(G-3424)***
M C Ward Inc....810 982-9720
4100 Griswold Rd Port Huron (48060) ***(G-12936)***
M Curry Corporation....989 777-7950
4475 Marlea Dr Saginaw (48601) ***(G-14080)***
M D Hubbard Spring Co Inc....248 628-2528
595 S Lapeer Rd Oxford (48371) ***(G-12358)***
M D I, Edwardsburg *Also called Mercury Displacement Inds Inc* ***(G-4766)***
M Den On Main....734 761-1030
3777 Plaza Dr Ste 5 Ann Arbor (48108) ***(G-537)***
M Forche Farms Inc....517 447-3488
1080 S Piotter Hwy Blissfield (49228) ***(G-1718)***
M J Day Machine Tool Company....313 730-1200
19231 Van Born Rd Allen Park (48101) ***(G-201)***
M J Diamonds, Dearborn *Also called Michels Inc* ***(G-3741)***
M J Mechanical Inc....989 865-9633
11787 Prior Rd Saint Charles (48655) ***(G-14195)***
M M P, Port Huron *Also called Michigan Manufactured Pdts Inc* ***(G-12941)***
M P C Awards....586 254-4660
52130 Van Dyke Ave Shelby Township (48316) ***(G-14629)***
M P D, Auburn Hills *Also called Multi-Precision Detail Inc* ***(G-951)***
M P D Welding Inc (PA)....248 340-0330
4200 S Lapeer Rd Orion (48359) ***(G-12184)***
M P I Coating, Riverview *Also called Materials Processing Inc* ***(G-13301)***
M P I International Inc (PA)....608 764-5416
2129 Austin Ave Rochester Hills (48309) ***(G-13463)***
M P Jackson LLC....517 782-0391
1824 River St Jackson (49202) ***(G-8503)***
M P Pumps Inc....586 293-8240
34800 Bennett Fraser (48026) ***(G-5688)***
M R A, Litchfield *Also called Michigan Rebuild & Automtn Inc* ***(G-9609)***
M R D Industries....269 623-8452
9755 Kingsbury Rd Delton (49046) ***(G-3818)***

M R G, Sterling Heights *Also called Michigan Rbr & Gasket Co Inc* ***(G-15421)***
M S Machining Systems Inc (PA)....517 546-1170
5833 Fisher Rd Howell (48855) ***(G-8059)***
M S Manufacturing Inc....586 463-2788
44431 Reynolds Dr Clinton Township (48036) ***(G-3161)***
M T E, Flint *Also called Monroe Truck Equipment Inc* ***(G-5470)***
M T S, Plymouth *Also called Miller Technical Services Inc* ***(G-12694)***
M T S Chenault LLC....269 861-0053
665 Pipestone St Benton Harbor (49022) ***(G-1523)***
M V A Enterprises Inc....906 282-6288
N7721 Six Mile Lake Rd Felch (49831) ***(G-5168)***
M&B Holdings LLC (PA)....734 677-0454
3035 Washtenaw Ave A322 Ann Arbor (48104) ***(G-538)***
M&D Dumpsters LLC....616 299-0234
6117 Polk St Hudsonville (49426) ***(G-8163)***
M&I Machine Inc....269 849-3624
5040 M 63 N Coloma (49038) ***(G-3358)***
M&M Mfg Inc....248 356-6543
29765 Briarbank Ct Southfield (48034) ***(G-14972)***
M&M Polishing Inc....269 468-4407
320 Park St Coloma (49038) ***(G-3359)***
M&S Printmedia Inc....248 601-1200
732 Brookwood Ln E Rochester Hills (48309) ***(G-13464)***
M-22 Challenge....231 392-2212
121 E Front St Ste 104 Traverse City (49684) ***(G-16029)***
M-52 Sand & Gravel LLC....734 453-3695
8483 Ann Arbor Rd W Plymouth (48170) ***(G-12680)***
M-57 Aggregate Company....810 639-7516
170 W State St Montrose (48457) ***(G-11103)***
M-A Metals Inc....989 268-5080
7470 N Crystal Rd Vestaburg (48891) ***(G-16826)***
M-B-M Manufacturing Inc....231 924-9614
9576 W 40th St Fremont (49412) ***(G-5778)***
M-Industries LLC....616 682-4642
6352 Fulton St E Ada (49301) ***(G-22)***
M-R Products Inc (PA)....231 378-2251
16612 Russo Dr Copemish (49625) ***(G-3573)***
M-Seal Products Co LLC....313 884-6147
55 Fairford Rd Grosse Pointe Shores (48236) ***(G-7200)***
M-Tek Inc....248 553-1581
29065 Cabot Dr 300 Novi (48377) ***(G-11931)***
M.R. Village Pizzeria, Middleton *Also called Shady Nook Farms* ***(G-10795)***
M1 Plant, Grand Rapids *Also called Roskam Baking Company* ***(G-6840)***
M2 Micro Machine, Kalamazoo *Also called Micro Machine Company LLC* ***(G-8824)***
M2 Plant, Grand Rapids *Also called Roskam Baking Company* ***(G-6841)***
M2 Scientifics LLC....616 379-9080
400 136th Ave Ste 100a Holland (49424) ***(G-7728)***
M4 CIC LLC....734 436-8507
719 W Ellsworth Rd Ste 1a Ann Arbor (48108) ***(G-539)***
MA MA La Rosa Foods Inc....734 946-7878
12100 Universal Dr Taylor (48180) ***(G-15736)***
Maas Enterprises Michigan LLC....616 875-8099
7938 112th Ave Holland (49424) ***(G-7729)***
Mabco, Madison Heights *Also called Michigan Auto Bending Corp* ***(G-10304)***
Mac Baits....616 392-2553
669 Douglas Ave Holland (49424) ***(G-7730)***
Mac Enterprises Inc (PA)....313 846-4567
11940 Hieber Rd Manchester (48158) ***(G-10407)***
Mac Lean Fasteners, Royal Oak *Also called Mac Lean-Fogg Company* ***(G-13945)***
Mac Lean-Fogg Company....248 280-0880
3200 W 14 Mile Rd Royal Oak (48073) ***(G-13945)***
Mac Material Acquisition Co....248 685-8393
1197 Craven Dr Highland (48356) ***(G-7496)***
Mac Valve Asia Inc (HQ)....248 624-7700
30569 Beck Rd Wixom (48393) ***(G-17851)***
Mac Valves Inc (PA)....248 624-7700
30569 Beck Rd Wixom (48393) ***(G-17852)***
Mac Valves Inc....734 529-5099
5555 N Ann Arbor Rd Dundee (48131) ***(G-4594)***
Mac-Mold Base Inc....586 752-1956
14921 32 Mile Rd Bruce Twp (48065) ***(G-2091)***
Mac-Tech Tooling Corporation....248 743-1400
1874 Larchwood Dr Troy (48083) ***(G-16468)***
Macair Inc....248 242-6860
3940 Loch Bend Dr Commerce Township (48382) ***(G-3425)***
Macali Inc....616 447-1202
1615 Monroe Ave Nw Ste 2 Grand Rapids (49505) ***(G-6639)***
Macarthur Corp (PA)....810 606-1777
3190 Tri Park Dr Grand Blanc (48439) ***(G-5975)***
Macatawa Bay Boat Works, Saugatuck *Also called N D R Enterprises Inc* ***(G-14460)***
Macauto U S A Inc....248 499-8208
3360 Crestwater Ct Rochester Hills (48309) ***(G-13465)***
Macauto Usa Inc....248 556-5256
2654 Elliott Dr Troy (48083) ***(G-16469)***
Macdermid Incorporated....248 399-3553
1221 Farrow St Ferndale (48220) ***(G-5298)***
Macdermid Incorporated....248 437-8161
29111 Milford Rd New Hudson (48165) ***(G-11547)***
Macdermid Ferndale Facility, Ferndale *Also called Macdermid Incorporated* ***(G-5298)***
Macdonald Publications Inc....989 875-4151
123 N Main St Ithaca (48847) ***(G-8363)***
Mach II Enterprises Inc....248 347-8822
200 S Main St Ste A Northville (48167) ***(G-11708)***
Mach II Tax Service, Northville *Also called Mach II Enterprises Inc* ***(G-11708)***
Mach Mold Incorporated....269 925-2044
360 Urbandale Ave Benton Harbor (49022) ***(G-1524)***
Machine Center, The, Albion *Also called Caster Concepts Inc* ***(G-119)***
Machine Control Technology....517 655-3506
4033 Vanneter Rd Williamston (48895) ***(G-17734)***
Machine Division, Romulus *Also called United Brass Manufacturers Inc* ***(G-13737)***
Machine Guard & Cover Co....616 392-8188
6187 136th Ave Holland (49424) ***(G-7731)***
Machine Shop, Whitmore Lake *Also called Michigan Cnc Tool Inc* ***(G-17704)***
Machine Tool & Gear Inc....989 723-5486
401 S Chestnut St Owosso (48867) ***(G-12299)***
Machine Tool & Gear Inc (HQ)....989 743-3936
1021 N Shiawassee St Corunna (48817) ***(G-3581)***
Machined Solutions....517 759-4075
360 Mulzer Ave Adrian (49221) ***(G-75)***
Machinery Prts Specialists LLC....989 662-7810
4533d Garfield Rd Auburn (48611) ***(G-756)***
Machining & Fabricating Inc....586 773-9288
30546 Groesbeck Hwy Roseville (48066) ***(G-13828)***
Machining Specialists Inc Mich....517 881-2863
2712 N Saginaw St Ofc Flint (48505) ***(G-5463)***
Machining Specialties, Madison Heights *Also called Central Gear Inc* ***(G-10208)***
Machining Technologies LLC....248 379-4201
9635 Davisburg Rd Clarkston (48348) ***(G-2935)***
Maci, Parma *Also called Michigan Auto Comprsr Inc* ***(G-12391)***
Mack Andrew & Son Brush Co....517 849-9272
216 E Chicago St Jonesville (49250) ***(G-8660)***
Mack Industries Michigan Inc....248 620-7400
8265 White Lake Rd White Lake (48386) ***(G-17634)***
Mack Oil Corporation....231 590-5903
7721 Outer Dr S Traverse City (49685) ***(G-16030)***
Mack's Ear Plugs, Warren *Also called McKeon Products Inc* ***(G-17146)***
Mackarynn Inc....616 263-9743
12175 Northland Dr Cedar Springs (49319) ***(G-2557)***
Mackellar Associates Inc....248 335-4440
1729 Northfield Dr Rochester Hills (48309) ***(G-13466)***
Mackellar Screenworks, Dimondale *Also called Trikala Inc* ***(G-4520)***
Mackenzies Bakery (PA)....269 343-8440
527 Harrison St Kalamazoo (49007) ***(G-8814)***
Mackinaw Power LLC....906 264-5025
102 W Washington St # 222 Marquette (49855) ***(G-10541)***
Maco Tool & Engineering Inc....989 224-6723
210 Spring St Saint Johns (48879) ***(G-14287)***
Macomb Business Forms Inc....586 790-8500
34895 Groesbeck Hwy Clinton Township (48035) ***(G-3162)***
Macomb County Republican Party....586 662-3703
41800 Prunum Dr Sterling Heights (48314) ***(G-15406)***
Macomb Daily, Clinton Township *Also called 21st Century Newspapers Inc* ***(G-3026)***
Macomb Daily, Mount Clemens *Also called Journal Register Company* ***(G-11137)***
Macomb Marketing Media, Clinton Township *Also called Macomb Printing Inc* ***(G-3163)***
Macomb North Clinton Advisor....586 731-1000
48075 Van Dyke Ave Shelby Township (48317) ***(G-14630)***
Macomb Printing Inc....586 463-2301
44272 N Groesbeck Hwy Clinton Township (48036) ***(G-3163)***
Macomb Sheet Metal Inc....586 790-4600
35195 Forton Ct Clinton Township (48035) ***(G-3164)***
Macomb Smoked Meats LLC....313 842-2375
2450 Wyoming St Dearborn (48120) ***(G-3735)***
Macomb Stairs Inc....586 226-2800
51032 Oro Dr Shelby Township (48315) ***(G-14631)***
Macomb Tube Fabricating Co....586 445-6770
13403 E 9 Mile Rd Warren (48089) ***(G-17135)***
Macsteel Monroe, Monroe *Also called Gerdau Macsteel Inc* ***(G-11034)***
Madar Metal Fabricating LLC....517 267-9610
3310 Ranger Rd Lansing (48906) ***(G-9243)***
Madden Enterprises Inc....734 284-5330
3557 Fort St Wyandotte (48192) ***(G-17966)***
Maddox Industries Inc....517 369-8665
900 W Chicago Rd Bronson (49028) ***(G-2032)***
Madison Electric Company (PA)....586 825-0200
31855 Van Dyke Ave Warren (48093) ***(G-17136)***
Madison Electric Company....586 294-8300
17930 E 14 Mile Rd Fraser (48026) ***(G-5689)***
Madison Electronics, Warren *Also called Madison Electric Company* ***(G-17136)***
Madison Machine Company....517 265-8532
2815 Sharp Rd Adrian (49221) ***(G-76)***
Madison Street Holdings LLC....517 252-2031
1408 E Church St Adrian (49221) ***(G-77)***
Maeder Bros Inc....989 644-2235
5016 W Weidman Rd Weidman (48893) ***(G-17459)***
Maeder Bros Qlty WD Pllets Inc....989 644-3500
5180 W Weidman Rd Weidman (48893) ***(G-17460)***
Maeder Bros Saw Mill, Weidman *Also called Maeder Bros Inc* ***(G-17459)***

A L P H A B E T I C

Maes Tool & Die Co Inc 517 750-3131
1074 Toro Dr Jackson (49201) ***(G-8504)***
Maestro Media Print Solutions, Bloomfield Hills *Also called Logan Marketing Group LLC* ***(G-1778)***
Mag Automotive LLC (HQ) 586 446-7000
6015 Center Dr Sterling Heights (48312) ***(G-15407)***
Mag Automotive LLC 586 446-7000
2555 20th St Port Huron (48060) ***(G-12937)***
Mag-Powertrain 586 446-7000
6015 Center Dr Sterling Heights (48312) ***(G-15408)***
Mag-TEC Casting Corporation 517 789-8505
2411 Research Dr Jackson (49203) ***(G-8505)***
Magazines In Motion Inc 248 310-7647
35451 Valley Crk Farmington Hills (48335) ***(G-5048)***
Maggie's Organics, Dexter *Also called Clean Clothes Inc* ***(G-4482)***
Magic City Heating & Cooling 269 467-6406
27290 Marvin Rd Centreville (49032) ***(G-2596)***
Magic Treatz LLC 248 989-9956
24245 Coolidge Hwy Oak Park (48237) ***(G-12080)***
Magiera Holdings Inc 269 685-1768
950 Lincoln Pkwy Plainwell (49080) ***(G-12529)***
Magiglide Inc 906 822-7321
257 Industrial Park Rd Crystal Falls (49920) ***(G-3611)***
Magline Inc (PA) 800 624-5463
1205 W Cedar St Standish (48658) ***(G-15221)***
Magline Inc 800 624-5463
1205 W Cedar St Standish (48658) ***(G-15222)***
Magline International LLC 989 512-1000
1205 W Cedar St Standish (48658) ***(G-15223)***
Magna 616 786-7403
3401 128th Ave Holland (49424) ***(G-7732)***
Magna Car Top Systems Amer Inc (HQ) 248 836-4500
2725 Commerce Pkwy Auburn Hills (48326) ***(G-932)***
Magna Car Top Systems Amer Inc 248 619-8133
1200 Chicago Rd Troy (48083) ***(G-16470)***
Magna E-Car USA LLC (HQ) 248 606-0600
10410 N Holly Rd Holly (48442) ***(G-7885)***
Magna E-Car USA LLC 248 606-0600
10410 N Holly Rd Holly (48442) ***(G-7886)***
Magna Electronics Inc 810 606-0444
1465 Combermere Dr Troy (48083) ***(G-16471)***
Magna Electronics Inc (HQ) 248 729-2643
2050 Auburn Rd Auburn Hills (48326) ***(G-933)***
Magna Electronics Inc 248 606-0606
2050 Auburn Rd Auburn Hills (48326) ***(G-934)***
Magna Electronics Tech Inc (HQ) 810 606-0145
10410 N Holly Rd Holly (48442) ***(G-7887)***
Magna Engineered Glass, Grand Rapids *Also called Magna Mirrors America Inc* ***(G-6640)***
Magna Exteriors America Inc 248 844-5446
2050 Auburn Rd Auburn Hills (48326) ***(G-935)***
Magna Exteriors America Inc (HQ) 248 631-1100
750 Tower Dr Troy (48098) ***(G-16472)***
Magna Exteriors America Inc 248 409-1817
1750 Brown Rd Auburn Hills (48326) ***(G-936)***
Magna Extrors Intrors Amer Inc 616 786-7000
5085 Kraft Ave Se Kentwood (49512) ***(G-9018)***
Magna Extrors Intrors Amer Inc 248 729-2400
750 Tower Dr Troy (48098) ***(G-16473)***
Magna International Amer Inc 616 786-7000
3501 John F Donnelly Dr Holland (49424) ***(G-7733)***
Magna International Amer Inc (HQ) 248 729-2400
750 Tower Dr 7000 Troy (48098) ***(G-16474)***
Magna International Amer Inc 313 422-6000
12800 Oakland Pkwy Detroit (48203) ***(G-4214)***
Magna International Inc 248 617-3200
54725 Grand River Ave New Hudson (48165) ***(G-11548)***
Magna Mirrors America Inc (HQ) 616 786-5120
5085 Kraft Ave Se Grand Rapids (49512) ***(G-6640)***
Magna Mirrors America Inc 616 786-7000
49 W 3rd St Holland (49423) ***(G-7734)***
Magna Mirrors America Inc 616 786-7300
414 E 40th St Holland (49423) ***(G-7735)***
Magna Mirrors America Inc 616 942-0163
579 S Park St Newaygo (49337) ***(G-11573)***
Magna Mirrors America Inc 616 738-0115
3601 John F Donnelly Dr Holland (49424) ***(G-7736)***
Magna Mirrors America Inc 616 786-7000
1800 Hayes St Grand Haven (49417) ***(G-6052)***
Magna Mirrors America Inc 616 786-7000
3401 128th Ave Holland (49424) ***(G-7737)***
Magna Mirrors America Inc 616 786-7000
5085 Kraft Ave Se Kentwood (49512) ***(G-9019)***
Magna Mirrors America Inc 616 786-7772
3501 John F Donnelly Dr Holland (49424) ***(G-7738)***
Magna Mirrors America Inc 616 868-6122
6151 Bancroft Ave Se Alto (49302) ***(G-328)***
Magna Mirrors America Inc 231 652-4450
700 Park St Newaygo (49337) ***(G-11574)***
Magna Mirrors Newaygo Division, Newaygo *Also called Magna Mirrors America Inc* ***(G-11573)***
Magna Mirrors North Amer LLC (HQ) 616 868-6122
6151 Bancroft Ave Se Alto (49302) ***(G-329)***
Magna Mirros Lowell, Alto *Also called Magna Mirrors America Inc* ***(G-328)***
Magna Modular Systems LLC 586 279-2000
14253 Frazho Rd Warren (48089) ***(G-17137)***
Magna Powertrain America Inc 517 316-1013
3140 Spanish Oak Dr Lansing (48911) ***(G-9394)***
Magna Powertrain America Inc (HQ) 248 597-7811
1870 Technology Dr Troy (48083) ***(G-16475)***
Magna Powertrain Lansing, Lansing *Also called Mpt Lansing LLC* ***(G-9403)***
Magna Powertrain Troy, Troy *Also called Magna Powertrain Usa Inc* ***(G-16476)***
Magna Powertrain Usa Inc 586 264-8180
6363 E 14 Mile Rd Sterling Heights (48312) ***(G-15409)***
Magna Powertrain Usa Inc (HQ) 248 680-4900
1870 Technology Dr Troy (48083) ***(G-16476)***
Magna Powertrain Usa Inc 248 524-1397
1875 Research Dr Troy (48083) ***(G-16477)***
Magna Sealing & Glass Systems, Holland *Also called Magna Mirrors America Inc* ***(G-7738)***
Magna Seating America Inc 248 243-7158
3800 Lapeer Rd Auburn Hills (48326) ***(G-937)***
Magna Seating America Inc (HQ) 248 567-4000
30020 Cabot Dr Novi (48377) ***(G-11932)***
Magna Seating America Inc 586 816-1400
6200 26 Mile Rd Shelby Township (48316) ***(G-14632)***
Magna Seating Auburn Hills, Auburn Hills *Also called Magna Seating America Inc* ***(G-937)***
Magna Seating Detriot, Detroit *Also called Magna International Amer Inc* ***(G-4214)***
Magna Steyr LLC 248 740-0214
1965 Research Dr Ste 100 Troy (48083) ***(G-16478)***
Magna Steyr North America, Troy *Also called Magna Steyr LLC* ***(G-16478)***
Magnecor Australia Limited 248 471-9505
24581 Crestview Ct Farmington Hills (48335) ***(G-5049)***
Magnesium Alum Machining LLC 616 309-1202
533 Godfrey St Lowell (49331) ***(G-10036)***
Magnesium Products America Inc 517 663-2700
2001 Industrial Dr Eaton Rapids (48827) ***(G-4728)***
Magnesium Products America Inc (HQ) 734 416-8600
47805 Galleon Dr Plymouth (48170) ***(G-12681)***
Magnetech Corporation 248 426-8840
22809 Heslip Dr Novi (48375) ***(G-11933)***
Magneti Marelli Holdg USA LLC (HQ) 248 418-3000
3900 Automation Ave Auburn Hills (48326) ***(G-938)***
Magneti Marelli North Amer Inc (HQ) 248 418-3000
3900 Automation Ave Auburn Hills (48326) ***(G-939)***
Magneti Mrlli Sspnsons USA LLC, Troy *Also called Marelli Tennessee USA LLC* ***(G-16485)***
Magnetic Chuck Services Co Inc 586 822-9441
9391 Lindsey Rd Casco (48064) ***(G-2502)***
Magnetic Michigan 734 922-7068
101 N Main St Ann Arbor (48104) ***(G-540)***
Magnetic Products Inc 248 887-5600
683 Town Center Dr Highland (48356) ***(G-7497)***
Magnetic Systems International 231 582-9600
3890 Charlevoix Rd Petoskey (49770) ***(G-12455)***
Magnetic Systems Intl Inc 231 582-9600
1095 Dam Rd Boyne City (49712) ***(G-1828)***
Magnetic Ventures LLC 313 670-3036
445 Nightingale St Dearborn (48128) ***(G-3736)***
Magnetool Inc 248 588-5400
505 Elmwood Dr Troy (48083) ***(G-16479)***
Magni Group Inc (PA) 248 647-4500
390 Park St Ste 300 Birmingham (48009) ***(G-1690)***
Magni-Industries Inc (HQ) 313 843-7855
2771 Hammond St Detroit (48209) ***(G-4215)***
Magnum Fabricating 734 484-5800
1754 E Michigan Ave Ypsilanti (48198) ***(G-18087)***
Magnum Induction Inc 586 716-4700
51517 Industrial Dr New Baltimore (48047) ***(G-11488)***
Magnum Machine and Tool Inc 616 844-1940
13744 172nd Ave Grand Haven (49417) ***(G-6053)***
Magnum Powder Coating Inc 616 785-3155
5500 West River Dr Ne Comstock Park (49321) ***(G-3495)***
Magnum Toolscom LLC 734 595-4600
30690 Cypress Rd Romulus (48174) ***(G-13703)***
Magnumm Corporation (PA) 586 427-9420
3839 E 10 Mile Rd Warren (48091) ***(G-17138)***
Magnus Precision Tool LLC 586 285-2500
34082 James J Pompo Dr Fraser (48026) ***(G-5690)***
Magnus Software Inc 517 294-0315
3883 Hogback Rd Fowlerville (48836) ***(G-5574)***
Mahale, Troy *Also called Hbpo North America Inc* ***(G-16392)***
Mahindra Automotive N Amer Mfg, Auburn Hills *Also called Mahindra North American* ***(G-940)***
Mahindra Genze, Ann Arbor *Also called Mahindra Tractor Assembly Inc* ***(G-541)***
Mahindra N Amrcn Technical Ctr, Auburn Hills *Also called Mahindra Vehicle Mfrs Ltd* ***(G-941)***
Mahindra North American (HQ) 248 268-6600
275 Rex Blvd Auburn Hills (48326) ***(G-940)***
Mahindra Tractor Assembly Inc 734 274-2239
1901 E Ellsworth Rd Ann Arbor (48108) ***(G-541)***

Mahindra Vehicle Mfrs Ltd 248 268-6600
275 Rex Blvd Auburn Hills (48326) *(G-941)*
Mahle Inc 248 305-8200
23030 Mahle Dr Farmington Hills (48335) *(G-5050)*
Mahle Aftermarket Inc (HQ) 248 347-9700
23030 Mahle Dr Farmington (48335) *(G-4904)*
Mahle Behr Industy America Lp 616 647-3490
5858 Safety Dr Ne Belmont (49306) *(G-1468)*
Mahle Behr Mfg MGT Inc 248 735-3623
2700 Daley Dr Troy (48083) *(G-16480)*
Mahle Behr Troy Inc (HQ) 248 743-3700
2700 Daley Dr Troy (48083) *(G-16481)*
Mahle Behr Troy Inc 248 735-3623
5820 Innovation Dr Troy (48098) *(G-16482)*
Mahle Behr USA Inc (HQ) 248 743-3700
2700 Daley Dr Troy (48083) *(G-16483)*
Mahle Eng Components USA Inc 248 305-8200
23030 Haggerty Rd Farmington Hills (48335) *(G-5051)*
Mahle Industries Incorporated 989 224-5423
916 W State St Ste B Saint Johns (48879) *(G-14288)*
Mahle Industries Incorporated (HQ) 248 305-8200
23030 Mahle Dr Farmington Hills (48335) *(G-5052)*
Mahle Industries Incorporated (HQ) 248 305-8200
23030 Mahle Dr Farmington Hills (48335) *(G-5053)*
Mahle Industries Incorporated 231 722-1300
2020 Sanford St Muskegon (49444) *(G-11372)*
Mahle Manufacturing MGT Inc 248 735-3623
23030 Mahle Dr Farmington Hills (48335) *(G-5054)*
Mahle Powertrain 248 473-6511
23030 Haggerty Rd Farmington Hills (48335) *(G-5055)*
Mahle Powertrain LLC (HQ) 248 305-8200
23030 Mahle Dr Farmington Hills (48335) *(G-5056)*
Mahnke Machine Inc 231 775-0581
1551 Filmore Ave Ste A Cadillac (49601) *(G-2262)*
Mahoney & Associates Inc 517 669-4300
12750 Escanaba Dr Ste 1 Dewitt (48820) *(G-4464)*
Main & Company 517 789-7183
2700 Cooper St Jackson (49201) *(G-8506)*
Main Street Portraits 269 321-3310
7586 Foxwood Richland (49083) *(G-13251)*
Main Street Printing 517 851-3816
119 W Main St Stockbridge (49285) *(G-15591)*
Maine Ornamental LLC 800 556-8449
68956 Us Highway 131 White Pigeon (49099) *(G-17652)*
Maine Plastics Incorporated 269 679-3988
3939 Emerald Dr Kalamazoo (49001) *(G-8815)*
Majeske Machine Inc 319 273-8905
44650 Pinetree Dr Plymouth (48170) *(G-12682)*
Majestic Industries Inc 586 786-9100
15378 Hallmark Ct Macomb (48042) *(G-10138)*
Majestic Pattern Company Inc 313 892-5800
20400 Sherwood St Detroit (48234) *(G-4216)*
Majik Graphics Inc 586 792-8055
19751 15 Mile Rd Clinton Township (48035) *(G-3165)*
Major Industries Ltd 810 985-9372
511 Fort St Rm 445 Port Huron (48060) *(G-12938)*
Major Products, Allen Park *Also called Riviera Industries Inc* *(G-206)*
Makaveli Cnstr & Assoc Inc 810 892-3412
20131 James Detroit (48235) *(G-4217)*
Make It Yours 517 990-6799
6982 Surrey Ln Jackson (49201) *(G-8507)*
Makinaw Fudge Co, Naubinway *Also called D A U P Corp* *(G-11465)*
Makkedah Mt Proc & Bulk Fd Str 231 873-2113
1813 N 136th Ave Hart (49420) *(G-7376)*
MAKS INCORPORATED 248 733-9771
1150 Rankin Dr Troy (48083) *(G-16484)*
Malabar Manufacturing Inc 517 448-2155
4255 Munson Hwy Hudson (49247) *(G-8135)*
Malachi Printing LLC 517 395-4813
444 E Prospect St Jackson (49203) *(G-8508)*
Maleports Sault Prtg Co Inc 906 632-3369
314 Osborn Blvd Sault Sainte Marie (49783) *(G-14468)*
Mall City Aluminum Inc 269 349-5088
850 E Crosstown Pkwy Kalamazoo (49001) *(G-8816)*
Mall City Containers Inc (PA) 269 381-2706
2710 N Pitcher St Kalamazoo (49004) *(G-8817)*
Mall City Containers Inc 616 249-3657
88 54th St Sw Unit 105 Grand Rapids (49548) *(G-6641)*
Mall Tooling & Engineering 586 463-6520
150 Grand Ave Mount Clemens (48043) *(G-11140)*
Mallory Pole Buildings Inc 269 668-2627
24359 Red Arrow Hwy Ste A Mattawan (49071) *(G-10665)*
Malloy Incorporated 734 665-6113
5411 Jackson Rd Ann Arbor (48103) *(G-542)*
Malmac Tool and Fixture Inc 517 448-8244
4255 Munson Hwy Hudson (49247) *(G-8136)*
Mammoth, Holland *Also called Nortek Air Solutions LLC* *(G-7759)*
Mammoth Distilling LLC 773 841-4242
1554 N East Torch Lake Dr Central Lake (49622) *(G-2592)*
Man Store, The, Livonia *Also called Gags and Games Inc* *(G-9747)*
Man U TEC Inc 586 262-4085
6522 Diplomat Dr Sterling Heights (48314) *(G-15410)*
Management Insight Analytics, Ann Arbor *Also called Visiun Inc* *(G-693)*
Manchester Industries Inc VA 269 496-2715
26920 M 60 Mendon (49072) *(G-10716)*
Maness Petroleum Corp 989 773-5475
1425 S Mission Rd Mount Pleasant (48858) *(G-11203)*
Manhattan Container, Romulus *Also called Packaging Specialties Inc* *(G-13718)*
Manigg Enterprises Inc (PA) 989 356-4986
1010 Us Highway 23 N Alpena (49707) *(G-296)*
Manistee News Advocate 231 723-3592
75 Maple St Manistee (49660) *(G-10427)*
Manistee News-Advocate, Manistee *Also called Pgi Holdings Inc* *(G-10435)*
Manistee Wldg & Piping Svc Inc (PA) 231 723-2551
325 Oakgrove St Manistee (49660) *(G-10428)*
Manistique Machine, Negaunee *Also called U P Fabricating Co Inc* *(G-11478)*
Manistique Pioneer Tribune, Manistique *Also called Four Seasons Publishing Inc* *(G-10440)*
Manistique Rentals Inc 906 341-6955
415 Chippewa Ave Manistique (49854) *(G-10443)*
Manly Innovations LLC 734 548 0200
19735 Deerfield Ct Chelsea (48118) *(G-2716)*
Mann + Hummel Inc (HQ) 269 329-3900
6400 S Sprinkle Rd Portage (49002) *(G-13013)*
Mann + Hummel Usa Inc 248 857-8500
2285 Franklin Rd Ste 200 Bloomfield Hills (48302) *(G-1780)*
Mann + Hummel Usa Inc 248 857-8501
3411 Ctr Park Plz Kalamazoo (49048) *(G-8818)*
Mann + Hummel Usa Inc (HQ) 269 329-3900
6400 S Sprinkle Rd Portage (49002) *(G-13014)*
Mann Metal Finishing Inc 269 621-6359
200 Prospect St Hartford (49057) *(G-7385)*
Mannetron 269 962-3475
74 Leonard Wood Rd Battle Creek (49037) *(G-1225)*
Mannetron Animatronics, Battle Creek *Also called Mannetron* *(G-1225)*
Manning Enterprises Inc 269 657-2346
45872 30th St Paw Paw (49079) *(G-12408)*
Manning Marine, Rockford *Also called Shore-Mate Products LLC* *(G-13590)*
Mannino Tile & Marble Inc 586 978-3390
38790 Hartwell Dr Sterling Heights (48312) *(G-15411)*
Mannisto Forest Products Inc 906 387-3836
E7720 Knuttila Rd Munising (49862) *(G-11245)*
Mannix RE Holdings LLC 231 972-0088
8965 Midstate Dr Mecosta (49332) *(G-10689)*
Manor Industries Inc 586 463-4604
24400 Maplehurst Dr Clinton Township (48036) *(G-3166)*
Manos Authentic LLC 800 242-2796
22599 15 Mile Rd Clinton Township (48035) *(G-3167)*
Manta Group LLC 248 325-8264
35 W Huron St Ste 10 Pontiac (48342) *(G-12847)*
Manthei Inc 231 347-4672
3996 Charlevoix Rd Petoskey (49770) *(G-12456)*
Manthei Development Corp 231 347-6282
3996 Charlevoix Rd Petoskey (49770) *(G-12457)*
Manthei Veneer Mill Inc 231 347-4688
5491 Manthei Rd Petoskey (49770) *(G-12458)*
Mantissa Industries Inc 517 694-2260
2362 Jarco Dr Holt (48842) *(G-7915)*
Manufactured Homes Inc 269 781-2887
330 S Kalamazoo Ave Marshall (49068) *(G-10574)*
Manufacturers / Mch Bldrs Svcs 734 748-3706
13035 Wayne Rd Livonia (48150) *(G-9821)*
Manufacturers Services Inds (PA) 906 493-6685
40014 S Cream City Pt Rd Drummond Island (49726) *(G-4565)*
Manufacturing & Indus Tech Inc 248 814-8544
525 Goldengate St Ste 100 Lake Orion (48362) *(G-9147)*
Manufacturing Associates Inc 248 421-4943
39201 Amrhein Rd Livonia (48150) *(G-9822)*
Manufacturing Center, Sterling Heights *Also called Proto Gage Inc* *(G-15454)*
Manufacturing Ctrl Systems Inc 248 853-7400
1928 Star Batt Dr Ste C Rochester Hills (48309) *(G-13467)*
Manufacturing Products & Svcs 734 927-1964
260 Ann Arbor Rd W Plymouth (48170) *(G-12683)*
Manufax Inc 231 929-3226
1324 Barlow St Ste D Traverse City (49686) *(G-16031)*
Manufctring Partners Group LLC 517 749-4050
1639 Horton Lake Rd Lapeer (48446) *(G-9473)*
Manufctring Solutions Tech LLC 734 744-5050
1975 Alpha St Commerce Township (48382) *(G-3426)*
Manufcturing Assembly Intl LLC 248 549-4700
2521 Torquay Ave Royal Oak (48073) *(G-13946)*
Manus Tool Inc 989 724-7171
510 S 3rd St Harrisville (48740) *(G-7365)*
Manutec, Sterling Heights *Also called Man U TEC Inc* *(G-15410)*
Mapal Inc (HQ) 810 364-8020
4032 Dove Rd Port Huron (48060) *(G-12939)*
Mapco Manufacturing, Canton *Also called Merchants Automatic Pdts Inc* *(G-2401)*
Maple Industries, New Hudson *Also called TEC Industries Inc* *(G-11558)*
Maple Lane Ag-Bag, Kawkawlin *Also called Glenn Knochel* *(G-8971)*

ALPHABETIC

(PA)=Parent Co (HQ)=Headquarters (DH)=Div Headquarters
2020 Harris Michigan Industrial Directory
1011

Maple Leaf Press Inc ... 616 846-8844
1215 S Beechtree St Grand Haven (49417) ***(G-6054)***
Maple Mold Technologies, Rochester Hills *Also called Precision Masters Inc* ***(G-13497)***
Maple Mold Technologies, Auburn Hills *Also called Precision Masters Inc* ***(G-979)***
Maple Press LLC ... 248 733-9669
31211 Stephenson Hwy # 100 Madison Heights (48071) ***(G-10301)***
Maple Ridge Companies Inc ... 989 356-4807
9528 S Bolton Rd Posen (49776) ***(G-13070)***
Maple Ridge Hardwoods Inc ... 989 873-5305
2270 Dobler Rd Sterling (48659) ***(G-15244)***
Maple Row Sugarhouse, Jones *Also called Daniel Olson* ***(G-8651)***
Maple Valley Concrete Products ... 517 852-1900
725 Durkee St Nashville (49073) ***(G-11460)***
Maple Valley Pallet Co ... 231 228-6641
9285 S Nash Rd Maple City (49664) ***(G-10463)***
Maple Valley Plastics LLC ... 810 346-3040
4119 Main St Brown City (48416) ***(G-2055)***
Maple Valley Truss Co ... 989 389-4267
4287 E West Branch Rd Prudenville (48651) ***(G-13085)***
Maples Sawmill Inc ... 906 484-3926
2736 Chard Rd Hessel (49745) ***(G-7481)***
Maquet Monthly ... 906 226-6500
810 N 3rd St Marquette (49855) ***(G-10542)***
Mar Cor Purification Inc ... 248 373-7844
180 Engelwood Dr Ste D Lake Orion (48359) ***(G-9148)***
Mar-Med Co., Grand Rapids *Also called Mar-Med Inc* ***(G-6642)***
Mar-Med Inc ... 616 454-3000
333 Fuller Ave Ne Grand Rapids (49503) ***(G-6642)***
Mar-Vo Mineral Company Inc ... 517 523-2669
115 E Bacon St Hillsdale (49242) ***(G-7529)***
Marana Group, Kalamazoo *Also called Lake Michigan Mailers Inc* ***(G-8804)***
Marand Products Company Inc ... 313 369-2000
17243 Filer St Detroit (48212) ***(G-4218)***
Marathon Oil, Flushing *Also called Fuel Tobacco Stop* ***(G-5535)***
Marathon Weld Group LLC ... 517 782-8040
5750 Marathon Dr Jackson (49201) ***(G-8509)***
Marbelite Corp ... 248 348-1900
22500 Heslip Dr Novi (48375) ***(G-11934)***
Marbels Outdoors, Gladstone *Also called Crl Inc* ***(G-5910)***
Marble Arms, Gladstone *Also called Marbles Gun Sights Inc* ***(G-5916)***
Marble Deluxe A C ... 248 668-8200
1820 W West Maple Rd Commerce Township (48390) ***(G-3427)***
Marble ERA Products Inc ... 989 742-4513
2146 Deepwoods Dr Gaylord (49735) ***(G-5876)***
Marble Grinding & Polishing ... 586 321-0543
57885 Romeo Plank Rd Ray (48096) ***(G-13134)***
Marblecast Kitchens & Baths, Oak Park *Also called Marblecast of Michigan Inc* ***(G-12081)***
Marblecast of Michigan Inc ... 248 398-0600
14831 W 11 Mile Rd Oak Park (48237) ***(G-12081)***
Marbles Gun Sights Inc ... 906 428-3710
420 Indl Pk Dr Gladstone (49837) ***(G-5916)***
Marc Schrreiber & Company LLC ... 734 222-9930
120 E Liberty St Ste 370 Ann Arbor (48104) ***(G-543)***
Marceau Enterprises Inc ... 586 697-8100
11517 Laurel Woods Dr Washington (48094) ***(G-17307)***
Marcellus News, Marcellus *Also called Moormann Printing Inc* ***(G-10466)***
March Coatings Inc (PA) ... 810 229-6464
160 Summit St Brighton (48116) ***(G-1953)***
Marcie Electric Inc ... 248 486-1200
8190 Boardwalk Rd Ste B Brighton (48116) ***(G-1954)***
Marco Rollo Inc ... 269 279-5246
415 W Cushman St Three Rivers (49093) ***(G-15869)***
Marcon Technologies LLC ... 269 279-1701
1 Industrial Park Dr Constantine (49042) ***(G-3538)***
Marcus Automotive LLC ... 616 494-6400
257 W Lakewood Blvd # 20 Holland (49424) ***(G-7739)***
Marelli North America Inc ... 248 848-4800
27000 Hills Tech Ct # 100 Farmington Hills (48331) ***(G-5057)***
Marelli Tennessee USA LLC ... 248 418-3000
3900 Automation Ave Auburn Hills (48326) ***(G-942)***
Marelli Tennessee USA LLC ... 248 680-8872
1389 Wheaton Dr Troy (48083) ***(G-16485)***
Margate Industries Inc ... 810 387-4300
129 N Main St Yale (48097) ***(G-18046)***
Marhar Snowboards LLC ... 616 432-3104
5693 Airline Rd Fruitport (49415) ***(G-5796)***
Mari Leather Works, Inc., Madison Heights *Also called Universal Trim Inc* ***(G-10374)***
Mari Villa Vineyards ... 231 935-4513
8175 Center Rd Traverse City (49686) ***(G-16032)***
Mariah Industries Inc (PA) ... 248 237-0404
1407 Allen Dr Ste E Troy (48083) ***(G-16486)***
Marias House Made Salsa ... 313 733-8406
23425 Blackstone Ave Warren (48089) ***(G-17139)***
Marias Italian Bakery Inc ... 734 981-1200
115 N Haggerty Rd Canton (48187) ***(G-2396)***
Marie Louise Moon, Berrien Springs *Also called All About Quilting and Design* ***(G-1591)***
Marie Minnie Bakers Inc ... 734 522-1100
12301 Farmington Rd Livonia (48150) ***(G-9823)***
Marilyn's Needlework, Grand Rapids *Also called Stoney Creek Collection Inc* ***(G-6893)***
Marimba Auto LLC ... 734 398-9000
41150 Van Born Rd Canton (48188) ***(G-2397)***
Marine Automated Doc System ... 989 539-9010
2900 Doc Dr Harrison (48625) ***(G-7315)***
Marine Industries Inc ... 989 635-3644
2900 Boyne Rd Marlette (48453) ***(G-10500)***
Marine Machining and Mfg ... 586 791-8800
33475 Giftos Dr Clinton Township (48035) ***(G-3168)***
Marion Pallet ... 231 743-6124
7414 20 Mile Rd Marion (49665) ***(G-10491)***
Marix Specialty Welding Co ... 586 754-9685
3822 Kiefer Ave Warren (48091) ***(G-17140)***
Marjo Plastics Company Inc ... 734 455-4130
1081 Cherry Plymouth (48170) ***(G-12684)***
Mark 4 Automotive, Troy *Also called Dayco Products LLC* ***(G-16298)***
Mark 7 Machine Inc ... 989 922-7335
535 S Tuscola Rd Bay City (48708) ***(G-1327)***
Mark A Nelson ... 989 305-5769
332 Oneil Rd Lupton (48635) ***(G-10092)***
Mark Adler Homes ... 586 850-0630
401 S Old Woodward Ave # 3 Birmingham (48009) ***(G-1691)***
Mark Barclay Ministries, Midland *Also called Living Word International Inc* ***(G-10882)***
Mark Beem ... 231 510-8122
861 N Green Rd Lake City (49651) ***(G-9092)***
Mark Carbide Co ... 248 545-0606
1830 Brinston Dr Troy (48083) ***(G-16487)***
Mark Four CAM Inc ... 586 204-5906
22926 W Industrial Dr Saint Clair Shores (48080) ***(G-14261)***
Mark Griessel ... 810 378-6060
7068 Jordan Rd Melvin (48454) ***(G-10691)***
Mark Honkala Logging Inc ... 906 485-1570
18261 County Road Cd Ishpeming (49849) ***(G-8349)***
Mark II Enterprises, Northville *Also called Northville Stitching Post* ***(G-11717)***
Mark Maker Company Inc (PA) ... 616 538-6980
4157 Stafford Ave Sw Grand Rapids (49548) ***(G-6643)***
Mark Mold and Engineering ... 989 687-9786
773 W Beamish Rd Sanford (48657) ***(G-14451)***
Mark One Corporation ... 989 732-2427
517 Alpine Rd Gaylord (49735) ***(G-5877)***
Mark Schwager Inc ... 248 275-1978
13170 W Star Dr Shelby Township (48315) ***(G-14633)***
Mark Sikorski MD ... 586 786-1800
16800 24 Mile Rd Macomb (48042) ***(G-10139)***
Mark-Pack Inc (PA) ... 616 837-5400
776 Main St Coopersville (49404) ***(G-3564)***
Marked Tool Inc ... 616 669-3201
2934 Highland Blvd Hudsonville (49426) ***(G-8164)***
Markerboard People Inc ... 517 372-1666
1611 N Grand River Ave # 1 Lansing (48906) ***(G-9244)***
Market Novelty Products, Traverse City *Also called Visual Identification Products* ***(G-16139)***
Marketing Communications Inc ... 616 784-4488
950 Vitality Dr Nw Ste A Comstock Park (49321) ***(G-3496)***
Marketing Displays Inc ... 248 553-1900
38271 W 12 Mile Rd Farmington Hills (48331) ***(G-5058)***
Marketing Displays Intl, Farmington Hills *Also called Marketing Displays Inc* ***(G-5058)***
Marketing Impact, Flint *Also called Printcomm Inc* ***(G-5484)***
Marketing VI Group Inc ... 989 793-3933
4414 Bay Rd Ste 1 Saginaw (48603) ***(G-14081)***
Marketlab Inc ... 616 656-5359
5220 68th St Se Caledonia (49316) ***(G-2306)***
Marketlab Inc ... 866 237-3722
6850 Southbelt Dr Se Caledonia (49316) ***(G-2307)***
Marketplace Signs ... 248 393-1609
681 Brown Rd Orion (48359) ***(G-12185)***
Marketplus Software Inc (PA) ... 269 968-4240
2821 Wilbur St Springfield (49037) ***(G-15198)***
Markham Peat Corp ... 800 851-7230
9475 Jefferson Rd Lakeview (48850) ***(G-9175)***
Marking Machine Co ... 517 767-4155
286 Spires Pkwy Tekonsha (49092) ***(G-15820)***
Markit Products ... 616 458-7881
2430 Turner Ave Nw Ste D Grand Rapids (49544) ***(G-6644)***
Marks Fuel Dock ... 586 445-8525
24200 Jefferson Ave Saint Clair Shores (48080) ***(G-14262)***
Marland Clutch, Warren *Also called Formsprag LLC* ***(G-17043)***
Marley Precision Inc (HQ) ... 269 963-7374
455 Fritz Keiper Blvd Battle Creek (49037) ***(G-1226)***
Marlin Corporation ... 248 683-1536
5243 Latimer St Orchard Lake (48324) ***(G-12167)***
Maro Precision Tool Company ... 734 261-3100
5041 Pheasant Cv West Bloomfield (48323) ***(G-17483)***
Marquee Engraving Inc ... 810 686-7550
600 S Mill St Ste A Clio (48420) ***(G-3275)***
Marquette Castings LLC ... 248 798-8035
123 W 5th St Royal Oak (48067) ***(G-13947)***
Marquette Distillery ... 906 869-4933
844 W Bluff St Marquette (49855) ***(G-10543)***

ALPHABETIC SECTION
Master Data Center Inc

Marquette Fence Company Inc 906 249-8000
1446 State Highway M28 E Marquette (49855) ***(G-10544)***
Marquette Machining & Fabg, Marquette *Also called Clair Sawyer* ***(G-10523)***
Marquette Maple Company, Marquette *Also called Levi Ohman Micah* ***(G-10540)***
Marquette Meats In City LLC 906 226-8333
3060 Us Highway 41 W Marquette (49855) ***(G-10545)***
Marquis Industries Inc 616 842-2810
17310 Teunis Dr Spring Lake (49456) ***(G-15160)***
Marquis Jewelers Ltd 586 725-3990
34748 23 Mile Rd Chesterfield (48047) ***(G-2801)***
Marrel Corporation 616 863-9155
4750 14 Mile Rd Ne Rockford (49341) ***(G-13578)***
Marrone Michigan Manufactoring 269 427-0300
700 Industrial Park Rd Bangor (49013) ***(G-1093)***
Marrs Discount Furniture 989 720-5436
1544 E M 21 Owosso (48867) ***(G-12300)***
Marsack Sand & Gravel Inc 586 293-4414
20900 E 14 Mile Rd Roseville (48066) ***(G-13829)***
Marsh Brothers Inc 517 869-2653
9800 Youngs Rd Quincy (49082) ***(G-13096)***
Marsh Industrial Services Inc 231 258-4870
135 E Mile Rd Kalkaska (49646) ***(G-8949)***
Marsh Plating Corporation (PA) 734 483-5767
103 N Grove St Ypsilanti (48198) ***(G-18088)***
Marsh Welding, Kalkaska *Also called Marsh Industrial Services Inc* ***(G-8949)***
Marshal E Hyman and Associates 248 643-0642
3250 W Big Beaver Rd # 529 Troy (48084) ***(G-16488)***
Marshall Bldg Components Corp 269 781-4236
1605 Brooks Dr Marshall (49068) ***(G-10575)***
Marshall Brass Co, Marshall *Also called SH Leggitt Company* ***(G-10588)***
Marshall Clayton & Sons Log 269 623-8898
8101 Keller Rd Delton (49046) ***(G-3819)***
Marshall Excelsior Co 269 789-6700
1508 George Brown Dr Marshall (49068) ***(G-10576)***
Marshall Excelsior Co (HQ) 269 789-6700
1506 George Brown Dr Marshall (49068) ***(G-10577)***
Marshall Gas Controls Inc 269 781-3901
450 Leggitt Rd Marshall (49068) ***(G-10578)***
Marshall Metal Products Inc 269 781-3924
1006 E Michigan Ave Marshall (49068) ***(G-10579)***
Marshall Middleby Holding LLC 906 863-4401
5600 13th St Menominee (49858) ***(G-10743)***
Marshall Plastic Film, Martin *Also called Mpf Acquisitions Inc* ***(G-10596)***
Marshall Ryerson Co 616 299-1751
7440 Lime Hollow Dr Se Grand Rapids (49546) ***(G-6645)***
Marshall Tool Service Inc 989 777-3137
2700 Iowa Ave Saginaw (48601) ***(G-14082)***
Marshall Welding & Fabrication 269 781-4010
817 Industrial Rd Marshall (49068) ***(G-10580)***
Marshall's Fudge, Mackinaw City *Also called Marshalls Trail Inc* ***(G-10099)***
Marshall-Gruber Company LLC (HQ) 248 353-4100
26776 W 12 Mile Rd Southfield (48034) ***(G-14973)***
Marshalls Crossing 810 639-4740
12050 Trident Blvd Montrose (48457) ***(G-11104)***
Marshalls Trail Inc 231 436-5082
308 E Central Ave Mackinaw City (49701) ***(G-10099)***
Martak Cultured Marble 313 891-5400
18841 John R St Detroit (48203) ***(G-4219)***
Martec Land Services Inc 231 929-3971
3335 S Arprt Rd W Ste A5 Traverse City (49684) ***(G-16033)***
Martel Tool Corporation 313 278-2420
5831 Pelham Rd Allen Park (48101) ***(G-202)***
Marten Models & Molds Inc 586 293-2260
18291 Mike C Ct Fraser (48026) ***(G-5691)***
Martin and Hattie Rasche Inc 616 245-1223
3353 Eastern Ave Se Grand Rapids (49508) ***(G-6646)***
Martin Bros Mill Fndry Sup Co 269 927-1355
289 Hinkley St Benton Harbor (49022) ***(G-1525)***
Martin Electric Mtr Sls & Svc, Carson City *Also called Martin Electric Mtrs Sls & Svc* ***(G-2492)***
Martin Electric Mtrs Sls & Svc 989 584-3850
10116 Cleveland Rd Carson City (48811) ***(G-2492)***
Martin Fluid Power Company (PA) 248 585-8170
900 E Whitcomb Ave Madison Heights (48071) ***(G-10302)***
Martin Mretta Magnesia Spc LLC 231 723-2577
1800 E Lake Rd Manistee (49660) ***(G-10429)***
Martin Products Company Inc 269 651-1721
66635 M 66 N Sturgis (49091) ***(G-15615)***
Martin Saw & Tool Inc (PA) 906 863-6812
1212 19th Ave Menominee (49858) ***(G-10744)***
Martin Structural Consult 810 633-9111
2300 Loree Rd Applegate (48401) ***(G-712)***
Martin Tool & Machine Inc 586 775-1800
29739 Groesbeck Hwy Roseville (48066) ***(G-13830)***
Martinrea Featherstone, Auburn Hills *Also called Martinrea Jonesville LLC* ***(G-943)***
Martinrea Hot Stampings Inc 859 509-3031
14401 Frazho Rd Warren (48089) ***(G-17141)***
Martinrea Industries Inc (HQ) 734 428-2400
10501 Mi State Road 52 Manchester (48158) ***(G-10408)***
Martinrea Industries Inc 231 832-5504
603 E Church Ave Reed City (49677) ***(G-13220)***
Martinrea Industries Inc 517 849-2195
260 Gaige St Jonesville (49250) ***(G-8661)***
Martinrea Jonesville LLC (HQ) 517 849-2195
260 Gaige St Jonesville (49250) ***(G-8662)***
Martinrea Jonesville LLC 248 630-7730
2325 Featherstone Rd Auburn Hills (48326) ***(G-943)***
Martinrea Metal Industries Inc 517 849-2195
4800 Knowles Rd North Adams (49262) ***(G-11656)***
Marton Tool & Die Co Inc 616 361-7337
610 Plymouth Ave Ne Grand Rapids (49505) ***(G-6647)***
Marvel Industries, Greenville *Also called Northland Corporation* ***(G-7147)***
Marvel Tool & Machine Company 810 329-2781
1096 River Rd Saint Clair (48079) ***(G-14227)***
Marvin Nelson Forest Products 906 384-6700
9868 County 426 E Rd Cornell (49818) ***(G-3575)***
Mary Boggs Baggs 586 731-2513
5218 Robert St Shelby Township (48316) ***(G-14634)***
Mary Pantely Associates 248 723-8771
2710 Ledgewood Ct Rochester (48306) ***(G-13333)***
Marygrove Awnings 734 422-7110
12700 Merriman Rd Livonia (48150) ***(G-9824)***
Marykay Software Inc 989 463-4385
5142 N State Rd Alma (48801) ***(G-239)***
Marysville Hydrocarbons LLC 586 445-2300
30078 Schoenherr Rd # 150 Warren (48088) ***(G-17142)***
Marysville Hydrocarbons LLC (HQ) 586 445-2300
2510 Busha Hwy Marysville (48040) ***(G-10606)***
Mas Inc 231 894-0409
2100 Cogswell Dr Whitehall (49461) ***(G-17677)***
Masco Building Products Corp (HQ) 313 274-7400
17450 College Pkwy Livonia (48152) ***(G-9825)***
Masco Cabinetry LLC 517 263-0771
4600 Arrowhead Dr Ann Arbor (48105) ***(G-544)***
Masco Cabinetry LLC 740 286-5033
4600 Arrowhead Dr Ann Arbor (48105) ***(G-545)***
Masco Cabinetry LLC (HQ) 734 205-4600
4600 Arrowhead Dr Ann Arbor (48105) ***(G-546)***
Masco Cabinetry LLC 239 561-7266
4600 Arrowhead Dr Ann Arbor (48105) ***(G-547)***
Masco Cabinetry LLC 407 857-4444
4600 Arrowhead Dr Ann Arbor (48105) ***(G-548)***
Masco Cabinetry LLC 517 263-0771
5353 W Us Highway 223 Adrian (49221) ***(G-78)***
Masco Cabinetry LLC 770 447-6363
4600 Arrowhead Dr Ann Arbor (48105) ***(G-549)***
Masco Corporation (PA) 313 274-7400
17450 College Pkwy Livonia (48152) ***(G-9826)***
Masco Corporation of Indiana 810 664-8501
211 Mccormick Dr Lapeer (48446) ***(G-9474)***
Masco De Puerto Rico Inc 313 274-7400
21001 Van Born Rd Taylor (48180) ***(G-15737)***
Masco Services Inc 313 274-7400
17450 College Pkwy Livonia (48152) ***(G-9827)***
Maslin Corporation (PA) 586 777-7500
20304 Harper Ave Harper Woods (48225) ***(G-7302)***
Maslo Fabrication LLC 616 298-7700
155 Manufacturers Dr Holland (49424) ***(G-7740)***
Mason Forge & Die Inc 517 676-2992
841 Hull Rd Mason (48854) ***(G-10645)***
Mason Specialty Forge, Mason *Also called Mason Forge & Die Inc* ***(G-10645)***
Mason Tackle Company 810 631-4571
11273 Center St Otisville (48463) ***(G-12233)***
Mason Tool and Gage Inc 248 344-0412
28800 Wall St Wixom (48393) ***(G-17853)***
Masonite International Corp 517 545-5811
5665 Sterling Dr Howell (48843) ***(G-8060)***
Masons Lumber & Hardware Inc 989 685-3999
2493 S M 33 Rose City (48654) ***(G-13763)***
Maspac International, Novi *Also called Clarkson Controls & Eqp Co* ***(G-11850)***
Massee Products Ltd 269 684-8255
2612 N 5th St Niles (49120) ***(G-11624)***
Massie Mfg Inc 906 353-6381
445 N Superior Ave Baraga (49908) ***(G-1109)***
Massive Mineral Mix LLC 517 857-4544
21110 29 1/2 Mile Rd Springport (49284) ***(G-15212)***
Massobrio Precision Products, Kimball *Also called Mpp Corp* ***(G-9045)***
Mast Mini Barns, Fremont *Also called K-Mar Structures LLC* ***(G-5777)***
Master Automatic Mch Co Inc (PA) 734 414-0500
40485 Schoolcraft Rd Plymouth (48170) ***(G-12685)***
Master Automatic Mch Co Inc 734 414-0500
12271 Globe St Livonia (48150) ***(G-9828)***
Master Coat LLC 734 405-2340
6120 Commerce Dr Westland (48185) ***(G-17578)***
Master Craft Extrusion Tls Inc 231 386-5149
771 N Mill St Northport (49670) ***(G-11670)***
Master Data Center Inc 248 352-5810
30200 Telg Rd Ste 300 Bingham Farms (48025) ***(G-1656)***

ALPHABETIC

Master Finish Co — 877 590-5819
2020 Nelson Ave Se # 103 Grand Rapids (49507) *(G-6648)*

Master Handyman Press Inc — 248 616-0810
1224 Rankin Dr Troy (48083) *(G-16489)*

Master Jig Grinding & Gage Co — 248 380-8515
43050 W 10 Mile Rd Novi (48375) *(G-11935)*

Master Machine & Tool Co Inc — 586 469-4243
23414 Reynolds Ct Clinton Township (48036) *(G-3169)*

Master Machining Inc — 248 454-9890
1960 Thunderbird Troy (48084) *(G-16490)*

Master Mfg Inc — 248 628-9400
3287 Metamora Rd Oxford (48371) *(G-12359)*

Master Mix Company — 734 487-7870
612 S Mansfield St Ypsilanti (48197) *(G-18089)*

Master Model & Fixture Inc — 586 532-1153
51731 Oro Dr Shelby Township (48315) *(G-14635)*

Master Precision Molds, Greenville Also called Master Precision Products Inc *(G-7145)*

Master Precision Products Inc — 616 754-5483
1212 E Fairplains St Greenville (48838) *(G-7145)*

Master Precision Tool Corp — 586 739-3240
7362 19 Mile Rd Sterling Heights (48314) *(G-15412)*

Master Pump Service, Canton Also called Water Master Inc *(G-2443)*

Master Robotics LLC — 586 484-7710
7300 Danielle Dr Almont (48003) *(G-262)*

Master Tag, Montague Also called International Master Pdts Corp *(G-11091)*

Master Unit Die Products, Inc., Greenville Also called D-M-E USA Inc *(G-7126)*

Master Woodworks — 269 240-3262
2916 Veronica Ct Saint Joseph (49085) *(G-14328)*

Masterbilt Products Corp — 269 749-4841
719 N Main St Olivet (49076) *(G-12142)*

Masterline Design & Mfg — 586 463-5888
41580 Production Dr Harrison Township (48045) *(G-7339)*

Mastermix, Ypsilanti Also called Master Mix Company *(G-18089)*

Masters Millwork LLC — 248 987-4511
37644 Hills Tech Dr Farmington Hills (48331) *(G-5059)*

Masters Tool & Die Inc — 989 777-2450
4485 Marlea Dr Saginaw (48601) *(G-14083)*

Mastertag, Montague Also called International Master Pdts Corp *(G-11092)*

Mastery Technologies Inc — 248 888-8420
41214 Bridge St Novi (48375) *(G-11936)*

Mat Tek Inc — 810 659-0322
175 Industrial Dr Ste A Flushing (48433) *(G-5540)*

Matcor Automotive Michigan Inc — 616 527-4050
401 S Steele St Ionia (48846) *(G-8248)*

Matech Lighting Systems, Holland Also called GT Solutions LLC *(G-7655)*

Matelski Lumber Company — 231 549-2780
2617 M 75 S Boyne Falls (49713) *(G-1841)*

Material Cnversion Systems Div, Fenton Also called Atlas Technologies LLC *(G-5183)*

Material Control Inc (PA) — 630 892-4274
130 Seltzer Rd Croswell (48422) *(G-3600)*

Material Difference Tech LLC — 888 818-1283
51195 Regency Center Dr Macomb (48042) *(G-10140)*

Material Handling Tech Inc — 586 725-5546
9023 Marine City Hwy B Ira (48023) *(G-8260)*

Material Sciences Corporation (PA) — 734 207-4444
6855 Commerce Blvd Canton (48187) *(G-2398)*

Material Transfer and Stor Inc — 800 836-7068
1214 Lincoln Rd Allegan (49010) *(G-176)*

Materialise Usa LLC — 734 259-6445
44650 Helm Ct Plymouth (48170) *(G-12686)*

Materials Processing Inc — 734 282-1888
17423 Jefferson Riverview (48193) *(G-13301)*

Materion Brush Inc — 586 443-4925
27555 College Park Dr Warren (48088) *(G-17143)*

Materion Brush Prfmce Alloys, Warren Also called Materion Brush Inc *(G-17143)*

Materne North America Corp — 231 346-6600
6331 Us Highway 31 Grawn (49637) *(G-7099)*

Matheson — 586 498-8315
26415 Gratiot Ave Roseville (48066) *(G-13831)*

Matheson Tri-Gas Inc — 734 425-8870
5913 Middlebelt Rd Garden City (48135) *(G-5833)*

Mathew Parmelee — 248 894-5955
707 W Hamlin Rd Rochester Hills (48307) *(G-13468)*

Mathie Energy Supply Co Inc — 517 625-3646
7840 Gale Rd Morrice (48857) *(G-11120)*

Mathworks Inc — 248 596-7920
39555 Orchard Hill Pl # 280 Novi (48375) *(G-11937)*

Matrix Engineering and Sls Inc — 734 981-7321
44330 Duchess Dr Canton (48187) *(G-2399)*

Matrix Engineering Inc — 810 231-0212
8830 Whitmore Lake Rd Brighton (48116) *(G-1955)*

Matrix Manufacturing Inc — 616 532-6000
862 47th St Sw Ste B2 Grand Rapids (49509) *(G-6649)*

Matrix Metalcraft, Auburn Hills Also called TEC International II *(G-1014)*

Matrix Metalcraft, Macomb Also called TEC International II *(G-10166)*

Matrix North Amercn Cnstr Inc — 734 847-4605
6945 Crabb Rd Temperance (48182) *(G-15836)*

Matrix Printing & Mailing, Grand Rapids Also called Graphic Impressions Inc *(G-6474)*

Matrix Tool Co — 586 296-6010
40577 Sunfield Ct Clinton Township (48038) *(G-3170)*

Matt and Dave LLC — 734 439-1988
4706 N Ann Arbor Rd Dundee (48131) *(G-4595)*

Matteson Manufacturing Inc — 231 779-2898
1480 Potthoff St Cadillac (49601) *(G-2263)*

Matthews Mill Inc — 989 257-3271
6400 E County Line Rd South Branch (48761) *(G-14749)*

Matthews Plating Inc — 517 784-3535
405 N Mechanic St Jackson (49201) *(G-8510)*

Matthews Software Inc — 248 593-6999
145 Larchlea Dr Birmingham (48009) *(G-1692)*

Mattress Mart, Waterford Also called Midwest Quality Bedding Inc *(G-17359)*

Mattress Wholesale — 248 968-2200
14510 W 8 Mile Rd Oak Park (48237) *(G-12082)*

Mattson Tool & Die Corp — 616 447-9012
4174 5 Mile Rd Ne Grand Rapids (49525) *(G-6650)*

Matuschek Welding Products Inc — 586 991-2434
42378 Yearego Dr Sterling Heights (48314) *(G-15413)*

Maureen I Martin Caster — 810 233-0484
2013 Ridgecliffe Dr Flint (48532) *(G-5464)*

Maurell Products Inc — 989 725-5188
2710 S M 52 Owosso (48867) *(G-12301)*

Maurer Meat Processors Inc — 989 658-8185
4075 Purdy Rd Ubly (48475) *(G-16719)*

Mauser — 248 795-2330
4750 Clawson Tank Dr Clarkston (48346) *(G-2936)*

Maven Drive LLC — 313 667-1541
300 Renaissance Ctr Detroit (48243) *(G-4220)*

Maverick Building Systems LLC — 248 366-9410
3190 Walnut Lake Rd Commerce Township (48390) *(G-3428)*

Maverick Exploration Prod Inc — 231 929-3923
3301 Veterans Dr Ste 107 Traverse City (49684) *(G-16034)*

Maverick Machine Tool — 269 789-1617
101 E Oliver Dr Marshall (49068) *(G-10581)*

Maw Ventures Inc — 231 798-8324
6230 Norton Center Dr Norton Shores (49441) *(G-11772)*

Mawby, L Vineyards, Suttons Bay Also called L Mawby LLC *(G-15653)*

Max 3 LLC — 269 925-2044
360 Urbandale Ave Benton Harbor (49022) *(G-1526)*

Max Casting Company Inc — 269 925-8081
116 Paw Paw Ave Benton Harbor (49022) *(G-1527)*

Max Endura Inc — 989 356-1593
3490 Us Highway 23 S Alpena (49707) *(G-297)*

Max Manufacturing — 517 990-9180
205 Watts Rd Jackson (49203) *(G-8511)*

Max2 LLC — 269 468-3452
320 Park St Coloma (49038) *(G-3360)*

Maxable Inc — 517 592-5638
202 Sherman St Brooklyn (49230) *(G-2039)*

Maxal Hobart Brothers, Traverse City Also called Hobart Brothers Company *(G-15998)*

Maxi-Grip, Warren Also called Rens LLC *(G-17220)*

Maxim Integrated Products Inc — 408 601-1000
10355 Citation Dr Ste 100 Brighton (48116) *(G-1956)*

Maximum Mold Inc — 269 468-6291
1440 Territorial Rd Benton Harbor (49022) *(G-1528)*

Maximum Oilfield Service Inc — 989 731-0099
7929 Alba Hwy Elmira (49730) *(G-4791)*

Maxion Fumagalli Auto USA — 734 737-5000
39500 Orchard Hill Pl Novi (48375) *(G-11938)*

Maxion Import LLC — 734 737-5000
39500 Orchard Hill Pl # 500 Novi (48375) *(G-11939)*

Maxion Wheels (HQ) — 734 737-5000
39500 Orchard Hill Pl # 500 Novi (48375) *(G-11940)*

Maxion Wheels Akron LLC — 734 737-5000
39500 Orchard Hill Pl # 500 Novi (48375) *(G-11941)*

Maxion Wheels USA LLC (HQ) — 734 737-5000
39500 Orchard Hill Pl # 500 Novi (48375) *(G-11942)*

Maxitrol Company — 517 486-2820
235 Sugar St Blissfield (49228) *(G-1719)*

Maxitrol Company — 269 432-3291
1000 E State St Colon (49040) *(G-3374)*

Maxitrol Company (PA) — 248 356-1400
23555 Telegraph Rd Southfield (48033) *(G-14974)*

Maxs Concrete Inc — 231 972-7558
15323 75th Ave Mecosta (49332) *(G-10690)*

Maxum LLC — 248 726-7110
600 Oliver Dr Rochester Hills (48309) *(G-13469)*

May Mobility Inc — 312 869-2711
650 Avis Dr Ste 100 Ann Arbor (48108) *(G-550)*

May-Day Window Manufacturing — 989 348-2809
403 N Wilcox Bridge Rd Grayling (49738) *(G-7111)*

Maya Gage Co., Farmington Hills Also called Maya Jig Grinding & Gage Co *(G-5060)*

Maya Jig Grinding & Gage Co — 248 471-0820
20770 Parker St Farmington (48336) *(G-5060)*

Maya Plastics Inc — 586 997-6000
13179 W Star Dr Shelby Township (48315) *(G-14636)*

Mayard Professional Center De, East Lansing Also called Fbe Corp *(G-4656)*

Mayco International LLC — 586 803-6000
34501 Harper Ave Clinton Township (48035) *(G-3171)*

Mayco International LLC ... 586 803-6000
1020 Doris Rd Auburn Hills (48326) ***(G-944)***
Mayco International LLC (PA) ... 586 803-6000
42400 Merrill Rd Sterling Heights (48314) ***(G-15414)***
Mayco Plastics, Sterling Heights *Also called Stonebridge Industries Inc* ***(G-15513)***
Mayco Tool ... 616 785-7350
5880 Comstock Park Dr Nw Comstock Park (49321) ***(G-3497)***
Mayer Alloys Corporation (PA) ... 248 399-2233
10711 Northend Ave Ferndale (48220) ***(G-5299)***
Mayer Metals Corporation ... 248 742-0077
10711 Northend Ave Ferndale (48220) ***(G-5300)***
Mayer Tool & Engineering Inc ... 269 651-1428
1404 N Centerville Rd Sturgis (49091) ***(G-15616)***
Mayfair Accessories Inc ... 989 732-8400
1639 Calkins Dr Gaylord (49735) ***(G-5878)***
Mayfair Golf Accessories ... 989 732-8400
1639 Calkins Dr Gaylord (49735) ***(G-5879)***
Mayfair Plastics Inc ... 989 732-2441
845 Dickerson Rd Gaylord (49735) ***(G-5880)***
Maygrove Awning Co., Livonia *Also called American Roll Shutter Awng Co* ***(G-9645)***
Maynard L Maclean L C ... 586 949-0471
50855 E Russell Schmidt Chesterfield (48051) ***(G-2802)***
Mayo Welding & Fabricating Co ... 248 435-2730
5061 Delemere Ave Royal Oak (48073) ***(G-13948)***
Mayser Usa Inc ... 734 858-1290
6200 Schooner St Van Buren Twp (48111) ***(G-16771)***
Maytag Appliances, Benton Harbor *Also called Maytag Corporation* ***(G-1529)***
Maytag Corporation (HQ) ... 269 923-5000
2000 N M 63 Benton Harbor (49022) ***(G-1529)***
Mayville Engineering Co Inc ... 616 878-5235
990 84th St Sw Byron Center (49315) ***(G-2197)***
Mayville Engineering Co Inc ... 989 748-6031
1444 Alexander Rd Vanderbilt (49795) ***(G-16806)***
Mayville Engineering Co Inc ... 616 877-2073
4714 Circuit Ct Wayland (49348) ***(G-17406)***
Mayville Engineering Co Inc ... 989 983-3911
8276 Yuill Rd Vanderbilt (49795) ***(G-16807)***
Mazzella Lifting Tech Inc ... 734 953-7300
12671 Richfield Ct Livonia (48150) ***(G-9829)***
Mazzella Lifting Tech Inc ... 248 585-1063
31623 Stephenson Hwy Madison Heights (48071) ***(G-10303)***
MB, Capac *Also called Miller Broach Inc* ***(G-2449)***
MB Aerospace Sterling Hts Inc (PA) ... 586 977-9200
38111 Comm Dr Sterling Heights (48312) ***(G-15415)***
MB Aerospace Warren LLC ... 586 772-2500
25250 Easy St Warren (48089) ***(G-17144)***
MB Fluid Services LLC ... 616 392-7036
11372 E Lakewood Blvd Holland (49424) ***(G-7741)***
MB Liquidating Corporation ... 810 638-5388
7162 Sheridan Rd Flushing (48433) ***(G-5541)***
MBA Printing Inc ... 616 243-1600
90 Windflower St Ne Comstock Park (49321) ***(G-3498)***
Mbcd Inc ... 517 484-4426
1520 E Malcolm X St Lansing (48912) ***(G-9395)***
Mbm Fabricators Co Inc ... 734 941-0100
36333 Northline Rd Romulus (48174) ***(G-13704)***
Mbs, Jackson *Also called Modern Builders Supply Inc* ***(G-8535)***
Mbwwproducts Inc ... 616 464-1650
825 Buchanan Ave Sw Grand Rapids (49507) ***(G-6651)***
Mc Creadie Sales, Midland *Also called MHR Investments Inc* ***(G-10884)***
Mc Donald Computer Corporation ... 248 350-9290
21411 Civic Center Dr # 100 Southfield (48076) ***(G-14975)***
Mc Guire Mill & Lumber ... 989 735-3851
4499 Ford Rd Glennie (48737) ***(G-5945)***
Mc Guire Spring Corporation ... 517 546-7311
6135 Grand River Rd Brighton (48114) ***(G-1957)***
Mc Nally Elevator Company (PA) ... 269 381-1860
223 W Ransom St Kalamazoo (49007) ***(G-8819)***
Mc Pherson Industrial Corp ... 586 752-5555
120 E Pond Dr Romeo (48065) ***(G-13633)***
Mc Pherson Plastics Inc ... 269 694-9487
1347 E M 89 89 M Otsego (49078) ***(G-12244)***
Mc REA Corporation ... 734 420-2116
40422 Cove Ct Plymouth (48170) ***(G-12687)***
McBf, Warren *Also called Melody Digiglio* ***(G-17147)***
McCallum Fabricating LLC ... 586 784-5555
13927 Hough Rd Allenton (48002) ***(G-229)***
McCann ... 734 429-2781
6187 Wild Currant Way Se Caledonia (49316) ***(G-2308)***
McCarthy Group Incorporated (PA) ... 616 977-2900
5505 52nd St Se Grand Rapids (49512) ***(G-6652)***
McClatchy Newspapers Inc ... 734 525-2224
31572 Industrial Rd # 400 Livonia (48150) ***(G-9830)***
McClure Metals Group Inc ... 616 957-5955
6161 28th St Se Ste 5 Grand Rapids (49546) ***(G-6653)***
McClure Tables Inc ... 616 662-5974
4939 Big Bass Dr Hudsonville (49426) ***(G-8165)***
McClure Tables Inc (PA) ... 616 662-5974
6661 Roger Dr Ste C Jenison (49428) ***(G-8633)***
McClures Pickles LLC ... 248 837-9323
8201 Saint Aubin St Detroit (48211) ***(G-4221)***
McClures Pickles LLC ... 248 837-9323
212 Royal Ave Royal Oak (48073) ***(G-13949)***
McCoig Materials LLC ... 734 414-6179
40500 Ann Arbor Rd E Plymouth (48170) ***(G-12688)***
McComb County Legal News ... 586 463-4300
148 S Main St Ste 100 Mount Clemens (48043) ***(G-11141)***
McConnell & Scully Inc (PA) ... 517 568-4104
146 W Main St Homer (49245) ***(G-7945)***
McCormick & Company Inc ... 586 558-8424
28650 Dequindre Rd Warren (48092) ***(G-17145)***
McCoy Craftsman LLC ... 616 634-7455
1642 Broadway Ave Nw Grand Rapids (49504) ***(G-6654)***
McCray Press ... 989 792-8681
2710 State St Saginaw (48602) ***(G-14084)***
McCullys Wldg Fabrication LLC ... 231 499-3842
3916 E Old State Rd East Jordan (49727) ***(G-4639)***
McDivitt Road Facility, Jackson *Also called Advance Turning and Mfg Inc* ***(G-8374)***
McDonald Acquisitions LLC ... 616 878-7800
8074 Clyde Park Ave Sw Byron Center (49315) ***(G-2198)***
McDonald Enterprises Inc ... 734 464-4664
36650 Plymouth Rd Livonia (48150) ***(G-9831)***
McDonald Modular Solutions, Milford *Also called 4d Building Inc* ***(G-10952)***
McDonald Wholesale Distributor ... 313 273-2870
19536 W Davison St Detroit (48223) ***(G-4222)***
McElroy Metal Mill Inc ... 269 781-8313
311 Oliver Dr Marshall (49068) ***(G-10582)***
McEsson Drug Company, Livonia *Also called McKesson Corporation* ***(G-9833)***
McG Plastics Inc ... 989 667-4349
3661 N Euclid Ave Bay City (48706) ***(G-1328)***
McGean-Rohco Inc ... 216 441-4900
38521 Schoolcraft Rd Livonia (48150) ***(G-9832)***
McIntyre Softwater Service ... 810 735-5778
1014 N Bridge St Linden (48451) ***(G-9593)***
McKay Press Inc ... 989 631-2360
7600 W Wackerly St Midland (48642) ***(G-10883)***
McKechnie Tooling and Engrg, Roseville *Also called McKechnie Vhcl Cmpnnts USA Inc* ***(G-13832)***
McKechnie Vhcl Cmpnnts USA Inc ... 218 894-1218
27087 Gratiot Ave 2 Roseville (48066) ***(G-13832)***
McKechnie Vhcl Cmpnnts USA Inc (HQ) ... 586 491-2600
27087 Gratiot Ave Fl 2 Roseville (48066) ***(G-13833)***
McKenna Enterprises Inc ... 248 375-3388
3128 Walton Blvd Rochester Hills (48309) ***(G-13470)***
McKeon Products Inc (PA) ... 586 427-7560
25460 Guenther Warren (48091) ***(G-17146)***
McKesson Corporation ... 734 953-2523
38220 Plymouth Rd Livonia (48150) ***(G-9833)***
McKesson Pharmacy Systems LLC (HQ) ... 800 521-1758
30881 Schoolcraft Rd Livonia (48150) ***(G-9834)***
McLaren Inc ... 989 720-4328
2170 W M 21 Owosso (48867) ***(G-12302)***
McLaren Engineering, Livonia *Also called Linamar Holding Nevada Inc* ***(G-9807)***
McLaren Plumbing Htg & Coolg, Owosso *Also called McLaren Inc* ***(G-12302)***
McLeod Wood and Christmas Pdts ... 989 777-4800
6794 Dixie Hwy Bridgeport (48722) ***(G-1853)***
McM, Novi *Also called Michigan Custom Machines Inc* ***(G-11946)***
McM Disposal LLC ... 616 656-4049
978 64th St Sw Byron Center (49315) ***(G-2199)***
McMillan Printing, Springfield *Also called Pro Connections LLC* ***(G-15201)***
MCN Oil & Gas, Traverse City *Also called DTE Gas & Oil Company* ***(G-15958)***
McNamara & Mcnamara ... 906 293-5281
13123 State Highway M123 Newberry (49868) ***(G-11580)***
McNaughton & Gunn Inc (PA) ... 734 429-5411
960 Woodland Dr Saline (48176) ***(G-14399)***
McNees Manufacturing Inc ... 616 675-7480
750 Canada Rd Bailey (49303) ***(G-1080)***
McNic Oil & Gas Properties ... 313 256-5500
2000 2nd Ave Detroit (48226) ***(G-4223)***
McNichols Conveyor Company ... 248 357-6077
21411 Civic Center Dr # 204 Southfield (48076) ***(G-14976)***
McNichols Polsg & Anodizing (PA) ... 313 538-3470
12139 Woodbine Redford (48239) ***(G-13171)***
McNichols Polsg & Anodizing ... 313 538-3470
12139 Wormer Redford (48239) ***(G-13172)***
MCO, Mount Clemens *Also called J B Cutting Inc* ***(G-11135)***
McPhails Pallets Inc ... 810 384-6458
9871 Bryce Rd Kenockee (48006) ***(G-8985)***
McPp-Detroit, LLC, Warren *Also called Mitsubishi Chls Perf Plyrs Inc* ***(G-17157)***
MCS Consultants Inc ... 810 229-4222
1347 Rickett Rd Brighton (48116) ***(G-1958)***
MCS Custom Design, Westland *Also called Mikes Cabinet Shop Inc* ***(G-17580)***
MCS Industries Inc ... 517 568-4161
124 W Platt St Homer (49245) ***(G-7946)***
MD Hiller Corp ... 877 751-9010
2021 Monroe St Ste 103 Dearborn (48124) ***(G-3737)***
Mdc, Bingham Farms *Also called Master Data Center Inc* ***(G-1656)***

ALPHABETIC

Mdg Commercial Kitchen LLC 269 207-1344
2312 Hemlock Ave Portage (49024) ***(G-13015)***
Mdhearingaid, Southfield *Also called SC Industries Inc* ***(G-15023)***
Mdm Enterprises Inc 616 452-1591
3829 Roger B Chaffee Mem Grand Rapids (49548) ***(G-6655)***
Mead Johnson & Company LLC 616 748-7100
725 E Main Ave Zeeland (49464) ***(G-18162)***
Mead Westvaco Paper Div 906 233-2362
1800 20th Ave N Escanaba (49829) ***(G-4841)***
Meal and More Incorporated 517 625-3186
130 W 3rd Ave Morrice (48857) ***(G-11121)***
Mean Erectors Inc 989 737-3285
1928 Wilson Ave Saginaw (48638) ***(G-14085)***
Means Industries Inc (HQ) 989 754-1433
3715 E Washington Rd Saginaw (48601) ***(G-14086)***
Means Industries Inc 989 754-3300
1860 S Jefferson Ave Saginaw (48601) ***(G-14087)***
Measuring Tool Services 734 261-1107
8984 Russell St Livonia (48150) ***(G-9835)***
Meca-Systeme Usa Inc 616 843-5566
101 Washington Ave Grand Haven (49417) ***(G-6055)***
Mecaplast Usa LLC 248 594-8082
19575 Victor Pkwy Ste 400 Livonia (48152) ***(G-9836)***
Meccom Corporation 313 895-4900
5945 Martin St Detroit (48210) ***(G-4224)***
Meccom Industrial Products Co 586 463-2828
22797 Morelli Dr Clinton Township (48036) ***(G-3172)***
Mechanical Air System Inc 248 346-7995
1994 Dorchester Dr Commerce Township (48390) ***(G-3429)***
Mechanical Engineer, Troy *Also called Tata Autocomp Systems Limited* ***(G-16632)***
Mechanical Fabricators Inc 810 765-8853
770 Degurse Ave Marine City (48039) ***(G-10477)***
Mechanical Products Co, Jackson *Also called Mp Hollywood LLC* ***(G-8537)***
Mechanical Sheet Metal Co 734 284-1006
723 Walnut St Wyandotte (48192) ***(G-17967)***
Mechanical Supply A Division 906 789-0355
1701 N 26th St Escanaba (49829) ***(G-4842)***
Mechanical Transplanter Co LLC 616 396-8738
1150 Central Ave Holland (49423) ***(G-7742)***
Mectron Engineering Co Inc 734 944-8777
400 S Industrial Dr Saline (48176) ***(G-14400)***
Med Share Inc 888 266-3567
1039 Washington St Dearborn (48124) ***(G-3738)***
Med-Kas Hydraulics Inc 248 585-3220
1419 John R Rd Troy (48083) ***(G-16491)***
Med-Tek, Troy *Also called Tilco Inc* ***(G-16643)***
Medallion Instrumentation 616 847-3700
17150 Hickory St Spring Lake (49456) ***(G-15161)***
Medbio Inc (PA) 616 245-0214
5346 36th St Se Grand Rapids (49512) ***(G-6656)***
Media Solutions Inc 313 831-3152
4715 Woodward Ave Fl 2 Detroit (48201) ***(G-4225)***
Media Swing LLC 313 885-2525
14 Radnor Cir Grosse Pointe Farms (48236) ***(G-7186)***
Media Tecnologies, Eaton Rapids *Also called Hoag & Sons Book Bindery Inc* ***(G-4726)***
Mediaform LLC 248 548-0260
623 E 6th St Royal Oak (48067) ***(G-13950)***
Mediatechnologies, Shelby *Also called Silver Street Incorporated* ***(G-14536)***
Medical ACC & Reseach Co, Zeeland *Also called Artisan Medical Displays LLC* ***(G-18113)***
Medical Cmfort Specialists LLC 810 229-4222
919 Garden Ln Fowlerville (48836) ***(G-5575)***
Medical Engineering & Dev 517 563-2352
4910 Dancer Rd Horton (49246) ***(G-7969)***
Medical Infrmtics Slutions LLC 248 851-3124
7285 Cathedral Dr Bloomfield Hills (48301) ***(G-1781)***
Medical Laser Group, Oxford *Also called Medical Laser Resources LLC* ***(G-12360)***
Medical Laser Resources LLC 248 628-8120
610 Gallagher Ct Oxford (48371) ***(G-12360)***
Medical Product Manufacturer, Ann Arbor *Also called Tissue Seal LLC* ***(G-675)***
Medical Systems Resource Group 248 476-5400
26105 Orchard Lake Rd Farmington Hills (48334) ***(G-5061)***
Medimage Inc 734 665-5400
331 Metty Dr Ste 1 Ann Arbor (48103) ***(G-551)***
Medisurge LLC 888 307-1144
333 Bridge St Nw Ste 1125 Grand Rapids (49504) ***(G-6657)***
Medsker Electric Inc 248 855-3383
28650 Grand River Ave Farmington Hills (48336) ***(G-5062)***
Medtest Dx Inc 866 540-2715
5449 Research Dr Canton (48188) ***(G-2400)***
Medtronic Inc 248 349-6987
41850 W 11 Mile Rd Novi (48375) ***(G-11943)***
Medtronic Inc 616 643-5200
620 Watson St Sw Grand Rapids (49504) ***(G-6658)***
Medtronic Inc 616 643-5200
520 Watson St Sw Grand Rapids (49504) ***(G-6659)***
Medtronic Usa Inc 248 449-5027
39555 Orchard Hill Pl # 500 Novi (48375) ***(G-11944)***
Medusa's Antidote, Detroit *Also called Nicole Acarter LLC* ***(G-4270)***
Meeders Dim & Lbr Pdts Co 231 587-8611
7810 S M 88 Hwy Mancelona (49659) ***(G-10394)***
Meeders Lumber Co 231 587-8611
7810 S M 88 Hwy Mancelona (49659) ***(G-10395)***
Mega Mania Diversions LLC 888 322-9076
3747 Loch Bend Dr Commerce Township (48382) ***(G-3430)***
MEGA Precast Inc 586 477-5959
14670 23 Mile Rd Shelby Township (48315) ***(G-14637)***
Mega Printing Inc 248 624-6065
1600 W West Maple Rd D Walled Lake (48390) ***(G-16898)***
Mega Screen Corp 517 849-7057
549 Industrial Pkwy Jonesville (49250) ***(G-8663)***
Mega Wall Inc 616 647-4190
5340 6 Mile Ct Nw Comstock Park (49321) ***(G-3499)***
Megaplast North America, Shelby Township *Also called Moller Group North America Inc* ***(G-14647)***
Megapro Marketing Usa Inc 866 522-3652
2710 S 3rd St Niles (49120) ***(G-11625)***
Megee Print Document Solutions, Kalamazoo *Also called Megee Printing Inc* ***(G-8820)***
Megee Printing Inc 269 344-3226
509 Mills St Kalamazoo (49001) ***(G-8820)***
Meh Logging Co, Nashville *Also called Mike Hughes* ***(G-11461)***
Mehring Books Inc 248 967-2924
25900 Greenfield Rd # 258 Oak Park (48237) ***(G-12083)***
Meiden America Inc (HQ) 734 459-1781
15800 Centennial Dr Northville (48168) ***(G-11709)***
Meiers Signs Inc 906 786-3424
1717 N Lincoln Rd Escanaba (49829) ***(G-4843)***
Meijer Inc 269 556-2400
5019 Red Arrow Hwy Stevensville (49127) ***(G-15577)***
Meiki Corporation 248 680-4638
200 E Big Beaver Rd Troy (48083) ***(G-16492)***
Meints Glass Blowing 269 349-1958
436 N Park St Ste 119 Kalamazoo (49007) ***(G-8821)***
Mejenta Systems Inc 248 434-2583
30233 Southfield Rd # 113 Southfield (48076) ***(G-14977)***
Mel Media Group, Taylor *Also called Mel Printing Co Inc* ***(G-15738)***
Mel Printing Co Inc 313 928-5440
6000 Pardee Rd Taylor (48180) ***(G-15738)***
Melange Computer Services Inc 517 321-8434
808 Century Blvd Ste 100 Lansing (48917) ***(G-9310)***
Melco Dctg & Furn Restoration 989 723-3335
526 N Dewey St Owosso (48867) ***(G-12303)***
Melco Engraving Inc 248 656-9000
1800 Production Dr Rochester Hills (48309) ***(G-13471)***
Melco Interior, Owosso *Also called Melco Dctg & Furn Restoration* ***(G-12303)***
Melix Services Inc 248 387-9303
2359 Livernois Rd Ste 300 Hamtramck (48212) ***(G-7244)***
Mellemas Cut Stone 616 984-2493
16610 Findley Dr Sand Lake (49343) ***(G-14424)***
Melling Automotive Products, Jackson *Also called Melling Tool Co* ***(G-8514)***
Melling Industries Inc 517 787-8172
2620 Saradan Dr Jackson (49202) ***(G-8512)***
Melling Manufacturing Inc 517 750-3580
4901 James Mcdevitt St Jackson (49201) ***(G-8513)***
Melling Products North LLC 989 588-6147
333 Grace St Farwell (48622) ***(G-5164)***
Melling Tool Co (PA) 517 787-8172
2620 Saradan Dr Jackson (49202) ***(G-8514)***
Mello Meats Inc (PA) 800 852-5019
270 Rex Blvd Auburn Hills (48326) ***(G-945)***
Melody Digiglio 586 754-4405
8088 E 9 Mile Rd Warren (48089) ***(G-17147)***
Melody Farms LLC 734 261-7980
31770 Enterprise Dr Livonia (48150) ***(G-9837)***
Meltex, Benton Harbor *Also called Martin Bros Mill Fndry Sup Co* ***(G-1525)***
Memcon North America LLC 269 281-0478
6000 Red Arrow Hwy Unit I Stevensville (49127) ***(G-15578)***
Memories Manor 810 329-2800
613 N Riverside Ave Saint Clair (48079) ***(G-14228)***
Memtech Inc (PA) 734 455-8550
9033 General Dr Plymouth (48170) ***(G-12689)***
Memtron Technologies Co 989 652-2656
530 N Franklin St Frankenmuth (48734) ***(G-5593)***
Men of Steel Inc 989 635-4866
2920 Municipal Dr Marlette (48453) ***(G-10501)***
Menasha Packaging Company LLC 800 253-1526
238 N West St Coloma (49038) ***(G-3361)***
Mendenhall Associates Inc 734 741-4710
1500 Cedar Bend Dr Ann Arbor (48105) ***(G-552)***
Mendota Mantels LLC 651 271-7544
E6638 Maple Creek Rd Ironwood (49938) ***(G-8335)***
Mendoza Enterprises 248 792-9120
6905 Telegraph Rd Ste 117 Bloomfield Hills (48301) ***(G-1782)***
Mennel Milling Co of Mich Inc 269 782-5175
301 S Mill St Dowagiac (49047) ***(G-4550)***
Menominee Acquisition Corp 906 863-5595
144 1st St Menominee (49858) ***(G-10745)***

Menominee Carbide Cutting Tls, Menominee *Also called Menominee Saw and Supply Co* ***(G-10747)***
Menominee City of Michigan 906 863-3050
1301 5th Ave Menominee (49858) ***(G-10746)***
Menominee Cnty Jurnl Print Sp 906 753-2296
S322 Menominee St Stephenson (49887) ***(G-15237)***
Menominee Saw and Supply Co (PA) 906 863-2609
900 16th St Menominee (49858) ***(G-10747)***
Menominee Saw and Supply Co 906 863-8998
2134 13th St Menominee (49858) ***(G-10748)***
Menomnee Rver Lbr Dmnsions LLC 906 863-2682
2219 10th Ave Menominee (49858) ***(G-10749)***
Mensch Manufacturing LLC 269 945-5300
2333 S M 37 Hwy Hastings (49058) ***(G-7420)***
Mensch Mfg Mar Div Inc 269 945-5300
2499 S M 37 Hwy Hastings (49058) ***(G-7421)***
Menu Pulse Inc 989 708-1207
1901 Kollen St Saginaw (48602) ***(G-14088)***
Merc-O-Tronic Instruments Corp 586 894-9529
215 Branch St Almont (48003) ***(G-263)***
Mercedes-Benz Extra LLC 205 747-8006
36455 Corp Dr Ste 175 Farmington Hills (48331) ***(G-5063)***
Merchandising Productions 616 676-6000
7575 Fulton St E Ada (49356) ***(G-23)***
Merchant Holdings Inc 906 786-7120
440 N 10th St Escanaba (49829) ***(G-4844)***
Merchants Automatic Pdts Inc 734 829-0020
5740 S Beck Rd Canton (48188) ***(G-2401)***
Merchants Industries Inc 734 397-3031
5715 S Sheldon Rd Canton (48188) ***(G-2402)***
Merchants Metals Inc 810 227-3036
830 Grand Oaks Dr Howell (48843) ***(G-8061)***
Mercury Displacement Inds Inc 269 663-8574
25028 Us 12 E Edwardsburg (49112) ***(G-4766)***
Mercury Drugs LLC 248 545-3600
22150 Coolidge Hwy Oak Park (48237) ***(G-12084)***
Mercury Manufacturing Company 734 285-5150
1212 Grove St Wyandotte (48192) ***(G-17968)***
Mercury Stamping Div, Saint Johns *Also called Lupaul Industries Inc* ***(G-14286)***
Mercy Health Partners (HQ) 231 728-4032
1675 Leahy St Ste 101 Muskegon (49442) ***(G-11373)***
Mercy Health Partners 231 672-4886
1560 E Sherman Blvd # 145 Muskegon (49444) ***(G-11374)***
Merdel Game Manufacturing Co 231 845-1263
218 E Dowland St Ludington (49431) ***(G-10071)***
Meredith Lea Sand Gravel 517 930-3662
6703 Lansing Rd Charlotte (48813) ***(G-2659)***
Merhow Acquisition LLC 269 483-0010
617 S Miller Rd White Pigeon (49099) ***(G-17653)***
Merhow Industries, White Pigeon *Also called Merhow Acquisition LLC* ***(G-17653)***
Meridian Contg & Excvtg LLC 734 476-5933
5520 Huron Hills Dr Commerce Township (48382) ***(G-3431)***
Meridian Energy Corporation 517 339-8444
6009 Marsh Rd Haslett (48840) ***(G-7397)***
Meridian Lightweight Tech, Plymouth *Also called Magnesium Products America Inc* ***(G-12681)***
Meridian Lightweight Tech Inc 248 663-8100
47805 Galleon Dr Ste B Plymouth (48170) ***(G-12690)***
Meridian Mechatronics LLC 517 447-4587
120 W Keegan St Deerfield (49238) ***(G-3813)***
Meridian Reclamation, Commerce Township *Also called Meridian Contg & Excvtg LLC* ***(G-3431)***
Meridian Screen Prtg & Design, Okemos *Also called Meridian Screen Prtg & Design* ***(G-12130)***
Meridian Screen Prtg & Design 517 351-2525
3362 Hulett Rd Okemos (48864) ***(G-12130)***
Meridian Weekly, The, Ovid *Also called Hometown Publishing Inc* ***(G-12272)***
Meridianrx LLC 855 323-4580
1 Campus Martius Ste 750 Detroit (48226) ***(G-4226)***
Merillat Cabinets, Ann Arbor *Also called Masco Cabinetry LLC* ***(G-545)***
Merillat Industries LLC 517 263-0269
5353 W Us Highway 223 Adrian (49221) ***(G-79)***
Merillat LP (HQ) 517 263-0771
5353 W Us Highway 223 Adrian (49221) ***(G-80)***
Merit Energy Company 989 685-3446
749 E Hughes Lake Rd Rose City (48654) ***(G-13764)***
Merit Energy Company LLC 231 258-6401
1510 E Thomas Rd Kalkaska (49646) ***(G-8950)***
Merit Tech Worldwide LLC (HQ) 734 927-9520
7261 Commerce Blvd Canton (48187) ***(G-2403)***
Meritor Inc (PA) 248 435-1000
2135 W Maple Rd Troy (48084) ***(G-16493)***
Meritor Heavy Vhcl Systems LLC (HQ) 248 435-1000
2135 W Maple Rd Troy (48084) ***(G-16494)***
Meritor Indus Aftermarket LLC 248 658-7345
1400 Rochester Rd Troy (48083) ***(G-16495)***
Meritor Indus Intl Hldings LLC, Troy *Also called Meritor Industrial Pdts LLC* ***(G-16497)***
Meritor Indus Intl Hldings LLC 248 658-7345
1400 Rochester Rd Troy (48083) ***(G-16496)***
Meritor Industrial Pdts LLC (HQ) 248 658-7200
1400 Rochester Rd Troy (48083) ***(G-16497)***
Meritor Intl Holdings LLC (HQ) 248 435-1000
2135 W Maple Rd Troy (48084) ***(G-16498)***
Meritor Specialty Products LLC 248 435-1000
12623 Newburgh Rd Livonia (48150) ***(G-9838)***
Meritor Specialty Products LLC 517 545-5800
1045 Durant Dr Howell (48843) ***(G-8062)***
Meritt Tool & Die 517 726-1452
2354 N Pease Rd Vermontville (49096) ***(G-16822)***
Merlin Simulation Inc 703 560-7203
2135 Bishop Cir E Ste 6 Dexter (48130) ***(G-4498)***
Merrifield McHy Solutions Inc 248 494-7335
1651 Highwood E Pontiac (48340) ***(G-12848)***
Merrill Aviation & Defense, Saginaw *Also called Merrill Technologies Group* ***(G-14089)***
Merrill Fabricators, Alma *Also called Merrill Technologies Group Inc* ***(G-241)***
Merrill Institute Inc 989 462-0330
520 Republic Ave Alma (48801) ***(G-240)***
Merrill Technologies Group 989 921-1490
1023 S Wheeler St Saginaw (48602) ***(G-14089)***
Merrill Technologies Group Inc (PA) 989 791-6676
400 Florence St Saginaw (48602) ***(G-14090)***
Merrill Technologies Group Inc 989 462-0330
520 Republic Ave Alma (48801) ***(G-241)***
Merrill Technologies Group Inc 989 643-7981
21659 Gratiot Rd Merrill (48637) ***(G-10760)***
Merrill Tool & Machine, Merrill *Also called Merrill Technologies Group Inc* ***(G-10760)***
Merrill Tool Holding Company, Saginaw *Also called Merrill Technologies Group Inc* ***(G-14090)***
Merriman Products Inc 517 787-1825
1302 W Ganson St Jackson (49202) ***(G-8515)***
Merritt Press Inc 517 394-0118
6534 Aurelius Rd Lansing (48911) ***(G-9396)***
Merritt Raceway LLC 231 590-4431
7300 N Maple Valley Rd Ne Mancelona (49659) ***(G-10396)***
Mersen 989 894-2911
900 Harrison St Bay City (48708) ***(G-1329)***
Mersen USA Bay City-MI LLC 989 894-2911
900 Harrison St Bay City (48708) ***(G-1330)***
Mersen USA Greenville-Mi Corp 616 754-5671
712 Industrial Park Dr Greenville (48838) ***(G-7146)***
Mesick Mold Co 231 885-1304
4901 Industrial Dr Mesick (49668) ***(G-10771)***
Messenger Printing & Copy Svc 616 669-5620
5300 Plaza Ave Hudsonville (49426) ***(G-8166)***
Messenger Printing Service 313 381-0300
20136 Ecorse Rd Taylor (48180) ***(G-15739)***
Messersmith Manufacturing Inc 906 466-9010
2612 F Rd Bark River (49807) ***(G-1121)***
Messina Concrete Inc 734 783-1020
14675 Telegraph Rd Flat Rock (48134) ***(G-5357)***
Met Inc 231 845-1737
640 S Pere Marquette Hwy Ludington (49431) ***(G-10072)***
Met-L-Tec LLC (PA) 734 847-7004
7310 Express Rd Temperance (48182) ***(G-15837)***
Met-Pro Technologies LLC 989 725-8184
1172 S M 13 Lennon (48449) ***(G-9518)***
Meta4mat LLC 616 214-7418
320 Dodge Rd Ne Ste B Comstock Park (49321) ***(G-3500)***
Metabolic Solutions Dev Co LLC 269 343-6732
161 E Michigan Ave Fl 4 Kalamazoo (49007) ***(G-8822)***
Metal Arc Inc 231 865-3111
3792 E Ellis Rd Muskegon (49444) ***(G-11375)***
Metal Components LLC (PA) 616 252-1900
3281 Roger B Grand Rapids (49548) ***(G-6660)***
Metal Components Employment 616 252-1900
3281 Rog B Chaffee Mem Dr Grand Rapids (49548) ***(G-6661)***
Metal Craft Impression Die, Livonia *Also called Metalcraft Impression Die Co* ***(G-9839)***
Metal Fab Tool & Machine, Mio *Also called Metalfab Tool & Machine Inc* ***(G-11005)***
Metal Fbrication Machining Div, Fennville *Also called Harrington Construction Co* ***(G-5173)***
Metal Finishing Quotecom LLC 248 890-1096
10799 Plaza Dr Whitmore Lake (48189) ***(G-17703)***
Metal Finishing Technology 231 733-9736
2652 Hoyt St Muskegon (49444) ***(G-11376)***
Metal Flow Corporation 616 392-7976
11694 James St Holland (49424) ***(G-7743)***
Metal Forming & Coining Corp 586 731-2003
51810 Danview Tech Ct Shelby Township (48315) ***(G-14638)***
Metal Forming Technology Inc 586 949-4586
48630 Structural Dr Chesterfield (48051) ***(G-2803)***
Metal Improvement Company LLC 734 728-8600
30100 Cypress Rd Romulus (48174) ***(G-13705)***
Metal Mart USA Inc 586 977-5820
31164 Dequindre Rd Warren (48092) ***(G-17148)***
Metal Mates Inc (PA) 248 646-9831
20135 Elwood St Beverly Hills (48025) ***(G-1618)***
Metal Mechanics Inc 269 679-2525
350 S 14th St Schoolcraft (49087) ***(G-14499)***

ALPHABETIC

Metal Merchants of Michigan 248 293-0621
2691 Leach Rd Rochester Hills (48309) ***(G-13472)***
Metal Prep Technology Inc 313 843-2890
621 Nightingale St Dearborn (48128) ***(G-3739)***
Metal Punch Corporation 231 775-8391
907 Saunders St Cadillac (49601) ***(G-2264)***
Metal Quest Inc 989 733-2011
11739 M68-33 Hwy Onaway (49765) ***(G-12147)***
Metal Sales Manufacturing Corp 989 686-5879
5209 Mackinaw Rd Bay City (48706) ***(G-1331)***
Metal Standard Corp 616 396-6356
286 Hedcor St Holland (49423) ***(G-7744)***
Metal Stmping Spport Group LLC 586 777-7440
16660 E 13 Mile Rd Roseville (48066) ***(G-13834)***
Metal Tech Products Inc 313 533-5277
15720 Dale St Detroit (48223) ***(G-4227)***
Metal Technologies Inc 231 853-0300
3800 Adams Rd Ravenna (49451) ***(G-13124)***
Metal Technologies Indiana Inc 269 278-1765
429 4th St Three Rivers (49093) ***(G-15870)***
Metal Technologies Trg, Three Rivers *Also called Metal Technologies Indiana Inc* ***(G-15870)***
Metal Treat, Jackson *Also called Michner Plating Company* ***(G-8521)***
Metal Worxs Inc 586 484-9355
7374 Flamingo St Clay (48001) ***(G-2999)***
Metal-Line Corp 231 723-7041
2708 9th St Muskegon (49444) ***(G-11377)***
Metalbuilt LLC 586 786-9106
50171 E Russell Schmdt Bl Chesterfield (48051) ***(G-2804)***
Metalbuilt Tactical LLC 586 786-9106
51820 Regency Center Dr Macomb (48042) ***(G-10141)***
Metalcraft Impression Die Co 734 513-8058
11914 Brookfield St Livonia (48150) ***(G-9839)***
Metaldyne LLC (HQ) 734 207-6200
1 Dauch Dr Detroit (48211) ***(G-4228)***
Metaldyne Prfmce Group Inc (HQ) 248 727-1800
1 Towne Sq Ste 550 Southfield (48076) ***(G-14978)***
Metaldyne Pwrtrain Cmpnnts Inc 517 542-5555
917 Anderson Rd Litchfield (49252) ***(G-9607)***
Metaldyne Pwrtrain Cmpnnts Inc 517 542-5555
917 Anderson Rd Litchfield (49252) ***(G-9608)***
Metaldyne Pwrtrain Cmpnnts Inc (HQ) 313 758-2000
1 Dauch Dr Detroit (48211) ***(G-4229)***
Metaldyne Sintered Components 734 207-6200
47603 Halyard Dr Plymouth (48170) ***(G-12691)***
Metaldyne Tblar Components LLC 248 727-1800
1 Towne Sq Ste 550 Southfield (48076) ***(G-14979)***
Metalfab Inc (PA) 313 381-7579
6900 Chase Rd Dearborn (48126) ***(G-3740)***
Metalfab Manufacturing Inc 989 826-2301
378 Booth Rd Mio (48647) ***(G-11004)***
Metalfab Tool & Machine Inc 989 826-6044
55 W Kittle Rd Mio (48647) ***(G-11005)***
Metalform Industries LLC 248 462-0056
52830 Tuscany Grv Shelby Township (48315) ***(G-14639)***
Metalform LLC 517 569-3313
2223 Rives Eaton Rd Jackson (49201) ***(G-8516)***
Metallist Inc 517 437-4476
200 Development Dr Hillsdale (49242) ***(G-7530)***
Metallurgical High Vacuum Corp 269 543-4291
6708 124th Ave Fennville (49408) ***(G-5175)***
Metallurgical Processing Co., Warren *Also called Metallurgical Processing LLC* ***(G-17149)***
Metallurgical Processing LLC 586 758-3100
23075 Warner Ave Warren (48091) ***(G-17149)***
Metalmite Corporation 248 651-9415
194 S Elizabeth St Rochester (48307) ***(G-13334)***
Metals Division, Benton Harbor *Also called Siemens Industry Inc* ***(G-1547)***
Metals Preservation Group LLC 586 944-2720
20420 Stephens St Saint Clair Shores (48080) ***(G-14263)***
Metalsa SA De Cv, Sterling Heights *Also called Metalsa Structural Pdts Inc* ***(G-15416)***
Metalsa Structural Pdts Inc 248 669-3704
40117 Mitchell Dr Sterling Heights (48313) ***(G-15416)***
Metalsa Structural Pdts Inc (HQ) 248 669-3704
29545 Hudson Dr Novi (48377) ***(G-11945)***
Metaltec Steel Abrasive Co (HQ) 734 459-7900
41155 Joy Rd Canton (48187) ***(G-2404)***
Metalution Tool Die 616 355-9700
60 W 64th St Holland (49423) ***(G-7745)***
Metalworking Lubricants Co (PA) 248 332-3500
25 W Silverdome Indus Par Pontiac (48342) ***(G-12849)***
Metalworks Inc (PA) 231 845-5136
902 4th St Ludington (49431) ***(G-10073)***
Metaris Hydraulics 586 949-4240
48175 Gratiot Ave Chesterfield (48051) ***(G-2805)***
Metavation LLC (HQ) 248 351-1000
900 Wilshire Dr Ste 270 Troy (48084) ***(G-16499)***
Metcalf Machine Inc 616 837-8128
6439 Rollenhagen Rd Ravenna (49451) ***(G-13125)***
Meteor Web Marketing Inc 734 822-4999
3438 E Ellsworth Rd Ste A Ann Arbor (48108) ***(G-553)***
Meter Devices Company Inc 330 455-0301
23847 Industrial Park Dr Farmington Hills (48335) ***(G-5064)***
Meter of America Inc 810 216-6074
920 Military St 1 Port Huron (48060) ***(G-12940)***
Meter USA LLC 810 388-9373
1765 Michigan Ave Marysville (48040) ***(G-10607)***
Method Technology Service LLC (PA) 312 622-7697
100 W Big Beavr Rd # 200 Troy (48084) ***(G-16500)***
Method Tool, Saint Charles *Also called MTI Precision Machining Inc* ***(G-14197)***
Methods Machine Tools Inc 248 624-8601
50531 Varsity Ct Wixom (48393) ***(G-17854)***
Metra Inc 248 543-3500
24211 John R Rd Hazel Park (48030) ***(G-7443)***
Metrex Research LLC 734 947-6700
28210 Wick Rd Romulus (48174) ***(G-13706)***
Metric Hydrulic Components LLC 586 786-6990
13870 Cavaliere Dr Shelby Township (48315) ***(G-14640)***
Metric Manufacturing Co Inc 616 897-5959
1001 Foreman St Lowell (49331) ***(G-10037)***
Metric Tool Company Inc 313 369-9610
17144 Mount Elliott St Detroit (48212) ***(G-4230)***
Metrie Inc 313 299-1860
27025 Trolley Indus Dr Taylor (48180) ***(G-15740)***
Metro Broach Inc 586 758-2340
2160 E 9 Mile Rd Warren (48091) ***(G-17150)***
Metro Cast Corporation 734 728-0210
6170 Commerce Dr Westland (48185) ***(G-17579)***
Metro Duct Inc 517 783-2646
485 E South St Jackson (49203) ***(G-8517)***
Metro Engrg of Grnd Rapids 616 458-2823
845 Ottawa Ave Nw Grand Rapids (49503) ***(G-6662)***
Metro Graphic Arts Inc 616 245-2271
900 40th St Se Grand Rapids (49508) ***(G-6663)***
Metro Machine Works Inc 734 941-4571
11977 Harrison Romulus (48174) ***(G-13707)***
Metro Medical Eqp Mfg Inc 734 522-8400
38415 Schoolcraft Rd Livonia (48150) ***(G-9840)***
Metro Parent Media Group, Ferndale *Also called All Kids Considered Publishing* ***(G-5257)***
Metro Piping Inc 313 872-4330
1500b Trombly St Detroit (48211) ***(G-4231)***
Metro Printing Service Inc 248 545-4444
1950 Barrett Dr Troy (48084) ***(G-16501)***
Metro Prints Inc 586 979-9690
5580 Gatewood Dr Ste 103 Sterling Heights (48310) ***(G-15417)***
Metro Promotional Specialties, Troy *Also called Metro Printing Service Inc* ***(G-16501)***
Metro Rebar Inc 248 851-5894
4275 Middlebelt Rd West Bloomfield (48323) ***(G-17484)***
Metro Sign Fabricators Inc 586 493-0502
43984 N Groesbeck Hwy Clinton Township (48036) ***(G-3173)***
Metro Stamping & Mfg Co 313 538-6464
26955 Fullerton Redford (48239) ***(G-13173)***
Metro Technologies Ltd 248 528-9240
1462 E Big Beaver Rd Troy (48083) ***(G-16502)***
Metro Times Inc 313 961-4060
1200 Woodward Hts Ferndale (48220) ***(G-5301)***
Metro Turn Inc 313 937-1904
12081 Farley Redford (48239) ***(G-13174)***
Metro Wbe Associates Inc 248 504-7563
18353 W Mcnichols Rd Detroit (48219) ***(G-4232)***
Metro-Fabricating LLC 989 667-8100
1650 Tech Dr Bay City (48706) ***(G-1332)***
Metronom US, Ann Arbor *Also called Inora Technologies Inc* ***(G-506)***
Metropolitan Alloys Corp 313 366-4443
17385 Ryan Rd Detroit (48212) ***(G-4233)***
Metropolitan Baking Company 313 875-7246
8579 Lumpkin St Detroit (48212) ***(G-4234)***
Metropolitan Indus Lithography 269 323-9333
1116 W Centre Ave Portage (49024) ***(G-13016)***
Metropoulos Amplification Inc 810 614-3905
10460 N Holly Rd Holly (48442) ***(G-7888)***
Mettek LLC 616 895-2033
11480 53rd Ave Ste B Allendale (49401) ***(G-222)***
Metter Flooring LLC 517 914-2004
2531 W Territorial Rd Rives Junction (49277) ***(G-13309)***
Metter Flooring and Cnstr, Rives Junction *Also called Metter Flooring LLC* ***(G-13309)***
Mettes Printery Inc 734 261-6262
27454 Plymouth Rd Livonia (48150) ***(G-9841)***
Mettle Craft Manufacturing LLC 586 306-8962
3223 15 Mile Rd Sterling Heights (48310) ***(G-15418)***
Metzeler Auto Profile Systems, Auburn Hills *Also called Henniges Auto Sling Systems N* ***(G-897)***
Metzgar Conveyor Co 616 784-0930
5801 Clay Ave Sw Ste A Grand Rapids (49548) ***(G-6664)***
Metzger Sawmill 269 963-3022
3100 W Halbert Rd Battle Creek (49017) ***(G-1227)***
Mexamerica Foods LLC 814 781-1447
219 Canton St Sw Ste A Grand Rapids (49507) ***(G-6665)***
Mexican Food Specialties Inc 734 779-2370
21084 Bridge St Southfield (48033) ***(G-14980)***

Mexico Express 313 843-6717
7611 W Vernor Hwy Detroit (48209) *(G-4235)*
Meyer Wood Products 269 657-3450
32180 E Red Arrow Hwy Paw Paw (49079) *(G-12409)*
Meyers Boat Company Inc 517 265-9821
343 Lawrence Ave Adrian (49221) *(G-81)*
Meyers John 989 236-5400
5752 Cleveland Rd Middleton (48856) *(G-10793)*
Meyers Metal Fab Inc 248 620-5411
9665 Northwest Ct Clarkston (48346) *(G-2937)*
Meyers Metal Fabrications Co, Clarkston *Also called Meyers Metal Fab Inc (G-2937)*
Mfp Automation Engineering Inc 616 538-5700
4404 Central Pkwy Hudsonville (49426) *(G-8167)*
MGR Molds Inc 586 254-6020
6450 Cotter Ave Sterling Heights (48314) *(G-15419)*
Mh Industries Ltd 734 261-7560
6960 Orchard Lake Rd # 301 West Bloomfield (48322) *(G-17485)*
Mhr Inc 616 394-0191
78 Veterans Dr Holland (49423) *(G-7746)*
MHR Investments Inc 989 832-5395
601 S Saginaw Rd Midland (48640) *(G-10884)*
MI Brew LLC 616 361-9658
321 Northland Dr Ne Rockford (49341) *(G-13579)*
MI Custom Signs LLC 734 946-7446
20109 Northline Rd Taylor (48180) *(G-15741)*
MI Dynaco, Kingston *Also called Midynaco LLC (G-9073)*
MI Frozen Food LLC 231 357-4334
33 Lake St Manistee (49660) *(G-10430)*
MI News 26 ....231 577-1844
320 W 13th St Cadillac (49601) *(G-2265)*
Mi-Tech Tooling Inc 989 912-2440
6215 Garfield Ave Cass City (48726) *(G-2519)*
Mi030, Cheboygan *Also called Cheboygan Housing Commission (G-2679)*
Miba Hydramechanica Corp 586 264-3094
6625 Cobb Dr Sterling Heights (48312) *(G-15420)*
Mibiz, Norton Shores *Also called News One Inc (G-11780)*
Mica Crafters Inc 517 548-2924
1400 Old Pinckney Rd Howell (48843) *(G-8063)*
Mica TEC Inc 586 758-4404
21325 Hoover Rd Warren (48089) *(G-17151)*
Miccus Inc 616 604-4449
3336 Lakewood Shores Dr Howell (48843) *(G-8064)*
Michael Anderson 231 652-5717
4933 E Croton Dr Newaygo (49337) *(G-11575)*
Michael Chris Storms 231 263-7516
1401 W Center Rd Kingsley (49649) *(G-9072)*
Michael Engineering Ltd 989 772-4073
5625 Venture Way Mount Pleasant (48858) *(G-11204)*
Michael Graves Logging 906 387-2852
N3293 Buckhorn Rd Wetmore (49895) *(G-17615)*
Michael Nadeau Cabinet Making 989 356-0229
4357 M 32 W Alpena (49707) *(G-298)*
Michael Niederpruem 231 935-0241
880 Lake Dr Ne Kalkaska (49646) *(G-8951)*
Michael R Burzynski 989 732-1820
1636 Big Lake Rd Gaylord (49735) *(G-5881)*
Michael Schafer and Associates, Wixom *Also called Midwest Sales Associates Inc (G-17855)*
Michael-Stephens Company 248 583-7767
1206 E Maple Rd Troy (48083) *(G-16503)*
Michaelene's Gourmet Granola, Clarkston *Also called Michaelenes Inc (G-2938)*
Michaelenes Inc 248 625-0156
7415 Deer Forest Ct Clarkston (48348) *(G-2938)*
Michalski Enterprises Inc 517 703-0777
16733 Industrial Pkwy Lansing (48906) *(G-9245)*
Michalski Wilbert Vault Co, Pickford *Also called Robinson Fence Co Inc (G-12483)*
Michcor Container Inc 616 452-7089
1151 Sheldon Ave Se Grand Rapids (49507) *(G-6666)*
Michelle's Restaurant, Harper Woods *Also called Sweetheart Bakery of Michigan (G-7306)*
Michels Inc (PA) 313 441-3620
18900 Michigan Ave K103 Dearborn (48126) *(G-3741)*
Michiana Aggregate Inc 269 695-7669
3265 W Us Highway 12 Niles (49120) *(G-11626)*
Michiana Corrugated Pdts Co 269 651-5225
110 N Franks Ave Sturgis (49091) *(G-15617)*
Michigan Acdemy Fmly Physcians 517 347-0098
2164 Commons Pkwy Okemos (48864) *(G-12131)*
Michigan Adhesive Mfg Inc 616 850-0507
14851 Michael Ln Spring Lake (49456) *(G-15162)*
Michigan AG Services Inc (PA) 616 374-8803
3587 W Tupper Lake Rd Lake Odessa (48849) *(G-9117)*
Michigan Aggr Sand/Gravel Haul 231 258-8237
765 Rabourn Rd Ne Kalkaska (49646) *(G-8952)*
Michigan Agricultural Fuel 419 490-6599
2411 Santigo Ave Se Grand Rapids (49546) *(G-6667)*
Michigan Aluminum Extrusion 517 764-5400
205 Watts Rd Jackson (49203) *(G-8518)*
Michigan Ammo LLC 313 383-4430
4680 High St Detroit (48229) *(G-4236)*
Michigan Apple Packers Coop 616 887-9933
10740 Peach Tree Sparta (49345) *(G-15102)*
Michigan ATF Holdings LLC (HQ) 734 941-2220
11850 Wayne Rd Romulus (48174) *(G-13708)*
Michigan Auto Bending Corp 248 528-1150
1700 E 14 Mile Rd Madison Heights (48071) *(G-10304)*
Michigan Auto Comprsr Inc (HQ) 517 796-3200
2400 N Dearing Rd Parma (49269) *(G-12391)*
Michigan Baking Co., Detroit *Also called Metropolitan Baking Company (G-4234)*
Michigan Banker Magazine 517 484-0775
1430 E Michigan Ave Lansing (48912) *(G-9397)*
Michigan Beer Growler Company 248 385-3773
31221 Southfield Rd Beverly Hills (48025) *(G-1619)*
Michigan Bingo Bugle 616 784-9344
2604 Pohens Ave Nw Grand Rapids (49544) *(G-6668)*
Michigan Biodiesel LLC 269 427-0804
2813 W Main St Kalamazoo (49006) *(G-8823)*
Michigan Biofuels, Kalamazoo *Also called Energy Suppliers LLC (G-8738)*
Michigan Box Company (PA) 313 873-9500
1910 Trombly St Detroit (48211) *(G-4237)*
Michigan Brass Division, Spring Lake *Also called Marquis Industries Inc (G-15160)*
Michigan Brlle Trnscrbing Fund 517 780-5096
3500 N Elm Ave Jackson (49201) *(G-8519)*
Michigan Brush Mfg Co 313 834-1070
7446 Central St Detroit (48210) *(G-4238)*
Michigan Btlg & Cstm Pack Co 313 846-1717
13940 Tireman St Detroit (48228) *(G-4239)*
Michigan Carbide Company Inc 586 264-8780
1263 Souter Dr Troy (48083) *(G-16504)*
Michigan Carton Paper Boy 269 963-4004
79 Fountain St E Battle Creek (49017) *(G-1228)*
Michigan Celery Promotion Coop 616 669-1250
5009 40th Ave Hudsonville (49426) *(G-8168)*
Michigan Chese Prtein Pdts LLC 517 403-5247
10015 Wisner Hwy Tipton (49287) *(G-15884)*
Michigan Chronicle Pubg Co 313 963-5522
1452 Randolph St Ste 400 Detroit (48226) *(G-4240)*
Michigan Church Supply Co Inc (PA) 810 686-8877
7166 N Saginaw Rd Mount Morris (48458) *(G-11165)*
Michigan Cnc Tool Inc 734 449-9590
11710 Green Oak Indus Dr Whitmore Lake (48189) *(G-17704)*
Michigan Coating Products Inc 616 456-8800
3761 Eastern Ave Se Grand Rapids (49508) *(G-6669)*
Michigan Counter Tops Company 313 369-1511
2929 John B Ave Warren (48091) *(G-17152)*
Michigan Crane Parts & Svc Co, Rochester Hills *Also called Crane Technologies Group Inc (G-13397)*
Michigan Custom Machines Inc 248 347-7900
22750 Heslip Dr Novi (48375) *(G-11946)*
Michigan Deburring Tool LLC 810 227-1000
2155 Pless Dr Ste B Brighton (48114) *(G-1959)*
Michigan Dessert Corporation 248 544-4574
10750 Capital St Oak Park (48237) *(G-12085)*
Michigan Development Corp 734 302-4600
3520 Green Ct Ste 300 Ann Arbor (48105) *(G-554)*
Michigan Die Casting LLC 269 471-7715
51241 M 51 N Dowagiac (49047) *(G-4551)*
Michigan Diversfd Holdings Inc 248 280-0450
700 E Whitcomb Ave Madison Heights (48071) *(G-10305)*
Michigan Diversified Metals 517 223-7730
144 Veterans Dr Fowlerville (48836) *(G-5576)*
Michigan Drill Corporation (PA) 248 689-5050
1863 Larchwood Dr Troy (48083) *(G-16505)*
Michigan Dutch Barns Inc 616 693-2754
9811 Thompson Rd Lake Odessa (48849) *(G-9118)*
Michigan East Side Sales LLC 989 354-6867
4220 Us Highway 23 S Alpena (49707) *(G-299)*
Michigan Engine Pro, Livonia *Also called Perfit Corporation (G-9886)*
Michigan Envelope Inc 616 554-3404
6650 Clay Ave Sw Grand Rapids (49548) *(G-6670)*
Michigan Ethanol LLC 989 672-1222
1551 Empire Dr Caro (48723) *(G-2471)*
Michigan Extruded Aluminum, Jackson *Also called Michigan Aluminum Extrusion (G-8518)*
Michigan Farm To Freezer, Manistee *Also called MI Frozen Food LLC (G-10430)*
Michigan Fire Estinguishers, Detroit *Also called Fire Equipment Company (G-4059)*
Michigan Flame Hardening, Detroit *Also called Detroit Edge Tool Company (G-3983)*
Michigan Foam Products Inc 616 452-9611
1820 Chicago Dr Sw Grand Rapids (49519) *(G-6671)*
Michigan Forge Company LLC 815 758-6400
2807 S Martin L Kng Jr Bl Lansing (48910) *(G-9398)*
Michigan Freeze Pack, Hart *Also called Hart Freeze Pack LlC (G-7373)*
Michigan Front Page LLC 313 963-5522
479 Ledyard St Detroit (48201) *(G-4241)*
Michigan Fuels 313 886-7110
20700 Mack Ave Grosse Pointe Woods (48236) *(G-7207)*
Michigan Gear & Engineering, Gregory *Also called Boos Products Inc (G-7164)*
Michigan General Grinding LLC 616 454-5089
328 Winter Ave Nw Grand Rapids (49504) *(G-6672)*

Michigan Glass Lined Storage, Lake Odessa *Also called Michigan AG Services Inc* ***(G-9117)***
Michigan Graphic Arts.......517 278-4120
131 N Angola Rd Coldwater (49036) ***(G-3315)***
Michigan Graphics & Awards, Berkley *Also called Michigan Plaques & Awards Inc* ***(G-1587)***
Michigan Graphics & Signs.......989 224-1936
1110 E Steel Rd Saint Johns (48879) ***(G-14289)***
Michigan Grower Products Inc.......269 665-7071
251 Mccollum Galesburg (49053) ***(G-5813)***
Michigan Gypsum Co.......989 792-8734
6105 Jefferson Ave Midland (48640) ***(G-10885)***
Michigan Highway Signs Inc (PA).......810 695-7529
5182 S Saginaw Rd Flint (48507) ***(G-5465)***
Michigan Hockey, Farmington Hills *Also called Suburban Hockey LLC* ***(G-5133)***
Michigan Hrdwood Vneer Lbr Div, Munising *Also called Timber Products Co Ltd Partnr* ***(G-11250)***
Michigan Indus Met Pdts Inc.......616 786-3922
1674 S Getty St Muskegon (49442) ***(G-11378)***
Michigan Industrial Finishes.......248 553-7014
29463 Shenandoah Dr Farmington Hills (48331) ***(G-5065)***
Michigan Industrial Pdts Co, Port Huron *Also called Graphtek Inc* ***(G-12923)***
Michigan Industrial Tools, Grand Rapids *Also called Tekton Inc* ***(G-6919)***
Michigan Industrial Trim Inc (PA).......734 947-0344
12400 Universal Dr Taylor (48180) ***(G-15742)***
Michigan Institute For Elect, Livonia *Also called Brenner Orthtic Prsthetic Labs* ***(G-9670)***
Michigan Interactive LLC.......517 241-4341
30600 Telg Rd Ste 2345 Bingham Farms (48025) ***(G-1657)***
Michigan Journal, The, Dearborn *Also called Univesity Michigan-Dearborn* ***(G-3767)***
Michigan Kitchen Distributors, Marshall *Also called W S Townsend Company* ***(G-10593)***
Michigan Kitchen Distributors, Lansing *Also called W S Townsend Company* ***(G-9433)***
Michigan Ladder Company LLC.......734 482-5946
12 E Forest Ave Ypsilanti (48198) ***(G-18090)***
Michigan Lasercut, Grand Rapids *Also called Lasercutting Services Inc* ***(G-6619)***
Michigan Legal Publishing Ltd.......877 525-1990
2885 Sanford Ave Sw Grandville (49418) ***(G-7057)***
Michigan Lightning Protection.......616 453-1174
2401 O Brien Rd Sw Grand Rapids (49534) ***(G-6673)***
Michigan Live Inc.......734 997-7090
339 E Liberty St Ste 210 Ann Arbor (48104) ***(G-555)***
Michigan Lumber & Wood Fiber I.......989 848-2100
4776 N Abbe Rd Comins (48619) ***(G-3383)***
Michigan Machining Inc.......810 686-6655
3322 E Mount Morris Rd Mount Morris (48458) ***(G-11166)***
Michigan Manufactured Pdts Inc.......586 770-2584
3605 32nd St Port Huron (48060) ***(G-12941)***
Michigan Maps Inc.......231 264-6800
104 Dexter St Elk Rapids (49629) ***(G-4779)***
Michigan Masonry Materials, Detroit *Also called Land Star Inc* ***(G-4193)***
Michigan Mattress Limited LLC.......248 669-6345
3168 Welch Rd Commerce Township (48390) ***(G-3432)***
Michigan Meat Processing.......906 786-7010
1120 S Lincoln Rd Escanaba (49829) ***(G-4845)***
Michigan Med Innovations LLC.......616 682-4848
481 Pettis Ave Se Ada (49301) ***(G-24)***
Michigan Medical Society, East Lansing *Also called Michigan State Medical Society* ***(G-4670)***
Michigan Metal Coatings Co.......810 966-9240
2015 Dove St Port Huron (48060) ***(G-12942)***
Michigan Metal Fabricators.......586 754-0421
24575 Hoover Rd Warren (48089) ***(G-17153)***
Michigan Metal Tech Inc.......586 598-7800
50250 E Russell Schmidt Chesterfield (48051) ***(G-2806)***
Michigan Metals and Mfg Inc.......248 910-7674
29100 Northwestern Hwy Southfield (48034) ***(G-14981)***
Michigan Milk Producers Assn (PA).......248 474-6672
41310 Bridge St Novi (48375) ***(G-11947)***
Michigan Milk Producers Assn.......989 834-2221
431 W Williams St Ovid (48866) ***(G-12273)***
Michigan Milk Producers Assn.......269 435-2835
125 Depot St Constantine (49042) ***(G-3539)***
Michigan Modular Service, Kalkaska *Also called Patton Welding Inc* ***(G-8957)***
Michigan Mold Inc.......269 468-3346
320 Park St Coloma (49038) ***(G-3362)***
Michigan Motor Exchange, Detroit *Also called Navarre Inc* ***(G-4264)***
Michigan Movie Magazine LLC.......734 726-5299
9040 N Territorial Rd Dexter (48130) ***(G-4499)***
Michigan Oil and Gas Assn.......517 487-0480
124 W Allegan St Ste 1610 Lansing (48933) ***(G-9399)***
Michigan Ornamental Ir & Fabg.......616 899-2441
219 Roosevelt St Conklin (49403) ***(G-3530)***
Michigan Overhead Door.......734 425-0295
11615 Inkster Rd Livonia (48150) ***(G-9842)***
Michigan Packaging Company (HQ).......517 676-8700
700 Eden Rd Mason (48854) ***(G-10646)***
Michigan Pallet Inc.......517 543-0606
1100 Packard Hwy Charlotte (48813) ***(G-2660)***
Michigan Pallet Inc (PA).......989 865-9915
1225 N Saginaw St Saint Charles (48655) ***(G-14196)***
Michigan Pallet Inc.......269 685-8802
957 Industrial Pkwy Plainwell (49080) ***(G-12530)***
Michigan Paper Die Inc.......313 873-0404
632 Harper Ave Detroit (48202) ***(G-4242)***
Michigan Pattern Works Inc.......616 245-9259
872 Grandville Ave Sw Grand Rapids (49503) ***(G-6674)***
Michigan Paving and Mtls Co.......517 787-4200
1600 N Elm Ave Jackson (49202) ***(G-8520)***
Michigan Paving and Mtls Co (HQ).......734 397-2050
2575 S Haggerty Rd # 100 Canton (48188) ***(G-2405)***
Michigan Paving and Mtls Co.......734 485-1717
1785 Rawsonville Rd Van Buren Twp (48111) ***(G-16772)***
Michigan Paving and Mtls Co.......989 463-1323
1950 Williams Rd Alma (48801) ***(G-242)***
Michigan Paving and Mtls Co.......616 459-9545
1100 Market Ave Sw Grand Rapids (49503) ***(G-6675)***
Michigan Peak Company, Sandusky *Also called Bay-Houston Towing Company* ***(G-14430)***
Michigan Pipe Company, Grand Ledge *Also called Michigan Poly Pipe Inc* ***(G-6111)***
Michigan Plaques & Awards Inc.......248 398-6400
3742 12 Mile Rd Berkley (48072) ***(G-1587)***
Michigan Plating LLC.......248 544-3500
21733 Dequindre Rd Hazel Park (48030) ***(G-7444)***
Michigan Playground Safety, Swartz Creek *Also called J C Walker & Sons Corp* ***(G-15668)***
Michigan Poly Pipe Inc.......517 709-8100
10242 W Grand River Hwy Grand Ledge (48837) ***(G-6111)***
Michigan Poly Supplies Inc.......734 282-5554
26060 Northline Rd Taylor (48180) ***(G-15743)***
Michigan Polymer Reclaim Inc.......989 227-0497
107 E Walker Rd Saint Johns (48879) ***(G-14290)***
Michigan Power Cleaning, Kalamazoo *Also called Becktold Enterprises Inc* ***(G-8694)***
Michigan Precision Swiss Prts.......810 329-2270
2145 Wadhams Rd Saint Clair (48079) ***(G-14229)***
Michigan Precision Tl & Engrg, Dowagiac *Also called Michigan Precision Tl & Engrg* ***(G-4552)***
Michigan Precision Tl & Engrg.......269 783-1300
613 Rudy Rd Dowagiac (49047) ***(G-4552)***
Michigan Printer Service, Ann Arbor *Also called M & M Typewriter Service Inc* ***(G-536)***
Michigan Printing Impressions, Shelby Township *Also called Peg-Master Business Forms Inc* ***(G-14662)***
Michigan Prod Machining Inc (PA).......586 228-9700
16700 23 Mile Rd Macomb (48044) ***(G-10142)***
Michigan Protein Inc.......616 696-7854
15030 Stout Ave Ne Cedar Springs (49319) ***(G-2558)***
Michigan Pump, Melvindale *Also called Core Electric Company Inc* ***(G-10694)***
Michigan Pure Ice Co LLC.......231 420-9896
126 N Straits Hwy Indian River (49749) ***(G-8220)***
Michigan Rbr & Gasket Co Inc.......586 323-4100
7447 19 Mile Rd Sterling Heights (48314) ***(G-15421)***
Michigan Rebuild & Automtn Inc.......517 542-6000
7460 Herring Rd Litchfield (49252) ***(G-9609)***
Michigan Reef Development.......989 288-2172
8252 E Lansing Rd Durand (48429) ***(G-4609)***
Michigan Rifle and Pistol Assn.......269 781-1223
215 N Linden St Marshall (49068) ***(G-10583)***
Michigan Rod Products Inc (PA).......517 552-9812
1326 Grand Oaks Dr Howell (48843) ***(G-8065)***
Michigan Roll Form Inc (PA).......248 669-3700
1132 Ladd Rd Commerce Township (48390) ***(G-3433)***
Michigan Roller Inc.......269 651-2304
1113 N Clay St Sturgis (49091) ***(G-15618)***
Michigan Satellite.......989 792-6666
3215 Christy Way S Saginaw (48603) ***(G-14091)***
Michigan Scientific Corp (PA).......248 685-3939
321 E Huron St Milford (48381) ***(G-10969)***
Michigan Scientific Corp.......231 547-5511
8500 Ance Rd Charlevoix (49720) ***(G-2620)***
Michigan Screen Printing.......810 687-5550
204 S Railway St Clio (48420) ***(G-3276)***
Michigan Seamless Tube LLC.......248 486-0100
400 Mcmunn St South Lyon (48178) ***(G-14801)***
Michigan Shippers Supply Inc (PA).......616 935-6680
17369 Taft Rd Spring Lake (49456) ***(G-15163)***
Michigan Sign Supplies, Lansing *Also called Alpine Sign and Prtg Sup Inc* ***(G-9275)***
Michigan Signs Inc.......734 662-1503
5527 Gallery Park Dr Ann Arbor (48103) ***(G-556)***
Michigan Slotting Company Inc.......586 772-1270
22214 Schoenherr Rd Warren (48089) ***(G-17154)***
Michigan Soft Water of Centr.......517 339-0722
2075 E M 78 East Lansing (48823) ***(G-4669)***
Michigan Soy Products Company.......248 544-7742
1213 N Main St Royal Oak (48067) ***(G-13951)***
Michigan Spline Gage Co Inc.......248 544-7303
1626 E 9 Mile Rd Hazel Park (48030) ***(G-7445)***
Michigan Spring & Stamp.......248 344-1459
41850 W 11 Mile Rd # 105 Novi (48375) ***(G-11948)***
Michigan Spring & Stamping LLC (HQ).......231 755-1691
2700 Wickham Dr Muskegon (49441) ***(G-11379)***
Michigan State Medical Society (PA).......517 337-1351
120 W Saginaw St East Lansing (48823) ***(G-4670)***
Michigan State Univ Press.......517 355-9543
Manly Miles Building East Lansing (48823) ***(G-4671)***

ALPHABETIC SECTION

Michigan State University Pape, East Lansing *Also called State News Inc (G-4676)*
Michigan Steel and Trim Inc 517 647-4555
　349 N Water St Portland (48875) *(G-13063)*
Michigan Steel Fabricators Inc 810 785-1478
　5225 Energy Dr Flint (48505) *(G-5466)*
Michigan Steel Finishing Co 313 838-3925
　12850 Mansfield St Detroit (48227) *(G-4243)*
MICHIGAN STEEL SPRING COMPANY, Detroit *Also called Michigan Steel Finishing Co (G-4243)*
Michigan Sugar Beet Growers, Bay City *Also called Michigan Sugar Company (G-1333)*
Michigan Sugar Company 989 673-3126
　725 S Almer St Caro (48723) *(G-2472)*
Michigan Sugar Company 989 883-3200
　763 N Beck St Sebewaing (48759) *(G-14516)*
Michigan Sugar Company 810 679-2241
　159 S Howard Ave Croswell (48422) *(G-3601)*
Michigan Sugar Company (PA) 989 686-0161
　122 Uptown Dr Unit 300 Bay City (48708) *(G-1333)*
Michigan Sugar Company 989 673-2223
　819 Peninsular St Caro (48723) *(G-2473)*
Michigan Tape Inc 734 582-9800
　41016 Concept Dr Plymouth (48170) *(G-12692)*
Michigan Tile and Marble Co (PA) 313 931-1700
　9317 Freeland St Detroit (48228) *(G-4244)*
Michigan Tool & Engineering 586 786-0540
　16963 Crystal Dr Macomb (48042) *(G-10143)*
Michigan Tool & Gauge Inc 517 548-4604
　1010 Packard Dr Howell (48843) *(G-8066)*
Michigan Tool Works LLC 269 651-5139
　618 N Centerville Rd Sturgis (49091) *(G-15619)*
Michigan Tube Swagers & Fab (PA) 734 847-3875
　7100 Industrial Dr Temperance (48182) *(G-15838)*
Michigan Turkey Producers (PA) 616 245-2221
　2140 Chicago Dr Sw Wyoming (49519) *(G-18020)*
Michigan Turkey Producers 616 875-1838
　9983 Polk St Zeeland (49464) *(G-18163)*
Michigan Turkey Producers 616 245-2221
　1100 Hall St Sw Grand Rapids (49503) *(G-6676)*
Michigan Veal Inc 616 669-6688
　3007 Van Buren St Hudsonville (49426) *(G-8169)*
Michigan Vehicle Solutions LLC 734 720-7649
　16600 Fort St Southgate (48195) *(G-15081)*
Michigan Vue Magazine 248 681-2410
　5865 Crescent Rd Waterford (48327) *(G-17357)*
Michigan Wheel Marine, Grand Rapids *Also called Michigan Wheel Operations LLC (G-6677)*
Michigan Wheel Operations LLC (HQ) 616 452-6941
　1501 Buchanan Ave Sw Grand Rapids (49507) *(G-6677)*
Michigan Wholesale Prtg Inc 248 350-8230
　24653 Halsted Rd Farmington Hills (48335) *(G-5066)*
Michigan Wire EDM Services 616 742-0940
　1246 Scribner Ave Nw Grand Rapids (49504) *(G-6678)*
Michigan Wireline Service 989 772-5075
　4854 E River Rd Mount Pleasant (48858) *(G-11205)*
Michigan Wood Fibers Llc 616 875-2241
　9426 Henry Ct Zeeland (49464) *(G-18164)*
Michigan Wood Fuels LLC 616 355-4955
　1125 Industrial Ave Holland (49423) *(G-7747)*
Michigan Wood Pellet LLC 989 348-4100
　2211 Industrial Dr Grayling (49738) *(G-7112)*
Michigan Woodwork 517 204-4394
　1234 Christian Way Mason (48854) *(G-10647)*
Michigrain Distillery 517 580-8624
　523 E Shiawassee St Lansing (48912) *(G-9400)*
Michiwest Energy Inc 989 772-2107
　1425 S Mission Rd Ste 2 Mount Pleasant (48858) *(G-11206)*
Michner Plating Company 517 789-6627
　1690 Shoemaker Dr Jackson (49203) *(G-8521)*
Mico Industries Inc (PA) 616 245-6426
　2929 32nd St Se Ste 8 Grand Rapids (49512) *(G-6679)*
Mico Industries Inc 616 245-6426
　2725 Prairie St Sw Grand Rapids (49519) *(G-6680)*
Mico Industries Inc 616 514-1143
　219 Canton St Sw Ste B Grand Rapids (49507) *(G-6681)*
Micrgraphics Printing Inc (PA) 231 739-6575
　2637 Emerson Blvd Norton Shores (49441) *(G-11773)*
Micro Belmont, Byron Center *Also called Micro Engineering Inc (G-2200)*
Micro EDM Co LLC 989 872-4306
　6172 Main St Cass City (48726) *(G-2520)*
Micro Engineering Inc 616 534-9681
　257 Sorrento Dr Se Byron Center (49315) *(G-2200)*
Micro Focus Software Inc 248 353-8010
　26677 W 12 Mile Rd Ste 1 Southfield (48034) *(G-14982)*
Micro Form Inc 517 750-3660
　180 Teft Rd Spring Arbor (49283) *(G-15126)*
Micro Gauge Inc 248 446-3720
　7350 Kensington Rd Brighton (48116) *(G-1960)*
Micro Gind, Hazel Park *Also called Micro Grind Co Inc (G-7446)*

Micro Grind Co Inc 248 398-9770
　1648 E 9 Mile Rd Hazel Park (48030) *(G-7446)*
Micro Logic 248 432-7209
　4710 Rolling Ridge Rd West Bloomfield (48323) *(G-17486)*
Micro Machine Company LLC 269 388-2440
　2429 N Burdick St Kalamazoo (49007) *(G-8824)*
Micro Manufacturing Inc 616 554-9200
　6900 Dtton Indus Pk Dr Se Caledonia (49316) *(G-2309)*
Micro Plastics Mfg & Sls 517 320-2488
　2944 Lakeview Ct Hillsdale (49242) *(G-7531)*
Micro Platers Sales Inc 313 865-2293
　221 Victor St Detroit (48203) *(G-4245)*
Micro Precision Molds Inc 269 344-2044
　3915 Ravine Rd Kalamazoo (49006) *(G-8825)*
Micro Rim Corporation 313 865-1090
　221 Victor St Detroit (48203) *(G-4246)*
Micro-Systems Inc 616 481-1601
　129 Woodslee Ct Norton Shores (49444) *(G-11774)*
Microcide Inc 248 526-9663
　2209 Niagara Dr Troy (48083) *(G-16506)*
Microdental Laboratories Inc (PA) 877 711-8778
　500 Stephenson Hwy Troy (48083) *(G-16507)*
Microform Tool Company Inc 586 776-4840
　20601 Stephens St Saint Clair Shores (48080) *(G-14264)*
Microforms Inc 586 939-7900
　30706 Georgetown Dr Beverly Hills (48025) *(G-1620)*
Microgauge Machining Inc 248 446-3720
　7350 Kensington Rd Brighton (48116) *(G-1961)*
Micromatic Screw Products Inc 517 787-3666
　825 Carroll Ave Jackson (49202) *(G-8522)*
Micromet Corp 231 885-1047
　3790 Burning Tree Dr Bloomfield Hills (48302) *(G-1783)*
Micron Holdings Inc 616 698-0707
　4436 Broadmoor Ave Se Kentwood (49512) *(G-9020)*
Micron Mfg Company 616 453-5486
　1722 Kloet St Nw Grand Rapids (49504) *(G-6682)*
Micron Precision Machining Inc (PA) 989 759-1030
　225 E Morley Dr Saginaw (48601) *(G-14092)*
Micron Precision Machining Inc 989 790-2425
　2824 Universal Dr Saginaw (48603) *(G-14093)*
Microphoto Incorporated 586 772-1999
　30499 Edison Dr Roseville (48066) *(G-13835)*
Microprecision Cleaning 586 997-6960
　6145 Wall St Sterling Heights (48312) *(G-15422)*
Microtap USA Inc 248 852-8277
　1854 Star Batt Dr Rochester Hills (48309) *(G-13473)*
Microtech Gaging LLC 517 750-2169
　4801 W Michigan Ave Jackson (49201) *(G-8523)*
Microtech Machine Company 517 750-4422
　4801 W Michigan Ave Jackson (49201) *(G-8524)*
Microtemp Fluid Systems LLC 248 703-5056
　23900 Haggerty Rd Farmington Hills (48335) *(G-5067)*
Mid America Building Pdts Div, Wixom *Also called Tapco Holdings Inc (G-17905)*
Mid America Commodities LLC 810 936-0108
　7420 Majestic Woods Dr Linden (48451) *(G-9594)*
Mid American AEL LLC 810 229-5483
　1375 Rickett Rd Brighton (48116) *(G-1962)*
Mid McHgan Feed Ingrdients LLC 989 236-5014
　4585 S Garfield Rd Middleton (48856) *(G-10794)*
Mid Michigan Industries, Clare *Also called Mid-Michigan Industries Inc (G-2877)*
Mid Michigan Logging 231 229-4501
　9620 N Nelson Rd Lake City (49651) *(G-9093)*
Mid Michigan Pipe Inc 989 772-5664
　977 Ada Place Dr Se Ste A Grand Rapids (49546) *(G-6683)*
Mid Michigan Repair Service 989 835-6014
　680 S Poseyville Rd Midland (48640) *(G-10886)*
Mid Michigan Wood Specialites 989 855-3667
　1370 Divine Hwy Lyons (48851) *(G-10094)*
Mid North Printing Inc 989 732-1313
　316 W 2nd St Gaylord (49735) *(G-5882)*
Mid State Oil Tools Inc (PA) 989 773-4114
　1934 Commercial Dr Mount Pleasant (48858) *(G-11207)*
Mid State Seawall Inc 989 435-3887
　4418 Jones Rd Beaverton (48612) *(G-1389)*
Mid West Pallet 810 919-3072
　2206 E Parkwood Ave Burton (48529) *(G-2158)*
Mid-America Machining Inc 517 592-4945
　11530 Brooklyn Rd Brooklyn (49230) *(G-2040)*
Mid-American Rubber Co, Three Rivers *Also called Marco Rollo Inc (G-15869)*
Mid-Michigan Industries Inc (PA) 989 773-6918
　2426 Parkway Dr Mount Pleasant (48858) *(G-11208)*
Mid-Michigan Industries Inc 989 386-7707
　790 Industrial Dr Clare (48617) *(G-2877)*
Mid-Michigan Screen Printing 989 624-9827
　11917 Conquest St Birch Run (48415) *(G-1666)*
Mid-Michigan Truss Components, Saginaw *Also called CHR W LLC (G-14017)*
Mid-State Distributors Inc 989 793-1820
　3137 Boardwalk Dr Saginaw (48603) *(G-14094)*
Mid-State Plating Co Inc 810 767-1622
　602 Kelso St Flint (48506) *(G-5467)*

Mid-State Printing Inc......989 875-4163
145 Industrial Pkwy Ithaca (48847) ***(G-8364)***
Mid-States Bolt & Screw Co......989 732-3265
1069 Orourke Blvd Gaylord (49735) ***(G-5883)***
Mid-Tech Inc......734 426-4327
175 Dino Dr Ann Arbor (48103) ***(G-557)***
Mid-West Innovators Inc......989 358-7147
3810 Us Highway 23 N Alpena (49707) ***(G-300)***
Mid-West Instrument Company, Sterling Heights *Also called Astra Associates Inc* ***(G-15266)***
Mid-West Mfg., Alpena *Also called Mid-West Innovators Inc* ***(G-300)***
Mid-West Screw Products Co......734 591-1800
11975 Globe St Livonia (48150) ***(G-9843)***
Mid-West Spring & Stamping Inc......231 777-2707
1935 E Laketon Ave Muskegon (49442) ***(G-11380)***
Mid-West Truck Accessories......313 592-1788
26425 Grand River Ave Detroit (48240) ***(G-4247)***
Mid-West Wire Products Inc......248 548-3200
1109 Brompton Rd Rochester Hills (48309) ***(G-13474)***
MIDAS FOODS INTERNATIONAL, Oak Park *Also called Michigan Dessert Corporation* ***(G-12085)***
Midbrook Inc (PA)......800 966-9274
2621 E Kimmel Rd Jackson (49201) ***(G-8525)***
Midbrook Medical Dist Inc......517 787-3481
2080 Brooklyn Rd Jackson (49203) ***(G-8526)***
Midco 2 Inc......517 467-2222
11703 Pentecost Hwy Onsted (49265) ***(G-12154)***
Middlebury Trailers, Vandalia *Also called LA East Inc* ***(G-16801)***
Middleby Corporation......906 863-4401
5600 13th St Menominee (49858) ***(G-10750)***
Middleton Printing Inc......616 247-8742
200 32nd St Se Ste A Grand Rapids (49548) ***(G-6684)***
Middleville Tool & Die Co Inc......269 795-3646
1900 Patterson Rd Middleville (49333) ***(G-10805)***
Midland Brewing Co LLC......989 631-3041
5011 N Saginaw Rd Midland (48642) ***(G-10887)***
Midland Cmpnding Cnsulting Inc......989 495-9367
3802 James Savage Rd Midland (48642) ***(G-10888)***
Midland Daily News, Midland *Also called Midland Publishing Company* ***(G-10891)***
Midland Iron Works Inc......989 832-3041
57 W Chippewa River Rd Midland (48640) ***(G-10889)***
Midland Mold & Machining Inc......989 832-9534
1406 E Pine St Ste 5 Midland (48640) ***(G-10890)***
Midland Publishing Company......989 835-7171
124 S Mcdonald St Midland (48640) ***(G-10891)***
Midland Silicon Company LLC......248 674-3736
3840 Island Park Dr Waterford (48329) ***(G-17358)***
Midnight Scoop, South Lyon *Also called Mykin Inc* ***(G-14804)***
Midstates Industrial Group Inc......586 307-3414
21299 Carlo Dr Clinton Township (48038) ***(G-3174)***
Midtown Bar......989 584-6212
116 W Main Carson City (48811) ***(G-2493)***
Midw Inc......269 343-7090
2734 Miller Rd Kalamazoo (49001) ***(G-8826)***
Midway Group LLC......586 264-5380
6227 Metropolitan Pkwy Sterling Heights (48312) ***(G-15423)***
Midway Machine Tech Inc......616 772-0808
555 N State St Zeeland (49464) ***(G-18165)***
Midway Products Group Inc (PA)......734 241-7242
1 Lyman E Hoyt Dr Monroe (48161) ***(G-11052)***
Midway Rotary Die Solutions, Williamston *Also called Seeley Inc* ***(G-17740)***
Midway Strl Pipe & Sup Inc (PA)......517 787-1350
1611 Clara St Jackson (49203) ***(G-8527)***
Midwest Acorn Nut Company (PA)......800 422-6887
256 Minnesota Dr Troy (48083) ***(G-16508)***
Midwest Air Products Co Inc......231 941-5865
281 Hughes Dr Traverse City (49696) ***(G-16035)***
Midwest Aquatics Group Inc......734 426-4155
8930 Dexter Pinckney Rd Pinckney (48169) ***(G-12500)***
Midwest Brake Bond Co......586 775-3000
26255 Groesbeck Hwy Warren (48089) ***(G-17155)***
Midwest Build Center LLC......989 672-1388
1750 Speirs Rd Caro (48723) ***(G-2474)***
Midwest Bus Corporation (PA)......989 723-5241
1940 W Stewart St Owosso (48867) ***(G-12304)***
Midwest Cabinet Counters......248 586-4260
650 E Mandoline Ave Madison Heights (48071) ***(G-10306)***
Midwest Circuits, Ferndale *Also called I Parth Inc* ***(G-5293)***
Midwest Custom Embroidery Co......269 381-7660
621 E North St Kalamazoo (49007) ***(G-8827)***
Midwest Defense Corp......231 590-6857
15543 Birch Dr Traverse City (49686) ***(G-16036)***
Midwest Die Corp......269 422-2171
9220 First St Baroda (49101) ***(G-1127)***
Midwest Direct Transport Inc......616 698-8900
1144 73rd St Sw Ste A Byron Center (49315) ***(G-2201)***
Midwest Diversified Products, Ferndale *Also called L Barge & Associates Inc* ***(G-5297)***
Midwest Electric Motor, Kalamazoo *Also called Midw Inc* ***(G-8826)***
Midwest Fabricating Inc......734 921-3914
26465 Northline Rd Taylor (48180) ***(G-15744)***
Midwest Fbrglas Fbricators Inc......810 765-7445
1796 S Parker St Marine City (48039) ***(G-10478)***
Midwest Fire Protection, Sturgis *Also called Con-De Manufacturing Inc* ***(G-15601)***
Midwest Flex Systems Inc......810 424-0060
415 Sb Chavez Dr Flint (48503) ***(G-5468)***
Midwest Fruit Package Co., Benton Harbor *Also called Mpc Company Inc* ***(G-1534)***
Midwest Gear & Tool Inc......586 779-1300
15700 Common Rd Roseville (48066) ***(G-13836)***
Midwest Graphics & Awards Inc......734 424-3700
2135 Bishop Cir E Ste 8 Dexter (48130) ***(G-4500)***
Midwest II Inc......734 856-5200
6194 Section Rd Ottawa Lake (49267) ***(G-12266)***
Midwest International Dist LLC......616 901-4621
433 Union St Ionia (48846) ***(G-8249)***
Midwest International Wines, Macomb *Also called Andretta & Associates Inc* ***(G-10107)***
Midwest Intl Std Pdts Inc......231 547-4073
105 Stover Rd Charlevoix (49720) ***(G-2621)***
Midwest Lift Trucks, Clarkston *Also called Midwest National LLC* ***(G-2939)***
Midwest Machining Inc......616 837-0165
526 Omalley Dr Coopersville (49404) ***(G-3565)***
Midwest Marketing Inc......989 793-9393
105 Lyon St Saginaw (48602) ***(G-14095)***
Midwest Media Management Div, Grand Rapids *Also called Rbc Ministries* ***(G-6812)***
MIDWEST MEDIA MANAGEMENT DIV, Grand Rapids *Also called Discovery House Publishers* ***(G-6355)***
Midwest Mold Services Inc......586 888-8800
29900 Hayes Rd Roseville (48066) ***(G-13837)***
Midwest National LLC......260 894-0963
9951 Norman Rd Clarkston (48348) ***(G-2939)***
Midwest Panel Systems Inc......517 486-4844
9012 E Us Highway 223 Blissfield (49228) ***(G-1720)***
Midwest Plastic Engineering......269 651-5223
1501 Progress St Sturgis (49091) ***(G-15620)***
Midwest Plating Company Inc......616 451-2007
613 North Ave Ne Grand Rapids (49503) ***(G-6685)***
Midwest Press and Automtn LLC......586 212-1937
20417 Calumet Dr Clinton Township (48038) ***(G-3175)***
Midwest Product Spc Inc......231 767-9942
2190 Aurora Dr Muskegon (49442) ***(G-11381)***
Midwest Products Finshg Co Inc......734 856-5200
6194 Section Rd Ottawa Lake (49267) ***(G-12267)***
Midwest Quality Bedding Inc......614 504-5971
1384 Glenview Dr Waterford (48327) ***(G-17359)***
Midwest Regional Office, Jackson *Also called Union Built PC Inc* ***(G-8598)***
Midwest Resin Inc......586 803-3417
15320 Common Rd Roseville (48066) ***(G-13838)***
Midwest Rubber Company (PA)......810 376-2085
3525 Range Line Rd Deckerville (48427) ***(G-3809)***
Midwest Safety Products Inc......616 554-5155
4929 East Paris Ave Se Grand Rapids (49512) ***(G-6686)***
Midwest Sales Associates Inc......248 348-9600
29445 Beck Rd Ste A103 Wixom (48393) ***(G-17855)***
Midwest Seating Solutions Inc......616 222-0636
2234 Burning Tree Dr Se Grand Rapids (49546) ***(G-6687)***
Midwest Stainless Fabricating......248 476-4502
32433 8 Mile Rd Livonia (48152) ***(G-9844)***
Midwest Steel Inc (PA)......313 873-2220
2525 E Grand Blvd Detroit (48211) ***(G-4248)***
Midwest Superior Abrasives......248 202-0454
24517 Cavendish Ave E Novi (48375) ***(G-11949)***
Midwest Timber Inc......269 663-5315
190 Kraus Rd Edwardsburg (49112) ***(G-4767)***
Midwest Timer Service Inc......269 849-2800
4815 M63 N Benton Harbor (49022) ***(G-1530)***
Midwest Tool and Cutlery Co (PA)......269 651-2476
1210 Progress St Sturgis (49091) ***(G-15621)***
Midwest Tool and Cutlery Co......231 258-2341
222 Seeley Rd Ne Kalkaska (49646) ***(G-8953)***
Midwest Tractor & Equipment Co......231 269-4100
10736 N M 37 Buckley (49620) ***(G-2130)***
Midwest Tube Fabricators Inc......586 264-9898
36845 Metro Ct Sterling Heights (48312) ***(G-15424)***
Midwest Vibro Inc......616 532-7670
3715 28th St Sw Grandville (49418) ***(G-7058)***
Midwest Wall Company LLC......517 881-3701
13753 Cottonwood Dr Dewitt (48820) ***(G-4465)***
Midynaco LLC......989 550-8552
3719 Ross St Kingston (48741) ***(G-9073)***
Mien Company Inc......616 818-1970
2547 3 Mile Rd Nw Ste F Grand Rapids (49534) ***(G-6688)***
Mif Custom Coatings, Farmington Hills *Also called Michigan Industrial Finishes* ***(G-5065)***
Mig Molding LLC......810 660-8435
3778 Van Dyke Rd Almont (48003) ***(G-264)***
Mig Molding LLC......810 724-7400
611 Industrial Park Dr Imlay City (48444) ***(G-8208)***
Migatron Precision Products (PA)......989 739-1439
4296 E River Rd Oscoda (48750) ***(G-12214)***
Mighty Co......616 822-1013
50 Louis St Nw 520 Hudsonville (49426) ***(G-8170)***

ALPHABETIC SECTION — Minland Machine Inc

Mighty In The Midwest, Hudsonville *Also called Mighty Co (G-8170)*
Mighty Legal LLC 800 870-4605
329 Burr Oak Dr Ann Arbor (48103) *(G-558)*
MII Disposition Inc 616 554-9696
4717 Talon Ct Se Grand Rapids (49512) *(G-6689)*
Mika Tool & Die Inc 989 662-6979
5127 Garfield Rd Auburn (48611) *(G-757)*
Mikan Corporation 734 944-9447
1271 Industrial Dr Ste 3 Saline (48176) *(G-14401)*
Mike Degrow 734 353-4752
327 Seymour Ave Lansing (48933) *(G-9401)*
Mike Haas, Detroit *Also called Carco Inc (G-3930)*
Mike Hughes 269 377-3578
6054 Marshall Rd Nashville (49073) *(G-11461)*
Mike Manufacturing Corporation (PA) 586 759-1140
7214 Murthum Ave Warren (48092) *(G-17156)*
Mike Vaughn Custom Sports Inc 248 969-8956
550 S Glaspie St Oxford (48371) *(G-12361)*
Mikes Cabinet Shop Inc 734 722-1800
37100 Enterprise Dr Westland (48186) *(G-17580)*
Mikes Garage 734 779-7383
20080 Sumpter Rd Belleville (48111) *(G-1448)*
Mikes Steamer Service Inc 231 258-8500
355 Columbus Dr Ne Kalkaska (49646) *(G-8954)*
Milacron LLC 517 424-8981
5550 S Occidental Rd Tecumseh (49286) *(G-15802)*
Milair, Sterling Heights *Also called Horstman Inc (G-15368)*
Milair LLC 513 576-0123
44215 Phoenix Dr Sterling Heights (48314) *(G-15425)*
Milan Burial Vault Inc 734 439-1538
10475 N Ann Arbor Rd Milan (48160) *(G-10946)*
Milan Cast Metal Corporation 734 439-0510
13905 N Sanford Rd Milan (48160) *(G-10947)*
Milan Metal Systems LLC 734 439-1546
555 S Platt Rd Milan (48160) *(G-10948)*
Milan Metal Worx LLC 734 369-7115
16779 Ida West Rd Petersburg (49270) *(G-12437)*
Milan Screw Products Inc 734 439-2431
291 Squires Dr Milan (48160) *(G-10949)*
Milan Supply Company 231 238-9200
6031 S Straits Hwy Indian River (49749) *(G-8221)*
Milan Vault, Milan *Also called Milan Burial Vault Inc (G-10946)*
Milano Bakery Inc 313 833-3500
3500 Russell St Detroit (48207) *(G-4249)*
Milcare Inc (HQ) 616 654-8000
855 E Main Ave Zeeland (49464) *(G-18166)*
Miles Cake Candy Supplies 586 783-9252
44885 Morley Dr Clinton Township (48036) *(G-3176)*
Miles Cake Decorating Supply, Clinton Township *Also called Miles Cake Candy Supplies (G-3176)*
Milford Jewelers Inc 248 676-0721
441 N Main St Milford (48381) *(G-10970)*
Milford Redi-Mix Company 248 684-1465
800 Concrete Dr Milford (48381) *(G-10971)*
Milford Sand & Gravel, Detroit *Also called Edw C Levy Co (G-4028)*
Military & Veterans Affairs 231 775-7222
415 Haynes St Cadillac (49601) *(G-2266)*
Miljevich Corporation 906 229-5367
511 Putnam St Wakefield (49968) *(G-16853)*
Miljoco Corp (PA) 586 777-4280
200 Elizabeth St Mount Clemens (48043) *(G-11142)*
Mill Assist Services Inc 269 692-3211
141 N Farmer St Otsego (49078) *(G-12245)*
Mill Creek Industries, Lexington *Also called Patton Tool and Die Inc (G-9559)*
Mill Steel Co (PA) 616 949-6700
2905 Lucerne Dr Se # 100 Grand Rapids (49546) *(G-6690)*
Mill Steel Company, Grand Rapids *Also called Mill Steel Co (G-6690)*
Mill Town Woodworks, Bay City *Also called A & B Display Systems Inc (G-1269)*
Millbrook Press Works 517 323-2111
517 S Waverly Rd Lansing (48917) *(G-9311)*
Millbrook Printing Co 517 627-4078
3540 Jefferson Hwy Grand Ledge (48837) *(G-6112)*
Millendo Therapeutics Inc (PA) 734 845-9000
110 Miller Ave Ste 100 Ann Arbor (48104) *(G-559)*
Millendo Transactionsub Inc 734 845-9300
301 N Main St Ste 100 Ann Arbor (48104) *(G-560)*
Millennium Adhesive Products (PA) 800 248-4010
4401 Page Ave Michigan Center (49254) *(G-10787)*
Millennium Filters, Farmington Hills *Also called Millennium Planet LLC (G-5068)*
Millennium Machine Inc 810 687-0671
2232 Hayward St Clio (48420) *(G-3277)*
Millennium Machining & Asm, Auburn Hills *Also called TI Automotive LLC (G-1021)*
Millennium Mold & Tool Inc 586 791-1711
35225 Automation Dr Clinton Township (48035) *(G-3177)*
Millennium Planet LLC 248 835-2331
27300 Haggerty Rd Ste F28 Farmington Hills (48331) *(G-5068)*
Millennium Screw Machine Inc 734 525-5235
13311 Stark Rd Livonia (48150) *(G-9845)*

Millennium Steering LLC 989 872-8823
6285 Garfield Ave Cass City (48726) *(G-2521)*
Millennium Technology II Inc 734 479-4440
28888 Goddard Rd Ste 200 Romulus (48174) *(G-13709)*
Millennm-The Inside Sltion Inc 248 645-9005
24748 Crestview Ct Farmington Hills (48335) *(G-5069)*
Miller Broach Inc 810 395-8810
14510 Bryce Rd Capac (48014) *(G-2449)*
Miller Designworks LLC 313 562-4000
3001 S Gulley Rd Ste D Dearborn (48124) *(G-3742)*
Miller Energy Inc 269 352-5960
277 S Rose St Ste 3300 Kalamazoo (49007) *(G-8828)*
Miller Exploration Company (PA) 231 941-0004
3104 Logan Valley Rd Traverse City (49684) *(G-16037)*
Miller Industrial Products Inc 517 783-2756
801 Water St Jackson (49203) *(G-8528)*
Miller Investment Company LLC 231 933-3233
10850 E Traverse Hwy # 5595 Traverse City (49684) *(G-16038)*
Miller Machine & Technologies, Jackson *Also called Miller Tool & Die Co (G-8529)*
Miller Machine Inc 734 455-5333
41250 Joy Rd Plymouth (48170) *(G-12693)*
Miller Mold Co 989 793-8881
690 Wren Rd Frankenmuth (48734) *(G-5594)*
Miller Prod & Machining Inc 810 395-8810
14510 Bryce Rd Capac (48014) *(G-2450)*
Miller Products & Supply Co 906 774-1243
1801 N Stephenson Ave Iron Mountain (49801) *(G-8290)*
Miller Sand & Gravel Company 269 672-5601
1466 120th Ave Hopkins (49328) *(G-7959)*
Miller Technical Services Inc 734 207-3159
47801 W Anchor Ct Plymouth (48170) *(G-12694)*
Miller Tool & Die Co 517 782-0347
829 Belden Rd Jackson (49203) *(G-8529)*
Miller Transit Mix, Richmond *Also called Mirkwood Properties Inc (G-13266)*
Millers Canvas Shop 231 821-0771
6531 Meinert Rd Holton (49425) *(G-7934)*
Millers Custom Boat Top Inc 586 468-5533
41700 Conger Bay Dr Harrison Township (48045) *(G-7340)*
Millers Redi-Mix Inc 989 587-6511
6218 S Wright Rd Fowler (48835) *(G-5554)*
Millers Shoe Parlor Inc 517 783-1258
103 W Michigan Ave Jackson (49201) *(G-8530)*
Millers Woodworking 989 386-8110
3378 E Beaverton Rd Clare (48617) *(G-2878)*
Milliken and Company, Southfield *Also called Morris Associates Inc (G-14987)*
Milliman Communications Inc (PA) 517 327-8407
4601 W Saginaw Hwy Apt 2 Lansing (48917) *(G-9312)*
Millplex Machine Products Inc 734 497-0763
23539 W Ditner Dr Rockwood (48173) *(G-13608)*
Mills Phrm & Apothecary LLC 248 633-2872
1740 W Maple Rd Birmingham (48009) *(G-1693)*
Millstar, Lake Orion *Also called Cole Tooling Systems Inc (G-9130)*
Millwork Inc 586 791-2330
17420 15 Mile Rd Fraser (48026) *(G-5692)*
Millwork Design Group LLC 248 472-2178
1280 Holden Ave Ste 127 Milford (48381) *(G-10972)*
Millworks Engineering Inc 517 741-5511
584 W Girard Rd Union City (49094) *(G-16735)*
Milo Boring & Machining Inc 586 293-8611
34275 Riviera Fraser (48026) *(G-5693)*
Milsco LLC 517 787-3650
2313 Brooklyn Rd Jackson (49203) *(G-8531)*
Milton Chili Company Inc 248 585-0300
511 E Whitcomb Ave Madison Heights (48071) *(G-10307)*
Milton Manufacturing Inc 313 366-2450
301 E Grixdale Detroit (48203) *(G-4250)*
Miltons Cabinet Shop Inc 269 473-2743
10331 Us Highway 31 Berrien Springs (49103) *(G-1599)*
Mind Fuel LLC 248 414-5296
2120 N Connecticut Ave Royal Oak (48073) *(G-13952)*
Minden City Herald 989 864-3630
1524 Main St Minden City (48456) *(G-11000)*
Mineral Cosmetics Inc 248 542-7733
21314 Hilltop St Southfield (48033) *(G-14983)*
Minerals Processing Corp 906 352-4024
414 10th Ave Menominee (49858) *(G-10751)*
Minerals Processing Corp 906 753-9602
N9373 River Rd Stephenson (49887) *(G-15238)*
Minerals Technology, Quinnesec *Also called Specialty Minerals Inc (G-13102)*
Minerick Logging Inc 906 542-3583
N10670 State Highway M95 Sagola (49881) *(G-14187)*
Mini-Mix Inc 586 792-2260
33600 Kelly Rd Clinton Township (48035) *(G-3178)*
Miniature Custom Mfg LLC 269 998-1277
170 N Leja Dr Vicksburg (49097) *(G-16839)*
Mining Journal, Marquette *Also called Ogden Newspapers Inc (G-10548)*
Mining Jrnl Bsness Offc-Dtrial 906 228-2500
249 W Washington St Marquette (49855) *(G-10546)*
Minland Machine Inc 269 641-7998
19801 Old 205 Edwardsburg (49112) *(G-4768)*

(PA)=Parent Co (HQ)=Headquarters (DH)=Div Headquarters

ALPHABETIC SECTION

Minor Creations Incorporated 517 347-2900
693 W Grand River Ave Okemos (48864) *(G-12132)*
Minowitz Manufacturing Co (PA) 586 779-5940
26311 Woodward Ave Huntington Woods (48070) *(G-8190)*
Mint Steel Forge Inc 248 276-9000
162 Northpointe Dr Lake Orion (48359) *(G-9149)*
Minth North America Inc 248 259-7468
51331 Pontiac Trl Wixom (48393) *(G-17856)*
Minute Maid Co 269 657-3171
38279 W Red Arrow Hwy Paw Paw (49079) *(G-12410)*
Minuteman Metal Works Inc 989 269-8342
1600 Patterson St Bad Axe (48413) *(G-1069)*
Miracle Petroleum LLC 231 946-8090
2780 Garfield Rd N Traverse City (49686) *(G-16039)*
Mirkwood Properties Inc 586 727-3363
35555 Division Rd Richmond (48062) *(G-13266)*
Mirrage Ltd 734 697-6447
8300 Belleville Rd Van Buren Twp (48111) *(G-16773)*
Mirror Image 231 775-2939
10797 Pine Shore Dr Cadillac (49601) *(G-2267)*
Mirror Image Inc 248 446-8440
3700 S Mile Rd South Lyon (48178) *(G-14802)*
Mirs News, Lansing *Also called Infoguys Inc (G-9385)*
Mis Associates Inc 844 225-8156
1735 Highwood W Pontiac (48340) *(G-12850)*
Mis Controls Inc 586 339-3900
2890 Technology Dr Rochester Hills (48309) *(G-13475)*
Misc Products 586 263-3300
16730 Enterprise Dr Macomb (48044) *(G-10144)*
Mishigama Brewing Company 734 547-5840
124 Pearl St Ypsilanti (48197) *(G-18091)*
Missaukee Molded Rubber Inc 231 839-5309
6400 W Blue Rd Lake City (49651) *(G-9094)*
Mission Critical Firearms LLC 586 232-5185
48380 Van Dyke Ave Shelby Township (48317) *(G-14641)*
Mistequay Group Ltd 989 752-7700
1212 N Niagara St Saginaw (48602) *(G-14096)*
Mistequay Group Ltd 989 846-1000
1015 W Cedar St Standish (48658) *(G-15224)*
Mistequay Group Ltd (PA) 989 752-7700
1156 N Niagara St Saginaw (48602) *(G-14097)*
Mistequay NDT Center, Saginaw *Also called Mistequay Group Ltd (G-14097)*
Misumi Investment USA Corp 989 875-5400
255 Industrial Pkwy Ithaca (48847) *(G-8365)*
Mit, Lake Orion *Also called Manufacturing & Indus Tech Inc (G-9147)*
Mitc St Clair, China *Also called Antolin Interiors Usa Inc (G-2858)*
Mitchart Inc 989 835-3964
2611 Schuette Rd Ste A Midland (48642) *(G-10892)*
Mitchell Coates 231 582-5878
5293 Korthase Rd Boyne City (49712) *(G-1829)*
Mitchell Equipment Corporation 734 529-3400
5275 N Ann Arbor Rd Dundee (48131) *(G-4596)*
Mitchell Graphics Inc (PA) 231 347-4635
2363 Mitchell Park Dr Petoskey (49770) *(G-12459)*
Mitchell Rail Gear, Dundee *Also called Mitchell Equipment Corporation (G-4596)*
Mitchell Welding Co LLC 517 265-8105
2708 E Maumee St Adrian (49221) *(G-82)*
Mitchells Fabrication Co 248 373-2199
2238 E Walton Blvd Auburn Hills (48326) *(G-946)*
Mitech Electronics Corporation 269 694-9471
411 Washington St Otsego (49078) *(G-12246)*
Mitovation Inc 734 395-1635
1280 Wedgewood Cir Saline (48176) *(G-14402)*
Mitsubishi Chls Perf Plyrs Inc 586 755-1660
24060 Hoover Rd Warren (48089) *(G-17157)*
Mitsubishi Elc Auto Amer Inc 734 453-2617
15603 Centennial Dr Northville (48168) *(G-11710)*
Mitsubishi Electric Us Inc 734 453-6200
15603 Centennial Dr Northville (48168) *(G-11711)*
Mitsubishi Steel Mfg Co Ltd 248 502-8000
2040 Crooks Rd Ste A Troy (48084) *(G-16509)*
Mitten Brewing Company LLC 616 608-5612
527 Leonard St Nw Grand Rapids (49504) *(G-6691)*
Mitten Fruit Company LLC 269 585-8541
3680 Stadium Pkwy Kalamazoo (49009) *(G-8829)*
Mitten Fruit Company, The, Kalamazoo *Also called Mitten Fruit Company LLC (G-8829)*
Mittex Group 616 878-4090
8936 Conifer Ridge Dr Sw Byron Center (49315) *(G-2202)*
Miwi, Jackson *Also called Crown Industrial Services Inc (G-8425)*
Mix Factory One LLC 248 799-9390
27380 W 9 Mile Rd Southfield (48033) *(G-14984)*
Mix Head Repair, Holland *Also called Mhr Inc (G-7746)*
Mix Masters Inc 616 490-8520
530 76th St Sw Ste 400 Byron Center (49315) *(G-2203)*
Mix Street 616 241-6550
1328 Burton St Se Grand Rapids (49507) *(G-6692)*
Mizkan America Inc 616 794-0226
700 Kiddville St Belding (48809) *(G-1425)*

Mj Creative Printing LLC 248 891-1117
19566 Hardy St Livonia (48152) *(G-9846)*
Mj Mechanical Services, Saint Charles *Also called M J Mechanical Inc (G-14195)*
Mj Mfg Co 810 744-3840
2441 E Bristol Rd Burton (48529) *(G-2159)*
Mj-Hick Inc 989 345-7610
2367 S M 76 West Branch (48661) *(G-17513)*
MJB Concepts Inc 616 866-1470
113 Courtland St Rockford (49341) *(G-13580)*
MJB Creative Concepts, Rockford *Also called MJB Concepts Inc (G-13580)*
Mjc Industries Inc 313 838-2800
15701 Glendale St Detroit (48227) *(G-4251)*
Mjc Tool & Machine Co Inc 586 790-4766
35806 Groesbeck Hwy Clinton Township (48035) *(G-3179)*
MJL Publishing LLC 734 268-6187
2898 Masters Ct Pinckney (48169) *(G-12501)*
MK Chambers Company (PA) 810 688-3750
2251 Johnson Mill Rd North Branch (48461) *(G-11663)*
Mkg, Clarkston *Also called Mobile Knowlege Group Services (G-2940)*
MKI Products 517 748-5075
1410 W Ganson St Ste 9 Jackson (49202) *(G-8532)*
MKP Enterprises Inc 248 809-2525
19785 W 12 Mile Rd 338 Southfield (48076) *(G-14985)*
Mkr Fabricating Inc 989 753-8100
810 N Towerline Rd Saginaw (48601) *(G-14098)*
Mlc of Wakefield Inc 906 224-1120
893 Cemetery Rd Wakefield (49968) *(G-16854)*
Mlc Window Co Inc (PA) 586 731-3500
2001 Crystal Lake Dr Shelby Township (48316) *(G-14642)*
Mlcwindows & Doors, Shelby Township *Also called Mlc Window Co Inc (G-14642)*
Mle, Holland *Also called Graphix Signs & Embroidery (G-7650)*
Mlh Services LLC 313 768-4403
11310 Kenmoor St Detroit (48205) *(G-4252)*
Mlive Com 517 768-4984
214 S Jackson St Jackson (49201) *(G-8533)*
Mlive Media Group, Grand Rapids *Also called Herald Publishing Company LLC (G-6508)*
Mlp Mfg Inc 616 842-8767
18630 Trimble Ct Spring Lake (49456) *(G-15164)*
MLS Automotive Incorporated 844 453-3669
27280 Haggerty Rd Ste C-9 Farmington Hills (48331) *(G-5070)*
MLS Signs Inc 586 948-0200
50617 Plaza Dr Macomb (48042) *(G-10145)*
Mmbs, Livonia *Also called Manufacturers / Mch Bldrs Svcs (G-9821)*
Mmgg Inc (PA) 616 405-3807
120 Waldo Ave Midland (48642) *(G-10893)*
Mmgg Inc 989 495-9322
120 Waldo Ave Midland (48642) *(G-10894)*
Mmi Companies LLC 248 528-1680
1094 Naughton Dr Troy (48083) *(G-16510)*
Mmi Engineered Solutions Inc (HQ) 734 429-4664
1715 Woodland Dr Saline (48176) *(G-14403)*
Mmi Engineered Solutions Inc 734 429-5130
12700 Stephens Rd Warren (48089) *(G-17158)*
Mmi of Central Michigan, Mount Pleasant *Also called Mid-Michigan Industries Inc (G-11208)*
Mmm Meat LLC 616 669-6140
4598 Buttermilk Dr Hudsonville (49426) *(G-8171)*
Mmp Molded Magnesium Pdts LLC 517 789-8505
2336 E High St Jackson (49203) *(G-8534)*
Mmsp, Birch Run *Also called Mid-Michigan Screen Printing (G-1666)*
MNP Corporation (PA) 586 254-1320
44225 Utica Rd Utica (48317) *(G-16744)*
MNP Corporation 810 982-8996
2305 Beard St Port Huron (48060) *(G-12943)*
MNP Corporation 248 585-5010
1524 E 14 Mile Rd Madison Heights (48071) *(G-10308)*
MNP Corporation Division 2, Madison Heights *Also called MNP Corporation (G-10308)*
Mobile Haulaway LLC 616 402-7878
4365 Evanston Ave Muskegon (49442) *(G-11382)*
Mobile Installations, Holland *Also called Carry-All Products Inc (G-7585)*
Mobile Knowlege Group Services (PA) 248 625-3327
5750 Bella Rosa Blvd # 100 Clarkston (48348) *(G-2940)*
Mobile Mini Inc 586 759-4916
21900 Hoover Rd Warren (48089) *(G-17159)*
Mobile Mix 734 497-3256
15519 Westwood Dr Monroe (48161) *(G-11053)*
Mobile Office Vehicle Inc 616 971-0080
4053 Brockton Dr Se Ste A Grand Rapids (49512) *(G-6693)*
Mobile Pallet Service Inc (PA) 269 792-4200
858 S Main St Wayland (49348) *(G-17407)*
Mobile Prosthetics 989 875-7000
1326 E Center St Ste 200 Ithaca (48847) *(G-8366)*
Mobility Innovations LLC 586 843-3816
51277 Celeste Shelby Township (48315) *(G-14643)*
Mobility Products and Design, Shelby Township *Also called Veigel North America LLC (G-14717)*
Mobility Trnsp Svcs Inc 734 453-6452
42000 Koppernick Rd A3 Canton (48187) *(G-2406)*
Mobilitytrans, Canton *Also called Mobility Trnsp Svcs Inc (G-2406)*

Mobilitytrans LLC....734 453-6452
42000 Koppernick Rd A3 Canton (48187) ***(G-2407)***
Mobimogul Inc....313 575-2795
29193 Northwestern Hwy Southfield (48034) ***(G-14986)***
Mod Interiors Inc....586 725-8227
9301 Marine City Hwy Ira (48023) ***(G-8261)***
Mod Signs Inc....616 455-0260
7475 Division Ave S Grand Rapids (49548) ***(G-6694)***
Moda Manufacturing LLC....586 204-5120
39255 Country Club Dr B1 Farmington Hills (48331) ***(G-5071)***
Model Pattern Company Inc....616 878-9710
8499 Centre Indus Dr Sw Byron Center (49315) ***(G-2204)***
Model Printing Service Inc....989 356-0834
829 W Chisholm St Alpena (49707) ***(G-301)***
Model Shop Inc....734 645-8290
4659 Freedom Dr Ann Arbor (48108) ***(G-561)***
Model-Matic Inc....248 528-1680
1094 Naughton Dr Troy (48083) ***(G-16511)***
Models & Tools Inc....586 580-6900
51400 Bellestri Ct Shelby Township (48315) ***(G-14644)***
Modern Age Pattern Mfg Inc....231 788-1222
7265 Hall Rd Muskegon (49442) ***(G-11383)***
Modern Builders Supply Inc....517 787-3633
2401 Brooklyn Rd Jackson (49203) ***(G-8535)***
Modern CAM and Tool Co....734 946-9800
27272 Wick Rd Taylor (48180) ***(G-15745)***
Modern Concrete Products, Flint *Also called Modern Industries Inc* ***(G-5469)***
Modern Craft Winery LLC....989 876-4948
211 E Huron Rd Au Gres (48703) ***(G-747)***
Modern Diversified Products....989 736-3430
202 S Second St Lincoln (48742) ***(G-9567)***
Modern Fur Dressing LLC....517 589-5575
801 Rice St Leslie (49251) ***(G-9545)***
Modern Industries Inc....810 767-3330
3275 W Pasadena Ave Flint (48504) ***(G-5469)***
Modern Kitchen & Bath, Troy *Also called Korcast Products Incorporated* ***(G-16449)***
Modern Machine Co....989 895-8563
1111 S Water St Bay City (48708) ***(G-1334)***
Modern Machine Tool Co....517 788-9120
2005 Losey Ave Jackson (49203) ***(G-8536)***
Modern Machining Inc....269 964-4415
415 Upton Ave Battle Creek (49037) ***(G-1229)***
Modern Metal Processing Corp....517 655-4402
3448 Corwin Rd Williamston (48895) ***(G-17735)***
Modern Metalcraft Inc....989 835-3716
2033 Roxbury Ct Midland (48642) ***(G-10895)***
Modern Millwork Inc....248 347-4777
29020 S Wixom Rd Ste 100 Wixom (48393) ***(G-17857)***
Modern Neon Sign Co Inc....269 349-8636
1219 E Vine St Kalamazoo (49001) ***(G-8830)***
Modern Printing Services Inc....586 792-9700
8850 Dixie Hwy Ira (48023) ***(G-8262)***
Modern Tech Machining LLC....810 531-7992
3735 Lapeer Rd Ste C Port Huron (48060) ***(G-12944)***
Modern Tool and Tapping Inc....586 777-5144
33517 Kelly Rd Fraser (48026) ***(G-5694)***
Modern Woodsmith LLC....906 387-5577
E9998 State Highway M28 Wetmore (49895) ***(G-17616)***
Moderne Slate Inc....231 584-3499
8333 County Road 571 Ne Mancelona (49659) ***(G-10397)***
Modified Gear and Spline Inc....313 893-3511
18300 Mount Elliott St Detroit (48234) ***(G-4253)***
Modified Technologies Inc....586 725-0448
6500 Bethuy Rd Ira (48023) ***(G-8263)***
Modineer Co (PA)....269 683-2550
2190 Industrial Dr Niles (49120) ***(G-11627)***
Modineer Co....269 684-3138
1501 S 3rd St Niles (49120) ***(G-11628)***
Modineer Coatings Division....269 925-0702
2200 E Empire Ave Benton Harbor (49022) ***(G-1531)***
Modular Data Systems Inc....586 739-5870
53089 Bellamine Dr Shelby Township (48316) ***(G-14645)***
Modular Systems Inc....231 865-3167
169 Park St Fruitport (49415) ***(G-5797)***
Modulated Metals Inc....586 749-8400
56409 Precision Dr Chesterfield (48051) ***(G-2807)***
Modzel Screen Printing....231 941-0911
1017 Washington St Traverse City (49686) ***(G-16040)***
Moehrle Inc....734 761-2000
4305 Pontiac Trl Ann Arbor (48105) ***(G-562)***
Moeller Aerospace Tech Inc....231 347-9575
8725 Moeller Dr Harbor Springs (49740) ***(G-7289)***
Moeller Manufacturing Co, Grand Rapids *Also called Moeller Mfg Company LLC* ***(G-6695)***
Moeller Mfg Company LLC....616 285-5012
3757 Broadmoor Ave Se Grand Rapids (49512) ***(G-6695)***
Mogul Minds LLC....682 217-9506
3019 S Wayne Rd 23 Wayne (48184) ***(G-17438)***
Moguitech LLC....734 944-5053
1454 Judd Rd Saline (48176) ***(G-14404)***
Mohawk Industries Inc....248 486-4075
28435 Automation Blvd A Wixom (48393) ***(G-17858)***
Moheco Products Company....734 855-4194
34410 Rosati Ave Livonia (48150) ***(G-9847)***
Mohr Engineering Inc....810 227-4598
1351 Rickett Rd Brighton (48116) ***(G-1963)***
Mohyi Labs LLC....248 973-7321
2649 Cove Ln West Bloomfield (48323) ***(G-17487)***
Moiron Branch 0918, Sparta *Also called Leggett Platt Components Inc* ***(G-15101)***
Mol Belting Company, Grand Rapids *Also called Mol Belting Systems Inc* ***(G-6696)***
Mol Belting Systems Inc....616 453-2484
2532 Waldorf Ct Nw Grand Rapids (49544) ***(G-6696)***
Mol-Son Inc....269 668-3377
53196 N Main St Mattawan (49071) ***(G-10666)***
Mold Masters Co....810 245-4100
1455 Imlay City Rd Lapeer (48446) ***(G-9475)***
Mold Matter....231 933-6653
1650 Barlow St Traverse City (49686) ***(G-16041)***
Mold Specialties Inc....586 247-4660
51232 Oro Dr Shelby Township (48315) ***(G-14646)***
Mold Tech Michigan, Fraser *Also called Standex International Corp* ***(G-5735)***
Mold Tooling Systems Inc....616 735-6653
2972 Wilson Dr Nw Grand Rapids (49534) ***(G-6697)***
Mold-Msters Injctioneering LLC....905 877-0185
29111 Stephenson Hwy Madison Heights (48071) ***(G-10309)***
Mold-Rite LLC (PA)....586 296-3970
33830 Riviera Fraser (48026) ***(G-5695)***
Molded Plastic Industries Inc....517 694-7434
2382 Jarco Dr Holt (48842) ***(G-7916)***
Molded Plastics & Tooling....517 268-0849
2200 Depot St Holt (48842) ***(G-7917)***
Moldex Crank Shaft Inc....313 561-7676
12255 Wormer Redford (48239) ***(G-13175)***
Moldex3d Northern America Inc (HQ)....248 946-4570
27725 Stansbury Blvd Farmington Hills (48334) ***(G-5072)***
Molding Concepts Inc....586 264-6990
6700 Sims Dr Sterling Heights (48313) ***(G-15426)***
Molding Solutions Inc....616 847-6822
1734 Airpark Dr Ste F Grand Haven (49417) ***(G-6056)***
Moller Group North America Inc (HQ)....586 532-0860
13877 Teresa Dr Shelby Township (48315) ***(G-14647)***
Mollers North America Inc....616 942-6504
5215 52nd St Se Grand Rapids (49512) ***(G-6698)***
Mollertech LLC....586 532-0860
13877 Teresa Dr Shelby Township (48315) ***(G-14648)***
Mollewood Export Inc....248 624-1885
46921 Enterprise Ct Wixom (48393) ***(G-17859)***
Momentum Industries Inc....989 681-5735
100 Woodside Dr Saint Louis (48880) ***(G-14366)***
Monarch Electric Apparatus Svc, Melvindale *Also called Monarch Electric Service Co* ***(G-10702)***
Monarch Electric Service Co....313 388-7800
18800 Meginnity St Melvindale (48122) ***(G-10702)***
Monarch Metal Mfg Inc....616 247-0412
3303 Union Ave Se Grand Rapids (49548) ***(G-6699)***
Monarch Millwork Inc (PA)....989 348-8292
2211 Industrial Dr Grayling (49738) ***(G-7113)***
Monarch Powder Coating Inc....231 798-1422
5906 Grand Haven Rd Norton Shores (49441) ***(G-11775)***
Monarch Print and Mail LLC....734 620-8378
1461 Selma St Westland (48186) ***(G-17581)***
Monarch Print Solutions LLC....517 522-8457
4000 Page Ave Ste E Michigan Center (49254) ***(G-10788)***
Monarch Welding & Engrg Inc....231 733-7222
519 W Hackley Ave Muskegon (49444) ***(G-11384)***
Mondrella Process Systems LLC....616 281-9836
2049 Innwood Dr Se Grand Rapids (49508) ***(G-6700)***
Monitec Services Incorporated....231 943-2227
4459 Lakeview Trl Traverse City (49696) ***(G-16042)***
Monnier, Clay *Also called Nu-ERA Holdings Inc* ***(G-3000)***
Mono Ceramics Inc....269 925-0212
2235 Pipestone Rd Benton Harbor (49022) ***(G-1532)***
Monoco Inc....616 459-9800
351 Ney Ave Sw Grand Rapids (49503) ***(G-6701)***
Monogram Etc....989 743-5999
231 N Shiawassee St Corunna (48817) ***(G-3582)***
Monograms & More Inc....313 299-3140
8914 Telegraph Rd Taylor (48180) ***(G-15746)***
Monroe LLC....616 942-9820
4490 44th St Se Ste A Grand Rapids (49512) ***(G-6702)***
Monroe Environmental Corp....734 242-2420
810 W Front St Monroe (48161) ***(G-11054)***
Monroe Evening News....734 242-1100
7460 White Horse Cir Monroe (48161) ***(G-11055)***
Monroe Fuel Company LLC....734 302-4824
414 S Main St Ste 600 Ann Arbor (48104) ***(G-563)***
Monroe Inc....616 284-3358
4490 44th St Se Ste A Grand Rapids (49512) ***(G-6703)***
Monroe Mold, Monroe *Also called DD Parker Enterprises Inc* ***(G-11027)***

A L P H A B E T I C

Monroe Mold LLC ... 734 241-6898
1402 W 7th St Monroe (48161) *(G-11056)*

Monroe Publishing Company (HQ) ... 734 242-1100
20 W 1st St Monroe (48161) *(G-11057)*

Monroe Sp Inc ... 517 374-6544
437 Lentz Ct Lansing (48917) *(G-9313)*

Monroe Success Vlc ... 734 682-3720
1000 S Monroe St Monroe (48161) *(G-11058)*

Monroe Truck and Auto ACC, Muskegon Also called Monroes Custom Campers Inc *(G-11385)*

Monroe Truck Equipment Inc ... 810 238-4603
2400 Reo Dr Flint (48507) *(G-5470)*

Monroes Custom Campers Inc ... 231 773-0005
2915 E Apple Ave Muskegon (49442) *(G-11385)*

Monsanto Company ... 269 483-1300
67760 Us 31 Constantine (49042) *(G-3540)*

Monsanto Company ... 517 676-2479
1440 Okemos Rd Mason (48854) *(G-10648)*

Montague Latch Company ... 810 687-4242
2000 W Dodge Rd Clio (48420) *(G-3278)*

Montague Metal Products Inc ... 231 893-0547
4101 Fruitvale Rd Montague (49437) *(G-11095)*

Montague Tool, Clio Also called Montague Latch Company *(G-3278)*

Montague Tool and Mfg Co ... 810 686-0000
11533 Liberty St Ste 3 Clio (48420) *(G-3279)*

Montaplast North America Inc ... 248 353-5553
1849 Pond Run Auburn Hills (48326) *(G-947)*

Montcalm Aggregates Inc ... 989 772-7038
2201 Commerce St Ste 4 Mount Pleasant (48858) *(G-11209)*

Monte Package Company LLC ... 269 849-1722
3752 Riverside Rd Riverside (49084) *(G-13285)*

Montina Manufacturing Inc ... 616 846-1080
13740 172nd Ave Grand Haven (49417) *(G-6057)*

Montmorency County Tribune, Atlanta Also called Montmorency Press Inc *(G-732)*

Montmorency Press Inc ... 989 785-4214
12625 State 33 N Atlanta (49709) *(G-732)*

Montronix Inc ... 734 213-6500
4343 Concourse Dr Ste 370 Ann Arbor (48108) *(G-564)*

Montrose Trailers Inc ... 810 639-7431
180 Ruth St Montrose (48457) *(G-11105)*

Moo-Ville Inc ... 517 852-9003
5875 S M 66 Hwy Nashville (49073) *(G-11462)*

Moo-Ville Creamery, Nashville Also called Moo-Ville Inc *(G-11462)*

Moody Bible Inst of Chicago ... 616 772-7300
3764 84th Ave Zeeland (49464) *(G-18167)*

Moody Sign Co ... 517 626-6404
14470 Howe Rd Portland (48875) *(G-13064)*

Moog Fcs, Plymouth Also called Moog Inc *(G-12695)*

Moog Inc ... 734 738-5862
47495 Clipper St Plymouth (48170) *(G-12695)*

Moomers Homemade Ice Cream LLC ... 231 941-4122
7263 N Long Lake Rd Traverse City (49685) *(G-16043)*

Moon River Soap Co LLC ... 248 930-9467
339 East St Ste 100 Rochester (48307) *(G-13335)*

Moon Roof Corporation America (PA) ... 586 772-8730
28117 Groesbeck Hwy Roseville (48066) *(G-13839)*

Moon Roof Corporation America ... 586 552-1901
30750 Edison Dr Roseville (48066) *(G-13840)*

Moonlight Graphics Inc ... 616 243-3166
3144 Broadmoor Ave Se Grand Rapids (49512) *(G-6704)*

Moonlight Tiffanies LLC ... 517 372-2795
1216 N Foster Ave Lansing (48912) *(G-9402)*

Moonpeace ... 616 456-1128
615 Parkwood St Ne Grand Rapids (49503) *(G-6705)*

Moore Brothers Electrical Co ... 810 232-2148
2602 Leith St Flint (48506) *(G-5471)*

Moore Flame Cutting Co ... 586 978-1090
1022 Top View Rd Bloomfield Hills (48304) *(G-1784)*

Moore Production Tool Spc, Farmington Also called Moore Production Tool Spc *(G-4905)*

Moore Production Tool Spc ... 248 476-1200
37531 Grand River Ave Farmington (48335) *(G-4905)*

Moore Products Inc ... 269 782-3957
58151 Park Pl Dowagiac (49047) *(G-4553)*

Moore Signs Investments Inc ... 586 783-9339
5220 Rail View Ct Apt 245 Shelby Township (48316) *(G-14649)*

Mooreco Inc ... 616 451-7800
549 Ionia Ave Sw Grand Rapids (49503) *(G-6706)*

Moormann Printing Inc (PA) ... 269 646-2101
149 W Main St Marcellus (49067) *(G-10466)*

Moormann Printing Inc ... 269 423-2411
121 S Phelps St Decatur (49045) *(G-3805)*

Moose Mfg & Machining LLC ... 586 765-4686
440 Burroughs St Ste 692 Detroit (48202) *(G-4254)*

Mopega LLC ... 231 631-2580
238 E Front St Traverse City (49684) *(G-16044)*

Mophie LLC ... 269 743-1340
6244 Technology Ave Kalamazoo (49009) *(G-8831)*

Mor-Dall Enterprises Inc ... 269 558-4915
511 S Kalamazoo Ave Marshall (49068) *(G-10584)*

Mor-Tech Design Inc (PA) ... 586 254-7982
6503 19 1/2 Mile Rd Sterling Heights (48314) *(G-15427)*

Mor-Tech Manufacturing Inc ... 586 254-7982
6503 19 1/2 Mile Rd Sterling Heights (48314) *(G-15428)*

Moran Iron Works Inc ... 989 733-2011
11739 M68-33 Hwy Onaway (49765) *(G-12148)*

Morbark LLC (PA) ... 989 866-2381
8507 S Winn Rd Winn (48896) *(G-17747)*

More Signature Cakes LLC ... 248 266-0504
5065 Livernois Rd Troy (48098) *(G-16512)*

Morenci Observer (PA) ... 517 458-6811
120 North St Morenci (49256) *(G-11113)*

Morgan Composting Inc (PA) ... 231 734-2451
4353 Us Highway 10 Sears (49679) *(G-14512)*

Morgan Composting Inc ... 231 734-2790
4281 Us Highway 10 Sears (49679) *(G-14513)*

Morgan Farm and Gardens, Sears Also called Morgan Composting Inc *(G-14513)*

Morgan Machine LLC ... 248 293-3277
2760 Auburn Rd Auburn Hills (48326) *(G-948)*

Morgan Olson LLC (HQ) ... 269 659-0200
1801 S Nottawa St Sturgis (49091) *(G-15622)*

Morgans Welding ... 517 523-3666
6520 Skuse Rd Osseo (49266) *(G-12227)*

Morgold Inc ... 269 445-3844
18409 Quaker St Cassopolis (49031) *(G-2534)*

Morin Boats ... 989 686-7353
377 State Park Dr Bay City (48706) *(G-1335)*

Morin Fireworks ... 906 353-6650
15781 Us Highway 41 N Baraga (49908) *(G-1110)*

Morkin and Sowards Inc ... 734 729-4242
38058 Van Born Rd Wayne (48184) *(G-17439)*

Morley Brands LLC ... 586 468-4300
23770 Hall Rd Clinton Township (48036) *(G-3180)*

Morning Star ... 989 755-2660
306 E Remington St Saginaw (48601) *(G-14099)*

Morning Star Land Company LLC ... 734 459-8022
7857 Ronda Dr Canton (48187) *(G-2408)*

Morning Star Publishing Co ... 989 463-6071
311 E Superior St Ste A Alma (48801) *(G-243)*

Morning Star Publishing Co (HQ) ... 989 779-6000
311 E Superior St Ste A Alma (48801) *(G-244)*

Morning Star Publishing Co ... 989 779-6000
311 E Superior St Ste A Alma (48801) *(G-245)*

Morning Star Publishing Co ... 989 732-5125
48 W Huron St Pontiac (48342) *(G-12851)*

Morrell Incorporated (PA) ... 248 373-1600
3333 Bald Mountain Rd Auburn Hills (48326) *(G-949)*

Morren Mold & Machine Inc ... 616 892-7474
10345 60th Ave Allendale (49401) *(G-223)*

Morren Plastic Molding Inc ... 616 997-7474
7677 Fillmore St Allendale (49401) *(G-224)*

Morris Associates Inc ... 248 355-9055
24007 Telegraph Rd Southfield (48033) *(G-14987)*

Morris Communications Co LLC ... 517 437-3253
33 Mccollum St Hillsdale (49242) *(G-7532)*

Morris Communications Co LLC ... 616 546-4200
54 W 8th St Holland (49423) *(G-7748)*

Morris Communications Corp ... 269 673-2141
595 Jenner Dr M40 Allegan (49010) *(G-177)*

Morris Excavating Inc ... 269 483-7773
69067 S Kalamazoo St White Pigeon (49099) *(G-17654)*

Morrison & Barnett Anesth ... 248 814-0609
830 Hemingway Rd Lake Orion (48362) *(G-9150)*

Morse Concrete & Excavating ... 989 826-3975
106 S Vine St Mio (48647) *(G-11006)*

Morse-Hemco, Holland Also called H E Morse Co *(G-7656)*

Morstar Inc ... 248 605-3291
12868 Farmington Rd Livonia (48150) *(G-9848)*

Morton Buildings Inc ... 616 696-4747
59924 S Us Highway 131 Three Rivers (49093) *(G-15871)*

Morton Salt Inc ... 231 398-0758
180 6th St Manistee (49660) *(G-10431)*

Moser Racing Inc ... 248 348-6502
43641 Serenity Dr Northville (48167) *(G-11712)*

Mosiac Potash Hersey LLC ... 231 832-3755
1395 135th Ave Hersey (49639) *(G-7474)*

Moss Audio Corporation ... 616 451-9933
561 Century Ave Sw Grand Rapids (49503) *(G-6707)*

Moss Telecommunications Svcs, Grand Rapids Also called Moss Audio Corporation *(G-6707)*

Mossworld Enterprises Inc ... 248 828-7460
3577 Orion Rd Oakland (48363) *(G-12107)*

Motan Inc ... 269 685-1050
320 Acorn St Plainwell (49080) *(G-12531)*

Motawi Tileworks Inc ... 734 213-0017
170 Enterprise Dr Ann Arbor (48103) *(G-565)*

Mote Industries Inc ... 248 613-3413
57446 River Oaks Dr New Haven (48048) *(G-11525)*

Motion Dynamics Corporation ... 231 865-7400
5621 Airline Rd Fruitport (49415) *(G-5798)*

ALPHABETIC SECTION

Motion Industries Inc 989 771-0200
   1646 Champagne Dr N Saginaw (48604) *(G-14100)*
Motion Industries Inc 269 926-7216
   2450 M 139 Ste B Benton Harbor (49022) *(G-1533)*
Motion Machine Company 810 664-9901
   524 Mccormick Dr Lapeer (48446) *(G-9476)*
Motion Systems Incorporated 586 774-5666
   21335 Schoenherr Rd Warren (48089) *(G-17160)*
Motivation Ideas Inc 989 356-1817
   1101 Dow Dr Alpena (49707) *(G-302)*
Motor City Aerospace 616 916-5473
   10500 Harvard Ave Ne Rockford (49341) *(G-13581)*
Motor City Bending & Rolling 313 368-4400
   17655 Filer St Detroit (48212) *(G-4255)*
Motor City Electric Tech Inc 313 921-5300
   9440 Grinnell St Detroit (48213) *(G-4256)*
Motor City Manufacturing Ltd 586 731-1086
   23440 Woodward Ave Ferndale (48220) *(G-5302)*
Motor City Metal Fab Inc 734 345-1001
   24340 Northline Rd Taylor (48180) *(G-15747)*
Motor City Naturals LLC 313 329-4071
   24201 Hoover Rd Warren (48089) *(G-17161)*
Motor City Products, Flint Also called U S Speedo Inc *(G-5516)*
Motor City Quick Lube One Inc 734 367-6457
   11900 Middlebelt Rd Ste A Livonia (48150) *(G-9849)*
Motor City Sewing 313 595-5275
   1651 Church St Detroit (48216) *(G-4257)*
Motor City Stampings Inc (PA) 586 949-8420
   47783 Gratiot Ave Chesterfield (48051) *(G-2808)*
Motor City Stampings Inc 586 949-8420
   47781 Gratiot Ave Chesterfield (48051) *(G-2809)*
Motor City Wash Works Inc 248 313-0272
   48285 Frank St Wixom (48393) *(G-17860)*
Motor City Wraps LLC 734 812-4580
   3510 Brophy Rd Howell (48855) *(G-8067)*
Motor Control Incorporated 313 389-4000
   17100 Francis St Melvindale (48122) *(G-10703)*
Motor Parts Inc of Michigan 248 852-1522
   2751 Commerce Dr Rochester Hills (48309) *(G-13476)*
Motor Products Corportation (HQ) 989 725-5151
   201 S Delaney Rd Owosso (48867) *(G-12305)*
Motor Tool Manufacturing Co 734 425-3300
   14710 Flamingo St Livonia (48154) *(G-9850)*
Motown Harley-Davidson Inc 734 947-4647
   14100 Telegraph Rd Taylor (48180) *(G-15748)*
Mott Media LLC (PA) 810 714-4280
   1130 Fenway Cir Fenton (48430) *(G-5226)*
Mottes Materials Inc 906 265-9955
   4084 Us Highway 2 Iron River (49935) *(G-8316)*
Motto Cedar Products Inc 906 753-4892
   Us Hwy 41 & County Rd 360 Daggett (49821) *(G-3622)*
Motus Holdings LLC (HQ) 616 422-7557
   88 E 48th St Holland (49423) *(G-7749)*
Motus Integrated Technologies, Holland Also called Motus LLC *(G-7750)*
Motus LLC (HQ) 616 422-7557
   88 E 48th St Holland (49423) *(G-7750)*
Motus LLC 734 266-3237
   13975 Farmington Rd Livonia (48154) *(G-9851)*
Mound Steel & Supply Inc 248 852-6630
   1450 Rochester Rd Troy (48083) *(G-16513)*
Mount Clemens Orthopedic Appls 586 463-3600
   24432 Crocker Blvd Clinton Township (48036) *(G-3181)*
Mount Clmens Orthopaedic Appls, Clinton Township Also called Mount Clemens Orthopedic Appls *(G-3181)*
Mount Mfg LLC 231 487-2118
   200 Air Industrial Pk Dr Boyne City (49712) *(G-1830)*
Mount of Olive Oil Company 989 928-9030
   1821 Ambrose Rd Mayville (48744) *(G-10675)*
Mount Pleasant Brewing Company 989 400-4666
   506 W Broadway St Mount Pleasant (48858) *(G-11210)*
Mount-N-Repair 248 647-8670
   205 Pierce St Ste 101 Birmingham (48009) *(G-1694)*
Mount-N-Repair Silver Jewelry, Birmingham Also called Mount-N-Repair *(G-1694)*
Mountain Machine LLC 734 480-2200
   7850 Rawsonville Rd Van Buren Twp (48111) *(G-16774)*
Mountain Town Stn Brew Pub LLC 989 775-2337
   506 W Broadway St Mount Pleasant (48858) *(G-11211)*
Mountain Town Stn Brewing Co &, Mount Pleasant Also called Mountain Town Stn Brew Pub LLC *(G-11211)*
Movellus Circuits Inc (PA) 877 321-7667
   220 E Huron St Ste 650 Ann Arbor (48104) *(G-566)*
Movie Collectors World, Fraser Also called Arena Publishing Co Inc *(G-5621)*
Moxies Boutique LLC 269 983-4273
   321 State St Saint Joseph (49085) *(G-14329)*
Moyle Lumber, Houghton Also called Thomas J Moyle Jr Incorporated *(G-7986)*
Mp Components, Byron Center Also called Model Pattern Company Inc *(G-2204)*
Mp Hollywood LLC 517 782-0391
   1824 River St Jackson (49202) *(G-8537)*

Mp Tool & Engineering Company 586 772-7730
   15850 Common Rd Roseville (48066) *(G-13841)*
Mp-Tec Inc 734 367-1284
   32920 Capitol St Livonia (48150) *(G-9852)*
Mp6 LLC 231 409-7530
   2488 Cass Rd Traverse City (49684) *(G-16045)*
Mpc Company Inc 269 927-3371
   1891 Territorial Rd Benton Harbor (49022) *(G-1534)*
Mpd Welding - Grand Rapids Inc 616 248-9353
   1903 Clyde Park Ave Sw Grand Rapids (49509) *(G-6708)*
Mpd Welding Center, Orion Also called M P D Welding Inc *(G-12184)*
Mpf Acquisitions Inc 269 672-5511
   904 E Allegan St Martin (49070) *(G-10596)*
Mpg Inc 734 207-6200
   47659 Halyard Dr Plymouth (48170) *(G-12696)*
Mpi, Highland Also called Magnetic Products Inc *(G-7497)*
Mpi, Holt Also called Molded Plastic Industries Inc *(G-7916)*
Mpi Plastics 201 502-1534
   51315 Regency Center Dr Macomb (48042) *(G-10146)*
Mpi Products Holdings LLC (HQ) 248 237-3007
   2129 Austin Ave Rochester Hills (48309) *(G-13477)*
Mpi Products LLC (HQ) 248 237-3007
   2129 Austin Ave Rochester Hills (48309) *(G-13478)*
Mpm, Macomb Also called Michigan Prod Machining Inc *(G-10142)*
Mpp Corp 810 364-2939
   82 Airport Dr Kimball (48074) *(G-9045)*
Mpr, Visitmpr, Saint Johns Also called Michigan Polymer Reclaim Inc *(G-14290)*
MPS, Saint Clair Also called Michigan Precision Swiss Prts *(G-14229)*
MPS Holdco Inc (HQ) 517 886-2526
   5800 W Grand River Ave Lansing (48906) *(G-9246)*
MPS Holdings, Lansing Also called MPS Holdco Inc *(G-9246)*
MPS Holland, Holland Also called Steketee-Van Huis Inc *(G-7814)*
MPS Hrl LLC 800 748-0517
   5800 W Grand River Ave Lansing (48906) *(G-9247)*
MPS Lansing Inc (HQ) 517 323-9000
   5800 W Grand River Ave Lansing (48906) *(G-9248)*
MPS Trading Group LLC 313 841-7588
   38755 Hills Tech Dr Farmington Hills (48331) *(G-5073)*
MPS/Ih LLC 517 323-9001
   5800 W Grand River Ave Lansing (48906) *(G-9249)*
Mpt Driveline Systems 248 680-3786
   1870 Technology Dr Troy (48083) *(G-16514)*
Mpt Lansing LLC 517 316-1013
   3140 Spanish Oak Dr Ste A Lansing (48911) *(G-9403)*
Mq Operating Company 906 337-1515
   416 6th St Calumet (49913) *(G-2330)*
Mr Axle 231 788-4624
   6336 E Apple Ave Muskegon (49442) *(G-11386)*
Mr Chain, Copemish Also called M-R Products Inc *(G-3573)*
Mr Chips Inc (HQ) 989 879-3555
   2628 N Huron Rd Pinconning (48650) *(G-12510)*
Mr Eds Sewer Cleaning Service 313 565-2740
   5673 Mckinley Ct Dearborn Heights (48125) *(G-3790)*
Mr Hydrogen, Oak Park Also called REB Research & Consulting Co *(G-12092)*
Mr Lube Inc 313 615-6161
   6915 Airport Hwy Wyandotte (48192) *(G-17969)*
Mr McGooz Products Inc 313 693-4003
   18911 W 7 Mile Rd Detroit (48219) *(G-4258)*
Mr Peel Inc 734 266-2022
   33975 Autry St Livonia (48150) *(G-9853)*
Mr TS Screenprinting, Grand Rapids Also called Robert J Lidzan *(G-6831)*
Mr. Hydrogen, Detroit Also called REB Research & Consulting Co *(G-3821)*
MRC Industries Inc (PA) 269 343-0747
   2538 S 26th St Kalamazoo (49048) *(G-8832)*
MRC Manufacturing, Roseville Also called Moon Roof Corporation America *(G-13839)*
Mri Consultants LLC 248 619-9771
   30785 Stephenson Hwy Madison Heights (48071) *(G-10310)*
Mri-PA, Benton Harbor Also called Siemens Vai Services LLC *(G-1548)*
Mrj Sign Company LLC 248 521-2431
   256 Narrin St Ortonville (48462) *(G-12200)*
MRM Ida Products Co Inc 313 834-0200
   8385 Lyndon St Detroit (48238) *(G-4259)*
MRM Industries Inc 989 723-7443
   1655 Industrial Dr Owosso (48867) *(G-12306)*
Mrpa, Marshall Also called Michigan Rifle and Pistol Assn *(G-10583)*
Ms Plastic Welders LLC 517 223-1059
   1101 Highview Dr Webberville (48892) *(G-17452)*
MSC Blinds & Shades Inc 269 489-5188
   1241 W Chicago Rd Bronson (49028) *(G-2033)*
MSC Pre Finish Metals Egv Inc 734 207-4400
   6855 Commerce Blvd Canton (48187) *(G-2409)*
Mscsoftware Corporation 734 994-3800
   201 Depot St Ste 100 Ann Arbor (48104) *(G-567)*
Msd Stamping, Livonia Also called Amanda Manufacturing LLC *(G-9641)*
MSE Fabrication LLC 586 991-6138
   6624 Burroughs Ave Sterling Heights (48314) *(G-15429)*
MSI, Boyne City Also called Magnetic Systems Intl Inc *(G-1828)*

MSI, Drummond Island ALPHABETIC SECTION

MSI, Drummond Island *Also called Manufacturers Services Inds* ***(G-4565)***
MSI Machine Tool Parts Inc 248 589-0515
1619 Donna Ave Madison Heights (48071) ***(G-10311)***
Msinc 248 275-1978
50463 Wing Dr Shelby Township (48315) ***(G-14650)***
Msmac Designs LLC 313 521-6289
11069 Nashville St Detroit (48205) ***(G-4260)***
Msnow, Plainwell *Also called Plastisnow LLC* ***(G-12539)***
MSP Industries Corporation 248 628-4150
45 W Oakwood Rd Oxford (48371) ***(G-12362)***
Mssc, Troy *Also called Mitsubishi Steel Mfg Co Ltd* ***(G-16509)***
Mssc Inc (HQ) 248 502-8000
2040 Crooks Rd Ste A Troy (48084) ***(G-16515)***
MST Steel Corp 586 359-2648
30360 Edison Dr Roseville (48066) ***(G-13842)***
Mstation, Kalamazoo *Also called Mophie LLC* ***(G-8831)***
Msw Print and Imaging 734 544-1626
3901 Bestech Rd Ypsilanti (48197) ***(G-18092)***
Msx International Inc 248 585-6654
30031 Stephenson Hwy Madison Heights (48071) ***(G-10312)***
Mt Clemens Glass & Mirror Co 586 465-1733
1231 S Gratiot Ave Clinton Township (48036) ***(G-3182)***
Mt. Clemens Crane, Harrison Township *Also called Crane 1 Services Inc* ***(G-7327)***
Mtg, Corunna *Also called Machine Tool & Gear Inc* ***(G-3581)***
MTI Precision Machining Inc 989 865-9880
11980 Beaver Rd Saint Charles (48655) ***(G-14197)***
MTI-Saline, Saline *Also called Crescive Die and Tool Inc* ***(G-14384)***
Mtm Machine Inc 586 443-5703
34575 Commerce Fraser (48026) ***(G-5696)***
Mtm Transport 989 709-0475
2173 Roseburgh Rd Alger (48610) ***(G-139)***
MTS, Benton Harbor *Also called Midwest Timer Service Inc* ***(G-1530)***
MTS Burgess LLC 734 847-2937
1244 W Dean Rd Temperance (48182) ***(G-15839)***
MTS Seating, Temperance *Also called Michigan Tube Swagers & Fab* ***(G-15838)***
Mtu America Inc (HQ) 248 560-8000
39525 Mackenzie Dr Novi (48377) ***(G-11950)***
Mtu America Incorporated 734 261-0309
30946 Industrial Rd Livonia (48150) ***(G-9854)***
Mtu America Incorporated 734 561-2040
19771 Brownstown Ctr Brownstown Township (48183) ***(G-2070)***
Mtu Onsite Energy Corporation 805 879-3499
1424 Crimson Way Walled Lake (48390) ***(G-16899)***
Mtw Performance & Fab 989 317-3301
706 W Pickard St Mount Pleasant (48858) ***(G-11212)***
Mubea Inc 248 393-9600
1701 Harmon Rd Auburn Hills (48326) ***(G-950)***
Mueller Brass, Belding *Also called Extruded Metals Inc* ***(G-1414)***
Mueller Brass Co 616 794-1200
302 Ashfield St Belding (48809) ***(G-1426)***
Mueller Brass Co 810 987-7770
2199 Lapeer Ave Port Huron (48060) ***(G-12945)***
Mueller Brass Forging Co Inc 810 987-7770
2199 Lapeer Ave Port Huron (48060) ***(G-12946)***
Mueller Brass Products, Belding *Also called Mueller Brass Co* ***(G-1426)***
Mueller Impacts Company Inc 810 364-3700
2409 Wills St Marysville (48040) ***(G-10608)***
Mueller Industrial Realty Co 810 987-7770
2199 Lapeer Ave Port Huron (48060) ***(G-12947)***
Mueller Industries Inc 248 446-3720
7350 Kensington Rd Brighton (48116) ***(G-1964)***
Mug Shots Burgers and Brews 616 895-2337
4633 Lake Michigan Dr Allendale (49401) ***(G-225)***
Muhleck Enterprises Inc 517 333-0713
2863 Jolly Rd Okemos (48864) ***(G-12133)***
Mull-It-Over Products Inc 616 843-6470
4275 White St Sw Grandville (49418) ***(G-7059)***
Multi Grinding Inc 586 268-7388
6877 Miller Dr Warren (48092) ***(G-17162)***
Multi McHning Capabilities Inc 734 955-5592
27482 Northline Rd # 100 Romulus (48174) ***(G-13710)***
Multi Packaging Solutions Inc 616 355-6024
13 W 4th St Holland (49423) ***(G-7751)***
Multi Packg Solutions Intl Ltd 517 323-9000
5800 W Grand River Ave Lansing (48906) ***(G-9250)***
Multi Tech Precision Inc 616 514-1415
3403 Lousma Dr Se Grand Rapids (49548) ***(G-6709)***
Multi Tech Systems, Troy *Also called MAKS INCORPORATED* ***(G-16484)***
Multi-Financial, Plymouth *Also called Plastipak Packaging Inc* ***(G-12719)***
Multi-Form Plastics Inc 586 786-4229
51315 Regency Center Dr Macomb (48042) ***(G-10147)***
Multi-Lab LLC 616 846-6990
18784 174th Ave Spring Lake (49456) ***(G-15165)***
Multi-Precision Detail Inc 248 373-3330
2635 Paldan Dr Auburn Hills (48326) ***(G-951)***
Multi-Sync Power LLC 734 658-3384
47561 Lindenhurst Blvd Canton (48188) ***(G-2410)***
Multiax International Inc 616 534-4530
3000 Remico St Sw Grandville (49418) ***(G-7060)***
Multifinish-Usa Inc 248 528-1154
1389 Wheaton Dr Ste 300 Troy (48083) ***(G-16516)***
Multiform Studios LLC 248 437-5964
12012 Doane Rd South Lyon (48178) ***(G-14803)***
Multimatic Michigan LLC 517 962-7190
2400 Enterprise St Jackson (49203) ***(G-8538)***
Munideals LLC 248 945-0991
29401 Stephenson Hwy Madison Heights (48071) ***(G-10313)***
Munideals.com, Madison Heights *Also called Munideals LLC* ***(G-10313)***
Munimula Inc 517 605-5343
548 Squires Rd Quincy (49082) ***(G-13097)***
Munn Manufacturing Company 616 765-3067
312 County Line Rd Freeport (49325) ***(G-5766)***
Munro Printing 586 773-9579
16145 E 10 Mile Rd Eastpointe (48021) ***(G-4707)***
Murdick's Fudge Kitchen, Mackinac Island *Also called Original Murdicks Fudge Co* ***(G-10097)***
Murleys Marine 586 725-7446
8174 Dixie Hwy Ira (48023) ***(G-8264)***
Murphy Software Company, Roseville *Also called Paul Murphy Plastics Co* ***(G-13851)***
Murphy USA 7601, Charlotte *Also called Murphy USA Inc* ***(G-2661)***
Murphy USA Inc 517 541-0502
1686 Packard Hwy Charlotte (48813) ***(G-2661)***
Murphy Water Well Bits (PA) 810 658-1554
3340 S State Rd Davison (48423) ***(G-3656)***
Murphys Custom Craftsmen Inc 989 205-7305
4125 W Shearer Rd Coleman (48618) ***(G-3349)***
Murray Equipment Company Inc (PA) 313 869-4444
6737 E 8 Mile Rd Warren (48091) ***(G-17163)***
Murray Grinding Inc 313 295-6030
5441 Sylvia St Dearborn Heights (48125) ***(G-3791)***
Murrays Worldwide Inc 248 691-9156
21841 Wyoming St Ste 1 Oak Park (48237) ***(G-12086)***
Murtech Energy Services LLC 810 653-5681
3097 Aberdeen Ct Port Huron (48060) ***(G-12948)***
Musashi Auto Parts Mich Inc 269 965-0057
195 Brydges Dr Battle Creek (49037) ***(G-1230)***
Museum Apparel 248 644-2303
40750 Woodward Ave Unit 3 Bloomfield Hills (48304) ***(G-1785)***
Musical Sneakers Incorporated (PA) 888 410-7050
2885 Snford Ave Sw 3533 Grandville (49418) ***(G-7061)***
Muskegon Awning & Fabrication, Muskegon *Also called Feb Inc* ***(G-11321)***
Muskegon Awning & Mfg Co 231 759-0911
2333 Henry St Muskegon (49441) ***(G-11387)***
Muskegon Brake & Distrg Co LLC (PA) 231 733-0874
848 E Broadway Ave Norton Shores (49444) ***(G-11776)***
Muskegon Brake & Parts, Norton Shores *Also called Muskegon Brake & Distrg Co LLC* ***(G-11776)***
Muskegon Castings LLC 231 777-3941
1985 E Laketon Ave Muskegon (49442) ***(G-11388)***
Muskegon Chronicle, Muskegon *Also called Herald Newspapers Company Inc* ***(G-11344)***
Muskegon Formulation Plant, Muskegon *Also called Bayer Cropscience LP* ***(G-11277)***
Muskegon Gas and Fuel, Muskegon *Also called Jet Fuel* ***(G-11353)***
Muskegon Heights Water Filter 231 780-3415
2323 Seminole Rd Norton Shores (49441) ***(G-11777)***
Muskegon Industrial Finishng 231 733-7663
2000 Sanford St Muskegon (49444) ***(G-11389)***
Muskegon Monument & Stone Co 231 722-2730
1396 Pine St Muskegon (49442) ***(G-11390)***
Muskegon Pioneer County Park, Muskegon *Also called County of Muskegon* ***(G-11302)***
Muskegon Tools LLC 231 788-4633
5142 Evanston Ave Muskegon (49442) ***(G-11391)***
Muslim Observer 248 426-7777
29004 W 8 Mile Rd Farmington Hills (48336) ***(G-5074)***
Mustang Aeronautics Inc 248 649-6818
1990 Heide Dr Troy (48084) ***(G-16517)***
Muzyl Oil Corp 989 732-8100
922 N Center Ave Gaylord (49735) ***(G-5884)***
Mv Metal Pdts & Solutions LLC 269 462-4010
51241 M 51 N Dowagiac (49047) ***(G-4554)***
Mv Metal Pdts & Solutions LLC (PA) 269 471-7715
3585 Bellflower Dr Portage (49024) ***(G-13017)***
Mvc, Roseville *Also called McKechnie Vhcl Cmpnnts USA Inc* ***(G-13833)***
Mvc Holdings LLC (PA) 586 491-2600
27087 Gratiot Ave Fl 2 Roseville (48066) ***(G-13843)***
Mvm7 LLC 989 317-3901
210 W Pickard St Mount Pleasant (48858) ***(G-11213)***
Mvp Sports Store 517 764-5165
5000 Ann Arbor Rd Jackson (49201) ***(G-8539)***
My Permit Pal Inc 248 432-2699
5030 Meadowbrook Dr West Bloomfield (48322) ***(G-17488)***
My-Can LLC 989 288-7779
989 N Saginaw St Durand (48429) ***(G-4610)***
Myco Enterprises Inc (PA) 248 348-3806
200 S Wing St Northville (48167) ***(G-11713)***

Myco Industries Inc ... 248 685-2496
510 Highland Ave 332 Milford (48381) **(G-10973)**
Mycrona Inc ... 734 453-9348
14777 Keel St Plymouth (48170) **(G-12697)**
Mykin Inc ... 248 667-8030
10081 Colonial Indus Dr South Lyon (48178) **(G-14804)**
Myles Group, Troy *Also called J E Myles Inc* **(G-16430)**
Mylockercom LLC ... 877 898-3366
1300 Rosa Parks Blvd Detroit (48216) **(G-4261)**
Mypac Inc ... 616 896-9359
1570 36th Ave Hudsonville (49426) **(G-8172)**
Myron Zucker Inc ... 586 979-9955
36825 Metro Ct Sterling Heights (48312) **(G-15430)**
Myrtle Industries Inc ... 517 784-8579
1810 E High St Ste 2 Jackson (49203) **(G-8540)**
N & K Fulbright LLC ... 269 695-4580
1760 Foundation Dr Niles (49120) **(G-11629)**
N A Actuaplast Inc ... 734 744-4010
31690 Glendale St Livonia (48150) **(G-9855)**
N A Sodecia Inc ... 586 879-8969
969 Chicago Rd Troy (48083) **(G-16518)**
N A Suez ... 734 379-3855
34001 W Jefferson Ave Rockwood (48173) **(G-13609)**
N A Visscher-Caravelle Inc ... 248 851-9800
2525 S Telg Rd Ste 302 Bloomfield Hills (48302) **(G-1786)**
N C Brighton Machine Corp ... 810 227-6190
7300 Whitmore Lake Rd Brighton (48116) **(G-1965)**
N D C Contracting, Petoskey *Also called Manthei Development Corp* **(G-12457)**
N D R Enterprises Inc ... 269 857-4556
297 S Maple St Saugatuck (49453) **(G-14460)**
N F P Inc ... 989 631-0009
7550 Eastman Ave Midland (48642) **(G-10896)**
N Forcer, Dearborn *Also called Die-Mold-Automation Component* **(G-3693)**
N G S G I Natural Gas Ser ... 989 786-3788
3690 County Road 491 Lewiston (49756) **(G-9553)**
N I S, Troy *Also called National Industrial Sup Co Inc* **(G-16520)**
N O C Industries, Cadillac *Also called Hope Network West Michigan* **(G-2252)**
N O F Metal Coatings N Amer ... 248 228-8610
26877 Northwestern Hwy Southfield (48033) **(G-14988)**
N Pack Ship Center ... 906 863-4095
1045 10th St Menominee (49858) **(G-10752)**
N S International Ltd (HQ) ... 248 251-1600
600 Wilshire Dr Troy (48084) **(G-16519)**
N S S Industries, Canton *Also called Nss Technologies Inc* **(G-2412)**
N-K Manufacturing Tech LLC (PA) ... 616 248-3200
1134 Freeman Ave Sw Grand Rapids (49503) **(G-6710)**
N-K Sealing Technologies LLC (PA) ... 616 248-3200
1134 Freeman Ave Sw Grand Rapids (49503) **(G-6711)**
N-P Grinding Inc ... 586 756-6262
3700 E 10 Mile Rd Warren (48091) **(G-17164)**
N. C. I., Rochester Hills *Also called Northville Circuits Inc* **(G-13484)**
N/C Production & Grinding Inc ... 586 731-2150
43758 Merrill Rd Sterling Heights (48314) **(G-15431)**
NA Publishing Inc ... 734 302-6500
6564 State Rd Saline (48176) **(G-14405)**
Naams LLC ... 586 285-5684
25141 Easy St Warren (48089) **(G-17165)**
Nabco Inc (HQ) ... 231 832-2001
660 Commerce Dr Reed City (49677) **(G-13221)**
Nadex of America Corporation (PA) ... 248 477-3900
24775 Crestview Ct Farmington Hills (48335) **(G-5075)**
Nagel Meat Processing ... 517 568-5035
3265 22 Mile Rd Homer (49245) **(G-7947)**
Nagel Paper Inc ... 989 753-4405
6437 Lennon Rd Swartz Creek (48473) **(G-15669)**
Nagel Precision Inc ... 734 426-5650
288 Dino Dr Ann Arbor (48103) **(G-568)**
Nagle Paving Company (PA) ... 248 553-0600
39525 W 13 Mile Rd # 300 Novi (48377) **(G-11951)**
Nagle Paving Company ... 734 591-1484
36780 Amrhein Rd Livonia (48150) **(G-9856)**
Nakagawa Special Stl Amer Inc ... 248 449-6050
42400 Grand River Ave # 102 Novi (48375) **(G-11952)**
Naked Fuel Juice Bar ... 248 325-9735
6718 Orchard Lake Rd West Bloomfield (48322) **(G-17489)**
Nalcor LLC (PA) ... 248 541-1140
1365 Jarvis St Ferndale (48220) **(G-5303)**
Nalpac Enterprises, Ferndale *Also called Nalcor LLC* **(G-5303)**
Naneva Inc ... 248 561-6425
5832 Naneva Ct West Bloomfield (48322) **(G-17490)**
Nankin Welding Co Inc ... 734 458-3980
12620 Fairlane St Livonia (48150) **(G-9857)**
Nano Innovations LLC ... 906 231-2101
22151 Ridge Rd Houghton (49931) **(G-7978)**
Nano Materials & Processes Inc ... 248 529-3873
659 Heritage Dr Milford (48381) **(G-10974)**
Nanocerox Inc (PA) ... 734 741-9522
712 State Cir Ann Arbor (48108) **(G-569)**
Nanomag LLC ... 734 261-2800
13753 Otterson Ct Livonia (48150) **(G-9858)**
Nanoplas, Grandville *Also called Lej Investments LLC* **(G-7056)**
Nanorete Inc ... 517 336-4680
3815 Tech Blvd Ste 1050 Lansing (48910) **(G-9404)**
Nanosynthons LLC ... 989 317-3737
1200 N Fancher Ave Mount Pleasant (48858) **(G-11214)**
Nanosystems Inc ... 734 274-0020
3588 Plymouth Rd Ann Arbor (48105) **(G-570)**
Napco, South Haven *Also called National Appliance Parts Co* **(G-14766)**
Napolitano Bakery, Saginaw *Also called Cesere Enterprises Inc* **(G-14015)**
Narens Associates Inc ... 248 304-0300
30903 Northwestern Hwy # 22 Farmington Hills (48334) **(G-5076)**
Nartron, Reed City *Also called Uusi LLC* **(G-13226)**
Nash Car Trailer Corporation ... 269 673-5776
1305 Lincoln Rd Allegan (49010) **(G-178)**
Nash Services ... 269 782-2016
57229 M 51 S Dowagiac (49047) **(G-4555)**
Nass Controls, New Baltimore *Also called Nass Corporation* **(G-11489)**
Nass Corporation ... 586 725-6610
51509 Birch St New Baltimore (48047) **(G-11489)**
Nassau Candy Midwest L L C ... 734 464-2787
35521 Industrial Rd Livonia (48150) **(G-9859)**
Nate Ronald ... 269 424-3777
50317 W Lakeshore Dr Dowagiac (49047) **(G-4556)**
Nathan Shetler ... 269 521-4554
44815 County Rd Ste 388 Bloomingdale (49026) **(G-1812)**
Nathan Slagter ... 616 648-7423
730 Lincoln Lake Ave Se Lowell (49331) **(G-10038)**
Nation Wide Fuel Inc ... 734 721-7110
6341 Barrie St Dearborn (48126) **(G-3743)**
National Advanced Mobility ... 734 995-3098
3025 Boardwalk St Ste 225 Ann Arbor (48108) **(G-571)**
National Aircraft Service Inc ... 517 423-7589
9133 Tecumseh Clinton Hwy Tecumseh (49286) **(G-15803)**
National Ambucs Inc ... 231 798-4244
708 Mapleway Dr Norton Shores (49441) **(G-11778)**
National Appliance Parts Co ... 269 639-1469
900 Indiana Ave South Haven (49090) **(G-14766)**
National Asphalt Products, Shelby Township *Also called Carlo John Inc* **(G-14557)**
National Bakery ... 313 891-7803
736 E State Fair Detroit (48203) **(G-4262)**
National Block Company ... 734 721-4050
39000 Ford Rd Westland (48185) **(G-17582)**
National Bronze Mfg Co, Roseville *Also called Conway Detroit Corporation* **(G-13786)**
National Bulk Equipment Inc (PA) ... 616 399-2220
12838 Stainless Dr Holland (49424) **(G-7752)**
National Carbon Tech LLC ... 651 330-4063
513 4th St Gwinn (49841) **(G-7220)**
National Case Corporation ... 586 726-1710
42710 Mound Rd Sterling Heights (48314) **(G-15432)**
National Chemical & Oil, Oak Park *Also called Ncoc Inc* **(G-12088)**
National Chili, Roseville *Also called National Coney Island Chili Co* **(G-13844)**
National Concrete Products Co ... 734 453-8448
939 S Mill St Plymouth (48170) **(G-12698)**
National Coney Island Chili Co ... 313 365-5611
27947 Groesbeck Hwy Roseville (48066) **(G-13844)**
National Control Systems Inc ... 810 231-2901
10737 Hamburg Rd Hamburg (48139) **(G-7226)**
National Crane & Hoist Service ... 248 789-4535
1630 Noble Rd Lakeville (48367) **(G-9179)**
National Credit Corporation (PA) ... 734 459-8100
7091 Orchard Lake Rd # 300 West Bloomfield (48322) **(G-17491)**
National Discount X-Ray Supply, Ann Arbor *Also called Associated Metals Inc* **(G-371)**
National Element Inc ... 248 486-1810
7939 Lochlin Dr Brighton (48116) **(G-1966)**
National Flag Football, Bloomfield Hills *Also called B4 Sports Inc* **(G-1749)**
National Flavors LLC ... 800 525-2431
3680 Stadium Park Way Kalamazoo (49009) **(G-8833)**
National Fleet Service LLC ... 313 923-1799
10100 Grinnell St Detroit (48213) **(G-4263)**
National Fuels Inc ... 734 895-7836
40401 Michigan Ave Canton (48188) **(G-2411)**
National Galvanizing LP ... 734 243-1882
1500 Telb St Monroe (48162) **(G-11059)**
National Industrial Sup Co Inc ... 248 588-1828
1201 Rochester Rd Troy (48083) **(G-16520)**
National Instruments Corp ... 734 464-2310
20255 Victor Pkwy Ste 195 Livonia (48152) **(G-9860)**
National Intgrated Systems Inc ... 734 927-3030
29241 Beck Rd Wixom (48393) **(G-17861)**
National Manufacturing Inc ... 586 755-8983
25426 Ryan Rd Warren (48091) **(G-17166)**
National Metal Sales Inc ... 734 942-3000
27400 Northline Rd Romulus (48174) **(G-13711)**
National Millwork Inc ... 248 307-1299
32350 Howard Ave Madison Heights (48071) **(G-10314)**
National Nail Corp (PA) ... 616 538-8000
2964 Clydon Ave Sw Wyoming (49519) **(G-18021)**

ALPHABETIC

(PA)=Parent Co (HQ)=Headquarters (DH)=Div Headquarters

2020 Harris Michigan Industrial Directory

1029

National Ordanace Auto Mfg LLC 248 853-8822
2900 Auburn Ct Auburn Hills (48326) ***(G-952)***
National Ordnance Auto Mfg LLC 248 853-8822
2900 Auburn Ct Auburn Hills (48326) ***(G-953)***
National Packaging Corporation 248 652-3600
1150 W Hamlin Rd Rochester Hills (48309) ***(G-13479)***
National Pattern Inc 989 755-6274
5900 Sherman Rd Saginaw (48604) ***(G-14101)***
National Plastek Inc 616 698-9559
7050 Dtton Indus Pk Dr Se Caledonia (49316) ***(G-2310)***
National Printing Services 616 813-0758
5360 Pine Slope Dr Sw Wyoming (49519) ***(G-18022)***
National Product Co 269 344-3640
1206 E Crosstown Pkwy Kalamazoo (49001) ***(G-8834)***
National Ready-Mix, Westland *Also called National Block Company* ***(G-17582)***
National Roofg & Shtmtl Co Inc 989 964-0557
200 Lee St Saginaw (48602) ***(G-14102)***
National Sign & Signal Co 269 963-2817
301 Armstrong Rd Battle Creek (49037) ***(G-1231)***
National Soap Company Inc 248 545-8180
1911 Bellaire Ave Royal Oak (48067) ***(G-13953)***
National Television Book Co, Troy *Also called Ntvb Media Inc* ***(G-16528)***
National Time and Signal Corp 248 291-5867
21800 Wyoming St Oak Park (48237) ***(G-12087)***
National Tool & Die Welding 734 522-0072
13340 Merriman Rd Livonia (48150) ***(G-9861)***
National Wholesale Prtg Corp 734 416-8400
41290 Joy Rd Plymouth (48170) ***(G-12699)***
National Zinc Processors Inc 269 926-1161
1256 Milton St Benton Harbor (49022) ***(G-1535)***
National-Standard LLC (HQ) 269 683-9902
1631 Lake St Niles (49120) ***(G-11630)***
Nationwide Communications LLC 517 990-1223
5263 Thames Ct Jackson (49201) ***(G-8541)***
Nationwide Design Inc 586 254-5493
6605 Burroughs Ave Sterling Heights (48314) ***(G-15433)***
Nationwide Envlope Spclsts Inc (PA) 248 354-5500
1225 E West Maple Rd Walled Lake (48390) ***(G-16900)***
Nationwide Intelligence, Saginaw *Also called Nationwide Network Inc* ***(G-14103)***
Nationwide Laser Technologies 248 488-0155
27600 Farmington Rd B1 Farmington Hills (48334) ***(G-5077)***
Nationwide Network Inc (PA) 989 793-0123
3401 Peale Dr Saginaw (48602) ***(G-14103)***
Nationwide Toner Cartridge, Farmington Hills *Also called Nationwide Laser Technologies* ***(G-5077)***
Native Green LLC 248 365-4200
180 Engelwood Dr Ste A Orion (48359) ***(G-12186)***
Natural Aggregate, Wixom *Also called American Aggregates Mich Inc* ***(G-17760)***
Natural Aggregates Corporation (PA) 248 685-1502
3362 Muir Rd Milford (48380) ***(G-10975)***
Natural American Foods Inc (PA) 517 467-2065
10464 Bryan Hwy Onsted (49265) ***(G-12155)***
Natural Attraction 231 398-0787
25 Cross St Manistee (49660) ***(G-10432)***
Natural Gas Compress (PA) 231 941-0107
2480 Aero Park Dr Traverse City (49686) ***(G-16046)***
Natures Best Top Soil Compost 810 657-9528
640 Old 51 Carsonville (48419) ***(G-2497)***
Natures Edge Stone Produ 231 943-3440
1776 Southpeak Dr Traverse City (49685) ***(G-16047)***
Natures Select Inc (PA) 616 956-1105
833 Kenmoor Ave Se Ste D Grand Rapids (49546) ***(G-6712)***
Nautical Knots 231 206-0400
301 N Harbor Dr Ste 12 Grand Haven (49417) ***(G-6058)***
Nauticraft Corporation 231 798-8440
5980 Grand Haven Rd Norton Shores (49441) ***(G-11779)***
Navarre Inc 313 892-7300
3500 E 8 Mile Rd Detroit (48234) ***(G-4264)***
Navistar Defense LLC 248 680-7505
1675 E Whitcomb Ave Madison Heights (48071) ***(G-10315)***
Navitas Systems LLC (HQ) 630 755-7920
4880 Venture Dr Ann Arbor (48108) ***(G-572)***
Navtech LLC 248 427-1080
47906 West Rd Wixom (48393) ***(G-17862)***
Nb Cement Co 313 278-8299
4203 Merrick St Dearborn Heights (48125) ***(G-3792)***
Nb Coatings Inc 248 365-1100
2851 High Meadow Cir # 140 Auburn Hills (48326) ***(G-954)***
NBC Truck Equipment Inc (PA) 586 774-4900
28130 Groesbeck Hwy Roseville (48066) ***(G-13845)***
Nbhx Trim USA Corporation 616 785-9400
3056 Wlker Ridge Ct Ste D Walker (49544) ***(G-16871)***
Nbhx Trim USA Corporation (HQ) 616 785-9400
1020 7 Mile Rd Nw Comstock Park (49321) ***(G-3501)***
Nci Mfg Inc 248 380-4151
12665 Richfield Ct Livonia (48150) ***(G-9862)***
Ncoc Inc 248 548-5950
21251 Meyers Rd Oak Park (48237) ***(G-12088)***
Ncp Coatings Inc (PA) 269 683-3377
225 Fort St Niles (49120) ***(G-11631)***
ND Industries Inc 248 288-0000
1819 Thunderbird Troy (48084) ***(G-16521)***
ND Industries Inc (PA) 248 288-0000
1000 N Crooks Rd Clawson (48017) ***(G-2982)***
ND Industries Inc 248 288-0000
1893 Barrett Dr Troy (48084) ***(G-16522)***
ND Technologies, Clawson *Also called ND Industries Inc* ***(G-2982)***
Ndex 248 432-9000
31440 Northwestern Hwy Farmington Hills (48334) ***(G-5078)***
Ndsay Nettell Logging 906 482-3549
47301 Janovosky Rd Atlantic Mine (49905) ***(G-738)***
Ne - Direct, Brighton *Also called New Echelon Direct Mktg LLC* ***(G-1967)***
Neapco Drivelines LLC 734 447-1316
6735 Haggerty Rd Van Buren Twp (48111) ***(G-16775)***
Neapco Drivelines LLC (HQ) 734 447-1300
6735 Haggerty Rd Van Buren Twp (48111) ***(G-16776)***
Neapco Holdings LLC (HQ) 248 699-6500
38900 Hills Tech Dr Farmington Hills (48331) ***(G-5079)***
Near's Septic, Whittemore *Also called Nears Inc* ***(G-17709)***
Nears Inc 989 756-2203
425 N M 65 Whittemore (48770) ***(G-17709)***
Nedrow Refractories Co 248 669-2500
150 Landrow Dr Wixom (48393) ***(G-17863)***
Needles N Pins Inc 734 459-0625
754 S Main St Plymouth (48170) ***(G-12700)***
Neenah Paper Inc 906 387-2700
501 E Munising Ave Munising (49862) ***(G-11246)***
Neetz Printing Inc 989 684-4620
700 S Euclid Ave Bay City (48706) ***(G-1336)***
Nefco, Jonesville *Also called North East Fabrication Co Inc* ***(G-8664)***
Neighborhood Artisans Inc 313 865-5373
85 Oakman Blvd Detroit (48203) ***(G-4265)***
Nelles Studios, Elk Rapids *Also called Allusion Star Inc* ***(G-4774)***
Nelms Technologies Inc 734 955-6500
15385 Pine Romulus (48174) ***(G-13712)***
Nelson Company 517 788-6117
654 Hupp Ave Jackson (49203) ***(G-8542)***
Nelson Farms 989 560-1303
7530 Madison Rd Elwell (48832) ***(G-4797)***
Nelson Hardware 269 327-3583
9029 Portage Rd Portage (49002) ***(G-13018)***
Nelson Iron Works Inc 313 925-5355
6350 Benham St Detroit (48211) ***(G-4266)***
Nelson Manufacturing Inc 810 648-0065
1240 W Sanilac Rd Ste A Sandusky (48471) ***(G-14440)***
Nelson Paint Co of Mich Inc (PA) 906 774-5566
1 Nelson Dr Kingsford (49802) ***(G-9063)***
Nelson Paint Company Ala Inc (PA) 906 774-5566
1 Nelson Dr Kingsford (49802) ***(G-9064)***
Nelson Paint Company Mich Inc 906 774-5566
1 Nelson Dr Iron Mountain (49802) ***(G-8291)***
Nelson Rapids Co Inc 616 691-8041
11834 Old Belding Rd Ne Belding (48809) ***(G-1427)***
Nelson Specialties Company 269 983-1878
211 Hilltop Rd Saint Joseph (49085) ***(G-14330)***
Nelson Steel Products Inc 616 396-1515
410 E 48th St Holland (49423) ***(G-7753)***
Nelson Technologies, Kingsford *Also called Nelson Paint Co of Mich Inc* ***(G-9063)***
Nelson Technologies Inc 906 774-5566
1 Nelson Dr Iron Mountain (49802) ***(G-8292)***
Nelsonite Chemical Products 616 456-7098
2320 Oak Industrial Dr Ne Grand Rapids (49505) ***(G-6713)***
Nelsons Saw Mill Inc 231 829-5220
8482 N Raymond Rd Tustin (49688) ***(G-16711)***
Nemak Commercial Services Inc 248 350-3999
2 Towne Sq Ste 300 Southfield (48076) ***(G-14989)***
Nematron, Ann Arbor *Also called D & C Investment Group Inc* ***(G-410)***
Nemo Capital Partners LLC (PA) 248 213-9899
28819 Franklin Rd Ste 130 Southfield (48034) ***(G-14990)***
Neo Manufacturing Inc 269 503-7630
21900 Us Highway 12 Sturgis (49091) ***(G-15623)***
Neo Trailers, Sturgis *Also called Neo Manufacturing Inc* ***(G-15623)***
Neogen Corporation (PA) 517 372-9200
620 Lesher Pl Lansing (48912) ***(G-9405)***
Neogen Corporation 800 327-5487
2620 S Cleveland Ave # 100 Saint Joseph (49085) ***(G-14331)***
Neopost Mailing Equipment, Grand Rapids *Also called D & D Business Machines Inc* ***(G-6329)***
Nephew Fabrication Inc 616 875-2121
10752 Polk St Zeeland (49464) ***(G-18168)***
Nepko Lake Nursery, Escanaba *Also called Plum Creek Timber Company Inc* ***(G-4852)***
Neptech Inc 810 225-2222
2000 E Highland Rd Highland (48356) ***(G-7498)***
Neptune Chemical Pump Company (HQ) 215 699-8700
1809 Century Ave Sw Grand Rapids (49503) ***(G-6714)***
Neptune Mixer, Grand Rapids *Also called Neptune Chemical Pump Company* ***(G-6714)***
Nesco Tool & Fixture LLC 517 618-7052
530 Fowler St Howell (48843) ***(G-8068)***

Nestle Infant Nutrition, Fremont *Also called Gerber Products Company* ***(G-5773)***
Nestle Purina Petcare Company..........888 202-4554
600 Executive Dr Troy (48083) ***(G-16523)***
Netcon Enterprises Inc..........248 673-7855
5085 Williams Lake Rd A Waterford (48329) ***(G-17360)***
Netshape International LLC..........616 846-8700
1900 Hayes St Grand Haven (49417) ***(G-6059)***
Nettleton Wood Products Inc..........906 297-5791
34882 S Mcadams Rd De Tour Village (49725) ***(G-3668)***
Netwave..........586 263-4469
20539 Country Side Dr Macomb (48044) ***(G-10148)***
Network Machinery Inc..........586 992-2459
54407 Woodcreek Blvd Shelby Township (48315) ***(G-14651)***
Networks Enterprises Inc..........248 446-8590
57450 Travis Rd New Hudson (48165) ***(G-11549)***
Neucadia LLC..........989 572-0324
404 S 2nd St Carson City (48811) ***(G-2494)***
Neumann Enterprises Inc..........906 293-8122
1011 Newberry Ave Newberry (49868) ***(G-11581)***
Neurable LLC..........206 696-4469
2260 Fuller Ct Apt 5 Ann Arbor (48105) ***(G-573)***
Neuvokas Corporation..........906 934-2661
32066 Rd Ahmeek (49901) ***(G-108)***
Nevill Supply Incorporated..........989 386-4522
8415 S Eberhart Ave Clare (48617) ***(G-2879)***
Nevis Energy, Traverse City *Also called Phoenix Technology Svcs USA* ***(G-16067)***
New 11 Inc..........616 494-9370
1886 Russel Ct Holland (49423) ***(G-7754)***
New 9 Inc..........616 459-8274
1411 Michigan St Ne Grand Rapids (49503) ***(G-6715)***
New Bolton Conductive Systems, Novi *Also called Conductive Bolton Systems LLC* ***(G-11852)***
New Boston Candle Company..........734 782-5809
21941 Merriman Rd New Boston (48164) ***(G-11504)***
New Boston Forge, New Boston *Also called Lc Manufacturing LLC* ***(G-11503)***
New Boston Rtm Inc..........734 753-9956
19155 Shook Rd New Boston (48164) ***(G-11505)***
New Buffalo Concrete Products..........269 469-2515
825 S Whittaker St New Buffalo (49117) ***(G-11516)***
New Buffalo Times..........269 469-1100
430 S Whittaker St New Buffalo (49117) ***(G-11517)***
New Center News, Warren *Also called Springer Publishing Co Inc* ***(G-17250)***
New Center Stamping Inc..........313 872-3500
950 E Milwaukee St Detroit (48211) ***(G-4267)***
New Century Heaters Ltd..........989 671-1994
4432 Ace Commercial Ct Bay City (48706) ***(G-1337)***
New Cnc Routercom Inc..........616 994-8844
510 E 40th St Holland (49423) ***(G-7755)***
New Concept Products Inc..........269 679-5970
277 E Lyons St Schoolcraft (49087) ***(G-14500)***
New Concepts Software Inc..........586 776-2855
28490 Bohn St Roseville (48066) ***(G-13846)***
New Delray Baking Co, Taylor *Also called Rainbow Pizza Inc* ***(G-15761)***
New Dimension Laser Inc..........586 415-6041
29540 Calahan Rd Roseville (48066) ***(G-13847)***
New Echelon Direct Mktg LLC..........248 809-2485
9825 Lyon Dr Brighton (48114) ***(G-1967)***
New ERA Canning Company..........231 861-2151
4856 1st St New ERA (49446) ***(G-11521)***
New Genesis Enterprise Inc..........313 220-0365
37774 Willow Ln Apt S2 Westland (48185) ***(G-17583)***
New Holland Brewery..........616 298-7727
690 Commerce Ct Holland (49424) ***(G-7756)***
New Holland Brewery..........616 202-7200
427 Bridge St Nw Grand Rapids (49504) ***(G-6716)***
New Holland Brewing Co LLC..........616 355-2941
684 Commerce Ct Holland (49424) ***(G-7757)***
New Image Dental P C..........586 727-1100
35000 Division Rd Ste 4 Richmond (48062) ***(G-13267)***
New Issues Poetry and Prose..........269 387-8185
1903 W Michigan Ave Kalamazoo (49008) ***(G-8835)***
New Issues Press, Kalamazoo *Also called New Issues Poetry and Prose* ***(G-8835)***
New Lfe Cppr & Brss Maint Free..........586 725-3286
9984 Marine City Hwy Casco (48064) ***(G-2503)***
New Line Inc..........586 228-4820
15164 Commercial Dr Shelby Township (48315) ***(G-14652)***
New Line Laminate Design, Shelby Township *Also called New Line Inc* ***(G-14652)***
New Martha Washington Bakery..........313 872-1988
10335 Joseph Campau St Detroit (48212) ***(G-4268)***
NEW MERIDIAN, Clinton *Also called Eden Foods Inc* ***(G-3019)***
New Method Steel Stamps Inc..........586 293-0200
17801 Helro Fraser (48026) ***(G-5697)***
New Mix 96..........231 941-0963
856 E Eighth St Traverse City (49686) ***(G-16048)***
New Monitor..........248 439-1863
23082 Reynolds Ave Hazel Park (48030) ***(G-7447)***
New Moon Noodle Incorporated..........269 962-8820
909 Stanley Dr Battle Creek (49037) ***(G-1232)***
New Ngc Inc..........989 756-2741
2375 S National City Rd National City (48748) ***(G-11464)***
New Product Development LLC..........616 399-6253
785 Mary Ave Holland (49424) ***(G-7758)***
New Rules Marketing Inc..........800 962-3119
540 Oak St Spring Lake (49456) ***(G-15166)***
New Technologies Tool & Mfg..........810 694-5426
4380 E Baldwin Rd Grand Blanc (48439) ***(G-5976)***
New Unison Corporation..........248 544-9500
1601 Wanda St Ferndale (48220) ***(G-5304)***
New Venture Foundry, Hillsdale *Also called Paragon Metals LLC* ***(G-7533)***
New Vintage Usa LLC..........248 259-4964
21840 Wyoming Pl Ste 1 Oak Park (48237) ***(G-12089)***
New Way Air Solution Company (PA)..........248 676-9418
4030 Sleeth Rd Milford (48380) ***(G-10976)***
New World Etching N Amer Ve..........586 296-8082
33870 Riviera Fraser (48026) ***(G-5698)***
New World Systems, Troy *Also called Brinston Acquisition LLC* ***(G-16246)***
New Yasmeen Bakery, Dearborn *Also called New Yasmeen Detroit Inc* ***(G-3744)***
New Yasmeen Detroit Inc..........313 582-6035
13900 W Warren Ave Dearborn (48126) ***(G-3744)***
New York Bagel Baking Co (PA)..........248 548-2580
23316 Woodward Ave Ferndale (48220) ***(G-5305)***
New-Matic Industries Inc..........586 415-9801
31256 Fraser Dr Fraser (48026) ***(G-5699)***
Newark Gravel Company..........810 796-3072
4290 Calkins Rd Dryden (48428) ***(G-4570)***
Newark High Pressure, Capac *Also called Imlay City High Pressure* ***(G-2448)***
Newark Morning Ledger Co..........517 487-8888
217 N Sycamore St Lansing (48933) ***(G-9406)***
Neway Manufacturing, Troy *Also called City Animation Co* ***(G-16268)***
Neway Manufacturing, Corunna *Also called City Animation Co* ***(G-3579)***
Neway Manufacturing Inc..........989 743-3458
1013 N Shiawassee St Corunna (48817) ***(G-3583)***
Newberry Bottling Co Inc (PA)..........906 293-5189
80 N Newberry Ave Newberry (49868) ***(G-11582)***
Newberry News Inc..........906 293-8401
316 Newberry Ave Newberry (49868) ***(G-11583)***
Newberry Redi-Mix Inc (PA)..........906 293-5178
307 E Victory Way Newberry (49868) ***(G-11584)***
Newberry Wood Enterprises Inc..........906 293-3131
7300 N County Road 403 Newberry (49868) ***(G-11585)***
Newco Industries LLC..........517 542-0105
900 Anderson Rd Litchfield (49252) ***(G-9610)***
Newcor Inc (HQ)..........248 537-0014
1021 N Shiawassee St Corunna (48817) ***(G-3584)***
Newcor, Deco Division, Clifford *Also called Deco Engineering Inc* ***(G-3010)***
Newell Brands Inc..........734 284-2528
20033 Eureka Rd Taylor (48180) ***(G-15749)***
Newkirk and Associates Inc..........616 863-9899
9767 Shaw Creek Ct Ne Rockford (49341) ***(G-13582)***
Newman Construction, Springfield *Also called Jn Newman Construction LLC* ***(G-15194)***
News One Inc..........231 798-4669
4080 Oak Hollow Ct Norton Shores (49441) ***(G-11780)***
Newsweb, Greenville *Also called Stafford Media Inc* ***(G-7154)***
Newtech 3 Inc..........248 912-0807
28373 Beck Rd Ste H7 Wixom (48393) ***(G-17864)***
Newton Well Service Inc..........269 945-5084
550 E Cloverdale Rd Hastings (49058) ***(G-7422)***
Nex Solutions, Litchfield *Also called Newco Industries LLC* ***(G-9610)***
Nexiq Technologies Inc..........248 293-8200
2950 Waterview Dr Rochester Hills (48309) ***(G-13480)***
Next Level Manufacturing LLC..........269 397-1220
6778 18th Ave Jenison (49428) ***(G-8634)***
Next Level Media Inc..........248 762-7043
15989 Addison St Southfield (48075) ***(G-14991)***
Next Specialty Resins Inc..........419 843-4600
215 N Talbot St Addison (49220) ***(G-37)***
Next Tool LLC..........734 405-7079
41200 Coca Cola Dr Belleville (48111) ***(G-1449)***
Nextcat Inc..........248 514-6742
2344 Fairway Dr Birmingham (48009) ***(G-1695)***
Nexteer - Plant 6, Saginaw *Also called Nexteer Automotive Corporation* ***(G-14108)***
Nexteer - Plant 6 E-Bike, Saginaw *Also called Nexteer Automotive Corporation* ***(G-14112)***
Nexteer - Saginaw Plant 1, Saginaw *Also called Nexteer Automotive Corporation* ***(G-14113)***
Nexteer - Saginaw Plant 3, Saginaw *Also called Nexteer Automotive Corporation* ***(G-14110)***
Nexteer - Saginaw Plant 4, Saginaw *Also called Nexteer Automotive Corporation* ***(G-14109)***
Nexteer - Saginaw Plant 5, Saginaw *Also called Nexteer Automotive Corporation* ***(G-14107)***
Nexteer - Saginaw Plant 7, Saginaw *Also called Nexteer Automotive Corporation* ***(G-14106)***
Nexteer Automotive Corporation..........989 757-5000
3900 E Holland Rd Saginaw (48601) ***(G-14104)***
Nexteer Automotive Corporation..........989 754-1920
2975 Nodular Dr Saginaw (48601) ***(G-14105)***
Nexteer Automotive Corporation..........989 757-5000
3900 E Holland Rd Saginaw (48601) ***(G-14106)***
Nexteer Automotive Corporation..........989 757-5000
3900 E Holland Rd Saginaw (48601) ***(G-14107)***

Nexteer Automotive Corporation 989 757-5000
3900 E Holland Rd Saginaw (48601) ***(G-14108)***
Nexteer Automotive Corporation 989 757-5000
3900 E Holland Rd Saginaw (48601) ***(G-14109)***
Nexteer Automotive Corporation 989 757-5000
3900 E Holland Rd Saginaw (48601) ***(G-14110)***
Nexteer Automotive Corporation 989 757-5000
3900 E Holland Rd Saginaw (48601) ***(G-14111)***
Nexteer Automotive Corporation 989 757-5000
3900 E Holland Rd Saginaw (48601) ***(G-14112)***
Nexteer Automotive Corporation 989 757-5000
3900 E Holland Rd Saginaw (48601) ***(G-14113)***
Nexteer Automotive Corporation 989 757-5000
5153 Hess Rd Saginaw (48601) ***(G-14114)***
Nexteer Automotive Corporation (HQ) 248 340-8200
1272 Doris Rd Auburn Hills (48326) ***(G-955)***
Nexteer Automotive Group Ltd 989 757-5000
3900 E Holland Rd Saginaw (48601) ***(G-14115)***
Nexteer Saginaw, Saginaw *Also called Nexteer Automotive Corporation* ***(G-14104)***
Nextek Power Systems Inc (PA) 313 887-1321
461 Burroughs St Detroit (48202) ***(G-4269)***
Nexthermal Corporation 269 964-0271
1045 Harts Lake Rd Battle Creek (49037) ***(G-1233)***
NGK Spark Plugs (usa) Inc (HQ) 248 926-6900
46929 Magellan Wixom (48393) ***(G-17865)***
NGK Spark Plugs USA, Wixom *Also called NGK Spark Plugs (usa) Inc* ***(G-17865)***
Nht Sales Inc 248 623-6114
2142 Pontiac Rd Ste 201 Auburn Hills (48326) ***(G-956)***
Niagara Machine, Hastings *Also called CNB International Inc* ***(G-7403)***
Nicholas Wine Sampling Room, Cheboygan *Also called Nicholass Black River Vineyar* ***(G-2687)***
Nicholass Black River Vineyar 231 436-5770
156 S Huron Ave Mackinaw City (49701) ***(G-10100)***
Nicholass Black River Vineyar (PA) 231 625-9060
6209 N Black River Rd Cheboygan (49721) ***(G-2687)***
Nicholson Terminal & Dock Co (PA) 313 842-4300
380 E Great Lakes St River Rouge (48218) ***(G-13279)***
Nicholson's, Ann Arbor *Also called Power Sports Ann Arbor LLC* ***(G-597)***
Nickels Boat Works Inc 810 767-4050
1871 Tower St Flint (48503) ***(G-5472)***
Nickels Logging 906 563-5880
1108 Railroad Ave Norway (49870) ***(G-11818)***
Nico Med Amersham, Grand Rapids *Also called GE Healthcare Inc* ***(G-6432)***
Nicole Acarter LLC 248 251-2800
551 Newport St Detroit (48215) ***(G-4270)***
Nicolet Sign & Construction, Iron River *Also called Nicolet Sign & Design* ***(G-8317)***
Nicolet Sign & Design 906 265-5220
612 W Adams St Iron River (49935) ***(G-8317)***
Nicro Finishing LLC 313 924-0661
6431 E Palmer St Detroit (48211) ***(G-4271)***
Nidec Motors & Actuators (usa) 248 340-9977
1800 Opdyke Ct Auburn Hills (48326) ***(G-957)***
Nieboer Electric Inc 231 924-0960
502 E Main St Fremont (49412) ***(G-5779)***
Nieboers Pit Stop 616 997-2026
288 Main St Coopersville (49404) ***(G-3566)***
Nieddu Drapery Mfg 586 977-0065
35532 Mound Rd Sterling Heights (48310) ***(G-15434)***
Niemela 906 523-4362
39466 Tapiola Rd Chassell (49916) ***(G-2674)***
Nihil Ultra Corporation 413 723-3218
55 E Long Lake Rd Troy (48085) ***(G-16524)***
Nike Retail Services Inc 248 858-9291
4000 Baldwin Rd Auburn Hills (48326) ***(G-958)***
Niki's Warehouse, Detroit *Also called Nikis Food Co Inc* ***(G-4272)***
Nikis Food Co Inc 313 925-0876
8844 Gratiot Ave Detroit (48213) ***(G-4272)***
Nikolic Industries Inc 586 254-4810
43252 Merrill Rd Sterling Heights (48314) ***(G-15435)***
Nikon Metrology Inc (HQ) 810 220-4360
12701 Grand River Rd Brighton (48116) ***(G-1968)***
Nikon Metrology Inc 810 220-4347
12589 Grand River Rd Brighton (48116) ***(G-1969)***
Nil-Cor LLC 616 554-3100
4855 Broadmoor Ave Se Kentwood (49512) ***(G-9021)***
Niles Aluminum Products Inc 269 683-1191
1434 S 9th St Niles (49120) ***(G-11632)***
Niles Daily Star, Niles *Also called Leader Publications LLC* ***(G-11623)***
Niles Machine & Tool Company 269 684-2594
2124 S 11th St Niles (49120) ***(G-11633)***
Niles Precision Company 269 683-0585
1308 Fort St Niles (49120) ***(G-11634)***
Nims Precision Machining Inc 248 446-1053
9493 Pontiac Trl South Lyon (48178) ***(G-14805)***
Nine Mile Dequindre Fuel Stop 586 757-7721
1940 E 9 Mile Rd Warren (48091) ***(G-17167)***
Ninja Tees N More 248 541-2547
505 W 9 Mile Rd Ste B Hazel Park (48030) ***(G-7448)***
Nipguards LLC 734 544-4490
2232 S Main St Ste 361 Ann Arbor (48103) ***(G-574)***
Nippa Sauna Stoves LLC 231 882-7707
8862 Us Highway 31 Beulah (49617) ***(G-1611)***
Nisshinbo Automotive Mfg Inc 586 997-1000
6100 19 Mile Rd Sterling Heights (48314) ***(G-15436)***
Nitrex Inc (HQ) 517 676-6370
822 Kim Dr Mason (48854) ***(G-10649)***
Nitro EDM and Machining Inc 586 247-8035
50606 Sabrina Dr Shelby Township (48315) ***(G-14653)***
Nitro Steel, Jackson *Also called Gerdau Macsteel Inc* ***(G-8456)***
Nitro-Vac Heat Treat Inc 586 754-4350
23080 Dequindre Rd Warren (48091) ***(G-17168)***
Nits Solutions Inc 248 231-2267
40850 Grand River Ave 100a Novi (48375) ***(G-11953)***
Nitto Inc 732 276-1039
36663 Van Born Rd Ste 360 Romulus (48174) ***(G-13713)***
Nitto Inc 734 729-7800
36663 Van Born Rd Ste 360 Romulus (48174) ***(G-13714)***
Nitto Inc 248 449-2300
45880 Dylan Dr Novi (48377) ***(G-11954)***
Nitto Denko Automotive, Romulus *Also called Nitto Inc* ***(G-13714)***
Nitto Seiko Co Ltd 248 588-0133
1301 Rankin Dr Troy (48083) ***(G-16525)***
Nitz Valve Hardware Inc 989 883-9500
8610 Unionville Rd Sebewaing (48759) ***(G-14517)***
Nivers Sand Gravel 231 743-6126
19937 M 115 Marion (49665) ***(G-10492)***
Nje Enterprises LLC 313 963-3600
400 Renaissance Ctr Lbby Detroit (48243) ***(G-4273)***
Njt Enterprises LLC, Clinton Township *Also called Mayco International LLC* ***(G-3171)***
Njt Enterprises LLC, Auburn Hills *Also called Mayco International LLC* ***(G-944)***
Njt Enterprises LLC, Sterling Heights *Also called Mayco International LLC* ***(G-15414)***
Nk Dockside Service & Repair 906 420-0777
1014 8th Ave S Escanaba (49829) ***(G-4846)***
Nmp Inc 231 798-8851
6170 Norton Center Dr Norton Shores (49441) ***(G-11781)***
No Limit Wireless-Michigan Inc 313 285-8402
6236 Michigan Ave Detroit (48210) ***(G-4274)***
Noack Ventures LLC 248 583-0311
1407 Allen Dr Ste G Troy (48083) ***(G-16526)***
Nobby Inc 810 984-3300
3950 Pine Grove Ave Fort Gratiot (48059) ***(G-5550)***
Noble Films Corporation 616 977-3770
967 Spaulding Ave Se B1 Ada (49301) ***(G-25)***
Noble Forestry Inc 989 866-6495
5012 Taylor Rd Blanchard (49310) ***(G-1711)***
Noble Polymers LLC 616 975-4800
4855 37th St Se Grand Rapids (49512) ***(G-6717)***
Nodel-Co 248 543-1325
2615 Wolcott St Ferndale (48220) ***(G-5306)***
Noelco Inc 586 846-4955
22303 Starks Dr Clinton Township (48036) ***(G-3183)***
Nof Metal Coatings N Amer Inc 810 966-9240
2015 Dove St Port Huron (48060) ***(G-12949)***
Noir Laser Company LLC 800 521-9746
4975 Technical Dr Milford (48381) ***(G-10977)***
Noir Manufacturing, South Lyon *Also called Noir Medical Technologies LLC* ***(G-14806)***
Noir Manufacturing Co, Milford *Also called Noir Medical Technologies LLC* ***(G-10978)***
Noir Medical Technologies LLC (PA) 734 769-5565
4975 Technical Dr Milford (48381) ***(G-10978)***
Noir Medical Technologies LLC 248 486-3760
10125 Colonial Indus Dr South Lyon (48178) ***(G-14806)***
Noisemeters Inc 248 840-6559
3233 Coolidge Hwy Berkley (48072) ***(G-1588)***
Nolan's Farm Equipment, Lapeer *Also called Nolans Outdoor Power Inc* ***(G-9477)***
Nolans Outdoor Power Inc 810 664-3798
3120 N Lapeer Rd Lapeer (48446) ***(G-9477)***
Nolans Top Tin Inc 586 899-3421
8428 Republic Ave Warren (48089) ***(G-17169)***
Non-Ferrous Cast Alloys Inc 231 799-0550
1146 N Gateway Blvd Norton Shores (49441) ***(G-11782)***
Nopras Technologies Inc 248 486-6684
13513 Windmoor Dr South Lyon (48178) ***(G-14807)***
Nor-Cote Inc 586 756-1200
11425 Timken Ave Warren (48089) ***(G-17170)***
Nor-Dic Tool Company Inc 734 326-3610
6577 Beverly Plz Romulus (48174) ***(G-13715)***
Noram Autobody Parts, Riverview *Also called North American Auto Inds Inc* ***(G-13302)***
Norbert Industries Inc 586 977-9200
38111 Commerce Dr Sterling Heights (48312) ***(G-15437)***
Norbord Panels USA Inc 248 608-0387
410 W University Dr # 210 Rochester (48307) ***(G-13336)***
Norbrook Plating Inc 586 755-4110
11400 E 9 Mile Rd Warren (48089) ***(G-17171)***
Norbrook Plating Inc 313 369-9304
19230 Mount Elliott St Detroit (48234) ***(G-4275)***
Norcold Inc 734 769-6000
7101 Jackson Rd Ann Arbor (48103) ***(G-575)***

Norcross Viscosity Controls...586 336-0700
12427 31 Mile Rd Washington (48095) *(G-17308)*
Nordic Label, Wixom *Also called Norman Industries Inc (G-17867)*
Nordson Corporation...734 459-8600
28775 Beck Rd Wixom (48393) *(G-17866)*
Norgren Automtn Solutions LLC (HQ)...734 429-4989
1325 Woodland Dr Saline (48176) *(G-14406)*
Norgren Automtn Solutions LLC...586 463-3000
2871 Bond St Rochester Hills (48309) *(G-13481)*
Norma Americas, Auburn Hills *Also called Norma Michigan Inc (G-959)*
Norma Group Craig Assembly...810 326-1374
1219 Fred Moore Hwy Saint Clair (48079) *(G-14230)*
Norma Michigan Inc (HQ)...248 373-4300
2430 E Walton Blvd Auburn Hills (48326) *(G-959)*
Norma Michigan Inc...248 373-4300
325 W Silverbell Rd Lake Orion (48359) *(G-9151)*
Normac Incorporated...248 349-2644
720 Baseline Rd Northville (48167) *(G-11714)*
Norman A Lewis...248 219-5736
27268 Pembridge Ln Farmington Hills (48331) *(G-5080)*
Norman Industries Inc...248 669-6213
47850 West Rd Wixom (48393) *(G-17867)*
Norman Township...231 848-4495
17201 6th St Wellston (49689) *(G-17463)*
Norman Township Fire Dept, Wellston *Also called Norman Township (G-17463)*
Normic Industries Inc...231 947-8860
1733 Park Dr Traverse City (49686) *(G-16049)*
Noron Composite Technologies...231 723-9277
650 W Hoague Rd Manistee (49660) *(G-10433)*
Norplas Industries Inc...517 999-1400
5589 W Mount Hope Hwy Lansing (48917) *(G-9314)*
Norris Graphics Inc...586 447-0646
33251 S Gratiot Ave Clinton Township (48035) *(G-3184)*
Nortech LLC...248 446-7575
30163 Research Dr New Hudson (48165) *(G-11550)*
Nortek Inc...616 719-5588
2547 3 Mile Rd Nw Ste A Grand Rapids (49534) *(G-6718)*
Nortek Air Solutions LLC...616 738-7148
4433 Holland Ave Holland (49424) *(G-7759)*
North America Fuel Systems R...616 541-1100
4232 Brockton Dr Se Grand Rapids (49512) *(G-6719)*
North American Aqua Envmtl LLC...269 476-2092
17397 Black St Vandalia (49095) *(G-16802)*
North American Asphalt...586 754-0014
11720 Susan Ave Warren (48093) *(G-17172)*
North American Assembly LLC...248 335-6702
4325 Giddings Rd Auburn Hills (48326) *(G-960)*
North American Auto Inds Inc...734 288-3877
18238 Fort St Riverview (48193) *(G-13302)*
North American Color Inc...269 323-0552
5960 S Sprinkle Rd Portage (49002) *(G-13019)*
North American Controls Inc...586 532-7140
13955 Teresa Dr Shelby Township (48315) *(G-14654)*
North American Forest Products (HQ)...269 663-8500
27263 May St Edwardsburg (49112) *(G-4769)*
North American Forest Products...269 663-8500
69708 Kraus Rd Edwardsburg (49112) *(G-4770)*
North American Graphics Inc...586 486-1110
24487 Gibson Dr Warren (48089) *(G-17173)*
North American Lighting Inc...248 553-6408
36600 Corporate Dr Farmington Hills (48331) *(G-5081)*
North American Machine & Engrg, Shelby Township *Also called North American Mch & Engrg Co (G-14655)*
North American Mch & Engrg Co...586 726-6700
13290 W Star Dr Shelby Township (48315) *(G-14655)*
North American Mold LLC (PA)...248 335-6702
4345 Giddings Rd Auburn Hills (48326) *(G-961)*
North American Oss Operations, Washington *Also called ZF Passive Safety (G-17316)*
North American Tool Inc...586 463-1746
43933 N Groesbeck Hwy Clinton Township (48036) *(G-3185)*
North Amrcn Frest Pdts Lqdtion, Edwardsburg *Also called North Amrcn Mlding Lqdtion LLC (G-4771)*
North Amrcn Masurement Systems...734 646-3458
44549 Clare Blvd Plymouth (48170) *(G-12701)*
North Amrcn Mlding Lqdtion LLC (HQ)...269 663-5300
70151 April St Edwardsburg (49112) *(G-4771)*
North Arrow Log Homes Inc...906 484-5524
5943 N 3 Mile Rd Pickford (49774) *(G-12482)*
North Attleboro Taps, Cheboygan *Also called Precision Threading Corp (G-2691)*
North Branch Machining & Engrg...989 795-2324
9318 Beech St Fostoria (48435) *(G-5552)*
North Central Machine, Houghton Lake *Also called Kuzimski Enterprises Inc (G-7994)*
North Central Welding Co...989 275-8054
402 Southline Rd Roscommon (48653) *(G-13751)*
North Coast Studios Inc...586 359-6630
29181 Calahan Rd Roseville (48066) *(G-13848)*
North Country Publishing Corp...231 526-2191
211 E 3rd St Harbor Springs (49740) *(G-7290)*
North East Fabrication Co Inc...517 849-8090
113 Deal Pkwy Jonesville (49250) *(G-8664)*
North End Electric Company...248 398-8187
2000 Bellaire Ave Royal Oak (48067) *(G-13954)*
North Group Inc...517 540-0038
2790 W Grand River Ave # 100 Howell (48843) *(G-8069)*
North Land Septic Tank Service, East Jordan *Also called Jordan Valley Concrete Service (G-4637)*
North Pier Brewing Company LLC...312 545-0446
3266 Estates Dr Saint Joseph (49085) *(G-14332)*
North Post Inc...906 482-5210
120 Quincy St Hancock (49930) *(G-7254)*
North Sails Group LLC...586 776-1330
22600 Greater Mack Ave Saint Clair Shores (48080) *(G-14265)*
North Sails-Detroit, Saint Clair Shores *Also called North Sails Group LLC (G-14265)*
North Shore Machine Works Inc...616 842-8360
595 W 2nd St Ferrysburg (49409) *(G-5336)*
North Shore Mfg Corp...269 849-2551
4706 M 63 N Coloma (49038) *(G-3363)*
North State Sales...989 681-2806
6298 N State Rd Saint Louis (48880) *(G-14367)*
North Wind Student Newspaper...906 227-2545
2310 University Ctr Marquette (49855) *(G-10547)*
North Woods Industrial...616 784-2840
3644 Mill Creek Dr Ne Comstock Park (49321) *(G-3502)*
North-East Gage Inc...586 792-6790
33398 Kelly Rd Clinton Township (48035) *(G-3186)*
Northamerican Reproduction...734 421-6800
34943 6 Mile Rd Livonia (48152) *(G-9863)*
Northeastern Products Corp...906 265-6241
85 Brady Ave Caspian (49915) *(G-2509)*
Northern A 1 Services Inc...231 258-9961
3947 Us Highway 131 Ne Kalkaska (49646) *(G-8955)*
Northern Building Components, Bloomingdale *Also called Nathan Shetler (G-1812)*
Northern Cable & Automtn LLC (PA)...231 937-8000
5822 Henkel Rd Howard City (49329) *(G-8004)*
Northern Chain Specialties...231 889-3151
7329 Chief Rd Kaleva (49645) *(G-8934)*
Northern Classics Trucks Inc...586 254-2835
3136 Norton Lawn Rochester Hills (48307) *(G-13482)*
Northern Coatings & Chem Co...906 863-2641
705 6th Ave Menominee (49858) *(G-10753)*
Northern Concrete Pipe Inc...517 645-2777
5281 Lansing Rd Charlotte (48813) *(G-2662)*
Northern Concrete Pipe Inc (PA)...989 892-3545
401 Kelton St Bay City (48706) *(G-1338)*
Northern Design Services Inc...231 258-9900
424 E Dresden St Kalkaska (49646) *(G-8956)*
Northern Express Publications, Traverse City *Also called Express Publications Inc (G-15967)*
Northern Extrusion Inc...989 386-7556
4915 E Colonville Rd Clare (48617) *(G-2880)*
Northern Fab & Machine LLC...906 863-8506
5601 13th St Menominee (49858) *(G-10754)*
Northern Hardwoods Oper Co LLC...860 632-3505
45807 Hwy M 26 South Range (49963) *(G-14818)*
Northern Industrial Mfg Corp...586 468-2790
41000 Executive Dr Harrison Township (48045) *(G-7341)*
Northern Industrial Wood Inc...989 736-6192
507 State St Lincoln (48742) *(G-9568)*
Northern Label Inc...231 854-6301
265 S Division St Hesperia (49421) *(G-7479)*
Northern Logistics LLC...989 386-2389
805 Industrial Dr Clare (48617) *(G-2881)*
Northern Machine Tool Company...231 755-1603
761 Alberta Ave Norton Shores (49441) *(G-11783)*
Northern Machining & Repr Inc...906 786-0526
1701 N 26th St Escanaba (49829) *(G-4847)*
Northern Metalcraft Inc...586 997-9630
50490 Corporate Dr Shelby Township (48315) *(G-14656)*
Northern Mich Aggregates LLC...989 354-3502
51445 W12 Mile Rd Wixom (48393) *(G-17868)*
Northern Mich Chrstn Cunseling...989 278-2590
5010 Beaushaw Rd Lachine (49753) *(G-9075)*
Northern Mich Endocrine Pllc...989 281-1125
103 Misty Meadow Ct Roscommon (48653) *(G-13752)*
Northern Mich Hardwoods Inc...231 347-4575
5151 Manthei Rd Petoskey (49770) *(G-12460)*
Northern Mich Mmrals Monuments...231 290-2333
2754 Old Mackinaw Rd Cheboygan (49721) *(G-2688)*
Northern Mich Pain Specialist...231 487-4650
1890 Us Highway 131 Petoskey (49770) *(G-12461)*
Northern Mich Residential Svcs...231 547-6144
9571 Rajasi Cir Vanderbilt (49795) *(G-16808)*
Northern Mich Rgional Hlth Sys...231 487-4094
416 Connable Ave Petoskey (49770) *(G-12462)*
Northern Mich Supportive Hsing...231 929-1309
250 E Front St Traverse City (49684) *(G-16050)*
Northern Mich Wdding Offciants...231 938-1683
4617 Bartlett Rd Williamsburg (49690) *(G-17715)*

A L P H A B E T I C

Northern Michig....989 340-1272
12595 Long Rapids Rd Lachine (49753) ***(G-9076)***
Northern Michigan Glass LLC....231 941-0050
1101 Hammond Rd W Traverse City (49686) ***(G-16051)***
Northern Michigan Publishing....231 946-7878
2438 Potter Rd E Traverse City (49696) ***(G-16052)***
Northern Michigan Review Inc (PA)....231 547-6558
319 State St Petoskey (49770) ***(G-12463)***
Northern Michigan Review Inc....231 547-6558
319 State St Petoskey (49770) ***(G-12464)***
Northern Michigan Sawmill....231 409-1314
4593 Hampshire Dr Williamsburg (49690) ***(G-17716)***
Northern Michigan Veneers Inc....906 428-1082
710 Rains Dr Gladstone (49837) ***(G-5917)***
Northern Millwork Co....313 365-7733
7201 E Mcnichols Rd Detroit (48212) ***(G-4276)***
Northern Oak Brewery Inc....248 634-7515
806 N Saginaw St Holly (48442) ***(G-7889)***
Northern Orthotics Prosthetics (PA)....906 353-7161
509 S Superior Ave Baraga (49908) ***(G-1111)***
Northern Packaging Mi Inc....734 692-4700
27665 Elba Dr Grosse Ile (48138) ***(G-7174)***
Northern Pallet....989 386-7556
4915 E Colonville Rd Clare (48617) ***(G-2882)***
Northern Plastics Inc....586 979-7737
6137 Product Dr Sterling Heights (48312) ***(G-15438)***
Northern Precision Inc....989 736-6322
601 S Lake St Lincoln (48742) ***(G-9569)***
Northern Precision Pdts Inc....231 768-4435
4790 Mackinaw Trl Leroy (49655) ***(G-9534)***
Northern Process Systems Inc....810 714-5200
235 Industrial Way Fenton (48430) ***(G-5227)***
Northern Processes & Sales LLC....248 669-3918
49700 Martin Dr Wixom (48393) ***(G-17869)***
Northern Products of Wisconsin....715 589-4417
W8969 Frei Dr Iron Mountain (49801) ***(G-8293)***
Northern Promotions, Lachine *Also called Northern Michig* ***(G-9076)***
Northern Pure Ice Co L L C....989 344-2088
1755 Yeager St Port Huron (48060) ***(G-12950)***
Northern Rfractories Insul Div, Brownstown Twp *Also called Cerco Inc* ***(G-2071)***
Northern Sand & Gravel, Sault Sainte Marie *Also called Van Sloten Enterprises Inc* ***(G-14477)***
Northern Sawmills Inc....231 547-9452
7250 Dalton Rd Charlevoix (49720) ***(G-2622)***
Northern Screen Printing & EMB....906 786-0373
1001 Ludington St Escanaba (49829) ***(G-4848)***
Northern Sierra Corporation....989 777-4784
5450 East Rd Saginaw (48601) ***(G-14116)***
Northern Specialty Co....906 376-8165
146 Evergreen St Republic (49879) ***(G-13246)***
Northern Staircase Co Inc....248 836-0652
630 Cesar E Chavez Ave Pontiac (48342) ***(G-12852)***
Northern Stampings Inc (PA)....586 598-6969
1853 Rochester Indus Ct Rochester Hills (48309) ***(G-13483)***
Northern Star, Pontiac *Also called Morning Star Publishing Co* ***(G-12851)***
Northern Tank Truck Service....989 732-7531
10764 Old Us Highway 27 S Gaylord (49735) ***(G-5885)***
Northern Tire Inc....906 486-4463
1880 Us Highway 41 W Ishpeming (49849) ***(G-8350)***
Northern Tool & Engineering, Baraga *Also called Laser North Inc* ***(G-1107)***
Northern Trading Group LLC....248 885-8750
284 W Maple Rd Birmingham (48009) ***(G-1696)***
Northern Wings Repair Inc (PA)....906 477-6176
6679 County Road 392 Newberry (49868) ***(G-11586)***
Northern Wire & Cable, Oakland Township *Also called Anwc LLC* ***(G-12110)***
Northern Woodcrafters....989 348-2553
4562 W N Down River Rd Grayling (49738) ***(G-7114)***
Northern Woods Finishing LLC....231 536-9640
2425 M 32 East Jordan (49727) ***(G-4640)***
Northfield Block Company....989 777-2575
6045 Dixie Hwy Bridgeport (48722) ***(G-1854)***
Northfield Manufacturing Inc....734 729-2890
38549 Webb Dr Westland (48185) ***(G-17584)***
Northfork Readi Mix Inc....906 341-3445
5665w Us Highway 2 Manistique (49854) ***(G-10444)***
Northland....231 775-3101
903 N Mitchell St Cadillac (49601) ***(G-2268)***
Northland Ad-Liner, West Branch *Also called Ogemaw County Herald Inc* ***(G-17514)***
Northland Castings Corporation (PA)....231 873-4974
4130 W Tyler Rd Hart (49420) ***(G-7377)***
Northland Corporation....616 754-5601
1260 E Van Deinse St Greenville (48838) ***(G-7147)***
Northland Corporation (HQ)....616 754-5601
1260 E Van Deinse St Greenville (48838) ***(G-7148)***
Northland Die Engineering, Clay *Also called D Michael Services* ***(G-2996)***
Northland Maintenace, Sault Sainte Marie *Also called Northland Maintenance Co Inc* ***(G-14469)***
Northland Maintenance Co Inc....906 253-9161
2366 E 3 Mile Rd Sault Sainte Marie (49783) ***(G-14469)***
Northland Publishers Inc....906 265-9927
801 W Adams St Iron River (49935) ***(G-8318)***
Northland Refrigeration, Greenville *Also called Northland Corporation* ***(G-7148)***
Northland Tool & Die Inc....616 866-4451
10399 Northland Dr Ne Rockford (49341) ***(G-13583)***
Northland Trailers, Cadillac *Also called Northland* ***(G-2268)***
Northline Express, Roscommon *Also called Ace Consulting & MGT Inc* ***(G-13747)***
Northport Manufacturing Inc....616 874-6455
8553 Browmyer Ct Ne Rockford (49341) ***(G-13584)***
Northport Naturals....231 420-9448
8627 N Straits Hwy Cheboygan (49721) ***(G-2689)***
Northrop Grmmn Spce & Mssn Sys....734 266-2600
12025 Tech Center Dr Livonia (48150) ***(G-9864)***
Northrop Grumman Innovation....313 424-9411
2845 Plymouth Dr Shelby Township (48316) ***(G-14657)***
Northshore Pontoon....517 547-8877
3985 Munson Hwy Hudson (49247) ***(G-8137)***
Northside Noodle....906 779-2181
609 Vulcan St Iron Mountain (49801) ***(G-8294)***
Northstar Sourcing LLC....313 782-4749
1399 Combermere Dr Troy (48083) ***(G-16527)***
Northstar Wholesale....517 545-2379
5818 Sterling Dr Howell (48843) ***(G-8070)***
Northview Window & Door....231 889-4565
9844 Milarch Rd Bear Lake (49614) ***(G-1379)***
Northville Cider Mill Inc....248 349-3181
714 Baseline Rd Northville (48167) ***(G-11715)***
Northville Circuits Inc....248 853-3232
1689 W Hamlin Rd Rochester Hills (48309) ***(G-13484)***
Northville Laboratories, Northville *Also called Jogue Inc* ***(G-11703)***
Northville Laboratories, Plymouth *Also called Jogue Inc* ***(G-12654)***
Northville Laboratories Inc....248 349-1500
100 Rural Hill St Northville (48167) ***(G-11716)***
Northville Stitching Post....248 347-7622
200 S Main St Ste A Northville (48167) ***(G-11717)***
Northville Winery....248 320-6507
630 Baseline Rd Northville (48167) ***(G-11718)***
Northwest Advertising, Rochester Hills *Also called Northwest Graphic Services* ***(G-13485)***
Northwest Fabrication Inc....231 536-3229
450 Griffin Rd East Jordan (49727) ***(G-4641)***
Northwest Graphic Services....248 349-9480
145 S Livernois Rd 277 Rochester Hills (48307) ***(G-13485)***
Northwest Hardwoods Inc....989 786-6100
3293 County Road 491 Lewiston (49756) ***(G-9554)***
Northwest Market....517 787-5005
7051 Standish Rd Jackson (49201) ***(G-8543)***
Northwest Metal Products Inc....616 453-0556
2055 Walker Ct Nw Grand Rapids (49544) ***(G-6720)***
Northwest Orthotics-Prosthetic....248 477-1443
39830 Grand River Ave B1d Novi (48375) ***(G-11955)***
Northwest Pattern Company....248 477-7070
29473 Medbury St Farmington Hills (48336) ***(G-5082)***
Northwest Polishing & Buffing....616 899-2682
3738 Walker Ave Nw Grand Rapids (49544) ***(G-6721)***
Northwest Tool & Machine Inc....517 750-1332
1014 Hurst Rd Jackson (49201) ***(G-8544)***
Northwods Prperty Holdings LLC....231 334-3000
6053 S Glen Lake Rd Glen Arbor (49636) ***(G-5941)***
Northwood Lumber....989 826-1751
937 W Kittle Rd Mio (48647) ***(G-11007)***
Northwood Signs Inc....231 843-3956
5111 W Us Highway 10 # 4 Ludington (49431) ***(G-10074)***
Northwoods Hardware, Glen Arbor *Also called Northwods Prperty Holdings LLC* ***(G-5941)***
Northwoods Hot Sprng Spas Inc....231 347-1134
2050 M 119 Petoskey (49770) ***(G-12465)***
Northwoods Manufacturing Inc....906 779-2370
850 East Blvd Kingsford (49802) ***(G-9065)***
Northwoods Products, Brethren *Also called Tracy Wilk* ***(G-1847)***
Northwoods Soda & Syrup, Williamsburg *Also called Northwoods Soda and Syrup Co* ***(G-17717)***
Northwoods Soda and Syrup Co....231 267-5853
5450 N Broomhead Rd Williamsburg (49690) ***(G-17717)***
Northwoods Trading Post, Hancock *Also called North Post Inc* ***(G-7254)***
Northwoods Wreathing Company....906 202-2888
143 E Johnson Lake Rd Gwinn (49841) ***(G-7221)***
Norton Equipment Corporation (PA)....517 486-2113
203 E Adrian St Blissfield (49228) ***(G-1721)***
Nortronic Company....313 893-3730
20210 Sherwood St Detroit (48234) ***(G-4277)***
Norway Granite Marble, Norway *Also called Steinbrecher Stone Corp* ***(G-11820)***
Nostrum Energy LLC....734 548-8677
330 E Liberty St Fl 4 Ann Arbor (48104) ***(G-576)***
Notes From Man Cave LLC....586 604-1997
3680 Seminole St Detroit (48214) ***(G-4278)***
Notions Marketing....616 243-8424
1500 Buchanan Ave Sw Grand Rapids (49507) ***(G-6722)***
Nova Industries Inc....586 294-9182
34180 Klein Rd Fraser (48026) ***(G-5700)***

Nova-Tron Controls Corp 989 358-6126
111 S Second Ave Alpena (49707) *(G-303)*
Novacare Prosthetics Orthotics, Monroe *Also called Swanson Orthtic Prsthetics Ctr (G-11071)*
Novaceuticals LLC 248 309-3402
3201 University Dr # 250 Auburn Hills (48326) *(G-962)*
Novares Corporation US Inc (HQ) 248 449-6100
19575 Victor Pkwy Ste 400 Livonia (48152) *(G-9865)*
Novares Group, Livonia *Also called Novares US LLC (G-9866)*
Novares US Eng Components Inc 248 799-8949
29200 Northwestern Hwy Southfield (48034) *(G-14992)*
Novares US LLC (HQ) 248 449-6100
19575 Victor Pkwy Ste 400 Livonia (48152) *(G-9866)*
Novares US LLC 517 546-1900
1301 Mcpherson Park Dr Howell (48843) *(G-8071)*
Novares US LLC 616 554-3555
5375 Intl Pkwy Se Grand Rapids (49512) *(G-6723)*
Novation Analytics LLC 313 910-3280
2851 High Meadow Cir Auburn Hills (48326) *(G-963)*
Novatron Corporation (PA) 609 815-2100
6000 Rinke Ave Warren (48091) *(G-17174)*
Novavax Inc 248 656-5336
870 Parkdale Rd Rochester (48307) *(G-13337)*
Novelis Corporation 248 668-5111
39550 W 13 Mile Rd # 150 Novi (48377) *(G-11956)*
Novell, Southfield *Also called Micro Focus Software Inc (G-14982)*
Novex Tool Division, Brighton *Also called Federal Screw Works (G-1922)*
Novi Crushed Concrete LLC 248 305-6020
46900 W 12 Mile Rd Novi (48377) *(G-11957)*
Novi Manufacturing Co 248 476-4350
25555 Seeley Rd Novi (48375) *(G-11958)*
Novi Matic Valves, Redford *Also called Novi Tool & Machine Company (G-13176)*
Novi Precision Products Inc 810 227-1024
11777 Grand River Rd Brighton (48116) *(G-1970)*
Novi Spring Inc 248 486-4220
7735 Boardwalk Rd Brighton (48116) *(G-1971)*
Novi Tool & Machine Company 313 532-0900
12202 Woodbine Redford (48239) *(G-13176)*
Novo Building Products LLC (HQ) 800 253-9000
8181 Logistics Dr Zeeland (49464) *(G-18169)*
Novus Corporation 248 545-8600
3077 Chard Ave Warren (48092) *(G-17175)*
Now Hear This, Auburn Hills *Also called Nht Sales Inc (G-956)*
Now Ogden News Pubg of Mich 906 774-3708
421 S Stephenson Ave Iron Mountain (49801) *(G-8295)*
Nowak Cabinets Inc 231 264-8603
11744 S Us Highway 31 Williamsburg (49690) *(G-17718)*
Nowak Machine Products, Norton Shores *Also called Nmp Inc (G-11781)*
Nowaks Window Door & Cab Co 989 734-2808
4003 Us Highway 23 S Rogers City (49779) *(G-13617)*
Npi 248 478-0010
23910 Freeway Park Dr Farmington Hills (48335) *(G-5083)*
Npi Wireless (PA) 231 922-9273
3054 Cass Rd Traverse City (49684) *(G-16053)*
Npo Synergy Donor Management, Southfield *Also called Mejenta Systems Inc (G-14977)*
NPR of America Inc 248 449-8955
41650 Gardenbrook Rd # 180 Novi (48375) *(G-11959)*
Nsi, Rochester Hills *Also called Northern Stampings Inc (G-13483)*
NSK Americas Inc (HQ) 734 913-7500
4200 Goss Rd Ann Arbor (48105) *(G-577)*
NSK Steering Systems Amer Inc (HQ) 734 913-7500
4200 Goss Rd Ann Arbor (48105) *(G-578)*
Nss Technologies Inc (HQ) 734 459-9500
8680 N Haggerty Rd Canton (48187) *(G-2412)*
Nss Technologies Inc 734 459-9500
8101 Ronda Dr Canton (48187) *(G-2413)*
Nssa Hq, Ann Arbor *Also called NSK Steering Systems Amer Inc (G-578)*
Nssc America Incorporated 248 449-6050
42400 Grand River Ave # 102 Novi (48375) *(G-11960)*
Ntf Filter, Oscoda *Also called Ntf Manufacturing Usa LLC (G-12215)*
Ntf Manufacturing Usa LLC 989 739-8560
4691 Industrial Row Oscoda (48750) *(G-12215)*
Ntvb Media Inc (PA) 248 583-4190
213 Park Dr Troy (48083) *(G-16528)*
Ntz Micro Filtration LLC 248 449-8700
28221 Beck Rd Ste A1 Wixom (48393) *(G-17870)*
Nu Art Designs Sign Fabg, Traverse City *Also called Lobo Signs Inc (G-16027)*
Nu Con Corporation 734 525-0770
34100 Industrial Rd Livonia (48150) *(G-9867)*
Nu Tek Sales 616 258-0631
3366 Kraft Ave Se Ste A Grand Rapids (49512) *(G-6724)*
Nu-Core, Inkster *Also called Coppertec Inc (G-8226)*
Nu-Core Inc 231 547-2600
8833 Gibbons Dr Charlevoix (49720) *(G-2623)*
Nu-ERA Holdings Inc (PA) 810 794-4935
2034 Fruit St Clay (48001) *(G-3000)*
Nu-ERA Holdings Inc 248 477-2288
32613 Folsom Rd Farmington Hills (48336) *(G-5084)*
Nu-Fold Inc 313 898-4695
4444 Lawton St Detroit (48208) *(G-4279)*
Nu-Ice Age Inc 517 990-0665
9700 Myers Rd Clarklake (49234) *(G-2897)*
Nu-Pak Solutions Inc 231 755-1662
2850 Lincoln St Norton Shores (49441) *(G-11784)*
Nu-Tech North Inc 231 347-1992
445 E Mitchell St Ste 6 Petoskey (49770) *(G-12466)*
Nu-Tran LLC 616 350-9575
2947 Buchanan Ave Sw Wyoming (49548) *(G-18023)*
Nu-Vu Food Service Systems, Menominee *Also called Marshall Middleby Holding LLC (G-10743)*
Nu-Way Stove Inc 989 733-8792
6566 Rainey Lake Rd Onaway (49765) *(G-12149)*
Nu-Wool Co Inc 800 748-0128
2472 Port Sheldon St Jenison (49428) *(G-8635)*
Nuance Communications Inc 248 919-7700
39255 Country Club Dr Farmington Hills (48331) *(G-5085)*
Nubreed Nutrition Inc 734 272-7395
318 John R Rd Ste 310 Troy (48083) *(G-16529)*
Nucon Schokbeton 269 381-1550
3102 E Cork St Kalamazoo (49001) *(G-8836)*
Nucraft Furniture Company 616 784-6016
5151 West River Dr Ne Comstock Park (49321) *(G-3503)*
Nucraft Metal Products, Roscommon *Also called North Central Welding Co (G-13751)*
Nuestro, Adrian *Also called Venchurs Inc (G-99)*
Nuestro, Adrian *Also called Venchurs Inc (G-100)*
Nugent Sand Company Inc 231 755-1686
2925 Lincoln St Norton Shores (49441) *(G-11785)*
Nugentec Oilfield Chem LLC 517 518-2712
1105 Grand Oaks Dr Howell (48843) *(G-8072)*
Nuko Precision LLC 734 464-6856
35455 Schoolcraft Rd Livonia (48150) *(G-9868)*
Null Taphouse 734 792-9124
2319 Bishop Cir E Dexter (48130) *(G-4501)*
Numatics, Sandusky *Also called Asco LP (G-14428)*
Nustep LLC 734 769-3939
5111 Venture Dr Ste 1 Ann Arbor (48108) *(G-579)*
Nutco Inc (PA) 800 872-4006
2140 Wilkins St Detroit (48207) *(G-4280)*
Nutrien AG Solutions Inc 989 842-1185
8263 N Ransom Rd Breckenridge (48615) *(G-1844)*
Nutting Newspapers Inc 906 482-1500
206 Shelden Ave Houghton (49931) *(G-7979)*
Nuvar Inc 616 394-5779
895 E 40th St Holland (49423) *(G-7760)*
Nuvosun Inc 408 514-6200
2040 Abbott Rd Midland (48674) *(G-10897)*
Nuwave Medical Solutions, Saint Joseph *Also called Nuwave Technology Partners LLC (G-14333)*
Nuwave Medical Solutions, Kalamazoo *Also called Nuwave Technology Partners LLC (G-8837)*
Nuwave Technology Partners LLC 616 942-7520
4079 Park East Ct Se A Grand Rapids (49546) *(G-6725)*
Nuwave Technology Partners LLC 269 342-4400
2231 Mount Curve Ave Saint Joseph (49085) *(G-14333)*
Nuwave Technology Partners LLC 517 336-9915
2501 Coolidge Rd East Lansing (48823) *(G-4672)*
Nuwave Technology Partners LLC 517 322-2200
6709 Centurion Dr Ste 200 Lansing (48917) *(G-9315)*
Nuwave Technology Partners LLC (PA) 269 342-4400
5268 Azo Dr Kalamazoo (49048) *(G-8837)*
Nuwood Components 616 395-1905
759 E 48th St Holland (49423) *(G-7761)*
NV Labs Inc 248 358-9022
20777 East St Southfield (48033) *(G-14993)*
Nvent Thermal LLC 248 273-3359
900 Wilshire Dr Ste 150 Troy (48084) *(G-16530)*
Nyatex Chemical Company 517 546-4046
2112 Industrial Dr Howell (48843) *(G-8073)*
Nylok LLC (PA) 586 786-0100
15260 Hallmark Ct Macomb (48042) *(G-10149)*
Nyloncraft of Michigan Inc 517 849-9911
1640 E Chicago Rd Jonesville (49250) *(G-8665)*
Nylube Products Company LLC (PA) 248 852-6500
2299 Star Ct Rochester Hills (48309) *(G-13486)*
Nylube Products Div, Rochester Hills *Also called Nylube Products Company LLC (G-13486)*
Nyx Inc 734 464-0800
38700 Plymouth Rd Livonia (48150) *(G-9869)*
Nyx Inc 734 261-7535
28350 Plymouth Rd Livonia (48150) *(G-9870)*
Nyx LLC (PA) 734 462-2385
36111 Schoolcraft Rd Livonia (48150) *(G-9871)*
Nyx LLC 734 467-7200
1000 Manufacturers Dr Westland (48186) *(G-17585)*
Nyx LLC 734 421-3850
30111 Schoolcraft Rd Livonia (48150) *(G-9872)*
Nyx Cherryhill Division, Westland *Also called Nyx LLC (G-17585)*

(PA)=Parent Co (HQ)=Headquarters (DH)=Div Headquarters
2020 Harris Michigan Industrial Directory
1035

Nyx Livonia Plant II, Livonia *Also called Nyx Inc* ***(G-9870)***
Nyx Plymouth, Livonia *Also called Nyx Inc* ***(G-9869)***
Nyx Technologies, Livonia *Also called Nyx LLC* ***(G-9871)***
O & S Tool and Machine Inc 248 926-8045
50400 Dennis Ct Unit B Wixom (48393) ***(G-17871)***
O and P Sparton 517 220-4960
2947 Eyde Pkwy East Lansing (48823) ***(G-4673)***
O D L, Zeeland *Also called Odl Incorporated* ***(G-18170)***
O E M Company Inc 810 985-9070
3495 24th St Port Huron (48060) ***(G-12951)***
O E M Parts Supply Inc 313 729-4283
16583 Greenview Ave Detroit (48219) ***(G-4281)***
O I K Industries Inc 269 382-1210
7882 Douglas Ave Kalamazoo (49009) ***(G-8838)***
O Keller Tool Engrg Co LLC 734 425-4500
12701 Inkster Rd Livonia (48150) ***(G-9873)***
O N Minerals 906 484-2201
5093 E M 134 Cedarville (49719) ***(G-2569)***
O R T, Erie *Also called Ort Tool & Die Corporation* ***(G-4807)***
O TP Industrial Solutions 248 745-5503
895 Joslyn Ave Pontiac (48340) ***(G-12853)***
O-N Minerals Michigan Company 906 484-2201
5093 E M 134 134 M Cedarville (49719) ***(G-2570)***
O-N Minerals Michigan Company 989 734-2131
1035 Calcite Rd Rogers City (49779) ***(G-13618)***
O-N Minerals Michigan Company 906 484-2201
5093 E M 134 Cedarville (49719) ***(G-2571)***
O-N Minerals Michigan Company (PA) 989 734-2131
1035 Calcite Rd Rogers City (49779) ***(G-13619)***
O. Keller Tool Engineering Co., Livonia *Also called Keller Tool Ltd* ***(G-9794)***
O2/Specialty Mfg Holdings LLC (PA) 248 554-4228
40900 Woodward Ave # 130 Bloomfield Hills (48304) ***(G-1787)***
Oak Division, Mount Pleasant *Also called Refrigeration Research Inc* ***(G-11223)***
Oak Frost Kennel, Marshall *Also called Harvey Richard John* ***(G-10571)***
Oak Mountain Industries 734 941-7000
14770 5 M Center Dr Romulus (48174) ***(G-13716)***
Oak North Manufacturing Inc 906 475-7992
114 Us Highway 41 E Negaunee (49866) ***(G-11472)***
Oak Press Solutions Inc 269 651-8513
504 Wade Rd Sturgis (49091) ***(G-15624)***
Oak Tree Cabinet & Woodworking, Reese *Also called Rohloff Builders Inc* ***(G-13232)***
Oakes Carton Company, Kalamazoo *Also called S & C Industries Inc* ***(G-8880)***
Oakland Automation LLC 810 874-3061
25475 Trans X Rd Novi (48375) ***(G-11961)***
Oakland Bolt & Nut Co LLC 313 659-1677
8977 Lyndon St Detroit (48238) ***(G-4282)***
Oakland Engineering Filtration, Pontiac *Also called United Fbrcnts Strainrite Corp* ***(G-12873)***
Oakland Machine Company 248 674-2201
4865 Highland Rd Ste G Waterford (48328) ***(G-17361)***
Oakland Orthopedic Appls Inc (PA) 989 893-7544
515 Mulholland St Bay City (48708) ***(G-1339)***
Oakland Orthopedic Appls Inc 989 839-9241
422 W Wackerly St Midland (48640) ***(G-10898)***
OAKLAND POST, Rochester *Also called Oakland Sail Inc* ***(G-13338)***
Oakland Sail Inc 248 370-4268
61 Oakland Ctr Rochester (48309) ***(G-13338)***
Oakland Sand & Gravel, Dearborn *Also called Lyon Sand & Gravel Co* ***(G-3734)***
Oakland Stamping LLC 313 867-3700
17757 Woodland Dr New Boston (48164) ***(G-11506)***
Oakland Stamping LLC (HQ) 734 397-6300
1200 Woodland St Detroit (48211) ***(G-4283)***
Oakland Stamping LLC 248 340-2520
4555 Giddings Rd Lake Orion (48359) ***(G-9152)***
Oakley Industries Inc (PA) 586 791-3194
35166 Automation Dr Clinton Township (48035) ***(G-3187)***
Oakley Industries Inc 586 792-1261
35224 Automation Dr Clinton Township (48035) ***(G-3188)***
Oakley Industries Saub Assembl, Flint *Also called Oakley Sub Assembly Inc* ***(G-5474)***
Oakley Industries Sub Assembly 586 754-5555
25295 Guenther Ste 200 Warren (48091) ***(G-17176)***
Oakley Industries Sub Assembly (PA) 810 720-4444
4333 Matthew Flint (48507) ***(G-5473)***
Oakley Sub Assembly Inc 810 720-4444
4333 Matthew Flint (48507) ***(G-5474)***
Oakley Sub Assembly Intl Inc 810 720-4444
4333 Matthew Flint (48507) ***(G-5475)***
Oakridge Supermarket, Royal Oak *Also called Raleigh & Ron Corporation* ***(G-13961)***
Oaks Concrete Products Inc 248 684-5004
51744 Pontiac Trl Wixom (48393) ***(G-17872)***
Oakwood Custom Coating Inc 313 561-7740
1100 Oakwood Blvd Dearborn (48124) ***(G-3745)***
Oakwood Energy Management Inc (HQ) 734 947-7700
9755 Inkster Rd Taylor (48180) ***(G-15750)***
Oakwood Expansion, Taylor *Also called Oakwood Energy Management Inc* ***(G-15750)***
Oakwood Group, The, Dearborn *Also called Oakwood Metal Fabricating Co* ***(G-3746)***
Oakwood Metal Fabricating Co (PA) 313 561-7740
1100 Oakwood Blvd Dearborn (48124) ***(G-3746)***
Oakwood Metal Fabricating Co 734 947-7740
9755 Inkster Rd Taylor (48180) ***(G-15751)***
Oakwood Sports Inc (PA) 517 321-6852
1025 Clark Rd Lansing (48917) ***(G-9316)***
Oakwood Veneer Company 248 720-0288
1830 Stephenson Hwy Ste A Troy (48083) ***(G-16531)***
Oasis Fuel Corporation 906 486-4126
417 E Hematite Dr Ishpeming (49849) ***(G-8351)***
Obara Corporation USA (HQ) 586 755-1250
26800 Meadowbrook Rd # 111 Novi (48377) ***(G-11962)***
Obep, Deerfield *Also called OBrien Engineered Products* ***(G-3814)***
Obertron Electronic Mfg Inc 734 428-0722
10098 Mi State Road 52 Manchester (48158) ***(G-10409)***
Oblut Ltd 248 645-9130
7111 Dixie Hwy Clarkston (48346) ***(G-2941)***
OBrien Engineered Products 517 447-3602
420 Carey St Deerfield (49238) ***(G-3814)***
OBrien Harris Woodworks LLc 616 248-0779
1125 41st St Se Ste A Grand Rapids (49507) ***(G-6726)***
OCC Systems, Ferndale *Also called Overhead Conveyor Company* ***(G-5307)***
Occasions (PA) 517 694-6437
3575 Scholar Ln Holt (48842) ***(G-7918)***
Occidental Chemical Corp 231 845-4411
1600 S Madison St Ludington (49431) ***(G-10075)***
Ocean Express Powerboats Inc 810 794-5551
9483 Smith St Algonac (48001) ***(G-145)***
Oceana Foods, Shelby *Also called Cherry Central Cooperative Inc* ***(G-14524)***
Oceana Foods Inc 231 861-2141
168 Lincoln St Shelby (49455) ***(G-14531)***
Oceana Forest Products Inc 231 861-6115
2033 Loop Rd Shelby (49455) ***(G-14532)***
Oceanas Herald-Journal Inc 231 873-5602
123 S State St Hart (49420) ***(G-7378)***
Oceans Sands Scuba 616 396-0068
780 Columbia Ave Holland (49423) ***(G-7762)***
Octapharma Plasma Inc 248 597-0314
401 E 13 Mile Rd Madison Heights (48071) ***(G-10316)***
Ocusano Inc 734 730-5407
600 Union Ave Se 1 Grand Rapids (49503) ***(G-6727)***
Oden Machinery Inc 716 874-3000
185 S Jebavy Dr Ludington (49431) ***(G-10076)***
Odin Defense Industries Inc 248 434-5072
2145 Crooks Rd Ste 210 Troy (48084) ***(G-16532)***
Odl Incorporated (PA) 616 772-9111
215 E Roosevelt Ave Zeeland (49464) ***(G-18170)***
Odl Incorporated 616 772-9111
100 Mulder Rd Zeeland (49464) ***(G-18171)***
Odonnells Docks 269 244-1446
12097 M 60 Jones (49061) ***(G-8652)***
Odor Gone Inc 888 636-7292
2849 Air Park Dr Zeeland (49464) ***(G-18172)***
Odt Research, Rochester *Also called Odt Systems Inc* ***(G-13339)***
Odt Systems Inc 248 953-9512
741 Ridgewood Rd Rochester (48306) ***(G-13339)***
Odyssey Electronics Inc 734 421-8340
12886 Fairlane St Livonia (48150) ***(G-9874)***
Odyssey Industries LLC 248 814-8800
3020 Indianwood Rd Lake Orion (48362) ***(G-9153)***
Odyssey Tool LLC 586 468-6696
22373 Starks Dr Clinton Township (48036) ***(G-3189)***
Oerlikon Blzers Cating USA Inc 248 409-5900
199 Kay Industrial Dr Lake Orion (48359) ***(G-9154)***
Oerlikon Blzers Cating USA Inc 989 463-6268
7800 N Alger Rd Alma (48801) ***(G-246)***
Oerlikon Blzers Cating USA Inc 586 465-0412
42728 Executive Dr Harrison Township (48045) ***(G-7342)***
Oerlikon Blzers Cating USA Inc 248 960-9055
46947 West Rd Wixom (48393) ***(G-17873)***
Oerlikon Blzers Cating USA Inc 989 362-3515
980 Aulerich Rd East Tawas (48730) ***(G-4691)***
Oerlikon Metco (us) Inc 248 288-0027
1972 Meijer Dr Troy (48084) ***(G-16533)***
Oex, Inc., Troy *Also called Office Express Inc* ***(G-16534)***
Off Grid LLC 734 780-4434
2950 Trillium Ln Ann Arbor (48103) ***(G-580)***
Off Site Manufacturing Tech, Chesterfield *Also called Offsite Manufacturing Inc* ***(G-2811)***
Off Site Mfg Tech Inc (PA) 586 598-3110
50350 E Russell Sch Chesterfield (48051) ***(G-2810)***
Office Connection Inc (PA) 248 871-2003
37676 Enterprise Ct Farmington Hills (48331) ***(G-5086)***
Office Design & Furn LLC 734 217-2717
417 S Huron St Ypsilanti (48197) ***(G-18093)***
Office Express Inc 248 307-1850
1280 E Big Beaver Rd A Troy (48083) ***(G-16534)***
Office Furniture Accessories, Grand Rapids *Also called Proos Manufacturing Inc* ***(G-6791)***
Office Services Division, Lansing *Also called Technology MGT & Budgt Dept* ***(G-9430)***
Office Updating 248 770-4769
2275 Reidsview E White Lake (48383) ***(G-17635)***
Office Ways, Ypsilanti *Also called Office Design & Furn LLC* ***(G-18093)***

Offsite Manufacturing Inc 586 598-8850
750 Structural Dr Chesterfield (48051) *(G-2811)*
Oflow-Rite Controls Ltd 616 583-1700
960 74th St Sw Byron Center (49315) *(G-2205)*
Og Technologies Inc 734 973-7500
4480 Varsity Dr Ste G Ann Arbor (48108) *(G-581)*
Ogden Newspapers Inc 906 786-2021
600 Ludington St Escanaba (49829) *(G-4849)*
Ogden Newspapers Inc 906 497-5652
W3985 2nd St Powers (49874) *(G-13078)*
Ogden Newspapers Inc 906 774-2772
215 E Ludington St Iron Mountain (49801) *(G-8296)*
Ogden Newspapers Inc 906 228-2500
249 W Washington St Marquette (49855) *(G-10548)*
Ogden Newspapers Inc 906 789-9122
600 2 Ludington St Escanaba (49829) *(G-4850)*
Ogden Newspapers Virginia LLC 906 228-8920
249 W Washington St Marquette (49855) *(G-10549)*
Ogemaw County Herald Inc (PA) 989 345-0044
215 W Houghton Ave West Branch (48661) *(G-17514)*
Ogilvie Manufacturing Company 810 793-6598
2445 Henry Rd Lapeer (48446) *(G-9478)*
Ogura Corporation 586 749-1900
55025 Gratiot Ave Chesterfield (48051) *(G-2812)*
Ohio Transmission Corporation 616 784-3228
5706 West River Dr Ne Belmont (49306) *(G-1469)*
Ohler Machine 517 852-1900
725 Durkee St Nashville (49073) *(G-11463)*
Oil Chem Inc 810 235-3040
711 W 12th St Flint (48503) *(G-5476)*
Oil City Venture Inc 989 832-8071
172 N 11 Mile Rd Midland (48640) *(G-10899)*
OIL Energy Corp (PA) 231 933-3600
954 Businemi Pk Dr Ste 5 Traverse City (49686) *(G-16054)*
Oil Exchange 6 Inc 734 641-4310
140 Middlebelt Rd Inkster (48141) *(G-8230)*
Oil Patch Machine & Tool, Mount Pleasant *Also called Oilpatch Machine Tool Inc* *(G-11215)*
Oiles America Corporation 734 414-7400
44099 Plymouth Oaks Blvd Plymouth (48170) *(G-12702)*
Oilgear Company (HQ) 231 929-1660
1424 International Dr Traverse City (49686) *(G-16055)*
Oilpatch Machine Tool Inc 989 772-0637
6773 E Pickard Rd Mount Pleasant (48858) *(G-11215)*
Oji Intertech Inc 248 373-7733
1091 Centre Rd Ste 110 Auburn Hills (48326) *(G-964)*
OKeefe Centre Ltd (PA) 231 223-7355
12239 Center Rd Traverse City (49686) *(G-16056)*
Oktober LLC 231 750-1998
1657 S Getty St Ste 17 Muskegon (49442) *(G-11392)*
Okuno International Corp 248 536-2727
40000 Grand River Ave # 103 Novi (48375) *(G-11963)*
Old Dura Inc (HQ) 248 299-7500
1780 Pond Run Auburn Hills (48326) *(G-965)*
Old Europe Cheese Inc 269 925-5003
1330 E Empire Ave Benton Harbor (49022) *(G-1536)*
Old Mission Gazette 231 590-4715
12875 Bluff Rd Traverse City (49686) *(G-16057)*
Old Mission Multigrain LLC 231 366-4121
1515 Chimney Ridge Dr Traverse City (49686) *(G-16058)*
Old Orchard Brands LLC 616 887-1745
1991 12 Mile Rd Nw Sparta (49345) *(G-15103)*
Old Sawmill Woodworking Co 248 366-6245
4552 Newcroft St Commerce Township (48382) *(G-3434)*
Old Xembedded LLC 734 975-0577
3915 Res Pk Dr Ste A8 Ann Arbor (48108) *(G-582)*
Oldcastle Buildingenvelope Inc 616 896-8341
4257 30th St Burnips (49314) *(G-2133)*
Oldcastle Buildingenvelope Inc 734 947-9670
26471 Nrthline Cmmerce Dr Taylor (48180) *(G-15752)*
Oldcastle Materials Inc 269 343-4659
2300 Glendenning Rd Kalamazoo (49001) *(G-8839)*
Oldcastle Materials Inc 248 625-5891
4751 White Lake Rd Clarkston (48346) *(G-2942)*
Oleco Inc (PA) 616 842-6790
18683 Trimble Ct Spring Lake (49456) *(G-15167)*
Oles Meat Processing 989 866-6442
11800 S Winn Rd Vestaburg (48891) *(G-16827)*
Olive Engineering Company 616 399-1756
14354 Blair St W West Olive (49460) *(G-17533)*
Olive Vinegar 248 923-2310
205 S Main St Ste C Rochester (48307) *(G-13340)*
Olive Vinegar 586 484-4700
44230 Apple Blossom Dr Sterling Heights (48314) *(G-15439)*
Oliver Carbide Products, Cottrellville *Also called L R Oliver and Company Inc* *(G-3590)*
Oliver Healthcare Packaging, Grand Rapids *Also called Oliver Products Company* *(G-6728)*
Oliver Industries Inc 586 977-7750
6070 18 Mile Rd Sterling Heights (48314) *(G-15440)*
Oliver of Adrian Inc 517 263-2132
1111 E Beecher St Adrian (49221) *(G-83)*
Oliver Packaging and Eqp Co 616 356-2950
3236 Wilson Dr Nw Walker (49534) *(G-16872)*
Oliver Products Company (HQ) 616 456-7711
445 6th St Nw Grand Rapids (49504) *(G-6728)*
Oliver Racing Parts, Charlevoix *Also called Baldwin Precision Inc* *(G-2608)*
Olivet Machine Tool Engrg Co 269 749-2671
423 N Main St Olivet (49076) *(G-12143)*
Olivo LLC 313 573-7202
1609 Applewood Ave Lincoln Park (48146) *(G-9582)*
Olympian Tool LLC 989 224-4817
604 N Us Highway 27 Saint Johns (48879) *(G-14291)*
Omaha Automation Inc 313 557-3565
8301 Saint Aubin St Detroit (48211) *(G-4284)*
Omaha Plant, Southfield *Also called Grede Omaha LLC* *(G-14928)*
Omara Sprung Floors Inc 810 743-8281
3130 Eugene St Burton (48519) *(G-2160)*
Omc Archtrim 517 482-9411
810 E Mount Hope Ave Lansing (48910) *(G-9407)*
Omega Industries Michigan LLC 616 460-0500
3744 Linden Ave Se Grand Rapids (49548) *(G-6729)*
Omega Plastics Inc 586 954-2100
24401 Capital Blvd Clinton Township (48036) *(G-3190)*
Omega Resources Inc 231 941-4838
415 S Union St Fl 1-2 Traverse City (49684) *(G-16059)*
Omega Steel Incorporated 616 877-3782
1232 Ingle Rd Ste A Wayland (49348) *(G-17408)*
Omega Surgical Instruments 810 695-9800
1072 S Elms Rd Ste E Flint (48532) *(G-5477)*
Omimex Energy Inc 231 845-7358
4854 W Angling Rd Ludington (49431) *(G-10077)*
Omimex Energy Inc 517 628-2820
3505 W Barnes Rd Mason (48854) *(G-10650)*
Omlor Enterprises Inc 616 837-6361
135 Mason Dr Coopersville (49404) *(G-3567)*
Omni Die & Engineering, Holland *Also called Karr Spring Company* *(G-7707)*
Omni Ergonomics, Saint Johns *Also called Omni Technical Services Inc* *(G-14292)*
Omni Metalcraft Corp (PA) 989 354-4075
4040 Us Highway 23 N Alpena (49707) *(G-304)*
Omni Technical Services Inc 989 227-8900
203 E Tolles Dr Saint Johns (48879) *(G-14292)*
Omni United (usa) Inc (HQ) 231 943-9804
5350 Birch Point Dr Interlochen (49643) *(G-8244)*
Omnilink Communications Corp 517 336-1800
3101 Technology Blvd Lansing (48910) *(G-9408)*
Omron Automotive Electronics 248 893-0200
29185 Cabot Dr Novi (48377) *(G-11964)*
Omron Automotive Electronics 248 893-0200
29185 Cabot Dr Novi (48377) *(G-11965)*
Omt Veyhl 616 738-6688
4430 136th Ave Ste 3 Holland (49424) *(G-7763)*
Omt-Veyhl USA Corporation 616 738-6688
11511 James St Holland (49424) *(G-7764)*
Omteco, Olivet *Also called Olivet Machine Tool Engrg Co* *(G-12143)*
Omtron Inc 248 673-3896
2560 Silverside Rd Waterford (48328) *(G-17362)*
On Green Logos 616 669-1928
2430 Chicago Dr Hudsonville (49426) *(G-8173)*
On Sight Armory, Niles *Also called Performance Machining Inc* *(G-11638)*
On The Mark Inc 989 317-8033
801 Industrial Dr Mount Pleasant (48858) *(G-11216)*
On The Side Sign Dsign Grphics 810 266-7446
15216 Murray Rd Byron (48418) *(G-2174)*
On-The-Spot-engraving, Lansing *Also called Applause Inc* *(G-9338)*
Oncofusion Therapeutics Inc 248 361-3341
120 W Main St Ste 300 Northville (48167) *(G-11719)*
One Beer At A Time LLC 616 719-1604
925 Cherry St Se Ste 1-2 Grand Rapids (49506) *(G-6730)*
One Stop Store 15, Flint *Also called D M J Corp* *(G-5412)*
One-Way Tool & Die Inc 248 477-2964
32845 8 Mile Rd Livonia (48152) *(G-9875)*
Onegene America Inc 734 855-4460
38777 6 Mile Rd Livonia (48152) *(G-9876)*
Oneida Tool Corporation 313 537-0770
12700 Inkster Rd Redford (48239) *(G-13177)*
Oneiric Systems Inc (PA) 248 554-3090
31711 Sherman Ave Madison Heights (48071) *(G-10317)*
Onesian Enterprises Inc 313 382-5875
10520 Balfour Ave Allen Park (48101) *(G-203)*
Onestream Software Corp 248 841-1356
425 S Main St Ste 203 Rochester (48307) *(G-13341)*
Onestream Software LLC (PA) 248 342-1541
362 S St Rochester Rochester (48307) *(G-13342)*
ONiel Metal Forming Inc 248 960-1804
1098 Rig St Commerce Township (48390) *(G-3435)*
Onion Crock of Michigan Inc 616 458-2922
1221 Mcreynolds Ave Nw Grand Rapids (49504) *(G-6731)*
Onl Therapeutics LLC 734 998-8339
1600 Huron Pkwy Ann Arbor (48109) *(G-583)*

A
L
P
H
A
B
E
T
I
C

Online Engineering Inc ... 906 341-0090
400 N Cedar St Manistique (49854) ***(G-10445)***
Onodi Tool & Engineering Co ... 313 386-6682
19150 Meginnity St Melvindale (48122) ***(G-10704)***
Ontario Die Company America (HQ) ... 810 987-5060
1755 Busha Hwy Marysville (48040) ***(G-10609)***
Ontonagon Herald Co Inc ... 906 884-2826
326 River St Ontonagon (49953) ***(G-12163)***
Onyx Manufacturing Inc ... 248 687-8611
1663 Star Batt Dr Rochester Hills (48309) ***(G-13487)***
Opco Lubrication Systems Inc ... 231 924-6160
9569 W 40th St Fremont (49412) ***(G-5780)***
Open Air Lifestyles LLC ... 586 716-2233
16009 Leone Dr Bldg A Macomb (48042) ***(G-10150)***
Openings Inc ... 248 623-6899
6145 Delfield Dr Waterford (48329) ***(G-17363)***
Opensystems Publishing LLC (PA) ... 586 415-6500
30233 Jefferson Ave Saint Clair Shores (48082) ***(G-14266)***
Opeo Inc ... 248 299-4000
2700 Auburn Ct Auburn Hills (48326) ***(G-966)***
Opeo Automotive, Auburn Hills *Also called Opeo Inc* ***(G-966)***
Operations Research Tech LLC ... 248 626-8960
4050 Hanover Ct West Bloomfield (48323) ***(G-17492)***
Operator Specialty Company Inc ... 616 675-5050
2547 3 Mile Rd Nw Grand Rapids (49534) ***(G-6732)***
Ophir Crafts LLC ... 734 794-7777
1522 N Maple Rd Ann Arbor (48103) ***(G-584)***
Ophir Yarn and Fiber, Ann Arbor *Also called Ophir Crafts LLC* ***(G-584)***
Opio LLc ... 313 433-1098
35000 Van Born Rd Wayne (48184) ***(G-17440)***
Oplogic, Clawson *Also called Wilson Technologies Inc* ***(G-2989)***
Ops Solutions LLC (PA) ... 248 374-8000
48443 Alpha Dr Ste 175 Wixom (48393) ***(G-17874)***
Optec Inc ... 616 897-9351
199 Smith St Lowell (49331) ***(G-10039)***
Opteos Inc ... 734 929-3333
775 Technology Dr Ste 200 Ann Arbor (48108) ***(G-585)***
Opti Temp Inc ... 231 946-2931
1500 International Dr Traverse City (49686) ***(G-16060)***
Optic Edge Corporation ... 231 547-6090
6279 Us Highway 31 S Charlevoix (49720) ***(G-2624)***
Optical Supply, Grand Rapids *Also called Essilor Laboratories Amer Inc* ***(G-6386)***
Optimems Technology Inc ... 248 660-0380
43422 W Oaks Dr Ste 183 Novi (48377) ***(G-11966)***
Optimizerx Corporation (PA) ... 248 651-6568
400 Water St Ste 200 Rochester (48307) ***(G-13343)***
Optimystic Enterprises Inc ... 269 695-7741
600 S Oak St Buchanan (49107) ***(G-2124)***
Option Energy LLC ... 269 329-4317
102 E River Rd Traverse City (49696) ***(G-16061)***
Options Cabinetry Inc ... 248 669-0000
2121 Easy St Commerce Township (48390) ***(G-3436)***
Optishot Golf, Northville *Also called Edens Technologies LLC* ***(G-11689)***
Opto Solutions Inc ... 269 254-9716
140 E Bridge St Plainwell (49080) ***(G-12532)***
Optrand Inc ... 734 451-3480
46155 Five Mile Rd Plymouth (48170) ***(G-12703)***
Opus Mach LLC ... 586 270-5170
31845 Denton Dr Warren (48092) ***(G-17177)***
Opus Packaging, Caledonia *Also called Action Packaging LLC* ***(G-2287)***
Oracle America Inc ... 989 495-0465
2200 Salzburg St Midland (48640) ***(G-10900)***
Oracle America Inc ... 248 273-1934
755 W Big Beavr Rd # 245 Troy (48084) ***(G-16535)***
Oracle Brewing Company ... 989 401-7446
122 N Michigan Ave Saginaw (48602) ***(G-14117)***
Oracle Brewing Company LLC ... 989 401-7446
1411 W Pine River Rd Breckenridge (48615) ***(G-1845)***
Oracle Corporation ... 248 393-2498
3216 Hickory Dr Orion (48359) ***(G-12187)***
Oracle Systems Corporation ... 248 614-5139
1365 N Fairview Ln Rochester Hills (48306) ***(G-13488)***
Oracle Systems Corporation ... 248 816-8050
3290 W Big Beaver Rd # 300 Troy (48084) ***(G-16536)***
Orangebox Us Inc ... 616 988-8624
4595 Broadmoor Ave Se # 120 Grand Rapids (49512) ***(G-6733)***
Orbis Corporation ... 248 616-3232
999 Chicago Rd Troy (48083) ***(G-16537)***
Orbit Technology Inc ... 906 776-7248
100 W Brown St Iron Mountain (49801) ***(G-8297)***
Orbitform Group, Jackson *Also called Smsg LLC* ***(G-8574)***
Orbitform Group LLC ... 800 957-4838
1600 Executive Dr Jackson (49203) ***(G-8545)***
Orchid Connecticut, Holt *Also called Orchid Orthpd Sltons Organ Inc* ***(G-7919)***
Orchid Lansing, Holt *Also called Orchid Orthpd Solutions LLC* ***(G-7920)***
Orchid Orthopedic Solutions, Holt *Also called Tulip US Holdings Inc* ***(G-7931)***
Orchid Orthpd Sltons Organ Inc ... 203 877-3341
1489 Cedar St Holt (48842) ***(G-7919)***
Orchid Orthpd Solutions LLC ... 989 746-0780
6688 Dixie Hwy Bridgeport (48722) ***(G-1855)***
Orchid Orthpd Solutions LLC (HQ) ... 517 694-2300
1489 Cedar St Holt (48842) ***(G-7920)***
Ore Dock Brewing Company LLC ... 906 228-8888
14 Spring St Marquette (49855) ***(G-10550)***
Organicorp Inc ... 616 540-0295
11455 36th St Se Lowell (49331) ***(G-10040)***
Organized Crime Entertainment, Pullman *Also called Paul F Hester* ***(G-13087)***
Original Footwear Company ... 231 796-5828
1005 Baldwin St Big Rapids (49307) ***(G-1639)***
Original Murdicks Fudge Co (PA) ... 906 847-3530
7363 Main St Mackinac Island (49757) ***(G-10097)***
Original Stay Cool Cap, The, Detroit *Also called Brintley Enterprises* ***(G-3918)***
Orin Jewelers Inc (PA) ... 734 422-7030
29317 Ford Rd Garden City (48135) ***(G-5834)***
Orion Bus Accnting Sltions LLC ... 248 893-1060
1611 Ford Ave Wyandotte (48192) ***(G-17970)***
Orion Machine Inc ... 231 728-1229
392 Irwin Ave Muskegon (49442) ***(G-11393)***
Orion Manufacturing Inc ... 616 527-5994
480 Apple Tree Dr Ionia (48846) ***(G-8250)***
Orion Test Systems Inc ... 248 373-9097
4260 Giddings Rd Auburn Hills (48326) ***(G-967)***
Orion Test Systems & Engrg, Auburn Hills *Also called Orion Test Systems Inc* ***(G-967)***
Orlandi Gear Company Inc ... 586 285-9900
17755 Masonic Fraser (48026) ***(G-5701)***
Oronoko Iron Works Inc ... 269 326-7045
9243 First St Baroda (49101) ***(G-1128)***
Orotex Corporation ... 248 773-8630
22475 Venture Dr Novi (48375) ***(G-11967)***
Orr Lumber, North Branch *Also called Production Threaded Parts Co* ***(G-11665)***
Orri Corp ... 248 618-1104
5385 Perry Dr Waterford (48329) ***(G-17364)***
Orsco Inc ... 314 679-4200
69900 Powell Rd Armada (48005) ***(G-721)***
Ort Tool & Die Corporation (PA) ... 419 242-9553
6555 S Dixie Hwy Erie (48133) ***(G-4807)***
Ortho-Clinical Diagnostics Inc ... 248 797-8087
2128 Lancer Dr Troy (48084) ***(G-16538)***
Orthopaedic Associates Mich, Grand Rapids *Also called Orthopaedic Associates Mich* ***(G-6734)***
Orthopaedic Associates Mich (PA) ... 616 459-7101
4665 44th St Se Ste A190 Grand Rapids (49512) ***(G-6734)***
Orthopedic Network News, Ann Arbor *Also called Mendenhall Associates Inc* ***(G-552)***
Orthotic Insoles LLC ... 517 641-4166
12390 Center Rd Bath (48808) ***(G-1135)***
Orthotic Shop Inc ... 800 309-0412
14200 Industrial Ctr Dr Shelby Township (48315) ***(G-14658)***
Orthotics & Prosthetics Center, Ann Arbor *Also called Regents of The University Mich* ***(G-618)***
Orthotics and Prosthetics, Muskegon *Also called Mercy Health Partners* ***(G-11374)***
Orthotool LLC (PA) ... 734 455-8103
50325 Ann Arbor Rd W Plymouth (48170) ***(G-12704)***
Orthoview LLC ... 800 318-0923
44650 Helm Ct Plymouth (48170) ***(G-12705)***
Ortus Enterprises LLC ... 269 491-1447
2527 Rolling Hill Ave Portage (49024) ***(G-13020)***
Orvis Machine Tool Inc ... 517 548-7638
5253 Clyde Rd Howell (48855) ***(G-8074)***
Orwood Precision Pdts Caratron, Fraser *Also called Bmt Aerospace Usa Inc* ***(G-5630)***
Os Holdings LLc (PA) ... 734 397-6300
17757 Woodland Dr New Boston (48164) ***(G-11507)***
Osbern Racing ... 313 538-8933
16751 Riverview St Detroit (48219) ***(G-4285)***
Osborne Concrete Co ... 734 941-3008
37500 Northline Rd Romulus (48174) ***(G-13717)***
Osborne Materials Company ... 906 493-5211
23311 E Haul Rd Drummond Island (49726) ***(G-4566)***
Osborne Transformer Corp ... 586 218-6900
33258 Groesbeck Hwy Fraser (48026) ***(G-5702)***
Oscar W Larson Company ... 248 575-0320
10080 Dixie Hwy Clarkston (48348) ***(G-2943)***
Oscar's Printing, Saint Joseph *Also called Tuteur Inc* ***(G-14344)***
Osceola Addition, Reed City *Also called Conine Publishing Company* ***(G-13212)***
Osco, Grand Rapids *Also called Operator Specialty Company Inc* ***(G-6732)***
Osco Inc ... 248 852-7310
2937 Waterview Dr Rochester Hills (48309) ***(G-13489)***
Oscoda Plastics Inc (PA) ... 989 739-6900
5585 N Huron Ave Oscoda (48750) ***(G-12216)***
Oscoda Press, Oscoda *Also called Iosco News Press Publishing Co* ***(G-12212)***
Oshkosh Defense LLC ... 586 576-8301
27600 Donald Ct Warren (48092) ***(G-17178)***
Osmi Inc ... 561 504-3924
777 Eight Mile Rd Whitmore Lake (48189) ***(G-17705)***
Ossineke Industries Inc ... 989 471-2197
10401 Piper Rd Ossineke (49766) ***(G-12230)***
Oster Pipe Threaders, Owosso *Also called Superior Threading Inc* ***(G-12319)***

Ostrander Company Inc...248 646-6680
1200 W 12 Mile Rd Madison Heights (48071) *(G-10318)*
Ot Dynamics LLC...734 984-7022
27100 Hall Rd Flat Rock (48134) *(G-5358)*
Oth Consultants Inc...586 598-0100
46480 Continental Dr Chesterfield (48047) *(G-2813)*
Otsego County Herald Times...989 732-1111
2058 S Otsego Ave Gaylord (49735) *(G-5886)*
Otsego Paper, Otsego *Also called United States Gypsum Company (G-12257)*
Otsego Paper Inc...269 692-6141
320 N Farmer St Otsego (49078) *(G-12247)*
Otsuka America Foods Inc...231 383-3124
1123 Main St Frankfort (49635) *(G-5604)*
Ottawa Forest Products Inc...906 932-9701
1243 Wall St Ironwood (49938) *(G-8336)*
Ottawa Tool & Machine LLC...616 677-1743
2188 Leonard St Nw Grand Rapids (49534) *(G-6735)*
Otter Company...248 566-3235
2687 Amberly Ln Troy (48084) *(G-16539)*
Otters Oasis...269 788-9987
36 Grand Blvd Battle Creek (49015) *(G-1234)*
Otto Bock, Rochester Hills *Also called Foampartner Americas Inc (G-13426)*
Outdoor Systems Advertising, Grand Rapids *Also called Outfront Media LLC (G-6736)*
Outfront Media LLC...616 452-3171
1355 Century Ave Sw Grand Rapids (49503) *(G-6736)*
Outline Industries LLC...303 632-6782
100 Industrial Parkway Dr Boyne City (49712) *(G-1831)*
Ova Science Inc...617 758-8605
301 N Main St Ste 100 Ann Arbor (48104) *(G-586)*
OVASCIENCE, Ann Arbor *Also called Millendo Therapeutics Inc (G-559)*
Over Top Steel Coating LLC...616 647-9140
931 W River Center Dr Ne B Comstock Park (49321) *(G-3504)*
Overhead Conveyer, Ferndale *Also called Structural Equipment Co (G-5320)*
Overhead Conveyor Company (PA)...248 547-3800
1330 Hilton Rd Ferndale (48220) *(G-5307)*
Overhead Door Company Alpena...989 354-8316
2550 Us Highway 23 S Alpena (49707) *(G-305)*
Overkill Research & Dev Labs...517 768-8155
2010 Micor Dr Jackson (49203) *(G-8546)*
Overseas Auto Parts Inc...734 427-4840
32400 Plymouth Rd Livonia (48150) *(G-9877)*
Overstreet Management, Benton Harbor *Also called Overstreet Property MGT Co (G-1537)*
Overstreet Property MGT Co...269 252-1560
1852 Commonwealth Rd Benton Harbor (49022) *(G-1537)*
Ovidon Manufacturing LLC...517 548-4005
1200 Grand Oaks Dr Howell (48843) *(G-8075)*
Ovshinsky Technologies LLC...248 390-3564
1 N Saginaw St Pontiac (48342) *(G-12854)*
Owens Building Co Inc...989 835-1293
1928 N Stark Rd Midland (48642) *(G-10901)*
Owens Cabinet & Trim, Midland *Also called Owens Building Co Inc (G-10901)*
Owens Classic International, Saint Joseph *Also called Worldwide Marketing Services (G-14355)*
Owens Corning Sales LLC...248 668-7500
46500 Humboldt Dr Novi (48377) *(G-11968)*
Owens Products Inc...269 651-2300
1107 Progress St Sturgis (49091) *(G-15625)*
Owens-Brockway Glass Cont Inc...269 435-2535
950 Industrial Park Dr Constantine (49042) *(G-3541)*
Owl Leasing, Springfield *Also called Marketplus Software Inc (G-15198)*
Own Lumber Mill, Gwinn *Also called Potlatchdeltic Corporation (G-7222)*
Owosso Automation Inc...989 725-8804
1650 E South St 488 Owosso (48867) *(G-12307)*
Owosso Country Club Pro Shop...989 723-1470
4200 N Chipman Rd Owosso (48867) *(G-12308)*
Owosso Fabrication and Design, Owosso *Also called Transit Bus Rebuilders Inc (G-12324)*
Owosso Graphic Arts Inc...989 725-7112
151 N Delaney Rd Owosso (48867) *(G-12309)*
Owosso Ready Mix Co...989 723-1295
441 Cleveland Ave Owosso (48867) *(G-12310)*
Owosso Soft Trim, Saint Louis *Also called American Soft Trim Inc (G-14357)*
Ox Engineered Products LLC (PA)...248 289-9950
22260 Haggerty Rd Ste 365 Northville (48167) *(G-11720)*
Ox Engineered Products LLC...269 435-2425
700 Centreville St Constantine (49042) *(G-3542)*
Ox Paperboard Michigan LLC...800 345-8881
700 Centreville St Constantine (49042) *(G-3543)*
Oxbow Machine Products Inc (PA)...734 422-7730
12743 Merriman Rd Livonia (48150) *(G-9878)*
Oxbowindo...248 698-9400
10195 Highland Rd White Lake (48386) *(G-17636)*
Oxford Biomedical Research Inc (PA)...248 852-8815
4600 Gardner Rd Metamora (48455) *(G-10779)*
Oxford Instruments America Inc...734 821-3003
120 Enterprise Dr Ann Arbor (48103) *(G-587)*
Oxford Leader, Oxford *Also called Sherman Publications Inc (G-12372)*
Oxford Manufacturing Facility, Oxford *Also called MSP Industries Corporation (G-12362)*
Oxid Corporation...248 474-9817
25325 Regency Dr Novi (48375) *(G-11969)*
Oxmaster Inc (PA)...810 987-7600
1105 24th St Port Huron (48060) *(G-12952)*
Oxus America Inc...248 475-0925
2676 Paldan Dr Auburn Hills (48326) *(G-968)*
Oxygenplus LLC...586 221-9112
15760 19 Mile Rd Ste E Clinton Township (48038) *(G-3191)*
Ozinga Ready Mix, New Buffalo *Also called New Buffalo Concrete Products (G-11516)*
Ozland Enterprises Inc...269 649-0706
603 W Prairie St Vicksburg (49097) *(G-16840)*
P & A Conveyor Sales Inc...734 285-7970
18999 Quarry St Riverview (48193) *(G-13303)*
P & C Group I Inc (PA)...248 442-6800
37000 W 12 Mile Rd Farmington Hills (48331) *(G-5087)*
P & D Uniforms and ACC Inc...313 881-3881
20936 Kelly Rd Eastpointe (48021) *(G-4708)*
P & F Enterprises LLC...616 340-1265
4095 Oak Valley Ave Sw Wyoming (49519) *(G-18024)*
P & G Technologies Inc...248 399-3135
938 E 10 Mile Rd Hazel Park (48030) *(G-7449)*
P & K Technologies Inc...586 336-9545
111 Shafer Dr Romeo (48065) *(G-13634)*
P & M Industries Inc...517 223-1000
5901 Weller Rd Gregory (48137) *(G-7165)*
P & O Services Inc...248 809-3072
24293 Telg Rd Ste 140 Southfield (48033) *(G-14994)*
P & P Manufacturing Co Inc...810 667-2712
260 Mccormick Dr Lapeer (48446) *(G-9479)*
P A Products, Livonia *Also called PA Products Inc (G-9880)*
P C S Companies Inc...616 754-2229
1251 Callaghan St Greenville (48838) *(G-7149)*
P D E Systems Inc...586 725-3330
37230 26 Mile Rd Chesterfield (48047) *(G-2814)*
P D P LLC...616 437-9618
2675 Chicago Dr Sw Wyoming (49519) *(G-18025)*
P D Q Press Inc...586 725-1888
7752 Dixie Hwy Ira (48023) *(G-8265)*
P D Q Signs Inc...248 669-8600
9578 Buckingham St White Lake (48386) *(G-17637)*
P E T S, Auburn Hills *Also called Plastic Engrg Tchncal Svcs Inc (G-974)*
P G K Enterprises LLC...248 535-4411
23450 Telegraph Rd Southfield (48033) *(G-14995)*
P G S Inc...248 526-3800
1600 E Big Beaver Rd Troy (48083) *(G-16540)*
P I W Corporation...989 448-2501
1492 Orourke Blvd Gaylord (49735) *(G-5887)*
P J Printing...269 673-3372
633 114th Ave Ste 5 Allegan (49010) *(G-179)*
P J Wallbank Springs Inc...810 987-2992
2121 Beard St Port Huron (48060) *(G-12953)*
P L Schmitt Crbide Tooling LLC...313 706-5756
8865 Seymour Rd Grass Lake (49240) *(G-7090)*
P M R Industries Inc...810 989-5020
2311 16th St Port Huron (48060) *(G-12954)*
P M Z Technology Inc...248 471-0447
33302 7 Mile Rd Livonia (48152) *(G-9879)*
P S Monograms...616 698-1177
160 84th St Sw Ste 4 Byron Center (49315) *(G-2206)*
P T M Corporation (PA)...586 725-2211
6560 Bethuy Rd Ira (48023) *(G-8266)*
P T T, Fraser *Also called Product and Tooling Tech Inc (G-5710)*
P X Tool Co...248 585-9330
32354 Edward Ave Madison Heights (48071) *(G-10319)*
P&L Development & Mfg LLC...989 739-5203
4025 Arrow St Oscoda (48750) *(G-12217)*
P&L Development and Mfg, Oscoda *Also called P&L Development & Mfg LLC (G-12217)*
P-S Business Acquisition Inc (HQ)...616 887-8837
122 S Aspen St Sparta (49345) *(G-15104)*
P-T Stamping Co Ltd...517 278-5961
460 Race St Coldwater (49036) *(G-3316)*
P.A.w Hardwood Flooring & Sups, Kalamazoo *Also called PAW Enterprises LLC (G-8845)*
P2r Metal Fabrication Inc...888 727-5587
49620 Hayes Rd Macomb (48044) *(G-10151)*
P3 Product Solutions Inc...248 703-7724
1225 Spartan St Madison Heights (48071) *(G-10320)*
P3 Vending, Garden City *Also called Gail Parker (G-5825)*
PA Products Inc...734 421-1060
33709 Schoolcraft Rd Livonia (48150) *(G-9880)*
Pac-Cnc Inc...616 288-3389
4045 Remembrance Rd Nw Grand Rapids (49534) *(G-6737)*
Pace Grinding Inc...231 861-0448
8647 W Shelby Rd Shelby (49455) *(G-14533)*
Pace Industries LLC...231 777-3941
2121 Latimer Dr Muskegon (49442) *(G-11394)*
Pace Industries LLC...231 773-4491
1868 Port City Blvd Muskegon (49442) *(G-11395)*
Pace Industries LLC...231 777-3941
1985 E Laketon Ave Muskegon (49442) *(G-11396)*

A L P H A B E T I C

Pace Industries LLC ALPHABETIC SECTION

Pace Industries LLC 231 777-5615
2350 Black Creek Rd Muskegon (49444) ***(G-11397)***
Pace Machine Tool Inc 248 960-9903
1144 Rig St Commerce Township (48390) ***(G-3437)***
Pace Software Systems Inc 586 727-3189
5345 Meldrum Rd Casco (48064) ***(G-2504)***
Pacific Engineering Corp 248 359-7823
39555 Orchard Hill Pl Novi (48375) ***(G-11970)***
Pacific Epoxy Polymers Inc 616 949-1634
3450 Charlevoix Dr Se Grand Rapids (49546) ***(G-6738)***
Pacific Industrial Dev Corp (PA) 734 930-9292
4788 Runway Blvd Ann Arbor (48108) ***(G-588)***
Pacific Industrial Furnace Div, Wixom *Also called Afc-Holcroft LLC* ***(G-17754)***
Pacific Insight Elec Corp 248 344-2569
25650 W 11 Mile Rd # 100 Southfield (48034) ***(G-14996)***
Pacific Oil Resources Inc 734 397-1120
44141 Yost Rd Van Buren Twp (48111) ***(G-16777)***
Pacific Stamex Clg Systems Inc 231 773-1330
2259 S Sheridan Dr Muskegon (49442) ***(G-11398)***
Pacific Tool & Engineering Ltd (PA) 586 737-2710
6410 19 Mile Rd Sterling Heights (48314) ***(G-15441)***
Package Design & Mfg Inc (PA) 248 486-4390
12424 Emerson Dr Brighton (48116) ***(G-1972)***
Packaging Corporation America 616 530-5700
3251 Chicago Dr Sw Grandville (49418) ***(G-7062)***
Packaging Corporation America 734 453-6262
936 N Sheldon Rd Plymouth (48170) ***(G-12706)***
Packaging Corporation America 734 266-1877
28330 Plymouth Rd Livonia (48150) ***(G-9881)***
Packaging Corporation America 231 723-1442
2246 Udell St Filer City (49634) ***(G-5345)***
Packaging Corporation America 231 947-2220
1106 Industrial Park Dr Edmore (48829) ***(G-4753)***
Packaging Corporation America 989 427-5129
1106 Industrial Park Dr Edmore (48829) ***(G-4754)***
Packaging Engineering LLC 248 437-9444
7138 Kensington Rd Brighton (48116) ***(G-1973)***
Packaging Engineering-Brighton, Brighton *Also called Packaging Engineering LLC* ***(G-1973)***
Packaging Personified Inc 616 887-8837
122 S Aspen St Sparta (49345) ***(G-15105)***
Packaging Specialties Inc (HQ) 586 473-6703
8111 Middlebelt Rd Romulus (48174) ***(G-13718)***
Packard Farms LLC 989 386-3816
6584 S Brand Ave Clare (48617) ***(G-2883)***
Packerland Packing Co 269 685-6886
11 11th St Plainwell (49080) ***(G-12533)***
Packers Canning Co Inc 269 624-4681
72100 M 40 Lawton (49065) ***(G-9513)***
Pacora River Defense LLC 248 546-1142
21323 John R Rd Hazel Park (48030) ***(G-7450)***
Paddle Hard Distributing LLC 513 309-1192
118 E Michigan Ave Grayling (49738) ***(G-7115)***
Paddle King Inc 989 235-6776
7110 S Crystal Rd Carson City (48811) ***(G-2495)***
Paddlesports Warehouse Inc 231 757-9051
467 W Us Highway 10 31 Scottville (49454) ***(G-14510)***
Paddletek LLC 269 340-5967
1990 S 11th St Ste 3 Niles (49120) ***(G-11635)***
Padnos Leitelt Inc 616 363-3817
2301 Turner Ave Nw Grand Rapids (49544) ***(G-6739)***
Pag, Troy *Also called Product Assembly Group LLC* ***(G-16565)***
Page Components Corporation 231 922-3600
15 Whispering Woods Dr Traverse City (49696) ***(G-16062)***
Page Litho Inc 313 885-8555
7 Wellington Pl Grosse Pointe (48230) ***(G-7181)***
Page One Inc 810 724-0254
594 N Almont Ave Imlay City (48444) ***(G-8209)***
Pageant Homes Inc 517 694-0431
4000 Holt Rd Holt (48842) ***(G-7921)***
Pages In Time, Grand Rapids *Also called Janelle Peterson* ***(G-6552)***
Pageworks, Grand Rapids *Also called Custom Printers Inc* ***(G-6326)***
Paice Technologies LLC 248 376-1115
5843 Bravo Ct Orchard Lake (48324) ***(G-12168)***
Paich Railworks Inc 734 397-2424
41275 Van Born Rd Van Buren Twp (48111) ***(G-16778)***
Paine Press LLC 231 645-1970
209 S Lake St Boyne City (49712) ***(G-1832)***
Painex Corporation 313 863-1200
18307 James Couzens Fwy Detroit (48235) ***(G-4286)***
Painexx Corporation 313 863-1200
18307 James Couzens Fwy Detroit (48235) ***(G-4287)***
Paint Finishing Div, Belding *Also called Belco Industries Inc* ***(G-1399)***
Paint Work Incorporated 586 759-6640
2088 Riggs Ave Warren (48091) ***(G-17179)***
Pak-Rite Industries Inc 313 388-6400
4270 High St Ecorse (48229) ***(G-4744)***
Pak-Rite Michigan, Wixom *Also called Mollewood Export Inc* ***(G-17859)***
Pak-Sak Industries, Sparta *Also called P-S Business Acquisition Inc* ***(G-15104)***
Pal-TEC Inc 906 788-4229
14 Ln W5886 Wallace (49893) ***(G-16887)***
Paladin Attachments, Dexter *Also called Paladin Brands Group Inc* ***(G-4502)***
Paladin Brands Group Inc (HQ) 319 378-3696
2800 Zeeb Rd Dexter (48130) ***(G-4502)***
Paladin Ind Inc 616 698-7495
4990 W Greenbrooke Dr Se Grand Rapids (49512) ***(G-6740)***
Palazzolo's Gelato, Fennville *Also called PGI of Saugatuck Inc* ***(G-5176)***
Palfam Industries Inc 248 922-0590
1959 Viola Dr Ortonville (48462) ***(G-12201)***
Pall Life Sciences, Ann Arbor *Also called Gelman Sciences Inc* ***(G-469)***
Pallet Man 269 274-8825
555 Upton Ave Springfield (49037) ***(G-15199)***
Pallet Masters 313 995-1131
16352 Farmington Rd Livonia (48154) ***(G-9882)***
Pallet Pros LLC 586 864-3353
8233 Sterling Center Line (48015) ***(G-2581)***
Palm Industries LLC 248 444-7922
4285 Clair Dr South Lyon (48178) ***(G-14808)***
Palm Industries LLC 248 444-7921
9135 General Ct Plymouth (48170) ***(G-12707)***
Palm Sweets LLC 586 554-7979
3605 15 Mile Rd Sterling Heights (48310) ***(G-15442)***
Palm Sweets Bakery & Cafe, Sterling Heights *Also called Palm Sweets LLC* ***(G-15442)***
Palmer Distributors Inc 586 772-4225
33525 Groesbeck Hwy Fraser (48026) ***(G-5703)***
Palmer Engineering Inc 517 321-3600
3525 Capitol City Blvd Lansing (48906) ***(G-9251)***
Palmer Envelope Co 269 965-1336
309 Fritz Keiper Blvd Battle Creek (49037) ***(G-1235)***
Palmer Paint Products Inc 248 588-4500
1291 Rochester Rd Troy (48083) ***(G-16541)***
Palmer Printing Co, Detroit *Also called Zak Brothers Printing LLC* ***(G-4456)***
Palmer Promotional Products, Fraser *Also called Palmer Distributors Inc* ***(G-5703)***
Palo Alto Manufacturing LLC 248 266-3669
2700 Auburn Ct Auburn Hills (48326) ***(G-969)***
Pan-Teck Corporation 989 792-2422
248 Stoneham Rd Saginaw (48638) ***(G-14118)***
Panagon Systems Inc 586 786-3920
51375 Regency Center Dr Macomb (48042) ***(G-10152)***
Pancheck LLC 989 288-6886
221 N Saginaw St Durand (48429) ***(G-4611)***
Panda King Express 616 796-3286
520 Butternut Dr Ste 30 Holland (49424) ***(G-7765)***
Pando Leather Craft, Gaylord *Also called Grozdanovski Vasilka* ***(G-5862)***
Panel Pro LLC 734 427-1691
16809 Ryan Rd Livonia (48154) ***(G-9883)***
Panel Processing Inc 517 279-8051
681 Race St Coldwater (49036) ***(G-3317)***
Panel Processing of Coldwater, Coldwater *Also called Panel Processing Inc* ***(G-3317)***
Panel Processing Oregon Inc (HQ) 989 356-9007
120 N Industrial Hwy Alpena (49707) ***(G-306)***
Pannell S-Erynn 248 692-3192
31831 Grand River Ave Farmington (48336) ***(G-4906)***
Panoplate Lithographics Inc 269 343-4644
101 N Riverview Dr Kalamazoo (49004) ***(G-8840)***
Panter Company Inc 313 537-5700
26029 W 8 Mile Rd Detroit (48240) ***(G-4288)***
Panter Master Controls Inc 810 687-5600
3060 S Dye Rd Ste A Flint (48507) ***(G-5478)***
Panther James LLC 248 850-7522
28822 Woodward Ave Royal Oak (48067) ***(G-13955)***
Pantless Jams LLC 419 283-8470
6937 Maplewood Dr Temperance (48182) ***(G-15840)***
Paper Image Printing Centres, Holt *Also called Printing Centre Inc* ***(G-7922)***
Paper Machine Service Inds (PA) 989 695-2646
3075 Shattuck Rd Ste 801 Saginaw (48603) ***(G-14119)***
Papertech, Bingham Farms *Also called Pressed Paperboard Tech LLC* ***(G-1658)***
Pappas Cutlery-Grinding Inc 800 521-0888
575 E Milwaukee St Detroit (48202) ***(G-4289)***
Pappys Pad LLC 231 894-0888
8812 Ferry St Montague (49437) ***(G-11096)***
Par Molds Inc 616 396-5249
850 Maple Ave Holland (49423) ***(G-7766)***
Par Pharmaceutical, Rochester *Also called Par Sterile Products LLC* ***(G-13344)***
Par Sterile Products LLC 248 651-9081
870 Parkdale Rd Rochester (48307) ***(G-13344)***
Paradigm Conveyor LLC 616 520-1926
15342 24th Ave Marne (49435) ***(G-10510)***
Paradigm Engineering Inc 586 776-5910
16470 E 13 Mile Rd Roseville (48066) ***(G-13849)***
Paragon D&E, Grand Rapids *Also called Paragon Die & Engineering Co* ***(G-6741)***
Paragon Die & Engineering Co (PA) 616 949-2220
5225 33rd St Se Grand Rapids (49512) ***(G-6741)***
Paragon Manufacturing Corp 810 629-4100
2046 W Thompson Rd Fenton (48430) ***(G-5228)***
Paragon Metals LLC (PA) 517 639-4629
3010 Mechanic Rd Hillsdale (49242) ***(G-7533)***

Paragon Model and Tool Inc......248 960-1223
46934 Magellan Wixom (48393) **(G-17875)**
Paragon Model Shop Inc......616 693-3224
10083 Thompson Rd Freeport (49325) **(G-5767)**
Paragon Molds Corporation......586 294-7630
33997 Riviera Fraser (48026) **(G-5704)**
Paragon Ready Mix Inc (PA)......586 731-8000
48000 Hixson Ave Shelby Township (48317) **(G-14659)**
Paragon Tempered Glass LLC (PA)......269 684-5060
1830 Terminal Rd Niles (49120) **(G-11636)**
Paragon Tool, Wixom *Also called Paragon Model and Tool Inc* **(G-17875)**
Paragon Tool Company......734 326-1702
36130 Ecorse Rd Romulus (48174) **(G-13719)**
Paramelt, Norton Shores *Also called M Argueso & Co Inc* **(G-11771)**
Paramelt Usa Inc (HQ)......231 759-7304
2817 Mccracken St Norton Shores (49441) **(G-11786)**
Parameter Driven Software Inc (PA)......248 553-6410
32605 W 12 Mile Rd # 275 Farmington Hills (48334) **(G-5088)**
Paramont Machine Co LLC......330 339-3489
2810 N Burdick St Kalamazoo (49004) **(G-8841)**
Paramount Baking Company......313 690-4844
29790 Little Mack Ave Roseville (48066) **(G-13850)**
Paramount Coffee Co., Lansing *Also called Inter State Foods Inc* **(G-9237)**
Paramount Solutions Inc......586 914-0708
59285 Elizabeth Ln Ray (48096) **(G-13135)**
Paramount Technologies Inc......248 960-0909
1374 E West Maple Rd Walled Lake (48390) **(G-16901)**
Paramount Tool and Die Inc......616 677-0000
1245 Comstock St Marne (49435) **(G-10511)**
Paravis Industries Inc......248 393-2300
1597 Atlantic Blvd Auburn Hills (48326) **(G-970)**
Pardon Inc......906 428-3494
3510 State Highway M35 Gladstone (49837) **(G-5918)**
Paris North Hardwood Lumber......231 584-2500
542 Tobias Rd Elmira (49730) **(G-4792)**
Pariseaus Printing Inc......810 653-8420
218 Mill St Davison (48423) **(G-3657)**
Parjana Distribution LLC......313 915-5406
1274 Library St Ste 600 Detroit (48226) **(G-4290)**
Park Molded Specialties Inc......906 225-0385
150 Huron Woods Dr Marquette (49855) **(G-10551)**
Park Street Machine Inc......231 739-9165
2201 Park St Muskegon (49444) **(G-11399)**
Parkedale Pharmaceuticals Inc......248 650-6400
1200 Parkdale Rd Rochester (48307) **(G-13345)**
Parker & Associates......269 694-6709
338 W Franklin St Otsego (49078) **(G-12248)**
Parker Engineering Amer Co Ltd......734 326-7630
38147 Abruzzi Dr Westland (48185) **(G-17586)**
Parker Engineering and Mfg Co......616 784-6500
11 N Park St Nw Grand Rapids (49544) **(G-6742)**
Parker Excvtg Grav & Recycle......616 784-1681
295 Hayes Rd Nw Comstock Park (49321) **(G-3505)**
Parker HSD......269 384-3915
2220 Palmer Ave Kalamazoo (49001) **(G-8842)**
Parker Machine & Engineering......734 692-4600
25028 Research Way Woodhaven (48183) **(G-17940)**
Parker Pattern Inc......586 466-5900
195 Malow St Mount Clemens (48043) **(G-11143)**
Parker Property Dev Inc......616 842-6118
12589 104th Ave Grand Haven (49417) **(G-6060)**
Parker Tooling & Design Inc......616 791-1080
2563 3 Mile Rd Nw Grand Rapids (49534) **(G-6743)**
Parker's Hilltop Brewery, Clarkston *Also called Clarkston Courts LLC* **(G-2913)**
Parker-Hannifin Corporation......269 384-3459
2220 Palmer Ave Kalamazoo (49001) **(G-8843)**
Parker-Hannifin Corporation......269 694-9411
300 Parker Dr Otsego (49078) **(G-12249)**
Parker-Hannifin Corporation......269 629-5000
8676 M 89 Richland (49083) **(G-13252)**
Parker-Hannifin Corporation......517 694-0491
1355 N Cedar Rd Mason (48854) **(G-10651)**
Parker-Hannifin Corporation......734 455-1700
900 Plymouth Rd Plymouth (48170) **(G-12708)**
Parker-Hannifin Corporation......269 692-6254
100 Parker Dr Otsego (49078) **(G-12250)**
Parker-Hannifin Corporation......330 253-5239
601 S Wilmott St Otsego (49078) **(G-12251)**
Parker-Hannifin Corporation......269 384-3400
2220 Palmer Ave Kalamazoo (49001) **(G-8844)**
Parks Sawmill Products......231 229-4551
9775 N Vander Meulen Rd Lake City (49651) **(G-9095)**
Parkside Printing Inc......810 765-4500
611 Broadway St Marine City (48039) **(G-10479)**
Parkside Speedy Print Inc......810 985-8484
1319 Military St Port Huron (48060) **(G-12955)**
Parkway Contract Group, Livonia *Also called Parkway Drapery & Uphl Co Inc* **(G-9884)**
Parkway Drapery & Uphl Co Inc......734 779-1300
12784 Currie Ct Livonia (48150) **(G-9884)**
Parkway Elc Communications LLC (PA)......616 392-2788
11952 James St Ste A Holland (49424) **(G-7767)**
Parkway Tool Die......248 889-3490
4576 Bretton Ln Highland (48356) **(G-7499)**
Parma Diversified Technologies, Rochester Hills *Also called Mathew Parmelee* **(G-13468)**
Parma Manufacturing Co Inc......517 531-4111
120 N Union St Parma (49269) **(G-12392)**
Parma Tube Corp......269 651-2351
1008 Progress St Sturgis (49091) **(G-15626)**
Parmalat Grand Rapids, Grand Rapids *Also called Agropur Inc* **(G-6154)**
Parousia Plastics Inc......989 832-4054
2412 Judith Ct Midland (48642) **(G-10902)**
Parry Precision Inc......248 585-1234
845 E Mandoline Ave Madison Heights (48071) **(G-10321)**
Parshallville Cider Mill......810 629-9079
8507 Parshallville Rd Fenton (48430) **(G-5229)**
Parson Adhesives Inc (PA)......248 299-5585
3345 W Auburn Rd Ste 107 Rochester Hills (48309) **(G-13490)**
Parsons Centennial Farm LLC......231 547-2038
61 Parsons Rd Charlevoix (49720) **(G-2625)**
Parton & Preble Inc......586 773-6000
23507 Groesbeck Hwy Warren (48089) **(G-17180)**
Parts Finishing Group, Detroit *Also called Bellevue Proc Met Prep Inc* **(G-3900)**
Party Time Ice Co, Port Huron *Also called Knowlton Enterprises Inc* **(G-12935)**
Paschal Burial Vault Svc LLC......517 448-8868
431 School St Hudson (49247) **(G-8138)**
Paschal Burial Vaults, Hudson *Also called Paschal Burial Vault Svc LLC* **(G-8138)**
Paslin Company......586 755-1693
23655 Hoover Rd Warren (48089) **(G-17181)**
Paslin Company (HQ)......586 758-0200
25303 Ryan Rd Warren (48091) **(G-17182)**
Paslin Company......248 953-8419
52550 Shelby Pkwy Shelby Township (48315) **(G-14660)**
Paslin Company......586 755-3606
3400 E 10 Mile Rd Warren (48091) **(G-17183)**
Paslin Controls Group, Warren *Also called Paslin Company* **(G-17183)**
Passport Health of Michigan, Farmington Hills *Also called Bruce Kane Enterprises LLC* **(G-4948)**
Pasty Oven Inc (PA)......906 774-2328
W7279 Us Highway 2 Quinnesec (49876) **(G-13101)**
Pat McArdle......989 375-4321
60 Mullen St Elkton (48731) **(G-4782)**
Patch Master Services, Sterling Heights *Also called Rite Way Asphalt Inc* **(G-15472)**
Patch Works Farms Inc......989 430-3610
9710 E Monroe Rd Wheeler (48662) **(G-17617)**
Patchwood Products Inc (PA)......989 742-2605
14797 State St Hillman (49746) **(G-7509)**
Patchwood Products Inc......989 742-2605
105 Stagecoach Dr Lachine (49753) **(G-9077)**
Patco Air Tool Inc......248 648-8830
100 Engelwood Dr Ste G Orion (48359) **(G-12188)**
Patent Lcnsing Clringhouse LLC......248 299-7500
2791 Research Dr Rochester Hills (48309) **(G-13491)**
Paterek Mold & Engineering......586 784-8030
74081 Church St Armada (48005) **(G-722)**
Pathway Publishers, Bloomingdale *Also called Pathway Publishing Corporation* **(G-1813)**
Pathway Publishing Corporation (HQ)......269 521-3025
43632 County Road 390 Bloomingdale (49026) **(G-1813)**
Patio Land Mfg Inc......586 758-5660
8407 E 9 Mile Rd Warren (48089) **(G-17184)**
Patmai Company Inc......586 294-0370
31425 Fraser Dr Fraser (48026) **(G-5705)**
Patricia Huellmantel Pubg......248 634-9894
2323 Academy Rd Holly (48442) **(G-7890)**
Patrick Carbide Die LLC......517 546-5646
840 Victory Dr Ste 200 Howell (48843) **(G-8076)**
Patrick Exploration Company......517 787-6633
301 W Michigan Ave Jackson (49201) **(G-8547)**
Patrick Newland Logging Ltd......906 524-2255
14738 Pequaming Rd Lanse (49946) **(G-9199)**
Patrick Wyman......810 227-2199
7892 Winfield Dr Brighton (48116) **(G-1974)**
Patriot Manufacturing LLC (PA)......734 259-2059
45345 Five Mile Rd Plymouth (48170) **(G-12709)**
Patriot Pyrotechnics......989 831-7788
5735 S Townhall Rd B Sheridan (48884) **(G-14733)**
Patriot Sensors & Contrls Corp......810 378-5511
6380 Brockway Rd Peck (48466) **(G-12420)**
Patriot Sensors & Contrls Corp (HQ)......248 435-0700
1080 N Crooks Rd Clawson (48017) **(G-2983)**
Patriot Solar Group LLC......517 629-9292
708 Valhalla Dr Albion (49224) **(G-128)**
Patriot Solutions LLC......616 240-8164
525 Ottawa Ave Nw Lvl Grand Rapids (49503) **(G-6744)**
Patriot Tool & Die Inc......269 687-9024
2116 Progressive Dr Niles (49120) **(G-11637)**
Patriot Tool Inc......313 299-1400
5310 Bayham St Dearborn Heights (48125) **(G-3793)**

A
L
P
H
A
B
E
T
I
C

Patten Monument Company (PA)..........616 785-4141
3980 West River Dr Ne Comstock Park (49321) ***(G-3506)***
Pattern Monument, Comstock Park *Also called Patten Monument Company* ***(G-3506)***
Patterson Precision Mfg Inc..........231 733-1913
1188 E Broadway Ave Norton Shores (49444) ***(G-11787)***
Patton Printing Inc..........313 535-9099
24625 Capitol Redford (48239) ***(G-13178)***
Patton Tool and Die Inc..........810 359-5336
7185 Baker Rd Lexington (48450) ***(G-9559)***
Patton Welding, Kalkaska *Also called D J and G Enterprise Inc* ***(G-8941)***
Patton Welding Inc..........231 258-9925
402 E Dresden St Kalkaska (49646) ***(G-8957)***
Paul Bunyon Saw Mill, Ubly *Also called Lanny Bensinger* ***(G-16718)***
Paul C Doerr..........734 242-2058
407 E Front St Monroe (48161) ***(G-11060)***
Paul F Hester..........616 302-6039
954 Maple St Pullman (49450) ***(G-13087)***
Paul Horn and Associates..........248 682-8490
2525 Sylvan Shores Dr Waterford (48328) ***(G-17365)***
Paul J Baroni Co..........906 337-3920
512 6th St Calumet (49913) ***(G-2331)***
Paul Jeffrey Kenny..........989 828-6109
1345 E Pleasant Valley Rd Shepherd (48883) ***(G-14730)***
Paul Marshall & Son Log LLC..........269 998-4440
7120 Marsh Rd Plainwell (49080) ***(G-12534)***
Paul Murphy Plastics Co (PA)..........586 774-4880
15301 E 11 Mile Rd Roseville (48066) ***(G-13851)***
Paul Tousley Inc..........313 841-5400
131 S Military St Detroit (48209) ***(G-4291)***
Paul W Marino Gages Inc..........586 772-2400
30744 Groesbeck Hwy Roseville (48066) ***(G-13852)***
Paul W Reed DDS..........231 347-4145
414 Petoskey St Petoskey (49770) ***(G-12467)***
Paul W Reed DDS Ms, Petoskey *Also called Paul W Reed DDS* ***(G-12467)***
Paulstra C R C-Cadillac Div, Cadillac *Also called Hutchinson Antivibration* ***(G-2254)***
Paumac Tubing LLC (PA)..........810 985-9400
315 Cuttle Rd Marysville (48040) ***(G-10610)***
PAW Enterprises LLC..........269 329-1865
3308 Covington Rd Ste 1 Kalamazoo (49001) ***(G-8845)***
Paw Paw Everlast Label Company..........269 657-4921
47161 M 40 Paw Paw (49079) ***(G-12411)***
Paw Paw Flashes, Paw Paw *Also called Vineyard Press Inc* ***(G-12416)***
Paw Paw Fuel Stop..........269 657-7357
60902 M 51 Paw Paw (49079) ***(G-12412)***
Paws Workholding, Clio *Also called Montague Tool and Mfg Co* ***(G-3279)***
Paxton Countertops, Lansing *Also called Paxton Products Inc* ***(G-9317)***
Paxton Media Group LLC..........269 429-2400
3450 Hollywood Rd Saint Joseph (49085) ***(G-14334)***
Paxton Products Inc..........517 627-3688
1340 S Waverly Rd Lansing (48917) ***(G-9317)***
Pazzel Inc..........616 291-0257
100 Stevens St Sw Grand Rapids (49507) ***(G-6745)***
Pbg Michigan LLC..........989 345-2595
610 Parkway Dr West Branch (48661) ***(G-17515)***
PBM Nutritionals LLC..........269 673-8451
515 Eastern Ave Allegan (49010) ***(G-180)***
PC Complete Inc..........248 545-4211
742 Livernois St Ferndale (48220) ***(G-5308)***
PC Solutions..........517 787-9934
1200 S West Ave Jackson (49203) ***(G-8548)***
PC Solutions of Michigan, Jackson *Also called PC Solutions* ***(G-8548)***
PC Techs On Wheels..........734 262-4424
8418 Brooke Park Dr # 111 Canton (48187) ***(G-2414)***
PCA, Livonia *Also called Packaging Corporation America* ***(G-9881)***
PCA Grandville, Grandville *Also called Packaging Corporation America* ***(G-7062)***
PCA/Edmore 321, Edmore *Also called Packaging Corporation America* ***(G-4754)***
PCA/Edmore 321a, Edmore *Also called Packaging Corporation America* ***(G-4753)***
PCA/Filer City 640, Filer City *Also called Packaging Corporation America* ***(G-5345)***
Pcb Load & Torque Inc..........248 471-0065
24350 Indoplex Cir Farmington Hills (48335) ***(G-5089)***
Pcb Piezotronics Inc..........888 684-0014
4000 Grand River Blvd Novi (48375) ***(G-11971)***
Pcb Piezotronics Inc..........716 684-0001
24350 Indoplex Cir Farmington Hills (48335) ***(G-5090)***
PCI, Melvindale *Also called Piping Components Inc* ***(G-10705)***
PCI Industries Inc..........248 542-2570
21717 Republic Ave Oak Park (48237) ***(G-12090)***
PCI Procal Inc..........989 358-7070
3810 Us Highway 23 N Alpena (49707) ***(G-307)***
Pcm US Steering Holding LLC (HQ)..........313 556-5000
300 Renaissance Ctr Detroit (48243) ***(G-4292)***
Pcmi Manufacturing Integration, Shelby Township *Also called Prototype Cast Mfg Inc* ***(G-14674)***
Pcnphone.com, Livonia *Also called Plymouth Computer &* ***(G-9890)***
PCS Company (HQ)..........586 294-7780
34488 Doreka Fraser (48026) ***(G-5706)***
Pct Security Inc..........888 567-3287
34668 Nova Dr Clinton Township (48035) ***(G-3192)***
PDC (PA)..........269 651-9975
69701 White St Sturgis (49091) ***(G-15627)***
Pdf Mfg Inc..........517 522-8431
11000 Cedar Knoll Dr Grass Lake (49240) ***(G-7091)***
PDM, Brighton *Also called Package Design & Mfg Inc* ***(G-1972)***
PDM Company..........231 946-4444
2563 S Sandy Ridge Rd Lake Leelanau (49653) ***(G-9105)***
PDM Industries Inc..........231 943-9601
1124 Stepke Ct Traverse City (49685) ***(G-16063)***
PDM Lumber Co, Lake Leelanau *Also called PDM Company* ***(G-9105)***
PDQ Ink Inc..........810 229-2989
7475 Grand River Rd Brighton (48114) ***(G-1975)***
Pds Plastics Inc..........616 896-1109
3297 140th Ave Dorr (49323) ***(G-4525)***
Peacocks Eco Log & Sawmill LLC..........231 250-3462
14823 4 Mile Rd Morley (49336) ***(G-11117)***
Peak Edm Inc..........248 380-0871
28221 Beck Rd Ste A2 Wixom (48393) ***(G-17876)***
Peak Industries Co Inc..........313 846-8666
5320 Oakman Blvd Dearborn (48126) ***(G-3747)***
Peak Manufacturing Inc..........517 769-6900
11855 Bunkerhill Rd Pleasant Lake (49272) ***(G-12553)***
Peake Asphalt Inc..........586 254-4567
48181 Ryan Rd Shelby Township (48317) ***(G-14661)***
Peaker Services, Brighton *Also called PSI Holding Company* ***(G-1982)***
Peaker Services Inc..........248 437-4174
8080 Kensington Ct Brighton (48116) ***(G-1976)***
Peaktronics Inc..........248 542-5640
1363 Anderson Rd Ste A Clawson (48017) ***(G-2984)***
Peanut Shop Inc..........517 374-0008
117 S Washington Sq Ste 1 Lansing (48933) ***(G-9409)***
Pearce Plastics LLC..........231 519-5994
4898 W 80th St Fremont (49412) ***(G-5781)***
Pearson Dean Excavating & Log..........906 932-3513
E3233 Lake Rd Ironwood (49938) ***(G-8337)***
Pearson Precast Concrete Pdts..........517 486-4060
7951 E Us Highway 223 Blissfield (49228) ***(G-1722)***
Pease Packing, Scotts *Also called Cole Carter Inc* ***(G-14504)***
Pease Packing, Scotts *Also called Scotts Hook & Cleaver Inc* ***(G-14507)***
Pebco Sales, Clinton Township *Also called Meccom Industrial Products Co* ***(G-3172)***
PEC of America, Novi *Also called Pacific Engineering Corp* ***(G-11970)***
PEC of America Corporation (HQ)..........248 675-3130
39555 Orchard Hill Pl # 220 Novi (48375) ***(G-11972)***
Peck Engineering Inc..........313 534-2950
12660 Farley Redford (48239) ***(G-13179)***
Peckham Vocational Inds Inc (PA)..........517 316-4000
3510 Capitol City Blvd Lansing (48906) ***(G-9252)***
Peckham Vocational Inds Inc..........517 316-4478
2511 N Martin Lthr King J Lansing (48906) ***(G-9253)***
Pedmic Converting Inc..........810 679-9600
7241 Wildcat Rd Croswell (48422) ***(G-3602)***
Pedri Mold Inc..........586 598-0882
46429 Continental Dr Chesterfield (48047) ***(G-2815)***
Peerless Canvas Products Inc..........269 429-0600
2355 Niles Rd Saint Joseph (49085) ***(G-14335)***
Peerless Metal Powders..........313 841-5400
6307 W Fort St Detroit (48209) ***(G-4293)***
Peerless Quality Products..........313 933-7525
7707 Lyndon St Detroit (48238) ***(G-4294)***
Peerless Steel Company..........616 530-6695
3280 Century Center St Sw Grandville (49418) ***(G-7063)***
Peerless Tooling Components, Madison Heights *Also called P X Tool Co* ***(G-10319)***
Peerless Waste Solutions LLC..........616 355-2800
510 E 40th St Holland (49423) ***(G-7768)***
Peg-Master Business Forms Inc..........586 566-8694
15018 Technology Dr Shelby Township (48315) ***(G-14662)***
Pegasus Industries Inc..........313 937-0770
12380 Beech Daly Rd Redford (48239) ***(G-13180)***
Pegasus Mold & Die Inc..........517 423-2009
415 E Russell Rd Tecumseh (49286) ***(G-15804)***
Pegasus Tool LLC..........313 255-5900
12680 Farley Detroit (48239) ***(G-4295)***
Peiseler LLC..........616 235-8460
601 Crosby St Nw Grand Rapids (49504) ***(G-6746)***
Pelhams Construction LLC..........517 549-8276
10800 Concord Rd Jonesville (49250) ***(G-8666)***
Pellow Printing Co..........906 475-9431
318 Iron St Negaunee (49866) ***(G-11473)***
Peloton Inc..........269 694-9702
124 E Allegan St Otsego (49078) ***(G-12252)***
Penchura LLC..........810 229-6245
889 S Old Us 23 Brighton (48114) ***(G-1977)***
Penguin Juice Co (PA)..........734 467-6991
39002 Webb Ct Westland (48185) ***(G-17587)***
Penguin LLC..........269 651-9488
1855 W Chicago Rd Sturgis (49091) ***(G-15628)***

Penguin Molding LLC 847 297-0560
1855 W Chicago Rd Sturgis (49091) ***(G-15629)***
Penguin-Iceberg Enterprises, Sturgis *Also called Penguin LLC* ***(G-15628)***
Penin Oil & Gas Compan Michiga 616 676-2090
555 Ada Dr Se Ada (49301) ***(G-26)***
Peninsula Copper Industries, Hubbell *Also called Koppers Performance Chem Inc* ***(G-8126)***
Peninsula Plastics Company Inc (PA) 248 852-3731
2800 Auburn Ct Auburn Hills (48326) ***(G-971)***
Peninsula Powder Coating Inc 906 353-7234
128 Hemlock St Baraga (49908) ***(G-1112)***
Peninsula Prestress Company, Wyoming *Also called P D P LLC* ***(G-18025)***
Peninsula Products Inc 906 296-9801
54385 Cemetery Rd Lake Linden (49945) ***(G-9109)***
Peninsular Inc 586 775-7211
27650 Groesbeck Hwy Roseville (48066) ***(G-13853)***
Peninsular Cylinder Company, Roseville *Also called Peninsular Inc* ***(G-13853)***
Peninsular Technologies LLC 616 676-9811
555 Ada Dr Se Ada (49301) ***(G-27)***
Penka Cutter Grinding, Madison Heights *Also called Penka Tool Corporation* ***(G-10322)***
Penka Tool Corporation 248 543-3940
1717 E 10 Mile Rd Madison Heights (48071) ***(G-10322)***
Penn Automotive Inc 313 299-8500
7845 Middlebelt Rd # 200 Romulus (48174) ***(G-13720)***
Penn Automotive Inc (HQ) 248 599-3700
5331 Dixie Hwy Waterford (48329) ***(G-17366)***
Penn Engineering & Mfg Corp 313 299-8500
5331 Dixie Hwy Waterford (48329) ***(G-17367)***
Pennisular Packaging LLC 313 304-4724
13505 N Haggerty Rd Plymouth (48170) ***(G-12710)***
Penny Saver, Three Rivers *Also called Three Rivers Commercial News* ***(G-15880)***
Penrose Therapeutix LLC 847 370-0303
46701 Commerce Center Dr Plymouth (48170) ***(G-12711)***
Penske Company LLC (HQ) 248 648-2000
2555 S Telegraph Rd Bloomfield Hills (48302) ***(G-1788)***
Penstone Inc 734 379-3160
31605 Gossett Dr Rockwood (48173) ***(G-13610)***
Penta Associates, Petoskey *Also called Boese Associates Inc* ***(G-12443)***
Pentagon Mold Co 269 496-7072
21015 M 60 Mendon (49072) ***(G-10717)***
Pentamere Winery 517 423-9000
131 E Chicago Blvd Ste 1 Tecumseh (49286) ***(G-15805)***
Pentar Stamping Inc 517 782-0700
1821 Wildwood Ave Jackson (49202) ***(G-8549)***
Pentech Industries Inc 586 445-1070
15645 Sturgeon St Roseville (48066) ***(G-13854)***
Pentel Tool & Die Inc 734 782-9500
26531 King Rd Romulus (48174) ***(G-13721)***
Pentier Group Inc 810 664-7997
587 S Court St Ste 300 Lapeer (48446) ***(G-9480)***
Penzel Oil Quick Change, Grand Haven *Also called Joy-Max Inc* ***(G-6040)***
Penzo America Inc 248 723-0802
6335 Thorncrest Dr Bloomfield Hills (48301) ***(G-1789)***
Pepin-Ireco Inc 906 486-4473
9045 County Road 476 Ishpeming (49849) ***(G-8352)***
Pepperidge Farm Incorporated 734 953-6729
29115 8 Mile Rd Livonia (48152) ***(G-9885)***
Pepperidge Farm Thrift Store, Livonia *Also called Pepperidge Farm Incorporated* ***(G-9885)***
Pepro Enterprises Inc 989 658-3200
2147 Leppek Rd Ubly (48475) ***(G-16720)***
Pepro Enterprises Inc (HQ) 989 658-3200
4385 Garfield St Ubly (48475) ***(G-16721)***
Pepsi 231 627-2290
6303 N Straits Hwy Cheboygan (49721) ***(G-2690)***
Pepsi Beverages Co 989 754-0435
100 S Outer Dr Saginaw (48601) ***(G-14120)***
Pepsi Beverages Company 248 596-9028
28345 Beck Rd Wixom (48393) ***(G-17877)***
Pepsi Bottling Group 810 966-8060
2111 Wadhams Rd Kimball (48074) ***(G-9046)***
Pepsi Bottling Group 517 546-2777
404 Mason Rd Howell (48843) ***(G-8077)***
Pepsi Cola Botling Co Houghton 906 482-0161
309 E Sharon Ave Houghton (49931) ***(G-7980)***
Pepsi-Cola Metro Btlg Co Inc 517 272-2800
3101 Grand Oak Dr Lansing (48911) ***(G-9410)***
Pepsi-Cola Metro Btlg Co Inc 517 321-0231
4900 W Grand River Ave Lansing (48906) ***(G-9254)***
Pepsi-Cola Metro Btlg Co Inc 248 335-3528
960 Featherstone St Pontiac (48342) ***(G-12855)***
Pepsi-Cola Metro Btlg Co Inc 989 345-2595
610 Parkway Dr West Branch (48661) ***(G-17516)***
Pepsi-Cola Metro Btlg Co Inc 231 946-0452
2550 Cass Rd Traverse City (49684) ***(G-16064)***
Pepsi-Cola Metro Btlg Co Inc 989 755-1020
736 N Outer Dr Saginaw (48601) ***(G-14121)***
Pepsi-Cola Metro Btlg Co Inc 517 546-2777
725 Mcpherson St Howell (48843) ***(G-8078)***
Pepsi-Cola Metro Btlg Co Inc 269 226-6400
2725 E Kilgore Rd Kalamazoo (49001) ***(G-8846)***
Pepsi-Cola Metro Btlg Co Inc 810 232-3925
6200g Taylor Dr Flint (48507) ***(G-5479)***
Pepsi-Cola Metro Btlg Co Inc 616 285-8200
3700 Kraft Ave Se Grand Rapids (49512) ***(G-6747)***
Pepsi-Cola Metro Btlg Co Inc 517 279-8436
101 Treat Dr Coldwater (49036) ***(G-3318)***
Pepsi-Cola Metro Btlg Co Inc 810 987-2181
2111 Wadhams Rd Kimball (48074) ***(G-9047)***
Pepsi-Cola Metro Btlg Co Inc 313 832-0910
1555 Mack Ave Detroit (48207) ***(G-4296)***
Pepsi-Cola Metro Btlg Co Inc 231 798-1274
4900 Paul Ct Norton Shores (49441) ***(G-11788)***
Pepsi-New Bern-Howell-151 ....517 546-7542
755 Mcpherson Park Dr Howell (48843) ***(G-8079)***
Pepsico, Kimball *Also called Pepsi Bottling Group* ***(G-9046)***
Pepsico, Wixom *Also called Pepsi Beverages Company* ***(G-17877)***
Pepsico, Cheboygan *Also called Pepsi* ***(G-2690)***
Pepsico, Howell *Also called Pepsi Bottling Group* ***(G-8077)***
Pepsico, Houghton *Also called Pepsi Cola Botling Co Houghton* ***(G-7980)***
Pepsico Inc 734 374-9841
12862 Reeck Rd Southgate (48195) ***(G-15082)***
Pepsico Inc 586 276-4102
6600 17 Mile Rd Sterling Heights (48313) ***(G-15443)***
Pepsicola, Newberry *Also called Newberry Bottling Co Inc* ***(G-11582)***
Perception Anlytics Rbtics LLC 734 846-5650
3239 Kilburn Park Cir Ann Arbor (48105) ***(G-589)***
Perceptive Controls Inc 269 685-3040
140 E Bridge St Plainwell (49080) ***(G-12535)***
Perceptive Industries Inc 269 204-6768
951 Industrial Pkwy Plainwell (49080) ***(G-12536)***
Perceptive Machining Inc 248 577-0380
297 Elmwood Dr Troy (48083) ***(G-16542)***
Perceptron Inc (PA) 734 414-6100
47827 Halyard Dr Plymouth (48170) ***(G-12712)***
Percor Manufacturing Inc 616 554-1668
4203 Roger B Chaffee Mem Wyoming (49548) ***(G-18026)***
Peregrine Wood Products, Muskegon *Also called Quality Pallet Inc* ***(G-11409)***
Perennial Software 734 414-0760
45185 Joy Rd Ste 102 Canton (48187) ***(G-2415)***
Perfect Dish LLC 313 784-3976
21867 Kings Pte Blvd Taylor (48180) ***(G-15753)***
Perfect Expressions 248 640-1287
3643 W Maple Rd Bloomfield Hills (48301) ***(G-1790)***
Perfect Fit Brdal Tuxedos Prom, Clio *Also called Demmem Enterprises LLC* ***(G-3269)***
Perfect Impressions Inc 248 478-2644
24580 N Industrial Dr Farmington Hills (48335) ***(G-5091)***
Perfect Signs 231 233-3721
338 4th St Manistee (49660) ***(G-10434)***
Perfected Grave Vault Co 616 243-3375
2500 3 Mile Rd Nw Grand Rapids (49534) ***(G-6748)***
Perfection Bakeries Inc 269 343-1217
807 Palmer Ave Kalamazoo (49001) ***(G-8847)***
Perfection Bakeries Inc 810 653-2378
3330 S State Rd Davison (48423) ***(G-3658)***
Perfection Bakeries Inc 517 278-2370
189 W Garfield Ave Coldwater (49036) ***(G-3319)***
Perfection Bakeries Inc 231 779-5365
7701 E 34 Rd Cadillac (49601) ***(G-2269)***
Perfection Bakeries Inc 517 750-1818
1001 Hurst Rd Jackson (49201) ***(G-8550)***
Perfection Bakery, Kalamazoo *Also called Perfection Bakeries Inc* ***(G-8847)***
Perfection Industries Inc (PA) 313 272-4040
18571 Weaver St Detroit (48228) ***(G-4297)***
Perfection Industries Inc 231 779-5325
218 Hanthorn St Cadillac (49601) ***(G-2270)***
Perfection Sprinkler Company 734 761-5110
2077 S State St Ann Arbor (48104) ***(G-590)***
Perfecto Industries Inc (PA) 989 732-2941
1567 Calkins Dr Gaylord (49735) ***(G-5888)***
Perfit Corporation 734 524-9208
13090 Fairlane St Livonia (48150) ***(G-9886)***
Perforated Tubes Inc 616 942-4550
4850 Fulton St E Ada (49301) ***(G-28)***
Perform3-D LLC 734 604-4100
411 Huronview Blvd # 200 Ann Arbor (48103) ***(G-591)***
Performance Cnc Inc 269 624-3206
75289 M 40 Lawton (49065) ***(G-9514)***
Performance Crankshaft Inc 586 549-7557
8829 Northend Ave Ferndale (48220) ***(G-5309)***
Performance Engrg Racg Engs 616 669-5800
2176 Center Industrial Ct Jenison (49428) ***(G-8636)***
Performance Fuels Systems Inc 248 202-1789
3108 Newport Ct Troy (48084) ***(G-16543)***
Performance Induction 734 658-1676
1475 Four Seasons Dr Howell (48843) ***(G-8080)***
Performance Machining Inc 269 683-4370
919 Michigan St Niles (49120) ***(G-11638)***
Performance Plus, Prudenville *Also called Viking Oil LLC* ***(G-13086)***

ALPHABETIC

Performance Print and Mktg — 517 896-9682
1907 Burkley Rd Williamston (48895) *(G-17736)*

Performance Sailing Inc — 586 790-7500
24227 Sorrentino Ct Clinton Township (48035) *(G-3193)*

Performance Springs Inc — 248 486-3372
57575 Travis Rd New Hudson (48165) *(G-11551)*

Performance Systematix Inc (PA) — 616 949-9090
5569 33rd St Se Grand Rapids (49512) *(G-6749)*

Performance Tool Inc — 231 943-9338
731 Mizar Ct Traverse City (49685) *(G-16065)*

Performcoat of Michigan LLC — 269 282-7030
319 Mcintyre Ln Springfield (49037) *(G-15200)*

Performnce Assmbly Sltions LLC — 734 466-6380
28190 Plymouth Rd Livonia (48150) *(G-9887)*

Performnce Dcutting Finshg LLC — 616 245-3636
955 Godfrey Ave Sw Grand Rapids (49503) *(G-6750)*

Peribambini Services LLC — 318 466-2881
13505 N Haggerty Rd Plymouth (48170) *(G-12713)*

Perigee Manufacturing Co Inc — 313 933-4420
7519 Intervale St Detroit (48238) *(G-4298)*

Permabilt Homes, Marshall Also called Manufactured Homes Inc *(G-10574)*

Permacel Corporation — 248 347-2843
45880 Dylan Dr Novi (48377) *(G-11973)*

Permacoat Inc — 313 388-7798
14868 Champaign Rd Allen Park (48101) *(G-204)*

Permaloc Aluminum Edging, Holland Also called Permaloc Corporation *(G-7769)*

Permaloc Corporation — 616 399-9600
13505 Barry St Holland (49424) *(G-7769)*

Perman Industries LLC — 586 991-5600
51523 Celeste Shelby Township (48315) *(G-14663)*

Permawick Company Inc (PA) — 248 433-3500
255 E Brown St Ste 100 Birmingham (48009) *(G-1697)*

Perpetual Measurement Inc — 248 343-2952
3185 Seebaldt Ave Waterford (48329) *(G-17368)*

Perrigo Brnded Phrmcticals Inc, Allegan Also called PMI Branded Pharmaceuticals *(G-185)*

Perrigo Company — 269 686-1973
900 Industrial Dr Allegan (49010) *(G-181)*

Perrigo Company (HQ) — 269 673-8451
515 Eastern Ave Allegan (49010) *(G-182)*

Perrigo Company — 616 396-0941
3896 58th St Holland (49423) *(G-7770)*

Perrigo Company — 269 673-7962
515 Eastern Ave Allegan (49010) *(G-183)*

Perrigo Logistics Center, Allegan Also called Perrigo Company *(G-181)*

Perrigo Pharmaceuticals Co — 269 673-8451
515 Eastern Ave Allegan (49010) *(G-184)*

Perrigo Printing Inc — 616 454-6761
125 Ottawa Ave Nw Ste 160 Grand Rapids (49503) *(G-6751)*

Perrin Screen Printing Inc — 616 785-9900
5320 Rusche Dr Nw Comstock Park (49321) *(G-3507)*

Perrin Souvenir Distrs Inc — 616 785-9700
5320 Rusche Dr Nw Comstock Park (49321) *(G-3508)*

Perry Tool Company Inc — 734 283-7393
12329 Hale St Riverview (48193) *(G-13304)*

Persico Usa Inc — 248 299-5100
50450 Wing Dr Shelby Township (48315) *(G-14664)*

Personal & Home Defense LLC — 517 596-3027
8795 Portage Lake Rd Munith (49259) *(G-11253)*

Personal Graphics — 231 347-6347
270 Creekside Dr Petoskey (49770) *(G-12468)*

Personal Tuch By AP Imprssions, Livonia Also called AP Impressions Inc *(G-9650)*

Personalized Embroidery Co — 208 263-1267
645 Clyde Lee Dr Traverse City (49696) *(G-16066)*

Persons Inc — 989 734-3835
285 S Bradley Hwy Ste 2 Rogers City (49779) *(G-13620)*

Perspective Enterprises Inc — 269 327-0869
7829 S Sprinkle Rd Ste A Portage (49002) *(G-13021)*

Perspectives Cabinetry, Troy Also called Perspectives Custom Cabinetry *(G-16544)*

Perspectives Custom Cabinetry — 248 288-4100
1401 Axtell Dr Troy (48084) *(G-16544)*

Pet Supplies Plus — 616 554-3600
6159 Kalamazoo Ave Se Grand Rapids (49508) *(G-6752)*

Pet Treats Plus — 313 533-1701
14141 Marion Redford (48239) *(G-13181)*

Pete Pullum Company Inc — 313 837-9440
15330 Castleton St Detroit (48227) *(G-4299)*

Peter-Lacke Usa LLC (HQ) — 248 588-9400
865 Stephenson Hwy Troy (48083) *(G-16545)*

Peterman Concrete Co, Portage Also called Peterman Mobile Concrete Inc *(G-13022)*

Peterman Mobile Concrete Inc (PA) — 269 324-1211
333 Peterman Ln Portage (49002) *(G-13022)*

Petersen Products Inc — 248 446-0500
7915 Kensington Ct Brighton (48116) *(G-1978)*

Peterson American Corporation — 269 279-7421
16805 Heimbach Rd Three Rivers (49093) *(G-15872)*

Peterson American Corporation — 248 616-3380
32601 Industrial Dr Madison Heights (48071) *(G-10323)*

Peterson American Corporation (PA) — 248 799-5400
21200 Telegraph Rd Southfield (48033) *(G-14997)*

Peterson American Corporation — 248 799-5400
679 E Mandoline Ave Madison Heights (48071) *(G-10324)*

Peterson American Corporation — 269 279-7421
16805 Heimbach Rd Three Rivers (49093) *(G-15873)*

Peterson American Corporation — 248 799-5410
3285 Martin Rd Ste N106 Commerce Township (48390) *(G-3438)*

Peterson Farms Inc — 231 861-6333
3104 W Baseline Rd Shelby (49455) *(G-14534)*

Peterson Jig & Fixture Inc (PA) — 616 866-8296
301 Rockford Park Dr Ne Rockford (49341) *(G-13585)*

Peterson Publishing Inc — 906 387-3282
132 E Superior St Munising (49862) *(G-11247)*

Peterson Spring Cima, Three Rivers Also called Peterson American Corp *(G-15872)*

Peterson Spring-Tech Pdts Ctr, Southfield Also called Peterson American Corporation *(G-14997)*

Petnet Solutions Inc — 865 218-2000
3601 W 13 Mile Rd Royal Oak (48073) *(G-13956)*

Petoskey News Review, Petoskey Also called Northern Michigan Review Inc *(G-12463)*

Petoskey Plastics Inc (PA) — 231 347-2602
1 Petoskey St Petoskey (49770) *(G-12469)*

Petoskey Plastics Inc — 231 347-2602
4226 Us Highway 31 S Petoskey (49770) *(G-12470)*

Petra Electronic Mfg Inc — 616 877-1991
3440 Windquest Dr Holland (49424) *(G-7771)*

Petroleum Environmental Tech — 231 258-0400
5681 Rapid City Rd Nw Rapid City (49676) *(G-13110)*

Petroleum Resources Inc (PA) — 586 752-7856
134 W Saint Clair St Romeo (48065) *(G-13635)*

Petronis Industries, Wixom Also called Squires Industries Inc *(G-17895)*

Pets Supplys Plus, Grand Rapids Also called Sk Enterprises Inc *(G-6867)*

Petschke Manufacturing Company — 586 463-0841
187 Hubbard St Mount Clemens (48043) *(G-11144)*

Petter Investments Inc — 269 637-1997
233 Veterans Blvd South Haven (49090) *(G-14767)*

Pettibone/Traverse Lift LLC (HQ) — 906 353-4800
1100 S Superior Ave Baraga (49908) *(G-1113)*

Pettibone/Traverse Lift LLC — 906 353-6668
16243 Main St Baraga (49908) *(G-1114)*

Petty Machine & Tool Inc — 517 782-9355
4035 Morrill Rd Jackson (49201) *(G-8551)*

Pewabic Pottery, Detroit Also called Pewabic Society Inc *(G-4300)*

Pewabic Society Inc — 313 626-2000
10125 E Jefferson Ave Detroit (48214) *(G-4300)*

Pezco Industries Inc — 248 589-1140
380 E Mandoline Ave Madison Heights (48071) *(G-10325)*

Pfb Manufacturing LLC — 517 486-4844
9012 E Us Highway 223 Blissfield (49228) *(G-1723)*

Pfg Enterprises Inc (PA) — 586 755-1053
50271 E Rssell Smith Blvd Chesterfield (48051) *(G-2816)*

Pfizer Inc — 248 867-9067
7064 Oak Meadows Dr Clarkston (48348) *(G-2944)*

Pfizer Inc — 248 650-6400
1200 Parkdale Rd Rochester (48307) *(G-13346)*

Pfizer Inc — 734 679-7368
18141 Meridian Rd Grosse Ile (48138) *(G-7175)*

Pfizer Inc — 734 671-9315
3495 Margarette Dr Trenton (48183) *(G-16156)*

Pfizer Inc — 269 833-5143
7171 Portage Rd Kalamazoo (49001) *(G-8848)*

Pfs, Taylor Also called Precision Framing Systems Inc *(G-15755)*

Pfs - Pnt Fnal Assmbly Systems, Southfield Also called Durr Systems Inc *(G-14889)*

Pft Industries, Romulus Also called J L International Inc *(G-13690)*

Pgf Technology Group Inc — 248 852-2800
2993 Technology Dr Rochester Hills (48309) *(G-13492)*

Pgi Holdings Inc (HQ) — 231 796-4831
115 N Michigan Ave Big Rapids (49307) *(G-1640)*

Pgi Holdings Inc — 231 723-3592
75 Maple St Manistee (49660) *(G-10435)*

Pgi Holdings Inc — 231 745-4635
851 Michigan Ave Baldwin (49304) *(G-1085)*

Pgi Holdings Inc — 231 937-4740
115 N Michigan Ave Big Rapids (49307) *(G-1641)*

PGI of Saugatuck Inc — 269 561-2000
413 3rd St Fennville (49408) *(G-5176)*

Pgm Products Inc — 586 757-4400
21034 Ryan Rd Warren (48091) *(G-17185)*

Pgw, Rochester Hills Also called Pittsburgh Glass Works LLC *(G-13494)*

Pharmacia & Upjohn Company LLC — 908 901-8000
7000 Portage Rd Kalamazoo (49001) *(G-8849)*

Phase III Graphics Inc (PA) — 616 949-9290
255 Colrain St Sw Ste 1 Grand Rapids (49548) *(G-6753)*

Phenosynthesis LLC, Grand Rapids Also called Light Speed Usa LLC *(G-6627)*

Pherotech, Grand Rapids Also called Contech (us) Inc *(G-6303)*

Phil Brown Welding Corporation — 616 784-3046
4689 8 Mile Rd Conklin (49403) *(G-3531)*

Phil Elenbaas Millwork Inc — 231 526-8399
341 Franklin Park Harbor Springs (49740) *(G-7291)*

ALPHABETIC SECTION

Piolax Corporation

Phil Elenbaas Millwork Inc (PA) 616 791-1616
3000 Wilson Dr Nw Grand Rapids (49534) ***(G-6754)***
Philips Automotive Ltg N Amer, Farmington Hills *Also called Philips North America LLC* ***(G-5092)***
Philips Machining Company 616 997-7777
80 Mason Dr Coopersville (49404) ***(G-3568)***
Philips North America LLC 248 553-9080
34119 W 12 Mile Rd # 102 Farmington Hills (48331) ***(G-5092)***
Phillip Anderson 269 687-7166
2536 Detroit Rd Niles (49120) ***(G-11639)***
Phillips Bros Screw Pdts Co 517 882-0279
2909 S Martin Luther King Lansing (48910) ***(G-9411)***
Phillips Enterprises Inc 586 615-6208
51245 Filomena Dr Shelby Township (48315) ***(G-14665)***
Phillips Service Inds Inc (PA) 734 853-5000
14492 N Sheldon Rd # 300 Plymouth (48170) ***(G-12714)***
Phillips-Medisize LLC 616 878-5030
8140 Cool Ridge Dr Sw Byron Center (49315) ***(G-2207)***
Phillips-Medisize LLC 248 592-2144
5706 Stonington Ct West Bloomfield (48322) ***(G-17493)***
Phoenix Cmposite Solutions LLC 989 739-7108
5911 Mission St Oscoda (48750) ***(G-12218)***
Phoenix Color, Chelsea *Also called Al Corp* ***(G-2701)***
Phoenix Countertops LLC 586 254-1450
7322 19 Mile Rd Sterling Heights (48314) ***(G-15444)***
Phoenix Data Incorporated 248 281-0054
28588 Northwestern Hwy # 280 Southfield (48034) ***(G-14998)***
Phoenix Data Systems, Southfield *Also called Phoenix Data Incorporated* ***(G-14998)***
Phoenix Dental Inc 810 750-2328
3452 W Thompson Rd Fenton (48430) ***(G-5230)***
Phoenix Fixtures LLC (az) 616 847-0895
16910 148th Ave Spring Lake (49456) ***(G-15168)***
Phoenix Imaging Inc 248 476-4578
36853 Heatherton Dr Farmington (48335) ***(G-4907)***
Phoenix Imaging Inc (PA) 248 476-4200
29865 6 Mile Rd Livonia (48152) ***(G-9888)***
Phoenix Imaging Machine Vision, Livonia *Also called Phoenix Imaging Inc* ***(G-9888)***
Phoenix Induction Corporation 248 486-7377
10132 Colonial Indus Dr South Lyon (48178) ***(G-14809)***
Phoenix Innovate, Troy *Also called Phoenix Press Incorporated* ***(G-16546)***
Phoenix Operating Company Inc 231 929-7171
4480b Mount Hope Rd Williamsburg (49690) ***(G-17719)***
Phoenix Packaging Corporation, Chesterfield *Also called Anchor Bay Packaging Corp* ***(G-2738)***
Phoenix Packaging Corporation 734 944-3916
600 W Michigan Ave Ste A Saline (48176) ***(G-14407)***
Phoenix Press Incorporated 248 435-8040
1775 Bellingham Dr Troy (48083) ***(G-16546)***
Phoenix Safety Systems, Troy *Also called Phoenix Wire Cloth Inc* ***(G-16547)***
Phoenix Sound Systems 734 662-6405
3514 W Liberty Rd Ann Arbor (48103) ***(G-592)***
Phoenix Technology Svcs USA 231 995-0100
327 E Welch Ct Ste A Traverse City (49686) ***(G-16067)***
Phoenix Trailer & Body Company 248 360-7184
4751 Juniper Dr Commerce Township (48382) ***(G-3439)***
Phoenix Trailers LLC 231 536-9760
6165 M 32 East Jordan (49727) ***(G-4642)***
Phoenix Wire Cloth Inc 248 585-6350
585 Stephenson Hwy Troy (48083) ***(G-16547)***
Phone Guide, Petoskey *Also called Review Directories Inc* ***(G-12472)***
Phone Guy LLC 248 361-0132
570 Golf Villa Dr Oxford (48371) ***(G-12363)***
Photo Offset Inc 906 786-5800
109 S Lincoln Rd Escanaba (49829) ***(G-4851)***
Photo Systems Inc (PA) 734 424-9625
7200 Huron River Dr Ste B Dexter (48130) ***(G-4503)***
Photo-Offset Printing, Escanaba *Also called Photo Offset Inc* ***(G-4851)***
Photo-Tron Corp 248 852-5200
1854 Star Batt Dr Rochester Hills (48309) ***(G-13493)***
Photodon LLC 847 377-1185
2682 Garfield Rd N Traverse City (49686) ***(G-16068)***
Photographic Support Inc 586 264-9957
6210 Product Dr Sterling Heights (48312) ***(G-15445)***
Physicians Compounding Phrm 248 758-9100
1900 S Telg Rd Ste 102 Bloomfield Hills (48302) ***(G-1791)***
Physicians Technology LLC 734 241-5060
23 E Front St Ste 200 Monroe (48161) ***(G-11061)***
PI Optima Inc 616 772-2138
2734 84th Ave Zeeland (49464) ***(G-18173)***
PI Optima Manufacturing LLC 616 931-9750
2734 84th Ave Zeeland (49464) ***(G-18174)***
Pic-Turn, Detroit *Also called Tri-Vision LLC* ***(G-4407)***
Pickle Print & Marketing LLC 231 668-4148
525 W Fourteenth St D Traverse City (49684) ***(G-16069)***
Picko Ferrum Fabricating LLC 810 626-7086
10800 Featherly Dr Hamburg (48139) ***(G-7227)***
Picpatch LLC 248 670-2681
2488 Pearson Rd Milford (48380) ***(G-10979)***
Picwood USA, Kalamazoo *Also called Picwood USA LLC* ***(G-8850)***
Picwood USA LLC 844 802-1599
2002 Charles Ave Kalamazoo (49048) ***(G-8850)***
Piedmont Concrete Inc 248 474-7740
29934 W 8 Mile Rd Farmington Hills (48336) ***(G-5093)***
Pier One Polymers Incorporated 810 326-1456
2011 Christian B Haas Dr Saint Clair (48079) ***(G-14231)***
Pierburg Instruments 734 414-9600
47519 Halyard Dr Plymouth (48170) ***(G-12715)***
Pierburg Pump Tech US LLC 864 688-1322
975 S Opdyke Rd Ste 100 Auburn Hills (48326) ***(G-972)***
Pierburg Us LLC 864 688-1322
975 S Opdyke Rd Ste 100 Auburn Hills (48326) ***(G-973)***
Pierce Engineers Inc 517 321-5051
5122 N Grand River Ave # 1 Lansing (48906) ***(G-9255)***
Pierian Press Inc 734 434-4074
3196 Maple Dr Ypsilanti (48197) ***(G-18094)***
Pierino Frozen Foods Inc 313 928-0950
1695 Southfield Rd Lincoln Park (48146) ***(G-9583)***
Pierson Fine Art 269 385-4974
3415 Meadowcroft Ave Kalamazoo (49004) ***(G-8851)***
Piezonix LLC 517 231-9586
325 E Grand River Ave East Lansing (48823) ***(G-4674)***
Pifers Airmotive Inc 248 674-0909
1660 Airport Rd Waterford (48327) ***(G-17369)***
Pilgrim Printing 586 752-9664
64007 Van Dyke Rd Ste 1 Washington (48095) ***(G-17309)***
Pilkington Glass - Niles, Niles *Also called Pilkington North America Inc* ***(G-11640)***
Pilkington North America Inc 989 754-2956
1400 Weiss St Saginaw (48602) ***(G-14122)***
Pilkington North America Inc 248 542-8300
1920 Bellaire Ave Royal Oak (48067) ***(G-13957)***
Pilkington North America Inc 269 687-2100
2121 W Chicago Rd Ste E Niles (49120) ***(G-11640)***
Pillar Induction 586 254-8470
30100 Stephenson Hwy Madison Heights (48071) ***(G-10326)***
Pillar Manufacturing Inc 269 628-5605
35620 County Road 388 Gobles (49055) ***(G-5948)***
Pims Co 313 665-8837
300 Renaissance Ctr Detroit (48243) ***(G-4301)***
Pin Point Welding Inc 586 598-7382
50505 Metzen Dr Chesterfield (48051) ***(G-2817)***
Pin-Key Manufacturing Co, Montague *Also called Dyer Corporation* ***(G-11090)***
Pinckney Automatic & Mfg 734 878-3430
6128 Cedar Lake Rd Pinckney (48169) ***(G-12502)***
Pinconning Journal 989 879-3811
110 E 3rd St Pinconning (48650) ***(G-12511)***
Pinconning Metals Inc 989 879-3144
1140 E Cody Estey Rd Pinconning (48650) ***(G-12512)***
Pine Needle People LLC 517 242-4752
934 Clark St Ste 4 Lansing (48906) ***(G-9256)***
Pine River Inc 231 758-3400
5339 M 66 N Charlevoix (49720) ***(G-2626)***
Pine River Group, Saint Clair *Also called Biewer Lumber LLC* ***(G-14206)***
Pine Tech Inc (PA) 989 426-0006
14941 Cleat St Plymouth (48170) ***(G-12716)***
Pinecrest Farms, Galien *Also called Pinecrest Industries* ***(G-5819)***
Pinecrest Industries 269 545-8125
4355 Spring Creek Rd Galien (49113) ***(G-5819)***
Pinetree Trading LLC 313 584-2700
10540 W Warren Ave Dearborn (48126) ***(G-3748)***
Pingree Detroit, Detroit *Also called Pingree Mfg L3c* ***(G-4302)***
Pingree Mfg L3c 313 444-8428
6438 Woodward Ave Detroit (48202) ***(G-4302)***
Pink Pallet LLC 586 873-2982
4176 Knollwood Dr Grand Blanc (48439) ***(G-5977)***
Pink Pin Lady LLC 586 731-1532
47768 Barclay Ct Shelby Township (48317) ***(G-14666)***
Pinnacle Cabinet Company Inc 989 772-3866
1121 N Fancher Ave Mount Pleasant (48858) ***(G-11217)***
Pinnacle Energy LLC 248 623-6091
5071 Timber Ridge Trl Clarkston (48346) ***(G-2945)***
Pinnacle Engineering Co Inc 734 428-7039
10250 Mi State Road 52 Manchester (48158) ***(G-10410)***
Pinnacle Foods Group LLC 810 724-6144
415 S Blacks Corners Rd Imlay City (48444) ***(G-8210)***
Pinnacle Mold & Machine Inc 616 892-9018
9900 Lake Michigan Dr West Olive (49460) ***(G-17534)***
Pinnacle Printing & Promotions, Southfield *Also called Rar Group Inc* ***(G-15010)***
Pinnacle Technology Group 734 568-6600
7076 Schnipke Dr Ottawa Lake (49267) ***(G-12268)***
Pinnacle Tool Incorporated 616 257-2700
1150 Gezon Pkwy Sw Wyoming (49509) ***(G-18027)***
Pinneys Logging Inc 231 536-7730
4226 Healey Rd East Jordan (49727) ***(G-4643)***
Pinto Products Inc 269 383-0015
2525 Miller Rd Kalamazoo (49001) ***(G-8852)***
Piolax Corporation 734 668-6005
47075 Five Mile Rd Plymouth (48170) ***(G-12717)***

ALPHABETIC

Pioneer Broach Midwest Inc.....231 768-5800
13957 Pioneer Ave Leroy (49655) ***(G-9535)***
Pioneer Cabinetry Inc.....810 658-2075
301 W Rising St Ste 2 Davison (48423) ***(G-3659)***
Pioneer Die Sets, Byron Center *Also called Pioneer Steel Corporation* ***(G-2208)***
Pioneer Foundry Company Inc (PA).....517 782-9469
606 Water St Jackson (49203) ***(G-8552)***
Pioneer Group, Big Rapids *Also called Pioneer Press* ***(G-1642)***
Pioneer Group, Inc., The, Big Rapids *Also called Pgi Holdings Inc* ***(G-1640)***
Pioneer Group, The, Manistee *Also called Pioneer Press* ***(G-10436)***
Pioneer Machine and Tech Inc.....248 546-4451
1167 E 10 Mile Rd Madison Heights (48071) ***(G-10327)***
Pioneer Meats LLC.....248 862-1988
915 E Maple Rd Birmingham (48009) ***(G-1698)***
Pioneer Metal Finishing LLC.....734 384-9000
525 Ternes Dr Monroe (48162) ***(G-11062)***
Pioneer Metal Finishing LLC.....877 721-1100
13251 Stephens Rd Warren (48089) ***(G-17186)***
Pioneer Michigan Broach Co.....231 768-5800
13957 Pioneer Ave Leroy (49655) ***(G-9536)***
Pioneer Molded Products Inc.....616 977-4172
5505 52nd St Se Grand Rapids (49512) ***(G-6755)***
Pioneer Molding, Warren *Also called Pioneer Plastics Inc* ***(G-17187)***
Pioneer North America Inc.....248 449-6799
22630 Haggerty Rd Farmington Hills (48335) ***(G-5094)***
Pioneer Oil Tools Inc.....989 644-6999
5179 W Weidman Rd Mount Pleasant (48858) ***(G-11218)***
Pioneer Plastics Inc.....586 262-0159
51650 Oro Dr Shelby Township (48315) ***(G-14667)***
Pioneer Plastics Inc (PA).....586 262-0159
2295 Bart Ave Warren (48091) ***(G-17187)***
Pioneer Pole Buildings N Inc.....989 386-2570
7400 S Clare Ave Clare (48617) ***(G-2884)***
Pioneer Press (PA).....231 796-8072
22405 18 Mile Rd Big Rapids (49307) ***(G-1642)***
Pioneer Press.....231 723-3592
75 Maple St Manistee (49660) ***(G-10436)***
Pioneer Press Printing (PA).....231 864-2404
12326 Virginia St Bear Lake (49614) ***(G-1380)***
Pioneer Publishing, Baldwin *Also called Pgi Holdings Inc* ***(G-1085)***
Pioneer Steel Corporation (PA).....313 933-9400
7447 Intervale St Detroit (48238) ***(G-4303)***
Pioneer Steel Corporation.....616 878-5800
8700 Byron Commerce Dr Sw Byron Center (49315) ***(G-2208)***
Pioneer Surgical Tech Inc (HQ).....906 226-9909
375 River Park Cir Marquette (49855) ***(G-10552)***
Pioneer Technologies Corp.....702 806-3152
7998 W 90th St Fremont (49412) ***(G-5782)***
Pipe Fabricators Inc.....269 345-8657
1018 Staples Ave Kalamazoo (49007) ***(G-8853)***
Pipeline Packaging.....248 743-0248
1421 Piedmont Dr Troy (48083) ***(G-16548)***
Piper Industries Inc.....586 771-5100
15930 Common Rd Roseville (48066) ***(G-13855)***
Piping Components Inc.....313 382-6400
4205 Oakwood Blvd Melvindale (48122) ***(G-10705)***
Pipp Mobil Stora Syste Holdi C.....616 735-9100
2966 Wilson Dr Nw Walker (49534) ***(G-16873)***
Pippa Custom Design Printing.....734 552-1598
22025 King Rd Woodhaven (48183) ***(G-17941)***
Pira International, Lansing *Also called Pira Testing LLC* ***(G-9318)***
Pira Testing LLC.....517 574-4297
6539 Westland Way Ste 24 Lansing (48917) ***(G-9318)***
Piranha Hose Products Inc.....231 779-4390
2500 Weigel St Cadillac (49601) ***(G-2271)***
Pisces Fish Machinery Inc (PA).....906 789-1636
7036 Us Highway 2 41 M35 Gladstone (49837) ***(G-5919)***
Piston Automotive LLC (HQ).....313 541-8674
12723 Telegraph Rd Ste 1 Redford (48239) ***(G-13182)***
Piston Automotive LLC.....313 541-8789
8500 Haggerty Rd Van Buren Twp (48111) ***(G-16779)***
Piston Automotive LLC.....313 541-8789
4015 Michigan Ave Detroit (48210) ***(G-4304)***
Piston Group LLC (PA).....248 226-3976
3000 Town Ctr Ste 3250 Southfield (48075) ***(G-14999)***
Pitchford Bertie.....517 627-1151
7821 W Grand River Hwy Grand Ledge (48837) ***(G-6113)***
Pitchfords Auto Parts & Svc, Grand Ledge *Also called Pitchford Bertie* ***(G-6113)***
Pitney Bowes Inc.....248 625-1666
9915 Boulder Ct Davisburg (48350) ***(G-3637)***
Pitney Bowes Inc.....203 356-5000
23594 Prescott Ln W South Lyon (48178) ***(G-14810)***
Pitney Bowes Inc.....248 591-2800
30200 Stephenson Hwy Madison Heights (48071) ***(G-10328)***
Pitss America LLC.....248 740-0935
570 Kirts Blvd Ste 207 Troy (48084) ***(G-16549)***
Pitstop Engineering, Livonia *Also called Carlson Technology Inc* ***(G-9677)***
Pittsburgh Glass Works LLC.....248 371-1700
3255 W Hamlin Rd Rochester Hills (48309) ***(G-13494)***
Pittsfield of Indiana, Ann Arbor *Also called Pittsfield Products Inc* ***(G-593)***
Pittsfield Products Inc (PA).....734 665-3771
5741 Jackson Rd Ann Arbor (48103) ***(G-593)***
Piwarski Brothers Logging Inc.....906 265-2914
941 Gibbs City Rd Iron River (49935) ***(G-8319)***
Pizza Crust Company Inc.....517 482-3368
728 E Cesar E Chavez Ave Lansing (48906) ***(G-9257)***
Pk Fabricating Inc.....248 398-4500
1975 Hilton Rd Ferndale (48220) ***(G-5310)***
Pk Global Logistics, Pontiac *Also called Manta Group LLC* ***(G-12847)***
Pkc Group, Farmington Hills *Also called Aees Inc* ***(G-4920)***
Pkc Group USA Inc (HQ).....248 489-4700
36555 Corp Dr Ste 300 Farmington Hills (48331) ***(G-5095)***
PL Schmitt Crbide Toling LLC.....517 522-6891
133 Drake St Grass Lake (49240) ***(G-7092)***
Plainwell Ice Cream Co.....269 685-8586
621 E Bridge St Plainwell (49080) ***(G-12537)***
Plamondon Oil Co Inc.....231 256-9261
525 W Main St Lake Leelanau (49653) ***(G-9106)***
Planet Neon, Wixom *Also called Harmon Sign Inc* ***(G-17824)***
Planewave Instruments Inc.....310 639-1662
1375 N Main St Adrian (49221) ***(G-84)***
Planning & Zoning Center Inc.....517 886-0555
715 N Cedar St Ste 2 Lansing (48906) ***(G-9258)***
Planning & Zoning News, Lansing *Also called Planning & Zoning Center Inc* ***(G-9258)***
Plant 1, Portage *Also called Summit Polymers Inc* ***(G-13047)***
Plant 2, Chesterfield *Also called Motor City Stampings Inc* ***(G-2809)***
Plant 2, Shelby Township *Also called Schwab Industries Inc* ***(G-14687)***
Plant 2, Chesterfield *Also called Prototech Laser Inc* ***(G-2826)***
Plant 2, Mendon *Also called Th Plastics Inc* ***(G-10720)***
Plant 27, Warren *Also called Shiloh Manufacturing LLC* ***(G-17239)***
Plant 28, Roseville *Also called Shiloh Manufacturing LLC* ***(G-13868)***
Plant 4, Blissfield *Also called L & W Inc* ***(G-1717)***
Plant Df.....734 397-0397
41133 Van Born Rd Ste 205 Van Buren Twp (48111) ***(G-16780)***
Plas-Labs Incorporated.....517 372-7178
401 E North St Ste 1 Lansing (48906) ***(G-9259)***
Plas-TEC Inc.....248 853-7777
1926 Northfield Dr Rochester Hills (48309) ***(G-13495)***
Plas-Tech Mold and Design Inc.....269 225-1223
946 Industrial Pkwy Plainwell (49080) ***(G-12538)***
Plasan Carbon Composites Inc (HQ).....616 965-9450
3195 Wilson Dr Nw Walker (49534) ***(G-16874)***
Plasan North America Inc.....616 559-0032
3236 Wilson Dr Nw Ste B Walker (49534) ***(G-16875)***
Plasan Us Inc (HQ).....616 559-0032
3236 Wilson Dr Nw Ste B Walker (49534) ***(G-16876)***
Plasco Formulating Division.....586 281-3714
14951 32 Mile Rd Bruce Twp (48065) ***(G-2092)***
Plascon Inc.....231 935-1580
2375 Traversefield Dr Traverse City (49686) ***(G-16070)***
Plascon Films Inc.....231 935-1580
2375 Traversefield Dr Traverse City (49686) ***(G-16071)***
Plascon Packaging Inc.....231 935-1580
2375 Traversefield Dr Traverse City (49686) ***(G-16072)***
Plascore Inc.....616 772-1220
581 E Roosevelt Ave Zeeland (49464) ***(G-18175)***
Plascore Inc.....616 772-1220
500a E Roosevelt Ave Zeeland (49464) ***(G-18176)***
Plasma Biolife Services L P.....616 667-0264
6331 Kenowa Ave Sw Grandville (49418) ***(G-7064)***
Plasma Biolife Services L P.....906 226-9080
175 Hawley St Marquette (49855) ***(G-10553)***
Plasma Pros.....734 354-6737
8179 Parkside Dr Westland (48185) ***(G-17588)***
Plasma-Tec Inc.....616 455-2593
1119 Morren Ct Wayland (49348) ***(G-17409)***
Plason Scraping Co Inc.....248 588-7280
32825 Dequindre Rd Madison Heights (48071) ***(G-10329)***
Plasport Inc.....231 935-1580
2375 Traversefield Dr Traverse City (49686) ***(G-16073)***
Plast-O-Foam LLC.....586 307-3790
24601 Capital Blvd Clinton Township (48036) ***(G-3194)***
Plastatech Engineering Ltd (PA).....989 754-6500
725 E Morley Dr Saginaw (48601) ***(G-14123)***
Plastatech Engineering Ltd.....989 754-6500
825 W Morley Dr Saginaw (48601) ***(G-14124)***
Plastech, Detroit *Also called Yanfeng US Automotive* ***(G-4454)***
Plastech Holding Corp.....313 565-5927
21551 Cherry Hill St Dearborn (48124) ***(G-3749)***
Plastech Weld.....313 963-3194
2364 17th St Detroit (48216) ***(G-4305)***
Plastechs LLC.....734 429-3129
1270 Barnes Ct Saline (48176) ***(G-14408)***
Plasteel Corporation.....313 562-5400
26970 Princeton St Inkster (48141) ***(G-8231)***
Plastgage Cstm Fabrication LLC.....517 817-0719
250 W Monroe St Jackson (49202) ***(G-8553)***

Plasti - Paint Inc (PA)....989 285-2280
801 Woodside Dr Saint Louis (48880) ***(G-14368)***
Plasti-Co Equipment Co, Brighton *Also called Applied Instruments Company* ***(G-1886)***
Plasti-Fab Inc....248 543-1415
2305 Hilton Rd Ferndale (48220) ***(G-5311)***
Plastic Dress-Up Service Inc....586 727-7878
2735 20th St Port Huron (48060) ***(G-12956)***
Plastic Engrg Tchncal Svcs Inc....248 373-0800
4141 Luella Ln Auburn Hills (48326) ***(G-974)***
Plastic Flow LLC....906 483-0691
540 Depot St Hancock (49930) ***(G-7255)***
Plastic Mold Technology Inc (PA)....616 698-9810
4201 Broadmoor Ave Se Kentwood (49512) ***(G-9022)***
Plastic Mold Technology Inc....616 698-9810
3870 Model Ct Se Grand Rapids (49512) ***(G-6756)***
Plastic Molding Development....586 739-4500
42400 Yearego Dr Sterling Heights (48314) ***(G-15446)***
Plastic Ominium Auto Inergy....734 753-1350
36000 Bruelle Ave New Boston (48164) ***(G-11508)***
Plastic Ominium Auto Inergy....517 265-1100
1549 W Beecher Rd Adrian (49221) ***(G-85)***
Plastic Omnium Inc....248 458-0772
2710 Bellingham Dr # 400 Troy (48083) ***(G-16550)***
Plastic Omnium Auto Exteriors (HQ)....248 458-0700
2710 Bellingham Dr # 400 Troy (48083) ***(G-16551)***
Plastic Omnium Auto Inergy LLC....248 743-5700
2585 W Maple Rd Troy (48084) ***(G-16552)***
Plastic Omnium Auto Inergy LLC (HQ)....248 743-5700
2710 Bellingham Dr Troy (48083) ***(G-16553)***
Plastic Plaque Inc....810 982-9591
1635 Poplar St Port Huron (48060) ***(G-12957)***
Plastic Plate LLC (HQ)....616 455-5240
3500 Raleigh Dr Se Grand Rapids (49512) ***(G-6757)***
Plastic Plate LLC....616 698-3678
5675 Kraft Ave Se Kentwood (49512) ***(G-9023)***
Plastic Plate LLC....616 949-6570
3505 Kraft Ave Se Kentwood (49512) ***(G-9024)***
Plastic Plate Plt 2, Grand Rapids *Also called Lacks Enterprises Inc* ***(G-6597)***
Plastic Solutions LLC....231 824-7350
1300 Stepke Ct Traverse City (49685) ***(G-16074)***
Plastic Tag & Trade Check Co....989 892-7913
252 Killarney Beach Rd Bay City (48706) ***(G-1340)***
Plastic Tool Company American, Howell *Also called Unified Industries Inc* ***(G-8118)***
Plastic Trends Inc....586 232-4167
56400 Mound Rd Shelby Township (48316) ***(G-14668)***
Plastic Trim Inc....937 429-1100
905 Cedar St Tawas City (48763) ***(G-15676)***
Plastic Trim International Inc (HQ)....248 259-7468
935 Aulerich Rd East Tawas (48730) ***(G-4692)***
Plastic Trim International Inc....989 362-4419
935 Aulerich Rd East Tawas (48730) ***(G-4693)***
Plastic-Plate Inc....616 698-2030
5460 Cascade Rd Se Grand Rapids (49546) ***(G-6758)***
Plastico Industries Inc (PA)....616 304-6289
320 W Main St Carson City (48811) ***(G-2496)***
Plasticos Inc....586 493-1908
21445 Carlo Dr Ste B Clinton Township (48038) ***(G-3195)***
Plasticrafts Inc....313 532-1900
25675 W 8 Mile Rd Redford (48240) ***(G-13183)***
Plastics Plus Inc (PA)....800 975-8694
4237 N Atlantic Blvd Auburn Hills (48326) ***(G-975)***
Plastics Technology Co....586 421-0479
48325 Gratiot Ave Chesterfield (48051) ***(G-2818)***
Plastipak Holdings Inc (PA)....734 455-3600
41605 Ann Arbor Rd E Plymouth (48170) ***(G-12718)***
Plastipak Packaging Inc (HQ)....734 455-3600
41605 Ann Arbor Rd E Plymouth (48170) ***(G-12719)***
Plastipak Packaging Inc....734 529-2475
500 Dunham St Dundee (48131) ***(G-4597)***
Plastipak Packaging Inc....734 326-6184
1351 N Hix Rd Westland (48185) ***(G-17589)***
Plastipak Packaging Inc....734 467-7519
36445 Van Born Rd Ste 200 Romulus (48174) ***(G-13722)***
Plastisnow LLC....414 397-1233
200 Prince St Plainwell (49080) ***(G-12539)***
Plastomer Corporation....734 464-0700
37819 Schoolcraft Rd Livonia (48150) ***(G-9889)***
Platemate, Clarklake *Also called Your Home Town USA Inc* ***(G-2902)***
Platform Computing Inc....248 359-7825
2000 Town Ctr Ste 1900 Southfield (48075) ***(G-15000)***
Platformsh Inc....734 707-9124
106 S Main St Ste 4 Brooklyn (49230) ***(G-2041)***
Plating Specialties Inc (PA)....248 547-8660
1625 E 10 Mile Rd Madison Heights (48071) ***(G-10330)***
Plating Systems and Tech Inc....517 783-4776
317 N Mechanic St Jackson (49201) ***(G-8554)***
Platinum Skin Care Inc....586 598-6075
20556 Hall Rd Clinton Township (48038) ***(G-3196)***
Platt Mounts - Usa Inc....586 202-2920
100 Engelwood Dr Ste D Lake Orion (48359) ***(G-9155)***
Player Prints LLC....844 774-7773
5904 Warbler Dr Clarkston (48346) ***(G-2946)***
Pleasant Graphics Inc....989 773-7777
6835 Lea Pick Dr Mount Pleasant (48858) ***(G-11219)***
Plesh Industries, Brighton *Also called Allor Manufacturing Inc* ***(G-1883)***
Plesh Industries Inc (PA)....716 873-4916
12534 Emerson Dr Brighton (48116) ***(G-1979)***
Plesko Sheet Metal Inc....989 847-3771
8980 S Ransom Rd Ashley (48806) ***(G-728)***
Plexicase Inc....616 246-6400
2431 Clyde Park Ave Sw Wyoming (49509) ***(G-18028)***
Pliant Plastics Corp (PA)....616 844-0300
17000 Taft Rd Spring Lake (49456) ***(G-15169)***
Pliant Plastics Corp....616 844-3215
17024 Taft Rd Spring Lake (49456) ***(G-15170)***
Plow Point Brewing Co....734 562-9102
6447 Stillwater Dr Chelsea (48118) ***(G-2717)***
Plum Brothers LLC....734 947-8100
9350 Harrison Romulus (48174) ***(G-13723)***
Plum Creek Timber Company Inc....715 453-7952
2831 N Lincoln Rd Escanaba (49829) ***(G-4852)***
Plum Tree....269 469-5980
16337 Red Arrow Hwy Union Pier (49129) ***(G-16738)***
Plush Apparel Cstm Impressions, Ferndale *Also called Troy Haygood* ***(G-5322)***
Pluskate Boarding Company....248 426-0899
33335 Grand River Ave Farmington (48336) ***(G-4908)***
Plutchak Fab....906 864-4650
N1715 Us Highway 41 Menominee (49858) ***(G-10755)***
Ply-Forms Incorporated....989 686-5681
4684 Fraser Rd Bay City (48706) ***(G-1341)***
Plymouth Brazing Inc....734 453-6274
6140 N Hix Rd Westland (48185) ***(G-17590)***
Plymouth Computer &....734 744-9563
27840 Plymouth Rd Livonia (48150) ***(G-9890)***
Plymouth Plating Works Inc....734 453-1560
42200 Joy Rd Plymouth (48170) ***(G-12720)***
Plymouth Technology Inc....248 537-0081
2700 Bond St Rochester Hills (48309) ***(G-13496)***
Plymouth-Canton Cmnty Crier (PA)....734 453-6900
821 Penniman Ave Plymouth (48170) ***(G-12721)***
Plymouth-Canton Cmnty Crier....734 453-6900
306 S Main St Ste 100 Plymouth (48170) ***(G-12722)***
PM Power Group Inc....906 885-7100
29639 Willow Rd White Pine (49971) ***(G-17658)***
PME - Croswell, Warren *Also called Proper Polymers - Warren LLC* ***(G-17207)***
PMI Branded Pharmaceuticals....269 673-8451
515 Eastern Ave Allegan (49010) ***(G-185)***
PMS Products Inc....616 355-6615
76 Veterans Dr Ste 110 Holland (49423) ***(G-7772)***
Pneumatic Feed Service, Clinton Township *Also called Caliber Industries LLC* ***(G-3074)***
Pneumatic Innovations LLC....989 734-3435
5369 Main St Millersburg (49759) ***(G-10992)***
Pneumatic Tube Products Co....503 968-0200
17108 S Hemlock Rd Oakley (48649) ***(G-12111)***
Poco Inc....313 220-6752
4850 S Sheldon Rd Canton (48188) ***(G-2416)***
Poet Biorefining- Caro 25200, Caro *Also called Michigan Ethanol LLC* ***(G-2471)***
Poetry Factory Ltd....586 296-3125
34028 James J Pompo Dr Fraser (48026) ***(G-5707)***
Pohl's Cstm Cnter Tops Cbnetry, Fowler *Also called Pohls Custom Counter Tops* ***(G-5555)***
Pohls Custom Counter Tops....989 593-2174
12185 W Colony Rd Fowler (48835) ***(G-5555)***
Pointe Printing Inc....313 821-0030
1103 Balfour St Grosse Pointe Park (48230) ***(G-7195)***
Pointe Scientific Inc....734 487-8300
5449 Research Dr Canton (48188) ***(G-2417)***
Polaris Engineering Inc....586 296-1603
17540 15 Mile Rd Fraser (48026) ***(G-5708)***
Poligon, Holland *Also called Porter Corp* ***(G-7773)***
Polish Daily News Inc....313 365-1990
11903 Joseph Campau St Detroit (48212) ***(G-4306)***
Polish Weekly, Detroit *Also called Polish Daily News Inc* ***(G-4306)***
Polk Gas Producer LLC....734 913-2970
414 S Main St Ste 600 Ann Arbor (48104) ***(G-594)***
Pollack Glass Co....517 349-6380
2360 Jolly Rd Okemos (48864) ***(G-12134)***
Pollington Machine Tool Inc....231 743-2003
20669 30th Ave Marion (49665) ***(G-10493)***
Pollums Natural Resources....810 245-7268
732 S Elba Rd Lapeer (48446) ***(G-9481)***
Pollution Control Services, Kalkaska *Also called Northern A 1 Services Inc* ***(G-8955)***
Polly Products, Mulliken *Also called Air Products Inc* ***(G-11238)***
Polsorb Sales, Sterling Heights *Also called Global Wholesale & Marketing* ***(G-15361)***
Poly Flex Products Inc (PA)....734 458-4194
23093 Commerce Dr Farmington Hills (48335) ***(G-5096)***
Poly Tech Industries Inc....248 589-9950
395 W Lincoln Ave Ste B Madison Heights (48071) ***(G-10331)***
Poly-Green Foam LLC....517 279-8019
325 Jay St Coldwater (49036) ***(G-3320)***

ALPHABETIC

Polycem LLC..231 799-1040
1271 Judson Rd Norton Shores (49456) *(G-11813)*
Polyhedron LLC..313 318-4807
203 Lakeland St Grosse Pointe (48230) *(G-7182)*
Polymer Inc (PA)..248 353-3035
24671 Telegraph Rd Southfield (48033) *(G-15001)*
Polymer Process Dev LLC...............................586 464-6400
11969 Shelby Tech Dr Shelby Township (48315) *(G-14669)*
Polymer Products Group Inc..........................989 723-9510
3670 N M 52 Owosso (48867) *(G-12311)*
Polymerica Limited Company (PA)..................248 542-2000
26909 Woodward Ave Huntington Woods (48070) *(G-8191)*
Polyply Composites LLC.................................616 842-6330
1540 Marion Ave Grand Haven (49417) *(G-6061)*
Polytec Foha Inc (HQ)....................................586 978-9386
7020 Murthum Ave Warren (48092) *(G-17188)*
Polytorx LLC (HQ)..734 322-2114
2300 Washtenaw Ave # 200 Ann Arbor (48104) *(G-595)*
Polyvalve Inc..616 656-2264
4855 Broadmoor Ave Se Kentwood (49512) *(G-9025)*
Polyworks USA Training Center......................216 226-1617
41700 Gardenbrook Rd Novi (48375) *(G-11974)*
Pomeroy Forest Products Inc..........................906 474-6780
9577 Ee.25 Rd Rapid River (49878) *(G-13113)*
Poncraft Door Co Inc.......................................248 373-6060
2005 Pontiac Rd Auburn Hills (48326) *(G-976)*
Ponder Industrial Incorporated.......................989 684-9841
287 S River Rd Bay City (48708) *(G-1342)*
Pontiac Coil Inc (PA)......................................248 922-1100
5800 Moody Dr Clarkston (48348) *(G-2947)*
Pontiac Electric Motor Works..........................248 332-4622
224 W Sheffield Ave Pontiac (48340) *(G-12856)*
Pontoon Rentals..906 387-2685
1330 Commercial St Munising (49862) *(G-11248)*
Poof-Slinky LLC..734 454-9552
45605 Helm St Plymouth (48170) *(G-12723)*
Pooles Meat Processing..................................989 846-6348
3084 Grove Street Rd Standish (48658) *(G-15225)*
Poor Boy Woodworks Inc...............................989 799-9440
1903 S Michigan Ave Saginaw (48602) *(G-14125)*
Popcorn Press Inc..248 588-4444
32400 Edward Ave Ste A Madison Heights (48071) *(G-10332)*
Porcupine Press Inc..906 439-5111
3720 Munising St E Chatham (49816) *(G-2675)*
Porex Technologies Corporation.....................989 865-8200
5301 S Graham Rd Saint Charles (48655) *(G-14198)*
Porite USA Co Ltd..248 597-9988
1295 Combermere Dr Troy (48083) *(G-16554)*
Porky Press, Chatham *Also called Porcupine Press Inc (G-2675)*
Port Austin Level & TI Mfg Co.........................989 738-5291
130 Arthur St Port Austin (48467) *(G-12878)*
Port City Custom Plastics, Muskegon *Also called Pace Industries LLC (G-11395)*
Port City Custom Plastics, Muskegon *Also called Cel Plastics Inc (G-11292)*
Port City Die Cast, Muskegon *Also called Pace Industries LLC (G-11394)*
Port City Group Inc (HQ)................................231 777-3941
1985 E Laketon Ave Muskegon (49442) *(G-11400)*
Port City Industrial Finishing..........................231 726-4288
1867 Huizenga St Muskegon (49442) *(G-11401)*
Port City Metal Products, Muskegon *Also called Pace Industries LLC (G-11397)*
Port City Paints Mfg Inc..................................231 726-5911
1250 9th St Muskegon (49440) *(G-11402)*
Port City Redi-Mix, Grand Rapids *Also called Grand Rapids Gravel Company (G-6454)*
Port City Redi-Mix Co, Muskegon *Also called Grand Rapids Gravel Company (G-11332)*
Port Cy Archtctral Signage LLC......................231 739-3463
2350 S Getty St Muskegon (49444) *(G-11403)*
Port Huron Building Supply Co.......................810 987-2666
3555 Electric Ave Port Huron (48060) *(G-12958)*
Port Huron Medical Assoc...............................810 982-0100
3825 24th Ave Fort Gratiot (48059) *(G-5551)*
Portable Factory..586 883-6843
7205 Sterling Ponds Ct Sterling Heights (48312) *(G-15447)*
Portage Printing, Portage *Also called Metropolitan Indus Lithography (G-13016)*
Portage Wire Systems Inc...............................231 889-4215
4853 Joseph Rd Onekama (49675) *(G-12151)*
Portage Yacht Club, Pinckney *Also called Midwest Aquatics Group Inc (G-12500)*
Portal Architects, Ann Arbor *Also called Skysync Inc (G-636)*
Portenga Manufacturing Company.................616 846-2691
220 5th St Ferrysburg (49409) *(G-5337)*
Porter Corp..616 399-1963
4240 136th Ave Holland (49424) *(G-7773)*
Porter Steel & Welding Company....................231 733-4495
831 E Hovey Ave Muskegon (49444) *(G-11404)*
Porters Orchards Farm Market........................810 636-7156
12160 Hegel Rd Goodrich (48438) *(G-5956)*
Portland Plastics Co..517 647-4115
3 Industrial Dr Portland (48875) *(G-13065)*
Pos Complete, Ferndale *Also called PC Complete Inc (G-5308)*
Posa-Cut Corporation......................................248 474-5620
23600 Haggerty Rd Farmington Hills (48335) *(G-5097)*
Poseidon Industries Inc...................................586 949-3550
25700 Dhondt Ct Chesterfield (48051) *(G-2819)*
Positech Inc...616 949-4024
4134 36th St Se Grand Rapids (49512) *(G-6759)*
Positive Tool & Engineering Co.......................313 532-1674
26025 W 7 Mile Rd Redford (48240) *(G-13184)*
Possibilities For Change LLC.........................810 333-1347
674 S Wagner Rd Ann Arbor (48103) *(G-596)*
Post Foods LLC..269 966-1000
275 Cliff St Battle Creek (49014) *(G-1236)*
Post Hardwoods Inc..269 751-2221
3544 38th St Hamilton (49419) *(G-7237)*
Post Production Solutions LLC.......................734 428-7000
110 Division St Ste 1 Manchester (48158) *(G-10411)*
Postal Savers, Flint *Also called Postal Savings Direct Mktg (G-5480)*
Postal Savings Direct Mktg.............................810 238-8866
1035 Ann Arbor St Flint (48503) *(G-5480)*
Postema Sign Co, Grand Rapids *Also called Japhil Inc (G-6553)*
Postema Signs & Graphics, Grand Rapids *Also called Mod Signs Inc (G-6694)*
Postguard, Farmington Hills *Also called Encore Commercial Products Inc (G-4986)*
Postle Extrusions, Cassopolis *Also called Dw Aluminum LLC (G-2528)*
Postma Brothers Maple Syrup........................906 478-3051
10702 W Ploegstra Rd Rudyard (49780) *(G-13985)*
Potatoe Ball LLC...313 483-0901
42160 Lochmoor St Clinton Township (48038) *(G-3197)*
Potlatchdeltic Corporation..............................906 346-3215
650 Avenue A Gwinn (49841) *(G-7222)*
Potteryland Inc..586 781-4425
7045 Emerson Washington (48094) *(G-17310)*
Powco Inc..269 646-5385
56165 Moorlag Rd Marcellus (49067) *(G-10467)*
Powder Coating Services, Greenville *Also called P C S Companies Inc (G-7149)*
Powder Cote II Inc (PA).................................586 463-7040
50 N Rose St Mount Clemens (48043) *(G-11145)*
Powder Cote II Inc...586 463-7040
60 N Rose St Mount Clemens (48043) *(G-11146)*
Powder It Inc...586 949-0395
46070 Edgewater St Chesterfield (48047) *(G-2820)*
Powell & Crisp Plankters LLC..........................231 271-6769
109 W Fourth St Suttons Bay (49682) *(G-15654)*
Powell Fabrication & Mfg Inc..........................989 681-2158
740 E Monroe Rd Saint Louis (48880) *(G-14369)*
Power Cleaning Systems Inc..........................248 347-7727
28294 Beck Rd Wixom (48393) *(G-17878)*
Power Components, Plymouth *Also called Dadco Inc (G-12604)*
Power Control Systems Inc.............................517 339-1442
2861 Jolly Rd Ste C Okemos (48864) *(G-12135)*
Power Controllers LLC...................................248 888-9896
23900 Freeway Park Dr Farmington Hills (48335) *(G-5098)*
Power Industries Corp.....................................586 783-3818
42279 Irwin Dr Harrison Township (48045) *(G-7343)*
Power Manufacturing, Holland *Also called New 11 Inc (G-7754)*
Power Marine LLC...586 344-1192
38303 Mast St Harrison Township (48045) *(G-7344)*
Power Precision Industries Inc........................586 997-0600
43545 Utica Rd Sterling Heights (48314) *(G-15448)*
Power Process Engrg Co Inc............................248 473-8450
24300 Catherne Ind Dr # 403 Novi (48375) *(G-11975)*
Power Process Piping Inc (PA).......................734 451-0130
45780 Port St Plymouth (48170) *(G-12724)*
Power Seal International LLC..........................248 537-1103
250 Park Dr Troy (48083) *(G-16555)*
Power Solutions International, Madison Heights *Also called Powertrain Integration LLC (G-10333)*
Power Sports Ann Arbor LLC..........................734 585-3300
4405 Jackson Rd Ann Arbor (48103) *(G-597)*
Power Without Wires, Detroit *Also called Creative Power Systems Inc (G-3954)*
Power-Brite of Michigan Inc............................734 591-7911
12053 Levan Rd Livonia (48150) *(G-9891)*
Power-Technology-Solutions, Pinckney *Also called Ptspower LLC (G-12503)*
Powergrid Inc...586 484-7185
28845 Inkster Rd Farmington Hills (48334) *(G-5099)*
Powerlase Photonics Inc..................................248 305-2963
26800 Meadowbrook Rd # 113 Novi (48377) *(G-11976)*
Powerplus Mouthguard...................................231 357-2167
10850 E Traverse Hwy Traverse City (49684) *(G-16075)*
Powers Printing, Powers *Also called Ogden Newspapers Inc (G-13078)*
Powerscreen USA LLC......................................989 288-3121
212 S Oak St Durand (48429) *(G-4612)*
Powersports Dales LLC....................................248 682-4200
2142 Beechmont St Keego Harbor (48320) *(G-8981)*
Powerthru Inc..734 583-5004
11825 Mayfield St Livonia (48150) *(G-9892)*
Powerthru Inc..734 853-5004
11825 Mayfield St Livonia (48150) *(G-9893)*
Powertrain Integration LLC (PA).....................248 577-0010
32505 Industrial Dr Madison Heights (48071) *(G-10333)*

ALPHABETIC SECTION
Precision Jig & Fixture Inc

Powertran Corporation 248 399-4300
1605 Bonner St Ferndale (48220) ***(G-5312)***

Ppc Design, Novi *Also called Programmed Products Corp* ***(G-11983)***

PPG 5622, Novi *Also called PPG Industries Inc* ***(G-11977)***

PPG 5624, Shelby Township *Also called PPG Industries Inc* ***(G-14670)***

PPG 5625, Southfield *Also called PPG Industries Inc* ***(G-15002)***

PPG 5628, Warren *Also called PPG Industries Inc* ***(G-17189)***

PPG 5629, Waterford *Also called PPG Industries Inc* ***(G-17370)***

PPG 5637, Clarkston *Also called PPG Industries Inc* ***(G-2948)***

PPG 9356, Jackson *Also called PPG Industries Inc* ***(G-8555)***

PPG Automotive, Flint *Also called PPG Industries Inc* ***(G-5481)***

PPG Coating Services 313 922-8433
6334 Lynch Rd Detroit (48234) ***(G-4307)***

PPG Coating Services (HQ) 586 575-9800
5875 New King Ct Troy (48098) ***(G-16556)***

PPG Coating Services 734 421-7300
31774 Enterprise Dr Livonia (48150) ***(G-9894)***

PPG Industrial Coatings 616 844-4391
14295 172nd Ave Grand Haven (49417) ***(G-6062)***

PPG Industries Inc 248 640-4174
54197 Myrica Dr Macomb (48042) ***(G-10153)***

PPG Industries Inc 517 394-9093
5633 Lamone Dr Ste B Lansing (48911) ***(G-9412)***

PPG Industries Inc 248 641-2000
5875 New King Ct Troy (48098) ***(G-16557)***

PPG Industries Inc 517 263-7831
961 Division St Adrian (49221) ***(G-86)***

PPG Industries Inc 810 767-8030
3601 James P Cole Blvd Flint (48505) ***(G-5481)***

PPG Industries Inc 616 846-4400
1855 Industrial Park Dr Grand Haven (49417) ***(G-6063)***

PPG Industries Inc 248 625-7282
5860 Sashabaw Rd Clarkston (48346) ***(G-2948)***

PPG Industries Inc 517 784-6138
167 W North St Jackson (49202) ***(G-8555)***

PPG Industries Inc 248 478-1300
40400 Grand River Ave C Novi (48375) ***(G-11977)***

PPG Industries Inc 586 566-3789
13651 23 Mile Rd Shelby Township (48315) ***(G-14670)***

PPG Industries Inc 248 357-4817
23361 Telegraph Rd Southfield (48033) ***(G-15002)***

PPG Industries Inc 734 287-2110
22673 Northline Rd Taylor (48180) ***(G-15754)***

PPG Industries Inc 248 683-8052
497 Elizabeth Lake Rd Waterford (48328) ***(G-17370)***

PPG Industries Inc 586 755-2011
13344 E 11 Mile Rd Warren (48089) ***(G-17189)***

Ppi, Flint *Also called Premiere Packaging Inc* ***(G-5483)***

Ppi LLC (PA) 586 772-7736
23514 Groesbeck Hwy Warren (48089) ***(G-17190)***

Ppi LLC 248 841-7721
5868 Hilmore Dr Troy (48085) ***(G-16558)***

Ppi Aerospace, Warren *Also called Ppi LLC* ***(G-17190)***

Pr39 Industries LLC 248 481-8512
2005 Pontiac Rd Auburn Hills (48326) ***(G-977)***

PRA Company (PA) 989 846-1029
1415 W Cedar St Standish (48658) ***(G-15226)***

Prab, Kalamazoo *Also called Kalamazoo Mfg Corp Globl* ***(G-8792)***

Prab Inc (HQ) 269 382-8200
5944 E N Ave Kalamazoo (49048) ***(G-8854)***

Prab Inc 269 343-1675
5944 E N Ave Kalamazoo (49048) ***(G-8855)***

Prab and Hapman, Kalamazoo *Also called Prab Inc* ***(G-8854)***

Practical Paper Inc 616 887-1723
98 E Division St Sparta Cedar Springs (49319) ***(G-2559)***

Practical Power 866 385-2961
202 South St Rochester (48307) ***(G-13347)***

Practical Solar 586 864-6686
23276 Doremus St Saint Clair Shores (48080) ***(G-14267)***

Praet Tool & Engineering Inc 586 677-3800
51214 Industrial Dr Macomb (48042) ***(G-10154)***

Prairie Pride Carrier, Troy *Also called Sadia Enterprises Inc* ***(G-16588)***

Prairie Wood Products Inc 269 659-1163
506 Prairie St Sturgis (49091) ***(G-15630)***

Praise Sign Company 616 439-0315
3404 Busch Dr Sw Ste F Grandville (49418) ***(G-7065)***

Pratt & Whitney Autoair Inc 517 393-4040
5640 Enterprise Dr Lansing (48911) ***(G-9413)***

Pratt Burnerd America, Kalamazoo *Also called Clausing Industrial Inc* ***(G-8707)***

Pratt Industries Inc 269 465-7676
11365 Red Arrow Hwy Bridgman (49106) ***(G-1872)***

Pratt Industries Inc 616 452-2111
2000 Beverly Ave Sw Grand Rapids (49519) ***(G-6760)***

Pratt Industries Inc 734 853-3000
32432 Capitol St Livonia (48150) ***(G-9895)***

Praxair Inc 586 751-7400
30600 Dequindre Rd Warren (48092) ***(G-17191)***

Praxair Inc 269 276-0442
1119 E Walnut St Kalamazoo (49001) ***(G-8856)***

Praxair Inc 231 796-3266
1000 Scribner Ave Nw Grand Rapids (49504) ***(G-6761)***

Praxair Inc 269 926-8296
2320 Meadowbrook Rd Benton Harbor (49022) ***(G-1538)***

Praxair Inc 231 722-3773
363 Ottawa St Muskegon (49442) ***(G-11405)***

Praxair Inc 313 319-6220
5825 Wyoming St Dearborn (48126) ***(G-3750)***

Praxair Inc 313 849-4200
300 E Great Lakes St River Rouge (48218) ***(G-13280)***

Praxair Distribution Inc 616 451-3055
1000 Scribner Ave Nw Grand Rapids (49504) ***(G-6762)***

Praxair Distribution Inc 313 778-7085
12820 Evergreen Rd Detroit (48223) ***(G-4308)***

Praxair Distribution Inc 586 598-9020
46025 Gratiot St Macomb (48042) ***(G-10155)***

Pre-Cut Patterns Inc 616 392-4415
76 Veterans Dr Ste 130 Holland (49423) ***(G-7774)***

Precious Furs Llc 734 262-6262
35912 Joy Rd Livonia (48150) ***(G-9896)***

Precise Cnc Routing Inc 616 538-8608
2605 Thornwood St Sw A Grand Rapids (49519) ***(G-6763)***

Precise Finishing Systems Inc 517 552-9200
1650 N Burkhart Rd Howell (48855) ***(G-8081)***

Precise Machining Inc 231 937-7957
17279 Almy Rd Howard City (49329) ***(G-8005)***

Precise Metal Components Inc 734 769-0790
91 Enterprise Dr Ste A Ann Arbor (48103) ***(G-598)***

Precise Power Systems LLC 248 709-4750
10520 Plaza Dr Whitmore Lake (48189) ***(G-17706)***

Precise Tool & Cutter Inc 248 684-8480
51143 Pontiac Trl Wixom (48393) ***(G-17879)***

Precision Aerospace Corp 616 243-8112
5300 Corporate Grv Grand Rapids (49512) ***(G-6764)***

Precision Automotive Mch Sp 616 534-6946
2320 Chicago Dr Sw Wyoming (49519) ***(G-18029)***

Precision Boring and Machine 248 371-9140
2238 E Walton Blvd Auburn Hills (48326) ***(G-978)***

Precision Boring Company 586 463-3900
24400 Maplehurst Dr Clinton Township (48036) ***(G-3198)***

Precision Coatings Inc (PA) 248 363-8361
8120 Goldie St Commerce Township (48390) ***(G-3440)***

Precision Components 248 588-5650
324 Robbins Dr Troy (48083) ***(G-16559)***

Precision Concepts Inc 989 673-8555
1220 W Sanilac Rd Caro (48723) ***(G-2475)***

Precision Controls Company 734 663-3104
107 Enterprise Dr Ann Arbor (48103) ***(G-599)***

Precision Devices Inc 734 439-2462
606 County St Milan (48160) ***(G-10950)***

Precision Dial Co 269 375-5601
7240 W Kl Ave Kalamazoo (49009) ***(G-8857)***

Precision Die Cast Inc 586 463-1800
44396 Reynolds Dr Clinton Township (48036) ***(G-3199)***

Precision Edge Srgcal Pdts LLC 231 459-4304
1448 Lexamar Dr Boyne City (49712) ***(G-1833)***

Precision Edge Srgcal Pdts LLC (PA) 906 632-5600
415 W 12th Ave Sault Sainte Marie (49783) ***(G-14470)***

Precision Engrg & Mfg Inc 616 837-6764
16913 Power Dr Nunica (49448) ***(G-12041)***

Precision Extraction Corp 855 420-0020
2468 Industrial Row Dr Troy (48084) ***(G-16560)***

Precision Extraction Solutions, Troy *Also called Precision Extraction Corp* ***(G-16560)***

Precision Finishing Co Inc 616 245-2255
1010 Chicago Dr Sw Grand Rapids (49509) ***(G-6765)***

Precision Forestry 989 619-1016
4285 S County Line Rd Onaway (49765) ***(G-12150)***

Precision Framing Systems Inc 704 588-6680
21001 Van Born Rd Taylor (48180) ***(G-15755)***

Precision Gage Inc 517 439-1690
256 Industrial Dr Hillsdale (49242) ***(G-7534)***

Precision Global Systems, Troy *Also called P G S Inc* ***(G-16540)***

Precision Guides LLC 517 536-7234
151 Factory Rd Michigan Center (49254) ***(G-10789)***

Precision Heat Treating Co 269 382-4660
660 Gull Rd Kalamazoo (49007) ***(G-8858)***

Precision Hone & Tool Inc 313 493-9760
13600 Evergreen Rd Detroit (48223) ***(G-4309)***

Precision Honing 586 757-0304
2029 Riggs Ave Warren (48091) ***(G-17192)***

Precision Hrdwood Rsources Inc 734 475-0144
680 E Industrial Dr Chelsea (48118) ***(G-2718)***

Precision Industries Inc 810 239-5816
3002 E Court St Flint (48506) ***(G-5482)***

Precision Jig & Fixture, Rockford *Also called Peterson Jig & Fixture Inc* ***(G-13585)***

Precision Jig & Fixture Inc 616 696-2595
4030 Cedar Coml Dr Ne Cedar Springs (49319) ***(G-2560)***

ALPHABETIC

Precision Jig Grinding Inc 989 865-7953
165 Entrepreneur Dr Saint Charles (48655) ***(G-14199)***
Precision Label Inc 616 534-9935
4181 Spartan Indus Dr Sw Grandville (49418) ***(G-7066)***
Precision Label Specialist 248 673-5010
4887 Highland Rd Waterford (48328) ***(G-17371)***
Precision Laser & Mfg LLC 519 733-8422
5690 18 Mile Rd Sterling Heights (48314) ***(G-15449)***
Precision Machine Co S Haven 269 637-2372
435 66th St South Haven (49090) ***(G-14768)***
Precision Machining 248 669-2660
4998 Mccarthy Dr Milford (48381) ***(G-10980)***
Precision Machining 269 925-5321
2809 Yore Ave Sodus (49126) ***(G-14746)***
Precision Machining Company 810 688-8674
6637 Bernie Kohler Dr North Branch (48461) ***(G-11664)***
Precision Manufacturing Svcs 734 995-3505
3738 W Liberty Rd Ann Arbor (48103) ***(G-600)***
Precision Masking Inc 734 848-4200
721 La Voy Rd Erie (48133) ***(G-4808)***
Precision Masters Inc (PA) 248 853-0308
1985 Northfield Dr Rochester Hills (48309) ***(G-13497)***
Precision Masters Inc 248 648-8071
2441 N Opdyke Rd Auburn Hills (48326) ***(G-979)***
Precision Measurement Co 734 995-0041
885 Oakdale Rd Ann Arbor (48105) ***(G-601)***
Precision Metal Finishing, Jackson *Also called Classic Metal Finishing Inc* ***(G-8411)***
Precision Metals Plus Inc 269 342-6330
7574 E Mich Ave Kalamazoo Kalamazoo (49048) ***(G-8859)***
Precision Metrology Inspection, Flint *Also called Bobier Tool Supply Inc* ***(G-5392)***
Precision Mfg Group Inc 616 837-6764
16913 Power Dr Nunica (49448) ***(G-12042)***
Precision Mold & Engineering 586 774-2421
13143 E 9 Mile Rd Warren (48089) ***(G-17193)***
Precision Mtl Hdlg Eqp LLC (HQ) 313 789-8101
26700 Princeton St Inkster (48141) ***(G-8232)***
Precision Mtl Hdlg Eqp LLC 734 351-7350
36663 Van Born Rd Ste 350 Romulus (48174) ***(G-13724)***
Precision Optical Mfg, Auburn Hills *Also called The Pom Group Inc* ***(G-1018)***
Precision Packing Corporation 586 756-8700
2145 Centerwood Dr Warren (48091) ***(G-17194)***
Precision Pallet LLC 252 943-5193
17195 Beck Rd Charlevoix (49720) ***(G-2627)***
Precision Parts Holdings Inc 248 853-9010
2129 Austin Ave Rochester Hills (48309) ***(G-13498)***
Precision Plumbing - T (PA) 269 695-2402
317 Post Rd Buchanan (49107) ***(G-2125)***
Precision Plus 906 553-7900
6911 County 426 M.5 Rd Escanaba (49829) ***(G-4853)***
Precision Polymer Mfg Inc 269 344-2044
3915 Ravine Rd Kalamazoo (49006) ***(G-8860)***
Precision Power Inc 517 371-4274
630 Park Pl Lansing (48912) ***(G-9414)***
Precision Printer Services Inc 269 384-5725
9185 Portage Indus Dr Portage (49024) ***(G-13023)***
Precision Prototype & Mfg Inc 517 663-4114
500 Marilin Ave Eaton Rapids (48827) ***(G-4729)***
Precision Race Services Inc 248 634-4010
16749 Dixie Hwy Ste 9 Davisburg (48350) ***(G-3638)***
Precision Resource Inc 248 478-3704
3250 W Big Beaver Rd # 231 Troy (48084) ***(G-16561)***
Precision Speed Equipment Inc 269 651-4303
1400 W Lafayette St Sturgis (49091) ***(G-15631)***
Precision Spindle Service Co 248 544-0100
836 Woodward Hts Ferndale (48220) ***(G-5313)***
Precision Stamping Co Inc 517 546-5656
1244 Grand Oaks Dr Howell (48843) ***(G-8082)***
Precision Threading Corp 231 627-3133
1306 Higgins Dr Cheboygan (49721) ***(G-2691)***
Precision Tool Inc 517 726-1060
519 Allegan Rd Vermontville (49096) ***(G-16823)***
Precision Tool & Machine Inc 989 291-3365
154 E Condensery Rd Sheridan (48884) ***(G-14734)***
Precision Tool & Mold LLC 906 932-3440
620 Easy St Ironwood (49938) ***(G-8338)***
Precision Tool Company Inc 231 733-0811
2839 Henry St Muskegon (49441) ***(G-11406)***
Precision Torque Control Inc 989 495-9330
220 Arrow Cv Midland (48642) ***(G-10903)***
Precision USA Mfg, Burton *Also called Hollander Machine Co Inc* ***(G-2156)***
Precision Wire EDM Service 616 453-4360
3180 3 Mile Rd Nw Grand Rapids (49534) ***(G-6766)***
Precision Wire Forms Inc (PA) 269 279-0053
1100 W Broadway St Three Rivers (49093) ***(G-15874)***
Precisioncraft Co 586 954-9510
44395 Reynolds Dr Clinton Township (48036) ***(G-3200)***
Predxion Bio Inc 734 353-0191
7455 Dexter Ann Arbor Rd Dexter (48130) ***(G-4504)***
Preeminence Inc 313 737-7920
12889 Leverne Redford (48239) ***(G-13185)***
Preferred Avionics Instrs LLC 800 521-5130
3679 Bowen Rd Howell (48855) ***(G-8083)***
Preferred Engineering, Rochester *Also called CPR III Inc* ***(G-13318)***
Preferred Industries Inc 810 364-4090
11 Ash Dr Kimball (48074) ***(G-9048)***
Preferred Machine LLC 616 272-6334
6673 Pine Ridge Ct Sw C Jenison (49428) ***(G-8637)***
Preferred Plastics Inc (PA) 269 685-5873
800 E Bridge St Plainwell (49080) ***(G-12540)***
Preferred Printing Inc (PA) 269 782-5488
304 E Division St Dowagiac (49047) ***(G-4557)***
Preferred Products Inc 248 255-0200
1200 Benstein Rd Commerce Township (48390) ***(G-3441)***
Preferred Screen Printing, Commerce Township *Also called Preferred Products Inc* ***(G-3441)***
Preferred Tool & Die Co Inc 616 784-6789
5400 West River Dr Ne Comstock Park (49321) ***(G-3509)***
Preferred Tool & Machine Ltd 248 399-6919
595 E 10 Mile Rd Madison Heights (48071) ***(G-10334)***
Pregis Film, Grand Rapids *Also called Pregis LLC* ***(G-6767)***
Pregis LLC 616 520-1550
1100 Hynes Ave Sw Ste B Grand Rapids (49507) ***(G-6767)***
Pregis LLC 810 320-3005
2700 Wills St Marysville (48040) ***(G-10611)***
Pregnancy Resource Center, Grand Rapids *Also called Frontlines Publishing* ***(G-6419)***
Prehab Technologies LLC 734 368-9983
103 E Liberty St Ste 201 Ann Arbor (48104) ***(G-602)***
Prell's Sawmill, Hawks *Also called Prells Saw Mill Inc* ***(G-7430)***
Prells Saw Mill Inc 989 734-2939
8571 F-21 Hwy Hawks (49743) ***(G-7430)***
Premier Casing Crews Inc 989 775-7436
5580 Venture Way Mount Pleasant (48858) ***(G-11220)***
Premier Corrugated Inc 517 629-5700
916 Burstein Dr Albion (49224) ***(G-129)***
Premier Finishing Inc 616 785-3070
3180 Fruit Ridge Ave Nw Grand Rapids (49544) ***(G-6768)***
Premier Fireplace Co LLC 586 949-4315
46566 Erb Dr Macomb (48042) ***(G-10156)***
Premier Imaging Center 248 594-3201
31500 Telg Rd Ste 225 Franklin (48025) ***(G-5608)***
Premier Industries, Monroe *Also called Thomas L Snarey & Assoc Inc* ***(G-11075)***
Premier International, Wixom *Also called Ds Sales Inc* ***(G-17796)***
Premier Malt Products Inc 586 443-3355
25760 Groesbeck Hwy # 103 Warren (48089) ***(G-17195)***
Premier Panel Company 734 427-1700
12300 Merriman Rd Livonia (48150) ***(G-9897)***
Premier Promotions, Saint Joseph *Also called Twin City Engraving Company* ***(G-14346)***
Premier Prototype Inc 586 323-6114
7775 18 1/2 Mile Rd Sterling Heights (48314) ***(G-15450)***
Premier Software Inc 616 940-8601
3501 Lake Dr Se Ste 140 Grand Rapids (49546) ***(G-6769)***
Premier Software Systems, Grand Rapids *Also called Premier Software Inc* ***(G-6769)***
Premier Sound, Troy *Also called Audio Technologies Inc* ***(G-16229)***
Premier Tooling Systems, Grand Blanc *Also called Selmuro Ltd* ***(G-5983)***
Premiere Packaging Inc (PA) 810 239-7650
6220 Lehman Dr Flint (48507) ***(G-5483)***
Premiere Tool & Die Cast 269 782-3030
6146 W Main St Ste C Kalamazoo (49009) ***(G-8861)***
Premium Air Systems Inc 248 680-8800
1051 Naughton Dr Troy (48083) ***(G-16562)***
Premium Machine & Tool Inc 989 855-3326
207 Water St Lyons (48851) ***(G-10095)***
Premiums Plus More 734 485-2423
2080 Whittaker Rd 222 Ypsilanti (48197) ***(G-18095)***
Prenovo, Ann Arbor *Also called Prehab Technologies LLC* ***(G-602)***
Prepress Services, Traverse City *Also called Johnson-Clark Printers Inc* ***(G-16014)***
Prescott Products Inc (HQ) 517 787-8172
2620 Saradan Dr Jackson (49202) ***(G-8556)***
Presidium Energy LLC 231 933-6373
3760 N Us Highway 31 S B Traverse City (49684) ***(G-16076)***
Presque Isle Newspapers Inc 989 734-2105
104 S 3rd St Rogers City (49779) ***(G-13621)***
Press On Juice 231 409-9971
305 Knollwood Dr Traverse City (49686) ***(G-16077)***
Press Play LLC 248 802-3837
2123 Willot Rd Auburn Hills (48326) ***(G-980)***
Press Room Eqp Sls & Svc Co 248 334-1880
244 W Sheffield Ave Pontiac (48340) ***(G-12857)***
Press-Way Inc 586 790-3324
19101 15 Mile Rd Clinton Township (48035) ***(G-3201)***
Presscraft Papers Inc 231 882-5505
5140 River Rd Benzonia (49616) ***(G-1576)***
Pressed Paperboard Tech LLC 248 646-6500
30400 Telg Rd Ste 386 Bingham Farms (48025) ***(G-1658)***
Pressing Point 810 387-3441
8870 Arendt Rd Brockway (48097) ***(G-2020)***
Pressure Releases Corporation (PA) 616 531-8116
2035 Porter St Sw Grand Rapids (49519) ***(G-6770)***

ALPHABETIC SECTION

Pressure Vessel Service Inc (PA)......................................313 921-1200
10900 Harper Ave Detroit (48213) *(G-4310)*

Pressweld Manufacturing Co......................................734 675-8282
11290 Charlotte Hwy Portland (48875) *(G-13066)*

Prest Sales Co......................................586 566-6900
14963 Park View Ct Sterling Heights (48313) *(G-15451)*

Prestige Advance, Madison Heights Also called Prestige Engrg Rsrces Tech Inc *(G-10336)*

Prestige Advanced Inc......................................586 868-4000
30031 Stephenson Hwy Madison Heights (48071) *(G-10335)*

Prestige Engrg Rsrces Tech Inc (PA)......................................586 573-3070
24700 Capital Blvd Clinton Township (48036) *(G-3202)*

Prestige Engrg Rsrces Tech Inc......................................586 573-3070
30031 Stephenson Hwy Madison Heights (48071) *(G-10336)*

Prestige Pet Products Inc......................................248 615-1526
30410 Balewood St Southfield (48076) *(G-15003)*

Prestige Printing Inc......................................616 532-5133
4437 Eastern Ave Se Ste 1 Grand Rapids (49508) *(G-6771)*

Prestige Stamping LLC......................................586 773-2700
23513 Groesbeck Hwy Warren (48089) *(G-17196)*

Prestige Warehouse & Assembly......................................586 777-1820
26155 Groesbeck Hwy Warren (48089) *(G-17197)*

Presto Print Inc......................................616 364-7132
3409 Plainfield Ave Ne Grand Rapids (49525) *(G-6772)*

Prestolite Electric LLC (HQ)......................................248 313-3807
30120 Hudson Dr Novi (48377) *(G-11978)*

Prestolite Electric Holding......................................248 313-3807
30120 Hudson Dr Novi (48377) *(G-11979)*

Prestolite Electric Inc (HQ)......................................866 463-7078
30120 Hudson Dr Novi (48377) *(G-11980)*

Prestolite International Holdg, Novi Also called Prestolite Electric Holding *(G-11979)*

Prestolite Wire LLC (HQ)......................................248 355-4422
200 Galleria Officentre Southfield (48034) *(G-15004)*

Prestwick Group LLP......................................248 360-6113
4057 Pioneer Dr Commerce Township (48390) *(G-3442)*

Preusser Jewelers......................................616 458-1425
125 Ottawa Ave Nw Ste 195 Grand Rapids (49503) *(G-6773)*

Pribusin Inc......................................734 677-0459
3938 Trade Center Dr Ann Arbor (48108) *(G-603)*

Pride Printing Inc......................................906 228-8182
2847 Us Highway 41 W Marquette (49855) *(G-10554)*

Pride Source Corporation......................................734 293-7200
20222 Farmington Rd Livonia (48152) *(G-9898)*

Pridgeon & Clay Inc (PA)......................................616 241-5675
50 Cottage Grove St Sw Grand Rapids (49507) *(G-6774)*

Prima Technologies Inc......................................586 759-0250
24837 Sherwood Center Line (48015) *(G-2582)*

Prima Welding & Experimental......................................586 415-8873
31000 Fraser Dr Fraser (48026) *(G-5709)*

Primary Tool & Cutter Grinding......................................248 588-1530
32388 Edward Ave Madison Heights (48071) *(G-10337)*

Prime Assemblies Inc......................................906 875-6420
2525 Us Highway 2 Crystal Falls (49920) *(G-3612)*

Prime Cuts of Jackson LLC......................................517 768-8090
1821 Horton Rd Jackson (49203) *(G-8557)*

Prime Industries Inc......................................734 946-8588
12350 Universal Dr Taylor (48180) *(G-15756)*

Prime Mold LLC......................................586 221-2512
44645 Macomb Indus Dr Clinton Township (48036) *(G-3203)*

Prime Products Inc......................................616 531-8970
2755 Remico St Sw Grand Rapids (49519) *(G-6775)*

Prime Solution Inc......................................269 694-6666
610 S Platt St Otsego (49078) *(G-12253)*

Prime Technologies, Novi Also called Kubica Corp *(G-11922)*

Prime Wheel Corporation......................................248 207-4739
6250 N Haggerty Rd Canton (48187) *(G-2418)*

Prime Wood Products Inc (PA)......................................616 399-4700
308 N River Ave Holland (49424) *(G-7775)*

Primera Pathways, Zeeland Also called Primera Plastics Inc *(G-18177)*

Primera Plastics Inc (PA)......................................616 748-6248
3424 Production Ct Zeeland (49464) *(G-18177)*

Primetals Technologies USA LLC......................................269 927-3591
470 Paw Paw Ave Benton Harbor (49022) *(G-1539)*

Primeway Inc......................................248 583-6922
4250 Normandy Ct Royal Oak (48073) *(G-13958)*

Primo Crafts......................................248 373-3229
1304 University Dr Pontiac (48342) *(G-12858)*

Primo Tool & Manufacturing......................................231 592-5262
20070 19 Mile Rd Big Rapids (49307) *(G-1643)*

Primore Inc (PA)......................................517 263-2220
2300 W Beecher Rd Adrian (49221) *(G-87)*

Primore Inc......................................517 263-2220
2304 W Beecher Rd Adrian (49221) *(G-88)*

Principal Diamond Works......................................248 589-1111
32750 Townley St Madison Heights (48071) *(G-10338)*

Print All......................................586 430-4383
69347 N Main St Richmond (48062) *(G-13268)*

Print Express Office Products, Saginaw Also called Hawk Design Inc *(G-14055)*

Print Haus......................................616 786-4030
295 120th Ave Ste 10 Holland (49424) *(G-7776)*

Print House Inc......................................248 473-1414
23014 Commerce Dr Farmington Hills (48335) *(G-5100)*

Print Masters Inc......................................248 548-7100
26039 Dequindre Rd Madison Heights (48071) *(G-10339)*

Print Masters Printing Co, Madison Heights Also called Print Masters Inc *(G-10339)*

Print Max, Troy Also called BCI Group Inc *(G-16234)*

Print Metro, Cedar Springs Also called Practical Paper Inc *(G-2559)*

Print Metro Inc......................................616 887-1723
98 E Division St Sparta (49345) *(G-15106)*

Print n go......................................989 362-6041
1769 E Us 23 East Tawas (48730) *(G-4694)*

Print Plus Inc......................................586 888-8000
28324 Elmdale St Saint Clair Shores (48081) *(G-14268)*

Print Shop......................................231 347-2000
324 Michigan St Petoskey (49770) *(G-12471)*

Print Shop 4u LLC......................................810 721-7500
110 N Almont Ave Imlay City (48444) *(G-8211)*

Print Shop, The, Imlay City Also called Print Shop 4u LLC *(G-8211)*

Print Shop, The, Houghton Also called Litsenberger Print Shop *(G-7976)*

Print Shop, The, Saginaw Also called Gombar Corp *(G-14048)*

Print Shop, The, Clarkston Also called G G & D Inc *(G-2924)*

Print Shop, The, Kalkaska Also called Michael Niederpruem *(G-8951)*

Print Tech Printing Place Inc......................................989 772-6109
1610 W Lyons St Mount Pleasant (48858) *(G-11221)*

Print Xpress......................................313 886-6850
20373 Mack Ave Grosse Pointe Woods (48236) *(G-7208)*

Print-Tech Inc......................................734 996-2345
6800 Jackson Rd Ann Arbor (48103) *(G-604)*

Printastic LLC......................................248 761-5697
46555 Humboldt Dr Ste 200 Novi (48377) *(G-11981)*

Printcomm Inc (PA)......................................810 239-5763
2929 Davison Rd Flint (48506) *(G-5484)*

Printed Impressions Inc......................................248 473-5333
32210 W 8 Mile Rd Farmington Hills (48336) *(G-5101)*

Printek Inc (PA)......................................269 925-3200
3515 Lakeshore Dr Ste 1 Saint Joseph (49085) *(G-14336)*

Printer Ink Warehousecom LLC......................................269 649-5492
109 E Prairie St Vicksburg (49097) *(G-16841)*

Printer Source Plus, Jackson Also called Psp Office Solutions LLC *(G-8558)*

Printery Inc......................................616 396-4655
79 Clover St Holland (49423) *(G-7777)*

Printex Printing & Graphics......................................269 629-0122
8988 E D Ave Richland (49083) *(G-13253)*

Printing & Auxiliary Services, Ann Arbor Also called Regents of The University Mich *(G-615)*

Printing Buying Service......................................586 907-2011
28108 Roy St Saint Clair Shores (48081) *(G-14269)*

Printing Buying Services, Saint Clair Shores Also called Printing Buying Service *(G-14269)*

Printing By Marc......................................248 355-0848
25960 Franklin Pointe Dr Southfield (48034) *(G-15005)*

Printing Centre Inc......................................517 694-2400
1900 Cedar St Holt (48842) *(G-7922)*

Printing Consolidation Co LLC (PA)......................................616 233-3161
190 Monroe Ave Nw Ste 600 Grand Rapids (49503) *(G-6776)*

Printing Cylinders Inc......................................586 791-5231
22045 Olson St Clinton Township (48035) *(G-3204)*

Printing Industries of Mich......................................248 946-5895
41300 Beacon Rd Novi (48375) *(G-11982)*

Printing Perspectives LLC......................................810 410-8186
1916 Owen St Flint (48503) *(G-5485)*

Printing Place, The, Traverse City Also called Copy Central Inc *(G-15947)*

Printing Plus Inc......................................734 482-1680
989 James L Hart Pkwy Ypsilanti (48197) *(G-18096)*

Printing Productions Ink......................................616 871-9292
3852 44th St Se Grand Rapids (49512) *(G-6777)*

Printing Service Inc......................................586 718-4103
7257 Parklane Dr Clay (48001) *(G-3001)*

Printing Services......................................269 321-9826
8815 S Sprinkle Rd Portage (49002) *(G-13024)*

Printing Services Inc......................................734 944-1404
1283 Industrial Dr Saline (48176) *(G-14409)*

Printing Systems Inc......................................734 946-5111
12005 Beech Daly Rd Taylor (48180) *(G-15757)*

Printlink Short Run......................................269 965-1336
309 Fritz Keiper Blvd Battle Creek (49037) *(G-1237)*

Printmasters, Cadillac Also called William C Fox Enterprises Inc *(G-2286)*

Printmill Inc......................................269 382-0428
4001 Portage St Kalamazoo (49001) *(G-8862)*

Printwand Inc......................................248 738-7225
22 W Huron St Pontiac (48342) *(G-12859)*

Printwell Acquisition Co Inc......................................734 941-6300
26975 Northline Rd Taylor (48180) *(G-15758)*

Printwell Printing, Taylor Also called Printwell Acquisition Co Inc *(G-15758)*

Printxpress Inc......................................313 846-1644
7120 Chase Rd Dearborn (48126) *(G-3751)*

Priorat Importers Corporation......................................248 217-4608
815 Baldwin Ave Royal Oak (48067) *(G-13959)*

Priority One Emergency Inc......................................734 398-5900
5755 Belleville Rd Canton (48188) *(G-2419)*

Priority Tool Inc — 616 847-1337
 1650 Marion Ave Grand Haven (49417) *(G-6064)*
Priority Waste LLC — 586 228-1200
 42822 Garfield Rd Clinton Township (48038) *(G-3205)*
Prism, Port Huron Also called Jgr Plastics LLC *(G-12932)*
Prism Plastics Inc (HQ) — 810 292-6300
 52111 Sierra Dr Chesterfield (48047) *(G-2821)*
Prism Plastics Inc — 810 292-6300
 50581 Sabrina Dr Shelby Township (48315) *(G-14671)*
Prism Printing — 586 786-1250
 51168 Milano Dr Macomb (48042) *(G-10157)*
Prism Publications Inc — 231 941-8174
 125 S Park St Ste 155 Traverse City (49684) *(G-16078)*
Pristine Glass Company — 616 454-2092
 647 Ottawa Ave Nw Grand Rapids (49503) *(G-6778)*
Pritech Corporation — 248 488-9120
 46036 Michigan Ave # 188 Canton (48188) *(G-2420)*
Pro - Tech Graphics Ltd — 586 791-6363
 34851 Groesbeck Hwy Clinton Township (48035) *(G-3206)*
Pro Body, Holland Also called Autoform Development Inc *(G-7561)*
Pro Bottle LLC — 248 345-9224
 805 Linn Rd Williamston (48895) *(G-17737)*
Pro Coatings Inc — 616 887-8808
 233 1/2 Prospect St Sparta (49345) *(G-15107)*
Pro Connections LLC — 269 962-4219
 4550 Wayne Rd Springfield (49037) *(G-15201)*
Pro Floor Service — 517 663-5012
 11636 Columbia Hwy Eaton Rapids (48827) *(G-4730)*
Pro Image Design — 231 322-8052
 331 W South Airport Rd Traverse City (49686) *(G-16079)*
Pro Lighting Group Inc — 810 229-5600
 716 Advance St Ste A Brighton (48116) *(G-1980)*
Pro Polymers Inc — 734 222-8820
 4974 Bird Dr Stockbridge (49285) *(G-15592)*
Pro Precision Inc — 586 247-6160
 14178 Randall Dr Sterling Heights (48313) *(G-15452)*
Pro Release Inc — 810 512-4120
 420 S Water St 275 Marine City (48039) *(G-10480)*
Pro Sealants — 616 318-6067
 3683 Maplebrook Dr Nw Grand Rapids (49534) *(G-6779)*
Pro Search — 248 553-7700
 37761 Baywood Dr Farmington Hills (48335) *(G-5102)*
Pro Shop The/P S Graphics — 517 448-8490
 309 W Main St Hudson (49247) *(G-8139)*
Pro Slot Ltd — 616 897-6000
 12 W Main St Hartford (49057) *(G-7386)*
Pro Source Manufacturing Inc — 616 607-2990
 12880 N Cedar Dr Ste A Grand Haven (49417) *(G-6065)*
Pro Stamp Plus LLC — 616 447-2988
 1988 Alpine Ave Nw Grand Rapids (49504) *(G-6780)*
Pro Tool LLC — 616 850-0556
 14714 Indian Trails Dr Grand Haven (49417) *(G-6066)*
Pro-Built Mfg — 989 354-1321
 820 Long Lake Ave Alpena (49707) *(G-308)*
Pro-CAM Services LLC — 616 748-4200
 323 E Roosevelt Ave Zeeland (49464) *(G-18178)*
Pro-Face America LLC (HQ) — 734 477-0600
 1050 Highland Dr Ste D Ann Arbor (48108) *(G-605)*
Pro-Finish Powder Coating Inc — 616 245-7550
 1000 Kn O Sha Indus Dr Se Grand Rapids (49508) *(G-6781)*
Pro-Motion Tech Group LLC — 248 668-3100
 29755 Beck Rd Wixom (48393) *(G-17880)*
Pro-Powersports — 734 457-0829
 7779 Townway Dr Monroe (48161) *(G-11063)*
Pro-Soil Site Services Inc — 517 267-8767
 3323 N East St Lansing (48906) *(G-9260)*
Pro-Tech Machine Inc — 810 743-1854
 3085 Joyce St Burton (48529) *(G-2161)*
Pro-Vision Solutions LLC — 616 583-1520
 8625b Byron Cmmerce Dr Sw Byron Center (49315) *(G-2209)*
Pro-Vision Video Systems, Byron Center Also called Pro-Vision Solutions LLC *(G-2209)*
Pro-Weld, Chesterfield Also called Camryn Fabrication LLC *(G-2751)*
Probe-TEC — 765 252-0257
 48454 Harbor Dr Chesterfield (48047) *(G-2822)*
Probotic Services LLC — 586 524-9589
 17920 Country Club Dr Macomb (48042) *(G-10158)*
Probus Technical Services Inc — 876 226-5692
 2424 Crooks Rd Apt 21 Troy (48084) *(G-16563)*
Procal, Alpena Also called Punching Concepts Inc *(G-309)*
Process Partners Inc — 616 875-2156
 3770 Chicago Dr Hudsonville (49426) *(G-8174)*
Process Systems Inc (HQ) — 586 757-5711
 23633 Pinewood St Warren (48091) *(G-17198)*
Process Technology & Controls, Novi Also called Venture Technology Groups Inc *(G-12025)*
Prochimir Inc — 248 457-4538
 200 E Big Beaver Rd Mi Troy (48083) *(G-16564)*
Procraft Custom Builder — 586 323-1605
 901 Markwood Dr Oxford (48370) *(G-12364)*
Proctor Logging Inc — 231 775-3820
 298 Bramblewood Cadillac (49601) *(G-2272)*

Product and Tooling Tech Inc — 586 293-1810
 33222 Groesbeck Hwy Fraser (48026) *(G-5710)*
Product Assembly Group LLC — 586 549-8601
 1080 Naughton Dr Troy (48083) *(G-16565)*
Product Resource Company — 517 484-8400
 2220 Raymond Dr Lansing (48906) *(G-9261)*
Product Saver, Holland Also called General Processing Systems Inc *(G-7640)*
Production & Prototype Svc LLC — 586 924-7479
 35820 31 Mile Rd Lenox (48050) *(G-9523)*
Production Accessories Co — 313 366-1500
 123 E Golden Gate Detroit (48203) *(G-4311)*
Production Dev Systems LLC — 810 648-2111
 245 Campbell Rd Sandusky (48471) *(G-14441)*
Production Fabricators Inc — 231 777-3822
 1608 Creston St Muskegon (49442) *(G-11407)*
Production Honing Company Inc — 586 757-1800
 24101 Wahl St Warren (48089) *(G-17199)*
Production Industries II Inc — 231 352-7500
 3535 Rennie School Rd Traverse City (49685) *(G-16080)*
Production Machining of Alma — 989 463-1495
 6595 N Jerome Rd Alma (48801) *(G-247)*
Production Saw & Machine Co — 517 529-4014
 9091 S Meridian Rd Clarklake (49234) *(G-2898)*
Production Spring LLC — 248 583-0036
 1151 Allen Dr Troy (48083) *(G-16566)*
Production Threaded Parts Co — 810 688-3186
 6829 Lincoln St North Branch (48461) *(G-11665)*
Production Tooling Inc — 269 668-6789
 23650 French Rd Mattawan (49071) *(G-10667)*
Production Tube Company Inc — 313 259-3990
 481 Beaufait St Detroit (48207) *(G-4312)*
Productivity Technologies (PA) — 810 714-0200
 3100 Copper Ave Fenton (48430) *(G-5231)*
Products Engineered Daley — 616 748-0162
 913 Mid Bluff Dr Zeeland (49464) *(G-18179)*
Profab, Muskegon Also called Production Fabricators Inc *(G-11407)*
Proface America, Ann Arbor Also called Pro-Face America LLC *(G-605)*
Professional Fabricating Inc — 616 531-1240
 902 47th St Sw Ste A Grand Rapids (49509) *(G-6782)*
Professional Fabricating & Mfg, Grand Rapids Also called Professional Fabricating Inc *(G-6782)*
Professional Instant Printing — 248 335-1117
 949 W Huron St Waterford (48328) *(G-17372)*
Professional Metal Finishers — 616 365-2620
 2474 Turner Ave Nw Ste 4 Grand Rapids (49544) *(G-6783)*
Professional Metal Works Inc — 517 351-7411
 8109 Old M 78 Haslett (48840) *(G-7398)*
Professional Rug Works Inc — 248 577-1400
 1020 Livernois Rd Troy (48083) *(G-16567)*
Professional Sftwr Assoc Inc — 727 724-0000
 2517 Imlay City Rd Lapeer (48446) *(G-9482)*
Proficient Machine & Tool, Byron Center Also called McDonald Acquisitions LLC *(G-2198)*
Proficient Machining Inc — 616 453-9496
 3455 3 Mile Rd Nw Grand Rapids (49534) *(G-6784)*
Proficient Products Inc — 586 977-8630
 6283 Millett Ave Sterling Heights (48312) *(G-15453)*
Profile EDM LLC — 586 949-4586
 50571 E Rssll Schmdt Blvd Chesterfield (48051) *(G-2823)*
Profile Films, Grand Rapids Also called Profile Industrial Packg Corp *(G-6785)*
Profile Gear Inc — 810 324-2731
 4777 Brott Rd North Street (48049) *(G-11668)*
Profile Inc — 517 224-8012
 345 Wright Indus Pkwy Potterville (48876) *(G-13075)*
Profile Industrial Packg Corp — 616 245-7260
 1976 Avastar Pkwy Nw Grand Rapids (49544) *(G-6785)*
Profile Mfg Inc — 586 598-0007
 50790 Richard W Blvd Chesterfield (48051) *(G-2824)*
Profile Steel and Wire, Waterford Also called Penn Automotive Inc *(G-17366)*
Profiles Magazine — 313 531-9041
 18250 Redfern St Detroit (48219) *(G-4313)*
Proforma, Williamston Also called Performance Print and Mktg *(G-17736)*
Proforma Pltnum Prtg Prmotions — 248 341-3814
 143 W Tacoma St Clawson (48017) *(G-2985)*
Programmed Products Corp — 248 348-7755
 44311 Grand River Ave Novi (48375) *(G-11983)*
Progress Chemical Inc — 616 534-6103
 3015 Dormax St Sw Grandville (49418) *(G-7067)*
Progress Custom Screen Prtg, Ferndale Also called Progress Custom Screen Prtg *(G-5314)*
Progress Custom Screen Prtg — 248 982-4247
 364 Hilton Rd Ferndale (48220) *(G-5314)*
Progress Machine & Tool Inc — 231 798-3410
 1155 Judson Rd Norton Shores (49456) *(G-11814)*
Progress Printers Inc — 231 947-5311
 1445 Woodmere Ave Traverse City (49686) *(G-16081)*
Progressive Cabinets Inc — 810 631-4611
 112 S State Rd Otisville (48463) *(G-12234)*
Progressive Cutter Grinding Co — 586 580-2367
 14207 Rick Dr Shelby Township (48315) *(G-14672)*

Progressive Dynamics Inc 269 781-4241
507 Industrial Rd Marshall (49068) ***(G-10585)***
Progressive Finishing Inc 586 949-6961
50800 E Russell S Chesterfield (48051) ***(G-2825)***
Progressive Graphics 269 945-9249
115 S Jefferson St Hastings (49058) ***(G-7423)***
Progressive Manufacturing LLC 231 924-9975
425 Connie Ave Fremont (49412) ***(G-5783)***
Progressive Metal Mfg Co (PA) 248 546-2827
3100 E 10 Mile Rd Warren (48091) ***(G-17200)***
Progressive Panel Systems 616 748-1384
8095 Riley St Zeeland (49464) ***(G-18180)***
Progressive Paper Corp 269 279-6320
1111 3rd St Three Rivers (49093) ***(G-15875)***
PROGRESSIVE PRINTING, Plymouth *Also called Kimprint Inc* ***(G-12668)***
Progressive Prtg & Graphics 269 965-8909
148 Columbia Ave E Battle Creek (49015) ***(G-1238)***
Progressive Surface Inc (PA) 616 957-0871
4695 Danvers Dr Se Grand Rapids (49512) ***(G-6786)***
Progressive Surface Inc 616 957-0871
4671 Danvers Dr Se Grand Rapids (49512) ***(G-6787)***
Progressive Tool Machinery, Elkton *Also called Pat McArdle* ***(G-4782)***
Project Die and Mold Inc 616 862-8689
228 Wesley St Se Grand Rapids (49548) ***(G-6788)***
Prolighting, Brighton *Also called Pro Lighting Group Inc* ***(G-1980)***
Promax Engineering LLC 734 979-0888
6035 E Executive Dr Westland (48185) ***(G-17591)***
Promess Inc (PA) 810 229-9334
11429 Grand River Rd Brighton (48116) ***(G-1981)***
Promess Dimensions, Brighton *Also called Promess Inc* ***(G-1981)***
Promethient Inc 231 525-0500
2382 Cass Rd Traverse City (49684) ***(G-16082)***
Promogarden.com, Holland *Also called Walters Seed Co LLC* ***(G-7852)***
Prompt Pattern, Warren *Also called Equivalent Base Co* ***(G-17019)***
Prompt Pattern Inc 586 759-2030
4175 E 10 Mile Rd Warren (48091) ***(G-17201)***
Prompt Plastics 586 307-8525
5524 E 10 Mile Rd Warren (48091) ***(G-17202)***
Pronav Marine, Hancock *Also called Superior Marine Products LLC* ***(G-7257)***
Prong Horn 616 456-1903
6757 Cascade Rd Se # 164 Grand Rapids (49546) ***(G-6789)***
Pronghorn Imprinting Co, Grand Rapids *Also called Prong Horn* ***(G-6789)***
Proof & Union LLC 312 919-0191
605 Greenwood Ave Se Grand Rapids (49506) ***(G-6790)***
Proos Manufacturing Inc 616 454-5622
2140 Oak Industrial Dr Ne Grand Rapids (49505) ***(G-6791)***
Prop Art Studio Inc 313 824-2200
112 E Grand Blvd Detroit (48207) ***(G-4314)***
Proper Arospc & Machining LLC 586 779-8787
13870 E 11 Mile Rd Warren (48089) ***(G-17203)***
Proper Group International Inc 586 552-5267
14575 E 11 Mile Rd Warren (48088) ***(G-17204)***
Proper Group International Inc (PA) 586 779-8787
13870 E 11 Mile Rd Warren (48089) ***(G-17205)***
Proper Polymers, Warren *Also called Proper Group International Inc* ***(G-17204)***
Proper Polymers - Anderson LLC 586 408-9120
13870 E 11 Mile Rd Warren (48089) ***(G-17206)***
Proper Polymers - Warren LLC (PA) 586 552-5267
13870 E 11 Mile Rd Warren (48089) ***(G-17207)***
Proper Polymers - Warren LLC 586 552-5267
14575 E 11 Mile Rd Warren (48088) ***(G-17208)***
Proper Polymers-Pulaski LLC 931 371-3147
13870 E 11 Mile Rd Warren (48089) ***(G-17209)***
Proper Tooling, Warren *Also called Proper Group International Inc* ***(G-17205)***
Prophotonix Limited 586 778-1100
15935 Sturgeon St Roseville (48066) ***(G-13856)***
Propride Inc 810 695-1127
8538 Old Plank Rd Grand Blanc (48439) ***(G-5978)***
Propur USA, Commerce Township *Also called Lincoln-Remi Group LLC* ***(G-3421)***
Proquest Outdoor Solutions Inc 734 761-4700
789 E Eisenhower Pkwy Ann Arbor (48108) ***(G-606)***
Pros-Tech Inc 248 680-2800
1717 Stephenson Hwy Troy (48083) ***(G-16568)***
Proservice Machine Ltd 734 317-7266
10835 Telegraph Rd Erie (48133) ***(G-4809)***
Prospectors LLC 616 634-8260
5035 W Greenbrooke Dr Se # 2 Grand Rapids (49512) ***(G-6792)***
Prospectors Cold Brew Coffee, Grand Rapids *Also called Prospectors LLC* ***(G-6792)***
Prosper-Tech Machine & Tl LLC 586 727-8800
69160 Skinner Dr Richmond (48062) ***(G-13269)***
Prosthetic & Implant Dentistry 248 254-3945
31396 Northwestern Hwy Farmington Hills (48334) ***(G-5103)***
Prosthetic Center Inc 517 372-7007
7343 Dupre Ave Dimondale (48821) ***(G-4519)***
Prosys Industries Inc 734 207-3710
7666 Market Dr Canton (48187) ***(G-2421)***
Protean Electric Inc 248 504-4940
1700 Harmon Rd Ste 3 Auburn Hills (48326) ***(G-981)***
Protean Holdings Corp (PA) 248 504-4940
1700 Harmon Rd Ste 3 Auburn Hills (48326) ***(G-982)***
Protective Coating & Assoc, Bronson *Also called Hice and Summey Inc* ***(G-2030)***
Protective Coating Associates, Bronson *Also called Hice and Summey Inc* ***(G-2029)***
Protective Ctngs Epoxy Systems 517 223-1192
971 Arlene Ct Fowlerville (48836) ***(G-5577)***
Protective Land & Sea Systems, Chesterfield *Also called SL Holdings Inc* ***(G-2841)***
Protecto Horse Equipment Inc 586 754-4820
22722 Dequindre Rd Warren (48091) ***(G-17210)***
Protege Concepts Corp 248 419-5330
28230 Orchard Lake Rd # 204 Farmington Hills (48334) ***(G-5104)***
Protein Magnet Corp 616 844-1545
15450 Oak Dr Spring Lake (49456) ***(G-15171)***
Protein Procurement Svcs Inc (PA) 248 738-7970
1750 S Telg Rd Ste 310 Bloomfield Hills (48302) ***(G-1792)***
Proto Crafts Inc (PA) 810 376-3665
4740 Shabbona Rd Deckerville (48427) ***(G-3810)***
Proto Design & Manufacturing 419 346-8416
31140 Fraser Dr Fraser (48026) ***(G-5711)***
Proto Gage Inc 586 978-2783
5972 Product Dr Sterling Heights (48312) ***(G-15454)***
Proto Manufacturing Inc 734 946-0974
12350 Universal Dr Taylor (48180) ***(G-15759)***
Proto Shapes Inc 517 278-3947
125 Industrial Ave Coldwater (49036) ***(G-3321)***
Proto Spec 269 934-8615
1419 Townline Rd Benton Harbor (49022) ***(G-1540)***
Proto Tool & Gage Inc 734 487-0830
300 S Ford Blvd Ypsilanti (48198) ***(G-18097)***
Proto Tool Company 248 471-0577
29660 W 9 Mile Rd Farmington Hills (48336) ***(G-5105)***
Proto-CAM Inc 616 454-9810
1009 Ottawa Ave Nw Grand Rapids (49503) ***(G-6793)***
Proto-Cast Inc 313 565-5400
2699 John Daly St Inkster (48141) ***(G-8233)***
Proto-Form Engineering Inc 586 727-9803
10312 Gratiot Ave Columbus (48063) ***(G-3381)***
Proto-TEC Inc 616 772-9511
260 N Church St Zeeland (49464) ***(G-18181)***
Proto-Tek Manufacturing Inc 586 772-2663
16094 Common Rd Roseville (48066) ***(G-13857)***
Protocon Rm, Sterling Heights *Also called Midway Group LLC* ***(G-15423)***
Protodesign Inc 586 739-4340
50495 Corporate Dr Ste 10 Shelby Township (48315) ***(G-14673)***
Protofab Corporation 248 689-3730
2835 Daley Dr Troy (48083) ***(G-16569)***
Protojet LLC 810 956-8000
17850 E 14 Mile Rd Fraser (48026) ***(G-5712)***
Protomatic Inc 734 426-3655
2125 Bishop Cir W Dexter (48130) ***(G-4505)***
Prototech Laser Inc 586 948-3032
46340 Continental Dr Chesterfield (48047) ***(G-2826)***
Prototech Laser Inc (PA) 586 598-6900
46340 Continental Dr Chesterfield (48047) ***(G-2827)***
Prototype Cast Mfg Inc (PA) 586 739-0180
51292 Danview Tech Ct Shelby Township (48315) ***(G-14674)***
Prototype Cast Mfg Inc 586 615-8524
42872 Mound Rd Sterling Heights (48314) ***(G-15455)***
Prototypes Plus Inc 269 751-7141
3537 Lincoln Rd Hamilton (49419) ***(G-7238)***
Protxs Inc (PA) 989 255-3836
7974 Parkside Ct Jenison (49428) ***(G-8638)***
Providence Worldwide LLC 313 586-4144
39005 Webb Dr Westland (48185) ***(G-17592)***
Prs Manufacturing Inc 616 784-4409
3745 Dykstra Dr Nw Grand Rapids (49544) ***(G-6794)***
PS & T, Jackson *Also called Plating Systems and Tech Inc* ***(G-8554)***
Psa, Lapeer *Also called Professional Sftwr Assoc Inc* ***(G-9482)***
PSC Industrial Outsourcing LP 313 824-5859
515 Lycaste St Detroit (48214) ***(G-4315)***
Psg Dover, Grand Rapids *Also called Blackmer* ***(G-6229)***
PSI, Plymouth *Also called Phillips Service Inds Inc* ***(G-12714)***
PSI Automotive Support Group, Sterling Heights *Also called Photographic Support Inc* ***(G-15445)***
PSI Holding Company (PA) 248 437-4174
8080 Kensington Ct Brighton (48116) ***(G-1982)***
PSI Hydraulics 734 261-4160
14492 N Sheldon Rd # 374 Plymouth (48170) ***(G-12725)***
PSI Labs 734 369-6273
3970 Varsity Dr Ann Arbor (48108) ***(G-607)***
PSI Marine Inc 989 695-2646
3075 Shattuck Rd Ste 801 Saginaw (48603) ***(G-14126)***
PSI Repair Services Inc (HQ) 734 853-5000
11900 Mayfield St Livonia (48150) ***(G-9899)***
PSI Satellite, Alger *Also called Zk Enterprises Inc* ***(G-140)***
PSI Semicon Services, Livonia *Also called PSI Repair Services Inc* ***(G-9899)***
Psp Office Solutions LLC 517 817-0680
1737 Spring Arbor Rd # 219 Jackson (49203) ***(G-8558)***

ALPHABETIC

Pt Tech Stamping Inc 586 293-1810
33222 Groesbeck Hwy Fraser (48026) **(G-5713)**
Pt Woody, Mount Clemens *Also called Auto-Tech Plastics Inc* **(G-11124)**
PT&t Precise Machining LLC 517 748-9325
325 Watts Rd Jackson (49203) **(G-8559)**
PT&t Properties, Jackson *Also called PT&t Precise Machining LLC* **(G-8559)**
Pti Engineered Plastics Inc 586 263-5100
50900 Corporate Dr Macomb (48044) **(G-10159)**
Pti International, Wixom *Also called Minth North America Inc* **(G-17856)**
PTL Engineering Inc 810 664-2310
3333 John Conley Dr # 2 Lapeer (48446) **(G-9483)**
Ptm-Electronics Inc 248 987-4446
39205 Country Club Dr C40 Farmington Hills (48331) **(G-5106)**
Ptspower LLC 734 268-6076
10000 Stnchfield Woods Rd Pinckney (48169) **(G-12503)**
Public Works Dept, Taylor *Also called City of Taylor* **(G-15700)**
Pubsof Chicago LLC 312 448-8282
1766 Lake Pointe Dr Traverse City (49686) **(G-16083)**
Puff Baby LLC 734 620-9991
6250 Middlebelt Rd Garden City (48135) **(G-5835)**
Pull Our Own Weight 313 686-4685
12811 Ardmore St Detroit (48227) **(G-4316)**
Pull-Buoy Inc 586 997-0900
6515 Cotter Ave Sterling Heights (48314) **(G-15456)**
Pullman Company (HQ) 734 243-8000
1 International Dr Monroe (48161) **(G-11064)**
Pulpwood & Forestry Products 231 788-3088
131 S Maple Island Rd Muskegon (49442) **(G-11408)**
Pulverdryer Usa LLC 269 552-5290
126 Avenue C Springfield (49037) **(G-15202)**
Pummill Print Services Lc 616 785-7960
960 W River Center Dr Ne Comstock Park (49321) **(G-3510)**
Pump House 616 647-5481
2090 Celebration Dr Ne # 120 Grand Rapids (49525) **(G-6795)**
Pump Solutions Group 616 241-1611
1809 Century Ave Sw Grand Rapids (49503) **(G-6796)**
Pump Solutions Group 616 241-1611
1809 Century Ave Sw Grand Rapids (49503) **(G-6797)**
Punati Chemical Corp 248 276-0101
1160 N Opdyke Rd Auburn Hills (48326) **(G-983)**
Punch Tech 810 364-4811
2701 Busha Hwy Marysville (48040) **(G-10612)**
Punchcraft McHning Tooling LLC 586 573-4840
30500 Ryan Rd Warren (48092) **(G-17211)**
Punching Concepts Inc 989 358-7070
3810 Us Highway 23 N Alpena (49707) **(G-309)**
Punkin Dsign Seds Orgnlity LLC 313 347-8488
633 Burlingame St Detroit (48202) **(G-4317)**
Pur E Clat 313 208-5763
27640 Gateway Dr E C106 Farmington Hills (48334) **(G-5107)**
Pure & Simple Solutions LLC 248 398-4600
1187 Souter Dr Troy (48083) **(G-16570)**
Pure Herbs Ltd 586 446-8200
33410 Sterling Ponds Blvd Sterling Heights (48312) **(G-15457)**
Pure Liberty Manufacturing LLC 734 224-0333
7075 Schnipke Dr Ottawa Lake (49267) **(G-12269)**
Pure Products International In 989 471-1104
11925 Us Highway 23 S Ossineke (49766) **(G-12231)**
Pure Pulp Products Inc 269 385-5050
600 Plastics Pl Kalamazoo (49001) **(G-8863)**
Pure Virtual Studios LLC (PA) 248 250-4070
24281 Ridgedale St Oak Park (48237) **(G-12091)**
Pure Water Tech of Mid-MI (PA) 888 310-9848
8173 Embury Rd Grand Blanc (48439) **(G-5979)**
Pureflex Inc 616 554-1100
4855 Broadmoor Ave Se Kentwood (49512) **(G-9026)**
Purforms Inc 616 897-3000
615 Chatham St Ste 1 Lowell (49331) **(G-10041)**
Purina Mills LLC 517 322-0200
5620 Millett Hwy Lansing (48917) **(G-9319)**
Puritan Automation LLC 248 668-1114
28389 Beck Rd Ste J2 Wixom (48393) **(G-17881)**
Puritan Magnetics Inc 248 628-3808
533 S Lapeer Rd Ste C Oxford (48371) **(G-12365)**
Purity Cylinder Gases Inc 517 321-9555
1035 Mak Tech Dr Ste A Lansing (48906) **(G-9262)**
Purity Foods Inc 517 448-7440
417 S Meridian Rd Hudson (49247) **(G-8140)**
Puroclean Restoration Services, Washington *Also called Marceau Enterprises Inc* **(G-17307)**
Purple Cow Creamery 616 494-1933
234 Charles St Holland (49424) **(G-7778)**
Pushard Welding LLC 269 760-9611
25222 Red Arrow Hwy Mattawan (49071) **(G-10668)**
Pushman Manufacturing Co Inc 810 629-9688
1044 Grant St Fenton (48430) **(G-5232)**
Putnam Cabinetry 248 442-0118
29233 Scotten St Farmington Hills (48336) **(G-5108)**
Putnam Machine Products Inc 517 278-2364
35 Cecil Dr Coldwater (49036) **(G-3322)**

Puzzleman Toys, The, Chesaning *Also called Charlies Wood Shop* **(G-2722)**
Pvh Corp 989 624-5575
8925 Market Place Dr # 450 Birch Run (48415) **(G-1667)**
Pvh Corp 989 345-7939
2990 Cook Rd Ste 104 West Branch (48661) **(G-17517)**
Pvh Corp 989 624-5651
12245 S Beyer Rd Ste A060 Birch Run (48415) **(G-1668)**
PVS Chemical Solutions Inc (HQ) 313 921-1200
10900 Harper Ave Detroit (48213) **(G-4318)**
PVS Chemicals, Detroit *Also called Pressure Vessel Service Inc* **(G-4310)**
PVS Chemicals, Inc. Illinois, Detroit *Also called PVS Chemical Solutions Inc* **(G-4318)**
PVS Holdings Inc (HQ) 313 921-1200
10900 Harper Ave Detroit (48213) **(G-4319)**
Pvs-Nolwood Chemicals Inc (HQ) 313 921-1200
10900 Harper Ave Detroit (48213) **(G-4320)**
Pwgg 989 506-9402
1040 Pueblo Pass Weidman (48893) **(G-17461)**
Pwr-Arm, Cassopolis *Also called Schwintek Inc* **(G-2535)**
Pwv Studios Ltd 616 361-5659
1650 Broadway Ave Nw Grand Rapids (49504) **(G-6798)**
Pyper Products Corporation, Battle Creek *Also called Systex Products Corporation* **(G-1257)**
Pyramid Paving and Contg Co (PA) 989 895-5861
600 N Jefferson St Bay City (48708) **(G-1343)**
Pyramid Paving Co, Bay City *Also called Pyramid Paving and Contg Co* **(G-1343)**
Pyramid Tool Company Inc 248 549-0602
4512 Fernlee Ave Royal Oak (48073) **(G-13960)**
Pyramid Tubular Tech Inc 810 732-6335
3214 S Dye Rd Ste C Flint (48507) **(G-5486)**
Pyrinas LLC 810 422-7535
10574 Waterford Rd Traverse City (49684) **(G-16084)**
Pyro Service Company 248 547-2552
25812 John R Rd Madison Heights (48071) **(G-10340)**
Pyxis Technologies LLC 734 414-0261
45911 Port St Plymouth (48170) **(G-12726)**
Q C I, Ann Arbor *Also called Quad City Innovations LLC* **(G-610)**
Q M E Inc 269 422-2137
9070 First St Baroda (49101) **(G-1129)**
Q M I, Madison Heights *Also called Qmi Group Inc* **(G-10342)**
Q P S Printing, Ypsilanti *Also called Printing Plus Inc* **(G-18096)**
Q-Photonics LLC 734 477-0133
3830 Packard St Ste 170 Ann Arbor (48108) **(G-608)**
Qc American LLC 734 961-0300
575 S Mansfield St Ypsilanti (48197) **(G-18098)**
Qc Tech LLC 248 597-3984
1605 E Avis Dr Madison Heights (48071) **(G-10341)**
Qcr Tech, Madison Heights *Also called Qc Tech LLC* **(G-10341)**
Qdc Plastics, Lansing *Also called Quality Dairy Company* **(G-9416)**
Qe, Walker *Also called Quality Edge Inc* **(G-16877)**
Qe Tools LLC 734 330-4707
417 8th St Ann Arbor (48103) **(G-609)**
QEd Envmtl Systems Inc 734 995-2547
2355 Bishop Cir W Dexter (48130) **(G-4506)**
Qfd Recycling 810 733-2335
4450 Linden Creek Pkwy Flint (48507) **(G-5487)**
Qg LLC 989 496-3333
1700 James Savage Rd Midland (48642) **(G-10904)**
Qmi Group Inc 248 589-0505
1645 E Avis Dr Madison Heights (48071) **(G-10342)**
Qp Acquisition 2 Inc 248 594-7432
2000 Town Ctr Ste 2450 Southfield (48075) **(G-15006)**
Qps Printing, Ann Arbor *Also called K & S Printing Centers Inc* **(G-514)**
Qrp Inc (PA) 989 496-2955
94 Ashman Cir Midland (48640) **(G-10905)**
Qrp Inc 989 496-2955
3000 James Savage Rd Midland (48642) **(G-10906)**
Qsdg Manufacturing LLC 231 941-1222
1576 International Dr Traverse City (49686) **(G-16085)**
Qsr Outdoor Products Inc 989 354-0777
600 W Campbell St Alpena (49707) **(G-310)**
Qsti, Coldwater *Also called Quality Spring/Togo Inc* **(G-3323)**
Qsv Pharma LLC 269 324-2358
3585 Bellflower Dr Portage (49024) **(G-13025)**
Qts, Muskegon *Also called Quality Tool & Stamping Co Inc* **(G-11410)**
Quad City Innovations LLC 513 200-6980
600 S Wagner Rd Ann Arbor (48103) **(G-610)**
Quad Electronics Inc (PA) 800 969-9220
359 Robbins Dr Troy (48083) **(G-16571)**
Quad Precision Tool Co Inc 248 608-2400
1763 W Hamlin Rd Rochester Hills (48309) **(G-13499)**
Quad/Graphics Inc 248 637-9950
3250 W Big Beaver Rd # 127 Troy (48084) **(G-16572)**
Quad/Graphics Inc 989 698-5598
1700 James Savage Rd Midland (48642) **(G-10907)**
Quad/Graphics Inc 616 754-3672
1321 E Van Deinse St Greenville (48838) **(G-7150)**
Quadra Manufacturing Inc (PA) 269 483-9633
305 Us Highway 131 S White Pigeon (49099) **(G-17655)**

Quaker Chemical Corporation....313 931-6910
14301 Birwood St Detroit (48238) ***(G-4321)***
Quaker Chemical Corporation....586 826-6454
41111 Van Dyke Ave Sterling Heights (48314) ***(G-15458)***
Qualcomm Incorporated....248 853-2017
359 Jonathan Dr Rochester Hills (48307) ***(G-13500)***
Quali Tone Corporation....269 426-3664
13092 Red Arrow Hwy Sawyer (49125) ***(G-14487)***
Quali Tone Pwdr Cating Sndblst, Sawyer *Also called Quali Tone Corporation* ***(G-14487)***
Qualite Inc....517 439-4316
215 W Mechanic St Hillsdale (49242) ***(G-7535)***
Qualite Sports Lighting, Hillsdale *Also called Qualite Inc* ***(G-7535)***
Quality Alum Acquisition LLC....734 783-0990
14544 Telegraph Rd Ste 1 Flat Rock (48134) ***(G-5359)***
Quality Alum Acquisition LLC (PA)....800 550-1667
429 S Michigan Ave Hastings (49058) ***(G-7424)***
Quality Assured Plastics Inc....269 674-3888
1200 Crandall Pkwy Lawrence (49064) ***(G-9506)***
Quality Awning Shops Inc....517 882-2491
4512 S Martin Luther King Lansing (48910) ***(G-9415)***
Quality Bending Threading Inc....313 898-5100
5100 Stanton St Detroit (48208) ***(G-4322)***
Quality Cabinets, Ann Arbor *Also called Masco Cabinetry LLC* ***(G-548)***
Quality Castings Co....269 349-7449
903 Hotop Ave Kalamazoo (49048) ***(G-8864)***
Quality Cavity Inc....248 344-9995
47955 Anna Ct Wixom (48393) ***(G-17882)***
Quality Chaser Co Div, Romeo *Also called Mc Pherson Industrial Corp* ***(G-13633)***
Quality Clutches Inc....734 782-0783
3966 Dauncy Rd Flat Rock (48134) ***(G-5360)***
Quality Container, Ypsilanti *Also called Alpha Packaging Michigan Inc* ***(G-18050)***
Quality Cylinder Service....269 345-0699
106 W Mosel Ave Kalamazoo (49004) ***(G-8865)***
Quality Dairy Company....517 319-4302
111 W Mount Hope Ave 3a Lansing (48910) ***(G-9416)***
Quality Dairy Company....517 367-2400
1400 S Washington Ave Lansing (48910) ***(G-9417)***
Quality Door & More Inc....989 317-8314
1102 Packard Rd Ste B Mount Pleasant (48858) ***(G-11222)***
Quality Edge Inc (HQ)....616 735-3833
2712 Walkent Dr Nw Walker (49544) ***(G-16877)***
Quality Engineering Company....248 351-9000
30194 S Wixom Rd Wixom (48393) ***(G-17883)***
Quality Engraving Service....269 781-4822
221 W Michigan Ave Marshall (49068) ***(G-10586)***
Quality Eqp Installations....616 249-3649
3404 Busch Dr Sw Ste A Grandville (49418) ***(G-7068)***
Quality Fabg & Erection Co....989 288-5210
8531 S Reed Rd Durand (48429) ***(G-4613)***
Quality Filters Inc....734 668-0211
7215 Jackson Rd Ste 3 Ann Arbor (48103) ***(G-611)***
Quality Finishing Systems....231 834-9131
333 W 136th St Grant (49327) ***(G-7081)***
Quality First Fire Alarm....810 736-4911
4286 Pheasant Dr Flint (48506) ***(G-5488)***
Quality First Systems Inc....248 922-4780
10301 Enterprise Dr Davisburg (48350) ***(G-3639)***
Quality Grinding Inc....586 293-3780
33950 Riviera Fraser (48026) ***(G-5714)***
Quality Guest Publishing Inc....616 894-1111
12920 Algoma Ave Ne Cedar Springs (49319) ***(G-2561)***
Quality Industries Inc....517 439-1591
215 W Mechanic St Hillsdale (49242) ***(G-7536)***
Quality Inspections Inc....586 323-6135
7563 19 Mile Rd Sterling Heights (48314) ***(G-15459)***
Quality Liquid Feeds Inc....616 784-2930
5715 Comstock Park Dr Nw Comstock Park (49321) ***(G-3511)***
Quality Lock & Door, Detroit *Also called Lorenzo White* ***(G-4210)***
Quality Lube Express Inc....586 421-0600
50900 Donner Rd Chesterfield (48047) ***(G-2828)***
Quality Machine & Automation....616 399-4415
184 Manufacturers Dr Holland (49424) ***(G-7779)***
Quality Manufacturing....989 736-8121
481 W Traverse Bay Rd Lincoln (48742) ***(G-9570)***
Quality Marine Electronics LLC....616 566-2101
10692 Chicago Dr Zeeland (49464) ***(G-18182)***
Quality Metal Fabricating....616 901-5510
1324 Burke Ave Ne Grand Rapids (49505) ***(G-6799)***
Quality Metalcraft Inc (HQ)....734 261-6700
28101 Schoolcraft Rd Livonia (48150) ***(G-9900)***
Quality Model & Pattern Co....616 791-1156
2663 Elmridge Dr Nw Grand Rapids (49534) ***(G-6800)***
Quality Models Intl Inc....519 727-4255
17516 Dix Rd Melvindale (48122) ***(G-10706)***
Quality Mold and Engineering, Baroda *Also called Q M E Inc* ***(G-1129)***
Quality Pallet Inc....231 788-5161
7220 Hall Rd Muskegon (49442) ***(G-11409)***
Quality Pallets LLC....231 825-8361
9773 S Burkett Rd Mc Bain (49657) ***(G-10683)***
Quality Pipe Products Inc....734 606-5100
17275 Huron River Dr New Boston (48164) ***(G-11509)***
Quality Precast Inc....269 342-0539
7800 Adobe Kalamazoo (49009) ***(G-8866)***
Quality Printing & Graphics....616 949-3400
3109 Broadmoor Ave Se Grand Rapids (49512) ***(G-6801)***
Quality Socks, Fraser *Also called Soyad Brothers Textile Corp* ***(G-5726)***
Quality Spring/Togo Inc....517 278-2391
355 Jay St Coldwater (49036) ***(G-3323)***
Quality Stainless Mfg Co....248 546-4141
1150 E 11 Mile Rd Madison Heights (48071) ***(G-10343)***
Quality Steel....989 823-1524
4021 W Saginaw Rd Vassar (48768) ***(G-16814)***
Quality Steel Products Inc....248 684-0555
4978 Technical Dr Milford (48381) ***(G-10981)***
Quality Time Components....231 947-1071
343 Hughes Dr Traverse City (49696) ***(G-16086)***
Quality Tool & Gear Inc....734 266-1500
12693 Marlin Dr Redford (48239) ***(G-13186)***
Quality Tool & Stamping Co Inc....231 733-2538
541 E Sherman Blvd Muskegon (49444) ***(G-11410)***
Quality Tool Company Inc....517 869-2490
6577 W Chicago Rd Allen (49227) ***(G-193)***
Quality Transparent Bag Inc (PA)....989 893-3561
110 Mcgraw St Bay City (48708) ***(G-1344)***
Quality Way Products LLC....248 634-2401
407 Hadley St Holly (48442) ***(G-7891)***
Quality Wood Products Inc....989 658-2160
3399 Bay Cy Frestville Rd Ubly (48475) ***(G-16722)***
Qualtek Inc....269 781-2835
1611 Brooks Dr Marshall (49068) ***(G-10587)***
Quanenergy Systems Inc....248 859-5587
2655 E Oakley Park Rd # 105 Commerce Township (48390) ***(G-3443)***
Quanta Containers LLC (PA)....734 282-3044
15801 Huron St Taylor (48180) ***(G-15760)***
Quantam Solutions LLC....248 395-2200
18877 W 10 Mile Rd # 108 Southfield (48075) ***(G-15007)***
Quantum Chemical LLC....734 429-0033
12944 Farmington Rd Livonia (48150) ***(G-9901)***
Quantum Compliance Systems....734 930-0009
2111 Golfside Rd Ste B Ypsilanti (48197) ***(G-18099)***
Quantum Composites Inc....989 922-3863
1310 S Valley Center Dr Bay City (48706) ***(G-1345)***
Quantum Digital Ventures LLC....248 292-5686
24680 Mound Rd Warren (48091) ***(G-17212)***
Quantum Graphics Inc....586 566-5656
50720 Corporate Dr Shelby Township (48315) ***(G-14675)***
Quantum Innovations LLC....734 576-2000
33680 5 Mile Rd Livonia (48154) ***(G-9902)***
Quantum Labs LLC....248 262-7731
24555 Southfield Rd Southfield (48075) ***(G-15008)***
Quantum Machining Inc (PA)....810 796-2035
5573 North St Dryden (48428) ***(G-4571)***
Quantum Mold & Engineering LLC....586 276-0100
35700 Stanley Dr Sterling Heights (48312) ***(G-15460)***
Quantum Sails Design Group LLC (PA)....231 941-1222
1576 International Dr Traverse City (49686) ***(G-16087)***
Quantum Ventures LLC....248 325-8380
18055 Fish Lake Rd Holly (48442) ***(G-7892)***
Quarry Ridge Stone Inc....616 827-8244
555 Ste B Sw Byron Center (49315) ***(G-2210)***
Quarrystone Inc....906 786-0343
6851 County 426 M.5 Rd Escanaba (49829) ***(G-4854)***
Quartech Corporation....586 781-0373
15923 Angelo Dr Macomb (48042) ***(G-10160)***
Quarter Mania....734 368-2765
22080 Elwell Rd Belleville (48111) ***(G-1450)***
Quarter To 5, Sault Sainte Marie *Also called Canusa LLC* ***(G-14462)***
Quarters LLC....313 510-5555
1415 Sheridan St Plymouth (48170) ***(G-12727)***
Quarters Vending LLC....313 510-5555
3174 Old Farm Ln Commerce Township (48390) ***(G-3444)***
Quasar Industries Inc (PA)....248 844-7190
1911 Northfield Dr Rochester Hills (48309) ***(G-13501)***
Quasar Industries Inc....248 852-0300
2687 Commerce Dr Rochester Hills (48309) ***(G-13502)***
Quasar Prototype and Tool Co., Ira *Also called P T M Corporation* ***(G-8266)***
Quest - IV Incorporated....734 847-5487
7116 Summerfield Rd Lambertville (48144) ***(G-9184)***
Quest Industries Inc....810 245-4535
3309 John Conley Dr Lapeer (48446) ***(G-9484)***
Questor Partners Fund II LP (PA)....248 593-1930
101 Southfield Rd 2 Birmingham (48009) ***(G-1699)***
Questron Packaging LLC....313 657-1630
7650 W Chicago Detroit (48204) ***(G-4323)***
Quick - Burn LLC....616 402-4874
14518 Edmeer Dr Holland (49424) ***(G-7780)***
Quick and Reliable Printing, Midland *Also called Qrp Inc* ***(G-10905)***
Quick Beverages, Southfield *Also called Viva Beverages LLC* ***(G-15062)***

ALPHABETIC

Quick Built ALPHABETIC SECTION

Quick Built...586 286-2900
51450 Oro Dr Shelby Township (48315) ***(G-14676)***
Quick Caller, The, Saint Clair Shores *Also called Fourth Seacoast Publishing Co* ***(G-14252)***
Quick Draw Tarpaulin Systems...313 561-0554
26125 Trowbridge St Inkster (48141) ***(G-8234)***
Quick Draw Tarpaulin Systems (PA)...313 945-0766
10200 Ford Rd Dearborn (48126) ***(G-3752)***
Quick Print, Adrian *Also called Quickprint of Adrian Inc* ***(G-89)***
Quick Printing Company Inc...616 241-0506
2642 Division Ave S Grand Rapids (49507) ***(G-6802)***
Quick Reliable Printing, Midland *Also called Qrp Inc* ***(G-10906)***
Quickmitt Inc...517 849-2141
2400 E Chicago Rd Jonesville (49250) ***(G-8667)***
Quickprint of Adrian Inc...517 263-2290
142 N Main St Adrian (49221) ***(G-89)***
Quickrete, Walker *Also called Quikrete Companies Inc* ***(G-16878)***
Quicktrophy LLC...906 228-2604
446 E Crescent St Marquette (49855) ***(G-10555)***
Quiet Concepts, Oak Park *Also called PCI Industries Inc* ***(G-12090)***
Quiet Moose, Petoskey *Also called Compass Interiors LLC* ***(G-12446)***
Quigley Co...989 983-3911
8276 Mill St Vanderbilt (49795) ***(G-16809)***
Quigley Industries Inc (HQ)...248 426-8600
38880 Grand River Ave Farmington Hills (48335) ***(G-5109)***
Quigley Lumber Inc...989 257-5116
5874 Heath Rd South Branch (48761) ***(G-14750)***
Quigley Manufacturing Inc (PA)...248 426-8600
38880 Grand River Ave Farmington Hills (48335) ***(G-5110)***
Quikrete Companies Inc...616 784-5790
20 N Park St Nw Walker (49544) ***(G-16878)***
Quikrete Gibraltar National, Holly *Also called Gibraltar National Corporation* ***(G-7881)***
Quilters Garden Inc...810 750-8104
1347 Lake Valley Dr Fenton (48430) ***(G-5233)***
Quilting By Cheryl...616 669-5636
8092 Emberly Dr Jenison (49428) ***(G-8639)***
Quincy Street Inc...616 399-3330
13350 Quincy St Holland (49424) ***(G-7781)***
Quincy Woodwrights LLC (PA)...808 397-0818
408 E Montezuma Ave Houghton (49931) ***(G-7981)***
Quinlan Lumber Co...810 743-0700
2470 E Bristol Rd Burton (48529) ***(G-2162)***
Quirkroberts Publishing Ltd...248 879-2598
6219 Seminole Dr Troy (48085) ***(G-16573)***
Qwik Tool & Mfg Inc...231 739-8849
480 W Hume Ave Muskegon (49444) ***(G-11411)***
R & A Tool & Engineering Co...734 981-2000
39127 Ford Rd Westland (48185) ***(G-17593)***
R & B Electronics Inc (PA)...906 632-1542
1520 Industrial Park Dr Sault Sainte Marie (49783) ***(G-14471)***
R & B Grinding Service Inc...231 824-6798
641 R W Harris Dr Manton (49663) ***(G-10457)***
R & B Industries Inc...734 462-9478
12055 Globe St Livonia (48150) ***(G-9903)***
R & B Plastics Machinery LLC...734 429-9421
1605 Woodland Dr Saline (48176) ***(G-14410)***
R & C Redi-Mix Inc...616 636-5650
11991 Elm St Sand Lake (49343) ***(G-14425)***
R & D Cnc Machining Inc...269 751-4171
3506 Lincoln Rd Hamilton (49419) ***(G-7239)***
R & D Enterprises Inc...248 349-7077
46900 Port St Plymouth (48170) ***(G-12728)***
R & D Machine and Tool Inc...231 798-8500
6059 Norton Center Dr Norton Shores (49441) ***(G-11789)***
R & D Screw Products Inc...517 546-2380
810 Fowler St Howell (48843) ***(G-8084)***
R & DS Manufacturing LLC...586 716-9900
51690 Birch St New Baltimore (48047) ***(G-11490)***
R & H Machine Products, Three Rivers *Also called Denny Grice Inc* ***(G-15860)***
R & I Repair Shop...906 283-6000
1129n N Gulliver Rd Gulliver (49840) ***(G-7212)***
R & J Almonds Inc...810 767-6887
G4254 Fenton Rd Flint (48507) ***(G-5489)***
R & J Manufacturing Company...248 669-2460
3200 Martin Rd Commerce Township (48390) ***(G-3445)***
R & J Quality Screenprinting...989 345-8614
266 S M 33 West Branch (48661) ***(G-17518)***
R & J Screen Printing, West Branch *Also called R & J Quality Screenprinting* ***(G-17518)***
R & L Color Graphics Inc...313 345-3838
18709 Meyers Rd Detroit (48235) ***(G-4324)***
R & L Frye...989 821-6661
9435 N Cut Rd Roscommon (48653) ***(G-13753)***
R & L Machine Products Inc...734 992-2574
15995 S Huron River Dr Romulus (48174) ***(G-13725)***
R & M Machine Inc...586 754-8447
23895 Regency Park Dr Warren (48089) ***(G-17213)***
R & M Machine Tool Inc...989 695-6601
7920 Webster Rd Freeland (48623) ***(G-5758)***
R & M Manufacturing Company...269 683-9550
2424 N 5th St Niles (49120) ***(G-11641)***
R & N Lumber...989 848-5553
1388 Caldwell Rd Mio (48647) ***(G-11008)***
R & R Broach Inc...586 779-2227
29680 Parkway Roseville (48066) ***(G-13858)***
R & R Forest Products Inc...989 766-8227
8622 M 65 Posen (49776) ***(G-13071)***
R & R Harwood Inc...616 669-6400
2688 Edward St Jenison (49428) ***(G-8640)***
R & R Ready-Mix Inc...810 686-5570
14151 N Saginaw Rd Clio (48420) ***(G-3280)***
R & R Ready-Mix Inc (PA)...989 753-3862
6050 Melbourne Rd Saginaw (48604) ***(G-14127)***
R & R Ready-Mix Inc...989 892-9313
1601 W Youngs Ditch Rd Bay City (48708) ***(G-1346)***
R & R Tool Inc...616 394-4200
192 E 48th St Holland (49423) ***(G-7782)***
R & S Cutter Grind Inc...989 791-3100
2870 Universal Dr Saginaw (48603) ***(G-14128)***
R & S Propeller Inc...616 636-8202
212 S 3rd St Sand Lake (49343) ***(G-14426)***
R & S Propeller Repair, Sand Lake *Also called R & S Propeller Inc* ***(G-14426)***
R & S Tool & Die Inc...989 673-8511
545 Columbia St Ste B Caro (48723) ***(G-2476)***
R A Miller Industries Inc...888 845-9450
14500 168th Ave Grand Haven (49417) ***(G-6067)***
R A Townsend Company...989 498-7000
2845 Mccarty Rd Saginaw (48603) ***(G-14129)***
R and J Dumpsters LLC...248 863-8579
5886 Lange Rd Howell (48843) ***(G-8085)***
R and Js Gravel...906 663-4571
108 N Cedar Ave Bessemer (49911) ***(G-1606)***
R and T Sporting Clays Inc...586 215-9861
37853 Elmlane Harrison Township (48045) ***(G-7345)***
R and T West Michigan Inc...616 698-9931
6955 E Paris Indus Ct Se Caledonia (49316) ***(G-2311)***
R Andrews Pallet Co Inc...616 677-3270
1035 Comstock St Marne (49435) ***(G-10512)***
R B Christian Inc (PA)...269 963-9327
525 24th St N Battle Creek (49037) ***(G-1239)***
R B I Mechanical Inc...231 582-2970
204 Industrial Parkway Dr Boyne City (49712) ***(G-1834)***
R B L Plastics Incorporated...313 873-8800
6040 Russell St Detroit (48211) ***(G-4325)***
R B Machine...616 928-8690
5904 142nd Ave Lot 93 Holland (49423) ***(G-7783)***
R Betker & Associates...269 927-3233
1400 Territorial Rd Benton Harbor (49022) ***(G-1541)***
R C Grinding and Tool Company...586 949-4373
49669 Leona Dr Chesterfield (48051) ***(G-2829)***
R C M Inc...586 336-1237
14901 32 Mile Rd Bruce Twp (48065) ***(G-2093)***
R C M S Inc...269 422-1617
10981 Hills Rd Baroda (49101) ***(G-1130)***
R C Plastics Inc...517 523-2112
4790 Hudson Rd Osseo (49266) ***(G-12228)***
R Concepts Incorporated...810 632-4857
10083 Bergin Rd Howell (48843) ***(G-8086)***
R Cushman & Associates Inc...248 477-9900
12623 Newburgh Rd Livonia (48150) ***(G-9904)***
R D M Enterprises Co Inc...810 985-4721
4045 Griswold Rd Port Huron (48060) ***(G-12959)***
R D Tool & Mfg, Erie *Also called Concentric Industries Inc* ***(G-4802)***
R E B Tool Inc...734 397-9116
5910 Belleville Rd Van Buren Twp (48111) ***(G-16781)***
R E D Industries Inc...248 542-2211
1671 E 9 Mile Rd Hazel Park (48030) ***(G-7451)***
R E Gallaher Corp...586 725-3333
9601 Marine City Hwy Ira (48023) ***(G-8267)***
R E Glancy Inc (PA)...989 362-0997
124 W M 55 Tawas City (48763) ***(G-15677)***
R E Glancy Inc...989 876-6030
5278 Turner Rd Tawas City (48763) ***(G-15678)***
R F M Incorporated...810 229-4567
2001 Orndorf Dr Brighton (48116) ***(G-1983)***
R G Ray Corporation...248 373-4300
2430 E Walton Blvd Auburn Hills (48326) ***(G-984)***
R H & Company Inc...269 345-7814
4510 W Kl Ave Kalamazoo (49006) ***(G-8867)***
R H Cross Enterprises Inc...269 488-4009
731 Porter St Kalamazoo (49007) ***(G-8868)***
R H Huhtala Aggregates Inc...906 524-7758
18154 Us Highway 41 Lanse (49946) ***(G-9200)***
R H K Technology Inc...248 577-5426
1233 Chicago Rd Troy (48083) ***(G-16574)***
R H M Rubber & Manufacturing...248 624-8277
203 Bernstadt St Novi (48377) ***(G-11984)***
R J Designers Inc...517 750-1990
8032 Spring Arbor Rd Spring Arbor (49283) ***(G-15127)***
R J Flood Professional Co...269 930-3608
2691 Orchard Ln Stevensville (49127) ***(G-15579)***

R J Manufacturing 810 610-0205
4196 S Irish Rd Davison (48423) ***(G-3660)***
R J Manufacturing Incorporated 906 779-9151
110 Forest Gtwy Crystal Falls (49920) ***(G-3613)***
R J Marshall Company (PA) 248 353-4100
26776 W 12 Mile Rd # 201 Southfield (48034) ***(G-15009)***
R J Marshall Company 734 379-4044
21220 Huron River Dr Rockwood (48173) ***(G-13611)***
R J Marshall Company 734 848-5325
1740 E Erie Rd Erie (48133) ***(G-4810)***
R J Michaels Inc 517 783-2637
515 S West Ave Jackson (49203) ***(G-8560)***
R J Reynolds Tobacco Company 616 949-3740
3156 Breton Rd Se Kentwood (49512) ***(G-9027)***
R J S, Birmingham *Also called R J S Tool & Gage Co* ***(G-1700)***
R J S Tool & Gage Co 248 642-8620
1081 S Eton St Birmingham (48009) ***(G-1700)***
R J Woodworking Inc 231 766-2511
3108 Whitehall Rd Muskegon (49445) ***(G-11412)***
R K C Corporation 231 627-9131
600 Riggs Dr Cheboygan (49721) ***(G-2692)***
R K Parts, Detroit *Also called Kirks Automotive Incorporated* ***(G-4179)***
R L Adams Plastics Inc 616 261-4400
5955 Crossroads Commerce Grand Rapids (49519) ***(G-6803)***
R L Hume Award Co 269 324-3063
2226 Kalarama Ave Portage (49024) ***(G-13026)***
R L M Industries Inc 248 628-5103
100 Hummer Lake Rd Oxford (48371) ***(G-12366)***
R L Schmitt Company Inc 734 525-9310
34506 Glendale St Livonia (48150) ***(G-9905)***
R M Brewer & Son Inc 517 531-3022
215 S Harrington Rd Parma (49269) ***(G-12393)***
R M I, Madison Heights *Also called Rotary Multiforms Inc* ***(G-10344)***
R M N Machining & Fabricating 616 772-4111
3252 88th Ave Zeeland (49464) ***(G-18183)***
R M Wright Company Inc (PA) 248 476-9800
23910 Freeway Park Dr Farmington Hills (48335) ***(G-5111)***
R M Young Company 231 946-3980
2801 Aero Park Dr Traverse City (49686) ***(G-16088)***
R N B Machine & Tool Inc 616 784-6868
5200 West River Dr Ne Comstock Park (49321) ***(G-3512)***
R N E Business Enterprises (PA) 313 963-3600
400 Renaissance Ctr Lbby Detroit (48243) ***(G-4326)***
R N Fink Manufacturing Co 517 655-4351
1530 Noble Rd Williamston (48895) ***(G-17738)***
R P T Cincinnati Inc 313 382-5880
1636 John A Papalas Dr Lincoln Park (48146) ***(G-9584)***
R R Donnelley & Sons Company 313 964-1330
3031 W Grand Blvd Ste 400 Detroit (48202) ***(G-4327)***
R S C Productions 586 532-9200
7811 24 Mile Rd Shelby Township (48316) ***(G-14677)***
R S L Tool LLC 616 786-2880
13417 New Hlland St Ste 2 Holland (49424) ***(G-7784)***
R S V P Inc 734 455-7229
833 Penniman Ave Ste A Plymouth (48170) ***(G-12729)***
R Smith and Sons, Allegan *Also called Southwest Gravel Inc* ***(G-188)***
R T C Enviro Fab Inc 517 596-2987
9043 M 106 Munith (49259) ***(G-11254)***
R T Gordon Inc 586 294-6100
33792 Doreka Fraser (48026) ***(G-5715)***
R T London Company (PA) 616 364-4800
1642 Broadway Ave Nw # 1 Grand Rapids (49504) ***(G-6804)***
R V Wolverine 989 426-9241
1088 N M 18 Gladwin (48624) ***(G-5934)***
R W Fernstrum & Company 906 863-5553
1716 11th Ave Menominee (49858) ***(G-10756)***
R W Patterson Printing Co 269 925-2177
1550 Territorial Rd Benton Harbor (49022) ***(G-1542)***
R WI Sign Co, Kalamazoo *Also called Rwl Sign Co LLC* ***(G-8877)***
R&R Tool & Gage, Mount Clemens *Also called Rebecca Eiben* ***(G-11148)***
R+r Mfg/Eng Inc 586 758-4420
21448 Mullin Ave Warren (48089) ***(G-17214)***
R-Bo Co Inc 616 748-9733
150 W Washington Ave Zeeland (49464) ***(G-18184)***
R.T. Baldwin Hardwood Floors, Hudsonville *Also called Rt Baldwin Enterprises Inc* ***(G-8181)***
Ra Prcsion Grnding Mtlwrks Inc 586 783-7776
40801 Irwin Dr Harrison Township (48045) ***(G-7346)***
Raal Industries Inc 734 782-6216
24802 Christian Dr Flat Rock (48134) ***(G-5361)***
Rabaut Printing Co, Shelby Township *Also called Complete Home Adv Media/Promo* ***(G-14565)***
Race Ramps LLC 866 464-2788
2003 23rd Ave N Ste A Escanaba (49829) ***(G-4855)***
Racelogic USA Corporation 248 994-9050
27260 Haggerty Rd Ste A2 Farmington Hills (48331) ***(G-5112)***
Racers Inc 586 727-4069
9627 Crawford Rd Columbus (48063) ***(G-3382)***
Rack & Pinion Inc 517 563-8872
7595 Moscow Rd Horton (49246) ***(G-7970)***
Rack Engineering Division, Alpena *Also called Corr-Fac Corporation* ***(G-284)***
Radam Motors LLC 269 365-4982
545 Washington St Otsego (49078) ***(G-12254)***
Radar Mexican Investments LLC 586 779-0300
27101 Groesbeck Hwy Warren (48089) ***(G-17215)***
Radar Tool & Manufacturing Co 586 759-2800
23201 Blackstone Ave Warren (48089) ***(G-17216)***
Radiant Electric Sign Corp 313 835-1400
14500 Schoolcraft St Detroit (48227) ***(G-4328)***
Radiolgical Fabrication Design 810 632-6000
10187 Bergin Rd Howell (48843) ***(G-8087)***
Radius LLC 248 685-0773
4922 Technical Dr Milford (48381) ***(G-10982)***
Radley Corp of Grand Rapids, Grand Rapids *Also called Radley Corporation* ***(G-6805)***
Radley Corporation 616 554-9060
4595 Broadmoor Ave Se # 115 Grand Rapids (49512) ***(G-6805)***
Radtke Farms, Berrien Springs *Also called Fairview Farms* ***(G-1595)***
Rae Manufacturing Company 810 987-9170
1327 Cedar St Port Huron (48060) ***(G-12960)***
Rae Precision Products Inc 810 987-9170
1327 Cedar St Port Huron (48060) ***(G-12961)***
Raenell Press LLC 616 534-8890
3637 Clyde Park Ave Sw # 6 Grand Rapids (49509) ***(G-6806)***
Rafalski CPA 248 689-1685
1607 E Big Beaver Rd # 103 Troy (48083) ***(G-16575)***
Rainbow Cleaning System, Troy *Also called Rexair LLC* ***(G-16579)***
Rainbow Pizza Inc 734 246-4250
14702 Allen Rd Taylor (48180) ***(G-15761)***
Rainbow Seamless Systems Inc (PA) 231 933-8888
4107 Manor Wood Dr S Traverse City (49685) ***(G-16089)***
Rainbow Tape & Label Inc 734 941-6090
11600 Wayne Rd Romulus (48174) ***(G-13726)***
Rainbow Wrap 586 949-3976
46440 Jefferson Ave Chesterfield (48047) ***(G-2830)***
Rainmaker Food Solutions LLC 313 530-1321
22857 Saint Andrews Dr South Lyon (48178) ***(G-14811)***
Rajason International Corp 248 506-4456
1207 Hartland Dr Troy (48083) ***(G-16576)***
Rak Welding 231 651-0732
7739 Valley Rd Honor (49640) ***(G-7953)***
Ral Technologies, Sterling Heights *Also called Rose-A-Lee Technologies Inc* ***(G-15479)***
Ralco Industries Inc (PA) 248 853-3200
2720 Auburn Ct Auburn Hills (48326) ***(G-985)***
Ralco Industries Inc 248 853-3200
1025 Doris Rd Auburn Hills (48326) ***(G-986)***
Ralco Industries Inc 248 853-3200
2860 Auburn Ct Auburn Hills (48326) ***(G-987)***
Raleigh & Ron Corporation (PA) 248 280-2820
2560 Crooks Rd Royal Oak (48073) ***(G-13961)***
Ralrube Inc 734 429-0033
8423 Boettner Rd Saline (48176) ***(G-14411)***
Ralston Foods, Battle Creek *Also called Treehouse Private Brands Inc* ***(G-1260)***
Ralyas Auto Body Incorporated 517 694-6512
1250 N Cedar Rd Mason (48854) ***(G-10652)***
Ram Die Corp 616 647-2855
2980 3 Mile Rd Nw Grand Rapids (49534) ***(G-6807)***
Ram Electronics, Fruitport *Also called Bralyn Inc* ***(G-5790)***
Ram Electronics Inc 231 865-3186
259 N 3rd Ave Fruitport (49415) ***(G-5799)***
Ram Meter Inc (HQ) 248 362-0990
1815 Bellaire Ave Ste B Royal Oak (48067) ***(G-13962)***
Ramco, Jenison *Also called Tannewitz Inc* ***(G-8644)***
Ramer Products Inc 269 409-8583
400 Post Rd Buchanan (49107) ***(G-2126)***
Rami, Grand Haven *Also called R A Miller Industries Inc* ***(G-6067)***
Ramparts LLC 616 656-2250
4855 Broadmoor Ave Se Kentwood (49512) ***(G-9028)***
Ramtec Corp 586 752-9270
409 E Saint Clair St Romeo (48065) ***(G-13636)***
Ran-Mark Co 231 873-5103
2978 E Hazel Rd Hart (49420) ***(G-7379)***
Ranch Life Plastics Inc 517 663-2350
5260 S Clinton Trl Eaton Rapids (48827) ***(G-4731)***
Ranch Production LLC 231 869-2050
3908 W Hogan Rd Pentwater (49449) ***(G-12430)***
Rand L Industries Inc 989 657-5175
2046 Partridge St Alpena (49707) ***(G-311)***
Rand Worldwide Subsidiary Inc 616 261-8183
4445 Wilson Ave Sw Ste 4 Grandville (49418) ***(G-7069)***
Randall Foods Inc 517 767-3247
401 S Main St Tekonsha (49092) ***(G-15821)***
Randall Tool & Manufacturing, Jenison *Also called Randall Tool & Mfg LLC* ***(G-8641)***
Randall Tool & Mfg LLC 616 669-1260
2514 Port Sheldon St # 3 Jenison (49428) ***(G-8641)***
Randalls Bakery 906 224-5401
505 Sunday Lake St Wakefield (49968) ***(G-16855)***
Randell, Weidman *Also called Unified Brands Inc* ***(G-17462)***
Randlis Manufacturing Co 313 368-0220
19669 John R St Detroit (48203) ***(G-4329)***

ALPHABETIC

Randy L Palmer   **ALPHABETIC SECTION**

Randy L Palmer 586 298-7629
   9915 Reese Rd Clarkston (48348) *(G-2949)*
Randy's Catering, Pontiac *Also called Unique Food Management Inc (G-12872)*
Rane Innovation LLC 419 577-2126
   2016 Crescent Dr Bay City (48706) *(G-1347)*
Range Cards 248 880-8444
   5680 Golf Pointe Dr Clarkston (48348) *(G-2950)*
Ranger Die, Coopersville *Also called Kinney Tool and Die Inc (G-3562)*
Ranger Products, Detroit *Also called Randlis Manufacturing Co (G-4329)*
Ranger Tool & Die Co 989 754-1403
   317 S Westervelt Rd Saginaw (48604) *(G-14130)*
Ranir LLC (PA) 616 698-8880
   4701 East Paris Ave Se Grand Rapids (49512) *(G-6808)*
Ranir Global Holdings   LLC 616 698-8880
   4701 East Paris Ave Se Grand Rapids (49512) *(G-6809)*
Rankin Biomedical Corporation 248 625-4104
   14515 Mackey Rd Holly (48442) *(G-7893)*
Rap Electronics & Machines 616 846-1437
   13353 Green St Grand Haven (49417) *(G-6068)*
Rap Products Inc 989 893-5583
   500 Germania St Bay City (48706) *(G-1348)*
Rapa Electric Inc 269 673-3157
   1173 Lincoln Rd Allegan (49010) *(G-186)*
Rapid Cnc Solutions 586 850-6385
   9605 Buffalo St Hamtramck (48212) *(G-7245)*
Rapid EDM Service Inc 616 243-5781
   3051 Hillcroft Ave Sw Grand Rapids (49548) *(G-6810)*
Rapid Engineering LLC (PA) 616 784-0500
   1100 7 Mile Rd Nw Comstock Park (49321) *(G-3513)*
Rapid Graphics Inc 269 925-7087
   2185 M 139 Benton Harbor (49022) *(G-1543)*
Rapid Grinding & Machine Co 989 753-1744
   3500 Janes Ave Saginaw (48601) *(G-14131)*
Rapid Printing, Benton Harbor *Also called Rapid Graphics Inc (G-1543)*
Rapid River Loghome, Rapid River *Also called Rapid River Rustic Inc (G-13114)*
Rapid River Rustic Inc (PA) 906 474-6404
   9211 County 511 22 And Rapid River (49878) *(G-13114)*
Rapid-Packaging Corporation 616 949-0950
   5151 52nd St Se Grand Rapids (49512) *(G-6811)*
Rapid-Veyor, Hudsonville *Also called Rapidtek LLC (G-8175)*
Rapids Tool & Engineering 517 663-8721
   10618 Petrieville Hwy Eaton Rapids (48827) *(G-4732)*
Rapids Tool & Engnrng, Eaton Rapids *Also called Rapids Tool & Engineering (G-4732)*
Rapidtek   LLC 616 662-0954
   3825 Central Pkwy Ste A Hudsonville (49426) *(G-8175)*
Rapp & Son Inc (PA) 734 283-1000
   3767 11th St Wyandotte (48192) *(G-17971)*
Raq LLC 313 473-7271
   392 S Sanford St Pontiac (48342) *(G-12860)*
Rar Group Inc 248 353-2266
   21421 Hilltop St Ste 12 Southfield (48033) *(G-15010)*
Rare Bird Holdings LLC 616 335-9463
   849 Allen Dr Holland (49423) *(G-7785)*
Rare Earth Hardwoods Inc 231 946-0043
   5800 Denali Dr Traverse City (49684) *(G-16090)*
Rare Tool Inc 517 423-5000
   300 E Russell Rd Tecumseh (49286) *(G-15806)*
Rassey Industries Inc 586 803-9500
   50375 Central Indus Dr Shelby Township (48315) *(G-14678)*
Rassini Brakes LLC 810 780-4600
   4175 Pier North Blvd Flint (48504) *(G-5490)*
Rathco Safety Supply Inc 269 323-0153
   6742 Lovers Ln Portage (49002) *(G-13027)*
Ratio Machining Inc 313 531-5155
   12214 Woodbine Redford (48239) *(G-13187)*
Rattunde Corporation (PA) 616 940-3340
   5080 Beltway Dr Se Caledonia (49316) *(G-2312)*
Raval USA Inc 248 260-4050
   1939 Northfield Dr Rochester Hills (48309) *(G-13503)*
Rave Computer Association Inc 586 939-8230
   7171 Sterling Ponds Ct Sterling Heights (48312) *(G-15461)*
Raven Carbide Die LLC 313 228-8776
   17901 Wdlnd Dr Ste 1100 New Boston (48164) *(G-11510)*
Raven Engineering Inc 248 969-9450
   725 S Glaspie St Oxford (48371) *(G-12367)*
Ravenna Casting Center Inc 231 853-0300
   3800 Adams Rd Ravenna (49451) *(G-13126)*
Ravenna Ductile Iron, Ravenna *Also called Metal Technologies Inc (G-13124)*
RAVENNA HYDRAULICS, Ravenna *Also called Ravenna Pattern & Mfg (G-13127)*
Ravenna Pattern & Mfg 231 853-2264
   13101 Apple Ave Ravenna (49451) *(G-13127)*
Ravenwood 231 421-5682
   503 Devonshire Ct Traverse City (49686) *(G-16091)*
Ray Printing Company Inc 517 787-4130
   201 Brookley Ave Jackson (49202) *(G-8561)*
Ray Scott Industries   Inc 248 535-2528
   3921 32nd St Port Huron (48060) *(G-12962)*
Ray's Big Game Processing, Brown City *Also called Rays Game (G-2056)*
Raybend, Rochester *Also called Sales Driven Services LLC (G-13350)*

Raybend, Kalamazoo *Also called Sales Driven Ltd Liability Co (G-8881)*
Rayco Manufacturing Inc 586 795-2884
   5520 Bridgewood Dr Sterling Heights (48310) *(G-15462)*
Rayconnect Inc 248 265-4000
   2350 Austin Ave Ste 100 Rochester Hills (48309) *(G-13504)*
Raydiance, West Bloomfield *Also called Tru-Fit International Inc (G-17502)*
Raymond S Ross 231 922-0235
   9740 E Avondale Ln Traverse City (49684) *(G-16092)*
Raynor Overhead Door, Livonia *Also called Michigan Overhead Door (G-9842)*
Rayomar Enterprises Inc 313 415-9102
   28600 Norwood Ave Warren (48092) *(G-17217)*
Rays Game 810 346-2628
   4101 Maple St Brown City (48416) *(G-2056)*
Rays Ice Cream Co Inc 248 549-5256
   4233 Coolidge Hwy Royal Oak (48073) *(G-13963)*
Rays Welding Co Inc 269 473-1140
   8469 Hollywood Rd Berrien Springs (49103) *(G-1600)*
Raze-It Printing 248 543-3813
   24221 John R Rd Hazel Park (48030) *(G-7452)*
RB Construction Company (PA) 586 264-9478
   249 Cass Ave Mount Clemens (48043) *(G-11147)*
RB Oil Enterprises LLC 734 354-0700
   Plymouth Mi Plymouth (48170) *(G-12730)*
Rbc Enterprises Inc (PA) 313 491-3350
   12301 Hubbell St Detroit (48227) *(G-4330)*
Rbc Ministries (PA) 616 942-6770
   3000 Kraft Ave Se Grand Rapids (49512) *(G-6812)*
Rbd Creative 313 259-5507
   705 S Main St Ste 220 Plymouth (48170) *(G-12731)*
Rbl Products Inc 313 873-8806
   6040 Russell St Detroit (48211) *(G-4331)*
Rbt Mfg LLC 800 691-8204
   9033 General Dr Plymouth (48170) *(G-12732)*
RC Directional Boring Inc 517 545-4887
   3402 Cedar Lake Rd Howell (48843) *(G-8088)*
RC Metal Products Inc 616 696-1694
   4365 21 Mile Rd Sand Lake (49343) *(G-14427)*
RCO Aerospace Products LLC 586 774-8400
   15725 E 12 Mile Rd Roseville (48066) *(G-13859)*
RCO Engineering Inc 586 620-4133
   15725 E 12 Mile Rd Roseville (48066) *(G-13860)*
Rcs Services Company LLC 989 732-7999
   10850 Hetherton Rd Johannesburg (49751) *(G-8650)*
Rdc, Grand Rapids *Also called Ram Die Corp (G-6807)*
Rdc Machine Inc 810 695-5587
   7503 Fenton Rd Grand Blanc (48439) *(G-5980)*
RDM Associates, Clarkston *Also called Export Service International (G-2919)*
Rdr Books, Muskegon *Also called Roger D Rapoport (G-11416)*
Rdz Racing Incorporated 517 468-3254
   9642 Sober Rd Fowlerville (48836) *(G-5578)*
Re-Sol LLC 248 270-7777
   1771 Harmon Rd Ste 150 Auburn Hills (48326) *(G-988)*
RE-Source Industries Inc 231 728-1155
   1485 S Getty St Muskegon (49442) *(G-11413)*
Re-Verber-Ray, Warren *Also called Detroit Radiant Products Co (G-17000)*
Ready Boring & Tooling, Farmington Hills *Also called Ready Molds Inc (G-5113)*
Ready Molds Inc (PA) 248 474-4007
   32645 Folsom Rd Farmington Hills (48336) *(G-5113)*
Readysetmail 810 982-1924
   64 S Range Rd 8 Saint Clair (48079) *(G-14232)*
Reagan Testing Tools 248 894-3423
   2171 Avon Industrial Dr Rochester Hills (48309) *(G-13505)*
Real Alloy Recycling LLC 517 279-9596
   267 N Fillmore Rd Coldwater (49036) *(G-3324)*
Real Alloy Recycling LLC 517 279-9596
   368 W Garfield Ave Coldwater (49036) *(G-3325)*
Real Detroit Weekly LLC 248 591-7325
   1200 Woodward Hts Ferndale (48220) *(G-5315)*
Real Estate Book, Farmington Hills *Also called Dynamic Color Publications (G-4976)*
Real Estate One Inc 248 851-2600
   3100 Old Farm Ln Ste 10 Commerce Township (48390) *(G-3446)*
Real Estate One Licensing Co, Commerce Township *Also called Real Estate One Inc (G-3446)*
Real Flavors LLC 855 443-9685
   135 Washington Ave Bay City (48708) *(G-1349)*
Real Green Systems Inc (PA) 888 345-2154
   4375 Pineview Dr Commerce Township (48390) *(G-3447)*
Real Love Printwear 248 327-7181
   28475 Greenfield Rd # 212 Southfield (48076) *(G-15011)*
Real Steel Manufacturing LLC 231 457-4673
   304 W Delano Ave Muskegon (49444) *(G-11414)*
Real Time Diagnostics, Warren *Also called Tambra Investments Inc (G-17261)*
Realbio Technology Inc 269 544-1088
   8390 Canary Dr Kalamazoo (49009) *(G-8869)*
Realm 313 706-4401
   34950 Van Born Rd Wayne (48184) *(G-17441)*
Rearden Development Corp 616 464-4434
   5960 Tahoe Dr Se Ste 103 Grand Rapids (49546) *(G-6813)*

Reau Manufacturing Co 734 823-5603
100 Research Pkwy Dundee (48131) ***(G-4598)***
REB Research & Consulting Co 248 545-0155
12851 Capital St Oak Park (48237) ***(G-12092)***
REB Research & Consulting Co (PA) 248 547-7942
25451 Gardner St Detroit (48237) ***(G-3821)***
REB Tool Company, Van Buren Twp *Also called R E B Tool Inc* ***(G-16781)***
Rebeats (PA) 989 463-4757
219 Prospect Ave Alma (48801) ***(G-248)***
Rebecca Eiben 586 231-0548
191 Grand Ave Mount Clemens (48043) ***(G-11148)***
Rebel Nell L3c 716 640-4267
4731 Grand River Ave Detroit (48208) ***(G-4332)***
Rebo Lighting & Elec LLC 734 213-4159
3990 Research Park Dr Ann Arbor (48108) ***(G-612)***
Rec Boat Holdings LLC (HQ) 231 775-1351
925 Frisbie St Cadillac (49601) ***(G-2273)***
Recaro North America Inc 313 842-3479
4617 W Fort St Detroit (48209) ***(G-4333)***
Recaro North America Inc (HQ) 734 254-5000
49200 Halyard Dr Plymouth (48170) ***(G-12733)***
Recco Products Inc 269 792-2243
702 S Main St Wayland (49348) ***(G-17410)***
Recognition Robotics Inc 440 590-0499
29445 Beck Rd Ste A106 Wixom (48393) ***(G-17884)***
Recollections Co 989 734-0566
7956 F-21 Hwy Hawks (49743) ***(G-7431)***
Recon Technologies LLC 616 241-1877
1522 Madison Ave Se Grand Rapids (49507) ***(G-6814)***
Recticel Foam Corporation (HQ) 248 241-9100
5600 Bow Pointe Dr Clarkston (48346) ***(G-2951)***
Recycled Paperboard Pdts Corp 313 579-6608
10400 Devine St Detroit (48213) ***(G-4334)***
Recycled Polymetric Materials 313 957-6373
15477 Woodrow Wilson St Detroit (48238) ***(G-4335)***
Recycledlps Com 810 623-4498
6320 Superior Dr Brighton (48116) ***(G-1984)***
Recycletech Products Inc 517 649-2243
12 Charlotte St Mulliken (48861) ***(G-11240)***
Recycling Concepts W Mich Inc 616 942-8888
5015 52nd St Se Grand Rapids (49512) ***(G-6815)***
Recycling Fluid Technologies 269 788-0488
4039 Columbia Ave W Battle Creek (49015) ***(G-1240)***
Recycling Rizzo Services LLC 248 541-4020
414 E Hudson Ave Royal Oak (48067) ***(G-13964)***
Red Carpet Capital Inc 248 952-8583
3514 Arrowvale Dr Orchard Lake (48324) ***(G-12169)***
Red Door Digital, Detroit *Also called Group 7500 Inc* ***(G-4107)***
Red Iron Strl Consulting Corp 810 364-5100
170 Royalview Rd Harbor Springs (49740) ***(G-7292)***
Red Laser Inc 517 540-1300
5684 E Highland Rd Howell (48843) ***(G-8089)***
Red Rock Industries Inc 734 992-3522
16705 Ecorse Rd Allen Park (48101) ***(G-205)***
Red Rose Flooring Shop, Sturgis *Also called Dave Brand* ***(G-15603)***
Red Spot Westland Inc 734 729-1913
550 Edwin St Westland (48186) ***(G-17594)***
RED Stamp Inc 616 878-7771
3800 Patterson Ave Se Grand Rapids (49512) ***(G-6816)***
Red Tie Group Inc 734 458-2011
11898 Belden Ct Livonia (48150) ***(G-9906)***
Red Tin Boat 734 239-3796
4081 Thornoaks Dr Ann Arbor (48104) ***(G-613)***
Red Wing Bags, Holland *Also called Rj Corp* ***(G-7788)***
Redbud Roots Lab I LLC 312 656-3823
215 Post Rd Buchanan (49107) ***(G-2127)***
Redeem Power Services 248 679-5277
43422 W Oaks Dr Ste 178 Novi (48377) ***(G-11985)***
Redi-Crete, Negaunee *Also called Rudy Goupille & Sons Inc* ***(G-11476)***
Redline Fabrications 810 984-5621
4752 Walker Rd Clyde (48049) ***(G-3284)***
Redtail Software 231 587-0720
1414 Plum Valley Rd Ne Mancelona (49659) ***(G-10398)***
Redviking, Plymouth *Also called Superior Controls Inc* ***(G-12763)***
Reed City Group LLC 231 832-7500
603 E Church Ave Reed City (49677) ***(G-13222)***
Reed Fuel LLC 574 520-3101
1445 S 3rd St Niles (49120) ***(G-11642)***
Reed Sportswear Mfg Co (PA) 313 963-7980
1601 W Lafayette Blvd Detroit (48216) ***(G-4336)***
Reed Sportswear Mfg Co 313 963-7980
1601 W Lafayette Blvd Detroit (48216) ***(G-4337)***
Reed Yacht Sales LLC (PA) 419 304-4405
11840 Toledo Beach Rd La Salle (48145) ***(G-9074)***
Reed Yacht Sales LLC 616 842-8899
1333 Madison St Blgd A St Grand Haven (49417) ***(G-6069)***
Reef Tool & Gage Co 586 468-3000
44800 Macomb Indus Dr Clinton Township (48036) ***(G-3207)***
Reeling Systems LLC 810 364-3900
5323 Gratiot Ave Saint Clair (48079) ***(G-14233)***
Reemco Incorporated 734 522-8988
11801 Belden Ct Livonia (48150) ***(G-9907)***
Reeves Plastics LLC 616 997-0777
507 Omalley Dr Coopersville (49404) ***(G-3569)***
Refab LLC 616 842-9705
1811 Hayes St Ste D Grand Haven (49417) ***(G-6070)***
Refinery Corporation America 877 881-0336
20008 Kelly Rd Harper Woods (48225) ***(G-7303)***
Reflection Medical Inc 734 850-0777
3200 W Temperance Rd B Temperance (48182) ***(G-15841)***
Reflective Art Inc 616 452-0712
4030 Eastern Ave Se Grand Rapids (49508) ***(G-6817)***
Reforma, Southfield *Also called NV Labs Inc* ***(G-14993)***
Refreshment Product Svcs Inc 906 475-7003
201 Summit St Bldg 53 Negaunee (49866) ***(G-11474)***
Refrigerant Services LLC 248 586-6988
54000 Grand River Ave New Hudson (48165) ***(G-11552)***
Refrigeration Concepts Inc 616 785-7335
5959 Comstock Park Dr Nw Comstock Park (49321) ***(G-3514)***
Refrigeration Research Inc (PA) 810 227-1151
525 N 5th St Brighton (48116) ***(G-1985)***
Refrigeration Research Inc 989 773-7540
2174 Commerce St Mount Pleasant (48858) ***(G-11223)***
Refrigeration Sales Inc 517 784-8579
1810 E High St Ste 2 Jackson (49203) ***(G-8562)***
Regal Finishing Co Inc 269 849-2963
3927 Bessemer Rd Coloma (49038) ***(G-3364)***
Regency Construction Corp 586 741-8000
35240 Forton Ct Clinton Township (48035) ***(G-3208)***
Regency Dki, Clinton Township *Also called Regency Construction Corp* ***(G-3208)***
Regency Plastics - Ubly Inc (HQ) 989 658-8504
4147 N Ubly Rd Ubly (48475) ***(G-16723)***
Regener-Eyes LLC 248 207-4641
330 E Liberty St Ll Ann Arbor (48104) ***(G-614)***
Regents of The University Mich 734 764-6230
1919 Green Rd Ann Arbor (48109) ***(G-615)***
Regents of The University Mich 734 764-4388
839 Greene St Ann Arbor (48104) ***(G-616)***
Regents of The University Mich 734 936-0435
3003 S State St Spc 1272 Ann Arbor (48109) ***(G-617)***
Regents of The University Mich 734 973-2400
2850 S Industrial Hwy # 400 Ann Arbor (48104) ***(G-618)***
Reger Manufacturing Company 586 293-5096
31375 Fraser Dr Fraser (48026) ***(G-5716)***
Reggie McKenzie Indus Mtls 734 261-0844
34401 Schoolcraft Rd Livonia (48150) ***(G-9908)***
Rehau Incorporated 269 651-7845
1110 N Clay St Sturgis (49091) ***(G-15632)***
Rehmann Industries Inc 810 748-7793
23051 Roseberry Ave Warren (48089) ***(G-17218)***
Rehrig Pacific Company 517 278-9808
500 Jonesville Rd Coldwater (49036) ***(G-3326)***
Reid Contractors Inc 906 632-2936
11969 S Mackinac Trl Dafter (49724) ***(G-3620)***
Reid Industries Inc 586 776-2070
28440 Groesbeck Hwy Roseville (48066) ***(G-13861)***
Reid Manufacturing, Fremont *Also called White River Knife and Tool* ***(G-5786)***
Reif Carbide Tool Co Inc 586 754-1890
11055 E 9 Mile Rd Warren (48089) ***(G-17219)***
Reilchz Inc 231 421-9600
600 W Front St Traverse City (49684) ***(G-16093)***
Reilly & Associates Inc 248 605-9393
7754 Parkcrest Cir Clarkston (48348) ***(G-2952)***
Reilly Craft Creamery LLC 313 300-9859
4731 Bellevue St Detroit (48207) ***(G-4338)***
Reimold Printing Corporation 989 799-0784
5171 Blackbeak Dr Saginaw (48604) ***(G-14132)***
Reinhart Industries, Livonia *Also called SB Investments LLC* ***(G-9921)***
Reis Custom Cabinets 586 791-4925
1398 S Bradford Rd Reese (48757) ***(G-13231)***
Rejoice International Corp 855 345-5575
21800 Haggerty Rd Ste 203 Northville (48167) ***(G-11721)***
Reklein Plastics Incorporated 586 739-8850
42130 Mound Rd Sterling Heights (48314) ***(G-15463)***
Rekmakker Millwork Inc 616 546-3680
6035 145th Ave Holland (49423) ***(G-7786)***
Reko International Holdings (HQ) 519 737-6974
6001 N Adams Rd Ste 251 Bloomfield Hills (48304) ***(G-1793)***
Rel Machine Inc 906 337-3018
57640 11th St Calumet (49913) ***(G-2332)***
Relative Path LLC 217 840-6376
4775 Commons Dr Unit Gg09 Mount Pleasant (48858) ***(G-11224)***
Releaf Michigan Inc 734 662-6350
1100 N Main St Ste 105 Ann Arbor (48104) ***(G-619)***
Reliable Architectural Mtls Co, Detroit *Also called Reliable Glass Company* ***(G-4339)***
Reliable Concepts Management, Bruce Twp *Also called R C M Inc* ***(G-2093)***
Reliable Freight Fwdg Inc 734 595-6165
30300 Cypress Rd Romulus (48174) ***(G-13727)***
Reliable Glass Company 313 924-9750
9751 Erwin St Detroit (48213) ***(G-4339)***

A
L
P
H
A
B
E
T
I
C

Reliable Reasonable TI Svc LLC 586 630-6016
21356 Carlo Dr Clinton Township (48038) *(G-3209)*
Reliable Sales Co 248 969-0943
660 Lakes Edge Dr Oxford (48371) *(G-12368)*
Reliance Electric Machine Co 810 232-3355
2601 Leith St Flint (48506) *(G-5491)*
Reliance Finishing Co 616 241-4436
1236 Judd Ave Sw Grand Rapids (49509) *(G-6818)*
Reliance Metal Products Inc 734 641-3334
1157 Mfrs Dr Ste B Westland (48186) *(G-17595)*
Reliance Rubber Industries Inc 734 641-4100
38230 N Executive Dr Westland (48185) *(G-17596)*
Reliance Spray Mask Co Inc 616 784-3664
2825 Northridge Dr Nw Grand Rapids (49544) *(G-6819)*
Reliance Tool Company Inc 734 946-9130
39110 Pennsylvania Rd Romulus (48174) *(G-13728)*
Reliant Industries Inc 586 275-0479
6119 15 Mile Rd Sterling Heights (48312) *(G-15464)*
Religious Communications LLC 313 822-3361
5590 Coplin St Detroit (48213) *(G-4340)*
Remacon Compressors Inc 313 842-8219
7939 Mcgraw St Detroit (48210) *(G-4341)*
Reminder Shopping Guide Inc 269 427-7474
416 Railroad St Bangor (49013) *(G-1094)*
Reminder, The, Hastings Also called J-Ad Graphics Inc *(G-7416)*
Remnant Publications Inc 517 279-1304
649 E Chicago Rd Ste B Coldwater (49036) *(G-3327)*
Remote Tank Monitors, Saginaw Also called Advance Tech Solutions LLC *(G-13992)*
Rempco Acquisition Inc 231 775-0108
251 Bell Ave Cadillac (49601) *(G-2274)*
Rena DRane Enterprises Inc 248 796-2765
24150 Philip Dr Southfield (48075) *(G-15012)*
Renaissance Media LLC 248 354-6060
29200 Northwstrn Hwy 11 Southfield (48034) *(G-15013)*
Rendon & Sons Machining Inc 269 628-2200
21870 M 40 Gobles (49055) *(G-5949)*
Renew Valve & Machine Co., Carleton Also called Fcx Performance Inc *(G-2454)*
Renewable World Energies LLC 906 828-0808
1001 Stephenson St Ste C Norway (49870) *(G-11819)*
Renosol Seating, Farwell Also called Lear Corporation *(G-5163)*
Rens LLC 586 756-6777
24871 Gibson Dr Warren (48089) *(G-17220)*
Renucell 888 400-6032
41 Washington Ave Ste 345 Grand Haven (49417) *(G-6071)*
REO Fab LLC (PA) 810 969-4667
1567 Imlay City Rd Ste A Lapeer (48446) *(G-9485)*
REO Hydraulic & Mfg Inc 313 891-2244
18475 Sherwood St Detroit (48234) *(G-4342)*
REO Hydro-Pierce Inc 313 891-2244
18475 Sherwood St Detroit (48234) *(G-4343)*
Repair Industries Michigan Inc 313 365-5300
6501 E Mcnichols Rd Detroit (48212) *(G-4344)*
Repair Rite Machine Inc 616 681-9711
1946 142nd Ave Dorr (49323) *(G-4526)*
Repcolite Decorating Center, Holland Also called Repcolite Paints Inc *(G-7787)*
Repcolite Paints Inc (PA) 616 396-5213
473 W 17th St Holland (49423) *(G-7787)*
Replacement Brush Tables, Plymouth Also called Rbt Mfg LLC *(G-12732)*
Reply Inc (HQ) 248 686-2481
691 N Squirrel Rd Ste 202 Auburn Hills (48326) *(G-989)*
Reporter & Shoppers Guide, Iron River Also called Northland Publishers Inc *(G-8318)*
Reporter Papers Inc 734 429-5428
106 W Michigan Ave Saline (48176) *(G-14412)*
Reproductions Resource, Saint Clair Shores Also called Print Plus Inc *(G-14268)*
Reprographics One, Livonia Also called M & J Graphics Enterprises Inc *(G-9820)*
Republic Die & Tool Co 734 699-3400
45000 Van Born Rd Van Buren Twp (48111) *(G-16782)*
Republic Roller Corporation 269 273-9591
205 S Us Highway 131 Three Rivers (49093) *(G-15876)*
Rescar Inc 517 486-3130
11440 Cemetery Rd Blissfield (49228) *(G-1724)*
Resco Pet Products, Commerce Township Also called Tecla Company Inc *(G-3453)*
Research & Developement, Cadillac Also called Fiamm Technologies LLC *(G-2247)*
Research and Development, Ypsilanti Also called Suematek *(G-18103)*
Research and Development Off, Escanaba Also called Emp Advanced Development LLC *(G-4824)*
Research Tool Corporation 989 834-2246
1401 S Main St Ovid (48866) *(G-12274)*
Resetar Equipment Inc 313 291-0500
26950 Van Born Rd Dearborn Heights (48125) *(G-3794)*
Resin Services, Sterling Heights Also called Reklein Plastics Incorporated *(G-15463)*
Resin Services Inc 586 254-6770
5959 18 1/2 Mile Rd Sterling Heights (48314) *(G-15465)*
Resinate Materials Group Inc 800 891-2955
46701 Commerce Center Dr C Plymouth (48170) *(G-12734)*
Resistance Welding Machne & AC 269 428-4770
255 Palladium Dr Saint Joseph (49085) *(G-14337)*
Resolute Forest Products, Menominee Also called Fibrek Inc *(G-10733)*

Resort + Recreation Magazine 616 891-5747
9820 Ravine Rdg Se Caledonia (49316) *(G-2313)*
Resource Rcovery Solutions Inc 248 454-3442
100 W Sheffield Ave Pontiac (48340) *(G-12861)*
Response Welding Inc 586 795-8090
40785 Brentwood Dr Sterling Heights (48310) *(G-15466)*
Restraint Systems Division, Auburn Hills Also called Joyson Safety Systems *(G-922)*
Retail Sign Systems, Belmont Also called Jant Group LLC *(G-1463)*
Retro Enterprises Inc 269 435-8583
1045 Parkview St Constantine (49042) *(G-3544)*
Retro-A-Go-go LLC 734 476-0300
214 S Michigan Ave Howell (48843) *(G-8090)*
Retrosense Therapeutics LLC 734 369-9333
330 E Liberty St Ll Ann Arbor (48104) *(G-620)*
Returnable Packaging Corp 586 206-8050
1917 S Riveerhill Dr Clinton Township (48038) *(G-3210)*
Reuland Electric Co 517 546-4400
4500 E Grand River Ave Howell (48843) *(G-8091)*
Reurink Roof Maint & Coating 269 795-2337
12795 Jackson Rd Middleville (49333) *(G-10806)*
Reurink Roofing and Siding Sls, Ionia Also called Reurink Sales & Service LLC *(G-8251)*
Reurink Sales & Service LLC 616 522-9100
1243 W Lincoln Ave Ionia (48846) *(G-8251)*
Reutter LLC (HQ) 248 621-9220
30150 Telg Rd Ste 172 Bingham Farms (48025) *(G-1659)*
Revak Precision Grinding Inc 313 388-2626
20188 Lorne St Taylor (48180) *(G-15762)*
Revealed Engineering LLC 734 642-5551
13177 Briar Hill Rd Carleton (48117) *(G-2461)*
Revere Plastics Systems LLC 586 415-4823
18401 Malyn Blvd Fraser (48026) *(G-5717)*
Revere Plastics Systems LLC (HQ) 419 547-6918
39555 Orchard Hill Pl # 362 Novi (48375) *(G-11986)*
Review Directories Inc 231 347-8606
311 E Mitchell St Petoskey (49770) *(G-12472)*
Revolutions Signs Designs LLC 248 439-0727
2429 N Connecticut Ave Royal Oak (48073) *(G-13965)*
Revstone Industries LLC 248 351-1000
900 Wilshire Dr Ste 270 Troy (48084) *(G-16577)*
Revstone Industries LLC 248 351-8800
2000 Town Ctr Ste 2100 Southfield (48075) *(G-15014)*
Revue Holding Company 616 608-6170
2422 Burton St Se Grand Rapids (49546) *(G-6820)*
Revue Magazine, Grand Rapids Also called Revue Holding Company *(G-6820)*
Revwires LLC 269 683-8100
1631 Lake St Niles (49120) *(G-11643)*
Rew Industries Inc 586 803-1150
51572 Danview Tech Ct Shelby Township (48315) *(G-14679)*
Rex M Tubbs 734 459-3180
1205 S Main St Plymouth (48170) *(G-12735)*
Rex Materials Inc (PA) 517 223-3787
1600 Brewer Rd Howell (48855) *(G-8092)*
Rex Printing Company 586 323-4002
7472 19 Mile Rd Sterling Heights (48314) *(G-15467)*
Rex Rush Inc 248 684-0221
4330 Cooley Lake Rd Commerce Township (48382) *(G-3448)*
Rexair Holdings Inc 248 643-7222
50 W Big Beavr Rd Ste 350 Troy (48084) *(G-16578)*
Rexair LLC (PA) 248 643-7222
50 W Big Beaver Rd # 350 Troy (48084) *(G-16579)*
Rexam Plastic Containers, Constantine Also called Owens-Brockway Glass Cont Inc *(G-3541)*
Reyers Advertising, Spring Lake Also called Reyers Company Inc *(G-15172)*
Reyers Company Inc 616 414-5530
700 E Savidge St Spring Lake (49456) *(G-15172)*
Reynolds Bus Solutions LLC 616 293-6449
3610 Sandy Lane Ct Se Grand Rapids (49546) *(G-6821)*
Reynolds Water Conditioning Co 248 888-5000
24545 Hathaway St Farmington Hills (48335) *(G-5114)*
Rezoop LLC 248 952-8070
1270 Romney Rd Bloomfield (48304) *(G-1735)*
Rf Design, Howell Also called Radiolgical Fabrication Design *(G-8087)*
Rf System Lab, Traverse City Also called Seneca Enterprises LLC *(G-16100)*
RGI Brands LLC (PA) 312 253-7400
3950 Wabeek Lake Dr E Bloomfield Hills (48302) *(G-1794)*
Rgm New Ventures Inc (PA) 248 624-5050
48230 West Rd Wixom (48393) *(G-17885)*
Rh Spies Group, Sterling Heights Also called Letnan Industries Inc *(G-15397)*
Rhe-Tech LLC 517 223-4874
9201 W Grand River Rd Fowlerville (48836) *(G-5579)*
Rhema Products Inc 313 561-6800
24141 Ann Arbor Trl Ste 5 Dearborn Heights (48127) *(G-3795)*
Rhinevault Olsen Machine & TI 989 753-4363
2533 Carrollton Rd Saginaw (48604) *(G-14133)*
Rhino Linings of Grand Rapids 616 361-9786
1520 Rupert St Ne Grand Rapids (49525) *(G-6822)*
Rhino Products Inc 269 674-8309
57100 48th Ave Lawrence (49064) *(G-9507)*

Rhino Seed & Landscape Sup LLC (PA) ... 800 482-3130
1093 129th Ave Wayland (49348) *(G-17411)*
Rhino Strapping Products Inc ... 734 442-4040
24341 Brest Taylor (48180) *(G-15763)*
Rhm Fluid Power, Westland *Also called Flodraulic Group Incorporated (G-17558)*
Rhombus Energy Solutions Inc ... 313 406-3292
15201 Century Dr Dearborn (48120) *(G-3753)*
Rice Juice Company Inc ... 906 774-1733
873 Evergreen Ct Iron Mountain (49802) *(G-8298)*
Richard Bennett & Associates ... 313 831-4262
470 Brainard St Detroit (48201) *(G-4345)*
Richard L Martin Construction, Higgins Lake *Also called Classic Log Homes Incorporated (G-7482)*
Richard Larabee ... 248 827-7755
22132 W 9 Mile Rd Southfield (48033) *(G-15015)*
Richard Reproductions, Southfield *Also called Richard Larabee (G-15015)*
Richard Tool & Die Corporation ... 248 486-0900
29700 Wk Smith Dr New Hudson (48165) *(G-11553)*
Richard-Allan Scientific Co (HQ) ... 269 544-5600
4481 Campus Dr Kalamazoo (49008) *(G-8870)*
Richards Printing ... 906 786-3540
718 Ludington St Escanaba (49829) *(G-4856)*
Richards Quality Bedding Co ... 616 363-0070
3443 Manderley Dr Ne Grand Rapids (49525) *(G-6823)*
Richardson Acqstions Group Inc ... 248 624-2272
961 Decker Rd Walled Lake (48390) *(G-16902)*
Richcoat LLC ... 586 978-1311
40573 Brentwood Dr Sterling Heights (48310) *(G-15468)*
Richelieu America Ltd (HQ) ... 586 264-1240
7021 Sterling Ponds Ct Sterling Heights (48312) *(G-15469)*
Richfield Industries, Flint *Also called Transportation Tech Group Inc (G-5512)*
Richfield Industries Inc ... 810 233-0440
3022 Airpark Dr S Flint (48507) *(G-5492)*
Richland Machine & Pump Co ... 269 629-4344
9854 M 89 Richland (49083) *(G-13254)*
Richman Company Products Inc ... 989 686-6251
3474 W Pressler Dr Bay City (48706) *(G-1350)*
Richmond Bros Fabrication LLC ... 989 551-1996
7911 Murdoch Rd Bay Port (48720) *(G-1374)*
Richmond Instrs & Systems Inc ... 586 954-3770
21392 Carlo Dr Clinton Township (48038) *(G-3211)*
Richmond Meat Packers Inc ... 586 727-1450
68104 S Main St Richmond (48062) *(G-13270)*
Richmond Millwork Inc ... 586 727-6747
66375 S Forest Ave Lenox (48050) *(G-9524)*
Richmond Steel Inc ... 586 948-4700
50570 E Russell Schmidt Chesterfield (48051) *(G-2831)*
Richmonds Steel Inc ... 989 453-7010
6767 Pigeon Rd Pigeon (48755) *(G-12492)*
Richter Precision Inc ... 586 465-0500
17741 Malyn Blvd Fraser (48026) *(G-5718)*
Richter Sawmill ... 231 829-3071
20408 18 Mile Rd Leroy (49655) *(G-9537)*
Richwood Industries Inc (PA) ... 616 243-2700
2700 Buchanan Ave Sw Grand Rapids (49548) *(G-6824)*
Rick Owen & Jason Vogel Partnr ... 734 417-3401
10475 N Territorial Rd Dexter (48130) *(G-4507)*
Rick Wykle LLC ... 734 839-6376
12502 Globe St Livonia (48150) *(G-9909)*
Rick's Deer Processing, Eaton Rapids *Also called Ricks Meat Processing LLC (G-4733)*
Ricks Cove Inc ... 734 283-7505
467 Biddle Ave Wyandotte (48192) *(G-17972)*
Ricks Custom Cycle LLP ... 734 762-2077
31532 Ford Rd Garden City (48135) *(G-5836)*
Ricks Meat Processing LLC ... 517 628-2263
3320 Onondaga Rd Eaton Rapids (48827) *(G-4733)*
Ride Control LLC (HQ) ... 248 247-7600
39300 Country Club Dr Farmington Hills (48331) *(G-5115)*
Rider Report Magazine ... 248 854-8460
3906 Baldwin Rd Auburn Hills (48321) *(G-990)*
Rider Type & Design ... 989 839-0015
3600 E Mary Jane Dr Midland (48642) *(G-10908)*
Ridge & Kramer Motor Supply Co ... 269 685-5838
1286 M 89 Plainwell (49080) *(G-12541)*
Ridge Cider ... 231 674-2040
351 W 136th St Grant (49327) *(G-7082)*
Ridgeview Industries Inc ... 616 453-8636
2727 3 Mile Rd Nw Grand Rapids (49534) *(G-6825)*
Ridgeview Industries Inc ... 616 414-6500
16933 144th Ave Nunica (49448) *(G-12043)*
Ridgeview Industries Inc (PA) ... 616 453-8636
3093 Northridge Dr Nw Grand Rapids (49544) *(G-6826)*
Ridgeview Metals Incorporated ... 850 259-1808
71 S Main St Casnovia (49318) *(G-2508)*
Ridgewood Stoves LLC ... 989 488-3397
1293 170th Ave Hersey (49639) *(G-7475)*
Ridgid Slotting LLC ... 616 847-0332
12046 120th Ave Grand Haven (49417) *(G-6072)*
Riedel USA Inc ... 734 595-9820
2315 Cambridge Dr Kalamazoo (49001) *(G-8871)*
Riegle Press Inc (PA) ... 810 653-9631
1282 N Gale Rd Davison (48423) *(G-3661)*
Rieke-Arminak Corp ... 248 631-5450
39400 Woodward Ave # 130 Bloomfield Hills (48304) *(G-1795)*
Rieth-Riley Cnstr Co Inc ... 231 263-2100
4435 S M 37 Grawn (49637) *(G-7100)*
Rieth-Riley Cnstr Co Inc ... 616 248-0920
2100 Chicago Dr Sw Wyoming (49519) *(G-18030)*
Rigaku Innovative Tech Inc ... 248 232-6400
1900 Taylor Rd Auburn Hills (48326) *(G-991)*
Right Brain Brewery ... 231 922-9662
1837 Carlisle Rd Traverse City (49696) *(G-16094)*
Rilas & Rogers LLC ... 937 901-4228
44440 Meadowcreek Ln Canton (48187) *(G-2422)*
Riley Enterprises LLC ... 517 263-9115
1703 E Gier Rd Adrian (49221) *(G-90)*
Rim Custom Racks, Detroit *Also called Repair Industries Michigan Inc (G-4344)*
Rim Guard Inc ... 616 608-7745
1575 Gezon Pkwy Sw Ste E Wyoming (49509) *(G-18031)*
Rima Manufacturing Company (PA) ... 517 448-8921
3850 Munson Hwy Hudson (49247) *(G-8141)*
Ring Screw, Holly *Also called Acument Global Tech Inc (G-7868)*
Ring Screw LLC ... 810 629-6602
2480 Owen Rd Fenton (48430) *(G-5234)*
Ring Screw LLC ... 810 695-0800
4146 Baldwin Rd Holly (48442) *(G-7894)*
Ring Screw LLC (HQ) ... 586 997-5600
6125 18 Mile Rd Sterling Heights (48314) *(G-15470)*
Ringmaster Robin Oil, Detroit *Also called Painex Corporation (G-4286)*
Ringmaster Software Corp ... 802 383-1050
631 E Big Beaver Rd # 109 Troy (48083) *(G-16580)*
Ringmasters Mfg LLC ... 734 729-6110
36502 Van Born Rd Wayne (48184) *(G-17442)*
Ripley Products Company Inc ... 906 482-1380
21194 Royce Rd Hancock (49930) *(G-7256)*
Rippa Products Inc ... 906 337-0010
25256 Renaissance Rd Calumet (49913) *(G-2333)*
Ripper Ventures LLC ... 248 808-2325
14708 Keel St Plymouth (48170) *(G-12736)*
Ripple Science Corporation ... 919 451-0241
303 Detroit St Ste 100 Ann Arbor (48104) *(G-621)*
Rise Machine Company Inc ... 989 772-2151
905 N Kinney Ave Mount Pleasant (48858) *(G-11225)*
Rite Machine Products Inc ... 586 465-9393
44795 Enterprise Dr Clinton Township (48038) *(G-3212)*
Rite Mark Stamp Company ... 248 391-7600
4141 N Atlantic Blvd Auburn Hills (48326) *(G-992)*
Rite Tool Company Inc ... 586 264-1900
36740 Metro Ct Sterling Heights (48312) *(G-15471)*
Rite Way Asphalt Inc ... 586 264-1020
6699 16 Mile Rd Ste B Sterling Heights (48312) *(G-15472)*
Rite Way Printing ... 734 721-2746
5821 Essex St Romulus (48174) *(G-13729)*
Ritsema Prcision Machining Inc ... 269 344-8882
3221 Redmond Ave Kalamazoo (49001) *(G-8872)*
Ritz Craft Corp of Michigan, Jonesville *Also called Ritz-Craft Corp PA Inc (G-8668)*
Ritz-Craft Corp PA Inc ... 517 849-7425
118 Deal Pkwy Jonesville (49250) *(G-8668)*
Rivas Inc (PA) ... 586 566-0326
12146 Monsbrook Dr Sterling Heights (48312) *(G-15473)*
Riveer Environmental, The, South Haven *Also called Petter Investments Inc (G-14767)*
River Bend Driving Range, Harrison Township *Also called J E Enterprises (G-7333)*
River City Studios Ltd ... 616 456-1404
1935 Monroe Ave Nw Grand Rapids (49505) *(G-6827)*
River Raisin Models ... 248 366-9621
6160 Upper Straits Blvd West Bloomfield (48324) *(G-17494)*
River Raisin Publications ... 517 486-2400
121 Newspaper St Blissfield (49228) *(G-1725)*
River Run Press Inc ... 269 349-7603
600 Shoppers Ln Kalamazoo (49004) *(G-8873)*
River Valley Machine Inc ... 269 673-8070
600 N Eastern Ave Allegan (49010) *(G-187)*
River Valley Shopper, Big Rapids *Also called Pgi Holdings Inc (G-1641)*
Riverbend Timber Framing Inc ... 517 486-3629
9012 E Us Highway 223 Blissfield (49228) *(G-1726)*
Riverbend Woodworing ... 231 869-4965
1293 W Adams Rd Pentwater (49449) *(G-12431)*
Rivercity Rollform Inc ... 231 799-9550
1130 E Mount Garfield Rd Norton Shores (49441) *(G-11790)*
Riverfront Cycle Inc ... 517 482-8585
507 E Shiawassee St Lansing (48912) *(G-9418)*
Riverhill Publications & Prtg ... 586 468-6011
8850 Dixie Hwy Ira (48023) *(G-8268)*
Riverside Block Co Inc ... 989 865-9951
1024 N Saginaw St Saint Charles (48655) *(G-14200)*
Riverside Cnc LLC ... 616 246-6000
3331 Lousma Dr Se Wyoming (49548) *(G-18032)*
Riverside Computer, Newaygo *Also called Riverside Internet Services (G-11576)*

A
L
P
H
A
B
E
T
I
C

Riverside Defense Training LLC 231 825-2895
5360 S Dickerson Rd Lake City (49651) *(G-9096)*
Riverside Electric Service Inc 269 849-1222
3864 Riverside Rd Riverside (49084) *(G-13286)*
Riverside Energy Michigan LLC 231 995-4000
10691 E Carter Rd Ste 201 Traverse City (49684) *(G-16095)*
Riverside Grinding Co, Jackson Also called Alro Riverside LLC *(G-8382)*
Riverside Internet Services (PA) 231 652-2562
45 W Gene Furgason Ln Newaygo (49337) *(G-11576)*
Riverside Plastic Co 231 937-7333
138 Washburn St Howard City (49329) *(G-8006)*
Riverside Prtg of Grnd Rapids 616 458-8011
1375 Monroe Ave Nw Grand Rapids (49505) *(G-6828)*
Riverside Screw Mch Pdts Inc 269 962-5449
52 Edison St S Battle Creek (49014) *(G-1241)*
Riverside Spline & Gear Inc 810 765-8302
1390 S Parker St Marine City (48039) *(G-10481)*
Riverside Tank & Mfg Corp 810 329-7143
1230 Clinton Ave Saint Clair (48079) *(G-14234)*
Riverside Tool & Mold Inc 989 435-9142
5819 Calhoun Rd Beaverton (48612) *(G-1390)*
Riverside Tool Corp 616 241-1424
88 54th St Sw Unit 106 Grand Rapids (49548) *(G-6829)*
Riverside Vans Inc 269 432-3212
57951 Farrand Rd Colon (49040) *(G-3375)*
Riverview Products Inc 616 866-1305
201 Byrne Industrial Dr Rockford (49341) *(G-13586)*
Rives Manufacturing Inc 517 569-3380
4000 Rives Eaton Rd Rives Junction (49277) *(G-13310)*
Rivian Automotive Inc (PA) 734 855-4350
13250 N Haggerty Rd Plymouth (48170) *(G-12737)*
Rivian Automotive Inc 408 483-1987
41100 Plymouth Rd 4ne Plymouth (48170) *(G-12738)*
Rivian Automotive LLC (HQ) 734 855-4350
13250 N Haggerty Rd Plymouth (48170) *(G-12739)*
Riviera Industries Inc 313 381-5500
16038 Southfield Rd Allen Park (48101) *(G-206)*
Rivmax Manufacturing Inc 517 784-2556
2218 E High St Ste C Jackson (49203) *(G-8563)*
Rivore Metals LLC (PA) 800 248-1250
850 Stephenson Hwy # 200 Troy (48083) *(G-16581)*
Rivore Metals LLC 248 397-8724
7900 Dix St Detroit (48209) *(G-4346)*
Rivore Metals LLC 248 397-8724
500 South Blvd E Ste 200 Pontiac (48341) *(G-12862)*
Rizk National Industries Inc 586 757-4700
24422 Ryan Rd Warren (48091) *(G-17221)*
Rizzo Environmental Services, Southfield Also called Gfl Envronmental Real Property *(G-14919)*
Rizzo Packaging Inc 269 685-5808
930 Lincoln Pkwy Plainwell (49080) *(G-12542)*
Rj Acquisition Corp 586 268-2300
5585 Gatewood Dr Sterling Heights (48310) *(G-15474)*
Rj Corp 616 396-0552
2127 112th Ave Holland (49424) *(G-7788)*
Rj Operating Company 616 392-7101
217 E 24th St Ste 102 Holland (49423) *(G-7789)*
Rj USA, Sterling Heights Also called Rj Acquisition Corp *(G-15474)*
Rj's Custom Plowing, Fremont Also called Two Feathers Enterprise LLC *(G-5785)*
Rjg Technologies Inc (PA) 231 947-3111
3111 Park Dr Traverse City (49686) *(G-16096)*
RJL Sciences Inc 800 528-4513
33939 Harper Ave Clinton Township (48035) *(G-3213)*
Rjl Systems, Clinton Township Also called RJL Sciences Inc *(G-3213)*
Rk Boring Inc 734 542-7920
35425 Schoolcraft Rd Livonia (48150) *(G-9910)*
RK Tool Inc (PA) 586 731-5640
44443 Phoenix Dr Ste B Sterling Heights (48314) *(G-15475)*
RK Wojan Inc 231 347-1160
6336 Us Highway 31 N Charlevoix (49720) *(G-2628)*
Rkaa Business LLC 231 734-5517
5843 100th Ave Evart (49631) *(G-4886)*
RKP Consulting Inc 616 698-0300
3286 Hnna Lk Ind Pk Dr Se Caledonia (49316) *(G-2314)*
Rl Flo-Master, Lowell Also called Root-Lowell Manufacturing Co *(G-10042)*
Rlh Industries Inc 989 732-0493
1574 Calkins Dr Gaylord (49735) *(G-5889)*
Rls Interventional Inc 616 301-7800
4375 Donkers Ct Se Kentwood (49512) *(G-9029)*
Rm Machine & Mold 734 721-8800
30399 Ecorse Rd Romulus (48174) *(G-13730)*
Rmcs Wings Enterprise 269 426-3559
12421 Flynn Rd Sawyer (49125) *(G-14488)*
Rmg Family Sugar Bush Inc 906 478-3038
11866 W Thompson Rd Rudyard (49780) *(G-13986)*
Rmt Acquisition Company LLC 248 353-5487
20941 East St Southfield (48033) *(G-15016)*
Rmt Acquisition Company LLC (PA) 248 353-4229
45755 Five Mile Rd Plymouth (48170) *(G-12740)*
Rmt Woodworth, Southfield Also called Rmt Acquisition Company LLC *(G-15016)*
Rmt Woodworth, Plymouth Also called Rmt Acquisition Company LLC *(G-12740)*
Rmt Woodworth, Plymouth Also called Savanna Inc *(G-12750)*
Rmt Woodworth Heat Treating, Southfield Also called Savanna Inc *(G-15022)*
Rnd Engineering LLC 734 328-8277
46036 Michigan Ave # 201 Canton (48188) *(G-2423)*
Rnj Services Inc 906 786-0585
2003 23rd Ave N Ste A Escanaba (49829) *(G-4857)*
Rob Enterprises Inc 269 685-5827
156 10th St Plainwell (49080) *(G-12543)*
Robb Machine Tool Co 616 532-6642
4301 Clyde Park Ave Sw Grand Rapids (49509) *(G-6830)*
Robbie Dean Press LLC 734 973-9511
2910 E Eisenhower Pkwy Ann Arbor (48108) *(G-622)*
Robbins Inc 513 619-5936
844 Highway M 28 Negaunee (49866) *(G-11475)*
Robert & Son Black Ox Special 586 778-7633
30665 Edison Dr Roseville (48066) *(G-13862)*
Robert A Nelson 231 597-9225
11118 N Straits Hwy Cheboygan (49721) *(G-2693)*
Robert Bosch Btry Systems LLC (HQ) 248 620-5700
3740 S Lapeer Rd Orion (48359) *(G-12189)*
Robert Bosch Fuel Systems LLC 616 554-6500
4700 S Broadmoor Ste 100 Kentwood (49512) *(G-9030)*
Robert Bosch LLC 616 466-4063
9890 Red Arrow Hwy Bridgman (49106) *(G-1873)*
Robert Bosch LLC 734 302-2000
3021 Miller Rd Ann Arbor (48103) *(G-623)*
Robert Bosch LLC 248 921-9054
Novi Research Park Novi (48377) *(G-11987)*
Robert Bosch LLC 734 979-3000
15000 N Haggerty Rd Plymouth (48170) *(G-12741)*
Robert Bosch LLC 734 979-3412
39775 Five Mile Rd Plymouth (48170) *(G-12742)*
Robert Bosch LLC 269 429-3221
3737 Red Arrow Hwy Saint Joseph (49085) *(G-14338)*
Robert Crawford & Son Logging 989 379-2712
15490 Green Farm Rd Lachine (49753) *(G-9078)*
Robert J Lidzan 616 361-6446
2147 Airway St Ne Grand Rapids (49525) *(G-6831)*
Robert McIntyre Logging 906 446-3158
6427 E Maple Rdg Rd Rapid River (49878) *(G-13115)*
Roberts Movable Walls Inc 269 626-0227
9611 32nd St S Scotts (49088) *(G-14506)*
Roberts Sinto Corporation 517 371-2471
150 Orchard St Grand Ledge (48837) *(G-6114)*
Roberts Sinto Corporation (HQ) 517 371-2460
3001 W Main St Lansing (48917) *(G-9320)*
Roberts Tool Company 517 423-6691
800 S Maumee St Tecumseh (49286) *(G-15807)*
Robertson Tool & Engineering 248 624-3838
1054 Rig St Commerce Township (48390) *(G-3449)*
Robertson-Stewart Inc 810 227-4500
1351 Rickett Rd Brighton (48116) *(G-1986)*
Robicon, Livonia Also called Speedway Ordering Systems Inc *(G-9939)*
Robinson Fence Co Inc 906 647-3301
24254 S Clegg Rd Pickford (49774) *(G-12483)*
Robinson Industries Inc 989 465-6111
3051 W Curtis Rd Coleman (48618) *(G-3350)*
Roblaw Industries, Taylor Also called AJM Packaging Corporation *(G-15685)*
Robmar Plastics Inc 989 386-9600
1385 E Maple Rd Clare (48617) *(G-2885)*
Robmar Precision Mfg Inc 734 326-2664
38189 Abruzzi Dr Westland (48185) *(G-17597)*
Robogistics LLC 409 234-1033
100 Industrial Dr Adrian (49221) *(G-91)*
Robot Space, The, Lapeer Also called Cypress Computer Systems Inc *(G-9453)*
Robotic System Integration, Wixom Also called Allfi Robotics Inc *(G-17757)*
Robotic Welded Parts Inc 989 386-5376
314 E 4th St Clare (48617) *(G-2886)*
Robovent Products Group Inc (HQ) 586 698-1800
37900 Mound Rd Sterling Heights (48310) *(G-15476)*
Robroy Enclosures Inc 616 794-0700
505 W Maple St Belding (48809) *(G-1428)*
Robroy Industries Inc 616 794-0700
505 W Maple St Belding (48809) *(G-1429)*
Rocar Precision Inc 586 226-2711
31207 Stricker Dr Warren (48088) *(G-17222)*
Rochester Cider Mill 248 651-4224
5215 N Rochester Rd Rochester (48306) *(G-13348)*
Rochester Gear Inc (HQ) 989 659-2899
9900 Main St Clifford (48727) *(G-3011)*
Rochester Grinding, Rochester Also called Special Mold Engineering Inc *(G-13516)*
Rochester Hills Facility, Rochester Hills Also called Lear Corporation *(G-13459)*
Rochester Mlls Prod Brewry LLC 248 377-3130
3275 Lapeer Rd W Auburn Hills (48326) *(G-993)*
Rochester Pallet 248 266-1094
2641 W Auburn Rd Rochester Hills (48309) *(G-13506)*

ALPHABETIC SECTION

Rook Metering Equipment, Mount Pleasant

Rochester Sports LLC..248 608-6000
1900 S Rochester Rd Rochester Hills (48307) *(G-13507)*
Rochester Tube Products Ltd......................................586 726-4816
51366 Fischer Park Dr Shelby Township (48316) *(G-14680)*
Rochester Tube Products Rtp, Shelby Township Also called Rochester Tube Products Ltd *(G-14680)*
Rochester Welding Company Inc................................248 628-0801
2793 Metamora Rd Oxford (48371) *(G-12369)*
Rock Construction, Bloomfield Hills Also called Rock Industries Inc *(G-1796)*
Rock Industries Inc (PA)...248 338-2800
6125 Old Orchard Dr Bloomfield Hills (48301) *(G-1796)*
Rock Products, The, Carrollton Also called Rock Redi-Mix Inc *(G-2486)*
Rock Redi-Mix Inc...989 752-0795
2820 Carrollton Rd Carrollton (48724) *(G-2486)*
Rock River Fabrications Inc.......................................616 281-5769
7670 Caterpillar Ct Sw Grand Rapids (49548) *(G-6832)*
Rock Tool & Machine Co Inc......................................734 455-9840
45145 Five Mile Rd Plymouth (48170) *(G-12743)*
Rock-Way LLC..734 357-2112
40500 Ann Arbor Rd E R Plymouth (48170) *(G-12744)*
Rockery...734 281-4629
1175 Eureka Rd Uppr Wyandotte (48192) *(G-17973)*
Rocket Fuel, Troy Also called Sizmek Dsp Inc *(G-16606)*
Rocket Print Copy Ship Center..................................248 336-3636
605 S Washington Ave Royal Oak (48067) *(G-13966)*
Rockford Carving Co, Marine City Also called Klingler Consulting & Mfg *(G-10476)*
Rockford Contract Mfg...616 304-3837
198 Rollingwood Dr Rockford (49341) *(G-13587)*
Rockford Molding & Trim..616 874-8997
8317 Woodcrest Dr Ne Rockford (49341) *(G-13588)*
Rockman & Sons Publishing LLC..............................810 750-6011
240 N Fenway Dr Fenton (48430) *(G-5235)*
Rockman Communications Inc.................................810 433-6800
256 N Fenway Dr Fenton (48430) *(G-5236)*
Rockstar Digital Inc..888 808-5868
6520 Cotter Ave Sterling Heights (48314) *(G-15477)*
Rockstar Group, Sterling Heights Also called Rockstar Digital Inc *(G-15477)*
Rocktech Systems LLC...586 330-9031
50250 E Russell Schmidt Chesterfield (48051) *(G-2832)*
Rockwell Automation Inc..248 696-1200
1441 W Long Lake Rd # 150 Troy (48098) *(G-16582)*
Rockwell Automation Inc..269 792-9137
1121 133rd Ave Wayland (49348) *(G-17412)*
Rockwell Medical Inc (PA)...248 960-9009
30142 S Wixom Rd Wixom (48393) *(G-17886)*
Rockwell Team Sports, Mount Morris Also called Kinder Company Inc *(G-11163)*
Rockwood Quarry LLC (PA)......................................734 783-7415
5699 Ready Rd South Rockwood (48179) *(G-14822)*
Rockwood Quarry LLC..734 783-7400
7500 Reaume Rd Newport (48166) *(G-11590)*
Rocky Mountain Chocolate, Troy Also called Elsa Enterprises Inc *(G-16340)*
Rocky Mountain Rv..435 713-4242
7145 Division Ave S Grand Rapids (49548) *(G-6833)*
Rocky Mtn Choclat Fctry Inc.....................................810 606-8550
12821 S Saginaw St Grand Blanc (48439) *(G-5981)*
Rocky Mtn Choclat Fctry Inc.....................................989 624-4784
8825 Market Place Dr # 425 Birch Run (48415) *(G-1669)*
Rocky Top Farm's, Ellsworth Also called Thomas Cooper *(G-4789)*
Rocon LLC..248 542-9635
1755 E 9 Mile Rd Hazel Park (48030) *(G-7453)*
Rod Chomper Inc...616 392-9677
4249 58th St Holland (49423) *(G-7790)*
Rodan Tool & Mold LLC..248 926-9200
3185 Old Farm Ln Commerce Township (48390) *(G-3450)*
Rodco Ltd..517 244-0200
2118 Cedar St Holt (48842) *(G-7923)*
Rodenhouse Door & Window, Comstock Park Also called Ken Rodenhouse Door & Window *(G-3488)*
Rodenhouse Inc..616 454-3100
974 Front Ave Nw Ste 4 Grand Rapids (49504) *(G-6834)*
Rodney E Harter...231 796-6734
12880 190th Ave Big Rapids (49307) *(G-1644)*
Rodriguez Printing Services (PA).............................248 651-7774
24649 Halsted Rd Farmington Hills (48335) *(G-5116)*
Rods Prints & Promotions...269 639-8814
67654 M 43 South Haven (49090) *(G-14769)*
Rodzina Industries Inc...810 235-2341
3518 Fenton Rd Flint (48507) *(G-5493)*
Roe LLC...231 755-5043
1446 Randolph Ave Muskegon (49441) *(G-11415)*
Roe Publishing Department.....................................517 522-3598
2535 Grey Tower Rd Jackson (49201) *(G-8564)*
Roesch Manufacturing, Tecumseh Also called Roesch Manufacturing Co LLC *(G-15808)*
Roesch Maufacturing Co LLC...................................517 424-6300
904 Industrial Dr Tecumseh (49286) *(G-15808)*
Rofin-Sinar Technologies LLC (HQ).........................734 416-0200
40984 Concept Dr Plymouth (48170) *(G-12745)*

Roger Bazuin & Sons Inc...231 825-2889
8750 W Stoney Corners Rd Mc Bain (49657) *(G-10684)*
Roger D Rapoport..231 755-6665
1487 Glen Ave Muskegon (49441) *(G-11416)*
Roger Mix Storage...231 352-9762
1218 Elm St Frankfort (49635) *(G-5605)*
Roger Randall Bakery, Wakefield Also called Randalls Bakery *(G-16855)*
Roger Zatkoff Company (PA)....................................248 478-2400
23230 Industrial Park Dr Farmington Hills (48335) *(G-5117)*
Roger Zatkoff Company..586 264-3593
31773 Denton Dr Warren (48092) *(G-17223)*
Rogers Athletic...989 386-7393
495 Pioneer Pkwy Clare (48617) *(G-2887)*
Rogers Athletic Company Inc...................................989 386-2950
3760 W Ludington Dr Farwell (48622) *(G-5165)*
Rogers Beef Farms...906 632-1584
6917 S Nicolet Rd Sault Sainte Marie (49783) *(G-14472)*
Rogers Foam Automotive Corp (HQ)......................810 820-6323
501 W Kearsley St Flint (48503) *(G-5494)*
Rogers Printing Inc..231 853-2244
3350 Main St Ravenna (49451) *(G-13128)*
Rogue Industrial Service, Atlanta Also called Bruno Wojcik *(G-730)*
Rohloff Builders Inc...989 868-3191
9916 Saginaw St Reese (48757) *(G-13232)*
Rohm Haas Dnmark Invstmnts LLC........................989 636-1463
2030 Dow Ctr Midland (48674) *(G-10909)*
Rohmann Iron Works Inc...810 233-5611
201 Kelso St Flint (48506) *(G-5495)*
Rokan Corp...810 735-9170
5929 Deerfield Indus Dr Linden (48451) *(G-9595)*
Rolfs Jewelers Ltd..586 739-3906
52930 Van Dyke Ave Shelby Township (48316) *(G-14681)*
Roll Rite Corporation..989 345-3434
650 Indl Pk Ave Gladwin (48624) *(G-5935)*
Roll Rite Group Holdings, Gladwin Also called Roll-Rite LLC *(G-5936)*
Roll Tech Inc...517 283-3811
104 Enterprise St Reading (49274) *(G-13137)*
Roll-Rite LLC..989 345-3434
650 Industrial Dr Gladwin (48624) *(G-5936)*
Rolled Alloys Inc (PA)..800 521-0332
125 W Sterns Rd Temperance (48182) *(G-15842)*
Rolleigh Inc...517 283-3811
104 Enterprise St Reading (49274) *(G-13138)*
Rollie Williams Paint Spot..616 791-6100
2570 Walker Ave Nw Grand Rapids (49544) *(G-6835)*
Rollstock Inc...616 803-5370
3680 44th St Se Ste 100a Grand Rapids (49512) *(G-6836)*
Rolston Hockey Academy LLC..................................248 450-5300
13950 Oak Park Blvd Oak Park (48237) *(G-12093)*
Roma Bakery & Imported Foods.............................517 485-9466
1928 Vassar Dr Lansing (48912) *(G-9419)*
Roma Bakery Deli & Fine Foods, Lansing Also called Roma Bakery & Imported Foods *(G-9419)*
Roma Tool Inc..248 218-1889
50 Northpointe Dr Lake Orion (48359) *(G-9156)*
Roman Engineering...231 238-7644
1715 E M 68 Hwy Afton (49705) *(G-106)*
Romeo Mold Technologies Inc.................................586 336-1245
121 Mclean Bruce Twp (48065) *(G-2094)*
Romeo North, Bruce Twp Also called L & L Products Inc *(G-2088)*
Romeo Printing Company Inc..................................586 752-9003
225 N Main St Romeo (48065) *(G-13637)*
Romeo South, Bruce Twp Also called L & L Products Inc *(G-2089)*
Romeo Technologies Inc...586 336-5015
101 Mclean Bruce Twp (48065) *(G-2095)*
Romeo-Rim Inc..586 336-5800
74000 Van Dyke Rd Bruce Twp (48065) *(G-2096)*
Romulus Division, Romulus Also called Penn Automotive Inc *(G-13720)*
Romulus Nut Division, Romulus Also called Federal Screw Works *(G-13677)*
Ron Fisk Hardwoods Inc (PA)...................................616 887-3826
10700 Low Lake Dr Ne Sparta (49345) *(G-15108)*
Ron Pair Enterprises Inc...231 547-4000
105 Stover Rd Charlevoix (49720) *(G-2629)*
Ron Rowe (PA)...231 652-2642
8140 S Mason Dr Newaygo (49337) *(G-11577)*
Ron Watkins..517 439-5451
4080 State Rd Hillsdale (49242) *(G-7537)*
Ronal Industries Inc..248 616-9691
6615 19 Mile Rd Sterling Heights (48314) *(G-15478)*
Ronald Bradley...989 422-5609
224 Welch Rd Houghton Lake (48629) *(G-7996)*
Ronald M Davis Co Inc...313 864-5588
16260 Meyers Rd Detroit (48235) *(G-4347)*
Ronald R Wellington...586 488-3087
141 Mclean Bruce Twp (48065) *(G-2097)*
Ronningen Research and Dev Co............................269 649-0520
6700 E Yz Ave Vicksburg (49097) *(G-16842)*
Rook Metering Equipment, Mount Pleasant Also called Michael Engineering Ltd *(G-11204)*

(PA)=Parent Co (HQ)=Headquarters (DH)=Div Headquarters

Rooms of Grand Rapids LLC 616 260-1452
17971 N Fruitport Rd Spring Lake (49456) ***(G-15173)***
Roost Oil Company, Coldwater *Also called Warner Oil Company* ***(G-3341)***
Root Spring Scraper Co 269 382-2025
527 W North St Kalamazoo (49007) ***(G-8874)***
Root-Lowell Manufacturing Co 616 897-9211
1000 Foreman St Lowell (49331) ***(G-10042)***
Rooto Corporation 517 546-8330
3505 W Grand River Ave Howell (48855) ***(G-8093)***
Ropp Orthopedic Clinic LLC 248 669-9222
2075 E West Maple Rd B207 Commerce Township (48390) ***(G-3451)***
Rosary Workshop 906 788-4846
5209 W 16 5 Ln Stephenson (49887) ***(G-15239)***
Rosati Specialties LLC 586 783-3866
24300 Capital Blvd Clinton Township (48036) ***(G-3214)***
Rose Acres Pallets LLC 989 268-3074
4769 N Bollinger Rd Vestaburg (48891) ***(G-16828)***
Rose Acres Tallets 989 268-3074
9932 E Kendaville Rd Vestaburg (48891) ***(G-16829)***
Rose Business Forms Company 734 424-5200
22008 W 8 Mile Rd Southfield (48033) ***(G-15017)***
Rose Computer Consulting, Troy *Also called Rose Mobile Computer Repr LLC* ***(G-16583)***
Rose Corporation 734 426-0005
2467 Bishop Cir E Dexter (48130) ***(G-4508)***
Rose Engraving Company 616 243-3108
1971 E Beltline Ave Ne # 240 Grand Rapids (49525) ***(G-6837)***
Rose Medical, Grand Rapids *Also called Rose Technologies Company* ***(G-6838)***
Rose Mobile Computer Repr LLC 248 653-0865
200 E Big Beaver Rd Troy (48083) ***(G-16583)***
Rose Printing Services, Southfield *Also called Rose Business Forms Company* ***(G-15017)***
Rose Technologies Company 616 233-3000
1440 Front Ave Nw Grand Rapids (49504) ***(G-6838)***
Rose Tool & Die Inc 989 343-1015
640 S Valley St West Branch (48661) ***(G-17519)***
Rose-A-Lee Technologies Inc 586 799-4555
6550 Sims Dr Sterling Heights (48313) ***(G-15479)***
Rosedale Products Inc (PA) 734 665-8201
3730 W Liberty Rd Ann Arbor (48103) ***(G-624)***
Rosenthal Logging 231 348-8168
577 Blanchard Rd Petoskey (49770) ***(G-12473)***
Roses Susies Feather 989 689-6570
7191 Middle Rd Hope (48628) ***(G-7956)***
Roskam Baking Company (PA) 616 574-5757
4880 Corp Exch Blvd Se Grand Rapids (49512) ***(G-6839)***
Roskam Baking Company 616 574-5757
3225 32nd St Se Grand Rapids (49512) ***(G-6840)***
Roskam Baking Company 616 574-5757
3035 32nd St Se Grand Rapids (49512) ***(G-6841)***
Roskam Baking Company 616 554-9160
4855 52nd St Se Grand Rapids (49512) ***(G-6842)***
Roskam Baking Company 616 574-5757
5353 Broadmoor Ave Se Grand Rapids (49512) ***(G-6843)***
Rosler Metal Finishing USA LLC (PA) 269 441-3000
1551 Denso Rd Battle Creek (49037) ***(G-1242)***
Rospatch Jessco Corporation 269 782-8661
202 Spaulding St Dowagiac (49047) ***(G-4558)***
Ross Cabinets II Inc 586 752-7750
50169 Hayes Rd Shelby Township (48315) ***(G-14682)***
Ross Decco Company 248 764-1845
1250 Stephenson Hwy Troy (48083) ***(G-16584)***
Ross Design & Engineering Inc (PA) 517 547-6033
14445 E Chicago Rd Cement City (49233) ***(G-2575)***
Ross Pallet Co 810 966-4945
3360 Petit St Port Huron (48060) ***(G-12963)***
Ross Sheet Metal Inc 248 543-1170
2300 Hilton Rd Ferndale (48220) ***(G-5316)***
Rosta USA Corp 269 841-5448
797 Ferguson Dr Benton Harbor (49022) ***(G-1544)***
Rotary Multiforms Inc 586 558-7960
1340 E 11 Mile Rd Madison Heights (48071) ***(G-10344)***
Rotational Levitation Levi, Bay City *Also called Twm Technology LLC* ***(G-1365)***
Roth Fabricating Inc 517 458-7541
9600 Skyline Dr Morenci (49256) ***(G-11114)***
Roth-Williams Industries Inc 586 792-0090
34335 Groesbeck Hwy Clinton Township (48035) ***(G-3215)***
Rothbury Farms Inc 616 574-5757
3061 Shaffer Ave Se Grand Rapids (49512) ***(G-6844)***
Rothig Forest Products Inc 231 266-8292
3600 N M 37 Irons (49644) ***(G-8322)***
Roto Flo, Rochester Hills *Also called U S Equipment Co* ***(G-13533)***
Roto-Feeders Inc 269 782-2456
28691 Middle Crossing Rd Dowagiac (49047) ***(G-4559)***
Roto-Finish Company Inc 269 327-7071
1600 Douglas Ave Kalamazoo (49007) ***(G-8875)***
Roto-Plastics Corporation 517 263-8981
1001 Division St Adrian (49221) ***(G-92)***
Rottman Manufacturing Group 586 693-5676
35566 Mound Rd Sterling Heights (48310) ***(G-15480)***
Rouch Enterprises, Farmington *Also called Roush Manufacturing Inc* ***(G-4910)***
Round Lake Sand & Gravel Inc 517 467-4458
8707 Round Lake Hwy Addison (49220) ***(G-38)***
Roura Acquisition Inc (PA) 586 790-6100
35355 Forton Ct Clinton Township (48035) ***(G-3216)***
Roura Material Handling, Clinton Township *Also called Roura Acquisition Inc* ***(G-3216)***
Roush Enterprises Inc 734 779-7006
12447 Levan Rd Livonia (48150) ***(G-9911)***
Roush Enterprises Inc 313 294-8200
16630 Southfield Rd Allen Park (48101) ***(G-207)***
Roush Enterprises Inc (PA) 734 805-4400
34300 W 9 Mile Rd Farmington (48335) ***(G-4909)***
Roush Industries Inc 734 779-7016
36580 Commerce St Livonia (48150) ***(G-9912)***
Roush Industries Inc 734 779-7013
11874 Market St Livonia (48150) ***(G-9913)***
Roush Industries Inc 734 779-7000
12447 Levan Rd Bldg 6 Livonia (48150) ***(G-9914)***
Roush Manufacturing Inc 734 805-4400
34300 W 9 Mile Rd Farmington (48335) ***(G-4910)***
Roush Manufacturing Inc (HQ) 734 779-7006
12447 Levan Rd Livonia (48150) ***(G-9915)***
Roussin M & Ubelhor R Inc 586 783-6015
41903 Irwin Dr Harrison Township (48045) ***(G-7347)***
Route One 616 455-4883
7290 Division Ave S Grand Rapids (49548) ***(G-6845)***
Rowe & Associates 231 932-9716
13685 S West Bay Shore Dr # 115 Traverse City (49684) ***(G-16097)***
Rowland Mold & Machine Inc 616 875-5400
9395 Henry Ct Zeeland (49464) ***(G-18185)***
Rowsey Construction & Dev LLC 313 675-2464
607 Shelby St Ste 722 Detroit (48226) ***(G-4348)***
Rowster Coffee Inc 616 780-7777
100 Stevens St Sw Grand Rapids (49507) ***(G-6846)***
Roxbury Creek LLC 989 731-2062
207 Arrowhead Trl Gaylord (49735) ***(G-5890)***
Roy A Hutchins Company 248 437-3470
57455 Travis Rd New Hudson (48165) ***(G-11554)***
Royal Accoutrements Inc 517 347-7983
172 W Sherwood Rd Okemos (48864) ***(G-12136)***
Royal Adhesives & Sealants LLC 517 764-0334
4401 Page Ave Michigan Center (49254) ***(G-10790)***
Royal Aluminum and Steel Inc 586 421-0057
51401 Chesterfield Rd Chesterfield (48051) ***(G-2833)***
Royal ARC Crane Service, Flat Rock *Also called Royal ARC Welding Company* ***(G-5362)***
Royal ARC Inc 586 758-0718
520 Sheffield Dr Madison Heights (48071) ***(G-10345)***
Royal ARC Welding Company (PA) 734 789-9099
23851 Vreeland Rd Flat Rock (48134) ***(G-5362)***
Royal Building Products, Shelby Township *Also called Plastic Trends Inc* ***(G-14668)***
Royal Cabinet Inc 517 787-2940
3900 Francis St Jackson (49203) ***(G-8565)***
Royal Cabinets 313 541-1190
15730 Telegraph Rd Redford (48239) ***(G-13188)***
Royal Coffee Maker, Okemos *Also called Royal Accoutrements Inc* ***(G-12136)***
Royal Container Inc 248 967-0910
21100 Hubbell St Oak Park (48237) ***(G-12094)***
Royal Container Services Inc (PA) 586 775-7600
22510 Hoover Rd Warren (48089) ***(G-17224)***
Royal Crest Inc 248 399-2476
14851 W 11 Mile Rd Oak Park (48237) ***(G-12095)***
Royal Design, Madison Heights *Also called J H P Inc* ***(G-10280)***
Royal Design & Manufacturing 248 588-0110
32401 Stephenson Hwy Madison Heights (48071) ***(G-10346)***
Royal Flex-N-Gate Oak LLC 248 549-3800
5663 E 9 Mile Rd Warren (48091) ***(G-17225)***
Royal Food Foods, Madison Heights *Also called Great Lakes Food Center LLC* ***(G-10261)***
Royal Lux Magazine 248 602-6565
25055 Champlaign Dr Southfield (48034) ***(G-15018)***
Royal Oak & Birmingham Tent (PA) 248 542-5552
2625 W 14 Mile Rd Royal Oak (48073) ***(G-13967)***
Royal Oak Industries Inc 248 628-2830
700 S Glaspie St Oxford (48371) ***(G-12370)***
Royal Oak Millwork Company LLC 248 547-1210
226 E Hudson Ave Royal Oak (48067) ***(G-13968)***
Royal Oak Name Plate Company 586 774-8500
16560 Industrial St Roseville (48066) ***(G-13863)***
Royal Oak Recycling, Royal Oak *Also called Recycling Rizzo Services LLC* ***(G-13964)***
Royal Oak Waste Ppr Met No 2, Royal Oak *Also called V & M Corporation* ***(G-13980)***
Royal Plastics LLC 616 669-3393
3765 Quincy St Hudsonville (49426) ***(G-8176)***
Royal Rod Co, Portland *Also called Pressweld Manufacturing Co* ***(G-13066)***
Royal Stewart Enterprises 734 224-7994
7355 Lewis Ave Ste B Temperance (48182) ***(G-15843)***
Royal Stone LLC 248 343-6232
3014 Dietz Rd Williamston (48895) ***(G-17739)***
Royal Technologies Corporation 616 667-4102
3133 Highland Blvd Hudsonville (49426) ***(G-8177)***
Royal Technologies Corporation (PA) 616 669-3393
3765 Quincy St Hudsonville (49426) ***(G-8178)***

ALPHABETIC SECTION — S & M Machining Company

Royal Technologies Corporation 616 667-4102
3712 Quincy St Hudsonville (49426) *(G-8179)*
Royal Technologies Corporation 616 669-3393
2905 Corporate Grove Dr Hudsonville (49426) *(G-8180)*
Royce Corporation 586 758-1500
23042 Sherwood Ave Warren (48091) *(G-17226)*
Royce Rolls Ringer Company 616 361-9266
16 Riverview Ter Ne Grand Rapids (49505) *(G-6847)*
Rpb Safety LLC 866 494-4599
2807 Samoset Rd Royal Oak (48073) *(G-13969)*
RPC Company 989 752-3618
1708 N Michigan Ave Saginaw (48602) *(G-14134)*
Rpd Manufacturing LLC 248 760-4796
3171 Rolling Green Ct Milford (48380) *(G-10983)*
Rps Bar 810 235-8876
533 Kelso St Flint (48506) *(G-5496)*
RPS Tool and Engineering Inc (PA) 586 298-6590
16149 Common Rd Roseville (48066) *(G-13864)*
RR, Bruce Twp Also called Romeo-Rim Inc *(G-2096)*
Rs Defense Tactics 248 693-2337
31 Beebe St Lake Orion (48362) *(G-9157)*
Rs Technologies Ltd 248 888-8260
25286 Witherspoon St Farmington Hills (48335) *(G-5118)*
Rsb North America LLC (HQ) 517 568-4171
24425 W M 60 Homer (49245) *(G-7948)*
Rsb Transmissions Na Inc (HQ) 517 568-4171
24425 W M 60 Homer (49245) *(G-7949)*
RSI Global Sourcing LLC 734 604-2448
43630 Wendingo Ct Novi (48375) *(G-11988)*
Rsls Corp 248 726-0675
51084 Filomena Dr Shelby Township (48315) *(G-14683)*
RSM & Associates Co 517 750-9330
4107 W Michigan Ave Jackson (49202) *(G-8566)*
RSM Auto Co., Jackson Also called RSM & Associates Co *(G-8566)*
RSR Industries, Ann Arbor Also called RSR Sales Inc *(G-625)*
RSR Sales Inc 734 668-8166
232 Haeussler Ct Ann Arbor (48103) *(G-625)*
Rt Baldwin Enterprises Inc 616 669-1626
4322 Cent Pkwy Ste A Hudsonville (49426) *(G-8181)*
Rt London, Grand Rapids Also called R T London Company *(G-6804)*
Rt Manufacturing Inc 906 233-9158
2522 14th Ave N Escanaba (49829) *(G-4858)*
Rt Swanson Inc 517 627-4955
1030 Tulip St Grand Ledge (48837) *(G-6115)*
Rta Water Treatment, Athens Also called Teachout and Associates Inc *(G-729)*
RTD Manufacturing Inc 517 783-1550
1150 S Elm Ave Jackson (49203) *(G-8567)*
Rtg Products Inc 734 323-8916
15924 Centralia Redford (48239) *(G-13189)*
Rti Products LLC 269 684-9960
1451 Lake St Niles (49120) *(G-11644)*
Rti Surgical, Marquette Also called Pioneer Surgical Tech Inc *(G-10552)*
Rtlf-Hope LLC 313 538-1700
1401 Abbott St Detroit (48216) *(G-4349)*
Rtr Alpha Inc 248 377-4060
2285 N Opdyke Rd Ste G Auburn Hills (48326) *(G-994)*
RTS Cutting Tools Inc 586 954-1900
24100 Capital Blvd Clinton Township (48036) *(G-3217)*
Rubbair LLC 269 327-7003
9229 Shaver Rd Portage (49024) *(G-13028)*
Rubber & Plastics Co (PA) 248 370-0700
3650 Lapeer Rd Auburn Hills (48326) *(G-995)*
Rubber Rope Products Company 906 358-4133
25760 Old Hwy 2e 2 E Watersmeet (49969) *(G-17389)*
Rubber Round-Up, Hastings Also called Mensch Mfg Mar Div Inc *(G-7421)*
Rubber Stamps Unlimited Inc 734 451-7300
334 S Harvey St Ste 1 Plymouth (48170) *(G-12746)*
Rucci Forged Wheels Inc (PA) 248 577-3500
2003 E 14 Mile Rd Sterling Heights (48310) *(G-15481)*
Rudy Goupille & Sons Inc 906 475-9816
118 Midway Dr Negaunee (49866) *(G-11476)*
Ruelle Industries Inc 248 618-0333
5425 Perry Dr Ste 108 Waterford (48329) *(G-17373)*
Ruess Winchester Inc 989 725-5809
705 Mcmillan Rd Owosso (48867) *(G-12312)*
Ruff Life LLC 231 347-1214
309 Howard St Petoskey (49770) *(G-12474)*
Rugged Liner Inc 989 725-8354
200 Universal Dr Owosso (48867) *(G-12313)*
Ruhlman Race Cars 517 529-4661
2132 Jefferson Rd Clarklake (49234) *(G-2899)*
Ruleau Brothers Inc (PA) 906 753-4767
W521 Stephenson S Dr Stephenson (49887) *(G-15240)*
Rumler Brothers Inc 517 437-2990
72 W Carleton Rd Hillsdale (49242) *(G-7538)*
Runguards, Ann Arbor Also called Nipguards LLC *(G-574)*
Runnin Gears, Harrison Also called James L Miller *(G-7313)*
Runway Liquidation LLC 989 624-4756
12150 S Beyer Rd Birch Run (48415) *(G-1670)*

Runyan Pottery Supply Inc 810 687-4500
820 Tacoma Ct Clio (48420) *(G-3281)*
Ruppe Manufacturing Company (PA) 906 932-3540
100 Mill St Ironwood (49938) *(G-8339)*
Rusas Printing Co Inc 313 952-2977
26770 Grand River Ave Redford (48240) *(G-13190)*
Rush Air Inc 810 694-5763
200 Quality Way Holly (48442) *(G-7895)*
Rush Machining Inc 248 583-0550
256 Minnesota Dr Troy (48083) *(G-16585)*
Rush Stationers Printers Inc 989 891-9305
1310 N Johnson St Bay City (48708) *(G-1351)*
Rush Technologies, Holly Also called Rush Air Inc *(G-7895)*
Russ Parke Awnings, Warren Also called Patio Land Mfg Inc *(G-17184)*
Russell Farms Inc 269 349-6120
5616 N Riverview Dr Kalamazoo (49004) *(G-8876)*
Russell R Peters Co LLC 989 732-0660
1370 Pineview St Gaylord (49735) *(G-5891)*
Russells Technical Pdts Inc 616 392-3161
1883 Russel Ct Holland (49423) *(G-7791)*
Russo Bros Inc 906 485-5250
1710 Us Highway 41 W Ishpeming (49849) *(G-8353)*
Russos Bakery Inc 586 791-7320
35160 Forton Ct Clinton Township (48035) *(G-3218)*
Rustic Cking Dsigns StrIng Hts 586 795-4897
5352 Northlawn Dr Sterling Heights (48310) *(G-15482)*
RUSTIC ROOM, Escanaba Also called Lakestate Industries Inc *(G-4838)*
Rustop Technologies LLC (PA) 517 223-5098
4831 W Grand River Ave Howell (48855) *(G-8094)*
Ruth Drain Tile Inc 989 864-3406
4551 Ruth Rd Ruth (48470) *(G-13989)*
Rutherford & Associates Inc 616 392-5000
1009 Productions Ct Holland (49423) *(G-7792)*
Rvm Company of Toledo 734 654-2201
845 Monroe St Carleton (48117) *(G-2462)*
Rwc Inc (PA) 989 684-4030
2105 S Euclid Ave Bay City (48706) *(G-1352)*
Rwi Manufacturing, Owosso Also called Ruess Winchester Inc *(G-12312)*
Rwl Sign Co LLC 269 372-3629
6185 W Kl Ave Kalamazoo (49009) *(G-8877)*
RWS & Associates LLC 517 278-3134
305 W Chicago Rd Coldwater (49036) *(G-3328)*
Rx Optical Laboratories Inc (PA) 269 342-5958
1825 S Park St Kalamazoo (49001) *(G-8878)*
Rx Optical Laboratories Inc 269 349-7627
5349 W Main St Ofc Kalamazoo (49009) *(G-8879)*
Rx Optical Laboratories Inc 269 965-5106
65 Columbia Ave E Battle Creek (49015) *(G-1243)*
Rx-Rite Optical Co 586 294-8500
32925 Groesbeck Hwy Fraser (48026) *(G-5719)*
Ryan Polishing Corporation 248 548-6832
10709 Capital St Oak Park (48237) *(G-12096)*
Ryan Reynolds Golf Shop LLC 269 629-9311
112 Walnut Blvd Unit 307 Rochester (48307) *(G-13349)*
Ryans Equipment Inc 989 427-2829
111 Quicksilver Ln Edmore (48829) *(G-4755)*
Ryder Automatic & Mfg 586 293-2109
16636 Admiral Fraser (48026) *(G-5720)*
Ryder Integrated Logistics Inc 517 492-4446
2901 S Canal Rd Lansing (48917) *(G-9321)*
Rydin & Associates, Clinton Township Also called Rydin and Associates Inc *(G-3219)*
Rydin and Associates Inc 586 783-9772
44604 Macomb Indus Dr Clinton Township (48036) *(G-3219)*
Ryson Tube Inc 810 227-4567
2095 Euler Rd Brighton (48114) *(G-1987)*
Rytam Technolgy, Rochester Hills Also called Dl Engineering & Tech Inc *(G-13409)*
S & B Roofing Services Inc 248 334-5372
184 W Sheffield Ave Pontiac (48340) *(G-12863)*
S & C Industries Inc 269 381-6022
5575 Collingwood Ave Kalamazoo (49004) *(G-8880)*
S & C Plastic Coating, Grand Rapids Also called Simmons & Courtright Plastic *(G-6866)*
S & C Tool & Manufacturing 313 378-1003
30954 Industrial Rd Ste A Livonia (48150) *(G-9916)*
S & G Erection Company 517 546-9240
2055 N Lima Center Dr Howell (48843) *(G-8095)*
S & G Prototype Inc 586 716-3600
51540 Industrial Dr New Baltimore (48047) *(G-11491)*
S & H Trophy & Sports 616 754-0005
1224 Blackburn St Greenville (48838) *(G-7151)*
S & J Inc 248 299-0822
1860 Star Batt Dr Rochester Hills (48309) *(G-13508)*
S & K Tool & Die Company Inc 269 345-2174
4401 Environmental Dr Portage (49002) *(G-13029)*
S & L Machine Products Inc 248 543-6633
30250 Stephenson Hwy Madison Heights (48071) *(G-10347)*
S & L Tool Inc 734 464-4200
11833 Brookfield St Livonia (48150) *(G-9917)*
S & M Machining Company 248 348-0310
47590 Avante Dr Wixom (48393) *(G-17887)*

(PA)=Parent Co (HQ)=Headquarters (DH)=Div Headquarters

S & N Aziza Inc ... 248 879-9396
6974 Brunswick Dr Troy (48085) *(G-16586)*
S & N Graphic Solutions LLC ... 734 495-3314
1818 Stonebridge Way Canton (48188) *(G-2424)*
S & N Machine & Fabricating ... 231 894-2658
7989 S Michigan Ave Rothbury (49452) *(G-13895)*
S & S Die Co ... 517 272-1100
2727 Lyons Ave Lansing (48910) *(G-9420)*
S & S Forest Products ... 906 892-8268
905 W Munising Ave Munising (49862) *(G-11249)*
S & S Machine Tool Repair LLC ... 616 877-4930
1664 144th Ave Dorr (49323) *(G-4527)*
S & S Mold & Tool, Grand Junction Also called Sollman & Son Mold & Tool *(G-6098)*
S & S Mowing Inc ... 906 466-9009
1460 15.5 Rd Bark River (49807) *(G-1122)*
S & S Parts LLC ... 517 467-6511
11000 Woerner Rd Onsted (49265) *(G-12156)*
S & S Specialties, Dorr Also called S & S Machine Tool Repair LLC *(G-4527)*
S & S Tool Inc ... 616 458-3219
1310 Taylor Ave N Grand Rapids (49505) *(G-6848)*
S & S Tube Inc ... 989 656-7211
9938 Pigeon Rd Bay Port (48720) *(G-1375)*
S & W Holdings Ltd (PA) ... 248 723-2870
114 S Old Woodward Ave Birmingham (48009) *(G-1701)*
S & W Marine System, Greenville Also called Wells Helicopter Service Inc *(G-7160)*
S 2 Yachts Inc (PA) ... 616 392-7163
725 E 40th St Holland (49423) *(G-7793)*
S A S ... 586 725-6381
33614 Lakeview St Chesterfield (48047) *(G-2834)*
S and P Drctnal Boring Svc LLC ... 989 832-7716
801 W Meadowbrook Dr Midland (48640) *(G-10910)*
S and S Enterprise LLC ... 989 894-7002
123 Webster St Bay City (48708) *(G-1353)*
S and S Enterprises, Bay City Also called S and S Enterprise LLC *(G-1353)*
S B C Holdings Inc ... 313 446-2000
300 River Place Dr # 5000 Detroit (48207) *(G-4350)*
S C Johnson & Son Inc ... 248 822-2174
3001 W Big Beaver Rd # 402 Troy (48084) *(G-16587)*
S C Johnson & Son Inc ... 989 667-0211
4867 Wilder Rd Bay City (48706) *(G-1354)*
S C Johnson Wax, Troy Also called S C Johnson & Son Inc *(G-16587)*
S C Johnson Wax, Bay City Also called S C Johnson & Son Inc *(G-1354)*
S C S, Ann Arbor Also called Strategic Computer Solutions *(G-648)*
S E S, Charlevoix Also called Seelye Equipment Specialist *(G-2630)*
S F Gilmore Inc ... 616 475-5100
321 Terminal St Sw Grand Rapids (49548) *(G-6849)*
S F R Precision Turning Inc ... 517 709-3367
2200 Depot St Holt (48842) *(G-7924)*
S F S Carbide Tool ... 989 777-3890
4480 Marlea Dr Saginaw (48601) *(G-14135)*
S G Publications Inc (PA) ... 517 676-5100
140 E Ash St Mason (48854) *(G-10653)*
S H A, Wixom Also called Semicndctor Hybrid Assmbly Inc *(G-17893)*
S M W, Holland Also called SMW Tooling Inc *(G-7808)*
S Main Company LLC ... 248 960-1540
50489 Pontiac Trl Wixom (48393) *(G-17888)*
S N D Steel Fabrication Inc ... 586 997-1500
11611 Park Ct Shelby Township (48315) *(G-14684)*
S P Jig Grinding ... 734 525-6335
32465 Schoolcraft Rd Livonia (48150) *(G-9918)*
S P Kish Industries Inc ... 517 543-2650
600 W Seminary St Charlotte (48813) *(G-2663)*
S P P D, Fenton Also called Creative Foam Corporation *(G-5198)*
S R P Inc ... 517 784-3153
1927 Wildwood Ave Jackson (49202) *(G-8568)*
S S Graphics Inc ... 734 246-4420
4176 6th St Wyandotte (48192) *(G-17974)*
S T A Inc ... 248 328-5000
4150 Grange Hall Rd Holly (48442) *(G-7896)*
S T I, Waterford Also called Safety Technology Intl Inc *(G-17375)*
S T M, Holland Also called Stm Mfg Inc *(G-7815)*
S& A Fuel LLC ... 313 945-6555
10005 W Warren Ave Dearborn (48126) *(G-3754)*
S&M Logging LLC ... 231 821-0588
6141 16th St Twin Lake (49457) *(G-16714)*
S&N Fabricating, Rothbury Also called S & N Machine & Fabricating *(G-13895)*
S&S Precision LLC ... 248 266-4770
1378 Cherrystone Ct Wixom (48393) *(G-17889)*
S-3 Engineering Inc ... 734 996-2303
95 Enterprise Dr Ann Arbor (48103) *(G-626)*
S1 Plant, Grand Rapids Also called Roskam Baking Company *(G-6843)*
S2 Games LLC ... 269 344-8020
950 Trade Centre Way # 200 Portage (49002) *(G-13030)*
SA Automotive Ltd (PA) ... 517 521-4205
1307 Highview Dr Webberville (48892) *(G-17453)*
SA Automotive Ltd LLC ... 989 723-0425
751 S Delaney Rd Owosso (48867) *(G-12314)*

SA Industries 2 Inc (PA) ... 248 693-9100
1081 Indianwood Rd Lake Orion (48362) *(G-9158)*
SA Sport, Lansing Also called Spieth Anderson USA Lc *(G-9265)*
Saa Tech Inc ... 313 933-4960
7420 Intervale St Detroit (48238) *(G-4351)*
Saad Fuels Inc ... 734 425-2829
8755 N Middlebelt Rd Westland (48185) *(G-17598)*
Saagara LLC ... 734 658-4693
709 W Ellsworth Rd # 200 Ann Arbor (48108) *(G-627)*
Saarsteel Incorporated ... 248 608-0849
445 S Livernois Rd # 222 Rochester Hills (48307) *(G-13509)*
Sab America Inc ... 313 363-3392
10800 W Wrren Ave Ste 260 Dearborn (48126) *(G-3755)*
Saba Software Inc ... 248 228-7300
26999 Centrl Pk Blvd # 210 Southfield (48076) *(G-15019)*
Saber Tool Company Inc ... 231 779-4340
1553 N Mitchell St Cadillac (49601) *(G-2275)*
Sabertooth Enterprises LLC ... 989 539-9842
2725 Larch Rd Harrison (48625) *(G-7316)*
Sabre Manufacturing ... 269 945-4120
2324 S M 37 Hwy Hastings (49058) *(G-7425)*
Sabre-TEC Inc ... 586 949-5386
48705 Structural Dr Chesterfield (48051) *(G-2835)*
Sac, Spring Arbor Also called Spring Arbor Coatings LLC *(G-15128)*
Sac Plastics Inc ... 616 846-0820
17259 Hickory St Spring Lake (49456) *(G-15174)*
Sadia Enterprises Inc ... 248 854-4666
3373 Rochester Rd Troy (48083) *(G-16588)*
SAE International ... 248 273-2455
755 W Big Beaver Rd # 1600 Troy (48084) *(G-16589)*
Saf-Air Products Inc ... 734 522-8360
32839 Manor Park Garden City (48135) *(G-5837)*
Saf-Holland Inc ... 616 396-6501
467 Ottawa Ave Holland (49423) *(G-7794)*
Saf-Holland Inc (HQ) ... 231 773-3271
1950 Industrial Blvd Muskegon (49442) *(G-11417)*
Saf-Holland Inc ... 616 396-6501
430 W 18th St Holland (49423) *(G-7795)*
Saf-Holland USA, Muskegon Also called Saf-Holland Inc *(G-11417)*
Safari Circuit, Otsego Also called Mitech Electronics Corporation *(G-12246)*
Safari Circuits Inc (PA) ... 269 694-9471
411 Washington St Otsego (49078) *(G-12255)*
Safari Meats Llc ... 313 539-3367
24570 Oneida Blvd Oak Park (48237) *(G-12097)*
Safe N Simple LLC ... 248 875-0840
5827 Terex Clarkston (48346) *(G-2953)*
Safecutters Inc ... 866 865-7171
800 E Ellis Rd Ste 245 Norton Shores (49441) *(G-11791)*
Safety Decals, Ludington Also called Tyes Inc *(G-10083)*
Safety Technology Holdings Inc ... 415 983-2706
23300 Haggerty Rd Farmington Hills (48335) *(G-5119)*
Safety Technology Intl, Waterford Also called Safety Technology Intl Inc *(G-17374)*
Safety Technology Intl Inc (PA) ... 248 673-9898
2306 Airport Rd Waterford (48327) *(G-17374)*
Safety Technology Intl Inc ... 248 673-9898
3777 Airport Rd Waterford (48329) *(G-17375)*
Safety-Kleen Systems Inc ... 989 753-3261
3899 Wolf Rd Saginaw (48601) *(G-14136)*
Safie Specialty Foods Co Inc ... 586 598-8282
25565 Terra Industrial Dr Chesterfield (48051) *(G-2836)*
Saflok, Madison Heights Also called Computerized SEC Systems Inc *(G-10219)*
Safran Group, The, Beverly Hills Also called Microforms Inc *(G-1620)*
Safran Printing Company Inc ... 586 939-7600
30706 Georgetown Dr Beverly Hills (48025) *(G-1621)*
Sage Acoustics LLC ... 269 861-5593
55962 M 43 Bangor (49013) *(G-1095)*
Sage Automotive Interiors Inc ... 248 355-9055
24007 Telegraph Rd Southfield (48033) *(G-15020)*
Sage Control Ordnance Inc ... 989 739-2200
3455 Kings Corner Rd Oscoda (48750) *(G-12219)*
Sage Direct Inc ... 616 940-8311
3400 Raleigh Dr Se Grand Rapids (49512) *(G-6850)*
Sage International Inc (HQ) ... 972 623-2004
26600 Heyn Dr Novi (48374) *(G-11989)*
Sage International Limited ... 989 739-7000
3455 Kings Corner Rd Oscoda (48750) *(G-12220)*
Saginaw, Saginaw Also called Bluewater Thermal Solutions *(G-14008)*
Saginaw Asphalt Paving Co ... 989 755-8147
2981 Carrollton Rd Carrollton (48724) *(G-2487)*
Saginaw Bay Plastics Inc ... 989 686-7860
2768 S Huron Rd Kawkawlin (48631) *(G-8975)*
Saginaw Bearing Company ... 989 752-3169
1400 Agricola Dr Saginaw (48604) *(G-14137)*
Saginaw Control & Engrg Inc (PA) ... 989 799-6871
95 Midland Rd Saginaw (48638) *(G-14138)*
Saginaw Industries LLC ... 989 752-5514
1622 Champagne Dr N Saginaw (48604) *(G-14139)*
Saginaw Knitting Mills Inc ... 989 695-2481
8788 Carter Rd Freeland (48623) *(G-5759)*

ALPHABETIC SECTION Sassy 14 LLC (HQ)

Saginaw Machine Systems Inc.....989 753-8465
800 N Hamilton St Saginaw (48602) *(G-14140)*
Saginaw News, Flint *Also called Herald Newspapers Company Inc (G-5445)*
Saginaw Products Corporation (PA).....989 753-1411
68 Williamson St Saginaw (48601) *(G-14141)*
Saginaw Products Corporation.....989 753-1411
5763 Dixie Hwy Saginaw (48601) *(G-14142)*
Saginaw Products Corporation.....989 753-1411
1320 S Graham Rd Saginaw (48609) *(G-14143)*
Saginaw Rock Products Co.....989 754-6589
1701 N 1st St Saginaw (48601) *(G-14144)*
Saginaw Valley Inst Mtls Inc.....989 496-2307
4800 James Savage Rd Midland (48642) *(G-10911)*
Saginaw Valley Shopper Inc.....989 842-3164
221 E Saginaw St Breckenridge (48615) *(G-1846)*
Saginaw Vly Rehabilitation Ctr, Saginaw *Also called Svrc Industries Inc (G-14159)*
Sagola Hardwoods Inc.....906 542-7200
N10640 State Highway M95 Sagola (49881) *(G-14188)*
Saint Gobain Glass Corporation.....248 816-0060
1651 W Big Beaver Rd Troy (48084) *(G-16590)*
Saint Johns Computer Machining, Saint Johns *Also called St Johns Computer Machining (G-14296)*
Saint Laurent Brothers, Bay City *Also called St Laurent Brothers Inc (G-1360)*
Saint-Gobain Delaware Corp.....734 941-1300
27588 Northline Rd Romulus (48174) *(G-13731)*
Saint-Gobain Prfmce Plas Corp.....989 435-9533
3910 Terry Dianne St Beaverton (48612) *(G-1391)*
Saint-Gobain Prfmce Plas Corp.....231 264-0101
11590 S Us Highway 31 Williamsburg (49690) *(G-17720)*
Saint-Gobain Prfmce Plas Corp.....989 435-9533
3910 Industrial Dr Beaverton (48612) *(G-1392)*
Saint-Gobain Sekurit Usa Inc (HQ).....586 264-1072
35801 Mound Rd Sterling Heights (48310) *(G-15483)*
Sakaiya Company America Ltd.....517 521-5633
901 Highview Dr Webberville (48892) *(G-17454)*
Sakor Technologies Inc.....989 720-2700
1900 Krouse Rd Owosso (48867) *(G-12315)*
Salco Engineering and Mfg Inc.....517 789-9010
2030 Micor Dr Jackson (49203) *(G-8569)*
Saldet Sales and Services Inc.....586 469-4312
44810 Vic Wertz Dr Clinton Township (48036) *(G-3220)*
Saleen Special Vehicles Inc.....909 978-6700
1225 E Maple Rd Troy (48083) *(G-16591)*
Salem Tool Company.....248 349-2632
7811 Salem Rd Northville (48168) *(G-11722)*
Salem/Savard Industries LLC.....313 931-6880
8561 W Chicago Detroit (48204) *(G-4352)*
Salenbien Welding Service Inc.....734 529-3280
460 Roosevelt St Dundee (48131) *(G-4599)*
Salerno Tool Works Inc.....586 755-5000
21034 Ryan Rd Warren (48091) *(G-17227)*
Sales & Engineering Inc.....734 525-9030
32920 Industrial Rd Livonia (48150) *(G-9919)*
Sales Driven Ltd Liability Co.....269 254-8497
2723 Kersten Ct Kalamazoo (49048) *(G-8881)*
Sales Driven Services LLC.....586 854-9494
3128 Walt Blvd Ste 216 Rochester (48309) *(G-13350)*
Sales Page Technologies Inc.....269 567-7401
227 N Rose St Kalamazoo (49007) *(G-8882)*
Salesman Inc.....517 563-8860
102 S Main St Concord (49237) *(G-3524)*
Salesman Publications, Concord *Also called Salesman Inc (G-3524)*
Salespage Technologies LLC (PA).....269 567-7400
600 E Michigan Ave # 103 Kalamazoo (49007) *(G-8883)*
Saline Lectronics Inc.....734 944-1972
710 N Maple Rd Saline (48176) *(G-14413)*
Saline Manufacturing Inc.....586 294-4701
15890 Sturgeon Ct Roseville (48066) *(G-13865)*
Salk Communications Inc.....248 342-7109
40 W Howard St Ste 204 Pontiac (48342) *(G-12864)*
Salk Sound, Pontiac *Also called Salk Communications Inc (G-12864)*
Salvo Tool & Engineering Co (PA).....810 346-2727
3948 Burnsline Rd Brown City (48416) *(G-2057)*
Sam, Clinton Township *Also called Synergy Additive Mfg LLC (G-3241)*
Sam Brown Sales LLC (HQ).....248 358-2626
33106 W 8 Mile Rd Farmington (48336) *(G-4911)*
Samco Industries LLC.....586 447-3900
15985 Sturgeon St Roseville (48066) *(G-13866)*
Sames Kremlin Inc (HQ).....734 979-0100
45001 Five Mile Rd Plymouth (48170) *(G-12747)*
Sames Kremlin Inc.....734 979-0100
45001 Five Mile Rd Plymouth (48170) *(G-12748)*
Sampling Bag Technologies LLC.....734 525-8600
27491 Schoolcraft Rd Livonia (48150) *(G-9920)*
Sampo Company LLC.....734 664-9761
41218 Greenbriar Ln Plymouth (48170) *(G-12749)*
Sampson Tool Incorporated.....248 651-3313
383 South St Rochester (48307) *(G-13351)*
Sams Suit Fctry & Alteration.....248 424-8666
25040 Southfield Rd Southfield (48075) *(G-15021)*
Samuel Son & Co (usa) Inc.....414 486-1556
580 Kirts Blvd Ste 300 Troy (48084) *(G-16592)*
Samvardhana Mtherson Reflectec, Marysville *Also called SMR Automotive Systems USA Inc (G-10616)*
San Marino Iron Company.....313 526-9255
21401 Hoover Rd Warren (48089) *(G-17228)*
Sand Castle For Kids, The, Holland *Also called Sandcastle For Kids Inc (G-7796)*
Sand Products Corporation.....906 292-5432
W5021 Us Hwy 2 Moran (49760) *(G-11108)*
Sand Products Wisconsin LLC.....231 722-6691
560 Mart St Muskegon (49440) *(G-11418)*
Sand Traxx.....616 460-5137
12956 Valley Dr Wayland (49348) *(G-17413)*
Sandbox Solutions Inc.....248 349-7010
1001 Doheny Dr Northville (48167) *(G-11723)*
Sandcastle For Kids Inc.....616 396-5955
2 E 8th St Holland (49423) *(G-7796)*
Sanders Candy LLC (HQ).....800 651-7263
23770 Hall Rd Clinton Township (48036) *(G-3221)*
Sanderson Insulation.....269 496-7660
840 Avery Dr Mendon (49072) *(G-10718)*
Sandlot Sports.....989 835-9696
2900 Universal Dr Saginaw (48603) *(G-14145)*
Sandlot Sports (PA).....989 391-9684
600 N Euclid Ave Bay City (48706) *(G-1355)*
Sandman Inc.....248 652-3432
5877 Livernois Rd Ste 103 Troy (48098) *(G-16593)*
Sandusky Concrete & Supply.....810 648-2627
376 E Sanilac Rd Sandusky (48471) *(G-14442)*
Sandvik Inc.....989 345-6138
510 Griffin Rd West Branch (48661) *(G-17520)*
Sandvik Inc.....269 926-7241
2235 Dewey Ave Benton Harbor (49022) *(G-1545)*
Sandys Contracting.....810 629-2259
10464 Circle J Ct Fenton (48430) *(G-5237)*
Sanford Whippy Dip, Sanford *Also called Farm Country Frz Custard & Kit (G-14450)*
Sanglo International Inc.....248 894-1900
21600 Wyoming St Oak Park (48237) *(G-12098)*
Sanilac Drain and Tile Co.....810 648-4100
61 Orval St Sandusky (48471) *(G-14443)*
Sanilac Steel Inc.....989 635-2992
2487 S Van Dyke Rd Marlette (48453) *(G-10502)*
Saninocencio Logging.....269 945-3567
2900 Roush Rd Hastings (49058) *(G-7426)*
Sanitation Strategies LLC.....517 268-3303
1798 Holloway Dr Ste A Holt (48842) *(G-7925)*
Sanitor Mfg Co.....269 327-3001
1221 W Centre Ave Portage (49024) *(G-13031)*
Sankuer Composite Tech Inc.....586 264-1880
36850 Metro Ct Sterling Heights (48312) *(G-15484)*
Sans Serif Inc.....734 944-1190
75 E Henry St Saline (48176) *(G-14414)*
Santanna Tool & Design LLC.....248 541-3500
25880 Commerce Dr Madison Heights (48071) *(G-10348)*
Santti Brothers Inc.....906 355-2347
26339 Ford Rd Watton (49970) *(G-17395)*
Sanvik Materials Technology, Benton Harbor *Also called Sandvik Inc (G-1545)*
Sanyo Machine America Corp.....248 651-5911
950 S Rochester Rd Rochester Hills (48307) *(G-13510)*
Sappington Crude Oil Inc.....989 345-1052
123 N 6th St West Branch (48661) *(G-17521)*
Sappington Henry Machine & Tl.....989 345-0711
222 Thomas St West Branch (48661) *(G-17522)*
Sappington Machine & Tool, West Branch *Also called Walter Sappington (G-17527)*
Sara Lee Bakery Group, Flint *Also called Bimbo Bakeries Usa Inc (G-5390)*
Sara Lee Bakery Outlet, Traverse City *Also called Bimbo Bakeries Usa Inc (G-15912)*
Saranac Tank Inc.....616 642-9481
100 W Main St Saranac (48881) *(G-14455)*
Sargent Sand Co.....989 792-8734
6105 Jefferson Ave Midland (48640) *(G-10912)*
Sarns Industries Inc.....586 463-5829
41451 Irwin Dr Harrison Twp (48045) *(G-7360)*
Sarns Machine, Harrison Twp *Also called Sarns Industries Inc (G-7360)*
Sas Automotive Systems, Sterling Heights *Also called Sas Automotive Usa Inc (G-15485)*
Sas Automotive Usa Inc.....248 606-1152
17801 E 14 Mile Rd Fraser (48026) *(G-5721)*
Sas Automotive Usa Inc (HQ).....248 606-1152
42555 Merrill Rd Sterling Heights (48314) *(G-15485)*
Sas Global Corporation (PA).....248 414-4470
21601 Mullin Ave Warren (48089) *(G-17229)*
Sas Global Corporation.....248 414-4470
21601 Mullin Ave Warren (48089) *(G-17230)*
Sashabaw Bead Co.....248 969-1353
2730 S Sashabaw Rd Oxford (48371) *(G-12371)*
Sassafras Tees, Ludington *Also called M & M Associates (G-10070)*
Sassy 14 LLC (HQ).....616 243-0767
3729 Patterson Ave Se Kentwood (49512) *(G-9031)*

ALPHABETIC

Sassy Fabrics Inc (PA)......810 694-0440
11805 S Saginaw St Grand Blanc (48439) ***(G-5982)***
Sat Plating LLC, Troy *Also called Surface Activation Tech LLC* ***(G-16628)***
Satellite Tracking Systems......248 627-3334
2160 S Ortonville Rd Ortonville (48462) ***(G-12202)***
Satori E-Technology Inc......408 517-9130
33533 W 12 Mile Rd # 305 Farmington Hills (48331) ***(G-5120)***
Sattler Inc......586 725-1140
6024 Corporate Dr Ira (48023) ***(G-8269)***
Saturn Electronics Corp......734 941-8100
28450 Northline Rd Romulus (48174) ***(G-13732)***
Saturn Printing & Mailing, Livonia *Also called Ameri-Print Inc* ***(G-9642)***
Saucony Inc......616 866-5500
9341 Courtland Dr Ne Rockford (49351) ***(G-13589)***
Saugatuck Brewing Co Inc......269 857-7222
2948 Blue Star Hwy Douglas (49406) ***(G-4532)***
Sault Tribe News......906 632-6398
531 Ashmun St Sault Sainte Marie (49783) ***(G-14473)***
Savair, Chesterfield *Also called Aro Welding Technologies Inc* ***(G-2742)***
Savanna Inc......734 254-0566
45755 Five Mile Rd Plymouth (48170) ***(G-12750)***
Savanna Inc (PA)......248 353-8180
20941 East St Southfield (48033) ***(G-15022)***
Savard Corporation......313 931-6880
8561 W Chicago Detroit (48204) ***(G-4353)***
Save On Everything Inc (PA)......248 362-9119
1000 W Maple Rd Ste 200 Troy (48084) ***(G-16594)***
Savers Wholesale Printing, Madison Heights *Also called Just Wing It Inc* ***(G-10286)***
Savory Foods Inc......616 241-2583
900 Hynes Ave Sw Ofc Grand Rapids (49507) ***(G-6851)***
Savoy Energy, Traverse City *Also called Savoy Exploration Inc* ***(G-16098)***
Savoy Exploration Inc......231 941-9552
920 Hastings St Ste A Traverse City (49686) ***(G-16098)***
Savs Welding Services Inc......313 841-3430
11811 Pleasant St Detroit (48217) ***(G-4354)***
Saw Tubergen Service Inc......616 534-0701
5252 Division Ave S Grand Rapids (49548) ***(G-6852)***
Sawdust Bin Inc......906 932-5518
629 W Cloverland Dr Ste 5 Ironwood (49938) ***(G-8340)***
Sawing Logz LLC......586 883-5649
28634 Milton Ave Warren (48092) ***(G-17231)***
Sawmill Bill Lumber Inc......231 275-3000
18657 Us Highway 31 Interlochen (49643) ***(G-8245)***
Sawmill Estates......269 792-7500
1185 Eagle Dr Wayland (49348) ***(G-17414)***
Saylor-Beall Manufacturing Co......989 224-2371
400 N Kibbee St Saint Johns (48879) ***(G-14293)***
SB Investments LLC......734 462-9478
12055 Globe St Livonia (48150) ***(G-9921)***
Sb3 LLC......877 978-6286
967 Spaulding Ave Se B Ada (49301) ***(G-29)***
Sbhpp, Novi *Also called Bakelite N Sumitomo Amer Inc* ***(G-11837)***
Sbn Enterprises LLC......586 839-4782
72901 Sorrel Dr Bruce Twp (48065) ***(G-2098)***
SBR LLC......313 350-8799
19872 Kelly Rd Harper Woods (48225) ***(G-7304)***
SBR Printing USA Inc......810 388-9441
2101 Cypress St Port Huron (48060) ***(G-12964)***
Sbsi Software Inc (PA)......248 567-3044
23570 Haggerty Rd Farmington Hills (48335) ***(G-5121)***
Sbti Company......586 726-5756
50600 Corporate Dr Shelby Township (48315) ***(G-14685)***
Sbz Corporation......248 649-1166
3001 W Big Beaver Rd # 402 Troy (48084) ***(G-16595)***
SC Custom Display Inc......616 940-0563
3010 Shaffer Ave Se Ste 1 Kentwood (49512) ***(G-9032)***
SC Industries Inc (PA)......312 366-3899
24151 Telg Rd Ste 100 Southfield (48033) ***(G-15023)***
SC Johnson & Son......989 667-0235
4867 Wilder Rd Bay City (48706) ***(G-1356)***
Scaff-All Inc......888 204-9990
7269 Cardinal St Clay (48001) ***(G-3002)***
SCE, Saginaw *Also called Saginaw Control & Engrg Inc* ***(G-14138)***
Scenario Systems Ltd......586 532-1320
50466 Rizzo Dr Shelby Township (48315) ***(G-14686)***
Scentmatchers LLC......800 859-9878
514 Camp Ten Rd Gaylord (49735) ***(G-5892)***
Schad Boiler Setting Company......313 273-2235
15240 Castleton St Detroit (48227) ***(G-4355)***
Schad Refractory Cnstr Co, Detroit *Also called Schad Boiler Setting Company* ***(G-4355)***
Schaefer Screw Products Co......734 522-0020
32832 Indl Rd Garden City (48135) ***(G-5838)***
Schaeffler Group USA Inc......810 360-0294
4574 Windswept Dr Milford (48380) ***(G-10984)***
Schaenzle Tool and Die Inc......248 656-0596
1785 E Hamlin Rd Rochester Hills (48307) ***(G-13511)***
Schafer Products Co (PA)......517 238-2266
714 S Angola Rd Coldwater (49036) ***(G-3329)***
Schafers Elevator Co......517 263-7202
4105 Country Club Rd Adrian (49221) ***(G-93)***
Schaffner Manufacturing Co......248 735-8900
19414 Gerald St Northville (48167) ***(G-11724)***
Schaller Corporation (PA)......586 949-6000
49495 Gratiot Ave Chesterfield (48051) ***(G-2837)***
Schaller Tool & Die Co......586 949-5500
49505 Gratiot Ave Chesterfield (48051) ***(G-2838)***
Schallips Inc......906 635-0941
17592 S Simonsen Rd Barbeau (49710) ***(G-1117)***
Schantz LLC......616 887-0517
9 Loomis St Sparta (49345) ***(G-15109)***
Schap Specialty Machine Inc (PA)......616 846-6530
17309 Taft Rd Ste A Spring Lake (49456) ***(G-15175)***
Schawk, Battle Creek *Also called Sgk LLC* ***(G-1245)***
Schawk Inc (PA)......269 381-3820
2325 N Burdick St Kalamazoo (49007) ***(G-8884)***
Scheduling, Troy *Also called Inteva Products LLC* ***(G-16422)***
Scheels Concrete Inc......734 782-1464
33146 Grennada St Livonia (48154) ***(G-9922)***
Schefenalker Vision Systems......810 388-2511
1855 Busha Hwy Marysville (48040) ***(G-10613)***
Schenck USA Corp......248 377-2100
26801 Northwestern Hwy Southfield (48033) ***(G-15024)***
Schepeler Corporation......517 592-6811
160 S Main St Brooklyn (49230) ***(G-2042)***
Scherdel Sales & Tech Inc (HQ)......231 777-7774
3440 E Laketon Ave Muskegon (49442) ***(G-11419)***
Schienke Electric & Mch Svcs I, Bruce Twp *Also called Schienke Products Inc* ***(G-2099)***
Schienke Products Inc......586 752-5454
120 Mclean Bruce Twp (48065) ***(G-2099)***
Schill U.S., Brighton *Also called Guys Timing Inc* ***(G-1936)***
Schimmelmanns Tool......586 795-0538
32408 Dequindre Rd Warren (48092) ***(G-17232)***
Schindler Elevator Corporation......517 272-1234
3135 Pinetree Rd Ste 2b Lansing (48911) ***(G-9421)***
Schlafer Iron & Steel Co, Detroit *Also called Fpt Schlafer* ***(G-4071)***
Schleben Forest Products Inc......989 734-2858
3302 S Ward Branch Rd Rogers City (49779) ***(G-13622)***
Schleben Rhinold Forest Pdts, Rogers City *Also called Schleben Forest Products Inc* ***(G-13622)***
Schmald Tool & Die Inc (PA)......810 743-1600
G4206 S Saginaw St Burton (48529) ***(G-2163)***
Schmidt Grinding......269 649-4604
202 E Raymond St Vicksburg (49097) ***(G-16843)***
Schmieding Saw Mill Inc......231 861-4189
1820 S 124th Ave Shelby (49455) ***(G-14535)***
Schmieding Sawmill, Shelby *Also called Schmieding Saw Mill Inc* ***(G-14535)***
Schmitz Foam Products LLC......517 781-6615
188 Treat Dr Coldwater (49036) ***(G-3330)***
Schmude Oil Inc......231 947-4410
2150 Ste B S Airport Rd W Traverse City (49684) ***(G-16099)***
Schneider Electric Usa Inc......810 733-9400
4110 Pier North Blvd D Flint (48504) ***(G-5497)***
Schneider Fabrication Inc......989 224-6937
3200 W M 21 Saint Johns (48879) ***(G-14294)***
Schneider Iron & Metal Inc......906 774-0644
100 E Superior St Iron Mountain (49801) ***(G-8299)***
Schneider National Inc......810 636-2220
10316 Gale Rd Goodrich (48438) ***(G-5957)***
Schneider Sheet Metal Sup Inc......517 694-7661
6836 Aurelius Rd Lansing (48911) ***(G-9422)***
Schnitzelstein Baking Co......616 988-2316
1305 Fulton St E Grand Rapids (49503) ***(G-6853)***
Schott Saw Co......269 782-3203
54813 M 51 N Dowagiac (49047) ***(G-4560)***
Schrader Bellows, Otsego *Also called Parker-Hannifin Corporation* ***(G-12251)***
Schramms Mead......248 439-5000
327 W 9 Mile Rd Ferndale (48220) ***(G-5317)***
Schreur Printing, Holland *Also called Generation Press Inc* ***(G-7642)***
Schrier Plastics Corp......616 669-7174
2019 Pine Ridge Dr Sw Jenison (49428) ***(G-8642)***
Schroth Enterprises Inc......586 939-0770
40736 Brentwood Dr Sterling Heights (48310) ***(G-15486)***
Schroth Enterprises Inc (PA)......586 759-4240
95 Tonnacour Pl Grosse Pointe Farms (48236) ***(G-7187)***
Schuette Farms......989 550-0563
2679 N Elkton Rd Elkton (48731) ***(G-4783)***
Schuler Hydroforming, Canton *Also called Schuler Incorporated* ***(G-2425)***
Schuler Incorporated (HQ)......734 207-7200
7145 Commerce Blvd Canton (48187) ***(G-2425)***
Schuler Tool & Die Company......269 489-2900
319 S 2nd St Burr Oak (49030) ***(G-2137)***
Schultz Bindery Inc......586 771-0777
14495 E 8 Mile Rd Warren (48089) ***(G-17233)***
Schultz Motors, Dundee *Also called Matt and Dave LLC* ***(G-4595)***
Schultz Sand Gravel LLC......269 720-7225
173 8th St Plainwell (49080) ***(G-12544)***

Schunk Oil Field Service Inc 517 676-8900
4161 Legion Dr Mason (48854) ***(G-10654)***
Schutte MSA LLC 517 782-3600
4055 Morrill Rd Jackson (49201) ***(G-8570)***
Schwab Industries Inc 586 566-8090
50750 Rizzo Dr Shelby Township (48315) ***(G-14687)***
Schwab Industries Inc (PA) 586 566-8090
50850 Rizzo Dr Shelby Township (48315) ***(G-14688)***
Schwartz Blast & Paint, Cheboygan *Also called Schwartz Boiler Shop Inc* ***(G-2694)***
Schwartz Boiler Shop Inc 231 627-2556
850 Lahaie Rd Cheboygan (49721) ***(G-2694)***
Schwartz Machine Co 586 756-2300
4441 E 8 Mile Rd Warren (48091) ***(G-17234)***
Schwartz Precision Gear Co 586 754-4600
38525 Woodward Ave # 2000 Bloomfield Hills (48304) ***(G-1797)***
Schwintek Inc 269 445-9999
310 Ranger Dr Cassopolis (49031) ***(G-2535)***
SCI Consulting, Sterling Heights *Also called Standard Components LLC* ***(G-15509)***
Scic LLC (PA) 800 248-5960
500 Hogsback Rd Mason (48854) ***(G-10655)***
Sciemetric Inc (HQ) 248 509-2209
1670 Star Batt Dr Rochester Hills (48309) ***(G-13512)***
Scientemp Corp 517 263-6020
3565 S Adrian Hwy Adrian (49221) ***(G-94)***
Scientific Notebook Company 269 429-8285
3295 W Linco Rd Stevensville (49127) ***(G-15580)***
Scitex LLC 517 694-7449
2046 Depot St Bldg B Holt (48842) ***(G-7926)***
Scitex LLC 517 694-7449
3982 Holt Rd Holt (48842) ***(G-7927)***
Scitex Trick Titanium LLC 517 349-3736
4251 Hulett Rd Okemos (48864) ***(G-12137)***
Scodeller Construction Inc 248 374-1102
51722 Grand River Ave Wixom (48393) ***(G-17890)***
Scooters Refuse Service Inc 269 962-2201
1185 Raymond Rd N Battle Creek (49014) ***(G-1244)***
Scorpion Reloads LLC 586 214-3843
34054 James J Pompo Dr Fraser (48026) ***(G-5722)***
Scott Roberts 269 668-5355
3711 Gembrit Cir Kalamazoo (49001) ***(G-8885)***
Scott & ITOH Machine Company 248 585-5385
31690 Stephenson Hwy Madison Heights (48071) ***(G-10349)***
Scott Enterprises 734 279-2078
3000 Petersburg Rd Dundee (48131) ***(G-4600)***
Scott Group Custom Carpets LLC (PA) 616 954-3200
3232 Kraft Ave Se Ste A Grand Rapids (49512) ***(G-6854)***
Scott Group Studio, Grand Rapids *Also called Scott Group Custom Carpets LLC* ***(G-6854)***
Scott Iron Works Inc 248 548-2822
24529 John R Rd Hazel Park (48030) ***(G-7454)***
Scott Johnson Forest Pdts Co 906 482-3978
43850 Superior Rd Houghton (49931) ***(G-7982)***
Scott Machine Inc 517 787-6616
4025 Morrill Rd Jackson (49201) ***(G-8571)***
Scott's Wood Products, Roscommon *Also called Scotts Enterprises Inc* ***(G-13754)***
Scott-Systems, Clay *Also called Scaff-All Inc* ***(G-3002)***
Scotten Steel Processing Inc 313 897-8837
3545 Scotten St Detroit (48210) ***(G-4356)***
Scotts Company LLC 586 254-6849
6575 Arrow Dr Sterling Heights (48314) ***(G-15487)***
Scotts Enterprises Inc 989 275-5011
554 W Federal Hwy Roscommon (48653) ***(G-13754)***
Scotts Hook & Cleaver Inc 269 626-8891
8713 38th St S Scotts (49088) ***(G-14507)***
Scotts Signs 616 532-2034
3386 Olivet St Sw Grandville (49418) ***(G-7070)***
Scranton Machine Inc 517 437-6000
266 Industrial Dr Hillsdale (49242) ***(G-7539)***
Scrapaloo 269 623-7310
6590 S M 43 Hwy Delton (49046) ***(G-3820)***
Scrappy Chic 248 426-9020
33523 8 Mile Rd Ste C1 Livonia (48152) ***(G-9923)***
Screen Graphics Co Inc 231 238-4499
5859 S Straits Hwy Indian River (49749) ***(G-8222)***
Screen Ideas Inc 616 458-5119
3257 Union Ave Se Grand Rapids (49548) ***(G-6855)***
Screen Print Department 616 235-2200
1181 Taylor Ave N Grand Rapids (49503) ***(G-6856)***
Screen Vaccine, Wyoming *Also called P & F Enterprises LLC* ***(G-18024)***
Screen Works, Novi *Also called Ar2 Engineering LLC* ***(G-11829)***
Screened Image Graphic Design 906 226-6112
149 W Washington St Marquette (49855) ***(G-10556)***
Screentek Imaging 586 759-4850
12934 E 10 Mile Rd Warren (48089) ***(G-17235)***
Screenworks Cstm Scrn Printg & 616 754-7762
9470 Sw Greenville Rd Greenville (48838) ***(G-7152)***
Scs Embedded Tech LLC 248 615-2244
41100 Bridge St Novi (48375) ***(G-11990)***
Scs Fasteners LLC 586 563-0865
23205 Gratiot Ave Eastpointe (48021) ***(G-4709)***
SD Oil Enterprises Inc 248 688-1419
28851 Hoover Rd Warren (48093) ***(G-17236)***
SE Tools, Lapeer *Also called Shaws Enterprises Inc* ***(G-9486)***
Se-Kure Controls Inc 269 651-9351
1139 Haines Blvd Sturgis (49091) ***(G-15633)***
Se-Kure Domes & Mirrors Inc 269 651-9351
1139 Haines Blvd Sturgis (49091) ***(G-15634)***
Sea Fare Foods Inc 313 568-0223
2127 Brewster St Detroit (48207) ***(G-4357)***
Sea Wolf, Howard City *Also called Inflatable Marine Products Inc* ***(G-8002)***
Seaberg Pontoon Rentals, Munising *Also called Pontoon Rentals* ***(G-11248)***
Seabrook Plastics Inc 231 759-8820
1869 Lindberg Dr Norton Shores (49441) ***(G-11792)***
Seadrift Pipeline Corp 989 636-6636
2030 Dow Ctr Midland (48674) ***(G-10913)***
Seagate Plastics Company 517 547-8123
320 S Steer St Addison (49220) ***(G-39)***
Seal All Aluminum Pdts Corp 248 585-6061
23200 Ranch Hill Dr E Southfield (48033) ***(G-15025)***
Seal Bond, Spring Lake *Also called Michigan Adhesive Mfg Inc* ***(G-15162)***
Seal Pots, Romeo *Also called Seal Support Systems Inc* ***(G-13638)***
Seal Right Services Inc 231 357-5595
141 W Wexford Ave Buckley (49620) ***(G-2131)***
Seal Support Systems Inc (HQ) 586 331-7251
141 Shafer Dr Romeo (48065) ***(G-13638)***
Sealex Inc 231 348-5020
8850 Moeller Dr Harbor Springs (49740) ***(G-7293)***
Sealmaster/Michigan, Romulus *Also called Laser Mfg Inc* ***(G-13699)***
Seaman Industries Inc 586 776-9620
16500 E 13 Mile Rd Roseville (48066) ***(G-13867)***
Searles Construction Inc (PA) 989 224-3297
1213 N Us 127 Saint Johns (48879) ***(G-14295)***
Seasoned Home LLC 616 392-8350
43 E 8th St Ste 100 Holland (49423) ***(G-7797)***
Seaver Finishing, Grand Haven *Also called Seaver-Smith Inc* ***(G-6075)***
Seaver Finishing Inc 616 844-4360
16900 Hayes St Grand Haven (49417) ***(G-6073)***
Seaver Industrial Finishing Co 616 842-8560
1645 Marion Ave Grand Haven (49417) ***(G-6074)***
Seaver-Smith Inc (PA) 616 842-8560
1645 Marion Ave Grand Haven (49417) ***(G-6075)***
Seaway Plastics Corporation 810 765-8864
814 Degurse Ave Marine City (48039) ***(G-10482)***
Sebawaing Flow Control, Sebewaing *Also called Sebewaing Tool and Engrg Co* ***(G-14519)***
Sebewa Sand & Gravel LLC 517 647-4296
11858 Keefer Hwy Portland (48875) ***(G-13067)***
Sebewaing Concrete Pdts Inc 989 883-3860
8552 Unionville Rd Sebewaing (48759) ***(G-14518)***
Sebewaing Tool and Engrg Co 989 883-2000
415 Union St Sebewaing (48759) ***(G-14519)***
Sebright Machining Inc 616 399-0445
613 Commerce Ct Holland (49424) ***(G-7798)***
Sebright Products Inc (PA) 269 793-7183
127 N Water St Hopkins (49328) ***(G-7960)***
Sebright Products Inc 269 792-6229
2631 12th St Wayland (49348) ***(G-17415)***
Sebro Plastics Inc (HQ) 248 348-4121
29200 Wall St Wixom (48393) ***(G-17891)***
Seco Holding Co Inc 248 528-5200
2805 Bellingham Dr Troy (48083) ***(G-16596)***
Second Nature Self Defense 734 775-6257
25015 Meadows Ave Flat Rock (48134) ***(G-5363)***
Secord Solutions LLC 734 363-8887
240 Southfield Rd Ecorse (48229) ***(G-4745)***
Secure Crossing RES & Dev Inc 248 535-3800
1122 Mason St Dearborn (48124) ***(G-3756)***
Secure Door LLC 586 792-2402
75 Lafayette St Mount Clemens (48043) ***(G-11149)***
Securecom Inc 989 837-4005
3079 E Commercial Dr Midland (48642) ***(G-10914)***
Securit Metal Products Co 269 782-7076
55905 92nd Ave Dowagiac (49047) ***(G-4561)***
Security Countermeasures Tech 248 237-6263
37637 5 Mile Rd Livonia (48154) ***(G-9924)***
Security Steelcraft Corp 231 733-1101
2636 Sanford St Muskegon (49444) ***(G-11420)***
Securitysnares Inc 734 308-5106
10683 Bitz Rd Maybee (48159) ***(G-10672)***
Sedco Inc 517 263-2220
2304 W Beecher Rd Adrian (49221) ***(G-95)***
Sedco Division Primore, Adrian *Also called Primore Inc* ***(G-87)***
Seeley Inc 517 655-5631
811 Progress Ct Williamston (48895) ***(G-17740)***
Seelye Equipment Specialist 231 547-9430
1217 State St Charlevoix (49720) ***(G-2630)***
Seelye Group Ltd 517 267-2001
912 E Michigan Ave Lansing (48912) ***(G-9423)***
Seeo Inc 510 782-7336
3740 S Lapeer Rd Lake Orion (48359) ***(G-9159)***

A L P H A B E T I C

Seewald Industries..................586 322-1042
6960 Hollow Corners Rd Almont (48003) ***(G-265)***
Seg Automotive North Amer LLC (HQ)..................248 465-2602
27275 Haggerty Rd Ste 420 Novi (48377) ***(G-11991)***
SEI, Gwinn *Also called Superior Extrusion Inc* ***(G-7223)***
Seifert City-Wide Printing Co..................248 477-9525
30789 Shiawassee Rd # 12 Farmington (48336) ***(G-4912)***
Sejasmi Industries Inc..................586 725-5300
6100 Bethuy Rd Ira (48023) ***(G-8270)***
Sekisui America Corporation..................517 279-7587
17 Allen Ave Coldwater (49036) ***(G-3331)***
Sekisui Plastics US A Inc..................248 308-3000
28345 Beck Rd Ste 406 Wixom (48393) ***(G-17892)***
Sekisui Polymr Innovations LLC..................616 392-9004
1305 Lincoln Ave Holland (49423) ***(G-7799)***
Sekisui Voltek LLC..................517 279-7587
17 Allen Ave Coldwater (49036) ***(G-3332)***
Select Building Supplies, Holland *Also called American Classic Homes Inc* ***(G-7558)***
Select Dental Groupcom..................734 459-3200
47299 Five Mile Rd Plymouth (48170) ***(G-12751)***
Select Distributors LLC..................586 510-4647
2324 Morrissey Ave Warren (48091) ***(G-17237)***
Select Fire LLC..................586 924-1974
32037 29 Mile Rd Lenox (48050) ***(G-9525)***
Select Hinges, Portage *Also called Select Products Limited* ***(G-13032)***
Select Products Limited..................269 323-4433
9770 Shaver Rd Portage (49024) ***(G-13032)***
Select Steel Fabricators Inc..................248 945-9582
23281 Telegraph Rd Southfield (48033) ***(G-15026)***
Select Tool and Die Inc..................269 422-2812
9170 First St Baroda (49101) ***(G-1131)***
Selective Industries Inc..................810 765-4666
6100 King Rd Marine City (48039) ***(G-10483)***
Selector Spline Products Co..................586 254-4020
6576 Diplomat Dr Sterling Heights (48314) ***(G-15488)***
Self Lube, Coopersville *Also called Midwest Machining Inc* ***(G-3565)***
Selfies 2 Helpease Inc..................517 769-6900
11855 Bunkerhill Rd Pleasant Lake (49272) ***(G-12554)***
Selfridge Plating Inc..................586 469-3141
42081 Irwin Dr Harrison Township (48045) ***(G-7348)***
Selfridge Technologies, Harrison Township *Also called Selfridge Plating Inc* ***(G-7348)***
Selkey Fabricators LLC..................906 353-7104
13170 Lindblom Rd Baraga (49908) ***(G-1115)***
Selkirk Corporation (HQ)..................616 656-8200
5030 Corp Exch Blvd Se Grand Rapids (49512) ***(G-6857)***
Selmuro Ltd..................810 603-2117
3111 Tri Park Dr Grand Blanc (48439) ***(G-5983)***
Semicndctor Hybrid Assmbly Inc..................248 668-9050
49113 Wixom Tech Dr Wixom (48393) ***(G-17893)***
Semmler Electric LLC..................517 869-2211
2500 Mechanic Rd Hillsdale (49242) ***(G-7540)***
Semperian Collection Center, Detroit *Also called Ally Servicing LLC* ***(G-3859)***
Semtron Inc..................810 732-9080
6465 Corunna Rd Flint (48532) ***(G-5498)***
Seneca Enterprises LLC..................231 943-1171
1745 Barlow St Ste A Traverse City (49686) ***(G-16100)***
Senneker Enterprises Inc..................616 877-4440
1585 142nd Ave Dorr (49323) ***(G-4528)***
Senneker Excavating, Dorr *Also called Senneker Enterprises Inc* ***(G-4528)***
Sensata Technologies Inc..................805 523-2000
235 E Main St Ste 102a Northville (48167) ***(G-11725)***
Senscomp Inc..................734 953-4783
36704 Commerce St Livonia (48150) ***(G-9925)***
Sensible Technologies, Livonia *Also called Bell and Howell LLC* ***(G-9664)***
Sensient Flavors LLC..................989 479-3211
79 State St Harbor Beach (48441) ***(G-7270)***
Sensient Technologies Corp..................989 479-3211
79 State St Harbor Beach (48441) ***(G-7271)***
Sensigma LLC..................734 998-8328
3660 Plaza Dr Ann Arbor (48108) ***(G-628)***
Sensitile Systems LLC..................313 872-6314
1735 Holmes Rd Ypsilanti (48198) ***(G-18100)***
Sensor Connection, The, Bloomfield Hills *Also called Harold G Schaevitz Inds LLC* ***(G-1772)***
Sensor Manufacturing Company..................248 474-7300
40750 Grand River Ave Novi (48375) ***(G-11992)***
Sensordata Technologies Inc..................586 739-4254
50207 Hayes Rd Shelby Township (48315) ***(G-14689)***
Senstronic Inc..................586 466-4108
44990 Vic Wertz Dr Ste A Clinton Township (48036) ***(G-3222)***
Sentio, Wixom *Also called Innovtive Srgcal Solutions LLC* ***(G-17834)***
Seoul International Inc..................586 275-2494
40622 Mound Rd Sterling Heights (48310) ***(G-15489)***
Sequoia Molding..................586 463-4400
820 Lakeland St Grosse Pointe (48230) ***(G-7183)***
Sequoia Tool Inc..................586 463-4400
44831 N Groesbeck Hwy Clinton Township (48036) ***(G-3223)***
SER Inc..................586 725-0192
51529 Birch St New Baltimore (48047) ***(G-11492)***
Serapid Inc..................586 274-0774
34100 Mound Rd Sterling Heights (48310) ***(G-15490)***
Serapid Scenic Technologies, Sterling Heights *Also called Serapid Inc* ***(G-15490)***
Serenus Johnson Portables LLC..................989 839-2324
1928 N Stark Rd Midland (48642) ***(G-10915)***
Serma Coat LLC..................810 229-0829
1279 Rickett Rd Brighton (48116) ***(G-1988)***
Serra Spring & Mfg LLC..................586 932-2202
7515 19 Mile Rd Sterling Heights (48314) ***(G-15491)***
Serta Restokraft Mat Co Inc..................734 727-9000
38025 Jay Kay Dr Romulus (48174) ***(G-13733)***
Service & Technical Assoc LLC..................248 233-3761
318 John R Rd Ste 323 Troy (48083) ***(G-16597)***
Service Diamond Tool Company..................248 669-3100
46590 Ryan Ct Novi (48377) ***(G-11993)***
Service Extrusion Die Co Inc..................616 784-6933
3648 Mill Creek Dr Ne Comstock Park (49321) ***(G-3515)***
Service File Sharpening, Saginaw *Also called S F S Carbide Tool* ***(G-14135)***
Service Iron Works Inc..................248 446-9750
245 S Mill St South Lyon (48178) ***(G-14812)***
Service Physical Testers Div, Novi *Also called Service Diamond Tool Company* ***(G-11993)***
Service Steel Co - Detroit, Detroit *Also called Van Pelt Corporation* ***(G-4422)***
Service Steel Company, Sterling Heights *Also called Van Pelt Corporation* ***(G-15538)***
Service Tectonics Inc..................517 263-0758
2827 Treat St Adrian (49221) ***(G-96)***
Services To Enhance Potential (PA)..................313 278-3040
2941 S Gulley Rd Dearborn (48124) ***(G-3757)***
Services Unlimited, White Cloud *Also called E Power Remote Ltd* ***(G-17621)***
Serviscreen Inc..................616 669-1640
1765 Chicago Dr Jenison (49428) ***(G-8643)***
Servo Innovations LLC..................269 792-9279
2560 Patterson Rd Wayland (49348) ***(G-17416)***
Servotech Industries Inc (PA)..................734 697-5555
25580 Brest Taylor (48180) ***(G-15764)***
Sesco Products Group Inc..................586 979-4400
40549 Brentwood Dr Sterling Heights (48310) ***(G-15492)***
Set Duct Manufacturing LLC..................313 491-4380
7800 Intervale St Detroit (48238) ***(G-4358)***
Set Duct Manufacturing, Inc., Detroit *Also called Set Duct Manufacturing LLC* ***(G-4358)***
Set Enterprises Inc (PA)..................586 573-3600
38600 Van Dy Sterling Heights (48312) ***(G-15493)***
Set Enterprises of Mi Inc (HQ)..................586 573-3600
38600 Van Dyke Ave # 325 Sterling Heights (48312) ***(G-15494)***
Set Liquidation Inc (PA)..................517 694-2300
1489 Cedar St Holt (48842) ***(G-7928)***
Setco Inc..................616 459-6311
314 Straight Ave Sw Grand Rapids (49504) ***(G-6858)***
Setco Sales Company..................248 888-8989
41129 Jo Dr Novi (48375) ***(G-11994)***
Seven Mile and Grnd River Fuel..................313 535-3000
5099 Fredro St Hamtramck (48212) ***(G-7246)***
Seven-Up of Detroit, Detroit *Also called Keurig Dr Pepper Inc* ***(G-4176)***
Severance Tool Industries Inc (PA)..................989 777-5500
3790 Orange St Saginaw (48601) ***(G-14146)***
Severance Tool Industries Inc..................989 777-5500
2150 Iowa Ave Saginaw (48601) ***(G-14147)***
Severstal Dearborn, Dearborn *Also called AK Steel Corporation* ***(G-3673)***
Sexton Enterprize Inc..................248 545-5880
2638 Hilton Rd Ferndale (48220) ***(G-5318)***
Seymour Dehaan..................269 672-7377
1613 10th St Martin (49070) ***(G-10597)***
SF Holdings Group Inc (HQ)..................800 248-5960
500 Hogsback Rd Mason (48854) ***(G-10656)***
SFE, Portage *Also called Stainless Fabg & Engrg Inc* ***(G-13034)***
Sfi Acquisition Inc..................248 471-1500
30550 W 8 Mile Rd Farmington Hills (48336) ***(G-5122)***
Sfs LLC..................734 947-4377
12621 Universal Dr Taylor (48180) ***(G-15765)***
SGC Industries Inc..................586 293-5260
17430 Malyn Blvd Fraser (48026) ***(G-5723)***
SGI Manufacturing Inc..................734 425-2680
32832 Manor Park Garden City (48135) ***(G-5839)***
Sgk LLC..................269 381-3820
70 Michigan Ave W Ste 400 Battle Creek (49017) ***(G-1245)***
Sgl Carbon Group, Shelby Township *Also called Sgl Technic Inc* ***(G-14690)***
Sgl Technic Inc..................248 540-9508
2156 Willow Cir Shelby Township (48316) ***(G-14690)***
Sgo Corporate Center LLC (PA)..................248 596-8626
47581 Galleon Dr Plymouth (48170) ***(G-12752)***
Sgp Technologies..................810 744-1715
2097 Amy St Burton (48519) ***(G-2164)***
SGS Inc..................989 239-1726
11195 Dixie Hwy Birch Run (48415) ***(G-1671)***
SH Leggitt Company..................269 781-3901
450 Leggitt Rd Marshall (49068) ***(G-10588)***
Shadko Enterprises Inc..................248 816-1712
1701 Lexington Dr Troy (48084) ***(G-16598)***
Shadowood Technology Inc..................810 358-2569
4221 Meadow Pond Ln Metamora (48455) ***(G-10780)***

Shady Lane Cellars, Suttons Bay *Also called Shady Lane Orchards Inc* ***(G-15655)***
Shady Lane Orchards Inc 231 935-1620
9580 E Shady Ln Suttons Bay (49682) ***(G-15655)***
Shady Nook Farms (PA) 989 236-7240
129 S Newton St Middleton (48856) ***(G-10795)***
Shafer Bros Inc 517 629-4800
29150 C Dr N Albion (49224) ***(G-130)***
Shafer Brothers, Albion *Also called Shafer Redi-Mix Inc* ***(G-131)***
Shafer Redi-Mix Inc (PA) 517 629-4800
29150 C Dr N Albion (49224) ***(G-131)***
Shafer Redi-Mix Inc 517 764-0517
5405 E Michigan Ave Jackson (49201) ***(G-8572)***
Shaftmasters 313 383-6347
1668 John A Papalas Dr Lincoln Park (48146) ***(G-9585)***
Shais Ldscpg Snow Plowing LLC 248 234-3663
995 N Pontiac Trl Walled Lake (48390) ***(G-16903)***
Shalco Systems, Lansing *Also called Roberts Sinto Corporation* ***(G-9320)***
Shamco Inc 906 265-5065
4128 Us Highway 2 Iron River (49935) ***(G-8320)***
Shamion Brothers 906 265-5065
4128 Us Highway 2 Iron River (49935) ***(G-8321)***
Shamrock Fabricating Inc 810 744-0677
2347 E Bristol Rd Burton (48529) ***(G-2165)***
Shamrock Printing 586 752-8580
109 Peyerk Ct Bruce Twp (48065) ***(G-2100)***
Shane Group LLC (HQ) 517 439-4316
215 W Mechanic St Hillsdale (49242) ***(G-7541)***
Shannon Distribution Center, Madison Heights *Also called Shannon Precision Fastener LLC* ***(G-10350)***
Shannon Distribution Center, Madison Heights *Also called Shannon Precision Fastener LLC* ***(G-10351)***
Shannon Precision Fastener LLC 248 658-3015
800 E 14 Mile Rd Madison Heights (48071) ***(G-10350)***
Shannon Precision Fastener LLC 248 589-9670
4425 Purks Rd Auburn Hills (48326) ***(G-996)***
Shannon Precision Fastener LLC (PA) 248 589-9670
31600 Stephenson Hwy Madison Heights (48071) ***(G-10351)***
Shannons Innovative Creat LLC 313 282-2724
20410 Lochmoor St Harper Woods (48225) ***(G-7305)***
Shape Corp 616 296-6300
14600 172nd Ave Grand Haven (49417) ***(G-6076)***
Shape Corp (PA) 616 846-8700
1900 Hayes St Grand Haven (49417) ***(G-6077)***
Shape Corp 616 846-8700
17155 Van Wagoner Rd Spring Lake (49456) ***(G-15176)***
Shape Corp 616 846-8700
1218 E Pontaluna Rd Ste D Norton Shores (49456) ***(G-11815)***
Shape Corp 616 844-3215
1825 Industrial Park Dr Grand Haven (49417) ***(G-6078)***
Shape Corp 616 846-8700
16344 Comstock St Grand Haven (49417) ***(G-6079)***
Shape Corp 248 788-8444
39625 Lewis Dr Ste 700 Novi (48377) ***(G-11995)***
Shape Corp 616 842-2825
16933 144th Ave Spring Lake (49456) ***(G-15177)***
Shape Corp 616 846-8700
1835 Hayes St Grand Haven (49417) ***(G-6080)***
Shape Dynamics Intl Inc 231 733-2164
500 W Sherman Blvd Muskegon (49444) ***(G-11421)***
Shape Process Automation, Auburn Hills *Also called Dynamic Robotic Solutions Inc* ***(G-848)***
Shape Stampings, Spring Lake *Also called Shape Corp* ***(G-15177)***
Shapeshift LLC 517 910-3078
4500 Empire Way Ste 11 Lansing (48917) ***(G-9322)***
Sharadans Leather Goods Inc 586 468-0666
237 N River Rd R19 Mount Clemens (48043) ***(G-11150)***
Sharedbook Inc 734 302-6500
4750 Venture Dr Ste 400 Ann Arbor (48108) ***(G-629)***
Sharewell, Grosse Ile *Also called Douglas West Company Inc* ***(G-7171)***
Shark Tool & Die Inc 586 749-7400
29500 25 Mile Rd Chesterfield (48051) ***(G-2839)***
Sharp Die & Mold Co 586 293-8660
34480 Commerce Fraser (48026) ***(G-5724)***
Sharp Industries Incorporated 810 229-6305
5975 Ford Ct Brighton (48116) ***(G-1989)***
Sharp Model Co (PA) 586 752-3099
70745 Powell Rd Bruce Twp (48065) ***(G-2101)***
Sharp Screw Products Inc 586 598-0440
49650 Leona Dr Chesterfield (48051) ***(G-2840)***
Sharp Tooling and Assembly, Fraser *Also called JF Hubert Enterprises Inc* ***(G-5675)***
Sharp Tooling Solutions, Bruce Twp *Also called Sharp Model Co* ***(G-2101)***
Sharpco Wldg & Fabrication LLC 989 915-0556
26 Consumers Energy Pkwy Clare (48617) ***(G-2888)***
Sharpe Fabricating Inc 586 465-4468
44049 N Groesbeck Hwy Clinton Township (48036) ***(G-3224)***
Sharpertek, Pontiac *Also called Gvn Group Corp* ***(G-12831)***
Shatila Food Products Inc (PA) 313 934-1520
8505 W Warren Ave Dearborn (48126) ***(G-3758)***
Shaun Jackson Design Inc 734 975-7500
134 S Industrial Dr Saline (48176) ***(G-14415)***
Shaw & Slavsky Inc (PA) 313 834-3990
13821 Elmira St Detroit (48227) ***(G-4359)***
Shaw & Slavsky Inc 313 834-3990
13639 Elmira St Detroit (48227) ***(G-4360)***
Shaw Design, Detroit *Also called Shaw & Slavsky Inc* ***(G-4360)***
Shaw Design Group, Detroit *Also called Shaw & Slavsky Inc* ***(G-4359)***
Shaw's Pharmacy, Durand *Also called Pancheck LLC* ***(G-4611)***
Shawmut Corporation 810 987-2222
2770 Dove St Port Huron (48060) ***(G-12965)***
Shawmut Mills, Port Huron *Also called Shawmut Corporation* ***(G-12965)***
Shawn Muma 989 426-9505
2315 Dassay Rd Gladwin (48624) ***(G-5937)***
Shawn Muma Logging 989 426-6852
2315 Dassay Rd Gladwin (48624) ***(G-5938)***
Shaws Enterprises Inc 810 664-2981
415 Howard St Lapeer (48446) ***(G-9486)***
Shay Water Co Inc 989 755-3221
320 W Bristol St Saginaw (48602) ***(G-14148)***
Shayleslie Corporation 517 694-4115
2385 Delhi Commerce Dr # 1 Holt (48842) ***(G-7929)***
Shayn Allen Marquetry 586 991-0445
14009 Simone Dr Shelby Township (48315) ***(G-14691)***
Sheba Professional Nail Pdts 313 291-8010
5681 S Beech Daly St Dearborn Heights (48125) ***(G-3796)***
Sheet Metal Division, Kalamazoo *Also called W Soule & Co* ***(G-8920)***
Sheffler Manufacturing LLC 248 409-0966
6338 Sashabaw Rd Clarkston (48346) ***(G-2954)***
Shefit Inc 616 209-7003
5340 Plaza Ave Ste B Hudsonville (49426) ***(G-8182)***
Shelby Antolin Inc 734 395-0328
52888 Shelby Pkwy Shelby Township (48315) ***(G-14692)***
Shelby Auto Trim Inc 586 939-9090
40430 Mound Rd Sterling Heights (48310) ***(G-15495)***
Shelby Foam Systems, Shelby Township *Also called Magna Seating America Inc* ***(G-14632)***
Shelby Operations 1, Sterling Heights *Also called General Dynamics Land* ***(G-15357)***
Shelby Signarama Township 586 843-3702
51084 Filomena Dr Shelby Township (48315) ***(G-14693)***
Shelby Trim Auto Uphl Cnvrtibl, Sterling Heights *Also called Shelby Auto Trim Inc* ***(G-15495)***
Shelby Utica News, The, Warren *Also called C & G News Inc* ***(G-16970)***
Sheler Corporation 586 979-8560
37885 Commerce Dr Sterling Heights (48312) ***(G-15496)***
Shelfactory LLC 734 709-3615
1750 N Gulley Rd Dearborn (48128) ***(G-3759)***
Shell Oil Company 248 693-0036
378 S Broadway St Lake Orion (48362) ***(G-9160)***
Shellback Manufacturing Co 248 544-4600
1320 E Elza Ave Hazel Park (48030) ***(G-7455)***
Shellcast Inc 231 893-8245
5230 Industrial Park Rd Montague (49437) ***(G-11097)***
Shelly Meehof 231 775-3065
1156 Plett Rd Ste 1 Cadillac (49601) ***(G-2276)***
Shellys Pins N Needles 517 861-7110
484 Brighton Rd Howell (48843) ***(G-8096)***
Shelter Carpet Specialties 616 475-4944
2025 Calvin Ave Se Grand Rapids (49507) ***(G-6859)***
Shelti Inc 989 893-1739
3020 N Water St Bay City (48708) ***(G-1357)***
Shepherd Caster Corp 269 668-4800
22186 Woodhenge Dr Mattawan (49071) ***(G-10669)***
Shepherd Hardware Products Inc 269 756-3830
6961 Us Highway 12 Three Oaks (49128) ***(G-15850)***
Shepherd Speciality Papers Inc (PA) 269 629-8001
10211 M 89 Ste 230 Richland (49083) ***(G-13255)***
Sheptime Music 586 806-9058
27035 Lorraine Ave Warren (48093) ***(G-17238)***
Sheren Plumbing & Heating Inc 231 943-7916
3801 Rennie School Rd Traverse City (49685) ***(G-16101)***
Sheri Boston 248 627-9576
1119 Briar Ridge Ln Ortonville (48462) ***(G-12203)***
Sheridan Books Inc (HQ) 734 475-9145
613 E Industrial Dr Chelsea (48118) ***(G-2719)***
Sheridan Pubg Grnd Rapids Inc 616 957-5100
5100 33rd St Se Grand Rapids (49512) ***(G-6860)***
Sherman Dairy Bar, South Haven *Also called Sherman Dairy Products Co Inc* ***(G-14770)***
Sherman Dairy Products Co Inc 269 637-8251
1601 Phoenix St South Haven (49090) ***(G-14770)***
Sherman Publications Inc (PA) 248 628-4801
666 S Lapeer Rd Oxford (48371) ***(G-12372)***
Sherman Publications Inc 248 625-3370
5 S Main St Ste 1 Clarkston (48346) ***(G-2955)***
Sherman Publications Inc 248 693-8331
30 N Broadway St Lake Orion (48362) ***(G-9161)***
Sherman Publications Inc 248 627-4332
12 South St Ortonville (48462) ***(G-12204)***
Sherwood Furniture, West Bloomfield *Also called Sherwood Studios Inc* ***(G-17495)***
Sherwood Manufacturing Corp 231 386-5132
922 N Mill St Northport (49670) ***(G-11671)***

ALPHABETIC

Sherwood Prototype Inc 313 883-3880
124 Victor St Highland Park (48203) *(G-7507)*
Sherwood Studios Inc (PA) 248 855-1600
6644 Orchard Lake Rd West Bloomfield (48322) *(G-17495)*
Sheski Logging 906 786-1886
2875 18th Rd Escanaba (49829) *(G-4859)*
Shetler Family Dairy LLC 231 258-8216
5436 Tyler Rd Se Kalkaska (49646) *(G-8958)*
Shiawassee County Independent, Owosso *Also called Indepndent Advsor Nwsppr Group (G-12296)*
Shiawssee Rhbilitation Program, Owosso *Also called Svrc Industries Inc (G-12320)*
Shield Material Handling Inc 248 418-0986
4280 N Atlantic Blvd Auburn Hills (48326) *(G-997)*
Shields & Shields Enterprises 269 345-7744
4302 S Westnedge Ave Kalamazoo (49008) *(G-8886)*
Shields Acquisition Co Inc (PA) 734 782-4454
26601 W Huron River Dr Flat Rock (48134) *(G-5364)*
Shikoku Cable North Amer Inc 248 488-8620
28175 Haggerty Rd Novi (48377) *(G-11996)*
Shiloh Industries Inc 989 463-6166
250 Adams St Alma (48801) *(G-249)*
Shiloh Industries Inc 734 454-4000
7295 N Haggerty Rd Canton (48187) *(G-2426)*
Shiloh Manufacturing LLC 586 873-2835
28101 Grsbeck Hwy Rsville Roseville Roseville (48066) *(G-13868)*
Shiloh Manufacturing LLC 586 779-0300
27101 Groesbeck Hwy Warren (48089) *(G-17239)*
Shinola/Detroit LLC (PA) 888 304-2534
485 W Milwaukee St Detroit (48202) *(G-4361)*
Shipping Container Corporation 313 937-2411
26000 Capitol Redford (48239) *(G-13191)*
Shipston Alum Tech Mich Inc 616 842-3500
14638 Apple Dr Fruitport (49415) *(G-5800)*
Shirt Tails Inc 906 774-3370
408 S Stephenson Ave Iron Mountain (49801) *(G-8300)*
Shirts n More Inc 269 963-3266
131 Grand Trunk Ave Battle Creek (49037) *(G-1246)*
Shively Corp 269 683-9503
2604 S 11th St Niles (49120) *(G-11645)*
Shock-Tek LLC 313 886-0530
21 Kercheval Ave Ste 225 Grosse Pointe Farms (48236) *(G-7188)*
Shoe Shop 231 739-2174
3324 Glade St Muskegon (49444) *(G-11422)*
Shomo Tool Company Inc 734 422-5588
28834 Cambridge St Garden City (48135) *(G-5840)*
Shooks Asphalt Paving Co Inc (PA) 989 236-7740
3588 W Cleveland Rd Perrinton (48871) *(G-12432)*
Shop IV Sbusid Inv Grede LLC 248 727-1800
1 Towne Sq Ste 550 Southfield (48076) *(G-15027)*
Shop Makarios LLC 800 479-0032
4390 104th St Sw Byron Center (49315) *(G-2211)*
Shopper's Guide, Coldwater *Also called Harold K Schultz (G-3308)*
Shoppers Fair Inc 231 627-7144
308 N Main St Cheboygan (49721) *(G-2695)*
Shore-Mate Products LLC 616 874-5438
9260 Belding Rd Ne Rockford (49341) *(G-13590)*
Shorecrest Enterprises Inc 586 948-9226
33251 S Gratiot Ave Clinton Township (48035) *(G-3225)*
Shoreline Container Inc (PA) 616 399-2088
4450 136th Ave Holland (49424) *(G-7800)*
Shoreline Container and Packg, Holland *Also called Shoreline Container Inc (G-7800)*
Shoreline Creations Ltd (PA) 616 393-2077
2465 112th Ave Holland (49424) *(G-7801)*
Shoreline Fruit LLC (PA) 231 941-4336
10850 E Traverse Hwy Traverse City (49684) *(G-16102)*
Shoreline Manufacturing LLC 616 834-1503
155 Manufacturers Dr Holland (49424) *(G-7802)*
Shoreline Media, Ludington *Also called Ludington Daily News Inc (G-10069)*
Shoreline Mold & Engrg LLC 269 926-2223
1530 Townline Rd Benton Harbor (49022) *(G-1546)*
Shoreline Mtal Fabricators Inc 231 722-4443
1880 Park St Muskegon (49441) *(G-11423)*
Shoreline Recycling & Supply 231 722-6081
259 Ottawa St Muskegon (49442) *(G-11424)*
Shores Engineering Co Inc 586 792-2748
34632 Nova Dr Clinton Township (48035) *(G-3226)*
Shores Tool and Mfg, Harrison Township *Also called Roussin M & Ubelhor R Inc (G-7347)*
Shorts Brewing Company LLC (PA) 231 498-2300
211 Industrial Park Dr Elk Rapids (49629) *(G-4780)*
Shoulder Innovations Inc 616 294-1029
13827 Port Sheldon St Holland (49424) *(G-7803)*
Shoulders LLC 248 843-1536
487 N Perry St Pontiac (48342) *(G-12865)*
Shouldice Indus Mfrs Cntrs Inc 269 962-5579
182 Elm St Battle Creek (49014) *(G-1247)*
Shouse Tool Inc 810 629-0391
290 N Alloy Dr Fenton (48430) *(G-5238)*
Showcase Cabinetry Inc 810 798-9966
4005 Van Dyke Rd Almont (48003) *(G-266)*
Shred-Pac Inc 269 793-7978
2982 22nd St Hopkins (49328) *(G-7961)*
Shuert Industries Inc 586 254-4590
6600 Dobry Dr Sterling Heights (48314) *(G-15497)*
Shuert Technologies, Sterling Heights *Also called Shuert Industries Inc (G-15497)*
Shure Star LLC (PA) 248 365-4382
15200 Century Dr Dearborn (48120) *(G-3760)*
Shure Star LLC 248 365-4382
2498 Commercial Dr Auburn Hills (48326) *(G-998)*
Shutterbooth 734 680-6067
4972 S Ridgeside Cir Ann Arbor (48105) *(G-630)*
Shutterbooth 586 747-4110
2441 Burleigh St West Bloomfield (48324) *(G-17496)*
Shutters Chandeliers LLC 989 773-0929
600 S Mission St Ste B Mount Pleasant (48858) *(G-11226)*
Shwayder Company 248 645-9511
2335 E Lincoln St Birmingham (48009) *(G-1702)*
Sidley Diamond Tool Company (PA) 734 261-7970
32320 Ford Rd Garden City (48135) *(G-5841)*
Siemens AG 248 307-3400
777 Chicago Rd Troy (48083) *(G-16599)*
Siemens Industry Inc 269 927-3591
470 Paw Paw Ave Benton Harbor (49022) *(G-1547)*
Siemens Industry Inc 616 913-7700
4147 Eastern Ave Se Grand Rapids (49508) *(G-6861)*
Siemens Product Life Mgmt Sftw 313 317-6100
1555 Fairlane Dr Ste 300 Allen Park (48101) *(G-208)*
Siemens Product Life Mgmt Sftw 734 953-2700
38695 7 Mile Rd Ste 300 Livonia (48152) *(G-9926)*
Siemens Product Life Mgmt Sftw 734 994-7300
2600 Green Rd Ste 100 Ann Arbor (48105) *(G-631)*
Siemens Vai Services LLC 269 927-3591
470 Paw Paw Ave Benton Harbor (49022) *(G-1548)*
Sierra 3 Defense LLC 248 343-1066
2830 Tall Oaks Ct Apt 23 Auburn Hills (48326) *(G-999)*
Sierra Plastics Inc 989 269-6272
175 Thompson Rd Ste A Bad Axe (48413) *(G-1070)*
Sightline Display, Comstock Park *Also called Marketing Communications Inc (G-3496)*
Sigma Diagnostics Inc 734 744-4846
14155 Farmington Rd Ste D Livonia (48154) *(G-9927)*
Sigma International Inc (PA) 248 230-9681
36800 Plymouth Rd Livonia (48150) *(G-9928)*
Sigma Luminous LLC 800 482-1327
36800 Plymouth Rd Livonia (48150) *(G-9929)*
Sigma Machine Inc 269 345-6316
3358 Center Park Pl Kalamazoo (49048) *(G-8887)*
Sigma Stamping Division, Royal Oak *Also called Koppy Corporation (G-13942)*
Sigma Tool Mfg Inc 586 792-3300
35280 Forton Ct Clinton Township (48035) *(G-3227)*
Sign & Art Inc 734 522-0520
12321 Stark Rd Ste 2 Livonia (48150) *(G-9930)*
Sign & Graphics Operations LLC 248 596-8626
47585 Galleon Dr Plymouth (48170) *(G-12753)*
Sign A Rama Canton 734 844-9068
18073 Ray St Riverview (48193) *(G-13305)*
Sign A Rama Inc 810 494-7446
5050 S Old Us Highway 23 # 200 Brighton (48114) *(G-1990)*
Sign and Design 231 348-9256
427 Creekside Dr Petoskey (49770) *(G-12475)*
Sign Art Inc (PA) 269 381-3012
5757 E Cork St Kalamazoo (49048) *(G-8888)*
Sign Cabinets Inc 231 725-7187
2000 9th St Muskegon (49444) *(G-11425)*
Sign Center, Kalamazoo *Also called Sign On Inc (G-8892)*
Sign Center of Kalamazoo Inc 269 381-6869
711 Portage St Kalamazoo (49001) *(G-8889)*
Sign City Inc 269 375-1385
7178 Stadium Dr Kalamazoo (49009) *(G-8890)*
Sign Concepts Corporation 248 680-8970
1119 Wheaton Dr Troy (48083) *(G-16600)*
Sign Depot, Kalamazoo *Also called Scott Roberts (G-8885)*
Sign Fabricators Inc 586 468-7360
37675 Lakeville St Harrison Township (48045) *(G-7349)*
Sign Image Inc 989 781-5229
8155 Gratiot Rd Saginaw (48609) *(G-14149)*
Sign Impressions Inc 269 382-5152
3929 Ravine Rd Kalamazoo (49006) *(G-8891)*
Sign of The Loon Gifts Inc 231 436-5155
311 W Central Ave Mackinaw City (49701) *(G-10101)*
Sign On Inc 269 381-6869
711 Portage St Kalamazoo (49001) *(G-8892)*
Sign Screen Inc 810 239-1100
408 S Center Rd Flint (48506) *(G-5499)*
Sign Shop, The, Kalamazoo *Also called Shields & Shields Enterprises (G-8886)*
Sign Solutions, Marquette *Also called Landers Drafting Inc (G-10539)*
Sign Specialties Co Inc 313 928-4230
17140 Ecorse Rd Allen Park (48101) *(G-209)*
Sign Stuff Inc 734 458-1055
13604 Merriman Rd Livonia (48150) *(G-9931)*

Sign Up Inc....906 789-7446
1300 Ludington St Escanaba (49829) *(G-4860)*
Sign Up Schumann Outdoor Arts, Escanaba *Also called Sign Up Inc (G-4860)*
Sign Works Inc....517 546-3620
5380 E Grand River Ave Howell (48843) *(G-8097)*
Sign-A-Rama, Brighton *Also called Sign A Rama Inc (G-1990)*
Sign-A-Rama, Flint *Also called D & G Signs LLC (G-5411)*
Sign-A-Rama, Grand Rapids *Also called K-Bur Enterprises Inc (G-6566)*
Sign-A-Rama, Riverview *Also called Sign A Rama Canton (G-13305)*
Sign-A-Rama....586 792-7446
36886 Harper Ave Clinton Township (48035) *(G-3228)*
Sign-A-Rama Inc....734 522-6661
6641 Middlebelt Rd Garden City (48135) *(G-5842)*
Signa Group Inc....231 845-5101
5175 W 6th St Ludington (49431) *(G-10078)*
Signal Conditioning Solutions, Novi *Also called Scs Embedded Tech LLC (G-11990)*
Signal Group LLC....248 479-1517
22285 Roethel Dr Novi (48375) *(G-11997)*
Signal Medical Corporation (PA)....810 364-7070
400 Pyramid Dr Ste 2 Marysville (48040) *(G-10614)*
Signal-Return Inc....313 567-8970
1345 Division St Ste 102 Detroit (48207) *(G-4362)*
Signalx Technologies LLC....248 935-4237
41100 Plymouth Rd Plymouth (48170) *(G-12754)*
Signarama Ann Arbor....734 221-5141
4655 Washtenaw Ave Ann Arbor (48108) *(G-632)*
Signarama Troy Metro Detroit, Troy *Also called Signproco Inc (G-16601)*
Signature Cnstr Svcs LLC....616 451-0549
3704 Mill Creek Dr Ne Comstock Park (49321) *(G-3516)*
Signature Designs Inc....248 426-9735
24357 Indoplex Cir Farmington Hills (48335) *(G-5123)*
Signature Glass Inc....586 447-9000
26415 Gratiot Ave Roseville (48066) *(G-13869)*
Signature Signs Inc....989 777-8701
6578 Dixie Hwy Bridgeport (48722) *(G-1856)*
Signature Stone Tops, Comstock Park *Also called Signature Cnstr Svcs LLC (G-3516)*
Signature Wall Solutions Inc....616 366-4242
1928 N Stark Rd Midland (48642) *(G-10916)*
Signcomp LLC....616 784-0405
3032 Walker Ridge Dr Nw Grand Rapids (49544) *(G-6862)*
Signcrafters Inc....231 773-3343
2325 Black Creek Rd Muskegon (49444) *(G-11426)*
Signet Machine Inc....616 261-2939
3119 Chicago Dr Sw Grandville (49418) *(G-7071)*
Signmakers Ltd....616 455-4220
7290 Division Ave S Ste A Grand Rapids (49548) *(G-6863)*
Signmeupcom Inc....312 343-1263
1285 N Telegraph Rd Monroe (48162) *(G-11065)*
Signoutfitters.com, Wyandotte *Also called S S Graphics Inc (G-17974)*
Signplicity Sign Systems Inc....231 943-3800
1555 S M 37 Traverse City (49685) *(G-16103)*
Signproco Inc....248 585-6880
1017 Naughton Dr Troy (48083) *(G-16601)*
Signs & Designs Inc....248 549-4850
30414 Woodward Ave Royal Oak (48073) *(G-13970)*
Signs & Designs Inc....269 968-8909
260 30th St N Springfield (49037) *(G-15203)*
Signs & Laser Engraving....248 577-6191
1221 E 14 Mile Rd Troy (48083) *(G-16602)*
Signs & More, Troy *Also called Fosters Ventures LLC (G-16371)*
Signs By Crannie Inc (PA)....810 487-0000
4145 Market Pl Flint (48507) *(G-5500)*
Signs By Tomorrow, Clinton Township *Also called Norris Graphics Inc (G-3184)*
Signs By Tomorrow, Plymouth *Also called Sign & Graphics Operations LLC (G-12753)*
Signs By Tomorrow, Clinton Township *Also called Shorecrest Enterprises Inc (G-3225)*
Signs By Tomorrow, Royal Oak *Also called JD Hemp Inc (G-13938)*
Signs By Tomorrow....810 225-7446
2150 Pless Dr Ste 3a Brighton (48114) *(G-1991)*
Signs By Tomorrow....734 822-0537
3965 Varsity Dr Ann Arbor (48108) *(G-633)*
Signs Etc....734 941-6991
1439 Fort St Wyandotte (48192) *(G-17975)*
Signs Letters & Graphics Inc....231 536-7929
4095 Jonathon Dr East Jordan (49727) *(G-4644)*
Signs Now, Negaunee *Also called 5 Pyn Inc (G-11466)*
Signs Now, Holland *Also called C T L Enterprises Inc (G-7583)*
Signs Now, Traverse City *Also called Auxier & Associates LLC (G-15901)*
Signs Now....248 623-4966
5425 Perry Dr Ste 110 Waterford (48329) *(G-17376)*
Signs Plus (PA)....810 987-7446
1604 Stone St Port Huron (48060) *(G-12966)*
Signs Unlimited....906 226-7446
1401 S Front St Marquette (49855) *(G-10557)*
Signs365com LLC....800 265-8830
51245 Filomena Dr Shelby Township (48315) *(G-14694)*
Signtech, Grand Rapids *Also called Signcomp LLC (G-6862)*
Signtext Incorporated....248 442-9080
24333 Indoplex Cir Farmington Hills (48335) *(G-5124)*
Signtext 2, Farmington Hills *Also called Signtext Incorporated (G-5124)*
Signworks of Michigan Inc (PA)....616 954-2554
4612 44th St Se Grand Rapids (49512) *(G-6864)*
Signz LLC....586 940-9891
40307 Denbigh Dr Sterling Heights (48310) *(G-15498)*
Sigvaris Inc....616 741-4281
13055 Riley St Ste 30 Holland (49424) *(G-7804)*
Sika Advanced Resins US, Madison Heights *Also called Sika Auto Eaton Rapids Inc (G-10352)*
Sika Auto Eaton Rapids Inc (HQ)....248 588-2270
30800 Stephenson Hwy Madison Heights (48071) *(G-10352)*
Sika Corporation....248 577-0020
30800 Stephenson Hwy Madison Heights (48071) *(G-10353)*
Sika Industry, Madison Heights *Also called Sika Corporation (G-10353)*
Siko Products Inc....734 426-3476
2155 Bishop Cir E Dexter (48130) *(G-4509)*
Silbond Corporation....517 436-3171
9901 Sand Creek Hwy Weston (49289) *(G-17613)*
Silent Call Communications, Waterford *Also called Silent Call Corporation (G-17377)*
Silent Call Corporation....248 673-7353
5095 Williams Lake Rd Waterford (48329) *(G-17377)*
Silent Observer, Greenville *Also called City of Greenville (G-7124)*
Silent Observer....616 392-4443
89 W 8th St Holland (49423) *(G-7805)*
Silent Observer....269 966-3550
20 Division St N Battle Creek (49014) *(G-1248)*
Siler Precision Machine Inc....989 643-7793
136 E Saginaw St Merrill (48637) *(G-10761)*
Siliconature Corporation....312 987-1848
4255 68th St Se Caledonia (49316) *(G-2315)*
Silikids Inc....866 789-7454
153 1/2 E Front St Ste B Traverse City (49684) *(G-16104)*
Silk Reflections....313 292-1150
22018 Haig St Taylor (48180) *(G-15766)*
Silk Screenstuff....517 543-7716
2860 S Cochran Rd Charlotte (48813) *(G-2664)*
Silkroute Global Inc....248 854-3409
950 Stephenson Hwy Troy (48083) *(G-16603)*
Sill Farms & Market Inc....269 674-3755
50241 Red Arrow Hwy Lawrence (49064) *(G-9508)*
Silver Bear Manufacturing, Atlantic Mine *Also called Halonen Mfg Group Inc (G-736)*
Silver Creek Manufacturing Inc....231 798-3003
696 Airport Pl Norton Shores (49441) *(G-11793)*
Silver Leaf Sawmill....231 584-2003
542 Tobias Rd Elmira (49730) *(G-4793)*
Silver Slate LLC....248 486-3989
4964 Technical Dr Milford (48381) *(G-10985)*
Silver Street Incorporated....231 861-2194
892 Industrial Park Dr Shelby (49455) *(G-14536)*
Silver Tortoise Sound Lab, Ann Arbor *Also called Logical Digital Audio Video (G-534)*
Silverglide Surgical Tech,, Portage *Also called Link Technology Inc (G-13009)*
Silvery Sawmill, Elmira *Also called Paris North Hardwood Lumber (G-4792)*
Simco Automotive Trim....800 372-3172
51362 Quadrate Dr Macomb (48042) *(G-10161)*
Simco Automotive Trim Inc....616 608-9818
3831 Patterson Ave Se Grand Rapids (49512) *(G-6865)*
Simerics Inc....248 513-3200
39500 Orchard Hill Pl # 155 Novi (48375) *(G-11998)*
Simiron Inc....248 585-7500
32700 Industrial Dr Madison Heights (48071) *(G-10354)*
Simmons & Courtright Plastic....616 365-0045
2701a West River Dr Nw Grand Rapids (49544) *(G-6866)*
Simmons Gravel Co....616 754-7073
5123 Youngman Rd Greenville (48838) *(G-7153)*
Simmys Edm LLC....989 802-2516
3018 Crockett Rd Beaverton (48612) *(G-1393)*
Simna Solutions LLC....313 442-7305
31500 W 13 Mile Rd Farmington Hills (48334) *(G-5125)*
Simolex Rubber Corporation....734 453-4500
14505 Keel St Plymouth (48170) *(G-12755)*
Simonds Industries, Big Rapids *Also called Simonds International LLC (G-1645)*
Simonds International LLC....231 527-2322
120 E Pere Marquette St Big Rapids (49307) *(G-1645)*
Simplicabinets, Wixom *Also called Belash Inc (G-17772)*
Simplified Control Solutions....248 652-1449
500 E Buell Rd Oakland (48306) *(G-12108)*
Simply Divine Baking LLC....313 903-2881
25162 Coral Gables St Southfield (48033) *(G-15028)*
Simply Green Outdoor Svcs LLC....734 385-6190
1535 Baker Rd Dexter (48130) *(G-4510)*
Simply Suzanne LLC....917 364-4549
200 River Place Dr Apt 10 Detroit (48207) *(G-4363)*
Simpson Industrial Svcs LLC....810 392-2717
9020 Green Rd Wales (48027) *(G-16860)*
Simpsons Enterprises Inc....269 279-7237
55255 Franklin Dr Three Rivers (49093) *(G-15877)*

ALPHABETIC

Sims Software II Inc...586 491-0058
44668 Morley Dr Clinton Township (48036) ***(G-3229)***
Sinclair Graphics LLC...269 621-3651
315 N Center St Hartford (49057) ***(G-7387)***
Sine Systems Corporation (HQ)...586 465-3131
44724 Morley Dr Clinton Township (48036) ***(G-3230)***
Sineramics Incorporated...248 879-0812
2062 Chancery Dr Troy (48085) ***(G-16604)***
Singh Senior Living LLC (PA)...248 865-1600
7125 Orchard Lake Rd # 200 West Bloomfield (48322) ***(G-17497)***
Single Shot Rifle Journal, Marquette *Also called Assra* ***(G-10518)***
Single Source Inc...765 825-4111
27100 Hall Rd Flat Rock (48134) ***(G-5365)***
Sink Rite Die Company...586 268-0000
6170 Wall St Sterling Heights (48312) ***(G-15499)***
Sinoscan Inc...269 966-0932
965 Capital Ave Sw Battle Creek (49015) ***(G-1249)***
Sintel Inc...616 842-6960
18437 171st Ave Spring Lake (49456) ***(G-15178)***
Sinto America Inc (HQ)...517 371-2460
3001 W Main St Lansing (48917) ***(G-9323)***
Sir Speedy, Saint Clair Shores *Also called Thomas Kenyon Inc* ***(G-14272)***
Sir Speedy, Royal Oak *Also called C S L Inc* ***(G-13912)***
Sir Speedy, Sterling Heights *Also called T J K Inc* ***(G-15518)***
Sir Speedy, Port Huron *Also called Bowman Printing Inc* ***(G-12904)***
Sir Speedy, Harper Woods *Also called Maslin Corporation* ***(G-7302)***
Sir Speedy, Saginaw *Also called Marketing VI Group Inc* ***(G-14081)***
Sir Speedy, Grand Rapids *Also called Derk Pieter Co Inc* ***(G-6343)***
Sistahs Braid Too...248 552-6202
17600 W 8 Mile Rd Ste 3 Southfield (48075) ***(G-15029)***
Sisu Mouthguards, Saline *Also called Akervall Technologies Inc* ***(G-14373)***
Sixteen Crooks BP Fuel...248 643-7272
2989 Crooks Rd Troy (48084) ***(G-16605)***
Size Reduction Specialists...517 333-2605
3510 West Rd East Lansing (48823) ***(G-4675)***
Sizmek Dsp Inc...313 516-4482
101 W Big Beaver Rd Troy (48084) ***(G-16606)***
Sizzl LLC...201 454-1938
721 S Forest Ave Apt 309 Ann Arbor (48104) ***(G-634)***
Sk Enterprises Inc...616 785-1070
3593 Alpine Ave Nw Grand Rapids (49544) ***(G-6867)***
Skater Boats, Douglas *Also called Douglas Marine Corporation* ***(G-4530)***
Skechers Factory Outlet 235, Birch Run *Also called Skechers USA Inc* ***(G-1672)***
Skechers USA Inc...989 624-9336
12240 S Beyer Rd Birch Run (48415) ***(G-1672)***
SKF Lnear Mtion Precision Tech, Armada *Also called SKF Motion Technologies LLC* ***(G-723)***
SKF Motion Technologies LLC...586 752-0060
69900 Powell Rd Armada (48005) ***(G-723)***
SKF USA Inc...734 414-6585
46815 Port St Plymouth (48170) ***(G-12756)***
Skg International Inc...248 620-4139
7550 Deerhill Dr Clarkston (48346) ***(G-2956)***
Skidmore, Benton Harbor *Also called Vent-Rite Valve Corp* ***(G-1560)***
Skill-Craft Company Inc...586 716-4300
10125 Radiance Dr Ira (48023) ***(G-8271)***
Skilled Manufacturing Inc (PA)...231 941-0290
3680 Cass Rd Traverse City (49684) ***(G-16105)***
Skilled Manufacturing Inc...231 941-0032
2440 Aero Park Dr Traverse City (49686) ***(G-16106)***
Skin Bar VII LLC...313 701-7958
18951 Livernois Ave Detroit (48221) ***(G-4364)***
Skinny Kid Race Cars...248 668-1040
3170 E Oakley Park Rd A Commerce Township (48390) ***(G-3452)***
Skip Printing and Dup Co...586 779-2640
28032 Groesbeck Hwy Roseville (48066) ***(G-13870)***
Skip Printing Co., Roseville *Also called Skip Printing and Dup Co* ***(G-13870)***
Skokie Castings LLC...248 727-1800
1 Towne Sq Ste 550 Southfield (48076) ***(G-15030)***
Sks Industries Inc (PA)...517 546-1117
1551 N Burkhart Rd Howell (48855) ***(G-8098)***
Sky Electric Northern Michigan, Traverse City *Also called William Shaw Inc* ***(G-16146)***
Sky Promotions...248 613-1637
3990 Calgary Ct Ann Arbor (48108) ***(G-635)***
Skyblade Fan Company...586 806-5107
24501 Hoover Rd Warren (48089) ***(G-17240)***
Skylark Machine Inc...616 931-1010
501 E Roosevelt Ave Zeeland (49464) ***(G-18186)***
Skyline Fall Protection, West Olive *Also called Skyline Window Cleaning Inc* ***(G-17535)***
Skyline Screen Printing & EMB, Madison Heights *Also called Authority Customwear Ltd* ***(G-10199)***
Skyline Window Cleaning Inc...616 813-0536
9790 Winans St West Olive (49460) ***(G-17535)***
Skypersonic LLC (PA)...248 648-4822
1667 Picadilly Dr Troy (48084) ***(G-16607)***
Skysync Inc...734 822-6858
801 W Ellsworth Rd # 200 Ann Arbor (48108) ***(G-636)***
Skyway Precision Inc (PA)...734 454-3550
41225 Plymouth Rd Plymouth (48170) ***(G-12757)***
Skyworks LLC...972 284-9093
15461 Bay Hill Dr Northville (48168) ***(G-11726)***
SL America Corporation...586 731-8511
4375 Giddings Rd Auburn Hills (48326) ***(G-1000)***
SL Holdings Inc...586 949-0818
50625 Richard W Blvd Chesterfield (48051) ***(G-2841)***
SL Wheels Inc...734 744-8500
38701 7 Mile Rd Ste 155 Livonia (48152) ***(G-9932)***
Slaco Tool and Manufacturing...248 449-9911
46089 Grand River Ave Novi (48374) ***(G-11999)***
Slades Printing Company Inc...248 334-6257
1502 Baldwin Ave Pontiac (48340) ***(G-12866)***
Slater Tools Inc...586 465-5000
44725 Trinity Dr Clinton Township (48038) ***(G-3231)***
Slaughter Instrument Company...269 428-7471
4356 N Roosevelt Rd Stevensville (49127) ***(G-15581)***
SLC Meter LLC...248 625-0667
595 Bradford St Pontiac (48341) ***(G-12867)***
Sled Shed Enterprises LLC...517 783-5136
1150 S Elm Ave Jackson (49203) ***(G-8573)***
Sledgehammer Construction Inc...313 478-5648
17706 Greenview Ave Detroit (48219) ***(G-4365)***
Sleep Diagnosis Northern Mich...231 935-9275
550 Munson Ave Ste 202 Traverse City (49686) ***(G-16107)***
Sleeping Bear Apiaries Ltd...231 882-4456
971 S Pioneer Rd Beulah (49617) ***(G-1612)***
Sleeping Bear Farms, Beulah *Also called Sleeping Bear Apiaries Ltd* ***(G-1612)***
Sleeping Bear Press, Ann Arbor *Also called Cbm LLC* ***(G-396)***
Slick Shirts Screen Printing...517 371-3600
805 Vine St Lansing (48912) ***(G-9424)***
Sliding Systems Inc...517 339-1455
8080 E Old M Haslett (48840) ***(G-7399)***
Slip Defense Inc...248 366-4423
10279 Lakeside Dr White Lake (48386) ***(G-17638)***
Slipnot Metal Safety Flooring, Detroit *Also called WS Molnar Co* ***(G-4451)***
SLM Solutions Na Inc...248 243-5400
48561 Alpha Dr Ste 300 Wixom (48393) ***(G-17894)***
Sloan Transportation Pdts Inc...616 395-5600
534 E 48th St Holland (49423) ***(G-7806)***
Sloan Transportation Products, Holland *Also called Tramec Sloan LLC* ***(G-7833)***
Sloan Valve Company...248 446-5300
30075 Research Dr New Hudson (48165) ***(G-11555)***
Slotting Ingram & Machine...248 478-2430
32175 Industrial Rd Livonia (48150) ***(G-9933)***
Slpt Global Pump Group, Rochester Hills *Also called Slw Automotive Inc* ***(G-13513)***
Slsi, Freeland *Also called Front Line Services Inc* ***(G-5757)***
Sludgehammer Group Ltd...231 348-5866
4772 Us Highway 131 Petoskey (49770) ***(G-12476)***
Slw Automotive Inc (HQ)...248 464-6200
1955 W Hamlin Rd Rochester Hills (48309) ***(G-13513)***
SM Smith Co...906 774-8258
1105 Westwood Ave Kingsford (49802) ***(G-9066)***
Small Scale Defense...616 238-2671
2779 132nd Ave Holland (49424) ***(G-7807)***
Smart Automation Systems Inc (PA)...248 651-5911
950 S Rochester Rd Rochester Hills (48307) ***(G-13514)***
Smart Diet Scale LLC...586 383-6734
75903 Peters Dr Bruce Twp (48065) ***(G-2102)***
Smart Label Solutions LLC...800 996-7343
2287 Grand Commerce Dr Howell (48855) ***(G-8099)***
Smart Swatter LLC...989 763-2626
3229 Valleyview Trl Harbor Springs (49740) ***(G-7294)***
Smart Vision Lights LLC...231 722-1199
5113 Robert Hunter Dr Norton Shores (49441) ***(G-11794)***
Smartcoast LLC...231 571-2020
3200 Broadmoor Ave Se Grand Rapids (49512) ***(G-6868)***
Smarteye Corporation...248 853-4495
2637 Bond St Rochester Hills (48309) ***(G-13515)***
Smartscape, Detroit *Also called Dynatrace LLC* ***(G-4022)***
Smartstart Medical LLC...616 227-4560
4334 Brockton Dr Se Ste E Grand Rapids (49512) ***(G-6869)***
Sme Holdings LLC...586 254-5310
6750 19 Mile Rd Sterling Heights (48314) ***(G-15500)***
Smede-Son Steel and Sup Co Inc (PA)...313 937-8300
12584 Inkster Rd Redford (48239) ***(G-13192)***
Smede-Son Steel and Sup Co Inc...248 332-0300
1097 Cesar E Chavez Ave Pontiac (48340) ***(G-12868)***
Smeko Inc...586 254-5310
6750 19 Mile Rd Sterling Heights (48314) ***(G-15501)***
Smeltzer Companies Inc...231 882-4421
6032 Joyfield Rd Frankfort (49635) ***(G-5606)***
Smeltzer Orchard Company, Frankfort *Also called Smeltzer Companies Inc* ***(G-5606)***
SMI American Inc...313 438-0096
6835 Monroe Blvd Taylor (48180) ***(G-15767)***
SMI Automotive, Traverse City *Also called Skilled Manufacturing Inc* ***(G-16105)***
SMI Evaporative Systems, Midland *Also called Snow Machines Incorporated* ***(G-10917)***
SMI- Aerospace, Traverse City *Also called Skilled Manufacturing Inc* ***(G-16106)***

Smigelski Properties LLC 989 255-6252
712 N Second Ave Alpena (49707) *(G-312)*
Smith & Sons Meat Proc Inc 989 772-6048
5080 E Broadway Rd Mount Pleasant (48858) *(G-11227)*
Smith - Sons ME 989 772-6048
5080 E Broadway Rd Mount Pleasant (48858) *(G-11228)*
Smith Bros. Tool Company, Shelby Township *Also called Sbti Company (G-14685)*
Smith Brothers Tool Company 586 726-5756
50600 Corporate Dr Shelby Township (48315) *(G-14695)*
Smith Castings Inc 906 774-4956
Ford Plant Iron Mountain (49802) *(G-8301)*
Smith Concrete Products 989 875-4687
3282 S Crapo Rd North Star (48862) *(G-11667)*
Smith Dumpsters 616 675-9399
13546 Kenowa Ave Kent City (49330) *(G-8994)*
Smith Logging LLC 616 558-0729
2717 134th Ave Hopkins (49328) *(G-7962)*
Smith Manufacturing Co Inc 269 925-8155
1636 Red Arrow Hwy Benton Harbor (49022) *(G-1549)*
Smith Meat Packing Inc 810 985-5900
2043 International Way Port Huron (48060) *(G-12967)*
Smith Metal LLC 269 731-5211
211 S Webster St Augusta (49012) *(G-1054)*
Smith Metal Turning Inc 269 731-5211
211 S Webster St Augusta (49012) *(G-1055)*
Smith Metal Turning Service, Augusta *Also called Smith Metal Turning Inc (G-1055)*
Smith Wa Inc 313 883-6977
14650 Dequindre St Detroit (48212) *(G-4366)*
Smith Welding and Repair LLC 616 374-1445
7430 Velte Rd Lake Odessa (48849) *(G-9119)*
Smith Well & Pump 269 721-3118
499 E Shore Dr Battle Creek (49017) *(G-1250)*
Smiths Machine & Grinding Inc 269 665-4231
203 E Battle Creek St Galesburg (49053) *(G-5814)*
Smo International Inc 248 275-1091
31745 Mound Rd Warren (48092) *(G-17241)*
Smoker Butts 586 362-2451
34541 Utica Rd Fraser (48026) *(G-5725)*
Smooches Blend Bar LLC 734 756-7152
636 Onandago St Ypsilanti (48198) *(G-18101)*
Smooth Logics, Holland *Also called Solid Logic LLC (G-7810)*
Smoothies 231 498-2374
11937 Stone Circle Dr Kewadin (49648) *(G-9040)*
Smoracy LLC 989 561-2270
6750 W Millbrook Rd Remus (49340) *(G-13241)*
Smp, Sturgis *Also called Sturgis Molded Products Co (G-15636)*
SMR Atmtive Mrror Intl USA Inc (HQ) 810 364-4141
1855 Busha Hwy Marysville (48040) *(G-10615)*
SMR Automotive Systems USA Inc 810 937-2456
2611 16th St Port Huron (48060) *(G-12968)*
SMR Automotive Systems USA Inc (HQ) 810 364-4141
1855 Busha Hwy Marysville (48040) *(G-10616)*
SMR Automotive Technology (HQ) 810 364-4141
1855 Busha Hwy Marysville (48040) *(G-10617)*
SMS, Saginaw *Also called Saginaw Machine Systems Inc (G-14140)*
SMS Elotherm North America LLC 586 469-8324
13129 23 Mile Rd Shelby Township (48315) *(G-14696)*
SMS Group, Saginaw *Also called SMS Holding Co Inc (G-14150)*
SMS Group Inc 734 246-8230
15200 Huron St Taylor (48180) *(G-15768)*
SMS Holding Co Inc (PA) 989 753-8465
800 N Hamilton St Saginaw (48602) *(G-14150)*
SMS Modern Hard Chrome LLC 586 445-0330
12880 E 9 Mile Rd Warren (48089) *(G-17242)*
SMS Technical Services 586 445-0330
12880 E 9 Mile Rd Warren (48089) *(G-17243)*
SMS-Mhc, Warren *Also called SMS Modern Hard Chrome LLC (G-17242)*
Smsg LLC (PA) 517 787-9447
1600 Executive Dr Jackson (49203) *(G-8574)*
Smullen Fire App Sales & Svcs 517 546-8898
3680 W Grand River Ave Howell (48855) *(G-8100)*
Smw Mfg Inc (PA) 517 596-3300
8707 Samuel Barton Dr Van Buren Twp (48111) *(G-16783)*
Smw Mfg Inc 517 596-3300
25575 Brest Taylor (48180) *(G-15769)*
SMW Tooling Inc 616 355-9822
11781 Greenway Dr Holland (49424) *(G-7808)*
Snackwerks of Michigan LLC 269 719-8282
180 Goodale Ave E Battle Creek (49037) *(G-1251)*
Snake Island, Detroit *Also called Zemis 5 LLC (G-4457)*
Snap Jaws Manufacturing Inc 248 588-1099
33215 Dequindre Rd Troy (48083) *(G-16608)*
Snap Quickprint, Traverse City *Also called Gary Cork Incorporated (G-15976)*
Snap-Back Shuffleboard, Commerce Township *Also called Mega Mania Diversions LLC (G-3430)*
Snd Manufacturing LLC 313 996-5088
23000 Arlington St Dearborn (48128) *(G-3761)*
Snider Construction Inc 231 537-4851
6711 E Levering Rd Levering (49755) *(G-9546)*

Sniffer Robotics LLC 855 476-4333
330 E Liberty St Ann Arbor (48104) *(G-637)*
Snoeks Automotive N Amer Inc 586 716-9588
35035 Cricklewood Blvd New Baltimore (48047) *(G-11493)*
Snook Inc 231 799-3333
6430 Norton Center Dr Norton Shores (49441) *(G-11795)*
Snow Machines Incorporated (PA) 989 631-6091
1512 Rockwell Dr Midland (48642) *(G-10917)*
Snow Technologies Incorporated 734 425-3600
13015 Fairlane St Livonia (48150) *(G-9934)*
Snyder Corporation 586 726-4300
13231 23 Mile Rd Shelby Township (48315) *(G-14697)*
Snyder Plastics Inc 989 684-8355
1707 Lewis St Bay City (48706) *(G-1358)*
Soaring Concepts Aerospace LLC 574 286-9670
3001 W Airport Rd Hastings (49058) *(G-7427)*
Sobaks Pharmacy Inc (PA) 989 725-2785
112 W Exchange St Owosso (48867) *(G-12316)*
Soccer World's, Rochester Hills *Also called Rochester Sports LLC (G-13507)*
Society of Saint John Inc 906 289-4484
6559 State Highway M26 Eagle Harbor (49950) *(G-4618)*
Socks & Associates Development 231 421-5150
516 Hidden Ridge Dr Traverse City (49686) *(G-16108)*
Socks Galore Wholesale Inc 248 545-7625
10355 Capital St Oak Park (48237) *(G-12099)*
Socks Kick LLC 231 222-2402
117 S Lake St East Jordan (49727) *(G-4645)*
Sodecia Auto Detroit Corp 586 759-2200
42600 Merrill Rd Sterling Heights (48314) *(G-15502)*
Sodecia Auto Detroit Corp 586 759-2200
15260 Common Rd Roseville (48066) *(G-13871)*
Sodecia Auto Detroit Corp (HQ) 586 759-2200
969 Chicago Rd Troy (48083) *(G-16609)*
Sodecia Auto Detroit Corp 586 759-2200
325 W Silverbell Rd Lake Orion (48359) *(G-9162)*
Sodecia Auto Detroit Corp 248 276-6647
4555 Giddings Rd 1 Orion (48359) *(G-12190)*
Sodecia Auto Detroit Corp 586 759-2200
23993 Sherwood Center Line (48015) *(G-2583)*
Sodecia Group, Troy *Also called N A Sodecia Inc (G-16518)*
Sodecia Group, Troy *Also called Sodecia Auto Detroit Corp (G-16609)*
Sodecia North America, Sterling Heights *Also called Sodecia Auto Detroit Corp (G-15502)*
Sodecia North America, Lake Orion *Also called Sodecia Auto Detroit Corp (G-9162)*
Sodius Corporation 720 507-7078
418 N Main St Ste 200 Royal Oak (48067) *(G-13971)*
Sodus Hard Chrome Inc 269 925-2077
3085 Yore Ave Sodus (49126) *(G-14747)*
Sofpoint, Livonia *Also called Giv LLC (G-9752)*
Softaire Diffusers Inc 810 730-1668
4198 Neal Ct Linden (48451) *(G-9596)*
Software Advantage Consulting 586 264-5632
8814 Pemberton Dr Sterling Heights (48312) *(G-15503)*
Software Finesse LLC (PA) 248 737-8990
31224 Mulfordton St # 200 Farmington Hills (48334) *(G-5126)*
Sohner Plastics LLC 734 222-4847
7275 Joy Rd Ste D Dexter (48130) *(G-4511)*
Soils and Structures Inc 800 933-3959
6480 Grand Haven Rd Norton Shores (49441) *(G-11796)*
Sol-I-Cor Industries 248 476-0670
30795 8 Mile Rd Livonia (48152) *(G-9935)*
Solaire Medical Storage LLC 888 435-2256
1239 Comstock St Marne (49435) *(G-10513)*
Solar Control Systems 734 671-6899
8463 Thorntree Dr Grosse Ile (48138) *(G-7176)*
Solar EZ Inc 989 773-3347
5340 E Jordan Rd Mount Pleasant (48858) *(G-11229)*
Solar Research Division, Brighton *Also called Refrigeration Research Inc (G-1985)*
Solar Solutions, Midland *Also called Dow Silicones Corporation (G-10853)*
Solar Street Lights Usa LLC 616 399-6166
169 Manufacturers Dr # 1 Holland (49424) *(G-7809)*
Solar Tonic LLC (PA) 734 368-0215
2232 S Main St Ste 364 Ann Arbor (48103) *(G-638)*
Solarbos 616 588-7270
2685 Northridge Dr Nw A Grand Rapids (49544) *(G-6870)*
Solaronics Inc 248 651-5333
704 Woodward Ave Rochester (48307) *(G-13352)*
Soleo Health Inc 248 513-8687
26800 Meadowbrook Rd # 119 Novi (48377) *(G-12000)*
Soli-Bond Inc (PA) 989 684-9611
2377 2 Mile Rd Bay City (48706) *(G-1359)*
Solid Logic LLC 616 738-8922
3455 John F Donnelly Dr Holland (49424) *(G-7810)*
Solid Manufacturing Inc 517 522-5895
125 W Michigan Ave Grass Lake (49240) *(G-7093)*
Solid Signal, Novi *Also called Signal Group LLC (G-11997)*
Solidbody Technology Company 248 709-7901
395 Elmwood Dr Troy (48083) *(G-16610)*
Solidica Inc 734 222-4680
5840 Interface Dr Ste 200 Ann Arbor (48103) *(G-639)*

ALPHABETIC

Sollman & Son Mold & Tool..........269 236-6700
254 58th St Grand Junction (49056) ***(G-6098)***
Solo Cup, Mason *Also called SF Holdings Group Inc* ***(G-10656)***
Solo Cup Company LLC (HQ)..........800 248-5960
500 Hogsback Rd Mason (48854) ***(G-10657)***
Solo Cup Operating Corporation (HQ)..........800 248-5960
500 Hogsback Rd Mason (48854) ***(G-10658)***
Solohill Engineering Inc..........734 973-2956
4370 Varsity Dr Ste B Ann Arbor (48108) ***(G-640)***
Soltis Plastics Corp..........248 698-1440
10479 Highland Rd White Lake (48386) ***(G-17639)***
Solus Innovations LLC..........231 744-9832
4275 Ford Rd Muskegon (49445) ***(G-11427)***
Solutia Inc..........734 676-4400
5100 W Jefferson Ave Trenton (48183) ***(G-16157)***
Solution Steel Treating LLC..........586 247-9250
51689 Oro Dr Shelby Township (48315) ***(G-14698)***
Solutions 4 Automation Inc..........989 790-2778
2124 S Michigan Ave Saginaw (48602) ***(G-14151)***
Solutions For Industry Inc..........517 448-8608
13240 Egypt Rd Hudson (49247) ***(G-8142)***
Solutions In Stone Inc..........734 453-4444
41980 Ann Arbor Rd E Plymouth (48170) ***(G-12758)***
Solutionsnowbiz..........269 321-5062
8675 Portage Rd Ste 7 Portage (49002) ***(G-13033)***
Somanetics..........248 689-3050
1653 E Maple Rd Troy (48083) ***(G-16611)***
Somero Enterprises Inc (PA)..........906 482-7252
46980 State Hwy M 26 26 M Houghton (49931) ***(G-7983)***
Somers Steel..........734 729-3700
6221 Commerce Dr Westland (48185) ***(G-17599)***
Sommer Co., Warren *Also called Midwest Brake Bond Co* ***(G-17155)***
Sommers Marine, Harrison Township *Also called Arthur R Sommers* ***(G-7322)***
Somoco Inc..........231 946-0200
13685 S West Bay Shore Dr Traverse City (49684) ***(G-16109)***
Sonetics Ultrasound Inc..........734 260-4800
2890 Carptr Rd Ste 1800 Ann Arbor (48108) ***(G-641)***
Sonic Alert, Troy *Also called R H K Technology Inc* ***(G-16574)***
Sonic Edm LLC..........248 379-2888
29970 Calahan Rd Roseville (48066) ***(G-13872)***
Sonima Corp..........302 450-6452
325 W Silverbell Rd # 250 Lake Orion (48359) ***(G-9163)***
Sonoco Products Company..........269 408-0182
500 Renaissance Dr # 102 Saint Joseph (49085) ***(G-14339)***
Sonoco Prtective Solutions Inc..........989 723-3720
123 N Chipman St Owosso (48867) ***(G-12317)***
Sonrize LLC..........586 329-3225
48051 Book Ct Chesterfield (48047) ***(G-2842)***
Sonus Engineered Solutions LLC..........586 427-3838
23031 Sherwood Ave Warren (48091) ***(G-17244)***
SOO Welding Inc..........906 632-8241
934 E Portage Ave Sault Sainte Marie (49783) ***(G-14474)***
Soper Manufacturing Company..........269 429-5245
3638 Bacon School Rd Saint Joseph (49085) ***(G-14340)***
Sophias Bakery Inc..........313 582-6992
8421 Michigan Ave Detroit (48210) ***(G-4367)***
Sophias Textiles & Furn Inc..........586 759-6231
24170 Sherwood Center Line (48015) ***(G-2584)***
Soroc Products Inc..........810 743-2660
4349 S Dort Hwy Burton (48529) ***(G-2166)***
Sort-Tek Insptn Systems Inc..........248 273-5200
1784 Larchwood Dr Troy (48083) ***(G-16612)***
SOS Engineering Inc..........616 846-5767
1901 Hayes St Grand Haven (49417) ***(G-6081)***
Soul of The City Classics Socc, Wyoming *Also called Buster Mathis Foundation* ***(G-17990)***
Soulfull Earth Herbals..........517 316-0547
1131 S Washington Ave Lansing (48910) ***(G-9425)***
Sound Productions Entrmt..........989 386-2221
1601 E Maple Rd Clare (48617) ***(G-2889)***
Sound-Off Signal, Hudsonville *Also called Emergency Technology Inc* ***(G-8155)***
Soundcase, Clare *Also called Sound Productions Entrmt* ***(G-2889)***
Soundtech Inc..........616 575-0866
3880 Soundtech Ct Se Grand Rapids (49512) ***(G-6871)***
Soupcan Inc..........269 381-2101
9406 E K Ave Ste 5 Galesburg (49053) ***(G-5815)***
Source Capital Backyard LLC..........734 242-6900
1000 Ternes Dr Monroe (48162) ***(G-11066)***
Source One Digital LLC..........231 799-4040
1137 N Gateway Blvd Norton Shores (49441) ***(G-11797)***
Source One Dist Svcs Inc..........248 399-5060
900 Tech Row Madison Heights (48071) ***(G-10355)***
Source Point Press..........269 501-3690
3603 Orchard Dr Midland (48640) ***(G-10918)***
Source Vending, Lansing *Also called Kansmackers Manufacturing Co* ***(G-9239)***
Sourcehub LLC..........800 246-1844
1875 Stephenson Hwy Troy (48083) ***(G-16613)***
Sourceone Imaging LLC..........616 452-2001
3223 Kraft Ave Se Grand Rapids (49512) ***(G-6872)***
Souris Enterprises Inc..........810 664-2964
2045 N Lapeer Rd Lapeer (48446) ***(G-9487)***
Soutec Div of Andritz Bricmont..........248 305-2955
26800 Meadowbrook Rd # 113 Novi (48377) ***(G-12001)***
South Flint Gravel Inc..........810 232-8911
6090 Belford Rd Holly (48442) ***(G-7897)***
South Haven Coil Inc (HQ)..........269 637-5201
05585 Blue Star Mem Hwy South Haven (49090) ***(G-14771)***
South Haven Finishing Inc..........269 637-2047
1610 Stieve Dr South Haven (49090) ***(G-14772)***
South Haven Packaging, South Haven *Also called Loope Enterprises Inc* ***(G-14763)***
South Haven Packaging Inc..........269 639-1567
73475 8th Ave South Haven (49090) ***(G-14773)***
South Haven Tribune..........269 637-1104
308 Kalamazoo St South Haven (49090) ***(G-14774)***
South Hill Sand and Gravel (PA)..........248 828-1726
5877 Livernois Rd Ste 103 Troy (48098) ***(G-16614)***
South Hill Sand and Gravel..........248 685-7020
4303 S Hill Rd Milford (48381) ***(G-10986)***
South Kent Gravel Inc..........269 795-3500
3700 Patterson Rd Middleville (49333) ***(G-10807)***
South Park Sales & Mfg Inc..........313 381-7579
6900 Chase Rd Dearborn (48126) ***(G-3762)***
South Park Welding Sups LLC (PA)..........810 364-6521
50 Gratiot Blvd Marysville (48040) ***(G-10618)***
South Range Bottling Works Inc..........906 370-2295
23 Champion St South Range (49963) ***(G-14819)***
South Shore Tool & Die Inc..........269 925-9660
2460 Meadowbrook Rd Benton Harbor (49022) ***(G-1550)***
Southast Berrien Cnty Landfill..........269 695-2500
1540 Mayflower Rd Niles (49120) ***(G-11646)***
Southeastern Equipment Co Inc..........248 349-9922
48545 Grand River Ave Novi (48374) ***(G-12002)***
Southeastern Packaging, Mason *Also called Michigan Packaging Company* ***(G-10646)***
Southern Auto Wholesalers Inc..........248 335-5555
597 N Saginaw St Pontiac (48342) ***(G-12869)***
Southern Lithoplate Inc..........616 957-2650
4150 Danvers Ct Se Grand Rapids (49512) ***(G-6873)***
Southfield Machining Inc..........313 871-8200
1831 Clay St Detroit (48211) ***(G-4368)***
Southtec LLC..........734 397-6300
17757 Woodland Dr New Boston (48164) ***(G-11511)***
Southtec LLC (HQ)..........734 397-6300
17757 Woodland Dr New Boston (48164) ***(G-11512)***
Southwest Broach..........714 356-2967
311 E Harris St Cadillac (49601) ***(G-2277)***
Southwest Gravel Inc..........269 673-4665
3641 108th Ave Allegan (49010) ***(G-188)***
Southwest Metals Incorporated..........313 842-2700
8122 W Fort St Detroit (48209) ***(G-4369)***
Southwest Mich Innovation Ctr..........269 353-1823
4717 Campus Dr Ste 100 Kalamazoo (49008) ***(G-8893)***
Southwest Michigan Living..........269 344-7438
1346 Floral Dr Kalamazoo (49008) ***(G-8894)***
Southwestern Foam Tech Inc (HQ)..........616 726-1677
1700 Alpine Ave Nw Grand Rapids (49504) ***(G-6874)***
Southwestern Hardwoods LLC..........269 795-0004
4450 Village Edge Dr Middleville (49333) ***(G-10808)***
Southwestern Mich Dust Ctrl..........269 521-7638
110 E Spring St Bloomingdale (49026) ***(G-1814)***
Southwin Ltd..........734 525-9000
11800 Sears St Livonia (48150) ***(G-9936)***
Sovereign Machine, Grand Rapids *Also called Macali Inc* ***(G-6639)***
Soyad Brothers Textile Corp..........586 755-5700
34272 Doreka Fraser (48026) ***(G-5726)***
Sp Industries, Hopkins *Also called Shred-Pac Inc* ***(G-7961)***
Spacerak, Marysville *Also called Heartland Steel Products LLC* ***(G-10603)***
Spamstopshere, Ann Arbor *Also called Greenview Data Inc* ***(G-479)***
Span America Detroit Inc..........734 957-1600
41775 Ecorse Rd Ste 100 Van Buren Twp (48111) ***(G-16784)***
Spancrete Great Lakes, Grandville *Also called Kerkstra Precast Inc* ***(G-7054)***
Spare Die Inc..........734 522-2508
30948 Industrial Rd Livonia (48150) ***(G-9937)***
Spare Time Studios..........810 653-2337
2310 N State Rd Davison (48423) ***(G-3662)***
Spark Games LLC..........269 303-7201
5243 Torrey Pines Dr Kalamazoo (49009) ***(G-8895)***
Sparkeology, Holland *Also called Jrt Enterprises LLC* ***(G-7703)***
Sparks Belting Company Inc..........800 451-4537
17237 Van Wagoner Rd Spring Lake (49456) ***(G-15179)***
Sparks Belting Company Inc (HQ)..........616 949-2750
3800 Stahl Dr Se Grand Rapids (49546) ***(G-6875)***
Sparks Exhbits Envrnments Corp..........248 291-0007
600 E 11 Mile Rd Royal Oak (48067) ***(G-13972)***
Sparta Outlets..........616 887-6010
470 E Division St Sparta (49345) ***(G-15110)***
Sparta Sheet Metal Inc..........616 784-9035
2200 Bristol Ave Nw Grand Rapids (49544) ***(G-6876)***

ALPHABETIC SECTION

Sparta Wash & Storage LLC 616 887-1034
  510 S State St Sparta (49345) *(G-15111)*
Spartan Automation Inc 586 206-7231
  50508 Central Indus Dr Shelby Township (48315) *(G-14699)*
Spartan Barricading 313 292-2488
  27730 Ecorse Rd Romulus (48174) *(G-13734)*
Spartan Carbide Inc 586 285-9786
  34110 Riviera Fraser (48026) *(G-5727)*
Spartan Central Kitchen 616 878-8940
  463 44th St Se Grand Rapids (49548) *(G-6877)*
Spartan Chassis, Charlotte Also called Spartan Motors Chassis Inc *(G-2666)*
Spartan Corner, East Lansing Also called Student Book Store Inc *(G-4677)*
Spartan Erv, Charlotte Also called Spartan Motors Usa Inc *(G-2667)*
Spartan Flag Company Inc 231 386-5150
  323 S Shabwasung St Northport (49670) *(G-11672)*
Spartan Forms Inc 313 278-6960
  24215 Ann Arbor Trl Dearborn Heights (48127) *(G-3797)*
Spartan Grinding Inc 586 774-1970
  28186 Hayes Rd Roseville (48066) *(G-13873)*
Spartan Industries, Benton Harbor Also called Anbren Inc *(G-1481)*
Spartan Metal Fab LLC 517 322-9050
  4905 N Grand River Ave Lansing (48906) *(G-9263)*
Spartan Motors Inc (PA) 517 543-6400
  1541 Reynolds Rd Charlotte (48813) *(G-2665)*
Spartan Motors Chassis Inc 517 543-6400
  1541 Reynolds Rd Charlotte (48813) *(G-2666)*
Spartan Motors Usa Inc (HQ) 517 543-6400
  1541 Reynolds Rd Charlotte (48813) *(G-2667)*
Spartan Pallet LLC 586 291-8898
  22387 Starks Dr Clinton Township (48036) *(G-3232)*
Spartan Paperboard Company Inc 269 381-0192
  8062 Stadium Dr Kalamazoo (49009) *(G-8896)*
Spartan Polymers LLC 586 255-5644
  11186 Chapman Ct Bruce Twp (48065) *(G-2103)*
Spartan Printing Inc 517 372-6910
  15551 S Us Highway 27 Lansing (48906) *(G-9264)*
Spartan Steel Coating LLC 734 289-5400
  3300 Wolverine Monroe (48162) *(G-11067)*
Spartan Tool LLC (HQ) 815 539-7411
  1618 Terminal Rd Niles (49120) *(G-11647)*
Spartan Tool Sales Inc 586 268-1556
  13715 Heritage Rd Sterling Heights (48312) *(G-15504)*
Spartannash Company 517 629-6313
  1406 N Eaton St Albion (49224) *(G-132)*
Spartannash Company 517 278-8963
  410 Marshall St Coldwater (49036) *(G-3333)*
Spatz Bakery Inc 989 755-5551
  1120 State St Saginaw (48602) *(G-14152)*
Spaulding Machine Co Inc 989 777-0694
  5366 East Rd Saginaw (48601) *(G-14153)*
Spaulding Mfg Inc 989 777-4550
  5366 East Rd Saginaw (48601) *(G-14154)*
Spec Abrasives and Finishing 231 722-1926
  543 W Southern Ave Muskegon (49441) *(G-11428)*
Spec Abrasive, Muskegon Also called Spec Abrasives and Finishing *(G-11428)*
Spec Check, Shelby Township Also called Spec Technologies Inc *(G-14700)*
Spec Corporation 517 529-4105
  4701 Industrial Dr Clarklake (49234) *(G-2900)*
Spec International Inc 616 248-9116
  739 Cottage Grove St Se Grand Rapids (49507) *(G-6878)*
Spec International Inc (PA) 616 248-3022
  1530 Eastern Ave Se Grand Rapids (49507) *(G-6879)*
Spec Technologies Inc 586 726-0000
  51455 Schoenherr Rd Shelby Township (48315) *(G-14700)*
Spec Tool Company (PA) 888 887-1717
  389 E Div St Sparta (49345) *(G-15112)*
Special Div, Westland Also called Thermal One Inc *(G-17603)*
Special Drill and Reamer Corp 248 588-5333
  408 E 14 Mile Rd Madison Heights (48071) *(G-10356)*
Special Fabricators Inc 248 588-6717
  31649 Stephenson Hwy Madison Heights (48071) *(G-10357)*
Special Mold Engineering Inc (PA) 248 652-6600
  1900 Production Dr Rochester Hills (48309) *(G-13516)*
Special Projects Engineering 517 676-8525
  2072 Tomlinson Rd Mason (48854) *(G-10659)*
Special Projects Inc 734 455-7130
  45901 Helm St Plymouth (48170) *(G-12759)*
Special T Custom Products 810 654-9602
  1492 Newcastle Dr Davison (48423) *(G-3663)*
Special Tool & Engineering Inc (PA) 586 285-5900
  33910 James J Pompo Dr Fraser (48026) *(G-5728)*
Special Tooling Service, Inc., Commerce Township Also called Fitz-Rite Products Inc *(G-3405)*
Special Welding Services, Saginaw Also called Sws - Trimac Inc *(G-14162)*
Special-Lite Inc 800 821-6531
  860 S Williams St Decatur (49045) *(G-3806)*
Speciality Grinding Co., Grand Rapids Also called Graphic Arts Service & Sup Inc *(G-6473)*
Specialty Castings, Springport Also called JP Castings Inc *(G-15211)*
Specialty Coatings Inc (PA) 586 294-8343
  33835 Kelly Rd Fraser (48026) *(G-5729)*
Specialty Eng Components LLC (PA) 734 955-6500
  25940 Northline Rd Taylor (48180) *(G-15770)*
Specialty Fabrication Services, Taylor Also called Sfs LLC *(G-15765)*
Specialty Hardwood Moldings 734 847-3997
  1244 W Dean Rd Temperance (48182) *(G-15844)*
Specialty Manufacturing Inc 989 790-9011
  2210 Midland Rd Saginaw (48603) *(G-14155)*
Specialty Metal Fabricators 616 698-9020
  6975 Dtton Indus Pk Dr Se Caledonia (49316) *(G-2316)*
Specialty Minerals Inc 906 779-9138
  W6705 Us Highway 2 Quinnesec (49876) *(G-13102)*
Specialty Pdts & Polymers Inc 269 684-5931
  2100 Progressive Dr Niles (49120) *(G-11648)*
Specialty Products Us LLC (HQ) 989 636-4341
  2211 H H Dow Way Midland (48642) *(G-10919)*
Specialty Steel Treating Inc 586 293-5355
  31610 W 8 Mile Rd Farmington Hills (48336) *(G-5127)*
Specialty Steel Treating Inc (PA) 586 293-5355
  34501 Commerce Fraser (48026) *(G-5730)*
Specialty Steel Treating Inc 586 415-8346
  17495 Malyn Blvd Fraser (48026) *(G-5731)*
Specialty Steel Treating Inc 586 415-8346
  17555 Malyn Blvd Fraser (48026) *(G-5732)*
Specialty Steel Treating Inc 586 415-8346
  17505 Malyn Blvd Fraser (48026) *(G-5733)*
Specialty Tool & Mold Inc 616 531-3870
  4542 Roger B Chaffee Mem Grand Rapids (49548) *(G-6880)*
Specialty Tooling Systems Inc 616 784-2353
  4315 3 Mile Rd Nw Grand Rapids (49534) *(G-6881)*
Specialty Tube LLC 616 949-5990
  3515 Raleigh Dr Se Grand Rapids (49512) *(G-6882)*
Specialty Tube Solutions 989 848-0880
  339 E Miller Rd Mio (48647) *(G-11009)*
Specialty Vehicle Engineering, Auburn Hills Also called Magna Exteriors America Inc *(G-936)*
Specialty Welding 517 627-5566
  12703 Melody Rd Grand Ledge (48837) *(G-6116)*
Specifications Service Company 248 353-0244
  5444 Saint Martins Ct Bloomfield (48302) *(G-1736)*
Specilty Adhesives Coating Inc 269 345-3801
  3334 N Pitcher St Kalamazoo (49004) *(G-8897)*
Specilty Vhcl Acquisition Corp 586 446-4701
  6115 E 13 Mile Rd Warren (48092) *(G-17245)*
Specs Office Supply, Bloomfield Also called Specifications Service Company *(G-1736)*
Spectra Link 313 417-3723
  21885 River Rd Grosse Pointe Woods (48236) *(G-7209)*
Spectra Lmp LLC (PA) 313 571-2100
  6501 Lynch Rd Detroit (48234) *(G-4370)*
Spectrum Automation Company 734 522-2160
  34447 Schoolcraft Rd Livonia (48150) *(G-9938)*
Spectrum Cubic, Grand Rapids Also called Spectrum Industries Inc *(G-6884)*
Spectrum Cubic Inc (PA) 616 459-8751
  13 Mcconnell St Sw Grand Rapids (49503) *(G-6883)*
Spectrum Graphics, Grand Rapids Also called Wolverine Printing Company LLC *(G-6999)*
Spectrum Graphics Inc 248 589-2795
  301 Park Dr Troy (48083) *(G-16615)*
Spectrum Illumination Co Inc 231 894-4590
  5114 Industrial Park Rd Montague (49437) *(G-11098)*
Spectrum Industries, Grand Rapids Also called Wealthy Street Corporation *(G-6980)*
Spectrum Industries Inc (PA) 616 451-0784
  700 Wealthy St Sw Grand Rapids (49504) *(G-6884)*
Spectrum Metal Products Inc 734 595-7600
  38289 Abruzzi Dr Westland (48185) *(G-17600)*
Spectrum Neon Co 248 246-1142
  1280 Kempar Ave Madison Heights (48071) *(G-10358)*
Spectrum Neon Company 313 366-7333
  3750 E Outer Dr Detroit (48234) *(G-4371)*
Spectrum Printers Inc 517 423-5735
  400 E Russell Rd Ste 1 Tecumseh (49286) *(G-15809)*
Spectrum Printing 248 625-5014
  4758 Clarkston Rd Clarkston (48348) *(G-2957)*
Spectrum Signs & Designs, Dearborn Also called Miller Designworks LLC *(G-3742)*
Spectrum Wireless (usa) Inc 586 693-7525
  27601 Little Mack Ave Saint Clair Shores (48081) *(G-14270)*
Specular LLC 248 680-1720
  6210 Product Dr Sterling Heights (48312) *(G-15505)*
Speed Cinch Inc 269 646-2016
  22724 96th Ave Marcellus (49067) *(G-10468)*
Speed Industry LLC 248 458-1335
  1668 Thorncroft Dr Troy (48084) *(G-16616)*
Speedline, Livonia Also called SL Wheels Inc *(G-9932)*
Speedrack Products Group Ltd 517 639-8781
  42 Cole St Quincy (49082) *(G-13098)*
Speedrack Products Group Ltd (PA) 616 887-0002
  7903 Venture Ave Nw Sparta (49345) *(G-15113)*
Speedway 8863, Taylor Also called Speedway LLC *(G-15771)*

Speedway LLC 586 727-2638
67371 Gratiot Ave Richmond (48062) *(G-13271)*
Speedway LLC 313 291-3710
21943 Ecorse Rd Taylor (48180) *(G-15771)*
Speedway LLC 231 775-8101
2010 N Mitchell St Cadillac (49601) *(G-2278)*
Speedway Ordering Systems Inc 734 420-0482
27601 Schoolcraft Rd C Livonia (48150) *(G-9939)*
Speedway Superamerica 3570, Cadillac *Also called Speedway LLC (G-2278)*
Spen-Tech Machine Engrg Corp 810 275-6800
2851 James P Cole Blvd Flint (48505) *(G-5501)*
Spence Industries Inc 586 758-3800
23888 Dequindre Rd Warren (48091) *(G-17246)*
Spencer Forest Products 906 341-6791
1110n Townline Rd Gulliver (49840) *(G-7213)*
Spencer Manufacturing Inc 269 637-9459
165 Veterans Dr South Haven (49090) *(G-14775)*
Spencer Plastics Inc 231 942-7100
2300 Gary E Schwach St Cadillac (49601) *(G-2279)*
Spencer Zdanowitz Inc 517 841-9380
120 S Dwight St Jackson (49203) *(G-8575)*
Speyside Real Estate LLC 248 354-7700
26555 Northwestern Hwy Southfield (48033) *(G-15031)*
Spheros North America Inc 734 218-7350
5536 Research Dr Canton (48188) *(G-2427)*
SPI Blow Molding LLC 269 849-3200
3930 Bessemer Rd Coloma (49038) *(G-3365)*
SPI LLC 586 566-5870
51370 Celeste Shelby Township (48315) *(G-14701)*
Spicer's, Iron River *Also called James Spicer Inc (G-8311)*
Spicers Boat Cy of Houghton Lk 989 366-8384
4165 W Houghton Lake Dr Houghton Lake (48629) *(G-7997)*
Spiders Software Solutions LLC 248 305-3225
49831 Parkside Dr Northville (48168) *(G-11727)*
Spieth Anderson USA Lc 817 536-3366
3327 Ranger Rd Lansing (48906) *(G-9265)*
Spike Bros Natures Treasures 989 833-5443
11230 W Saint Charles Rd Sumner (48889) *(G-15643)*
Spillson Ltd 734 384-0284
878 Regents Park Dr Monroe (48161) *(G-11068)*
Spina Electric Company 586 771-8080
26801 Groesbeck Hwy Warren (48089) *(G-17247)*
Spina Wind LLC 586 771-8080
26801 Groesbeck Hwy Warren (48089) *(G-17248)*
Spindance Inc 616 355-7000
150 E 8th St Holland (49423) *(G-7811)*
Spindel Corp Specialized 616 554-2200
4517 Broadmoor Ave Se Grand Rapids (49512) *(G-6885)*
Spindel Electronics, Grand Rapids *Also called Spindel Corp Specialized (G-6885)*
Spine Align Inc 616 395-5407
741 Chicago Dr Holland (49423) *(G-7812)*
Spinform Inc 810 767-4660
1848 Tower St Flint (48503) *(G-5502)*
Spinnaker Forms Systems Corp 616 956-7677
6812 Old 28th St Se Ste L Grand Rapids (49546) *(G-6886)*
Spiral Industries Inc 810 632-6300
1572 N Old Hwy Us23 Howell (48843) *(G-8101)*
Spiral-Matic Inc 248 486-5080
7772 Park Pl Brighton (48116) *(G-1992)*
Spiratex Company 734 289-4800
1916 Frenchtown Ctr Dr Monroe (48162) *(G-11069)*
SPIRATEX COMPANY THE, Monroe *Also called Spiratex Company (G-11069)*
Spirit Industries Inc 517 371-7840
2900 7th Ave Lansing (48906) *(G-9266)*
Spirit of Apparel, The, Kalamazoo *Also called Pierson Fine Art (G-8851)*
Spirit of Livingston Inc 517 545-8831
3280 W Grand River Ave Howell (48855) *(G-8102)*
Spirit Shoppe, Kalamazoo *Also called R H & Company Inc (G-8867)*
Spirit Steel Co Inc 517 750-4885
212 W Monroe St Jackson (49202) *(G-8576)*
Spirits of Detroit, The, Detroit *Also called Detroit City Distillery LLC (G-3977)*
Splash In Time LLC 269 775-1204
2015 Lake St Kalamazoo (49001) *(G-8898)*
Spline Specialist Inc 586 731-4569
7346 19 Mile Rd Sterling Heights (48314) *(G-15506)*
Split Second Defense LLC 586 709-1385
34024 James J Pompo Dr Fraser (48026) *(G-5734)*
Spm Industries Inc 586 758-1100
2455 E 10 Mile Rd Warren (48091) *(G-17249)*
Spoiler Wing King 810 733-9464
5042 Exchange Dr Flint (48507) *(G-5503)*
Sportcap, Farmington Hills *Also called American Silk Screen & EMB (G-4930)*
Sporting Image Inc 269 657-5646
37174 W Red Arrow Hwy Paw Paw (49079) *(G-12413)*
Sports Inc 734 728-1313
34904 W Michigan Ave Wayne (48184) *(G-17443)*
Sports Ink Screen Prtg EMB LLC 231 723-5696
316 W Parkdale Ave Manistee (49660) *(G-10437)*

Sports Junction (PA) 989 791-5900
5605 State St Saginaw (48603) *(G-14156)*
Sports Junction 989 835-9696
6823 Eastman Ave Ste 11 Midland (48642) *(G-10920)*
Sports Resorts International 989 725-8354
200 Universal Dr Owosso (48867) *(G-12318)*
Sports Stop 517 676-2199
124 W Ash St Mason (48854) *(G-10660)*
Sports Stop Sportswear, Mason *Also called Sports Stop (G-10660)*
Sportswear Specialties Inc 734 416-9941
7930 N Lilley Rd Canton (48187) *(G-2428)*
Spot Imaging Solutions, Sterling Heights *Also called Diagnostic Instruments Inc (G-15316)*
Spotted Cow 517 265-6188
1336 N Main St Ste 1 Adrian (49221) *(G-97)*
Spotted Dog Winery 734 944-9463
5743 Ping Dr Ann Arbor (48108) *(G-642)*
Spray Booth Products Inc 313 766-4400
26211 W 7 Mile Rd Redford (48240) *(G-13193)*
Spray Foam Fabrication LLC 517 745-7885
3627 Pickett Rd Parma (49269) *(G-12394)*
Spray Metal Mold Technology 269 781-7151
200 Woolley Dr Marshall (49068) *(G-10589)*
Spray Right, Grandville *Also called Industrial Innovations Inc (G-7052)*
Spraying Systems Co 248 473-1331
30701 W 10 Mile Rd # 200 Farmington Hills (48336) *(G-5128)*
Spraytek Inc (PA) 248 546-3551
2535 Wolcott St Ferndale (48220) *(G-5319)*
Spring Air Mattress Company, Grand Rapids *Also called Grand Rapids Bedding Co (G-6451)*
Spring Arbor Coatings LLC 517 750-2903
190 W Main St Spring Arbor (49283) *(G-15128)*
Spring Design and Mfg Inc 586 566-9741
14105 Industrial Ctr Dr D Shelby Township (48315) *(G-14702)*
Spring Dynamics Inc 810 798-2622
7378 Research Dr Almont (48003) *(G-267)*
Spring Saginaw Company 989 624-9333
11008 Dixie Hwy Birch Run (48415) *(G-1673)*
Springboard Manufacturing, Bridgman *Also called Kruger Plastic Products LLC (G-1869)*
Springdale Automatics Inc 517 523-2424
7201 Hudson Rd Osseo (49266) *(G-12229)*
Springer Prsthtic Orthtic Svcs (PA) 517 337-0300
200 N Homer St Lansing (48912) *(G-9426)*
Springer Publishing Co Inc (PA) 586 939-6800
31201 Chicago Rd S A101 Warren (48093) *(G-17250)*
Springfield Landscape Mtls 269 965-6748
700 20th St N Springfield (49037) *(G-15204)*
Springfield Machine and TI Inc 269 968-8223
257 30th St N Springfield (49037) *(G-15205)*
Spry Publishing Llc 877 722-2264
315 E Eisenhower Pkwy # 2 Ann Arbor (48108) *(G-643)*
Spry Sign & Graphics Co LLC 517 524-7685
12123 Spring Arbor Rd Concord (49237) *(G-3525)*
Spurt Industries LLC 616 688-5575
5204 Adams St Zeeland (49464) *(G-18187)*
SPX Corporation 586 574-2332
28635 Mound Rd Warren (48092) *(G-17251)*
SPX Corporation 989 652-6136
6950 Junction Rd Bridgeport (48722) *(G-1857)*
SPX Corporation 313 768-2103
13324 Farmington Rd Livonia (48150) *(G-9940)*
SPX Corporation 704 752-4400
700 Terrace Point Dr Muskegon (49440) *(G-11429)*
SPX Corporation 586 574-2332
28635 Mines Rd Warren (48092) *(G-17252)*
Squires Industries Inc 248 449-6092
29181 Beck Rd Wixom (48393) *(G-17895)*
Sr Injection Molding Inc 586 260-2360
41565 Production Dr Harrison Township (48045) *(G-7350)*
Srg Global Inc (HQ) 248 509-1100
800 Stephenson Hwy Troy (48083) *(G-16617)*
Srg Global Inc 586 757-7800
12620 Delta St Taylor (48180) *(G-15772)*
Srg Global Coatings Inc (HQ) 248 509-1100
800 Stephenson Hwy Troy (48083) *(G-16618)*
Srose Publishing Company 248 208-7073
29100 Pointe O Woods Pl # 207 Southfield (48034) *(G-15032)*
SRS Manufacturing Inc 586 792-5693
18840 Kelly Ct Clinton Township (48035) *(G-3233)*
Srw Inc 989 732-8884
10691 E Carter Rd Ste 201 Traverse City (49684) *(G-16110)*
Srw Inc (PA) 989 269-8528
175 Thompson Rd Ste A Bad Axe (48413) *(G-1071)*
Ss Services 616 866-6453
2431 13 Mile Rd Ne Rockford (49341) *(G-13591)*
SS&e Metalcraft, Grand Rapids *Also called Steel Supply & Engineering Co (G-6888)*
Ssa Global, Grand Rapids *Also called Infor (us) Inc (G-6534)*
Ssb Holdings Inc 586 755-1660
2619 Bond St Rochester Hills (48309) *(G-13517)*
Ssi Electronics Inc 616 866-8880
8080 Graphic Dr Ne Belmont (49306) *(G-1470)*

Ssi Technology Inc 248 582-0600
35715 Stanley Dr Sterling Heights (48312) **(G-15507)**
Ssrm Machine Shop Inc 989 379-4075
4346 S Herron Rd Herron (49744) **(G-7470)**
SSS Spring & Wire, Grand Rapids *Also called Stump Schlele Somappa Sprng* **(G-6895)**
Ssw Holding Company LLC 231 780-0230
902 N Rowe St Ste 200 Ludington (49431) **(G-10079)**
St Charles Hardwood Michigan 989 865-9299
10500 Mckeighan Rd Saint Charles (48655) **(G-14201)**
St Clair Packaging Inc 810 364-4230
2121 Busha Hwy Marysville (48040) **(G-10619)**
St Evans Inc 269 663-6100
27383 May St Edwardsburg (49112) **(G-4772)**
St Gobain Abrasives, Romulus *Also called Saint-Gobain Delaware Corp* **(G-13731)**
St Ignace News 906 643-9150
359 Reagon St Saint Ignace (49781) **(G-14279)**
St Joe Tool Co 269 426-4300
11521 Red Arrow Hwy Bridgman (49106) **(G-1874)**
St Joe Valley Grinding Inc 269 925-0709
396 E Main St Benton Harbor (49022) **(G-1551)**
St John 313 576-8212
4100 John R St Detroit (48201) **(G-4372)**
St John 313 499-4065
1056 Yorkshire Rd Grosse Pointe Park (48230) **(G-7196)**
St Johns Computer Machining 989 224-7664
501 E Steel St Saint Johns (48879) **(G-14296)**
St Johns Reminder, Alma *Also called Morning Star Publishing Co* **(G-245)**
St Julian Wine Company Inc (PA) 269 657-5568
716 S Kalamazoo St Paw Paw (49079) **(G-12414)**
St Julian Wine Company Inc 734 529-3700
700 Freedom Ct Dundee (48131) **(G-4601)**
St Julian Wine Company Inc 989 652-3281
127 S Main St Frankenmuth (48734) **(G-5595)**
St Laurent Brothers Inc 989 893-7522
1101 N Water St Bay City (48708) **(G-1360)**
St Lawrence Boring, Ypsilanti *Also called B & W Tool Co* **(G-18054)**
St Marys Cement Inc (us) 616 846-8553
555 W 2nd St Ferrysburg (49409) **(G-5338)**
St Marys Cement Inc (us) 269 679-5253
640 South St Schoolcraft (49087) **(G-14501)**
St Marys Cement US LLC 231 547-9971
16000 Bells Bay Rd Charlevoix (49720) **(G-2631)**
St Pierre Inc 248 620-2755
9649 Northwest Ct Clarkston (48346) **(G-2958)**
St Regis Culvert Inc (PA) 517 543-3430
202 Morrell St Charlotte (48813) **(G-2668)**
St USA Holding Corp (PA) 517 278-7144
491 W Garfield Ave Coldwater (49036) **(G-3334)**
St USA Holding Corp 800 637-3303
575 Race St Coldwater (49036) **(G-3335)**
St. Clair Paper & Supply, Marysville *Also called St Clair Packaging Inc* **(G-10619)**
Stable ARC, Novi *Also called RSI Global Sourcing LLC* **(G-11988)**
Stachnik Logging LLC 231 275-7641
5664 S Townline Rd Cedar (49621) **(G-2542)**
Stackpole International, Auburn Hills *Also called Stackpole Pwrtrn Intl USA LLC* **(G-1001)**
Stackpole Pwrtrn Intl USA LLC 248 481-4600
3201 University Dr # 350 Auburn Hills (48326) **(G-1001)**
Stadium Bleachers LLC 810 245-6258
3597 Lippincott Rd Lapeer (48446) **(G-9488)**
Stafford Media Inc (PA) 616 754-9301
109 N Lafayette St Greenville (48838) **(G-7154)**
Stafford Media Inc 616 754-1178
1005 E Fairplains St Greenville (48838) **(G-7155)**
Stage 5 Coatings, Wayne *Also called Lenawee Industrial Pnt Sup Inc* **(G-17436)**
Stage Right, Clare *Also called Stageright Corporation* **(G-2890)**
Stage Stop 989 838-4039
5348 Us 127 S Ithaca (48847) **(G-8367)**
Stageright Corporation (PA) 989 386-7393
495 Pioneer Pkwy Clare (48617) **(G-2890)**
Stagg Machine Products Inc 231 775-2355
11711 W Cadillac Rd Cadillac (49601) **(G-2280)**
Stahlin Division, Belding *Also called Robroy Industries Inc* **(G-1429)**
Stahlin Enclosures, Belding *Also called Robroy Enclosures Inc* **(G-1428)**
Stahls Inc (PA) 800 478-2457
6353 E 14 Mile Rd Sterling Heights (48312) **(G-15508)**
Stained Glass and Gifts 810 736-6766
4290 N Genesee Rd Flint (48506) **(G-5504)**
Stainless Fabg & Engrg Inc 269 329-6142
9718 Portage Rd Portage (49002) **(G-13034)**
Stair Specialist Inc 269 964-2351
2257 Columbia Ave W Battle Creek (49015) **(G-1252)**
Stamatopolos & Sons 734 369-2995
869 W Eisenhower Pkwy Ann Arbor (48103) **(G-644)**
Stamp-Rite Incorporated 517 487-5071
2822 N M Luther King Jr Lansing (48906) **(G-9267)**
Stampede Die & Engineering, Wayland *Also called Stampede Die Corp* **(G-17417)**
Stampede Die Corp 616 877-0100
1142 Electric Ave Wayland (49348) **(G-17417)**
Stamping Grounds Inc (PA) 248 851-6764
6827 Crestway Dr Bloomfield Hills (48301) **(G-1798)**
Stamprite Supersine, Lansing *Also called Stamp-Rite Incorporated* **(G-9267)**
Stan Kell Inc 734 283-0005
12045 Dix Toledo Rd Southgate (48195) **(G-15083)**
Stan Sax Corp (PA) 248 683-9199
10900 Harper Ave Detroit (48213) **(G-4373)**
Stanco Metal Products Inc (PA) 616 842-5000
2101 168th Ave Grand Haven (49417) **(G-6082)**
Stanco Metal Products Company, Grand Haven *Also called Stanco Metal Products Inc* **(G-6082)**
Standale Lumber and Supply Co 616 530-8200
2971 Franklin Ave Sw Grandville (49418) **(G-7072)**
Standale Smoothie LLC 810 691-9625
1028 N Leroy St Fenton (48430) **(G-5239)**
Standard Coating Inc 248 297-6650
32565 Dequindre Rd Madison Heights (48071) **(G-10359)**
Standard Components LLC 586 323-9700
44208 Phoenix Dr Sterling Heights (48314) **(G-15509)**
Standard Die International Inc (PA) 800 838-5464
12980 Wayne Rd Livonia (48150) **(G-9941)**
Standard Electric Company 906 774-4455
701 Valsam St Kingsford (49802) **(G-9067)**
Standard Plaque Incorporated 313 383-7233
17271 Francis St Melvindale (48122) **(G-10707)**
Standard Printing 734 483-0339
120 E Cross St Ypsilanti (48198) **(G-18102)**
Standard Printing of Warren 586 771-3770
13647 E 10 Mile Rd Warren (48089) **(G-17253)**
Standard Provision LLC 989 354-4975
1505 Greenhaven Ln Alpena (49707) **(G-313)**
Standard Sand Corporation 616 538-3667
14201 Lakeshore Dr Grand Haven (49417) **(G-6083)**
Standard Scale & Supply Co (PA) 313 255-6700
25421 Glendale Detroit (48239) **(G-4374)**
Standard Spring, Royal Oak *Also called American Industrial Gauge Inc* **(G-13901)**
Standard Tool & Die Inc 269 465-6004
2950 Johnson Rd Stevensville (49127) **(G-15582)**
Standby Power USA LLC 586 716-9610
7770 Bouvier Blvd Ira (48023) **(G-8272)**
Standex International Corp 586 296-5500
34497 Kelly Rd Fraser (48026) **(G-5735)**
Standfast Industries Inc 248 380-3223
13570 Wayne Rd Livonia (48150) **(G-9942)**
Standing Company 989 746-9100
5848 Dixie Hwy Saginaw (48601) **(G-14157)**
Standing Dani, Flint *Also called Davismade Inc* **(G-5415)**
Standing Wheelchair Company, Saginaw *Also called Standing Company* **(G-14157)**
Standish Magline, Standish *Also called Magline Inc* **(G-15222)**
Stanecki Inc (PA) 734 432-9900
7550 Walnut Lake Rd West Bloomfield (48323) **(G-17498)**
Stanek Rack Company, Detroit *Also called Fmmb LLC* **(G-4065)**
Stanford Dental Pllc 248 476-4500
34441 8 Mile Rd Ste 114 Livonia (48152) **(G-9943)**
Stange Company, Grand Rapids *Also called Terryberry Company LLC* **(G-6923)**
Stanhope Tool Inc 248 585-5711
395 W Girard Ave Madison Heights (48071) **(G-10360)**
Stanisci Design and Mfg Inc 586 752-3368
700 S Glaspie St Oxford (48371) **(G-12373)**
STANLEY ENGINEERED FASTENING, Troy *Also called Emhart Teknologies LLC* **(G-16342)**
Stanley Engineered Fastening, Troy *Also called Emhart Teknologies LLC* **(G-16343)**
Stans Affordable Videography 734 671-2975
4290 Ponderosa St Trenton (48183) **(G-16158)**
Stansley Industries Inc 810 515-1919
4171 Holiday Dr Flint (48507) **(G-5505)**
Stansley Mineral Resources Inc 517 456-6310
13500 Allen Rd Clinton (49236) **(G-3025)**
Stant USA Corp 765 827-8104
1955 Enterprise Dr Rochester Hills (48309) **(G-13518)**
Stapels Manufacturing LLC 248 577-5570
2612 Elliott Dr Troy (48083) **(G-16619)**
Star 10 Inc 231 830-8070
575 W Hume Ave Ste 1 Muskegon (49444) **(G-11430)**
Star Board ATT Tev, Grand Haven *Also called Star Board Multi Media Inc* **(G-6084)**
Star Board Multi Media Inc 616 296-0823
41 Washington Ave Ste 395 Grand Haven (49417) **(G-6084)**
Star Buyers Guide 989 366-8341
4772 W Houghton Lake Dr Houghton Lake (48629) **(G-7998)**
Star Crane Hist Svc of Klmazoo 269 321-8882
8722 Portage Indus Dr Portage (49024) **(G-13035)**
Star Cutter Co (PA) 248 474-8200
23461 Industrial Park Dr Farmington Hills (48335) **(G-5129)**
Star Cutter Co 248 474-8200
4210 Doyle Lewiston (49756) **(G-9555)**
Star Cutter Company, Farmington Hills *Also called Star Cutter Co* **(G-5129)**
Star Design Metro Detroit LLC 734 740-0189
32401 8 Mile Rd Ste 1-1 Livonia (48152) **(G-9944)**

ALPHABETIC

(PA)=Parent Co (HQ)=Headquarters (DH)=Div Headquarters
2020 Harris Michigan Industrial Directory
1079

Star Line Commercial Printing......810 733-1152
6122 W Pierson Rd Unit 5 Flushing (48433) ***(G-5542)***
Star Lite International LLC......248 546-4489
14131 Ludlow Pl Oak Park (48237) ***(G-12100)***
Star of West Milling Company (PA)......989 652-9971
121 E Tuscola St Frankenmuth (48734) ***(G-5596)***
Star of West Milling Company......517 639-3165
14 Church St Quincy (49082) ***(G-13099)***
Star of West Milling Company......989 872-5847
4073 N Cemetery Rd Cass City (48726) ***(G-2522)***
Star Paper Converters Inc......313 963-5200
1717 17th St Detroit (48216) ***(G-4375)***
Star Paper Products, Detroit *Also called Star Paper Converters Inc* ***(G-4375)***
Star Publication, Gaylord *Also called Upper Michigan Newspapers LLC* ***(G-5898)***
Star Ringmaster......734 641-7147
1261 S Lotz Rd Canton (48188) ***(G-2429)***
Star Shade Cutter Co......269 983-2403
2028 Washington Ave Saint Joseph (49085) ***(G-14341)***
Star Su Company LLC......248 474-8200
23461 Industrial Park Dr Farmington Hills (48335) ***(G-5130)***
Star Textile Inc......888 527-5700
1000 Tech Row Madison Heights (48071) ***(G-10361)***
Star Tickets Plus, Grand Rapids *Also called Tickets Plus Inc* ***(G-6931)***
Starbuck Machining Inc......616 399-9720
13413 New Holland St Holland (49424) ***(G-7813)***
Stardock Systems Inc (PA)......734 927-0677
15090 N Beck Rd Ste 300 Plymouth (48170) ***(G-12760)***
Starlight Technologies Inc......248 250-9607
2055 Applewood Dr Troy (48085) ***(G-16620)***
Starlite Coatings, Canton *Also called Innovative Solutions Tech Inc* ***(G-2387)***
Starlite Tool & Die Welding......313 533-3462
12091 Woodbine Detroit (48239) ***(G-4376)***
Starr Puff Factory, Grand Rapids *Also called Roskam Baking Company* ***(G-6839)***
Startech Services Inc......586 752-2460
111 E Pond Dr Romeo (48065) ***(G-13639)***
Startech Software Systems Inc......248 344-2266
39500 High Pointe Blvd # 400 Novi (48375) ***(G-12003)***
Startech-Solutions LLC......248 419-0650
6689 Orchard Lake Rd # 267 West Bloomfield (48322) ***(G-17499)***
Startech-Solutions LLC......248 419-0650
26300 Telg Rd Ste 101 Southfield (48033) ***(G-15033)***
State Building Product Inc......586 772-8878
21751 Schmeman Ave Warren (48089) ***(G-17254)***
State Crushing Inc......248 332-6210
2260 Auburn Rd Auburn Hills (48326) ***(G-1002)***
State Fabricators, Inc., Farmington Hills *Also called Sfi Acquisition Inc* ***(G-5122)***
State Heat Treating Company......616 243-0178
520 32nd St Se Grand Rapids (49548) ***(G-6887)***
State Line Observer, The, Morenci *Also called Morenci Observer* ***(G-11113)***
State News Inc......517 295-1680
435 E Grand River Ave # 100 East Lansing (48823) ***(G-4676)***
State Screw Products Corp......586 463-3892
44605 Macomb Indus Dr Clinton Township (48036) ***(G-3234)***
State Tool & Manufacturing Co (PA)......269 927-3153
1650 E Empire Ave Benton Harbor (49022) ***(G-1552)***
State Wide Grinding Co......586 778-5700
27980 Groesbeck Hwy Roseville (48066) ***(G-13874)***
Statewide Boring and Mch Inc......734 397-5950
6401 Haggerty Rd Van Buren Twp (48111) ***(G-16785)***
Statewide Printing LLC......517 485-4466
16230 S Lowell Rd Lansing (48906) ***(G-9268)***
Static Controls Corp......248 926-4400
30460 S Wixom Rd Wixom (48393) ***(G-17896)***
Statistical Processed Products (PA)......586 792-6900
35409 Groesbeck Hwy Clinton Township (48035) ***(G-3235)***
Status Transportation, Grand Rapids *Also called Pressure Releases Corporation* ***(G-6770)***
Steadfast Engineered Pdts LLC......616 846-4747
775 Woodlawn Ave Grand Haven (49417) ***(G-6085)***
Steadfast Lab......248 242-2291
21928 John R Rd Hazel Park (48030) ***(G-7456)***
Steadfast Tool & Machine Inc......989 856-8127
6601 Limerick Rd Caseville (48725) ***(G-2506)***
Steadypower, Grand Rapids *Also called Coffman Electrical Eqp Co* ***(G-6286)***
Stealth Medical Technologies, Holt *Also called Set Liquidation Inc* ***(G-7928)***
Stearns & Stafford Inc......269 624-4541
33081 County Road 358 Lawton (49065) ***(G-9515)***
Stec Usa Inc (PA)......248 307-1440
31900 Sherman Ave Madison Heights (48071) ***(G-10362)***
Stechschulte/Wegerly AG LLC......586 739-0101
42250 Yearego Dr Sterling Heights (48314) ***(G-15510)***
Stedman Corp......269 629-5930
10301 M 89 Richland (49083) ***(G-13256)***
Steel 21 LLC......616 884-2121
11786 White Creek Ave Ne Cedar Springs (49319) ***(G-2562)***
STEEL AND WIRE, Utica *Also called MNP Corporation* ***(G-16744)***
Steel Craft Inc......989 358-7196
1086 Hamilton Rd Alpena (49707) ***(G-314)***
Steel Craft Technologies Inc......616 866-4400
8057 Graphic Dr Ne Belmont (49306) ***(G-1471)***
Steel Fab, Flint *Also called Wpw Inc* ***(G-5527)***
Steel Forming Systems, Grand Haven *Also called Trainer Metal Forming Co Inc* ***(G-6089)***
Steel Industries Inc......313 535-8505
12600 Beech Daly Rd Redford (48239) ***(G-13194)***
Steel Master LLC......810 771-4943
8018 Embury Rd Ste 1 Grand Blanc (48439) ***(G-5984)***
Steel Mill Components Inc......586 920-2595
22522 Hoover Rd Warren (48089) ***(G-17255)***
Steel Mill Components Inc (PA)......313 386-0893
17000 Ecorse Rd Allen Park (48101) ***(G-210)***
Steel Processing Company Inc......586 772-3310
23605 Groesbeck Hwy Warren (48089) ***(G-17256)***
Steel Products, Homer *Also called MCS Industries Inc* ***(G-7946)***
Steel Skinz Graphics, Howell *Also called Steel Skinz LLC* ***(G-8103)***
Steel Skinz LLC......517 545-9955
4836 Pinckney Rd Howell (48843) ***(G-8103)***
Steel Supply & Engineering Co (PA)......616 452-3281
2020 Newark Ave Se Grand Rapids (49507) ***(G-6888)***
Steel Tank & Fabricating Co (PA)......248 625-8700
4701 White Lake Rd Clarkston (48346) ***(G-2959)***
Steel Tank & Fabricating Co......231 587-8412
9517 Lake St Mancelona (49659) ***(G-10399)***
Steel Tool & Engineering Co......734 692-8580
28005 Fort St Brownstown Twp (48183) ***(G-2072)***
Steel-Fab Wilson & Machine......989 773-6046
1219 N Mission St Mount Pleasant (48858) ***(G-11230)***
Steel-Guard Company LLC......586 232-3909
51407 Milano Dr Macomb (48042) ***(G-10162)***
Steelcase Inc (PA)......616 247-2710
901 44th St Se Grand Rapids (49508) ***(G-6889)***
Steelcase Inc......616 247-2710
1120 S 36th Grand Rapids (49508) ***(G-6890)***
Steelcraft Tool Co Inc......734 522-7130
12930 Wayne Rd Livonia (48150) ***(G-9945)***
Steele Supply Co......269 983-0920
3413 Hill St Saint Joseph (49085) ***(G-14342)***
Steelhead Industries LLC......989 506-7416
121 E Broadway St Mount Pleasant (48858) ***(G-11231)***
Steeltech Ltd (PA)......616 243-7920
1251 Phillips Ave Sw Grand Rapids (49507) ***(G-6891)***
Steeltech Ltd......616 696-1130
69 Maple Cedar Springs (49319) ***(G-2563)***
Steenson Enterprises......248 628-0036
4444 Forest St Leonard (48367) ***(G-9528)***
Steeplechase Tool & Die Inc......989 352-5544
9307 Howard Cy Edmore Rd Lakeview (48850) ***(G-9176)***
Steering Solutions Corporation (HQ)......989 757-5000
3900 E Holland Rd Saginaw (48601) ***(G-14158)***
Steffens Enterprises Inc......616 656-6886
4045 Korona Ct Se Caledonia (49316) ***(G-2317)***
Stegman Tool Co Inc......248 588-4634
1985 Ring Dr Troy (48083) ***(G-16621)***
Stegner Controls LLC......248 904-0400
3333 Bald Mountain Rd Auburn Hills (48326) ***(G-1003)***
Steigers Timber Operations......906 667-0266
401 S Tamarack Ave Bessemer (49911) ***(G-1607)***
Steinbauer Performance LLC......704 587-0856
22790 Fosdick St Dowagiac (49047) ***(G-4562)***
Steinbrecher Stone Corp (PA)......906 563-5852
N1443 Forest Dr Norway (49870) ***(G-11820)***
Steiner Tractor Parts Inc......810 621-3000
1660 S M 13 Lennon (48449) ***(G-9519)***
Steinke-Fenton Fabricators......517 782-8174
1355 Page Ave Jackson (49203) ***(G-8577)***
Steketee-Van Huis Inc......616 392-2326
13 W 4th St Holland (49423) ***(G-7814)***
Stel Technologies LLC......248 802-9457
600 S Wagner Rd Ste 142 Ann Arbor (48103) ***(G-645)***
Stella-Maris, Pellston *Also called Vte Inc* ***(G-12426)***
Stellar Computer Services LLC......989 732-7153
633 Crestwood Dr Gaylord (49735) ***(G-5893)***
Stellar Forge Products Inc (PA)......313 535-7631
13050 Inkster Rd Redford (48239) ***(G-13195)***
Stellar Materials Intl LLC......561 504-3924
777 Eight Mile Rd Whitmore Lake (48189) ***(G-17707)***
Stellar Plastics Corporation......313 527-7337
14121 Gratiot Ave Detroit (48205) ***(G-4377)***
Stellar Plastics Fabg LLC......313 527-7337
14121 Gratiot Ave Detroit (48205) ***(G-4378)***
Stellar Scents......989 868-3477
8110 W Caro Rd Reese (48757) ***(G-13233)***
Stelmatic Industries Inc......586 949-0160
50575 Richard W Blvd Chesterfield (48051) ***(G-2843)***
Stemco Products Inc......888 854-6474
4641 Industrial Dr Millington (48746) ***(G-10998)***
Step, Dearborn *Also called Services To Enhance Potential* ***(G-3757)***
Step Into Success Inc......734 426-1075
9940 Sunrise Dr Pinckney (48169) ***(G-12504)***
Stephen A James......269 641-5879
68730 Calvin Center Rd Cassopolis (49031) ***(G-2536)***

Stephen Haas.....906 475-4826
96 Croix St Apt 6 Negaunee (49866) *(G-11477)*
Stephens Fence Supply, Grand Rapids *Also called Stephens Pipe & Steel LLC (G-6892)*
Stephens Pipe & Steel LLC.....616 248-3433
3400 Roger B Chaffee Mem Grand Rapids (49548) *(G-6892)*
Sterling, Shelby Township *Also called SPI LLC (G-14701)*
Sterling Contracting, Farmington Hills *Also called Sterling Millwork Inc (G-5131)*
Sterling Diagnostics Inc.....586 979-2141
36645 Metro Ct Sterling Heights (48312) *(G-15511)*
Sterling Die & Engineering Inc.....586 677-0707
15767 Claire Ct Macomb (48042) *(G-10163)*
Sterling Edge Inc.....248 438-6034
50230 Dennis Ct Wixom (48393) *(G-17897)*
Sterling Laboratories Inc.....248 233-1190
19270 W 8 Mile Rd Southfield (48075) *(G-15034)*
Sterling Manufacturing & Engrg, Sterling Heights *Also called Sme Holdings LLC (G-15500)*
Sterling Metal Works LLC.....586 977-9577
35705 Beattie Dr Sterling Heights (48312) *(G-15512)*
Sterling Millwork Inc.....248 427-1400
23350 Commerce Dr Farmington Hills (48335) *(G-5131)*
Sterling Oil & Chemical Co (PA).....248 298-2973
702 E 11 Mile Rd Royal Oak (48067) *(G-13973)*
Sterling Performance Inc.....248 685-7811
54420 Pontiac Trl Milford (48381) *(G-10987)*
Sterling Printing & Graphics, Troy *Also called DGa Printing Inc (G-16315)*
Sterling Prod Machining LLC.....586 493-0633
42522 Executive Dr Harrison Township (48045) *(G-7351)*
Sterling Scale Company (PA).....248 358-0590
20955 Boening Dr Southfield (48075) *(G-15035)*
Sterling Software Inc.....248 528-6500
525 E Big Beaver Rd # 204 Troy (48083) *(G-16622)*
Sterling Spring LLC.....517 782-2479
2001 Wellworth Jackson (49203) *(G-8578)*
Sterling Truck and Wstn Star (HQ).....313 592-4200
13400 W Outer Dr Redford (48239) *(G-13196)*
Sterling Trucking, Redford *Also called Sterling Truck and Wstn Star (G-13196)*
Steve's Back Room, Harper Woods *Also called SBR LLC (G-7304)*
Steven Crandell.....231 582-7445
10436 Burnett Rd Charlevoix (49720) *(G-2632)*
Steven J Devlin.....734 439-1325
268 S Platt St Milan (48160) *(G-10951)*
Steven Schadler, Saint Joseph *Also called Neogen Corporation (G-14331)*
Stevens Custom Fabrication.....989 340-1184
928 Lockwood St Alpena (49707) *(G-315)*
Stevens Custom Fabrication.....989 340-1184
615 W Campbell St Alpena (49707) *(G-316)*
Stevenson Building and Sup Co.....734 856-3931
8197 Secor Rd Lambertville (48144) *(G-9185)*
Steves Backroom LLC.....313 527-7240
13250 Rotunda Dr Dearborn (48120) *(G-3763)*
Steves Custom Signs Inc.....734 662-5964
4676 Freedom Dr Ann Arbor (48108) *(G-646)*
Stewart Components, Escanaba *Also called Emp Racing Inc (G-4825)*
Stewart Industries LLC.....269 660-9290
150 Mcquiston Dr Battle Creek (49037) *(G-1253)*
Stewart Knives LLC.....906 789-1801
6911 County 426 M.5 Rd Escanaba (49829) *(G-4861)*
Stewart Manufacturing LLC.....906 498-7600
N16415 Earle Dr Hermansville (49847) *(G-7466)*
Stewart Metrology LLC.....269 660-9290
150 Mcquiston Dr Battle Creek (49037) *(G-1254)*
Stewart Printing Company Inc.....734 283-8440
2715 Fort St Wyandotte (48192) *(G-17976)*
Stewart Reed Inc.....616 846-2550
747 Grant Ave Grand Haven (49417) *(G-6086)*
Stewart Steel Specialties.....248 477-0680
20755 Whitlock St Farmington Hills (48336) *(G-5132)*
Stewart Sutherland Inc.....269 649-0530
5411 E V Ave Vicksburg (49097) *(G-16844)*
Stexley-Brake LLC.....231 421-3092
164 Carpenter Hill Rd Traverse City (49686) *(G-16111)*
Stickmann Baeckerei.....269 205-2444
11332 W M 179 Hwy Middleville (49333) *(G-10809)*
Stilson Die-Draulic, Roseville *Also called Prophotonix Limited (G-13856)*
Stilson Products LLC.....586 778-1100
28400 Groesbeck Hwy Roseville (48066) *(G-13875)*
Stirnemann Tool & Mch Co Inc.....248 435-4040
1457 N Main St Clawson (48017) *(G-2986)*
Stm Mfg Inc (PA).....616 392-4656
494 E 64th St Holland (49423) *(G-7815)*
Stm Power Inc (PA).....734 214-1448
275 Metty Dr Ann Arbor (48103) *(G-647)*
Stockbridge Manufacturing Co.....517 851-7865
4859 E Main St Stockbridge (49285) *(G-15593)*
Stokes Steel Treating Company.....810 235-3573
624 Kelso St Flint (48506) *(G-5506)*
Stokosa Prosthetic Clinic, Okemos *Also called American Prosthetic Institute (G-12112)*
Stone For You.....248 651-9940
111 W 2nd St Ste A Rochester (48307) *(G-13353)*
Stone House Bread LLC (PA).....231 933-8864
4200 Us Highway 31 S Traverse City (49685) *(G-16112)*
Stone House Bread Inc.....231 933-8864
4200 Us Highway 31 S Traverse City (49685) *(G-16113)*
Stone Plastics and Mfg Inc.....616 748-9740
8245 Riley St Ste 100 Zeeland (49464) *(G-18188)*
Stone Shop Inc.....248 852-4700
2920 Wright St Port Huron (48060) *(G-12969)*
Stone Soap Company Inc.....248 706-1000
2000 Pontiac Dr Sylvan Lake (48320) *(G-15672)*
Stone Specialists Inc.....810 744-2278
4231 Davison Rd Burton (48509) *(G-2167)*
Stonebrdge Technical Entps Ltd.....810 750-0040
14165 N Fenton Rd 102c Fenton (48430) *(G-5240)*
Stonebridge Industries Inc.....586 323-0348
42400 Merrill Rd Sterling Heights (48314) *(G-15513)*
Stonebridge Technical Services, Fenton *Also called Stonebrdge Technical Entps Ltd (G-5240)*
Stoneco Inc.....734 587-7125
6837 Scofield Rd Maybee (48159) *(G-10673)*
Stoneco of Michigan Inc.....734 236-6538
7250 Reaume Rd Newport (48166) *(G-11591)*
Stoneco of Michigan Inc (PA).....734 241-8966
15203 S Telegraph Rd Monroe (48161) *(G-11070)*
Stonecrafters Inc.....517 529-4990
4807 Industrial Dr Clarklake (49234) *(G-2901)*
Stonehedge Farm.....231 536-2779
2246 Pesek Rd East Jordan (49727) *(G-4646)*
Stoneridge Inc (PA).....248 489-9300
39675 Mackenzie Dr # 400 Novi (48377) *(G-12004)*
Stoneridge Control Devices Inc.....248 489-9300
39675 Mackenzie Dr # 400 Novi (48377) *(G-12005)*
Stoneway Marble Granite & Tile, Grand Haven *Also called Parker Property Dev Inc (G-6060)*
Stoney Acres Winery.....989 356-1041
4268 Truckey Rd Alpena (49707) *(G-317)*
Stoney Creek Collection Inc.....616 363-4858
4336 Plnfeld Ave Ne Ste H Grand Rapids (49525) *(G-6893)*
Stoney Crest Regrind Service.....989 777-7190
6243 Dixie Hwy Bridgeport (48722) *(G-1858)*
Stony Creek Essential Oils.....989 227-5500
6718 W Centerline Rd Saint Johns (48879) *(G-14297)*
Stony Lake Corporation.....734 944-9426
5115 Saline Waterworks Rd Saline (48176) *(G-14416)*
Stop & Go No 10 Inc.....734 281-7500
13785 Allen Rd Southgate (48195) *(G-15084)*
Stop & Go Transportation LLC.....313 346-7114
13425 Amberglen Dr Washington (48094) *(G-17311)*
Storage Control Systems Inc (PA).....616 887-7994
100 Applewood Dr Sparta (49345) *(G-15114)*
Storch Magnetics, Livonia *Also called Storch Products Company Inc (G-9946)*
Storch Products Company Inc.....734 591-2200
11827 Globe St Livonia (48150) *(G-9946)*
Storm Seal Co Inc.....248 689-1900
2789 Rochester Rd Troy (48083) *(G-16623)*
Stoutenburg Inc.....810 648-4400
121 Campbell Rd Sandusky (48471) *(G-14444)*
Stovall Drilling, Grand Rapids *Also called Stovall Well Drilling Co (G-6894)*
Stovall Well Drilling Co.....616 364-4144
2132 4 Mile Rd Ne Grand Rapids (49525) *(G-6894)*
Stow Company (PA).....616 399-3311
130 Central Ave Ste 400 Holland (49423) *(G-7816)*
Str Company.....517 206-6058
6442 Wooster Rd Grass Lake (49240) *(G-7094)*
Straatsma Associates Inc.....810 735-6957
110 S Bridge St Linden (48451) *(G-9597)*
Straight Line Design.....616 296-0920
18055 174th Ave Spring Lake (49456) *(G-15180)*
Straitoplane Inc.....616 997-2211
7193 Arthur St Coopersville (49404) *(G-3570)*
Straits Area Printing Corp.....231 627-5647
313 Lafayette Ave Cheboygan (49721) *(G-2696)*
Straits Corporation (PA).....989 684-5088
616 Oak St Tawas City (48763) *(G-15679)*
Straits Corporation.....989 684-3584
4804 Wilder Rd Bay City (48706) *(G-1361)*
Straits Operations Company.....989 684-5088
616 Oak St Tawas City (48763) *(G-15680)*
Straits Service Corporation.....989 684-5088
616 Oak St Tawas City (48763) *(G-15681)*
Straits Steel and Wire Company (HQ).....231 843-3416
902 N Rowe St Ste 100 Ludington (49431) *(G-10080)*
Straits Wood Treating Inc (HQ).....989 684-5088
616 Oak St Tawas City (48763) *(G-15682)*
Straitsland Resorter.....231 238-7362
3636 S Straits Hwy Indian River (49749) *(G-8223)*
Strata Design, Traverse City *Also called Cerny Industries LLC (G-15935)*
Strategic Computer Solutions.....248 888-0666
2625 Shefman Ter Ste 200 Ann Arbor (48105) *(G-648)*
Stratos Technologies Inc.....248 808-2117
617 Detroit St Ann Arbor (48104) *(G-649)*

ALPHABETIC

Strattec Power Access LLC (HQ) — 248 649-9742
2998 Dutton Rd Auburn Hills (48326) *(G-1004)*

Strattec Security Corporation — 248 649-9742
2998 Dutton Rd Auburn Hills (48326) *(G-1005)*

Strauss Tool Inc — 989 743-4741
410 S Shiawassee St Corunna (48817) *(G-3585)*

Street Denim & Co — 313 837-1200
15530 Grand River Ave Detroit (48227) *(G-4379)*

Strema Sales Corp — 248 645-0626
31000 Telg Rd Ste 240 Bingham Farms (48025) *(G-1660)*

Stress Con Industries Inc — 269 381-1550
3102 E Cork St Kalamazoo (49001) *(G-8899)*

Stridepost, Ann Arbor Also called AK Rewards LLC *(G-349)*

Strider Software Inc — 906 863-7798
1605 7th St Menominee (49858) *(G-10757)*

Strik-Wstfen-Dynarad Frnc Corp (HQ) — 616 355-2327
301 Hoover Blvd Ste 200 Holland (49423) *(G-7817)*

Striker Tools LLC — 248 990-7767
210 Park St Manitou Beach (49253) *(G-10449)*

Striko Dynarad, Holland Also called Strik-Wstfen-Dynarad Fmc Corp *(G-7817)*

Stringo, Southfield Also called Famek Inc *(G-14902)*

Strive O&P, Sterling Heights Also called Strive Orthtics Prsthetics LLC *(G-15514)*

Strive Orthtics Prsthetics LLC — 586 803-4325
41400 Dequindre Rd # 105 Sterling Heights (48314) *(G-15514)*

Stroh Companies Inc (PA) — 313 446-2000
300 River Place Dr # 5000 Detroit (48207) *(G-4380)*

Strohs — 734 285-5480
3162 Biddle Ave Wyandotte (48192) *(G-17977)*

Stromberg-Carlson Products Inc — 231 947-8600
2323 Traversefield Dr Traverse City (49686) *(G-16114)*

Strong Steel Products LLC — 313 267-3300
6464 Strong St Detroit (48211) *(G-4381)*

Structural Concepts Corp (PA) — 231 798-8888
888 E Porter Rd Norton Shores (49441) *(G-11798)*

Structural Equipment Co — 248 547-3800
1330 Hilton Rd Ferndale (48220) *(G-5320)*

Structural Plastics Inc — 810 953-9400
3401 Chief Holly (48442) *(G-7898)*

Structural Standards Inc — 616 813-1798
465 Apple Jack Ct Sparta (49345) *(G-15115)*

Stryker Australia LLC (HQ) — 269 385-2600
2825 Airview Blvd Portage (49002) *(G-13036)*

Stryker Corporation — 269 389-3741
6300 S Sprinkle Rd Portage (49002) *(G-13037)*

Stryker Corporation (PA) — 269 385-2600
2825 Airview Blvd Portage (49002) *(G-13038)*

Stryker Corporation — 269 324-5346
750 Trade Centre Way # 200 Portage (49002) *(G-13039)*

Stryker Corporation — 248 374-6352
27275 Haggerty Rd Ste 680 Novi (48377) *(G-12006)*

Stryker Corporation — 269 329-2100
3800 E Centre Ave Portage (49002) *(G-13040)*

Stryker Corporation — 269 389-2300
1901 Romence Road Pkwy Portage (49002) *(G-13041)*

Stryker Corporation — 269 323-1027
4100 E Milham Ave Portage (49002) *(G-13042)*

Stryker Customs Brokers LLC — 269 389-2300
1901 Romence Road Pkwy Portage (49002) *(G-13043)*

Stryker Far East Inc (HQ) — 269 385-2600
2825 Airview Blvd Portage (49002) *(G-13044)*

Stryker Instrs A Div Stryker, Portage Also called Stryker Corporation *(G-13042)*

Stryker Medical A Div Stryker, Portage Also called Stryker Corporation *(G-13040)*

Strzynski Signs, Cadillac Also called Donald Francis Strzynski *(G-2244)*

STS, Mio Also called Specialty Tube Solutions *(G-11009)*

STS, Grand Rapids Also called Specialty Tooling Systems Inc *(G-6881)*

Stt Usa Inc — 248 522-9655
47815 West Rd Ste D-101 Wixom (48393) *(G-17898)*

Stuarts of Novi — 248 615-2955
41390 W 10 Mile Rd Novi (48375) *(G-12007)*

Stud Boy Traction, Ravenna Also called Liberty Products Inc *(G-13123)*

Student Book Store Inc — 517 351-6768
103 E Grand River Ave East Lansing (48823) *(G-4677)*

Student Publications, Mount Pleasant Also called Central Michigan University *(G-11186)*

Studio 626, Marysville Also called Thorpe Printing Services Inc *(G-10622)*

Studio of Fine Arts Inc — 313 280-1177
4921 Leafdale Blvd Royal Oak (48073) *(G-13974)*

Studio One Midwest Inc — 269 962-3475
74 Leonard Wood Rd Battle Creek (49037) *(G-1255)*

Studiocraft, Kentwood Also called SC Custom Display Inc *(G-9032)*

Studtmans Stuff (PA) — 269 673-3126
422 N Cedar St Allegan (49010) *(G-189)*

Stuff A Pal — 734 646-3775
14401 Cone Rd Maybee (48159) *(G-10674)*

Stump Schlele Somappa Sprng — 616 361-2791
5161 Woodfield Ct Ne Grand Rapids (49525) *(G-6895)*

Stumpp Schuele Somappa USA Inc — 616 361-2791
5161 Woodfield Ct Ne Grand Rapids (49525) *(G-6896)*

Stunt3 Multimedia LLC — 313 417-0909
829 Rivard Blvd Grosse Pointe (48230) *(G-7184)*

Sturak Brothers Inc — 269 345-2929
2450 S Sprinkle Rd Kalamazoo (49001) *(G-8900)*

Sturdy Grinding Machining Inc — 586 463-8880
58600 Rosell Rd New Haven (48048) *(G-11526)*

Sturgeon Controls, Roseville Also called Dominion Tech Group Inc *(G-13797)*

Sturgis Electric Motor Service — 269 651-2955
703 N Centerville Rd Sturgis (49091) *(G-15635)*

Sturgis Molded Products Co — 269 651-9381
70343 Clark Rd Sturgis (49091) *(G-15636)*

Sturgis Tool and Die Inc — 269 651-5435
817 Broadus St Sturgis (49091) *(G-15637)*

Stus Welding & Fabrication — 616 392-8459
4249 58th St Holland (49423) *(G-7818)*

Style Craft Prototype Inc — 248 619-9048
1820 Brinston Dr Troy (48083) *(G-16624)*

Stylecraft Printing & Graphics, Canton Also called Stylecraft Printing Co *(G-2430)*

Stylecraft Printing Co (PA) — 734 455-5500
8472 Ronda Dr Canton (48187) *(G-2430)*

Stylerite Label Corporation (PA) — 248 853-7977
2140 Avon Industrial Dr Rochester Hills (48309) *(G-13519)*

Su-Dan Company (PA) — 248 651-6035
190 Northpointe Dr Lake Orion (48359) *(G-9164)*

Su-Dan Plastics Inc — 248 651-6035
4693 Gallagher Rd Rochester (48306) *(G-13354)*

Su-Dan Plastics Inc (PA) — 248 651-6035
190 Northpointe Dr Lake Orion (48359) *(G-9165)*

Su-Dan Plastics Inc — 248 651-6035
1949 Rochester Indus Dr Rochester Hills (48309) *(G-13520)*

Su-Tec Inc — 248 852-4711
1852 Star Batt Dr Rochester Hills (48309) *(G-13521)*

Subassembly Plus Inc — 616 395-2075
11359 James St Holland (49424) *(G-7819)*

Submerge Camera, Portage Also called Livbig LLC *(G-13010)*

Subterranean Press — 810 232-1489
913 Beard St Flint (48503) *(G-5507)*

Suburban Hockey LLC (PA) — 248 478-1600
23995 Freeway Park Dr # 200 Farmington Hills (48335) *(G-5133)*

Suburban Industries Inc — 734 676-6141
28093 Fort St Brownstown Twp (48183) *(G-2073)*

Subway Restaurant — 248 625-5739
7743 Sashabaw Rd Ste B Clarkston (48348) *(G-2960)*

Success By Design Inc — 800 327-0057
3741 Linden Ave Se Wyoming (49548) *(G-18033)*

Sudan, Lake Orion Also called Su-Dan Company *(G-9164)*

Suematek — 517 614-2235
4255 Lilac Ln Ypsilanti (48197) *(G-18103)*

SUEZ N.A., Rockwood Also called N A Suez *(G-13609)*

Sugar Berry — 517 321-0177
5451 W Saginaw Hwy Lansing (48917) *(G-9324)*

Sugar Bush Printing Inc — 248 373-8888
281 Enterprise Ct Ste 100 Bloomfield Hills (48302) *(G-1799)*

Sugar Free Specialties LLC (PA) — 616 734-6999
5320 West River Dr Ne Comstock Park (49321) *(G-3517)*

Sugar Kissed Cupcakes LLC — 231 421-9156
127 E Front St Traverse City (49684) *(G-16115)*

Sugru Inc — 877 990-9888
38120 Amrhein Rd Livonia (48150) *(G-9947)*

Suite 600 T-Shirts LLC — 866 712-7749
277 Gratiot Ave Ste 600 Detroit (48226) *(G-4382)*

Suite Spa Manufacturing LLC — 616 560-2713
464 Stanton Farms Dr Caledonia (49316) *(G-2318)*

Sulfo-Technologies LLC — 248 307-9150
32300 Howard Ave Madison Heights (48071) *(G-10363)*

Sullivan Reproductions Inc — 313 965-3666
241 W Congress St Detroit (48226) *(G-4383)*

Sulzer Mixpac USA Inc (HQ) — 517 339-3330
8181 Coleman Rd Haslett (48840) *(G-7400)*

Sumika Polymers North Amer LLC (HQ) — 248 284-4797
27555 Executive Dr # 380 Farmington Hills (48331) *(G-5134)*

Sumitomo Chemical America Inc — 248 284-4797
45525 Grand River Ave # 200 Novi (48374) *(G-12008)*

Sumitomo Electric Carbide Inc — 734 451-0200
14496 N Sheldon Rd # 230 Plymouth (48170) *(G-12761)*

Summers Rd Gravel, Almont Also called Summers Road Gravel & Dev LLC *(G-268)*

Summers Road Gravel & Dev LLC — 810 798-8533
3620 Van Dyke Rd Almont (48003) *(G-268)*

Summertime Concrete Inc (PA) — 517 641-6966
15765 Chandler Rd Bath (48808) *(G-1136)*

Summertime Precast, Bath Also called Summertime Concrete Inc *(G-1136)*

Summit Cutting Tools and Mfg — 248 859-2625
50210 Dennis Ct Wixom (48393) *(G-17899)*

Summit Plastic Molding Inc — 586 262-4500
51340 Celeste Shelby Township (48315) *(G-14703)*

Summit Plastic Molding II Inc — 586 977-8300
5985 Wall St Sterling Heights (48312) *(G-15515)*

Summit Plastic Molding II Inc (PA) — 586 262-4500
51340 Celeste Shelby Township (48315) *(G-14704)*

ALPHABETIC SECTION
Superior Imaging, Kalamazoo

Summit Polymers Inc (PA) 269 324-9330
6715 S Sprinkle Rd Portage (49002) ***(G-13045)***
Summit Polymers Inc 269 324-9320
6615 S Sprinkle Rd Portage (49002) ***(G-13046)***
Summit Polymers Inc 269 324-9330
5858 E N Ave Kalamazoo (49048) ***(G-8901)***
Summit Polymers Inc 269 323-1301
4750 Executive Dr Portage (49002) ***(G-13047)***
Summit Polymers Inc 269 651-1643
1211 Progress St Sturgis (49091) ***(G-15638)***
Summit Polymers Inc 269 649-4900
115 S Leja Dr Vicksburg (49097) ***(G-16845)***
Summit Printing & Graphics 989 892-2267
205 4th St Bay City (48708) ***(G-1362)***
Summit Services Inc 586 977-8300
51340 Celeste Shelby Township (48315) ***(G-14705)***
Summit Tooling & Mfg Inc 231 856-7037
451 N Cass St Morley (49336) ***(G-11118)***
Summit Training Source Inc (PA) 800 842-0466
4170 Embassy Dr Se Grand Rapids (49546) ***(G-6897)***
Summit Truss, Holton *Also called Joseph Miller* ***(G-7933)***
Summit-Reed City Inc 989 433-5716
4147 E Monroe St Rosebush (48878) ***(G-13765)***
Sun Chemical Corporation 513 681-5950
5025 Evanston Ave Muskegon (49442) ***(G-11431)***
Sun Chemical Corporation 231 788-2371
4835 Evanston Ave Muskegon (49442) ***(G-11432)***
Sun Coating Co, Plymouth *Also called Sun Plastics Coating Company* ***(G-12762)***
Sun Communities Inc (PA) 248 208-2500
27777 Franklin Rd Ste 200 Southfield (48034) ***(G-15036)***
Sun Daily 248 842-2925
4226 Cherry Hill Dr Orchard Lake (48323) ***(G-12170)***
Sun Gro Horticulture Dist Inc 517 639-3115
1150 E Chicago Rd Quincy (49082) ***(G-13100)***
Sun Microsystems, Troy *Also called Oracle America Inc* ***(G-16535)***
Sun Pharmaceutical Inds Inc 248 346-7302
29714 Orion Ct Farmington Hills (48334) ***(G-5135)***
Sun Pharmaceutical Inds Inc 609 495-2800
1150 Elijah Mccoy Dr Detroit (48202) ***(G-4384)***
Sun Plastics Coating Company 734 453-0822
42105 Postiff Ave Plymouth (48170) ***(G-12762)***
Sun Ray Sign Group Inc 616 392-2824
376 Roost Ave Holland (49424) ***(G-7820)***
Sun Steel Treating Inc 877 471-0844
550 N Mill St South Lyon (48178) ***(G-14813)***
Sun Tool Company 313 837-2442
18505 Weaver St Detroit (48228) ***(G-4385)***
Sun-Tec Corp (PA) 248 669-3100
46590 Ryan Ct Novi (48377) ***(G-12009)***
Sunaire Window Manufacturing 248 437-5870
7936 Boardwalk Rd Brighton (48116) ***(G-1993)***
Sunbeam, Livonia *Also called American Household Inc* ***(G-9643)***
Sunburst Shutters 248 674-4600
5499 Perry Dr Ste M Waterford (48329) ***(G-17378)***
Sunchime Company, Brighton *Also called Technacraft Corp* ***(G-1995)***
Sundance Beverage Company, Warren *Also called Sundance Beverages Inc* ***(G-17257)***
Sundance Beverages Inc 586 755-9470
6600 E 9 Mile Rd Warren (48091) ***(G-17257)***
Sundog Construction Heaters, Birmingham *Also called U S Distributing Inc* ***(G-1707)***
Sundown Sheet Metal Inc 616 846-7674
16929 148th Ave Spring Lake (49456) ***(G-15181)***
Sunek Co 231 421-5317
3125 Buttermilk Loop Traverse City (49686) ***(G-16116)***
Sunera Technologies Inc (PA) 248 524-0222
631 E Big Beaver Rd # 105 Troy (48083) ***(G-16625)***
Sunglass Hut 4711, Birch Run *Also called Luxottica of America Inc* ***(G-1665)***
Sungwoo Hitech Co Ltd 248 509-0445
3321 W Big Beaver Rd # 303 Troy (48084) ***(G-16626)***
Sunhill America LLC (PA) 616 249-3600
5300 Broadmoor Ave Se B Grand Rapids (49512) ***(G-6898)***
Sunlite Market Inc 586 792-9870
34705 S Gratiot Ave Clinton Township (48035) ***(G-3236)***
Sunmed LLC (HQ) 616 259-8400
2710 Northridge Dr Nw A Grand Rapids (49544) ***(G-6899)***
Sunmed Holdings LLC (PA) 616 259-8400
2710 Northridge Dr Nw Grand Rapids (49544) ***(G-6900)***
Sunopta Ingredients Inc 502 587-7999
16369 Us Highway 131 S Schoolcraft (49087) ***(G-14502)***
Sunraise Inc 810 359-7301
6547 Lakeshore Rd Lexington (48450) ***(G-9560)***
Sunrise Bread Co, Grand Rapids *Also called Gr Baking Company* ***(G-6449)***
Sunrise Print Cmmnications Inc 989 345-4475
118 W Houghton Ave West Branch (48661) ***(G-17523)***
Sunrise Printed Embroidered AP, Ann Arbor *Also called Sunrise Screen Printing Inc* ***(G-650)***
Sunrise Screen Printing Inc 734 769-3888
5277 Jackson Rd Ste C Ann Arbor (48103) ***(G-650)***
Sunrise Tool Products Inc 989 724-6688
604 S 3rd St Harrisville (48740) ***(G-7366)***
Sunsation Boats, Clay *Also called Sunsation Products Inc* ***(G-3003)***
Sunsation Products Inc 810 794-4888
9666 Kretz Dr Clay (48001) ***(G-3003)***
Sunset Enterprises Inc (PA) 269 373-6440
633 W Michigan Ave Kalamazoo (49007) ***(G-8902)***
Sunset Sportswear Inc 248 437-7611
676 Shady Maple Dr Wixom (48393) ***(G-17900)***
Sunshine Systems Inc 616 363-9272
3700 Buchanan Ave Sw B Grand Rapids (49548) ***(G-6901)***
Sunshine Water Conditioner, Linden *Also called McIntyre Softwater Service* ***(G-9593)***
Sunstone Granite & Marble Co, Grand Rapids *Also called Grand Valley Wood Products Inc* ***(G-6471)***
Suntech Industrials LLC 734 678-5922
5137 Colonial Ct Ann Arbor (48108) ***(G-651)***
Super Book, Portage *Also called Llomen Inc* ***(G-13011)***
Super Bowl 50 Book, Traverse City *Also called Jkr Ventures LLC* ***(G-16013)***
Super Fluids LLC 313 409-6522
8838 3rd St Detroit (48202) ***(G-4386)***
Super Sidebar Inc 989 709-0048
1396 Autumn Trl West Branch (48661) ***(G-17524)***
Super Steel Treating Inc 586 755-9140
6227 Rinke Ave Warren (48091) ***(G-17258)***
Super Video Service Center 248 358-4794
26561 W 12 Mile Rd # 102 Southfield (48034) ***(G-15037)***
Superabrasives Inc 248 348-7670
28047 Grand Oaks Ct Wixom (48393) ***(G-17901)***
Superb Machine Repair Inc (PA) 586 749-8800
59180 Havenridge Rd New Haven (48048) ***(G-11527)***
Superfly Manufacturing Co 313 454-1492
31505 Grand River Ave 7c Farmington (48336) ***(G-4913)***
Superior Abrasive Products 248 969-4090
85 S Glaspie St Ste A Oxford (48371) ***(G-12374)***
Superior Attachment Inc 906 864-1708
N3522 Us Highway 41 Menominee (49858) ***(G-10758)***
Superior Auto Glass of Mich 989 366-9691
7006 W Houghton Lake Dr Houghton Lake (48629) ***(G-7999)***
Superior Automotive Eqp Inc 231 829-9902
18153 150th Ave Leroy (49655) ***(G-9538)***
Superior Block Company Inc 906 482-2731
100 Isle Royale St Houghton (49931) ***(G-7984)***
Superior Brass & Alum Cast Co 517 351-7534
4893 Dawn Ave East Lansing (48823) ***(G-4678)***
Superior Cam Inc 248 588-1100
31240 Stephenson Hwy Madison Heights (48071) ***(G-10364)***
Superior Casket Co 313 592-3190
26789 Fullerton Redford (48239) ***(G-13197)***
Superior Cedar Products Inc 906 639-2132
101 Fence Factory Rd Carney (49812) ***(G-2464)***
Superior Collision Inc 231 946-4983
9419 Westwood Dr Traverse City (49685) ***(G-16117)***
Superior Controls Inc 734 454-0500
46247 Five Mile Rd Plymouth (48170) ***(G-12763)***
Superior Country Wood Truss 906 499-3354
Railroad St Seney (49883) ***(G-14522)***
Superior Cutter Grinding Inc 586 781-2365
54631 Franklin Dr Shelby Township (48316) ***(G-14706)***
Superior Cutting Service Inc 616 796-0114
4740 136th Ave Holland (49424) ***(G-7821)***
Superior Design & Mfg 810 678-3950
4180 Pleasant St Metamora (48455) ***(G-10781)***
Superior Distribution Svcs LLC 616 453-6358
4001 3 Mile Rd Nw Grand Rapids (49534) ***(G-6902)***
Superior Elc Mtr Sls & Svc, Marquette *Also called Superior Elc Mtr Sls & Svc Inc* ***(G-10558)***
Superior Elc Mtr Sls & Svc Inc 906 226-9051
1740 Presque Isle Ave Marquette (49855) ***(G-10558)***
Superior Equipment & Supply Co 906 774-1789
1515 S Stephenson Ave Iron Mountain (49801) ***(G-8302)***
Superior Equipment LLC 269 388-2871
7008 E N Ave Kalamazoo (49048) ***(G-8903)***
Superior Extrusion Inc 906 346-7308
118 Avenue G Gwinn (49841) ***(G-7223)***
Superior Fabricating Inc 989 354-8877
320 N Eleventh Ave Alpena (49707) ***(G-318)***
Superior Fabrication Co LLC 906 495-5634
17499 S Dolan St Bldg 434 Kincheloe (49788) ***(G-9053)***
Superior Fixture & Tooling LLC 616 828-1566
425 36th St Se Grand Rapids (49548) ***(G-6903)***
Superior Fluid Systems 734 246-4550
7804 Beech Daly Rd Taylor (48180) ***(G-15773)***
Superior Furniture Company, Grand Rapids *Also called Van Zee Acquisitions Inc* ***(G-6958)***
Superior Graphics Studios Ltd 906 482-7891
19923 W Sharon Ave Houghton (49931) ***(G-7985)***
Superior Growers Supply, Lansing *Also called Growgeneration Michigan Corp* ***(G-9379)***
Superior Gun Drilling 810 744-1112
1830 Kelso St Flint (48503) ***(G-5508)***
Superior Heat Treat LLC 586 792-9500
36125 Groesbeck Hwy Clinton Township (48035) ***(G-3237)***
Superior Hockey LLC (PA) 906 225-9008
401 E Fair Ave Marquette (49855) ***(G-10559)***
Superior Imaging, Kalamazoo *Also called Superior Typesetting Service* ***(G-8905)***

ALPHABETIC

Superior Imaging Services Inc 269 382-0428
4001 Portage St Kalamazoo (49001) *(G-8904)*

Superior Industries Intl Inc (PA) 248 352-7300
26600 Telg Rd Ste 400 Southfield (48033) *(G-15038)*

Superior Industries N Amer LLC 248 352-7300
26600 Telegraph Rd # 400 Southfield (48033) *(G-15039)*

Superior Information Tech LLC 734 666-9963
38701 7 Mile Rd Ste 285 Livonia (48152) *(G-9948)*

Superior Inspection Svc 231 258-9400
1864 Prough Rd Sw Kalkaska (49646) *(G-8959)*

Superior Lumber Inc 906 786-1638
8000 County 426 M.5 Rd Gladstone (49837) *(G-5920)*

Superior Machining Inc 248 446-9451
55378 Lyon Industrial Dr New Hudson (48165) *(G-11556)*

Superior Manufacturing Corp (PA) 313 935-1550
431 Stephenson Hwy Troy (48083) *(G-16627)*

Superior Mar & Envmtl Svcs LLC 906 253-9448
3779 S Riverside Dr Sault Sainte Marie (49783) *(G-14475)*

Superior Marine Products LLC 906 370-9908
20134 Gagnon Cir Hancock (49930) *(G-7257)*

Superior Materials LLC 734 941-2479
39001 W Huron River Dr Romulus (48174) *(G-13735)*

Superior Materials LLC (PA) 248 788-8000
30701 W 10 Mile Rd Farmington Hills (48336) *(G-5136)*

Superior Materials Inc 888 988-4400
20565 Hoover St Detroit (48205) *(G-4387)*

Superior Materials Inc (PA) 248 788-8000
585 Stewart Ave Farmington Hills (48333) *(G-5137)*

Superior Mold Services Inc 586 264-9570
6100 15 Mile Rd Sterling Heights (48312) *(G-15516)*

Superior Monuments Co 616 844-1700
1003 S Beacon Blvd Grand Haven (49417) *(G-6087)*

Superior Monuments Co (PA) 231 728-2211
354 Ottawa St Muskegon (49442) *(G-11433)*

Superior Mtal Finshg Rustproof 313 893-1050
3510 E Mcnichols Rd Detroit (48212) *(G-4388)*

Superior Mtls Holdings LLC 248 788-8000
30701 W 10 Mile Rd Farmington Hills (48336) *(G-5138)*

Superior Non-Ferrous Inc 586 791-7988
35475 Forton Ct Clinton Township (48035) *(G-3238)*

Superior Polymer Products, Calumet Also called Kiilunen Mfg Group Inc *(G-2328)*

Superior Polyolefin Films Inc 248 334-8074
465 Fox River Dr Bloomfield Hills (48304) *(G-1800)*

Superior Products Mfg Inc 810 679-4479
124 Louise St Croswell (48422) *(G-3603)*

Superior Receipt Book Co Inc 269 467-8265
215 S Clark St Centreville (49032) *(G-2597)*

Superior Roll LLC 734 279-1831
399 E Center St Petersburg (49270) *(G-12438)*

Superior Roll & Turning, Petersburg Also called Superior Roll LLC *(G-12438)*

Superior Spindle Services LLC 734 946-4646
25377 Brest Taylor (48180) *(G-15774)*

Superior Steel Components Inc (PA) 616 866-4759
180 Monroe Ave Nw Ste 2r Grand Rapids (49503) *(G-6904)*

Superior Suppliers Network LLC 906 284-1561
1307 Harrison Ave Crystal Falls (49920) *(G-3614)*

Superior Surface Protection Co 517 206-1541
3728 Luella St Jackson (49201) *(G-8579)*

Superior Synchronized Sys 906 863-7824
W4365 Pinewoods Loop 12 Wallace (49893) *(G-16888)*

Superior Text LLC 866 482-8762
151 Airport Industrial Dr Ypsilanti (48198) *(G-18104)*

Superior Threading Inc 989 729-1160
1535 N Hickory Rd Owosso (48867) *(G-12319)*

Superior Tool & Fabg LLC 906 353-7588
13529 Old 41 Rd Keweenaw Bay (49908) *(G-9041)*

Superior Typesetting Service 269 382-0428
4001 Portage St Kalamazoo (49001) *(G-8905)*

Superior Vault Co 989 643-4200
345 E Mahoney Merrill (48637) *(G-10762)*

Superior Water Screen Company, Farmington Hills Also called Protege Concepts Corp *(G-5104)*

Superior Waterjet Service, Chesterfield Also called American Brake and Clutch Inc *(G-2736)*

Superior Welding & Mfg Inc 906 498-7616
5704 Old Us 2 Rd 43 Hermansville (49847) *(G-7467)*

Superior Wood Products Inc 616 453-4100
7584 Warner St Allendale (49401) *(G-226)*

Supermarket Liquidation, Grand Rapids Also called Hilco Fixture Finders LLC *(G-6511)*

Supersine Company 313 892-6200
27634 Rackham Dr Lathrup Village (48076) *(G-9501)*

Supertramp Custom Trampoline 616 634-2010
5161 Woodfield Ct Ne # 1 Grand Rapids (49525) *(G-6905)*

Supplement Group Inc 248 588-2055
32787 Stephenson Hwy Madison Heights (48071) *(G-10365)*

Supply Line International LLC 248 242-7140
42350 Grand River Ave Novi (48375) *(G-12010)*

Supported Intelligence Inc 517 908-4420
1555 Watertower Pl # 300 East Lansing (48823) *(G-4679)*

Supreme Bakery & Deli, Detroit Also called Supreme Baking Company *(G-4389)*

Supreme Baking Company 313 894-0222
5401 Proctor St Detroit (48210) *(G-4389)*

Supreme Casting Inc 269 465-5757
3389 W Linco Rd Stevensville (49127) *(G-15583)*

Supreme Domestic Intl Sls Corp 616 842-6550
18686 172nd Ave Spring Lake (49456) *(G-15182)*

Supreme Gear Co (PA) 586 775-6325
17430 Malyn Blvd Fraser (48026) *(G-5736)*

Supreme Industries LLC 586 725-2500
6015 Corporate Dr Ira (48023) *(G-8273)*

Supreme Machined Pdts Co Inc (PA) 616 842-6550
18686 172nd Ave Spring Lake (49456) *(G-15183)*

Supreme Machined Pdts Co Inc 616 842-6550
18686 172nd Ave Spring Lake (49456) *(G-15184)*

Supreme Media Blasting and Pow 586 792-7705
36427 Groesbeck Hwy Clinton Township (48035) *(G-3239)*

Supreme Tool & Machine Inc 248 673-8408
5409 Perry Dr Waterford (48329) *(G-17379)*

Supreme Welding Inc 586 791-8860
34727 Nova Dr Clinton Township (48035) *(G-3240)*

Sur-Form LLC 586 221-1950
50320 E Russell Schmidt Chesterfield (48051) *(G-2844)*

Surclean Inc 248 791-2226
7974 Lochlin Dr Ste B1 Brighton (48116) *(G-1994)*

Sure -Loc Edging-Wolverine Tls, Holland Also called Sure-Loc Aluminum Edging Inc *(G-7822)*

Sure Alloy Steel, Warren Also called Sas Global Corporation *(G-17230)*

Sure Conveyors Inc 248 926-2100
48155 West Rd Ste 6 Wixom (48393) *(G-17902)*

Sure Solutions Corporation 248 674-7210
40 Corporate Dr Auburn Hills (48326) *(G-1006)*

Sure-Fit Glove & Safety 734 729-4960
38241 Abruzzi Dr Westland (48185) *(G-17601)*

Sure-Flo Fittings, Ann Arbor Also called Perfection Sprinkler Company *(G-590)*

Sure-Loc Aluminum Edging Inc 616 392-3209
310 E 64th St Holland (49423) *(G-7822)*

Sure-Plating Rack Co, Southfield Also called Sure-Weld & Plating Rack Co *(G-15040)*

Sure-Weld & Plating Rack Co (PA) 248 304-9430
21680 W 8 Mile Rd Southfield (48075) *(G-15040)*

Surefil, Kentwood Also called Abaco Partners LLC *(G-8997)*

Surface Activation Tech LLC 248 273-0037
1837 Thunderbird Troy (48084) *(G-16628)*

Surface Blasting Systems LLC 616 384-3351
90 Mason Dr Coopersville (49404) *(G-3571)*

Surface Coatings Company, Auburn Hills Also called Bonsal American Inc *(G-794)*

Surface Encounters LLC 586 566-7557
16280 23 Mile Rd Macomb (48044) *(G-10164)*

Surface Expressions LLC 231 843-8282
904 1st St Ludington (49431) *(G-10081)*

Surface Mausoleum Company Inc 989 864-3460
1799 Main St Minden City (48456) *(G-11001)*

Surfalloy, Troy Also called Alloying Surfaces Inc *(G-16191)*

Surge Cardiovascular, Grand Rapids Also called Medisurge LLC *(G-6657)*

Surgitech Surgical Svcs Inc 248 593-0797
1477 Schooner Cv Highland (48356) *(G-7500)*

Surplus Steel Inc 248 338-0000
321 Collier Rd Auburn Hills (48326) *(G-1007)*

Suse Linux, Southfield Also called Suse LLC *(G-15041)*

Suse LLC 248 353-8010
26677 W 12 Mile Rd Ste 1 Southfield (48034) *(G-15041)*

Suspa Incorporated (HQ) 616 241-4200
3970 R B Chaffee Mem Dr Grand Rapids (49548) *(G-6906)*

Suspension Solutions, Lansing Also called Air Lift Company *(G-9272)*

Sustainable Industries LLC 248 213-6599
16800 Plainview Ave Detroit (48219) *(G-4390)*

Sutherland Felt Co, Madison Heights Also called Michigan Diversfd Holdings Inc *(G-10305)*

Suttons Bay Ciders 734 646-3196
10530 E Hilltop Rd Suttons Bay (49682) *(G-15656)*

Suttons Bay Tasting Room, Suttons Bay Also called Black Star Farms LLC *(G-15650)*

Svn Inc 734 707-7131
6763 Heatheridge Dr Saline (48176) *(G-14417)*

Svrc Industries Inc (PA) 989 280-3038
203 S Washington Ave # 310 Saginaw (48607) *(G-14159)*

Svrc Industries Inc 989 723-8205
2009 Corunna Ave Owosso (48867) *(G-12320)*

Swagelok Michigan Toledo, Farmington Hills Also called Lennon Fluid Systems LLC *(G-5043)*

Swain Meter Company 989 773-3700
220 E Ludington Dr Farwell (48622) *(G-5166)*

Swan Creek Candle, Dundee Also called Ambrosia Inc *(G-4575)*

Swanson Grading & Brining Inc 231 853-2289
11561 Heights Ravenna Rd Ravenna (49451) *(G-13129)*

Swanson Orthtic Prsthetics Ctr 734 241-4397
1174 W Front St Monroe (48161) *(G-11071)*

Swanson Pickle Co Inc 231 853-2289
11561 Heights Ravenna Rd Ravenna (49451) *(G-13130)*

Swansons Excavating Inc 989 873-4419
2733 Greenwood Rd Prescott (48756) *(G-13081)*

ALPHABETIC SECTION T W S Wldg & Cstm Fabrication, Kalkaska

Swarovski North America Ltd 248 874-0753
4000 Baldwin Rd Auburn Hills (48326) *(G-1008)*
Swarovski North America Ltd 616 977-5008
3175 28th St Se Grand Rapids (49512) *(G-6907)*
Swartzmiller Lumber Company (PA) 989 845-6625
802 W Broad St Chesaning (48616) *(G-2728)*
Swat Environmental Inc (PA) 517 322-2999
2607 Eaton Rapids Rd Lansing (48911) *(G-9427)*
Sway Magazine Publishing 517 394-4295
3612 W Miller Rd Lansing (48911) *(G-9428)*
Sweeney Metalworking LLC 989 401-6531
4450 Marlea Dr Saginaw (48601) *(G-14160)*
Sweepster Attachments LLC 734 996-9116
2800 Zeeb Rd Dexter (48130) *(G-4512)*
Sweet & Sweeter Inc 586 977-9338
4059 17 Mile Rd Sterling Heights (48310) *(G-15517)*
Sweet & Sweeter By Linda, Sterling Heights *Also called Sweet & Sweeter Inc* *(G-15517)*
Sweet Creations 989 327-1157
1375 Lathrup Ave Saginaw (48638) *(G-14161)*
Sweet Earth 248 850-8031
313 S Main St Royal Oak (48067) *(G-13975)*
Sweet Essentials LLC 248 398-7933
3233 12 Mile Rd Berkley (48072) *(G-1589)*
Sweet Harvest Foods, Onsted *Also called Natural American Foods Inc* *(G-12155)*
Sweet Manufacturing Inc 269 344-2086
3421 S Burdick St Kalamazoo (49001) *(G-8906)*
Sweet Mellisas Cupcakes 616 889-3998
4413 Causeway Dr Ne Lowell (49331) *(G-10043)*
Sweet Potato Sensations Inc 313 532-7996
17337 Lahser Rd Detroit (48219) *(G-4391)*
Sweet Street Motor Car, Paw Paw *Also called Ambiance LLC* *(G-12396)*
Sweet Tmpttons Ice Cream Prlor 616 842-8108
1003 S Beacon Blvd Grand Haven (49417) *(G-6088)*
Sweetheart Bakery Inc (PA) 313 839-6330
19200 Kelly Rd Detroit (48225) *(G-4392)*
Sweetheart Bakery of Michigan 586 795-1660
19200 Kelly Rd Harper Woods (48225) *(G-7306)*
Sweetie Pie Pantry (PA) 517 669-9300
108 N Bridge St Dewitt (48820) *(G-4466)*
Sweetwater Brew LLC 616 805-5077
1760 44th St Sw Wyoming (49519) *(G-18034)*
Sweetwaters Donut Mill 269 979-1944
2807 Capital Ave Sw Battle Creek (49015) *(G-1256)*
Sweney-Kern Manufacturing, Saginaw *Also called Midwest Marketing Inc* *(G-14095)*
Swift Biosciences Inc 734 330-2568
674 S Wagner Rd Ste 100 Ann Arbor (48103) *(G-652)*
Swift Printing and Comm, Grand Rapids *Also called Swift Printing Co* *(G-6908)*
Swift Printing Co 616 459-4263
404 Bridge St Nw Grand Rapids (49504) *(G-6908)*
Swiftwall Solutions, Midland *Also called Signature Wall Solutions Inc* *(G-10916)*
Swing-Lo Suspended Scaffold Co 269 764-8989
75609 County Road 376 Covert (49043) *(G-3591)*
Swing-Lo System, Covert *Also called Swing-Lo Suspended Scaffold Co* *(G-3591)*
Swirlberry 734 779-0830
17382 Haggerty Rd Livonia (48152) *(G-9949)*
Swiss American Screw Pdts Inc 734 397-1600
5740 S Sheldon Rd Canton (48188) *(G-2431)*
Swiss Industries Inc 517 437-3682
305 Arch Ave Hillsdale (49242) *(G-7542)*
Swiss Precision Machining Inc 586 677-7558
54370 Oconee Dr Macomb (48042) *(G-10165)*
Swivl - Eze Marine 616 897-9241
1016 N Monroe St Lowell (49331) *(G-10044)*
Swoboda Inc 616 554-6161
4108 52nd St Se Grand Rapids (49512) *(G-6909)*
Sws - Trimac Inc 989 791-4595
5225 Davis Rd Saginaw (48604) *(G-14162)*
Sy Fuel Inc 313 531-5894
27360 Grand River Ave Redford (48240) *(G-13198)*
Sycron Technologies Inc 810 694-4007
8130 Industrial Park Dr Grand Blanc (48439) *(G-5985)*
Syd Enterprises 517 719-2740
3850 E Grand River Ave Howell (48843) *(G-8104)*
Sydeline Corporation 734 675-9330
9155 Groh Rd Grosse Ile (48138) *(G-7177)*
Sydney Bogg's Sweet Essentials, Berkley *Also called Sweet Essentials LLC* *(G-1589)*
Sylvania Minerals, South Rockwood *Also called Great Lakes Aggregates LLC* *(G-14821)*
Sylvesters (PA) 989 348-9097
5610 W M 72 Hwy Grayling (49738) *(G-7116)*
Symbiosis International, Okemos *Also called Umakanth Consultants Inc* *(G-12139)*
Symbiote Inc 616 772-1790
300 N Centennial St Zeeland (49464) *(G-18189)*
Symmetry Medical Inc 517 887-3424
5212 Aurelius Rd Lansing (48911) *(G-9429)*
Symonds Machine Co Inc 269 782-8051
414 West St Dowagiac (49047) *(G-4563)*
Symorex Ltd 734 971-6000
3728 Plaza Dr Ste 3 Ann Arbor (48108) *(G-653)*
Synchronous Manufacturing Inc 517 764-6930
4050 Page Ave Michigan Center (49254) *(G-10791)*
Syncon Inc 313 914-4481
31001 Schoolcraft Rd Livonia (48150) *(G-9950)*
Syncreon Acquisition Corp (HQ) 248 377-4700
2851 High Meadow Cir # 250 Auburn Hills (48326) *(G-1009)*
Syncreonus Inc 586 754-4100
12350 E 9 Mile Rd Warren (48089) *(G-17259)*
Syncreonus Inc (HQ) 248 377-4700
2851 High Meadow Cir # 250 Auburn Hills (48326) *(G-1010)*
Syndevco Inc 248 356-2839
24205 Telegraph Rd Southfield (48033) *(G-15042)*
Synergy Additive Mfg LLC (HQ) 248 719-2194
22792 Macomb Indus Dr Clinton Township (48036) *(G-3241)*
Synergy Prototype Stamping LLC (PA) 586 961-6109
22778 Macomb Indus Dr Clinton Township (48036) *(G-3242)*
Synex Wolverine LLC 989 689-3161
6000 S M 30 Edenville (48620) *(G-4748)*
Synod of Great Lakes 616 698-7071
4500 60th St Se Grand Rapids (49512) *(G-6910)*
Syntech Plant, Sturgis *Also called Summit Polymers Inc* *(G-15638)*
Synthetic Lubricants Inc 616 754-1050
1411 Callaghan St Greenville (48838) *(G-7156)*
System 2/90 Inc 616 656-4310
5350 Corprte Grv Dr Se Grand Rapids (49512) *(G-6911)*
System Components Inc 269 637-2191
1635 Stieve Dr South Haven (49090) *(G-14776)*
System Controls Inc 734 427-0440
35245 Schoolcraft Rd Livonia (48150) *(G-9951)*
Systemation, Grand Ledge *Also called Roberts Sinto Corporation* *(G-6114)*
Systems Design & Installation 269 543-4204
2091 66th St Fennville (49408) *(G-5177)*
Systems Duplicating Co Inc 248 585-7590
358 Robbins Dr Troy (48083) *(G-16629)*
Systems Unlimited Inc 517 279-8407
300 Jay St Coldwater (49036) *(G-3336)*
Systex Products Corporation (HQ) 269 964-8800
300 Buckner Rd Battle Creek (49037) *(G-1257)*
Systrand Manufacturing Corp (PA) 734 479-8100
19050 Allen Rd Brownstown Twp (48183) *(G-2074)*
Systrand Prsta Eng Systems LLC 734 479-8100
19050 Allen Rd Ste 200 Brownstown Twp (48183) *(G-2075)*
T & C Tool & Sales Inc 586 677-8390
60950 Van Dyke Rd Washington (48094) *(G-17312)*
T & D Machine Inc 517 423-0778
2485 E Monroe Rd Tecumseh (49286) *(G-15810)*
T & J Uphl Sp & Marathon Svc, Moran *Also called Gustafson Smoked Fish* *(G-11107)*
T & L Products 989 868-4428
2586 S Bradleyville Rd Reese (48757) *(G-13234)*
T & L Transport Inc 313 350-1535
13801 Westbrook Rd Plymouth (48170) *(G-12764)*
T & W Tool & Die Corporation 248 548-5400
21770 Wyoming Pl Oak Park (48237) *(G-12101)*
T - Shirt Printing Plus Inc 269 383-3666
8608 W Main St Ste B Kalamazoo (49009) *(G-8907)*
T C H Industries Incorporated (HQ) 616 942-0505
7441 Div Ave S Ste A1 Grand Rapids (49548) *(G-6912)*
T C V S, Ann Arbor *Also called Terumo Crdvscular Systems Corp* *(G-666)*
T D A, Kalamazoo *Also called Buddy Tda Inc* *(G-8702)*
T D I C, Sterling Heights *Also called TD Industrial Coverings Inc* *(G-15521)*
T D Vinette Company 906 786-1884
1212 N 19th St Escanaba (49829) *(G-4862)*
T E C Boring 586 443-5437
15645 Sturgeon St Roseville (48066) *(G-13876)*
T E L, Ann Arbor *Also called Thalner Electronic Labs Inc* *(G-668)*
T E Technology Inc 231 929-3966
1590 Keane Dr Traverse City (49696) *(G-16118)*
T F Boyer Industries Inc 248 674-8420
5489 Perry Dr Ste C Waterford (48329) *(G-17380)*
T F G Gage Components 734 427-2274
11901 Brookfield St Livonia (48150) *(G-9952)*
T J K Inc 586 731-9639
39370 Bella Vista Dr Sterling Heights (48313) *(G-15518)*
T L V Inc 989 773-4362
5747 W Isabella Rd Mount Pleasant (48858) *(G-11232)*
T M P, Hudsonville *Also called Topcraft Metal Products Inc* *(G-8184)*
T M Shea Products Inc 800 992-5233
1950 Austin Dr Troy (48083) *(G-16630)*
T M Smith Tool Intl Corp (PA) 586 468-1465
360 Hubbard St Mount Clemens (48043) *(G-11151)*
T Q Machining Inc 231 726-5914
450 W Hackley Ave Muskegon (49444) *(G-11434)*
T R S Fieldbus Systems Inc 586 826-9696
666 Baldwin Ct Birmingham (48009) *(G-1703)*
T S M Foods LLC 313 262-6556
1241 Woodward Ave Detroit (48226) *(G-4393)*
T S Manufacturing & Design 517 543-5368
2250 Otto Rd Charlotte (48813) *(G-2669)*
T W S Wldg & Cstm Fabrication, Kalkaska *Also called Todds Welding Service Inc* *(G-8964)*

ALPHABETIC

(PA)=Parent Co (HQ)=Headquarters (DH)=Div Headquarters
2020 Harris Michigan Industrial Directory
1085

T Warren Sawmill 989 619-0840
6187 Warren Trl Grayling (49738) *(G-7117)*
T Wigley Inc 313 831-6881
1537 Hale St Detroit (48207) *(G-4394)*
T&M Usa Inc 517 789-9420
4115 County Farm Rd Jackson (49201) *(G-8580)*
T-Mach Industries LLC 734 673-6964
7941 Margaret St Taylor (48180) *(G-15775)*
T-Print USA 269 751-4603
3410 136th Ave Hamilton (49419) *(G-7240)*
T-Shirt World 313 387-2023
25351 Grand River Ave Redford (48240) *(G-13199)*
Ta Delaware Inc (PA) 248 675-6000
17672 N Laure Park Dr Ste Novi (48377) *(G-12011)*
TA Systems Inc 248 656-5150
1842 Rochester Indus Dr Rochester Hills (48309) *(G-13522)*
Tabletting Inc 616 957-0281
4201 Danvers Ct Se Grand Rapids (49512) *(G-6913)*
Tabor Hill Champagne Cellar, Bridgman Also called CHI Co/Tabor Hill Winery *(G-1861)*
Tabor Hill Winery & Restaurant, Buchanan Also called CHI Co/Tabor Hill Winery *(G-2113)*
Tabs Wall Systems LLC 616 554-5400
4515 Airwest Dr Se Grand Rapids (49512) *(G-6914)*
TAC Industrial Group LLC 517 917-8976
1164 Lexington Blvd Jackson (49201) *(G-8581)*
TAC Manufacturing Inc (HQ) 517 789-7000
4111 County Farm Rd Jackson (49201) *(G-8582)*
Tachi-S Engineering USA Inc (HQ) 248 478-5050
23227 Commerce Dr Farmington Hills (48335) *(G-5139)*
Tachyon Corporation 586 598-4320
48705 Gratiot Ave Chesterfield (48051) *(G-2845)*
Tacs Automation LLC (PA) 586 446-8828
1856 Star Batt Dr Rochester Hills (48309) *(G-13523)*
Tactical Simplicity LLC 248 410-4523
2817 Beck Rd Ste E-16 Wixom (48393) *(G-17903)*
Tade Publishing Group, Troy Also called Timothy J Tade Inc *(G-16644)*
Tadey Frank R Radian Tool Co 586 754-7422
23823 Blackstone Ave Warren (48089) *(G-17260)*
Tafcor Inc 269 471-2351
9918 N Tudor Rd Berrien Springs (49103) *(G-1601)*
Tai Consulting, Franklin Also called Talbot & Associates Inc *(G-5609)*
Tait Grinding Service Inc 248 437-5100
57401 Travis Rd New Hudson (48165) *(G-11557)*
Taiz Fuel Inc 313 485-2972
4630 S Beech Daly St Dearborn Heights (48125) *(G-3798)*
Tajco North America Inc 248 418-7550
2851 High Meadow Cir # 190 Auburn Hills (48326) *(G-1011)*
Takata Americas (HQ) 336 547-1600
2500 Takata Dr Ste 300 Auburn Hills (48326) *(G-1012)*
Take A Label, Nunica Also called Converting Systems Inc *(G-12034)*
Take Us-4-Granite Inc 586 803-1305
13000 23 Mile Rd Shelby Township (48315) *(G-14707)*
Take-A-Label Inc 616 698-1882
16900 Power Dr Nunica (49448) *(G-12044)*
Talbot & Associates Inc 248 723-9700
30400 Telg Rd Ste 479 Franklin (48025) *(G-5609)*
Talco Industries 989 269-6260
705 E Woodworth St Bad Axe (48413) *(G-1072)*
Talent Industries Inc 313 531-4700
12950 Inkster Rd Redford (48239) *(G-13200)*
Talicor Inc (PA) 269 685-2345
901 Lincoln Pkwy Plainwell (49080) *(G-12545)*
Talkin Tackle LLC 517 474-6241
205 S Sandstone Rd Jackson (49201) *(G-8583)*
Tall City LLC 248 854-0713
3386 Countryside Cir Auburn Hills (48326) *(G-1013)*
Tallman Industries Inc 231 879-4755
6592 Lund Rd Sw Fife Lake (49633) *(G-5343)*
Tallulahs Satchels 231 775-4082
615 White Pine Dr Cadillac (49601) *(G-2281)*
Talon LLC 313 392-1000
350 Talon Centre Dr Detroit (48207) *(G-4395)*
Tamara Tool Inc 269 273-1463
1234 William R Monroe Blv Three Rivers (49093) *(G-15878)*
Tamarack Uphl & Interiors 616 866-2922
9024 Algoma Ave Ne Rockford (49341) *(G-13592)*
Tambra Investments Inc 866 662-7897
23247 Pinewood St Warren (48091) *(G-17261)*
Tamsco Inc 586 415-1500
17580 Helro Fraser (48026) *(G-5737)*
Tandis LLC 248 345-3448
6357 Branford Dr West Bloomfield (48322) *(G-17500)*
Tanfaster Inc 248 669-3312
813 Saint Charles Pl Wixom (48393) *(G-17904)*
Tanis Technologies Inc 616 796-2712
645 Commerce Ct Ste 10 Holland (49424) *(G-7823)*
Tank Truck Service & Sales Inc 989 731-4887
1981 Engel Ave Gaylord (49735) *(G-5894)*
Tank Truck Service & Sales Inc (PA) 586 757-6500
25150 Dequindre Rd Warren (48091) *(G-17262)*

Tannewitz Inc 616 457-5999
794 Chicago Dr Jenison (49428) *(G-8644)*
Tanning Trends, Jackson Also called International Smart Tan Netwrk *(G-8472)*
Tapco Group, The, Wixom Also called Boral Building Products Inc *(G-17777)*
Tapco Holdings Inc (HQ) 248 668-6400
29797 Beck Rd Wixom (48393) *(G-17905)*
Tape Master, Troy Also called Lavalier Corp *(G-16458)*
Tape Wrangler, Traverse City Also called Stexley-Brake LLC *(G-16111)*
Taper-Line Inc (PA) 586 775-5960
23426 Reynolds Ct Clinton Township (48036) *(G-3243)*
Tapestry Inc 616 538-5802
3700 Rivertown Pkwy Sw # 1184 Grandville (49418) *(G-7073)*
Tapestry Inc 631 724-8066
14000 Lakeside Cir Sterling Heights (48313) *(G-15519)*
Tapex American Corporation 810 987-4722
2626 20th St Port Huron (48060) *(G-12970)*
Tapoos LLC 619 319-4872
21813 Hunter Cir S Taylor (48180) *(G-15776)*
Tara Industries Inc (PA) 248 477-6520
30105 8 Mile Rd Livonia (48152) *(G-9953)*
Target Construction Inc 616 866-7728
3850 Russell St Cedar Springs (49319) *(G-2564)*
Target Mold Corporation 231 798-3535
4088 Treeline Dr Norton Shores (49441) *(G-11799)*
Target Oil Tools LLC 231 258-4960
3540 Us Highway 131 Ne Kalkaska (49646) *(G-8960)*
Tarifa, Almont Also called Inter-Power Corporation *(G-259)*
Tarpon Automation & Design Co 586 774-8020
26692 Groesbeck Hwy Warren (48089) *(G-17263)*
Tarpon Industries Inc 810 364-7421
2420 Wills St Marysville (48040) *(G-10620)*
Tarps Now, Saint Joseph Also called Industrial Fabric Products Inc *(G-14318)*
Tarrs Tree Service Inc 248 528-3313
2009 Milverton Dr Troy (48083) *(G-16631)*
Tartan Industries Inc 810 387-4255
2 1st St Yale (48097) *(G-18047)*
Tarus Products Inc (PA) 586 977-1400
38100 Commerce Dr Sterling Heights (48312) *(G-15520)*
Tassier Boat Works Inc 906 484-2573
1011 S Islington Rd Cedarville (49719) *(G-2572)*
Tata Autocomp Systems Limited 248 680-4608
200 E Big Beaver Rd # 145 Troy (48083) *(G-16632)*
Tatum Bindery Company 616 458-8991
666 Wealthy St Se Grand Rapids (49503) *(G-6915)*
Tatum Bookbinding, Grand Rapids Also called Tatum Bindery Company *(G-6915)*
TAW Plastics LLC (PA) 616 302-0954
1118 S Edgewood St Greenville (48838) *(G-7157)*
Tawas Plating Company 989 362-2011
510 Industrial Ave Tawas City (48763) *(G-15683)*
Tawas Powder Coating Inc 989 362-2011
510 Industrial Ave Tawas City (48763) *(G-15684)*
Tawas Tool Co Inc (HQ) 989 362-6121
756 Aulerich Rd East Tawas (48730) *(G-4695)*
Tawas Tool Co Inc 989 362-0414
980 Aulerich Rd East Tawas (48730) *(G-4696)*
Tawas Tools Plant 2, East Tawas Also called Tawas Tool Co Inc *(G-4696)*
Taxtime USA Inc 248 642-7070
30800 Telegraph Rd Bingham Farms (48025) *(G-1661)*
Taylor Building Products Inc (PA) 989 345-5110
631 N 1st St West Branch (48661) *(G-17525)*
Taylor Communications Inc 248 304-4800
24800 Denso Dr Ste 140 Southfield (48033) *(G-15043)*
Taylor Company, The, Grand Rapids Also called Van Zee Corporation *(G-6959)*
Taylor Controls Inc 269 637-8521
10529 Blue Star Mem Hwy South Haven (49090) *(G-14777)*
Taylor Freezer Michigan Inc 616 453-0531
2111 Walker Ct Nw Grand Rapids (49544) *(G-6916)*
Taylor Machine Products Inc 734 287-3550
176 S Harvey St Plymouth (48170) *(G-12765)*
Taylor Screw Products Company 734 697-8018
16894 Haggerty Rd Van Buren Twp (48111) *(G-16786)*
Taylor Supply Company, The, Detroit Also called Detroit Nipple Works Inc *(G-3996)*
Taylor Tooling Group LLC 616 805-3917
4303 3 Mile Rd Nw Grand Rapids (49534) *(G-6917)*
Taylor Turning Inc 248 960-7920
29632 West Tech Dr Wixom (48393) *(G-17906)*
Tazz Broach and Machine Inc 586 296-7755
41565 Production Dr Harrison Township (48045) *(G-7352)*
Tbf Graphics, Saginaw Also called Turner Business Forms Inc *(G-14171)*
Tbf Graphics, Flint Also called Turner Business Forms Inc *(G-5515)*
Tbl Fabrications Inc 586 294-2087
28178 Hayes Rd Roseville (48066) *(G-13877)*
Tc Flying Adventures, Traverse City Also called Traverse City Helicopters LLC *(G-16126)*
Tc Moulding 248 588-2333
31811 Sherman Ave Madison Heights (48071) *(G-10366)*
Tc Sports, Tecumseh Also called Turkey Creek Inc *(G-15814)*
Tcwc LLC (HQ) 231 922-8292
201 E Fourteenth St Traverse City (49684) *(G-16119)*

ALPHABETIC SECTION Temo Inc

TD Industrial Coverings Inc 586 731-2080
6220 18 1/2 Mile Rd Sterling Heights (48314) ***(G-15521)***
Tdrn Inc 906 497-5510
N16187 N Balsam Lane I.5 Spalding (49886) ***(G-15087)***
Te Connectivity Corporation 248 273-3344
900 Wilshire Dr Ste 150 Troy (48084) ***(G-16633)***
Teachout and Associates Inc 269 729-4440
1887 M 66 Athens (49011) ***(G-729)***
Team Acquistions, Kalkaska *Also called Team Spooling Services LLC* ***(G-8962)***
Team Breadwinner LLC 313 460-0152
14414 Mansfield St Detroit (48227) ***(G-4396)***
Team Pharma 269 344-8326
2022 Fulford St Kalamazoo (49001) ***(G-8908)***
Team Services LLC 231 258-9130
1587 Enterprise Dr Kalkaska (49646) ***(G-8961)***
Team Spankys, Alanson *Also called K & J Enterprises Inc* ***(G-111)***
Team Spooling Services LLC 231 258-9130
209 E Park Dr Kalkaska (49646) ***(G-8962)***
Teamtech Motorsports Safety 989 792-4880
6285 Bay Rd Ste 7 Saginaw (48604) ***(G-14163)***
Tebis America Inc 248 524-0430
400 E Big Beaver Rd # 200 Troy (48083) ***(G-16634)***
TEC Industries Inc 248 446-9560
55309 Lyon Industrial Dr New Hudson (48165) ***(G-11558)***
TEC International II (PA) 248 724-1800
68 S Squirrel Rd Auburn Hills (48326) ***(G-1014)***
TEC International II 586 469-9611
15721 Leone Dr Macomb (48042) ***(G-10166)***
TEC-3 Prototypes Inc 810 678-8909
4321 Blood Rd Metamora (48455) ***(G-10782)***
Tec-Option Inc 517 486-6055
334 Sherman St Blissfield (49228) ***(G-1727)***
Tecart Industries Inc 248 624-8880
28059 Center Oaks Ct Wixom (48393) ***(G-17907)***
Tecat Performance Systems LLC 248 615-9862
705 Technology Dr Ann Arbor (48108) ***(G-654)***
Tech Electric Co LLC 586 697-5095
16177 Leone Dr Macomb (48042) ***(G-10167)***
Tech Engineering International, Saint Clair Shores *Also called Lord Laboratories* ***(G-14260)***
Tech Enterprises, Saint Clair Shores *Also called Technology Network Svcs Inc* ***(G-14271)***
Tech Forms Metal Ltd 616 956-0430
2437 Coit Ave Ne Grand Rapids (49505) ***(G-6918)***
Tech Group, Wayne *Also called Cul-Mac Industries Inc* ***(G-17429)***
Tech Group Grand Rapids Inc 616 643-6001
3116 N Wilson Ct Nw Walker (49534) ***(G-16879)***
Tech Tool Company Inc 313 836-4131
18235 Weaver St Detroit (48228) ***(G-4397)***
Tech Tool Supply LLC 734 207-7700
9060 General Dr Plymouth (48170) ***(G-12766)***
Tech Tooling Specialties Inc 517 782-8898
1708 Cooper St Jackson (49202) ***(G-8584)***
Tech-Source International Inc 231 652-9100
1000 Park St Newaygo (49337) ***(G-11578)***
Techna Systems Inc 248 681-1717
6850 Torybrooke Cir Orchard Lake (48323) ***(G-12171)***
Technacraft Corp 810 227-8281
2635 Pady Ln Brighton (48114) ***(G-1995)***
Techncal Audio Video Solutions 810 899-5546
5695 Whispering Oaks Dr Howell (48855) ***(G-8105)***
Techni CAM and Manufacturing 734 261-6477
30633 Schoolcraft Rd A Livonia (48150) ***(G-9954)***
Technical Air Products LLC 616 863-9115
8069 Belmont Ave Ne Belmont (49306) ***(G-1472)***
Technical Auto Parts, Battle Creek *Also called Musashi Auto Parts Mich Inc* ***(G-1230)***
Technical Center, Farmington Hills *Also called Gleason Works* ***(G-5009)***
Technical Center, Portage *Also called Summit Polymers Inc* ***(G-13045)***
Technical Illustration Corp 313 982-9660
46177 Windridge Ln Canton (48188) ***(G-2432)***
Technical Rotary Services Inc 586 772-6755
14020 Hovey Ave Warren (48089) ***(G-17264)***
Technical Stamping Inc 586 948-3285
50600 E Russell Schmidt Chesterfield (48051) ***(G-2846)***
Technickel Inc 269 926-8505
1200 S Crystal Ave Benton Harbor (49022) ***(G-1553)***
Techniplas LLC 517 849-9911
1640 E Chicago Rd Jonesville (49250) ***(G-8669)***
Technique Inc 517 789-8988
1500 Technology Dr Jackson (49201) ***(G-8585)***
Technisand Inc 269 465-5833
400 Riverview Dr Ste 300 Benton Harbor (49022) ***(G-1554)***
Techno Urban 3d LLC 313 740-8110
20299 Greenview Ave Detroit (48219) ***(G-4398)***
Techno-Coat Inc 616 396-6446
861 E 40th St Holland (49423) ***(G-7824)***
Technology & Manufacturing Inc 248 755-1444
3190 Pine Cone Ct Milford (48381) ***(G-10988)***
Technology MGT & Budgt Dept 517 322-1897
7461 Crowner Dr Lansing (48913) ***(G-9430)***
Technology Network Svcs Inc (PA) 586 294-7771
31375 Harper Ave Saint Clair Shores (48082) ***(G-14271)***
Technology Plus Trailers Inc 734 928-0001
7780 Ronda Dr Canton (48187) ***(G-2433)***
Technotrim Inc 734 254-5243
40600 Ann Arbor Rd E Plymouth (48170) ***(G-12767)***
Technova Corporation 517 485-1402
3927 Dobie Rd Okemos (48864) ***(G-12138)***
Tecla Company Inc (PA) 248 624-8200
1250 Ladd Rd Commerce Township (48390) ***(G-3453)***
Teclab Inc (PA) 269 372-6000
6450 Valley Industrial Dr Kalamazoo (49009) ***(G-8909)***
Tecniq Inc 269 629-4440
9100 E Michigan Ave Galesburg (49053) ***(G-5816)***
Tecomet Inc 517 882-4311
5212 Aurelius Rd Lansing (48911) ***(G-9431)***
Tecra Systems Inc (PA) 248 888-1116
6005 E Executive Dr Westland (48185) ***(G-17602)***
Tecstar LP 734 604-8962
7075 Dort Hwy 600b Grand Blanc (48439) ***(G-5986)***
Tecstar Grand Blanc Facility, Grand Blanc *Also called Tecstar LP* ***(G-5986)***
Tectonics Industries LLC (PA) 248 597-1600
1681 Harmon Rd Auburn Hills (48326) ***(G-1015)***
Tectum Holdings Inc (HQ) 734 677-0444
5400 Data Ct Ann Arbor (48108) ***(G-655)***
Tectum Holdings Inc 734 926-2362
4670 Runway Blvd Ann Arbor (48108) ***(G-656)***
Tecumseh Compressor Co LLC 662 566-2231
5683 Hines Dr Ann Arbor (48108) ***(G-657)***
Tecumseh Compressor Company 734 585-9500
1136 Oak Valley Dr Ann Arbor (48108) ***(G-658)***
Tecumseh Division, Tecumseh *Also called Tecumseh Packg Solutions Inc* ***(G-15811)***
Tecumseh Herald, Tecumseh *Also called Herald Publishing Company* ***(G-15797)***
Tecumseh Packg Solutions Inc (PA) 517 423-2126
707 S Evans St Tecumseh (49286) ***(G-15811)***
Tecumseh Products Company 734 973-1359
4220 Varsity Dr Ste C Ann Arbor (48108) ***(G-659)***
Tecumseh Products Company 734 769-0650
5683 Hines Dr Ann Arbor (48108) ***(G-660)***
Tecumseh Products Company LLC (HQ) 734 585-9500
5683 Hines Dr Ann Arbor (48108) ***(G-661)***
Tecumseh Products Company LLC 734 585-9500
5683 Hines Dr Ann Arbor (48108) ***(G-662)***
Tecumseh Products Holdings LLC (PA) 734 585-9500
5683 Hines Dr Ann Arbor (48108) ***(G-663)***
Tecumseh Signals LLC 517 301-2064
805 S Maumee St Tecumseh (49286) ***(G-15812)***
Ted Senk Tooling Inc 989 725-6067
1117 E Henderson Rd Owosso (48867) ***(G-12321)***
Ted Voss & Sons Inc 616 396-8344
995 Lincoln Ave Holland (49423) ***(G-7825)***
Tedson Industries Inc 248 588-9230
1408 Allen Dr Troy (48083) ***(G-16635)***
Tee To Green Print & Promo Pro 517 322-3088
3030 Sanders Rd Ste 1 Lansing (48917) ***(G-9325)***
Teijin Advan Compo Ameri Inc 248 365-6600
1200 Harmon Rd Auburn Hills (48326) ***(G-1016)***
Tekkra Systems Inc 517 568-4121
300 S Elm St Homer (49245) ***(G-7950)***
Teknicolors Inc 734 414-9900
43319 Joy Rd Canton (48187) ***(G-2434)***
Teknikut Corporation 586 778-7150
46036 Michigan Ave Canton (48188) ***(G-2435)***
Teksid Inc (HQ) 734 846-5897
36524 Grand River Ave B-1 Farmington (48335) ***(G-4914)***
Tekton Inc 616 243-2443
3707 R B Chaffee Memrl Dr Grand Rapids (49548) ***(G-6919)***
Tel-X Corporation 734 425-2225
32400 Ford Rd Garden City (48135) ***(G-5843)***
Telco Tools 616 296-0253
510 Elm St Spring Lake (49456) ***(G-15185)***
Telegram Newspaper 313 928-2955
10748 W Jefferson Ave River Rouge (48218) ***(G-13281)***
Telespector Corporation 248 373-5400
1460 N Opdyke Rd Auburn Hills (48326) ***(G-1017)***
Telic Corporation 219 406-2164
581 Upton Dr Saint Joseph (49085) ***(G-14343)***
Telmar Manufacturing Company 810 577-7050
2121 W Thompson Rd Fenton (48430) ***(G-5241)***
Telo 810 845-8051
707 Hickory St Fenton (48430) ***(G-5242)***
Telocyte LLC 616 570-4515
9464 Conservation St Ne Ada (49301) ***(G-30)***
Telsonic Ultrasonics Inc (HQ) 586 802-0033
14120 Industrial Ctr Dr Shelby Township (48315) ***(G-14708)***
Tem-Press Division, Saint Joseph *Also called Leco Corporation* ***(G-14324)***
Temcor Systems Inc 810 229-0006
1341 Rickett Rd Brighton (48116) ***(G-1996)***
Temo Inc 800 344-8366
20400 Hall Rd Clinton Township (48038) ***(G-3244)***

ALPHABETIC

Temo Sunrooms, Clinton Township *Also called Temo Inc* ***(G-3244)***

Temp Rite Steel Treating Inc 586 469-3071
42386 Executive Dr Harrison Township (48045) ***(G-7353)***

Temperance Distilling Company 734 847-5262
177 Reed Dr Temperance (48182) ***(G-15845)***

Temperance Fuel Stop Inc 734 206-2676
2110 Anita Ave Grosse Pointe Woods (48236) ***(G-7210)***

Temperance Printing 419 290-6846
3363 Hemmingway Ln Lambertville (48144) ***(G-9186)***

Temperform LLC 248 349-5230
25425 Trans X Rd Novi (48375) ***(G-12012)***

Temperform Corp 248 851-9611
1975 Tuckaway Dr Bloomfield Hills (48302) ***(G-1801)***

Temprel Inc 231 582-6585
206 Industrial Parkway Dr Boyne City (49712) ***(G-1835)***

Tempro Industries Inc 734 451-5900
47808 Galleon Dr Plymouth (48170) ***(G-12768)***

Ten X Plastics LLC 616 813-3037
610 Maryland Ave Ne Ste A Grand Rapids (49505) ***(G-6920)***

Tenants Tolerance Tooling 269 349-6907
3704 Wedgwood Dr Portage (49024) ***(G-13048)***

Tengam Engineering Inc 269 694-9466
545 Washington St Otsego (49078) ***(G-12256)***

Tenibac-Graphion Inc (HQ) 586 792-0150
35155 Automation Dr Clinton Township (48035) ***(G-3245)***

Tenibac-Graphion Inc 616 647-3333
2925 Northridge Dr Nw Grand Rapids (49544) ***(G-6921)***

Tenmec, Howell *Also called North Group Inc* ***(G-8069)***

Tennant & Associates Inc 248 643-6140
1700 Stutz Dr Ste 61 Troy (48084) ***(G-16636)***

Tennant Commercial 616 994-4000
12875 Ransom St Holland (49424) ***(G-7826)***

Tennant Company 616 994-4000
12875 Ransom St Holland (49424) ***(G-7827)***

Tenneco Automotive Oper Co 248 849-1258
15701 Technology Dr Northville (48168) ***(G-11728)***

Tenneco Automotive Oper Co Inc 517 522-5520
3901 Willis Rd Grass Lake (49240) ***(G-7095)***

Tenneco Automotive Oper Co Inc 734 243-8000
4722 Grand Riv Lansing (48906) ***(G-9269)***

Tenneco Automotive Oper Co Inc 734 243-8039
13910 Lake Dr Monroe (48161) ***(G-11072)***

Tenneco Automotive Oper Co Inc 269 781-1350
904 Industrial Rd Marshall (49068) ***(G-10590)***

Tenneco Automotive Oper Co Inc 517 542-5511
929 Anderson Rd Litchfield (49252) ***(G-9611)***

Tenneco Automotive Oper Co Inc 517 522-5525
2701 N Dettman Rd Jackson (49201) ***(G-8586)***

Tenneco Automotive Oper Co Inc 734 243-4615
1 International Dr Monroe (48161) ***(G-11073)***

Tenneco Automotive Oper Co Inc 734 243-8000
1 International Dr Monroe (48161) ***(G-11074)***

Tenneco Clean Air US Inc (HQ) 734 384-7867
18765 Seaway Dr Lansing (48911) ***(G-9432)***

Tenneco Inc 734 254-1122
44099 Plymouth Oaks Blvd Plymouth (48170) ***(G-12769)***

Tenneco Inc 248 354-7700
27300 W 11 Mile Rd Southfield (48034) ***(G-15044)***

Tenneco Inc 248 354-7700
26555 Northwestern Hwy Southfield (48033) ***(G-15045)***

Tennessee Fabricators LLC 615 793-4444
35900 Mound Rd Sterling Heights (48310) ***(G-15522)***

Tepel Brothers, Troy *Also called C2 Imaging LLC* ***(G-16251)***

Tepso Gen-X Plastics LLC 248 869-2130
28525 Beck Rd Unit 111 Wixom (48393) ***(G-17908)***

Ter Molen & Hart Inc 616 458-4832
3056 Eastern Ave Se Ste C Grand Rapids (49508) ***(G-6922)***

Teradyne Inc 313 425-3900
1800 Fairlane Dr Ste 200 Allen Park (48101) ***(G-211)***

Teradyne Diagnostic Solutions, Allen Park *Also called Teradyne Inc* ***(G-211)***

Terametrix LLC 540 769-8430
2725 S Industrial Hwy # 100 Ann Arbor (48104) ***(G-664)***

Terex Canica, Durand *Also called Terex Corporation* ***(G-4614)***

Terex Corporation 360 993-0515
212 S Oak St Durand (48429) ***(G-4614)***

Terex Simplicity, Durand *Also called Powerscreen USA LLC* ***(G-4612)***

Terratrike, Grand Rapids *Also called Wiz Wheelz Inc* ***(G-6995)***

Terrell Assoc Signs & Disp 517 726-0455
8939 Spore St Vermontville (49096) ***(G-16824)***

Terrell Manufacturing Svcs Inc 231 788-2000
7245 Hall Rd Muskegon (49442) ***(G-11435)***

Terry Hanover 269 426-4199
4102 Hanover Rd New Troy (49119) ***(G-11560)***

Terry Heiden 906 753-6248
N8745 Us Highway 41 Stephenson (49887) ***(G-15241)***

Terry Tool & Die Co 517 750-1771
1080 Toro Dr Jackson (49201) ***(G-8587)***

Terryberry Company LLC (PA) 616 458-1391
2033 Oak Industrial Dr Ne Grand Rapids (49505) ***(G-6923)***

Terrys Precast Products Inc 616 396-7042
4248 58th St Holland (49423) ***(G-7828)***

Terumo Americas Holding Inc 734 663-4145
6200 Jackson Rd Ann Arbor (48103) ***(G-665)***

Terumo Cardiovascular Systems, Ann Arbor *Also called Terumo Americas Holding Inc* ***(G-665)***

Terumo Crdvscular Systems Corp (HQ) 734 663-4145
6200 Jackson Rd Ann Arbor (48103) ***(G-666)***

Tesa Tape Inc 616 785-6970
2945 Walkent Ct Nw Grand Rapids (49544) ***(G-6924)***

Tesa Tape Inc 616 887-3107
324 S Union St Sparta (49345) ***(G-15116)***

Tesca Usa Inc 586 991-0744
2638 Bond St Rochester Hills (48309) ***(G-13524)***

Tesla Inc 248 205-3206
2850 W Big Beaver Rd Troy (48084) ***(G-16637)***

Tesla Motors, Troy *Also called Tesla Inc* ***(G-16637)***

Teslir LLC 248 644-5500
100 W Long Lake Rd # 102 Bloomfield Hills (48304) ***(G-1802)***

Tesma Instruments LLC 517 940-1362
8770 Giovanni Ct Howell (48855) ***(G-8106)***

Tessonics Corp 248 885-8335
2019 Hazel St Birmingham (48009) ***(G-1704)***

Test Products Incorporated 586 997-9600
41255 Technology Park Dr Sterling Heights (48314) ***(G-15523)***

Testek LLC 248 573-4980
28320 Lakeview Dr Wixom (48393) ***(G-17909)***

Testron Incorporated 734 513-6820
34153 Industrial Rd Livonia (48150) ***(G-9955)***

Teta Foods, Grosse Pointe *Also called Gourmet Holdings LLC* ***(G-7179)***

Teter Orthotics & Prosthetics 231 779-8022
8865 Professional Dr C Cadillac (49601) ***(G-2282)***

Tetra Corporation 401 529-1630
1606 Hults Dr Eaton Rapids (48827) ***(G-4734)***

Tetra Pak Inc 517 629-2163
1104 Industrial Blvd Albion (49224) ***(G-133)***

Tetradyn Ltd 202 415-7295
9833 E Cherry Bend Rd Traverse City (49684) ***(G-16120)***

Texas Corners Brewing Company, Kalamazoo *Also called Apple Blossom Winery LLC* ***(G-8679)***

Texas Instruments Incorporated 248 305-5718
39555 Orchard Hill Pl # 525 Novi (48375) ***(G-12013)***

Texas Metal Industries Inc 586 261-0090
2305 E 9 Mile Rd Warren (48091) ***(G-17265)***

Texas Transformer, Grand Haven *Also called Gti Liquidating Inc* ***(G-6028)***

Textron Inc 248 545-2035
25225 Dequindre Rd Madison Heights (48071) ***(G-10367)***

Tfi Inc 231 728-2310
2620 Park St Muskegon (49444) ***(G-11436)***

Tg Fluid Systems USA Corp 810 220-6161
100 Brighton Interior Dr Brighton (48116) ***(G-1997)***

Tg Manufacturing LLC 616 842-1503
146 Monroe Center St Nw # 710 Grand Rapids (49503) ***(G-6925)***

Tg Manufacturing LLC (PA) 616 935-7575
8197 Clyde Park Ave Sw Byron Center (49315) ***(G-2212)***

Tg North America, Brighton *Also called Tg Fluid Systems USA Corp* ***(G-1997)***

TGI Direct Inc (PA) 810 239-5553
5365 Hill 23 Dr Flint (48507) ***(G-5509)***

TGI Direct Inc 810 239-5553
1225 Rosewood St Ann Arbor (48104) ***(G-667)***

Tgw Systems Inc (HQ) 231 798-4547
1300 E Mount Garfield Rd Norton Shores (49441) ***(G-11800)***

Th Plastics Inc (PA) 269 496-8495
106 E Main St Mendon (49072) ***(G-10719)***

Th Plastics Inc 269 496-8495
106 E Main St Mendon (49072) ***(G-10720)***

Tha Shopp LLC 734 231-9991
162 S Ford Blvd Ypsilanti (48198) ***(G-18105)***

Thai Summit America Corp (HQ) 517 548-4900
1480 Mcpherson Park Dr Howell (48843) ***(G-8107)***

Thalner Electronic Labs Inc 734 761-4506
7235 Jackson Rd Ann Arbor (48103) ***(G-668)***

Thangbom LLC 517 862-0144
336 W 1st St Ste 113 Flint (48502) ***(G-5510)***

That French Place 231 437-6037
212 Bridge St Charlevoix (49720) ***(G-2633)***

Thayne Art Mart, Battle Creek *Also called W W Thayne Advertising Cons* ***(G-1264)***

The Daily Tribune, Mount Clemens *Also called Independent Newspapers Inc* ***(G-11134)***

The Envelope Printery Inc (PA) 734 398-7700
8979 Samuel Barton Dr Van Buren Twp (48111) ***(G-16787)***

The Gluten Free Bar, The, Grand Rapids *Also called West Thomas Partners LLC* ***(G-6989)***

The Pom Group Inc 248 409-7900
2350 Pontiac Rd Auburn Hills (48326) ***(G-1018)***

The Shopping Guide, Mason *Also called S G Publications Inc* ***(G-10653)***

The Signwriter, Kalamazoo *Also called Sunset Enterprises Inc* ***(G-8902)***

The South Main Company, Wixom *Also called S Main Company LLC* ***(G-17888)***

The Spott 269 459-6462
550 E Cork St Kalamazoo (49001) ***(G-8910)***

Theradapt Products Inc 231 480-4008
922 N Washington Ave Ludington (49431) ***(G-10082)***
Therapyline Technologies Inc 734 407-9626
21635 Adams Dr Brownstown (48193) ***(G-2068)***
Therm Technology Corp 616 530-6540
2879 Remico St Sw Grandville (49418) ***(G-7074)***
Therm-O-Disc Incorporated 231 799-4100
851 E Porter Rd Norton Shores (49441) ***(G-11801)***
Therm-O-Disc Midwest Inc 231 799-4100
851 E Porter Rd Norton Shores (49441) ***(G-11802)***
Therma-Tech Engineering Inc 313 537-5330
24900 Capitol Redford (48239) ***(G-13201)***
Thermal Designs & Manufacturng 586 773-5231
16660 E 13 Mile Rd Roseville (48066) ***(G-13878)***
Thermal Designs & Mfg 248 476-2978
41069 Vincenti Ct Novi (48375) ***(G-12014)***
Thermal One Inc (PA) 734 721-8500
39026 Webb Ct Westland (48185) ***(G-17603)***
Thermal Products, Saint Clair *Also called Dana Limited* ***(G-14213)***
Thermal Solutions Mfg (PA) 734 655-7145
35255 Glendale St Livonia (48150) ***(G-9956)***
Thermal Trends, Alto *Also called Coral Corporation* ***(G-326)***
Thermal Wave Imaging Inc 248 414-3730
845 Livernois St Ferndale (48220) ***(G-5321)***
Thermalfab Products Inc 517 486-2073
10005 E Us Highway 223 Blissfield (49228) ***(G-1728)***
Thermfrmer Parts Suppliers LLC 989 435-3800
3818 Terry Dianne St Beaverton (48612) ***(G-1394)***
Thermo Arl US Inc 313 336-3901
15300 Rotunda Dr Ste 301 Dearborn (48120) ***(G-3764)***
Thermo Fischer Scientific, Kalamazoo *Also called Richard-Allan Scientific Co* ***(G-8870)***
Thermo Fisher Scientific Inc 231 932-0242
6270 S West Bay Shore Dr Traverse City (49684) ***(G-16121)***
Thermo Fisher Scientific Inc 800 346-4364
4169 Commercial Ave Portage (49002) ***(G-13049)***
Thermo Fisher Scientific Inc 269 544-5600
4481 Campus Dr Kalamazoo (49008) ***(G-8911)***
Thermo Fisher Scientific Inc 734 662-4117
2868 W Delhi Rd Ann Arbor (48103) ***(G-669)***
Thermo Pressed Laminates, Alpena *Also called Panel Processing Oregon Inc* ***(G-306)***
Thermo Shandon Inc 269 544-7500
4481 Campus Dr Kalamazoo (49008) ***(G-8912)***
Thermo Vac Inc 248 969-0300
201 W Oakwood Rd Oxford (48371) ***(G-12375)***
Thermo-Shield Window Mfg, Alpena *Also called Overhead Door Company Alpena* ***(G-305)***
Thermoforming Tech Group LLC (HQ) 989 435-7741
330 N Ross St Beaverton (48612) ***(G-1395)***
Thermoforms Inc 616 974-0055
4374 Donkers Ct Se Kentwood (49512) ***(G-9033)***
Thermotron Industries Inc 616 928-9044
875 Brooks Ave Holland (49423) ***(G-7829)***
Thermotron Industries Inc (HQ) 616 392-1491
291 Kollen Park Dr Holland (49423) ***(G-7830)***
Thesnowmobilestore.com, Gladstone *Also called Bucks Sports Products Inc* ***(G-5908)***
Thetford Corporation 734 769-6000
800 Baker Rd Dexter (48130) ***(G-4513)***
Thetford Corporation (HQ) 734 769-6000
7101 Jackson Rd Ann Arbor (48103) ***(G-670)***
Theut Concrete Products Inc 810 679-3376
138 E Harrington Rd Croswell (48422) ***(G-3604)***
Theut Products Inc 810 364-7132
1444 Gratiot Blvd Marysville (48040) ***(G-10621)***
Theut Products Inc 810 765-9321
1910 S Parker St Marine City (48039) ***(G-10484)***
Theut Products Inc 586 949-1300
47875 Gratiot Ave Chesterfield (48051) ***(G-2847)***
Thi Equipment, Grand Rapids *Also called Thierica Equipment Corporation* ***(G-6928)***
Thielenhaus Microfinish Corp (HQ) 248 349-9450
42925 W 9 Mile Rd Novi (48375) ***(G-12015)***
Thierica Inc (HQ) 616 458-1538
900 Clancy Ave Ne Grand Rapids (49503) ***(G-6926)***
Thierica Controls Inc 616 956-5500
4400 Donkers Ct Se Grand Rapids (49512) ***(G-6927)***
Thierica Display Products, Grand Rapids *Also called Thierica Inc* ***(G-6926)***
Thierica Equipment Corporation 616 453-6570
3147 N Wilson Ct Nw Grand Rapids (49534) ***(G-6928)***
Thin Line Pump 231 258-2692
208 Court St Kalkaska (49646) ***(G-8963)***
Think NA, Dearborn *Also called Think North America Inc* ***(G-3765)***
Think North America Inc (PA) 313 565-6781
22226 Garrison St Dearborn (48124) ***(G-3765)***
Third Coast Manufacturing, Stevensville *Also called Great Lakes Wire Packaging LLC* ***(G-15568)***
Third Vault Inc 248 353-5555
7300 Deep Run Apt 1613 Bloomfield Hills (48301) ***(G-1803)***
Third Wave Computing 616 855-5501
2176 Wealthy St Se 2 Grand Rapids (49506) ***(G-6929)***
Thk Rhythm Auto Mich Corp 517 647-4121
902 Lyons Rd Portland (48875) ***(G-13068)***
Thoman Tool Inc 517 768-0114
313 Oak St Jackson (49201) ***(G-8588)***
Thomas A Despres Inc 313 633-9648
4229 Williamston Ct Williamsburg (49690) ***(G-17721)***
Thomas and Milliken Mllwk Inc (PA) 231 386-7236
931 N Mill St Northport (49670) ***(G-11673)***
Thomas Cake Shop, Troy *Also called More Signature Cakes LLC* ***(G-16512)***
Thomas Cheal 906 288-3487
40240 Aspen Rd Toivola (49965) ***(G-15885)***
Thomas Construction, Belding *Also called Hunt Hoppough Custom Crafted* ***(G-1418)***
Thomas Cooper 231 599-2251
11486 Essex Rd Ellsworth (49729) ***(G-4789)***
Thomas Dale Noble & Noble, Blanchard *Also called Noble Forestry Inc* ***(G-1711)***
Thomas Frankini 517 783-2400
1415 S Cooper St Jackson (49203) ***(G-8589)***
Thomas Industrial Rolls Inc 313 584-9696
8526 Brandt St Dearborn (48126) ***(G-3766)***
Thomas J Moyle Jr Incorporated (PA) 906 482-3000
46702 Hwy M 26 Houghton (49931) ***(G-7986)***
Thomas Kenyon Inc 248 476-8130
22704 Harper Ave Saint Clair Shores (48080) ***(G-14272)***
Thomas L Snarey & Assoc Inc (PA) 734 241-8474
513 N Dixie Hwy Monroe (48162) ***(G-11075)***
Thomas Logging LLC 269 838-2020
11777 Reflection Dr Woodland (48897) ***(G-17943)***
Thomas Toys Inc 810 629-8707
2017 Bly Dr Fenton (48430) ***(G-5243)***
Thomas-Ward Systems LLC 734 929-0644
314 Pauline Blvd Ann Arbor (48103) ***(G-671)***
Thomasine D Jones LLC 773 726-1404
9974 Town Line Rd Union Pier (49129) ***(G-16739)***
Thompson Art Glass Inc 810 225-8766
6815 Grand River Rd Brighton (48114) ***(G-1998)***
Thompson Fabrication Inds, Muskegon *Also called Tfi Inc* ***(G-11436)***
Thompson Glass Co, Howell *Also called Thompson John* ***(G-8108)***
Thompson I.G., Fenton *Also called Tig Entity LLC* ***(G-5244)***
Thompson John 810 225-8780
5345 Crooked Lake Rd Howell (48843) ***(G-8108)***
Thompson Surgical Instrs Inc 231 922-0177
10170 E Cherry Bend Rd Traverse City (49684) ***(G-16122)***
Thompson Surgical Instrs Inc 231 922-5169
10341 E Cherry Bend Rd Traverse City (49684) ***(G-16123)***
Thompson Well Drilling 616 754-5032
12300 Stultz St Ne Rockford (49341) ***(G-13593)***
Thomson Aerospace & Defense, Saginaw *Also called Linear Motion LLC* ***(G-14078)***
Thomson Plastics Inc 517 545-5026
3970 Parsons Rd Howell (48855) ***(G-8109)***
Thomson Reuters Corporation 734 913-3930
100 Phoenix Dr Ann Arbor (48108) ***(G-672)***
Thomson-Shore Inc 734 426-3939
7300 Joy Rd Dexter (48130) ***(G-4514)***
Thor Tool and Machine LLC 248 628-3185
401 E Elmwood Lakeville (48367) ***(G-9180)***
Thoratec Corporation 734 827-7422
6190 Jackson Rd Ann Arbor (48103) ***(G-673)***
Thoreson-Mc Cosh Inc 248 362-0960
1885 Thunderbird Troy (48084) ***(G-16638)***
Thorn Creek Lumber LLC 231 832-1600
9676 S Hawkins Rd Reed City (49677) ***(G-13223)***
Thorpe Printing Services Inc 810 364-6222
604 Busha Hwy Marysville (48040) ***(G-10622)***
Thread Grinding Service Inc 248 474-5350
32420 W 8 Mile Rd Farmington Hills (48336) ***(G-5140)***
Thread-Craft Inc 586 323-1116
43643 Utica Rd Sterling Heights (48314) ***(G-15524)***
Threaded Products Co 586 727-3435
68750 Oak St Richmond (48062) ***(G-13272)***
Threads, Traverse City *Also called Get In Game Marketing LLC* ***(G-15979)***
Threadworks Ltd Inc 517 548-9745
29907 N Park Ct New Boston (48164) ***(G-11513)***
Three 60 Corporation 517 545-3600
741 Victory Dr Howell (48843) ***(G-8110)***
Three Chairs Co 734 665-2796
215 S Ashley St Ann Arbor (48104) ***(G-674)***
Three D Precision Tool 810 765-9418
5405 Starville Rd China (48054) ***(G-2862)***
Three Dogs One Cat 313 285-8371
2472 Riopelle St Detroit (48207) ***(G-4399)***
Three M Tool & Machine Inc 248 363-0982
8135 Richardson Rd Commerce Township (48390) ***(G-3454)***
Three Oaks Engraving & Engrg 269 469-2124
14381 Three Oaks Rd Three Oaks (49128) ***(G-15851)***
Three Rivers Coffee Company 269 244-0083
1501 Kdf Dr Three Rivers (49093) ***(G-15879)***
Three Rivers Commercial News 269 279-7488
124 N Main St Three Rivers (49093) ***(G-15880)***
Three Rivers Driveline Fcilty, Three Rivers *Also called American Axle & Mfg Inc* ***(G-15853)***
Three-Dimensional Services Inc 248 852-1333
2547 Product Dr Rochester Hills (48309) ***(G-13525)***

A L P H A B E T I C

Throbak Electronics, Grand Rapids *Also called Gundry Media Inc* ***(G-6486)***
Thumb Bioenergy LLC 810 404-2466
155 Orval St Sandusky (48471) ***(G-14445)***
Thumb Blanket 989 269-9918
55 Westland Dr Bad Axe (48413) ***(G-1073)***
Thumb Plastics Inc 989 269-9791
400 Liberty St Bad Axe (48413) ***(G-1074)***
Thumb Tool & Engineering Co 989 269-9731
354 Liberty St Bad Axe (48413) ***(G-1075)***
Thumb Truck and Trailer Co 989 453-3133
8305 Geiger Rd Pigeon (48755) ***(G-12493)***
Thumbprint News 810 794-2300
8061 Marsh Rd Clay (48001) ***(G-3004)***
Thunder Bay Concrete Products, Alpena *Also called Clay & Graham Inc* ***(G-283)***
Thunder Bay Pattern Works Inc 586 783-1126
44345 Macomb Indus Dr Clinton Township (48036) ***(G-3246)***
Thunder Bay Press Inc 517 694-3205
2325 Jarco Dr Holt (48842) ***(G-7930)***
Thunder Technologies LLC 248 844-4875
1618 Star Batt Dr Rochester Hills (48309) ***(G-13526)***
Thunderdome Media LLC 800 978-0206
6218 Valleyfield Dr Plymouth (48170) ***(G-12770)***
Thunderhead Enterprises LLC 248 210-1146
26916 Gornada St Novi (48377) ***(G-12016)***
Thunderhead Gaming, Novi *Also called Thunderhead Enterprises LLC* ***(G-12016)***
Thyssenkrupp Automotive Sales 248 530-2991
3331 W Big Beaver Rd # 300 Troy (48084) ***(G-16639)***
Thyssenkrupp Automotive Sales (HQ) 248 530-2902
3155 W Big Beaver Rd # 260 Troy (48084) ***(G-16640)***
Thyssenkrupp Bilstein Amer Inc 248 530-2900
3155 W Big Beaver Rd # 125 Troy (48084) ***(G-16641)***
Thyssenkrupp Components, Troy *Also called Thyssenkrupp Automotive Sales* ***(G-16639)***
Thyssenkrupp Elevator Corp 616 942-4710
5169 Northland Dr Ne Grand Rapids (49525) ***(G-6930)***
Thyssenkrupp System Engrg (HQ) 248 340-8000
901 Doris Rd Auburn Hills (48326) ***(G-1019)***
TI Automotive LLC 586 948-6036
30600 Commerce Blvd New Haven (48048) ***(G-11528)***
TI Automotive LLC (HQ) 248 494-5000
2020 Taylor Rd Auburn Hills (48326) ***(G-1020)***
TI Automotive LLC 248 393-4525
1700 Harmon Rd Ste 2 Auburn Hills (48326) ***(G-1021)***
TI Automotive Systems, Chesterfield *Also called TI Group Auto Systems LLC* ***(G-2848)***
TI Group Auto Systems LLC (HQ) 248 296-8000
2020 Taylor Rd Auburn Hills (48326) ***(G-1022)***
TI Group Auto Systems LLC 859 235-5420
2020 Taylor Rd Auburn Hills (48326) ***(G-1023)***
TI Group Auto Systems LLC 989 672-1200
630 Columbia St Caro (48723) ***(G-2477)***
TI Group Auto Systems LLC 248 494-5000
1272 Doris Rd 100 Auburn Hills (48326) ***(G-1024)***
TI Group Auto Systems LLC 989 673-7727
630 Columbia St Caro (48723) ***(G-2478)***
TI Group Auto Systems LLC 517 437-7462
200 Arch Ave Hillsdale (49242) ***(G-7543)***
TI Group Auto Systems LLC 248 475-4663
1227 Centre Rd Auburn Hills (48326) ***(G-1025)***
TI Group Auto Systems LLC 248 494-5000
100 W Big Beaver Rd Troy (48084) ***(G-16642)***
TI Group Auto Systems LLC 810 364-3277
184 Gratiot Blvd Marysville (48040) ***(G-10623)***
TI Group Auto Systems LLC 586 948-6006
30600 Commerce Blvd Chesterfield (48051) ***(G-2848)***
Ti-Coating Inc 586 726-1900
50500 Corporate Dr Shelby Township (48315) ***(G-14709)***
Tial Products Inc 989 729-8553
450 S Shiawassee St Owosso (48867) ***(G-12322)***
Tial Sport, Owosso *Also called Tial Products Inc* ***(G-12322)***
Tianhai Electric N Amer Inc (HQ) 248 987-2100
70 E Silverdome Indus Par Pontiac (48342) ***(G-12870)***
Tiara Yachts, Holland *Also called S 2 Yachts Inc* ***(G-7793)***
Ticglobal, Canton *Also called Technical Illustration Corp* ***(G-2432)***
Tickets Plus Inc (PA) 616 222-4000
620 Century Ave Sw # 300 Grand Rapids (49503) ***(G-6931)***
Ticona Polymers Inc 248 377-6868
2600 N Opdyke Rd Auburn Hills (48326) ***(G-1026)***
Tide Rings LLC 586 206-3142
14150 Hough Rd Allenton (48002) ***(G-230)***
Tideslide Mooring Products, Saginaw *Also called PSI Marine Inc* ***(G-14126)***
Tidy Mro Enterprises LLC 734 649-1122
520 Wolverine St Manchester (48158) ***(G-10412)***
Tienda San Rafael LLC 989 681-2020
321 N Mill St Saint Louis (48880) ***(G-14370)***
Tig Entity LLC 810 629-9558
3196 W Thompson Rd Fenton (48430) ***(G-5244)***
Tiger Neuroscience LLC 872 903-1904
200 Viridian Dr Muskegon (49440) ***(G-11437)***
Tigmaster Co 800 824-4830
9283 First St Baroda (49101) ***(G-1132)***
Tigner Printing Inc 989 465-6916
221 E Railway St Coleman (48618) ***(G-3351)***
Tijer Inc 586 741-0308
44326 Macomb Indus Dr Clinton Township (48036) ***(G-3247)***
Tilco Inc 248 644-0901
401 Elmwood Dr Troy (48083) ***(G-16643)***
Tilden Mine, Ishpeming *Also called Tilden Mining Company LC* ***(G-8354)***
Tilden Mining Company LC 906 475-3400
2 Miles S Of Ishpeming Ishpeming (49849) ***(G-8354)***
Tile By Bill & Sondra 616 554-5413
6873 Rosecrest Dr Se Caledonia (49316) ***(G-2319)***
Tile Craft Inc (PA) 231 929-7207
1430 Trade Center Dr Traverse City (49696) ***(G-16124)***
Tile Installation, Sterling Heights *Also called Mannino Tile & Marble Inc* ***(G-15411)***
Tiller Tool and Die Inc 517 458-6602
555 W Main St Morenci (49256) ***(G-11115)***
Tillerman Jfp LLC (PA) 616 443-8346
10451 W Garbow Rd Middleville (49333) ***(G-10810)***
Tim's Cabinet Shop, Pinconning *Also called Tims Cabinet Inc* ***(G-12513)***
Timber Pdts Mich Ltd Partnr (PA) 906 779-2000
104 E B St Iron Mountain (49801) ***(G-8303)***
Timber Products Co Ltd Partnr 906 452-6221
Hwy M 28 E Munising (49862) ***(G-11250)***
Timberland Forestry 906 387-4350
E6971 Wildwood Rd Munising (49862) ***(G-11251)***
Timberline Logging Inc 989 731-2794
855 Dickerson Rd Gaylord (49735) ***(G-5895)***
Timbertech Inc 231 348-2750
8796 Moeller Dr Harbor Springs (49740) ***(G-7295)***
Timco Engine Center Inc 989 739-2194
3921 Arrow St Oscoda (48750) ***(G-12221)***
Time For Blinds Inc 248 363-9174
9633 Highland Rd White Lake (48386) ***(G-17640)***
Time Machines Unlimited, Ellsworth *Also called Dts Enterprises Inc* ***(G-4787)***
Times Herald Company (HQ) 810 985-7171
911 Military St Port Huron (48060) ***(G-12971)***
Times Indicator Publications 231 924-4400
44 W Main St Fremont (49412) ***(G-5784)***
Timkensteel Corporation 248 994-4422
28125 Cabot Dr Ste 204 Novi (48377) ***(G-12017)***
Timkensteel Detroit Off Novi, Novi *Also called Timkensteel Corporation* ***(G-12017)***
Timothy J Tade Inc (PA) 248 552-8583
4798 Butler Dr Troy (48085) ***(G-16644)***
Tims Cabinet Inc 989 846-9831
5309 S Huron Rd Pinconning (48650) ***(G-12513)***
Tims Underbody 231 347-9146
1702 Standish Ave Ste 1 Petoskey (49770) ***(G-12477)***
Tin Can Dewitt 517 624-2078
13175 Schavey Rd Dewitt (48820) ***(G-4467)***
Tindall Packaging Inc 269 649-1163
9718 Portage Rd Portage (49002) ***(G-13050)***
Tip Top Drilling LLC 616 291-8006
8274 Alpine Ave Sparta (49345) ***(G-15117)***
Tip Top Gravel Co Inc 616 897-8342
9741 Fulton St E Ada (49301) ***(G-31)***
Tip Top Screw Manufacturi 989 739-5157
725 W Morley Dr Saginaw (48601) ***(G-14164)***
Tip-Top Screw Mfg Inc 989 739-5157
4183 Forest St Oscoda (48750) ***(G-12222)***
Tipaloy Inc 313 875-5145
1435 E Milwaukee St Detroit (48211) ***(G-4400)***
Tire Wholesalers Company 269 349-9401
3883 Emerald Dr Kalamazoo (49001) ***(G-8913)***
Tischco Signs 231 755-5529
2107 Henry St Ste 1 Muskegon (49441) ***(G-11438)***
Tischco Signs & Service, Muskegon *Also called Tischco Signs* ***(G-11438)***
Tissue Seal LLC 734 213-5530
4401 Varsity Dr Ste D Ann Arbor (48108) ***(G-675)***
Titan Coatings International, Detroit *Also called Titan Sales International LLC* ***(G-4401)***
Titan Global Oil Services Inc 248 594-5983
401 S Old Woodward Ave # 308 Birmingham (48009) ***(G-1705)***
Titan Sales International LLC 313 469-7105
1497 E Grand Blvd Detroit (48211) ***(G-4401)***
Titan Sprinkler LLC 517 540-1851
1987 Sundance Rdg Howell (48843) ***(G-8111)***
Titan Tool & Die Inc 231 799-8680
6435 Schamber Dr Norton Shores (49444) ***(G-11803)***
Titania Software LLC 734 786-8225
2232 S Main St Ste 454 Ann Arbor (48103) ***(G-676)***
Titanium Building Co Inc 586 634-8580
53355 Fairchild Rd Macomb (48042) ***(G-10168)***
Titanium Industries Inc 973 983-1185
14505 Keel St Ste B Plymouth (48170) ***(G-12771)***
Titanium Operations LLC 616 717-0218
5199 Mountain Ridge Dr Ne Ada (49301) ***(G-32)***
Titanium Products Corp 810 326-4325
2855 E Mill Creek Rd Saint Clair (48079) ***(G-14235)***
Titanium Sports LLC 734 818-0904
13705 Stowell Rd Dundee (48131) ***(G-4602)***

Titanium Technologies Inc 248 836-2100
4280 Giddings Rd Auburn Hills (48326) *(G-1027)*
Tite Neon Cat 734 755-7349
3175 Comboni Way Monroe (48162) *(G-11076)*
Titus Welding Company 248 476-9366
20750 Sunnydale St Farmington Hills (48336) *(G-5141)*
Tj Rampit Usa Inc 517 278-9015
338 Bidwell Rd Coldwater (49036) *(G-3337)*
Tjb Industries 248 690-9608
3622 Sweet Bay Ct Oakland (48363) *(G-12109)*
Tk Enterprises Inc 989 865-9915
1225 N Saginaw St Saint Charles (48655) *(G-14202)*
Tk Holdings, Auburn Hills *Also called Takata Americas* *(G-1012)*
Tk Holdings Inc 517 545-9535
1199 Austin Ct Howell (48843) *(G-8112)*
Tk Mexico Inc 248 373-8040
2500 Innovation Dr Auburn Hills (48326) *(G-1028)*
Tk Mold & Engineering Inc 586 752-5840
131 Shafer Dr Romeo (48065) *(G-13640)*
Tks Industrial Company (HQ) 248 786-5000
901 Tower Dr Ste 300 Troy (48098) *(G-16645)*
TLC Printing 248 620-3228
7826 High Ridge Ct Clarkston (48348) *(G-2961)*
Tls Productions Inc 810 220-8577
78 Jackson Plz Ann Arbor (48103) *(G-677)*
Tmb Trends Inc 866 445-2344
100 W Big Beaver Rd Troy (48084) *(G-16646)*
TMC Furniture Inc 734 622-0080
119 E Ann St Ann Arbor (48104) *(G-678)*
TMC Furniture Inc (PA) 734 622-0080
4525 Airwest Dr Se Kentwood (49512) *(G-9034)*
TMC Group Inc 248 819-6063
26 Elm Park Blvd Pleasant Ridge (48069) *(G-12556)*
Tmd Machining Inc 269 685-3091
751 Wakefield Plainwell (49080) *(G-12546)*
TMI Climate Solutions Inc (HQ) 810 603-3300
200 Quality Way Holly (48442) *(G-7899)*
TMJ Manufacturing LLC 248 987-7857
26842 Haggerty Rd Farmington Hills (48331) *(G-5142)*
Tms International LLC 734 241-3007
3000 E Front St Monroe (48161) *(G-11077)*
Tms International LLC 517 764-5123
3100 Brooklyn Rd Jackson (49203) *(G-8590)*
Tms International LLC 313 378-6502
1 Quality Dr Ecorse (48229) *(G-4746)*
Tms International LLC 734 241-3007
3000 E Front St Monroe (48161) *(G-11078)*
TN Michigan LLC 906 632-7310
1390 Industrial Park Dr Sault Sainte Marie (49783) *(G-14476)*
Tnr Machine Inc 269 623-2827
2050 W Dowling Rd Dowling (49050) *(G-4564)*
TNT Marble and Stone Inc 248 887-8237
1240 Bogie Lake Rd Hartland (48353) *(G-7394)*
TNT Well Service Ltd 989 939-7098
6310 Ranger Lake Rd Gaylord (49735) *(G-5896)*
TNT-Edm Inc 734 459-1700
47689 E Anchor Ct Plymouth (48170) *(G-12772)*
To Willow Harbor Vineyard 269 369-3900
3223 Kaiser Rd Three Oaks (49128) *(G-15852)*
Toastmasters International 810 385-5477
6415 State Rd Burtchville (48059) *(G-2141)*
Toastmasters International 517 651-6507
6687 Westview Dr Laingsburg (48848) *(G-9081)*
Toda America Incorporated 269 962-0353
4750 W Dickman Rd Battle Creek (49037) *(G-1258)*
Today Publications, Indian River *Also called G L Nelson Inc* *(G-8218)*
Todds Welding Service Inc 231 587-9969
8604 Us 131 N Kalkaska (49646) *(G-8964)*
Toefco Engineering Inc 269 683-0188
1220 N 14th St Niles (49120) *(G-11649)*
Toefco Engnred Coating Systems, Niles *Also called Toefco Engineering Inc* *(G-11649)*
Toggled, Troy *Also called Ilumisys Inc* *(G-16411)*
Togreencleancom 269 428-4812
4791 S Cedar Trl Stevensville (49127) *(G-15584)*
Tokai Rika Group, Battle Creek *Also called Trmi Inc* *(G-1261)*
Tokusen Hytech Inc 269 685-1768
950 Lincoln Pkwy Plainwell (49080) *(G-12547)*
Tokusen Hytech Inc 269 658-1768
950 Lincoln Pkwy Plainwell (49080) *(G-12548)*
Tolas Brothers, Mount Pleasant *Also called Tolas Oil Gas Exploration Co* *(G-11233)*
Tolas Oil Gas Exploration Co 989 772-2599
306 E Broadway St Ste 1 Mount Pleasant (48858) *(G-11233)*
Toledo Molding & Die Inc 734 233-6338
47912 Halyard Dr Plymouth (48170) *(G-12773)*
Tolerance Tool & Engineering 313 592-4011
20541 Glendale St Detroit (48223) *(G-4402)*
Tolman Meat Processing, Hudsonville *Also called Tolmans Processing* *(G-8183)*
Tolman's Wholesale Meats, Hudsonville *Also called Mmm Meat LLC* *(G-8171)*
Tolmans Processing 616 875-8598
7405 Port Sheldon St Hudsonville (49426) *(G-8183)*
Tom Clisch Logging Inc 906 338-2900
Hwy 134700 Pelkie (49958) *(G-12423)*
Tom Nickels 248 348-7974
22000 Garfield Rd Northville (48167) *(G-11729)*
Tom's Sign, Rochester Hills *Also called Toms Sign Service* *(G-13527)*
Toman Industries Inc 734 289-1393
1652 E Hurd Rd Monroe (48162) *(G-11079)*
Tomas Plastics Inc 734 455-4706
9833 Tennyson Dr Plymouth (48170) *(G-12774)*
Tomco Fabricating & Engrg Inc 248 669-2900
50853 Century Ct Wixom (48393) *(G-17910)*
Tommark Lansing, Lansing *Also called 2 Brothers Holdings LLC* *(G-9330)*
Tommy Joe Reed 989 291-5768
6551 S Townhall Rd Sheridan (48884) *(G-14735)*
Tompkins Products Inc (PA) 313 894-2222
1040 W Grand Blvd Detroit (48208) *(G-4403)*
Toms Sign Service 248 852-3550
2926 Grant Rd Rochester Hills (48309) *(G-13527)*
Toms World of Wood 517 264-2836
105 Sand Creek Hwy Adrian (49221) *(G-98)*
Tomtek Hvac Inc 517 546-0357
627 Dearborn St Howell (48843) *(G-8113)*
Tomukun Noodle Bar 734 995-8668
505 E Liberty St Ste 200 Ann Arbor (48104) *(G-679)*
Ton-Tex Corporation (PA) 616 957-3200
4029 E Grv Unit 7 Greenville (48838) *(G-7158)*
Ton-Tex Corporation 616 957-3200
4245 44th St Se Ste 1 Grand Rapids (49512) *(G-6932)*
Tony S Die Machine Company 586 773-7379
24358 Groesbeck Hwy Warren (48089) *(G-17266)*
Tool & Die Futures Initiative 586 336-1237
14901 32 Mile Rd Bruce Twp (48065) *(G-2104)*
Tool & Die Systems Inc 248 446-1499
30529 Anderson Ct Wixom (48393) *(G-17911)*
Tool and Die, Muskegon *Also called Freedom Tool & Mfg Co* *(G-11327)*
Tool Company Inc 586 598-1519
48707 Gratiot Ave Chesterfield (48051) *(G-2849)*
Tool Craft, Lansing *Also called Michalski Enterprises Inc* *(G-9245)*
Tool North Inc 231 941-1150
2475 N Aero Park Ct Traverse City (49686) *(G-16125)*
Tool Organisations Service, Lapeer *Also called Dads Panels Inc* *(G-9455)*
Tool Sales & Engineering 810 714-5000
1045 Grant St Fenton (48430) *(G-5245)*
Tool Service Company Inc 586 296-2500
34150 Riviera Fraser (48026) *(G-5738)*
Tool-Craft Industries Inc 248 549-0077
6101 Product Dr Sterling Heights (48312) *(G-15525)*
Toolco Inc 734 453-9911
47709 Galleon Dr Plymouth (48170) *(G-12775)*
Toolcraft Machine Co Inc 517 223-9265
5390 Weller Rd Gregory (48137) *(G-7166)*
Tooling & Equipment Intl Corp 734 522-1422
12550 Tech Center Dr Livonia (48150) *(G-9957)*
Tooling Cncepts Design Not Inc 810 444-9807
3921 32nd St Port Huron (48060) *(G-12972)*
Tooling Solutions Plus, Port Huron *Also called Tooling Cncepts Design Not Inc* *(G-12972)*
Tooling Systems Enterprises, Grand Rapids *Also called Tooling Systems Group Inc* *(G-6933)*
Tooling Systems Group Inc (PA) 616 863-8623
555 Plymouth Ave Ne Grand Rapids (49505) *(G-6933)*
Tooling Tech Group, Macomb *Also called Tooling Technology LLC* *(G-10169)*
Tooling Technology LLC (PA) 937 381-9211
51223 Quadrate Dr Macomb (48042) *(G-10169)*
Tooltech Machinery Inc (PA) 248 628-1813
625 S Glaspie St Oxford (48371) *(G-12376)*
Top Craft Tool Inc 586 461-4600
33674 Giftos Dr Clinton Township (48035) *(G-3248)*
Top Deck Systems Inc 586 263-1550
44753 Centre Ct Clinton Township (48038) *(G-3249)*
Top Form Inc 815 653-9616
4165 River Rd Twin Lake (49457) *(G-16715)*
Top Notch Cookies & Cakes Inc 734 467-9550
1849 Knolson St Westland (48185) *(G-17604)*
Top Notch Tree Service, Holland *Also called Maas Enterprises Michigan LLC* *(G-7729)*
Top of Line Crane Service LLC 231 267-5326
6925 M 72 E Williamsburg (49690) *(G-17722)*
Top OMichigan Reclaimers Inc 989 705-7983
620 E Main St Gaylord (49735) *(G-5897)*
Top Shelf Barber Supplies LLC (PA) 586 453-6809
5400 Pierson Hwy W Lansing (48917) *(G-9326)*
Top Shelf Painter Inc 586 465-0867
34400 Klein Rd Fraser (48026) *(G-5739)*
Top Shop Inc 517 323-9085
2526 N Grand River Ave Lansing (48906) *(G-9270)*
Topcraft Metal Products Inc 616 669-1790
5112 40th Ave Hudsonville (49426) *(G-8184)*
Topduck Products LLC 517 322-3202
2902 Sanders Rd Lansing (48917) *(G-9327)*

A L P H A B E T I C

(PA)=Parent Co (HQ)=Headquarters (DH)=Div Headquarters
2020 Harris Michigan Industrial Directory
1091

Topors Pickle Co Inc 313 237-0288
5407 Pocono Dr West Bloomfield (48323) *(G-17501)*
Tops All Clamps Inc 313 533-7500
26627 W 8 Mile Rd Redford (48240) *(G-13202)*
Toray Resin Company (HQ) 248 269-8800
2800 Livernois Rd D115 Troy (48083) *(G-16647)*
Torch Steel Processing LLC 313 571-7000
8103 Lynch Rd Detroit (48234) *(G-4404)*
Torenzo Inc 313 732-7874
6632 Telegraph Rd Ste 122 Bloomfield Hills (48301) *(G-1804)*
Toro Company 888 492-6841
2007-2010 Boss Way Iron Mountain (49801) *(G-8304)*
Torque-Tight, Boyne City Also called Outline Industries LLC *(G-1831)*
Torsion Control Products Inc 248 537-1900
1900 Northfield Dr Rochester Hills (48309) *(G-13528)*
Tortillas Tita LLC 734 756-7646
3763 Commerce Ct Wayne (48184) *(G-17444)*
Toshiba Amer Bus Solutions Inc 248 427-8100
29100 Northwstn Hwy 300 Southfield (48034) *(G-15046)*
Toshiba America Electronic 248 347-2608
48679 Alpha Dr Ste 120 Wixom (48393) *(G-17912)*
Total Business Systems Inc (PA) 248 307-1076
30800 Montpelier Dr Madison Heights (48071) *(G-10368)*
Total Chips Company Inc 989 866-2610
11285 S Winn Rd Shepherd (48883) *(G-14731)*
Total Door An Openings, Waterford Also called Openings Inc *(G-17363)*
Total Door II Inc 866 781-2069
6145 Delfield Dr Waterford (48329) *(G-17381)*
Total Flow Products Inc 248 588-4490
1197 Rochester Rd Ste N Troy (48083) *(G-16648)*
Total Health Colon Care 586 268-5444
38245 Mound Rd E Sterling Heights (48310) *(G-15526)*
Total Innovative Mfg LLC 616 399-9903
13395 Tyler St Holland (49424) *(G-7831)*
Total Lee Sports Inc 989 772-6121
1575 Airway Dr Mount Pleasant (48858) *(G-11234)*
Total Local Acquisitions LLC 517 663-2405
117 E Knight St Eaton Rapids (48827) *(G-4735)*
Total MGT Reclamation Svcs LLC 734 384-3500
8400 Beech Daly Rd Taylor (48180) *(G-15777)*
Total Molding Solutions Inc 517 424-5900
416 E Cummins St Tecumseh (49286) *(G-15813)*
Total Packaging Solutions LLC 248 519-2376
775 W Big Beavr Rd # 2020 Troy (48084) *(G-16649)*
Total Plastics International, Kalamazoo Also called Total Plastics Resources LLC *(G-8914)*
Total Plastics Resources LLC (HQ) 269 344-0009
2810 N Burdick St Ste A Kalamazoo (49004) *(G-8914)*
Total Plastics Resources LLC 248 299-9500
1661 Northfield Dr Rochester Hills (48309) *(G-13529)*
Total Quality Machining Inc 231 767-1825
2620 Park St Muskegon (49444) *(G-11439)*
Total Repair Express MI LLC 248 690-9410
118 Indianwood Rd Ste C Lake Orion (48362) *(G-9166)*
Total Security Solutions Inc 517 223-7807
935 Garden Ln Fowlerville (48836) *(G-5580)*
Total Tennis LLC 248 594-1749
2519 W Maple Rd Bloomfield Hills (48301) *(G-1805)*
Total Tooling Concepts Inc 616 785-8402
4870 West River Dr Ne A Comstock Park (49321) *(G-3518)*
Total Toxicology Labs LLC 248 352-7171
24525 Southfield Rd Southfield (48075) *(G-15047)*
Totd, Grand Rapids Also called Treat of Day LLC *(G-6936)*
Totle Inc 248 645-1111
260 E Brown St Ste 200 Birmingham (48009) *(G-1706)*
TOUCH REVOLUTION, Holland Also called Tpk America LLC *(G-7832)*
Touchstone Distributing Inc 517 669-8200
103 S Bridge St Ste B Dewitt (48820) *(G-4468)*
Touchstone Pottery, Dewitt Also called Touchstone Distributing Inc *(G-4468)*
Touchstone Systems & Svcs Inc 616 532-0060
1817 Porter St Sw Wyoming (49519) *(G-18035)*
Tough Coatings, Sturgis Also called Collier Enterprise III *(G-15600)*
Toughbuoy Co 989 465-6111
3051 W Curtis Rd Coleman (48618) *(G-3352)*
Tow-Line Trailer Sales, Saginaw Also called Tow-Line Trailers *(G-14165)*
Tow-Line Trailers 989 752-0055
4854 E Holland Rd Saginaw (48601) *(G-14165)*
Tower Acquisition Co II LLC 248 675-6000
17672 N Laurel Park Dr Livonia (48152) *(G-9958)*
Tower Autmtve Oprtns USA III (HQ) 248 675-6000
17672 N Laurel Park Dr Livonia (48152) *(G-9959)*
Tower Auto Holdings I LLC 248 675-6000
17672 N Laurel Park Dr 400e Livonia (48152) *(G-9960)*
Tower Auto Holdings II A LLC 248 675-6000
17672 N Laurel Park Dr 400e Livonia (48152) *(G-9961)*
Tower Auto Holdings II B LLC 248 675-6000
17672 N Laurel Park Dr Livonia (48152) *(G-9962)*
Tower Auto Holdings USA LLC (HQ) 248 675-6000
17672 N Laurel Park Dr 400e Livonia (48152) *(G-9963)*
Tower Automotive Operations (HQ) 248 675-6000
17672 N Laurel Park Dr 400e Livonia (48152) *(G-9964)*
Tower Automotive Operations (HQ) 248 675-6000
17672 N Laurel Park Dr 400e Livonia (48152) *(G-9965)*
Tower Automotive Operations I 989 375-2201
81 Drettman St Elkton (48731) *(G-4784)*
Tower Automotive Operations I 616 802-1600
4695 44th St Se Ste B175 Grand Rapids (49512) *(G-6934)*
Tower Automotive Operations I 586 465-5158
44850 N Groesbeck Hwy Clinton Township (48036) *(G-3250)*
Tower Automotive Operations I 734 414-3100
43955 Plymouth Oaks Blvd Plymouth (48170) *(G-12776)*
Tower Defense & Aerospace LLC 248 675-6000
17672 N Laurel Park Dr Livonia (48152) *(G-9966)*
Tower International, Livonia Also called Tower Auto Holdings USA LLC *(G-9963)*
Tower International, Novi Also called Ta Delaware Inc *(G-12011)*
Tower International Inc 989 623-2174
81 Drettman St Elkton (48731) *(G-4785)*
Tower International Inc 616 802-1600
4695 44th St Se Ste B175 Grand Rapids (49512) *(G-6935)*
Tower International Inc (HQ) 248 675-6000
17672 N Laurel Park Dr Livonia (48152) *(G-9967)*
Tower Tag & Label LLC 269 927-1065
1300 E Empire Ave Benton Harbor (49022) *(G-1555)*
Towerline Software LLC 517 669-8112
240 S Bridge St Ste 110 Dewitt (48820) *(G-4469)*
Towing & Equipment Magazine 248 601-1385
1700 W Hamlin Rd Ste 100 Rochester Hills (48309) *(G-13530)*
Town & Country Cedar Homes 231 347-4360
4740 Skop Rd Boyne Falls (49713) *(G-1842)*
Town & Country Log Homes Mill, Boyne Falls Also called Town & Country Cedar Homes *(G-1842)*
Town Crier, Saint Ignace Also called St Ignace News *(G-14279)*
Townline Ciderworks LLC 231 883-5330
11595 S Us Highway 31 Williamsburg (49690) *(G-17723)*
Township of Saline 734 429-4440
205 E Michigan Ave Saline (48176) *(G-14418)*
Tox Presso Technik 248 374-1877
28287 Beck Rd Ste D12 Wixom (48393) *(G-17913)*
Toyo Seat USA Corporation (HQ) 606 849-3009
2155 S Almont Ave Imlay City (48444) *(G-8212)*
Toyoda Gosei North Amer Corp (HQ) 248 280-2100
1400 Stephenson Hwy Troy (48083) *(G-16650)*
Toyota Industries Elctc Sys N 248 489-7700
28700 Cabot Dr Ste 100 Novi (48377) *(G-12018)*
Tpa Inc 248 302-9131
1360 Oakman Blvd Detroit (48238) *(G-4405)*
Tpi Industries LLC 810 987-2222
2770 Dove St Port Huron (48060) *(G-12973)*
Tpi Powder Metallurgy Inc (PA) 989 865-9921
12030 Beaver Rd Saint Charles (48655) *(G-14203)*
Tpk America LLC 616 786-5300
215 Central Ave Ste 200 Holland (49423) *(G-7832)*
Tps, Beaverton Also called Thermfrmer Parts Suppliers LLC *(G-1394)*
Tps LLC 269 849-2700
3827 Riverside Rd Riverside (49084) *(G-13287)*
Tps North America LLC, Troy Also called Tubular PDT Solutions NA LLC *(G-16656)*
TR Timber Co 989 345-5350
502 E State Rd West Branch (48661) *(G-17526)*
Trace Zero Inc 248 289-1277
2740 Auburn Ct Auburn Hills (48326) *(G-1029)*
Tractech Inc (HQ) 248 226-6800
26201 Northwestern Hwy Southfield (48076) *(G-15048)*
Tracy Wilk 231 477-5135
15840 Dickson Rd Brethren (49619) *(G-1847)*
Trade Bindery Service Inc 734 425-7500
35400 Plymouth Rd Livonia (48150) *(G-9968)*
Trade Specific Solutions LLC 734 752-7124
13092 Superior St Southgate (48195) *(G-15085)*
Trademark Die & Engineering 616 863-6660
8060 Graphic Dr Ne Unit 1 Belmont (49306) *(G-1473)*
TRAFFIC & SAFETY, Wixom Also called Traffic Sfety Ctrl Systems Inc *(G-17914)*
Traffic Displays LLC 616 225-8865
9363 S Grow Rd Greenville (48838) *(G-7159)*
Traffic Engineering, Saginaw Also called City of Saginaw *(G-14019)*
Traffic Sfety Ctrl Systems Inc 248 348-0570
48584 Downing St Wixom (48393) *(G-17914)*
Traffic Signs Inc 269 964-7511
341 Helmer Rd N Springfield (49037) *(G-15206)*
Trailer Tech Holdings LLC 248 960-9700
48282 Frank St Wixom (48393) *(G-17915)*
Trailer Tech One, Plymouth Also called Trailer Tech Repair Inc *(G-12777)*
Trailer Tech Repair Inc 734 354-6680
13101 Eckles Rd Plymouth (48170) *(G-12777)*
Trainer Metal Forming Co Inc 616 844-9982
14080 172nd Ave Grand Haven (49417) *(G-6089)*
Trainingmask LLC 888 407-7555
1140 Plett Rd Cadillac (49601) *(G-2283)*

ALPHABETIC SECTION — Tri-Star Engineering, Sterling Heights

Tram Inc (HQ) 734 254-8500
47200 Port St Plymouth (48170) *(G-12778)*

Tramec Sloan LLC (HQ) 616 395-5600
534 E 48th St Holland (49423) *(G-7833)*

Tramm Tech Inc 989 723-2944
807 S Delaney Rd Owosso (48867) *(G-12323)*

Trane US Inc 800 245-3964
5335 Hill 23 Dr Flint (48507) *(G-5511)*

Trane US Inc 734 367-0700
33725 Schoolcraft Rd Livonia (48150) *(G-9969)*

Trane US Inc 734 452-2000
37001 Industrial Rd Livonia (48150) *(G-9970)*

Tranor Industries LLC 313 733-4888
19365 Sherwood St Detroit (48234) *(G-4406)*

Tranquil Systems Intl LLC 800 631-0212
528 Pioneer Pkwy Clare (48617) *(G-2891)*

Trans Industries Plastics LLC (PA) 248 310-0008
414 East St Rochester (48307) *(G-13355)*

Trans Parts Plus Inc 734 427-6844
32816 Manor Park Garden City (48135) *(G-5844)*

Trans Tube Inc 248 334-5720
34 W Sheffield Ave Pontiac (48340) *(G-12871)*

Trans-Matic Mfg Co Inc (PA) 616 820-2500
300 E 48th St Holland (49423) *(G-7834)*

Trans-Matic Mfg Co Inc 616 820-2541
471 E 40th St Holland (49423) *(G-7835)*

Transcontinental US LLC 269 964-7137
155 Brook St Battle Creek (49037) *(G-1259)*

Transet, Grand Rapids *Also called Northwest Metal Products Inc (G-6720)*

Transfer Tool Products, Grand Haven *Also called Transfer Tool Systems Inc (G-6090)*

Transfer Tool Systems Inc 616 846-8510
14444 168th Ave Grand Haven (49417) *(G-6090)*

Transform Automotive LLC 586 826-8500
52400 Shelby Pkwy Shelby Township (48315) *(G-14710)*

Transform Automotive LLC (HQ) 586 826-8500
7026 Sterling Ponds Ct Sterling Heights (48312) *(G-15527)*

Transglobal Design & Mfg LLC (PA) 734 525-2651
1020 Doris Rd Auburn Hills (48326) *(G-1030)*

Transign LLC 248 623-6400
281 Collier Rd Auburn Hills (48326) *(G-1031)*

Transit Bus Rebuilders Inc 989 277-3645
500 Smith Ave Owosso (48867) *(G-12324)*

Transit Solutions LLC 989 893-3230
1322 Washington Ave Bay City (48708) *(G-1363)*

Transnav Holdings Inc (PA) 586 716-5600
35105 Cricklewood Blvd New Baltimore (48047) *(G-11494)*

Transnav Technologies Inc (HQ) 888 249-9955
35105 Cricklewood Blvd New Baltimore (48047) *(G-11495)*

Transology Associates 517 694-8645
2915 Crestwood Dr East Lansing (48823) *(G-4680)*

Transpak Inc 586 264-2064
34400 Mound Rd Sterling Heights (48310) *(G-15528)*

Transporation Automation Conve, Rochester Hills *Also called Tacs Automation LLC (G-13523)*

Transport Trailers Co 269 543-4405
2166 68th St Fennville (49408) *(G-5178)*

Transportation Tech Group Inc (PA) 810 233-0440
3020 Airpark Dr S Flint (48507) *(G-5512)*

Transtar Autobody Tech Inc, Brighton *Also called Transtar Autobody Tech LLC (G-1999)*

Transtar Autobody Tech LLC 810 220-3000
2040 Heiserman Dr Brighton (48114) *(G-1999)*

Transtechbio Inc 734 994-4728
5001 Quincy Ct Saline (48176) *(G-14419)*

Travel Information Services 989 275-8042
101 E Federal Hwy Roscommon (48653) *(G-13755)*

Traverse Bay Canvas Inc 231 347-3001
787 W Conway Rd Harbor Springs (49740) *(G-7296)*

Traverse Bay Manufacturing Inc 231 264-8111
8980 Cairn Hwy Elk Rapids (49629) *(G-4781)*

Traverse City Helicopters LLC (HQ) 231 668-6000
1190 Airport Access Rd B Traverse City (49686) *(G-16126)*

Traverse City Pie Company LLC 231 929-7437
2911 Garfield Rd N Traverse City (49686) *(G-16127)*

Traverse City Print & Copy, Traverse City *Also called Kwikie Inc (G-16019)*

Traverse City Products Inc 231 946-4414
501 Hughes Dr Traverse City (49696) *(G-16128)*

Traverse City Record-Eagle, Traverse City *Also called Traverse Cy Record-Eagle Inc (G-16129)*

Traverse City Whiskey Co., Traverse City *Also called Tcwc LLC (G-16119)*

Traverse Cy Record-Eagle Inc 231 946-2000
120 W Front St Traverse City (49684) *(G-16129)*

Traverse Nthrn Michigans Mag, Traverse City *Also called Prism Publications Inc (G-16078)*

Travis Creek Tooling 269 685-2000
923 Industrial Pkwy Plainwell (49080) *(G-12549)*

Treasure Enterprise LLC 810 233-7141
1161 N Ballenger Hwy # 7 Flint (48504) *(G-5513)*

Treat of Day LLC 616 706-1717
2540 Ridgemoor Dr Se Grand Rapids (49512) *(G-6936)*

Tree Tech 248 543-2166
820 S Washington Ave Royal Oak (48067) *(G-13976)*

Treehouse Private Brands Inc 269 968-6181
150 Mccamly St S Battle Creek (49017) *(G-1260)*

Tregets Tool & Engineering Co 517 782-0044
1021 Airport Rd Jackson (49202) *(G-8591)*

Treib Inc (PA) 989 752-4821
850 S Outer Dr Saginaw (48601) *(G-14166)*

Trelan Manufacturing 989 561-2280
498 8 Mile Rd Remus (49340) *(G-13242)*

Trelleborg Sling Sltions US Inc 269 639-4217
1042 N Crystal Ave Benton Harbor (49022) *(G-1556)*

Trelleborg Sling Sltions US Inc 734 354-1250
15701 Centennial Dr Northville (48168) *(G-11730)*

Trelleborg Automotive, South Haven *Also called Vibracoustic Usa Inc (G-14781)*

Trelleborg Automotive, Sandusky *Also called Vibracoustic Usa Inc (G-14446)*

Trelleborg Automotive USA Inc 734 254-9140
15701 Centennial Dr Northville (48168) *(G-11731)*

Trelleborg Corporation (HQ) 269 639-9891
200 Veterans Blvd Ste 3 South Haven (49090) *(G-14778)*

Trenary Wood Products, Trenary *Also called Holmquist Feed Mill (G-16151)*

Trend Millwork LLC 313 383-6300
1300 John A Papalas Dr Lincoln Park (48146) *(G-9586)*

Trend Performance Products 586 792-6620
23003 Diamond Dr Clinton Township (48035) *(G-3251)*

Trend Services Company 231 258-9951
311 Maple St Kalkaska (49646) *(G-8965)*

Trendway Corporation (HQ) 616 399-3900
13467 Quincy St Holland (49424) *(G-7836)*

Trendway Svcs Organization LLC 616 994-5327
13467 Quincy St Holland (49424) *(G-7837)*

Trendwell Energy Corporation 616 866-5024
10 E Bridge St Ste 200 Rockford (49341) *(G-13594)*

Trenton Corporation (PA) 734 424-3600
7700 Jackson Rd Ann Arbor (48103) *(G-680)*

Trenton Forging Company 734 675-1620
5523 Hoover St Trenton (48183) *(G-16159)*

Trenton Hearthside Shop Inc 734 558-5860
2447 3rd St Trenton (48183) *(G-16160)*

Trenton Jewelers Ltd 734 676-0188
2355 West Rd Trenton (48183) *(G-16161)*

Trestle Plastic Services LLC 616 262-5484
3393 Lincoln Rd Hamilton (49419) *(G-7241)*

Tri City Aggregates, Burton *Also called Genoak Materials Inc (G-2155)*

Tri City Blinds Inc 989 695-5699
10976 W Freeland Rd Freeland (48623) *(G-5760)*

Tri City Record LLC 269 463-6397
138 N Main St Watervliet (49098) *(G-17394)*

Tri City Times, Imlay City *Also called Page One Inc (G-8209)*

Tri County Precision Grinding 586 776-6600
21960 Schmeman Ave Warren (48089) *(G-17267)*

Tri County Sand & Stone Shop, Alden *Also called Tri County Sand and Stone Inc (G-137)*

Tri County Sand and Stone Inc 231 331-6549
5318 Bebb Rd Alden (49612) *(G-137)*

Tri K Cylinder Service Inc 269 965-3981
4539 Wayne Rd Springfield (49037) *(G-15207)*

Tri Matics Mfg Inc 586 469-3150
25500 Henry B Joy Blvd Harrison Township (48045) *(G-7354)*

Tri State Optical Inc 517 279-2701
350 Marshall St Ste B Coldwater (49036) *(G-3338)*

Tri Tech Tooling Inc 616 396-6000
11615 Greenway Dr Holland (49424) *(G-7838)*

Tri-City Aggregates Inc 248 634-8276
14300 Shields Rd Holly (48442) *(G-7900)*

Tri-City Repair Company 989 835-4784
6700 Middle Rd Hope (48628) *(G-7957)*

Tri-City Vinyl Inc 989 401-7992
640 E Morley Dr Saginaw (48601) *(G-14167)*

Tri-County Diversified Inds, Lansing *Also called Community Mental Health (G-9210)*

Tri-County Equip-Sandusky, Sandusky *Also called Bader & Co (G-14429)*

Tri-County Fab Inc 586 443-5130
16153 Common Rd Roseville (48066) *(G-13879)*

Tri-County Logging, Clinton *Also called Hmi Hardwoods LLC (G-3023)*

Tri-County Precision Grinding, Warren *Also called Tri County Precision Grinding (G-17267)*

Tri-County Times, Fenton *Also called Rockman Communications Inc (G-5236)*

Tri-Dim Filter Corporation 734 229-0877
11800 Hannan Rd Van Buren Twp (48111) *(G-16788)*

Tri-Forestry 906 474-9379
10222 15.25 Rd Rapid River (49878) *(G-13116)*

Tri-M-Mold Inc 269 465-3301
3390 W Linco Rd Stevensville (49127) *(G-15585)*

Tri-Matic Screw Products Co 517 548-6414
5684 E Highland Rd Howell (48843) *(G-8114)*

Tri-Mation Industries Inc 269 668-4333
53160 N Main St Plant 12 Mattawan (49071) *(G-10670)*

Tri-Power Manufacturing Inc 734 414-8084
9229 General Dr Ste B Plymouth (48170) *(G-12779)*

Tri-Star Engineering, Sterling Heights *Also called Tri-Star Tooling LLC (G-15529)*

Tri-Star Molding Inc 269 646-0062
  51540 M 40 Marcellus (49067) *(G-10469)*
Tri-Star Tool & Machine Co 734 729-5700
  613 Manufacturers Dr Westland (48186) *(G-17605)*
Tri-Star Tooling LLC 586 978-0435
  35640 Beattie Dr Sterling Heights (48312) *(G-15529)*
Tri-State Aluminum LLC (HQ) 231 722-7825
  1060 E Keating Ave Muskegon (49442) *(G-11440)*
Tri-State Cast Technologies Co (PA) 231 582-0452
  926 N Lake St Boyne City (49712) *(G-1836)*
Tri-State Flame Hardening Co 586 776-0035
  27150 Gloede Dr Warren (48088) *(G-17268)*
Tri-State Technical Services 517 563-8743
  9659 Grover Rd Hanover (49241) *(G-7262)*
Tri-TEC Seal LLC (HQ) 810 655-3900
  2111 W Thompson Rd Fenton (48430) *(G-5246)*
Tri-Tech Engineering Inc 734 283-3700
  3663 11th St Wyandotte (48192) *(G-17978)*
Tri-Tool Boring Machine Co 586 598-0036
  46440 Continental Dr Chesterfield (48047) *(G-2850)*
Tri-Vision LLC (PA) 313 526-6020
  12326 E Mcnichols Rd Detroit (48205) *(G-4407)*
Tri-Way Manufacturing Inc 586 776-0700
  15363 E 12 Mile Rd Roseville (48066) *(G-13880)*
TRI-WAY MOLD & ENGINEERING, Roseville *Also called Tri-Way Manufacturing Inc (G-13880)*
Triad Industrial Corp 989 358-7191
  11656 Reimann Rd Atlanta (49709) *(G-733)*
Triad Manufacturing Co Inc 248 583-9636
  32020 Edward Ave Madison Heights (48071) *(G-10369)*
Triad Process Equipment Inc 248 685-9938
  4922 Technical Dr Milford (48381) *(G-10989)*
Triangle Broach Company 313 838-2150
  18404 Fitzpatrick St Detroit (48228) *(G-4408)*
Triangle Grinding Company Inc 586 749-6540
  57877 Main St New Haven (48048) *(G-11529)*
Triangle Printing Inc 586 293-7530
  30520 Gratiot Ave Roseville (48066) *(G-13881)*
Triangle Product Distributors 970 609-9001
  5750 Lakeshore Dr Holland (49424) *(G-7839)*
Triangle Window Fashions Inc 616 538-9676
  2625 Buchanan Ave Sw A Wyoming (49548) *(G-18036)*
Trianon Industries Corporation 586 759-2200
  24331 Sherwood Center Line (48015) *(G-2585)*
Tribal Manufacturing Inc (PA) 269 781-3901
  450 Leggitt Rd Marshall (49068) *(G-10591)*
Tribar Manufacturing LLC 248 669-0077
  30517 Anderson Ct Wixom (48393) *(G-17916)*
Tribar Manufacturing LLC 248 374-5870
  29883 Beck Rd Wixom (48393) *(G-17917)*
Tribar Manufacturing LLC (HQ) 248 516-1600
  2211 Grand Commerce Dr Howell (48855) *(G-8115)*
Tribar Technologies Inc (PA) 248 516-1600
  48668 Alpha Dr Wixom (48393) *(G-17918)*
Tribar Technologies Inc 248 516-1600
  48668 Alpha Dr Wixom (48393) *(G-17919)*
Tribune Recorder, Sandusky *Also called Eldon Publishing LLC (G-14433)*
Tric Tool Ltd 616 395-1530
  3760 John F Donnelly Dr Holland (49424) *(G-7840)*
Trick Titanium, Holt *Also called Scitex LLC (G-7927)*
Trick Titanium, Holt *Also called Scitex LLC (G-7926)*
Trico Incorporated 517 764-1780
  7401 Foxworth Ct Jackson (49201) *(G-8592)*
Trico Products Corporation (HQ) 248 371-1700
  3255 W Hamlin Rd Rochester Hills (48309) *(G-13531)*
Trident Lighting LLC 616 957-9500
  2929 32nd St Se Grand Rapids (49512) *(G-6937)*
Trig Tool Inc 248 543-2550
  1143 E 10 Mile Rd Madison Heights (48071) *(G-10370)*
Trigon Metal Products, Livonia *Also called A&G Corporate Holdings LLC (G-9620)*
Trigon Metal Products Inc 734 513-3488
  12725 Inkster Rd Livonia (48150) *(G-9971)*
Trigon Steel Components Inc 616 834-0506
  1448 Lincoln Ave Holland (49423) *(G-7841)*
Trijicon Inc (PA) 248 960-7700
  49385 Shafer Ct Wixom (48393) *(G-17920)*
Trikala Inc 517 646-8188
  11546 Ransom Hwy Dimondale (48821) *(G-4520)*
Trillacorpe Construction, Bingham Farms *Also called Trillacorpe/Bk LLC (G-1662)*
Trillacorpe/Bk LLC 248 433-0585
  30100 Telg Rd Ste 366 Bingham Farms (48025) *(G-1662)*
Trim Pac Inc 269 279-9498
  315 7th Ave Three Rivers (49093) *(G-15881)*
Trim Star Warehouse, Almont *Also called Ligon Helicopter Corporation (G-261)*
Trimas Company LLC (HQ) 248 631-5450
  39400 Woodward Ave # 130 Bloomfield Hills (48304) *(G-1806)*
Trimas Corporation (PA) 248 631-5450
  38505 Woodward Ave # 200 Bloomfield Hills (48304) *(G-1807)*

Trimet Industries Inc 231 929-9100
  829 Duell Rd Traverse City (49686) *(G-16130)*
Trims Unlimited, Almont *Also called Inplast Interior Tech LLC (G-258)*
Trin Jnc 260 587-9282
  47200 Port St Plymouth (48170) *(G-12780)*
Trin-Mac Company Inc 586 774-1900
  24825 Little Mack Ave # 200 Saint Clair Shores (48080) *(G-14273)*
Trinco, Fraser *Also called Trinity Tool Co (G-5741)*
Trinity Equipment Co 231 719-1813
  3918 Holton Rd Muskegon (49445) *(G-11441)*
Trinity Holding Inc (PA) 517 787-3100
  420 Ingham St Jackson (49201) *(G-8593)*
Trinity Industries Inc 586 285-1692
  33910 James J Pompo Dr Fraser (48026) *(G-5740)*
Trinity Industries Inc 517 741-4300
  594 M 60 Union City (49094) *(G-16736)*
Trinity Seven Enterprises Inc 216 906-0984
  4398 Pond Run Canton (48188) *(G-2436)*
Trinity Tool Co 586 296-5900
  34600 Commerce Fraser (48026) *(G-5741)*
Trinseo 989 636-5409
  3700 James Savage Rd Midland (48642) *(G-10921)*
Trinseo LLC 888 789-7661
  409 Ashman St Ste 1 Midland (48640) *(G-10922)*
Triple C Geothermal Inc 517 282-7249
  487 W Forest Ave Muskegon (49441) *(G-11442)*
Triple Creek Shirts and More 269 273-5154
  54 N Main St Three Rivers (49093) *(G-15882)*
Triple Ddd Firewood 231 734-5215
  9533 90th Ave Evart (49631) *(G-4887)*
Triple E LLC 517 531-4481
  8535 E Michigan Ave Parma (49269) *(G-12395)*
Triple K Farms Inc 517 458-9741
  13648 Wabash Rd Morenci (49256) *(G-11116)*
Triple R Precision Boring Co, West Bloomfield *Also called Maro Precision Tool Company (G-17483)*
Triple Thread 248 321-7757
  25 W 14 Mile Rd Clawson (48017) *(G-2987)*
Triple Tool 586 795-1785
  40715 Brentwood Dr Sterling Heights (48310) *(G-15530)*
Trisco Chemical Co 586 779-8260
  21125 Yale St Saint Clair Shores (48081) *(G-14274)*
Trisco Products, Saint Clair Shores *Also called Trisco Chemical Co (G-14274)*
Trison Tool and Machine Inc 248 628-8770
  925 S Glaspie St Oxford (48371) *(G-12377)*
Trispec Precision Products Inc 248 308-3231
  47580 Avante Dr Wixom (48393) *(G-17921)*
Tristone Flowtech USA Inc (HQ) 248 560-1724
  2000 Town Ctr Ste 660 Southfield (48075) *(G-15049)*
Tritec Performance Solutions, Fenton *Also called Tri-TEC Seal LLC (G-5246)*
Triton Global Sources Inc 734 668-7107
  2111 Golfside Rd Ypsilanti (48197) *(G-18106)*
Triumph Gear Systems - Macomb 586 781-2800
  15375 23 Mile Rd Macomb (48042) *(G-10170)*
Triunfar Industries Inc 313 790-5592
  10813 Bouldercrest Dr South Lyon (48178) *(G-14814)*
Trmi Inc 269 966-0800
  100 Hill Brady Rd Battle Creek (49037) *(G-1261)*
Trojan Heat Treat Inc 517 568-4403
  809 S Byron St Homer (49245) *(G-7951)*
Trojan Heat Treat Company, Homer *Also called Trojan Heat Treat Inc (G-7951)*
Trolley Rebuilders Inc 810 364-4820
  1765 Michigan Ave Marysville (48040) *(G-10624)*
Tronox Incorporated 231 328-4986
  4176 N Dorr Rd Merritt (49667) *(G-10765)*
Trophy Center West Michigan 231 893-1686
  8060 Whitehall Rd Whitehall (49461) *(G-17678)*
Troy Design & Manufacturing Co (HQ) 734 738-2300
  14425 N Sheldon Rd Plymouth (48170) *(G-12781)*
Troy Haygood 313 478-3308
  2871 Hilton Rd Ferndale (48220) *(G-5322)*
Troy Industries Inc 586 739-7760
  13300 W Star Dr Shelby Township (48315) *(G-14711)*
Troy Laser & Fab LLC 586 510-4570
  23720 Dequindre Rd Warren (48091) *(G-17269)*
Troy Millwork Inc 248 852-8383
  1841 Northfield Dr Rochester Hills (48309) *(G-13532)*
Troy Mixing Plant, Troy *Also called Barrett Paving Materials Inc (G-16233)*
Troy Orthopedic Associates PLC 248 244-9426
  1350 Kirts Blvd Ste 160 Troy (48084) *(G-16651)*
Troy Somerset Gazette, Troy *Also called Gazette Newspapers Inc (G-16380)*
Troy Tube & Manufacturing Co 586 949-8700
  50100 E Russell Schmidt B Chesterfield (48051) *(G-2851)*
Trp Enterprises Inc 810 329-4027
  6267 Saint Clair Hwy East China (48054) *(G-4625)*
Trp Sand & Gravel, East China *Also called Trp Enterprises Inc (G-4625)*
Tru Blu Industries LLC 269 684-4989
  1920 Industrial Dr Niles (49120) *(G-11650)*

ALPHABETIC SECTION Turchetti Spaghetti Co LLC

Tru Custom Blends Inc 810 407-6207
2321 Branch Rd Flint (48506) ***(G-5514)***
Tru Die Cast Corporation 269 426-3361
13066 California Rd New Troy (49119) ***(G-11561)***
Tru Flo Carbide Inc 989 658-8515
3999 N Ubly Rd Ubly (48475) ***(G-16724)***
Tru Point Corporation 313 897-9100
6707 W Warren Ave Detroit (48210) ***(G-4409)***
Tru Tech Systems LLC (HQ) 586 469-2700
24550 N River Rd Mount Clemens (48043) ***(G-11152)***
Tru-Bore Machine Tool Co Inc 734 729-9590
6262 E Executive Dr Westland (48185) ***(G-17606)***
Tru-Coat Inc 810 785-3331
10428 Seymour Rd Montrose (48457) ***(G-11106)***
Tru-Fit International Inc 248 855-8845
5799 W Maple Rd Ste 167 West Bloomfield (48322) ***(G-17502)***
Tru-Line Metal Products, Livonia *Also called Tru-Line Screw Products Inc* ***(G-9973)***
Tru-Line Metal Products Co, Livonia *Also called Tru-Line Screw Products Inc* ***(G-9972)***
Tru-Line Screw Products Inc (PA) 734 261-8780
15223 Farmington Rd Ste 5 Livonia (48154) ***(G-9972)***
Tru-Line Screw Products Inc 734 261-8780
30649 Schoolcraft Rd Livonia (48150) ***(G-9973)***
Tru-Syzygy Inc 248 622-7211
1151 Sunset Hills Dr Lake Orion (48360) ***(G-9167)***
Tru-Thread Co Inc 248 399-0255
1600 Hilton Rd Ferndale (48220) ***(G-5323)***
Truans Candies Inc (PA) 313 281-0185
4251 Fleming Way Plymouth (48170) ***(G-12782)***
Truarx Inc 248 538-7809
2000 Town Ctr Ste 2050 Southfield (48075) ***(G-15050)***
Trucent Inc (PA) 734 426-9015
7400 Newman Blvd Dexter (48130) ***(G-4515)***
Trucent Separation Tech LLC 734 426-9015
7400 Newman Blvd Dexter (48130) ***(G-4516)***
Truck Trailer Transit Inc 313 516-7151
1400 Rochester Rd Troy (48083) ***(G-16652)***
Truck Acquisition Inc (HQ) 877 875-4376
5400 Data Ct Ann Arbor (48108) ***(G-681)***
Truck Hero Inc (HQ) 877 875-4376
5400 Data Ct Ste 100 Ann Arbor (48108) ***(G-682)***
Truck Hero Ann Arbor, Ann Arbor *Also called Tectum Holdings Inc* ***(G-656)***
Truck Holdings Inc (PA) 877 875-4376
5400 Data Ct Ste 100 Ann Arbor (48108) ***(G-683)***
Trucksforsalecom 989 883-3382
8440 Unionville Rd Sebewaing (48759) ***(G-14520)***
True Anlytics Mfg Slutions LLC 517 902-9700
5400 Douglas Rd Ida (48140) ***(G-8194)***
True Built Woodworking (PA) 517 626-6482
11672 W Herbison Rd Eagle (48822) ***(G-4617)***
True Built Woodworking 989 587-3041
6140 S Wright Rd Fowler (48835) ***(G-5556)***
True Fabrications & Machine 248 288-0140
1731 Thorncroft Dr Troy (48084) ***(G-16653)***
True Industrial Corporation (PA) 586 771-3500
15300 E 12 Mile Rd Roseville (48066) ***(G-13882)***
True Teknit Inc 616 656-5111
5300 Corprte Grv Dr Se De Grand Rapids (49512) ***(G-6938)***
True Tool Cnc Regrinding & Mfg 616 677-1751
14110 Ironwood Dr Nw Grand Rapids (49534) ***(G-6939)***
Truemner Enterprises Inc 586 756-6470
25418 Ryan Rd Warren (48091) ***(G-17270)***
Truform Machine Inc 517 782-8523
2510 Precision St Jackson (49202) ***(G-8594)***
Truing Systems Inc 248 588-9060
1060 Chicago Rd Troy (48083) ***(G-16654)***
Trulife 800 492-1088
2010 E High St Jackson (49203) ***(G-8595)***
Trulife Inc (HQ) 517 787-1600
2010 E High St Jackson (49203) ***(G-8596)***
Trumpf Inc 734 354-9770
47711 Clipper St Plymouth (48170) ***(G-12783)***
Trusco, Grand Rapids *Also called Ginsan Liquidating Company LLC* ***(G-6443)***
Truss Development 248 624-8100
1573 S Telegraph Rd Bloomfield Hills (48302) ***(G-1808)***
Truss Technologies Inc 231 788-6330
404 S Maple Island Rd Muskegon (49442) ***(G-11443)***
Trussway 713 691-6900
8450 Winona Dr Jenison (49428) ***(G-8645)***
Trusted Tool Mfg Inc 810 750-6000
8075 Old Us 23 Fenton (48430) ***(G-5247)***
Trutron Corporation 248 583-9166
274 Executive Dr Troy (48083) ***(G-16655)***
TRW Atmtive Stering Suspension, Washington *Also called ZF Active Safety US Inc* ***(G-17315)***
TRW Auto Holdings Inc (HQ) 734 855-2600
12001 Tech Center Dr Livonia (48150) ***(G-9974)***
TRW Automotive Inc., Livonia *Also called ZF Active Safety US Inc* ***(G-10015)***
TRW Automotive JV LLC (HQ) 734 855-2787
12001 Tech Center Dr Livonia (48150) ***(G-9975)***
TRW Automotive US LLC 248 426-3901
23855 Research Dr Farmington Hills (48335) ***(G-5143)***
TRW East Inc 734 855-2600
12001 Tech Center Dr Livonia (48150) ***(G-9976)***
TRW Engineered Fas Components, Livonia *Also called Illinois Tool Works Inc* ***(G-9779)***
TRW Odyssey Mexico LLC 734 855-2600
12001 Tech Center Dr Livonia (48150) ***(G-9977)***
TRW Oss, Romeo *Also called ZF Passive Safety Systems US* ***(G-13643)***
Try Square Design, Troy *Also called Four-Way Tool and Die Inc* ***(G-16373)***
Tryco Inc 734 953-6800
23800 Research Dr Farmington Hills (48335) ***(G-5144)***
Trynex International LLC 248 586-3500
531 Ajax Dr Madison Heights (48071) ***(G-10371)***
TS Carbide Inc 248 486-8330
3131 Ruler Dr Commerce Township (48390) ***(G-3455)***
TS Enterprise Associates Inc 248 348-2963
110 W Main St Northville (48167) ***(G-11732)***
TS Silkscreen, Fremont *Also called HI-Lites Graphic Inc* ***(G-5776)***
Tsg Tooling Systems Group, Comstock Park *Also called Advanced Tooling Systems Inc* ***(G-3459)***
Tsg Tooling Systems Group.com, Grand Rapids *Also called Engineered Tooling Systems Inc* ***(G-6380)***
Tsk of America Inc (HQ) 517 542-2955
152 Simpson Dr Litchfield (49252) ***(G-9612)***
Tsm Corporation 248 276-4700
1175 N Opdyke Rd Auburn Hills (48326) ***(G-1032)***
TSS, Warren *Also called TSS Inc* ***(G-17271)***
TSS Inc 586 427-0070
21000 Hoover Rd Warren (48089) ***(G-17271)***
TST Tooling Software Tech LLC (PA) 248 922-9293
6547 Dixie Hwy Clarkston (48346) ***(G-2962)***
Tsunami Inc 989 497-5200
6235 Gratiot Rd Saginaw (48638) ***(G-14168)***
Ttg Automation, Temperance *Also called Bel-Kur Inc* ***(G-15823)***
Tu Way, Troy *Also called Tuway American Group Inc* ***(G-16658)***
Tube Assembly Manufacturing Co, Lexington *Also called Huron Inc* ***(G-9558)***
Tube Fab/Roman Engrg Co Inc 231 238-9366
1715 Michigan 68 Afton Afton (49705) ***(G-107)***
Tube Forming and Machine Inc 989 739-3323
4614 Industrial Row Oscoda (48750) ***(G-12223)***
Tube Wright Inc 810 227-4567
2111 Euler Rd Brighton (48114) ***(G-2000)***
Tube-Co Inc 586 775-0244
23094 Schoenherr Rd Warren (48089) ***(G-17272)***
Tubelite Inc (HQ) 800 866-2227
3056 Walker Ridge Dr Nw G Walker (49544) ***(G-16880)***
Tubelite Inc 800 866-2227
4878 Mackinaw Trl Reed City (49677) ***(G-13224)***
Tubergen Cutting Tools, Grand Rapids *Also called Saw Tubergen Service Inc* ***(G-6852)***
Tubesource Manufacturing Inc 248 543-4746
1600 E 9 Mile Rd Ferndale (48220) ***(G-5324)***
Tubular Metal Systems LLC (HQ) 989 879-2611
401 E 5th St Pinconning (48650) ***(G-12514)***
Tubular PDT Solutions NA LLC 248 388-4664
700 E Big Beaver Rd Ste F Troy (48083) ***(G-16656)***
Tubular Products Division, Grand Rapids *Also called Benteler Automotive Corp* ***(G-6212)***
Tuckey Concrete Products 989 872-4779
6062 Cass City Rd Cass City (48726) ***(G-2523)***
Tuff Automation Inc 616 735-3939
2751 Courier Dr Nw Grand Rapids (49534) ***(G-6940)***
Tuff Body Padding Company, Adrian *Also called Roto-Plastics Corporation* ***(G-92)***
Tulip US Holdings Inc (PA) 517 694-2300
1489 Cedar St Holt (48842) ***(G-7931)***
Tumbl Trak, Mount Pleasant *Also called T L V Inc* ***(G-11232)***
Tumblweed Weld/Fab 313 277-6860
3904 Campbell St Dearborn Heights (48125) ***(G-3799)***
Tunkers Inc 734 744-5990
36200 Mound Rd Sterling Heights (48310) ***(G-15531)***
Tunkers-Mastech, Sterling Heights *Also called Tunkers Inc* ***(G-15531)***
Tunnel Vision Brewery, Harbor Springs *Also called Harbor Sprng Vnyrds Winery LLC* ***(G-7283)***
Tunnel Vision Pipeline Svcs, Escanaba *Also called Upper Peninsula Rubber Co Inc* ***(G-4864)***
Tuocai America LLC 248 346-5910
5700 Crooks Rd Ste 222 Troy (48098) ***(G-16657)***
Tupes of Saginaw Inc 989 799-1550
2858 Enterprise Ct Saginaw (48603) ***(G-14169)***
Turbine Conversions Ltd 616 837-9428
18155 120th Ave Nunica (49448) ***(G-12045)***
Turbine Tool & Gage Inc 734 427-2270
11901 Brookfield St Livonia (48150) ***(G-9978)***
Turbo-Spray Midwest Inc (PA) 517 548-9096
1172 Fendt Dr Ste 3 Howell (48843) ***(G-8116)***
Turbosocks Performance 586 864-3252
50765 Cedargrove Rd Shelby Township (48317) ***(G-14712)***
Turchetti Spaghetti Co LLC 616 706-4766
1535 Industrial Park Dr Hart (49420) ***(G-7380)***

ALPHABETIC

(PA)=Parent Co (HQ)=Headquarters (DH)=Div Headquarters
2020 Harris Michigan Industrial Directory
1095

Turkey Creek Inc....517 451-5221
7279 Smith Rd Tecumseh (49286) *(G-15814)*
Turn Key Automotive LLC....248 628-5556
3200 Adventure Ln 32-64 Oxford (48371) *(G-12378)*
Turn Key Harness & Wire LLC....248 236-9915
465 S Glaspie St Oxford (48371) *(G-12379)*
Turn Key/Redico, Oxford *Also called Turn Key Automotive LLC (G-12378)*
Turn One Inc....989 652-2778
1260 S Beyer Rd Saginaw (48601) *(G-14170)*
Turn Tech Inc....586 415-8090
33901 Riviera Fraser (48026) *(G-5742)*
Turner Business Forms Inc (PA)....989 752-5540
19 Slatestone Dr Saginaw (48603) *(G-14171)*
Turner Business Forms Inc....810 244-6980
1016 Professional Dr Flint (48532) *(G-5515)*
Turnkey Fabrication LLC....616 248-9116
1530 Eastern Ave Se Grand Rapids (49507) *(G-6941)*
Turpeinen Bros Inc....906 338-2870
12920 State Highway M38 Pelkie (49958) *(G-12424)*
Turris Italian Foods Inc (PA)....586 773-6010
16695 Common Rd Roseville (48066) *(G-13883)*
Tuscarora Inc -Vs....989 729-2780
123 N Chipman St Owosso (48867) *(G-12325)*
Tuscola County Advertiser Inc (PA)....989 673-3181
344 N State St Caro (48723) *(G-2479)*
Tuscola County Advertiser Inc....517 673-3181
344 N State St Caro (48723) *(G-2480)*
Tuscola County Advertiser Inc....989 823-8651
5881 Frankenmuth Rd Vassar (48768) *(G-16815)*
Tuscola Energy....989 894-5815
920 N Water St Ste 204 Bay City (48708) *(G-1364)*
Tuteur Inc....269 983-1246
1721 Lakeshore Dr Saint Joseph (49085) *(G-14344)*
Tuthill Farms & Composting....248 437-7354
10505 Tuthill Rd South Lyon (48178) *(G-14815)*
Tuttle Forest Products....906 283-3871
1964 W Hwy Us 2 Gulliver (49840) *(G-7214)*
Tuway American Group Inc....248 205-9999
3155 W Big Beaver Rd # 104 Troy (48084) *(G-16658)*
Tva Kane Inc (PA)....248 946-4670
45380 W 10 Mile Rd # 100 Novi (48375) *(G-12019)*
Tvb Inc....616 456-9629
544 Richmond St Nw Grand Rapids (49504) *(G-6942)*
Twb Company LLC (HQ)....734 289-6400
1600 Nadeau Rd Monroe (48162) *(G-11080)*
Twb of Indiana Inc....734 289-6400
1600 Nadeau Rd Monroe (48162) *(G-11081)*
Tweddle Group Inc (PA)....586 307-3700
24700 Maplehurst Dr Clinton Township (48036) *(G-3252)*
Tweddle Group Inc....586 840-3275
2111 Woodward Ave 8f Detroit (48201) *(G-4410)*
TWI, Ferndale *Also called Thermal Wave Imaging Inc (G-5321)*
Twin Ash Frms Organic Proc LLC....810 404-1943
4175 Mushroom Rd Snover (48472) *(G-14744)*
Twin Bay Dock and Products....231 943-8420
982 E Commerce Dr Ste B Traverse City (49685) *(G-16131)*
Twin Bay Medical, Williamsburg *Also called Saint-Gobain Prfmce Plas Corp (G-17720)*
Twin Beginnings LLC (PA)....248 542-6250
13308 Lasalle Blvd Huntington Woods (48070) *(G-8192)*
Twin Cities Orthotic & Prosthe....269 428-2910
3538 Magnolia Ln Saint Joseph (49085) *(G-14345)*
Twin City Engraving Company....269 983-0601
1232 Broad St Saint Joseph (49085) *(G-14346)*
Twin City Foods Inc....616 374-4002
801 Lincoln St Lake Odessa (48849) *(G-9120)*
Twin City Optical, Traverse City *Also called Essilor Laboratories Amer Inc (G-15966)*
Twin Mold and Engineering LLC....586 532-8558
51738 Filomena Dr Shelby Township (48315) *(G-14713)*
Twin Pines, Detroit *Also called C F Burger Creamery Co (G-3925)*
Twinlab Holdings Inc....800 645-5626
3133 Orchard Vista Dr Se Grand Rapids (49546) *(G-6943)*
Twist....248 859-2169
6331 Haggerty Rd West Bloomfield (48322) *(G-17503)*
Twm Technology LLC....989 684-7050
3490 E North Union Rd Bay City (48706) *(G-1365)*
Two Feathers Enterprise LLC....231 924-3612
1117 S Baldwin Ave Fremont (49412) *(G-5785)*
Two James Spirits LLC....313 964-4800
2445 Michigan Ave Detroit (48216) *(G-4411)*
Two Mitts Inc (PA)....800 888-5054
600 Plastics Pl Kalamazoo (49001) *(G-8915)*
Tyde Group Worldwide LLC....248 879-7656
5700 Crooks Rd Ste 207 Troy (48098) *(G-16659)*
Tyes Inc....888 219-6301
5236 W 1st St Ludington (49431) *(G-10083)*
Tyght Defense....616 427-3760
4409 Carol Ave Sw Wyoming (49519) *(G-18037)*
Tygrus LLC....248 218-0347
1134 E Big Beaver Rd Troy (48083) *(G-16660)*

Tyler Crockett Marine Engines....810 324-2720
4600 Brott Rd North Street (48049) *(G-11669)*
Tyler Technologies Inc....734 677-0550
525 Avis Dr Ste 3 Ann Arbor (48108) *(G-684)*
Tyrone Tool Company Inc....810 742-4762
3336 Associates Dr Burton (48529) *(G-2168)*
Tyson....231 922-3214
2314 Sybrant Rd Traverse City (49684) *(G-16132)*
Tyson Foods Inc....231 929-2456
845 Bertina Ln Traverse City (49696) *(G-16133)*
Tyson Foods /Hr....616 875-2311
8300 96th Ave Zeeland (49464) *(G-18190)*
Tyson Fresh Meats Inc....248 213-1000
26999 Central Park Blvd Southfield (48076) *(G-15051)*
Tzamco Inc (PA)....248 624-7710
1060 W West Maple Rd Walled Lake (48390) *(G-16904)*
U C P, Grand Rapids *Also called Universal Consumer Pdts Inc (G-6953)*
U E I, Grand Rapids *Also called Uei Inc (G-6944)*
U K Edm Ltd....248 437-9500
8192 Boardwalk Rd Brighton (48116) *(G-2001)*
U K Sailmakers, Clinton Township *Also called Performance Sailing Inc (G-3193)*
U P Concrete Pipe, Escanaba *Also called Upper Peninsula Con Pipe Co (G-4863)*
U P Fabricating Co Inc (PA)....906 475-4400
120 Us Highway 41 E Ste A Negaunee (49866) *(G-11478)*
U P Fabricating Co Inc....906 341-2868
342 Elm St Manistique (49854) *(G-10446)*
U P Machine & Engineering Co....906 497-5278
N15930 Main St Powers (49874) *(G-13079)*
U S Baird Corporation....616 826-5013
8121 108th St Se Middleville (49333) *(G-10811)*
U S Distributing Inc....248 646-0550
2333 Cole St Birmingham (48009) *(G-1707)*
U S Engineering, Grand Rapids *Also called J W Holdings Inc (G-6549)*
U S Equipment Co (HQ)....313 526-8300
3667 Merriweather Ln Rochester Hills (48306) *(G-13533)*
U S Fabrication & Design LLC....248 919-2910
32890 Capitol St Livonia (48150) *(G-9979)*
U S Farathane Port Huron LLC....248 754-7000
2700 High Meadow Cir Auburn Hills (48326) *(G-1033)*
U S Graphite Inc (PA)....989 755-0441
1620 E Holland Ave Saginaw (48601) *(G-14172)*
U S Group Inc (PA)....313 372-7900
3667 Merriweather Ln Rochester Hills (48306) *(G-13534)*
U S Ice Corp....313 862-3344
10625 W 8 Mile Rd Detroit (48221) *(G-4412)*
U S Speedo Inc....810 244-0909
6050 Birch Rd Flint (48507) *(G-5516)*
U S Target Inc....586 445-3131
16472 Common Rd Roseville (48066) *(G-13884)*
U S Tool & Cutter Co....248 553-7745
42525 W 11 Mile Rd Novi (48375) *(G-12020)*
U-Haul, Novi *Also called Novi Manufacturing Co (G-11958)*
U-Shin America Inc....248 449-3155
40000 Grand River Ave # 105 Novi (48375) *(G-12021)*
U.P. Action News, Escanaba *Also called Ogden Newspapers Inc (G-4850)*
U.P. Machine, Powers *Also called U P Machine & Engineering Co (G-13079)*
U.S. Farathane Corp, Shelby Township *Also called US Farathane Holdings Corp (G-14714)*
U.S. Wire & Rope, Detroit *Also called US Wire Rope Supply Inc (G-4417)*
Uacj Auto Whitehall Inds Inc....231 845-5101
801 S Madison St Ludington (49431) *(G-10084)*
Uacj Automotive Whitehall Inds....231 845-5101
4960 Progress Dr Ludington (49431) *(G-10085)*
Ualoy, Roseville *Also called Upton Industries Inc (G-13887)*
Uantum Lifecare, Holly *Also called Quantum Ventures LLC (G-7892)*
Ube Industries, Ann Arbor *Also called Ube Machinery Inc (G-685)*
Ube Machinery Inc....734 741-7000
5700 S State Rd Ann Arbor (48108) *(G-685)*
Uc Holdings Inc (PA)....248 728-8642
300 Galleria Officentre Southfield (48034) *(G-15052)*
Ucb Advertising....269 808-2411
12047 Oakridge Rd Plainwell (49080) *(G-12550)*
Uchiyama Mktg & Dev Amer LLC....248 859-3986
46805 Magellan Dr Novi (48377) *(G-12022)*
Uckele Health & Nutrition, Blissfield *Also called Uckele Health and Nutrition (G-1729)*
Uckele Health and Nutrition (PA)....800 248-0330
5600 Silberhorn Hwy Blissfield (49228) *(G-1729)*
Ucp, White Pigeon *Also called Universal Consumer Pdts Inc (G-17656)*
Uei Inc....616 361-6093
2771 West River Dr Nw Grand Rapids (49544) *(G-6944)*
Ufi Filters Usa Inc....248 376-0441
50 W Big Beavr Rd Ste 440 Troy (48084) *(G-16661)*
Ufi Filters Usa Inc....248 376-0441
50 W Big Beavr Rd Ste 440 Troy (48084) *(G-16662)*
Ufm, Hazel Park *Also called Universal Flow Monitors Inc (G-7457)*
Ufp Atlantic LLC....616 364-6161
2801 E Beltline Ave Ne Grand Rapids (49525) *(G-6945)*
Ufp Eastern Division Inc (HQ)....616 364-6161
2801 E Beltline Ave Ne Grand Rapids (49525) *(G-6946)*

Ufp Grand Rapids LLC 616 464-1650
825 Buchanan Ave Sw Grand Rapids (49507) ***(G-6947)***

Ufp Lansing LLC 517 322-0025
2509 Snow Rd Lansing (48917) ***(G-9328)***

Ufp Technologies, Grand Rapids *Also called Simco Automotive Trim Inc* ***(G-6865)***

Ufp Technologies Inc 616 949-8100
3831 Patterson Ave Se Grand Rapids (49512) ***(G-6948)***

Ufp West Central LLC 616 364-6161
2801 E Beltline Ave Ne Grand Rapids (49525) ***(G-6949)***

Ugs, Troy *Also called United Global Sourcing Inc* ***(G-16663)***

Uis Industries LLC 734 443-3737
39111 6 Mile Rd Livonia (48152) ***(G-9980)***

Ultimate Bed, Menominee *Also called Anderson Manufacturing Co Inc* ***(G-10723)***

Ultimate Highway Solutions, Grand Haven *Also called Alternate Number Five Inc* ***(G-5991)***

Ultimate Manufacturing Inc 313 538-6212
12125 Dixie Redford (48239) ***(G-13203)***

Ultimate Software Group Inc 517 540-9718
809 E Grand River Ave A Howell (48843) ***(G-8117)***

Ultimate Systems, Madison Heights *Also called Usi Inc* ***(G-10375)***

Ultimate Turf of Flint LLC 810 202-0203
1054 W Schumacher Ave Flint (48507) ***(G-5517)***

Ultimation Industries LLC 586 771-1881
15935 Sturgeon St Roseville (48066) ***(G-13885)***

Ultra Derm Systems, Saginaw *Also called J & B Products Ltd* ***(G-14065)***

Ultra Fab & Machine Inc 248 628-7065
465 S Glaspie St Ste D Oxford (48371) ***(G-12380)***

Ultra Forms Plus Inc 269 337-6000
301 Peekstock Rd Kalamazoo (49001) ***(G-8916)***

Ultra Printing 248 352-7238
22850 Inkster Rd Southfield (48033) ***(G-15053)***

Ultra Stitch Embroidery 586 498-5600
16627 Eastland St Roseville (48066) ***(G-13886)***

Ultra-Dex Tooling Systems, Flushing *Also called MB Liquidating Corporation* ***(G-5541)***

Ultra-Dex USA LLC 810 638-5388
7144 Sheridan Rd Flushing (48433) ***(G-5543)***

Ultra-Grip International Div, Commerce Township *Also called Three M Tool & Machine Inc* ***(G-3454)***

Ultra-Sonic Extrusion Dies Inc 586 791-8550
34863 Groesbeck Hwy Clinton Township (48035) ***(G-3253)***

Ultra-Tech Printing Co 616 249-0500
5851 Crossrds Cmmrce Pkwy Wyoming (49519) ***(G-18038)***

Ultra-Temp Corporation 810 794-4709
7270 Flamingo St Clay (48001) ***(G-3005)***

Ultraform Industries Inc 586 752-4508
150 Peyerk Ct Bruce Twp (48065) ***(G-2105)***

Ultralight Prosthetics Inc 313 538-8500
24781 5 Mile Rd Redford (48239) ***(G-13204)***

Ultramouse Ltd 734 761-1144
1442 E Park Pl Ann Arbor (48104) ***(G-686)***

Um Orthotics Pros Cntr 734 764-3100
2500 Green Rd Ste 100 Ann Arbor (48105) ***(G-687)***

Umakanth Consultants Inc 517 347-7500
3581 Cabaret Trl Okemos (48864) ***(G-12139)***

Umi, Holland *Also called United Manufacturing Inc* ***(G-7842)***

Umix Dissoultion Corp 586 446-9950
6050 15 Mile Rd Sterling Heights (48312) ***(G-15532)***

Uncle Eds Oil Shoppes Inc 269 962-0999
2050 Columbia Ave W Battle Creek (49015) ***(G-1262)***

Uncle Eds Oil Shoppes Inc 248 288-4738
1116 W 14 Mile Rd Clawson (48017) ***(G-2988)***

Uncle Johns Cider Mill Inc 989 224-3686
8614 N Us Highway 27 Saint Johns (48879) ***(G-14298)***

Uncle Rays LLC 313 739-6035
14300 Ilene St Detroit (48238) ***(G-4413)***

Uncle Rays LLC (HQ) 313 834-0800
14245 Birwood St Detroit (48238) ***(G-4414)***

Uncle Rons Woodworking 248 585-7837
611 W Girard Ave Madison Heights (48071) ***(G-10372)***

Unco Automotive Products, Livonia *Also called Mid-West Screw Products Co* ***(G-9843)***

Under Pressure Pwr Washers LLC 616 292-4289
885 Meyer Ln Marne (49435) ***(G-10514)***

Undercar Products Group Inc 616 719-4571
4247 Eastern Ave Se Wyoming (49508) ***(G-18039)***

Underground Bev Brands LLC 248 336-9383
800 N Rembrandt Ave Royal Oak (48067) ***(G-13977)***

Underground Printing, Ann Arbor *Also called A-1 Screenprinting LLC* ***(G-335)***

Underhill Logging, Big Rapids *Also called Chris Underhill* ***(G-1624)***

Understated Corrugated LLC 248 880-5767
635 Horton St Northville (48167) ***(G-11733)***

Ungar Frozen Food Product 248 626-3148
1556 Lone Pine Rd Bloomfield Hills (48302) ***(G-1809)***

UNI Vue Inc 248 545-0810
2424 Wolcott St Ferndale (48220) ***(G-5325)***

UNI-Bond Brake, Ferndale *Also called Grattan Family Enterprises LLC* ***(G-5290)***

Uniband Usa LLC 616 676-6011
2555 Oak Industrial Dr Ne C Grand Rapids (49505) ***(G-6950)***

Unicor, Norton Shores *Also called Dama Tool & Gauge Company* ***(G-11747)***

Unicote Corporation 586 296-0700
33165 Groesbeck Hwy Fraser (48026) ***(G-5743)***

Unifab Cages, Portage *Also called Unifab Corporation* ***(G-13051)***

Unifab Corporation 269 382-2803
5260 Lovers Ln Portage (49002) ***(G-13051)***

Unified Brands Inc 989 644-3331
525 S Coldwater Rd Weidman (48893) ***(G-17462)***

Unified Industries Inc (HQ) 517 546-3220
1033 Sutton St Howell (48843) ***(G-8118)***

Unified Screening and Crushing 888 464-9473
305 E Walker Rd Saint Johns (48879) ***(G-14299)***

Unified Tool and Die Inc 517 768-8070
2010 Micor Dr Jackson (49203) ***(G-8597)***

Unifilter Company, Novi *Also called Unifilter Inc* ***(G-12023)***

Unifilter Inc 248 476-5100
43800 Grand River Ave Novi (48375) ***(G-12023)***

Uniflex Inc 248 486-6000
7830 Lochlin Dr Brighton (48116) ***(G-2002)***

Unigraphics 517 337-9316
6049 Skyline Dr East Lansing (48823) ***(G-4681)***

Unigraphics Print & Copy, East Lansing *Also called Unigraphics* ***(G-4681)***

Unilock Michigan Inc 248 437-1380
12591 Emerson Dr Brighton (48116) ***(G-2003)***

Uniloy Inc 514 424-8900
5550 S Occidental Rd B Tecumseh (49286) ***(G-15815)***

Unimerco Group A/S, Saline *Also called Kyocera Unimerco Tooling Inc* ***(G-14397)***

Union Built PC Inc 248 910-3955
4202 Ann Arbor Rd Jackson (49202) ***(G-8598)***

Union Commissary LLC 248 795-2483
64 S Main St Clarkston (48346) ***(G-2963)***

Union First Promotions, Grand Rapids *Also called Versatility Inc* ***(G-6967)***

Union Kitchen, Clarkston *Also called Union Commissary LLC* ***(G-2963)***

Union Pallet & Cont Co Inc 517 279-4888
161 Race St Coldwater (49036) ***(G-3339)***

Unique Fabricating Inc (PA) 248 853-2333
800 Standard Pkwy Auburn Hills (48326) ***(G-1034)***

Unique Fabricating Inc 248 853-2333
2817 Bond St Rochester Hills (48309) ***(G-13535)***

Unique Fabricating Na Inc (HQ) 248 853-2333
800 Standard Pkwy Auburn Hills (48326) ***(G-1035)***

Unique Fabricating Na Inc 517 524-9010
13221 Allman Rd Concord (49237) ***(G-3526)***

Unique Food Management Inc 248 738-9393
248 S Telegraph Rd Pontiac (48341) ***(G-12872)***

Unique Molded Foam Tech Inc 517 524-9010
13221 Allman Rd Concord (49237) ***(G-3527)***

Unique Namecraft Inc 906 863-3644
N297 River Dr Menominee (49858) ***(G-10759)***

Unique Products 616 794-3800
7205 Whites Bridge Rd Belding (48809) ***(G-1430)***

Unique Reproductions Inc 248 788-2887
5470 Carol Run S West Bloomfield (48322) ***(G-17504)***

Unique Shape Fabricating, Clarkston *Also called Oblut Ltd* ***(G-2941)***

Unique Tool & Mfg Co Inc 734 850-1050
100 Reed Dr Temperance (48182) ***(G-15846)***

Unique Truck Accessories, Sturgis *Also called Lake Fabricators Inc* ***(G-15611)***

Unique-Intasco Usa Inc 810 982-3360
800 Standard Pkwy Auburn Hills (48326) ***(G-1036)***

Unirak, Taylor *Also called F & F Industries Inc* ***(G-15718)***

Unislat LLC 616 844-4211
13660 172nd Ave Grand Haven (49417) ***(G-6091)***

Unisorb Inc (HQ) 517 764-6060
4117 Felters Rd Ste A Michigan Center (49254) ***(G-10792)***

Unisorb Installation Tech, Michigan Center *Also called Unisorb Inc* ***(G-10792)***

Unist Inc (PA) 616 949-0853
4134 36th St Se Grand Rapids (49512) ***(G-6951)***

Unistrut, Wayne *Also called Allied Support Systems* ***(G-17421)***

Unistrut Diversified Products, Wayne *Also called Unistrut International Corp* ***(G-17445)***

Unistrut International Corp 734 721-4040
4205 Elizabeth St Wayne (48184) ***(G-17445)***

Unit Step Company Inc 989 684-9361
3788 S Huron Rd Bay City (48706) ***(G-1366)***

United Abrasive Inc (PA) 906 563-9249
19100 Industrial Dr Vulcan (49892) ***(G-16846)***

United Brass Manufacturers Inc (PA) 734 941-0700
35030 Goddard Rd Romulus (48174) ***(G-13736)***

United Brass Manufacturers Inc 734 942-9224
39000 W Huron River Dr Romulus (48174) ***(G-13737)***

United Collision 269 792-7274
125 Railroad St Wayland (49348) ***(G-17418)***

United Dowel Pin Mfg Co, Fraser *Also called United States Socket* ***(G-5744)***

United Engineered Tooling 231 947-3650
1974 Cass Hartman Ct Traverse City (49685) ***(G-16134)***

United Fabricating Company 248 887-7289
160 N Saint John Rd Highland (48357) ***(G-7501)***

United Fabrications, Livonia *Also called J & J United Industries LLC* ***(G-9787)***

United Fbrcnts Strainrite Corp 800 487-3136
481 N Saginaw St Ste A Pontiac (48342) ***(G-12873)***

United Foam A Ufp Tech Brnd...616 949-8100
3831 Patterson Ave Se Grand Rapids (49512) ***(G-6952)***
United Foam Products, Grand Rapids *Also called Ufp Technologies Inc* ***(G-6948)***
United Fr Survl St Joseph Recy...269 983-3820
2215 Wilson Ct Saint Joseph (49085) ***(G-14347)***
United Global Sourcing Inc (PA)...248 952-5700
5607 New King Dr Ste 100 Troy (48098) ***(G-16663)***
United Kennel Club Inc...269 343-9020
100 E Kilgore Rd Portage (49002) ***(G-13052)***
United Lighting Standards Inc (PA)...586 774-5650
23171 Groesbeck Hwy Warren (48089) ***(G-17273)***
United Machining Inc (HQ)...586 323-4300
6300 18 1/2 Mile Rd Sterling Heights (48314) ***(G-15533)***
United Machining Inc...586 323-4300
51362 Quadrate Dr Macomb (48042) ***(G-10171)***
United Manufacturing Inc...616 738-8888
4150 Sunnyside Dr Holland (49424) ***(G-7842)***
United Metal Products, Detroit *Also called A & R Specialty Services Corp* ***(G-3826)***
United Metal Technology Inc...517 787-7940
144 W Monroe St Jackson (49202) ***(G-8599)***
United Mfg Netwrk Inc...586 321-7887
14500 E 11 Mile Rd Warren (48089) ***(G-17274)***
United Mill & Cabinet Company...734 482-1981
8842 Bunton Rd Willis (48191) ***(G-17745)***
United Paint & Chemical, Southfield *Also called Polymer Inc* ***(G-15001)***
United Paint and Chemical Corp...248 353-3035
24671 Telegraph Rd Southfield (48033) ***(G-15054)***
United Paravis Cnc, Auburn Hills *Also called Paravis Industries Inc* ***(G-970)***
United Precision Pdts Co Inc...313 292-0100
25040 Van Born Rd Dearborn Heights (48125) ***(G-3800)***
United Resin Inc (PA)...800 521-4757
4359 Normandy Ct Royal Oak (48073) ***(G-13978)***
United Shield Intl LLC...231 933-1179
1462 International Dr Traverse City (49686) ***(G-16135)***
United State Phrm Group...734 462-3685
39209 6 Mile Rd Livonia (48152) ***(G-9981)***
United States Gypsum Company...269 384-6335
320 N Farmer St Otsego (49078) ***(G-12257)***
United States Gypsum Company...313 624-4232
10090 W Jefferson Ave River Rouge (48218) ***(G-13282)***
United States Gypsum Company...313 842-4455
10090 W Jefferson Ave Detroit (48218) ***(G-4415)***
United States Marble, Remus *Also called Usm Acquisition LLC* ***(G-13243)***
United States Ski Pole Company, Cheboygan *Also called Liebner Enterprises LLC* ***(G-2686)***
United States Socket (PA)...586 469-8811
33675 Riviera Fraser (48026) ***(G-5744)***
United States Steel Corp...313 749-2100
1 Quality Dr Ecorse (48229) ***(G-4747)***
United Systems...248 583-9670
525 Elmwood Dr Troy (48083) ***(G-16664)***
United Systems Group LLC (PA)...810 227-4567
2111 Euler Rd Brighton (48114) ***(G-2004)***
United Technologies, Taylor *Also called Lear Corporation* ***(G-15734)***
United Tool, Traverse City *Also called United Engineered Tooling* ***(G-16134)***
Universal / Devlieg Inc...989 752-3077
1270 Agricola Dr Saginaw (48604) ***(G-14173)***
Universal Brick System, Charlotte *Also called K-Tel Corporation* ***(G-2657)***
Universal Casket Co...269 476-2163
17664 Chain Lake St Cassopolis (49031) ***(G-2537)***
Universal Coating Inc...810 785-7555
5204 Energy Dr Flint (48505) ***(G-5518)***
Universal Coating Technology...616 847-6036
16891 Johnson St Ste A Grand Haven (49417) ***(G-6092)***
Universal Components LLC...517 861-7064
510 S Hughes Rd Howell (48843) ***(G-8119)***
Universal Consumer Pdts Inc...616 365-4201
68956 Us Highway 131 White Pigeon (49099) ***(G-17656)***
Universal Consumer Pdts Inc (HQ)...616 364-6161
2801 E Beltline Ave Ne Grand Rapids (49525) ***(G-6953)***
Universal Container Corp...248 543-2788
10750 Galaxie Ave Ferndale (48220) ***(G-5326)***
Universal Fabricators Inc...248 399-7565
25855 Commerce Dr Madison Heights (48071) ***(G-10373)***
Universal Flow Monitors Inc (PA)...248 542-9635
1755 E 9 Mile Rd Hazel Park (48030) ***(G-7457)***
Universal Forest Products, Lansing *Also called Ufp Lansing LLC* ***(G-9328)***
Universal Forest Products, Grand Rapids *Also called Ufp Eastern Division Inc* ***(G-6946)***
Universal Forest Products Inc (PA)...616 364-6161
2801 E Beltline Ave Ne Grand Rapids (49525) ***(G-6954)***
Universal Handling Eqpt, Owosso *Also called Universal Hdlg Eqp Owosso LLC* ***(G-12326)***
Universal Hdlg Eqp Owosso LLC...989 720-1650
1650 Industrial Dr Owosso (48867) ***(G-12326)***
Universal Heating and Cooling...734 216-5826
6301 Pontiac Trl South Lyon (48178) ***(G-14816)***
Universal Impex Inc...734 306-6684
1619 Mclaine St Canton (48188) ***(G-2437)***
Universal Induction Inc...269 925-9890
352 W Britain Ave Benton Harbor (49022) ***(G-1557)***

Universal Laundry Machinery, Westland *Also called Kah* ***(G-17576)***
Universal Led, Detroit *Also called Lighting Enterprises Inc* ***(G-4205)***
Universal Magnetics Inc...231 937-5555
5555 N Amy School Rd Howard City (49329) ***(G-8007)***
Universal Manufacturing Co...586 463-2560
43900 N Groesbeck Hwy Clinton Township (48036) ***(G-3254)***
Universal Print...989 525-5055
2758 E Fisher Rd Bay City (48706) ***(G-1367)***
Universal Printing Company Inc...989 671-9409
1200 Woodside Ave Bay City (48708) ***(G-1368)***
Universal Product Mktg LLC...248 585-9959
854 Edgemont Park Grosse Pointe Park (48230) ***(G-7197)***
Universal Products Inc...231 937-5555
210 Rockford Park Dr Ne Rockford (49341) ***(G-13595)***
Universal Sftwr Solutions Inc...810 653-5000
1334 S Irish Rd Davison (48423) ***(G-3664)***
Universal Sign Inc...616 554-9999
5001 Falcon View Ave Se Grand Rapids (49512) ***(G-6955)***
Universal Spiral Air, Walker *Also called Krupp Industries LLC* ***(G-16870)***
Universal Sprial Air, Livonia *Also called Krupp Industries LLC* ***(G-9801)***
Universal Stamping Inc...269 925-5300
1570 Townline Rd Benton Harbor (49022) ***(G-1558)***
Universal Tire Recycling Inc (PA)...313 429-1212
19106 Livernois Ave Detroit (48221) ***(G-4416)***
Universal Tl Eqp & Contrls Inc...586 268-4380
42409 Van Dyke Ave Sterling Heights (48314) ***(G-15534)***
Universal Tool Inc...248 733-9800
552 Robbins Dr Troy (48083) ***(G-16665)***
Universal Trim Inc...248 586-3300
1451 E Lincoln Ave Madison Heights (48071) ***(G-10374)***
Universal Tube Inc...248 853-5100
2607 Bond St Rochester Hills (48309) ***(G-13536)***
Universal Warranty Corpor...248 263-6900
300 Galleria Officentre Southfield (48034) ***(G-15055)***
Universal/Devlieg LLC...989 752-7700
1270 Agricola Dr Saginaw (48604) ***(G-14174)***
University Michigan Software, Ann Arbor *Also called Regents of The University Mich* ***(G-617)***
University of Michigan Press, Ann Arbor *Also called Regents of The University Mich* ***(G-616)***
University Plastics Inc...734 668-8773
7150 Jackson Rd Ann Arbor (48103) ***(G-688)***
Univesity Michigan-Dearborn...313 593-5428
4901 Evergreen Rd # 2130 Dearborn (48128) ***(G-3767)***
Unlimited Marine Inc...248 249-0222
7775 Highland Rd White Lake (48383) ***(G-17641)***
Unoco Exploration Co...231 829-3235
23382 17 Mile Rd Leroy (49655) ***(G-9539)***
Unytrex Inc...810 796-9074
5901 Dryden Rd Dryden (48428) ***(G-4572)***
Up Catholic Newspaper...906 226-8821
347 Rock St Marquette (49855) ***(G-10560)***
UP Coin & Cultivation LLC (PA)...906 341-4769
321 Deer St Manistique (49854) ***(G-10447)***
Up North Publications Inc...231 587-8471
112 E State St Mancelona (49659) ***(G-10400)***
Up North Spices Inc...419 346-4155
612 E 4th St Royal Oak (48067) ***(G-13979)***
Up Officeexpress LLC...906 281-0089
53091 Dover Rd Calumet (49913) ***(G-2334)***
Up To Date Painting, Millington *Also called Home Style Co* ***(G-10996)***
UP Truck Center Inc...906 774-0098
4920 Menominee St Quinnesec (49876) ***(G-13103)***
Upcycle Polymers LLC...248 446-8750
1145 Sutton St Howell (48843) ***(G-8120)***
UPF Group PLC, Flint *Also called UPF Inc* ***(G-5519)***
UPF Inc...810 768-0001
2851 James P Cole Blvd Flint (48505) ***(G-5519)***
Upnorth Design & Repair Inc...231 824-6025
10811 E 20 Rd Manton (49663) ***(G-10458)***
Upper Level Graphics Inc...734 525-7111
13193 Wayne Rd Livonia (48150) ***(G-9982)***
Upper Michigan Newspapers LLC...989 732-5125
1966 S Otsego Ave Gaylord (49735) ***(G-5898)***
Upper Peninsula Con Pipe Co (PA)...906 786-0934
6480 Us Hwy 2 Escanaba (49829) ***(G-4863)***
Upper Peninsula Rubber Co Inc...906 786-0460
2101 N 19th St Bldg B Escanaba (49829) ***(G-4864)***
UPS Stores , The, Eastpointe *Also called Crk Ltd* ***(G-4699)***
Upston Associates Inc...269 349-2782
5 Minges Ln Battle Creek (49015) ***(G-1263)***
Upton Industries Inc...586 771-1200
30435 Groesbeck Hwy Ste 2 Roseville (48066) ***(G-13887)***
Urban Specialty Apparel Inc...248 395-9500
29540 Southfield Rd # 102 Southfield (48076) ***(G-15056)***
Urefer Inc...734 585-5684
912 N Main St Ste 100 Ann Arbor (48104) ***(G-689)***
Urgent Design and Mfg Inc...810 245-1300
2547 Product Dr Lapeer (48446) ***(G-9489)***
Urgent Plastic Services Inc (PA)...248 852-8999
2777 Product Dr Rochester Hills (48309) ***(G-13537)***

ALPHABETIC SECTION — Valeo North America Inc

URS Energy & Construction Inc 989 642-4190
12334 Geddes Rd Hemlock (48626) *(G-7464)*

US 223 Inland Marine LLC 517 547-2628
17250 Us Highway 223 Addison (49220) *(G-40)*

US Bio Carbon LLC 616 334-9862
435 N Lake Dr Caledonia (49316) *(G-2320)*

US Boring Inc 586 756-7511
24895 Mound Rd Ste D Warren (48091) *(G-17275)*

US Energia LLC 248 669-1462
400 Water St Ste 250 Rochester (48307) *(G-13356)*

US Energy Systems Inc 248 765-7995
1761 John R Rd Rochester Hills (48307) *(G-13538)*

US Farathane Corp 248 754-7000
2700 High Meadow Cir Auburn Hills (48326) *(G-1037)*

US Farathane Holdings Corp 586 726-1200
38000 Mound Rd Sterling Heights (48310) *(G-15535)*

US Farathane Holdings Corp (PA) 586 726-1200
11650 Park Ct Shelby Township (48315) *(G-14714)*

US Farathane Holdings Corp 586 978-2800
750 W Maple Rd Troy (48084) *(G-16666)*

US Farathane Holdings Corp 248 754-7000
2133 Petit St Port Huron (48060) *(G-12974)*

US Farathane Holdings Corp 248 754-7000
11650 Park Ct Bldg B Shelby Township (48315) *(G-14715)*

US Farathane Holdings Corp 248 754-7000
325 W Silverbell Rd # 220 Lake Orion (48359) *(G-9168)*

US Farathane Holdings Corp 586 991-6922
6543 Arrow Dr Sterling Heights (48314) *(G-15536)*

US Farathane Holdings Corp 780 246-1034
1350 Harmon Rd Auburn Hills (48326) *(G-1038)*

US Farathane Holdings Corp 248 391-6801
2082 Brown Rd Auburn Hills (48326) *(G-1039)*

US Farathane Holdings Corp 586 978-2800
39200 Ford Rd Westland (48185) *(G-17607)*

US Farathane Holdings Corp 586 685-4000
42155 Merrill Rd Sterling Heights (48314) *(G-15537)*

US Farathane Holdings Corp 248 754-7000
2700 High Meadow Cir Auburn Hills (48326) *(G-1040)*

US Farathane Holdings Corp 248 754-7000
4872 S Lapeer Rd Orion (48359) *(G-12191)*

US Farathane Merrill Plant, Sterling Heights Also called US Farathane Holdings Corp *(G-15537)*

US Green Energy Solutions LLC 810 955-2992
9532 Harrison St Livonia (48150) *(G-9983)*

US Guys Deer Processing LLC 616 642-0967
7661 Bluewater Hwy Saranac (48881) *(G-14456)*

US Gypsum Co 313 842-5800
10090 W Jefferson Ave River Rouge (48218) *(G-13283)*

US Jack Company 269 925-7777
1125 Industrial Ct Benton Harbor (49022) *(G-1559)*

US Printers 906 639-3100
W4763 Okwood Rd 30 Daggett (49821) *(G-3623)*

US Salon Supply LLC 616 365-5790
760 S Kalamazoo St Paw Paw (49079) *(G-12415)*

US Trade LLC 800 676-0208
29145 Warren Rd Garden City (48135) *(G-5845)*

US Wire Rope Supply Inc 313 925-0444
6555 Sherwood St Detroit (48211) *(G-4417)*

Us-Bingo.com, Ann Arbor Also called Meteor Web Marketing Inc *(G-553)*

USA Carbide 248 817-5137
1395 Wheaton Dr Ste 500 Troy (48083) *(G-16667)*

USA Hq Michigan, Plymouth Also called Varroc Lighting Systems Inc *(G-12786)*

USA Quality Metal Finshg LLC 269 427-9000
67131 56th St Lawrence (49064) *(G-9509)*

USA Sign Frame & Stake Inc 616 662-9100
2150 Center Industrial Ct Jenison (49428) *(G-8646)*

USA Summit Plas Silao 1 LLC (HQ) 269 324-9330
6715 S Sprinkle Rd Portage (49002) *(G-13053)*

USA Switch Inc (PA) 248 960-8500
49030 Pontiac Trl Ste 100 Wixom (48393) *(G-17922)*

USA Today, Detroit Also called Gannett Stllite Info Ntwrk Inc *(G-4077)*

USA Today Advertising 248 680-6530
2800 Livernois Rd Ste 600 Troy (48083) *(G-16668)*

Used Car News, Saint Clair Shores Also called General Media LLC *(G-14254)*

Uses, Rochester Hills Also called US Energy Systems Inc *(G-13538)*

USF Delta Tooling LLC (HQ) 248 391-6800
1350 Harmon Rd Auburn Hills (48326) *(G-1041)*

USF Westland LLC 248 754-7000
2700 High Meadow Cir Auburn Hills (48326) *(G-1042)*

Usher Enterprises Inc 313 834-7055
9000 Roselawn St Detroit (48204) *(G-4418)*

Usher Logging LLC 906 238-4261
4423 Cty Rd 557 Arnold (49819) *(G-725)*

Usher Logging LLC 906 238-4261
14443 Sa Rd 426 Sa Cornell (49818) *(G-3576)*

Usher Oil Company, Detroit Also called Usher Enterprises Inc *(G-4418)*

Usher Tool & Die Inc 616 583-9160
1015 84th St Sw Byron Center (49315) *(G-2213)*

Usi Inc 248 583-9337
31302 Stephenson Hwy A Madison Heights (48071) *(G-10375)*

Usm Acquisition LLC (HQ) 989 561-2293
7839 Costabella Ave Remus (49340) *(G-13243)*

Usmats Inc 810 765-4545
6347 King Rd Marine City (48039) *(G-10485)*

Usmfg Inc (HQ) 269 637-6392
28400 Northwestern Hwy # 2 Southfield (48034) *(G-15057)*

Usmfg Inc 262 993-9197
1500 Kalamazoo St South Haven (49090) *(G-14779)*

Usui International Corporation (HQ) 734 354-3626
44780 Helm St Plymouth (48170) *(G-12784)*

Utec, Sterling Heights Also called Universal Tl Eqp & Contrls Inc *(G-15534)*

Utica Aerospace Inc 586 598-9300
26950 23 Mile Rd Chesterfield (48051) *(G-2852)*

Utica Body & Assembly Inc (HQ) 586 726-4330
5750 New King Dr Ste 200 Troy (48098) *(G-16669)*

Utica Enterprises Inc (PA) 586 726-4300
5750 New King Dr Ste 200 Troy (48098) *(G-16670)*

Utica International Inc (HQ) 586 726-4330
5750 New King Dr Ste 200 Troy (48098) *(G-16671)*

Utica Laeser Systems, Troy Also called Utica Enterprises Inc *(G-16670)*

Utica Steel Inc 586 949-1900
48000 Structural Dr Chesterfield (48051) *(G-2853)*

Utica Washers 313 571-1568
3105 Beaufait St Detroit (48207) *(G-4419)*

Utilitec, Troy Also called Ancor Information MGT LLC *(G-16201)*

Utility Supply and Cnstr Co (PA) 231 832-2297
420 S Roth St Ste A Reed City (49677) *(G-13225)*

Utley Brothers Inc 248 585-1700
567 Robbins Dr Troy (48083) *(G-16672)*

Uusi LLC 231 832-5513
5000 N Us 131 Reed City (49677) *(G-13226)*

Uv Angel, Livonia Also called Uv Partners Inc *(G-9984)*

Uv Partners Inc (PA) 616 204-5416
38099 Schoolcraft Rd # 165 Livonia (48150) *(G-9984)*

V & M Corporation (PA) 248 541-4020
414 E Hudson Ave Royal Oak (48067) *(G-13980)*

V & S Detroit Galvanizing LLC 313 535-2600
12600 Arnold Redford (48239) *(G-13205)*

V & V Inc 616 842-8611
1703 Eaton Dr Grand Haven (49417) *(G-6093)*

V & V Industries Inc 248 624-7943
48553 West Rd Wixom (48393) *(G-17923)*

V D B, Holland Also called John A Van Den Bosch Co *(G-7695)*

V E S T Inc 248 649-9550
3250 W Big Beaver Rd # 440 Troy (48084) *(G-16673)*

V J Industries Inc 810 364-6470
827 Degurse Ave Marine City (48039) *(G-10486)*

V S America Inc 248 585-6715
1000 John R Rd Ste 111 Troy (48083) *(G-16674)*

V V P Auto Glass, Westland Also called Vitro Automotriz SA De CV *(G-17608)*

V&R Enterprize 313 837-5545
16011 W Mcnichols Rd Detroit (48235) *(G-4420)*

V-Line Precision Products, Walled Lake Also called Richardson Acqstions Group Inc *(G-16902)*

V.P.M., Eastpointe Also called Valade Precision Machining Inc *(G-4710)*

Vac-Met Inc 586 264-8100
7236 Murthum Ave Warren (48092) *(G-17276)*

Vachon Industries Inc (PA) 517 278-2354
580 Race St Coldwater (49036) *(G-3340)*

Vaclovers Inc 616 246-1700
3611 3 Mile Rd Nw Grand Rapids (49534) *(G-6956)*

Vacuum Farm Tools, Grand Rapids Also called Parker Tooling & Design Inc *(G-6743)*

Vacuum Orna Metal Company Inc 734 941-9100
11380 Harrison Romulus (48174) *(G-13738)*

Vade Nutrition, Williamston Also called Pro Bottle LLC *(G-17737)*

Vaive Wood Products Co 586 949-4900
24935 21 Mile Rd Macomb (48042) *(G-10172)*

Val Valley Inc 248 474-7335
24409 Halsted Rd Farmington Hills (48335) *(G-5145)*

Valade Precision Machining Inc 586 771-7705
17155 Stephens Dr Eastpointe (48021) *(G-4710)*

Valassis Communications Inc (HQ) 734 591-3000
19975 Victor Pkwy Livonia (48152) *(G-9985)*

Valassis Communications Inc 734 432-8000
38905 6 Mile Rd Livonia (48152) *(G-9986)*

Valassis International Inc (HQ) 734 591-3000
19975 Victor Pkwy Livonia (48152) *(G-9987)*

Valentine Distilling 248 629-9951
161 Vester St Ferndale (48220) *(G-5327)*

Valentine Distilling Co 646 286-2690
965 Wanda St Ferndale (48220) *(G-5328)*

Valeo Friction Materials Inc (HQ) 248 619-8300
150 Stephenson Hwy Troy (48083) *(G-16675)*

Valeo Inc Eng Coolg Auto Div, Auburn Hills Also called Valeo North America Inc *(G-1043)*

Valeo North America Inc 248 209-8253
4100 N Atlantic Blvd Auburn Hills (48326) *(G-1043)*

Valeo North America Inc 248 619-8300
150 Stephenson Hwy Troy (48083) ***(G-16676)***
Valeo North America Inc (HQ) 248 619-8300
150 Stephenson Hwy Troy (48083) ***(G-16677)***
Valeo North America Inc 313 883-8850
12240 Oakland Pkwy Detroit (48203) ***(G-4421)***
Valeo Radar Systems Inc 248 340-3126
3000 University Dr Auburn Hills (48326) ***(G-1044)***
Valeo Radar Systems Inc (HQ) 248 619-8300
150 Stephenson Hwy Troy (48083) ***(G-16678)***
Valeo Service Center, Troy *Also called Valeo North America Inc* ***(G-16676)***
Valeo Switches & Dete (HQ) 248 619-8300
150 Stephenson Hwy Troy (48083) ***(G-16679)***
Valeo Wiper Systems, Troy *Also called Valeo Friction Materials Inc* ***(G-16675)***
Valeo Wiper Systems, Troy *Also called Valeo North America Inc* ***(G-16677)***
Valero Renewable Fuels Co LLC 517 486-6190
7025 Silberhorn Hwy Blissfield (49228) ***(G-1730)***
Valero Riga Ethanol Plant, Blissfield *Also called Valero Renewable Fuels Co LLC* ***(G-1730)***
Valiant Specialties Inc 248 656-1001
301 Hacker St Unit 3 Rochester Hills (48307) ***(G-13539)***
Valley City Plating Company, Grand Rapids *Also called Martin and Hattie Rasche Inc* ***(G-6646)***
Valley City Sign Company 616 784-5711
5009 West River Dr Ne Comstock Park (49321) ***(G-3519)***
Valley Enterprises, Ubly *Also called Pepro Enterprises Inc* ***(G-16720)***
Valley Enterprises Ubly Inc 989 269-6272
4175 N Ubly Rd Ubly (48475) ***(G-16725)***
Valley Enterprises Ubly Inc (HQ) 989 658-3200
2147 Leppek Rd Ubly (48475) ***(G-16726)***
Valley Gear and Machine Inc 989 269-8177
514 Chickory St Bad Axe (48413) ***(G-1076)***
Valley Glass Co Inc 989 790-9342
2424 Midland Rd Saginaw (48603) ***(G-14175)***
Valley Group of Companies 989 799-9669
548 Shattuck Rd Ste B Saginaw (48604) ***(G-14176)***
Valley Publishing 989 671-1200
5215 Mackinaw Rd Bay City (48706) ***(G-1369)***
Valley Services, Saginaw *Also called Valley Group of Companies* ***(G-14176)***
Valley Steel Company 989 799-2600
1322 King St Saginaw (48602) ***(G-14177)***
Valley Truck Parts Inc (PA) 616 241-5431
1900 Chicago Dr Sw Wyoming (49519) ***(G-18040)***
Valley Truck Parts Inc 269 429-9953
305 Palladium Dr Saint Joseph (49085) ***(G-14348)***
Valmec Inc 810 629-8750
12487 Thornbury Dr Fenton (48430) ***(G-5248)***
Valtec LLC 810 724-5048
565 S Cedar St Imlay City (48444) ***(G-8213)***
Valves D S S, Niles *Also called Dss Valve Products Inc* ***(G-11609)***
Vamp Company, Brownstown Twp *Also called Vamp Screw Products Company* ***(G-2076)***
Vamp Screw Products Company 734 676-8020
28055 Fort St Brownstown Twp (48183) ***(G-2076)***
Van Beeks Custom Wood Products 616 583-9002
7950 Clyde Park Ave Sw Byron Center (49315) ***(G-2214)***
Van Boven Incorporated 734 665-7228
326 S State St Ann Arbor (48104) ***(G-690)***
Van Boven Clothing, Ann Arbor *Also called Van Boven Incorporated* ***(G-690)***
Van Buren Steel, Belleville *Also called Very Best Steel LLC* ***(G-1451)***
Van Daeles Inc 734 587-7165
8830 Ida Maybee Rd Monroe (48162) ***(G-11082)***
Van Dam Iron Works Inc 616 452-8627
1813 Chicago Dr Sw Grand Rapids (49519) ***(G-6957)***
Van Dam Marine Co 231 582-2323
970 E Division St Boyne City (49712) ***(G-1837)***
Van Dam Wood Craft, Boyne City *Also called Van Dam Marine Co* ***(G-1837)***
Van Dellen Steel Inc 616 698-9950
6945 Dtton Indus Pk Dr Se Caledonia (49316) ***(G-2321)***
Van Duinen Forest Products 231 328-4507
4680 E Houghton Lake Rd Lake City (49651) ***(G-9097)***
Van Dyke Fuell 586 758-0120
21715 Van Dyke Ave Warren (48089) ***(G-17277)***
Van Dyken Mechanical Inc 616 224-7030
4275 Spartan Indus Dr Sw Grandville (49418) ***(G-7075)***
Van Eck Diesel Services, Grand Rapids *Also called Creek Diesel Services Inc* ***(G-6316)***
Van Emon Bruce 269 467-7803
501 S Clark St Centreville (49032) ***(G-2598)***
Van Enk Woodcrafters LLC 616 931-0090
500 E Washington Ave # 50 Zeeland (49464) ***(G-18191)***
Van F Belknap Company, Wixom *Also called Hank Thorn Co* ***(G-17823)***
Van Heusen, West Branch *Also called Pvh Corp* ***(G-17517)***
Van Heusen, Birch Run *Also called Pvh Corp* ***(G-1668)***
Van Horn Bros Inc (PA) 248 623-4830
3700 Airport Rd Waterford (48329) ***(G-17382)***
Van Horn Bros Inc 248 623-6000
3770 Airport Rd Waterford (48329) ***(G-17383)***
Van Horn Concrete, Waterford *Also called Van Horn Bros Inc* ***(G-17382)***
Van Horn Concrete, Waterford *Also called Van Horn Bros Inc* ***(G-17383)***

Van Industries Inc 248 398-6990
1285 Wordsworth St Ferndale (48220) ***(G-5329)***
Van Kam Inc 231 744-2658
1316 Whitehall Rd Muskegon (49445) ***(G-11444)***
Van Kehrberg Vern 810 364-1066
914 Gratiot Blvd Ste 3 Marysville (48040) ***(G-10625)***
Van Loon Industries Inc 586 532-8530
51583 Filomena Dr Shelby Township (48315) ***(G-14716)***
Van Machine Co 269 729-9540
131 2nd St East Leroy (49051) ***(G-4685)***
Van Paemel Mini-Storage, Armada *Also called Van Paemels Equipment Company* ***(G-724)***
Van Paemels Equipment Company 586 784-5295
75357 North Ave Armada (48005) ***(G-724)***
Van Peete Enterprises 517 369-2123
897 W Chicago Rd Bronson (49028) ***(G-2034)***
Van Pelt Corporation (PA) 313 365-3600
36155 Mound Rd Sterling Heights (48310) ***(G-15538)***
Van Pelt Corporation 313 365-6500
13700 Sherwood St Ste 1 Detroit (48212) ***(G-4422)***
Van Pelt Industries LLC 616 842-1200
720 Taylor Ave Grand Haven (49417) ***(G-6094)***
Van Rob Lansing, Lansing *Also called Van-Rob Inc* ***(G-9271)***
Van Ron Steel Services LLC 616 813-6907
1100 Comstock St Marne (49435) ***(G-10515)***
Van S Fabrications Inc 810 679-2115
4446 Peck Rd Croswell (48422) ***(G-3605)***
Van Sloten Enterprises Inc (PA) 906 635-5151
1320 W 3 Mile Rd Sault Sainte Marie (49783) ***(G-14477)***
Van Straten Brothers Inc 906 353-6490
14908 Us Highway 41 Baraga (49908) ***(G-1116)***
Van Zee Acquisitions Inc 616 855-7000
4047 Eastern Ave Se Grand Rapids (49508) ***(G-6958)***
Van Zee Corporation 616 245-9000
4047 Eastern Ave Se Grand Rapids (49508) ***(G-6959)***
Van's Fabrications, Croswell *Also called Van S Fabrications Inc* ***(G-3605)***
Van-Dies Engineering Inc 586 293-1430
17525 Helro Ste A Fraser (48026) ***(G-5745)***
Van-Mark Products Corporation 248 478-1200
24145 Industrial Park Dr Farmington Hills (48335) ***(G-5146)***
Van-Rob Inc 517 657-2450
16325 Felton Rd Lansing (48906) ***(G-9271)***
Van-Rob USA Holdings (HQ) 517 423-2400
1200 E Chicago Blvd Tecumseh (49286) ***(G-15816)***
Vanaire Inc 906 428-4656
840 Clark Dr Gladstone (49837) ***(G-5921)***
Vancho Tool and Engineering, Sterling Heights *Also called Vince Krstevski* ***(G-15540)***
Vanco Steel Inc 810 688-4333
6573 Bernie Kohler Dr North Branch (48461) ***(G-11666)***
Vandco Incorporated 906 482-1550
200 Hancock St Hancock (49930) ***(G-7258)***
Vander Mill LLC (PA) 616 259-8828
505 Ball Ave Ne Grand Rapids (49503) ***(G-6960)***
Vander Roest Homes Fine Wdwkg 269 353-3175
2419 N 3rd St Kalamazoo (49009) ***(G-8917)***
Vander Wall Bros, Spring Lake *Also called Ludvanwall Inc* ***(G-15159)***
Vandervest Electric Mtr & Fabg 231 843-6196
5635 W Dewey Rd Ludington (49431) ***(G-10086)***
Vanerum Stelter, Grand Rapids *Also called Mooreco Inc* ***(G-6706)***
Vanex Mold Inc 616 662-4100
2240 Pine Ridge Dr Sw Jenison (49428) ***(G-8647)***
Vanguard Publications Inc 517 336-1600
4440 Hagadorn Rd Okemos (48864) ***(G-12140)***
Vanity Fur 810 744-3000
1184 S Belsay Rd Ste B Burton (48509) ***(G-2169)***
Vankam Trailer Sales & Mfg, Muskegon *Also called Van Kam Inc* ***(G-11444)***
Vanmeer Corporation 269 694-6090
1754 106th Ave Otsego (49078) ***(G-12258)***
Vanova Technologies LLC 734 476-7204
5403 Waldenhill Ct Superior Township (48198) ***(G-15648)***
Vanroth LLC 734 929-5268
401 S Maple Rd Ann Arbor (48103) ***(G-691)***
Vans Car Wash Inc 231 744-4831
1600 Whitehall Rd Muskegon (49445) ***(G-11445)***
Vans Pattern Corp 616 364-9483
11 Sweet St Nw Grand Rapids (49505) ***(G-6961)***
Vantage Plastics, Standish *Also called Airpark Plastics LLC* ***(G-15215)***
Vantage Plastics, Standish *Also called PRA Company* ***(G-15226)***
Varatech Inc 616 393-6408
1141 Ambertrace Ln Apt 8 Holland (49424) ***(G-7843)***
Vargas & Sons 989 754-4636
125 S Park Ave Saginaw (48607) ***(G-14178)***
Vari-Data Co., Galesburg *Also called Impact Label Corporation* ***(G-5811)***
Variable Machining & Tool Inc 586 778-8803
21443 Groesbeck Hwy Warren (48089) ***(G-17278)***
Variety Die & Stamping Co 734 426-4488
2221 Bishop Cir E Dexter (48130) ***(G-4517)***
Variety Foods Inc (PA) 586 268-4900
7001 Chicago Rd Warren (48092) ***(G-17279)***

Varn International Inc 734 781-4600
14909 N Beck Rd Plymouth (48170) *(G-12785)*
Varneys Fab & Weld LLC 231 865-6856
5967 Maple Island Rd Nunica (49448) *(G-12046)*
Varroc Lighting Systems Inc (HQ) 734 446-4400
47828 Halyard Dr Plymouth (48170) *(G-12786)*
Varsity Monthly Thumb 810 404-5297
251 N State St Caro (48723) *(G-2481)*
Vassar Welding & Machine Co 989 823-8266
769 Birch Rd Vassar (48768) *(G-16816)*
Vaughan Industries Inc 313 935-2040
8490 Lyndon St Detroit (48238) *(G-4423)*
Vaupell Molding & Tooling Inc 269 435-8414
485 Florence Rd Constantine (49042) *(G-3545)*
Vb Chesaning LLC 989 323-2333
624 Brady St Chesaning (48616) *(G-2729)*
Vci Inc (PA) 269 659-3676
1500 Progress St Sturgis (49091) *(G-15639)*
Vci Inc 269 659-3676
1301 W Dresser Dr Sturgis (49091) *(G-15640)*
Vconverter Corporation (PA) 248 388-0549
10505 Plaza Dr Ste C Whitmore Lake (48189) *(G-17708)*
VDO Automotive, Auburn Hills *Also called Continental Auto Systems Inc* *(G-821)*
Vectech Pharmaceutical Cons (PA) 248 478-5820
12501 Grand River Rd Brighton (48116) *(G-2005)*
Vector Distribution LLC 616 361-2021
1642 Broadway Ave Nw Grand Rapids (49504) *(G-6962)*
Vector North America Inc 248 449-9290
39500 Orchard Hill Pl Novi (48375) *(G-12024)*
Vectorall Manufacturing Inc 248 486-4570
7675 Lochlin Dr Brighton (48116) *(G-2006)*
Veet Axelson Liberty Industry 586 776-3000
14322 E 9 Mile Rd Warren (48089) *(G-17280)*
Veet Industries Inc 586 776-3000
14322 E 9 Mile Rd Warren (48089) *(G-17281)*
Vega Manufacturing LLC 231 668-6365
526 W Fourteenth St # 150 Traverse City (49684) *(G-16136)*
Vehicles, Southfield *Also called Eaton Corporation* *(G-14894)*
Vehma International Amer Inc 248 585-4800
1230 Chicago Rd Troy (48083) *(G-16680)*
Vehma International Amer Inc (HQ) 248 631-2800
750 Tower Dr 4000 Troy (48098) *(G-16681)*
Veigel North America LLC 586 843-3816
51277 Celeste Shelby Township (48315) *(G-14717)*
Veit Tool & Gage Inc 810 658-4949
303 S Dayton St Davison (48423) *(G-3665)*
Velcro USA Inc 248 583-6060
1210 Souter Dr Troy (48083) *(G-16682)*
Veldheer Tulip Garden Inc 616 399-1900
12755 Quincy St Holland (49424) *(G-7844)*
Velesco Phrm Svcs Inc 734 545-0696
28036 Oakland Oaks Ct Wixom (48393) *(G-17924)*
Velesco Phrm Svcs Inc (PA) 734 527-9125
46701 Commerce Center Dr Plymouth (48170) *(G-12787)*
Velocity Manufacturing LLC 517 630-0408
921 Elliott St Albion (49224) *(G-134)*
Velocity USA, Grand Rapids *Also called Velocity Worldwide Inc* *(G-6963)*
Velocity Worldwide Inc 616 243-3400
2280 29th St Se Grand Rapids (49508) *(G-6963)*
Veltri Tooling Company, Warren *Also called Flex-N-Gate Michigan LLC* *(G-17039)*
Venchurs Inc 517 263-1206
800 Tabor St Adrian (49221) *(G-99)*
Venchurs Inc 517 263-8937
751 S Center St Adrian (49221) *(G-100)*
Vendco LLC 800 764-8245
50613 Central Indus Dr Shelby Township (48315) *(G-14718)*
Venntis Technologies LLC 616 395-8254
1261 S Waverly Rd Holland (49423) *(G-7845)*
Venom Motorsports Inc 616 635-2519
5174 Plainfield Ave Ne Grand Rapids (49525) *(G-6964)*
Vent-Rite Valve Corp 269 925-8812
1875 Dewey Ave Benton Harbor (49022) *(G-1560)*
Ventcon Inc 313 336-4000
500 Enterprise Dr Allen Park (48101) *(G-212)*
Ventech, Wixom *Also called Puritan Automation LLC* *(G-17881)*
Ventilation + Plus Eqp Inc 231 487-1156
670 W Conway Rd 1 Harbor Springs (49740) *(G-7297)*
Ventower Industries, Monroe *Also called Great Lakes Towers LLC* *(G-11037)*
Ventra Evart LLC 231 734-9000
601 W 7th St Evart (49631) *(G-4888)*
Ventra Grand Rapids 5 LLC 616 222-3296
3075 Breton Rd Se Grand Rapids (49512) *(G-6965)*
Ventra Greenwich Holdings Corp 586 759-8900
5663 E 9 Mile Rd Warren (48091) *(G-17282)*
Ventra Greenwich Tooling Co, Warren *Also called Ventra Greenwich Holdings Corp* *(G-17282)*
Ventra Ionia Main LLC 616 597-3220
1790 E Bluewater Hwy Ionia (48846) *(G-8252)*
Ventra Ionia Main LLC (HQ) 616 597-3220
14 Beardsley St Ionia (48846) *(G-8253)*
Ventra Plastics, Warren *Also called Flex-N-Gate LLC* *(G-17036)*
Ventuor LLC 248 790-8700
336 W 1st St Ste 113 Flint (48502) *(G-5520)*
Ventura Aerospace LLC 734 357-0114
51170 Grand River Ave A Wixom (48393) *(G-17925)*
Ventura Industries Inc 734 357-0114
46301 Port St Plymouth (48170) *(G-12788)*
Ventura Manufacturing Inc (PA) 616 772-7405
471 E Roosevelt Ave # 100 Zeeland (49464) *(G-18192)*
Venture Grafix LLC 248 449-1330
47757 West Rd Ste C-105 Wixom (48393) *(G-17926)*
Venture Label Inc 313 928-2545
3380 Baseline Rd Detroit (48231) *(G-4424)*
Venture Labels USA Inc 313 928-2545
855 Southfield Rd Lincoln Park (48146) *(G-9587)*
Venture Manufacturing Inc 269 429-6337
3542 Crestview Rd Saint Joseph (49085) *(G-14349)*
Venture Technology Groups Inc (PA) 248 473-8450
24300 Catherine Industria Novi (48375) *(G-12025)*
Venture Tool & Metalizing 989 883-9121
42 E Main St Sebewaing (48759) *(G-14521)*
Venturedyne Ltd 616 392-1491
291 Kollen Park Dr Holland (49423) *(G-7846)*
Venturedyne Ltd 616 392-6550
836 Brooks Ave Holland (49423) *(G-7847)*
Venus Controls Inc 248 477-0448
30105 8 Mile Rd Livonia (48152) *(G-9988)*
Veoneer Inc (PA) 248 223-0600
26360 American Dr Southfield (48034) *(G-15058)*
Veoneer Southfield, Southfield *Also called Veoneer Us Inc* *(G-15060)*
Veoneer Us Inc (HQ) 248 223-8074
26360 American Dr Southfield (48034) *(G-15059)*
Veoneer Us Inc 248 223-0600
26360 American Dr Southfield (48034) *(G-15060)*
Ver Duins Inc 616 842-0730
623 Washington Ave Grand Haven (49417) *(G-6095)*
Verbio North America Corp (PA) 866 306-4777
17199 N Laurel Park Dr # 409 Livonia (48152) *(G-9989)*
Verdoni Productions Inc 989 790-0845
5090 Overhill Dr Saginaw (48603) *(G-14179)*
Verduyn Tarps Detroit Inc 313 270-4890
19231 W Davison St Detroit (48223) *(G-4425)*
Verellen Orchards 586 752-2989
63260 Van Dyke Rd Washington (48095) *(G-17313)*
Verellen Orchards & Cider Mill, Washington *Also called Verellen Orchards* *(G-17313)*
Verimation Technology Inc 248 471-0000
23883 Industrial Park Dr Farmington Hills (48335) *(G-5147)*
Veritas USA Corporation 248 374-5019
39555 Orchard Hill Pl # 600 Novi (48375) *(G-12026)*
Veritas Vineyard LLC 517 474-9026
2199 N Concord Rd Albion (49224) *(G-135)*
Veritas Vineyard LLC 517 592-4663
11000 Silver Lake Hwy Brooklyn (49230) *(G-2043)*
Veritas Vineyard LLC (PA) 517 962-2427
117 W Louis Glick Hwy Jackson (49201) *(G-8600)*
Vermeulen & Associates Inc 616 291-1255
4665 Cascade Rd Se # 140 Grand Rapids (49546) *(G-6966)*
Verndale Products Inc 313 834-4190
8445 Lyndon St Detroit (48238) *(G-4426)*
Versa Handling Co (PA) 313 491-0500
12995 Hillview St Detroit (48227) *(G-4427)*
Versa Handling Co 313 891-1420
17265 Gable St Detroit (48212) *(G-4428)*
Versa Tech Technologies, Roseville *Also called Versi-Tech Incorporated* *(G-13888)*
Versa-Craft Inc 586 465-5999
35117 Automation Dr Clinton Township (48035) *(G-3255)*
Versacut Industries, Morenci *Also called Tiller Tool and Die Inc* *(G-11115)*
Versant Medical Physics 888 316-3644
116 S Riverview Dr Kalamazoo (49004) *(G-8918)*
Versatile Fabrication Co Inc 231 739-7115
2708 9th St Muskegon (49444) *(G-11446)*
Versatile Manufacturing, Muskegon *Also called Metal-Line Corp* *(G-11377)*
Versatile Systems LLC 734 397-3957
8347 Ronda Dr Canton (48187) *(G-2438)*
Versatility Inc 616 957-5555
2610 Berwyck Rd Se Grand Rapids (49506) *(G-6967)*
Versatranz, Plymouth *Also called Designshirtscom Inc* *(G-12609)*
Versatube Corporation 248 524-0299
4755 Rochester Rd Ste 200 Troy (48085) *(G-16683)*
Versi-Tech Incorporated 586 944-2230
29901 Calahan Rd Roseville (48066) *(G-13888)*
Versicor LLC 734 306-9137
333 W 7th St Royal Oak (48067) *(G-13981)*
Verso Corporation 906 786-1660
7100 County 426 M.5 Rd Escanaba (49829) *(G-4865)*
Verso Corporation 906 779-3371
Us Hwy 2 Norway (49870) *(G-11821)*

ALPHABETIC

Verso Paper Holding LLC 906 779-3200
W6791 Us Highway 2 Quinnesec (49876) ***(G-13104)***
Verso Paper Holding LLC 906 396-2358
W6705 Us Highway 2 Quinnesec (49876) ***(G-13105)***
Verso Quinnesec LLC 877 447-2737
W6791 Us Highway 2 Quinnesec (49876) ***(G-13106)***
Verso Quinnesec Rep LLC 906 779-3200
W6705 Us Highway 2 Quinnesec (49876) ***(G-13107)***
Verstar Group Inc (PA) 586 465-5033
50305 Patricia St Chesterfield (48051) ***(G-2854)***
Verstraete Conveyability Inc 800 798-0410
2889 Northridge Dr Nw Grand Rapids (49544) ***(G-6968)***
Vertellus Hlth Spclty Pdts LLC 616 772-2193
215 N Centennial St Zeeland (49464) ***(G-18193)***
Vertellus LLC 616 772-2193
215 N Centennial St Zeeland (49464) ***(G-18194)***
Vertellus Specialty Materials, Zeeland *Also called Vertellus Hlth Spclty Pdts LLC* ***(G-18193)***
Vertellus Zeeland, Zeeland *Also called Vertellus LLC* ***(G-18194)***
Vertex Steel Inc 248 684-4177
2175 Fyke Dr Milford (48381) ***(G-10990)***
Vertical Solutions Company 517 655-8164
1436 E Grand River Rd Williamston (48895) ***(G-17741)***
Vertical Technologies LLC 586 619-0141
12901 Stephens Rd Warren (48089) ***(G-17283)***
Vertical Vics, Mount Clemens *Also called Detroit Custom Services Inc* ***(G-11129)***
Vertigee Corporation 313 999-1020
1722 Wildwood Trl Saline (48176) ***(G-14420)***
Vertigo 910 381-8925
1006 Lake Ave Quinnesec (49876) ***(G-13108)***
Very Best Steel LLC 734 697-8609
327 Davis St Belleville (48111) ***(G-1451)***
Vetionx, Grand Rapids *Also called Ionxhealth Inc* ***(G-6544)***
Vetionx, Grand Rapids *Also called Hello Life Inc* ***(G-6504)***
Vets Access LLC 810 639-2222
1449 E Pierson Rd Ste B Flushing (48433) ***(G-5544)***
Vetta LLC (PA) 517 521-2525
1200 Mason Ct Webberville (48892) ***(G-17455)***
Vgage LLC 248 589-7455
13250 Northend Ave Oak Park (48237) ***(G-12102)***
Vgkids Inc 734 485-5128
884 Railroad St Ste C Ypsilanti (48197) ***(G-18107)***
Vhb-123 Corporation 248 623-4830
3770 Airport Rd Waterford (48329) ***(G-17384)***
Vi-Chem Corp 616 247-8501
55 Cottage Grove St Sw Grand Rapids (49507) ***(G-6969)***
Via-Tech Corp 989 358-7028
11715 M 32 W Lachine (49753) ***(G-9079)***
Viable Inc 616 774-2022
44 Grandville Ave Sw Grand Rapids (49503) ***(G-6970)***
Viant Medical Inc 616 643-5200
620 Watson St Sw Grand Rapids (49504) ***(G-6971)***
Viaus Super Market 906 786-1950
1519 Sheridan Rd Escanaba (49829) ***(G-4866)***
Vibra-Tite, Troy *Also called ND Industries Inc* ***(G-16522)***
Vibracoustic North America L P (HQ) 269 637-2116
400 Aylworth Ave South Haven (49090) ***(G-14780)***
Vibracoustic North America LP 248 410-5066
32605 W 12 Mile Rd # 350 Farmington Hills (48334) ***(G-5148)***
Vibracoustic Usa Inc (HQ) 269 637-2116
400 Aylworth Ave South Haven (49090) ***(G-14781)***
Vibracoustic Usa Inc 810 648-2100
180 Dawson St Sandusky (48471) ***(G-14446)***
Vibracoustic Usa Inc 810 648-2100
370 Industrial St Sandusky (48471) ***(G-14447)***
Vibration Controls Tech LLC 248 822-8010
2075 W Big Beaver Rd # 500 Troy (48084) ***(G-16684)***
Vibration Research Corporation 616 669-3028
1294 Chicago Dr Jenison (49428) ***(G-8648)***
Vic Bond Sales Inc 517 548-0107
2225 W Grand River Ave Howell (48843) ***(G-8121)***
Vic Freed Logging 906 477-9933
W13745 Hahn Rd Engadine (49827) ***(G-4799)***
Vickers Engineering Inc 269 426-8545
3604 Glendora Rd New Troy (49119) ***(G-11562)***
Vico Company 734 453-3777
41555 Ann Arbor Rd E Plymouth (48170) ***(G-12789)***
Vico Products Co (PA) 734 453-3777
41555 Ann Arbor Rd E Plymouth (48170) ***(G-12790)***
Vicount Industries Inc 248 471-5071
24704 Hathaway St Farmington Hills (48335) ***(G-5149)***
Victor Screw Products Co 269 489-2760
235 S 4th St Burr Oak (49030) ***(G-2138)***
Victora Usa Inc 810 798-0253
3776 Van Dyke Rd Almont (48003) ***(G-269)***
Victoria Tool & Machine Div, Warren *Also called Jordan Tool Corporation* ***(G-17117)***
Vidatak LLC 877 392-6273
1327 Jones Dr Ste 203 Ann Arbor (48105) ***(G-692)***
Video Service Center, Livonia *Also called P M Z Technology Inc* ***(G-9879)***
Vidon Plastics Inc 810 667-0634
3171 John Conley Dr Lapeer (48446) ***(G-9490)***
Vierson Boiler & Repair Co 616 949-0500
3700 Patterson Ave Se Grand Rapids (49512) ***(G-6972)***
View Newspaper 734 697-8255
159 Main St Belleville (48111) ***(G-1452)***
View, The, Belleville *Also called Action Ad Newspapers Inc* ***(G-1439)***
Vigel North America Inc (HQ) 734 947-9900
32375 Howard Ave Madison Heights (48071) ***(G-10376)***
Vihi LLC (HQ) 734 710-2277
1 Village Center Dr Van Buren Twp (48111) ***(G-16789)***
Viking Boat Harbor Inc 906 484-3303
1121 S Islington Rd Cedarville (49719) ***(G-2573)***
Viking Corporation (HQ) 269 945-9501
210 Industrial Park Dr Hastings (49058) ***(G-7428)***
Viking Fabrication Svcs LLC (HQ) 269 945-9501
210 Industrial Park Dr Hastings (49058) ***(G-7429)***
Viking Group Inc (HQ) 616 432-6800
5150 Beltway Dr Se Caledonia (49316) ***(G-2322)***
Viking Industries Inc 734 421-5416
6012 Hubbard St Garden City (48135) ***(G-5846)***
Viking Oil LLC 989 366-4772
55 W Houghton Lake Dr Prudenville (48651) ***(G-13086)***
Viking Sales Inc 810 227-2222
169 Summit St Brighton (48116) ***(G-2007)***
Viking Spas Inc 616 248-7800
2725 Prairie St Sw Wyoming (49519) ***(G-18041)***
Viking Technologies Inc 586 914-0819
25169 Dequindre Rd Madison Heights (48071) ***(G-10377)***
Viking Tool & Engineering Inc 231 893-0031
2780 Colby Rd Whitehall (49461) ***(G-17679)***
Viladon Corporation 248 548-0043
10411 Capital St Oak Park (48237) ***(G-12103)***
Viladon Laboratories, Oak Park *Also called Viladon Corporation* ***(G-12103)***
Village & Country Water Trtmnt (PA) 810 632-7880
2875 N Old Us Highway 23 Hartland (48353) ***(G-7395)***
Village Automatics Inc 269 663-8521
69576 Section St Edwardsburg (49112) ***(G-4773)***
Village Cabinet Shoppe Inc 586 264-6464
37975 Commerce Dr Sterling Heights (48312) ***(G-15539)***
Village Graphics Inc 231 547-4172
111 Antrim St Charlevoix (49720) ***(G-2634)***
Village Press Inc 231 946-3712
2779 Aero Park Dr Traverse City (49686) ***(G-16137)***
Village Printing & Supply Inc 810 664-2270
349 Mccormick Dr Lapeer (48446) ***(G-9491)***
Village Shop Inc 231 946-3712
2779 Aero Park Dr Traverse City (49686) ***(G-16138)***
Villanuevo Soledad 989 770-4309
2855 E Burt Rd Burt (48417) ***(G-2139)***
Vin-Lee-Ron Meat Packing LLC 574 353-1386
54501 Griffis Rd Cassopolis (49031) ***(G-2538)***
Vince Joes Frt Mkt - Shlby Inc 586 786-9230
55178 Van Dyke Ave Shelby Township (48316) ***(G-14719)***
Vince Krstevski 586 739-7600
43450 Merrill Rd Sterling Heights (48314) ***(G-15540)***
Vinco Tool Inc 586 465-1961
44616 Macomb Indus Dr Clinton Township (48036) ***(G-3256)***
Vinecroft Studios, Grand Rapids *Also called Bivins Graphics* ***(G-6227)***
Vinette Boatworks, Escanaba *Also called T D Vinette Company* ***(G-4862)***
Vinewood Metalcraft Inc 734 946-8733
9501 Inkster Rd Taylor (48180) ***(G-15778)***
Vineyard 2121 LLC 269 429-0555
2121 Kerlikowske Rd Benton Harbor (49022) ***(G-1561)***
Vineyard Press Inc 269 657-5080
32280 E Red Arrow Hwy Paw Paw (49079) ***(G-12416)***
Vineyards Gourmet 269 468-4778
6841 High St Coloma (49038) ***(G-3366)***
Vinnies Machining Tool Die 231 546-3290
3507 Buell Rd Elmira (49730) ***(G-4794)***
Vintage Views Press 616 475-7662
959 Ogden Ave Se Grand Rapids (49506) ***(G-6973)***
Vintech Industries Inc (PA) 810 724-7400
611 Industrial Park Dr Imlay City (48444) ***(G-8214)***
Vintech Mexico Holdings LLC (PA) 810 387-3224
611 Industrial Park Dr Imlay City (48444) ***(G-8215)***
Vinyl Craft Window LLC 231 832-8905
14654 Hersey Rd Hersey (49639) ***(G-7476)***
Vinyl Express 269 469-5165
19654 Ash Ct New Buffalo (49117) ***(G-11518)***
Vinyl Graphix Inc 586 774-1188
24731 Harper Ave Saint Clair Shores (48080) ***(G-14275)***
Vinyl Industrial Paints Inc 734 284-3536
1401 Sycamore St Wyandotte (48192) ***(G-17979)***
Vinyl Sash of Flint Inc (PA) 810 234-4831
5433 Fenton Rd G Flint (48507) ***(G-5521)***
Vinyl Tech Window Systems Inc 248 634-8900
405 Cogshall St Holly (48442) ***(G-7901)***
Vipers Den Winery LLC 734 644-0213
3228 W Philadelphia St Detroit (48206) ***(G-4429)***

ALPHABETIC SECTION — Vulcan Wood Products Inc

Viron International Corp (PA) 254 773-9292
505 N Hintz Rd Owosso (48867) *(G-12327)*

Virotech Biomaterials Inc 313 421-1648
8260 Dartmouth Dr Warren (48093) *(G-17284)*

Virtec Manufacturing LLC 313 590-2367
28302 Hayes Rd Roseville (48066) *(G-13889)*

Virtec Manufacturing LLC 313 369-4858
17565 W P Chrysler Fwy Detroit (48203) *(G-4430)*

Virtual Advantage LLc 877 772-6886
3290 W Big Beavr Rd # 310 Troy (48084) *(G-16685)*

Virtual Emergency Services LLC 734 324-2299
1400 Biddle Ave Wyandotte (48192) *(G-17980)*

Virtual Technology Inc 248 528-6565
1345 Wheaton Dr Troy (48083) *(G-16686)*

Virtue Cider 269 455-0526
2180 62nd St Fennville (49408) *(G-5179)*

Virtuoso Custom Creations LLC 313 332-1299
1111 Bellevue St Unit 201 Detroit (48207) *(G-4431)*

Visalus Sciences 877 847-2587
340 E Big Beaver Rd # 280 Troy (48083) *(G-16687)*

Viscount Equipment Co Inc 586 293-5900
33743 Groesbeck Hwy Fraser (48026) *(G-5746)*

Visible Ink Press LLC 734 667-3211
43311 Joy Rd 414 Canton (48187) *(G-2439)*

Vision Designs Inc 616 994-7054
774 Columbia Ave Holland (49423) *(G-7848)*

Vision Fuels LLC 586 997-3286
51969 Van Dyke Ave Shelby Township (48316) *(G-14720)*

Vision Global Industries 248 390-5805
16041 Leone Dr Macomb (48042) *(G-10173)*

Vision Solutions Inc 810 695-9569
4417 Brighton Dr Grand Blanc (48439) *(G-5987)*

Vision-Craft Inc 248 669-1130
3285 Martin Rd Ste 110 Commerce Township (48390) *(G-3456)*

Visionary Landscaping, Shelby Township *Also called Huntler Industries Inc (G-14601)*

Visionary Vitamin Co 734 788-5934
3205 Mckitrick St Melvindale (48122) *(G-10708)*

Visioncraft 586 949-6540
28161 Kehrig St Chesterfield (48047) *(G-2855)*

Visioneering Inc (PA) 248 622-5600
2055 Taylor Rd Auburn Hills (48326) *(G-1045)*

Visioneering Inc 248 622-5600
17085 Masonic Fraser (48026) *(G-5747)*

Visionit Supplies and Svcs Inc 313 664-5650
3031 W Grand Blvd Ste 600 Detroit (48202) *(G-4432)*

Visions Car & Truck Acc 269 342-2962
8250 Douglas Ave Kalamazoo (49009) *(G-8919)*

Visiun Inc 734 741-0356
3865 S Michael Rd Ann Arbor (48103) *(G-693)*

Visor Frames LLC 586 864-6058
6400 Sterling Dr N Ste B Sterling Heights (48312) *(G-15541)*

Visotek Inc 734 427-4800
11700 Belden Ct Livonia (48150) *(G-9990)*

Vista Manufacturing Inc 616 719-5520
3110 Wilson Dr Nw Walker (49534) *(G-16881)*

Visteon Corporation 734 718-8927
45004 Lothrop Ct Canton (48188) *(G-2440)*

Visteon Corporation (PA) 800 847-8366
1 Village Center Dr Van Buren Twp (48111) *(G-16790)*

Visteon Electronics Corp 800 847-8366
1 Village Center Dr Van Buren Twp (48111) *(G-16791)*

Visteon Global Electronics Inc (HQ) 800 847-8366
1 Village Center Dr Van Buren Twp (48111) *(G-16792)*

Visteon Global Electronics Inc 734 710-5000
1 Village Center Dr Van Buren Twp (48111) *(G-16793)*

Visteon International Business, Van Buren Twp *Also called Visteon Intl Holdings Inc (G-16794)*

Visteon Intl Holdings Inc (HQ) 734 710-2000
1 Village Center Dr Van Buren Twp (48111) *(G-16794)*

Visteon Systems LLC 313 755-9500
5500 Auto Club Dr Dearborn (48126) *(G-3768)*

Visteon Systems LLC (HQ) 800 847-8366
1 Village Center Dr Van Buren Twp (48111) *(G-16795)*

Visual Chimera 586 585-1210
23082 Saxony Ave Eastpointe (48021) *(G-4711)*

Visual Components N Amer Corp 855 823-3746
2633 S Lapeer Rd Ste G Orion (48360) *(G-12192)*

Visual Identification Products 231 941-7272
1733 Park Dr Traverse City (49686) *(G-16139)*

Visual Precision Inc 248 546-7984
111 E 10 Mile Rd Madison Heights (48071) *(G-10378)*

Visual Productions Inc 248 356-4399
24050 Northwestern Hwy Southfield (48075) *(G-15061)*

Visual Workplace LLC 616 583-9400
1300 Richfield Ct Sw Byron Center (49315) *(G-2215)*

Vita Plus Corporation 989 665-0013
6506 Mill St Gagetown (48735) *(G-5803)*

Vita Plus Gagetown, Gagetown *Also called Vita Plus Corporation (G-5803)*

Vital Signs Inc (PA) 313 491-2010
6753 Kings Mill Dr Canton (48187) *(G-2441)*

Vital Signs Michigan Inc 906 632-7602
751 Peck St Sault Sainte Marie (49783) *(G-14478)*

Vital Technologies 231 352-9364
1152 Martin Dr Frankfort (49635) *(G-5607)*

Vital Test, Frankfort *Also called Vital Technologies (G-5607)*

Vitec LLC 313 633-2254
2801 Clark St Detroit (48210) *(G-4433)*

Vitesco Technologies 313 583-5980
15001 N Commerce Dr Dearborn (48120) *(G-3769)*

Vitesco Technologies 248 393-5880
18615 Sherwood St Detroit (48234) *(G-4434)*

Vitesco Technologies 704 442-8000
1 Continental Dr Auburn Hills (48326) *(G-1046)*

Vitesco Technologies Usa LLC (HQ) 248 209-4000
2400 Executive Hills Dr Auburn Hills (48326) *(G-1047)*

Vitro Automotriz SA De CV 734 727-5001
1515 S Newburgh Rd Unit B Westland (48186) *(G-17608)*

Vitullo & Associates, Commerce Township *Also called Manufctring Solutions Tech LLC (G-3426)*

Viva Beverages LLC 248 746-7044
27777 Franklin Rd # 1640 Southfield (48034) *(G-15062)*

Vivatar Inc 616 928-0750
935 E 40th St Holland (49423) *(G-7849)*

Vivian Enterprises LLC 248 792-9925
29111 Telegraph Rd Southfield (48034) *(G-15063)*

Vizcom Media, Grand Rapids *Also called Sourceone Imaging LLC (G-6872)*

Vocational Strategies Inc 906 482-6142
23390 Airpark Blvd Calumet (49913) *(G-2335)*

Vochaska Engineering 269 637-5670
66935 County Road 388 South Haven (49090) *(G-14782)*

Vogel Engineering Inc 231 821-2125
6688 Maple Island Rd Holton (49425) *(G-7935)*

Vogel Tooling & Machine LLC 517 414-7635
2010 Micor Dr Jackson (49203) *(G-8601)*

Vogt Industries Inc 616 531-4830
4530 Roger B Chaffee Se Grand Rapids (49548) *(G-6974)*

Voice Communications Corp (PA) 586 716-8100
19176 Hall Rd Ste 200 Clinton Township (48038) *(G-3257)*

Voice Newspapers, The, Clinton Township *Also called Voice Communications Corp (G-3257)*

Voigt & Schweitzer LLC 313 535-2600
12600 Arnold Redford (48239) *(G-13206)*

Voigt Schwtzer Galvanizers Inc 313 535-2600
12600 Arnold Redford (48239) *(G-13207)*

Voila Print Inc 866 942-1677
37000 Industrial Rd Livonia (48150) *(G-9991)*

Volcor Finishing Inc 616 527-5555
510 Apple Tree Dr Ionia (48846) *(G-8254)*

Volk Corporation 616 940-9900
23936 Industrial Park Dr Farmington Hills (48335) *(G-5150)*

Volkswagen Auto Securitization, Auburn Hills *Also called Volkswagen Group America Inc (G-1048)*

Volkswagen Group, Auburn Hills *Also called Autombili Lamborghini Amer LLC (G-787)*

Volkswagen Group America Inc 248 754-5000
3800 Hamlin Rd Auburn Hills (48326) *(G-1048)*

Vollmer Ready-Mix Inc (PA) 989 453-2262
196 S Caseville Rd 204 Pigeon (48755) *(G-12494)*

Vollwerth & Co, Hancock *Also called Vandco Incorporated (G-7258)*

Volos Tube Form Inc 586 416-3600
50395 Corporate Dr Macomb (48044) *(G-10174)*

Volta Power Systems LLC 616 226-4224
12550 Superior Ct 40 Holland (49424) *(G-7850)*

Vomela Specialty Company 269 927-6500
375 Urbandale Ave Benton Harbor (49022) *(G-1562)*

Von Weise LLC (HQ) 517 618-9763
402 Haven St Ste H Eaton Rapids (48827) *(G-4736)*

Voorheis Hausbeck Excavating 989 752-9666
2695 W Vassar Rd Reese (48757) *(G-13235)*

Vortec 616 292-2401
201 W Washington Ave # 110 Zeeland (49464) *(G-18195)*

Vortech Pharmaceutical Ltd 313 584-4088
6851 Chase Rd Dearborn (48126) *(G-3770)*

Vortek 248 767-2992
440 S Dexter St Pinckney (48169) *(G-12505)*

Voss T & Sons Septic Tanks, Holland *Also called Ted Voss & Sons Inc (G-7825)*

Voxeljet America Inc 734 709-8237
41430 Haggerty Cir S Canton (48188) *(G-2442)*

Vp Demand Creation Services, Traverse City *Also called Village Press Inc (G-16137)*

Vs Products 989 831-4861
2075 Lakeside Dr Stanton (48888) *(G-15230)*

VSI Archtectural Signs Systems, Canton *Also called Vital Signs Inc (G-2441)*

VSR Technologies Inc 734 425-7172
12270 Belden Ct Livonia (48150) *(G-9992)*

Vte Inc 231 539-8000
5437 Robinson Rd Pellston (49769) *(G-12426)*

Vtec Graphics Inc (PA) 734 953-9729
12487 Globe St Livonia (48150) *(G-9993)*

Vulcan Wood Products Inc 906 563-8995
N1549 Sturgeon Mill Rd Vulcan (49892) *(G-16847)*

Vulcanmasters Welding Inc....313 843-5043
2094 Hampton St White Lake (48386) ***(G-17642)***
Vx-LLC....734 854-8700
8336 Monroe Rd Rm 201 Lambertville (48144) ***(G-9187)***
W & S Development Inc....989 724-5463
4957 Main St Greenbush (48738) ***(G-7121)***
W & W Tool and Die Inc....989 835-5522
1508 E Grove St Midland (48640) ***(G-10923)***
W A Thomas Company....734 475-8626
446 Congdon St Chelsea (48118) ***(G-2720)***
W A Thomas Company....734 955-6500
25940 Northline Rd Taylor (48180) ***(G-15779)***
W B Mason Co Inc....734 947-6370
25299 Brest Taylor (48180) ***(G-15780)***
W Bay Cupcakes....231 632-2010
524 W Thirteenth St Traverse City (49684) ***(G-16140)***
W G Benjey Inc (PA)....989 356-0016
2293 Werth Rd Alpena (49707) ***(G-319)***
W G Benjey Inc....989 356-0027
108 E Herman St Alpena (49707) ***(G-320)***
W G Benjey North, Alpena *Also called W G Benjey Inc* ***(G-320)***
W Industries, Livonia *Also called Tower Defense & Aerospace LLC* ***(G-9966)***
W J Z & Sons Harvesting Inc....906 586-6360
481 Lustila Rd Germfask (49836) ***(G-5902)***
W L Hamilton & Co....269 781-6941
325 Cherry St Marshall (49068) ***(G-10592)***
W L Snow Enterprises Inc....989 732-9501
2017 Dickerson Rd Gaylord (49735) ***(G-5899)***
W M Enterprises....810 694-4384
3487 Esson Dr Grand Blanc (48439) ***(G-5988)***
W M G, Taylor *Also called Windsor Mch & Stamping 2009* ***(G-15782)***
W M H Fluidpower, Portage *Also called Wmh Fluidpower Inc* ***(G-13058)***
W News....231 946-4446
300 E Front St Traverse City (49684) ***(G-16141)***
W S Townsend Company (PA)....269 781-5131
106 E Oliver Dr Marshall (49068) ***(G-10593)***
W S Townsend Company....517 393-7300
5320 S Pennsylvania Ave Lansing (48911) ***(G-9433)***
W Soule & Co (PA)....269 324-7001
7125 S Sprinkle Rd Portage (49002) ***(G-13054)***
W Soule & Co....269 344-0139
5175 King Hwy Kalamazoo (49048) ***(G-8920)***
W Soule & Co....616 975-6272
4925 Kendrick St Se Grand Rapids (49512) ***(G-6975)***
W Soule & Co Service Group, Portage *Also called W Soule & Co* ***(G-13054)***
W Soule & Company, Grand Rapids *Also called W Soule & Co* ***(G-6975)***
W T & M Inc....313 533-7888
12635 Arnold Redford (48239) ***(G-13208)***
W T Beresford Co....248 350-2900
26400 Lahser Rd Ste 408 Southfield (48033) ***(G-15064)***
W T C, Farmington Hills *Also called Nadex of America Corporation* ***(G-5075)***
W T C, Farmington Hills *Also called Welding Technology Corp* ***(G-5151)***
W T P, Coloma *Also called Witchcraft Tape Products Inc* ***(G-3368)***
W Vbh....269 927-1527
78 W Wall St Benton Harbor (49022) ***(G-1563)***
W W J Form Tool Company Inc....313 565-0015
26122 Michigan Ave Inkster (48141) ***(G-8235)***
W W Thayne Advertising Cons....269 979-1411
4642 Capital Ave Sw Battle Creek (49015) ***(G-1264)***
W W Williams Company LLC....313 584-6150
4000 Stecker St Dearborn (48126) ***(G-3771)***
W-Lok Corporation....616 355-4015
861 Productions Pl Holland (49423) ***(G-7851)***
W.A. Kates Company, The, Madison Heights *Also called Custom Valve Concepts Inc* ***(G-10225)***
W.K. Kellogg Institute, Battle Creek *Also called Kellogg Company* ***(G-1210)***
W2 Inc....517 764-3141
233 N Jackson St Jackson (49201) ***(G-8602)***
W2fuel Adrian, Adrian *Also called Adrian Lva Biofuel LLC* ***(G-44)***
W2fuel Adrian II, Adrian *Also called II Adrian LLC W2fuel* ***(G-68)***
W2fuel Keokuk I, Adrian *Also called W2fuel LLC* ***(G-101)***
W2fuel LLC (PA)....517 920-4868
1571 W Beecher Rd Adrian (49221) ***(G-101)***
Waanders Concrete Co....269 673-6352
3169 Babylon Rd Allegan (49010) ***(G-190)***
Wab, The, Ferndale *Also called Woodward Avenue Brewers* ***(G-5330)***
Wabco Holdings Inc (PA)....248 270-9300
1220 Pacific Dr Auburn Hills (48326) ***(G-1049)***
Waber Tool & Engineering Co....269 342-0765
1335 Ravine Rd Kalamazoo (49004) ***(G-8921)***
Wachler, David & Sons Jewelers, Birmingham *Also called David Wachler & Sons Inc* ***(G-1681)***
Wachtel Tool & Broach Inc....586 758-0110
6676 Fred W Moore Hwy Saint Clair (48079) ***(G-14236)***
Wacker Biochem Corporation....517 264-8500
3301 Sutton Rd Adrian (49221) ***(G-102)***
Wacker Chemical Corporation (HQ)....517 264-8500
3301 Sutton Rd Adrian (49221) ***(G-103)***
Wacker Neuson Corporation....231 799-4500
1300 E Mount Garfield Rd Norton Shores (49441) ***(G-11804)***
Waco Classic Aircraft Corp....269 565-1000
15955 South Airport Rd Battle Creek (49015) ***(G-1265)***
Waddell Electric Company....616 791-4860
4279 3 Mile Rd Nw Grand Rapids (49534) ***(G-6976)***
Wade Logging....231 463-0363
7108 W Sharon Rd Sw Fife Lake (49633) ***(G-5344)***
Wagon Automotive Inc....248 262-2020
28025 Oakland Oaks Ct Wixom (48393) ***(G-17927)***
Wahmhoff Farms LLC....269 628-4308
11121 M 40 Gobles (49055) ***(G-5950)***
Wahoo Composites LLC....734 424-0966
7190 Huron River Dr Dexter (48130) ***(G-4518)***
Wakefield News....906 224-9561
405 Sunday Lake St Wakefield (49968) ***(G-16856)***
Wal Fuel Systems (usa) Inc....248 579-4147
39111 6 Mile Rd Ste 167 Livonia (48152) ***(G-9994)***
Wal-Vac Inc....616 241-6717
900 47th St Sw Ste A Wyoming (49509) ***(G-18042)***
Walbro LLC....989 872-2131
6242 Garfield Ave Cass City (48726) ***(G-2524)***
Waldron's Exhaust, Centreville *Also called Waldrons Antique Exhaust* ***(G-2599)***
Waldrons Antique Exhaust....269 467-7185
208 W Main St Centreville (49032) ***(G-2599)***
Walker Printery Inc....248 548-5100
13351 Cloverdale St Oak Park (48237) ***(G-12104)***
Walker Telecommunications....989 274-7384
1375 S Center Rd Saginaw (48638) ***(G-14180)***
Walker Tool & Die Inc....616 453-5471
2411 Walker Ave Nw Grand Rapids (49544) ***(G-6977)***
Walker Tool & Manufacturing, Redford *Also called W T & M Inc* ***(G-13208)***
Walker Wire (ispat) Inc....248 399-4800
42744 Mound Rd Sterling Heights (48314) ***(G-15542)***
Wall Co Incorporated (PA)....248 585-6400
101 W Girard Ave Madison Heights (48071) ***(G-10379)***
Wall Colmonoy Corporation (HQ)....248 585-6400
101 W Girard Ave Madison Heights (48071) ***(G-10380)***
Wall Street Journal Gate A 20....734 941-4139
1 Detroit Metro Airport Detroit (48242) ***(G-4435)***
Wallace Publishing LLC....248 416-7259
1127 E Pearl Ave Hazel Park (48030) ***(G-7458)***
Wallace Stone Plant, Bay Port *Also called Falcon Trucking Company* ***(G-1373)***
Wallace Studios LLC....248 917-2459
17260 Madison St Southfield (48076) ***(G-15065)***
Waller Machine Co Inc....517 789-7707
433 Condad Ave Jackson (49202) ***(G-8603)***
Wallin Brothers Inc....734 525-7750
35270 Glendale St Ste 1 Livonia (48150) ***(G-9995)***
Walls Holding Company, Harbor Springs *Also called Central Industrial Mfg Inc* ***(G-7277)***
Wallside Inc....313 292-4400
27000 Trolley Indus Dr Taylor (48180) ***(G-15781)***
Wallside Window Factory, Taylor *Also called Wallside Inc* ***(G-15781)***
Walmart Inc....517 541-1481
1680 Packard Hwy Charlotte (48813) ***(G-2670)***
Walsworth Print Group, Saint Joseph *Also called Walsworth Publishing Co Inc* ***(G-14350)***
Walsworth Publishing Co Inc....269 428-2054
2180 Maiden Ln Saint Joseph (49085) ***(G-14350)***
Walter Sappington....989 345-1052
483 N 1st St West Branch (48661) ***(G-17527)***
Walters Plumbing & Htg Sups, Battle Creek *Also called Walters Plumbing Company* ***(G-1266)***
Walters Plumbing Company....269 962-6253
189 20th St N Battle Creek (49015) ***(G-1266)***
Walters Seed Co LLC....616 355-7333
65 Veterans Dr Holland (49423) ***(G-7852)***
Walther Trowal LLC....616 455-8940
4540 East Paris Ave Se F Grand Rapids (49512) ***(G-6978)***
Walther Trowal GMBH & Co KG....616 871-0031
4540 East Paris Ave Se Grand Rapids (49512) ***(G-6979)***
Walton Electronics, East Lansing *Also called Charles Walton* ***(G-4654)***
Walton Wood, West Bloomfield *Also called Singh Senior Living LLC* ***(G-17497)***
Waltons Sawmill....517 841-5241
1004 Hamilton St Jackson (49202) ***(G-8604)***
Waltz-Holst Blow Pipe Company....616 676-8119
230 Alta Dale Ave Se Ada (49301) ***(G-33)***
Wamu Fuel LLC....313 386-8700
17151 Middlebelt Rd Livonia (48152) ***(G-9996)***
Wandas Barium Cookie LLC....906 281-1788
25770 Elm St Calumet (49913) ***(G-2336)***
Wandres Corporation....734 214-9903
719 W Ellsworth Rd Ste 7 Ann Arbor (48108) ***(G-694)***
Wapc Holdings Inc....586 939-0770
40736 Brentwood Dr Sterling Heights (48310) ***(G-15543)***
Wara Construction Company LLC....248 299-2410
2927 Waterview Dr Rochester Hills (48309) ***(G-13540)***

ALPHABETIC SECTION
Weber Bros & White Metal Works

Ward-Williston Company (PA) 248 594-6622
36700 Woodward Ave # 101 Bloomfield (48304) ***(G-1737)***
Wardcraft Industries LLC 517 750-9100
1 Wardcraft Dr Spring Arbor (49283) ***(G-15129)***
Wards Automotive International, Southfield *Also called Informa Business Media Inc* ***(G-14947)***
Warfield Electric Company Inc 734 722-4044
5920 N Hix Rd Westland (48185) ***(G-17609)***
Warm Rain Corporation (PA) 906 482-3750
51675 Industrial Dr Calumet (49913) ***(G-2337)***
Warmerscom 800 518-0938
365 84th St Sw Ste 4 Byron Center (49315) ***(G-2216)***
Warmilu LLC 855 927-6458
8186 Jackson Rd Ste C Ann Arbor (48103) ***(G-695)***
Warn Industries Inc 734 953-9870
37002 Industrial Rd Livonia (48150) ***(G-9997)***
Warner Door 989 823-8397
397 Division St Vassar (48768) ***(G-16817)***
Warner Instruments 616 843-5342
1320 Fulton Ave Grand Haven (49417) ***(G-6096)***
Warner Oil Company 517 278-5844
400 Race St Coldwater (49036) ***(G-3341)***
Warner Vineyards Inc (PA) 269 657-3165
706 S Kalamazoo St Paw Paw (49079) ***(G-12417)***
Warner Vineyards Inc 269 637-6900
515 Williams St South Haven (49090) ***(G-14783)***
Warren Abrasives Inc 586 772-0002
25800 Groesbeck Hwy Warren (48089) ***(G-17285)***
Warren Autometric Fasteners, Livonia *Also called Warren Screw Works Inc* ***(G-9998)***
Warren Broach & Machine Corp 586 254-7080
6541 Diplomat Dr Sterling Heights (48314) ***(G-15544)***
Warren Chassix 248 728-8700
23300 Blackstone Ave Warren (48089) ***(G-17286)***
Warren City Fuel 586 759-4759
134 N Silvery Ln Dearborn (48128) ***(G-3772)***
Warren Industrial Welding Co (PA) 586 756-0230
24275 Hoover Rd Warren (48089) ***(G-17287)***
Warren Industrial Welding Co 586 463-6600
44441 N Groesbeck Hwy Clinton Township (48036) ***(G-3258)***
Warren Industries Inc (PA) 586 741-0420
22805 Interstate Dr Clinton Township (48035) ***(G-3259)***
Warren Manufacturing 269 483-0603
68635 Suszek Rd White Pigeon (49099) ***(G-17657)***
Warren Mfg Facility, Warren *Also called Punchcraft McHning Tooling LLC* ***(G-17211)***
Warren Screw Products Inc 586 757-1280
13201 Stephens Rd Warren (48089) ***(G-17288)***
Warren Screw Works Inc 734 525-2920
13360 Wayne Rd Livonia (48150) ***(G-9998)***
Warren Scrw Products Inc 586 994-0342
1733 Mead Rd Rochester Hills (48306) ***(G-13541)***
Warren Stamping Plant, Warren *Also called FCA US LLC* ***(G-17029)***
Warrior Sports Inc (HQ) 800 968-7845
32125 Hollingsworth Ave Warren (48092) ***(G-17289)***
Wartian Lock Company 586 777-2244
20525 E 9 Mile Rd Saint Clair Shores (48080) ***(G-14276)***
Wartrom Machine Systems 586 469-1915
22786 Patmore Dr Clinton Township (48036) ***(G-3260)***
Warwick Mas & Equipment Co 810 966-3431
1621 Pine Grove Ave Port Huron (48060) ***(G-12975)***
Washburn Woodwork & Cabinet, Otsego *Also called George Washburn* ***(G-12240)***
Washers Incorporated (PA) 734 523-1000
33375 Glendale St Livonia (48150) ***(G-9999)***
Washers Incorporated 734 523-1000
32711 Glendale St Livonia (48150) ***(G-10000)***
Washington Street Printers LLC 734 240-5541
17 Washington St Monroe (48161) ***(G-11083)***
Washtenaw Communications Inc 734 662-7138
1510 Saunders Cres Ann Arbor (48103) ***(G-696)***
Washtenaw Legal News, Ann Arbor *Also called Detroit Legal News Pubg LLC* ***(G-418)***
Washtenaw Voice 734 677-5405
4800 E Huron River Dr Ann Arbor (48105) ***(G-697)***
Waste and Water Trtmnt Plant, Port Huron *Also called City of Port Huron* ***(G-12908)***
Waste Management, Ontonagon *Also called K and W Landfill Inc* ***(G-12160)***
Waste Water Treatment, Menominee *Also called Menominee City of Michigan* ***(G-10746)***
Watchdog Quarterly Inc 734 593-7039
19 Chestnut Dr Chelsea (48118) ***(G-2721)***
Water Department 313 943-2307
2951 Greenfield Rd Dearborn (48120) ***(G-3773)***
Water Master Inc 313 255-3930
41747 Joy Rd Canton (48187) ***(G-2443)***
Waterfall Jewelers, Waterford *Also called C T & T Inc* ***(G-17328)***
Waterjetplus, Gaylord *Also called P I W Corporation* ***(G-5887)***
Waterman and Sons Prtg Co Inc 313 864-5562
17134 Wyoming St Detroit (48221) ***(G-4436)***
Waterman Tool & Machine Corp 989 823-8181
1032 E Huron Ave Vassar (48768) ***(G-16818)***
Watkins Products 586 774-3187
15734 Camden Ave Eastpointe (48021) ***(G-4712)***
Watson Sales 517 296-4275
7821 Topinabee Dr Montgomery (49255) ***(G-11100)***
Wattsson & Wattsson Jewelers 906 228-5775
118 W Washington St # 100 Marquette (49855) ***(G-10561)***
Wave, Benton Harbor *Also called Worthington Armstrong Venture* ***(G-1572)***
Way Bakery (HQ) 517 787-6720
2100 Enterprise St Jackson (49203) ***(G-8605)***
Wayne Allen Lambert 269 467-4624
231 N Clark St Centreville (49032) ***(G-2600)***
Wayne County Laboratory 734 285-5215
797 Central St Wyandotte (48192) ***(G-17981)***
Wayne Craft, Livonia *Also called Wayne-Craft Inc* ***(G-10001)***
Wayne Novick 269 685-9818
113 4th St Plainwell (49080) ***(G-12551)***
Wayne Steel Tech, Farmington *Also called Detroit Materials Inc* ***(G-4897)***
Wayne Stmping Intrntnal- Sbsid, Detroit *Also called Milton Manufacturing Inc* ***(G-4250)***
Wayne Wire A Bag Cmponents Inc 231 258-9187
200 E Dresden St Kalkaska (49646) ***(G-8966)***
Wayne Wire Airbag Components, Kalkaska *Also called Wayne Wire Cloth Products Inc* ***(G-8967)***
Wayne Wire Cloth Products Inc 989 742-4591
221 Garfield St Hillman (49746) ***(G-7510)***
Wayne Wire Cloth Products Inc (PA) 231 258-9187
200 E Dresden St Kalkaska (49646) ***(G-8967)***
Wayne Wire Cloths, Bingham Farms *Also called Strema Sales Corp* ***(G-1660)***
Wayne-Craft Inc 734 421-8800
13525 Wayne Rd Livonia (48150) ***(G-10001)***
Wb, Roseville *Also called Wolverine Bronze Company* ***(G-13891)***
WB Pallets Inc 616 669-3000
4440 Chicago Dr Hudsonville (49426) ***(G-8185)***
Wcec, Shelby Township *Also called World Class Equipment Company* ***(G-14723)***
Wcg Design, Detroit *Also called Whiteside Consulting Group LLC* ***(G-4440)***
Wcscarts LLC (PA) 248 901-0965
900 Wilshire Dr Ste 202 Troy (48084) ***(G-16688)***
We Print Everything Inc 989 723-6499
215 N Ball St Owosso (48867) ***(G-12328)***
We're Rolling Pretzel Company, Howell *Also called Syd Enterprises* ***(G-8104)***
Wealthy Street Corporation 616 451-0784
700 Wealthy St Sw Grand Rapids (49504) ***(G-6980)***
Weather King of Indiana, Farmington *Also called Weather King Windows Doors Inc* ***(G-4915)***
Weather King Windows Doors Inc (PA) 313 933-1234
20775 Chesley Dr Farmington (48336) ***(G-4915)***
Weather King Windows Doors Inc 248 478-7788
20775 Chesley Dr Farmington (48336) ***(G-4916)***
Weather Pane Inc 810 798-8695
6209 Bordman Rd Almont (48003) ***(G-270)***
Weather-Rite LLC 612 338-1401
1100 7 Mile Rd Nw Comstock Park (49321) ***(G-3520)***
Weathergard Window Company Inc 248 967-8822
14350 W 8 Mile Rd Oak Park (48237) ***(G-12105)***
Weathergard Window Factory, Oak Park *Also called Weathergard Window Company Inc* ***(G-12105)***
Weatherproof Inc 517 764-1330
385 Watts Rd Jackson (49203) ***(G-8606)***
Weathervane Vinyards Inc 231 228-4800
6530 S Lake Shore Dr Cedar (49621) ***(G-2543)***
Weave Alloy Products Company, Sterling Heights *Also called Wapc Holdings Inc* ***(G-15543)***
Weaver Instructional Systems 616 942-2891
6161 28th St Se Ste 9 Grand Rapids (49546) ***(G-6981)***
Web Litho Inc 586 803-9000
560 John R Rd Rochester Hills (48307) ***(G-13542)***
Web Printing & Mktg Concepts 269 983-4646
4086 Red Arrow Hwy Saint Joseph (49085) ***(G-14351)***
Webasto Assembly, Rochester Hills *Also called Webasto Roof Systems Inc* ***(G-13545)***
Webasto Convertibles USA Inc (HQ) 734 582-5900
14988 Pilot Dr Plymouth (48170) ***(G-12791)***
Webasto Convertibles USA Inc 734 582-5900
14967 Pilot Dr Plymouth (48170) ***(G-12792)***
Webasto Roof Systems Inc 734 452-2600
36930 Industrial Rd Livonia (48150) ***(G-10002)***
Webasto Roof Systems Inc (HQ) 248 997-5100
1757 Northfield Dr Rochester Hills (48309) ***(G-13543)***
Webasto Roof Systems Inc 248 299-2000
2700 Product Dr Rochester Hills (48309) ***(G-13544)***
Webasto Roof Systems Inc 248 997-5100
1757 Northfield Dr Rochester Hills (48309) ***(G-13545)***
Webasto Roofing, Rochester Hills *Also called Webasto Roof Systems Inc* ***(G-13543)***
Webasto Sunroofs, Rochester Hills *Also called Webasto Roof Systems Inc* ***(G-13544)***
Webasto-Group, Plymouth *Also called Webasto Convertibles USA Inc* ***(G-12791)***
Webb Partners Inc 734 727-0560
39140 Webb Dr Westland (48185) ***(G-17610)***
Webcor Packaging Corporation (PA) 810 767-2806
1220 N Center Rd Burton (48509) ***(G-2170)***
Weber Automotive Corporation 248 393-5520
1750 Summit Dr Auburn Hills (48326) ***(G-1050)***
Weber Bros & White Metal Works 269 751-5193
4715 136th Ave Hamilton (49419) ***(G-7242)***

ALPHABETIC

Weber Bros Sawmill Inc ALPHABETIC SECTION

Weber Bros Sawmill Inc 989 644-2206
2862 N Winn Rd Mount Pleasant (48858) **(G-11235)**
Weber Electric Mfg Co 586 323-9000
2465 23 Mile Rd Shelby Township (48316) **(G-14721)**
Weber Machine (usa) Inc 207 947-4990
4717 Broadmoor Ave Se B Grand Rapids (49512) **(G-6982)**
Weber Precision Grinding Inc 616 842-1634
18438 171st Ave Spring Lake (49456) **(G-15186)**
Weber Sand and Gravel Inc (PA) 248 373-0900
1401 E Silverbell Rd Lake Orion (48360) **(G-9169)**
Weber Security Group Inc 586 582-0000
95 S Rose St Ste A Mount Clemens (48043) **(G-11153)**
Weber Steel & Body, Vassar *Also called Weber Steel Inc* **(G-16819)**
Weber Steel Inc 989 868-4162
3000 Bradford Rd Vassar (48768) **(G-16819)**
Weber Ultrasonics America LLC 248 620-5142
7478 Gateway Park Dr Clarkston (48346) **(G-2964)**
Webo Detroit Corp 586 268-8900
6221 Progress Dr Sterling Heights (48312) **(G-15545)**
Webster Cold Forge Co 313 554-4500
47652 Pine Creek Ct Northville (48168) **(G-11734)**
Websto Stamping, Livonia *Also called Webasto Roof Systems Inc* **(G-10002)**
Wec Group LLC 248 260-4252
1850 Northfield Dr Rochester Hills (48309) **(G-13546)**
Weco International Inc 810 686-7221
235 S Seymour Rd Flushing (48433) **(G-5545)**
Wedin International Inc (PA) 231 779-8650
1111 6th Ave Cadillac (49601) **(G-2284)**
Wefa Cedar Inc 616 696-0873
104 W Beech St Cedar Springs (49319) **(G-2565)**
Weiderman Motorsports 269 689-0264
28386 Witt Lake Rd Sturgis (49091) **(G-15641)**
Weighman Enterprises Inc 989 755-2116
1131 E Genesee Ave Saginaw (48607) **(G-14181)**
Weinschel An API Technolo, Ann Arbor *Also called API Technologies Corp* **(G-361)**
Weiser Metal Products Inc 989 736-6055
3040 E Carbide Dr Harrisville (48740) **(G-7367)**
Weiser Metal Products Inc 989 736-8151
3431 E M 72 Lincoln (48742) **(G-9571)**
Weiss Technik North Amer Inc (HQ) 616 554-5020
3881 N Greenbrooke Dr Se Grand Rapids (49512) **(G-6983)**
Welch Foods Inc A Cooperative 269 624-4141
400 Walker St Lawton (49065) **(G-9516)**
Welch Land & Timber Inc 989 848-5197
2708 N Reeves Rd Curran (48728) **(G-3617)**
Welchdry Inc 616 399-2711
4270 Sunnyside Dr Holland (49424) **(G-7853)**
Weld Tech Unlimited Inc 231 627-7531
10983 Townline Rd Cheboygan (49721) **(G-2697)**
Weld-Aid Products, Detroit *Also called CRC Industries Inc* **(G-3953)**
Weldall Corporation 989 375-2251
2295 Hartsell Rd Elkton (48731) **(G-4786)**
Weldaloy Products Company 586 758-5550
24011 Hoover Rd Warren (48089) **(G-17290)**
Weldcraft Inc 734 779-1303
11881 Belden Ct Livonia (48150) **(G-10003)**
Welders & Presses Inc 586 948-4300
27295 Luckino Dr Chesterfield (48047) **(G-2856)**
Welders and Presses, Chesterfield *Also called 1271 Associates Inc* **(G-2730)**
Welding & Joining Tech LLC 248 625-3045
5439 Bristol Parke Dr Clarkston (48348) **(G-2965)**
Welding Fabricating Inc 616 877-4345
3989 9th St Wayland (49348) **(G-17419)**
Welding Technology Corp (HQ) 248 477-3900
24775 Crestview Ct Farmington Hills (48335) **(G-5151)**
Weldmet Industries Inc 586 773-0533
21799 Schmeman Ave Warren (48089) **(G-17291)**
Weldore Manufacturing, Hazel Park *Also called Fox Aluminum Products Inc* **(G-7438)**
Weldpower, Clarkston *Also called Welding & Joining Tech LLC* **(G-2965)**
Welform Electrodes Inc 586 755-1184
2147 Kenney Ave Warren (48091) **(G-17292)**
Welk-Ko Fabricators Inc 248 486-2598
53655 Grand River Ave New Hudson (48165) **(G-11559)**
Welk-Ko Fabricators Inc (PA) 734 425-6840
11885 Mayfield St Livonia (48150) **(G-10004)**
Welk-Ko Fabricators Inc 810 227-7500
11777 Grand River Rd Brighton (48116) **(G-2008)**
Wellard Inc 312 752-0155
10377 Mesic Dr West Olive (49460) **(G-17536)**
Weller Truck Parts, Grand Rapids *Also called Jasper Weller LLC* **(G-6554)**
Wellington Fragrance 734 261-5531
33306 Glendale St Livonia (48150) **(G-10005)**
Wellington Industries Inc (PA) 734 942-1060
39555 S I 94 Servce Dr Van Buren Twp (48111) **(G-16796)**
Wellington Industries Inc 734 403-6112
39635 S I 94 Servce Dr Van Buren Twp (48111) **(G-16797)**
Wellington-Almont LLC (HQ) 734 942-1060
39555 S Interstate 94 Ser Van Buren Twp (48111) **(G-16798)**
Wellman's Bait and Tackle, Oscoda *Also called Wellmans Sport Center* **(G-12224)**
Wellmans Sport Center 989 739-2869
910 S State St Oscoda (48750) **(G-12224)**
Wellmaster Consulting Inc 231 893-9266
2658 W Winston Rd Rothbury (49452) **(G-13896)**
Wells Equipment Sales Inc 517 542-2376
534 Homer Rd Litchfield (49252) **(G-9613)**
Wells Helicopter Service Inc 616 874-6255
10860 11 Mile Rd Ne Greenville (48838) **(G-7160)**
Wells Index Division, Muskegon *Also called A & D Run Off Inc* **(G-11256)**
Wellsaw, Kalamazoo *Also called Coxline Inc* **(G-8720)**
Wellsense USA Inc 888 335-0995
199 W Brown St Ste 110 Birmingham (48009) **(G-1708)**
Welz Tool Mch & Boring Co Inc 734 425-3920
11952 Hubbard St Livonia (48150) **(G-10006)**
Wemco, Shelby Township *Also called Weber Electric Mfg Co* **(G-14721)**
Wender Logging Inc 906 779-1483
W7487 Upper Pine Creek Dr Iron Mountain (49801) **(G-8305)**
Wendling Sheet Metal Inc 989 753-5286
2633 Carrollton Rd Saginaw (48604) **(G-14182)**
Wendricks Truss Inc 906 635-8822
6142 S Mackinac Trl Sault Sainte Marie (49783) **(G-14479)**
Wendricks Truss Inc (PA) 906 498-7709
W5728 Old Us 2 Road No 43 Hermansville (49847) **(G-7468)**
Wenz & Gibbens Enterprises 248 333-7938
101 E Walton Blvd Pontiac (48340) **(G-12874)**
Wepco Energy LLC (PA) 231 932-8615
250 E Front St Ste 402 Traverse City (49684) **(G-16142)**
Werkema Machine Company Inc 616 455-7650
7300 Division Ave S Grand Rapids (49548) **(G-6984)**
Werner Electric Co 313 561-0854
20520 Van Born Rd Dearborn Heights (48125) **(G-3801)**
Wes Corp 231 536-2500
5900 Airport Rd East Jordan (49727) **(G-4647)**
Wes Stabeck Industries, LLC, Troy *Also called Stapels Manufacturing LLC* **(G-16619)**
West Bay Exploration Company (PA) 231 946-3529
13685 S West Bay Shore Dr Traverse City (49684) **(G-16143)**
West Bay Geophysical Inc 231 946-3529
13685 W Bay Shr 116 Traverse City (49684) **(G-16144)**
West Branch Wood Treating Inc 989 343-0066
3800 S M 30 West Branch (48661) **(G-17528)**
West Brothers LLC 734 457-0083
815 Scarlet Oak Dr Monroe (48162) **(G-11084)**
West Colony Graphic Inc 269 375-6625
2519 Summerdale Ave Kalamazoo (49004) **(G-8922)**
West Colony Printing, Kalamazoo *Also called West Colony Graphic Inc* **(G-8922)**
West Mich Auto Stl & Engrg Inc 616 560-8198
550 E Ellis Ave Belding (48809) **(G-1431)**
West Mich Awning, Holland *Also called West Michigan Canvas Company* **(G-7855)**
West Mich Flcking Assembly LLC 269 639-1634
78277 County Road 378 Covert (49043) **(G-3592)**
West Mich Off Interiors Inc 269 344-0768
3308 S Westnedge Ave Kalamazoo (49008) **(G-8923)**
West Mich Prcsion McHining Inc 616 791-1970
2500 Waldorf Ct Nw Grand Rapids (49544) **(G-6985)**
West Michigan Aerial LLc 269 998-4455
62422 M 40 Lawton (49065) **(G-9517)**
West Michigan Alpacas 616 990-0556
15747 Greenly St Holland (49424) **(G-7854)**
West Michigan Cabinet Supply 616 896-6990
4366 Central Pkwy Hudsonville (49426) **(G-8186)**
West Michigan Canvas Company 616 355-7855
11041 Paw Paw Dr Holland (49424) **(G-7855)**
West Michigan Coating LLC 616 647-9509
3150 Fruit Ridge Ave Nw Grand Rapids (49544) **(G-6986)**
West Michigan Compounding, Greenville *Also called Wmc LLC* **(G-7161)**
West Michigan Crematory Svc, Muskegon *Also called Wilbert Burial Vault Company* **(G-11449)**
West Michigan Fab Corp 616 794-3750
321 Root St 3ph Belding (48809) **(G-1432)**
West Michigan Forklift Inc 616 262-4949
4155 12th St Wayland (49348) **(G-17420)**
West Michigan Gage Inc 616 735-0585
4055 Rmmbrnce Rd Nw Ste 1 Walker (49534) **(G-16882)**
West Michigan Grinding Svc Inc 231 739-4245
1188 E Broadway Ave Norton Shores (49444) **(G-11805)**
West Michigan Medical 269 673-2141
595 Jenner Dr Allegan (49010) **(G-191)**
West Michigan Metals LLC 269 978-7021
1168 33rd St Allegan (49010) **(G-192)**
West Michigan Molding Inc 616 846-4950
1425 Aerial View Dr Grand Haven (49417) **(G-6097)**
West Michigan Nail & Wire Co, Wyoming *Also called National Nail Corp* **(G-18021)**
West Michigan Pedorthics, Muskegon *Also called Shoe Shop* **(G-11422)**
West Michigan Printing Inc 616 676-2190
513 Pine Land Dr Se Ada (49301) **(G-34)**
West Michigan Sawmill 616 693-0044
7760 Nash Hwy Clarksville (48815) **(G-2967)**
West Michigan Spline Inc 616 399-4078
156 Manufacturers Dr Holland (49424) **(G-7856)**

West Michigan Stamp & Seal 269 323-1913
10330 Portage Rd Portage (49002) ***(G-13055)***
West Michigan Tag & Label Inc 616 235-0120
5300 Broadmoor Ave Se F Grand Rapids (49512) ***(G-6987)***
West Michigan Technical Supply 616 735-0991
11331 3rd Ave Nw Grand Rapids (49534) ***(G-6988)***
West Michigan Tool & Die, Benton Harbor *Also called Bulk AG Innovations LLC* ***(G-1488)***
West Michigan Tool & Die Co 269 925-0900
1007 Nickerson Ave Benton Harbor (49022) ***(G-1564)***
West Michigan Truss Company, Muskegon *Also called Truss Technologies Inc* ***(G-11443)***
West Michigan Wire Co 231 845-1281
211 E Dowland St Ludington (49431) ***(G-10087)***
West Plant, Grand Rapids *Also called Cascade Engineering Inc* ***(G-6262)***
West River Machine, Niles *Also called Shively Corp* ***(G-11645)***
West Shore Services Inc (PA) 616 895-4347
6620 Lake Michigan Dr Allendale (49401) ***(G-227)***
West Shore Signs Inc 734 324-7076
18600 Krause St Riverview (48193) ***(G-13306)***
West Side Flamehardening Inc 734 729-1665
38200 N Executive Dr Westland (48185) ***(G-17611)***
West Side Mfg Fabrication Inc 248 380-6640
28776 Wall St Wixom (48393) ***(G-17928)***
West System Inc 989 684-7286
102 Patterson Ave Bay City (48706) ***(G-1370)***
West Thomas Partners LLC 616 430-7585
4053 Brockton Dr Se Ste A Grand Rapids (49512) ***(G-6989)***
West/Win Ltd 734 525-9000
11800 Sears St Livonia (48150) ***(G-10007)***
Westco Metalcraft Inc 734 425-0900
31846 Glendale St Livonia (48150) ***(G-10008)***
Westcott Displays Inc (PA) 313 872-1200
450 Amsterdam St Detroit (48202) ***(G-4437)***
Westcott Paper Products, Detroit *Also called Westcott Displays Inc* ***(G-4437)***
Westech Corp 231 766-3914
2357 Whitehall Rd Muskegon (49445) ***(G-11447)***
Westendorff Redi-Mix, Pewamo *Also called Westendorff Transit Mix* ***(G-12480)***
Westendorff Transit Mix 989 593-2488
3344 N Hubbardston Rd Pewamo (48873) ***(G-12480)***
Western Adhesive Inc 616 874-5869
6768 Kitson Dr Ne Rockford (49341) ***(G-13596)***
Western Diversified, Mattawan *Also called Mol-Son Inc* ***(G-10666)***
Western Diversified Plas LLC (PA) 269 668-3393
53150 N Main St Mattawan (49071) ***(G-10671)***
Western Engineered Products 248 371-9259
540 N Lapeer Rd Ste 390 Lake Orion (48362) ***(G-9170)***
Western Global, Troy *Also called Western International Inc* ***(G-16689)***
Western International Inc 866 814-2470
1707 Northwood Dr Troy (48084) ***(G-16689)***
Western Land Services Inc (PA) 231 843-8878
1100 Conrad Industrial Dr Ludington (49431) ***(G-10088)***
Western Michigan Plastics 616 394-9269
5745 143rd Ave Holland (49423) ***(G-7857)***
Western Pegasus Inc (PA) 616 393-9580
728 E 8th St Ste 3 Holland (49423) ***(G-7858)***
Western Press, Troy *Also called United Systems* ***(G-16664)***
Western Reflections LLC 616 772-9111
215 E Roosevelt Ave Zeeland (49464) ***(G-18196)***
Westgood Manufacturing Co (PA) 586 771-3970
15211 E 11 Mile Rd Roseville (48066) ***(G-13890)***
Westlund Mfg, Jackson *Also called Thomas Frankini* ***(G-8589)***
Westool Corporation 734 847-2520
7383 Sulier Dr Temperance (48182) ***(G-15847)***
Westpack Inc 231 725-9200
1204 W Western Ave Ste 3 Muskegon (49441) ***(G-11448)***
Westrock Company 734 453-6700
11333 General Dr Plymouth (48170) ***(G-12793)***
Westrock Cp LLC 810 787-6503
1409 E Pierson Rd Flint (48505) ***(G-5522)***
Westrock Rkt LLC 269 963-5511
177 Angell St Battle Creek (49037) ***(G-1267)***
Westshore Design, Holland *Also called Hgc Westshore LLC* ***(G-7664)***
Westshore Testing, Holland *Also called Parkway Elc Communications LLC* ***(G-7767)***
Westside Powder Coat LLC 734 729-1667
35777 Genron Ct Romulus (48174) ***(G-13739)***
Westside Tool & Gage LLC 734 728-9520
5682 Morley St Westland (48185) ***(G-17612)***
Wet N Rugged Sports, Galesburg *Also called Soupcan Inc* ***(G-5815)***
Wetzel Tool & Engineering Inc 248 960-0430
46952 Liberty Dr Wixom (48393) ***(G-17929)***
Wexford Wood Workings LLC 231 876-9663
407 Goode Ave Cadillac (49601) ***(G-2285)***
Weyerhaeuser Company 989 348-2881
4111 W 4 Mile Rd Grayling (49738) ***(G-7118)***
Weyhing Bros Manufacturing Co 313 567-0600
3040 Gratiot Ave Detroit (48207) ***(G-4438)***
Weyv Inc 248 614-2400
1820 E Big Beaver Rd Troy (48083) ***(G-16690)***
Wfl Millturn Technologies Inc 440 729-0896
48152 West Rd Wixom (48393) ***(G-17930)***
WG Sweis Investments LLC 313 477-8433
57155 Covington Dr Washington (48094) ***(G-17314)***
Wgnb, Zeeland *Also called Moody Bible Inst of Chicago* ***(G-18167)***
Wgs Global Services LC (PA) 810 239-4947
6350 Taylor Dr Flint (48507) ***(G-5523)***
Wgs Global Services LC 810 694-3843
7075 Dort Hwy Grand Blanc (48439) ***(G-5989)***
Wh Manufacturing Inc 616 534-7560
2606 Thornwood St Sw Grand Rapids (49519) ***(G-6990)***
Whats Scoop 616 662-6423
3667 Baldwin St Hudsonville (49426) ***(G-8187)***
Whats Your Mix Menchies LLC 248 840-1668
2168 Scarboro Ct Shelby Township (48316) ***(G-14722)***
Wheat Jewelers, Okemos *Also called Kevin Wheat & Assoc Ltd* ***(G-12127)***
Wheel Truing Brake Shoe Co, Rochester *Also called Gorang Industries Inc* ***(G-13322)***
Wheelchair Carrier, Lambertville *Also called Innovative Cargo Systems LLC* ***(G-9183)***
Wheeler Insulation, Battle Creek *Also called Insulation Wholesale Supply* ***(G-1200)***
Wheelers Wolf Lake Sawmill 231 745-7078
195 N M 37 # 137 Baldwin (49304) ***(G-1086)***
Wheelhouse Graphix LLC 800 732-0815
445 Enterprise Ct Bloomfield Hills (48302) ***(G-1810)***
Wheelock & Son Welding Shop 231 947-6557
9954 N Long Lake Rd Traverse City (49685) ***(G-16145)***
Wheelock & Sons Welding, Traverse City *Also called Wheelock & Son Welding Shop* ***(G-16145)***
Whimsical Fusions LLC 248 956-0952
2326 E 7 Mile Rd Detroit (48234) ***(G-4439)***
Whipple Printing Inc 313 382-8033
17140 Ecorse Rd Allen Park (48101) ***(G-213)***
Whirlpool Corporation (PA) 269 923-5000
2000 N M 63 Benton Harbor (49022) ***(G-1565)***
Whirlpool Corporation 269 923-7441
500 Renaissance Dr # 102 Saint Joseph (49085) ***(G-14352)***
Whirlpool Corporation 269 923-5000
600 W Main St Benton Harbor (49022) ***(G-1566)***
Whirlpool Corporation 269 923-7400
1800 Paw Paw Ave Benton Harbor (49022) ***(G-1567)***
Whirlpool Corporation 269 849-0907
3694 Kerlikowske Rd Coloma (49038) ***(G-3367)***
Whirlpool Corporation 269 923-5000
750 Monte Rd Benton Harbor (49022) ***(G-1568)***
Whirlpool Corporation 269 923-6057
303 Upton Dr Saint Joseph (49085) ***(G-14353)***
Whirlpool Corporation 269 923-6486
151 Riverview Dr Benton Harbor (49022) ***(G-1569)***
Whirlpool Corporation 269 923-5000
2000 N M 63 Benton Harbor (49022) ***(G-1570)***
Whirlpool Corporation 269 923-3009
150 Hilltop Rd Mldrop7590 7590 Maildrop Benton Harbor (49022) ***(G-1571)***
Whisper Creative Products Inc (PA) 734 529-2734
1585 Wells Rd Dundee (48131) ***(G-4603)***
Whitcomb and Sons Sign Co Inc 586 752-3576
315 E Lafayette St Romeo (48065) ***(G-13641)***
Whitcomb Sign, Romeo *Also called Whitcomb and Sons Sign Co Inc* ***(G-13641)***
White Automation & Tool Co 734 947-9822
28888 Goddard Rd Ste 100 Romulus (48174) ***(G-13740)***
White Cloud Manufacturing Co (PA) 231 796-8603
123 N Dekraft Ave Big Rapids (49307) ***(G-1646)***
White Cloud Mfg Co 231 689-6087
19 N Charles St White Cloud (49349) ***(G-17627)***
White Dress The LLC 810 588-6147
209 W Main St Ste 101 Brighton (48116) ***(G-2009)***
White Engineering Inc 269 695-0825
3000 E Geyer Rd Niles (49120) ***(G-11651)***
White Lake Beacon Inc 231 894-5356
432 E Spring St Whitehall (49461) ***(G-17680)***
White Lake Excavating Inc 231 894-6918
2571 Holton Whitehall Rd Whitehall (49461) ***(G-17681)***
White Lotus Farms Inc 734 904-1379
7217 W Liberty Rd Ann Arbor (48103) ***(G-698)***
White Pallet Chair 989 424-8771
4961 E Colonville Rd Clare (48617) ***(G-2892)***
White Pigeon Paper Co, White Pigeon *Also called Artistic Carton Company* ***(G-17644)***
White Pine Copper Refinery Inc 906 885-7100
29784 Willow Rd White Pine (49971) ***(G-17659)***
White Pines Corporation 734 761-2670
5204 Jackson Rd Ste 1 Ann Arbor (48103) ***(G-699)***
White River 231 894-9216
7386 Post Rd Montague (49437) ***(G-11099)***
White River Knife and Tool 616 997-0026
515 Industrial Dr Fremont (49412) ***(G-5786)***
White River Sugar Bush 231 861-4860
2840 E Garfield Rd Hesperia (49421) ***(G-7480)***
White Tool & Engineering, Niles *Also called White Engineering Inc* ***(G-11651)***
Whiteboard Depot, Rockford *Also called Newkirk and Associates Inc* ***(G-13582)***
Whitehall Industries, Ludington *Also called Signa Group Inc* ***(G-10078)***

A L P H A B E T I C

Whitehall Products LLC 231 894-2688
1625 Warner St Whitehall (49461) *(G-17682)*
Whitehouse Logging & Hardwood, Manton *Also called Allen Whitehouse (G-10450)*
Whitens Kiln & Lumber Inc 906 498-2116
125801 Coney Rd Hermansville (49847) *(G-7469)*
Whites Bridge Tooling Inc 616 897-4151
1395 Bowes Rd Lowell (49331) *(G-10045)*
Whites Industrial Service 616 291-3706
5010 Abraham Dr Ne Lowell (49331) *(G-10046)*
Whitesell Frmed Components Inc 313 299-1178
5331 Dixie Hwy Waterford (48329) *(G-17385)*
Whiteside Consulting Group LLC 313 288-6598
19341 Stansbury St Detroit (48235) *(G-4440)*
Whitesville Mill Service Co, Detroit *Also called Butler Mill Service Company (G-3922)*
Whiting Corporation 734 451-0400
48961 Thoreau Dr Plymouth (48170) *(G-12794)*
Whiting Petroleum Corporation 989 345-7903
2251 Simmons Rd West Branch (48661) *(G-17529)*
Whitlam Group Inc (PA) 586 757-5100
24800 Sherwood Center Line (48015) *(G-2586)*
Whitlock Business Systems Inc 248 548-1040
275 E 12 Mile Rd Madison Heights (48071) *(G-10381)*
Whitlock Distribution Svcs LLC 248 548-1040
275 E 12 Mile Rd Madison Heights (48071) *(G-10382)*
Whittaker Timber Corporation 989 872-3065
3623 Elmwood Rd Cass City (48726) *(G-2525)*
Wholesale Ticket Co Inc 616 642-9476
41 Parsonage St Saranac (48881) *(G-14457)*
Wholesale Weave Inc 800 762-2037
3130 E 8 Mile Rd Detroit (48234) *(G-4441)*
Wickedglow Industries Inc 586 776-4132
248 Nrthbound Gratiot Ave Mount Clemens (48043) *(G-11154)*
Wickey Custom Cabinets 517 858-1119
807 N Matteson St Bronson (49028) *(G-2035)*
Wico Metal Products Company (PA) 586 755-9600
23500 Sherwood Ave Warren (48091) *(G-17293)*
Wico Metal Products Company 586 755-9600
24400 Sherwood Center Line (48015) *(G-2587)*
Wicwas Press 269 344-8027
1620 Miller Rd Kalamazoo (49001) *(G-8924)*
Widell Industries Inc 989 742-4528
24601 Veterans Mem Hwy Hillman (49746) *(G-7511)*
Wiesen EDM Inc 616 794-9870
8630 Storey Rd Belding (48809) *(G-1433)*
Wieske Tool Inc 989 288-2648
202 S Hagle St Durand (48429) *(G-4615)*
Wigton Pipe Organs Inc 810 796-3311
4848 General Squier Rd Dryden (48428) *(G-4573)*
Wikoff Color Corporation 616 245-3930
3410 Jefferson Ave Se Grand Rapids (49548) *(G-6991)*
Wil-Kast Inc 616 281-2850
8025 Division Ave S Grand Rapids (49548) *(G-6992)*
Wilbert Burial Vault Co, Traverse City *Also called Bostwick Enterprises Inc (G-15917)*
Wilbert Burial Vault Company (PA) 231 773-6631
1510 S Getty St Muskegon (49442) *(G-11449)*
Wilbert Burial Vault Company 231 773-6631
1546 S Getty St Muskegon (49442) *(G-11450)*
Wilbert Burial Vault Works 906 786-0261
609 S Carpenter Ave Kingsford (49802) *(G-9068)*
Wilbert Plastic Services, Troy *Also called Enginred Plstic Components Inc (G-16347)*
Wilbert Saginaw Vault Corp (PA) 989 753-3065
2810 Hess Ave Saginaw (48601) *(G-14183)*
Wilbur Products Inc 231 755-3805
950 W Broadway Ave Muskegon (49441) *(G-11451)*
Wilco Tooling & Mfg LLC 517 901-0147
105 Enterprise St Reading (49274) *(G-13139)*
Wild Flavors Inc 269 216-2603
1717 Douglas Ave Kalamazoo (49007) *(G-8925)*
Wild Mitten LLC 616 795-1610
2037 Holliday Dr Sw Wyoming (49519) *(G-18043)*
Wildcat Buildings Inc 231 824-6406
656 Rw Hrris Indus Prk Dr Manton (49663) *(G-10459)*
Wilde Group, Muskegon *Also called Wilde Signs (G-11452)*
Wilde Signs 231 727-1200
771 Access Hwy Muskegon (49442) *(G-11452)*
Wiley & Co 616 361-7110
4186 Plainfield Ave Ne Grand Rapids (49525) *(G-6993)*
Wilfred Swartz & Swartz G 989 652-6322
11465 Holland Rd Reese (48757) *(G-13236)*
Wilkie Bros Conveyors Inc 810 364-4820
1765 Michigan Ave Ste 2 Marysville (48040) *(G-10626)*
Wilkie Brothers, Marysville *Also called American Metal Restoration (G-10598)*
Wilkinson Chemical Corporation 989 843-6163
8290 Lapeer Rd Mayville (48744) *(G-10676)*
Will Lent Horseshoe Co 231 861-5033
5800 W Woodrow Rd Shelby (49455) *(G-14537)*
Willbee Concrete Products Co 517 782-8246
2323 Brooklyn Rd Jackson (49203) *(G-8607)*
Willbee Transit-Mix Co Inc 517 782-9493
2323 Brooklyn Rd Jackson (49203) *(G-8608)*
Willc, Pontiac *Also called Williams International Co LLC (G-12875)*
Willco Extrusion LLC 248 817-2373
1107 Naughton Dr Troy (48083) *(G-16691)*
Willenborg Associates Inc 810 724-5678
620 Industrial Park Dr Imlay City (48444) *(G-8216)*
William B Eerdmans Pubg Co 616 459-4591
4035 Park East Ct Se Grand Rapids (49546) *(G-6994)*
William C Fox Enterprises Inc 231 775-2732
1215 N Mitchell St Cadillac (49601) *(G-2286)*
William Cosgriff Electrc 313 832-6958
4761 Avery St Detroit (48208) *(G-4442)*
William Penn Systems Inc 313 383-8299
3510 Helen Ave Lincoln Park (48146) *(G-9588)*
William R Hall Kimberly 989 426-4605
4083 Cassidy Rd Gladwin (48624) *(G-5939)*
William S Wixtrom 906 376-8247
2131 County Road 601 Republic (49879) *(G-13247)*
William Shaw Inc 231 536-3569
402 Wadsworth St Traverse City (49684) *(G-16146)*
Williams Business Services 248 280-0073
551 Brittany Ct Rochester Hills (48309) *(G-13547)*
Williams Cheese Co 989 697-4492
998 N Huron Rd Linwood (48634) *(G-9599)*
Williams Diversified Inc 734 421-6100
13170 Merriman Rd Livonia (48150) *(G-10009)*
Williams Finishing Inc 734 421-6100
13170 Merriman Rd Livonia (48150) *(G-10010)*
Williams Form Engineering Corp (PA) 616 866-0815
8165 Graphic Dr Ne Belmont (49306) *(G-1474)*
Williams Gun Sight Company 800 530-9028
7389 Lapeer Rd Davison (48423) *(G-3666)*
Williams International Co LLC (PA) 248 624-5200
2000 Centerpoint Pkwy Pontiac (48341) *(G-12875)*
Williams International Co LLC 248 762-8713
7201 Astro Dr N Waterford (48327) *(G-17386)*
Williams Milling & Moulding In 906 474-9222
10304 Bay Shore Dr Rapid River (49878) *(G-13117)*
Williams Reddi Mix Inc 906 875-6952
1345 Us Highway 2 Crystal Falls (49920) *(G-3615)*
Williams Redi Mix 906 875-6839
170 Williams Rd Crystal Falls (49920) *(G-3616)*
Williams Tooling & Mfg 616 681-2093
1856 142nd Ave Dorr (49323) *(G-4529)*
Williams Welding and Repair 517 783-3977
2445 Brooklyn Rd Jackson (49203) *(G-8609)*
Williamston Products Inc (PA) 517 655-2131
845 Progress Ct Williamston (48895) *(G-17742)*
Williamston Products Inc 517 655-2273
1560 Noble Rd Williamston (48895) *(G-17743)*
Williamston Products Inc 989 723-0149
615 N Delany Rd Owosso (48867) *(G-12329)*
Willies Wicks 810 730-4176
1315 Kapp Ct Flushing (48433) *(G-5546)*
Willmar, Ada *Also called Drill Technology (G-14)*
Willoughby Press 989 723-3360
1407 Corunna Ave Owosso (48867) *(G-12330)*
Willow, Monroe *Also called Physicians Technology LLC (G-11061)*
Willow Mfg Inc 231 275-1026
11455 Us Highway 31 Interlochen (49643) *(G-8246)*
Willow Vineyards Inc 231 271-4810
10702 E Hilltop Rd Suttons Bay (49682) *(G-15657)*
Willsie Lumber Company 989 695-5094
9770 Pierce Rd Freeland (48623) *(G-5761)*
Wilson Stamping & Mfg Inc 989 823-8521
603 State Rd Vassar (48768) *(G-16820)*
Wilson Technologies Inc 248 655-0005
851 W Maple Rd Clawson (48017) *(G-2989)*
Wilson-Garner Company 586 466-5880
40935 Production Dr Harrison Township (48045) *(G-7355)*
Win Schuler Foods Inc 248 262-3450
27777 Franklin Rd # 1520 Southfield (48034) *(G-15066)*
Winans Inc 810 744-1240
494 S Comstock St Corunna (48817) *(G-3586)*
Winans Electric Motor Repair, Corunna *Also called Winans Inc (G-3586)*
Windmill Hill Farm LLC 810 378-5972
1686 Sheridan Line Rd Croswell (48422) *(G-3606)*
Window Designs Inc (PA) 616 396-5295
753 Lincoln Ave Holland (49423) *(G-7859)*
Windsong Mobile Home 248 758-2140
1750 S Telg Rd Ste 106 Bloomfield Hills (48302) *(G-1811)*
Windsor Mch & Stamping 2009 ....734 941-7320
26655 Northline Rd Taylor (48180) *(G-15782)*
Windsor Mold Saline, Saline *Also called Windsor Mold USA Inc (G-14421)*
Windsor Mold USA Inc 734 944-5080
1294 Beach Ct Saline (48176) *(G-14421)*
Windtronics Inc 231 332-1200
380 W Western Ave Ste 301 Muskegon (49440) *(G-11453)*
Windword Press 248 681-7905
3109 Portman St Keego Harbor (48320) *(G-8982)*

Wine Cellar Visions LLC 517 332-1026
500 Kedzie St East Lansing (48823) *(G-4682)*
Winery At Black Star Farms LLC 231 271-4882
10844 E Revold Rd Suttons Bay (49682) *(G-15658)*
Winford Engineering LLC 989 671-9721
4561 Garfield Rd Auburn (48611) *(G-758)*
Wing Pattern Inc 248 588-1121
6145 Wall St Ste D Sterling Heights (48312) *(G-15546)*
Winn Archery Equipment Co 269 637-2658
13757 64th St South Haven (49090) *(G-14784)*
Winsol Electronics LLC 810 767-2987
2000 N Saginaw St Flint (48505) *(G-5524)*
Winstanley Associates LLC 231 946-3552
2670 Garfield Rd N Ste 19 Traverse City (49686) *(G-16147)*
Winter Sausage Mfg Co Inc 586 777-9080
22011 Gratiot Ave Eastpointe (48021) *(G-4713)*
Wiper Shaker LLC 231 668-2418
6650 E Railway Cmn Williamsburg (49690) *(G-17724)*
Wirco Manufacturing LLC 810 984-5576
2550 20th St Port Huron (48060) *(G-12976)*
Wirco Products Inc 810 984-5576
2550 20th St Port Huron (48060) *(G-12977)*
Wire Dynamics Inc 586 879-0321
18210 Malyn Blvd Fraser (48026) *(G-5748)*
Wire Fab Inc 313 893-8816
18055 Sherwood St Detroit (48234) *(G-4443)*
Wire Wizard Welding Products, Jackson *Also called Elco Enterprises Inc (G-8443)*
Wired Technologies LLC 313 800-1611
31099 Schoolcraft Rd Livonia (48150) *(G-10011)*
Wireless 4 Less Inc 313 653-3345
9660 Greenfield Rd Detroit (48227) *(G-4444)*
Wireless Svcs Div Navy A Force, Taylor *Also called General Dynamics Corporation (G-15725)*
Wiretech Wire EDM Service Inc 810 966-9912
2243 Wadhams Rd Ste A Kimball (48074) *(G-9049)*
Wiric Corporation 248 598-5297
2781 Bond St Rochester Hills (48309) *(G-13548)*
Wirt Stone Dock, Bay City *Also called Doug Wirt Enterprises Inc (G-1305)*
Wirtz Manufacturing Co Inc (PA) 810 987-7600
1105 24th St Port Huron (48060) *(G-12978)*
Wisner Machine Works LLC 989 274-7690
7800 M 25 Akron (48701) *(G-109)*
Wit-O-Matic, Ortonville *Also called Palfam Industries Inc (G-12201)*
Wit-Son Carbide Tool Inc 231 536-2247
6490 Rogers Rd East Jordan (49727) *(G-4648)*
Witchcraft Tape Products Inc (PA) 269 468-3399
100 Klitchman Dr Coloma (49038) *(G-3368)*
Witco Inc 810 387-4231
6401 Bricker Rd Greenwood (48006) *(G-7163)*
Withers Corporation 586 758-2750
23801 Mound Rd Warren (48091) *(G-17294)*
Witson Quality Tools LLC 989 471-2317
5601 F 41 Spruce (48762) *(G-15214)*
Witzenmann Usa LLC (PA) 248 588-6033
1201 Stephenson Hwy Troy (48083) *(G-16692)*
Wixom Coating Center, Wixom *Also called Oerlikon Blzers Cating USA Inc (G-17873)*
Wixom Moving Boxes LLC 248 613-5078
27046 Sprucewood Dr # 204 Wixom (48393) *(G-17931)*
Wixtrom Lumber Co, Republic *Also called William S Wixtrom (G-13247)*
Wiz Wheelz Inc 616 455-5988
4460 40th St Se Grand Rapids (49512) *(G-6995)*
Wizard Electronics, Rockford *Also called Rockford Contract Mfg (G-13587)*
Wkw Erbsloeh N Amer Holdg Inc 205 338-4242
3310 W Big Beaver Rd Troy (48084) *(G-16693)*
Wkw Extrusion, Portage *Also called Erbsloeh Alum Solutions Inc (G-12993)*
Wkw Roof Rail Systems LLC 205 338-4242
6565 S Sprinkle Rd Portage (49002) *(G-13056)*
Wl Molding of Michigan LLC 269 327-3075
8212 Shaver Rd Portage (49024) *(G-13057)*
Wm Kloeffler Industries Inc 810 765-4068
6033 King Rd Marine City (48039) *(G-10487)*
WM Tube & Wire Forming Inc 231 830-9393
2724 9th St Muskegon (49444) *(G-11454)*
Wmc Lievense Company 231 946-3800
810 Hastings St Traverse City (49686) *(G-16148)*
Wmc LLC 616 560-4142
1300 Moore St Greenville (48838) *(G-7161)*
Wmc Sales LLC 616 813-7237
4455 Tiffany Ave Ne Ada (49301) *(G-35)*
Wmcs, Hudsonville *Also called West Michigan Cabinet Supply (G-8186)*
Wmgm, Norton Shores *Also called West Michigan Grinding Svc Inc (G-11805)*
Wmh Fluidpower Inc (PA) 269 327-7011
862 Lenox Ave Portage (49024) *(G-13058)*
Wmt Properties Inc 248 486-6400
7771 Kensington Ct Brighton (48116) *(G-2010)*
Wmtl, Grand Rapids *Also called West Michigan Tag & Label Inc (G-6987)*
Wmv Incorporated 248 333-1380
2187 Orchard Lake Rd # 205 Sylvan Lake (48320) *(G-15673)*
Wochen-Post 248 641-9944
12200 E 13 Mile Rd # 140 Warren (48093) *(G-17295)*
Woder Construction Inc 989 731-6371
3661 Nowak Rd Gaylord (49735) *(G-5900)*
Wojan Aluminum Products Corp (PA) 231 547-2931
217 Stover Rd Charlevoix (49720) *(G-2635)*
Wojan Window & Door, Charlevoix *Also called Wojan Aluminum Products Corp (G-2635)*
Wojo Associates, Commerce Township *Also called Highland Machine Design Inc (G-3412)*
Woldering Plastic Mold Tech, Grand Rapids *Also called Plastic Mold Technology Inc (G-6756)*
Wolf Log Home Buildings 231 757-7000
880 W Us Highway 10 31 Scottville (49454) *(G-14511)*
Wolfgang Moneta 269 422-2296
8903 Stvnsville Baroda Rd Baroda (49101) *(G-1133)*
Wolverine Advanced Mtls LLC (HQ) 313 749-6100
5850 Mercury Dr Ste 250 Dearborn (48126) *(G-3774)*
Wolverine Broach Co Inc (PA) 586 468-4445
41200 Executive Dr Harrison Township (48045) *(G-7356)*
Wolverine Bronze Company (PA) 586 776-8180
28178 Hayes Rd Roseville (48066) *(G-13891)*
Wolverine Carbide & Tool Inc 248 247-3888
684 Robbins Dr Troy (48083) *(G-16694)*
Wolverine Carbide Die Company 248 280-0300
2613 Industrial Row Dr Troy (48084) *(G-16695)*
Wolverine Coil Spring Company 616 459-3504
818 Front Ave Nw Grand Rapids (49504) *(G-6996)*
Wolverine Concrete Products 313 931-7189
9189 Central St Detroit (48204) *(G-4445)*
Wolverine Crane & Service Inc (PA) 616 538-4870
2557 Thornwood St Sw Grand Rapids (49519) *(G-6997)*
Wolverine Crane & Service Inc 734 467-9066
30777 Beverly Rd Ste 150 Romulus (48174) *(G-13741)*
Wolverine Die Cast Ltd Ptnshp 586 757-1900
22550 Nagel St Warren (48089) *(G-17296)*
Wolverine Gas and Oil Corp (PA) 616 458-1150
1 Riverfront Plz # 55 Grand Rapids (49503) *(G-6998)*
Wolverine Glass Products Inc 616 538-0100
3400 Wentworth Dr Sw Wyoming (49519) *(G-18044)*
Wolverine Grinding Inc 734 769-4499
160 N Staebler Rd Bldg B Ann Arbor (48103) *(G-700)*
Wolverine Hydraulics & Mfg Co 248 543-5261
25329 John R Rd Madison Heights (48071) *(G-10383)*
Wolverine Leathers, Rockford *Also called Wolverine World Wide Inc (G-13602)*
Wolverine Machine Products Co 248 634-9952
319 Cogshall St Holly (48442) *(G-7902)*
Wolverine Metal Stamping Inc (PA) 269 429-6600
3600 Tennis Ct Saint Joseph (49085) *(G-14354)*
Wolverine Orthotics Inc 248 360-3736
2028 Applebrook Dr Commerce Township (48382) *(G-3457)*
Wolverine Packing Co (PA) 313 259-7500
2535 Rivard St Detroit (48207) *(G-4446)*
Wolverine Plating Corporation 586 771-5000
29456 Groesbeck Hwy Roseville (48066) *(G-13892)*
Wolverine Printing Company LLC 616 451-2075
315 Grandville Ave Sw Grand Rapids (49503) *(G-6999)*
Wolverine Procurement Inc 616 866-9521
175 S Main St Rockford (49341) *(G-13597)*
Wolverine Procurement Inc (HQ) 616 866-5500
9341 Ne Courland Dr Rockford (49341) *(G-13598)*
Wolverine Production & Engrg 586 468-2890
41160 Executive Dr Harrison Township (48045) *(G-7357)*
Wolverine Products Inc 586 792-3740
35220 Groesbeck Hwy Clinton Township (48035) *(G-3261)*
Wolverine Slipper Group Inc (HQ) 616 866-5500
9341 Courtland Dr Ne Hb1141 Rockford (49351) *(G-13599)*
Wolverine Special Tool Inc 616 791-1027
1857 Waldorf St Nw Grand Rapids (49544) *(G-7000)*
Wolverine Tool & Engrg Co 616 785-9796
5641 West River Dr Ne Belmont (49306) *(G-1475)*
Wolverine Tool Co 810 664-2964
2045 N Lapeer Rd Lapeer (48446) *(G-9492)*
Wolverine Trailers Inc (PA) 517 782-4950
116 Frost St Jackson (49202) *(G-8610)*
Wolverine Trailers Inc 517 782-4950
1500 Chanter Rd Jackson (49201) *(G-8611)*
Wolverine Trailers Inc 517 782-4950
1500 Chanter Rd Jackson (49201) *(G-8612)*
Wolverine Water Trtmnt Systems, East Lansing *Also called Michigan Soft Water of Centr (G-4669)*
Wolverine Water Works Inc 248 673-4310
2469 Airport Rd Waterford (48327) *(G-17387)*
Wolverine Waterworks, Waterford *Also called Wolverine Water Works Inc (G-17387)*
Wolverine World Wide Inc (PA) 616 866-5500
9341 Courtland Dr Ne Rockford (49351) *(G-13600)*
Wolverine World Wide Inc 616 863-3983
9343 Courtland Dr Ne Rockford (49351) *(G-13601)*
Wolverine World Wide Inc 616 866-5500
123 N Main St Rockford (49341) *(G-13602)*
Wolverine Worldwide, Rockford *Also called Wolverine World Wide Inc (G-13600)*

ALPHABETIC

(PA)=Parent Co (HQ)=Headquarters (DH)=Div Headquarters
2020 Harris Michigan Industrial Directory
1109

Wolverine Worldwide, Rockford *Also called Wolverine Procurement Inc* ***(G-13597)***
Wolvering Fur 313 961-0620
2937 Russell St Detroit (48207) ***(G-4447)***
Women Lifestyle Northshore, Muskegon *Also called Roe LLC* ***(G-11415)***
Womens Lifestyle Inc 616 458-2121
3500 3 Mile Rd Nw A Grand Rapids (49534) ***(G-7001)***
Wonder Hostess Thrift Store, Cadillac *Also called Hostess Cake ITT Contntl Bkg* ***(G-2253)***
Wonder Makers Environmental 269 382-4154
2117 Lane Blvd Kalamazoo (49001) ***(G-8926)***
Wonderland Graphics Inc 616 452-0712
4030 Eastern Ave Se Grand Rapids (49508) ***(G-7002)***
Wood Brothers Logging 989 350-6064
5915 Gamble Rd Atlanta (49709) ***(G-734)***
Wood Burn LLC 810 614-4204
8106 Vassar Rd Millington (48746) ***(G-10999)***
Wood Dowel & Dimension, Nunica *Also called Doltek Enterprises Inc* ***(G-12036)***
Wood Graphics Signs, Greenville *Also called Woods Graphics* ***(G-7162)***
Wood Shop Inc 231 582-9835
111 N East St Boyne City (49712) ***(G-1838)***
Wood Smiths Inc 269 372-6432
1180 S 8th St Kalamazoo (49009) ***(G-8927)***
Wood Tech Inc 616 455-0800
670 76th St Sw Byron Center (49315) ***(G-2217)***
Wood-Cutters Tooling Inc 616 257-7930
4685 Spartan Indus Dr Sw Grandville (49418) ***(G-7076)***
Wood-N-Stuff Inc 616 677-0177
12151 Linden Dr Marne (49435) ***(G-10516)***
Woodard—Cm LLC 989 725-4265
210 S Delaney Rd Owosso (48867) ***(G-12331)***
Woodbridge Group, Romulus *Also called Woodbridge Holdings Inc* ***(G-13742)***
Woodbridge Group Inc 269 324-8993
2400 Meijer Dr Troy (48084) ***(G-16696)***
Woodbridge Holdings Inc (HQ) 248 288-0100
1515 Equity Dr Ste 100 Troy (48084) ***(G-16697)***
Woodbridge Holdings Inc 734 942-0458
15573 Oakwood Dr Romulus (48174) ***(G-13742)***
Woodbridge Sales & Engrg Inc (HQ) 248 288-0100
1515 Equity Dr Troy (48084) ***(G-16698)***
Woodcraft Customs LLC 248 987-4473
24790 Crestview Ct Farmington Hills (48335) ***(G-5152)***
Woodcraft Industries, Marine City *Also called Usmats Inc* ***(G-10485)***
Woodcrafters 517 741-7423
855 Athens Rd Sherwood (49089) ***(G-14737)***
Woodcrafters Custom Furniture, Sherwood *Also called Woodcrafters* ***(G-14737)***
Wooden Moon Studio 269 329-3229
10334 Portage Rd Portage (49002) ***(G-13059)***
Wooden Runabout Co 616 396-7248
4261 58th St Holland (49423) ***(G-7860)***
Woodhams Enterprises Inc 269 383-0600
11546 W County Line Rd Climax (49034) ***(G-3014)***
Woodhaven Log & Lumber, Mio *Also called Gilchrist Premium Lumber Pdts* ***(G-11002)***
Woodie Manufacturing Inc 517 782-7663
1400 Wildwood Ave Jackson (49202) ***(G-8613)***
Woodland Creek Furniture Inc (PA) 231 518-4084
546 M 72 E Kalkaska (49646) ***(G-8968)***
Woodland Industries 989 686-6176
112 S Huron Rd Kawkawlin (48631) ***(G-8976)***
Woodland Paving Co (PA) 616 784-5220
3566 Mill Creek Dr Ne Comstock Park (49321) ***(G-3521)***
Woodpecker Industries LLC 231 347-0970
375 Franklin Park 2 Harbor Springs (49740) ***(G-7298)***
Woods & Fields Community, Owosso *Also called Constine Inc* ***(G-12284)***
Woods Graphics 616 691-8025
9180 Wabasis Ave Ne Greenville (48838) ***(G-7162)***
Woodside Logging LLC 906 482-0150
23763 Woodside Ln Hancock (49930) ***(G-7259)***
Woodtech Builders Inc 906 932-8055
219 E Frederick St Ironwood (49938) ***(G-8341)***
Woodville Heights Enterprises 231 629-7750
7147 6 Mile Rd Big Rapids (49307) ***(G-1647)***
Woodward Inc 970 482-5811
331 Metty Dr Ste 4 Ann Arbor (48103) ***(G-701)***
Woodward Inc 616 772-9171
700 N Centennial St Zeeland (49464) ***(G-18197)***
Woodward Avenue Brewers 248 894-7665
22646 Woodward Ave Ferndale (48220) ***(G-5330)***
Woodward Energy Solutions LLC 888 967-4533
719 Griswold St Ste 720 Detroit (48226) ***(G-4448)***
Woodward Fst Inc 616 772-9171
700 N Centennial St Zeeland (49464) ***(G-18198)***
Woodward Printing Co, Troy *Also called Color Source Graphics Inc* ***(G-16272)***
Woodways Custom Built, Grand Rapids *Also called Woodways Industries LLC* ***(G-7003)***
Woodways Industries LLC (PA) 616 956-3070
4265 28th St Se Ste A Grand Rapids (49512) ***(G-7003)***
Woodworks & Design Company 517 482-6665
109 E South St Lansing (48910) ***(G-9434)***
Woodworth Inc 810 820-6780
4201 Pier North Blvd Flint (48504) ***(G-5525)***
Woodworth Inc (PA) 248 481-2354
500 Centerpoint Pkwy N Pontiac (48341) ***(G-12876)***
Wooley Industries Inc 810 341-8823
3034 S Ballenger Hwy Flint (48507) ***(G-5526)***
Woolly & Co LLC 248 480-4354
575 Stanley Blvd Birmingham (48009) ***(G-1709)***
Woolly and Co, Birmingham *Also called Woolly & Co LLC* ***(G-1709)***
Wooshin Safety Systems 248 615-4946
23255 Commerce Dr Farmington Hills (48335) ***(G-5153)***
Word Baron Inc 248 471-4080
315 E Eisenhower Pkwy # 2 Ann Arbor (48108) ***(G-702)***
Worden Company, The, Holland *Also called Everest Expedition LLC* ***(G-7627)***
Worden Farms, Beulah *Also called Leroy Worden* ***(G-1610)***
Worden Group LLC 616 392-1848
199 E 17th St Holland (49423) ***(G-7861)***
Work Apparel Division, Jackson *Also called Libra Industries Inc Michigan* ***(G-8499)***
Workblades Inc 586 778-0060
21535 Groesbeck Hwy Warren (48089) ***(G-17297)***
Workforce Payhub Inc 517 759-4026
104 E Maumee St Adrian (49221) ***(G-104)***
Workforce Software LLC (PA) 734 542-4100
38705 7 Mile Rd Ste 300 Livonia (48152) ***(G-10012)***
Working Bugs LLC 517 203-4744
2000 Merritt Rd East Lansing (48823) ***(G-4683)***
Workman Printing Inc 231 744-5500
1261 Holton Rd Muskegon (49445) ***(G-11455)***
Workshop Detroit, Detroit *Also called Alo LLC* ***(G-3860)***
World Class Equipment Company 586 331-2121
51515 Celeste Shelby Township (48315) ***(G-14723)***
World Class Prototypes Inc 616 355-0200
400 Center St Holland (49423) ***(G-7862)***
World Class Shopping Carts, Troy *Also called Wcscarts LLC* ***(G-16688)***
World Class Steel & Proc Inc 586 585-1734
2673 American Dr Troy (48083) ***(G-16699)***
World Corrugated Container Inc 517 629-9400
930 Elliott St Albion (49224) ***(G-136)***
World Etching North America Ve, Fraser *Also called New World Etching N Amer Ve* ***(G-5698)***
World Industries Inc (PA) 248 288-0000
1000 N Crooks Rd Clawson (48017) ***(G-2990)***
World Magnetics, Traverse City *Also called Wmc Lievense Company* ***(G-16148)***
World of Cd-Rom 269 382-3766
4026 S Westnedge Ave D Kalamazoo (49008) ***(G-8928)***
World of Cd-Rom , The, Kalamazoo *Also called World of Cd-Rom* ***(G-8928)***
World of Pallets and Trucking 313 899-2000
3420 Lovett St Detroit (48210) ***(G-4449)***
World Trade Press, Traverse City *Also called Edward G Hinkelman* ***(G-15960)***
World Wide Cabinets Inc 248 683-2680
2655 Orchard Lake Rd # 101 Sylvan Lake (48320) ***(G-15674)***
Worldcolor Midland, Midland *Also called Qg LLC* ***(G-10904)***
Worldtek Industries LLC 734 494-5204
36310 Eureka Rd Romulus (48174) ***(G-13743)***
Worldwide Company, Farmington Hills *Also called Jervis B Webb Company* ***(G-5032)***
Worldwide Marketing Services 269 556-2000
1776 Hilltop Rd Saint Joseph (49085) ***(G-14355)***
Worldwide Power Transm Div, Rochester Hills *Also called Gates Corporation* ***(G-13431)***
Worswick Mold & Tool Inc 810 765-1700
6232 King Rd Marine City (48039) ***(G-10488)***
Worten Copy Center Inc 231 845-7030
601 N Washington Ave Ludington (49431) ***(G-10089)***
Worthen Coated Fabrics, Grand Rapids *Also called Worthen Industries Inc* ***(G-7004)***
Worthen Industries Inc 616 742-8990
1125 41st St Se Grand Rapids (49508) ***(G-7004)***
Worthington Armstrong Venture 269 934-6200
745 Enterprise Way Benton Harbor (49022) ***(G-1572)***
Worthington Industries Inc 734 397-6187
5260 S Haggerty Rd Canton (48188) ***(G-2444)***
Worthington Steel of Michigan (HQ) 734 374-3260
11700 Worthington Dr Taylor (48180) ***(G-15783)***
Wow Factor Tables and Events 248 550-5922
4337 E Grand River Ave Howell (48843) ***(G-8122)***
Wow Plastics LLC 760 827-7800
3394 Carmel Mtn Rd 250 Caro (48723) ***(G-2482)***
Wow Products USA 989 672-1300
1111 S Colling Rd Caro (48723) ***(G-2483)***
Wowza ME LLC 734 636-4460
122 W Noble Ave Monroe (48162) ***(G-11085)***
Wpi, Williamston *Also called Williamston Products Inc* ***(G-17742)***
Wpw Inc 810 785-1478
5225 Energy Dr Flint (48505) ***(G-5527)***
Wranosky & Sons Inc 586 336-9761
105 S Main St Romeo (48065) ***(G-13642)***
Wreaths By Heather RE Nee 810 874-3119
4377 Staunton Dr Swartz Creek (48473) ***(G-15670)***
Wright & Filippis Inc 517 484-2624
1438 E Michigan Ave # 100 Lansing (48912) ***(G-9435)***
Wright & Filippis Inc 248 336-8460
23520 Woodward Ave Detroit (48220) ***(G-3822)***

ALPHABETIC SECTION
Yaskawa America Inc

Wright & Filippis Inc ... 586 756-4020
13384 E 11 Mile Rd Warren (48089) ***(G-17298)***
Wright & Filippis Inc ... 313 832-5020
4201 Saint Antoine St Detroit (48201) ***(G-4450)***
Wright & Filippis Inc ... 313 386-3330
4050 Fort St Lincoln Park (48146) ***(G-9589)***
Wright Brace & Limb Inc ... 989 343-0300
611 Court St Ste 102 West Branch (48661) ***(G-17530)***
Wright Communications Inc ... 248 585-3838
1229 Chicago Rd Troy (48083) ***(G-16700)***
Wright Plastic Products Co LLC ... 810 326-3000
2021 Christian B Haas Dr Saint Clair (48079) ***(G-14237)***
Wright Plastic Products Co LLC (PA) ... 989 291-3211
201 E Condensery Rd Sheridan (48884) ***(G-14736)***
Wright Sealant Restoration Inc ... 616 453-5914
3848 Sydney Ct Nw Walker (49534) ***(G-16883)***
Wright-K Spare Parts and Svcs, Saginaw *Also called Wright-K Technology Inc* ***(G-14184)***
Wright-K Technology Inc ... 989 752-2588
2025 E Genesee Ave Saginaw (48601) ***(G-14184)***
Wrkco Inc ... 269 964-7181
4075 Columbia Ave W Battle Creek (49015) ***(G-1268)***
WS Molnar Co ... 313 923-0400
2545 Beaufait St Detroit (48207) ***(G-4451)***
Ws Woodworks, Scottville *Also called Wolf Log Home Buildings* ***(G-14511)***
WSi Industrial Services Inc (PA) ... 734 942-9300
18555 Fort St Riverview (48193) ***(G-13307)***
Wsp Management LLC ... 586 447-2750
23600 Schoenherr Rd Warren (48089) ***(G-17299)***
Wyandotte Collet and Tool Inc ... 734 283-8055
4070 5th St Wyandotte (48192) ***(G-17982)***
Wyatt Services Inc ... 586 264-8000
6425 Sims Dr Sterling Heights (48313) ***(G-15547)***
Wyke Die & Engineering Inc ... 616 871-1175
4334 Brockton Dr Se Ste I Grand Rapids (49512) ***(G-7005)***
Wyman-Gordon Forgings Inc ... 810 229-9550
7250 Whitmore Lake Rd Brighton (48116) ***(G-2011)***
Wynalda Litho Inc (PA) ... 616 866-1561
8221 Graphic Dr Ne Belmont (49306) ***(G-1476)***
Wynalda Packaging, Belmont *Also called Wynalda Litho Inc* ***(G-1476)***
Wyse Glass Specialties Inc ... 989 496-3510
1100 Rockwell Dr Freeland (48623) ***(G-5762)***
Wyser Innovative Products LLC ... 616 583-9225
8560 Centre Indstrl Dr E Byron Center (49315) ***(G-2218)***
Wysong, Midland *Also called N F P Inc* ***(G-10896)***
Wysong Corporation ... 989 631-0009
7550 Eastman Ave Midland (48642) ***(G-10924)***
Wysong Medical Corporation ... 989 631-0009
7550 Eastman Ave Midland (48642) ***(G-10925)***
X L T Engineering Inc ... 989 684-4344
2595 S Huron Rd Kawkawlin (48631) ***(G-8977)***
X-Bar Automation Inc ... 248 616-9890
961 Elmsford Dr Troy (48083) ***(G-16701)***
X-Cel Industries Inc ... 248 226-6000
21121 Telegraph Rd Southfield (48033) ***(G-15067)***
X-L Machine Co Inc ... 269 279-5128
20481 M 60 Three Rivers (49093) ***(G-15883)***
X-Ray and Specialty Instrs ... 734 485-6300
1980 E Michigan Ave Ypsilanti (48198) ***(G-18108)***
X-Rite Company, The, Grand Rapids *Also called X-Rite Incorporated* ***(G-7006)***
X-Rite Incorporated (HQ) ... 616 803-2100
4300 44th St Se Grand Rapids (49512) ***(G-7006)***
X-Treme Printing Inc ... 810 232-3232
2638 Corunna Rd Flint (48503) ***(G-5528)***
Xaerus Performance Fluids Intl, Midland *Also called Xaerus Performance Fluids LLC* ***(G-10927)***
Xaerus Performance Fluids LLC ... 989 631-7871
2825 Schuette Rd Midland (48642) ***(G-10926)***
Xaerus Performance Fluids LLC (PA) ... 989 631-7871
1605 Ashman St Midland (48640) ***(G-10927)***
Xalt Energy LLC ... 248 409-5419
750 South Blvd E Pontiac (48341) ***(G-12877)***
Xalt Energy LLC (HQ) ... 989 486-8501
2700 S Saginaw Rd Midland (48640) ***(G-10928)***
Xalt Energy LLC ... 816 525-1153
2700 S Saginaw Rd Midland (48640) ***(G-10929)***
Xalt Energy Mi LLC ... 989 486-8501
2700 S Saginaw Rd Midland (48640) ***(G-10930)***
Xc LLC ... 586 755-1660
24060 Hoover Rd Warren (48089) ***(G-17300)***
Xcentric Mold & Engrg Inc ... 586 598-4636
24541 Maplehurst Dr Clinton Township (48036) ***(G-3262)***
Xenith LLC ... 866 888-2322
1201 Woodward Ave Fl 5 Detroit (48226) ***(G-4452)***
Xg Sciences Inc ... 517 316-2038
2100 S Washington Ave Lansing (48910) ***(G-9436)***
Xg Sciences Inc (PA) ... 517 703-1110
3101 Grand Oak Dr Lansing (48911) ***(G-9437)***
Xilinx Inc ... 248 344-0786
28345 Beck Rd Ste 400 Wixom (48393) ***(G-17932)***
Xl Engineering LLC ... 616 656-0324
6960 Hammond Ave Se Caledonia (49316) ***(G-2323)***
XMCO Inc ... 586 558-8510
5501 Entp Ct Ste 400 Warren (48092) ***(G-17301)***
Xoran Holdings LLC (PA) ... 734 418-5108
5210 S State Rd Ann Arbor (48108) ***(G-703)***
Xoran Technologies LLC ... 734 663-7194
5210 S State Rd Ann Arbor (48108) ***(G-704)***
Xplorer Motor Home Division, Brown City *Also called Frank Industries Inc* ***(G-2051)***
Xpo Cnw Inc (HQ) ... 734 757-1444
2211 Old Earhart Rd Ann Arbor (48105) ***(G-705)***
Xpo Nlm ... 866 251-3651
600 Galleria Officentre S Southfield (48034) ***(G-15068)***
Xpress Packaging Solutions LLC ... 231 629-0463
11655 Park Ct Shelby Township (48315) ***(G-14724)***
Xpress Printing, Saint Joseph *Also called Web Printing & Mktg Concepts* ***(G-14351)***
Xsi, Ypsilanti *Also called X-Ray and Specialty Instrs* ***(G-18108)***
Xstream Tackle, Imlay City *Also called Grapentin Specialties Inc* ***(G-8201)***
Xtol, Warren *Also called Hudson Industries Inc* ***(G-17082)***
Xytek Industries Inc ... 313 838-6961
19431 W Davison St Detroit (48223) ***(G-4453)***
XYZ McHine Tl Fabrications Inc ... 517 482-3668
2127 W Willow St Lansing (48917) ***(G-9329)***
Y M C A Family Center ... 269 428-9622
3665 Hollywood Rd Saint Joseph (49085) ***(G-14356)***
Yach Basin Marina, Holland *Also called Eldean Yacht Basin Ltd* ***(G-7620)***
Yacks Dry Dock ... 989 689-6749
6227 N Meridian Rd Hope (48628) ***(G-7958)***
Yakel Enterprises LLC ... 586 943-5885
8679 26 Mile Rd Ste 305 Washington Township (48094) ***(G-17320)***
Yakkertech Limited ... 734 568-6162
8000 Yankee Rd Ste 350 Ottawa Lake (49267) ***(G-12270)***
Yale Bologna, Yale *Also called C Roy Inc* ***(G-18045)***
Yale Expositor ... 810 387-2300
21 S Main St Yale (48097) ***(G-18048)***
Yale Steel Inc ... 810 387-2567
13334 Jeddo Rd Brockway (48097) ***(G-2021)***
Yale Tool & Engraving Inc ... 734 459-7171
1471 Gold Smith Plymouth (48170) ***(G-12795)***
Yamaha Logging ... 989 657-1706
2682 Sandy Trl Grayling (49738) ***(G-7119)***
Yamato International Corp ... 734 675-6055
22036 Commerce Dr Woodhaven (48183) ***(G-17942)***
Yanfeng Auto Intr Systems, Holland *Also called Yanfeng US Automotive* ***(G-7865)***
Yanfeng Automotive Interiors, Harrison Township *Also called Yanfeng US Automotive* ***(G-7358)***
Yanfeng US Automotive ... 616 392-5151
1776 Airport Park Ct Holland (49423) ***(G-7863)***
Yanfeng US Automotive ... 616 392-5151
915 E 32nd St Holland (49423) ***(G-7864)***
Yanfeng US Automotive ... 734 254-5000
49200 Halyard Dr Plymouth (48170) ***(G-12796)***
Yanfeng US Automotive (HQ) ... 248 319-7333
41935 W 12 Mile Rd Novi (48377) ***(G-12027)***
Yanfeng US Automotive ... 734 289-4841
1833 Frenchtown Ctr Dr Monroe (48162) ***(G-11086)***
Yanfeng US Automotive ... 616 394-1199
701 S Waverly Rd Holland (49423) ***(G-7865)***
Yanfeng US Automotive ... 616 394-1523
915 32nd St Tech Ctr Holland (49423) ***(G-7866)***
Yanfeng US Automotive ... 586 354-2101
42150 Executive Dr Harrison Township (48045) ***(G-7358)***
Yanfeng US Automotive ... 734 289-4841
1833 Frenchtown Ctr Dr Monroe (48162) ***(G-11087)***
Yanfeng US Automotive ... 517 721-0179
41935 W 12 Mile Rd Novi (48377) ***(G-12028)***
Yanfeng US Automotive ... 313 259-3226
2931 E Jefferson Ave Detroit (48207) ***(G-4454)***
Yanfeng US Automotive ... 734 946-0600
9800 Inkster Rd Romulus (48174) ***(G-13744)***
Yanfeng US Automotive ... 616 975-4000
5050 Kendrick St Se Kentwood (49512) ***(G-9035)***
Yanfeng USA Automotive Trim Sy (HQ) ... 586 354-2101
42150 Executive Dr Harrison Township (48045) ***(G-7359)***
Yankee Screw Products Company ... 248 634-3011
212 Elm St Holly (48442) ***(G-7903)***
Yapp USA Auto Systems Inc ... 248 404-8696
36320 Eureka Rd Romulus (48174) ***(G-13745)***
Yarbrough Precision Screws LLC ... 586 776-0752
17722 Rainbow Fraser (48026) ***(G-5749)***
Yard & Home LLC ... 844 927-3466
2801 E Beltline Ave Nw Grand Rapids (49525) ***(G-7007)***
Yard King, Cadillac *Also called Cadillac Fabrication Inc* ***(G-2238)***
Yarema Die & Engineering Co (PA) ... 248 585-2830
300 Minnesota Dr Troy (48083) ***(G-16702)***
Yarema Die & Engineering Co ... 248 689-5777
1855 Stephenson Hwy Troy (48083) ***(G-16703)***
Yaskawa America Inc ... 248 668-8800
2050 Austin Ave Rochester Hills (48309) ***(G-13549)***

ALPHABETIC

Yaskawa America Inc
ALPHABETIC SECTION

Yaskawa America Inc 248 668-8800
2050 Austin Ave Rochester Hills (48309) **(G-13550)**
Yates Cider Mill Inc 248 651-8300
1990 E Avon Rd Rochester Hills (48307) **(G-13551)**
Yates Cylinders, Saint Clair Shores *Also called Yates Industries Inc* **(G-14277)**
Yates Forest Products Inc 989 739-8412
7110 Woodlea Rd Oscoda (48750) **(G-12225)**
Yates Industries Inc (PA) 586 778-7680
23050 E Industrial Dr Saint Clair Shores (48080) **(G-14277)**
Yaw Gallery, Royal Oak *Also called Studio of Fine Arts Inc* **(G-13974)**
Yazaki International Corp (HQ) 734 983-1000
6801 N Haggerty Rd 4707e Canton (48187) **(G-2445)**
Yello Dumpster 616 915-0506
1505 Steele Ave Sw Grand Rapids (49507) **(G-7008)**
Yellowstone Products Inc 616 299-7855
310 Dodge Rd Ne Ste C Comstock Park (49321) **(G-3522)**
Yen Group LLC 810 201-6457
2340 Dove St Port Huron (48060) **(G-12979)**
Yerington Brothers Inc 269 695-7669
3265 W Us Highway 12 Niles (49120) **(G-11652)**
Yeungs Lotus Express 248 380-3820
27500 Novi Rd Novi (48377) **(G-12029)**
YMCA, Saint Joseph *Also called Y M C A Family Center* **(G-14356)**
Yoder Forest Products L L C 989 848-2437
7310 W M 72 Curran (48728) **(G-3618)**
Yoe Industries Inc 586 791-7660
24451 Sorrentino Ct Clinton Township (48035) **(G-3263)**
Yogurtown Inc 313 908-9376
22231 Watsonia St Dearborn (48128) **(G-3775)**
Yokohama Inds Americas Inc 248 276-0480
2285 N Opdyke Rd Ste F Auburn Hills (48326) **(G-1051)**
Yonker Welding Service Inc 616 534-2774
3975 Linden Ave Se Grand Rapids (49548) **(G-7009)**
Yooper WD Wrks Restoration LLC 906 203-0056
312 Barbeau St Sault Sainte Marie (49783) **(G-14480)**
Yooper Wood Works & Designs, Sault Sainte Marie *Also called Yooper WD Wrks Restoration LLC* **(G-14480)**
Yoplait USA 231 832-3285
128 E Slosson Ave Reed City (49677) **(G-13227)**
York Electric Inc (PA) 989 684-7460
611 Andre St Bay City (48706) **(G-1371)**
York Electric Inc 517 487-6400
1905 S Washington Ave Lansing (48910) **(G-9438)**
York Servo Motor Repair, Bay City *Also called York Electric Inc* **(G-1371)**
Yorkshire Edm Inc 248 349-3017
44825 Exeter Ct Novi (48375) **(G-12030)**
Yost Vises LLC 616 396-2063
388 W 24th St Holland (49423) **(G-7867)**
Young Cabinetry Inc 734 316-2896
1400 E Michigan Ave Saline (48176) **(G-14422)**
Young Diversified Industries 248 353-1867
21015 Bridge St Southfield (48033) **(G-15069)**
Young Ideas Enterprises, Troy *Also called Quirkroberts Publishing Ltd* **(G-16573)**
Young Manufacturing Inc 906 483-3851
23455 Hellman Ave Dollar Bay (49922) **(G-4522)**
Young Supply Company 313 875-3280
1177 W Baltimore St Detroit (48202) **(G-4455)**
Young, W & Son Lumber, Columbus *Also called Duane Young & Son Lumber* **(G-3378)**
Younggren Farm & Forest Inc 906 355-2272
34392 Younggren Rd Covington (49919) **(G-3593)**
Younggren Timber Company 906 355-2272
34392 Younggren Rd Covington (49919) **(G-3594)**
Youngtronics LLC 248 896-5790
49197 Wixom Tech Dr Ste A Wixom (48393) **(G-17933)**
Your Custom Image 989 621-2250
2021 E River Rd Mount Pleasant (48858) **(G-11236)**
Your Home Town USA Inc 517 529-9421
9301 Hyde Rd Clarklake (49234) **(G-2902)**
Your Hometown Shopper LLC 586 412-8500
55130 Shelby Rd Ste A Shelby Township (48316) **(G-14725)**
Your Shower Door 616 940-0900
2958 28th St Se Grand Rapids (49512) **(G-7010)**
Yoxheimer Tile Co 517 788-7542
919 E South St Jackson (49203) **(G-8614)**
Yti Office Express LLC 866 996-8952
1280 E Big Beaver Rd A Troy (48083) **(G-16704)**
Yukon Manufacturing 989 358-6248
167 N Industrial Hwy Alpena (49707) **(G-321)**
Z & A News 231 747-6232
1239 W Giles Rd Muskegon (49445) **(G-11456)**
Z & R Electric Service Inc 906 774-0468
619 Industrial Park Dr Iron Mountain (49801) **(G-8306)**
Z Mold & Engineering Inc 586 948-5000
46390 Continental Dr Chesterfield (48047) **(G-2857)**
Z Technologies Corporation 313 937-0710
26500 Capitol Redford (48239) **(G-13209)**
Z-Brite Metal Finishing Inc 269 422-2191
6979 Stvnsville Baroda Rd Stevensville (49127) **(G-15586)**
Z. Real Estate Company, Greenville *Also called Greenville Tool & Die Co* **(G-7135)**
Zajac Industries Inc 586 489-6746
21319 Carlo Dr Clinton Township (48038) **(G-3264)**
Zajac Packaging, Clinton Township *Also called Zajac Industries Inc* **(G-3264)**
Zak Brothers Printing LLC 313 831-3216
5480 Cass Ave Detroit (48202) **(G-4456)**
Zakron USA Inc 313 582-0462
3319 Greenfield Rd 365 Dearborn (48120) **(G-3776)**
Zander Colloids Lc (PA) 810 714-1623
2040 W Thompson Rd Fenton (48430) **(G-5249)**
Zareason Inc 510 868-5000
333 N Washington St Lapeer (48446) **(G-9493)**
Zatkoff Gasket Division, Warren *Also called Roger Zatkoff Company* **(G-17223)**
Zatkoff Seals & Packings, Farmington Hills *Also called Roger Zatkoff Company* **(G-5117)**
Zav-Tech Metal Finishing 269 422-2559
6979 Stvnsville Baroda Rd Stevensville (49127) **(G-15587)**
Zayna LLC 616 452-4522
1600 Marshall Ave Se Side Grand Rapids (49507) **(G-7011)**
Zcc USA Inc 734 997-3811
3622 W Liberty Rd Ann Arbor (48103) **(G-706)**
Zeeland Bio-Based Products LLC 616 748-1831
2525 84th Ave Zeeland (49464) **(G-18199)**
Zeeland Component Sales LLC 616 399-8614
138 W Washington Ave Zeeland (49464) **(G-18200)**
Zeeland Farm Services Inc (PA) 616 772-9042
2525 84th Ave Zeeland (49464) **(G-18201)**
Zeeland Freight Services, Zeeland *Also called Zeeland Farm Services Inc* **(G-18201)**
Zeeland Print Shop Co 616 772-6636
145 E Main Ave Zeeland (49464) **(G-18202)**
Zeeland Record Co 616 772-2131
16 S Elm St Zeeland (49464) **(G-18203)**
Zeilinger Wool Co LLC 989 652-2920
1130 Weiss St Frankenmuth (48734) **(G-5597)**
Zellar Forest Products 906 586-9817
462 Lustila Rd Germfask (49836) **(G-5903)**
Zellco Precision Inc 269 684-1720
1710 E Main St Niles (49120) **(G-11653)**
Zemis 5 LLC 317 946-7015
13207 Santa Clara St Detroit (48235) **(G-4457)**
Zenith Global LLC 517 546-7402
1100 Sutton St Howell (48843) **(G-8123)**
Zenwolf Technologies Group 517 618-2000
815 E Grand River Ave Howell (48843) **(G-8124)**
Zephyros Inc (PA) 586 336-1600
160 Mclean Bruce Twp (48065) **(G-2106)**
Zero Gage Division, Wixom *Also called Benny Gage Inc* **(G-17773)**
ZF Active Safety & Elec US LLC 586 843-2100
12025 Tech Center Dr Livonia (48150) **(G-10013)**
ZF Active Safety & Elec US LLC (HQ) 734 855-2600
12001 Tech Center Dr Livonia (48150) **(G-10014)**
ZF Active Safety US Inc 906 248-3882
21105 W M 28 Bldg 6 Brimley (49715) **(G-2017)**
ZF Active Safety US Inc (HQ) 734 855-2542
12001 Tech Center Dr Livonia (48150) **(G-10015)**
ZF Active Safety US Inc 517 223-8330
500 E Van Riper Rd Fowlerville (48836) **(G-5581)**
ZF Active Safety US Inc (HQ) 734 812-6979
12001 Tech Center Dr Livonia (48150) **(G-10016)**
ZF Active Safety US Inc 810 750-1036
9475 Center Rd Fenton (48430) **(G-5250)**
ZF Active Safety US Inc 586 232-7200
4585 26 Mile Rd Washington (48094) **(G-17315)**
ZF Active Safety US Inc 586 899-2807
42315 R Mancini Dr Sterling Heights (48314) **(G-15548)**
ZF Active Safety US Inc 734 855-2470
12200 Tech Center Dr Livonia (48150) **(G-10017)**
ZF Active Safety US Inc 248 863-2412
2828 E Genesee Ave Saginaw (48601) **(G-14185)**
ZF Axle Drives Marysville LLC 810 989-8702
2900 Busha Hwy Marysville (48040) **(G-10627)**
ZF Chassis Components LLC (HQ) 810 245-2000
3300 John Conley Dr Lapeer (48446) **(G-9494)**
ZF Chassis Components LLC 810 245-2000
930 S Saginaw St Lapeer (48446) **(G-9495)**
ZF Lemforder Corp 810 245-7136
3300 John Conley Dr Lapeer (48446) **(G-9496)**
ZF North America Inc 248 478-7210
34605 W 12 Mile Rd Farmington Hills (48331) **(G-5154)**
ZF North America Inc (HQ) 734 416-6200
15811 Centennial Dr 48 Northville (48168) **(G-11735)**
ZF North America Inc 734 416-6200
15811 Centennial Dr Northville (48168) **(G-11736)**
ZF Passive Safety 248 478-7210
24175 Research Dr Farmington Hills (48335) **(G-5155)**
ZF Passive Safety 734 855-3631
12075 Tech Center Dr Livonia (48150) **(G-10018)**
ZF Passive Safety 586 232-7200
4505 26 Mile Rd Washington (48094) **(G-17316)**
ZF Passive Safety Systems US 586 752-1409
14761 E32 Mile Rd Romeo (48065) **(G-13643)**

ALPHABETIC SECTION

ZF Passive Safety Systems US 586 781-5511
4505 26 Mile Rd Washington (48094) *(G-17317)*

ZF Passive Safety US Inc (HQ) 734 855-2600
12001 Tech Center Dr Livonia (48150) *(G-10019)*

ZF Passive Safety US Inc 586 232-7200
4505 26 Mile Rd Washington (48094) *(G-17318)*

ZF Passive Sfety Systems US In (HQ) 586 232-7200
4505 26 Mile Rd Washington (48094) *(G-17319)*

ZF String Active Safety US Inc (HQ) 734 855-2600
12001 Tech Center Dr Livonia (48150) *(G-10020)*

ZF TRW Auto Holdings Corp (HQ) 734 855-2600
12001 Tech Center Dr Livonia (48150) *(G-10021)*

ZF TRW Global Electronics, Farmington Hills Also called ZF North America Inc *(G-5154)*

Zferral Inc 248 792-3472
333 W 7th St Ste 310 Royal Oak (48067) *(G-13982)*

Zhi Publising, Onsted Also called Zonya Health International *(G-12157)*

Zhongding Saling Parts USA Inc (HQ) 734 241-8870
400 Detroit Ave Monroe (48162) *(G-11088)*

Zhongli North America Inc 248 733-9300
449 Executive Dr Troy (48083) *(G-16705)*

Zick's Meats, Berrien Springs Also called Zicks Specialty Meats Inc *(G-1602)*

Zicks Specialty Meats Inc 269 471-7121
215 N Mechanic St Berrien Springs (49103) *(G-1602)*

Ziebart International Corp (PA) 248 588-4100
1290 E Maple Rd Troy (48083) *(G-16706)*

Ziel Optics Inc 734 994-9803
7167 Jackson Rd Ann Arbor (48103) *(G-707)*

Zimbell House Publishing LLC 248 909-0143
1093 Irwin Dr Waterford (48327) *(G-17388)*

Zimmer Marble Co Inc 517 787-1500
1812 River St Jackson (49202) *(G-8615)*

Zimmermann Engineering Co Inc 248 358-0044
24260 Telegraph Rd Southfield (48033) *(G-15070)*

Zinger Sheet Metal Inc 616 532-3121
4005 Roger B Chaffee Mem Grand Rapids (49548) *(G-7012)*

Zingermans Bakehouse Inc 734 761-2095
3711 Plaza Dr Ste 5 Ann Arbor (48108) *(G-708)*

Zingermans Creamery LLC 734 929-0500
3723 Plaza Dr Ste 2 Ann Arbor (48108) *(G-709)*

Zion Industries Inc 517 622-3409
1180 Comet Ln Grand Ledge (48837) *(G-6117)*

Zip Cut, Kalamazoo Also called Waber Tool & Engineering Co *(G-8921)*

Zippers, Temperance Also called Temperance Distilling Company *(G-15845)*

Zk Enterprises Inc (PA) 989 728-4439
2382 M 33 Alger (48610) *(G-140)*

Zks Sales 810 360-0682
10315 Grand River Rd # 303 Brighton (48116) *(G-2012)*

Zkw Lighting Systems Usa Inc 248 525-4600
100 W Big Beavr Rd # 300 Troy (48084) *(G-16707)*

Zobl Quarter Horses 810 479-9534
4065 Abbottsford Rd Clyde (48049) *(G-3285)*

Zodiac Enterprises LLC 810 640-7146
1000 Church St Ste 1 Mount Morris (48458) *(G-11167)*

Zoe Health 616 485-1909
5715 Christie Ave Se Kentwood (49508) *(G-9036)*

Zoetis LLC 888 963-8471
2605 E Kilgore Rd Kalamazoo (49001) *(G-8929)*

Zomedica Pharmaceutical Inc 734 369-2555
100 Phoenix Dr Ste 190 Ann Arbor (48108) *(G-710)*

Zomedica Pharmaceuticals Corp (PA) 734 369-2555
100 Phoenix Dr Ste 190 Ann Arbor (48108) *(G-711)*

Zondervan Corporation LLC (HQ) 616 698-6900
3900 Sparks Dr Se Grand Rapids (49546) *(G-7013)*

Zondervan Publishing House, Grand Rapids Also called Zondervan Corporation LLC *(G-7013)*

Zonya Health International 517 467-6995
7134 Donegal Dr Onsted (49265) *(G-12157)*

Zoomer Display LLC 616 734-0300
522 Stocking Ave Nw Grand Rapids (49504) *(G-7014)*

Zoyes East Inc 248 584-3300
1280 Hilton Rd Ferndale (48220) *(G-5331)*

Zsi-Foster Inc (HQ) 734 844-0055
45065 Michigan Ave Canton (48188) *(G-2446)*

Zuckero & Sons Inc 586 772-3377
27450 Groesbeck Hwy Roseville (48066) *(G-13893)*

Zulski Lumber Inc 231 539-8909
2465 Zulski Rd Pellston (49769) *(G-12427)*

Zume It Inc 248 522-6868
34405 W 12 Mile Rd # 137 Farmington Hills (48331) *(G-5156)*

Zunairah Fuels Inc 647 405-1606
37109 Harper Ave Clinton Township (48036) *(G-3265)*

Zurn Industries LLC 313 864-2800
7431 W 8 Mile Rd Detroit (48221) *(G-4458)*

Zygot Operations Limited 810 736-2900
4301 Western Rd Flint (48506) *(G-5529)*

Zynp International Corp 734 947-1000
27501 Hldbrndt Rd Ste 300 Romulus (48174) *(G-13746)*

Zyongyuan International, Romulus Also called Zynp International Corp *(G-13746)*

PRODUCT INDEX

• Product categories are listed in alphabetical order.

A

ABRASIVES
ABRASIVES: Aluminum Oxide Fused
ABRASIVES: Steel Shot
ABRASIVES: Synthetic
ABRASIVES: Tungsten Carbide
ACADEMY
ACCELERATION INDICATORS & SYSTEM COMPONENTS: Aerospace
ACCELERATORS: Electrostatic Particle
ACCELEROMETERS
ACCOUNTING SVCS, NEC
ACIDS
ACIDS: Inorganic
ACIDS: Sulfuric, Oleum
ACOUSTICAL BOARD & TILE
ACRYLIC RESINS
ACTUATORS: Indl, NEC
ADDITIVE BASED PLASTIC MATERIALS: Plasticizers
ADHESIVES
ADHESIVES & SEALANTS
ADHESIVES & SEALANTS WHOLESALERS
ADHESIVES: Adhesives, plastic
ADHESIVES: Epoxy
ADULT DAYCARE CENTERS
ADVERTISING AGENCIES
ADVERTISING AGENCIES: Consultants
ADVERTISING CURTAINS
ADVERTISING DISPLAY PRDTS
ADVERTISING MATERIAL DISTRIBUTION
ADVERTISING REPRESENTATIVES: Electronic Media
ADVERTISING REPRESENTATIVES: Newspaper
ADVERTISING REPRESENTATIVES: Printed Media
ADVERTISING SPECIALTIES, WHOLESALE
ADVERTISING SVCS, NEC
ADVERTISING SVCS: Billboards
ADVERTISING SVCS: Direct Mail
ADVERTISING SVCS: Display
ADVERTISING SVCS: Outdoor
ADVERTISING SVCS: Poster, Outdoor
AERIAL WORK PLATFORMS
AGENTS, BROKERS & BUREAUS: Personal Service
AGRICULTURAL CHEMICALS: Trace Elements
AGRICULTURAL EQPT: BARN, SILO, POULTRY, DAIRY/LIVESTOCK MACH
AGRICULTURAL EQPT: Clippers, Animal, Hand Or Electric
AGRICULTURAL EQPT: Fertilizng, Sprayng, Dustng/Irrigatn Mach
AGRICULTURAL EQPT: Grounds Mowing Eqpt
AGRICULTURAL EQPT: Harvesters, Fruit, Vegetable, Tobacco
AGRICULTURAL EQPT: Irrigation Eqpt, Self-Propelled
AGRICULTURAL EQPT: Storage Bins, Crop
AGRICULTURAL EQPT: Tractors, Farm
AGRICULTURAL EQPT: Transplanters
AGRICULTURAL EQPT: Turf & Grounds Eqpt
AGRICULTURAL EQPT: Weeding Machines
AGRICULTURAL MACHINERY & EQPT: Wholesalers
AIR CLEANING SYSTEMS
AIR CONDITIONERS: Motor Vehicle
AIR CONDITIONING & VENTILATION EQPT & SPLYS: Wholesales
AIR CONDITIONING EQPT
AIR CONDITIONING UNITS: Complete, Domestic Or Indl
AIR MATTRESSES: Plastic
AIR POLLUTION CONTROL EQPT & SPLYS WHOLESALERS
AIR POLLUTION MEASURING SVCS
AIR PURIFICATION EQPT
AIRCRAFT & AEROSPACE FLIGHT INSTRUMENTS & GUIDANCE SYSTEMS
AIRCRAFT & HEAVY EQPT REPAIR SVCS
AIRCRAFT ASSEMBLY PLANTS
AIRCRAFT CLEANING & JANITORIAL SVCS
AIRCRAFT CONTROL SYSTEMS: Electronic Totalizing Counters
AIRCRAFT ENGINES & ENGINE PARTS: Cooling Systems
AIRCRAFT ENGINES & ENGINE PARTS: Mount Parts

AIRCRAFT ENGINES & ENGINE PARTS: Research & Development, Mfr
AIRCRAFT ENGINES & PARTS
AIRCRAFT EQPT & SPLYS WHOLESALERS
AIRCRAFT FLIGHT INSTRUMENTS
AIRCRAFT LIGHTING
AIRCRAFT MAINTENANCE & REPAIR SVCS
AIRCRAFT PARTS & AUXILIARY EQPT: Assys, Subassemblies/Parts
AIRCRAFT PARTS & AUXILIARY EQPT: Countermeasure Dispensers
AIRCRAFT PARTS & AUXILIARY EQPT: Gears, Power Transmission
AIRCRAFT PARTS & AUXILIARY EQPT: Lighting/Landing Gear Assy
AIRCRAFT PARTS & AUXILIARY EQPT: Military Eqpt & Armament
AIRCRAFT PARTS & AUXILIARY EQPT: Oxygen Systems
AIRCRAFT PARTS & AUXILIARY EQPT: Pontoons
AIRCRAFT PARTS & EQPT, NEC
AIRCRAFT SEATS
AIRCRAFT SERVICING & REPAIRING
AIRCRAFT TURBINES
AIRCRAFT: Airplanes, Fixed Or Rotary Wing
AIRCRAFT: Research & Development, Manufacturer
AIRPORTS, FLYING FIELDS & SVCS
ALARM SYSTEMS WHOLESALERS
ALARMS: Burglar
ALARMS: Fire
ALCOHOL: Ethyl & Ethanol
ALKALIES & CHLORINE
ALL-TERRAIN VEHICLE DEALERS
ALLOYS: Additive, Exc Copper Or Made In Blast Furnaces
ALTERNATORS & GENERATORS: Battery Charging
ALTERNATORS: Automotive
ALUMINUM
ALUMINUM PRDTS
ALUMINUM: Pigs
ALUMINUM: Rolling & Drawing
AMMUNITION: Cartridges Case, 30 mm & Below
AMMUNITION: Pellets & BB's, Pistol & Air Rifle
AMMUNITION: Small Arms
AMPLIFIERS
AMUSEMENT & RECREATION SVCS: Boating Club, Membership
AMUSEMENT & RECREATION SVCS: Mechanical Games, Coin-Operated
AMUSEMENT & RECREATION SVCS: Recreation Center
AMUSEMENT & RECREATION SVCS: Ski Instruction
AMUSEMENT MACHINES: Coin Operated
AMUSEMENT PARK DEVICES & RIDES
AMUSEMENT PARK DEVICES & RIDES: Ferris Wheels
AMUSEMENT/REC SVCS: Ticket Sales, Sporting Events, Contract
ANALGESICS
ANALYZERS: Coulometric, Exc Indl Process
ANALYZERS: Network
ANALYZERS: Respiratory
ANESTHESIA EQPT
ANIMAL BASED MEDICINAL CHEMICAL PRDTS
ANIMAL FEED & SUPPLEMENTS: Livestock & Poultry
ANIMAL FEED: Wholesalers
ANIMAL FOOD & SUPPLEMENTS: Alfalfa Or Alfalfa Meal
ANIMAL FOOD & SUPPLEMENTS: Bird Food, Prepared
ANIMAL FOOD & SUPPLEMENTS: Dog
ANIMAL FOOD & SUPPLEMENTS: Dog & Cat
ANIMAL FOOD & SUPPLEMENTS: Feed Premixes
ANIMAL FOOD & SUPPLEMENTS: Feed Supplements
ANIMAL FOOD & SUPPLEMENTS: Livestock
ANIMAL FOOD & SUPPLEMENTS: Mineral feed supplements
ANIMAL FOOD & SUPPLEMENTS: Pet, Exc Dog & Cat, Dry
ANIMAL FOOD & SUPPLEMENTS: Poultry
ANIMAL FOOD & SUPPLEMENTS: Specialty, Mice & Other Pets
ANIMAL FOOD/SUPPLEMENTS: Feeds Fm Meat/Meat/Veg Combnd Meals
ANIMAL OILS: Medicinal Grade, Refined Or Concentrated
ANNEALING: Metal

ANODIZING EQPT
ANODIZING SVC
ANTENNAS: Radar Or Communications
ANTENNAS: Receiving
ANTI-GLARE MATERIAL
ANTIBIOTICS
ANTIFREEZE
ANTIQUE REPAIR & RESTORATION SVCS, EXC FURNITURE & AUTOS
ANTIQUE SHOPS
APPAREL ACCESS STORES
APPAREL DESIGNERS: Commercial
APPLIANCE CORDS: Household Electrical Eqpt
APPLIANCE PARTS: Porcelain Enameled
APPLIANCES, HOUSEHOLD OR COIN OPERATED: Laundry Dryers
APPLIANCES, HOUSEHOLD: Kitchen, Major, Exc Refrigs & Stoves
APPLIANCES, HOUSEHOLD: Laundry Machines, Incl Coin-Operated
APPLIANCES, HOUSEHOLD: Refrigs, Mechanical & Absorption
APPLIANCES, HOUSEHOLD: Sewing Machines & Attchmnts, Domestic
APPLIANCES: Household, NEC
APPLIANCES: Household, Refrigerators & Freezers
APPLIANCES: Major, Cooking
APPLIANCES: Small, Electric
APPLICATIONS SOFTWARE PROGRAMMING
AQUARIUMS & ACCESS: Plastic
ARCHITECTURAL SVCS
ARMATURE REPAIRING & REWINDING SVC
ARMOR PLATES
ARRESTERS & COILS: Lightning
ART & ORNAMENTAL WARE: Pottery
ART DEALERS & GALLERIES
ART DESIGN SVCS
ART GALLERIES
ART GOODS & SPLYS WHOLESALERS
ART GOODS, WHOLESALE
ART SPLY STORES
ARTISTS' AGENTS & BROKERS
ARTISTS' MATERIALS: Boards, Drawing
ARTISTS' MATERIALS: Boxes, Sketching & Paint
ARTISTS' MATERIALS: Water Colors
ARTS & CRAFTS SCHOOL
ARTWORK: Framed
ASBESTOS PRDTS: Friction Materials
ASBESTOS PRDTS: Pipe Covering, Heat Insulatng Matl, Exc Felt
ASBESTOS REMOVAL EQPT
ASPHALT & ASPHALT PRDTS
ASPHALT COATINGS & SEALERS
ASPHALT MINING & BITUMINOUS STONE QUARRYING SVCS
ASPHALT MIXTURES WHOLESALERS
ASPHALT PLANTS INCLUDING GRAVEL MIX TYPE
ASSEMBLING SVC: Plumbing Fixture Fittings, Plastic
ASSOCIATIONS: Business
ASSOCIATIONS: Engineering
ASSOCIATIONS: Manufacturers'
ASSOCIATIONS: Real Estate Management
ASSOCIATIONS: Trade
ATOMIZERS
AUCTION ROOMS: General Merchandise
AUCTION SVCS: Motor Vehicle
AUCTIONEERS: Fee Basis
AUDIO & VIDEO EQPT, EXC COMMERCIAL
AUDIO COMPONENTS
AUDIO ELECTRONIC SYSTEMS
AUDIO-VISUAL PROGRAM PRODUCTION SVCS
AUDIOLOGICAL EQPT: Electronic
AUTO & HOME SUPPLY STORES: Auto & Truck Eqpt & Parts
AUTO & HOME SUPPLY STORES: Auto Air Cond Eqpt, Sell/Install
AUTO & HOME SUPPLY STORES: Automotive Access
AUTO & HOME SUPPLY STORES: Automotive parts

PRODUCT INDEX

AUTO & HOME SUPPLY STORES: Batteries, Automotive & Truck
AUTO & HOME SUPPLY STORES: Truck Eqpt & Parts
AUTO SPLYS & PARTS, NEW, WHSLE: Exhaust Sys, Mufflers, Etc
AUTOCLAVES: Laboratory
AUTOMATIC REGULATING CONTROL: Building Svcs Monitoring, Auto
AUTOMATIC REGULATING CONTROLS: AC & Refrigeration
AUTOMATIC REGULATING CONTROLS: Appliance Regulators
AUTOMATIC REGULATING CONTROLS: Appliance, Exc Air-Cond/Refr
AUTOMATIC REGULATING CONTROLS: Energy Cutoff, Residtl/Comm
AUTOMATIC REGULATING CONTROLS: Float, Residential Or Comm
AUTOMATIC REGULATING CONTROLS: Gas Burner, Automatic
AUTOMATIC REGULATING CONTROLS: Hardware, Environmental Reg
AUTOMATIC REGULATING CONTROLS: Hydronic Pressure Or Temp
AUTOMATIC REGULATING CONTROLS: Pneumatic Relays, Air-Cond
AUTOMATIC REGULATING CONTROLS: Thermocouples, Vacuum, Glass
AUTOMATIC REGULATING CONTROLS: Vapor Heating
AUTOMATIC REGULATING CTRLS: Damper, Pneumatic Or Electric
AUTOMATIC TELLER MACHINES
AUTOMOBILE FINANCE LEASING
AUTOMOBILES & OTHER MOTOR VEHICLES WHOLESALERS
AUTOMOBILES: Midget, Power Driven
AUTOMOBILES: Off-Road, Exc Recreational Vehicles
AUTOMOTIVE & TRUCK GENERAL REPAIR SVC
AUTOMOTIVE BATTERIES WHOLESALERS
AUTOMOTIVE BODY SHOP
AUTOMOTIVE BODY, PAINT & INTERIOR REPAIR & MAINTENANCE SVC
AUTOMOTIVE COLLISION SHOPS
AUTOMOTIVE CUSTOMIZING SVCS, NONFACTORY BASIS
AUTOMOTIVE EMISSIONS TESTING SVCS
AUTOMOTIVE EXTERIOR REPAIR SVCS
AUTOMOTIVE GLASS REPLACEMENT SHOPS
AUTOMOTIVE PARTS, ACCESS & SPLYS
AUTOMOTIVE PARTS: Plastic
AUTOMOTIVE PRDTS: Rubber
AUTOMOTIVE RADIATOR REPAIR SHOPS
AUTOMOTIVE REPAIR SHOPS: Diesel Engine Repair
AUTOMOTIVE REPAIR SHOPS: Electrical Svcs
AUTOMOTIVE REPAIR SHOPS: Engine Rebuilding
AUTOMOTIVE REPAIR SHOPS: Engine Repair
AUTOMOTIVE REPAIR SHOPS: Frame & Front End Repair Svcs
AUTOMOTIVE REPAIR SHOPS: Fuel System Repair
AUTOMOTIVE REPAIR SHOPS: Machine Shop
AUTOMOTIVE REPAIR SHOPS: Muffler Shop, Sale/Rpr/Installation
AUTOMOTIVE REPAIR SHOPS: Springs, Rebuilding & Repair
AUTOMOTIVE REPAIR SHOPS: Trailer Repair
AUTOMOTIVE REPAIR SHOPS: Truck Engine Repair, Exc Indl
AUTOMOTIVE REPAIR SVC
AUTOMOTIVE REPAIR SVCS, MISCELLANEOUS
AUTOMOTIVE SPLYS & PARTS, NEW, WHOL: Auto Servicing Eqpt
AUTOMOTIVE SPLYS & PARTS, NEW, WHOLESALE: Alternators
AUTOMOTIVE SPLYS & PARTS, NEW, WHOLESALE: Clutches
AUTOMOTIVE SPLYS & PARTS, NEW, WHOLESALE: Engines/Eng Parts
AUTOMOTIVE SPLYS & PARTS, NEW, WHOLESALE: Filters, Air & Oil
AUTOMOTIVE SPLYS & PARTS, NEW, WHOLESALE: Hardware
AUTOMOTIVE SPLYS & PARTS, NEW, WHOLESALE: Radiators
AUTOMOTIVE SPLYS & PARTS, NEW, WHOLESALE: Seat Belts
AUTOMOTIVE SPLYS & PARTS, NEW, WHOLESALE: Splys
AUTOMOTIVE SPLYS & PARTS, NEW, WHOLESALE: Stampings
AUTOMOTIVE SPLYS & PARTS, NEW, WHOLESALE: Tools & Eqpt
AUTOMOTIVE SPLYS & PARTS, NEW, WHOLESALE: Trim
AUTOMOTIVE SPLYS & PARTS, NEW, WHOLESALE: Wheels
AUTOMOTIVE SPLYS & PARTS, USED, WHOLESALE
AUTOMOTIVE SPLYS & PARTS, USED, WHOLESALE: Access, NEC
AUTOMOTIVE SPLYS & PARTS, WHOLESALE, NEC
AUTOMOTIVE SPLYS, USED, WHOLESALE & RETAIL
AUTOMOTIVE SPLYS/PART, NEW, WHOL: Spring, Shock Absorb/Strut
AUTOMOTIVE SPLYS/PARTS, NEW, WHOL: Body Rpr/Paint Shop Splys
AUTOMOTIVE SVCS, EXC REPAIR & CARWASHES: Customizing
AUTOMOTIVE SVCS, EXC REPAIR & CARWASHES: Fuel Sys Conv
AUTOMOTIVE SVCS, EXC REPAIR & CARWASHES: Glass Tinting
AUTOMOTIVE SVCS, EXC REPAIR & CARWASHES: Insp & Diagnostic
AUTOMOTIVE SVCS, EXC REPAIR & CARWASHES: Lubrication
AUTOMOTIVE SVCS, EXC REPAIR & CARWASHES: Maintenance
AUTOMOTIVE SVCS, EXC REPAIR & CARWASHES: Road Svc
AUTOMOTIVE SVCS, EXC REPAIR: Carwash, Automatic
AUTOMOTIVE SVCS, EXC REPAIR: Carwash, Self-Service
AUTOMOTIVE SVCS, EXC REPAIR: Truck Wash
AUTOMOTIVE SVCS, EXC REPAIR: Washing & Polishing
AUTOMOTIVE TRANSMISSION REPAIR SVC
AUTOMOTIVE UPHOLSTERY SHOPS
AUTOMOTIVE WELDING SVCS
AUTOMOTIVE: Bodies
AUTOMOTIVE: Seat Frames, Metal
AUTOMOTIVE: Seating
AUTOTRANSFORMERS: Electric
AWNINGS & CANOPIES
AWNINGS & CANOPIES: Awnings, Fabric, From Purchased Matls
AWNINGS & CANOPIES: Fabric
AWNINGS: Fiberglass
AWNINGS: Metal
AWNINGS: Wood
AXLES
AXLES: Rolled Or Forged, Made In Steel Mills

B

BABBITT (METAL)
BABY FORMULA
BACKFILLERS: Self-Propelled
BACKHOES
BADGES, WHOLESALE
BADGES: Identification & Insignia
BAGS & CONTAINERS: Textile, Exc Sleeping
BAGS & SACKS: Shipping & Shopping
BAGS: Canvas
BAGS: Cement, Made From Purchased Materials
BAGS: Food Storage & Trash, Plastic
BAGS: Garment Storage Exc Paper Or Plastic Film
BAGS: Garment, Plastic Film, Made From Purchased Materials
BAGS: Paper
BAGS: Paper, Made From Purchased Materials
BAGS: Plastic
BAGS: Plastic & Pliofilm
BAGS: Plastic, Made From Purchased Materials
BAGS: Shipping
BAGS: Shopping, Made From Purchased Materials
BAGS: Textile
BAGS: Trash, Plastic Film, Made From Purchased Materials
BAKERIES, COMMERCIAL: On Premises Baking Only
BAKERIES: On Premises Baking & Consumption
BAKERY FOR HOME SVC DELIVERY
BAKERY MACHINERY
BAKERY PRDTS: Bakery Prdts, Partially Cooked, Exc frozen
BAKERY PRDTS: Bread, All Types, Fresh Or Frozen
BAKERY PRDTS: Buns, Bread Type, Fresh Or Frozen
BAKERY PRDTS: Cakes, Bakery, Exc Frozen
BAKERY PRDTS: Cakes, Bakery, Frozen
BAKERY PRDTS: Cones, Ice Cream
BAKERY PRDTS: Cookies
BAKERY PRDTS: Cookies & crackers
BAKERY PRDTS: Doughnuts, Exc Frozen
BAKERY PRDTS: Doughnuts, Frozen
BAKERY PRDTS: Dry
BAKERY PRDTS: Frozen
BAKERY PRDTS: Pastries, Danish, Frozen
BAKERY PRDTS: Pastries, Exc Frozen
BAKERY PRDTS: Pies, Exc Frozen
BAKERY PRDTS: Pretzels
BAKERY PRDTS: Wholesalers
BAKERY: Wholesale Or Wholesale & Retail Combined
BALCONIES: Metal
BALERS
BALLASTS: Fluorescent
BALLOONS: Hot Air
BALLOONS: Novelty & Toy
BALLOONS: Toy & Advertising, Rubber
BANNERS: Fabric
BAR
BAR FIXTURES: Wood
BAR FIXTURES: Wood
BARBECUE EQPT
BARGES BUILDING & REPAIR
BARRELS: Shipping, Metal
BARRICADES: Metal
BARS & BAR SHAPES: Steel, Cold-Finished, Own Hot-Rolled
BARS & BAR SHAPES: Steel, Hot-Rolled
BARS, COLD FINISHED: Steel, From Purchased Hot-Rolled
BARS: Cargo, Stabilizing, Metal
BARS: Concrete Reinforcing, Fabricated Steel
BARS: Iron, Made In Steel Mills
BASES, BEVERAGE
BASKETS: Steel Wire
BATHROOM ACCESS & FITTINGS: Vitreous China & Earthenware
BATHROOM FIXTURES: Plastic
BATTERIES, EXC AUTOMOTIVE: Wholesalers
BATTERIES: Lead Acid, Storage
BATTERIES: Rechargeable
BATTERIES: Storage
BATTERIES: Wet
BATTERY CASES: Plastic Or Plastics Combination
BATTERY CHARGERS
BATTERY CHARGING GENERATORS
BATTERY REPAIR & SVCS
BATTS & BATTING: Cotton
BAUXITE MINING
BEARINGS
BEARINGS & PARTS Ball
BEARINGS: Ball & Roller
BEARINGS: Roller & Parts
BEAUTY & BARBER SHOP EQPT
BEAUTY & BARBER SHOP EQPT & SPLYS WHOLESALERS
BEAUTY CONTEST PRODUCTION
BED & BREAKFAST INNS
BED TICKINGS, COTTON
BEDDING & BEDSPRINGS STORES
BEDDING, BEDSPREADS, BLANKETS & SHEETS
BEDDING, BEDSPREADS, BLANKETS & SHEETS: Comforters & Quilts
BEDS & ACCESS STORES
BEDS: Hospital
BEEKEEPERS' SPLYS: Honeycomb Foundations
BEER & ALE WHOLESALERS
BEER, WINE & LIQUOR STORES
BEER, WINE & LIQUOR STORES: Beer, Packaged
BEER, WINE & LIQUOR STORES: Wine
BEER, WINE & LIQUOR STORES: Wine & Beer
BELLOWS
BELTING: Rubber
BELTS: Chain
BELTS: Conveyor, Made From Purchased Wire
BELTS: Seat, Automotive & Aircraft
BENCHES, WORK : Factory
BEVERAGE BASES & SYRUPS
BEVERAGE PRDTS: Brewers' Grain
BEVERAGE PRDTS: Malt Syrup
BEVERAGE STORES
BEVERAGE, NONALCOHOLIC: Iced Tea/Fruit Drink, Bottled/Canned
BEVERAGES, ALCOHOLIC: Ale
BEVERAGES, ALCOHOLIC: Applejack
BEVERAGES, ALCOHOLIC: Beer
BEVERAGES, ALCOHOLIC: Beer & Ale
BEVERAGES, ALCOHOLIC: Bourbon Whiskey
BEVERAGES, ALCOHOLIC: Cocktails

PRODUCT INDEX

BEVERAGES, ALCOHOLIC: Cordials & Premixed Cocktails
BEVERAGES, ALCOHOLIC: Distilled Liquors
BEVERAGES, ALCOHOLIC: Liquors, Malt
BEVERAGES, ALCOHOLIC: Near Beer
BEVERAGES, ALCOHOLIC: Rum
BEVERAGES, ALCOHOLIC: Vodka
BEVERAGES, ALCOHOLIC: Wines
BEVERAGES, MALT
BEVERAGES, NONALCOHOLIC: Bottled & canned soft drinks
BEVERAGES, NONALCOHOLIC: Carbonated
BEVERAGES, NONALCOHOLIC: Carbonated, Canned & Bottled, Etc
BEVERAGES, NONALCOHOLIC: Cider
BEVERAGES, NONALCOHOLIC: Flavoring extracts & syrups, nec
BEVERAGES, NONALCOHOLIC: Fruit Drnks, Under 100% Juice, Can
BEVERAGES, NONALCOHOLIC: Soft Drinks, Canned & Bottled, Etc
BEVERAGES, NONALCOHOLIC: Tea, Iced, Bottled & Canned, Etc
BEVERAGES, WINE & DISTILLED ALCOHOLIC, WHOLESALE: Wine
BEVERAGES, WINE/DISTILLED ALCOHOLIC, WHOL: Cocktls, Premixed
BICYCLE SHOPS
BICYCLES WHOLESALERS
BICYCLES, PARTS & ACCESS
BILLING & BOOKKEEPING SVCS
BINDING SVC: Books & Manuals
BINDING SVC: Pamphlets
BINDING SVC: Trade
BINS: Prefabricated, Metal Plate
BIOLOGICAL PRDTS: Blood Derivatives
BIOLOGICAL PRDTS: Exc Diagnostic
BIOLOGICAL PRDTS: Vaccines
BIOLOGICAL PRDTS: Vaccines & Immunizing
BIOLOGICAL PRDTS: Venoms
BIOLOGICAL PRDTS: Veterinary
BLACKSMITH SHOP
BLADES: Saw, Chain Type
BLANKBOOKS & LOOSELEAF BINDERS
BLANKBOOKS: Receipt
BLANKBOOKS: Scrapbooks
BLANKETS, FROM PURCHASED MATERIALS
BLANKETS: Horse
BLASTING SVC: Sand, Metal Parts
BLINDS & SHADES: Vertical
BLINDS : Window
BLINDS, WOOD
BLOCKS & BRICKS: Concrete
BLOCKS: Brush, Wood, Turned & Shaped
BLOCKS: Landscape Or Retaining Wall, Concrete
BLOCKS: Paving, Cut Stone
BLOCKS: Standard, Concrete Or Cinder
BLOWERS & FANS
BLUEPRINTING SVCS
BOAT & BARGE COMPONENTS: Metal, Prefabricated
BOAT BUILDING & REPAIR
BOAT BUILDING & REPAIRING: Fiberglass
BOAT BUILDING & REPAIRING: Houseboats
BOAT BUILDING & REPAIRING: Jet Skis
BOAT BUILDING & REPAIRING: Motorboats, Inboard Or Outboard
BOAT BUILDING & REPAIRING: Motorized
BOAT BUILDING & REPAIRING: Non-Motorized
BOAT BUILDING & REPAIRING: Pontoons, Exc Aircraft & Inflat
BOAT BUILDING & REPAIRING: Rigid, Plastic
BOAT BUILDING & REPAIRING: Yachts
BOAT DEALERS
BOAT DEALERS: Canoe & Kayak
BOAT DEALERS: Inflatable
BOAT DEALERS: Marine Splys & Eqpt
BOAT DEALERS: Motor
BOAT DEALERS: Sailboats & Eqpt
BOAT LIFTS
BOAT REPAIR SVCS
BOAT YARD: Boat yards, storage & incidental repair
BOATS & OTHER MARINE EQPT: Plastic
BOATS: Plastic, Nonrigid
BODIES: Truck & Bus
BODY PARTS: Automobile, Stamped Metal
BOILER & HEATING REPAIR SVCS
BOILERS & BOILER SHOP WORK
BOILERS: Low-Pressure Heating, Steam Or Hot Water
BOLTS: Metal
BONDERIZING: Bonderizing, Metal Or Metal Prdts
BOOK STORES
BOOK STORES: College
BOOK STORES: Foreign
BOOK STORES: Religious
BOOKING AGENCIES, THEATRICAL
BOOKS, WHOLESALE
BOOTHS: Spray, Sheet Metal, Prefabricated
BOOTS: Men's
BORING MILL
BOTTLE CAPS & RESEALERS: Plastic
BOTTLED GAS DEALERS: Propane
BOTTLES: Plastic
BOWLING EQPT & SPLY STORES
BOWLING EQPT & SPLYS
BOX & CARTON MANUFACTURING EQPT
BOXES & CRATES: Rectangular, Wood
BOXES & SHOOK: Nailed Wood
BOXES: Corrugated
BOXES: Filing, Paperboard Made From Purchased Materials
BOXES: Outlet, Electric Wiring Device
BOXES: Packing & Shipping, Metal
BOXES: Paperboard, Folding
BOXES: Paperboard, Set-Up
BOXES: Plastic
BOXES: Solid Fiber
BOXES: Wirebound, Wood
BOXES: Wooden
BRAKES & BRAKE PARTS
BRAKES: Bicycle, Friction Clutch & Other
BRAKES: Electromagnetic
BRAKES: Metal Forming
BRAKES: Press
BRASS & BRONZE PRDTS: Die-casted
BRASS FOUNDRY, NEC
BRASS GOODS, WHOLESALE
BRAZING SVCS
BRAZING: Metal
BRIC-A-BRAC
BRICK, STONE & RELATED PRDTS WHOLESALERS
BRICKS & BLOCKS: Structural
BRICKS : Ceramic Glazed, Clay
BRICKS: Clay
BRICKS: Concrete
BRIDAL SHOPS
BROACHING MACHINES
BROADCASTING & COMMS EQPT: Antennas, Transmitting/Comms
BROADCASTING & COMMS EQPT: Trnsmttng TV Antennas/Grndng Eqpt
BROADCASTING & COMMUNICATIONS EQPT: Studio Eqpt, Radio & TV
BROKERS & DEALERS: Securities
BROKERS' SVCS
BROKERS: Automotive
BROKERS: Commodity Contracts
BROKERS: Food
BROKERS: Printing
BRONZE FOUNDRY, NEC
BROOMS
BROOMS & BRUSHES
BROOMS & BRUSHES: Household Or Indl
BROOMS & BRUSHES: Paintbrushes
BROOMS & BRUSHES: Street Sweeping, Hand Or Machine
BUCKLES & PARTS
BUFFING FOR THE TRADE
BUILDING & OFFICE CLEANING SVCS
BUILDING & STRUCTURAL WOOD MEMBERS
BUILDING CLEANING & MAINTENANCE SVCS
BUILDING COMPONENTS: Structural Steel
BUILDING ITEM REPAIR SVCS, MISCELLANEOUS
BUILDING MAINTENANCE SVCS, EXC REPAIRS
BUILDING PRDTS & MATERIALS DEALERS
BUILDING PRDTS: Concrete
BUILDING SCALES MODELS
BUILDINGS & COMPONENTS: Prefabricated Metal
BUILDINGS: Mobile, For Commercial Use
BUILDINGS: Portable
BUILDINGS: Prefabricated, Metal
BUILDINGS: Prefabricated, Plastic
BUILDINGS: Prefabricated, Wood
BUILDINGS: Prefabricated, Wood
BULLETPROOF VESTS
BUMPERS: Motor Vehicle
BURIAL VAULTS, FIBERGLASS
BURIAL VAULTS: Concrete Or Precast Terrazzo
BURIAL VAULTS: Stone
BURNERS: Gas, Indl
BURNING: Metal
BUSHINGS & BEARINGS: Brass, Exc Machined
BUSHINGS: Cast Steel, Exc Investment
BUSHINGS: Rubber
BUSINESS ACTIVITIES: Non-Commercial Site
BUSINESS FORMS WHOLESALERS
BUSINESS FORMS: Printed, Continuous
BUSINESS FORMS: Printed, Manifold
BUSINESS MACHINE REPAIR, ELECTRIC
BUTTER WHOLESALERS
BUTYL RUBBER: Isobutylene-Isoprene Rubbers

C

CABINETS & CASES: Show, Display & Storage, Exc Wood
CABINETS: Bathroom Vanities, Wood
CABINETS: Entertainment
CABINETS: Entertainment Units, Household, Wood
CABINETS: Factory
CABINETS: Filing, Wood
CABINETS: Kitchen, Wood
CABINETS: Office, Metal
CABINETS: Office, Wood
CABINETS: Radio & Television, Metal
CABINETS: Show, Display, Etc, Wood, Exc Refrigerated
CABLE & OTHER PAY TELEVISION DISTRIBUTION
CABLE & PAY TV SVCS: Satellite Master Antenna Sys/SMATV
CABLE WIRING SETS: Battery, Internal Combustion Engines
CABLE: Coaxial
CABLE: Fiber Optic
CABLE: Noninsulated
CABLE: Steel, Insulated Or Armored
CAFES
CAGES: Wire
CALCAREOUS TUFA: Crushed & Broken
CALCIUM META-PHOSPHATE
CALIBRATING SVCS, NEC
CAMERA & PHOTOGRAPHIC SPLYS STORES
CAMERAS & RELATED EQPT: Photographic
CAMPERS: Truck Mounted
CAMPERS: Truck, Slide-In
CAMSHAFTS
CANDLE SHOPS
CANDLES
CANDY & CONFECTIONS: Candy Bars, Including Chocolate Covered
CANDY & CONFECTIONS: Chocolate Candy, Exc Solid Chocolate
CANDY & CONFECTIONS: Cough Drops, Exc Pharmaceutical Preps
CANDY & CONFECTIONS: Fruit & Fruit Peel
CANDY & CONFECTIONS: Fudge
CANDY & CONFECTIONS: Nuts, Candy Covered
CANDY, NUT & CONFECTIONERY STORE: Popcorn, Incl Caramel Corn
CANDY, NUT & CONFECTIONERY STORES: Candy
CANDY, NUT & CONFECTIONERY STORES: Nuts
CANDY, NUT & CONFECTIONERY STORES: Produced For Direct Sale
CANDY: Chocolate From Cacao Beans
CANDY: Hard
CANNED SPECIALTIES
CANS: Aluminum
CANS: Composite Foil-Fiber, Made From Purchased Materials
CANS: Metal
CANS: Tin
CANVAS PRDTS
CANVAS PRDTS: Boat Seats
CANVAS PRDTS: Convertible Tops, Car/Boat, Fm Purchased Mtrl
CANVAS PRDTS: Shades, Made From Purchased Materials
CAPS: Plastic
CAR WASH EQPT
CAR WASH EQPT & SPLYS WHOLESALERS
CARBIDES
CARBON & GRAPHITE PRDTS, NEC
CARBON SPECIALTIES Electrical Use
CARBURETORS
CARDBOARD PRDTS, EXC DIE-CUT

PRODUCT INDEX

CARDS: Color
CARDS: Greeting
CARDS: Identification
CARNIVAL & AMUSEMENT PARK EQPT WHOLESALERS
CARPET & RUG CLEANING & REPAIRING PLANTS
CARPET & UPHOLSTERY CLEANING SVCS
CARPETS & RUGS: Tufted
CARPETS, RUGS & FLOOR COVERING
CARPETS: Textile Fiber
CARPORTS: Prefabricated Metal
CARRIAGES: Horse Drawn
CARS: Electric
CARTS: Grocery
CARVING SETS, STAINLESS STEEL
CASES, WOOD
CASES: Carrying
CASES: Carrying, Clothing & Apparel
CASES: Packing, Nailed Or Lock Corner, Wood
CASES: Shipping, Nailed Or Lock Corner, Wood
CASH REGISTER REPAIR SVCS
CASH REGISTERS WHOLESALERS
CASINGS: Sheet Metal
CASKETS & ACCESS
CASKETS WHOLESALERS
CAST STONE: Concrete
CASTERS
CASTINGS GRINDING: For The Trade
CASTINGS: Aerospace Investment, Ferrous
CASTINGS: Aerospace, Aluminum
CASTINGS: Aerospace, Nonferrous, Exc Aluminum
CASTINGS: Aluminum
CASTINGS: Brass, Bronze & Copper
CASTINGS: Brass, NEC, Exc Die
CASTINGS: Bronze, NEC, Exc Die
CASTINGS: Commercial Investment, Ferrous
CASTINGS: Die, Aluminum
CASTINGS: Die, Copper & Copper Alloy
CASTINGS: Die, Lead & Zinc
CASTINGS: Die, Magnesium & Magnesium-Base Alloy
CASTINGS: Die, Nonferrous
CASTINGS: Die, Zinc
CASTINGS: Ductile
CASTINGS: Gray Iron
CASTINGS: Machinery, Aluminum
CASTINGS: Machinery, Copper Or Copper-Base Alloy
CASTINGS: Machinery, Nonferrous, Exc Die or Aluminum Copper
CASTINGS: Precision
CASTINGS: Steel
CASTINGS: Titanium
CASTINGS: Zinc
CATALOG & MAIL-ORDER HOUSES
CATALOG SALES
CATALOG SHOWROOMS
CATERERS
CATS, WHOLESALE
CEILING SYSTEMS: Luminous, Commercial
CEMENT & CONCRETE RELATED PRDTS & EQPT: Bituminous
CEMENT ROCK: Crushed & Broken
CEMENT, EXC LINOLEUM & TILE
CEMENT: High Temperature, Refractory, Nonclay
CEMENT: Hydraulic
CEMENT: Magnesia
CEMENT: Masonry
CEMENT: Portland
CEMETERIES: Real Estate Operation
CEMETERY MEMORIAL DEALERS
CERAMIC FIBER
CERAMIC FLOOR & WALL TILE WHOLESALERS
CESSPOOL CLEANING SVCS
CHAIN: Welded, Made From Purchased Wire
CHAINS: Forged
CHAMBERS OF COMMERCE
CHARCOAL
CHARCOAL: Activated
CHASSIS: Automobile Trailer
CHASSIS: Motor Vehicle
CHECK VALIDATION SVCS
CHEESE WHOLESALERS
CHEMICAL ELEMENTS
CHEMICAL PROCESSING MACHINERY & EQPT
CHEMICAL SPLYS FOR FOUNDRIES
CHEMICAL: Sodm Compnds/Salts, Inorg, Exc Rfnd Sodm Chloride

CHEMICALS & ALLIED PRDTS WHOLESALERS, NEC
CHEMICALS & ALLIED PRDTS, WHOL: Gases, Compressed/Liquefied
CHEMICALS & ALLIED PRDTS, WHOLESALE: Acids
CHEMICALS & ALLIED PRDTS, WHOLESALE: Alcohols
CHEMICALS & ALLIED PRDTS, WHOLESALE: Anti-Corrosion Prdts
CHEMICALS & ALLIED PRDTS, WHOLESALE: Aromatic
CHEMICALS & ALLIED PRDTS, WHOLESALE: Chemical Additives
CHEMICALS & ALLIED PRDTS, WHOLESALE: Chemicals, Indl
CHEMICALS & ALLIED PRDTS, WHOLESALE: Chemicals, Rustproofing
CHEMICALS & ALLIED PRDTS, WHOLESALE: Compressed Gas
CHEMICALS & ALLIED PRDTS, WHOLESALE: Detergent/Soap
CHEMICALS & ALLIED PRDTS, WHOLESALE: Oil Additives
CHEMICALS & ALLIED PRDTS, WHOLESALE: Oxygen
CHEMICALS & ALLIED PRDTS, WHOLESALE: Plastics Prdts, NEC
CHEMICALS & ALLIED PRDTS, WHOLESALE: Plastics Sheets & Rods
CHEMICALS & ALLIED PRDTS, WHOLESALE: Polyurethane Prdts
CHEMICALS & ALLIED PRDTS, WHOLESALE: Resins, Plastics
CHEMICALS & ALLIED PRDTS, WHOLESALE: Rubber, Synthetic
CHEMICALS & ALLIED PRDTS, WHOLESALE: Spec Clean/Sanitation
CHEMICALS & OTHER PRDTS DERIVED FROM COKING
CHEMICALS: Agricultural
CHEMICALS: Boron Compounds, Not From Mines, NEC
CHEMICALS: Calcium Chloride
CHEMICALS: Chromates & Bichromates
CHEMICALS: Copper Compounds Or Salts, Inorganic
CHEMICALS: Fire Retardant
CHEMICALS: Fuel Tank Or Engine Cleaning
CHEMICALS: High Purity Grade, Organic
CHEMICALS: High Purity, Refined From Technical Grade
CHEMICALS: Inorganic, NEC
CHEMICALS: Medicinal
CHEMICALS: Medicinal, Organic, Uncompounded, Bulk
CHEMICALS: NEC
CHEMICALS: Nonmetallic Compounds
CHEMICALS: Organic, NEC
CHEMICALS: Phenol
CHEMICALS: Phosphates, Defluorinated/Ammoniated, Exc Fertlr
CHEMICALS: Reagent Grade, Refined From Technical Grade
CHEMICALS: Silica Compounds
CHEMICALS: Tanning Agents, Synthetic Inorganic
CHEMICALS: Water Treatment
CHESTS: Bank, Metal
CHILD RESTRAINT SEATS, AUTOMOTIVE, WHOLESALE
CHILDREN'S & INFANTS' CLOTHING STORES
CHILDREN'S WEAR STORES
CHIMNEY CLEANING SVCS
CHINA & GLASS REPAIR SVCS
CHLORINE
CHOCOLATE, EXC CANDY FROM BEANS: Chips, Powder, Block, Syrup
CHOCOLATE, EXC CANDY FROM PURCH CHOC: Chips, Powder, Block
CHRISTMAS NOVELTIES, WHOLESALE
CHRISTMAS TREE LIGHTING SETS: Electric
CHRISTMAS TREES: Artificial
CHUCKS
CHUTES: Metal Plate
CIGARETTE FILTERS
CIGARETTE LIGHTERS
CIRCUIT BOARD REPAIR SVCS
CIRCUIT BOARDS, PRINTED: Television & Radio
CIRCUIT BREAKERS
CIRCUITS, INTEGRATED: Hybrid
CIRCUITS: Electronic
CIRCULAR KNIT FABRICS DYEING & FINISHING
CLAMPS & COUPLINGS: Hose
CLAMPS: Metal
CLAY PRDTS: Architectural
CLAY: Ground Or Treated
CLEANERS: Boiler Tube
CLEANING & DESCALING SVC: Metal Prdts

CLEANING COMPOUNDS: Rifle Bore
CLEANING EQPT: Blast, Dustless
CLEANING EQPT: Commercial
CLEANING EQPT: Dirt Sweeping Units, Indl
CLEANING EQPT: Floor Washing & Polishing, Commercial
CLEANING EQPT: Mop Wringers
CLEANING OR POLISHING PREPARATIONS, NEC
CLEANING PRDTS: Automobile Polish
CLEANING PRDTS: Bleaches, Household, Dry Or Liquid
CLEANING PRDTS: Degreasing Solvent
CLEANING PRDTS: Disinfectants, Household Or Indl Plant
CLEANING PRDTS: Drain Pipe Solvents Or Cleaners
CLEANING PRDTS: Dusting Cloths, Chemically Treated
CLEANING PRDTS: Floor Waxes
CLEANING PRDTS: Indl Plant Disinfectants Or Deodorants
CLEANING PRDTS: Polishing Preparations & Related Prdts
CLEANING PRDTS: Rug, Upholstery/Dry Clng Detergents/Spotters
CLEANING PRDTS: Sanitation Preparations
CLEANING PRDTS: Sanitation Preps, Disinfectants/Deodorants
CLEANING PRDTS: Specialty
CLEANING PRDTS: Window Cleaning Preparations
CLEANING SVCS
CLEANING SVCS: Industrial Or Commercial
CLIPS & FASTENERS, MADE FROM PURCHASED WIRE
CLOCKS
CLOSURES: Closures, Stamped Metal
CLOSURES: Plastic
CLOTHESPINS: Plastic
CLOTHING & ACCESS STORES
CLOTHING & ACCESS, WOMEN, CHILD & INFANT, WHSLE: Sportswear
CLOTHING & ACCESS, WOMEN, CHILD/INFANT, WHOLESALE: Child
CLOTHING & ACCESS, WOMEN, CHILDREN & INFANT, WHOL: Uniforms
CLOTHING & ACCESS, WOMEN, CHILDREN/INFANT, WHOL: Underwear
CLOTHING & ACCESS: Costumes, Theatrical
CLOTHING & ACCESS: Handicapped
CLOTHING & ACCESS: Handkerchiefs, Exc Paper
CLOTHING & ACCESS: Men's Miscellaneous Access
CLOTHING & ACCESS: Regalia
CLOTHING & APPAREL STORES: Custom
CLOTHING & FURNISHINGS, MEN'S & BOYS', WHOLESALE: Caps
CLOTHING & FURNISHINGS, MEN'S & BOYS', WHOLESALE: Uniforms
CLOTHING & FURNISHINGS, MENS & BOYS, WHOL: Sportswear/Work
CLOTHING & FURNISHINGS, MENS & BOYS, WHOLESALE: Lined
CLOTHING STORES: Designer Apparel
CLOTHING STORES: Formal Wear
CLOTHING STORES: Shirts, Custom Made
CLOTHING STORES: T-Shirts, Printed, Custom
CLOTHING STORES: Unisex
CLOTHING STORES: Work
CLOTHING: Access
CLOTHING: Access, Women's & Misses'
CLOTHING: Athletic & Sportswear, Men's & Boys'
CLOTHING: Athletic & Sportswear, Women's & Girls'
CLOTHING: Baker, Barber, Lab/Svc Ind Apparel, Washable, Men
CLOTHING: Bathing Suits & Swimwear, Knit
CLOTHING: Beachwear, Knit
CLOTHING: Belts
CLOTHING: Blouses, Women's & Girls'
CLOTHING: Brassieres
CLOTHING: Children's, Girls'
CLOTHING: Coats & Jackets, Leather & Sheep-Lined
CLOTHING: Coats & Suits, Men's & Boys'
CLOTHING: Costumes
CLOTHING: Culottes & Shorts, Children's
CLOTHING: Disposable
CLOTHING: Dresses
CLOTHING: Furs
CLOTHING: Garments, Indl, Men's & Boys
CLOTHING: Gowns & Dresses, Wedding
CLOTHING: Hats & Caps, NEC
CLOTHING: Hosiery, Anklets
CLOTHING: Hospital, Men's
CLOTHING: Jeans, Men's & Boys'
CLOTHING: Men's & boy's underwear & nightwear

PRODUCT INDEX

CLOTHING: Outerwear, Lthr, Wool/Down-Filled, Men, Youth/Boy
CLOTHING: Outerwear, Women's & Misses' NEC
CLOTHING: Overalls & Coveralls
CLOTHING: Shirts
CLOTHING: Shirts & T-Shirts, Knit
CLOTHING: Shirts, Dress, Men's & Boys'
CLOTHING: Socks
CLOTHING: Sportswear, Women's
CLOTHING: Sweatshirts & T-Shirts, Men's & Boys'
CLOTHING: Swimwear, Men's & Boys'
CLOTHING: Swimwear, Women's & Misses'
CLOTHING: T-Shirts & Tops, Knit
CLOTHING: Tights & Leg Warmers
CLOTHING: Uniforms, Firemen's, From Purchased Materials
CLOTHING: Uniforms, Men's & Boys'
CLOTHING: Uniforms, Team Athletic
CLOTHING: Uniforms, Work
CLOTHING: Vests, Sport, Suede, Leatherette, Etc, Mens & Boys
CLOTHING: Work, Men's
CLOTHS: Dust, Made From Purchased Materials
CLUTCHES OR BRAKES: Electromagnetic
CLUTCHES, EXC VEHICULAR
COAL MINING SERVICES
COAL MINING: Bituminous Coal & Lignite-Surface Mining
COAL, MINERALS & ORES, WHOLESALE: Coal
COATED OR PLATED PRDTS
COATING SVC
COATING SVC: Aluminum, Metal Prdts
COATING SVC: Electrodes
COATING SVC: Hot Dip, Metals Or Formed Prdts
COATING SVC: Metals & Formed Prdts
COATING SVC: Metals, With Plastic Or Resins
COATING SVC: Rust Preventative
COATING SVC: Silicon
COATINGS: Epoxy
COATINGS: Polyurethane
COCKTAIL LOUNGE
COFFEE SVCS
COILS & TRANSFORMERS
COILS: Electric Motors Or Generators
COILS: Pipe
COLLETS
COLOR LAKES OR TONERS
COLORING & FINISHING SVC: Aluminum Or Formed Prdts
COLORS: Pigments, Inorganic
COLORS: Pigments, Organic
COLUMNS: Concrete
COMMERCIAL & OFFICE BUILDINGS RENOVATION & REPAIR
COMMERCIAL ART & GRAPHIC DESIGN SVCS
COMMERCIAL ART & ILLUSTRATION SVCS
COMMERCIAL CONTAINERS WHOLESALERS
COMMERCIAL EQPT WHOLESALERS, NEC
COMMERCIAL EQPT, WHOLESALE: Bakery Eqpt & Splys
COMMERCIAL EQPT, WHOLESALE: Coffee Brewing Eqpt & Splys
COMMERCIAL EQPT, WHOLESALE: Comm Cooking & Food Svc Eqpt
COMMERCIAL EQPT, WHOLESALE: Restaurant, NEC
COMMERCIAL EQPT, WHOLESALE: Scales, Exc Laboratory
COMMERCIAL EQPT, WHOLESALE: Store Fixtures & Display Eqpt
COMMERCIAL EQPT, WHOLESALE: Teaching Machines, Electronic
COMMERCIAL LAUNDRY EQPT
COMMERCIAL PRINTING & NEWSPAPER PUBLISHING COMBINED
COMMERCIAL REFRIGERATORS WHOLESALERS
COMMODITY INSPECTION SVCS
COMMON SAND MINING
COMMUNICATIONS CARRIER: Wired
COMMUNICATIONS EQPT & SYSTEMS, NEC
COMMUNICATIONS EQPT REPAIR & MAINTENANCE
COMMUNICATIONS EQPT WHOLESALERS
COMMUNICATIONS SVCS
COMMUNICATIONS SVCS, NEC
COMMUNICATIONS SVCS: Cellular
COMMUNICATIONS SVCS: Data
COMMUNICATIONS SVCS: Electronic Mail
COMMUNICATIONS SVCS: Facsimile Transmission
COMMUNICATIONS SVCS: Internet Connectivity Svcs
COMMUNICATIONS SVCS: Internet Host Svcs
COMMUNICATIONS SVCS: Proprietary Online Svcs Networks
COMMUNICATIONS SVCS: Telephone Or Video
COMMUNICATIONS SVCS: Telephone, Data
COMMUNITY DEVELOPMENT GROUPS
COMPARATORS: Machinists
COMPARATORS: Optical
COMPASSES & ACCESS
COMPOST
COMPRESSORS: Air & Gas
COMPRESSORS: Air & Gas, Including Vacuum Pumps
COMPRESSORS: Refrigeration & Air Conditioning Eqpt
COMPRESSORS: Repairing
COMPRESSORS: Wholesalers
COMPUTER & COMPUTER SOFTWARE STORES
COMPUTER & COMPUTER SOFTWARE STORES: Peripheral Eqpt
COMPUTER & COMPUTER SOFTWARE STORES: Personal Computers
COMPUTER & COMPUTER SOFTWARE STORES: Printers & Plotters
COMPUTER & COMPUTER SOFTWARE STORES: Software & Access
COMPUTER & COMPUTER SOFTWARE STORES: Software, Bus/Non-Game
COMPUTER & COMPUTER SOFTWARE STORES: Word Process Eqpt/Splys
COMPUTER & DATA PROCESSING EQPT REPAIR & MAINTENANCE
COMPUTER & OFFICE MACHINE MAINTENANCE & REPAIR
COMPUTER CALCULATING SVCS
COMPUTER FACILITIES MANAGEMENT SVCS
COMPUTER FORMS
COMPUTER GRAPHICS SVCS
COMPUTER INTERFACE EQPT: Indl Process
COMPUTER PERIPHERAL EQPT REPAIR & MAINTENANCE
COMPUTER PERIPHERAL EQPT, NEC
COMPUTER PERIPHERAL EQPT, WHOLESALE
COMPUTER PERIPHERAL EQPT: Graphic Displays, Exc Terminals
COMPUTER PERIPHERAL EQPT: Input Or Output
COMPUTER PLOTTERS
COMPUTER PROCESSING SVCS
COMPUTER PROGRAMMING SVCS
COMPUTER PROGRAMMING SVCS: Custom
COMPUTER RELATED MAINTENANCE SVCS
COMPUTER SOFTWARE DEVELOPMENT
COMPUTER SOFTWARE DEVELOPMENT & APPLICATIONS
COMPUTER SOFTWARE SYSTEMS ANALYSIS & DESIGN: Custom
COMPUTER SOFTWARE WRITERS
COMPUTER STORAGE DEVICES, NEC
COMPUTER SYSTEMS ANALYSIS & DESIGN
COMPUTER TERMINALS
COMPUTER-AIDED DESIGN SYSTEMS SVCS
COMPUTER-AIDED MANUFACTURING SYSTEMS SVCS
COMPUTERS, NEC
COMPUTERS, NEC, WHOLESALE
COMPUTERS, PERIPH & SOFTWARE, WHLSE: Personal & Home Entrtn
COMPUTERS, PERIPHERALS & SOFTWARE, WHOLESALE: Printers
COMPUTERS, PERIPHERALS & SOFTWARE, WHOLESALE: Software
COMPUTERS: Mainframe
COMPUTERS: Mini
COMPUTERS: Personal
CONCENTRATES, DRINK
CONCRETE BUILDING PRDTS WHOLESALERS
CONCRETE CURING & HARDENING COMPOUNDS
CONCRETE MIXERS
CONCRETE PLANTS
CONCRETE PRDTS
CONCRETE PRDTS, PRECAST, NEC
CONCRETE REINFORCING MATERIAL
CONCRETE: Bituminous
CONCRETE: Dry Mixture
CONCRETE: Ready-Mixed
CONDENSERS & CONDENSING UNITS: Air Conditioner
CONDENSERS: Heat Transfer Eqpt, Evaporative
CONDENSERS: Motors Or Generators
CONFECTIONERY PRDTS WHOLESALERS
CONFECTIONS & CANDY
CONNECTORS & TERMINALS: Electrical Device Uses
CONNECTORS: Electrical
CONNECTORS: Electronic
CONNECTORS: Power, Electric
CONSTRUCTION & MINING MACHINERY WHOLESALERS
CONSTRUCTION EQPT: Attachments
CONSTRUCTION EQPT: Attachments, Backhoe Mounted, Hyd Pwrd
CONSTRUCTION EQPT: Attachments, Snow Plow
CONSTRUCTION EQPT: Blade, Grader, Scraper, Dozer/Snow Plow
CONSTRUCTION EQPT: Buckets, Excavating, Clamshell, Etc
CONSTRUCTION EQPT: Cranes
CONSTRUCTION EQPT: Finishers & Spreaders
CONSTRUCTION EQPT: Grinders, Stone, Portable
CONSTRUCTION EQPT: Soil compactors, Vibratory
CONSTRUCTION EQPT: Subgraders
CONSTRUCTION EQPT: Tractors
CONSTRUCTION EQPT: Wellpoint Systems
CONSTRUCTION EQPT: Wrecker Hoists, Automobile
CONSTRUCTION MATERIALS, WHOL: Concrete/Cinder Bldg Prdts
CONSTRUCTION MATERIALS, WHOLESALE: Aggregate
CONSTRUCTION MATERIALS, WHOLESALE: Air Ducts, Sheet Metal
CONSTRUCTION MATERIALS, WHOLESALE: Architectural Metalwork
CONSTRUCTION MATERIALS, WHOLESALE: Asphalt Felts & coating
CONSTRUCTION MATERIALS, WHOLESALE: Awnings
CONSTRUCTION MATERIALS, WHOLESALE: Block, Concrete & Cinder
CONSTRUCTION MATERIALS, WHOLESALE: Brick, Exc Refractory
CONSTRUCTION MATERIALS, WHOLESALE: Building Stone
CONSTRUCTION MATERIALS, WHOLESALE: Building Stone, Granite
CONSTRUCTION MATERIALS, WHOLESALE: Building Stone, Marble
CONSTRUCTION MATERIALS, WHOLESALE: Building, Interior
CONSTRUCTION MATERIALS, WHOLESALE: Cement
CONSTRUCTION MATERIALS, WHOLESALE: Concrete Mixtures
CONSTRUCTION MATERIALS, WHOLESALE: Doors, Sliding
CONSTRUCTION MATERIALS, WHOLESALE: Glass
CONSTRUCTION MATERIALS, WHOLESALE: Gravel
CONSTRUCTION MATERIALS, WHOLESALE: Insulation, Thermal
CONSTRUCTION MATERIALS, WHOLESALE: Limestone
CONSTRUCTION MATERIALS, WHOLESALE: Millwork
CONSTRUCTION MATERIALS, WHOLESALE: Pallets, Wood
CONSTRUCTION MATERIALS, WHOLESALE: Paving Materials
CONSTRUCTION MATERIALS, WHOLESALE: Prefabricated Structures
CONSTRUCTION MATERIALS, WHOLESALE: Roof, Asphalt/Sheet Metal
CONSTRUCTION MATERIALS, WHOLESALE: Roofing & Siding Material
CONSTRUCTION MATERIALS, WHOLESALE: Sand
CONSTRUCTION MATERIALS, WHOLESALE: Septic Tanks
CONSTRUCTION MATERIALS, WHOLESALE: Sewer Pipe, Clay
CONSTRUCTION MATERIALS, WHOLESALE: Siding, Exc Wood
CONSTRUCTION MATERIALS, WHOLESALE: Stone, Crushed Or Broken
CONSTRUCTION MATERIALS, WHOLESALE: Windows
CONSTRUCTION MATLS, WHOL: Lumber, Rough, Dressed/Finished
CONSTRUCTION MATLS, WHOLESALE: Struct Assy, Prefab, NonWood
CONSTRUCTION SAND MINING
CONSTRUCTION SITE PREPARATION SVCS
CONSTRUCTION: Agricultural Building
CONSTRUCTION: Apartment Building
CONSTRUCTION: Athletic & Recreation Facilities
CONSTRUCTION: Athletic & Recreation Facilities
CONSTRUCTION: Commercial & Institutional Building
CONSTRUCTION: Commercial & Office Building, New
CONSTRUCTION: Drainage System
CONSTRUCTION: Electric Power Line

PRODUCT INDEX

CONSTRUCTION: Farm Building
CONSTRUCTION: Food Prdts Manufacturing or Packing Plant
CONSTRUCTION: Heavy Highway & Street
CONSTRUCTION: Indl Building & Warehouse
CONSTRUCTION: Indl Buildings, New, NEC
CONSTRUCTION: Institutional Building
CONSTRUCTION: Marine
CONSTRUCTION: Nonresidential Buildings, Custom
CONSTRUCTION: Parade Float
CONSTRUCTION: Parking Lot
CONSTRUCTION: Pipeline, NEC
CONSTRUCTION: Railroad & Subway
CONSTRUCTION: Refineries
CONSTRUCTION: Residential, Nec
CONSTRUCTION: Roads, Gravel or Dirt
CONSTRUCTION: Sewer Line
CONSTRUCTION: Silo, Agricultural
CONSTRUCTION: Single-Family Housing
CONSTRUCTION: Single-family Housing, New
CONSTRUCTION: Single-family Housing, Prefabricated
CONSTRUCTION: Steel Buildings
CONSTRUCTION: Street Surfacing & Paving
CONSTRUCTION: Swimming Pools
CONSTRUCTION: Utility Line
CONSTRUCTION: Waste Water & Sewage Treatment Plant
CONSTRUCTION: Water Main
CONSULTING SVC: Business, NEC
CONSULTING SVC: Chemical
CONSULTING SVC: Computer
CONSULTING SVC: Data Processing
CONSULTING SVC: Educational
CONSULTING SVC: Engineering
CONSULTING SVC: Financial Management
CONSULTING SVC: Management
CONSULTING SVC: Marketing Management
CONSULTING SVC: Online Technology
CONSULTING SVC: Productivity Improvement
CONSULTING SVC: Sales Management
CONSULTING SVC: Telecommunications
CONSULTING SVCS, BUSINESS: Communications
CONSULTING SVCS, BUSINESS: Energy Conservation
CONSULTING SVCS, BUSINESS: Environmental
CONSULTING SVCS, BUSINESS: Safety Training Svcs
CONSULTING SVCS, BUSINESS: Sys Engnrg, Exc Computer/Prof
CONSULTING SVCS, BUSINESS: Systems Analysis & Engineering
CONSULTING SVCS, BUSINESS: Systems Analysis Or Design
CONSULTING SVCS, BUSINESS: Test Development & Evaluation
CONSULTING SVCS: Oil
CONSULTING SVCS: Scientific
CONTACT LENSES
CONTACTS: Electrical
CONTAINERS: Air Cargo, Metal
CONTAINERS: Cargo, Wood
CONTAINERS: Cargo, Wood & Metal Combination
CONTAINERS: Cargo, Wood & Wood With Metal
CONTAINERS: Corrugated
CONTAINERS: Foil, Bakery Goods & Frozen Foods
CONTAINERS: Glass
CONTAINERS: Metal
CONTAINERS: Plastic
CONTAINERS: Plywood & Veneer, Wood
CONTAINERS: Sanitary, Food
CONTAINERS: Shipping & Mailing, Fiber
CONTAINERS: Shipping, Bombs, Metal Plate
CONTAINERS: Wood
CONTRACT DIVING SVC
CONTRACTOR: Dredging
CONTRACTOR: Rigging & Scaffolding
CONTRACTORS: Access Control System Eqpt
CONTRACTORS: Acoustical & Insulation Work
CONTRACTORS: Antenna Installation
CONTRACTORS: Asphalt
CONTRACTORS: Awning Installation
CONTRACTORS: Boiler & Furnace
CONTRACTORS: Boiler Maintenance Contractor
CONTRACTORS: Building Eqpt & Machinery Installation
CONTRACTORS: Building Front Installation, Metal
CONTRACTORS: Building Movers
CONTRACTORS: Building Sign Installation & Mntnce
CONTRACTORS: Building Site Preparation
CONTRACTORS: Carpentry Work
CONTRACTORS: Carpentry, Cabinet & Finish Work
CONTRACTORS: Carpentry, Cabinet Building & Installation
CONTRACTORS: Carpet Laying
CONTRACTORS: Closed Circuit Television Installation
CONTRACTORS: Closet Organizers, Installation & Design
CONTRACTORS: Coating, Caulking & Weather, Water & Fire
CONTRACTORS: Commercial & Office Building
CONTRACTORS: Computer Installation
CONTRACTORS: Computerized Controls Installation
CONTRACTORS: Concrete
CONTRACTORS: Concrete Repair
CONTRACTORS: Construction Caulking
CONTRACTORS: Construction Site Cleanup
CONTRACTORS: Construction Site Metal Structure Coating
CONTRACTORS: Countertop Installation
CONTRACTORS: Demolition, Building & Other Structures
CONTRACTORS: Directional Oil & Gas Well Drilling Svc
CONTRACTORS: Dock Eqpt Installation, Indl
CONTRACTORS: Drapery Track Installation
CONTRACTORS: Driveway
CONTRACTORS: Electrical
CONTRACTORS: Electronic Controls Installation
CONTRACTORS: Energy Management Control
CONTRACTORS: Erection & Dismantling, Poured Concrete Forms
CONTRACTORS: Excavating
CONTRACTORS: Excavating Slush Pits & Cellars Svcs
CONTRACTORS: Exterior Wall System Installation
CONTRACTORS: Fence Construction
CONTRACTORS: Fire Detection & Burglar Alarm Systems
CONTRACTORS: Fire Sprinkler System Installation Svcs
CONTRACTORS: Floor Laying & Other Floor Work
CONTRACTORS: Flooring
CONTRACTORS: Food Svcs Eqpt Installation
CONTRACTORS: Foundation Building
CONTRACTORS: Gas Field Svcs, NEC
CONTRACTORS: Gasoline Condensation Removal Svcs
CONTRACTORS: General Electric
CONTRACTORS: Glass, Glazing & Tinting
CONTRACTORS: Gutters & Downspouts
CONTRACTORS: Heating & Air Conditioning
CONTRACTORS: Heating Systems Repair & Maintenance Svc
CONTRACTORS: Highway & Street Construction, General
CONTRACTORS: Highway & Street Paving
CONTRACTORS: Highway & Street Resurfacing
CONTRACTORS: Home & Office Intrs Finish, Furnish/Remodel
CONTRACTORS: Hot Shot Svcs
CONTRACTORS: Hydraulic Eqpt Installation & Svcs
CONTRACTORS: Indl Building Renovation, Remodeling & Repair
CONTRACTORS: Insulation Installation, Building
CONTRACTORS: Kitchen & Bathroom Remodeling
CONTRACTORS: Lighting Syst
CONTRACTORS: Lightweight Steel Framing Installation
CONTRACTORS: Machine Rigging & Moving
CONTRACTORS: Machinery Installation
CONTRACTORS: Marble Masonry, Exterior
CONTRACTORS: Masonry & Stonework
CONTRACTORS: Mechanical
CONTRACTORS: Mobile Home Site Set-Up
CONTRACTORS: Oil & Gas Building, Repairing & Dismantling Svc
CONTRACTORS: Oil & Gas Field Geophysical Exploration Svcs
CONTRACTORS: Oil & Gas Field Tools Fishing Svcs
CONTRACTORS: Oil & Gas Well Casing Cement Svcs
CONTRACTORS: Oil & Gas Well Drilling Svc
CONTRACTORS: Oil & Gas Well Foundation Grading Svcs
CONTRACTORS: Oil & Gas Well On-Site Foundation Building Svcs
CONTRACTORS: Oil & Gas Wells Svcs
CONTRACTORS: Oil Field Haulage Svcs
CONTRACTORS: Oil Field Lease Tanks: Erectg, Clng/Rprg Svcs
CONTRACTORS: Oil Field Mud Drilling Svcs
CONTRACTORS: Oil Field Pipe Testing Svcs
CONTRACTORS: Oil Sampling Svcs
CONTRACTORS: Oil/Gas Field Casing,Tube/Rod Running,Cut/Pull
CONTRACTORS: Oil/Gas Well Construction, Rpr/Dismantling Svcs
CONTRACTORS: On-Site Welding
CONTRACTORS: Ornamental Metal Work
CONTRACTORS: Painting & Wall Covering
CONTRACTORS: Painting, Commercial
CONTRACTORS: Painting, Commercial, Interior
CONTRACTORS: Painting, Indl
CONTRACTORS: Painting, Residential
CONTRACTORS: Parking Facility Eqpt Installation
CONTRACTORS: Parking Lot Maintenance
CONTRACTORS: Patio & Deck Construction & Repair
CONTRACTORS: Pipe & Boiler Insulating
CONTRACTORS: Playground Construction & Eqpt Installation
CONTRACTORS: Plumbing
CONTRACTORS: Pollution Control Eqpt Installation
CONTRACTORS: Precast Concrete Struct Framing & Panel Placing
CONTRACTORS: Prefabricated Fireplace Installation
CONTRACTORS: Prefabricated Window & Door Installation
CONTRACTORS: Process Piping
CONTRACTORS: Pulpwood, Engaged In Cutting
CONTRACTORS: Refrigeration
CONTRACTORS: Rigging, Theatrical
CONTRACTORS: Roofing
CONTRACTORS: Roustabout Svcs
CONTRACTORS: Safety & Security Eqpt
CONTRACTORS: Sandblasting Svc, Building Exteriors
CONTRACTORS: Seismograph Survey Svcs
CONTRACTORS: Septic System
CONTRACTORS: Sheet Metal Work, NEC
CONTRACTORS: Sheet metal Work, Architectural
CONTRACTORS: Siding
CONTRACTORS: Single-family Home General Remodeling
CONTRACTORS: Skylight Installation
CONTRACTORS: Solar Energy Eqpt
CONTRACTORS: Sound Eqpt Installation
CONTRACTORS: Special Trades, NEC
CONTRACTORS: Storage Tank Erection, Metal
CONTRACTORS: Store Fixture Installation
CONTRACTORS: Store Front Construction
CONTRACTORS: Structural Iron Work, Structural
CONTRACTORS: Structural Steel Erection
CONTRACTORS: Stucco, Interior
CONTRACTORS: Svc Well Drilling Svcs
CONTRACTORS: Tile Installation, Ceramic
CONTRACTORS: Tuck Pointing & Restoration
CONTRACTORS: Underground Utilities
CONTRACTORS: Ventilation & Duct Work
CONTRACTORS: Wall Covering, Residential
CONTRACTORS: Warm Air Heating & Air Conditioning
CONTRACTORS: Water Intake Well Drilling Svc
CONTRACTORS: Water Well Drilling
CONTRACTORS: Waterproofing
CONTRACTORS: Well Acidizing Svcs
CONTRACTORS: Window Treatment Installation
CONTROL CIRCUIT DEVICES
CONTROL EQPT: Buses Or Trucks, Electric
CONTROL EQPT: Electric
CONTROL EQPT: Noise
CONTROL PANELS: Electrical
CONTROLS & ACCESS: Indl, Electric
CONTROLS & ACCESS: Motor
CONTROLS: Air Flow, Refrigeration
CONTROLS: Automatic Temperature
CONTROLS: Crane & Hoist, Including Metal Mill
CONTROLS: Environmental
CONTROLS: Marine & Navy, Auxiliary
CONTROLS: Numerical
CONTROLS: Relay & Ind
CONTROLS: Thermostats
CONTROLS: Voice
CONVENIENCE STORES
CONVENTION & TRADE SHOW SVCS
CONVERTERS: Data
CONVERTERS: Frequency
CONVERTERS: Phase Or Rotary, Electrical
CONVERTERS: Power, AC to DC
CONVERTERS: Rotary, Electrical
CONVERTERS: Torque, Exc Auto
CONVEYOR SYSTEMS
CONVEYOR SYSTEMS: Belt, General Indl Use
CONVEYOR SYSTEMS: Bucket Type
CONVEYOR SYSTEMS: Bulk Handling
CONVEYOR SYSTEMS: Pneumatic Tube
CONVEYOR SYSTEMS: Robotic
CONVEYORS & CONVEYING EQPT
CONVEYORS: Overhead
COOKING & FOOD WARMING EQPT: Commercial

PRODUCT INDEX

COOKING & FOODWARMING EQPT: Coffee Brewing
COOKING & FOODWARMING EQPT: Commercial
COOKING EQPT, HOUSEHOLD: Convection Ovens, Incldg Portable
COOKING EQPT, HOUSEHOLD: Indoor
COOKING EQPT, HOUSEHOLD: Ranges, Gas
COOKING SCHOOL
COOKWARE, STONEWARE: Coarse Earthenware & Pottery
COOLERS & ICE CHESTS: Metal
COOLERS & ICE CHESTS: Polystyrene Foam
COOLING TOWERS: Metal
COPPER ORE MILLING & PREPARATION
COPPER ORE MINING
COPPER: Cakes, Primary
COPPER: Rolling & Drawing
COPY MACHINES WHOLESALERS
CORD & TWINE
CORK & CORK PRDTS
CORRUGATED PRDTS: Boxes, Partition, Display Items, Sheet/Pad
COSMETIC PREPARATIONS
COSMETICS & TOILETRIES
COSMETOLOGIST
COSMETOLOGY & PERSONAL HYGIENE SALONS
COSTUME JEWELRY & NOVELTIES: Apparel, Exc Precious Metals
COSTUME JEWELRY & NOVELTIES: Exc Semi & Precious
COSTUME JEWELRY & NOVELTIES: Rosaries & Sm Religious Items
COUNTER & SINK TOPS
COUNTERS & COUNTING DEVICES
COUNTERS OR COUNTER DISPLAY CASES, EXC WOOD
COUNTERS OR COUNTER DISPLAY CASES, WOOD
COUNTING DEVICES: Controls, Revolution & Timing
COUNTING DEVICES: Electromechanical
COUNTING DEVICES: Electronic Totalizing
COUNTING DEVICES: Gauges, Press Temp Corrections Computing
COUNTING DEVICES: Speedometers
COUNTING DEVICES: Vehicle Instruments
COUPLINGS, EXC PRESSURE & SOIL PIPE
COUPLINGS: Pipe
COUPLINGS: Shaft
COUPON REDEMPTION SVCS
COURIER SVCS: Ground
COVERS: Automobile Seat
COVERS: Automotive, Exc Seat & Tire
COVERS: Canvas
CRACKED CASTING REPAIR SVCS
CRANE & AERIAL LIFT SVCS
CRANES & MONORAIL SYSTEMS
CRANES: Indl Plant
CRANES: Overhead
CRANKSHAFTS & CAMSHAFTS: Machining
CRANKSHAFTS: Motor Vehicle
CRATES: Fruit, Wood Wirebound
CREDIT AGENCIES: Federal & Federally Sponsored
CREDIT INST, SHORT-TERM BUSINESS: Accts Receiv & Coml Paper
CREDIT INST, SHORT-TERM BUSINESS: Financing Dealers
CREDIT INSTITUTIONS: Personal
CREDIT INSTITUTIONS: Short-Term Business
CREMATORIES
CROWNS & CLOSURES
CRUDE PETROLEUM & NATURAL GAS PRODUCTION
CRUDE PETROLEUM & NATURAL GAS PRODUCTION
CRUDE PETROLEUM PRODUCTION
CRYSTALS
CUBICLES: Electric Switchboard Eqpt
CULVERTS: Sheet Metal
CUPS & PLATES: Foamed Plastics
CUPS: Plastic Exc Polystyrene Foam
CURBING: Granite Or Stone
CURTAIN & DRAPERY FIXTURES: Poles, Rods & Rollers
CURTAINS & BEDDING: Knit
CURTAINS: Window, From Purchased Materials
CUSHIONS & PILLOWS
CUSHIONS & PILLOWS: Bed, From Purchased Materials
CUSHIONS & PILLOWS: Boat
CUSTOM COMPOUNDING OF RUBBER MATERIALS
CUT STONE & STONE PRODUCTS
CUTLERY
CUTLERY WHOLESALERS
CUTOUTS: Cardboard, Die-Cut, Made From Purchased Materials

CUTOUTS: Distribution
CUTTING SVC: Paperboard
CYCLIC CRUDES & INTERMEDIATES
CYLINDER & ACTUATORS: Fluid Power
CYLINDERS: Pressure
CYLINDERS: Pump

D

DAIRY EQPT
DAIRY PRDTS STORE: Cheese
DAIRY PRDTS STORE: Ice Cream, Packaged
DAIRY PRDTS STORES
DAIRY PRDTS WHOLESALERS: Fresh
DAIRY PRDTS: Butter
DAIRY PRDTS: Cheese
DAIRY PRDTS: Condensed Milk
DAIRY PRDTS: Cream Substitutes
DAIRY PRDTS: Dietary Supplements, Dairy & Non-Dairy Based
DAIRY PRDTS: Dips & Spreads, Cheese Based
DAIRY PRDTS: Dried Milk
DAIRY PRDTS: Fermented & Cultured Milk Prdts
DAIRY PRDTS: Frozen Desserts & Novelties
DAIRY PRDTS: Ice Cream & Ice Milk
DAIRY PRDTS: Ice Cream, Bulk
DAIRY PRDTS: Ice Cream, Packaged, Molded, On Sticks, Etc.
DAIRY PRDTS: Milk, Chocolate
DAIRY PRDTS: Milk, Condensed & Evaporated
DAIRY PRDTS: Milk, Fluid
DAIRY PRDTS: Milk, Processed, Pasteurized, Homogenized/Btld
DAIRY PRDTS: Natural Cheese
DAIRY PRDTS: Powdered Milk
DAIRY PRDTS: Processed Cheese
DAIRY PRDTS: Sherbets, Dairy Based
DAIRY PRDTS: Yogurt, Exc Frozen
DAIRY PRDTS: Yogurt, Frozen
DATA PROCESSING & PREPARATION SVCS
DATA PROCESSING SVCS
DECORATIVE WOOD & WOODWORK
DEFENSE SYSTEMS & EQPT
DEGREASING MACHINES
DEHUMIDIFIERS: Electric
DEHYDRATION EQPT
DELIVERY SVCS, BY VEHICLE
DENTAL EQPT
DENTAL EQPT & SPLYS
DENTAL EQPT & SPLYS WHOLESALERS
DENTAL EQPT & SPLYS: Cabinets
DENTAL EQPT & SPLYS: Compounds
DENTAL EQPT & SPLYS: Dental Materials
DENTAL EQPT & SPLYS: Enamels
DENTAL EQPT & SPLYS: Impression Materials
DENTAL EQPT & SPLYS: Metal
DENTISTS' OFFICES & CLINICS
DERMATOLOGICALS
DESIGN SVCS, NEC
DESIGN SVCS: Commercial & Indl
DESIGN SVCS: Computer Integrated Systems
DESIGN SVCS: Hand Tools
DETECTION APPARATUS: Electronic/Magnetic Field, Light/Heat
DETECTION EQPT: Aeronautical Electronic Field
DETECTIVE & ARMORED CAR SERVICES
DEVELOPING & PRINTING: Motion Picture Film, Commercial
DIAGNOSTIC SUBSTANCES
DIAGNOSTIC SUBSTANCES OR AGENTS: Blood Derivative
DIAGNOSTIC SUBSTANCES OR AGENTS: In Vitro
DIAGNOSTIC SUBSTANCES OR AGENTS: Microbiology & Virology
DIAGNOSTIC SUBSTANCES OR AGENTS: Radioactive
DIAGNOSTIC SUBSTANCES OR AGENTS: Veterinary
DIAMOND SETTER SVCS
DIE CUTTING SVC: Paper
DIE SETS: Presses, Metal Stamping
DIES & TOOLS: Special
DIES: Cutting, Exc Metal
DIES: Extrusion
DIES: Plastic Forming
DIES: Steel Rule
DIFFERENTIAL ASSEMBLIES & PARTS
DIMENSION STONE: Buildings
DIODES: Light Emitting
DIRECT SELLING ESTABLISHMENTS, NEC

DIRECT SELLING ESTABLISHMENTS: Milk Delivery
DISC JOCKEYS
DISCOUNT DEPARTMENT STORES
DISHWASHING EQPT: Commercial
DISHWASHING EQPT: Household
DISINFECTING & PEST CONTROL SERVICES
DISINFECTING SVCS
DISK & DRUM DRIVES & COMPONENTS: Computers
DISK DRIVES: Computer
DISPENSING EQPT & PARTS, BEVERAGE: Fountain/Other Beverage
DISPLAY FIXTURES: Showcases, Wood, Exc Refrigerated
DISPLAY FIXTURES: Wood
DISPLAY ITEMS: Corrugated, Made From Purchased Materials
DISPLAY ITEMS: Solid Fiber, Made From Purchased Materials
DISPLAY LETTERING SVCS
DISPLAY STANDS: Merchandise, Exc Wood
DISTILLERS DRIED GRAIN & SOLUBLES
DISTRIBUTORS: Motor Vehicle Engine
DIVING EQPT STORES
DOCK EQPT & SPLYS, INDL
DOCK OPERATION SVCS, INCL BLDGS, FACILITIES, OPERS & MAINT
DOCKS: Floating, Wood
DOCKS: Prefabricated Metal
DOOR & WINDOW REPAIR SVCS
DOOR FRAMES: Wood
DOOR OPERATING SYSTEMS: Electric
DOORS & WINDOWS WHOLESALERS: All Materials
DOORS & WINDOWS: Screen & Storm
DOORS & WINDOWS: Storm, Metal
DOORS: Fiberglass
DOORS: Folding, Plastic Or Plastic Coated Fabric
DOORS: Garage, Overhead, Metal
DOORS: Garage, Overhead, Wood
DOORS: Glass
DOORS: Louver, Wood
DOORS: Rolling, Indl Building Or Warehouse, Metal
DOORS: Wooden
DOWELS & DOWEL RODS
DRAFTING SPLYS WHOLESALERS
DRAFTING SVCS
DRAINAGE PRDTS: Concrete
DRAPERIES & CURTAINS
DRAPERIES & DRAPERY FABRICS, COTTON
DRAPERIES: Plastic & Textile, From Purchased Materials
DRAPERY & UPHOLSTERY STORES: Curtains
DRAPERY & UPHOLSTERY STORES: Draperies
DRAPES & DRAPERY FABRICS, FROM MANMADE FIBER
DRILL BITS
DRILLING MACHINERY & EQPT: Water Well
DRINKING PLACES: Alcoholic Beverages
DRINKING PLACES: Bars & Lounges
DRINKING PLACES: Beer Garden
DRINKING PLACES: Tavern
DRIVE CHAINS: Bicycle Or Motorcycle
DRIVE SHAFTS
DRIVES: High Speed Indl, Exc Hydrostatic
DRIVES: Hydrostatic
DRUG STORES
DRUGS & DRUG PROPRIETARIES, WHOL: Biologicals/Allied Prdts
DRUGS & DRUG PROPRIETARIES, WHOLESALE
DRUGS & DRUG PROPRIETARIES, WHOLESALE: Medical Rubber Goods
DRUGS & DRUG PROPRIETARIES, WHOLESALE: Pharmaceuticals
DRUMS: Brake
DRUMS: Fiber
DRYERS & REDRYERS: Indl
DUCTING: Metal Plate
DUCTS: Sheet Metal
DUMBWAITERS
DUMPSTERS: Garbage
DUST OR FUME COLLECTING EQPT: Indl
DYES & PIGMENTS: Organic
DYES & TINTS: Household
DYNAMOMETERS

E

EARTH SCIENCE SVCS
EATING PLACES
EDUCATIONAL SVCS

PRODUCT INDEX

EDUCATIONAL SVCS, NONDEGREE GRANTING: Continuing Education
ELASTOMERS
ELECTRIC & OTHER SERVICES COMBINED
ELECTRIC MOTOR REPAIR SVCS
ELECTRIC POWER GENERATION: Fossil Fuel
ELECTRIC POWER, COGENERATED
ELECTRIC SERVICES
ELECTRIC SVCS, NEC: Power Generation
ELECTRICAL APPARATUS & EQPT WHOLESALERS
ELECTRICAL APPLIANCES, TELEVISIONS & RADIOS WHOLESALERS
ELECTRICAL CONSTRUCTION MATERIALS WHOLESALERS
ELECTRICAL CURRENT CARRYING WIRING DEVICES
ELECTRICAL DEVICE PARTS: Porcelain, Molded
ELECTRICAL DISCHARGE MACHINING, EDM
ELECTRICAL EQPT & SPLYS
ELECTRICAL EQPT FOR ENGINES
ELECTRICAL EQPT REPAIR & MAINTENANCE
ELECTRICAL EQPT REPAIR SVCS: High Voltage
ELECTRICAL EQPT: Automotive, NEC
ELECTRICAL GOODS, WHOLESALE: Alarms & Signaling Eqpt
ELECTRICAL GOODS, WHOLESALE: Batteries, Storage, Indl
ELECTRICAL GOODS, WHOLESALE: Electrical Appliances, Major
ELECTRICAL GOODS, WHOLESALE: Electrical Entertainment Eqpt
ELECTRICAL GOODS, WHOLESALE: Electronic Parts
ELECTRICAL GOODS, WHOLESALE: Facsimile Or Fax Eqpt
ELECTRICAL GOODS, WHOLESALE: Generators
ELECTRICAL GOODS, WHOLESALE: Light Bulbs & Related Splys
ELECTRICAL GOODS, WHOLESALE: Lighting Fixtures, Comm & Indl
ELECTRICAL GOODS, WHOLESALE: Modems, Computer
ELECTRICAL GOODS, WHOLESALE: Motor Ctrls, Starters & Relays
ELECTRICAL GOODS, WHOLESALE: Motors
ELECTRICAL GOODS, WHOLESALE: Security Control Eqpt & Systems
ELECTRICAL GOODS, WHOLESALE: Signaling, Eqpt
ELECTRICAL GOODS, WHOLESALE: Switchboards
ELECTRICAL GOODS, WHOLESALE: Telephone Eqpt
ELECTRICAL GOODS, WHOLESALE: Time Switches
ELECTRICAL GOODS, WHOLESALE: Video Eqpt
ELECTRICAL GOODS, WHOLESALE: Wire & Cable
ELECTRICAL GOODS, WHOLESALE: Wire & Cable, Electronic
ELECTRICAL HOUSEHOLD APPLIANCE REPAIR
ELECTRICAL INDL APPARATUS, NEC
ELECTRICAL SPLYS
ELECTRICAL SUPPLIES: Porcelain
ELECTRODES: Indl Process
ELECTROMEDICAL EQPT
ELECTROMETALLURGICAL PRDTS
ELECTRON BEAM: Cutting, Forming, Welding
ELECTRONIC COMPONENTS
ELECTRONIC DEVICES: Solid State, NEC
ELECTRONIC EQPT REPAIR SVCS
ELECTRONIC LOADS & POWER SPLYS
ELECTRONIC PARTS & EQPT WHOLESALERS
ELECTRONIC SHOPPING
ELECTRONIC TRAINING DEVICES
ELECTROPLATING & PLATING SVC
ELEVATOR: Bean, Storage Only
ELEVATORS & EQPT
ELEVATORS WHOLESALERS
ELEVATORS: Installation & Conversion
ELEVATORS: Stair, Motor Powered
EMBALMING FLUID
EMBLEMS: Embroidered
EMBOSSING SVC: Paper
EMBROIDERING & ART NEEDLEWORK FOR THE TRADE
EMBROIDERING SVC
EMBROIDERING SVC: Schiffli Machine
EMBROIDERY ADVERTISING SVCS
EMBROIDERY KITS
EMERGENCY & RELIEF SVCS
EMERGENCY ALARMS
EMPLOYEE LEASING SVCS
EMPLOYMENT AGENCY SVCS
EMPLOYMENT SVCS: Labor Contractors
ENAMELING SVC: Metal Prdts, Including Porcelain

ENCLOSURES: Electronic
ENCLOSURES: Screen
ENGINE PARTS & ACCESS: Internal Combustion
ENGINE REBUILDING: Diesel
ENGINE REBUILDING: Gas
ENGINEERING HELP SVCS
ENGINEERING SVCS
ENGINEERING SVCS: Acoustical
ENGINEERING SVCS: Aviation Or Aeronautical
ENGINEERING SVCS: Building Construction
ENGINEERING SVCS: Construction & Civil
ENGINEERING SVCS: Electrical Or Electronic
ENGINEERING SVCS: Industrial
ENGINEERING SVCS: Machine Tool Design
ENGINEERING SVCS: Marine
ENGINEERING SVCS: Mechanical
ENGINEERING SVCS: Pollution Control
ENGINEERING SVCS: Professional
ENGINEERING SVCS: Sanitary
ENGINEERING SVCS: Structural
ENGINES & ENGINE PARTS: Guided Missile
ENGINES: Diesel & Semi-Diesel Or Duel Fuel
ENGINES: Gasoline, NEC
ENGINES: Hydrojet, Marine
ENGINES: Internal Combustion, NEC
ENGINES: Marine
ENGINES: Steam
ENGRAVING SVC, NEC
ENGRAVING SVC: Jewelry & Personal Goods
ENGRAVING SVCS
ENGRAVING: Steel line, For The Printing Trade
ENGRAVINGS: Plastic
ENTERTAINMENT PROMOTION SVCS
ENTERTAINMENT SVCS
ENVELOPES
ENZYMES
EPOXY RESINS
EQUIPMENT: Pedestrian Traffic Control
EQUIPMENT: Rental & Leasing, NEC
ESCALATORS: Passenger & Freight
ETCHING & ENGRAVING SVC
ETHERS
ETHYLENE-PROPYLENE RUBBERS: EPDM Polymers
EXHAUST SYSTEMS: Eqpt & Parts
EXPANSION JOINTS: Rubber
EXPLOSIVES
EXPLOSIVES, EXC AMMO & FIREWORKS WHOLESALERS
EXPLOSIVES: Plastic
EXTRACTS, FLAVORING
EYEGLASSES
EYEGLASSES: Sunglasses

F

FABRIC STORES
FABRICATED METAL PRODUCTS, NEC
FABRICS & CLOTH: Quilted
FABRICS: Alpacas, Mohair, Woven
FABRICS: Apparel & Outerwear, Cotton
FABRICS: Automotive, From Manmade Fiber
FABRICS: Broadwoven, Synthetic Manmade Fiber & Silk
FABRICS: Broadwoven, Wool
FABRICS: Canvas
FABRICS: Chenilles, Tufted Textile
FABRICS: Coated Or Treated
FABRICS: Cords
FABRICS: Denims
FABRICS: Dress, From Manmade Fiber Or Silk
FABRICS: Fiberglass, Broadwoven
FABRICS: Furniture Denim
FABRICS: Laminated
FABRICS: Laundry, Cotton
FABRICS: Luggage, Cotton
FABRICS: Metallized
FABRICS: Osnaburgs
FABRICS: Resin Or Plastic Coated
FABRICS: Rubberized
FABRICS: Scrub Cloths
FABRICS: Seat Cover, Automobile, Cotton
FABRICS: Trimmings
FABRICS: Upholstery, Cotton
FABRICS: Window Shade, Cotton
FABRICS: Woven Wire, Made From Purchased Wire
FABRICS: Woven, Narrow Cotton, Wool, Silk
FACILITIES SUPPORT SVCS
FAMILY CLOTHING STORES

FANS, BLOWING: Indl Or Commercial
FANS, VENTILATING: Indl Or Commercial
FARM & GARDEN MACHINERY WHOLESALERS
FARM PRDTS, RAW MATERIALS, WHOLESALE: Skins
FARM SPLY STORES
FARM SPLYS WHOLESALERS
FARM SPLYS, WHOLESALE: Feed
FARM SPLYS, WHOLESALE: Fertilizers & Agricultural Chemicals
FARM SPLYS, WHOLESALE: Flower & Field Bulbs
FARM SPLYS, WHOLESALE: Garden Splys
FASTENERS WHOLESALERS
FASTENERS: Brads, Alum, Brass/Other Nonferrous Metal/Wire
FASTENERS: Metal
FASTENERS: Metal
FASTENERS: Notions, NEC
FASTENERS: Wire, Made From Purchased Wire
FAUCETS & SPIGOTS: Metal & Plastic
FELT, WHOLESALE
FELT: Acoustic
FENCES & FENCING MATERIALS
FENCES OR POSTS: Ornamental Iron Or Steel
FENCING DEALERS
FENCING MATERIALS: Docks & Other Outdoor Prdts, Wood
FENCING MATERIALS: Plastic
FENCING MATERIALS: Snow Fence, Wood
FENCING MATERIALS: Wood
FENCING: Chain Link
FENDERS: Automobile, Stamped Or Pressed Metal
FERROTITANIUM
FERTILIZER, AGRICULTURAL: Wholesalers
FERTILIZERS: NEC
FERTILIZERS: Nitrogenous
FERTILIZERS: Phosphatic
FIBER & FIBER PRDTS: Acrylic
FIBER & FIBER PRDTS: Anidex
FIBER & FIBER PRDTS: Organic, Noncellulose
FIBER & FIBER PRDTS: Protein
FIBER & FIBER PRDTS: Synthetic Cellulosic
FIBERS: Carbon & Graphite
FIGURES, WAX
FILE FOLDERS
FILLERS & SEALERS: Wood
FILM & SHEET: Unsuppported Plastic
FILM DEVELOPING & PRINTING SVCS
FILTER ELEMENTS: Fluid & Hydraulic Line
FILTERS
FILTERS & SOFTENERS: Water, Household
FILTERS & STRAINERS: Pipeline
FILTERS: Air
FILTERS: Air Intake, Internal Combustion Engine, Exc Auto
FILTERS: General Line, Indl
FILTERS: Motor Vehicle
FILTERS: Oil, Internal Combustion Engine, Exc Auto
FILTRATION DEVICES: Electronic
FILTRATION SAND MINING
FINANCIAL INVESTMENT ADVICE
FINANCIAL SVCS
FINDINGS & TRIMMINGS: Fabric
FINDINGS & TRIMMINGS: Furniture, Fabric
FINGERNAILS, ARTIFICIAL
FIRE ALARM MAINTENANCE & MONITORING SVCS
FIRE ARMS, SMALL: Guns Or Gun Parts, 30 mm & Below
FIRE ARMS, SMALL: Pellet & BB guns
FIRE ARMS, SMALL: Pistols Or Pistol Parts, 30 mm & below
FIRE ARMS, SMALL: Shotguns Or Shotgun Parts, 30 mm & Below
FIRE CONTROL OR BOMBING EQPT: Electronic
FIRE EXTINGUISHER CHARGES
FIRE EXTINGUISHER SVC
FIRE EXTINGUISHERS, WHOLESALE
FIRE EXTINGUISHERS: Portable
FIRE OR BURGLARY RESISTIVE PRDTS
FIRE PROTECTION EQPT
FIRE PROTECTION SVCS: Contracted
FIRE PROTECTION, EXC CONTRACT
FIREARMS: Small, 30mm or Less
FIREPLACE & CHIMNEY MATERIAL: Concrete
FIREPLACE EQPT & ACCESS
FIREWOOD, WHOLESALE
FIREWORKS
FIREWORKS SHOPS
FISH & SEAFOOD PROCESSORS: Fresh Or Frozen
FISH FOOD

PRODUCT INDEX

FISHING EQPT: Lures
FISHING EQPT: Nets & Seines
FITTINGS & ASSEMBLIES: Hose & Tube, Hydraulic Or Pneumatic
FITTINGS & SPECIALTIES: Steam
FITTINGS: Pipe
FITTINGS: Pipe, Fabricated
FIXTURES & EQPT: Kitchen, Metal, Exc Cast Aluminum
FIXTURES & EQPT: Kitchen, Porcelain Enameled
FIXTURES: Bank, Metal, Ornamental
FIXTURES: Cut Stone
FLAGS: Fabric
FLAKEBOARD
FLAT GLASS: Building
FLAT GLASS: Construction
FLAT GLASS: Laminated
FLAT GLASS: Plate, Polished & Rough
FLAT GLASS: Tempered
FLAT GLASS: Window, Clear & Colored
FLAVORS OR FLAVORING MATERIALS: Synthetic
FLOATING DRY DOCKS
FLOCKING METAL PRDTS
FLOOR COVERING STORES
FLOOR COVERING STORES: Carpets
FLOOR COVERING: Plastic
FLOOR COVERINGS WHOLESALERS
FLOORING & GRATINGS: Open, Construction Applications
FLOORING & SIDING: Metal
FLOORING: Baseboards, Wood
FLOORING: Hard Surface
FLOORING: Hardwood
FLOORING: Tile
FLORIST: Flowers, Fresh
FLORISTS
FLOWER ARRANGEMENTS: Artificial
FLOWER POTS Plastic
FLOWERS & FLORISTS' SPLYS WHOLESALERS
FLOWERS: Artificial & Preserved
FLUES & PIPES: Stove Or Furnace
FLUID METERS & COUNTING DEVICES
FLUID POWER PUMPS & MOTORS
FLUID POWER VALVES & HOSE FITTINGS
FLUXES
FLYSWATTERS
FOAM RUBBER
FOAMS & RUBBER, WHOLESALE
FOIL & LEAF: Metal
FOIL: Aluminum
FOOD CONTAMINATION TESTING OR SCREENING KITS
FOOD PRDTS, BREAKFAST: Cereal, Corn Flakes
FOOD PRDTS, CANNED OR FRESH PACK: Fruit Juices
FOOD PRDTS, CANNED OR FRESH PACK: Vegetable Juices
FOOD PRDTS, CANNED: Applesauce
FOOD PRDTS, CANNED: Barbecue Sauce
FOOD PRDTS, CANNED: Beans, Baked With Meat
FOOD PRDTS, CANNED: Chili
FOOD PRDTS, CANNED: Ethnic
FOOD PRDTS, CANNED: Fruit Juices, Concentrated
FOOD PRDTS, CANNED: Fruit Juices, Fresh
FOOD PRDTS, CANNED: Fruits
FOOD PRDTS, CANNED: Fruits
FOOD PRDTS, CANNED: Fruits & Fruit Prdts
FOOD PRDTS, CANNED: Italian
FOOD PRDTS, CANNED: Jams, Including Imitation
FOOD PRDTS, CANNED: Jams, Jellies & Preserves
FOOD PRDTS, CANNED: Maraschino Cherries
FOOD PRDTS, CANNED: Mexican, NEC
FOOD PRDTS, CANNED: Soups
FOOD PRDTS, CANNED: Tomato Sauce.
FOOD PRDTS, CANNED: Tomatoes
FOOD PRDTS, CANNED: Vegetables
FOOD PRDTS, CONFECTIONERY, WHOLESALE: Candy
FOOD PRDTS, CONFECTIONERY, WHOLESALE: Nuts, Salted/Roasted
FOOD PRDTS, CONFECTIONERY, WHOLESALE: Snack Foods
FOOD PRDTS, DAIRY, WHOLESALE: Frozen Dairy Desserts
FOOD PRDTS, DAIRY, WHOLESALE: Milk & Cream, Fluid
FOOD PRDTS, FISH & SEAFOOD: Fish, Salted
FOOD PRDTS, FISH & SEAFOOD: Fish, Smoked
FOOD PRDTS, FISH & SEAFOOD: Herring, Cured, NEC
FOOD PRDTS, FROZEN, WHOLESALE: Vegetables & Fruit Prdts
FOOD PRDTS, FROZEN: Dinners, Packaged
FOOD PRDTS, FROZEN: Ethnic Foods, NEC
FOOD PRDTS, FROZEN: Fruits
FOOD PRDTS, FROZEN: Fruits & Vegetables
FOOD PRDTS, FROZEN: Fruits, Juices & Vegetables
FOOD PRDTS, FROZEN: NEC
FOOD PRDTS, FROZEN: Pizza
FOOD PRDTS, FROZEN: Potato Prdts
FOOD PRDTS, FROZEN: Snack Items
FOOD PRDTS, FROZEN: Vegetables, Exc Potato Prdts
FOOD PRDTS, FROZEN: Waffles
FOOD PRDTS, FRUITS & VEGETABLES, FRESH, WHOLESALE
FOOD PRDTS, FRUITS & VEGETABLES, FRESH, WHOLESALE: Fruits
FOOD PRDTS, FRUITS & VEGETABLES, FRESH, WHOLESALE: Vegetable
FOOD PRDTS, MEAT & MEAT PRDTS, WHOLESALE: Fresh
FOOD PRDTS, WHOLESALE: Beans, Field
FOOD PRDTS, WHOLESALE: Beverage Concentrates
FOOD PRDTS, WHOLESALE: Beverages, Exc Coffee & Tea
FOOD PRDTS, WHOLESALE: Coffee, Green Or Roasted
FOOD PRDTS, WHOLESALE: Diet
FOOD PRDTS, WHOLESALE: Flavorings & Fragrances
FOOD PRDTS, WHOLESALE: Grain Elevators
FOOD PRDTS, WHOLESALE: Grains
FOOD PRDTS, WHOLESALE: Honey
FOOD PRDTS, WHOLESALE: Juices
FOOD PRDTS, WHOLESALE: Natural & Organic
FOOD PRDTS, WHOLESALE: Pasta & Rice
FOOD PRDTS, WHOLESALE: Pizza Splys
FOOD PRDTS, WHOLESALE: Specialty
FOOD PRDTS, WHOLESALE: Spices & Seasonings
FOOD PRDTS, WHOLESALE: Tea
FOOD PRDTS, WHOLESALE: Water, Distilled
FOOD PRDTS, WHOLESALE: Wheat
FOOD PRDTS, WHOLESALE: Wine Makers' Eqpt & Splys
FOOD PRDTS: Animal & marine fats & oils
FOOD PRDTS: Box Lunches, For Sale Off Premises
FOOD PRDTS: Bread Crumbs, Exc Made In Bakeries
FOOD PRDTS: Breakfast Bars
FOOD PRDTS: Butter, Renovated & Processed
FOOD PRDTS: Cake Flour
FOOD PRDTS: Cereals
FOOD PRDTS: Chewing Gum Base
FOOD PRDTS: Chocolate Bars, Solid
FOOD PRDTS: Coconut Oil
FOOD PRDTS: Coffee
FOOD PRDTS: Coffee Roasting, Exc Wholesale Grocers
FOOD PRDTS: Coffee, Ground, Mixed With Grain Or Chicory
FOOD PRDTS: Corn Oil, Refined
FOOD PRDTS: Desserts, Ready-To-Mix
FOOD PRDTS: Dips, Exc Cheese & Sour Cream Based
FOOD PRDTS: Doughs & Batters From Purchased Flour
FOOD PRDTS: Doughs, Frozen Or Refrig From Purchased Flour
FOOD PRDTS: Dressings, Salad, Raw & Cooked Exc Dry Mixes
FOOD PRDTS: Dried & Dehydrated Fruits, Vegetables & Soup Mix
FOOD PRDTS: Edible Oil Prdts, Exc Corn Oil
FOOD PRDTS: Edible fats & oils
FOOD PRDTS: Eggs, Processed
FOOD PRDTS: Emulsifiers
FOOD PRDTS: Flour
FOOD PRDTS: Flour & Other Grain Mill Products
FOOD PRDTS: Flour Mixes & Doughs
FOOD PRDTS: Freeze-Dried Coffee
FOOD PRDTS: Frosting Mixes, Dry, For Cakes, Cookies, Etc.
FOOD PRDTS: Fruit Juices
FOOD PRDTS: Fruits & Vegetables, Pickled
FOOD PRDTS: Fruits, Dried Or Dehydrated, Exc Freeze-Dried
FOOD PRDTS: Granola & Energy Bars, Nonchocolate
FOOD PRDTS: Honey
FOOD PRDTS: Horseradish, Exc Sauce
FOOD PRDTS: Hydrol
FOOD PRDTS: Ice, Blocks
FOOD PRDTS: Ice, Cubes
FOOD PRDTS: Instant Coffee
FOOD PRDTS: Macaroni, Noodles, Spaghetti, Pasta, Etc
FOOD PRDTS: Malt
FOOD PRDTS: Mixes, Doughnut From Purchased Flour
FOOD PRDTS: Mixes, Flour
FOOD PRDTS: Nuts & Seeds
FOOD PRDTS: Olive Oil
FOOD PRDTS: Oriental Noodles
FOOD PRDTS: Pasta, Rice/Potatoes, Uncooked, Pkgd
FOOD PRDTS: Pasta, Uncooked, Packaged With Other Ingredients
FOOD PRDTS: Peanut Butter
FOOD PRDTS: Pickles, Vinegar
FOOD PRDTS: Pizza Doughs From Purchased Flour
FOOD PRDTS: Pizza, Refrigerated
FOOD PRDTS: Pork Rinds
FOOD PRDTS: Potato & Corn Chips & Similar Prdts
FOOD PRDTS: Potato Chips & Other Potato-Based Snacks
FOOD PRDTS: Poultry, Processed, Smoked
FOOD PRDTS: Preparations
FOOD PRDTS: Prepared Meat Sauces Exc Tomato & Dry
FOOD PRDTS: Prepared Sauces, Exc Tomato Based
FOOD PRDTS: Raw cane sugar
FOOD PRDTS: Relishes, Fruit & Vegetable
FOOD PRDTS: Salads
FOOD PRDTS: Sandwiches
FOOD PRDTS: Sauerkraut, Bulk
FOOD PRDTS: Seasonings & Spices
FOOD PRDTS: Shortening & Solid Edible Fats
FOOD PRDTS: Soybean Oil, Refined, Exc Made In Mills
FOOD PRDTS: Soybean Protein Concentrates & Isolates
FOOD PRDTS: Spices, Including Ground
FOOD PRDTS: Sugar, Beet
FOOD PRDTS: Sugar, Cane
FOOD PRDTS: Sugar, Granulated Sugar Beet
FOOD PRDTS: Sugar, Maple, Indl
FOOD PRDTS: Sugar, Refined Sugar Beet
FOOD PRDTS: Syrup, Maple
FOOD PRDTS: Tea
FOOD PRDTS: Tortilla Chips
FOOD PRDTS: Tortillas
FOOD PRDTS: Vegetable Oil Mills, NEC
FOOD PRDTS: Vinegar
FOOD PRDTS: Wheat Flour
FOOD PRDTS: Yeast
FOOD PRODUCTS MACHINERY
FOOD STORES: Convenience, Chain
FOOD STORES: Grocery, Independent
FOOD STORES: Supermarket, More Than 100K Sq Ft, Hypermrkt
FOOD STORES: Supermarkets
FOOD STORES: Supermarkets, Chain
FOOD STORES: Supermarkets, Independent
FOOTWEAR, WHOLESALE: Shoes
FOOTWEAR: Cut Stock
FORESTRY RELATED EQPT
FORGINGS
FORGINGS: Aluminum
FORGINGS: Automotive & Internal Combustion Engine
FORGINGS: Gear & Chain
FORGINGS: Iron & Steel
FORGINGS: Machinery, Ferrous
FORGINGS: Nonferrous
FORMS: Concrete, Sheet Metal
FOUNDRIES: Aluminum
FOUNDRIES: Brass, Bronze & Copper
FOUNDRIES: Gray & Ductile Iron
FOUNDRIES: Iron
FOUNDRIES: Nonferrous
FOUNDRIES: Steel
FOUNDRIES: Steel Investment
FOUNDRY MACHINERY & EQPT
FOUNDRY SAND MINING
FOUNTAIN PEN REPAIR SHOP
FOUNTAINS: Concrete
FRACTIONATION PRDTS OF CRUDE PETROLEUM, HYDROCARBONS, NEC
FRAMES & FRAMING WHOLESALE
FRANCHISES, SELLING OR LICENSING
FREEZERS: Household
FREIGHT FORWARDING ARRANGEMENTS: Domestic
FREIGHT TRANSPORTATION ARRANGEMENTS
FREON
FRICTION MATERIAL, MADE FROM POWDERED METAL
FRUIT & VEGETABLE MARKETS
FRUIT STANDS OR MARKETS
FUEL ADDITIVES
FUEL CELLS: Solid State
FUEL DEALERS: Coal
FUEL OIL DEALERS
FUELS: Diesel
FUELS: Ethanol

PRODUCT INDEX

FUELS: Jet
FUELS: Oil
FUNGICIDES OR HERBICIDES
FUR APPAREL STORES
FUR: Apparel
FURNACE CASINGS: Sheet Metal
FURNACES & OVENS: Fuel-Fired
FURNACES & OVENS: Indl
FURNACES: Indl, Electric
FURNITURE & CABINET STORES: Cabinets, Custom Work
FURNITURE & FIXTURES Factory
FURNITURE COMPONENTS: Porcelain Enameled
FURNITURE PARTS: Metal
FURNITURE REFINISHING SVCS
FURNITURE REPAIR & MAINTENANCE SVCS
FURNITURE STOCK & PARTS: Carvings, Wood
FURNITURE STOCK & PARTS: Dimension Stock, Hardwood
FURNITURE STOCK & PARTS: Hardwood
FURNITURE STOCK & PARTS: Turnings, Wood
FURNITURE STORES
FURNITURE STORES: Cabinets, Kitchen, Exc Custom Made
FURNITURE STORES: Custom Made, Exc Cabinets
FURNITURE STORES: Juvenile
FURNITURE STORES: Office
FURNITURE UPHOLSTERY REPAIR SVCS
FURNITURE WHOLESALERS
FURNITURE, HOUSEHOLD: Wholesalers
FURNITURE, MATTRESSES: Wholesalers
FURNITURE, OFFICE: Wholesalers
FURNITURE, WHOLESALE: Racks
FURNITURE: Altars & Pulpits
FURNITURE: Assembly Hall
FURNITURE: Bedroom, Wood
FURNITURE: Bookcases, Office, Wood
FURNITURE: Camp, Wood
FURNITURE: Chairs & Couches, Wood, Upholstered
FURNITURE: Chairs, Bentwood
FURNITURE: Chairs, Household Upholstered
FURNITURE: Chairs, Household, Metal
FURNITURE: Chairs, Office Exc Wood
FURNITURE: Console Tables, Wood
FURNITURE: Cut Stone
FURNITURE: Desks & Tables, Office, Exc Wood
FURNITURE: Desks & Tables, Office, Wood
FURNITURE: Desks, Wood
FURNITURE: Dining Room, Wood
FURNITURE: Dressers, Household, Wood
FURNITURE: Fiberglass & Plastic
FURNITURE: Foundations & Platforms
FURNITURE: Game Room, Wood
FURNITURE: Hospital
FURNITURE: Hotel
FURNITURE: Household, Metal
FURNITURE: Household, Upholstered, Exc Wood Or Metal
FURNITURE: Household, Wood
FURNITURE: Hydraulic Barber & Beauty Shop Chairs
FURNITURE: Institutional, Exc Wood
FURNITURE: Juvenile, Wood
FURNITURE: Kitchen & Dining Room
FURNITURE: Laboratory
FURNITURE: Lawn & Garden, Metal
FURNITURE: Lawn, Wood
FURNITURE: Library
FURNITURE: Living Room, Upholstered On Wood Frames
FURNITURE: Mattresses & Foundations
FURNITURE: Mattresses, Box & Bedsprings
FURNITURE: Mattresses, Innerspring Or Box Spring
FURNITURE: Novelty, Wood
FURNITURE: Office Panel Systems, Exc Wood
FURNITURE: Office Panel Systems, Wood
FURNITURE: Office, Exc Wood
FURNITURE: Office, Wood
FURNITURE: Outdoor, Wood
FURNITURE: Pews, Church
FURNITURE: Picnic Tables Or Benches, Park
FURNITURE: Play Pens, Children's, Wood
FURNITURE: Restaurant
FURNITURE: School
FURNITURE: Stands & Chests, Exc Bedside Stands, Wood
FURNITURE: Stools, Household, Wood
FURNITURE: Storage Chests, Household, Wood
FURNITURE: Table Tops, Marble
FURNITURE: Tables & Table Tops, Wood
FURNITURE: Unfinished, Wood
FURNITURE: Upholstered
FURNITURE: Vehicle
FURRIERS
FUSES: Electric
Furs

G

GAMES & TOYS: Bingo Boards
GAMES & TOYS: Board Games, Children's & Adults'
GAMES & TOYS: Craft & Hobby Kits & Sets
GAMES & TOYS: Dolls, Exc Stuffed Toy Animals
GAMES & TOYS: Electronic
GAMES & TOYS: Game Machines, Exc Coin-Operated
GAMES & TOYS: Kits, Science, Incl Microscopes/Chemistry Sets
GAMES & TOYS: Trains & Eqpt, Electric & Mechanical
GAMES & TOYS: Tricycles
GARBAGE CONTAINERS: Plastic
GARBAGE DISPOSERS & COMPACTORS: Commercial
GAS & HYDROCARBON LIQUEFACTION FROM COAL
GAS & OIL FIELD EXPLORATION SVCS
GAS & OIL FIELD SVCS, NEC
GAS STATIONS
GASES & LIQUIFIED PETROLEUM GASES
GASES: Acetylene
GASES: Argon
GASES: Carbon Dioxide
GASES: Helium
GASES: Hydrogen
GASES: Indl
GASES: Neon
GASES: Nitrogen
GASES: Oxygen
GASKET MATERIALS
GASKETS
GASKETS & SEALING DEVICES
GASOLINE FILLING STATIONS
GATES: Ornamental Metal
GAUGE BLOCKS
GAUGES
GEARS
GEARS & GEAR UNITS: Reduction, Exc Auto
GEARS: Power Transmission, Exc Auto
GENERAL COUNSELING SVCS
GENERAL MERCHANDISE, NONDURABLE, WHOLESALE
GENERATION EQPT: Electronic
GENERATOR REPAIR SVCS
GENERATORS: Electric
GENERATORS: Electrochemical, Fuel Cell
GENERATORS: Ultrasonic
GENERATORS: Vehicles, Gas-Electric Or Oil-Electric
GIFT SHOP
GIFT, NOVELTY & SOUVENIR STORES: Gift Baskets
GIFT, NOVELTY & SOUVENIR STORES: Party Favors
GIFTS & NOVELTIES: Wholesalers
GIFTWARE: Copper
GLASS FABRICATORS
GLASS PRDTS, FROM PURCHASED GLASS: Art
GLASS PRDTS, FROM PURCHASED GLASS: Glassware
GLASS PRDTS, FROM PURCHASED GLASS: Glassware, Indl
GLASS PRDTS, FROM PURCHASED GLASS: Insulating
GLASS PRDTS, FROM PURCHASED GLASS: Mirrored
GLASS PRDTS, FROM PURCHASED GLASS: Windshields
GLASS PRDTS, FROM PURCHD GLASS: Strengthened Or Reinforced
GLASS PRDTS, PRESSED OR BLOWN: Blocks & Bricks
GLASS PRDTS, PRESSED OR BLOWN: Bulbs, Electric Lights
GLASS PRDTS, PRESSED OR BLOWN: Glassware, Art Or Decorative
GLASS PRDTS, PRESSED OR BLOWN: Lighting Eqpt Parts
GLASS PRDTS, PRESSED OR BLOWN: Reflector, Lighting Eqpt
GLASS PRDTS, PRESSED/BLOWN: Glassware, Art, Decor/Novelty
GLASS PRDTS, PRESSED/BLOWN: Lenses, Lantern, Flshlght, Etc
GLASS PRDTS, PURCHSD GLASS: Ornamental, Cut, Engraved/Décor
GLASS STORE: Leaded Or Stained
GLASS STORES
GLASS, AUTOMOTIVE: Wholesalers
GLASS: Fiber
GLASS: Flat
GLASS: Insulating
GLASS: Pressed & Blown, NEC
GLASS: Stained
GLASS: Tempered
GLASSWARE: Cut & Engraved
GLASSWARE: Indl
GLASSWARE: Laboratory
GLOVES: Fabric
GLOVES: Leather, Work
GLOVES: Safety
GLUE
GOLD ORE MINING
GOLF EQPT
GOLF GOODS & EQPT
GOURMET FOOD STORES
GRANITE: Crushed & Broken
GRANITE: Cut & Shaped
GRANITE: Dimension
GRANITE: Dimension
GRAPHIC ARTS & RELATED DESIGN SVCS
GRASSES: Artificial & Preserved
GRAVE MARKERS: Concrete
GRAVEL & PEBBLE MINING
GRAVEL MINING
GREASE CUPS: Metal
GREASES & INEDIBLE FATS, RENDERED
GREASES: Lubricating
GREENHOUSES: Prefabricated Metal
GREETING CARD SHOPS
GRILLS & GRILLWORK: Woven Wire, Made From Purchased Wire
GRINDING BALLS: Ceramic
GRINDING SVC: Precision, Commercial Or Indl
GRINDING SVCS: Ophthalmic Lens, Exc Prescription
GRINDS: Electric
GRIPS OR HANDLES: Rubber
GROCERIES WHOLESALERS, NEC
GROCERIES, GENERAL LINE WHOLESALERS
GROUTING EQPT: Concrete
GUARDS: Machine, Sheet Metal
GUIDED MISSILES & SPACE VEHICLES
GUM & WOOD CHEMICALS
GUN SIGHTS: Optical
GUTTERS
GUTTERS: Sheet Metal
GYPSUM MINING
GYPSUM PRDTS

H

HAIR & HAIR BASED PRDTS
HAIR ACCESS WHOLESALERS
HAIR CARE PRDTS
HAIR CURLERS: Beauty Shop
HALL EFFECT DEVICES
HAMPERS: Laundry, Sheet Metal
HAND TOOLS, NEC: Wholesalers
HANDBAGS
HANDBAGS: Women's
HANDCUFFS & LEG IRONS
HANDLES: Wood
HANGERS: Garment, Home & Store, Wooden
HANGERS: Garment, Plastic
HANGERS: Garment, Wire
HARDWARE
HARDWARE & BUILDING PRDTS: Plastic
HARDWARE & EQPT: Stage, Exc Lighting
HARDWARE STORES
HARDWARE STORES: Builders'
HARDWARE STORES: Door Locks & Lock Sets
HARDWARE STORES: Pumps & Pumping Eqpt
HARDWARE STORES: Tools
HARDWARE STORES: Tools, Power
HARDWARE WHOLESALERS
HARDWARE, WHOLESALE: Bolts
HARDWARE, WHOLESALE: Builders', NEC
HARDWARE, WHOLESALE: Casters & Glides
HARDWARE, WHOLESALE: Chains
HARDWARE, WHOLESALE: Nozzles
HARDWARE, WHOLESALE: Rivets
HARDWARE, WHOLESALE: Screws
HARDWARE, WHOLESALE: Security Devices, Locks
HARDWARE, WHOLESALE: Staples
HARDWARE: Aircraft
HARDWARE: Builders'
HARDWARE: Cabinet
HARDWARE: Door Opening & Closing Devices, Exc Electrical

PRODUCT INDEX

HARDWARE: Furniture
HARDWARE: Furniture, Builders' & Other Household
HARDWARE: Locking Systems, Security Cable
HARDWARE: Padlocks
HARDWARE: Rubber
HARNESS ASSEMBLIES: Cable & Wire
HARNESS WIRING SETS: Internal Combustion Engines
HARNESSES, HALTERS, SADDLERY & STRAPS
HARVESTING MACHINERY & EQPT WHOLESALERS
HEADPHONES: Radio
HEADS-UP DISPLAY & HUD SYSTEMS Aeronautical
HEALTH & ALLIED SERVICES, NEC
HEALTH AIDS: Exercise Eqpt
HEALTH AIDS: Vaporizers
HEALTH FOOD & SUPPLEMENT STORES
HEALTH SCREENING SVCS
HEARING AIDS
HEAT EMISSION OPERATING APPARATUS
HEAT EXCHANGERS: After Or Inter Coolers Or Condensers, Etc
HEAT TREATING: Metal
HEATERS: Room, Gas
HEATING & AIR CONDITIONING EQPT & SPLYS WHOLESALERS
HEATING & AIR CONDITIONING UNITS, COMBINATION
HEATING EQPT & SPLYS
HEATING EQPT: Complete
HEATING EQPT: Induction
HEATING SYSTEMS: Radiant, Indl Process
HEATING UNITS & DEVICES: Indl, Electric
HELICOPTERS
HELMETS: Athletic
HELP SUPPLY SERVICES
HERMETICS REPAIR SVCS
HIGHWAY & STREET MAINTENANCE SVCS
HITCHES: Trailer
HOBBY & CRAFT SPLY STORES
HOBBY, TOY & GAME STORES: Arts & Crafts & Splys
HOBBY, TOY & GAME STORES: Dolls & Access
HOBBY, TOY & GAME STORES: Hobbies, NEC
HOBBY, TOY & GAME STORES: Toys & Games
HOISTING SLINGS
HOISTS
HOISTS: Hand
HOLDERS, PAPER TOWEL, GROCERY BAG, ETC: Plastic
HOLDING COMPANIES: Investment, Exc Banks
HOLDING COMPANIES: Personal, Exc Banks
HOME CENTER STORES
HOME DELIVERY NEWSPAPER ROUTES
HOME ENTERTAINMENT EQPT: Electronic, NEC
HOME FURNISHINGS WHOLESALERS
HOME HEALTH CARE SVCS
HOME IMPROVEMENT & RENOVATION CONTRACTOR AGENCY
HOMEBUILDERS & OTHER OPERATIVE BUILDERS
HOMEFURNISHING STORE: Bedding, Sheet, Blanket,Spread/Pillow
HOMEFURNISHING STORES: Closet organizers & shelving units
HOMEFURNISHING STORES: Fireplaces & Wood Burning Stoves
HOMEFURNISHING STORES: Pictures, Wall
HOMEFURNISHING STORES: Pottery
HOMEFURNISHING STORES: Vertical Blinds
HOMEFURNISHING STORES: Window Furnishings
HOMEFURNISHING STORES: Window Shades, NEC
HOMEFURNISHINGS & SPLYS, WHOLESALE: Decorative
HOMEFURNISHINGS, WHOLESALE: Blankets
HOMEFURNISHINGS, WHOLESALE: Blinds, Venetian
HOMEFURNISHINGS, WHOLESALE: Carpets
HOMEFURNISHINGS, WHOLESALE: Mirrors/Pictures, Framed/Unframd
HOMEFURNISHINGS, WHOLESALE: Pottery
HOMEMAKERS' SVCS
HOMES, MODULAR: Wooden
HOMES: Log Cabins
HONES
HONING & LAPPING MACHINES
HOODS: Range, Sheet Metal
HOPPERS: End Dump
HOPPERS: Sheet Metal
HORNS: Marine, Compressed Air Or Steam
HORSE & PET ACCESSORIES: Textile
HORSESHOES
HOSE: Air Line Or Air Brake, Rubber Or Rubberized Fabric

HOSE: Automobile, Plastic
HOSE: Fire, Rubber
HOSE: Flexible Metal
HOSE: Plastic
HOSE: Pneumatic, Rubber Or Rubberized Fabric, NEC
HOSE: Rubber
HOSES & BELTING: Rubber & Plastic
HOSPITAL EQPT REPAIR SVCS
HOSPITAL HOUSEKEEPING SVCS
HOSTELS
HOT TUBS
HOT TUBS: Plastic & Fiberglass
HOUSEHOLD ANTENNA INSTALLATION & SVCS
HOUSEHOLD APPLIANCE STORES
HOUSEHOLD APPLIANCE STORES: Electric Household, Major
HOUSEHOLD ARTICLES, EXC FURNITURE: Cut Stone
HOUSEHOLD ARTICLES: Metal
HOUSEHOLD FURNISHINGS, NEC
HOUSEWARE STORES
HOUSEWARES, ELECTRIC, EXC COOKING APPLIANCES & UTENSILS
HOUSEWARES, ELECTRIC: Blankets
HOUSEWARES, ELECTRIC: Blenders
HOUSEWARES, ELECTRIC: Heaters, Immersion
HOUSEWARES, ELECTRIC: Heaters, Sauna
HOUSEWARES, ELECTRIC: Heaters, Space
HOUSEWARES, ELECTRIC: Heating Units, Electric Appliances
HOUSEWARES, ELECTRIC: Humidifiers, Household
HOUSEWARES, ELECTRIC: Massage Machines, Exc Beauty/Barber
HOUSEWARES: Bowls, Wood
HOUSEWARES: Dishes, Plastic
HOUSEWARES: Dishes, Wooden
HOUSEWARES: Food Dishes & Utensils, Pressed & Molded Pulp
HOUSEWARES: Plates, Pressed/Molded Pulp, From Purchased Mtrl
HOUSINGS: Business Machine, Sheet Metal
HUB CAPS: Automobile, Stamped Metal
HUMIDIFYING EQPT, EXC PORTABLE
HYDRAULIC EQPT REPAIR SVC
HYDRAULIC FLUIDS: Synthetic Based
HYDROPONIC EQPT
Hard Rubber & Molded Rubber Prdts

I

ICE
ICE CREAM & ICES WHOLESALERS
ICE WHOLESALERS
IDENTIFICATION PLATES
IDENTIFICATION TAGS, EXC PAPER
IGNITION APPARATUS & DISTRIBUTORS
IGNITION COILS: Automotive
IGNITION SYSTEMS: High Frequency
INCINERATORS
INDL & PERSONAL SVC PAPER WHOLESALERS
INDL & PERSONAL SVC PAPER, WHOL: Bags, Paper/Disp Plastic
INDL & PERSONAL SVC PAPER, WHOL: Boxes, Corrugtd/Solid Fiber
INDL & PERSONAL SVC PAPER, WHOL: Cups, Disp, Plastic/Paper
INDL & PERSONAL SVC PAPER, WHOL: Paper, Wrap/Coarse/Prdts
INDL & PERSONAL SVC PAPER, WHOLESALE: Press Sensitive Tape
INDL & PERSONAL SVC PAPER, WHOLESALE: Shipping Splys
INDL EQPT CLEANING SVCS
INDL EQPT SVCS
INDL GASES WHOLESALERS
INDL MACHINERY & EQPT WHOLESALERS
INDL MACHINERY REPAIR & MAINTENANCE
INDL PATTERNS: Foundry Patternmaking
INDL PROCESS INSTRUMENTS: Control
INDL PROCESS INSTRUMENTS: Controllers, Process Variables
INDL PROCESS INSTRUMENTS: Data Loggers
INDL PROCESS INSTRUMENTS: Digital Display, Process Variables
INDL PROCESS INSTRUMENTS: Draft Gauges
INDL PROCESS INSTRUMENTS: Elements, Primary

INDL PROCESS INSTRUMENTS: Fluidic Devices, Circuit & Systems
INDL PROCESS INSTRUMENTS: Indl Flow & Measuring
INDL PROCESS INSTRUMENTS: Level & Bulk Measuring
INDL PROCESS INSTRUMENTS: Temperature
INDL PROCESS INSTRUMENTS: Water Quality Monitoring/Cntrl Sys
INDL SALTS WHOLESALERS
INDL SPLYS WHOLESALERS
INDL SPLYS, WHOL: Fasteners, Incl Nuts, Bolts, Screws, Etc
INDL SPLYS, WHOLESALE: Abrasives
INDL SPLYS, WHOLESALE: Abrasives & Adhesives
INDL SPLYS, WHOLESALE: Adhesives, Tape & Plasters
INDL SPLYS, WHOLESALE: Bearings
INDL SPLYS, WHOLESALE: Fasteners & Fastening Eqpt
INDL SPLYS, WHOLESALE: Filters, Indl
INDL SPLYS, WHOLESALE: Fittings
INDL SPLYS, WHOLESALE: Gaskets & Seals
INDL SPLYS, WHOLESALE: Glass Bottles
INDL SPLYS, WHOLESALE: Hydraulic & Pneumatic Pistons/Valves
INDL SPLYS, WHOLESALE: Mill Splys
INDL SPLYS, WHOLESALE: Plastic, Pallets
INDL SPLYS, WHOLESALE: Power Transmission, Eqpt & Apparatus
INDL SPLYS, WHOLESALE: Rubber Goods, Mechanical
INDL SPLYS, WHOLESALE: Seals
INDL SPLYS, WHOLESALE: Signmaker Eqpt & Splys
INDL SPLYS, WHOLESALE: Tools
INDL SPLYS, WHOLESALE: Tools, NEC
INDL SPLYS, WHOLESALE: Valves & Fittings
INDL TOOL GRINDING SVCS
INDUCTORS
INDUSTRIAL & COMMERCIAL EQPT INSPECTION SVCS
INFORMATION RETRIEVAL SERVICES
INFRARED OBJECT DETECTION EQPT
INGOT, EXTRUSION: Extrusion ingot, aluminum: rolling mills
INK OR WRITING FLUIDS
INK: Duplicating
INK: Printing
INNER TUBES: Indl
INNER TUBES: Truck Or Bus
INSECT LAMPS: Electric
INSECTICIDES & PESTICIDES
INSPECTION & TESTING SVCS
INSTR, MEASURE & CONTROL: Gauge, Oil Pressure & Water Temp
INSTRUMENTS, LABORATORY: Spectrometers
INSTRUMENTS, MEASURING & CNTRL: Gauges, Auto, Computer
INSTRUMENTS, MEASURING & CNTRL: Geophysical & Meteorological
INSTRUMENTS, MEASURING & CNTRL: Testing, Abrasion, Etc
INSTRUMENTS, MEASURING & CNTRLG: Aircraft & Motor Vehicle
INSTRUMENTS, MEASURING & CNTRLG: Fatigue Test, Indl, Mech
INSTRUMENTS, MEASURING & CNTRLG: Stress, Strain & Measure
INSTRUMENTS, MEASURING & CNTRLNG: Press & Vac Ind, Acft Eng
INSTRUMENTS, MEASURING & CONTROLLING: Dosimetry, Personnel
INSTRUMENTS, MEASURING & CONTROLLING: Gas Detectors
INSTRUMENTS, MEASURING & CONTROLLING: Ultrasonic Testing
INSTRUMENTS, MEASURING/CNTRL: Gauging, Ultrasonic Thickness
INSTRUMENTS, MEASURING/CNTRLG: Fire Detect Sys, Non-Electric
INSTRUMENTS, MEASURING/CNTRLNG: Med Diagnostic Sys, Nuclear
INSTRUMENTS, OPTICAL: Lens Mounts
INSTRUMENTS, OPTICAL: Lenses, All Types Exc Ophthalmic
INSTRUMENTS, OPTICAL: Sighting & Fire Control
INSTRUMENTS, OPTICAL: Test & Inspection
INSTRUMENTS, SURGICAL & MED: Needles & Syringes, Hypodermic
INSTRUMENTS, SURGICAL & MEDICAL: Biopsy
INSTRUMENTS, SURGICAL & MEDICAL: Blood & Bone Work
INSTRUMENTS, SURGICAL & MEDICAL: Lasers, Ophthalmic
INSTRUMENTS, SURGICAL & MEDICAL: Lasers, Surgical

PRODUCT INDEX

INSTRUMENTS, SURGICAL & MEDICAL: Needles, Suture
INSTRUMENTS, SURGICAL & MEDICAL: Ophthalmic
INSTRUMENTS, SURGICAL & MEDICAL: Plates & Screws, Bone
INSTRUMENTS, SURGICAL & MEDICAL: Skin Grafting
INSTRUMENTS: Ammeters, NEC
INSTRUMENTS: Analytical
INSTRUMENTS: Combustion Control, Indl
INSTRUMENTS: Differential Pressure, Indl
INSTRUMENTS: Electronic, Analog-Digital Converters
INSTRUMENTS: Endoscopic Eqpt, Electromedical
INSTRUMENTS: Flow, Indl Process
INSTRUMENTS: Frequency Meters, Electrical, Mech & Electronic
INSTRUMENTS: Indl Process Control
INSTRUMENTS: Infrared, Indl Process
INSTRUMENTS: Laser, Scientific & Engineering
INSTRUMENTS: Measurement, Indl Process
INSTRUMENTS: Measuring & Controlling
INSTRUMENTS: Measuring Electricity
INSTRUMENTS: Measuring, Current, NEC
INSTRUMENTS: Measuring, Electrical Energy
INSTRUMENTS: Measuring, Electrical Power
INSTRUMENTS: Medical & Surgical
INSTRUMENTS: Meteorological
INSTRUMENTS: Meters, Integrating Electricity
INSTRUMENTS: Microwave Test
INSTRUMENTS: Nautical
INSTRUMENTS: Photographic, Electronic
INSTRUMENTS: Power Measuring, Electrical
INSTRUMENTS: Pressure Measurement, Indl
INSTRUMENTS: Radio Frequency Measuring
INSTRUMENTS: Temperature Measurement, Indl
INSTRUMENTS: Test, Digital, Electronic & Electrical Circuits
INSTRUMENTS: Test, Electrical, Engine
INSTRUMENTS: Test, Electronic & Electric Measurement
INSTRUMENTS: Test, Electronic & Electrical Circuits
INSTRUMENTS: Testing, Semiconductor
INSTRUMENTS: Thermal Conductive, Indl
INSTRUMENTS: Thermal Property Measurement
INSTRUMENTS: Viscometer, Indl Process
INSULATING BOARD, CELLULAR FIBER
INSULATING COMPOUNDS
INSULATION & CUSHIONING FOAM: Polystyrene
INSULATION & ROOFING MATERIALS: Wood, Reconstituted
INSULATION MATERIALS WHOLESALERS
INSULATION: Fiberglass
INSULATORS & INSULATION MATERIALS: Electrical
INSURANCE CARRIERS: Automobile
INSURANCE CARRIERS: Direct Accident & Health
INSURANCE CARRIERS: Property & Casualty
INTEGRATED CIRCUITS, SEMICONDUCTOR NETWORKS, ETC
INTERCOMMUNICATIONS SYSTEMS: Electric
INTERIOR DECORATING SVCS
INTERIOR DESIGN SVCS, NEC
INTERIOR DESIGNING SVCS
INVENTORY STOCKING SVCS
INVERTERS: Nonrotating Electrical
INVESTMENT FUNDS, NEC
INVESTORS, NEC
IRON & STEEL PRDTS: Hot-Rolled
IRON ORES
IRRIGATION SYSTEMS, NEC Water Distribution Or Sply Systems

J

JACKS: Hydraulic
JANITORIAL & CUSTODIAL SVCS
JANITORIAL EQPT & SPLYS WHOLESALERS
JAR RINGS: Rubber
JEWELERS' FINDINGS & MATERIALS
JEWELERS' FINDINGS & MATERIALS: Castings
JEWELRY & PRECIOUS STONES WHOLESALERS
JEWELRY APPAREL
JEWELRY FINDINGS & LAPIDARY WORK
JEWELRY REPAIR SVCS
JEWELRY STORES
JEWELRY STORES: Precious Stones & Precious Metals
JEWELRY, PRECIOUS METAL: Bracelets
JEWELRY, PRECIOUS METAL: Cigar & Cigarette Access
JEWELRY, PRECIOUS METAL: Rings, Finger
JEWELRY, PRECIOUS METAL: Settings & Mountings
JEWELRY, WHOLESALE
JEWELRY: Decorative, Fashion & Costume
JEWELRY: Precious Metal
JIGS & FIXTURES
JIGS: Welding Positioners
JOB PRINTING & NEWSPAPER PUBLISHING COMBINED
JOB TRAINING & VOCATIONAL REHABILITATION SVCS
JOINTS & COUPLINGS
JOINTS OR FASTENINGS: Rail
JOINTS: Expansion
JOINTS: Expansion, Pipe
JOISTS: Fabricated Bar
JOISTS: Long-Span Series, Open Web Steel

K

KEYS: Machine
KILNS & FURNACES: Ceramic
KITCHEN CABINET STORES, EXC CUSTOM
KITCHEN CABINETS WHOLESALERS
KITCHEN UTENSILS: Bakers' Eqpt, Wood
KITCHEN UTENSILS: Food Handling & Processing Prdts, Wood
KNIVES: Agricultural Or indl

L

LABELS: Paper, Made From Purchased Materials
LABOR RESOURCE SVCS
LABORATORIES, TESTING: Automobile Proving & Testing Ground
LABORATORIES, TESTING: Prdt Certification, Sfty/Performance
LABORATORIES, TESTING: Product Testing
LABORATORIES, TESTING: Product Testing, Safety/Performance
LABORATORIES: Biological Research
LABORATORIES: Biotechnology
LABORATORIES: Commercial Nonphysical Research
LABORATORIES: Dental
LABORATORIES: Dental, Artificial Teeth Production
LABORATORIES: Dental, Crown & Bridge Production
LABORATORIES: Electronic Research
LABORATORIES: Environmental Research
LABORATORIES: Medical
LABORATORIES: Noncommercial Research
LABORATORIES: Physical Research, Commercial
LABORATORIES: Testing
LABORATORY APPARATUS & FURNITURE
LABORATORY APPARATUS, EXC HEATING & MEASURING
LABORATORY APPARATUS: Evaporation
LABORATORY APPARATUS: Granulators
LABORATORY APPARATUS: Microtomes
LABORATORY APPARATUS: Physics, NEC
LABORATORY APPARATUS: Time Interval Measuring, Electric
LABORATORY CHEMICALS: Organic
LABORATORY EQPT, EXC MEDICAL: Wholesalers
LABORATORY EQPT: Centrifuges
LABORATORY EQPT: Clinical Instruments Exc Medical
LABORATORY EQPT: Incubators
LABORATORY EQPT: Measuring
LABORATORY EQPT: Sterilizers
LACQUERING SVC: Metal Prdts
LADDER & WORKSTAND COMBINATION ASSEMBLIES: Metal
LADDERS: Metal
LADDERS: Portable, Metal
LADDERS: Wood
LAMINATED PLASTICS: Plate, Sheet, Rod & Tubes
LAMINATING MATERIALS
LAMINATING SVCS
LAMP & LIGHT BULBS & TUBES
LAMP BULBS & TUBES, ELECTRIC: Electric Light
LAMP BULBS & TUBES, ELECTRIC: For Specialized Applications
LAMP BULBS & TUBES, ELECTRIC: Glow Lamp
LAMP BULBS & TUBES, ELECTRIC: Light, Complete
LAMP BULBS & TUBES, ELECTRIC: Vapor
LAMP BULBS & TUBES/PARTS, ELECTRIC: Generalized Applications
LAMP REPAIR & MOUNTING SVCS
LAMPS: Desk, Commercial
LAMPS: Table, Residential
LAND SUBDIVISION & DEVELOPMENT
LANGUAGE SCHOOLS
LASER SYSTEMS & EQPT
LASERS: Welding, Drilling & Cutting Eqpt
LATEX: Foamed
LATHES
LAUNDRY & DRYCLEANING SVCS, EXC COIN-OPERATED: Retail Agent
LAUNDRY & GARMENT SVCS, NEC: Garment Making, Alter & Repair
LAUNDRY & GARMENT SVCS, NEC: Reweaving, Textiles
LAUNDRY & GARMENT SVCS, NEC: Seamstress
LAUNDRY EQPT: Commercial
LAUNDRY EQPT: Household
LAWN & GARDEN EQPT
LAWN & GARDEN EQPT: Blowers & Vacuums
LAWN & GARDEN EQPT: Edgers
LAWN & GARDEN EQPT: Grass Catchers, Lawn Mower
LAWN & GARDEN EQPT: Tractors & Eqpt
LAWN MOWER REPAIR SHOP
LEAD
LEAD & ZINC ORES
LEAD PENCILS & ART GOODS
LEASING & RENTAL SVCS: Cranes & Aerial Lift Eqpt
LEASING & RENTAL SVCS: Earth Moving Eqpt
LEASING & RENTAL: Construction & Mining Eqpt
LEASING & RENTAL: Medical Machinery & Eqpt
LEASING & RENTAL: Mobile Home Sites
LEASING & RENTAL: Other Real Estate Property
LEASING & RENTAL: Trucks, Without Drivers
LEASING & RENTAL: Utility Trailers & RV's
LEASING: Passenger Car
LEASING: Shipping Container
LEATHER GOODS: Aprons, Welders', Blacksmiths', Etc
LEATHER GOODS: Belting & Strapping
LEATHER GOODS: Embossed
LEATHER GOODS: Garments
LEATHER GOODS: Harnesses Or Harness Parts
LEATHER GOODS: Money Holders
LEATHER GOODS: NEC
LEATHER GOODS: Personal
LEATHER GOODS: Saddles Or Parts
LEATHER GOODS: Straps
LEATHER TANNING & FINISHING
LEATHER: Cut
LEATHER: Die-cut
LEATHER: Indl Prdts
LEATHER: Processed
LECTURING SVCS
LEGAL OFFICES & SVCS
LENS COATING: Ophthalmic
LICENSE TAGS: Automobile, Stamped Metal
LIGHT OIL CRUDE: From Chemical Recovery Coke Ovens
LIGHT SENSITIVE DEVICES
LIGHTING EQPT: Area & Sports Luminaries
LIGHTING EQPT: Motor Vehicle
LIGHTING EQPT: Motor Vehicle, Dome Lights
LIGHTING EQPT: Motor Vehicle, Headlights
LIGHTING EQPT: Motor Vehicle, NEC
LIGHTING EQPT: Motor Vehicle, Taillights
LIGHTING EQPT: Outdoor
LIGHTING FIXTURES WHOLESALERS
LIGHTING FIXTURES, NEC
LIGHTING FIXTURES: Decorative Area
LIGHTING FIXTURES: Fluorescent, Commercial
LIGHTING FIXTURES: Indl & Commercial
LIGHTING FIXTURES: Motor Vehicle
LIGHTING FIXTURES: Public
LIGHTING FIXTURES: Residential
LIGHTING FIXTURES: Residential, Electric
LIGHTING FIXTURES: Street
LIGHTS: Trouble lights
LIME ROCK: Ground
LIMESTONE & MARBLE: Dimension
LIMESTONE: Crushed & Broken
LIMESTONE: Dimension
LIMESTONE: Ground
LINEN SPLY SVC
LINEN SPLY SVC: Coat
LINEN SPLY SVC: Uniform
LINENS & TOWELS WHOLESALERS
LINERS & COVERS: Fabric
LINERS & LINING
LINERS: Indl, Metal Plate
LITHOGRAPHIC PLATES
LOADS: Electronic
LOCK & KEY SVCS
LOCKERS: Refrigerated
LOCKS
LOCKSMITHS

PRODUCT INDEX

LOG SPLITTERS
LOGGING
LOGGING CAMPS & CONTRACTORS
LOGGING: Fuel Wood Harvesting
LOGGING: Pulpwood Camp, Exc Pulp Mill At Same Site
LOGGING: Saw Logs
LOGGING: Skidding Logs
LOGGING: Stump Harvesting
LOGGING: Timber, Cut At Logging Camp
LOGGING: Wheel stock, Hewn
LOGGING: Wood Chips, Produced In The Field
LOGGING: Wooden Logs
LOOSELEAF BINDERS
LOTIONS OR CREAMS: Face
LOTIONS: SHAVING
LOUDSPEAKERS
LOVING CUPS, STAINLESS STEEL
LUBRICANTS: Corrosion Preventive
LUBRICATING EQPT: Indl
LUBRICATING OIL & GREASE WHOLESALERS
LUBRICATING SYSTEMS: Centralized
LUBRICATION SYSTEMS & EQPT
LUGGAGE & BRIEFCASES
LUGGAGE & LEATHER GOODS STORES: Leather, Exc Luggage & Shoes
LUGGAGE: Traveling Bags
LUMBER & BLDG MATLS DEALER, RET: Garage Doors, Sell/Install
LUMBER & BLDG MATLS DEALERS, RET: Energy Conservation Prdts
LUMBER & BLDG MATRLS DEALERS, RETAIL: Doors, Wood/Metal
LUMBER & BLDG MTRLS DEALERS, RET: Doors, Storm, Wood/Metal
LUMBER & BLDG MTRLS DEALERS, RET: Planing Mill Prdts/Lumber
LUMBER & BLDG MTRLS DEALERS, RET: Windows, Storm, Wood/Metal
LUMBER & BUILDING MATERIALS DEALER, RET: Door & Window Prdts
LUMBER & BUILDING MATERIALS DEALER, RET: Masonry Matls/Splys
LUMBER & BUILDING MATERIALS DEALERS, RETAIL: Brick
LUMBER & BUILDING MATERIALS DEALERS, RETAIL: Cement
LUMBER & BUILDING MATERIALS DEALERS, RETAIL: Countertops
LUMBER & BUILDING MATERIALS DEALERS, RETAIL: Modular Homes
LUMBER & BUILDING MATERIALS DEALERS, RETAIL: Paving Stones
LUMBER & BUILDING MATERIALS DEALERS, RETAIL: Sand & Gravel
LUMBER & BUILDING MATERIALS DEALERS, RETAIL: Siding
LUMBER & BUILDING MATERIALS RET DEALERS: Millwork & Lumber
LUMBER & BUILDING MATLS DEALERS, RET: Concrete/Cinder Block
LUMBER & BUILDING MTRLS DEALERS, RET: Insulation Mtrl, Bldg
LUMBER: Cants, Resawn
LUMBER: Dimension, Hardwood
LUMBER: Furniture Dimension Stock, Softwood
LUMBER: Hardwood Dimension
LUMBER: Hardwood Dimension & Flooring Mills
LUMBER: Kiln Dried
LUMBER: Plywood, Hardwood
LUMBER: Plywood, Hardwood or Hardwood Faced
LUMBER: Plywood, Prefinished, Hardwood
LUMBER: Plywood, Softwood
LUMBER: Resawn, Small Dimension
LUMBER: Stacking Or Sticking
LUMBER: Treated
LUMBER: Veneer, Hardwood
LUNCHROOMS & CAFETERIAS

M

MACHINE PARTS: Stamped Or Pressed Metal
MACHINE SHOPS
MACHINE TOOL ACCESS: Arbors
MACHINE TOOL ACCESS: Balancing Machines
MACHINE TOOL ACCESS: Boring Attachments
MACHINE TOOL ACCESS: Broaches
MACHINE TOOL ACCESS: Cams
MACHINE TOOL ACCESS: Counterbores, Metalworking
MACHINE TOOL ACCESS: Cutting
MACHINE TOOL ACCESS: Diamond Cutting, For Turning, Etc
MACHINE TOOL ACCESS: Dies, Thread Cutting
MACHINE TOOL ACCESS: Dresser, Abrasive Wheel Or Other
MACHINE TOOL ACCESS: Dressing/Wheel Crushing Attach, Diamond
MACHINE TOOL ACCESS: Drill Bushings, Drilling Jig
MACHINE TOOL ACCESS: Drills
MACHINE TOOL ACCESS: End Mills
MACHINE TOOL ACCESS: Files
MACHINE TOOL ACCESS: Hobs
MACHINE TOOL ACCESS: Honing Heads
MACHINE TOOL ACCESS: Hopper Feed Devices
MACHINE TOOL ACCESS: Knives, Metalworking
MACHINE TOOL ACCESS: Machine Attachments & Access, Drilling
MACHINE TOOL ACCESS: Milling Machine Attachments
MACHINE TOOL ACCESS: Pushers
MACHINE TOOL ACCESS: Rotary Tables
MACHINE TOOL ACCESS: Shaping Tools
MACHINE TOOL ACCESS: Sockets
MACHINE TOOL ACCESS: Threading Tools
MACHINE TOOL ACCESS: Tool Holders
MACHINE TOOL ACCESS: Tools & Access
MACHINE TOOL ACCESS: Wheel Turning Eqpt, Diamond Point, Etc
MACHINE TOOL ATTACHMENTS & ACCESS
MACHINE TOOLS & ACCESS
MACHINE TOOLS, METAL CUTTING: Brushing
MACHINE TOOLS, METAL CUTTING: Cutoff
MACHINE TOOLS, METAL CUTTING: Die Sinking
MACHINE TOOLS, METAL CUTTING: Drilling
MACHINE TOOLS, METAL CUTTING: Drilling & Boring
MACHINE TOOLS, METAL CUTTING: Electrochemical Milling
MACHINE TOOLS, METAL CUTTING: Electron-Discharge
MACHINE TOOLS, METAL CUTTING: Exotic, Including Explosive
MACHINE TOOLS, METAL CUTTING: Grind, Polish, Buff, Lapp
MACHINE TOOLS, METAL CUTTING: Home Workshop
MACHINE TOOLS, METAL CUTTING: Jig, Boring & Grinding
MACHINE TOOLS, METAL CUTTING: Lathes
MACHINE TOOLS, METAL CUTTING: Numerically Controlled
MACHINE TOOLS, METAL CUTTING: Pipe Cutting & Threading
MACHINE TOOLS, METAL CUTTING: Plasma Process
MACHINE TOOLS, METAL CUTTING: Pointing & Burring
MACHINE TOOLS, METAL CUTTING: Regrinding, Crankshaft
MACHINE TOOLS, METAL CUTTING: Robot, Drilling, Cutting, Etc
MACHINE TOOLS, METAL CUTTING: Saws, Power
MACHINE TOOLS, METAL CUTTING: Tool Replacement & Rpr Parts
MACHINE TOOLS, METAL CUTTING: Turret Lathes
MACHINE TOOLS, METAL CUTTING: Ultrasonic
MACHINE TOOLS, METAL CUTTING: Vertical Turning & Boring
MACHINE TOOLS, METAL FORMING: Beaders, Metal
MACHINE TOOLS, METAL FORMING: Bending
MACHINE TOOLS, METAL FORMING: Die Casting & Extruding
MACHINE TOOLS, METAL FORMING: Electroforming
MACHINE TOOLS, METAL FORMING: Forging Machinery & Hammers
MACHINE TOOLS, METAL FORMING: Forming, Metal Deposit
MACHINE TOOLS, METAL FORMING: Lathes, Spinning
MACHINE TOOLS, METAL FORMING: Magnetic Forming
MACHINE TOOLS, METAL FORMING: Mechanical, Pneumatic Or Hyd
MACHINE TOOLS, METAL FORMING: Plasma Jet Spray
MACHINE TOOLS, METAL FORMING: Presses, Arbor
MACHINE TOOLS, METAL FORMING: Presses, Hyd & Pneumatic
MACHINE TOOLS, METAL FORMING: Punching & Shearing
MACHINE TOOLS, METAL FORMING: Rebuilt
MACHINE TOOLS, METAL FORMING: Robots, Pressing, Extrudg, Etc
MACHINE TOOLS, METAL FORMING: Spinning, Spline Rollg/Windg
MACHINE TOOLS, METAL FORMING: Spline Rolling
MACHINE TOOLS: Metal Cutting
MACHINE TOOLS: Metal Forming
MACHINERY & EQPT FINANCE LEASING
MACHINERY & EQPT, AGRICULTURAL, WHOL: Farm Eqpt Parts/Splys
MACHINERY & EQPT, AGRICULTURAL, WHOL: Poultry/Livestock Eqpt
MACHINERY & EQPT, AGRICULTURAL, WHOLESALE: Farm Implements
MACHINERY & EQPT, AGRICULTURAL, WHOLESALE: Landscaping Eqpt
MACHINERY & EQPT, AGRICULTURAL, WHOLESALE: Livestock Eqpt
MACHINERY & EQPT, INDL, WHOL: Brewery Prdts Mfrg, Commercial
MACHINERY & EQPT, INDL, WHOL: Controlling Instruments/Access
MACHINERY & EQPT, INDL, WHOL: Environ Pollution Cntrl, Air
MACHINERY & EQPT, INDL, WHOL: Environ Pollution Cntrl, Water
MACHINERY & EQPT, INDL, WHOL: Meters, Consumption Registerng
MACHINERY & EQPT, INDL, WHOLESALE: Conveyor Systems
MACHINERY & EQPT, INDL, WHOLESALE: Cranes
MACHINERY & EQPT, INDL, WHOLESALE: Engines & Parts, Diesel
MACHINERY & EQPT, INDL, WHOLESALE: Engines, Gasoline
MACHINERY & EQPT, INDL, WHOLESALE: Engs & Parts, Air-Cooled
MACHINERY & EQPT, INDL, WHOLESALE: Engs/Transportation Eqpt
MACHINERY & EQPT, INDL, WHOLESALE: Food Manufacturing
MACHINERY & EQPT, INDL, WHOLESALE: Food Product Manufacturng
MACHINERY & EQPT, INDL, WHOLESALE: Fuel Injection Systems
MACHINERY & EQPT, INDL, WHOLESALE: Hoists
MACHINERY & EQPT, INDL, WHOLESALE: Hydraulic Systems
MACHINERY & EQPT, INDL, WHOLESALE: Indl Machine Parts
MACHINERY & EQPT, INDL, WHOLESALE: Instruments & Cntrl Eqpt
MACHINERY & EQPT, INDL, WHOLESALE: Lift Trucks & Parts
MACHINERY & EQPT, INDL, WHOLESALE: Machine Tools & Access
MACHINERY & EQPT, INDL, WHOLESALE: Machine Tools & Metalwork
MACHINERY & EQPT, INDL, WHOLESALE: Measure/Test, Electric
MACHINERY & EQPT, INDL, WHOLESALE: Metal Refining
MACHINERY & EQPT, INDL, WHOLESALE: Paint Spray
MACHINERY & EQPT, INDL, WHOLESALE: Petroleum Industry
MACHINERY & EQPT, INDL, WHOLESALE: Plastic Prdts Machinery
MACHINERY & EQPT, INDL, WHOLESALE: Pneumatic Tools
MACHINERY & EQPT, INDL, WHOLESALE: Processing & Packaging
MACHINERY & EQPT, INDL,,WHOLESALE: Recycling
MACHINERY & EQPT, INDL, WHOLESALE: Robots
MACHINERY & EQPT, INDL, WHOLESALE: Safety Eqpt
MACHINERY & EQPT, INDL, WHOLESALE: Sawmill
MACHINERY & EQPT, INDL, WHOLESALE: Screening
MACHINERY & EQPT, INDL, WHOLESALE: Sewing
MACHINERY & EQPT, INDL, WHOLESALE: Textile
MACHINERY & EQPT, INDL, WHOLESALE: Tool & Die Makers
MACHINERY & EQPT, INDL, WHOLESALE: Water Pumps
MACHINERY & EQPT, WHOLESALE: Blades, Graders, Scrapers, Etc
MACHINERY & EQPT, WHOLESALE: Construction & Mining, Ladders
MACHINERY & EQPT, WHOLESALE: Construction & Mining, Pavers
MACHINERY & EQPT, WHOLESALE: Construction, General
MACHINERY & EQPT, WHOLESALE: Logging & Forestry
MACHINERY & EQPT, WHOLESALE: Masonry
MACHINERY & EQPT, WHOLESALE: Oil Field Eqpt
MACHINERY & EQPT: Electroplating
MACHINERY & EQPT: Farm
MACHINERY & EQPT: Gas Producers, Generators/Other Rltd Eqpt

PRODUCT INDEX

MACHINERY & EQPT: Liquid Automation
MACHINERY & EQPT: Metal Finishing, Plating Etc
MACHINERY & EQPT: Vibratory Parts Handling Eqpt
MACHINERY BASES
MACHINERY, COMMERCIAL LAUNDRY & Drycleaning: Ironers
MACHINERY, EQPT & SUPPLIES: Parking Facility
MACHINERY, FOOD PRDTS: Biscuit Cutters
MACHINERY, FOOD PRDTS: Cutting, Chopping, Grinding, Mixing
MACHINERY, FOOD PRDTS: Dairy & Milk
MACHINERY, FOOD PRDTS: Food Processing, Smokers
MACHINERY, FOOD PRDTS: Grinders, Commercial
MACHINERY, FOOD PRDTS: Juice Extractors, Fruit & Veg, Comm
MACHINERY, FOOD PRDTS: Ovens, Bakery
MACHINERY, FOOD PRDTS: Pasta
MACHINERY, FOOD PRDTS: Processing, Fish & Shellfish
MACHINERY, FOOD PRDTS: Roasting, Coffee, Peanut, Etc.
MACHINERY, FOOD PRDTS: Slicers, Commercial
MACHINERY, LUBRICATION: Automatic
MACHINERY, MAILING: Mailing
MACHINERY, MAILING: Postage Meters
MACHINERY, METALWORKING: Assembly, Including Robotic
MACHINERY, METALWORKING: Coiling
MACHINERY, METALWORKING: Cutting & Slitting
MACHINERY, METALWORKING: Rotary Slitters, Metalworking
MACHINERY, OFFICE: Paper Handling
MACHINERY, PACKAGING: Carton Packing
MACHINERY, PACKAGING: Packing & Wrapping
MACHINERY, PACKAGING: Vacuum
MACHINERY, PACKAGING: Wrapping
MACHINERY, PAPER INDUSTRY: Coating & Finishing
MACHINERY, PAPER INDUSTRY: Converting, Die Cutting & Stampng
MACHINERY, PAPER INDUSTRY: Cutting
MACHINERY, PAPER INDUSTRY: Paper Mill, Plating, Etc
MACHINERY, PRINTING TRADES: Bookbinding Machinery
MACHINERY, PRINTING TRADES: Copy Holders
MACHINERY, PRINTING TRADES: Type & Type Making
MACHINERY, PRINTING TRADES: Type Casting, Founding/Melting
MACHINERY, SEWING: Sewing & Hat & Zipper Making
MACHINERY, TEXTILE: Embroidery
MACHINERY, TEXTILE: Finishing
MACHINERY, TEXTILE: Heddles, Wire, For Loom Harnesses
MACHINERY, TEXTILE: Opening
MACHINERY, TEXTILE: Printing
MACHINERY, TEXTILE: Silk Screens
MACHINERY, TEXTILE: Thread Making Or Spinning
MACHINERY, WOODWORKING: Bandsaws
MACHINERY, WOODWORKING: Cabinet Makers'
MACHINERY, WOODWORKING: Furniture Makers
MACHINERY, WOODWORKING: Pattern Makers'
MACHINERY, WOODWORKING: Planers
MACHINERY/EQPT, INDL, WHOL: Cleaning, High Press, Sand/Steam
MACHINERY/EQPT, INDL, WHOL: Machinist Precision Measrng Tool
MACHINERY: Ammunition & Explosives Loading
MACHINERY: Assembly, Exc Metalworking
MACHINERY: Automotive Maintenance
MACHINERY: Automotive Related
MACHINERY: Binding
MACHINERY: Bottling & Canning
MACHINERY: Centrifugal
MACHINERY: Concrete Prdts
MACHINERY: Construction
MACHINERY: Custom
MACHINERY: Deburring
MACHINERY: Die Casting
MACHINERY: Dredging
MACHINERY: Drill Presses
MACHINERY: Electrical Discharge Erosion
MACHINERY: Electronic Component Making
MACHINERY: Electronic Teaching Aids
MACHINERY: Extruding
MACHINERY: Fiber Optics Strand Coating
MACHINERY: Folding
MACHINERY: Gear Cutting & Finishing
MACHINERY: General, Industrial, NEC
MACHINERY: Glass Cutting
MACHINERY: Glassmaking
MACHINERY: Grinding
MACHINERY: Ice Cream
MACHINERY: Ice Crushers
MACHINERY: Ice Making
MACHINERY: Industrial, NEC
MACHINERY: Kilns
MACHINERY: Kilns, Lumber
MACHINERY: Labeling
MACHINERY: Lapping
MACHINERY: Marking, Metalworking
MACHINERY: Metalworking
MACHINERY: Milling
MACHINERY: Mining
MACHINERY: Packaging
MACHINERY: Paint Making
MACHINERY: Paper Industry Miscellaneous
MACHINERY: Pharmacuitical
MACHINERY: Photographic Reproduction
MACHINERY: Plastic Working
MACHINERY: Polishing & Buffing
MACHINERY: Printing Presses
MACHINERY: Recycling
MACHINERY: Riveting
MACHINERY: Road Construction & Maintenance
MACHINERY: Robots, Molding & Forming Plastics
MACHINERY: Rubber Working
MACHINERY: Saw & Sawing
MACHINERY: Screening Eqpt, Electric
MACHINERY: Semiconductor Manufacturing
MACHINERY: Separation Eqpt, Magnetic
MACHINERY: Sheet Metal Working
MACHINERY: Snow Making
MACHINERY: Specialty
MACHINERY: Tapping
MACHINERY: Textile
MACHINERY: Thread Rolling
MACHINERY: Tire Shredding
MACHINERY: Wire Drawing
MACHINERY: Woodworking
MACHINES: Forming, Sheet Metal
MACHINISTS' TOOLS & MACHINES: Measuring, Metalworking Type
MACHINISTS' TOOLS: Measuring, Precision
MACHINISTS' TOOLS: Precision
MAGNESIUM
MAGNETIC INK & OPTICAL SCANNING EQPT
MAGNETIC RESONANCE IMAGING DEVICES: Nonmedical
MAGNETIC SHIELDS, METAL
MAGNETIC TAPE, AUDIO: Prerecorded
MAGNETS: Ceramic
MAGNETS: Permanent
MAIL-ORDER HOUSE, NEC
MAIL-ORDER HOUSES: Computer Software
MAIL-ORDER HOUSES: Cosmetics & Perfumes
MAIL-ORDER HOUSES: Educational Splys & Eqpt
MAIL-ORDER HOUSES: Fitness & Sporting Goods
MAIL-ORDER HOUSES: Fruit
MAIL-ORDER HOUSES: Record & Tape, Music Or Video Club
MAIL-ORDER HOUSES: Tools & Hardware
MAIL-ORDER HOUSES: Women's Apparel
MAILBOX RENTAL & RELATED SVCS
MAILING & MESSENGER SVCS
MAILING LIST: Compilers
MAILING SVCS, NEC
MANAGEMENT CONSULTING SVCS: Administrative
MANAGEMENT CONSULTING SVCS: Automation & Robotics
MANAGEMENT CONSULTING SVCS: Business
MANAGEMENT CONSULTING SVCS: Construction Project
MANAGEMENT CONSULTING SVCS: Hospital & Health
MANAGEMENT CONSULTING SVCS: Industrial
MANAGEMENT CONSULTING SVCS: Industrial & Labor
MANAGEMENT CONSULTING SVCS: Industrial Hygiene
MANAGEMENT CONSULTING SVCS: Industry Specialist
MANAGEMENT CONSULTING SVCS: Maintenance
MANAGEMENT CONSULTING SVCS: Management Engineering
MANAGEMENT CONSULTING SVCS: Manufacturing
MANAGEMENT CONSULTING SVCS: Quality Assurance
MANAGEMENT CONSULTING SVCS: Retail Trade Consultant
MANAGEMENT SERVICES
MANAGEMENT SVCS, FACILITIES SUPPORT: Environ Remediation
MANAGEMENT SVCS: Business
MANAGEMENT SVCS: Construction
MANAGEMENT SVCS: Hospital
MANAGEMENT SVCS: Restaurant
MANHOLES & COVERS: Metal
MANHOLES COVERS: Concrete
MANICURE PREPARATIONS
MANIFOLDS: Pipe, Fabricated From Purchased Pipe
MANNEQUINS
MANUFACTURED & MOBILE HOME DEALERS
MANUFACTURING INDUSTRIES, NEC
MAPS
MAPS & CHARTS, WHOLESALE
MARBLE, BUILDING: Cut & Shaped
MARINAS
MARINE BASIN OPERATIONS
MARINE CARGO HANDLING SVCS: Marine Terminal
MARINE CARGO HANDLING SVCS: Waterfront Terminal Operations
MARINE ENGINE REPAIR SVCS
MARINE HARDWARE
MARINE PROPELLER REPAIR SVCS
MARINE RELATED EQPT
MARINE SPLY DEALERS
MARINE SPLYS WHOLESALERS
MARKERS
MARKETS: Meat & fish
MARKING DEVICES
MARKING DEVICES: Embossing Seals & Hand Stamps
MARKING DEVICES: Printing Dies, Marking Mach, Rubber/Plastic
MARKING DEVICES: Screens, Textile Printing
MARKING DEVICES: Seal Presses, Notary & Hand
MASKS: Gas
MASQUERADE OR THEATRICAL COSTUMES STORES
MASSAGE MACHINES, ELECTRIC: Barber & Beauty Shops
MATERIAL GRINDING & PULVERIZING SVCS NEC
MATERIALS HANDLING EQPT WHOLESALERS
MATS, MATTING & PADS: Nonwoven
MEAL DELIVERY PROGRAMS
MEAT & MEAT PRDTS WHOLESALERS
MEAT CUTTING & PACKING
MEAT MARKETS
MEAT PRDTS: Boxed Beef, From Slaughtered Meat
MEAT PRDTS: Canned Exc Baby Food, From Slaughtered Meat
MEAT PRDTS: Cooked Meats, From Purchased Meat
MEAT PRDTS: Corned Beef, From Purchased Meat
MEAT PRDTS: Cured, From Slaughtered Meat
MEAT PRDTS: Frankfurters, From Purchased Meat
MEAT PRDTS: Lamb, From Slaughtered Meat
MEAT PRDTS: Luncheon Meat, From Purchased Meat
MEAT PRDTS: Meat By-Prdts, From Slaughtered Meat
MEAT PRDTS: Pork, From Slaughtered Meat
MEAT PRDTS: Prepared Beef Prdts From Purchased Beef
MEAT PRDTS: Prepared Pork Prdts, From Purchased Meat
MEAT PRDTS: Sausages & Related Prdts, From Purchased Meat
MEAT PRDTS: Sausages, From Purchased Meat
MEAT PRDTS: Sausages, From Slaughtered Meat
MEAT PRDTS: Smoked
MEAT PRDTS: Snack Sticks, Incl Jerky, From Purchased Meat
MEAT PRDTS: Veal, From Slaughtered Meat
MEAT PROCESSED FROM PURCHASED CARCASSES
MEAT PROCESSING MACHINERY
MEATS, PACKAGED FROZEN: Wholesalers
MEDIA: Magnetic & Optical Recording
MEDICAL & HOSPITAL EQPT WHOLESALERS
MEDICAL & HOSPITAL SPLYS: Radiation Shielding Garments
MEDICAL & SURGICAL SPLYS: Abdominal Support, Braces/Trusses
MEDICAL & SURGICAL SPLYS: Absorbent Cotton, Sterilized
MEDICAL & SURGICAL SPLYS: Bandages & Dressings
MEDICAL & SURGICAL SPLYS: Belts, Surg, Sanitary & Corrective
MEDICAL & SURGICAL SPLYS: Braces, Orthopedic
MEDICAL & SURGICAL SPLYS: Clothing, Fire Resistant & Protect
MEDICAL & SURGICAL SPLYS: Cosmetic Restorations
MEDICAL & SURGICAL SPLYS: Crutches & Walkers
MEDICAL & SURGICAL SPLYS: Ear Plugs
MEDICAL & SURGICAL SPLYS: Foot Appliances, Orthopedic
MEDICAL & SURGICAL SPLYS: Hydrotherapy
MEDICAL & SURGICAL SPLYS: Limbs, Artificial
MEDICAL & SURGICAL SPLYS: Models, Anatomical
MEDICAL & SURGICAL SPLYS: Orthopedic Appliances

PRODUCT INDEX

MEDICAL & SURGICAL SPLYS: Personal Safety Eqpt
MEDICAL & SURGICAL SPLYS: Prosthetic Appliances
MEDICAL & SURGICAL SPLYS: Respiratory Protect Eqpt, Personal
MEDICAL & SURGICAL SPLYS: Technical Aids, Handicapped
MEDICAL & SURGICAL SPLYS: Traction Apparatus
MEDICAL & SURGICAL SPLYS: Trusses, Orthopedic & Surgical
MEDICAL & SURGICAL SPLYS: Walkers
MEDICAL & SURGICAL SPLYS: Welders' Hoods
MEDICAL EQPT: Cardiographs
MEDICAL EQPT: Diagnostic
MEDICAL EQPT: Dialyzers
MEDICAL EQPT: Electromedical Apparatus
MEDICAL EQPT: Electrotherapeutic Apparatus
MEDICAL EQPT: Heart-Lung Machines, Exc Iron Lungs
MEDICAL EQPT: Laser Systems
MEDICAL EQPT: TENS Units/Transcutaneous Elec Nerve Stimulatr
MEDICAL EQPT: Ultrasonic Scanning Devices
MEDICAL HELP SVCS
MEDICAL SUNDRIES: Rubber
MEDICAL SVCS ORGANIZATION
MEDICAL, DENTAL & HOSP EQPT, WHOLESALE: X-ray Film & Splys
MEDICAL, DENTAL & HOSPITAL EQPT, WHOL: Hospital Eqpt & Splys
MEDICAL, DENTAL & HOSPITAL EQPT, WHOL: Hosptl Eqpt/Furniture
MEDICAL, DENTAL & HOSPITAL EQPT, WHOLESALE: Diagnostic, Med
MEDICAL, DENTAL & HOSPITAL EQPT, WHOLESALE: Hosp Furniture
MEDICAL, DENTAL & HOSPITAL EQPT, WHOLESALE: Med Eqpt & Splys
MEDICAL, DENTAL & HOSPITAL EQPT, WHOLESALE: Medical Lab
MEDICAL, DENTAL & HOSPITAL EQPT, WHOLESALE: Orthopedic
MEDICAL, DENTAL & HOSPITAL EQPT, WHOLESALE: Therapy
MEDICAL, DENTAL/HOSPITAL EQPT, WHOL: Tech Aids, Handicapped
MEMBERSHIP ORGANIZATIONS, BUSINESS: Growers' Association
MEMBERSHIP ORGANIZATIONS, NEC: Amateur Sports Promotion
MEMBERSHIP ORGANIZATIONS, NEC: Automobile Owner Association
MEMBERSHIP ORGANIZATIONS, NEC: Charitable
MEMBERSHIP ORGANIZATIONS, PROFESSIONAL: Health Association
MEMBERSHIP ORGANIZATIONS, REL: Covenant & Evangelical Church
MEMBERSHIP ORGANIZATIONS, RELIGIOUS: Catholic Church
MEMBERSHIP ORGANIZATIONS, RELIGIOUS: Reformed Church
MEMBERSHIP ORGS, CIVIC, SOCIAL & FRATERNAL: Protection
MEMBERSHIP SPORTS & RECREATION CLUBS
MEMORIES: Solid State
MEN'S & BOYS' CLOTHING ACCESS STORES
MEN'S & BOYS' CLOTHING STORES
MEN'S & BOYS' CLOTHING WHOLESALERS, NEC
MEN'S & BOYS' SPORTSWEAR CLOTHING STORES
MEN'S & BOYS' SPORTSWEAR WHOLESALERS
MEN'S & BOYS' UNDERWEAR WHOLESALERS
MEN'S & BOYS' WORK CLOTHING WHOLESALERS
MEN'S SUITS STORES
MERCHANDISING MACHINE OPERATORS: Vending
METAL & STEEL PRDTS: Abrasive
METAL COMPONENTS: Prefabricated
METAL CUTTING SVCS
METAL FABRICATORS: Architechtural
METAL FABRICATORS: Plate
METAL FABRICATORS: Sheet
METAL FABRICATORS: Structural, Ship
METAL FABRICATORS: Structural, Ship
METAL FINISHING SVCS
METAL MINING SVCS
METAL RESHAPING & REPLATING SVCS
METAL SERVICE CENTERS & OFFICES
METAL SLITTING & SHEARING
METAL SPINNING FOR THE TRADE
METAL STAMPING, FOR THE TRADE
METAL STAMPINGS: Ornamental
METAL STAMPINGS: Patterned
METAL STAMPINGS: Perforated
METAL TREATING COMPOUNDS
METALS SVC CENTERS & WHOL: Structural Shapes, Iron Or Steel
METALS SVC CENTERS & WHOLESALERS: Bars, Metal
METALS SVC CENTERS & WHOLESALERS: Casting, Rough,Iron/Steel
METALS SVC CENTERS & WHOLESALERS: Copper
METALS SVC CENTERS & WHOLESALERS: Copper Prdts
METALS SVC CENTERS & WHOLESALERS: Ferroalloys
METALS SVC CENTERS & WHOLESALERS: Ferrous Metals
METALS SVC CENTERS & WHOLESALERS: Flat Prdts, Iron Or Steel
METALS SVC CENTERS & WHOLESALERS: Foundry Prdts
METALS SVC CENTERS & WHOLESALERS: Iron & Steel Prdt, Ferrous
METALS SVC CENTERS & WHOLESALERS: Misc Nonferrous Prdts
METALS SVC CENTERS & WHOLESALERS: Pipe & Tubing, Steel
METALS SVC CENTERS & WHOLESALERS: Plates, Metal
METALS SVC CENTERS & WHOLESALERS: Rope, Wire, Exc Insulated
METALS SVC CENTERS & WHOLESALERS: Stampings, Metal
METALS SVC CENTERS & WHOLESALERS: Steel
METALS SVC CENTERS & WHOLESALERS: Zinc
METALS SVC CNTRS & WHOL: Metal Wires, Ties, Cables/Screening
METALS SVC CTRS & WHOLESALERS: Aluminum Bars, Rods, Etc
METALS: Antifriction Bearing, Lead-Base
METALS: Precious NEC
METALS: Precious, Secondary
METALS: Primary Nonferrous, NEC
METALWORK: Miscellaneous
METALWORK: Ornamental
METEOROLOGIC TRACKING SYSTEMS
METERING DEVICES: Water Quality Monitoring & Control Systems
METERS: Liquid
METERS: Pyrometers, Indl Process
METERS: Solarimeters
MGMT CONSULTING SVCS: Matls, Incl Purch, Handle & Invntry
MICA PRDTS
MICROCIRCUITS, INTEGRATED: Semiconductor
MICROFILM SVCS
MICROPHONES
MICROPROCESSORS
MICROSCOPES: Electron & Proton
MICROWAVE COMPONENTS
MILITARY INSIGNIA
MILLING: Chemical
MILLING: Corn Grits & Flakes, For Brewers' Use
MILLWORK
MINE DEVELOPMENT SVCS: Nonmetallic Minerals
MINERAL MINING: Nonmetallic
MINERAL WOOL
MINERALS: Ground Or Otherwise Treated
MINERALS: Ground or Treated
MINIATURES
MINING EXPLORATION & DEVELOPMENT SVCS
MINING MACHINERY & EQPT WHOLESALERS
MINING MACHINES & EQPT: Grinders, Stone, Stationary
MINING MACHINES & EQPT: Pellet Mills
MINING MACHINES & EQPT: Rock Crushing, Stationary
MINING MACHINES & EQPT: Stamping Mill Machinery
MIRRORS: Motor Vehicle
MISCELLANEOUS FINANCIAL INVEST ACT: Oil/Gas Lease Brokers
MISSILES: Ballistic, Complete
MIXING EQPT
MIXTURES & BLOCKS: Asphalt Paving
MOBILE COMMUNICATIONS EQPT
MOBILE HOME REPAIR SVCS
MOBILE HOMES
MOBILE HOMES, EXC RECREATIONAL
MOBILE HOMES: Personal Or Private Use
MODELS
MODELS: Airplane, Exc Toy
MODELS: General, Exc Toy
MODELS: Railroad, Exc Toy
MODULES: Computer Logic
MODULES: Solid State
MOLDED RUBBER PRDTS
MOLDING COMPOUNDS
MOLDING SAND MINING
MOLDINGS & TRIM: Metal, Exc Automobile
MOLDINGS & TRIM: Wood
MOLDINGS OR TRIM: Automobile, Stamped Metal
MOLDINGS: Picture Frame
MOLDS: Indl
MOLDS: Plastic Working & Foundry
MONASTERIES
MONUMENTS & GRAVE MARKERS, EXC TERRAZZO
MONUMENTS & GRAVE MARKERS, WHOLESALE
MONUMENTS: Cut Stone, Exc Finishing Or Lettering Only
MOPS: Floor & Dust
MOTEL: Franchised
MOTION PICTURE & VIDEO PRODUCTION SVCS
MOTOR & GENERATOR PARTS: Electric
MOTOR HOME DEALERS
MOTOR HOMES
MOTOR REBUILDING SVCS, EXC AUTOMOTIVE
MOTOR REPAIR SVCS
MOTOR VEHICLE ASSEMBLY, COMPLETE: Ambulances
MOTOR VEHICLE ASSEMBLY, COMPLETE: Autos, Incl Specialty
MOTOR VEHICLE ASSEMBLY, COMPLETE: Buses, All Types
MOTOR VEHICLE ASSEMBLY, COMPLETE: Cars, Armored
MOTOR VEHICLE ASSEMBLY, COMPLETE: Fire Department Vehicles
MOTOR VEHICLE ASSEMBLY, COMPLETE: Hearses
MOTOR VEHICLE ASSEMBLY, COMPLETE: Military Motor Vehicle
MOTOR VEHICLE ASSEMBLY, COMPLETE: Motor Homes, Self Contained
MOTOR VEHICLE ASSEMBLY, COMPLETE: Scout Cars
MOTOR VEHICLE ASSEMBLY, COMPLETE: Snow Plows
MOTOR VEHICLE ASSEMBLY, COMPLETE: Truck & Tractor Trucks
MOTOR VEHICLE ASSEMBLY, COMPLETE: Truck Tractors, Highway
MOTOR VEHICLE ASSEMBLY, COMPLETE: Trucks, Pickup
MOTOR VEHICLE ASSEMBLY, COMPLETE: Universal Carriers, Mil
MOTOR VEHICLE ASSEMBLY, COMPLETE: Wreckers, Tow Truck
MOTOR VEHICLE DEALERS: Automobiles, New & Used
MOTOR VEHICLE DEALERS: Cars, Used Only
MOTOR VEHICLE DEALERS: Pickups, New & Used
MOTOR VEHICLE DEALERS: Trucks, Tractors/Trailers, New & Used
MOTOR VEHICLE PARTS & ACCESS: Air Conditioner Parts
MOTOR VEHICLE PARTS & ACCESS: Axel Housings & Shafts
MOTOR VEHICLE PARTS & ACCESS: Ball Joints
MOTOR VEHICLE PARTS & ACCESS: Bearings
MOTOR VEHICLE PARTS & ACCESS: Body Components & Frames
MOTOR VEHICLE PARTS & ACCESS: Brakes, Air
MOTOR VEHICLE PARTS & ACCESS: Brakes, Vacuum
MOTOR VEHICLE PARTS & ACCESS: Clutches
MOTOR VEHICLE PARTS & ACCESS: Connecting Rods
MOTOR VEHICLE PARTS & ACCESS: Cylinder Heads
MOTOR VEHICLE PARTS & ACCESS: Defrosters
MOTOR VEHICLE PARTS & ACCESS: Directional Signals
MOTOR VEHICLE PARTS & ACCESS: Electrical Eqpt
MOTOR VEHICLE PARTS & ACCESS: Engines & Parts
MOTOR VEHICLE PARTS & ACCESS: Engs & Trans,Factory, Rebuilt
MOTOR VEHICLE PARTS & ACCESS: Frames
MOTOR VEHICLE PARTS & ACCESS: Fuel Pumps
MOTOR VEHICLE PARTS & ACCESS: Fuel Systems & Parts
MOTOR VEHICLE PARTS & ACCESS: Gas Tanks
MOTOR VEHICLE PARTS & ACCESS: Gears
MOTOR VEHICLE PARTS & ACCESS: Heaters
MOTOR VEHICLE PARTS & ACCESS: Horns
MOTOR VEHICLE PARTS & ACCESS: Instrument Board Assemblies
MOTOR VEHICLE PARTS & ACCESS: Manifolds
MOTOR VEHICLE PARTS & ACCESS: Mufflers, Exhaust
MOTOR VEHICLE PARTS & ACCESS: Oil Pumps
MOTOR VEHICLE PARTS & ACCESS: Pickup Truck Bed Liners
MOTOR VEHICLE PARTS & ACCESS: Power Steering Eqpt

PRODUCT INDEX

MOTOR VEHICLE PARTS & ACCESS: Pumps, Hydraulic Fluid Power
MOTOR VEHICLE PARTS & ACCESS: Rear Axel Housings
MOTOR VEHICLE PARTS & ACCESS: Thermostats
MOTOR VEHICLE PARTS & ACCESS: Tops
MOTOR VEHICLE PARTS & ACCESS: Trailer Hitches
MOTOR VEHICLE PARTS & ACCESS: Transmission Housings Or Parts
MOTOR VEHICLE PARTS & ACCESS: Transmissions
MOTOR VEHICLE PARTS & ACCESS: Universal Joints
MOTOR VEHICLE PARTS & ACCESS: Water Pumps
MOTOR VEHICLE PARTS & ACCESS: Wheel rims
MOTOR VEHICLE PARTS & ACCESS: Wiring Harness Sets
MOTOR VEHICLE RADIOS WHOLESALERS
MOTOR VEHICLE SPLYS & PARTS WHOLESALERS: New
MOTOR VEHICLE: Hardware
MOTOR VEHICLE: Radiators
MOTOR VEHICLE: Shock Absorbers
MOTOR VEHICLE: Steering Mechanisms
MOTOR VEHICLE: Wheels
MOTOR VEHICLES & CAR BODIES
MOTOR VEHICLES, WHOLESALE: Fire Trucks
MOTOR VEHICLES, WHOLESALE: Snowmobiles
MOTOR VEHICLES, WHOLESALE: Trailers, Truck, New & Used
MOTOR VEHICLES, WHOLESALE: Truck bodies
MOTOR VEHICLES, WHOLESALE: Trucks, commercial
MOTORCYCLE & BICYCLE PARTS: Frames
MOTORCYCLE ACCESS
MOTORCYCLE DEALERS
MOTORCYCLE PARTS & ACCESS DEALERS
MOTORCYCLE REPAIR SHOPS
MOTORCYCLES & RELATED PARTS
MOTORS: Electric
MOTORS: Generators
MOTORS: Pneumatic
MOTORS: Starting, Automotive & Aircraft
MOUTHWASHES
MUCILAGE
MUSEUMS
MUSIC BOXES
MUSIC BROADCASTING SVCS
MUSIC DISTRIBUTION APPARATUS
MUSIC RECORDING PRODUCER
MUSICAL INSTRUMENT LESSONS
MUSICAL INSTRUMENTS & ACCESS: NEC
MUSICAL INSTRUMENTS & ACCESS: Pipe Organs
MUSICAL INSTRUMENTS & PARTS: String
MUSICAL INSTRUMENTS & SPLYS STORES
MUSICAL INSTRUMENTS & SPLYS STORES: String instruments
MUSICAL INSTRUMENTS/SPLYS STORE: Drums/Rltd Percussion Instr
MUSICAL INSTRUMENTS: Autophones/Organs W/Perfrtd Music Rolls
MUSICAL INSTRUMENTS: Fretted Instruments & Parts
MUSICAL INSTRUMENTS: Guitars & Parts, Electric & Acoustic
MUSICAL INSTRUMENTS: Organ Parts & Materials
MUSICAL INSTRUMENTS: Organs
MUSICAL INSTRUMENTS: Saxophones & Parts
MUSICAL INSTRUMENTS: Strings, Instrument
MUSICAL INSTRUMENTS: Violins & Parts

N

NAILS: Steel, Wire Or Cut
NAME PLATES: Engraved Or Etched
NAMEPLATES
NATIONAL SECURITY FORCES
NATURAL GAS COMPRESSING SVC, On-Site
NATURAL GAS DISTRIBUTION TO CONSUMERS
NATURAL GAS LIQUIDS PRODUCTION
NATURAL GAS PRODUCTION
NATURAL GAS STORAGE SVCS
NATURAL GAS TRANSMISSION & DISTRIBUTION
NATURAL GASOLINE PRODUCTION
NATURAL LIQUEFIED PETROLEUM GAS PRODUCTION
NATURAL RESOURCE PRESERVATION SVCS
NAUTICAL REPAIR SVCS
NAVIGATIONAL SYSTEMS & INSTRUMENTS
NEIGHBORHOOD DEVELOPMENT GROUP
NETTING: Cargo
NEW & USED CAR DEALERS
NEWS DEALERS & NEWSSTANDS
NEWSPAPERS & PERIODICALS NEWS REPORTING SVCS
NEWSPAPERS, WHOLESALE
NICKEL ALLOY
NONCURRENT CARRYING WIRING DEVICES
NONDAIRY BASED FROZEN DESSERTS
NONFERROUS: Rolling & Drawing, NEC
NONMETALLIC MINERALS: Support Activities, Exc Fuels
NOTEBOOKS, MADE FROM PURCHASED MATERIALS
NOTIONS: Buttons, Collar Or Cuff, Exc Semi & Precious
NOTIONS: Fasteners, Glove
NOVELTIES
NOVELTIES, DURABLE, WHOLESALE
NOVELTIES: Plastic
NOZZLES & SPRINKLERS Lawn Hose
NOZZLES: Fire Fighting
NOZZLES: Spray, Aerosol, Paint Or Insecticide
NURSERIES & LAWN & GARDEN SPLY STORE, RET: Lawn/Garden Splys
NURSERIES & LAWN & GARDEN SPLY STORES, RETAIL: Fertilizer
NURSERIES & LAWN/GARDEN SPLY STORE, RET: Lawn-mowers/Tractors
NURSERIES & LAWN/GARDEN SPLY STORES, RET: Garden Splys/Tools
NURSERIES/LAWN/GRDN SPLY STORE, RET: Nursery Stck, Seed/Bulb
NURSERY & GARDEN CENTERS
NURSERY STOCK, WHOLESALE
NURSING CARE FACILITIES: Skilled
NUTRITION SVCS
NUTS: Metal

O

OFFICE EQPT WHOLESALERS
OFFICE EQPT, WHOLESALE: Photocopy Machines
OFFICE SPLY & STATIONERY STORES
OFFICE SPLY & STATIONERY STORES: Office Forms & Splys
OFFICE SPLYS, NEC, WHOLESALE
OFFICES & CLINICS OF DOCTORS OF MEDICINE: Dermatologist
OFFICES & CLINICS OF DOCTORS OF MEDICINE: Psychiatrist
OFFICES & CLINICS OF DOCTORS OF MEDICINE: Surgeon, Plastic
OFFICES & CLINICS OF DRS OF MED: Cardiologist & Vascular
OFFICES & CLINICS OF DRS OF MED: Health Maint Org Or HMO
OFFICES & CLINICS OF DRS OF MEDICINE: Physician, Orthopedic
OFFICES & CLINICS OF HEALTH PRACTITIONERS: Nutrition
OFFICES & CLINICS OF HEALTH PRACTITIONERS: Occu Therapist
OFFICES & CLINICS OF HEALTH PRACTITIONERS: Physical Therapy
OFFICES & CLINICS OF OPTOMETRISTS: Specialist, Optometrists
OIL & GAS FIELD MACHINERY
OIL FIELD MACHINERY & EQPT
OIL FIELD SVCS, NEC
OILS & ESSENTIAL OILS
OILS & GREASES: Blended & Compounded
OILS & GREASES: Lubricating
OILS: Cutting
OILS: Essential
OILS: Lubricating
OILS: Lubricating
OILS: Magnetic Inspection Or Powder
OPERATOR: Apartment Buildings
OPERATOR: Nonresidential Buildings
OPHTHALMIC GOODS
OPHTHALMIC GOODS WHOLESALERS
OPHTHALMIC GOODS, NEC, WHOLESALE: Frames
OPHTHALMIC GOODS: Frames, Lenses & Parts, Eyeglasses
OPHTHALMIC GOODS: Lenses, Ophthalmic
OPHTHALMIC GOODS: Protectors, Eye
OPTICAL GOODS STORES
OPTICAL GOODS STORES: Eyeglasses, Prescription
OPTICAL GOODS STORES: Opticians
OPTICAL INSTRUMENTS & APPARATUS
OPTICAL INSTRUMENTS & LENSES
OPTICAL SCANNING SVCS
OPTOMETRIC EQPT & SPLYS WHOLESALERS
OPTOMETRISTS' OFFICES
ORDNANCE
ORGAN TUNING & REPAIR SVCS
ORGANIZATIONS & UNIONS: Labor
ORGANIZATIONS: Medical Research
ORGANIZATIONS: Noncommercial Biological Research
ORGANIZATIONS: Physical Research, Noncommercial
ORGANIZATIONS: Religious
ORGANIZATIONS: Research Institute
ORGANIZATIONS: Scientific Research Agency
ORGANIZERS, CLOSET & DRAWER Plastic
ORNAMENTS: Christmas Tree, Exc Electrical & Glass
ORNAMENTS: Lawn
OUTBOARD MOTOR DEALERS
OUTLETS: Electric, Convenience
OVENS: Infrared
OVENS: Paint Baking & Drying
OVENS: Smelting

P

PACKAGING & LABELING SVCS
PACKAGING MATERIALS, INDL: Wholesalers
PACKAGING MATERIALS, WHOLESALE
PACKAGING MATERIALS: Paper
PACKAGING MATERIALS: Paper, Coated Or Laminated
PACKAGING MATERIALS: Plastic Film, Coated Or Laminated
PACKAGING MATERIALS: Polystyrene Foam
PACKAGING: Blister Or Bubble Formed, Plastic
PACKING & CRATING SVC
PACKING & CRATING SVCS: Containerized Goods For Shipping
PACKING MATERIALS: Mechanical
PACKING SVCS: Shipping
PADDING: Foamed Plastics
PADS & PADDING: Insulator, Cordage
PADS: Athletic, Protective
PAILS: Shipping, Metal
PAINT & PAINTING SPLYS STORE
PAINT & PAINTING SPLYS STORE: Brushes, Rollers, Sprayers
PAINT STORE
PAINTING SVC: Metal Prdts
PAINTS & ADDITIVES
PAINTS & ALLIED PRODUCTS
PAINTS, VARNISHES & SPLYS WHOLESALERS
PAINTS, VARNISHES & SPLYS, WHOLESALE: Colors & Pigments
PAINTS, VARNISHES & SPLYS, WHOLESALE: Paints
PAINTS: Oil Or Alkyd Vehicle Or Water Thinned
PAINTS: Waterproof
PALLET REPAIR SVCS
PALLETIZERS & DEPALLETIZERS
PALLETS
PALLETS & SKIDS: Wood
PALLETS: Metal
PALLETS: Plastic
PALLETS: Wood & Metal Combination
PALLETS: Wooden
PANEL & DISTRIBUTION BOARDS & OTHER RELATED APPARATUS
PANEL & DISTRIBUTION BOARDS: Electric
PANELS, FLAT: Plastic
PANELS: Building, Metal
PANELS: Building, Plastic, NEC
PANELS: Building, Wood
PANELS: Switchboard, Slate
PANELS: Wood
PAPER & BOARD: Die-cut
PAPER CONVERTING
PAPER MANUFACTURERS: Exc Newsprint
PAPER PRDTS: Book Covers
PAPER PRDTS: Infant & Baby Prdts
PAPER PRDTS: Sanitary
PAPER PRDTS: Sanitary Tissue Paper
PAPER PRDTS: Toilet Paper, Made From Purchased Materials
PAPER PRDTS: Toweling Tissue
PAPER PRDTS: Towels, Napkins/Tissue Paper, From Purchd Mtrls
PAPER: Adhesive
PAPER: Book
PAPER: Building, Insulating & Packaging
PAPER: Cardboard
PAPER: Coated & Laminated, NEC
PAPER: Corrugated
PAPER: Packaging

PRODUCT INDEX

PAPER: Printer
PAPER: Specialty
PAPER: Waxed, Made From Purchased Materials
PAPER: Wrapping & Packaging
PAPERBOARD
PAPERBOARD CONVERTING
PAPERBOARD PRDTS: Coated & Treated Board
PAPERBOARD PRDTS: Container Board
PAPERBOARD PRDTS: Packaging Board
PAPERBOARD: Boxboard
PAPERBOARD: Chipboard
PAPERBOARD: Coated
PARKING LOTS & GARAGES
PARTICLEBOARD
PARTICLEBOARD: Laminated, Plastic
PARTITIONS & FIXTURES: Except Wood
PARTITIONS: Solid Fiber, Made From Purchased Materials
PARTITIONS: Wood & Fixtures
PARTS: Metal
PATTERNS: Indl
PAVING BREAKERS
PAVING MATERIALS: Prefabricated, Concrete
PAWN SHOPS
PAYROLL SVCS
PEARLS, WHOLESALE
PEAT GRINDING SVCS
PEAT MINING SVCS
PERFORMANCE RIGHTS, PUBLISHING & LICENSING
PERFUMES
PERLITE: Processed
PERSONAL & HOUSEHOLD GOODS REPAIR, NEC
PERSONAL CREDIT INSTITUTIONS: Financing, Autos, Furniture
PESTICIDES
PESTICIDES WHOLESALERS
PET & PET SPLYS STORES
PET ACCESS: Collars, Leashes, Etc, Exc Leather
PET SPLYS
PETROLEUM & PETROLEUM PRDTS, WHOLESALE Fuel Oil
PETROLEUM BULK STATIONS & TERMINALS
PETROLEUM PRDTS WHOLESALERS
PHARMACEUTICAL PREPARATIONS: Adrenal
PHARMACEUTICAL PREPARATIONS: Druggists' Preparations
PHARMACEUTICAL PREPARATIONS: Emulsions
PHARMACEUTICAL PREPARATIONS: Medicines, Capsule Or Ampule
PHARMACEUTICAL PREPARATIONS: Powders
PHARMACEUTICAL PREPARATIONS: Proprietary Drug PRDTS
PHARMACEUTICAL PREPARATIONS: Solutions
PHARMACEUTICAL PREPARATIONS: Tablets
PHARMACEUTICALS
PHARMACEUTICALS: Medicinal & Botanical Prdts
PHARMACIES & DRUG STORES
PHOSPHORIC ACID ESTERS
PHOTO RECONNAISSANCE SYSTEMS
PHOTOCOPY MACHINE REPAIR SVCS
PHOTOCOPYING & DUPLICATING SVCS
PHOTOENGRAVING SVC
PHOTOGRAMMATIC MAPPING SVCS
PHOTOGRAPHIC EQPT & SPLYS
PHOTOGRAPHIC EQPT & SPLYS WHOLESALERS
PHOTOGRAPHIC EQPT & SPLYS, WHOLESALE: Printing Apparatus
PHOTOGRAPHIC EQPT & SPLYS: Cameras, Aerial
PHOTOGRAPHIC EQPT & SPLYS: Densitometers
PHOTOGRAPHIC EQPT & SPLYS: Printing Eqpt
PHOTOGRAPHIC EQPT & SPLYS: Printing Frames
PHOTOGRAPHIC EQPT & SPLYS: Toners, Prprd, Not Chem Plnts
PHOTOGRAPHY SVCS: Commercial
PHOTOGRAPHY SVCS: Portrait Studios
PHOTOGRAPHY SVCS: School
PHOTOGRAPHY SVCS: Still Or Video
PHOTOTYPESETTING SVC
PHOTOVOLTAIC Solid State
PHYSICAL FITNESS CENTERS
PHYSICIANS' OFFICES & CLINICS: Medical doctors
PICTURE FRAMES: Wood
PIECE GOODS & NOTIONS WHOLESALERS
PIECE GOODS, NOTIONS & DRY GOODS, WHOL: Textile Converters

PIECE GOODS, NOTIONS & OTHER DRY GOODS, WHOL: Fabric, Coated
PIECE GOODS, NOTIONS & OTHER DRY GOODS, WHOL: Flags/Banners
PIECE GOODS, NOTIONS & OTHER DRY GOODS, WHOLESALE: Fabrics
PIECE GOODS, NOTIONS/DRY GOODS, WHOL: Drapery Mtrl, Woven
PIECE GOODS, NOTIONS/DRY GOODS, WHOL: Silk Piece, Woven
PIGMENTS, INORGANIC: Bone Black
PILLOW FILLING MTRLS: Curled Hair, Cotton Waste, Moss
PINS
PINS: Dowel
PIPE & FITTING: Fabrication
PIPE & FITTINGS: Cast Iron
PIPE & FITTINGS: Pressure, Cast Iron
PIPE & TUBES: Copper & Copper Alloy
PIPE & TUBES: Seamless
PIPE FITTINGS: Plastic
PIPE JOINT COMPOUNDS
PIPE SECTIONS, FABRICATED FROM PURCHASED PIPE
PIPE, SEWER: Concrete
PIPE: Brass & Bronze
PIPE: Concrete
PIPE: Plastic
PIPE: Sewer, Cast Iron
PIPE: Sheet Metal
PIPELINE TERMINAL FACILITIES: Independent
PIPES & TUBES
PIPES & TUBES: Steel
PIPES & TUBES: Welded
PIPES: Steel & Iron
PIPES: Tobacco
PISTONS & PISTON RINGS
PLANING MILL, NEC
PLANING MILLS: Millwork
PLANTERS: Plastic
PLANTS: Artificial & Preserved
PLAQUES: Clay, Plaster/Papier-Mache, Factory Production
PLAQUES: Picture, Laminated
PLASMAS
PLASTIC COLORING & FINISHING
PLASTIC PRDTS
PLASTICS FILM & SHEET
PLASTICS FILM & SHEET: Polyethylene
PLASTICS FILM & SHEET: Vinyl
PLASTICS FINISHED PRDTS: Laminated
PLASTICS FOAM, WHOLESALE
PLASTICS MATERIAL & RESINS
PLASTICS MATERIALS, BASIC FORMS & SHAPES WHOLESALERS
PLASTICS PROCESSING
PLASTICS SHEET: Packing Materials
PLASTICS: Blow Molded
PLASTICS: Cast
PLASTICS: Extruded
PLASTICS: Finished Injection Molded
PLASTICS: Injection Molded
PLASTICS: Molded
PLASTICS: Polystyrene Foam
PLASTICS: Thermoformed
PLATE WORK: For Nuclear Industry
PLATE WORK: Metalworking Trade
PLATEMAKING SVC: Color Separations, For The Printing Trade
PLATEMAKING SVC: Embossing, For The Printing Trade
PLATEMAKING SVC: Gravure
PLATEMAKING SVC: Gravure, Plates Or Cylinders
PLATEMAKING SVC: Letterpress
PLATES
PLATES: Paper, Made From Purchased Materials
PLATES: Plastic Exc Polystyrene Foam
PLATES: Sheet & Strip, Exc Coated Prdts
PLATES: Steel
PLATES: Truss, Metal
PLATING & FINISHING SVC: Decorative, Formed Prdts
PLATING & POLISHING SVC
PLATING COMPOUNDS
PLATING SVC: Chromium, Metals Or Formed Prdts
PLATING SVC: Electro
PLATING SVC: NEC
PLAYGROUND EQPT
PLEATING & STITCHING FOR THE TRADE: Decorative & Novelty

PLEATING & STITCHING SVC
PLUGS: Electric
PLUMBING & HEATING EQPT & SPLY, WHOL: Htg Eqpt/Panels, Solar
PLUMBING & HEATING EQPT & SPLY, WHOLESALE: Hydronic Htg Eqpt
PLUMBING & HEATING EQPT & SPLYS WHOLESALERS
PLUMBING & HEATING EQPT & SPLYS, WHOL: Plumbing Fitting/Sply
PLUMBING & HEATING EQPT & SPLYS, WHOL: Water Purif Eqpt
PLUMBING & HEATING EQPT & SPLYS, WHOLESALE: Brass/Fittings
PLUMBING & HEATING EQPT & SPLYS, WHOLESALE: Gas Burners
PLUMBING & HEATING EQPT & SPLYS, WHOLESALE: Sanitary Ware
PLUMBING & HEATING EQPT/SPLYS, WHOL: Boilers, Hot Water Htg
PLUMBING FIXTURES
PLUMBING FIXTURES: Brass, Incl Drain Cocks, Faucets/Spigots
PLUMBING FIXTURES: Plastic
POINT OF SALE DEVICES
POLISHING SVC: Metals Or Formed Prdts
POLYMETHYL METHACRYLATE RESINS: Plexiglas
POLYOXYMETHYLENE RESINS
POLYPROPYLENE RESINS
POLYSTYRENE RESINS
POLYURETHANE RESINS
POLYVINYL CHLORIDE RESINS
PONTOONS: Rubber
POPULAR MUSIC GROUPS OR ARTISTS
POSTAL EQPT: Locker Boxes, Exc Wood
POSTERS
POSTERS, WHOLESALE
POTPOURRI
POTTING SOILS
POULTRY & SMALL GAME SLAUGHTERING & PROCESSING
POWDER PUFFS & MITTS
POWDER: Metal
POWDER: Silver
POWER GENERATORS
POWER MOWERS WHOLESALERS
POWER SPLY CONVERTERS: Static, Electronic Applications
POWER SUPPLIES: All Types, Static
POWER TOOLS, HAND: Chain Saws, Portable
POWER TOOLS, HAND: Drills & Drilling Tools
POWER TOOLS, HAND: Drills, Port, Elec/Pneumatic, Exc Rock
POWER TOOLS, HAND: Grinders, Portable, Electric Or Pneumatic
POWER TOOLS, HAND: Guns, Pneumatic, Chip Removal
POWER TOOLS, HAND: Hammers, Portable, Elec/Pneumatic, Chip
POWER TRANSMISSION EQPT WHOLESALERS
POWER TRANSMISSION EQPT: Aircraft
POWER TRANSMISSION EQPT: Mechanical
PRECAST TERRAZZO OR CONCRETE PRDTS
PRECIOUS STONE MINING SVCS, NEC
PRERECORDED TAPE, COMPACT DISC & RECORD STORES
PRERECORDED TAPE, COMPACT DISC & RECORD STORES: Records
PRESSES
PRIMARY METAL PRODUCTS
PRIMARY ROLLING MILL EQPT
PRINT CARTRIDGES: Laser & Other Computer Printers
PRINTED CIRCUIT BOARDS
PRINTERS & PLOTTERS
PRINTERS' SVCS: Folding, Collating, Etc
PRINTERS: Computer
PRINTERS: Magnetic Ink, Bar Code
PRINTING & BINDING: Books
PRINTING & BINDING: Pamphlets
PRINTING & BINDING: Textbooks
PRINTING & EMBOSSING: Plastic Fabric Articles
PRINTING & ENGRAVING: Invitation & Stationery
PRINTING & STAMPING: Fabric Articles
PRINTING & WRITING PAPER WHOLESALERS
PRINTING INKS WHOLESALERS
PRINTING MACHINERY
PRINTING MACHINERY, EQPT & SPLYS: Wholesalers
PRINTING, COMMERCIAL Newspapers, NEC

PRODUCT INDEX

PRINTING, COMMERCIAL: Business Forms, NEC
PRINTING, COMMERCIAL: Calendars, NEC
PRINTING, COMMERCIAL: Cards, Visiting, Incl Business, NEC
PRINTING, COMMERCIAL: Catalogs, NEC
PRINTING, COMMERCIAL: Coupons, NEC
PRINTING, COMMERCIAL: Envelopes, NEC
PRINTING, COMMERCIAL: Imprinting
PRINTING, COMMERCIAL: Invitations, NEC
PRINTING, COMMERCIAL: Labels & Seals, NEC
PRINTING, COMMERCIAL: Letterpress & Screen
PRINTING, COMMERCIAL: Literature, Advertising, NEC
PRINTING, COMMERCIAL: Magazines, NEC
PRINTING, COMMERCIAL: Menus, NEC
PRINTING, COMMERCIAL: Music, Sheet, NEC
PRINTING, COMMERCIAL: Periodicals, NEC
PRINTING, COMMERCIAL: Post Cards, Picture, NEC
PRINTING, COMMERCIAL: Promotional
PRINTING, COMMERCIAL: Publications
PRINTING, COMMERCIAL: Ready
PRINTING, COMMERCIAL: Screen
PRINTING, COMMERCIAL: Tags, NEC
PRINTING, COMMERCIAL: Tickets, NEC
PRINTING, LITHOGRAPHIC: Advertising Posters
PRINTING, LITHOGRAPHIC: Catalogs
PRINTING, LITHOGRAPHIC: Decals
PRINTING, LITHOGRAPHIC: Forms & Cards, Business
PRINTING, LITHOGRAPHIC: Forms, Business
PRINTING, LITHOGRAPHIC: Newspapers
PRINTING, LITHOGRAPHIC: Offset & photolithographic printing
PRINTING, LITHOGRAPHIC: On Metal
PRINTING, LITHOGRAPHIC: Periodicals
PRINTING, LITHOGRAPHIC: Posters
PRINTING, LITHOGRAPHIC: Posters & Decals
PRINTING, LITHOGRAPHIC: Promotional
PRINTING, LITHOGRAPHIC: Tags
PRINTING, LITHOGRAPHIC: Transfers, Decalcomania Or Dry
PRINTING, LITHOGRAPHIC: Wrappers & Seals
PRINTING: Books
PRINTING: Books
PRINTING: Broadwoven Fabrics. Cotton
PRINTING: Commercial, NEC
PRINTING: Flexographic
PRINTING: Gravure, Forms, Business
PRINTING: Gravure, Job
PRINTING: Gravure, Labels
PRINTING: Gravure, Rotogravure
PRINTING: Gravure, Stationery & Invitation
PRINTING: Gravure, Wrapper & Seal
PRINTING: Laser
PRINTING: Letterpress
PRINTING: Lithographic
PRINTING: Offset
PRINTING: Photo-Offset
PRINTING: Photogravure
PRINTING: Photolithographic
PRINTING: Rotary Photogravure
PRINTING: Screen, Broadwoven Fabrics, Cotton
PRINTING: Screen, Fabric
PRINTING: Screen, Manmade Fiber & Silk, Broadwoven Fabric
PRINTING: Thermography
PRODUCT ENDORSEMENT SVCS
PROFESSIONAL EQPT & SPLYS, WHOLESALE: Analytical Instruments
PROFESSIONAL EQPT & SPLYS, WHOLESALE: Law Enforcement
PROFESSIONAL EQPT & SPLYS, WHOLESALE: Optical Goods
PROFESSIONAL EQPT & SPLYS, WHOLESALE: Precision Tools
PROFESSIONAL EQPT & SPLYS, WHOLESALE: Scientific & Engineerg
PROFESSIONAL INSTRUMENT REPAIR SVCS
PROFILE SHAPES: Unsupported Plastics
PROGRAMMERS: Indl Process
PROMOTERS OF SHOWS & EXHIBITIONS
PROMOTION SVCS
PROPELLERS: Boat & Ship, Machined
PROPELLERS: Ship, Cast Brass
PROPULSION UNITS: Guided Missiles & Space Vehicles
PUBLIC FINANCE, TAX & MONETARY POLICY OFFICES, GOVT: State
PUBLIC LIBRARY

PUBLIC RELATIONS & PUBLICITY SVCS
PUBLIC RELATIONS SVCS
PUBLISHERS: Art Copy & Poster
PUBLISHERS: Book
PUBLISHERS: Book Clubs, No Printing
PUBLISHERS: Books, No Printing
PUBLISHERS: Catalogs
PUBLISHERS: Directories, NEC
PUBLISHERS: Directories, Telephone
PUBLISHERS: Guides
PUBLISHERS: Magazines, No Printing
PUBLISHERS: Miscellaneous
PUBLISHERS: Music Book & Sheet Music
PUBLISHERS: Newsletter
PUBLISHERS: Newspaper
PUBLISHERS: Newspapers, No Printing
PUBLISHERS: Pamphlets, No Printing
PUBLISHERS: Periodical, With Printing
PUBLISHERS: Periodicals, Magazines
PUBLISHERS: Periodicals, No Printing
PUBLISHERS: Shopping News
PUBLISHERS: Technical Manuals
PUBLISHERS: Technical Manuals & Papers
PUBLISHERS: Telephone & Other Directory
PUBLISHERS: Textbooks, No Printing
PUBLISHERS: Trade journals, No Printing
PUBLISHING & BROADCASTING: Internet Only
PUBLISHING & PRINTING: Art Copy
PUBLISHING & PRINTING: Book Music
PUBLISHING & PRINTING: Books
PUBLISHING & PRINTING: Comic Books
PUBLISHING & PRINTING: Directories, NEC
PUBLISHING & PRINTING: Directories, Telephone
PUBLISHING & PRINTING: Guides
PUBLISHING & PRINTING: Magazines: publishing & printing
PUBLISHING & PRINTING: Newsletters, Business Svc
PUBLISHING & PRINTING: Newspapers
PUBLISHING & PRINTING: Pamphlets
PUBLISHING & PRINTING: Posters
PUBLISHING & PRINTING: Shopping News
PUBLISHING & PRINTING: Textbooks
PUBLISHING & PRINTING: Trade Journals
PUBLISHING & PRINTING: Yearbooks
PULLEYS: Metal
PULLEYS: Power Transmission
PULP MILLS
PULP MILLS: Chemical & Semichemical Processing
PULP MILLS: Mechanical & Recycling Processing
PULVERIZED EARTH
PUMICE: Abrasives
PUMP JACKS & OTHER PUMPING EQPT: Indl
PUMPS
PUMPS & PARTS: Indl
PUMPS & PUMPING EQPT REPAIR SVCS
PUMPS & PUMPING EQPT WHOLESALERS
PUMPS, HEAT: Electric
PUMPS: Domestic, Water Or Sump
PUMPS: Fluid Power
PUMPS: Gasoline, Measuring Or Dispensing
PUMPS: Hydraulic Power Transfer
PUMPS: Measuring & Dispensing
PUMPS: Vacuum, Exc Laboratory
PUNCHES: Forming & Stamping
PUPPETS & MARIONETTES
PURIFICATION & DUST COLLECTION EQPT
PURSES: Women's

Q

QUILTING SVC
QUILTING SVC & SPLYS, FOR THE TRADE

R

RACE CAR OWNERS
RACE TRACK OPERATION
RACETRACKS
RACEWAYS
RACKS: Display
RACKS: Garment, Exc Wood
RACKS: Pallet, Exc Wood
RACKS: Trash, Metal Rack
RADAR SYSTEMS & EQPT
RADIATORS: Stationary Engine
RADIO & TELEVISION COMMUNICATIONS EQUIPMENT
RADIO & TELEVISION RECEIVER INSTALLATION SVCS
RADIO & TELEVISION REPAIR

RADIO BROADCASTING & COMMUNICATIONS EQPT
RADIO BROADCASTING STATIONS
RADIO PRODUCERS
RADIO RECEIVER NETWORKS
RADIO REPAIR & INSTALLATION SVCS
RADIO, TELEVISION & CONSUMER ELECTRONICS STORES: Eqpt, NEC
RADIO, TELEVISION & CONSUMER ELECTRONICS STORES: TV Sets
RADIO, TV & CONSUMER ELEC STORES: Automotive Sound Eqpt
RADIO, TV & CONSUMER ELEC STORES: High Fidelity Stereo Eqpt
RADIO, TV & CONSUMER ELEC STORES: Radios, Receiver Type
RADIO, TV/CONSUMER ELEC STORES: Antennas, Satellite Dish
RAIL & STRUCTURAL SHAPES: Aluminum rail & structural shapes
RAILINGS: Prefabricated, Metal
RAILROAD CAR RENTING & LEASING SVCS
RAILROAD CAR REPAIR SVCS
RAILROAD CARGO LOADING & UNLOADING SVCS
RAILROAD CROSSINGS: Steel Or Iron
RAILROAD EQPT
RAILROAD EQPT & SPLYS WHOLESALERS
RAILROAD EQPT: Brakes, Air & Vacuum
RAILROAD EQPT: Cars & Eqpt, Dining
RAILROAD EQPT: Cars, Rebuilt
RAILROAD EQPT: Locomotives & Parts, Indl
RAILROAD EQPT: Street Cars & Eqpt
RAILROAD MAINTENANCE & REPAIR SVCS
RAILROAD RELATED EQPT
RAILROADS: Long Haul
RAILS: Steel Or Iron
RAMPS: Prefabricated Metal
RAZORS, RAZOR BLADES
REAL ESTATE AGENCIES & BROKERS
REAL ESTATE AGENCIES: Leasing & Rentals
REAL ESTATE AGENTS & MANAGERS
REAL ESTATE INVESTMENT TRUSTS
REAL ESTATE LISTING SVCS
REAL ESTATE OPERATORS, EXC DEVELOPERS: Commercial/Indl Bldg
RECLAIMED RUBBER: Reworked By Manufacturing Process
RECORD BLANKS: Phonographic
RECORDING & PLAYBACK HEADS: Magnetic
RECORDING TAPE: Video, Blank
RECORDS & TAPES: Prerecorded
RECORDS OR TAPES: Masters
RECOVERY SVCS: Metal
RECREATIONAL SPORTING EQPT REPAIR SVCS
RECREATIONAL VEHICLE DEALERS
RECREATIONAL VEHICLE PARTS & ACCESS STORES
RECREATIONAL VEHICLE REPAIRS
RECREATIONAL VEHICLE: Wholesalers
RECTIFIERS: Mercury Arc, Electrical
RECYCLING: Paper
REELS: Cable, Metal
REELS: Fiber, Textile, Made From Purchased Materials
REFINERS & SMELTERS: Aluminum
REFINERS & SMELTERS: Copper
REFINERS & SMELTERS: Copper, Secondary
REFINERS & SMELTERS: Gold, Secondary
REFINERS & SMELTERS: Lead, Secondary
REFINERS & SMELTERS: Nonferrous Metal
REFINERS & SMELTERS: Zinc, Primary, Including Zinc Residue
REFINERS & SMELTERS: Zinc, Secondary
REFINING LUBRICATING OILS & GREASES, NEC
REFINING: Petroleum
REFLECTIVE ROAD MARKERS, WHOLESALE
REFRACTORIES: Castable, Clay
REFRACTORIES: Cement
REFRACTORIES: Cement, nonclay
REFRACTORIES: Clay
REFRACTORIES: Graphite, Carbon Or Ceramic Bond
REFRACTORIES: Nonclay
REFRACTORIES: Tile & Brick, Exc Plastic
REFRIGERATION & HEATING EQUIPMENT
REFRIGERATION EQPT & SPLYS WHOLESALERS
REFRIGERATION EQPT & SPLYS, WHOLESALE: Beverage Coolers
REFRIGERATION EQPT & SPLYS, WHOLESALE: Ice Cream Cabinets

PRODUCT INDEX

REFRIGERATION EQPT: Complete
REFRIGERATION REPAIR SVCS
REFRIGERATION SVC & REPAIR
REFUSE SYSTEMS
REGISTERS: Air, Metal
REGULATORS: Power
REGULATORS: Transmission & Distribution Voltage
REHABILITATION CENTER, OUTPATIENT TREATMENT
RELAYS & SWITCHES: Indl, Electric
RELAYS: Control Circuit, Ind
RELAYS: Electronic Usage
RELIGIOUS SPLYS WHOLESALERS
REMOVERS & CLEANERS
REMOVERS: Paint
RENT-A-CAR SVCS
RENTAL SVCS: Audio-Visual Eqpt & Sply
RENTAL SVCS: Bicycle
RENTAL SVCS: Business Machine & Electronic Eqpt
RENTAL SVCS: Invalid Splys
RENTAL SVCS: Musical Instrument
RENTAL SVCS: Oil Eqpt
RENTAL SVCS: Personal Items, Exc Recreation & Medical
RENTAL SVCS: Pleasure Boat
RENTAL SVCS: Propane Eqpt
RENTAL SVCS: Sign
RENTAL SVCS: Sound & Lighting Eqpt
RENTAL SVCS: Tent & Tarpaulin
RENTAL SVCS: Tuxedo
RENTAL SVCS: Video Cassette Recorder & Access
RENTAL: Portable Toilet
REPLATING SHOP, EXC SILVERWARE
RESEARCH, DEV & TESTING SVCS, COMM: Chem Lab, Exc Testing
RESEARCH, DEVELOPMENT & TEST SVCS, COMM: Research, Exc Lab
RESEARCH, DEVELOPMENT & TESTING SVCS, COMM: Natural Resource
RESEARCH, DEVELOPMENT & TESTING SVCS, COMM: Research Lab
RESEARCH, DEVELOPMENT & TESTING SVCS, COMMERCIAL: Business
RESEARCH, DEVELOPMENT & TESTING SVCS, COMMERCIAL: Education
RESEARCH, DEVELOPMENT & TESTING SVCS, COMMERCIAL: Energy
RESEARCH, DEVELOPMENT & TESTING SVCS, COMMERCIAL: Food
RESEARCH, DEVELOPMENT & TESTING SVCS, COMMERCIAL: Medical
RESEARCH, DEVELOPMENT & TESTING SVCS, COMMERCIAL: Physical
RESEARCH, DEVELOPMENT SVCS, COMMERCIAL: Indl Lab
RESEARCH, DVLPT & TEST SVCS, COMM: Mkt Analysis or Research
RESEARCH, DVLPT & TESTING SVCS, COMM: Survey, Mktg
RESIDENTIAL REMODELERS
RESINS: Custom Compound Purchased
RESISTORS
RESPIRATORS
RESTAURANT EQPT REPAIR SVCS
RESTAURANT EQPT: Carts
RESTAURANT EQPT: Food Wagons
RESTAURANT EQPT: Sheet Metal
RESTAURANTS: Delicatessen
RESTAURANTS:Full Svc, American
RESTAURANTS:Full Svc, Family
RESTAURANTS:Full Svc, Family, Chain
RESTAURANTS:Full Svc, Family, Independent
RESTAURANTS:Full Svc, Steak
RESTAURANTS:Limited Svc, Coffee Shop
RESTAURANTS:Limited Svc, Drive-In
RESTAURANTS:Limited Svc, Fast-Food, Independent
RESTAURANTS:Limited Svc, Grill
RESTAURANTS:Limited Svc, Ice Cream Stands Or Dairy Bars
RESTAURANTS:Limited Svc, Pizza
RESTAURANTS:Limited Svc, Pizzeria, Chain
RESTAURANTS:Limited Svc, Pizzeria, Independent
RESTAURANTS:Limited Svc, Sandwiches & Submarines Shop
RESTAURANTS:Limited Svc, Snack Shop
RESTAURANTS:Ltd Svc, Ice Cream, Soft Drink/Fountain Stands

RETAIL BAKERY: Bagels
RETAIL BAKERY: Bread
RETAIL BAKERY: Cakes
RETAIL BAKERY: Cookies
RETAIL BAKERY: Doughnuts
RETAIL BAKERY: Pastries
RETAIL BAKERY: Pretzels
RETAIL FIREPLACE STORES
RETAIL LUMBER YARDS
RETAIL STORES: Alarm Signal Systems
RETAIL STORES: Alcoholic Beverage Making Eqpt & Splys
RETAIL STORES: Aquarium Splys
RETAIL STORES: Art & Architectural Splys
RETAIL STORES: Artificial Limbs
RETAIL STORES: Audio-Visual Eqpt & Splys
RETAIL STORES: Awnings
RETAIL STORES: Banners
RETAIL STORES: Batteries, Non-Automotive
RETAIL STORES: Business Machines & Eqpt
RETAIL STORES: Canvas Prdts
RETAIL STORES: Christmas Lights & Decorations
RETAIL STORES: Cleaning Eqpt & Splys
RETAIL STORES: Concrete Prdts, Precast
RETAIL STORES: Convalescent Eqpt & Splys
RETAIL STORES: Cosmetics
RETAIL STORES: Electronic Parts & Eqpt
RETAIL STORES: Engine & Motor Eqpt & Splys
RETAIL STORES: Farm Eqpt & Splys
RETAIL STORES: Farm Machinery, NEC
RETAIL STORES: Fire Extinguishers
RETAIL STORES: Flags
RETAIL STORES: Foam & Foam Prdts
RETAIL STORES: Hair Care Prdts
RETAIL STORES: Hearing Aids
RETAIL STORES: Hospital Eqpt & Splys
RETAIL STORES: Maps & Charts
RETAIL STORES: Medical Apparatus & Splys
RETAIL STORES: Mobile Telephones & Eqpt
RETAIL STORES: Monuments, Finished To Custom Order
RETAIL STORES: Motors, Electric
RETAIL STORES: Orthopedic & Prosthesis Applications
RETAIL STORES: Pet Splys
RETAIL STORES: Posters
RETAIL STORES: Religious Goods
RETAIL STORES: Rock & Stone Specimens
RETAIL STORES: Rubber Stamps
RETAIL STORES: Safety Splys & Eqpt
RETAIL STORES: Sales Barns
RETAIL STORES: Sauna Eqpt & Splys
RETAIL STORES: Spas & Hot Tubs
RETAIL STORES: Swimming Pools, Above Ground
RETAIL STORES: Technical Aids For The Handicapped
RETAIL STORES: Telephone & Communication Eqpt
RETAIL STORES: Telephone Eqpt & Systems
RETAIL STORES: Water Purification Eqpt
RETAIL STORES: Welding Splys
RETORTS: Indl, Smelting, Etc
RETREADING MATERIALS: Tire
REUPHOLSTERY & FURNITURE REPAIR
REUPHOLSTERY SVCS
REWINDING SVCS
RHEOSTATS: Electronic
RIVETS: Metal
ROBOTS, SERVICES OR NOVELTY, WHOLESALE
ROBOTS: Assembly Line
ROBOTS: Indl Spraying, Painting, Etc
ROD & BAR Aluminum
RODS: Steel & Iron, Made In Steel Mills
RODS: Welding
ROLL FORMED SHAPES: Custom
ROLLING MACHINERY: Steel
ROLLING MILL EQPT: Rod Mills
ROLLING MILL MACHINERY
ROLLING MILL ROLLS: Cast Iron
ROLLS & BLANKETS, PRINTERS': Rubber Or Rubberized Fabric
ROLLS & ROLL COVERINGS: Rubber
ROOF DECKS
ROOFING MATERIALS: Asphalt
ROOFING MATERIALS: Sheet Metal
ROOMING & BOARDING HOUSES: Furnished Room Rental
ROTORS: Motor
RUBBER
RUBBER PRDTS: Automotive, Mechanical
RUBBER PRDTS: Mechanical

RUBBER PRDTS: Reclaimed
RUBBER PRDTS: Silicone
RUBBER PRDTS: Sponge
RUBBER STAMP, WHOLESALE
RUBBER, CRUDE, WHOLESALE
RUGS : Hand & Machine Made
RUST PROOFING SVC: Hot Dipping, Metals & Formed Prdts
RUST REMOVERS
RUST RESISTING

S

SAFES & VAULTS: Metal
SAFETY EQPT & SPLYS WHOLESALERS
SAILBOAT BUILDING & REPAIR
SAILS
SALES PROMOTION SVCS
SALT
SALT & SULFUR MINING
SAND & GRAVEL
SAND LIME PRDTS
SAND MINING
SAND: Hygrade
SANDBLASTING EQPT
SANDBLASTING SVC: Building Exterior
SANDSTONE: Crushed & Broken
SANITARY SVC, NEC
SANITARY SVCS: Refuse Collection & Disposal Svcs
SANITARY SVCS: Sanitary Landfill, Operation Of
SANITARY SVCS: Waste Materials, Recycling
SANITARY WARE: Metal
SANITATION CHEMICALS & CLEANING AGENTS
SASHES: Door Or Window, Metal
SATCHELS
SATELLITE COMMUNICATIONS EQPT
SATELLITES: Communications
SAUNA ROOMS: Prefabricated
SAW BLADES
SAWING & PLANING MILLS
SAWING & PLANING MILLS: Custom
SAWS & SAWING EQPT
SAWS: Portable
SCAFFOLDS: Mobile Or Stationary, Metal
SCALE REPAIR SVCS
SCALES & BALANCES, EXC LABORATORY
SCALES: Indl
SCALES: Truck
SCHOOL SPLYS, EXC BOOKS: Wholesalers
SCHOOLS: Elementary & Secondary
SCHOOLS: Vocational, NEC
SCIENTIFIC EQPT REPAIR SVCS
SCIENTIFIC INSTRUMENTS WHOLESALERS
SCRAP & WASTE MATERIALS, WHOLESALE: Ferrous Metal
SCRAP & WASTE MATERIALS, WHOLESALE: Metal
SCRAP & WASTE MATERIALS, WHOLESALE: Nonferrous Metals Scrap
SCRAP & WASTE MATERIALS, WHOLESALE: Oil
SCRAP & WASTE MATERIALS, WHOLESALE: Paper
SCRAP & WASTE MATERIALS, WHOLESALE: Plastics Scrap
SCRAP STEEL CUTTING
SCREENS: Woven Wire
SCREW MACHINE PRDTS
SCREW MACHINES
SCREWS: Metal
SEALANTS
SEALING COMPOUNDS: Sealing, synthetic rubber or plastic
SEALS: Hermetic
SEALS: Oil, Rubber
SEARCH & DETECTION SYSTEMS, EXC RADAR
SEARCH & NAVIGATION SYSTEMS
SEAT BELTS: Automobile & Aircraft
SEATING: Bleacher, Portable
SEATING: Chairs, Table & Arm
SEATING: Stadium
SEATING: Transportation
SECRETARIAL & COURT REPORTING
SECURITY CONTROL EQPT & SYSTEMS
SECURITY DEVICES
SECURITY EQPT STORES
SECURITY PROTECTIVE DEVICES MAINTENANCE & MONITORING SVCS
SECURITY SYSTEMS SERVICES
SEMICONDUCTOR & RELATED DEVICES: Read-Only Memory Or ROM
SEMICONDUCTOR CIRCUIT NETWORKS

PRODUCT INDEX

SEMICONDUCTORS & RELATED DEVICES
SENSORS: Infrared, Solid State
SENSORS: Radiation
SENSORS: Temperature For Motor Windings
SEPTIC TANK CLEANING SVCS
SEPTIC TANKS: Concrete
SEWAGE & WATER TREATMENT EQPT
SEWAGE FACILITIES
SEWER CLEANING EQPT: Power
SEWING CONTRACTORS
SEWING MACHINE STORES
SEWING, NEEDLEWORK & PIECE GOODS STORE: Quilting Matls/Splys
SEWING, NEEDLEWORK & PIECE GOODS STORES: Sewing & Needlework
SHADES: Window
SHAFTS: Flexible
SHAPES & PILINGS, STRUCTURAL: Steel
SHAPES: Extruded, Aluminum, NEC
SHEET METAL SPECIALTIES, EXC STAMPED
SHEETING: Laminated Plastic
SHEETS & STRIPS: Aluminum
SHEETS: Fabric, From Purchased Materials
SHEETS: Hard Rubber
SHEETS: Solid Fiber, Made From Purchased Materials
SHELLAC
SHELTERED WORKSHOPS
SHELVES & SHELVING: Wood
SHELVING, MADE FROM PURCHASED WIRE
SHELVING: Office & Store, Exc Wood
SHIP BUILDING & REPAIRING: Cargo Vessels
SHIP BUILDING & REPAIRING: Rigging, Marine
SHIPBUILDING & REPAIR
SHIPPING AGENTS
SHIPS WHOLESALERS
SHOE & BOOT ACCESS
SHOE MATERIALS: Counters
SHOE MATERIALS: Quarters
SHOE MATERIALS: Rands
SHOE STORES
SHOE STORES: Athletic
SHOE STORES: Custom
SHOE STORES: Custom & Orthopedic
SHOE STORES: Men's
SHOE STORES: Orthopedic
SHOES & BOOTS WHOLESALERS
SHOES: Athletic, Exc Rubber Or Plastic
SHOES: Canvas, Rubber Soled
SHOES: Infants' & Children's
SHOES: Men's
SHOES: Orthopedic, Children's
SHOES: Orthopedic, Men's
SHOES: Orthopedic, Women's
SHOES: Plastic Or Rubber
SHOES: Plastic Or Rubber Soles With Fabric Uppers
SHOES: Women's
SHOES: Women's, Dress
SHOPPING CART REPAIR SVCS
SHOPPING CENTERS & MALLS
SHOT PEENING SVC
SHOW CARD & POSTER PAINTING
SHOWCASES & DISPLAY FIXTURES: Office & Store
SHOWER STALLS: Plastic & Fiberglass
SHREDDERS: Indl & Commercial
SHUNTS: Electric
SHUTTERS, DOOR & WINDOW: Metal
SHUTTERS, DOOR & WINDOW: Plastic
SIDING & STRUCTURAL MATERIALS: Wood
SIDING MATERIALS
SIDING: Plastic
SIDING: Sheet Metal
SIGN LETTERING & PAINTING SVCS
SIGN PAINTING & LETTERING SHOP
SIGNALING APPARATUS: Electric
SIGNALS: Traffic Control, Electric
SIGNS & ADVERTISING SPECIALTIES
SIGNS & ADVERTISING SPECIALTIES: Artwork, Advertising
SIGNS & ADVERTISING SPECIALTIES: Displays, Paint Process
SIGNS & ADVERTISING SPECIALTIES: Letters For Signs, Metal
SIGNS & ADVERTISING SPECIALTIES: Novelties
SIGNS & ADVERTISING SPECIALTIES: Scoreboards, Electric
SIGNS & ADVERTISING SPECIALTIES: Signs
SIGNS & ADVERTSG SPECIALTIES: Displays/Cutouts Window/Lobby
SIGNS, EXC ELECTRIC, WHOLESALE
SIGNS: Electrical
SIGNS: Neon
SILICON: Pure
SILICONE RESINS
SILICONES
SILK SCREEN DESIGN SVCS
SILLS: Concrete
SILVER ORE MINING
SILVERWARE & PLATED WARE
SIMULATORS: Flight
SIRENS: Vehicle, Marine, Indl & Warning
SKIDS: Wood
SKILL TRAINING CENTER
SKIN CARE PRDTS: Suntan Lotions & Oils
SKYLIGHTS
SLABS: Steel
SLAG PRDTS
SLAG: Crushed Or Ground
SLATE PRDTS
SLAUGHTERING & MEAT PACKING
SLINGS: Lifting, Made From Purchased Wire
SLINGS: Rope
SLIP RINGS
SLIPPERS: House
SMOKE DETECTORS
SNOW PLOWING SVCS
SNOW REMOVAL EQPT: Residential
SNOWMOBILE DEALERS
SNOWMOBILES
SOAPS & DETERGENTS
SOAPS & DETERGENTS: Scouring Compounds
SOAPS & DETERGENTS: Textile
SOCIAL CLUBS
SOCIAL SVCS, HANDICAPPED
SOCKETS: Electric
SOFT DRINKS WHOLESALERS
SOFTWARE PUBLISHERS: Application
SOFTWARE PUBLISHERS: Business & Professional
SOFTWARE PUBLISHERS: Computer Utilities
SOFTWARE PUBLISHERS: Education
SOFTWARE PUBLISHERS: NEC
SOFTWARE PUBLISHERS: Operating Systems
SOFTWARE PUBLISHERS: Publisher's
SOFTWARE TRAINING, COMPUTER
SOLAR CELLS
SOLAR HEATING EQPT
SOLDERING EQPT: Electrical, Exc Handheld
SOLDERING EQPT: Irons Or Coppers
SOLENOIDS
SOLID CONTAINING UNITS: Concrete
SOLVENTS
SOLVENTS: Organic
SONAR SYSTEMS & EQPT
SOUND EFFECTS & MUSIC PRODUCTION: Motion Picture
SOUND EQPT: Electric
SOUND RECORDING STUDIOS
SOUVENIRS, WHOLESALE
SOYBEAN PRDTS
SPACE VEHICLE EQPT
SPAS
SPEAKER SYSTEMS
SPECIAL EVENTS DECORATION SVCS
SPECIALTY FOOD STORES: Coffee
SPECIALTY FOOD STORES: Dietetic Foods
SPECIALTY FOOD STORES: Health & Dietetic Food
SPECIALTY OUTPATIENT CLINICS, NEC
SPECIALTY SAWMILL PRDTS
SPEED CHANGERS
SPICE & HERB STORES
SPINDLES: Textile
SPONGES, ANIMAL, WHOLESALE
SPONGES: Bleached & Dyed
SPONGES: Plastic
SPOOLS: Indl
SPORTING & ATHLETIC GOODS: Arrows, Archery
SPORTING & ATHLETIC GOODS: Balls, Baseball, Football, Etc
SPORTING & ATHLETIC GOODS: Bowling Alleys & Access
SPORTING & ATHLETIC GOODS: Bows, Archery
SPORTING & ATHLETIC GOODS: Camping Eqpt & Splys
SPORTING & ATHLETIC GOODS: Exercising Cycles
SPORTING & ATHLETIC GOODS: Fishing Bait, Artificial
SPORTING & ATHLETIC GOODS: Fishing Eqpt
SPORTING & ATHLETIC GOODS: Fishing Tackle, General
SPORTING & ATHLETIC GOODS: Football Eqpt & Splys, NEC
SPORTING & ATHLETIC GOODS: Gymnasium Eqpt
SPORTING & ATHLETIC GOODS: Hockey Eqpt & Splys, NEC
SPORTING & ATHLETIC GOODS: Hooks, Fishing
SPORTING & ATHLETIC GOODS: Hunting Eqpt
SPORTING & ATHLETIC GOODS: Masks, Hockey, Baseball, Etc
SPORTING & ATHLETIC GOODS: Protective Sporting Eqpt
SPORTING & ATHLETIC GOODS: Shafts, Golf Club
SPORTING & ATHLETIC GOODS: Shooting Eqpt & Splys, General
SPORTING & ATHLETIC GOODS: Shuffleboards & Shuffleboard Eqpt
SPORTING & ATHLETIC GOODS: Skateboards
SPORTING & ATHLETIC GOODS: Snow Skis
SPORTING & ATHLETIC GOODS: Strings, Tennis Racket
SPORTING & ATHLETIC GOODS: Targets, Archery & Rifle Shooting
SPORTING & ATHLETIC GOODS: Team Sports Eqpt
SPORTING & ATHLETIC GOODS: Trampolines & Eqpt
SPORTING & ATHLETIC GOODS: Water Sports Eqpt
SPORTING & RECREATIONAL GOODS & SPLYS WHOLESALERS
SPORTING & RECREATIONAL GOODS, WHOL: Sharpeners, Sporting
SPORTING & RECREATIONAL GOODS, WHOLESALE: Athletic Goods
SPORTING & RECREATIONAL GOODS, WHOLESALE: Boat Access & Part
SPORTING & RECREATIONAL GOODS, WHOLESALE: Canoes
SPORTING & RECREATIONAL GOODS, WHOLESALE: Fishing Tackle
SPORTING & RECREATIONAL GOODS, WHOLESALE: Fitness
SPORTING & RECREATIONAL GOODS, WHOLESALE: Golf
SPORTING & RECREATIONAL GOODS, WHOLESALE: Golf & Skiing
SPORTING & RECREATIONAL GOODS, WHOLESALE: Gymnasium
SPORTING & RECREATIONAL GOODS, WHOLESALE: Hunting
SPORTING FIREARMS WHOLESALERS
SPORTING GOODS
SPORTING GOODS STORES, NEC
SPORTING GOODS STORES: Archery Splys
SPORTING GOODS STORES: Camping & Backpacking Eqpt
SPORTING GOODS STORES: Firearms
SPORTING GOODS STORES: Fishing Eqpt
SPORTING GOODS STORES: Playground Eqpt
SPORTING GOODS STORES: Skiing Eqpt
SPORTING GOODS STORES: Soccer Splys
SPORTING GOODS STORES: Specialty Sport Splys, NEC
SPORTING GOODS STORES: Team sports Eqpt
SPORTING GOODS: Archery
SPORTING GOODS: Fishing Nets
SPORTING GOODS: Hammocks, Fabric, Made From Purchased Mat
SPORTS APPAREL STORES
SPORTS PROMOTION SVCS
SPOUTING: Plastic & Fiberglass Reinforced
SPRAYING & DUSTING EQPT
SPRAYING EQPT: Agricultural
SPRINGS: Automobile
SPRINGS: Clock, Precision
SPRINGS: Coiled Flat
SPRINGS: Cold Formed
SPRINGS: Instrument, Precision
SPRINGS: Leaf, Automobile, Locomotive, Etc
SPRINGS: Mechanical, Precision
SPRINGS: Precision
SPRINGS: Steel
SPRINGS: Torsion Bar
SPRINGS: Wire
SPRINKLER SYSTEMS: Field
SPRINKLING SYSTEMS: Fire Control
SPROCKETS: Power Transmission
STACKING MACHINES: Automatic
STADIUM EVENT OPERATOR SERVICES
STAFFING, EMPLOYMENT PLACEMENT
STAGE LIGHTING SYSTEMS
STAINLESS STEEL

PRODUCT INDEX

STAINLESS STEEL WARE
STAINS: Wood
STAIRCASES & STAIRS, WOOD
STAMPINGS: Automotive
STAMPINGS: Metal
STANDS & RACKS: Engine, Metal
STARTERS & CONTROLLERS: Motor, Electric
STARTERS: Electric Motor
STARTERS: Motor
STATIONARY & OFFICE SPLYS, WHOLESALE: Inked Ribbons
STATIONARY & OFFICE SPLYS, WHOLESALE: Office Filing Splys
STATIONERY & OFFICE SPLYS WHOLESALERS
STATIONERY PRDTS
STATORS REWINDING SVCS
STEEL & ALLOYS: Tool & Die
STEEL FABRICATORS
STEEL MILLS
STEEL SHEET: Cold-Rolled
STEEL WOOL
STEEL, COLD-ROLLED: Sheet Or Strip, From Own Hot-Rolled
STEEL, COLD-ROLLED: Strip NEC, From Purchased Hot-Rolled
STEEL, COLD-ROLLED: Strip Or Wire
STEEL, HOT-ROLLED: Sheet Or Strip
STEEL: Cold-Rolled
STEERING SYSTEMS & COMPONENTS
STENCILS
STERILIZERS, BARBER & BEAUTY SHOP
STITCHING SVCS
STITCHING SVCS: Custom
STOKERS: Mechanical, Domestic Or Indl
STONE: Crushed & Broken, NEC
STONE: Dimension, NEC
STONE: Quarrying & Processing, Own Stone Prdts
STOOLS: Factory
STORE FIXTURES: Exc Wood
STORE FIXTURES: Wood
STORES: Auto & Home Supply
STORES: Drapery & Upholstery
STOVES: Wood & Coal Burning
STRAIN GAGES: Solid State
STRAPS: Cotton Webbing
STRAPS: Spindle Banding
STRAWS: Drinking, Made From Purchased Materials
STRINGING BEADS
STRUCTURAL SUPPORT & BUILDING MATERIAL: Concrete
STUDIOS: Artists & Artists' Studios
STUDS & JOISTS: Sheet Metal
SUBMARINE BUILDING & REPAIR
SUBPRESSES, METALWORKING
SUNDRIES & RELATED PRDTS: Medical & Laboratory, Rubber
SUNGLASSES, WHOLESALE
SUNROOFS: Motor Vehicle
SUPERMARKETS & OTHER GROCERY STORES
SURFACE ACTIVE AGENTS
SURFACE ACTIVE AGENTS: Emulsifiers, Exc Food & Pharmaceuticl
SURFACE ACTIVE AGENTS: Textile Processing Assistants
SURFACERS: Concrete Grinding
SURGICAL APPLIANCES & SPLYS
SURGICAL APPLIANCES & SPLYS
SURGICAL EQPT: See Also Instruments
SURGICAL IMPLANTS
SURVEYING & MAPPING: Land Parcels
SUSPENSION SYSTEMS: Acoustical, Metal
SVC ESTABLISH EQPT, WHOLESALE: Carpet/Rug Clean Eqpt & Sply
SVC ESTABLISHMENT EQPT & SPLYS WHOLESALERS
SVC ESTABLISHMENT EQPT, WHOL: Cleaning & Maint Eqpt & Splys
SVC ESTABLISHMENT EQPT, WHOL: Concrete Burial Vaults & Boxes
SVC ESTABLISHMENT EQPT, WHOLESALE: Cemetery Splys & Eqpt
SVC ESTABLISHMENT EQPT, WHOLESALE: Firefighting Eqpt
SVC ESTABLISHMENT EQPT, WHOLESALE: Shredders, Indl & Comm
SVC ESTABLISHMENT EQPT, WHOLESALE: Vacuum Cleaning Systems
SVC ESTABLISHMENT EQPT, WHOLESALE: Vending Machines & Splys
SWEEPING COMPOUNDS
SWIMMING POOLS, EQPT & SPLYS: Wholesalers
SWITCHBOARDS & PARTS: Power
SWITCHES
SWITCHES: Electric Power
SWITCHES: Electronic
SWITCHES: Electronic Applications
SWITCHES: Solenoid
SWITCHES: Time, Electrical Switchgear Apparatus
SWITCHGEAR & SWITCHBOARD APPARATUS
SYNTHETIC RESIN FINISHED PRDTS, NEC
SYRUPS, DRINK
SYSTEMS ENGINEERING: Computer Related
SYSTEMS INTEGRATION SVCS
SYSTEMS INTEGRATION SVCS: Local Area Network
SYSTEMS INTEGRATION SVCS: Office Computer Automation
SYSTEMS SOFTWARE DEVELOPMENT SVCS

T

TABLE OR COUNTERTOPS, PLASTIC LAMINATED
TABLES: Lift, Hydraulic
TABLEWARE OR KITCHEN ARTICLES: Commercial, Fine Earthenware
TAGS & LABELS: Paper
TALLOW: Animal
TANK COMPONENTS: Military, Specialized
TANK REPAIR & CLEANING SVCS
TANK REPAIR SVCS
TANKS & OTHER TRACKED VEHICLE CMPNTS
TANKS: Concrete
TANKS: Cryogenic, Metal
TANKS: For Tank Trucks, Metal Plate
TANKS: Fuel, Including Oil & Gas, Metal Plate
TANKS: Lined, Metal
TANKS: Military, Amphibian
TANKS: Plastic & Fiberglass
TANKS: Standard Or Custom Fabricated, Metal Plate
TANNERIES: Leather
TANNING SALONS
TAPE PRINT UNITS: Computer
TAPES: Fabric
TAPES: Plastic Coated
TAPES: Pressure Sensitive
TAPES: Tie, Woven Or Braided
TAPS
TARPAULINS
TARPAULINS, WHOLESALE
TAX RETURN PREPARATION SVCS
TAXI CABS
TAXIDERMISTS
TECHNICAL WRITING SVCS
TELECOMMUNICATION EQPT REPAIR SVCS, EXC TELEPHONES
TELECOMMUNICATION SYSTEMS & EQPT
TELECOMMUNICATIONS CARRIERS & SVCS: Wired
TELEGRAPH OR TELEPHONE CARRIER & REPEATER EQPT
TELEMARKETING BUREAUS
TELEMETERING EQPT
TELEPHONE COUNSELING SVCS
TELEPHONE EQPT: Modems
TELEPHONE EQPT: NEC
TELEPHONE SVCS
TELEPHONE: Fiber Optic Systems
TELEPHONE: Headsets
TELESCOPES
TELEVISION BROADCASTING & COMMUNICATIONS EQPT
TELEVISION BROADCASTING STATIONS
TELEVISION SETS
TELEVISION: Closed Circuit Eqpt
TEMPERING: Metal
TEMPORARY HELP SVCS
TENT REPAIR SHOP
TENTS: All Materials
TEST BORING, METAL MINING
TESTERS: Battery
TESTERS: Environmental
TESTERS: Hardness
TESTERS: Physical Property
TESTERS: Water, Exc Indl Process
TESTING SVCS
TEXTILE & APPAREL SVCS
TEXTILE FINISHING: Embossing, Cotton, Broadwoven
TEXTILE PRDTS: Hand Woven & Crocheted
TEXTILE: Finishing, Cotton Broadwoven
TEXTILE: Finishing, Raw Stock NEC
TEXTILE: Goods, NEC
TEXTILES
TEXTILES: Linen Fabrics
TEXTILES: Linings, Carpet, Exc Felt
TEXTILES: Mill Waste & Remnant
TEXTILES: Tops, Manmade Fiber
THEATRICAL LIGHTING SVCS
THEATRICAL PRODUCERS & SVCS
THEATRICAL PRODUCTION SVCS
THERMOCOUPLES
THERMOCOUPLES: Indl Process
THERMOELECTRIC DEVICES: Solid State
THERMOMETERS: Indl
THERMOPLASTIC MATERIALS
THERMOPLASTICS
THERMOSETTING MATERIALS
THIN FILM CIRCUITS
THREAD: Embroidery
THREAD: Hand Knitting
THREAD: Natural Fiber
TIES, FORM: Metal
TILE: Brick & Structural, Clay
TILE: Clay Refractory
TILE: Clay, Drain & Structural
TILE: Stamped Metal, Floor Or Wall
TILE: Wall, Fiberboard
TIMBER PRDTS WHOLESALERS
TIMING DEVICES: Cycle & Program Controllers
TIN
TIRE & INNER TUBE MATERIALS & RELATED PRDTS
TIRE CORD & FABRIC
TIRE CORD & FABRIC: Cord, Rubber, Reinforcing
TIRE CORD & FABRIC: Steel
TIRE DEALERS
TIRE INNER-TUBES
TIRE RECAPPING & RETREADING
TIRES & INNER TUBES
TIRES & TUBES WHOLESALERS
TIRES: Cushion Or Solid Rubber
TITANIUM MILL PRDTS
TITLE ABSTRACT & SETTLEMENT OFFICES
TOBACCO & TOBACCO PRDTS WHOLESALERS
TOBACCO STORES & STANDS
TOBACCO: Cigarettes
TOBACCO: Smoking
TOILET SEATS: Wood
TOILETRIES, COSMETICS & PERFUME STORES
TOILETRIES, WHOLESALE: Razor Blades
TOILETRIES, WHOLESALE: Toilet Articles
TOILETRIES, WHOLESALE: Toilet Soap
TOILETRIES, WHOLESALE: Toiletries
TOILETRIES, WHOLESALE: Toothbrushes, Exc Electric
TOILETS: Portable Chemical, Plastics
TOLLS: Caulking
TOOL & DIE STEEL
TOOL REPAIR SVCS
TOOLS: Carpenters', Including Levels & Chisels, Exc Saws
TOOLS: Hand
TOOLS: Hand, Ironworkers'
TOOLS: Hand, Power
TOOLS: Hand, Shovels Or Spades
TOOLS: Soldering
TOOTHBRUSHES: Exc Electric
TOUR OPERATORS
TOWERS, SECTIONS: Transmission, Radio & Television
TOWING & TUGBOAT SVC
TOWING BARS & SYSTEMS
TOWING SVCS: Marine
TOWING SVCS: Mobile Homes
TOYS
TOYS & HOBBY GOODS & SPLYS, WHOLESALE: Arts/Crafts Eqpt/Sply
TOYS & HOBBY GOODS & SPLYS, WHOLESALE: Dolls
TOYS & HOBBY GOODS & SPLYS, WHOLESALE: Toys & Games
TOYS & HOBBY GOODS & SPLYS, WHOLESALE: Toys, NEC
TOYS, HOBBY GOODS & SPLYS WHOLESALERS
TOYS: Rubber
TRADE SHOW ARRANGEMENT SVCS
TRAILER PARKS

PRODUCT INDEX

TRAILERS & CHASSIS: Camping
TRAILERS & PARTS: Boat
TRAILERS & PARTS: Truck & Semi's
TRAILERS & TRAILER EQPT
TRAILERS OR VANS: Horse Transportation, Fifth-Wheel Type
TRAILERS: Bodies
TRAILERS: Bus, Tractor Type
TRAILERS: House, Exc Permanent Dwellings
TRAILERS: Semitrailers, Missile Transportation
TRAILERS: Semitrailers, Truck Tractors
TRAILERS: Truck, Chassis
TRANSDUCERS: Electrical Properties
TRANSDUCERS: Pressure
TRANSFORMERS: Control
TRANSFORMERS: Distribution
TRANSFORMERS: Distribution, Electric
TRANSFORMERS: Doorbell, Electric
TRANSFORMERS: Electric
TRANSFORMERS: Electronic
TRANSFORMERS: Fluorescent Lighting
TRANSFORMERS: Furnace, Electric
TRANSFORMERS: Power Related
TRANSFORMERS: Rectifier
TRANSFORMERS: Toy
TRANSFORMERS: Voltage Regulating
TRANSLATION & INTERPRETATION SVCS
TRANSMISSIONS: Motor Vehicle
TRANSPORTATION BROKERS: Truck
TRANSPORTATION EPQT & SPLYS, WHOLESALE: Marine Crafts/Splys
TRANSPORTATION EPQT & SPLYS, WHOLESALE: Tanks & Tank Compnts
TRANSPORTATION EQUIPMENT, NEC
TRANSPORTATION SVCS: Rental, Local
TRANSPORTATION: Bus Transit Systems
TRANSPORTATION: Local Passenger, NEC
TRANSPORTATION: Transit Systems, NEC
TRAPS: Animal, Iron Or Steel
TRAPS: Stem
TRAVEL AGENCIES
TRAVEL TRAILER DEALERS
TRAVEL TRAILERS & CAMPERS
TRAVERTINE: Crushed & Broken
TRAYS: Plastic
TROPHIES, NEC
TROPHIES, PLATED, ALL METALS
TROPHIES, WHOLESALE
TROPHIES: Metal, Exc Silver
TROPHY & PLAQUE STORES
TRUCK & BUS BODIES: Bus Bodies
TRUCK & BUS BODIES: Car Carrier
TRUCK & BUS BODIES: Cement Mixer
TRUCK & BUS BODIES: Dump Truck
TRUCK & BUS BODIES: Garbage Or Refuse Truck
TRUCK & BUS BODIES: Motor Vehicle, Specialty
TRUCK & BUS BODIES: Truck Beds
TRUCK & BUS BODIES: Truck, Motor Vehicle
TRUCK & BUS BODIES: Utility Truck
TRUCK & BUS BODIES: Van Bodies
TRUCK BODIES: Body Parts
TRUCK BODY SHOP
TRUCK GENERAL REPAIR SVC
TRUCK PAINTING & LETTERING SVCS
TRUCK PARTS & ACCESSORIES: Wholesalers
TRUCKING & HAULING SVCS: Animal & Farm Prdt
TRUCKING & HAULING SVCS: Contract Basis
TRUCKING & HAULING SVCS: Furniture, Local W/out Storage
TRUCKING & HAULING SVCS: Garbage, Collect/Transport Only
TRUCKING & HAULING SVCS: Lumber & Log, Local
TRUCKING & HAULING SVCS: Mail Carriers, Contract
TRUCKING & HAULING SVCS: Mobile Homes
TRUCKING & HAULING SVCS: Petroleum, Local
TRUCKING & HAULING SVCS: Steel, Local
TRUCKING & HAULING SVCS: Timber, Local
TRUCKING, AUTOMOBILE CARRIER
TRUCKING, DUMP
TRUCKING: Except Local
TRUCKING: Local, With Storage
TRUCKING: Local, Without Storage
TRUCKS & TRACTORS: Industrial
TRUCKS: Forklift
TRUCKS: Indl
TRUNKS

TRUSSES & FRAMING: Prefabricated Metal
TRUSSES: Wood, Floor
TRUSSES: Wood, Roof
TUBE & PIPE MILL EQPT
TUBE & TUBING FABRICATORS
TUBES: Extruded Or Drawn, Aluminum
TUBES: Finned, For Heat Transfer
TUBES: Gas Or Vapor
TUBES: Paper
TUBES: Steel & Iron
TUBES: Welded, Aluminum
TUBES: Wrought, Welded Or Lock Joint
TUBING: Copper
TUBING: Flexible, Metallic
TUBING: Plastic
TUBING: Rubber
TUBING: Seamless
TUMBLING
TUNGSTEN MILL PRDTS
TURBINE GENERATOR SET UNITS: Hydraulic, Complete
TURBINES & TURBINE GENERATOR SET UNITS, COMPLETE
TURBINES & TURBINE GENERATOR SETS
TURBINES: Hydraulic, Complete
TURKEY PROCESSING & SLAUGHTERING
TURNKEY VENDORS: Computer Systems
TWINE PRDTS
TWINE: Binder & Baler
TYPESETTING SVC
TYPESETTING SVC: Computer
TYPESETTING SVC: Hand Composition

U

ULTRASONIC EQPT: Cleaning, Exc Med & Dental
UMBRELLAS & CANES
UNDERGROUND IRON ORE MINING
UNIFORM STORES
UNIVERSITY
UNSUPPORTED PLASTICS: Tile
UPHOLSTERY FILLING MATERIALS
UPHOLSTERY MATERIAL
URNS: Cut Stone
USED CAR DEALERS
USED CLOTHING STORES
USED MERCHANDISE STORES
USED MERCHANDISE STORES: Office Furniture & Store Fixtures
UTENSILS: Household, Cooking & Kitchen, Metal
UTILITY TRAILER DEALERS

V

VACUUM CLEANER REPAIR SVCS
VACUUM CLEANER STORES
VACUUM CLEANERS: Household
VACUUM CLEANERS: Indl Type
VACUUM CLEANERS: Wholesalers
VALUE-ADDED RESELLERS: Computer Systems
VALVE REPAIR SVCS, INDL
VALVES
VALVES & PARTS: Gas, Indl
VALVES & PIPE FITTINGS
VALVES & REGULATORS: Pressure, Indl
VALVES: Aerosol, Metal
VALVES: Aircraft, Control, Hydraulic & Pneumatic
VALVES: Aircraft, Fluid Power
VALVES: Control, Automatic
VALVES: Engine
VALVES: Fluid Power, Control, Hydraulic & pneumatic
VALVES: Indl
VALVES: Plumbing & Heating
VALVES: Regulating & Control, Automatic
VALVES: Regulating, Process Control
VALVES: Water Works
VAN CONVERSIONS
VAN CONVERSIONS
VEHICLE DRIVING SCHOOL
VEHICLES: All Terrain
VEHICLES: Recreational
VENDING MACHINE OPERATORS: Sandwich & Hot Food
VENDING MACHINES & PARTS
VENETIAN BLINDS & SHADES
VENTILATING EQPT. Metal
VENTILATING EQPT: Sheet Metal
VESSELS: Process, Indl, Metal Plate
VETERINARY PHARMACEUTICAL PREPARATIONS

VETERINARY PRDTS: Instruments & Apparatus
VIBRATORS: Concrete Construction
VIBRATORS: Interrupter
VIDEO & AUDIO EQPT, WHOLESALE
VIDEO PRODUCTION SVCS
VIDEO REPAIR SVCS
VIDEO TAPE PRODUCTION SVCS
VINYL RESINS, NEC
VISES: Machine
VISUAL COMMUNICATIONS SYSTEMS
VITAMINS: Natural Or Synthetic, Uncompounded, Bulk
VITAMINS: Pharmaceutical Preparations
VOCATIONAL REHABILITATION AGENCY
VOCATIONAL TRAINING AGENCY

W

WALLBOARD, EXC GYPSUM
WALLS: Curtain, Metal
WAREHOUSING & STORAGE FACILITIES, NEC
WAREHOUSING & STORAGE, REFRIGERATED: Cold Storage Or Refrig
WAREHOUSING & STORAGE, REFRIGERATED: Frozen Or Refrig Goods
WAREHOUSING & STORAGE: Farm Prdts
WAREHOUSING & STORAGE: General
WAREHOUSING & STORAGE: General
WAREHOUSING & STORAGE: Liquid
WAREHOUSING & STORAGE: Miniwarehouse
WAREHOUSING & STORAGE: Self Storage
WAREHOUSING & STORAGE: Textile
WARM AIR HEATING & AC EQPT & SPLYS, WHOL: Dust Collecting
WARM AIR HEATING & AC EQPT & SPLYS, WHOLESALE Air Filters
WARM AIR HEATING & AC EQPT & SPLYS, WHOLESALE Furnaces, Elec
WARM AIR HEATING/AC EQPT/SPLYS, WHOL Dehumidifiers, Exc Port
WARM AIR HEATING/AC EQPT/SPLYS, WHOL Warm Air Htg Eqpt/Splys
WASHERS
WASHERS: Metal
WASHING MACHINES: Household
WATCH REPAIR SVCS
WATER HEATERS
WATER HEATERS WHOLESALERS EXCEPT ELECTRIC
WATER PURIFICATION EQPT: Household
WATER PURIFICATION PRDTS: Chlorination Tablets & Kits
WATER SOFTENER SVCS
WATER SOFTENING WHOLESALERS
WATER SPLY: Irrigation
WATER TREATMENT EQPT: Indl
WATER: Distilled
WATER: Mineral, Carbonated, Canned & Bottled, Etc
WATER: Pasteurized & Mineral, Bottled & Canned
WATER: Pasteurized, Canned & Bottled, Etc
WATERPROOFING COMPOUNDS
WAVEGUIDE STRUCTURES: Accelerating
WAX Sealing wax
WEATHER STRIP: Sponge Rubber
WEATHER VANES
WEDDING CONSULTING SVCS
WELDING & CUTTING APPARATUS & ACCESS, NEC
WELDING EQPT
WELDING EQPT & SPLYS WHOLESALERS
WELDING EQPT & SPLYS: Arc Welders, Transformer-Rectifier
WELDING EQPT & SPLYS: Electrodes
WELDING EQPT & SPLYS: Resistance, Electric
WELDING EQPT & SPLYS: Spot, Electric
WELDING EQPT & SPLYS: Wire, Bare & Coated
WELDING EQPT REPAIR SVCS
WELDING EQPT: Electric
WELDING EQPT: Electrical
WELDING MACHINES & EQPT: Ultrasonic
WELDING REPAIR SVC
WELDING SPLYS, EXC GASES: Wholesalers
WELDING TIPS: Heat Resistant, Metal
WELDMENTS
WET CORN MILLING
WHEEL BALANCING EQPT: Automotive
WHEELCHAIR LIFTS
WHEELCHAIRS
WHEELS
WHEELS & GRINDSTONES, EXC ARTIFICIAL: Abrasive

PRODUCT INDEX

WHEELS & PARTS
WHEELS, GRINDING: Artificial
WHEELS: Abrasive
WHEELS: Buffing & Polishing
WHEELS: Disc, Wheelbarrow, Stroller, Etc, Stamped Metal
WHEELS: Iron & Steel, Locomotive & Car
WICKER PRDTS
WICKING
WIGS & HAIRPIECES
WIGS, DOLL: Hair
WINCHES
WIND CHIMES
WINDINGS: Coil, Electronic
WINDMILLS: Electric Power Generation
WINDMILLS: Farm Type
WINDOW & DOOR FRAMES
WINDOW FRAMES & SASHES: Plastic
WINDOW FRAMES, MOLDING & TRIM: Vinyl
WINDOW FURNISHINGS WHOLESALERS
WINDOW SQUEEGEES
WINDOWS: Frames, Wood
WINDOWS: Louver, Glass, Wood Framed
WINDOWS: Storm, Wood
WINDOWS: Wood
WINDSHIELD WIPER SYSTEMS
WINE CELLARS, BONDED: Wine, Blended
WIRE
WIRE & CABLE: Aluminum
WIRE & CABLE: Aluminum
WIRE & CABLE: Nonferrous, Automotive, Exc Ignition Sets
WIRE & CABLE: Nonferrous, Building
WIRE & WIRE PRDTS
WIRE CLOTH & WOVEN WIRE PRDTS, MADE FROM PURCHASED WIRE
WIRE CLOTH: Cylinder, Made From Purchased Wire
WIRE FABRIC: Welded Steel
WIRE FENCING & ACCESS WHOLESALERS
WIRE MATERIALS: Steel
WIRE PRDTS: Steel & Iron
WIRE WHOLESALERS
WIRE: Communication
WIRE: Magnet
WIRE: Mesh
WIRE: Nonferrous
WIRE: Wire, Ferrous Or Iron
WOMEN'S & CHILDREN'S CLOTHING WHOLESALERS, NEC
WOMEN'S & GIRLS' SPORTSWEAR WHOLESALERS
WOMEN'S CLOTHING STORES
WOMEN'S SPORTSWEAR STORES
WOOD CARVINGS, WHOLESALE
WOOD CHIPS, PRODUCED AT THE MILL
WOOD FENCING WHOLESALERS
WOOD PRDTS
WOOD PRDTS: Applicators
WOOD PRDTS: Barrels & Barrel Parts
WOOD PRDTS: Beekeeping Splys
WOOD PRDTS: Engraved
WOOD PRDTS: Hampers, Laundry
WOOD PRDTS: Laundry
WOOD PRDTS: Mantels
WOOD PRDTS: Moldings, Unfinished & Prefinished
WOOD PRDTS: Mulch Or Sawdust
WOOD PRDTS: Mulch, Wood & Bark
WOOD PRDTS: Novelties, Fiber
WOOD PRDTS: Oars & Paddles
WOOD PRDTS: Outdoor, Structural
WOOD PRDTS: Paint Sticks
WOOD PRDTS: Poles
WOOD PRDTS: Shoe & Boot Prdts
WOOD PRDTS: Signboards
WOOD PRDTS: Survey Stakes
WOOD PRDTS: Trim
WOOD PRDTS: Veneer Work, Inlaid
WOOD PRODUCTS: Reconstituted
WOOD TREATING: Bridges & Trestles
WOOD TREATING: Creosoting
WOOD TREATING: Flooring, Block
WOOD TREATING: Structural Lumber & Timber
WOODWORK & TRIM: Interior & Ornamental
WOODWORK: Carved & Turned
WOODWORK: Interior & Ornamental, NEC
WOODWORK: Ornamental, Cornices, Mantels, Etc.
WOVEN WIRE PRDTS, NEC
WREATHS: Artificial
WRENCHES

X

X-RAY EQPT & TUBES

Y

YARN : Crochet, Spun
YARN MILLS: Texturizing, Throwing & Twisting
YARN WHOLESALERS
YARN: Knitting, Spun
YOGURT WHOLESALERS

Z

ZINC ORE MINING

PRODUCT SECTION

Indicates approximate employment figure
A = Over 500 employees, B = 251-500
C = 101-250, D = 51-100, E = 20-50
F = 10-19, G = 3-9

Product category ──→ **BOXES:** *Folding*
Edgar & Son Paperboard ....G....... 999 999-9999
Yourtown *(G-11480)*
Ready Box Co............................E....... 999 999-9999
City ──→ Anytown *(G-7097)*

- Business phone
- Geographic Section entry number where full company information appears.

See footnotes for symbols and codes identification.
- Refer to the Industrial Product Index preceding this section to locate product headings.

ABRASIVES

3M Company.................................E....... 313 372-4200
 Detroit *(G-3824)*
Abrasive Diamond Tool Company...E....... 248 588-4800
 Madison Heights *(G-10179)*
Abrasive Finishing Inc.....................G....... 734 433-9236
 Chelsea *(G-2698)*
Abrasive Materials LLC...................G....... 517 437-4796
 Hillsdale *(G-7512)*
Auto Quip Inc................................F....... 810 364-3366
 Kimball *(G-9042)*
Belanger Inc................................G....... 248 349-7010
 Northville *(G-11678)*
Botsg Inc....................................D....... 231 929-2121
 Traverse City *(G-15918)*
Cdp Diamond Products Inc..............E....... 734 591-1041
 Livonia *(G-9678)*
Crippen Manufacturing Company.......E....... 989 681-4323
 Saint Louis *(G-14361)*
Detroit Abrasives Company..............G....... 989 725-2405
 Owosso *(G-12289)*
Di-Coat Corporation......................E....... 248 349-1211
 Novi *(G-11868)*
Diamond Tool Manufacturing Inc........E....... 734 416-1900
 Plymouth *(G-12611)*
E C Moore Company.....................D....... 313 581-7878
 Dearborn *(G-3696)*
Ervin Industries Inc.......................E....... 517 423-5477
 Tecumseh *(G-15792)*
Even-Cut Abrasive Company............D....... 216 881-9595
 Grand Rapids *(G-6390)*
Ferro Industries Inc......................E....... 586 792-6001
 Harrison Township *(G-7330)*
Finishing Technologies Inc..............F....... 616 794-4001
 Belding *(G-1415)*
Hammond Machinery Inc.................D....... 269 345-7151
 Kalamazoo *(G-8759)*
IGA Abrasives LLC........................E....... 616 243-5566
 Grand Rapids *(G-6526)*
International Abrasives Inc..............G....... 586 778-8490
 Roseville *(G-13820)*
Kalamazoo Company.....................E....... 269 345-7151
 Kalamazoo *(G-8786)*
Kevin S Macaddino.......................G....... 248 642-0333
 Birmingham *(G-1687)*
L R Oliver and Company Inc............E....... 810 765-1000
 Cottrellville *(G-3590)*
Roto-Finish Company Inc...............G....... 269 327-7071
 Kalamazoo *(G-8875)*
Saint-Gobain Delaware Corp...........G....... 734 941-1300
 Romulus *(G-13731)*
Sam Brown Sales LLC..................E....... 248 358-2626
 Farmington *(G-4911)*
Sandbox Solutions Inc...................C....... 248 349-7010
 Northville *(G-11723)*
Sidley Diamond Tool Company.........E....... 734 261-7970
 Garden City *(G-5841)*
Stan Sax Corp.............................F....... 248 683-9199
 Detroit *(G-4373)*
Superabrasives Inc......................E....... 248 348-7670
 Wixom *(G-17901)*
Superior Abrasive Products.............E....... 248 969-4090
 Oxford *(G-12374)*
Trinity Tool Co.............................E....... 586 296-5900
 Fraser *(G-5741)*
United Abrasive Inc......................F....... 906 563-9249
 Vulcan *(G-16846)*

ABRASIVES: Aluminum Oxide Fused

Detroit Abrasives Company..............G....... 734 475-1651
 Chelsea *(G-2706)*

ABRASIVES: Steel Shot

Ervin Industries Inc.......................D....... 517 265-6118
 Adrian *(G-62)*
Ervin Industries Inc.......................E....... 734 769-4600
 Ann Arbor *(G-447)*
GMA Industries Inc.......................E....... 734 595-7300
 Romulus *(G-13682)*
Metaltec Steel Abrasive Co.............E....... 734 459-7900
 Canton *(G-2404)*

ABRASIVES: Synthetic

D R W Systems............................G....... 989 874-4663
 Filion *(G-5346)*

ABRASIVES: Tungsten Carbide

Michigan Carbide Company Inc.........F....... 586 264-8780
 Troy *(G-16504)*

ACADEMY

Detroit Fd Entrprnrship Acdemy..........F....... 248 894-8941
 Detroit *(G-3984)*

ACCELERATION INDICATORS & SYSTEM COMPONENTS: Aerospace

Beaver Aerospace & Defense Inc......D....... 734 853-5003
 Livonia *(G-9662)*
Demmer Corporation.....................C....... 517 321-3600
 Lansing *(G-9217)*
Elite Tooling LLC..........................G....... 269 383-9714
 Kalamazoo *(G-8734)*
Utica Aerospace Inc.....................F....... 586 598-9300
 Chesterfield *(G-2852)*

ACCELERATORS: Electrostatic Particle

Elite Electro Coaters Inc.................G....... 517 886-1020
 Lansing *(G-9223)*

ACCELEROMETERS

Patriot Sensors & Cntrls Corp...........D....... 248 435-0700
 Clawson *(G-2983)*

ACCOUNTING SVCS, NEC

Orion Bus Accnting Sltions LLC........G....... 248 893-1060
 Wyandotte *(G-17970)*

ACIDS

Trace Zero Inc.............................F....... 248 289-1277
 Auburn Hills *(G-1029)*

ACIDS: Inorganic

Sterling Diagnostics Inc..................F....... 586 979-2141
 Sterling Heights *(G-15511)*

ACIDS: Sulfuric, Oleum

Pressure Vessel Service Inc............E....... 313 921-1200
 Detroit *(G-4310)*

ACOUSTICAL BOARD & TILE

Certainteed Gypsum Inc..................C....... 906 524-6101
 Lanse *(G-9189)*
Integrated Interiors Inc...................F....... 586 756-4840
 Warren *(G-17094)*

ACRYLIC RESINS

Allnex USA Inc.............................D....... 269 385-1205
 Kalamazoo *(G-8675)*
Marketlab Inc..............................F....... 616 656-5359
 Caledonia *(G-2306)*
Spartan Polymers LLC...................G....... 586 255-5644
 Bruce Twp *(G-2103)*

ACTUATORS: Indl, NEC

Acculift Inc..................................G....... 313 382-5121
 Melvindale *(G-10692)*
Arvinmeritor Inc............................E....... 248 435-1000
 Troy *(G-16222)*
Burr Engineering & Dev Co..............G....... 269 965-2371
 Battle Creek *(G-1160)*
Ctc Acquisition Company LLC...........C....... 616 884-7100
 Rockford *(G-13564)*
Meritor Inc..................................C....... 248 435-1000
 Troy *(G-16493)*
Radius LLC.................................G....... 248 685-0773
 Milford *(G-10982)*
Saginaw Products Corporation..........E....... 989 753-1411
 Saginaw *(G-14141)*
Serapid Inc.................................F....... 586 274-0774
 Sterling Heights *(G-15490)*
Stoneridge Inc.............................G....... 248 489-9300
 Novi *(G-12004)*
Von Weise LLC............................F....... 517 618-9763
 Eaton Rapids *(G-4736)*

ADDITIVE BASED PLASTIC MATERIALS: Plasticizers

Sulfo-Technologies LLC..................G....... 248 307-9150
 Madison Heights *(G-10363)*

ADHESIVES

Action Fabricators Inc....................C....... 616 957-2032
 Grand Rapids *(G-6136)*
Adco Global Inc............................B....... 517 764-0334
 Michigan Center *(G-10783)*
Adhesives and Processes Tech.......G....... 231 737-4418
 Norton Shores *(G-11807)*
Argent International Inc...................C....... 734 582-9800
 Plymouth *(G-12572)*
Chem Link Inc.............................D....... 269 679-4440
 Schoolcraft *(G-14491)*
Clair Evans-St Inc........................G....... 313 259-2266
 Detroit *(G-3938)*
Covalent Medical Inc.....................G....... 734 604-0688
 Ann Arbor *(G-406)*
Daring Company..........................G....... 248 340-0741
 Orion *(G-12179)*
Diversitak Inc..............................E....... 313 869-8500
 Detroit *(G-4012)*
Eternabond Inc............................G....... 847 540-0600
 Michigan Center *(G-10786)*
Fairmount Santrol Inc....................G....... 440 279-0204
 Detroit *(G-4051)*
HB Fuller Company......................E....... 616 453-8271
 Grand Rapids *(G-6500)*
Henkel Loctite Corporation..............G....... 787 264-7534
 Madison Heights *(G-10264)*
Kent Manufacturing Company...........D....... 616 454-9495
 Grand Rapids *(G-6577)*
Kleiberit Adhesives USA Inc............G....... 248 709-9308
 Royal Oak *(G-13941)*
Lenderink Inc..............................F....... 616 887-8257
 Belmont *(G-1466)*
Master Mix Company.....................F....... 734 487-7870
 Ypsilanti *(G-18089)*

ADHESIVES

PRODUCT SECTION

Millennium Adhesive Products ....G...... 800 248-4010
  Michigan Center *(G-10787)*
Nyatex Chemical Company ....F...... 517 546-4046
  Howell *(G-8073)*
Parson Adhesives Inc ....G...... 248 299-5585
  Rochester Hills *(G-13490)*
PPG Industries Inc ....E...... 517 263-7831
  Adrian *(G-86)*
Specilty Adhesives Coating Inc ....F...... 269 345-3801
  Kalamazoo *(G-8897)*
Stahls Inc ....D...... 800 478-2457
  Sterling Heights *(G-15508)*
Western Adhesive Inc ....F...... 616 874-5869
  Rockford *(G-13596)*
Worthen Industries Inc ....E...... 616 742-8990
  Grand Rapids *(G-7004)*

ADHESIVES & SEALANTS

A & B Display Systems Inc ....F...... 989 893-6642
  Bay City *(G-1269)*
Adco Products LLC ....C...... 517 841-7238
  Michigan Center *(G-10784)*
Alco Products LLC ....E...... 313 823-7500
  Detroit *(G-3853)*
AM Tech Services LLC ....G...... 734 762-7209
  Livonia *(G-9640)*
Applied Molecules LLC ....G...... 810 355-1475
  Whitmore Lake *(G-17688)*
Cass Polymers ....E...... 517 543-7510
  Charlotte *(G-2636)*
Dawson Manufacturing ....G...... 269 639-4213
  Sandusky *(G-14432)*
Dow Chemical Company ....C...... 517 439-4400
  Hillsdale *(G-7523)*
Dyna Tech ....G...... 248 358-3962
  Southfield *(G-14891)*
Eftec North America LLC ....D...... 248 585-2200
  Taylor *(G-15713)*
Henniges Auto Holdings Inc ....B...... 248 340-4100
  Auburn Hills *(G-896)*
Henniges Auto Sling Systems N .....C...... 248 340-4100
  Auburn Hills *(G-897)*
Kiilunen Mfg Group Inc ....G...... 906 337-2433
  Calumet *(G-2328)*
L & L Products Inc ....B...... 586 752-6681
  Bruce Twp *(G-2088)*
Lj/Hah Holdings Corporation ....G...... 248 340-4100
  Auburn Hills *(G-929)*
Materials Processing Inc ....D...... 734 282-1888
  Riverview *(G-13301)*
Michigan Adhesive Mfg Inc ....E...... 616 850-0507
  Spring Lake *(G-15162)*
Ncoc Inc ....E...... 248 548-5950
  Oak Park *(G-12088)*
ND Industries Inc ....C...... 248 288-0000
  Clawson *(G-2982)*
Paramelt Usa Inc ....C...... 231 759-7304
  Norton Shores *(G-11786)*
Portland Plastics Co ....E...... 517 647-4115
  Portland *(G-13065)*
Seal Support Systems Inc ....E...... 586 331-7251
  Romeo *(G-13638)*
Sealex Inc ....G...... 231 348-5020
  Harbor Springs *(G-7293)*
Sika Corporation ....D...... 248 577-0020
  Madison Heights *(G-10353)*
Transtar Autobody Tech LLC ....C...... 810 220-3000
  Brighton *(G-1999)*
Wall Colmonoy Corporation ....E...... 248 585-6400
  Madison Heights *(G-10380)*
Wilbur Products Inc ....F...... 231 755-3805
  Muskegon *(G-11451)*
Ziebart International Corp ....C...... 248 588-4100
  Troy *(G-16706)*

ADHESIVES & SEALANTS WHOLESALERS

Quantum Chemical LLC ....G...... 734 429-0033
  Livonia *(G-9901)*

ADHESIVES: Adhesives, plastic

Conley Composites LLC ....E...... 918 299-5051
  Grand Rapids *(G-6300)*
Highland Industrial Inc ....G...... 989 391-9992
  Bay City *(G-1320)*

ADHESIVES: Epoxy

Plasco Formulating Division ....G...... 586 281-3714
  Bruce Twp *(G-2092)*

West System Inc ....E...... 989 684-7286
  Bay City *(G-1370)*

ADULT DAYCARE CENTERS

Services To Enhance Potential ....G...... 313 278-3040
  Dearborn *(G-3757)*

ADVERTISING AGENCIES

All Seasons Agency Inc ....G...... 586 752-6381
  Bruce Twp *(G-2077)*
Berline Group Inc ....E...... 248 203-0492
  Royal Oak *(G-13907)*
Bowman Enterprises Inc ....G...... 269 720-1946
  Portage *(G-12987)*
Fusion Design Group Ltd ....G...... 269 469-8226
  New Buffalo *(G-11514)*
Interntonal Innovative Systems ....G...... 248 524-2222
  Troy *(G-16421)*
Kissman Consulting LLC ....G...... 517 256-1077
  Okemos *(G-12128)*
Pioneer Press ....E...... 231 723-3592
  Manistee *(G-10436)*
Pioneer Press Printing ....G...... 231 864-2404
  Bear Lake *(G-1380)*
Printwand Inc ....G...... 248 738-7225
  Pontiac *(G-12859)*
Rtr Alpha Inc ....G...... 248 377-4060
  Auburn Hills *(G-994)*
Total Local Acquisitions LLC ....G...... 517 663-2405
  Eaton Rapids *(G-4735)*
Your Home Town USA Inc ....E...... 517 529-9421
  Clarklake *(G-2902)*
Your Hometown Shopper LLC ....F...... 586 412-8500
  Shelby Township *(G-14725)*

ADVERTISING AGENCIES: Consultants

Ampm Inc ....F...... 989 837-8800
  Midland *(G-10814)*
Northwest Graphic Services ....G...... 248 349-9480
  Rochester Hills *(G-13485)*
R J Michaels Inc ....F...... 517 783-2637
  Jackson *(G-8560)*
W W Thayne Advertising Cons ....G...... 269 979-1411
  Battle Creek *(G-1264)*
Zenwolf Technologies Group ....E...... 517 618-2000
  Howell *(G-8124)*

ADVERTISING CURTAINS

World Class Steel & Proc Inc ....G...... 586 585-1734
  Troy *(G-16699)*

ADVERTISING DISPLAY PRDTS

A & B Display Systems Inc ....F...... 989 893-6642
  Bay City *(G-1269)*
Altus Brands LLC ....F...... 231 421-3810
  Grawn *(G-7096)*
Charter House Holdings LLC ....C...... 616 399-6000
  Zeeland *(G-18124)*
Design Manufacturing LLC ....E...... 616 647-2229
  Comstock Park *(G-3476)*
Dover Metals Inc ....G...... 269 849-1411
  Hartford *(G-7383)*
Flexi Display Marketing Inc ....G...... 800 875-1725
  Farmington Hills *(G-5003)*
Sizmek Dsp Inc ....G...... 313 516-4482
  Troy *(G-16606)*
Sparks Exhbits Envrnments Corp ....G...... 248 291-0007
  Royal Oak *(G-13972)*

ADVERTISING MATERIAL DISTRIBUTION

All Dealer Inventory LLC ....G...... 231 342-9823
  Lake Ann *(G-9083)*
MKP Enterprises Inc ....G...... 248 809-2525
  Southfield *(G-14985)*
Valassis Communications Inc ....C...... 734 591-3000
  Livonia *(G-9985)*
Valassis Communications Inc ....C...... 734 432-8000
  Livonia *(G-9986)*

ADVERTISING REPRESENTATIVES: Electronic Media

All Dealer Inventory LLC ....G...... 231 342-9823
  Lake Ann *(G-9083)*

ADVERTISING REPRESENTATIVES: Newspaper

Fowlerville News & Views ....G...... 517 223-8760
  Fowlerville *(G-5567)*
Herald Newspapers Company Inc ....C...... 989 752-7171
  Flint *(G-5445)*
Herald Newspapers Company Inc ....E...... 989 895-8551
  Flint *(G-5447)*
Maquet Monthly ....G...... 906 226-6500
  Marquette *(G-10542)*
Morning Star Publishing Co ....G...... 989 779-6000
  Alma *(G-245)*
Newark Morning Ledger Co ....E...... 517 487-8888
  Lansing *(G-9406)*
Nutting Newspapers Inc ....E...... 906 482-1500
  Houghton *(G-7979)*
Tuscola County Advertiser Inc ....F...... 989 823-8651
  Vassar *(G-16815)*

ADVERTISING REPRESENTATIVES: Printed Media

Commercial Graphics Company ......G...... 517 278-2159
  Coldwater *(G-3299)*

ADVERTISING SPECIALTIES, WHOLESALE

Adco Specialties Inc ....G...... 616 452-6882
  Grand Rapids *(G-6143)*
Advertising Accents Inc ....E...... 313 937-3890
  Redford *(G-13142)*
Alex Delvecchio Entps Inc ....E...... 248 619-9600
  Troy *(G-16184)*
Armada Printwear Inc ....G...... 586 784-5553
  Armada *(G-715)*
Bay Supply & Marketing Inc ....G...... 231 943-3249
  Traverse City *(G-15908)*
Classic Images Embroidery ....G...... 616 844-1702
  Grand Haven *(G-6004)*
Creative Promotions ....G...... 734 854-2292
  Lambertville *(G-9181)*
Dealer Aid Enterprises ....G...... 313 331-5800
  Detroit *(G-3965)*
Eclipse Print Emporium Inc ....G...... 248 477-8337
  Livonia *(G-9720)*
Edwards Sign & Screen Printing .....E...... 989 725-2988
  Owosso *(G-12290)*
Embroidery House Inc ....G...... 616 669-6400
  Jenison *(G-8625)*
Exposure Unlimited Inc ....G...... 248 459-9104
  Fenton *(G-5205)*
Faubles Prtg & Specialities ....G...... 231 775-4973
  Cadillac *(G-2246)*
Foresight Group Inc ....E...... 517 485-5700
  Lansing *(G-9230)*
Fun Promotion LLC ....G...... 616 453-4245
  Grand Rapids *(G-6424)*
GLS Enterprises Inc ....G...... 616 243-2574
  Comstock Park *(G-3482)*
Helm Incorporated ....D...... 734 468-3700
  Plymouth *(G-12637)*
Image Factory Inc ....G...... 989 732-2712
  Gaylord *(G-5866)*
Imprint House LLC ....G...... 810 985-8203
  Port Huron *(G-12929)*
Mahoney & Associates Inc ....G...... 517 669-4300
  Dewitt *(G-4464)*
Metro Printing Service Inc ....G...... 248 545-4444
  Troy *(G-16501)*
Monograms & More Inc ....E...... 313 299-3140
  Taylor *(G-15746)*
Northern Specialty Co ....G...... 906 376-8165
  Republic *(G-13246)*
Premiums Plus More ....G...... 734 485-2423
  Ypsilanti *(G-18095)*
Prest Sales Co ....G...... 586 566-6900
  Sterling Heights *(G-15451)*
Pride Printing Inc ....G...... 906 228-8182
  Marquette *(G-10554)*
R & R Harwood Inc ....G...... 616 669-6400
  Jenison *(G-8640)*
Screen Ideas Inc ....G...... 616 458-5119
  Grand Rapids *(G-6855)*
Shayleslie Corporation ....G...... 517 694-4115
  Holt *(G-7929)*
Shirts n More Inc ....F...... 269 963-3266
  Battle Creek *(G-1246)*
Spinnaker Forms Systems Corp ......G...... 616 956-7677
  Grand Rapids *(G-6886)*

PRODUCT SECTION

Tilco Inc .... G 248 644-0901
  Troy *(G-16643)*
Twin City Engraving Company .... G 269 983-0601
  Saint Joseph *(G-14346)*
Ver Duins Inc .... G 616 842-0730
  Grand Haven *(G-6095)*
Web Printing & Mktg Concepts .... G 269 983-4646
  Saint Joseph *(G-14351)*

ADVERTISING SVCS, NEC

Direct Aim Media LLC .... E 800 817-7101
  Grand Rapids *(G-6353)*
Kenewell Group .... G 810 714-4290
  Fenton *(G-5222)*

ADVERTISING SVCS: Billboards

Adams Outdoor Advg Ltd Partnr .... E 517 321-2121
  Lansing *(G-9201)*
Douglas E Fulk .... G 517 482-2090
  Lansing *(G-9362)*
R J Designers Inc .... G 517 750-1990
  Spring Arbor *(G-15127)*

ADVERTISING SVCS: Direct Mail

ADS Plus Printing .... G 810 659-7190
  Flushing *(G-5530)*
Ancor Information MGT LLC .... D 248 740-8866
  Troy *(G-16201)*
Econo Print Inc .... G 734 878-5806
  Pinckney *(G-12496)*
Logan Marketing Group LLC .... F 248 731-7650
  Bloomfield Hills *(G-1778)*
National Wholesale Prtg Corp .... G 734 416-8400
  Plymouth *(G-12699)*
P D Q Press Inc .... G 586 725-1888
  Ira *(G-8265)*
Print Masters Inc .... F 248 548-7100
  Madison Heights *(G-10339)*
Printwell Acquisition Co Inc .... D 734 941-6300
  Taylor *(G-15758)*
Ray Printing Company Inc .... F 517 787-4130
  Jackson *(G-8561)*
Real Green Systems Inc .... D 888 345-2154
  Commerce Township *(G-3447)*
Temperance Printing .... G 419 290-6846
  Lambertville *(G-9186)*
Valassis Communications Inc .... C 734 591-3000
  Livonia *(G-9985)*
Valassis Communications Inc .... C 734 432-8000
  Livonia *(G-9986)*

ADVERTISING SVCS: Display

A & B Display Systems Inc .... F 989 893-6642
  Bay City *(G-1269)*
Complete Source Inc .... G 616 285-9110
  Grand Rapids *(G-6293)*
Religious Communications LLC .... G 313 822-3361
  Detroit *(G-4340)*
Sign Image Inc .... F 989 781-5229
  Saginaw *(G-14149)*
Venture Grafix LLC .... G 248 449-1330
  Wixom *(G-17926)*

ADVERTISING SVCS: Outdoor

Edwards Outdoor Science .... G 906 353-7375
  Baraga *(G-1102)*
Graphic Resource Group Inc .... E 248 588-6100
  Troy *(G-16386)*
Outfront Media LLC .... F 616 452-3171
  Grand Rapids *(G-6736)*
Steel Skinz LLC .... G 517 545-9955
  Howell *(G-8103)*

ADVERTISING SVCS: Poster, Outdoor

Bruce Inc .... G 517 371-5205
  Lansing *(G-9352)*

AERIAL WORK PLATFORMS

West Michigan Aerial LLc .... E 269 998-4455
  Lawton *(G-9517)*

AGENTS, BROKERS & BUREAUS: Personal Service

Mission Critical Firearms LLC .... G 586 232-5185
  Shelby Township *(G-14641)*

Rockwell Automation Inc .... D 248 696-1200
  Troy *(G-16582)*
Township of Saline .... F 734 429-4440
  Saline *(G-14418)*

AGRICULTURAL CHEMICALS: Trace Elements

Dow Agrosciences LLC .... E 989 636-4400
  Midland *(G-10833)*

AGRICULTURAL EQPT: BARN, SILO, POULTRY, DAIRY/LIVESTOCK MACH

Burly Oak Builders Inc .... G 734 368-4912
  Dexter *(G-4480)*
Do-Mor Products .... G 269 651-7362
  Burr Oak *(G-2135)*
Packard Farms LLC .... E 989 386-3816
  Clare *(G-2883)*
Roto-Feeders Inc .... G 269 782-2456
  Dowagiac *(G-4559)*

AGRICULTURAL EQPT: Clippers, Animal, Hand Or Electric

Stuff A Pal .... G 734 646-3775
  Maybee *(G-10674)*

AGRICULTURAL EQPT: Fertilizng, Sprayng, Dustng/Irrigatn Mach

Logan Diesel Incorporated .... G 517 589-8811
  Leslie *(G-9544)*

AGRICULTURAL EQPT: Grounds Mowing Eqpt

Brilar LLC .... D 248 547-6439
  Oak Park *(G-12053)*
Overstreet Property MGT Co .... G 269 252-1560
  Benton Harbor *(G-1537)*
S & S Mowing Inc .... G 906 466-9009
  Bark River *(G-1122)*

AGRICULTURAL EQPT: Harvesters, Fruit, Vegetable, Tobacco

BEI International LLC .... E 616 204-8274
  Holland *(G-7566)*

AGRICULTURAL EQPT: Irrigation Eqpt, Self-Propelled

Triple K Farms Inc .... G 517 458-9741
  Morenci *(G-11116)*

AGRICULTURAL EQPT: Storage Bins, Crop

Glenn Knochel .... G 989 684-7869
  Kawkawlin *(G-8971)*

AGRICULTURAL EQPT: Tractors, Farm

Ebels Hardware Inc .... F 231 826-3334
  Falmouth *(G-4892)*
Mahindra Tractor Assembly Inc .... E 734 274-2239
  Ann Arbor *(G-541)*

AGRICULTURAL EQPT: Transplanters

Holland Transplanter Co Inc .... E 616 392-3579
  Holland *(G-7680)*
Liver Transplant/Univ of Mich .... G 734 936-7670
  Ann Arbor *(G-531)*
Mechanical Transplanter Co LLC .... E 616 396-8738
  Holland *(G-7742)*

AGRICULTURAL EQPT: Turf & Grounds Eqpt

Ultimate Turf of Flint LLC .... G 810 202-0203
  Flint *(G-5517)*

AGRICULTURAL EQPT: Weeding Machines

Buddingh Weeder Co .... G 616 698-8613
  Caledonia *(G-2293)*

AGRICULTURAL MACHINERY & EQPT: Wholesalers

Steiner Tractor Parts Inc .... E 810 621-3000
  Lennon *(G-9519)*

AIR CLEANING SYSTEMS

Clarkson Controls & Eqp Co .... G 248 380-9915
  Novi *(G-11850)*
Expert Air Cleaner Maint .... G 248 889-3760
  Highland *(G-7492)*
Robovent Products Group Inc .... E 586 698-1800
  Sterling Heights *(G-15476)*
Technical Air Products LLC .... F 616 863-9115
  Belmont *(G-1472)*
Waltz-Holst Blow Pipe Company .... E 616 676-8119
  Ada *(G-33)*

AIR CONDITIONERS: Motor Vehicle

Air International (us) Inc .... D 248 391-7970
  Auburn Hills *(G-762)*
Espar Inc .... G 248 994-7010
  Novi *(G-11885)*
Evans Tempcon Delaware LLC .... E 616 361-2681
  Grand Rapids *(G-6388)*
Mahle Behr Troy Inc .... C 248 743-3700
  Troy *(G-16481)*
Marelli North America Inc .... E 248 848-4800
  Farmington Hills *(G-5057)*
Michigan Auto Comprsr Inc .... B 517 796-3200
  Parma *(G-12391)*

AIR CONDITIONING & VENTILATION EQPT & SPLYS: Wholesales

Spheros North America Inc .... G 734 218-7350
  Canton *(G-2427)*

AIR CONDITIONING EQPT

Cdgjl Inc .... E 517 787-2100
  Jackson *(G-8404)*
Milair LLC .... G 513 576-0123
  Sterling Heights *(G-15425)*
Murtech Energy Services LLC .... G 810 653-5681
  Port Huron *(G-12948)*
Rush Air Inc .... F 810 694-5763
  Holly *(G-7895)*
TI Automotive LLC .... C 248 494-5000
  Auburn Hills *(G-1020)*

AIR CONDITIONING UNITS: Complete, Domestic Or Indl

U S Distributing Inc .... E 248 646-0550
  Birmingham *(G-1707)*
Whirlpool Corporation .... B 269 923-5000
  Benton Harbor *(G-1570)*
Whirlpool Corporation .... A 269 923-5000
  Benton Harbor *(G-1565)*
Whirlpool Corporation .... G 269 923-5000
  Benton Harbor *(G-1566)*
Whirlpool Corporation .... C 269 849-0907
  Coloma *(G-3367)*
Whirlpool Corporation .... C 269 923-3009
  Benton Harbor *(G-1571)*

AIR MATTRESSES: Plastic

Denali Incorporated .... G 517 574-0047
  Hartland *(G-7389)*
Proper Polymers - Warren LLC .... E 586 552-5267
  Warren *(G-17207)*
Proper Polymers - Warren LLC .... E 586 552-5267
  Warren *(G-17208)*
Rehrig Pacific Company .... G 517 278-9808
  Coldwater *(G-3326)*
Trinseo LLC .... E 888 789-7661
  Midland *(G-10922)*

AIR POLLUTION CONTROL EQPT & SPLYS WHOLESALERS

Robovent Products Group Inc .... E 586 698-1800
  Sterling Heights *(G-15476)*

AIR POLLUTION MEASURING SVCS

Advanced Recovery Tech Corp .... F 231 788-2911
  Nunica *(G-12031)*

AIR PURIFICATION EQPT

AIR PURIFICATION EQPT
Advanced Air Technologies Inc		G	989 743-5544
Corunna *(G-3577)*			
Air and Liquid Systems Inc		E	248 656-3610
Rochester Hills *(G-13367)*			
Cdgjl Inc		E	517 787-2100
Jackson *(G-8404)*			
Control Manufacturing Corp		E	734 283-4300
Riverview *(G-13292)*			
Gallagher-Kaiser Corporation		D	313 368-3100
Troy *(G-16378)*			
Gelman Sciences Inc		A	734 665-0651
Ann Arbor *(G-469)*			
Met-Pro Technologies LLC		D	989 725-8184
Lennon *(G-9518)*			
Midwest Air Products Co Inc		E	231 941-5865
Traverse City *(G-16035)*			
Tanis Technologies LLC		G	616 796-2712
Holland *(G-7823)*			
Viron International Corp		D	254 773-9292
Owosso *(G-12327)*			

AIRCRAFT & AEROSPACE FLIGHT INSTRUMENTS & GUIDANCE SYSTEMS
- General Dynamics Corporation .... E 615 427-5768
  Taylor *(G-15725)*
- Herrmann Aerospace .... G 810 695-1758
  Grand Blanc *(G-5969)*
- Interactive Aerial Inc .... G 231 715-1422
  Traverse City *(G-16007)*
- Ppi LLC .... G 248 841-7721
  Troy *(G-16558)*
- Preferred Avionics Instrs LLC .... F 800 521-5130
  Howell *(G-8083)*

AIRCRAFT & HEAVY EQPT REPAIR SVCS
- Cascade Equipment Company .... G 734 697-7870
  Van Buren Twp *(G-16750)*
- Grand Rapids Machine Repr Inc .... E 616 245-9102
  Grand Rapids *(G-6459)*
- Liebherr Aerospace Saline Inc .... C 734 429-7225
  Saline *(G-14398)*
- Woodward Inc .... B 616 772-9171
  Zeeland *(G-18197)*

AIRCRAFT ASSEMBLY PLANTS
- Aero Inspection & Tool LLC .... G 517 525-7373
  Leslie *(G-9540)*
- Ascent Aerospace Holdings LLC .... G 212 916-8142
  Macomb *(G-10109)*
- Boeing Company .... G 248 258-7191
  Bloomfield Hills *(G-1753)*
- C H Industries Inc .... F 586 997-1717
  Shelby Township *(G-14556)*
- Eaton Aerospace LLC .... F 517 787-8121
  Jackson *(G-8438)*
- Manufacturing & Indus Tech Inc .... E 248 814-8544
  Lake Orion *(G-9147)*
- Mustang Aeronautics Inc .... G 248 649-6818
  Troy *(G-16517)*
- P2r Metal Fabrication Inc .... G 888 727-5587
  Macomb *(G-10151)*
- Sika Corporation .... D 248 577-0020
  Madison Heights *(G-10353)*
- Soaring Concepts Aerospace LLC .... F 574 286-9670
  Hastings *(G-7427)*
- Textron Inc .... G 248 545-2035
  Madison Heights *(G-10367)*

AIRCRAFT CLEANING & JANITORIAL SVCS
- Wells Helicopter Service Inc .... G 616 874-6255
  Greenville *(G-7160)*

AIRCRAFT CONTROL SYSTEMS: Electronic Totalizing Counters
- GE Aviation Systems LLC .... E 616 224-6480
  Grand Rapids *(G-6431)*

AIRCRAFT ENGINES & ENGINE PARTS: Cooling Systems
- Dry Coolers Inc .... E 248 969-3400
  Oxford *(G-12344)*
- Stm Power Inc .... F 734 214-1448
  Ann Arbor *(G-647)*

AIRCRAFT ENGINES & ENGINE PARTS: Mount Parts
- Rapp & Son Inc .... C 734 283-1000
  Wyandotte *(G-17971)*

AIRCRAFT ENGINES & ENGINE PARTS: Research & Development, Mfr
- Eaton Corporation .... B 269 781-0200
  Marshall *(G-10566)*
- Steven J Devlin .... G 734 439-1325
  Milan *(G-10951)*

AIRCRAFT ENGINES & PARTS
- AAR Corp .... F 231 779-4859
  Cadillac *(G-2219)*
- Advance Turning and Mfg Inc .... C 517 783-2713
  Jackson *(G-8373)*
- Aerovision Aircraft Svcs LLC .... E 231 799-9000
  Norton Shores *(G-11737)*
- Aerovision International LLC .... E 231 799-9000
  Norton Shores *(G-11738)*
- Aircraft Precision Pdts Inc .... D 989 875-4186
  Ithaca *(G-8356)*
- Approved Aircraft Accessories .... G 734 946-9000
  Romulus *(G-13651)*
- AVI Inventory Services LLC .... E 231 799-9000
  Norton Shores *(G-11740)*
- Barnes Group Inc .... A 517 393-5110
  Lansing *(G-9346)*
- Dorris Company .... E 586 293-5260
  Fraser *(G-5644)*
- Expernced Prcsion McHining Inc .... G 989 635-2299
  Marlette *(G-10496)*
- Filtration Machine .... G 810 845-0536
  Davison *(G-3649)*
- Honeywell International Inc .... E 989 792-8707
  Saginaw *(G-14061)*
- Honeywell International Inc .... A 586 777-7870
  Fraser *(G-5665)*
- Honeywell International Inc .... E 734 392-5501
  Plymouth *(G-12641)*
- LAY Precision Machine Inc .... G 989 726-5022
  West Branch *(G-17511)*
- Manufacturing & Indus Tech Inc .... E 248 814-8544
  Lake Orion *(G-9147)*
- MB Aerospace Warren LLC .... C 586 772-2500
  Warren *(G-17144)*
- Merrill Technologies Group .... F 989 921-1490
  Saginaw *(G-14089)*
- Merrill Technologies Group Inc .... D 989 791-6676
  Saginaw *(G-14090)*
- Moeller Aerospace Tech Inc .... C 231 347-9575
  Harbor Springs *(G-7289)*
- Niles Precision Company .... C 269 683-0585
  Niles *(G-11634)*
- Nu Con Corporation .... E 734 525-0770
  Livonia *(G-9867)*
- Pratt & Whitney Autoair Inc .... B 517 393-4040
  Lansing *(G-9413)*
- SGC Industries Inc .... E 586 293-5260
  Fraser *(G-5723)*
- Steel Tool & Engineering Co .... P2r 734 692-8580
  Brownstown Twp *(G-2072)*
- Supreme Gear Co .... E 586 775-6325
  Fraser *(G-5736)*
- T Q Machining Inc .... E 231 726-5914
  Muskegon *(G-11434)*
- Tidy Mro Enterprises LLC .... G 734 649-1122
  Manchester *(G-10412)*
- United Precision Pdts Co Inc .... E 313 292-0100
  Dearborn Heights *(G-3800)*
- Woodward Fst Inc .... C 616 772-9171
  Zeeland *(G-18198)*

AIRCRAFT EQPT & SPLYS WHOLESALERS
- Great Lakes Aero Products .... F 810 235-1402
  Flint *(G-5441)*

AIRCRAFT FLIGHT INSTRUMENTS
- Flight Management Corporation .... G 517 327-0400
  Lansing *(G-9229)*
- Grand Rapids Machine Repr Inc .... E 616 245-9102
  Grand Rapids *(G-6459)*
- L3 Aviation Products Inc .... B 616 949-6600
  Grand Rapids *(G-6593)*
- Thierica Inc .... D 616 458-1538
  Grand Rapids *(G-6926)*

AIRCRAFT LIGHTING
- B/E Aerospace Inc .... G 734 425-6200
  Livonia *(G-9658)*

AIRCRAFT MAINTENANCE & REPAIR SVCS
- Aerovision International LLC .... E 231 799-9000
  Norton Shores *(G-11738)*
- Beaver Aerospace & Defense Inc .... D 734 853-5003
  Livonia *(G-9662)*
- Northern Wings Repair Inc .... E 906 477-6176
  Newberry *(G-11586)*

AIRCRAFT PARTS & AUXILIARY EQPT: Assys, Subassemblies/Parts
- Bradley-Thompson Tool Company .... E 248 352-1466
  Southfield *(G-14855)*
- Phoeñix Cmposite Solutions LLC .... C 989 739-7108
  Oscoda *(G-12218)*
- Pifers Airmotive Inc .... G 248 674-0909
  Waterford *(G-17369)*
- R & B Electronics Inc .... D 906 632-1542
  Sault Sainte Marie *(G-14471)*
- Ventura Aerospace LLC .... E 734 357-0114
  Wixom *(G-17925)*
- Ventura Industries Inc .... E 734 357-0114
  Plymouth *(G-12788)*
- Visioneering Inc .... E 248 622-5600
  Fraser *(G-5747)*
- Waller Machine Co Inc .... G 517 789-7707
  Jackson *(G-8603)*

AIRCRAFT PARTS & AUXILIARY EQPT: Countermeasure Dispensers
- Intergrted Dspnse Slutions LLC .... F 586 554-7404
  Shelby Township *(G-14605)*

AIRCRAFT PARTS & AUXILIARY EQPT: Gears, Power Transmission
- Beaver Aerospace & Defense Inc .... D 734 853-5003
  Livonia *(G-9662)*
- Bmt Aerospace Usa Inc .... D 586 285-7700
  Fraser *(G-5630)*
- Dorris Company .... E 586 293-5260
  Fraser *(G-5644)*
- Gear Master Inc .... F 810 798-9254
  Almont *(G-257)*
- SGC Industries Inc .... E 586 293-5260
  Fraser *(G-5723)*
- Triumph Gear Systems - Macomb .... C 586 781-2800
  Macomb *(G-10170)*

AIRCRAFT PARTS & AUXILIARY EQPT: Lighting/Landing Gear Assy
- Liebherr Aerospace Saline Inc .... C 734 429-7225
  Saline *(G-14398)*

AIRCRAFT PARTS & AUXILIARY EQPT: Military Eqpt & Armament
- Eagle Industrial Group Inc .... E 616 647-9904
  Comstock Park *(G-3481)*
- Lapeer Industries Inc .... C 810 664-1816
  Lapeer *(G-9467)*
- Military & Veterans Affairs .... D 231 775-7222
  Cadillac *(G-2266)*

AIRCRAFT PARTS & AUXILIARY EQPT: Oxygen Systems
- Air Craft Industries Inc .... G 269 663-8544
  Edwardsburg *(G-4757)*

AIRCRAFT PARTS & AUXILIARY EQPT: Pontoons
- Pontoon Rentals .... G 906 387-2685
  Munising *(G-11248)*

AIRCRAFT PARTS & EQPT, NEC
- 360 Group Au Pty Ltd .... G 586 219-2005
  Rochester Hills *(G-13357)*
- Advanced Integration Tech LP .... G 586 749-5525
  Chesterfield *(G-2734)*

PRODUCT SECTION

ALUMINUM PRDTS

Aero Train Corp ....G..... 810 230-8096
  Flint *(G-5372)*
Aerostatica Inc ....F..... 734 426-5525
  Dexter *(G-4473)*
Aerovision Aircraft Svcs LLC ....E..... 231 799-9000
  Norton Shores *(G-11737)*
Aerovision International LLC ....E..... 231 799-9000
  Norton Shores *(G-11738)*
Aircraft Precision Pdts Inc ....D..... 989 875-4186
  Ithaca *(G-8356)*
Aj Aircraft ....G..... 734 244-4015
  Monroe *(G-11014)*
American Aircraft Parts Mfg Co ....E..... 586 294-3300
  Clinton Township *(G-3046)*
AVI Inventory Services LLC ....E..... 231 799-9000
  Norton Shores *(G-11740)*
B/E Aerospace Inc ....G..... 734 425-6200
  Livonia *(G-9658)*
Bgt Aerospace LLC ....G..... 989 225-5812
  Bay City *(G-1290)*
Chardam Gear Company Inc ....D..... 586 795-8900
  Sterling Heights *(G-15287)*
Detail Precision Products Inc ....E..... 248 544-3390
  Ferndale *(G-5271)*
Detroit Coil Co ....E..... 248 658-1543
  Ferndale *(G-5274)*
Dolphin Manufacturing Inc ....E..... 734 946-6322
  Taylor *(G-15707)*
Eaton-Aeroquip Llc ....B..... 949 452-9575
  Jackson *(G-8440)*
Extreme Precision Screw Pdts ....E..... 810 744-1980
  Flint *(G-5427)*
Fema Corporation of Michigan ....C..... 269 323-1369
  Portage *(G-12996)*
Flow-Rite Controls Ltd ....E..... 616 583-1700
  Byron Center *(G-2191)*
General Dynamics Glbl IMG Tech .....F..... 248 293-2929
  Rochester Hills *(G-13433)*
Grand Rapids Technologies Inc ....G..... 616 245-7700
  Grand Rapids *(G-6465)*
Hart Precision Products Inc ....E..... 313 537-0490
  Redford *(G-13165)*
Honeywell International Inc ....C..... 231 582-5686
  Boyne City *(G-1822)*
Hytrol Manufacturing Inc ....E..... 734 261-8030
  Jackson *(G-8468)*
Jedco Inc ....C..... 616 459-5161
  Grand Rapids *(G-6557)*
Liberty Tool Inc ....E..... 586 726-2449
  Sterling Heights *(G-15398)*
Linear Motion LLC ....C..... 989 759-8300
  Saginaw *(G-14078)*
Manufacturing & Indus Tech Inc ....E..... 248 814-8544
  Lake Orion *(G-9147)*
Mas Inc ....G..... 231 894-0409
  Whitehall *(G-17677)*
Masterbilt Products Corp ....E..... 269 749-4841
  Olivet *(G-12142)*
Melling Manufacturing Inc ....E..... 517 750-3580
  Jackson *(G-8513)*
Merrill Technologies Group ....E..... 989 921-1490
  Saginaw *(G-14089)*
Moose Mfg & Machining LLC ....G..... 586 765-4686
  Detroit *(G-4254)*
Motor City Aerospace ....E..... 616 916-5473
  Rockford *(G-13581)*
National Aircraft Service Inc ....F..... 517 423-7589
  Tecumseh *(G-15803)*
Niles Precision Company ....C..... 269 683-0585
  Niles *(G-11634)*
Northern Wings Repair Inc ....E..... 906 477-6176
  Newberry *(G-11586)*
Nu Con Corporation ....E..... 734 525-0770
  Livonia *(G-9867)*
Odyssey Industries LLC ....C..... 248 814-8800
  Lake Orion *(G-9153)*
Parker-Hannifin Corporation ....B..... 269 384-3459
  Kalamazoo *(G-8843)*
Prime Products Inc ....E..... 616 531-8970
  Grand Rapids *(G-6775)*
Saf-Air Products Inc ....G..... 734 522-8360
  Garden City *(G-5837)*
Scott Machine Inc ....E..... 517 787-6616
  Jackson *(G-8571)*
Teamtech Motorsports Safety ....G..... 989 792-4880
  Saginaw *(G-14163)*
United Precision Pdts Co Inc ....E..... 313 292-0100
  Dearborn Heights *(G-3800)*
Veet Industries Inc ....F..... 586 776-3000
  Warren *(G-17281)*

Wmh Fluidpower Inc ....F..... 269 327-7011
  Portage *(G-13058)*

AIRCRAFT SEATS

B/E Aerospace Inc ....G..... 734 425-6200
  Livonia *(G-9658)*

AIRCRAFT SERVICING & REPAIRING

Liebherr Aerospace Saline Inc ....C..... 734 429-7225
  Saline *(G-14398)*

AIRCRAFT TURBINES

GE Aviation Muskegon ....F..... 231 777-2685
  Norton Shores *(G-11757)*
Johnson Technology Inc ....B..... 231 777-2685
  Muskegon *(G-11354)*
Metro Machine Works Inc ....D..... 734 941-4571
  Romulus *(G-13707)*
Moeller Mfg Company LLC ....G..... 616 285-5012
  Grand Rapids *(G-6695)*
Turbine Conversions Ltd ....G..... 616 837-9428
  Nunica *(G-12045)*
Williams International Co LLC ....B..... 248 624-5200
  Pontiac *(G-12875)*
Williams International Co LLC ....C..... 248 762-8713
  Waterford *(G-17386)*

AIRCRAFT: Airplanes, Fixed Or Rotary Wing

Great Lakes Aviaiton Svcs LLC ....G..... 586 770-3450
  Clinton Township *(G-3129)*
Midwest Build Center LLC ....G..... 989 672-1388
  Caro *(G-2474)*
Waco Classic Aircraft Corp ....E..... 269 565-1000
  Battle Creek *(G-1265)*

AIRCRAFT: Research & Development, Manufacturer

Mohyi Labs LLC ....G..... 248 973-7321
  West Bloomfield *(G-17487)*

AIRPORTS, FLYING FIELDS & SVCS

Approved Aircraft Accessories ....G..... 734 946-9000
  Romulus *(G-13651)*

ALARM SYSTEMS WHOLESALERS

Dice Corporation ....E..... 989 891-2800
  Bay City *(G-1301)*

ALARMS: Burglar

Controller Systems Corporation ....E..... 586 772-6100
  Eastpointe *(G-4698)*
Engineered Control Systems Inc ....E..... 509 483-6215
  Washington *(G-17303)*
Safety Technology Intl Inc ....E..... 248 673-9898
  Waterford *(G-17374)*
Safety Technology Intl Inc ....G..... 248 673-9898
  Waterford *(G-17375)*

ALARMS: Fire

Gentex Corporation ....C..... 616 392-7195
  Zeeland *(G-18142)*
Select Fire LLC ....G..... 586 924-1974
  Lenox *(G-9525)*

ALCOHOL: Ethyl & Ethanol

Carbon Green Bioenergy LLC ....E..... 616 374-4000
  Lake Odessa *(G-9112)*
Michigan Ethanol LLC ....E..... 989 672-1222
  Caro *(G-2471)*
Valero Renewable Fuels Co LLC ......E..... 517 486-6190
  Blissfield *(G-1730)*

ALKALIES & CHLORINE

Dow Chemical Company ....B..... 989 636-1000
  Midland *(G-10834)*
Dow Chemical Company ....D..... 989 636-5409
  Midland *(G-10848)*
Jci Jones Chemicals Inc ....E..... 734 283-0677
  Wyandotte *(G-17963)*
Pittsburgh Glass Works LLC ....C..... 248 371-1700
  Rochester Hills *(G-13494)*
PPG Industries Inc ....F..... 248 641-2000
  Troy *(G-16557)*

ALL-TERRAIN VEHICLE DEALERS

Lumberjack Shack Inc ....G..... 810 724-7230
  Imlay City *(G-8207)*

ALLOYS: Additive, Exc Copper Or Made In Blast Furnaces

Alloying Surfaces Inc ....G..... 248 524-9200
  Troy *(G-16191)*
Cannon-Muskegon Corporation ....C..... 231 755-1681
  Norton Shores *(G-11744)*

ALTERNATORS & GENERATORS: Battery Charging

Arotech Corporation ....E..... 800 281-0356
  Ann Arbor *(G-368)*

ALTERNATORS: Automotive

Denso International Amer Inc ....G..... 248 359-4177
  Van Buren Twp *(G-16757)*
Don Duff Rebuilding ....G..... 734 522-7700
  Livonia *(G-9714)*
Prestolite Electric Inc ....F..... 866 463-7078
  Novi *(G-11980)*
Seg Automotive North Amer LLC ....F..... 248 465-2602
  Novi *(G-11991)*

ALUMINUM

Aleris International Inc ....E..... 517 279-9596
  Coldwater *(G-3287)*
Arconic Inc ....F..... 231 981-3002
  Whitehall *(G-17661)*
Arconic Inc ....G..... 231 894-5686
  Whitehall *(G-17662)*
Constellium Automotive USA LLC .....C..... 734 879-9700
  Van Buren Twp *(G-16752)*
Fritz Enterprises ....E..... 313 841-9460
  Detroit *(G-4073)*
General Motors LLC ....B..... 989 757-0528
  Saginaw *(G-14044)*
Kaiser Aluminum Fab Pdts LLC ....D..... 269 250-8400
  Kalamazoo *(G-8784)*
Kkt Inc ....E..... 734 425-5330
  Livonia *(G-9798)*
Nemak Commercial Services Inc ....E..... 248 350-3999
  Southfield *(G-14989)*
United Global Sourcing Inc ....F..... 248 952-5700
  Troy *(G-16663)*
Viking Industries Inc ....F..... 734 421-5416
  Garden City *(G-5846)*
Wayne-Craft Inc ....F..... 734 421-8800
  Livonia *(G-10001)*

ALUMINUM PRDTS

Aacoa Extrusions Inc ....C..... 269 697-6063
  Niles *(G-11592)*
Air Conditioning Products Co ....D..... 734 326-0050
  Romulus *(G-13649)*
Aluminum Textures Inc ....E..... 616 538-3144
  Grandville *(G-7020)*
Arconic Inc ....E..... 248 489-4900
  Farmington Hills *(G-4932)*
Austin Tube Products Inc ....E..... 231 745-2741
  Baldwin *(G-1082)*
Benteler Aluminium Systems ....E..... 616 396-6591
  Holland *(G-7568)*
C & C Manufacturing Inc ....F..... 586 268-3650
  Sterling Heights *(G-15278)*
D & W Awning and Window Co ....E..... 810 742-0340
  Davison *(G-3645)*
Erbsloeh Alum Solutions Inc ....B..... 269 323-2565
  Portage *(G-12993)*
Extruded Aluminum Corporation ....F..... 616 794-0300
  Belding *(G-1413)*
Flotronics Inc ....G..... 248 620-1820
  Clarkston *(G-2921)*
General Structures Inc ....E..... 586 774-6105
  Warren *(G-17054)*
Hancock Enterprises Inc ....D..... 734 287-8840
  Taylor *(G-15728)*
Hydro Extrusion North Amer LLC ......B..... 269 349-6626
  Kalamazoo *(G-8772)*
International Extrusions Inc ....C..... 734 427-8700
  Garden City *(G-5830)*
Kaiser Aluminum Corporation ....F..... 269 488-0957
  Kalamazoo *(G-8783)*

Employee Codes: A=Over 500 employees, B=251-500
C=101-250, D=51-100, E=20-50, F=10-19, G=3-9

ALUMINUM PRDTS

Light Metals Corporation ....B...... 616 538-3030
  Wyoming *(G-18016)*
Lippert Components Mfg Inc ....C...... 989 845-3061
  Chesaning *(G-2725)*
Loftis Alumi-TEC Inc ....E...... 616 846-1990
  Grand Haven *(G-6050)*
Marketing Displays Inc ....C...... 248 553-1900
  Farmington Hills *(G-5058)*
Michigan Aluminum Extrusion ....D...... 517 764-5400
  Jackson *(G-8518)*
Mike Manufacturing Corporation......G...... 586 759-1140
  Warren *(G-17156)*
Minerals Processing Corp................E...... 906 753-9602
  Stephenson *(G-15238)*
Mueller Impacts Company Inc ....C...... 810 364-3700
  Marysville *(G-10608)*
Plascore Inc ....F...... 616 772-1220
  Zeeland *(G-18175)*
Quality Alum Acquisition LLC ....F...... 734 783-0990
  Flat Rock *(G-5359)*
Quality Alum Acquisition LLC ....D...... 800 550-1667
  Hastings *(G-7424)*
Quality Model & Pattern Co ....E...... 616 791-1156
  Grand Rapids *(G-6800)*
Signcomp LLC ....E...... 616 784-0405
  Grand Rapids *(G-6862)*
Special-Lite Inc ....C...... 800 821-6531
  Decatur *(G-3806)*
Superior Extrusion Inc ....C...... 906 346-7308
  Gwinn *(G-7223)*
Tubelite Inc ....D...... 800 866-2227
  Walker *(G-16880)*
Uacj Auto Whitehall Inds Inc ....C...... 231 845-5101
  Ludington *(G-10084)*
Ube Machinery Inc ....D...... 734 741-7000
  Ann Arbor *(G-685)*

ALUMINUM: Pigs

Real Alloy Recycling LLC ....C...... 517 279-9596
  Coldwater *(G-3325)*

ALUMINUM: Rolling & Drawing

AAR Manufacturing Inc ....E...... 231 779-8800
  Cadillac *(G-2220)*
General Structures Inc ....E...... 586 774-6105
  Warren *(G-17054)*

AMMUNITION: Cartridges Case, 30 mm & Below

Scorpion Reloads LLC ....G...... 586 214-3843
  Fraser *(G-5722)*

AMMUNITION: Pellets & BB's, Pistol & Air Rifle

Michigan Rifle and Pistol Assn ....G...... 269 781-1223
  Marshall *(G-10583)*

AMMUNITION: Small Arms

Bold Ammo & Guns Inc ....G...... 616 826-0913
  Rockford *(G-13559)*
General Dynamics Land ....B...... 586 825-4805
  Sterling Heights *(G-15356)*
Michigan Ammo LLC ....G...... 313 383-4430
  Detroit *(G-4236)*
On The Mark Inc ....G...... 989 317-8033
  Mount Pleasant *(G-11216)*
Sage Control Ordnance Inc ....F...... 989 739-2200
  Oscoda *(G-12219)*
Tactical Simplicity LLC ....G...... 248 410-4523
  Wixom *(G-17903)*

AMPLIFIERS

Harman Becker Auto Systems Inc ..D...... 248 848-0393
  Farmington Hills *(G-5016)*
Mitsubishi Elc Auto Amer Inc ....D...... 734 453-2617
  Northville *(G-11710)*

AMUSEMENT & RECREATION SVCS: Boating Club, Membership

Midwest Aquatics Group Inc ....G...... 734 426-4155
  Pinckney *(G-12500)*

AMUSEMENT & RECREATION SVCS: Mechanical Games, Coin-Operated

Pannell S-Erynn ....G...... 248 692-3192
  Farmington *(G-4906)*

AMUSEMENT & RECREATION SVCS: Recreation Center

Y M C A Family Center ....G...... 269 428-9622
  Saint Joseph *(G-14356)*

AMUSEMENT & RECREATION SVCS: Ski Instruction

Plastisnow LLC ....G...... 414 397-1233
  Plainwell *(G-12539)*

AMUSEMENT MACHINES: Coin Operated

AMI Entertainment Network Inc ......G...... 877 762-6765
  Wyoming *(G-17986)*
Spec International Inc ....F...... 616 248-3022
  Grand Rapids *(G-6879)*

AMUSEMENT PARK DEVICES & RIDES

Autosport Development LLC ....G...... 734 675-1620
  Trenton *(G-16152)*
Classic Turning Inc ....D...... 517 764-1335
  Jackson *(G-8412)*
Elkins Machine & Tool Co Inc ....E...... 734 941-0266
  Romulus *(G-13671)*
M & M Machining Inc ....G...... 586 997-9910
  Sterling Heights *(G-15404)*
Magnus Precision Tool LLC ....G...... 586 285-2500
  Fraser *(G-5690)*
Prestige Engrg Rsrces Tech Inc ......F...... 586 573-3070
  Clinton Township *(G-3202)*
Prestige Engrg Rsrces Tech Inc ......E...... 586 573-3070
  Madison Heights *(G-10336)*
S & M Machining Company ....G...... 248 348-0310
  Wixom *(G-17887)*
Tec-Option Inc ....F...... 517 486-6055
  Blissfield *(G-1727)*
TI Automotive LLC ....C...... 248 494-5000
  Auburn Hills *(G-1020)*

AMUSEMENT PARK DEVICES & RIDES: Ferris Wheels

D Michael Services ....G...... 810 794-2407
  Clay *(G-2996)*

AMUSEMENT/REC SVCS: Ticket Sales, Sporting Events, Contract

Tickets Plus Inc ....E...... 616 222-4000
  Grand Rapids *(G-6931)*

ANALGESICS

L Perrigo Company ....D...... 248 687-1036
  Troy *(G-16453)*
Perrigo Company ....A...... 269 673-8451
  Allegan *(G-182)*

ANALYZERS: Coulometric, Exc Indl Process

Neptech Inc ....E...... 810 225-2222
  Highland *(G-7498)*

ANALYZERS: Network

Medical Infrmtics Slutions LLC ....G...... 248 851-3124
  Bloomfield Hills *(G-1781)*
Netwave ....F...... 586 263-4469
  Macomb *(G-10148)*
Network Machinery Inc ....G...... 586 992-2459
  Shelby Township *(G-14651)*

ANALYZERS: Respiratory

Healthcare Dme LLC ....G...... 734 975-6668
  Ann Arbor *(G-485)*

ANESTHESIA EQPT

Morrison & Barnett Anesth ....G...... 248 814-0609
  Lake Orion *(G-9150)*

ANIMAL BASED MEDICINAL CHEMICAL PRDTS

Little Silver Corp ....G...... 248 642-0860
  Birmingham *(G-1688)*

ANIMAL FEED & SUPPLEMENTS: Livestock & Poultry

Active Feed Company ....D...... 989 453-2472
  Pigeon *(G-12485)*
Belle Feeds ....G...... 269 628-1231
  Paw Paw *(G-12397)*
Cargill Incorporated ....F...... 608 868-5150
  Owosso *(G-12281)*
Custom Blend Feeds Inc ....G...... 810 798-3265
  Bruce Twp *(G-2081)*
Darling Ingredients Inc ....C...... 517 279-9731
  Coldwater *(G-3301)*
Darling Ingredients Inc ....D...... 313 928-7400
  Melvindale *(G-10695)*
Darling Ingredients Inc ....G...... 269 751-0560
  Hamilton *(G-7231)*
Endres Processing LLC ....D...... 616 878-4230
  Byron Center *(G-2189)*
Endres Processing Michigan LLC ...F...... 269 965-0427
  Battle Creek *(G-1177)*
Hearthside Food Solutions LLC ......C...... 616 871-6240
  Kentwood *(G-9009)*
Mid McHgan Feed Ingrdients LLC ..G...... 989 236-5014
  Middleton *(G-10794)*
N F P Inc ....G...... 989 631-0009
  Midland *(G-10896)*
Pet Treats Plus ....F...... 313 533-1701
  Redford *(G-13181)*
Purina Mills LLC ....E...... 517 322-0200
  Lansing *(G-9319)*
Schantz LLC ....G...... 616 887-0517
  Sparta *(G-15109)*

ANIMAL FEED: Wholesalers

Custom Blend Feeds Inc ....G...... 810 798-3265
  Bruce Twp *(G-2081)*
Holmquist Feed Mill ....G...... 906 446-3325
  Trenary *(G-16151)*
Purina Mills LLC ....E...... 517 322-0200
  Lansing *(G-9319)*
Schantz LLC ....G...... 616 887-0517
  Sparta *(G-15109)*
Vita Plus Corporation ....F...... 989 665-0013
  Gagetown *(G-5803)*

ANIMAL FOOD & SUPPLEMENTS: Alfalfa Or Alfalfa Meal

Darwin Sneller ....G...... 989 977-3718
  Sebewaing *(G-14514)*

ANIMAL FOOD & SUPPLEMENTS: Bird Food, Prepared

Heath Manufacturing Company ......D...... 616 997-8181
  Coopersville *(G-3561)*
Markham Peat Corp ....F...... 800 851-7230
  Lakeview *(G-9175)*
Midwest Marketing Inc ....G...... 989 793-9393
  Saginaw *(G-14095)*

ANIMAL FOOD & SUPPLEMENTS: Dog

Free Rnge Ntrals Dog Trats Inc ......F...... 586 737-0797
  Sterling Heights *(G-15347)*
Happy Howies Inc ....F...... 313 537-7200
  Detroit *(G-4116)*
Harvey Richard John ....G...... 269 781-5801
  Marshall *(G-10571)*
Vita Plus Corporation ....F...... 989 665-0013
  Gagetown *(G-5803)*
Wysong Medical Corporation ....E...... 989 631-0009
  Midland *(G-10925)*

ANIMAL FOOD & SUPPLEMENTS: Dog & Cat

Archer-Daniels-Midland Company ...E...... 517 647-4155
  Portland *(G-13061)*
Blendco LLC ....F...... 269 350-2914
  Stevensville *(G-15557)*
Nestle Purina Petcare Company .....E...... 888 202-4554
  Troy *(G-16523)*

PRODUCT SECTION

Prestige Pet Products Inc ....G...... 248 615-1526
  Southfield (G-15003)
Three Dogs One One Cat ....G...... 313 285-8371
  Detroit (G-4399)

ANIMAL FOOD & SUPPLEMENTS: Feed Premixes

Corunna Mills Feed LLC ....G...... 989 743-3110
  Corunna (G-3580)
Finkbeiner L & D Feed & Farm ....G...... 734 429-9777
  Saline (G-14390)

ANIMAL FOOD & SUPPLEMENTS: Feed Supplements

Kemin Industries Inc ....F 248 869-3080
  Plymouth (G-12663)
Quality Liquid Feeds Inc ....G...... 616 784-2930
  Comstock Park (G-3511)

ANIMAL FOOD & SUPPLEMENTS: Livestock

Holmquist Feed Mill ....G...... 906 446-3325
  Trenary (G-16151)
John A Van Den Bosch Co ....E 616 848-2000
  Holland (G-7695)
Kent Nutrition Group Inc ....F 517 676-9544
  Mason (G-10643)
Meal and More Incorporated ....E 517 625-3186
  Morrice (G-11121)
Vita Plus Corporation ....F 989 665-0013
  Gagetown (G-5803)

ANIMAL FOOD & SUPPLEMENTS: Mineral feed supplements

Mar-Vo Mineral Company Inc ....G...... 517 523-2669
  Hillsdale (G-7529)

ANIMAL FOOD & SUPPLEMENTS: Pet, Exc Dog & Cat, Dry

Bake N Cakes LP ....G...... 517 337-2253
  Lansing (G-9345)

ANIMAL FOOD & SUPPLEMENTS: Poultry

Chippewa Farm Supply LLC ....G...... 989 471-5523
  Spruce (G-15213)

ANIMAL FOOD & SUPPLEMENTS: Specialty, Mice & Other Pets

Wysong Corporation ....G...... 989 631-0009
  Midland (G-10924)
Wysong Medical Corporation ....E 989 631-0009
  Midland (G-10925)

ANIMAL FOOD/SUPPLEMENTS: Feeds Fm Meat/Meat/Veg Combnd Meals

Armada Grain Co ....E 586 784-5911
  Armada (G-714)
Mathie Energy Supply Co Inc ....G...... 517 625-3646
  Morrice (G-11120)

ANIMAL OILS: Medicinal Grade, Refined Or Concentrated

Darling Ingredients Inc ....D 313 928-7400
  Melvindale (G-10695)

ANNEALING: Metal

Ajax Metal Processing Inc ....F 586 497-7000
  Warren (G-16922)
Atmosphere Annealing LLC ....D 517 485-5090
  Lansing (G-9342)
Atmosphere Annealing LLC ....E 517 482-1374
  Lansing (G-9343)
Austemper Inc ....E 616 458-7061
  Grand Rapids (G-6189)
Cyprium Induction LLC ....G...... 586 884-4982
  Sterling Heights (G-15305)
Emerald Consulting Group LLC ....E 248 720-0573
  Madison Heights (G-10245)
Gerdau Macsteel Atmosphere Ann ....F 517 782-0415
  Lansing (G-9373)
Hycal Corp ....F 216 671-6161
  Gibraltar (G-5904)

Mjc Industries Inc ....F 313 838-2800
  Detroit (G-4251)
Nor-Cote Inc ....E 586 756-1200
  Warren (G-17170)
Sun Steel Treating Inc ....D 877 471-0844
  South Lyon (G-14813)
Super Steel Treating Inc ....D 586 755-9140
  Warren (G-17258)
Western Engineered Products ....G...... 248 371-9259
  Lake Orion (G-9170)

ANODIZING EQPT

Protege Concepts Corp ....G...... 248 419-5330
  Farmington Hills (G-5104)

ANODIZING SVC

Allan Tool & Machine Co Inc ....D 248 585-2910
  Troy (G-16190)
Almond Products Inc ....D 616 844-1813
  Spring Lake (G-15132)
Aluminum Finishing Company ....G...... 269 382-4010
  Kalamazoo (G-8678)
Ano-Kal Company ....F 269 685-5743
  Plainwell (G-12518)
Changeover Integration LLC ....F 231 845-5320
  Ludington (G-10053)
Charlotte Anodizing Pdts Inc ....D 517 543-1911
  Charlotte (G-2638)
Classic Metal Finishing Inc ....E 517 990-0011
  Jackson (G-8411)
Di-Anodic Finishing Corp ....E 616 454-0470
  Grand Rapids (G-6348)
Erbsloeh Alum Solutions Inc ....B 269 323-2565
  Portage (G-12993)
Ihc Inc ....C 313 535-3210
  Detroit (G-4136)
Lorin Industries Inc ....D 231 722-1631
  Muskegon (G-11367)
McNichols Polsg & Anodizing ....F 313 538-3470
  Redford (G-13171)
McNichols Polsg & Anodizing ....G...... 313 538-3470
  Redford (G-13172)
Professional Metal Finishers ....F 616 365-2620
  Grand Rapids (G-6783)

ANTENNAS: Radar Or Communications

R A Miller Industries Inc ....C 888 845-9450
  Grand Haven (G-6067)

ANTENNAS: Receiving

Accessories Wholesale Inc ....F 248 755-7465
  Pontiac (G-12798)
Dynamic Supply Solutions Inc ....G...... 248 987-2205
  Grosse Pointe Shores (G-7198)
Mobile Knowlege Group Services ....G...... 248 625-3327
  Clarkston (G-2940)
Safari Circuits Inc ....C 269 694-9471
  Otsego (G-12255)

ANTI-GLARE MATERIAL

Rustop Technologies LLC ....G...... 517 223-5098
  Howell (G-8094)

ANTIBIOTICS

Aureogen Inc ....G...... 269 353-3805
  Kalamazoo (G-8688)

ANTIFREEZE

Recycling Fluid Technologies ....F 269 788-0488
  Battle Creek (G-1240)

ANTIQUE REPAIR & RESTORATION SVCS, EXC FURNITURE & AUTOS

A K Services Inc ....G...... 313 972-1010
  Detroit (G-3827)

ANTIQUE SHOPS

A K Services Inc ....G...... 313 972-1010
  Detroit (G-3827)
Plum Tree ....G...... 269 469-5980
  Union Pier (G-16738)

APPAREL ACCESS STORES

Brintley Enterprises ....G...... 248 991-4086
  Detroit (G-3918)

APPAREL DESIGNERS: Commercial

Flavored Group LLC ....G...... 517 775-4371
  Lansing (G-9289)
Real Love Printwear ....G...... 248 327-7181
  Southfield (G-15011)
Rena DRane Enterprises Inc ....G...... 248 796-2765
  Southfield (G-15012)
Retro-A-Go-go LLC ....G...... 734 476-0300
  Howell (G-8090)

APPLIANCE CORDS: Household Electrical Eqpt

Semmler Electric LLC ....G...... 517 869-2211
  Hillsdale (G-7540)

APPLIANCE PARTS: Porcelain Enameled

Precision Stamping Co Inc ....E 517 546-5656
  Howell (G-8082)
Su-Dan Company ....D 248 651-6035
  Lake Orion (G-9164)

APPLIANCES, HOUSEHOLD OR COIN OPERATED: Laundry Dryers

Maytag Corporation ....C 269 923-5000
  Benton Harbor (G-1529)

APPLIANCES, HOUSEHOLD: Kitchen, Major, Exc Refrigs & Stoves

J & E Appliance Company Inc ....G...... 248 642-9191
  Beverly Hills (G-1617)
Masco Building Products Corp ....G...... 313 274-7400
  Livonia (G-9825)
Nikis Food Co Inc ....G...... 313 925-0876
  Detroit (G-4272)

APPLIANCES, HOUSEHOLD: Laundry Machines, Incl Coin-Operated

Whirlpool Corporation ....C 269 923-7441
  Saint Joseph (G-14352)
Whirlpool Corporation ....C 269 849-0907
  Coloma (G-3367)
Whirlpool Corporation ....C 269 923-3009
  Benton Harbor (G-1571)

APPLIANCES, HOUSEHOLD: Refrigs, Mechanical & Absorption

Norcold Inc ....G...... 734 769-6000
  Ann Arbor (G-575)
Thetford Corporation ....C 734 769-6000
  Ann Arbor (G-670)
Whirlpool Corporation ....B 269 923-5000
  Benton Harbor (G-1570)
Whirlpool Corporation ....A 269 923-5000
  Benton Harbor (G-1565)
Whirlpool Corporation ....G...... 269 923-5000
  Benton Harbor (G-1566)
Whirlpool Corporation ....C 269 849-0907
  Coloma (G-3367)

APPLIANCES, HOUSEHOLD: Sewing Machines & Attchmnts, Domestic

Company Products Inc ....G...... 586 757-6160
  Warren (G-16989)

APPLIANCES: Household, NEC

Three D Precision Tool ....G...... 810 765-9418
  China (G-2862)

APPLIANCES: Household, Refrigerators & Freezers

Flow Gas Misture Solutions Inc ....G...... 810 216-9004
  Port Huron (G-12918)
Forma-Kool Manufacturing Inc ....E 586 949-4813
  Chesterfield (G-2778)
Maytag Corporation ....C 269 923-5000
  Benton Harbor (G-1529)

APPLIANCES: Household, Refrigerators & Freezers — PRODUCT SECTION

Scientemp Corp ....E..... 517 263-6020
  Adrian *(G-94)*
Whirlpool Corporation ....C..... 269 923-7400
  Benton Harbor *(G-1567)*

APPLIANCES: Major, Cooking

Delorean Associates Inc ....G..... 248 646-1930
  Bloomfield Hills *(G-1757)*

APPLIANCES: Small, Electric

E H Inc ....E..... 269 673-6456
  Allegan *(G-159)*
Eesco Inc ....G..... 517 265-5148
  Adrian *(G-61)*
National Element Inc ....E..... 248 486-1810
  Brighton *(G-1966)*
Thoreson-Mc Cosh Inc ....E..... 248 362-0960
  Troy *(G-16638)*

APPLICATIONS SOFTWARE PROGRAMMING

Adair Printing Company ....E..... 734 426-2822
  Dexter *(G-4472)*
Engtechnik Inc ....G..... 734 667-4237
  Canton *(G-2371)*
Ethnicemedia LLC ....G..... 248 762-8904
  Troy *(G-16352)*
Method Technology Service LLC .....E..... 312 622-7697
  Troy *(G-16500)*
Real Green Systems Inc ....D..... 888 345-2154
  Commerce Township *(G-3447)*
Rena DRane Enterprises Inc ....G..... 248 796-2765
  Southfield *(G-15012)*

AQUARIUMS & ACCESS: Plastic

Rbl Products Inc ....F..... 313 873-8806
  Detroit *(G-4331)*

ARCHITECTURAL SVCS

Architectural Planners Inc ....E..... 248 674-1340
  Waterford *(G-17322)*
Kreations Inc ....F..... 313 255-1230
  Detroit *(G-4183)*
Zoyes East Inc ....G..... 248 584-3300
  Ferndale *(G-5331)*

ARMATURE REPAIRING & REWINDING SVC

Heco Inc ....D..... 269 381-7200
  Kalamazoo *(G-8762)*
Industrial Elc Co Detroit Inc ....D..... 313 872-1133
  Detroit *(G-4139)*
Master Mfg Inc ....E..... 248 628-9400
  Oxford *(G-12359)*
Monarch Electric Service Co ....E..... 313 388-7800
  Melvindale *(G-10702)*
Setco Sales Company ....F..... 248 888-8989
  Novi *(G-11994)*
Valley Truck Parts Inc ....D..... 616 241-5431
  Wyoming *(G-18040)*

ARMOR PLATES

Central Lake Armor Express Inc ......C..... 231 544-6090
  Central Lake *(G-2588)*

ARRESTERS & COILS: Lightning

Gary L Melchi Inc ....G..... 810 231-0262
  Whitmore Lake *(G-17701)*

ART & ORNAMENTAL WARE: Pottery

Creative Arts Studio Royal Oak ....F..... 248 544-2234
  Royal Oak *(G-13916)*
Karla-Von Ceramics Inc ....G..... 616 866-0563
  Rockford *(G-13576)*
Make It Yours ....G..... 517 990-6799
  Jackson *(G-8507)*
Penzo America Inc ....G..... 248 723-0802
  Bloomfield Hills *(G-1789)*
Veldheer Tulip Garden Inc ....D..... 616 399-1900
  Holland *(G-7844)*

ART DEALERS & GALLERIES

Plum Tree ....G..... 269 469-5980
  Union Pier *(G-16738)*

ART DESIGN SVCS

Alpha 21 LLC ....G..... 248 352-7330
  Southfield *(G-14828)*
Arrow Printing LLC ....G..... 248 738-2222
  Waterford *(G-17323)*
DRae LLC ....G..... 313 923-7230
  Oak Park *(G-12060)*
Edwards Sign & Screen Printing .....G..... 989 725-2988
  Owosso *(G-12290)*
Mackellar Associates Inc ....F..... 248 335-4440
  Rochester Hills *(G-13466)*
Valeo North America Inc ....C..... 248 619-8300
  Troy *(G-16676)*
Vinyl Graphix Inc ....G..... 586 774-1188
  Saint Clair Shores *(G-14275)*

ART GALLERIES

Art of Custom Framing Inc ....G..... 248 435-3726
  Troy *(G-16218)*
Pierson Fine Art ....G..... 269 385-4974
  Kalamazoo *(G-8851)*

ART GOODS & SPLYS WHOLESALERS

G-M Wood Products Inc ....D..... 231 652-2201
  Newaygo *(G-11568)*
Studio of Fine Arts Inc ....G..... 313 280-1177
  Royal Oak *(G-13974)*

ART GOODS, WHOLESALE

Runyan Pottery Supply Inc ....G..... 810 687-4500
  Clio *(G-3281)*

ART SPLY STORES

Business Helper LLC ....G..... 231 271-4404
  Suttons Bay *(G-15651)*

ARTISTS' AGENTS & BROKERS

Houseparty ....G..... 616 422-1226
  Holland *(G-7681)*
Nicole Acarter LLC ....G..... 248 251-2800
  Detroit *(G-4270)*

ARTISTS' MATERIALS: Boards, Drawing

Markerboard People Inc ....E..... 517 372-1666
  Lansing *(G-9244)*

ARTISTS' MATERIALS: Boxes, Sketching & Paint

Pro Search ....G..... 248 553-7700
  Farmington Hills *(G-5102)*

ARTISTS' MATERIALS: Water Colors

J Cilluffo Son Studio ....G..... 810 794-2911
  Clay *(G-2998)*

ARTS & CRAFTS SCHOOL

Pewabic Society Inc ....E..... 313 626-2000
  Detroit *(G-4300)*

ARTWORK: Framed

RecycledIps Com ....G..... 810 623-4498
  Brighton *(G-1984)*

ASBESTOS PRDTS: Friction Materials

Cobalt Friction Technologies ....F..... 734 274-3030
  Ann Arbor *(G-402)*

ASBESTOS PRDTS: Pipe Covering, Heat Insulatng Matl, Exc Felt

K-Value Insulation LLC ....G..... 248 688-5816
  Troy *(G-16442)*

ASBESTOS REMOVAL EQPT

Aerospace America Inc ....E..... 989 684-2121
  Bay City *(G-1273)*
Lampco Industries Inc ....G..... 517 783-3414
  Jackson *(G-8494)*
Wonder Makers Environmental ....F..... 269 382-4154
  Kalamazoo *(G-8926)*

ASPHALT & ASPHALT PRDTS

Ajax Materials Corporation ....G..... 248 244-3300
  Troy *(G-16174)*
Ajax Materials Corporation ....F..... 248 244-3445
  Brighton *(G-1882)*
Ajax Paving Industries Inc ....C..... 248 244-3300
  Troy *(G-16175)*
Angelos Crushed Concrete Inc ....G..... 586 756-1070
  Warren *(G-16934)*
Edw C Levy Co ....G..... 248 634-0879
  Davisburg *(G-3631)*
Edw C Levy Co ....B..... 313 429-2200
  Dearborn *(G-3700)*
Edw C Levy Co ....D..... 313 843-7200
  Detroit *(G-4028)*
Hess Asphalt Pav Sand Cnstr Co ...F..... 810 984-4466
  Clyde *(G-3283)*
Hhj Holdings Limited ....F..... 248 652-9716
  Troy *(G-16396)*
Nagle Paving Company ....F..... 248 553-0600
  Novi *(G-11951)*
Oldcastle Materials Inc ....D..... 248 625-5891
  Clarkston *(G-2942)*
Rite Way Asphalt Inc ....G..... 586 264-1020
  Sterling Heights *(G-15472)*
Saginaw Asphalt Paving Co ....D..... 989 755-8147
  Carrollton *(G-2487)*
Woodland Paving Co ....E..... 616 784-5220
  Comstock Park *(G-3521)*

ASPHALT COATINGS & SEALERS

Arnt Asphalt Sealing Inc ....D..... 269 927-1532
  Benton Harbor *(G-1482)*
Curbco Inc ....D..... 810 232-2121
  Flint *(G-5409)*
Detroit Cornice & Slate Co Inc ....E..... 248 398-7690
  Ferndale *(G-5275)*
Genova Products Inc ....D..... 810 744-4500
  Davison *(G-3650)*
Liveroof LLC ....E..... 616 842-1392
  Nunica *(G-12040)*
McElroy Metal Mill Inc ....E..... 269 781-8313
  Marshall *(G-10582)*
Michigan Paving and Mtls Co ....D..... 517 787-4200
  Jackson *(G-8520)*
Over Top Steel Coating LLC ....G..... 616 647-9140
  Comstock Park *(G-3504)*

ASPHALT MINING & BITUMINOUS STONE QUARRYING SVCS

Eggers Excavating LLC ....F..... 989 695-5205
  Freeland *(G-5756)*

ASPHALT MIXTURES WHOLESALERS

Barrett Paving Materials Inc ....C..... 248 362-0850
  Troy *(G-16233)*

ASPHALT PLANTS INCLUDING GRAVEL MIX TYPE

Ajax Materials Corporation ....F..... 248 244-3445
  Brighton *(G-1882)*
Bob-O-Link Associates LLC ....G..... 616 891-6939
  Caledonia *(G-2292)*
Gerken Materials Inc ....G..... 734 243-1851
  Monroe *(G-11035)*
White Lake Excavating Inc ....F..... 231 894-6918
  Whitehall *(G-17681)*

ASSEMBLING SVC: Plumbing Fixture Fittings, Plastic

Fernco Inc ....C..... 810 503-9000
  Davison *(G-3648)*
Machine Guard & Cover Co ....G..... 616 392-8188
  Holland *(G-7731)*
Village & Country Water Trtmnt ....F..... 810 632-7880
  Hartland *(G-7395)*

ASSOCIATIONS: Business

Grand Rapids Gravel Company ....E..... 616 538-9000
  Holland *(G-7648)*
J-Ad Graphics Inc ....G..... 517 543-4041
  Charlotte *(G-2656)*
Michigan Milk Producers Assn ....E..... 248 474-6672
  Novi *(G-11947)*

PRODUCT SECTION

AUTO & HOME SUPPLY STORES: Truck Eqpt & Parts

ASSOCIATIONS: Engineering
American Soc AG Blgcal Engners ....E 269 429-0300
  Saint Joseph *(G-14300)*

ASSOCIATIONS: Manufacturers'
Ram Electronics Inc ....F 231 865-3186
  Fruitport *(G-5799)*
SA Automotive Ltd LLC ....F 989 723-0425
  Owosso *(G-12314)*

ASSOCIATIONS: Real Estate Management
Mj-Hick Inc ....G 989 345-7610
  West Branch *(G-17513)*
Stroh Companies Inc ....F 313 446-2000
  Detroit *(G-4380)*

ASSOCIATIONS: Trade
Michigan Oil and Gas Assn ....G 517 487-0480
  Lansing *(G-9399)*

ATOMIZERS
Aftermarket Industries LLC ....G 810 229-3200
  Brighton *(G-1879)*
Airman Inc ....E 248 960-1354
  Brighton *(G-1880)*
American MSC Inc ....E 248 589-7770
  Troy *(G-16198)*
Benteler Automotive Corp ....C 248 364-7190
  Auburn Hills *(G-792)*
Burr Oak Tool Inc ....C 269 651-9393
  Sturgis *(G-15599)*
Busch Machine Tool Supply LLC ....G 989 798-4794
  Freeland *(G-5753)*
Caflor Industries LLC ....G 734 604-1168
  Ypsilanti *(G-18059)*
Eagleburgmann Industries LP ....G 989 486-1571
  Midland *(G-10857)*
Ebinger Manufacturing Company ....F 248 486-8880
  Brighton *(G-1917)*
Emag LLC ....E 248 477-7440
  Farmington Hills *(G-4983)*
Emhart Teknologies LLC ....D 248 677-9693
  Troy *(G-16342)*
Esyntrk Industries LLC ....G 248 730-0640
  Orchard Lake *(G-12166)*
Faurecia Interior Systems Inc ....B 248 724-5100
  Auburn Hills *(G-861)*
Next Level Manufacturing LLC ....E 269 397-1220
  Jenison *(G-8634)*
Rayconnect Inc ....D 248 265-4000
  Rochester Hills *(G-13504)*
Venture Technology Groups Inc ....F 248 473-8450
  Novi *(G-12025)*
Vision Global Industries ....G 248 390-5805
  Macomb *(G-10173)*

AUCTION ROOMS: General Merchandise
Equipment Material Sales LLC ....G 734 284-8711
  Wyandotte *(G-17958)*

AUCTION SVCS: Motor Vehicle
G Tech Sales LLC ....G 586 803-9393
  Sterling Heights *(G-15353)*
KYB Americas Corporation ....G 248 374-0100
  Novi *(G-11923)*

AUCTIONEERS: Fee Basis
Auction Masters ....G 586 576-7777
  Oak Park *(G-12050)*
Fine Tool Journal LLC ....G 269 463-8255
  Watervliet *(G-17392)*

AUDIO & VIDEO EQPT, EXC COMMERCIAL
Alpine Electronics America Inc ....C 248 409-9444
  Auburn Hills *(G-766)*
Audio Technologies Inc ....G 586 323-3890
  Troy *(G-16229)*
BBC Communications Inc ....G 616 399-0432
  West Olive *(G-17531)*
Bluewater Tech Group Inc ....C 248 356-4399
  Southfield *(G-14854)*
Bluewater Tech Group Inc ....G 231 885-2600
  Mesick *(G-10767)*
Bluewater Tech Group Inc ....F 616 656-9380
  Grand Rapids *(G-6233)*

Cco Holdings LLC ....G 517 583-4125
  Tekonsha *(G-15817)*
Cco Holdings LLC ....G 616 244-2071
  Belding *(G-1406)*
Cco Holdings LLC ....G 616 384-2060
  Coopersville *(G-3551)*
Cco Holdings LLC ....G 517 639-1060
  Quincy *(G-13091)*
Cco Holdings LLC ....G 734 244-8028
  Monroe *(G-11024)*
Cco Holdings LLC ....G 734 868-5044
  Ida *(G-8193)*
Cco Holdings LLC ....G 810 270-1002
  North Branch *(G-11657)*
Cco Holdings LLC ....G 810 375-7020
  Dryden *(G-4568)*
Cco Holdings LLC ....G 810 545-4020
  Columbiaville *(G-3376)*
Cco Holdings LLC ....G 906 285-6497
  Ironwood *(G-8325)*
Cco Holdings LLC ....G 906 239-3763
  Iron Mountain *(G-8279)*
Cco Holdings LLC ....G 906 346-1000
  Gwinn *(G-7218)*
Cco Holdings LLC ....G 231 720-0688
  Muskegon *(G-11291)*
Cco Holdings LLC ....G 248 494-4550
  Auburn Hills *(G-811)*
Cco Holdings LLC ....G 269 202-3286
  Coloma *(G-3355)*
Cco Holdings LLC ....G 269 216-6680
  Kalamazoo *(G-8704)*
Cco Holdings LLC ....G 269 432-0052
  Colon *(G-3370)*
Cco Holdings LLC ....G 269 464-3454
  White Pigeon *(G-17646)*
Cco Holdings LLC ....G 989 328-4187
  Sidney *(G-14738)*
Cco Holdings LLC ....G 989 567-0151
  Shepherd *(G-14726)*
Cco Holdings LLC ....G 989 863-4023
  Reese *(G-13229)*
Cco Holdings LLC ....G 989 853-2008
  Muir *(G-11237)*
Digital Systems Adio Video LLC ....G 248 454-0387
  Bloomfield Hills *(G-1758)*
Lg Electronics USA Inc ....C 248 268-5100
  Troy *(G-16463)*
Logical Digital Audio Video ....G 734 572-0022
  Ann Arbor *(G-534)*
Pioneer North America Inc ....E 248 449-6799
  Farmington Hills *(G-5094)*
Pro-Vision Solutions LLC ....E 616 583-1520
  Byron Center *(G-2209)*
Startech-Solutions LLC ....G 248 419-0650
  Southfield *(G-15033)*

AUDIO COMPONENTS
Clarion Corporation America ....E 248 991-3100
  Farmington *(G-4896)*
Intaglio LLC ....F 616 243-3300
  Grand Rapids *(G-6539)*
Shinola/Detroit LLC ....C 888 304-2534
  Detroit *(G-4361)*

AUDIO ELECTRONIC SYSTEMS
Bluewater Tech Group Inc ....G 248 356-4399
  Farmington Hills *(G-4943)*
Cartalign Research Co ....G 248 681-6689
  West Bloomfield *(G-17468)*
Corporate AV Services LLC ....G 248 939-0900
  Commerce Township *(G-3395)*
Earbyte Inc ....G 734 418-8661
  Southfield *(G-14892)*
Fast Cash ....G 269 966-0079
  Battle Creek *(G-1185)*

AUDIO-VISUAL PROGRAM PRODUCTION SVCS
Verdoni Productions Inc ....G 989 790-0845
  Saginaw *(G-14179)*

AUDIOLOGICAL EQPT: Electronic
Bieri Hearing Instruments Inc ....F 989 793-2701
  Saginaw *(G-14007)*
E3 Diagnostics Inc ....G 734 981-3655
  Canton *(G-2369)*

AUTO & HOME SUPPLY STORES: Auto & Truck Eqpt & Parts
CC Industries LLC ....D 269 426-3342
  Sawyer *(G-14483)*
Horizon Global Corporation ....C 248 593-8820
  Troy *(G-16401)*
Joint Clutch & Gear Svc Inc ....E 734 641-7575
  Romulus *(G-13693)*
Nexteer Automotive Corporation ....B 989 757-5000
  Saginaw *(G-14104)*
Ventra Evart LLC ....G 231 734-9000
  Evart *(G-4888)*

AUTO & HOME SUPPLY STORES: Auto Air Cond Eqpt, Sell/Install
Fenton Radiator & Garage Inc ....G 810 629-0923
  Fenton *(G-5212)*

AUTO & HOME SUPPLY STORES: Automotive Access
Alliance Automation LLC ....G 810 953-9539
  Flint *(G-5375)*
Auto-Masters Inc ....E 616 455-4510
  Grand Rapids *(G-6190)*

AUTO & HOME SUPPLY STORES: Automotive parts
Aapico Detroit LLC ....D 313 551-6001
  Detroit *(G-3835)*
Afx Industries LLC ....G 810 966-4650
  Port Huron *(G-12881)*
Angstrom USA LLC ....E 313 295-0100
  Southfield *(G-14838)*
Axle of Dearborn Inc ....C 248 543-5995
  Ferndale *(G-5263)*
Canadian Amrcn Rstoration Sups ....E 248 853-8900
  Rochester Hills *(G-13384)*
Considine Sales & Marketing ....G 248 889-7887
  Highland *(G-7490)*
Dearborn Total Auto Svc Ctr ....F 313 291-6300
  Dearborn Heights *(G-3781)*
General Parts Inc ....E 989 686-3114
  Bay City *(G-1316)*
Howe Racing Enterprises Inc ....F 989 435-7080
  Beaverton *(G-1385)*
Ididit Inc ....E 517 424-0577
  Tecumseh *(G-15798)*
K & K Mfg Inc ....G 616 784-4286
  Sparta *(G-15100)*
Kurabe America Corporation ....A 248 939-5803
  Farmington Hills *(G-5039)*
Mr Axle ....F 231 788-4624
  Muskegon *(G-11386)*
Nci Mfg Inc ....F 248 380-4151
  Livonia *(G-9862)*
Opeo Inc ....F 248 299-4000
  Auburn Hills *(G-966)*
Yanfeng US Automotive ....D 616 392-5151
  Holland *(G-7864)*

AUTO & HOME SUPPLY STORES: Batteries, Automotive & Truck
G & L Powerup Inc ....G 586 200-2169
  Roseville *(G-13806)*
M & M Irish Enterprises Inc ....G 248 644-0666
  Birmingham *(G-1689)*

AUTO & HOME SUPPLY STORES: Truck Eqpt & Parts
Automotive Service Co ....F 517 784-6131
  Jackson *(G-8385)*
Carter Industries Inc ....E 510 324-6700
  Adrian *(G-53)*
Great Lakes Allied LLC ....G 231 924-5794
  White Cloud *(G-17622)*
Joes Trailer Manufacturing ....G 734 261-0050
  Livonia *(G-9793)*
UP Truck Center Inc ....E 906 774-0098
  Quinnesec *(G-13103)*

AUTO SPLYS & PARTS, NEW, WHSLE: Exhaust Sys, Mufflers, Etc

Technique Inc.................................D...... 517 789-8988
Jackson *(G-8585)*

AUTOCLAVES: Laboratory

Multi-Lab LLC.................................F...... 616 846-6990
Spring Lake *(G-15165)*

AUTOMATIC REGULATING CONTROL: Building Svcs Monitoring, Auto

Integrated Building Solutions..........F...... 616 889-3070
Chesaning *(G-2724)*
Johnson Controls Inc......................D...... 248 276-6000
Auburn Hills *(G-920)*

AUTOMATIC REGULATING CONTROLS: AC & Refrigeration

Siemens Industry Inc......................D...... 269 927-3591
Benton Harbor *(G-1547)*

AUTOMATIC REGULATING CONTROLS: Appliance Regulators

System Controls Inc.......................E...... 734 427-0440
Livonia *(G-9951)*

AUTOMATIC REGULATING CONTROLS: Appliance, Exc Air-Cond/Refr

Precision Speed Equipment Inc.......C...... 269 651-4303
Sturgis *(G-15631)*

AUTOMATIC REGULATING CONTROLS: Energy Cutoff, Residtl/Comm

Easi LLC..E...... 248 712-2750
Troy *(G-16334)*
Energy Development Assoc LLC.....G...... 313 354-2644
Dearborn *(G-3701)*
Rhombus Energy Solutions Inc......G...... 313 406-3292
Dearborn *(G-3753)*

AUTOMATIC REGULATING CONTROLS: Float, Residential Or Comm

Mercury Displacement Inds Inc......D...... 269 663-8574
Edwardsburg *(G-4766)*

AUTOMATIC REGULATING CONTROLS: Gas Burner, Automatic

Maxitrol Company..........................C...... 269 432-3291
Colon *(G-3374)*

AUTOMATIC REGULATING CONTROLS: Hardware, Environmental Reg

Control Systems & Service.............G...... 616 887-2738
Sparta *(G-15093)*
Swat Environmental Inc.................E...... 517 322-2999
Lansing *(G-9427)*

AUTOMATIC REGULATING CONTROLS: Hydronic Pressure Or Temp

Hydronix Ltd..................................G...... 231 439-5000
Harbor Springs *(G-7284)*

AUTOMATIC REGULATING CONTROLS: Pneumatic Relays, Air-Cond

Edmore Tool & Grinding Inc...........E...... 989 427-3790
Edmore *(G-4750)*

AUTOMATIC REGULATING CONTROLS: Thermocouples, Vacuum, Glass

Pyro Service Company...................G...... 248 547-2552
Madison Heights *(G-10340)*

AUTOMATIC REGULATING CONTROLS: Vapor Heating

Inland Vapor of Michigan LLC.........F...... 734 237-4389
Garden City *(G-5828)*

AUTOMATIC REGULATING CTRLS: Damper, Pneumatic Or Electric

Vibration Controls Tech LLC...........G...... 248 822-8010
Troy *(G-16684)*

AUTOMATIC TELLER MACHINES

Atm International Services LLC......F...... 734 524-9771
Westland *(G-17544)*
Cornelius Systems Inc....................E...... 248 545-5558
Berkley *(G-1582)*
Family Fare LLC.............................G...... 269 965-5631
Battle Creek *(G-1184)*
Great Lakes Atm............................G...... 248 542-2613
Ferndale *(G-5291)*

AUTOMOBILE FINANCE LEASING

General Motors LLC........................A...... 313 972-6000
Detroit *(G-4084)*
General Motors LLC........................E...... 248 456-5000
Pontiac *(G-12827)*

AUTOMOBILES & OTHER MOTOR VEHICLES WHOLESALERS

FCA Intrntional Operations LLC......E...... 800 334-9200
Auburn Hills *(G-865)*
General Motors LLC........................A...... 248 857-3500
Pontiac *(G-12828)*
Global Fleet Sales LLC...................G...... 248 327-6483
Southfield *(G-14920)*

AUTOMOBILES: Midget, Power Driven

RSM & Associates Co.....................F...... 517 750-9330
Jackson *(G-8566)*

AUTOMOBILES: Off-Road, Exc Recreational Vehicles

Yanfeng US Automotive..................C...... 616 975-4000
Kentwood *(G-9035)*

AUTOMOTIVE & TRUCK GENERAL REPAIR SVC

Aldez North America LLC...............G...... 810 577-3891
Almont *(G-251)*
Auto-Masters Inc............................E...... 616 455-4510
Grand Rapids *(G-6190)*
Dearborn Total Auto Svc Ctr..........F...... 313 291-6300
Dearborn Heights *(G-3781)*
Dts Enterprises Inc........................E...... 231 599-3123
Ellsworth *(G-4787)*
Emergency Services LLC................G...... 231 727-7400
Muskegon *(G-11317)*
Fenton Radiator & Garage Inc........G...... 810 629-0923
Fenton *(G-5212)*
Floss Automotive Group.................E...... 734 773-2524
Inkster *(G-8227)*
Front Line Services Inc..................F...... 989 695-6633
Freeland *(G-5757)*
Harrys Steering Gear Repair..........E...... 586 677-5580
Macomb *(G-10128)*
Hulet Body Co Inc..........................E...... 313 931-6000
Northville *(G-11699)*
Kirchhoff Automotive USA Inc........F...... 248 247-3740
Troy *(G-16446)*
Michigan Auto Bending Corp..........E...... 248 528-1150
Madison Heights *(G-10304)*
Nash Services...............................G...... 269 782-2016
Dowagiac *(G-4555)*
Pitchford Bertie.............................G...... 517 627-1151
Grand Ledge *(G-6113)*
Techni CAM and Manufacturing......F...... 734 261-6477
Livonia *(G-9954)*

AUTOMOTIVE BATTERIES WHOLESALERS

Contemporary Amperex Corp..........G...... 248 289-6200
Rochester Hills *(G-13395)*

AUTOMOTIVE BODY SHOP

Great Lakes Bath & Body Inc.........G...... 231 421-9160
Traverse City *(G-15991)*
Superior Collision Inc.....................G...... 231 946-4983
Traverse City *(G-16117)*

AUTOMOTIVE BODY, PAINT & INTERIOR REPAIR & MAINTENANCE SVC

Autoform Development Inc............F...... 616 392-4909
Holland *(G-7561)*
Cartex Corporation........................D...... 734 857-5961
Romulus *(G-13660)*
Lakeside Canvas & Upholstery.......G...... 231 755-2514
Muskegon *(G-11363)*
Midwest Bus Corporation...............D...... 989 723-5241
Owosso *(G-12304)*

AUTOMOTIVE COLLISION SHOPS

Eleven Mile Trck Frme & Ax..........D...... 248 399-7536
Madison Heights *(G-10244)*

AUTOMOTIVE CUSTOMIZING SVCS, NONFACTORY BASIS

On The Side Sign Dsign Grphics....G...... 810 266-7446
Byron *(G-2174)*
Qp Acquisition 2 Inc......................E...... 248 594-7432
Southfield *(G-15006)*

AUTOMOTIVE EMISSIONS TESTING SVCS

Diagnostic Systems Association.....F...... 269 544-9000
Kalamazoo *(G-8725)*
Intern Metals and Energy..............G...... 248 765-7747
Jackson *(G-8471)*

AUTOMOTIVE EXTERIOR REPAIR SVCS

Ralyas Auto Body Incorporated......G...... 517 694-6512
Mason *(G-10652)*

AUTOMOTIVE GLASS REPLACEMENT SHOPS

Superior Auto Glass of Mich..........G...... 989 366-9691
Houghton Lake *(G-7999)*

AUTOMOTIVE PARTS, ACCESS & SPLYS

3d Polymers Inc............................D...... 248 588-5562
Orchard Lake *(G-12164)*
A I Flint LLC..................................A...... 810 732-8760
Flint *(G-5367)*
A&M Assembly and Machining LLC..E...... 313 369-9475
Detroit *(G-3829)*
AAM Pwder Metal Components Inc..F...... 248 597-3800
Royal Oak *(G-13898)*
Aapico Detroit LLC........................D...... 313 551-6001
Detroit *(G-3835)*
Accel Performance Group LLC........F...... 248 380-2780
Wixom *(G-17750)*
Access Works Inc..........................G...... 231 777-2537
Muskegon *(G-11259)*
Adac Plastics Inc..........................C...... 616 957-0520
Muskegon *(G-11261)*
Adac Plastics Inc..........................B...... 616 957-0311
Muskegon *(G-11262)*
Adient US LLC...............................A...... 734 254-5000
Plymouth *(G-12564)*
Adient US LLC...............................B...... 734 414-9215
Plymouth *(G-12565)*
Adient US LLC...............................E...... 734 414-9215
Plymouth *(G-12566)*
Adient US LLC...............................C...... 616 394-8510
Holland *(G-7549)*
Adient US LLC...............................B...... 269 968-3000
Battle Creek *(G-1138)*
ADS Us Inc....................................C...... 989 871-4550
Millington *(G-10993)*
Advanced Assembly Products Inc...G...... 248 543-2427
Hazel Park *(G-7432)*
Advanced Auto Trends Inc.............E...... 248 628-4850
Oxford *(G-12334)*
Advanced Auto Trends Inc.............E...... 248 628-6111
Oxford *(G-12333)*
Advantage Truck ACC Inc..............E...... 800 773-3110
Ann Arbor *(G-347)*
ADW Industries Inc.......................E...... 989 466-4742
Alma *(G-231)*
Aer..G...... 517 345-7272
Grand Ledge *(G-6099)*
Affinia Group Inc..........................E...... 734 827-5400
Ann Arbor *(G-348)*
Aftech Inc.....................................G...... 616 866-1650
Grand Rapids *(G-6151)*

AGM Automotive Mexico LLC ... G ... 248 925-4152
Farmington Hills (G-4924)
Agritek Industries Inc ... D ... 616 786-9200
Holland (G-7551)
Air Lift Company ... E ... 517 322-2144
Lansing (G-9272)
Airboss Flexible Products Co ... C ... 248 852-5500
Auburn Hills (G-763)
Albion Automotive Limited ... B ... 313 758-2000
Detroit (G-3852)
Allegan Tubular Products Inc ... D ... 269 673-6636
Allegan (G-149)
Alma Products I LLC ... C ... 989 463-0290
Alma (G-235)
Alpha Technology Corporation ... E ... 517 546-9700
Howell (G-8011)
Aludyne Inc ... C ... 248 728-8642
Southfield (G-14831)
Aludyne Columbus LLC ... B ... 248 728-8642
Southfield (G-14832)
Aludyne East Michigan LLC ... D ... 810 987-7633
Port Huron (G-12888)
Aludyne Montague LLC ... A ... 248 479-6455
Southfield (G-14834)
Aludyne North America Inc ... G ... 248 728-8642
Southfield (G-14835)
Aludyne North America Inc ... C ... 248 728-8642
Howell (G-8012)
Aludyne US LLC ... C ... 586 782-0200
Warren (G-16927)
Aludyne US LLC ... D ... 810 987-1112
Port Huron (G-12889)
Aludyne West Michigan LLC ... F ... 248 728-8642
Stevensville (G-15555)
Amalgamated Uaw ... G ... 231 734-9286
Evart (G-4878)
American Axle & Mfg Inc ... E ... 248 299-2900
Rochester Hills (G-13368)
American Axle & Mfg Inc ... F ... 248 276-2328
Auburn Hills (G-769)
American Mitsuba Corporation ... B ... 989 779-4962
Mount Pleasant (G-11170)
Ameristeel Inc ... F ... 586 585-5250
Fraser (G-5619)
Anand Nvh North America Inc ... C ... 810 724-2400
Imlay City (G-8196)
Android Industries-Delta Towns ... C ... 517 322-0657
Lansing (G-9277)
Android Industries-Wixom LLC ... F ... 248 255-5434
Shelby Township (G-14546)
Android Industries-Wixom LLC ... E ... 248 732-0000
Auburn Hills (G-772)
Angstrom Automotive Group LLC ... E ... 248 627-2871
Ortonville (G-12193)
Anjun America Inc ... F ... 248 680-8825
Auburn Hills (G-773)
Anrod Screen Cylinder Company ... E ... 989 872-2101
Cass City (G-2511)
Antolin Interiors Usa Inc ... B ... 248 373-1749
Auburn Hills (G-775)
Antolin Interiors Usa Inc ... A ... 517 548-0052
Howell (G-8015)
Antolin Interiors Usa Inc ... G ... 248 567-4000
Troy (G-16203)
Applied Technology Group ... G ... 586 286-6442
Sterling Heights (G-15263)
Aptiv Corporation ... G ... 248 724-5900
Auburn Hills (G-777)
Aptiv Corporation ... A ... 248 813-2000
Troy (G-16207)
Aptiv Holdings (us) LLC ... E ... 248 813-2000
Troy (G-16208)
Aptiv Mexican Holdings US LLC ... G ... 248 813-2000
Troy (G-16209)
Aptiv PLC ... G ... 248 813-2000
Troy (G-16210)
Aptiv Services 3 (us) LLC ... G ... 248 813-2000
Troy (G-16212)
Aptiv Services Us LLC ... F ... 616 246-2471
Grand Rapids (G-6176)
Aptiv Services Us LLC ... G ... 313 322-6845
Dearborn (G-3677)
Aptiv Services Us LLC ... G ... 810 459-8809
Auburn Hills (G-778)
Aptiv Services Us LLC ... D ... 248 724-5900
Auburn Hills (G-779)
Aptiv Services Us LLC ... G ... 248 813-2000
Hudsonville (G-8146)
Aptiv Services Us LLC ... D ... 248 813-2000
Troy (G-16213)
Aptiv Services Us LLC ... B ... 248 813-2000
Troy (G-16214)
Aptiv Trade MGT Svcs US LLC ... G ... 248 813-2000
Troy (G-16215)
Arete Industries Inc ... F ... 231 582-4470
Boyne City (G-1815)
Argent Tape & Label Inc ... F ... 734 582-9956
Plymouth (G-12573)
Artisans Cstm Mmory Mattresses ... F ... 989 793-3208
Saginaw (G-13996)
Arvin Intl Holdings LLC ... G ... 248 435-1000
Troy (G-16221)
Arvinmeritor Oe LLC ... G ... 248 435-1000
Troy (G-16223)
Asmo Detroit Inc ... G ... 248 359-4440
Novi (G-11831)
Asp Grede Acquisitionco LLC ... G ... 248 727-1800
Southfield (G-14842)
Asp Grede Intrmdate Hldngs LLC ... A ... 313 758-2000
Detroit (G-3882)
Asp Hhi Acquisition Co Inc ... G ... 313 758-2000
Detroit (G-3883)
Asp Hhi Holdings Inc ... F ... 248 597-3800
Royal Oak (G-13906)
Asp Hhi Intermediate Holdings ... G ... 248 727-1800
Southfield (G-14843)
Asp Hhi Intrmdate Holdings Inc ... G ... 248 727-1800
Southfield (G-14844)
Aspra World Inc ... D ... 248 872-7030
Warren (G-16943)
Atf Inc ... E ... 989 685-2468
Rose City (G-13760)
Atlantic Boat Brokers ... G ... 231 941-8050
Traverse City (G-15899)
Auria Solutions USA Inc ... F ... 734 456-2800
Southfield (G-14845)
Auria St Clair LLC ... E ... 810 329-8400
Saint Clair (G-14205)
Auto-Tech Plastics Inc ... G ... 586 783-0103
Mount Clemens (G-11124)
Autocam Corporation ... C ... 616 698-0707
Kentwood (G-9001)
Autoform Development Inc ... F ... 616 392-4909
Holland (G-7561)
Autoliv Asp Inc ... C ... 248 761-0081
Pontiac (G-12805)
Autoliv Asp Inc ... B ... 248 475-9000
Auburn Hills (G-784)
Autoliv Holding Inc ... D ... 248 475-9000
Auburn Hills (G-785)
Automotive LLC ... C ... 248 712-1175
Southfield (G-14847)
Automotive Exteriors LLC ... G ... 248 458-0702
Auburn Hills (G-788)
Autoneum North America Inc ... D ... 248 848-0100
Novi (G-11836)
Avon Plastic Products Inc ... D ... 248 852-1000
Rochester Hills (G-13374)
Aztec Manufacturing Corp ... C ... 734 942-7433
Romulus (G-13653)
Barker Manufacturing Co ... E ... 269 965-2371
Battle Creek (G-1150)
Barker Manufacturing Co ... E ... 269 965-2371
Battle Creek (G-1151)
Bcs Automotive Interface Solut ... G ... 734 855-3297
Livonia (G-9661)
BDS Company Inc ... E ... 517 279-2135
Coldwater (G-3291)
Bearing Holdings LLC ... G ... 313 758-2000
Detroit (G-3896)
Benteler Aluminium Systems ... G ... 616 396-6591
Holland (G-7567)
Bentler Industries Inc ... G ... 269 665-4261
Galesburg (G-5808)
Best Products Inc ... E ... 313 538-7414
Redford (G-13148)
Borg Warner Automotive ... E ... 248 754-9200
Auburn Hills (G-795)
Borgwarner Inc ... G ... 248 371-0040
Auburn Hills (G-797)
Borgwarner Inc ... E ... 231 779-7500
Cadillac (G-2232)
Borgwarner Inc ... G ... 248 754-9600
Auburn Hills (G-798)
Borgwarner Inc ... B ... 248 754-9200
Auburn Hills (G-799)
Borgwarner Inc ... E ... 248 754-9600
Auburn Hills (G-800)
Borgwarner Inc ... E ... 248 754-9200
Auburn Hills (G-801)
Borgwarner Inv Holdg Inc ... G ... 248 754-9200
Auburn Hills (G-802)
Borgwarner Pds (usa) Inc ... B ... 248 754-9600
Auburn Hills (G-803)
Borgwarner Pds Anderson LLC ... G ... 248 641-3045
Troy (G-16245)
Borgwarner Thermal Systems Inc ... C ... 269 781-1228
Marshall (G-10563)
Bos Automotive Products Inc ... E ... 248 289-6072
Rochester Hills (G-13378)
Bosch Auto Svc Solutions Inc ... C ... 586 574-2332
Warren (G-16963)
Brembo North America Inc ... D ... 734 416-1275
Plymouth (G-12590)
Brose North America Inc ... C ... 248 339-4000
Auburn Hills (G-808)
Brugola Oeb Indstriale USA Inc ... F ... 734 468-0009
Plymouth (G-12591)
Bullseye Power ... G ... 231 788-5209
Muskegon (G-11286)
Burr Engineering & Dev Co ... G ... 269 965-2371
Battle Creek (G-1160)
Bushings Inc ... F ... 248 650-0603
Rochester Hills (G-13381)
Bwi Chassis Dynamics NA Inc ... G ... 937 455-5308
Brighton (G-1892)
Bwi North America Inc ... C ... 810 494-4584
Brighton (G-1893)
C W A Manufacturing Co Inc ... E ... 810 686-3030
Mount Morris (G-11159)
Cadillac Products Inc ... B ... 248 813-8200
Troy (G-16253)
Cadillac Products Inc ... D ... 586 774-1700
Roseville (G-13779)
Cadillac Products Inc ... D ... 989 766-2294
Rogers City (G-13613)
Cambridge Sharpe Inc ... D ... 248 613-5562
South Lyon (G-14788)
Carter Industries Inc ... E ... 510 324-6700
Adrian (G-53)
Casco Products Corporation ... F ... 248 957-0400
Novi (G-11844)
CC Industries LLC ... D ... 269 426-3342
Sawyer (G-14483)
Chassix Blackstone Operat ... G ... 586 782-7311
Warren (G-16979)
Check Technology Solutions LLC ... E ... 248 680-2323
Troy (G-16264)
Chicago Blow Pipe Company ... F ... 773 533-6100
Marquette (G-10522)
Cinnabar Engineering Inc ... F ... 810 648-2444
Sandusky (G-14431)
Cipa Usa Inc ... E ... 810 982-3555
Port Huron (G-12907)
Circuit Controls Corporation ... C ... 231 347-0760
Petoskey (G-12444)
Citation Lost Foam Pttrns LLC ... E ... 248 727-1800
Southfield (G-14868)
Cloyes Gear Holdings LLC ... G ... 313 758-2000
Detroit (G-3940)
Clutch Masters Inc ... G ... 586 759-1300
Warren (G-16984)
Con-Vel Inc ... G ... 864 281-2228
Lansing (G-9284)
Concent Grinding Inc ... G ... 517 787-8172
Jackson (G-8418)
Concorde Inc ... F ... 248 391-8177
Auburn Hills (G-817)
Continental Auto Systems Inc ... F ... 906 248-6700
Brimley (G-2015)
Continental Auto Systems Inc ... E ... 248 267-9408
Troy (G-16277)
Cooper-Standard Auto OH LLC ... G ... 248 596-5900
Novi (G-11853)
Cooper-Standard Automotive Inc ... B ... 248 596-5900
Novi (G-11854)
Cooper-Standard Automotive Inc ... D ... 734 542-6300
Livonia (G-9688)
Cooper-Standard Automotive Inc ... C ... 248 754-2000
Auburn Hills (G-827)
Cooper-Standard Fhs LLC ... G ... 248 596-5900
Novi (G-11855)
Cooper-Standard Holdings Inc ... G ... 248 596-5900
Novi (G-11856)
Corvac Composites LLC ... C ... 616 281-4059
Kentwood (G-9004)
Cosma International Amer Inc ... B ... 248 631-1100
Troy (G-16284)
Creative Controls Inc ... F ... 248 577-9800
Madison Heights (G-10222)

Employee Codes: A=Over 500 employees, B=251-500
C=101-250, D=51-100, E=20-50, F=10-19, G=3-9
2020 Harris Michigan Industrial Directory
1149

AUTOMOTIVE PARTS, ACCESS & SPLYS PRODUCT SECTION

Crowne Group LLC G 734 855-4512
Livonia *(G-9693)*

Csa Services Inc G 248 596-6184
Novi *(G-11859)*

Cutversion Technologies Corp G 586 634-1339
Sterling Heights *(G-15304)*

D2t America Inc F 248 680-9001
Rochester Hills *(G-13400)*

Daimay North America Auto Inc E 313 533-9680
Redford *(G-13156)*

Dakkota Integrated Systems LLC E 517 694-6500
Holt *(G-7907)*

Dana Driveshaft Mfg LLC C 248 623-2185
Auburn Hills *(G-835)*

Dana Limited D 810 329-2500
Saint Clair *(G-14213)*

Dana Thermal Products LLC D 810 329-2500
Saint Clair *(G-14214)*

Dana Thermal Products LLC C 810 329-2500
Saint Clair *(G-14215)*

Davco Manufacturing LLC D 734 429-5665
Saline *(G-14385)*

Dawson Manufacturing Company C 269 925-0100
Benton Harbor *(G-1493)*

Dayco Products LLC C 989 775-0689
Mount Pleasant *(G-11191)*

Dayco Products LLC E 517 439-0689
Hillsdale *(G-7522)*

Dearborn Total Auto Svc Ctr F 313 291-6300
Dearborn Heights *(G-3781)*

Debron Industrial Elec Inc E 248 588-7220
Troy *(G-16300)*

Delco Elec Overseas Corp G 248 813-2000
Troy *(G-16301)*

Delphi G 248 813-2000
Troy *(G-16302)*

Delphi Automotive Systems G 248 813-2000
Troy *(G-16303)*

Delphi Powertrain Corporation G 248 813-2000
Troy *(G-16304)*

Delphi Powertrain Systems LLC F 248 280-8340
Troy *(G-16305)*

Delphi Powertrain Systems LLC G 248 813-2000
Troy *(G-16306)*

Delphi Powertrain Systems LLC E 248 813-1549
Troy *(G-16307)*

Delphi Powertrain Systems LLC C 248 813-2000
Auburn Hills *(G-839)*

Delphi Powertrain Systems LLC C 248 813-2000
Troy *(G-16308)*

Delphi Powertrain Systems LLC D 248 280-8319
Troy *(G-16309)*

Delphi Powertrain Systems LLC E 800 521-4784
Troy *(G-16310)*

Delphi Pwertrain Intl Svcs LLC G 248 813-2000
Troy *(G-16311)*

Delphi Pwrtrain Tech Gen Prtnr G 248 813-2000
Troy *(G-16312)*

Delta Research Corporation E 734 261-6400
Livonia *(G-9705)*

Denso Sales Michigan Inc E 269 965-3322
Battle Creek *(G-1173)*

Design Usa Inc G 734 233-8677
Livonia *(G-9707)*

Detroit Technologies Inc F 248 647-0400
Macomb *(G-10117)*

Detroit Technologies Inc F 248 647-0400
Bingham Farms *(G-1651)*

Dgh Enterprises Inc E 269 925-0657
Benton Harbor *(G-1494)*

Dieomatic Incorporated F 269 966-4900
Battle Creek *(G-1174)*

Dieomatic Incorporated D 319 668-2031
Troy *(G-16319)*

Diesel Performance Products G 586 726-7478
Shelby Township *(G-14575)*

Dmi Edon LLC G 586 782-7311
Warren *(G-17003)*

Dmi Edon LLC G 248 728-8642
Southfield *(G-14884)*

Donnelly Corp F 231 652-8425
Newaygo *(G-11567)*

Dph LLC A 248 813-2000
Troy *(G-16323)*

Dph Holdings Corp C 248 813-2000
Troy *(G-16324)*

Dph-Das Global (holdings) LLC A 248 813-2000
Troy *(G-16325)*

Dph-Das LLC A 248 813-2000
Troy *(G-16326)*

Dreal Inc G 248 813-2000
Troy *(G-16328)*

Dse Industries LLC G 313 530-6668
Macomb *(G-10118)*

Dst Industries Inc F 734 941-0300
Clinton *(G-3018)*

Dura Brake Systems LLC G 248 299-7500
Rochester Hills *(G-13410)*

Dura Cables North LLC G 248 299-7500
Rochester Hills *(G-13411)*

Dura Cables South LLC G 248 299-7500
Rochester Hills *(G-13412)*

Dura Global Technologies Inc G 248 299-7500
Rochester Hills *(G-13413)*

Dura Shifter LLC G 248 299-7500
Rochester Hills *(G-13414)*

Durakon Industries Inc G 608 742-5301
Lapeer *(G-9457)*

E & E Manufacturing Co Inc F 248 616-1300
Clawson *(G-2977)*

E-T-M Enterprises I Inc C 517 627-8461
Grand Ledge *(G-6105)*

Eagle Assemblies Inc G 586 296-4836
Fraser *(G-5646)*

Eagle Thread Verifier LLC G 586 764-8218
Sterling Heights *(G-15327)*

Eaton Corporation E 248 226-6200
Southfield *(G-14894)*

Eberspaecher North America Inc E 248 778-5231
Novi *(G-11876)*

Ecotrons LLC G 248 891-6965
Wixom *(G-17799)*

Egr Incorporated G 248 848-1411
Farmington Hills *(G-4978)*

Elite Plastic Products Inc E 586 247-5800
Shelby Township *(G-14587)*

Elmwood Manufacturing Company G 313 571-1777
Detroit *(G-4034)*

Emergency Vehicle Products G 269 342-0973
Kalamazoo *(G-8736)*

Emma Sogoian Inc E 248 549-8690
Royal Oak *(G-13923)*

Engineered Machined Pdts Inc E 906 789-7497
Escanaba *(G-4827)*

Engineering Service of America D 248 357-3800
Southfield *(G-14899)*

Enovapremier LLC G 517 541-3200
Charlotte *(G-2646)*

Environmental Catalysts LLC G 248 813-2000
Troy *(G-16350)*

Ervins Group LLC G 248 203-2000
Bloomfield Hills *(G-1764)*

Erwin Quarder Inc D 616 575-1600
Grand Rapids *(G-6383)*

Etx Holdings Inc G 989 463-1151
Alma *(G-237)*

Euclid Industries Inc C 989 686-8920
Bay City *(G-1310)*

Excellence Manufacturing Inc D 616 456-9928
Grand Rapids *(G-6391)*

Expernced Prcsion McHining Inc G 989 635-2299
Marlette *(G-10496)*

Extang Corporation D 734 677-0444
Ann Arbor *(G-454)*

Fabulous Operating Pdts LLC G 810 245-5759
Lapeer *(G-9461)*

Fastime Racing Engines & Parts G 734 947-1600
Taylor *(G-15720)*

Faurecia G 248 917-1702
Southfield *(G-14904)*

Faurecia Emissions Contl Tech B 734 947-1688
Taylor *(G-15721)*

Faurecia Interior Systems Inc E 734 429-0030
Saline *(G-14389)*

FCA North America Holdings LLC E 248 512-2950
Auburn Hills *(G-866)*

FCA US LLC B 734 478-5658
Dundee *(G-4582)*

FCA US LLC A 586 497-2500
Warren *(G-17030)*

Fcaus Dundee Engine Plant A 734 529-9256
Dundee *(G-4583)*

Federal Screw Works C 231 796-7664
Big Rapids *(G-1627)*

Federal-Mogul Powertrain Inc C 616 887-8231
Sparta *(G-15094)*

Federal-Mogul Powertrain LLC C 734 254-0100
Plymouth *(G-12620)*

Federal-Mogul World Wide LLC G 248 354-7700
Southfield *(G-14913)*

Fft Sidney LLC F 248 647-0400
Sidney *(G-14739)*

Fisher & Company Incorporated E 586 746-2280
Saint Clair Shores *(G-14250)*

Fisher & Company Incorporated D 586 746-2101
Troy *(G-16364)*

Fleet Engineers Inc C 231 777-2537
Muskegon *(G-11324)*

Flex-N-Gate LLC C 800 398-1496
Warren *(G-17036)*

Flex-N-Gate Battle Creek LLC C 269 962-2982
Battle Creek *(G-1189)*

Flex-N-Gate Corporation E 586 773-0800
Warren *(G-17037)*

Flextronics Automotive USA Inc D 248 853-5724
Rochester Hills *(G-13425)*

Flextronics Intl USA Inc B 616 837-9711
Coopersville *(G-3558)*

Fluid Routing Solutions Inc E 231 592-1700
Big Rapids *(G-1628)*

Ford Motor Company A 313 594-0050
Dearborn *(G-3710)*

Ford Motor Company A 734 377-4954
Livonia *(G-9743)*

Ford Motor Company A 313 594-4090
Allen Park *(G-198)*

Ford Motor Company B 313 322-3000
Dearborn *(G-3709)*

Ford Motor Company A 734 523-3000
Livonia *(G-9744)*

Ford Motor Company A 734 942-6248
Brownstown *(G-2062)*

Forging Holdings LLC G 313 758-2000
Detroit *(G-4070)*

Formtech Inds Holdings LLC G 248 597-3800
Royal Oak *(G-13928)*

Frank Industries Inc E 810 346-3234
Brown City *(G-2051)*

Fremont L Dura L C G 248 299-7500
Auburn Hills *(G-878)*

Freudenberg N Amer Ltd Partnr G 734 354-5505
Plymouth *(G-12623)*

Freudenberg-Nok General Partnr C 734 451-0020
Plymouth *(G-12624)*

Fujikura Automotive Amer LLC E 248 957-0130
Farmington Hills *(G-5006)*

G P Dura G 248 299-7500
Rochester Hills *(G-13430)*

Gabriel Ride Control LLC D 248 247-7600
Farmington Hills *(G-5007)*

Gage Pattern & Model Inc E 248 361-6609
Madison Heights *(G-10255)*

Gates Corporation D 248 260-2300
Rochester Hills *(G-13431)*

Gearing Holdings LLC G 313 758-2000
Detroit *(G-4078)*

General Motors China Inc D 313 556-5000
Detroit *(G-4081)*

General Motors Company F 248 249-6347
Brownstown *(G-2063)*

General Motors Company B 586 218-9240
Warren *(G-17051)*

General Motors Company B 313 667-1500
Detroit *(G-4082)*

General Motors Holdings LLC E 313 556-5000
Detroit *(G-4083)*

General Motors LLC B 989 894-7210
Bay City *(G-1315)*

General Motors LLC F 586 731-2743
Sterling Heights *(G-15358)*

General Motors LLC A 517 885-6669
Lansing *(G-9290)*

General Motors LLC A 313 972-6000
Detroit *(G-4084)*

General Motors LLC F 931 486-5049
Warren *(G-17053)*

General Motors LLC C 248 874-1737
Pontiac *(G-12826)*

General Motors LLC C 313 410-2704
Detroit *(G-4085)*

General Motors LLC E 248 456-5000
Pontiac *(G-12827)*

General Motors LLC A 313 556-5000
Detroit *(G-4087)*

Gentex Corporation C 616 772-1800
Zeeland *(G-18138)*

Gestamp Mason LLC B 517 244-8800
Mason *(G-10641)*

Gestamp North America Inc C 248 743-3400
Troy *(G-16382)*

PRODUCT SECTION

AUTOMOTIVE PARTS, ACCESS & SPLYS

Ghsp Inc — Grand Haven (G-6018)	B	616 842-5500
Ghsp Inc — Grand Haven (G-6019)	D	248 588-5095
Ghsp Inc — Troy (G-16384)	D	248 581-0890
Ghsp Inc — Hart (G-7371)	F	231 873-3300
Glassmaster Controls Co Inc — Kalamazoo (G-8753)	E	269 382-2010
Global Fmi LLC — Fenton (G-5216)	D	810 964-5555
GM Components Holdings LLC — Detroit (G-4092)	C	313 665-4707
GM Laam Holdings LLC — Detroit (G-4093)	G	313 556-5000
Grede Machining LLC — Southfield (G-14927)	E	248 727-1800
Grede Omaha LLC — Southfield (G-14928)	E	248 727-1800
Grede Radford LLC — Southfield (G-14929)	E	248 727-1800
Ground Effects LLC — Flint (G-5443)	C	810 250-5560
GSC Riii - Grede LLC — Southfield (G-14933)	G	248 727-1800
H & L Manufacturing Co — Middleville (G-10804)	C	269 795-5000
H R P Motor Sports Inc — Rockford (G-13570)	G	616 874-6338
Hadley Products Corporation — Grandville (G-7043)	C	616 530-1717
Hamaton Inc — Wixom (G-17822)	G	248 308-3856
Hamlin Tool & Machine Co Inc — Rochester Hills (G-13438)	D	248 651-6302
Hanho America Co Ltd — Troy (G-16391)	G	248 422-6921
Hanwha Advanced Mtls Amer LLC — Monroe (G-11038)	E	810 629-2496
Harrys Steering Gear Repair — Macomb (G-10128)	G	586 677-5580
Harvey S Freeman — West Bloomfield (G-17479)	E	248 852-2222
Hayes Lemmerz Intl-GA LLC — Novi (G-11898)	C	734 737-5000
Hayes-Albion Corporation — Jackson (G-8463)	F	517 629-2141
Hdt Automotive Solutions LLC — Livonia (G-9767)	G	810 359-5344
Heavy Duty Radiator LLC — Riverview (G-13295)		800 525-0011
Henniges Auto Sling Systems N — Auburn Hills (G-897)	C	248 340-4100
Hhi Formtech LLC — Detroit (G-4121)	B	313 758-2000
Hhi Formtech LLC — Fraser (G-5662)	E	586 415-2000
Hhi Formtech Holdings LLC — Detroit (G-4122)	G	313 758-2000
Hhi Funding II LLC — Detroit (G-4123)	C	313 758-2000
Hhi Holdings LLC — Detroit (G-4124)	G	313 758-2000
Hi-Lex America Incorporated — Rochester Hills (G-13440)	D	248 844-0096
Hi-Lex Controls Incorporated — Hudson (G-8130)	C	517 448-2752
Hitachi America Ltd — Farmington Hills (G-5021)	E	248 477-5400
Honeywell International Inc — Southfield (G-14937)	G	248 827-6460
Hope Focus — Detroit (G-4128)	E	313 494-4500
Hope Focus — Detroit (G-4129)	C	313 494-4500
Hope Network West Michigan — Paris (G-12385)	C	231 796-4801
Horizon Intl Group LLC — Birmingham (G-1686)	D	734 341-9336
Howe Racing Enterprises Inc — Beaverton (G-1385)	F	989 435-7080
HP Pelzer Auto Systems Inc — Port Huron (G-12926)	E	810 987-4444
Huf North America Automoti — Farmington Hills (G-5022)	E	248 213-4605
Humphrey Companies LLC — Grandville (G-7048)	C	616 530-1717
Hutchinson Sealing Syst — Auburn Hills (G-904)	D	248 375-3721
Hydro-Craft Inc — Rochester Hills (G-13448)	E	248 652-8100
Impact Forge Holdings LLC — Detroit (G-4137)	G	313 758-2000
In Line Tube Inc — Shelby Township (G-14604)	F	586 532-1338
Inalfa Roof Systems Inc — Warren (G-17085)	C	586 758-6620
Inoac Usa Inc — Troy (G-16419)	E	248 619-7031
Integrated Program MGT LLC — Clarkston (G-2932)	G	248 241-9257
International Automotive Compo — Alma (G-238)	B	989 620-7649
International Automotive Compo — Port Huron (G-12930)	B	810 987-8500
Interstate Power Systems Inc — Iron Mountain (G-8285)	F	952 854-2044
Inteva Products LLC — Troy (G-16422)	F	248 655-8886
Inteva Products LLC — Troy (G-16423)	F	248 655-8886
Inteva Products LLC — Troy (G-16424)	B	248 655-8886
Inteva Products Usa LLC — Troy (G-16425)	G	248 655-8886
Inzi Controls Detroit LLC — Rochester Hills (G-13451)	G	334 282-4237
Iochpe Holdings LLC — Novi (G-11907)	D	734 737-5000
J G Kern Enterprises Inc — Sterling Heights (G-15378)	D	586 531-9472
J L International Inc — Romulus (G-13690)	C	734 941-0300
Jac Products Inc — Shelby Township (G-14608)	F	586 254-1534
Jac Products Inc — Pontiac (G-12840)	D	248 874-1800
Jay & Kay Manufacturing LLC — Croswell (G-3598)	E	810 679-2333
Jay & Kay Manufacturing LLC — Croswell (G-3599)	G	810 679-3079
Jernberg Holdings LLC — Detroit (G-4161)	G	313 758-2000
Johnson Controls Inc — Detroit (G-4165)	C	313 842-3300
Johnson Controls Inc — Plymouth (G-12656)	C	734 254-5000
Johnson Controls Inc — Plymouth (G-12657)	E	734 254-7200
Johnson Controls Inc — Holland (G-7697)	B	616 392-5151
Joint Clutch & Gear Svc Inc — Romulus (G-13693)	E	734 641-7575
Jomar Performance Products LLC — Pontiac (G-12841)	G	248 322-3080
Jorgensen Stl Mch & Fab Inc — Tekonsha (G-15819)	F	517 767-4600
Jost International Corp — Grand Haven (G-6039)	C	616 846-7700
Joyson Safety Systems — Auburn Hills (G-921)	G	248 364-6023
Joyson Sfety Systems Acqstion — Auburn Hills (G-923)	F	248 373-8040
Jtekt Automotive N Amer Inc — Plymouth (G-12659)	A	734 454-1500
Kar-Bones Inc — Detroit (G-4171)	G	313 582-5551
Katcon Usa Inc — Auburn Hills (G-924)	D	248 499-1500
Kay Manufacturing Company — Saint Joseph (G-14320)	E	269 408-8344
Kearsley Lake Terrace LLC — Flint (G-5453)	G	810 736-7000
Keihin Michigan Mfg LLC — Mussey (G-11457)	C	317 462-3015
Kenona Industries LLC — Grand Rapids (G-6574)	C	616 735-6228
Key Sfety Rstraint Systems Inc — Auburn Hills (G-927)	A	586 726-3800
Kiekert Usa Inc — Wixom (G-17841)	D	248 960-4100
Knoedler Manufacturers Inc — Battle Creek (G-1221)	F	269 969-7722
Kongsberg Holding I Inc — Novi (G-11919)	G	248 468-1300
Kongsberg Holding III Inc — Novi (G-11920)	E	248 468-1300
Kongsberg Intr Systems I Inc — Novi (G-11921)	F	956 465-4541
Kostal of America Inc — Troy (G-16450)	C	248 284-6500
Kyklos Holdings Inc — Detroit (G-4186)	G	313 758-2000
Kysor Industrial Corporation — Cadillac (G-2259)	C	231 779-7500
L & C Hanwha — Monroe (G-11046)	G	734 457-5600
L T C Roll & Engineering Co — Fraser (G-5682)	F	586 465-1023
Lab Tool and Engineering Corp — Spring Arbor (G-15124)	E	517 750-4131
Lacks Industries Inc — Grand Rapids (G-6606)	C	616 698-6890
Lacks Industries Inc — Grand Rapids (G-6612)	D	616 656-2910
Lakeland Finishing Corporation — Grand Rapids (G-6614)	D	616 949-8001
Laurmark Enterprises Inc — Ann Arbor (G-526)	E	818 365-9000
Lear Corp Eeds and Interiors — Southfield (G-14960)	F	248 447-1500
Lear Corporation — Southfield (G-14961)	A	313 852-7800
Lear Corporation — Rochester Hills (G-13458)	B	248 299-7100
Lear Corporation — Traverse City (G-16023)	C	231 947-0160
Lear Corporation — Taylor (G-15734)	C	734 946-1600
Lear Trim LP — Southfield (G-14966)	G	248 447-1500
Leon Interiors Inc — Holland (G-7721)	B	616 422-7479
Lippert Components Mfg Inc — Chesaning (G-2725)	C	989 845-3061
Lj/Hah Holdings Corporation — Auburn Hills (G-929)	G	248 340-4100
M-Tek Inc — Novi (G-11931)	F	248 553-1581
Mac Lean-Fogg Company — Royal Oak (G-13945)	C	248 280-0880
Machine Tool & Gear Inc — Corunna (G-3581)	D	989 743-3936
Machinery Prts Specialists LLC — Auburn (G-756)	G	989 662-7810
Magna Electronics Tech Inc — Holly (G-7887)	E	810 606-0145
Magna Exteriors America Inc — Auburn Hills (G-935)	C	248 844-5446
Magna Exteriors America Inc — Auburn Hills (G-936)	B	248 409-1817
Magna Extrors Intrors Amer Inc — Troy (G-16473)	C	248 729-2400
Magna International Amer Inc — Troy (G-16474)	C	248 729-2400
Magna International Amer Inc — Detroit (G-4214)	B	313 422-6000
Magna International Inc — New Hudson (G-11548)	F	248 617-3200
Magna Powertrain America Inc — Lansing (G-9394)	G	517 316-1013
Magna Powertrain America Inc — Troy (G-16475)	C	248 597-7811
Magna Powertrain Usa Inc — Sterling Heights (G-15409)	C	586 264-8180
Magna Seating America Inc — Auburn Hills (G-937)	D	248 243-7158
Magna Seating America Inc — Novi (G-11932)	B	248 567-4000
Magna Seating America Inc — Shelby Township (G-14632)	G	586 816-1400
Magnesium Products America Inc — Plymouth (G-12681)	B	734 416-8600
Magneti Marelli Holdg USA LLC — Auburn Hills (G-938)	E	248 418-3000
Mahle Inc — Farmington Hills (G-5050)	E	248 305-8200
Mahle Aftermarket Inc — Farmington (G-4904)	C	248 347-9700
Mahle Behr Troy Inc — Troy (G-16482)	D	248 735-3623
Mahle Industries Incorporated — Saint Johns (G-14288)	C	989 224-5423
Mahle Industries Incorporated — Farmington Hills (G-5053)	G	248 305-8200
Mahle Manufacturing MGT Inc — Farmington Hills (G-5054)	G	248 735-3623
Mann + Hummel Usa Inc — Bloomfield Hills (G-1780)	F	248 857-8500

Employee Codes: A=Over 500 employees, B=251-500
C=101-250, D=51-100, E=20-50, F=10-19, G=3-9

2020 Harris Michigan Industrial Directory

AUTOMOTIVE PARTS, ACCESS & SPLYS

Mann + Hummel Usa Inc, Kalamazoo (G-8818)	E	248 857-8501
Mann + Hummel Usa Inc, Portage (G-13014)	F	269 329-3900
Mariah Industries Inc, Troy (G-16486)	E	248 237-0404
Marley Precision Inc, Battle Creek (G-1226)	E	269 963-7374
Martinrea Industries Inc, Manchester (G-10408)	E	734 428-2400
Martinrea Industries Inc, Jonesville (G-8661)	F	517 849-2195
Master Mfg Inc, Oxford (G-12359)	E	248 628-9400
Maxable Inc, Brooklyn (G-2039)	E	517 592-5638
Maxion Import LLC, Novi (G-11939)	F	734 737-5000
Maxion Wheels Akron LLC, Novi (G-11941)	G	734 737-5000
Mayser Usa Inc, Van Buren Twp (G-16771)	D	734 858-1290
Mayville Engineering Co Inc, Vanderbilt (G-16807)	E	989 983-3911
Medallion Instrumentation, Spring Lake (G-15161)	C	616 847-3700
Melling Products North LLC, Farwell (G-5164)	D	989 588-6147
Meritor Industrial Pdts LLC, Troy (G-16497)	F	248 658-7200
Meritor Intl Holdings LLC, Troy (G-16498)	G	248 435-1000
Meritor Specialty Products LLC, Livonia (G-9838)	G	248 435-1000
Metaldyne LLC, Detroit (G-4228)	C	734 207-6200
Metaldyne Pwrtrain Cmpnnts Inc, Litchfield (G-9608)	F	517 542-5555
Metaldyne Pwrtrain Cmpnnts Inc, Litchfield (G-9607)	C	517 542-5555
Metaldyne Sintered Components, Plymouth (G-12691)	F	734 207-6200
Metalsa Structural Pdts Inc, Sterling Heights (G-15416)	G	248 669-3704
Metalsa Structural Pdts Inc, Novi (G-11945)	D	248 669-3704
Metavation LLC, Troy (G-16499)	E	248 351-1000
Michigan Auto Comprsr Inc, Parma (G-12391)	B	517 796-3200
Micron Holdings Inc, Kentwood (G-9020)	A	616 698-0707
Miller Industrial Products Inc, Jackson (G-8528)	E	517 783-2756
Mint Steel Forge Inc, Lake Orion (G-9149)	F	248 276-9000
Misc Products, Macomb (G-10144)	D	586 263-3300
Mistequay Group Ltd, Saginaw (G-14097)	F	989 752-7700
Mistequay Group Ltd, Standish (G-15224)	D	989 846-1000
Mj Mfg Co, Burton (G-2159)	G	810 744-3840
MNP Corporation, Madison Heights (G-10308)	E	248 585-5010
MNP Corporation, Utica (G-16744)	A	586 254-1320
Model-Matic Inc, Troy (G-16511)	F	248 528-1680
Montaplast North America Inc, Auburn Hills (G-947)	F	248 353-5553
Mpt Driveline Systems, Troy (G-16514)	G	248 680-3786
National Fleet Service LLC, Detroit (G-4263)	E	313 923-1799
National Ordnance Auto Mfg LLC, Auburn Hills (G-953)	G	248 853-8822
Nationwide Design Inc, Sterling Heights (G-15433)	F	586 254-5493
Nbhx Trim USA Corporation, Walker (G-16871)	F	616 785-9400
Nbhx Trim USA Corporation, Comstock Park (G-3501)	C	616 785-9400
Neapco Holdings LLC, Farmington Hills (G-5079)	C	248 699-6500
Nexteer Automotive Corporation, Saginaw (G-14105)	B	989 754-1920
Nexteer Automotive Corporation, Saginaw (G-14108)	A	989 757-5000
Nexteer Automotive Corporation, Saginaw (G-14110)	A	989 757-5000
Nexteer Automotive Corporation, Saginaw (G-14111)	D	989 757-5000
Nexteer Automotive Corporation, Saginaw (G-14112)	E	989 757-5000
Nexteer Automotive Corporation, Auburn Hills (G-955)	A	248 340-8200
Nitrex Inc, Mason (G-10649)	E	517 676-6370
Nitto Inc, Romulus (G-13713)	G	732 276-1039
Nodel-Co, Ferndale (G-5306)	E	248 543-1325
Norma Michigan Inc, Lake Orion (G-9151)	F	248 373-4300
Norma Michigan Inc, Auburn Hills (G-959)	C	248 373-4300
Northern Classics Trucks Inc, Rochester Hills (G-13482)	G	586 254-2835
Novares US LLC, Grand Rapids (G-6723)	B	616 554-3555
Nu Con Corporation, Livonia (G-9867)	E	734 525-0770
Nyx Inc, Livonia (G-9870)	B	734 261-7535
Nyx LLC, Livonia (G-9871)	C	734 462-2385
Oakley Sub Assembly Intl Inc, Flint (G-5475)	G	810 720-4444
Offsite Manufacturing Inc, Chesterfield (G-2811)	G	586 598-8850
Oiles America Corporation, Plymouth (G-12702)	D	734 414-7400
Orotex Corporation, Novi (G-11967)	C	248 773-8630
P T M Corporation, Ira (G-8266)	D	586 725-2211
Patent Lcnsing Clringhouse LLC, Rochester Hills (G-13491)	G	248 299-7500
PCI Procal Inc, Alpena (G-307)	F	989 358-7070
Pcm US Steering Holding LLC, Detroit (G-4292)	G	313 556-5000
Peckham Vocational Inds Inc, Lansing (G-9253)	C	517 316-4478
Performnce Assmbly Sltions LLC, Livonia (G-9887)	E	734 466-6380
Pims Co, Detroit (G-4301)	G	313 665-8837
Piston Automotive LLC, Redford (G-13182)	B	313 541-8674
Piston Automotive LLC, Van Buren Twp (G-16779)	D	313 541-8789
Piston Automotive LLC, Detroit (G-4304)	E	313 541-8789
Piston Group LLC, Southfield (G-14999)	D	248 226-3976
Plasan Carbon Composites Inc, Walker (G-16874)	C	616 965-9450
Plastic Ominium Auto Inergy, Adrian (G-85)	C	517 265-1100
Plastic Omnium Auto Inergy LLC, Troy (G-16552)	E	248 743-5700
Plastic Plate LLC, Grand Rapids (G-6757)	E	616 455-5240
Plastic Plate LLC, Kentwood (G-9023)	C	616 698-3678
Plastic Plate LLC, Kentwood (G-9024)	D	616 949-6570
Pontiac Coil Inc, Clarkston (G-2947)	C	248 922-1100
Powergrid Inc, Farmington Hills (G-5099)	G	586 484-7185
Prestige Warehouse & Assembly, Warren (G-17197)	F	586 777-1820
Pridgeon & Clay Inc, Grand Rapids (G-6774)	A	616 241-5675
Product Assembly Group LLC, Troy (G-16565)	G	586 549-8601
Profile Mfg Inc, Chesterfield (G-2824)	E	586 598-0007
Propride Inc, Grand Blanc (G-5978)	G	810 695-1127
Prototech Laser Inc, Chesterfield (G-2826)	F	586 948-3032
Prototypes Plus Inc, Hamilton (G-7238)	G	269 751-7141
Pullman Company, Monroe (G-11064)	F	734 243-8000
Quality Engineering Company, Wixom (G-17883)	F	248 351-9000
Quality Spring/Togo Inc, Coldwater (G-3323)	C	517 278-2391
Quality Steel Products Inc, Milford (G-10981)	E	248 684-0555
Ralco Industries Inc, Auburn Hills (G-985)	D	248 853-3200
Ralco Industries Inc, Auburn Hills (G-986)	E	248 853-3200
Rapp & Son Inc, Wyandotte (G-17971)	C	734 283-1000
Rassey Industries Inc, Shelby Township (G-14678)	E	586 803-9500
Ravenna Casting Center Inc, Ravenna (G-13126)	C	231 853-0300
RCO Engineering Inc, Roseville (G-13860)	D	586 620-4133
Regency Plastics - Ubly Inc, Ubly (G-16723)	D	989 658-8504
Rieke-Arminak Corp, Bloomfield Hills (G-1795)	G	248 631-5450
Rivas Inc, Sterling Heights (G-15473)	D	586 566-0326
Riverside Tank & Mfg Corp, Saint Clair (G-14234)	E	810 329-7143
Rivian Automotive LLC, Plymouth (G-12739)	D	734 855-4350
Robert Bosch LLC, Novi (G-11987)	E	248 921-9054
Robert Bosch LLC, Plymouth (G-12742)	B	734 979-3412
Robertson-Stewart Inc, Brighton (G-1986)	F	810 227-4500
Roush Enterprises Inc, Livonia (G-9911)	A	734 779-7006
Roush Enterprises Inc, Allen Park (G-207)	E	313 294-8200
Roush Industries Inc, Livonia (G-9912)	F	734 779-7016
Roush Manufacturing Inc, Farmington (G-4910)	D	734 805-4400
Roush Manufacturing Inc, Livonia (G-9915)	G	734 779-7006
Royce Corporation, Warren (G-17226)	G	586 758-1500
Rugged Liner Inc, Owosso (G-12313)	E	989 725-8354
Ryder Integrated Logistics Inc, Lansing (G-9321)	A	517 492-4446
SA Automotive Ltd LLC, Owosso (G-12314)	F	989 723-0425
Saf-Holland Inc, Holland (G-7794)	F	616 396-6501
Saf-Holland Inc, Holland (G-7795)	C	616 396-6501
Sam Brown Sales LLC, Farmington (G-4911)	E	248 358-2626
Sas Automotive Usa Inc, Fraser (G-5721)	G	248 606-1152
Sas Automotive Usa Inc, Sterling Heights (G-15485)	E	248 606-1152
Schwab Industries Inc, Shelby Township (G-14687)	F	586 566-8090
Seaman Industries Inc, Roseville (G-13867)	G	586 776-9620
Servotech Industries Inc, Taylor (G-15764)	F	734 697-5555
SH Leggitt Company, Marshall (G-10588)	C	269 781-3901
Sharp Model Co, Bruce Twp (G-2101)	D	586 752-3099
Shelby Antolin Inc, Shelby Township (G-14692)	F	734 395-0328
Shiloh Industries Inc, Alma (G-249)	D	989 463-6166
Shop IV Sbusid Inv Grede LLC, Southfield (G-15027)	B	248 727-1800
Skilled Manufacturing Inc, Traverse City (G-16105)	C	231 941-0290
Skilled Manufacturing Inc, Traverse City (G-16106)	E	231 941-0032
Skokie Castings LLC, Southfield (G-15030)	D	248 727-1800
SL America Corporation, Auburn Hills (G-1000)	E	586 731-8511
Sort-Tek Insptn Systems Inc, Troy (G-16612)	F	248 273-5200
Spartan Motors Inc, Charlotte (G-2665)	A	517 543-6400

Spectrum Cubic Inc D 616 459-8751
Grand Rapids *(G-6883)*

Stackpole Pwrtrn Intl USA LLC G 248 481-4600
Auburn Hills *(G-1001)*

Stant USA Corp E 765 827-8104
Rochester Hills *(G-13518)*

Steering Solutions Corporation E 989 757-5000
Saginaw *(G-14158)*

Steinbauer Performance LLC G 704 587-0856
Dowagiac *(G-4562)*

Strattec Security Corporation E 248 649-9742
Auburn Hills *(G-1005)*

Stromberg-Carlson Products Inc F 231 947-8600
Traverse City *(G-16114)*

Su-Dan Plastics Inc F 248 651-6035
Lake Orion *(G-9165)*

Supply Line International LLC F 248 242-7140
Novi *(G-12010)*

Swiss American Screw Pdts Inc F 734 397-1600
Canton *(G-2431)*

Sycron Technologies Inc G 810 694-4007
Grand Blanc *(G-5985)*

Synchronous Manufacturing Inc E 517 764-6930
Michigan Center *(G-10791)*

Syncreonus Inc D 248 377-4700
Auburn Hills *(G-1010)*

Takata Americas E 336 547-1600
Auburn Hills *(G-1012)*

Tata Autocomp Systems Limited G 248 680-4608
Troy *(G-16632)*

Teamtech Motorsports Safety G 989 792-4880
Saginaw *(G-14163)*

Teksid Inc F 734 846-5897
Farmington *(G-4914)*

Telmar Manufacturing Company G 810 577-7050
Fenton *(G-5241)*

Tenneco Automotive Oper Co Inc C 517 522-5520
Grass Lake *(G-7095)*

Tenneco Automotive Oper Co Inc D 517 522-5525
Jackson *(G-8586)*

Tenneco Automotive Oper Co Inc F 734 243-4615
Monroe *(G-11073)*

Tenneco Inc G 734 254-1122
Plymouth *(G-12769)*

Tenneco Inc G 248 354-7700
Southfield *(G-15045)*

Th Plastics Inc D 269 496-8495
Mendon *(G-10720)*

Thermal Solutions Mfg G 734 655-7145
Livonia *(G-9956)*

Thk Rhythm Auto Mich Corp C 517 647-4121
Portland *(G-13068)*

Thyssenkrupp Automotive Sales F 248 530-2991
Troy *(G-16639)*

Thyssenkrupp Automotive Sales E 248 530-2902
Troy *(G-16640)*

TI Group Auto Systems LLC B 989 672-1200
Caro *(G-2477)*

TI Group Auto Systems LLC D 989 673-7727
Caro *(G-2478)*

TI Group Auto Systems LLC C 810 364-3277
Marysville *(G-10623)*

TI Group Auto Systems LLC C 586 948-6006
Chesterfield *(G-2848)*

TI Group Auto Systems LLC C 859 235-5420
Auburn Hills *(G-1023)*

TI Group Auto Systems LLC B 248 475-4663
Auburn Hills *(G-1025)*

TI Group Auto Systems LLC D 517 437-7462
Hillsdale *(G-7543)*

Tianhai Electric N Amer Inc D 248 987-2100
Pontiac *(G-12870)*

Toyo Seat USA Corporation C 606 849-3009
Imlay City *(G-8212)*

Tractech Inc E 248 226-6800
Southfield *(G-15048)*

Tramec Sloan LLC D 616 395-5600
Holland *(G-7833)*

Transform Automotive LLC D 586 826-8500
Shelby Township *(G-14710)*

Transpak Inc E 586 264-2064
Sterling Heights *(G-15528)*

Trend Performance Products E 586 792-6620
Clinton Township *(G-3251)*

Trident Lighting LLC C 616 957-9500
Grand Rapids *(G-6937)*

Trimas Corporation E 248 631-5450
Bloomfield Hills *(G-1807)*

Trin Inc G 260 587-9282
Plymouth *(G-12780)*

Tristone Flowtech USA Inc G 248 560-1724
Southfield *(G-15049)*

TRW Auto Holdings Inc G 734 855-2600
Livonia *(G-9974)*

TRW East Inc G 734 855-2600
Livonia *(G-9976)*

TRW Odyssey Mexico LLC G 734 855-2600
Livonia *(G-9977)*

U-Shin America Inc G 248 449-3155
Novi *(G-12021)*

Ufp Technologies Inc D 616 949-8100
Grand Rapids *(G-6948)*

Unifilter Inc E 248 476-5100
Novi *(G-12023)*

Unique Fabricating Inc E 248 853-2333
Auburn Hills *(G-1034)*

United Foam A Ufp Tech Brnd D 616 949-8100
Grand Rapids *(G-6952)*

United Machining Inc C 586 323-4300
Sterling Heights *(G-15533)*

United Machining Inc G 586 323-4300
Macomb *(G-10171)*

United Metal Technology Inc F 517 787-7940
Jackson *(G-8599)*

US Farathane Holdings Corp E 586 991-6922
Sterling Heights *(G-15536)*

Usui International Corporation E 734 354-3626
Plymouth *(G-12784)*

Valeo North America Inc C 248 209-8253
Auburn Hills *(G-1043)*

Valeo Switches & Dete E 248 619-8300
Troy *(G-16679)*

Valley Truck Parts Inc G 269 429-9953
Saint Joseph *(G-14348)*

Veet Industries Inc F 586 776-3000
Warren *(G-17281)*

Vehma International Amer Inc D 248 631-2800
Troy *(G-16681)*

Vehma International Amer Inc C 248 585-4800
Troy *(G-16680)*

Venchurs Inc E 517 263-1206
Adrian *(G-99)*

Venchurs Inc F 517 263-8937
Adrian *(G-100)*

Veoneer Inc A 248 223-0600
Southfield *(G-15058)*

Vibracoustic North America L P E 269 637-2116
South Haven *(G-14780)*

Vihi LLC G 734 710-2277
Van Buren Twp *(G-16789)*

Visions Car & Truck Acc G 269 342-2962
Kalamazoo *(G-8919)*

Visteon Corporation D 734 718-8927
Canton *(G-2440)*

Visteon Electronics Corp G 800 847-8366
Van Buren Twp *(G-16791)*

Visteon Global Electronics Inc G 800 847-8366
Van Buren Twp *(G-16792)*

Visteon Global Electronics Inc G 734 710-5000
Van Buren Twp *(G-16793)*

Vitesco Technologies C 313 583-5980
Dearborn *(G-3769)*

Vitesco Technologies G 248 393-5880
Detroit *(G-4434)*

Vitesco Technologies G 704 442-8000
Auburn Hills *(G-1046)*

Vitesco Technologies Usa LLC F 248 209-4000
Auburn Hills *(G-1047)*

Vortek G 248 767-2992
Pinckney *(G-12505)*

Walbro LLC C 989 872-2131
Cass City *(G-2524)*

Waldrons Antique Exhaust G 269 467-7185
Centreville *(G-2599)*

Walter Sappington G 989 345-1052
West Branch *(G-17527)*

Walther Trowal GMBH & Co KG G 616 871-0031
Grand Rapids *(G-6979)*

Warn Industries Inc G 734 953-9870
Livonia *(G-9997)*

Warren Chassix G 248 728-8700
Warren *(G-17286)*

Warren Screw Products Inc C 586 757-1280
Warren *(G-17288)*

Webasto Roof Systems Inc F 248 997-5100
Rochester Hills *(G-13545)*

West Mich Auto Stl & Engrg Inc E 616 560-8198
Belding *(G-1431)*

West Michigan Gage Inc F 616 735-0585
Walker *(G-16882)*

Windsor Mch & Stamping 2009 D 734 941-7320
Taylor *(G-15782)*

Wkw Erbsloeh N Amer Holdg Inc D 205 338-4242
Troy *(G-16693)*

Wolfgang Moneta G 269 422-2296
Baroda *(G-1133)*

Yanfeng US Automotive E 616 392-5151
Holland *(G-7863)*

Yanfeng US Automotive D 616 392-5151
Holland *(G-7864)*

Young Diversified Industries G 248 353-1867
Southfield *(G-15069)*

ZF Active Safety & Elec US LLC A 586 843-2100
Livonia *(G-10013)*

ZF Active Safety US Inc G 906 248-3882
Brimley *(G-2017)*

ZF Active Safety US Inc C 517 223-8330
Fowlerville *(G-5581)*

ZF Active Safety US Inc C 810 750-1036
Fenton *(G-5250)*

ZF Active Safety US Inc A 586 232-7200
Washington *(G-17315)*

ZF Active Safety US Inc C 248 863-2412
Saginaw *(G-14185)*

ZF Axle Drives Marysville LLC B 810 989-8702
Marysville *(G-10627)*

ZF Lemforder Corp F 810 245-7136
Lapeer *(G-9496)*

ZF North America Inc B 734 416-6200
Northville *(G-11735)*

ZF North America Inc G 734 416-6200
Northville *(G-11736)*

ZF Passive Safety B 248 478-7210
Farmington Hills *(G-5155)*

ZF Passive Safety Systems US E 586 752-1409
Romeo *(G-13643)*

ZF Passive Safety Systems US B 586 781-5511
Washington *(G-17317)*

ZF Passive Safety US Inc F 734 855-2600
Livonia *(G-10019)*

ZF Passive Safety US Inc G 586 232-7200
Washington *(G-17318)*

ZF Passive Sfety Systems US In A 586 232-7200
Washington *(G-17319)*

ZF String Active Safety US Inc G 734 855-2600
Livonia *(G-10020)*

ZF TRW Auto Holdings Corp A 734 855-2600
Livonia *(G-10021)*

Zynp International Corp E 734 947-1000
Romulus *(G-13746)*

AUTOMOTIVE PARTS: Plastic

Adduxi E 248 564-2000
Rochester Hills *(G-13364)*

Advanced Composite Tech Inc G 248 709-9097
Rochester *(G-13311)*

Aktis Engrg Solutions Inc G 313 450-2420
Southfield *(G-14826)*

Anderton Machining LLC G 517 905-5155
Jackson *(G-8384)*

Blue Fire Manufacturing LLC E 248 714-7166
Waterford *(G-17325)*

Cadillac Products Inc D 989 766-2294
Rogers City *(G-13613)*

Capsonic Automotive Inc G 248 754-1100
Auburn Hills *(G-809)*

Conatus Inc G 810 494-6210
Brighton *(G-1901)*

Creed Development G 248 926-9811
Novi *(G-11857)*

Crescent Machining Inc G 248 541-7010
Oak Park *(G-12055)*

Crw Plastics Usa Inc C 517 545-0900
Howell *(G-8027)*

Dupearl Technology LLC D 248 390-9609
Bloomfield Hills *(G-1762)*

Enovapremier LLC G 517 541-3200
Charlotte *(G-2646)*

Fischer America Inc C 248 276-1940
Auburn Hills *(G-874)*

Flex-N Gate Shelby LLC C 586 759-8092
Warren *(G-17035)*

Flex-N-Gate Detroit LLC B 586 759-8092
Warren *(G-17038)*

Global Automotive Products Inc E 734 589-6179
Romulus *(G-13680)*

Henry Machine Shop G 989 777-8495
Saginaw *(G-14056)*

IAC Mexico Holdings Inc G 248 455-7000
Southfield *(G-14941)*

Employee Codes: A=Over 500 employees, B=251-500
C=101-250, D=51-100, E=20-50, F=10-19, G=3-9

2020 Harris Michigan
Industrial Directory

1153

AUTOMOTIVE PARTS: Plastic

IAC Plymouth LLC ....E 734 207-7000
  Plymouth *(G-12645)*
Illinois Tool Works Inc ....D 248 589-2500
  Troy *(G-16410)*
Ims/Chinatool Jv LLC ....G 734 466-5151
  Livonia *(G-9781)*
Inoac Interior Systems LLC ....E 248 488-7610
  Farmington Hills *(G-5028)*
International Automotive Compo ....B 734 456-2800
  Plymouth *(G-12648)*
International Automotive Compo ....B 586 795-7800
  Sterling Heights *(G-15376)*
International Automotive Compo ....A 248 455-7000
  Southfield *(G-14948)*
JD Plastics Inc ....G 517 264-6858
  Adrian *(G-72)*
Jvis - Usa LLC ....F 586 884-5700
  Shelby Township *(G-14613)*
Jvis Fh LLC ....E 248 478-2900
  Farmington Hills *(G-5036)*
Jvis International LLC ....D 586 739-9542
  Shelby Township *(G-14614)*
Keiper LLC ....C 248 655-5100
  Troy *(G-16445)*
Kyrie Enterprises LLC ....E 248 549-8690
  Royal Oak *(G-13943)*
Lacks Exterior Systems LLC ....C 616 949-6570
  Grand Rapids *(G-6602)*
Lacks Exterior Systems LLC ....C 616 949-6570
  Grand Rapids *(G-6603)*
Lacks Exterior Systems LLC ....C 616 949-6570
  Grand Rapids *(G-6604)*
Ligon Helicopter Corporation ....G 810 706-1885
  Almont *(G-261)*
Macauto U S A Inc ....G 248 499-8208
  Rochester Hills *(G-13465)*
Macauto Usa Inc ....G 248 556-5256
  Troy *(G-16469)*
Machine Tool & Gear Inc ....D 989 743-3936
  Corunna *(G-3581)*
McKechnie Vhcl Cmpnnts USA Inc .....F 586 491-2600
  Roseville *(G-13833)*
Moon Roof Corporation America ....E 586 772-8730
  Roseville *(G-13839)*
Mubea Inc ....D 248 393-9600
  Auburn Hills *(G-950)*
Noble Polymers LLC ....F 616 975-4800
  Grand Rapids *(G-6717)*
North American Assembly LLC ....E 248 335-6702
  Auburn Hills *(G-960)*
North American Mold LLC ....E 248 335-6702
  Auburn Hills *(G-961)*
Novares Corporation US Inc ....G 248 449-6100
  Livonia *(G-9865)*
Novares US LLC ....D 248 449-6100
  Livonia *(G-9866)*
NPR of America Inc ....F 248 449-8955
  Novi *(G-11959)*
Opeo Inc ....F 248 299-4000
  Auburn Hills *(G-966)*
Pierburg Pump Tech US LLC ....G 864 688-1322
  Auburn Hills *(G-972)*
Pioneer Plastics Inc ....E 586 262-0159
  Warren *(G-17187)*
Plastech Weld ....G 313 963-3194
  Detroit *(G-4305)*
Plastic Omnium Auto Exteriors ....B 248 458-0700
  Troy *(G-16551)*
Preferred Plastics Inc ....D 269 685-5873
  Plainwell *(G-12540)*
Prism Plastics Inc ....F 810 292-6300
  Chesterfield *(G-2821)*
Proper Group International Inc ....G 586 779-8787
  Warren *(G-17205)*
Roberts Tool Company ....F 517 423-6691
  Tecumseh *(G-15807)*
Rocktech Systems LLC ....E 586 330-9031
  Chesterfield *(G-2832)*
S&S Precision LLC ....G 248 266-4770
  Wixom *(G-17889)*
SA Automotive Ltd ....C 517 521-4205
  Webberville *(G-17453)*
Schwintek Inc ....G 269 445-9999
  Cassopolis *(G-2535)*
Summit Polymers Inc ....G 269 324-9320
  Portage *(G-13046)*
Svrc Industries Inc ....E 989 280-3038
  Saginaw *(G-14159)*
Tepso Gen-X Plastics LLC ....G 248 869-2130
  Wixom *(G-17908)*
Thunder Bay Pattern Works Inc ....E 586 783-1126
  Clinton Township *(G-3246)*
Toyoda Gosei North Amer Corp ....C 248 280-2100
  Troy *(G-16650)*
Tribar Technologies Inc ....B 248 516-1600
  Wixom *(G-17918)*
Tribar Technologies Inc ....A 248 516-1600
  Wixom *(G-17919)*
US Farathane Holdings Corp ....B 248 754-7000
  Shelby Township *(G-14715)*
US Farathane Holdings Corp ....C 780 246-1034
  Auburn Hills *(G-1038)*
US Farathane Holdings Corp ....F 248 391-6801
  Auburn Hills *(G-1039)*
Valley Enterprises Ubly Inc ....C 989 658-3200
  Ubly *(G-16726)*
Williamston Products Inc ....D 517 655-2131
  Williamston *(G-17742)*
Williamston Products Inc ....E 517 655-2273
  Williamston *(G-17743)*
Williamston Products Inc ....D 989 723-0149
  Owosso *(G-12329)*
Wow Plastics LLC ....G 760 827-7800
  Caro *(G-2482)*
Yapp USA Auto Systems Inc ....G 248 404-8696
  Romulus *(G-13745)*

AUTOMOTIVE PRDTS: Rubber

Airboss Flexible Products Co ....C 248 852-5500
  Auburn Hills *(G-763)*
Changan US RES & Dev Ctr Inc ....G 734 259-6440
  Plymouth *(G-12596)*
Evans Industries Inc ....G 313 259-2266
  Detroit *(G-4045)*
Henniges Auto Holdings Inc ....B 248 340-4100
  Auburn Hills *(G-896)*
Hutchinson Sealing Syst ....D 248 375-3721
  Auburn Hills *(G-904)*
Hutchinson Sealing Systems Inc ....D 248 375-3720
  Auburn Hills *(G-905)*
Inoac Interior Systems LLC ....E 248 488-7610
  Farmington Hills *(G-5028)*
Korens ....G 248 817-5188
  Rochester Hills *(G-13456)*
Nitto Inc ....F 734 729-7800
  Romulus *(G-13714)*
Northern Tire Inc ....F 906 486-4463
  Ishpeming *(G-8350)*
Opeo Inc ....F 248 299-4000
  Auburn Hills *(G-966)*
Rajason International Corp ....G 248 506-4456
  Troy *(G-16576)*

AUTOMOTIVE RADIATOR REPAIR SHOPS

Colberg Radiator & Welding ....G 810 742-0028
  Burton *(G-2149)*
Fenton Radiator & Garage Inc ....G 810 629-0923
  Fenton *(G-5212)*

AUTOMOTIVE REPAIR SHOPS: Diesel Engine Repair

Cummins Inc ....F 989 732-5055
  Gaylord *(G-5854)*
Cummins Inc ....E 313 843-6200
  Dearborn *(G-3688)*
Cummins Inc ....E 989 752-5200
  Saginaw *(G-14023)*
Detroit Diesel Corporation ....A 313 592-5000
  Detroit *(G-3980)*
Detroit Diesel Corporation ....F 313 592-8256
  Redford *(G-13157)*

AUTOMOTIVE REPAIR SHOPS: Electrical Svcs

Auto Clinic ....G 906 774-5780
  Iron Mountain *(G-8275)*
Creative Power Systems Inc ....E 313 961-2460
  Detroit *(G-3954)*
Dearborn Total Auto Svc Ctr ....F 313 291-6300
  Dearborn Heights *(G-3781)*
Precision Race Services Inc ....G 248 634-4010
  Davisburg *(G-3638)*
Solutions For Industry Inc ....G 517 448-8608
  Hudson *(G-8142)*

AUTOMOTIVE REPAIR SHOPS: Engine Rebuilding

Chesterfield Engines Inc ....G 586 949-5777
  Chesterfield *(G-2753)*
D & S Engine Specialist Inc ....F 248 583-9240
  Clawson *(G-2976)*
Daniel Pruitoff ....G 616 392-1371
  Holland *(G-7605)*
Falvey Limited ....G 517 263-2699
  Adrian *(G-64)*

AUTOMOTIVE REPAIR SHOPS: Engine Repair

Creek Diesel Services Inc ....F 800 974-4600
  Grand Rapids *(G-6316)*
Kyrie Enterprises LLC ....E 248 549-8690
  Royal Oak *(G-13943)*

AUTOMOTIVE REPAIR SHOPS: Frame & Front End Repair Svcs

Axle of Dearborn Inc ....G 313 581-3300
  Detroit *(G-3888)*

AUTOMOTIVE REPAIR SHOPS: Fuel System Repair

Howell Engine Developments Inc ....F 810 765-5100
  Cottrellville *(G-3587)*

AUTOMOTIVE REPAIR SHOPS: Machine Shop

Busche Southfield Inc ....C 248 357-5180
  Southfield *(G-14860)*
Chesterfield Engines Inc ....G 586 949-5777
  Chesterfield *(G-2753)*
Daniel Pruitoff ....G 616 392-1371
  Holland *(G-7605)*
David A Mohr Jr ....G 517 266-2694
  Adrian *(G-58)*
Experienced Concepts Inc ....F 586 752-4200
  Armada *(G-719)*
General Parts Inc ....E 989 686-3114
  Bay City *(G-1316)*
Midwest Fabricating Inc ....G 734 921-3914
  Taylor *(G-15744)*
Mjc Tool & Machine Co Inc ....G 586 790-4766
  Clinton Township *(G-3179)*
Mtm Machine Inc ....G 586 443-5703
  Fraser *(G-5696)*
New Concept Products Inc ....G 269 679-5970
  Schoolcraft *(G-14500)*
Oilpatch Machine Tool Inc ....G 989 772-0637
  Mount Pleasant *(G-11215)*
Peak Manufacturing Inc ....E 517 769-6900
  Pleasant Lake *(G-12553)*
Pitchford Bertie ....G 517 627-1151
  Grand Ledge *(G-6113)*
Senneker Enterprises Inc ....G 616 877-4440
  Dorr *(G-4528)*
Three-Dimensional Services Inc ....C 248 852-1333
  Rochester Hills *(G-13525)*
V J Industries Inc ....F 810 364-6470
  Marine City *(G-10486)*
Vochaska Engineering ....G 269 637-5670
  South Haven *(G-14782)*

AUTOMOTIVE REPAIR SHOPS: Muffler Shop, Sale/Rpr/Installation

Dearborn Total Auto Svc Ctr ....F 313 291-6300
  Dearborn Heights *(G-3781)*

AUTOMOTIVE REPAIR SHOPS: Springs, Rebuilding & Repair

Beattie Spring & Welding Svc ....G 810 239-9151
  Flint *(G-5386)*

AUTOMOTIVE REPAIR SHOPS: Trailer Repair

A and D Design Electronics ....G 989 493-1884
  Auburn *(G-748)*
Ajax Trailers Inc ....F 586 757-7676
  Warren *(G-16923)*
D & W Management Company Inc ....E 586 758-2284
  Warren *(G-16996)*

PRODUCT SECTION

AUTOMOTIVE SPLYS/PARTS, NEW, WHOL: Body Rpr/Paint Shop Splys

Lupa R A and Sons Repair ....G....... 810 346-3579
  Marlette *(G-10498)*
Transport Trailers Co ....G....... 269 543-4405
  Fennville *(G-5178)*

AUTOMOTIVE REPAIR SHOPS: Truck Engine Repair, Exc Indl

M R D Industries ....G....... 269 623-8452
  Delton *(G-3818)*
Midwest Tractor & Equipment Co ....F 231 269-4100
  Buckley *(G-2130)*

AUTOMOTIVE REPAIR SVC

Benlee Inc ....E....... 586 791-1830
  Romulus *(G-13656)*
Clydes Frame & Wheel Service ....F 248 338-0323
  Pontiac *(G-12810)*
Energy Products Inc ....D....... 248 545-7700
  Madison Heights *(G-10247)*
Energy Products Inc ....G....... 248 866-5622
  Troy *(G-16345)*
Kern Auto Sales and Svc LLC ....F 734 475-2722
  Chelsea *(G-2715)*
Kustom Creations Inc ....G....... 586 997-4141
  Sterling Heights *(G-15394)*
Muskegon Brake & Distrg Co LLC ....E....... 231 733-0874
  Norton Shores *(G-11776)*
Nash Services ....G....... 269 782-2016
  Dowagiac *(G-4555)*
Valley Truck Parts Inc ....D....... 616 241-5431
  Wyoming *(G-18040)*

AUTOMOTIVE REPAIR SVCS, MISCELLANEOUS

RB Oil Enterprises LLC ....G....... 734 354-0700
  Plymouth *(G-12730)*

AUTOMOTIVE SPLYS & PARTS, NEW, WHOL: Auto Servicing Eqpt

Magna Mirrors America Inc ....C....... 616 786-7000
  Holland *(G-7737)*
Single Source Inc ....G....... 765 825-4111
  Flat Rock *(G-5365)*

AUTOMOTIVE SPLYS & PARTS, NEW, WHOLESALE: Alternators

Nabco Inc ....G....... 231 832-2001
  Reed City *(G-13221)*

AUTOMOTIVE SPLYS & PARTS, NEW, WHOLESALE: Clutches

Ogura Corporation ....C....... 586 749-1900
  Chesterfield *(G-2812)*

AUTOMOTIVE SPLYS & PARTS, NEW, WHOLESALE: Engines/Eng Parts

Continental Auto Systems Inc ....B....... 248 209-4000
  Auburn Hills *(G-820)*
GKN Driveline North Amer Inc ....B....... 248 296-7000
  Auburn Hills *(G-885)*
Illinois Tool Works Inc ....D....... 248 589-2500
  Troy *(G-16410)*

AUTOMOTIVE SPLYS & PARTS, NEW, WHOLESALE: Filters, Air & Oil

Unifilter Inc ....E....... 248 476-5100
  Novi *(G-12023)*

AUTOMOTIVE SPLYS & PARTS, NEW, WHOLESALE: Hardware

Axle of Dearborn Inc ....C....... 248 543-5995
  Ferndale *(G-5263)*
D2t America Inc ....F 248 680-9001
  Rochester Hills *(G-13400)*

AUTOMOTIVE SPLYS & PARTS, NEW, WHOLESALE: Radiators

D & B Heat Transfer Pdts Inc ....F 616 827-0028
  Grand Rapids *(G-6327)*

AUTOMOTIVE SPLYS & PARTS, NEW, WHOLESALE: Seat Belts

Craig Assembly Inc ....C....... 810 326-1374
  Saint Clair *(G-14212)*

AUTOMOTIVE SPLYS & PARTS, NEW, WHOLESALE: Splys

Conatus Inc ....G....... 810 494-6210
  Brighton *(G-1901)*
Ziebart International Corp ....C....... 248 588-4100
  Troy *(G-16706)*

AUTOMOTIVE SPLYS & PARTS, NEW, WHOLESALE: Stampings

Matcor Automotive Michigan Inc ....C....... 616 527-4050
  Ionia *(G-8248)*

AUTOMOTIVE SPLYS & PARTS, NEW, WHOLESALE: Tools & Eqpt

K-Tool Corporation Michigan ....D....... 863 603-0777
  Plymouth *(G-12661)*
Tooling Cncepts Design Not Inc ....F 810 444-9807
  Port Huron *(G-12972)*

AUTOMOTIVE SPLYS & PARTS, NEW, WHOLESALE: Trim

Detroit Tarpaulin Repr Sp Inc ....E....... 734 955-8200
  Romulus *(G-13666)*

AUTOMOTIVE SPLYS & PARTS, NEW, WHOLESALE: Wheels

Hot Wheels City Inc ....E....... 248 589-8800
  Madison Heights *(G-10268)*

AUTOMOTIVE SPLYS & PARTS, USED, WHOLESALE

D & D Fabrications Inc ....G....... 810 798-2491
  Almont *(G-255)*
Mr Axle ....F 231 788-4624
  Muskegon *(G-11386)*
North American Auto Inds Inc ....G....... 734 288-3877
  Riverview *(G-13302)*
Valley Truck Parts Inc ....D....... 616 241-5431
  Wyoming *(G-18040)*

AUTOMOTIVE SPLYS & PARTS, USED, WHOLESALE: Access, NEC

Gemo Hopkins Usa Inc ....G....... 734 330-1271
  Auburn Hills *(G-882)*

AUTOMOTIVE SPLYS & PARTS, WHOLESALE, NEC

Aapico Detroit LLC ....D....... 313 551-6001
  Detroit *(G-3835)*
Alpha Technology Corporation ....E....... 517 546-9700
  Howell *(G-8011)*
American Furukawa Inc ....E....... 734 254-0344
  Plymouth *(G-12570)*
Asimco International Inc ....G....... 248 213-5200
  Southfield *(G-14841)*
Auto-Masters Inc ....E....... 616 455-4510
  Grand Rapids *(G-6190)*
Bentler Industries Inc ....G....... 269 665-4261
  Galesburg *(G-5808)*
Can-AM Engineered Products ....G....... 734 427-2020
  Livonia *(G-9673)*
Canadian Amrcn Rstoration Sups ....E....... 248 853-8900
  Rochester Hills *(G-13384)*
CC Industries LLC ....D....... 269 426-3342
  Sawyer *(G-14483)*
CCI Driveline LLC ....G....... 586 716-1160
  Casco *(G-2499)*
Cinnabar Engineering Inc ....F 810 648-2444
  Sandusky *(G-14431)*
Eagle Thread Verifier Inc ....G....... 586 764-8218
  Sterling Heights *(G-15327)*
Ena North America Corporation ....F 248 926-0011
  Wixom *(G-17803)*
Erin Industries Inc ....E....... 248 669-2050
  Walled Lake *(G-16893)*
Etx Holdings Inc ....G....... 989 463-1151
  Alma *(G-237)*
F J Lucido & Associates ....E....... 586 574-3577
  Warren *(G-17028)*
F M T Products Inc ....G....... 517 568-3373
  Homer *(G-7942)*
Faurecia Interior Systems Inc ....B....... 248 724-5100
  Auburn Hills *(G-861)*
Faurecia North America Inc ....F 248 288-1000
  Auburn Hills *(G-863)*
Federal-Mogul Powertrain LLC ....G....... 248 354-7700
  Southfield *(G-14910)*
General Parts Inc ....E....... 989 686-3114
  Bay City *(G-1316)*
Hella Corporate Center USA Inc ....E....... 586 232-4788
  Northville *(G-11697)*
Henniges Automotive N America ....C....... 248 340-4100
  Auburn Hills *(G-898)*
Horizon Intl Group LLC ....D....... 734 341-9336
  Birmingham *(G-1686)*
HP Pelzer Auto Systems Inc ....E....... 810 987-4444
  Port Huron *(G-12926)*
Ididit Inc ....E....... 517 424-0577
  Tecumseh *(G-15798)*
K & K Mfg Inc ....G....... 616 784-4286
  Sparta *(G-15100)*
Kirks Automotive Incorporated ....E....... 313 933-7030
  Detroit *(G-4179)*
Mahle Behr Mfg MGT Inc ....A....... 248 735-3623
  Troy *(G-16480)*
N S International Ltd ....C....... 248 251-1600
  Troy *(G-16519)*
NSK Americas Inc ....C....... 734 913-7500
  Ann Arbor *(G-577)*
Opeo Inc ....F 248 299-4000
  Auburn Hills *(G-966)*
Piolax Corporation ....F 734 668-6005
  Plymouth *(G-12717)*
Polytec Foha Inc ....F 586 978-9386
  Warren *(G-17188)*
Quality Spring/Togo Inc ....C....... 517 278-2391
  Coldwater *(G-3323)*
Robert Bosch LLC ....E....... 248 921-9054
  Novi *(G-11987)*
Robert Bosch LLC ....A....... 734 979-3000
  Plymouth *(G-12741)*
S&S Precision LLC ....G....... 248 266-4770
  Wixom *(G-17889)*
Toledo Molding & Die Inc ....G....... 734 233-6338
  Plymouth *(G-12773)*
Toyo Seat USA Corporation ....C....... 606 849-3009
  Imlay City *(G-8212)*
Transpak Inc ....E....... 586 264-2064
  Sterling Heights *(G-15528)*
Valley Truck Parts Inc ....D....... 616 241-5431
  Wyoming *(G-18040)*
Van-Rob Inc ....C....... 517 657-2450
  Lansing *(G-9271)*
Vectorall Manufacturing Inc ....E....... 248 486-4570
  Brighton *(G-2006)*
Woodbridge Sales & Engrg Inc ....C....... 248 288-0100
  Troy *(G-16698)*
Worldwide Marketing Services ....E....... 269 556-2000
  Saint Joseph *(G-14355)*
Yazaki International Corp ....G....... 734 983-1000
  Canton *(G-2445)*
ZF North America Inc ....B....... 734 416-6200
  Northville *(G-11735)*
ZF North America Inc ....G....... 734 416-6200
  Northville *(G-11736)*

AUTOMOTIVE SPLYS, USED, WHOLESALE & RETAIL

Innovation Unlimited LLC ....G....... 574 635-1064
  Bay City *(G-1322)*

AUTOMOTIVE SPLYS/PART, NEW, WHOL: Spring, Shock Absorb/Strut

Magneti Marelli North Amer Inc ....G....... 248 418-3000
  Auburn Hills *(G-939)*
Thyssenkrupp Bilstein Amer Inc ....F 248 530-2900
  Troy *(G-16641)*

AUTOMOTIVE SPLYS/PARTS, NEW, WHOL: Body Rpr/Paint Shop Splys

Auto Clinic ....G....... 906 774-5780
  Iron Mountain *(G-8275)*

Employee Codes: A=Over 500 employees, B=251-500
C=101-250, D=51-100, E=20-50, F=10-19, G=3-9

AUTOMOTIVE SPLYS/PARTS, NEW, WHOL: Body Rpr/Paint Shop Splys

Reliance Spray Mask Co Inc ....F....... 616 784-3664
  Grand Rapids (G-6819)

AUTOMOTIVE SVCS, EXC REPAIR & CARWASHES: Customizing

Priority One Emergency Inc ....G....... 734 398-5900
  Canton (G-2419)

AUTOMOTIVE SVCS, EXC REPAIR & CARWASHES: Fuel Sys Conv

Oscar W Larson Company ....G....... 248 575-0320
  Clarkston (G-2943)

AUTOMOTIVE SVCS, EXC REPAIR & CARWASHES: Glass Tinting

Car Audio Outlet LLC ....G....... 810 686-3300
  Clio (G-3266)

AUTOMOTIVE SVCS, EXC REPAIR & CARWASHES: Insp & Diagnostic

Bosch Auto Svc Solutions Inc ....C....... 586 574-2332
  Warren (G-16963)
P G S Inc ....C....... 248 526-3800
  Troy (G-16540)
Spec Technologies Inc ....D....... 586 726-0000
  Shelby Township (G-14700)

AUTOMOTIVE SVCS, EXC REPAIR & CARWASHES: Lubrication

Mark 7 Machine Inc ....G....... 989 922-7335
  Bay City (G-1327)
Ziebart International Corp ....C....... 248 588-4100
  Troy (G-16706)

AUTOMOTIVE SVCS, EXC REPAIR & CARWASHES: Maintenance

Dynamic Auto Test Engineering ....G....... 269 342-1334
  Portage (G-12991)

AUTOMOTIVE SVCS, EXC REPAIR & CARWASHES: Road Svc

Michigan Paving and Mtls Co ....D....... 517 787-4200
  Jackson (G-8520)

AUTOMOTIVE SVCS, EXC REPAIR: Carwash, Automatic

Treib Inc ....F....... 989 752-4821
  Saginaw (G-14166)

AUTOMOTIVE SVCS, EXC REPAIR: Carwash, Self-Service

Imlay City High Pressure ....G....... 810 395-7459
  Capac (G-2448)

AUTOMOTIVE SVCS, EXC REPAIR: Truck Wash

Interclean Equipment LLC ....E....... 734 961-3300
  Ypsilanti (G-18082)

AUTOMOTIVE SVCS, EXC REPAIR: Washing & Polishing

Floss Automotive Group ....G....... 734 773-2524
  Inkster (G-8227)

AUTOMOTIVE TRANSMISSION REPAIR SVC

Quaker Chemical Corporation ....G....... 586 826-6454
  Sterling Heights (G-15458)

AUTOMOTIVE UPHOLSTERY SHOPS

Dts Enterprises Inc ....E....... 231 599-3123
  Ellsworth (G-4787)
G&G Industries Inc ....E....... 586 726-6000
  Shelby Township (G-14595)
Lear Automotive Mfg LLC ....F....... 248 447-1603
  Detroit (G-4196)
Lear Automotive Mfg LLC ....F....... 248 447-1603
  Detroit (G-4197)

Shelby Auto Trim Inc ....F....... 586 939-9090
  Sterling Heights (G-15495)

AUTOMOTIVE WELDING SVCS

Angstrom Automotive Group LLC ....G....... 313 295-0100
  Taylor (G-15689)
Arcelormittal Tailored Blanks ....B....... 313 332-5300
  Detroit (G-3873)
Britten Metalworks LLC ....G....... 231 421-1615
  Traverse City (G-15921)
Classic Welding Inc ....F....... 586 758-2400
  Warren (G-16983)
David A Mohr Jr ....G....... 517 266-2694
  Adrian (G-58)
Gustos Quality Systems ....G....... 231 409-0219
  Fife Lake (G-5341)
Ianna Fab Inc ....G....... 586 739-2410
  Shelby Township (G-14603)
Joy Industries Inc ....F....... 248 334-4062
  Pontiac (G-12842)
Krause Welding Inc ....F....... 231 773-4443
  Muskegon (G-11358)
Mico Industries Inc ....D....... 616 245-6426
  Grand Rapids (G-6679)
Midwest Fabricating Inc ....G....... 734 921-3914
  Taylor (G-15744)
O E M Company Inc ....E....... 810 985-9070
  Port Huron (G-12951)
Response Welding Inc ....G....... 586 795-8090
  Sterling Heights (G-15466)
Technique Inc ....D....... 517 789-8988
  Jackson (G-8585)
UP Truck Center Inc ....E....... 906 774-0098
  Quinnesec (G-13103)
Virtec Manufacturing LLC ....F....... 313 590-2367
  Roseville (G-13889)
Wellington Industries Inc ....E....... 734 403-6112
  Van Buren Twp (G-16797)

AUTOMOTIVE: Bodies

Bordrin Motor Corporation Inc ....G....... 877 507-3267
  Oak Park (G-12052)
Detroit Mfg Systems LLC ....D....... 313 243-0700
  Detroit (G-3989)
HP Pelzer Automotive Systems ....E....... 810 987-0725
  Port Huron (G-12927)
Quality Inspections Inc ....G....... 586 323-6135
  Sterling Heights (G-15459)
Ralyas Auto Body Incorporated ....G....... 517 694-6512
  Mason (G-10652)
Special Projects Inc ....E....... 734 455-7130
  Plymouth (G-12759)

AUTOMOTIVE: Seat Frames, Metal

Camaco LLC ....E....... 248 442-6800
  Farmington Hills (G-4954)
Metalbuilt Tactical LLC ....E....... 586 786-9106
  Macomb (G-10141)
Nortech LLC ....E....... 248 446-7575
  New Hudson (G-11550)
P & C Group I Inc ....E....... 248 442-6800
  Farmington Hills (G-5087)

AUTOMOTIVE: Seating

Adient Inc ....D....... 734 254-5000
  Plymouth (G-12563)
American Metal Fab Inc ....D....... 269 279-5108
  Three Rivers (G-15854)
Bridgewater Interiors LLC ....F....... 517 322-4800
  Lansing (G-9279)
Bridgewater Interiors LLC ....A....... 586 582-0882
  Warren (G-16967)
Faurecia Auto Seating LLC ....B....... 248 563-9241
  Highland Park (G-7503)
Faurecia Auto Seating LLC ....C....... 248 563-9241
  Highland Park (G-7504)
Fisher & Company Incorporated ....B....... 586 746-2000
  Saint Clair Shores (G-14249)
Fisher & Company Incorporated ....G....... 248 280-0808
  Troy (G-16362)
Fisher Dynamics Corporation ....E....... 586 746-2000
  Saint Clair Shores (G-14251)
Greenfield Holdings LLC ....F....... 734 530-5600
  Brownstown (G-2064)
Hoover Universal Inc ....E....... 734 454-0994
  Plymouth (G-12642)
Integrated Mfg & Assembly LLC ....E....... 313 267-2634
  Detroit (G-4143)

Integrated Mfg & Assembly LLC ....B....... 734 530-5600
  Detroit (G-4144)
Isringhausen Inc ....C....... 269 484-5333
  Galesburg (G-5812)
Johnson Controls Inc ....D....... 616 283-5578
  Holland (G-7696)
Johnson Controls Inc ....G....... 269 226-4748
  Portage (G-13003)
Johnson Controls Inc ....G....... 866 252-3677
  Grand Rapids (G-6563)
Johnson Controls Inc ....E....... 616 847-2766
  Spring Lake (G-15156)
Johnson Controls Inc ....E....... 269 323-0988
  Kalamazoo (G-8781)
Lear Corporation ....B....... 269 496-2215
  Mendon (G-10715)
Lear Corporation ....B....... 248 447-1500
  Southfield (G-14962)
Lear European Operations Corp ....G....... 248 447-1500
  Southfield (G-14963)
Lear Mexican Seating Corp ....G....... 248 447-1500
  Southfield (G-14964)
Promax Engineering LLC ....C....... 734 979-0888
  Westland (G-17591)
Recaro North America Inc ....D....... 734 254-5000
  Plymouth (G-12733)
Tachi-S Engineering USA Inc ....D....... 248 478-5050
  Farmington Hills (G-5139)
Toyo Seat USA Corporation ....C....... 606 849-3009
  Imlay City (G-8212)
Woodbridge Holdings Inc ....G....... 248 288-0100
  Troy (G-16697)
Yanfeng US Automotive ....B....... 248 319-7333
  Novi (G-12027)
Yanfeng US Automotive ....E....... 616 394-1199
  Holland (G-7865)
Yanfeng US Automotive ....F....... 586 354-2101
  Harrison Township (G-7358)
Yanfeng US Automotive ....G....... 616 394-1523
  Holland (G-7866)

AUTOTRANSFORMERS: Electric

Controlled Magnetics Inc ....F....... 734 449-7225
  Whitmore Lake (G-17693)
Gti Power Acquisition LLC ....D....... 616 842-5430
  Grand Haven (G-6029)
Rizk National Industries Inc ....E....... 586 757-4700
  Warren (G-17221)

AWNINGS & CANOPIES

Case-Free Inc ....G....... 616 245-3136
  Grand Rapids (G-6265)
D & W Awning and Window Co ....E....... 810 742-0340
  Davison (G-3645)

AWNINGS & CANOPIES: Awnings, Fabric, From Purchased Matls

American Roll Shutter Awng Co ....E....... 734 422-7110
  Livonia (G-9645)
Battle Creek Tent & Awning Co ....G....... 269 964-1824
  Battle Creek (G-1152)
Benton Harbor Awning & Tent ....E....... 800 272-2187
  Benton Harbor (G-1485)
Case-Free Inc ....G....... 616 245-3136
  Grand Rapids (G-6265)
Dial Tent & Awning Co ....F....... 989 793-0741
  Saginaw (G-14027)
Dockside Canvas Co Inc ....F....... 586 463-1231
  Harrison Township (G-7329)
Feb Inc ....F....... 231 759-0911
  Muskegon (G-11321)
Golden Needle Awnings LLC ....G....... 517 404-6219
  Gaines (G-5804)
Grand Traverse Canvas Works ....F....... 231 947-3140
  Traverse City (G-15982)
Holiday Distributing Co ....E....... 517 782-7146
  Jackson (G-8466)
J & K Canvas Products ....G....... 810 635-7711
  Flint (G-5451)
Jackson Canvas Company ....E....... 517 768-8459
  Jackson (G-8475)
Jacquart Fabric Products Inc ....C....... 906 932-1339
  Ironwood (G-8332)
Muskegon Awning & Mfg Co ....E....... 231 759-0911
  Muskegon (G-11387)
Quality Awning Shops Inc ....G....... 517 882-2491
  Lansing (G-9415)
Royal Oak & Birmingham Tent ....F....... 248 542-5552
  Royal Oak (G-13967)

PRODUCT SECTION

Traverse Bay Canvas Inc............................G...... 231 347-3001
  Harbor Springs (G-7296)

AWNINGS & CANOPIES: Fabric

Canvas Kings..G...... 616 846-6220
  Spring Lake (G-15135)
Industrial Fabric Products Inc ....G...... 269 932-4440
  Saint Joseph (G-14318)

AWNINGS: Fiberglass

Case-Free Inc ....G...... 616 245-3136
  Grand Rapids (G-6265)
Golden Pointe Inc ....G...... 313 581-8284
  Detroit (G-4096)

AWNINGS: Metal

A-1 Awning Company ....G...... 734 421-0680
  Westland (G-17537)
American Roll Shutter Awng Co ....E...... 734 422-7110
  Livonia (G-9645)
Mike Manufacturing Corporation............G...... 586 759-1140
  Warren (G-17156)
Patio Land Mfg Inc ....G...... 586 758-5660
  Warren (G-17184)
Seal All Aluminum Pdts Corp ....G...... 248 585-6061
  Southfield (G-15025)

AWNINGS: Wood

Wayne-Craft Inc...F...... 734 421-8800
  Livonia (G-10001)

AXLES

American Axle & Mfg Inc ....A...... 269 278-0211
  Three Rivers (G-15853)
American Axle Mfg Holdings Inc ....C...... 313 758-2000
  Detroit (G-3866)
Benteler Automotive Corp ....B...... 269 665-4261
  Galesburg (G-5807)
Meritor Indus Aftermarket LLC ....G...... 248 658-7345
  Troy (G-16495)
Metcalf Machine Inc ....G...... 616 837-8128
  Ravenna (G-13125)
Mr Axle ....F...... 231 788-4624
  Muskegon (G-11386)
Nexteer Automotive Corporation ....B...... 989 757-5000
  Saginaw (G-14107)
Nexteer Automotive Corporation ....A...... 989 757-5000
  Saginaw (G-14109)

AXLES: Rolled Or Forged, Made In Steel Mills

Axle of Dearborn Inc.................................C...... 248 543-5995
  Ferndale (G-5263)

BABBITT (METAL)

Airtec Corporation ....G...... 313 892-7800
  Detroit (G-3849)

BABY FORMULA

Gerber Products Company ....C...... 231 928-2000
  Fremont (G-5773)

BACKFILLERS: Self-Propelled

Wacker Neuson Corporation ....F...... 231 799-4500
  Norton Shores (G-11804)

BACKHOES

Ss Services..G...... 616 866-6453
  Rockford (G-13591)

BADGES, WHOLESALE

Jbl Enterprises ....G...... 616 530-8647
  Grand Rapids (G-6555)

BADGES: Identification & Insignia

Rodzina Industries Inc ....G...... 810 235-2341
  Flint (G-5493)

BAGS & CONTAINERS: Textile, Exc Sleeping

Industrial Bag & Spc Inc............................F...... 248 559-5550
  Southfield (G-14945)

JAC Custom Pouches Inc ....E...... 269 782-3190
  Dowagiac (G-4544)

BAGS & SACKS: Shipping & Shopping

McKenna Enterprises Inc ....G...... 248 375-3388
  Rochester Hills (G-13470)

BAGS: Canvas

Birlon Group LLC ....G...... 313 551-5341
  Inkster (G-8225)
Foreward Logistics LLC ....G...... 877 488-9724
  Oak Park (G-12068)

BAGS: Cement, Made From Purchased Materials

Lisa Bain..G...... 313 389-9661
  Allen Park (G-200)

BAGS: Food Storage & Trash, Plastic

Olivo LLC...G...... 313 573-7202
  Lincoln Park (G-9582)

BAGS: Garment Storage Exc Paper Or Plastic Film

Vega Manufacturing LLC..........................G...... 231 668-6365
  Traverse City (G-16136)

BAGS: Garment, Plastic Film, Made From Purchased Materials

D&Js Plastics LLC ....G...... 616 745-5798
  Hudsonville (G-8154)
Packaging Personified Inc ....C...... 616 887-8837
  Sparta (G-15105)

BAGS: Paper

Acme Mills Company ....C...... 517 437-8940
  Hillsdale (G-7513)
Concorde Inc ....F...... 248 391-8177
  Auburn Hills (G-817)

BAGS: Paper, Made From Purchased Materials

AJM Packaging Corporation ....E...... 313 291-6500
  Taylor (G-15685)
AJM Packaging Corporation ....D...... 248 901-0040
  Bloomfield Hills (G-1743)
AJM Packaging Corporation ....C...... 313 842-7530
  Detroit (G-3851)
Stewart Sutherland Inc ....C...... 269 649-0530
  Vicksburg (G-16844)

BAGS: Plastic

A-Pac Manufacturing Company...............E...... 616 791-7222
  Grand Rapids (G-6126)
Bioplstic Plymers Cmpsites LLC..............G...... 517 349-2970
  Okemos (G-12117)
Cadillac Products Inc ....D...... 989 766-2294
  Rogers City (G-13613)
Coveris ....E...... 269 964-1130
  Battle Creek (G-1169)
Idea Mia LLC..G...... 248 891-8939
  Lathrup Village (G-9500)
Plasport Inc ....G...... 231 935-1580
  Traverse City (G-16073)
Transcontinental US LLC ....D...... 269 964-7137
  Battle Creek (G-1259)

BAGS: Plastic & Pliofilm

Superior Polyolefin Films Inc ....G...... 248 334-8074
  Bloomfield Hills (G-1800)

BAGS: Plastic, Made From Purchased Materials

Bear Packaging and Supply.....................G...... 989 772-2268
  Mount Pleasant (G-11177)
Cadillac Products Inc ....D...... 586 774-1700
  Roseville (G-13779)
Cadillac Products Inc ....B...... 248 813-8200
  Troy (G-16253)
Carroll Products Inc...................................E...... 586 254-6300
  Sterling Heights (G-15282)

BAKERIES, COMMERCIAL: On Premises Baking Only

Lbv Sales LLC...G...... 616 874-9390
  Belmont (G-1465)
P-S Business Acquisition Inc ....E...... 616 887-8837
  Sparta (G-15104)
Quality Transparent Bag Inc ....F...... 989 893-3561
  Bay City (G-1344)

BAGS: Shipping

Pak-Rite Industries Inc ....D...... 313 388-6400
  Ecorse (G-4744)

BAGS: Shopping, Made From Purchased Materials

Olivo LLC...G...... 313 573-7202
  Lincoln Park (G-9582)

BAGS: Textile

Acme Mills Company ....C...... 517 437-8940
  Hillsdale (G-7513)
Total Packaging Solutions LLC ....G...... 248 519-2376
  Troy (G-16649)

BAGS: Trash, Plastic Film, Made From Purchased Materials

Michigan Poly Supplies Inc......................G...... 734 282-5554
  Taylor (G-15743)

BAKERIES, COMMERCIAL: On Premises Baking Only

Achatzs Hand Made Pie Co ....D...... 586 749-2882
  Chesterfield (G-2731)
Almar Orchards LLC..................................E...... 810 659-6568
  Flushing (G-5531)
Apple Valley Natural Foods......................C...... 269 471-3234
  Berrien Springs (G-1592)
Barneys Bakery ....G...... 989 895-5466
  Bay City (G-1281)
Big Boy Restaurants Intl LLC ....D...... 586 263-6220
  Clinton Township (G-3067)
Bimbo Bakeries Usa Inc ....E...... 989 667-0551
  Bay City (G-1291)
Bimbo Bakeries Usa Inc ....E...... 586 772-0055
  Warren (G-16960)
Campbell Soup Company ....F...... 313 295-6884
  Taylor (G-15698)
Campbell Soup Company ....D...... 248 336-8486
  Ferndale (G-5265)
Care2share Baking Company ....G...... 810 280-0307
  Attica (G-739)
Carlson Enterprises Inc.............................G...... 248 656-1442
  Rochester Hills (G-13385)
Coles Quality Foods Inc ....E...... 231 722-1651
  Muskegon (G-11295)
Cottage Bakery...G...... 989 790-8135
  Saginaw (G-14021)
Country Mill Farms LLC ....E...... 517 543-1019
  Charlotte (G-2642)
Cupcake Station ....G...... 248 334-7927
  Pontiac (G-12812)
Dakota Cupcake Factory ....G...... 810 694-7198
  Grand Blanc (G-5964)
Evelyn Robertson Lett...............................G...... 248 569-8746
  Southfield (G-14901)
Farmington Bakery ....G...... 248 442-2360
  Farmington (G-4899)
For The Love of Cupcakes ....G...... 906 399-3004
  Bark River (G-1119)
G M Paris Bakery Inc ....E...... 734 425-2060
  Livonia (G-9746)
Great Harvest Bread Co ....G...... 586 566-9500
  Shelby Township (G-14598)
Home Bakery ....E...... 248 651-4830
  Rochester (G-13326)
Hostess Cake ITT Contntl Bkg.................G...... 231 775-4629
  Cadillac (G-2253)
Jaimes Cupcake Haven ....G...... 586 596-6809
  Warren (G-17111)
Jorgensens Inc..E...... 989 831-8338
  Greenville (G-7140)
Josefs French Pastry Shop Co ....E...... 313 881-5710
  Grosse Pointe Woods (G-7204)
Julian Brothers Inc ....E...... 248 588-0280
  Clawson (G-2981)
Keebler Company ....B...... 269 961-2000
  Battle Creek (G-1207)

Employee Codes: A=Over 500 employees, B=251-500
C=101-250, D=51-100, E=20-50, F=10-19, G=3-9

2020 Harris Michigan
Industrial Directory

BAKERIES, COMMERCIAL: On Premises Baking Only

Kellers Farm Bakery ....G..... 734 753-4360
  Belleville *(G-1446)*
Klaus Nixdorf ....E..... 269 429-3259
  Stevensville *(G-15573)*
Kroger Co ....C..... 586 727-4946
  Richmond *(G-13265)*
Looney Baker of Livonia Inc ....E..... 734 425-8569
  Livonia *(G-9818)*
Mackenzies Bakery ....E..... 269 343-8440
  Kalamazoo *(G-8814)*
Marias Italian Bakery Inc ....F..... 734 981-1200
  Canton *(G-2396)*
Marie Minnie Bakers Inc ....C..... 734 522-1100
  Livonia *(G-9823)*
Miles Cake Candy Supplies ....G..... 586 783-9252
  Clinton Township *(G-3176)*
New Yasmeen Detroit Inc ....E..... 313 582-6035
  Dearborn *(G-3744)*
New York Bagel Baking Co ....F..... 248 548-2580
  Ferndale *(G-5305)*
Perfection Bakeries Inc ....F..... 231 779-5365
  Cadillac *(G-2269)*
Perfection Bakeries Inc ....E..... 517 750-1818
  Jackson *(G-8550)*
Rainbow Pizza Inc ....G..... 734 246-4250
  Taylor *(G-15761)*
Raleigh & Ron Corporation ....D..... 248 280-2820
  Royal Oak *(G-13961)*
Randalls Bakery ....G..... 906 224-5401
  Wakefield *(G-16855)*
Roma Bakery & Imported Foods ....E..... 517 485-9466
  Lansing *(G-9419)*
Roskam Baking Company ....C..... 616 574-5757
  Grand Rapids *(G-6839)*
Roskam Baking Company ....D..... 616 574-5757
  Grand Rapids *(G-6840)*
Roskam Baking Company ....C..... 616 574-5757
  Grand Rapids *(G-6841)*
Roskam Baking Company ....B..... 616 574-5757
  Grand Rapids *(G-6843)*
Rothbury Farms Inc ....A..... 616 574-5757
  Grand Rapids *(G-6844)*
Shatila Food Products Inc ....E..... 313 934-1520
  Dearborn *(G-3758)*
Simply Divine Baking LLC ....G..... 313 903-2881
  Southfield *(G-15028)*
Spartannash Company ....C..... 517 629-6313
  Albion *(G-132)*
Spartannash Company ....D..... 517 278-8963
  Coldwater *(G-3333)*
Supreme Baking Company ....E..... 313 894-0222
  Detroit *(G-4389)*
Sweet Mellisas Cupcakes ....G..... 616 889-3998
  Lowell *(G-10043)*
Sweetheart Bakery Inc ....D..... 313 839-6330
  Detroit *(G-4392)*
Sweetheart Bakery of Michigan ....D..... 586 795-1660
  Harper Woods *(G-7306)*
Uncle Johns Cider Mill Inc ....D..... 989 224-3686
  Saint Johns *(G-14298)*
Vargas & Sons ....F..... 989 754-4636
  Saginaw *(G-14178)*
W Bay Cupcakes ....G..... 231 632-2010
  Traverse City *(G-16140)*
Walmart Inc ....B..... 517 541-1481
  Charlotte *(G-2670)*

BAKERIES: On Premises Baking & Consumption

Aldos Bakery Inc ....G..... 810 744-9123
  Flint *(G-5374)*
Bake N Cakes LP ....G..... 517 337-2253
  Lansing *(G-9345)*
Big Boy Restaurants Intl LLC ....D..... 586 263-6220
  Clinton Township *(G-3067)*
Bimbo Bakeries Usa Inc ....G..... 231 922-3296
  Traverse City *(G-15912)*
Campbell Soup Company ....F..... 313 295-6884
  Taylor *(G-15698)*
Campbell Soup Company ....D..... 248 336-8486
  Ferndale *(G-5265)*
Kellers Farm Bakery ....G..... 734 753-4360
  Belleville *(G-1446)*
New Martha Washington Bakery ....G..... 313 872-1988
  Detroit *(G-4268)*
Pepperidge Farm Incorporated ....G..... 734 953-6729
  Livonia *(G-9885)*
Rainbow Pizza Inc ....G..... 734 246-4250
  Taylor *(G-15761)*

Randalls Bakery ....G..... 906 224-5401
  Wakefield *(G-16855)*
Shatila Food Products Inc ....E..... 313 934-1520
  Dearborn *(G-3758)*
Spartannash Company ....C..... 517 629-6313
  Albion *(G-132)*
Spartannash Company ....D..... 517 278-8963
  Coldwater *(G-3333)*
Stone House Bread Inc ....E..... 231 933-8864
  Traverse City *(G-16113)*
Supreme Baking Company ....E..... 313 894-0222
  Detroit *(G-4389)*
Sweetheart Bakery Inc ....D..... 313 839-6330
  Detroit *(G-4392)*
Sweetheart Bakery of Michigan ....D..... 586 795-1660
  Harper Woods *(G-7306)*
Top Notch Cookies & Cakes Inc ....G..... 734 467-9550
  Westland *(G-17604)*

BAKERY FOR HOME SVC DELIVERY

Wow Factor Tables and Events ....G..... 248 550-5922
  Howell *(G-8122)*

BAKERY MACHINERY

Banner Engineering & Sales Inc ....F..... 989 755-0584
  Saginaw *(G-14000)*
Dawn Equipment Company Inc ....C..... 517 789-4500
  Jackson *(G-8427)*
Dawn Food Products Inc ....C..... 517 789-4400
  Jackson *(G-8429)*
Dawn Foods Inc ....C..... 517 789-4400
  Jackson *(G-8430)*
Lematic Inc ....D..... 517 787-3301
  Jackson *(G-8497)*
Oliver Packaging and Eqp Co ....D..... 616 356-2950
  Walker *(G-16872)*

BAKERY PRDTS: Bakery Prdts, Partially Cooked, Exc frozen

Dorothy Dawson Food Products ....E..... 517 788-9830
  Jackson *(G-8435)*

BAKERY PRDTS: Bread, All Types, Fresh Or Frozen

Aldos Bakery Inc ....G..... 810 744-9123
  Flint *(G-5374)*
Aunt Millies Bakeries Inc ....E..... 734 528-1475
  Ypsilanti *(G-18053)*
Bay Bread Co ....F..... 231 922-8022
  Traverse City *(G-15906)*
Bread of Life Bakery & Cafe ....F..... 906 663-4005
  Bessemer *(G-1603)*
Darwin Sneller ....G..... 989 977-3718
  Sebewaing *(G-14514)*
Embassy Distributing Company ....G..... 248 926-0590
  Commerce Township *(G-3404)*
Gr Baking Company ....F..... 616 245-3446
  Grand Rapids *(G-6449)*
Italian BTR Bread Sticks Bky ....G..... 313 893-4945
  Detroit *(G-4152)*
Knickerbocker Baking Inc ....E..... 248 541-2110
  Madison Heights *(G-10291)*
Metropolitan Baking Company ....D..... 313 875-7246
  Detroit *(G-4234)*
Milano Bakery Inc ....E..... 313 833-3500
  Detroit *(G-4249)*
Perfection Bakeries Inc ....G..... 810 653-2378
  Davison *(G-3658)*
Perfection Bakeries Inc ....D..... 517 278-2370
  Coldwater *(G-3319)*
Schnitzelstein Baking Co ....G..... 616 988-2316
  Grand Rapids *(G-6853)*
Schuette Farms ....G..... 989 550-0563
  Elkton *(G-4783)*
Spatz Bakery Inc ....F..... 989 755-5551
  Saginaw *(G-14152)*
Zingermans Bakehouse Inc ....D..... 734 761-2095
  Ann Arbor *(G-708)*

BAKERY PRDTS: Buns, Bread Type, Fresh Or Frozen

Way Bakery ....C..... 517 787-6720
  Jackson *(G-8605)*
White Lotus Farms Inc ....G..... 734 904-1379
  Ann Arbor *(G-698)*

BAKERY PRDTS: Cakes, Bakery, Exc Frozen

Baker & Baker ....G..... 810 982-2763
  Port Huron *(G-12897)*
Brothers Baking Company ....E..... 269 663-8591
  Edwardsburg *(G-4761)*
Cake Connection Tc LLC ....G..... 231 943-3531
  Traverse City *(G-15928)*
Ethels Edibles LLC ....F..... 586 552-5110
  Saint Clair Shores *(G-14247)*
James Ave Catering ....G..... 517 655-4532
  Williamston *(G-17731)*
Magic Treatz LLC ....G..... 248 989-9956
  Oak Park *(G-12080)*
More Signature Cakes LLC ....G..... 248 266-0504
  Troy *(G-16512)*
Palm Sweets LLC ....E..... 586 554-7979
  Sterling Heights *(G-15442)*
Top Notch Cookies & Cakes Inc ....G..... 734 467-9550
  Westland *(G-17604)*

BAKERY PRDTS: Cakes, Bakery, Frozen

Dawn Foods Inc ....C..... 517 789-4400
  Jackson *(G-8430)*
Julian Brothers Inc ....E..... 248 588-0280
  Clawson *(G-2981)*
Sweet Creations ....G..... 989 327-1157
  Saginaw *(G-14161)*

BAKERY PRDTS: Cones, Ice Cream

Cherry Cone LLC ....G..... 231 944-1036
  Traverse City *(G-15939)*

BAKERY PRDTS: Cookies

Among Friends LLC ....F..... 734 997-9720
  Ann Arbor *(G-354)*
Cherry Republic Inc ....D..... 231 334-3150
  Glen Arbor *(G-5940)*
Keebler Company ....B..... 269 961-2000
  Battle Creek *(G-1207)*
Keebler Company ....D..... 231 445-0335
  Cheboygan *(G-2684)*
Kellogg Company ....A..... 269 961-2000
  Battle Creek *(G-1211)*
Kellogg North America Company ....A..... 269 961-2000
  Battle Creek *(G-1218)*
Krumbsnatcher Enterprises LLC ....F..... 313 408-6802
  Detroit *(G-4184)*
Lotte USA Incorporated ....F..... 269 963-6664
  Battle Creek *(G-1223)*
Pepperidge Farm Incorporated ....G..... 734 953-6729
  Livonia *(G-9885)*
Top Notch Cookies & Cakes Inc ....G..... 734 467-9550
  Westland *(G-17604)*

BAKERY PRDTS: Cookies & crackers

Bimbo Bakeries Usa Inc ....B..... 616 252-2709
  Grand Rapids *(G-6222)*
Campbell Soup Company ....F..... 313 295-6884
  Taylor *(G-15698)*
Campbell Soup Company ....D..... 248 336-8486
  Ferndale *(G-5265)*
Dick and Jane Baking Co LLC ....G..... 248 519-2418
  Troy *(G-16317)*
Ludwicks Frozen Donuts Inc ....F..... 616 453-6880
  Grand Rapids *(G-6635)*
Marias Italian Bakery Inc ....F..... 734 981-1200
  Canton *(G-2396)*
Roma Bakery & Imported Foods ....E..... 517 485-9466
  Lansing *(G-9419)*
Savory Foods Inc ....D..... 616 241-2583
  Grand Rapids *(G-6851)*
Shatila Food Products Inc ....E..... 313 934-1520
  Dearborn *(G-3758)*
Stone House Bread Inc ....E..... 231 933-8864
  Traverse City *(G-16113)*
Supreme Baking Company ....E..... 313 894-0222
  Detroit *(G-4389)*
Sweet Potato Sensations Inc ....G..... 313 532-7996
  Detroit *(G-4391)*

BAKERY PRDTS: Doughnuts, Exc Frozen

Donutville ....G..... 616 396-1160
  Holland *(G-7610)*
Dunkin Donuts & Baskin-Robbins ....E..... 989 835-8412
  Midland *(G-10856)*
Sweetwaters Donut Mill ....F..... 269 979-1944
  Battle Creek *(G-1256)*

PRODUCT SECTION

BARS: Concrete Reinforcing, Fabricated Steel

BAKERY PRDTS: Doughnuts, Frozen

Ludwicks Frozen Donuts Inc ....F 616 453-6880
  Grand Rapids *(G-6635)*

BAKERY PRDTS: Dry

Bake Station Bakeries Mich Inc ....E 248 352-9000
  Southfield *(G-14849)*
Chewys Gourmet Kitchen LLC ....G 313 757-2595
  Detroit *(G-3934)*
Sweetie Pie Pantry ....G 517 669-9300
  Dewitt *(G-4466)*

BAKERY PRDTS: Frozen

Bakers Rhapsody ....G 269 767-1368
  Dowagiac *(G-4535)*
Bimbo Bakeries Usa Inc ....G 231 922-3296
  Traverse City *(G-15912)*
Bimbo Bakeries Usa Inc ....B 616 252-2709
  Grand Rapids *(G-6222)*
Marie Minnie Bakers Inc ....C 734 522-1100
  Livonia *(G-9823)*
Pepperidge Farm Incorporated ....G 734 953-6729
  Livonia *(G-9885)*
Savory Foods Inc ....D 616 241-2583
  Grand Rapids *(G-6851)*

BAKERY PRDTS: Pastries, Danish, Frozen

Jakes Cakes Inc ....G 734 522-2103
  Garden City *(G-5831)*

BAKERY PRDTS: Pastries, Exc Frozen

Kellogg Company ....A 269 961-2000
  Battle Creek *(G-1211)*

BAKERY PRDTS: Pies, Exc Frozen

Linwood Bakery ....G 989 697-4430
  Linwood *(G-9598)*

BAKERY PRDTS: Pretzels

Artisan Bread Co LLC ....E 586 756-0100
  Warren *(G-16940)*
Frito-Lay North America Inc ....E 989 754-0435
  Saginaw *(G-14040)*
Karemor Inc ....G 517 323-3042
  Lansing *(G-9303)*
Nautical Knots ....G 231 206-0400
  Grand Haven *(G-6058)*
Syd Enterprises ....G 517 719-2740
  Howell *(G-8104)*

BAKERY PRDTS: Wholesalers

Beirut Bakery Inc ....F 313 533-4422
  Redford *(G-13147)*
Bimbo Bakeries Usa Inc ....E 810 239-8070
  Flint *(G-5390)*
Dick and Jane Baking Co LLC ....G 248 519-2418
  Troy *(G-16317)*
New Yasmeen Detroit Inc ....E 313 582-6035
  Dearborn *(G-3744)*
New York Bagel Baking Co ....F 248 548-2580
  Ferndale *(G-5305)*
Rothbury Farms Inc ....A 616 574-5757
  Grand Rapids *(G-6844)*
Shatila Food Products Inc ....E 313 934-1520
  Dearborn *(G-3758)*
Supreme Baking Company ....E 313 894-0222
  Detroit *(G-4389)*

BAKERY: Wholesale Or Wholesale & Retail Combined

Aunt Millies Bakeries ....G 989 356-6688
  Alpena *(G-278)*
Bakewell Company ....G 269 459-8030
  Portage *(G-12983)*
Beirut Bakery Inc ....F 313 533-4422
  Redford *(G-13147)*
Bimbo Bakeries Usa Inc ....F 734 953-5741
  Livonia *(G-9665)*
Bimbo Bakeries Usa Inc ....E 906 786-4042
  Escanaba *(G-4819)*
Bimbo Bakeries Usa Inc ....B 616 252-2709
  Grand Rapids *(G-6222)*
Bimbo Bakeries Usa Inc ....E 810 239-8070
  Flint *(G-5390)*

Chewys Gourmet Kitchen LLC ....G 313 757-2595
  Detroit *(G-3934)*
Classroom Farming Ltd ....G 810 247-8410
  Owosso *(G-12283)*
Coles Quality Foods Inc ....C 231 722-1651
  Grand Rapids *(G-6288)*
Creme Curls Bakery Inc ....C 616 669-6230
  Hudsonville *(G-8151)*
Dough Masters ....E 248 585-0600
  Warren *(G-17005)*
Elegance of Season ....G 616 296-1059
  Spring Lake *(G-15140)*
Flatout Inc ....D 734 944-5445
  Saline *(G-14391)*
Grace Extended ....G 616 502-2078
  Grand Haven *(G-6020)*
Jt Bakers ....G 989 424-5102
  Clare *(G-2874)*
National Bakery ....G 313 891-7803
  Detroit *(G-4262)*
New Martha Washington Bakery ....G 313 872-1988
  Detroit *(G-4268)*
Old Mission Multigrain LLC ....G 231 366-4121
  Traverse City *(G-16058)*
Perfection Bakeries Inc ....D 269 343-1217
  Kalamazoo *(G-8847)*
Roskam Baking Company ....C 616 554-9160
  Grand Rapids *(G-6842)*
Russos Bakery Inc ....F 586 791-7320
  Clinton Township *(G-3218)*
Savory Foods Inc ....D 616 241-2583
  Grand Rapids *(G-6851)*
Stone House Bread LLC ....E 231 933-8864
  Traverse City *(G-16112)*
Telo ....G 810 845-8051
  Fenton *(G-5242)*
West Thomas Partners LLC ....E 616 430-7585
  Grand Rapids *(G-6989)*

BALCONIES: Metal

Stus Welding & Fabrication ....G 616 392-8459
  Holland *(G-7818)*

BALERS

Howey Tree Baler Corporation ....G 231 328-4321
  Merritt *(G-10763)*

BALLASTS: Fluorescent

Nextek Power Systems Inc ....E 313 887-1321
  Detroit *(G-4269)*

BALLOONS: Hot Air

Aerostatica Inc ....F 734 426-5525
  Dexter *(G-4473)*

BALLOONS: Novelty & Toy

Lachman Enterprises Inc ....G 248 948-9944
  Southfield *(G-14958)*

BALLOONS: Toy & Advertising, Rubber

Gaco Sourcing LLC ....G 248 633-2656
  Birmingham *(G-1684)*
Wiley & Co ....G 616 361-7110
  Grand Rapids *(G-6993)*

BANNERS: Fabric

Bannergalaxycom LLC ....G 231 941-8200
  Traverse City *(G-15903)*
Britten Pop LLC ....G 800 426-9496
  Traverse City *(G-15922)*
Consort Corporation ....E 269 388-4532
  Kalamazoo *(G-8713)*
Engineering Reproduction Inc ....F 313 366-3390
  Detroit *(G-4038)*
Jack Ripper & Associates Inc ....G 734 453-7333
  Plymouth *(G-12652)*

BAR

Bells Brewery Inc ....G 906 233-5000
  Escanaba *(G-4816)*

BAR FIXTURES: Wood

Ferrante Manufacturing Co ....E 313 571-1111
  Detroit *(G-4056)*

BAR FIXTURES: Wood

Glastender Inc ....C 989 752-4275
  Saginaw *(G-14045)*

BARBECUE EQPT

American Household Inc ....G 601 296-5000
  Livonia *(G-9643)*
Richmond Meat Packers Inc ....G 586 727-1450
  Richmond *(G-13270)*
Trenton Hearthside Shop Inc ....G 734 558-5860
  Trenton *(G-16160)*

BARGES BUILDING & REPAIR

Arcosa Shoring Products Inc ....E 517 741-4300
  Union City *(G-16731)*

BARRELS: Shipping, Metal

Mauser ....G 248 795-2330
  Clarkston *(G-2936)*
Rap Products Inc ....G 989 893-5583
  Bay City *(G-1348)*

BARRICADES: Metal

Avian Control Technologies LLC ....G 231 349-9050
  Stanwood *(G-15231)*
Give-Em A Brake Safety LLC ....E 616 531-8705
  Grandville *(G-7037)*
Poco Inc ....E 313 220-6752
  Canton *(G-2416)*
Signature Wall Solutions Inc ....G 616 366-4242
  Midland *(G-10916)*
Spartan Barricading ....G 313 292-2488
  Romulus *(G-13734)*

BARS & BAR SHAPES: Steel, Cold-Finished, Own Hot-Rolled

A B C Roll Co ....G 586 465-9125
  Mount Clemens *(G-11122)*
Eaton Steel Corporation ....D 248 398-3434
  Oak Park *(G-12064)*
Eaton Steel Corporation ....D 248 398-3434
  Livonia *(G-9719)*
Gerdau Macsteel Inc ....B 517 764-3920
  Jackson *(G-8455)*
Gerdau Macsteel Inc ....B 734 243-2446
  Monroe *(G-11034)*
Gerdau Macsteel Inc ....E 517 782-0415
  Jackson *(G-8456)*

BARS & BAR SHAPES: Steel, Hot-Rolled

Gerdau Macsteel Inc ....A 734 243-2446
  Monroe *(G-11033)*

BARS, COLD FINISHED: Steel, From Purchased Hot-Rolled

BR Safety Products Inc ....G 734 582-4499
  Plymouth *(G-12589)*

BARS: Cargo, Stabilizing, Metal

Atf Inc ....E 989 685-2468
  Rose City *(G-13760)*
Friendship Industries Inc ....E 586 323-0033
  Sterling Heights *(G-15349)*
Lock and Load Corp ....G 800 975-9658
  Marion *(G-10490)*

BARS: Concrete Reinforcing, Fabricated Steel

Bowling Enterprises Inc ....G 231 864-2653
  Kaleva *(G-8930)*
Corson Fabricating LLC ....F 810 326-0532
  Saint Clair *(G-14211)*
Cotson Fabricating Inc ....E 248 589-2758
  Sterling Heights *(G-15301)*
D & D Fabrications Inc ....G 810 798-2491
  Almont *(G-255)*
Daughtery Group Inc ....G 313 452-7918
  Detroit *(G-3961)*
Econ-O-Line Abrasive Products ....E 616 846-4150
  Grand Haven *(G-6011)*
Global Lift Corp ....F 989 269-5900
  Bad Axe *(G-1066)*

Employee Codes: A=Over 500 employees, B=251-500
C=101-250, D=51-100, E=20-50, F=10-19, G=3-9

BARS: Concrete Reinforcing, Fabricated Steel

Laser North Inc ....G...... 906 353-6090
  Baraga *(G-1107)*
Metro Rebar Inc ....G...... 248 851-5894
  West Bloomfield *(G-17484)*
N & K Fulbright LLC ....E...... 269 695-4580
  Niles *(G-11629)*
Superior Fabricating Inc ....F...... 989 354-8877
  Alpena *(G-318)*
Tennessee Fabricators LLC ....G...... 615 793-4444
  Sterling Heights *(G-15522)*
Ter Molen & Hart Inc ....G...... 616 458-4832
  Grand Rapids *(G-6922)*
Welk-Ko Fabricators Inc ....G...... 248 486-2598
  New Hudson *(G-11559)*

BARS: Iron, Made In Steel Mills

Primetals Technologies USA LLC ...G...... 269 927-3591
  Benton Harbor *(G-1539)*

BASES, BEVERAGE

Sensient Technologies Corp ....D...... 989 479-3211
  Harbor Beach *(G-7271)*

BASKETS: Steel Wire

Richfield Industries Inc ....F...... 810 233-0440
  Flint *(G-5492)*
Transportation Tech Group Inc ....E...... 810 233-0440
  Flint *(G-5512)*

BATHROOM ACCESS & FITTINGS: Vitreous China & Earthenware

Americast LLC ....G...... 989 681-4800
  Saint Louis *(G-14358)*
York Electric Inc ....E...... 517 487-6400
  Lansing *(G-9438)*

BATHROOM FIXTURES: Plastic

Lyons Industries Inc ....C...... 269 782-3404
  Dowagiac *(G-4548)*

BATTERIES, EXC AUTOMOTIVE: Wholesalers

A123 Systems LLC ....B...... 248 412-9249
  Novi *(G-11822)*
Auto Clinic ....G...... 906 774-5780
  Iron Mountain *(G-8275)*

BATTERIES: Lead Acid, Storage

Johnson Controls Inc ....G...... 734 995-3016
  Ann Arbor *(G-513)*

BATTERIES: Rechargeable

A123 Systems LLC ....C...... 734 466-6521
  Livonia *(G-9621)*
Adana Voltaics LLC ....G...... 734 622-0193
  Ann Arbor *(G-342)*
Arotech Corporation ....E...... 800 281-0356
  Ann Arbor *(G-368)*
Ematrix Energy Systems Inc ....G...... 248 629-9111
  Royal Oak *(G-13922)*
G & L Powerup Inc ....G...... 586 200-2169
  Roseville *(G-13806)*

BATTERIES: Storage

A123 Systems LLC ....C...... 734 772-0600
  Romulus *(G-13646)*
A123 Systems LLC ....B...... 248 412-9249
  Novi *(G-11822)*
Advanced Battery Concepts LLC ...E...... 989 424-6645
  Clare *(G-2863)*
Auto Clinic ....G...... 906 774-5780
  Iron Mountain *(G-8275)*
Batteries Shack ....G...... 586 580-2893
  Sterling Heights *(G-15273)*
Contemporary Amperex Corp ....G...... 248 289-6200
  Rochester Hills *(G-13395)*
East Penn Manufacturing Co ....F...... 586 979-5300
  Sterling Heights *(G-15329)*
Ematrix Energy Systems Inc ....G...... 248 797-2149
  Royal Oak *(G-13922)*
Energy Powercell LLC ....E...... 248 585-1000
  Pontiac *(G-12822)*
Exide Technologies ....F...... 248 853-5000
  Auburn Hills *(G-858)*

Harding Energy Inc ....E...... 231 798-7033
  Norton Shores *(G-11759)*
Httm LLC ....F...... 616 820-2500
  Holland *(G-7683)*
Innovative Weld Solutions LLC ....G...... 937 545-7695
  Rochester *(G-13329)*
Lg Chem Michigan Inc ....G...... 248 291-2385
  Troy *(G-16461)*
Lg Chem Michigan Inc ....G...... 248 307-1800
  Troy *(G-16462)*
Lg Chem Michigan Inc ....C...... 616 494-7100
  Holland *(G-7722)*
M & M Irish Enterprises Inc ....G...... 248 644-0666
  Birmingham *(G-1689)*
Navitas Systems LLC ....F...... 630 755-7920
  Ann Arbor *(G-572)*
Redeem Power Services ....G...... 248 679-5277
  Novi *(G-11985)*
Robert Bosch Btry Systems LLC ....D...... 248 620-5700
  Orion *(G-12189)*
Seeo Inc ....F...... 510 782-7336
  Lake Orion *(G-9159)*
TMC Group Inc ....F...... 248 819-6063
  Pleasant Ridge *(G-12556)*
Xalt Energy LLC ....G...... 248 409-5419
  Pontiac *(G-12877)*
Xalt Energy LLC ....F...... 989 486-8501
  Midland *(G-10928)*
Xalt Energy Mi LLC ....G...... 989 486-8501
  Midland *(G-10930)*

BATTERIES: Wet

Bargain Business Supplies Inc ....G...... 810 750-0999
  Fenton *(G-5186)*
G & L Powerup Inc ....G...... 586 200-2169
  Roseville *(G-13806)*
Mophie LLC ....D...... 269 743-1340
  Kalamazoo *(G-8831)*
Robert Bosch Btry Systems LLC ....D...... 248 620-5700
  Orion *(G-12189)*

BATTERY CASES: Plastic Or Plastics Combination

Akwel Cadillac Usa Inc ....E...... 248 848-9599
  Farmington Hills *(G-4926)*
D&Js Plastics LLC ....G...... 616 745-5798
  Hudsonville *(G-8154)*
US Farathane LLC ....E...... 248 754-7000
  Auburn Hills *(G-1037)*

BATTERY CHARGERS

Exide Technologies ....F...... 248 853-5000
  Auburn Hills *(G-858)*

BATTERY CHARGING GENERATORS

Electrodynamics Inc ....G...... 734 422-5420
  Livonia *(G-9723)*
Rizk National Industries Inc ....E...... 586 757-4700
  Warren *(G-17221)*

BATTERY REPAIR & SVCS

Energy Products Inc ....D...... 248 545-7700
  Madison Heights *(G-10247)*
Energy Products Inc ....G...... 248 866-5622
  Troy *(G-16345)*

BATTS & BATTING: Cotton

Zeilinger Wool Co LLC ....E...... 989 652-2920
  Frankenmuth *(G-5597)*

BAUXITE MINING

Arconic Inc ....G...... 231 894-5686
  Whitehall *(G-17662)*

BEARINGS

Craft Steel Products Inc ....E...... 616 935-7575
  Spring Lake *(G-15137)*

BEARINGS & PARTS Ball

ABC Acquisition Company LLC ......E...... 734 335-4083
  Livonia *(G-9624)*
Federal-Mogul Powertrain LLC ....E...... 734 930-1590
  Ann Arbor *(G-458)*

BEARINGS: Ball & Roller

Carter Manufacturing Co Inc ....D...... 616 842-8760
  Grand Haven *(G-6001)*
Cw Manufacturing LLC ....E...... 734 781-4000
  Northville *(G-11686)*
Frost Incorporated ....E...... 616 453-7781
  Grand Rapids *(G-6421)*
Independent Mfg Solutions Corp ....E...... 248 960-3550
  Wixom *(G-17833)*
Jtekt North America Corp ....E...... 734 454-1500
  Plymouth *(G-12660)*
Kaydon Corporation ....B...... 734 747-7025
  Ann Arbor *(G-516)*
Kaydon Corporation ....C...... 231 755-3741
  Norton Shores *(G-11766)*
SKF Motion Technologies LLC ....E...... 586 752-0060
  Armada *(G-723)*
SKF USA Inc ....D...... 734 414-6585
  Plymouth *(G-12756)*
Sunhill America LLC ....G...... 616 249-3600
  Grand Rapids *(G-6898)*
TN Michigan LLC ....D...... 906 632-7310
  Sault Sainte Marie *(G-14476)*

BEARINGS: Roller & Parts

Schaeffler Group USA Inc ....B...... 810 360-0294
  Milford *(G-10984)*
Stearns & Stafford Inc ....F...... 269 624-4541
  Lawton *(G-9515)*

BEAUTY & BARBER SHOP EQPT

Android Industries LLC ....G...... 517 322-0141
  Lansing *(G-9276)*
B T I Industries ....F...... 586 532-8411
  Shelby Township *(G-14554)*
Bloom Industries LLC ....G...... 616 890-8029
  Traverse City *(G-15913)*
Coventry Industries LLC ....G...... 248 761-8462
  Holly *(G-7872)*
Crescent Manufacturing Company ..E...... 517 486-2670
  Blissfield *(G-1715)*
Gearx LLC ....G...... 248 766-6903
  Sterling Heights *(G-15354)*
Innovative Thermal Systems LLC ...E...... 586 920-2900
  Warren *(G-17093)*
Intuitive Technology Inc ....G...... 602 249-5750
  Dexter *(G-4495)*
Jk Manufacturing Co ....F...... 231 258-2638
  Kalkaska *(G-8945)*
Karmann Manufacturing LLC ....E...... 734 582-5900
  Plymouth *(G-12662)*
Kims Mart Inc ....G...... 313 592-4929
  Detroit *(G-4178)*
Kriewall Enterprises Inc ....E...... 586 336-0600
  Romeo *(G-13631)*
Lee Beauty & Gen Mechandise ....G...... 586 294-4400
  Fraser *(G-5684)*
Northwoods Manufacturing Inc ......D...... 906 779-2370
  Kingsford *(G-9065)*
Patriot Manufacturing LLC ....G...... 734 259-2059
  Plymouth *(G-12709)*
Perfection Industries Inc ....G...... 231 779-5325
  Cadillac *(G-2270)*
Precision Engrg & Mfg Inc ....G...... 616 837-6764
  Nunica *(G-12041)*
Probus Technical Services Inc ....F...... 876 226-5692
  Troy *(G-16563)*
Qsdg Manufacturing LLC ....F...... 231 941-1222
  Traverse City *(G-16085)*
SPX Corporation ....G...... 704 752-4400
  Muskegon *(G-11429)*
Stewart Manufacturing LLC ....D...... 906 498-7600
  Hermansville *(G-7466)*
Top Shelf Barber Supplies LLC ......G...... 586 453-6809
  Lansing *(G-9326)*
US Salon Supply LLC ....G...... 616 365-5790
  Paw Paw *(G-12415)*
Willow Mfg Inc ....G...... 231 275-1026
  Interlochen *(G-8246)*

BEAUTY & BARBER SHOP EQPT & SPLYS WHOLESALERS

US Salon Supply LLC ....G...... 616 365-5790
  Paw Paw *(G-12415)*

PRODUCT SECTION

BEAUTY CONTEST PRODUCTION
Go Beyond Healthy LLC .... G 407 255-0314
  Grand Rapids *(G-6445)*

BED & BREAKFAST INNS
Black Star Farms LLC .... F 231 271-4970
  Suttons Bay *(G-15650)*
Chateau Operations Ltd .... E 231 223-4110
  Traverse City *(G-15937)*
R C M S Inc .... G 269 422-1617
  Baroda *(G-1130)*

BED TICKINGS, COTTON
Mackarynn Inc .... E 616 263-9743
  Cedar Springs *(G-2557)*

BEDDING & BEDSPRINGS STORES
Jonathan Stevens Mattress Co .... G 616 243-4342
  Grand Rapids *(G-6564)*

BEDDING, BEDSPREADS, BLANKETS & SHEETS
Grabber Inc .... E 616 940-1914
  Byron Center *(G-2193)*
Star Textile Inc .... E 888 527-5700
  Madison Heights *(G-10361)*

BEDDING, BEDSPREADS, BLANKETS & SHEETS: Comforters & Quilts
Custom Quilts .... G 517 626-6399
  Lansing *(G-9212)*
Down Inc .... E 616 241-3922
  Grand Rapids *(G-6360)*

BEDS & ACCESS STORES
Longstreet Group LLC .... F 517 278-4487
  Coldwater *(G-3314)*

BEDS: Hospital
Innovative Pdts Unlimited Inc .... E 269 684-5050
  Niles *(G-11620)*
Stryker Corporation .... E 269 385-2600
  Portage *(G-13038)*
Stryker Corporation .... B 269 329-2100
  Portage *(G-13040)*
Stryker Far East Inc .... E 269 385-2600
  Portage *(G-13044)*

BEEKEEPERS' SPLYS: Honeycomb Foundations
Grh Inc .... G 888 344-6639
  Lapeer *(G-9463)*
Jeremy Jelinek .... G 231 313-7124
  Traverse City *(G-16012)*
Spike Bros Natures Treasures .... G 989 833-5443
  Sumner *(G-15643)*

BEER & ALE WHOLESALERS
Clarkston Courts LLC .... C 248 383-8444
  Clarkston *(G-2913)*
Oracle Brewing Company LLC .... G 989 401-7446
  Breckenridge *(G-1845)*

BEER, WINE & LIQUOR STORES
Mpc Company Inc .... G 269 927-3371
  Benton Harbor *(G-1534)*
Spartannash Company .... C 517 629-6313
  Albion *(G-132)*
Two James Spirits LLC .... G 313 964-4800
  Detroit *(G-4411)*

BEER, WINE & LIQUOR STORES: Beer, Packaged
Brew Detroit LLC .... F 313 974-7366
  Detroit *(G-3915)*
Marias Italian Bakery Inc .... F 734 981-1200
  Canton *(G-2396)*
Mishigama Brewing Company .... G 734 547-5840
  Ypsilanti *(G-18091)*
Northwest Market .... G 517 787-5005
  Jackson *(G-8543)*

One Beer At A Time LLC .... E 616 719-1604
  Grand Rapids *(G-6730)*
Oracle Brewing Company LLC .... G 989 401-7446
  Breckenridge *(G-1845)*
Roma Bakery & Imported Foods .... E 517 485-9466
  Lansing *(G-9419)*
Russo Bros Inc .... E 906 485-5250
  Ishpeming *(G-8353)*
Sunlite Market Inc .... G 586 792-9870
  Clinton Township *(G-3236)*

BEER, WINE & LIQUOR STORES: Wine
Chateau Operations Ltd .... E 231 223-4110
  Traverse City *(G-15937)*
Fontaine Chateau .... G 231 256-0000
  Lake Leelanau *(G-9103)*
Howells Mainstreet Winery .... G 517 545-9463
  Howell *(G-8053)*
Lemon Creek Winery Ltd .... E 269 471-1321
  Berrien Springs *(G-1597)*
Northville Cider Mill Inc .... E 248 349-3181
  Northville *(G-11715)*
Shady Lane Orchards Inc .... F 231 935-1620
  Suttons Bay *(G-15655)*
St Julian Wine Company Inc .... G 989 652-3281
  Frankenmuth *(G-5595)*

BEER, WINE & LIQUOR STORES: Wine & Beer
Veritas Vineyard LLC .... E 517 962-2427
  Jackson *(G-8600)*

BELLOWS
Magnumm Corporation .... F 586 427-9420
  Warren *(G-17138)*
Sfs LLC .... G 734 947-4377
  Taylor *(G-15765)*

BELTING: Rubber
Factory Products Inc .... G 269 668-3329
  Mattawan *(G-10664)*
Gates Corporation .... D 248 260-2300
  Rochester Hills *(G-13431)*
Mol Belting Systems Inc .... D 616 453-2484
  Grand Rapids *(G-6696)*
Sparks Belting Company Inc .... D 616 949-2750
  Grand Rapids *(G-6875)*
Stephen A James .... G 269 641-5879
  Cassopolis *(G-2536)*

BELTS: Chain
Production Industries II Inc .... F 231 352-7500
  Traverse City *(G-16080)*

BELTS: Conveyor, Made From Purchased Wire
Lesco Design & Mfg Co Inc .... B 248 596-9301
  Wixom *(G-17846)*
Omni Technical Services Inc .... E 989 227-8900
  Saint Johns *(G-14292)*
Ton-Tex Corporation .... E 616 957-3200
  Greenville *(G-7158)*
Yokohama Inds Americas Inc .... C 248 276-0480
  Auburn Hills *(G-1051)*

BELTS: Seat, Automotive & Aircraft
Key Safety Systems Inc .... C 586 726-3800
  Auburn Hills *(G-926)*
Key Sfety Rstraint Systems Inc .... A 586 726-3800
  Auburn Hills *(G-927)*
Takata Americas .... E 336 547-1600
  Auburn Hills *(G-1012)*
Teamtech Motorsports Safety .... G 989 792-4880
  Saginaw *(G-14163)*
Tk Holdings Inc .... C 517 545-9535
  Howell *(G-8112)*
Wooshin Safety Systems .... G 248 615-4946
  Farmington Hills *(G-5153)*

BENCHES, WORK : Factory
Benchwork Inc .... G 586 464-6699
  Clinton Township *(G-3065)*

BEVERAGES, ALCOHOLIC: Beer

BEVERAGE BASES & SYRUPS
Farber Concessions Inc .... E 313 387-1600
  Redford *(G-13161)*
Penguin Juice Co .... F 734 467-6991
  Westland *(G-17587)*

BEVERAGE PRDTS: Brewers' Grain
One Beer At A Time LLC .... E 616 719-1604
  Grand Rapids *(G-6730)*
Ore Dock Brewing Company LLC ...... G 906 228-8888
  Marquette *(G-10550)*
Rochester Mlls Prod Brewry LLC .... G 248 377-3130
  Auburn Hills *(G-993)*

BEVERAGE PRDTS: Malt Syrup
Premier Malt Products Inc .... E 586 443-3355
  Warren *(G-17195)*

BEVERAGE STORES
Northville Cider Mill Inc .... E 248 349-3181
  Northville *(G-11715)*
Panther James LLC .... G 248 850-7522
  Royal Oak *(G-13955)*

BEVERAGE, NONALCOHOLIC: Iced Tea/Fruit Drink, Bottled/Canned
Ellis Infinity LLC .... G 313 570-0840
  Detroit *(G-4033)*
Warner Vineyards Inc .... G 269 657-3165
  Paw Paw *(G-12417)*

BEVERAGES, ALCOHOLIC: Ale
Clarkston Courts LLC .... C 248 383-8444
  Clarkston *(G-2913)*
Frankenmuth Brewery LLC .... C 989 262-8300
  Frankenmuth *(G-5585)*
Ml Brew LLC .... F 616 361-9658
  Rockford *(G-13579)*
Oracle Brewing Company LLC .... G 989 401-7446
  Breckenridge *(G-1845)*

BEVERAGES, ALCOHOLIC: Applejack
Mammoth Distilling LLC .... G 773 841-4242
  Central Lake *(G-2592)*
Temperance Distilling Company .... F 734 847-5262
  Temperance *(G-15845)*

BEVERAGES, ALCOHOLIC: Beer
5 Mile Brewing Company LLC .... G 313 348-1628
  Detroit *(G-3825)*
734 Brewing Company Inc .... G 734 649-6453
  Ypsilanti *(G-18049)*
Atwater In Park .... G 313 344-5104
  Grosse Pointe Park *(G-7191)*
Backdraft Brewing Company .... D 734 722-7639
  Wayne *(G-17427)*
Bells Brewery Inc .... F 269 382-1402
  Kalamazoo *(G-8695)*
Bells Brewery Inc .... E 269 382-2338
  Galesburg *(G-5806)*
Black Bottom Brewing Co Inc .... G 313 205-5493
  Detroit *(G-3905)*
Blackrocks Brewery LLC .... G 906 273-1333
  Marquette *(G-10520)*
Blackrocks Brewery LLC .... G 906 273-1333
  Marquette *(G-10521)*
Brew Detroit LLC .... F 313 974-7366
  Detroit *(G-3915)*
Canal Street Brewing Co LLC .... D 616 776-1195
  Grand Rapids *(G-6253)*
Corner Brewery LLC .... E 734 480-2739
  Ypsilanti *(G-18061)*
Eastside Spot Inc .... G 906 226-9431
  Marquette *(G-10528)*
Fabiano Bros Dev - Wscnsin LLC ...... G 989 509-0200
  Bay City *(G-1313)*
Frankenmuth Brewing Company .... D 989 262-8300
  Frankenmuth *(G-5586)*
Gpbc Inc .... C 734 741-7325
  Ann Arbor *(G-475)*
Im A Beer Hound .... G 517 331-0528
  Lansing *(G-9296)*
James Joy LLC .... G 989 317-6629
  Farwell *(G-5162)*

Employee Codes: A=Over 500 employees, B=251-500
C=101-250, D=51-100, E=20-50, F=10-19, G=3-9

BEVERAGES, ALCOHOLIC: Beer

Jolly Pumpkin Artisan Ales LLC .... G. 734 426-4962
  Dexter *(G-4496)*
Keweenaw Brewing Company LLC ...... F. 906 482-5596
  Houghton *(G-7973)*
Keweenaw Brewing Company LLC ...... G. 906 482-1937
  South Range *(G-14817)*
Loggers Brewing Co .... G. 989 401-3085
  Saginaw *(G-14079)*
Mor-Dall Enterprises Inc .... G. 269 558-4915
  Marshall *(G-10584)*
Mount Pleasant Brewing Company .... G. 989 400-4666
  Mount Pleasant *(G-11210)*
Mountain Town Stn Brew Pub LLC .... C. 989 775-2337
  Mount Pleasant *(G-11211)*
New Holland Brewing Co LLC .... C. 616 355-2941
  Holland *(G-7757)*
Northern Oak Brewery Inc .... F. 248 634-7515
  Holly *(G-7889)*
Paddle Hard Distributing LLC .... G. 513 309-1192
  Grayling *(G-7115)*
S B C Holdings Inc .... F. 313 446-2000
  Detroit *(G-4350)*
Saugatuck Brewing Co Inc .... E. 269 857-7222
  Douglas *(G-4532)*
Stony Lake Corporation .... G. 734 944-9426
  Saline *(G-14416)*
Stroh Companies Inc .... F. 313 446-2000
  Detroit *(G-4380)*
Woodward Avenue Brewers .... E. 248 894-7665
  Ferndale *(G-5330)*

BEVERAGES, ALCOHOLIC: Beer & Ale

127 Brewing 517 258-1346
  Jackson *(G-8368)*
51 North Brewing .... G. 248 690-7367
  Lake Orion *(G-9121)*
Abaco Partners LLC .... C. 616 532-1700
  Kentwood *(G-8997)*
Acoustic Tap Room .... G. 231 714-5028
  Traverse City *(G-15888)*
Bells Brewery Inc .... G. 906 233-5000
  Escanaba *(G-4816)*
Biere De Mac Brew Works LLC .... G. 616 862-8018
  Mackinaw City *(G-10098)*
Detroit Cycle Pub LLC .... G. 231 286-5257
  Macomb *(G-10116)*
Detroit Rivertwn Brewing Co LL .... C. 313 877-9205
  Detroit *(G-4000)*
Draught Horse Group LLC .... G. 231 631-5218
  New Hudson *(G-11538)*
Ghost Island Brewery .... G. 219 242-4800
  New Buffalo *(G-11515)*
Harville Associates Inc .... G. 313 839-5712
  Harper Woods *(G-7301)*
Knickerbocker .... G. 616 345-5642
  Grand Rapids *(G-6586)*
Kraftbrau Brewery Inc .... G. 269 384-0288
  Kalamazoo *(G-8803)*
Lucky Girl Brewing - Cross Rads .... G. 630 723-4285
  Paw Paw *(G-12407)*
M4 CIC LLC .... G. 734 436-8507
  Ann Arbor *(G-539)*
Marquette Distillery .... G. 906 869-4933
  Marquette *(G-10543)*
Michigan Beer Growler Company .... G. 248 385-3773
  Beverly Hills *(G-1619)*
Mishigama Brewing Company .... G. 734 547-5840
  Ypsilanti *(G-18091)*
Mitten Brewing Company LLC .... G. 616 608-5612
  Grand Rapids *(G-6691)*
Mug Shots Burgers and Brews .... G. 616 895-2337
  Allendale *(G-225)*
New Holland Brewery .... F. 616 298-7727
  Holland *(G-7756)*
New Holland Brewery .... G. 616 202-7200
  Grand Rapids *(G-6716)*
North Pier Brewing Company LLC .... G. 312 545-0446
  Saint Joseph *(G-14332)*
Null Taphouse .... G. 734 792-9124
  Dexter *(G-4501)*
Oracle Brewing Company .... G. 989 401-7446
  Saginaw *(G-14117)*
Plow Point Brewing Co .... G. 734 562-9102
  Chelsea *(G-2717)*
Rare Bird Holdings LLC .... G. 616 335-9463
  Holland *(G-7785)*
Shorts Brewing Company LLC .... D. 231 498-2300
  Elk Rapids *(G-4780)*
Sweetwater Brew LLC .... G. 616 805-5077
  Wyoming *(G-18034)*

Wild Mitten LLC .... G. 616 795-1610
  Wyoming *(G-18043)*

BEVERAGES, ALCOHOLIC: Bourbon Whiskey

RGI Brands LLC .... F. 312 253-7400
  Bloomfield Hills *(G-1794)*
Tcwc LLC .... F. 231 922-8292
  Traverse City *(G-16119)*

BEVERAGES, ALCOHOLIC: Cocktails

Rockery .... G. 734 281-4629
  Wyandotte *(G-17973)*

BEVERAGES, ALCOHOLIC: Cordials & Premixed Cocktails

Beverage Solution Technolgies .... G. 616 252-1700
  Grand Rapids *(G-6215)*
Proof & Union LLC .... G. 312 919-0191
  Grand Rapids *(G-6790)*

BEVERAGES, ALCOHOLIC: Distilled Liquors

Ann Arbor Distilling Co .... G. 734 769-6075
  Ann Arbor *(G-357)*
Bier Barrel Distillery LLC .... G. 616 633-8601
  Comstock Park *(G-3464)*
Detroit City Distillery LLC .... F. 313 338-3760
  Detroit *(G-3977)*
Detroit City Distillery LLC .... G. 734 904-3073
  Spring Lake *(G-15138)*
Distillery 9 LLC .... G. 517 990-2929
  Whitmore Lake *(G-17695)*
Les Cheneaux Distillers Inc .... G. 906 748-0505
  Cedarville *(G-2568)*
Michigrain Distillery .... G. 517 580-8624
  Lansing *(G-9400)*
Sunlite Market Inc .... G. 586 792-9870
  Clinton Township *(G-3236)*
Two James Spirits LLC .... G. 313 964-4800
  Detroit *(G-4411)*
Valentine Distilling Co .... G. 646 286-2690
  Ferndale *(G-5328)*

BEVERAGES, ALCOHOLIC: Liquors, Malt

Apple Blossom Winery LLC .... F. 269 668-3724
  Kalamazoo *(G-8679)*

BEVERAGES, ALCOHOLIC: Near Beer

Austin Brothers Beer Co LLC .... G. 909 213-4194
  Alpena *(G-279)*

BEVERAGES, ALCOHOLIC: Rum

Liquid Manufacturing LLC .... C. 810 220-2802
  Ann Arbor *(G-530)*

BEVERAGES, ALCOHOLIC: Vodka

Embrace Premium Vodka LLC .... G. 616 617-5602
  Ypsilanti *(G-18070)*
Valentine Distilling .... G. 248 629-9951
  Ferndale *(G-5327)*

BEVERAGES, ALCOHOLIC: Wines

45 North Vineyard & Winery .... F. 231 271-1188
  Lake Leelanau *(G-9098)*
Andretta & Associates Inc .... F. 586 557-6226
  Macomb *(G-10107)*
B Nektar LLC .... G. 313 999-5157
  Ferndale *(G-5264)*
Black Dragon LLC .... G. 269 277-4874
  Saint Joseph *(G-14302)*
Black Star Farms LLC .... F. 231 271-4970
  Suttons Bay *(G-15650)*
Blustone Partners LLC .... F. 231 256-0146
  Lake Leelanau *(G-9101)*
Bowers Harbor Vinyrd & Winery .... G. 231 223-7615
  Traverse City *(G-15919)*
Brys Estate Vineyard & Winery .... G. 231 223-9303
  Traverse City *(G-15923)*
Cellar 849 Winery .... G. 734 254-0275
  Plymouth *(G-12594)*
Chateau Aronautique Winery LLC .... G. 517 569-2132
  Jackson *(G-8407)*
Chateau Grand Travers Ltd .... G. 231 223-7355
  Traverse City *(G-15936)*

Chateau Operations Ltd .... E. 231 223-4110
  Traverse City *(G-15937)*
CHI Co/Tabor Hill Winery .... D. 269 422-1161
  Buchanan *(G-2113)*
CHI Co/Tabor Hill Winery .... G. 269 465-6566
  Bridgman *(G-1861)*
Circus Procession LLC .... G. 616 834-8048
  Holland *(G-7591)*
Cody Kresta Vineyard & Winery .... G. 269 668-3800
  Mattawan *(G-10663)*
Dablon Vineyards LLC .... G. 269 422-2846
  Baroda *(G-1123)*
Dunn Beverage Intl LLC .... G. 269 420-1547
  Battle Creek *(G-1176)*
End of Road Winery LLC .... G. 906 450-1541
  Germfask *(G-5901)*
Fenton Winery Brewery .... G. 810 373-4194
  Fenton *(G-5214)*
Flying Otter Winery LLC .... G. 517 424-7107
  Adrian *(G-65)*
Fontaine Chateau .... G. 231 256-0000
  Lake Leelanau *(G-9103)*
Garden Bay Winery LLC .... G. 906 361-0318
  Cooks *(G-3546)*
Garden Bay Winery LLC .... G. 906 361-6136
  Menominee *(G-10737)*
Great Meadhall Brewing Co LLC .... G. 269 427-0827
  Bangor *(G-1091)*
Harbor Sprng Vnyrds Winery LLC .... G. 231 242-4062
  Harbor Springs *(G-7283)*
Hickory Creek Winery LLC .... G. 269 422-1100
  Buchanan *(G-2120)*
Howells Mainstreet Winery .... G. 517 545-9463
  Howell *(G-8053)*
L Mawby LLC .... G. 231 271-3522
  Suttons Bay *(G-15653)*
Lawton Ridge Winery LLC .... G. 269 372-9463
  Kalamazoo *(G-8806)*
Lazy Ballerina Winery LLC .... G. 269 363-6218
  Saint Joseph *(G-14323)*
Lazy Ballerina Winery LLC .... F. 269 759-8486
  Bridgman *(G-1870)*
Leelanau Wine Cellars Ltd .... G. 231 386-5201
  Ann Arbor *(G-527)*
Leighs Garden Winery Inc .... G. 906 553-7799
  Escanaba *(G-4839)*
Lemon Creek Winery Ltd .... G. 616 844-1709
  Grand Haven *(G-6048)*
Lemon Creek Winery Ltd .... E. 269 471-1321
  Berrien Springs *(G-1597)*
Little Man Winery LLC .... G. 616 292-3983
  Holland *(G-7726)*
Mari Villa Vineyards .... G. 231 935-4513
  Traverse City *(G-16032)*
MI Brew LLC .... F. 616 361-9658
  Rockford *(G-13579)*
Modern Craft Winery LLC .... G. 989 876-4948
  Au Gres *(G-747)*
Nate Ronald .... E. 269 424-3777
  Dowagiac *(G-4556)*
Nicholass Black River Vineyard .... G. 231 436-5770
  Mackinaw City *(G-10100)*
Nicholass Black River Vineyar .... G. 231 625-9060
  Cheboygan *(G-2687)*
Northville Winery .... F. 248 320-6507
  Northville *(G-11718)*
OKeefe Centre Ltd .... G. 231 223-7355
  Traverse City *(G-16056)*
Pentamere Winery .... F. 517 423-9000
  Tecumseh *(G-15805)*
Schramms Mead .... G. 248 439-5000
  Ferndale *(G-5317)*
Shady Lane Orchards Inc .... F. 231 935-1620
  Suttons Bay *(G-15655)*
Spotted Dog Winery .... G. 734 944-9463
  Ann Arbor *(G-642)*
St Julian Wine Company Inc .... F. 734 529-3700
  Dundee *(G-4601)*
St Julian Wine Company Inc .... E. 269 657-5568
  Paw Paw *(G-12414)*
Suttons Bay Ciders .... G. 734 646-3196
  Suttons Bay *(G-15656)*
To Willow Harbor Vineyard .... G. 269 369-3900
  Three Oaks *(G-15852)*
Townline Ciderworks LLC .... G. 231 883-5330
  Williamsburg *(G-17723)*
Vander Mill LLC .... D. 616 259-8828
  Grand Rapids *(G-6960)*
Veritas Vineyard LLC .... G. 517 592-4663
  Brooklyn *(G-2043)*

PRODUCT SECTION

Veritas Vineyard LLC	E	517 962-2427
Jackson *(G-8600)*		
Virtue Cider	G	269 455-0526
Fennville *(G-5179)*		
Warner Vineyards Inc	G	269 657-3165
Paw Paw *(G-12417)*		
Warner Vineyards Inc	G	269 637-6900
South Haven *(G-14783)*		
Weathervane Vinyards Inc	G	231 228-4800
Cedar *(G-2543)*		
Willow Vineyards Inc	D	231 271-4810
Suttons Bay *(G-15657)*		
Winery At Black Star Farms LLC	E	231 271-4882
Suttons Bay *(G-15658)*		

BEVERAGES, MALT

Midland Brewing Co LLC	G	989 631-3041
Midland *(G-10887)*		

BEVERAGES, NONALCOHOLIC: Bottled & canned soft drinks

American Bottling Company	D	517 622-8605
Grand Ledge *(G-6100)*		
Binks Coca-Cola Bottling Co	E	906 786-4144
Escanaba *(G-4820)*		
Binks Coca-Cola Bottling Co	F	906 774-3202
Iron Mountain *(G-8277)*		
Bottling Group Inc	G	517 545-2624
Howell *(G-8017)*		
Coca-Cola Bottling Co	G	313 868-2167
Highland Park *(G-7502)*		
Coca-Cola Company	B	269 657-3171
Paw Paw *(G-12399)*		
Coca-Cola Company	C	734 397-2700
Belleville *(G-1443)*		
Coca-Cola Refreshments USA Inc	D	989 895-8537
Bay City *(G-1296)*		
Coca-Cola Refreshments USA Inc	D	231 947-4150
Traverse City *(G-15943)*		
Coca-Cola Refreshments USA Inc	D	616 458-4536
Grand Rapids *(G-6285)*		
Coca-Cola Refreshments USA Inc	E	231 347-3242
Petoskey *(G-12445)*		
Coca-Cola Refreshments USA Inc	D	269 657-8538
Paw Paw *(G-12400)*		
Coca-Cola Refreshments USA Inc	D	810 237-4000
Flint *(G-5398)*		
Coca-Cola Refreshments USA Inc	C	313 897-2176
Detroit *(G-3942)*		
Coca-Cola Refreshments USA Inc	C	517 322-2349
Lansing *(G-9283)*		
Coca-Cola Refreshments USA Inc	C	313 897-5000
Farmington Hills *(G-4964)*		
Coke Bottle	G	810 424-3352
Flint *(G-5399)*		
Diehls Orchard & Cider Mill	G	248 634-8981
Holly *(G-7876)*		
Dr Pepper Snapple Group	G	616 393-5800
Holland *(G-7611)*		
Florida Coca-Cola Bottling Co	F	906 495-2261
Kincheloe *(G-9051)*		
Hancock Bottling Co Inc	F	906 482-3701
Hancock *(G-7251)*		
Hill Brothers	G	616 784-2767
Grand Rapids *(G-6513)*		
Jbt Bottling LLC	G	269 377-4905
Kalamazoo *(G-8777)*		
Jumpin Johnnys Inc	G	989 832-0160
Midland *(G-10878)*		
Liquid Manufacturing LLC	C	810 220-2802
Ann Arbor *(G-530)*		
Michigan Btlg & Cstm Pack Co	D	313 846-1717
Detroit *(G-4239)*		
Minute Maid Co	G	269 657-3171
Paw Paw *(G-12410)*		
Northville Cider Mill Inc	E	248 349-3181
Northville *(G-11715)*		
Pbg Michigan LLC	G	989 345-2595
West Branch *(G-17515)*		
Select Distributors LLC	F	586 510-4647
Warren *(G-17237)*		
South Range Bottling Works Inc	G	906 370-2295
South Range *(G-14819)*		
St Julian Wine Company Inc	G	989 652-3281
Frankenmuth *(G-5595)*		
Super Sidebar Inc	G	989 709-0048
West Branch *(G-17524)*		
Underground Bev Brands LLC	G	248 336-9383
Royal Oak *(G-13977)*		

BEVERAGES, NONALCOHOLIC: Carbonated

Newberry Bottling Co Inc	G	906 293-5189
Newberry *(G-11582)*		
Pepsi	G	231 627-2290
Cheboygan *(G-2690)*		
Pepsi Beverages Co	G	989 754-0435
Saginaw *(G-14120)*		
Pepsi Beverages Company	E	248 596-9028
Wixom *(G-17877)*		
Pepsi Bottling Group	F	517 546-2777
Howell *(G-8077)*		
Pepsi Cola Bottling Co Houghton	F	906 482-0161
Houghton *(G-7980)*		
Pepsi-Cola Metro Btlg Co Inc	D	517 321-0231
Lansing *(G-9254)*		
Pepsi-Cola Metro Btlg Co Inc	C	248 335-3528
Pontiac *(G-12855)*		
Pepsi-Cola Metro Btlg Co Inc	E	989 345-2595
West Branch *(G-17516)*		
Pepsi-Cola Metro Btlg Co Inc	E	231 946-0452
Traverse City *(G-16064)*		
Pepsi-Cola Metro Btlg Co Inc	D	989 755-1020
Saginaw *(G-14121)*		
Pepsi-Cola Metro Btlg Co Inc	F	517 546-2777
Howell *(G-8078)*		
Pepsi-Cola Metro Btlg Co Inc	D	269 226-6400
Kalamazoo *(G-8846)*		
Pepsi-Cola Metro Btlg Co Inc	D	616 285-8200
Grand Rapids *(G-6747)*		
Pepsi-Cola Metro Btlg Co Inc	E	313 832-0910
Detroit *(G-4296)*		
Pepsi-New Bern-Howell-151	G	517 546-7542
Howell *(G-8079)*		
Pepsico Inc	G	734 374-9841
Southgate *(G-15082)*		
Pepsico Inc	G	586 276-4102
Sterling Heights *(G-15443)*		

BEVERAGES, NONALCOHOLIC: Carbonated, Canned & Bottled, Etc

Global Restaurant Group Inc	F	313 271-2777
Dearborn *(G-3716)*		
Pepsi-Cola Metro Btlg Co Inc	E	810 987-2181
Kimball *(G-9047)*		
Viva Beverages LLC	D	248 746-7044
Southfield *(G-15062)*		

BEVERAGES, NONALCOHOLIC: Cider

Aseltine Cider Company Inc	G	616 784-7676
Comstock Park *(G-3460)*		
Blakes Orchard Inc	G	586 784-5343
Armada *(G-717)*		
Dexter Cider Mill Inc	G	734 475-6419
Chelsea *(G-2707)*		
Hill Brothers	G	616 784-2767
Grand Rapids *(G-6513)*		
Mizkan America Inc	F	616 794-0226
Belding *(G-1425)*		
Parshallville Cider Mill	G	810 629-9079
Fenton *(G-5229)*		
Porters Orchards Farm Market	F	810 636-7156
Goodrich *(G-5956)*		
Ridge Cider	G	231 674-2040
Grant *(G-7082)*		
Rochester Cider Mill	G	248 651-4224
Rochester *(G-13348)*		
Uncle Johns Cider Mill Inc	D	989 224-3686
Saint Johns *(G-14298)*		
Verellen Orchards	G	586 752-2989
Washington *(G-17313)*		
Yates Cider Mill Inc	G	248 651-8300
Rochester Hills *(G-13551)*		

BEVERAGES, NONALCOHOLIC: Flavoring extracts & syrups, nec

Coffee Beanery Ltd	E	810 733-1020
Flushing *(G-5533)*		
Jogue Inc	F	248 349-1501
Northville *(G-11703)*		
Kalsec Inc	B	269 349-9711
Kalamazoo *(G-8799)*		
Leroy Worden	G	231 325-3837
Beulah *(G-1610)*		
National Product Co	G	269 344-3640
Kalamazoo *(G-8834)*		
Real Flavors LLC	F	855 443-9685
Bay City *(G-1349)*		
Sensient Flavors LLC	G	989 479-3211
Harbor Beach *(G-7270)*		
Sunopta Ingredients Inc	E	502 587-7999
Schoolcraft *(G-14502)*		

BEVERAGES, NONALCOHOLIC: Fruit Drnks, Under 100% Juice, Can

Everfresh Beverages Inc	D	586 755-9500
Warren *(G-17024)*		
S B C Holdings Inc	F	313 446-2000
Detroit *(G-4350)*		
Stroh Companies Inc	F	313 446-2000
Detroit *(G-4380)*		
Sundance Beverages Inc	E	586 755-9470
Warren *(G-17257)*		

BEVERAGES, NONALCOHOLIC: Soft Drinks, Canned & Bottled, Etc

American Bottling Company	D	810 564-1432
Mount Morris *(G-11157)*		
American Bottling Company	D	616 396-1281
Holland *(G-7556)*		
American Bottling Company	E	616 392-2124
Holland *(G-7557)*		
American Bottling Company	E	989 731-5392
Gaylord *(G-5848)*		
American Bottling Company	E	231 775-7393
Cadillac *(G-2227)*		
Faygo Beverages Inc	B	313 925-1600
Detroit *(G-4052)*		
Keurig Dr Pepper Inc	G	231 775-7393
Cadillac *(G-2257)*		
Keurig Dr Pepper Inc	D	313 937-3500
Detroit *(G-4176)*		
Pepsi Bottling Group	G	810 966-8060
Kimball *(G-9046)*		
Pepsi-Cola Metro Btlg Co Inc	D	810 232-3925
Flint *(G-5479)*		
Pepsi-Cola Metro Btlg Co Inc	E	517 279-8436
Coldwater *(G-3318)*		
Pepsi-Cola Metro Btlg Co Inc	E	231 798-1274
Norton Shores *(G-11788)*		
Refreshment Product Svcs Inc	G	906 475-7003
Negaunee *(G-11474)*		

BEVERAGES, NONALCOHOLIC: Tea, Iced, Bottled & Canned, Etc

Detroit Bubble Tea Company	G	248 239-1131
Ferndale *(G-5273)*		
Grandads Sweet Tea LLC	G	313 320-4446
Warren *(G-17062)*		

BEVERAGES, WINE & DISTILLED ALCOHOLIC, WHOLESALE: Wine

Fontaine Chateau	G	231 256-0000
Lake Leelanau *(G-9103)*		
Garden Bay Winery LLC	G	906 361-0318
Cooks *(G-3546)*		
Great Lakes Wine & Spirits LLC	C	313 278-5400
Highland Park *(G-7506)*		

BEVERAGES, WINE/DISTILLED ALCOHOLIC, WHOL: Cocktls, Premixed

RGI Brands LLC	F	312 253-7400
Bloomfield Hills *(G-1794)*		

BICYCLE SHOPS

Assenmacher Lightweight Cycles	G	810 635-7844
Swartz Creek *(G-15661)*		
Detroit Bikes LLC	G	313 646-4109
Detroit *(G-3971)*		
Riverfront Cycle Inc	G	517 482-8585
Lansing *(G-9418)*		

BICYCLES WHOLESALERS

Shinola/Detroit LLC	C	888 304-2534
Detroit *(G-4361)*		

BICYCLES, PARTS & ACCESS

Aerospoke Incorporated	G	248 685-9009
Brighton *(G-1878)*		
Alter Cycles Ltd	G	313 737-1196
Grandville *(G-7019)*		

BICYCLES, PARTS & ACCESS

Detroit Bikes LLC .... G 313 646-4109
 Detroit *(G-3971)*
Shinola/Detroit LLC .... C 888 304-2534
 Detroit *(G-4361)*
Velocity Worldwide Inc .... F 616 243-3400
 Grand Rapids *(G-6963)*
Wiz Wheelz Inc .... F 616 455-5988
 Grand Rapids *(G-6995)*

BILLING & BOOKKEEPING SVCS

Jax Services LLC .... G 586 703-3212
 Warren *(G-17112)*
N F P Inc .... G 989 631-0009
 Midland *(G-10896)*

BINDING SVC: Books & Manuals

A Koppel Color Image Company .... G 616 534-3600
 Grandville *(G-7015)*
Aladdin Printing .... G 248 360-2842
 Commerce Township *(G-3386)*
American Label & Tag Inc .... E 734 454-7600
 Canton *(G-2347)*
Americas Finest Prtg Graphics .... G 586 296-1312
 Fraser *(G-5618)*
An Corporate Center LLC .... E 248 669-1188
 Plymouth *(G-12571)*
Apb Inc .... G 248 528-2990
 Troy *(G-16204)*
Arrow Printing LLC .... G 248 738-2222
 Waterford *(G-17323)*
ASAP Printing Inc .... E 517 882-3500
 Okemos *(G-12114)*
Bastian Brothers & Company .... E 989 239-5107
 Freeland *(G-5752)*
Bayside Printing Inc .... G 231 352-4440
 Frankfort *(G-5598)*
Brd Printing Inc .... E 517 372-0268
 Lansing *(G-9350)*
Breck Graphics Incorporated .... E 616 248-4110
 Grand Rapids *(G-6235)*
Bronco Printing Company .... G 248 544-1120
 Hazel Park *(G-7435)*
Bruce Inc .... G 517 371-5205
 Lansing *(G-9352)*
Business Press Inc .... E 248 652-8855
 Rochester *(G-13316)*
Clark Graphic Service Inc .... D 586 772-4900
 Warren *(G-16981)*
Color Connection .... G 248 351-0920
 Southfield *(G-14870)*
Commercial Graphics of Mich .... G 810 744-2102
 Burton *(G-2150)*
Copy Central Inc .... G 231 941-2298
 Traverse City *(G-15947)*
Cushing-Malloy Inc .... E 734 663-8554
 Ann Arbor *(G-409)*
Custom Printers Inc .... D 616 454-9224
 Grand Rapids *(G-6326)*
David H Bosley & Associates .... G 734 261-8390
 Livonia *(G-9698)*
De Vru Printing Co .... G 616 452-5451
 Grand Rapids *(G-6339)*
Derk Pieter Co Inc .... G 616 554-7777
 Grand Rapids *(G-6343)*
Dobb Printing Inc .... E 231 722-1060
 Muskegon *(G-11306)*
DPrinter Inc .... G 517 423-6554
 Tecumseh *(G-15791)*
Earle Press Inc .... E 231 773-2111
 Muskegon *(G-11312)*
Econo Print Inc .... G 734 878-5806
 Pinckney *(G-12496)*
Edia Technologies Inc .... G 517 349-0322
 Okemos *(G-12120)*
Edwards Brothers Inc .... C 800 722-3231
 Ann Arbor *(G-436)*
F P Horak Company .... C 989 892-6505
 Bay City *(G-1312)*
Fedex Office & Print Svcs Inc .... E 248 443-2679
 Lathrup Village *(G-9499)*
Fedex Office & Print Svcs Inc .... E 616 336-1900
 Grand Rapids *(G-6404)*
Fedex Office & Print Svcs Inc .... F 734 761-4539
 Ann Arbor *(G-459)*
Fedex Office & Print Svcs Inc .... F 313 359-3124
 Dearborn *(G-3705)*
Fedex Office & Print Svcs Inc .... F 248 932-3373
 Farmington Hills *(G-4998)*
Fedex Office & Print Svcs Inc .... G 517 332-5855
 East Lansing *(G-4657)*

Fedex Office & Print Svcs Inc .... E 248 355-5670
 Southfield *(G-14915)*
Fedex Office & Print Svcs Inc .... E 269 344-7445
 Portage *(G-12995)*
Fedex Office & Print Svcs Inc .... F 734 522-7322
 Westland *(G-17555)*
Fedex Office & Print Svcs Inc .... F 313 271-8877
 Dearborn *(G-3706)*
Fedex Office & Print Svcs Inc .... F 248 680-0280
 Troy *(G-16361)*
Fedex Office & Print Svcs Inc .... F 517 347-8656
 Okemos *(G-12123)*
Fedex Office & Print Svcs Inc .... F 248 377-2222
 Auburn Hills *(G-870)*
Fedex Office & Print Svcs Inc .... E 586 296-4890
 Roseville *(G-13803)*
Fedex Office & Print Svcs Inc .... F 734 374-0225
 Taylor *(G-15722)*
Foremost Graphics LLC .... D 616 453-4747
 Grand Rapids *(G-6415)*
Forsons Inc .... G 517 787-4562
 Jackson *(G-8450)*
Frye Printing Company Inc .... F 517 456-4124
 Clinton *(G-3021)*
Future Reproductions Inc .... F 248 350-2060
 Southfield *(G-14916)*
Gombar Corp .... G 989 793-9427
 Saginaw *(G-14048)*
Grand Blanc Printing Inc .... E 810 694-1155
 Grand Blanc *(G-5968)*
Graphic Impressions Inc .... G 616 455-0303
 Grand Rapids *(G-6474)*
Graphic Specialties Inc .... E 616 247-0060
 Grand Rapids *(G-6475)*
Halsan Inc .... G 734 285-5420
 Southgate *(G-15078)*
Hamblin Company .... E 517 423-7491
 Tecumseh *(G-15796)*
Handy Bindery Co Inc .... E 586 469-2240
 Clinton Township *(G-3133)*
Hatteras Inc .... E 734 525-5500
 Dearborn *(G-3719)*
Hi-Lites Graphic Inc .... E 231 924-0630
 Fremont *(G-5775)*
Hodges & Irvine Inc .... F 810 329-4787
 Saint Clair *(G-14222)*
J-Ad Graphics Inc .... E 269 965-3955
 Battle Creek *(G-1202)*
J-Ad Graphics Inc .... D 800 870-7085
 Hastings *(G-7416)*
Kent Communications Inc .... D 616 957-2120
 Grand Rapids *(G-6575)*
Lee Industries Inc .... E 231 777-2537
 Muskegon *(G-11365)*
Litsenberger Print Shop .... G 906 482-3903
 Houghton *(G-7976)*
Logan Brothers Printing Inc .... F 517 485-3771
 Dewitt *(G-4463)*
Macomb Printing Inc .... E 586 463-2301
 Clinton Township *(G-3163)*
Maleports Sault Prtg Co Inc .... E 906 632-3369
 Sault Sainte Marie *(G-14468)*
Malloy Incorporated .... A 734 665-6113
 Ann Arbor *(G-542)*
McNaughton & Gunn Inc .... C 734 429-5411
 Saline *(G-14399)*
Mel Printing Co Inc .... E 313 928-5440
 Taylor *(G-15738)*
Metropolitan Indus Lithography .... G 269 323-9333
 Portage *(G-13016)*
Micrgraphics Printing Inc .... E 231 739-6575
 Norton Shores *(G-11773)*
Mid-State Printing Inc .... F 989 875-4163
 Ithaca *(G-8364)*
Millbrook Printing Co .... F 517 627-4078
 Grand Ledge *(G-6112)*
Mitchell Graphics Inc .... E 231 347-4635
 Petoskey *(G-12459)*
Ogemaw County Herald Inc .... E 989 345-0044
 West Branch *(G-17514)*
Owosso Graphic Arts Inc .... E 989 725-7112
 Owosso *(G-12309)*
Parkside Printing Inc .... G 810 765-4500
 Marine City *(G-10479)*
Parkside Speedy Print Inc .... G 810 985-8484
 Port Huron *(G-12955)*
Paul C Doerr .... G 734 242-2058
 Monroe *(G-11060)*
Phase III Graphics Inc .... G 616 949-9290
 Grand Rapids *(G-6753)*

PRODUCT SECTION

Print-Tech Inc .... E 734 996-2345
 Ann Arbor *(G-604)*
Printcomm Inc .... D 810 239-5763
 Flint *(G-5484)*
Printery Inc .... E 616 396-4655
 Holland *(G-7777)*
Printing Plus Inc .... G 734 482-1680
 Ypsilanti *(G-18096)*
Printwell Acquisition Co Inc .... D 734 941-6300
 Taylor *(G-15758)*
Qrp Inc .... E 989 496-2955
 Midland *(G-10906)*
Qrp Inc .... E 989 496-2955
 Midland *(G-10905)*
R & R Harwood Inc .... G 616 669-6400
 Jenison *(G-8640)*
R W Patterson Printing Co .... D 269 925-2177
 Benton Harbor *(G-1542)*
Reyers Company Inc .... F 616 414-5530
 Spring Lake *(G-15172)*
Riegle Press Inc .... E 810 653-9631
 Davison *(G-3661)*
River Run Press Inc .... E 269 349-7603
 Kalamazoo *(G-8873)*
Ron Rowe .... G 231 652-2642
 Newaygo *(G-11577)*
Spartan Printing Inc .... E 517 372-6910
 Lansing *(G-9264)*
Spectrum Printers Inc .... E 517 423-5735
 Tecumseh *(G-15809)*
T J K Inc .... G 586 731-9639
 Sterling Heights *(G-15518)*
Technology MGT & Budgt Dept .... D 517 322-1897
 Lansing *(G-9430)*
Thomas Kenyon Inc .... G 248 476-8130
 Saint Clair Shores *(G-14272)*
Thorpe Printing Services Inc .... G 810 364-6222
 Marysville *(G-10622)*
Tribar Manufacturing LLC .... E 248 669-0077
 Wixom *(G-17916)*
Turner Business Forms Inc .... E 989 752-5540
 Saginaw *(G-14171)*
Val Valley Inc .... G 248 474-7335
 Farmington Hills *(G-5145)*
Village Shop Inc .... D 231 946-3712
 Traverse City *(G-16138)*
Wolverine Printing Company LLC ..... E 616 451-2075
 Grand Rapids *(G-6999)*
Woodhams Enterprises Inc .... G 269 383-0600
 Climax *(G-3014)*

BINDING SVC: Pamphlets

Schultz Bindery Inc .... F 586 771-0777
 Warren *(G-17233)*

BINDING SVC: Trade

E & R Bindery Service Inc .... G 734 464-7954
 Livonia *(G-9717)*

BINS: Prefabricated, Metal Plate

Contract Welding and Fabg Inc .... E 734 699-5561
 Van Buren Twp *(G-16753)*
L & W Inc .... B 734 397-2212
 Van Buren Twp *(G-16770)*
L & W Inc .... C 616 394-9665
 Holland *(G-7715)*

BIOLOGICAL PRDTS: Blood Derivatives

Transtechbio Inc .... G 734 994-4728
 Saline *(G-14419)*

BIOLOGICAL PRDTS: Exc Diagnostic

Axonia Medical Inc .... G 269 615-6632
 Kalamazoo *(G-8689)*
Biosan Laboratories Inc .... F 586 755-8970
 Warren *(G-16961)*
Biosavita Inc .... G 734 233-3146
 Plymouth *(G-12587)*
Esperovax Inc .... G 248 667-1845
 Plymouth *(G-12619)*
Immuno Concepts NA Ltd .... E 734 464-0701
 Livonia *(G-9780)*
Koppert Biological Systems .... E 734 641-3763
 Howell *(G-8057)*
Oxford Biomedical Research Inc ...... G 248 852-8815
 Metamora *(G-10779)*

PRODUCT SECTION

BLOWERS & FANS

BIOLOGICAL PRDTS: Vaccines
Emergent Biodef Oper Lnsng LLC .... B 517 327-1500
  Lansing *(G-9224)*

BIOLOGICAL PRDTS: Vaccines & Immunizing
Bruce Kane Enterprises LLC .... G 410 727-0637
  Farmington Hills *(G-4948)*
Novavax Inc .... G 248 656-5336
  Rochester *(G-13337)*

BIOLOGICAL PRDTS: Venoms
Venom Motorsports Inc .... G 616 635-2519
  Grand Rapids *(G-6964)*

BIOLOGICAL PRDTS: Veterinary
Arbor Assays Inc .... F 734 677-1774
  Ann Arbor *(G-362)*
Neogen Corporation .... B 517 372-9200
  Lansing *(G-9405)*
Stel Technologies LLC .... G 248 802-9457
  Ann Arbor *(G-645)*

BLACKSMITH SHOP
Cooks Blacksmith Welding Inc .... G 231 796-6819
  Big Rapids *(G-1625)*

BLADES: Saw, Chain Type
Saw Tubergen Service Inc .... G 616 534-0701
  Grand Rapids *(G-6852)*

BLANKBOOKS & LOOSELEAF BINDERS
Microforms Inc .... D 586 939-7900
  Beverly Hills *(G-1620)*

BLANKBOOKS: Receipt
Superior Receipt Book Co Inc .... E 269 467-8265
  Centreville *(G-2597)*

BLANKBOOKS: Scrapbooks
Artful Scrapbooking & Rubber .... G 586 651-1577
  Washington *(G-17302)*
Janelle Peterson .... G 616 447-9070
  Grand Rapids *(G-6552)*
Memories Manor .... G 810 329-2800
  Saint Clair *(G-14228)*
Scrapaloo .... G 269 623-7310
  Delton *(G-3820)*
Scrappy Chic .... G 248 426-9020
  Livonia *(G-9923)*

BLANKETS, FROM PURCHASED MATERIALS
Cellulose Mtl Solutions LLC .... G 616 669-2990
  Jenison *(G-8620)*

BLANKETS: Horse
Huron Vlleys Hrse Blnket Hdqtr .... G 248 859-2398
  Wixom *(G-17831)*

BLASTING SVC: Sand, Metal Parts
Abrasive Solutions LLC .... G 517 592-2668
  Cement City *(G-2574)*
Beech & Rich Inc .... E 269 968-8012
  Springfield *(G-15188)*
J & L Products Inc .... G 248 544-8500
  Hazel Park *(G-7439)*
Northwest Fabrication Inc .... G 231 536-3229
  East Jordan *(G-4641)*
Schwartz Boiler Shop Inc .... G 231 627-2556
  Cheboygan *(G-2694)*
Spec Abrasives and Finishing .... F 231 722-1926
  Muskegon *(G-11428)*
Supreme Media Blasting and Pow .... G 586 792-7705
  Clinton Township *(G-3239)*

BLINDS & SHADES: Vertical
A ME Vertical Incorporated .... G 248 720-0245
  Troy *(G-16164)*
Custom Verticals Unlimited .... G 734 522-1615
  Oak Park *(G-12057)*

Kyler Industries Inc .... G 616 392-1042
  Holland *(G-7714)*
MSC Blinds & Shades Inc .... G 269 489-5188
  Bronson *(G-2033)*
Sophias Textiles & Furn Inc .... F 586 759-6231
  Center Line *(G-2584)*
Time For Blinds Inc .... G 248 363-9174
  White Lake *(G-17640)*
Triangle Window Fashions Inc .... E 616 538-9676
  Wyoming *(G-18036)*

BLINDS : Window
Blinds and Designs Inc .... D 770 971-5524
  Wixom *(G-17776)*
Dave Brand .... G 269 651-4693
  Sturgis *(G-15603)*
Detroit Custom Services Inc .... E 586 465-3631
  Mount Clemens *(G-11129)*
Parkway Drapery & Uphl Co Inc .... G 734 779-1300
  Livonia *(G-9884)*
Signature Designs Inc .... G 248 426-9735
  Farmington Hills *(G-5123)*
Sunburst Shutters .... G 248 674-4600
  Waterford *(G-17378)*
Tri City Blinds Inc .... G 989 695-5699
  Freeland *(G-5760)*

BLINDS, WOOD
Comfort Blinds .... G 248 926-9300
  Wixom *(G-17788)*

BLOCKS & BRICKS: Concrete
Carlesimo Products Inc .... E 248 474-0415
  Farmington Hills *(G-4957)*
Interlock Design .... F 616 784-5901
  Comstock Park *(G-3486)*
Kurtz Gravel Company Inc .... E 810 787-6543
  Farmington Hills *(G-5040)*
Maple Valley Concrete Products .... G 517 852-1900
  Nashville *(G-11460)*
Miller Products & Supply Co .... F 906 774-1243
  Iron Mountain *(G-8290)*
St Marys Cement Inc (us) .... G 269 679-5253
  Schoolcraft *(G-14501)*
Swartzmiller Lumber Company .... G 989 845-6625
  Chesaning *(G-2728)*
Waanders Concrete Co .... E 269 673-6352
  Allegan *(G-190)*

BLOCKS: Brush, Wood, Turned & Shaped
Southeastern Equipment Co Inc .... G 248 349-9922
  Novi *(G-12002)*

BLOCKS: Landscape Or Retaining Wall, Concrete
A2z Outside Services Inc .... G 586 430-1143
  Richmond *(G-13257)*
Declarks Landscaping Inc .... E 586 752-7200
  Bruce Twp *(G-2082)*
K-Tel Corporation .... F 517 543-6174
  Charlotte *(G-2657)*
Livingston County Concrete Inc .... F 810 632-3030
  Brighton *(G-1951)*
Simply Green Outdoor Svcs LLC .... G 734 385-6190
  Dexter *(G-4510)*
Springfield Landscape Mtls .... G 269 965-6748
  Springfield *(G-15204)*

BLOCKS: Paving, Cut Stone
Unilock Michigan Inc .... E 248 437-1380
  Brighton *(G-2003)*

BLOCKS: Standard, Concrete Or Cinder
Bark River Concrete Pdts Co .... F 906 466-9940
  Bark River *(G-1118)*
Best Block Company .... E 586 772-7000
  Warren *(G-16956)*
Branch West Concrete Products .... F 989 345-0794
  West Branch *(G-17507)*
Cheboygan Cement Products Inc .... E 231 627-5631
  Cheboygan *(G-2677)*
Clay & Graham Inc .... G 989 354-5292
  Alpena *(G-283)*
Consumers Concrete Corp .... E 616 243-3651
  Wyoming *(G-17993)*

Consumers Concrete Corp .... E 269 384-0977
  Kalamazoo *(G-8714)*
Consumers Concrete Corporation .... E 269 342-0136
  Kalamazoo *(G-8715)*
Consumers Concrete Corporation .... F 231 777-3981
  Muskegon *(G-11300)*
Fendt Builders Supply Inc .... F 734 663-4277
  Ann Arbor *(G-461)*
Fendt Builders Supply Inc .... F 248 474-3211
  Farmington Hills *(G-4999)*
Ferguson Block Co Inc .... F 810 653-2812
  Davison *(G-3647)*
Fraco .... F 906 249-1476
  Marquette *(G-10532)*
Grand Blanc Cement Pdts Inc .... E 810 694-7500
  Grand Blanc *(G-5967)*
Hagen Cement Products Inc .... G 269 483-9641
  White Pigeon *(G-17651)*
Hampton Block Co .... G 248 628-1333
  Oxford *(G-12348)*
Hobe Inc .... G 231 845-5196
  Ludington *(G-10065)*
Lafarge North America Inc .... F 703 480-3600
  Dundee *(G-4591)*
Ludvanwall Inc .... E 616 842-4500
  Spring Lake *(G-15159)*
National Block Company .... E 734 721-4050
  Westland *(G-17582)*
New Buffalo Concrete Products .... B 269 469-2515
  New Buffalo *(G-11516)*
Port Huron Building Supply Co .... F 810 987-2666
  Port Huron *(G-12958)*
Ruppe Manufacturing Company .... E 906 932-3540
  Ironwood *(G-8339)*
Superior Block Company Inc .... F 906 482-2731
  Houghton *(G-7984)*
Theut Concrete Products Inc .... F 810 679-3376
  Croswell *(G-3604)*

BLOWERS & FANS
AC Covers Inc .... F 313 541-7770
  Redford *(G-13141)*
Advance Products Corporation .... E 269 849-1000
  Benton Harbor *(G-1480)*
Anrod Screen Cylinder Company .... E 989 872-2101
  Cass City *(G-2511)*
Avl Test Systems Inc .... C 734 414-9600
  Plymouth *(G-12580)*
Borgwarner Thermal Systems Inc .... E 231 779-7500
  Cadillac *(G-2233)*
Chicago Blow Pipe Company .... F 773 533-6100
  Marquette *(G-10522)*
Clean Air Technology Inc .... E 734 459-6500
  Canton *(G-2362)*
Combustion Research Corp .... E 248 852-3611
  Rochester Hills *(G-13391)*
Compressor Technologies Inc .... F 616 949-7000
  Grand Rapids *(G-6296)*
Constructive Sheet Metal Inc .... E 616 245-5306
  Allendale *(G-215)*
Dcl Inc .... C 231 547-5600
  Charlevoix *(G-2613)*
Dexter Automatic Products Co .... C 734 426-8900
  Dexter *(G-4485)*
Forma-Kool Manufacturing Inc .... E 586 949-4813
  Chesterfield *(G-2778)*
Howden North America Inc .... G 313 931-4000
  Dearborn *(G-3721)*
Key Gas Components Inc .... E 269 673-2151
  Allegan *(G-169)*
Midwest Intl Std Pdts Inc .... G 231 547-4073
  Charlevoix *(G-2621)*
MKI Products .... G 517 748-5075
  Jackson *(G-8532)*
Murtech Energy Services LLC .... G 810 653-5681
  Port Huron *(G-12948)*
Nortek Air Solutions LLC .... D 616 738-7148
  Holland *(G-7759)*
Parker-Hannifin Corporation .... B 269 629-5000
  Richland *(G-13252)*
Pittsfield Products Inc .... E 734 665-3771
  Ann Arbor *(G-593)*
Process Systems Inc .... D 586 757-5711
  Warren *(G-17198)*
Quality Filters Inc .... F 734 668-0211
  Ann Arbor *(G-611)*
Ronal Industries Inc .... F 248 616-9691
  Sterling Heights *(G-15478)*
Rosedale Products Inc .... D 734 665-8201
  Ann Arbor *(G-624)*

Employee Codes: A=Over 500 employees, B=251-500
C=101-250, D=51-100, E=20-50, F=10-19, G=3-9

2020 Harris Michigan Industrial Directory

1165

BLOWERS & FANS

Salem/Savard Industries LLC ....E..... 313 931-6880
  Detroit *(G-4352)*
Wayne Wire Cloth Products Inc ....C..... 989 742-4591
  Hillman *(G-7510)*
West Mich Auto Stl & Engrg Inc ....E..... 616 560-8198
  Belding *(G-1431)*

BLUEPRINTING SVCS

American Reprographics Co LLC ....E..... 248 299-8900
  Clawson *(G-2973)*
Capital City Blue Print Inc ....G..... 517 482-5431
  Lansing *(G-9207)*
Capital Imaging Inc ....F..... 517 482-2292
  Lansing *(G-9355)*
Commercial Blueprint Inc ....E..... 517 372-8360
  Lansing *(G-9357)*
Copy Central Inc ....G..... 231 941-2298
  Traverse City *(G-15947)*
Daniel Ward ....G..... 810 965-6535
  Mount Morris *(G-11160)*
Engineering Reproduction Inc ....F..... 313 366-3390
  Detroit *(G-4038)*
PDQ Ink Inc ....F..... 810 229-2989
  Brighton *(G-1975)*

BOAT & BARGE COMPONENTS: Metal, Prefabricated

Dedoes Innovative Mfg Inc ....E..... 517 223-2500
  Fowlerville *(G-5562)*
K & M Industrial LLC ....G..... 906 420-8770
  Gladstone *(G-5914)*

BOAT BUILDING & REPAIR

A & B Tube Benders Inc ....E..... 586 773-0440
  Warren *(G-16905)*
Abrahamson Marine Inc ....G..... 231 843-2142
  Ludington *(G-10047)*
Andersen Boat Works ....G..... 616 836-2502
  South Haven *(G-14753)*
Artisans Cstm Mmory Mattresses ....F..... 989 793-3208
  Saginaw *(G-13996)*
Beacon Marine Sales & Service ....G..... 586 465-2539
  Harrison Township *(G-7323)*
Bingham Boat Works Ltd ....G..... 906 225-0050
  Marquette *(G-10519)*
C & C Sports Inc ....E..... 810 227-7068
  Brighton *(G-1895)*
D B A Richards Boatworks Mar ....G..... 906 789-4168
  Escanaba *(G-4823)*
Eldean Company ....E..... 616 335-5843
  Macatawa *(G-10096)*
Eldean Yacht Basin Ltd ....E..... 616 786-2205
  Holland *(G-7620)*
Glastron LLC ....B..... 800 354-3141
  Cadillac *(G-2249)*
Invision Boatworks LLC ....G..... 989 754-3341
  Saginaw *(G-14064)*
Irish Boat Shop Inc ....E..... 231 547-9967
  Charlevoix *(G-2619)*
Jans Sport Shop Inc ....F..... 810 636-2241
  Goodrich *(G-5954)*
Marsh Brothers Inc ....F..... 517 869-2653
  Quincy *(G-13096)*
Max Manufacturing ....F..... 517 990-9180
  Jackson *(G-8511)*
Meyers Boat Company Inc ....F..... 517 265-9821
  Adrian *(G-81)*
Mid-Tech Inc ....G..... 734 426-4327
  Ann Arbor *(G-557)*
Midwest Aquatics Group Inc ....G..... 734 426-4155
  Pinckney *(G-12500)*
Morin Boats ....G..... 989 686-7353
  Bay City *(G-1335)*
N D R Enterprises Inc ....G..... 269 857-4556
  Saugatuck *(G-14460)*
Powell & Crisp Plankters LLC ....G..... 231 271-6769
  Suttons Bay *(G-15654)*
Rec Boat Holdings LLC ....D..... 231 775-1351
  Cadillac *(G-2273)*
Ricks Cove Inc ....G..... 734 283-7505
  Wyandotte *(G-17972)*
Spicers Boat Cy of Houghton Lk ....E..... 989 366-8384
  Houghton Lake *(G-7997)*
Swivl - Eze Marine ....E..... 616 897-9241
  Lowell *(G-10044)*
T D Vinette Company ....G..... 906 786-1884
  Escanaba *(G-4862)*
Tassier Boat Works Inc ....G..... 906 484-2573
  Cedarville *(G-2572)*

Unlimited Marine Inc ....G..... 248 249-0222
  White Lake *(G-17641)*
Van Dam Marine Co ....F..... 231 582-2323
  Boyne City *(G-1837)*
Viking Boat Harbor Inc ....F..... 906 484-3303
  Cedarville *(G-2573)*
Wooden Runabout Co ....G..... 616 396-7248
  Holland *(G-7860)*

BOAT BUILDING & REPAIRING: Fiberglass

Advanced Fiberglass Services ....G..... 810 785-7541
  Flint *(G-5370)*
Bay City Fiberglass Inc ....G..... 989 751-9622
  Bay City *(G-1285)*
Northshore Pontoon ....G..... 517 547-8877
  Hudson *(G-8137)*
Ocean Express Powerboats Inc ....G..... 810 794-5551
  Algonac *(G-145)*
S 2 Yachts Inc ....A..... 616 392-7163
  Holland *(G-7793)*
Sunsation Products Inc ....E..... 810 794-4888
  Clay *(G-3003)*

BOAT BUILDING & REPAIRING: Houseboats

Maurell Products Inc ....C..... 989 725-5188
  Owosso *(G-12301)*

BOAT BUILDING & REPAIRING: Jet Skis

Powersports Dales LLC ....G..... 248 682-4200
  Keego Harbor *(G-8981)*

BOAT BUILDING & REPAIRING: Motorboats, Inboard Or Outboard

Douglas Marine Corporation ....E..... 269 857-1764
  Douglas *(G-4530)*
Sterling Performance Inc ....E..... 248 685-7811
  Milford *(G-10987)*

BOAT BUILDING & REPAIRING: Motorized

Murleys Marine ....G..... 586 725-7446
  Ira *(G-8264)*

BOAT BUILDING & REPAIRING: Non-Motorized

Ameriform Acquisition Co LLC ....B..... 231 733-2725
  Muskegon *(G-11269)*
Paddle King Inc ....F..... 989 235-6776
  Carson City *(G-2495)*
Rubber Rope Products Company ....G..... 906 358-4133
  Watersmeet *(G-17389)*

BOAT BUILDING & REPAIRING: Pontoons, Exc Aircraft & Inflat

American Pleasure Products Inc ....G..... 989 685-8484
  Rose City *(G-13758)*
Avalon & Tahoe Mfg Inc ....C..... 989 463-2112
  Alma *(G-236)*
Crest Marine LLC ....E..... 989 725-5188
  Owosso *(G-12285)*

BOAT BUILDING & REPAIRING: Rigid, Plastic

Nauticraft Corporation 231 798-8440
  Norton Shores *(G-11779)*

BOAT BUILDING & REPAIRING: Yachts

Beardslee Investments Inc ....F..... 810 748-9951
  Harsens Island *(G-7368)*
Reed Yacht Sales LLC ....G..... 419 304-4405
  La Salle *(G-9074)*
Reed Yacht Sales LLC ....F..... 616 842-8899
  Grand Haven *(G-6069)*

BOAT DEALERS

Irish Boat Shop Inc ....E..... 231 547-9967
  Charlevoix *(G-2619)*

BOAT DEALERS: Canoe & Kayak

Paddlesports Warehouse Inc ....G..... 231 757-9051
  Scottville *(G-14510)*

BOAT DEALERS: Inflatable

Inflatable Marine Products Inc ....G..... 616 723-8140
  Howard City *(G-8002)*

BOAT DEALERS: Marine Splys & Eqpt

Interlochen Boat Shop Inc ....G..... 231 275-7112
  Interlochen *(G-8243)*
Quality Marine Electronics LLC ....G..... 616 566-2101
  Zeeland *(G-18182)*
Tassier Boat Works Inc ....G..... 906 484-2573
  Cedarville *(G-2572)*

BOAT DEALERS: Motor

C & C Sports Inc ....E..... 810 227-7068
  Brighton *(G-1895)*
Jans Sport Shop Inc ....F..... 810 636-2241
  Goodrich *(G-5954)*
Northshore Pontoon ....G..... 517 547-8877
  Hudson *(G-8137)*
Spicers Boat Cy of Houghton Lk ....E..... 989 366-8384
  Houghton Lake *(G-7997)*

BOAT DEALERS: Sailboats & Eqpt

Midwest Aquatics Group Inc ....G..... 734 426-4155
  Pinckney *(G-12500)*

BOAT LIFTS

Bulmann Enterprises Inc ....E..... 231 549-5020
  Boyne City *(G-1818)*
Great Lakes Lift Inc ....G..... 989 673-2109
  Caro *(G-2469)*
Harbor Master Ltd ....F..... 616 669-3170
  Hudsonville *(G-8159)*
Interlochen Boat Shop Inc ....G..... 231 275-7112
  Interlochen *(G-8243)*
L & M Mfg Inc ....G..... 989 689-4010
  Hope *(G-7955)*
Odonnells Docks ....G..... 269 244-1446
  Jones *(G-8652)*
Shore-Mate Products LLC ....G..... 616 874-5438
  Rockford *(G-13590)*

BOAT REPAIR SVCS

Advanced Fiberglass Services ....G..... 810 785-7541
  Flint *(G-5370)*
Bay City Fiberglass Inc ....G..... 989 751-9622
  Bay City *(G-1285)*
Bingham Boat Works Ltd ....G..... 906 225-0050
  Marquette *(G-10519)*
Chesterfield Engines Inc ....G..... 586 949-5777
  Chesterfield *(G-2753)*
Tassier Boat Works Inc ....G..... 906 484-2573
  Cedarville *(G-2572)*
West Shore Signs Inc ....G..... 734 324-7076
  Riverview *(G-13306)*

BOAT YARD: Boat yards, storage & incidental repair

Eldean Company ....E..... 616 335-5843
  Macatawa *(G-10096)*
Irish Boat Shop Inc ....E..... 231 547-9967
  Charlevoix *(G-2619)*
Leco Corporation ....F..... 269 982-2230
  Saint Joseph *(G-14325)*
Spicers Boat Cy of Houghton Lk ....E..... 989 366-8384
  Houghton Lake *(G-7997)*
T D Vinette Company ....G..... 906 786-1884
  Escanaba *(G-4862)*
Van Dam Marine Co ....F..... 231 582-2323
  Boyne City *(G-1837)*

BOATS & OTHER MARINE EQPT: Plastic

Inflatable Marine Products Inc ....G..... 616 723-8140
  Howard City *(G-8002)*
Inplast Interior Tech LLC ....G..... 810 724-3500
  Almont *(G-258)*

BOATS: Plastic, Nonrigid

Meyers Boat Company Inc ....F..... 517 265-9821
  Adrian *(G-81)*

BODIES: Truck & Bus

AM General LLC ....B..... 734 523-8098
  Auburn Hills *(G-767)*

Armada Rubber Manufacturing Co .... D 586 784-9135
Armada *(G-716)*
Borgwarner Thermal Systems Inc .... E 231 779-7500
Cadillac *(G-2233)*
Cameron Kirk Forest Pdts Inc .... G 989 426-3439
Gladwin *(G-5926)*
Carter Industries Inc .... E 510 324-6700
Adrian *(G-53)*
D & W Management Company Inc .... E 586 758-2284
Warren *(G-16996)*
Durakon Industries Inc .... G 608 742-5301
Lapeer *(G-9457)*
E-T-M Enterprises I Inc .... C 517 627-8461
Grand Ledge *(G-6105)*
Eleven Mile Trck Frme & Ax .... D 248 399-7536
Madison Heights *(G-10244)*
Ford Motor Company .... B 313 322-3000
Dearborn *(G-3709)*
Ford Motor Company .... A 313 322-7715
Dearborn *(G-3711)*
Ford Motor Company .... E 910 381-7998
Taylor *(G-15723)*
Ford Motor Company .... A 734 523-3000
Livonia *(G-9744)*
Ford Motor Company .... A 734 942-6248
Brownstown *(G-2062)*
Hme Inc .... C 616 534-1463
Wyoming *(G-18011)*
Marsh Industrial Services Inc .... F 231 258-4870
Kalkaska *(G-8949)*
Midwest Bus Corporation .... D 989 723-5241
Owosso *(G-12304)*
Monroe Truck Equipment Inc .... E 810 238-4603
Flint *(G-5470)*
NBC Truck Equipment Inc .... E 586 774-4900
Roseville *(G-13845)*
Norma Michigan Inc .... C 248 373-4300
Auburn Hills *(G-959)*
Norma Michigan Inc .... F 248 373-4300
Lake Orion *(G-9151)*
Novi Manufacturing Co .... D 248 476-4350
Novi *(G-11958)*
Ralyas Auto Body Incorporated .... G 517 694-6512
Mason *(G-10652)*
Saf-Holland Inc .... F 616 396-6501
Holland *(G-7794)*
Tractech Inc .... E 248 226-6800
Southfield *(G-15048)*

BODY PARTS: Automobile, Stamped Metal

A G Simpson (usa) Inc .... D 586 268-4817
Sterling Heights *(G-15245)*
A G Simpson (usa) Inc .... F 586 268-4817
Sterling Heights *(G-15246)*
A G Simpson (usa) Inc .... E 586 268-5844
Sterling Heights *(G-15247)*
Aaron Incorporated .... G 586 791-0320
Clinton Township *(G-3031)*
Aludyne International Inc .... G 248 728-8642
Southfield *(G-14833)*
Aludyne US LLC .... D 810 987-1112
Port Huron *(G-12889)*
Aludyne US LLC .... D 810 966-9350
Port Huron *(G-12890)*
Aludyne US LLC .... F 248 728-8642
Warren *(G-16928)*
Anderton Equity LLC .... G 248 430-6650
Troy *(G-16202)*
Android Indstrs-Shreveport LLC .... C 248 454-0500
Auburn Hills *(G-771)*
Anjun America Inc .... F 248 680-8825
Auburn Hills *(G-773)*
Arcturian LLC .... G 313 643-5326
Dearborn *(G-3679)*
Automobili Lamborghini Amer LLC .... G 866 681-6276
Auburn Hills *(G-787)*
Autowares Inc .... G 248 473-0928
Farmington Hills *(G-4937)*
Avon Machining LLC .... D 586 884-2200
Shelby Township *(G-14551)*
Avon Machining Holdings Inc .... C 586 884-2200
Shelby Township *(G-14552)*
Bae Industries Inc .... C 586 754-3000
Warren *(G-16950)*
Bae Industries Inc .... F 248 475-9600
Auburn Hills *(G-790)*
Benesh Corporation .... E 734 244-4143
Monroe *(G-11023)*
Bopp-Busch Manufacturing Co .... E 989 876-7121
Au Gres *(G-744)*
Caparo Vehicle Components Inc .... D 734 513-2859
Livonia *(G-9674)*
Challenge Mfg Company LLC .... F 616 735-6500
Walker *(G-16863)*
Concord Tool and Mfg Inc .... C 586 465-6537
Mount Clemens *(G-11127)*
Cooper-Standard Automotive Inc .... G 248 630-7262
Auburn Hills *(G-826)*
D T M 1 Inc .... E 248 889-9210
Highland *(G-7491)*
Dajaco Industries Inc .... D 586 949-1590
Chesterfield *(G-2760)*
Dayco Incorporated .... G 248 404-6500
Troy *(G-16297)*
Dexter Stamping Company LLC .... D 517 750-3414
Jackson *(G-8432)*
Dongah America Inc .... E 248 918-5810
Troy *(G-16322)*
Dunne-Rite Performance Inc .... F 616 828-0908
Warren *(G-17007)*
Dynetics Inc .... G 248 619-1681
Troy *(G-16331)*
Faurecia Interior Systems Inc .... C 248 409-3500
Auburn Hills *(G-862)*
Flex-N-Gate Corporation .... C 517 223-5900
Fowlerville *(G-5564)*
Ford Global Technologies LLC .... F 313 312-3000
Bingham Farms *(G-1653)*
Forged Tubular .... G 313 843-4870
Detroit *(G-4068)*
Gestamp Alabama LLC .... C 810 245-3100
Lapeer *(G-9462)*
Gestamp Washtenaw LLC .... E 248 251-3004
Chelsea *(G-2711)*
Gns North America Inc .... G 616 796-0433
Holland *(G-7646)*
Grant Industries Incorporated .... D 586 293-9200
Fraser *(G-5657)*
Guelph Tool Sales Inc .... B 586 755-3333
Warren *(G-17071)*
Hatch Stamping Company LLC .... C 517 540-1021
Howell *(G-8047)*
Hatch Stamping Company LLC .... C 734 433-1903
Chelsea *(G-2713)*
Hbpo North America Inc .... C 248 823-7076
Troy *(G-16392)*
Invention Evolution Comp LLC .... G 517 219-0180
Fowlerville *(G-5570)*
Iroquois Industries Inc .... E 586 353-1410
Warren *(G-17102)*
K & K Sales Assoc LLC .... G 248 623-7378
Waterford *(G-17353)*
K&K Stamping Company .... E 586 443-7900
Saint Clair Shores *(G-14257)*
Kecy Products Inc .... D 517 448-8954
Hudson *(G-8134)*
Kirchhoff Auto Tecumseh Inc .... B 517 423-2400
Tecumseh *(G-15800)*
Kirchhoff Automotive USA Inc .... F 248 247-3740
Troy *(G-16446)*
Lacks Exterior Systems LLC .... E 616 554-7180
Kentwood *(G-9016)*
Manufcturing Assembly Intl LLC .... F 248 549-4700
Royal Oak *(G-13946)*
Martinrea Jonesville LLC .... D 517 849-2195
Jonesville *(G-8662)*
Martinrea Jonesville LLC .... G 248 630-7730
Auburn Hills *(G-943)*
Matcor Automotive Michigan Inc .... C 616 527-4050
Ionia *(G-8248)*
Means Industries Inc .... D 989 754-3300
Saginaw *(G-14087)*
Melling Products North LLC .... D 989 588-6147
Farwell *(G-5164)*
Merit Tech Worldwide LLC .... E 734 927-9520
Canton *(G-2403)*
Michigan Vehicle Solutions LLC .... G 734 720-7649
Southgate *(G-15081)*
Microgauge Machining Inc .... C 248 446-3720
Brighton *(G-1961)*
Milan Metal Systems LLC .... C 734 439-1546
Milan *(G-10948)*
Minth North America Inc .... D 248 259-7468
Wixom *(G-17856)*
Motor City Stampings Inc .... B 586 949-8420
Chesterfield *(G-2808)*
Motor City Stampings Inc .... C 586 949-8420
Chesterfield *(G-2809)*
Motus Holdings LLC .... A 616 422-7557
Holland *(G-7749)*
Motus LLC .... C 616 422-7557
Holland *(G-7750)*
N A Sodecia Inc .... B 586 879-8969
Troy *(G-16518)*
North American Auto Inds Inc .... G 734 288-3877
Riverview *(G-13302)*
Pacific Engineering Corp .... G 248 359-7823
Novi *(G-11970)*
Pinconning Metals Inc .... G 989 879-3144
Pinconning *(G-12512)*
Plastic Trim International Inc .... E 248 259-7468
East Tawas *(G-4692)*
Precision Stamping Co Inc .... E 517 546-5656
Howell *(G-8082)*
Press-Way Inc .... D 586 790-3324
Clinton Township *(G-3201)*
R D M Enterprises Co Inc .... G 810 985-4721
Port Huron *(G-12959)*
Royal Flex-N-Gate Oak LLC .... B 248 549-3800
Warren *(G-17225)*
Sales & Engineering Inc .... E 734 525-9030
Livonia *(G-9919)*
Sierra Plastics Inc .... E 989 269-6272
Bad Axe *(G-1070)*
Sodecia Auto Detroit Corp .... E 586 759-2200
Sterling Heights *(G-15502)*
Sodecia Auto Detroit Corp .... B 586 759-2200
Roseville *(G-13871)*
Sodecia Auto Detroit Corp .... C 586 759-2200
Troy *(G-16609)*
Sodecia Auto Detroit Corp .... C 248 276-6647
Orion *(G-12190)*
Sodecia Auto Detroit Corp .... C 586 759-2200
Center Line *(G-2583)*
Spheros North America Inc .... G 734 218-7350
Canton *(G-2427)*
Spoiler Wing King .... G 810 733-9464
Flint *(G-5503)*
Style Craft Prototype Inc .... F 248 619-9048
Troy *(G-16624)*
Su-Dan Company .... D 248 651-6035
Lake Orion *(G-9164)*
Superior Cam Inc .... D 248 588-1100
Madison Heights *(G-10364)*
Tajco North America Inc .... G 248 418-7550
Auburn Hills *(G-1011)*
Tower Acquisition Co II LLC .... G 248 675-6000
Livonia *(G-9958)*
Tower International Inc .... B 248 675-6000
Livonia *(G-9967)*
Tubular Metal Systems LLC .... E 989 879-2611
Pinconning *(G-12514)*
Ventra Grand Rapids 5 LLC .... B 616 222-3296
Grand Rapids *(G-6965)*
Visor Frames LLC .... F 586 864-6058
Sterling Heights *(G-15541)*
Wellington Industries Inc .... C 734 942-1060
Van Buren Twp *(G-16796)*
Wellington-Almont LLC .... D 734 942-1060
Van Buren Twp *(G-16798)*
Wirco Products Inc .... F 810 984-5576
Port Huron *(G-12977)*

BOILER & HEATING REPAIR SVCS

Johnson Controls Inc .... E 616 847-2766
Spring Lake *(G-15156)*

BOILERS & BOILER SHOP WORK

Vierson Boiler & Repair Co .... F 616 949-0500
Grand Rapids *(G-6972)*

BOILERS: Low-Pressure Heating, Steam Or Hot Water

Armstrong Hot Water Inc .... E 269 278-1413
Three Rivers *(G-15857)*
Crown Heating Inc .... G 248 352-1688
Detroit *(G-3955)*

BOLTS: Metal

A A Anchor Bolt Inc .... F 248 349-6565
Northville *(G-11675)*
B & D Thread Rolling Inc .... D 734 728-7070
Taylor *(G-15693)*
B & S Manufacturing Inc .... G 586 939-5130
Clinton Township *(G-3062)*
Cold Heading Co .... D 586 497-7000
Warren *(G-16985)*

PRODUCT

BOLTS: Metal

Cold Heading Co .... D 586 497-7016
  Warren *(G-16986)*
Connection Service Company .... F 269 926-2658
  Benton Harbor *(G-1491)*
Dexter Fastener Tech Inc .... C 734 426-0311
  Dexter *(G-4486)*
E M P Manufacturing Corp .... F 586 949-8277
  Chesterfield *(G-2769)*
Federal Screw Works .... C 231 796-7664
  Big Rapids *(G-1627)*
Federal Screw Works .... G 231 922-9500
  Traverse City *(G-15969)*
Federal Screw Works .... F 734 941-4211
  Romulus *(G-13676)*
Kamax Inc .... B 248 879-0200
  Rochester Hills *(G-13454)*
MNP Corporation .... A 586 254-1320
  Utica *(G-16744)*
Nss Technologies Inc .... E 734 459-9500
  Canton *(G-2412)*
Nss Technologies Inc .... E 734 459-9500
  Canton *(G-2413)*
Vico Products Co .... C 734 453-3777
  Plymouth *(G-12790)*
Wilson-Garner Company .... E 586 466-5880
  Harrison Township *(G-7355)*

BONDERIZING: Bonderizing, Metal Or Metal Prdts

Ionbond LLC .... D 248 398-9100
  Madison Heights *(G-10278)*

BOOK STORES

Baker Book House Company .... C 616 676-9185
  Ada *(G-10)*
Lighthouse Direct Buy LLC .... G 313 340-1850
  Detroit *(G-4204)*

BOOK STORES: College

Student Book Store Inc .... G 517 351-6768
  East Lansing *(G-4677)*

BOOK STORES: Foreign

Algo Especial Variety Str Inc .... G 313 963-9013
  Detroit *(G-3854)*

BOOK STORES: Religious

Diocese of Lansing .... F 517 484-4449
  Lansing *(G-9361)*

BOOKING AGENCIES, THEATRICAL

Paul F Hester .... F 616 302-6039
  Pullman *(G-13087)*

BOOKS, WHOLESALE

A B Publishing Inc .... G 989 875-4985
  Ithaca *(G-8355)*
Lost Horizons Inc .... G 248 366-6858
  Commerce Township *(G-3423)*
Mott Media LLC .... F 810 714-4280
  Fenton *(G-5226)*
Superior Text LLC .... F 866 482-8762
  Ypsilanti *(G-18104)*

BOOTHS: Spray, Sheet Metal, Prefabricated

Custom Metal Works Inc .... G 810 420-0390
  Marine City *(G-10472)*
Gallagher-Kaiser Corporation .... D 313 368-3100
  Troy *(G-16378)*

BOOTS: Men's

Hy-Test Inc .... G 616 866-5500
  Rockford *(G-13572)*
Original Footwear Company .... B 231 796-5828
  Big Rapids *(G-1639)*

BORING MILL

ABC Boring Co Inc .... E 586 751-2580
  Warren *(G-16911)*
Fair Industries LLC .... C 248 740-7841
  Troy *(G-16359)*
Kasper Machine Co .... F 248 547-3150
  Madison Heights *(G-10289)*

BOTTLE CAPS & RESEALERS: Plastic

Berry Global Inc .... C 269 435-2425
  Constantine *(G-3532)*
Berry Global Inc .... B 616 772-4635
  Zeeland *(G-18118)*

BOTTLED GAS DEALERS: Propane

Van S Fabrications Inc .... G 810 679-2115
  Croswell *(G-3605)*

BOTTLES: Plastic

Alpha Packaging Michigan Inc .... D 314 427-4300
  Ypsilanti *(G-18050)*
Graham Packaging Company LP .... E 616 355-0479
  Holland *(G-7647)*
Inoac Usa Inc .... E 248 619-7031
  Troy *(G-16419)*
Novares US LLC .... B 616 554-3555
  Grand Rapids *(G-6723)*
Plastipak Packaging Inc .... C 734 455-3600
  Plymouth *(G-12719)*
Plastipak Packaging Inc .... C 734 326-6184
  Westland *(G-17589)*
Plastipak Packaging Inc .... F 734 467-7519
  Romulus *(G-13722)*
R N Fink Manufacturing Co .... E 517 655-4351
  Williamston *(G-17738)*

BOWLING EQPT & SPLY STORES

W M Enterprises .... G 810 694-4384
  Grand Blanc *(G-5988)*

BOWLING EQPT & SPLYS

Bbp Investment Holdings LLC .... F 231 725-4966
  Muskegon *(G-11278)*
Brunswick Bowling Products LLC .... B 231 725-3300
  Muskegon *(G-11285)*

BOX & CARTON MANUFACTURING EQPT

Bell Packaging Corp .... D 616 452-2111
  Grand Rapids *(G-6208)*

BOXES & CRATES: Rectangular, Wood

Action Wood Technologies Inc .... E 586 468-2300
  Clinton Township *(G-3036)*
AS Property Management Inc .... F 586 427-8000
  Warren *(G-16941)*
Diversified Pdts & Svcs LLC .... G 616 836-6600
  Holland *(G-7608)*
Mollewood Export Inc .... E 248 624-1885
  Wixom *(G-17859)*
Northern Packaging Mi Inc .... F 734 692-4700
  Grosse Ile *(G-7174)*
Scotts Enterprises Inc .... E 989 275-5011
  Roscommon *(G-13754)*

BOXES & SHOOK: Nailed Wood

Anbren Inc .... G 269 944-5066
  Benton Harbor *(G-1481)*
Charlies Wood Shop .... F 989 845-2632
  Chesaning *(G-2722)*
Czuk Studio .... G 269 628-2568
  Kendall *(G-8983)*
Demeester Wood Products Inc .... F 616 677-5995
  Coopersville *(G-3556)*
Diversified Pdts & Svcs LLC .... G 616 836-6600
  Holland *(G-7608)*
Donald Gleason 269 673-6802
  Allegan *(G-158)*
Export Corporation .... D 810 227-6153
  Brighton *(G-1920)*
Mollewood Export Inc .... E 248 624-1885
  Wixom *(G-17859)*
Packaging Specialties Inc .... E 586 473-6703
  Romulus *(G-13718)*
Scotts Enterprises Inc .... E 989 275-5011
  Roscommon *(G-13754)*

BOXES: Corrugated

Advance Packaging Acquisition .... D 616 949-6610
  Grand Rapids *(G-6146)*
Advance Packaging Corporation .... C 616 949-6610
  Grand Rapids *(G-6147)*
Advance Packaging Corporation .... D 616 949-6610
  Jackson *(G-8372)*
Aero Box Company .... G 586 415-0000
  Roseville *(G-13769)*
Alma Container Corporation .... F 989 463-2106
  Alma *(G-233)*
Anchor Bay Packaging Corp .... E 586 949-4040
  Chesterfield *(G-2738)*
Anchor Bay Packaging Corp .... E 586 949-1500
  Chesterfield *(G-2739)*
Arvco Container Corporation .... E 269 381-0900
  Kalamazoo *(G-8685)*
Arvco Container Corporation .... C 269 381-0900
  Kalamazoo *(G-8686)*
Arvco Container Corporation .... E 269 381-0900
  Kalamazoo *(G-8687)*
Arvco Container Corporation .... F 231 876-0935
  Cadillac *(G-2228)*
Bay Corrugated Container Inc .... C 734 243-5400
  Monroe *(G-11020)*
Blossomland Container Corp .... F 269 926-8206
  Benton Harbor *(G-1487)*
Bramco Containers Inc .... G 906 428-2855
  Gladstone *(G-5907)*
C/W South Inc .... E 810 767-2806
  Burton *(G-2148)*
Caraustar Cstm Packg Group Inc .... E 616 247-0330
  Grand Rapids *(G-6255)*
Corr Pack In .... G 248 348-4188
  Northville *(G-11684)*
Delta Containers Inc .... C 810 742-2730
  Bay City *(G-1299)*
Dewitt Packaging Corporation .... E 616 698-0210
  Grand Rapids *(G-6347)*
Flint Boxmakers Inc .... E 810 743-0400
  Burton *(G-2154)*
Georgia-Pacific LLC .... G 989 725-5191
  Owosso *(G-12293)*
Grand Traverse Reels Inc .... C 231 946-1057
  Traverse City *(G-15987)*
Great Lakes-Triad Plastic .... D 616 241-6441
  Grand Rapids *(G-6480)*
Green Bay Packaging Inc .... C 269 552-1000
  Kalamazoo *(G-8757)*
Industrial Packaging Corp .... F 248 677-0084
  Berkley *(G-1584)*
Inter-Pack Corporation .... E 734 242-7755
  Monroe *(G-11042)*
Jet Box Co Inc .... F 248 362-1260
  Troy *(G-16437)*
Jetco Packaging Solutions LLC .... G 616 588-2492
  Grand Rapids *(G-6559)*
Kentwood Packaging Corporation ...... D 616 698-9000
  Walker *(G-16869)*
Kraft-Wrap Inc .... F 586 755-2050
  Warren *(G-17121)*
Loope Enterprises Inc .... F 269 639-1567
  South Haven *(G-14763)*
Mall City Containers Inc .... G 269 381-2706
  Kalamazoo *(G-8817)*
Mall City Containers Inc .... G 616 249-3657
  Grand Rapids *(G-6641)*
Menasha Packaging Company LLC .... F 800 253-1526
  Coloma *(G-3361)*
Michcor Container Inc .... E 616 452-7089
  Grand Rapids *(G-6666)*
Michiana Corrugated Pdts Co .... E 269 651-5225
  Sturgis *(G-15617)*
Michigan Box Company .... D 313 873-9500
  Detroit *(G-4237)*
Monte Package Company LLC .... E 269 849-1722
  Riverside *(G-13285)*
Packaging Corporation America .... C 616 530-5700
  Grandville *(G-7062)*
Packaging Corporation America .... D 734 453-6262
  Plymouth *(G-12706)*
Packaging Corporation America .... G 734 266-1877
  Livonia *(G-9881)*
Packaging Corporation America .... B 231 723-1442
  Filer City *(G-5345)*
Packaging Corporation America 231 947-2220
  Edmore *(G-4753)*
Packaging Corporation America .... D 989 427-5129
  Edmore *(G-4754)*
Packaging Specialties Inc .... E 586 473-6703
  Romulus *(G-13718)*
Patriot Solutions LLC .... G 616 240-8164
  Grand Rapids *(G-6744)*
Premier Corrugated Inc .... E 517 629-5700
  Albion *(G-129)*
Royal Container Inc .... E 248 967-0910
  Oak Park *(G-12094)*

PRODUCT SECTION

Shipping Container Corporation ....E 313 937-2411
  Redford *(G-13191)*
Shoreline Container Inc..........................C....... 616 399-2088
  Holland *(G-7800)*
South Haven Packaging Inc..................F....... 269 639-1567
  South Haven *(G-14773)*
St Clair Packaging Inc ....E....... 810 364-4230
  Marysville *(G-10619)*
Tecumseh Packg Solutions Inc ....E....... 517 423-2126
  Tecumseh *(G-15811)*
Universal Container Corp........................E....... 248 543-2788
  Ferndale *(G-5326)*
Webcor Packaging Corporation ....D....... 810 767-2806
  Burton *(G-2170)*
Westrock Company ....E....... 734 453-6700
  Plymouth *(G-12793)*
Westrock Cp LLC ....F....... 810 787-6503
  Flint *(G-5522)*
World Corrugated Container Inc ....E....... 517 629-9400
  Albion *(G-136)*
Wrkco Inc..E....... 269 964-7181
  Battle Creek *(G-1268)*

BOXES: Filing, Paperboard Made From Purchased Materials

Michigan Box Company ....D....... 313 873-9500
  Detroit *(G-4237)*

BOXES: Outlet, Electric Wiring Device

Masco Building Products Corp ....G....... 313 274-7400
  Livonia *(G-9825)*

BOXES: Packing & Shipping, Metal

Hollingsworth Container LLC ....G....... 313 768-1400
  Dearborn *(G-3720)*
Hyper Alloys Inc......................................E....... 586 772-0571
  Clinton Township *(G-3138)*
Yarema Die & Engineering Co ....E....... 248 689-5777
  Troy *(G-16703)*

BOXES: Paperboard, Folding

Americraft Carton Inc ....D....... 269 651-2365
  Sturgis *(G-15596)*
Caraustar Cstm Packg Group Inc.............E....... 616 247-0330
  Grand Rapids *(G-6255)*
Complete Packaging Inc ....E....... 734 241-2794
  Monroe *(G-11025)*
Graphic Packaging Intl LLC ....D....... 269 969-7446
  Battle Creek *(G-1194)*
Michigan Carton Paper Boy ....G....... 269 963-4004
  Battle Creek *(G-1228)*
Packaging Specialties Inc ....E....... 586 473-6703
  Romulus *(G-13718)*
Rapid-Packaging Corporation ....E....... 616 949-0950
  Grand Rapids *(G-6811)*
S & C Industries Inc ....F....... 269 381-6022
  Kalamazoo *(G-8880)*
Steketee-Van Huis Inc.............................C....... 616 392-2326
  Holland *(G-7814)*
Wrkco Inc..E....... 269 964-7181
  Battle Creek *(G-1268)*
Wynalda Litho Inc ....C....... 616 866-1561
  Belmont *(G-1476)*

BOXES: Paperboard, Set-Up

Packaging Specialties Inc ....E....... 586 473-6703
  Romulus *(G-13718)*

BOXES: Plastic

Datacover Inc ....G....... 844 875-4076
  Pontiac *(G-12814)*
Handley Industries Inc............................F....... 517 787-8821
  Jackson *(G-8462)*
National Case Corporation......................G....... 586 726-1710
  Sterling Heights *(G-15432)*

BOXES: Solid Fiber

General Wood Products Co ....F....... 248 221-0214
  Big Rapids *(G-1630)*
Phoenix Packaging Corporation ....G....... 734 944-3916
  Saline *(G-14407)*

BOXES: Wirebound, Wood

Industrial Wood Fab & Packg Co ....G....... 734 284-4808
  Riverview *(G-13298)*

BOXES: Wooden

Auto Pallets-Boxes Inc.............................F....... 248 559-7744
  Lathrup Village *(G-9498)*
C & K Box Company Inc...........................E....... 517 784-1779
  Jackson *(G-8397)*
Complete Packaging Inc ....E....... 734 241-2794
  Monroe *(G-11025)*
Crossroads Industries Inc........................D....... 989 732-1233
  Gaylord *(G-5853)*
Grigg Box Co Inc......................................E....... 313 273-9000
  Detroit *(G-4106)*
Home Shop..G....... 517 543-5325
  Charlotte *(G-2654)*
Michigan Box Company ....D....... 313 873-9500
  Detroit *(G-4237)*

BRAKES & BRAKE PARTS

Autocam Corporation ....B....... 616 698-0707
  Kentwood *(G-9000)*
Bpi Holdings International Inc ....G....... 815 363-9000
  Ann Arbor *(G-389)*
Braetec Inc..G....... 269 968-4711
  Battle Creek *(G-1156)*
Brembo North America Inc ....E....... 517 568-4398
  Homer *(G-7937)*
Cambro Products Inc...............................E....... 586 468-8847
  Harrison Township *(G-7326)*
Chassis Brakes Intl USA ....G....... 248 957-9997
  Farmington Hills *(G-4962)*
Continental Auto Systems Inc ....A....... 248 393-5300
  Auburn Hills *(G-819)*
Dura Auto Systems Cble Oprtons ....G....... 248 299-7500
  Auburn Hills *(G-844)*
Dura Automotive Systems LLC ....C....... 248 299-7500
  Auburn Hills *(G-845)*
Grattan Family Enterprises LLC ....D....... 248 547-3870
  Ferndale *(G-5290)*
Litebrake Tech LLC ....G....... 906 523-2007
  Houghton *(G-7975)*
Midwest Brake Bond Co ....E....... 586 775-3000
  Warren *(G-17155)*
Nisshinbo Automotive Mfg Inc ....D....... 586 997-1000
  Sterling Heights *(G-15436)*
Northrop Grmmn Spce & Mssn Sys ......A....... 734 266-2600
  Livonia *(G-9864)*
Old Dura Inc ....G....... 248 299-7500
  Auburn Hills *(G-965)*
Opeo Inc..F....... 248 299-4000
  Auburn Hills *(G-966)*
Robert Bosch LLC ....F....... 269 429-3221
  Saint Joseph *(G-14338)*
S & S Tube Inc ....F....... 989 656-7211
  Bay Port *(G-1375)*
Truck Trailer Transit Inc..........................E....... 313 516-7151
  Troy *(G-16652)*
Wabco Holdings Inc..................................C....... 248 270-9300
  Auburn Hills *(G-1049)*

BRAKES: Bicycle, Friction Clutch & Other

ITT Motion Tech Amer LLC......................F....... 248 863-2161
  Novi *(G-11909)*

BRAKES: Electromagnetic

Cusolar Industries Inc.............................E....... 586 949-3880
  Chesterfield *(G-2757)*
Magnetech Corporation...........................G....... 248 426-8840
  Novi *(G-11933)*

BRAKES: Metal Forming

Brake Roller Co Inc..................................E....... 269 965-2371
  Battle Creek *(G-1157)*

BRAKES: Press

Seg Automotive North Amer LLC ....F....... 248 465-2602
  Novi *(G-11991)*

BRASS & BRONZE PRDTS: Die-casted

Cooper Foundry Inc..................................F....... 269 343-2808
  Kalamazoo *(G-8717)*
Evans Industries Inc ....G....... 313 259-2266
  Detroit *(G-4045)*
Flare Fittings Incorporated ....E....... 269 344-7600
  Kalamazoo *(G-8744)*
Lubo Usa Inc ....G....... 810 244-5826
  Madison Heights *(G-10300)*
Wolverine Bronze Company ....D....... 586 776-8180
  Roseville *(G-13891)*

BRASS FOUNDRY, NEC

Ehc Inc ....G....... 313 259-2266
  Detroit *(G-4030)*
G M Brass & Alum Fndry Inc ....F....... 269 926-6366
  Benton Harbor *(G-1500)*
Mueller Brass Co......................................D....... 810 987-7770
  Port Huron *(G-12945)*
Non-Ferrous Cast Alloys Inc ....E....... 231 799-0550
  Norton Shores *(G-11782)*

BRASS GOODS, WHOLESALE

Stexley-Brake LLC ....G....... 231 421-3092
  Traverse City *(G-16111)*

BRAZING SVCS

Anderson Brazing Co Inc.........................G....... 248 399-5155
  Madison Heights *(G-10192)*
D K Enterprises Inc..................................G....... 586 756-7350
  Warren *(G-16997)*
KC Jones Brazing Inc ....G....... 586 755-4900
  Warren *(G-17118)*
Plymouth Brazing Inc ....D....... 734 453-6274
  Westland *(G-17590)*

BRAZING: Metal

Bell Induction Heating Inc......................G....... 734 697-0133
  Van Buren Twp *(G-16748)*
Bodycote Thermal Proc Inc ....G....... 313 442-2387
  Romulus *(G-13659)*
Bodycote Thermal Proc Inc ....E....... 734 451-0338
  Canton *(G-2354)*
Detroit Flame Hardening Co ....E....... 586 484-1726
  Clinton Township *(G-3101)*
Modern Metal Processing Corp ....G....... 517 655-4402
  Williamston *(G-17735)*
Nitro-Vac Heat Treat Inc..........................F....... 586 754-4350
  Warren *(G-17168)*
Specialty Steel Treating Inc ....E....... 586 293-5355
  Fraser *(G-5730)*
Vac-Met Inc ....E....... 586 264-8100
  Warren *(G-17276)*
Wall Co Incorporated ....E....... 248 585-6400
  Madison Heights *(G-10379)*
West Side Flamehardening Inc ....F....... 734 729-1665
  Westland *(G-17611)*

BRIC-A-BRAC

Services To Enhance Potential ....G....... 313 278-3040
  Dearborn *(G-3757)*

BRICK, STONE & RELATED PRDTS WHOLESALERS

Hagen Cement Products Inc ....G....... 269 483-9641
  White Pigeon *(G-17651)*
Holcim (us) Inc ....D....... 734 529-2411
  Dundee *(G-4587)*
Lakeshore Cement Products ....G....... 989 739-9341
  Oscoda *(G-12213)*
Motawi Tileworks Inc ....E....... 734 213-0017
  Ann Arbor *(G-565)*
Newark Gravel Company ....F....... 810 796-3072
  Dryden *(G-4570)*
Willbee Transit-Mix Co Inc ....E....... 517 782-9493
  Jackson *(G-8608)*

BRICKS & BLOCKS: Structural

Heb Development LLC.............................G....... 616 363-3825
  Grand Rapids *(G-6501)*

BRICKS : Ceramic Glazed, Clay

Sineramics Incorporated.........................G....... 248 879-0812
  Troy *(G-16604)*

BRICKS: Clay

Tabs Wall Systems LLC ....G....... 616 554-5400
  Grand Rapids *(G-6914)*

BRICKS: Concrete

Mbcd Inc ....E....... 517 484-4426
  Lansing *(G-9395)*

BRIDAL SHOPS

BRIDAL SHOPS
Bella Sposa Bridal & Prom .... G 616 364-0777
  Grand Rapids *(G-6209)*
Celebrations .... G 906 482-4946
  Hancock *(G-7250)*
Genesee County Herald Inc .... F 810 686-3840
  Clio *(G-3272)*
Progressive Prtg & Graphics .... G 269 965-8909
  Battle Creek *(G-1238)*

BROACHING MACHINES
American Broach & Machine Co .... E 734 961-0300
  Ypsilanti *(G-18051)*
Apex Broaching Systems Inc .... F 586 758-2626
  Warren *(G-16936)*
Federal Broach & Mch Co LLC .... C 989 539-7420
  Harrison *(G-7311)*
Forst-Usa Incorporated .... G 586 759-9380
  Warren *(G-17044)*
General Broach & Engrg Inc .... E 586 726-4300
  Troy *(G-16381)*
General Broach Company .... E 517 458-7555
  Morenci *(G-11109)*

BROADCASTING & COMMS EQPT: Antennas, Transmitting/Comms
Amphenol T&M Antennas Inc .... G 847 478-5600
  Brighton *(G-1885)*
Antenna Technologies Inc .... G 586 697-5626
  Shelby Township *(G-14547)*
Harada Industry America Inc .... D 248 374-2587
  Novi *(G-11894)*
R A Miller Industries Inc .... C 888 845-9450
  Grand Haven *(G-6067)*
Stanecki Inc .... D 734 432-9900
  West Bloomfield *(G-17498)*

BROADCASTING & COMMS EQPT: Trnsmttng TV Antennas/Grndng Eqpt
Livbig LLC .... G 888 519-8290
  Portage *(G-13010)*

BROADCASTING & COMMUNICATIONS EQPT: Studio Eqpt, Radio & TV
Community Access Center .... F 269 343-2211
  Kalamazoo *(G-8710)*
Livespace LLC .... F 616 929-0491
  Grand Rapids *(G-6629)*

BROKERS & DEALERS: Securities
Batts Group Ltd .... G 616 956-3053
  Grand Rapids *(G-6206)*

BROKERS' SVCS
Cardinal Group Industries Corp .... E 517 437-6000
  Hillsdale *(G-7521)*
Novation Analytics LLC .... G 313 910-3280
  Auburn Hills *(G-963)*
Rowe & Associates .... G 231 932-9716
  Traverse City *(G-16097)*

BROKERS: Automotive
Faurecia North America Inc .... F 248 288-1000
  Auburn Hills *(G-863)*

BROKERS: Commodity Contracts
Darling Ingredients Inc .... E 269 751-0560
  Hamilton *(G-7231)*

BROKERS: Food
Global Restaurant Group Inc .... F 313 271-2777
  Dearborn *(G-3716)*
Mexican Food Specialties Inc .... G 734 779-2370
  Southfield *(G-14980)*

BROKERS: Printing
Johnnie On Spot Inc .... G 248 673-2233
  Waterford *(G-17352)*
Lloyd Waters & Associates .... G 734 525-2777
  Livonia *(G-9817)*

BRONZE FOUNDRY, NEC
White Cloud Mfg Co .... G 231 689-6087
  White Cloud *(G-17627)*

BROOMS
Sweepster Attachments LLC .... A 734 996-9116
  Dexter *(G-4512)*

BROOMS & BRUSHES
Duff Brush LLC .... G 906 863-3319
  Menominee *(G-10730)*
Even Weight Brush LLC .... G 906 863-3319
  Menominee *(G-10732)*
Halonen Mfg Group Inc .... G 906 483-4077
  Atlantic Mine *(G-736)*
R J Manufacturing Incorporated .... G 906 779-9151
  Crystal Falls *(G-3613)*
Thierica Equipment Corporation .... E 616 453-6570
  Grand Rapids *(G-6928)*

BROOMS & BRUSHES: Household Or Indl
Brollytime Inc .... F 312 854-7606
  Royal Oak *(G-13911)*
Custom Built Brush Company .... F 269 463-3171
  Watervliet *(G-17390)*
Detroit Qulty Brush Mfg Co Inc .... D 734 525-5660
  Livonia *(G-9708)*
Laco Inc .... E 231 929-3300
  Traverse City *(G-16020)*
Michigan Brush Mfg Co .... E 313 834-1070
  Detroit *(G-4238)*
Rbt Mfg LLC .... G 800 691-8204
  Plymouth *(G-12732)*

BROOMS & BRUSHES: Paintbrushes
Mack Andrew & Son Brush Co .... G 517 849-9272
  Jonesville *(G-8660)*

BROOMS & BRUSHES: Street Sweeping, Hand Or Machine
City of Taylor .... E 734 374-1372
  Taylor *(G-15700)*
Eco Brushes and Fibers .... G 231 683-9202
  Muskegon *(G-11315)*
Shais Ldscpg Snow Plowing LLC .... G 248 234-3663
  Walled Lake *(G-16903)*
Superior Equipment LLC .... G 269 388-2871
  Kalamazoo *(G-8903)*

BUCKLES & PARTS
Michigan ATF Holdings LLC .... D 734 941-2220
  Romulus *(G-13708)*
Rhino Strapping Products Inc .... F 734 442-4040
  Taylor *(G-15763)*

BUFFING FOR THE TRADE
A-W Custom Chrome Inc .... G 586 775-2040
  Eastpointe *(G-4697)*
Apollo Plating Inc .... C 586 777-0070
  Roseville *(G-13773)*
B & K Buffing Inc .... G 734 941-2144
  Romulus *(G-13654)*
Martin and Hattie Rasche Inc .... D 616 245-1223
  Grand Rapids *(G-6646)*
Patmai Company Inc .... E 586 294-0370
  Fraser *(G-5705)*
Ryan Polishing Corporation .... F 248 548-6832
  Oak Park *(G-12096)*

BUILDING & OFFICE CLEANING SVCS
Services To Enhance Potential .... G 313 278-3040
  Dearborn *(G-3757)*
Svrc Industries Inc .... E 989 280-3038
  Saginaw *(G-14159)*

BUILDING & STRUCTURAL WOOD MEMBERS
Bay Wood Homes Inc .... E 989 245-4156
  Fenton *(G-5187)*
Better-Bilt Cabinet Co .... G 586 469-0080
  Mount Clemens *(G-11125)*
Calderwood WD Pdts & Svcs LLC .... G 906 852-3232
  Trout Creek *(G-16162)*

PRODUCT SECTION

Laketon Truss Inc .... G 231 798-3467
  Norton Shores *(G-11770)*
Midwest Panel Systems Inc .... E 517 486-4844
  Blissfield *(G-1720)*
North American Forest Products .... G 269 663-8500
  Edwardsburg *(G-4770)*
Rapid River Rustic Inc .... E 906 474-6404
  Rapid River *(G-13114)*
Riverbend Timber Framing Inc .... D 517 486-3629
  Blissfield *(G-1726)*
Truss Development .... G 248 624-8100
  Bloomfield Hills *(G-1808)*

BUILDING CLEANING & MAINTENANCE SVCS
Overstreet Property MGT Co .... G 269 252-1560
  Benton Harbor *(G-1537)*
Twin Ash Frms Organic Proc LLC .... G 810 404-1943
  Snover *(G-14744)*

BUILDING COMPONENTS: Structural Steel
Afco Manufacturing Corp .... F 248 634-4415
  Holly *(G-7869)*
Boomer Company .... E 313 832-5050
  Detroit *(G-3910)*
Bristol Steel & Conveyor Corp .... E 810 658-9510
  Davison *(G-3641)*
Busch Industries Inc .... G 616 957-3737
  Grand Rapids *(G-6246)*
Howard Structural Steel Inc .... E 989 752-3000
  Saginaw *(G-14062)*
J & S Livonia Inc .... G 734 793-9000
  Livonia *(G-9788)*
Lna Solutions Inc .... F 734 677-2305
  Ann Arbor *(G-532)*
Mechanical Fabricators Inc .... F 810 765-8853
  Marine City *(G-10477)*
Midco 2 Inc .... G 517 467-2222
  Onsted *(G-12154)*
Pk Fabricating Inc .... E 248 398-4500
  Ferndale *(G-5310)*
R Betker & Associates .... G 269 927-3233
  Benton Harbor *(G-1541)*
Rohmann Iron Works Inc .... E 810 233-5611
  Flint *(G-5495)*
Signa Group Inc .... B 231 845-5101
  Ludington *(G-10078)*
Spirit Steel Co Inc .... E 517 750-4885
  Jackson *(G-8576)*
Steel Mill Components Inc .... E 313 386-0893
  Allen Park *(G-210)*
Tbl Fabrications Inc .... E 586 294-2087
  Roseville *(G-13877)*
Van Dellen Steel Inc .... E 616 698-9950
  Caledonia *(G-2321)*
Vci Inc .... E 269 659-3676
  Sturgis *(G-15640)*
Vci Inc .... D 269 659-3676
  Sturgis *(G-15639)*
Very Best Steel LLC .... G 734 697-8609
  Belleville *(G-1451)*

BUILDING ITEM REPAIR SVCS, MISCELLANEOUS
Colombo Sales & Engrg Inc .... F 248 547-2820
  Davisburg *(G-3630)*
Johns Glass .... G 269 468-4227
  Coloma *(G-3357)*

BUILDING MAINTENANCE SVCS, EXC REPAIRS
Continental Bldg Svs of Cinci .... F 313 336-8543
  Grosse Pointe Woods *(G-7202)*

BUILDING PRDTS & MATERIALS DEALERS
Bozzer Brothers Inc .... G 989 732-9684
  Gaylord *(G-5851)*
Capital Steel & Builders Sup .... F 517 694-0451
  Holt *(G-7905)*
Daniel D Slater .... G 989 833-7135
  Riverdale *(G-13284)*
Deweys Lumberville Inc .... G 313 885-0960
  Grosse Pointe *(G-7178)*
Erickson Lumber & True Value .... G 906 524-6295
  Lanse *(G-9191)*

PRODUCT SECTION

BUSINESS ACTIVITIES: Non-Commercial Site

Fendt Builders Supply Inc ....F 734 663-4277
  Ann Arbor *(G-461)*
Fenton Concrete Inc ....G 810 629-0783
  Fenton *(G-5208)*
Jensen Bridge & Supply Company ......E 810 648-3000
  Sandusky *(G-14437)*
Land Star Inc ....G 313 834-2366
  Detroit *(G-4193)*
M 37 Concrete Products Inc ....G 231 689-1785
  White Cloud *(G-17626)*
Masons Lumber & Hardware Inc ....G 989 685-3999
  Rose City *(G-13763)*
Mc Guire Mill & Lumber ....G 989 735-3851
  Glennie *(G-5945)*
Motto Cedar Products Inc ....G 906 753-4892
  Daggett *(G-3622)*
Mound Steel & Supply Inc ....F 248 852-6630
  Troy *(G-16513)*
R B Christian Inc ....G 269 963-9327
  Battle Creek *(G-1239)*
Storm Seal Co Inc ....G 248 689-1900
  Troy *(G-16623)*
United Mill & Cabinet Company ....F 734 482-1981
  Willis *(G-17745)*
Yale Steel Inc ....G 810 387-2567
  Brockway *(G-2021)*

BUILDING PRDTS: Concrete

Bonsal American Inc ....F 734 753-4413
  New Boston *(G-11497)*
Everlast Concrete Tech LLC ....G 248 894-1900
  Farmington Hills *(G-4994)*

BUILDING SCALES MODELS

Sika Auto Eaton Rapids Inc ....F 248 588-2270
  Madison Heights *(G-10352)*

BUILDINGS & COMPONENTS: Prefabricated Metal

Classic Car Port & Canopies ....F 586 759-5490
  Warren *(G-16982)*
Compact Engineering Corp ....F 231 788-5470
  Muskegon *(G-11298)*
McElroy Metal Mill Inc ....E 269 781-8313
  Marshall *(G-10582)*
Morton Buildings Inc ....F 616 696-4747
  Three Rivers *(G-15871)*
Nathan Shetler ....F 269 521-4554
  Bloomingdale *(G-1812)*
Pioneer Pole Buildings N Inc ....E 989 386-2570
  Clare *(G-2884)*
RB Construction Company ....E 586 264-9478
  Mount Clemens *(G-11147)*
Serenus Johnson Portables LLC ....F 989 839-2324
  Midland *(G-10915)*
Thoreson-Mc Cosh Inc ....E 248 362-0960
  Troy *(G-16638)*

BUILDINGS: Mobile, For Commercial Use

CCI Arnheim Inc ....G 906 353-6330
  Baraga *(G-1099)*
Flex Building Systems LLC ....G 586 803-6000
  Sterling Heights *(G-15342)*

BUILDINGS: Portable

Brasco International Inc ....D 313 393-0393
  Madison Heights *(G-10206)*
Icon Shelters Inc ....E 616 396-0919
  Holland *(G-7686)*
Little Buildings Inc ....G 586 752-7100
  Romeo *(G-13632)*
Mark Adler Homes ....G 586 850-0630
  Birmingham *(G-1691)*
Mobile Mini Inc ....F 586 759-4916
  Warren *(G-17159)*
Wildcat Buildings Inc ....F 231 824-6406
  Manton *(G-10459)*

BUILDINGS: Prefabricated, Metal

Duo-Gard Industries Inc ....D 734 207-9700
  Canton *(G-2367)*
Temo Inc ....C 800 344-8366
  Clinton Township *(G-3244)*

BUILDINGS: Prefabricated, Plastic

Mollewood Export Inc ....E 248 624-1885
  Wixom *(G-17859)*

BUILDINGS: Prefabricated, Wood

/// 702 Cedar River Lbr Inc ....E 906 497-5365
  Powers *(G-13076)*
4d Building Inc ....F 248 799-7384
  Milford *(G-10952)*
Backyard Products LLC ....G 734 242-6900
  Monroe *(G-11015)*
Little Buildings Inc ....G 586 752-7100
  Romeo *(G-13632)*
Mallory Pole Buildings Inc ....F 269 668-2627
  Mattawan *(G-10665)*
Pioneer Pole Buildings N Inc ....E 989 386-2570
  Clare *(G-2884)*
Premier Panel Company ....E 734 427-1700
  Livonia *(G-9897)*
Source Capital Backyard LLC ....G 734 242-6900
  Monroe *(G-11066)*
Woodtech Builders Inc ....F 906 932-8055
  Ironwood *(G-8341)*

BUILDINGS: Prefabricated, Wood

Bay Wood Homes Inc ....E 989 245-4156
  Fenton *(G-5187)*
Manufactured Homes Inc ....E 269 781-2887
  Marshall *(G-10574)*
Meyer Wood Products ....G 269 657-3450
  Paw Paw *(G-12409)*
Michigan Dutch Barns Inc ....F 616 693-2754
  Lake Odessa *(G-9118)*
Pageant Homes Inc ....G 517 694-0431
  Holt *(G-7921)*

BULLETPROOF VESTS

Central Lake Armor Express Inc ....C 231 544-6090
  Central Lake *(G-2588)*

BUMPERS: Motor Vehicle

Flex-N-Gate Corporation ....B 616 222-3296
  Grand Rapids *(G-6411)*
Flex-N-Gate Michigan LLC ....E 586 759-8900
  Warren *(G-17039)*
Micro Rim Corporation ....F 313 865-1090
  Detroit *(G-4246)*
Norplas Industries Inc ....D 517 999-1400
  Lansing *(G-9314)*

BURIAL VAULTS, FIBERGLASS

Eternal Image Inc ....G 248 932-3333
  Farmington Hills *(G-4990)*

BURIAL VAULTS: Concrete Or Precast Terrazzo

Bostwick Enterprises Inc ....F 231 946-8613
  Traverse City *(G-15917)*
Brutsche Concrete Products Co ....E 269 963-1554
  Battle Creek *(G-1159)*
Burrell Tri-County Vaults Inc ....F 734 483-2024
  Ypsilanti *(G-18058)*
Central Michigan Crematory ....E 269 963-1554
  Battle Creek *(G-1165)*
Christy Vault Company Inc ....G 415 994-1378
  Grand Rapids *(G-6276)*
Cremation Service of Michigan ....G 586 465-1700
  Clinton Township *(G-3093)*
Detroit Wilbert Cremation Serv ....G 248 853-0559
  Rochester Hills *(G-13408)*
Fenton Memorials & Vaults Inc ....F 810 629-2858
  Fenton *(G-5210)*
Grand Rpids Wilbert Burial Vlt ....E 616 453-9429
  Grand Rapids *(G-6469)*
Jarvis Concrete Products Inc ....G 269 463-3000
  Watervliet *(G-17393)*
Milan Burial Vault Inc ....F 734 439-1538
  Milan *(G-10946)*
Paschal Burial Vault Svc LLC ....G 517 448-8868
  Hudson *(G-8138)*
Peninsula Products Inc ....G 906 296-9801
  Lake Linden *(G-9109)*
Smith Concrete Products ....G 989 875-4687
  North Star *(G-11667)*
Superior Vault Co ....G 989 643-4200
  Merrill *(G-10762)*

Surface Mausoleum Company Inc ......G 989 864-3460
  Minden City *(G-11001)*
Wilbert Burial Vault Company ....G 231 773-6631
  Muskegon *(G-11449)*
Wilbert Burial Vault Company ....G 231 773-6631
  Muskegon *(G-11450)*
Wilbert Burial Vault Works ....G 906 786-0261
  Kingsford *(G-9068)*
Wilbert Saginaw Vault Corp ....G 989 753-3065
  Saginaw *(G-14183)*
Willbee Concrete Products Co ....F 517 782-8246
  Jackson *(G-8607)*

BURIAL VAULTS: Stone

Pearson Precast Concrete Pdts ....G 517 486-4060
  Blissfield *(G-1722)*

BURNERS: Gas, Indl

Burners Inc ....G 248 676-9141
  Milford *(G-10957)*

BURNING: Metal

Induction Services Inc ....E 586 754-1640
  Warren *(G-17089)*

BUSHINGS & BEARINGS: Brass, Exc Machined

Parker-Hannifin Corporation ....B 269 694-9411
  Otsego *(G-12249)*
Threaded Products Co ....E 586 727-3435
  Richmond *(G-13272)*

BUSHINGS: Cast Steel, Exc Investment

Axly Production Machining Inc ....B 989 269-2444
  Bad Axe *(G-1057)*

BUSHINGS: Rubber

Bushings Inc ....F 248 650-0603
  Rochester Hills *(G-13381)*

BUSINESS ACTIVITIES: Non-Commercial Site

3-D Designs LLC ....G 313 658-1249
  Detroit *(G-3823)*
Advanced Altrntive Sltions LLC ....G 616 607-6956
  Wyoming *(G-17984)*
AMF-Nano Corporation ....G 734 726-0148
  Ann Arbor *(G-353)*
Amour Your Body LLC ....G 586 846-3100
  Clinton Township *(G-3049)*
Amrican Petro Inc ....G 313 520-8404
  Detroit *(G-3868)*
Barlows Gourmet Products Inc ....G 248 245-0393
  Holly *(G-7870)*
Bcs Creative LLC ....G 248 917-1660
  Davisburg *(G-3627)*
Boat Guard Inc ....G 989 424-1490
  Gladwin *(G-5923)*
Bramin Enterprises ....G 313 960-1528
  Detroit *(G-3913)*
Business Connect L3c ....G 616 443-8070
  Grandville *(G-7025)*
BV Technology LLC ....G 616 558-1746
  Alto *(G-323)*
Cambridge Foods LLC ....G 248 348-3800
  Northville *(G-11682)*
Causey Consulting LLC ....G 248 671-4979
  West Bloomfield *(G-17469)*
Center Mass Inc ....G 734 207-8934
  Canton *(G-2359)*
Christopher S Campion ....G 517 414-6796
  Jackson *(G-8409)*
Circle S Products Inc ....G 734 675-2960
  Woodhaven *(G-17938)*
Collier Enterprise III ....G 269 503-3402
  Sturgis *(G-15600)*
Construction Retail Svcs Inc ....G 586 469-2289
  Clinton Township *(G-3088)*
Cruux LLC ....G 248 515-8411
  Troy *(G-16288)*
Curvy LLC ....G 917 960-3774
  Northville *(G-11685)*
D&E Incorporated ....G 313 673-3284
  Southfield *(G-14876)*

Employee Codes: A=Over 500 employees, B=251-500
C=101-250, D=51-100, E=20-50, F=10-19, G=3-9

2020 Harris Michigan Industrial Directory

Delta 6 LLC ....G.... 248 778-6414
Livonia *(G-9703)*
Dse Industries LLC ....G.... 313 530-6668
Macomb *(G-10118)*
Eb Enterprises LLC ....G.... 231 768-5072
Leroy *(G-9532)*
Eco Brushes and Fibers ....G.... 231 683-9202
Muskegon *(G-11315)*
Ecovia Renewables Inc ....G.... 248 953-0594
Ann Arbor *(G-433)*
Edi Experts LLC ....G.... 734 844-7016
Canton *(G-2370)*
Elsie Publishing Institute ....F.... 517 371-5257
Lansing *(G-9365)*
Embrace Premium Vodka LLC ....G.... 616 617-5602
Ypsilanti *(G-18070)*
Ethnicemedia LLC ....G.... 248 762-8904
Troy *(G-16352)*
Ezbake Technologies LLC ....G.... 817 430-1621
Fenton *(G-5206)*
Flashplays Live LLC ....G.... 978 888-3935
Ann Arbor *(G-462)*
Forever Flooring and More LLC ....G.... 517 745-6194
Lowell *(G-10029)*
Garbage Man LLC ....G.... 810 225-3001
Brighton *(G-1927)*
Geartec Inc ....G.... 810 987-4700
Port Huron *(G-12922)*
Grace Contracting Services LLC ....G.... 906 630-4680
Mc Millan *(G-10685)*
Grand Rapids Graphix ....G.... 616 359-2383
Wyoming *(G-18005)*
High Touch Healthcare LLC ....G.... 248 513-2425
Novi *(G-11901)*
Hug-A-Plug Inc ....G.... 810 626-1224
Brighton *(G-1942)*
Innovative Packg Solutions LLC ....G.... 517 213-3169
Holt *(G-7914)*
Integrated Program MGT LLC ....G.... 248 241-9257
Clarkston *(G-2932)*
Integrity Sltons Feld Svcs Inc ....F.... 303 263-9522
East Lansing *(G-4664)*
Intra Business LLC ....G.... 269 262-0863
Niles *(G-11621)*
Inventev LLC ....G.... 248 535-0477
Detroit *(G-4148)*
IXL Graphics Inc ....G.... 313 350-2800
South Lyon *(G-14796)*
Jns Sawmill ....G.... 989 352-5430
Coral *(G-3574)*
Jr Larry Dudley ....G.... 313 721-3600
Detroit *(G-4166)*
Jrt Enterprises LLC ....G.... 877 318-7661
Holland *(G-7703)*
K&P Discount Pallets Inc ....G.... 616 835-1661
Belding *(G-1422)*
Ka-Wood Gear & Machine Co ....E.... 248 585-8870
Madison Heights *(G-10287)*
Kemari LLC ....G.... 248 348-7407
South Lyon *(G-14797)*
Kingsford Broach & Tool Inc ....E.... 906 774-4917
Kingsford *(G-9060)*
Kokaly Sports ....G.... 989 671-7412
Bay City *(G-1325)*
Kringer Industrial Corporation ....F.... 519 818-3509
Warren *(G-17122)*
Krumbsnatcher Enterprises LLC ....F.... 313 408-6802
Detroit *(G-4184)*
Live Track Productions Inc ....G.... 313 704-2224
Detroit *(G-4207)*
Luhu LLC ....G.... 320 469-3162
East Lansing *(G-4668)*
M-57 Aggregate Company ....G.... 810 639-7516
Montrose *(G-11103)*
M2 Scientifics LLC ....G.... 616 379-9080
Holland *(G-7728)*
Mark Beem ....G.... 231 510-8122
Lake City *(G-9092)*
Media Swing LLC ....G.... 313 885-2525
Grosse Pointe Farms *(G-7186)*
Mega Mania Diversions LLC ....G.... 888 322-9076
Commerce Township *(G-3430)*
Meridian Contg & Excvtg LLC ....G.... 734 476-5933
Commerce Township *(G-3431)*
Michigan Movie Magazine LLC ....G.... 734 726-5299
Dexter *(G-4499)*
Midwest Defense Corp ....G.... 231 590-6857
Traverse City *(G-16036)*
Mitovation Inc ....G.... 734 395-1635
Saline *(G-14402)*
National Ambucs Inc ....E.... 231 798-4244
Norton Shores *(G-11778)*
Off Grid LLC ....G.... 734 780-4434
Ann Arbor *(G-580)*
Onyx Manufacturing Inc ....G.... 248 687-8611
Rochester Hills *(G-13487)*
P & F Enterprises LLC ....G.... 616 340-1265
Wyoming *(G-18024)*
Photodon LLC ....G.... 847 377-1185
Traverse City *(G-16068)*
Pioneer Pole Buildings N Inc ....E.... 989 386-2570
Clare *(G-2884)*
Printing Perspectives LLC ....G.... 810 410-8186
Flint *(G-5485)*
Pull Our Own Weight ....G.... 313 686-4685
Detroit *(G-4316)*
Pur E Clat ....G.... 313 208-5763
Farmington Hills *(G-5107)*
Red Iron Strl Consulting Corp ....G.... 810 364-5100
Harbor Springs *(G-7292)*
Scentmatchers LLC ....G.... 800 859-9878
Gaylord *(G-5892)*
Sheptime Music ....F.... 586 806-9058
Warren *(G-17238)*
Simmys Edm LLC ....G.... 989 802-2516
Beaverton *(G-1393)*
Sizzl LLC ....F.... 201 454-1938
Ann Arbor *(G-634)*
Smart Diet Scale LLC ....G.... 586 383-6734
Bruce Twp *(G-2102)*
Striker Tools LLC ....G.... 248 990-7767
Manitou Beach *(G-10449)*
Talkin Tackle LLC ....G.... 517 474-6241
Jackson *(G-8583)*
Thangbom LLC ....G.... 517 862-0144
Flint *(G-5510)*
Tmb Trends Inc ....G.... 866 445-2344
Troy *(G-16646)*
True Anlytics Mfg Slutions LLC ....G.... 517 902-9700
Ida *(G-8194)*
Two Feathers Enterprise LLC ....G.... 231 924-3612
Fremont *(G-5785)*
Up Officeexpress LLC ....G.... 906 281-0089
Calumet *(G-2334)*
US Green Energy Solutions LLC ....G.... 810 955-2992
Livonia *(G-9983)*
Valmec Inc ....G.... 810 629-8750
Fenton *(G-5248)*
Vanova Technologies LLC ....G.... 734 476-7204
Superior Township *(G-15648)*
Ventuor LLC ....G.... 248 790-8700
Flint *(G-5520)*
Virotech Biomaterials Inc ....G.... 313 421-1648
Warren *(G-17284)*
Wayne Novick ....G.... 269 685-9818
Plainwell *(G-12551)*
Whiteside Consulting Group LLC ....G.... 313 288-6598
Detroit *(G-4440)*
Windmill Hill Farm LLC ....G.... 810 378-5972
Croswell *(G-3606)*
Winford Engineering LLC ....G.... 989 671-9721
Auburn *(G-758)*
Wowza ME LLC ....G.... 734 636-4460
Monroe *(G-11085)*

BUSINESS FORMS WHOLESALERS

Alpha Data Business Forms Inc ....G.... 248 540-5930
Birmingham *(G-1674)*
Complete Data Products Inc ....G.... 248 651-8602
Troy *(G-16275)*
Earle Press Inc ....E.... 231 773-2111
Muskegon *(G-11312)*
Kendall & Company Inc ....G.... 810 733-7330
Flint *(G-5454)*
Lepages 2000 Inc ....G.... 416 357-0041
Romulus *(G-13700)*
Local Printers Inc ....G.... 586 795-1290
Sterling Heights *(G-15402)*
Printcomm Inc ....D.... 810 239-5763
Flint *(G-5484)*
Rose Business Forms Company ....E.... 734 424-5200
Southfield *(G-15017)*
Shayleslie Corporation ....G.... 517 694-4115
Holt *(G-7929)*
Spinnaker Forms Systems Corp ....G.... 616 956-7677
Grand Rapids *(G-6886)*
Turner Business Forms Inc ....E.... 989 752-5540
Saginaw *(G-14171)*
Turner Business Forms Inc ....G.... 810 244-6980
Flint *(G-5515)*
Web Printing & Mktg Concepts ....G.... 269 983-4646
Saint Joseph *(G-14351)*
Whitlock Business Systems Inc ....E.... 248 548-1040
Madison Heights *(G-10381)*

BUSINESS FORMS: Printed, Continuous

Ultra Forms Plus Inc ....F.... 269 337-6000
Kalamazoo *(G-8916)*

BUSINESS FORMS: Printed, Manifold

Alpha Data Business Forms Inc ....G.... 248 540-5930
Birmingham *(G-1674)*
BCI Group Inc ....E.... 248 925-2000
Troy *(G-16234)*
Business Press Inc ....G.... 248 652-8855
Rochester *(G-13316)*
Earle Press Inc ....E.... 231 773-2111
Muskegon *(G-11312)*
Forms Trac Enterprises Inc ....G.... 248 524-0006
Sterling Heights *(G-15345)*
Frye Printing Company Inc ....F.... 517 456-4124
Clinton *(G-3021)*
Grand Traverse Continuous Inc ....E.... 231 941-5400
Traverse City *(G-15983)*
Hi-Speed Business Forms Inc ....G.... 269 927-3191
Benton Harbor *(G-1509)*
Imperial Clinical RES Svcs Inc ....C.... 616 784-0100
Grand Rapids *(G-6528)*
Micrgraphics Printing Inc ....E.... 231 739-6575
Norton Shores *(G-11773)*
Microforms Inc ....D.... 586 939-7900
Beverly Hills *(G-1620)*
Peg-Master Business Forms Inc ....G.... 586 566-8694
Shelby Township *(G-14662)*
Riegle Press Inc ....E.... 810 653-9631
Davison *(G-3661)*
Timbertech Inc ....E.... 231 348-2750
Harbor Springs *(G-7295)*
Total Business Systems Inc ....F.... 248 307-1076
Madison Heights *(G-10368)*
Whitlock Business Systems Inc ....E.... 248 548-1040
Madison Heights *(G-10381)*

BUSINESS MACHINE REPAIR, ELECTRIC

Cornelius Systems Inc ....E.... 248 545-5558
Berkley *(G-1582)*

BUTTER WHOLESALERS

Butterball Farms Inc ....C.... 616 243-0105
Grand Rapids *(G-6247)*

BUTYL RUBBER: Isobutylene-Isoprene Rubbers

A-Line Products Corporation ....F.... 313 571-8300
Detroit *(G-3830)*

CABINETS & CASES: Show, Display & Storage, Exc Wood

Childs Carpentry ....G.... 734 425-8783
Garden City *(G-5821)*
Impert Industries Inc ....G.... 269 694-2727
Otsego *(G-12241)*
Structural Concepts Corp ....B.... 231 798-8888
Norton Shores *(G-11798)*

CABINETS: Bathroom Vanities, Wood

Cabinet One Inc ....G.... 248 625-9440
Clarkston *(G-2910)*
Crystal Lake Apartments Family ....E.... 586 731-3500
Shelby Township *(G-14571)*
E & W Cabinet & Counter ....G.... 734 895-7497
Romulus *(G-13668)*
Gast Cabinet Co ....E.... 269 422-1587
Baroda *(G-1125)*
Janice Morse Inc ....E.... 248 624-7300
West Bloomfield *(G-17482)*
Jeff R Cabinets LLC ....G.... 989 233-0976
Gagetown *(G-5802)*
Masco Cabinetry LLC ....C.... 517 263-0771
Adrian *(G-78)*
Masco Corporation ....A.... 313 274-7400
Livonia *(G-9826)*
Owens Building Co Inc ....E.... 989 835-1293
Midland *(G-10901)*

PRODUCT SECTION

CABINETS: Radio & Television, Metal

Perspectives Custom Cabinetry .... E 248 288-4100
  Troy *(G-16544)*
Pioneer Cabinetry Inc .... D 810 658-2075
  Davison *(G-3659)*

CABINETS: Entertainment

European Cabinet Mfg Co .... E 586 445-8909
  Roseville *(G-13802)*
George Washburn .... G 269 694-2930
  Otsego *(G-12240)*
Pazzel Inc .... G 616 291-0257
  Grand Rapids *(G-6745)*
Ross Cabinets II Inc .... E 586 752-7750
  Shelby Township *(G-14682)*
Sterling Millwork Inc .... D 248 427-1400
  Farmington Hills *(G-5131)*

CABINETS: Entertainment Units, Household, Wood

A & A Woodwork Studio LLC .... G 248 691-8380
  Oak Park *(G-12047)*
Millennm-The Inside Sltion Inc ...... E 248 645-9005
  Farmington Hills *(G-5069)*

CABINETS: Factory

B & W Woodwork Inc .... G 616 772-4577
  Holland *(G-7564)*
M and G Laminated Products .... G 517 784-4974
  Jackson *(G-8502)*
Pinnacle Cabinet Company Inc ..... E 989 772-3866
  Mount Pleasant *(G-11217)*
Royal Oak Millwork Company LLC .. G 248 547-1210
  Royal Oak *(G-13968)*

CABINETS: Filing, Wood

H L F Furniture Incorporated .... E 734 697-3000
  Van Buren Twp *(G-16762)*
Tims Cabinet Inc .... G 989 846-9831
  Pinconning *(G-12513)*

CABINETS: Kitchen, Wood

A K Services Inc .... G 313 972-1010
  Detroit *(G-3827)*
AAM Wholesale Carpet Corp .... G 313 898-5101
  Detroit *(G-3832)*
Albers Cabinet Company .... G 586 727-9090
  Lenox *(G-9520)*
Avon Cabinets Atkins .... G 248 237-1103
  Rochester Hills *(G-13373)*
Bayshore Kitchen and Bath Inc ...... G 586 725-8800
  New Baltimore *(G-11481)*
Belash Inc .... G 248 379-4444
  Wixom *(G-17772)*
Berrien Custom Cabinet Inc .... G 269 473-3404
  Berrien Springs *(G-1593)*
Better-Bilt Cabinet Co .... G 586 469-0080
  Mount Clemens *(G-11125)*
Biotec Incorporated .... D 616 772-2133
  Zeeland *(G-18120)*
C&C Doors Inc .... G 586 232-4538
  Macomb *(G-10113)*
Cabinets By Robert Inc .... F 231 947-3261
  Traverse City *(G-15927)*
Carson Wood Specialties Inc .... G 269 465-6091
  Stevensville *(G-15559)*
Case Systems Inc .... C 989 496-9510
  Midland *(G-10822)*
CCM Modernization Co .... G 586 231-0396
  Clinton Township *(G-3076)*
Charlotte Cabinets Inc .... G 517 543-1522
  Charlotte *(G-2639)*
Classic Cabinets Interiors LLC .... G 517 817-5650
  Jackson *(G-8410)*
Classic Cabinets Interiors LLC .... G 517 423-2600
  Tecumseh *(G-15784)*
Cole Wagner Cabinetry .... G 248 642-5330
  Birmingham *(G-1677)*
Cole Wagner Cabinetry .... F 248 852-2406
  Rochester Hills *(G-13390)*
D & M Cabinet Shop Inc .... G 989 479-9271
  Ruth *(G-13988)*
David Hirn Cabinets and Contg ...... G 906 428-1935
  Gladstone *(G-5911)*
Designtech Custom Interiors .... G 989 695-6306
  Freeland *(G-5754)*
Edwards Building & HM Sup Inc .... G 313 368-9120
  Detroit *(G-4029)*

Elan Designs Inc .... G 248 682-3000
  Pontiac *(G-12820)*
Elite Woodworking LLC .... E 586 204-5882
  Saint Clair Shores *(G-14245)*
Euro-Craft Interiors Inc .... F 586 254-9130
  Sterling Heights *(G-15334)*
European Cabinet Mfg Co .... E 586 445-8909
  Roseville *(G-13802)*
Expo Kitchen & Bath Ltd .... G 734 741-5888
  Ann Arbor *(G-451)*
Farmington Cabinet Company .... F 248 476-2666
  Livonia *(G-9735)*
Flagg Distribution LLC .... F 248 926-0510
  Wixom *(G-17811)*
Flairwood Industries Inc .... E 231 798-8324
  Norton Shores *(G-11756)*
Fort Grtiot Cbnets Counter LLC ...... F 810 364-1924
  Port Huron *(G-12919)*
G & G Wood & Supply Inc .... F 586 293-0450
  Roseville *(G-13805)*
George Washburn .... G 269 694-2930
  Otsego *(G-12240)*
Great Lakes Fine Cabinetry .... G 906 493-5780
  Sault Sainte Marie *(G-14465)*
Greenia Custom Woodworking Inc .. E 989 868-9790
  Reese *(G-13230)*
Greenville Cabinet Distri .... G 616 225-2424
  Greenville *(G-7133)*
Handorn Inc .... E 616 241-6181
  Grand Rapids *(G-6490)*
I S Two .... G 616 396-5634
  Holland *(G-7685)*
Impressive Cabinets Inc .... F 248 542-1185
  Oak Park *(G-12074)*
Interior Spc of Holland .... E 616 396-5634
  Holland *(G-7690)*
Jmc Custom Cabinetry .... G 989 345-0475
  West Branch *(G-17509)*
Kaliniak Design LLC .... G 616 675-3850
  Kent City *(G-8992)*
Kurtis Mfg & Distrg Corp .... E 734 522-7600
  Livonia *(G-9802)*
Lafata Cabinet Shop .... E 586 247-6536
  Shelby Township *(G-14620)*
Lakeshore Marble Company Inc .... E 269 429-8241
  Stevensville *(G-15574)*
Lloyds Cabinet Shop Inc .... F 989 879-3015
  Pinconning *(G-12509)*
M and G Laminated Products .... G 517 784-4974
  Jackson *(G-8502)*
Marbelite Corp .... E 248 348-1900
  Novi *(G-11934)*
Masco Cabinetry LLC .... D 517 263-0771
  Ann Arbor *(G-544)*
Masco Cabinetry LLC .... B 740 286-5033
  Ann Arbor *(G-545)*
Masco Cabinetry LLC .... B 734 205-4600
  Ann Arbor *(G-546)*
Masco Cabinetry LLC .... F 239 561-7266
  Ann Arbor *(G-547)*
Masco Cabinetry LLC .... G 407 857-4444
  Ann Arbor *(G-548)*
Masco Cabinetry LLC .... D 770 447-6363
  Ann Arbor *(G-549)*
Masco Services Inc .... G 313 274-7400
  Livonia *(G-9827)*
Merillat Industries LLC .... G 517 263-0269
  Adrian *(G-79)*
Merillat LP .... C 517 263-0771
  Adrian *(G-80)*
Michigan Counter Tops Company ... F 313 369-1511
  Warren *(G-17152)*
Mid Michigan Wood Specialites ..... F 989 855-3667
  Lyons *(G-10094)*
Mikes Cabinet Shop Inc .... G 734 722-1800
  Westland *(G-17580)*
Millennm-The Inside Sltion Inc ...... E 248 645-9005
  Farmington Hills *(G-5069)*
Millwork Inc .... F 586 791-2330
  Fraser *(G-5692)*
Millwork Design Group LLC .... G 248 472-2178
  Milford *(G-10972)*
Miltons Cabinet Shop Inc .... G 269 473-2743
  Berrien Springs *(G-1599)*
Murphys Custom Craftsmen Inc .... G 989 205-7305
  Coleman *(G-3349)*
New Line Inc .... G 586 228-4820
  Shelby Township *(G-14652)*
North State Sales .... G 989 681-2806
  Saint Louis *(G-14367)*

Nowak Cabinets Inc .... G 231 264-8603
  Williamsburg *(G-17718)*
Oak North Manufacturing Inc .... F 906 475-7992
  Negaunee *(G-11472)*
OBrien Harris Woodworks LLc .... E 616 248-0779
  Grand Rapids *(G-6726)*
Pazzel Inc .... G 616 291-0257
  Grand Rapids *(G-6745)*
Pinnacle Cabinet Company Inc ..... E 989 772-3866
  Mount Pleasant *(G-11217)*
Prime Wood Products Inc .... G 616 399-4700
  Holland *(G-7775)*
Progressive Cabinets Inc .... G 810 631-4611
  Otisville *(G-12234)*
Putnam Cabinetry .... G 248 442-0118
  Farmington Hills *(G-5108)*
Rohloff Builders Inc .... E 989 868-3191
  Reese *(G-13232)*
Rose Corporation .... E 734 426-0005
  Dexter *(G-4508)*
Ross Cabinets II Inc .... E 586 752-7750
  Shelby Township *(G-14682)*
Royal Cabinets .... G 313 541-1190
  Redford *(G-13188)*
Sawdust Bin Inc .... F 906 932-5518
  Ironwood *(G-8340)*
Shayn Allen Marquetry .... G 586 991-0445
  Shelby Township *(G-14691)*
Showcase Cabinetry Inc .... G 810 798-9966
  Almont *(G-266)*
Stanisci Design and Mfg Inc .... G 586 752-3368
  Oxford *(G-12373)*
Straight Line Design .... G 616 296-0920
  Spring Lake *(G-15180)*
Surface Expressions LLC .... G 231 843-8282
  Ludington *(G-10081)*
Tims Cabinet Inc .... G 989 846-9831
  Pinconning *(G-12513)*
Van Daeles Inc .... G 734 587-7165
  Monroe *(G-11082)*
Village Cabinet Shoppe Inc .... G 586 264-6464
  Sterling Heights *(G-15539)*
W S Townsend Company .... G 517 393-7300
  Lansing *(G-9433)*
W S Townsend Company .... C 269 781-5131
  Marshall *(G-10593)*
West Michigan Cabinet Supply ...... F 616 896-6990
  Hudsonville *(G-8186)*
Wickey Custom Cabinets .... G 517 858-1119
  Bronson *(G-2035)*
Woodways Industries LLC .... E 616 956-3070
  Grand Rapids *(G-7003)*
World Wide Cabinets Inc .... F 248 683-2680
  Sylvan Lake *(G-15674)*
Young Cabinetry Inc .... G 734 316-2896
  Saline *(G-14422)*

CABINETS: Office, Metal

Cerny Industries LLC .... E 231 929-2140
  Traverse City *(G-15935)*
Greenfield Cabinetry Inc .... F 586 759-3300
  Warren *(G-17066)*
Mica TEC Inc .... G 586 758-4404
  Warren *(G-17151)*

CABINETS: Office, Wood

Case Systems Inc .... C 989 496-9510
  Midland *(G-10822)*
Cygnus Inc .... E 231 347-5404
  Petoskey *(G-12447)*
Debbink and Sons Inc .... G 231 845-6421
  Ludington *(G-10055)*
Farnell Contracting Inc .... F 810 714-3421
  Linden *(G-9590)*
Jsj Furniture Corporation .... E 616 847-6534
  Grand Haven *(G-6043)*
Konwinski Kabnets Inc .... G 989 773-2906
  Mount Pleasant *(G-11201)*
Pazzel Inc .... G 616 291-0257
  Grand Rapids *(G-6745)*
Phillip Anderson .... G 269 687-7166
  Niles *(G-11639)*

CABINETS: Radio & Television, Metal

Rivmax Manufacturing Inc .... F 517 784-2556
  Jackson *(G-8563)*

CABINETS: Show, Display, Etc, Wood, Exc Refrigerated

CABINETS: Show, Display, Etc, Wood, Exc Refrigerated

Dallas Design Inc	G	810 238-4546
Flint *(G-5413)*		
Grand Valley Wood Products Inc	E	616 475-5890
Grand Rapids *(G-6471)*		
Korcast Products Incorporated	G	248 740-2340
Troy *(G-16448)*		
Korcast Products Incorporated	G	248 740-2340
Troy *(G-16449)*		
Kreations Inc	F	313 255-1230
Detroit *(G-4183)*		
Lafata Cabinet Shop	E	586 247-6536
Shelby Township *(G-14620)*		
Royal Cabinet Inc	F	517 787-2940
Jackson *(G-8565)*		
Zuckero & Sons Inc	E	586 772-3377
Roseville *(G-13893)*		

CABLE & OTHER PAY TELEVISION DISTRIBUTION

Cco Holdings LLC	G	517 583-4125
Tekonsha *(G-15817)*		
Cco Holdings LLC	G	616 244-2071
Belding *(G-1406)*		
Cco Holdings LLC	G	616 384-2060
Coopersville *(G-3551)*		
Cco Holdings LLC	G	517 639-1060
Quincy *(G-13091)*		
Cco Holdings LLC	G	734 244-8028
Monroe *(G-11024)*		
Cco Holdings LLC	G	734 868-5044
Ida *(G-8193)*		
Cco Holdings LLC	G	810 270-1002
North Branch *(G-11657)*		
Cco Holdings LLC	G	810 375-7020
Dryden *(G-4568)*		
Cco Holdings LLC	G	810 545-4020
Columbiaville *(G-3376)*		
Cco Holdings LLC	G	906 285-6497
Ironwood *(G-8325)*		
Cco Holdings LLC	G	906 239-3763
Iron Mountain *(G-8279)*		
Cco Holdings LLC	G	906 346-1000
Gwinn *(G-7218)*		
Cco Holdings LLC	G	231 720-0688
Muskegon *(G-11291)*		
Cco Holdings LLC	G	248 494-4550
Auburn Hills *(G-811)*		
Cco Holdings LLC	G	269 202-3286
Coloma *(G-3355)*		
Cco Holdings LLC	G	269 216-6680
Kalamazoo *(G-8704)*		
Cco Holdings LLC	G	269 432-0052
Colon *(G-3370)*		
Cco Holdings LLC	G	269 464-3454
White Pigeon *(G-17646)*		
Cco Holdings LLC	G	989 328-4187
Sidney *(G-14738)*		
Cco Holdings LLC	G	989 567-0151
Shepherd *(G-14726)*		
Cco Holdings LLC	G	989 863-4023
Reese *(G-13229)*		
Cco Holdings LLC	G	989 853-2008
Muir *(G-11237)*		
Community Access Center	F	269 343-2211
Kalamazoo *(G-8710)*		

CABLE & PAY TV SVCS: Satellite Master Antenna Sys/SMATV

Digital Success Network	E	517 244-0771
Mason *(G-10636)*		

CABLE WIRING SETS: Battery, Internal Combustion Engines

Keystone Cable Corporation	G	313 924-9720
Detroit *(G-4177)*		
Prestolite Wire LLC	E	248 355-4422
Southfield *(G-15004)*		
Vte Inc	E	231 539-8000
Pellston *(G-12426)*		

CABLE: Coaxial

Shikoku Cable North Amer Inc	G	248 488-8620
Novi *(G-11996)*		

CABLE: Fiber Optic

American Furukawa Inc	E	734 254-0344
Plymouth *(G-12570)*		
T R S Fieldbus Systems Inc	G	586 826-9696
Birmingham *(G-1703)*		

CABLE: Noninsulated

Commercial Group Inc	E	313 931-6100
Taylor *(G-15704)*		
Detroit Wire Rope Splcing Corp	F	248 585-1063
Madison Heights *(G-10230)*		
Hi-Lex America Incorporated	B	269 968-0781
Battle Creek *(G-1198)*		
Hi-Lex America Incorporated	D	248 844-0096
Rochester Hills *(G-13440)*		
Jaslin Assembly Inc	G	248 528-3024
Troy *(G-16432)*		
Orri Corp	F	248 618-1104
Waterford *(G-17364)*		

CABLE: Steel, Insulated Or Armored

Benteler Defense Corp	G	248 377-9999
Auburn Hills *(G-793)*		

CAFES

Bread of Life Bakery & Cafe	F	906 663-4005
Bessemer *(G-1603)*		
Electric Eye Cafe	G	734 369-6904
Ann Arbor *(G-439)*		
Vivian Enterprises LLC	E	248 792-9925
Southfield *(G-15063)*		

CAGES: Wire

Corners Limited	G	269 353-8311
Kalamazoo *(G-8718)*		
Unifab Corporation	E	269 382-2803
Portage *(G-13051)*		

CALCAREOUS TUFA: Crushed & Broken

Grand Rapids Gravel Company	F	616 538-9000
Grand Rapids *(G-6454)*		

CALCIUM META-PHOSPHATE

F C Simpson Lime Co	G	810 367-3510
Kimball *(G-9043)*		

CALIBRATING SVCS, NEC

Gage Numerical Inc	G	231 328-4426
Lake City *(G-9087)*		

CAMERA & PHOTOGRAPHIC SPLYS STORES

Livbig LLC	G	888 519-8290
Portage *(G-13010)*		

CAMERAS & RELATED EQPT: Photographic

Just Rite Bracket	G	248 477-0592
Farmington Hills *(G-5035)*		

CAMPERS: Truck Mounted

Monroes Custom Campers Inc	G	231 773-0005
Muskegon *(G-11385)*		
Northland	G	231 775-3101
Cadillac *(G-2268)*		
R V Wolverine	F	989 426-9241
Gladwin *(G-5934)*		
Van Kam Inc	F	231 744-2658
Muskegon *(G-11444)*		

CAMPERS: Truck, Slide-In

Forest River Inc	D	269 471-6321
Centreville *(G-2594)*		

CAMSHAFTS

Camshaft Acquisition Inc	E	517 787-2040
Jackson *(G-8400)*		
Camshaft Machine Company LLC	E	517 787-2040
Jackson *(G-8401)*		
Engine Power Components Inc	B	616 846-0110
Grand Haven *(G-6015)*		
Kautex Inc	B	231 739-2704
Muskegon *(G-11357)*		

CANDLE SHOPS

Holland House Candles Inc	F	800 238-8467
Holland *(G-7672)*		

CANDLES

Ambrosia Inc	G	734 529-7174
Dundee *(G-4575)*		
Bee Dazzled Candle Works	G	231 882-7765
Benzonia *(G-1573)*		
Candela Products Inc	G	248 541-2547
Warren *(G-16976)*		
Candle Factory Grand Traverse	F	231 946-2280
Traverse City *(G-15929)*		
Candle Wick	G	248 547-2987
Ferndale *(G-5266)*		
Coventry Creations Inc	G	248 547-2987
Ferndale *(G-5268)*		
Holland House Candles Inc	F	800 238-8467
Holland *(G-7672)*		
J F McCaughin Co	E	231 759-7304
Norton Shores *(G-11765)*		
Kalamazoo Candle Company	F	269 532-9816
Kalamazoo *(G-8785)*		
New Boston Candle Company	F	734 782-5809
New Boston *(G-11504)*		
Preeminence Inc	G	313 737-7920
Redford *(G-13185)*		
Victora Usa Inc	G	810 798-0253
Almont *(G-269)*		
Willies Wicks	G	810 730-4176
Flushing *(G-5546)*		

CANDY & CONFECTIONS: Candy Bars, Including Chocolate Covered

Chocolate Vault Llc	G	517 688-3388
Horton *(G-7963)*		
Comstock Creamery LLC	G	269 929-7693
Kalamazoo *(G-8712)*		
Rps Bar		810 235-8876
Flint *(G-5496)*		
Truans Candies Inc	F	313 281-0185
Plymouth *(G-12782)*		

CANDY & CONFECTIONS: Chocolate Candy, Exc Solid Chocolate

Elsa Enterprises Inc	G	248 816-1454
Troy *(G-16340)*		
Gayles Chocolates Limited	E	248 398-0001
Royal Oak *(G-13929)*		

CANDY & CONFECTIONS: Cough Drops, Exc Pharmaceutical Preps

Berkley Pharmacy LLC	F	586 573-8300
Warren *(G-16955)*		

CANDY & CONFECTIONS: Fruit & Fruit Peel

Mr Peel Inc	G	734 266-2022
Livonia *(G-9853)*		

CANDY & CONFECTIONS: Fudge

Detroit Fudge Company Inc	G	734 369-8573
Ann Arbor *(G-417)*		
Doug Murdicks Fudge Inc	G	231 938-2330
Traverse City *(G-15957)*		
Original Murdicks Fudge Co	E	906 847-3530
Mackinac Island *(G-10097)*		

CANDY & CONFECTIONS: Nuts, Candy Covered

R & J Almonds Inc	F	810 767-6887
Flint *(G-5489)*		

CANDY, NUT & CONFECTIONERY STORE: Popcorn, Incl Caramel Corn

American Gourmet Snacks LLC	G	989 892-4856
Essexville *(G-4867)*		

CANDY, NUT & CONFECTIONERY STORES: Candy

Alinosi French Ice Cream Co	G	313 527-3195
Detroit *(G-3855)*		

PRODUCT SECTION

Chocolate Vault Llc..................................G......517 688-3388
  Horton (G-7963)
Donckers Candies & Gifts.........................G......906 226-6110
  Marquette (G-10526)
Doug Murdicks Fudge Inc.........................G......231 938-2330
  Traverse City (G-15957)
Elsa Enterprises Inc..................................G......248 816-1454
  Troy (G-16340)
Kemnitz Fine Candies..............................G......734 453-0480
  Plymouth (G-12665)
Koeze Company..E......616 724-2601
  Grand Rapids (G-6588)
Morley Brands LLC...................................D......586 468-4300
  Clinton Township (G-3180)
Original Murdicks Fudge Co......................E......906 847-3530
  Mackinac Island (G-10097)
Rocky Mtn Choclat Fctry Inc.....................G......989 624-4784
  Birch Run (G-1669)
Sanders Candy LLC..................................D......800 651-7263
  Clinton Township (G-3221)
Truans Candies Inc...................................F......313 281-0185
  Plymouth (G-12782)
W2 Inc...G......517 764-3141
  Jackson (G-8602)

CANDY, NUT & CONFECTIONERY STORES: Nuts

Nutco Inc...E......800 872-4006
  Detroit (G-4280)

CANDY, NUT & CONFECTIONERY STORES: Produced For Direct Sale

Gayles Chocolates Limited.......................E......248 398-0001
  Royal Oak (G-13929)
Marshalls Trail Inc.....................................F......231 436-5082
  Mackinaw City (G-10099)

CANDY: Chocolate From Cacao Beans

Alinosi French Ice Cream Co....................G......313 527-3195
  Detroit (G-3855)

CANDY: Hard

Liquid Otc LLC..G......248 214-7771
  Commerce Township (G-3422)

CANNED SPECIALTIES

American Spoon Foods Inc......................E......231 347-9030
  Petoskey (G-12440)
Amway International Inc...........................E......616 787-1000
  Ada (G-7)
Kraft Heinz Foods Company....................B......616 396-6557
  Holland (G-7713)

CANS: Aluminum

Oktober LLC...G......231 750-1998
  Muskegon (G-11392)

CANS: Composite Foil-Fiber, Made From Purchased Materials

Plasan Us Inc...F......616 559-0032
  Walker (G-16876)
Technova Corporation..............................F......517 485-1402
  Okemos (G-12138)

CANS: Metal

AAR Manufacturing Inc............................E......231 779-8800
  Cadillac (G-2220)
Contract Welding and Fabg Inc................E......734 699-5561
  Van Buren Twp (G-16753)
Delta Tube & Fabricating Corp................C......248 634-8267
  Holly (G-7875)
Mh Industries Ltd.....................................G......734 261-7560
  West Bloomfield (G-17485)
Royal Design & Manufacturing.................D......248 588-0110
  Madison Heights (G-10346)

CANS: Tin

Tin Can Dewitt...G......517 624-2078
  Dewitt (G-4467)

CANVAS PRDTS

Acme Mills Company...............................C......517 437-8940
  Hillsdale (G-7513)
Advanced Inc..G......231 938-2233
  Acme (G-2)
Anchor Bay Canv and Upholstery............G......810 512-4325
  Algonac (G-141)
Armstrong Display Concepts....................F......231 652-1675
  Newaygo (G-11563)
Belle Isle Awning Co Inc..........................E......586 294-6050
  Warren (G-16954)
Blanco Canvas Company Inc...................G......313 963-7787
  Farmington Hills (G-4942)
Bluewater Canvas LLC............................G......586 727-5345
  Columbus (G-3377)
Canco Inc..G......810 664-3520
  Lapeer (G-9449)
Canvas Concepts Inc...............................G......810 794-3305
  Algonac (G-142)
Canvas Shop..G......734 782-2222
  Flat Rock (G-5350)
JAC Custom Pouches Inc........................E......269 782-3190
  Dowagiac (G-4544)
Lakeside Canvas & Upholstery................G......231 755-2514
  Muskegon (G-11363)
Paddle King Inc..F......989 235-6776
  Carson City (G-2495)

CANVAS PRDTS: Boat Seats

Blue Water Sail & Canvas Inc..................G......231 941-5224
  Traverse City (G-15914)

CANVAS PRDTS: Convertible Tops, Car/Boat, Fm Purchased Mtrl

Boat Guard Inc...G......989 424-1490
  Gladwin (G-5923)
Magna Car Top Systems Amer Inc..........D......248 836-4500
  Auburn Hills (G-932)
Magna Car Top Systems Amer Inc..........F......248 619-8133
  Troy (G-16470)
Peerless Canvas Products Inc.................G......269 429-0600
  Saint Joseph (G-14335)
Shelby Auto Trim Inc................................F......586 939-9090
  Sterling Heights (G-15495)
Specilty Vhcl Acquisition Corp..................E......586 446-4701
  Warren (G-17245)

CANVAS PRDTS: Shades, Made From Purchased Materials

Kts Enterprises...G......269 624-3435
  Lawton (G-9512)

CAPS: Plastic

C M E Plastic Company...........................G......517 456-7722
  Clinton (G-3015)

CAR WASH EQPT

Admiral...G......989 356-6419
  Alpena (G-271)
Cascade Equipment Company................G......734 697-7870
  Van Buren Twp (G-16750)
Ginsan Liquidating Company LLC...........D......616 791-8100
  Grand Rapids (G-6443)
Great Lakes Ncw LLC.............................G......616 355-2626
  Holland (G-7653)
Interclean Equipment LLC.......................E......734 961-3300
  Ypsilanti (G-18082)
Motor City Wash Works Inc....................E......248 313-0272
  Wixom (G-17860)
Power-Brite of Michigan Inc.....................F......734 591-7911
  Livonia (G-9891)
Sparta Wash & Storage LLC..................G......616 887-1034
  Sparta (G-15111)
Vans Car Wash Inc..................................F......231 744-4831
  Muskegon (G-11445)

CAR WASH EQPT & SPLYS WHOLESALERS

Sam Brown Sales LLC.............................E......248 358-2626
  Farmington (G-4911)

CARBIDES

Cole King LLC..G......248 276-1278
  Orion (G-12176)
Continental Carbide Ltd Inc.....................F......586 463-9577
  Clinton Township (G-3090)
Drw Systems Carbide LLC......................G......810 392-3526
  Riley (G-13273)
Raven Carbide Die LLC...........................G......313 228-8776
  New Boston (G-11510)
Sumitomo Electric Carbide Inc................F......734 451-0200
  Plymouth (G-12761)
USA Carbide...G......248 817-5137
  Troy (G-16667)
Weiser Metal Products Inc......................G......989 736-6055
  Harrisville (G-7367)

CARBON & GRAPHITE PRDTS, NEC

American Graphite Corporation...............G......586 757-3540
  Warren (G-16930)
Astech Inc...E......989 823-7211
  Vassar (G-16811)
Bay Carbon Inc..E......989 686-8090
  Bay City (G-1282)
Bay Composites Inc.................................F......989 891-9159
  Essexville (G-4869)
Carbone of America.................................F......989 894-2911
  Bay City (G-1294)
Composite Builders LLC.........................E......616 377-7767
  Holland (G-7596)
Cummings-Moore Graphite Co...............E......313 841-1615
  Detroit (G-3957)
Graphite Electrodes Ltd..........................F......989 893-3635
  Bay City (G-1319)
Graphite Machining Inc...........................F......810 678-2227
  Metamora (G-10775)
Mersen..F......989 894-2911
  Bay City (G-1329)
Mersen USA Greenville-Mi Corp.............C......616 754-5671
  Greenville (G-7146)
U S Graphite Inc......................................C......989 755-0441
  Saginaw (G-14172)
Wahoo Composites LLC..........................F......734 424-0966
  Dexter (G-4518)

CARBON SPECIALTIES Electrical Use

National Carbon Tech LLC......................E......651 330-4063
  Gwinn (G-7220)

CARBURETORS

Tyde Group Worldwide LLC....................G......248 879-7656
  Troy (G-16659)
Walbro LLC..C......989 872-2131
  Cass City (G-2524)

CARDBOARD PRDTS, EXC DIE-CUT

Whisper Creative Products Inc................G......734 529-2734
  Dundee (G-4603)

CARDS: Color

Presscraft Papers Inc..............................E......231 882-5505
  Benzonia (G-1576)

CARDS: Greeting

Avanti Press Inc.......................................E......800 228-2684
  Detroit (G-3886)
Avanti Press Inc.......................................E......313 961-0022
  Taylor (G-15692)
Denali Seed Co..G......907 344-0347
  Pentwater (G-12429)
Design Design Inc...................................C......866 935-2648
  Grand Rapids (G-6345)
Katys Kards...G......989 793-4094
  Saginaw (G-14070)
Notes From Man Cave LLC....................G......586 604-1997
  Detroit (G-4278)
Reyers Company Inc...............................F......616 414-5530
  Spring Lake (G-15172)

CARDS: Identification

Greg Linska Sales Inc.............................G......248 765-6354
  Troy (G-16387)
Impact Label Corporation........................D......269 381-4280
  Galesburg (G-5811)
MPS Lansing Inc.....................................A......517 323-9000
  Lansing (G-9248)
W T Beresford Co....................................G......248 350-2900
  Southfield (G-15064)

CARNIVAL & AMUSEMENT PARK EQPT WHOLESALERS

Wiley & Co..G......616 361-7110
  Grand Rapids (G-6993)

CARPET & RUG CLEANING & REPAIRING PLANTS

Real Green Systems Inc .... D 888 345-2154
 Commerce Township *(G-3447)*

CARPET & UPHOLSTERY CLEANING SVCS

Dave Brand .... G 269 651-4693
 Sturgis *(G-15603)*

CARPETS & RUGS: Tufted

Mohawk Industries Inc .... G 248 486-4075
 Wixom *(G-17858)*

CARPETS, RUGS & FLOOR COVERING

Custom Marine Carpet .... G 269 684-1922
 Niles *(G-11604)*
Forever Flooring and More LLC .... G 517 745-6194
 Lowell *(G-10029)*
HP Pelzer Auto Systems Inc .... E 248 280-1010
 Troy *(G-16405)*
Marceau Enterprises Inc .... G 586 697-8100
 Washington *(G-17307)*
Plant Df .... E 734 397-0397
 Van Buren Twp *(G-16780)*
Prestwick Group LLP .... G 248 360-6113
 Commerce Township *(G-3442)*
Professional Rug Works Inc .... G 248 577-1400
 Troy *(G-16567)*
Pwv Studios Ltd .... F 616 361-5659
 Grand Rapids *(G-6798)*
Seelye Group Ltd .... G 517 267-2001
 Lansing *(G-9423)*
Shelter Carpet Specialties .... G 616 475-4944
 Grand Rapids *(G-6859)*
Usmats Inc .... G 810 765-4545
 Marine City *(G-10485)*
W A Thomas Company .... G 734 955-6500
 Taylor *(G-15779)*

CARPETS: Textile Fiber

James E Sullivan & Associates .... G 616 453-0345
 Grand Rapids *(G-6551)*
Scott Group Custom Carpets LLC .... C 616 954-3200
 Grand Rapids *(G-6854)*

CARPORTS: Prefabricated Metal

G & C Carports .... F 616 678-4308
 Kent City *(G-8990)*

CARRIAGES: Horse Drawn

Justin Carriage Works LLC .... G 517 852-9743
 Nashville *(G-11458)*

CARS: Electric

Axle of Dearborn Inc .... G 313 581-3300
 Detroit *(G-3888)*
Dynamic Corporation .... F 248 338-1100
 Auburn Hills *(G-847)*

CARTS: Grocery

US Wire Rope Supply Inc .... E 313 925-0444
 Detroit *(G-4417)*
Wcscarts LLC .... F 248 901-0965
 Troy *(G-16688)*

CARVING SETS, STAINLESS STEEL

Rivore Metals LLC .... D 800 248-1250
 Troy *(G-16581)*

CASES, WOOD

Bennett Wood Specialties Inc .... F 616 772-6683
 Zeeland *(G-18117)*
Garcia Company .... G 248 459-0952
 Holly *(G-7879)*

CASES: Carrying

Rhino Products Inc .... F 269 674-8309
 Lawrence *(G-9507)*
Sound Productions Entrmt .... E 989 386-2221
 Clare *(G-2889)*

CASES: Carrying, Clothing & Apparel

Birlon Group LLC .... G 313 551-5341
 Inkster *(G-8225)*

CASES: Packing, Nailed Or Lock Corner, Wood

National Case Corporation .... G 586 726-1710
 Sterling Heights *(G-15432)*

CASES: Shipping, Nailed Or Lock Corner, Wood

Vaive Wood Products Co .... E 586 949-4900
 Macomb *(G-10172)*

CASH REGISTER REPAIR SVCS

Great Lakes Weld LLC .... G 231 943-4180
 Traverse City *(G-15994)*
Lorna Icr LLC .... G 586 582-1500
 Warren *(G-17131)*

CASH REGISTERS WHOLESALERS

Speedway Ordering Systems Inc .... G 734 420-0482
 Livonia *(G-9939)*

CASINGS: Sheet Metal

Hart Acquisition Company LLC .... E 313 537-0490
 Redford *(G-13164)*
Progressive Manufacturing LLC .... G 231 924-9975
 Fremont *(G-5783)*

CASKETS & ACCESS

Genesis International LLC .... E 317 777-6700
 Mason *(G-10640)*
Superior Casket Co .... E 313 592-3190
 Redford *(G-13197)*
Universal Casket Co .... E 269 476-2163
 Cassopolis *(G-2537)*

CASKETS WHOLESALERS

American Vault Service .... G 989 366-8657
 Prudenville *(G-13084)*
Burrell Tri-County Vaults Inc .... F 734 483-2024
 Ypsilanti *(G-18058)*
Wilbert Burial Vault Company .... G 231 773-6631
 Muskegon *(G-11449)*
Willbee Concrete Products Co .... F 517 782-8246
 Jackson *(G-8607)*

CAST STONE: Concrete

Royal Stone LLC .... E 248 343-6232
 Williamston *(G-17739)*

CASTERS

Evans Industries Inc .... G 313 272-8200
 Detroit *(G-4046)*
Maureen I Martin Caster 810 233-0484
 Flint *(G-5464)*
Saginaw Products Corporation .... E 989 753-1411
 Saginaw *(G-14141)*
Shepherd Caster Corp .... G 269 668-4800
 Mattawan *(G-10669)*

CASTINGS GRINDING: For The Trade

A M Grinding .... G 616 847-8373
 Ferrysburg *(G-5332)*
A-OK Grinding Co .... G 248 589-3070
 Madison Heights *(G-10176)*
ABC Grinding Inc .... G 313 295-1060
 Dearborn Heights *(G-3777)*
Able Manufacturing Inc .... F 616 235-3322
 Grand Rapids *(G-6130)*
Alro Riverside LLC .... G 517 782-8322
 Jackson *(G-8382)*
American Grinding Machining Co .... F 313 388-0440
 Lincoln Park *(G-9572)*
C & C Grinding Corp .... G 248 689-1979
 Troy *(G-16249)*
Echo Quality Grinding Inc .... F 231 544-6637
 Central Lake *(G-2591)*
Edmore Tool & Grinding Inc .... E 989 427-3790
 Edmore *(G-4750)*
Grind-All Precision Tool Co .... F 586 954-3430
 Clinton Township *(G-3132)*
Grinding Specialists Inc .... E 734 729-1775
 Westland *(G-17565)*
Jem Jig Grinding Inc .... G 248 486-7006
 Wixom *(G-17838)*
Line Precision Inc .... E 248 474-5280
 Farmington Hills *(G-5044)*
Michigan General Grinding LLC .... G 616 454-5089
 Grand Rapids *(G-6672)*
Modified Gear and Spline Inc .... F 313 893-3511
 Detroit *(G-4253)*
Multi Grinding Inc .... E 586 268-7388
 Warren *(G-17162)*
Progressive Cutter Grinding Co .... G 586 580-2367
 Shelby Township *(G-14672)*
Quality Grinding Inc .... G 586 293-3780
 Fraser *(G-5714)*
R & B Grinding Service Inc .... G 231 824-6798
 Manton *(G-10457)*
R & S Cutter Grind Inc .... G 989 791-3100
 Saginaw *(G-14128)*
Rapid Grinding & Machine Co .... G 989 753-1744
 Saginaw *(G-14131)*
S P Jig Grinding .... G 734 525-6335
 Livonia *(G-9918)*
SMS Modern Hard Chrome LLC .... D 586 445-0330
 Warren *(G-17242)*
St Joe Valley Grinding Inc .... G 269 925-0709
 Benton Harbor *(G-1551)*
Superior Cutter Grinding Inc .... G 586 781-2365
 Shelby Township *(G-14706)*
Tait Grinding Service Inc .... G 248 437-5100
 New Hudson *(G-11557)*
True Tool Cnc Regrinding & Mfg .... G 616 677-1751
 Grand Rapids *(G-6939)*

CASTINGS: Aerospace Investment, Ferrous

Barron Industries Inc .... D 248 628-4300
 Oxford *(G-12337)*
Eps Industries Inc .... E 616 844-9223
 Ferrysburg *(G-5334)*
Onodi Tool & Engineering Co .... E 313 386-6682
 Melvindale *(G-10704)*

CASTINGS: Aerospace, Aluminum

Centracore LLC .... F 586 776-5700
 Saint Clair *(G-14209)*
Cytec Industries Inc .... C 269 349-6677
 Kalamazoo *(G-8722)*
Infinity Tech & Arospc Inc .... G 734 480-9001
 Ypsilanti *(G-18080)*
Onodi Tool & Engineering Co .... E 313 386-6682
 Melvindale *(G-10704)*
Tower Defense & Aerospace LLC .... C 248 675-6000
 Livonia *(G-9966)*

CASTINGS: Aerospace, Nonferrous, Exc Aluminum

Onodi Tool & Engineering Co .... E 313 386-6682
 Melvindale *(G-10704)*

CASTINGS: Aluminum

Algonac Marine Cast LLC .... F 810 794-9391
 Clay *(G-2992)*
Bernier Cast Metals Inc .... G 989 754-7571
 Saginaw *(G-14006)*
Birkhold Pattern Company Inc .... G 269 467-8705
 Centreville *(G-2593)*
Casting Industries Inc .... F 586 776-5700
 Saint Clair *(G-14208)*
Eagle Aluminum Cast Pdts Inc .... G 231 788-4884
 Muskegon *(G-11309)*
G M Brass & Alum Fndry Inc .... F 269 926-6366
 Benton Harbor *(G-1500)*
Hackett Brass Foundry Co .... E 313 331-6005
 Detroit *(G-4113)*
International Fenestration .... G 248 735-6880
 Northville *(G-11701)*
Mall City Aluminum Inc .... G 269 349-5088
 Kalamazoo *(G-8816)*
Max Casting Company Inc .... F 269 925-8081
 Benton Harbor *(G-1527)*
Milan Cast Metal Corporation .... E 734 439-0510
 Milan *(G-10947)*
Sterling Metal Works LLC .... G 586 977-9577
 Sterling Heights *(G-15512)*
Superior Non-Ferrous Inc .... G 586 791-7988
 Clinton Township *(G-3238)*

PRODUCT SECTION
CASTINGS: Machinery, Copper Or Copper-Base Alloy

Tooling & Equipment Intl Corp ....C 734 522-1422
  Livonia *(G-9957)*
Wolverine Bronze Company ....D 586 776-8180
  Roseville *(G-13891)*

CASTINGS: Brass, Bronze & Copper

L & L Pattern Inc ....G 231 733-2646
  Muskegon *(G-11359)*
Smith Castings Inc ....E 906 774-4956
  Iron Mountain *(G-8301)*

CASTINGS: Brass, NEC, Exc Die

Allusion Star Inc ....G 231 264-5858
  Elk Rapids *(G-4774)*
Bernier Cast Metals Inc ....G 989 754-7571
  Saginaw *(G-14006)*
Jsj Corporation ....E 616 842-6350
  Grand Haven *(G-6042)*
Lewkowicz Corporation ....F 734 941-0411
  Romulus *(G-13701)*

CASTINGS: Bronze, NEC, Exc Die

Barron Industries Inc ....D 248 628-4300
  Oxford *(G-12337)*

CASTINGS: Commercial Investment, Ferrous

Barron Industries Inc ....D 248 628-4300
  Oxford *(G-12338)*
Federal Group Usa Inc ....F 248 545-5000
  Southfield *(G-14905)*
Howmet Corporation ....E 231 894-5686
  Whitehall *(G-17669)*
Howmet Corporation ....D 231 894-7183
  Whitehall *(G-17670)*
Howmet Corporation ....C 231 894-7290
  Whitehall *(G-17671)*
Howmet Corporation ....E 231 981-3269
  Whitehall *(G-17672)*
Howmet Holdings Corporation ....G 231 894-5686
  Whitehall *(G-17676)*
Invecast Corporation ....E 586 755-4050
  Warren *(G-17096)*
Triton Global Sources Inc ....G 734 668-7107
  Ypsilanti *(G-18106)*

CASTINGS: Die, Aluminum

Aludyne Inc ....F 269 556-9236
  Stevensville *(G-15554)*
Aludyne Inc ....G 248 506-1692
  Warren *(G-16926)*
Angstrom Aluminum Castings LLC .....E 616 309-1208
  Grand Rapids *(G-6170)*
Cascade Die Casting Group Inc ....G 616 281-1774
  Grand Rapids *(G-6258)*
Cascade Die Casting Group Inc ....D 616 887-1771
  Sparta *(G-15089)*
Centracore De Mexico LLC ....E 586 776-5700
  Saint Clair *(G-14210)*
Charles Group Inc ....B 336 882-0186
  Grand Rapids *(G-6271)*
Connell Limited Partnership ....D 989 875-5135
  Ithaca *(G-8358)*
Cooper Foundry Inc ....F 269 343-2808
  Kalamazoo *(G-8717)*
Elco Inc ....G 586 778-6858
  Roseville *(G-13799)*
Evans Industries Inc ....G 313 259-2266
  Detroit *(G-4045)*
Federal Group Usa Inc ....F 248 545-5000
  Southfield *(G-14905)*
Great Lakes Die Cast Corp ....D 231 726-4002
  Muskegon *(G-11337)*
Hackett Brass Foundry Co ....E 313 822-1214
  Detroit *(G-4112)*
Hanson International Inc ....D 269 429-5555
  Saint Joseph *(G-14316)*
Hoffmann Die Cast LLC ....C 269 983-1102
  Saint Joseph *(G-14317)*
Homestead Tool and Machine ....E 989 465-6182
  Coleman *(G-3344)*
Husite Engineering Co Inc ....E 248 588-0337
  Clinton Township *(G-3136)*
Key Casting Company Inc ....G 269 426-3800
  Sawyer *(G-14486)*
Lakeshore Die Cast Inc ....F 269 422-1523
  Baroda *(G-1126)*
M & M Die Cast Inc ....E 269 465-6206
  Bridgman *(G-1871)*

Mag-TEC Casting Corporation ....E 517 789-8505
  Jackson *(G-8505)*
Michigan Die Casting LLC ....D 269 471-7715
  Dowagiac *(G-4551)*
Montague Metal Products Inc ....E 231 893-0547
  Montague *(G-11095)*
Muskegon Castings LLC ....C 231 777-3941
  Muskegon *(G-11388)*
Mv Metal Pdts & Solutions LLC ....D 269 462-4010
  Dowagiac *(G-4554)*
North Shore Mfg Corp ....E 269 849-2551
  Coloma *(G-3363)*
Pace Industries LLC ....C 231 777-3941
  Muskegon *(G-11394)*
Pace Industries LLC ....E 231 773-4491
  Muskegon *(G-11395)*
Paragon Metals LLC ....G 517 639-4629
  Hillsdale *(G-7533)*
Precision Die Cast Inc ....G 586 463-1800
  Clinton Township *(G-3199)*
Prototype Cast Mfg Inc ....G 586 739-0180
  Shelby Township *(G-14674)*
Prototype Cast Mfg Inc ....G 586 615-8524
  Sterling Heights *(G-15455)*
Quality Castings Co ....G 269 349-7449
  Kalamazoo *(G-8864)*
Shiloh Industries Inc ....D 989 463-6166
  Alma *(G-249)*
Soper Manufacturing Company ....E 269 429-5245
  Saint Joseph *(G-14340)*
Supreme Casting Inc ....D 269 465-5757
  Stevensville *(G-15583)*
T C H Industries Incorporated ....G 616 942-0505
  Grand Rapids *(G-6912)*
Tooling Technology LLC ....D 937 381-9211
  Macomb *(G-10169)*
Tri-State Aluminum LLC ....F 231 722-7825
  Muskegon *(G-11440)*
Triton Global Sources Inc ....G 734 668-7107
  Ypsilanti *(G-18106)*
Tru Die Cast Corporation ....E 269 426-3361
  New Troy *(G-11561)*
Ube Machinery Inc ....D 734 741-7000
  Ann Arbor *(G-685)*
Wolverine Die Cast Ltd Ptnshp ....E 586 757-1900
  Warren *(G-17296)*

CASTINGS: Die, Copper & Copper Alloy

Hackett Brass Foundry Co ....E 313 822-1214
  Detroit *(G-4112)*

CASTINGS: Die, Lead & Zinc

North Shore Mfg Corp ....E 269 849-2551
  Coloma *(G-3363)*

CASTINGS: Die, Magnesium & Magnesium-Base Alloy

Mag-TEC Casting Corporation ....E 517 789-8505
  Jackson *(G-8505)*
Magnesium Products America Inc ....B 734 416-8600
  Plymouth *(G-12681)*

CASTINGS: Die, Nonferrous

Cascade Die Casting Group Inc ....E 616 455-4010
  Grand Rapids *(G-6259)*
Cobra Patterns & Models Inc ....E 248 588-2669
  Madison Heights *(G-10215)*
Magnesium Products America Inc ....G 517 663-2700
  Eaton Rapids *(G-4728)*
Mv Metal Pdts & Solutions LLC ....A 269 471-7715
  Portage *(G-13017)*

CASTINGS: Die, Zinc

Cascade Die Casting Group Inc ....G 616 281-1774
  Grand Rapids *(G-6258)*
Cascade Die Casting Group Inc ....D 616 887-1771
  Sparta *(G-15089)*
Charles Group Inc ....B 336 882-0186
  Grand Rapids *(G-6271)*
Hoffmann Die Cast LLC ....C 269 983-1102
  Saint Joseph *(G-14317)*
Key Casting Company Inc ....G 269 426-3800
  Sawyer *(G-14486)*
Lakeshore Die Cast Inc ....F 269 422-1523
  Baroda *(G-1126)*
Mv Metal Pdts & Solutions LLC ....D 269 462-4010
  Dowagiac *(G-4554)*

Proto-Cast Inc ....E 313 565-5400
  Inkster *(G-8233)*
Superior Non-Ferrous Inc ....G 586 791-7988
  Clinton Township *(G-3238)*
T C H Industries Incorporated ....G 616 942-0505
  Grand Rapids *(G-6912)*
Tru Die Cast Corporation ....E 269 426-3361
  New Troy *(G-11561)*
Wolverine Die Cast Ltd Ptnshp ....E 586 757-1900
  Warren *(G-17296)*

CASTINGS: Ductile

Berne Enterprises Inc ....F 989 453-3235
  Pigeon *(G-12487)*
Betz Industries Inc ....D 616 453-4429
  Grand Rapids *(G-6214)*
Citation Camden Cast Ctr LLC ....C 248 727-1800
  Southfield *(G-14867)*
Global Technology Ventures Inc ....G 248 324-3707
  Farmington Hills *(G-5011)*
Grede II LLC ....E 248 727-1800
  Southfield *(G-14925)*
Kent Foundry Company ....E 616 754-1100
  Greenville *(G-7142)*
Ravenna Casting Center Inc ....C 231 853-0300
  Ravenna *(G-13126)*
Triton Global Sources Inc ....G 734 668-7107
  Ypsilanti *(G-18106)*

CASTINGS: Gray Iron

American Axle & Mfg Inc ....D 248 522-4500
  Southfield *(G-14836)*
Anstey Foundry Co Inc ....E 269 429-3229
  Stevensville *(G-15556)*
Awcco USA Incorporated ....G 586 336-9135
  Romeo *(G-13624)*
Blue Fire Manufacturing LLC ....E 248 714-7166
  Waterford *(G-17325)*
Brillion Iron Works Inc ....C 248 727-1800
  Southfield *(G-14858)*
Calhoun Foundry Company Inc ....D 517 568-4415
  Homer *(G-7940)*
Casting Industries Inc ....F 586 776-5700
  Saint Clair *(G-14208)*
Citation Michigan LLC ....E 248 522-4500
  Novi *(G-11848)*
Ej Usa Inc ....B 800 874-4100
  East Jordan *(G-4636)*
Federal Group Usa Inc ....F 248 545-5000
  Southfield *(G-14905)*
Great Lakes Castings LLC ....E 616 399-9710
  Holland *(G-7652)*
Grede Foundries Inc ....C 248 440-9500
  Southfield *(G-14923)*
Grede Holdings LLC ....E 248 440-9500
  Southfield *(G-14924)*
Grede LLC ....B 906 774-7250
  Kingsford *(G-9058)*
Grede LLC ....B 248 440-9500
  Southfield *(G-14926)*
Grede Wsncsin Subsidiaries LLC ....B 248 727-1800
  Southfield *(G-14930)*
Metal Technologies Inc ....C 231 853-0300
  Ravenna *(G-13124)*
Metal Technologies Indiana Inc ....C 269 278-1765
  Three Rivers *(G-15870)*
Midland Iron Works Inc ....F 989 832-3041
  Midland *(G-10889)*
Northland Castings Corporation ....F 231 873-4974
  Hart *(G-7377)*
Pioneer Foundry Company Inc ....F 517 782-9469
  Jackson *(G-8552)*
Smith Castings Inc ....E 906 774-4956
  Iron Mountain *(G-8301)*
Steeltech Ltd ....D 616 243-7920
  Grand Rapids *(G-6891)*

CASTINGS: Machinery, Aluminum

Century Foundry Inc ....E 231 733-1572
  Muskegon *(G-11293)*

CASTINGS: Machinery, Copper Or Copper-Base Alloy

Conway Detroit Corporation ....E 586 552-8413
  Roseville *(G-13786)*

CASTINGS: Machinery, Nonferrous, Exc Die or Aluminum Copper

Kuhlman Casting Co Inc ..... F 248 853-2382
Detroit (G-4185)

CASTINGS: Precision

Acra Cast Inc ..... E 989 893-3961
Bay City (G-1271)
Federal Group Usa Inc ..... F 248 545-5000
Southfield (G-14905)
Grosse Tool and Machine Co ..... E 586 773-6770
Warren (G-17068)
High-Tech Inds of Holland ..... E 616 399-5430
Holland (G-7666)
Holland Alloys Inc ..... E 616 396-6444
Holland (G-7667)
Holland Pattern Co ..... E 616 396-6348
Holland (G-7675)
Shellcast Inc ..... E 231 893-8245
Montague (G-11097)
Stegman Tool Co Inc ..... E 248 588-4634
Troy (G-16621)

CASTINGS: Steel

Alloying Surfaces Inc ..... G 248 524-9200
Troy (G-16191)
Arcanum Alloys Inc ..... G 312 810-4479
Kentwood (G-8999)
Axis Machining Inc ..... D 989 453-3943
Pigeon (G-12486)
Bay Cast Inc ..... D 989 892-0511
Bay City (G-1283)
Berne Enterprises Inc ..... F 989 453-3235
Pigeon (G-12487)
Huron Casting Inc ..... B 989 453-3933
Pigeon (G-12491)
Northfield Manufacturing Inc ..... E 734 729-2890
Westland (G-17584)
Steeltech Ltd ..... D 616 243-7920
Grand Rapids (G-6891)
Steeltech Ltd ..... F 616 696-1130
Cedar Springs (G-2563)
Temperform LLC ..... E 248 349-5230
Novi (G-12012)

CASTINGS: Titanium

Apollo Trick Titanium Inc ..... F 517 694-7449
Troy (G-16205)

CASTINGS: Zinc

Soper Manufacturing Company ..... E 269 429-5245
Saint Joseph (G-14340)
Triton Global Sources Inc ..... G 734 668-7107
Ypsilanti (G-18106)
Wil-Kast Inc ..... E 616 281-2850
Grand Rapids (G-6992)

CATALOG & MAIL-ORDER HOUSES

A W B Industries Inc ..... E 989 739-1447
Oscoda (G-12205)
Swartzmiller Lumber Company ..... G 989 845-6625
Chesaning (G-2728)

CATALOG SALES

Fitness Finders Inc ..... E 517 750-1500
Jackson (G-8449)

CATALOG SHOWROOMS

Pubsof Chicago LLC ..... G 312 448-8282
Traverse City (G-16083)

CATERERS

Evelyn Robertson Lett ..... G 248 569-8746
Southfield (G-14901)
Kellys Catering ..... G 231 796-5414
Big Rapids (G-1635)
Richmond Meat Packers Inc ..... G 586 727-1450
Richmond (G-13270)

CATS, WHOLESALE

Go Cat Feather Toys ..... G 517 543-7519
Charlotte (G-2652)

CEILING SYSTEMS: Luminous, Commercial

Skyworks LLC ..... F 972 284-9093
Northville (G-11726)

CEMENT & CONCRETE RELATED PRDTS & EQPT: Bituminous

Globe Industries Incorporated ..... F 906 932-3540
Ironwood (G-8329)

CEMENT ROCK: Crushed & Broken

C & L Concrete ..... G 231 829-3386
Tustin (G-16709)
State Crushing Inc ..... G 248 332-6210
Auburn Hills (G-1002)

CEMENT, EXC LINOLEUM & TILE

Concrete Manufacturing Inc ..... G 586 777-3320
Roseville (G-13785)

CEMENT: High Temperature, Refractory, Nonclay

Taylor Controls Inc ..... F 269 637-8521
South Haven (G-14777)

CEMENT: Hydraulic

Joe Davis Crushing Inc ..... G 586 757-3612
Sterling Heights (G-15381)
Lafarge North America Inc ..... E 989 399-1005
Saginaw (G-14076)
Lafarge North America Inc ..... G 989 894-0157
Essexville (G-4875)
Lafarge North America Inc ..... C 989 595-3820
Presque Isle (G-13083)
Lafarge North America Inc ..... E 216 566-0545
Essexville (G-4876)
Lafarge North America Inc ..... F 703 480-3649
Dundee (G-4592)
Lafarge North America Inc ..... G 989 755-7515
Saginaw (G-14077)
Nb Cement Co ..... G 313 278-8299
Dearborn Heights (G-3792)
St Marys Cement Inc (us) ..... G 616 846-8553
Ferrysburg (G-5338)

CEMENT: Magnesia

Martin Mretta Magnesia Spc LLC ..... E 231 723-2577
Manistee (G-10429)

CEMENT: Masonry

Knust Masonry ..... G 231 322-2587
Rapid City (G-13109)
St Marys Cement US LLC ..... E 231 547-9971
Charlevoix (G-2631)

CEMENT: Portland

Holcim (us) Inc ..... D 734 529-2411
Dundee (G-4587)
Holcim (us) Inc ..... G 734 529-4600
Dundee (G-4588)
Holcim (us) Inc ..... F 989 755-7515
Saginaw (G-14060)
Lafarge North America Inc ..... G 989 354-4171
Alpena (G-295)
Lafarge North America Inc ..... F 703 480-3600
Dundee (G-4591)

CEMETERIES: Real Estate Operation

Fenton Corporation ..... G 810 629-2858
Fenton (G-5209)

CEMETERY MEMORIAL DEALERS

Fenton Corporation ..... G 810 629-2858
Fenton (G-5209)
Fenton Memorials & Vaults Inc ..... F 810 629-2858
Fenton (G-5210)
Patten Monument Company ..... D 616 785-4141
Comstock Park (G-3506)

CERAMIC FIBER

HC Starck Inc ..... E 517 279-9511
Coldwater (G-3309)

Nano Innovations LLC ..... G 906 231-2101
Houghton (G-7978)

CERAMIC FLOOR & WALL TILE WHOLESALERS

Dal-Tile Corporation ..... F 248 471-7150
Farmington Hills (G-4968)

CESSPOOL CLEANING SVCS

Van Paemels Equipment Company ..... G 586 784-5295
Armada (G-724)

CHAIN: Welded, Made From Purchased Wire

Columbus McKinnon Corporation ..... G 800 955-5541
Muskegon (G-11296)

CHAINS: Forged

Allor Manufacturing Inc ..... D 248 486-4500
Brighton (G-1883)
Plesh Industries Inc ..... F 716 873-4916
Brighton (G-1979)
Shadko Enterprises Inc ..... G 248 816-1712
Troy (G-16598)

CHAMBERS OF COMMERCE

Fenton Chamber Commerce ..... G 810 629-5447
Fenton (G-5207)

CHARCOAL

Country Schoolhouse Kingsford ..... G 906 828-1971
Kingsford (G-9056)

CHARCOAL: Activated

US Bio Carbon LLC ..... G 616 334-9862
Caledonia (G-2320)

CHASSIS: Automobile Trailer

Composite Sign Products Inc ..... G 616 252-9110
Jenison (G-8621)
Precision Concepts Inc ..... G 989 673-8555
Caro (G-2475)

CHASSIS: Motor Vehicle

A & A Manufacturing Co ..... G 616 846-1730
Spring Lake (G-15130)
American Axle Mfg Holdings Inc ..... C 313 758-2000
Detroit (G-3866)
Detroit Chassis LLC ..... G 313 571-2100
Detroit (G-3974)
Detroit Custom Chassis LLC ..... C 313 571-2100
Detroit (G-3978)
Federal-Mogul Chassis LLC ..... F 248 354-7700
Southfield (G-14906)
Spartan Motors Inc ..... A 517 543-6400
Charlotte (G-2665)
Spartan Motors Chassis Inc ..... A 517 543-6400
Charlotte (G-2666)
Spectra Lmp LLC ..... C 313 571-2100
Detroit (G-4370)
UPF Inc ..... D 810 768-0001
Flint (G-5519)

CHECK VALIDATION SVCS

Stewart Metrology LLC ..... G 269 660-9290
Battle Creek (G-1254)

CHEESE WHOLESALERS

Langs Inc ..... G 248 634-6048
Holly (G-7884)
Williams Cheese Co ..... E 989 697-4492
Linwood (G-9599)

CHEMICAL ELEMENTS

Element 80 Engraving LLC ..... G 616 318-7407
Grand Rapids (G-6374)
Element Salon and Day Spa ..... G 989 708-6006
Midland (G-10860)
Element Services LLC ..... G 517 672-1005
Howell (G-8038)

PRODUCT SECTION

CHEMICALS: Fuel Tank Or Engine Cleaning

CHEMICAL PROCESSING MACHINERY & EQPT

B&P Littleford Day LLC	D	989 757-1300
Saginaw (G-13998)		
B&P Littleford LLC	E	989 757-1300
Saginaw (G-13999)		
Frontier Technology Inc	F	269 673-9464
Allegan (G-163)		
Innovative Cleaning Eqp Inc	E	616 656-9225
Grand Rapids (G-6537)		
Jcu International Inc	G	248 313-6630
Wixom (G-17837)		
Powell Fabrication & Mfg Inc	E	989 681-2158
Saint Louis (G-14369)		
Ti-Coating Inc	E	586 726-1900
Shelby Township (G-14709)		

CHEMICAL SPLYS FOR FOUNDRIES

Dow Credit Corporation	G	989 636-8949
Midland (G-10850)		

CHEMICAL: Sodm Compnds/Salts, Inorg, Exc Rfnd Sodm Chloride

Kage Group LLC	E	734 604-5052
Van Buren Twp (G-16767)		

CHEMICALS & ALLIED PRDTS WHOLESALERS, NEC

Dow Chemical Company	C	989 832-1000
Midland (G-10844)		
Ebonex Corporation	F	313 388-0063
Melvindale (G-10697)		
Flint Group US LLC	A	734 781-4600
Livonia (G-9741)		
General Tape Label Liquidating	D	248 437-5200
Wixom (G-17817)		
Great Lakes Laboratories Inc	G	734 525-8300
Livonia (G-9760)		
Idemitsu Chemicals USA Corp	G	248 355-0666
Southfield (G-14942)		
Jade Scientific Inc	F	734 207-3775
Westland (G-17572)		
R J Marshall Company	F	248 353-4100
Southfield (G-15009)		
Recycling Fluid Technologies	F	269 788-0488
Battle Creek (G-1240)		

CHEMICALS & ALLIED PRDTS, WHOL: Gases, Compressed/Liquefied

Purity Cylinder Gases Inc	G	517 321-9555
Lansing (G-9262)		

CHEMICALS & ALLIED PRDTS, WHOLESALE: Acids

Pressure Vessel Service Inc	E	313 921-1200
Detroit (G-4310)		

CHEMICALS & ALLIED PRDTS, WHOLESALE: Alcohols

Carbon Green Bioenergy LLC	E	616 374-4000
Lake Odessa (G-9112)		

CHEMICALS & ALLIED PRDTS, WHOLESALE: Anti-Corrosion Prdts

Trenton Corporation	E	734 424-3600
Ann Arbor (G-680)		

CHEMICALS & ALLIED PRDTS, WHOLESALE: Aromatic

Odor Gone Inc	F	888 636-7292
Zeeland (G-18172)		

CHEMICALS & ALLIED PRDTS, WHOLESALE: Chemical Additives

Tryco Inc	F	734 953-6800
Farmington Hills (G-5144)		

CHEMICALS & ALLIED PRDTS, WHOLESALE: Chemicals, Indl

Colfran Industrial Sales Inc	F	734 595-8920
Romulus (G-13663)		
Jci Jones Chemicals Inc	E	734 283-0677
Wyandotte (G-17963)		
Wacker Chemical Corporation	A	517 264-8500
Adrian (G-103)		

CHEMICALS & ALLIED PRDTS, WHOLESALE: Chemicals, Rustproofing

Condat Corporation	E	734 944-4994
Saline (G-14383)		

CHEMICALS & ALLIED PRDTS, WHOLESALE: Compressed Gas

S&S Precision LLC	G	248 266-4770
Wixom (G-17889)		

CHEMICALS & ALLIED PRDTS, WHOLESALE: Detergent/Soap

Access Business Group LLC	B	616 787-6000
Ada (G-3)		
Alticor Global Holdings Inc	F	616 787-1000
Ada (G-5)		
Alticor Inc	C	616 787-1000
Ada (G-6)		
Kmi Cleaning Solutions Inc	F	269 964-2557
Battle Creek (G-1220)		

CHEMICALS & ALLIED PRDTS, WHOLESALE: Oil Additives

Nano Materials & Processes Inc	G	248 529-3873
Milford (G-10974)		
Stony Creek Essential Oils	G	989 227-5500
Saint Johns (G-14297)		

CHEMICALS & ALLIED PRDTS, WHOLESALE: Oxygen

Tupes of Saginaw Inc	F	989 799-1550
Saginaw (G-14169)		

CHEMICALS & ALLIED PRDTS, WHOLESALE: Plastics Prdts, NEC

Champion Plastics Inc	F	248 373-8995
Auburn Hills (G-812)		
Curbell Plastics Inc	G	734 513-0531
Livonia (G-9694)		
Gibraltar Canvas Inc	G	734 675-4891
Rockwood (G-13604)		
Proto Shapes Inc	F	517 278-3947
Coldwater (G-3321)		
Stone Plastics and Mfg Inc	C	616 748-9740
Zeeland (G-18188)		
Uniflex Inc	G	248 486-6000
Brighton (G-2002)		
Woodbridge Sales & Engrg Inc	C	248 288-0100
Troy (G-16698)		
Wright Plastic Products Co LLC	D	810 326-3000
Saint Clair (G-14237)		

CHEMICALS & ALLIED PRDTS, WHOLESALE: Plastics Sheets & Rods

Ann Arbor Plastics Inc	G	734 944-0800
Saline (G-14377)		
Exotic Rubber & Plastics Corp	D	248 477-2122
Farmington Hills (G-4996)		
Humphrey Companies LLC	C	616 530-1717
Grandville (G-7048)		
Total Plastics Resources LLC	D	269 344-0009
Kalamazoo (G-8914)		
Total Plastics Resources LLC	F	248 299-9500
Rochester Hills (G-13529)		

CHEMICALS & ALLIED PRDTS, WHOLESALE: Polyurethane Prdts

Recycled Polymetric Materials	G	313 957-6373
Detroit (G-4335)		

CHEMICALS & ALLIED PRDTS, WHOLESALE: Resins, Plastics

Aci Plastics Inc	E	810 767-3800
Flint (G-5369)		
American Commodities Inc	E	810 767-3800
Flint (G-5376)		

CHEMICALS & ALLIED PRDTS, WHOLESALE: Rubber, Synthetic

Exotic Rubber & Plastics Corp	D	248 477-2122
Farmington Hills (G-4996)		

CHEMICALS & ALLIED PRDTS, WHOLESALE: Spec Clean/Sanitation

Able Solutions LLC	G	810 216-6106
Port Huron (G-12880)		
Advanced Fiberglass Services	G	810 785-7541
Flint (G-5370)		

CHEMICALS & OTHER PRDTS DERIVED FROM COKING

Woodbridge Group Inc	G	269 324-8993
Troy (G-16696)		

CHEMICALS: Agricultural

Avian Enterprises LLC	E	888 366-0709
Sylvan Lake (G-15671)		
Bayer Cropscience LP	D	231 744-4711
Muskegon (G-11277)		
Centen AG LLC	G	989 636-1000
Midland (G-10823)		
Dow Agrosciences LLC	D	989 479-3245
Harbor Beach (G-7265)		
Dow Chemical Company	D	989 636-0540
Midland (G-10845)		
E I Du Pont De Nemours & Co	B	248 549-4794
Royal Oak (G-13920)		
E I Du Pont De Nemours & Co	B	586 263-0258
Clinton Township (G-3107)		
Monsanto Company	E	269 483-1300
Constantine (G-3540)		
Monsanto Company	G	517 676-2479
Mason (G-10648)		
Rim Guard Inc	G	616 608-7745
Wyoming (G-18031)		

CHEMICALS: Boron Compounds, Not From Mines, NEC

Boropharm Inc	G	248 348-5776
Novi (G-11839)		
Boropharm Inc	G	734 585-0601
Ann Arbor (G-387)		

CHEMICALS: Calcium Chloride

Liquid Dustlayer Inc	G	231 723-3750
Manistee (G-10426)		
Wilkinson Chemical Corporation	F	989 843-6163
Mayville (G-10676)		

CHEMICALS: Chromates & Bichromates

Diazem Corp	G	989 832-3612
Midland (G-10832)		

CHEMICALS: Copper Compounds Or Salts, Inorganic

Koppers Performance Chem Inc	E	906 296-8271
Hubbell (G-8126)		

CHEMICALS: Fire Retardant

Lenderink Inc	F	616 887-8257
Belmont (G-1466)		
R J Marshall Company	E	734 379-4044
Rockwood (G-13611)		

CHEMICALS: Fuel Tank Or Engine Cleaning

American Jetway Corporation	D	734 721-5930
Wayne (G-17423)		
Questron Packaging LLC	G	313 657-1630
Detroit (G-4323)		

Employee Codes: A=Over 500 employees, B=251-500
C=101-250, D=51-100, E=20-50, F=10-19, G=3-9

CHEMICALS: High Purity Grade, Organic

CHEMICALS: High Purity Grade, Organic
Bioelectrica Inc .... G 517 884-4542
  East Lansing (G-4651)
Thumb Bioenergy LLC .... G 810 404-2466
  Sandusky (G-14445)
Tpa Inc .... G 248 302-9131
  Detroit (G-4405)

CHEMICALS: High Purity, Refined From Technical Grade
Chemico Systems Inc .... G 586 986-2343
  Warren (G-16980)
Chemico Systems Inc .... E 248 723-3263
  Southfield (G-14866)
Great Lakes Chemical Services .... E 269 372-6886
  Portage (G-12999)
ICM Products Inc .... E 269 445-0847
  Cassopolis (G-2531)
Nelsonite Chemical Products .... G 616 456-7098
  Grand Rapids (G-6713)

CHEMICALS: Inorganic, NEC
Airgas Usa LLC .... F 517 673-0997
  Blissfield (G-1712)
Albemarle Corporation .... C 269 637-8474
  South Haven (G-14751)
Algoma Products Inc .... F 616 285-6440
  Grand Rapids (G-6157)
Assay Designs Inc .... E 734 214-0923
  Ann Arbor (G-370)
Axchem Inc .... G 734 641-9842
  Wayne (G-17425)
Blue Cube Holding LLC .... E 989 636-1000
  Midland (G-10817)
Cal-Chlor Corp .... E 231 843-1147
  Ludington (G-10051)
Caravan Technologies Inc .... F 313 341-2551
  Detroit (G-3929)
Ceratizit Usa Inc .... C 586 759-2280
  Warren (G-16977)
Chemtrade Chemicals US LLC .... G 313 842-5222
  Detroit (G-3933)
Cytec Industries Inc .... C 269 349-6677
  Kalamazoo (G-8722)
Dando Chemicals US LLC .... G 248 629-9434
  Southfield (G-14878)
Haviland Products Company .... C 616 361-6691
  Grand Rapids (G-6498)
Haviland Products Company .... G 800 456-1134
  Grand Rapids (G-6499)
Henkel US Operations Corp .... C 586 759-5555
  Warren (G-17080)
Henkel US Operations Corp .... B 248 588-1082
  Madison Heights (G-10266)
High-Po-Chlor Inc .... G 734 942-1500
  Ann Arbor (G-490)
Hydro-Zone Inc .... G 734 247-4488
  Brownstown (G-2065)
Icmp Inc .... E 269 445-0847
  Cassopolis (G-2532)
Jade Scientific Inc .... F 734 207-3775
  Westland (G-17572)
Jci Jones Chemicals Inc .... E 734 283-0677
  Wyandotte (G-17963)
Lily Products Michigan Inc .... G 616 245-9193
  Grand Rapids (G-6628)
McGean-Rohco Inc .... E 216 441-4900
  Livonia (G-9832)
Metrex Research LLC .... D 734 947-6700
  Romulus (G-13706)
Nanocerox Inc .... F 734 741-9522
  Ann Arbor (G-569)
Nextcat Inc .... G 248 514-6742
  Birmingham (G-1695)
Nugentec Oilfield Chem LLC .... G 517 518-2712
  Howell (G-8072)
Oerlikon Metco (us) Inc .... E 248 288-0027
  Troy (G-16533)
Pacific Industrial Dev Corp .... D 734 930-9292
  Ann Arbor (G-588)
PVS Chemical Solutions Inc .... G 313 921-1200
  Detroit (G-4318)
Pvs-Nolwood Chemicals Inc .... E 313 921-1200
  Detroit (G-4320)
R L Schmitt Company Inc .... E 734 525-9310
  Livonia (G-9905)
Rap Products Inc .... G 989 893-5583
  Bay City (G-1348)
Sbz Corporation .... G 248 649-1166
  Troy (G-16595)
Silbond Corporation .... E 517 436-3171
  Weston (G-17613)
Solutia Inc .... B 734 676-4400
  Trenton (G-16157)
Specialty Minerals Inc .... F 906 779-9138
  Quinnesec (G-13102)
Transtar Autobody Tech LLC .... C 810 220-3000
  Brighton (G-1999)
United Abrasive Inc .... F 906 563-9249
  Vulcan (G-16846)
Xg Sciences Inc .... G 517 703-1110
  Lansing (G-9437)

CHEMICALS: Medicinal
Degrasyn Biosciences LLC .... G 713 582-3395
  Ann Arbor (G-413)
Solohill Engineering Inc .... F 734 973-2956
  Ann Arbor (G-640)

CHEMICALS: Medicinal, Organic, Uncompounded, Bulk
Pharmacia & Upjohn Company LLC ... D 908 901-8000
  Kalamazoo (G-8849)

CHEMICALS: NEC
Aapharmasyn LLC .... F 734 213-2123
  Ann Arbor (G-337)
American Chem Solutions LLC .... F 231 655-5840
  Muskegon (G-11267)
Bars Products Inc .... E 248 634-8278
  Holly (G-7871)
BASF .... G 231 719-3019
  Muskegon (G-11275)
BASF Corporation .... D 734 591-5560
  Livonia (G-9660)
Bohning Company Ltd .... E 231 229-4247
  Lake City (G-9085)
Bridge Organics Company .... E 269 649-4200
  Vicksburg (G-16831)
Brighton Laboratories Inc .... F 810 225-9520
  Brighton (G-1890)
Cabot Corporation .... E 989 495-2113
  Midland (G-10821)
Caravan Technologies Inc .... F 313 341-2551
  Detroit (G-3929)
Cau Acquisition Company LLC .... D 989 875-8133
  Ithaca (G-8357)
Cayman Chemical Company Inc .... D 734 971-3335
  Ann Arbor (G-395)
Cerco Inc .... E 734 362-8664
  Brownstown Twp (G-2071)
Chem-Trend Holding Inc .... G 517 545-7980
  Howell (G-8021)
Chem-Trend Limited Partnership .... C 517 546-4520
  Howell (G-8022)
Chem-Trend Limited Partnership .... F 517 546-4520
  Howell (G-8023)
Chemetall US Inc .... F 517 787-4846
  Jackson (G-8408)
Covaron Inc .... G 480 298-9433
  Ann Arbor (G-407)
Cows Locomotive Mfg Co .... E 248 583-7150
  Madison Heights (G-10221)
Cummings-Moore Graphite Co .... E 313 841-1615
  Detroit (G-3957)
Cytec Industries Inc .... C 269 349-6677
  Kalamazoo (G-8722)
Diversified Chemical Tech Inc .... C 313 867-5444
  Detroit (G-4011)
Dow Chemical Company .... C 517 439-4400
  Hillsdale (G-7523)
Eastern Oil Company .... E 248 333-1333
  Pontiac (G-12819)
Eftec North America LLC .... D 248 585-2200
  Taylor (G-15713)
H M Products Inc .... G 313 875-5148
  Detroit (G-4109)
Haltermann Carless Us Inc .... G 248 422-6548
  Troy (G-16390)
Haviland Enterprises Inc .... F 616 361-6691
  Grand Rapids (G-6497)
Henkel US Operations Corp .... C 586 759-5555
  Warren (G-17080)
Hercules LLC .... C 269 388-8676
  Kalamazoo (G-8767)
Houghton International Inc .... F 248 641-3231
  Livonia (G-9774)
Jones Chemical Inc .... G 734 283-0677
  Riverview (G-13299)
Khi Coating .... G 248 236-2100
  Oxford (G-12353)
Lymtal International Inc .... E 248 373-8100
  Orion (G-12183)
Macdermid Incorporated .... E 248 437-8161
  New Hudson (G-11547)
McGean-Rohco Inc .... E 216 441-4900
  Livonia (G-9832)
Nanosynthons LLC .... G 989 317-3737
  Mount Pleasant (G-11214)
Nelsonite Chemical Products .... G 616 456-7098
  Grand Rapids (G-6713)
Nof Metal Coatings N Amer Inc .... G 810 966-9240
  Port Huron (G-12949)
Northern Coatings & Chem Co .... E 906 863-2641
  Menominee (G-10753)
Petroleum Environmental Tech .... G 231 258-0400
  Rapid City (G-13110)
Photo Systems Inc .... E 734 424-9625
  Dexter (G-4503)
Pinecrest Industries .... G 269 545-8125
  Galien (G-5819)
Quaker Chemical Corporation .... D 313 931-6910
  Detroit (G-4321)
R J Marshall Company .... F 734 848-5325
  Erie (G-4810)
Ralrube Inc .... G 734 429-0033
  Saline (G-14411)
Rolled Alloys Inc .... D 800 521-0332
  Temperance (G-15842)
Sika Corporation .... D 248 577-0020
  Madison Heights (G-10353)
Smith Wa Inc .... E 313 883-6977
  Detroit (G-4366)
Thetford Corporation .... C 734 769-6000
  Ann Arbor (G-670)
Transtar Autobody Tech LLC .... C 810 220-3000
  Brighton (G-1999)
Varn International Inc .... C 734 781-4600
  Plymouth (G-12785)
Vertellus Hlth Spclty Pdts LLC .... G 616 772-2193
  Zeeland (G-18193)
Wacker Biochem Corporation .... B 517 264-8500
  Adrian (G-102)
Wilbur Products Inc .... F 231 755-3805
  Muskegon (G-11451)

CHEMICALS: Nonmetallic Compounds
I C S Corporation America Inc .... F 616 554-9300
  Grand Rapids (G-6522)

CHEMICALS: Organic, NEC
Aapharmasyn LLC .... F 734 213-2123
  Ann Arbor (G-337)
Advanced Urethanes Inc .... G 313 273-5705
  Detroit (G-3844)
Akzo Nobel Coatings Inc .... D 248 451-6231
  Pontiac (G-12800)
BASF Corporation .... D 810 639-0492
  Montrose (G-11101)
BASF Corporation .... C 734 324-6963
  Wyandotte (G-17947)
BASF Corporation .... G 313 382-4250
  Lincoln Park (G-9573)
BASF Corporation .... C 734 324-6000
  Wyandotte (G-17948)
BASF Corporation .... A 734 324-6100
  Wyandotte (G-17949)
BASF Corporation .... D 734 591-5560
  Livonia (G-9660)
BASF Corporation 248 827-4670
  Southfield (G-14850)
Berry & Associates Inc .... F 734 426-3787
  Dexter (G-4478)
Caravan Technologies Inc .... F 313 341-2551
  Detroit (G-3929)
CJ Chemicals LLC .... F 888 274-1044
  Perry (G-12433)
Clariant Plas Coatings USA LLC .... D 517 629-9101
  Albion (G-120)
Dow Chemical Company .... E 989 638-6571
  Beaverton (G-1384)
Dow Chemical Company .... C 989 496-2246
  Midland (G-10841)
Dow Chemical Company .... C 989 636-2636
  Midland (G-10842)
Dow Chemical Company .... D 989 695-2584
  Freeland (G-5755)

PRODUCT SECTION

Dow Chemical Company .... E 989 638-6441
  Midland *(G-10846)*
Dow Silicones Corporation .... C 989 496-4400
  Midland *(G-10853)*
Dow Silicones Corporation .... C 800 248-2481
  Hemlock *(G-7462)*
Dow Silicones Corporation .... B 989 895-3397
  Bay City *(G-1306)*
Draths Corporation .... E 517 349-0668
  Howell *(G-8035)*
Ecology Coatings .... G 248 723-2223
  Bloomfield *(G-1733)*
Ecovia Renewables Inc .... G 248 953-0594
  Ann Arbor *(G-433)*
Gage Products Company .... D 248 541-3824
  Ferndale *(G-5288)*
Georgia-Pacific LLC .... E 989 348-7275
  Grayling *(G-7107)*
Grm Corporation .... D 989 453-2322
  Pigeon *(G-12489)*
Henkel US Operations Corp .... B 248 588-1082
  Madison Heights *(G-10266)*
Hydrosciences LLC .... G 248 890-8116
  Keego Harbor *(G-8979)*
Metal Mates Inc .... G 248 646-9831
  Beverly Hills *(G-1618)*
Michigan Agricultural Fuel .... G 419 490-6599
  Grand Rapids *(G-6667)*
Microcide Inc .... G 248 526-9663
  Troy *(G-16506)*
Northern Coatings & Chem Co .... E 906 863-2641
  Menominee *(G-10753)*
Pira Testing LLC .... F 517 574-4297
  Lansing *(G-9318)*
Rap Products Inc .... G 989 893-5583
  Bay City *(G-1348)*
Specialty Products Us LLC .... G 989 636-4341
  Midland *(G-10919)*
Twin Ash Frms Organic Proc LLC ...... G 810 404-1943
  Snover *(G-14744)*
Tygrus LLC .... G 248 218-0347
  Troy *(G-16660)*
Vertellus LLC .... C 616 772-2193
  Zeeland *(G-18194)*
Working Bugs LLC .... G 517 203-4744
  East Lansing *(G-4683)*

CHEMICALS: Phenol

Durez Corporation .... C 248 313-7000
  Novi *(G-11874)*

CHEMICALS: Phosphates, Defluorinated/Ammoniated, Exc Fertlr

Freiborne Industries Inc .... E 248 333-2490
  Pontiac *(G-12825)*

CHEMICALS: Reagent Grade, Refined From Technical Grade

Empirical Bioscience Inc .... G 877 479-9949
  Grand Rapids *(G-6377)*

CHEMICALS: Silica Compounds

Alonzo Products Inc .... F 269 445-0847
  Cassopolis *(G-2526)*
Cabot Corporation .... E 989 495-2113
  Midland *(G-10821)*
Inpore Technologies Inc .... G 517 481-2270
  East Lansing *(G-4663)*

CHEMICALS: Tanning Agents, Synthetic Inorganic

Antonios Leather Experts .... G 734 762-5000
  Livonia *(G-9649)*

CHEMICALS: Water Treatment

Antimicrobial Specialist Assoc .... F 989 662-0377
  Auburn *(G-749)*
Aurora Spclty Chemistries Corp .... E 517 372-9121
  Lansing *(G-9344)*
Clearwater Treatment Systems .... G 517 688-9316
  Clarklake *(G-2896)*
Dsw Holdings Inc .... G 313 567-4500
  Detroit *(G-4018)*
Enerco Corporation .... E 517 627-1669
  Grand Ledge *(G-6106)*

Ginsan Liquidating Company LLC ...... D 616 791-8100
  Grand Rapids *(G-6443)*
Great Lakes Treatment Corp .... G 517 566-8008
  Sunfield *(G-15646)*
H-O-H Water Technology Inc .... F 248 669-6667
  Commerce Township *(G-3409)*
Hydro Chem Laboratories Inc .... G 248 348-1737
  Novi *(G-11904)*
N A Suez .... G 734 379-3855
  Rockwood *(G-13609)*
Pressure Vessel Service Inc .... E 313 921-1200
  Detroit *(G-4310)*
Teachout and Associates Inc .... G 269 729-4440
  Athens *(G-729)*

CHESTS: Bank, Metal

Gallatin Tank Works LLC .... G 734 856-5107
  Ottawa Lake *(G-12263)*

CHILD RESTRAINT SEATS, AUTOMOTIVE, WHOLESALE

Amway International Inc .... E 616 787-1000
  Ada *(G-7)*

CHILDREN'S & INFANTS' CLOTHING STORES

Bearcub Outfitters LLC .... F 231 439-9500
  Petoskey *(G-12441)*

CHILDREN'S WEAR STORES

Carters Inc .... G 616 647-9452
  Grand Rapids *(G-6257)*
Sandcastle For Kids Inc .... F 616 396-5955
  Holland *(G-7796)*

CHIMNEY CLEANING SVCS

Doctor Flue Inc .... G 517 423-2832
  Tecumseh *(G-15790)*

CHINA & GLASS REPAIR SVCS

Pristine Glass Company .... G 616 454-2092
  Grand Rapids *(G-6778)*

CHLORINE

Arkema Inc .... C 616 243-4578
  Grand Rapids *(G-6181)*
Kassouni Manufacturing Inc .... G 616 794-0989
  Belding *(G-1423)*
Occidental Chemical Corp .... E 231 845-4411
  Ludington *(G-10075)*

CHOCOLATE, EXC CANDY FROM BEANS: Chips, Powder, Block, Syrup

Gayles Chocolates Limited .... E 248 398-0001
  Royal Oak *(G-13929)*
Kemnitz Fine Candies .... G 734 453-0480
  Plymouth *(G-12665)*
Marshalls Trail Inc .... F 231 436-5082
  Mackinaw City *(G-10099)*
Original Murdicks Fudge Co .... E 906 847-3530
  Mackinac Island *(G-10097)*
Sanders Candy LLC .... D 800 651-7263
  Clinton Township *(G-3221)*
Sugar Free Specialties LLC .... F 616 734-6999
  Comstock Park *(G-3517)*

CHOCOLATE, EXC CANDY FROM PURCH CHOC: Chips, Powder, Block

Rocky Mtn Choclat Fctry Inc .... D 810 606-8550
  Grand Blanc *(G-5981)*
Rocky Mtn Choclat Fctry Inc .... G 989 624-4784
  Birch Run *(G-1669)*

CHRISTMAS NOVELTIES, WHOLESALE

Bronner Display Sign Advg Inc .... C 989 652-9931
  Frankenmuth *(G-5584)*

CHRISTMAS TREE LIGHTING SETS: Electric

Bronner Display Sign Advg Inc .... C 989 652-9931
  Frankenmuth *(G-5584)*

CIRCUITS: Electronic

CHRISTMAS TREES: Artificial

Fruit Haven Nursery Inc .... G 231 889-9973
  Kaleva *(G-8933)*

CHUCKS

Cap Collet & Tool Co Inc .... F 734 283-4040
  Wyandotte *(G-17951)*
Kalamazoo Chuck Mfg Svc Ctr Co ..... F 269 679-2325
  Schoolcraft *(G-14498)*
Magnetic Chuck Services Co Inc .... G 586 822-9441
  Casco *(G-2502)*
Skill-Craft Company Inc .... F 586 716-4300
  Ira *(G-8271)*

CHUTES: Metal Plate

Formrite Inc .... G 517 521-1373
  Webberville *(G-17449)*

CIGARETTE FILTERS

Nodel-Co .... F 248 543-1325
  Ferndale *(G-5306)*

CIGARETTE LIGHTERS

Select Distributors LLC .... F 586 510-4647
  Warren *(G-17237)*

CIRCUIT BOARD REPAIR SVCS

Phillips Service Inds Inc .... F 734 853-5000
  Plymouth *(G-12714)*
PSI Repair Services Inc .... C 734 853-5000
  Livonia *(G-9899)*

CIRCUIT BOARDS, PRINTED: Television & Radio

Hughes Electronics Pdts Corp .... E 734 427-8310
  Livonia *(G-9776)*
Ips Assembly Corp .... F 734 391-0080
  Livonia *(G-9786)*
K & F Electronic Inc .... E 586 294-8720
  Fraser *(G-5677)*
Nu Tek Sales .... F 616 258-0631
  Grand Rapids *(G-6724)*
Saturn Electronics Corp .... C 734 941-8100
  Romulus *(G-13732)*

CIRCUIT BREAKERS

M P Jackson LLC .... E 517 782-0391
  Jackson *(G-8503)*
Mp Hollywood LLC .... F 517 782-0391
  Jackson *(G-8537)*

CIRCUITS, INTEGRATED: Hybrid

Hewtech Electronics .... G 810 765-0820
  China *(G-2860)*

CIRCUITS: Electronic

Adco Circuits Inc .... C 248 853-6620
  Rochester Hills *(G-13363)*
Amptech Inc .... G 231 464-5492
  Manistee *(G-10415)*
Automotive Electronic Spc .... E 248 335-3229
  Bloomfield Hills *(G-1748)*
Aztecnology LLC .... G 734 857-2045
  Southgate *(G-15074)*
Circuits of Sound .... G 313 886-5599
  Grosse Pointe Woods *(G-7201)*
Code Systems Inc .... E 248 307-3884
  Auburn Hills *(G-816)*
Contract People Corporation .... F 248 304-9900
  Southfield *(G-14872)*
Debron Industrial Elec Inc .... E 248 588-7220
  Troy *(G-16300)*
Diversfied Tchncal Systems Inc .... E 248 513-6050
  Novi *(G-11870)*
Ebw Electronics Inc .... E 616 786-0575
  Holland *(G-7616)*
General Motors LLC .... F 931 486-1914
  Warren *(G-17052)*
Ghs Corporation .... B 269 968-3351
  Springfield *(G-15192)*
H and H Electronics .... G 586 725-5412
  Clay *(G-2997)*
Hirschmann Car Comm Inc .... F 248 373-7150
  Auburn Hills *(G-900)*

Employee Codes: A=Over 500 employees, B=251-500
C=101-250, D=51-100, E=20-50, F=10-19, G=3-9

2020 Harris Michigan
Industrial Directory

CIRCUITS: Electronic

Innotec Corp .... D 616 772-5959
  Zeeland *(G-18160)*
Intuitive Circuits LLC .... G 248 588-4400
  Troy *(G-16426)*
Kaydon Corporation .... B 734 747-7025
  Ann Arbor *(G-516)*
Lectronix Inc .... D 517 492-1900
  Lansing *(G-9391)*
Leoni Wiring Systems Inc .... F 586 782-4444
  Warren *(G-17128)*
Liberty Circuits Corporation .... G 269 226-8743
  Kalamazoo *(G-8809)*
Magna Electronics Inc .... E 248 606-0606
  Auburn Hills *(G-934)*
Magna Electronics Inc .... C 248 729-2643
  Auburn Hills *(G-933)*
Magnetech Corporation .... G 248 426-8840
  Novi *(G-11933)*
MAKS INCORPORATED .... E 248 733-9771
  Troy *(G-16484)*
Memtron Technologies Co .... D 989 652-2656
  Frankenmuth *(G-5593)*
Mitech Electronics Corporation .... C 269 694-9471
  Otsego *(G-12246)*
Movellus Circuits Inc .... G 877 321-7667
  Ann Arbor *(G-566)*
Nelson Specialties Company .... F 269 983-1878
  Saint Joseph *(G-14330)*
Nova-Tron Controls Corp .... G 989 358-6126
  Alpena *(G-303)*
Omtron Inc .... G 248 673-3896
  Waterford *(G-17362)*
Photo-Tron Corp .... G 248 852-5200
  Rochester Hills *(G-13493)*
Rockford Contract Mfg .... G 616 304-3837
  Rockford *(G-13587)*
TMC Group Inc .... F 248 819-6063
  Pleasant Ridge *(G-12556)*
Touchstone Systems & Svcs Inc .... G 616 532-0060
  Wyoming *(G-18035)*
Venntis Technologies LLC .... F 616 395-8254
  Holland *(G-7845)*

CIRCULAR KNIT FABRICS DYEING & FINISHING

Circular Motion LLC .... G 989 779-9040
  Mount Pleasant *(G-11188)*

CLAMPS & COUPLINGS: Hose

Aba of America Inc .... F 815 332-5170
  Auburn Hills *(G-759)*
Anchor Coupling Inc .... C 906 863-2672
  Menominee *(G-10722)*
Myrtle Industries Inc .... F 517 784-8579
  Jackson *(G-8540)*
Peterson American Corp .... D 269 279-7421
  Three Rivers *(G-15872)*

CLAMPS: Metal

Dover Energy Inc .... C 248 836-6700
  Auburn Hills *(G-843)*
Five Star Manufacturing Inc .... E 815 723-2245
  Auburn Hills *(G-875)*
Hydra-Zorb Company .... F 248 373-5151
  Auburn Hills *(G-906)*
R G Ray Corporation .... F 248 373-4300
  Auburn Hills *(G-984)*
Souris Enterprises Inc .... F 810 664-2964
  Lapeer *(G-9487)*
Zsi-Foster Inc .... D 734 844-0055
  Canton *(G-2446)*

CLAY PRDTS: Architectural

Architectural Bldg Pdts Inc .... G 248 680-1563
  Troy *(G-16216)*

CLAY: Ground Or Treated

Runyan Pottery Supply Inc .... G 810 687-4500
  Clio *(G-3281)*

CLEANERS: Boiler Tube

L A Burnhart Inc .... G 810 227-4567
  Brighton *(G-1948)*

CLEANING & DESCALING SVC: Metal Prdts

Deburring Company .... F 734 542-9800
  Livonia *(G-9702)*
Grand Rapids Stripping Co .... G 616 361-0794
  Grand Rapids *(G-6464)*
International Paint Stripping .... F 734 942-0500
  Romulus *(G-13687)*
International Paint Stripping .... F 734 942-0500
  Romulus *(G-13688)*
Synthetic Lubricants Inc .... G 616 754-1050
  Greenville *(G-7156)*
Togreencleancom .... G 269 428-4812
  Stevensville *(G-15584)*
WSi Industrial Services Inc .... E 734 942-9300
  Riverview *(G-13307)*

CLEANING COMPOUNDS: Rifle Bore

BV Technology LLC .... G 616 558-1746
  Alto *(G-323)*

CLEANING EQPT: Blast, Dustless

Dee-Blast Corporation .... F 269 428-2400
  Stevensville *(G-15563)*
Progressive Surface Inc .... D 616 957-0871
  Grand Rapids *(G-6786)*
Progressive Surface Inc .... E 616 957-0871
  Grand Rapids *(G-6787)*
Smart Diet Scale LLC .... G 586 383-6734
  Bruce Twp *(G-2102)*
Trinity Tool Co .... E 586 296-5900
  Fraser *(G-5741)*

CLEANING EQPT: Commercial

Creative Products Intl .... F 616 335-3333
  Holland *(G-7600)*
Custom Service & Design Inc .... E 248 340-9005
  Auburn Hills *(G-833)*
Easy Scrub LLC .... G 586 565-1777
  Roseville *(G-13798)*
Geerpres Inc .... E 231 773-3211
  Muskegon *(G-11329)*
Products Engineered Daley .... G 616 748-0162
  Zeeland *(G-18179)*
Tennant Commercial .... B 616 994-4000
  Holland *(G-7826)*
Tennant Company .... G 616 994-4000
  Holland *(G-7827)*

CLEANING EQPT: Dirt Sweeping Units, Indl

Sweepster Attachments LLC .... A 734 996-9116
  Dexter *(G-4512)*

CLEANING EQPT: Floor Washing & Polishing, Commercial

Hines Corporation .... F 231 799-6240
  Norton Shores *(G-11812)*
Pacific Stamex Clg Systems Inc .... E 231 773-1330
  Muskegon *(G-11398)*

CLEANING EQPT: Mop Wringers

Royce Rolls Ringer Company .... E 616 361-9266
  Grand Rapids *(G-6847)*

CLEANING OR POLISHING PREPARATIONS, NEC

All-Chem Corporation .... G 313 865-3600
  Detroit *(G-3857)*
Burge Incorporated .... G 616 791-2214
  Grand Rapids *(G-6242)*
Cal Chemical Manufacturing Co .... G 586 778-7006
  Saint Clair Shores *(G-14242)*
Chemloc Inc .... G 989 465-6541
  Coleman *(G-3342)*
Coastal Concierge .... G 269 639-1515
  South Haven *(G-14757)*
Colonial Chemical Corp .... G 517 789-8161
  Jackson *(G-8415)*
DSC Laboratories Inc .... E 800 492-5988
  Muskegon *(G-11307)*
Enviro-Brite Solutions LLC .... G 989 387-2758
  Oscoda *(G-12209)*
Great Lakes Laboratories Inc .... G 734 525-8300
  Livonia *(G-9760)*
Hydro-Chem Systems Inc .... E 616 531-6420
  Caledonia *(G-2301)*
Innovative Fluids LLC .... F 734 241-5699
  Milan *(G-10941)*
Ipax Atlantic LLC .... F 313 933-4211
  Detroit *(G-4149)*
Ipax Cleanogel Inc .... G 313 933-4211
  Detroit *(G-4150)*
Labtech Corporation .... F 313 862-1737
  Detroit *(G-4190)*
Peerless Quality Products .... F 313 933-7525
  Detroit *(G-4294)*
Progress Chemical Inc .... G 616 534-6103
  Grandville *(G-7067)*
Wilbur Products Inc .... F 231 755-3805
  Muskegon *(G-11451)*

CLEANING PRDTS: Automobile Polish

Rhino Linings of Grand Rapids .... G 616 361-9786
  Grand Rapids *(G-6822)*

CLEANING PRDTS: Bleaches, Household, Dry Or Liquid

Chemetall US Inc .... F 517 787-4846
  Jackson *(G-8408)*
High-Po-Chlor Inc .... G 734 942-1500
  Ann Arbor *(G-490)*

CLEANING PRDTS: Degreasing Solvent

Superior Manufacturing Corp .... F 313 935-1550
  Troy *(G-16627)*

CLEANING PRDTS: Disinfectants, Household Or Indl Plant

Arrow Chemical Products Inc .... E 313 237-0277
  Detroit *(G-3879)*
Cul-Mac Industries Inc .... E 734 728-9700
  Wayne *(G-17429)*

CLEANING PRDTS: Drain Pipe Solvents Or Cleaners

County of Muskegon .... G 231 724-6219
  Muskegon *(G-11301)*
Mr Eds Sewer Cleaning Service .... G 313 565-2740
  Dearborn Heights *(G-3790)*
Rooto Corporation .... F 517 546-8330
  Howell *(G-8093)*

CLEANING PRDTS: Dusting Cloths, Chemically Treated

Anchor Wiping Cloth Inc .... D 313 892-4000
  Detroit *(G-3870)*

CLEANING PRDTS: Floor Waxes

S C Johnson & Son Inc .... F 248 822-2174
  Troy *(G-16587)*
S C Johnson & Son Inc .... C 989 667-0211
  Bay City *(G-1354)*

CLEANING PRDTS: Indl Plant Disinfectants Or Deodorants

Punati Chemical Corp .... F 248 276-0101
  Auburn Hills *(G-983)*

CLEANING PRDTS: Polishing Preparations & Related Prdts

Premiere Packaging Inc .... D 810 239-7650
  Flint *(G-5483)*

CLEANING PRDTS: Rug, Upholstery/Dry Clng Detergents/Spotters

Chemeisters Inc .... G 313 538-5550
  Redford *(G-13152)*

CLEANING PRDTS: Sanitation Preparations

Healthcure LLC .... F 313 743-2331
  Detroit *(G-4119)*
Thetford Corporation .... C 734 769-6000
  Ann Arbor *(G-670)*

PRODUCT SECTION

CLOTHING: Athletic & Sportswear, Women's & Girls'

CLEANING PRDTS: Sanitation Preps, Disinfectants/Deodorants

Odor Gone Inc .... F 888 636-7292
  Zeeland *(G-18172)*

CLEANING PRDTS: Specialty

Able Solutions LLC .... G 810 216-6106
  Port Huron *(G-12880)*
American Jetway Corporation .... D 734 721-5930
  Wayne *(G-17423)*
Bio Kleen Products Inc .... G 269 567-9400
  Kalamazoo *(G-8697)*
Biosolutions LLC .... F 616 846-1210
  Grand Haven *(G-5997)*
Chrysan Industries Inc .... E 734 451-5411
  Plymouth *(G-12597)*
Grav Co LLC .... F 269 651-5467
  Sturgis *(G-15605)*
Liedel Power Cleaning .... F 734 848-2827
  Erie *(G-4805)*
Native Green LLC .... F 248 365-4200
  Orion *(G-12186)*
P & F Enterprises LLC .... G 616 340-1265
  Wyoming *(G-18024)*

CLEANING PRDTS: Window Cleaning Preparations

Diversified Davitco LLC .... F 248 681-9197
  Waterford *(G-17334)*
Southwin Ltd .... E 734 525-9000
  Livonia *(G-9936)*

CLEANING SVCS

Creative Products Intl .... F 616 335-3333
  Holland *(G-7600)*

CLEANING SVCS: Industrial Or Commercial

American Metal Restoration .... G 810 364-4820
  Marysville *(G-10598)*
DNR Inc .... G 734 722-4000
  Plymouth *(G-12613)*
Liedel Power Cleaning .... F 734 848-2827
  Erie *(G-4805)*
Seelye Group Ltd .... G 517 267-2001
  Lansing *(G-9423)*

CLIPS & FASTENERS, MADE FROM PURCHASED WIRE

Automatic Spring Products Corp .... C 616 842-2284
  Grand Haven *(G-5995)*
Industries Unlimited Inc .... E 586 949-4300
  Chesterfield *(G-2788)*
Law Enforcement Supply Inc .... G 616 895-7875
  Allendale *(G-220)*
Ultraform Industries Inc .... D 586 752-4508
  Bruce Twp *(G-2105)*

CLOCKS

Howard Miller Company .... B 616 772-9131
  Zeeland *(G-18154)*
Lumichron Inc .... G 616 245-8888
  Grand Rapids *(G-6637)*
National Time and Signal Corp .... E 248 291-5867
  Oak Park *(G-12087)*
Visual Identification Products .... G 231 941-7272
  Traverse City *(G-16139)*

CLOSURES: Closures, Stamped Metal

Roll Rite Corporation .... E 989 345-3434
  Gladwin *(G-5935)*
Roll-Rite LLC .... E 989 345-3434
  Gladwin *(G-5936)*

CLOSURES: Plastic

Reutter LLC .... G 248 621-9220
  Bingham Farms *(G-1659)*

CLOTHESPINS: Plastic

Dr Schneider Auto Systems Inc .... G 270 858-5400
  Brighton *(G-1912)*

CLOTHING & ACCESS STORES

Northern Screen Printing & EMB ...... G 906 786-0373
  Escanaba *(G-4848)*

CLOTHING & ACCESS, WOMEN, CHILD & INFANT, WHSLE: Sportswear

Heikkinen Productions Inc .... G 734 485-4020
  Ypsilanti *(G-18076)*
Ideal Wholesale Inc .... G 989 873-5850
  Prescott *(G-13080)*

CLOTHING & ACCESS, WOMEN, CHILD/INFANT, WHOLESALE: Child

Carters Inc .... G 616 647-9452
  Grand Rapids *(G-6257)*

CLOTHING & ACCESS, WOMEN, CHILDREN & INFANT, WHOL: Uniforms

Mvp Sports Store .... G 517 764-5165
  Jackson *(G-8539)*

CLOTHING & ACCESS, WOMEN, CHILDREN/INFANT, WHOL: Underwear

Lockett Enterprises LLC .... G 810 407-6644
  Flint *(G-5459)*

CLOTHING & ACCESS: Costumes, Theatrical

Excellent Designs Swimwear .... E 586 977-9140
  Warren *(G-17025)*

CLOTHING & ACCESS: Handicapped

Bioflex Inc .... G 734 327-2946
  Ann Arbor *(G-384)*

CLOTHING & ACCESS: Handkerchiefs, Exc Paper

GLS Enterprises Inc .... G 616 243-2574
  Comstock Park *(G-3482)*

CLOTHING & ACCESS: Men's Miscellaneous Access

Logofit LLC .... E 810 715-1980
  Flint *(G-5461)*

CLOTHING & ACCESS: Regalia

Kalamazoo Regalia Inc .... F 269 344-4299
  Kalamazoo *(G-8797)*

CLOTHING & APPAREL STORES: Custom

Embroidery Products LLC .... G 734 483-0293
  Ypsilanti *(G-18071)*
Hi-Tech Optical Inc .... E 989 799-9390
  Saginaw *(G-14057)*
JS Original Silkscreens LLC .... G 586 779-5456
  Eastpointe *(G-4705)*
Lazer Graphics .... E 269 926-1066
  Benton Harbor *(G-1522)*
Real Love Printwear .... G 248 327-7181
  Southfield *(G-15011)*
Shirt Tails Inc .... G 906 774-3370
  Iron Mountain *(G-8300)*
Tapestry Inc .... F 616 538-5802
  Grandville *(G-7073)*

CLOTHING & FURNISHINGS, MEN'S & BOYS', WHOLESALE: Caps

Gerald Froberg .... G 906 346-3311
  Gwinn *(G-7219)*

CLOTHING & FURNISHINGS, MEN'S & BOYS', WHOLESALE: Uniforms

Elite Arms Inc .... F 734 424-9955
  Chelsea *(G-2709)*
Lamacs Inc .... G 248 643-9210
  Troy *(G-16456)*

CLOTHING & FURNISHINGS, MENS & BOYS, WHOL: Sportswear/Work

Ideal Wholesale Inc .... G 989 873-5850
  Prescott *(G-13080)*

CLOTHING & FURNISHINGS, MENS & BOYS, WHOLESALE: Lined

Reed Sportswear Mfg Co .... E 313 963-7980
  Detroit *(G-4336)*

CLOTHING STORES: Designer Apparel

Bella Sposa Bridal & Prom .... G 616 364-0777
  Grand Rapids *(G-6209)*
Sports Ink Screen Prtg EMB LLC ..... G 231 723-5696
  Manistee *(G-10437)*

CLOTHING STORES: Formal Wear

Celebrations .... G 906 482-4946
  Hancock *(G-7250)*

CLOTHING STORES: Shirts, Custom Made

MHR Investments Inc .... F 989 832-5395
  Midland *(G-10884)*

CLOTHING STORES: T-Shirts, Printed, Custom

Adams Shirt Shack Inc .... G 269 964-3323
  Battle Creek *(G-1137)*
Christman Screenprint Inc .... F 800 962-9330
  Springfield *(G-15189)*
Graphics Unlimited Inc .... G 231 773-2696
  Muskegon *(G-11336)*

CLOTHING STORES: Unisex

Custom Giant LLC .... G 313 799-2085
  Southfield *(G-14875)*
Mopega LLC .... G 231 631-2580
  Traverse City *(G-16044)*

CLOTHING STORES: Work

RPC Company .... F 989 752-3618
  Saginaw *(G-14134)*

CLOTHING: Access

Bond Manufacturing LLC .... G 313 671-0799
  Detroit *(G-3909)*
Davis Girls .... G 586 781-6865
  Shelby Township *(G-14572)*
Fabjunky LLC .... G 323 572-4988
  Muskegon *(G-11319)*
Museum Apparel .... G 248 644-2303
  Bloomfield Hills *(G-1785)*
Retro-A-Go-go LLC .... G 734 476-0300
  Howell *(G-8090)*
Superfly Manufacturing Co .... F 313 454-1492
  Farmington *(G-4913)*

CLOTHING: Access, Women's & Misses'

Brintley Enterprises .... G 248 991-4086
  Detroit *(G-3918)*

CLOTHING: Athletic & Sportswear, Men's & Boys'

Harvard Clothing Company .... F 517 542-2986
  Litchfield *(G-9602)*
J America LLC .... E 517 521-2525
  Webberville *(G-17451)*
Traverse Bay Manufacturing Inc .... D 231 264-8111
  Elk Rapids *(G-4781)*
Van Boven Incorporated .... G 734 665-7228
  Ann Arbor *(G-690)*
Vega Manufacturing LLC .... G 231 668-6365
  Traverse City *(G-16136)*
Vetta LLC .... G 517 521-2525
  Webberville *(G-17455)*

CLOTHING: Athletic & Sportswear, Women's & Girls'

Baa Baa Zuzu .... G 231 256-7176
  Lake Leelanau *(G-9100)*

CLOTHING: Athletic & Sportswear, Women's & Girls'

Cliff Keen Wrestling Pdts Inc .... E 734 975-8800
  Ann Arbor *(G-401)*
Moxies Boutique LLC .... G 269 983-4273
  Saint Joseph *(G-14329)*
Natural Attraction .... G 231 398-0787
  Manistee *(G-10432)*
Reed Sportswear Mfg Co .... G 313 963-7980
  Detroit *(G-4337)*

CLOTHING: Baker, Barber, Lab/Svc Ind Apparel, Washable, Men

Tha Shopp LLC .... G 734 231-9991
  Ypsilanti *(G-18105)*

CLOTHING: Bathing Suits & Swimwear, Knit

M Den On Main .... G 734 761-1030
  Ann Arbor *(G-537)*

CLOTHING: Beachwear, Knit

Sb3 LLC .... G 877 978-6286
  Ada *(G-29)*

CLOTHING: Belts

Vega Manufacturing LLC .... G 231 668-6365
  Traverse City *(G-16136)*

CLOTHING: Blouses, Women's & Girls'

Peckham Vocational Inds Inc .... A 517 316-4000
  Lansing *(G-9252)*
Peckham Vocational Inds Inc .... C 517 316-4478
  Lansing *(G-9253)*

CLOTHING: Brassieres

Busted Bra Shop LLC .... G 313 288-0449
  Detroit *(G-3921)*
Shefit Inc .... F 616 209-7003
  Hudsonville *(G-8182)*

CLOTHING: Children's, Girls'

Carters Inc .... G 616 647-9452
  Grand Rapids *(G-6257)*
Mossworld Enterprises Inc .... G 248 828-7460
  Oakland *(G-12107)*

CLOTHING: Coats & Jackets, Leather & Sheep-Lined

Lee-Cobb Company .... G 269 553-0873
  Kalamazoo *(G-8808)*
Reed Sportswear Mfg Co .... E 313 963-7980
  Detroit *(G-4336)*

CLOTHING: Coats & Suits, Men's & Boys'

Baryames Tux Shop Inc .... G 517 349-6555
  Okemos *(G-12116)*
Peckham Vocational Inds Inc .... A 517 316-4000
  Lansing *(G-9252)*
Peckham Vocational Inds Inc .... C 517 316-4478
  Lansing *(G-9253)*

CLOTHING: Costumes

Gags and Games Inc .... E 734 591-1717
  Livonia *(G-9747)*
Lewmar Custom Designs Inc .... G 586 677-5135
  Shelby Township *(G-14626)*

CLOTHING: Culottes & Shorts, Children's

Just Girls LLC .... G 248 952-1967
  Troy *(G-16441)*

CLOTHING: Disposable

Mopega LLC .... G 231 631-2580
  Traverse City *(G-16044)*

CLOTHING: Dresses

G-III Apparel Group Ltd .... C 248 332-4922
  Auburn Hills *(G-879)*
Runway Liquidation LLC .... G 989 624-4756
  Birch Run *(G-1670)*

CLOTHING: Furs

Practical Solar .... G 586 864-6686
  Saint Clair Shores *(G-14267)*

CLOTHING: Garments, Indl, Men's & Boys

Vega Manufacturing LLC .... G 231 668-6365
  Traverse City *(G-16136)*

CLOTHING: Gowns & Dresses, Wedding

Demmem Enterprises LLC .... F 810 564-9500
  Clio *(G-3269)*
White Dress The LLC .... G 810 588-6147
  Brighton *(G-2009)*

CLOTHING: Hats & Caps, NEC

Bahama Souvenirs Inc .... G 269 964-8275
  Battle Creek *(G-1149)*

CLOTHING: Hosiery, Anklets

Grandview Foot & Ankle .... G 989 584-3916
  Carson City *(G-2489)*

CLOTHING: Hospital, Men's

Shoulders LLC .... G 248 843-1536
  Pontiac *(G-12865)*

CLOTHING: Jeans, Men's & Boys'

Guess Inc .... F 517 546-2933
  Howell *(G-8046)*

CLOTHING: Men's & boy's underwear & nightwear

Harrys Meme LLC .... G 248 977-0168
  Novi *(G-11897)*

CLOTHING: Outerwear, Lthr, Wool/Down-Filled, Men, Youth/Boy

Carhartt Inc .... B 313 271-8460
  Dearborn *(G-3686)*

CLOTHING: Outerwear, Women's & Misses' NEC

Clean Clothes Inc .... G 734 482-4000
  Dexter *(G-4482)*
Guess Inc .... F 517 546-2933
  Howell *(G-8046)*
Harvard Clothing Company .... F 517 542-2986
  Litchfield *(G-9602)*
Hemp Global Products Inc .... G 616 617-6476
  Holland *(G-7661)*
Otter Company .... G 248 566-3235
  Troy *(G-16539)*
Peckham Vocational Inds Inc .... A 517 316-4000
  Lansing *(G-9252)*
Pvh Corp .... E 989 624-5575
  Birch Run *(G-1667)*
Tall City LLC .... G 248 854-0713
  Auburn Hills *(G-1013)*
Traverse Bay Manufacturing Inc .... D 231 264-8111
  Elk Rapids *(G-4781)*

CLOTHING: Overalls & Coveralls

Carhartt Inc .... B 313 271-8460
  Dearborn *(G-3686)*

CLOTHING: Shirts

Pvh Corp .... G 989 345-7939
  West Branch *(G-17517)*

CLOTHING: Shirts & T-Shirts, Knit

T-Shirt World .... G 313 387-2023
  Redford *(G-13199)*

CLOTHING: Shirts, Dress, Men's & Boys'

Pvh Corp .... G 989 624-5651
  Birch Run *(G-1668)*

CLOTHING: Socks

5 Water Socks LLC .... G 248 735-1730
  Northville *(G-11674)*
Argyle Socks LLC .... G 269 615-0097
  Kalamazoo *(G-8683)*
Bold Endeavors LLC .... G 616 389-3902
  Wyoming *(G-17988)*
Skechers USA Inc .... F 989 624-9336
  Birch Run *(G-1672)*
Socks & Associates Development .... G 231 421-5150
  Traverse City *(G-16108)*
Socks Galore Wholesale Inc .... G 248 545-7625
  Oak Park *(G-12099)*
Socks Kick LLC .... G 231 222-2402
  East Jordan *(G-4645)*
Soyad Brothers Textile Corp .... E 586 755-5700
  Fraser *(G-5726)*
Turbosocks Performance .... G 586 864-3252
  Shelby Township *(G-14712)*

CLOTHING: Sportswear, Women's

St John .... G 313 576-8212
  Detroit *(G-4372)*
St John .... G 313 499-4065
  Grosse Pointe Park *(G-7196)*

CLOTHING: Sweatshirts & T-Shirts, Men's & Boys'

Zemis 5 LLC .... G 317 946-7015
  Detroit *(G-4457)*

CLOTHING: Swimwear, Men's & Boys'

Avidasports LLC .... G 313 447-5670
  Harper Woods *(G-7299)*

CLOTHING: Swimwear, Women's & Misses'

Excellent Designs Swimwear .... E 586 977-9140
  Warren *(G-17025)*

CLOTHING: T-Shirts & Tops, Knit

Fuzzybutz .... G 269 983-9663
  Saint Joseph *(G-14311)*
Wickedglow Industries Inc .... G 586 776-4132
  Mount Clemens *(G-11154)*

CLOTHING: Tights & Leg Warmers

Warmerscom .... G 800 518-0938
  Byron Center *(G-2216)*

CLOTHING: Uniforms, Firemen's, From Purchased Materials

Priority One Emergency Inc .... G 734 398-5900
  Canton *(G-2419)*
SM Smith Co .... G 906 774-8258
  Kingsford *(G-9066)*

CLOTHING: Uniforms, Men's & Boys'

Allie Brothers Inc .... F 248 477-4434
  Livonia *(G-9635)*
P & D Uniforms and ACC Inc .... G 313 881-3881
  Eastpointe *(G-4708)*

CLOTHING: Uniforms, Team Athletic

Cliff Keen Wrestling Pdts Inc .... E 734 975-8800
  Ann Arbor *(G-401)*
Graphic Gear Inc .... G 734 283-3864
  Lincoln Park *(G-9579)*

CLOTHING: Uniforms, Work

P & D Uniforms and ACC Inc .... G 313 881-3881
  Eastpointe *(G-4708)*

CLOTHING: Vests, Sport, Suede, Leatherette, Etc, Mens & Boys

Kinder Company Inc .... G 810 240-3065
  Mount Morris *(G-11163)*

CLOTHING: Work, Men's

Acme Mills Company .... C 517 437-8940
  Hillsdale *(G-7513)*
Carhartt Inc .... G 517 282-4193
  Dewitt *(G-4461)*
Gerald Froberg .... G 906 346-3311
  Gwinn *(G-7219)*

PRODUCT SECTION

COATING SVC: Metals & Formed Prdts

Peckham Vocational Inds Inc..............A....... 517 316-4000
  Lansing *(G-9252)*
Traverse Bay Manufacturing Inc..........D....... 231 264-8111
  Elk Rapids *(G-4781)*

CLOTHS: Dust, Made From Purchased Materials

K and J Absorbent Products LLC ....G....... 517 486-3110
  Blissfield *(G-1716)*

CLUTCHES OR BRAKES: Electromagnetic

American Brake and Clutch Inc............F....... 586 948-3730
  Chesterfield *(G-2736)*

CLUTCHES, EXC VEHICULAR

Altra Industrial Motion Corp ....D....... 586 758-5000
  Warren *(G-16925)*
Formsprag LLC ....C....... 586 758-5000
  Warren *(G-17043)*
Friction Control LLC ....G....... 586 741-8493
  Clinton Township *(G-3127)*
Great Lakes Industry Inc ....E....... 517 784-3153
  Jackson *(G-8459)*
S R P Inc ....D....... 517 784-3153
  Jackson *(G-8568)*

COAL MINING SERVICES

Peak Manufacturing Inc........................E....... 517 769-6900
  Pleasant Lake *(G-12553)*

COAL MINING: Bituminous Coal & Lignite-Surface Mining

Lotus International Company ....A....... 734 245-0140
  Canton *(G-2394)*
Silver Slate LLC ....E....... 248 486-3989
  Milford *(G-10985)*

COAL, MINERALS & ORES, WHOLESALE: Coal

Arbor Stone ....G....... 517 750-1340
  Spring Arbor *(G-15119)*

COATED OR PLATED PRDTS

Euridium Solutions LLC ....G....... 248 535-7005
  Troy *(G-16353)*

COATING SVC

A2z Coating ....G....... 616 805-3281
  Grand Rapids *(G-6127)*
Adrian Coatings Company ....E....... 517 438-8699
  Adrian *(G-43)*
Custom Anything LLC ....G....... 231 282-1981
  Stanwood *(G-15233)*
Custom Powder Coating LLC ....G....... 616 454-9730
  Grand Rapids *(G-6325)*
Eisele Connectors Inc ....G....... 616 726-7714
  Grand Rapids *(G-6370)*
Modineer Coatings Division.................G....... 269 925-0702
  Benton Harbor *(G-1531)*
Nano Materials & Processes Inc..........G....... 248 529-3873
  Milford *(G-10974)*
Protective Ctngs Epoxy Systems.........G....... 517 223-1192
  Fowlerville *(G-5577)*
Schmidt Grinding.................................G....... 269 649-4604
  Vicksburg *(G-16843)*

COATING SVC: Aluminum, Metal Prdts

Permacoat Inc ....F....... 313 388-7798
  Allen Park *(G-204)*
Reliance Finishing Co ....D....... 616 241-4436
  Grand Rapids *(G-6818)*

COATING SVC: Electrodes

Csquared Innovations Inc ....F....... 734 998-8330
  Novi *(G-11860)*

COATING SVC: Hot Dip, Metals Or Formed Prdts

Voigt & Schweitzer LLC ....E....... 313 535-2600
  Redford *(G-13206)*
Voigt Schwtzer Galvanizers Inc ....D....... 313 535-2600
  Redford *(G-13207)*

COATING SVC: Metals & Formed Prdts

Aactron Inc..E....... 248 543-6740
  Madison Heights *(G-10177)*
AB Custom Fabricating LLC................E....... 269 663-8100
  Edwardsburg *(G-4756)*
Action Asphalt LLC ....F....... 734 449-8565
  Whitmore Lake *(G-17684)*
Ajax Metal Processing Inc...................G....... 313 267-2100
  Detroit *(G-3850)*
Alpha Coatings Inc ....E....... 734 523-9000
  Livonia *(G-9636)*
Anchor Bay Powder Coat LLC.............F....... 586 725-3255
  New Baltimore *(G-11480)*
Applied Coatings Solutions LLC ....G....... 269 341-9757
  Kalamazoo *(G-8680)*
Aristo-Cote Inc....................................D....... 586 447-9049
  Fraser *(G-5622)*
Aristo-Cote Inc....................................E....... 586 336-9421
  Harrison Township *(G-7321)*
August Lighting Inc ....G....... 616 895-4951
  Zeeland *(G-18115)*
Beech & Rich Inc.................................E....... 269 968-8012
  Springfield *(G-15188)*
Bio-Vac Inc..E....... 248 350-2150
  Southfield *(G-14853)*
Bolyea Industries.................................F....... 586 293-8600
  Fraser *(G-5631)*
Burkard Industries Inc.........................C....... 586 791-6520
  Clinton Township *(G-3070)*
Carbide Surface Company ....G....... 586 465-6110
  Clinton Township *(G-3075)*
Cast Coatings Inc ....E....... 269 545-8373
  Galien *(G-5817)*
Coatings Plus Inc ....E....... 616 451-2427
  Grand Rapids *(G-6284)*
Commercial Steel Treating Corp ....D....... 248 588-3300
  Madison Heights *(G-10217)*
Cox Brothers Machining Inc ....E....... 517 796-4662
  Jackson *(G-8422)*
Custom Coating Technologies ....G....... 734 244-3610
  Flat Rock *(G-5352)*
Decc Company Inc..............................E....... 616 245-0431
  Grand Rapids *(G-6341)*
Eagle Powder Coating ....E....... 517 784-2556
  Jackson *(G-8437)*
Electro Chemical Finishing Co.............F....... 616 531-0670
  Wyoming *(G-17999)*
Engineered Prfmce Coatings Inc.........G....... 616 988-7927
  Grand Rapids *(G-6379)*
Evans Coatings L L C ....G....... 248 583-9890
  Troy *(G-16354)*
Fastener Coatings Inc ....F....... 269 279-5134
  Three Rivers *(G-15861)*
Finishing Services Inc ....C....... 734 484-1700
  Ypsilanti *(G-18073)*
Fricia Enterprises Inc ....G....... 586 977-1900
  Sterling Heights *(G-15348)*
Grand Haven Powder Coating Inc........E....... 616 850-8822
  Grand Haven *(G-6023)*
Great Lakes Powder Coating LLC ....F....... 248 522-6222
  Walled Lake *(G-16894)*
Gyro Powder Coating Inc....................F....... 616 846-2580
  Grand Haven *(G-6030)*
Hice and Summey Inc.........................F....... 269 651-6217
  Bronson *(G-2030)*
Howmet Corporation............................F....... 231 981-3000
  Whitehall *(G-17673)*
Howmet Corporation............................E....... 231 894-5686
  Whitehall *(G-17669)*
Howmet Holdings Corporation.............G....... 231 894-5686
  Whitehall *(G-17676)*
I S P Coatings Corp ....E....... 586 752-5020
  Romeo *(G-13630)*
Integricoat Inc......................................E....... 616 935-7878
  Spring Lake *(G-15154)*
Jackson Industrial Coating Svc............G....... 517 782-8169
  Jackson *(G-8477)*
JD Plating Company Inc......................E....... 248 547-5200
  Madison Heights *(G-10283)*
Kalb & Associates Inc ....E....... 586 949-2735
  Chesterfield *(G-2793)*
KC Jones Plating Co............................E....... 586 755-4900
  Warren *(G-17119)*
Kentwood Powder Coat Inc ....E....... 616 698-8181
  Grand Rapids *(G-6580)*
Lampco Manufacturing Company ....G....... 517 784-4393
  Jackson *(G-8495)*
Liberty Bell Powdr Coating LLC ....G....... 586 557-6328
  Lincoln Park *(G-9581)*
Magna Extrors Intrors Amer Inc ....G....... 616 786-7000
  Kentwood *(G-9018)*
Magnum Powder Coating Inc..............G....... 616 785-3155
  Comstock Park *(G-3495)*
Master Coat LLC ....F....... 734 405-2340
  Westland *(G-17578)*
Metal Finishing Technology ....E....... 231 733-9736
  Muskegon *(G-11376)*
Michigan Metal Coatings Co ....D....... 810 966-9240
  Port Huron *(G-12942)*
Mirrage Ltd ....F....... 734 697-6447
  Van Buren Twp *(G-16773)*
Monarch Powder Coating Inc..............G....... 231 798-1422
  Norton Shores *(G-11775)*
Motor City Metal Fab Inc ....E....... 734 345-1001
  Taylor *(G-15747)*
MSC Pre Finish Metals Egv Inc...........G....... 734 207-4400
  Canton *(G-2409)*
N O F Metal Coatings N Amer ....G....... 248 228-8610
  Southfield *(G-14988)*
ND Industries Inc ....E....... 248 288-0000
  Troy *(G-16522)*
ND Industries Inc ....C....... 248 288-0000
  Clawson *(G-2982)*
Oerlikon Blzers Cating USA Inc...........E....... 248 409-5900
  Lake Orion *(G-9154)*
Oerlikon Blzers Cating USA Inc...........E....... 586 465-0412
  Harrison Township *(G-7342)*
Oerlikon Blzers Cating USA Inc...........E....... 248 960-9055
  Wixom *(G-17873)*
Oerlikon Blzers Cating USA Inc...........E....... 989 362-3515
  East Tawas *(G-4691)*
P C S Companies Inc..........................G....... 616 754-2229
  Greenville *(G-7149)*
Peninsula Powder Coating Inc ....E....... 906 353-7234
  Baraga *(G-1112)*
Performcoat of Michigan LLC..............F....... 269 282-7030
  Springfield *(G-15200)*
Plasma-Tec Inc....................................E....... 616 455-2593
  Wayland *(G-17409)*
Plasti - Paint Inc..................................C....... 989 285-2280
  Saint Louis *(G-14368)*
Powco Inc ....F....... 269 646-5385
  Marcellus *(G-10467)*
Powder Cote II Inc...............................C....... 586 463-7040
  Mount Clemens *(G-11145)*
Powder Cote II Inc...............................G....... 586 463-7040
  Mount Clemens *(G-11146)*
PPG Coating Services ....E....... 586 575-9800
  Troy *(G-16556)*
PPG Coating Services ....D....... 734 421-7300
  Livonia *(G-9894)*
Precision Coatings Inc ....D....... 248 363-8361
  Commerce Township *(G-3440)*
Pro-Finish Powder Coating Inc............E....... 616 245-7550
  Grand Rapids *(G-6781)*
Richcoat LLC ....E....... 586 978-1311
  Sterling Heights *(G-15468)*
Richter Precision Inc ....E....... 586 465-0500
  Fraser *(G-5718)*
Sas Global Corporation ....C....... 248 414-4470
  Warren *(G-17229)*
Seaver Industrial Finishing Co ....D....... 616 842-8560
  Grand Haven *(G-6074)*
Serma Coat LLC ....F....... 810 229-0829
  Brighton *(G-1988)*
Spraytek Inc...F....... 248 546-3551
  Ferndale *(G-5319)*
Stechschulte/Wegerly AG LLC ....F....... 586 739-0101
  Sterling Heights *(G-15510)*
Sun Plastics Coating Company ....F....... 734 453-0822
  Plymouth *(G-12762)*
Superior Mtal Finshg Rustproof ....F....... 313 893-1050
  Detroit *(G-4388)*
Tawas Powder Coating Inc..................E....... 989 362-2011
  Tawas City *(G-15684)*
TEC International II ....G....... 248 724-1800
  Auburn Hills *(G-1014)*
Techno-Coat Inc..................................C....... 616 396-6446
  Holland *(G-7824)*
Thierica Inc..D....... 616 458-1538
  Grand Rapids *(G-6926)*
Ti-Coating Inc.......................................E....... 586 726-1900
  Shelby Township *(G-14709)*
Toefco Engineering Inc ....E....... 269 683-0188
  Niles *(G-11649)*
Unicote Corporation ....E....... 586 296-0075
  Fraser *(G-5743)*
Universal Coating Inc ....D....... 810 785-7555
  Flint *(G-5518)*

Employee Codes: A=Over 500 employees, B=251-500
C=101-250, D=51-100, E=20-50, F=10-19, G=3-9

2020 Harris Michigan Industrial Directory

1185

COATING SVC: Metals & Formed Prdts

Universal Coating Technology ....G...... 616 847-6036
  Grand Haven *(G-6092)*
Wealthy Street Corporation ....C...... 616 451-0784
  Grand Rapids *(G-6980)*
West Michigan Coating LLC ....E...... 616 647-9509
  Grand Rapids *(G-6986)*
X-Cel Industries Inc ....C...... 248 226-6000
  Southfield *(G-15067)*
Z Technologies Corporation ....E...... 313 937-0710
  Redford *(G-13209)*

COATING SVC: Metals, With Plastic Or Resins

C & M Coatings Inc ....F...... 616 842-1925
  Grand Haven *(G-5999)*
Dunnage Engineering Inc ....E...... 810 229-9501
  Brighton *(G-1913)*
Expert Coating Company Inc ....F...... 616 453-8261
  Grand Rapids *(G-6393)*
Godfrey & Wing Inc ....G...... 330 562-1440
  Saginaw *(G-14047)*
Instacote Inc ....G...... 734 847-5260
  Erie *(G-4804)*
Mdm Enterprises Inc ....F...... 616 452-1591
  Grand Rapids *(G-6655)*
PDM Industries Inc ....E...... 231 943-9601
  Traverse City *(G-6393)*
Simmons & Courtright Plastic ....G...... 616 365-0045
  Grand Rapids *(G-6866)*
Sure-Weld & Plating Rack Co ....G...... 248 304-9430
  Southfield *(G-15040)*

COATING SVC: Rust Preventative

Albah Manufacturing Tech Corp ....E...... 519 972-7222
  Troy *(G-16182)*
Cadillac Oil Company ....F...... 313 365-6200
  Detroit *(G-3926)*
Depor Industries Inc ....G...... 248 362-3900
  Troy *(G-16313)*
Magni Group Inc ....F...... 248 647-4500
  Birmingham *(G-1690)*
Master Mix Company ....F...... 734 487-7870
  Ypsilanti *(G-18089)*

COATING SVC: Silicon

Midland Silicon Company LLC ....F...... 248 674-3736
  Waterford *(G-17358)*

COATINGS: Epoxy

Creative Surfaces Inc ....F...... 586 226-2950
  Clinton Township *(G-3092)*
Epoxy Pro Flr Ctngs Rstoration ....G...... 248 990-8890
  Shelby Township *(G-14590)*
Gougeon Holding Co ....G...... 989 684-7286
  Bay City *(G-1317)*
Simiron Inc ....E...... 248 585-7500
  Madison Heights *(G-10354)*
Specialty Coatings Inc ....F...... 586 294-8343
  Fraser *(G-5729)*
Supreme Media Blasting and Pow ....G...... 586 792-7705
  Clinton Township *(G-3259)*
West System Inc ....E...... 989 684-7286
  Bay City *(G-1370)*

COATINGS: Polyurethane

Innovative Engineering Mich ....G...... 517 977-0460
  Lansing *(G-9236)*
Innovative Polymers Inc ....F...... 989 224-9500
  Saint Johns *(G-14284)*
Lancast Urethane Inc ....G...... 517 485-6070
  Commerce Township *(G-3419)*
Lymtal International Inc ....E...... 248 373-8100
  Orion *(G-12183)*
Marshall Ryerson Co ....F...... 616 299-1751
  Grand Rapids *(G-6645)*
Sun Chemical Corporation ....F...... 513 681-5950
  Muskegon *(G-11431)*

COCKTAIL LOUNGE

Kennedys Irish Pub Inc ....G...... 248 681-1050
  Waterford *(G-17354)*

COFFEE SVCS

Prospectors LLC ....G...... 616 634-8260
  Grand Rapids *(G-6792)*

Shay Water Co Inc ....E...... 989 755-3221
  Saginaw *(G-14148)*

COILS & TRANSFORMERS

Controlled Power Company ....C...... 248 528-3700
  Troy *(G-16281)*
Ford Motor Company ....A...... 734 484-8000
  Ypsilanti *(G-18074)*
H W Jencks Incorporated ....E...... 231 352-4422
  Frankfort *(G-5603)*
Heco Inc ....D...... 269 381-7200
  Kalamazoo *(G-8762)*
Induction Engineering Inc ....F...... 586 716-4700
  New Baltimore *(G-11486)*
Osborne Transformer Corp ....F...... 586 218-6900
  Fraser *(G-5702)*
Techna Systems Inc ....G...... 248 681-1717
  Orchard Lake *(G-12171)*

COILS: Electric Motors Or Generators

Magnetech Corporation ....G...... 248 426-8840
  Novi *(G-11933)*

COILS: Pipe

Alternative Components LLC ....E...... 586 755-9177
  Warren *(G-16924)*
Lapine Metal Products Inc ....F...... 269 388-5900
  Kalamazoo *(G-8805)*

COLLETS

Acg Services Inc ....G...... 586 232-4698
  Shelby Township *(G-14540)*
B C I Collet Inc ....E...... 734 326-1222
  Westland *(G-17546)*
Tru Point Corporation ....G...... 313 897-9100
  Detroit *(G-4409)*
Wyandotte Collet and Tool Inc ....F...... 734 283-8055
  Wyandotte *(G-17982)*

COLOR LAKES OR TONERS

Mis Associates Inc ....G...... 844 225-8156
  Pontiac *(G-12850)*

COLORING & FINISHING SVC: Aluminum Or Formed Prdts

Great Lakes Metal Finshg LLC ....E...... 517 764-1335
  Jackson *(G-8460)*
Spencer Zdanowitz Inc ....G...... 517 841-9380
  Jackson *(G-8575)*

COLORS: Pigments, Inorganic

Alloying Surfaces Inc ....G...... 248 524-9200
  Troy *(G-16191)*
Douglas Corp ....F...... 517 767-4112
  Tekonsha *(G-15818)*
Oerlikon Metco (us) Inc ....E...... 248 288-0027
  Troy *(G-16533)*
Sun Chemical Corporation ....C...... 231 788-2371
  Muskegon *(G-11432)*

COLORS: Pigments, Organic

Aubio Life Sciences LLC ....G...... 561 289-1888
  Wixom *(G-17767)*
Chromatech Inc ....F...... 734 451-1230
  Canton *(G-2361)*
Flint CPS Inks North Amer LLC ....G...... 734 781-4600
  Plymouth *(G-12621)*
Flint Group US LLC ....B...... 734 781-4600
  Livonia *(G-9740)*

COLUMNS: Concrete

Quality Way Products LLC ....F...... 248 634-2401
  Holly *(G-7891)*

COMMERCIAL & OFFICE BUILDINGS RENOVATION & REPAIR

Flor TEC Inc ....G...... 616 897-3122
  Lowell *(G-10028)*
S & B Roofing Services Inc ....D...... 248 334-5372
  Pontiac *(G-12863)*
Sterling Millwork Inc ....D...... 248 427-1400
  Farmington Hills *(G-5131)*

COMMERCIAL ART & GRAPHIC DESIGN SVCS

5 Pyn Inc ....G...... 906 228-2828
  Negaunee *(G-11466)*
A-1 Signs ....G...... 269 488-9411
  Portage *(G-12980)*
Agnew Grphics Signs Promotions ....G...... 989 723-4621
  Owosso *(G-12276)*
American Reprographics Co LLC ....E...... 248 299-8900
  Clawson *(G-2973)*
Ar2 Engineering LLC ....E...... 248 735-9999
  Novi *(G-11829)*
Art In Transit Inc ....G...... 248 585-5566
  Troy *(G-16217)*
C H M Graphics & Litho Inc ....G...... 586 777-4550
  Saint Clair Shores *(G-14241)*
Danmark Graphics LLC ....G...... 616 675-7499
  Casnovia *(G-2507)*
Domer Industries LLC ....F...... 269 226-4000
  Kalamazoo *(G-8731)*
Exclusive Imagery Inc ....E...... 248 436-2999
  Royal Oak *(G-13927)*
Fedex Office & Print Svcs Inc ....E...... 586 296-4890
  Roseville *(G-13803)*
Fusion Design Group Ltd ....G...... 269 469-8226
  New Buffalo *(G-11514)*
Iris Design & Print Inc ....G...... 313 277-0505
  Dearborn *(G-3727)*
Kent Communications Inc ....D...... 616 957-2120
  Grand Rapids *(G-6575)*
Lake Michigan Mailers Inc ....D...... 269 383-9333
  Kalamazoo *(G-8804)*
Lazer Graphics ....E...... 269 926-1066
  Benton Harbor *(G-1522)*
Mogul Minds LLC ....G...... 682 217-9506
  Wayne *(G-17438)*
Print Masters Inc ....F...... 248 548-7100
  Madison Heights *(G-10339)*
Sans Serif Inc ....G...... 734 944-1190
  Saline *(G-14414)*
Shelby Signarama Township ....G...... 586 843-3702
  Shelby Township *(G-14693)*
Sign Center of Kalamazoo Inc ....G...... 269 381-6869
  Kalamazoo *(G-8889)*
Star Design Metro Detroit LLC ....E...... 734 740-0189
  Livonia *(G-9944)*
Steel Skinz LLC ....G...... 517 545-9955
  Howell *(G-8103)*
Vision Designs Inc ....G...... 616 994-7054
  Holland *(G-7848)*
Wallace Studios LLC ....G...... 248 917-2459
  Southfield *(G-15065)*
Whiteside Consulting Group LLC ....G...... 313 288-6598
  Detroit *(G-4440)*
Word Baron Inc ....F...... 248 471-4080
  Ann Arbor *(G-702)*

COMMERCIAL ART & ILLUSTRATION SVCS

Northern Michig ....F...... 989 340-1272
  Lachine *(G-9076)*

COMMERCIAL CONTAINERS WHOLESALERS

Associated Metals Inc ....G...... 734 369-3851
  Ann Arbor *(G-371)*

COMMERCIAL EQPT WHOLESALERS, NEC

Bay Plastics Machinery Co LLC ....E...... 989 671-9630
  Bay City *(G-1288)*
Taylor Freezer Michigan Inc ....F...... 616 453-0531
  Grand Rapids *(G-6916)*

COMMERCIAL EQPT, WHOLESALE: Bakery Eqpt & Splys

Dawn Equipment Company Inc ....C...... 517 789-4500
  Jackson *(G-8427)*
Dawn Food Products Inc ....C...... 517 789-4400
  Jackson *(G-8429)*
Dawn Foods Inc ....C...... 517 789-4400
  Jackson *(G-8430)*

COMMERCIAL EQPT, WHOLESALE: Coffee Brewing Eqpt & Splys

Prospectors LLC ....G...... 616 634-8260
  Grand Rapids *(G-6792)*

COMMERCIAL EQPT, WHOLESALE: Comm Cooking & Food Svc Eqpt

Farber Concessions Inc .... E 313 387-1600
  Redford *(G-13161)*
Keglove LLC .... E 616 610-7289
  Holland *(G-7708)*

COMMERCIAL EQPT, WHOLESALE: Restaurant, NEC

Auction Masters .... G 586 576-7777
  Oak Park *(G-12050)*
Dominos Pizza LLC .... C 734 930-3030
  Ann Arbor *(G-424)*
PA Products Inc .... G 734 421-1060
  Livonia *(G-9880)*
Super Sidebar Inc .... G 989 709-0048
  West Branch *(G-17524)*

COMMERCIAL EQPT, WHOLESALE: Scales, Exc Laboratory

Dura-Pack Inc .... E 313 299-9600
  Taylor *(G-15711)*
Kanawha Scales & Systems Inc .... F 734 947-4030
  Romulus *(G-13695)*
Standard Scale & Supply Co .... G 313 255-6700
  Detroit *(G-4374)*

COMMERCIAL EQPT, WHOLESALE: Store Fixtures & Display Eqpt

G & W Display Fixtures Inc .... E 517 369-7110
  Bronson *(G-2026)*
Hudsonville Products LLC .... G 616 836-1904
  Grand Rapids *(G-6518)*

COMMERCIAL EQPT, WHOLESALE: Teaching Machines, Electronic

Weaver Instructional Systems .... G 616 942-2891
  Grand Rapids *(G-6981)*

COMMERCIAL LAUNDRY EQPT

Kah .... G 734 727-0478
  Westland *(G-17576)*

COMMERCIAL PRINTING & NEWSPAPER PUBLISHING COMBINED

C & G News Inc .... D 586 498-8000
  Warren *(G-16970)*
Calhoun Communications Inc .... F 517 629-0041
  Albion *(G-116)*
Conine Publishing Inc .... E 231 723-3592
  Manistee *(G-10418)*
County Journal Inc .... F 517 543-1099
  Charlotte *(G-2643)*
County Press .... G 517 531-4542
  Parma *(G-12389)*
Detroit Legal News Company .... D 313 961-6000
  Detroit *(G-3987)*
Detroit Newspaper Partnr LP .... A 586 826-7187
  Sterling Heights *(G-15314)*
Fedex Office & Print Svcs Inc .... G 248 651-2679
  Rochester *(G-13321)*
Gatehouse Media Mich Holdings ...... D 585 598-0030
  Coldwater *(G-3304)*
Gazelle Publishing .... G 734 529-2688
  Dundee *(G-4584)*
Grand Rapids Times Inc .... F 616 245-8737
  Grand Rapids *(G-6466)*
Iosco News Press Publishing Co ...... G 989 739-2054
  Oscoda *(G-12212)*
Italian Tribune .... G 586 783-3260
  Macomb *(G-10132)*
J-Ad Graphics Inc .... G 269 945-9554
  Marshall *(G-10573)*
Ludington Daily News Inc .... D 231 845-5181
  Ludington *(G-10069)*
Menominee Cnty Jurnl Print Sp .... F 906 753-2296
  Stephenson *(G-15237)*
Montmorency Press Inc .... G 989 785-4214
  Atlanta *(G-732)*
Northern Michigan Review Inc .... E 231 547-6558
  Petoskey *(G-12463)*
Ogden Newspapers Inc .... D 906 228-2500
  Marquette *(G-10548)*
Pgi Holdings Inc .... G 231 937-4740
  Big Rapids *(G-1641)*
Pgi Holdings Inc .... E 231 796-4831
  Big Rapids *(G-1640)*
Polish Daily News Inc .... G 313 365-1990
  Detroit *(G-4306)*
Shoppers Fair Inc .... E 231 627-7144
  Cheboygan *(G-2695)*
Splash In Time LLC .... G 269 775-1204
  Kalamazoo *(G-8898)*
St Ignace News .... F 906 643-9150
  Saint Ignace *(G-14279)*
Stafford Media Inc .... E 616 754-9301
  Greenville *(G-7154)*
Telegram Newspaper .... G 313 928-2955
  River Rouge *(G-13281)*
Thumbprint News .... G 810 794-2300
  Clay *(G-3004)*
Wakefield News .... G 906 224-9561
  Wakefield *(G-16856)*

COMMERCIAL REFRIGERATORS WHOLESALERS

Forma-Kool Manufacturing Inc .... E 586 949-4813
  Chesterfield *(G-2778)*

COMMODITY INSPECTION SVCS

Manufacturing Products & Svcs .... F 734 927-1964
  Plymouth *(G-12683)*

COMMON SAND MINING

Alpena Aggregate Inc .... F 989 595-2511
  Alpena *(G-273)*
Jack Millikin Inc .... G 989 348-8411
  Grayling *(G-7109)*
John R Sand & Gravel Co Inc .... G 810 678-3715
  Metamora *(G-10777)*
Lc Materials .... E 231 839-4319
  Lake City *(G-9091)*
Miller Sand & Gravel Company .... G 269 672-5601
  Hopkins *(G-7959)*
Round Lake Sand & Gravel Inc .... G 517 467-4458
  Addison *(G-38)*
Tri County Sand and Stone Inc .... G 231 331-6549
  Alden *(G-137)*
Van Sloten Enterprises Inc .... F 906 635-5151
  Sault Sainte Marie *(G-14477)*

COMMUNICATIONS CARRIER: Wired

Mexico Express .... F 313 843-6717
  Detroit *(G-4235)*

COMMUNICATIONS EQPT & SYSTEMS, NEC

Aaccess Entertainment .... G 734 260-1002
  Brighton *(G-1876)*
Techncal Audio Video Solutions .... G 810 899-5546
  Howell *(G-8105)*

COMMUNICATIONS EQPT REPAIR & MAINTENANCE

Central On Line Data Systems .... G 586 939-7000
  Sterling Heights *(G-15284)*

COMMUNICATIONS EQPT WHOLESALERS

Cincinnati Time Systems Inc .... F 248 615-8300
  Farmington Hills *(G-4963)*
Star Lite International LLC .... G 248 546-4489
  Oak Park *(G-12100)*

COMMUNICATIONS SVCS

Media Swing LLC .... G 313 885-2525
  Grosse Pointe Farms *(G-7186)*
Mophie LLC .... D 269 743-1340
  Kalamazoo *(G-8831)*

COMMUNICATIONS SVCS, NEC

Challenger Communications LLC ...... F 517 680-0125
  Springport *(G-15208)*

COMMUNICATIONS SVCS: Cellular

Abrasive Services Incorporated .... G 734 941-2144
  Romulus *(G-13647)*
Elite Business Services & Exec .... D 734 956-4550
  Bloomfield Hills *(G-1763)*
Mophie LLC .... D 269 743-1340
  Kalamazoo *(G-8831)*
No Limit Wireless-Michigan Inc .... G 313 285-8402
  Detroit *(G-4274)*

COMMUNICATIONS SVCS: Data

Black Box Corporation .... G 248 743-1320
  Troy *(G-16241)*
Causey Consulting LLC .... G 248 671-4979
  West Bloomfield *(G-17469)*
Intaglio LLC .... F 616 243-3300
  Grand Rapids *(G-6539)*

COMMUNICATIONS SVCS: Electronic Mail

Computer Mail Services Inc .... F 248 352-6700
  Sterling Heights *(G-15293)*

COMMUNICATIONS SVCS: Facsimile Transmission

Business Helper LLC .... G 231 271-4404
  Suttons Bay *(G-15651)*

COMMUNICATIONS SVCS: Internet Connectivity Svcs

Nutrien AG Solutions Inc .... G 989 842-1185
  Breckenridge *(G-1844)*
Rockman Communications Inc .... E 810 433-6800
  Fenton *(G-5236)*

COMMUNICATIONS SVCS: Internet Host Svcs

Fusion Design Group Ltd .... G 269 469-8226
  New Buffalo *(G-11514)*
Timothy J Tade Inc .... G 248 552-8583
  Troy *(G-16644)*
Zenwolf Technologies Group .... E 517 618-2000
  Howell *(G-8124)*

COMMUNICATIONS SVCS: Proprietary Online Svcs Networks

Interface Associates Inc .... G 734 327-9500
  Ann Arbor *(G-507)*

COMMUNICATIONS SVCS: Telephone Or Video

Startech-Solutions LLC .... G 248 419-0650
  Southfield *(G-15033)*
Startech-Solutions LLC .... G 248 419-0650
  West Bloomfield *(G-17499)*

COMMUNICATIONS SVCS: Telephone, Data

Abrasive Services Incorporated .... G 734 941-2144
  Romulus *(G-13647)*

COMMUNITY DEVELOPMENT GROUPS

Neighborhood Artisans Inc .... G 313 865-5373
  Detroit *(G-4265)*

COMPARATORS: Machinists

Costello Machine LLC .... E 586 749-0136
  Chesterfield *(G-2755)*
Five Star Industries Inc .... E 586 786-0500
  Macomb *(G-10122)*

COMPARATORS: Optical

Genx Corporation .... G 269 341-4242
  Kalamazoo *(G-8751)*
Visual Precision Inc .... G 248 546-7984
  Madison Heights *(G-10378)*

COMPASSES & ACCESS

Cammenga Company LLC .... G 313 914-7160
  Dearborn *(G-3685)*
Mercy Health Partners .... D 231 728-4032
  Muskegon *(G-11373)*

COMPOST

Indian Summer Recycling Inc .... G 586 725-1340
  Casco *(G-2500)*

Employee Codes: A=Over 500 employees, B=251-500
C=101-250, D=51-100, E=20-50, F=10-19, G=3-9

COMPOST

Morgan Composting Inc .... G 231 734-2451
  Sears *(G-14512)*
Morgan Composting Inc .... E 231 734-2790
  Sears *(G-14513)*
Natures Best Top Soil Compost .... G 810 657-9528
  Carsonville *(G-2497)*
Spurt Industries LLC .... G 616 688-5575
  Zeeland *(G-18187)*
Tuthill Farms & Composting .... G 248 437-7354
  South Lyon *(G-14815)*

COMPRESSORS: Air & Gas

Belco Industries Inc .... C 616 794-0410
  Belding *(G-1399)*
Blissfield Manufacturing Co .... B 517 486-2121
  Blissfield *(G-1713)*
Engineering Interests Inc .... G 248 461-6706
  Waterford *(G-17342)*
Harvey S Freeman .... E 248 852-2222
  West Bloomfield *(G-17479)*
Michigan Auto Comprsr Inc .... B 517 796-3200
  Parma *(G-12391)*
Millennium Planet LLC .... G 248 835-2331
  Farmington Hills *(G-5068)*
Natural Gas Compress .... E 231 941-0107
  Traverse City *(G-16046)*
Nordson Corporation .... D 734 459-8600
  Wixom *(G-17866)*
Pr39 Industries LLC .... G 248 481-8512
  Auburn Hills *(G-977)*
Primore Inc .... F 517 263-2220
  Adrian *(G-87)*
Stop & Go No 10 Inc .... G 734 281-7500
  Southgate *(G-15084)*
Thierica Equipment Corporation .... E 616 453-6570
  Grand Rapids *(G-6928)*
Unist Inc .... E 616 949-0853
  Grand Rapids *(G-6951)*

COMPRESSORS: Air & Gas, Including Vacuum Pumps

Correct Compression Inc .... G 231 864-2101
  Bear Lake *(G-1378)*
Gast Manufacturing Inc .... D 269 926-6171
  Benton Harbor *(G-1505)*
Metallurgical High Vacuum Corp ...... F 269 543-4291
  Fennville *(G-5175)*
Saylor-Beall Manufacturing Co .... B 989 224-2371
  Saint Johns *(G-14293)*

COMPRESSORS: Refrigeration & Air Conditioning Eqpt

Compressor Industries LLC .... F 313 389-2800
  Melvindale *(G-10693)*
Etx Holdings Inc .... G 989 463-1151
  Alma *(G-237)*
Great Lakes Air Products Inc .... E 734 326-7080
  Westland *(G-17563)*
Hanon Systems Usa LLC .... B 248 907-8000
  Novi *(G-11893)*
Remacon Compressors Inc .... G 313 842-8219
  Detroit *(G-4341)*
Tecumseh Compressor Co LLC .... A 662 566-2231
  Ann Arbor *(G-657)*
Tecumseh Compressor Company ..... G 734 585-9500
  Ann Arbor *(G-658)*

COMPRESSORS: Repairing

Air Supply Company Inc .... G 616 874-7751
  Rockford *(G-13556)*
Compressor Technologies Inc .... F 616 949-7000
  Grand Rapids *(G-6296)*
Correct Compression Inc .... G 231 864-2101
  Bear Lake *(G-1378)*

COMPRESSORS: Wholesalers

Compressor Technologies Inc .... F 616 949-7000
  Grand Rapids *(G-6296)*

COMPUTER & COMPUTER SOFTWARE STORES

EMC Corporation .... G 248 374-5009
  Novi *(G-11883)*
Lowry Holding Company Inc .... C 810 229-7200
  Brighton *(G-1952)*
Precision Printer Services Inc .... F 269 384-5725
  Portage *(G-13023)*
World of Cd-Rom .... F 269 382-3766
  Kalamazoo *(G-8928)*

COMPUTER & COMPUTER SOFTWARE STORES: Peripheral Eqpt

Automated Media Inc .... D 313 662-0185
  Redford *(G-13146)*
Jem Computers Inc .... F 586 783-3400
  Clinton Township *(G-3149)*
Photodon LLC .... G 847 377-1185
  Traverse City *(G-16068)*

COMPUTER & COMPUTER SOFTWARE STORES: Personal Computers

Christopher S Campion .... G 517 414-6796
  Jackson *(G-8409)*
Digilink Technology Inc .... F 517 381-8888
  Okemos *(G-12119)*

COMPUTER & COMPUTER SOFTWARE STORES: Printers & Plotters

M & J Graphics Enterprises Inc .... E 734 542-8800
  Livonia *(G-9820)*
Visionit Supplies and Svcs Inc .... A 313 664-5650
  Detroit *(G-4432)*

COMPUTER & COMPUTER SOFTWARE STORES: Software & Access

Industrial Service Tech Inc .... F 616 288-3352
  Grand Rapids *(G-6533)*
Materialise Usa LLC .... D 734 259-6445
  Plymouth *(G-12686)*

COMPUTER & COMPUTER SOFTWARE STORES: Software, Bus/Non-Game

Dynics Inc .... D 734 677-6100
  Ann Arbor *(G-428)*
Rutherford & Associates Inc .... E 616 392-5000
  Holland *(G-7792)*

COMPUTER & COMPUTER SOFTWARE STORES: Word Process Eqpt/Splys

Great Lakes Log & Firewd Co .... G 231 206-4073
  Twin Lake *(G-16712)*

COMPUTER & DATA PROCESSING EQPT REPAIR & MAINTENANCE

Bull Hn Info Systems Inc .... F 616 942-7126
  Grand Rapids *(G-6240)*
Stellar Computer Services LLC .... G 989 732-7153
  Gaylord *(G-5893)*

COMPUTER & OFFICE MACHINE MAINTENANCE & REPAIR

Active Solutions Group Inc .... G 313 278-4522
  Dearborn *(G-3671)*
Automated Media Inc .... D 313 662-0185
  Redford *(G-13146)*
Compucom Computers Inc .... G 989 837-1895
  Midland *(G-10826)*
Digilink Technology Inc .... F 517 381-8888
  Okemos *(G-12119)*
Geeks of Detroit LLC .... G 734 576-2363
  Detroit *(G-4079)*
Medical Systems Resource Group .... G 248 476-5400
  Farmington Hills *(G-5061)*
Precision Printer Services Inc .... F 269 384-5725
  Portage *(G-13023)*
Rap Electronics & Machines .... F 616 846-1437
  Grand Haven *(G-6068)*
Rose Mobile Computer Repr LLC ..... F 248 653-0865
  Troy *(G-16583)*
S T A Inc .... E 248 328-5000
  Holly *(G-7896)*

COMPUTER CALCULATING SVCS

Nits Solutions Inc .... F 248 231-2267
  Novi *(G-11953)*

COMPUTER FACILITIES MANAGEMENT SVCS

E-Con LLC .... E 248 766-9000
  Birmingham *(G-1682)*

COMPUTER FORMS

F P Horak Company .... C 989 892-6505
  Bay City *(G-1312)*
MPS Lansing Inc .... A 517 323-9000
  Lansing *(G-9248)*
Rotary Multiforms Inc .... G 586 558-7960
  Madison Heights *(G-10344)*

COMPUTER GRAPHICS SVCS

Eview 360 Corp .... E 248 306-5191
  Farmington Hills *(G-4995)*
H M Day Signs Inc .... G 231 946-7132
  Traverse City *(G-15996)*
Hypertek Corporation .... G 248 619-0395
  Troy *(G-16407)*
Religious Communications LLC .... G 313 822-3361
  Detroit *(G-4340)*
Star Board Multi Media Inc .... G 616 296-0823
  Grand Haven *(G-6084)*
Whiteside Consulting Group LLC ..... G 313 288-6598
  Detroit *(G-4440)*

COMPUTER INTERFACE EQPT: Indl Process

Allrout Inc .... G 616 748-7696
  Zeeland *(G-18111)*
D & C Investment Group Inc .... F 734 994-0591
  Ann Arbor *(G-410)*
Smarteye Corporation .... F 248 853-4495
  Rochester Hills *(G-13515)*

COMPUTER PERIPHERAL EQPT REPAIR & MAINTENANCE

Interface Associates Inc .... G 734 327-9500
  Ann Arbor *(G-507)*
Lasers Resource Inc .... E 616 554-5555
  Grand Rapids *(G-6620)*
Mikan Corporation .... F 734 944-9447
  Saline *(G-14401)*

COMPUTER PERIPHERAL EQPT, NEC

Acromag Incorporated .... D 248 624-1541
  Wixom *(G-17751)*
Advanced Integrated Mfg .... F 586 439-0300
  Fraser *(G-5613)*
Artic Technologies Intl .... G 248 689-9884
  Troy *(G-16220)*
Bbcm Inc .... G 248 410-2528
  Bloomfield Hills *(G-1750)*
Black Box Corporation .... G 248 743-1320
  Troy *(G-16241)*
Black Box Corporation .... F 616 246-1320
  Caledonia *(G-2290)*
Bull Hn Info Systems Inc .... F 616 942-7126
  Grand Rapids *(G-6240)*
Comptek Inc .... F 248 477-5215
  Farmington Hills *(G-4965)*
Computers Edge .... G 989 659-3179
  Munger *(G-11241)*
Daco Hand Controllers Inc .... F 248 982-3266
  Novi *(G-11861)*
Elite Engineering Inc .... F 517 304-3254
  Rochester Hills *(G-13417)*
Ensure Technologies Inc .... F 734 668-8800
  Ypsilanti *(G-18072)*
Innovative Support Svcs Inc .... E 248 585-3600
  Troy *(G-16418)*
Interface Associates Inc .... G 734 327-9500
  Ann Arbor *(G-507)*
Jem Computers Inc .... F 586 783-3400
  Clinton Township *(G-3149)*
Jo-Dan International Inc .... G 248 340-0300
  Auburn Hills *(G-919)*
Law Enforcement Development Co .. D 734 656-4100
  Plymouth *(G-12672)*
Lexmark International Inc .... F 248 352-0616
  Southfield *(G-14967)*
Mirror Image .... G 231 775-2939
  Cadillac *(G-2267)*
Pro-Face America LLC .... E 734 477-0600
  Ann Arbor *(G-605)*

PRODUCT SECTION — COMPUTER TERMINALS

Sakor Technologies Inc .... F 989 720-2700
  Owosso (G-12315)
Toshiba Amer Bus Solutions Inc .... F 248 427-8100
  Southfield (G-15046)
Triangle Product Distributors .... F 970 609-9001
  Holland (G-7839)
Winstanley Associates LLC .... G 231 946-3552
  Traverse City (G-16147)
Yakel Enterprises LLC .... G 586 943-5885
  Washington Township (G-17320)

COMPUTER PERIPHERAL EQPT, WHOLESALE

Jem Computers Inc .... F 586 783-3400
  Clinton Township (G-3149)
Mitsubishi Electric Us Inc .... D 734 453-6200
  Northville (G-11711)
Virtual Technology Inc .... F 248 528-6565
  Troy (G-16686)

COMPUTER PERIPHERAL EQPT: Graphic Displays, Exc Terminals

Ampm Inc .... F 989 837-8800
  Midland (G-10814)
Graphic Resource Group Inc .... E 248 588-6100
  Troy (G-16386)
Jant Group LLC .... G 616 863-6600
  Belmont (G-1463)

COMPUTER PERIPHERAL EQPT: Input Or Output

Scs Embedded Tech LLC .... G 248 615-2244
  Novi (G-11990)

COMPUTER PLOTTERS

Envisiontec Inc .... D 313 436-4300
  Dearborn (G-3702)

COMPUTER PROCESSING SVCS

Copy Central Inc .... G 231 941-2298
  Traverse City (G-15947)
Tru-Syzygy Inc .... G 248 622-7211
  Lake Orion (G-9167)

COMPUTER PROGRAMMING SVCS

21st Century Graphic Tech LLC .... G 586 463-9599
  Utica (G-16740)
Autodesk Inc .... D 248 347-9650
  Novi (G-11833)
Christopher S Campion .... G 517 414-6796
  Jackson (G-8409)
Core Technology Corporation .... F 517 627-1521
  Lansing (G-9285)
Dematic .... G 616 395-8671
  Holland (G-7607)
Egemin Automation Inc .... C 616 393-0101
  Holland (G-7619)
Enterprise Services LLC .... F 734 523-6525
  Livonia (G-9727)
Falcon Consulting Services LLC .... G 989 262-9325
  Alpena (G-288)
General Motors Company .... B 586 218-9240
  Warren (G-17051)
Great Lakes Infotronics Inc .... E 248 476-2500
  Northville (G-11695)
Intellibee Inc .... G 313 586-4122
  Detroit (G-4145)
International Machining Svc .... G 248 486-3600
  South Lyon (G-14795)
New Concepts Software Inc .... G 586 776-2855
  Roseville (G-13846)
Nuwave Technology Partners LLC .... F 616 942-7520
  Grand Rapids (G-6725)
Nuwave Technology Partners LLC .... G 269 342-4400
  Saint Joseph (G-14333)
Nuwave Technology Partners LLC .... F 269 342-4400
  Kalamazoo (G-8837)
Simna Solutions LLC .... G 313 442-7305
  Farmington Hills (G-5125)
Superior Information Tech LLC .... F 734 666-9963
  Livonia (G-9948)
Workforce Software LLC .... C 734 542-4100
  Livonia (G-10012)

COMPUTER PROGRAMMING SVCS: Custom

Ancor Information MGT LLC .... D 248 740-8866
  Troy (G-16201)
Stardock Systems Inc .... E 734 927-0677
  Plymouth (G-12760)
Technology Network Svcs Inc .... F 586 294-7771
  Saint Clair Shores (G-14271)

COMPUTER RELATED MAINTENANCE SVCS

Medimage Inc .... G 734 665-5400
  Ann Arbor (G-551)

COMPUTER SOFTWARE DEVELOPMENT

Amicus Software .... G 313 417-9550
  White Lake (G-17629)
Atos Syntel Inc .... C 248 619-2800
  Troy (G-16228)
Axis Tms Corp .... E 248 509-2440
  Troy (G-16231)
Braiq Inc .... G 858 729-4116
  Detroit (G-3912)
Competitive Cmpt Info Tech Inc .... E 732 829-9699
  Northville (G-11683)
Complete Data Products Inc .... G 248 651-8602
  Troy (G-16275)
Computer Mail Services Inc .... F 248 352-6700
  Sterling Heights (G-15293)
Compuware Corporation .... C 313 227-7300
  Detroit (G-3945)
E-Con LLC .... E 248 766-9000
  Birmingham (G-1682)
Elite Engineering Inc .... F 517 304-3254
  Rochester Hills (G-13417)
Empower Financials Inc .... F 734 747-9393
  Ann Arbor (G-443)
Engineering Tech Assoc Inc .... D 248 729-3010
  Troy (G-16346)
Global Supply Integrator LLC .... G 586 484-0734
  Davisburg (G-3635)
Harbor Software Intl Inc .... G 231 347-8866
  Petoskey (G-12451)
Imagen Orthopedics LLC .... G 616 294-1026
  Holland (G-7687)
Inovision Sftwr Solutions Inc .... G 586 598-8750
  Chesterfield (G-2791)
International Bus Mchs Corp .... B 517 391-5248
  East Lansing (G-4665)
Melange Computer Services Inc .... E 517 321-8434
  Lansing (G-9310)
Mendenhall Associates Inc .... G 734 741-4710
  Ann Arbor (G-552)
Nits Solutions Inc .... F 248 231-2267
  Novi (G-11953)
Panter Master Controls Inc .... F 810 687-5600
  Flint (G-5478)
Quantum Compliance Systems .... D 734 930-0009
  Ypsilanti (G-18099)
Radley Corporation .... E 616 554-9060
  Grand Rapids (G-6805)
Sciemetric Inc .... F 248 509-2209
  Rochester Hills (G-13512)
Silkroute Global Inc .... E 248 854-3409
  Troy (G-16603)
Tecra Systems Inc .... E 248 888-1116
  Westland (G-17602)
Tyler Technologies Inc .... F 734 677-0550
  Ann Arbor (G-684)
Union Built PC Inc .... G 248 910-3955
  Jackson (G-8598)

COMPUTER SOFTWARE DEVELOPMENT & APPLICATIONS

Coeus LLC .... F 248 564-1958
  Bloomfield Hills (G-1754)
El Informador LLC .... G 616 272-1092
  Wyoming (G-17998)
Ginkgotree Inc .... G 734 707-7191
  Detroit (G-4091)
Greenback Inc .... G 313 443-4272
  Birmingham (G-1685)
Ideation International Inc .... F 248 737-8854
  Farmington Hills (G-5025)
Kingston Educational Software .... G 248 895-4803
  Farmington Hills (G-5038)
Kubica Corp .... F 248 344-7750
  Novi (G-11922)
Lspedia LLC .... G 248 320-1909
  Farmington Hills (G-5046)

Prehab Technologies LLC .... G 734 368-9983
  Ann Arbor (G-602)
Professional Sftwr Assoc Inc .... G 727 724-0000
  Lapeer (G-9482)
Smart Diet Scale LLC .... G 586 383-6734
  Bruce Twp (G-2102)
Torenzo Inc .... F 313 732-7874
  Bloomfield Hills (G-1804)
Tweddle Group Inc .... C 586 307-3700
  Clinton Township (G-3252)
Ventuor LLC .... G 248 790-8700
  Flint (G-5520)

COMPUTER SOFTWARE SYSTEMS ANALYSIS & DESIGN: Custom

3dfx Interactive Inc .... E 918 938-8967
  Saginaw (G-13990)
3r Info LLC .... F 201 221-6133
  Canton (G-2342)
Beet LLC .... F 248 432-0052
  Plymouth (G-12584)
Chain-Sys Corporation .... F 517 627-1173
  Lansing (G-9281)
Compucare .... G 616 245-5371
  Grand Rapids (G-6297)
Cypress Computer Systems Inc .... F 810 245-2300
  Lapeer (G-9453)
Driven-4 LLC .... G 269 281-7567
  Saint Joseph (G-14307)
Dupearl Technology LLC .... D 248 390-9609
  Bloomfield Hills (G-1762)
E Z Logic Data Systems Inc .... E 248 817-8800
  Farmington Hills (G-4977)
Edi Experts LLC .... G 734 844-7016
  Canton (G-2370)
Innovative Programming Systems .... G 810 695-9332
  Grand Blanc (G-5971)
Lintech Global Inc .... D 248 553-8033
  Farmington Hills (G-5045)
Mejenta Systems Inc .... E 248 434-2583
  Southfield (G-14977)
Software Finesse LLC .... G 248 737-8990
  Farmington Hills (G-5126)
Strategic Computer Solutions .... G 248 888-0666
  Ann Arbor (G-648)
Sycron Technologies Inc .... G 810 694-4007
  Grand Blanc (G-5985)
Tru-Syzygy Inc .... G 248 622-7211
  Lake Orion (G-9167)

COMPUTER SOFTWARE WRITERS

Appliction Spclist Kompany Inc .... F 517 676-6633
  Lansing (G-9339)

COMPUTER STORAGE DEVICES, NEC

Aperion Information Tech Inc .... F 248 969-9791
  Oxford (G-12336)
Digilink Technology Inc .... F 517 381-8888
  Okemos (G-12119)
EMC Corporation .... C 248 957-5800
  Farmington Hills (G-4984)
International Bus Mchs Corp .... B 517 391-5248
  East Lansing (G-4665)
Quantam Solutions LLC .... G 248 395-2200
  Southfield (G-15007)
Quantum Innovations LLC .... G 734 576-2000
  Livonia (G-9902)
Quantum Labs LLC .... G 248 262-7731
  Southfield (G-15008)
Quantum Ventures LLC .... G 248 325-8380
  Holly (G-7892)
Rave Computer Association Inc .... E 586 939-8230
  Sterling Heights (G-15461)
Virtual Technology Inc .... F 248 528-6565
  Troy (G-16686)

COMPUTER SYSTEMS ANALYSIS & DESIGN

Design & Test Technology Inc .... G 734 665-4111
  Dexter (G-4484)
Design & Test Technology Inc .... F 734 665-4316
  Ann Arbor (G-416)
Export Service International .... G 248 620-7100
  Clarkston (G-2919)

COMPUTER TERMINALS

Geeks of Detroit LLC .... G 734 576-2363
  Detroit (G-4079)

Employee Codes: A=Over 500 employees, B=251-500
C=101-250, D=51-100, E=20-50, F=10-19, G=3-9

COMPUTER TERMINALS

Mobile Knowlege Group Services ....G....... 248 625-3327
  Clarkston *(G-2940)*
Pro-Face America LLC ....E....... 734 477-0600
  Ann Arbor *(G-605)*
Union Built PC Inc..................................G....... 248 910-3955
  Jackson *(G-8598)*

COMPUTER-AIDED DESIGN SYSTEMS SVCS

Adapt..G....... 989 343-9755
  West Branch *(G-17505)*
Advantage Industries Inc ....E....... 616 669-2400
  Jenison *(G-8616)*
Awcco USA Incorporated ....G....... 586 336-9135
  Romeo *(G-13624)*
Axsys Inc ....E....... 248 926-8810
  Wixom *(G-17769)*
Laser North Inc ....G....... 906 353-6090
  Baraga *(G-1106)*

COMPUTER-AIDED MANUFACTURING SYSTEMS SVCS

Garett Tunison ....G....... 248 330-9835
  Oakland *(G-12106)*
Onyx Manufacturing Inc ....G....... 248 687-8611
  Rochester Hills *(G-13487)*

COMPUTERS, NEC

Advanced Integrated Mfg ....F....... 586 439-0300
  Fraser *(G-5613)*
Artemis Technologies Inc ....E....... 517 336-9915
  East Lansing *(G-4650)*
Cypress Computer Systems Inc..........F....... 810 245-2300
  Lapeer *(G-9453)*
Disrupttech LLC ....G....... 248 225-8383
  Saint Clair Shores *(G-14244)*
Dynamic Software Group LLC ....F....... 734 716-0925
  Livonia *(G-9716)*
Enovate It..F....... 248 721-8104
  Ferndale *(G-5283)*
Entron Computer Systems Inc ....G....... 248 349-8898
  Northville *(G-11690)*
Ews Legacy LLC ....E....... 248 853-6363
  Rochester Hills *(G-13421)*
Exaconnect Corp ....G....... 810 232-1400
  Flint *(G-5426)*
I S My Department Inc ....G....... 248 622-0622
  Clarkston *(G-2928)*
Indocomp Systems Inc ....F....... 810 678-3990
  Metamora *(G-10776)*
Innovation Unlimited LLC ....G....... 574 635-1064
  Bay City *(G-1322)*
Innovtive Design Solutions Inc ....C....... 248 583-1010
  Sterling Heights *(G-15374)*
International Bus Mchs Corp ....E....... 989 832-6000
  Midland *(G-10873)*
Opto Solutions Inc ....G....... 269 254-9716
  Plainwell *(G-12532)*
PC Techs On Wheels ....G....... 734 262-4424
  Canton *(G-2414)*
PCI Procal Inc ....F....... 989 358-7070
  Alpena *(G-307)*
Protxs Inc...C....... 989 255-3836
  Jenison *(G-8638)*
Rave Computer Association Inc ....E....... 586 939-8230
  Sterling Heights *(G-15461)*
S T A Inc ....E....... 248 328-5000
  Holly *(G-7896)*
Secord Solutions LLC ....G....... 734 363-8887
  Ecorse *(G-4745)*
William Penn Systems Inc...................G....... 313 383-8299
  Lincoln Park *(G-9588)*
Zareason Inc ....F....... 510 868-5000
  Lapeer *(G-9493)*

COMPUTERS, NEC, WHOLESALE

Interface Associates Inc ....G....... 734 327-9500
  Ann Arbor *(G-507)*
Rave Computer Association Inc ....E....... 586 939-8230
  Sterling Heights *(G-15461)*
Technology Network Svcs Inc ....F....... 586 294-7771
  Saint Clair Shores *(G-14271)*

COMPUTERS, PERIPH & SOFTWARE, WHLSE: Personal & Home Entrtn

Computers Edge ....G....... 989 659-3179
  Munger *(G-11241)*

COMPUTERS, PERIPHERALS & SOFTWARE, WHOLESALE: Printers

Wright Communications Inc ....F....... 248 585-3838
  Troy *(G-16700)*

COMPUTERS, PERIPHERALS & SOFTWARE, WHOLESALE: Software

Axsys Inc ....E....... 248 926-8810
  Wixom *(G-17769)*
D2t America Inc ....F....... 248 680-9001
  Rochester Hills *(G-13400)*
Label Tech Inc ....F....... 586 247-6444
  Shelby Township *(G-14619)*
Spindance Inc..G....... 616 355-7000
  Holland *(G-7811)*
Triangle Product Distributors ....F....... 970 609-9001
  Holland *(G-7839)*

COMPUTERS: Mainframe

Bk Computing ....G....... 231 865-3558
  Fruitport *(G-5789)*
Bull Hn Info Systems Inc.....................F....... 616 942-7126
  Grand Rapids *(G-6240)*

COMPUTERS: Mini

Intellibee Inc ....G....... 313 586-4122
  Detroit *(G-4145)*
International Bus Mchs Corp ....B....... 517 391-5248
  East Lansing *(G-4665)*
Pro-Face America LLC ....E....... 734 477-0600
  Ann Arbor *(G-605)*

COMPUTERS: Personal

3dfx Interactive Inc ....E....... 918 938-8967
  Saginaw *(G-13990)*
Christopher S Campion ....G....... 517 414-6796
  Jackson *(G-8409)*
Compudyne Inc ....F....... 906 360-9081
  Marquette *(G-10525)*
Eaton Aerospace LLC..........................B....... 616 949-1090
  Grand Rapids *(G-6368)*
HP Inc ....E....... 650 857-1501
  Lansing *(G-9293)*
HP Inc ....E....... 248 614-6600
  Troy *(G-16404)*
Kismet Strategic Sourcing Part ....G....... 269 932-4990
  Saint Joseph *(G-14321)*
Lga Retail Inc ....G....... 248 910-1918
  South Lyon *(G-14800)*
Plymouth Computer & ....G....... 734 744-9563
  Livonia *(G-9890)*

CONCENTRATES, DRINK

Glcc Co ....E....... 269 657-3167
  Paw Paw *(G-12404)*
Refreshment Product Svcs Inc ....G....... 906 475-7003
  Negaunee *(G-11474)*

CONCRETE BUILDING PRDTS WHOLESALERS

Best Concrete & Supply Inc................G....... 734 283-7055
  Brownstown *(G-2059)*
Milford Redi-Mix Company ....E....... 248 684-1465
  Milford *(G-10971)*

CONCRETE CURING & HARDENING COMPOUNDS

BASF Construction Chem LLC............E....... 269 668-3371
  Mattawan *(G-10662)*
Rooto Corporation ....F....... 517 546-8330
  Howell *(G-8093)*

CONCRETE MIXERS

Oshkosh Defense LLC..........................E....... 586 576-8301
  Warren *(G-17178)*

CONCRETE PLANTS

Arcosa Shoring Products Inc ....E....... 517 741-4300
  Union City *(G-16731)*
Besser Company ....B....... 989 354-4111
  Alpena *(G-282)*

Thomas J Moyle Jr Incorporated........E....... 906 482-3000
  Houghton *(G-7986)*

CONCRETE PRDTS

Ajax Paving Industries Inc ....C....... 248 244-3300
  Troy *(G-16175)*
Best Block Company ....E....... 586 772-7000
  Warren *(G-16956)*
Bonsal American Inc ....F....... 248 338-0335
  Auburn Hills *(G-794)*
Cheboygan Cement Products Inc ......G....... 989 742-4107
  Hillman *(G-7508)*
Clancy Excavating Co ....G....... 586 294-2900
  Roseville *(G-13781)*
Concrete Manufacturing Inc ....G....... 586 777-3320
  Roseville *(G-13785)*
Concrete Pipe Northern.......................G....... 616 608-6025
  Wyoming *(G-17992)*
Consumers Concrete Corp ....E....... 616 243-3651
  Wyoming *(G-17993)*
Consumers Concrete Corporation .....F....... 517 784-9108
  Jackson *(G-8419)*
Cosella Dorken Products Inc ....G....... 888 433-5824
  Rochester *(G-13317)*
Darby Ready Mix Concrete Co............E....... 517 547-7004
  Addison *(G-36)*
E & M Cores Inc....................................G....... 989 386-9223
  Clare *(G-2869)*
Elastizell Corporation America ....G....... 734 426-6076
  Dexter *(G-4490)*
Eppert Concrete Products Inc ....G....... 248 647-1800
  Southfield *(G-14900)*
Fendt Builders Supply Inc...................E....... 248 474-3211
  Farmington Hills *(G-4999)*
Fraco Products Ltd ....G....... 248 667-9260
  Troy *(G-16374)*
Gambles Redi-Mix Inc.........................F....... 989 539-6460
  Harrison *(G-7312)*
Gibraltar National Corporation ....F....... 248 634-8257
  Holly *(G-7881)*
High Grade Materials Company ....E....... 616 754-5545
  Greenville *(G-7138)*
Holcim (us) Inc ....C....... 734 529-4600
  Dundee *(G-4588)*
Kurtz Gravel Company Inc ....E....... 810 787-6543
  Farmington Hills *(G-5040)*
Lafarge North America Inc ....F....... 703 480-3600
  Dundee *(G-4591)*
Lake Orion Concrete Orna Pdts ....G....... 248 693-8683
  Lake Orion *(G-9144)*
M 37 Concrete Products Inc...............G....... 231 689-1785
  White Cloud *(G-17626)*
Marquette Castings LLC ....E....... 248 798-8035
  Royal Oak *(G-13947)*
Mbcd Inc ....E....... 517 484-4426
  Lansing *(G-9395)*
McCann ....G....... 734 429-2781
  Caledonia *(G-2308)*
MEGA Precast Inc ....F....... 586 477-5959
  Shelby Township *(G-14637)*
Metro Cast Corporation.......................G....... 734 728-0210
  Westland *(G-17579)*
National Block Company.....................E....... 734 721-4050
  Westland *(G-17582)*
Northfield Block Company ....G....... 989 777-2575
  Bridgeport *(G-1854)*
Oaks Concrete Products Inc ....F....... 248 684-5004
  Wixom *(G-17872)*
Paul Murphy Plastics Co ....E....... 586 774-4880
  Roseville *(G-13851)*
Pearson Precast Concrete Pdts ....G....... 517 486-4060
  Blissfield *(G-1722)*
Polycem LLC ....E....... 231 799-1040
  Norton Shores *(G-11813)*
Port Huron Building Supply Co ....F....... 810 987-2666
  Port Huron *(G-12958)*
Sanglo International Inc ....G....... 248 894-1900
  Oak Park *(G-12098)*
Van Sloten Enterprises Inc.................F....... 906 635-5151
  Sault Sainte Marie *(G-14477)*
White Lake Excavating Inc ....F....... 231 894-6918
  Whitehall *(G-17681)*

CONCRETE PRDTS, PRECAST, NEC

ADL Systems Inc ....G....... 517 647-7543
  Portland *(G-13060)*
Advance Concrete Products Co ....E....... 248 887-4173
  Highland *(G-7484)*
Beck Mobile Concrete LLC ....G....... 517 655-4996
  Williamston *(G-17726)*

PRODUCT SECTION

CONCRETE: Ready-Mixed

Bush Concrete Products Inc ....F 231 733-1904
  Norton Shores (G-11742)
Concrete Step Co ....G 810 789-3061
  Flint (G-5402)
Fenton Corporation ....G 810 629-2858
  Fenton (G-5209)
Great Lakes Precast Systems ....E 616 784-5900
  Comstock Park (G-3484)
Interntnal Prcast Slutions LLC ....D 313 843-0073
  River Rouge (G-13278)
Mack Industries Michigan Inc ....C 248 620-7400
  White Lake (G-17634)
Nucon Schokbeton ....C 269 381-1550
  Kalamazoo (G-8836)
Terrys Precast Products Inc ....G 616 396-7042
  Holland (G-7828)
Wolverine Concrete Products ....G 313 931-7189
  Detroit (G-4445)

CONCRETE REINFORCING MATERIAL

Polytorx LLC ....G 734 322-2114
  Ann Arbor (G-595)

CONCRETE: Bituminous

Barrett Paving Materials Inc ....C 248 362-0850
  Troy (G-16233)

CONCRETE: Dry Mixture

Detroit Recycled Concrete Co ....G 248 553-0600
  Novi (G-11865)
Quikrete Companies Inc ....E 616 784-5790
  Walker (G-16878)

CONCRETE: Ready-Mixed

Aggregate Industries - Mwr Inc ....E 734 529-5876
  Dundee (G-4574)
Aggregate Industries - Mwr Inc ....E 269 321-3800
  Kalamazoo (G-8673)
Aggregate Industries - Mwr Inc ....E 269 685-5937
  Plainwell (G-12517)
Aggregate Industries - Mwr Inc ....G 734 475-2531
  Grass Lake (G-7083)
Aggregate Industries Centl Reg ....G 734 475-2531
  Grass Lake (G-7084)
Aggregate Industries-Wcr Inc ....G 269 963-7263
  Battle Creek (G-1143)
Ajax Paving Industries Inc ....C 248 244-3300
  Troy (G-16175)
Alma Concrete Products Company ......G 989 463-5476
  Alma (G-232)
American Concrete Products Inc ....G 517 546-2810
  Howell (G-8013)
Angelos Crushed Concrete Inc ....G 586 756-1070
  Warren (G-16934)
Arquette Concrete & Supply ....G 989 846-4131
  Standish (G-15216)
Associated Constructors LLC ....D 906 226-6505
  Negaunee (G-11467)
Baraga County Concrete Company ......G 906 353-6595
  Baraga (G-1097)
Bardon Inc ....E 734 529-5876
  Dundee (G-4576)
Beck Mobile Concrete LLC ....G 517 655-4996
  Williamston (G-17726)
Becker & Scrivens Con Pdts Inc ....E 517 437-4250
  Hillsdale (G-7517)
Beckman Brothers Inc ....E 231 861-2031
  Shelby (G-14523)
Beechbed Mix ....G 616 263-7422
  Holland (G-7565)
Best Concrete & Supply Inc ....G 734 283-7055
  Brownstown (G-2059)
Bichler Gravel & Concrete Co ....F 906 786-0343
  Escanaba (G-4818)
Bigos Precast ....G 517 223-5000
  Fowlerville (G-5561)
Bischer Ready-Mix Inc ....G 989 479-3267
  Ruth (G-13987)
Bogen Concrete Inc ....G 269 651-6751
  Sturgis (G-15598)
Bonsal American Inc ....F 734 753-4413
  New Boston (G-11497)
Bos Concrete Inc ....F 269 468-7267
  Coloma (G-3354)
Bozzer Brothers Inc ....G 989 732-9684
  Gaylord (G-5851)
Branch West Concrete Products ....F 989 345-0794
  West Branch (G-17507)

Brewers City Dock Inc ....E 616 396-6563
  Holland (G-7578)
Bwb LLC ....D 231 439-9200
  Farmington Hills (G-4950)
C F Long & Sons Inc ....F 248 624-1562
  Walled Lake (G-16892)
Carrollton Concrete Mix Inc ....G 989 753-7737
  Saginaw (G-14011)
Carrollton Paving Co ....F 989 752-7139
  Saginaw (G-14012)
Cemex Cement Inc ....C 231 547-9971
  Charlevoix (G-2610)
Central Concrete Products Inc ....F 810 659-7488
  Flushing (G-5532)
Cheboygan Cement Products Inc ....E 231 627-5631
  Cheboygan (G-2677)
Cheboygan Cement Products Inc ....G 989 742-4107
  Hillman (G-7508)
Coit Avenue Gravel Co Inc ....E 616 363-7777
  Grand Rapids (G-6287)
Concrete To Go ....G 734 455-3531
  Plymouth (G-12600)
Consumers Concrete Corp ....E 269 384-0977
  Kalamazoo (G-8714)
Consumers Concrete Corporation ......E 269 342-0136
  Kalamazoo (G-8715)
Consumers Concrete Corporation ......G 800 643-4235
  Plainwell (G-12520)
Consumers Concrete Corporation ......F 231 777-3981
  Muskegon (G-11300)
Consumers Concrete Corporation ......F 231 924-6131
  Fremont (G-5768)
Consumers Concrete Corporation ......F 616 827-0063
  Byron Center (G-2182)
Consumers Concrete Corporation ......F 269 342-5983
  Kalamazoo (G-8716)
Consumers Concrete Corporation ......G 616 392-6190
  Holland (G-7598)
Consumers Concrete Corporation ......G 269 684-8760
  Niles (G-11601)
Consumers Concrete Corporation ......F 231 894-2705
  Whitehall (G-17664)
Consumers Concrete Corporation ......F 517 784-9108
  Jackson (G-8419)
Cornillie Acquisitions LLC ....F 231 946-5600
  Cadillac (G-2242)
Cornillie Acquisitions LLC ....F 231 946-5600
  Bear Lake (G-1377)
Cornillie Concrete ....E 231 439-9200
  Harbor Springs (G-7279)
Crete Dry-Mix & Supply Co ....F 616 784-5790
  Comstock Park (G-3473)
Darby Ready Mix Concrete Co ....E 517 547-7004
  Addison (G-36)
Darby Ready Mix-Dundee LLC ....F 734 529-7100
  Dundee (G-4578)
Daves Concrete Products Inc ....F 269 624-4100
  Lawton (G-9511)
Dekes Concrete Inc ....E 810 686-5570
  Clarkston (G-2916)
Detroit Ready Mix Concrete ....F 313 931-7043
  Detroit (G-3998)
Dewent Redi-Mix LLC ....G 616 457-2100
  Jenison (G-8623)
Doan Construction Co ....F 734 971-4678
  Ypsilanti (G-18067)
Downriver Crushed Concrete ....G 734 283-1833
  Taylor (G-15708)
Drayton Iron & Metal Inc ....F 248 673-1269
  Waterford (G-17339)
E A Wood Inc ....F 989 739-9118
  Oscoda (G-12208)
Edw C Levy Co ....F 248 334-4302
  Auburn Hills (G-851)
Edw C Levy Co ....D 313 843-7200
  Detroit (G-4028)
Edward E Yates ....G 517 467-4961
  Onsted (G-12152)
Elmers Crane and Dozer Inc ....C 231 943-3443
  Traverse City (G-15962)
Fenton Concrete Inc ....G 810 629-0783
  Fenton (G-5208)
Ferguson Block Co Inc ....F 810 653-2812
  Davison (G-3647)
Fisher Redi Mix Concrete ....F 989 723-1622
  Owosso (G-12291)
Fisher Sand and Gravel Company ....E 989 835-7187
  Midland (G-10861)
Fraco ....F 906 249-1476
  Marquette (G-10532)

Gale Briggs Inc ....G 517 543-1320
  Charlotte (G-2651)
Gambles Redi-Mix Inc ....F 989 539-6460
  Harrison (G-7312)
Gene Brow & Sons Inc ....F 906 635-0859
  Sault Sainte Marie (G-14464)
Gildners Concrete ....G 989 356-5156
  Alpena (G-292)
Gotts Transit Mix Inc ....E 734 439-1528
  Milan (G-10939)
Grand Rapids Gravel Company ....F 616 538-9000
  Grand Rapids (G-6454)
Grand Rapids Gravel Company ....F 616 538-9000
  Grandville (G-7038)
Grand Rapids Gravel Company ....F 616 538-9000
  Belmont (G-1462)
Grand Rapids Gravel Company ....F 616 538-9000
  Holland (G-7648)
Grand Rapids Gravel Company ....E 231 777-2777
  Muskegon (G-11332)
Great Lakes Sand & Gravel LLC ....F 616 374-3169
  Lake Odessa (G-9115)
Guidobono Concrete Inc ....F 810 229-2666
  Brighton (G-1935)
Hamilton Block & Ready Mix Co ....F 269 751-5129
  Hamilton (G-7232)
Hardcrete Inc ....G 989 644-5543
  Weidman (G-17457)
Hart Concrete LLC ....G 231 873-2183
  Spring Lake (G-15150)
High Grade Materials Company ....E 616 554-8828
  Caledonia (G-2299)
High Grade Materials Company ....E 616 754-5545
  Greenville (G-7138)
High Grade Materials Company ....E 269 926-6900
  Benton Harbor (G-1510)
High Grade Materials Company ....F 269 349-8222
  Kalamazoo (G-8769)
High Grade Materials Company ....F 616 677-1271
  Grand Rapids (G-6510)
High Grade Materials Company ....F 517 374-1029
  Lansing (G-9235)
High Grade Materials Company ....G 989 584-6004
  Carson City (G-2491)
High Grade Materials Company ....G 989 365-3010
  Six Lakes (G-14740)
High Grade Materials Company ....G 616 696-9540
  Sand Lake (G-14423)
Huizenga & Sons Inc ....E 616 772-6241
  Zeeland (G-18155)
Hunderman & Sons Redi-Mix Inc ....G 616 453-5999
  Walker (G-16868)
Imlay City Concrete Inc ....F 810 724-3905
  Imlay City (G-8203)
Ironwood Ready Mix & Trucking ....G 906 932-4531
  Ironwood (G-8331)
Ishpeming Concrete Corporation ....F 906 485-5851
  Ishpeming (G-8347)
Jordan Valley Concrete Service ....F 231 536-7701
  East Jordan (G-4637)
Kens Redi Mix Inc ....F 810 687-6000
  Clio (G-3273)
Kens Redi Mix Inc ....G 810 238-4931
  Goodrich (G-5955)
Koenig Fuel & Supply Co ....G 313 368-1870
  Wayne (G-17433)
Kuhlman Concrete Inc ....G 517 265-2722
  Adrian (G-74)
Kuhlman Corporation ....G 734 241-8692
  Monroe (G-11045)
Kurtz Gravel Company Inc ....E 810 787-6543
  Farmington Hills (G-5040)
L & S Transit Mix Concrete Co ....F 989 354-5363
  Alpena (G-294)
Lafarge North America Inc ....G 269 983-6333
  Saint Joseph (G-14322)
Lafarge North America Inc ....F 703 480-3600
  Dundee (G-4591)
Lafarge North America Inc ....G 231 726-3291
  Muskegon (G-11362)
Lafarge North America Inc ....G 313 842-9258
  Detroit (G-4191)
Lakeside Building Products ....G 248 349-3500
  Detroit (G-4192)
Land Star Inc ....G 313 834-2366
  Detroit (G-4193)
Lattimore Material ....G 972 837-2462
  Dundee (G-4593)
Lc Materials ....G 231 796-8685
  Big Rapids (G-1638)

Employee Codes: A=Over 500 employees, B=251-500
C=101-250, D=51-100, E=20-50, F=10-19, G=3-9

CONCRETE: Ready-Mixed

Lc Materials .... G 989 422-4202
  Houghton Lake *(G-7995)*
Lc Materials .... G 231 825-2473
  Cadillac *(G-2260)*
Lc Materials .... G 231 775-9301
  Cadillac *(G-2261)*
Lc Materials .... F 231 258-8633
  Kalkaska *(G-8948)*
Lc Materials .... G 231 832-5460
  Reed City *(G-13219)*
Lc Materials .... G 989 344-0235
  Grayling *(G-7110)*
Leelanau Redi-Mix Inc .... G 231 228-5005
  Maple City *(G-10462)*
Lees Ready Mix Inc .... G 989 734-7666
  Rogers City *(G-13616)*
Lewiston Concrete Inc .... G 989 786-3722
  Lewiston *(G-9551)*
Little Bay Concrete Products .... G 906 428-9859
  Gladstone *(G-5915)*
Livingston County Concrete Inc .... F 810 632-3030
  Brighton *(G-1951)*
M 37 Concrete Products Inc .... E 231 733-8247
  Muskegon *(G-11371)*
M 37 Concrete Products Inc .... G 231 689-1785
  White Cloud *(G-17626)*
Manistique Rentals Inc .... G 906 341-6955
  Manistique *(G-10443)*
Manthei Development Corp .... G 231 347-6282
  Petoskey *(G-12457)*
Massive Mineral Mix LLC .... G 517 857-4544
  Springport *(G-15212)*
Maxs Concrete Inc .... G 231 972-7558
  Mecosta *(G-10690)*
McCoig Materials LLC .... E 734 414-6179
  Plymouth *(G-12688)*
Meredith Lea Sand Gravel .... G 517 930-3662
  Charlotte *(G-2659)*
Messina Concrete Inc .... E 734 783-1020
  Flat Rock *(G-5357)*
Midway Group LLC .... E 586 264-5380
  Sterling Heights *(G-15423)*
Milford Redi-Mix Company .... E 248 684-1465
  Milford *(G-10971)*
Miller Sand & Gravel Company ..... G 269 672-5601
  Hopkins *(G-7959)*
Millers Redi-Mix Inc .... F 989 587-6511
  Fowler *(G-5554)*
Mini-Mix Inc .... E 586 792-2260
  Clinton Township *(G-3178)*
Mirkwood Properties Inc .... G 586 727-3363
  Richmond *(G-13266)*
Mix Factory One LLC .... G 248 799-9390
  Southfield *(G-14984)*
Mix Masters Inc .... G 616 490-8520
  Byron Center *(G-2203)*
Mix Street .... G 616 241-6550
  Grand Rapids *(G-6692)*
Mobile Mix .... G 734 497-3256
  Monroe *(G-11053)*
Modern Industries Inc .... E 810 767-3330
  Flint *(G-5469)*
Morse Concrete & Excavating ..... F 989 826-3975
  Mio *(G-11006)*
Mottes Materials Inc .... E 906 265-9955
  Iron River *(G-8316)*
National Block Company .... E 734 721-4050
  Westland *(G-17582)*
New Buffalo Concrete Products .... B 269 469-2515
  New Buffalo *(G-11516)*
New Mix 96 .... G 231 941-0963
  Traverse City *(G-16048)*
Newberry Redi-Mix Inc .... G 906 293-5178
  Newberry *(G-11584)*
Northfork Readi Mix Inc .... G 906 341-3445
  Manistique *(G-10444)*
Novi Crushed Concrete LLC .... G 248 305-6020
  Novi *(G-11957)*
Osborne Concrete Co .... G 734 941-3008
  Romulus *(G-13717)*
Owosso Ready Mix Co .... G 989 723-1295
  Owosso *(G-12310)*
P D P LLC .... F 616 437-9618
  Wyoming *(G-18025)*
Paragon Ready Mix Inc .... E 586 731-8000
  Shelby Township *(G-14659)*
Peterman Mobile Concrete Inc .... E 269 324-1211
  Portage *(G-13022)*
Piedmont Concrete Inc .... F 248 474-7740
  Farmington Hills *(G-5093)*

Port Huron Building Supply Co ..... F 810 987-2666
  Port Huron *(G-12958)*
Quarrystone Inc .... E 906 786-0343
  Escanaba *(G-4854)*
R & C Redi-Mix Inc .... G 616 636-5650
  Sand Lake *(G-14425)*
R & R Ready-Mix Inc .... G 810 686-5570
  Clio *(G-3280)*
R & R Ready-Mix Inc .... F 989 753-3862
  Saginaw *(G-14127)*
R & R Ready-Mix Inc .... G 989 892-9313
  Bay City *(G-1346)*
Readysetmail .... G 810 982-1924
  Saint Clair *(G-14232)*
Riverside Block Co Inc .... G 989 865-9951
  Saint Charles *(G-14200)*
Rock Redi-Mix Inc .... G 989 752-0795
  Carrollton *(G-2486)*
Roger Mix Storage .... G 231 352-9762
  Frankfort *(G-5605)*
Rudy Goupille & Sons Inc .... G 906 475-9816
  Negaunee *(G-11476)*
Ruppe Manufacturing Company ... E 906 932-3540
  Ironwood *(G-8339)*
Ruth Drain Tile Inc .... G 989 864-3406
  Ruth *(G-13989)*
Saginaw Rock Products Co .... E 989 754-6589
  Saginaw *(G-14144)*
Scheels Concrete Inc .... G 734 782-1464
  Livonia *(G-9922)*
Sebewaing Concrete Pdts Inc .... F 989 883-3860
  Sebewaing *(G-14518)*
Shafer Bros Inc .... G 517 629-4800
  Albion *(G-130)*
Shafer Redi-Mix Inc .... D 517 629-4800
  Albion *(G-131)*
Shafer Redi-Mix Inc .... D 517 764-0517
  Jackson *(G-8572)*
St Marys Cement Inc (us) .... G 616 846-8553
  Ferrysburg *(G-5338)*
Stevenson Building and Sup Co ... G 734 856-3931
  Lambertville *(G-9185)*
Summertime Concrete Inc .... E 517 641-6966
  Bath *(G-1136)*
Superior Materials LLC .... E 248 788-8000
  Farmington Hills *(G-5136)*
Superior Materials LLC .... C 734 941-2479
  Romulus *(G-13735)*
Superior Materials Inc .... F 888 988-4400
  Detroit *(G-4387)*
Superior Materials Inc .... E 248 788-8000
  Farmington Hills *(G-5137)*
Superior Mtls Holdings LLC .... E 248 788-8000
  Farmington Hills *(G-5138)*
Swansons Excavating Inc .... G 989 873-4419
  Prescott *(G-13081)*
Swartzmiller Lumber Company .... G 989 845-6625
  Chesaning *(G-2728)*
Theut Concrete Products Inc .... F 810 679-3376
  Croswell *(G-3604)*
Theut Products Inc .... F 810 765-9321
  Marine City *(G-10484)*
Theut Products Inc .... E 586 949-1300
  Chesterfield *(G-2847)*
Tuckey Concrete Products .... G 989 872-4779
  Cass City *(G-2523)*
Van Horn Bros Inc .... E 248 623-4830
  Waterford *(G-17382)*
Van Horn Bros Inc .... E 248 623-6000
  Waterford *(G-17383)*
Van Sloten Enterprises Inc .... F 906 635-5151
  Sault Sainte Marie *(G-14477)*
Vhb-123 Corporation .... E 248 623-4830
  Waterford *(G-17384)*
Vollmer Ready-Mix Inc .... G 989 453-2262
  Pigeon *(G-12494)*
Voorheis Hausbeck Excavating .... F 989 752-9666
  Reese *(G-13235)*
Waanders Concrete Co .... E 269 673-6352
  Allegan *(G-190)*
Westendorff Transit Mix .... G 989 593-2488
  Pewamo *(G-12480)*
Whats Your Mix Menchies LLC ..... G 248 840-1668
  Shelby Township *(G-14722)*
Willbee Transit-Mix Co Inc .... E 517 782-9493
  Jackson *(G-8608)*
Williams Reddi Mix Inc .... G 906 875-6952
  Crystal Falls *(G-3615)*
Williams Redi Mix .... G 906 875-6839
  Crystal Falls *(G-3616)*

CONDENSERS & CONDENSING UNITS: Air Conditioner

Clear Advantage Mechanical .... G 616 520-5884
  Grand Rapids *(G-6279)*

CONDENSERS: Heat Transfer Eqpt, Evaporative

D & B Heat Transfer Pdts Inc .... F 616 827-0028
  Grand Rapids *(G-6327)*
Stahls Inc .... D 800 478-2457
  Sterling Heights *(G-15508)*

CONDENSERS: Motors Or Generators

Blissfield Manufacturing Co .... B 517 486-2121
  Blissfield *(G-1713)*

CONFECTIONERY PRDTS WHOLESALERS

Asao LLC .... F 734 522-6333
  Livonia *(G-9653)*
Happy Candy .... G 248 629-9819
  Warren *(G-17076)*

CONFECTIONS & CANDY

American Gourmet Snacks LLC .... G 989 892-4856
  Essexville *(G-4867)*
D A U P Corp .... G 906 477-1148
  Naubinway *(G-11465)*
Donckers Candies & Gifts .... G 906 226-6110
  Marquette *(G-10526)*
Fretty Media LLC .... G 231 894-8055
  Whitehall *(G-17667)*
Gerbers Home Made Sweets .... G 231 348-3743
  Charlevoix *(G-2615)*
Gki Foods LLC .... D 248 486-0055
  Brighton *(G-1931)*
Happy Candy .... G 248 629-9819
  Warren *(G-17076)*
Klopp Group LLC .... G 877 256-4528
  Saginaw *(G-14073)*
Lotte USA Incorporated .... F 269 963-6664
  Battle Creek *(G-1223)*
Maas Enterprises Michigan LLC ... G 616 875-8099
  Holland *(G-7729)*
Marshalls Trail Inc .... F 231 436-5082
  Mackinaw City *(G-10099)*
Morley Brands LLC .... D 586 468-4300
  Clinton Township *(G-3180)*
Nassau Candy Midwest L L C .... D 734 464-2787
  Livonia *(G-9859)*
Rocky Mtn Choclat Fctry Inc .... D 810 606-8550
  Grand Blanc *(G-5981)*
Sanders Candy LLC .... D 800 651-7263
  Clinton Township *(G-3221)*
Sugar Free Specialties LLC .... F 616 734-6999
  Comstock Park *(G-3517)*
Sweet Essentials LLC .... G 248 398-7933
  Berkley *(G-1589)*
Vineyards Gourmet .... G 269 468-4778
  Coloma *(G-3366)*
W2 Inc .... G 517 764-3141
  Jackson *(G-8602)*
White River Sugar Bush .... G 231 861-4860
  Hesperia *(G-7480)*

CONNECTORS & TERMINALS: Electrical Device Uses

American Pwr Cnnection Systems ... F 989 686-6302
  Bay City *(G-1275)*
Cardell Corporation .... F 248 371-9700
  Auburn Hills *(G-810)*
Emm Inc .... G 248 478-1182
  Farmington Hills *(G-4985)*
Frank Condon Inc .... E 517 849-2505
  Hillsdale *(G-7525)*
Sine Systems Corporation 586 465-3131
  Clinton Township *(G-3230)*
Syndevco Inc .... F 248 356-2839
  Southfield *(G-15042)*
Teradyne Inc .... C 313 425-3900
  Allen Park *(G-211)*

CONNECTORS: Electrical

JST Sales America Inc .... E 248 324-1957
  Farmington Hills *(G-5034)*

CONNECTORS: Electronic

Aees Power Systems Ltd Partnr............F 269 668-4429
  Farmington Hills *(G-4921)*
Amphenol Corporation.........................G....... 256 417-4338
  Novi *(G-11825)*
Amphenol Corporation.........................B 586 465-3131
  Clinton Township *(G-3050)*
Cardell Corporation ....F 248 371-9700
  Auburn Hills *(G-810)*
Harsco Corporation ....D....... 231 843-3431
  Ludington *(G-10062)*
Hirschmann Auto N Amer LLC ....G....... 248 495-2677
  Rochester Hills *(G-13444)*
Iriso USA Inc.......................................E 248 324-9780
  Farmington Hills *(G-5030)*
Kostal Kontakt Systeme Inc.................C....... 248 284-7600
  Rochester Hills *(G-13457)*
Mac Lean-Fogg Company ....C....... 248 280-0880
  Royal Oak *(G-13945)*
Midwest Sales Associates Inc ....G....... 248 348-9600
  Wixom *(G-17855)*
Norma Group Craig Assembly..............G....... 810 326-1374
  Saint Clair *(G-14230)*
Nvent Thermal LLC ....D....... 248 273-3359
  Troy *(G-16530)*
Rapp & Son Inc ....C....... 734 283-1000
  Wyandotte *(G-17971)*
Sine Systems Corporation ....C....... 586 465-3131
  Clinton Township *(G-3230)*
Te Connectivity Corporation.................C....... 248 273-3344
  Troy *(G-16633)*
Teradyne Inc ....C....... 313 425-3900
  Allen Park *(G-211)*
Winford Engineering LLC....................G....... 989 671-9721
  Auburn *(G-758)*

CONNECTORS: Power, Electric

Power Controllers LLC ....G....... 248 888-9896
  Farmington Hills *(G-5098)*

CONSTRUCTION & MINING MACHINERY WHOLESALERS

D & G Equipment Inc ....C....... 517 655-4606
  Williamston *(G-17729)*
Dimond Machinery Company Inc ....E 269 945-5908
  Hastings *(G-7407)*
Hitachi America Ltd ....E 248 477-5400
  Farmington Hills *(G-5021)*
Lappans of Gaylord Inc ....G....... 989 732-3274
  Gaylord *(G-5874)*
Magnum Toolscom LLC ....F 734 595-4600
  Romulus *(G-13703)*

CONSTRUCTION EQPT: Attachments

Ryans Equipment Inc ....E 989 427-2829
  Edmore *(G-4755)*

CONSTRUCTION EQPT: Attachments, Backhoe Mounted, Hyd Pwrd

Lang Tool Company ....G....... 989 435-9864
  Beaverton *(G-1387)*

CONSTRUCTION EQPT: Attachments, Snow Plow

JG Distributing Inc..............................G....... 906 225-0882
  Marquette *(G-10537)*
Jolman & Jolman Enterprises ....G....... 231 744-4500
  Muskegon *(G-11355)*
Kaufman Custom Sheet M ....G....... 906 932-2130
  Ironwood *(G-8333)*
Root Spring Scraper Co ....E 269 382-2025
  Kalamazoo *(G-8874)*
Toro Company ....B 888 492-6841
  Iron Mountain *(G-8304)*

CONSTRUCTION EQPT: Blade, Grader, Scraper, Dozer/Snow Plow

Great Lakes Snow & Ice Inc ....G....... 989 584-1211
  Carson City *(G-2490)*

CONSTRUCTION EQPT: Buckets, Excavating, Clamshell, Etc

Eagle Buckets Inc................................G....... 517 787-0385
  Jackson *(G-8436)*
Lyonnais Inc ....G....... 616 868-6625
  Lowell *(G-10035)*

CONSTRUCTION EQPT: Cranes

Simpson Industrial Svcs LLC ....G....... 810 392-2717
  Wales *(G-16860)*
Terex Corporation ....G....... 360 993-0515
  Durand *(G-4614)*
Top of Line Crane Service LLC............G....... 231 267-5326
  Williamsburg *(G-17722)*
Wmc Sales LLC ....G....... 616 813-7237
  Ada *(G-35)*

CONSTRUCTION EQPT: Finishers & Spreaders

Drag Finishing Tech LLC......................G....... 616 785-0400
  Comstock Park *(G-3479)*
Paladin Brands Group Inc ....F 319 378-3696
  Dexter *(G-4502)*
Wmv Incorporated ....G....... 248 333-1380
  Sylvan Lake *(G-15673)*

CONSTRUCTION EQPT: Grinders, Stone, Portable

ABI International ....G....... 248 583-7150
  Madison Heights *(G-10178)*

CONSTRUCTION EQPT: Soil compactors, Vibratory

Weber Machine (usa) Inc.....................G....... 207 947-4990
  Grand Rapids *(G-6982)*

CONSTRUCTION EQPT: Subgraders

Zeeland Component Sales LLC ....G....... 616 399-8614
  Zeeland *(G-18200)*

CONSTRUCTION EQPT: Tractors

Capital Equipment Clare LLC ....F 517 669-5533
  Dewitt *(G-4460)*

CONSTRUCTION EQPT: Wellpoint Systems

Big Foot Manufacturing Co ....F 231 775-5588
  Cadillac *(G-2231)*

CONSTRUCTION EQPT: Wrecker Hoists, Automobile

AME For Auto Dealers Inc ....G....... 248 720-0245
  Auburn Hills *(G-768)*

CONSTRUCTION MATERIALS, WHOL: Concrete/Cinder Bldg Prdts

Arbor Stone ....G....... 517 750-1340
  Spring Arbor *(G-15119)*
M 37 Concrete Products Inc.................G....... 231 689-1785
  White Cloud *(G-17626)*

CONSTRUCTION MATERIALS, WHOLESALE: Aggregate

Edw C Levy Co ....B 313 429-2200
  Dearborn *(G-3700)*
Edw C Levy Co ....D....... 313 843-7200
  Detroit *(G-4028)*
Saginaw Rock Products Co ....E 989 754-6589
  Saginaw *(G-14144)*

CONSTRUCTION MATERIALS, WHOLESALE: Air Ducts, Sheet Metal

Conquest Manufacturing LLC...............D....... 586 576-7600
  Warren *(G-16991)*

CONSTRUCTION MATERIALS, WHOLESALE: Architectural Metalwork

R J Designers Inc................................G....... 517 750-1990
  Spring Arbor *(G-15127)*

CONSTRUCTION MATERIALS, WHOLESALE: Asphalt Felts & coating

Full Spektrem LLC ....G....... 313 910-1920
  Saint Clair Shores *(G-14253)*

CONSTRUCTION MATERIALS, WHOLESALE: Awnings

Wayne-Craft Inc...................................F 734 421-8800
  Livonia *(G-10001)*

CONSTRUCTION MATERIALS, WHOLESALE: Block, Concrete & Cinder

C F Long & Sons Inc ....F 248 624-1562
  Walled Lake *(G-16892)*
Fisher Sand and Gravel Company ....E 989 835-7187
  Midland *(G-10861)*
Miller Products & Supply Co................F 906 774-1243
  Iron Mountain *(G-8290)*
Theut Concrete Products Inc...............F 810 679-3376
  Croswell *(G-3604)*

CONSTRUCTION MATERIALS, WHOLESALE: Brick, Exc Refractory

Boomer Company ....E 313 832-5050
  Detroit *(G-3910)*

CONSTRUCTION MATERIALS, WHOLESALE: Building Stone

Genesee Cut Stone & Marble Co ....E 810 743-1800
  Flint *(G-5437)*

CONSTRUCTION MATERIALS, WHOLESALE: Building Stone, Granite

Granite City Inc ....F 248 478-0033
  Livonia *(G-9756)*
Surface Encounters LLC ....D....... 586 566-7557
  Macomb *(G-10164)*
Yoxheimer Tile Co ....F 517 788-7542
  Jackson *(G-8614)*

CONSTRUCTION MATERIALS, WHOLESALE: Building Stone, Marble

Classic Stone MBL & Gran Inc ....G....... 248 588-1599
  Troy *(G-16269)*

CONSTRUCTION MATERIALS, WHOLESALE: Building, Interior

Reliable Glass Company ....E 313 924-9750
  Detroit *(G-4339)*

CONSTRUCTION MATERIALS, WHOLESALE: Cement

Holcim (us) Inc ....F 989 755-7515
  Saginaw *(G-14060)*
Lafarge North America Inc ....G....... 989 354-4171
  Alpena *(G-295)*
St Marys Cement Inc (us) ....G....... 269 679-5253
  Schoolcraft *(G-14501)*

CONSTRUCTION MATERIALS, WHOLESALE: Concrete Mixtures

Angelos Crushed Concrete Inc ....G....... 586 756-1070
  Warren *(G-16934)*
Gotts Transit Mix Inc...........................E 734 439-1528
  Milan *(G-10939)*
Sandusky Concrete & Supply ....G....... 810 648-2627
  Sandusky *(G-14442)*

CONSTRUCTION MATERIALS, WHOLESALE: Doors, Sliding

Antcliff Windows & Doors Inc...............F 810 742-5963
  Burton *(G-2144)*

CONSTRUCTION MATERIALS, WHOLESALE: Glass

I2 International Dev LLC ....F 616 534-8100
  Grandville *(G-7050)*

CONSTRUCTION MATERIALS, WHOLESALE: Glass

Oldcastle Buildingenvelope Inc .... E 616 896-8341
  Burnips (G-2133)

CONSTRUCTION MATERIALS, WHOLESALE: Gravel

Bently Sand & Gravel .... G 810 629-6172
  Fenton (G-5189)
Consumers Concrete Corporation .... E 269 342-0136
  Kalamazoo (G-8715)
Consumers Concrete Corporation .... F 231 777-3981
  Muskegon (G-11300)
Parker Excvtg Grav & Recycle .... F 616 784-1681
  Comstock Park (G-3505)
Thomas J Moyle Jr Incorporated .... E 906 482-3000
  Houghton (G-7986)
White Lake Excavating Inc .... F 231 894-6918
  Whitehall (G-17681)

CONSTRUCTION MATERIALS, WHOLESALE: Insulation, Thermal

Marshall Ryerson Co .... F 616 299-1751
  Grand Rapids (G-6645)

CONSTRUCTION MATERIALS, WHOLESALE: Limestone

Atlas Cut Stone Company .... G 248 545-5100
  Oak Park (G-12049)
Doug Wirt Enterprises Inc .... G 989 684-5777
  Bay City (G-1305)
O-N Minerals Michigan Company .... C 989 734-2131
  Rogers City (G-13619)

CONSTRUCTION MATERIALS, WHOLESALE: Millwork

D & D Building Inc .... F 616 248-7908
  Grand Rapids (G-6328)
Maple Valley Concrete Products .... G 517 852-1900
  Nashville (G-11460)
W S Townsend Company .... C 269 781-5131
  Marshall (G-10593)

CONSTRUCTION MATERIALS, WHOLESALE: Pallets, Wood

Mobile Pallet Service Inc .... E 269 792-4200
  Wayland (G-17407)

CONSTRUCTION MATERIALS, WHOLESALE: Paving Materials

Falcon Trucking Company .... F 248 634-9471
  Davisburg (G-3633)

CONSTRUCTION MATERIALS, WHOLESALE: Prefabricated Structures

Jensen Bridge & Supply Company .... E 810 648-3000
  Sandusky (G-14437)
K-Tel Corporation .... F 517 543-6174
  Charlotte (G-2657)
Morton Buildings Inc .... F 616 696-4747
  Three Rivers (G-15871)

CONSTRUCTION MATERIALS, WHOLESALE: Roof, Asphalt/Sheet Metal

Howard Structural Steel Inc .... E 989 752-3000
  Saginaw (G-14062)

CONSTRUCTION MATERIALS, WHOLESALE: Roofing & Siding Material

Caliber Metals Inc .... E 586 465-7650
  New Baltimore (G-11482)

CONSTRUCTION MATERIALS, WHOLESALE: Sand

American Aggregate Inc .... G 269 683-6160
  Niles (G-11594)
Brewers City Dock Inc .... E 616 396-6563
  Holland (G-7578)

CONSTRUCTION MATERIALS, WHOLESALE: Septic Tanks

Jack Millikin Inc .... G 989 348-8411
  Grayling (G-7109)

CONSTRUCTION MATERIALS, WHOLESALE: Sewer Pipe, Clay

Northern Concrete Pipe Inc .... D 517 645-2777
  Charlotte (G-2662)

CONSTRUCTION MATERIALS, WHOLESALE: Siding, Exc Wood

Astro Building Products Inc .... G 231 941-0324
  Traverse City (G-15898)

CONSTRUCTION MATERIALS, WHOLESALE: Stone, Crushed Or Broken

Bichler Gravel & Concrete Co .... F 906 786-0343
  Escanaba (G-4818)
Springfield Landscape Mtls .... G 269 965-6748
  Springfield (G-15204)

CONSTRUCTION MATERIALS, WHOLESALE: Windows

EZ Vent LLC .... G 616 874-2787
  Rockford (G-13568)
MRM Ida Products Co Inc .... G 313 834-0200
  Detroit (G-4080)
Pete Pullum Company Inc .... G 313 837-9440
  Detroit (G-4299)

CONSTRUCTION MATLS, WHOL: Lumber, Rough, Dressed/Finished

Banks Hardwoods Inc .... D 269 483-2323
  White Pigeon (G-17645)
Breiten Box & Packaging Co Inc .... G 586 469-0800
  Harrison Township (G-7324)
Daniel D Slater .... G 989 833-7135
  Riverdale (G-13284)
Empire Company LLC .... C 800 253-9000
  Zeeland (G-18134)
General Hardwood Company .... F 313 365-7733
  Detroit (G-4080)
Interntonal Hardwoods Michiana .... G 517 278-8446
  Coldwater (G-3310)
L & M Hardwood & Skids LLC .... G 734 281-3043
  Southgate (G-15079)
Maine Ornamental LLC .... F 800 556-8449
  White Pigeon (G-17652)
North American Forest Products .... C 269 663-8500
  Edwardsburg (G-4769)
PDM Company .... F 231 946-4444
  Lake Leelanau (G-9105)
Rare Earth Hardwoods Inc .... F 231 946-0043
  Traverse City (G-16090)
Rothig Forest Products Inc .... E 231 266-8292
  Irons (G-8322)
Schleben Forest Products Inc .... G 989 734-2858
  Rogers City (G-13622)
William S Wixtrom .... G 906 376-8247
  Republic (G-13247)

CONSTRUCTION MATLS, WHOLESALE: Struct Assy, Prefab, NonWood

Reliable Glass Company .... E 313 924-9750
  Detroit (G-4339)

CONSTRUCTION SAND MINING

Bdk Group Northern Mich Inc .... E 574 875-5183
  Charlevoix (G-2609)
Bunting Sand & Gravel Products .... E 989 345-2373
  West Branch (G-17508)
Cliffs Sand & Gravel Inc .... G 989 422-3463
  Houghton Lake (G-7989)
Crandell Bros Trucking Co .... E 517 543-2930
  Charlotte (G-2644)
Delhi Leasing Inc .... G 517 694-8578
  Holt (G-7910)
Fuoss Gravel Company .... F 989 725-2084
  Owosso (G-12292)
Halliday Sand & Gravel Inc .... E 989 422-3463
  Houghton Lake (G-7990)
Ironwood Ready Mix & Trucking .... G 906 932-4531
  Ironwood (G-8331)
Kasson Sand & Gravel Co Inc .... F 231 228-5455
  Maple City (G-10461)
Lc Materials .... G 231 825-2473
  Cadillac (G-2260)
Natural Aggregates Corporation .... F 248 685-1502
  Milford (G-10975)
R H Huhtala Aggregates Inc .... G 906 524-7758
  Lanse (G-9200)
Ruppe Manufacturing Company .... G 906 932-3540
  Ironwood (G-8339)
Sandman Inc .... G 248 652-3432
  Troy (G-16593)
Southwest Gravel Inc .... G 269 673-4665
  Allegan (G-188)

CONSTRUCTION SITE PREPARATION SVCS

Helsels Tree Service Inc .... G 231 879-3666
  Manton (G-10454)
St Charles Hardwood Michigan .... F 989 865-9299
  Saint Charles (G-14201)

CONSTRUCTION: Agricultural Building

Lumber & Truss Inc .... E 810 664-7290
  Lapeer (G-9472)

CONSTRUCTION: Apartment Building

Kearsley Lake Terrace LLC .... G 810 736-7000
  Flint (G-5453)

CONSTRUCTION: Athletic & Recreation Facilities

Fidelis Contracting LLC .... G 313 361-1000
  Detroit (G-4057)

CONSTRUCTION: Athletic & Recreation Facilities

Spartan Barricading .... G 313 292-2488
  Romulus (G-13734)
Systems Design & Installation .... G 269 543-4204
  Fennville (G-5177)

CONSTRUCTION: Commercial & Institutional Building

Buckeys Contracting & Service .... G 989 835-9512
  Midland (G-10819)
Clean Air Technology Inc .... E 734 459-6320
  Canton (G-2362)
Jn Newman Construction LLC .... G 269 968-1290
  Springfield (G-15194)
Keeler-Glasgow Company Inc .... E 269 621-2415
  Hartford (G-7384)
Michigan Indus Met Pdts Inc .... E 616 786-3922
  Muskegon (G-11378)
Sandbox Solutions Inc .... C 248 349-7010
  Northville/ (G-11723)

CONSTRUCTION: Commercial & Office Building, New

Architectural Planners Inc .... E 248 674-1340
  Waterford (G-17322)
Metter Flooring LLC .... G 517 914-2004
  Rives Junction (G-13309)
RB Construction Company .... E 586 264-9478
  Mount Clemens (G-11147)
Thomas J Moyle Jr Incorporated .... E 906 482-3000
  Houghton (G-7986)

CONSTRUCTION: Drainage System

County of Muskegon .... G 231 724-6219
  Muskegon (G-11301)

CONSTRUCTION: Electric Power Line

A1 Utility Contractor Inc .... D 989 324-8581
  Evart (G-4877)

CONSTRUCTION: Farm Building

Pioneer Pole Buildings N Inc .... E 989 386-2570
  Clare (G-2884)

PRODUCT SECTION

CONSTRUCTION: Food Prdts Manufacturing or Packing Plant
Harrison Partners Inv Group..............G...... 419 708-8154
  Milan *(G-10940)*

CONSTRUCTION: Heavy Highway & Street
A Lindberg & Sons Inc..............E...... 906 485-5705
  Ishpeming *(G-8342)*
D J McQuestion & Sons Inc..............F...... 231 768-4403
  Leroy *(G-9530)*
Michigan Paving and Mtls Co..............E...... 734 485-1717
  Van Buren Twp *(G-16772)*

CONSTRUCTION: Indl Building & Warehouse
Dcr Services & Cnstr Inc..............F...... 313 297-6544
  Detroit *(G-3962)*
E Power Remote Ltd..............G...... 231 689-5448
  White Cloud *(G-17621)*
Elevated Technologies Inc..............F...... 616 288-9817
  Grand Rapids *(G-6375)*
Emhart Teknologies LLC..............D...... 248 677-9693
  Troy *(G-16342)*

CONSTRUCTION: Indl Buildings, New, NEC
K & M Industrial LLC..............G...... 906 420-8770
  Gladstone *(G-5914)*
Michigan Paving and Mtls Co..............E...... 734 397-2050
  Canton *(G-2405)*

CONSTRUCTION: Institutional Building
Rock Industries Inc..............E...... 248 338-2800
  Bloomfield Hills *(G-1796)*

CONSTRUCTION: Marine
Oceans Sands Scuba..............G...... 616 396-0068
  Holland *(G-7762)*

CONSTRUCTION: Nonresidential Buildings, Custom
IKEA Chip LLC..............G...... 877 218-9931
  Troy *(G-16409)*

CONSTRUCTION: Parade Float
Prop Art Studio Inc..............G...... 313 824-2200
  Detroit *(G-4314)*

CONSTRUCTION: Parking Lot
Woodland Paving Co..............E...... 616 784-5220
  Comstock Park *(G-3521)*

CONSTRUCTION: Pipeline, NEC
Mid Michigan Pipe Inc..............G...... 989 772-5664
  Grand Rapids *(G-6683)*

CONSTRUCTION: Railroad & Subway
Delta Tube & Fabricating Corp..............C...... 248 634-8267
  Holly *(G-7875)*
Plymouth Technology Inc..............F...... 248 537-0081
  Rochester Hills *(G-13496)*

CONSTRUCTION: Refineries
URS Energy & Construction Inc..............C...... 989 642-4190
  Hemlock *(G-7464)*

CONSTRUCTION: Residential, Nec
Buster Mathis Foundation..............G...... 616 843-4433
  Wyoming *(G-17990)*
Jn Newman Construction LLC..............G...... 269 968-1290
  Springfield *(G-15194)*
Michigan Paving and Mtls Co..............E...... 734 397-2050
  Canton *(G-2405)*
Top Shelf Painter Inc..............G...... 586 465-0867
  Fraser *(G-5739)*

CONSTRUCTION: Roads, Gravel or Dirt
White Lake Excavating Inc..............F...... 231 894-6918
  Whitehall *(G-17681)*

CONSTRUCTION: Sewer Line
Bdk Group Northern Mich Inc..............E...... 574 875-5183
  Charlevoix *(G-2609)*

CONSTRUCTION: Silo, Agricultural
Michigan AG Services Inc..............F...... 616 374-8803
  Lake Odessa *(G-9117)*

CONSTRUCTION: Single-Family Housing
A-1 Awning Company..............G...... 734 421-0680
  Westland *(G-17537)*
Debbink and Sons Inc..............G...... 231 845-6421
  Ludington *(G-10055)*
G B Wolfgram and Sons Inc..............F...... 231 238-4638
  Indian River *(G-8217)*
Jn Newman Construction LLC..............G...... 269 968-1290
  Springfield *(G-15194)*
Makaveli Cnstr & Assoc Inc..............G...... 810 892-3412
  Detroit *(G-4217)*
Midwest Panel Systems Inc..............E...... 517 486-4844
  Blissfield *(G-1720)*
P C S Companies Inc..............G...... 616 754-2229
  Greenville *(G-7149)*
Red Carpet Capital Inc..............G...... 248 952-8583
  Orchard Lake *(G-12169)*
Riverbend Timber Framing Inc..............D...... 517 486-3629
  Blissfield *(G-1726)*

CONSTRUCTION: Single-family Housing, New
Burly Oak Builders Inc..............G...... 734 368-4912
  Dexter *(G-4480)*
Champion Home Builders Inc..............D...... 248 614-8200
  Troy *(G-16263)*
Harman Lumber & Supply Inc..............G...... 269 641-5424
  Union *(G-16729)*
Kampers Woodfire Company Inc..............G...... 906 478-7902
  Rudyard *(G-13984)*
Koskis Log Homes Inc..............G...... 906 884-4937
  Ontonagon *(G-12162)*
Thomas J Moyle Jr Incorporated..............E...... 906 482-3000
  Houghton *(G-7986)*
Woodtech Builders Inc..............F...... 906 932-8055
  Ironwood *(G-8341)*

CONSTRUCTION: Single-family Housing, Prefabricated
North Arrow Log Homes Inc..............G...... 906 484-5524
  Pickford *(G-12482)*

CONSTRUCTION: Steel Buildings
Scott Enterprises..............G...... 734 279-2078
  Dundee *(G-4600)*

CONSTRUCTION: Street Surfacing & Paving
Asphalt Paving Inc..............F...... 231 733-1409
  Muskegon *(G-11272)*
Barrett Paving Materials Inc..............E...... 734 985-9480
  Ypsilanti *(G-18055)*
D O W Asphalt Paving LLC..............F...... 810 743-2633
  Swartz Creek *(G-15665)*
Hd Selcating Pav Solutions LLC..............G...... 248 241-6526
  Clarkston *(G-2925)*
Nagle Paving Company..............F...... 248 553-0600
  Novi *(G-11951)*
Rieth-Riley Cnstr Co Inc..............F...... 231 263-2100
  Grawn *(G-7100)*
Rieth-Riley Cnstr Co Inc..............E...... 616 248-0920
  Wyoming *(G-18030)*
RWS & Associates LLC..............F...... 517 278-3134
  Coldwater *(G-3328)*
Woodland Paving Co..............E...... 616 784-5220
  Comstock Park *(G-3521)*

CONSTRUCTION: Swimming Pools
Solar EZ Inc..............F...... 989 773-3347
  Mount Pleasant *(G-11229)*

CONSTRUCTION: Utility Line
Forbes Sanitation & Excavation..............F...... 231 723-2311
  Manistee *(G-10422)*
Genoak Materials Inc..............C...... 248 634-8276
  Holly *(G-7880)*
Lgc Global Inc..............E...... 313 989-4141
  Detroit *(G-4202)*

CONSTRUCTION: Waste Water & Sewage Treatment Plant
Digested Organics LLC..............G...... 844 934-4378
  Farmington Hills *(G-4973)*

CONSTRUCTION: Water Main
A Lindberg & Sons Inc..............E...... 906 485-5705
  Ishpeming *(G-8342)*

CONSULTING SVC: Business, NEC
ADS LLC..............G...... 248 740-9593
  Troy *(G-16168)*
Art Glass Inc..............G...... 586 731-8627
  Sterling Heights *(G-15264)*
Autoneum North America Inc..............D...... 248 848-0100
  Farmington Hills *(G-4936)*
Cg & D Group..............G...... 248 310-9166
  Farmington Hills *(G-4960)*
Dcr Services & Cnstr Inc..............F...... 313 297-6544
  Detroit *(G-3962)*
Ernie Romanco..............E...... 517 531-3686
  Albion *(G-123)*
Global Impact Group LLC..............G...... 248 895-9900
  Grand Blanc *(G-5966)*
GT Solutions LLC..............G...... 616 259-0700
  Holland *(G-7655)*
IKEA Chip LLC..............G...... 877 218-9931
  Troy *(G-16409)*
Innovative Weld Solutions LLC..............G...... 937 545-7695
  Rochester *(G-13329)*
Kage Group LLC..............E...... 734 604-5052
  Van Buren Twp *(G-16767)*
Metro Wbe Associates Inc..............G...... 248 504-7563
  Detroit *(G-4232)*
PMS Products Inc..............G...... 616 355-6615
  Holland *(G-7772)*
Regency Construction Corp..............E...... 586 741-8000
  Clinton Township *(G-3208)*
Reply Inc..............F...... 248 686-2481
  Auburn Hills *(G-989)*
Steelcase Inc..............A...... 616 247-2710
  Grand Rapids *(G-6889)*
Suburban Hockey LLC..............G...... 248 478-1600
  Farmington Hills *(G-5133)*
Up Officeexpress LLC..............G...... 906 281-0089
  Calumet *(G-2334)*
Virtual Emergency Services LLC..............F...... 734 324-2299
  Wyandotte *(G-17980)*
Visual Productions Inc..............E...... 248 356-4399
  Southfield *(G-15061)*
Welding & Joining Tech LLC..............G...... 248 625-3045
  Clarkston *(G-2965)*
Wyser Innovative Products LLC..............G...... 616 583-9225
  Byron Center *(G-2218)*

CONSULTING SVC: Chemical
V & V Industries Inc..............F...... 248 624-7943
  Wixom *(G-17923)*

CONSULTING SVC: Computer
3r Info LLC..............F...... 201 221-6133
  Canton *(G-2342)*
Aperion Information Tech Inc..............F...... 248 969-9791
  Oxford *(G-12336)*
Chain-Sys Corporation..............F...... 517 627-1173
  Lansing *(G-9281)*
Competitive Cmpt Info Tech Inc..............E...... 732 829-9699
  Northville *(G-11683)*
E-Con LLC..............E...... 248 766-9000
  Birmingham *(G-1682)*
Edi Experts LLC..............G...... 734 844-7016
  Canton *(G-2370)*
Export Service International..............G...... 248 620-7100
  Clarkston *(G-2919)*
Intellibee Inc..............G...... 313 586-4122
  Detroit *(G-4145)*
International Bus Mchs Corp..............B...... 517 391-5248
  East Lansing *(G-4665)*
Rose Mobile Computer Repr LLC..............F...... 248 653-0865
  Troy *(G-16583)*
Signalx Technologies LLC..............F...... 248 935-4237
  Plymouth *(G-12754)*
Simerics Inc..............G...... 248 513-3200
  Novi *(G-11998)*

CONSULTING SVC: Computer

Software Advantage Consulting............G...... 586 264-5632
  Sterling Heights (G-15503)
Spiders Software Solutions LLC............E...... 248 305-3225
  Northville (G-11727)
Strategic Computer Solutions................G...... 248 888-0666
  Ann Arbor (G-648)
Sunera Technologies Inc..........................E...... 248 524-0222
  Troy (G-16625)
Torenzo Inc...F...... 313 732-7874
  Bloomfield Hills (G-1804)
Tru-Syzygy Inc..G...... 248 622-7211
  Lake Orion (G-9167)

CONSULTING SVC: Data Processing

Tecra Systems Inc.......................................E...... 248 888-1116
  Westland (G-17602)

CONSULTING SVC: Educational

Effective Schools Products ....G...... 517 349-8841
  Okemos (G-12121)
Esl Supplies LLC...G...... 517 525-7877
  Mason (G-10637)
Quirkroberts Publishing Ltd.....................G...... 248 879-2598
  Troy (G-16573)

CONSULTING SVC: Engineering

Amerivet Engineering LLC........................G...... 269 751-9092
  Hamilton (G-7230)
Arboc Ltd..G...... 248 684-2895
  Commerce Township (G-3390)
Binsfeld Engineering Inc..........................F...... 231 334-4383
  Maple City (G-10460)
Boyd Manufacturing LLC.........................G...... 734 649-9765
  Muskegon (G-11284)
Commonwealth Associates Inc...............C...... 517 788-3000
  Jackson (G-8416)
Data Acquisition Ctrl Systems.................F...... 248 437-6096
  Brighton (G-1909)
Design Safety Engineering Inc................G...... 734 483-2033
  Ypsilanti (G-18065)
Disrupttech LLC...G...... 248 225-8383
  Saint Clair Shores (G-14244)
Dynamic Corporation.................................D...... 616 399-9391
  Holland (G-7613)
Electrical Design and Ctrl Co...................E...... 248 743-2400
  Troy (G-16338)
Elite Engineering Inc.................................F...... 517 304-3254
  Rochester Hills (G-13417)
Experienced Concepts Inc.......................F...... 586 752-4200
  Armada (G-719)
GM Gdls Defense Group LLC..................G...... 586 825-4000
  Sterling Heights (G-15362)
Jad Products Inc..G...... 517 456-4810
  Clinton (G-3024)
Jax Services LLC.......................................G...... 586 703-3212
  Warren (G-17112)
John Lamantia Corporation......................G...... 269 428-8100
  Stevensville (G-15572)
Kubica Corp..F...... 248 344-7750
  Novi (G-11922)
Lotus International Company ....A...... 734 245-0140
  Canton (G-2394)
Lube - Power Inc.......................................D...... 586 247-6500
  Shelby Township (G-14628)
Maness Petroleum Corp............................G...... 989 773-5475
  Mount Pleasant (G-11203)
Mejenta Systems Inc.................................E...... 248 434-2583
  Southfield (G-14977)
Minth North America Inc..........................D...... 248 259-7468
  Wixom (G-17856)
Piping Components Inc............................G...... 313 382-6400
  Melvindale (G-10705)
Roush Enterprises Inc..............................C...... 734 805-4400
  Farmington (G-4909)
Secord Solutions LLC...............................G...... 734 363-8887
  Ecorse (G-4745)
Spen-Tech Machine Engrg Corp.............D...... 810 275-6800
  Flint (G-5501)
Superior Controls Inc...............................C...... 734 454-0500
  Plymouth (G-12763)
T E Technology Inc...................................E...... 231 929-3966
  Traverse City (G-16118)
Varatech Inc...F...... 616 393-6408
  Holland (G-7843)
Venntis Technologies LLC........................F...... 616 395-8254
  Holland (G-7845)
W G Benjey Inc..F...... 989 356-0016
  Alpena (G-319)

CONSULTING SVC: Financial Management

Cygnet Financial Planning Inc.................G...... 248 673-2900
  Waterford (G-17331)

CONSULTING SVC: Management

American Journal Hlth Prom Inc..............G...... 248 682-0707
  Troy (G-16196)
Aqpe LLC..G...... 810 329-9259
  Saint Clair (G-14204)
Bpc Acquisition Company........................D...... 231 798-1310
  Norton Shores (G-11809)
Cardinal Group Industries Corp..............E...... 517 437-6000
  Hillsdale (G-7521)
Cg & D Group...G...... 248 310-9166
  Farmington Hills (G-4960)
Christian Schools Intl................................E...... 616 957-1070
  Grand Rapids (G-6275)
Complete Services LLC...........................F...... 248 470-8247
  Livonia (G-9686)
Ervins Group LLC.....................................G...... 248 203-2000
  Bloomfield Hills (G-1764)
Geolean USA LLC....................................F...... 313 859-9780
  Livonia (G-9751)
Gnutti Carlo Usa Inc................................B...... 517 223-1059
  Webberville (G-17450)
Horizon Intl Group LLC............................D...... 734 341-9336
  Birmingham (G-1686)
Lowry Holding Company Inc..................C...... 810 229-7200
  Brighton (G-1952)
Mendenhall Associates Inc.....................G...... 734 741-4710
  Ann Arbor (G-552)
Petroleum Environmental Tech...............G...... 231 258-0400
  Rapid City (G-13110)
Questor Partners Fund II LP...................G...... 248 593-1930
  Birmingham (G-1699)
Sika Corporation..D...... 248 577-0020
  Madison Heights (G-10353)
Systrand Manufacturing Corp.................C...... 734 479-8100
  Brownstown Twp (G-2074)
Toyo Seat USA Corporation.....................C...... 606 849-3009
  Imlay City (G-8212)
Verdoni Productions Inc..........................G...... 989 790-0845
  Saginaw (G-14179)
Welding & Joining Tech LLC...................G...... 248 625-3045
  Clarkston (G-2965)

CONSULTING SVC: Marketing Management

Adair Printing Company...........................E...... 734 426-2822
  Dexter (G-4472)
Arbor Press LLC...D...... 248 549-0150
  Royal Oak (G-13904)
Blue Pony LLC...G...... 616 291-5554
  Hudsonville (G-8149)
Contemporary Industries Inc..................G...... 248 478-8850
  Farmington Hills (G-4966)
D Find Corporation....................................G...... 248 641-2858
  Troy (G-16293)
Elm International Inc.................................E...... 517 332-4900
  Okemos (G-12122)
Fusion Design Group Ltd.........................G...... 269 469-8226
  New Buffalo (G-11514)
Graphic Resource Group Inc.................E...... 248 588-6100
  Troy (G-16386)
High Impact Solutions Inc........................G...... 248 473-9804
  Farmington Hills (G-5019)
Integrated Program MGT LLC.................G...... 248 241-9257
  Clarkston (G-2932)
Marshall Ryerson Co.................................F...... 616 299-1751
  Grand Rapids (G-6645)
Media Swing LLC......................................G...... 313 885-2525
  Grosse Pointe Farms (G-7186)
Menu Pulse Inc..G...... 989 708-1207
  Saginaw (G-14088)
New Rules Marketing Inc.........................E...... 800 962-3119
  Spring Lake (G-15166)
Phoenix Press Incorporated...................G...... 248 435-8040
  Troy (G-16546)
Rtr Alpha Inc..G...... 248 377-4060
  Auburn Hills (G-994)
Sage Direct Inc..F...... 616 940-8311
  Grand Rapids (G-6850)
Solutionsnowbiz..G...... 269 321-5062
  Portage (G-13033)
Technova Corporation...............................F...... 517 485-1402
  Okemos (G-12138)
Wellard Inc...G...... 312 752-0155
  West Olive (G-17536)

CONSULTING SVC: Online Technology

Ginkgotree Inc..G...... 734 707-7191
  Detroit (G-4091)
Lowery Corporation...................................C...... 616 554-5200
  Grand Rapids (G-6633)

CONSULTING SVC: Productivity Improvement

Link Tech Inc..G...... 269 427-8297
  Bangor (G-1092)
Quality Engineering Company................F...... 248 351-9000
  Wixom (G-17883)

CONSULTING SVC: Sales Management

Considine Sales & Marketing..................G...... 248 889-7887
  Highland (G-7490)
Emhart Teknologies LLC.........................D...... 248 677-9693
  Troy (G-16342)

CONSULTING SVC: Telecommunications

Causey Consulting LLC...........................G...... 248 671-4979
  West Bloomfield (G-17469)
No Limit Wireless-Michigan Inc.............G...... 313 285-8402
  Detroit (G-4274)

CONSULTING SVCS, BUSINESS: Communications

Blue Pony LLC...G...... 616 291-5554
  Hudsonville (G-8149)
Forum and Link Inc..................................G...... 313 945-5465
  Dearborn (G-3713)
Satellite Tracking Systems.....................G...... 248 627-3334
  Ortonville (G-12202)

CONSULTING SVCS, BUSINESS: Energy Conservation

Volta Power Systems LLC.......................G...... 616 226-4224
  Holland (G-7850)

CONSULTING SVCS, BUSINESS: Environmental

Baygeo Inc..E...... 231 941-7660
  Traverse City (G-15909)
Environmental Protection Inc.................F...... 231 943-2265
  Traverse City (G-15965)
Lgc Global Inc...E...... 313 989-4141
  Detroit (G-4202)
Lyman Thornton...G...... 248 762-8433
  Wixom (G-17847)

CONSULTING SVCS, BUSINESS: Safety Training Svcs

Versant Medical Physics..........................E...... 888 316-3644
  Kalamazoo (G-8918)

CONSULTING SVCS, BUSINESS: Sys Engnrg, Exc Computer/Prof

Braiq Inc...G...... 858 729-4116
  Detroit (G-3912)
Christopher S Campion.............................G...... 517 414-6796
  Jackson (G-8409)
Secord Solutions LLC...............................G...... 734 363-8887
  Ecorse (G-4745)

CONSULTING SVCS, BUSINESS: Systems Analysis & Engineering

Apis North America LLC..........................G...... 800 470-8970
  Royal Oak (G-13903)
Atos Syntel Inc..C...... 248 619-2800
  Troy (G-16228)
Beet LLC..F...... 248 432-0052
  Plymouth (G-12584)
Inora Technologies Inc............................F...... 734 302-7488
  Ann Arbor (G-506)
Light Speed Usa LLC...............................A...... 616 308-0054
  Grand Rapids (G-6627)
Pioneer Technologies Corp.....................E...... 702 806-3152
  Fremont (G-5782)
Precision Laser & Mfg LLC.....................G...... 519 733-8422
  Sterling Heights (G-15449)

PRODUCT SECTION

Torenzo Inc ....F 313 732-7874
Bloomfield Hills *(G-1804)*

CONSULTING SVCS, BUSINESS: Systems Analysis Or Design

Corporate AV Services LLC ....G 248 939-0900
Commerce Township *(G-3395)*
National Element Inc ....E 248 486-1810
Brighton *(G-1966)*
Specilty Vhcl Acquisition Corp ....E 586 446-4701
Warren *(G-17245)*
Stonebrdge Technical Entps Ltd ....F 810 750-0040
Fenton *(G-5240)*

CONSULTING SVCS, BUSINESS: Test Development & Evaluation

Tectum Holdings Inc ....D 734 926-2362
Ann Arbor *(G-656)*

CONSULTING SVCS: Oil

Wellmaster Consulting Inc ....F 231 893-9266
Rothbury *(G-13896)*

CONSULTING SVCS: Scientific

Consoldted Rsource Imaging LLC ....E 616 735-2080
Grand Rapids *(G-6301)*
Light Speed Usa LLC ....A 616 308-0054
Grand Rapids *(G-6627)*
Welding & Joining Tech LLC ....G 248 625-3045
Clarkston *(G-2965)*

CONTACT LENSES

Art Optical Contact Lens Inc ....C 616 453-1888
Grand Rapids *(G-6183)*
Essilor Laboratories Amer Inc ....C 616 361-6000
Grand Rapids *(G-6386)*

CONTACTS: Electrical

Mike Degrow ....G 734 353-4752
Lansing *(G-9401)*

CONTAINERS: Air Cargo, Metal

American Fabricated Pdts Inc ....F 616 607-8785
Spring Lake *(G-15133)*
Lock and Load Corp ....G 800 975-9658
Marion *(G-10490)*

CONTAINERS: Cargo, Wood

Grand Industries Inc ....E 616 846-7120
Grand Haven *(G-6026)*

CONTAINERS: Cargo, Wood & Metal Combination

Karjo Trucking Inc ....F 248 597-3700
Troy *(G-16443)*
Lock and Load Corp ....G 800 975-9658
Marion *(G-10490)*

CONTAINERS: Cargo, Wood & Wood With Metal

Just Cover It Up ....G 734 247-4729
Romulus *(G-13694)*
Tamsco Inc ....F 586 415-1500
Fraser *(G-5737)*

CONTAINERS: Corrugated

Aldez North America LLC ....G 810 577-3891
Almont *(G-251)*
All Packaging Solutions Inc ....G 248 880-1548
Madison Heights *(G-10187)*
Classic Container Corporation ....E 734 853-3000
Livonia *(G-9684)*
Coastal Container Corporation ....D 616 355-9800
Holland *(G-7593)*
Complete Packaging Inc ....E 734 241-2794
Monroe *(G-11025)*
Corrugated Options LLC ....G 734 850-1300
Temperance *(G-15825)*
Corrugated Pratt ....G 734 853-3030
Livonia *(G-9690)*
D T Fowler Mfg Co Inc ....G 810 245-9336
Lapeer *(G-9454)*

Delta Containers Inc ....E 810 742-2730
Bay City *(G-1300)*
Eco Paper ....G 248 652-3601
Rochester Hills *(G-13415)*
Genesee Group Inc ....E 810 235-8041
Flint *(G-5439)*
Genesee Group Inc ....D 810 235-6120
Flint *(G-5440)*
Georgia-Pacific LLC ....D 734 439-2441
Milan *(G-10938)*
Lepages 2000 Inc ....G 416 357-0041
Romulus *(G-13700)*
MRC Industries Inc ....D 269 343-0747
Kalamazoo *(G-8832)*
National Packaging Corporation ....F 248 652-3600
Rochester Hills *(G-13479)*
Pratt Industries Inc ....C 616 452-2111
Grand Rapids *(G-6760)*
Pratt Industries Inc ....G 734 853-3000
Livonia *(G-9895)*
Scotts Enterprises Inc ....E 989 275-5011
Roscommon *(G-13754)*
Understated Corrugated LLC ....G 248 880-5767
Northville *(G-11733)*
Westrock Rkt LLC ....C 269 963-5511
Battle Creek *(G-1267)*

CONTAINERS: Foil, Bakery Goods & Frozen Foods

Ungar Frozen Food Product ....G 248 626-3148
Bloomfield Hills *(G-1809)*

CONTAINERS: Glass

Owens-Brockway Glass Cont Inc ....G 269 435-2535
Constantine *(G-3541)*

CONTAINERS: Metal

Actron Steel Inc ....E 231 947-3981
Traverse City *(G-15890)*
Advance Packaging Corporation ....C 616 949-6610
Grand Rapids *(G-6147)*
Associated Metals Inc ....G 734 369-3851
Ann Arbor *(G-371)*
Chemtool Incorporated ....G 734 439-7010
Milan *(G-10934)*
Delta Tube & Fabricating Corp ....C 248 634-8267
Holly *(G-7875)*
Eagle Buckets Inc ....G 517 787-0385
Jackson *(G-8436)*
Geerpres Inc ....E 231 773-3211
Muskegon *(G-11329)*
Georgia-Pacific LLC ....D 734 439-2441
Milan *(G-10938)*
Georgia-Pacific LLC ....C 989 725-5191
Owosso *(G-12293)*
Green Bay Packaging Inc ....C 269 552-1000
Kalamazoo *(G-8757)*
Repair Industries Michigan Inc ....C 313 365-5300
Detroit *(G-4344)*
Royal ARC Welding Company ....E 734 789-9099
Flat Rock *(G-5362)*
Zayna LLC ....G 616 452-4522
Grand Rapids *(G-7011)*

CONTAINERS: Plastic

Advanced Fibermolding Inc ....E 231 768-5177
Leroy *(G-9529)*
Amcor Rigid Packaging Usa LLC ....C 734 336-3812
Manchester *(G-10401)*
Amcor Rigid Packaging Usa LLC ....D 734 428-9741
Plymouth *(G-12569)*
Decade Products LLC ....F 616 975-4965
Grand Rapids *(G-6340)*
Eliason Corporation ....D 269 327-7003
Portage *(G-12992)*
Genova-Minnesota Inc ....D 810 744-4500
Davison *(G-3651)*
Global Enterprise Limited ....G 586 948-4100
Chesterfield *(G-2782)*
Global Mfg & Assembly Corp ....B 517 789-8116
Jackson *(G-8458)*
Graham Packaging Company LP ....E 616 355-0479
Holland *(G-7647)*
Hold It Products Corporation ....G 248 624-1195
Commerce Township *(G-3413)*
Huhtamaki Inc ....C 989 465-9046
Coleman *(G-3345)*

CONTAINERS: Wood

Imperial Industries Inc ....F 734 397-1400
Saline *(G-14395)*
Kautex Inc ....B 313 633-2254
Detroit *(G-4173)*
Kent City Plastics LLC ....F 616 678-4900
Kent City *(G-8993)*
Lacks Industries Inc ....D 616 554-7134
Grand Rapids *(G-6610)*
Letica Corporation ....C 248 652-0557
Rochester Hills *(G-13460)*
Martinrea Industries Inc ....E 734 428-2400
Manchester *(G-10408)*
Osco Inc ....E 248 852-7310
Rochester Hills *(G-13489)*
Performance Systematix Inc ....D 616 949-9090
Grand Rapids *(G-6749)*
Plasticrafts Inc ....G 313 532-1900
Redford *(G-13183)*
Polytec Foha Inc ....F 586 978-9386
Warren *(G-17188)*
Retro Enterprises Inc ....G 269 435-8583
Constantine *(G-3544)*
Sonus Engineered Solutions LLC ....C 586 427-3838
Warren *(G-17244)*
Sur-Form LLC ....E 586 221-1950
Chesterfield *(G-2844)*
Th Plastics Inc ....D 269 496-8495
Mendon *(G-10720)*
Thomson Plastics Inc ....D 517 545-5026
Howell *(G-8109)*
Yanfeng US Automotive ....C 734 289-4841
Monroe *(G-11087)*
Yanfeng US Automotive ....E 734 946-0600
Romulus *(G-13744)*
Zayna LLC ....G 616 452-4522
Grand Rapids *(G-7011)*

CONTAINERS: Plywood & Veneer, Wood

Delta Packaging International ....G 517 321-6548
Lansing *(G-9214)*

CONTAINERS: Sanitary, Food

Acumedia Manufacturers Inc ....E 517 372-9200
Lansing *(G-9332)*
Huhtamaki Inc ....B 989 633-8900
Coleman *(G-3346)*
Letica Corporation ....C 248 652-0557
Rochester Hills *(G-13460)*

CONTAINERS: Shipping & Mailing, Fiber

Action Packaging LLC ....E 616 871-5200
Caledonia *(G-2287)*
Xpress Packaging Solutions LLC ....G 231 629-0463
Shelby Township *(G-14724)*

CONTAINERS: Shipping, Bombs, Metal Plate

Big Steel Rack LLC ....G 517 740-5428
Jackson *(G-8389)*
Industrial Container Inc ....F 313 923-8778
Detroit *(G-4138)*

CONTAINERS: Wood

AAR Manufacturing Inc ....E 231 779-8800
Cadillac *(G-2220)*
Black River Pallet Company ....E 616 772-6211
Zeeland *(G-18121)*
C & K Box Company Inc ....E 517 784-1779
Jackson *(G-8397)*
Classic Container Corporation ....E 734 853-3000
Livonia *(G-9684)*
Demeester Wood Products Inc ....F 616 677-5995
Coopersville *(G-3556)*
Kamps Inc ....F 517 645-2800
Potterville *(G-13074)*
Luberda Wood Products Inc ....G 989 876-4334
Omer *(G-12144)*
Millers Woodworking ....G 989 386-8110
Clare *(G-2878)*
Quinlan Lumber Co ....G 810 743-0700
Burton *(G-2162)*
Setco Inc ....G 616 459-6311
Grand Rapids *(G-6858)*
Union Pallet & Cont Co Inc ....E 517 279-4888
Coldwater *(G-3339)*

CONTRACT DIVING SVC

Superior Mar & Envmtl Svcs LLC ....G....... 906 253-9448
  Sault Sainte Marie *(G-14475)*

CONTRACTOR: Dredging

K & M Industrial LLC ....G....... 906 420-8770
  Gladstone *(G-5914)*

CONTRACTOR: Rigging & Scaffolding

Dobson Industrial Inc ....E....... 800 298-6063
  Bay City *(G-1304)*

CONTRACTORS: Access Control System Eqpt

Cornelius Systems Inc ....E....... 248 545-5558
  Berkley *(G-1582)*
D Find Corporation ....G....... 248 641-2858
  Troy *(G-16293)*

CONTRACTORS: Acoustical & Insulation Work

Masco Corporation ....A....... 313 274-7400
  Livonia *(G-9826)*

CONTRACTORS: Antenna Installation

Cjg LLC ....F....... 734 793-1400
  Livonia *(G-9683)*

CONTRACTORS: Asphalt

Action Asphalt LLC ....F....... 734 449-8565
  Whitmore Lake *(G-17684)*
Arnt Asphalt Sealing Inc ....D....... 269 927-1532
  Benton Harbor *(G-1482)*
Carrollton Paving Co ....F....... 989 752-7139
  Saginaw *(G-14012)*
D O W Asphalt Paving LLC ....F....... 810 743-2633
  Swartz Creek *(G-15665)*
Lite Load Services LLC ....F....... 269 751-6037
  Hamilton *(G-7236)*
Michigan Paving and Mtls Co ....F....... 989 463-1323
  Alma *(G-242)*
Nagle Paving Company ....C....... 734 591-1484
  Livonia *(G-9856)*
RWS & Associates LLC ....F....... 517 278-3134
  Coldwater *(G-3328)*

CONTRACTORS: Awning Installation

Royal Oak & Birmingham Tent ....F....... 248 542-5552
  Royal Oak *(G-13967)*

CONTRACTORS: Boiler & Furnace

Dfc Inc ....G....... 734 285-6749
  Riverview *(G-13293)*

CONTRACTORS: Boiler Maintenance Contractor

Detroit Boiler Company ....F....... 313 921-7060
  Detroit *(G-3972)*
Diversified Mech Svcs Inc ....F....... 616 785-2735
  Comstock Park *(G-3478)*
Vierson Boiler & Repair Co ....F....... 616 949-0500
  Grand Rapids *(G-6972)*

CONTRACTORS: Building Eqpt & Machinery Installation

Amtrade Systems Inc ....G....... 734 522-9500
  Livonia *(G-9647)*
Assa Abloy Entrance Systems US ....E....... 734 462-2348
  Livonia *(G-9654)*
Constructive Sheet Metal Inc ....E....... 616 245-5306
  Allendale *(G-215)*
Morton Buildings Inc ....F....... 616 696-4747
  Three Rivers *(G-15871)*
Thyssenkrupp Elevator Corp ....F....... 616 942-4710
  Grand Rapids *(G-6930)*
Ufp Atlantic LLC ....G....... 616 364-6161
  Grand Rapids *(G-6945)*
Ufp West Central LLC ....G....... 616 364-6161
  Grand Rapids *(G-6949)*
Universal Forest Products Inc ....C....... 616 364-6161
  Grand Rapids *(G-6954)*

Vierson Boiler & Repair Co ....F....... 616 949-0500
  Grand Rapids *(G-6972)*
Waltz-Holst Blow Pipe Company ....E....... 616 676-8119
  Ada *(G-33)*
Yard & Home LLC ....G....... 844 927-3466
  Grand Rapids *(G-7007)*

CONTRACTORS: Building Front Installation, Metal

West Michigan Metals LLC ....G....... 269 978-7021
  Allegan *(G-192)*

CONTRACTORS: Building Movers

West Shore Services Inc ....E....... 616 895-4347
  Allendale *(G-227)*

CONTRACTORS: Building Sign Installation & Mntnce

Bill Daup Signs Inc ....G....... 810 235-4080
  Swartz Creek *(G-15663)*
H M Day Signs Inc ....G....... 231 946-7132
  Traverse City *(G-15996)*
Huron Advertising Company Inc ....E....... 734 483-2000
  Ypsilanti *(G-18077)*
Media Swing LLC ....G....... 313 885-2525
  Grosse Pointe Farms *(G-7186)*
Meiers Signs Inc ....G....... 906 786-3424
  Escanaba *(G-4843)*
Michigan Signs Inc ....G....... 734 662-1503
  Ann Arbor *(G-556)*
Modern Neon Sign Co Inc ....F....... 269 349-8636
  Kalamazoo *(G-8830)*
Signs Plus ....F....... 810 987-7446
  Port Huron *(G-12966)*
Wenz & Gibbens Enterprises ....G....... 248 333-7938
  Pontiac *(G-12874)*

CONTRACTORS: Building Site Preparation

Frenchys Skirting Inc ....G....... 734 721-3013
  Wayne *(G-17430)*

CONTRACTORS: Carpentry Work

Arnold & Sautter Co ....F....... 989 684-7557
  Bay City *(G-1276)*
Brunt Associates Inc ....E....... 248 960-8295
  Wixom *(G-17779)*
Grand Traverse Garage Doors ....E....... 231 943-9897
  Traverse City *(G-15985)*
Greenia Custom Woodworking Inc ....E....... 989 868-9790
  Reese *(G-13230)*
Nuwood Components ....G....... 616 395-1905
  Holland *(G-7761)*
PCI Industries Inc ....D....... 248 542-2570
  Oak Park *(G-12090)*
W S Townsend Company ....C....... 269 781-5131
  Marshall *(G-10593)*
Woodways Industries LLC ....E....... 616 956-3070
  Grand Rapids *(G-7003)*
Woodworks & Design Company ....F....... 517 482-6665
  Lansing *(G-9434)*

CONTRACTORS: Carpentry, Cabinet & Finish Work

A & B Display Systems Inc ....F....... 989 893-6642
  Bay City *(G-1269)*
Charlotte Cabinets Inc ....G....... 517 543-1522
  Charlotte *(G-2639)*
Custom Crafters ....G....... 269 763-9180
  Bellevue *(G-1453)*
Gast Cabinet Co ....G....... 269 422-1587
  Baroda *(G-1125)*
Great Lakes Fine Cabinetry ....G....... 906 493-5780
  Sault Sainte Marie *(G-14465)*
Owens Building Co Inc ....E....... 989 835-1293
  Midland *(G-10901)*
Terry Hanover ....G....... 269 426-4199
  New Troy *(G-11560)*

CONTRACTORS: Carpentry, Cabinet Building & Installation

Designtech Custom Interiors ....G....... 989 695-6306
  Freeland *(G-5754)*
Mod Interiors Inc ....E....... 586 725-8227
  Ira *(G-8261)*

Progressive Cabinets Inc ....G....... 810 631-4611
  Otisville *(G-12234)*
Thomas and Milliken Mllwk Inc ....F....... 231 386-7236
  Northport *(G-11673)*
Tims Cabinet Inc ....G....... 989 846-9831
  Pinconning *(G-12513)*
Village Cabinet Shoppe Inc ....G....... 586 264-6464
  Sterling Heights *(G-15539)*

CONTRACTORS: Carpet Laying

Grand River Interiors Inc ....E....... 616 454-2800
  Grand Rapids *(G-6468)*
Seelye Group Ltd ....G....... 517 267-2001
  Lansing *(G-9423)*

CONTRACTORS: Closed Circuit Television Installation

Thalner Electronic Labs Inc ....E....... 734 761-4506
  Ann Arbor *(G-668)*

CONTRACTORS: Closet Organizers, Installation & Design

W S Townsend Company ....C....... 269 781-5131
  Marshall *(G-10593)*

CONTRACTORS: Coating, Caulking & Weather, Water & Fire

Rock Industries Inc ....E....... 248 338-2800
  Bloomfield Hills *(G-1796)*

CONTRACTORS: Commercial & Office Building

Crown Heating Inc ....G....... 248 352-1688
  Detroit *(G-3955)*
E Power Remote Ltd ....G....... 231 689-5448
  White Cloud *(G-17621)*
Fidelis Contracting LLC ....G....... 313 361-1000
  Detroit *(G-4057)*
Red Carpet Capital Inc ....G....... 248 952-8583
  Orchard Lake *(G-12169)*
Trolley Rebuilders Inc ....A....... 810 364-4820
  Marysville *(G-10624)*

CONTRACTORS: Computer Installation

Huron Valley Telecom ....G....... 734 995-9780
  Ann Arbor *(G-497)*

CONTRACTORS: Computerized Controls Installation

Union Built PC Inc ....G....... 248 910-3955
  Jackson *(G-8598)*

CONTRACTORS: Concrete

Barrett Paving Materials Inc ....E....... 734 985-9480
  Ypsilanti *(G-18055)*
Bdk Group Northern Mich Inc ....E....... 574 875-5183
  Charlevoix *(G-2609)*
Central Asphalt Inc ....F....... 989 772-0720
  Mount Pleasant *(G-11183)*
Concrete Lifters Inc ....G....... 616 669-0400
  Jenison *(G-8622)*
Consumers Concrete Corporation ....F....... 517 784-9108
  Jackson *(G-8419)*
Gildners Concrete ....G....... 989 356-5156
  Alpena *(G-292)*
Pyramid Paving and Contg Co ....E....... 989 895-5861
  Bay City *(G-1343)*
Simply Green Outdoor Svcs LLC ....G....... 734 385-6190
  Dexter *(G-4510)*
Snider Construction Inc ....G....... 231 537-4851
  Levering *(G-9546)*

CONTRACTORS: Concrete Repair

All About Drainage LLC ....G....... 248 921-0766
  Commerce Township *(G-3387)*
Scodeller Construction Inc ....D....... 248 374-1102
  Wixom *(G-17890)*

CONTRACTORS: Construction Caulking

DC Byers Co/Grand Rapids Inc ....F....... 616 538-7300
  Grand Rapids *(G-6338)*

CONTRACTORS: Construction Site Cleanup

Gloria C Williams ....G...... 313 220-2735
  Southfield *(G-14922)*
Pro-Soil Site Services Inc..................G...... 517 267-8767
  Lansing *(G-9260)*

CONTRACTORS: Construction Site Metal Structure Coating

Corotech Acquisition Co ....F...... 616 456-5557
  Grand Rapids *(G-6312)*

CONTRACTORS: Countertop Installation

Classic Stone MBL & Gran Inc ....G...... 248 588-1599
  Troy *(G-16269)*
Howes Custom Counter Tops ....G...... 989 498-4044
  Saginaw *(G-14063)*
Korcast Products Incorporated ....G...... 248 740-2340
  Troy *(G-16448)*
Mica Crafters Inc................................E...... 517 548-2924
  Howell *(G-8063)*
Owens Building Co Inc......................E...... 989 835-1293
  Midland *(G-10901)*

CONTRACTORS: Demolition, Building & Other Structures

Grace Contracting Services LLC.........G...... 906 630-4680
  Mc Millan *(G-10685)*
Morse Concrete & Excavating ....F...... 989 826-3975
  Mio *(G-11006)*
Reid Contractors Inc..........................G...... 906 632-2936
  Dafter *(G-3620)*

CONTRACTORS: Directional Oil & Gas Well Drilling Svc

5 Star Drctional Drlg Svcs Ind ....G...... 231 263-2050
  Kingsley *(G-9069)*
Alexander Directional Boring ....G...... 989 362-9506
  East Tawas *(G-4686)*
Alpha Directional Boring ....G...... 586 405-0171
  Davisburg *(G-3624)*
Bigard & Huggard Drilling Inc............D...... 989 775-6608
  Mount Pleasant *(G-11178)*
Diamondbck-Directional Drlg LLC......F...... 231 943-3000
  Traverse City *(G-15956)*
Energy Acquisition Corp ....F...... 517 339-0249
  Holt *(G-7911)*
Phoenix Technology Svcs USA ....F...... 231 995-0100
  Traverse City *(G-16067)*
RC Directional Boring Inc ....F...... 517 545-4887
  Howell *(G-8088)*
S and P Drctnal Boring Svc LLC ....G...... 989 832-7716
  Midland *(G-10910)*
Tip Top Drilling LLC..........................G...... 616 291-8006
  Sparta *(G-15117)*

CONTRACTORS: Dock Eqpt Installation, Indl

Con-De Manufacturing Inc ....G...... 269 651-3756
  Sturgis *(G-15601)*

CONTRACTORS: Drapery Track Installation

Apple Fence Co.................................F...... 231 276-9888
  Grawn *(G-7097)*
Detroit Custom Services Inc ....E...... 586 465-3631
  Mount Clemens *(G-11129)*

CONTRACTORS: Driveway

Delta Paving Inc ....F...... 810 232-0220
  Flint *(G-5417)*

CONTRACTORS: Electrical

Advanced Electric..............................G...... 517 529-9050
  Clarklake *(G-2893)*
Advantage Industries Inc ....E...... 616 669-2400
  Jenison *(G-8616)*
HI Tech Mechanical Svcs LLC ....G...... 734 847-1831
  Temperance *(G-15831)*
Meiers Signs Inc................................G...... 906 786-3424
  Escanaba *(G-4843)*
Michigan Satellite..............................E...... 989 792-6666
  Saginaw *(G-14091)*
Tech Electric Co LLC.........................G...... 586 697-5095
  Macomb *(G-10167)*

CONTRACTORS: Electronic Controls Installation

Control One Inc.................................G...... 586 979-6106
  Sterling Heights *(G-15297)*
Energy Efficient Ltg LLC Eel..............G...... 586 214-5557
  West Bloomfield *(G-17476)*

CONTRACTORS: Energy Management Control

Global Green Corporation...................F...... 734 560-1743
  Ann Arbor *(G-473)*

CONTRACTORS: Erection & Dismantling, Poured Concrete Forms

Grace Contracting Services LLC.........G...... 906 630-4680
  Mc Millan *(G-10685)*

CONTRACTORS: Excavating

A Lindberg & Sons Inc ....E...... 906 485-5705
  Ishpeming *(G-8342)*
Carr Brothers and Sons Inc ....E...... 517 629-3549
  Albion *(G-117)*
Carr Brothers and Sons Inc ....F...... 517 531-3358
  Albion *(G-118)*
D J McQuestion & Sons Inc ....F...... 231 768-4403
  Leroy *(G-9530)*
Eggers Excavating LLC......................F...... 989 695-5205
  Freeland *(G-5756)*
Elmers Crane and Dozer Inc ....C...... 231 943-3443
  Traverse City *(G-15962)*
Franke Salisbury Virginia ....G...... 231 775-7014
  Cadillac *(G-2248)*
Jack Millikin Inc.................................G...... 989 348-8411
  Grayling *(G-7109)*
Jordan Valley Concrete Service ....F...... 231 536-7701
  East Jordan *(G-4637)*
Lewiston Sand & Gravel Inc...............G...... 989 786-2742
  Lewiston *(G-9552)*
Manigg Enterprises Inc ....F...... 989 356-4986
  Alpena *(G-296)*
Mid Michigan Pipe Inc ....G...... 989 772-5664
  Grand Rapids *(G-6683)*
Morris Excavating Inc........................F...... 269 483-7773
  White Pigeon *(G-17654)*
Morse Concrete & Excavating ....F...... 989 826-3975
  Mio *(G-11006)*
Northern Tank Truck Service ....G...... 989 732-7531
  Gaylord *(G-5885)*
Rudy Goupille & Sons Inc ....G...... 906 475-9816
  Negaunee *(G-11476)*
Senneker Enterprises Inc...................G...... 616 877-4440
  Dorr *(G-4528)*
Swansons Excavating Inc ....G...... 989 873-4419
  Prescott *(G-13081)*
Tip Top Gravel Co Inc ....G...... 616 897-8342
  Ada *(G-31)*
White Lake Excavating Inc.................F...... 231 894-6918
  Whitehall *(G-17681)*
Zellar Forest Products ....G...... 906 586-9817
  Germfask *(G-5903)*

CONTRACTORS: Excavating Slush Pits & Cellars Svcs

Burkholder Excavating Inc..................G...... 269 426-4227
  Sawyer *(G-14482)*
Hobys Contracting.............................G...... 989 631-4263
  Bentley *(G-1477)*
Meridian Contg & Excvtg LLC ....G...... 734 476-5933
  Commerce Township *(G-3431)*
Reid Contractors Inc..........................G...... 906 632-2936
  Dafter *(G-3620)*

CONTRACTORS: Exterior Wall System Installation

Signature Wall Solutions Inc ....G...... 616 366-4242
  Midland *(G-10916)*

CONTRACTORS: Fence Construction

Bradys Fence Company Inc................G...... 313 492-8804
  South Rockwood *(G-14820)*
Contractors Fence Service ....E...... 313 592-1300
  Detroit *(G-3947)*
Mark Beem...G...... 231 510-8122
  Lake City *(G-9092)*
Marquette Fence Company Inc...........G...... 906 249-8000
  Marquette *(G-10544)*
Metter Flooring LLC...........................G...... 517 914-2004
  Rives Junction *(G-13309)*
Nevill Supply Incorporated ....G...... 989 386-4522
  Clare *(G-2879)*
Ranch Life Plastics Inc......................F...... 517 663-2350
  Eaton Rapids *(G-4731)*
Robinson Fence Co Inc......................G...... 906 647-3301
  Pickford *(G-12483)*
Spartan Metal Fab LLC......................G...... 517 322-9050
  Lansing *(G-9263)*

CONTRACTORS: Fire Detection & Burglar Alarm Systems

Dice Corporation................................E...... 989 891-2800
  Bay City *(G-1301)*
Gentex Corporation............................C...... 616 392-7195
  Zeeland *(G-18142)*

CONTRACTORS: Fire Sprinkler System Installation Svcs

B L Harroun and Son Inc ....E...... 269 345-8657
  Kalamazoo *(G-8692)*
Exquise Inc..G...... 248 220-9048
  Detroit *(G-4047)*
Gallagher Fire Equipment Co ....E...... 248 477-1540
  Livonia *(G-9748)*

CONTRACTORS: Floor Laying & Other Floor Work

Collier Enterprise III..........................G...... 269 503-3402
  Sturgis *(G-15600)*
Homespun Furniture Inc ....F...... 734 284-6277
  Riverview *(G-13297)*
PCI Industries Inc.............................D...... 248 542-2570
  Oak Park *(G-12090)*
Whites Industrial Service ....G...... 616 291-3706
  Lowell *(G-10046)*

CONTRACTORS: Flooring

Leelanau Redi-Mix Inc ....E...... 231 228-5005
  Maple City *(G-10462)*

CONTRACTORS: Food Svcs Eqpt Installation

D C Norris North America LLC ....G...... 231 935-1519
  Traverse City *(G-15955)*

CONTRACTORS: Foundation Building

Cerco Inc...E...... 734 362-8664
  Brownstown Twp *(G-2071)*

CONTRACTORS: Gas Field Svcs, NEC

Columbus Oil & Gas LLC ....G...... 810 385-9140
  Burtchville *(G-2140)*
DTE Energy Resources Inc................C...... 313 297-4203
  Detroit *(G-4020)*
DTE Energy Resources Inc................D...... 734 302-4800
  Ann Arbor *(G-426)*
Eastport Group Inc ....F...... 989 732-0030
  Johannesburg *(G-8649)*
El Paso LLC ....G...... 231 587-0704
  Mancelona *(G-10389)*
Harmonie International LLC...............E...... 248 737-9933
  Farmington Hills *(G-5017)*
Pelhams Construction LLC.................G...... 517 549-8276
  Jonesville *(G-8666)*

CONTRACTORS: Gasoline Condensation Removal Svcs

Gas Recovery Systems LLC ....F...... 248 305-7774
  Northville *(G-11693)*

CONTRACTORS: General Electric

Aerobee Electric Inc..........................G...... 248 549-2044
  Ferndale *(G-5252)*
Ainsworth Electric Inc.......................E...... 810 984-5768
  Port Huron *(G-12883)*
H & R Electrical Contrs LLC..............G...... 517 669-2102
  Dewitt *(G-4462)*
Industrial Elc Co Detroit Inc...............D...... 313 872-1133
  Detroit *(G-4139)*

CONTRACTORS: General Electric

John V Gedda Jr ....G...... 906 482-5037
  Hancock *(G-7253)*
Nieboer Electric Inc ....F...... 231 924-0960
  Fremont *(G-5779)*
Parkway Elc Communications LLC ....D...... 616 392-2788
  Holland *(G-7767)*
PM Power Group Inc ....G...... 906 885-7100
  White Pine *(G-17658)*
Praise Sign Company ....G...... 616 439-0315
  Grandville *(G-7065)*
Waddell Electric Company ....G...... 616 791-4860
  Grand Rapids *(G-6976)*

CONTRACTORS: Glass, Glazing & Tinting

Arnold & Sautter Co ....F...... 989 684-7557
  Bay City *(G-1276)*
Double Otis Inc ....E...... 616 878-3998
  Grand Rapids *(G-6359)*
Knight Tonya ....G...... 313 255-3434
  Southfield *(G-14956)*
Lenox Cement Products Inc ....G...... 586 727-1488
  Lenox *(G-9521)*
Mt Clemens Glass & Mirror Co ....F...... 586 465-1733
  Clinton Township *(G-3182)*
Northern Michigan Glass LLC ....E...... 231 941-0050
  Traverse City *(G-16051)*
Thompson John ....G...... 810 225-8780
  Howell *(G-8108)*
Valley Glass Co Inc ....G...... 989 790-9342
  Saginaw *(G-14175)*

CONTRACTORS: Gutters & Downspouts

Makaveli Cnstr & Assoc Inc ....G...... 810 892-3412
  Detroit *(G-4217)*
Rainbow Seamless Systems Inc ....F...... 231 933-8888
  Traverse City *(G-16089)*
SGS Inc ....G...... 989 239-1726
  Birch Run *(G-1671)*

CONTRACTORS: Heating & Air Conditioning

Grand Traverse Mech Contg LLC ....G...... 231 943-7400
  Interlochen *(G-8241)*

CONTRACTORS: Heating Systems Repair & Maintenance Svc

Crown Heating Inc ....G...... 248 352-1688
  Detroit *(G-3955)*

CONTRACTORS: Highway & Street Construction, General

Bdk Group Northern Mich Inc ....E...... 574 875-5183
  Charlevoix *(G-2609)*
Fidelis Contracting LLC ....G...... 313 361-1000
  Detroit *(G-4057)*
Oldcastle Materials Inc ....E...... 269 343-4659
  Kalamazoo *(G-8839)*
R H Huhtala Aggregates Inc ....G...... 906 524-7758
  Lanse *(G-9200)*
Stoneco Inc ....E...... 734 587-7125
  Maybee *(G-10673)*

CONTRACTORS: Highway & Street Paving

Ajax Paving Industries Inc ....C...... 248 244-3300
  Troy *(G-16175)*
Clancy Excavating Co ....G...... 586 294-2900
  Roseville *(G-13781)*
Edw C Levy Co ....E...... 248 349-8600
  Novi *(G-11880)*
Edw C Levy Co ....D...... 313 843-7200
  Detroit *(G-4028)*
Elmers Crane and Dozer Inc ....C...... 231 943-3443
  Traverse City *(G-15962)*
Genoak Materials Inc ....C...... 248 634-8276
  Holly *(G-7880)*
Hess Asphalt Pav Sand Cnstr Co ....F...... 810 984-4466
  Clyde *(G-3283)*
Hhj Holdings Limited ....F...... 248 652-9716
  Troy *(G-16396)*
Oldcastle Materials Inc ....D...... 248 625-5891
  Clarkston *(G-2942)*
Saginaw Asphalt Paving Co ....D...... 989 755-6228
  Carrollton *(G-2487)*
Shooks Asphalt Paving Co Inc ....F...... 989 236-7740
  Perrinton *(G-12432)*

CONTRACTORS: Highway & Street Resurfacing

Central Asphalt Inc ....F...... 989 772-0720
  Mount Pleasant *(G-11183)*
Pyramid Paving and Contg Co ....E...... 989 895-5861
  Bay City *(G-1343)*

CONTRACTORS: Home & Office Intrs Finish, Furnish/Remodel

Installations Inc ....F...... 313 532-9000
  Redford *(G-13166)*

CONTRACTORS: Hot Shot Svcs

Guided Per Bus & Prof Svcs LLC ....G...... 248 567-2121
  Livonia *(G-9762)*

CONTRACTORS: Hydraulic Eqpt Installation & Svcs

Control One Inc ....G...... 586 979-6106
  Sterling Heights *(G-15297)*

CONTRACTORS: Indl Building Renovation, Remodeling & Repair

Manistee Wldg & Piping Svc Inc ....G...... 231 723-2551
  Manistee *(G-10428)*

CONTRACTORS: Insulation Installation, Building

Insulation Wholesale Supply ....G...... 269 968-9746
  Battle Creek *(G-1200)*
Knauf Insulation Inc ....C...... 517 630-2000
  Albion *(G-127)*
Valley Group of Companies ....F...... 989 799-9669
  Saginaw *(G-14176)*

CONTRACTORS: Kitchen & Bathroom Remodeling

J & J Laminate Connection Inc ....G...... 810 227-1824
  Brighton *(G-1944)*
Korcast Products Incorporated ....G...... 248 740-2340
  Troy *(G-16449)*
Surface Expressions LLC ....G...... 231 843-8282
  Ludington *(G-10081)*
W S Townsend Company ....G...... 517 393-7300
  Lansing *(G-9433)*

CONTRACTORS: Lighting Syst

Band-Ayd Systems Intl Inc ....F...... 586 294-8851
  Madison Heights *(G-10200)*

CONTRACTORS: Lightweight Steel Framing Installation

West Michigan Metals LLC ....G...... 269 978-7021
  Allegan *(G-192)*

CONTRACTORS: Machine Rigging & Moving

FD Lake Company ....F...... 616 241-5639
  Grand Rapids *(G-6403)*
Quality Fabg & Erection Co ....G...... 989 288-5210
  Durand *(G-4613)*

CONTRACTORS: Machinery Installation

Ase Industries Inc ....D...... 586 754-7480
  Warren *(G-16942)*
Best Industrial Group Inc ....F...... 586 826-8800
  Warren *(G-16957)*
J I B Properties LLC ....G...... 313 382-3234
  Melvindale *(G-10701)*
Siemens Industry Inc ....G...... 616 913-7700
  Grand Rapids *(G-6861)*
Tachyon Corporation ....E...... 586 598-4320
  Chesterfield *(G-2845)*
West Mich Auto Stl & Engrg Inc ....E...... 616 560-8198
  Belding *(G-1431)*

CONTRACTORS: Marble Masonry, Exterior

Surface Encounters LLC ....D...... 586 566-7557
  Macomb *(G-10164)*

CONTRACTORS: Masonry & Stonework

Knust Masonry ....G...... 231 322-2587
  Rapid City *(G-13109)*

CONTRACTORS: Mechanical

Access Heating & Cooling Inc ....G...... 734 464-0566
  Livonia *(G-9625)*
Gee & Missler Inc ....E...... 734 284-1224
  Wyandotte *(G-17959)*
Great Lakes Mechanical Corp ....C...... 313 581-1400
  Dearborn *(G-3717)*
Johnson Systems Inc ....G...... 616 455-1900
  Caledonia *(G-2304)*
Monarch Welding & Engrg Inc ....F...... 231 733-7222
  Muskegon *(G-11384)*
Quality Stainless Mfg Co ....F...... 248 546-4141
  Madison Heights *(G-10343)*
RC Directional Boring Inc ....F...... 517 545-4887
  Howell *(G-8088)*
Spray Booth Products Inc ....E...... 313 766-4400
  Redford *(G-13193)*
W Soule & Co ....C...... 269 344-0139
  Kalamazoo *(G-8920)*

CONTRACTORS: Mobile Home Site Set-Up

Sunshine Systems Inc ....G...... 616 363-9272
  Grand Rapids *(G-6901)*

CONTRACTORS: Oil & Gas Building, Repairing & Dismantling Svc

Great Lakes Wellhead Inc ....G...... 231 943-9100
  Grawn *(G-7098)*
Pioneer Oil Tools Inc ....G...... 989 644-6999
  Mount Pleasant *(G-11218)*
Stovall Well Drilling Co ....G...... 616 364-4144
  Grand Rapids *(G-6894)*
Wara Construction Company LLC ....D...... 248 299-2410
  Rochester Hills *(G-13540)*

CONTRACTORS: Oil & Gas Field Geophysical Exploration Svcs

CMS Enterprises Company ....C...... 517 788-0550
  Jackson *(G-8413)*

CONTRACTORS: Oil & Gas Field Tools Fishing Svcs

Land Services Incorporated ....G...... 231 947-9400
  Traverse City *(G-16021)*

CONTRACTORS: Oil & Gas Well Casing Cement Svcs

Central Mich Cmenting Svcs LLC ....G...... 989 775-0940
  Mount Pleasant *(G-11184)*
Miller Investment Company LLC ....G...... 231 933-3233
  Traverse City *(G-16038)*
Verbio North America Corp ....G...... 866 306-4777
  Livonia *(G-9989)*

CONTRACTORS: Oil & Gas Well Drilling Svc

Advanced Energy Services LLC ....D...... 231 369-2602
  South Boardman *(G-14748)*
Arrow Drilling Services LLC ....E...... 231 258-4596
  Kalkaska *(G-8936)*
Bob Fleming Well Drilling ....G...... 248 627-3511
  Ortonville *(G-12195)*
Crystal Flash Inc ....G...... 269 781-8221
  Marshall *(G-10565)*
Eis Inc ....F...... 734 266-6500
  Livonia *(G-9722)*
Fortis Energy Services Inc ....E...... 231 258-4596
  Bloomfield Hills *(G-1766)*
Fortis Energy Services Inc ....D...... 248 283-7100
  Troy *(G-16370)*
Gage Well Drilling Inc ....G...... 989 389-4372
  Saint Helen *(G-14278)*
Industrial Control Systems LLC ....G...... 269 689-3241
  Sturgis *(G-15607)*
Key Energy Services Inc ....E...... 231 258-9637
  Kalkaska *(G-8947)*
Michiwest Energy Inc ....G...... 989 772-2107
  Mount Pleasant *(G-11206)*
Rafalski CPA ....G...... 248 689-1685
  Troy *(G-16575)*

PRODUCT SECTION

CONTRACTORS: Plumbing

Srw Inc ....F....... 989 732-8884
  Traverse City *(G-16110)*
Srw Inc ....F....... 989 269-8528
  Bad Axe *(G-1071)*
Stovall Well Drilling Co.......................G....... 616 364-4144
  Grand Rapids *(G-6894)*
Thompson Well Drilling........................G....... 616 754-5032
  Rockford *(G-13593)*

CONTRACTORS: Oil & Gas Well Foundation Grading Svcs

Grace Contracting Services LLC...........G....... 906 630-4680
  Mc Millan *(G-10685)*

CONTRACTORS: Oil & Gas Well On-Site Foundation Building Svcs

Badger Pipe & Piling LLC....................G....... 989 965-0126
  Harrison *(G-7308)*

CONTRACTORS: Oil & Gas Wells Svcs

Acme Septic Tank Co ....F....... 989 684-3852
  Kawkawlin *(G-8969)*
Integrity Sltons Feld Svcs Inc...............F....... 303 263-9522
  East Lansing *(G-4664)*
JO Well Service and Tstg Inc...............G....... 989 772-4221
  Mount Pleasant *(G-11200)*
Jones Ray Well Servicing Inc ....E....... 989 832-8071
  Midland *(G-10877)*
Lease Management Inc........................G....... 989 773-5948
  Mount Pleasant *(G-11202)*
Northern A 1 Services Inc ....E....... 231 258-9961
  Kalkaska *(G-8955)*
Sappington Crude Oil Inc....................G....... 989 345-1052
  West Branch *(G-17521)*
Team Services LLC...............................E....... 231 258-9130
  Kalkaska *(G-8961)*
Team Spooling Services LLC................G....... 231 258-9130
  Kalkaska *(G-8962)*
TNT Well Service Ltd...........................G....... 989 939-7098
  Gaylord *(G-5896)*

CONTRACTORS: Oil Field Haulage Svcs

1st Choice Trckg & Rentl Inc...............G....... 231 258-0417
  Kalkaska *(G-8935)*
B & H Tractor & Truck Inc....................G....... 989 773-5975
  Mount Pleasant *(G-11173)*

CONTRACTORS: Oil Field Lease Tanks: Erectg, Clng/Rprg Svcs

Central Michigan Tank Rental................G....... 989 681-5963
  Saint Louis *(G-14360)*

CONTRACTORS: Oil Field Mud Drilling Svcs

Concrete Lifters Inc.............................G....... 616 669-0400
  Jenison *(G-8622)*

CONTRACTORS: Oil Field Pipe Testing Svcs

5 By 5 LLC ....F....... 855 369-6757
  Traverse City *(G-15886)*

CONTRACTORS: Oil Sampling Svcs

Oil Exchange 6 Inc ....G....... 734 641-4310
  Inkster *(G-8230)*

CONTRACTORS: Oil/Gas Field Casing,Tube/Rod Running,Cut/Pull

Superior Mar & Envmtl Svcs LLC..........G....... 906 253-9448
  Sault Sainte Marie *(G-14475)*

CONTRACTORS: Oil/Gas Well Construction, Rpr/Dismantling Svcs

917 Chittock Street LLC ....F....... 866 945-0269
  Lansing *(G-9331)*
Bach Services & Mfg Co LLC...............E....... 231 263-2777
  Kingsley *(G-9070)*
Baker Hughes A GE Company LLC.......G....... 989 506-2167
  Mount Pleasant *(G-11176)*
Exodus Pressure Control......................G....... 231 258-8001
  Kalkaska *(G-8942)*
Fiore Construction................................G....... 517 404-0000
  Howell *(G-8041)*
Gloria C Williams.................................G....... 313 220-2735
  Southfield *(G-14922)*
Greenlight Home Inspection Svc...........G....... 313 885-5616
  Saint Clair Shores *(G-14255)*
Jn Newman Construction LLC...............G....... 269 968-1290
  Springfield *(G-15194)*
Jr Larry Dudley....................................G....... 313 721-3600
  Detroit *(G-4166)*
Jrj Energy Services LLC.......................C....... 231 823-2171
  Stanwood *(G-15234)*
Kadant Johnson LLC............................C....... 269 278-1715
  Three Rivers *(G-15867)*
Kdk Downhole Tooling LLC..................G....... 231 590-3137
  Williamsburg *(G-17714)*
Lgc Global Inc ....E....... 313 989-4141
  Detroit *(G-4202)*
Melix Services Inc................................G....... 248 387-9303
  Hamtramck *(G-7244)*
Premier Casing Crews Inc....................G....... 989 775-7436
  Mount Pleasant *(G-11220)*
Red Carpet Capital Inc.........................G....... 248 952-8583
  Orchard Lake *(G-12169)*
Rock Industries Inc..............................E....... 248 338-2800
  Bloomfield Hills *(G-1796)*
Sledgehammer Construction Inc............G....... 313 478-5648
  Detroit *(G-4365)*
Superior Inspection Svc........................G....... 231 258-9400
  Kalkaska *(G-8959)*
Tims Underbody...................................G....... 231 347-9146
  Petoskey *(G-12477)*
Top Shelf Painter Inc ....G....... 586 465-0867
  Fraser *(G-5739)*
Trend Services Company ....G....... 231 258-9951
  Kalkaska *(G-8965)*

CONTRACTORS: On-Site Welding

All-Fab Corporation ....G....... 269 673-6572
  Allegan *(G-147)*
Anderson Welding & Mfg Inc ....F....... 906 523-4661
  Chassell *(G-2671)*
B & B Custom and Prod Wldg ....F....... 517 524-7121
  Spring Arbor *(G-15120)*
B & B Holdings Groesbeck LLC ....F....... 586 554-7600
  Sterling Heights *(G-15269)*
Bnb Welding & Fabrication Inc.............G....... 810 820-1508
  Burton *(G-2145)*
Case Welding & Fabrication Inc ....G....... 517 278-2729
  Coldwater *(G-3294)*
Custom Design & Manufacturing ....F....... 989 754-9962
  Carrollton *(G-2484)*
Dunns Welding Inc...............................G....... 248 356-3866
  Southfield *(G-14887)*
JS Welding Inc ....G....... 517 451-2098
  Britton *(G-2018)*
K & S Welding ....G....... 517 629-7842
  Albion *(G-126)*
Lakeside Mechanical Contrs..................E....... 616 786-0211
  Allegan *(G-174)*
Marsh Industrial Services Inc ....F....... 231 258-4870
  Kalkaska *(G-8949)*
Marshall Welding & Fabrication ....G....... 269 781-4010
  Marshall *(G-10580)*
Nephew Fabrication Inc........................G....... 616 875-2121
  Zeeland *(G-18168)*
Nor-Dic Tool Company Inc ....F....... 734 326-3610
  Romulus *(G-13715)*
Reau Manufacturing Co........................G....... 734 823-5603
  Dundee *(G-4598)*
Sexton Enterprize Inc ....G....... 248 545-5880
  Ferndale *(G-5318)*
Sparta Sheet Metal Inc........................F....... 616 784-9035
  Grand Rapids *(G-6876)*
Specialty Welding ....G....... 517 627-5566
  Grand Ledge *(G-6116)*
TEC International II ....G....... 248 724-1800
  Auburn Hills *(G-1014)*
United Systems ....G....... 248 583-9670
  Troy *(G-16664)*
Van S Fabrications Inc.........................G....... 810 679-2115
  Croswell *(G-3605)*
Varneys Fab & Weld LLC.....................G....... 231 865-6856
  Nunica *(G-12046)*
Yonker Welding Service Inc ....G....... 616 534-2774
  Grand Rapids *(G-7009)*

CONTRACTORS: Ornamental Metal Work

Cramblits Welding LLC ....G....... 906 932-1908
  Ironwood *(G-8326)*

CONTRACTORS: Painting & Wall Covering

Boss Electro Static Inc ....E....... 616 575-0577
  Wyoming *(G-17989)*
Elite Electro Coaters Inc......................G....... 517 886-1020
  Lansing *(G-9223)*
Home Style Co.....................................G....... 989 871-3654
  Millington *(G-10996)*
Makaveli Cnstr & Assoc Inc ....G....... 810 892-3412
  Detroit *(G-4217)*
PCI Industries Inc................................D....... 248 542-2570
  Oak Park *(G-12090)*

CONTRACTORS: Painting, Commercial

Abrasive Solutions LLC ....G....... 517 592-2668
  Cement City *(G-2574)*
Gj Prey Cml & Indus Pntg Cov ....G....... 248 250-4792
  Clawson *(G-2980)*
Horizon Bros Painting Corp..................G....... 810 632-3362
  Howell *(G-8051)*

CONTRACTORS: Painting, Commercial, Interior

Tks Industrial Company ....E....... 248 786-5000
  Troy *(G-16645)*

CONTRACTORS: Painting, Indl

Beech & Rich Inc.................................E....... 269 968-8012
  Springfield *(G-15188)*
CPS LLC..F....... 517 639-1464
  Quincy *(G-13093)*
Finishing Touch Inc ....E....... 517 542-5581
  Litchfield *(G-9601)*
Luans Welding LLC..............................G....... 248 787-5735
  Oak Park *(G-12078)*
P C S Companies Inc ....G....... 616 754-2229
  Greenville *(G-7149)*

CONTRACTORS: Painting, Residential

Top Shelf Painter Inc ....G....... 586 465-0867
  Fraser *(G-5739)*

CONTRACTORS: Parking Facility Eqpt Installation

Traffic Sfety Ctrl Systems Inc ....E....... 248 348-0570
  Wixom *(G-17914)*

CONTRACTORS: Parking Lot Maintenance

Hd Selcating Pav Solutions LLC ....G....... 248 241-6526
  Clarkston *(G-2925)*

CONTRACTORS: Patio & Deck Construction & Repair

Ranch Life Plastics Inc.........................F....... 517 663-2350
  Eaton Rapids *(G-4731)*
Vinyl Sash of Flint Inc..........................E....... 810 234-4831
  Flint *(G-5521)*

CONTRACTORS: Pipe & Boiler Insulating

Valley Group of Companies ....F....... 989 799-9669
  Saginaw *(G-14176)*

CONTRACTORS: Playground Construction & Eqpt Installation

J C Walker & Sons Corp......................G....... 248 752-8165
  Swartz Creek *(G-15668)*

CONTRACTORS: Plumbing

McLaren Inc...G....... 989 720-4328
  Owosso *(G-12302)*
Mr Eds Sewer Cleaning Service ....G....... 313 565-2740
  Dearborn Heights *(G-3790)*
Precision Plumbing - T.........................G....... 269 695-6402
  Buchanan *(G-2125)*
Sheren Plumbing & Heating Inc ....E....... 231 943-7916
  Traverse City *(G-16101)*
Walters Plumbing Company ....F....... 269 962-6253
  Battle Creek *(G-1266)*

CONTRACTORS: Pollution Control Eqpt Installation

CONTRACTORS: Pollution Control Eqpt Installation
- Advanced Recovery Tech Corp .... F 231 788-2911
  Nunica *(G-12031)*
- Forrest Brothers Inc .... C 989 356-4011
  Gaylord *(G-5859)*

CONTRACTORS: Precast Concrete Struct Framing & Panel Placing
- Grace Contracting Services LLC .... G 906 630-4680
  Mc Millan *(G-10685)*

CONTRACTORS: Prefabricated Fireplace Installation
- Premier Fireplace Co LLC .... G 586 949-4315
  Macomb *(G-10156)*

CONTRACTORS: Prefabricated Window & Door Installation
- Architectural Design Wdwrk Inc .... G 586 726-9050
  Shelby Township *(G-14548)*
- Architectural Glass & Mtls Inc .... F 269 375-6165
  Kalamazoo *(G-8682)*
- Chames LLC .... G 616 363-0000
  Grand Rapids *(G-6269)*
- Lsd Investments Inc .... G 248 333-9085
  Bloomfield Hills *(G-1779)*
- Vinyl Sash of Flint Inc .... E 810 234-4831
  Flint *(G-5521)*
- Wallside Inc .... F 313 292-4400
  Taylor *(G-15781)*

CONTRACTORS: Process Piping
- W Soule & Co .... D 269 324-7001
  Portage *(G-13054)*

CONTRACTORS: Pulpwood, Engaged In Cutting
- Bundy Logging .... G 231 824-6054
  Manton *(G-10451)*
- Casselman Logging .... G 231 885-1040
  Mesick *(G-10768)*

CONTRACTORS: Refrigeration
- Duquaine Incorporated .... G 906 228-7290
  Marquette *(G-10527)*
- Refrigeration Concepts Inc .... E 616 785-7335
  Comstock Park *(G-3514)*

CONTRACTORS: Rigging, Theatrical
- Tls Productions Inc .... E 810 220-8577
  Ann Arbor *(G-677)*

CONTRACTORS: Roofing
- CPS LLC .... F 517 639-1464
  Quincy *(G-13093)*
- Detroit Cornice & Slate Co Inc .... E 248 398-7690
  Ferndale *(G-5275)*
- Laduke Corporation .... E 248 414-6600
  Oak Park *(G-12077)*
- Michigan Steel and Trim Inc .... G 517 647-4555
  Portland *(G-13063)*
- National Roofg & Shtmtl Co Inc ...... D 989 964-0557
  Saginaw *(G-14102)*
- Reurink Roof Maint & Coating .... G 269 795-2337
  Middleville *(G-10806)*
- S & B Roofing Services Inc .... D 248 334-5372
  Pontiac *(G-12863)*

CONTRACTORS: Roustabout Svcs
- Ally Servicing LLC .... F 248 948-7702
  Detroit *(G-3859)*

CONTRACTORS: Safety & Security Eqpt
- Executive Operations LLC .... E 313 312-0653
  Canton *(G-2373)*
- Rpb Safety LLC .... E 866 494-4599
  Royal Oak *(G-13969)*

CONTRACTORS: Sandblasting Svc, Building Exteriors
- Kardux Welding & Fabricating .... G 231 873-4648
  Hart *(G-7375)*
- Trin-Mac Company Inc .... G 586 774-1900
  Saint Clair Shores *(G-14273)*

CONTRACTORS: Seismograph Survey Svcs
- Baker Hghes Olfld Oprtions LLC ...... F 989 773-7992
  Mount Pleasant *(G-11175)*
- Emerson Geophysical LLC .... E 231 943-1400
  Traverse City *(G-15963)*
- West Bay Geophysical Inc .... F 231 946-3529
  Traverse City *(G-16144)*

CONTRACTORS: Septic System
- Acme Septic Tank Co .... F 989 684-3852
  Kawkawlin *(G-8969)*
- Deforest & Bloom Septic Tanks ...... G 231 544-3599
  Central Lake *(G-2590)*
- Forbes Sanitation & Excavation ...... F 231 723-2311
  Manistee *(G-10422)*
- Lenox Cement Products Inc .... G 586 727-1488
  Lenox *(G-9521)*
- Morse Concrete & Excavating .... F 989 826-3975
  Mio *(G-11006)*
- Snider Construction Inc .... G 231 537-4851
  Levering *(G-9546)*

CONTRACTORS: Sheet Metal Work, NEC
- Bauer Sheet Metal & Fabg Inc .... E 231 773-3244
  Muskegon *(G-11276)*
- C & T Fabrication LLC .... G 616 678-5133
  Kent City *(G-8988)*
- Custom Fab Inc .... G 586 755-7260
  Warren *(G-16995)*
- Designers Sheet Metal Inc .... G 269 429-4133
  Saint Joseph *(G-14306)*
- East Muskegon Roofg Shtmtl Co .... D 231 744-2461
  Muskegon *(G-11313)*
- East Muskegon Roofg Shtmtl Co .... F 616 791-6900
  Grand Rapids *(G-6367)*
- Gallagher-Kaiser Corporation .... D 313 368-3100
  Troy *(G-16378)*
- Harris Sheet Metal Co .... F 989 496-3080
  Midland *(G-10867)*
- J M L Contracting & Sales Inc .... F 586 756-4133
  Warren *(G-17108)*
- Kalamazoo Mechanical Inc .... F 269 343-5351
  Kalamazoo *(G-8790)*
- Kaufman Custom Sheet M .... G 906 932-2130
  Ironwood *(G-8333)*
- Shouldice Indus Mfrs Cntrs Inc ...... D 269 962-5579
  Battle Creek *(G-1247)*
- Thermal Designs & Manufacturng .. E 586 773-5231
  Roseville *(G-13878)*
- Turnkey Fabrication LLC .... G 616 248-9116
  Grand Rapids *(G-6941)*
- Young Manufacturing Inc .... G 906 483-3851
  Dollar Bay *(G-4522)*

CONTRACTORS: Sheet metal Work, Architectural
- Custo Arch Shee Meta .... F 313 571-2277
  Detroit *(G-3958)*

CONTRACTORS: Siding
- C L Rieckhoff Company Inc .... C 734 946-8220
  Taylor *(G-15697)*
- Sanderson Insulation .... G 269 496-7660
  Mendon *(G-10718)*
- Vinyl Sash of Flint Inc .... E 810 234-4831
  Flint *(G-5521)*

CONTRACTORS: Single-family Home General Remodeling
- Arnold & Sautter Co .... F 989 684-7557
  Bay City *(G-1276)*
- Bestway Building Supply Co .... G 810 732-6280
  Flint *(G-5388)*
- CCM Modernization Co .... G 586 231-0396
  Clinton Township *(G-3076)*
- Constine Inc .... E 989 723-6043
  Owosso *(G-12284)*

- Lorencz Construction Co .... G 989 798-3151
  Chesaning *(G-2727)*
- Overhead Door Company Alpena ...... G 989 354-8316
  Alpena *(G-305)*
- Regency Construction Corp .... E 586 741-8000
  Clinton Township *(G-3208)*
- S & B Roofing Services Inc .... D 248 334-5372
  Pontiac *(G-12863)*
- Terry Hanover .... G 269 426-4199
  New Troy *(G-11560)*
- Woodworks & Design Company .... F 517 482-6665
  Lansing *(G-9434)*

CONTRACTORS: Skylight Installation
- Northern Michigan Glass LLC .... E 231 941-0050
  Traverse City *(G-16051)*

CONTRACTORS: Solar Energy Eqpt
- Option Energy LLC .... F 269 329-4317
  Traverse City *(G-16061)*

CONTRACTORS: Sound Eqpt Installation
- Audio Technologies Inc .... G 586 323-3890
  Troy *(G-16229)*

CONTRACTORS: Special Trades, NEC
- Bohley Industries .... G 734 455-3430
  Northville *(G-11680)*

CONTRACTORS: Storage Tank Erection, Metal
- Corotech Acquisition Co .... F 616 456-5557
  Grand Rapids *(G-6312)*

CONTRACTORS: Store Fixture Installation
- Fab Concepts .... G 586 466-6411
  Clinton Township *(G-3111)*

CONTRACTORS: Store Front Construction
- Northern Michigan Glass LLC .... E 231 941-0050
  Traverse City *(G-16051)*

CONTRACTORS: Structural Iron Work, Structural
- Bristol Steel & Conveyor Corp .... E 810 658-9510
  Davison *(G-3641)*
- Douglas Steel Fabricating Corp .... D 517 322-2050
  Lansing *(G-9288)*
- Empire Machine & Conveyors Inc .... F 989 541-2060
  Durand *(G-4608)*
- Mean Erectors Inc .... E 989 737-3285
  Saginaw *(G-14085)*

CONTRACTORS: Structural Steel Erection
- Campbell & Shaw Steel Inc .... F 810 364-5100
  Marysville *(G-10600)*
- Corson Fabricating LLC .... F 810 326-0532
  Saint Clair *(G-14211)*
- Davis Iron Works Inc .... E 248 624-5960
  Commerce Township *(G-3398)*
- Dobson Industrial Inc .... E 800 298-6063
  Bay City *(G-1304)*
- Elevated Technologies Inc .... F 616 288-9817
  Grand Rapids *(G-6375)*
- Ferguson Steel Inc .... E 810 984-3918
  Fort Gratiot *(G-5549)*
- G & G Steel Fabricating Co .... G 586 979-4112
  Warren *(G-17048)*
- Howard Structural Steel Inc .... E 989 752-3000
  Saginaw *(G-14062)*
- Imm Inc .... E 989 344-7662
  Grayling *(G-7108)*
- Mbm Fabricators Co Inc .... C 734 941-0100
  Romulus *(G-13704)*
- Men of Steel Inc .... F 989 635-4866
  Marlette *(G-10501)*
- Midwest Steel Inc .... E 313 873-2220
  Detroit *(G-4248)*
- Steel Supply & Engineering Co .... E 616 452-3281
  Grand Rapids *(G-6888)*
- Titus Welding Company .... F 248 476-9366
  Farmington Hills *(G-5141)*

PRODUCT SECTION

CONTRACTORS: Stucco, Interior
Rowsey Construction & Dev LLC ....G....... 313 675-2464
  Detroit *(G-4348)*

CONTRACTORS: Svc Well Drilling Svcs
GTM Steamer Service Inc ....G....... 989 732-7678
  Gaylord *(G-5863)*

CONTRACTORS: Tile Installation, Ceramic
Tile Craft Inc ....F....... 231 929-7207
  Traverse City *(G-16124)*
Yoxheimer Tile Co ....F....... 517 788-7542
  Jackson *(G-8614)*

CONTRACTORS: Tuck Pointing & Restoration
Libra Industries Inc Michigan ....G....... 517 787-5675
  Jackson *(G-8499)*

CONTRACTORS: Underground Utilities
Morris Excavating Inc............................F....... 269 483-7773
  White Pigeon *(G-17654)*

CONTRACTORS: Ventilation & Duct Work
Dee Cramer Inc..................................E....... 517 485-5519
  Lansing *(G-9286)*
R B I Mechanical Inc ....E....... 231 582-2970
  Boyne City *(G-1834)*

CONTRACTORS: Wall Covering, Residential
Crown Heating Inc ....G....... 248 352-1688
  Detroit *(G-3955)*

CONTRACTORS: Warm Air Heating & Air Conditioning
Fhc Holding Company..........................G....... 616 538-3231
  Wyoming *(G-18001)*
Kalamazoo Mechanical Inc ....F....... 269 343-5351
  Kalamazoo *(G-8790)*
Premium Air Systems Inc ....D....... 248 680-8800
  Troy *(G-16562)*
Tomtek Hvac Inc..................................G....... 517 546-0357
  Howell *(G-8113)*
Van Dyken Mechanical Inc ....D....... 616 224-7030
  Grandville *(G-7075)*

CONTRACTORS: Water Intake Well Drilling Svc
Newton Well Service Inc......................G....... 269 945-5084
  Hastings *(G-7422)*
R M Brewer & Son Inc..........................G....... 517 531-3022
  Parma *(G-12393)*
Smith Well & Pump..............................G....... 269 721-3118
  Battle Creek *(G-1250)*
Walters Plumbing Company ....F....... 269 962-6253
  Battle Creek *(G-1266)*

CONTRACTORS: Water Well Drilling
Bob Fleming Well Drilling ....G....... 248 627-3511
  Ortonville *(G-12195)*
Gage Well Drilling Inc ....G....... 989 389-4372
  Saint Helen *(G-14278)*
Grace Contracting Services LLC..........G....... 906 630-4680
  Mc Millan *(G-10685)*
Thompson Well Drilling ....G....... 616 754-5032
  Rockford *(G-13593)*

CONTRACTORS: Waterproofing
Rowsey Construction & Dev LLC ....G....... 313 675-2464
  Detroit *(G-4348)*

CONTRACTORS: Well Acidizing Svcs
Atlas Oil Transportation Inc ....F....... 800 878-2000
  Taylor *(G-15690)*
Baker Hughes A GE Company LLC........G....... 989 732-2082
  Gaylord *(G-5849)*

CONTRACTORS: Window Treatment Installation
Melody Digiglio ....F....... 586 754-4405
  Warren *(G-17147)*

CONTROL CIRCUIT DEVICES
Emergency Technology Inc ....D....... 616 896-7100
  Hudsonville *(G-8155)*
M P Jackson LLC ....E....... 517 782-0391
  Jackson *(G-8503)*

CONTROL EQPT: Buses Or Trucks, Electric
Eltek Inc ....G....... 616 363-6397
  Belmont *(G-1461)*

CONTROL EQPT: Electric
Borgwarner Thermal Systems Inc........E....... 231 779-7500
  Cadillac *(G-2233)*
Burners Inc ....G....... 248 676-9141
  Milford *(G-10957)*
Electrojet Inc ....G....... 734 272-4709
  Wixom *(G-17800)*
Hewtech Electronics ....G....... 810 765-0820
  China *(G-2860)*
ITT Motion Tech Amer LLC..................F....... 248 863-2161
  Novi *(G-11909)*
Motor Control Incorporated ....G....... 313 389-4000
  Melvindale *(G-10703)*
Nadex of America Corporation ....E....... 248 477-3900
  Farmington Hills *(G-5075)*
Solutions For Industry Inc ....G....... 517 448-8608
  Hudson *(G-8142)*
Stegner Controls LLC..........................E....... 248 904-0400
  Auburn Hills *(G-1003)*
Versatile Systems LLC ....F....... 734 397-3957
  Canton *(G-2438)*

CONTROL EQPT: Noise
Fortis Energy Services Inc..................E....... 231 258-4596
  Bloomfield Hills *(G-1766)*
Fortis Energy Services Inc..................D....... 248 283-7100
  Troy *(G-16370)*
Noisemeters Inc ....G....... 248 840-6559
  Berkley *(G-1588)*
Valley Group of Companies ....F....... 989 799-9669
  Saginaw *(G-14176)*
Vibracoustic Usa Inc...........................C....... 269 637-2116
  South Haven *(G-14781)*

CONTROL PANELS: Electrical
AB Electrical Wires Inc........................E....... 231 737-9200
  Muskegon *(G-11258)*
Alpha Tran Engineering Co..................E....... 616 837-7341
  Nunica *(G-12032)*
C L Design Inc....................................G....... 248 474-4220
  Farmington Hills *(G-4951)*
Clarkston Control Products ....G....... 248 394-1430
  Clarkston *(G-2912)*
Command Electronics Inc....................E....... 269 679-4011
  Schoolcraft *(G-14492)*
Conductive Bolton Systems LLC ....D....... 248 669-7080
  Novi *(G-11852)*
Control Technique Incorporated ....D....... 586 997-3200
  Sterling Heights *(G-15298)*
Danlyn Controls Inc..............................G....... 586 773-6797
  Chesterfield *(G-2761)*
Die Heat Systems Inc..........................G....... 586 749-9756
  Chesterfield *(G-2767)*
Electrical Design and Ctrl Co................E....... 248 743-2400
  Troy *(G-16338)*
Generl-Lctrical-Mechanical Inc ....G....... 248 698-1110
  White Lake *(G-17633)*
Harlo Corporation ....C....... 616 538-0550
  Grandville *(G-7045)*
Indicon Corporation..............................C....... 586 274-0505
  Sterling Heights *(G-15372)*
Infra Corporation..................................F....... 248 623-0400
  Waterford *(G-17351)*
Intec Automated Controls Inc..............E....... 586 532-8881
  Sterling Heights *(G-15375)*
Jervis B Webb Company......................B....... 248 553-1000
  Novi *(G-11912)*
Kirk Enterprises Inc ....G....... 248 357-5070
  Southfield *(G-14955)*
M & N Controls Inc..............................G....... 734 850-2127
  Temperance *(G-15835)*
Magnetech Corporation ....G....... 248 426-8840
  Novi *(G-11933)*
Metro-Fabricating LLC ....D....... 989 667-8100
  Bay City *(G-1332)*
Motor City Electric Tech Inc................D....... 313 921-5300
  Detroit *(G-4256)*

CONTROLS: Environmental

Spec Corporation..................................G....... 517 529-4105
  Clarklake *(G-2900)*
Superior Controls Inc ....C....... 734 454-0500
  Plymouth *(G-12763)*
Thierica Controls Inc............................F....... 616 956-5500
  Grand Rapids *(G-6927)*
US Energia LLC ....D....... 248 669-1462
  Rochester *(G-13356)*
X-Bar Automation Inc ....E....... 248 616-9890
  Troy *(G-16701)*

CONTROLS & ACCESS: Indl, Electric
Altair Systems Inc................................F....... 248 668-0116
  Wixom *(G-17758)*
Amtex Inc...G....... 586 792-7888
  Clinton Township *(G-3051)*
Automated Control Systems Inc ....G....... 248 476-9490
  Novi *(G-11834)*
Balogh Tag Inc ....G....... 248 486-7343
  Brighton *(G-1888)*
Complete Dsign Automtn Systems ......G....... 734 424-2789
  Dexter *(G-4483)*
Concentric Labs Inc............................G....... 517 969-3038
  Mason *(G-10629)*
Data Acquisition Ctrl Systems.............F....... 248 437-6096
  Brighton *(G-1909)*
Ghsp Inc..D....... 248 588-5095
  Grand Haven *(G-6019)*
Jenda Controls Inc...............................E....... 248 656-0090
  Rochester *(G-13331)*
Lor Manufacturing Co Inc ....G....... 866 644-8622
  Weidman *(G-17458)*
Patriot Sensors & Contrls Corp............D....... 810 378-5511
  Peck *(G-12420)*
Prestolite Electric LLC.........................G....... 248 313-3807
  Novi *(G-11978)*
Southern Auto Wholesalers Inc............F....... 248 335-5555
  Pontiac *(G-12869)*
Stonebrdge Technical Entps Ltd..........F....... 810 750-0040
  Fenton *(G-5240)*
Tachyon Corporation............................E....... 586 598-4320
  Chesterfield *(G-2845)*
Valmec Inc ....G....... 810 629-8750
  Fenton *(G-5248)*

CONTROLS & ACCESS: Motor
Advanced Automation Group LLC ....G....... 248 299-8100
  Rochester Hills *(G-13366)*
Eaton Aerospace LLC..........................B....... 616 949-1090
  Grand Rapids *(G-6368)*
Great Lakes Electric LLC ....G....... 269 408-8276
  Saint Joseph *(G-14313)*
Hydraulic Systems Technology............G....... 248 656-5810
  Rochester Hills *(G-13447)*
Innovative Support Svcs Inc................E....... 248 585-3600
  Troy *(G-16418)*

CONTROLS: Air Flow, Refrigeration
Softaire Diffusers Inc...........................G....... 810 730-1668
  Linden *(G-9596)*

CONTROLS: Automatic Temperature
Century Instrument Company ....E....... 734 427-0340
  Livonia *(G-9681)*
Control Solutions Inc............................D....... 616 247-9422
  Byron Center *(G-2183)*
James G Gallagher ....G....... 989 832-3458
  Midland *(G-10874)*
Maxitrol Company.................................D....... 248 356-1400
  Southfield *(G-14974)*

CONTROLS: Crane & Hoist, Including Metal Mill
AB Electrical Wires Inc........................E....... 231 737-9200
  Muskegon *(G-11258)*
National Crane & Hoist Service ....G....... 248 789-4535
  Lakeville *(G-9179)*

CONTROLS: Environmental
Ademco Inc..G....... 586 759-1455
  Warren *(G-16918)*
Ademco Inc..E....... 248 926-5510
  Wixom *(G-17752)*
Astra Associates Inc............................E....... 586 254-6500
  Sterling Heights *(G-15266)*
Commonwealth Associates Inc ....C....... 517 788-3000
  Jackson *(G-8416)*

Employee Codes: A=Over 500 employees, B=251-500
C=101-250, D=51-100, E=20-50, F=10-19, G=3-9

CONTROLS: Environmental

Crewbotiq LLC	E	248 939-4229
Troy (G-16287)		
Eaton Corporation	A	248 226-6347
Southfield (G-14893)		
Enertemp Inc	E	616 243-2752
Grand Rapids (G-6378)		
Hart & Cooley Inc	C	616 656-8200
Grand Rapids (G-6495)		
Hella Corporate Center USA Inc	E	586 232-4788
Northville (G-11697)		
Industrial Temperature Control	G	734 451-8740
Canton (G-2384)		
Kanawha Scales & Systems Inc	F	734 947-4030
Romulus (G-13695)		
Lyman Thornton	G	248 762-8433
Wixom (G-17847)		
Peak Industries Co Inc	D	313 846-8666
Dearborn (G-3747)		
Refrigerant Services LLC	G	248 586-6988
New Hudson (G-11552)		
Releaf Michigan Inc	G	734 662-6350
Ann Arbor (G-619)		
Seelye Equipment Specialist	G	231 547-9430
Charlevoix (G-2630)		
T E Technology Inc	E	231 929-3966
Traverse City (G-16118)		
Warner Instruments	G	616 843-5342
Grand Haven (G-6096)		

CONTROLS: Marine & Navy, Auxiliary

Jered LLC	G	906 776-1800
Iron Mountain (G-8286)		
Precise Power Systems LLC	G	248 709-4750
Whitmore Lake (G-17706)		

CONTROLS: Numerical

Fidia Co	F	248 680-0700
Rochester Hills (G-13424)		
Fitz-Rite Products Inc	E	248 528-8440
Troy (G-16366)		

CONTROLS: Relay & Ind

Acromag Incorporated	D	248 624-1541
Wixom (G-17751)		
AG Davis Gage & Engrg Co	E	586 977-9000
Sterling Heights (G-15256)		
Amx Corp	G	469 624-8000
Sterling Heights (G-15261)		
Apollo America Inc	D	248 332-3900
Auburn Hills (G-776)		
Comptek Inc	F	248 477-5215
Farmington Hills (G-4965)		
Control One Inc	G	586 979-6106
Sterling Heights (G-15297)		
Controls For Industries Inc	F	517 468-3385
Webberville (G-17448)		
Custom Engineering & Design	G	248 680-1435
Troy (G-16289)		
Dura Operating LLC	B	231 924-0930
Fremont (G-5770)		
Eaton Corporation	C	586 228-2029
Clinton Township (G-3108)		
Energy Products Inc	G	248 866-5622
Troy (G-16345)		
Energy Products Inc	D	248 545-7700
Madison Heights (G-10247)		
Fenton Systems Inc	G	810 636-6318
Goodrich (G-5953)		
Ford Motor Company	A	734 484-8000
Ypsilanti (G-18074)		
Galco Industrial Elec Inc	G	248 542-9090
Madison Heights (G-10256)		
Glassmaster Controls Co Inc	E	269 382-2010
Kalamazoo (G-8753)		
H&H Automation Controls	G	616 457-5994
Jenison (G-8628)		
HI-Lex Controls Incorporated	C	517 448-2752
Hudson (G-8130)		
Hydro-Logic Inc	E	586 757-7477
Warren (G-17083)		
Incoe Corporation	C	248 616-0220
Auburn Hills (G-910)		
Indicon Corporation	C	586 274-0505
Sterling Heights (G-15372)		
Industrial Computer & Controls	F	734 697-4152
Van Buren Twp (G-16765)		
Industrial Temperature Control	G	734 451-8740
Canton (G-2384)		
Inertia Cycleworks	G	269 684-2000
Niles (G-11618)		
Mahle Powertrain LLC	D	248 305-8200
Farmington Hills (G-5056)		
Maxitrol Company	D	248 356-1400
Southfield (G-14974)		
Maxitrol Company	C	269 432-3291
Colon (G-3374)		
Maxitrol Company	E	517 486-2820
Blissfield (G-1719)		
Melling Tool Co	B	517 787-8172
Jackson (G-8514)		
Murray Equipment Company Inc	F	313 869-4444
Warren (G-17163)		
Nabco Inc	G	231 832-2001
Reed City (G-13221)		
National Control Systems Inc	G	810 231-2901
Hamburg (G-7226)		
Noelco Inc	G	586 846-4955
Clinton Township (G-3183)		
Parker-Hannifin Corporation	B	269 384-3459
Kalamazoo (G-8843)		
Peak Industries Co Inc	D	313 846-8666
Dearborn (G-3747)		
Peaker Services Inc	D	248 437-4174
Brighton (G-1976)		
Precision Controls Company	E	734 663-3104
Ann Arbor (G-599)		
Rick Wykle LLC	G	734 839-6376
Livonia (G-9909)		
Rjg Technologies Inc	C	231 947-3111
Traverse City (G-16096)		
Rockwell Automation Inc	D	248 696-1200
Troy (G-16582)		
Rockwell Automation Inc	D	269 792-9137
Wayland (G-17412)		
Ross Decco Company	E	248 764-1845
Troy (G-16584)		
Seelye Equipment Specialist	G	231 547-9430
Charlevoix (G-2630)		
Sloan Transportation Pdts Inc	D	616 395-5600
Holland (G-7806)		
Ssi Technology Inc	D	248 582-0600
Sterling Heights (G-15507)		
Superior Controls Inc	C	734 454-0500
Plymouth (G-12763)		
Sycron Technologies Inc	G	810 694-4007
Grand Blanc (G-5985)		
Symorex Ltd	F	734 971-6000
Ann Arbor (G-653)		
Synchronous Manufacturing Inc	E	517 764-6930
Michigan Center (G-10791)		
TAC Manufacturing Inc	B	517 789-7000
Jackson (G-8582)		
Temcor Systems Inc	G	810 229-0006
Brighton (G-1996)		
Tramec Sloan LLC	D	616 395-5600
Holland (G-7833)		
Venus Controls Inc	F	248 477-0448
Livonia (G-9988)		
Warner Instruments	G	616 843-5342
Grand Haven (G-6096)		

CONTROLS: Thermostats

AMF-Nano Corporation	G	734 726-0148
Ann Arbor (G-353)		
Energy Control Solutions Inc	G	810 735-2800
Fenton (G-5202)		
Taylor Controls Inc	F	269 637-8521
South Haven (G-14777)		

CONTROLS: Voice

Parkway Elc Communications LLC	D	616 392-2788
Holland (G-7767)		

CONVENIENCE STORES

Admiral	G	989 356-6419
Alpena (G-271)		
Agenda 2020 Inc	F	616 581-6271
Grand Rapids (G-6153)		
D M J Corp	G	810 239-9071
Flint (G-5412)		
Kern Auto Sales and Svc LLC	F	734 475-2722
Chelsea (G-2715)		

CONVENTION & TRADE SHOW SVCS

Art Craft Display Inc	D	517 485-2221
Lansing (G-9278)		
Nationwide Network Inc	E	989 793-0123
Saginaw (G-14103)		

CONVERTERS: Data

Berkshire & Associates Inc	F	734 719-1822
Canton (G-2351)		
Cisco Systems Inc	A	800 553-6387
Detroit (G-3937)		
Startech-Solutions LLC	G	248 419-0650
Southfield (G-15033)		

CONVERTERS: Frequency

Revealed Engineering LLC	G	734 642-5551
Carleton (G-2461)		

CONVERTERS: Phase Or Rotary, Electrical

Elite Industrial Mfg LLC	G	616 895-1873
Allendale (G-216)		

CONVERTERS: Power, AC to DC

Controlled Power Company	C	248 528-3700
Troy (G-16281)		
Ssi Technology Inc	D	248 582-0600
Sterling Heights (G-15507)		
Winford Engineering LLC	G	989 671-9721
Auburn (G-758)		

CONVERTERS: Rotary, Electrical

Acat Global LLC	F	231 437-5000
White Cloud (G-17618)		

CONVERTERS: Torque, Exc Auto

Alma Products Company	G	989 463-1151
Alma (G-234)		

CONVEYOR SYSTEMS

Altron Automation Inc	D	616 669-7711
Hudsonville (G-8144)		
Bradford Company	C	616 399-3000
Holland (G-7575)		
GMI Packaging Co	G	734 972-7389
Ann Arbor (G-474)		
Intersrce Recovery Systems Inc	E	269 375-5100
Kalamazoo (G-8774)		
Motion Machine Company	F	810 664-9901
Lapeer (G-9476)		
Production Accessories Co	G	313 366-1500
Detroit (G-4311)		
Spectrum Automation Company	E	734 522-2160
Livonia (G-9938)		
Steel Master LLC	E	810 771-4943
Grand Blanc (G-5984)		
Systems Unlimited Inc	E	517 279-8407
Coldwater (G-3336)		
Wardcraft Industries LLC	E	517 750-9100
Spring Arbor (G-15129)		
Whiting Corporation	G	734 451-0400
Plymouth (G-12794)		

CONVEYOR SYSTEMS: Belt, General Indl Use

Arrowhead Systems Inc	G	810 720-4770
Flint (G-5377)		
Chip Systems International	F	269 626-8000
Scotts (G-14503)		
Livonia Magnetics LLC	F	734 397-8844
Canton (G-2393)		
National Element Inc	E	248 486-1810
Brighton (G-1966)		
Uniband Usa LLC	F	616 676-6011
Grand Rapids (G-6950)		
Versa-Craft Inc	G	586 465-5999
Clinton Township (G-3255)		

CONVEYOR SYSTEMS: Bucket Type

Material Control Inc	G	630 892-4274
Croswell (G-3600)		

CONVEYOR SYSTEMS: Bulk Handling

Alternative Engineering Inc	E	616 785-7200
Belmont (G-1455)		
Ensign Equipment Inc	G	616 738-9000
Holland (G-7623)		

RK Wojan Inc....E.... 231 347-1160
Charlevoix (G-2628)

CONVEYOR SYSTEMS: Pneumatic Tube

Colombo Sales & Engrg Inc....F.... 248 547-2820
Davisburg (G-3630)
Lrh & Associates Inc....G.... 517 784-1055
Jackson (G-8500)
Pneumatic Tube Products Co....G.... 503 968-0200
Oakley (G-12111)

CONVEYOR SYSTEMS: Robotic

Dimension Machine Tech LLC....F.... 586 649-4747
Bloomfield Hills (G-1759)
Esys Automation LLC....D.... 248 754-1900
Auburn Hills (G-856)
Fibro Laepple Technology Inc....G.... 248 591-4494
Sterling Heights (G-15340)
Simplified Control Solutions....G.... 248 652-1449
Oakland (G-12108)
Tacs Automation LLC....F.... 586 446-8828
Rochester Hills (G-13523)

CONVEYORS & CONVEYING EQPT

ADW Industries Inc....E.... 989 466-4742
Alma (G-231)
Allied Indus Solutions LLC....G.... 810 422-5093
Fenton (G-5180)
Allor Manufacturing Inc....D.... 248 486-4500
Brighton (G-1883)
Ally Equipment LLC....G.... 810 422-5093
Fenton (G-5182)
Anchor Conveyor Products Inc....G.... 313 582-5045
Dearborn (G-3676)
Ase Industries Inc....D.... 586 754-7480
Warren (G-16942)
Automated Systems Inc....E.... 248 373-5600
Auburn Hills (G-786)
Automatic Handling Intl Inc....D.... 734 847-0633
Erie (G-4800)
Automtion Mdlar Components Inc....D.... 248 922-4740
Davisburg (G-3625)
Bay Manufacturing Corporation....E.... 989 358-7198
Alpena (G-281)
Belco Industries Inc....C.... 616 794-0410
Belding (G-1399)
Belco Industries Inc....E.... 616 794-0410
Belding (G-1400)
Benesh Corporation....E.... 734 244-4143
Monroe (G-11023)
Best Industrial Group Inc....F.... 586 826-8800
Warren (G-16957)
Blue Water Manufacturing Inc....F.... 810 364-6170
Marysville (G-10599)
Bos Manufacturing LLC....G.... 231 398-3328
Manistee (G-10417)
Bristol Steel & Conveyor Corp....E.... 810 658-9510
Davison (G-3641)
C T & G Enterprises Inc....G.... 810 798-8661
Almont (G-253)
Caliber Industries LLC....F.... 586 774-6775
Clinton Township (G-3074)
Central Conveyor Company LLC....D.... 248 446-0118
Wixom (G-17782)
Change Parts Incorporated....E.... 231 845-5107
Ludington (G-10052)
Cignys Inc....G.... 989 753-1411
Saginaw (G-14018)
Clinton Machine Inc....E.... 989 834-2235
Ovid (G-12271)
Columbus McKinnon Corporation....G.... 800 955-5541
Muskegon (G-11296)
Constructive Sheet Metal Inc....E.... 616 245-5306
Allendale (G-215)
Continental Crane & Service....F.... 586 294-7900
Fraser (G-5639)
Conveyor Concepts Michigan LLC....F.... 616 997-5200
Coopersville (G-3553)
Cornerstone Fabg & Cnstr Inc....E.... 989 642-5241
Hemlock (G-7460)
CPI Products Inc....C.... 231 547-6064
Auburn Hills (G-829)
Crippen Manufacturing Company....E.... 989 681-4323
Saint Louis (G-14361)
Daifuku North America Holdg Co....E.... 248 553-1000
Novi (G-11862)
Dcl Inc....C.... 231 547-5600
Charlevoix (G-2613)
Dearborn Mid West Conveyor Co....G.... 313 273-2804
Detroit (G-3966)
Dearborn Mid-West Company LLC....C.... 734 288-4400
Taylor (G-15706)
Dematic....G.... 616 395-8671
Holland (G-7607)
Diamond Automation Ltd....G.... 734 838-7138
Livonia (G-9710)
Dunkley International Inc....C.... 269 343-5583
Kalamazoo (G-8732)
Durr Systems Inc....E.... 586 755-7500
Warren (G-17010)
Dynamic Conveyor Corporation....E.... 231 798-0014
Norton Shores (G-11748)
Eagle Buckets Inc....G.... 517 787-0385
Jackson (G-8436)
Eagle Engineering & Supply Co....E.... 989 356-4526
Alpena (G-286)
Egemin Automation Inc....C.... 616 393-0101
Holland (G-7619)
Empire Machine & Conveyors Inc....F.... 989 541-2060
Durand (G-4608)
Endura-Veyor Inc....F.... 989 358-7060
Alpena (G-287)
Ermanco....F.... 231 798-4547
Norton Shores (G-11754)
Fata Automation Inc....D.... 248 724-7660
Auburn Hills (G-860)
Fraser Fab and Machine Inc....E.... 248 852-9050
Rochester Hills (G-13428)
Frost Links....G.... 616 785-9030
Grand Rapids (G-6422)
Gonzalez Prod Systems Inc....C.... 248 745-1200
Pontiac (G-12829)
Great Lakes Tech & Mfg LLC....G.... 810 593-0257
Fenton (G-5217)
Gudel Inc....D.... 734 214-0000
Ann Arbor (G-480)
Hapman....F.... 269 343-1675
Kalamazoo (G-8760)
Harry Major Machine & Tool Co....D.... 586 783-7030
Clinton Township (G-3134)
Harvey S Freeman....E.... 248 852-2222
West Bloomfield (G-17479)
Herkules Equipment Corporation....E.... 248 960-7100
Commerce Township (G-3411)
Highland Engineering Inc....E.... 517 548-4372
Howell (G-8048)
Hines Corporation....F.... 231 799-6240
Norton Shores (G-11812)
HMS Products Co....D.... 248 689-8120
Troy (G-16398)
Howard Structural Steel Inc....E.... 989 752-3000
Saginaw (G-14062)
Integrated Conveyor Ltd....G.... 231 747-6430
Muskegon (G-11349)
International Material Co....F.... 616 355-2800
Holland (G-7691)
Intralox LLC....G.... 616 259-7471
Grand Rapids (G-6543)
Jantec Incorporated....E.... 231 941-4339
Traverse City (G-16009)
Jervis B Webb Company....B.... 248 553-1222
Farmington Hills (G-5032)
Jervis B Webb Company....C.... 231 347-3931
Harbor Springs (G-7285)
Jervis B Webb Company....D.... 231 582-6558
Boyne City (G-1825)
Kalamazoo Mfg Corp Globl....C.... 269 382-8200
Kalamazoo (G-8792)
Lenawee Tool & Automation Inc....G.... 517 458-7222
Morenci (G-11112)
Loudon Steel Inc....D.... 989 871-9353
Millington (G-10997)
Magline Inc....D.... 800 624-5463
Standish (G-15222)
Magnetic Products Inc....D.... 248 887-5600
Highland (G-7497)
Mark One Corporation....D.... 989 732-2427
Gaylord (G-5877)
Material Transfer and Stor Inc....E.... 800 836-7068
Allegan (G-176)
Max Endura Inc....E.... 989 356-1593
Alpena (G-297)
McNichols Conveyor Company....F.... 248 357-6077
Southfield (G-14976)
Metzgar Conveyor Co....E.... 616 784-0930
Grand Rapids (G-6664)
Milan Metal Worx LLC....G.... 734 369-7115
Petersburg (G-12437)
Mol Belting Systems Inc....D.... 616 453-2484
Grand Rapids (G-6696)
Mondrella Process Systems LLC....G.... 616 281-9836
Grand Rapids (G-6700)
Motan Inc....E.... 269 685-1050
Plainwell (G-12531)
Motion Industries Inc....G.... 989 771-0200
Saginaw (G-14100)
New Technologies Tool & Mfg....F.... 810 694-5426
Grand Blanc (G-5976)
North Woods Industrial....G.... 616 784-2840
Comstock Park (G-3502)
Omni Metalcraft Corp....E.... 989 354-4075
Alpena (G-304)
Overhead Conveyor Company....E.... 248 547-3800
Ferndale (G-5307)
P & A Conveyor Sales Inc....G.... 734 285-7970
Riverview (G-13303)
Paradigm Conveyor LLC....G.... 616 520-1926
Marne (G-10510)
Paslin Company....C.... 248 953-8419
Shelby Township (G-14660)
PCI Procal Inc....F.... 989 358-7070
Alpena (G-307)
Peak Industries Co Inc....D.... 313 846-8666
Dearborn (G-3747)
Powerscreen USA LLC....G.... 989 288-3121
Durand (G-4612)
Prab Inc....C.... 269 382-8200
Kalamazoo (G-8854)
Prab Inc....D.... 269 343-1675
Kalamazoo (G-8855)
Pressure Vessel Service Inc....E.... 313 921-1200
Detroit (G-4310)
PVS Holdings Inc....G.... 313 921-1200
Detroit (G-4319)
Roberts Sinto Corporation....D.... 517 371-2471
Grand Ledge (G-6114)
Roberts Sinto Corporation....C.... 517 371-2460
Lansing (G-9320)
Saginaw Products Corporation....E.... 989 753-1411
Saginaw (G-14141)
Santanna Tool & Design LLC....D.... 248 541-3500
Madison Heights (G-10348)
Siemens Industry Inc....C.... 616 913-7700
Grand Rapids (G-6861)
Sinto America Inc....E.... 517 371-2460
Lansing (G-9323)
Sparks Belting Company Inc....G.... 800 451-4537
Spring Lake (G-15179)
Sparks Belting Company Inc....D.... 616 949-2750
Grand Rapids (G-6875)
Steel Craft Inc....E.... 989 358-7196
Alpena (G-314)
Storch Products Company Inc....F.... 734 591-2200
Livonia (G-9946)
Straatsma Associates Inc....G.... 810 735-6957
Linden (G-9597)
Structural Equipment Co....E.... 248 547-3800
Ferndale (G-5320)
Sure Conveyors Inc....G.... 248 926-2100
Wixom (G-17902)
Symbiote Inc....E.... 616 772-1790
Zeeland (G-18189)
Symorex Ltd....F.... 734 971-6000
Ann Arbor (G-653)
Tgw Systems Inc....C.... 231 798-4547
Norton Shores (G-11800)
Thoreson-Mc Cosh Inc....E.... 248 362-0960
Troy (G-16638)
Ton-Tex Corporation....E.... 616 957-3200
Greenville (G-7158)
Triad Industrial Corp....F.... 989 358-7191
Atlanta (G-733)
Ultimation Industries LLC....E.... 586 771-1881
Roseville (G-13885)
Unified Screening and Crushing....F.... 888 464-9473
Saint Johns (G-14299)
Versa Handling Co....G.... 313 491-0500
Detroit (G-4427)
Versa Handling Co....G.... 313 891-1420
Detroit (G-4428)
Verstraete Conveyability Inc....E.... 800 798-0410
Grand Rapids (G-6968)
Via-Tech Corp....F.... 989 358-7028
Lachine (G-9079)
W Soule & Co....C.... 269 344-0139
Kalamazoo (G-8920)
Wedin International Inc....D.... 231 779-8650
Cadillac (G-2284)

Employee Codes: A=Over 500 employees, B=251-500
C=101-250, D=51-100, E=20-50, F=10-19, G=3-9

CONVEYORS & CONVEYING EQPT

Whites Bridge Tooling Inc .... E 616 897-4151
  Lowell *(G-10045)*

CONVEYORS: Overhead

Auto/Con Services LLC .... E 586 791-7474
  Fraser *(G-5624)*
Frost Inc .... G 616 785-9030
  Grand Rapids *(G-6420)*
Frost Incorporated .... E 616 453-7781
  Grand Rapids *(G-6421)*
Jervis B Webb Company .... B 248 553-1000
  Novi *(G-11912)*
Wilkie Bros Conveyors Inc .... E 810 364-4820
  Marysville *(G-10626)*

COOKING & FOOD WARMING EQPT: Commercial

Delfield Company LLC .... A 989 773-7981
  Mount Pleasant *(G-11192)*
H & R Electrical Contrs LLC .... G 517 669-2102
  Dewitt *(G-4462)*
Midwest Stainless Fabricating .... G 248 476-4502
  Livonia *(G-9844)*
Sandbox Solutions Inc .... C 248 349-7010
  Northville *(G-11723)*

COOKING & FOODWARMING EQPT: Coffee Brewing

Royal Accoutrements Inc .... G 517 347-7983
  Okemos *(G-12136)*

COOKING & FOODWARMING EQPT: Commercial

Solaronics Inc .... E 248 651-5353
  Rochester *(G-13352)*

COOKING EQPT, HOUSEHOLD: Convection Ovens, Incldg Portable

Lockett Enterprises LLC .... G 810 407-6644
  Flint *(G-5459)*

COOKING EQPT, HOUSEHOLD: Indoor

M & D Distribution Inc .... G 313 592-1467
  Redford *(G-13170)*

COOKING EQPT, HOUSEHOLD: Ranges, Gas

Maytag Corporation .... C 269 923-5000
  Benton Harbor *(G-1529)*
Whirlpool Corporation .... B 269 923-5000
  Benton Harbor *(G-1570)*

COOKING SCHOOL

Detroit Fd Entrprnrship Acdemy .... F 248 894-8941
  Detroit *(G-3984)*

COOKWARE, STONEWARE: Coarse Earthenware & Pottery

Reilchz Inc .... G 231 421-9600
  Traverse City *(G-16093)*

COOLERS & ICE CHESTS: Metal

Keglove LLC .... E 616 610-7289
  Holland *(G-7708)*

COOLERS & ICE CHESTS: Polystyrene Foam

Joy Products Inc .... G 269 683-1662
  Niles *(G-11622)*

COOLING TOWERS: Metal

Bosch Auto Svc Solutions Inc .... E 586 574-1820
  Warren *(G-16964)*
Great Lakes Gauge Company .... F 989 652-6136
  Bridgeport *(G-1852)*
SPX Corporation .... C 586 574-2332
  Warren *(G-17251)*
SPX Corporation .... D 989 652-6136
  Bridgeport *(G-1857)*
SPX Corporation .... D 313 768-2103
  Livonia *(G-9940)*

COPPER ORE MILLING & PREPARATION

Eagle Mine LLC .... B 906 339-7000
  Champion *(G-2602)*

COPPER ORE MINING

Copperwood Resources Inc .... F 906 229-3115
  Wakefield *(G-16848)*
Trelleborg Corporation .... G 269 639-9891
  South Haven *(G-14778)*

COPPER: Cakes, Primary

Center Cupcakes .... G 248 302-6503
  West Bloomfield *(G-17470)*

COPPER: Rolling & Drawing

Aluminum Blanking Co Inc .... D 248 338-4422
  Pontiac *(G-12802)*
Anchor Lamina America Inc .... C 231 533-8646
  Bellaire *(G-1434)*
J M L Contracting & Sales Inc .... F 586 756-4133
  Warren *(G-17108)*
Materion Brush Inc .... F 586 443-4925
  Warren *(G-17143)*
Vx-LLC .... G 734 854-8700
  Lambertville *(G-9187)*

COPY MACHINES WHOLESALERS

Lowery Corporation .... C 616 554-5200
  Grand Rapids *(G-6633)*
Orbit Technology Inc .... G 906 776-7248
  Iron Mountain *(G-8297)*

CORD & TWINE

Great Lakes Cordage Inc .... F 616 842-4455
  Spring Lake *(G-15148)*

CORK & CORK PRDTS

Blade Industrial Products Inc .... G 248 773-7400
  Wixom *(G-17774)*
Derby Fabg Solutions LLC .... D 616 866-1650
  Rockford *(G-13566)*

CORRUGATED PRDTS: Boxes, Partition, Display Items, Sheet/Pad

Roberts Movable Walls Inc .... G 269 626-0227
  Scotts *(G-14506)*
Russell R Peters Co LLC .... G 989 732-0660
  Gaylord *(G-5891)*

COSMETIC PREPARATIONS

Agrestal Hygienics LLC .... G 800 410-9053
  Kalamazoo *(G-8674)*
Bio Source Naturals LLC .... G 734 335-6798
  Canton *(G-2352)*
Merchandising Productions .... E 616 676-6000
  Ada *(G-23)*
Mineral Cosmetics Inc .... G 248 542-7733
  Southfield *(G-14983)*
Smooches Blend Bar LLC .... G 734 756-7152
  Ypsilanti *(G-18101)*
Stone Soap Company Inc .... G 248 706-1000
  Sylvan Lake *(G-15672)*

COSMETICS & TOILETRIES

Amway International Dev Inc .... F 616 787-6000
  Ada *(G-8)*
Art of Shaving - Fl LLC .... G 248 649-5872
  Troy *(G-16219)*
Brun Laboratories Inc .... G 616 456-1114
  Grand Rapids *(G-6237)*
Can You Handlebar LLC .... F 248 821-2171
  Mount Clemens *(G-11126)*
Conquest Scents .... E 810 653-2759
  Davison *(G-3643)*
Homedics Usa LLC .... B 248 863-3000
  Commerce Township *(G-3414)*
Jogue Inc .... G 313 921-4802
  Detroit *(G-4163)*
Northport Naturals .... G 231 420-9448
  Cheboygan *(G-2689)*
NV Labs Inc .... F 248 358-9022
  Southfield *(G-14993)*
Platinum Skin Care Inc .... G 586 598-6075
  Clinton Township *(G-3196)*
Ravenwood .... G 231 421-5682
  Traverse City *(G-16091)*
Rejoice International Corp .... G 855 345-5575
  Northville *(G-11721)*
Smo International Inc .... F 248 275-1091
  Warren *(G-17241)*
Soulfull Earth Herbals .... G 517 316-0547
  Lansing *(G-9425)*
Stellar Scents .... G 989 868-3477
  Reese *(G-13233)*
Whimsical Fusions LLC .... G 248 956-0952
  Detroit *(G-4439)*

COSMETOLOGIST

Luma Laser and Medi Spa .... G 248 817-5499
  Troy *(G-16466)*

COSMETOLOGY & PERSONAL HYGIENE SALONS

Skin Bar VII LLC .... G 313 701-7958
  Detroit *(G-4364)*

COSTUME JEWELRY & NOVELTIES: Apparel, Exc Precious Metals

Bead Gallery .... F 734 663-6800
  Ann Arbor *(G-381)*

COSTUME JEWELRY & NOVELTIES: Exc Semi & Precious

Amalgamations Ltd .... G 248 879-7345
  Troy *(G-16194)*

COSTUME JEWELRY & NOVELTIES: Rosaries & Sm Religious Items

Rosary Workshop .... G 906 788-4846
  Stephenson *(G-15239)*

COUNTER & SINK TOPS

Cameo Countertops Inc .... E 616 458-8745
  Grand Rapids *(G-6252)*
Custom Crafters .... G 269 763-9180
  Bellevue *(G-1453)*
Eagle Marble & Granite .... G 586 421-1912
  Chesterfield *(G-2770)*
Granite Planet LLC .... G 734 522-0190
  Livonia *(G-9757)*
J & J Laminate Connection Inc .... G 810 227-1824
  Brighton *(G-1944)*
KS Liquidating LLC .... E 248 577-8220
  Madison Heights *(G-10295)*
Mica Crafters Inc .... E 517 548-2924
  Howell *(G-8063)*
Natures Edge Stone Produ .... G 231 943-3440
  Traverse City *(G-16047)*
Paxton Products Inc .... E 517 627-3688
  Lansing *(G-9317)*
Phoenix Countertops LLC .... G 586 254-1450
  Sterling Heights *(G-15444)*
Top Form Inc .... G 815 653-9616
  Twin Lake *(G-16715)*
Village Cabinet Shoppe Inc .... G 586 264-6464
  Sterling Heights *(G-15539)*

COUNTERS & COUNTING DEVICES

Ernest Industries Acquisition, ... E 734 595-9500
  Westland *(G-17554)*

COUNTERS OR COUNTER DISPLAY CASES, EXC WOOD

Grand Valley Wood Products Inc .... E 616 475-5890
  Grand Rapids *(G-6471)*
Top Shop Inc .... G 517 323-9085
  Lansing *(G-9270)*

COUNTERS OR COUNTER DISPLAY CASES, WOOD

Howes Custom Counter Tops .... G 989 498-4044
  Saginaw *(G-14063)*
Pohls Custom Counter Tops .... G 989 593-2174
  Fowler *(G-5555)*

PRODUCT SECTION

CRUDE PETROLEUM & NATURAL GAS PRODUCTION

COUNTING DEVICES: Controls, Revolution & Timing

Micro-Systems Inc ....G....... 616 481-1601
  Norton Shores *(G-11774)*
Rap Electronics & Machines...................F....... 616 846-1437
  Grand Haven *(G-6068)*

COUNTING DEVICES: Electromechanical

Modular Data Systems Inc ....F....... 586 739-5870
  Shelby Township *(G-14645)*
Prestolite Electric LLC..............................G....... 248 313-3807
  Novi *(G-11978)*
Southern Auto Wholesalers Inc............F....... 248 335-5555
  Pontiac *(G-12869)*

COUNTING DEVICES: Electronic Totalizing

L Thompson Co LLC.................................F....... 616 844-1135
  Grand Haven *(G-6044)*

COUNTING DEVICES: Gauges, Press Temp Corrections Computing

Essex Brass Corporation ....F....... 586 757-8200
  Warren *(G-17020)*

COUNTING DEVICES: Speedometers

U S Speedo Inc ....F....... 810 244-0909
  Flint *(G-5516)*

COUNTING DEVICES: Vehicle Instruments

Clark Brothers Instrument Co.................F....... 586 781-7000
  Shelby Township *(G-14563)*
New Vintage Usa LLC ....G....... 248 259-4964
  Oak Park *(G-12089)*

COUPLINGS, EXC PRESSURE & SOIL PIPE

O2/Specialty Mfg Holdings LLC.............G....... 248 554-4228
  Bloomfield Hills *(G-1787)*

COUPLINGS: Pipe

Invent Detroit R&D Collaborati ....G....... 313 451-2658
  Detroit *(G-4147)*
Norma Michigan Inc.................................C....... 248 373-4300
  Auburn Hills *(G-959)*

COUPLINGS: Shaft

Evans Industries Inc.................................G....... 313 272-8200
  Detroit *(G-4046)*
Hayes Manufacturing Inc ....E....... 231 879-3372
  Fife Lake *(G-5342)*
Liquid Drive Corporation........................E....... 248 634-5382
  Mount Clemens *(G-11139)*
Lovejoy Inc ....D....... 269 637-3017
  South Haven *(G-14764)*
Lovejoy Curtis LLC ....G....... 269 637-5132
  South Haven *(G-14765)*
System Components Inc ....G....... 269 637-2191
  South Haven *(G-14776)*

COUPON REDEMPTION SVCS

Epi Printers Inc..E....... 269 964-4600
  Battle Creek *(G-1182)*
Epi Printers Inc..C....... 269 968-2221
  Battle Creek *(G-1180)*

COURIER SVCS: Ground

Aunt Millies Bakeries Inc........................E....... 734 528-1475
  Ypsilanti *(G-18053)*
Kolossos Printing Inc ....F....... 734 994-5400
  Ann Arbor *(G-517)*

COVERS: Automobile Seat

Sage Automotive Interiors Inc ....F....... 248 355-9055
  Southfield *(G-15020)*
Technotrim Inc ....A....... 734 254-5243
  Plymouth *(G-12767)*
Tk Mexico Inc ....G....... 248 373-8040
  Auburn Hills *(G-1028)*

COVERS: Automotive, Exc Seat & Tire

AGM Automotive LLC ....D....... 248 776-0600
  Farmington Hills *(G-4923)*

Faurecia North America Inc ....F....... 248 288-1000
  Auburn Hills *(G-863)*
McCarthy Group Incorporated.............G....... 616 977-2900
  Grand Rapids *(G-6652)*
Michigan Industrial Trim Inc ....F....... 734 947-0344
  Taylor *(G-15742)*
Snoeks Automotive N Amer Inc............G....... 586 716-9588
  New Baltimore *(G-11493)*
Verduyn Tarps Detroit Inc ....G....... 313 270-4890
  Detroit *(G-4425)*

COVERS: Canvas

Millers Canvas Shop................................G....... 231 821-0771
  Holton *(G-7934)*
TD Industrial Coverings Inc ....D....... 586 731-2080
  Sterling Heights *(G-15521)*

CRACKED CASTING REPAIR SVCS

Elden Industries Corporation ....F....... 734 946-6900
  Taylor *(G-15715)*

CRANE & AERIAL LIFT SVCS

Continental Crane & Service.................F....... 586 294-7900
  Fraser *(G-5639)*
Crane Technologies Group Inc............E....... 248 652-8700
  Rochester Hills *(G-13397)*
Loshaw Bros Inc ....G....... 989 732-7263
  Gaylord *(G-5875)*
Star Crane Hist Svc of Klmazoo ....G....... 269 321-8882
  Portage *(G-13035)*

CRANES & MONORAIL SYSTEMS

Jervis B Webb Company ....B....... 248 553-1000
  Novi *(G-11912)*
Star Crane Hist Svc of Klmazoo ....G....... 269 321-8882
  Portage *(G-13035)*

CRANES: Indl Plant

Crane Technologies Group Inc............E....... 248 652-8700
  Rochester Hills *(G-13397)*
Royal ARC Welding Company ....E....... 734 789-9099
  Flat Rock *(G-5362)*

CRANES: Overhead

C R B Crane & Service Co......................G....... 586 757-1222
  Warren *(G-16973)*
Grand Traverse Crane Corp ....G....... 231 943-7787
  Traverse City *(G-15984)*
Unified Industries Inc ....F....... 517 546-3220
  Howell *(G-8118)*
Versa Handling Co ....G....... 313 491-0500
  Detroit *(G-4427)*
Wolverine Crane & Service Inc ....E....... 616 538-4870
  Grand Rapids *(G-6997)*
Wolverine Crane & Service Inc ....F....... 734 467-9066
  Romulus *(G-13741)*

CRANKSHAFTS & CAMSHAFTS: Machining

Daniel Pruitoff ....G....... 616 392-1371
  Holland *(G-7605)*
Ddks Industries LLC................................G....... 586 323-5909
  Shelby Township *(G-14573)*
Iq Manufacturing LLC ....G....... 586 634-7185
  Auburn Hills *(G-915)*
Systrand Prsta Eng Systems LLC ....F....... 734 479-8100
  Brownstown Twp *(G-2075)*
TAC Industrial Group LLC ....G....... 517 917-8976
  Jackson *(G-8581)*
Yen Group LLC..F....... 810 201-6457
  Port Huron *(G-12979)*

CRANKSHAFTS: Motor Vehicle

Kellogg Crankshaft Co............................D....... 517 788-9200
  Jackson *(G-8488)*
Moldex Crank Shaft Inc ....G....... 313 561-7676
  Redford *(G-13175)*

CRATES: Fruit, Wood Wirebound

Monte Package Company LLC ....E....... 269 849-1722
  Riverside *(G-13285)*
Tk Enterprises Inc....................................E....... 989 865-9915
  Saint Charles *(G-14202)*

CREDIT AGENCIES: Federal & Federally Sponsored

National Credit Corporation..................F....... 734 459-8100
  West Bloomfield *(G-17491)*

CREDIT INST, SHORT-TERM BUSINESS: Accts Receiv & Coml Paper

National Credit Corporation..................F....... 734 459-8100
  West Bloomfield *(G-17491)*

CREDIT INST, SHORT-TERM BUSINESS: Financing Dealers

Ford Motor Company...............................B....... 313 322-3000
  Dearborn *(G-3709)*
Ford Motor Company...............................A....... 734 523-3000
  Livonia *(G-9744)*
Ford Motor Company...............................A....... 734 942-6248
  Brownstown *(G-2062)*
General Motors LLC.................................A....... 313 972-6000
  Detroit *(G-4084)*

CREDIT INSTITUTIONS: Personal

General Motors LLC.................................E....... 248 456-5000
  Pontiac *(G-12827)*

CREDIT INSTITUTIONS: Short-Term Business

General Motors LLC.................................E....... 248 456-5000
  Pontiac *(G-12827)*

CREMATORIES

American Vault Service ....G....... 989 366-8657
  Prudenville *(G-13084)*
Arnets Inc ....F....... 734 665-3650
  Ann Arbor *(G-367)*
W L Snow Enterprises Inc......................G....... 989 732-9501
  Gaylord *(G-5899)*
Wilbert Burial Vault Company..............G....... 231 773-6631
  Muskegon *(G-11449)*
Wilbert Burial Vault Works ....G....... 906 786-0261
  Kingsford *(G-9068)*
Wilbert Saginaw Vault Corp ....G....... 989 753-3065
  Saginaw *(G-14183)*
Willbee Concrete Products Co ....F....... 517 782-8246
  Jackson *(G-8607)*

CROWNS & CLOSURES

Adcaa LLC ....G....... 734 623-4236
  Ann Arbor *(G-343)*

CRUDE PETROLEUM & NATURAL GAS PRODUCTION

Columbus Oil & Gas LLC ....G....... 810 385-9140
  Burtchville *(G-2140)*
Omimex Energy Inc ....G....... 517 628-2820
  Mason *(G-10650)*
Wepco Energy LLC ....G....... 231 932-8615
  Traverse City *(G-16142)*

CRUDE PETROLEUM & NATURAL GAS PRODUCTION

Aztec Producing Co Inc.........................G....... 269 792-0505
  Wayland *(G-17398)*
Cima Energy LP ....G....... 231 941-0633
  Traverse City *(G-15941)*
Dicks Sporting Goods Inc ....G....... 248 581-8028
  Troy *(G-16318)*
DTE Energy Company ....E....... 313 235-4000
  Detroit *(G-4019)*
DTE Energy Trust II ....G....... 313 235-8822
  Detroit *(G-4021)*
Kelly Oil & Gas Inc ....G....... 231 929-0591
  Traverse City *(G-16017)*
Michigan Reef Development ....G....... 989 288-2172
  Durand *(G-4609)*
Miller Exploration Company ....F....... 231 941-0004
  Traverse City *(G-16037)*
Oil City Venture Inc ....G....... 989 832-8071
  Midland *(G-10899)*
SD Oil Enterprises Inc ....G....... 248 688-1419
  Warren *(G-17236)*

Employee Codes: A=Over 500 employees, B=251-500
C=101-250, D=51-100, E=20-50, F=10-19, G=3-9

2020 Harris Michigan Industrial Directory

1207

CRUDE PETROLEUM & NATURAL GAS PRODUCTION

Shell Oil Company ....G...... 248 693-0036
  Lake Orion (G-9160)
Summit-Reed City Inc ....E...... 989 433-5716
  Rosebush (G-13765)
Tronox Incorporated ....G...... 231 328-4986
  Merritt (G-10765)
William R Hall Kimberly ....G...... 989 426-4605
  Gladwin (G-5939)

CRUDE PETROLEUM PRODUCTION

Bailer and De Shaw ....G...... 989 684-3610
  Kawkawlin (G-8970)
Black River Oil Corp ....G...... 231 723-6502
  Manistee (G-10416)
Blarney Castle Inc ....G...... 231 864-3111
  Bear Lake (G-1376)
Christian Oil Company ....F...... 269 673-2218
  Allegan (G-152)
Dart Energy Corporation ....F...... 231 885-1665
  Mesick (G-10769)
Devonian Energy Inc ....G...... 989 732-9400
  Gaylord (G-5855)
Federated Oil & Gas Prpts Inc ....G...... 231 929-4466
  Traverse City (G-15970)
Force Energy Inc ....G...... 989 732-0724
  Gaylord (G-5858)
Goodale Enterprises LLC ....G...... 616 453-7690
  Grand Rapids (G-6448)
Jordan Exploration Co LLC ....F...... 231 935-4220
  Traverse City (G-16015)
Lease Management Inc ....G...... 989 773-5948
  Mount Pleasant (G-11202)
Mack Oil Corporation ....G...... 231 590-5903
  Traverse City (G-16030)
Merit Energy Company ....G...... 989 685-3446
  Rose City (G-13764)
Merit Energy Company LLC ....E...... 231 258-6401
  Kalkaska (G-8950)
Omega Resources Inc ....G...... 231 941-4838
  Traverse City (G-16059)
Omimex Energy Inc ....F...... 231 845-7358
  Ludington (G-10077)
Petroleum Resources Inc ....G...... 586 752-7856
  Romeo (G-13635)
Presidium Energy LLC ....G...... 231 933-6373
  Traverse City (G-16076)
Sappington Crude Oil Inc ....G...... 989 345-1052
  West Branch (G-17521)
Somoco Inc ....E...... 231 946-0200
  Traverse City (G-16109)
Southwestern Mich Dust Ctrl ....F...... 269 521-7638
  Bloomingdale (G-1814)
Speedway LLC ....F...... 586 727-2638
  Richmond (G-13271)
Speedway LLC ....G...... 313 291-3710
  Taylor (G-15771)
Speedway LLC ....F...... 231 775-8101
  Cadillac (G-2278)
Tolas Oil Gas Exploration Co ....G...... 989 772-2599
  Mount Pleasant (G-11233)
Trendwell Energy Corporation ....F...... 616 866-5024
  Rockford (G-13594)
West Bay Exploration Company ....F...... 231 946-3529
  Traverse City (G-16143)

CRYSTALS

Kyocera International Inc ....F...... 734 416-8500
  Plymouth (G-12670)

CUBICLES: Electric Switchboard Eqpt

Continental Electrical Pdts ....G...... 248 589-2758
  Sterling Heights (G-15296)

CULVERTS: Sheet Metal

Jensen Bridge & Supply Company ....E...... 810 648-3000
  Sandusky (G-14437)
Schneider Iron & Metal Inc ....F...... 906 774-0644
  Iron Mountain (G-8299)

CUPS & PLATES: Foamed Plastics

Dart Container Corp Kentucky ....B...... 517 676-3800
  Mason (G-10632)
Dart Container Michigan LLC ....E...... 800 248-5960
  Mason (G-10634)
Dart Container Michigan LLC ....E...... 517 694-9455
  Holt (G-7909)
Dart Container Michigan LLC ....C...... 517 676-3803
  Mason (G-10635)

CUPS: Plastic Exc Polystyrene Foam

Dart Container Corp Georgia ....B...... 517 676-3800
  Mason (G-10631)
Scic LLC ....E...... 800 248-5960
  Mason (G-10655)
Solo Cup Company LLC ....C...... 800 248-5960
  Mason (G-10657)

CURBING: Granite Or Stone

Ardo Granite LLC ....F...... 517 253-7139
  Lansing (G-9204)
Granite City Inc ....F...... 248 478-0033
  Livonia (G-9756)
Stone Specialists Inc ....F...... 810 744-2278
  Burton (G-2167)

CURTAIN & DRAPERY FIXTURES: Poles, Rods & Rollers

Lorne Hanley ....G...... 248 547-9865
  Huntington Woods (G-8189)
Melody Digiglio ....F...... 586 754-4405
  Warren (G-17147)
Muskegon Awning & Mfg Co ....E...... 231 759-0911
  Muskegon (G-11387)
PCI Industries Inc ....D...... 248 542-2570
  Oak Park (G-12090)

CURTAINS & BEDDING: Knit

Star Textile Inc ....E...... 888 527-5700
  Madison Heights (G-10361)

CURTAINS: Window, From Purchased Materials

Barons Inc ....E...... 517 484-1366
  Lansing (G-9347)
Hospital Curtain Solutions Inc ....G...... 248 293-9785
  Rochester Hills (G-13445)

CUSHIONS & PILLOWS

Arden Companies LLC ....E...... 248 415-8500
  Bingham Farms (G-1648)
Krams Enterprises Inc ....A...... 248 415-8500
  Bingham Farms (G-1655)

CUSHIONS & PILLOWS: Bed, From Purchased Materials

Jacquart Fabric Products Inc ....C...... 906 932-1339
  Ironwood (G-8332)

CUSHIONS & PILLOWS: Boat

Inplast Interior Tech LLC ....G...... 810 724-3500
  Almont (G-258)

CUSTOM COMPOUNDING OF RUBBER MATERIALS

Jedtco Corp ....E...... 734 326-3010
  Westland (G-17573)
Mykin Inc ....F...... 248 667-8030
  South Lyon (G-14804)
Rex M Tubbs ....G...... 734 459-3180
  Plymouth (G-12735)
Specialty Pdts & Polymers Inc ....E...... 269 684-5931
  Niles (G-11648)

CUT STONE & STONE PRODUCTS

Atlas Tile & Stone LLC ....G...... 586 264-7720
  Warren (G-16945)
Booms Stone Company ....D...... 313 531-3000
  Redford (G-13150)
Botsg Inc ....D...... 231 929-2121
  Traverse City (G-15918)
Cig Jan Products Ltd ....F...... 616 698-9070
  Caledonia (G-2294)
Farnese North America Inc ....G...... 616 844-8651
  Grand Rapids (G-6398)
Gmr Stone Products LLC ....F...... 586 739-2700
  Sterling Heights (G-15363)
Korcast Products Incorporated ....G...... 248 740-2340
  Troy (G-16449)
Landscape Stone Supply Inc ....G...... 616 953-2028
  Holland (G-7719)
Mellemas Cut Stone ....G...... 616 984-2493
  Sand Lake (G-14424)
Michigan Tile and Marble Co ....E...... 313 931-1700
  Detroit (G-4244)
Parker Property Dev Inc ....F...... 616 842-6118
  Grand Haven (G-6060)
Patten Monument Company ....D...... 616 785-4141
  Comstock Park (G-3506)
Royal Stone LLC ....E...... 248 343-6232
  Williamston (G-17739)
Superior Monuments Co ....G...... 616 844-1700
  Grand Haven (G-6087)
Superior Monuments Co ....G...... 231 728-2211
  Muskegon (G-11433)

CUTLERY

Crl Inc ....E...... 906 428-3710
  Gladstone (G-5910)

CUTLERY WHOLESALERS

PA Products Inc ....G...... 734 421-1060
  Livonia (G-9880)

CUTOUTS: Cardboard, Die-Cut, Made From Purchased Materials

Rizzo Packaging Inc ....E...... 269 685-5808
  Plainwell (G-12542)

CUTOUTS: Distribution

West Michigan Technical Supply ......G...... 616 735-0991
  Grand Rapids (G-6988)

CUTTING SVC: Paperboard

Design Converting Inc ....F...... 616 942-7780
  Grand Rapids (G-6344)

CYCLIC CRUDES & INTERMEDIATES

Diversified Chem Technologies ....C...... 313 867-5444
  Detroit (G-4010)
Esco Company LLC ....D...... 231 726-3106
  Grand Rapids (G-6384)
Sun Chemical Corporation ....C...... 231 788-2371
  Muskegon (G-11432)

CYLINDER & ACTUATORS: Fluid Power

Beaver Aerospace & Defense Inc ....D...... 734 853-5003
  Livonia (G-9662)
Best Metal Products Co Inc ....C...... 616 942-7141
  Grand Rapids (G-6213)
Cpj Company Inc ....E...... 616 784-6355
  Comstock Park (G-3472)
Dadco Inc ....D...... 734 207-1100
  Plymouth (G-12604)
Dadco Inc ....G...... 616 785-2888
  Comstock Park (G-3475)
E J M Ball Screw LLC ....F...... 989 893-7674
  Bay City (G-1307)
E K Hydraulics Inc ....G...... 800 632-7112
  Petoskey (G-12448)
Eaton Corporation ....C...... 517 787-7220
  Jackson (G-8439)
Hilite International Inc ....C...... 231 894-3200
  Whitehall (G-17668)
Ksb Dubric Inc ....E...... 616 784-6355
  Comstock Park (G-3492)
Lor Manufacturing Co Inc ....G...... 866 644-8622
  Weidman (G-17458)
Npi ....G...... 248 478-0010
  Farmington Hills (G-5083)
Pacora River Defense LLC ....G...... 248 546-1142
  Hazel Park (G-7450)
Parker-Hannifin Corporation ....B...... 269 629-5000
  Richland (G-13252)
Parker-Hannifin Corporation ....B...... 269 384-3459
  Kalamazoo (G-8843)
Peninsular Inc ....E...... 586 775-7211
  Roseville (G-13853)
R M Wright Company Inc ....E...... 248 476-9800
  Farmington Hills (G-5111)
Suspa Incorporated ....C...... 616 241-4200
  Grand Rapids (G-6906)

CYLINDERS: Pressure

E K Hydraulics Inc ....G...... 800 632-7112
  Petoskey (G-12448)

PRODUCT SECTION

DAIRY PRDTS: Milk, Processed, Pasteurized, Homogenized/Btld

Elden Cylinder Testing Inc ....E....... 734 946-6900
  Taylor *(G-15714)*
Mahle Eng Components USA Inc ....F....... 248 305-8200
  Farmington Hills *(G-5051)*
Peninsular Inc ....E....... 586 775-7211
  Roseville *(G-13853)*
Printing Cylinders Inc ....G....... 586 791-5231
  Clinton Township *(G-3204)*

CYLINDERS: Pump

K & M Industrial LLC ....G....... 906 420-8770
  Gladstone *(G-5914)*
Standfast Industries Inc ....E....... 248 380-3223
  Livonia *(G-9942)*
Yoe Industries Inc ....G....... 586 791-7660
  Clinton Township *(G-3263)*

DAIRY EQPT

Recon Technologies LLC ....G....... 616 241-1877
  Grand Rapids *(G-6814)*

DAIRY PRDTS STORE: Cheese

Reilchz Inc ....G....... 231 421-9600
  Traverse City *(G-16093)*

DAIRY PRDTS STORE: Ice Cream, Packaged

Alinosi French Ice Cream Co ....G....... 313 527-3195
  Detroit *(G-3855)*
Moo-Ville Inc ....E....... 517 852-9003
  Nashville *(G-11462)*

DAIRY PRDTS STORES

Guernsey Dairy Stores Inc ....C....... 248 349-1466
  Northville *(G-11696)*

DAIRY PRDTS WHOLESALERS: Fresh

C F Burger Creamery Co ....D....... 313 584-4040
  Detroit *(G-3925)*
Michigan Milk Producers Assn ....D....... 989 834-2221
  Ovid *(G-12273)*

DAIRY PRDTS: Butter

Blank Slate Creamery LLC ....G....... 734 218-3242
  Whitmore Lake *(G-17690)*
Brinks Family Creamery LLC ....G....... 231 826-0099
  Mc Bain *(G-10680)*
Browndog Creamery LLC ....G....... 248 361-3759
  Northville *(G-11681)*
Greenville Ventr Partners LLC ....E....... 616 303-2400
  Greenville *(G-7137)*
Inverness Dairy Inc ....E....... 231 627-4655
  Cheboygan *(G-2681)*
Michigan Milk Producers Assn ....E....... 269 435-2835
  Constantine *(G-3539)*
Michigan Milk Producers Assn ....E....... 248 474-6672
  Novi *(G-11947)*
Michigan Milk Producers Assn ....D....... 989 834-2221
  Ovid *(G-12273)*
Moo-Ville Inc ....E....... 517 852-9003
  Nashville *(G-11462)*
Purple Cow Creamery ....G....... 616 494-1933
  Holland *(G-7778)*

DAIRY PRDTS: Cheese

Agropur Inc ....D....... 616 538-3822
  Grand Rapids *(G-6154)*
Country Home Creations Inc ....E....... 810 244-7348
  Flint *(G-5405)*
Evergreen Lane Farm LLC ....G....... 269 543-9900
  Fennville *(G-5171)*
Greenville Ventr Partners LLC ....E....... 616 303-2400
  Greenville *(G-7137)*
Liberty Dairy Company ....C....... 800 632-5552
  Evart *(G-4885)*
Litehouse Inc ....C....... 616 897-5911
  Lowell *(G-10034)*
Michigan Chese Prtein Pdts LLC ......G....... 517 403-5247
  Tipton *(G-15884)*
Williams Cheese Co ....E....... 989 697-4492
  Linwood *(G-9599)*
Win Schuler Foods Inc ....G....... 248 262-3450
  Southfield *(G-15066)*
Zingermans Creamery LLC ....F....... 734 929-0500
  Ann Arbor *(G-709)*

DAIRY PRDTS: Condensed Milk

Greenville Ventr Partners LLC ....E....... 616 303-2400
  Greenville *(G-7137)*

DAIRY PRDTS: Cream Substitutes

Bay Valley Foods LLC ....C....... 269 792-2277
  Wayland *(G-17399)*

DAIRY PRDTS: Dietary Supplements, Dairy & Non-Dairy Based

Artjen Complexus Usa LLC ....G....... 519 919-0814
  Detroit *(G-3881)*
Castle Remedies Inc ....F....... 734 973-8990
  Ann Arbor *(G-394)*
Enrinity Supplements Inc ....G....... 734 322-4966
  Westland *(G-17553)*
Green Room Michigan LLC ....F....... 248 289-3288
  Farmington Hills *(G-5015)*
Visalus Sciences ....G....... 877 847-2587
  Troy *(G-16687)*

DAIRY PRDTS: Dips & Spreads, Cheese Based

Baracoa Dips ....G....... 616 643-3204
  Grand Rapids *(G-6204)*

DAIRY PRDTS: Dried Milk

Michigan Milk Producers Assn ....E....... 248 474-6672
  Novi *(G-11947)*

DAIRY PRDTS: Fermented & Cultured Milk Prdts

Langs Inc ....G....... 248 634-6048
  Holly *(G-7884)*
Old Europe Cheese Inc ....D....... 269 925-5003
  Benton Harbor *(G-1536)*

DAIRY PRDTS: Frozen Desserts & Novelties

Blossom Berry ....G....... 517 775-6978
  Novi *(G-11838)*
Cold Stone Creamery ....G....... 313 886-4020
  Grosse Pointe Park *(G-7192)*
Comstock Creamery LLC ....G....... 269 929-7693
  Kalamazoo *(G-8712)*
Custard Corner Inc ....G....... 734 771-4396
  Grosse Ile *(G-7168)*
Dairy Freezzz Too LLC ....G....... 248 629-6666
  Madison Heights *(G-10226)*
Dairy Queen ....F....... 616 235-0102
  Grand Rapids *(G-6333)*
Farm Country Frz Custard & Kit ....G....... 989 687-6700
  Sanford *(G-14450)*
Guernsey Dairy Stores Inc ....C....... 248 349-1466
  Northville *(G-11696)*
Hattiegirl Ice Cream Foods LLC ....G....... 877 444-3738
  Detroit *(G-4118)*
International Brands Inc ....G....... 248 644-2701
  Bloomfield Hills *(G-1775)*
Loven Spoonful ....G....... 517 522-3953
  Grass Lake *(G-7089)*
Moo-Ville Inc ....E....... 517 852-9003
  Nashville *(G-11462)*
Plainwell Ice Cream Co ....F....... 269 685-8586
  Plainwell *(G-12537)*
Pump House ....G....... 616 647-5481
  Grand Rapids *(G-6795)*
Quality Dairy Company ....F....... 517 367-2400
  Lansing *(G-9417)*
Sweet Tmpttons Ice Cream Prlor ......G....... 616 842-8108
  Grand Haven *(G-6088)*
That French Place ....F....... 231 437-6037
  Charlevoix *(G-2633)*
WG Sweis Investments LLC ....E....... 313 477-8433
  Washington *(G-17314)*

DAIRY PRDTS: Ice Cream & Ice Milk

Moomers Homemade Ice Cream LLC ...E....... 231 941-4122
  Traverse City *(G-16043)*
Shetler Family Dairy LLC ....F....... 231 258-8216
  Kalkaska *(G-8958)*

DAIRY PRDTS: Ice Cream, Bulk

Alinosi French Ice Cream Co ....G....... 313 527-3195
  Detroit *(G-3855)*

Berkley Frosty Freeze Inc ....G....... 248 336-2634
  Berkley *(G-1581)*
Corner Cone ....G....... 810 412-4433
  Davison *(G-3644)*
Deans Ice Cream Inc ....F....... 269 685-6641
  Plainwell *(G-12522)*
Frosty Cove ....G....... 231 343-6643
  Muskegon *(G-11328)*
Hudsonville Crmry Ice Cream LLC ....E....... 616 546-4005
  Holland *(G-7684)*
Independent Dairy Inc ....G....... 734 241-6016
  Monroe *(G-11041)*
PGI of Saugatuck Inc ....G....... 269 561-2000
  Fennville *(G-5176)*
Rays Ice Cream Co Inc ....E....... 248 549-5256
  Royal Oak *(G-13963)*
Sherman Dairy Products Co Inc ....F....... 269 637-8251
  South Haven *(G-14770)*
Strohs ....G....... 734 285-5480
  Wyandotte *(G-17977)*
Swirlberry ....G....... 734 779-0830
  Livonia *(G-9949)*
Whats Scoop ....G....... 616 662-6423
  Hudsonville *(G-8187)*

DAIRY PRDTS: Ice Cream, Packaged, Molded, On Sticks, Etc.

House of Flavors Inc ....C....... 231 845-7369
  Ludington *(G-10066)*

DAIRY PRDTS: Milk, Chocolate

Chocolate Vault Llc ....G....... 517 688-3388
  Horton *(G-7963)*

DAIRY PRDTS: Milk, Condensed & Evaporated

Continental Dar Facilities LLC ....D....... 616 837-7641
  Coopersville *(G-3552)*
Dairy Farmers America Inc ....E....... 517 265-5045
  Adrian *(G-57)*
Gerber Products Company ....E....... 231 928-2076
  Fremont *(G-5772)*
Kerry Inc ....D....... 616 871-9940
  Detroit *(G-4175)*
Michigan Milk Producers Assn ....D....... 989 834-2221
  Ovid *(G-12273)*
Michigan Milk Producers Assn ....E....... 269 435-2835
  Constantine *(G-3539)*

DAIRY PRDTS: Milk, Fluid

Bay Valley Foods LLC ....C....... 269 792-2277
  Wayland *(G-17399)*
Calder Bros Dairy Inc ....E....... 313 381-8858
  Lincoln Park *(G-9575)*
Country Dairy Inc ....D....... 231 861-4636
  New ERA *(G-11520)*
Country Fresh LLC ....C....... 734 261-7980
  Livonia *(G-9691)*
Dairy Farmers America Inc ....E....... 517 265-5045
  Adrian *(G-57)*
Greenville Ventr Partners LLC ....E....... 616 303-2400
  Greenville *(G-7137)*
Melody Farms LLC ....E....... 734 261-7980
  Livonia *(G-9837)*
Michigan Milk Producers Assn ....E....... 248 474-6672
  Novi *(G-11947)*
Shetler Family Dairy LLC ....F....... 231 258-8216
  Kalkaska *(G-8958)*
Yoplait USA ....F....... 231 832-3285
  Reed City *(G-13227)*

DAIRY PRDTS: Milk, Processed, Pasteurized, Homogenized/Btld

C F Burger Creamery Co ....D....... 313 584-4040
  Detroit *(G-3925)*
Cream Cup Dairy ....G....... 231 889-4158
  Kaleva *(G-8931)*
Inverness Dairy Inc ....E....... 231 627-4655
  Cheboygan *(G-2681)*
Liberty Dairy Company ....C....... 800 632-5552
  Evart *(G-4885)*
Michigan Milk Producers Assn ....D....... 989 834-2221
  Ovid *(G-12273)*
Michigan Milk Producers Assn ....E....... 269 435-2835
  Constantine *(G-3539)*

Employee Codes: A=Over 500 employees, B=251-500
C=101-250, D=51-100, E=20-50, F=10-19, G=3-9

DAIRY PRDTS: Milk, Processed, Pasteurized, Homogenized/Btld

Quality Dairy Company .... E 517 367-2400
  Lansing *(G-9417)*

DAIRY PRDTS: Natural Cheese

Farm Country Cheese House .... F 989 352-7779
  Lakeview *(G-9172)*
Leprino Foods Company .... D 989 967-3635
  Remus *(G-13239)*
Leprino Foods Company .... C 616 895-5800
  Allendale *(G-221)*
Reilly Craft Creamery LLC .... G 313 300-9859
  Detroit *(G-4338)*
White Lotus Farms Inc .... G 734 904-1379
  Ann Arbor *(G-698)*

DAIRY PRDTS: Powdered Milk

Verndale Products Inc .... E 313 834-4190
  Detroit *(G-4426)*

DAIRY PRDTS: Processed Cheese

Kraft Heinz .... G 616 940-2260
  Grand Rapids *(G-6589)*
Krafts & Thingz .... G 810 689-2457
  Chesterfield *(G-2799)*

DAIRY PRDTS: Sherbets, Dairy Based

Reilly Craft Creamery LLC .... G 313 300-9859
  Detroit *(G-4338)*

DAIRY PRDTS: Yogurt, Exc Frozen

Bloomberry .... G 586 212-9510
  East China *(G-4621)*
Fruit Fro Yo .... G 517 580-3967
  Okemos *(G-12124)*
General Mills Inc .... E 231 832-3285
  Reed City *(G-13213)*
Rocky Mtn Choclat Fctry Inc .... D 810 606-8550
  Grand Blanc *(G-5981)*
Sugar Berry .... G 517 321-0177
  Lansing *(G-9324)*
Sweet Earth .... G 248 850-8031
  Royal Oak *(G-13975)*
Twist .... G 248 859-2169
  West Bloomfield *(G-17503)*
Yogurtown Inc .... G 313 908-9376
  Dearborn *(G-3775)*

DAIRY PRDTS: Yogurt, Frozen

Froyo Pinckney LLC .... G 248 310-4465
  Pinckney *(G-12498)*
Stuarts of Novi .... G 248 615-2955
  Novi *(G-12007)*

DATA PROCESSING & PREPARATION SVCS

Beljan Ltd Inc .... F 734 426-3503
  Dexter *(G-4476)*
Mejenta Systems Inc .... E 248 434-2583
  Southfield *(G-14977)*

DATA PROCESSING SVCS

Ancor Information MGT LLC .... D 248 740-8866
  Troy *(G-16201)*
Covisint Corporation .... D 248 483-2000
  Southfield *(G-14874)*
Datamatic Processing Inc .... E 517 882-4401
  Lansing *(G-9359)*
Enterprise Services LLC .... F 734 523-6525
  Livonia *(G-9727)*
Master Data Center Inc .... D 248 352-5810
  Bingham Farms *(G-1656)*
Mc Donald Computer Corporation .... F 248 350-9290
  Southfield *(G-14975)*
Melange Computer Services Inc ...... E 517 321-8434
  Lansing *(G-9310)*
NA Publishing Inc .... E 734 302-6500
  Saline *(G-14405)*
New Echelon Direct Mktg LLC .... G 248 809-2485
  Brighton *(G-1967)*
Sage Direct Inc .... F 616 940-8311
  Grand Rapids *(G-6850)*
TGI Direct Inc .... E 810 239-5553
  Flint *(G-5509)*
Uniband Usa LLC .... F 616 676-6011
  Grand Rapids *(G-6950)*

DECORATIVE WOOD & WOODWORK

Ausable Upholstery .... G 989 366-5219
  Cadillac *(G-2229)*
Ausable Woodworking Co Inc .... E 989 348-7086
  Frederic *(G-5750)*
Cards of Wood Inc .... G 616 887-8680
  Belmont *(G-1460)*
CHR W LLC .... E 989 755-4000
  Saginaw *(G-14017)*
Custom Rustic Flags LLC .... G 906 203-6935
  Sault Sainte Marie *(G-14463)*
Dynamic Wood Solutions .... G 616 935-7727
  Spring Lake *(G-15139)*
Hillside Creations LLC .... G 269 496-7041
  Mendon *(G-10713)*
Koetje Wood Products Inc .... G 616 393-9191
  Holland *(G-7712)*
Michael Nadeau Cabinet Making ..... G 989 356-0229
  Alpena *(G-298)*
Nuwood Components .... G 616 395-1905
  Holland *(G-7761)*
Oakwood Sports Inc .... G 517 321-6852
  Lansing *(G-9316)*
Silver Street Incorporated .... E 231 861-2194
  Shelby *(G-14536)*
Smith Manufacturing Co Inc .... F 269 925-8155
  Benton Harbor *(G-1549)*
T&M Usa Inc .... F 517 789-9420
  Jackson *(G-8580)*
Thompson Art Glass Inc .... G 810 225-8766
  Brighton *(G-1998)*
Toms World of Wood .... G 517 264-2836
  Adrian *(G-98)*
Unique Namecraft Inc .... G 906 863-3644
  Menominee *(G-10759)*

DEFENSE SYSTEMS & EQPT

Adept Defense LLC .... G 231 758-2792
  Petoskey *(G-12439)*
Aerospace Mfg Svcs Inc .... G 269 697-4800
  Buchanan *(G-2108)*
AMF Defense .... G 586 684-3365
  New Baltimore *(G-11479)*
Antrim Machine Products Inc .... E 231 587-9114
  Mancelona *(G-10386)*
Bg Defense Co LLC .... F 616 710-0609
  Grand Rapids *(G-6217)*
Burtek Enterprises Inc .... C 586 421-8000
  Chesterfield *(G-2749)*
Defense Company of America .... G 248 763-6509
  Rochester Hills *(G-13403)*
Defense Material Recapitalizat .... G 248 698-9333
  White Lake *(G-17632)*
G Defense Company B .... G 616 202-4500
  Grand Rapids *(G-6428)*
His & Her Self Defense .... G 248 767-9085
  Bloomfield Hills *(G-1773)*
Kba Defense .... G 586 552-9268
  Lakeville *(G-9178)*
Kings Self Defense LLC .... G 910 890-4322
  Grand Rapids *(G-6584)*
Leviathan Defense Group .... G 419 575-7792
  Newport *(G-11589)*
Navistar Defense LLC .... G 248 680-7505
  Madison Heights *(G-10315)*
Personal & Home Defense LLC .... G 517 596-3027
  Munith *(G-11253)*
Riverside Defense Training LLC ...... G 231 825-2895
  Lake City *(G-9096)*
Rs Defense Tactics .... G 248 693-2337
  Lake Orion *(G-9157)*
Second Nature Self Defense .... G 734 775-6257
  Flat Rock *(G-5363)*
Sierra 3 Defense LLC .... G 248 343-1066
  Auburn Hills *(G-999)*
Slip Defense Inc .... G 248 366-4423
  White Lake *(G-17638)*
Small Scale Defense .... G 616 238-2671
  Holland *(G-7807)*
Split Second Defense LLC .... G 586 709-1385
  Fraser *(G-5734)*
Superior Fabrication Co LLC .... D 906 495-5634
  Kincheloe *(G-9053)*
Tyght Defense .... G 616 427-3760
  Wyoming *(G-18037)*

DEGREASING MACHINES

Federal-Mogul Powertrain LLC .... G 616 754-1272
  Greenville *(G-7131)*

Kimastle Corporation .... D 586 949-2355
  Chesterfield *(G-2797)*
Midbrook Inc .... D 800 966-9274
  Jackson *(G-8525)*
Oneiric Systems Inc .... G 248 554-3090
  Madison Heights *(G-10317)*
Safety-Kleen Systems Inc .... E 989 753-3261
  Saginaw *(G-14136)*
Tenneco Inc .... F 248 354-7700
  Southfield *(G-15044)*

DEHUMIDIFIERS: Electric

Mann + Hummel Inc .... G 269 329-3900
  Portage *(G-13013)*

DEHYDRATION EQPT

Indian Summer Cooperative Inc ...... E 231 873-7504
  Hart *(G-7374)*

DELIVERY SVCS, BY VEHICLE

Detroit Ready Mix Concrete .... F 313 931-7043
  Detroit *(G-3998)*
Pressure Releases Corporation .... F 616 531-8116
  Grand Rapids *(G-6770)*
Wolverine Concrete Products .... G 313 931-7189
  Detroit *(G-4445)*

DENTAL EQPT

Axsys Inc .... E 248 926-8810
  Wixom *(G-17769)*
Garrison Dental Solutions LLC .... E 616 842-2035
  Spring Lake *(G-15144)*
Kalamazoo Dental Supply .... G 269 345-0260
  Kalamazoo *(G-8787)*

DENTAL EQPT & SPLYS

Air Force Inc .... G 616 399-8511
  Holland *(G-7553)*
Akervall Technologies Inc .... F 800 444-0570
  Saline *(G-14373)*
Dental Art Laboratories Inc .... D 517 485-2200
  Lansing *(G-9222)*
End Product Results LLC .... F 586 585-1210
  Roseville *(G-13801)*
Ghost Mfg LLC .... G 269 281-0489
  Saint Joseph *(G-14312)*
Ktr Dental Lab & Pdts LLC .... F 248 224-9158
  Southfield *(G-14957)*
Liquid Otc LLC .... G 248 214-7771
  Commerce Township *(G-3422)*
Microdental Laboratories Inc .... G 877 711-8778
  Troy *(G-16507)*
Patrick Wyman .... G 810 227-2199
  Brighton *(G-1974)*
Ranir LLC .... B 616 698-8880
  Grand Rapids *(G-6808)*
Ranir Global Holdings LLC .... A 616 698-8880
  Grand Rapids *(G-6809)*
Visual Chimera .... F 586 585-1210
  Eastpointe *(G-4711)*

DENTAL EQPT & SPLYS WHOLESALERS

Kalamazoo Dental Supply .... G 269 345-0260
  Kalamazoo *(G-8787)*

DENTAL EQPT & SPLYS: Cabinets

Biotec Incorporated .... D 616 772-2133
  Zeeland *(G-18120)*

DENTAL EQPT & SPLYS: Compounds

Phoenix Dental Inc .... G 810 750-2328
  Fenton *(G-5230)*

DENTAL EQPT & SPLYS: Dental Materials

Kerr Corporation .... C 734 946-7800
  Romulus *(G-13696)*

DENTAL EQPT & SPLYS: Enamels

Andrew J Reisterer D D S Pllc .... G 231 845-8989
  Ludington *(G-10049)*
Dental Impressions .... G 231 719-0033
  Muskegon *(G-11305)*
New Image Dental P C .... G 586 727-1100
  Richmond *(G-13267)*

PRODUCT SECTION

DIE SETS: Presses, Metal Stamping

Select Dental Groupcom .... G 734 459-3200
  Plymouth *(G-12751)*
Stanford Dental Pllc .... G 248 476-4500
  Livonia *(G-9943)*

DENTAL EQPT & SPLYS: Impression Materials

Aluwax Dental Products Co Inc .... G 616 895-4385
  Allendale *(G-214)*

DENTAL EQPT & SPLYS: Metal

Tokusen Hytech Inc .... C 269 685-1768
  Plainwell *(G-12547)*

DENTISTS' OFFICES & CLINICS

Dental Art Laboratories Inc .... D 517 485-2200
  Lansing *(G-9222)*
Paul W Reed DDS .... F 231 347-4145
  Petoskey *(G-12467)*

DERMATOLOGICALS

Affiliated Troy Dermatologist .... F 248 267-5020
  Troy *(G-16171)*
Harper Dermatology PC .... G 586 776-7546
  Grosse Pointe Shores *(G-7199)*

DESIGN SVCS, NEC

A and D Design Electronics .... G 989 493-1884
  Auburn *(G-748)*
Adam Electronics Incorporated .... E 248 583-2000
  Madison Heights *(G-10181)*
Advanced Research Company .... F 248 475-4770
  Orion *(G-12173)*
All About Quilting and Design .... G 269 471-7359
  Berrien Springs *(G-1591)*
Auto/Con Services LLC .... E 586 791-7474
  Fraser *(G-5624)*
Automotive Manufacturing .... G 517 566-8174
  Sunfield *(G-15645)*
Bbcm Inc .... G 248 410-2528
  Bloomfield Hills *(G-1750)*
Blackbox Visual Design Inc .... G 734 459-1307
  Plymouth *(G-12588)*
CCS Design LLC .... G 248 313-9178
  Wixom *(G-17781)*
Glov Enterprises LLC .... D 517 423-9700
  Tecumseh *(G-15794)*
Gonzalez Prod Systems Inc .... D 313 297-6682
  Detroit *(G-4097)*
Liberty Circuits Corporation .... G 269 226-8743
  Kalamazoo *(G-8809)*
New Echelon Direct Mktg LLC .... G 248 809-2485
  Brighton *(G-1967)*
Novares Corporation US Inc .... G 248 449-6100
  Livonia *(G-9865)*
Paslin Company .... E 586 755-3606
  Warren *(G-17183)*
Phoenix Trailer & Body Company .... F 248 360-7184
  Commerce Township *(G-3439)*
Ram Die Corp .... F 616 647-2855
  Grand Rapids *(G-6807)*
Straight Line Design .... G 616 296-0920
  Spring Lake *(G-15180)*
Window Designs Inc .... F 616 396-5295
  Holland *(G-7859)*

DESIGN SVCS: Commercial & Indl

Design Fabrications Inc .... D 248 597-0988
  Madison Heights *(G-10229)*
Electrodynamics Inc .... G 734 422-5420
  Livonia *(G-9723)*
Icon Industries Inc .... G 616 241-1877
  Grand Rapids *(G-6524)*
Kostal of America Inc .... C 248 284-6500
  Troy *(G-16450)*
Micro-Systems Inc .... G 616 481-1601
  Norton Shores *(G-11774)*
Refrigeration Concepts Inc .... E 616 785-7335
  Comstock Park *(G-3514)*
RTD Manufacturing Inc .... E 517 783-1550
  Jackson *(G-8567)*
Shaun Jackson Design Inc .... G 734 975-7500
  Saline *(G-14415)*
T S Manufacturing & Design .... G 517 543-5368
  Charlotte *(G-2669)*

DESIGN SVCS: Computer Integrated Systems

Active Solutions Group Inc .... G 313 278-4522
  Dearborn *(G-3671)*
AMF-Nano Corporation .... G 734 726-0148
  Ann Arbor *(G-353)*
Cypress Computer Systems Inc .... F 810 245-2300
  Lapeer *(G-9453)*
Driven-4 LLC .... G 269 281-7567
  Saint Joseph *(G-14307)*
Freedom Technologies Corp .... E 810 227-3737
  Brighton *(G-1926)*
Inovision Sftwr Solutions Inc .... G 586 598-8750
  Chesterfield *(G-2791)*
Intellibee Inc .... G 313 586-4122
  Detroit *(G-4145)*
Moog Inc .... E 734 738-5862
  Plymouth *(G-12695)*
Reply Inc .... F 248 686-2481
  Auburn Hills *(G-989)*
Startech-Solutions LLC .... G 248 419-0650
  West Bloomfield *(G-17499)*
Sycron Technologies Inc .... G 810 694-4007
  Grand Blanc *(G-5985)*
Vector North America Inc .... D 248 449-9290
  Novi *(G-12024)*
Winstanley Associates LLC .... G 231 946-3552
  Traverse City *(G-16147)*

DESIGN SVCS: Hand Tools

Drill Technology .... G 616 676-1287
  Ada *(G-14)*
Umix Dissoultion Corp .... G 586 446-9950
  Sterling Heights *(G-15532)*

DETECTION APPARATUS: Electronic/Magnetic Field, Light/Heat

Electronic Design & Packg Co .... F 734 591-9176
  Livonia *(G-9724)*
N S International Ltd .... C 248 251-1600
  Troy *(G-16519)*
Tetradyn Ltd .... G 202 415-7295
  Traverse City *(G-16120)*

DETECTION EQPT: Aeronautical Electronic Field

Universal Magnetics Inc .... G 231 937-5555
  Howard City *(G-8007)*

DETECTIVE & ARMORED CAR SERVICES

Ernie Romanco .... E 517 531-3686
  Albion *(G-123)*

DEVELOPING & PRINTING: Motion Picture Film, Commercial

Star Design Metro Detroit LLC .... E 734 740-0189
  Livonia *(G-9944)*

DIAGNOSTIC SUBSTANCES

Connies Clutter .... G 517 684-7291
  Bay City *(G-1298)*
Everist Genomics Inc .... F 734 929-9475
  Ann Arbor *(G-450)*
Greenmark Biomedical Inc .... G 517 336-4665
  Lansing *(G-9378)*
Lynx Dx Inc .... G 734 274-3144
  Northville *(G-11707)*
Med Share Inc .... F 888 266-3567
  Dearborn *(G-3738)*
Neogen Corporation .... G 800 327-5487
  Saint Joseph *(G-14331)*
Ova Science Inc .... G 617 758-8605
  Ann Arbor *(G-586)*
Retrosense Therapeutics LLC .... G 734 369-9333
  Ann Arbor *(G-620)*
Sigma Diagnostics Inc .... G 734 744-4846
  Livonia *(G-9927)*
Swift Biosciences Inc .... G 734 330-2568
  Ann Arbor *(G-652)*

DIAGNOSTIC SUBSTANCES OR AGENTS: Blood Derivative

Ortho-Clinical Diagnostics Inc .... C 248 797-8087
  Troy *(G-16538)*
Plasma Biolife Services L P .... E 906 226-9080
  Marquette *(G-10553)*
Plasma Biolife Services L P .... G 616 667-0264
  Grandville *(G-7064)*

DIAGNOSTIC SUBSTANCES OR AGENTS: In Vitro

Anatech Ltd .... F 269 964-6450
  Battle Creek *(G-1146)*
Isensium .... G 517 580-9022
  East Lansing *(G-4666)*
Nanorete Inc .... G 517 336-4680
  Lansing *(G-9404)*

DIAGNOSTIC SUBSTANCES OR AGENTS: Microbiology & Virology

Biosan Laboratories Inc .... F 586 755-8970
  Warren *(G-16961)*
Cooper Genomics .... G 313 579-9650
  Plymouth *(G-12602)*

DIAGNOSTIC SUBSTANCES OR AGENTS: Radioactive

Petnet Solutions Inc .... G 865 218-2000
  Royal Oak *(G-13956)*
Versant Medical Physics .... E 888 316-3644
  Kalamazoo *(G-8918)*

DIAGNOSTIC SUBSTANCES OR AGENTS: Veterinary

Neogen Corporation .... B 517 372-9200
  Lansing *(G-9405)*

DIAMOND SETTER SVCS

C T & T Inc .... F 248 623-9422
  Waterford *(G-17328)*

DIE CUTTING SVC: Paper

Diecutting Service Inc .... F 734 426-0290
  Dexter *(G-4489)*

DIE SETS: Presses, Metal Stamping

Acme Carbide Die Inc .... E 734 722-2303
  Westland *(G-17538)*
Anchor Lamina America Inc .... E 248 489-9122
  Novi *(G-11826)*
Artiflex Manufacturing LLC .... C 616 459-8285
  Grand Rapids *(G-6185)*
Concord Tool and Mfg Inc .... C 586 465-6537
  Mount Clemens *(G-11127)*
Connell Limited Partnership .... D 989 875-5135
  Ithaca *(G-8358)*
Danly IEM .... G 800 243-2659
  Grand Rapids *(G-6335)*
De Luxe Die Set Inc .... G 810 227-2556
  Brighton *(G-1910)*
Hardy-Reed Tool & Die Co Inc .... F 517 547-7107
  Manitou Beach *(G-10448)*
Jbl Systems Inc .... G 586 802-6700
  Shelby Township *(G-14609)*
Kraftube Inc .... C 231 832-5562
  Reed City *(G-13217)*
Misumi Investment USA Corp .... F 989 875-5400
  Ithaca *(G-8365)*
Pioneer Steel Corporation .... E 616 878-5800
  Byron Center *(G-2208)*
Pioneer Steel Corporation .... E 313 933-9400
  Detroit *(G-4303)*
Precision Parts Holdings Inc .... A 248 853-9010
  Rochester Hills *(G-13498)*
R & S Tool & Die Inc .... G 989 673-8511
  Caro *(G-2476)*
R D M Enterprises Co Inc .... G 810 985-4721
  Port Huron *(G-12959)*
Schwab Industries Inc .... C 586 566-8090
  Shelby Township *(G-14688)*
True Industrial Corporation .... D 586 771-3500
  Roseville *(G-13882)*

DIE SETS: Presses, Metal Stamping

Vogel Tooling & Machine LLC ....G...... 517 414-7635
 Jackson *(G-8601)*
Williams Tooling & Mfg ....F...... 616 681-2093
 Dorr *(G-4529)*
Wolverine Tool & Engrg Co ....E...... 616 785-9796
 Belmont *(G-1475)*
Yarema Die & Engineering Co ....D...... 248 585-2830
 Troy *(G-16702)*

DIES & TOOLS: Special

A B M Tool & Die Inc ....G...... 734 432-6060
 Livonia *(G-9619)*
A J Tool Co ....F...... 517 787-5755
 Jackson *(G-8369)*
A S A P Tool Inc ....G...... 586 790-6550
 Clinton Township *(G-3029)*
Action Die & Tool Inc ....G...... 616 538-2326
 Grandville *(G-7016)*
Action Tool & Machine Inc ....E...... 810 229-6300
 Brighton *(G-1877)*
Ada Gage Inc ....G...... 616 676-3338
 Ada *(G-4)*
Adrian Precision Machining LLC ....E...... 517 263-4564
 Adrian *(G-45)*
Advanced Tooling Systems Inc ....F...... 616 784-7513
 Comstock Park *(G-3459)*
Advantage Design & Tool Inc ....G...... 586 463-2800
 Clinton Township *(G-3039)*
Aero Foil International Inc ....E...... 231 773-0200
 Muskegon *(G-11263)*
Aggressive Tooling Inc ....E...... 616 754-1404
 Greenville *(G-7122)*
Airmetal Corporation ....F...... 517 784-6000
 Jackson *(G-8378)*
Alcona Tool & Machine Inc ....E...... 989 736-8151
 Harrisville *(G-7362)*
Alcona Tool & Machine Inc ....G...... 989 736-8151
 Lincoln *(G-9561)*
Alliance Tool and Machine Co ....F...... 586 427-6411
 Saint Clair Shores *(G-14239)*
Allied Tool and Machine Co ....E...... 989 755-5384
 Saginaw *(G-13995)*
Amber Manufacturing Inc ....G...... 586 218-6080
 Fraser *(G-5615)*
American Die Corporation ....E...... 810 794-4080
 Clay *(G-2993)*
American Tooling Center Inc ....G...... 517 522-8411
 Lansing *(G-9202)*
American Tooling Center Inc ....G...... 517 522-8411
 Jackson *(G-8383)*
American Tooling Center Inc ....D...... 517 522-8411
 Grass Lake *(G-7085)*
Anitom Automation LLC ....E...... 517 278-6205
 Coldwater *(G-3288)*
Applied Mechanics Corporation ....G...... 616 677-1355
 Grand Rapids *(G-6174)*
Argus Corporation ....E...... 313 937-2900
 Redford *(G-13144)*
Athey Precision Inc ....G...... 989 386-4523
 Clare *(G-2864)*
Atlantic Tool Inc ....G...... 586 954-9268
 Clinton Township *(G-3057)*
Autodie LLC ....C...... 616 454-9361
 Grand Rapids *(G-6192)*
Axis Machine & Tool Inc ....G...... 616 738-2196
 Holland *(G-7563)*
B & B Mold & Engineering Inc ....G...... 586 773-6664
 Warren *(G-16946)*
B & M Machine & Tool Company ......G...... 989 288-2934
 Durand *(G-4605)*
B C Manufacturing Inc ....F...... 248 344-0101
 Wixom *(G-17770)*
Baxter Machine & Tool Co ....E...... 517 782-2808
 Jackson *(G-8388)*
Bay Products Inc ....G...... 586 296-7130
 Fraser *(G-5628)*
Bel-Kur Inc ....E...... 734 847-0651
 Temperance *(G-15823)*
Bernal LLC ....D...... 248 299-3600
 Rochester Hills *(G-13377)*
Bessey Tool & Die Inc ....F...... 616 887-8820
 Sparta *(G-15088)*
Betz Contracting Inc ....G...... 269 746-3320
 Climax *(G-3012)*
Big 3 Precision Products Inc ....E...... 313 846-6601
 Dearborn *(G-3682)*
Blackledge Tool Inc ....G...... 989 865-8393
 Saint Charles *(G-14190)*
Boda Corporation ....G...... 906 353-7320
 Chassell *(G-2672)*

Bolman Die Services Inc ....F...... 810 919-2262
 Sterling Heights *(G-15276)*
Borgia Die & Engineering Inc ....F...... 616 677-3595
 Marne *(G-10505)*
Boyers Tool and Die Inc ....G...... 517 782-7869
 Jackson *(G-8394)*
Bradford Tool & Die Company ....G...... 810 664-8653
 Lapeer *(G-9444)*
Bradley-Thompson Tool Company .....E...... 248 352-1466
 Southfield *(G-14855)*
Bravo Machine and Tool Inc ....F...... 586 790-3463
 Clinton Township *(G-3069)*
Bridge Tool and Die LLC ....G...... 231 269-3200
 Buckley *(G-2129)*
Briggs Mold & Die Inc ....G...... 517 784-6908
 Jackson *(G-8395)*
Btmc Holdings Inc ....G...... 616 794-0100
 Belding *(G-1405)*
Buckingham Tool Corp ....F...... 734 591-2333
 Livonia *(G-9671)*
Buiter Tool & Die Inc ....E...... 616 455-7410
 Grand Rapids *(G-6239)*
C & H Stamping Inc ....E...... 517 750-3600
 Jackson *(G-8396)*
C & M Tool LLC ....G...... 734 944-3355
 Saline *(G-14380)*
C & R Tool Die ....G...... 231 584-3588
 Alba *(G-112)*
Cad CAM Services Inc ....F...... 616 554-5222
 Grand Rapids *(G-6250)*
Cadillac Tool and Die Inc ....G...... 231 775-9007
 Cadillac *(G-2240)*
Cambria Tool and Machine Inc ....F...... 517 437-3500
 Hillsdale *(G-7520)*
Cambron Engineering Inc ....E...... 989 684-5890
 Bay City *(G-1293)*
Cameron Tool Corporation ....D...... 517 487-3671
 Lansing *(G-9353)*
Carlet Tool Inc ....G...... 248 435-0319
 Clawson *(G-2974)*
Carroll Tool and Die Co ....E...... 586 949-7670
 Macomb *(G-10114)*
Cascade Metal Works Inc ....F...... 616 868-0668
 Alto *(G-325)*
Cascade Tool & Die Inc ....G...... 269 429-2210
 Saint Joseph *(G-14304)*
Cav Tool Company ....F...... 248 349-7860
 Novi *(G-11845)*
Central Industrial Mfg Inc ....F...... 231 347-5920
 Harbor Springs *(G-7277)*
Certified Metal Products Inc ....F...... 586 598-1000
 Clinton Township *(G-3077)*
CG Automation & Fixture Inc ....E...... 616 785-5400
 Comstock Park *(G-3467)*
Circle Engineering Inc ....G...... 586 978-8120
 Sterling Heights *(G-15289)*
Coles Machine Service Inc ....E...... 810 658-5373
 Davison *(G-3642)*
Corban Industries Inc ....D...... 248 393-2720
 Orion *(G-12177)*
Crash Tool Inc ....F...... 517 552-0250
 Howell *(G-8025)*
CTS Manufacturing Inc ....G...... 586 465-4594
 Clinton Township *(G-3094)*
Custom Tool & Die Service Inc ....G...... 616 662-1068
 Hudsonville *(G-8153)*
Custom Tooling Systems Inc ....D...... 616 748-9880
 Zeeland *(G-18130)*
D & F Mold LLC ....F...... 269 465-6633
 Bridgman *(G-1862)*
Datum Industries LLC ....G...... 616 977-1995
 Grand Rapids *(G-6336)*
Davis Steel Rule Die ....G...... 269 492-9908
 Kalamazoo *(G-8723)*
Diamond Die and Mold Company ......F...... 586 791-0700
 Clinton Township *(G-3102)*
Die & Slide Technologies Inc ....G...... 810 326-0986
 China *(G-2859)*
Die-Mold-Automation Component .....G...... 313 581-6510
 Dearborn *(G-3693)*
Die-Namic Inc ....C...... 734 710-3200
 Van Buren Twp *(G-16759)*
Die-Namic Tool & Design Llc ....F...... 517 787-4900
 Jackson *(G-8433)*
Die-Namic Tool Corp ....G...... 616 954-7882
 Grand Rapids *(G-6350)*
Die-Tech and Engineering Inc ....E...... 616 530-9030
 Grand Rapids *(G-6351)*
Diversified Tool & Engineering ....F...... 734 692-1260
 Grosse Ile *(G-7170)*

Dlt Industries Inc ....G...... 616 754-2762
 Greenville *(G-7128)*
Do Rite Tool Inc ....G...... 734 522-7510
 Garden City *(G-5822)*
DPM Manufacturing LLC ....F...... 248 349-6375
 Livonia *(G-9715)*
Dura Mold Inc ....D...... 269 465-3301
 Stevensville *(G-15565)*
E Z Tool Inc ....G...... 269 429-0070
 Stevensville *(G-15566)*
E-T-M Enterprises I Inc ....C...... 517 627-8461
 Grand Ledge *(G-6105)*
Eagle Indus Group Federal LLC ....G...... 616 863-8623
 Grand Rapids *(G-6365)*
East River Machine & Tool Inc ....G...... 231 767-1701
 Muskegon *(G-11314)*
Eclipse Tool & Die Inc ....E...... 616 877-3717
 Wayland *(G-17405)*
Ekstrom Industries Inc ....D...... 248 477-0040
 Novi *(G-11881)*
Ellis Machine & Tool Co Inc ....G...... 734 847-4113
 Temperance *(G-15827)*
Emcor Inc ....F...... 989 667-0652
 Bay City *(G-1308)*
Emmie Die and Engineering Corp .....G...... 810 346-2914
 Brown City *(G-2050)*
Empire Machine Company ....F...... 269 684-3713
 Saint Joseph *(G-14309)*
Engineered Tooling Systems Inc ....F...... 616 647-5063
 Grand Rapids *(G-6380)*
Enmark Tool Company ....E...... 586 293-2797
 Fraser *(G-5651)*
Enterprise Tool & Die LLC ....D...... 616 538-0920
 Grandville *(G-7033)*
ERA Tool & Engineering Co ....E...... 810 227-3509
 Livonia *(G-9730)*
Evolution Tool Inc ....G...... 810 664-5500
 Lapeer *(G-9460)*
Excell Machine & Tool Co LLC ....E...... 231 728-1210
 Muskegon *(G-11318)*
Expert Machine & Tool Inc ....G...... 810 984-2323
 Port Huron *(G-12917)*
Extreme Wire EDM Service Inc ....G...... 616 249-3901
 Grandville *(G-7035)*
Fairlane Co ....E...... 586 294-6100
 Fraser *(G-5653)*
Falcon Corporation ....E...... 616 842-7071
 Spring Lake *(G-15141)*
Falcon Industry Inc ....F...... 586 468-7010
 Clinton Township *(G-3113)*
Fischer Tool & Die Corp ....D...... 734 847-4788
 Temperance *(G-15828)*
Flannery Machine & Tool Inc ....E...... 231 587-5076
 Mancelona *(G-10391)*
Forrest Company ....G...... 269 384-6120
 Kalamazoo *(G-8747)*
Four Star Tooling & Engrg Inc ....G...... 586 264-4090
 Sterling Heights *(G-15346)*
Four-Way Tool and Die Inc ....E...... 248 585-8255
 Troy *(G-16372)*
Frankfort Manufacturing Inc ....E...... 231 352-7551
 Frankfort *(G-5601)*
Freedom Tool & Mfg Co ....G...... 231 788-2898
 Muskegon *(G-11327)*
Freer Tool & Die Inc ....E...... 586 463-3200
 Clinton Township *(G-3124)*
Freer Tool & Die Inc ....G...... 586 741-5274
 Clinton Township *(G-3125)*
Frimo Inc ....C...... 248 668-3160
 Wixom *(G-17814)*
Fulgham Machine & Tool Company ..G...... 517 937-8316
 Jackson *(G-8453)*
G & F Tool Products ....E...... 517 663-3646
 Eaton Rapids *(G-4724)*
G & L Tool Inc ....F...... 734 728-1990
 Westland *(G-17559)*
G A Machine Company Inc ....G...... 313 836-5646
 Detroit *(G-4074)*
G F Proto-Type Plaster Inc ....E...... 586 296-2750
 Fraser *(G-5656)*
General Die & Engineering Inc ....E...... 616 698-6961
 Grand Rapids *(G-6435)*
Gill Holding Company Inc ....E...... 616 559-2700
 Grand Rapids *(G-6440)*
Gill Industries Inc ....C...... 616 559-2700
 Grand Rapids *(G-6441)*
Gladwin Machine Inc ....G...... 989 426-8753
 Gladwin *(G-5930)*
Gleason Holbrook Mfg Co ....F...... 586 749-5519
 Ray *(G-13133)*

PRODUCT SECTION — DIES & TOOLS: Special

Company	Emp	Phone
Gollnick Tool Co, Warren *(G-17061)*	G	586 755-0100
Grandville Industries Inc, Grandville *(G-7039)*	D	616 538-0920
Granite Precision Tool Corp, Rochester Hills *(G-13435)*	G	248 299-8317
Gray Bros Stamping & Mch Inc, White Pigeon *(G-17649)*	E	269 483-7615
Greenfield Die & Mfg Corp, Canton *(G-2379)*	C	734 454-4000
Greenville Tool & Die Co, Greenville *(G-7135)*	C	616 754-5693
Griffin Tool Inc, Stevensville *(G-15569)*	E	269 429-4077
H B D M Inc, Three Rivers *(G-15864)*	G	269 273-1976
H B D M Inc, Three Rivers *(G-15865)*	F	269 273-1976
H S Die & Engineering Inc, Grand Rapids *(G-6488)*	C	616 453-5451
Hacker Machine Inc, Rives Junction *(G-13308)*	F	517 569-3348
Hallmark Tool and Gage Co Inc, Wixom *(G-17821)*	E	248 669-4010
Hanson International Inc, Saint Joseph *(G-14315)*	G	269 429-5555
Harbrook Tool Inc, Novi *(G-11895)*	F	248 477-8040
Hard Milling Solutions Inc, Bruce Twp *(G-2083)*	G	586 286-2300
Harper Machine Tool Inc, Warren *(G-17077)*	G	586 756-0140
Harris Tooling, Stevensville *(G-15571)*	G	269 465-5870
Hatch Stamping Company LLC, Howell *(G-8047)*	C	517 540-1021
Havercroft Tool & Die Inc, Greenbush *(G-7120)*	G	989 724-5913
Heinzmann D Tool & Die Inc, Commerce Township *(G-3410)*	F	248 363-5115
Hill Machinery Co, Grand Rapids *(G-6514)*	D	616 940-2800
Hillman Extrusion Tool Inc, Lincoln *(G-9563)*	G	989 736-8010
Holland Tool & Die LLC, Holland *(G-7679)*	G	269 751-5862
Homestead Tool and Machine, Coleman *(G-3344)*	E	989 465-6182
HQT Inc, Madison Heights *(G-10270)*	G	248 589-7960
Huron Tool & Gage Co Inc, Wixom *(G-17830)*	G	313 381-1900
Idel LLC, Traverse City *(G-16001)*	G	231 929-3195
Imperial Engineering Inc, Troy *(G-16412)*	G	248 588-2022
Independent Die Association, Warren *(G-17087)*	G	586 773-9000
Industrial Tooling Tech Inc, Muskegon *(G-11347)*	F	231 766-2155
ITT Gage Inc, Muskegon *(G-11350)*	G	231 766-2155
J C Manufacturing Company, Warren *(G-17106)*	G	586 757-2713
J M Kusch Inc, Bay City *(G-1323)*	E	989 684-8820
JCs Tool & Mfg Co Inc, Essexville *(G-4873)*	E	989 892-8975
Jeffery Tool & Mfg Co, Clinton Township *(G-3148)*	F	586 307-8846
Jemar Tool Inc, Shelby Township *(G-14610)*	E	586 726-6960
Jerrys Tool & Die, Gaylord *(G-5868)*	G	989 732-4689
Jet Gage & Tool Inc, Fraser *(G-5674)*	E	586 294-3770
Jirgens Modern Tool Corp, Kalamazoo *(G-8778)*	F	269 381-5588
Jo-Ad Industries Inc, Madison Heights *(G-10284)*	E	248 588-4810
Jo-Mar Industries Inc, Troy *(G-16439)*	F	248 588-9625
Joggle Tool & Die Co Inc, Clinton Township *(G-3150)*	G	586 792-7477
John Lamantia Corporation, Stevensville *(G-15572)*	G	269 428-8100
Jolico/J-B Tool Inc, Shelby Township *(G-14611)*	E	586 739-5555
Jordan Tool Corporation, Warren *(G-17117)*	E	586 755-6700
K & K Precision Tool LLC, Sterling Heights *(G-15385)*	G	586 294-1030
K & T Tool and Die Inc, Rockford *(G-13575)*	F	616 884-5900
K&K Stamping Company, Saint Clair Shores *(G-14257)*	E	586 443-7900
K-B Tool Corporation, Sterling Heights *(G-15386)*	G	586 795-9003
Karr Unlimited Inc, Newaygo *(G-11571)*	G	231 652-9045
Katai Machine Shop, Bridgman *(G-1868)*	F	269 465-6051
KDI Technologies Inc, Jenison *(G-8631)*	D	616 667-1600
Kent Tool and Die Inc, Chesterfield *(G-2796)*	F	586 949-6600
Kentwater Tool & Mfg Co, Comstock Park *(G-3489)*	F	616 784-7171
Kenyon Specialties Inc, Clio *(G-3274)*	G	810 686-3190
Kern Industries Inc, Novi *(G-11914)*	E	248 349-4866
Ketchum Machine Corporated, Freeport *(G-5765)*	F	616 765-5101
Key Casting Company Inc, Sawyer *(G-14486)*	E	269 426-3800
Kinney Tool and Die Inc, Coopersville *(G-3562)*	D	616 997-0901
Kirmin Die & Tool Inc, Romulus *(G-13697)*	E	734 722-9210
Koch Limited, Fraser *(G-5679)*	G	586 296-3103
Komarnicki Tool & Die Company, Roseville *(G-13825)*	E	586 776-9300
Koppy Corporation, Royal Oak *(G-13942)*	D	248 373-1900
Krt Precision Tool & Mfg Co, Jackson *(G-8490)*	G	517 783-5715
Kurek Tool Inc, Saginaw *(G-14075)*	F	989 777-5300
Kwik Tech Inc, Shelby Township *(G-14617)*	E	586 268-6201
L & L Machine & Tool Inc, Jackson *(G-8491)*	E	517 784-5575
Lab Tool and Engineering Corp, Spring Arbor *(G-15124)*	E	517 750-4131
Lake Design and Mfg Co, Belding *(G-1424)*	G	616 794-0290
Lakeside Manufacturing Inc, Stevensville *(G-15576)*	E	269 429-6193
Lakeview Quality Tool Inc, Gaylord *(G-5873)*	G	989 732-6417
Lambert Industries Inc, Ann Arbor *(G-525)*	F	734 668-6864
Lapeer Industries Inc, Lapeer *(G-9467)*	C	810 664-1816
Lc Manufacturing LLC, Lake City *(G-9090)*	C	231 839-7102
Lca Mold & Engineering Inc, Sturgis *(G-15612)*	G	269 651-1193
Leader Tool Company - HB Inc, Harbor Beach *(G-7269)*	D	989 479-3281
Lincoln Park Die & Tool Co, Brownstown *(G-2067)*	E	734 285-1680
Lomar Machine & Tool Co, Horton *(G-7966)*	E	517 563-8136
LP Products, Coleman *(G-3347)*	F	989 465-0287
LP Products, Coleman *(G-3348)*	G	989 465-1485
Lupaul Industries Inc, Saint Johns *(G-14286)*	F	517 783-3223
Lyons Tool & Engineering Inc, Warren *(G-17133)*	E	586 200-3003
M & M Services Inc, Troy *(G-16467)*	G	248 619-9861
Maco Tool & Engineering Inc, Saint Johns *(G-14287)*	E	989 224-6723
Maddox Industries Inc, Bronson *(G-2032)*	E	517 369-8665
Maes Tool & Die Co Inc, Jackson *(G-8504)*	F	517 750-3131
Majestic Industries Inc, Macomb *(G-10138)*	D	586 786-9100
Mark Carbide Co, Troy *(G-16487)*	G	248 545-0606
Mark Mold and Engineering, Sanford *(G-14451)*	F	989 687-9786
Martin Tool & Machine Inc, Roseville *(G-13830)*	G	586 775-1800
Marton Tool & Die Co Inc, Grand Rapids *(G-6647)*	G	616 361-7337
Marvel Tool & Machine Company, Saint Clair *(G-14227)*	G	810 329-2781
Master Craft Extrusion Tls Inc, Northport *(G-11670)*	F	231 386-5149
Matrix Engineering Inc, Brighton *(G-1955)*	G	810 231-0212
Matrix Tool Co, Clinton Township *(G-3170)*	G	586 296-6010
Mattson Tool & Die Corp, Grand Rapids *(G-6650)*	G	616 447-9012
Maya Jig Grinding & Gage Co, Farmington Hills *(G-5060)*	F	248 471-0820
Met-L-Tec LLC, Temperance *(G-15837)*	E	734 847-7004
Metalcraft Impression Die Co, Livonia *(G-9839)*	E	734 513-8058
Metalfab Tool & Machine Inc, Mio *(G-11005)*	G	989 826-6044
Michigan Auto Bending Corp, Madison Heights *(G-10304)*	E	248 528-1150
Michigan Precision Tl & Engrg, Dowagiac *(G-4552)*	E	269 783-1300
Michigan Tool & Engineering, Macomb *(G-10143)*	G	586 786-0540
Michigan Tool & Gauge Inc, Howell *(G-8066)*	E	517 548-4604
Mid Michigan Pipe Inc, Grand Rapids *(G-6683)*	G	989 772-5664
Mid-Tech Inc, Ann Arbor *(G-557)*	G	734 426-4327
Middleville Tool & Die Co Inc, Middleville *(G-10805)*	D	269 795-3646
Midwest Machining Inc, Coopersville *(G-3565)*	E	616 837-0165
Millennium Mold & Tool Inc, Clinton Township *(G-3177)*	G	586 791-1711
Mistequay Group Ltd, Saginaw *(G-14096)*	E	989 752-7700
Models & Tools Inc, Shelby Township *(G-14644)*	C	586 580-6900
Modineer Co, Niles *(G-11627)*	C	269 683-2550
Modineer Co, Niles *(G-11628)*	C	269 684-3138
Mol-Son Inc, Mattawan *(G-10666)*	D	269 668-3377
Mold Tooling Systems Inc, Grand Rapids *(G-6697)*	F	616 735-6653
Momentum Industries Inc, Saint Louis *(G-14366)*	E	989 681-5735
Multi-Precision Detail Inc, Auburn Hills *(G-951)*	E	248 373-3330
Nesco Tool & Fixture LLC, Howell *(G-8068)*	G	517 618-7052
Next Tool LLC, Belleville *(G-1449)*	F	734 405-7079
Northern Machine Tool Company, Norton Shores *(G-11783)*	E	231 755-1603
Northern Precision Inc, Lincoln *(G-9569)*	E	989 736-6322
Northland Tool & Die Inc, Rockford *(G-13583)*	G	616 866-4451
Northwest Tool & Machine Inc, Jackson *(G-8544)*	E	517 750-1332
Oakwood Custom Coating Inc, Dearborn *(G-3745)*	F	313 561-7740
Oakwood Energy Management Inc, Taylor *(G-15750)*	C	734 947-7700
Odyssey Tool LLC, Clinton Township *(G-3189)*	F	586 468-6696
Olivet Machine Tool Engrg Co, Olivet *(G-12143)*	F	269 749-2671
Olympian Tool LLC, Saint Johns *(G-14291)*	E	989 224-4817
Ontario Die Company America, Marysville *(G-10609)*	D	810 987-5060
Paragon Die & Engineering Co, Grand Rapids *(G-6741)*	C	616 949-2220
Parkway Tool Die, Highland *(G-7499)*	G	248 889-3490
Paterek Mold & Engineering, Armada *(G-722)*	G	586 784-8030
Patriot Tool & Die Inc, Niles *(G-11637)*	G	269 687-9024
Pentel Tool & Die Inc, Romulus *(G-13721)*	G	734 782-9500
Peterson Jig & Fixture Inc, Rockford *(G-13585)*	E	616 866-8296

Employee Codes: A=Over 500 employees, B=251-500
C=101-250, D=51-100, E=20-50, F=10-19, G=3-9

DIES & TOOLS: Special

Pinnacle Engineering Co Inc ....F 734 428-7039
  Manchester *(G-10410)*
Plas-TEC Inc ....G..... 248 853-7777
  Rochester Hills *(G-13495)*
Positive Tool & Engineering Co............G..... 313 532-1674
  Redford *(G-13184)*
Praet Tool & Engineering Inc ....E..... 586 677-3800
  Macomb *(G-10154)*
Precision Machining ....G..... 269 925-5321
  Sodus *(G-14746)*
Precision Masking Inc ....E..... 734 848-4200
  Erie *(G-4808)*
Preferred Industries Inc........................E..... 810 364-4090
  Kimball *(G-9048)*
Preferred Tool & Die Co Inc ....E..... 616 784-6789
  Comstock Park *(G-3509)*
Product and Tooling Tech Inc ....E..... 586 293-1810
  Fraser *(G-5710)*
Proto Gage Inc ....D..... 586 978-2783
  Sterling Heights *(G-15454)*
Punchcraft McHning Tooling LLC........E..... 586 573-4840
  Warren *(G-17211)*
Quad Precision Tool Co Inc ....F..... 248 608-2400
  Rochester Hills *(G-13499)*
Quality Metalcraft Inc..........................C..... 734 261-6700
  Livonia *(G-9900)*
R C M Inc ....G..... 586 336-1237
  Bruce Twp *(G-2093)*
R E B Tool Inc ....C..... 734 397-9116
  Van Buren Twp *(G-16781)*
R S L Tool LLC ....G..... 616 786-2880
  Holland *(G-7784)*
Radar Tool & Manufacturing Co ....G..... 586 759-2800
  Warren *(G-17216)*
Ralco Industries Inc..............................D..... 248 853-3200
  Auburn Hills *(G-985)*
Ranger Tool & Die Co ....E..... 989 754-1403
  Saginaw *(G-14130)*
Rapids Tool & Engineering ....G..... 517 663-8721
  Eaton Rapids *(G-4732)*
Rdc Machine Inc....................................G..... 810 695-5587
  Grand Blanc *(G-5980)*
Reagan Testing Tools............................G..... 248 894-3423
  Rochester Hills *(G-13505)*
Reef Tool & Gage Co ....F..... 586 468-3000
  Clinton Township *(G-3207)*
Reger Manufacturing Company............G..... 586 293-5096
  Fraser *(G-5716)*
Reliance Tool Company Inc..................G..... 734 946-9130
  Romulus *(G-13728)*
Republic Die & Tool Co ....E..... 734 699-3400
  Van Buren Twp *(G-16782)*
Research Tool Corporation....................E..... 989 834-2246
  Ovid *(G-12274)*
Resistance Welding Machne & AC......F..... 269 428-4770
  Saint Joseph *(G-14337)*
Richard Tool & Die Corporation..........D..... 248 486-0900
  New Hudson *(G-11553)*
Rivercity Rollform Inc..........................F..... 231 799-9550
  Norton Shores *(G-11790)*
Rk Boring Inc ....G..... 734 542-7920
  Livonia *(G-9910)*
Rkaa Business LLC ....E..... 231 734-5517
  Evart *(G-4886)*
Roth-Williams Industries Inc................F..... 586 792-0090
  Clinton Township *(G-3215)*
S & S Die Co ....E..... 517 272-1100
  Lansing *(G-9420)*
Sampson Tool Incorporated ....G..... 248 651-3313
  Rochester *(G-13351)*
Schaenzle Tool and Die Inc..................G..... 248 656-0596
  Rochester Hills *(G-13511)*
Schaller Tool & Die Co ....E..... 586 949-5500
  Chesterfield *(G-2838)*
Schmald Tool & Die Inc ....F..... 810 743-1600
  Burton *(G-2163)*
Shark Tool & Die Inc ....G..... 586 749-7400
  Chesterfield *(G-2839)*
Sharp Model Co....................................D..... 586 752-3099
  Bruce Twp *(G-2101)*
Sigma Tool Mfg Inc ....G..... 586 792-3300
  Clinton Township *(G-3227)*
Sink Rite Die Company ....F..... 586 268-0000
  Sterling Heights *(G-15499)*
Smith Brothers Tool Company..............D..... 586 726-5756
  Shelby Township *(G-14695)*
Sollman & Son Mold & Tool ....G..... 269 236-6700
  Grand Junction *(G-6098)*
Spare Die Inc ....G..... 734 522-2508
  Livonia *(G-9937)*

Specialty Tool & Mold Inc....................G..... 616 531-3870
  Grand Rapids *(G-6880)*
Stampede Die Corp ....D..... 616 877-0100
  Wayland *(G-17417)*
Standard Components LLC ....D..... 586 323-9700
  Sterling Heights *(G-15509)*
Standard Die International Inc............E..... 800 838-5464
  Livonia *(G-9941)*
Steeplechase Tool & Die Inc ....E..... 989 352-5544
  Lakeview *(G-9176)*
Stellar Forge Products Inc ....F..... 313 535-7631
  Redford *(G-13195)*
Stm Mfg Inc..D..... 616 392-4656
  Holland *(G-7815)*
Suburban Industries Inc ....F..... 734 676-6141
  Brownstown Twp *(G-2073)*
Supreme Tool & Machine Inc ....F..... 248 673-8408
  Waterford *(G-17379)*
T & C Tool & Sales Inc ....F..... 586 677-8390
  Washington *(G-17312)*
T & W Tool & Die Corporation............F..... 248 548-5400
  Oak Park *(G-12101)*
Talent Industries Inc ....F..... 313 531-4700
  Redford *(G-13200)*
Tamara Tool Inc....................................F..... 269 273-1463
  Three Rivers *(G-15878)*
Taylor Turning Inc ....E..... 248 960-7920
  Wixom *(G-17906)*
Tech Tooling Specialties Inc ....F..... 517 782-8898
  Jackson *(G-8584)*
Telco Tools..F..... 616 296-0253
  Spring Lake *(G-15185)*
Thumb Tool & Engineering Co ....C..... 989 269-9731
  Bad Axe *(G-1075)*
Tiller Tool and Die Inc..........................F..... 517 458-6602
  Morenci *(G-11115)*
Titan Tool & Die Inc..............................G..... 231 799-8680
  Norton Shores *(G-11803)*
Tnr Machine Inc....................................F..... 269 623-2827
  Dowling *(G-4564)*
Tolerance Tool & Engineering ....E..... 313 592-4011
  Detroit *(G-4402)*
Tool & Die Systems Inc ....F..... 248 446-1499
  Wixom *(G-17911)*
Tool Company Inc ....G..... 586 598-1519
  Chesterfield *(G-2849)*
Toolco Inc ....E..... 734 453-9911
  Plymouth *(G-12775)*
Top Craft Tool Inc ....F..... 586 461-4600
  Clinton Township *(G-3248)*
Trademark Die & Engineering ....F..... 616 863-6660
  Belmont *(G-1473)*
Tranor Industries LLC..........................F..... 313 733-4888
  Detroit *(G-4406)*
Tregets Tool & Engineering Co............G..... 517 782-0044
  Jackson *(G-8591)*
Tri Tech Tooling Inc..............................F..... 616 396-6000
  Holland *(G-7838)*
Tri-M-Mold Inc......................................D..... 269 465-3301
  Stevensville *(G-15585)*
Trianon Industries Corporation............A..... 586 759-2200
  Center Line *(G-2585)*
Tric Tool Ltd ....E..... 616 395-1530
  Holland *(G-7839)*
Trispec Precision Products Inc ....F..... 248 308-3231
  Wixom *(G-17921)*
Tru Flo Carbide Inc ....D..... 989 658-8515
  Ubly *(G-16724)*
Trutron Corporation..............................E..... 248 583-9166
  Troy *(G-16655)*
U K Edm Ltd ....F..... 248 437-9500
  Brighton *(G-2001)*
Uei Inc ....E..... 616 361-6093
  Grand Rapids *(G-6944)*
Unified Tool and Die Inc ....F..... 517 768-8070
  Jackson *(G-8597)*
US Boring Inc..G..... 586 756-7511
  Warren *(G-17275)*
Utica Enterprises Inc ....C..... 586 726-4300
  Troy *(G-16670)*
Veit Tool & Gage Inc ....F..... 810 658-4949
  Davison *(G-3665)*
Velocity Manufacturing LLC................F..... 517 630-0408
  Albion *(G-134)*
Venture Manufacturing Inc ....G..... 269 429-6337
  Saint Joseph *(G-14349)*
Vertical Technologies LLC ....E..... 586 619-0141
  Warren *(G-17283)*
Vicount Industries Inc ....D..... 248 471-5071
  Farmington Hills *(G-5149)*

Viking Tool & Engineering Inc ....E..... 231 893-0031
  Whitehall *(G-17679)*
Wallin Brothers Inc ....G..... 734 525-7750
  Livonia *(G-9995)*
Waterman Tool & Machine Corp..........F..... 989 823-8181
  Vassar *(G-16818)*
West Michigan Tool & Die Co ....E..... 269 925-0900
  Benton Harbor *(G-1564)*
Westool Corporation ....E..... 734 847-2520
  Temperance *(G-15847)*
Wetzel Tool & Engineering Inc............F..... 248 960-0430
  Wixom *(G-17929)*
White Automation & Tool Co ....E..... 734 947-9822
  Romulus *(G-13740)*
White Engineering Inc..........................G..... 269 695-0825
  Niles *(G-11651)*
Wico Metal Products Company ....F..... 586 755-9600
  Center Line *(G-2587)*
Widell Industries Inc............................E..... 989 742-4528
  Hillman *(G-7511)*
Wieske Tool Inc ....F..... 989 288-2648
  Durand *(G-4615)*
Withers Corporation ....E..... 586 758-2750
  Warren *(G-17294)*
Wolverine Carbide Die Company ....E..... 248 280-0300
  Troy *(G-16695)*
Wolverine Tool Co ....F..... 810 664-2964
  Lapeer *(G-9492)*
Worswick Mold & Tool Inc ....F..... 810 765-1700
  Marine City *(G-10488)*
Wyke Die & Engineering Inc ....F..... 616 871-1175
  Grand Rapids *(G-7005)*
X-L Machine Co Inc ....E..... 269 279-5128
  Three Rivers *(G-15883)*

DIES: Cutting, Exc Metal

Performnce Dcutting Finshg LLC........G..... 616 245-3636
  Grand Rapids *(G-6750)*

DIES: Extrusion

Centennial Technologies Inc ....E..... 989 752-6167
  Saginaw *(G-14013)*
Link Tool & Mfg Co LLC ....D..... 734 710-0010
  Westland *(G-17577)*
Ovidon Manufacturing LLC................D..... 517 548-4005
  Howell *(G-8075)*
Service Extrusion Die Co Inc ....G..... 616 784-6933
  Comstock Park *(G-3515)*
Ultra-Sonic Extrusion Dies Inc ....E..... 586 791-8550
  Clinton Township *(G-3253)*
Wefa Cedar Inc ....F..... 616 696-0873
  Cedar Springs *(G-2565)*

DIES: Plastic Forming

Atra Plastics Inc ....F..... 734 237-3393
  Plymouth *(G-12576)*
Byrnes Manufacturing Co LLC ....G..... 810 664-3686
  Lapeer *(G-9446)*
Complete Surface Technologies ....E..... 586 493-5800
  Clinton Township *(G-3086)*
Elite Mold & Engineering Inc ....E..... 586 873-1770
  Shelby Township *(G-14586)*
Enkon LLC..F..... 937 890-5678
  Manchester *(G-10405)*
Incoe Corporation ....C..... 248 616-0220
  Auburn Hills *(G-910)*
Incoe International Inc ....G..... 248 616-0220
  Auburn Hills *(G-911)*
Manufax Inc..G..... 231 929-3226
  Traverse City *(G-16031)*
Pinnacle Mold & Machine Inc..............G..... 616 892-9018
  West Olive *(G-17534)*
Prima Technologies Inc........................F..... 586 759-0250
  Center Line *(G-2582)*
Shoreline Mold & Engrg LLC ....G..... 269 926-2223
  Benton Harbor *(G-1546)*

DIES: Steel Rule

A C Steel Rule Dies Inc........................G..... 248 588-5600
  Madison Heights *(G-10175)*
Champion Die Incorporated ....E..... 616 784-2397
  Comstock Park *(G-3469)*
Creative Steel Rule Dies Inc................F..... 630 307-8880
  Grand Rapids *(G-6315)*
Diecrafters Inc......................................G..... 734 425-8000
  Livonia *(G-9711)*
Exco Extrusion Dies Inc ....C..... 586 749-5400
  Chesterfield *(G-2774)*

PRODUCT SECTION

Fowlerville Machine Tool Inc ....G....... 517 223-8871
  Fowlerville (G-5566)
Jacobsen Industries Inc ....D....... 734 591-6111
  Livonia (G-9791)
Kendor Steel Rule Die Inc ....E....... 586 293-7111
  Fraser (G-5678)
Lasercutting Services Inc ....F....... 616 975-2000
  Grand Rapids (G-6619)
Rolleigh Inc ....F....... 517 283-3811
  Reading (G-13138)

DIFFERENTIAL ASSEMBLIES & PARTS

P G S Inc ....C....... 248 526-3800
  Troy (G-16540)

DIMENSION STONE: Buildings

Genesee Cut Stone & Marble Co ....E....... 810 743-1800
  Flint (G-5437)

DIODES: Light Emitting

Kimberly Lighting LLC ....E....... 888 480-0070
  Clarkston (G-2933)
Nihil Ultra Corporation ....G....... 413 723-3218
  Troy (G-16524)
Sigma Luminous LLC ....G....... 800 482-1327
  Livonia (G-9929)
US Trade LLC ....G....... 800 676-0208
  Garden City (G-5845)

DIRECT SELLING ESTABLISHMENTS, NEC

Ace Vending Service Inc ....E....... 616 243-7983
  Grand Rapids (G-6135)
Alticor Global Holdings Inc ....F....... 616 787-1000
  Ada (G-5)
Alticor Inc ....C....... 616 787-1000
  Ada (G-6)
Amway International Inc ....E....... 616 787-1000
  Ada (G-7)
Cognisys Inc ....G....... 231 943-2425
  Traverse City (G-15944)
Hollow Metal Services LLC ....G....... 248 394-0233
  Clarkston (G-2926)

DIRECT SELLING ESTABLISHMENTS: Milk Delivery

Calder Bros Dairy Inc ....E....... 313 381-8858
  Lincoln Park (G-9575)

DISC JOCKEYS

Sound Productions Entrmt ....E....... 989 386-2221
  Clare (G-2889)

DISCOUNT DEPARTMENT STORES

Walmart Inc ....B....... 517 541-1481
  Charlotte (G-2670)

DISHWASHING EQPT: Commercial

Glastender Inc ....C....... 989 752-4275
  Saginaw (G-14045)

DISHWASHING EQPT: Household

Maytag Corporation ....C....... 269 923-5000
  Benton Harbor (G-1529)
Whirlpool Corporation ....B....... 269 923-5000
  Benton Harbor (G-1570)
Whirlpool Corporation ....B....... 269 923-3009
  Benton Harbor (G-1571)

DISINFECTING & PEST CONTROL SERVICES

Swat Environmental Inc ....E....... 517 322-2999
  Lansing (G-9427)

DISINFECTING SVCS

Marceau Enterprises Inc ....G....... 586 697-8100
  Washington (G-17307)

DISK & DRUM DRIVES & COMPONENTS: Computers

American Furukawa Inc ....E....... 734 254-0344
  Plymouth (G-12570)
Autocam Corporation ....B....... 616 698-0707
  Kentwood (G-9000)

DISK DRIVES: Computer

Piolax Corporation ....F....... 734 668-6005
  Plymouth (G-12717)

DISPENSING EQPT & PARTS, BEVERAGE: Fountain/Other Beverage

Auction Masters ....G....... 586 576-7777
  Oak Park (G-12050)

DISPLAY FIXTURES: Showcases, Wood, Exc Refrigerated

Flairwood Industries Inc ....E....... 231 798-8324
  Norton Shores (G-11756)
Maw Ventures Inc ....E....... 231 798-8324
  Norton Shores (G-11772)

DISPLAY FIXTURES: Wood

Great Lakes Woodworking Co Inc ....E....... 313 892-8500
  Detroit (G-4101)
H & R Wood Specialties Inc ....E....... 269 628-2181
  Gobles (G-5947)
Harbor Industries Inc ....D....... 616 842-5330
  Grand Haven (G-6032)
Harbor Industries Inc ....D....... 616 842-5330
  Charlevoix (G-2618)
PDC ....F....... 269 651-9975
  Sturgis (G-15627)
Unislat LLC ....G....... 616 844-4211
  Grand Haven (G-6091)

DISPLAY ITEMS: Corrugated, Made From Purchased Materials

Compak Inc ....G....... 810 767-2806
  Burton (G-2151)
Compak Inc ....G....... 989 288-3199
  Burton (G-2152)

DISPLAY ITEMS: Solid Fiber, Made From Purchased Materials

Armstrong Display Concepts ....F....... 231 652-1675
  Newaygo (G-11563)
Zoomer Display LLC ....G....... 616 734-0300
  Grand Rapids (G-7014)

DISPLAY LETTERING SVCS

Sign Impressions Inc ....G....... 269 382-5152
  Kalamazoo (G-8891)

DISPLAY STANDS: Merchandise, Exc Wood

Shaw & Slavsky Inc ....E....... 313 834-3990
  Detroit (G-4360)

DISTILLERS DRIED GRAIN & SOLUBLES

Artesian Distillers ....G....... 616 252-1700
  Grand Rapids (G-6184)
Long Road Distillers LLC ....G....... 616 356-1770
  Grand Rapids (G-6630)

DISTRIBUTORS: Motor Vehicle Engine

Digital Dimensions Inc ....G....... 419 630-4343
  Camden (G-2341)
Electro-Matic Products Inc ....G....... 248 478-1182
  Farmington Hills (G-4980)
Meritor Indus Intl Hldings LLC ....G....... 248 658-7345
  Troy (G-16496)
Midwest International Dist LLC ....G....... 616 901-4621
  Ionia (G-8249)

DIVING EQPT STORES

Livbig LLC ....G....... 888 519-8290
  Portage (G-13010)
Oceans Sands Scuba ....G....... 616 396-0068
  Holland (G-7762)

DOCK EQPT & SPLYS, INDL

Admin Industries LLC ....F....... 989 685-3438
  Rose City (G-13756)
American Marine Shore Control ....F....... 248 887-7855
  White Lake (G-17628)
Berlin Holdings LLC ....G....... 517 523-2444
  Pittsford (G-12515)

DOORS & WINDOWS: Storm, Metal

Brumley Tools Inc ....G....... 586 260-8326
  Warren (G-16969)
Deluxe Technologies LLC ....E....... 586 294-2340
  Fraser (G-5642)

DOCK OPERATION SVCS, INCL BLDGS, FACILITIES, OPERS & MAINT

Odonnells Docks ....G....... 269 244-1446
  Jones (G-8652)

DOCKS: Floating, Wood

Paddle King Inc ....F....... 989 235-6776
  Carson City (G-2495)

DOCKS: Prefabricated Metal

4ever Aluminum Products Inc ....F....... 517 368-0000
  Coldwater (G-3286)
Berlin Holdings LLC ....G....... 517 523-2444
  Pittsford (G-12515)
Classic Dock & Lift LLC ....G....... 231 882-4374
  Beulah (G-1609)
Con-De Manufacturing Inc ....G....... 269 651-3756
  Sturgis (G-15601)
Great Lakes Lift Inc ....G....... 989 673-2109
  Caro (G-2469)
Instant Marine Inc ....G....... 248 398-1011
  Clarkston (G-2931)
Marine Automated Doc System ....F....... 989 539-9010
  Harrison (G-7315)
Shore-Mate Products LLC ....G....... 616 874-5438
  Rockford (G-13590)
Twin Bay Dock and Products ....G....... 231 943-8420
  Traverse City (G-16131)
Wheelock & Son Welding Shop ....G....... 231 947-6557
  Traverse City (G-16145)

DOOR & WINDOW REPAIR SVCS

Grand Traverse Garage Doors ....E....... 231 943-9897
  Traverse City (G-15985)
Seal All Aluminum Pdts Corp ....G....... 248 585-6061
  Southfield (G-15025)
Wood Smiths Inc ....F....... 269 372-6432
  Kalamazoo (G-8927)

DOOR FRAMES: Wood

Crossroads Industries Inc ....D....... 989 732-1233
  Gaylord (G-5853)
Idp Inc ....E....... 248 352-0044
  Southfield (G-14944)
Sunek Co ....F....... 231 421-5317
  Traverse City (G-16116)

DOOR OPERATING SYSTEMS: Electric

Assa Abloy Entrance Systems US ....E....... 734 462-2348
  Livonia (G-9654)
Computerized SEC Systems Inc ....C....... 248 837-3700
  Madison Heights (G-10219)
Magna Mirrors America Inc ....B....... 231 652-4450
  Newaygo (G-11574)
Operator Specialty Company Inc ....D....... 616 675-5050
  Grand Rapids (G-6732)
Quality Door & More Inc ....G....... 989 317-8314
  Mount Pleasant (G-11222)

DOORS & WINDOWS WHOLESALERS: All Materials

Antcliff Windows & Doors Inc ....F....... 810 742-5963
  Burton (G-2144)
Daiek Products Inc ....F....... 248 816-1360
  Troy (G-16295)
Double Otis Inc ....E....... 616 878-3998
  Grand Rapids (G-6359)
Lippert Components Mfg Inc ....C....... 989 845-3061
  Chesaning (G-2725)
Weathergard Window Company Inc ....D....... 248 967-8822
  Oak Park (G-12105)

DOORS & WINDOWS: Screen & Storm

PTL Engineering Inc ....F....... 810 664-2310
  Lapeer (G-9483)

DOORS & WINDOWS: Storm, Metal

Fox Aluminum Products Inc ....E....... 248 399-4288
  Hazel Park (G-7438)

DOORS & WINDOWS: Storm, Metal

Ken Rodenhouse Door & Window ....F 616 784-3365
  Comstock Park *(G-3488)*
National Nail Corp ....C 616 538-8000
  Wyoming *(G-18021)*
Scott Iron Works Inc ....F 248 548-2822
  Hazel Park *(G-7454)*
Seal All Aluminum Pdts Corp ....G 248 585-6061
  Southfield *(G-15025)*
Storm Seal Co Inc ....G 248 689-1900
  Troy *(G-16623)*
Weather King Windows Doors Inc .....D 313 933-1234
  Farmington *(G-4915)*
Weather King Windows Doors Inc .....E 248 478-7788
  Farmington *(G-4916)*
Weatherproof Inc ....E 517 764-1330
  Jackson *(G-8606)*
Wojan Aluminum Products Corp ....D 231 547-2931
  Charlevoix *(G-2635)*

DOORS: Fiberglass

Daiek Products Inc ....F 248 816-1360
  Troy *(G-16295)*

DOORS: Folding, Plastic Or Plastic Coated Fabric

Poncraft Door Co Inc ....F 248 373-6060
  Auburn Hills *(G-976)*
Special-Lite Inc ....C 800 821-6531
  Decatur *(G-3806)*

DOORS: Garage, Overhead, Metal

Integrity Door LLC ....G 616 896-8077
  Dorr *(G-4524)*

DOORS: Garage, Overhead, Wood

Area Exteriors ....G 248 544-0706
  Leonard *(G-9526)*
Michigan Overhead Door ....F 734 425-0295
  Livonia *(G-9842)*

DOORS: Glass

City Auto Glass Co ....G 616 842-3235
  Grand Haven *(G-6003)*
Vitro Automotriz SA De CV ....F 734 727-5001
  Westland *(G-17608)*

DOORS: Louver, Wood

Beechcraft Products Inc ....E 989 288-2606
  Durand *(G-4606)*

DOORS: Rolling, Indl Building Or Warehouse, Metal

Alliance Engnred Sltons NA Ltd ....C 586 291-3694
  Detroit *(G-3858)*

DOORS: Wooden

Andoor Craftmaster ....G 989 672-2020
  Caro *(G-2465)*
B & W Woodwork Inc ....G 616 772-4577
  Holland *(G-7564)*
E-Zee Set Wood Products Inc ....G 248 398-0090
  Oak Park *(G-12063)*
Five Lakes Manufacturing Inc ....E 586 463-4123
  Clinton Township *(G-3120)*
Gibouts Sash & Door ....G 906 863-2224
  Menominee *(G-10738)*
Jeld-Wen Inc ....C 616 554-3551
  Caledonia *(G-2303)*
Jeld-Wen Inc ....D 616 531-5440
  Grand Rapids *(G-6558)*
Lemica Corporation ....F 313 839-2150
  Detroit *(G-4198)*
Magiglide Inc ....F 906 822-7321
  Crystal Falls *(G-3611)*
Masonite International Corp ....F 517 545-5811
  Howell *(G-8060)*
Monarch Millwork Inc ....G 989 348-8292
  Grayling *(G-7113)*
Moore Products Inc ....G 269 782-3957
  Dowagiac *(G-4553)*
Van Beeks Custom Wood Products ...F 616 583-9002
  Byron Center *(G-2214)*

DOWELS & DOWEL RODS

Doltek Enterprises Inc ....E 616 837-7828
  Nunica *(G-12036)*

DRAFTING SPLYS WHOLESALERS

Commercial Blueprint Inc ....E 517 372-8360
  Lansing *(G-9357)*

DRAFTING SVCS

Fairchilds Daughters & Son LLC ....G 906 239-6061
  Iron Mountain *(G-8283)*
Soils and Structures Inc ....E 800 933-3959
  Norton Shores *(G-11796)*

DRAINAGE PRDTS: Concrete

All About Drainage LLC ....G 248 921-0766
  Commerce Township *(G-3387)*
Sanilac Drain and Tile Co ....G 810 648-4100
  Sandusky *(G-14443)*

DRAPERIES & CURTAINS

Benton Harbor Awning & Tent ....E 800 272-2187
  Benton Harbor *(G-1485)*
Lorne Hanley ....G 248 547-9865
  Huntington Woods *(G-8189)*
Sassy Fabrics Inc 810 694-0440
  Grand Blanc *(G-5982)*

DRAPERIES & DRAPERY FABRICS, COTTON

Drapery Workroom ....G 269 463-5633
  Watervliet *(G-17391)*
Window Designs Inc ....F 616 396-5295
  Holland *(G-7859)*

DRAPERIES: Plastic & Textile, From Purchased Materials

Cardinal Custom Designs Inc ....G 586 296-2060
  Fraser *(G-5635)*
Detroit Custom Services Inc ....E 586 465-3631
  Mount Clemens *(G-11129)*
Melco Dctg & Furn Restoration ....G 989 723-3335
  Owosso *(G-12303)*
Niedda Drapery Mfg 586 977-0065
  Sterling Heights *(G-15434)*
Parkway Drapery & Uphl Co Inc ....G 734 779-1300
  Livonia *(G-9884)*
Signature Designs Inc ....G 248 426-9735
  Farmington Hills *(G-5123)*
Triangle Window Fashions Inc ....E 616 538-9676
  Wyoming *(G-18036)*

DRAPERY & UPHOLSTERY STORES: Curtains

Barons Inc ....E 517 484-1366
  Lansing *(G-9347)*

DRAPERY & UPHOLSTERY STORES: Draperies

Detroit Custom Services Inc ....E 586 465-3631
  Mount Clemens *(G-11129)*
Tamarack Uphl & Interiors ....G 616 866-2922
  Rockford *(G-13592)*
Window Designs Inc ....F 616 396-5295
  Holland *(G-7859)*

DRAPES & DRAPERY FABRICS, FROM MANMADE FIBER

Window Designs Inc ....F 616 396-5295
  Holland *(G-7859)*

DRILL BITS

Hougen Manufacturing Inc ....C 810 635-7111
  Swartz Creek *(G-15667)*

DRILLING MACHINERY & EQPT: Water Well

Milan Supply Company ....G 231 238-9200
  Indian River *(G-8221)*
Murphy Water Well Bits ....G 810 658-1554
  Davison *(G-3656)*

DRINKING PLACES: Alcoholic Beverages

Backdraft Brewing Company ....D 734 722-7639
  Wayne *(G-17427)*
New Holland Brewing Co LLC ....C 616 355-2941
  Holland *(G-7757)*

DRINKING PLACES: Bars & Lounges

Blackrocks Brewery LLC ....G 906 273-1333
  Marquette *(G-10521)*
Blackrocks Brewery LLC ....G 906 273-1333
  Marquette *(G-10520)*
Midland Brewing Co LLC ....G 989 631-3041
  Midland *(G-10887)*
Northern Oak Brewery Inc ....F 248 634-7515
  Holly *(G-7889)*
Oracle Brewing Company LLC ....G 989 401-7446
  Breckenridge *(G-1845)*

DRINKING PLACES: Beer Garden

Acoustic Tap Room ....G 231 714-5028
  Traverse City *(G-15888)*

DRINKING PLACES: Tavern

Gpbc Inc ....C 734 741-7325
  Ann Arbor *(G-475)*

DRIVE CHAINS: Bicycle Or Motorcycle

Baker Inc ....E 517 339-3835
  Haslett *(G-7396)*

DRIVE SHAFTS

Arvinmeritor Inc ....E 248 435-1000
  Troy *(G-16222)*
Cambria Tool and Machine Inc ....F 517 437-3500
  Hillsdale *(G-7520)*
Erae AMS America Corp ....F 419 386-8876
  Pontiac *(G-12823)*
Meritor Inc ....C 248 435-1000
  Troy *(G-16493)*
Minowitz Manufacturing Co ....E 586 779-5940
  Huntington Woods *(G-8190)*
Shaftmasters ....G 313 383-6347
  Lincoln Park *(G-9585)*

DRIVES: High Speed Indl, Exc Hydrostatic

Dama Tool & Gauge Company ....F 616 842-9631
  Norton Shores *(G-11747)*

DRIVES: Hydrostatic

Flint Hydrostatics Inc ....F 901 794-2462
  Chesterfield *(G-2777)*
Hydraulex Intl Holdings Inc ....E 914 682-2700
  Chesterfield *(G-2786)*

DRUG STORES

Diplomat Spclty Phrm Flint LLC ....B 810 768-9000
  Flint *(G-5419)*
Hackley Health Ventures Inc ....G 231 728-5720
  Muskegon *(G-11342)*

DRUGS & DRUG PROPRIETARIES, WHOL: Biologicals/Allied Prdts

Oxford Biomedical Research Inc ....G 248 852-8815
  Metamora *(G-10779)*

DRUGS & DRUG PROPRIETARIES, WHOLESALE

Smo International Inc ....F 248 275-1091
  Warren *(G-17241)*

DRUGS & DRUG PROPRIETARIES, WHOLESALE: Medical Rubber Goods

Mykin Inc ....F 248 667-8030
  South Lyon *(G-14804)*

DRUGS & DRUG PROPRIETARIES, WHOLESALE: Pharmaceuticals

Central Admxture Phrm Svcs Inc ......E 734 953-6760
  Livonia *(G-9680)*
Diplomat Spclty Phrm Flint LLC ....B 810 768-9000
  Flint *(G-5419)*

PRODUCT SECTION

McKesson Corporation ....D....... 734 953-2523
  Livonia *(G-9833)*
McKesson Pharmacy Systems LLC ......A....... 800 521-1758
  Livonia *(G-9834)*
Special Mold Engineering Inc ....E....... 248 652-6600
  Rochester Hills *(G-13516)*

DRUMS: Brake

Stemco Products Inc ....G....... 888 854-6474
  Millington *(G-10998)*

DRUMS: Fiber

Eteron Inc ....E....... 248 478-2900
  Farmington Hills *(G-4991)*

DRYERS & REDRYERS: Indl

Macair Inc ....G....... 248 242-6860
  Commerce Township *(G-3425)*
Pulverdryer Usa LLC ....E....... 269 552-5290
  Springfield *(G-15202)*

DUCTING: Metal Plate

Conquest Manufacturing LLC................D....... 586 576-7600
  Warren *(G-16991)*

DUCTS: Sheet Metal

Constructive Sheet Metal Inc.................E....... 616 245-5306
  Allendale *(G-215)*
Ecolo-Tech Inc..F....... 248 541-1100
  Madison Heights *(G-10238)*
Harris Sheet Metal Co ....F....... 989 496-3080
  Midland *(G-10867)*
Integrated Industries Inc ....D....... 586 790-1550
  Clinton Township *(G-3141)*
J & J Metal Products Inc ....G....... 586 792-2680
  Clinton Township *(G-3146)*
Jbs Sheet Metal Inc..................................G....... 231 777-2802
  Muskegon *(G-11352)*
Krupp Industries LLC ....D....... 734 261-0410
  Livonia *(G-9801)*
Krupp Industries LLC ....E....... 616 475-5905
  Walker *(G-16870)*
Magic City Heating & Cooling ....G....... 269 467-6406
  Centreville *(G-2596)*
Schneider Sheet Metal Sup Inc..............G....... 517 694-7661
  Lansing *(G-9422)*

DUMBWAITERS

Schindler Elevator Corporation..............F....... 517 272-1234
  Lansing *(G-9421)*

DUMPSTERS: Garbage

Actron Steel Inc.......................................E....... 231 947-3981
  Traverse City *(G-15890)*
American Dumpster Services LLC ....G....... 586 501-3600
  Center Line *(G-2578)*
Best Rate Dumpster Rental Inc ....G....... 248 391-5956
  Ortonville *(G-12194)*
Brian A Broomfield ....G....... 989 309-0709
  Remus *(G-13238)*
Detroit Dumpster Inc ....G....... 313 466-3174
  Detroit *(G-3982)*
Dino S Dumpsters LLC............................G....... 989 225-5635
  Bay City *(G-1303)*
Dmg Dumpsters Inc.................................G....... 313 610-3476
  Farmington Hills *(G-4974)*
Dolphin Dumpsters LLC..........................G....... 734 272-8981
  Farmington Hills *(G-4975)*
Dumpster Express LLC ....G....... 855 599-7255
  Holly *(G-7877)*
Hammars Contracting LLC ....F....... 810 367-3037
  Kimball *(G-9044)*
K and W Landfill Inc................................F....... 906 883-3504
  Ontonagon *(G-12160)*
M&D Dumpsters LLC ....G....... 616 299-0234
  Hudsonville *(G-8163)*
McM Disposal LLC....................................G....... 616 656-4049
  Byron Center *(G-2199)*
Priority Waste LLC ....E....... 586 228-1200
  Clinton Township *(G-3205)*
R and J Dumpsters LLC ....G....... 248 863-8579
  Howell *(G-8085)*
Smith Dumpsters ....G....... 616 675-9399
  Kent City *(G-8994)*
Yello Dumpster...G....... 616 915-0506
  Grand Rapids *(G-7008)*

DUST OR FUME COLLECTING EQPT: Indl

Baker Enterprises Inc..............................E....... 989 354-2189
  Alpena *(G-280)*
Beckert & Hiester Inc ....G....... 989 793-2420
  Saginaw *(G-14003)*
Besser Company ....B....... 989 354-4111
  Alpena *(G-282)*
Forrest Brothers Inc ....C....... 989 356-4011
  Gaylord *(G-5859)*
Hammond Machinery Inc ....D....... 269 345-7151
  Kalamazoo *(G-8759)*
Madison Street Holdings LLC................E....... 517 252-2031
  Adrian *(G-77)*
Ron Pair Enterprises Inc ....E....... 231 547-4000
  Charlevoix *(G-2629)*

DYES & PIGMENTS: Organic

Cut-Tech...G....... 269 687-9005
  Niles *(G-11605)*
Sun Chemical Corporation......................F....... 513 681-5950
  Muskegon *(G-11431)*

DYES & TINTS: Household

Chames LLC ....G....... 616 363-0000
  Grand Rapids *(G-6269)*

DYNAMOMETERS

Froude Inc...G....... 248 579-4295
  Novi *(G-11888)*
Greening Incorporated ....G....... 313 366-7160
  Detroit *(G-4104)*
Greening Associates Inc ....E....... 313 366-7160
  Detroit *(G-4105)*
Superior Controls Inc ....C....... 734 454-0500
  Plymouth *(G-12763)*

EARTH SCIENCE SVCS

Baygeo Inc..E....... 231 941-7660
  Traverse City *(G-15909)*

EATING PLACES

Arbor Kitchen LLC ....G....... 248 921-4602
  Ann Arbor *(G-364)*
Backdraft Brewing Company..................D....... 734 722-7639
  Wayne *(G-17427)*
Bowers Harbor Vinyrd & Winery ....G....... 231 223-7615
  Traverse City *(G-15919)*
Cherry Hut Products LLC........................G....... 231 882-4431
  Benzonia *(G-1574)*
Country Mill Farms LLC ....E....... 517 543-1019
  Charlotte *(G-2642)*
Gpbc Inc...C....... 734 741-7325
  Ann Arbor *(G-475)*
Jabars Complements LLC.......................G....... 810 966-8371
  Port Huron *(G-12931)*
Jorgensens Inc..E....... 989 831-8338
  Greenville *(G-7140)*
Marias Italian Bakery Inc ....F....... 734 981-1200
  Canton *(G-2396)*
Mexamerica Foods LLC..........................E....... 814 781-1447
  Grand Rapids *(G-6665)*
Midwest Aquatics Group Inc..................G....... 734 426-4155
  Pinckney *(G-12500)*
New Holland Brewing Co LLC ....C....... 616 355-2941
  Holland *(G-7757)*
SBR LLC ....E....... 313 350-8799
  Harper Woods *(G-7304)*
The Spott ....G....... 269 459-6462
  Kalamazoo *(G-8910)*
Walmart Inc...B....... 517 541-1481
  Charlotte *(G-2670)*

EDUCATIONAL SVCS

Arbor Press LLC ....D....... 248 549-0150
  Royal Oak *(G-13904)*
Hope Focus ....C....... 313 494-5500
  Detroit *(G-4129)*
Royal ARC Welding Company ....E....... 734 789-9099
  Flat Rock *(G-5362)*
Step Into Success Inc..............................G....... 734 426-1075
  Pinckney *(G-12504)*
Svrc Industries Inc ....E....... 989 280-3038
  Saginaw *(G-14159)*
Techno Urban 3d LLC ....F....... 313 740-8110
  Detroit *(G-4398)*

EDUCATIONAL SVCS, NONDEGREE GRANTING: Continuing Education

Toastmasters International ....F....... 810 385-5477
  Burtchville *(G-2141)*
Toastmasters International ....E....... 517 651-6507
  Laingsburg *(G-9081)*

ELASTOMERS

Argonics Inc..D....... 906 226-9747
  Gwinn *(G-7215)*
Sika Auto Eaton Rapids Inc ....F....... 248 588-2270
  Madison Heights *(G-10352)*

ELECTRIC & OTHER SERVICES COMBINED

Lgc Global Inc..E....... 313 989-4141
  Detroit *(G-4202)*

ELECTRIC MOTOR REPAIR SVCS

A & C Electric Company..........................E....... 586 773-2746
  Harrison Township *(G-7317)*
All City Electric Motor Repair ....G....... 734 284-2268
  Riverview *(G-13289)*
American Electric Motor Corp ....F....... 810 743-6080
  Burton *(G-2143)*
Arrow Motor & Pump Inc ....E....... 734 285-7860
  Wyandotte *(G-17946)*
Barry Electric-Rovill Co...........................G....... 810 985-8960
  Port Huron *(G-12898)*
Bay United Motors Inc ....F....... 989 684-3972
  Bay City *(G-1289)*
Birclar Electric and Elec LLC ....F....... 734 941-7400
  Romulus *(G-13658)*
Commercial Electric Co...........................G....... 269 731-3350
  Augusta *(G-1052)*
Commonwealth Service Sls Corp...........G....... 313 581-8050
  Rochester Hills *(G-13392)*
Complete Electric.....................................G....... 517 629-9267
  Albion *(G-121)*
Core Electric Company Inc ....F....... 313 382-7140
  Melvindale *(G-10694)*
DMS Electric Apparatus Service ....E....... 269 349-7000
  Kalamazoo *(G-8729)*
Electric Equipment Company ....G....... 269 925-3266
  Benton Harbor *(G-1496)*
Electric Motor & Contg Co ....F....... 313 871-3775
  Detroit *(G-4031)*
Electric Motor Service ....G....... 269 945-5113
  Hastings *(G-7408)*
Electric Motor Service Ctr Inc................G....... 616 532-6007
  Grandville *(G-7030)*
Fife Pearce Electric Company ....F....... 313 369-2560
  Detroit *(G-4058)*
Fixall Electric Motor Service..................G....... 616 454-6863
  Grand Rapids *(G-6409)*
Franklin Electric Corporation ....F....... 248 442-8000
  Garden City *(G-5824)*
Gower Corporation ....G....... 989 249-5938
  Saginaw *(G-14050)*
Grand Rapids Elc Mtr Svc LLC ....G....... 616 243-8866
  Grand Rapids *(G-6453)*
Hamilton Electric Co................................F....... 989 799-6291
  Saginaw *(G-14053)*
Holland Electric Motor Co ....G....... 616 392-1115
  Holland *(G-7671)*
Jones Electric Company ....F....... 231 726-5001
  Muskegon *(G-11356)*
Kalamazoo Electric Motor Inc................G....... 269 345-7802
  Kalamazoo *(G-8788)*
Martin Electric Mtrs Sls & Svc ....G....... 989 584-3850
  Carson City *(G-2492)*
Medsker Electric Inc................................E....... 248 855-3383
  Farmington Hills *(G-5062)*
Midw Inc..G....... 269 343-7090
  Kalamazoo *(G-8826)*
Moore Brothers Electrical Co ....G....... 810 232-2148
  Flint *(G-5471)*
Nieboer Electric Inc ....F....... 231 924-0960
  Fremont *(G-5779)*
North End Electric Company ....G....... 248 398-8187
  Royal Oak *(G-13954)*
Phillips Service Inds Inc.........................F....... 734 853-5000
  Plymouth *(G-12714)*
Pontiac Electric Motor Works ....G....... 248 332-4622
  Pontiac *(G-12856)*
PSI Repair Services Inc..........................C....... 734 853-5000
  Livonia *(G-9899)*
Rapa Electric Inc.....................................E....... 269 673-3157
  Allegan *(G-186)*

Employee Codes: A=Over 500 employees, B=251-500
C=101-250, D=51-100, E=20-50, F=10-19, G=3-9

ELECTRIC MOTOR REPAIR SVCS

Reliance Electric Machine Co ....F 810 232-3355
  Flint *(G-5491)*
Riverside Electric Service Inc ....G 269 849-1222
  Riverside *(G-13286)*
Spina Electric Company ....E 586 771-8080
  Warren *(G-17247)*
Sturgis Electric Motor Service ....G 269 651-2955
  Sturgis *(G-15635)*
Superior Elc Mtr Sls & Svc Inc ....G 906 226-9051
  Marquette *(G-10558)*
Waddell Electric Company ....G 616 791-4860
  Grand Rapids *(G-6976)*
Werner Electric Co ....G 313 561-0854
  Dearborn Heights *(G-3801)*
Winans Inc ....G 810 744-1240
  Corunna *(G-3586)*
York Electric Inc ....D 989 684-7460
  Bay City *(G-1371)*
York Electric Inc ....E 517 487-6400
  Lansing *(G-9438)*
Z & R Electric Service Inc ....F 906 774-0468
  Iron Mountain *(G-8306)*

ELECTRIC POWER GENERATION: Fossil Fuel

DTE Energy Company ....E 313 235-4000
  Detroit *(G-4019)*
DTE Energy Trust II ....G 313 235-8822
  Detroit *(G-4021)*

ELECTRIC POWER, COGENERATED

Option Energy LLC ....F 269 329-4317
  Traverse City *(G-16061)*

ELECTRIC SERVICES

Diamond Electric ....G 734 995-5525
  Ann Arbor *(G-419)*
DTE Energy Resources Inc ....C 313 297-4203
  Detroit *(G-4020)*
DTE Energy Resources Inc ....D 734 302-4800
  Ann Arbor *(G-426)*
Engtechnik Inc ....G 734 667-4237
  Canton *(G-2371)*
Fremont Community Digester LLC ....F 248 735-6684
  Novi *(G-11887)*
General Electric Company ....D 734 728-1472
  Wayne *(G-17431)*

ELECTRIC SVCS, NEC: Power Generation

CMS Enterprises Company ....C 517 788-0550
  Jackson *(G-8413)*

ELECTRICAL APPARATUS & EQPT WHOLESALERS

AA Anderson & Co Inc ....G 734 432-9800
  Livonia *(G-9622)*
Ademco Inc ....G 586 759-1455
  Warren *(G-16918)*
Ademco Inc ....E 248 926-5510
  Wixom *(G-17752)*
Electro-Matic Products Inc ....G 248 478-1182
  Farmington Hills *(G-4980)*
Energy Design Svc Systems LLC ....F 810 227-3377
  Whitmore Lake *(G-17697)*
Genco Alliance LLC ....E 269 216-5500
  Kalamazoo *(G-8748)*
Hitachi America Ltd ....E 248 477-5400
  Farmington Hills *(G-5021)*
Interntonal Innovative Systems ....G 248 524-2222
  Troy *(G-16421)*
Monarch Electric Service Co ....E 313 388-7800
  Melvindale *(G-10702)*
Osborne Transformer Corp ....F 586 218-6900
  Fraser *(G-5702)*
Quad Electronics Inc ....D 800 969-9220
  Troy *(G-16571)*
Seelye Equipment Specialist ....G 231 547-9430
  Charlevoix *(G-2630)*

ELECTRICAL APPLIANCES, TELEVISIONS & RADIOS WHOLESALERS

Bluewater Tech Group Inc ....G 231 885-2600
  Mesick *(G-10767)*
Bluewater Tech Group Inc ....F 616 656-9380
  Grand Rapids *(G-6233)*

Cco Holdings LLC ....G 517 583-4125
  Tekonsha *(G-15817)*
Cco Holdings LLC ....G 616 244-2071
  Belding *(G-1406)*
Cco Holdings LLC ....G 616 384-2060
  Coopersville *(G-3551)*
Cco Holdings LLC ....G 517 639-1060
  Quincy *(G-13091)*
Cco Holdings LLC ....G 734 244-8028
  Monroe *(G-11024)*
Cco Holdings LLC ....G 734 868-5044
  Ida *(G-8193)*
Cco Holdings LLC ....G 810 270-1002
  North Branch *(G-11657)*
Cco Holdings LLC ....G 810 375-7020
  Dryden *(G-4568)*
Cco Holdings LLC ....G 810 545-4020
  Columbiaville *(G-3376)*
Cco Holdings LLC ....G 906 285-6497
  Ironwood *(G-8325)*
Cco Holdings LLC ....G 906 239-3763
  Iron Mountain *(G-8279)*
Cco Holdings LLC ....G 906 346-1000
  Gwinn *(G-7218)*
Cco Holdings LLC ....G 231 720-0688
  Muskegon *(G-11291)*
Cco Holdings LLC ....G 248 494-4550
  Auburn Hills *(G-811)*
Cco Holdings LLC ....G 269 202-3286
  Coloma *(G-3355)*
Cco Holdings LLC ....G 269 216-6680
  Kalamazoo *(G-8704)*
Cco Holdings LLC ....G 269 432-0052
  Colon *(G-3370)*
Cco Holdings LLC ....G 269 464-3454
  White Pigeon *(G-17646)*
Cco Holdings LLC ....G 989 328-4187
  Sidney *(G-14738)*
Cco Holdings LLC ....G 989 567-0151
  Shepherd *(G-14726)*
Cco Holdings LLC ....G 989 863-4023
  Reese *(G-13229)*
Cco Holdings LLC ....G 989 853-2008
  Muir *(G-11237)*
Scientemp Corp ....E 517 263-6020
  Adrian *(G-94)*

ELECTRICAL CONSTRUCTION MATERIALS WHOLESALERS

Madison Electric Company ....D 586 825-0200
  Warren *(G-17136)*

ELECTRICAL CURRENT CARRYING WIRING DEVICES

Aees Power Systems Ltd Partnr ....F 269 668-4429
  Farmington Hills *(G-4921)*
Armada Rubber Manufacturing Co ....D 586 784-9135
  Armada *(G-716)*
Astra Associates Inc ....E 586 254-6500
  Sterling Heights *(G-15266)*
Break-A-Beam ....F 586 758-7790
  Warren *(G-16966)*
Coppertec Inc ....E 313 278-0139
  Inkster *(G-8226)*
Ekstrom Industries Inc ....D 248 477-0040
  Novi *(G-11881)*
Electrical Concepts Inc ....E 616 847-0293
  Grand Haven *(G-6013)*
Electrical Product Sales Inc ....F 248 583-6100
  Troy *(G-16339)*
Electrocom Midwest Sales Inc ....G 248 449-2643
  Madison Heights *(G-10243)*
Ews Legacy LLC ....E 248 853-6363
  Rochester Hills *(G-13421)*
Flextronics Automotive USA Inc ....D 248 853-5724
  Rochester Hills *(G-13425)*
Flextronics Intl USA Inc ....B 616 837-9711
  Coopersville *(G-3558)*
Four-Way Tool and Die Inc ....E 248 585-8255
  Troy *(G-16372)*
H W Jencks Incorporated ....E 231 352-4422
  Frankfort *(G-5603)*
Harman Corporation ....E 248 651-4477
  Rochester *(G-13324)*
Hi-Lex America Incorporated ....D 248 844-0096
  Rochester Hills *(G-13440)*
Imperial Industries Inc ....F 734 397-1400
  Saline *(G-14395)*

Kostal of America Inc ....C 248 284-6500
  Troy *(G-16450)*
Lear Corporation ....B 248 447-1500
  Southfield *(G-14962)*
Mercury Displacement Inds Inc ....D 269 663-8574
  Edwardsburg *(G-4766)*
Meter Devices Company Inc ....A 330 455-0301
  Farmington Hills *(G-5064)*
Metropolitan Alloys Corp ....E 313 366-4443
  Detroit *(G-4233)*
National Zinc Processors Inc ....F 269 926-1161
  Benton Harbor *(G-1535)*
NGK Spark Plugs (usa) Inc ....C 248 926-6900
  Wixom *(G-17865)*
Nyx Inc ....B 734 464-0800
  Livonia *(G-9869)*
Owosso Graphic Arts Inc ....E 989 725-7112
  Owosso *(G-12309)*
Patriot Sensors & Contrls Corp ....D 810 378-5511
  Peck *(G-12420)*
Patriot Sensors & Contrls Corp ....D 248 435-0700
  Clawson *(G-2983)*
Prime Assemblies Inc ....F 906 875-6420
  Crystal Falls *(G-3612)*
Ssi Electronics Inc ....E 616 866-8880
  Belmont *(G-1470)*
Testron Incorporated ....F 734 513-6820
  Livonia *(G-9955)*
TI Group Auto Systems LLC ....C 586 948-6006
  Chesterfield *(G-2848)*
Tram Inc ....C 734 254-8500
  Plymouth *(G-12778)*
Yazaki International Corp ....G 734 983-1000
  Canton *(G-2445)*

ELECTRICAL DEVICE PARTS: Porcelain, Molded

NGK Spark Plugs (usa) Inc ....C 248 926-6900
  Wixom *(G-17865)*

ELECTRICAL DISCHARGE MACHINING, EDM

AA EDM Corporation ....F 734 253-2784
  Dexter *(G-4470)*
Accutronic Incorporated ....G 586 756-2510
  Warren *(G-16913)*
C L Design Inc ....G 248 474-4220
  Farmington Hills *(G-4951)*
Chief EDM ....G 586 752-5078
  Bruce Twp *(G-2079)*
Cleary Developments Inc ....E 248 588-7011
  Madison Heights *(G-10210)*
Damick Enterprises ....F 248 652-7500
  Rochester Hills *(G-13401)*
Damm Company Inc ....G 248 427-9060
  Farmington Hills *(G-4969)*
Detail Technologies LLC ....E 616 261-1313
  Wyoming *(G-17996)*
Diversified E D M Inc ....G 248 547-2320
  Madison Heights *(G-10231)*
E D M Cut-Rite Inc ....F 586 566-0100
  Shelby Township *(G-14584)*
E D M Shuttle Inc ....G 586 468-9880
  Clinton Township *(G-3106)*
Electro-Way Co ....G 586 771-9450
  Fraser *(G-5649)*
EMD Wire Tek ....G 810 235-5344
  Flint *(G-5424)*
J C Manufacturing Company ....G 586 757-2713
  Warren *(G-17106)*
Micro EDM Co LLC ....G 989 872-4306
  Cass City *(G-2520)*
Pdf Mfg Inc ....Gws ... 517 522-8431
  Grass Lake *(G-7091)*
Ramtec Corp ....F 586 752-9270
  Romeo *(G-13636)*
Rapid EDM Service Inc ....G 616 243-5781
  Grand Rapids *(G-6810)*
Simmys Edm LLC ....G 989 802-2516
  Beaverton *(G-1393)*
Superior Cutting Service Inc ....F 616 796-0114
  Holland *(G-7821)*
Tri-Way Manufacturing Inc ....E 586 776-0700
  Roseville *(G-13880)*
Wiretech Wire EDM Service Inc ....G 810 966-9912
  Kimball *(G-9049)*
Wolverine Carbide Die Company ......E 248 280-0300
  Troy *(G-16695)*

PRODUCT SECTION

ELECTRICAL GOODS, WHOLESALE: Facsimile Or Fax Eqpt

ELECTRICAL EQPT & SPLYS

Advanced Research Company	F	248 475-4770
Orion *(G-12173)*		
Aerobee Electric Inc	G	248 549-2044
Ferndale *(G-5252)*		
Asco Power Technologies LP	G	248 957-9050
Farmington Hills *(G-4933)*		
BT Engineering LLC	G	734 417-2218
Spring Lake *(G-15134)*		
Challenger Communications LLC	F	517 680-0125
Springport *(G-15208)*		
Comptek Inc	F	248 477-5215
Farmington Hills *(G-4965)*		
Connolly	G	248 683-7985
Waterford *(G-17329)*		
Csh Incorporated	F	989 723-8985
Owosso *(G-12286)*		
Dare Products Inc	E	269 965-2307
Springfield *(G-15190)*		
Diamond Electric	G	734 995-5525
Ann Arbor *(G-419)*		
Dm3d Technology LLC	F	248 409-7900
Auburn Hills *(G-841)*		
Eesco Inc	G	517 265-5148
Adrian *(G-61)*		
Electric Eye Cafe	G	734 369-6904
Ann Arbor *(G-439)*		
Electronic Design & Packg Co	F	734 591-9176
Livonia *(G-9724)*		
Faac Incorporated	G	734 761-5836
Ann Arbor *(G-455)*		
General Electric Company	D	734 728-1472
Wayne *(G-17431)*		
Grt Avionics Inc	G	616 245-7700
Wyoming *(G-18006)*		
Harold G Schaevitz Inds LLC	G	248 636-1515
Bloomfield Hills *(G-1772)*		
Heco Inc	D	269 381-7200
Kalamazoo *(G-8762)*		
Iaec Corporation	D	586 354-5996
Armada *(G-720)*		
Insulation Wholesale Supply	G	269 968-9746
Battle Creek *(G-1200)*		
Jervis B Webb Company	D	231 582-6558
Boyne City *(G-1825)*		
Kore Inc	E	616 785-5900
Comstock Park *(G-3491)*		
Lakepoint Elec	G	586 983-2510
Shelby Township *(G-14621)*		
Lighthouse Elec Protection LLC	G	586 932-2690
Sterling Heights *(G-15400)*		
Magna Electronics Inc	E	810 606-0444
Troy *(G-16471)*		
Metropoulos Amplification Inc	G	810 614-3905
Holly *(G-7888)*		
Midwest Sales Associates Inc	G	248 348-9600
Wixom *(G-17855)*		
Montronix Inc	G	734 213-6500
Ann Arbor *(G-564)*		
Oleco Inc	E	616 842-6790
Spring Lake *(G-15167)*		
Peak Edm Inc	G	248 380-0871
Wixom *(G-17876)*		
Quad City Innovations LLC	G	513 200-6980
Ann Arbor *(G-610)*		
Ram Electronics Inc	F	231 865-3186
Fruitport *(G-5799)*		
Robroy Industries Inc	D	616 794-0700
Belding *(G-1429)*		
Saginaw Control & Engrg Inc	B	989 799-6871
Saginaw *(G-14138)*		
Sensigma LLC	G	734 998-8328
Ann Arbor *(G-628)*		
Tech Electric Co LLC	G	586 697-5095
Macomb *(G-10167)*		
Tech-Source International Inc	E	231 652-9100
Newaygo *(G-11578)*		
Tenneco Automotive Oper Co Inc	E	734 243-8000
Lansing *(G-9269)*		
Testek LLC	D	248 573-4980
Wixom *(G-17909)*		
Walker Telecommunications	G	989 274-7384
Saginaw *(G-14180)*		
Welk-Ko Fabricators Inc	F	734 425-6840
Livonia *(G-10004)*		

ELECTRICAL EQPT FOR ENGINES

Aees Power Systems Ltd Partnr	F	269 668-4429
Farmington Hills *(G-4921)*		
Blade Welding Service Inc	G	734 941-4253
Van Buren Twp *(G-16749)*		
Bontaz Centre Usa Inc	F	248 588-8113
Troy *(G-16244)*		
Calsonickansei North Amer Inc	G	248 848-4727
West Bloomfield *(G-17467)*		
Cignet LLC	E	586 307-3790
Clinton Township *(G-3080)*		
Continental Auto Systems Inc	B	248 253-2969
Auburn Hills *(G-818)*		
Cusolar Industries Inc	E	586 949-3880
Chesterfield *(G-2757)*		
Ford Motor Company	A	734 484-8000
Ypsilanti *(G-18074)*		
H & L Manufacturing Co	C	269 795-5000
Middleville *(G-10804)*		
Kirks Automotive Incorporated	E	313 933-7030
Detroit *(G-4179)*		
Magnecor Australia Limited	F	248 471-9505
Farmington Hills *(G-5049)*		
Minowitz Manufacturing Co	E	586 779-5940
Huntington Woods *(G-8190)*		
Nabco Inc	G	231 832-2001
Reed City *(G-13221)*		
USA Switch Inc	F	248 960-8500
Wixom *(G-17922)*		
Walbro LLC	C	989 872-2131
Cass City *(G-2524)*		
Walther Trowal LLC	F	616 455-8940
Grand Rapids *(G-6978)*		

ELECTRICAL EQPT REPAIR & MAINTENANCE

Aero Grinding Inc	D	586 774-6450
Roseville *(G-13770)*		
American Wldg & Press Repr Inc	F	248 358-2050
Southfield *(G-14837)*		
Bond Bailey and Smith Company	G	313 496-0177
Detroit *(G-3908)*		
C & B Machinery Company	E	734 462-0600
Brighton *(G-1894)*		
Cpj Company Inc	E	616 784-6355
Comstock Park *(G-3472)*		
D & G Equipment Inc	C	517 655-4606
Williamston *(G-17729)*		
Douglas Corp	F	517 767-4112
Tekonsha *(G-15818)*		
Genco Alliance LLC	E	269 216-5500
Kalamazoo *(G-8748)*		
Hamilton Industrial Products	E	269 751-5153
Hamilton *(G-7233)*		
Hel Inc	F	616 774-9032
Grand Rapids *(G-6503)*		
Jones Electric Company	F	231 726-5001
Muskegon *(G-11356)*		
Ksb Dubric Inc	E	616 784-6355
Comstock Park *(G-3492)*		
Mq Operating Company	E	906 337-1515
Calumet *(G-2330)*		
Pepsi-Cola Metro Btlg Co Inc	D	517 272-2800
Lansing *(G-9410)*		
PSI Hydraulics	C	734 261-4160
Plymouth *(G-12725)*		
Spina Electric Company	E	586 771-8080
Warren *(G-17247)*		
U S Equipment Co	E	313 526-8300
Rochester Hills *(G-13533)*		

ELECTRICAL EQPT REPAIR SVCS: High Voltage

Franklin Electric Corporation	F	248 442-8000
Garden City *(G-5824)*		

ELECTRICAL EQPT: Automotive, NEC

3con Corporation	E	248 859-5440
Wixom *(G-17748)*		
Aptiv Services 2 Us Inc	E	248 813-2000
Troy *(G-16211)*		
Brose New Boston Inc	G	248 339-4000
Auburn Hills *(G-807)*		
Brose New Boston Inc	C	248 339-4021
New Boston *(G-11498)*		
Continental Auto Systems Inc	A	248 874-2597
Auburn Hills *(G-821)*		
Crosscon Industries LLC	F	248 852-5888
Rochester Hills *(G-13398)*		
Daimay North America Auto Inc	G	313 533-9860
Redford *(G-13155)*		
Electra Cable & Communication	G	586 754-3479
Warren *(G-17017)*		
Kathrein Automotive N Amer Inc	G	248 230-2951
Rochester Hills *(G-13455)*		
Lg Electronics Vehicle Compone	C	248 268-5851
Hazel Park *(G-7441)*		
Lg Electronics Vehicle Compone	C	248 268-5851
Troy *(G-16464)*		
Omron Automotive Electronics	E	248 893-0200
Novi *(G-11964)*		
Omron Automotive Electronics	E	248 893-0200
Novi *(G-11965)*		
Overseas Auto Parts Inc	F	734 427-4840
Livonia *(G-9877)*		
Portable Factory	F	586 883-6843
Sterling Heights *(G-15447)*		
Precision Power Inc	G	517 371-4274
Lansing *(G-9414)*		
Protean Electric Inc	D	248 504-4940
Auburn Hills *(G-981)*		
Protean Holdings Corp	G	248 504-4940
Auburn Hills *(G-982)*		
Veoneer Inc	A	248 223-0600
Southfield *(G-15058)*		
Veoneer Us Inc	C	248 223-8074
Southfield *(G-15059)*		
Veoneer Us Inc	B	248 223-0600
Southfield *(G-15060)*		
Wiric Corporation	E	248 598-5297
Rochester Hills *(G-13548)*		
Wolverine Advanced Mtls LLC	E	313 749-6100
Dearborn *(G-3774)*		
Xytek Industries Inc	F	313 838-6961
Detroit *(G-4453)*		

ELECTRICAL GOODS, WHOLESALE: Alarms & Signaling Eqpt

Exquise Inc	G	248 220-9048
Detroit *(G-4047)*		

ELECTRICAL GOODS, WHOLESALE: Batteries, Storage, Indl

Energy Products Inc	G	248 866-5622
Troy *(G-16345)*		
Energy Products Inc	D	248 545-7700
Madison Heights *(G-10247)*		

ELECTRICAL GOODS, WHOLESALE: Electrical Appliances, Major

Lg Electronics USA Inc	C	248 268-5100
Troy *(G-16463)*		
Nu-Way Stove Inc	G	989 733-8792
Onaway *(G-12149)*		

ELECTRICAL GOODS, WHOLESALE: Electrical Entertainment Eqpt

Bluewater Tech Group Inc	C	248 356-4399
Southfield *(G-14854)*		
Star Lite International LLC	G	248 546-4489
Oak Park *(G-12100)*		

ELECTRICAL GOODS, WHOLESALE: Electronic Parts

Advanced-Cable LLC	F	586 491-3073
Troy *(G-16170)*		
American Furukawa Inc	E	734 254-0344
Plymouth *(G-12570)*		
Galco Industrial Elec Inc	G	248 542-9090
Madison Heights *(G-10256)*		
Ghi Electronics LLC	F	248 397-8856
Madison Heights *(G-10257)*		
Morrell Incorporated	D	248 373-1600
Auburn Hills *(G-949)*		
Rave Computer Association Inc	E	586 939-8230
Sterling Heights *(G-15461)*		
Static Controls Corp	E	248 926-4400
Wixom *(G-17896)*		

ELECTRICAL GOODS, WHOLESALE: Facsimile Or Fax Eqpt

Technology Network Svcs Inc	F	586 294-7771
Saint Clair Shores *(G-14271)*		

ELECTRICAL GOODS, WHOLESALE: Generators

ELECTRICAL GOODS, WHOLESALE: Generators

Ainsworth Electric Inc	E	810 984-5768
Port Huron *(G-12883)*		
Amtrade Systems Inc	G	734 522-9500
Livonia *(G-9647)*		
Coffman Electrical Eqp Co	E	616 452-8708
Grand Rapids *(G-6286)*		
Cummins Inc	E	616 281-2211
Grand Rapids *(G-6321)*		
Cummins Npower LLC	E	906 475-8800
Negaunee *(G-11469)*		
Holland Electric Motor Co	G	616 392-1115
Holland *(G-7671)*		

ELECTRICAL GOODS, WHOLESALE: Light Bulbs & Related Splys

G & L Powerup Inc	G	586 200-2169
Roseville *(G-13806)*		
Lumecon LLC	G	248 505-1090
Farmington Hills *(G-5047)*		
M & M Irish Enterprises Inc	G	248 644-0666
Birmingham *(G-1689)*		

ELECTRICAL GOODS, WHOLESALE: Lighting Fixtures, Comm & Indl

Global Green Corporation	F	734 560-1743
Ann Arbor *(G-473)*		
H & R Electrical Contrs LLC	G	517 669-2102
Dewitt *(G-4462)*		

ELECTRICAL GOODS, WHOLESALE: Modems, Computer

Viking Technologies Inc	G	586 914-0819
Madison Heights *(G-10377)*		

ELECTRICAL GOODS, WHOLESALE: Motor Ctrls, Starters & Relays

Nabco Inc	G	231 832-2001
Reed City *(G-13221)*		

ELECTRICAL GOODS, WHOLESALE: Motors

A & C Electric Company	E	586 773-2746
Harrison Township *(G-7317)*		
Alpena Electric Motor Service	G	989 354-8780
Alpena *(G-275)*		
Arrow Motor & Pump Inc	E	734 285-7860
Wyandotte *(G-17946)*		
Bay United Motors Inc	F	989 684-3972
Bay City *(G-1289)*		
Commonwealth Service Sls Corp	G	313 581-8050
Rochester Hills *(G-13392)*		
Core Electric Company Inc	F	313 382-7140
Melvindale *(G-10694)*		
Cummins Inc	F	989 732-5055
Gaylord *(G-5854)*		
DMS Electric Apparatus Service	E	269 349-7000
Kalamazoo *(G-8729)*		
Eagle Engineering & Supply Co	E	989 356-4526
Alpena *(G-286)*		
Edwards Industrial Sales Inc	G	517 887-6100
Lansing *(G-9363)*		
Electric Equipment Company	G	269 925-3266
Benton Harbor *(G-1496)*		
Electric Motor Service	G	269 945-5113
Hastings *(G-7408)*		
Gower Corporation	G	989 249-5938
Saginaw *(G-14050)*		
Hamilton Electric Co	F	989 799-6291
Saginaw *(G-14053)*		
Heco Inc	D	269 381-7200
Kalamazoo *(G-8762)*		
Johnson Electric N Amer Inc	D	734 392-5300
Plymouth *(G-12658)*		
Kalamazoo Electric Motor Inc	G	269 345-7802
Kalamazoo *(G-8788)*		
Lincoln Service LLC	G	734 793-0083
Livonia *(G-9808)*		
Midw Inc	G	269 343-7090
Kalamazoo *(G-8826)*		
Motor Control Incorporated	G	313 389-4000
Melvindale *(G-10703)*		
North End Electric Company	G	248 398-8187
Royal Oak *(G-13954)*		
Pontiac Electric Motor Works	G	248 332-4622
Pontiac *(G-12856)*		
Rapa Electric Inc	E	269 673-3157
Allegan *(G-186)*		
Reliance Electric Machine Co	F	810 232-3355
Flint *(G-5491)*		
Riverside Electric Service Inc	G	269 849-1222
Riverside *(G-13286)*		
Spina Electric Company	E	586 771-8080
Warren *(G-17247)*		
Superior Elc Mtr Sls & Svc Inc	G	906 226-9051
Marquette *(G-10558)*		
Werner Electric Co	G	313 561-0854
Dearborn Heights *(G-3801)*		
Winans Inc	G	810 744-1240
Corunna *(G-3586)*		
York Electric Inc	D	989 684-7460
Bay City *(G-1371)*		
Z & R Electric Service Inc	F	906 774-0468
Iron Mountain *(G-8306)*		

ELECTRICAL GOODS, WHOLESALE: Security Control Eqpt & Systems

Code Blue Corporation	E	616 392-8296
Holland *(G-7594)*		
Pct Security Inc	G	888 567-3287
Clinton Township *(G-3192)*		
Traffic Sfety Ctrl Systems Inc	E	248 348-0570
Wixom *(G-17914)*		

ELECTRICAL GOODS, WHOLESALE: Signaling, Eqpt

Carrier & Gable Inc	E	248 477-8700
Farmington Hills *(G-4958)*		
Rathco Safety Supply Inc	E	269 323-0153
Portage *(G-13027)*		

ELECTRICAL GOODS, WHOLESALE: Switchboards

Advanced Electric	G	517 529-9050
Clarklake *(G-2893)*		
Memcon North America LLC	F	269 281-0478
Stevensville *(G-15578)*		

ELECTRICAL GOODS, WHOLESALE: Telephone Eqpt

J L International Inc	C	734 941-0300
Romulus *(G-13690)*		

ELECTRICAL GOODS, WHOLESALE: Time Switches

Balogh Tag Inc	G	248 486-7343
Brighton *(G-1888)*		

ELECTRICAL GOODS, WHOLESALE: Video Eqpt

Corporate AV Services LLC	G	248 939-0900
Commerce Township *(G-3395)*		

ELECTRICAL GOODS, WHOLESALE: Wire & Cable

Pro-Motion Tech Group LLC	D	248 668-3100
Wixom *(G-17880)*		

ELECTRICAL GOODS, WHOLESALE: Wire & Cable, Electronic

Wh Manufacturing Inc	E	616 534-7560
Grand Rapids *(G-6990)*		

ELECTRICAL HOUSEHOLD APPLIANCE REPAIR

Advanced Blnding Solutions LLC	F	906 914-4180
Menominee *(G-10721)*		

ELECTRICAL INDL APPARATUS, NEC

Sparta Outlets	G	616 887-6010
Sparta *(G-15110)*		

ELECTRICAL SPLYS

Eesco Inc	G	517 265-5148
Adrian *(G-61)*		
Electro-Matic Ventures Inc	D	248 478-1182
Farmington Hills *(G-4981)*		
Standard Electric Company	E	906 774-4455
Kingsford *(G-9067)*		
Utility Supply and Cnstr Co	G	231 832-2297
Reed City *(G-13225)*		

ELECTRICAL SUPPLIES: Porcelain

Leco Corporation	B	269 983-5531
Saint Joseph *(G-14324)*		
Leco Corporation	F	269 982-2230
Saint Joseph *(G-14325)*		
Tengam Engineering Inc	E	269 694-9466
Otsego *(G-12256)*		

ELECTRODES: Indl Process

Debron Industrial Elec Inc	E	248 588-7220
Troy *(G-16300)*		

ELECTROMEDICAL EQPT

Benesh Corporation	E	734 244-4143
Monroe *(G-11023)*		
Cerephex Corporation	G	517 719-0414
Bancroft *(G-1087)*		
Helping Hands Therapy	G	313 492-6007
Southfield *(G-14936)*		
Isensium	G	517 580-9022
East Lansing *(G-4666)*		
Medtronic Inc	G	616 643-5200
Grand Rapids *(G-6658)*		
Metrex Research LLC	D	734 947-6700
Romulus *(G-13706)*		
MII Disposition Inc	E	616 554-9696
Grand Rapids *(G-6689)*		
Rofin-Sinar Technologies LLC	F	734 416-0206
Plymouth *(G-12745)*		
Somanetics	F	248 689-3050
Troy *(G-16611)*		
Terumo Crdvsculary Systems Corp	C	734 663-4145
Ann Arbor *(G-666)*		
Thoratec Corporation	C	734 827-7422
Ann Arbor *(G-673)*		
Uv Partners Inc	G	616 204-5416
Livonia *(G-9984)*		

ELECTROMETALLURGICAL PRDTS

Alpha Resources LLC	E	269 465-5559
Stevensville *(G-15553)*		
Miccus Inc	F	616 604-4449
Howell *(G-8064)*		

ELECTRON BEAM: Cutting, Forming, Welding

Hirose Electric USA Inc	D	734 542-9963
Livonia *(G-9771)*		
Tandis LLC	G	248 345-3448
West Bloomfield *(G-17500)*		

ELECTRONIC COMPONENTS

Ace Electronics LLC Michigan	G	443 327-6100
Troy *(G-16167)*		
Control Electronics	E	734 941-5008
Romulus *(G-13664)*		

ELECTRONIC DEVICES: Solid State, NEC

Regener-Eyes LLC	G	248 207-4641
Ann Arbor *(G-614)*		
Ziel Optics Inc	G	734 994-9803
Ann Arbor *(G-707)*		

ELECTRONIC EQPT REPAIR SVCS

Consoldted Rsource Imaging LLC	E	616 735-2080
Grand Rapids *(G-6301)*		
Galco Industrial Elec Inc	G	248 542-9090
Madison Heights *(G-10256)*		
H and H Electronics	G	586 725-5412
Clay *(G-2997)*		
Industrial Service Tech Inc	F	616 288-3352
Grand Rapids *(G-6533)*		
Innovative Support Svcs Inc	E	248 585-3600
Troy *(G-16418)*		

PRODUCT SECTION

Monitec Services Incorporated .... G 231 943-2227
  Traverse City *(G-16042)*

ELECTRONIC LOADS & POWER SPLYS

Aees Inc .... B 248 489-4700
  Farmington Hills *(G-4920)*
High Effcncy Pwr Solutions Inc .... G 800 833-7094
  Whitmore Lake *(G-17702)*
Onegene America Inc .... G 734 855-4460
  Livonia *(G-9876)*
Renewable World Energies LLC .... F 906 828-0808
  Norway *(G-11819)*

ELECTRONIC PARTS & EQPT WHOLESALERS

Automotive Electronic Spc .... E 248 335-3229
  Bloomfield Hills *(G-1748)*
B Company Inc .... F 734 283-7080
  Riverview *(G-13291)*
Great Lakes Infotronics Inc .... E 248 476-2500
  Northville *(G-11695)*
Hitachi America Ltd .... E 248 477-5400
  Farmington Hills *(G-5021)*
Hydraulic Systems Technology .... G 248 656-5810
  Rochester Hills *(G-13447)*
Imagepro Inc .... G 231 723-7906
  Manistee *(G-10424)*
Jo-Dan International Inc .... G 248 340-0300
  Auburn Hills *(G-919)*
Mitsubishi Electric Us Inc .... D 734 453-6200
  Northville *(G-11711)*
Odyssey Electronics Inc .... D 734 421-8340
  Livonia *(G-9874)*
Ram Meter Inc .... F 248 362-0990
  Royal Oak *(G-13962)*
Rena DRane Enterprises Inc .... G 248 796-2765
  Southfield *(G-15012)*
Rick Wykle LLC .... G 734 839-6376
  Livonia *(G-9909)*
Scs Embedded Tech LLC .... G 248 615-2244
  Novi *(G-11990)*

ELECTRONIC SHOPPING

Fabjunky LLC .... G 323 572-4988
  Muskegon *(G-11319)*
Meteor Web Marketing Inc .... F 734 822-4999
  Ann Arbor *(G-553)*

ELECTRONIC TRAINING DEVICES

Combat Action LLC .... G 810 772-3758
  Brighton *(G-1900)*
Farr & Faron Associates Inc .... G 810 229-7730
  Brighton *(G-1921)*
Parker Engineering and Mfg Co .... G 616 784-6500
  Grand Rapids *(G-6742)*

ELECTROPLATING & PLATING SVC

Abrasive Services Incorporated .... G 734 941-2144
  Romulus *(G-13647)*
Heidtman Steel Products Inc .... D 734 848-2115
  Erie *(G-4803)*
Howard Finishing LLC .... D 586 777-0070
  Roseville *(G-13816)*
Nicro Finishing LLC .... F 313 924-0661
  Detroit *(G-4271)*
Sigma International Inc .... E 248 230-9681
  Livonia *(G-9928)*
Spring Arbor Coatings LLC .... D 517 750-2903
  Spring Arbor *(G-15128)*
Vacuum Orna Metal Company Inc .... E 734 941-9100
  Romulus *(G-13738)*

ELEVATOR: Bean, Storage Only

Nutrien AG Solutions Inc .... G 989 842-1185
  Breckenridge *(G-1844)*

ELEVATORS & EQPT

Central Elevator Co Inc .... F 269 329-0705
  Vicksburg *(G-16833)*
Chelsea Grain LLC .... G 734 475-1386
  Chelsea *(G-2703)*
Detroit Elevator Company .... E 248 591-7484
  Ferndale *(G-5276)*
Mc Nally Elevator Company .... F 269 381-1860
  Kalamazoo *(G-8819)*

Nylube Products Company LLC .... E 248 852-6500
  Rochester Hills *(G-13486)*
Schafers Elevator Co .... G 517 263-7202
  Adrian *(G-93)*
Vertical Solutions Company .... G 517 655-8164
  Williamston *(G-17741)*

ELEVATORS WHOLESALERS

Schindler Elevator Corporation .... F 517 272-1234
  Lansing *(G-9421)*

ELEVATORS: Installation & Conversion

Detroit Elevator Company .... E 248 591-7484
  Ferndale *(G-5276)*
Elevated Technologies Inc .... F 616 288-9817
  Grand Rapids *(G-6375)*
Mc Nally Elevator Company .... F 269 381-1860
  Kalamazoo *(G-8819)*
Mitsubishi Electric Us Inc .... D 734 453-6200
  Northville *(G-11711)*
Schindler Elevator Corporation .... F 517 272-1234
  Lansing *(G-9421)*

ELEVATORS: Stair, Motor Powered

Elevated Technologies Inc .... F 616 288-9817
  Grand Rapids *(G-6375)*

EMBALMING FLUID

Trisco Chemical Co .... G 586 779-8260
  Saint Clair Shores *(G-14274)*

EMBLEMS: Embroidered

1365267 Ontario Inc .... G 888 843-5245
  Port Huron *(G-12879)*
Aisin Holdings America Inc .... G 734 453-5551
  Northville *(G-11676)*
Dun Mor Embroidery & Designs .... F 248 577-1155
  Troy *(G-16329)*
Inkpressions LLC .... E 248 461-2555
  Commerce Township *(G-3416)*
Sports Stop .... G 517 676-2199
  Mason *(G-10660)*

EMBOSSING SVC: Paper

Amazing Engraving .... G 989 652-8503
  Frankenmuth *(G-5582)*
Graphic Specialties Inc .... E 616 247-0060
  Grand Rapids *(G-6475)*
Graphics Embossed Images Inc .... G 616 791-0404
  Grand Rapids *(G-6476)*

EMBROIDERING & ART NEEDLEWORK FOR THE TRADE

A Design Line Embroidery LLC .... G 734 697-3545
  Van Buren Twp *(G-16745)*
Advanced Printwear Inc .... G 248 585-4412
  Madison Heights *(G-10182)*
Apparel Sales Inc .... G 616 842-5650
  Jenison *(G-8617)*
C R Stitching .... G 313 538-1660
  Redford *(G-13151)*
Creative Promotions .... G 734 854-2292
  Lambertville *(G-9181)*
Custom Embroidery Plus LLC .... G 989 227-9432
  Saint Johns *(G-14282)*
Design Tech LLC .... G 616 459-2885
  Grand Rapids *(G-6346)*
E Q R 2 Inc .... G 586 731-3383
  Sterling Heights *(G-15324)*
Earthbound Inc .... G 616 774-0096
  Grand Rapids *(G-6366)*
Embroidery Shoppe LLC .... G 734 595-7612
  Westland *(G-17552)*
Heikkinen Productions Inc .... G 734 485-4020
  Ypsilanti *(G-18076)*
Jean Smith Designs .... E 616 942-9212
  Grand Rapids *(G-6556)*
Mach II Enterprises Inc .... G 248 347-8822
  Northville *(G-11708)*
Meridian Screen Prtg & Design .... G 517 351-2525
  Okemos *(G-12130)*
MJB Concepts Inc .... G 616 866-1470
  Rockford *(G-13580)*
Monograms & More Inc .... E 313 299-3140
  Taylor *(G-15746)*

On Green Logos .... G 616 669-1928
  Hudsonville *(G-8173)*
P S Monograms .... G 616 698-1177
  Byron Center *(G-2206)*
Pierson Fine Art .... G 269 385-4974
  Kalamazoo *(G-8851)*
Special T Custom Products .... G 810 654-9602
  Davison *(G-3663)*
Sportswear Specialties Inc .... G 734 416-9941
  Canton *(G-2428)*
Sylvesters .... G 989 348-9097
  Grayling *(G-7116)*
T - Shirt Printing Plus Inc .... F 269 383-3666
  Kalamazoo *(G-8907)*
Threadworks Ltd Inc .... G 517 548-9745
  New Boston *(G-11513)*
Trophy Center West Michigan .... G 231 893-1686
  Whitehall *(G-17678)*
Ultra Stitch Embroidery .... F 586 498-5600
  Roseville *(G-13886)*

EMBROIDERING SVC

Adams Shirt Shack Inc .... G 269 964-3323
  Battle Creek *(G-1137)*
Adlib Grafix & Apparel .... G 269 964-2810
  Battle Creek *(G-1139)*
Alfie Embroidery Inc .... F 231 935-1488
  Traverse City *(G-15892)*
Bay Supply & Marketing Inc .... G 231 943-3249
  Traverse City *(G-15908)*
Bd Classic Sewing .... G 231 825-2628
  Mc Bain *(G-10677)*
Beck & Boys Custom Apparel .... G 734 458-4015
  Livonia *(G-9663)*
Charlevoix Screen Masters Inc .... G 231 547-5111
  Charlevoix *(G-2612)*
Classic Images Embroidery .... G 616 844-1702
  Grand Haven *(G-6004)*
Classy Threadz .... G 989 479-9595
  Harbor Beach *(G-7264)*
Colorful Stitches .... G 269 683-6442
  Niles *(G-11600)*
Creative Loop .... G 231 629-8228
  Paris *(G-12383)*
Custom Embroidery & Sewing .... G 586 749-7669
  Ray *(G-13132)*
D & M Silkscreening .... G 517 694-4199
  Holt *(G-7906)*
Delta Sports Service & EMB .... G 517 482-6565
  Lansing *(G-9215)*
Designs By Bean .... G 989 845-4371
  Chesaning *(G-2723)*
Embroidery & Much More LLC .... F 586 771-3832
  Saint Clair Shores *(G-14246)*
Embroidery House Inc .... G 616 669-6400
  Jenison *(G-8625)*
Embroidery Products LLC .... G 734 483-0293
  Ypsilanti *(G-18071)*
Embroidery Wearhouse .... G 906 228-5818
  Marquette *(G-10529)*
Ensign Emblem Ltd .... D 231 946-7703
  Traverse City *(G-15964)*
Exposure Unlimited Inc .... G 248 459-9104
  Fenton *(G-5205)*
Grasel Graphics Inc .... G 989 652-5151
  Frankenmuth *(G-5589)*
I D Pro Embroidery LLC .... G 734 847-6650
  Temperance *(G-15832)*
Ideal Wholesale Inc .... G 989 873-5850
  Prescott *(G-13080)*
Imprint House LLC .... G 810 985-8203
  Port Huron *(G-12929)*
Initial Artistry .... G 313 277-6300
  Dearborn Heights *(G-3787)*
J America LLC .... E 517 521-2525
  Webberville *(G-17451)*
Janet Kelly .... F 231 775-2313
  Cadillac *(G-2256)*
Jene Holly Designs Inc .... G 586 954-0255
  Harrison Township *(G-7334)*
JJ Jinkleheimer & Co Inc .... F 517 546-4345
  Howell *(G-8056)*
Keeping You In Stitches .... G 586 421-9509
  Chesterfield *(G-2794)*
Lansing Athletics .... G 517 327-8828
  Lansing *(G-9305)*
Logospot .... G 616 785-7170
  Belmont *(G-1467)*
Markit Products .... G 616 458-7881
  Grand Rapids *(G-6644)*

Employee Codes: A=Over 500 employees, B=251-500
C=101-250, D=51-100, E=20-50, F=10-19, G=3-9

2020 Harris Michigan
Industrial Directory

EMBROIDERING SVC

Michigan Graphic Arts	G	517 278-4120
Coldwater (G-3315)		
Midwest Custom Embroidery Co	G	269 381-7660
Kalamazoo (G-8827)		
Monogram Etc	G	989 743-5999
Corunna (G-3582)		
Northville Stitching Post	G	248 347-7622
Northville (G-11717)		
Personal Graphics	G	231 347-6347
Petoskey (G-12468)		
Personalized Embroidery Co	G	208 263-1267
Traverse City (G-16066)		
Royal Stewart Enterprises	G	734 224-7994
Temperance (G-15843)		
S & H Trophy & Sports	G	616 754-0005
Greenville (G-7151)		
Saginaw Knitting Mills Inc	F	989 695-2481
Freeland (G-5759)		
Shelly Meehof	G	231 775-3065
Cadillac (G-2276)		
Shirts n More Inc	F	269 963-3266
Battle Creek (G-1246)		
Silk Screenstuff	G	517 543-7716
Charlotte (G-2664)		
Slick Shirts Screen Printing	F	517 371-3600
Lansing (G-9424)		
Spirit of Livingston Inc	G	517 545-8831
Howell (G-8102)		
Sporting Image Inc	F	269 657-5646
Paw Paw (G-12413)		
Sports Junction	G	989 791-5900
Saginaw (G-14156)		
Sports Junction	G	989 835-9696
Midland (G-10920)		
Student Book Store Inc	G	517 351-6768
East Lansing (G-4677)		

EMBROIDERING SVC: Schiffli Machine

Chromatic Graphics Inc	G	616 393-0034
Holland (G-7590)		
Circles Way To Go Around Inc	F	313 384-1193
Clinton Township (G-3081)		
Ideal Wholesale Inc	G	989 873-5850
Prescott (G-13080)		

EMBROIDERY ADVERTISING SVCS

Adco Specialties Inc	G	616 452-6882
Grand Rapids (G-6143)		
Authority Customwear Ltd	E	248 588-8075
Madison Heights (G-10199)		
R H & Company Inc	F	269 345-7814
Kalamazoo (G-8867)		
Sign Screen Inc	G	810 239-1100
Flint (G-5499)		
Wellard Inc	G	312 752-0155
West Olive (G-17536)		

EMBROIDERY KITS

Heritage	G	734 414-0343
Plymouth (G-12638)		

EMERGENCY & RELIEF SVCS

Virtual Emergency Services LLC	F	734 324-2299
Wyandotte (G-17980)		

EMERGENCY ALARMS

Ademco Inc	G	586 759-1455
Warren (G-16918)		
Ademco Inc	E	248 926-5510
Wixom (G-17752)		
Aero Systems	F	253 269-3000
Livonia (G-9630)		
Causey Consulting LLC	G	248 671-4979
West Bloomfield (G-17469)		
Code Blue Corporation	E	616 392-8296
Holland (G-7594)		
Emergency Technology Inc	D	616 896-7100
Hudsonville (G-8155)		
Monitec Services Incorporated	G	231 943-2227
Traverse City (G-16042)		

EMPLOYEE LEASING SVCS

Contract People Corporation	F	248 304-9900
Southfield (G-14872)		

EMPLOYMENT AGENCY SVCS

Douglas Autotech Corporation	E	517 369-2315
Bronson (G-2025)		
F J Lucido & Associates	E	586 574-3577
Warren (G-17028)		
RCO Engineering Inc	D	586 620-4133
Roseville (G-13860)		

EMPLOYMENT SVCS: Labor Contractors

Die Tech Services Inc	E	616 363-6604
Walker (G-16865)		

ENAMELING SVC: Metal Prdts, Including Porcelain

American Porcelain Enamel Co	E	231 744-3013
Muskegon (G-11268)		
B & J Enmeling Inc A Mich Corp	F	313 365-6620
Detroit (G-3892)		
Hope Network West Michigan	C	231 796-4801
Paris (G-12385)		
Spectrum Industries Inc	D	616 451-0784
Grand Rapids (G-6884)		

ENCLOSURES: Electronic

Brooks Utility Products Group	E	248 477-0250
Novi (G-11841)		
Innovation Fab Inc	F	586 752-3092
Bruce Twp (G-2084)		

ENCLOSURES: Screen

All Season Enclosures	G	248 650-8020
Shelby Township (G-14545)		

ENGINE PARTS & ACCESS: Internal Combustion

Ash Industries Inc	F	269 672-9630
Martin (G-10594)		
Extreme Machine Inc	D	810 231-0521
Whitmore Lake (G-17699)		
Katech Inc	E	586 791-4120
Clinton Township (G-3153)		
Metaldyne Pwrtrain Cmpnnts Inc	C	517 542-5555
Litchfield (G-9607)		
Metaldyne Pwrtrain Cmpnnts Inc	C	313 758-2000
Detroit (G-4229)		
Minowitz Manufacturing Co	E	586 779-5940
Huntington Woods (G-8190)		
Perfit Corporation	G	734 524-9208
Livonia (G-9886)		
R & D Enterprises Inc	E	248 349-7077
Plymouth (G-12728)		

ENGINE REBUILDING: Diesel

Logan Diesel Incorporated	G	517 589-8811
Leslie (G-9544)		
Mtu America Incorporated	G	734 261-0309
Livonia (G-9854)		
Peaker Services Inc	D	248 437-4174
Brighton (G-1976)		
PSI Holding Company	D	248 437-4174
Brighton (G-1982)		

ENGINE REBUILDING: Gas

D & S Engine Specialist Inc	F	248 583-9240
Clawson (G-2976)		
Falvey Limited	E	517 263-2699
Adrian (G-64)		
Wilson Stamping & Mfg Inc	G	989 823-8521
Vassar (G-16820)		

ENGINEERING HELP SVCS

Bpg International Fin Co LLC	G	616 855-1480
Ada (G-11)		
Gonzalez Prod Systems Inc	D	313 297-6682
Detroit (G-4097)		

ENGINEERING SVCS

4d Systems LLC	E	800 380-9165
Flint (G-5366)		
ADS LLC	G	248 740-9593
Troy (G-16168)		
Alcotec Wire Corporation	D	800 228-0750
Traverse City (G-15891)		
Altair Engineering Inc	C	248 614-2400
Troy (G-16192)		
AM General LLC	B	734 523-8098
Auburn Hills (G-767)		
AMS Co Ltd	G	248 712-4435
Troy (G-16199)		
Amtex Inc	G	586 792-7888
Clinton Township (G-3051)		
Aom Engineering Solutions LLC	G	313 406-8130
Dearborn Heights (G-3778)		
Aphase II Inc	D	586 977-0790
Sterling Heights (G-15262)		
Atmo-Seal Inc	G	248 528-9640
Troy (G-16227)		
Automotive Lighting LLC	E	248 418-3000
Auburn Hills (G-789)		
Bel-Kur Inc	E	734 847-0651
Temperance (G-15823)		
Bpg International Fin Co LLC	G	616 855-1480
Ada (G-11)		
Broaching Industries Inc	E	586 949-3775
Chesterfield (G-2748)		
Cambric Corporation	B	801 415-7300
Novi (G-11842)		
Capsonic Automotive Inc	G	248 754-1100
Auburn Hills (G-809)		
Classic Systems LLC	C	248 588-2738
Troy (G-16270)		
Clean Air Technology Inc	E	734 459-6320
Canton (G-2362)		
Cold Heading Co	D	586 497-7000
Warren (G-16985)		
Compunetics Incorporated	E	248 524-6376
Troy (G-16276)		
Contract People Corporation	F	248 304-9900
Southfield (G-14872)		
Controlled Power Company	C	248 528-3700
Troy (G-16281)		
Corotech Acquisition Co	F	616 456-5557
Grand Rapids (G-6312)		
Covaron Inc	G	480 298-9433
Ann Arbor (G-407)		
Creative Composites Inc	E	906 474-9941
Rapid River (G-13111)		
Dayco Products LLC	D	248 404-6506
Troy (G-16298)		
Dlhbowles Inc	F	248 569-0652
Southfield (G-14883)		
Dse Industries LLC	G	313 530-6668
Macomb (G-10118)		
E D P Technical Services Inc	G	734 591-9176
Livonia (G-9718)		
Eaton Corporation	F	517 787-8121
Ann Arbor (G-430)		
Ecorse McHy Sls & Rbldrs Inc	E	313 383-2100
Wyandotte (G-17956)		
Emp Advanced Development LLC	D	906 789-7497
Escanaba (G-4824)		
Energy Design Svc Systems LLC	F	810 227-3377
Whitmore Lake (G-17697)		
Engineered Control Systems Inc	E	509 483-6215
Washington (G-17303)		
Engineered Tools Corp	D	989 673-8733
Caro (G-2468)		
Engineering Tech Assoc Inc	D	248 729-3010
Troy (G-16346)		
Ernie Romanco	E	517 531-3686
Albion (G-123)		
Esys Automation LLC	D	248 754-1900
Auburn Hills (G-856)		
Etcs Inc	F	586 268-4870
Warren (G-17022)		
Extreme Machine Inc	D	810 231-0521
Whitmore Lake (G-17700)		
Faac Incorporated	C	734 761-5836
Ann Arbor (G-456)		
Fev Test Systems Inc	G	248 373-6000
Auburn Hills (G-872)		
Global Fleet Sales LLC	G	248 327-6483
Southfield (G-14920)		
Global Strgc Sup Solutions LLC	D	734 525-9100
Livonia (G-9753)		
Global Supply Integrator LLC	G	586 484-0734
Davisburg (G-3635)		
Glov Enterprises LLC	D	517 423-9700
Tecumseh (G-15794)		
Hawk Design Inc	G	989 781-1152
Saginaw (G-14055)		
Hbpo North America Inc	C	248 823-7076
Troy (G-16392)		

PRODUCT SECTION

ENGINEERING SVCS: Pollution Control

Helios Solar LLC ....G..... 269 343-5581
  Kalamazoo *(G-8763)*
Hi-Tech Furnace Systems Inc ....F..... 586 566-0600
  Shelby Township *(G-14600)*
Hj Manufacturing Inc ....F..... 906 233-1500
  Escanaba *(G-4833)*
Industrial Service Tech Inc ....F..... 616 288-3352
  Grand Rapids *(G-6533)*
Infinity Controls & Engrg Inc ....G..... 248 397-8267
  Lake Orion *(G-9139)*
Innovative Thermal Systems LLC ....G..... 586 920-2900
  Warren *(G-17093)*
Innovative Weld Solutions LLC ....G..... 937 545-7695
  Rochester *(G-13329)*
Inoac Interior Systems LLC ....E..... 248 488-7610
  Farmington Hills *(G-5028)*
Island Machine and Engrg LLC ....G..... 810 765-8228
  Marine City *(G-10475)*
Johnson Electric N Amer Inc ....D..... 734 392-5300
  Plymouth *(G-12658)*
K & K Technology Inc ....G..... 989 399-9910
  Flushing *(G-5538)*
Katcon Usa Inc ....D..... 248 499-1500
  Auburn Hills *(G-924)*
Kaydon Corporation ....C..... 231 755-3741
  Norton Shores *(G-11766)*
Limo-Reid Inc ....G..... 517 447-4164
  Deerfield *(G-3812)*
Lord Laboratories ....G..... 586 447-8955
  Saint Clair Shores *(G-14260)*
Magna Exteriors America Inc ....A..... 248 631-1100
  Troy *(G-16472)*
Magna Exteriors America Inc ....B..... 248 409-1817
  Auburn Hills *(G-936)*
Magnetech Corporation ....G..... 248 426-8840
  Novi *(G-11933)*
Mahle Powertrain LLC ....D..... 248 305-8200
  Farmington Hills *(G-5056)*
Manufacturing & Indus Tech Inc ....E..... 248 814-8544
  Lake Orion *(G-9147)*
Marelli North America Inc ....C..... 248 848-4800
  Farmington Hills *(G-5057)*
Memtech Inc ....F..... 734 455-8550
  Plymouth *(G-12689)*
Merrill Technologies Group Inc ....D..... 989 791-6676
  Saginaw *(G-14090)*
Method Technology Service LLC ....E..... 312 622-7697
  Troy *(G-16500)*
Michigan Scientific Corp ....E..... 248 685-3939
  Milford *(G-10969)*
Midstates Industrial Group Inc ....E..... 586 307-3414
  Clinton Township *(G-3174)*
Mmi Engineered Solutions Inc ....D..... 734 429-4664
  Saline *(G-14403)*
Mmi Engineered Solutions Inc ....E..... 734 429-5130
  Warren *(G-17158)*
Motor City Electric Tech Inc ....D..... 313 921-5300
  Detroit *(G-4256)*
Northville Circuits Inc ....G..... 248 853-3232
  Rochester Hills *(G-13484)*
Oakland Automation LLC ....F..... 810 874-3061
  Novi *(G-11961)*
Omaha Automation Inc ....G..... 313 557-3565
  Detroit *(G-4284)*
Opus Mach LLC ....G..... 586 270-5170
  Warren *(G-17177)*
P2r Metal Fabrication Inc ....G..... 888 727-5587
  Macomb *(G-10151)*
Pacific Engineering Corp ....G..... 248 359-7823
  Novi *(G-11970)*
Peloton Inc ....G..... 269 694-9702
  Otsego *(G-12252)*
Plasan Us Inc ....F..... 616 559-0032
  Walker *(G-16876)*
Portable Factory ....F..... 586 883-6843
  Sterling Heights *(G-15447)*
Praet Tool & Engineering Inc ....E..... 586 677-3800
  Macomb *(G-10154)*
Process Partners Inc ....G..... 616 875-2156
  Hudsonville *(G-8174)*
Pyrinas LLC ....G..... 810 422-7535
  Traverse City *(G-16084)*
Quality Engineering Company ....F..... 248 351-9000
  Wixom *(G-17883)*
Recaro North America Inc ....D..... 734 254-5000
  Plymouth *(G-12733)*
Rhombus Energy Solutions Inc ....G..... 313 406-3292
  Dearborn *(G-3753)*
Roman Engineering ....D..... 231 238-7644
  Afton *(G-106)*
Romeo Technologies Inc ....D..... 586 336-5015
  Bruce Twp *(G-2095)*
Ross Design & Engineering Inc ....E..... 517 547-6033
  Cement City *(G-2575)*
Rosta USA Corp ....F..... 269 841-5448
  Benton Harbor *(G-1544)*
Roush Industries Inc ....E..... 734 779-7016
  Livonia *(G-9912)*
Roush Industries Inc ....E..... 734 779-7013
  Livonia *(G-9913)*
Roush Manufacturing Inc ....C..... 734 779-7006
  Livonia *(G-9915)*
RPS Tool and Engineering Inc ....E..... 586 298-6590
  Roseville *(G-13864)*
Set Liquidation Inc ....D..... 517 694-2300
  Holt *(G-7928)*
Siemens Industry Inc ....C..... 616 913-7700
  Grand Rapids *(G-6861)*
Soils and Structures Inc ....E..... 800 933-3959
  Norton Shores *(G-11796)*
Sws - Trimac Inc ....E..... 989 791-4595
  Saginaw *(G-14162)*
Tecat Performance Systems LLC ....F..... 248 615-9862
  Ann Arbor *(G-654)*
Testek LLC ....D..... 248 573-4980
  Wixom *(G-17909)*
Therma-Tech Engineering Inc ....E..... 313 537-5330
  Redford *(G-13201)*
Three-Dimensional Services Inc ....C..... 248 852-1333
  Rochester Hills *(G-13525)*
Torsion Control Products Inc ....C..... 248 537-1900
  Rochester Hills *(G-13528)*
Turn Key Automotive LLC ....E..... 248 628-5556
  Oxford *(G-12378)*
Uniflex Inc ....C..... 248 486-6000
  Brighton *(G-2002)*
US Energia LLC ....D..... 248 669-1462
  Rochester *(G-13356)*
Van Dyken Mechanical Inc ....C..... 616 224-7030
  Grandville *(G-7075)*
Yates Industries Inc ....D..... 586 778-7680
  Saint Clair Shores *(G-14277)*

ENGINEERING SVCS: Acoustical

Progressive Panel Systems ....F..... 616 748-1384
  Zeeland *(G-18180)*

ENGINEERING SVCS: Aviation Or Aeronautical

Ascent Aerospace LLC ....A..... 586 726-0500
  Macomb *(G-10108)*
Chandas Engineering Inc ....F..... 313 582-8666
  Dearborn *(G-3687)*
Pioneer Technologies Corp ....E..... 702 806-3152
  Fremont *(G-5782)*
Schallips Inc ....G..... 906 635-0941
  Barbeau *(G-1117)*

ENGINEERING SVCS: Building Construction

Advanced Altrntive Sltions LLC ....G..... 616 607-6956
  Wyoming *(G-17984)*
Boral Building Products Inc ....C..... 248 668-6400
  Wixom *(G-17777)*
K & M Industrial LLC ....G..... 906 420-8770
  Gladstone *(G-5914)*

ENGINEERING SVCS: Construction & Civil

Kadant Johnson LLC ....C..... 269 278-1715
  Three Rivers *(G-15867)*
Lgc Global Inc ....E..... 313 989-4141
  Detroit *(G-4202)*

ENGINEERING SVCS: Electrical Or Electronic

Complete Dsign Automtn Systems ....G..... 734 424-2789
  Dexter *(G-4483)*
Consoldted Rsource Imaging LLC ....E..... 616 735-2080
  Grand Rapids *(G-6301)*
Debron Industrial Elec Inc ....E..... 248 588-7220
  Troy *(G-16300)*
Eberspecher Contrls N Amer Inc ....G..... 248 994-7010
  Brighton *(G-1916)*
Energy Development Assoc LLC ....E..... 313 354-2644
  Dearborn *(G-3701)*
Fairchilds Daughters & Son LLC ....G..... 906 239-6061
  Iron Mountain *(G-8283)*
Flextronics Intl USA Inc ....B..... 616 837-9711
  Coopersville *(G-3558)*
Lectronix Inc ....D..... 517 492-1900
  Lansing *(G-9391)*
MAKS INCORPORATED ....E..... 248 733-9771
  Troy *(G-16484)*
Manufacturing Ctrl Systems Inc ....G..... 248 853-7400
  Rochester Hills *(G-13467)*
Nadex of America Corporation ....E..... 248 477-3900
  Farmington Hills *(G-5075)*
Nextek Power Systems Inc ....E..... 313 887-1321
  Detroit *(G-4269)*
Spec Corporation ....G..... 517 529-4105
  Clarklake *(G-2900)*
Xytek Industries Inc ....F..... 313 838-6961
  Detroit *(G-4453)*

ENGINEERING SVCS: Industrial

Chemincon Inc ....G..... 734 439-2478
  Milan *(G-10933)*
Clarkston Control Products ....G..... 248 394-1430
  Clarkston *(G-2912)*
DTe Hankin Inc ....F..... 734 279-1831
  Petersburg *(G-12435)*
Henshaw Inc ....E..... 586 752-0700
  Romeo *(G-13629)*
International Mech Design ....E..... 248 546-5740
  Royal Oak *(G-13936)*
Leading Edge Engineering Inc ....F..... 586 786-0382
  Shelby Township *(G-14625)*
R Cushman & Associates Inc ....E..... 248 477-9900
  Livonia *(G-9904)*

ENGINEERING SVCS: Machine Tool Design

Advanced Integration Tech LP ....G..... 586 749-5525
  Chesterfield *(G-2734)*
Center Line Gage Inc ....G..... 810 387-4300
  Brockway *(G-2019)*
Enkon LLC ....F..... 937 890-5678
  Manchester *(G-10405)*
Highland Machine Design Inc ....G..... 248 669-6150
  Commerce Township *(G-3412)*
Integrity Design & Mfg LLC ....G..... 248 628-6927
  Oxford *(G-12352)*
JF Hubert Enterprises Inc ....F..... 586 293-8660
  Fraser *(G-5675)*
Metalform Industries LLC ....G..... 248 462-0056
  Shelby Township *(G-14639)*
Onyx Manufacturing Inc ....G..... 248 687-8611
  Rochester Hills *(G-13487)*
Ort Tool & Die Corporation ....D..... 419 242-9553
  Erie *(G-4807)*
Solutions For Industry Inc ....G..... 517 448-8608
  Hudson *(G-8142)*
Stonebrdge Technical Entps Ltd ....F..... 810 750-0040
  Fenton *(G-5240)*
Terrell Manufacturing Svcs Inc ....F..... 231 788-2000
  Muskegon *(G-11435)*
World Class Equipment Company ....F..... 586 331-2121
  Shelby Township *(G-14723)*

ENGINEERING SVCS: Marine

Dts Enterprises Inc ....E..... 231 599-3123
  Ellsworth *(G-4787)*

ENGINEERING SVCS: Mechanical

Backos Engineering Co ....G..... 734 513-0020
  Livonia *(G-9659)*
Competitive Edge Designs Inc ....G..... 616 257-0565
  Grand Rapids *(G-6292)*
Ford Motor Company ....E..... 313 805-5938
  Dearborn *(G-3712)*
Mahindra North American ....C..... 248 268-6600
  Auburn Hills *(G-940)*
Mahindra Vehicle Mfrs Ltd ....C..... 248 268-6600
  Auburn Hills *(G-941)*
Mor-Tech Design Inc ....E..... 586 254-7982
  Sterling Heights *(G-15427)*
Mor-Tech Manufacturing Inc ....E..... 586 254-7982
  Sterling Heights *(G-15428)*
Omni Technical Services Inc ....E..... 989 227-8900
  Saint Johns *(G-14292)*
Revealed Engineering LLC ....G..... 734 642-5551
  Carleton *(G-2461)*

ENGINEERING SVCS: Pollution Control

Dipsol of America Inc ....E..... 734 367-0530
  Livonia *(G-9713)*

ENGINEERING SVCS: Professional

Infrared Telemetrics Inc .... F 906 482-0012
  Hancock *(G-7252)*
TMC Group Inc .... F 248 819-6063
  Pleasant Ridge *(G-12556)*
Vision Global Industries .... G 248 390-5805
  Macomb *(G-10173)*

ENGINEERING SVCS: Sanitary

Douglas Steel Fabricating Corp .... D 517 322-2050
  Lansing *(G-9288)*
Stegman Tool Co Inc .... E 248 588-4634
  Troy *(G-16621)*

ENGINEERING SVCS: Structural

Composite Techniques Inc .... F 616 878-9745
  Byron Center *(G-2181)*

ENGINES & ENGINE PARTS: Guided Missile

Federal-Mogul Powertrain LLC .... E 734 930-1590
  Ann Arbor *(G-458)*
Hytrol Manufacturing Inc .... E 734 261-8030
  Jackson *(G-8468)*
Williams International Co LLC .... B 248 624-5200
  Pontiac *(G-12875)*
Williams International Co LLC .... C 248 762-8713
  Waterford *(G-17386)*

ENGINES: Diesel & Semi-Diesel Or Duel Fuel

Detroit Diesel Corporation .... A 313 592-5000
  Detroit *(G-3980)*
Detroit Diesel Corporation .... F 313 592-8256
  Redford *(G-13157)*
Double H Mfg Inc .... E 734 729-3450
  Westland *(G-17551)*
Engine Guru LLC .... G 616 430-3114
  Wyoming *(G-18000)*
FCA US LLC .... C 313 957-7000
  Detroit *(G-4054)*

ENGINES: Gasoline, NEC

Powertrain Integration LLC .... F 248 577-0010
  Madison Heights *(G-10333)*

ENGINES: Hydrojet, Marine

Pinnacle Technology Group .... D 734 568-6600
  Ottawa Lake *(G-12268)*

ENGINES: Internal Combustion, NEC

Chandas Engineering Inc .... F 313 582-8666
  Dearborn *(G-3687)*
Combat Advanced Propulsion LLC ...... G 231 724-2100
  Muskegon *(G-11297)*
Cosworth LLC .... E 586 353-5403
  Shelby Township *(G-14569)*
Creek Diesel Services Inc .... F 800 974-4600
  Grand Rapids *(G-6316)*
Cummins Bridgeway Grove Cy LLC .... G 614 604-6000
  New Hudson *(G-11535)*
Cummins Inc .... F 586 469-2010
  Clinton Township *(G-3095)*
Cummins Inc .... E 616 281-2211
  Grand Rapids *(G-6321)*
Cummins Inc .... E 313 843-6200
  Dearborn *(G-3688)*
Cummins Inc .... E 248 573-1900
  New Hudson *(G-11536)*
Cummins Inc .... F 989 732-5055
  Gaylord *(G-5854)*
Cummins Inc .... E 989 752-5200
  Saginaw *(G-14023)*
Cummins Npower LLC .... E 906 475-8800
  Negaunee *(G-11469)*
Emp Racing Inc .... G 906 786-8404
  Escanaba *(G-4825)*
Engineered Machined Pdts Inc .... B 906 786-8404
  Escanaba *(G-4826)*
Extreme Machine Inc .... D 810 231-0521
  Whitmore Lake *(G-17700)*
Fev Test Systems Inc .... G 248 373-6000
  Auburn Hills *(G-872)*
Geislinger Corporation .... F 269 441-7000
  Battle Creek *(G-1192)*
Global Fmi LLC .... D 810 964-5555
  Fenton *(G-5216)*

GM Components Holdings LLC .... E 616 246-2000
  Grand Rapids *(G-6444)*
GM Powertrain-Romulus Engine .... G 734 595-5203
  Romulus *(G-13681)*
Hdp Inc .... G 248 674-4967
  Waterford *(G-17349)*
Holbrook Racing Engines .... F 734 762-4315
  Livonia *(G-9772)*
Impco Technologies Inc .... E 586 264-1200
  Sterling Heights *(G-15370)*
K & S Property Inc .... A 248 573-1600
  New Hudson *(G-11546)*
Navarre Inc .... E 313 892-7300
  Detroit *(G-4264)*
Paice Technologies LLC .... G 248 376-1115
  Orchard Lake *(G-12168)*
Trend Performance Products .... E 586 792-6620
  Clinton Township *(G-3251)*
W W Williams Company LLC .... E 313 584-6150
  Dearborn *(G-3771)*

ENGINES: Marine

Ehc Inc .... G 313 259-2266
  Detroit *(G-4030)*

ENGINES: Steam

Elderberry Steam Engines .... G 989 245-0652
  Saginaw *(G-14034)*

ENGRAVING SVC, NEC

Bk Mattson Enterprises Inc .... G 906 774-0097
  Iron Mountain *(G-8278)*
Marking Machine Co .... F 517 767-4155
  Tekonsha *(G-15820)*
Marquee Engraving Inc .... G 810 686-7550
  Clio *(G-3275)*
Melco Engraving Inc .... G 248 656-9000
  Rochester Hills *(G-13471)*
MJB Concepts Inc .... G 616 866-1470
  Rockford *(G-13580)*
New World Etching N Amer Ve .... G 586 296-8082
  Fraser *(G-5698)*
Quality Engraving Service .... G 269 781-4822
  Marshall *(G-10586)*
Rodzina Industries Inc .... G 810 235-2341
  Flint *(G-5493)*

ENGRAVING SVC: Jewelry & Personal Goods

Bk Mattson Enterprises Inc .... G 906 774-0097
  Iron Mountain *(G-8278)*
Engrave & Graphic Inc .... G 616 245-8082
  Grand Rapids *(G-6381)*
Imagecraft .... G 517 750-0077
  Jackson *(G-8469)*
Jandron II .... G 906 225-9600
  Marquette *(G-10536)*
Jbl Enterprises .... G 616 530-8647
  Grand Rapids *(G-6555)*
Three Oaks Engraving & Engrg .... G 269 469-2124
  Three Oaks *(G-15851)*

ENGRAVING SVCS

A D Johnson Engraving Co Inc .... F 269 385-0044
  Kalamazoo *(G-8672)*
American Awards & Engrv LLC .... G 810 229-5911
  Milford *(G-10954)*
Applause Inc .... G 517 485-9880
  Lansing *(G-9338)*
Bk Mattson Enterprises Inc .... G 906 774-0097
  Iron Mountain *(G-8278)*
Garden City Products Inc .... F 269 684-6264
  Niles *(G-11614)*
M P C Awards .... G 586 254-4660
  Shelby Township *(G-14629)*
Rex M Tubbs .... G 734 459-3180
  Plymouth *(G-12735)*
Trophy Center West Michigan .... G 231 893-1686
  Whitehall *(G-17678)*
Twin City Engraving Company .... G 269 983-0601
  Saint Joseph *(G-14346)*

ENGRAVING: Steel line, For The Printing Trade

Rose Engraving Company .... G 616 243-3108
  Grand Rapids *(G-6837)*

ENGRAVINGS: Plastic

Ejs Engraving .... G 616 534-8104
  Grandville *(G-7029)*

ENTERTAINMENT PROMOTION SVCS

Pull Our Own Weight .... G 313 686-4685
  Detroit *(G-4316)*

ENTERTAINMENT SVCS

Ball Hard Music Group LLC .... G 734 636-0038
  Monroe *(G-11018)*
Intellitech Systems Inc .... G 586 219-3737
  Troy *(G-16420)*
Nationwide Network Inc .... E 989 793-0123
  Saginaw *(G-14103)*
New Genesis Enterprise Inc .... F 313 220-0365
  Westland *(G-17583)*

ENVELOPES

F M Envelope Inc .... E 313 899-4065
  Detroit *(G-4048)*
Husky Envelope Products Inc .... D 248 624-7070
  Walled Lake *(G-16895)*
Michigan Envelope Inc .... G 616 554-3404
  Grand Rapids *(G-6670)*
The Envelope Printery Inc .... D 734 398-7700
  Van Buren Twp *(G-16787)*

ENZYMES

American Farm Products Inc .... F 734 484-4180
  Saline *(G-14374)*

EPOXY RESINS

Cass Polymers .... E 517 543-7510
  Charlotte *(G-2636)*
Nano Materials & Processes Inc .... G 248 529-3873
  Milford *(G-10974)*
Pacific Epoxy Polymers Inc .... E 616 949-1634
  Grand Rapids *(G-6738)*
Resin Services Inc .... F 586 254-6770
  Sterling Heights *(G-15465)*
United Resin Inc .... E 800 521-4757
  Royal Oak *(G-13978)*

EQUIPMENT: Pedestrian Traffic Control

Em A Give Break Safety .... F 231 263-6625
  Kingsley *(G-9071)*

EQUIPMENT: Rental & Leasing, NEC

4d Building Inc .... F 248 799-7384
  Milford *(G-10952)*
Bluewater Tech Group Inc .... G 231 885-2600
  Mesick *(G-10767)*
Bluewater Tech Group Inc .... F 616 656-9380
  Grand Rapids *(G-6233)*
Boomer Company .... E 313 832-5050
  Detroit *(G-3910)*
Farber Concessions Inc .... E 313 387-1600
  Redford *(G-13161)*
GKN North America Inc .... A 248 296-7200
  Auburn Hills *(G-886)*
Global Pump Company LLC .... G 810 653-4828
  Davison *(G-3652)*
Jetech Inc .... E 269 965-6311
  Battle Creek *(G-1204)*
Jones & Hollands Inc .... G 810 364-6400
  Marysville *(G-10605)*
Leonard Fountain Spc Inc .... D 313 891-4141
  Detroit *(G-4199)*
Marketplus Software Inc .... F 269 968-4240
  Springfield *(G-15198)*
Midwest Vibro Inc .... G 616 532-7670
  Grandville *(G-7058)*
Safety-Kleen Systems Inc .... E 989 753-3261
  Saginaw *(G-14136)*
Sterling Scale Company .... G 248 358-0590
  Southfield *(G-15035)*
Visual Productions Inc .... E 248 356-4399
  Southfield *(G-15061)*

ESCALATORS: Passenger & Freight

Mitsubishi Electric Us Inc .... D 734 453-6200
  Northville *(G-11711)*

PRODUCT SECTION

ETCHING & ENGRAVING SVC

A & K Finishing Inc .... E 616 949-9100
  Grand Rapids *(G-6122)*
Baron Acquisition LLC .... G 248 585-0444
  Madison Heights *(G-10202)*
Boss Electro Static Inc .... E 616 575-0577
  Wyoming *(G-17989)*
Changeover Integration LLC .... F 231 845-5320
  Ludington *(G-10053)*
Done Right Engraving Inc .... G 248 332-3133
  Pontiac *(G-12818)*
Ejs Engraving .... G 616 534-8104
  Grandville *(G-7029)*
Exclusive Imagery Inc .... G 248 436-2999
  Royal Oak *(G-13927)*
Lacks Exterior Systems LLC .... C 616 554-3419
  Grand Rapids *(G-6599)*
Normic Industries Inc .... E 231 947-8860
  Traverse City *(G-16049)*
On The Side Sign Dsign Grphics .... G 810 266-7446
  Byron *(G-2174)*
Pro - Tech Graphics Ltd .... F 586 791-6363
  Clinton Township *(G-3206)*
West Michigan Stamp & Seal .... G 269 323-1913
  Portage *(G-13055)*
WS Molnar Co. .... E 313 923-0400
  Detroit *(G-4451)*
Yale Tool & Engraving Inc .... G 734 459-7171
  Plymouth *(G-12795)*

ETHERS

Ether LLC .... G 248 795-8830
  Ortonville *(G-12199)*

ETHYLENE-PROPYLENE RUBBERS: EPDM Polymers

Dendritech Inc .... G 989 496-1152
  Midland *(G-10830)*

EXHAUST SYSTEMS: Eqpt & Parts

Acat Global LLC .... F 231 330-2553
  Charlevoix *(G-2605)*
Benteler Automotive Corp .... A 616 245-4607
  Grand Rapids *(G-6212)*
Bosal Industries-Georgia Inc .... E 734 547-7022
  Ypsilanti *(G-18056)*
Classic Design Concepts LLC .... F 248 504-5202
  Milford *(G-10958)*
Eberspaecher North America Inc .... E 248 994-7010
  Novi *(G-11877)*
Eberspaecher North America Inc .... E 517 303-1775
  Wixom *(G-17780)*
Interntional Catalyst Tech Inc .... G 248 340-1040
  Auburn Hills *(G-914)*
Jet Industries Inc .... E 734 641-0900
  Westland *(G-17574)*
Technique Inc .... D 517 789-8988
  Jackson *(G-8585)*

EXPANSION JOINTS: Rubber

Meccom Industrial Products Co .... F 586 463-2828
  Clinton Township *(G-3172)*

EXPLOSIVES

Austin Powder Company .... F 989 595-2400
  Presque Isle *(G-13082)*
Dyno Nobel Inc .... F 906 486-4473
  Ishpeming *(G-8344)*
Pepin-Ireco Inc .... E 906 486-4473
  Ishpeming *(G-8352)*

EXPLOSIVES, EXC AMMO & FIREWORKS WHOLESALERS

Mission Critical Firearms LLC .... G 586 232-5185
  Shelby Township *(G-14641)*
Pepin-Ireco Inc .... E 906 486-4473
  Ishpeming *(G-8352)*

EXPLOSIVES: Plastic

Mission Critical Firearms LLC .... G 586 232-5185
  Shelby Township *(G-14641)*

EXTRACTS, FLAVORING

Jogue Inc .... E 734 207-0100
  Plymouth *(G-12654)*
Jogue Inc .... G 313 921-4802
  Detroit *(G-4163)*
John L Hinkle Holding Co Inc .... E 269 344-3640
  Kalamazoo *(G-8780)*
Northville Laboratories Inc .... F 248 349-1500
  Northville *(G-11716)*
Pure Herbs Ltd .... F 586 446-8200
  Sterling Heights *(G-15457)*
Watkins Products .... G 586 774-3187
  Eastpointe *(G-4712)*
Wild Flavors Inc .... E 269 216-2603
  Kalamazoo *(G-8925)*

EYEGLASSES

Dennis OBryan Od .... G 231 348-1255
  Harbor Springs *(G-7282)*

EYEGLASSES: Sunglasses

Noir Medical Technologies LLC .... E 734 769-5565
  Milford *(G-10978)*
Noir Medical Technologies LLC .... F 248 486-3760
  South Lyon *(G-14806)*

FABRIC STORES

J America Licensed Pdts Inc .... G 517 655-8800
  Fowlerville *(G-5571)*
Sassy Fabrics Inc .... G 810 694-0440
  Grand Blanc *(G-5982)*

FABRICATED METAL PRODUCTS, NEC

AAA Waterjet and Machining Inc .... G 586 759-3736
  Warren *(G-16910)*
Advanced Metal Fabricators .... G 616 570-4847
  Lowell *(G-10022)*
Arrowhead Industries Inc .... E 231 238-9366
  Afton *(G-105)*
Dag R&D .... G 248 444-0575
  Milford *(G-10959)*
Focal Point Metal Fab LLC .... G 616 844-7670
  Spring Lake *(G-15142)*
J Solutions LLC .... G 586 477-0127
  Chesterfield *(G-2792)*
Lafave Hydraulics & Metal .... G 989 872-2163
  Cass City *(G-2517)*
Magnum Fabricating .... G 734 484-5800
  Ypsilanti *(G-18087)*
Ottawa Tool & Machine LLC .... G 616 677-1743
  Grand Rapids *(G-6735)*
Proper Arospc & Machining LLC .... G 586 779-8787
  Warren *(G-17203)*
Quality Metal Fabricating .... G 616 901-5510
  Grand Rapids *(G-6799)*
Quick - Burn LLC .... G 616 402-4874
  Holland *(G-7780)*
Specialty Metal Fabricators .... G 616 698-9020
  Caledonia *(G-2316)*
Virtec Manufacturing LLC .... G 313 369-4858
  Detroit *(G-4430)*

FABRICS & CLOTH: Quilted

Quilters Garden Inc .... G 810 750-8104
  Fenton *(G-5233)*

FABRICS: Alpacas, Mohair, Woven

West Michigan Alpacas .... G 616 990-0556
  Holland *(G-7854)*

FABRICS: Apparel & Outerwear, Cotton

American Sales Co .... G 517 750-4070
  Spring Arbor *(G-15118)*
Bearcub Outfitters LLC .... F 231 439-9500
  Petoskey *(G-12441)*

FABRICS: Automotive, From Manmade Fiber

Advanced Composite Tech Inc .... G 248 709-9097
  Rochester *(G-13311)*
C & J Fabrication Inc .... G 586 791-6269
  Clinton Township *(G-3071)*
Takata Americas .... E 336 547-1600
  Auburn Hills *(G-1012)*

FABRICS: Broadwoven, Synthetic Manmade Fiber & Silk

Airhug LLC .... G 734 262-0431
  Canton *(G-2346)*
J America Licensed Pdts Inc .... G 517 655-8800
  Fowlerville *(G-5571)*
JAC Custom Pouches Inc .... E 269 782-3190
  Dowagiac *(G-4544)*
Performance Sailing Inc .... F 586 790-7500
  Clinton Township *(G-3193)*
Sassy Fabrics Inc .... G 810 694-0440
  Grand Blanc *(G-5982)*

FABRICS: Broadwoven, Wool

Stonehedge Farm .... G 231 536-2779
  East Jordan *(G-4646)*

FABRICS: Canvas

Canvas Co Inc .... G 231 276-3083
  Interlochen *(G-8238)*
Canvas Innovations LLC .... G 616 393-4400
  Holland *(G-7584)*
Carry-All Products Inc .... F 616 399-8080
  Holland *(G-7585)*
Great Lakes Canvas Co .... G 954 439-3090
  Fennville *(G-5172)*

FABRICS: Chenilles, Tufted Textile

Floracraft Corporation .... C 231 845-5127
  Ludington *(G-10059)*
G T Jerseys LLC .... G 248 588-3231
  Troy *(G-16376)*

FABRICS: Coated Or Treated

Elden Industries Corporation .... F 734 946-6900
  Taylor *(G-15715)*
Worthen Industries Inc .... E 616 742-8990
  Grand Rapids *(G-7004)*

FABRICS: Cords

Tapex American Corporation .... F 810 987-4722
  Port Huron *(G-12970)*

FABRICS: Denims

Denim Baby LLC .... G 313 539-5309
  Roseville *(G-13791)*
Detroit Denim LLC .... G 313 626-9216
  Detroit *(G-3979)*
Street Denim & Co .... G 313 837-1200
  Detroit *(G-4379)*

FABRICS: Dress, From Manmade Fiber Or Silk

Nickels Boat Works Inc .... F 810 767-4050
  Flint *(G-5472)*

FABRICS: Fiberglass, Broadwoven

Bay City Fiberglass Inc .... G 989 751-9622
  Bay City *(G-1285)*
Fulcrum Composites Inc .... G 989 636-1025
  Midland *(G-10863)*
Glassline Incorporated .... F 734 453-2728
  Plymouth *(G-12628)*
P I W Corporation .... G 989 448-2501
  Gaylord *(G-5887)*

FABRICS: Furniture Denim

Rooms of Grand Rapids LLC .... F 616 260-1452
  Spring Lake *(G-15173)*

FABRICS: Laminated

Plastatech Engineering Ltd .... D 989 754-6500
  Saginaw *(G-14123)*
Plastatech Engineering Ltd .... E 989 754-6500
  Saginaw *(G-14124)*
Shawmut Corporation .... C 810 987-2222
  Port Huron *(G-12965)*
Tpi Industries LLC .... G 810 987-2222
  Port Huron *(G-12973)*

FABRICS: Laundry, Cotton

Great Lkes Tex Restoration LLC .... G 989 448-8600
  Gaylord *(G-5861)*
Joan Arnoudse .... G 616 364-9075
  Grand Rapids *(G-6561)*

FABRICS: Luggage, Cotton

Peribambini Services LLC .... G 318 466-2881
  Plymouth *(G-12713)*

FABRICS: Metallized

APS Machine LLC .... F 906 212-5600
  Escanaba *(G-4814)*

FABRICS: Osnaburgs

D&E Incorporated .... G 313 673-3284
  Southfield *(G-14876)*

FABRICS: Resin Or Plastic Coated

Bentzer Enterprises .... G 269 663-2289
  Edwardsburg *(G-4758)*
Duro-Last Inc .... B 800 248-0280
  Saginaw *(G-14031)*
Duro-Last Inc .... D 800 248-0280
  Saginaw *(G-14032)*
Duro-Last Inc .... D 800 248-0280
  Saginaw *(G-14033)*
Haartz Corporation .... G 248 646-8200
  Bloomfield Hills *(G-1771)*
Hig Recovery Fund Inc .... G 269 435-8414
  Constantine *(G-3537)*
Mp-Tec Inc .... E 734 367-1284
  Livonia *(G-9852)*
Pioneer Plastics Inc .... E 586 262-0159
  Shelby Township *(G-14667)*
Tri-City Vinyl Inc .... E 989 401-7992
  Saginaw *(G-14167)*

FABRICS: Rubberized

PRA Company .... D 989 846-1029
  Standish *(G-15226)*

FABRICS: Scrub Cloths

Ace-Tex Enterprises Inc .... E 313 834-4000
  Detroit *(G-3839)*
Apogee Technologies Inc .... F 269 639-1616
  South Haven *(G-14754)*

FABRICS: Seat Cover, Automobile, Cotton

Simco Automotive Trim .... D 800 372-3172
  Macomb *(G-10161)*

FABRICS: Trimmings

Advance Graphic Systems Inc .... E 248 656-8000
  Rochester Hills *(G-13365)*
Advanced Composite Tech Inc .... G 248 709-9097
  Rochester *(G-13311)*
American Twisting Company .... E 269 637-8581
  South Haven *(G-14752)*
AP Impressions Inc .... G 734 464-8009
  Livonia *(G-9650)*
Applause Inc .... G 517 485-9880
  Lansing *(G-9338)*
Authority Customwear Ltd .... E 248 588-8075
  Madison Heights *(G-10199)*
Bivins Graphics .... G 616 453-2211
  Grand Rapids *(G-6226)*
Bivins Graphics .... G 616 453-2211
  Grand Rapids *(G-6227)*
Blts Wearable Art Inc .... G 517 669-9659
  Dewitt *(G-4459)*
Britten Inc .... C 231 941-8200
  Traverse City *(G-15920)*
Cadillac Prsentation Solutions .... E 248 288-9777
  Troy *(G-16255)*
Celia Corporation .... D 616 887-7341
  Sparta *(G-15091)*
Detroit Name Plate Etching Inc .... E 248 543-5200
  Ferndale *(G-5278)*
E Q R 2 Inc .... G 586 731-3383
  Sterling Heights *(G-15324)*
Fibre Converters Inc .... E 269 279-1700
  Constantine *(G-3535)*
Hexon Corporation .... F 248 585-7585
  Farmington Hills *(G-5018)*
HI-Lites Graphic Inc .... G 231 924-4540
  Fremont *(G-5776)*
Innovative Material Handling .... F 586 291-3694
  Detroit *(G-4141)*
Irvin Acquisition LLC .... F 248 451-4100
  Pontiac *(G-12837)*
Irvin Automotive Products LLC .... C 248 451-4100
  Pontiac *(G-12838)*
J America LLC .... E 517 521-2525
  Webberville *(G-17451)*
J2 Licensing Inc .... G 586 307-3400
  Troy *(G-16431)*
Janet Kelly .... F 231 775-2313
  Cadillac *(G-2256)*
Jean Smith Designs .... E 616 942-9212
  Grand Rapids *(G-6556)*
Kalamazoo Regalia Inc .... F 269 344-4299
  Kalamazoo *(G-8797)*
Kay Screen Printing Inc .... C 248 377-4999
  Lake Orion *(G-9141)*
Lacks Exterior Systems LLC .... B 616 949-6570
  Grand Rapids *(G-6605)*
Larsen Graphics Inc .... E 989 823-3000
  Vassar *(G-16812)*
Lazer Graphics .... E 269 926-1066
  Benton Harbor *(G-1522)*
Lear Corporation .... A 248 447-1500
  Mason *(G-10644)*
Lear Corporation .... B 248 447-1500
  Southfield *(G-14962)*
Logofit LLC .... E 810 715-1980
  Flint *(G-5461)*
Mackellar Associates Inc .... F 248 335-4440
  Rochester Hills *(G-13466)*
Marketing Displays Inc .... C 248 553-1900
  Farmington Hills *(G-5058)*
Michael Anderson .... G 231 652-5717
  Newaygo *(G-11575)*
Mid-Michigan Industries Inc .... D 989 773-6918
  Mount Pleasant *(G-11208)*
Mid-Michigan Industries Inc .... E 989 386-7707
  Clare *(G-2877)*
Nalcor LLC .... D 248 541-1140
  Ferndale *(G-5303)*
Neighborhood Artisans Inc .... G 313 865-5373
  Detroit *(G-4265)*
Nobby Inc .... E 810 984-3300
  Fort Gratiot *(G-5550)*
Perrin Souvenir Distrs Inc .... B 616 785-9700
  Comstock Park *(G-3508)*
Plasti-Fab Inc .... E 248 543-1415
  Ferndale *(G-5311)*
Qmi Group Inc .... E 248 589-0505
  Madison Heights *(G-10342)*
Regents Of The University Mich .... E 734 764-6230
  Ann Arbor *(G-615)*
Rtlf-Hope LLC .... E 313 538-1700
  Detroit *(G-4349)*
Sign Screen Inc .... G 810 239-1100
  Flint *(G-5499)*
Srg Global Inc .... C 248 509-1100
  Troy *(G-16617)*
Srg Global Inc .... F 586 757-7800
  Taylor *(G-15772)*
Strattec Power Access LLC .... F 248 649-9742
  Auburn Hills *(G-1004)*
Tempro Industries Inc .... F 734 451-5900
  Plymouth *(G-12768)*
Timbertech Inc .... E 231 348-2750
  Harbor Springs *(G-7295)*
Twin City Engraving Company .... G 269 983-0601
  Saint Joseph *(G-14346)*
V&R Enterprize .... G 313 837-5545
  Detroit *(G-4420)*
Vomela Specialty Company .... E 269 927-6500
  Benton Harbor *(G-1562)*
Wec Group LLC .... F 248 260-4252
  Rochester Hills *(G-13546)*
Yanfeng USA Automotive Trim Sy ...... D 586 354-2101
  Harrison Township *(G-7359)*

FABRICS: Upholstery, Cotton

American Soft Trim Inc .... E 989 681-0037
  Saint Louis *(G-14357)*

FABRICS: Window Shade, Cotton

Allender & Company .... G 248 398-5776
  Ferndale *(G-5258)*

FABRICS: Woven Wire, Made From Purchased Wire

Fabric Patch Ltd .... G 906 932-5260
  Ironwood *(G-8328)*

FABRICS: Woven, Narrow Cotton, Wool, Silk

Car-Min-Vu Farm .... G 517 749-9112
  Webberville *(G-17447)*
Rhino Products Inc .... F 269 674-8309
  Lawrence *(G-9507)*
Sistahs Braid Too .... G 248 552-6202
  Southfield *(G-15029)*

FACILITIES SUPPORT SVCS

Dynamic Corporation .... D 616 399-9391
  Holland *(G-7613)*
Guelph Tool Sales Inc .... B 586 755-3333
  Warren *(G-17071)*
Quality Engineering Company .... F 248 351-9000
  Wixom *(G-17883)*

FAMILY CLOTHING STORES

Gerald Froberg .... G 906 346-3311
  Gwinn *(G-7219)*
Sports Inc .... G 734 728-1313
  Wayne *(G-17443)*

FANS, BLOWING: Indl Or Commercial

Entrepreneurial Pursuits .... G 248 829-6903
  Rochester Hills *(G-13418)*
Skyblade Fan Company .... G 586 806-5107
  Warren *(G-17240)*
Thermo Vac Inc .... D 248 969-0300
  Oxford *(G-12375)*

FANS, VENTILATING: Indl Or Commercial

Airmaster Fan Company .... D 517 764-2300
  Clarklake *(G-2894)*
Clean Rooms International Inc .... E 616 452-8700
  Grand Rapids *(G-6278)*

FARM & GARDEN MACHINERY WHOLESALERS

Jones & Hollands Inc .... G 810 364-6400
  Marysville *(G-10605)*

FARM PRDTS, RAW MATERIALS, WHOLESALE: Skins

Berry & Sons-Rababeh .... G 313 259-6925
  Detroit *(G-3901)*

FARM SPLY STORES

Corunna Mills Feed LLC .... G 989 743-3110
  Corunna *(G-3580)*

FARM SPLYS WHOLESALERS

Andersons Inc .... G 989 642-5291
  Hemlock *(G-7459)*

FARM SPLYS, WHOLESALE: Feed

Active Feed Company .... D 989 453-2472
  Pigeon *(G-12485)*

FARM SPLYS, WHOLESALE: Fertilizers & Agricultural Chemicals

Chippewa Farm Supply LLC .... G 989 471-5523
  Spruce *(G-15213)*
Ittner Bean & Grain Inc .... F 989 662-4461
  Auburn *(G-753)*

FARM SPLYS, WHOLESALE: Flower & Field Bulbs

Veldheer Tulip Garden Inc .... D 616 399-1900
  Holland *(G-7844)*

FARM SPLYS, WHOLESALE: Garden Splys

Interntonal Innovative Systems .... G 248 524-2222
  Troy *(G-16421)*

FASTENERS WHOLESALERS

Elkay Industries Inc .... F 269 381-4266
  Kalamazoo *(G-8735)*
Mid-States Bolt & Screw Co .... F 989 732-3265
  Gaylord *(G-5883)*
ND Industries Inc .... C 248 288-0000
  Clawson *(G-2982)*
ND Industries Inc .... E 248 288-0000
  Troy *(G-16522)*
Warren Screw Works Inc .... G 734 525-2920
  Livonia *(G-9998)*

FASTENERS: Brads, Alum, Brass/Other Nonferrous Metal/Wire

Mueller Brass Co .... E 616 794-1200
  Belding *(G-1426)*
Revwires LLC .... G 269 683-8100
  Niles *(G-11643)*

FASTENERS: Metal

Arch Global Precision LLC .... F 734 266-6900
  Bloomfield Hills *(G-1747)*
Cox Industries Inc .... F 586 749-6650
  Chesterfield *(G-2756)*
Lisi Automotive HI Vol Inc .... F 734 266-6958
  Livonia *(G-9812)*
Nitto Seiko Co Ltd .... E 248 588-0133
  Troy *(G-16525)*
Nylok LLC .... G 586 786-0100
  Macomb *(G-10149)*
Tapex American Corporation .... F 810 987-4722
  Port Huron *(G-12970)*

FASTENERS: Metal

Bauer Products Inc .... E 616 245-4540
  Grand Rapids *(G-6207)*
Caillau Usa Inc .... G 248 446-1900
  Brighton *(G-1896)*
Consort Corporation .... E 269 388-4532
  Kalamazoo *(G-8713)*
Flexible Steel Lacing Company .... D 616 459-3196
  Grand Rapids *(G-6413)*
Jay Cee Sales & Rivet Inc .... F 248 478-2150
  Farmington *(G-4901)*
Penn Automotive Inc .... B 248 599-3700
  Waterford *(G-17366)*
Penn Engineering & Mfg Corp .... B 313 299-8500
  Waterford *(G-17367)*
Rayomar Enterprises Inc .... G 313 415-9102
  Warren *(G-17217)*
Shark Tool & Die Inc .... G 586 749-7400
  Chesterfield *(G-2839)*

FASTENERS: Notions, NEC

A Raymond Tinnerman Mexico .... G 248 537-3404
  Rochester Hills *(G-13361)*
Acument Global Tech Inc .... E 586 254-3900
  Sterling Heights *(G-15252)*
Baker Fastening Systems Inc .... G 616 669-7400
  Hudsonville *(G-8147)*
Decoties Inc .... G 906 285-1286
  Bessemer *(G-1604)*
Elkay Industries Inc .... F 269 381-4266
  Kalamazoo *(G-8735)*
Fas N Nedschroef Amer Inc .... G 586 795-1220
  Sterling Heights *(G-15336)*
Fourslides Inc .... F 313 564-5600
  Chesterfield *(G-2779)*
Ortus Enterprises LLC .... G 269 491-1447
  Portage *(G-13020)*
Penn Automotive Inc .... B 248 599-3700
  Waterford *(G-17366)*
Penn Engineering & Mfg Corp .... B 313 299-8500
  Waterford *(G-17367)*
Rayomar Enterprises Inc .... G 313 415-9102
  Warren *(G-17217)*
Rodenhouse Inc .... G 616 454-3100
  Grand Rapids *(G-6834)*
Scs Fasteners LLC .... G 586 563-0865
  Eastpointe *(G-4709)*
Universal Components LLC .... G 517 861-7064
  Howell *(G-8119)*

FASTENERS: Wire, Made From Purchased Wire

King Hughes Fasteners Inc .... E 810 721-0300
  Imlay City *(G-8206)*

FAUCETS & SPIGOTS: Metal & Plastic

American Beverage Equipment Co .... E 586 773-0094
  Roseville *(G-13772)*
Epic Fine Arts Company Inc .... G 313 274-7400
  Taylor *(G-15716)*
Masco Corporation .... A 313 274-7400
  Livonia *(G-9826)*

FELT, WHOLESALE

Michigan Diversfd Holdings Inc .... F 248 280-0450
  Madison Heights *(G-10305)*

FELT: Acoustic

Acoufelt LLC .... G 800 966-8557
  Clawson *(G-2969)*
Auto Tex .... G 248 340-0844
  Auburn Hills *(G-783)*

FENCES & FENCING MATERIALS

Merchants Metals Inc .... E 810 227-3036
  Howell *(G-8061)*
Robinson Fence Co Inc .... G 906 647-3301
  Pickford *(G-12483)*
Royal Aluminum and Steel Inc .... F 586 421-0057
  Chesterfield *(G-2833)*

FENCES OR POSTS: Ornamental Iron Or Steel

Bradys Fence Company Inc .... G 313 492-8804
  South Rockwood *(G-14820)*

FENCING DEALERS

Apple Fence Co .... F 231 276-9888
  Grawn *(G-7097)*
Contractors Fence Service .... E 313 592-1300
  Detroit *(G-3947)*
Nevill Supply Incorporated .... G 989 386-4522
  Clare *(G-2879)*

FENCING MATERIALS: Docks & Other Outdoor Prdts, Wood

Heath Manufacturing Company .... D 616 997-8181
  Coopersville *(G-3561)*
Mark Beem .... G 231 510-8122
  Lake City *(G-9092)*

FENCING MATERIALS: Plastic

Bradys Fence Company Inc .... G 313 492-8804
  South Rockwood *(G-14820)*
Universal Consumer Pdts Inc .... D 616 365-4201
  White Pigeon *(G-17656)*

FENCING MATERIALS: Snow Fence, Wood

Nevill Supply Incorporated .... G 989 386-4522
  Clare *(G-2879)*

FENCING MATERIALS: Wood

Apple Fence Co .... F 231 276-9888
  Grawn *(G-7097)*
Cherry Creek Post LLC .... G 231 734-2466
  Evart *(G-4880)*
Contractors Fence Service .... E 313 592-1300
  Detroit *(G-3947)*
Maine Ornamental LLC .... F 800 556-8449
  White Pigeon *(G-17652)*
Newberry Wood Enterprises Inc .... F 906 293-3131
  Newberry *(G-11585)*
Rapid River Rustic Inc .... E 906 474-6404
  Rapid River *(G-13114)*
Ufp Lansing LLC .... F 517 322-0025
  Lansing *(G-9328)*

FENCING: Chain Link

Metter Flooring LLC .... G 517 914-2004
  Rives Junction *(G-13309)*

FENDERS: Automobile, Stamped Or Pressed Metal

Dst Industries Inc .... C 734 941-0300
  Romulus *(G-13667)*
Schwab Industries Inc .... C 586 566-8090
  Shelby Township *(G-14688)*

FERROTITANIUM

Kena Corporation .... G 586 873-4761
  Chesterfield *(G-2795)*

FERTILIZER, AGRICULTURAL: Wholesalers

Star of West Milling Company .... D 989 652-9971
  Frankenmuth *(G-5596)*

FERTILIZERS: NEC

Bay-Houston Towing Company .... E 810 648-2210
  Sandusky *(G-14430)*
Cog Marketers Ltd .... F 434 455-3209
  Ashley *(G-727)*
Cog Marketers Ltd .... F 989 224-4117
  Saint Johns *(G-14281)*
Hydrodynamics International .... G 517 887-2007
  Lansing *(G-9383)*
Hyponex Corporation .... E 810 724-2875
  Imlay City *(G-8202)*
Markham Peat Corp .... F 800 851-7230
  Lakeview *(G-9175)*
Michigan Grower Products Inc .... F 269 665-7071
  Galesburg *(G-5813)*
Nutrien AG Solutions Inc .... G 989 842-1185
  Breckenridge *(G-1844)*

FERTILIZERS: Nitrogenous

Harmony Products .... G 906 387-5411
  Munising *(G-11243)*

FERTILIZERS: Phosphatic

Andersons Inc .... G 989 642-5291
  Hemlock *(G-7459)*
Cog Marketers Ltd .... E 989 224-4117
  Saint Johns *(G-14280)*

FIBER & FIBER PRDTS: Acrylic

Cytec Industries Inc .... C 269 349-6677
  Kalamazoo *(G-8722)*

FIBER & FIBER PRDTS: Anidex

ABC Nails LLC .... G 616 776-6000
  Grand Rapids *(G-6129)*

FIBER & FIBER PRDTS: Organic, Noncellulose

Dal-Tile Corporation .... F 248 471-7150
  Farmington Hills *(G-4968)*
Solutia Inc .... B 734 676-4400
  Trenton *(G-16157)*

FIBER & FIBER PRDTS: Protein

Protein Procurement Svcs Inc .... G 248 738-7970
  Bloomfield Hills *(G-1792)*

FIBER & FIBER PRDTS: Synthetic Cellulosic

Applegate Insul Systems Inc .... E 517 521-3545
  Webberville *(G-17446)*
J Rettenmaier USA LP .... C 269 679-2340
  Schoolcraft *(G-14497)*
Kraig Biocraft Labs Inc .... G 734 619-8066
  Ann Arbor *(G-520)*

FIBERS: Carbon & Graphite

Acp Technologies LLC .... G 586 322-3511
  Sterling Heights *(G-15251)*
Fortress Stblztion Systems LLC .... G 616 355-1421
  Holland *(G-7636)*
Sankuer Composite Tech Inc .... F 586 264-1880
  Sterling Heights *(G-15484)*

FIGURES, WAX

Studio One Midwest Inc .... F 269 962-3475
  Battle Creek *(G-1255)*

FILE FOLDERS

Nu-Fold Inc .... F 313 898-4695
Detroit *(G-4279)*

FILLERS & SEALERS: Wood

Conway-Cleveland Corp .... G 616 458-0056
Grand Rapids *(G-6309)*

FILM & SHEET: Unsuppported Plastic

Berry Global Inc .... C 269 435-2425
Constantine *(G-3532)*
Cadillac Products Inc .... D 989 766-2294
Rogers City *(G-13613)*
Corotech Acquisition Co .... F 616 456-5557
Grand Rapids *(G-6312)*
Dow Chemical Company .... D 989 636-0540
Midland *(G-10845)*
Durakon Industries Inc .... G 608 742-5301
Lapeer *(G-9457)*
Encore Commercial Products Inc .... F 248 354-4090
Farmington Hills *(G-4986)*
Filcon Inc .... F 989 386-2986
Clare *(G-2870)*
Great Lakes Containment Inc .... F 231 258-8800
Kalkaska *(G-8943)*
Kraft-Wrap Inc .... F 586 755-2050
Warren *(G-17121)*
Loose Plastics Inc .... C 989 246-1880
Gladwin *(G-5933)*
Quality Transparent Bag Inc .... F 989 893-3561
Bay City *(G-1344)*
Zenith Global LLC .... G 517 546-7402
Howell *(G-8123)*

FILM DEVELOPING & PRINTING SVCS

P D Q Press Inc .... G 586 725-1888
Ira *(G-8265)*

FILTER ELEMENTS: Fluid & Hydraulic Line

Bulldog Fabricating Corp .... G 734 761-3111
Ann Arbor *(G-392)*
Flodraulic Group Incorporated .... D 734 326-5400
Westland *(G-17558)*
Hydraulic Systems Inc .... E 517 787-7818
Jackson *(G-8467)*
Parker-Hannifin Corporation .... D 330 253-5239
Otsego *(G-12251)*

FILTERS

Acme Mills Company .... E 517 437-8940
Hillsdale *(G-7514)*
Acme Mills Company .... G 800 521-8585
Bloomfield Hills *(G-1741)*
Advanced Recovery Tech Corp .... F 231 788-2911
Nunica *(G-12031)*
Boulding Filtration Co LLC .... G 313 300-2388
Detroit *(G-3911)*
Bratten Enterprises Inc .... D 248 427-9090
Farmington Hills *(G-4946)*
Buhler Technologies LLC .... F 248 652-1546
Rochester Hills *(G-13379)*
D B Tool Company Inc .... G 989 453-2429
Pigeon *(G-12488)*
Duperon Corporation .... D 800 383-8479
Saginaw *(G-14030)*
Fergin & Associates Inc .... G 906 477-0040
Engadine *(G-4798)*
Filtra-Systems Company LLC .... F 248 427-9090
Farmington Hills *(G-5001)*
Harloff Manufacturing Co LLC .... G 269 655-1097
Paw Paw *(G-12405)*
Kdf Fluid Treatment Inc .... G 269 273-3300
Three Rivers *(G-15868)*
Lampco Industries Inc .... G 517 783-3414
Jackson *(G-8494)*
Mahle Powertrain .... E 248 473-6511
Farmington Hills *(G-5055)*
Millennium Planet LLC .... G 248 835-2331
Farmington Hills *(G-5068)*
Muskegon Heights Water Filter ...... G 231 780-3415
Norton Shores *(G-11777)*
Ohio Transmission Corporation ...... E 616 784-3228
Belmont *(G-1469)*
Petter Investments Inc .... F 269 637-1997
South Haven *(G-14767)*
REB Research & Consulting Co ...... G 248 545-0155
Oak Park *(G-12092)*
REB Research & Consulting Co ...... G 248 547-7942
Detroit *(G-3821)*
Wal Fuel Systems (usa) Inc .... G 248 579-4147
Livonia *(G-9994)*
Wayne Wire Cloth Products Inc ..... C 989 742-4591
Hillman *(G-7510)*

FILTERS & SOFTENERS: Water, Household

Bauer Soft Water Co .... G 269 695-7900
Niles *(G-11596)*
Doulton & Co .... G 248 258-6977
Southfield *(G-14886)*
Environmental Resources .... G 248 446-9639
New Hudson *(G-11540)*
Lane Soft Water .... G 269 673-3272
Allegan *(G-175)*
Lincoln-Remi Group LLC .... G 248 255-0200
Commerce Township *(G-3421)*
McIntyre Softwater Service .... E 810 735-5778
Linden *(G-9593)*
Michigan Soft Water of Centr .... D 517 339-0722
East Lansing *(G-4669)*
Plymouth Technology Inc .... F 248 537-0081
Rochester Hills *(G-13496)*

FILTERS & STRAINERS: Pipeline

Barbron Corporation .... E 586 716-3530
Kalkaska *(G-8937)*
Beswick Corporation .... F 248 589-0562
Troy *(G-16239)*
Everest Energy Fund L L C .... G 586 445-2300
Warren *(G-17023)*
Microphoto Incorporated .... E 586 772-1999
Roseville *(G-13835)*
William Shaw Inc .... F 231 536-3569
Traverse City *(G-16146)*

FILTERS: Air

Aero Filter Inc .... E 248 837-4100
Madison Heights *(G-10183)*
Air Filter & Equipment Inc .... G 734 261-1860
Livonia *(G-9632)*
American Cooling Systems LLC ..... E 616 954-0280
Grand Rapids *(G-6165)*
Complete Filtration Inc .... F 248 693-0500
Lake Orion *(G-9132)*
D-Mark Inc .... E 586 949-3610
Mount Clemens *(G-11128)*
General Filters Inc .... E 248 476-5100
Novi *(G-11890)*
SER Inc .... E 586 725-0192
New Baltimore *(G-11492)*
Tri-Dim Filter Corporation .... F 734 229-0877
Van Buren Twp *(G-16788)*

FILTERS: Air Intake, Internal Combustion Engine, Exc Auto

Engineered Machined Pdts Inc .... B 906 786-8404
Escanaba *(G-4826)*
Esco Group Inc .... G 616 453-5458
Grand Rapids *(G-6385)*
Ronal Industries Inc .... F 248 616-9691
Sterling Heights *(G-15478)*
Superb Machine Repair Inc .... F 586 749-8800
New Haven *(G-11527)*

FILTERS: General Line, Indl

Flow Ezy Filters Inc .... F 734 665-8777
Ann Arbor *(G-463)*
Gelman Sciences Inc .... A 734 665-0651
Ann Arbor *(G-469)*
Hoff Engineering Co Inc .... G 248 969-8272
Oxford *(G-12349)*
Hoffmann Filter Corporation .... F 248 486-8430
Brighton *(G-1939)*
Jomesa North America Inc .... G 248 457-0023
Troy *(G-16440)*
K and J Absorbent Products LLC ... G 517 486-3110
Blissfield *(G-1716)*
Kaydon Corporation .... B 734 747-7025
Ann Arbor *(G-516)*
Ntz Micro Filtration LLC .... F 248 449-8700
Wixom *(G-11870)*
Nu-ERA Holdings Inc .... E 810 794-4935
Clay *(G-3000)*
Pittsfield Products Inc .... E 734 665-3771
Ann Arbor *(G-593)*
Quality Filters Inc .... F 734 668-0211
Ann Arbor *(G-611)*
Recco Products Inc .... E 269 792-2243
Wayland *(G-17410)*
Rosedale Products Inc .... D 734 665-8201
Ann Arbor *(G-624)*
United Fbrcnts Strainrite Corp .... E 800 487-3136
Pontiac *(G-12873)*

FILTERS: Motor Vehicle

ABC Precision Machining Inc .... G 269 926-6322
Benton Harbor *(G-1478)*
Champion Laboratories Inc .... D 586 247-9044
Shelby Township *(G-14561)*
Cusolar Industries Inc .... E 586 949-3880
Chesterfield *(G-2757)*
Hengst of North America Inc .... G 586 757-2995
Novi *(G-11899)*
Hoff Engineering Co Inc .... G 248 969-8272
Oxford *(G-12349)*
M&M Mfg Inc .... G 248 356-6543
Southfield *(G-14972)*
TI Automotive LLC .... C 248 494-5000
Auburn Hills *(G-1020)*
Ufi Filters Usa Inc .... G 248 376-0441
Troy *(G-16661)*
Ufi Filters Usa Inc .... F 248 376-0441
Troy *(G-16662)*
Uncle Eds Oil Shoppes Inc .... G 248 288-4738
Clawson *(G-2988)*

FILTERS: Oil, Internal Combustion Engine, Exc Auto

Hudson Industries Inc .... G 800 459-1077
Warren *(G-17082)*
Rex Materials Inc .... E 517 223-3787
Howell *(G-8092)*
Viking Oil LLC .... G 989 366-4772
Prudenville *(G-13086)*

FILTRATION DEVICES: Electronic

Ecoclean Inc .... C 248 450-2000
Southfield *(G-14897)*
Innovative Air Management LLC .... G 586 201-3513
Highland *(G-7495)*
La Solucion Corp .... G 313 893-9760
Detroit *(G-4188)*
Ntf Manufacturing Usa LLC .... F 989 739-8560
Oscoda *(G-12215)*
Trucent Inc .... G 734 426-9015
Dexter *(G-4515)*
Trucent Separation Tech LLC .... D 734 426-9015
Dexter *(G-4516)*

FILTRATION SAND MINING

Barnes International .... G 586 978-2880
Sterling Heights *(G-15272)*

FINANCIAL INVESTMENT ADVICE

Batts Group Ltd .... G 616 956-3053
Grand Rapids *(G-6206)*

FINANCIAL SVCS

Joyce Zahradnik .... G 616 874-3350
Rockford *(G-13574)*
Totle Inc .... G 248 645-1111
Birmingham *(G-1706)*

FINDINGS & TRIMMINGS: Fabric

AGM Automotive LLC .... D 248 776-0600
Farmington Hills *(G-4923)*
Automotive Trim Technologies .... E 734 947-0344
Taylor *(G-15691)*
Canadian Amrcn Rstoration Sups ... E 248 853-8900
Rochester Hills *(G-13384)*
Cni Enterprises Inc .... G 248 586-3300
Madison Heights *(G-10212)*
Cni-Owosso LLC .... G 248 586-3300
Madison Heights *(G-10213)*
Eissmann Auto Port Huron LLC ..... C 810 216-6300
Port Huron *(G-12916)*
Eissmann Auto Port Huron LLC ..... E 248 829-4990
Rochester Hills *(G-13416)*
Futuris Automotive (us) Inc .... E 248 439-7800
Oak Park *(G-12069)*

PRODUCT SECTION — FIXTURES & EQPT: Kitchen, Metal, Exc Cast Aluminum

Futuris Global Holdings LLC ....D....... 248 439-7800
Oak Park *(G-12070)*
Gst Autoleather Inc ....F....... 248 436-2300
Rochester Hills *(G-13436)*
Hayes-Albion Corporation ....F....... 517 629-2141
Jackson *(G-8463)*
Inplast Interior Tech LLC ....G....... 810 724-3500
Almont *(G-258)*
International Automotive Compo ....B....... 810 987-8500
Port Huron *(G-12930)*
Lacks Industries Inc ....C....... 616 698-9852
Grand Rapids *(G-6609)*
Peckham Vocational Inds Inc................A....... 517 316-4000
Lansing *(G-9252)*
Peckham Vocational Inds Inc................C....... 517 316-4478
Lansing *(G-9253)*
Takata Americas ....E....... 336 547-1600
Auburn Hills *(G-1012)*
Tesca Usa Inc ....E....... 586 991-0744
Rochester Hills *(G-13524)*
Universal Trim Inc ....E....... 248 586-3300
Madison Heights *(G-10374)*

FINDINGS & TRIMMINGS: Furniture, Fabric

Tennant & Associates Inc.....................G....... 248 643-6140
Troy *(G-16636)*

FINGERNAILS, ARTIFICIAL

Sheba Professional Nail Pdts ....G....... 313 291-8010
Dearborn Heights *(G-3796)*

FIRE ALARM MAINTENANCE & MONITORING SVCS

Gallagher Fire Equipment Co ....E....... 248 477-1540
Livonia *(G-9748)*

FIRE ARMS, SMALL: Guns Or Gun Parts, 30 mm & Below

AB Weapons Division Inc......................G....... 616 696-2008
Cedar Springs *(G-2544)*
Manly Innovations LLC.........................G....... 734 548-0200
Chelsea *(G-2716)*
Marbles Gun Sights Inc ....G....... 906 428-3710
Gladstone *(G-5916)*
Pierce Engineers Inc.............................G....... 517 321-5051
Lansing *(G-9255)*
Sbn Enterprises LLC ....G....... 586 839-4782
Bruce Twp *(G-2098)*

FIRE ARMS, SMALL: Pellet & BB guns

Kirtland Products LLC...........................F....... 231 582-7505
Boyne City *(G-1826)*

FIRE ARMS, SMALL: Pistols Or Pistol Parts, 30 mm & below

Olivo LLC...G....... 313 573-7202
Lincoln Park *(G-9582)*

FIRE ARMS, SMALL: Shotguns Or Shotgun Parts, 30 mm & Below

Crl Inc..E....... 906 428-3710
Gladstone *(G-5910)*

FIRE CONTROL OR BOMBING EQPT: Electronic

Fire Equipment Company ....E....... 313 891-3164
Detroit *(G-4059)*

FIRE EXTINGUISHER CHARGES

Ernie Romanco......................................E....... 517 531-3686
Albion *(G-123)*

FIRE EXTINGUISHER SVC

Fire Equipment Company ....E....... 313 891-3164
Detroit *(G-4059)*
Gallagher Fire Equipment Co ....E....... 248 477-1540
Livonia *(G-9748)*

FIRE EXTINGUISHERS, WHOLESALE

Exquise Inc..G....... 248 220-9048
Detroit *(G-4047)*

FIRE EXTINGUISHERS: Portable

Exquise Inc..G....... 248 220-9048
Detroit *(G-4047)*
Kidde Safety ....G....... 800 880-6788
Novi *(G-11915)*
Product Resource Company.................G....... 517 484-8400
Lansing *(G-9261)*

FIRE OR BURGLARY RESISTIVE PRDTS

A & S Enterprises LLC..........................G....... 906 482-9007
Laurium *(G-9502)*
Ace Controls Inc ....C....... 248 476-0213
Farmington Hills *(G-4919)*
Campbell & Shaw Steel Inc..................F....... 810 364-5100
Marysville *(G-10600)*
Fab-Alloy Company ....G....... 517 787-4313
Jackson *(G-8447)*
Jokab Safety North America Inc...........F....... 888 282-2123
Westland *(G-17575)*
Northwoods Manufacturing Inc.............D....... 906 779-2370
Kingsford *(G-9065)*
Prs Manufacturing Inc...........................G....... 616 784-4409
Grand Rapids *(G-6794)*
Synchronous Manufacturing Inc...........E....... 517 764-6930
Michigan Center *(G-10791)*
Tpi Powder Metallurgy Inc ....D....... 989 865-9921
Saint Charles *(G-14203)*
Van Dyken Mechanical Inc ....D....... 616 224-7030
Grandville *(G-7075)*
Viking Corporation.................................B....... 269 945-9501
Hastings *(G-7428)*
Viking Fabrication Svcs LLC ....B....... 269 945-9501
Hastings *(G-7429)*

FIRE PROTECTION EQPT

First Due Fire Supply Company ....G....... 517 969-3065
Mason *(G-10638)*
Front Line Services Inc ....F....... 989 695-6633
Freeland *(G-5757)*
New 9 Inc ....E....... 616 459-8274
Grand Rapids *(G-6715)*
Norman Township..................................E....... 231 848-4495
Wellston *(G-17463)*

FIRE PROTECTION SVCS: Contracted

Fire Safety Displays Co ....G....... 313 274-7888
Dearborn Heights *(G-3785)*
Invent Detroit R&D Collaborati ....G....... 313 451-2658
Detroit *(G-4147)*

FIRE PROTECTION, EXC CONTRACT

Township of Saline ....F....... 734 429-4440
Saline *(G-14418)*

FIREARMS: Small, 30mm or Less

Aerospace America Inc ....E....... 989 684-2121
Bay City *(G-1273)*
Combat Action LLC ....G....... 810 772-3758
Brighton *(G-1900)*
Sage International Limited ....F....... 989 739-7000
Oscoda *(G-12220)*

FIREPLACE & CHIMNEY MATERIAL: Concrete

Espinoza Bros.......................................G....... 313 468-7775
Detroit *(G-4041)*
Premier Fireplace Co LLC ....G....... 586 949-4315
Macomb *(G-10156)*

FIREPLACE EQPT & ACCESS

Custom Fireplace Doors Inc.................F....... 248 673-3121
Waterford *(G-17330)*
Doctor Flue Inc......................................G....... 517 423-2832
Tecumseh *(G-15790)*
Flue Sentinel LLC..................................E....... 586 739-4373
Shelby Township *(G-14594)*
Hearth-N-Home Inc ....G....... 517 625-5586
Owosso *(G-12295)*

FIREWOOD, WHOLESALE

Great Lakes Log & Firewd Co...............G....... 231 206-4073
Twin Lake *(G-16712)*
Triple Ddd Firewood ....G....... 231 734-5215
Evart *(G-4887)*

FIREWORKS

Bay City Fireworks Festival ....G....... 989 892-2264
Bay City *(G-1286)*
Morin Fireworks ....G....... 906 353-6650
Baraga *(G-1110)*
Patriot Pyrotechnics ....G....... 989 831-7788
Sheridan *(G-14733)*
St Evans Inc..G....... 269 663-6100
Edwardsburg *(G-4772)*

FIREWORKS SHOPS

Morin Fireworks ....G....... 906 353-6650
Baraga *(G-1110)*

FISH & SEAFOOD PROCESSORS: Fresh Or Frozen

Collins Caviar Company........................G....... 269 469-4576
Union Pier *(G-16737)*
Ruleau Brothers Inc ....E....... 906 753-4767
Stephenson *(G-15240)*
Sea Fare Foods Inc ....E....... 313 568-0223
Detroit *(G-4357)*

FISH FOOD

Big Jon Sports Inc.................................G....... 231 275-1010
Interlochen *(G-8236)*
Hatfield Enterprises ....G....... 616 677-5215
Marne *(G-10508)*
Mac Baits ....G....... 616 392-2553
Holland *(G-7730)*

FISHING EQPT: Lures

Bay De Noc Lure Company ....F....... 906 428-1133
Gladstone *(G-5906)*

FISHING EQPT: Nets & Seines

Mason Tackle Company ....E....... 810 631-4571
Otisville *(G-12233)*

FITTINGS & ASSEMBLIES: Hose & Tube, Hydraulic Or Pneumatic

Austin Tube Products Inc ....E....... 231 745-2741
Baldwin *(G-1082)*
Burgaflex North America LLC...............E....... 810 714-3285
Fenton *(G-5192)*
Central Industrial Corporation...............G....... 616 784-9612
Grand Rapids *(G-6267)*
Kord Industrial Inc ....G....... 248 374-8900
Wixom *(G-17843)*
Loryco Inc..G....... 248 674-4673
Pontiac *(G-12845)*
Spiral Industries Inc..............................E....... 810 632-6300
Howell *(G-8101)*

FITTINGS & SPECIALTIES: Steam

Kadant Johnson LLC.............................C....... 269 278-1715
Three Rivers *(G-15867)*

FITTINGS: Pipe

Creform Corporation ....F....... 248 926-2555
Novi *(G-11858)*
Metro Piping Inc....................................F....... 313 872-4330
Detroit *(G-4231)*
Parker-Hannifin Corporation.................C....... 517 694-0491
Mason *(G-10651)*
Perfection Sprinkler Company ....G....... 734 761-5110
Ann Arbor *(G-590)*
Piper Industries Inc...............................D....... 586 771-5100
Roseville *(G-13855)*

FITTINGS: Pipe, Fabricated

Ferguson Enterprises Inc.....................E....... 989 790-2220
Saginaw *(G-14037)*
Hosco Inc...F....... 248 912-1750
Wixom *(G-17828)*

FIXTURES & EQPT: Kitchen, Metal, Exc Cast Aluminum

Duquaine Incorporated..........................G....... 906 228-7290
Marquette *(G-10527)*

FIXTURES & EQPT: Kitchen, Porcelain Enameled

New Line Inc .... G 586 228-4820
  Shelby Township *(G-14652)*

FIXTURES: Bank, Metal, Ornamental

Arnold & Sautter Co .... F 989 684-7557
  Bay City *(G-1276)*

FIXTURES: Cut Stone

Marbelite Corp .... E 248 348-1900
  Novi *(G-11934)*
Marblecast of Michigan Inc .... F 248 398-0600
  Oak Park *(G-12081)*

FLAGS: Fabric

American Flag & Banner Company .... G 248 288-3010
  Clawson *(G-2972)*
Bay Supply & Marketing Inc .... G 231 943-3249
  Traverse City *(G-15908)*
Spartan Flag Company Inc .... F 231 386-5150
  Northport *(G-11672)*

FLAKEBOARD

Arauco North America Inc .... C 800 261-4896
  Grayling *(G-7103)*
Norbord Panels USA Inc .... A 248 608-0387
  Rochester *(G-13336)*

FLAT GLASS: Building

Furniture City Glass Corp .... E 616 784-5500
  Grand Rapids *(G-6425)*
Johnson Glass Cleaning Inc .... G 906 361-0361
  Negaunee *(G-11471)*

FLAT GLASS: Construction

I2 International Dev LLC .... F 616 534-8100
  Grandville *(G-7050)*
Pilkington North America Inc .... B 269 687-2100
  Niles *(G-11640)*

FLAT GLASS: Laminated

Magna International Amer Inc .... G 616 786-7000
  Holland *(G-7733)*

FLAT GLASS: Plate, Polished & Rough

Guardian Fabrication LLC .... G 248 340-1800
  Auburn Hills *(G-892)*

FLAT GLASS: Tempered

Lippert Components Mfg Inc .... C 323 663-1261
  Chesaning *(G-2726)*
Superior Auto Glass of Mich .... G 989 366-9691
  Houghton Lake *(G-7999)*

FLAT GLASS: Window, Clear & Colored

Astro Lite Window Company Inc .... E 734 326-2455
  Romulus *(G-13652)*
Ford Motor Company .... A 313 446-5945
  Detroit *(G-4067)*

FLAVORS OR FLAVORING MATERIALS: Synthetic

Wild Flavors Inc .... E 269 216-2603
  Kalamazoo *(G-8925)*

FLOATING DRY DOCKS

Floatation Docking Inc .... E 906 484-3422
  Cedarville *(G-2567)*

FLOCKING METAL PRDTS

West Mich Flcking Assembly LLC .... D 269 639-1634
  Covert *(G-3592)*

FLOOR COVERING STORES

Standale Lumber and Supply Co .... D 616 530-8200
  Grandville *(G-7072)*

FLOOR COVERING STORES: Carpets

AAM Wholesale Carpet Corp .... G 313 898-5101
  Detroit *(G-3832)*
Dave Brand .... G 269 651-4693
  Sturgis *(G-15603)*
Homespun Furniture Inc .... F 734 284-6277
  Riverview *(G-13297)*

FLOOR COVERING: Plastic

Oscoda Plastics Inc .... E 989 739-6900
  Oscoda *(G-12216)*

FLOOR COVERINGS WHOLESALERS

Grand River Interiors Inc .... E 616 454-2800
  Grand Rapids *(G-6468)*

FLOORING & GRATINGS: Open, Construction Applications

Alro Steel Corporation .... F 989 893-9553
  Bay City *(G-1274)*
Harbor Steel and Supply Corp .... F 616 786-0002
  Holland *(G-7657)*
Land Enterprises Inc .... E 248 398-7276
  Madison Heights *(G-10297)*

FLOORING & SIDING: Metal

Longstreet Group LLC .... F 517 278-4487
  Coldwater *(G-3314)*

FLOORING: Baseboards, Wood

Black Creek Timber LLC .... G 517 202-2169
  Rudyard *(G-13983)*
Shayn Allen Marquetry .... G 586 991-0445
  Shelby Township *(G-14691)*

FLOORING: Hard Surface

Floorcovering Engineers LLC .... G 616 299-1007
  Grand Rapids *(G-6414)*
Flor TEC Inc .... G 616 897-3122
  Lowell *(G-10028)*
Innovative Surface Works .... F 734 261-3010
  Farmington Hills *(G-5027)*
Pro Floor Service .... G 517 663-5012
  Eaton Rapids *(G-4730)*

FLOORING: Hardwood

Connor Sports Flooring Corp .... F 906 822-7311
  Amasa *(G-330)*
Horner Flooring Company Inc .... D 906 482-1180
  Dollar Bay *(G-4521)*
Interntonal Hardwoods Michiana .... G 517 278-8446
  Coldwater *(G-3310)*
McLeod Wood and Christmas Pdts .... G 989 777-4800
  Bridgeport *(G-1853)*
Omara Sprung Floors Inc .... G 810 743-8281
  Burton *(G-2160)*
PAW Enterprises LLC .... F 269 329-1865
  Kalamazoo *(G-8845)*
Rare Earth Hardwoods Inc .... F 231 946-0043
  Traverse City *(G-16090)*
Robbins Inc .... G 513 619-5936
  Negaunee *(G-11475)*
Rt Baldwin Enterprises Inc .... G 616 669-1626
  Hudsonville *(G-8181)*

FLOORING: Tile

Yoxheimer Tile Co .... F 517 788-7542
  Jackson *(G-8614)*

FLORIST: Flowers, Fresh

Birmingham Jewelry Inc .... G 586 939-5100
  Sterling Heights *(G-15274)*
Flowers By Kevin .... G 810 376-4600
  Deckerville *(G-3808)*
Harry Miller Flowers Inc .... G 313 581-2328
  Dearborn *(G-3718)*
Veldheer Tulip Garden Inc .... D 616 399-1900
  Holland *(G-7844)*

FLORISTS

Neumann Enterprises Inc .... G 906 293-8122
  Newberry *(G-11581)*

Spartannash Company .... D 517 278-8963
  Coldwater *(G-3333)*

FLOWER ARRANGEMENTS: Artificial

Classic Sea Scapes .... G 517 323-7775
  Lansing *(G-9282)*
Eileen Smeltzer .... G 269 629-8056
  Richland *(G-13248)*
Flowers By Kevin .... G 810 376-4600
  Deckerville *(G-3808)*
Sheri Boston .... G 248 627-9576
  Ortonville *(G-12203)*

FLOWER POTS Plastic

Harry Miller Flowers Inc .... G 313 581-2328
  Dearborn *(G-3718)*
New Product Development LLC .... G 616 399-6253
  Holland *(G-7758)*

FLOWERS & FLORISTS' SPLYS WHOLESALERS

Wahmhoff Farms LLC .... F 269 628-4308
  Gobles *(G-5950)*

FLOWERS: Artificial & Preserved

Aurora Preserved Flowers .... G 989 498-0290
  Bay City *(G-1278)*
Roses Susies Feather .... G 989 689-6570
  Hope *(G-7956)*

FLUES & PIPES: Stove Or Furnace

Chicago Blow Pipe Company .... F 773 533-6100
  Marquette *(G-10522)*

FLUID METERS & COUNTING DEVICES

Advanced Integrated Mfg .... F 586 439-0300
  Fraser *(G-5613)*
Dearborn Collision Service Inc .... G 734 455-3299
  Northville *(G-11687)*
Medallion Instrumentation .... C 616 847-3700
  Spring Lake *(G-15161)*
Northville Circuits Inc .... G 248 853-3232
  Rochester Hills *(G-13484)*
Pierburg Instruments .... C 734 414-9600
  Plymouth *(G-12715)*
Re-Sol LLC .... F 248 270-7777
  Auburn Hills *(G-988)*
Royal Design & Manufacturing .... D 248 588-0110
  Madison Heights *(G-10346)*
Woodward Inc .... B 616 772-9171
  Zeeland *(G-18197)*

FLUID POWER PUMPS & MOTORS

Dare Auto Inc .... E 734 228-6243
  Plymouth *(G-12605)*
Ddks Industries LLC .... G 586 323-5909
  Shelby Township *(G-14573)*
Eaton Corporation .... C 517 787-7220
  Jackson *(G-8439)*
Eaton-Aeroquip Llc .... B 949 452-9575
  Jackson *(G-8440)*
Flow-Rite Controls Ltd .... E 616 583-1700
  Byron Center *(G-2191)*
Gds Enterprises .... G 989 644-3115
  Lake *(G-9082)*
GM Components Holdings LLC .... E 616 246-2000
  Grand Rapids *(G-6444)*
Great Lakes Hydra Corporation .... F 616 949-8844
  Grand Rapids *(G-6479)*
Hilite International Inc .... C 231 894-3200
  Whitehall *(G-17668)*
Hydro-Craft Inc .... E 248 652-8100
  Rochester Hills *(G-13448)*
J H Bennett and Company Inc .... E 248 596-5100
  Novi *(G-11910)*
Kawasaki Prcision McHy USA Inc .... E 616 975-3100
  Grand Rapids *(G-6570)*
Loftis Alumi-TEC Inc .... E 616 846-1990
  Grand Haven *(G-6050)*
M P Pumps Inc .... D 586 293-8240
  Fraser *(G-5688)*
Med-Kas Hydraulics Inc .... F 248 585-3220
  Troy *(G-16491)*
Metaris Hydraulics .... G 586 949-4240
  Chesterfield *(G-2805)*

PRODUCT SECTION

FOOD PRDTS, CANNED: Fruits

Mfp Automation Engineering Inc............D...... 616 538-5700
  Hudsonville *(G-8167)*
Npi ....G...... 248 478-0010
  Farmington Hills *(G-5083)*
Parker HSD ....F...... 269 384-3915
  Kalamazoo *(G-8842)*
Parker-Hannifin Corporation...................D...... 734 455-1700
  Plymouth *(G-12708)*
Parker-Hannifin Corporation...................C...... 269 692-6254
  Otsego *(G-12250)*
Parker-Hannifin Corporation...................B...... 269 384-3459
  Kalamazoo *(G-8843)*
Piper Industries Inc.................................D...... 586 771-5100
  Roseville *(G-13855)*
Prophotonix Limited ....E...... 586 778-1100
  Roseville *(G-13856)*
REO Hydraulic & Mfg Inc........................E...... 313 891-2244
  Detroit *(G-4342)*
Robert Bosch LLC ....F...... 269 429-3221
  Saint Joseph *(G-14338)*
Truform Machine Inc...............................E...... 517 782-8523
  Jackson *(G-8594)*
Wmh Fluidpower Inc................................F...... 269 327-7011
  Portage *(G-13058)*
Wolverine Water Works Inc....................G...... 248 673-4310
  Waterford *(G-17387)*
Yates Industries Inc................................D...... 586 778-7680
  Saint Clair Shores *(G-14277)*

FLUID POWER VALVES & HOSE FITTINGS

A Raymond Corp N Amer Inc..................G...... 810 964-7994
  Rochester Hills *(G-13359)*
Aircraft Precision Pdts Inc.....................D...... 989 875-4186
  Ithaca *(G-8356)*
Alco Manufacturing Corp........................E...... 734 426-3941
  Dexter *(G-4474)*
Automatic Valve Corp ....E...... 248 474-6761
  Novi *(G-11835)*
Bucher Hydraulics Inc.............................C...... 616 458-1306
  Grand Rapids *(G-6238)*
Bucher Hydraulics Inc.............................E...... 231 652-2773
  Newaygo *(G-11564)*
Craig Assembly Inc..................................C...... 810 326-1374
  Saint Clair *(G-14212)*
Dadco Inc...D...... 734 207-1100
  Plymouth *(G-12604)*
Dutchman Mfg Co LLC ....G...... 734 922-5803
  Traverse City *(G-15959)*
Fluid Hutchinson Management..............D...... 248 679-1327
  Auburn Hills *(G-876)*
GM Components Holdings LLC..............E...... 616 246-2000
  Grand Rapids *(G-6444)*
Hilite International Inc...........................C...... 231 894-3200
  Whitehall *(G-17668)*
Hosco Fittings LLC ....E...... 248 912-1750
  Wixom *(G-17829)*
Northland Maintenance Co Inc ....G...... 906 253-9161
  Sault Sainte Marie *(G-14469)*
Novi Tool & Machine Company ....D...... 313 532-0900
  Redford *(G-13176)*
Parker-Hannifin Corporation..................B...... 269 629-5000
  Richland *(G-13252)*
Pinckney Automatic & Mfg......................G...... 734 878-3430
  Pinckney *(G-12502)*
Piper Industries Inc.................................D...... 586 771-5100
  Roseville *(G-13855)*
Precision Packing Corporation...............E...... 586 756-8700
  Warren *(G-17194)*
Quaker Chemical Corporation ....G...... 586 826-6454
  Sterling Heights *(G-15458)*
Sames Kremlin Inc...................................C...... 734 979-0100
  Plymouth *(G-12747)*
Scott Machine Inc....................................E...... 517 787-6616
  Jackson *(G-8571)*
Thomas Toys Inc......................................G...... 810 629-8707
  Fenton *(G-5243)*

FLUXES

CRC Industries Inc...................................E...... 313 883-6977
  Detroit *(G-3953)*
Selkey Fabricators LLC...........................F...... 906 353-7104
  Baraga *(G-1115)*

FLYSWATTERS

Smart Swatter LLC..................................G...... 989 763-2626
  Harbor Springs *(G-7294)*

FOAM RUBBER

Cartex Corporation..................................G...... 610 759-1650
  Troy *(G-16261)*
Creative Foam Corporation....................C...... 810 629-4149
  Fenton *(G-5198)*
Ds Sales Inc..G...... 248 960-6411
  Wixom *(G-17796)*
Great Lake Foam Technologies.............F...... 517 563-8030
  Hanover *(G-7260)*
Massee Products Ltd..............................G...... 269 684-8255
  Niles *(G-11624)*
Milsco LLC...B...... 517 787-3650
  Jackson *(G-8531)*

FOAMS & RUBBER, WHOLESALE

Envirolite LLC...F...... 248 792-3184
  Troy *(G-16349)*
Envirolite LLC...D...... 888 222-2191
  Coldwater *(G-3302)*

FOIL & LEAF: Metal

Barbron Corporation................................E...... 586 716-3530
  Kalkaska *(G-8937)*
Graphic Specialties Inc..........................E...... 616 247-0060
  Grand Rapids *(G-6475)*
Illinois Tool Works Inc ....D...... 231 258-5521
  Kalkaska *(G-8944)*

FOIL: Aluminum

Novelis Corporation.................................G...... 248 668-5111
  Novi *(G-11956)*

FOOD CONTAMINATION TESTING OR SCREENING KITS

Svn Inc...G...... 734 707-7131
  Saline *(G-14417)*

FOOD PRDTS, BREAKFAST: Cereal, Corn Flakes

Kellogg Company ....A...... 269 961-6693
  Battle Creek *(G-1216)*
Kellogg Company ....A...... 269 961-2000
  Battle Creek *(G-1211)*

FOOD PRDTS, CANNED OR FRESH PACK: Fruit Juices

Burnette Foods Inc..................................D...... 231 264-8116
  Elk Rapids *(G-4776)*
Everfresh Beverages Inc........................D...... 586 755-9500
  Warren *(G-17024)*
Old Orchard Brands LLC.........................D...... 616 887-1745
  Sparta *(G-15103)*
Rice Juice Company Inc.........................G...... 906 774-1733
  Iron Mountain *(G-8298)*
St Julian Wine Company Inc..................E...... 269 657-5568
  Paw Paw *(G-12414)*
Welch Foods Inc A Cooperative ....D...... 269 624-4141
  Lawton *(G-9516)*

FOOD PRDTS, CANNED OR FRESH PACK: Vegetable Juices

J House LLC..G...... 313 220-4449
  Grosse Pointe Farms *(G-7185)*
Panther James LLC.................................G...... 248 850-7522
  Royal Oak *(G-13955)*

FOOD PRDTS, CANNED: Applesauce

Indian Summer Cooperative Inc............C...... 231 845-6248
  Ludington *(G-10067)*
Materne North America Corp.................E...... 231 346-6600
  Grawn *(G-7099)*
Michigan Apple Packers Coop ....G...... 616 887-9933
  Sparta *(G-15102)*

FOOD PRDTS, CANNED: Barbecue Sauce

Cherry Republic Inc................................D...... 231 334-3150
  Glen Arbor *(G-5940)*

FOOD PRDTS, CANNED: Beans, Baked With Meat

Randall Foods Inc....................................F...... 517 767-3247
  Tekonsha *(G-15821)*

FOOD PRDTS, CANNED: Chili

Detroit Chili Co Inc..................................G...... 313 521-6323
  Detroit *(G-3975)*
National Coney Island Chili Co..............F...... 313 365-5611
  Roseville *(G-13844)*

FOOD PRDTS, CANNED: Ethnic

Global Restaurant Group Inc.................F...... 313 271-2777
  Dearborn *(G-3716)*

FOOD PRDTS, CANNED: Fruit Juices, Concentrated

Integrity Beverage Inc............................E...... 248 348-1010
  Wixom *(G-17836)*

FOOD PRDTS, CANNED: Fruit Juices, Fresh

Knouse Foods Cooperative Inc.............D...... 269 657-5524
  Paw Paw *(G-12406)*
Mitten Fruit Company LLC....................G...... 269 585-8541
  Kalamazoo *(G-8829)*
Mizkan America Inc.................................F...... 616 794-0226
  Belding *(G-1425)*
Peterson Farms Inc.................................B...... 231 861-6333
  Shelby *(G-14534)*

FOOD PRDTS, CANNED: Fruits

Burnette Foods Inc..................................D...... 269 621-3181
  Hartford *(G-7382)*
Burnette Foods Inc..................................E...... 231 536-2284
  East Jordan *(G-4626)*
Cherry Central Cooperative Inc............D...... 231 861-2141
  Shelby *(G-14524)*
Cherry Growers Inc.................................C...... 231 276-9241
  Birmingham *(G-1676)*
Cherry Growers Inc.................................G...... 231 947-2502
  Traverse City *(G-15940)*
Mpc Company Inc....................................G...... 269 927-3371
  Benton Harbor *(G-1534)*
New ERA Canning Company ....C...... 231 861-2151
  New ERA *(G-11521)*
Oceana Foods Inc....................................E...... 231 861-2141
  Shelby *(G-14531)*
Packers Canning Co Inc.........................D...... 269 624-4681
  Lawton *(G-9513)*

FOOD PRDTS, CANNED: Fruits

Almar Orchards LLC................................E...... 810 659-6568
  Flushing *(G-5531)*
Birds Eye Foods Inc................................C...... 269 561-8211
  Fennville *(G-5170)*
Blakes Orchard Inc..................................G...... 586 784-5343
  Armada *(G-717)*
Brownwood Acres Foods Inc.................F...... 231 599-3101
  Eastport *(G-4714)*
Burnette Foods Inc..................................C...... 231 861-2151
  New ERA *(G-11519)*
Campbell Soup Company ....F...... 313 295-6884
  Taylor *(G-15698)*
Campbell Soup Company ....D...... 248 336-8486
  Ferndale *(G-5265)*
Cherry Central Cooperative Inc............E...... 231 946-1860
  Traverse City *(G-15938)*
Country Mill Farms LLC..........................E...... 517 543-1019
  Charlotte *(G-2642)*
Great Lakes Packing Co.........................E...... 231 264-5561
  Kewadin *(G-9039)*
Hopeful Harvest Foods Inc ....G...... 248 967-1500
  Oak Park *(G-12073)*
Jt Foods Inc..G...... 810 772-9035
  Owosso *(G-12297)*
Kraft Heinz Foods Company..................B...... 616 447-0481
  Grand Rapids *(G-6590)*
Kraft Heinz Foods Company..................B...... 616 396-6557
  Holland *(G-7713)*
McClures Pickles LLC.............................E...... 248 837-9323
  Detroit *(G-4221)*
Northville Cider Mill Inc.........................E...... 248 349-3181
  Northville *(G-11715)*
Randall Foods Inc....................................F...... 517 767-3247
  Tekonsha *(G-15821)*

FOOD PRDTS, CANNED: Fruits

Twin City Foods Inc .... C 616 374-4002
  Lake Odessa (G-9120)
Uncle Johns Cider Mill Inc .... D 989 224-3686
  Saint Johns (G-14298)

FOOD PRDTS, CANNED: Fruits & Fruit Prdts

Food For Thought Inc .... E 231 326-5444
  Traverse City (G-15971)

FOOD PRDTS, CANNED: Italian

Charidimos Inc .... G 248 827-7733
  Southfield (G-14865)
Paul J Baroni Co .... G 906 337-3920
  Calumet (G-2331)
SBR LLC .... E 313 350-8799
  Harper Woods (G-7304)
Turchetti Spaghetti Co LLC .... G 616 706-4766
  Hart (G-7380)

FOOD PRDTS, CANNED: Jams, Including Imitation

Cherry Hut Products LLC .... G 231 882-4431
  Benzonia (G-1574)
Fairview Farms .... G 269 449-0500
  Berrien Springs (G-1595)

FOOD PRDTS, CANNED: Jams, Jellies & Preserves

I Jams LLC .... G 248 756-1380
  Keego Harbor (G-8980)
Pantless Jams LLC .... G 419 283-8470
  Temperance (G-15840)
Society of Saint John Inc .... G 906 289-4484
  Eagle Harbor (G-4618)

FOOD PRDTS, CANNED: Maraschino Cherries

Gray & Company .... C 231 873-5628
  Hart (G-7372)

FOOD PRDTS, CANNED: Mexican, NEC

Tienda San Rafael LLC .... G 989 681-2020
  Saint Louis (G-14370)

FOOD PRDTS, CANNED: Soups

Onion Crock of Michigan Inc .... G 616 458-2922
  Grand Rapids (G-6731)

FOOD PRDTS, CANNED: Tomato Sauce.

La Rozinas Inc .... G 906 779-2181
  Iron Mountain (G-8287)

FOOD PRDTS, CANNED: Tomatoes

M Forche Farms Inc .... F 517 447-3488
  Blissfield (G-1718)

FOOD PRDTS, CANNED: Vegetables

Crazy Joes Enterprises LLC .... G 906 395-1522
  Baraga (G-1100)

FOOD PRDTS, CONFECTIONERY, WHOLESALE: Candy

W2 Inc .... G 517 764-3141
  Jackson (G-8602)

FOOD PRDTS, CONFECTIONERY, WHOLESALE: Nuts, Salted/Roasted

Kar Nut Products Company LLC .... C 248 588-1903
  Madison Heights (G-10288)
Nutco Inc .... E 800 872-4006
  Detroit (G-4280)

FOOD PRDTS, CONFECTIONERY, WHOLESALE: Snack Foods

Frito-Lay North America Inc .... E 989 754-0435
  Saginaw (G-14040)
Win Schuler Foods Inc .... G 248 262-3450
  Southfield (G-15066)

FOOD PRDTS, DAIRY, WHOLESALE: Frozen Dairy Desserts

Blossom Berry .... G 517 775-6978
  Novi (G-11838)

FOOD PRDTS, DAIRY, WHOLESALE: Milk & Cream, Fluid

Independent Dairy Inc .... E 734 241-6016
  Monroe (G-11041)
Michigan Milk Producers Assn .... E 248 474-6672
  Novi (G-11947)

FOOD PRDTS, FISH & SEAFOOD: Fish, Salted

Ruleau Brothers Inc .... E 906 753-4767
  Stephenson (G-15240)

FOOD PRDTS, FISH & SEAFOOD: Fish, Smoked

Big O Smokehouse .... F 616 891-5555
  Caledonia (G-2289)
Gustafson Smoked Fish .... G 906 292-5424
  Moran (G-11107)

FOOD PRDTS, FISH & SEAFOOD: Herring, Cured, NEC

Sea Fare Foods Inc .... E 313 568-0223
  Detroit (G-4357)

FOOD PRDTS, FROZEN, WHOLESALE: Vegetables & Fruit Prdts

Ungar Frozen Food Product .... G 248 626-3148
  Bloomfield Hills (G-1809)

FOOD PRDTS, FROZEN: Dinners, Packaged

Mid America Commodities LLC .... G 810 936-0108
  Linden (G-9594)

FOOD PRDTS, FROZEN: Ethnic Foods, NEC

Cole King Foods .... E 313 872-0220
  Detroit (G-3943)
Pasty Oven Inc .... G 906 774-2328
  Quinnesec (G-13101)
Turris Italian Foods Inc .... D 586 773-6010
  Roseville (G-13883)

FOOD PRDTS, FROZEN: Fruits

Cherry Growers Inc .... C 231 276-9241
  Birmingham (G-1676)
Cherry Growers Inc .... G 231 947-2502
  Traverse City (G-15940)
Dole Packaged Foods LLC .... E 269 423-6375
  Decatur (G-3803)
Graceland Fruit Inc .... C 231 352-7181
  Frankfort (G-5602)
Hart Freeze Pack LIC .... F 231 873-2175
  Hart (G-7373)
Peterson Farms Inc .... B 231 861-6333
  Shelby (G-14534)
Sill Farms & Market Inc .... E 269 674-3755
  Lawrence (G-9508)
Smeltzer Companies Inc .... C 231 882-4421
  Frankfort (G-5606)

FOOD PRDTS, FROZEN: Fruits & Vegetables

Coloma Frozen Foods Inc .... D 269 849-0500
  Coloma (G-3356)

FOOD PRDTS, FROZEN: Fruits, Juices & Vegetables

All American Whse & Cold Stor .... E 313 865-3870
  Detroit (G-3856)
Clarkson Smoothie Inc .... G 248 620-8005
  Clarkston (G-2911)
Clio Smoothie LLC .... G 810 691-9620
  Fenton (G-5195)
Farber Concessions Inc .... E 313 387-1600
  Redford (G-13161)
Jar-ME LLC .... G 313 319-7765
  Detroit (G-4158)

MI Frozen Food LLC .... G 231 357-4334
  Manistee (G-10430)
Old Orchard Brands LLC .... D 616 887-1745
  Sparta (G-15103)
Smoothies .... G 231 498-2374
  Kewadin (G-9040)
Standale Smoothie LLC .... G 810 691-9625
  Fenton (G-5239)
Welch Foods Inc A Cooperative .... D 269 624-4141
  Lawton (G-9516)

FOOD PRDTS, FROZEN: NEC

Achatzs Hand Made Pie Co .... D 586 749-2882
  Chesterfield (G-2731)
Campbell Soup Company .... F 313 295-6884
  Taylor (G-15698)
Campbell Soup Company .... D 248 336-8486
  Ferndale (G-5265)
Coles Quality Foods Inc .... E 231 722-1651
  Muskegon (G-11295)
Detroit Chili Co Inc .... G 248 440-5933
  Southfield (G-14880)
DForte Inc .... F 269 657-6996
  Paw Paw (G-12402)
Kring Pizza Inc .... G 586 792-0049
  Harrison Township (G-7336)
Pierino Frozen Foods Inc .... E 313 928-0950
  Lincoln Park (G-9583)
Pinnacle Foods Group LLC .... B 810 724-6144
  Imlay City (G-8210)
Rays Ice Cream Co Inc .... E 248 549-5256
  Royal Oak (G-13963)
Twin City Foods Inc .... C 616 374-4002
  Lake Odessa (G-9120)

FOOD PRDTS, FROZEN: Pizza

Dina Mia Kitchens Inc .... F 906 265-9082
  Iron River (G-8308)
Frandale Sub Shop .... F 616 446-6311
  Allendale (G-217)
Paul J Baroni Co .... G 906 337-3920
  Calumet (G-2331)

FOOD PRDTS, FROZEN: Potato Prdts

Potatoe Ball LLC .... G 313 483-0901
  Clinton Township (G-3197)

FOOD PRDTS, FROZEN: Snack Items

Farber Concessions Inc .... E 313 387-1600
  Redford (G-13161)

FOOD PRDTS, FROZEN: Vegetables, Exc Potato Prdts

Twin City Foods Inc .... C 616 374-4002
  Lake Odessa (G-9120)

FOOD PRDTS, FROZEN: Waffles

Kellogg Company .... A 269 961-2000
  Battle Creek (G-1211)

FOOD PRDTS, FRUITS & VEGETABLES, FRESH, WHOLESALE

Burnette Foods Inc .... E 231 223-4282
  Traverse City (G-15924)

FOOD PRDTS, FRUITS & VEGETABLES, FRESH, WHOLESALE: Fruits

Blakes Orchard Inc .... G 586 784-5343
  Armada (G-717)
Mpc Company Inc .... G 269 927-3371
  Benton Harbor (G-1534)

FOOD PRDTS, FRUITS & VEGETABLES, FRESH, WHOLESALE: Vegetable

Home Style Foods Inc .... F 313 874-3250
  Detroit (G-4126)
Michigan Celery Promotion Coop ...... E 616 669-1250
  Hudsonville (G-8168)

PRODUCT SECTION

FOOD PRDTS: Coffee Roasting, Exc Wholesale Grocers

FOOD PRDTS, MEAT & MEAT PRDTS, WHOLESALE: Fresh

Cornbelt Beef Corporation .... E 313 237-0087
  Oak Park *(G-12054)*
Erlas Inc .... D 989 872-2191
  Cass City *(G-2514)*
Richmond Meat Packers Inc .... G 586 727-1450
  Richmond *(G-13270)*
Wolverine Packing Co .... D 313 259-7500
  Detroit *(G-4446)*

FOOD PRDTS, WHOLESALE: Beans, Field

Ittner Bean & Grain Inc .... F 989 662-4461
  Auburn *(G-753)*

FOOD PRDTS, WHOLESALE: Beverage Concentrates

Penguin Juice Co .... F 734 467-6991
  Westland *(G-17587)*

FOOD PRDTS, WHOLESALE: Beverages, Exc Coffee & Tea

C F Burger Creamery Co .... D 313 584-4040
  Detroit *(G-3925)*
Global Restaurant Group Inc .... F 313 271-2777
  Dearborn *(G-3716)*
Viva Beverages LLC .... D 248 746-7044
  Southfield *(G-15062)*

FOOD PRDTS, WHOLESALE: Coffee, Green Or Roasted

Becharas Bros Coffee Co .... E 313 869-4700
  Detroit *(G-3897)*
Coffee Beanery Ltd .... E 810 733-1020
  Flushing *(G-5533)*
Good Sense Coffee LLC .... G 810 355-2349
  Brighton *(G-1932)*
Hermans Boy .... G 616 866-2900
  Rockford *(G-13571)*

FOOD PRDTS, WHOLESALE: Diet

Hacienda Mexican Foods LLC .... D 313 895-8823
  Detroit *(G-4110)*

FOOD PRDTS, WHOLESALE: Flavorings & Fragrances

Preeminence Inc .... G 313 737-7920
  Redford *(G-13185)*

FOOD PRDTS, WHOLESALE: Grain Elevators

Archer-Daniels-Midland Company .... G 810 672-9221
  Snover *(G-14743)*
Vita Plus Corporation .... F 989 665-0013
  Gagetown *(G-5803)*

FOOD PRDTS, WHOLESALE: Grains

Andersons Inc .... G 989 642-5291
  Hemlock *(G-7459)*
Armada Grain Co .... E 586 784-5911
  Armada *(G-714)*
Citizens LLC .... G 517 541-1449
  Charlotte *(G-2640)*
Corunna Mills Feed LLC .... G 989 743-3110
  Corunna *(G-3580)*
Purity Foods Inc .... F 517 448-7440
  Hudson *(G-8140)*
Schafers Elevator Co .... G 517 263-7202
  Adrian *(G-93)*
Star of West Milling Company .... D 989 652-9971
  Frankenmuth *(G-5596)*
Zeeland Farm Services Inc .... C 616 772-9042
  Zeeland *(G-18201)*

FOOD PRDTS, WHOLESALE: Honey

Windmill Hill Farm LLC .... G 810 378-5972
  Croswell *(G-3606)*

FOOD PRDTS, WHOLESALE: Juices

Go Beyond Healthy LLC .... G 407 255-0314
  Grand Rapids *(G-6445)*

Rice Juice Company Inc .... G 906 774-1733
  Iron Mountain *(G-8298)*
Rochester Cider Mill .... G 248 651-4224
  Rochester *(G-13348)*

FOOD PRDTS, WHOLESALE: Natural & Organic

Aubio Life Sciences LLC .... G 561 289-1888
  Wixom *(G-17767)*

FOOD PRDTS, WHOLESALE: Pasta & Rice

Purity Foods Inc .... F 517 448-7440
  Hudson *(G-8140)*

FOOD PRDTS, WHOLESALE: Pizza Splys

Dominos Pizza LLC .... C 734 930-3030
  Ann Arbor *(G-424)*

FOOD PRDTS, WHOLESALE: Specialty

Coles Quality Foods Inc .... E 231 722-1651
  Muskegon *(G-11295)*
Reilchz Inc .... G 231 421-9600
  Traverse City *(G-16093)*

FOOD PRDTS, WHOLESALE: Spices & Seasonings

Asmus Seasoning Inc .... F 586 939-4505
  Sterling Heights *(G-15265)*

FOOD PRDTS, WHOLESALE: Tea

Ellis Infinity LLC .... G 313 570-0840
  Detroit *(G-4033)*

FOOD PRDTS, WHOLESALE: Water, Distilled

Seymour Dehaan .... G 269 672-7377
  Martin *(G-10597)*

FOOD PRDTS, WHOLESALE: Wheat

Cargill Incorporated .... F 608 868-5150
  Owosso *(G-12281)*

FOOD PRDTS, WHOLESALE: Wine Makers' Eqpt & Splys

R C M S Inc .... G 269 422-1617
  Baroda *(G-1130)*

FOOD PRDTS: Animal & marine fats & oils

Asao LLC .... F 734 522-6333
  Livonia *(G-9653)*
Darling Ingredients Inc .... E 269 751-0560
  Hamilton *(G-7231)*
Evergreen Grease Service Inc .... G 517 264-9913
  Adrian *(G-63)*
Protein Magnet Corp .... G 616 844-1545
  Spring Lake *(G-15171)*

FOOD PRDTS: Box Lunches, For Sale Off Premises

Stephen Haas .... G 906 475-4826
  Negaunee *(G-11477)*

FOOD PRDTS: Bread Crumbs, Exc Made In Bakeries

Pepperidge Farm Incorporated .... G 734 953-6729
  Livonia *(G-9885)*

FOOD PRDTS: Breakfast Bars

Junkless Foods Inc .... G 616 560-7895
  Kalamazoo *(G-8782)*

FOOD PRDTS: Butter, Renovated & Processed

Butterball Farms Inc .... C 616 243-0105
  Grand Rapids *(G-6247)*

FOOD PRDTS: Cake Flour

Cake Flour .... G 231 571-3054
  Norton Shores *(G-11743)*

FOOD PRDTS: Cereals

Bay Valley Foods LLC .... C 269 792-2277
  Wayland *(G-17399)*
General Mills Inc .... D 763 764-7600
  Kalamazoo *(G-8749)*
Hearthside Food Solutions LLC .... C 616 871-6240
  Kentwood *(G-9009)*
Hearthside Food Solutions LLC .... B 616 574-2000
  Kentwood *(G-9010)*
K-Two Inc .... F 269 961-2000
  Battle Creek *(G-1206)*
Kellogg (thailand) Limited .... G 269 969-8937
  Battle Creek *(G-1208)*
Kellogg Chile Inc .... G 269 961-2000
  Battle Creek *(G-1209)*
Kellogg Company .... B 269 961-2000
  Battle Creek *(G-1210)*
Kellogg Company .... B 810 653-5625
  Davison *(G-3655)*
Kellogg Company .... B 269 961-9387
  Mulliken *(G-11239)*
Kellogg Company .... B 269 964-8525
  Battle Creek *(G-1212)*
Kellogg Company .... G 269 969-8107
  Battle Creek *(G-1213)*
Kellogg Company .... B 901 373-6115
  Battle Creek *(G-1214)*
Kellogg Company .... C 269 961-2000
  Battle Creek *(G-1217)*
Kellogg Company .... D 269 961-2000
  Battle Creek *(G-1215)*
Kellogg USA Inc .... C 269 961-2000
  Battle Creek *(G-1219)*
Michaelenes Inc .... G 248 625-0156
  Clarkston *(G-2938)*
Post Foods LLC .... C 269 966-1000
  Battle Creek *(G-1236)*
Roskam Baking Company .... C 616 574-5757
  Grand Rapids *(G-6839)*
Rothbury Farms Inc .... A 616 574-5757
  Grand Rapids *(G-6844)*
Snackwerks of Michigan LLC .... F 269 719-8282
  Battle Creek *(G-1251)*
Treehouse Private Brands Inc .... C 269 968-6181
  Battle Creek *(G-1260)*

FOOD PRDTS: Chewing Gum Base

Lotte USA Incorporated .... F 269 963-6664
  Battle Creek *(G-1223)*

FOOD PRDTS: Chocolate Bars, Solid

Heather N Holly .... G 989 832-6460
  Midland *(G-10869)*
Kilwins Qulty Confections Inc .... G 231 347-3800
  Petoskey *(G-12452)*

FOOD PRDTS: Coconut Oil

Go Beyond Healthy LLC .... G 407 255-0314
  Grand Rapids *(G-6445)*

FOOD PRDTS: Coffee

Becharas Bros Coffee Co .... E 313 869-4700
  Detroit *(G-3897)*
Coffee Beanery Ltd .... E 810 733-1020
  Flushing *(G-5533)*
Coffee Express Co .... F 734 459-4900
  Plymouth *(G-12599)*
Farmer Bros Co .... F 989 791-7985
  Saginaw *(G-14036)*
Infusco Coffee Roasters LLC .... G 269 213-5282
  Sawyer *(G-14485)*
Koeze Company .... E 616 724-2601
  Grand Rapids *(G-6588)*
La Colombe Torrefaction .... G 231 798-9853
  Norton Shores *(G-11769)*
Stickmann Baeckerei .... G 269 205-2444
  Middleville *(G-10809)*
Three Rivers Coffee Company .... G 269 244-0083
  Three Rivers *(G-15879)*

FOOD PRDTS: Coffee Roasting, Exc Wholesale Grocers

Cadillac Coffee Company .... G 800 438-6900
  Troy *(G-16252)*
Cozy Cup Coffee Company Llc .... G 989 984-7619
  Oscoda *(G-12207)*

Employee Codes: A=Over 500 employees, B=251-500
C=101-250, D=51-100, E=20-50, F=10-19, G=3-9

FOOD PRDTS: Coffee Roasting, Exc Wholesale Grocers

Good Sense Coffee LLC .... G 810 355-2349
Brighton *(G-1932)*
Hermans Boy .... G 616 866-2900
Rockford *(G-13571)*
Inter State Foods Inc .... F 517 372-5500
Lansing *(G-9237)*
Rowster Coffee Inc .... E 616 780-7777
Grand Rapids *(G-6846)*
Treat of Day LLC .... F 616 706-1717
Grand Rapids *(G-6936)*

FOOD PRDTS: Coffee, Ground, Mixed With Grain Or Chicory

Caffina Coffee Co .... G 313 584-3584
Dearborn *(G-3683)*

FOOD PRDTS: Corn Oil, Refined

Cargill Incorporated .... F 608 868-5150
Owosso *(G-12281)*

FOOD PRDTS: Desserts, Ready-To-Mix

Michigan Dessert Corporation .... E 248 544-4574
Oak Park *(G-12085)*

FOOD PRDTS: Dips, Exc Cheese & Sour Cream Based

Grand Rapids Salsa .... G 616 780-1801
Grand Rapids *(G-6463)*
Marias House Made Salsa .... G 313 733-8406
Warren *(G-17139)*

FOOD PRDTS: Doughs & Batters From Purchased Flour

Dawn Food Products Inc .... C 800 654-4843
Grand Rapids *(G-6337)*

FOOD PRDTS: Doughs, Frozen Or Refrig From Purchased Flour

Big Dipper Dough Co Inc .... G 231 883-6035
Traverse City *(G-15911)*

FOOD PRDTS: Dressings, Salad, Raw & Cooked Exc Dry Mixes

DForte Inc .... F 269 657-6996
Paw Paw *(G-12402)*
Litehouse Inc .... C 616 897-5911
Lowell *(G-10034)*

FOOD PRDTS: Dried & Dehydrated Fruits, Vegetables & Soup Mix

American Spoon Foods Inc .... E 231 347-9030
Petoskey *(G-12440)*
Apple Quest Inc .... C 616 299-4834
Conklin *(G-3528)*
Cherry Central Cooperative Inc .... D 231 861-2141
Shelby *(G-14524)*
Smeltzer Companies Inc .... E 231 882-4421
Frankfort *(G-5606)*
Up North Spices Inc .... G 419 346-4155
Royal Oak *(G-13979)*

FOOD PRDTS: Edible Oil Prdts, Exc Corn Oil

Cozart Producers .... G 810 736-1046
Flint *(G-5406)*

FOOD PRDTS: Edible fats & oils

Frank Smith .... G 313 443-8882
Detroit *(G-4072)*

FOOD PRDTS: Eggs, Processed

Farmers Egg Cooperative .... G 517 649-8957
Charlotte *(G-2648)*

FOOD PRDTS: Emulsifiers

Russo Bros Inc .... E 906 485-5250
Ishpeming *(G-8353)*

FOOD PRDTS: Flour

Knappen Milling Company .... E 269 731-4141
Augusta *(G-1053)*

Star of West Milling Company .... D 989 652-9971
Frankenmuth *(G-5596)*

FOOD PRDTS: Flour & Other Grain Mill Products

Archer-Daniels-Midland Company .... C 269 968-2900
Battle Creek *(G-1147)*
Archer-Daniels-Midland Company .... G 810 672-9221
Snover *(G-14743)*
Archer-Daniels-Midland Company .... F 517 627-4017
Grand Ledge *(G-6101)*
Archer-Daniels-Midland Company .... E 517 647-4155
Portland *(G-13061)*
Citizens LLC 517 541-1449
Charlotte *(G-2640)*
Dorothy Dawson Food Products .... E 517 788-9830
Jackson *(G-8435)*
Freeport Milling .... G 616 765-8421
Freeport *(G-5764)*
Ittner Bean & Grain Inc .... F 989 662-4461
Auburn *(G-753)*
Kellogg Company .... A 269 961-2000
Battle Creek *(G-1211)*
Kelloggs Corporation .... F 616 219-6100
Grand Rapids *(G-6572)*
Purity Foods Inc .... F 517 448-7440
Hudson *(G-8140)*
Star of West Milling Company .... E 517 639-3165
Quincy *(G-13099)*
Star of West Milling Company .... F 989 872-5847
Cass City *(G-2522)*
Williams Milling & Moulding In .... G 906 474-9222
Rapid River *(G-13117)*

FOOD PRDTS: Flour Mixes & Doughs

Advanced Food Technologies Inc .... D 616 574-4144
Grand Rapids *(G-6148)*
Bektrom Foods Inc .... F 734 241-3796
Monroe *(G-11021)*
Dawn Foods International Corp .... C 517 789-4400
Jackson *(G-8431)*
Dominos Pizza LLC .... C 734 930-3030
Ann Arbor *(G-424)*
Dorothy Dawson Food Products .... E 517 788-9830
Jackson *(G-8435)*
Dough & Spice Inc .... G 586 756-6100
Warren *(G-17004)*
Ezbake Technologies LLC .... G 817 430-1621
Fenton *(G-5206)*
Fry Krisp Food Products Inc .... F 517 784-8531
Jackson *(G-8452)*

FOOD PRDTS: Freeze-Dried Coffee

Prospectors LLC .... G 616 634-8260
Grand Rapids *(G-6792)*

FOOD PRDTS: Frosting Mixes, Dry, For Cakes, Cookies, Etc.

Among Friends LLC .... F 734 997-9720
Ann Arbor *(G-354)*

FOOD PRDTS: Fruit Juices

Juvenex Inc .... F 248 436-2866
Southfield *(G-14953)*
Super Fluids LLC .... G 313 409-6522
Detroit *(G-4386)*

FOOD PRDTS: Fruits & Vegetables, Pickled

Bessinger Pickle Co Inc .... G 989 876-8008
Au Gres *(G-743)*
Hausbeck Pickle Company .... D 989 754-4721
Saginaw *(G-14054)*
Vince Joes Frt Mkt - Shlby Inc .... E 586 786-9230
Shelby Township *(G-14719)*

FOOD PRDTS: Fruits, Dried Or Dehydrated, Exc Freeze-Dried

Graceland Fruit Inc .... C 231 352-7181
Frankfort *(G-5602)*
Shoreline Fruit LLC .... D 231 941-4336
Traverse City *(G-16102)*

FOOD PRDTS: Granola & Energy Bars, Nonchocolate

Detroit Fd Entrprnrship Acdemy .... F 248 894-8941
Detroit *(G-3984)*
Simply Suzanne LLC .... G 917 364-4549
Detroit *(G-4363)*

FOOD PRDTS: Honey

Natural American Foods Inc .... E 517 467-2065
Onsted *(G-12155)*
Priorat Importers Corporation .... G 248 217-4608
Royal Oak *(G-13959)*
Sleeping Bear Apiaries Ltd .... F 231 882-4456
Beulah *(G-1612)*
Windmill Hill Farm LLC .... G 810 378-5972
Croswell *(G-3606)*

FOOD PRDTS: Horseradish, Exc Sauce

Brede Inc .... G 313 273-1079
Detroit *(G-3914)*

FOOD PRDTS: Hydrol

Synex Wolverine LLC .... G 989 689-3161
Edenville *(G-4748)*

FOOD PRDTS: Ice, Blocks

Arctic Glacier Texas Inc .... G 517 999-3500
Lansing *(G-9340)*
Knowlton Enterprises Inc .... D 810 987-7100
Port Huron *(G-12935)*

FOOD PRDTS: Ice, Cubes

Home City Ice Company .... E 734 955-9094
Romulus *(G-13685)*
Imlay City High Pressure .... G 810 395-7459
Capac *(G-2448)*
Michigan Pure Ice Co LLC .... G 231 420-9896
Indian River *(G-8220)*
Northern Pure Ice Co L L C .... F 989 344-2088
Port Huron *(G-12950)*
U S Ice Corp .... E 313 862-3344
Detroit *(G-4412)*

FOOD PRDTS: Instant Coffee

Fireside Coffee Company Inc .... F 810 635-9196
Swartz Creek *(G-15666)*

FOOD PRDTS: Macaroni, Noodles, Spaghetti, Pasta, Etc

Dina Mia Kitchens Inc .... F 906 265-9082
Iron River *(G-8308)*
Pierino Frozen Foods Inc .... E 313 928-0950
Lincoln Park *(G-9583)*
Turris Italian Foods Inc .... D 586 773-6010
Roseville *(G-13883)*

FOOD PRDTS: Malt

Apple Blossom Winery LLC .... F 269 668-3724
Kalamazoo *(G-8679)*

FOOD PRDTS: Mixes, Doughnut From Purchased Flour

Dawn Food Products Inc .... C 517 789-4400
Jackson *(G-8428)*
Dawn Food Products Inc .... C 517 789-4400
Jackson *(G-8429)*
Dawn Foods Inc .... C 517 789-4400
Jackson *(G-8430)*

FOOD PRDTS: Mixes, Flour

Advanced Food Technologies Inc .... D 616 574-4144
Grand Rapids *(G-6148)*
General Mills Inc .... E 231 832-3285
Reed City *(G-13213)*
General Mills Inc .... G 269 337-0288
Kalamazoo *(G-8750)*

FOOD PRDTS: Nuts & Seeds

Koeze Company .... E 616 724-2601
Grand Rapids *(G-6588)*
Nutco Inc .... E 800 872-4006
Detroit *(G-4280)*

PRODUCT SECTION

FOOD PRDTS: Salads

St Laurent Brothers Inc .... E 989 893-7522
 Bay City *(G-1360)*
Variety Foods Inc .... E 586 268-4900
 Warren *(G-17279)*

FOOD PRDTS: Olive Oil

Mount of Olive Oil Company .... G 989 928-9030
 Mayville *(G-10675)*
Priorat Importers Corporation .... G 248 217-4608
 Royal Oak *(G-13959)*
Stamatopolos & Sons .... G 734 369-2995
 Ann Arbor *(G-644)*

FOOD PRDTS: Oriental Noodles

New Moon Noodle Incorporated .... E 269 962-8820
 Battle Creek *(G-1232)*

FOOD PRDTS: Pasta, Rice/Potatoes, Uncooked, Pkgd

Pierino Frozen Foods Inc .... E 313 928-0950
 Lincoln Park *(G-9583)*

FOOD PRDTS: Pasta, Uncooked, Packaged With Other Ingredients

Al Dente Inc .... E 734 449-8522
 Whitmore Lake *(G-17686)*

FOOD PRDTS: Peanut Butter

St Laurent Brothers Inc .... E 989 893-7522
 Bay City *(G-1360)*

FOOD PRDTS: Pickles, Vinegar

Custom Foods Inc .... E 989 249-8061
 Saginaw *(G-14024)*
Harrison Packing Co Inc .... F 269 381-3837
 Kalamazoo *(G-8761)*
Kaiser Foods Inc .... F 989 879-2087
 Pinconning *(G-12508)*
McClures Pickles LLC .... G 248 837-9323
 Royal Oak *(G-13949)*

FOOD PRDTS: Pizza Doughs From Purchased Flour

MA MA La Rosa Foods Inc .... F 734 946-7878
 Taylor *(G-15736)*
Pizza Crust Company Inc .... F 517 482-3368
 Lansing *(G-9257)*

FOOD PRDTS: Pizza, Refrigerated

Artisan Bread Co LLC .... E 586 756-0100
 Warren *(G-16940)*
Champion Foods LLC .... B 734 753-3663
 New Boston *(G-11499)*
Shady Nook Farms .... G 989 236-7240
 Middleton *(G-10795)*

FOOD PRDTS: Pork Rinds

Grandpapas Inc .... E 313 891-6830
 Detroit *(G-4099)*

FOOD PRDTS: Potato & Corn Chips & Similar Prdts

Cambridge Sharpe Inc .... D 248 613-5562
 South Lyon *(G-14788)*
Campbell Soup Company .... F 313 295-6884
 Taylor *(G-15698)*
Campbell Soup Company .... D 248 336-8486
 Ferndale *(G-5265)*
Dedinas & Franzak Entps Inc .... D 616 784-6095
 Grand Rapids *(G-6342)*
Great Lkes Fstida Holdings Inc .... G 616 241-0400
 Grand Rapids *(G-6481)*
Manos Authentic LLC .... G 800 242-2796
 Clinton Township *(G-3167)*
Mexamerica Foods LLC .... E 814 781-1447
 Grand Rapids *(G-6665)*
Rainmaker Food Solutions LLC .... G 313 530-1321
 South Lyon *(G-14811)*

FOOD PRDTS: Potato Chips & Other Potato-Based Snacks

Better Made Snack Foods Inc .... C 313 925-4774
 Detroit *(G-3902)*
Detroit Frnds Potato Chips LLC .... G 313 924-0085
 Detroit *(G-3985)*
Downeys Potato Chips-Waterford ..... G 248 673-3636
 Waterford *(G-17338)*
Pepsi-Cola Metro Btlg Co Inc .... D 517 272-2800
 Lansing *(G-9410)*
Uncle Rays LLC .... G 313 739-6035
 Detroit *(G-4413)*
Uncle Rays LLC .... D 313 834-0800
 Detroit *(G-4414)*
Variety Foods Inc .... E 586 268-4900
 Warren *(G-17279)*

FOOD PRDTS: Poultry, Processed, Smoked

Detroit Smoke House LLC .... G 313 622-9714
 Ecorse *(G-4743)*

FOOD PRDTS: Preparations

18th Street Deli Inc .... G 313 921-7710
 Hamtramck *(G-7243)*
A La Don Seasonings .... G 734 532-7862
 Southgate *(G-15072)*
Ace Vending Service Inc .... E 616 243-7983
 Grand Rapids *(G-6135)*
American Classics Corp .... G 231 843-0523
 Ludington *(G-10048)*
American Soy Products Inc .... D 734 429-2310
 Saline *(G-14375)*
Amway International Inc .... E 616 787-1000
 Ada *(G-7)*
Arbre Farms Corporation .... B 231 873-3337
 Walkerville *(G-16884)*
B & B Pretzels Inc .... E 248 358-1655
 Southfield *(G-14848)*
Better Made Snack Foods Inc .... C 313 925-4774
 Detroit *(G-3902)*
Big Boy Restaurants Intl LLC .... C 586 759-6000
 Warren *(G-16958)*
Bimbo Bakeries Usa Inc .... B 616 252-2709
 Grand Rapids *(G-6222)*
Brians Foods LLC .... G 248 739-5280
 Southfield *(G-14857)*
Burnette Foods Inc .... E 231 223-4282
 Traverse City *(G-15924)*
Canadian Harvest LP .... G 952 835-6429
 Schoolcraft *(G-14490)*
Cherry Blossom .... G 231 342-3635
 Williamsburg *(G-17710)*
Coffee Beanery Ltd .... E 810 733-1020
 Flushing *(G-5533)*
Conagra Brands Inc .... E 402 240-8210
 Quincy *(G-13092)*
Conagra Foods .... G 616 392-2359
 Holland *(G-7597)*
Custom Foods Inc .... E 989 249-8061
 Saginaw *(G-14024)*
Dedinas & Franzak Entps Inc .... D 616 784-6095
 Grand Rapids *(G-6342)*
DForte Inc .... F 269 657-6996
 Paw Paw *(G-12402)*
Dorothy Dawson Food Products .... E 517 788-9830
 Jackson *(G-8435)*
Downeys Potato Chips-Waterford ..... G 248 673-3636
 Waterford *(G-17338)*
Eden Foods Inc .... C 517 456-7424
 Clinton *(G-3019)*
Giovannis Apptzing Fd Pdts Inc .... F 586 727-9355
 Richmond *(G-13263)*
Global Quality Ingredients Inc .... G 651 337-2028
 Onsted *(G-12153)*
Gourmet Kitchen Qiuyang LLC .... G 517 332-8866
 East Lansing *(G-4659)*
Green Zebra Foods Incorporated ..... G 248 291-7339
 Grosse Pointe Park *(G-7194)*
Gt Foods Inc .... G 734 934-2729
 Southgate *(G-15077)*
Hillshire Brands Company .... A 231 947-2100
 Traverse City *(G-15997)*
Hillshire Brands Company .... A 616 875-8131
 Zeeland *(G-18150)*
Honey Tree .... G 734 697-1000
 Van Buren Twp *(G-16764)*
Indian Summer Cooperative Inc .... E 231 873-7504
 Hart *(G-7374)*
International Noodle Co Inc .... G 248 583-2479
 Madison Heights *(G-10277)*
J B Dough Co .... G 269 944-4160
 Benton Harbor *(G-1514)*
Jogue Inc .... F 248 349-1501
 Northville *(G-11703)*
Jogue Inc .... E 734 207-0100
 Plymouth *(G-12654)*
Kerry Foods .... G 616 871-9940
 Grand Rapids *(G-6582)*
Knouse Foods Cooperative Inc .... D 269 657-5524
 Paw Paw *(G-12406)*
L & J Enterprises Inc .... G 586 995-4153
 Metamora *(G-10778)*
L & J Products K Huntington .... G 810 919-3550
 Brighton *(G-1947)*
Lesley Elizabeth Inc .... G 810 667-0706
 Lapeer *(G-9469)*
Litehouse Inc .... C 616 897-5911
 Lowell *(G-10034)*
Marshalls Trail Inc .... F 231 436-5082
 Mackinaw City *(G-10099)*
McClures Pickles LLC .... E 248 837-9323
 Detroit *(G-4221)*
Mead Johnson & Company LLC ...... E 616 748-7100
 Zeeland *(G-18162)*
Michigan Celery Promotion Coop ..... E 616 669-1250
 Hudsonville *(G-8168)*
Milton Chili Company Inc .... G 248 585-0300
 Madison Heights *(G-10307)*
N F P Inc .... G 989 631-0009
 Midland *(G-10896)*
Natures Select Inc .... G 616 956-1105
 Grand Rapids *(G-6712)*
Otsuka America Foods Inc .... G 231 383-3124
 Frankfort *(G-5604)*
Rays Ice Cream Co Inc .... E 248 549-5256
 Royal Oak *(G-13963)*
Safie Specialty Foods Co Inc .... E 586 598-8282
 Chesterfield *(G-2836)*
Savory Foods Inc .... G 616 241-2583
 Grand Rapids *(G-6851)*
Spartan Central Kitchen .... G 616 878-8940
 Grand Rapids *(G-6877)*
Sunopta Ingredients Inc .... E 502 587-7999
 Schoolcraft *(G-14502)*
Twin City Foods Inc .... C 616 374-4002
 Lake Odessa *(G-9120)*
Union Commissary LLC .... F 248 795-2483
 Clarkston *(G-2963)*
Unique Food Management Inc .... E 248 738-9393
 Pontiac *(G-12872)*
Variety Foods Inc .... E 586 268-4900
 Warren *(G-17279)*
Villanuevo Soledad .... E 989 770-4309
 Burt *(G-2139)*
Wysong Medical Corporation .... E 989 631-0009
 Midland *(G-10925)*

FOOD PRDTS: Prepared Meat Sauces Exc Tomato & Dry

Barlows Gourmet Products Inc .... G 248 245-0393
 Holly *(G-7870)*

FOOD PRDTS: Prepared Sauces, Exc Tomato Based

Great Lakes Food Center LLC .... E 248 397-8166
 Madison Heights *(G-10261)*

FOOD PRDTS: Raw cane sugar

Michigan Sugar Company .... D 989 883-3200
 Sebewaing *(G-14516)*
Michigan Sugar Company .... D 989 673-2223
 Caro *(G-2473)*

FOOD PRDTS: Relishes, Fruit & Vegetable

Flamm Pickle and Packaging Co ...... F 269 461-6916
 Eau Claire *(G-4739)*

FOOD PRDTS: Salads

Countryside Foods LLC .... B 586 447-3500
 Warren *(G-16994)*
Subway Restaurant .... G 248 625-5739
 Clarkston *(G-2960)*

Employee Codes: A=Over 500 employees, B=251-500
C=101-250, D=51-100, E=20-50, F=10-19, G=3-9

FOOD PRDTS: Sandwiches
- Frandale Sub Shop .... F 616 446-6311
  Allendale *(G-217)*

FOOD PRDTS: Sauerkraut, Bulk
- Cultured Love LLC .... G 703 362-5991
  Zeeland *(G-18128)*

FOOD PRDTS: Seasonings & Spices
- Asmus Seasoning Inc .... F 586 939-4505
  Sterling Heights *(G-15265)*
- Azz On Fire LLC .... G 248 470-3742
  Detroit *(G-3889)*
- Lesley Elizabeth Inc .... F 810 667-0706
  Lapeer *(G-9470)*

FOOD PRDTS: Shortening & Solid Edible Fats
- Asao LLC .... F 734 522-6333
  Livonia *(G-9653)*

FOOD PRDTS: Soybean Oil, Refined, Exc Made In Mills
- Michigan Biodiesel LLC .... G 269 427-0804
  Kalamazoo *(G-8823)*

FOOD PRDTS: Soybean Protein Concentrates & Isolates
- Nubreed Nutrition Inc .... G 734 272-7395
  Troy *(G-16529)*

FOOD PRDTS: Spices, Including Ground
- Bektrom Foods Inc .... G 734 241-3711
  Monroe *(G-11022)*
- Country Home Creations Inc .... E 810 244-7348
  Flint *(G-5405)*
- Kalamazoo Holdings Inc .... G 269 349-9711
  Kalamazoo *(G-8789)*
- Kalsec Inc .... B 269 349-9711
  Kalamazoo *(G-8799)*
- Kring Pizza Inc .... G 586 792-0049
  Harrison Township *(G-7336)*
- McCormick & Company Inc .... C 586 558-8424
  Warren *(G-17145)*

FOOD PRDTS: Sugar, Beet
- Michigan Sugar Company .... D 989 883-3200
  Sebewaing *(G-14516)*
- Michigan Sugar Company .... D 989 686-0161
  Bay City *(G-1333)*
- Michigan Sugar Company .... D 989 673-2223
  Caro *(G-2473)*

FOOD PRDTS: Sugar, Cane
- Americane Sugar Refining LLC .... G 313 299-1300
  Taylor *(G-15687)*
- Farber Concessions Inc .... E 313 387-1600
  Redford *(G-13161)*
- Michigan Sugar Company .... C 989 673-3126
  Caro *(G-2472)*

FOOD PRDTS: Sugar, Granulated Sugar Beet
- Darwin Sneller .... G 989 977-3718
  Sebewaing *(G-14514)*
- Schuette Farms .... G 989 550-0563
  Elkton *(G-4783)*

FOOD PRDTS: Sugar, Maple, Indl
- Jaspers Sugar Bush LLC .... G 906 639-2588
  Carney *(G-2463)*

FOOD PRDTS: Sugar, Refined Sugar Beet
- Michigan Sugar Company .... C 989 673-3126
  Caro *(G-2472)*
- Michigan Sugar Company .... D 810 679-2241
  Croswell *(G-3601)*

FOOD PRDTS: Syrup, Maple
- Daniel Olson .... G 269 816-1838
  Jones *(G-8651)*
- Grandpa Hanks Maple Syrup LLC .... G 231 826-4494
  Falmouth *(G-4893)*
- Haighs Maple Syrup & Sups LLC .... F 517 202-6975
  Vermontville *(G-16821)*
- Herman Hillbillies Farm LLC .... G 906 201-0760
  Lanse *(G-9192)*
- Levi Ohman Micah .... G 612 251-1293
  Marquette *(G-10540)*
- Parsons Centennial Farm LLC .... G 231 547-2038
  Charlevoix *(G-2625)*
- Postma Brothers Maple Syrup .... G 906 478-3051
  Rudyard *(G-13985)*
- Rmg Family Sugar Bush Inc .... G 906 478-3038
  Rudyard *(G-13986)*
- White River Sugar Bush .... G 231 861-4860
  Hesperia *(G-7480)*

FOOD PRDTS: Tea
- Twinlab Holdings Inc .... G 800 645-5626
  Grand Rapids *(G-6943)*

FOOD PRDTS: Tortilla Chips
- Hacienda Mexican Foods LLC .... D 313 895-8823
  Detroit *(G-4110)*
- Hacienda Mexican Foods LLC .... F 313 843-7007
  Detroit *(G-4111)*

FOOD PRDTS: Tortillas
- Del Pueblo Tortillas .... G 248 858-9835
  Pontiac *(G-12815)*
- El Milagro of Michigan .... G 616 452-6625
  Grand Rapids *(G-6371)*
- Hacienda Mexican Foods LLC .... F 313 843-7007
  Detroit *(G-4111)*
- La Jalisciense Inc .... F 313 237-0008
  Farmington Hills *(G-5041)*
- Lafrontera Tortillas Inc .... G 734 231-1701
  Rockwood *(G-13606)*
- Las Brazas Tortillas .... G 616 886-0737
  Holland *(G-7720)*
- Mexamerica Foods LLC .... E 814 781-1447
  Grand Rapids *(G-6665)*
- Mexican Food Specialties Inc .... G 734 779-2370
  Southfield *(G-14980)*
- Tortillas Tita LLC .... G 734 756-7646
  Wayne *(G-17444)*

FOOD PRDTS: Vegetable Oil Mills, NEC
- Darling Ingredients Inc .... D 313 928-7400
  Melvindale *(G-10695)*
- Darling Ingredients Inc .... E 269 751-0560
  Hamilton *(G-7231)*
- Grand Trvrse Culinary Oils LLC .... G 231 590-2180
  Traverse City *(G-15990)*

FOOD PRDTS: Vinegar
- Bliss & Vinegar LLC .... G 616 970-0732
  Grand Rapids *(G-6231)*
- Intl Giuseppes Oils & Vinegars .... G 586 698-2754
  Sterling Hts *(G-15550)*
- Intl Giuseppes Oils & Vinegars .... G 586 263-4200
  Clinton Township *(G-3144)*
- Kraft Heinz Foods Company .... B 616 396-6557
  Holland *(G-7713)*
- Olive Vinegar .... G 248 923-2310
  Rochester *(G-13340)*
- Olive Vinegar .... G 586 484-4700
  Sterling Heights *(G-15439)*

FOOD PRDTS: Wheat Flour
- King Milling Company .... D 616 897-9264
  Lowell *(G-10033)*
- Mennel Milling Co of Mich Inc .... C 269 782-5175
  Dowagiac *(G-4550)*

FOOD PRDTS: Yeast
- Sensient Flavors LLC .... G 989 479-3211
  Harbor Beach *(G-7270)*
- Sensient Technologies Corp .... D 989 479-3211
  Harbor Beach *(G-7271)*

FOOD PRODUCTS MACHINERY
- APV Baker .... G 616 784-3111
  Grand Rapids *(G-6177)*
- Automated Process Equipment .... E 616 374-1000
  Lake Odessa *(G-9111)*
- B&P Littleford Day LLC .... D 989 757-1300
  Saginaw *(G-13998)*
- D C Norris North America LLC .... G 231 935-1519
  Traverse City *(G-15955)*
- Frontier Technology Inc .... F 269 673-9464
  Allegan *(G-163)*
- Marshall Middleby Holding LLC .... F 906 863-4401
  Menominee *(G-10743)*
- Process Partners Inc .... G 616 875-2156
  Hudsonville *(G-8174)*
- Spiral-Matic Inc .... G 248 486-5080
  Brighton *(G-1992)*
- Vendco LLC .... G 800 764-8245
  Shelby Township *(G-14718)*

FOOD STORES: Convenience, Chain
- Independent Dairy Inc .... E 734 241-6016
  Monroe *(G-11041)*

FOOD STORES: Grocery, Independent
- Algo Especial Variety Str Inc .... G 313 963-9013
  Detroit *(G-3854)*
- Kerns Sausages Inc .... E 989 652-2684
  Frankenmuth *(G-5590)*
- Marias Italian Bakery Inc .... F 734 981-1200
  Canton *(G-2396)*
- Raleigh & Ron Corporation .... D 248 280-2820
  Royal Oak *(G-13961)*
- Roma Bakery & Imported Foods .... E 517 485-9466
  Lansing *(G-9419)*
- Spartannash Company .... C 517 629-6313
  Albion *(G-132)*
- Sunlite Market Inc .... G 586 792-9870
  Clinton Township *(G-3236)*
- Supreme Baking Company .... E 313 894-0222
  Detroit *(G-4389)*
- Viaus Super Market .... G 906 786-1950
  Escanaba *(G-4866)*

FOOD STORES: Supermarket, More Than 100K Sq Ft, Hypermrkt
- Walmart Inc .... B 517 541-1481
  Charlotte *(G-2670)*

FOOD STORES: Supermarkets
- Spartannash Company .... D 517 278-8963
  Coldwater *(G-3333)*

FOOD STORES: Supermarkets, Chain
- Kroger Co .... C 586 727-4946
  Richmond *(G-13265)*

FOOD STORES: Supermarkets, Independent
- Erlas Inc .... D 989 872-2191
  Cass City *(G-2514)*

FOOTWEAR, WHOLESALE: Shoes
- Kalamazoo Orthotics & Dbtc .... F 269 349-2247
  Kalamazoo *(G-8793)*

FOOTWEAR: Cut Stock
- David Epstein Inc .... F 248 542-0802
  Ferndale *(G-5270)*
- Paul Murphy Plastics Co .... E 586 774-4880
  Roseville *(G-13851)*
- S A S .... G 586 725-6381
  Chesterfield *(G-2834)*
- Wolverine Procurement Inc .... E 616 866-9521
  Rockford *(G-13597)*

FORESTRY RELATED EQPT
- JP Skidmore LLC .... G 906 424-4127
  Menominee *(G-10740)*
- K2 Engineering Inc .... G 906 356-6303
  Rock *(G-13553)*
- Timberland Forestry .... F 906 387-4350
  Munising *(G-11251)*

FORGINGS
- Bjerke Forgings Inc .... A 313 382-2600
  Taylor *(G-15696)*
- Borgwarner Powdered Metals Inc .... E 734 261-5322
  Livonia *(G-9668)*

PRODUCT SECTION

FOUNDRIES: Gray & Ductile Iron

Buchanan Metal Forming Inc .... E 269 695-3836
  Buchanan *(G-2111)*
Chardam Gear Company Inc .... D 586 795-8900
  Sterling Heights *(G-15287)*
Composite Forgings Ltd Partnr .... D 313 496-1226
  Detroit *(G-3944)*
Computer Operated Mfg .... E 989 686-1333
  Bay City *(G-1297)*
Detail Precision Products Inc .... E 248 544-3390
  Ferndale *(G-5271)*
Dorris Company .... E 586 293-5260
  Fraser *(G-5644)*
Enterprise Tool and Gear Inc .... D 989 269-9797
  Bad Axe *(G-1060)*
Gage Eagle Spline Inc .... D 586 776-7240
  Warren *(G-17049)*
Great Lakes Forge Inc .... G 231 947-4931
  Traverse City *(G-15992)*
Great Lakes Industry Inc .... E 517 784-3153
  Jackson *(G-8459)*
Hephaestus Holdings LLC .... G 248 479-2700
  Novi *(G-11900)*
Hhi Formtech LLC .... E 586 415-2000
  Fraser *(G-5662)*
Hhi Formtech Industries LLC .... A 248 597-3800
  Royal Oak *(G-13934)*
Invo Spline Inc .... E 586 757-8840
  Warren *(G-17097)*
Jervis B Webb Company .... B 248 553-1000
  Novi *(G-11912)*
Kendor Steel Rule Die Inc .... E 586 293-7111
  Fraser *(G-5678)*
Lansing Forge Inc .... F 517 882-2056
  Lansing *(G-9388)*
Lansing Holding Company Inc .... G 517 882-2056
  Lansing *(G-9390)*
Lc Manufacturing LLC .... E 734 753-3990
  New Boston *(G-11503)*
Linear Mold & Engineering LLC .... E 734 744-4548
  Livonia *(G-9809)*
Lisi Automotive HI Vol Inc .... C 734 266-6900
  Livonia *(G-9813)*
Lyons Tool & Engineering Inc .... E 586 200-3003
  Warren *(G-17133)*
Mat Tek Inc .... G 810 659-0322
  Flushing *(G-5540)*
Metal Forming & Coining Corp .... G 586 731-2003
  Shelby Township *(G-14638)*
Michigan Forge Company LLC .... E 815 758-6400
  Lansing *(G-9398)*
Rack & Pinion Inc .... G 517 563-8872
  Horton *(G-7970)*
Ringmasters Mfg LLC .... E 734 729-6110
  Wayne *(G-17442)*
Schwartz Precision Gear Co .... E 586 754-4600
  Bloomfield Hills *(G-1797)*
Sinoscan Inc .... G 269 966-0932
  Battle Creek *(G-1249)*
Somers Steel .... G 734 729-3700
  Westland *(G-17599)*
Stonebridge Industries Inc .... A 586 323-0348
  Sterling Heights *(G-15513)*
Trenton Forging Company .... D 734 675-1620
  Trenton *(G-16159)*
Triumph Gear Systems - Macomb .... C 586 781-2800
  Macomb *(G-10170)*
Vectorall Manufacturing Inc .... E 248 486-4570
  Brighton *(G-2006)*
Wartian Lock Company .... G 586 777-2244
  Saint Clair Shores *(G-14276)*
Webster Cold Forge Co .... F 313 554-4500
  Northville *(G-11734)*
Wedin International Inc .... D 231 779-8650
  Cadillac *(G-2284)*
Wilkie Bros Conveyors Inc .... E 810 364-4820
  Marysville *(G-10626)*
Wyman-Gordon Forgings Inc .... E 810 229-9550
  Brighton *(G-2011)*

FORGINGS: Aluminum

Lincoln Park Die & Tool Co .... E 734 285-1680
  Brownstown *(G-2067)*
Mat Tek Inc .... G 810 659-0322
  Flushing *(G-5540)*
Mueller Brass Forging Co Inc .... D 810 987-7770
  Port Huron *(G-12946)*
Wonder Makers Environmental .... F 269 382-4154
  Kalamazoo *(G-8926)*

FORGINGS: Automotive & Internal Combustion Engine

Cambric Corporation .... B 801 415-7300
  Novi *(G-11842)*
Global Engine Mfg Aliance LLC .... G 734 529-9888
  Dundee *(G-4585)*
Hhi Form Tech LLC .... B 248 597-3800
  Royal Oak *(G-13933)*
Hy Lift Johnson Inc .... G 231 722-1100
  Muskegon *(G-11345)*
Linear Mold & Engineering LLC .... F 734 422-6060
  Livonia *(G-9810)*
Tenneco Inc .... F 248 354-7700
  Southfield *(G-15044)*

FORGINGS: Gear & Chain

Decker Gear Inc .... F 810 388-1500
  Saint Clair *(G-14216)*
Formax Precision Gear Inc .... E 586 323-9067
  Sterling Heights *(G-15344)*
Global Gear Inc .... E 734 979-0888
  Westland *(G-17562)*
Riverside Spline & Gear Inc .... E 810 765-8302
  Marine City *(G-10481)*
Tech Tool Company Inc .... G 313 836-4131
  Detroit *(G-4397)*

FORGINGS: Iron & Steel

American Axle Oxford .... E 248 361-6044
  Oxford *(G-12335)*
Stage Stop .... G 989 838-4039
  Ithaca *(G-8367)*
Steel Industries Inc .... C 313 535-8505
  Redford *(G-13194)*

FORGINGS: Machinery, Ferrous

Power Industries Corp .... G 586 783-3818
  Harrison Township *(G-7343)*

FORGINGS: Nonferrous

Borgwarner Powdered Metals Inc .... E 734 261-5322
  Livonia *(G-9668)*
Global Fmi LLC .... D 810 964-5555
  Fenton *(G-5216)*
Greenseed LLC .... G 313 295-0100
  Taylor *(G-15727)*
Hephaestus Holdings LLC .... G 248 479-2700
  Novi *(G-11900)*
Hhi Formtech LLC .... E 586 415-2000
  Fraser *(G-5662)*
Mueller Impacts Company Inc .... C 810 364-3700
  Marysville *(G-10608)*
Mueller Industries Inc .... D 248 446-3720
  Brighton *(G-1964)*
Resistance Welding Machne & AC .... F 269 428-4770
  Saint Joseph *(G-14337)*
United Brass Manufacturers Inc .... E 734 942-9224
  Romulus *(G-13737)*
United Brass Manufacturers Inc .... D 734 941-0700
  Romulus *(G-13736)*
Weldaloy Products Company .... D 586 758-5550
  Warren *(G-17290)*

FORMS: Concrete, Sheet Metal

EMI Construction Products .... G 800 603-9965
  Holland *(G-7622)*
Metal Merchants of Michigan .... E 248 293-0621
  Rochester Hills *(G-13472)*

FOUNDRIES: Aluminum

Acra Cast Inc .... E 989 893-3961
  Bay City *(G-1271)*
Cascade Die Casting Group Inc .... D 616 887-1771
  Sparta *(G-15089)*
Castalloy Corporation .... G 517 265-2452
  Adrian *(G-54)*
Dundee Castings Company .... D 734 529-2455
  Dundee *(G-4579)*
Ehc Inc .... G 313 259-2266
  Detroit *(G-4030)*
Eps Industries Inc .... E 616 844-9220
  Ferrysburg *(G-5533)*
Hoffmann Die Cast LLC .... C 269 983-1102
  Saint Joseph *(G-14317)*
Holland Alloys Inc .... E 616 396-6444
  Holland *(G-7667)*
IBC Precision Inc .... G 248 373-8202
  Auburn Hills *(G-907)*
J & M Machine Products Inc .... D 231 755-1622
  Norton Shores *(G-11764)*
Line Precision Inc .... E 248 474-5280
  Farmington Hills *(G-5044)*
Non-Ferrous Cast Alloys Inc .... D 231 799-0550
  Norton Shores *(G-11782)*
Prompt Pattern Inc .... E 586 759-2030
  Warren *(G-17201)*
RCO Engineering Inc .... D 586 620-4133
  Roseville *(G-13860)*
Shipston Alum Tech Mich Inc .... G 616 842-3500
  Fruitport *(G-5800)*
Specialty Steel Treating Inc .... E 586 293-5355
  Fraser *(G-5730)*
Supreme Casting Inc .... D 269 465-5757
  Stevensville *(G-15583)*
Tooling Technology LLC .... D 937 381-9211
  Macomb *(G-10169)*
Tri-State Cast Technologies Co .... G 231 582-0452
  Boyne City *(G-1836)*
Whitehall Products LLC .... D 231 894-2688
  Whitehall *(G-17682)*
Wolverine Die Cast Ltd Ptnshp .... E 586 757-1900
  Warren *(G-17296)*

FOUNDRIES: Brass, Bronze & Copper

Anchor Lamina America Inc .... C 231 533-8646
  Bellaire *(G-1434)*
Anchor Lamina America Inc .... E 248 489-9122
  Novi *(G-11826)*
Axly Production Machining Inc .... B 989 269-2444
  Bad Axe *(G-1057)*
Belwith Products LLC .... F 616 247-4000
  Grandville *(G-7022)*
Duplicast Corporation .... G 586 756-5900
  Warren *(G-17008)*
Enterprise Tool and Gear Inc .... D 989 269-9797
  Bad Axe *(G-1060)*
Eps Industries Inc .... E 616 844-9220
  Ferrysburg *(G-5334)*
GKN Sinter Metals LLC .... G 248 296-7832
  Auburn Hills *(G-888)*
Global CNC Industries Ltd .... E 734 464-1920
  Plymouth *(G-12629)*
Hackett Brass Foundry Co .... E 313 331-6005
  Detroit *(G-4113)*
Holland Alloys Inc .... E 616 396-6444
  Holland *(G-7667)*
Huron Tool & Engineering Co .... E 989 269-9927
  Bad Axe *(G-1068)*
Production Tube Company Inc .... G 313 259-3990
  Detroit *(G-4312)*
Prompt Pattern Inc .... E 586 759-2030
  Warren *(G-17201)*
Sterling Metal Works LLC .... G 586 977-9577
  Sterling Heights *(G-15512)*

FOUNDRIES: Gray & Ductile Iron

Bernier Cast Metals Inc .... G 989 754-7571
  Saginaw *(G-14006)*
Cadillac Casting Inc .... D 231 779-9600
  Cadillac *(G-2235)*
E & M Cores Inc .... G 989 386-9223
  Clare *(G-2869)*
Eagle Quest International Ltd .... F 616 850-2630
  Norton Shores *(G-11750)*
Ej Co .... E 231 536-4527
  East Jordan *(G-4632)*
Elco Inc .... G 586 778-6858
  Roseville *(G-13799)*
Eqi Ltd .... G 616 850-2630
  Norton Shores *(G-11753)*
Federal-Mogul Powertrain Inc .... C 616 887-8231
  Sparta *(G-15094)*
General Motors LLC .... B 989 757-0528
  Saginaw *(G-14044)*
Great Lakes Castings LLC .... C 231 843-2501
  Ludington *(G-10061)*
Holland Alloys Inc .... E 616 396-6444
  Holland *(G-7667)*
JP Castings Inc .... E 517 857-3660
  Springport *(G-15211)*
Paragon Metals LLC .... G 517 639-4629
  Hillsdale *(G-7533)*
Robert Bosch LLC .... F 269 429-3221
  Saint Joseph *(G-14338)*
Steeltech Ltd .... F 616 696-1130
  Cedar Springs *(G-2563)*

Employee Codes: A=Over 500 employees, B=251-500
C=101-250, D=51-100, E=20-50, F=10-19, G=3-9

FOUNDRIES: Gray & Ductile Iron — PRODUCT SECTION

Triumph Gear Systems - Macomb .... C 586 781-2800
  Macomb *(G-10170)*

FOUNDRIES: Iron

Grede LLC .... B 906 774-7250
  Kingsford *(G-9058)*
Holland Alloys Inc .... E 616 396-6444
  Holland *(G-7667)*
International Casting Corp .... F 586 293-8220
  Roseville *(G-13821)*
Kramer International Inc .... G 586 726-4300
  Troy *(G-16451)*
Paragon Metals LLC .... G 517 639-4629
  Hillsdale *(G-7533)*
Peerless Steel Company .... E 616 530-6695
  Grandville *(G-7063)*
Prompt Pattern Inc .... E 586 759-2030
  Warren *(G-17201)*
Robert Bosch LLC .... F 269 429-3221
  Saint Joseph *(G-14338)*
Smith Castings Inc .... E 906 774-4956
  Iron Mountain *(G-8301)*
Teksid Inc .... F 734 846-5897
  Farmington *(G-4914)*
Tooling Technology LLC .... D 937 381-9211
  Macomb *(G-10169)*
Wolverine Bronze Company .... D 586 776-8180
  Roseville *(G-13891)*

FOUNDRIES: Nonferrous

Algonac Marine Cast LLC .... F 810 794-9391
  Clay *(G-2992)*
Alloy Machining LLC .... G 517 204-3306
  Lansing *(G-9274)*
Ascent Integrated Platforms .... F 586 726-0500
  Macomb *(G-10110)*
Astech Inc .... E 989 823-7211
  Vassar *(G-16811)*
Awcco USA Incorporated .... G 586 336-9135
  Romeo *(G-13624)*
Barron Industries Inc .... D 248 628-4300
  Oxford *(G-12337)*
Berne Enterprises Inc .... F 989 453-3235
  Pigeon *(G-12487)*
Computer Operated Mfg .... E 989 686-1333
  Bay City *(G-1297)*
Douglas King Industries Inc .... E 989 642-2865
  Hemlock *(G-7461)*
Dundee Castings Company .... D 734 529-2455
  Dundee *(G-4579)*
Elden Industries Corporation .... F 734 946-6900
  Taylor *(G-15715)*
Federal-Mogul Piston Rings Inc .... F 248 354-7700
  Southfield *(G-14909)*
GKN Sinter Metals LLC .... G 248 296-7832
  Auburn Hills *(G-888)*
Gokoh Coldwater Incorporated .... F 517 279-1080
  Coldwater *(G-3305)*
Hackett Brass Foundry Co .... E 313 331-6005
  Detroit *(G-4113)*
Hoffmann Die Cast LLC .... C 269 983-1102
  Saint Joseph *(G-14317)*
Huron Casting Inc .... B 989 453-3933
  Pigeon *(G-12491)*
Husite Engineering Co Inc .... E 248 588-0337
  Clinton Township *(G-3136)*
Inland Lakes Machine Inc .... E 231 775-6543
  Cadillac *(G-2255)*
Invecast Corporation .... E 586 755-4050
  Warren *(G-17096)*
Line Precision Inc .... E 248 474-5280
  Farmington Hills *(G-5044)*
Magnesium Products America Inc .... B 734 416-8600
  Plymouth *(G-12681)*
Non-Ferrous Cast Alloys Inc .... D 231 799-0550
  Norton Shores *(G-11782)*
Paragon Metals LLC .... G 517 639-4629
  Hillsdale *(G-7533)*
Premiere Tool & Die Cast .... G 269 782-3030
  Kalamazoo *(G-8861)*
Prompt Pattern Inc .... E 586 759-2030
  Warren *(G-17201)*
Proto-Cast Inc .... E 313 565-5400
  Inkster *(G-8233)*
Rolled Alloys Inc .... D 800 521-0332
  Temperance *(G-15842)*
Smith Castings Inc .... E 906 774-4956
  Iron Mountain *(G-8301)*
Superior Brass & Alum Cast Co .... F 517 351-7534
  East Lansing *(G-4678)*

Trin-Mac Company Inc .... G 586 774-1900
  Saint Clair Shores *(G-14273)*
White Cloud Manufacturing Co .... E 231 796-8603
  Big Rapids *(G-1646)*

FOUNDRIES: Steel

Allied Metals Corp .... E 248 680-2400
  Auburn Hills *(G-765)*
Astech Inc .... E 989 823-7211
  Vassar *(G-16811)*
Bico Michigan Inc .... E 616 453-2400
  Grand Rapids *(G-6218)*
Detroit Materials Inc .... G 248 924-5436
  Farmington *(G-4897)*
Federal Screw Works .... G 231 922-9500
  Traverse City *(G-15969)*
G M Brass & Alum Fndry Inc .... F 269 926-6366
  Benton Harbor *(G-1500)*
GAL Gage Co .... E 269 465-5750
  Bridgman *(G-1863)*
General Motors Company .... E 989 757-1576
  Saginaw *(G-14043)*
General Motors LLC .... B 989 757-0528
  Saginaw *(G-14044)*
Hackett Brass Foundry Co .... E 313 331-6005
  Detroit *(G-4113)*
Heckett Multiserve .... G 313 842-2120
  Detroit *(G-4120)*
Holland Alloys Inc .... E 616 396-6444
  Holland *(G-7667)*
International Casting Corp .... F 586 293-8220
  Roseville *(G-13821)*
Invecast Corporation .... E 586 755-4050
  Warren *(G-17096)*
J & M Machine Products Inc .... D 231 755-1622
  Norton Shores *(G-11764)*
Mannix RE Holdings LLC .... G 231 972-0088
  Mecosta *(G-10689)*
Pal-TEC Inc .... G 906 788-4229
  Wallace *(G-16887)*
Paragon Metals LLC .... G 517 639-4629
  Hillsdale *(G-7533)*
Pennisular Packaging LLC .... G 313 304-4724
  Plymouth *(G-12710)*
RCO Engineering Inc .... D 586 620-4133
  Roseville *(G-13860)*
Saarsteel Incorporated .... G 248 608-0849
  Rochester Hills *(G-13509)*
Smith Castings Inc .... E 906 774-4956
  Iron Mountain *(G-8301)*
Temperform Corp .... G 248 851-9611
  Bloomfield Hills *(G-1801)*
Torch Steel Processing LLC .... E 313 571-7000
  Detroit *(G-4404)*
Usmfg Inc .... G 262 993-9197
  South Haven *(G-14779)*

FOUNDRIES: Steel Investment

Acra Cast Inc .... E 989 893-3961
  Bay City *(G-1271)*
Barber Steel Foundry Corp .... F 231 894-1830
  Rothbury *(G-13894)*
Chain Industries Inc .... E 248 348-7722
  Wixom *(G-17783)*
Douglas King Industries Inc .... E 989 642-2865
  Hemlock *(G-7461)*
Eagle Precision Cast Parts Inc .... E 231 788-3318
  Muskegon *(G-11310)*
Eutectic Engineering Co Inc .... E 313 892-2248
  Bloomfield Hills *(G-1765)*
Paragon Metals LLC .... G 517 639-4629
  Hillsdale *(G-7533)*
R L M Industries Inc .... D 248 628-5103
  Oxford *(G-12366)*

FOUNDRY MACHINERY & EQPT

Centennial Technologies Inc .... E 989 752-6167
  Saginaw *(G-14013)*
Corr-Fac Corporation .... G 989 358-7050
  Alpena *(G-284)*
Fata Aluminum LLC° .... F 248 724-7669
  Auburn Hills *(G-859)*
Koins Corp .... G 248 548-3038
  Madison Heights *(G-10293)*
Roberts Sinto Corporation .... E 517 371-2460
  Lansing *(G-9320)*
Sinto America Inc .... E 517 371-2460
  Lansing *(G-9323)*

FOUNDRY SAND MINING

Fairmount Santrol Inc .... E 800 255-7263
  Benton Harbor *(G-1497)*
Sand Products Corporation .... G 906 292-5432
  Moran *(G-11108)*
Sargent Sand Co .... G 989 792-8734
  Midland *(G-10912)*
Standard Sand Corporation .... G 616 538-3667
  Grand Haven *(G-6083)*

FOUNTAIN PEN REPAIR SHOP

Curbco Inc .... D 810 232-2121
  Flint *(G-5409)*

FOUNTAINS: Concrete

Felicity Fountains .... G 517 663-1324
  Eaton Rapids *(G-4723)*

FRACTIONATION PRDTS OF CRUDE PETROLEUM, HYDROCARBONS, NEC

Marysville Hydrocarbons LLC .... E 586 445-2300
  Marysville *(G-10606)*

FRAMES & FRAMING WHOLESALE

Tc Moulding .... G 248 588-2333
  Madison Heights *(G-10366)*

FRANCHISES, SELLING OR LICENSING

Coffee Beanery Ltd .... E 810 733-1020
  Flushing *(G-5533)*
Dominos Pizza LLC .... C 734 930-3030
  Ann Arbor *(G-424)*
Rocky Mtn Choclat Fctry Inc .... D 810 606-8550
  Grand Blanc *(G-5981)*
Ziebart International Corp .... E 248 588-4100
  Troy *(G-16706)*

FREEZERS: Household

Northland Corporation .... C 616 754-5601
  Greenville *(G-7148)*
Whirlpool Corporation .... C 269 923-3009
  Benton Harbor *(G-1571)*

FREIGHT FORWARDING ARRANGEMENTS: Domestic

Xpo Cnw Inc .... C 734 757-1444
  Ann Arbor *(G-705)*

FREIGHT TRANSPORTATION ARRANGEMENTS

Blujay Solutions Co .... G 616 738-6400
  Holland *(G-7571)*
Boskage Commerce Publications .... G 269 673-7242
  Portage *(G-12986)*
Business Helper LLC .... G 231 271-4404
  Suttons Bay *(G-15651)*
Fourth Seacoast Publishing Co .... G 586 779-5570
  Saint Clair Shores *(G-14252)*
Harrison Partners Inv Group .... G 419 708-8154
  Milan *(G-10940)*
Kolossos Printing Inc .... G 734 741-1600
  Ann Arbor *(G-518)*
World of Pallets and Trucking .... G 313 899-2000
  Detroit *(G-4449)*

FREON

Cjg LLC .... F 734 793-1400
  Livonia *(G-9683)*
J&J Freon Removal .... G 586 264-6379
  Warren *(G-17110)*

FRICTION MATERIAL, MADE FROM POWDERED METAL

Greene Manufacturing Tech LLC .... C 810 982-9720
  Port Huron *(G-12924)*
Miba Hydramechanica Corp .... D 586 264-3094
  Sterling Heights *(G-15420)*

FRUIT & VEGETABLE MARKETS

Porters Orchards Farm Market .... F 810 636-7156
  Goodrich *(G-5956)*

PRODUCT SECTION

Verellen Orchards .... G 586 752-2989
Washington *(G-17313)*

FRUIT STANDS OR MARKETS

Northville Cider Mill Inc .... E 248 349-3181
Northville *(G-11715)*
Uncle Johns Cider Mill Inc .... D 989 224-3686
Saint Johns *(G-14298)*
Yates Cider Mill Inc .... G 248 651-8300
Rochester Hills *(G-13551)*

FUEL ADDITIVES

Fortech Products Inc .... E 248 446-9500
Brighton *(G-1925)*
Nano Materials & Processes Inc .... G 248 529-3873
Milford *(G-10974)*

FUEL CELLS: Solid State

Fuel Cell System Mfg LLC .... G 313 319-5571
Brownstown Township *(G-2069)*

FUEL DEALERS: Coal

Arbor Stone .... G 517 750-1340
Spring Arbor *(G-15119)*

FUEL OIL DEALERS

Koenig Fuel & Supply Co .... G 313 368-1870
Wayne *(G-17433)*
Lansing Ice and Fuel Company .... F 517 372-3850
Lansing *(G-9240)*
M R D Industries .... G 269 623-8452
Delton *(G-3818)*

FUELS: Diesel

W2fuel LLC .... E 517 920-4868
Adrian *(G-101)*

FUELS: Ethanol

Adrian Lva Biofuel LLC .... F 517 920-4863
Adrian *(G-44)*
Albasara Fuel LLC .... G 313 443-6581
Dearborn *(G-3674)*
Ana Fuel Inc .... G 810 422-5659
Ann Arbor *(G-355)*
Assi Fuel Inc .... G 586 759-4759
Warren *(G-16944)*
Beebe Fuel Systems Inc .... G 248 437-3322
South Lyon *(G-14786)*
BKM Fuels LLC .... G 269 342-9576
Kalamazoo *(G-8698)*
BP Gas/ JB Fuel .... G 517 531-3400
Parma *(G-12387)*
Camerons of Jackson LLC .... G 517 531-3400
Parma *(G-12388)*
Century Fuel Products .... F 734 728-0300
Van Buren Twp *(G-16751)*
Chouteau Fuels Company LLC .... G 734 302-4800
Ann Arbor *(G-399)*
D M J Corp .... G 810 239-9071
Flint *(G-5412)*
Elite Fuels LLC .... G 313 871-6308
Detroit *(G-4032)*
EZ Fuel Inc .... G 810 744-4452
Flint *(G-5428)*
Fit Fuel By Kt LLC .... G 517 643-8827
East Lansing *(G-4658)*
Fk Fuel Inc .... G 313 383-6005
Lincoln Park *(G-9577)*
Freal Fuel Inc .... G 248 790-7202
Chesterfield *(G-2780)*
Frontier Rnwable Resources LLC .... G 906 228-7960
Marquette *(G-10533)*
Fuel Tobacco Stop .... G 810 487-2040
Flushing *(G-5535)*
Fuel Woodfire Grill LLC .... G 810 479-4933
Port Huron *(G-12920)*
Gb Dynamics Inc .... E 313 400-3570
Port Huron *(G-12921)*
Green Fuels Llc .... G 734 735-6802
Carleton *(G-2455)*
Ibidltd-Blue Green Energy .... G 909 547-5160
Dearborn *(G-3723)*
Il Adrian LLC W2fuel .... G 517 920-4863
Adrian *(G-68)*
Inkster Fuel & Food Inc .... G 313 565-8230
Inkster *(G-8228)*

K&S Fuel Ventures .... G 248 360-0055
Commerce Township *(G-3418)*
Kentwood Fuel Inc .... G 616 455-2387
Kentwood *(G-9013)*
Kern Auto Sales and Svc LLC .... F 734 475-2722
Chelsea *(G-2715)*
Lansing Fuel Ventures Inc .... G 517 371-1198
Lansing *(G-9389)*
Lillian Fuel Inc .... G 734 439-8505
Milan *(G-10945)*
Lin Adam Fuel Inc .... G 313 733-6631
Detroit *(G-4206)*
M and A Fuels .... G 313 397-7141
Detroit *(G-4213)*
Marks Fuel Dock .... G 586 445-8525
Saint Clair Shores *(G-14262)*
Michigan Fuels .... G 313 886-7110
Grosse Pointe Woods *(G-7207)*
Mind Fuel LLC .... G 248 414-5296
Royal Oak *(G-13952)*
Monroe Fuel Company LLC .... G 734 302-4824
Ann Arbor *(G-563)*
Naked Fuel Juice Bar .... G 248 325-9735
West Bloomfield *(G-17489)*
Nation Wide Fuel Inc .... G 734 721-7110
Dearborn *(G-3743)*
National Fuels Inc .... G 734 895-7836
Canton *(G-2411)*
Nine Mile Dequindre Fuel Stop .... G 586 757-7721
Warren *(G-17167)*
Oasis Fuel Corporation .... G 906 486-4126
Ishpeming *(G-8351)*
Organicorp Inc .... G 616 540-0295
Lowell *(G-10040)*
Paw Paw Fuel Stop .... G 269 657-7357
Paw Paw *(G-12412)*
Performance Fuels Systems Inc .... G 248 202-1789
Troy *(G-16543)*
Reed Fuel LLC .... G 574 520-3101
Niles *(G-11642)*
S& A Fuel LLC .... G 313 945-6555
Dearborn *(G-3754)*
Saad Fuels Inc .... G 734 425-2829
Westland *(G-17598)*
Seven Mile and Grnd River Fuel .... G 313 535-3000
Hamtramck *(G-7246)*
Sixteen Crooks BP Fuel .... G 248 643-7272
Troy *(G-16605)*
Sy Fuel Inc .... G 313 531-5894
Redford *(G-13198)*
Taiz Fuel Inc .... G 313 485-2972
Dearborn Heights *(G-3798)*
Temperance Fuel Stop Inc .... G 734 206-2676
Grosse Pointe Woods *(G-7210)*
Van Dyke Fuell .... G 586 758-0120
Warren *(G-17277)*
Vision Fuels LLC .... G 586 997-3286
Shelby Township *(G-14720)*
Wamu Fuel LLC .... G 313 386-8700
Livonia *(G-9996)*
Warren City Fuel .... G 586 759-4795
Dearborn *(G-3772)*
Zunairah Fuels Inc .... G 647 405-1606
Clinton Township *(G-3265)*

FUELS: Jet

Avflight Corporation .... G 734 663-6466
Ann Arbor *(G-376)*
Jet Fuel .... G 231 767-9566
Muskegon *(G-11353)*

FUELS: Oil

Corrigan Enterprises Inc .... E 810 229-6323
Brighton *(G-1904)*
Motor City Quick Lube One Inc .... G 734 367-6457
Livonia *(G-9849)*
Pacific Oil Resources Inc .... E 734 397-1120
Van Buren Twp *(G-16777)*

FUNGICIDES OR HERBICIDES

Dow Chemical Company .... C 989 636-4406
Midland *(G-10836)*
Dow Chemical Company .... B 989 636-1000
Midland *(G-10834)*
Dow Chemical Company .... D 989 636-5409
Midland *(G-10848)*

FUR APPAREL STORES

Birlon Group LLC .... G 313 551-5341
Inkster *(G-8225)*
Holloway Fur Dressing .... G 231 258-5200
Lake City *(G-9088)*

FUR: Apparel

Wolvering Fur .... G 313 961-0620
Detroit *(G-4447)*

FURNACE CASINGS: Sheet Metal

Kraftube Inc .... C 231 832-5562
Reed City *(G-13217)*

FURNACES & OVENS: Fuel-Fired

Kolene Corporation .... E 313 273-9220
Detroit *(G-4180)*

FURNACES & OVENS: Indl

Able Htng Clng & Plmbng .... G 231 779-5430
Cadillac *(G-2221)*
Afc-Holcroft LLC .... D 248 624-8191
Wixom *(G-17754)*
Allegan Tubular Products Inc .... D 269 673-6636
Allegan *(G-149)*
Atmosphere Group Inc .... G 248 624-8191
Wixom *(G-17763)*
Belco Industries Inc .... C 616 794-0410
Belding *(G-1399)*
Ce II Holdings Inc .... F 248 305-7700
Brighton *(G-1899)*
Clark Granco Inc .... D 616 794-2600
Belding *(G-1407)*
Complete Filtration Inc .... F 248 693-0500
Lake Orion *(G-9132)*
Detroit Steel Treating Company .... E 248 334-7436
Pontiac *(G-12816)*
Dfc Inc .... G 734 285-6749
Riverview *(G-13293)*
Efd Induction Inc .... F 248 658-0700
Madison Heights *(G-10240)*
Fluid Hutchinson Management .... D 248 679-1327
Auburn Hills *(G-876)*
Fluidtherm Corp Michigan .... G 989 344-1500
Frederic *(G-5751)*
Gemini Precision Machining Inc .... D 989 269-9702
Bad Axe *(G-1065)*
Gerref Industries Inc .... E 616 794-3110
Belding *(G-1416)*
Industrial Temperature Control .... G 734 451-8740
Canton *(G-2384)*
J L Becker Acquisition LLC .... E 734 656-2000
Plymouth *(G-12651)*
Jackson Oven Supply Inc .... F 517 784-9660
Jackson *(G-8478)*
Nortek Air Solutions LLC .... D 616 738-7148
Holland *(G-7759)*
North Woods Industrial .... G 616 784-2840
Comstock Park *(G-3502)*
Perceptive Industries Inc .... E 269 204-6768
Plainwell *(G-12536)*
Salem/Savard Industries LLC .... E 313 931-6880
Detroit *(G-4352)*
Thermal Designs & Manufacturng .... E 586 773-5231
Roseville *(G-13878)*
Thermalfab Products Inc .... F 517 486-2073
Blissfield *(G-1728)*
Thoreson-Mc Cosh Inc .... E 248 362-0960
Troy *(G-16638)*
Tomtek Hvac Inc .... G 517 546-0357
Howell *(G-8113)*
Tps LLC .... D 269 849-2700
Riverside *(G-13287)*
Ultra-Temp Corporation .... G 810 794-4709
Clay *(G-3005)*
Upton Industries Inc .... E 586 771-1200
Roseville *(G-13887)*
Vconverter Corporation .... D 248 388-0549
Whitmore Lake *(G-17708)*

FURNACES: Indl, Electric

Ajax Tocco Magnethermic Corp .... E 248 589-2524
Madison Heights *(G-10185)*
Ajax Tocco Magnethermic Corp .... F 248 585-1140
Madison Heights *(G-10186)*
Strik-Wstfen-Dynarad Frnc Corp .... G 616 355-2327
Holland *(G-7817)*

FURNITURE & CABINET STORES: Cabinets, Custom Work

FURNITURE & CABINET STORES: Cabinets, Custom Work

G & G Wood & Supply Inc .... F 586 293-0450
  Roseville *(G-13805)*
Kurtis Mfg & Distrg Corp .... E 734 522-7600
  Livonia *(G-9802)*
Moda Manufacturing LLC .... G 586 204-5120
  Farmington Hills *(G-5071)*
Phillip Anderson .... G 269 687-7166
  Niles *(G-11639)*
Reis Custom Cabinets .... G 586 791-4925
  Reese *(G-13231)*
Rose Corporation .... E 734 426-0005
  Dexter *(G-4508)*
Van Daeles Inc .... G 734 587-7165
  Monroe *(G-11082)*

FURNITURE & FIXTURES Factory

Banta Furniture Company .... F 616 575-8180
  Grand Rapids *(G-6203)*
Consort Corporation .... E 269 388-4532
  Kalamazoo *(G-8713)*
Firehouse Woodworks LLC .... G 616 285-2300
  Grand Rapids *(G-6407)*
Frank Terlecki Company Inc .... F 586 759-5770
  Warren *(G-17045)*
Paladin Ind Inc .... E 616 698-7495
  Grand Rapids *(G-6740)*
Pinetree Trading LLC .... F 313 584-2700
  Dearborn *(G-3748)*
Superior Fixture & Tooling LLC .... G 616 828-1566
  Grand Rapids *(G-6903)*
Symbiote Inc .... E 616 772-1790
  Zeeland *(G-18189)*
West Michigan Gage Inc .... F 616 735-0585
  Walker *(G-16882)*
Woodard—Cm LLC .... E 989 725-4265
  Owosso *(G-12331)*

FURNITURE COMPONENTS: Porcelain Enameled

Forward Metal Craft Inc .... F 616 459-6051
  Grand Rapids *(G-6417)*

FURNITURE PARTS: Metal

Fournier Enterprises Inc .... G 586 323-9160
  Mount Clemens *(G-11131)*
Gibraltar Inc .... E 616 748-4857
  Zeeland *(G-18144)*
Metalworks Inc .... C 231 845-5136
  Ludington *(G-10073)*
Omt Veyhl .... G 616 738-6688
  Holland *(G-7763)*

FURNITURE REFINISHING SVCS

Industrial Finishing Co LLC .... G 616 784-5737
  Comstock Park *(G-3485)*

FURNITURE REPAIR & MAINTENANCE SVCS

Ausable Upholstery .... G 989 366-5219
  Cadillac *(G-2229)*
Irwin Seating Holding Company .... B 616 574-7400
  Grand Rapids *(G-6545)*

FURNITURE STOCK & PARTS: Carvings, Wood

Gem Wood Products Inc .... G 616 384-3460
  Coopersville *(G-3559)*
IKEA Chip LLC .... G 877 218-9931
  Troy *(G-16409)*
Warner Door .... G 989 823-8397
  Vassar *(G-16817)*
Yooper WD Wrks Restoration LLC .... G 906 203-0056
  Sault Sainte Marie *(G-14480)*
Zemis 5 LLC .... G 317 946-7015
  Detroit *(G-4457)*

FURNITURE STOCK & PARTS: Dimension Stock, Hardwood

Grand Rapids Carvers Inc .... E 616 538-0022
  Grand Rapids *(G-6452)*
Matelski Lumber Company .... E 231 549-2780
  Boyne Falls *(G-1841)*

Meeders Dim & Lbr Pdts Co .... G 231 587-8611
  Mancelona *(G-10394)*

FURNITURE STOCK & PARTS: Hardwood

De Meester Saw Mill .... G 616 677-3144
  Coopersville *(G-3555)*
Demeester Wood Products Inc .... F 616 677-5995
  Coopersville *(G-3556)*
Doltek Enterprises Inc .... E 616 837-7828
  Nunica *(G-12036)*
Forestry Management Svcs Inc .... C 517 456-7431
  Clinton *(G-3020)*
H & R Wood Specialties Inc .... E 269 628-2181
  Gobles *(G-5947)*
Jarvis Saw Mill Inc .... G 231 861-2078
  Shelby *(G-14526)*
Motto Cedar Products Inc .... G 906 753-4892
  Daggett *(G-3622)*

FURNITURE STOCK & PARTS: Turnings, Wood

Solaire Medical Storage LLC .... D 888 435-2256
  Marne *(G-10513)*

FURNITURE STORES

Artisans Cstm Mmory Mattresses .... F 989 793-3208
  Saginaw *(G-13996)*
Compass Interiors LLC .... G 231 348-5353
  Petoskey *(G-12446)*
H L F Furniture Incorporated .... E 734 697-3000
  Van Buren Twp *(G-16762)*
Homespun Furniture Inc .... F 734 284-6277
  Riverview *(G-13297)*
Izzy Plus .... G 574 821-1200
  Grand Haven *(G-6038)*
Koegel Meats Inc .... C 810 238-3685
  Flint *(G-5456)*
La-Z-Boy Incorporated .... A 734 242-1444
  Monroe *(G-11049)*
Marrs Discount Furniture .... G 989 720-5436
  Owosso *(G-12300)*
Richards Quality Bedding Co .... E 616 363-0070
  Grand Rapids *(G-6823)*
Straits Corporation .... F 989 684-5088
  Tawas City *(G-15679)*
Tvb Inc .... F 616 456-9629
  Grand Rapids *(G-6942)*
West Mich Off Interiors Inc .... G 269 344-0768
  Kalamazoo *(G-8923)*

FURNITURE STORES: Cabinets, Kitchen, Exc Custom Made

Farmington Cabinet Company .... F 248 476-2666
  Livonia *(G-9735)*

FURNITURE STORES: Custom Made, Exc Cabinets

Woodland Creek Furniture Inc .... E 231 518-4084
  Kalkaska *(G-8968)*

FURNITURE STORES: Juvenile

Van Peete Enterprises .... G 517 369-2123
  Bronson *(G-2034)*

FURNITURE STORES: Office

Garants Office Sups & Prtg Inc .... G 989 356-3930
  Alpena *(G-291)*
Office Design & Furn LLC .... G 734 217-2717
  Ypsilanti *(G-18093)*
W B Mason Co Inc .... D 734 947-6370
  Taylor *(G-15780)*
Yti Office Express LLC .... G 866 996-8952
  Troy *(G-16704)*

FURNITURE UPHOLSTERY REPAIR SVCS

Banta Furniture Company .... F 616 575-8180
  Grand Rapids *(G-6203)*
Custom Interiors of Toledo .... G 419 865-3090
  Ottawa Lake *(G-12261)*
Jacquart Fabric Products Inc .... C 906 932-1339
  Ironwood *(G-8332)*

FURNITURE WHOLESALERS

AAM Wholesale Carpet Corp .... G 313 898-5101
  Detroit *(G-3832)*
Alticor Global Holdings Inc .... F 616 787-1000
  Ada *(G-5)*
Alticor Inc .... C 616 787-1000
  Ada *(G-6)*
Casual Ptio Furn Rfnishing Inc .... G 586 254-1900
  Canton *(G-2358)*
Richwood Industries Inc .... E 616 243-2700
  Grand Rapids *(G-6824)*
West Mich Off Interiors Inc .... G 269 344-0768
  Kalamazoo *(G-8923)*

FURNITURE, HOUSEHOLD: Wholesalers

Kurtis Mfg & Distrg Corp .... E 734 522-7600
  Livonia *(G-9802)*

FURNITURE, MATTRESSES: Wholesalers

Mattress Wholesale .... F 248 968-2200
  Oak Park *(G-12082)*

FURNITURE, OFFICE: Wholesalers

Electra-Tec Inc .... G 269 694-6652
  Otsego *(G-12238)*
Maleports Sault Prtg Co Inc .... E 906 632-3369
  Sault Sainte Marie *(G-14468)*
Office Connection Inc .... E 248 871-2003
  Farmington Hills *(G-5086)*
Rush Stationers Printers Inc .... F 989 891-9305
  Bay City *(G-1351)*

FURNITURE, WHOLESALE: Racks

Repair Industries Michigan Inc .... C 313 365-5300
  Detroit *(G-4344)*

FURNITURE: Altars & Pulpits

Bracy & Associates Ltd .... G 616 298-8120
  Holland *(G-7574)*

FURNITURE: Assembly Hall

Subassembly Plus Inc .... E 616 395-2075
  Holland *(G-7819)*

FURNITURE: Bedroom, Wood

Rooms of Grand Rapids LLC .... F 616 260-1452
  Spring Lake *(G-15173)*

FURNITURE: Bookcases, Office, Wood

T F Boyer Industries Inc .... G 248 674-8420
  Waterford *(G-17380)*

FURNITURE: Camp, Wood

G&J Products & Services .... G 734 522-2984
  Westland *(G-17560)*

FURNITURE: Chairs & Couches, Wood, Upholstered

Leland International Inc .... E 616 975-9260
  Grand Rapids *(G-6626)*

FURNITURE: Chairs, Bentwood

Picwood USA LLC .... G 844 802-1599
  Kalamazoo *(G-8850)*

FURNITURE: Chairs, Household Upholstered

La-Z-Boy Global Limited .... G 734 241-2438
  Monroe *(G-11048)*
La-Z-Boy Incorporated .... A 734 242-1444
  Monroe *(G-11049)*

FURNITURE: Chairs, Household, Metal

MTS Burgess LLC .... D 734 847-2937
  Temperance *(G-15839)*

FURNITURE: Chairs, Office Exc Wood

Jsj Corporation .... E 616 842-6350
  Grand Haven *(G-6042)*

PRODUCT SECTION — FURNITURE: Kitchen & Dining Room

FURNITURE: Console Tables, Wood
Dorel Home Furnishings Inc .... B 269 782-8661
  Dowagiac *(G-4540)*

FURNITURE: Cut Stone
A E G M Inc .... G 313 304-5279
  Dearborn *(G-3670)*

FURNITURE: Desks & Tables, Office, Exc Wood
Autoexec Inc .... G 616 971-0080
  Grand Rapids *(G-6193)*
Office Updating .... G 248 770-4769
  White Lake *(G-17635)*

FURNITURE: Desks & Tables, Office, Wood
R J Woodworking Inc .... F 231 766-2511
  Muskegon *(G-11412)*

FURNITURE: Desks, Wood
Cornerstone Furniture Inc .... G 269 795-3379
  Middleville *(G-10801)*
Rj Operating Company .... F 616 392-7101
  Holland *(G-7789)*

FURNITURE: Dining Room, Wood
Context Furniture L L C .... G 248 200-0724
  Ferndale *(G-5267)*
Kindel Furniture Company LLC .... C 616 243-3676
  Grand Rapids *(G-6583)*

FURNITURE: Dressers, Household, Wood
Anderson Manufacturing Co Inc .... F 906 863-8223
  Menominee *(G-10723)*

FURNITURE: Fiberglass & Plastic
D & R Fabrication Inc .... D 616 794-1130
  Belding *(G-1408)*
Innovative Pdts Unlimited Inc .... E 269 684-5050
  Niles *(G-11620)*
New Line Inc .... G 586 228-4820
  Shelby Township *(G-14652)*

FURNITURE: Foundations & Platforms
Helping Hearts Helping Hands .... G 248 980-5090
  Constantine *(G-3536)*

FURNITURE: Game Room, Wood
Mega Mania Diversions LLC .... G 888 322-9076
  Commerce Township *(G-3430)*

FURNITURE: Hospital
Hmi Liquidating Company Inc .... G 616 654-5055
  Zeeland *(G-18151)*

FURNITURE: Hotel
Custom Components Corporation .... F 616 523-1111
  Ionia *(G-8247)*

FURNITURE: Household, Metal
Industrial Reflections Inc .... G 734 782-4454
  Flat Rock *(G-5355)*
M C M Fixture Company Inc .... E 248 547-9280
  Hazel Park *(G-7442)*
Martin and Hattie Rasche Inc .... D 616 245-1223
  Grand Rapids *(G-6646)*
Premium Machine & Tool Inc .... F 989 855-3326
  Lyons *(G-10095)*
Spec International Inc .... F 616 248-3022
  Grand Rapids *(G-6879)*

FURNITURE: Household, Upholstered, Exc Wood Or Metal
Dozy Dotes LLC .... G 866 870-1048
  Grand Blanc *(G-5965)*

FURNITURE: Household, Wood
A K Services Inc .... G 313 972-1010
  Detroit *(G-3827)*
Alo LLC .... G 313 318-9029
  Detroit *(G-3860)*
Boese Associates Inc .... G 231 347-3995
  Petoskey *(G-12443)*
Center of World Woodshop Inc .... G 269 469-5687
  Sawyer *(G-14484)*
Charles Phipps and Sons Ltd .... F 810 359-7141
  Lexington *(G-9556)*
Charlies Wood Shop .... F 989 845-2632
  Chesaning *(G-2722)*
Charlotte Cabinets Inc .... G 517 543-1522
  Charlotte *(G-2639)*
Compass Interiors LLC .... G 231 348-5353
  Petoskey *(G-12446)*
Craftwood Industries Inc .... E 616 796-1209
  Holland *(G-7599)*
Custom Interiors of Toledo .... G 419 865-3090
  Ottawa Lake *(G-12261)*
Czuk Studio .... G 269 628-2568
  Kendall *(G-8983)*
Ejw Contract Inc .... G 616 293-5181
  Whitmore Lake *(G-17696)*
Essilor Laboratories Amer Inc .... C 616 361-6000
  Grand Rapids *(G-6386)*
European Cabinet Mfg Co .... E 586 445-8909
  Roseville *(G-13802)*
Flairwood Industries Inc .... E 231 798-8324
  Norton Shores *(G-11756)*
Genesis Seating Inc .... G 616 954-1040
  Grand Rapids *(G-6436)*
Genesis Seating Inc .... G 616 954-1040
  Grand Rapids *(G-6437)*
Grand Rapids Carvers Inc .... E 616 538-0022
  Grand Rapids *(G-6452)*
Grand Rapids Chair Company .... C 616 774-0561
  Byron Center *(G-2194)*
H L F Furniture Incorporated .... E 734 697-3000
  Van Buren Twp *(G-16762)*
Hekman Furniture Company .... E 616 748-2660
  Zeeland *(G-18146)*
Industrial Woodworking Corp .... E 616 741-9663
  Zeeland *(G-18158)*
J B Cutting Inc .... G 586 468-4765
  Mount Clemens *(G-11135)*
Jack-Post Corporation .... F 269 695-7000
  Buchanan *(G-2121)*
Janice Morse Inc .... E 248 624-7300
  West Bloomfield *(G-17482)*
Kaliniak Design LLC .... G 616 675-3850
  Kent City *(G-8992)*
Kentwood Manufacturing Co .... E 616 698-6370
  Grand Rapids *(G-6579)*
La-Z-Boy Casegoods Inc .... E 734 242-1444
  Monroe *(G-11047)*
La-Z-Boy Incorporated .... A 734 242-1444
  Monroe *(G-11049)*
M C M Fixture Company Inc .... E 248 547-9280
  Hazel Park *(G-7442)*
Meeders Dim & Lbr Pdts Co .... G 231 587-8611
  Mancelona *(G-10394)*
Merdel Game Manufacturing Co .... G 231 845-1263
  Ludington *(G-10071)*
Mid-State Distributors Inc .... G 989 793-1820
  Saginaw *(G-14094)*
Mien Company Inc .... F 616 818-1970
  Grand Rapids *(G-6688)*
Millennm-The Inside Sltion Inc .... E 248 645-9005
  Farmington Hills *(G-5069)*
Nu-Tran LLC .... G 616 350-9575
  Wyoming *(G-18023)*
Nuvar Inc .... E 616 394-5779
  Holland *(G-7760)*
Perspectives Custom Cabinetry .... E 248 288-4100
  Troy *(G-16544)*
Plum Tree .... G 269 469-5980
  Union Pier *(G-16738)*
Prime Wood Products Inc .... G 616 399-4700
  Holland *(G-7775)*
R-Bo Co Inc .... E 616 748-9753
  Zeeland *(G-18184)*
Rgm New Ventures Inc .... D 248 624-5050
  Wixom *(G-17885)*
Rospatch Jessco Corporation .... B 269 782-8661
  Dowagiac *(G-4558)*
Shop Makarios LLC .... G 800 479-0032
  Byron Center *(G-2211)*
Stow Company .... C 616 399-3311
  Holland *(G-7816)*
Terry Hanover .... G 269 426-4199
  New Troy *(G-11560)*
Theradapt Products Inc .... G 231 480-4008
  Ludington *(G-10082)*
Van Zee Acquisitions Inc .... E 616 855-7000
  Grand Rapids *(G-6958)*
Woodard—Cm LLC .... E 989 725-4265
  Owosso *(G-12331)*
Woodcraft Customs LLC .... E 248 987-4473
  Farmington Hills *(G-5152)*
Woodcrafters .... G 517 741-7423
  Sherwood *(G-14737)*
Woodland Creek Furniture Inc .... E 231 518-4084
  Kalkaska *(G-8968)*
Woodways Industries LLC .... E 616 956-3070
  Grand Rapids *(G-7003)*

FURNITURE: Hydraulic Barber & Beauty Shop Chairs
Young Manufacturing Inc .... G 906 483-3851
  Dollar Bay *(G-4522)*

FURNITURE: Institutional, Exc Wood
Alr Products Inc .... E 517 649-2243
  Mulliken *(G-11238)*
Big Bear Products Inc .... G 269 657-3550
  Paw Paw *(G-12398)*
Bridgewater Interiors LLC .... C 313 842-3300
  Detroit *(G-3916)*
Brill Company Inc .... E 231 843-2430
  Ludington *(G-10050)*
Counterpoint By Hlf .... D 734 699-7100
  Van Buren Twp *(G-16754)*
Craftwood Industries Inc .... E 616 796-1209
  Holland *(G-7599)*
Furniture Partners LLC .... D 616 355-3051
  Holland *(G-7638)*
Grand Rapids Carvers Inc .... E 616 538-0022
  Grand Rapids *(G-6452)*
Herman Miller Inc .... B 616 654-3000
  Zeeland *(G-18147)*
Interkal LLC .... G 989 486-1788
  Midland *(G-10872)*
ITW Dahti Seating .... E 616 866-1323
  Rockford *(G-13573)*
Johnson Controls Inc .... B 734 254-5000
  Plymouth *(G-12655)*
Jrt Enterprises LLC .... G 877 318-7661
  Holland *(G-7703)*
Kawkawlin Manufacturing Co .... G 989 684-5470
  Kawkawlin *(G-8974)*
Knoedler Manufacturers Inc .... F 269 969-7722
  Battle Creek *(G-1221)*
Lear Corporation .... A 248 447-1500
  Mason *(G-10644)*
Milcare Inc .... B 616 654-8000
  Zeeland *(G-18166)*
Multiform Studios LLC .... G 248 437-5964
  South Lyon *(G-14803)*
R T London Company .... D 616 364-4800
  Grand Rapids *(G-6804)*
RCO Aerospace Products LLC .... D 586 774-8400
  Roseville *(G-13859)*
RCO Engineering Inc .... D 586 620-4133
  Roseville *(G-13860)*
Recaro North America Inc .... B 313 842-3479
  Detroit *(G-4333)*
Syncreonus Inc .... D 248 377-4700
  Auburn Hills *(G-1010)*
TMC Furniture Inc .... G 734 622-0080
  Ann Arbor *(G-678)*
Woodard—Cm LLC .... E 989 725-4265
  Owosso *(G-12331)*
Woodbridge Holdings Inc .... C 734 942-0458
  Romulus *(G-13742)*
Yanfeng US Automotive .... D 734 289-4841
  Monroe *(G-11086)*

FURNITURE: Juvenile, Wood
Van Peete Enterprises .... G 517 369-2123
  Bronson *(G-2034)*

FURNITURE: Kitchen & Dining Room
Contract Furn Solutions Inc .... E 734 941-2750
  Brownstown *(G-2061)*
Distinctive Custom Furniture .... G 248 399-9175
  Ferndale *(G-5279)*

FURNITURE: Laboratory

Counter Reaction LLC	G	248 624-7900	
Wixom (G-17790)			
Impert Industries Inc	G	269 694-2727	
Otsego (G-12241)			
Metal Arc Inc	E	231 865-3111	
Muskegon (G-11375)			
Security Steelcraft Corp	E	231 733-1101	
Muskegon (G-11420)			
Teclab Inc	E	269 372-6000	
Kalamazoo (G-8909)			

FURNITURE: Lawn & Garden, Metal

Flanders Industries Inc	C	906 863-4491	
Menominee (G-10736)			
Jack-Post Corporation	F	269 695-7000	
Buchanan (G-2121)			

FURNITURE: Lawn, Wood

Lapointe Cedar Products Inc	F	906 753-4072	
Ingalls (G-8224)			

FURNITURE: Library

Everest Expedition LLC	D	616 392-1848	
Holland (G-7627)			
Worden Group LLC	D	616 392-1848	
Holland (G-7861)			

FURNITURE: Living Room, Upholstered On Wood Frames

Singh Senior Living LLC	E	248 865-1600	
West Bloomfield (G-17497)			

FURNITURE: Mattresses & Foundations

Artisans Cstm Mmory Mattresses	F	989 793-3208	
Saginaw (G-13996)			
Indratech LLC	D	248 377-1877	
Troy (G-16416)			
Marrs Discount Furniture	G	989 720-5436	
Owosso (G-12300)			
Spine Align Inc	G	616 395-5407	
Holland (G-7812)			

FURNITURE: Mattresses, Box & Bedsprings

Mattress Wholesale	F	248 968-2200	
Oak Park (G-12082)			
Michigan Mattress Limited LLC	G	248 669-6345	
Commerce Township (G-3432)			
Midwest Quality Bedding Inc	F	614 504-5971	
Waterford (G-17359)			

FURNITURE: Mattresses, Innerspring Or Box Spring

Clare Bedding Mfg Co	E	906 789-9902	
Escanaba (G-4822)			
Comfort Mattress Co	D	586 293-4000	
Roseville (G-13784)			
Grand Rapids Bedding Co	E	616 459-8234	
Grand Rapids (G-6451)			
Jonathan Stevens Mattress Co	G	616 243-4342	
Grand Rapids (G-6564)			
Serta Restokraft Mat Co Inc	C	734 727-9000	
Romulus (G-13733)			

FURNITURE: Novelty, Wood

Home Shop	G	517 543-5325	
Charlotte (G-2654)			

FURNITURE: Office Panel Systems, Exc Wood

Total Innovative Mfg LLC	E	616 399-9903	
Holland (G-7831)			
Trendway Corporation	B	616 399-3900	
Holland (G-7836)			
West Mich Off Interiors Inc	G	269 344-0768	
Kalamazoo (G-8923)			

FURNITURE: Office Panel Systems, Wood

Trendway Corporation	B	616 399-3900	
Holland (G-7836)			
West Mich Off Interiors Inc	G	269 344-0768	
Kalamazoo (G-8923)			

FURNITURE: Office, Exc Wood

Agritek Industries Inc	D	616 786-9200	
Holland (G-7551)			
Altus Industries Inc	F	616 233-9530	
Walker (G-16861)			
American Seating Company	B	616 732-6600	
Grand Rapids (G-6166)			
Amneon Acquisitions LLC	E	616 895-6640	
Holland (G-7559)			
Anso Products	G	248 357-2300	
Southfield (G-14839)			
Avantis Inc	G	616 285-8000	
Grand Rapids (G-6195)			
Bostontec Inc	F	989 496-9510	
Midland (G-10818)			
Compact Engineering Corp	F	231 788-5470	
Muskegon (G-11298)			
Contract Source & Assembly Inc	F	616 897-2185	
Grand Rapids (G-6305)			
Counterpoint By Hlf	D	734 699-7100	
Van Buren Twp (G-16754)			
Craftwood Industries Inc	E	616 796-1209	
Holland (G-7599)			
Custom Components Corporation	F	616 523-1111	
Ionia (G-8247)			
Electra-Tec Inc	G	269 694-6652	
Otsego (G-12238)			
Essilor Laboratories Amer Inc	C	616 361-6000	
Grand Rapids (G-6386)			
Haskell Office	G	616 988-0880	
Wyoming (G-18008)			
Haworth Inc	A	616 393-3000	
Holland (G-7659)			
Haworth Inc	B	231 796-1400	
Big Rapids (G-1633)			
Haworth Inc	D	231 845-0607	
Ludington (G-10064)			
Haworth International Ltd	A	616 393-3000	
Holland (G-7660)			
Herman Miller Inc	B	616 654-3000	
Zeeland (G-18147)			
Hmi Liquidating Company Inc	G	616 654-5055	
Zeeland (G-18151)			
Interior Concepts Corporation	E	616 842-5550	
Spring Lake (G-15155)			
Jem Computers Inc	F	586 783-3400	
Clinton Township (G-3149)			
Knoll Inc	E	231 755-2270	
Norton Shores (G-11767)			
Metal Arc Inc	E	231 865-3111	
Muskegon (G-11375)			
Metal Components LLC	D	616 252-1900	
Grand Rapids (G-6660)			
Mobile Office Vehicle Inc	G	616 971-0080	
Grand Rapids (G-6693)			
Mooreco Inc	E	616 451-7800	
Grand Rapids (G-6706)			
Office Design & Furn LLC	G	734 217-2717	
Ypsilanti (G-18093)			
Premium Machine & Tool Inc	F	989 855-3326	
Lyons (G-10095)			
Rj Operating Company	F	616 392-7101	
Holland (G-7789)			
Srg Global Coatings Inc	C	248 509-1100	
Troy (G-16618)			
Steelcase Inc	A	616 247-2710	
Grand Rapids (G-6889)			
Steelcase Inc	D	616 247-2710	
Grand Rapids (G-6890)			
Systems Design & Installation	G	269 543-4204	
Fennville (G-5177)			
Trendway Svcs Organization LLC	G	616 994-5327	
Holland (G-7837)			
Tvb Inc	F	616 456-9629	
Grand Rapids (G-6942)			
Up Officeexpress LLC	G	906 281-0089	
Calumet (G-2334)			

FURNITURE: Office, Wood

Boese Associates Inc	G	231 347-3995	
Petoskey (G-12443)			
Bold Companies Inc	D	231 773-8026	
Muskegon (G-11282)			
Bourne Industries Inc	E	989 743-3461	
Corunna (G-3578)			
Counterpoint By Hlf	D	734 699-7100	
Van Buren Twp (G-16754)			
Craftwood Industries Inc	E	616 796-1209	
Holland (G-7599)			
Custom Components Corporation	F	616 523-1111	
Ionia (G-8247)			
Custom Crafters	G	269 763-9180	
Bellevue (G-1453)			
D & M Cabinet Shop Inc	G	989 479-9271	
Ruth (G-13988)			
Designtec Services Inc	G	734 216-6051	
Howell (G-8028)			
Dynamic Wood Products Inc	G	616 897-8114	
Saranac (G-14454)			
Flairwood Industries Inc	E	231 798-8324	
Norton Shores (G-11756)			
Genesis Seating Inc	G	616 954-1040	
Grand Rapids (G-6437)			
Grand Rapids Carvers Inc	E	616 538-0022	
Grand Rapids (G-6452)			
Grand Valley Wood Products Inc	E	616 475-5890	
Grand Rapids (G-6471)			
Haworth Inc	A	616 393-3000	
Holland (G-7659)			
Haworth Inc	B	231 796-1400	
Big Rapids (G-1633)			
Haworth International Ltd	A	616 393-3000	
Holland (G-7660)			
Hekman Furniture Company	D	616 735-3905	
Grand Rapids (G-6502)			
Herman Miller	F	616 296-3422	
Spring Lake (G-15151)			
Herman Miller Inc	B	616 654-3000	
Zeeland (G-18147)			
Herman Miller Inc	G	616 846-0280	
Spring Lake (G-15152)			
Herman Miller Inc	E	616 654-7456	
Holland (G-7662)			
Herman Miller Inc	E	616 654-3716	
Van Buren Twp (G-16763)			
Herman Miller Inc	E	616 654-8078	
Holland (G-7663)			
Holland Stitchcraft Inc	F	616 399-3868	
Holland (G-7678)			
Howe US Inc	D	616 419-2226	
Grand Rapids (G-6517)			
Interior Concepts Corporation	E	616 842-5550	
Spring Lake (G-15155)			
Izzy Plus	G	574 821-1200	
Grand Haven (G-6038)			
Jsj Corporation	C	616 847-7000	
Spring Lake (G-15157)			
Knoll Inc	C	616 949-1050	
Grand Rapids (G-6587)			
Knoll Inc	E	231 755-2270	
Norton Shores (G-11767)			
Michigan Tube Swagers & Fab	B	734 847-3875	
Temperance (G-15838)			
Mooreco Inc	E	616 451-7800	
Grand Rapids (G-6706)			
Nucraft Furniture Company	D	616 784-6016	
Comstock Park (G-3503)			
Omt-Veyhl USA Corporation	E	616 738-6688	
Holland (G-7764)			
Paladin Ind Inc	E	616 698-7495	
Grand Rapids (G-6740)			
Primeway Inc	F	248 583-6922	
Royal Oak (G-13958)			
R T London Company	D	616 364-4800	
Grand Rapids (G-6804)			
Rose Corporation	E	734 426-0005	
Dexter (G-4508)			
S & J Inc	G	248 299-0822	
Rochester Hills (G-13508)			
S F Gilmore Inc	C	616 475-5100	
Grand Rapids (G-6849)			
Silver Street Incorporated	E	231 861-2194	
Shelby (G-14536)			
Steelcase Inc	A	616 247-2710	
Grand Rapids (G-6889)			
Tranquil Systems Intl LLC	F	800 631-0212	
Clare (G-2891)			
Viable Inc	G	616 774-2022	
Grand Rapids (G-6970)			
West Shore Services Inc	E	616 895-4347	
Allendale (G-227)			
Woodard—Cm LLC	E	989 725-4265	
Owosso (G-12331)			

FURNITURE: Outdoor, Wood

Eb Enterprises LLC	G	231 768-5072	
Leroy (G-9532)			
Great Lakes Wood Products	G	906 228-3737	
Negaunee (G-11470)			

PRODUCT SECTION

Lakeland Mills Inc .... E 989 427-5133
  Edmore *(G-4752)*
Meyer Wood Products .... G 269 657-3450
  Paw Paw *(G-12409)*

FURNITURE: Pews, Church

Kawkawlin Manufacturing Co .... G 989 684-5470
  Midland *(G-10879)*

FURNITURE: Picnic Tables Or Benches, Park

Joes Tables LLC .... G 989 846-4970
  Standish *(G-15220)*
Recycletech Products Inc .... E 517 649-2243
  Mulliken *(G-11240)*

FURNITURE: Play Pens, Children's, Wood

Backyard Products LLC .... G 734 242-6900
  Monroe *(G-11015)*
Source Capital Backyard LLC .... G 734 242-6900
  Monroe *(G-11066)*

FURNITURE: Restaurant

Billco Acquisition LLC .... E 616 928-0637
  Holland *(G-7570)*
Brill Company Inc .... E 231 843-2430
  Ludington *(G-10050)*
Harborfront Interiors Inc .... F 231 777-3838
  Muskegon *(G-11343)*
La Rosa Refrigeration & Eqp Co .... E 313 368-6620
  Detroit *(G-4187)*

FURNITURE: School

Bourne Industries Inc .... E 989 743-3461
  Corunna *(G-3578)*
Greene Manufacturing Inc .... E 734 428-8304
  Chelsea *(G-2712)*
Irwin Seating Holding Company .... B 616 574-7400
  Grand Rapids *(G-6545)*
TMC Furniture Inc .... E 734 622-0080
  Kentwood *(G-9034)*

FURNITURE: Stands & Chests, Exc Bedside Stands, Wood

Sawdust Bin Inc .... F 906 932-5518
  Ironwood *(G-8340)*

FURNITURE: Stools, Household, Wood

Two Feathers Enterprise LLC .... G 231 924-3612
  Fremont *(G-5785)*

FURNITURE: Storage Chests, Household, Wood

Backyard Services LLC .... C 734 242-6900
  Monroe *(G-11016)*
Best Self Storage .... G 810 227-7050
  Brighton *(G-1889)*

FURNITURE: Table Tops, Marble

Classic Stone Creations Inc .... G 269 637-9497
  South Haven *(G-14756)*
Stonecrafters Inc .... F 517 529-4990
  Clarklake *(G-2901)*
TNT Marble and Stone Inc .... G 248 887-8237
  Hartland *(G-7394)*

FURNITURE: Tables & Table Tops, Wood

Audia Woodworking & Fine Furn ...... F 586 296-6330
  Clinton Township *(G-3058)*

FURNITURE: Unfinished, Wood

Deweys Lumberville Inc .... G 313 885-0960
  Grosse Pointe *(G-7178)*

FURNITURE: Upholstered

Debbink and Sons Inc .... G 231 845-6421
  Ludington *(G-10055)*
Homespun Furniture Inc .... F 734 284-6277
  Riverview *(G-13297)*
International Seating Co .... G 586 293-2201
  Fraser *(G-5672)*
Lzb Manufacturing Inc .... G 734 242-1444
  Monroe *(G-11051)*

Plum Tree .... G 269 469-5980
  Union Pier *(G-16738)*
Sherwood Studios Inc .... E 248 855-1600
  West Bloomfield *(G-17495)*
Tamarack Uphl & Interiors .... G 616 866-2922
  Rockford *(G-13592)*

FURNITURE: Vehicle

American Seating Company .... B 616 732-6600
  Grand Rapids *(G-6166)*
Lanzen Incorporated .... D 586 771-7070
  Bruce Twp *(G-2090)*
Milsco LLC .... B 517 787-3650
  Jackson *(G-8531)*

FURRIERS

Wolvering Fur .... G 313 961-0620
  Detroit *(G-4447)*

FUSES: Electric

PEC of America Corporation .... F 248 675-3130
  Novi *(G-11972)*

Furs

Burtrum Furs .... G 810 771-4563
  Grand Blanc *(G-5962)*
H & H Wildlife Desgn & Furng I .... F 231 832-7002
  Reed City *(G-13214)*
Inglis Farms Inc .... G 989 727-8727
  Alpena *(G-293)*
Precious Furs Llc .... G 734 262-6262
  Livonia *(G-9896)*
Vanity Fur .... G 810 744-3000
  Burton *(G-2169)*

GAMES & TOYS: Bingo Boards

Meteor Web Marketing Inc .... F 734 822-4999
  Ann Arbor *(G-553)*
Spark Games LLC .... G 269 303-7201
  Kalamazoo *(G-8895)*

GAMES & TOYS: Board Games, Children's & Adults'

Hallwell Games LLC .... G 586 879-3404
  Southfield *(G-14935)*
Lost Horizons Inc .... G 248 366-6858
  Commerce Township *(G-3423)*
Talicor Inc .... E 269 685-2345
  Plainwell *(G-12545)*

GAMES & TOYS: Craft & Hobby Kits & Sets

American Plastic Toys Inc .... B 248 624-4881
  Walled Lake *(G-16890)*
Au Gres Sheep Factory .... F 989 876-8787
  Au Gres *(G-742)*
Mac Enterprises Inc .... F 313 846-4567
  Manchester *(G-10407)*

GAMES & TOYS: Dolls, Exc Stuffed Toy Animals

Dolls By Maurice Inc .... G 586 739-5147
  Utica *(G-16741)*
Marshal E Hyman and Associates ... G 248 643-0642
  Troy *(G-16488)*

GAMES & TOYS: Electronic

Pannell S-Erynn .... G 248 692-3192
  Farmington *(G-4906)*

GAMES & TOYS: Game Machines, Exc Coin-Operated

Hampton Company Inc .... G 517 765-2222
  Burlington *(G-2132)*

GAMES & TOYS: Kits, Science, Incl Microscopes/Chemistry Sets

Eca Educational Services Inc .... E 248 669-7170
  Commerce Township *(G-3403)*

GAMES & TOYS: Trains & Eqpt, Electric & Mechanical

American Models .... G 248 437-6800
  Whitmore Lake *(G-17687)*

GAMES & TOYS: Tricycles

National Ambucs Inc .... E 231 798-4244
  Norton Shores *(G-11778)*

GARBAGE CONTAINERS: Plastic

Little Traverse Disposal LLC .... G 231 487-0780
  Harbor Springs *(G-7287)*
Royal Container Services Inc .... G 586 775-7600
  Warren *(G-17224)*

GARBAGE DISPOSERS & COMPACTORS: Commercial

Garbage Man LLC .... G 810 225-3001
  Brighton *(G-1927)*
MRM Ida Products Co Inc .... G 313 834-0200
  Detroit *(G-4259)*
Sebright Products Inc .... E 269 793-7183
  Hopkins *(G-7960)*
Shred-Pac Inc .... E 269 793-7978
  Hopkins *(G-7961)*

GAS & HYDROCARBON LIQUEFACTION FROM COAL

Refinery Corporation America .... G 877 881-0336
  Harper Woods *(G-7303)*

GAS & OIL FIELD EXPLORATION SVCS

Arbor Operating LLC .... G 231 941-2237
  Traverse City *(G-15896)*
Baygeo Inc .... E 231 941-7660
  Traverse City *(G-15909)*
Beckman Production Svcs Inc .... E 989 539-7126
  Harrison *(G-7309)*
Bobcat Oil & Gas Inc .... G 989 426-4375
  Gladwin *(G-5924)*
Core Energy LLC .... G 231 946-2419
  Traverse City *(G-15948)*
Dart Energy Corporation .... F 231 885-1665
  Mesick *(G-10769)*
Dcr Services & Cnstr Inc .... F 313 297-6544
  Detroit *(G-3962)*
Don Yohe Enterprises Inc .... F 586 784-5556
  Armada *(G-718)*
DTE Gas & Oil Company .... E 231 995-4000
  Traverse City *(G-15958)*
Dynamic Development Inc .... G 231 723-8318
  Manistee *(G-10419)*
Energy Exploration .... G 248 579-6531
  Novi *(G-11884)*
Express Care of South Lyon .... G 248 437-6919
  South Lyon *(G-14791)*
Forward Distributing Inc .... G 989 846-4501
  Standish *(G-15218)*
Geostar Corporation .... E 989 773-7050
  Mount Pleasant *(G-11194)*
Howard Energy Co Inc .... E 231 995-7850
  Traverse City *(G-15999)*
HRF Exploration & Prod LLC .... F 989 732-6950
  Gaylord *(G-5865)*
Innova Exploration Inc .... G 231 929-3985
  Traverse City *(G-16004)*
J R Productions Inc .... G 989 732-2905
  Gaylord *(G-5867)*
John T Stoliker Enterprises .... G 586 727-1402
  Columbus *(G-3379)*
Loneys Welding & Excvtg Inc .... G 231 328-4408
  Merritt *(G-10764)*
Maness Petroleum Corp .... G 989 773-5475
  Mount Pleasant *(G-11203)*
Martec Land Services Inc .... F 231 929-3971
  Traverse City *(G-16033)*
Maverick Exploration Prod Inc .... G 231 929-3923
  Traverse City *(G-16034)*
Meridian Energy Corporation .... F 517 339-8444
  Haslett *(G-7397)*
Miller Energy Inc .... F 269 352-5960
  Kalamazoo *(G-8828)*
Miracle Petroleum LLC .... G 231 946-8090
  Traverse City *(G-16039)*
Muzyl Oil Corp .... G 989 732-8100
  Gaylord *(G-5884)*

GAS & OIL FIELD EXPLORATION SVCS

OIL Energy Corp .... F 231 933-3600
  Traverse City *(G-16054)*
Patrick Exploration Company .... G 517 787-6633
  Jackson *(G-8547)*
Penin Oil & Gas Compan Michiga .... G 616 676-2090
  Ada *(G-26)*
Pinnacle Energy LLC .... G 248 623-6091
  Clarkston *(G-2945)*
Rowe & Associates .... G 231 932-9716
  Traverse City *(G-16097)*
Savoy Exploration Inc .... G 231 941-9552
  Traverse City *(G-16098)*
Schmude Oil Inc .... G 231 947-4410
  Traverse City *(G-16099)*
Sturak Brothers Inc .... G 269 345-2929
  Kalamazoo *(G-8900)*
Unoco Exploration Co .... G 231 829-3235
  Leroy *(G-9539)*
Wara Construction Company LLC ..... D 248 299-2410
  Rochester Hills *(G-13540)*
Ward-Williston Company .... F 248 594-6622
  Bloomfield *(G-1737)*
Wepco Energy LLC .... G 231 932-8615
  Traverse City *(G-16142)*
Western Land Services Inc .... D 231 843-8878
  Ludington *(G-10088)*
Whiting Petroleum Corporation .... G 989 345-7903
  West Branch *(G-17529)*
Wolverine Gas and Oil Corp .... E 616 458-1150
  Grand Rapids *(G-6998)*

GAS & OIL FIELD SVCS, NEC

Unoco Exploration Co .... G 231 829-3235
  Leroy *(G-9539)*

GAS STATIONS

Admiral .... G 989 356-6419
  Alpena *(G-271)*
Blarney Castle Inc .... G 231 864-3111
  Bear Lake *(G-1376)*
Murphy USA Inc .... F 517 541-0502
  Charlotte *(G-2661)*

GASES & LIQUIFIED PETROLEUM GASES

Amrican Petro Inc .... G 313 520-8404
  Detroit *(G-3868)*

GASES: Acetylene

Greenville Trck Wldg Sups LLC .... F 616 754-6120
  Greenville *(G-7136)*

GASES: Argon

Argon Group LLC .... G 248 370-0003
  Rochester Hills *(G-13370)*

GASES: Carbon Dioxide

Caseq Technologies Inc .... G 734 730-5407
  Holland *(G-7586)*
Praxair Distribution Inc .... E 616 451-3055
  Grand Rapids *(G-6762)*
Praxair Distribution Inc .... E 313 778-7085
  Detroit *(G-4308)*

GASES: Helium

Helium Home Base LLC .... G 734 895-3608
  Westland *(G-17568)*

GASES: Hydrogen

Hydrogen Assist Development .... G 734 823-4969
  Dundee *(G-4589)*

GASES: Indl

Air Products and Chemicals Inc .... E 313 297-2006
  Detroit *(G-3847)*
Airgas Usa LLC .... F 517 673-0997
  Blissfield *(G-1712)*
Fremont Community Digester LLC .... F 248 735-6684
  Novi *(G-11887)*
Linde Inc .... G 517 541-2473
  Charlotte *(G-2658)*
Matheson .... G 586 498-8315
  Roseville *(G-13831)*
Matheson Tri-Gas Inc .... F 734 425-8870
  Garden City *(G-5833)*

Praxair Inc .... F 586 751-7400
  Warren *(G-17191)*
Praxair Inc .... E 269 276-0442
  Kalamazoo *(G-8856)*
Praxair Inc .... E 231 796-3266
  Grand Rapids *(G-6761)*
Praxair Inc .... E 269 926-8296
  Benton Harbor *(G-1538)*
Praxair Inc .... E 231 722-3773
  Muskegon *(G-11405)*
Praxair Inc .... G 313 319-6220
  Dearborn *(G-3750)*
Praxair Inc .... E 313 849-4200
  River Rouge *(G-13280)*
South Park Welding Sups LLC .... F 810 364-6521
  Marysville *(G-10618)*

GASES: Neon

Affordable Neon Ent .... G 906 356-6168
  Rock *(G-13552)*
Great Lakes Neon .... G 517 582-7451
  Grand Ledge *(G-6108)*
Spectrum Neon Co .... G 248 246-1142
  Madison Heights *(G-10358)*
Tite Neon Cat .... G 734 755-7349
  Monroe *(G-11076)*

GASES: Nitrogen

Linde Gas LLC .... G 616 754-7575
  Greenville *(G-7144)*
Linde Gas North America LLC .... F 616 475-0203
  Wyoming *(G-18017)*

GASES: Oxygen

Airserve LLC .... G 586 427-5349
  Center Line *(G-2576)*
Linde Gas North America LLC .... G 630 857-6460
  Southfield *(G-14969)*
Linde Gas North America LLC .... G 734 397-7373
  Canton *(G-2392)*

GASKET MATERIALS

Michigan Rbr & Gasket Co Inc .... E 586 323-4100
  Sterling Heights *(G-15421)*
Upper Peninsula Rubber Co Inc .... G 906 786-0460
  Escanaba *(G-4864)*

GASKETS

Basic Rubber and Plastics Co .... E 248 360-7400
  Walled Lake *(G-16891)*
Champion Gasket & Rubber Inc .... E 248 624-6140
  Commerce Township *(G-3394)*
Derby Fabg Solutions LLC .... D 616 866-1650
  Rockford *(G-13566)*
Garco Gaskets Inc .... G 734 728-4912
  Livonia *(G-9749)*
Grand Haven Gasket Company .... F 616 842-7682
  Grand Haven *(G-6022)*
Lamons .... G 989 488-4580
  Midland *(G-10881)*
Plastomer Corporation .... C 734 464-0700
  Livonia *(G-9889)*
Tri-TEC Seal LLC .... E 810 655-3900
  Fenton *(G-5246)*
Unique Fabricating Inc .... E 248 853-2333
  Auburn Hills *(G-1034)*
Unique Fabricating Inc .... E 248 853-2333
  Rochester Hills *(G-13535)*
Unique Fabricating Na Inc .... B 248 853-2333
  Auburn Hills *(G-1035)*
Unique Fabricating Na Inc .... C 517 524-9010
  Concord *(G-3526)*

GASKETS & SEALING DEVICES

Action Fabricators Inc .... C 616 957-2032
  Grand Rapids *(G-6136)*
Copeland-Gibson Products Corp .... F 248 740-4400
  Troy *(G-16282)*
Energy Manufacturing Inc .... G 248 360-0065
  Wixom *(G-17804)*
Federal-Mogul Ignition LLC .... E 248 354-7700
  Southfield *(G-14907)*
Federal-Mogul Piston Rings Inc .... F 248 354-7700
  Southfield *(G-14909)*
Federal-Mogul Powertrain Inc .... C 616 887-8231
  Sparta *(G-15094)*

Federal-Mogul Powertrain LLC .... G 248 354-7700
  Southfield *(G-14910)*
Federal-Mogul Powertrain LLC .... E 734 930-1590
  Ann Arbor *(G-458)*
Gasket Holdings Inc .... G 248 354-7700
  Southfield *(G-14918)*
Grm Corporation .... G 989 453-2322
  Pigeon *(G-12490)*
Ishino Gasket North Amer LLC .... G 734 451-0020
  Plymouth *(G-12650)*
Kaydon Corporation .... B 734 747-7025
  Ann Arbor *(G-516)*
Kent Manufacturing Company .... D 616 454-9495
  Grand Rapids *(G-6577)*
L & L Products Inc .... A 586 336-1600
  Bruce Twp *(G-2087)*
L & L Products Inc .... B 586 336-1600
  Bruce Twp *(G-2089)*
Martin Fluid Power Company .... D 248 585-8170
  Madison Heights *(G-10302)*
Memtech Inc .... F 734 455-8550
  Plymouth *(G-12689)*
N-K Sealing Technologies LLC .... G 616 248-3200
  Grand Rapids *(G-6711)*
Parker-Hannifin Corporation .... D 330 253-5239
  Otsego *(G-12251)*
R & J Manufacturing Company .... E 248 669-2460
  Commerce Township *(G-3445)*
Rhino Strapping Products Inc .... F 734 442-4040
  Taylor *(G-15763)*
Roger Zatkoff Company .... E 586 264-3593
  Warren *(G-17223)*
Roger Zatkoff Company .... E 248 478-2400
  Farmington Hills *(G-5117)*
SKF USA Inc .... F 734 414-6585
  Plymouth *(G-12756)*
Speyside Real Estate LLC .... F 248 354-7700
  Southfield *(G-15031)*
Zephyros Inc .... A 586 336-1600
  Bruce Twp *(G-2106)*

GASOLINE FILLING STATIONS

Gustafson Smoked Fish .... G 906 292-5424
  Moran *(G-11107)*
Treib Inc .... F 989 752-4821
  Saginaw *(G-14166)*

GATES: Ornamental Metal

Ideal Wrought Iron .... G 313 581-1324
  Detroit *(G-4135)*
Scott Iron Works Inc .... F 248 548-2822
  Hazel Park *(G-7454)*

GAUGE BLOCKS

Gage Numerical Inc .... G 231 328-4426
  Lake City *(G-9087)*
Zakron USA Inc .... F 313 582-0462
  Dearborn *(G-3776)*

GAUGES

Accell Technologies Inc .... G 248 360-3762
  Commerce Township *(G-3384)*
Advantage Design and Tool .... G 586 801-7413
  Richmond *(G-13258)*
AG Davis Gage & Engrg Co .... E 586 977-9000
  Sterling Heights *(G-15256)*
Alberts Machine Tool Inc .... G 231 743-2457
  Marion *(G-10489)*
American Industrial Gauge Inc .... G 248 280-0048
  Royal Oak *(G-13901)*
Artcraft Pattern Works Inc .... F 734 729-0022
  Westland *(G-17543)*
Benny Gage Inc .... E 734 455-3080
  Wixom *(G-17773)*
Bilco Tool Corporation .... G 586 574-9300
  Warren *(G-16959)*
Bower Tool & Manufacturing Inc .... G 734 522-0444
  Livonia *(G-9669)*
Comau LLC .... B 248 353-8888
  Southfield *(G-14871)*
Component Engrg Solutions LLC ..... F 616 514-1343
  Grand Rapids *(G-6294)*
Cross Paths Corp .... G 616 248-5371
  Grand Rapids *(G-6318)*
Douglas Gage Inc .... F 586 727-2089
  Richmond *(G-13261)*
Dura Thread Gage Inc .... F 248 545-2890
  Madison Heights *(G-10236)*

PRODUCT SECTION — GLASS FABRICATORS

Emtron Corporation Inc .... F 248 347-3333
  New Hudson (G-11539)
Enmark Tool Company .... E 586 293-2797
  Fraser (G-5651)
Fraser Tool & Gauge LLC .... G 313 882-9192
  Grosse Pointe Park (G-7193)
Gage Eagle Spline Inc .... D 586 776-7240
  Warren (G-17049)
GAL Gage Co .... E 269 465-5750
  Bridgman (G-1863)
H E Morse Co .... D 616 396-4604
  Holland (G-7656)
Hanlo Gauges & Engineering Co .... G 734 422-4224
  Livonia (G-9766)
Huron Tool & Gage Co Inc .... G 313 381-1900
  Wixom (G-17830)
Invo Spline Inc .... E 586 757-8840
  Warren (G-17097)
Keller Tool Ltd .... D 734 425-4500
  Livonia (G-9794)
Leader Corporation .... E 586 566-7114
  Shelby Township (G-14624)
Martel Tool Corporation .... F 313 278-2420
  Allen Park (G-202)
Master Jig Grinding & Gage Co .... G 248 380-8515
  Novi (G-11935)
North-East Gage Inc .... G 586 792-6790
  Clinton Township (G-3186)
O Keller Tool Engrg Co LLC .... E 734 425-4500
  Livonia (G-9873)
Perry Tool Company Inc .... G 734 283-7393
  Riverview (G-13304)
R & S Tool & Die Inc .... G 989 673-8511
  Caro (G-2476)
Reef Tool & Gage Co .... F 586 468-3000
  Clinton Township (G-3207)
Smeko Inc .... E 586 254-5310
  Sterling Heights (G-15501)
Spartan Tool Sales Inc .... F 586 268-1556
  Sterling Heights (G-15504)
Spence Industries Inc .... G 586 758-3800
  Warren (G-17246)
Stanhope Tool Inc .... F 248 585-5711
  Madison Heights (G-10360)
Target Mold Corporation .... F 231 798-3535
  Norton Shores (G-11799)
Trusted Tool Mfg Inc .... G 810 750-6000
  Fenton (G-5247)
Turbine Tool & Gage Inc .... F 734 427-2270
  Livonia (G-9978)
Western Pegasus Inc .... G 616 393-9580
  Holland (G-7858)
Westside Tool & Gage LLC .... G 734 728-9520
  Westland (G-17612)

GEARS

Avon Machining LLC .... D 586 884-2200
  Shelby Township (G-14551)
Avon Machining Holdings Inc .... C 586 884-2200
  Shelby Township (G-14552)
Boos Products Inc .... F 734 498-2207
  Gregory (G-7164)
Equitable Engineering Co Inc .... E 248 689-9700
  Troy (G-16351)
Gearx LLC .... G 248 766-6903
  Sterling Heights (G-15354)
HI Tech Gear Inc .... G 248 548-8649
  Huntington Woods (G-8188)
Midwest Gear & Tool Inc .... E 586 779-1300
  Roseville (G-13836)
Motion Systems Incorporated .... F 586 774-5666
  Warren (G-17160)

GEARS & GEAR UNITS: Reduction, Exc Auto

Cone Drive Operations Inc .... E 231 843-3393
  Ludington (G-10054)
Geartec Inc .... G 810 987-4700
  Port Huron (G-12922)

GEARS: Power Transmission, Exc Auto

American Gear & Engrg Co Inc .... E 734 595-6400
  Westland (G-17541)
Atlas Gear Company .... F 248 583-2964
  Madison Heights (G-10198)
Custom Gears Inc .... G 616 243-2723
  Grand Rapids (G-6324)
Decker Gear Inc .... F 810 388-1500
  Saint Clair (G-14216)

Fairlane Gear Inc .... G 734 459-2440
  Canton (G-2374)
J G Kern Enterprises Inc .... D 586 531-9472
  Sterling Heights (G-15378)
Porite USA Co Ltd .... G 248 597-9988
  Troy (G-16554)
Tri-TEC Seal LLC .... E 810 655-3900
  Fenton (G-5246)
Truemner Enterprises Inc .... G 586 756-6470
  Warren (G-17270)

GENERAL COUNSELING SVCS

Amplified Life Network LLC .... G 800 453-7733
  Byron Center (G-2176)

GENERAL MERCHANDISE, NONDURABLE, WHOLESALE

American Sales Co .... G 517 750-4070
  Spring Arbor (G-15118)
AP Impressions Inc .... G 734 464-8009
  Livonia (G-9650)
Hemp Global Products Inc .... G 616 617-6476
  Holland (G-7661)
L & P LLC .... F 231 733-1415
  Muskegon (G-11360)
L & S Products LLC .... G 517 238-4645
  Coldwater (G-3313)
Travel Information Services .... F 989 275-8042
  Roscommon (G-13755)

GENERATION EQPT: Electronic

Adam Electronics Incorporated .... E 248 583-2000
  Madison Heights (G-10181)
Equipment Material Sales LLC .... G 734 284-8711
  Wyandotte (G-17958)
Jem Computers Inc .... F 586 783-3400
  Clinton Township (G-3149)
Xalt Energy LLC .... G 816 525-1153
  Midland (G-10929)

GENERATOR REPAIR SVCS

Ainsworth Electric Inc .... E 810 984-5768
  Port Huron (G-12883)

GENERATORS: Electric

Global Fleet Sales LLC .... G 248 327-6483
  Southfield (G-14920)
Jlm Elec .... G 989 486-3788
  Midland (G-10875)
Standby Power USA LLC .... G 586 716-9610
  Ira (G-8272)

GENERATORS: Electrochemical, Fuel Cell

Gei Global Energy Corp .... G 810 610-2816
  Flint (G-5433)

GENERATORS: Ultrasonic

Ace Filtration Inc .... G 248 624-6300
  Commerce Township (G-3385)
B & M Sonics and Machine LLC .... G 810 793-1236
  Lapeer (G-9441)

GENERATORS: Vehicles, Gas-Electric Or Oil-Electric

Ev Anywhere LLC .... G 313 653-9870
  Detroit (G-4044)

GIFT SHOP

Bk Mattson Enterprises Inc .... G 906 774-0097
  Iron Mountain (G-8278)
Country Home Creations Inc .... E 810 244-7348
  Flint (G-5405)
Donckers Candies & Gifts .... G 906 226-6110
  Marquette (G-10526)
Gast Cabinet Co .... E 269 422-1587
  Baroda (G-1125)
Harry Miller Flowers Inc .... G 313 581-2328
  Dearborn (G-3718)
Lighthouse Direct Buy LLC .... G 313 340-1850
  Detroit (G-4204)
Marshalls Trail Inc .... G 231 436-5082
  Mackinaw City (G-10099)
R H & Company Inc .... F 269 345-7814
  Kalamazoo (G-8867)

R S V P Inc .... G 734 455-7229
  Plymouth (G-12729)
Sandcastle For Kids Inc .... F 616 396-5955
  Holland (G-7796)
Sign of The Loon Gifts Inc .... G 231 436-5155
  Mackinaw City (G-10101)
Sobaks Pharmacy Inc .... F 989 725-2785
  Owosso (G-12316)

GIFT, NOVELTY & SOUVENIR STORES: Gift Baskets

Carlson Enterprises Inc .... G 248 656-1442
  Rochester Hills (G-13385)

GIFT, NOVELTY & SOUVENIR STORES: Party Favors

Gags and Games Inc .... E 734 591-1717
  Livonia (G-9747)

GIFTS & NOVELTIES: Wholesalers

Amway International Inc .... E 616 787-1000
  Ada (G-7)
Graphic Resource Group Inc .... E 248 588-6100
  Troy (G-16386)
Ideal Wholesale Inc .... G 989 873-5850
  Prescott (G-13080)
Lighthouse Direct Buy LLC .... G 313 340-1850
  Detroit (G-4204)
Nalcor LLC .... D 248 541-1140
  Ferndale (G-5303)

GIFTWARE: Copper

Lsr Incorporated .... F 734 455-6530
  Plymouth (G-12679)

GLASS FABRICATORS

A & B Display Systems Inc .... F 989 893-6642
  Bay City (G-1269)
C & B Glass Inc .... G 248 625-4376
  Clarkston (G-2909)
Case Island Glass LLC .... G 810 252-1704
  Flint (G-5396)
Duo-Gard Industries Inc .... D 734 207-9700
  Canton (G-2367)
Fox Fire Glass LLC .... E 248 332-2442
  Fenton (G-5215)
Furniture City Glass Corp .... E 616 784-5500
  Grand Rapids (G-6425)
Glass Recyclers Ltd .... D 313 584-3434
  Dearborn (G-3715)
Guardian Fabrication LLC .... G 248 340-1800
  Auburn Hills (G-892)
Guardian Industries LLC .... B 734 654-4285
  Carleton (G-2456)
Heritage Glass Inc .... G 248 887-1010
  Highland (G-7493)
Inalfa Road System Inc .... B 248 371-3060
  Auburn Hills (G-908)
Keeler-Glasgow Company Inc .... E 269 621-2415
  Hartford (G-7384)
Kentwood Manufacturing Co .... E 616 698-6370
  Grand Rapids (G-6579)
Knight Tonya .... G 313 255-3434
  Southfield (G-14956)
Lippert Components Mfg Inc .... C 323 663-1261
  Chesaning (G-2726)
Louis Padnos Iron and Metal Co .... E 616 459-4208
  Grand Rapids (G-6631)
Luxottica of America Inc .... G 989 624-8958
  Birch Run (G-1665)
Magna .... G 616 786-7403
  Holland (G-7732)
Magna Mirrors America Inc .... C 616 868-6122
  Alto (G-328)
Oldcastle Buildingenvelope Inc .... E 616 896-8341
  Burnips (G-2133)
On The Side Sign Dsign Grphics .... G 810 266-7446
  Byron (G-2174)
Paragon Tempered Glass LLC .... E 269 684-5060
  Niles (G-11636)
Penstone Inc .... E 734 379-3160
  Rockwood (G-13610)
Polymer Process Dev LLC .... D 586 464-6400
  Shelby Township (G-14669)
Schefenalker Vision Systems .... G 810 388-2511
  Marysville (G-10613)

Employee Codes: A=Over 500 employees, B=251-500
C=101-250, D=51-100, E=20-50, F=10-19, G=3-9

2020 Harris Michigan Industrial Directory

GLASS FABRICATORS

PRODUCT SECTION

Se-Kure Controls Inc .... E 269 651-9351
  Sturgis *(G-15633)*
Signature Glass Inc .... G 586 447-9000
  Roseville *(G-13869)*
SMR Atmtive Mrror Intl USA Inc .... B 810 364-4141
  Marysville *(G-10615)*
SMR Automotive Systems USA Inc ... F 810 937-2456
  Port Huron *(G-12968)*
SMR Automotive Technology .... F 810 364-4141
  Marysville *(G-10617)*
Solutia Inc .... B 734 676-4400
  Trenton *(G-16157)*
Stained Glass and Gifts .... G 810 736-6766
  Flint *(G-5504)*
Syncreonus Inc .... D 248 377-4700
  Auburn Hills *(G-1010)*
Valley Glass Co Inc .... G 989 790-9342
  Saginaw *(G-14175)*
Wolverine Glass Products Inc ...... E 616 538-0100
  Wyoming *(G-18044)*

GLASS PRDTS, FROM PURCHASED GLASS: Art

Boyer Glassworks Inc .... G 231 526-6359
  Harbor Springs *(G-7275)*

GLASS PRDTS, FROM PURCHASED GLASS: Glassware

Etched Glass Works & A Bldg Co ... G 517 819-4343
  Lansing *(G-9367)*
Grand River Interiors Inc .... E 616 454-2800
  Grand Rapids *(G-6468)*

GLASS PRDTS, FROM PURCHASED GLASS: Glassware, Indl

Sydeline Corporation .... G 734 675-9330
  Grosse Ile *(G-7177)*
Wyse Glass Specialties Inc .... G 989 496-3510
  Freeland *(G-5762)*

GLASS PRDTS, FROM PURCHASED GLASS: Insulating

Classic Glass Battle Creek Inc ..... F 269 968-2791
  Battle Creek *(G-1167)*

GLASS PRDTS, FROM PURCHASED GLASS: Mirrored

Alexanders Custom GL & Mirror ... G 734 513-5850
  Garden City *(G-5820)*
Hensley Mfg Inc .... F 810 653-3226
  Davison *(G-3653)*
Magna Mirrors America Inc .... B 616 738-0115
  Holland *(G-7736)*
Magna Mirrors America Inc .... E 616 786-7000
  Grand Haven *(G-6052)*
Rgm New Ventures Inc .... D 248 624-5050
  Wixom *(G-17885)*
Se-Kure Domes & Mirrors Inc ...... E 269 651-9351
  Sturgis *(G-15634)*

GLASS PRDTS, FROM PURCHASED GLASS: Windshields

Exatec LLC .... E 248 926-4200
  Wixom *(G-17807)*
Lippert Components Mfg Inc .... C 989 845-3061
  Chesaning *(G-2725)*

GLASS PRDTS, FROM PURCHD GLASS: Strengthened Or Reinforced

PPG Industries Inc .... F 248 641-2000
  Troy *(G-16557)*

GLASS PRDTS, PRESSED OR BLOWN: Blocks & Bricks

Knickerbocker R Yr Brickr Blk ..... G 517 531-5369
  Parma *(G-12390)*

GLASS PRDTS, PRESSED OR BLOWN: Bulbs, Electric Lights

Lumecon LLC .... G 248 505-1090
  Farmington Hills *(G-5047)*

GLASS PRDTS, PRESSED OR BLOWN: Glassware, Art Or Decorative

Jordan Valley Glassworks .... G 231 536-0539
  East Jordan *(G-4638)*
Meints Glass Blowing .... G 269 349-1958
  Kalamazoo *(G-8821)*

GLASS PRDTS, PRESSED OR BLOWN: Lighting Eqpt Parts

Laidco Sales Inc .... G 231 832-1327
  Hersey *(G-7473)*

GLASS PRDTS, PRESSED OR BLOWN: Reflector, Lighting Eqpt

Light Speed Usa LLC .... A 616 308-0054
  Grand Rapids *(G-6627)*

GLASS PRDTS, PRESSED/BLOWN: Glassware, Art, Decor/Novelty

Glassicart Decorative Glwr .... G 231 739-5956
  Muskegon *(G-11330)*
Pubsof Chicago LLC .... G 312 448-8282
  Traverse City *(G-16083)*

GLASS PRDTS, PRESSED/BLOWN: Lenses, Lantern, Flshlght, Etc

Hudson Industries Inc .... G 800 459-1077
  Warren *(G-17082)*

GLASS PRDTS, PURCHSD GLASS: Ornamental, Cut, Engraved/Décor

A K Services Inc .... G 313 972-1010
  Detroit *(G-3827)*
Pristine Glass Company .... G 616 454-2092
  Grand Rapids *(G-6778)*

GLASS STORE: Leaded Or Stained

Full Spectrum Stained GL Inc ...... G 269 432-2610
  Colon *(G-3373)*

GLASS STORES

Jene Holly Designs Inc .... G 586 954-0255
  Harrison Township *(G-7334)*
Knight Tonya 313 255-3434
  Southfield *(G-14956)*
Lenox Cement Products Inc .... G 586 727-1488
  Lenox *(G-9521)*
Oldcastle Buildingenvelope Inc ... F 734 947-9670
  Taylor *(G-15752)*
Pollack Glass Co .... F 517 349-6380
  Okemos *(G-12134)*
Valley Glass Co Inc .... G 989 790-9342
  Saginaw *(G-14175)*

GLASS, AUTOMOTIVE: Wholesalers

Oldcastle Buildingenvelope Inc ... E 616 896-8341
  Burnips *(G-2133)*
Vitro Automotriz SA De CV .... F 734 727-5001
  Westland *(G-17608)*

GLASS: Fiber

Keweenaw Bay Indian Community ... F 906 524-5757
  Baraga *(G-1104)*
Optrand Inc .... F 734 451-3480
  Plymouth *(G-12703)*
PPG Industries Inc .... F 248 641-2000
  Troy *(G-16557)*
Robroy Enclosures Inc .... C 616 794-0700
  Belding *(G-1428)*
Thompson John .... G 810 225-8780
  Howell *(G-8108)*

GLASS: Flat

Beechcraft Products Inc .... E 989 288-2606
  Durand *(G-4606)*
Carlex Glass America LLC .... A 248 824-8800
  Troy *(G-16258)*
Guardian Fabrication Inc .... A 248 340-1800
  Auburn Hills *(G-893)*
Guardian Industries LLC .... F 517 629-9464
  Albion *(G-125)*
Guardian Industries LLC .... B 734 654-4285
  Carleton *(G-2456)*
Guardian Industries LLC .... B 248 340-1800
  Auburn Hills *(G-894)*
Guardian Industries LLC .... D 734 654-1111
  Carleton *(G-2457)*
Mirror Image Inc .... G 248 446-8440
  South Lyon *(G-14802)*
Pilkington North America Inc ...... F 989 754-2956
  Saginaw *(G-14122)*
Pilkington North America Inc ...... F 248 542-8300
  Royal Oak *(G-13957)*
Pittsburgh Glass Works LLC .... C 248 371-1700
  Rochester Hills *(G-13494)*
Pollack Glass Co .... F 517 349-6380
  Okemos *(G-12134)*
PPG Industries Inc .... F 248 641-2000
  Troy *(G-16557)*
Saint Gobain Glass Corporation ... G 248 816-0060
  Troy *(G-16590)*
Saint-Gobain Sekurit Usa Inc ...... F 586 264-1072
  Sterling Heights *(G-15483)*
Valley Glass Co Inc .... G 989 790-9342
  Saginaw *(G-14175)*

GLASS: Insulating

Weatherproof Inc .... E 517 764-1330
  Jackson *(G-8606)*

GLASS: Pressed & Blown, NEC

Dare Products Inc .... E 269 965-2307
  Springfield *(G-15190)*
Essilor Laboratories Amer Inc .... C 616 361-6000
  Grand Rapids *(G-6386)*
General Scientific Corporation .... E 734 996-9200
  Ann Arbor *(G-471)*
Great Lakes Aero Products .... F 810 235-1402
  Flint *(G-5441)*
Guardian Industries LLC .... B 734 654-4285
  Carleton *(G-2456)*
Precision Polymer Mfg Inc .... E 269 344-2044
  Kalamazoo *(G-8860)*
Rgm New Ventures Inc .... D 248 624-5050
  Wixom *(G-17885)*

GLASS: Stained

Full Spectrum Stained GL Inc ...... G 269 432-2610
  Colon *(G-3373)*
Jordan Valley Glassworks .... G 231 536-0539
  East Jordan *(G-4638)*
Thompson Art Glass Inc .... G 810 225-8766
  Brighton *(G-1998)*

GLASS: Tempered

Oldcastle Buildingenvelope Inc ... F 734 947-9670
  Taylor *(G-15752)*

GLASSWARE: Cut & Engraved

Engrave A Remembrance Inc ..... G 586 772-7480
  Warren *(G-17018)*

GLASSWARE: Indl

City Auto Glass Co .... G 616 842-3235
  Grand Haven *(G-6003)*
Tig Entity LLC .... G 810 629-9558
  Fenton *(G-5244)*

GLASSWARE: Laboratory

M2 Scientifics LLC .... G 616 379-9080
  Holland *(G-7728)*

GLOVES: Fabric

Kaul Glove and Mfg Co .... E 313 894-9494
  Detroit *(G-4172)*

GLOVES: Leather, Work

Kaul Glove and Mfg Co .... E 313 894-9494
  Detroit *(G-4172)*

GLOVES: Safety

A and J Industries .... G 616 877-4845
  Wayland *(G-17396)*
Cooper Glove and Safety LLC .... G 706 512-0486
  Bridgeport *(G-1851)*

GLUE

Adhesive Systems Inc ....E 313 865-4448
  Detroit *(G-3843)*
Genova Products Inc ....D 810 744-4500
  Davison *(G-3650)*
Sugru Inc ....G 877 990-9888
  Livonia *(G-9947)*

GOLD ORE MINING

Trelleborg Corporation ....G 269 639-9891
  South Haven *(G-14778)*

GOLF EQPT

Accessories & Specialties Inc ....G 989 235-3331
  Crystal *(G-3607)*
Consumer Advntage Rference Svc ....G 586 783-1806
  Clinton Township *(G-3089)*
Edens Technologies LLC ....F 517 304-1324
  Northville *(G-11689)*
Golf Store ....G 517 347-8733
  Okemos *(G-12125)*
James D Frisbie ....F 616 868-0092
  Alto *(G-327)*
King Par, LLC ....D 810 732-2470
  Flushing *(G-5539)*
Ryan Reynolds Golf Shop LLC ....G 269 629-9311
  Rochester *(G-13349)*

GOLF GOODS & EQPT

Great Lakes Allied LLC ....G 231 924-5794
  White Cloud *(G-17622)*
Owosso Country Club Pro Shop ....G 989 723-1470
  Owosso *(G-12308)*

GOURMET FOOD STORES

Cherry Republic Inc ....D 231 334-3150
  Glen Arbor *(G-5940)*
Crazy Joes Enterprises LLC ....G 906 395-1522
  Baraga *(G-1100)*
Downeys Potato Chips-Waterford ....G 248 673-3636
  Waterford *(G-17338)*
SBR LLC ....E 313 350-8799
  Harper Woods *(G-7304)*

GRANITE: Crushed & Broken

Genesee Cut Stone & Marble Co ....E 810 743-1800
  Flint *(G-5437)*
Graniteonecom Inc ....G 616 452-8372
  Grand Rapids *(G-6472)*

GRANITE: Cut & Shaped

Classic Stone MBL & Gran Inc ....G 248 588-1599
  Troy *(G-16269)*
Ecogranite LLC ....G 248 820-9196
  Livonia *(G-9721)*
Grand River Granite Inc ....G 616 399-9324
  Holland *(G-7649)*
Leonardos Marble & Granite ....F 248 468-2900
  Wixom *(G-17845)*
Solutions In Stone Inc ....G 734 453-4444
  Plymouth *(G-12758)*
Yellowstone Products Inc ....G 616 299-7855
  Comstock Park *(G-3522)*

GRANITE: Dimension

Surface Encounters LLC ....D 586 566-7557
  Macomb *(G-10164)*

GRANITE: Dimension

Take Us-4-Granite Inc ....G 586 803-1305
  Shelby Township *(G-14707)*

GRAPHIC ARTS & RELATED DESIGN SVCS

Action Printech Inc ....E 734 207-6000
  Plymouth *(G-12561)*
Bivins Graphics ....G 616 453-2211
  Grand Rapids *(G-6227)*
Book Concern Printers ....G 906 482-1250
  Hancock *(G-7248)*
Commercial Graphics Company ....G 517 278-2159
  Coldwater *(G-3299)*
Commercial Graphics of Mich ....G 810 744-2102
  Burton *(G-2150)*
Different By Design Inc ....E 248 588-4840
  Farmington Hills *(G-4972)*
Fonts About Inc ....G 248 767-7504
  Northville *(G-11692)*
Freshwater Dgtal Mdia Prtnrs ....F 616 446-1771
  Kentwood *(G-9007)*
Genesis Service Associates LLC ....G 734 994-3900
  Dexter *(G-4493)*
Graphic Enterprises Inc ....D 248 616-4900
  Madison Heights *(G-10258)*
Graphic Resource Group Inc ....E 248 588-6100
  Troy *(G-16386)*
Graphic Visions Inc ....F 248 347-3355
  Farmington Hills *(G-5013)*
Graphics Unlimited Inc ....G 231 773-2696
  Muskegon *(G-11336)*
Grigg Graphic Services Inc ....F 248 356-5005
  Southfield *(G-14932)*
Hycorr LLC ....F 269 381-6349
  Kalamazoo *(G-8771)*
Kalamazoo Photo Comp Svcs ....E 269 345-3706
  Kalamazoo *(G-8794)*
Kendall & Company Inc ....G 810 733-7330
  Flint *(G-5454)*
Kenewell Group ....G 810 714-4290
  Fenton *(G-5222)*
Lloyd Waters & Associates ....G 734 525-2777
  Livonia *(G-9817)*
M Beshara Inc ....G 248 542-9220
  Oak Park *(G-12079)*
Media Solutions Inc ....G 313 831-3152
  Detroit *(G-4225)*
Meridian Screen Prtg & Design ....G 517 351-2525
  Okemos *(G-12130)*
Modzel Screen Printing ....G 231 941-0911
  Traverse City *(G-16040)*
Printxpress Inc ....G 313 846-1644
  Dearborn *(G-3751)*
Skip Printing and Dup Co ....G 586 779-2640
  Roseville *(G-13870)*
Star Board Multi Media Inc ....G 616 296-0823
  Grand Haven *(G-6084)*
Startech Services Inc ....G 586 752-2460
  Romeo *(G-13639)*
Thorpe Printing Services Inc ....G 810 364-6222
  Marysville *(G-10622)*
Vomela Specialty Company ....E 269 927-6500
  Benton Harbor *(G-1562)*
Vtec Graphics Inc ....G 734 953-9729
  Livonia *(G-9993)*
Whitcomb and Sons Sign Co Inc ....G 586 752-3576
  Romeo *(G-13641)*

GRASSES: Artificial & Preserved

Fieldturf Usa Inc ....G 706 625-6533
  Auburn Hills *(G-873)*

GRAVE MARKERS: Concrete

Arnets Inc ....F 734 665-3650
  Ann Arbor *(G-367)*
Perfected Grave Vault Co ....G 616 243-3375
  Grand Rapids *(G-6748)*

GRAVEL & PEBBLE MINING

Genoak Materials Inc ....G 810 742-0050
  Burton *(G-2155)*

GRAVEL MINING

A Lindberg & Sons Inc ....E 906 485-5705
  Ishpeming *(G-8342)*
Albrecht Sand & Gravel Co ....E 810 672-9272
  Snover *(G-14742)*
American Aggregate Inc ....G 269 683-6160
  Niles *(G-11594)*
Barber Creek Sand & Gravel ....F 616 675-7619
  Kent City *(G-8987)*
Bechtel Sand & Gravel ....G 810 346-2041
  Brown City *(G-2046)*
Bently Sand & Gravel ....G 810 629-6172
  Fenton *(G-5189)*
Bischer Ready-Mix Inc ....G 989 479-3267
  Ruth *(G-13987)*
Branch West Concrete Products ....F 989 345-0794
  West Branch *(G-17507)*
Carr Brothers and Sons Inc ....E 517 629-3549
  Albion *(G-117)*
Carr Brothers and Sons Inc ....F 517 531-3358
  Albion *(G-118)*
Chippewa Stone & Gravel Inc ....G 231 867-5757
  Rodney *(G-13612)*
Flushing Sand and Gravel ....G 810 577-8260
  Flint *(G-5431)*
Genoak Materials Inc ....C 248 634-8276
  Holly *(G-7880)*
Gerken Materials Inc ....G 517 567-4406
  Waldron *(G-16858)*
Hubscher & Son Inc ....G 989 773-5369
  Mount Pleasant *(G-11196)*
Hubscher & Son Inc ....G 989 875-2151
  Sumner *(G-15642)*
Huizenga Gravel Company Inc ....G 616 457-1030
  Jenison *(G-8629)*
Kurtz Gravel Company Inc ....E 810 787-6543
  Farmington Hills *(G-5040)*
Lyon Sand & Gravel Co ....G 313 843-7200
  Dearborn *(G-3734)*
Lyon Sand & Gravel Co ....D 248 348-8511
  Wixom *(G-17848)*
Morris Excavating Inc ....F 269 483-7773
  White Pigeon *(G-17654)*
Newark Gravel Company ....F 810 796-3072
  Dryden *(G-4570)*
Parker Excvtg Grav & Recycle ....F 616 784-1681
  Comstock Park *(G-3505)*
R E Glancy Inc ....G 989 876-6030
  Tawas City *(G-15678)*
Simmons Gravel Co ....G 616 754-7073
  Greenville *(G-7153)*
Snider Construction Inc ....G 231 537-4851
  Levering *(G-9546)*
South Flint Gravel Inc ....G 810 232-8911
  Holly *(G-7897)*
South Hill Sand and Gravel ....G 248 828-1726
  Troy *(G-16614)*
South Hill Sand and Gravel ....G 248 685-7020
  Milford *(G-10986)*
Tip Top Gravel Co Inc ....G 616 897-8342
  Ada *(G-31)*
Top OMichigan Reclaimers Inc ....G 989 705-7983
  Gaylord *(G-5897)*
Weber Sand and Gravel Inc ....F 248 373-0900
  Lake Orion *(G-9169)*

GREASE CUPS: Metal

Essex Brass Corporation ....F 586 757-8200
  Warren *(G-17020)*

GREASES & INEDIBLE FATS, RENDERED

Darling Ingredients Inc ....D 313 928-7400
  Melvindale *(G-10695)*
Darling Ingredients Inc ....C 517 279-9731
  Coldwater *(G-3301)*
Michigan Protein Inc ....G 616 696-7854
  Cedar Springs *(G-2558)*

GREASES: Lubricating

Huron Industries Inc ....G 810 984-4213
  Port Huron *(G-12928)*

GREENHOUSES: Prefabricated Metal

Control Dekk LLC ....G 616 828-4862
  Wyoming *(G-17994)*
Keeler-Glasgow Company Inc ....E 269 621-2415
  Hartford *(G-7384)*
Luiten Greenhouse Tech ....G 269 381-4020
  Kalamazoo *(G-8811)*

GREETING CARD SHOPS

Katys Kards ....G 989 793-4094
  Saginaw *(G-14070)*

GRILLS & GRILLWORK: Woven Wire, Made From Purchased Wire

Benmill LLC ....E 616 243-7555
  Grand Rapids *(G-6210)*
Great Lakes Grilling Co ....F 616 791-8600
  Grand Rapids *(G-6478)*

GRINDING BALLS: Ceramic

Afi Enterprises Inc ....E 734 475-9111
  Chelsea *(G-2700)*
Internal Grinding Abrasives ....E 616 243-5566
  Grand Rapids *(G-6540)*

GRINDING SVC: Precision, Commercial Or Indl

Automated Precision Eqp LLC	G	517 481-2414
Eaton Rapids (G-4717)		
Detroit Chrome Inc	E	313 341-9478
Detroit (G-3976)		
Diversified Precision Pdts Inc	E	517 750-2310
Spring Arbor (G-15121)		
Fega Tool & Gage Company	F	586 469-4400
Clinton Township (G-3114)		
Gear Master Inc	F	810 798-9254
Almont (G-257)		
Grand Rapids Metaltek Inc	E	616 791-2373
Grand Rapids (G-6460)		
Jordan Tool Corporation	E	586 755-6700
Warren (G-17211)		
Momentum Industries Inc	E	989 681-5735
Saint Louis (G-14366)		
Precise Metal Components Inc	G	734 769-0790
Ann Arbor (G-598)		
Ramtec Corp	F	586 752-9270
Romeo (G-13636)		
Sodus Hard Chrome Inc	F	269 925-2077
Sodus (G-14747)		
Tazz Broach and Machine Inc	G	586 296-7755
Harrison Township (G-7352)		
Tru Tech Systems LLC	D	586 469-2700
Mount Clemens (G-11152)		
West Michigan Grinding Svc Inc	F	231 739-4245
Norton Shores (G-11805)		
Wolverine Special Tool Inc	E	616 791-1027
Grand Rapids (G-7000)		

GRINDING SVCS: Ophthalmic Lens, Exc Prescription

Rx-Rite Optical Co	E	586 294-8500
Fraser (G-5719)		

GRINDS: Electric

Morstar Inc	F	248 605-3291
Livonia (G-9848)		

GRIPS OR HANDLES: Rubber

Hold-It Inc	G	810 984-4213
Port Huron (G-12925)		

GROCERIES WHOLESALERS, NEC

American Bottling Company	D	517 622-8605
Grand Ledge (G-6100)		
Coca-Cola Refreshments USA Inc	C	517 322-2349
Lansing (G-9283)		
Fireside Coffee Company Inc	F	810 635-9196
Swartz Creek (G-15666)		
Greenfield Noodle Specialty Co	F	313 873-2212
Detroit (G-4103)		
Home Style Foods Inc	F	313 874-3250
Detroit (G-4126)		
New Moon Noodle Incorporated	E	269 962-8820
Battle Creek (G-1232)		
Pepsi-Cola Metro Btlg Co Inc	E	517 279-8436
Coldwater (G-3318)		
Pepsi-Cola Metro Btlg Co Inc	D	616 285-8200
Grand Rapids (G-6747)		
Purina Mills LLC	E	517 322-0200
Lansing (G-9319)		
Stone House Bread Inc	E	231 933-8864
Traverse City (G-16113)		
Uncle Johns Cider Mill Inc	D	989 224-3686
Saint Johns (G-14298)		

GROCERIES, GENERAL LINE WHOLESALERS

18th Street Deli Inc	G	313 921-7710
Hamtramck (G-7243)		
Achatzs Hand Made Pie Co	D	586 749-2882
Chesterfield (G-2731)		
Countryside Foods LLC	B	586 447-3500
Warren (G-16994)		
Vandco Incorporated	E	906 482-1550
Hancock (G-7258)		

GROUTING EQPT: Concrete

K&H Supply of Lansing Inc	G	517 482-7600
Lansing (G-9301)		

GUARDS: Machine, Sheet Metal

Steel-Guard Company LLC	G	586 232-3909
Macomb (G-10162)		

GUIDED MISSILES & SPACE VEHICLES

Telic Corporation	G	219 406-2164
Saint Joseph (G-14343)		

GUM & WOOD CHEMICALS

Conway-Cleveland Corp	G	616 458-0056
Grand Rapids (G-6309)		

GUN SIGHTS: Optical

Leapers Inc	E	734 542-1500
Livonia (G-9805)		
Trijicon Inc	C	248 960-7700
Wixom (G-17920)		
Williams Gun Sight Company	D	800 530-9028
Davison (G-3666)		

GUTTERS

Genova Products Inc	D	810 744-4500
Davison (G-3650)		

GUTTERS: Sheet Metal

Rainbow Seamless Systems Inc	F	231 933-8888
Traverse City (G-16089)		

GYPSUM MINING

Michigan Gypsum Co	F	989 792-8734
Midland (G-10885)		

GYPSUM PRDTS

New Ngc Inc	E	989 756-2741
National City (G-11464)		
United States Gypsum Company	C	269 384-6335
Otsego (G-12257)		
United States Gypsum Company	F	313 624-4232
River Rouge (G-13282)		
United States Gypsum Company	C	313 842-4455
Detroit (G-4415)		
US Gypsum Co	D	313 842-5800
River Rouge (G-13283)		

HAIR & HAIR BASED PRDTS

American Laser Centers LLC	A	248 426-8250
Farmington Hills (G-4929)		
Kevin Larkin Inc	G	248 736-8203
Waterford (G-17355)		
Rena DRane Enterprises Inc	D	248 796-2765
Southfield (G-15012)		

HAIR ACCESS WHOLESALERS

Brintley Enterprises	G	248 991-4086
Detroit (G-3918)		

HAIR CARE PRDTS

Detroit Fine Products LLC	F	877 294-5826
Ferndale (G-5277)		
Murrays Worldwide Inc	F	248 691-9156
Oak Park (G-12086)		
Viladon Corporation	G	248 548-0043
Oak Park (G-12103)		

HAIR CURLERS: Beauty Shop

Head Over Heels	G	248 435-2954
Troy (G-16393)		

HALL EFFECT DEVICES

White River	G	231 894-9216
Montague (G-11099)		

HAMPERS: Laundry, Sheet Metal

Metro-Fabricating LLC	D	989 667-8100
Bay City (G-1332)		

HAND TOOLS, NEC: Wholesalers

Hank Thorn Co	F	248 348-7800
Wixom (G-17823)		
Tekton Inc	D	616 243-2443
Grand Rapids (G-6919)		

HANDBAGS

Accessories By Gigi LLC	G	248 242-0036
Clawson (G-2968)		
Nicole Acarter LLC	G	248 251-2800
Detroit (G-4270)		
Tmb Trends Inc	G	866 445-2344
Troy (G-16646)		

HANDBAGS: Women's

Mary Boggs Baggs	G	586 731-2513
Shelby Township (G-14634)		
Tapestry Inc	F	631 724-8066
Sterling Heights (G-15519)		

HANDCUFFS & LEG IRONS

C & S Security Inc	G	989 821-5759
Roscommon (G-13748)		

HANDLES: Wood

Home Style Co	G	989 871-3654
Millington (G-10996)		

HANGERS: Garment, Home & Store, Wooden

Hangers Plus LLC	G	616 997-4264
Coopersville (G-3560)		
Setco Inc	G	616 459-6311
Grand Rapids (G-6858)		

HANGERS: Garment, Plastic

Batts Group Ltd	G	616 956-3053
Grand Rapids (G-6206)		
Do-It Corporation	D	269 637-1121
South Haven (G-14758)		
Hangers Plus LLC	G	616 997-4264
Coopersville (G-3560)		
Tower Tag & Label LLC	F	269 927-1065
Benton Harbor (G-1555)		

HANGERS: Garment, Wire

Hangers Plus LLC	G	616 997-4264
Coopersville (G-3560)		

HARDWARE

Acme Mills Company	C	517 437-8940
Hillsdale (G-7513)		
Admat Manufacturing Inc	F	269 641-7453
Union (G-16727)		
ADS Us Inc	C	989 871-4550
Millington (G-10993)		
Albion Industries LLC	C	800 835-8911
Albion (G-113)		
Antolin Interiors Usa Inc	A	517 548-0052
Howell (G-8015)		
Apex Spring & Stamping Corp	D	616 453-5463
Grand Rapids (G-6171)		
B & B Electrical Inc	G	248 391-3800
Keego Harbor (G-8978)		
BDS Company Inc	E	517 279-2135
Coldwater (G-3291)		
Berkley Screw Machine Pdts Inc	E	248 853-0044
Rochester Hills (G-13376)		
Brauer Clamps USA	C	586 427-5304
Warren (G-16965)		
Caster Concepts Inc	G	517 629-2456
Albion (G-119)		
Clamptech LLC	G	989 832-8027
Bay City (G-1295)		
Consolidated Clips Clamps Inc	D	734 455-0880
Plymouth (G-12601)		
Dgh Enterprises Inc	G	269 925-0657
Benton Harbor (G-1495)		
Die Cast Press Mfg Co Inc	E	269 657-6060
Paw Paw (G-12403)		
Dolphin Manufacturing Inc	E	734 946-6322
Taylor (G-15707)		
Dowding Industries Inc	E	517 663-5455
Eaton Rapids (G-4720)		
E K Hydraulics Inc	G	800 632-7112
Petoskey (G-12448)		
Eaton-Aeroquip Llc	B	949 452-9575
Jackson (G-8440)		
Ervins Group LLC	G	248 203-2000
Bloomfield Hills (G-1764)		
Evans Industries Inc	G	313 272-8200
Detroit (G-4046)		

PRODUCT SECTION

HARDWARE, WHOLESALE: Chains

Flextronics Intl USA Inc ....B 616 837-9711
  Coopersville (G-3558)
Fluid Hutchinson Management ....D 248 679-1327
  Auburn Hills (G-876)
Franklin Fastener Company ....E 313 537-8900
  Redford (G-13162)
G T Gundrilling Inc ....G 586 992-3301
  Macomb (G-10124)
G&G Industries Inc ....E 586 726-6000
  Shelby Township (G-14595)
GAL Gage Co ....E 269 465-5750
  Bridgman (G-1863)
Gates Corporation ....D 248 260-2300
  Rochester Hills (G-13431)
General Dynamics Glbl IMG Tech ....F 248 293-2929
  Rochester Hills (G-13433)
Grant Industries Incorporated ....D 586 293-9200
  Fraser (G-5657)
Great Lakes Trim Inc ....D 231 267-3000
  Williamsburg (G-17713)
Guardian Automotive Corp ....C 586 757-7800
  Sterling Heights (G-15365)
Hella Corporate Center USA Inc ....E 586 232-4788
  Northville (G-11697)
Hydro-Craft Inc ....E 248 652-8100
  Rochester Hills (G-13448)
Incoe Corporation ....C 248 616-0220
  Auburn Hills (G-910)
International Automotive Compo ....B 810 987-8500
  Port Huron (G-12930)
International Engrg & Mfg Inc ....D 989 689-4911
  Hope (G-7954)
Jay & Kay Manufacturing LLC ....G 810 679-3079
  Croswell (G-3599)
K & W Manufacturing Co Inc ....F 517 369-9708
  Bronson (G-2031)
Kriewall Enterprises Inc ....E 586 336-0600
  Romeo (G-13631)
L & W Inc ....D 734 397-6300
  New Boston (G-11502)
Lacks Industries Inc ....C 616 698-6890
  Grand Rapids (G-6606)
Michigan Wheel Operations LLC ....E 616 452-6941
  Grand Rapids (G-6677)
Milan Screw Products Inc ....E 734 439-2431
  Milan (G-10949)
Milton Manufacturing Inc ....E 313 366-2450
  Detroit (G-4250)
Mvc Holdings LLC ....F 586 491-2600
  Roseville (G-13843)
Norma Michigan Inc ....F 248 373-4300
  Lake Orion (G-9151)
Norma Michigan Inc ....C 248 373-4300
  Auburn Hills (G-959)
Orion Manufacturing Inc ....F 616 527-5994
  Ionia (G-8250)
Peninsular Inc ....E 586 775-7211
  Roseville (G-13853)
Penn Automotive Inc ....D 313 299-8500
  Romulus (G-13720)
Penstone Inc ....E 734 379-3160
  Rockwood (G-13610)
Pressweld Manufacturing Co ....G 734 675-8282
  Portland (G-13066)
Probe-TEC ....G 765 252-0257
  Chesterfield (G-2822)
Probotic Services LLC ....G 586 524-9589
  Macomb (G-10158)
R & D Enterprises Inc ....E 248 349-7077
  Plymouth (G-12728)
R M Wright Company Inc ....E 248 476-9800
  Farmington Hills (G-5111)
R T Gordon Inc ....E 586 294-6100
  Fraser (G-5715)
R W Fernstrum & Company ....E 906 863-5553
  Menominee (G-10756)
Refrigeration Sales Inc ....G 517 784-8579
  Jackson (G-8562)
Regency Construction Corp ....E 586 741-8000
  Clinton Township (G-3208)
River Valley Machine Inc ....E 269 673-8070
  Allegan (G-187)
RSR Sales Inc ....E 734 668-8166
  Ann Arbor (G-625)
Scaff-All Inc ....G 888 204-9990
  Clay (G-3002)
Shepherd Hardware Products Inc ....D 269 756-3830
  Three Oaks (G-15850)
Spiral Industries Inc ....E 810 632-6300
  Howell (G-8101)

Sterling Die & Engineering Inc ....E 586 677-0707
  Macomb (G-10163)
Stromberg-Carlson Products Inc ....F 231 947-8600
  Traverse City (G-16114)
TEC-3 Prototypes Inc ....E 810 678-8909
  Metamora (G-10782)
TI Group Auto Systems LLC ....C 248 494-5000
  Auburn Hills (G-1024)
TI Group Auto Systems LLC ....C 586 948-6006
  Chesterfield (G-2848)
Toyo Seat USA Corporation ....C 606 849-3009
  Imlay City (G-8212)
Unist Inc ....E 616 949-0853
  Grand Rapids (G-6951)
Vacuum Orna Metal Company Inc ....E 734 941-9100
  Romulus (G-13738)
Vogt Industries Inc ....G 616 531-4830
  Grand Rapids (G-6974)
Wico Metal Products Company ....C 586 755-9600
  Warren (G-17293)

HARDWARE & BUILDING PRDTS: Plastic

Beechcraft Products Inc ....E 989 288-2606
  Durand (G-4606)
Datacover Inc ....F 248 391-2163
  Lake Orion (G-9134)
Deluxe Frame Company Inc ....E 248 373-8811
  Auburn Hills (G-840)
Lacks Exterior Systems LLC ....A 616 949-6570
  Grand Rapids (G-6600)
Lacks Exterior Systems LLC ....E 616 949-6570
  Grand Rapids (G-6601)
Lacks Exterior Systems LLC ....F 248 351-0555
  Novi (G-11926)
Lacks Exterior Systems LLC ....F 616 554-7805
  Kentwood (G-9015)
Lacks Industries Inc ....D 616 656-2910
  Grand Rapids (G-6612)
Qfd Recycling ....F 810 733-2335
  Flint (G-5487)
Schrier Plastics Corp ....E 616 669-7174
  Jenison (G-8642)
Standard Plaque Incorporated ....F 313 383-7233
  Melvindale (G-10707)
US Farathane Holdings Corp ....D 586 978-2800
  Westland (G-17607)

HARDWARE & EQPT: Stage, Exc Lighting

North Coast Studios Inc ....F 586 359-6630
  Roseville (G-13848)
Stageright Corporation ....C 989 386-7393
  Clare (G-2890)

HARDWARE STORES

A W B Industries Inc ....E 989 739-1447
  Oscoda (G-12205)
Ebels Hardware Inc ....F 231 826-3334
  Falmouth (G-4892)
Erickson Lumber & True Value ....G 906 524-6295
  Lanse (G-9191)
Houseart LLC ....E 248 651-8124
  Rochester (G-13327)
J Kaltz & Co ....G 616 942-6070
  Grand Rapids (G-6547)
Kalamazoo Electric Motor Inc ....G 269 345-7802
  Kalamazoo (G-8788)
Masons Lumber & Hardware Inc ....G 989 685-3999
  Rose City (G-13763)
McLaren Inc ....G 989 720-4328
  Owosso (G-12302)
Nelson Hardware ....G 269 327-3583
  Portage (G-13018)
Northwods Prperty Holdings LLC ....G 231 334-3000
  Glen Arbor (G-5941)
Port Huron Building Supply Co ....F 810 987-2666
  Port Huron (G-12958)
Toms World of Wood ....G 517 264-2836
  Adrian (G-98)
Weber Steel Inc ....F 989 868-4162
  Vassar (G-16819)

HARDWARE STORES: Builders'

Smede-Son Steel and Sup Co Inc ....D 313 937-3200
  Redford (G-13192)

HARDWARE STORES: Door Locks & Lock Sets

Acorn Stamping Inc ....F 248 628-5216
  Oxford (G-12332)

HARDWARE STORES: Pumps & Pumping Eqpt

Etna Distributors LLC ....G 906 273-2331
  Marquette (G-10530)
Jet Subsurface Rod Pumps Corp ....G 989 732-7513
  Gaylord (G-5869)
Vic Bond Sales Inc ....G 517 548-0107
  Howell (G-8121)

HARDWARE STORES: Tools

Arm Tooling Systems Inc ....F 586 759-5677
  Warren (G-16938)
Busch Machine Tool Supply LLC ....G 989 798-4794
  Freeland (G-5753)
Loon Lake Precision Inc ....G 810 953-0732
  Grand Blanc (G-5974)
Marshall Tool Service Inc ....G 989 777-3137
  Saginaw (G-14082)
Mmp Molded Magnesium Pdts LLC ....G 517 789-8505
  Jackson (G-8534)
S F S Carbide Tool ....G 989 777-3890
  Saginaw (G-14135)
Tool Sales & Engineering ....G 810 714-5000
  Fenton (G-5245)
Triple Tool ....F 586 795-1785
  Sterling Heights (G-15530)
Widell Industries Inc ....E 989 742-4528
  Hillman (G-7511)

HARDWARE STORES: Tools, Power

Great Lakes Wood Products ....G 906 228-3737
  Negaunee (G-11470)

HARDWARE WHOLESALERS

Acument Global Tech Inc ....E 586 254-3900
  Sterling Heights (G-15252)
All Tool Sales Inc ....F 231 941-4302
  Traverse City (G-15893)
Dgh Enterprises Inc ....E 269 925-0657
  Benton Harbor (G-1494)
Fixtureworks LLC ....G 586 294-6100
  Fraser (G-5654)
G & T Industries Inc ....D 616 452-8611
  Byron Center (G-2192)
K-Tool Corporation Michigan ....D 863 603-0777
  Plymouth (G-12661)
La Force Inc ....G 248 588-5601
  Troy (G-16455)
Patco Air Tool Inc ....F 248 648-8830
  Orion (G-12188)
Rae Manufacturing Company ....F 810 987-9170
  Port Huron (G-12960)
Roger Zatkoff Company ....E 248 478-2400
  Farmington Hills (G-5117)
RSR Sales Inc ....E 734 668-8166
  Ann Arbor (G-625)

HARDWARE, WHOLESALE: Bolts

Connection Service Company ....F 269 926-2658
  Benton Harbor (G-1491)
Federal Group Usa Inc ....F 248 545-5000
  Southfield (G-14905)
MNP Corporation ....A 586 254-1320
  Utica (G-16744)

HARDWARE, WHOLESALE: Builders', NEC

Modern Builders Supply Inc ....G 517 787-3633
  Jackson (G-8535)
Richelieu America Ltd ....E 586 264-1240
  Sterling Heights (G-15469)

HARDWARE, WHOLESALE: Casters & Glides

Shepherd Hardware Products Inc ....D 269 756-3830
  Three Oaks (G-15850)

HARDWARE, WHOLESALE: Chains

Serapid Inc ....F 586 274-0774
  Sterling Heights (G-15490)

Employee Codes: A=Over 500 employees, B=251-500
C=101-250, D=51-100, E=20-50, F=10-19, G=3-9

HARDWARE, WHOLESALE: Nozzles

Signet Machine Inc ....G...... 616 261-2939
  Grandville *(G-7071)*

HARDWARE, WHOLESALE: Rivets

Jay Cee Sales & Rivet Inc ....F...... 248 478-2150
  Farmington *(G-4901)*

HARDWARE, WHOLESALE: Screws

United States Socket ....F...... 586 469-8811
  Fraser *(G-5744)*

HARDWARE, WHOLESALE: Security Devices, Locks

A & L Metal Products ....G...... 734 654-8990
  Carleton *(G-2451)*
Cincinnati Time Systems Inc ....F...... 248 615-8300
  Farmington Hills *(G-4963)*
Cypress Computer Systems Inc............F...... 810 245-2300
  Lapeer *(G-9453)*

HARDWARE, WHOLESALE: Staples

Aactus Inc ....G...... 734 425-1212
  Livonia *(G-9623)*

HARDWARE: Aircraft

Precision Polymer Mfg Inc ....E...... 269 344-2044
  Kalamazoo *(G-8860)*
Teamtech Motorsports Safety ....G...... 989 792-4880
  Saginaw *(G-14163)*

HARDWARE: Builders'

Dundee Manufacturing Co Inc ....E...... 734 529-2540
  Dundee *(G-4580)*
Engineered Products Company ....E...... 810 767-2050
  Flint *(G-5425)*
Enterprise Hinge Inc ....G...... 269 857-2111
  Douglas *(G-4531)*
Masco Corporation ....A...... 313 274-7400
  Livonia *(G-9826)*

HARDWARE: Cabinet

Options Cabinetry Inc..............................F...... 248 669-0000
  Commerce Township *(G-3436)*

HARDWARE: Door Opening & Closing Devices, Exc Electrical

D A C Industries Inc ....G...... 616 235-0140
  Grand Rapids *(G-6331)*
Magna Mirrors America Inc ....B...... 231 652-4450
  Newaygo *(G-11574)*
Select Products Limited ....E...... 269 323-4433
  Portage *(G-13032)*

HARDWARE: Furniture

Belwith Products LLC ....F...... 616 247-4000
  Grandville *(G-7022)*
H & L Advantage Inc ....E...... 616 532-1012
  Grandville *(G-7042)*
Herman Miller Inc ....G...... 616 453-5995
  Grand Rapids *(G-6509)*
Moheco Products Company ....G...... 734 855-4194
  Livonia *(G-9847)*
Northwest Metal Products Inc ....F...... 616 453-0556
  Grand Rapids *(G-6720)*

HARDWARE: Furniture, Builders' & Other Household

Knape & Vogt Manufacturing Co ....A...... 616 459-3311
  Grand Rapids *(G-6585)*
Polytec Foha Inc ....F...... 586 978-9386
  Warren *(G-17188)*

HARDWARE: Locking Systems, Security Cable

Startech-Solutions LLC ....G...... 248 419-0650
  Southfield *(G-15233)*

HARDWARE: Padlocks

Solidbody Technology Company ....G...... 248 709-7901
  Troy *(G-16610)*

HARDWARE: Rubber

Armada Rubber Manufacturing Co ....D...... 586 784-9135
  Armada *(G-716)*
Blade Industrial Products Inc ....G...... 248 773-7400
  Wixom *(G-17774)*
Derby Fabg Solutions LLC......................D...... 616 866-1650
  Rockford *(G-13566)*

HARNESS ASSEMBLIES: Cable & Wire

A B Electrical Inc....................................E...... 231 737-9200
  Muskegon *(G-11257)*
AB Electrical Wires Inc ....E...... 231 737-9200
  Muskegon *(G-11258)*
Alpine Electronics America Inc ....C...... 248 409-9444
  Auburn Hills *(G-766)*
Amphenol Borisch Tech Inc...................G...... 616 554-9820
  Grand Rapids *(G-6168)*
Assem-Tech Inc......................................E...... 616 846-3410
  Grand Haven *(G-5993)*
Bay Electronics Inc ....E...... 586 296-0900
  Roseville *(G-13776)*
Byrne Elec Specialists Inc ....C...... 616 866-3461
  Rockford *(G-13560)*
Byrne Elec Specialists Inc ....G...... 616 866-3461
  Rockford *(G-13561)*
Connect With Us LLC ....E...... 586 262-4359
  Shelby Township *(G-14566)*
Ctc Acquisition Company LLC ....C...... 616 884-7100
  Rockford *(G-13564)*
Direct Connect Systems LLC.................G...... 248 694-0130
  Commerce Township *(G-3400)*
Dupearl Technology LLC........................D...... 248 390-9609
  Bloomfield Hills *(G-1762)*
Electro Panel Inc ....G...... 989 832-2110
  Midland *(G-10859)*
Electro-Matic Integrated Inc..................G...... 248 478-1182
  Farmington Hills *(G-4979)*
Enertech Corporation ....F...... 231 832-5587
  Hersey *(G-7472)*
Madison Electric Company ....D...... 586 825-0200
  Warren *(G-17136)*
Netcon Enterprises Inc...........................E...... 248 673-7855
  Waterford *(G-17360)*
Pkc Group USA Inc ....F...... 248 489-4700
  Farmington Hills *(G-5095)*
Saldet Sales and Services Inc ....E...... 586 469-4312
  Clinton Township *(G-3220)*
Stoneridge Inc...G...... 248 489-9300
  Novi *(G-12004)*
Turn Key Harness & Wire LLC ....G...... 248 236-9915
  Oxford *(G-12379)*
Wh Manufacturing Inc ....E...... 616 534-7560
  Grand Rapids *(G-6990)*

HARNESS WIRING SETS: Internal Combustion Engines

Aees Power Systems Ltd Partnr............D...... 248 489-4900
  Allen Park *(G-194)*
Electrical Concepts Inc ....E...... 616 847-0293
  Grand Haven *(G-6013)*
Portage Wire Systems Inc ....E...... 231 889-4215
  Onekama *(G-12151)*
Starlight Technologies Inc ....G...... 248 250-9607
  Troy *(G-16620)*

HARNESSES, HALTERS, SADDLERY & STRAPS

Birlon Group LLC....................................G...... 313 551-5341
  Inkster *(G-8225)*

HARVESTING MACHINERY & EQPT WHOLESALERS

Gregory M Boese ....F...... 989 754-2990
  Saginaw *(G-14052)*

HEADPHONES: Radio

Chrouch Communications Inc................G...... 231 972-0339
  Mecosta *(G-10687)*
Fka Distributing Co LLC.........................B...... 248 863-3000
  Commerce Township *(G-3406)*
Gadget Locker LLC.................................G...... 702 901-1440
  Detroit *(G-4075)*
House of Marley LLC ....G...... 248 863-3000
  Commerce Township *(G-3415)*
No Limit Wireless-Michigan Inc.............G...... 313 285-8402
  Detroit *(G-4274)*

HEADS-UP DISPLAY & HUD SYSTEMS Aeronautical

Cheboygan Housing Commission ....G...... 231 627-7189
  Cheboygan *(G-2679)*

HEALTH & ALLIED SERVICES, NEC

Lift Aid Inc ....G...... 248 345-5110
  Farmington *(G-4903)*
Total Health Colon Care ....G...... 586 268-5444
  Sterling Heights *(G-15526)*

HEALTH AIDS: Exercise Eqpt

National Credit Corporation....................F...... 734 459-8100
  West Bloomfield *(G-17491)*
Nustep LLC...D...... 734 769-3939
  Ann Arbor *(G-579)*
Riverfront Cycle Inc ....F...... 517 482-8585
  Lansing *(G-9418)*
Y M C A Family Center ....G...... 269 428-9622
  Saint Joseph *(G-14356)*

HEALTH AIDS: Vaporizers

Detroit Buyers Club LLC ....G...... 248 871-7827
  Detroit *(G-3973)*

HEALTH FOOD & SUPPLEMENT STORES

Apple Valley Natural Foods...................C...... 269 471-3234
  Berrien Springs *(G-1592)*

HEALTH SCREENING SVCS

Cotton Concepts Printing LLC ....G...... 313 444-3857
  Detroit *(G-3949)*

HEARING AIDS

Audionet America Inc ....G...... 586 944-0043
  Clinton Township *(G-3059)*
SC Industries Inc....................................F...... 312 366-3899
  Southfield *(G-15023)*

HEAT EMISSION OPERATING APPARATUS

Advanced Avionics Inc...........................G...... 734 259-5300
  Plymouth *(G-12567)*
Hanon Systems Usa LLC ....B...... 248 907-8000
  Novi *(G-11893)*

HEAT EXCHANGERS: After Or Inter Coolers Or Condensers, Etc

Acorn Stamping Inc................................F...... 248 628-5216
  Oxford *(G-12332)*
R & D Enterprises Inc ....E...... 248 349-7077
  Plymouth *(G-12728)*

HEAT TREATING: Metal

Advanced Heat Treat Corp ....E...... 734 243-0063
  Monroe *(G-11013)*
Ajax Metal Processing Inc.....................G...... 313 267-2100
  Detroit *(G-3850)*
Al-Fe Heat Treating Inc ....E...... 989 752-2819
  Saginaw *(G-13994)*
Ald Thermal Treatment Inc ....C...... 810 357-0693
  Port Huron *(G-12884)*
Alloy Steel Treating Company ....F...... 269 628-2154
  Gobles *(G-5946)*
Almar Industries Inc ....G...... 248 541-5617
  Hazel Park *(G-7433)*
Alpha Steel Treating Inc ....E...... 734 523-1035
  Livonia *(G-9637)*
American Metal Processing Co ....E...... 586 757-7144
  Warren *(G-16931)*
American Metallurgical Svcs ....F...... 313 893-8328
  Detroit *(G-3867)*
Anstey Foundry Co Inc..........................E...... 269 429-3229
  Stevensville *(G-15556)*
Apollo Heat Treating Proc LLC ....E...... 248 398-3434
  Oak Park *(G-12048)*
Applied Process Inc...............................E...... 734 464-8000
  Livonia *(G-9651)*
Atmosphere Group Inc ....G...... 248 624-8191
  Wixom *(G-17763)*
Atmosphere Heat Treating Inc ....F...... 248 960-4700
  Wixom *(G-17764)*
Austemper Inc...E...... 586 293-4554
  Wixom *(G-17768)*

Authority Flame Hardening & St............F 586 598-5887
Chesterfield *(G-2743)*
Autocam-Pax Inc....................................E 269 782-5186
Dowagiac *(G-4534)*
Bellaire Log Homes Indus Hm...............G....... 231 533-6669
Bellaire *(G-1435)*
Bellevue Proc Met Prep Inc...................E 313 921-1931
Detroit *(G-3900)*
Benton Harbor LLC................................G....... 269 925-6581
Benton Harbor *(G-1486)*
Bluewater Thermal Solutions ....G....... 989 753-7770
Saginaw *(G-14008)*
Bodycote Thermal Proc Inc ....D....... 616 399-6880
Holland *(G-7573)*
Bodycote Thermal Proc Inc ....D....... 616 245-0465
Grand Rapids *(G-6234)*
Bodycote Thermal Proc Inc ....E 734 459-8514
Canton *(G-2353)*
Bodycote Thermal Proc Inc ....F 734 427-6814
Livonia *(G-9666)*
Bodycote Thermal Proc Inc ....F 734 427-6814
Livonia *(G-9667)*
Burkk Inc..G....... 616 365-0354
Grand Rapids *(G-6244)*
Century Inc...C....... 231 947-6400
Traverse City *(G-15932)*
Century Inc...D....... 231 941-7800
Traverse City *(G-15934)*
Curtis Metal Finishing Co.......................G....... 248 588-3300
Madison Heights *(G-10224)*
Darby Metal Treating Inc ....F 269 204-6504
Plainwell *(G-12521)*
Detroit Edge Tool Company...................G....... 586 776-3727
Roseville *(G-13793)*
Detroit Steel Treating Company ....E 248 334-7436
Pontiac *(G-12816)*
Die Heat Systems Inc.............................G....... 586 749-9756
Chesterfield *(G-2767)*
Dynamic Mtal Treating Intl Inc ....E 734 459-8022
Canton *(G-2368)*
East - Lind Heat Treat Inc.......................E 248 585-1415
Madison Heights *(G-10237)*
Eltro Services Inc...................................G....... 248 628-9790
Oxford *(G-12345)*
Engineered Heat Treat Inc......................E 248 588-5141
Madison Heights *(G-10248)*
Fire-Rite Inc ....E 313 273-3730
Detroit *(G-4060)*
Gerdau Macsteel Atmosphere Ann ....E 517 482-1374
Lansing *(G-9374)*
Gestamp Mason LLC ....B 517 244-8800
Mason *(G-10641)*
Grand Blanc Processing LLC ....D....... 810 694-6000
Holly *(G-7882)*
Heat Treating Svcs Corp Amer ....E 248 858-2230
Pontiac *(G-12832)*
Heat Treating Svcs Corp Amer ....E 248 332-1510
Pontiac *(G-12833)*
Heat Treating Svcs Corp Amer ....E 248 253-9560
Waterford *(G-17350)*
Hi-Tech Steel Treating Inc ....D....... 800 835-8294
Saginaw *(G-14058)*
Induction Engineering Inc......................F 586 716-4700
New Baltimore *(G-11486)*
Induction Processing Inc ....F 586 756-5101
Warren *(G-17088)*
Industrial Steel Treating Co ....D....... 517 787-6312
Jackson *(G-8470)*
Ionbond LLC...D....... 248 398-9100
Madison Heights *(G-10278)*
J Hansen-Balk Stl Treating Co...............E 616 458-1414
Grand Rapids *(G-6546)*
L & L Machine & Tool Inc........................G....... 517 784-5575
Jackson *(G-8491)*
Laydon Enterprises Inc ....E 906 774-4633
Iron Mountain *(G-8288)*
Magnum Induction Inc...........................E 586 716-4700
New Baltimore *(G-11488)*
MB Aerospace Warren LLC...................C....... 586 772-2500
Warren *(G-17144)*
Metallurgical Processing LLC................E 586 758-3100
Warren *(G-17149)*
Metro Machine Works Inc......................D....... 734 941-4571
Romulus *(G-13707)*
Mpd Welding - Grand Rapids Inc...........E 616 248-9353
Grand Rapids *(G-6708)*
Ncoc Inc..E 248 548-5950
Oak Park *(G-12088)*
Nitrex Inc...E 517 676-6370
Mason *(G-10649)*
Nssc America Incorporated ....G....... 248 449-6050
Novi *(G-11960)*
Omc Archtrim..E 517 482-9411
Lansing *(G-9407)*
Pioneer Metal Finishing LLC.................C....... 734 384-9000
Monroe *(G-11062)*
Precision Heat Treating Co ....E 269 382-4660
Kalamazoo *(G-8858)*
Production Tube Company Inc ....G....... 313 259-3990
Detroit *(G-4312)*
Richter Precision Inc.............................E 586 465-0500
Fraser *(G-5718)*
Rmt Acquisition Company LLC ....G....... 248 353-5487
Southfield *(G-15016)*
Rmt Acquisition Company LLC ....G....... 248 353-4229
Plymouth *(G-12740)*
Savanna Inc..E 734 254-0566
Plymouth *(G-12750)*
Savanna Inc..D....... 248 353-8180
Southfield *(G-15022)*
Schroth Enterprises Inc ....E 586 759-4240
Grosse Pointe Farms *(G-7187)*
Solution Steel Treating LLC...................F 586 247-9250
Shelby Township *(G-14698)*
South Haven Finishing Inc....................E 269 637-2047
South Haven *(G-14772)*
Specialty Steel Treating Inc ....E 586 293-5355
Farmington Hills *(G-5127)*
Specialty Steel Treating Inc ....F 586 415-8346
Fraser *(G-5731)*
Specialty Steel Treating Inc ....E 586 415-8346
Fraser *(G-5732)*
Specialty Steel Treating Inc ....F 586 415-8346
Fraser *(G-5733)*
Steel Industries Inc................................C....... 313 535-8505
Redford *(G-13194)*
Stokes Steel Treating Company ....E 810 235-3573
Flint *(G-5506)*
Superior Heat Treat LLC........................E 586 792-9500
Clinton Township *(G-3237)*
Thermal One Inc......................................F 734 721-8500
Westland *(G-17603)*
Tri-State Flame Hardening Co...............G....... 586 776-0035
Warren *(G-17268)*
Trojan Heat Treat Inc.............................E 517 568-4403
Homer *(G-7951)*
Universal Induction Inc ....G....... 269 925-9890
Benton Harbor *(G-1557)*
Walker Wire (ispat) Inc ....G....... 248 399-4800
Sterling Heights *(G-15542)*
Woodworth Inc..E 810 820-6780
Flint *(G-5525)*
Woodworth Inc..E 248 481-2354
Pontiac *(G-12876)*
Wyatt Services Inc ....F 586 264-8000
Sterling Heights *(G-15547)*
Zion Industries Inc..................................F 517 622-3409
Grand Ledge *(G-6117)*

HEATERS: Room, Gas

Detroit Radiant Products Co..................E 586 756-0950
Warren *(G-17000)*
U S Distributing Inc................................E 248 646-0550
Birmingham *(G-1707)*

HEATING & AIR CONDITIONING EQPT & SPLYS WHOLESALERS

2 Brothers Holdings LLC........................G....... 517 487-3900
Lansing *(G-9330)*
Honeywell International Inc ....D....... 248 926-4800
Wixom *(G-17827)*
Marelli North America Inc......................C....... 248 848-4800
Farmington Hills *(G-5057)*
Young Supply Company.........................E 313 875-3280
Detroit *(G-4455)*

HEATING & AIR CONDITIONING UNITS, COMBINATION

Crown Heating Inc ....G....... 248 352-1688
Detroit *(G-3955)*
Kelley Brothers Lc ....F 734 462-6266
Livonia *(G-9795)*
Mechanical Air System Inc.....................G....... 248 346-7995
Commerce Township *(G-3429)*
Northstar Wholesale...............................G....... 517 545-2379
Howell *(G-8070)*
Universal Heating and Cooling..............G....... 734 216-5826
South Lyon *(G-14816)*

HEATING EQPT & SPLYS

Alhern-Martin Indus Frnc Co ....E 248 689-6363
Troy *(G-16187)*
Banner Engineering & Sales Inc............F 989 755-0584
Saginaw *(G-14000)*
Commercial Works ....C....... 269 795-2060
Middleville *(G-10800)*
Dempsey Manufacturing Co ....G....... 810 346-2273
Brown City *(G-2049)*
Marshall Excelsior Co.............................G....... 269 789-6700
Marshall *(G-10576)*
Marshall Excelsior Co.............................E 269 789-6700
Marshall *(G-10577)*
Milair LLC..G....... 513 576-0123
Sterling Heights *(G-15425)*
River Valley Machine Inc ....E 269 673-8070
Allegan *(G-187)*
Rlh Industries Inc...................................F 989 732-0493
Gaylord *(G-5889)*
Seelye Equipment Specialist.................G....... 231 547-9430
Charlevoix *(G-2630)*
Solaronics Inc ....E 248 651-5333
Rochester *(G-13352)*
Ventura Aerospace LLC ....E 734 357-0114
Wixom *(G-17925)*

HEATING EQPT: Complete

Check Technology Solutions LLC.........E 248 680-2323
Troy *(G-16264)*
Combustion Research Corp ....E 248 852-3611
Rochester Hills *(G-13391)*
Rapid Engineering LLC ....D....... 616 784-0500
Comstock Park *(G-3513)*
Snow Technologies Incorporated ....G....... 734 425-3600
Livonia *(G-9934)*
Weather-Rite LLC....................................D....... 612 338-1401
Comstock Park *(G-3520)*

HEATING EQPT: Induction

Capital Induction Inc..............................F 586 322-1444
Sterling Heights *(G-15280)*
Cyprium Induction LLC ....G....... 586 884-4982
Sterling Heights *(G-15305)*
D K Enterprises Inc.................................G....... 586 756-7350
Warren *(G-16997)*
Eldec LLC ....F 248 364-4750
Auburn Hills *(G-852)*
Electroheat Technologies LLC ....E 810 798-2400
Auburn Hills *(G-853)*
Heating Induction Services Inc..............G....... 586 791-3160
Clinton Township *(G-3135)*
Inter-Power Corporation.........................E 810 798-7050
Almont *(G-259)*
Interpower Induction Svcs Inc...............G....... 586 296-7697
Fraser *(G-5673)*
Phoenix Induction Corporation ....F 248 486-7377
South Lyon *(G-14809)*
Pillar Induction...G....... 586 254-8470
Madison Heights *(G-10326)*
Sheler Corporation ....F 586 979-8560
Sterling Heights *(G-15496)*
SMS Elotherm North America LLC........G....... 586 469-8324
Shelby Township *(G-14696)*

HEATING SYSTEMS: Radiant, Indl Process

Florheat Company ....G....... 517 272-4441
Lansing *(G-9368)*
Jensen Industries Inc. ....F 810 224-5005
Fenton *(G-5221)*
Solaronics Inc ....E 248 651-5333
Rochester *(G-13352)*

HEATING UNITS & DEVICES: Indl, Electric

Alhern-Martin Indus Frnc Co ....E 248 689-6363
Troy *(G-16187)*
Custom Electric Mfg LLC ....E 248 305-7700
Wixom *(G-17793)*
Ddr Heating Inc ....E 269 673-2145
Allegan *(G-155)*
Ddr Heating Inc ....G....... 269 673-2145
Allegan *(G-156)*
E H Inc..E 269 673-6456
Allegan *(G-159)*
Great Lkes Indus Frnc Svcs Inc ....F 586 323-9200
Sterling Heights *(G-15364)*
Hi-Tech Furnace Systems Inc ....F 586 566-0600
Shelby Township *(G-14600)*

Employee Codes: A=Over 500 employees, B=251-500
C=101-250, D=51-100, E=20-50, F=10-19, G=3-9
2020 Harris Michigan
Industrial Directory
1251

HEATING UNITS & DEVICES: Indl, Electric

Industrial Frnc Interiors Inc ....G....... 586 977-9600
  Sterling Heights (G-15373)
National Appliance Parts Co ....F....... 269 639-1469
  South Haven (G-14766)
National Element Inc..............................E....... 248 486-1810
  Brighton (G-1966)
Nexthermal Corporation ....D....... 269 964-0271
  Battle Creek (G-1233)

HELICOPTERS

Enstrom Helicopter Corporation ....C....... 906 863-1200
  Menominee (G-10731)
G-Force Tooling LLC ....G....... 517 541-2747
  Charlotte (G-2650)
G-Force Tooling LLC ....G....... 517 712-8177
  Grand Ledge (G-6107)
Traverse City Helicopters LLC ....G....... 231 668-6000
  Traverse City (G-16126)

HELMETS: Athletic

Xenith LLC ....E....... 866 888-2322
  Detroit (G-4452)

HELP SUPPLY SERVICES

Msx International Inc ....D....... 248 585-6654
  Madison Heights (G-10312)

HERMETICS REPAIR SVCS

Gustos Quality Systems..........................G....... 231 409-0219
  Fife Lake (G-5341)

HIGHWAY & STREET MAINTENANCE SVCS

Southwestern Mich Dust Ctrl..................F....... 269 521-7638
  Bloomingdale (G-1814)

HITCHES: Trailer

Hensley Mfg Inc......................................F....... 810 653-3226
  Davison (G-3653)
Horizon Global Americas Inc ....C....... 734 656-3000
  Plymouth (G-12643)
Rieke-Arminak Corp ....G....... 248 631-5450
  Bloomfield Hills (G-1795)
Trimas Corporation ....E....... 248 631-5450
  Bloomfield Hills (G-1807)

HOBBY & CRAFT SPLY STORES

Ophir Crafts LLC ....G....... 734 794-7777
  Ann Arbor (G-584)

HOBBY, TOY & GAME STORES: Arts & Crafts & Splys

Runyan Pottery Supply Inc ....G....... 810 687-4500
  Clio (G-3281)
Toms World of Wood ....G....... 517 264-2836
  Adrian (G-98)

HOBBY, TOY & GAME STORES: Dolls & Access

Dolls By Maurice Inc................................G....... 586 739-5147
  Utica (G-16741)

HOBBY, TOY & GAME STORES: Hobbies, NEC

Hadd Enterprises ....G....... 586 773-4260
  Eastpointe (G-4702)

HOBBY, TOY & GAME STORES: Toys & Games

Dog Might LLC ....F....... 734 679-0646
  Ann Arbor (G-423)
Sandcastle For Kids Inc ....F....... 616 396-5955
  Holland (G-7796)
Thomas Toys Inc.....................................G....... 810 629-8707
  Fenton (G-5243)

HOISTING SLINGS

K&S Consultants LLC.............................G....... 269 240-7767
  Buchanan (G-2122)

HOISTS

Besser Company USA..............................E....... 616 399-5215
  Zeeland (G-18119)
Detroit Hoist & Crane Co L L C ....E....... 586 268-2600
  Sterling Heights (G-15312)

HOISTS: Hand

Frost Incorporated..................................E....... 616 453-7781
  Grand Rapids (G-6421)

HOLDERS, PAPER TOWEL, GROCERY BAG, ETC: Plastic

Able Solutions LLC..................................G....... 810 216-6106
  Port Huron (G-12880)

HOLDING COMPANIES: Investment, Exc Banks

A Raymond Corp N Amer Inc ....E....... 248 853-2500
  Rochester Hills (G-13358)
Anderton Equity LLC ....G....... 248 430-6650
  Troy (G-16202)
Avon Machining Holdings Inc.................C....... 586 884-2200
  Shelby Township (G-14552)
Bbp Investment Holdings LLC................F....... 231 725-4966
  Muskegon (G-11278)
Dawn Foods Inc ....C....... 517 789-4400
  Jackson (G-8430)
Ej Americas LLC ....G....... 231 536-2261
  East Jordan (G-4629)
Erae AMS America Corp..........................F....... 419 386-8876
  Pontiac (G-12823)
Flint Group Packaging Inks ....G....... 734 781-4600
  Livonia (G-9739)
Gns North America Inc ....G....... 616 796-0433
  Holland (G-7646)
Knpc Holdco LLC ....G....... 248 588-1903
  Madison Heights (G-10292)
L Thompson Co LLC................................F....... 616 844-1135
  Grand Haven (G-6044)
Motus Holdings LLC ....A....... 616 422-7557
  Holland (G-7749)
Sandbox Solutions Inc ....C....... 248 349-7010
  Northville (G-11723)
Sunmed Holdings LLC ....F....... 616 259-8400
  Grand Rapids (G-6900)
Tecumseh Products Holdings LLC ....F....... 734 585-9500
  Ann Arbor (G-663)
Truck Holdings Inc..................................G....... 877 875-4376
  Ann Arbor (G-683)

HOLDING COMPANIES: Personal, Exc Banks

Howa USA Holdings Inc ....G....... 248 715-4000
  Novi (G-11902)

HOME CENTER STORES

Swartzmiller Lumber Company ....G....... 989 845-6625
  Chesaning (G-2728)

HOME DELIVERY NEWSPAPER ROUTES

Pathway Publishing Corporation ....G....... 269 521-3025
  Bloomingdale (G-1813)

HOME ENTERTAINMENT EQPT: Electronic, NEC

B Company Inc.......................................F....... 734 283-7080
  Riverview (G-13291)
Intellitech Systems Inc ....G....... 586 219-3737
  Troy (G-16420)
M A S Information Age Tech...................G....... 248 352-0162
  Southfield (G-14971)

HOME FURNISHINGS WHOLESALERS

Humphrey Companies LLC.....................C....... 616 530-1717
  Grandville (G-7048)

HOME HEALTH CARE SVCS

Landra Prsthtics Orthotics Inc ....G....... 586 294-7188
  Saint Clair Shores (G-14259)

HOME IMPROVEMENT & RENOVATION CONTRACTOR AGENCY

Houseparty ....G....... 616 422-1226
  Holland (G-7681)
Overstreet Property MGT Co ....G....... 269 252-1560
  Benton Harbor (G-1537)

HOMEBUILDERS & OTHER OPERATIVE BUILDERS

Lumber & Truss Inc ....E....... 810 664-7290
  Lapeer (G-9472)

HOMEFURNISHING STORE: Bedding, Sheet, Blanket, Spread/Pillow

Shop Makarios LLC ....G....... 800 479-0032
  Byron Center (G-2211)

HOMEFURNISHING STORES: Closet organizers & shelving units

Home Niches Inc ....G....... 734 330-9189
  Ann Arbor (G-494)
Pipp Mobil Stora Syste Holdi C ....C....... 616 735-9100
  Walker (G-16873)

HOMEFURNISHING STORES: Fireplaces & Wood Burning Stoves

Premier Fireplace Co LLC ....G....... 586 949-4315
  Macomb (G-10156)
Trenton Hearthside Shop Inc ....G....... 734 558-5860
  Trenton (G-16160)

HOMEFURNISHING STORES: Pictures, Wall

A&Lb Custom Framing LLC....................G....... 517 783-3810
  Jackson (G-8370)

HOMEFURNISHING STORES: Pottery

Karla-Von Ceramics Inc ....G....... 616 866-0563
  Rockford (G-13576)

HOMEFURNISHING STORES: Vertical Blinds

Detroit Custom Services Inc ....E....... 586 465-3631
  Mount Clemens (G-11129)

HOMEFURNISHING STORES: Window Furnishings

Time For Blinds Inc.................................G....... 248 363-9174
  White Lake (G-17640)

HOMEFURNISHING STORES: Window Shades, NEC

Tri City Blinds Inc....................................G....... 989 695-5699
  Freeland (G-5760)

HOMEFURNISHINGS & SPLYS, WHOLESALE: Decorative

Pubsof Chicago LLC................................G....... 312 448-8282
  Traverse City (G-16083)

HOMEFURNISHINGS, WHOLESALE: Blankets

Grabber Inc..E....... 616 940-1914
  Byron Center (G-2193)

HOMEFURNISHINGS, WHOLESALE: Blinds, Venetian

Custom Verticals Unlimited ....G....... 734 522-1615
  Oak Park (G-12057)
Elsie Inc ....F....... 734 421-8844
  Livonia (G-9726)
Sunburst Shutters..................................G....... 248 674-4600
  Waterford (G-17378)

HOMEFURNISHINGS, WHOLESALE: Carpets

Floorcovering Engineers LLC..................G....... 616 299-1007
  Grand Rapids (G-6414)
James E Sullivan & Associates ....G....... 616 453-0345
  Grand Rapids (G-6551)

PRODUCT SECTION

HOUSEWARES, ELECTRIC: Blankets

Parkway Drapery & Uphl Co Inc .... G 734 779-1300
Livonia *(G-9884)*

HOMEFURNISHINGS, WHOLESALE: Mirrors/Pictures, Framed/Unframd

Prime Wood Products Inc .... G 616 399-4700
Holland *(G-7775)*

HOMEFURNISHINGS, WHOLESALE: Pottery

Penzo America Inc .... G 248 723-0802
Bloomfield Hills *(G-1789)*

HOMEMAKERS' SVCS

Shoulders LLC .... G 248 843-1536
Pontiac *(G-12865)*

HOMES, MODULAR: Wooden

Dickinson Homes Inc .... E 906 774-5800
Kingsford *(G-9057)*
E B I Inc .... G 810 227-8180
Brighton *(G-1914)*
Hunt Hoppough Custom Crafted .... E 616 794-3455
Belding *(G-1418)*
Marshalls Crossing .... G 810 639-4740
Montrose *(G-11104)*
Ritz-Craft Corp PA Inc .... E 517 849-7425
Jonesville *(G-8668)*

HOMES: Log Cabins

Beaver Log Homes Inc .... F 231 258-5020
Kalkaska *(G-8938)*
Classic Log Homes Incorporated .... F 989 821-6118
Higgins Lake *(G-7482)*
G B Wolfgram and Sons Inc .... F 231 238-4638
Indian River *(G-16729)*
Harman Lumber & Supply Inc .... G 269 641-5424
Union *(G-16729)*
Hiawatha Log Homes Inc .... E 877 275-9090
Munising *(G-11244)*
J B Log Homes Inc .... G 906 875-6581
Crystal Falls *(G-3610)*
Koskis Log Homes Inc .... G 906 884-4937
Ontonagon *(G-12162)*
Lorencz Construction Co .... G 989 798-3151
Chesaning *(G-2727)*
Masons Lumber & Hardware Inc .... G 989 685-3999
Rose City *(G-13763)*
North Arrow Log Homes Inc .... G 906 484-5524
Pickford *(G-12482)*
Riverbend Timber Framing Inc .... D 517 486-3629
Blissfield *(G-1726)*
Wolf Log Home Buildings .... G 231 757-7000
Scottville *(G-14511)*

HONES

Howell Tool Service Inc .... F 517 548-1114
Howell *(G-8052)*

HONING & LAPPING MACHINES

Nagel Precision Inc .... C 734 426-5650
Ann Arbor *(G-568)*

HOODS: Range, Sheet Metal

Curbs & Damper Products Inc .... F 586 776-7890
Roseville *(G-13788)*

HOPPERS: End Dump

Bondfire Company .... F 231 834-5696
Bailey *(G-1078)*

HOPPERS: Sheet Metal

Material Handling Tech Inc .... D 586 725-5546
Ira *(G-8260)*

HORNS: Marine, Compressed Air Or Steam

Dts Enterprises Inc .... E 231 599-3123
Ellsworth *(G-4787)*

HORSE & PET ACCESSORIES: Textile

Hamilton Equine Products LLC .... G 616 842-2406
Grand Haven *(G-6031)*

HORSESHOES

Goodyear Horseshoe Supply Inc .... G 810 639-2591
Montrose *(G-11102)*
Lincoln Park Die & Tool Co .... E 734 285-1680
Brownstown *(G-2067)*
Will Lent Horseshoe Co .... G 231 861-5033
Shelby *(G-14537)*

HOSE: Air Line Or Air Brake, Rubber Or Rubberized Fabric

Andronaco Inc .... G 616 554-4600
Kentwood *(G-8998)*

HOSE: Automobile, Plastic

Continental Plastics Co .... A 586 294-4600
Shelby Township *(G-14567)*
Dayco Products LLC .... D 248 404-6506
Troy *(G-16298)*
Sejasmi Industries Inc .... C 586 725-5300
Ira *(G-8270)*

HOSE: Fire, Rubber

Douglass Safety Systems LLC .... G 989 687-7600
Sanford *(G-14449)*

HOSE: Flexible Metal

Northern Fab & Machine LLC .... F 906 863-8506
Menominee *(G-10754)*
TI Group Auto Systems LLC .... B 248 296-8000
Auburn Hills *(G-1022)*

HOSE: Plastic

Haviland Contoured Plastics .... G 616 361-6691
Walker *(G-16866)*
Piranha Hose Products Inc .... E 231 779-4390
Cadillac *(G-2271)*
TI Automotive LLC .... C 248 494-5000
Auburn Hills *(G-1020)*
TI Group Auto Systems LLC .... B 248 296-8000
Auburn Hills *(G-1022)*

HOSE: Pneumatic, Rubber Or Rubberized Fabric, NEC

Snook Inc .... F 231 799-3333
Norton Shores *(G-11795)*

HOSE: Rubber

Akwel Cadillac Usa Inc .... G 231 876-1361
Cadillac *(G-2225)*
Dayco Products LLC .... C 248 404-6537
Roseville *(G-13789)*
Kadant Johnson LLC .... C 269 278-1715
Three Rivers *(G-15867)*
Pureflex Inc .... C 616 554-1100
Kentwood *(G-9026)*
TI Group Auto Systems LLC .... D 517 437-7462
Hillsdale *(G-7543)*

HOSES & BELTING: Rubber & Plastic

Akwel Cadillac Usa Inc .... E 248 848-9599
Farmington Hills *(G-4926)*
Anand Nvh North America Inc .... C 810 724-2400
Imlay City *(G-8196)*
Atcoflex Inc .... F 616 842-4661
Grand Haven *(G-5994)*
Eaton-Aeroquip Llc .... B 949 452-9575
Jackson *(G-8440)*
Ena North America Corporation .... F 248 926-0011
Wixom *(G-17803)*
Fabricated Flex & Hose Sup Inc .... G 269 342-2221
Kalamazoo *(G-8741)*
Flexfab LLC .... E 269 945-3533
Grand Rapids *(G-6412)*
Flexfab Horizons Intl Inc .... E 269 945-4700
Hastings *(G-7409)*
Flexfab LLC .... E 269 945-2433
Hastings *(G-7410)*
Thunder Technologies LLC .... F 248 844-4875
Rochester Hills *(G-13526)*
Ton-Tex Corporation .... F 616 957-3200
Greenville *(G-7158)*

HOSPITAL EQPT REPAIR SVCS

Vets Access LLC .... G 810 639-2222
Flushing *(G-5544)*

HOSPITAL HOUSEKEEPING SVCS

Shoulders LLC .... G 248 843-1536
Pontiac *(G-12865)*

HOSTELS

Soutec Div of Andritz Bricmont .... G 248 305-2955
Novi *(G-12001)*

HOT TUBS

Conway Products Corporation .... E 616 698-2601
Grand Rapids *(G-6308)*
Viking Spas Inc .... F 616 248-7800
Wyoming *(G-18041)*

HOT TUBS: Plastic & Fiberglass

Aquatic Co .... D 269 279-7461
Three Rivers *(G-15855)*

HOUSEHOLD ANTENNA INSTALLATION & SVCS

Plymouth Computer & .... G 734 744-9563
Livonia *(G-9890)*

HOUSEHOLD APPLIANCE STORES

Lockett Enterprises LLC .... G 810 407-6644
Flint *(G-5459)*
Wal-Vac Inc .... G 616 241-6717
Wyoming *(G-18042)*

HOUSEHOLD APPLIANCE STORES: Electric Household, Major

Marrs Discount Furniture .... G 989 720-5436
Owosso *(G-12300)*

HOUSEHOLD ARTICLES, EXC FURNITURE: Cut Stone

Marble ERA Products Inc .... E 989 742-4513
Gaylord *(G-5876)*

HOUSEHOLD ARTICLES: Metal

Bulman Products Inc .... E 616 363-4416
Grand Rapids *(G-6241)*
Heath Manufacturing Company .... D 616 997-8181
Coopersville *(G-3561)*
Toughbuoy Co .... G 989 465-6111
Coleman *(G-3352)*

HOUSEHOLD FURNISHINGS, NEC

Anchor Wiping Cloth Inc .... D 313 892-4000
Detroit *(G-3870)*
Gamco Inc .... F 269 683-4280
Niles *(G-11613)*
Intramode LLC .... G 313 964-6990
Detroit *(G-4146)*
Jackson Manufacturing & Distrg .... G 616 451-3030
Grand Rapids *(G-6550)*
Preferred Products Inc .... E 248 255-0200
Commerce Township *(G-3441)*
Three Chairs Co .... G 734 665-2796
Ann Arbor *(G-674)*

HOUSEWARE STORES

Candle Factory Grand Traverse .... F 231 946-2280
Traverse City *(G-15929)*

HOUSEWARES, ELECTRIC, EXC COOKING APPLIANCES & UTENSILS

Distinctive Appliances Distrg .... F 248 380-2007
Wixom *(G-17795)*

HOUSEWARES, ELECTRIC: Blankets

Neptech Inc .... E 810 225-2222
Highland *(G-7498)*
Sampling Bag Technologies LLC .... G 734 525-8600
Livonia *(G-9920)*

Employee Codes: A=Over 500 employees, B=251-500
C=101-250, D=51-100, E=20-50, F=10-19, G=3-9

HOUSEWARES, ELECTRIC: Blenders

Advanced Blnding Solutions LLC ....F 906 914-4180
  Menominee *(G-10721)*

HOUSEWARES, ELECTRIC: Heaters, Immersion

New Century Heaters Ltd ....G....... 989 671-1994
  Bay City *(G-1337)*

HOUSEWARES, ELECTRIC: Heaters, Sauna

Nippa Sauna Stoves LLC ....G....... 231 882-7707
  Beulah *(G-1611)*

HOUSEWARES, ELECTRIC: Heaters, Space

Therm Technology Corp.........................G....... 616 530-6540
  Grandville *(G-7074)*

HOUSEWARES, ELECTRIC: Heating Units, Electric Appliances

Ogilvie Manufacturing Company...........G....... 810 793-6598
  Lapeer *(G-9478)*
Weco International Inc.............................G....... 810 686-7221
  Flushing *(G-5545)*

HOUSEWARES, ELECTRIC: Humidifiers, Household

Cdgjl Inc...E....... 517 787-2100
  Jackson *(G-8404)*

HOUSEWARES, ELECTRIC: Massage Machines, Exc Beauty/Barber

Fka Distributing Co LLC........................B....... 248 863-3000
  Commerce Township *(G-3406)*

HOUSEWARES: Bowls, Wood

Holland Bowl Mill ....E....... 616 396-6513
  Holland *(G-7669)*

HOUSEWARES: Dishes, Plastic

D&W Fine Pack LLC...............................G....... 866 296-2020
  Gladwin *(G-5928)*
Idrink Products Inc ....G....... 734 531-6324
  Ann Arbor *(G-500)*
Munimula Inc..G....... 517 605-5343
  Quincy *(G-13097)*
Solo Cup Operating Corporation...........D....... 800 248-5960
  Mason *(G-10658)*

HOUSEWARES: Dishes, Wooden

Mbwwproducts Inc.................................F....... 616 464-1650
  Grand Rapids *(G-6651)*

HOUSEWARES: Food Dishes & Utensils, Pressed & Molded Pulp

Pressed Paperboard Tech LLC..............D....... 248 646-6500
  Bingham Farms *(G-1658)*

HOUSEWARES: Plates, Pressed/Molded Pulp, From Purchased Mtrl

AJM Packaging Corporation..................E....... 313 291-6500
  Taylor *(G-15685)*

HOUSINGS: Business Machine, Sheet Metal

Diversified Fabricators Inc....................F....... 586 868-1000
  Clinton Township *(G-3104)*

HUB CAPS: Automobile, Stamped Metal

Capco Automovite ....G....... 248 616-8888
  Troy *(G-16257)*
Stemco Products Inc ....G....... 888 854-6474
  Millington *(G-10998)*

HUMIDIFYING EQPT, EXC PORTABLE

General Filters Inc.................................E....... 248 476-5100
  Novi *(G-11890)*

HYDRAULIC EQPT REPAIR SVC

American Electric Motor Corp ....F....... 810 743-6080
  Burton *(G-2143)*
Cpj Company Inc...................................E....... 616 784-6355
  Comstock Park *(G-3472)*
E K Hydraulics Inc ....G....... 800 632-7112
  Petoskey *(G-12448)*
Gds Enterprises ....G....... 989 644-3115
  Lake *(G-9082)*
Great Lakes Hydra Corporation............F....... 616 949-8844
  Grand Rapids *(G-6479)*
Ksb Dubric Inc..E....... 616 784-6355
  Comstock Park *(G-3492)*
Npi ....G....... 248 478-0010
  Farmington Hills *(G-5083)*
Sarns Industries Inc..............................F....... 586 463-5829
  Harrison Twp *(G-7360)*
Tri-Tech Engineering Inc ....E....... 734 283-3700
  Wyandotte *(G-17978)*
Yates Industries Inc ....D....... 586 778-7680
  Saint Clair Shores *(G-14277)*
Yoe Industries Inc ....G....... 586 791-7660
  Clinton Township *(G-3263)*

HYDRAULIC FLUIDS: Synthetic Based

American Chemical Tech Inc ....E....... 517 223-0300
  Fowlerville *(G-5557)*
Chem-Trend Limited Partnership ....C....... 517 546-4520
  Howell *(G-8022)*

HYDROPONIC EQPT

Cultivation Stn - Detroit Inc....................G....... 313 383-1766
  Allen Park *(G-196)*
Grany Greenthumbs LLC.......................G....... 517 223-1302
  Fowlerville *(G-5568)*

Hard Rubber & Molded Rubber Prdts

Americo Corporation ....G....... 313 565-6550
  Dearborn *(G-3675)*
Ehc Inc ....G....... 313 259-2266
  Detroit *(G-4030)*
Minowitz Manufacturing Co ....E....... 586 779-5940
  Huntington Woods *(G-8190)*
Procraft Custom Builder ....G....... 586 323-1605
  Oxford *(G-12364)*

ICE

Agi Ccaa Inc ....G....... 715 355-0856
  Port Huron *(G-12882)*
Arctic Glacier Grayling Inc.....................F....... 810 987-7100
  Port Huron *(G-12892)*
Arctic Glacier Inc ....E....... 734 485-0430
  Port Huron *(G-12893)*
Arctic Glacier PA Inc..............................E....... 610 494-8200
  Port Huron *(G-12894)*
Daneks Goodtime Ice Co Inc ....G....... 989 725-5920
  Owosso *(G-12287)*
Gold Coast Ice Makers LLC ....G....... 231 845-2745
  Ludington *(G-10060)*
Hanson Cold Storage Co.......................F....... 269 982-1390
  Saint Joseph *(G-14314)*
Home City Ice Company........................E....... 269 926-2490
  Sodus *(G-14745)*
Kelly Bros Inc ....G....... 989 723-4543
  Owosso *(G-12298)*
Lansing Ice and Fuel Company ....F....... 517 372-3850
  Lansing *(G-9240)*

ICE CREAM & ICES WHOLESALERS

Cold Stone Creamery ....G....... 313 886-4020
  Grosse Pointe Park *(G-7192)*
Moomers Homemade Ice Cream LLC ...E....... 231 941-4122
  Traverse City *(G-16043)*

ICE WHOLESALERS

Arctic Glacier Inc ....E....... 734 485-0430
  Port Huron *(G-12893)*

IDENTIFICATION PLATES

Keyes-Davis Company ....E....... 269 962-7505
  Springfield *(G-15195)*

IDENTIFICATION TAGS, EXC PAPER

Industrial Mtal Idntfction Inc ....G....... 616 847-0060
  Spring Lake *(G-15153)*

IGNITION APPARATUS & DISTRIBUTORS

Borgwrner Emssions Systems LLC......G....... 248 754-9600
  Auburn Hills *(G-805)*

IGNITION COILS: Automotive

Daewon America Inc..............................G....... 334 364-1630
  Troy *(G-16294)*
Diamond Electric Mfg Corp ....F....... 734 995-5525
  Ann Arbor *(G-420)*
Eldor Automotive N Amer Inc ....G....... 248 878-9193
  Troy *(G-16337)*

IGNITION SYSTEMS: High Frequency

Emp Racing Inc......................................G....... 906 786-8404
  Escanaba *(G-4825)*

INCINERATORS

Durr Inc ....G....... 734 459-6800
  Southfield *(G-14888)*
Durr Systems Inc ....B....... 248 450-2000
  Southfield *(G-14889)*

INDL & PERSONAL SVC PAPER WHOLESALERS

ABC Packaging Equipment & Mtls........F 616 784-2330
  Comstock Park *(G-3458)*
Associated Metals Inc ....G....... 734 369-3851
  Ann Arbor *(G-371)*
Fibers of Kalamazoo Inc.......................E....... 269 344-3122
  Kalamazoo *(G-8743)*
Mark-Pack Inc...E....... 616 837-5400
  Coopersville *(G-3564)*

INDL & PERSONAL SVC PAPER, WHOL: Bags, Paper/Disp Plastic

Chelsea Milling Company ....F 269 781-2823
  Marshall *(G-10564)*

INDL & PERSONAL SVC PAPER, WHOL: Boxes, Corrugtd/Solid Fiber

All American Container Corp ....F....... 586 949-0000
  Macomb *(G-10105)*
Compak Inc...G....... 989 288-3199
  Burton *(G-2152)*
Delta Containers Inc ....E....... 810 742-2730
  Bay City *(G-1300)*
National Packaging Corporation...........F....... 248 652-3600
  Rochester Hills *(G-13479)*
Phoenix Packaging Corporation ....G....... 734 944-3916
  Saline *(G-14407)*
Russell R Peters Co LLC......................G....... 989 732-0660
  Gaylord *(G-5891)*
St Clair Packaging Inc ....E....... 810 364-4230
  Marysville *(G-10619)*
Wrkco Inc..E....... 269 964-7181
  Battle Creek *(G-1268)*

INDL & PERSONAL SVC PAPER, WHOL: Cups, Disp, Plastic/Paper

Michigan Poly Supplies Inc...................G....... 734 282-5554
  Taylor *(G-15743)*

INDL & PERSONAL SVC PAPER, WHOL: Paper, Wrap/Coarse/Prdts

Practical Paper Inc................................F 616 887-1723
  Cedar Springs *(G-2559)*

INDL & PERSONAL SVC PAPER, WHOLESALE: Press Sensitive Tape

Aactus Inc...G....... 734 425-1212
  Livonia *(G-9623)*
Elliott Tape Inc.......................................E....... 248 475-2000
  Auburn Hills *(G-854)*

INDL & PERSONAL SVC PAPER, WHOLESALE: Shipping Splys

Volk Corporation ....G....... 616 940-9900
  Farmington Hills *(G-5150)*

INDL EQPT CLEANING SVCS

Chemico Systems Inc ... E ... 248 723-3263
Southfield *(G-14866)*

INDL EQPT SVCS

American Steel Works Inc ... F ... 734 282-0300
Riverview *(G-13290)*
Back Machine Shop LLC ... G ... 269 963-7061
Springfield *(G-15187)*
Bulk AG Innovations LLC ... F ... 269 925-0900
Benton Harbor *(G-1488)*
C R B Crane & Service Co ... G ... 586 757-1222
Warren *(G-16973)*
Clarkston Control Products ... G ... 248 394-1430
Clarkston *(G-2912)*
Equitable Engineering Co Inc ... E ... 248 689-9700
Troy *(G-16351)*
F&B Technologies ... F ... 734 856-2118
Ottawa Lake *(G-12262)*
Fidia Co ... F ... 248 680-0700
Rochester Hills *(G-13424)*
Franklin Electric Corporation ... F ... 248 442-8000
Garden City *(G-5824)*
Grand Traverse Crane Corp ... G ... 231 943-7787
Traverse City *(G-15984)*
Great Lkes Indus Frnc Svcs Inc ... F ... 586 323-9200
Sterling Heights *(G-15364)*
Hammars Contracting LLC ... F ... 810 367-3037
Kimball *(G-9044)*
Island Machine and Engrg LLC ... G ... 810 765-8228
Marine City *(G-10475)*
Jensen Industries Inc. ... F ... 810 224-5005
Fenton *(G-5221)*
Mahle Industries Incorporated ... E ... 248 305-8200
Farmington Hills *(G-5052)*
Stirnemann Tool & Mch Co Inc ... G ... 248 435-4040
Clawson *(G-2986)*
TEC International II ... G ... 248 724-1800
Auburn Hills *(G-1014)*
Wolverine Crane & Service Inc ... E ... 616 538-4870
Grand Rapids *(G-6997)*
Wolverine Crane & Service Inc ... F ... 734 467-9066
Romulus *(G-13741)*

INDL GASES WHOLESALERS

Airgas Usa LLC ... F ... 517 673-0997
Blissfield *(G-1712)*
Praxair Inc ... F ... 586 751-7400
Warren *(G-17191)*

INDL MACHINERY & EQPT WHOLESALERS

AA Anderson & Co Inc ... E ... 248 476-7782
Plymouth *(G-12559)*
Ability Mfg & Engrg Co ... F ... 269 227-3292
Fennville *(G-5169)*
Advanced Feedlines LLC ... D ... 248 583-9400
Troy *(G-16169)*
Aero Grinding Inc ... G ... 586 774-6450
Roseville *(G-13771)*
AG Davis Gage & Engrg Co ... E ... 586 977-9000
Sterling Heights *(G-15256)*
Becktold Enterprises Inc ... G ... 269 349-3656
Kalamazoo *(G-8694)*
Belco Industries Inc ... E ... 616 794-0410
Belding *(G-1400)*
Benny Gage Inc ... E ... 734 455-3080
Wixom *(G-17773)*
Bobier Tool Supply Inc ... F ... 810 732-4030
Flint *(G-5392)*
Brawn Mixer Inc ... F ... 616 399-5600
Holland *(G-7576)*
Campbell Inc Press Repair ... E ... 517 371-1034
Lansing *(G-9354)*
Custom Valve Concepts Inc ... E ... 248 597-8999
Madison Heights *(G-10225)*
Dadco Inc ... D ... 734 207-1100
Plymouth *(G-12604)*
Dcl Inc ... C ... 231 547-5600
Charlevoix *(G-2613)*
Dee-Blast Corporation ... F ... 269 428-2400
Stevensville *(G-15563)*
Dimond Machinery Company Inc ... E ... 269 945-5908
Hastings *(G-7407)*
Douglas Water Conditioning ... E ... 248 363-8383
Waterford *(G-17336)*
Dupearl Technology LLC ... D ... 248 390-9609
Bloomfield Hills *(G-1762)*
Energy Products Inc ... G ... 248 866-5622
Troy *(G-16345)*
Energy Products Inc ... D ... 248 545-7700
Madison Heights *(G-10247)*
Esoc Inc ... F ... 248 624-7992
Wixom *(G-17806)*
Fata Aluminum LLC ... F ... 248 724-7669
Auburn Hills *(G-859)*
Fisher-Baker Corporation ... G ... 810 765-3548
Marine City *(G-10473)*
Fitz-Rite Products Inc ... E ... 248 528-8440
Troy *(G-16366)*
Flint Hydrostatics Inc ... F ... 901 794-2462
Chesterfield *(G-2777)*
Flow Ezy Filters Inc ... F ... 734 665-8777
Ann Arbor *(G-463)*
General Processing Systems Inc ... F ... 630 554-7804
Holland *(G-7640)*
Global CNC Industries Ltd ... E ... 734 464-1920
Plymouth *(G-12629)*
Gluco Inc ... G ... 616 457-1212
Jenison *(G-8627)*
Green Age Products & Svcs LLC ... F ... 586 207-5724
Washington *(G-17304)*
Haller International Tech Inc ... G ... 313 821-0809
Detroit *(G-4114)*
Heck Industries Incorporated ... F ... 810 632-5400
Hartland *(G-7390)*
Hitachi America Ltd ... E ... 248 477-5400
Farmington Hills *(G-5021)*
Hoffmann Filter Corporation ... F ... 248 486-8430
Brighton *(G-1939)*
Hot Melt Technologies Inc ... E ... 248 853-2011
Rochester Hills *(G-13446)*
Htc Sales Corporation ... E ... 800 624-2027
Ira *(G-8257)*
Hydraulex Intl Holdings Inc ... E ... 914 682-2700
Chesterfield *(G-2786)*
I M F Inc ... G ... 269 948-2345
Hastings *(G-7415)*
Icon Industries Inc ... G ... 616 241-1877
Grand Rapids *(G-6524)*
Independent Mfg Solutions Corp ... E ... 248 960-3550
Wixom *(G-17833)*
Industrial Automation LLC ... D ... 248 598-5900
Rochester Hills *(G-13449)*
Integrated Conveyor Ltd ... G ... 231 747-6430
Muskegon *(G-11349)*
Interstate Power Systems Inc ... F ... 952 854-2044
Iron Mountain *(G-8285)*
Iron River Mfg Co Inc ... E ... 906 265-5121
Iron River *(G-8310)*
Ivan Doverspike ... E ... 313 579-3000
Detroit *(G-4153)*
Jetech Inc ... E ... 269 965-6311
Battle Creek *(G-1204)*
Johnson Controls Inc ... D ... 248 276-6000
Auburn Hills *(G-920)*
Kalamazoo Mfg Corp Globl ... C ... 269 382-8200
Kalamazoo *(G-8792)*
Kalamazoo Packg Systems LLC ... F ... 616 534-2600
Wyoming *(G-18013)*
Kecy Products Inc ... D ... 517 448-8954
Hudson *(G-8134)*
Kuka US Holding Company LLC ... F ... 586 795-2000
Sterling Heights *(G-15393)*
Lubecon Systems Inc ... D ... 231 689-0002
White Cloud *(G-17625)*
Mac Material Acquisition Co ... G ... 248 685-8393
Highland *(G-7496)*
Madison Street Holdings LLC ... E ... 517 252-2031
Adrian *(G-77)*
Meiki Corporation ... G ... 248 680-4638
Troy *(G-16492)*
Merrifield McHy Solutions Inc ... E ... 248 494-7335
Pontiac *(G-12848)*
Metaris Hydraulics ... G ... 586 949-4240
Chesterfield *(G-2805)*
Metzgar Conveyor Co ... E ... 616 784-0930
Grand Rapids *(G-6664)*
Mhr Inc ... F ... 616 394-0191
Holland *(G-7746)*
Michigan Shippers Supply Inc ... F ... 616 935-6680
Spring Lake *(G-15163)*
Mobile Knowlege Group Services ... G ... 248 625-3327
Clarkston *(G-2940)*
Montronix Inc ... G ... 734 213-6500
Ann Arbor *(G-564)*
National Bulk Equipment Inc ... C ... 616 399-2220
Holland *(G-7752)*
North American Mch & Engrg Co ... G ... 586 726-6700
Shelby Township *(G-14655)*
Oliver of Adrian Inc ... G ... 517 263-2132
Adrian *(G-83)*
Omni Metalcraft Corp ... E ... 989 354-4075
Alpena *(G-304)*
Posa-Cut Corporation ... E ... 248 474-5620
Farmington Hills *(G-5097)*
Prab Inc ... C ... 269 382-8200
Kalamazoo *(G-8854)*
Praxair Distribution Inc ... F ... 586 598-9020
Macomb *(G-10155)*
Press Room Eqp Sls & Svc Co ... G ... 248 334-1880
Pontiac *(G-12857)*
Puritan Magnetics Inc ... F ... 248 628-3808
Oxford *(G-12365)*
R Concepts Incorporated ... G ... 810 632-4857
Howell *(G-8086)*
R M Wright Company Inc ... E ... 248 476-9800
Farmington Hills *(G-5111)*
Rapidtek LLC ... G ... 616 662-0954
Hudsonville *(G-8175)*
Reif Carbide Tool Co Inc ... F ... 586 754-1890
Warren *(G-17219)*
Reko International Holdings ... G ... 519 737-6974
Bloomfield Hills *(G-1793)*
Reliable Sales Co ... G ... 248 969-0943
Oxford *(G-12368)*
Rempco Acquisition Inc ... E ... 231 775-0108
Cadillac *(G-2274)*
Rocon LLC ... G ... 248 542-9635
Hazel Park *(G-7453)*
Roesch Maufacturing Co LLC ... G ... 517 424-6300
Tecumseh *(G-15808)*
Roy A Hutchins Company ... G ... 248 437-3470
New Hudson *(G-11554)*
Schuler Incorporated ... D ... 734 207-7200
Canton *(G-2425)*
Sebright Products Inc ... E ... 269 793-7183
Hopkins *(G-7960)*
Sinto America Inc ... E ... 517 371-2460
Lansing *(G-9323)*
Spray Booth Products Inc ... E ... 313 766-4400
Redford *(G-13193)*
Superior Equipment & Supply Co ... G ... 906 774-1789
Iron Mountain *(G-8302)*
T F G Gage Components ... G ... 734 427-2274
Livonia *(G-9952)*
TAC Industrial Group LLC ... G ... 517 917-8976
Jackson *(G-8581)*
Tool-Craft Industries Inc ... F ... 248 549-0077
Sterling Heights *(G-15525)*
Tops All Clamps Inc ... G ... 313 533-7500
Redford *(G-13202)*
Trinity Holding Inc ... F ... 517 787-3100
Jackson *(G-8593)*
Trucent Inc ... G ... 734 426-9015
Dexter *(G-4515)*
U S Equipment Co ... E ... 313 526-8300
Rochester Hills *(G-13533)*
U S Group Inc ... G ... 313 372-7900
Rochester Hills *(G-13534)*
Ube Machinery Inc ... D ... 734 741-7000
Ann Arbor *(G-685)*
Warren Manufacturing ... G ... 269 483-0603
White Pigeon *(G-17657)*
Western International Inc ... E ... 866 814-2470
Troy *(G-16689)*

INDL MACHINERY REPAIR & MAINTENANCE

1271 Associates Inc ... D ... 586 948-4300
Chesterfield *(G-2730)*
Ajax Tocco Magnethermic Corp ... E ... 248 589-2524
Madison Heights *(G-10185)*
Ajax Tocco Magnethermic Corp ... F ... 248 585-1140
Madison Heights *(G-10186)*
American Pride Machining Inc ... G ... 586 294-6404
Fraser *(G-5617)*
American Wldg & Press Repr Inc ... F ... 248 358-2050
Southfield *(G-14837)*
Ase Industries Inc ... D ... 586 754-7480
Warren *(G-16942)*
Bell Fork Lift Inc ... F ... 313 841-1220
Detroit *(G-3899)*
C & B Machinery Company ... E ... 734 462-0600
Brighton *(G-1894)*
Certified Reducer Rbldrs Inc ... F ... 248 585-0883
Sterling Heights *(G-15285)*
Cochran Corporation ... F ... 517 857-2211
Springport *(G-15209)*

Employee Codes: A=Over 500 employees, B=251-500
C=101-250, D=51-100, E=20-50, F=10-19, G=3-9
2020 Harris Michigan
Industrial Directory
1255

INDL MACHINERY REPAIR & MAINTENANCE

Crane 1 Services Inc .... E 586 468-0909
  Harrison Township (G-7327)
Dimension Machine Tech LLC .... F 586 649-4747
  Bloomfield Hills (G-1759)
Electric Motor & Contg Co .... F 313 871-3775
  Detroit (G-4031)
Fortune Tool & Machine Inc .... E 248 669-9119
  Wixom (G-17813)
Heating Induction Services Inc .... G 586 791-3160
  Clinton Township (G-3135)
Hel Inc .... F 616 774-9032
  Grand Rapids (G-6503)
J I B Properties LLC .... G 313 382-3234
  Melvindale (G-10701)
M P D Welding Inc .... E 248 340-0330
  Orion (G-12184)
Mac Material Acquisition Co .... G 248 685-8393
  Highland (G-7496)
Macali Inc .... G 616 447-1202
  Grand Rapids (G-6639)
Machine Control Technology .... G 517 655-3506
  Williamston (G-17734)
Magnetic Chuck Services Co Inc .... G 586 822-9441
  Casco (G-2502)
Mhr Inc .... F 616 394-0191
  Holland (G-7746)
Michigan Rebuild & Automtn Inc .... F 517 542-6000
  Litchfield (G-9609)
Mjc Tool & Machine Co Inc .... G 586 790-4766
  Clinton Township (G-3179)
Monarch Electric Service Co .... E 313 388-7800
  Melvindale (G-10702)
Mq Operating Company .... E 906 337-1515
  Calumet (G-2330)
Nedrow Refractories Co .... E 248 669-2500
  Wixom (G-17863)
North American Mch & Engrg Co .... G 586 726-6700
  Shelby Township (G-14655)
Padnos Leitelt Inc .... F 616 363-3817
  Grand Rapids (G-6739)
Pgm Products Inc .... F 586 757-4400
  Warren (G-17185)
Plason Scraping Co Inc .... G 248 588-7280
  Madison Heights (G-10329)
Progressive Surface Inc .... D 616 957-0871
  Grand Rapids (G-6786)
Progressive Surface Inc .... E 616 957-0871
  Grand Rapids (G-6787)
Richland Machine & Pump Co .... G 269 629-4344
  Richland (G-13204)
Star Crane Hist Svc of Klmazoo .... G 269 321-8882
  Portage (G-13035)
Surclean Inc .... G 248 791-2226
  Brighton (G-1994)
Thyssenkrupp System Engrg .... C 248 340-8000
  Auburn Hills (G-1019)
Tindall Packaging Inc .... G 269 649-1163
  Portage (G-13050)
Tri-City Repair Company .... G 989 835-4784
  Hope (G-7957)
Trispec Precision Products Inc .... G 248 308-3231
  Wixom (G-17921)

INDL PATTERNS: Foundry Patternmaking

Acme Casting Enterprises Inc .... G 586 755-0300
  Warren (G-16916)
Anderson Global Inc .... C 231 733-2164
  Muskegon (G-11270)
Azko Manufacturing Inc .... G 231 733-0888
  Muskegon (G-11273)
D & K Pattern Inc .... G 989 865-9955
  Saint Charles (G-14191)
Harvey Pattern Works Inc .... F 906 774-4285
  Kingsford (G-9059)
Quality Model & Pattern Co .... E 616 791-1156
  Grand Rapids (G-6800)

INDL PROCESS INSTRUMENTS: Control

Acromag Incorporated .... D 248 624-1541
  Wixom (G-17751)
Banner Engineering & Sales Inc .... F 989 755-0584
  Saginaw (G-14000)
Emitted Energy Inc .... F 855 752-3347
  Sterling Heights (G-15332)
Henkel US Operations Corp .... B 248 588-1082
  Madison Heights (G-10266)
Kubica Corp .... F 248 344-7750
  Novi (G-11922)

INDL PROCESS INSTRUMENTS: Controllers, Process Variables

ABB Enterprise Software Inc .... D 248 471-0888
  Farmington Hills (G-4917)
Forefront Control Systems LLC .... G 616 796-3495
  Holland (G-7634)
Patriot Sensors & Contrls Corp .... D 248 435-0700
  Clawson (G-2983)
Patriot Sensors & Contrls Corp .... D 810 378-5511
  Peck (G-12420)
QEd Envmtl Systems Inc .... D 734 995-2547
  Dexter (G-4506)
Superior Controls Inc .... C 734 454-0500
  Plymouth (G-12763)

INDL PROCESS INSTRUMENTS: Data Loggers

Digital Performance Tech .... F 877 983-4230
  Troy (G-16320)

INDL PROCESS INSTRUMENTS: Digital Display, Process Variables

Tech Tool Supply LLC .... G 734 207-7700
  Plymouth (G-12766)

INDL PROCESS INSTRUMENTS: Draft Gauges

Turbine Tool & Gage Inc .... F 734 427-2270
  Livonia (G-9978)

INDL PROCESS INSTRUMENTS: Elements, Primary

Beet LLC .... F 248 432-0052
  Plymouth (G-12584)

INDL PROCESS INSTRUMENTS: Fluidic Devices, Circuit & Systems

Hines Corporation .... F 231 799-6240
  Norton Shores (G-11812)
Metric Hydrulic Components LLC .... F 586 786-6990
  Shelby Township (G-14640)
Toledo Molding & Die Inc .... G 734 233-6338
  Plymouth (G-12773)

INDL PROCESS INSTRUMENTS: Indl Flow & Measuring

Complete Auto-Mation Inc .... D 248 693-0500
  Lake Orion (G-9131)
Nordson Corporation .... G 734 459-8600
  Wixom (G-17866)

INDL PROCESS INSTRUMENTS: Level & Bulk Measuring

Air Pump Valve Corporation .... G 810 655-6444
  Swartz Creek (G-15660)

INDL PROCESS INSTRUMENTS: Temperature

Incoe Corporation .... C 248 616-0220
  Auburn Hills (G-910)
International Temperature Ctrl .... G 989 876-8075
  Au Gres (G-746)
K-TEC Systems Inc .... F 248 414-4100
  Ferndale (G-5296)
Maxitrol Company .... D 248 356-1400
  Southfield (G-14974)
Warner Instruments .... G 616 843-5342
  Grand Haven (G-6096)

INDL PROCESS INSTRUMENTS: Water Quality Monitoring/Cntrl Sys

Geotech Environmental Eqp Inc .... G 517 655-5616
  Williamston (G-17730)
Integrated Marketing Svcs LLC .... F 248 625-7444
  Pontiac (G-12836)
Parjana Distribution LLC .... G 313 915-5406
  Detroit (G-4290)

INDL SALTS WHOLESALERS

Cargill Incorporated .... B 810 329-2736
  Saint Clair (G-14207)

INDL SPLYS WHOLESALERS

Aactus Inc .... G 734 425-1212
  Livonia (G-9623)
Acumen Technologies Inc .... F 586 566-8600
  Shelby Township (G-14541)
Airgas Usa LLC .... F 248 545-9353
  Ferndale (G-5255)
All Tool Sales Inc .... F 231 941-4302
  Traverse City (G-15893)
American Blower Supply Inc .... F 586 771-7337
  Warren (G-16929)
Cleary Developments Inc .... E 248 588-7011
  Madison Heights (G-10210)
Coleman Bowman & Associates .... G 248 642-8221
  Bloomfield Hills (G-1755)
Colonial Engineering Inc .... F 269 323-2495
  Portage (G-12989)
Commercial Group Inc .... E 313 931-6100
  Taylor (G-15704)
Continental Carbide Ltd Inc .... F 586 463-9577
  Clinton Township (G-3090)
Covenant Cpitl Investments Inc .... F 248 477-4230
  Farmington Hills (G-4967)
Dow Chemical Company .... C 517 439-4400
  Hillsdale (G-7523)
Gravel Flow Inc .... F 269 651-5467
  Sturgis (G-15606)
Inteva Products LLC .... B 248 655-8886
  Troy (G-16424)
Jtekt North America Corp .... E 734 454-1500
  Plymouth (G-12660)
K-C Welding Supply Inc .... F 989 893-6509
  Essexville (G-4874)
Kaydon Corporation .... C 231 755-3741
  Norton Shores (G-11766)
Ltek Industries Inc .... G 734 747-6105
  Ann Arbor (G-535)
Magnetic Products Inc .... D 248 887-5600
  Highland (G-7497)
Marshall-Gruber Company LLC .... F 248 353-4100
  Southfield (G-14973)
Maximum Mold Inc .... G 269 468-6291
  Benton Harbor (G-1528)
Motion Industries Inc .... G 989 771-0200
  Saginaw (G-14100)
Northern Processes & Sales LLC .... G 248 669-3918
  Wixom (G-17869)
NSK Americas Inc .... G 734 913-7500
  Ann Arbor (G-577)
Orsco Inc .... G 314 679-4200
  Armada (G-721)
Primore Inc .... E 517 263-2220
  Adrian (G-88)
Quality Pipe Products Inc .... E 734 606-5100
  New Boston (G-11509)
Rock Industries Inc .... E 248 338-2800
  Bloomfield Hills (G-1796)
Scs Embedded Tech LLC .... G 248 615-2244
  Novi (G-11990)
Sourcehub LLC .... G 800 246-1844
  Troy (G-16613)
Symorex Ltd .... F 734 971-6000
  Ann Arbor (G-653)
Triad Process Equipment Inc .... G 248 685-9938
  Milford (G-10989)
United Abrasive Inc .... F 906 563-9249
  Vulcan (G-16846)
Venture Technology Groups Inc .... F 248 473-8450
  Novi (G-12025)

INDL SPLYS, WHOL: Fasteners, Incl Nuts, Bolts, Screws, Etc

Henrob Corporation .... D 248 493-3800
  New Hudson (G-11543)
Hexagon Enterprises Inc .... E 248 583-0550
  Troy (G-16395)
Rush Machining Inc .... F 248 583-0550
  Troy (G-16585)

INDL SPLYS, WHOLESALE: Abrasives

Finishing Technologies Inc .... F 616 794-4001
  Belding (G-1415)
Grand Northern Products .... G 800 968-1811
  Grand Rapids (G-6450)

PRODUCT SECTION

Kalamazoo Company..............................E...... 269 345-7151
  Kalamazoo *(G-8786)*
Roto-Finish Company Inc ....E...... 269 327-7071
  Kalamazoo *(G-8875)*
Vachon Industries Inc...........................F...... 517 278-2354
  Coldwater *(G-3340)*

INDL SPLYS, WHOLESALE: Abrasives & Adhesives

Jay Cee Sales & Rivet Inc ....F...... 248 478-2150
  Farmington *(G-4901)*
Quantum Chemical LLC ....G...... 734 429-0033
  Livonia *(G-9901)*

INDL SPLYS, WHOLESALE: Adhesives, Tape & Plasters

General Tape Label Liquidating............D...... 248 437-5200
  Wixom *(G-17817)*

INDL SPLYS, WHOLESALE: Bearings

Break-A-Beam ....F...... 586 758-7790
  Warren *(G-16966)*
Edwards Industrial Sales Inc ....G...... 517 887-6100
  Lansing *(G-9363)*

INDL SPLYS, WHOLESALE: Fasteners & Fastening Eqpt

A Raymond Corp N Amer Inc ....E...... 248 853-2500
  Rochester Hills *(G-13358)*
Penn Automotive Inc ....B...... 248 599-3700
  Waterford *(G-17366)*
Penn Engineering & Mfg Corp ....B...... 313 299-8500
  Waterford *(G-17367)*

INDL SPLYS, WHOLESALE: Filters, Indl

Bulldog Fabricating Corp ....G...... 734 761-3111
  Ann Arbor *(G-392)*
Lub-Tech Inc ....G...... 616 299-3540
  Grand Rapids *(G-6634)*
Millennium Planet LLC ....G...... 248 835-2331
  Farmington Hills *(G-5068)*
Omega Industries Michigan LLC ....G...... 616 460-0500
  Grand Rapids *(G-6729)*

INDL SPLYS, WHOLESALE: Fittings

Fixtureworks LLC ....G...... 586 294-6100
  Fraser *(G-5654)*
Global Hoses & Fittings LLC ....G...... 248 219-9581
  Farmington Hills *(G-5010)*
National Industrial Sup Co Inc............F...... 248 588-1828
  Troy *(G-16520)*

INDL SPLYS, WHOLESALE: Gaskets & Seals

Flaretite Inc..G...... 810 750-4140
  Brighton *(G-1923)*

INDL SPLYS, WHOLESALE: Glass Bottles

Recycling Concepts W Mich Inc..........D...... 616 942-8888
  Grand Rapids *(G-6815)*

INDL SPLYS, WHOLESALE: Hydraulic & Pneumatic Pistons/Valves

J E Myles Inc ....E...... 248 583-1020
  Troy *(G-16430)*
Morgold Inc...G...... 269 445-3844
  Cassopolis *(G-2534)*

INDL SPLYS, WHOLESALE: Mill Splys

Tryco Inc ....F...... 734 953-6800
  Farmington Hills *(G-5144)*

INDL SPLYS, WHOLESALE: Plastic, Pallets

Pfb Manufacturing LLC ....E...... 517 486-4844
  Blissfield *(G-1723)*

INDL SPLYS, WHOLESALE: Power Transmission, Eqpt & Apparatus

Idc Industries Inc ....E...... 586 427-4321
  Clinton Township *(G-3139)*

INDL SPLYS, WHOLESALE: Rubber Goods, Mechanical

Advanced Rubber & Plastic ....G...... 586 754-7398
  Warren *(G-16920)*
Four Star Rubber Inc ....G...... 810 632-3335
  Commerce Township *(G-3407)*

INDL SPLYS, WHOLESALE: Seals

Ksb Dubric Inc.....................................E...... 616 784-6355
  Comstock Park *(G-3492)*
Martin Fluid Power Company ....D...... 248 585-8170
  Madison Heights *(G-10302)*
Mechanical Supply A Division ....E...... 906 789-0355
  Escanaba *(G-4842)*
Memtech Inc ....F...... 734 455-8550
  Plymouth *(G-12689)*
Roger Zatkoff Company ....E...... 248 478-2400
  Farmington Hills *(G-5117)*

INDL SPLYS, WHOLESALE: Signmaker Eqpt & Splys

C M S Sales Company Inc ....G...... 248 853-7446
  Rochester Hills *(G-13383)*

INDL SPLYS, WHOLESALE: Tools

Jomat Industries Ltd............................F...... 586 336-1801
  Bruce Twp *(G-2085)*
Star Lite International LLC ....G...... 248 546-4489
  Oak Park *(G-12100)*

INDL SPLYS, WHOLESALE: Tools, NEC

Busch Machine Tool Supply LLC ....G...... 989 798-4794
  Freeland *(G-5753)*
Patco Air Tool Inc................................G...... 248 648-8830
  Orion *(G-12188)*

INDL SPLYS, WHOLESALE: Valves & Fittings

Automatic Valve Corp..........................E...... 248 474-6761
  Novi *(G-11835)*
Detroit Nipple Works Inc ....F...... 313 872-6370
  Detroit *(G-3996)*
Ferguson Enterprises Inc....................E...... 989 790-2220
  Saginaw *(G-14037)*
Fluid Systems Engineering Inc............E...... 586 790-8880
  Clinton Township *(G-3123)*
Kennedy Industries Inc ....D...... 248 684-1200
  Wixom *(G-17840)*
Mac Valves Inc....................................E...... 734 529-5099
  Dundee *(G-4594)*
Meccom Industrial Products Co ....F...... 586 463-2828
  Clinton Township *(G-3172)*
Nass Corporation ....F...... 586 725-6610
  New Baltimore *(G-11489)*
Northland Maintenance Co Inc ....G...... 906 253-9161
  Sault Sainte Marie *(G-14469)*
R M Wright Company Inc ....E...... 248 476-9800
  Farmington Hills *(G-5111)*
Rvm Company of Toledo.....................E...... 734 654-2201
  Carleton *(G-2462)*

INDL TOOL GRINDING SVCS

Lincoln Tool Co Inc..............................G...... 989 736-8711
  Harrisville *(G-7364)*
R & S Cutter Grind Inc ....G...... 989 791-3100
  Saginaw *(G-14128)*
West Michigan Grinding Svc Inc ....F...... 231 739-4245
  Norton Shores *(G-11805)*

INDUCTORS

Performance Induction.........................G...... 734 658-1676
  Howell *(G-8080)*

INDUSTRIAL & COMMERCIAL EQPT INSPECTION SVCS

Aldez North America LLC....................G...... 810 577-3891
  Almont *(G-251)*

INFORMATION RETRIEVAL SERVICES

Gottch-Ya Graphix USA.......................G...... 269 979-7587
  Battle Creek *(G-1193)*

INFRARED OBJECT DETECTION EQPT

Consoldted Rsource Imaging LLC ....E...... 616 735-2080
  Grand Rapids *(G-6301)*
Teslir LLC..G...... 248 644-5500
  Bloomfield Hills *(G-1802)*

INGOT, EXTRUSION: Extrusion ingot, aluminum: rolling mills

CPM Acquisition Corp ....G...... 231 947-6400
  Traverse City *(G-15950)*
Dw Aluminum LLC ....E...... 269 445-5601
  Cassopolis *(G-2528)*
Extrunet America Inc ....G...... 517 301-4504
  Tecumseh *(G-15793)*
Northern Extrusion Inc ....G...... 989 386-7556
  Clare *(G-2880)*

INK OR WRITING FLUIDS

Carco Inc..F...... 313 925-1053
  Detroit *(G-3930)*
Dell Marking Systems Inc...................G...... 248 547-7750
  Rochester Hills *(G-13407)*

INK: Duplicating

D & D Business Machines Inc.............G...... 616 364-8446
  Grand Rapids *(G-6329)*

INK: Printing

America Ink and Technology ....G...... 269 345-4657
  Portage *(G-12981)*
Celia Corporation.................................G...... 616 887-7387
  Sparta *(G-15090)*
Flint CPS Inks North Amer LLC ....G...... 734 781-4600
  Plymouth *(G-12621)*
Flint Group LLC...................................G...... 734 641-3062
  Westland *(G-17557)*
Flint Group North America LLC ....C...... 734 781-4600
  Livonia *(G-9737)*
Flint Group US LLC.............................G...... 313 538-0479
  Detroit *(G-4063)*
Flint Group US LLC.............................E...... 269 381-1955
  Kalamazoo *(G-8745)*
Flint Group US LLC.............................B...... 734 781-4600
  Livonia *(G-9740)*
Flint Ink Receivables Corp ....G...... 734 781-4600
  Plymouth *(G-12622)*
Grand Rapids Printing Ink Co ....F...... 616 241-5681
  Grand Rapids *(G-6462)*
Graphics Unlimited Inc.........................G...... 616 662-0455
  Hudsonville *(G-8157)*
Great Lakes Toll Services ....G...... 616 847-1868
  Spring Lake *(G-15149)*
Intra Business LLC..............................G...... 269 262-0863
  Niles *(G-11621)*
Pittsburgh Glass Works LLC ....C...... 248 371-1700
  Rochester Hills *(G-13494)*
Red Tie Group Inc ....F...... 734 458-2011
  Livonia *(G-9906)*
Wikoff Color Corporation ....E...... 616 245-3930
  Grand Rapids *(G-6991)*

INNER TUBES: Indl

Fastube LLC..F...... 734 398-0474
  Canton *(G-2376)*

INNER TUBES: Truck Or Bus

Avon Machining LLC ....D...... 586 884-2200
  Shelby Township *(G-14551)*
Avon Machining Holdings Inc..............C...... 586 884-2200
  Shelby Township *(G-14552)*

INSECT LAMPS: Electric

Gelman Sciences Inc ....A...... 734 665-0651
  Ann Arbor *(G-469)*

INSECTICIDES & PESTICIDES

Envirodine Inc......................................G...... 231 723-5905
  Manistee *(G-10420)*
Hpi Products Inc ....G...... 248 773-7460
  Northville *(G-11698)*

INSPECTION & TESTING SVCS

P G S Inc ....C...... 248 526-3800
  Troy *(G-16540)*

INSPECTION & TESTING SVCS

Schallips Inc ....G...... 906 635-0941
  Barbeau (G-1117)
Tri-Star Tooling LLC ....F...... 586 978-0435
  Sterling Heights (G-15529)
Vectorall Manufacturing Inc ....E...... 248 486-4570
  Brighton (G-2006)

INSTR, MEASURE & CONTROL: Gauge, Oil Pressure & Water Temp

D & N Gage Inc ....F...... 586 336-2110
  Romeo (G-13627)
Quigley Manufacturing Inc ....C...... 248 426-8600
  Farmington Hills (G-5110)

INSTRUMENTS, LABORATORY: Spectrometers

Thermo Arl US Inc ....F...... 313 336-3901
  Dearborn (G-3764)

INSTRUMENTS, MEASURING & CNTRL: Gauges, Auto, Computer

Novatron Corporation ....C...... 609 815-2100
  Warren (G-17174)

INSTRUMENTS, MEASURING & CNTRL: Geophysical & Meteorological

Abletech Industries LLC ....G...... 734 677-2420
  Dexter (G-4471)

INSTRUMENTS, MEASURING & CNTRL: Testing, Abrasion, Etc

Balance Technology Inc ....D...... 734 769-2100
  Whitmore Lake (G-17689)
Bti Measurement Tstg Svcs LLC ....G...... 734 769-2100
  Whitmore Lake (G-17691)
Bti Measurement Tstg Svcs LLC ....G...... 734 769-2100
  Dexter (G-4479)
Comau LLC ....B...... 248 353-8888
  Southfield (G-14871)
Demmer Investments Inc ....G...... 517 321-3600
  Lansing (G-9221)
Dietert Foundry Testing Eqp ....G...... 313 491-4680
  Detroit (G-4008)
Humantics Innvtive Sltions Inc .....C...... 734 451-7878
  Farmington Hills (G-5023)
Innkeeper LLC ....G...... 734 743-1707
  Canton (G-2386)
Jgs Machining LLC ....G...... 810 329-4210
  Saint Clair (G-14223)
Kuka Assembly and Test Corp ......C...... 989 220-3088
  Saginaw (G-14074)
M Antonik ....G...... 248 236-0333
  Oxford (G-12357)
Michigan Scientific Corp ....E...... 248 685-3939
  Milford (G-10969)
Michigan Scientific Corp ....D...... 231 547-5511
  Charlevoix (G-2620)
R & J Manufacturing Company .....E...... 248 669-2460
  Commerce Township (G-3445)
Safety Technology Holdings Inc ....G...... 415 983-2706
  Farmington Hills (G-5119)
Schenck USA Corp ....E...... 248 377-2100
  Southfield (G-15024)
Thermal Wave Imaging Inc ....F...... 248 414-3730
  Ferndale (G-5321)

INSTRUMENTS, MEASURING & CNTRLG: Aircraft & Motor Vehicle

Adcole Corporation ....G...... 508 485-9100
  Orion (G-12172)
Advanced Systems & Contrls Inc ...E...... 586 992-9684
  Macomb (G-10103)
Ambiance LLC ....G...... 269 657-6027
  Paw Paw (G-12396)
Beet LLC ....F...... 248 432-0052
  Plymouth (G-12584)
Creative Engineering Inc ....G...... 734 996-5900
  Ann Arbor (G-408)
F I D Corporation ....F...... 248 373-7005
  Rochester Hills (G-13422)
Inora Technologies Inc ....F...... 734 302-7488
  Ann Arbor (G-506)
Parker-Hannifin Corporation ....D...... 330 253-5239
  Otsego (G-12251)

Pinto Products Inc ....G...... 269 383-0015
  Kalamazoo (G-8852)
Schap Specialty Machine Inc ....E...... 616 846-6530
  Spring Lake (G-15175)
Ssi Technology Inc ....D...... 248 582-0600
  Sterling Heights (G-15507)
Vgage LLC ....D...... 248 589-7455
  Oak Park (G-12102)

INSTRUMENTS, MEASURING & CNTRLG: Fatigue Test, Indl, Mech

Fatigue Dynamics Inc ....G...... 248 641-9487
  Troy (G-16360)
Promess Inc ....C...... 810 229-9334
  Brighton (G-1981)
Quality First Systems Inc ....F...... 248 922-4780
  Davisburg (G-3639)

INSTRUMENTS, MEASURING & CNTRLG: Stress, Strain & Measure

Bonal International Inc ....F...... 248 582-0900
  Royal Oak (G-13909)
Bonal Technologies Inc ....F...... 248 582-0900
  Royal Oak (G-13910)
K-Space Associates Inc ....E...... 734 426-7977
  Dexter (G-4497)
Tecat Performance Systems LLC ..F...... 248 615-9862
  Ann Arbor (G-654)

INSTRUMENTS, MEASURING & CNTRLNG: Press & Vac Ind, Acft Eng

Wmc Lievense Company ....E...... 231 946-3800
  Traverse City (G-16148)

INSTRUMENTS, MEASURING & CONTROLLING: Dosimetry, Personnel

Endectra LLC ....G...... 734 476-9381
  Ann Arbor (G-444)

INSTRUMENTS, MEASURING & CONTROLLING: Gas Detectors

Analytical Process Systems Inc ....E...... 248 393-0700
  Auburn Hills (G-770)
Family Safety Products Inc ....G...... 616 530-6540
  Grandville (G-7036)
Gfg Instrumentation Inc ....E...... 734 769-0573
  Ann Arbor (G-472)
Invertech Inc ....F...... 734 944-4400
  Saline (G-14396)

INSTRUMENTS, MEASURING & CONTROLLING: Ultrasonic Testing

Inventron Inc ....G...... 248 473-9250
  Livonia (G-9785)

INSTRUMENTS, MEASURING/CNTRL: Gauging, Ultrasonic Thickness

Verimation Technology Inc ....F...... 248 471-0000
  Farmington Hills (G-5147)

INSTRUMENTS, MEASURING/CNTRLG: Fire Detect Sys, Non-Electric

Exquise Inc ....G...... 248 220-9048
  Detroit (G-4047)

INSTRUMENTS, MEASURING/CNTRLNG: Med Diagnostic Sys, Nuclear

Assay Designs Inc ....E...... 734 214-0923
  Ann Arbor (G-370)
Avidhrt Inc ....G...... 517 214-9041
  Okemos (G-12115)
Gravikor Inc ....G...... 734 302-3200
  Ann Arbor (G-477)
Mri Consultants LLC ....G...... 248 619-9771
  Madison Heights (G-10310)
Oxford Instruments America Inc ..F...... 734 821-3003
  Ann Arbor (G-587)

PRODUCT SECTION

INSTRUMENTS, OPTICAL: Lens Mounts

Kwik-Site Corporation ....F...... 734 326-1500
  Wayne (G-17434)

INSTRUMENTS, OPTICAL: Lenses, All Types Exc Ophthalmic

General Scientific Corporation ......E...... 734 996-9200
  Ann Arbor (G-471)

INSTRUMENTS, OPTICAL: Sighting & Fire Control

L-3 Communications Eotech Inc ....C...... 734 741-8868
  Ann-Arbor (G-522)

INSTRUMENTS, OPTICAL: Test & Inspection

Data Optics Inc ....G...... 734 483-8228
  Ypsilanti (G-18064)
Integral Vision Inc ....G...... 248 668-9230
  Wixom (G-17835)
Kaiser Optical Systems Inc ....D...... 734 665-8083
  Ann Arbor (G-515)
Phoenix Imaging Inc ....G...... 248 476-4578
  Farmington (G-4907)
Phoenix Imaging Inc ....G...... 248 476-4200
  Livonia (G-9888)

INSTRUMENTS, SURGICAL & MED: Needles & Syringes, Hypodermic

Assuramed Inc ....G...... 616 419-2020
  Wyoming (G-17987)

INSTRUMENTS, SURGICAL & MEDICAL: Biopsy

Rls Interventional Inc ....F...... 616 301-7800
  Kentwood (G-9029)

INSTRUMENTS, SURGICAL & MEDICAL: Blood & Bone Work

J Sterling Industries LLC ....F...... 269 492-6922
  Kalamazoo (G-8776)
Marketlab Inc ....D...... 866 237-3722
  Caledonia (G-2307)
Oxygenplus LLC ....G...... 586 221-9112
  Clinton Township (G-3191)
Sonetics Ultrasound Inc ....G...... 734 260-4800
  Ann Arbor (G-641)
Tesma Instruments LLC ....G...... 517 940-1362
  Howell (G-8106)
Virotech Biomaterials Inc ....G...... 313 421-1648
  Warren (G-17284)

INSTRUMENTS, SURGICAL & MEDICAL: Lasers, Ophthalmic

Jodon Engineering Assoc Inc ....F...... 734 761-4044
  Ann Arbor (G-511)

INSTRUMENTS, SURGICAL & MEDICAL: Lasers, Surgical

Medical Laser Resources LLC ......G...... 248 628-8120
  Oxford (G-12360)

INSTRUMENTS, SURGICAL & MEDICAL: Needles, Suture

Terumo Americas Holding Inc ......B...... 734 663-4145
  Ann Arbor (G-665)

INSTRUMENTS, SURGICAL & MEDICAL: Ophthalmic

Myco Industries Inc ....G...... 248 685-2496
  Milford (G-10973)

INSTRUMENTS, SURGICAL & MEDICAL: Plates & Screws, Bone

Orchid Orthpd Sltons Organ Inc ...D...... 203 877-3341
  Holt (G-7919)

PRODUCT SECTION

INSTRUMENTS: Laser, Scientific & Engineering

INSTRUMENTS, SURGICAL & MEDICAL: Skin Grafting

American Laser Centers LLC	A	248 426-8250
Farmington Hills *(G-4929)*		
Barron Precision Instruments	E	810 695-2080
Grand Blanc *(G-5959)*		

INSTRUMENTS: Ammeters, NEC

Swain Meter Company	G	989 773-3700
Farwell *(G-5166)*		

INSTRUMENTS: Analytical

Auric Enterprises Inc	G	231 882-7251
Beulah *(G-1608)*		
Best Products Inc	E	313 538-7414
Redford *(G-13148)*		
Burke E Porter Machinery Co	C	616 234-1200
Grand Rapids *(G-6243)*		
Essen Instruments Inc	D	734 769-1600
Ann Arbor *(G-449)*		
Hiden Analytical Inc	G	734 542-6666
Livonia *(G-9769)*		
Horiba Instruments Inc	D	734 213-6555
Ann Arbor *(G-495)*		
Hti Usa Inc	E	248 358-5533
Farmington *(G-4900)*		
Lake Erie Med Surgical Sup Inc	E	734 847-3847
Temperance *(G-15833)*		
Leco Corporation	B	269 983-5531
Saint Joseph *(G-14324)*		
Leco Corporation	F	269 982-2230
Saint Joseph *(G-14325)*		
Lumigen Inc	E	248 351-5600
Southfield *(G-14970)*		
Mectron Engineering Co Inc	E	734 944-8777
Saline *(G-14400)*		
Proto Manufacturing Inc	E	734 946-0974
Taylor *(G-15759)*		
R H K Technology Inc	E	248 577-5426
Troy *(G-16574)*		
Richard-Allan Scientific Co	E	269 544-5600
Kalamazoo *(G-8870)*		
Rigaku Innovative Tech Inc	C	248 232-6400
Auburn Hills *(G-991)*		
Srg Global Coatings Inc	C	248 509-1100
Troy *(G-16618)*		
Thermo Fisher Scientific Inc	G	231 932-0242
Traverse City *(G-16121)*		
Thermo Fisher Scientific Inc	F	800 346-4364
Portage *(G-13049)*		
Thermo Fisher Scientific Inc	B	269 544-5600
Kalamazoo *(G-8911)*		
Thermo Fisher Scientific Inc	F	734 662-4117
Ann Arbor *(G-669)*		
Thermo Shandon Inc	G	269 544-7500
Kalamazoo *(G-8912)*		
TS Enterprise Associates Inc	F	248 348-2963
Northville *(G-11732)*		
X-Ray and Specialty Instrs	G	734 485-6300
Ypsilanti *(G-18108)*		
X-Rite Incorporated	C	616 803-2100
Grand Rapids *(G-7006)*		

INSTRUMENTS: Combustion Control, Indl

Engineered Combustn Systems LLC	G	248 549-1703
Royal Oak *(G-13925)*		
Ptspower LLC	G	734 268-6076
Pinckney *(G-12503)*		

INSTRUMENTS: Differential Pressure, Indl

Astra Associates Inc	E	586 254-6500
Sterling Heights *(G-15266)*		

INSTRUMENTS: Electronic, Analog-Digital Converters

Elmet LLC	G	248 473-2924
Novi *(G-11882)*		

INSTRUMENTS: Endoscopic Eqpt, Electromedical

Endoscopic Solutions	G	248 625-4055
Clarkston *(G-2918)*		
Iha Vsclar Endvsclar Spcalists	G	734 712-8150
Ypsilanti *(G-18078)*		

INSTRUMENTS: Flow, Indl Process

ADS LLC	G	248 740-9593
Troy *(G-16168)*		
Airflow Sciences Equipment LLC	E	734 525-0300
Livonia *(G-9633)*		
Custom Valve Concepts Inc	E	248 597-8999
Madison Heights *(G-10225)*		
Piping Components Inc	G	313 382-6400
Melvindale *(G-10705)*		
Universal Flow Monitors Inc	E	248 542-9635
Hazel Park *(G-7457)*		

INSTRUMENTS: Frequency Meters, Electrical, Mech & Electronic

Standard Electric Company	E	906 774-4455
Kingsford *(G-9067)*		

INSTRUMENTS: Indl Process Control

A&D Technology Inc	D	734 973-1111
Ann Arbor *(G-333)*		
ABB Enterprise Software Inc	D	313 965-8900
Detroit *(G-3837)*		
Advanced Integrated Mfg	F	586 439-0300
Fraser *(G-5613)*		
AG Davis Gage & Engrg Co	E	586 977-9000
Sterling Heights *(G-15256)*		
Altair Systems Inc	F	248 668-0116
Wixom *(G-17758)*		
Auric Enterprises Inc	G	231 882-7251
Beulah *(G-1608)*		
Avl Michigan Holding Corp	E	734 414-9600
Plymouth *(G-12578)*		
Avl Test Systems Inc	C	734 414-9600
Plymouth *(G-12580)*		
Balance Technology Inc	D	734 769-2100
Whitmore Lake *(G-17689)*		
Benny Gage Inc	E	734 455-3080
Wixom *(G-17773)*		
Bisbee Infrared Services Inc	G	517 787-4620
Jackson *(G-8391)*		
Broadteq Incorporated	G	248 794-9323
Waterford *(G-17327)*		
Burke E Porter Machinery Co	C	616 234-1200
Grand Rapids *(G-6243)*		
C E C Controls Company Inc	D	586 779-0222
Warren *(G-16972)*		
C E C Controls Company Inc	G	248 926-5701
Wixom *(G-17780)*		
Clarkson Controls & Eqp Co	G	248 380-9915
Novi *(G-11850)*		
D2t America Inc	F	248 680-9001
Rochester Hills *(G-13400)*		
Dura Thread Gage Inc	F	248 545-2890
Madison Heights *(G-10236)*		
Electronic Apps Speclsts Inc	G	248 491-4988
Milford *(G-10963)*		
Emerson Electric Co	E	616 846-3950
Grand Haven *(G-6014)*		
Emerson Electric Co	E	586 268-3104
Sterling Heights *(G-15331)*		
Emerson Electric Co	E	734 420-0832
Plymouth *(G-12617)*		
Emerson Process Management	C	313 874-0860
Detroit *(G-4037)*		
Fannon Products LLC	F	810 794-2000
Algonac *(G-143)*		
Flow-Rite Controls Ltd	E	616 583-1700
Byron Center *(G-2191)*		
Forrest Brothers Inc	C	989 356-4011
Gaylord *(G-5859)*		
Gic LLC	F	231 237-7000
Charlevoix *(G-2616)*		
Gordinier Electronics Corp	G	586 778-0426
Roseville *(G-13809)*		
Henshaw Inc	E	586 752-0700
Romeo *(G-13629)*		
Hexagon Metrology Inc	D	248 662-1740
Wixom *(G-17826)*		
Hines Industries Inc	E	734 769-2300
Ann Arbor *(G-492)*		
Honeywell International Inc	C	231 582-5686
Boyne City *(G-1822)*		
Horiba Instruments Inc	D	734 213-6555
Ann Arbor *(G-495)*		
Howard Miller Company	B	616 772-9131
Zeeland *(G-18154)*		
Infrared Telemetrics Inc	F	906 482-0012
Hancock *(G-7252)*		
Innovative Support Svcs Inc	E	248 585-3600
Troy *(G-16418)*		
Integral Vision Inc	G	248 668-9230
Wixom *(G-17835)*		
Integrated Security Corp	F	248 624-0700
Novi *(G-11906)*		
Jay/Enn Corporation	D	248 588-2393
Troy *(G-16433)*		
Jcp LLC	E	989 754-7496
Saginaw *(G-14066)*		
Jdl Enterprises Inc	F	586 977-8863
Sterling Heights *(G-15380)*		
Labortrio Elttrofisico USA Inc	G	248 340-7040
Lake Orion *(G-9143)*		
Leader Corporation	E	586 566-7114
Shelby Township *(G-14624)*		
Leco Corporation	B	269 983-5531
Saint Joseph *(G-14324)*		
Leco Corporation	F	269 982-2230
Saint Joseph *(G-14325)*		
Maes Tool & Die Co Inc	F	517 750-3131
Jackson *(G-8504)*		
Mahle Powertrain LLC	D	248 305-8200
Farmington Hills *(G-5056)*		
Martel Tool Corporation	F	313 278-2420
Allen Park *(G-202)*		
Maxitrol Company	E	517 486-2820
Blissfield *(G-1719)*		
Montague Latch Company	F	810 687-4242
Clio *(G-3278)*		
Mycrona Inc	F	734 453-9348
Plymouth *(G-12697)*		
Norcross Viscosity Controls	G	586 336-0700
Washington *(G-17308)*		
Oflow-Rite Controls Ltd	D	616 583-1700
Byron Center *(G-2205)*		
Online Engineering Inc	F	906 341-0090
Manistique *(G-10445)*		
Peaker Services Inc	D	248 437-4174
Brighton *(G-1976)*		
Peaktronics Inc	G	248 542-5640
Clawson *(G-2984)*		
Pierburg Instruments	C	734 414-9600
Plymouth *(G-12715)*		
R Concepts Incorporated	G	810 632-4857
Howell *(G-8086)*		
Rjg Technologies Inc	C	231 947-3111
Traverse City *(G-16096)*		
Service & Technical Assoc LLC	F	248 233-3761
Troy *(G-16597)*		
Sinto America Inc	E	517 371-2460
Lansing *(G-9323)*		
Ssi Technology Inc	D	248 582-0600
Sterling Heights *(G-15507)*		
Taylor Controls Inc	F	269 637-8521
South Haven *(G-14777)*		
Temprel Inc	E	231 582-6585
Boyne City *(G-1835)*		
Terametrix LLC	C	540 769-8430
Ann Arbor *(G-664)*		
Testron Incorporated	F	734 513-6820
Livonia *(G-9955)*		
Therm-O-Disc Incorporated	B	231 799-4100
Norton Shores *(G-11801)*		
Therm-O-Disc Midwest Inc	F	231 799-4100
Norton Shores *(G-11802)*		
Thermo Arl US Inc	F	313 336-3901
Dearborn *(G-3764)*		
Welding Technology Corp	F	248 477-3900
Farmington Hills *(G-5151)*		
Welform Electrodes Inc	D	586 755-1184
Warren *(G-17292)*		
X-Rite Incorporated	C	616 803-2100
Grand Rapids *(G-7006)*		

INSTRUMENTS: Infrared, Indl Process

Dexter Research Center Inc	D	734 426-3921
Dexter *(G-4488)*		

INSTRUMENTS: Laser, Scientific & Engineering

Clark-Mxr Inc	E	734 426-2803
Dexter *(G-4481)*		
Jodon Engineering Assoc Inc	F	734 761-4044
Ann Arbor *(G-511)*		
Pioneer Technologies Corp	E	702 806-3152
Fremont *(G-5782)*		
Q-Photonics LLC	G	734 477-0133
Ann Arbor *(G-608)*		

Employee Codes: A=Over 500 employees, B=251-500
C=101-250, D=51-100, E=20-50, F=10-19, G=3-9

INSTRUMENTS: Measurement, Indl Process

Atmo-Seal Inc....G.... 248 528-9640
Troy *(G-16227)*
Binsfeld Engineering Inc....F.... 231 334-4383
Maple City *(G-10460)*
Harvest Energy Inc....F.... 269 838-4595
Grand Rapids *(G-6496)*
Hitec Sensor Developments Inc....E.... 313 506-2460
Plymouth *(G-12640)*
Horiba Instruments Inc....D.... 248 689-9000
Troy *(G-16400)*
IMC Dataworks LLC....G.... 248 356-4311
Novi *(G-11905)*
Perceptive Controls Inc....E.... 269 685-3040
Plainwell *(G-12535)*
Perpetual Measurement Inc....G.... 248 343-2952
Waterford *(G-17368)*
Stewart Metrology LLC....G.... 269 660-9290
Battle Creek *(G-1254)*
Transology Associates....G.... 517 694-8645
East Lansing *(G-4680)*

INSTRUMENTS: Measuring & Controlling

2 Brothers Holdings LLC....G.... 517 487-3900
Lansing *(G-9330)*
A S I Instruments Inc....G.... 586 756-1222
Warren *(G-16909)*
A&D Technology Inc....D.... 734 973-1111
Ann Arbor *(G-333)*
Acromag Incorporated....D.... 248 624-1541
Wixom *(G-17751)*
Apollo America Inc....D.... 248 332-3900
Auburn Hills *(G-776)*
Astra Associates Inc....E.... 586 254-6500
Sterling Heights *(G-15266)*
Ateq Corporation....F.... 734 838-3100
Livonia *(G-9655)*
Ats Assembly and Test Inc....D.... 734 266-4713
Livonia *(G-9657)*
Auric Enterprises Inc....G.... 231 882-7251
Beulah *(G-1608)*
Avl Test Systems Inc....C.... 734 414-9600
Plymouth *(G-12580)*
Benesh Corporation....E.... 734 244-4143
Monroe *(G-11023)*
Biosan Laboratories Inc....F.... 586 755-8970
Warren *(G-16961)*
Calhoun County Med Care Fcilty....E.... 269 962-5458
Battle Creek *(G-1162)*
Cammenga & Associates LLC....E.... 313 914-7160
Dearborn *(G-3684)*
Clark Instrument Inc....F.... 248 669-3100
Novi *(G-11849)*
Control Power-Reliance LLC....G.... 248 583-1020
Troy *(G-16280)*
Conway-Cleveland Corp....G.... 616 458-0056
Grand Rapids *(G-6309)*
Crippen Manufacturing Company....E.... 989 681-4323
Saint Louis *(G-14361)*
D2t America Inc....F.... 248 680-9001
Rochester Hills *(G-13400)*
Data Optics Inc....G.... 734 483-8228
Ypsilanti *(G-18064)*
Detroit Testing Machine Co....G.... 248 669-3100
Novi *(G-11866)*
Dimension Products Corporation....F.... 616 842-6050
Grand Haven *(G-6010)*
Equitable Engineering Co Inc....E.... 248 689-9700
Troy *(G-16351)*
Ezm LLC....F.... 248 438-6570
Novi *(G-11886)*
Force Dynamics Inc....G.... 248 673-9878
Waterford *(G-17344)*
Gage Eagle Spline Inc....D.... 586 776-7240
Warren *(G-17049)*
General Inspection LLC....F.... 248 625-0529
Davisburg *(G-3634)*
Gic LLC....F.... 231 237-7000
Charlevoix *(G-2616)*
Hines Industries Inc....E.... 734 769-2300
Ann Arbor *(G-492)*
Horiba Instruments Inc....D.... 734 213-6555
Ann Arbor *(G-495)*
Howard Miller Company....B.... 616 772-9131
Zeeland *(G-18154)*
Ibg Nbt Systems Corp....G.... 248 478-9490
Farmington Hills *(G-5024)*
Infrared Telemetrics Inc....F.... 906 482-0012
Hancock *(G-7252)*
Instrumented Sensor Tech Inc....G.... 517 349-8487
Okemos *(G-12126)*
Integrated Sensing Systems Inc....E.... 734 547-9896
Ypsilanti *(G-18081)*
Intelligent Dynamics LLC....F.... 313 727-9920
Dearborn *(G-3725)*
Intra Corporation....C.... 734 326-7030
Westland *(G-17571)*
Invo Spline Inc....E.... 586 757-8840
Warren *(G-17097)*
J E Myles Inc....E.... 248 583-1020
Troy *(G-16430)*
Jomat Industries Ltd....F.... 586 336-1801
Bruce Twp *(G-2085)*
Kistler Instrument Corporation....D.... 248 668-6900
Novi *(G-11916)*
KLC Enterprises Inc....F.... 989 753-0496
Saginaw *(G-14072)*
Labortrio Elttrofisico USA Inc....G.... 248 340-7040
Lake Orion *(G-9143)*
M&B Holdings LLC....G.... 734 677-0454
Ann Arbor *(G-538)*
Martel Tool Corporation....F.... 313 278-2420
Allen Park *(G-202)*
Michael Engineering Ltd....E.... 989 772-4073
Mount Pleasant *(G-11204)*
Michigan Spline Gage Co Inc....F.... 248 544-7303
Hazel Park *(G-7445)*
Midwest Flex Systems Inc....F.... 810 424-0060
Flint *(G-5468)*
Miljoco Corp....D.... 586 777-4280
Mount Clemens *(G-11142)*
Montronix Inc....G.... 734 213-6500
Ann Arbor *(G-564)*
Nikon Metrology Inc....G.... 810 220-4347
Brighton *(G-1969)*
North American Controls Inc....E.... 586 532-7140
Shelby Township *(G-14654)*
North Amrcn Masurement Systems....G.... 734 646-3458
Plymouth *(G-12701)*
Og Technologies Inc....F.... 734 973-7500
Ann Arbor *(G-581)*
Pcb Piezotronics Inc....F.... 888 684-0014
Novi *(G-11971)*
Pcb Piezotronics Inc....G.... 716 684-0001
Farmington Hills *(G-5090)*
Perceptron Inc....C.... 734 414-6100
Plymouth *(G-12712)*
Pierburg Instruments....C.... 734 414-9600
Plymouth *(G-12715)*
Port Austin Level & Tl Mfg Co....F.... 989 738-5291
Port Austin *(G-12878)*
Ram Meter Inc....F.... 248 362-0990
Royal Oak *(G-13962)*
Ramer Products Inc....G.... 269 409-8583
Buchanan *(G-2126)*
Rayco Manufacturing Inc....F.... 586 795-2884
Sterling Heights *(G-15462)*
Richmond Instrs & Systems Inc....F.... 586 954-3770
Clinton Township *(G-3211)*
Russells Technical Pdts Inc....E.... 616 392-3161
Holland *(G-7791)*
Saginaw Machine Systems Inc....D.... 989 753-8465
Saginaw *(G-14140)*
Sensordata Technologies Inc....F.... 586 739-4254
Shelby Township *(G-14689)*
Shield Material Handling Inc....F.... 248 418-0986
Auburn Hills *(G-997)*
Siko Products Inc....G.... 734 426-3476
Dexter *(G-4509)*
Storage Control Systems Inc....E.... 616 887-7994
Sparta *(G-15114)*
T E Technology Inc....E.... 231 929-3966
Traverse City *(G-16118)*
T-Mach Industries LLC....G.... 734 673-6964
Taylor *(G-15775)*
Teradyne Inc....C.... 313 425-3900
Allen Park *(G-211)*
Tessonics Corp....G.... 248 885-8335
Birmingham *(G-1704)*
Thermotron Industries Inc....B.... 616 392-1491
Holland *(G-7830)*
Thielenhaus Microfinish Corp....E.... 248 349-9450
Novi *(G-12015)*
Thierica Inc....D.... 616 458-1538
Grand Rapids *(G-6926)*
Triangle Broach Company....F.... 313 838-2150
Detroit *(G-4408)*
United Abrasive Inc....F.... 906 563-9249
Vulcan *(G-16846)*
Versicor LLC....F.... 734 306-9137
Royal Oak *(G-13981)*
Vibration Research Corporation....E.... 616 669-3028
Jenison *(G-8648)*
Waber Tool & Engineering Co....E.... 269 342-0765
Kalamazoo *(G-8921)*
Wellsense USA Inc....G.... 888 335-0995
Birmingham *(G-1708)*

INSTRUMENTS: Measuring Electricity

A&D Technology Inc....D.... 734 973-1111
Ann Arbor *(G-333)*
Advanced Systems & Contrls Inc....E.... 586 992-9684
Macomb *(G-10103)*
AG Davis Gage & Engrg Co....E.... 586 977-9000
Sterling Heights *(G-15256)*
Ats Assembly and Test Inc....B.... 937 222-3030
Wixom *(G-17766)*
Auric Enterprises Inc....G.... 231 882-7251
Beulah *(G-1608)*
Balance Technology Inc....D.... 734 769-2100
Whitmore Lake *(G-17689)*
Benesh Corporation....E.... 734 244-4143
Monroe *(G-11023)*
Burke E Porter Machinery Co....C.... 616 234-1200
Grand Rapids *(G-6243)*
Classic Instruments Inc....G.... 231 582-0461
Boyne City *(G-1820)*
CSM Products Inc....G.... 248 836-4995
Auburn Hills *(G-830)*
D2t America Inc....F.... 248 680-9001
Rochester Hills *(G-13400)*
Dynamic Auto Test Engineering....G.... 269 342-1334
Portage *(G-12991)*
Global Electronics Limited....E.... 248 353-0100
Bloomfield Hills *(G-1770)*
Greening Associates Inc....E.... 313 366-7160
Detroit *(G-4105)*
Hole Industries Incorporated....G.... 517 548-4229
Howell *(G-8050)*
Honeywell International Inc....C.... 231 582-5686
Boyne City *(G-1822)*
Horiba Instruments Inc....D.... 734 213-6555
Ann Arbor *(G-495)*
Infrared Telemetrics Inc....F.... 906 482-0012
Hancock *(G-7252)*
Instrumented Sensor Tech Inc....G.... 517 349-8487
Okemos *(G-12126)*
Ix Innovations LLC....G....
Ann Arbor *(G-508)*
Leco Corporation....B.... 269 983-5531
Saint Joseph *(G-14324)*
Leco Corporation....F.... 269 982-2230
Saint Joseph *(G-14325)*
Merc-O-Tronic Instruments Corp....F.... 586 894-9529
Almont *(G-263)*
Michigan Scientific Corp....D.... 231 547-5511
Charlevoix *(G-2620)*
Nanorete Inc....G.... 517 336-4680
Lansing *(G-9404)*
Racelogic USA Corporation....G.... 248 994-9050
Farmington Hills *(G-5112)*
Ram Meter Inc....F.... 248 362-0990
Royal Oak *(G-13962)*
Sciemetric Inc....F.... 248 509-2209
Rochester Hills *(G-13512)*
Seneca Enterprises LLC....G.... 231 943-1171
Traverse City *(G-16100)*
Srg Global Coatings Inc....C.... 248 509-1100
Troy *(G-16618)*
Testron Incorporated....F.... 734 513-6820
Livonia *(G-9955)*

INSTRUMENTS: Measuring, Current, NEC

Nadex of America Corporation....E.... 248 477-3900
Farmington Hills *(G-5075)*

INSTRUMENTS: Measuring, Electrical Energy

Ezm LLC....F.... 248 438-6570
Novi *(G-11886)*

INSTRUMENTS: Measuring, Electrical Power

Hale Manufacturing Inc....G.... 231 529-6271
Alanson *(G-110)*

INSTRUMENTS: Medical & Surgical

Aees Power Systems Ltd Partnr....F.... 269 668-4429
Farmington Hills *(G-4921)*

PRODUCT SECTION

INSTRUMENTS: Test, Electronic & Electric Measurement

Alliant Enterprises LLC ....E...... 269 629-0300
　Grand Rapids *(G-6162)*
Animal Medical Ctr of Lapeer ....F...... 989 631-3350
　Midland *(G-10815)*
Artisan Medical Displays LLC..........E...... 616 748-8950
　Zeeland *(G-18113)*
Autocam Corporation ....B...... 616 698-0707
　Kentwood *(G-9000)*
Autocam Med DVC Holdings LLC .....G...... 616 541-8080
　Kentwood *(G-9002)*
Autocam Medical Devices LLC ....E...... 877 633-8080
　Grand Rapids *(G-6191)*
Bonwrx Ltd ....G...... 517 481-2924
　Lansing *(G-9206)*
Brio Device LLC ....G...... 734 945-5728
　Ann Arbor *(G-390)*
C2dx Inc ....F...... 269 409-0068
　Schoolcraft *(G-14489)*
Capnesity Inc ....G...... 317 401-6766
　Lapeer *(G-9450)*
Cardiac Assist Holdings LLC ....G...... 781 727-1391
　Plymouth *(G-12593)*
Cardinal Health Inc ....C...... 248 685-9655
　Highland *(G-7487)*
Clear Image Devices LLC ....G...... 734 645-6459
　Ann Arbor *(G-400)*
Cnd Products LLC ....G...... 616 361-1000
　Grand Rapids *(G-6282)*
Crippen Manufacturing Company .....E...... 989 681-4323
　Saint Louis *(G-14361)*
David Epstein Inc ....F...... 248 542-0802
　Ferndale *(G-5270)*
Delphinus Medical Technologies ......E...... 248 522-9600
　Novi *(G-11863)*
DForte Inc ....F...... 269 657-6996
　Paw Paw *(G-12402)*
Di-Coat Corporation ....E...... 248 349-1211
　Novi *(G-11868)*
Domico Med-Device LLC ....D...... 810 750-5300
　Fenton *(G-5200)*
Ferndale Pharma Group Inc ....B...... 248 548-0900
　Ferndale *(G-5285)*
Filter Plus Inc ....F...... 734 475-7403
　Chelsea *(G-2710)*
Flexdex Inc ....F...... 810 522-9009
　Brighton *(G-1924)*
Grace Engineering Corp ....D...... 810 392-2181
　Memphis *(G-10710)*
Hanna Instruments Inc ....G...... 734 971-8160
　Ann Arbor *(G-481)*
Hart Enterprises USA Inc ....D...... 616 887-0400
　Sparta *(G-15098)*
Healthcare Dme LLC ....G...... 734 975-6668
　Ann Arbor *(G-485)*
Healthmark Industries Co Inc ....C...... 586 774-7600
　Fraser *(G-5660)*
Helix Devices LLC ....G...... 724 681-0975
　East Lansing *(G-4660)*
Imagen Orthopedics LLC ....G...... 616 294-1026
　Holland *(G-7687)*
Infusystem Holdings Inc ....D...... 248 291-1210
　Madison Heights *(G-10274)*
Keystone Manufacturing LLC ....F...... 269 343-4108
　Kalamazoo *(G-8801)*
Krasitys Med Surgical Sup Inc ....F...... 313 274-2210
　Dearborn *(G-3731)*
Lake Erie Med Surgical Sup Inc ....E...... 734 847-3847
　Temperance *(G-15833)*
Lake Lansing ASC Partners LLC ......F...... 517 708-3333
　Lansing *(G-9386)*
Link Technology Inc ....F...... 269 324-8212
　Portage *(G-13009)*
Mar-Med Inc ....G...... 616 454-3000
　Grand Rapids *(G-6642)*
Medical Engineering & Dev ....G...... 517 563-2450
　Horton *(G-7969)*
Medisurge LLC ....F...... 888 307-1144
　Grand Rapids *(G-6657)*
Medtronic Inc ....G...... 248 349-6987
　Novi *(G-11943)*
Medtronic Inc ....G...... 616 643-5200
　Grand Rapids *(G-6658)*
Medtronic Inc ....G...... 616 643-5200
　Grand Rapids *(G-6659)*
Medtronic Usa Inc ....G...... 248 449-5027
　Novi *(G-11944)*
Melling Manufacturing Inc ....E...... 517 750-3580
　Jackson *(G-8513)*
Metro Wbe Associates Inc ....G...... 248 504-7563
　Detroit *(G-4232)*

Mitovation Inc ....G...... 734 395-1635
　Saline *(G-14402)*
Operations Research Tech LLC ....G...... 248 626-8960
　West Bloomfield *(G-17492)*
Orchid Orthpd Solutions LLC ....F...... 989 746-0780
　Bridgeport *(G-1855)*
Orchid Orthpd Solutions LLC ....C...... 517 694-2300
　Holt *(G-7920)*
Oxus America Inc ....G...... 248 475-0925
　Auburn Hills *(G-968)*
Performance Systematix Inc ....D...... 616 949-9090
　Grand Rapids *(G-6749)*
Perspective Enterprises Inc ....G...... 269 327-0869
　Portage *(G-13021)*
Pioneer Surgical Tech Inc ....C...... 906 226-9909
　Marquette *(G-10552)*
Plasma Biolife Services L P ....G...... 616 667-0264
　Grandville *(G-7064)*
Precision Edge Srgcal Pdts LLC ......C...... 231 459-4304
　Boyne City *(G-1833)*
Precision Edge Srgcal Pdts LLC ......D...... 906 632-5600
　Sault Sainte Marie *(G-14470)*
Progressive Dynamics Inc ....D...... 269 781-4241
　Marshall *(G-10585)*
Protomatic Inc ....E...... 734 426-3655
　Dexter *(G-4505)*
R H Cross Enterprises Inc ....G...... 269 488-4009
　Kalamazoo *(G-8868)*
RJL Sciences Inc ....F...... 800 528-4513
　Clinton Township *(G-3213)*
Rose Technologies Company ....E...... 616 233-3000
　Grand Rapids *(G-6838)*
Saint-Gobain Prfmce Plas Corp........F...... 231 264-0101
　Williamsburg *(G-17720)*
SGC Industries Inc ....E...... 586 293-5260
　Fraser *(G-5723)*
Shoulder Innovations Inc ....G...... 616 294-1029
　Holland *(G-7803)*
Steele Supply Co ....G...... 269 983-0920
　Saint Joseph *(G-14342)*
Stryker Corporation ....C...... 269 324-5346
　Portage *(G-13039)*
Stryker Corporation ....G...... 248 374-6352
　Novi *(G-12006)*
Stryker Corporation ....E...... 269 389-3741
　Portage *(G-13037)*
Stryker Corporation ....E...... 269 323-1027
　Portage *(G-13042)*
Sunmed LLC ....D...... 616 259-8400
　Grand Rapids *(G-6899)*
Sunmed Holdings LLC ....F...... 616 259-8400
　Grand Rapids *(G-6900)*
Supreme Gear Co ....E...... 586 775-6325
　Fraser *(G-5736)*
Surgitech Surgical Svcs Inc ....E...... 248 593-0797
　Highland *(G-7500)*
Symmetry Medical Inc ....F...... 517 887-3424
　Lansing *(G-9429)*
Tecomet Inc ....B...... 517 882-4311
　Lansing *(G-9431)*
Terumo Crdvscular Systems Corp ...C...... 734 663-4145
　Ann Arbor *(G-666)*
Thompson Surgical Instrs Inc ....E...... 231 922-0177
　Traverse City *(G-16122)*
Thompson Surgical Instrs Inc ....G...... 231 922-5169
　Traverse City *(G-16123)*
Thoratec Corporation ....C...... 734 827-7422
　Ann Arbor *(G-673)*
Tiger Neuroscience LLC ....G...... 872 903-1904
　Muskegon *(G-11437)*
Tilco Inc ....G...... 248 644-0901
　Troy *(G-16643)*
TMJ Manufacturing LLC ....E...... 248 987-7857
　Farmington Hills *(G-5142)*
Truform Machine Inc ....E...... 517 782-8523
　Jackson *(G-8594)*
Viant Medical Inc ....D...... 616 643-5200
　Grand Rapids *(G-6971)*
Warmilu LLC ....G...... 855 927-6458
　Ann Arbor *(G-695)*
Wright & Filippis Inc ....E...... 248 336-8460
　Detroit *(G-3822)*
Wright & Filippis Inc ....E...... 313 386-3330
　Lincoln Park *(G-9589)*
Wysong Medical Corporation ....E...... 989 631-0009
　Midland *(G-10925)*

INSTRUMENTS: Meteorological

Intelligent Vision Systems LLC ....G...... 734 426-3921
　Dexter *(G-4494)*

Nikon Metrology Inc ....C...... 810 220-4360
　Brighton *(G-1968)*
R M Young Company ....E...... 231 946-3980
　Traverse City *(G-16088)*

INSTRUMENTS: Meters, Integrating Electricity

Volta Power Systems LLC ....G...... 616 226-4224
　Holland *(G-7850)*

INSTRUMENTS: Microwave Test

API / Inmet Inc ....C...... 734 426-5553
　Ann Arbor *(G-360)*
Cobham McRlctrnic Slutions Inc .....G...... 734 426-1230
　Ann Arbor *(G-403)*
Jodon Engineering Assoc Inc ....F...... 734 761-4044
　Ann Arbor *(G-511)*

INSTRUMENTS: Nautical

Novatron Corporation ....C...... 609 815-2100
　Warren *(G-17174)*

INSTRUMENTS: Photographic, Electronic

Cognisys Inc ....G...... 231 943-2425
　Traverse City *(G-15944)*

INSTRUMENTS: Power Measuring, Electrical

Creative Power Systems Inc ....E...... 313 961-2460
　Detroit *(G-3954)*

INSTRUMENTS: Pressure Measurement, Indl

Ateq Tpms Tools Lc ....F...... 734 838-3104
　Livonia *(G-9656)*

INSTRUMENTS: Radio Frequency Measuring

Eagile Incorporated ....F...... 616 243-1200
　Grand Rapids *(G-6364)*
Smart Label Solutions LLC ....G...... 800 996-7343
　Howell *(G-8099)*

INSTRUMENTS: Temperature Measurement, Indl

H O Trerice Co Inc ....E...... 248 399-8000
　Oak Park *(G-12072)*
Precise Finishing Systems Inc ....E...... 517 552-9200
　Howell *(G-8081)*

INSTRUMENTS: Test, Digital, Electronic & Electrical Circuits

Orion Test Systems Inc ....D...... 248 373-9097
　Auburn Hills *(G-967)*

INSTRUMENTS: Test, Electrical, Engine

Concept Technology Inc ....E...... 248 765-0100
　Birmingham *(G-1678)*
Diagnostic Systems Association ......F...... 269 544-9000
　Kalamazoo *(G-8725)*
Mahle Powertrain LLC ....D...... 248 305-8200
　Farmington Hills *(G-5056)*
Meiden America Inc ....F...... 734 459-1781
　Northville *(G-11709)*

INSTRUMENTS: Test, Electronic & Electric Measurement

Accurate Technologies Inc ....D...... 248 848-9200
　Novi *(G-11823)*
Debron Industrial Elec Inc ....E...... 248 588-7220
　Troy *(G-16300)*
Design & Test Technology Inc ....G...... 734 665-4111
　Dexter *(G-4484)*
Design & Test Technology Inc ....F...... 734 665-4316
　Ann Arbor *(G-416)*
Industrial Optical Measurement ......G...... 734 975-0436
　Ann Arbor *(G-504)*
Opteos Inc ....G...... 734 929-3333
　Ann Arbor *(G-585)*
Test Products Incorporated ....E...... 586 997-9600
　Sterling Heights *(G-15523)*
VSR Technologies Inc ....F...... 734 425-7172
　Livonia *(G-9992)*

INSTRUMENTS: Test, Electronic & Electrical Circuits

Aerospace America Inc ....E...... 989 684-2121
Bay City *(G-1273)*
Brothers Mead 3 LLC ....G...... 269 883-6241
Battle Creek *(G-1158)*
CPR III Inc ....F...... 248 652-2900
Rochester *(G-13318)*
Electronic Apps Specists Inc ....G...... 248 491-4988
Milford *(G-10963)*
Ptm-Electronics Inc ....F...... 248 987-4446
Farmington Hills *(G-5106)*
Tengam Engineering Inc ....E...... 269 694-9466
Otsego *(G-12256)*

INSTRUMENTS: Testing, Semiconductor

Abtech Installation & Svc Inc ...E...... 800 548-2381
Southgate *(G-15073)*
Esirpal Inc ....G...... 586 337-7848
Macomb *(G-10120)*
Teradyne Inc ....C...... 313 425-3900
Allen Park *(G-211)*

INSTRUMENTS: Thermal Conductive, Indl

Advance Engineering Company ..D...... 313 537-3500
Canton *(G-2344)*

INSTRUMENTS: Thermal Property Measurement

Marshall Ryerson Co ....F...... 616 299-1751
Grand Rapids *(G-6645)*

INSTRUMENTS: Viscometer, Indl Process

Kaltec Scientific Inc ....G...... 248 349-8100
Novi *(G-11913)*

INSULATING BOARD, CELLULAR FIBER

Nu-Wool Co Inc ....D...... 800 748-0128
Jenison *(G-8635)*

INSULATING COMPOUNDS

Midland Cmpnding Cnsulting Inc ..G...... 989 495-9367
Midland *(G-10888)*
Pfb Manufacturing LLC ....E...... 517 486-4844
Blissfield *(G-1723)*

INSULATION & CUSHIONING FOAM: Polystyrene

Atlas Roofing Corporation ....C...... 616 878-1568
Byron Center *(G-2177)*
Everest Manufacturing Inc ....F...... 313 401-2608
Farmington Hills *(G-4993)*
G & T Industries Inc ....D...... 616 452-8611
Byron Center *(G-2192)*
Harbor Foam Inc ....G...... 616 855-8150
Grandville *(G-7044)*
High Tech Insulators Inc ....E...... 734 525-9030
Livonia *(G-9770)*
Janesville LLC ....B...... 248 948-1811
Southfield *(G-14950)*
Jason Incorporated ....E...... 248 948-1811
Southfield *(G-14951)*
Michigan Foam Products Inc ....G...... 616 452-9611
Grand Rapids *(G-6671)*
Plasteel Corporation ....F...... 313 562-5400
Inkster *(G-8231)*

INSULATION & ROOFING MATERIALS: Wood, Reconstituted

Applegate Insul Systems Inc .....E...... 517 521-3545
Webberville *(G-17446)*

INSULATION MATERIALS WHOLESALERS

Rex Materials Inc ....E...... 517 223-3787
Howell *(G-8092)*

INSULATION: Fiberglass

Dgp Inc ....E...... 989 635-7531
Marlette *(G-10495)*
Fiberglass Concepts West Mich ..G...... 616 392-4909
Holland *(G-7630)*
Knauf Insulation Inc ....C...... 517 630-2000
Albion *(G-127)*
Midwest Fbrglas Fbricators Inc ..F...... 810 765-7445
Marine City *(G-10478)*

INSULATORS & INSULATION MATERIALS: Electrical

Dare Products Inc ....E...... 269 965-2307
Springfield *(G-15190)*
Monoco Inc ....G...... 616 459-9800
Grand Rapids *(G-6701)*

INSURANCE CARRIERS: Automobile

General Motors LLC ....A...... 313 972-6000
Detroit *(G-4084)*

INSURANCE CARRIERS: Direct Accident & Health

Enterprise Services LLC ....F...... 734 523-6525
Livonia *(G-9727)*

INSURANCE CARRIERS: Property & Casualty

General Motors LLC ....E...... 248 456-5000
Pontiac *(G-12827)*

INTEGRATED CIRCUITS, SEMICONDUCTOR NETWORKS, ETC

Qualcomm Incorporated ....B...... 248 853-2017
Rochester Hills *(G-13500)*

INTERCOMMUNICATIONS SYSTEMS: Electric

Axis Tms Corp ....E...... 248 509-2440
Troy *(G-16231)*
Curbell Plastics Inc ....G...... 734 513-0531
Livonia *(G-9694)*
R A Miller Industries Inc ....C...... 888 845-9450
Grand Haven *(G-6067)*
Vidatak LLC ....G...... 877 392-6273
Ann Arbor *(G-692)*

INTERIOR DECORATING SVCS

Homespun Furniture Inc ....F...... 734 284-6277
Riverview *(G-13297)*

INTERIOR DESIGN SVCS, NEC

Sherwood Studios Inc ....E...... 248 855-1600
West Bloomfield *(G-17495)*

INTERIOR DESIGNING SVCS

Home Style Co ....G...... 989 871-3654
Millington *(G-10996)*

INVENTORY STOCKING SVCS

Jasco International LLC ....F...... 313 841-5000
Detroit *(G-4159)*

INVERTERS: Nonrotating Electrical

Redeem Power Services ....G...... 248 679-5277
Novi *(G-11985)*

INVESTMENT FUNDS, NEC

Evans Industries Inc ....G...... 313 259-2266
Detroit *(G-4045)*

INVESTORS, NEC

Ascent Aerospace Holdings LLC ..G...... 212 916-8142
Macomb *(G-10109)*

IRON & STEEL PRDTS: Hot-Rolled

Fritz Enterprises ....G...... 734 283-7272
Trenton *(G-16154)*
Iron Clad Security Inc ....G...... 313 837-0390
Detroit *(G-4151)*
Refab LLC ....G...... 616 842-9705
Grand Haven *(G-6070)*

IRON ORES

Cleveland-Cliffs Inc ....A...... 906 475-3547
Ishpeming *(G-8343)*
Empire Iron Mining Partnership ..A...... 906 475-3600
Palmer *(G-12381)*
Tilden Mining Company LC ....A...... 906 475-3400
Ishpeming *(G-8354)*

IRRIGATION SYSTEMS, NEC Water Distribution Or Sply Systems

Engineering Interests Inc ....G...... 248 461-6706
Waterford *(G-17342)*
Village & Country Water Trtmnt ..F...... 810 632-7880
Hartland *(G-7395)*

JACKS: Hydraulic

Arbor International Inc ....G...... 734 761-5200
Ann Arbor *(G-363)*
Jack Weaver Corp ....G...... 517 263-6500
Adrian *(G-71)*
US Jack Company ....G...... 269 925-7777
Benton Harbor *(G-1559)*

JANITORIAL & CUSTODIAL SVCS

Lockett Enterprises LLC ....G...... 810 407-6644
Flint *(G-5459)*
Regency Construction Corp ......E...... 586 741-8000
Clinton Township *(G-3208)*

JANITORIAL EQPT & SPLYS WHOLESALERS

National Soap Company Inc ......G...... 248 545-8180
Royal Oak *(G-13953)*

JAR RINGS: Rubber

Hutchinson Seal Corporation .....G...... 248 375-4190
Auburn Hills *(G-903)*

JEWELERS' FINDINGS & MATERIALS

Finger Fit Co ....G...... 734 522-2935
Saint Clair Shores *(G-14248)*
Trenton Jewelers Ltd ....G...... 734 676-0188
Trenton *(G-16161)*

JEWELERS' FINDINGS & MATERIALS: Castings

Au Enterprises Inc ....F...... 248 544-9700
Berkley *(G-1580)*
L N T Inc ....G...... 248 347-6006
Novi *(G-11925)*

JEWELRY & PRECIOUS STONES WHOLESALERS

Kevin Wheat & Assoc Ltd ....G...... 517 349-0101
Okemos *(G-12127)*

JEWELRY APPAREL

Abracadabra Jewelry ....G...... 734 994-4848
Ann Arbor *(G-338)*
Bednarsh Mrris Jwly Design Mfg ..F...... 248 671-0087
Bloomfield *(G-1732)*
Daves Diamond Inc ....F...... 248 693-2482
Lake Orion *(G-9135)*
Glitterbug USA ....G...... 586 247-7569
Macomb *(G-10126)*
La Gold Mine Inc ....G...... 517 540-1050
Brighton *(G-1949)*
LLC Stahl Cross ....G...... 810 688-2505
Lapeer *(G-9471)*
Michels Inc ....G...... 313 441-3620
Dearborn *(G-3741)*
Wattsson & Wattsson Jewelers ..F...... 906 228-5775
Marquette *(G-10561)*

JEWELRY FINDINGS & LAPIDARY WORK

Alex and Ani LLC ....G...... 248 649-7348
Troy *(G-16183)*
Jostens Inc ....G...... 734 308-3879
Ada *(G-19)*
Kevin Wheat & Assoc Ltd ....G...... 517 349-0101
Okemos *(G-12127)*

PRODUCT SECTION

JEWELRY REPAIR SVCS

Abracadabra Jewelry .... G 734 994-4848
  Ann Arbor *(G-338)*
Bauble Patch Inc .... G 616 785-1100
  Comstock Park *(G-3462)*
Diamond Setters Inc .... G 734 439-8655
  Milan *(G-10936)*
Discount Jewelry Center Inc .... G 734 266-8200
  Westland *(G-17549)*
Jewelers Workshop .... G 616 791-6500
  Grand Rapids *(G-6560)*
Kayayan Hayk Jewelry Mfg Co .... E 248 626-3060
  Bloomfield *(G-1734)*
Kevin Wheat & Assoc Ltd .... G 517 349-0101
  Okemos *(G-12127)*
Novus Corporation .... E 248 545-8600
  Warren *(G-17175)*
Orin Jewelers Inc .... F 734 422-7030
  Garden City *(G-5834)*
Trenton Jewelers Ltd .... G 734 676-0188
  Trenton *(G-16161)*
Wattsson & Wattsson Jewelers .... F 906 228-5775
  Marquette *(G-10561)*

JEWELRY STORES

Alexander J Bongiorno Inc .... G 248 689-7766
  Troy *(G-16185)*
Aurum Design Inc .... G 248 651-9040
  Rochester *(G-13314)*
Bead Gallery .... F 734 663-6800
  Ann Arbor *(G-381)*
Finger Fit Co .... G 734 522-2935
  Saint Clair Shores *(G-14248)*
Kevin Wheat & Assoc Ltd .... G 517 349-0101
  Okemos *(G-12127)*
Mount-N-Repair .... G 248 647-8670
  Birmingham *(G-1694)*
Weyhing Bros Manufacturing Co .... F 313 567-0600
  Detroit *(G-4438)*

JEWELRY STORES: Precious Stones & Precious Metals

Abracadabra Jewelry .... G 734 994-4848
  Ann Arbor *(G-338)*
Bauble Patch Inc .... G 616 785-1100
  Comstock Park *(G-3462)*
Bednarsh Mrris Jwly Design Mfg .... F 248 671-0087
  Bloomfield *(G-1732)*
C T & T Inc .... F 248 623-9422
  Waterford *(G-17328)*
Daves Diamond Inc .... F 248 693-2482
  Lake Orion *(G-9135)*
Discount Jewelry Center Inc .... G 734 266-8200
  Westland *(G-17549)*
George Koueiter Jewelers .... G 313 882-1110
  Grosse Pointe Woods *(G-7203)*
Jewelers Workshop .... G 616 791-6500
  Grand Rapids *(G-6560)*
Jostens Inc .... G 734 308-3879
  Ada *(G-19)*
Just Jewelers .... G 248 476-9011
  Farmington *(G-4902)*
Kayayan Hayk Jewelry Mfg Co .... E 248 626-3060
  Bloomfield *(G-1734)*
La Gold Mine Inc .... G 517 540-1050
  Brighton *(G-1949)*
Michels Inc .... G 313 441-3620
  Dearborn *(G-3741)*
Milford Jewelers Inc .... G 248 676-0721
  Milford *(G-10970)*
Novus Corporation .... E 248 545-8600
  Warren *(G-17175)*
Orin Jewelers Inc .... F 734 422-7030
  Garden City *(G-5834)*
Preusser Jewelers .... G 616 458-1425
  Grand Rapids *(G-6773)*
Rex M Tubbs .... G 734 459-3180
  Plymouth *(G-12735)*
Trenton Jewelers Ltd .... G 734 676-0188
  Trenton *(G-16161)*
Tva Kane Inc .... G 248 946-4670
  Novi *(G-12019)*
Wattsson & Wattsson Jewelers .... F 906 228-5775
  Marquette *(G-10561)*

JEWELRY, PRECIOUS METAL: Bracelets

Pure & Simple Solutions LLC .... E 248 398-4600
  Troy *(G-16570)*

JEWELRY, PRECIOUS METAL: Cigar & Cigarette Access

Otters Oasis .... G 269 788-9987
  Battle Creek *(G-1234)*

JEWELRY, PRECIOUS METAL: Rings, Finger

Herff Jones LLC .... G 810 632-6500
  Hartland *(G-7391)*
Terryberry Company LLC .... C 616 458-1391
  Grand Rapids *(G-6923)*

JEWELRY, PRECIOUS METAL: Settings & Mountings

Diamond Setters Inc .... G 734 439-8655
  Milan *(G-10936)*

JEWELRY, WHOLESALE

Bahama Souvenirs Inc .... G 269 964-8275
  Battle Creek *(G-1149)*
Bauble Patch Inc .... G 616 785-1100
  Comstock Park *(G-3462)*
Candela Products Inc .... G 248 541-2547
  Warren *(G-16976)*
Pure & Simple Solutions LLC .... E 248 398-4600
  Troy *(G-16570)*

JEWELRY: Decorative, Fashion & Costume

HL Manufacturing Inc .... F 586 731-2800
  Utica *(G-16742)*
Preusser Jewelers .... G 616 458-1425
  Grand Rapids *(G-6773)*
Swarovski North America Ltd .... E 248 874-0753
  Auburn Hills *(G-1008)*
Swarovski North America Ltd .... G 616 977-5008
  Grand Rapids *(G-6907)*

JEWELRY: Precious Metal

Alex and Ani LLC .... G 248 649-7348
  Troy *(G-16183)*
Alexander J Bongiorno Inc .... G 248 689-7766
  Troy *(G-16185)*
Amalgamations Ltd .... G 248 879-7345
  Troy *(G-16194)*
Aurum Design Inc .... G 248 651-9040
  Rochester *(G-13314)*
Bauble Patch Inc .... G 616 785-1100
  Comstock Park *(G-3462)*
Birmingham Jewelry Inc .... G 586 939-5100
  Sterling Heights *(G-15274)*
C I I Ltd .... G 248 585-9905
  Troy *(G-16250)*
C T & T Inc .... F 248 623-9422
  Waterford *(G-17328)*
Combine International Inc .... C 248 585-9900
  Troy *(G-16273)*
David Wachler & Sons Inc .... F 248 540-4622
  Birmingham *(G-1681)*
Discount Jewelry Center Inc .... G 734 266-8200
  Westland *(G-17549)*
George Koueiter Jewelers .... G 313 882-1110
  Grosse Pointe Woods *(G-7203)*
HL Manufacturing Inc .... F 586 731-2800
  Utica *(G-16742)*
Jewelers Workshop .... G 616 791-6500
  Grand Rapids *(G-6560)*
Joseph A Dimaggio .... G 313 881-5353
  Grosse Pointe Woods *(G-7205)*
Just Jewelers .... G 248 476-9011
  Farmington *(G-4902)*
Kayayan Hayk Jewelry Mfg Co .... E 248 626-3060
  Bloomfield *(G-1734)*
Marquis Jewelers Ltd .... G 586 725-3990
  Chesterfield *(G-2801)*
Milford Jewelers Inc .... G 248 676-0721
  Milford *(G-10970)*
Mount-N-Repair .... G 248 647-8670
  Birmingham *(G-1694)*
Newell Brands Inc .... G 734 284-2528
  Taylor *(G-15749)*
Novus Corporation .... E 248 545-8600
  Warren *(G-17175)*
Orin Jewelers Inc .... F 734 422-7030
  Garden City *(G-5834)*
Rebel Nell L3c .... G 716 640-4267
  Detroit *(G-4332)*
Rolfs Jewelers Ltd .... G 586 739-3906
  Shelby Township *(G-14681)*
Seoul International Inc .... G 586 275-2494
  Sterling Heights *(G-15489)*
Touchstone Distributing Inc .... G 517 669-8200
  Dewitt *(G-4468)*
Tva Kane Inc .... G 248 946-4670
  Novi *(G-12019)*
Weyhing Bros Manufacturing Co .... F 313 567-0600
  Detroit *(G-4438)*

JIGS & FIXTURES

Advantage Design and Tool .... G 586 801-7413
  Richmond *(G-13258)*
Auto Metal Craft Inc .... E 248 398-2240
  Oak Park *(G-12051)*
Bilco Tool Corporation .... G 586 574-9300
  Warren *(G-16959)*
Enterprise Tool and Gear Inc .... D 989 269-9797
  Bad Axe *(G-1060)*
Experienced Concepts Inc .... F 586 752-4200
  Armada *(G-719)*
Feg Gage Inc .... F 248 616-3631
  Madison Heights *(G-10252)*
Futuramic Tool & Engrg Co .... C 586 758-2200
  Warren *(G-17046)*
Gage Pattern & Model Inc .... E 248 361-6609
  Madison Heights *(G-10255)*
Generation Tool Inc .... G 734 641-6937
  Westland *(G-17561)*
H & M Machining Inc .... F 586 778-5028
  Roseville *(G-13814)*
Hub Tool and Machine Inc .... G 586 772-7866
  Chesterfield *(G-2785)*
I E & E Industries Inc .... F 248 544-8181
  Madison Heights *(G-10272)*
Keller Tool Ltd .... D 734 425-4500
  Livonia *(G-9794)*
Lane Tool and Mfg Corp .... G 248 528-1606
  Troy *(G-16457)*
Lonero Engineering Co Inc .... E 248 689-9120
  Troy *(G-16465)*
Master Machine & Tool Co Inc .... G 586 469-4243
  Clinton Township *(G-3169)*
Masters Tool & Die Inc .... G 989 777-2450
  Saginaw *(G-14083)*
Merriman Products Inc .... G 517 787-1825
  Jackson *(G-8515)*
Michalski Enterprises Inc .... F 517 703-0777
  Lansing *(G-9245)*
O Keller Tool Engrg Co LLC .... E 734 425-4500
  Livonia *(G-9873)*
Olive Engineering Company .... G 616 399-1756
  West Olive *(G-17533)*
P X Tool Co .... G 248 585-9330
  Madison Heights *(G-10319)*
Parry Precision Inc .... F 248 585-1234
  Madison Heights *(G-10321)*
Paslin Company .... A 586 758-0200
  Warren *(G-17182)*
Paslin Company .... C 248 953-8419
  Shelby Township *(G-14660)*
Patton Tool and Die Inc .... F 810 359-5336
  Lexington *(G-9559)*
Peak Industries Co Inc .... D 313 846-8666
  Dearborn *(G-3747)*
Proto-Tek Manufacturing Inc .... E 586 772-2663
  Roseville *(G-13857)*
Rens LLC .... F 586 756-6777
  Warren *(G-17220)*
Skylark Machine Inc .... G 616 931-1010
  Zeeland *(G-18186)*
Ssrm Machine Shop Inc .... G 989 379-4075
  Herron *(G-7470)*
Tri-Star Tool & Machine Co .... F 734 729-5700
  Westland *(G-17605)*
Triangle Broach Company .... F 313 838-2150
  Detroit *(G-4408)*
Tru Point Corporation .... G 313 897-9100
  Detroit *(G-4409)*
Turbine Tool & Gage Inc .... F 734 427-2270
  Livonia *(G-9978)*
Usher Tool & Die Inc .... F 616 583-9160
  Byron Center *(G-2213)*
Visioneering Inc .... B 248 622-5600
  Auburn Hills *(G-1045)*
Wire Dynamics Inc .... G 586 879-0321
  Fraser *(G-5748)*

Employee Codes: A=Over 500 employees, B=251-500
C=101-250, D=51-100, E=20-50, F=10-19, G=3-9

JIGS: Welding Positioners
American Vault Service ....G...... 989 366-8657
  Prudenville *(G-13084)*

JOB PRINTING & NEWSPAPER PUBLISHING COMBINED
Crawford County Avalanche ....G...... 989 348-6811
  Grayling *(G-7104)*
Genesee County Herald Inc ....F...... 810 686-3840
  Clio *(G-3272)*
Oceanas Herald-Journal Inc ....F...... 231 873-5602
  Hart *(G-7378)*
Ontonagon Herald Co Inc............G...... 906 884-2826
  Ontonagon *(G-12163)*
Peterson Publishing Inc ....G...... 906 387-3282
  Munising *(G-11247)*
Presque Isle Newspapers Inc ....F...... 989 734-2105
  Rogers City *(G-13621)*
Tri City Record LLC ....G...... 269 463-6397
  Watervliet *(G-17394)*

JOB TRAINING & VOCATIONAL REHABILITATION SVCS
Buster Mathis Foundation............G...... 616 843-4433
  Wyoming *(G-17990)*
Complete Services LLC............F...... 248 470-8247
  Livonia *(G-9686)*
Services To Enhance Potential............G...... 313 278-3040
  Dearborn *(G-3757)*

JOINTS & COUPLINGS
Con-Vel Inc ....G...... 864 281-2228
  Lansing *(G-9284)*

JOINTS OR FASTENINGS: Rail
A Raymond Tinnerman Auto Inc ....F...... 248 537-3147
  Rochester Hills *(G-13360)*

JOINTS: Expansion
Meccom Corporation............G...... 313 895-4900
  Detroit *(G-4224)*

JOINTS: Expansion, Pipe
J D Russell Company ....E...... 586 254-8500
  Utica *(G-16743)*

JOISTS: Fabricated Bar
Creform Corporation ....F...... 248 926-2555
  Novi *(G-11858)*

JOISTS: Long-Span Series, Open Web Steel
Jaimes Liquidation Inc ....F...... 248 356-8600
  Southfield *(G-14949)*

KEYS: Machine
Basch Olovson Engineering Co ....G...... 231 865-2027
  Fruitport *(G-5788)*

KILNS & FURNACES: Ceramic
Evenheat Kiln Inc............F...... 989 856-2281
  Caseville *(G-2505)*

KITCHEN CABINET STORES, EXC CUSTOM
A & B Display Systems Inc ....F...... 989 893-6642
  Bay City *(G-1269)*
Charlotte Cabinets Inc............G...... 517 543-1522
  Charlotte *(G-2639)*
D & M Cabinet Shop Inc ....G...... 989 479-9271
  Ruth *(G-13988)*
Dallas Design Inc ....G...... 810 238-4546
  Flint *(G-5413)*
Howes Custom Counter Tops............G...... 989 498-4044
  Saginaw *(G-14063)*
Interior Spc of Holland ....E...... 616 396-5634
  Holland *(G-7690)*
Lafata Cabinet Shop ....E...... 586 247-6536
  Shelby Township *(G-14620)*
Lloyds Cabinet Shop Inc ....F...... 989 879-3015
  Pinconning *(G-12509)*
Masco Cabinetry LLC ....D...... 770 447-6363
  Ann Arbor *(G-549)*
Millwork Design Group LLC............G...... 248 472-2178
  Milford *(G-10972)*
Owens Building Co Inc............E...... 989 835-1293
  Midland *(G-10901)*
Reis Custom Cabinets ....G...... 586 791-4925
  Reese *(G-13231)*

KITCHEN CABINETS WHOLESALERS
Greenfield Cabinetry Inc ....F...... 586 759-3300
  Warren *(G-17066)*
Kurtis Mfg & Distrg Corp............E...... 734 522-7600
  Livonia *(G-9802)*
M and G Laminated Products ....G...... 517 784-4974
  Jackson *(G-8502)*
Modern Woodsmith LLC ....G...... 906 387-5577
  Wetmore *(G-17616)*
Richelieu America Ltd ....E...... 586 264-1240
  Sterling Heights *(G-15469)*

KITCHEN UTENSILS: Bakers' Eqpt, Wood
Bremer Authentic Ingredients ....G...... 616 772-9100
  Zeeland *(G-18123)*
Buck-Spica Equipment Ltd ....F...... 269 792-2251
  Wayland *(G-17402)*

KITCHEN UTENSILS: Food Handling & Processing Prdts, Wood
M C Products............G...... 248 960-0590
  Commerce Township *(G-3424)*
Russell Farms Inc ....G...... 269 349-6120
  Kalamazoo *(G-8876)*

KNIVES: Agricultural Or indl
Ontario Die Company America ....D...... 810 987-5060
  Marysville *(G-10609)*

LABELS: Paper, Made From Purchased Materials
Artex Label & Graphics Inc............E...... 616 748-9655
  Zeeland *(G-18112)*
Macarthur Corp ....E...... 810 606-1777
  Grand Blanc *(G-5975)*
Venture Label Inc ....G...... 313 928-2545
  Detroit *(G-4424)*
Venture Labels USA Inc............G...... 313 928-2545
  Lincoln Park *(G-9587)*

LABOR RESOURCE SVCS
E-Con LLC ....E...... 248 766-9000
  Birmingham *(G-1682)*

LABORATORIES, TESTING: Automobile Proving & Testing Ground
E D P Technical Services Inc ....G...... 734 591-9176
  Livonia *(G-9718)*
Roush Enterprises Inc............C...... 734 805-4400
  Farmington *(G-4909)*
Roush Industries Inc ....E...... 734 779-7013
  Livonia *(G-9913)*

LABORATORIES, TESTING: Prdt Certification, Sfty/Performance
Dynamic Corporation ....D...... 616 399-9391
  Holland *(G-7613)*

LABORATORIES, TESTING: Product Testing
Hydraulic Systems Technology............G...... 248 656-5810
  Rochester Hills *(G-13447)*

LABORATORIES, TESTING: Product Testing, Safety/Performance
Ford Motor Company............A...... 313 446-5945
  Detroit *(G-4067)*
Greening Incorporated ....G...... 313 366-7160
  Detroit *(G-4104)*
J E Myles Inc............E...... 248 583-1020
  Troy *(G-16430)*

LABORATORIES: Biological Research
Biosan Laboratories Inc............F...... 586 755-8970
  Warren *(G-16961)*
Metabolic Solutions Dev Co LLC............F...... 269 343-6732
  Kalamazoo *(G-8822)*
Onl Therapeutics LLC............G...... 734 998-8339
  Ann Arbor *(G-583)*
Oxford Biomedical Research Inc............G...... 248 852-8815
  Metamora *(G-10779)*

LABORATORIES: Biotechnology
Retrosense Therapeutics LLC............G...... 734 369-9333
  Ann Arbor *(G-620)*
Tetradyn Ltd ....G...... 202 415-7295
  Traverse City *(G-16120)*

LABORATORIES: Commercial Nonphysical Research
Technova Corporation............F...... 517 485-1402
  Okemos *(G-12138)*

LABORATORIES: Dental
Ktr Dental Lab & Pdts LLC ....F...... 248 224-9158
  Southfield *(G-14957)*

LABORATORIES: Dental, Artificial Teeth Production
Dental Art Laboratories Inc............D...... 517 485-2200
  Lansing *(G-9222)*

LABORATORIES: Dental, Crown & Bridge Production
Davis Dental Laboratory............G...... 616 261-9191
  Wyoming *(G-17995)*

LABORATORIES: Electronic Research
Consoldted Rsource Imaging LLC............E...... 616 735-2080
  Grand Rapids *(G-6301)*
Ebw Electronics Inc ....E...... 616 786-0575
  Holland *(G-7616)*
Kore Inc............E...... 616 785-5900
  Comstock Park *(G-3491)*
Sensigma LLC ....G...... 734 998-8328
  Ann Arbor *(G-628)*

LABORATORIES: Environmental Research
Environmental Protection Inc............F...... 231 943-2265
  Traverse City *(G-15965)*

LABORATORIES: Medical
Holland Community Hosp Aux Inc............E...... 616 355-3926
  Holland *(G-7670)*

LABORATORIES: Noncommercial Research
Bioplstic Plymers Cmpsites LLC............G...... 517 349-2970
  Okemos *(G-12117)*
Kellogg Company ....D...... 269 961-2000
  Battle Creek *(G-1215)*

LABORATORIES: Physical Research, Commercial
Akzo Nobel Coatings Inc............E...... 248 637-0400
  Pontiac *(G-12801)*
Aurora Spclty Chemistries Corp ....E...... 517 372-9121
  Lansing *(G-9344)*
Bioelectrica Inc ....G...... 517 884-4542
  East Lansing *(G-4651)*
Bwi North America Inc............C...... 810 494-4584
  Brighton *(G-1893)*
Contract People Corporation............F...... 248 304-9900
  Southfield *(G-14872)*
Csquared Innovations Inc ....F...... 734 998-8330
  Novi *(G-11860)*
Eftec North America LLC............D...... 248 585-2200
  Taylor *(G-15713)*
Ervin Industries Inc............E...... 517 423-5477
  Tecumseh *(G-15792)*
Feg Gage Inc ....F...... 248 616-3631
  Madison Heights *(G-10252)*
Gates Corporation ....D...... 248 260-2300
  Rochester Hills *(G-13431)*
Innovative Weld Solutions LLC ....G...... 937 545-7695
  Rochester *(G-13329)*
Medical Engineering & Dev ....G...... 517 563-2352
  Horton *(G-7969)*

PRODUCT SECTION

LAMP BULBS & TUBES, ELECTRIC: Electric Light

Metrex Research LLC .... D 734 947-6700
  Romulus *(G-13706)*
Sika Corporation .... D 248 577-0020
  Madison Heights *(G-10353)*
Trico Products Corporation .... C 248 371-1700
  Rochester Hills *(G-13531)*
Valeo North America Inc .... C 248 619-8300
  Troy *(G-16676)*

LABORATORIES: Testing

Anchor Bay Packaging Corp .... E 586 949-4040
  Chesterfield *(G-2738)*
Avomeen LLC .... E 734 222-1090
  Ann Arbor *(G-377)*
Bwi North America Inc .... C 810 494-4584
  Brighton *(G-1893)*
Eaton Corporation .... B 269 781-0200
  Marshall *(G-10566)*
Elden Industries Corporation .... F 734 946-6900
  Taylor *(G-15715)*
Holland Community Hosp Aux Inc .... E 616 355-3926
  Holland *(G-7670)*
Industrial Temperature Control .... G 734 451-8740
  Canton *(G-2384)*
Marelli North America Inc .... C 248 848-4800
  Farmington Hills *(G-5057)*
Medsker Electric Inc .... E 248 855-3383
  Farmington Hills *(G-5062)*
Merrill Technologies Group .... E 989 921-1490
  Saginaw *(G-14089)*
Merrill Technologies Group Inc .... D 989 791-6676
  Saginaw *(G-14090)*
Michigan Scientific Corp .... D 231 547-5511
  Charlevoix *(G-2620)*
PSI Labs .... G 734 369-6273
  Ann Arbor *(G-607)*
Roush Industries Inc .... E 734 779-7016
  Livonia *(G-9912)*
Saginaw Valley Inst Mtls Inc .... G 989 496-2307
  Midland *(G-10911)*
SKF USA Inc .... D 734 414-6585
  Plymouth *(G-12756)*
Thermal Wave Imaging Inc .... F 248 414-3730
  Ferndale *(G-5321)*
Trico Products Corporation .... C 248 371-1700
  Rochester Hills *(G-13531)*
Weiss Technik North Amer Inc .... D 616 554-5020
  Grand Rapids *(G-6983)*
Xytek Industries Inc .... F 313 838-6961
  Detroit *(G-4453)*

LABORATORY APPARATUS & FURNITURE

Absolute Nano LLC .... G 617 319-9617
  Ann Arbor *(G-339)*
AG Davis Gage & Engrg Co .... E 586 977-9000
  Sterling Heights *(G-15256)*
Alpha Resources LLC .... E 269 465-5559
  Stevensville *(G-15553)*
Balance Technology Inc .... D 734 769-2100
  Whitmore Lake *(G-17689)*
Case Systems Inc .... C 989 496-9510
  Midland *(G-10822)*
Coy Laboratory Products Inc .... E 734 433-9296
  Grass Lake *(G-7086)*
Marketlab Inc .... D 866 237-3722
  Caledonia *(G-2307)*
Symbiote Inc .... E 616 772-1790
  Zeeland *(G-18189)*

LABORATORY APPARATUS, EXC HEATING & MEASURING

Accuri Cytometers Inc .... E 734 994-8000
  Ann Arbor *(G-340)*
Gelman Sciences Inc .... A 734 665-0651
  Ann Arbor *(G-469)*
Leco Corporation .... B 269 983-5531
  Saint Joseph *(G-14324)*
Leco Corporation .... F 269 982-2230
  Saint Joseph *(G-14325)*

LABORATORY APPARATUS: Evaporation

Snow Machines Incorporated .... E 989 631-6091
  Midland *(G-10917)*

LABORATORY APPARATUS: Granulators

Cmg America Inc .... G 810 686-3064
  Clio *(G-3268)*

LABORATORY APPARATUS: Microtomes

Rankin Biomedical Corporation .... F 248 625-4104
  Holly *(G-7893)*

LABORATORY APPARATUS: Physics, NEC

Boyd Manufacturing LLC .... G 734 649-9765
  Muskegon *(G-11284)*

LABORATORY APPARATUS: Time Interval Measuring, Electric

Total Toxicology Labs LLC .... G 248 352-7171
  Southfield *(G-15047)*

LABORATORY CHEMICALS: Organic

Boropharm Inc .... E 517 455-7847
  Ann Arbor *(G-386)*
Burhani Labs Inc .... G 313 212-3842
  Detroit *(G-3920)*
Dynamic Staffing Solutions .... F 616 399-5220
  Holland *(G-7614)*
Jade Scientific Inc .... F 734 207-3775
  Westland *(G-17572)*
Kemai (usa) Chemical Co Ltd .... G 248 924-2225
  Northville *(G-11704)*
Medtest Dx Inc .... D 866 540-2715
  Canton *(G-2400)*

LABORATORY EQPT, EXC MEDICAL: Wholesalers

Alpha Resources LLC .... E 269 465-5559
  Stevensville *(G-15553)*
Boyd Manufacturing LLC .... G 734 649-9765
  Muskegon *(G-11284)*
Healthcare Dme LLC .... G 734 975-6668
  Ann Arbor *(G-485)*
Rankin Biomedical Corporation .... F 248 625-4104
  Holly *(G-7893)*

LABORATORY EQPT: Centrifuges

M2 Scientifics LLC .... G 616 379-9080
  Holland *(G-7728)*

LABORATORY EQPT: Clinical Instruments Exc Medical

Holland Community Hosp Aux Inc .... E 616 355-3926
  Holland *(G-7670)*

LABORATORY EQPT: Incubators

Southwest Mich Innovation Ctr .... G 269 353-1823
  Kalamazoo *(G-8893)*

LABORATORY EQPT: Measuring

Sleep Diagnosis Northern Mich .... G 231 935-9275
  Traverse City *(G-16107)*

LABORATORY EQPT: Sterilizers

Peerless Waste Solutions LLC .... G 616 355-2800
  Holland *(G-7768)*

LACQUERING SVC: Metal Prdts

Gladwin Metal Processing Inc .... G 989 426-9038
  Gladwin *(G-5931)*

LADDER & WORKSTAND COMBINATION ASSEMBLIES: Metal

Jershon Inc .... G 231 861-2900
  Shelby *(G-14527)*

LADDERS: Metal

Laddertech LLC .... F 248 437-7100
  Brighton *(G-1950)*
Ultimate Manufacturing Inc .... G 313 538-6212
  Redford *(G-13203)*

LADDERS: Portable, Metal

Aquarius Recreational Products .... G 586 469-4600
  Harrison Township *(G-7320)*
Con-De Manufacturing Inc .... G 269 651-3756
  Sturgis *(G-15601)*

LADDERS: Wood

Ladder Carolina Company Inc .... F 734 482-5946
  Ypsilanti *(G-18083)*
Michigan Ladder Company LLC .... F 734 482-5946
  Ypsilanti *(G-18090)*

LAMINATED PLASTICS: Plate, Sheet, Rod & Tubes

Advanced Drainage Systems Inc .... D 989 723-5208
  Owosso *(G-12275)*
Bangor Plastics Inc .... E 269 427-7971
  Bangor *(G-1088)*
Basic Rubber and Plastics Co .... E 248 360-7400
  Walled Lake *(G-16891)*
Bordener Engnred Laminates Inc ..... G 989 835-6881
  Bay City *(G-1292)*
Duo-Gard Industries Inc .... D 734 207-9700
  Canton *(G-2367)*
J Kaltz & Co .... G 616 942-6070
  Grand Rapids *(G-6547)*
Kent Manufacturing Company .... D 616 454-9495
  Grand Rapids *(G-6577)*
McKechnie Vhcl Cmpnnts USA Inc ... E 218 894-1218
  Roseville *(G-13832)*
Paul Murphy Plastics Co .... E 586 774-4880
  Roseville *(G-13851)*
Plascore Inc .... D 616 772-1220
  Zeeland *(G-18176)*
Polyply Composites LLC .... E 616 842-6330
  Grand Haven *(G-6061)*
Rehau Incorporated .... E 269 651-7845
  Sturgis *(G-15632)*
Ronald M Davis Co Inc .... G 313 864-5588
  Detroit *(G-4347)*
Scooters Refuse Service Inc .... G 269 962-2201
  Battle Creek *(G-1244)*
Shawmut Corporation .... C 810 987-2222
  Port Huron *(G-12965)*
Spiratex Company .... D 734 289-4800
  Monroe *(G-11069)*
Summit Polymers Inc .... B 269 323-1301
  Portage *(G-13047)*
Summit Polymers Inc .... B 269 651-1643
  Sturgis *(G-15638)*
Total Plastics Resources LLC .... D 269 344-0009
  Kalamazoo *(G-8914)*
Vidon Plastics Inc .... D 810 667-0634
  Lapeer *(G-9490)*

LAMINATING MATERIALS

Dico Manufacturing LLC .... G 586 731-3008
  Chesterfield *(G-2766)*

LAMINATING SVCS

Celia Corporation .... G 616 887-7387
  Sparta *(G-15090)*
Engineering Reproduction Inc .... F 313 366-3390
  Detroit *(G-4038)*
F & A Enterprises of Michigan .... G 906 228-3222
  Marquette *(G-10531)*

LAMP & LIGHT BULBS & TUBES

Chicl LLC .... A 859 294-5590
  Troy *(G-16266)*
Energy Efficient Ltg LLC Eel .... G 586 214-5557
  West Bloomfield *(G-17476)*
Ews Legacy LLC .... E 248 853-6363
  Rochester Hills *(G-13421)*
High Q Lighting Inc .... E 616 396-3591
  Holland *(G-7665)*
Ilumisys Inc .... G 844 864-4533
  Troy *(G-16411)*
Inland Vapor of Michigan LLC .... G 734 738-6312
  Canton *(G-2385)*
Philips North America LLC .... E 248 553-9080
  Farmington Hills *(G-5092)*
Trident Lighting LLC .... C 616 957-9500
  Grand Rapids *(G-6937)*

LAMP BULBS & TUBES, ELECTRIC: Electric Light

Johnico LLC .... E 248 895-7820
  Detroit *(G-4164)*

Employee Codes: A=Over 500 employees, B=251-500
C=101-250, D=51-100, E=20-50, F=10-19, G=3-9

LAMP BULBS & TUBES, ELECTRIC: For Specialized Applications

LAMP BULBS & TUBES, ELECTRIC: For Specialized Applications
Emitted Energy Inc ....F 855 752-3347
  Sterling Heights *(G-15332)*

LAMP BULBS & TUBES, ELECTRIC: Glow Lamp
Wickedglow Industries Inc ....G...... 586 776-4132
  Mount Clemens *(G-11154)*

LAMP BULBS & TUBES, ELECTRIC: Light, Complete
Earthtronics Inc ....E 231 332-1188
  Norton Shores *(G-11751)*
Elumigen LLC ....G...... 855 912-0477
  Troy *(G-16341)*
G & L Powerup Inc ....G...... 586 200-2169
  Roseville *(G-13806)*

LAMP BULBS & TUBES, ELECTRIC: Vapor
Inland Vapor of Michigan LLC ....F 734 237-4389
  Garden City *(G-5828)*

LAMP BULBS & TUBES/PARTS, ELECTRIC: Generalized Applications
Optic Edge Corporation ....G...... 231 547-6090
  Charlevoix *(G-2624)*

LAMP REPAIR & MOUNTING SVCS
Beltone Skoric Hearng Aid Cntr ....G...... 906 379-0606
  Sault Sainte Marie *(G-14461)*
Beltone Skoric Hearng Aid Cntr ....G...... 906 553-4660
  Escanaba *(G-4817)*

LAMPS: Desk, Commercial
Light Corp Inc ....C 616 842-5100
  Grand Haven *(G-6049)*

LAMPS: Table, Residential
Lighting Enterprises Inc ....G...... 313 693-9504
  Detroit *(G-4205)*

LAND SUBDIVISION & DEVELOPMENT
Marshalls Crossing ....G...... 810 639-4740
  Montrose *(G-11104)*
Stroh Companies Inc ....F 313 446-2000
  Detroit *(G-4380)*

LANGUAGE SCHOOLS
Complete Services LLC ....F 248 470-8247
  Livonia *(G-9686)*

LASER SYSTEMS & EQPT
Boyd Manufacturing LLC ....G...... 734 649-9765
  Muskegon *(G-11284)*
Cortar Laser and Fab LLC ....G...... 248 446-1110
  Brighton *(G-1905)*
Fabrilaser Mfg LLC ....E 269 789-9490
  Marshall *(G-10567)*
Fusion Laser Services ....G...... 586 739-7716
  Sterling Heights *(G-15352)*
Imperial Laser Inc ....G...... 616 735-9315
  Grand Rapids *(G-6529)*
Imra America Inc ....E 734 669-7377
  Ann Arbor *(G-503)*
Ipg Photonics Corporation ....F 248 863-5001
  Novi *(G-11908)*
Laser Fab Inc ....G...... 586 415-8090
  Fraser *(G-5683)*
Laser Marking Technologies LLC ....F 989 673-6690
  Caro *(G-2470)*
Laser Mechanisms Inc ....D...... 248 474-9480
  Novi *(G-11929)*
Laser Product Development LLC ....G...... 800 765-4424
  Center Line *(G-2580)*
Rofin-Sinar Technologies LLC ....F 734 416-0206
  Plymouth *(G-12745)*

LASERS: Welding, Drilling & Cutting Eqpt
Andex Laser Inc ....G...... 734 947-9840
  Taylor *(G-15688)*
Arin Inc ....F 586 779-3410
  Roseville *(G-13774)*
Laser Access Inc ....C 616 459-5496
  Grand Rapids *(G-6618)*
Macomb Sheet Metal Inc ....E 586 790-4600
  Clinton Township *(G-3164)*
Reau Manufacturing Co ....G...... 734 823-5603
  Dundee *(G-4598)*
Rydin and Associates Inc ....F 586 783-9772
  Clinton Township *(G-3219)*
SLM Solutions Na Inc ....E 248 243-5400
  Wixom *(G-17894)*
Troy Laser & Fab LLC ....G...... 586 510-4570
  Warren *(G-17269)*
Trumpf Inc ....E 734 354-9770
  Plymouth *(G-12783)*
Visotek Inc ....F 734 427-4800
  Livonia *(G-9990)*

LATEX: Foamed
Trinseo LLC ....E 888 789-7661
  Midland *(G-10922)*

LATHES
Advanced Maintenance Tech ....G...... 810 820-2554
  Flint *(G-5371)*

LAUNDRY & DRYCLEANING SVCS, EXC COIN-OPERATED: Retail Agent
Bella Sposa Bridal & Prom ....G...... 616 364-0777
  Grand Rapids *(G-6209)*

LAUNDRY & GARMENT SVCS, NEC: Garment Making, Alter & Repair
Demmem Enterprises LLC ....F 810 564-9500
  Clio *(G-3269)*

LAUNDRY & GARMENT SVCS, NEC: Reweaving, Textiles
Zeilinger Wool Co LLC ....E 989 652-2920
  Frankenmuth *(G-5597)*

LAUNDRY & GARMENT SVCS, NEC: Seamstress
Bella Sposa Bridal & Prom ....G...... 616 364-0777
  Grand Rapids *(G-6209)*

LAUNDRY EQPT: Commercial
AEC Systems Usa Inc ....E 616 257-9502
  Grandville *(G-7018)*

LAUNDRY EQPT: Household
Whirlpool Corporation ....A 269 923-5000
  Benton Harbor *(G-1565)*
Whirlpool Corporation ....G...... 269 923-5000
  Benton Harbor *(G-1566)*
Whirlpool Corporation ....C 269 923-7400
  Benton Harbor *(G-1567)*
Whirlpool Corporation ....D...... 269 923-5000
  Benton Harbor *(G-1568)*
Whirlpool Corporation ....C 269 923-6057
  Saint Joseph *(G-14353)*
Whirlpool Corporation ....B 269 923-6486
  Benton Harbor *(G-1569)*

LAWN & GARDEN EQPT
Big Green Tomato LLC ....G...... 269 282-1593
  Battle Creek *(G-1154)*
Buyers Development Group LLC ....F 734 677-0009
  Ann Arbor *(G-393)*
Contech (us) Inc ....E 616 459-4139
  Grand Rapids *(G-6303)*
Harrells LLC ....G...... 248 446-8070
  New Hudson *(G-11542)*
Hydro Giant 4 Inc ....F 248 661-0034
  West Bloomfield *(G-17480)*
Milsco LLC ....B 517 787-3650
  Jackson *(G-8531)*
Nolans Outdoor Power Inc ....G...... 810 664-3798
  Lapeer *(G-9477)*
Root Spring Scraper Co ....E 269 382-2025
  Kalamazoo *(G-8874)*
Superior Cedar Products Inc ....E 906 639-2132
  Carney *(G-2464)*
UP Coin & Cultivation LLC ....G...... 906 341-4769
  Manistique *(G-10447)*
Whitehall Products LLC ....D...... 231 894-2688
  Whitehall *(G-17682)*

LAWN & GARDEN EQPT: Blowers & Vacuums
Dynamic Manufacturing LLC ....E 989 644-8109
  Weidman *(G-17456)*

LAWN & GARDEN EQPT: Edgers
Sure-Loc Aluminum Edging Inc ....G...... 616 392-3209
  Holland *(G-7822)*

LAWN & GARDEN EQPT: Grass Catchers, Lawn Mower
Cjm Maintenance ....G...... 734 285-0247
  Wyandotte *(G-17952)*
Ebels Hardware Inc ....F 231 826-3334
  Falmouth *(G-4892)*

LAWN & GARDEN EQPT: Tractors & Eqpt
Wells Equipment Sales Inc ....F 517 542-2376
  Litchfield *(G-9613)*

LAWN MOWER REPAIR SHOP
Bader & Co ....E 810 648-2404
  Sandusky *(G-14429)*
D P Equipment Co ....F 517 368-5266
  Camden *(G-2340)*
Ebels Hardware Inc ....F 231 826-3334
  Falmouth *(G-4892)*

LEAD
Mayer Alloys Corporation ....G...... 248 399-2233
  Ferndale *(G-5299)*

LEAD & ZINC ORES
Lee Industries Inc ....E 231 777-2537
  Muskegon *(G-11365)*
National Zinc Processors Inc ....F 269 926-1161
  Benton Harbor *(G-1535)*

LEAD PENCILS & ART GOODS
Mac Enterprises Inc ....F 313 846-4567
  Manchester *(G-10407)*
Panoplate Lithographics Inc ....G...... 269 343-4644
  Kalamazoo *(G-8840)*

LEASING & RENTAL SVCS: Cranes & Aerial Lift Eqpt
Bristol Manufacturing Inc ....E 810 658-9510
  Davison *(G-3640)*
Joseph A Dimaggio ....G...... 313 881-5353
  Grosse Pointe Woods *(G-7205)*
Schwartz Boiler Shop Inc ....G...... 231 627-2556
  Cheboygan *(G-2694)*

LEASING & RENTAL SVCS: Earth Moving Eqpt
D P Equipment Co ....F 517 368-5266
  Camden *(G-2340)*

LEASING & RENTAL: Construction & Mining Eqpt
Arcosa Shoring Products Inc ....F 800 292-1225
  Lansing *(G-9203)*
Capital Equipment Clare LLC ....F 517 669-5533
  Dewitt *(G-4460)*
Delhi Leasing Inc ....G...... 517 694-8578
  Holt *(G-7910)*
Garrisons Hitch Center Inc ....G...... 810 239-5728
  Flint *(G-5432)*
Jones & Hollands Inc ....G...... 810 364-6400
  Marysville *(G-10605)*
Modern Industries Inc ....E 810 767-3330
  Flint *(G-5469)*

PRODUCT SECTION — LIGHTING FIXTURES, NEC

LEASING & RENTAL: Medical Machinery & Eqpt
Metro Medical Eqp Mfg Inc .... D 734 522-8400
  Livonia *(G-9840)*
Wright & Filippis Inc .... F 586 756-4020
  Warren *(G-17298)*

LEASING & RENTAL: Mobile Home Sites
Kearsley Lake Terrace LLC .... G 810 736-7000
  Flint *(G-5453)*

LEASING & RENTAL: Other Real Estate Property
J M Longyear Heirs Inc .... G 906 228-7960
  Marquette *(G-10535)*
Overstreet Property MGT Co .... G 269 252-1560
  Benton Harbor *(G-1537)*

LEASING & RENTAL: Trucks, Without Drivers
Area Cycle Inc .... G 989 777-0850
  Bridgeport *(G-1849)*

LEASING & RENTAL: Utility Trailers & RV's
Spartan Motors Inc .... A 517 543-6400
  Charlotte *(G-2665)*

LEASING: Passenger Car
Ford Motor Company .... A 734 942-6248
  Brownstown *(G-2062)*
Ford Motor Company .... B 313 322-3000
  Dearborn *(G-3709)*
Ford Motor Company .... A 734 523-3000
  Livonia *(G-9744)*

LEASING: Shipping Container
Corsair Engineering Inc .... F 810 233-0440
  Flint *(G-5403)*

LEATHER GOODS: Aprons, Welders', Blacksmiths', Etc
Sharadans Leather Goods Inc .... G 586 468-0666
  Mount Clemens *(G-11150)*

LEATHER GOODS: Belting & Strapping
C W Marsh Company .... E 231 722-3781
  Muskegon *(G-11288)*

LEATHER GOODS: Embossed
Tapestry Inc .... F 616 538-5802
  Grandville *(G-7073)*

LEATHER GOODS: Garments
Grozdanovski Vasilka .... G 989 731-0723
  Gaylord *(G-5862)*
Leathercrafts By Bear .... G 616 453-8308
  Grand Rapids *(G-6623)*

LEATHER GOODS: Harnesses Or Harness Parts
C I M Product .... G 269 983-5348
  Saint Joseph *(G-14303)*
Low Cost Surcing Solutions LLC .... G 248 535-7721
  Washington *(G-17306)*

LEATHER GOODS: Money Holders
Birlon Group LLC .... G 313 551-5341
  Inkster *(G-8225)*

LEATHER GOODS: NEC
Ihicore LLC .... G 800 960-0448
  Lansing *(G-9384)*

LEATHER GOODS: Personal
C W Marsh Company .... E 231 722-3781
  Muskegon *(G-11288)*
Charlies Wood Shop .... F 989 845-2632
  Chesaning *(G-2722)*
Original Footwear Company .... B 231 796-5828
  Big Rapids *(G-1639)*

LEATHER GOODS: Saddles Or Parts
Protecto Horse Equipment Inc .... G 586 754-4820
  Warren *(G-17210)*

LEATHER GOODS: Straps
Shinola/Detroit LLC .... C 888 304-2534
  Detroit *(G-4361)*

LEATHER TANNING & FINISHING
Horn Corp .... G 248 358-8883
  Brighton *(G-1940)*
Lear Corporation .... E 248 853-3122
  Rochester Hills *(G-13459)*
Mexico Express .... F 313 843-6717
  Detroit *(G-4235)*
Modern Fur Dressing LLC .... G 517 589-5575
  Leslie *(G-9545)*
Wolverine World Wide Inc .... C 616 866-5500
  Rockford *(G-13600)*

LEATHER: Cut
Afx Industries LLC .... G 517 768-8993
  Jackson *(G-8376)*

LEATHER: Die-cut
Michigan Diversfd Holdings Inc .... F 248 280-0450
  Madison Heights *(G-10305)*

LEATHER: Indl Prdts
Afx Industries LLC .... G 810 966-4650
  Port Huron *(G-12881)*
Lynn Noyes Industries Inc .... G 313 841-3130
  Ypsilanti *(G-18086)*
National Manufacturing Inc .... G 586 755-8983
  Warren *(G-17166)*

LEATHER: Processed
Transnav Holdings Inc .... C 586 716-5600
  New Baltimore *(G-11494)*

LECTURING SVCS
Step Into Success Inc .... G 734 426-1075
  Pinckney *(G-12504)*

LEGAL OFFICES & SVCS
Detroit Legal News Pubg LLC .... E 248 577-6100
  Troy *(G-16314)*
Marshal E Hyman and Associates .... G 248 643-0642
  Troy *(G-16488)*

LENS COATING: Ophthalmic
Hi-Tech Optical Inc .... E 989 799-9390
  Saginaw *(G-14057)*

LICENSE TAGS: Automobile, Stamped Metal
Southtec LLC .... G 734 397-6300
  New Boston *(G-11511)*
Southtec LLC .... C 734 397-6300
  New Boston *(G-11512)*

LIGHT OIL CRUDE: From Chemical Recovery Coke Ovens
Alan Bruce Enterprises .... G 616 262-4609
  Byron Center *(G-2175)*

LIGHT SENSITIVE DEVICES
Alsentis LLC .... G 616 395-8254
  Holland *(G-7555)*

LIGHTING EQPT: Area & Sports Luminaries
Qualite Inc .... E 517 439-4316
  Hillsdale *(G-7535)*

LIGHTING EQPT: Motor Vehicle
A S Auto Lights Inc .... G 734 941-1164
  Romulus *(G-13644)*
Emergency Technology Inc .... D 616 896-7100
  Hudsonville *(G-8155)*
F M T Products Inc .... G 517 568-3373
  Homer *(G-7942)*
Gyb LLC .... F 586 218-3222
  Warren *(G-17072)*
HA Automotive Systems Inc .... F 248 781-0001
  Troy *(G-16388)*

LIGHTING EQPT: Motor Vehicle, Dome Lights
Magna Mirrors America Inc .... E 616 786-5120
  Grand Rapids *(G-6640)*
Magna Mirrors America Inc .... G 616 786-7000
  Holland *(G-7734)*
Magna Mirrors America Inc .... D 616 786-7300
  Holland *(G-7735)*
Magna Mirrors America Inc .... C 616 942-0163
  Newaygo *(G-11573)*

LIGHTING EQPT: Motor Vehicle, Headlights
Automotive Lighting LLC .... G 248 418-3000
  Clarkston *(G-2908)*
Automotive Lighting LLC .... E 248 418-3000
  Auburn Hills *(G-789)*

LIGHTING EQPT: Motor Vehicle, NEC
Autosystems America Inc .... B 734 582-2300
  Plymouth *(G-12577)*
Eto Magnetic Corp .... D 616 957-2570
  Grand Rapids *(G-6387)*
Fisher-Baker Corporation .... G 810 765-3548
  Marine City *(G-10473)*
Il Stanley Co Inc .... A 269 660-7777
  Battle Creek *(G-1199)*
International Automotive Compo .... D 231 734-9000
  Evart *(G-4884)*
MLS Automotive Incorporated .... F 844 453-3669
  Farmington Hills *(G-5070)*
North American Lighting Inc .... D 248 553-6408
  Farmington Hills *(G-5081)*
Rebo Lighting & Elec LLC .... F 734 213-4159
  Ann Arbor *(G-612)*
Trident Lighting LLC .... C 616 957-9500
  Grand Rapids *(G-6937)*
Zkw Lighting Systems Usa Inc .... G 248 525-4600
  Troy *(G-16707)*

LIGHTING EQPT: Motor Vehicle, Taillights
Tecniq Inc .... E 269 629-4440
  Galesburg *(G-5816)*

LIGHTING EQPT: Outdoor
D & G Equipment Inc .... C 517 655-4606
  Williamston *(G-17729)*

LIGHTING FIXTURES WHOLESALERS
Full Spectrum Solutions Inc .... E 517 783-3800
  Jackson *(G-8454)*
Houseart LLC .... G 248 651-8124
  Rochester *(G-13327)*
Nextek Power Systems Inc .... E 313 887-1321
  Detroit *(G-4269)*

LIGHTING FIXTURES, NEC
Affordable OEM Autolighting .... G 989 400-6106
  Stanton *(G-15227)*
Ci Lighting LLC .... G 248 997-4415
  Auburn Hills *(G-813)*
Coreled Systems LLC .... G 734 516-2060
  Livonia *(G-9689)*
Dakkota Lighting Tech LLC .... E 517 993-7700
  Holt *(G-7908)*
Emergency Technology Inc .... D 616 896-7100
  Hudsonville *(G-8155)*
Energy Design Svc Systems LLC .... F 810 227-3377
  Whitmore Lake *(G-17697)*
Gadget Factory LLC .... G 517 449-1444
  Lansing *(G-9370)*
General Structures Inc .... E 586 774-6105
  Warren *(G-17054)*
Global Green Corporation .... F 734 560-1743
  Ann Arbor *(G-473)*
GT Solutions LLC .... G 616 259-0700
  Holland *(G-7655)*
High Q Lighting Inc .... E 616 396-3591
  Holland *(G-7665)*
I Parth Inc .... G 248 548-9722
  Ferndale *(G-5293)*
Infection Prevention Tech LLC .... G 248 340-8800
  Grand Blanc *(G-5970)*

Employee Codes: A=Over 500 employees, B=251-500
C=101-250, D=51-100, E=20-50, F=10-19, G=3-9

LIGHTING FIXTURES, NEC

J & B Products Ltd.................................F...... 989 792-6119
 Saginaw *(G-14065)*
J & M Products and Service LLC..........G..... 517 263-3082
 Adrian *(G-70)*
Lumasmart Technology Intl Inc...............C..... 586 232-4125
 Macomb *(G-10137)*
Lumerica Corporation ....F...... 248 543-8085
 Warren *(G-17132)*
Michigan Lightning Protection ....G..... 616 453-1174
 Grand Rapids *(G-6673)*
Off Grid LLC ....G..... 734 780-4434
 Ann Arbor *(G-580)*
Phoenix Imaging Inc ....G..... 248 476-4200
 Livonia *(G-9888)*
Randy L Palmer.....................................G..... 586 298-7629
 Clarkston *(G-2949)*
Sonrize LLC..G..... 586 329-3225
 Chesterfield *(G-2842)*
Sound Productions Entrmt ....E..... 989 386-2221
 Clare *(G-2889)*
Spectrum Illumination Co Inc ....G..... 231 894-4590
 Montague *(G-11098)*
Steelcase Inc ....A..... 616 247-2710
 Grand Rapids *(G-6889)*

LIGHTING FIXTURES: Decorative Area

Wayne Novick.......................................G..... 269 685-9818
 Plainwell *(G-12551)*

LIGHTING FIXTURES: Fluorescent, Commercial

High Q Lighting Inc................................E..... 616 396-3591
 Holland *(G-7665)*

LIGHTING FIXTURES: Indl & Commercial

Alumalight LLC ....E..... 248 457-9302
 Troy *(G-16193)*
Burst Led ....G..... 248 321-6262
 Farmington Hills *(G-4949)*
Command Electronics Inc......................E..... 269 679-4011
 Schoolcraft *(G-14492)*
E-Light LLC ....G..... 734 427-0600
 Commerce Township *(G-3402)*
Energy Design Svc Systems LLC..........F..... 810 227-3377
 Whitmore Lake *(G-17697)*
Global Green Corporation.....................F..... 734 560-1743
 Ann Arbor *(G-473)*
GT Solutions LLC.................................G..... 616 259-0700
 Holland *(G-7655)*
Haworth Inc ....D..... 231 845-0607
 Ludington *(G-10064)*
Hazloc Industries LLC ....G..... 810 679-2551
 Croswell *(G-3597)*
Johnico LLC...E..... 248 895-7820
 Detroit *(G-4164)*
Landmark Energy Development Co ......G..... 586 457-0200
 Sterling Heights *(G-15395)*
Leif Distribution LLC ....E..... 517 481-2122
 Lansing *(G-9308)*
Lumificent Corporation ....F..... 763 424-3702
 Oxford *(G-12356)*
Lyte Poles Incorporated ....D..... 586 771-4610
 Warren *(G-17134)*
Nylube Products Company LLC............E..... 248 852-6500
 Rochester Hills *(G-13486)*
Pro Lighting Group Inc..........................G..... 810 229-5600
 Brighton *(G-1980)*
R-Bo Co Inc..E..... 616 748-9733
 Zeeland *(G-18184)*
Robogistics LLC ....F...... 409 234-1033
 Adrian *(G-91)*
Smart Vision Lights LLC ....F...... 231 722-1199
 Norton Shores *(G-11794)*
Sound Productions Entrmt ....E..... 989 386-2221
 Clare *(G-2889)*
Suntech Industrials LLC........................G..... 734 678-5922
 Ann Arbor *(G-651)*
Woodward Energy Solutions LLC ....F..... 888 967-4533
 Detroit *(G-4448)*

LIGHTING FIXTURES: Motor Vehicle

Mid American AEL LLC ....G..... 810 229-5483
 Brighton *(G-1962)*
Penske Company LLC..........................G..... 248 648-2000
 Bloomfield Hills *(G-1788)*
Progressive Dynamics Inc ....D..... 269 781-4241
 Marshall *(G-10585)*

LIGHTING FIXTURES: Public

Johnico LLC...E..... 248 895-7820
 Detroit *(G-4164)*

LIGHTING FIXTURES: Residential

A & D Lighting ....G..... 269 327-1126
 Kalamazoo *(G-8670)*
Full Spectrum Solutions Inc ....E..... 517 783-3800
 Jackson *(G-8454)*
H U R Enterprises Inc ....G..... 906 774-0833
 Iron Mountain *(G-8284)*
R-Bo Co Inc..E..... 616 748-9733
 Zeeland *(G-18184)*

LIGHTING FIXTURES: Residential, Electric

Universal Manufacturing Co..................F..... 586 463-2560
 Clinton Township *(G-3254)*

LIGHTING FIXTURES: Street

Leif Distribution LLC ....E..... 517 481-2122
 Lansing *(G-9308)*
Solar Tonic LLC....................................G..... 734 368-0215
 Ann Arbor *(G-638)*

LIGHTS: Trouble lights

Arkin Automotive Inc ....G..... 248 542-1192
 Ferndale *(G-5262)*

LIME ROCK: Ground

Great Lakes Aggregates LLC...............D...... 734 379-0311
 South Rockwood *(G-14821)*

LIMESTONE & MARBLE: Dimension

Doug Wirt Enterprises Inc.....................G..... 989 684-5777
 Bay City *(G-1305)*

LIMESTONE: Crushed & Broken

Aggregate and Developing LLC ....G..... 269 217-5492
 Allegan *(G-146)*
Carmeuse Lime Inc ....E..... 906 484-2201
 Cedarville *(G-2566)*
Carmeuse Lime Inc ....E..... 313 849-9268
 River Rouge *(G-13274)*
Carmeuse Lime & Stone Inc ....G..... 989 734-2131
 Rogers City *(G-13614)*
Eggers Excavating LLC........................F..... 989 695-5205
 Freeland *(G-5756)*
F G Cheney Limestone Co ....G..... 269 763-9541
 Bellevue *(G-1454)*
Falcon Trucking Company ....E..... 989 656-2831
 Bay Port *(G-1373)*
Flint Lime Industries Inc........................G..... 313 843-6050
 Detroit *(G-4064)*
Genesee Cut Stone & Marble Co ....E..... 810 743-1800
 Flint *(G-5437)*
O N Minerals ....G..... 906 484-2201
 Cedarville *(G-2569)*
O-N Minerals Michigan Company ....G..... 989 734-2131
 Rogers City *(G-13618)*
O-N Minerals Michigan Company ....G..... 906 484-2201
 Cedarville *(G-2571)*
O-N Minerals Michigan Company ....C..... 989 734-2131
 Rogers City *(G-13619)*
Stoneco Inc..E..... 734 587-7125
 Maybee *(G-10673)*
Waanders Concrete Co ....E..... 269 673-6352
 Allegan *(G-190)*

LIMESTONE: Dimension

Levy Indiana Slag Co ....F..... 313 843-7200
 Dearborn *(G-3733)*
Manigg Enterprises Inc ....F..... 989 356-4986
 Alpena *(G-296)*
Northern Mich Aggregates LLC ....F..... 989 354-3502
 Wixom *(G-17868)*
O-N Minerals Michigan Company ....C..... 989 734-2131
 Rogers City *(G-13619)*

LIMESTONE: Ground

Carmeuse Lime & Stone Inc ....D..... 906 283-3456
 Gulliver *(G-7211)*
O-N Minerals Michigan Company ....D..... 906 484-2201
 Cedarville *(G-2570)*

R E Glancy Inc......................................E..... 989 362-0997
 Tawas City *(G-15677)*
R E Glancy Inc......................................G..... 989 876-6030
 Tawas City *(G-15678)*

LINEN SPLY SVC

Reilchz Inc..G..... 231 421-9600
 Traverse City *(G-16093)*

LINEN SPLY SVC: Coat

Transtar Autobody Tech LLC ....C..... 810 220-3000
 Brighton *(G-1999)*

LINEN SPLY SVC: Uniform

Apparelmaster-Muskegon Inc...............E..... 231 728-5406
 Muskegon *(G-11271)*

LINENS & TOWELS WHOLESALERS

Jackson Manufacturing & Distrg...........G..... 616 451-3030
 Grand Rapids *(G-6550)*

LINERS & COVERS: Fabric

Canvas Shoppe Inc...............................G..... 810 733-1841
 Flint *(G-5395)*
Gibraltar Canvas Inc.............................G..... 734 675-4891
 Rockwood *(G-13604)*
Industrial Bag & Spc Inc........................F..... 248 559-5550
 Southfield *(G-14945)*
Millers Custom Boat Top Inc.................G..... 586 468-5533
 Harrison Township *(G-7340)*

LINERS & LINING

Geomembrane Services Inc..................F..... 231 264-9030
 Kewadin *(G-9038)*
Plesh Industries Inc..............................F..... 716 873-4916
 Brighton *(G-1979)*
Rlh Industries Inc.................................F..... 989 732-0493
 Gaylord *(G-5889)*

LINERS: Indl, Metal Plate

Diversified Tooling Group Inc................F..... 248 837-5828
 Madison Heights *(G-10232)*
Ian Davidson & Assoc Inc.....................G..... 269 925-7552
 Benton Harbor *(G-1512)*

LITHOGRAPHIC PLATES

Adgravers Inc.......................................E..... 313 259-3780
 Detroit *(G-3842)*
Panoplate Lithographics Inc..................G..... 269 343-4644
 Kalamazoo *(G-8840)*
Southern Lithoplate Inc.........................D..... 616 957-2650
 Grand Rapids *(G-6873)*

LOADS: Electronic

Affinity Electronics Inc..........................G..... 586 477-4920
 Fraser *(G-5614)*
Sensor Manufacturing Company...........F..... 248 474-7300
 Novi *(G-11992)*

LOCK & KEY SVCS

Hacks Key Shop Inc..............................F..... 517 485-9488
 Lansing *(G-9380)*

LOCKERS: Refrigerated

Wilson Stamping & Mfg Inc...................G..... 989 823-8521
 Vassar *(G-16820)*

LOCKS

Adjustable Locking Tech LLC................D..... 248 443-9664
 Bloomfield Hills *(G-1742)*
Commando Lock Company LLC ....F..... 248 709-7901
 Troy *(G-16274)*
Euro-Locks Inc ....F..... 616 994-0490
 Holland *(G-7626)*
Strattec Security Corporation................E..... 248 649-9742
 Auburn Hills *(G-1005)*
Weber Security Group Inc....................G..... 586 582-0000
 Mount Clemens *(G-11153)*

LOCKSMITHS

Northwoods Prperty Holdings LLC ....G..... 231 334-3000
 Glen Arbor *(G-5941)*

LOG SPLITTERS

Milan Metal Worx LLC ..... G 734 369-7115
Petersburg *(G-12437)*

LOGGING

Bear Creek Logging ..... G 269 317-7475
Ceresco *(G-2601)*

Bennett Sawmill ..... G 231 734-5733
Evart *(G-4879)*

Bixby Logging ..... G 231 348-9794
Petoskey *(G-12442)*

Bourdo Logging ..... G 269 623-4981
Delton *(G-3816)*

Brent Bastian Logging LLC ..... G 906 482-6378
Hancock *(G-7249)*

Bryan K Sergent ..... G 231 670-2106
Stanwood *(G-15232)*

Budd Logging LLC ..... G 989 329-1578
Farwell *(G-5159)*

Bugay Logging ..... G 906 428-2125
Gladstone *(G-5909)*

Cal Park Logging LLC ..... G 231 796-4662
Big Rapids *(G-1623)*

Cg Logging ..... G 906 322-1018
Brimley *(G-2014)*

Chris Underhill ..... G 231 349-5228
Big Rapids *(G-1624)*

Dale Routley Logging ..... G 231 861-2596
Hart *(G-7370)*

Darrell A Curtice ..... G 231 745-9890
Bitely *(G-1710)*

David Boyd ..... G 517 567-2302
Waldron *(G-16857)*

David Gauss Logging ..... G 517 851-8102
Stockbridge *(G-15588)*

Dawzye Excavation Inc ..... G 906 786-5276
Gladstone *(G-5912)*

Dees Logging ..... G 616 796-8050
Holland *(G-7606)*

Dehaan Forest Products Inc ..... F 906 883-3417
Mass City *(G-10661)*

DJL Logging Inc ..... G 231 590-2012
Manton *(G-10453)*

Donald LII Sons Logging ..... G 231 420-3800
Pellston *(G-12425)*

Doyle Forest Products Inc ..... E 231 832-5586
Paris *(G-12384)*

Duane F Proehl Inc ..... G 906 474-6630
Rapid River *(G-13112)*

Duane Young & Son Lumber ..... G 586 727-1470
Columbus *(G-3378)*

Earl St John Forest Products ..... E 906 497-5667
Spalding *(G-15086)*

East Branch Forest Products ..... G 906 852-3315
Kenton *(G-8995)*

Ej Timber Producers Inc ..... F 231 544-9866
East Jordan *(G-4635)*

Forest Blake Products Inc ..... G 231 879-3913
Fife Lake *(G-5340)*

H & N Hauling ..... G 989 640-3847
Elsie *(G-4796)*

Heritage Forestry LLC ..... G 231 689-5721
White Cloud *(G-17624)*

Holli Forest Products ..... E 906 486-9352
Ishpeming *(G-8346)*

James L Miller ..... G 989 539-5540
Harrison *(G-7313)*

Jerome Miller Lumber Co ..... G 231 745-3694
Baldwin *(G-1084)*

Jesse James Logging ..... G 906 395-6819
Lanse *(G-9193)*

Jim Detweiler ..... G 269 467-7728
Sturgis *(G-15608)*

John Barnes ..... G 231 885-1561
Copemish *(G-3572)*

John Vuk & Son Inc ..... G 906 524-6074
Lanse *(G-9194)*

Johnson Logging Firewoo ..... G 231 578-5833
Ravenna *(G-13122)*

Jungnitsch Bros Logging ..... G 989 233-8091
Saint Charles *(G-14193)*

Keith Falan ..... G 231 834-7358
Grant *(G-7080)*

Kells Sawmill Inc ..... G 906 753-2778
Stephenson *(G-15236)*

Kenneth A Gould ..... G 231 828-4705
Twin Lake *(G-16713)*

Lake Superior Logging ..... G 906 440-3567
Brimley *(G-2016)*

Laws & Ponies Logging Show ..... G 269 838-3942
Delton *(G-3817)*

Lee J Cummings ..... G 906 932-3298
Ironwood *(G-8334)*

Leep Logging Inc ..... G 517 852-1540
Nashville *(G-11459)*

Leonard J Hill Logging Co ..... F 906 337-3435
Calumet *(G-2329)*

Lindsay Nettell Inc ..... G 906 482-3549
Atlantic Mine *(G-737)*

Long Lake Forest Products ..... G 989 239-6527
Harrison *(G-7314)*

Low Impact Logging Inc ..... G 906 250-5117
Iron River *(G-8315)*

Mannisto Forest Products Inc ..... G 906 387-3836
Munising *(G-11245)*

Mark A Nelson ..... G 989 305-5769
Lupton *(G-10092)*

Noble Forestry Inc ..... G 989 866-6495
Blanchard *(G-1711)*

Pinneys Logging Inc ..... G 231 536-7730
East Jordan *(G-4643)*

Pomeroy Forest Products Inc ..... G 906 474-6780
Rapid River *(G-13113)*

Proctor Logging Inc ..... G 231 775-3820
Cadillac *(G-2272)*

Rapid River Rustic Inc ..... E 906 474-6404
Rapid River *(G-13114)*

Rex Rush Inc ..... G 248 684-0221
Commerce Township *(G-3448)*

Robert McIntyre Logging ..... G 906 446-3158
Rapid River *(G-13115)*

Rodney E Harter ..... G 231 796-6734
Big Rapids *(G-1644)*

Rothig Forest Products Inc ..... E 231 266-8292
Irons *(G-8322)*

Roxbury Creek LLC ..... G 989 731-2062
Gaylord *(G-5890)*

S & S Forest Products ..... G 906 892-8268
Munising *(G-11249)*

S&M Logging LLC ..... G 231 821-0588
Twin Lake *(G-16714)*

Saninocencio Logging ..... G 269 945-3567
Hastings *(G-7426)*

Shawn Muma ..... G 989 426-9505
Gladwin *(G-5937)*

Sheski Logging ..... G 906 786-1886
Escanaba *(G-4859)*

Stachnik Logging LLC ..... G 231 275-7641
Cedar *(G-2542)*

Steven Crandell ..... G 231 582-7445
Charlevoix *(G-2632)*

Tarrs Tree Service Inc ..... F 248 528-3313
Troy *(G-16631)*

Thomas Logging LLC ..... G 269 838-2020
Woodland *(G-17943)*

Total Chips Company Inc ..... F 989 866-2610
Shepherd *(G-14731)*

TR Timber Co ..... F 989 345-5350
West Branch *(G-17526)*

Triple Ddd Firewood ..... G 231 734-5215
Evart *(G-4887)*

Usher Logging LLC ..... G 906 238-4261
Arnold *(G-725)*

Utility Supply and Cnstr Co ..... G 231 832-2297
Reed City *(G-13225)*

Van Duinen Forest Products ..... F 231 328-4507
Lake City *(G-9097)*

Vic Freed Logging ..... G 906 477-9933
Engadine *(G-4799)*

Wade Logging ..... G 231 463-0363
Fife Lake *(G-5344)*

Whittaker Timber Corporation ..... G 989 872-3065
Cass City *(G-2525)*

Yamaha Logging ..... G 989 657-1706
Grayling *(G-7119)*

Yates Forest Products Inc ..... G 989 739-8412
Oscoda *(G-12225)*

Younggren Timber Company ..... G 906 355-2272
Covington *(G-3594)*

Zellar Forest Products ..... G 906 586-9817
Germfask *(G-5903)*

LOGGING CAMPS & CONTRACTORS

Aj Logging ..... F 989 725-9610
Henderson *(G-7465)*

Alexa Forest Products ..... G 906 265-2347
Iron River *(G-8307)*

Allen Whitehouse ..... G 231 824-3000
Manton *(G-10450)*

Anderson Logging Inc ..... G 906 482-7505
Houghton *(G-7971)*

Antilla Logging Inc ..... G 906 376-2374
Republic *(G-13244)*

Atwood Forest Products Inc ..... E 616 696-0081
Cedar Springs *(G-2545)*

Beacom Enterprises Inc ..... G 906 647-3831
Pickford *(G-12481)*

Bosanic Lwrnce Sons Tmber Pdts ..... G 906 341-5609
Manistique *(G-10439)*

C D C Logging ..... G 906 524-6369
Lanse *(G-9188)*

Cain Brothers Logging Inc ..... G 906 345-9252
Negaunee *(G-11468)*

Cdn Loading Inc ..... G 906 338-2630
Pelkie *(G-12421)*

Charles William Carr Sr ..... G 231 854-3643
Hesperia *(G-7477)*

Danny K Bundy ..... G 231 590-6924
Manton *(G-10452)*

David Jenks ..... G 810 793-7340
North Branch *(G-11659)*

Davis Logging ..... G 517 617-4550
Bronson *(G-2023)*

Doug Anderson Logging ..... G 906 337-3707
Calumet *(G-2327)*

Duberville Logging ..... G 906 586-6267
Curtis *(G-3619)*

E H Tulgestka & Sons Inc ..... F 989 734-2129
Rogers City *(G-13615)*

Erickson Logging Inc ..... G 906 523-4049
Chassell *(G-2673)*

Fahl Forest Products Inc ..... D 231 258-9734
Mancelona *(G-10390)*

GA Dalbeck Logging LLC ..... F 906 364-3300
Wakefield *(G-16852)*

Gendzwill Co ..... G 906 786-9321
Escanaba *(G-4830)*

Giguere Logging Inc ..... G 906 786-3975
Escanaba *(G-4832)*

Gordon Hackworth Logging ..... G 517 589-9218
Leslie *(G-9541)*

Great Lakes Log & Firewd Co ..... G 231 206-4073
Twin Lake *(G-16712)*

Gustafson Logging ..... G 906 250-2482
Trout Creek *(G-16163)*

Heidtman Logging Inc ..... G 906 249-3914
Marquette *(G-10534)*

Hincka Logging LLC ..... G 989 766-8893
Posen *(G-13069)*

Inman Forest Products Inc ..... G 989 370-4473
Glennie *(G-5943)*

J & D Logging ..... G 517 543-3873
Charlotte *(G-2655)*

J Carey Logging Inc ..... F 906 542-3420
Channing *(G-2603)*

James Pollard Logging ..... G 906 884-6744
Ontonagon *(G-12158)*

James Spicer Inc ..... G 906 265-2385
Iron River *(G-8311)*

Jason Lutke ..... E 231 824-6655
Manton *(G-10456)*

Jeffery Lucas ..... G 231 797-5152
Luther *(G-10093)*

Jeffrey L Hackworth ..... G 517 589-5884
Leslie *(G-9543)*

John Sivula Logging & Cnstr ..... G 906 639-2714
Daggett *(G-3621)*

Joseph Lakosky Logging ..... G 906 573-2783
Manistique *(G-10442)*

Kanerva Forest Products Inc ..... G 906 356-6061
Rock *(G-13554)*

Karttunen Logging ..... G 906 884-4312
Ontonagon *(G-12161)*

Kelly St Amour ..... G 231 625-9789
Cheboygan *(G-2685)*

Ketola Logging ..... G 906 524-6479
Lanse *(G-9196)*

Kk Logging ..... G 906 524-6047
Lanse *(G-9197)*

Kostamo Logging ..... G 906 353-6171
Pelkie *(G-12422)*

Lake Brothers Forest Products ..... G 906 485-5639
Ishpeming *(G-8348)*

Lawrence Beaudoin Logging ..... G 906 296-0549
Lake Linden *(G-9108)*

Logging Long Branch ..... G 231 549-3031
Boyne Falls *(G-1840)*

Lucas Logging ..... G 906 246-3629
Bark River *(G-1120)*

LOGGING CAMPS & CONTRACTORS — PRODUCT SECTION

Lumberjack Logging LLC .... G ... 616 799-4657
Pierson *(G-12484)*
M V A Enterprises Inc .... G ... 906 282-6288
Felch *(G-5168)*
Mark Honkala Logging Inc .... G ... 906 485-1570
Ishpeming *(G-8349)*
Marshall Clayton & Sons Log .... G ... 269 623-8898
Delton *(G-3819)*
Marvin Nelson Forest Products .... F ... 906 384-6700
Cornell *(G-3575)*
McNamara & Mcnamara .... F ... 906 293-5281
Newberry *(G-11580)*
Michael Graves Logging .... G ... 906 387-2852
Wetmore *(G-17615)*
Mid Michigan Logging .... F ... 231 229-4501
Lake City *(G-9093)*
Mike Hughes .... G ... 269 377-3578
Nashville *(G-11461)*
Miljevich Corporation .... F ... 906 229-5367
Wakefield *(G-16853)*
Ndsay Nettell Logging .... G ... 906 482-3549
Atlantic Mine *(G-738)*
Nickels Logging .... G ... 906 563-5880
Norway *(G-11818)*
Patrick Newland Logging Ltd .... G ... 906 524-2255
Lanse *(G-9199)*
Paul Marshall & Son Log LLC .... G ... 269 998-4440
Plainwell *(G-12534)*
Peacocks Eco Log & Sawmill LLC .... G ... 231 250-3462
Morley *(G-11117)*
Pearson Dean Excavating & Log .... G ... 906 932-3513
Ironwood *(G-8337)*
Piwarski Brothers Logging Inc .... G ... 906 265-2914
Iron River *(G-8319)*
Precision Forestry .... G ... 989 619-1016
Onaway *(G-12150)*
Robert Crawford & Son Logging .... G ... 989 379-2712
Lachine *(G-9078)*
Roger Bazuin & Sons Inc .... E ... 231 825-2889
Mc Bain *(G-10684)*
Rosenthal Logging .... G ... 231 348-8168
Petoskey *(G-12473)*
Santti Brothers Inc .... G ... 906 355-2347
Watton *(G-17395)*
Scott Johnson Forest Pdts Co .... G ... 906 482-3978
Houghton *(G-7982)*
Shamco Inc .... G ... 906 265-5065
Iron River *(G-8320)*
Shamion Brothers .... E ... 906 265-5065
Iron River *(G-8321)*
Shawn Muma Logging .... G ... 989 426-6852
Gladwin *(G-5938)*
Smith Logging LLC .... G ... 616 558-0729
Hopkins *(G-7962)*
Spencer Forest Products .... G ... 906 341-6791
Gulliver *(G-7213)*
Steigers Timber Operations .... G ... 906 667-0266
Bessemer *(G-1607)*
Timberline Logging Inc .... F ... 989 731-2794
Gaylord *(G-5895)*
Tom Clisch Logging Inc .... G ... 906 338-2900
Pelkie *(G-12423)*
Tri-Forestry .... G ... 906 474-9379
Rapid River *(G-13116)*
Tuttle Forest Products .... G ... 906 283-3871
Gulliver *(G-7214)*
Usher Logging LLC .... G ... 906 238-4261
Cornell *(G-3576)*
W J Z & Sons Harvesting Inc .... E ... 906 586-6360
Germfask *(G-5902)*
Welch Land & Timber Inc .... G ... 989 848-5197
Curran *(G-3617)*
Wender Logging Inc .... G ... 906 779-1483
Iron Mountain *(G-8305)*
Wood Brothers Logging .... G ... 989 350-6064
Atlanta *(G-734)*
Younggren Farm & Forest Inc .... G ... 906 355-2272
Covington *(G-3593)*

LOGGING: Fuel Wood Harvesting

Dales LLC .... G ... 734 444-4620
Lapeer *(G-9456)*
Vulcan Wood Products Inc .... F ... 906 563-8995
Vulcan *(G-16847)*

LOGGING: Pulpwood Camp, Exc Pulp Mill At Same Site

Dillon Charles Logging & Cnstr .... G ... 906 376-8470
Republic *(G-13245)*

Minerick Logging Inc .... E ... 906 542-3583
Sagola *(G-14187)*

LOGGING: Saw Logs

Gentz Forest Robert Products .... F ... 231 398-9194
Manistee *(G-10423)*
Jns Sawmill .... G ... 989 352-5430
Coral *(G-3574)*

LOGGING: Skidding Logs

Joe Bosanic Forest Products .... G ... 906 341-2037
Manistique *(G-10441)*

LOGGING: Stump Harvesting

Plum Creek Timber Company Inc .... G ... 715 453-7952
Escanaba *(G-4852)*

LOGGING: Timber, Cut At Logging Camp

Bruning Forest Products .... C ... 989 733-2880
Onaway *(G-12145)*
Hytec Equipment .... G ... 906 789-5811
Escanaba *(G-4835)*
K & M Industrial LLC .... G ... 906 420-8770
Gladstone *(G-5914)*
Woodside Logging LLC .... G ... 906 482-0150
Hancock *(G-7259)*

LOGGING: Wheel stock, Hewn

P G K Enterprises LLC .... G ... 248 535-4411
Southfield *(G-14995)*

LOGGING: Wood Chips, Produced In The Field

Chris Muma Forest Products .... F ... 989 426-5916
Gladwin *(G-5927)*
Manigg Enterprises Inc .... F ... 989 356-4986
Alpena *(G-296)*
Turpeinen Bros Inc .... F ... 906 338-2870
Pelkie *(G-12424)*

LOGGING: Wooden Logs

Abcor Partners LLC .... E ... 616 994-9577
Holland *(G-7546)*
Hiawatha Log Homes Inc .... E ... 877 275-9090
Munising *(G-11244)*
Yoder Forest Products L L C .... G ... 989 848-2437
Curran *(G-3618)*

LOOSELEAF BINDERS

Cadillac Prsentation Solutions .... E ... 248 288-9777
Troy *(G-16255)*
Hexon Corporation .... F ... 248 585-7585
Farmington Hills *(G-5018)*

LOTIONS OR CREAMS: Face

Pur E Clat .... G ... 313 208-5763
Farmington Hills *(G-5107)*

LOTIONS: SHAVING

Amour Your Body LLC .... G ... 586 846-3100
Clinton Township *(G-3049)*

LOUDSPEAKERS

Salk Communications Inc .... G ... 248 342-7109
Pontiac *(G-12864)*

LOVING CUPS, STAINLESS STEEL

Isby Industry LLC .... G ... 313 269-4213
Sterling Heights *(G-15377)*

LUBRICANTS: Corrosion Preventive

Doerken Corporation .... G ... 517 522-4600
Grass Lake *(G-7087)*
Henkel US Operations Corp .... B ... 248 588-1082
Madison Heights *(G-10266)*
Sks Industries Inc .... F ... 517 546-1117
Howell *(G-8098)*
Topduck Products LLC .... F ... 517 322-3202
Lansing *(G-9327)*
Xaerus Performance Fluids LLC .... G ... 989 631-7871
Midland *(G-10926)*

LUBRICATING EQPT: Indl

Acumen Technologies Inc .... F ... 586 566-8600
Shelby Township *(G-14541)*
Essex Brass Corporation .... F ... 586 757-8200
Warren *(G-17020)*
G P Reeves Inc .... E ... 616 399-8893
Holland *(G-7639)*
Intellichem LLC .... F ... 810 765-4075
Marine City *(G-10474)*
Lube - Power Inc .... D ... 586 247-6500
Shelby Township *(G-14628)*
M-B-M Manufacturing Inc .... G ... 231 924-9614
Fremont *(G-5778)*
Opco Lubrication Systems Inc .... G ... 231 924-6160
Fremont *(G-5780)*

LUBRICATING OIL & GREASE WHOLESALERS

American Chemical Tech Inc .... E ... 517 223-0300
Fowlerville *(G-5557)*
Bva Inc .... E ... 248 348-4920
New Hudson *(G-11533)*
Condat Corporation .... E ... 734 944-4994
Saline *(G-14383)*
Eastern Oil Company .... E ... 248 333-1333
Pontiac *(G-12819)*
Lubecon Systems Inc .... D ... 231 689-0002
White Cloud *(G-17625)*
Metalworking Lubricants Co .... E ... 248 332-3500
Pontiac *(G-12849)*
Oil Chem Inc .... E ... 810 235-3040
Flint *(G-5476)*
Unist Inc .... E ... 616 949-0853
Grand Rapids *(G-6951)*

LUBRICATING SYSTEMS: Centralized

Pan-Teck Corporation .... G ... 989 792-2422
Saginaw *(G-14118)*

LUBRICATION SYSTEMS & EQPT

Amcol Corporation .... E ... 248 414-5700
Hazel Park *(G-7434)*
E Power Remote Ltd .... G ... 231 689-5448
White Cloud *(G-17621)*
Intersrce Recovery Systems Inc .... E ... 269 375-5100
Kalamazoo *(G-8774)*
Mark One Corporation .... D ... 989 732-2427
Gaylord *(G-5877)*
Orsco Inc .... G ... 314 679-4200
Armada *(G-721)*
Permawick Company Inc .... G ... 248 433-3500
Birmingham *(G-1697)*

LUGGAGE & BRIEFCASES

Mary Boggs Baggs .... G ... 586 731-2513
Shelby Township *(G-14634)*

LUGGAGE & LEATHER GOODS STORES: Leather, Exc Luggage & Shoes

Birlon Group LLC .... G ... 313 551-5341
Inkster *(G-8225)*

LUGGAGE: Traveling Bags

Shaun Jackson Design Inc .... G ... 734 975-7500
Saline *(G-14415)*

LUMBER & BLDG MATLS DEALER, RET: Garage Doors, Sell/Install

Overhead Door Company Alpena .... G ... 989 354-8316
Alpena *(G-305)*

LUMBER & BLDG MATLS DEALERS, RET: Energy Conservation Prdts

Detroit Renewable Energy LLC .... C ... 313 972-5700
Detroit *(G-3999)*

LUMBER & BLDG MATRLS DEALERS, RETAIL: Doors, Wood/Metal

Architectural Design Wdwrk Inc .... G ... 586 726-9050
Shelby Township *(G-14548)*
Quality Door & More Inc .... G ... 989 317-8314
Mount Pleasant *(G-11222)*

PRODUCT SECTION

LUMBER: Hardwood Dimension & Flooring Mills

Wood Smiths Inc ....F 269 372-6432
   Kalamazoo *(G-8927)*

LUMBER & BLDG MTRLS DEALERS, RET: Doors, Storm, Wood/Metal

Bestway Building Supply Co ....G 810 732-6280
   Flint *(G-5388)*
Lsd Investments Inc ....G 248 333-9085
   Bloomfield Hills *(G-1779)*

LUMBER & BLDG MTRLS DEALERS, RET: Planing Mill Prdts/Lumber

Duane Young & Son Lumber ....G 586 727-1470
   Columbus *(G-3378)*
Menomnee Rver Lbr Dmnsions LLC .....E 906 863-2682
   Menominee *(G-10749)*

LUMBER & BLDG MTRLS DEALERS, RET: Windows, Storm, Wood/Metal

Fox Aluminum Products Inc ....E 248 399-4288
   Hazel Park *(G-7438)*
MRM Ida Products Co Inc ....G 313 834-0200
   Detroit *(G-4259)*
Nowaks Window Door & Cab Co ....G 989 734-2808
   Rogers City *(G-13617)*

LUMBER & BUILDING MATERIALS DEALER, RET: Door & Window Prdts

Genex Window Inc ....G 586 754-2917
   Warren *(G-17055)*
Grand Traverse Garage Doors ....E 231 943-9897
   Traverse City *(G-15985)*
Sunburst Shutters ....G 248 674-4600
   Waterford *(G-17378)*
Weathergard Window Company Inc .....D 248 967-8822
   Oak Park *(G-12105)*

LUMBER & BUILDING MATERIALS DEALER, RET: Masonry Matls/Splys

Advance Concrete Products Co ....E 248 887-4173
   Highland *(G-7484)*
Clay & Graham Inc ....G 989 354-5292
   Alpena *(G-283)*
E M I Construction Products ....D 616 392-7207
   Holland *(G-7615)*
Fendt Builders Supply Inc ....E 248 474-3211
   Farmington Hills *(G-4999)*
Genesee Cut Stone & Marble Co ....E 810 743-1800
   Flint *(G-5437)*
L & S Transit Mix Concrete Co ....F 989 354-5363
   Alpena *(G-294)*
Lakeshore Cement Products ....G 989 739-9341
   Oscoda *(G-12213)*
Stevenson Building and Sup Co ....G 734 856-3931
   Lambertville *(G-9185)*

LUMBER & BUILDING MATERIALS DEALERS, RETAIL: Brick

Arquette Concrete & Supply ....G 989 846-4131
   Standish *(G-15216)*
Grand Blanc Cement Pdts Inc ....E 810 694-7500
   Grand Blanc *(G-5967)*
Ludvanwall Inc ....E 616 842-4500
   Spring Lake *(G-15159)*
Newberry Redi-Mix Inc ....G 906 293-5178
   Newberry *(G-11584)*

LUMBER & BUILDING MATERIALS DEALERS, RETAIL: Cement

Darby Ready Mix-Dundee LLC ....F 734 529-7100
   Dundee *(G-4578)*
National Block Company ....E 734 721-4050
   Westland *(G-17582)*
R & R Ready-Mix Inc ....G 989 892-9313
   Bay City *(G-1346)*
Superior Materials LLC ....C 734 941-2479
   Romulus *(G-13735)*

LUMBER & BUILDING MATERIALS DEALERS, RETAIL: Countertops

Kurtis Mfg & Distrg Corp ....E 734 522-7600
   Livonia *(G-9802)*

Rose Corporation ....E 734 426-0005
   Dexter *(G-4508)*

LUMBER & BUILDING MATERIALS DEALERS, RETAIL: Modular Homes

Ritz-Craft Corp PA Inc ....E 517 849-7425
   Jonesville *(G-8668)*

LUMBER & BUILDING MATERIALS DEALERS, RETAIL: Paving Stones

White Lake Excavating Inc ....F 231 894-6918
   Whitehall *(G-17681)*

LUMBER & BUILDING MATERIALS DEALERS, RETAIL: Sand & Gravel

Bouchey and Sons Inc ....G 989 588-4118
   Farwell *(G-5158)*
Lewiston Sand & Gravel Inc ....G 989 786-2742
   Lewiston *(G-9552)*
Maple Valley Concrete Products ....G 517 852-1900
   Nashville *(G-11460)*

LUMBER & BUILDING MATERIALS DEALERS, RETAIL: Siding

Astro Building Products Inc ....G 231 941-0324
   Traverse City *(G-15898)*

LUMBER & BUILDING MATERIALS RET DEALERS: Millwork & Lumber

B & W Woodwork Inc ....G 616 772-4577
   Holland *(G-7564)*
Goodrich Brothers Inc ....E 989 593-2104
   Pewamo *(G-12479)*
Greenia Custom Woodworking Inc ......E 989 868-9790
   Reese *(G-13230)*
Maeder Bros Inc ....E 989 644-2235
   Weidman *(G-17459)*
Phil Elenbaas Millwork Inc ....E 616 791-1616
   Grand Rapids *(G-6754)*
Rare Earth Hardwoods Inc ....F 231 946-0043
   Traverse City *(G-16090)*
W S Townsend Company ....G 517 393-7300
   Lansing *(G-9433)*
Warner Door ....G 989 823-8397
   Vassar *(G-16817)*

LUMBER & BUILDING MATLS DEALERS, RET: Concrete/Cinder Block

Arbor Stone ....G 517 750-1340
   Spring Arbor *(G-15119)*
Best Block Company ....E 586 772-7000
   Warren *(G-16956)*
Burrell Tri-County Vaults Inc ....F 734 483-2024
   Ypsilanti *(G-18058)*
Ferguson Block Co Inc ....F 810 653-2812
   Davison *(G-3647)*
Fisher Sand and Gravel Company ....E 989 835-7187
   Midland *(G-10861)*
Gildners Concrete ....G 989 356-5156
   Alpena *(G-292)*
Guidobono Concrete Inc ....F 810 229-2666
   Brighton *(G-1935)*
Sandusky Concrete & Supply ....G 810 648-2627
   Sandusky *(G-14442)*

LUMBER & BUILDING MTRLS DEALERS, RET: Insulation Mtrl, Bldg

Insulation Wholesale Supply ....G 269 968-9746
   Battle Creek *(G-1200)*
Northwoods Manufacturing Inc ....D 906 779-2370
   Kingsford *(G-9065)*

LUMBER: Cants, Resawn

Diversified Pdts & Svcs LLC ....G 616 836-6600
   Holland *(G-7608)*

LUMBER: Dimension, Hardwood

Menomnee Rver Lbr Dmnsions LLC .....E 906 863-2682
   Menominee *(G-10749)*

LUMBER: Furniture Dimension Stock, Softwood

Met Inc ....G 231 845-1737
   Ludington *(G-10072)*
Pine Tech Inc ....E 989 426-0006
   Plymouth *(G-12716)*

LUMBER: Hardwood Dimension

Component Solutions LLC ....E 906 863-2682
   Menominee *(G-10729)*
Devereaux Saw Mill Inc ....D 989 593-2552
   Pewamo *(G-12478)*
Timber Pdts Mich Ltd Partnr ....G 906 779-2000
   Iron Mountain *(G-8303)*

LUMBER: Hardwood Dimension & Flooring Mills

Atwood Forest Products Inc ....E 616 696-0081
   Cedar Springs *(G-2545)*
B & B Heartwoods Inc ....G 734 332-9525
   Ann Arbor *(G-379)*
Banks Hardwoods Inc ....D 269 483-2323
   White Pigeon *(G-17645)*
Besse Forest Products Inc ....E 906 353-7193
   Baraga *(G-1098)*
Burt Moeke & Son Hardwoods ....E 231 587-5388
   Mancelona *(G-10388)*
Counterpoint By Hlf ....D 734 699-7100
   Van Buren Twp *(G-16754)*
Craftwood Industries Inc ....E 616 796-1209
   Holland *(G-7599)*
Duane Young & Son Lumber ....G 586 727-1470
   Columbus *(G-3378)*
Dyers Sawmill Inc ....E 231 768-4438
   Leroy *(G-9531)*
Erickson Lumber & True Value ....G 906 524-6295
   Lanse *(G-9191)*
Forest Elders Products Inc ....F 616 866-9317
   Rockford *(G-13569)*
Forte Industries Mill Inc ....F 906 753-6256
   Stephenson *(G-15235)*
Genesis Seating Inc ....E 616 954-1040
   Grand Rapids *(G-6436)*
Genesis Seating Inc ....G 616 954-1040
   Grand Rapids *(G-6437)*
Grants Woodshop Inc ....E 517 543-1116
   Charlotte *(G-2653)*
Jaroche Brothers Inc ....F 231 525-8100
   Wolverine *(G-17934)*
John A Biewer Lumber Company ....D 231 825-2855
   Mc Bain *(G-10682)*
Kentwood Manufacturing Co ....E 616 698-6370
   Grand Rapids *(G-6579)*
Lumber Jack Hardwoods Inc ....F 906 863-7090
   Menominee *(G-10742)*
Maple Ridge Hardwoods Inc ....E 989 873-5305
   Sterling *(G-15244)*
Metter Flooring LLC ....G 517 914-2004
   Rives Junction *(G-13309)*
Nettleton Wood Products Inc ....G 906 297-5791
   De Tour Village *(G-3668)*
North American Forest Products ....G 269 663-8500
   Edwardsburg *(G-4770)*
Northern Mich Hardwoods Inc ....F 231 347-4575
   Petoskey *(G-12460)*
Ottawa Forest Products Inc ....E 906 932-9701
   Ironwood *(G-8336)*
Paris North Hardwood Lumber ....E 231 584-2500
   Elmira *(G-4792)*
Pine Tech Inc ....E 989 426-0006
   Plymouth *(G-12716)*
Potlatchdeltic Corporation ....C 906 346-3215
   Gwinn *(G-7222)*
Quigley Lumber Inc ....G 989 257-5116
   South Branch *(G-14750)*
Richwood Industries Inc ....E 616 243-2700
   Grand Rapids *(G-6824)*
Ron Fisk Hardwoods Inc ....G 616 887-3826
   Sparta *(G-15108)*
Vocational Strategies Inc ....E 906 482-6142
   Calumet *(G-2335)*
Weber Bros Sawmill Inc ....E 989 644-2206
   Mount Pleasant *(G-11235)*
Whitens Kiln & Lumber Inc ....F 906 498-2116
   Hermansville *(G-7469)*
William S Wixtrom ....G 906 376-8247
   Republic *(G-13247)*

LUMBER: Kiln Dried

Banks Hardwoods Inc .... D 269 483-2323
White Pigeon *(G-17645)*
Forestry Management Svcs Inc .... C 517 456-7431
Clinton *(G-3020)*
Lumber Jack Hardwoods Inc .... F 906 863-7090
Menominee *(G-10742)*
PDM Company .... F 231 946-4444
Lake Leelanau *(G-9105)*

LUMBER: Plywood, Hardwood

Bay Wood Homes Inc .... E 989 245-4156
Fenton *(G-5187)*
Coldwater Veneer Inc .... C 517 278-5676
Coldwater *(G-3297)*
Dyers Sawmill Inc .... E 231 768-4438
Leroy *(G-9531)*
Forest Corullo Products Corp .... E 906 667-0275
Bessemer *(G-1605)*
Forte Industries Mill Inc .... F 906 753-6256
Stephenson *(G-15235)*
Manthei Veneer Mill Inc .... G 231 347-4688
Petoskey *(G-12458)*
Midwest Panel Systems Inc .... E 517 486-4844
Blissfield *(G-1720)*
Northern Mich Chrstn Cunseling .... G 989 278-2590
Lachine *(G-9075)*
Northern Mich Endocrine Pllc .... G 989 281-1125
Roscommon *(G-13752)*
Northern Mich Hardwoods Inc .... F 231 347-4575
Petoskey *(G-12460)*
Northern Mich Mmrals Monuments ... G 231 290-2333
Cheboygan *(G-2688)*
Northern Mich Pain Specialist .... G 231 487-4650
Petoskey *(G-12461)*
Northern Mich Residential Svcs .... G 231 547-6144
Vanderbilt *(G-16808)*
Northern Mich Rgional Hlth Sys .... F 231 487-4094
Petoskey *(G-12462)*
Northern Mich Supportive Hsing .... G 231 929-1309
Traverse City *(G-16050)*
Northern Mich Wdding Offciants .... G 231 938-1683
Williamsburg *(G-17715)*
Ply-Forms Incorporated .... F 989 686-5681
Bay City *(G-1341)*
Programmed Products Corp .... D 248 348-7755
Novi *(G-11983)*
Timber Products Co Ltd Partnr .... C 906 452-6221
Munising *(G-11250)*

LUMBER: Plywood, Hardwood or Hardwood Faced

Decatur Wood Products Inc .... E 269 657-6041
Decatur *(G-3802)*

LUMBER: Plywood, Prefinished, Hardwood

Rosati Specialties LLC .... G 586 783-3866
Clinton Township *(G-3214)*

LUMBER: Plywood, Softwood

Forest Corullo Products Corp .... E 906 667-0275
Bessemer *(G-1605)*
Forte Industries Mill Inc .... F 906 753-6256
Stephenson *(G-15235)*
Ply-Forms Incorporated .... F 989 686-5681
Bay City *(G-1341)*

LUMBER: Resawn, Small Dimension

Nelsons Saw Mill Inc .... G 231 829-5220
Tustin *(G-16711)*
North American Forest Products .... C 269 663-8500
Edwardsburg *(G-4769)*

LUMBER: Stacking Or Sticking

Rapid River Rustic Inc .... E 906 474-6404
Rapid River *(G-13114)*

LUMBER: Treated

/// 702 Cedar River Lbr Inc .... E 906 497-5365
Powers *(G-13076)*
Paris North Hardwood Lumber .... E 231 584-2500
Elmira *(G-4792)*
Riverbend Woodwroring .... G 231 869-4965
Pentwater *(G-12431)*

Straits Corporation .... F 989 684-5088
Tawas City *(G-15679)*
Straits Operations Company .... G 989 684-5088
Tawas City *(G-15680)*
Straits Service Corporation .... F 989 684-5088
Tawas City *(G-15681)*
Straits Wood Treating Inc .... G 989 684-5088
Tawas City *(G-15682)*
Ufp Lansing LLC .... F 517 322-0025
Lansing *(G-9328)*
Utility Supply and Cnstr Co .... G 231 832-2297
Reed City *(G-13225)*
West Branch Wood Treating Inc .... F 989 343-0066
West Branch *(G-17528)*
Yooper WD Wrks Restoration LLC ...... G 906 203-0056
Sault Sainte Marie *(G-14480)*

LUMBER: Veneer, Hardwood

J A S Veneer & Lumber Inc .... E 906 635-0710
Sault Sainte Marie *(G-14466)*
Manthei Inc .... C 231 347-4672
Petoskey *(G-12456)*
Northern Michigan Veneers Inc .... D 906 428-1082
Gladstone *(G-5917)*
Quincy Woodwrights LLC .... G 808 397-0818
Houghton *(G-7981)*
Timber Pdts Mich Ltd Partnr .... C 906 779-2000
Iron Mountain *(G-8303)*

LUNCHROOMS & CAFETERIAS

Bay Bread Co .... F 231 922-8022
Traverse City *(G-15906)*

MACHINE PARTS: Stamped Or Pressed Metal

Allen Tool .... G 517 566-2200
Sunfield *(G-15644)*
Bay Manufacturing Corporation .... E 989 358-7198
Alpena *(G-281)*
Burnside Industries LLC .... D 231 798-3394
Norton Shores *(G-11811)*
Covenant Cpitl Investments Inc .... F 248 477-4230
Farmington Hills *(G-4967)*
D & D Driers Timber Product .... G 906 224-7251
Wakefield *(G-16849)*
Diversfied Prcurement Svcs LLC .... G 248 821-1147
Ferndale *(G-5280)*
Echo Quality Grinding Inc .... G 231 544-6637
Central Lake *(G-2591)*
Hti Associates LLC .... E 616 399-5430
Holland *(G-7682)*
Hz Industries Inc .... B 616 453-4491
Grand Rapids *(G-6521)*
Jad Products Inc .... G 517 456-4810
Clinton *(G-3024)*
Ka-Wood Gear & Machine Co .... E 248 585-8870
Madison Heights *(G-10287)*
L Barge & Associates Inc .... F 248 582-3430
Ferndale *(G-5297)*
Max2 LLC .... F 269 468-3452
Coloma *(G-3360)*
Metal Stmping Spport Group LLC .... F 586 777-7440
Roseville *(G-13834)*
Nelson Manufacturing Inc .... G 810 648-0065
Sandusky *(G-14440)*
Ort Tool & Die Corporation .... D 419 242-9553
Erie *(G-4807)*
P-T Stamping Co Ltd .... G 517 278-5961
Coldwater *(G-3316)*
Paradigm Engineering Inc .... E 586 776-5910
Roseville *(G-13849)*
PEC of America Corporation .... F 248 675-3130
Novi *(G-11972)*
Pentar Stamping Inc .... E 517 782-0700
Jackson *(G-8549)*
Pinnacle Tool Incorporated .... E 616 257-2700
Wyoming *(G-18027)*
R & L Machine Products Inc .... G 734 992-2574
Romulus *(G-13725)*
Rel Machine Inc .... G 906 337-3018
Calumet *(G-2332)*
Reliance Metal Products Inc .... G 734 641-3334
Westland *(G-17595)*
Riverside Tool & Mold Inc .... F 989 435-9142
Beaverton *(G-1390)*
Rj Acquisition Corp .... E 586 268-2300
Sterling Heights *(G-15474)*
Schaller Corporation .... C 586 949-6000
Chesterfield *(G-2837)*

Sharp Industries Incorporated .... G 810 229-6305
Brighton *(G-1989)*
Unique Products .... G 616 794-3800
Belding *(G-1430)*
West Mich Auto Stl & Engrg Inc .... E 616 560-8198
Belding *(G-1431)*

MACHINE SHOPS

Advanced Automotive Group LLC .... F 586 206-2478
Clay *(G-2991)*
Aero Marine Inc .... G 734 721-6241
Westland *(G-17539)*
American Axle & Mfg Inc .... D 248 522-4500
Southfield *(G-14836)*
Art Laser Inc .... F 248 391-6600
Auburn Hills *(G-780)*
B & B Custom and Prod Wldg .... F 517 524-7121
Spring Arbor *(G-15120)*
Benzie Manufacturing LLC .... G 231 631-0498
Frankfort *(G-5599)*
Breco LLC .... G 517 317-2211
Quincy *(G-13090)*
Burrow Industries Inc .... F 734 847-1842
Temperance *(G-15824)*
David A Mohr Jr .... G 517 266-2694
Adrian *(G-58)*
Demmer Corporation .... D 517 703-3116
Lansing *(G-9216)*
Demmer Corporation .... G 517 703-3163
Lansing *(G-9218)*
Demmer Corporation .... D 517 703-3131
Lansing *(G-9219)*
Demmer Corporation .... E 517 321-3600
Lansing *(G-9287)*
Detroit Edge Tool Company .... D 313 366-4120
Detroit *(G-3983)*
Detroit Edge Tool Company .... E 586 776-1598
Roseville *(G-13794)*
Dorr Industries Inc .... F 616 681-9440
Dorr *(G-4523)*
Dowding Industries Inc .... E 517 663-5455
Eaton Rapids *(G-4720)*
E & C Manufacturing LLC .... F 248 330-0400
Troy *(G-16332)*
E & D Engineering Systems LLC .... G 989 246-0770
Gladwin *(G-5929)*
Elco Inc .... E 586 778-6858
Roseville *(G-13799)*
Enkon LLC .... F 937 890-5678
Manchester *(G-10405)*
Extreme Machine Inc .... D 810 231-0521
Whitmore Lake *(G-17699)*
Falcon Consulting Services LLC .... G 989 262-9325
Alpena *(G-288)*
Hart Industries LLC .... F 313 588-1837
Sterling Heights *(G-15366)*
Independent Machine Co Inc .... E 906 428-4524
Escanaba *(G-4836)*
Jems of Litchfield Inc .... F 517 542-5367
Litchfield *(G-9605)*
Johnson Precision Mold & Engrg .... G 269 651-2553
Sturgis *(G-15609)*
Knapp Manufacturing Inc .... F 517 279-9538
Coldwater *(G-3311)*
L & L Pattern Inc .... G 231 733-2646
Muskegon *(G-11359)*
Lakeside Boring Inc .... G 586 286-8883
Clinton Township *(G-3159)*
Letty Manufacturing Inc .... G 248 461-6604
Commerce Township *(G-3420)*
M & M Services Inc .... G 248 619-9861
Troy *(G-16467)*
Merchants Automatic Pdts Inc .... E 734 829-0020
Canton *(G-2401)*
Merrill Technologies Group Inc .... D 989 791-6676
Saginaw *(G-14090)*
Metal Arc Inc .... E 231 865-3111
Muskegon *(G-11375)*
Michigan Slotting Company Inc .... F 586 772-1270
Warren *(G-17154)*
Morren Mold & Machine Inc .... G 616 892-7474
Allendale *(G-223)*
Mountain Machine LLC .... F 734 480-2200
Van Buren Twp *(G-16774)*
Nephew Fabrication Inc .... G 616 875-2121
Zeeland *(G-18168)*
P2r Metal Fabrication Inc .... G 888 727-5587
Macomb *(G-10151)*
Production Dev Systems LLC .... F 810 648-2111
Sandusky *(G-14441)*

Prototech Laser Inc ....E.... 586 598-6900
Chesterfield (G-2827)
Prototype Cast Mfg Inc ....G.... 586 739-0180
Shelby Township (G-14674)
Quality Cavity Inc ....F.... 248 344-9995
Wixom (G-17882)
Roush Industries Inc ....C.... 734 779-7000
Livonia (G-9914)
Spec Technologies Inc ....D.... 586 726-0000
Shelby Township (G-14700)
Stanhope Tool Inc ....F.... 248 585-5711
Madison Heights (G-10360)
Thermotron Industries Inc ....E.... 616 928-9044
Holland (G-7829)
Thierica Equipment Corporation ....E.... 616 453-6570
Grand Rapids (G-6928)
Trend Performance Products ....E.... 586 792-6620
Clinton Township (G-3251)
West Michigan Grinding Svc Inc ....F.... 231 739-4245
Norton Shores (G-11805)

MACHINE TOOL ACCESS: Arbors

Hydra-Lock Corporation ....E.... 586 783-5007
Mount Clemens (G-11133)
SB Investments LLC ....E.... 734 462-9478
Livonia (G-9921)

MACHINE TOOL ACCESS: Balancing Machines

Schenck USA Corp ....E.... 248 377-2100
Southfield (G-15024)

MACHINE TOOL ACCESS: Boring Attachments

Borite Manufacturing Corp ....G.... 248 588-7260
Madison Heights (G-10205)
Harroun Enterprises Inc ....G.... 810 629-9885
Fenton (G-5219)
Johan Van De Weerd Co Inc ....G.... 517 542-3817
Litchfield (G-9606)
Lightning Machine Holland LLC ....F.... 616 786-9280
Holland (G-7725)
Raal Industries Inc ....G.... 734 782-6216
Flat Rock (G-5361)
Riviera Industries Inc ....G.... 313 381-5500
Allen Park (G-206)

MACHINE TOOL ACCESS: Broaches

Admiral Broach Company Inc ....E.... 586 468-8411
Clinton Township (G-3037)
Apollo Broach Inc ....G.... 734 467-5750
Westland (G-17542)
Associated Broach Corporation ....E.... 810 798-9112
Almont (G-252)
Avon Broach & Prod Co LLC ....E.... 248 650-8080
Rochester Hills (G-13372)
Diamond Broach Company ....G.... 586 757-5131
Warren (G-17002)
Federal Broach & Mch Co LLC ....C.... 989 539-7420
Harrison (G-7311)
General Broach & Engrg Inc ....E.... 586 726-4300
Troy (G-16381)
General Broach Company ....E.... 517 458-7555
Morenci (G-11109)
General Broach Company ....E.... 517 458-7555
Morenci (G-11110)
J & L Turning Inc ....F.... 810 765-5755
East China (G-4623)
Kingsford Broach & Tool Inc ....E.... 906 774-4917
Kingsford (G-9060)
Laydon Enterprises Inc ....E.... 906 774-4633
Iron Mountain (G-8288)
Miller Broach Inc ....D.... 810 395-8810
Capac (G-2449)
Pioneer Michigan Broach Co ....F.... 231 768-5800
Leroy (G-9536)
Tazz Broach and Machine Inc ....G.... 586 296-7755
Harrison Township (G-7352)
Triangle Broach Company ....F.... 313 838-2150
Detroit (G-4408)
Utica Enterprises Inc ....C.... 586 726-4300
Troy (G-16670)
Wachtel Tool & Broach Inc ....G.... 586 758-0110
Saint Clair (G-14236)
Warren Broach & Machine Corp ....F.... 586 254-7080
Sterling Heights (G-15544)
Wolverine Broach Co Inc ....E.... 586 468-4445
Harrison Township (G-7356)

MACHINE TOOL ACCESS: Cams

Modern CAM and Tool Co ....G.... 734 946-9800
Taylor (G-15745)
Techni CAM and Manufacturing ....F.... 734 261-6477
Livonia (G-9954)

MACHINE TOOL ACCESS: Counterbores, Metalworking

V J Industries Inc ....F.... 810 364-6470
Marine City (G-10486)

MACHINE TOOL ACCESS: Cutting

Accurate Carbide Tool Co Inc ....F.... 989 755-0429
Saginaw (G-13991)
Acme Grooving Tool Co ....F.... 800 633-8828
Clarkston (G-2903)
Action Tool & Machine Inc ....E.... 810 229-6300
Brighton (G-1877)
Adaptable Tool Supply LLC ....F.... 248 439-0866
Clawson (G-2970)
American Lap Company ....G.... 231 526-7121
Harbor Springs (G-7273)
Apollo Tool & Engineering Inc ....F.... 616 735-4934
Grand Rapids (G-6172)
Aw Carbide Fabricators Inc ....F.... 586 294-1850
Fraser (G-5626)
Bitner Tooling Technologies ....F.... 586 803-1100
Sterling Heights (G-15275)
Breckers ABC Tool Company Inc ....F.... 586 779-1122
Roseville (G-13778)
Breesport Holdings Inc ....C.... 248 685-9500
Milford (G-10956)
Bullion Tool Technology LLC ....G.... 313 881-1404
Harper Woods (G-7300)
Carbide Form Master Inc ....G.... 248 625-9373
Davisburg (G-3629)
Carbide Technologies Inc ....E.... 586 296-5200
Fraser (G-5634)
Caro Carbide Corporation ....E.... 248 588-4252
Troy (G-16260)
Ceratizit Usa Inc ....C.... 586 759-2280
Warren (G-16977)
Champion Tool Company ....G.... 248 474-6200
Farmington Hills (G-4961)
Clymer Manufacturing Company ....G.... 248 853-5555
Rochester Hills (G-13389)
Cogsdill Tool Products Inc ....G.... 734 744-4500
Livonia (G-9685)
Cole Carbide Industries Inc ....F.... 248 276-1278
Lake Orion (G-9129)
Cole Carbide Industries Inc ....D.... 989 872-4348
Cass City (G-2513)
Colonial Tool Sales & Svc LLC ....F.... 734 946-2733
Taylor (G-15703)
Complete Cutting Tl & Mfg Inc ....G.... 248 662-9811
Wixom (G-17789)
Cougar Cutting Tools Inc ....F.... 586 469-1310
Clinton Township (G-3091)
Dijet Incorporated ....G.... 734 454-9100
Plymouth (G-12612)
Dumbarton Tool Inc ....F.... 231 775-4342
Cadillac (G-2245)
Ecco Tool Co Inc ....G.... 248 349-0840
Novi (G-11878)
Elk Lake Tool Co ....E.... 231 264-5616
Elk Rapids (G-4777)
Ellsworth Cutting Tools LLC ....F.... 586 598-6040
Chesterfield (G-2772)
Engineered Tools Corp ....D.... 989 673-8733
Caro (G-2468)
Evans Tool & Engineering Inc ....F.... 616 791-6333
Grand Rapids (G-6389)
Fab-Jet Services LLC ....G.... 586 463-9622
Clinton Township (G-3112)
Fsp Inc ....F.... 248 585-0760
Troy (G-16375)
Global CNC Industries Ltd ....E.... 734 464-1920
Plymouth (G-12629)
Global Tooling Systems LLC ....E.... 586 726-0500
Macomb (G-10127)
Guhring Inc ....E.... 262 784-6730
Novi (G-11892)
Howell Tool Service Inc ....F.... 517 548-1114
Howell (G-8052)
I & G Tool Co Inc ....E.... 586 777-7690
New Baltimore (G-11485)
Ideal Heated Knives Inc ....G.... 248 437-1510
New Hudson (G-11545)
Indexable Cutter Engineering ....G.... 586 598-1540
Chesterfield (G-2787)
J E Wood Co ....F.... 248 585-5711
Madison Heights (G-10279)
Joint Production Tech Inc ....E.... 586 786-0080
Macomb (G-10133)
Kel Tool Inc ....G.... 517 750-4515
Spring Arbor (G-15123)
Kennametal Inc ....D.... 231 946-2100
Traverse City (G-16018)
Krebs Tool Inc ....G.... 734 697-8611
Van Buren Twp (G-16768)
Kyocera Unimerco Tooling Inc ....E.... 734 944-4433
Saline (G-14397)
M C Carbide Tool Co ....F.... 248 486-9590
Wixom (G-17850)
Mac-Tech Tooling Corporation ....G.... 248 743-1400
Troy (G-16468)
Mapal Inc ....D.... 810 364-8020
Port Huron (G-12939)
Motor Tool Manufacturing Co ....G.... 734 425-3300
Livonia (G-9850)
Pace Grinding Inc ....G.... 231 861-0448
Shelby (G-14533)
PL Schmitt Crbide Toling LLC ....G.... 517 522-6891
Grass Lake (G-7092)
Precision Tool Company Inc ....E.... 231 733-0811
Muskegon (G-11406)
Primary Tool & Cutter Grinding ....F.... 248 588-1530
Madison Heights (G-10337)
Pyramid Tool Company Inc ....G.... 248 549-0602
Royal Oak (G-13960)
Qc American LLC ....G.... 734 961-0300
Ypsilanti (G-18098)
R L Schmitt Company Inc ....E.... 734 525-9310
Livonia (G-9905)
Reif Carbide Tool Co Inc ....F.... 586 754-1890
Warren (G-17219)
RTS Cutting Tools Inc ....E.... 586 954-1900
Clinton Township (G-3217)
S F S Carbide Tool ....G.... 989 777-3890
Saginaw (G-14135)
Seco Holding Co Inc ....A.... 248 528-5200
Troy (G-16596)
Selmuro Ltd ....E.... 810 603-2117
Grand Blanc (G-5983)
Severance Tool Industries Inc ....E.... 989 777-5500
Saginaw (G-14146)
Severance Tool Industries Inc ....G.... 989 777-5500
Saginaw (G-14147)
Shape Dynamics Intl Inc ....G.... 231 733-2164
Muskegon (G-11421)
Shouse Tool Inc ....F.... 810 629-0391
Fenton (G-5238)
Simonds International LLC ....D.... 231 527-2322
Big Rapids (G-1645)
Southwest Broach ....G.... 714 356-2967
Cadillac (G-2277)
Spartan Carbide Inc ....E.... 586 285-9786
Fraser (G-5727)
Star Cutter Co ....E.... 248 474-8200
Farmington Hills (G-5129)
Steelcraft Tool Co Inc ....E.... 734 522-7130
Livonia (G-9945)
Sterling Edge Inc ....G.... 248 438-6034
Wixom (G-17897)
Stoney Crest Regrind Service ....F.... 989 777-7190
Bridgeport (G-1858)
Teknikut Corporation ....G.... 586 778-7150
Canton (G-2435)
Tool Service Company Inc ....G.... 586 296-2500
Fraser (G-5738)
Tool-Craft Industries Inc ....F.... 248 549-0077
Sterling Heights (G-15525)
TS Carbide Inc ....G.... 248 486-8330
Commerce Township (G-3455)
Universal / Devlieg Inc ....F.... 989 752-3077
Saginaw (G-14173)
Wit-Son Carbide Tool Inc ....E.... 231 536-2247
East Jordan (G-4648)
Wolverine Special Tool Inc ....E.... 616 791-1027
Grand Rapids (G-7000)
Wood-Cutters Tooling Inc ....G.... 616 257-7930
Grandville (G-7076)
Workblades Inc ....E.... 586 778-0060
Warren (G-17297)
Wyser Innovative Products LLC ....G.... 616 583-9225
Byron Center (G-2218)

PRODUCT

Employee Codes: A=Over 500 employees, B=251-500
C=101-250, D=51-100, E=20-50, F=10-19, G=3-9

2020 Harris Michigan
Industrial Directory

1273

MACHINE TOOL ACCESS: Cutting

Zimmermann Engineering Co Inc.........G...... 248 358-0044
Southfield *(G-15070)*

MACHINE TOOL ACCESS: Diamond Cutting, For Turning, Etc

Crystal Cut Tool Inc ....G...... 734 494-5076
Romulus *(G-13665)*
Di-Coat Corporation.............................E...... 248 349-1211
Novi *(G-11868)*
Diamond Tool Manufacturing Inc ......E...... 734 416-1900
Plymouth *(G-12611)*
Principal Diamond Works ....G...... 248 589-1111
Madison Heights *(G-10338)*
Service Diamond Tool Company ....G...... 248 669-3100
Novi *(G-11993)*
Sidley Diamond Tool Company ....E...... 734 261-7970
Garden City *(G-5841)*

MACHINE TOOL ACCESS: Dies, Thread Cutting

M & M Thread & Assembly Inc............G...... 248 583-9696
Sterling Heights *(G-15405)*
Mc Pherson Industrial Corp ....D...... 586 752-5555
Romeo *(G-13633)*

MACHINE TOOL ACCESS: Dresser, Abrasive Wheel Or Other

Abrasive Diamond Tool Company........E...... 248 588-4800
Madison Heights *(G-10179)*

MACHINE TOOL ACCESS: Dressing/Wheel Crushing Attach, Diamond

Truing Systems Inc ....F...... 248 588-9060
Troy *(G-16654)*

MACHINE TOOL ACCESS: Drill Bushings, Drilling Jig

Carbide Surface Company ....G...... 586 465-6110
Clinton Township *(G-3075)*
Colonial Bushings Inc ....F...... 586 954-3880
Clinton Township *(G-3082)*
M Curry Corporation ....E...... 989 777-7950
Saginaw *(G-14080)*

MACHINE TOOL ACCESS: Drills

Ace Drill Corporation............................G...... 517 265-5184
Adrian *(G-42)*
Drill Technology ....G...... 616 676-1287
Ada *(G-14)*
Fulgham Machine & Tool Company ....G...... 517 937-8316
Jackson *(G-8453)*
Link Manufacturing Inc........................E...... 231 238-8741
Indian River *(G-8219)*
Ossineke Industries Inc........................D...... 989 471-2197
Ossineke *(G-12230)*

MACHINE TOOL ACCESS: End Mills

Award Cutter Company Inc..................F...... 616 531-0430
Grand Rapids *(G-6196)*
Conical Cutting Tools Inc.....................E...... 616 531-8500
Grand Rapids *(G-6299)*
P L Schmitt Crbide Tooling LLC ....G...... 313 706-5756
Grass Lake *(G-7090)*
Precision Components ....F...... 248 588-5650
Troy *(G-16559)*

MACHINE TOOL ACCESS: Files

Fullerton Tool Company Inc ....C...... 989 799-4550
Saginaw *(G-14041)*

MACHINE TOOL ACCESS: Hobs

Tawas Tool Co Inc ....D...... 989 362-6121
East Tawas *(G-4695)*
Tawas Tool Co Inc ....D...... 989 362-0414
East Tawas *(G-4696)*

MACHINE TOOL ACCESS: Honing Heads

Nagel Precision Inc..............................C...... 734 426-5650
Ann Arbor *(G-568)*

MACHINE TOOL ACCESS: Hopper Feed Devices

Owsso Automation Inc........................G...... 989 725-8804
Owosso *(G-12307)*

MACHINE TOOL ACCESS: Knives, Metalworking

Detroit Edge Tool Company ....E...... 586 776-1598
Roseville *(G-13794)*
Detroit Edge Tool Company ....D...... 313 366-4120
Detroit *(G-3983)*

MACHINE TOOL ACCESS: Machine Attachments & Access, Drilling

Special Drill and Reamer Corp ....F...... 248 588-5333
Madison Heights *(G-10356)*

MACHINE TOOL ACCESS: Milling Machine Attachments

A & D Run Off Inc.................................G...... 231 759-0950
Muskegon *(G-11256)*
Bob G Machining LLC ....G...... 586 285-1400
Clinton Township *(G-3068)*
Moehrle Inc...F...... 734 761-2000
Ann Arbor *(G-562)*

MACHINE TOOL ACCESS: Pushers

Excel Screw Machine Tools ....G...... 313 383-4200
Taylor *(G-15717)*

MACHINE TOOL ACCESS: Rotary Tables

Technical Rotary Services Inc ....G...... 586 772-6755
Warren *(G-17264)*

MACHINE TOOL ACCESS: Shaping Tools

Hanchett Manufacturing Inc................C...... 231 796-7678
Big Rapids *(G-1632)*

MACHINE TOOL ACCESS: Sockets

G A Machine Company Inc ....G...... 313 836-5646
Detroit *(G-4074)*
Lance Industries LLC ....G...... 248 549-1968
Madison Heights *(G-10296)*
Universal Tool Inc ....G...... 248 733-9800
Troy *(G-16665)*

MACHINE TOOL ACCESS: Threading Tools

A A Anchor Bolt Inc ....F...... 248 349-6565
Northville *(G-11675)*

MACHINE TOOL ACCESS: Tool Holders

Active Tooling LLC ....F...... 616 875-8111
Zeeland *(G-18109)*
FL Tool Holders LLC ....E...... 734 591-0134
Livonia *(G-9736)*
Jade Tool Inc ....E...... 231 946-7710
Traverse City *(G-16008)*
T M Smith Tool Intl Corp......................E...... 586 468-1465
Mount Clemens *(G-11151)*
TEC Industries Inc ....G...... 248 446-9560
New Hudson *(G-11558)*
Universal/Devlieg LLC ....F...... 989 752-7700
Saginaw *(G-14174)*

MACHINE TOOL ACCESS: Tools & Access

American Broach & Machine Co ....E...... 734 961-0300
Ypsilanti *(G-18051)*
Briggs Industries Inc ....E...... 586 749-5191
Chesterfield *(G-2747)*
Buddy Tda Inc ....G...... 269 349-8105
Kalamazoo *(G-8702)*
Century Inc...G...... 231 946-7500
Traverse City *(G-15933)*
Champagne Grinding & Mfg Co...........F...... 734 459-1759
Canton *(G-2360)*
Contour Tool and Machine Inc............G...... 517 787-6806
Jackson *(G-8420)*
Etcs Inc ....F...... 586 268-4870
Warren *(G-17022)*
Green Manufacturing Inc.....................G...... 517 458-1500
Morenci *(G-11111)*
Groholski Mfg Solutions LLC ....E...... 517 278-9339
Coldwater *(G-3307)*
H & G Tool Company ....F...... 586 573-7040
Warren *(G-17073)*
Hardy-Reed Tool & Die Co Inc ....F...... 517 547-7107
Manitou Beach *(G-10448)*
Indepndnce Tling Solutions LLC ....E...... 586 274-2300
Troy *(G-16414)*
Knight Carbide Inc ....E...... 586 598-4888
Chesterfield *(G-2798)*
Kwik Tech Inc ....E...... 586 268-6201
Shelby Township *(G-14617)*
Machining & Fabricating Inc ....E...... 586 773-9288
Roseville *(G-13828)*
Malmac Tool and Fixture Inc...............G...... 517 448-8244
Hudson *(G-8136)*
Mp Tool & Engineering Company........E...... 586 772-7730
Roseville *(G-13841)*
Nexteer Automotive Corporation ....B...... 989 757-5000
Saginaw *(G-14104)*
P & P Manufacturing Co Inc................E...... 810 667-2712
Lapeer *(G-9479)*
P T M Corporation ....D...... 586 725-2211
Ira *(G-8266)*
R & A Tool & Engineering Co ....E...... 734 981-2000
Westland *(G-17593)*
R J S Tool & Gage Co ....E...... 248 642-8620
Birmingham *(G-1700)*
Rhinevault Olsen Machine & Tl ....G...... 989 753-4363
Saginaw *(G-14133)*
Rodan Tool & Mold LLC ....G...... 248 926-9200
Commerce Township *(G-3450)*
Tooltech Machinery Inc ....G...... 248 628-1813
Oxford *(G-12376)*
Wire Fab Inc..F...... 313 893-8816
Detroit *(G-4443)*
Wolverine Tool Co ....F...... 810 664-2964
Lapeer *(G-9492)*

MACHINE TOOL ACCESS: Wheel Turning Eqpt, Diamond Point, Etc

Dianamic Abrasive Products ....F...... 248 280-1185
Troy *(G-16316)*

MACHINE TOOL ATTACHMENTS & ACCESS

Advance Products Corporation............E...... 269 849-1000
Benton Harbor *(G-1480)*
American Gator Tool Company ....G...... 231 347-3222
Harbor Springs *(G-7272)*
Cardinal Machine Co ....E...... 810 686-1190
Clio *(G-3267)*
E & E Special Products LLC ....F...... 586 978-3377
Warren *(G-17012)*
F & S Tool & Gauge Co Inc..................G...... 517 787-2661
Jackson *(G-8446)*
Fega Tool & Gage Company ....F...... 586 469-4400
Clinton Township *(G-3114)*
Gt Technologies Inc ....E...... 734 467-8371
Westland *(G-17566)*
Haller International Tech Inc ....G...... 313 821-0809
Detroit *(G-4114)*
Hydro-Craft Inc.....................................E...... 248 652-8100
Rochester Hills *(G-13448)*
Kasper Machine Co..............................F...... 248 547-3150
Madison Heights *(G-10289)*
Lamina Inc ....C...... 248 489-9122
Farmington Hills *(G-5042)*
Marshall-Gruber Company LLC..........F...... 248 353-4100
Southfield *(G-14973)*
Reid Industries Inc...............................G...... 586 776-2070
Roseville *(G-13861)*
Sesco Products Group Inc...................D...... 586 979-4400
Sterling Heights *(G-15492)*
Snap Jaws Manufacturing Inc.............G...... 248 588-1099
Troy *(G-16608)*
Van Emon Bruce ....G...... 269 467-7803
Centreville *(G-2598)*

MACHINE TOOLS & ACCESS

Acme Carbide Die Inc ....E...... 734 722-2303
Westland *(G-17538)*
Advanced Feedlines LLC ....D...... 248 583-9400
Troy *(G-16169)*
American Gear & Engrg Co Inc ....E...... 734 595-6400
Westland *(G-17541)*
Anchor Lamina America Inc ....C...... 231 533-8646
Bellaire *(G-1434)*
Anderson-Cook Inc..............................D...... 586 954-0700
Clinton Township *(G-3053)*

Anderson-Cook Inc ... D ... 586 293-0800 Fraser *(G-5620)*
Apex Broaching Systems Inc ... F ... 586 758-2626 Warren *(G-16936)*
Art Laser Inc ... F ... 248 391-6600 Auburn Hills *(G-780)*
Atlas Thread Gage Inc ... G ... 248 477-3230 Farmington Hills *(G-4935)*
Baxter Machine & Tool Co ... E ... 517 782-2808 Jackson *(G-8388)*
Broaching Industries Inc ... E ... 586 949-3775 Chesterfield *(G-2748)*
Capitol Tool Grinding Co ... G ... 517 321-8230 Lansing *(G-9280)*
Cdp Diamond Products Inc ... E ... 734 591-1041 Livonia *(G-9678)*
Center Line Gage Inc ... G ... 810 387-4300 Brockway *(G-2019)*
Coles Machine Service Inc ... E ... 810 658-5373 Davison *(G-3642)*
Complex Tool & Machine Inc ... G ... 248 625-0664 Clarkston *(G-2915)*
Cows Locomotive Mfg Co ... E ... 248 583-7150 Madison Heights *(G-10221)*
Coyne Machine & Tool LLC ... G ... 231 944-8755 Kewadin *(G-9037)*
Cz Industries Inc ... G ... 248 475-4415 Auburn Hills *(G-834)*
D & F Corporation ... D ... 586 254-5300 Sterling Heights *(G-15306)*
Davison-Rite Products Co ... E ... 734 513-0505 Livonia *(G-9699)*
Detail Precision Products Inc ... E ... 248 544-3390 Ferndale *(G-5271)*
Die Services International LLC ... D ... 734 699-3400 Van Buren Twp *(G-16758)*
Dixon & Ryan Corporation ... F ... 248 549-4000 Royal Oak *(G-13919)*
Dobday Manufacturing Co Inc ... E ... 586 254-6777 Sterling Heights *(G-15320)*
Dowding Machining LLC ... F ... 517 663-5455 Eaton Rapids *(G-4721)*
Dynamic Jig Grinding Corp ... E ... 248 589-3110 Troy *(G-16330)*
Elmhirst Industries Inc ... E ... 586 731-8663 Sterling Heights *(G-15330)*
Enterprise Tool and Gear Inc ... D ... 989 269-9797 Bad Axe *(G-1060)*
Equitable Engineering Co Inc ... E ... 248 689-9700 Troy *(G-16351)*
Erdman Machine Co ... E ... 231 894-1010 Whitehall *(G-17665)*
Est Tools America Inc ... G ... 810 824-3323 Ira *(G-8255)*
Express Machine & Tool Co ... G ... 586 758-5080 Warren *(G-17027)*
Falcon Motorsports Inc ... G ... 248 328-2222 Holly *(G-7878)*
Feed - Lease Corp ... E ... 248 377-0000 Auburn Hills *(G-871)*
Fitz-Rite Products Inc ... E ... 248 528-8440 Troy *(G-16366)*
Fontijne Grotnes Inc ... E ... 269 262-4700 Niles *(G-11611)*
Forkardt Inc ... E ... 231 995-8300 Traverse City *(G-15973)*
Formula One Tool & Engineering ... G ... 810 794-3617 Algonac *(G-144)*
Gemini Precision Machining Inc ... D ... 989 269-9702 Bad Axe *(G-1065)*
Global Engineering Inc ... E ... 586 566-0423 Shelby Township *(G-14596)*
Global Retool Group Amer LLC ... F ... 248 289-5820 Wixom *(G-17818)*
Gr Innovations LLC ... G ... 248 618-3813 Waterford *(G-17347)*
Great Lakes Tool LLC ... F ... 586 759-5253 Warren *(G-17064)*
Green Oak Tool and Svcs Inc ... G ... 586 531-2255 Brighton *(G-1934)*
Guardian Manufacturing Corp ... E ... 734 591-1454 Livonia *(G-9761)*
Hank Thorn Co ... F ... 248 348-7800 Wixom *(G-17823)*
Htc Sales Corporation ... E ... 800 624-2027 Ira *(G-8257)*
Hti Cybernetics Inc ... E ... 586 826-8346 Sterling Heights *(G-15369)*
Huron Tool & Engineering Co ... E ... 989 269-9927 Bad Axe *(G-1068)*
Illinois Tool Works Inc ... D ... 231 947-5755 Traverse City *(G-16002)*
Illinois Tool Works Inc ... G ... 231 947-5755 Traverse City *(G-16003)*
International Mech Design ... E ... 248 546-5740 Royal Oak *(G-13936)*
K-Tool Corporation Michigan ... D ... 863 603-0777 Plymouth *(G-12661)*
Karr Spring Company ... E ... 616 394-1277 Holland *(G-7707)*
Keo Cutters Inc ... E ... 586 771-2050 Warren *(G-17120)*
Krmc LLC ... G ... 734 955-9311 Romulus *(G-13698)*
Kurek Tool Inc ... F ... 989 777-5300 Saginaw *(G-14075)*
L & M Tool Co Inc ... F ... 586 677-4700 Macomb *(G-10136)*
L E Jones Company ... B ... 906 863-1043 Menominee *(G-10741)*
Lab Tool and Engineering Corp ... E ... 517 750-4131 Spring Arbor *(G-15124)*
Lavalier Corp ... E ... 248 616-8880 Troy *(G-16458)*
Legacy Tool LLC ... G ... 231 335-8983 Newaygo *(G-11572)*
Lester Detterbeck Entps Ltd ... E ... 906 265-5121 Iron River *(G-8314)*
Lincoln Precision Carbide Inc ... E ... 989 736-8113 Lincoln *(G-9566)*
Lumco Manufacturing Company ... F ... 810 724-0582 Lum *(G-10090)*
Lyons Tool & Engineering Inc ... E ... 586 200-3003 Warren *(G-17133)*
Maes Tool & Die Co Inc ... F ... 517 750-3131 Jackson *(G-8504)*
MB Liquidating Corporation ... D ... 810 638-5388 Flushing *(G-5541)*
Merrifield McHy Solutions Inc ... E ... 248 494-7335 Pontiac *(G-12848)*
Metal Punch Corporation ... E ... 231 775-8391 Cadillac *(G-2264)*
Metro Machine Works Inc ... D ... 734 941-4571 Romulus *(G-13707)*
Michigan Drill Corporation ... F ... 248 689-5050 Troy *(G-16505)*
Midwest Tool and Cutlery Co ... D ... 269 651-2476 Sturgis *(G-15621)*
Millennium Technology II Inc ... F ... 734 479-4440 Romulus *(G-13709)*
Miller Tool & Die Co ... E ... 517 782-0347 Jackson *(G-8529)*
Milo Boring & Machining Inc ... G ... 586 293-8611 Fraser *(G-5693)*
Mistequay Group Ltd ... F ... 989 752-7700 Saginaw *(G-14097)*
Mjc Tool & Machine Co Inc ... G ... 586 790-4766 Clinton Township *(G-3179)*
MNP Corporation ... F ... 810 982-8996 Port Huron *(G-12943)*
Montague Tool and Mfg Co ... E ... 810 686-0000 Clio *(G-3279)*
Northern Precision Inc ... E ... 989 736-6322 Lincoln *(G-9569)*
Olivet Machine Tool Engrg Co ... F ... 269 749-2671 Olivet *(G-12143)*
Olympian Tool LLC ... E ... 989 224-4817 Saint Johns *(G-14291)*
Oneida Tool Corporation ... E ... 313 537-0770 Redford *(G-13177)*
P&L Development & Mfg LLC ... D ... 989 739-5203 Oscoda *(G-12217)*
Paslin Company ... E ... 586 755-1693 Warren *(G-17181)*
Paslin Company ... A ... 586 758-0200 Warren *(G-17182)*
Patriot Manufacturing LLC ... G ... 734 259-2059 Plymouth *(G-12709)*
Peak Industries Co Inc ... D ... 313 846-8666 Dearborn *(G-3747)*
Philips Machining Company ... F ... 616 997-7777 Coopersville *(G-3568)*
Pioneer Broach Midwest Inc ... F ... 231 768-5800 Leroy *(G-9535)*
Posa-Cut Corporation ... E ... 248 474-5620 Farmington Hills *(G-5097)*
Precision Gage Inc ... D ... 517 439-1690 Hillsdale *(G-7534)*
Precision Threading Corp ... G ... 231 627-3133 Cheboygan *(G-2691)*
Prime Industries Inc ... E ... 734 946-8588 Taylor *(G-15756)*
Productivity Technologies ... C ... 810 714-0200 Fenton *(G-5231)*
Proto Design & Manufacturing ... G ... 419 346-8416 Fraser *(G-5711)*
Proto Tool & Gage Inc ... G ... 734 487-0830 Ypsilanti *(G-18097)*
R & B Industries Inc ... E ... 734 462-9478 Livonia *(G-9903)*
R T Gordon Inc ... E ... 586 294-6100 Fraser *(G-5715)*
Riverside Spline & Gear Inc ... E ... 810 765-8302 Marine City *(G-10481)*
Roesch Maufacturing Co LLC ... G ... 517 424-6300 Tecumseh *(G-15808)*
Rose Tool & Die Inc ... E ... 989 343-1015 West Branch *(G-17519)*
Roth-Williams Industries Inc ... F ... 586 792-0090 Clinton Township *(G-3215)*
Royal Design & Manufacturing ... D ... 248 588-0110 Madison Heights *(G-10346)*
Sbti Company ... D ... 586 726-5756 Shelby Township *(G-14685)*
Schaller Tool & Die Co ... E ... 586 949-5500 Chesterfield *(G-2838)*
Select Steel Fabricators Inc ... F ... 248 945-9582 Southfield *(G-15026)*
Setco Sales Company ... F ... 248 888-8989 Novi *(G-11994)*
Shwayder Company ... G ... 248 645-9511 Birmingham *(G-1702)*
Stapels Manufacturing LLC ... F ... 248 577-5570 Troy *(G-16619)*
Star Ringmaster ... G ... 734 641-7147 Canton *(G-2429)*
Superior Controls Inc ... C ... 734 454-0500 Plymouth *(G-12763)*
Superior Design & Mfg ... F ... 810 678-3950 Metamora *(G-10781)*
Taylor Turning Inc ... E ... 248 960-7920 Wixom *(G-17906)*
Tenants Tolerance Tooling ... G ... 269 349-6907 Portage *(G-13048)*
Thielenhaus Microfinish Corp ... E ... 248 349-9450 Novi *(G-12015)*
Thread-Craft Inc ... D ... 586 323-1116 Sterling Heights *(G-15524)*
Three-Dimensional Services Inc ... C ... 248 852-1333 Rochester Hills *(G-13525)*
Tolerance Tool & Engineering ... E ... 313 592-4011 Detroit *(G-4402)*
Total Tooling Concepts Inc ... G ... 616 785-8402 Comstock Park *(G-3518)*
Trig Tool Inc ... G ... 248 543-2550 Madison Heights *(G-10370)*
Trimas Corporation ... E ... 248 631-5450 Bloomfield Hills *(G-1807)*
Tru Flo Carbide Inc ... D ... 989 658-8515 Ubly *(G-16724)*
Vigel North America Inc ... G ... 734 947-9900 Madison Heights *(G-10376)*
Weber Precision Grinding Inc ... G ... 616 842-1634 Spring Lake *(G-15186)*
Wedin International Inc ... D ... 231 779-8650 Cadillac *(G-2284)*
West Michigan Gage Inc ... F ... 616 735-0585 Walker *(G-16882)*
Westech Corp ... E ... 231 766-3914 Muskegon *(G-11447)*
Wilco Tooling & Mfg LLC ... F ... 517 901-0147 Reading *(G-13139)*
Wolverine Production & Engrg ... F ... 586 468-2890 Harrison Township *(G-7357)*
Zcc USA Inc ... F ... 734 997-3811 Ann Arbor *(G-706)*

MACHINE TOOLS, METAL CUTTING: Brushing

Steadfast Tool & Machine Inc ... G ... 989 856-8127 Caseville *(G-2506)*

MACHINE TOOLS, METAL CUTTING: Cutoff

Allfi Robotics Inc ... G ... 586 248-1198 Wixom *(G-17757)*
Modern Machine Tool Co ... F ... 517 788-9120 Jackson *(G-8536)*
Novi Tool & Machine Company ... D ... 313 532-0900 Redford *(G-13176)*

PRODUCT

Employee Codes: A=Over 500 employees, B=251-500 C=101-250, D=51-100, E=20-50, F=10-19, G=3-9

2020 Harris Michigan Industrial Directory

1275

MACHINE TOOLS, METAL CUTTING: Cutoff

P M R Industries Inc .... F 810 989-5020
  Port Huron *(G-12954)*

MACHINE TOOLS, METAL CUTTING: Die Sinking

J C Manufacturing Company .... G 586 757-2713
  Warren *(G-17106)*

MACHINE TOOLS, METAL CUTTING: Drilling

Exlterra Inc .... G 248 268-2336
  Hazel Park *(G-7437)*
Govro-Nelson Co .... G 810 329-4727
  Commerce Township *(G-3408)*
Infra Corporation .... F 248 623-0400
  Waterford *(G-17351)*
J & W Machine Inc .... G 989 773-9951
  Mount Pleasant *(G-11199)*
Viscount Equipment Co Inc .... G 586 293-5900
  Fraser *(G-5746)*
Wright-K Technology Inc .... E 989 752-2588
  Saginaw *(G-14184)*

MACHINE TOOLS, METAL CUTTING: Drilling & Boring

Antech Tool Inc .... F 734 207-3622
  Canton *(G-2348)*
Esco Group Inc .... F 616 453-5458
  Grand Rapids *(G-6385)*
Industrial Boring Company .... G 586 756-9110
  Warren *(G-17090)*
Mag-Powertrain .... F 586 446-7000
  Sterling Heights *(G-15408)*
Raven Engineering Inc .... E 248 969-9450
  Oxford *(G-12367)*
Richardson Acqstions Group Inc .... E 248 624-2272
  Walled Lake *(G-16902)*
Roy A Hutchins Company .... G 248 437-3470
  New Hudson *(G-11554)*
Saginaw Machine Systems Inc .... D 989 753-8465
  Saginaw *(G-14140)*
SMS Holding Co Inc .... C 989 753-8465
  Saginaw *(G-14150)*
Soils and Structures Inc .... E 800 933-3959
  Norton Shores *(G-11796)*
Systems Unlimited Inc .... E 517 279-8407
  Coldwater *(G-3336)*
T E C Boring .... G 586 443-5437
  Roseville *(G-13876)*

MACHINE TOOLS, METAL CUTTING: Electrochemical Milling

A & D Run Off Inc .... G 231 759-0950
  Muskegon *(G-11256)*

MACHINE TOOLS, METAL CUTTING: Electron-Discharge

Liquid Drive Corporation .... E 248 634-5382
  Mount Clemens *(G-11139)*

MACHINE TOOLS, METAL CUTTING: Exotic, Including Explosive

Carb-A-Tron Tool Co .... G 517 782-2249
  Jackson *(G-8402)*
Electro ARC Manufacturing Co .... E 734 483-4233
  Dexter *(G-4491)*
Lester Detterbeck Entps Ltd .... E 906 265-5121
  Iron River *(G-8314)*
Paragon Tool Company .... G 734 326-1702
  Romulus *(G-13719)*
Roussin M & Ubelhor R Inc .... G 586 783-6015
  Harrison Township *(G-7347)*
W W J Form Tool Company Inc .... G 313 565-0015
  Inkster *(G-8235)*

MACHINE TOOLS, METAL CUTTING: Grind, Polish, Buff, Lapp

Acme Manufacturing Company .... D 248 393-7300
  Auburn Hills *(G-760)*
Boride Engineered Abr Inc .... F 231 929-2121
  Traverse City *(G-15916)*
Tru Tech Systems LLC .... D 586 469-2700
  Mount Clemens *(G-11152)*

MACHINE TOOLS, METAL CUTTING: Home Workshop

David A Mohr Jr .... G 517 266-2694
  Adrian *(G-58)*
Mi-Tech Tooling Inc .... E 989 912-2440
  Cass City *(G-2519)*

MACHINE TOOLS, METAL CUTTING: Jig, Boring & Grinding

Leader Corporation .... E 586 566-7114
  Shelby Township *(G-14624)*
Precision Jig Grinding Inc .... G 989 865-7953
  Saint Charles *(G-14199)*

MACHINE TOOLS, METAL CUTTING: Lathes

High-Star Corporation .... G 734 743-1503
  Westland *(G-17569)*
J & R Tool Inc .... G 989 662-0026
  Auburn *(G-754)*
New Dimension Laser Inc .... G 586 415-6041
  Roseville *(G-13847)*
Riverside Tool Corp .... E 616 241-1424
  Grand Rapids *(G-6829)*

MACHINE TOOLS, METAL CUTTING: Numerically Controlled

Cellular Concepts Co Inc .... E 313 371-4800
  Rochester Hills *(G-13388)*
M S Machining Systems Inc .... F 517 546-1170
  Howell *(G-8059)*
Morgan Machine LLC .... G 248 293-3277
  Auburn Hills *(G-948)*
Pro Precision Inc .... G 586 247-6160
  Sterling Heights *(G-15452)*
Rapid Cnc Solutions .... G 586 850-6385
  Hamtramck *(G-7245)*
Sabre-TEC Inc .... F 586 949-5386
  Chesterfield *(G-2835)*
Schienke Products Inc .... G 586 752-5454
  Bruce Twp *(G-2099)*
Snap Jaws Manufacturing Inc .... G 248 588-1099
  Troy *(G-16608)*
Soaring Concepts Aerospace LLC .... F 574 286-9670
  Hastings *(G-7427)*
True Fabrications & Machine .... E 248 288-0140
  Troy *(G-16653)*
U S Equipment Co .... E 313 526-8300
  Rochester Hills *(G-13533)*
Warren Industries Inc .... D 586 741-0420
  Clinton Township *(G-3259)*

MACHINE TOOLS, METAL CUTTING: Pipe Cutting & Threading

Quality Pipe Products Inc .... E 734 606-5100
  New Boston *(G-11509)*

MACHINE TOOLS, METAL CUTTING: Plasma Process

RSI Global Sourcing LLC .... F 734 604-2448
  Novi *(G-11988)*

MACHINE TOOLS, METAL CUTTING: Pointing & Burring

Schenck USA Corp .... E 248 377-2100
  Southfield *(G-15024)*

MACHINE TOOLS, METAL CUTTING: Regrinding, Crankshaft

Crankshaft Machine Company .... E 517 787-3791
  Jackson *(G-8423)*
Performance Crankshaft Inc .... G 586 549-7557
  Ferndale *(G-5309)*

MACHINE TOOLS, METAL CUTTING: Robot, Drilling, Cutting, Etc

Dynamic Robotic Solutions Inc .... C 248 829-2800
  Auburn Hills *(G-848)*

MACHINE TOOLS, METAL CUTTING: Saws, Power

Reggie McKenzie Indus Mtls .... G 734 261-0844
  Livonia *(G-9908)*

MACHINE TOOLS, METAL CUTTING: Tool Replacement & Rpr Parts

ABC Precision Machining Inc .... G 269 926-6322
  Benton Harbor *(G-1478)*
Accra Tool Inc .... G 248 680-9936
  Lake Orion *(G-9122)*
Accubilt Automated Systems LLC .... E 517 787-9353
  Jackson *(G-8371)*
Alto Manufacturing Inc .... F 734 641-8800
  Westland *(G-17540)*
American Gear & Engrg Co Inc .... E 734 595-6400
  Westland *(G-17541)*
American Pride Machining Inc .... G 586 294-6404
  Fraser *(G-5617)*
Donald E Rogers Associates .... E 248 673-9878
  Waterford *(G-17335)*
Emcor Inc .... F 989 667-0652
  Bay City *(G-1308)*
Faro Technologies Inc .... F 248 669-8620
  Wixom *(G-17809)*
Great Lakes Waterjet Laser LLC .... G 517 629-9900
  Albion *(G-124)*
Huron Tool & Engineering Co .... E 989 269-9927
  Bad Axe *(G-1068)*
K&S Consultants LLC .... G 269 240-7767
  Buchanan *(G-2122)*
Liberty Steel Fabricating Inc .... E 269 556-9792
  Saint Joseph *(G-14327)*
Michigan Cnc Tool Inc .... F 734 449-9590
  Whitmore Lake *(G-17704)*
MNP Corporation .... F 810 982-8996
  Port Huron *(G-12943)*
Normac Incorporated .... F 248 349-2644
  Northville *(G-11714)*
Precision Honing .... G 586 757-0304
  Warren *(G-17192)*
Punch Tech .... E 810 364-4811
  Marysville *(G-10612)*
R P T Cincinnati Inc .... G 313 382-5880
  Lincoln Park *(G-9584)*
S & S Machine Tool Repair LLC .... G 616 877-4930
  Dorr *(G-4527)*
Tank Truck Service & Sales Inc .... E 586 757-6500
  Warren *(G-17262)*
Transfer Tool Systems Inc .... D 616 846-8510
  Grand Haven *(G-6090)*
Ultra-Dex USA LLC .... G 810 638-5388
  Flushing *(G-5543)*

MACHINE TOOLS, METAL CUTTING: Turret Lathes

D W Machine Inc .... F 517 787-9929
  Jackson *(G-8426)*

MACHINE TOOLS, METAL CUTTING: Ultrasonic

Telsonic Ultrasonics Inc .... E 586 802-0033
  Shelby Township *(G-14708)*

MACHINE TOOLS, METAL CUTTING: Vertical Turning & Boring

Bob G Machining LLC .... G 586 285-1400
  Clinton Township *(G-3068)*

MACHINE TOOLS, METAL FORMING: Beaders, Metal

Van-Mark Products Corporation .... E 248 478-1200
  Farmington Hills *(G-5146)*

MACHINE TOOLS, METAL FORMING: Bending

B & M Bending & Forging Inc .... G 586 731-3332
  Shelby Township *(G-14553)*
CNB International Inc .... D 269 948-3300
  Hastings *(G-7403)*
Hti Cybernetics Inc .... E 586 826-8346
  Sterling Heights *(G-15369)*

PRODUCT SECTION

MACHINE TOOLS, METAL FORMING: Die Casting & Extruding

Digital Die Solutions Inc ....F...... 734 542-2222
  Livonia (G-9712)
Pace Industries LLC ....A...... 231 777-3941
  Muskegon (G-11396)
Port City Group Inc ....F...... 231 777-3941
  Muskegon (G-11400)
Product and Tooling Tech Inc.......E...... 586 293-1810
  Fraser (G-5710)

MACHINE TOOLS, METAL FORMING: Electroforming

Bmax USA LLC ....E...... 248 794-4176
  Pontiac (G-12807)

MACHINE TOOLS, METAL FORMING: Forging Machinery & Hammers

Midwest Tool and Cutlery Co........F...... 231 258-2341
  Kalkaska (G-8953)
P M R Industries Inc ....F...... 810 989-5020
  Port Huron (G-12954)

MACHINE TOOLS, METAL FORMING: Forming, Metal Deposit

Titanium Industries Inc..................G....... 973 983-1185
  Plymouth (G-12771)

MACHINE TOOLS, METAL FORMING: Lathes, Spinning

M & M Turning Co ....E...... 586 791-7188
  Fraser (G-5686)

MACHINE TOOLS, METAL FORMING: Magnetic Forming

Magnetool Inc..............................E...... 248 588-5400
  Troy (G-16479)

MACHINE TOOLS, METAL FORMING: Mechanical, Pneumatic Or Hyd

Dimond Machinery Company Inc....E...... 269 945-5908
  Hastings (G-7407)

MACHINE TOOLS, METAL FORMING: Plasma Jet Spray

American Brake and Clutch Inc.....F...... 586 948-3730
  Chesterfield (G-2736)

MACHINE TOOLS, METAL FORMING: Presses, Arbor

Green Oak Tool and Svcs Inc ....G...... 586 531-2455
  Brighton (G-1934)

MACHINE TOOLS, METAL FORMING: Presses, Hyd & Pneumatic

Air-Hydraulics Inc ....F...... 517 787-9444
  Jackson (G-8377)
Burton Press Co Inc ....G...... 248 853-0212
  Rochester Hills (G-13380)
Lloyd Tool & Mfg Corp................E...... 810 694-3519
  Grand Blanc (G-5973)
Metal Mechanics Inc ....F...... 269 679-2525
  Schoolcraft (G-14499)

MACHINE TOOLS, METAL FORMING: Punching & Shearing

United States Socket ....F...... 586 469-8811
  Fraser (G-5744)

MACHINE TOOLS, METAL FORMING: Rebuilt

Centerless Rebuilders Inc............E...... 586 749-6529
  New Haven (G-11523)
Reliable Sales Co ....G...... 248 969-0943
  Oxford (G-12368)
S & L Tool Inc ....G...... 734 464-4200
  Livonia (G-9917)

MACHINE TOOLS, METAL FORMING: Robots, Pressing, Extrudg, Etc

Buster Mathis Foundation.............G...... 616 843-4433
  Wyoming (G-17990)
Fanuc America Corporation..........B...... 248 377-7000
  Rochester Hills (G-13423)
RC Directional Boring Inc ....F...... 517 545-4887
  Howell (G-8088)

MACHINE TOOLS, METAL FORMING: Spinning, Spline Rollg/Windg

Automated Indus Motion Inc........F...... 231 865-1800
  Fruitport (G-5787)
Michigan Roll Form Inc ....E...... 248 669-3700
  Commerce Township (G-3433)
U S Baird Corporation ....F...... 616 826-5013
  Middleville (G-10811)

MACHINE TOOLS, METAL FORMING: Spline Rolling

Anderson-Cook Inc......................D...... 586 954-0700
  Clinton Township (G-3053)
Anderson-Cook Inc......................D...... 586 293-0800
  Fraser (G-5620)
Anderson-Cook Inc......................E...... 586 954-0700
  Clinton Township (G-3054)
Spline Specialist Inc ....G...... 586 731-4569
  Sterling Heights (G-15506)
West Michigan Spline Inc ....F...... 616 399-4078
  Holland (G-7856)

MACHINE TOOLS: Metal Cutting

AAA Industries Inc.......................E...... 313 255-0420
  Redford (G-13140)
Acme Manufacturing Company ....F...... 248 393-7300
  Lake Orion (G-9123)
Advanced Stage Tooling LLC ......G...... 810 444-9807
  East China (G-4620)
Alliance Tool ....G...... 586 465-3960
  Harrison Township (G-7318)
Ascent Aerospace LLC ....A...... 586 726-0500
  Macomb (G-10108)
Atlas Technologies LLC ....D...... 810 714-2128
  Fenton (G-5183)
Aw Carbide Fabricators Inc ....F...... 586 294-1850
  Fraser (G-5626)
Axly Production Machining Inc ....B...... 989 269-2444
  Bad Axe (G-1057)
Belco Industries Inc ....C...... 616 794-0410
  Belding (G-1399)
Belco Industries Inc ....E...... 616 794-0410
  Belding (G-1400)
Berg Tool Inc ....F...... 586 646-7100
  Chesterfield (G-2745)
Bielomatik USA Inc ....E...... 248 446-9910
  New Hudson (G-11532)
Broaching Industries Inc..............E...... 586 949-3775
  Chesterfield (G-2748)
Bulk AG Innovations LLC............F...... 269 925-0900
  Benton Harbor (G-1488)
CBS Tool Inc................................F...... 586 566-5945
  Shelby Township (G-14558)
CDM Machine Co........................F...... 313 538-9100
  Southfield (G-14864)
City Animation Co ....E...... 248 589-0600
  Troy (G-16268)
City Animation Co ....F...... 989 743-3458
  Corunna (G-3579)
Clas Carbide ....G...... 248 236-8353
  Oxford (G-12342)
Clear Cut Water Jet Machining ...G...... 616 534-9119
  Grand Rapids (G-6280)
Cleary Developments Inc ....E...... 248 588-7011
  Madison Heights (G-10210)
Craft Industries Inc......................A...... 586 726-4300
  Shelby Township (G-14570)
Cutex Inc......................................G...... 734 953-8908
  Livonia (G-9696)
D & D Production Inc ....F...... 248 334-2112
  Waterford (G-17332)
Davison-Rite Products Co...........E...... 734 513-0505
  Livonia (G-9699)
Design Services Unlimited Inc.....F...... 586 463-3225
  Chesterfield (G-2765)
Detroit Boring & Mch Co LLC .....G...... 586 604-6506
  Sterling Heights (G-15311)
Detroit Edge Tool Company ....E...... 586 776-1598
  Roseville (G-13794)
Dikar Tool Company Inc ....F...... 248 348-0010
  Novi (G-11869)
Dimond Machinery Company Inc ..E...... 269 945-5908
  Hastings (G-7407)
Dvs Technology America Inc ......G...... 734 656-2080
  Plymouth (G-12614)
Dyna-Bignell Products LLC ....G...... 989 418-5050
  Clare (G-2868)
Ecorse McHy Sls & Rbldrs Inc ...E...... 313 383-2100
  Wyandotte (G-17956)
Elite Tooling LLC ....G...... 269 383-9714
  Kalamazoo (G-8734)
Elk Rapids Engineering Inc.........E...... 231 264-5661
  Elk Rapids (G-4778)
Emhart Teknologies LLC ....E...... 586 949-0440
  Chesterfield (G-2773)
Emhart Teknologies LLC ....F...... 800 783-6427
  Troy (G-16343)
Esr ....G...... 989 619-7160
  Harrisville (G-7363)
Falcon Motorsports Inc ....G...... 248 328-2222
  Holly (G-7878)
Fitz-Rite Products Inc ....G...... 248 360-3730
  Commerce Township (G-3405)
Five Star Industries Inc ....E...... 586 786-0500
  Macomb (G-10122)
Fortune Tool & Machine Inc ....E...... 248 669-9119
  Wixom (G-17813)
Fourway Machinery Sales Co .....F...... 517 782-9371
  Jackson (G-8451)
Framon Mfg Co Inc ....G...... 989 356-6296
  Alpena (G-290)
G & W Machine Co ....G...... 616 363-4435
  Grand Rapids (G-6426)
Gehring Corporation....................D...... 248 478-8060
  Farmington Hills (G-5008)
Gerald Harris ....G...... 985 774-0261
  Detroit (G-4089)
Globe Tech LLC ....E...... 734 656-2200
  Plymouth (G-12630)
Godin Tool Inc ....G...... 231 946-2210
  Traverse City (G-15980)
Graflex Inc ....F...... 616 842-3654
  Spring Lake (G-15146)
H & G Tool Company ....F...... 586 573-7040
  Warren (G-17073)
Hal International Inc.....................G...... 248 488-0440
  Livonia (G-9763)
Hegenscheidt-Mfd Corporation ...E...... 586 274-4900
  Sterling Heights (G-15367)
Heller Inc......................................E...... 248 288-5000
  Troy (G-16394)
Highland Machine Design Inc ....G...... 248 669-6150
  Commerce Township (G-3412)
Hot Tool Cutter Grinding Co ....E...... 586 790-4867
  Fraser (G-5666)
Hougen Manufacturing Inc..........C...... 810 635-7111
  Swartz Creek (G-15667)
Hydro-Craft Inc............................E...... 248 652-8100
  Rochester Hills (G-13448)
Ideal Tool Inc ....F...... 989 893-8336
  Bay City (G-1321)
Ingersoll CM Systems LLC..........D...... 989 495-5000
  Midland (G-10870)
Inland Lakes Machine Inc............E...... 231 775-6543
  Cadillac (G-2255)
Integrity Design & Mfg LLC........G...... 248 628-6927
  Oxford (G-12352)
Internal Grinding Abrasives ....E...... 616 243-5566
  Grand Rapids (G-6540)
Iron River Mfg Co Inc..................E...... 906 265-5121
  Iron River (G-8310)
Ivan Doverspike ....E...... 313 579-3000
  Detroit (G-4153)
J W Holdings Inc ....E...... 616 530-9889
  Grand Rapids (G-6549)
Jdl Enterprises Inc.......................G...... 586 977-8863
  Warren (G-17113)
Jdl Enterprises Inc.......................F...... 586 977-8863
  Sterling Heights (G-15380)
JF Hubert Enterprises Inc ....F...... 586 293-8660
  Fraser (G-5675)
JPS Mfg Inc.................................G...... 586 415-8702
  Fraser (G-5676)
Jtekt Toyoda Americas Corp.......F...... 847 506-2415
  Wixom (G-17839)
K-Tool Corporation Michigan ......D...... 863 603-0777
  Plymouth (G-12661)

Employee Codes: A=Over 500 employees, B=251-500
C=101-250, D=51-100, E=20-50, F=10-19, G=3-9

2020 Harris Michigan Industrial Directory

1277

Kadia Inc ... G ... 248 446-1970
Brighton *(G-1945)*
Kalamazoo Machine Tool Co Inc ... G ... 269 321-8860
Portage *(G-13004)*
Kbe Precision Products LLC ... G ... 586 725-4200
New Baltimore *(G-11487)*
Kelm Acubar Lc ... F ... 269 927-3000
Benton Harbor *(G-1516)*
Koch Limited ... G ... 586 296-3103
Fraser *(G-5679)*
Krmc LLC ... G ... 734 955-9311
Romulus *(G-13698)*
Laydon Enterprises Inc ... E ... 906 774-4633
Iron Mountain *(G-8288)*
Liberty Tool Inc ... E ... 586 726-2449
Sterling Heights *(G-15398)*
Lincoln Precision Carbide Inc ... E ... 989 736-8113
Lincoln *(G-9566)*
Lloyd Tool & Mfg Corp ... E ... 810 694-3519
Grand Blanc *(G-5973)*
Loc Performance Products Inc ... C ... 734 453-2300
Plymouth *(G-12674)*
Loc Performance Products Inc ... C ... 734 453-2300
Lansing *(G-9242)*
Loc Performance Products Inc ... G ... 734 453-2300
Sterling Heights *(G-15401)*
Loon Lake Precision Inc ... G ... 810 953-0732
Grand Blanc *(G-5974)*
Love Machinery Inc ... G ... 734 427-0824
Livonia *(G-9819)*
M C Carbide Tool Co ... F ... 248 486-9590
Wixom *(G-17850)*
Maes Tool & Die Co Inc ... F ... 517 750-3131
Jackson *(G-8504)*
MB Liquidating Corporation ... D ... 810 638-5388
Flushing *(G-5541)*
Mc Pherson Industrial Corp ... D ... 586 752-5555
Romeo *(G-13633)*
Menominee Saw and Supply Co ... E ... 906 863-2609
Menominee *(G-10747)*
Metal-Line Corp ... E ... 231 723-7041
Muskegon *(G-11377)*
Methods Machine Tools Inc ... E ... 248 624-8601
Wixom *(G-17854)*
Microform Tool Company Inc ... G ... 586 776-4840
Saint Clair Shores *(G-14264)*
Microtap USA Inc ... G ... 248 852-8277
Rochester Hills *(G-13473)*
Migatron Precision Products ... F ... 989 739-1439
Oscoda *(G-12214)*
Millennium Screw Machine Inc ... G ... 734 525-5235
Livonia *(G-9845)*
Miller Broach Inc ... D ... 810 395-8810
Capac *(G-2449)*
Miller Tool & Die Co ... E ... 517 782-0347
Jackson *(G-8529)*
Moore Production Tool Spc ... E ... 248 476-1200
Farmington *(G-4905)*
Neway Manufacturing Inc ... G ... 989 743-3458
Corunna *(G-3583)*
Oliver of Adrian Inc ... G ... 517 263-2132
Adrian *(G-83)*
Peiseler LLC ... G ... 616 235-8460
Grand Rapids *(G-6746)*
Pentech Industries Inc ... E ... 586 445-1070
Roseville *(G-13854)*
Petty Machine & Tool Inc ... E ... 517 782-9355
Jackson *(G-8551)*
Pinnacle Engineering Co Inc ... F ... 734 428-7039
Manchester *(G-10410)*
Pioneer Broach Midwest Inc ... F ... 231 768-5800
Leroy *(G-9535)*
Plason Scraping Co Inc ... G ... 248 588-7280
Madison Heights *(G-10329)*
Posa-Cut Corporation ... E ... 248 474-5620
Farmington Hills *(G-5097)*
Precision Guides LLC ... G ... 517 536-7234
Michigan Center *(G-10789)*
Prime Industries Inc ... E ... 734 946-8588
Taylor *(G-15756)*
Production Threaded Parts Co ... F ... 810 688-3186
North Branch *(G-11665)*
Productivity Technologies ... C ... 810 714-0200
Fenton *(G-5231)*
R F M Incorporated ... F ... 810 229-4567
Brighton *(G-1983)*
Rae Manufacturing Company ... F ... 810 987-9170
Port Huron *(G-12960)*
Rapid Grinding & Machine Co ... G ... 989 753-1744
Saginaw *(G-14131)*
Riverside Spline & Gear Inc ... E ... 810 765-8302
Marine City *(G-10481)*
Rnd Engineering LLC ... G ... 734 328-8277
Canton *(G-2423)*
Rod Chomper Inc ... F ... 616 392-9677
Holland *(G-7790)*
Roto-Finish Company Inc ... E ... 269 327-7071
Kalamazoo *(G-8875)*
RTS Cutting Tools Inc ... E ... 586 954-1900
Clinton Township *(G-3217)*
Rwc Inc ... D ... 989 684-4030
Bay City *(G-1352)*
S & L Tool Inc ... G ... 734 464-4200
Livonia *(G-9917)*
Schutte MSA LLC ... F ... 517 782-3600
Jackson *(G-8570)*
Select Steel Fabricators Inc ... F ... 248 945-9582
Southfield *(G-15026)*
Snyder Corporation ... E ... 586 726-4300
Shelby Township *(G-14697)*
Solidica Inc ... F ... 734 222-4680
Ann Arbor *(G-639)*
Stanhope Tool Inc ... F ... 248 585-5711
Madison Heights *(G-10360)*
Star Cutter Co ... G ... 248 474-8200
Lewiston *(G-9555)*
Star Cutter Co ... E ... 248 474-8200
Farmington Hills *(G-5129)*
Star Su Company LLC ... E ... 248 474-8200
Farmington Hills *(G-5130)*
Stoney Crest Regrind Service ... F ... 989 777-7190
Bridgeport *(G-1858)*
Sunrise Tool Products Inc ... F ... 989 724-6688
Harrisville *(G-7366)*
Tank Truck Service & Sales Inc ... G ... 989 731-4887
Gaylord *(G-5894)*
Tawas Tool Co Inc ... D ... 989 362-0414
East Tawas *(G-4696)*
Tech Tooling Specialties Inc ... F ... 517 782-8898
Jackson *(G-8584)*
Thielenhaus Microfinish Corp ... E ... 248 349-9450
Novi *(G-12015)*
Thyssenkrupp System Engrg ... C ... 248 340-8000
Auburn Hills *(G-1019)*
Tri-Power Manufacturing Inc ... G ... 734 414-8084
Plymouth *(G-12779)*
Triangle Broach Company ... F ... 313 838-2150
Detroit *(G-4408)*
Trispec Precision Products Inc ... G ... 248 308-3231
Wixom *(G-17921)*
Troy Industries Inc ... F ... 586 739-7760
Shelby Township *(G-14711)*
U S Tool & Cutter Co ... F ... 248 553-7745
Novi *(G-12020)*
Utica Body & Assembly Inc ... E ... 586 726-4330
Troy *(G-16669)*
Utica Enterprises Inc ... C ... 586 726-4300
Troy *(G-16670)*
Van-Mark Products Corporation ... E ... 248 478-1200
Farmington Hills *(G-5146)*
Ventra Greenwich Holdings Corp ... G ... 586 759-8900
Warren *(G-17282)*
Waber Tool & Engineering Co ... E ... 269 342-0765
Kalamazoo *(G-8921)*
Warren Broach & Machine Corp ... F ... 586 254-7080
Sterling Heights *(G-15544)*
Wfl Millturn Technologies Inc ... G ... 440 729-0896
Wixom *(G-17930)*
Wolverine Carbide Die Company ... E ... 248 280-0300
Troy *(G-16695)*
Wolverine Machine Products Co ... E ... 248 634-9952
Holly *(G-7902)*

MACHINE TOOLS: Metal Forming

3M Company ... E ... 248 926-2500
Wixom *(G-17749)*
A W B Industries Inc ... E ... 989 739-1447
Oscoda *(G-12205)*
Advanced Feedlines LLC ... D ... 248 583-9400
Troy *(G-16169)*
American Wldg & Press Repr Inc ... F ... 248 358-2050
Southfield *(G-14837)*
B&P Littleford LLC ... E ... 989 757-1300
Saginaw *(G-13999)*
Baldauf Enterprises Inc ... E ... 989 686-0350
Bay City *(G-1280)*
Birdsall Tool & Gage Co ... E ... 248 474-5150
Farmington Hills *(G-4941)*
Century Inc ... C ... 231 947-6400
Traverse City *(G-15932)*
Cold Forming Technology Inc ... F ... 586 254-4600
Sterling Heights *(G-15291)*
Columbia Marking Tools Inc ... E ... 586 949-8400
Chesterfield *(G-2754)*
Contractors Steel Company ... E ... 616 531-4000
Grand Rapids *(G-6306)*
Die Cast Press Mfg Co Inc ... G ... 269 427-5408
Bangor *(G-1090)*
Dm Tool & Fab Inc ... D ... 586 726-8390
Sterling Heights *(G-15319)*
Eagle Machine Tool Corporation ... G ... 231 798-8473
Norton Shores *(G-11749)*
Enprotech Industrial Tech LLC ... C ... 517 372-0950
Lansing *(G-9226)*
Enprotech Industrial Tech LLC ... E ... 517 319-5306
Lansing *(G-9366)*
Feed - Lease Corp ... E ... 248 377-0000
Auburn Hills *(G-871)*
Fontijne Grotnes Inc ... E ... 269 262-4700
Niles *(G-11611)*
Global Strgc Sup Solutions LLC ... D ... 734 525-9100
Livonia *(G-9753)*
Globe Tech LLC ... E ... 734 656-2200
Plymouth *(G-12630)*
Hamilton Industrial Products ... E ... 269 751-5153
Hamilton *(G-7233)*
HMS Products Co ... D ... 248 689-8120
Troy *(G-16398)*
Howmet Corporation ... E ... 231 894-5686
Whitehall *(G-17669)*
Howmet Holdings Corporation ... G ... 231 894-5686
Whitehall *(G-17676)*
Jier North America Inc ... F ... 734 404-6683
Plymouth *(G-12653)*
Koppy Corporation ... D ... 248 373-1900
Royal Oak *(G-13942)*
M C Molds Inc ... E ... 517 655-5481
Williamston *(G-17733)*
Martinrea Industries Inc ... C ... 231 832-5504
Reed City *(G-13220)*
Miller Tool & Die Co ... E ... 517 782-0347
Jackson *(G-8529)*
Monroe LLC ... B ... 616 942-9820
Grand Rapids *(G-6702)*
Moore Production Tool Spc ... E ... 248 476-1200
Farmington *(G-4905)*
Mor-Tech Design Inc ... E ... 586 254-7982
Sterling Heights *(G-15427)*
Mor-Tech Manufacturing Inc ... E ... 586 254-7982
Sterling Heights *(G-15428)*
Penka Tool Corporation ... G ... 248 543-3940
Madison Heights *(G-10322)*
Press Room Eqp Sls & Svc Co ... G ... 248 334-1880
Pontiac *(G-12857)*
Production Fabricators Inc ... E ... 231 777-3822
Muskegon *(G-11407)*
Productivity Technologies ... C ... 810 714-0200
Fenton *(G-5231)*
Prophotonix Limited ... E ... 586 778-1100
Roseville *(G-13856)*
Pt Tech Stamping Inc ... E ... 586 293-1810
Fraser *(G-5713)*
R and T West Michigan Inc ... E ... 616 698-9931
Caledonia *(G-2311)*
Rempco Acquisition Inc ... E ... 231 775-0108
Cadillac *(G-2274)*
Shannon Precision Fastener LLC ... E ... 248 658-3015
Madison Heights *(G-10350)*
Shape Dynamics Intl Inc ... G ... 231 733-2164
Muskegon *(G-11421)*
Stilson Products LLC ... E ... 586 778-1100
Roseville *(G-13875)*
T & D Machine Inc ... G ... 517 423-0778
Tecumseh *(G-15810)*
Tech Tooling Specialties Inc ... F ... 517 782-8898
Jackson *(G-8584)*
Triple Tool ... F ... 586 795-1785
Sterling Heights *(G-15530)*

MACHINERY & EQPT FINANCE LEASING

Enterprise Services LLC ... F ... 734 523-6525
Livonia *(G-9727)*
Ervin Industries Inc ... E ... 734 769-4600
Ann Arbor *(G-447)*
Mistequay Group Ltd ... D ... 989 846-1000
Standish *(G-15224)*

PRODUCT SECTION

MACHINERY & EQPT, INDL, WHOLESALE: Machine Tools & Access

MACHINERY & EQPT, AGRICULTURAL, WHOL: Farm Eqpt Parts/Splys

Tupes of Saginaw Inc ....F 989 799-1550
  Saginaw *(G-14169)*

MACHINERY & EQPT, AGRICULTURAL, WHOL: Poultry/Livestock Eqpt

Ozland Enterprises Inc ....G 269 649-0706
  Vicksburg *(G-16840)*

MACHINERY & EQPT, AGRICULTURAL, WHOLESALE: Farm Implements

Van Paemels Equipment Company ......G 586 784-5295
  Armada *(G-724)*

MACHINERY & EQPT, AGRICULTURAL, WHOLESALE: Landscaping Eqpt

Bay-Houston Towing Company ....E 810 648-2210
  Sandusky *(G-14430)*
Doug Wirt Enterprises Inc ....G 989 684-5777
  Bay City *(G-1305)*
Michigan Wood Fibers Llc ....G 616 875-2241
  Zeeland *(G-18164)*
Springfield Landscape Mtls ....G 269 965-6748
  Springfield *(G-15204)*

MACHINERY & EQPT, AGRICULTURAL, WHOLESALE: Livestock Eqpt

Anderson Welding & Mfg Inc ....F 906 523-4661
  Chassell *(G-2671)*

MACHINERY & EQPT, INDL, WHOL: Brewery Prdts Mfrg, Commercial

Keglove LLC ....E 616 610-7289
  Holland *(G-7708)*
Loggers Brewing Co ....G 989 401-3085
  Saginaw *(G-14079)*

MACHINERY & EQPT, INDL, WHOL: Controlling Instruments/Access

Applied Instruments Company ....E 810 227-5510
  Brighton *(G-1886)*
Cammenga & Associates LLC ....E 313 914-7160
  Dearborn *(G-3684)*

MACHINERY & EQPT, INDL, WHOL: Environ Pollution Cntrl, Air

Swat Environmental Inc ....E 517 322-2999
  Lansing *(G-9427)*

MACHINERY & EQPT, INDL, WHOL: Environ Pollution Cntrl, Water

Antimicrobial Specialist Assoc ....F 989 662-0377
  Auburn *(G-749)*
Lyman Thornton ....G 248 762-8433
  Wixom *(G-17847)*

MACHINERY & EQPT, INDL, WHOL: Meters, Consumption Registerng

Vaughan Industries Inc ....F 313 935-2040
  Detroit *(G-4423)*

MACHINERY & EQPT, INDL, WHOLESALE: Conveyor Systems

Best Industrial Group Inc ....F 586 826-8800
  Warren *(G-16957)*
Corr-Fac Corporation ....G 989 358-7050
  Alpena *(G-284)*
P & A Conveyor Sales Inc ....G 734 285-7970
  Riverview *(G-13303)*
Pneumatic Innovations LLC ....G 989 734-3435
  Millersburg *(G-10992)*
Siemens Industry Inc ....C 616 913-7700
  Grand Rapids *(G-6861)*
Valmec Inc ....G 810 629-8750
  Fenton *(G-5248)*
W G Benjey Inc ....G 989 356-0027
  Alpena *(G-320)*

MACHINERY & EQPT, INDL, WHOLESALE: Cranes

C R B Crane & Service Co ....G 586 757-1222
  Warren *(G-16973)*
Crane 1 Services Inc ....E 586 468-0909
  Harrison Township *(G-7327)*
Crane Technologies Group Inc ....E 248 652-8700
  Rochester Hills *(G-13397)*
Plutchak Fab ....G 906 864-4650
  Menominee *(G-10755)*

MACHINERY & EQPT, INDL, WHOLESALE: Engines & Parts, Diesel

Chesterfield Engines Inc ....G 586 949-5777
  Chesterfield *(G-2753)*
Cummins Bridgeway Grove Cy LLC .....G 614 604-6000
  New Hudson *(G-11535)*
Cummins Inc ....F 586 469-2010
  Clinton Township *(G-3095)*
Cummins Inc ....E 989 752-5200
  Saginaw *(G-14023)*
Cummins Inc ....E 248 573-1900
  New Hudson *(G-11536)*
Cummins Npower LLC ....E 906 475-8800
  Negaunee *(G-11469)*
K & S Property Inc ....A 248 573-1600
  New Hudson *(G-11546)*
Kraft Power Corporation ....F 989 748-4040
  Gaylord *(G-5872)*

MACHINERY & EQPT, INDL, WHOLESALE: Engines, Gasoline

Area Cycle Inc ....G 989 777-0850
  Bridgeport *(G-1849)*

MACHINERY & EQPT, INDL, WHOLESALE: Engs & Parts, Air-Cooled

D & S Engine Specialist Inc ....F 248 583-9240
  Clawson *(G-2976)*

MACHINERY & EQPT, INDL, WHOLESALE: Engs/Transportation Eqpt

Martin Electric Mtrs Sls & Svc ....G 989 584-3850
  Carson City *(G-2492)*

MACHINERY & EQPT, INDL, WHOLESALE: Food Manufacturing

Pappas Cutlery-Grinding Inc ....G 800 521-0888
  Detroit *(G-4289)*

MACHINERY & EQPT, INDL, WHOLESALE: Food Product Manufacturng

D C Norris North America LLC ....G 231 935-1519
  Traverse City *(G-15955)*
Harrison Partners Inv Group ....G 419 708-8154
  Milan *(G-10940)*

MACHINERY & EQPT, INDL, WHOLESALE: Fuel Injection Systems

Autocam Corporation ....B 616 698-0707
  Kentwood *(G-9000)*
Lisi Automotive HI Vol Inc ....F 734 266-6958
  Livonia *(G-9812)*

MACHINERY & EQPT, INDL, WHOLESALE: Hoists

Whiting Corporation ....G 734 451-0400
  Plymouth *(G-12794)*

MACHINERY & EQPT, INDL, WHOLESALE: Hydraulic Systems

Behco Inc ....F 586 755-0200
  Madison Heights *(G-10203)*
E K Hydraulics Inc ....G 800 632-7112
  Petoskey *(G-12448)*
Flodraulic Group Incorporated ....D 734 326-5400
  Westland *(G-17558)*
Great Lakes Hydra Corporation ....F 616 949-8844
  Grand Rapids *(G-6479)*
Gregory M Boese ....F 989 754-2990
  Saginaw *(G-14052)*
Hydra-Tech Inc ....G 586 232-4479
  Macomb *(G-10130)*
J H Bennett and Company Inc ....E 248 596-5100
  Novi *(G-11910)*
Kord Industrial Inc ....G 248 374-8900
  Wixom *(G-17843)*
Lube - Power Inc ....D 586 247-6500
  Shelby Township *(G-14628)*
Marrel Corporation ....G 616 863-9155
  Rockford *(G-13578)*
Mfp Automation Engineering Inc ....D 616 538-5700
  Hudsonville *(G-8167)*
Morrell Incorporated ....D 248 373-1600
  Auburn Hills *(G-949)*
Wmh Fluidpower Inc ....F 269 327-7011
  Portage *(G-13058)*

MACHINERY & EQPT, INDL, WHOLESALE: Indl Machine Parts

Eagle Quest International Ltd ....F 616 850-2630
  Norton Shores *(G-11750)*
Electro ARC Manufacturing Co ....E 734 483-4233
  Dexter *(G-4491)*
Equipment Material Sales LLC ....G 734 284-8711
  Wyandotte *(G-17958)*
Hti Associates LLC ....E 616 399-5430
  Holland *(G-7682)*
Jomat Industries Ltd ....F 586 336-1801
  Bruce Twp *(G-2085)*
Kenrie Inc ....F 616 494-3200
  Holland *(G-7710)*
Paradigm Engineering Inc ....G 586 776-5910
  Roseville *(G-13849)*

MACHINERY & EQPT, INDL, WHOLESALE: Instruments & Cntrl Eqpt

Balogh Tag Inc ....G 248 486-7343
  Brighton *(G-1888)*
Medsker Electric Inc ....E 248 855-3383
  Farmington Hills *(G-5062)*

MACHINERY & EQPT, INDL, WHOLESALE: Lift Trucks & Parts

4ever Aluminum Products Inc ....F 517 368-0000
  Coldwater *(G-3286)*
Alta Equipment Holdings Inc ....E 248 449-6700
  Livonia *(G-9638)*

MACHINERY & EQPT, INDL, WHOLESALE: Machine Tools & Access

Adaptable Tool Supply LLC ....F 248 439-0866
  Clawson *(G-2970)*
All-Fab Corporation ....G 269 673-6572
  Allegan *(G-147)*
Antech Tool Inc ....F 734 207-3622
  Canton *(G-2348)*
Champion Screw Mch Engrg Inc ....F 248 624-4545
  Wixom *(G-17785)*
Clausing Industrial Inc ....E 269 345-7155
  Kalamazoo *(G-8706)*
Clausing Industrial Inc ....D 269 345-7155
  Kalamazoo *(G-8707)*
Cleary Developments Inc ....E 248 588-7011
  Madison Heights *(G-10210)*
E & E Special Products LLC ....F 586 978-3377
  Warren *(G-17012)*
Ebinger Manufacturing Company ....F 248 486-8880
  Brighton *(G-1917)*
Fluid Systems Engineering Inc ....E 586 790-8880
  Clinton Township *(G-3123)*
Fourway Machinery Sales Co ....F 517 782-9371
  Jackson *(G-8451)*
Henrob Corporation ....D 248 493-3800
  New Hudson *(G-11543)*
Kyocera Unimerco Tooling Inc ....E 734 944-4433
  Saline *(G-14397)*
Machine Control Technology ....G 517 655-3506
  Williamston *(G-17734)*
Mq Operating Company ....E 906 337-1515
  Calumet *(G-2330)*
Peak Edm Inc ....G 248 380-0871
  Wixom *(G-17876)*
Punchcraft McHning Tooling LLC ....E 586 573-4840
  Warren *(G-17211)*

MACHINERY & EQPT, INDL, WHOLESALE: Machine Tools & Access

Schutte MSA LLC ....F 517 782-3600
  Jackson *(G-8570)*
South Park Sales & Mfg Inc ....G 313 381-7579
  Dearborn *(G-3762)*
Sycron Technologies Inc ....G 810 694-4007
  Grand Blanc *(G-5985)*
Teknikut Corporation ....G 586 778-7150
  Canton *(G-2435)*
Viscount Equipment Co Inc ....G 586 293-5900
  Fraser *(G-5746)*

MACHINERY & EQPT, INDL, WHOLESALE: Machine Tools & Metalwork

Aero Grinding Inc...............................D 586 774-6450
  Roseville *(G-13770)*
Arm Tooling Systems Inc ....F 586 759-5677
  Warren *(G-16938)*
Die Cast Press Mfg Co Inc ....E 269 657-6060
  Paw Paw *(G-12403)*
Hougen Manufacturing Inc ....C 810 635-7111
  Swartz Creek *(G-15667)*
Letts Industries Inc ....G 313 579-1100
  Detroit *(G-4200)*
Micro EDM Co LLC ....G 989 872-4306
  Cass City *(G-2520)*
Roberts Sinto Corporation ....C 517 371-2460
  Lansing *(G-9320)*
Walther Trowal LLC ....F 616 455-8940
  Grand Rapids *(G-6978)*
Wolverine Special Tool Inc ....E 616 791-1027
  Grand Rapids *(G-7000)*

MACHINERY & EQPT, INDL, WHOLESALE: Measure/Test, Electric

Analytical Process Systems Inc ....E 248 393-0700
  Auburn Hills *(G-770)*
Mycrona Inc ....F 734 453-9348
  Plymouth *(G-12697)*

MACHINERY & EQPT, INDL, WHOLESALE: Metal Refining

Ied Inc ....G 231 728-9154
  Muskegon *(G-11346)*

MACHINERY & EQPT, INDL, WHOLESALE: Paint Spray

Herkules Equipment Corporation.........E 248 960-7100
  Commerce Township *(G-3411)*
Sames Kremlin Inc ....C 734 979-0100
  Plymouth *(G-12747)*
Sames Kremlin Inc ....F 734 979-0100
  Plymouth *(G-12748)*

MACHINERY & EQPT, INDL, WHOLESALE: Petroleum Industry

D & W Flow Testing Inc ....G 231 258-4926
  Kalkaska *(G-8940)*
Lube-Tech Inc ....G 269 329-1269
  Portage *(G-13012)*

MACHINERY & EQPT, INDL, WHOLESALE: Plastic Prdts Machinery

Gt Plastics & Equipment LLC ....F 616 678-7445
  Kent City *(G-8991)*

MACHINERY & EQPT, INDL, WHOLESALE: Pneumatic Tools

REO Hydraulic & Mfg Inc ....E 313 891-2244
  Detroit *(G-4342)*

MACHINERY & EQPT, INDL, WHOLESALE: Processing & Packaging

Mark-Pack Inc ....E 616 837-5400
  Coopersville *(G-3564)*
Oliver Products Company ....D 616 456-7711
  Grand Rapids *(G-6728)*

MACHINERY & EQPT, INDL, WHOLESALE: Recycling

Libra Industries Michigan ....G 517 787-5675
  Jackson *(G-8499)*

MACHINERY & EQPT, INDL, WHOLESALE: Robots

National Advanced Mobility ....G 734 995-3098
  Ann Arbor *(G-571)*
Realm ....G 313 706-4401
  Wayne *(G-17441)*

MACHINERY & EQPT, INDL, WHOLESALE: Safety Eqpt

C & C Enterprises Inc ....G 989 772-5095
  Mount Pleasant *(G-11182)*
Douglass Safety Systems LLC ....G 989 687-7600
  Sanford *(G-14449)*
Rpb Safety LLC ....E 866 494-4599
  Royal Oak *(G-13969)*

MACHINERY & EQPT, INDL, WHOLESALE: Sawmill

Menominee Saw and Supply Co ....E 906 863-2609
  Menominee *(G-10747)*

MACHINERY & EQPT, INDL, WHOLESALE: Screening

Northern Process Systems Inc ....G 810 714-5200
  Fenton *(G-5227)*

MACHINERY & EQPT, INDL, WHOLESALE: Sewing

William Cosgriff Electrc ....G 313 832-6958
  Detroit *(G-4442)*

MACHINERY & EQPT, INDL, WHOLESALE: Textile

Oerlikon Metco (us) Inc ....E 248 288-0027
  Troy *(G-16533)*

MACHINERY & EQPT, INDL, WHOLESALE: Tool & Die Makers

Eagle Industrial Group Inc ....E 616 647-9904
  Comstock Park *(G-3481)*

MACHINERY & EQPT, INDL, WHOLESALE: Water Pumps

Kerr Pump and Supply Inc ....E 248 543-3880
  Oak Park *(G-12076)*
Sales Driven Services LLC ....G 586 854-9494
  Rochester *(G-13350)*

MACHINERY & EQPT, WHOLESALE: Blades, Graders, Scrapers, Etc

Trynex International LLC ....F 248 586-3500
  Madison Heights *(G-10371)*

MACHINERY & EQPT, WHOLESALE: Construction & Mining, Ladders

Michigan Ladder Company LLC ....F 734 482-5946
  Ypsilanti *(G-18090)*
Ortus Enterprises LLC ....G 269 491-1447
  Portage *(G-13020)*

MACHINERY & EQPT, WHOLESALE: Construction & Mining, Pavers

Petter Investments Inc ....F 269 637-1997
  South Haven *(G-14767)*

MACHINERY & EQPT, WHOLESALE: Construction, General

Boomer Company ....E 313 832-5050
  Detroit *(G-3910)*
Eagle Industrial Group Inc ....E 616 647-9904
  Comstock Park *(G-3481)*
Hines Corporation ....F 231 799-6240
  Norton Shores *(G-11812)*

MACHINERY & EQPT, WHOLESALE: Logging & Forestry

Bandit Industries Inc ....B 989 561-2270
  Remus *(G-13237)*
James L Miller ....G 989 539-5540
  Harrison *(G-7313)*

MACHINERY & EQPT, WHOLESALE: Masonry

E M I Construction Products ....D 616 392-7207
  Holland *(G-7615)*

MACHINERY & EQPT, WHOLESALE: Oil Field Eqpt

Great Lakes Wellhead Inc ....G 231 943-9100
  Grawn *(G-7098)*

MACHINERY & EQPT: Electroplating

Vanova Technologies LLC ....G 734 476-7204
  Superior Township *(G-15648)*

MACHINERY & EQPT: Farm

A & B Packing Equipment Inc ....C 269 539-4700
  Lawrence *(G-9504)*
Advanced Drainage Systems Inc ....D 989 723-5208
  Owosso *(G-12275)*
Advanced Farm Equipment LLC ....F 989 268-5711
  Vestaburg *(G-16825)*
Agritek Industries Inc ....D 616 786-9200
  Holland *(G-7551)*
Andersen Oakleaf Inc ....G 517 546-1805
  Howell *(G-8014)*
Bader & Co ....E 810 648-2404
  Sandusky *(G-14429)*
Big Foot Manufacturing Co ....F 231 775-5588
  Cadillac *(G-2231)*
Boxer Equipment/Morbark Inc ....G 989 866-2381
  Winn *(G-17746)*
CPM Acquisition Corp ....G 231 947-6400
  Traverse City *(G-15950)*
Diamond Moba Americas Inc ....C 248 476-7100
  Farmington Hills *(G-4971)*
Eagle Group II Ltd ....E 616 754-7777
  Greenville *(G-7129)*
Express Welding Inc ....G 906 786-8808
  Escanaba *(G-4829)*
Gillisons Var Fabrication Inc ....E 231 882-5921
  Benzonia *(G-1575)*
Heath Manufacturing Company ....D 616 997-8181
  Coopersville *(G-3561)*
Mensch Manufacturing LLC ....C 269 945-5300
  Hastings *(G-7420)*
Mensch Mfg Mar Div Inc ....E 269 945-5300
  Hastings *(G-7421)*
Michigan AG Services Inc ....F 616 374-8803
  Lake Odessa *(G-9117)*
Morbark LLC ....B 989 866-2381
  Winn *(G-17747)*
Phil Brown Welding Corporation ....F 616 784-3046
  Conklin *(G-3531)*
Steiner Tractor Parts Inc ....E 810 621-3000
  Lennon *(G-9519)*
Stephens Pipe & Steel LLC ....E 616 248-3433
  Grand Rapids *(G-6892)*
Superior Attachment Inc ....G 906 864-1708
  Menominee *(G-10758)*
Tindall Packaging Inc ....G 269 649-1163
  Portage *(G-13050)*
Turkey Creek Inc ....F 517 451-5221
  Tecumseh *(G-15814)*
Van Paemels Equipment Company ....G 586 784-5295
  Armada *(G-724)*

MACHINERY & EQPT: Gas Producers, Generators/Other Rltd Eqpt

Global Tooling Systems LLC ....E 586 726-0500
  Macomb *(G-10127)*
Plamondon Oil Co Inc ....G 231 256-9261
  Lake Leelanau *(G-9106)*
Polk Gas Producer LLC ....G 734 913-2970
  Ann Arbor *(G-594)*

MACHINERY & EQPT: Liquid Automation

AA Anderson & Co Inc ....E 248 476-7782
  Plymouth *(G-12559)*

PRODUCT SECTION

MACHINERY, METALWORKING: Assembly, Including Robotic

Alberts Machine Tool Inc..................G...... 231 743-2457
  Marion *(G-10489)*
Avl North Amer Corp Svcs Inc ....A...... 734 414-9600
  Plymouth *(G-12579)*
Dispense Technologies LLC ....G...... 248 486-6244
  Brighton *(G-1911)*
Inovatech Automation Inc ....F...... 586 210-9010
  Macomb *(G-10131)*
Solutions 4 Automation Inc ....F...... 989 790-2778
  Saginaw *(G-14151)*
Terrell Manufacturing Svcs Inc ....F...... 231 788-2000
  Muskegon *(G-11435)*

MACHINERY & EQPT: Metal Finishing, Plating Etc

Ctmf Inc...E....... 734 482-3086
  Ypsilanti *(G-18063)*
Dipsol of America Inc ....E....... 734 367-0530
  Livonia *(G-9713)*
Durr Inc ....G....... 734 459-6800
  Southfield *(G-14888)*
Durr Systems Inc ....B....... 248 450-2000
  Southfield *(G-14889)*
Durr Systems Inc ....C....... 248 745-8500
  Southfield *(G-14890)*
Fanuc America Corporation..................B....... 248 377-7000
  Rochester Hills *(G-13423)*
Giffin Inc ....D....... 248 494-9600
  Auburn Hills *(G-884)*
Grav Co LLC ....F....... 269 651-5467
  Sturgis *(G-15605)*
Gravel Flow Inc ....G....... 269 651-5467
  Sturgis *(G-15606)*
Ied Inc ....G....... 231 728-9154
  Muskegon *(G-11346)*
Met-L-Tec LLC ....E....... 734 847-7004
  Temperance *(G-15837)*
Morrell Incorporated ....D....... 248 373-1600
  Auburn Hills *(G-949)*
Mp Tool & Engineering Company..........E....... 586 772-7730
  Roseville *(G-13841)*
Omega Industries Michigan LLC ....G....... 616 460-0500
  Grand Rapids *(G-6729)*
Pioneer Metal Finishing LLC ....G....... 877 721-1100
  Warren *(G-17186)*
Tks Industrial Company ....E....... 248 786-5000
  Troy *(G-16645)*
Upton Industries Inc ....E....... 586 771-1200
  Roseville *(G-13887)*
Z-Brite Metal Finishing Inc ....F....... 269 422-2191
  Stevensville *(G-15586)*

MACHINERY & EQPT: Vibratory Parts Handling Eqpt

Great Lakes Allied LLC......................G....... 231 924-5794
  White Cloud *(G-17622)*
Rosler Metal Finishing USA LLC ....D....... 269 441-3000
  Battle Creek *(G-1242)*

MACHINERY BASES

A&G Corporate Holdings LLC ....G....... 734 513-3488
  Livonia *(G-9620)*
A2 Energy Systems ....G....... 734 622-9800
  Plymouth *(G-12558)*
Great Lakes Laser Dynamics Inc..........D....... 616 892-7070
  Allendale *(G-218)*
Johnson Systems Inc ....G....... 616 455-1900
  Caledonia *(G-2304)*
M & J Manufacturing Inc ....G....... 586 778-6352
  Roseville *(G-13827)*
Neucadia LLC ....G....... 989 572-0324
  Carson City *(G-2494)*
Prototech Laser Inc ....E....... 586 598-6900
  Chesterfield *(G-2827)*
Unisorb Inc ....E....... 517 764-6060
  Michigan Center *(G-10792)*

MACHINERY, COMMERCIAL LAUNDRY & Drycleaning: Ironers

Pressing Point ....G....... 810 387-3441
  Brockway *(G-2020)*

MACHINERY, EQPT & SUPPLIES: Parking Facility

Cincinnati Time Systems Inc ....F....... 248 615-8300
  Farmington Hills *(G-4963)*

Perfected Grave Vault Co....................G...... 616 243-3375
  Grand Rapids *(G-6748)*
Traffic Sfety Ctrl Systems Inc ....E...... 248 348-0570
  Wixom *(G-17914)*

MACHINERY, FOOD PRDTS: Biscuit Cutters

Schallips Inc ....G...... 906 635-0941
  Barbeau *(G-1117)*

MACHINERY, FOOD PRDTS: Cutting, Chopping, Grinding, Mixing

Carb-A-Tron Tool Co............................G...... 517 782-2249
  Jackson *(G-8402)*
Kitchenaid..G...... 800 541-6390
  Benton Harbor *(G-1519)*

MACHINERY, FOOD PRDTS: Dairy & Milk

J J Steel Inc ....E...... 269 964-0474
  Battle Creek *(G-1201)*
Twin Beginnings LLC ....G...... 248 542-6250
  Huntington Woods *(G-8192)*

MACHINERY, FOOD PRDTS: Food Processing, Smokers

Baker Perkins Inc................................D....... 616 784-3111
  Grand Rapids *(G-6202)*

MACHINERY, FOOD PRDTS: Grinders, Commercial

Pappas Cutlery-Grinding Inc ....G...... 800 521-0888
  Detroit *(G-4289)*

MACHINERY, FOOD PRDTS: Juice Extractors, Fruit & Veg, Comm

Dunkley International Inc ....C...... 269 343-5583
  Kalamazoo *(G-8732)*
Precision Extraction Corp....................G...... 855 420-0020
  Troy *(G-16560)*

MACHINERY, FOOD PRDTS: Ovens, Bakery

Middleby Corporation...........................C...... 906 863-4401
  Menominee *(G-10750)*
Rustic Cking Dsigns Strlng Hts............G...... 586 795-4897
  Sterling Heights *(G-15482)*

MACHINERY, FOOD PRDTS: Pasta

Blackmer Dover Resources Inc ....G....... 616 475-9285
  Grand Rapids *(G-6230)*

MACHINERY, FOOD PRDTS: Processing, Fish & Shellfish

Pisces Fish Machinery Inc ....E...... 906 789-1636
  Gladstone *(G-5919)*

MACHINERY, FOOD PRDTS: Roasting, Coffee, Peanut, Etc.

Duke De Jong LLC..............................G...... 734 403-1708
  Taylor *(G-15710)*
Infusco Coffee Roasters LLC...............G...... 269 213-5282
  Sawyer *(G-14485)*
Peanut Shop Inc..................................G...... 517 374-0008
  Lansing *(G-9409)*

MACHINERY, FOOD PRDTS: Slicers, Commercial

Foodtools Inc ....E....... 269 637-9969
  South Haven *(G-14759)*

MACHINERY, LUBRICATION: Automatic

Advance Products Corporation............E....... 269 849-1000
  Benton Harbor *(G-1480)*
Positech Inc...G...... 616 949-4024
  Grand Rapids *(G-6759)*

MACHINERY, MAILING: Mailing

Pitney Bowes Inc ....D....... 203 356-5000
  South Lyon *(G-14810)*

Pitney Bowes Inc ....E...... 248 348-0570
  (G-17914)

MACHINERY, MAILING: Postage Meters

Pitney Bowes Inc ....D...... 248 625-1666
  Davisburg *(G-3637)*
Pitney Bowes Inc ....F...... 248 591-2800
  Madison Heights *(G-10328)*

MACHINERY, METALWORKING: Assembly, Including Robotic

Ais Automation Systems Inc ....F...... 734 365-2384
  Rockwood *(G-13603)*
Allied Tool and Machine Co ....E...... 989 755-5384
  Saginaw *(G-13995)*
Apollo Seiko Ltd...................................F...... 269 465-3400
  Bridgman *(G-1859)*
Atlas Technologies LLC ....D...... 810 714-2128
  Fenton *(G-5183)*
Auto/Con Corp ....D...... 586 791-7474
  Fraser *(G-5623)*
Burton Industries Inc ....E...... 906 932-5970
  Ironwood *(G-8323)*
Creative Automation Inc.......................E...... 734 780-3175
  Whitmore Lake *(G-17694)*
Dane Systems LLC ....D...... 269 465-3263
  Stevensville *(G-15562)*
Das Group Inc ....G...... 248 670-2718
  Royal Oak *(G-13917)*
Diamond Automation Ltd ....G...... 734 838-7138
  Livonia *(G-9710)*
Dominion Tech Group Inc ....C...... 586 773-3303
  Roseville *(G-13797)*
Duo Robotic Solutions Inc ....F...... 586 883-7559
  Sterling Heights *(G-15322)*
Esys Automation LLC..........................D...... 248 754-1900
  Auburn Hills *(G-856)*
Fives Cinetic Corp ....D...... 248 477-0800
  Farmington Hills *(G-5002)*
Fluid Innovations Inc ....G...... 810 241-0990
  Sterling Heights *(G-15343)*
Hanwha Techm Usa LLC ....G...... 248 588-1242
  Rochester Hills *(G-13439)*
Ideal Tool Inc ....F...... 989 893-8336
  Bay City *(G-1321)*
J W Froehlich Inc ....E...... 586 580-0025
  Sterling Heights *(G-15379)*
J W Holdings Inc ....E...... 616 530-9889
  Grand Rapids *(G-6549)*
JR Automation Tech LLC ....C...... 616 399-2168
  Holland *(G-7698)*
JR Automation Tech LLC ....G...... 616 399-2168
  Holland *(G-7699)*
JR Automation Tech LLC ....G...... 616 399-2168
  Holland *(G-7700)*
JR Automation Tech LLC ....G...... 616 399-2168
  Holland *(G-7701)*
Jr Technology Group LLC ....C...... 616 399-2168
  Holland *(G-7702)*
Kuka Assembly and Test Corp ....C...... 989 220-3088
  Saginaw *(G-14074)*
Kuka Systems North America LLC.......B...... 586 795-2000
  Sterling Heights *(G-15392)*
Kuka Systems North America LLC.......... 586 726-4300
  Shelby Township *(G-14616)*
Kuka US Holding Company LLC ....F...... 586 795-2000
  Sterling Heights *(G-15393)*
L & H Diversified Mfg USA LLC ....G...... 586 615-4873
  Shelby Township *(G-14618)*
Lab Tool and Engineering Corp............E...... 517 750-4131
  Spring Arbor *(G-15124)*
Letnan Industries Inc ....E...... 586 726-1155
  Sterling Heights *(G-15397)*
Lomar Machine & Tool Co ....E...... 517 563-8136
  Horton *(G-7966)*
Mark One Corporation ....D...... 989 732-2427
  Gaylord *(G-5877)*
National Advanced Mobility ....G...... 734 995-3098
  Ann Arbor *(G-571)*
Norgren Automtn Solutions LLC ....E...... 734 429-4989
  Saline *(G-14406)*
Novi Precision Products Inc ....E...... 810 227-1024
  Brighton *(G-1970)*
Pro-Tech Machine Inc ....E...... 810 743-1854
  Burton *(G-2161)*
Prosys Industries Inc...........................E....... 734 207-3710
  Canton *(G-2421)*
Rock Tool & Machine Co Inc................E...... 734 455-9840
  Plymouth *(G-12743)*
Roma Tool Inc ....F...... 248 218-1889
  Lake Orion *(G-9156)*

Employee Codes: A=Over 500 employees, B=251-500
C=101-250, D=51-100, E=20-50, F=10-19, G=3-9

2020 Harris Michigan Industrial Directory

1281

MACHINERY, METALWORKING: Assembly, Including Robotic

Schenck USA Corp .... E 248 377-2100
  Southfield *(G-15024)*
Smartcoast LLC .... G 231 571-2020
  Grand Rapids *(G-6868)*
Spen-Tech Machine Engrg Corp .... D 810 275-6800
  Flint *(G-5501)*
TA Systems Inc .... D 248 656-5150
  Rochester Hills *(G-13522)*
Tarpon Automation & Design Co .... E 586 774-8020
  Warren *(G-17263)*
Toman Industries Inc .... G 734 289-1393
  Monroe *(G-11079)*
Utica Body & Assembly Inc .... E 586 726-4330
  Troy *(G-16669)*
Utica Enterprises Inc .... C 586 726-4300
  Troy *(G-16670)*
Utica International Inc .... C 586 726-4330
  Troy *(G-16671)*
Wright-K Technology Inc .... E 989 752-2588
  Saginaw *(G-14184)*
Yaskawa America Inc .... F 248 668-8800
  Rochester Hills *(G-13549)*

MACHINERY, METALWORKING: Coiling

Feed - Lease Corp .... E 248 377-0000
  Auburn Hills *(G-871)*
Heidtman Steel Products Inc .... D 734 848-2115
  Erie *(G-4803)*
Perfecto Industries Inc .... E 989 732-2941
  Gaylord *(G-5888)*

MACHINERY, METALWORKING: Cutting & Slitting

Bay Plastics Machinery Co LLC .... E 989 671-9630
  Bay City *(G-1288)*

MACHINERY, METALWORKING: Rotary Slitters, Metalworking

Van-Mark Products Corporation .... E 248 478-1200
  Farmington Hills *(G-5146)*

MACHINERY, OFFICE: Paper Handling

Central Michigan Engravers .... G 517 485-5865
  Lansing *(G-9208)*

MACHINERY, PACKAGING: Carton Packing

Elopak Inc .... C 248 486-4600
  Wixom *(G-17801)*
Elopak-Americas Inc .... C 248 486-4600
  Wixom *(G-17802)*

MACHINERY, PACKAGING: Packing & Wrapping

Kalamazoo Packg Systems LLC .... F 616 534-2600
  Wyoming *(G-18013)*
RED Stamp Inc .... E 616 878-7771
  Grand Rapids *(G-6816)*

MACHINERY, PACKAGING: Vacuum

Ameri-Serv Group .... F 734 426-9700
  Troy *(G-16195)*
Industrial Model Inc .... G 586 254-0450
  Auburn Hills *(G-913)*

MACHINERY, PACKAGING: Wrapping

Highlight Industries Inc .... D 616 531-2464
  Wyoming *(G-18010)*

MACHINERY, PAPER INDUSTRY: Coating & Finishing

Euclid Coating Systems Inc .... F 989 922-4789
  Bay City *(G-1309)*

MACHINERY, PAPER INDUSTRY: Converting, Die Cutting & Stampng

Challenge Machinery Company .... E 231 799-8484
  Norton Shores *(G-11745)*
S & W Holdings Ltd .... G 248 723-2870
  Birmingham *(G-1701)*

MACHINERY, PAPER INDUSTRY: Cutting

Graphic Art Service & Supply .... G 810 229-4700
  Brighton *(G-1933)*
Graphic Arts Service & Sup Inc .... F 616 698-9300
  Grand Rapids *(G-6473)*

MACHINERY, PAPER INDUSTRY: Paper Mill, Plating, Etc

Hycorr LLC .... F 269 381-6349
  Kalamazoo *(G-8771)*

MACHINERY, PRINTING TRADES: Bookbinding Machinery

F P Rosback Co .... E 269 983-2582
  Saint Joseph *(G-14310)*

MACHINERY, PRINTING TRADES: Copy Holders

M & M Typewriter Service Inc .... G 734 995-4033
  Ann Arbor *(G-536)*

MACHINERY, PRINTING TRADES: Type & Type Making

Varn International Inc .... G 734 781-4600
  Plymouth *(G-12785)*

MACHINERY, PRINTING TRADES: Type Casting, Founding/Melting

Haynie and Hess Realty Co LLC .... F 586 296-2750
  Fraser *(G-5659)*

MACHINERY, SEWING: Sewing & Hat & Zipper Making

Ace Controls Inc .... C 248 476-0213
  Farmington Hills *(G-4919)*
Imperial Industries Inc .... F 734 397-1400
  Saline *(G-14395)*
Knight Industries Inc .... G 248 377-4950
  Auburn Hills *(G-928)*

MACHINERY, TEXTILE: Embroidery

All American Embroidery Inc .... F 734 421-9292
  Livonia *(G-9634)*
Fabri-Tech Inc .... E 616 662-0150
  Jenison *(G-8626)*
Needles N Pins Inc .... G 734 459-0625
  Plymouth *(G-12700)*
Tri-State Technical Services .... G 517 563-8743
  Hanover *(G-7262)*

MACHINERY, TEXTILE: Finishing

Oji Intertech Inc .... G 248 373-7733
  Auburn Hills *(G-964)*

MACHINERY, TEXTILE: Heddles, Wire, For Loom Harnesses

Orri Corp .... F 248 618-1104
  Waterford *(G-17364)*

MACHINERY, TEXTILE: Opening

Bpg International Fin Co LLC .... G 616 855-1480
  Ada *(G-11)*

MACHINERY, TEXTILE: Printing

Becmar Corp .... G 616 675-7479
  Bailey *(G-1077)*

MACHINERY, TEXTILE: Silk Screens

Carry-All Products Inc .... F 616 399-8080
  Holland *(G-7585)*
Craft Press Printing Inc .... G 269 683-9694
  Niles *(G-11602)*

MACHINERY, TEXTILE: Thread Making Or Spinning

Superior Threading Inc .... F 989 729-1160
  Owosso *(G-12319)*

MACHINERY, WOODWORKING: Bandsaws

Coxline Inc .... E 269 345-1132
  Kalamazoo *(G-8720)*
Parma Manufacturing Co Inc .... G 517 531-4111
  Parma *(G-12392)*

MACHINERY, WOODWORKING: Cabinet Makers'

Moda Manufacturing LLC .... G 586 204-5120
  Farmington Hills *(G-5071)*
R J Flood Professional Co .... G 269 930-3608
  Stevensville *(G-15579)*

MACHINERY, WOODWORKING: Furniture Makers

Northern Woodcrafters .... G 989 348-2553
  Grayling *(G-7114)*

MACHINERY, WOODWORKING: Pattern Makers'

Bespro Pattern Inc .... F 586 268-6970
  Madison Heights *(G-10204)*
Northwest Pattern Company .... G 248 477-7070
  Farmington Hills *(G-5082)*
Saginaw Industries LLC .... F 989 752-5514
  Saginaw *(G-14139)*
Wing Pattern Inc .... G 248 588-1121
  Sterling Heights *(G-15546)*

MACHINERY, WOODWORKING: Planers

Straitoplane Inc .... G 616 997-2211
  Coopersville *(G-3570)*

MACHINERY/EQPT, INDL, WHOL: Cleaning, High Press, Sand/Steam

H & R Industries Inc .... F 616 247-1165
  Grand Rapids *(G-6487)*
Kmi Cleaning Solutions Inc .... F 269 964-2557
  Battle Creek *(G-1220)*

MACHINERY/EQPT, INDL, WHOL: Machinist Precision Measrng Tool

Landis Precision Inc .... G 248 685-8032
  Milford *(G-10968)*

MACHINERY: Ammunition & Explosives Loading

Genix LLC .... C 248 761-3030
  West Bloomfield *(G-17478)*

MACHINERY: Assembly, Exc Metalworking

+vantage Corporation .... E 734 432-5055
  Livonia *(G-9614)*
Airtificial Intelligent Robots .... G 989 799-6669
  Saginaw *(G-13993)*
Asw Amerca Inc .... G 248 957-9638
  Farmington Hills *(G-4934)*
Ats Assembly and Test Inc .... B 937 222-3030
  Wixom *(G-17766)*
Auto/Con Services LLC .... E 586 791-7474
  Fraser *(G-5624)*
Baird Investments LLC .... G 586 665-0154
  Orion *(G-12174)*
Baird Investments LLC .... G 586 665-0154
  Sterling Heights *(G-15271)*
Bme Inc .... G 810 937-2974
  Port Huron *(G-12903)*
Change Parts Incorporated .... E 231 845-5107
  Ludington *(G-10052)*
Craft Industries Inc .... A 586 726-4300
  Shelby Township *(G-14570)*
Esirpal Inc .... G 586 337-7848
  Macomb *(G-10120)*
Fec Inc .... E 586 580-2622
  Shelby Township *(G-14592)*
General Electric Company .... F 616 676-0870
  Ada *(G-16)*
Global Hoses & Fittings LLC .... G 248 219-9581
  Farmington Hills *(G-5010)*
Hanson Systems LLC .... C 269 465-6986
  Bridgman *(G-1866)*

PRODUCT SECTION — MACHINERY: Construction

Haosen Automation N Amer Inc .... G 248 556-6398
  Auburn Hills *(G-895)*
Harvey S Freeman .... E 248 852-2222
  West Bloomfield *(G-17479)*
Haven Innovation Inc .... E 616 935-1040
  Grand Haven *(G-6034)*
Hirotec America Inc .... B 248 836-5100
  Auburn Hills *(G-899)*
Hot Melt Technologies Inc .... E 248 853-2011
  Rochester Hills *(G-13446)*
Independent Mfg Solutions Corp .... E 248 960-3550
  Wixom *(G-17833)*
Infra Corporation .... F 248 623-0400
  Waterford *(G-17351)*
Metalform Industries LLC .... G 248 462-0056
  Shelby Township *(G-14639)*
Mhr Inc .... F 616 394-0191
  Holland *(G-7746)*
New Cnc Routercom Inc .... G 616 994-8844
  Holland *(G-7755)*
Northern Processes & Sales LLC .... G 248 669-3918
  Wixom *(G-17869)*
Puritan Automation LLC .... F 248 668-1114
  Wixom *(G-17881)*
Sanyo Machine America Corp .... D 248 651-5911
  Rochester Hills *(G-13510)*
Schap Specialty Machine Inc .... E 616 846-6530
  Spring Lake *(G-15175)*
Service Tectonics Inc .... F 517 263-0758
  Adrian *(G-96)*
SMS Group Inc .... D 734 246-8230
  Taylor *(G-15768)*
Superior Design & Mfg .... F 810 678-3950
  Metamora *(G-10781)*
Surclean Inc .... G 248 791-2226
  Brighton *(G-1994)*
Tool North Inc .... E 231 941-1150
  Traverse City *(G-16125)*
Volos Tube Form Inc .... E 586 416-3600
  Macomb *(G-10174)*
Wartrom Machine Systems .... E 586 469-1915
  Clinton Township *(G-3260)*
West Mich Flcking Assembly LLC .... D 269 639-1634
  Covert *(G-3592)*
Whites Bridge Tooling Inc .... E 616 897-4151
  Lowell *(G-10045)*
Wolverine Water Works Inc .... G 248 673-4310
  Waterford *(G-17387)*
Youngtronics LLC .... F 248 896-5790
  Wixom *(G-17933)*

MACHINERY: Automotive Maintenance

AGC Grand Haven LLC .... G 616 842-1820
  Grand Haven *(G-5990)*
Alliance Automation LLC .... G 810 953-9539
  Flint *(G-5375)*
B & J Tool Services Inc .... G 810 629-8577
  Fenton *(G-5185)*
Berghof Group North Amer Inc .... F 313 720-6884
  Troy *(G-16237)*
Burke E Porter Machinery Co .... C 616 234-1200
  Grand Rapids *(G-6243)*
Burton Industries Inc .... E 906 932-5970
  Ironwood *(G-8323)*
Busche Southfield Inc .... C 248 357-5180
  Southfield *(G-14860)*
Considine Sales & Marketing .... G 248 889-7887
  Highland *(G-7490)*
D Marsh Company Inc .... G 616 677-5276
  Marne *(G-10506)*
Drew Technologies Inc .... G 734 222-5228
  Ann Arbor *(G-425)*
Esoc Inc .... F 248 624-7992
  Wixom *(G-17806)*
Liberty Fabricators Inc .... F 810 877-7117
  Flint *(G-5458)*
RB Oil Enterprises LLC .... G 734 354-0700
  Plymouth *(G-12730)*
Rnj Services Inc .... F 906 786-0585
  Escanaba *(G-4857)*
Stec Usa Inc .... F 248 307-1440
  Madison Heights *(G-10362)*
Superior Automotive Eqp Inc .... G 231 829-9902
  Leroy *(G-9538)*

MACHINERY: Automotive Related

Air-Hydraulics Inc .... F 517 787-9444
  Jackson *(G-8377)*
Aisin Technical Ctr Amer Inc .... D 734 453-5551
  Northville *(G-11677)*
Amerivet Engineering LLC .... G 269 751-9092
  Hamilton *(G-7230)*
AMI Industries Inc .... D 989 786-3755
  Lewiston *(G-9547)*
AMI Industries Inc .... F 989 872-8823
  Cass City *(G-2510)*
Anwar Atwa Prism Autobody .... F 313 655-0000
  Detroit *(G-3872)*
Automotive Component Mfg .... G 705 549-7406
  Sterling Heights *(G-15267)*
Automotive Technology LLC .... C 586 446-7000
  Sterling Heights *(G-15268)*
Best Mfg Tooling Solutions Ltd .... G 616 877-0504
  Wayland *(G-17400)*
CCS Design LLC .... G 248 313-9178
  Wixom *(G-17781)*
Centracore LLC .... F 586 776-5700
  Saint Clair *(G-14209)*
Corvac Composites LLC .... E 812 256-2287
  Grand Rapids *(G-6313)*
Corvac Composites LLC .... C 616 281-2430
  Grand Rapids *(G-6314)*
Corvac Composites LLC .... E 616 281-4026
  Byron Center *(G-2184)*
Creative Performance Racg LLC .... G 248 250-6187
  Troy *(G-16285)*
D & F Corporation .... D 586 254-5300
  Sterling Heights *(G-15306)*
Dayco Products LLC .... C 989 775-0689
  Mount Pleasant *(G-11191)*
Dayco Products LLC .... E 517 439-0689
  Hillsdale *(G-7522)*
Detroit Tech Innovation LLC .... G 734 259-4168
  Redford *(G-13158)*
Eberspaecher North America Inc .... C 810 225-4582
  Brighton *(G-1915)*
Erae AMS Usa LLC .... F 419 386-8876
  Farmington Hills *(G-4989)*
Erae AMS USA Manufacturing LLC ..... F 248 770-6969
  Pontiac *(G-12824)*
Extol Inc .... D 616 741-0231
  Zeeland *(G-18136)*
Gd Enterprises LLC .... G 248 486-9800
  Brighton *(G-1928)*
Generation Tool Inc .... G 734 641-6937
  Westland *(G-17561)*
Genix LLC .... F 248 419-0231
  Sterling Heights *(G-15360)*
Global Strgc Sup Solutions LLC .... D 734 525-9100
  Livonia *(G-9753)*
H A Eckhart & Associates Inc .... E 517 321-7700
  Lansing *(G-9233)*
HP Pelzer Auto Systems Inc .... E 810 987-4444
  Port Huron *(G-12926)*
Hti Cybernetics Inc .... E 586 826-8346
  Sterling Heights *(G-15369)*
Ims/Chinatool Jv LLC .... G 734 466-5151
  Livonia *(G-9781)*
Iroquois Assembly Systems Inc .... F 586 771-5734
  Warren *(G-17099)*
J H P Inc .... G 248 588-0110
  Madison Heights *(G-10280)*
Jvis - Usa LLC .... B 586 803-6056
  Clinton Township *(G-3151)*
K & K Technology Inc .... G 989 399-9910
  Flushing *(G-5538)*
Kmj Boring Co Inc .... G 586 465-8771
  Clinton Township *(G-3155)*
Kolco Industries Inc .... G 248 486-1690
  South Lyon *(G-14799)*
Lumen North America Inc .... G 248 289-6100
  Rochester Hills *(G-13462)*
Mag Automotive LLC .... D 586 446-7000
  Sterling Heights *(G-15407)*
Mag Automotive LLC .... G 586 446-7000
  Port Huron *(G-12937)*
Martinrea Metal Industries Inc .... D 517 849-2195
  North Adams *(G-11656)*
Master Automatic Mch Co Inc .... E 734 414-0500
  Livonia *(G-9828)*
Modern Diversified Products .... G 989 736-3430
  Lincoln *(G-9567)*
Mountain Machine LLC .... F 734 480-2200
  Van Buren Twp *(G-16774)*
New-Matic Industries Inc .... G 586 415-9801
  Fraser *(G-5699)*
Nyx Inc .... B 734 464-0800
  Livonia *(G-9869)*
Operations Research Tech LLC .... G 248 626-8960
  West Bloomfield *(G-17492)*
Oxmaster Inc .... G 810 987-7600
  Port Huron *(G-12952)*
Palm Industries LLC .... G 248 444-7922
  South Lyon *(G-14808)*
R B Machine .... G 616 928-8690
  Holland *(G-7783)*
Race Ramps LLC .... G 866 464-2788
  Escanaba *(G-4855)*
Royal Design & Manufacturing .... D 248 588-0110
  Madison Heights *(G-10346)*
Sarns Industries Inc .... F 586 463-5829
  Harrison Twp *(G-7360)*
Schneider National Inc .... F 810 636-2220
  Goodrich *(G-5957)*
SGC Industries Inc .... E 586 293-5260
  Fraser *(G-5723)*
Spartan Automation Inc .... G 586 206-7231
  Shelby Township *(G-14699)*
Sungwoo Hitech Co Ltd .... G 248 509-0445
  Troy *(G-16626)*
Sure Solutions Corporation .... G 248 674-7210
  Auburn Hills *(G-1006)*
Surface Blasting Systems LLC .... G 616 384-3351
  Coopersville *(G-3571)*
Syncreon Acquisition Corp .... F 248 377-4700
  Auburn Hills *(G-1009)*
Technology & Manufacturing Inc .... G 248 755-1444
  Milford *(G-10988)*
Thomas-Ward Systems LLC .... G 734 929-0644
  Ann Arbor *(G-671)*
Van-Rob USA Holdings .... E 517 423-2400
  Tecumseh *(G-15816)*
W G Benjey Inc .... F 989 356-0016
  Alpena *(G-319)*
Webasto Convertibles USA Inc .... G 734 582-5900
  Plymouth *(G-12792)*
Wirtz Manufacturing Co Inc .... D 810 987-7600
  Port Huron *(G-12978)*
Wolverine Advanced Mtls LLC .... E 313 749-6100
  Dearborn *(G-3774)*

MACHINERY: Binding

Digital Finishing Corp .... G 586 427-6003
  Shelby Township *(G-14576)*

MACHINERY: Bottling & Canning

XI Engineering LLC .... G 616 656-0324
  Caledonia *(G-2323)*

MACHINERY: Centrifugal

Centrum Force Fabrication LLC .... G 517 857-4774
  Ann Arbor *(G-398)*
Chip Systems International .... F 269 626-8000
  Scotts *(G-14503)*

MACHINERY: Concrete Prdts

Besser Company .... B 989 354-4111
  Alpena *(G-282)*
Blockmatic Inc .... G 269 683-1655
  Niles *(G-11597)*
Somero Enterprises Inc .... D 906 482-7252
  Houghton *(G-7983)*
Williams Form Engineering Corp .... D 616 866-0815
  Belmont *(G-1474)*

MACHINERY: Construction

Ais Construction Eqp Svc Corp .... E 616 538-2400
  Grand Rapids *(G-6155)*
All-Lift Systems Inc .... F 906 779-1620
  Iron Mountain *(G-8274)*
Alta Construction Eqp LLC .... D 248 356-5200
  New Hudson *(G-11530)*
Amw Machine Control Inc .... G 616 642-9514
  Saranac *(G-14453)*
Arcosa Shoring Products Inc .... F 800 292-1225
  Lansing *(G-9203)*
B&P Littleford LLC .... E 989 757-1300
  Saginaw *(G-13999)*
Bme Inc .... G 810 937-2974
  Port Huron *(G-12903)*
Boral Building Products Inc .... C 248 668-6400
  Wixom *(G-17777)*
Border City Tool and Mfg Co .... E 586 758-5574
  Warren *(G-16962)*
Contract Welding and Fabg Inc .... E 734 699-5561
  Van Buren Twp *(G-16753)*
D P Equipment Co .... F 517 368-5266
  Camden *(G-2340)*

Employee Codes: A=Over 500 employees, B=251-500
C=101-250, D=51-100, E=20-50, F=10-19, G=3-9

Di-Coat Corporation....E....248 349-1211
Novi (G-11868)
E M I Construction Products....D....616 392-7207
Holland (G-7615)
Fleming Fabrication Machining....G....906 542-3573
Sagola (G-14186)
Fw Shoring Company....D....517 676-8800
Mason (G-10639)
Harsco Corporation....D....231 843-3431
Ludington (G-10062)
Harsco Corporation....F....231 843-3431
Ludington (G-10063)
Hines Corporation....F....231 799-6240
Norton Shores (G-11812)
Keizer-Morris Intl Inc....E....810 688-1234
North Branch (G-11661)
Lawrence J Julio LLC....G....906 483-4781
Houghton (G-7974)
Magnum Toolscom LLC....F....734 595-4600
Romulus (G-13703)
Mid State Seawall Inc....G....989 435-3887
Beaverton (G-1389)
Mmgg Inc....G....616 405-3807
Midland (G-10893)
Mmgg Inc....E....989 495-9332
Midland (G-10894)
Mull-It-Over Products Inc....G....616 843-6470
Grandville (G-7059)
Nordson Corporation....D....734 459-8600
Wixom (G-17866)
Petter Investments Inc....F....269 637-1997
South Haven (G-14767)
Plastech Holding Corp....F....313 565-5927
Dearborn (G-3749)
Repair Rite Machine Inc....G....616 681-9711
Dorr (G-4526)
Shred-Pac Inc....E....269 793-7978
Hopkins (G-7961)
Stoneco of Michigan Inc....G....734 236-6538
Newport (G-11591)
Stoneco of Michigan Inc....E....734 241-8966
Monroe (G-11070)
Superior Fabrication Co LLC....D....906 495-5634
Kincheloe (G-9053)
Tapco Holdings Inc....C....248 668-6400
Wixom (G-17905)
U P Fabricating Co Inc....E....906 475-4400
Negaunee (G-11478)

MACHINERY: Custom

A M Manufacturing LLC....G....231 437-3377
Charlevoix (G-2604)
Ability Mfg & Engrg Co....F....269 227-3292
Fennville (G-5169)
Accuworx LLC....E....734 847-6115
Temperance (G-15822)
All Metal Designs Inc....G....616 392-3696
Holland (G-7554)
Ase Industries Inc....D....586 754-7480
Warren (G-16942)
Auto Builders Inc....E....586 948-3780
Chesterfield (G-2744)
Automated Indus Motion Inc....F....231 865-1800
Fruitport (G-5787)
Automated Techniques LLC....G....810 346-4670
Brown City (G-2045)
Azon Usa Inc....F....269 385-5942
Kalamazoo (G-8690)
Azon Usa Inc....E....269 385-5942
Kalamazoo (G-8691)
Belding Tool Acquisition LLC....F....586 816-4450
Belding (G-1402)
Belding Tool Acquisition LLC....G....616 794-0100
Belding (G-1403)
Cambria Tool and Machine Inc....F....517 437-3500
Hillsdale (G-7520)
Centech Inc....F....517 546-9185
Howell (G-8020)
Clipper Belt Lacer Company....D....616 459-3196
Grand Rapids (G-6281)
Coles Machine Service Inc....E....810 658-5373
Davison (G-3642)
Cousins Manufacturing Inc....G....586 323-6033
Sterling Heights (G-15302)
Creative Machine Company....E....248 669-4230
Wixom (G-17792)
D B Mattson Co....G....734 697-8056
Van Buren Twp (G-16755)
Deshler Group Inc....C....734 525-9100
Livonia (G-9706)
Directional Regulated Systems....G....734 451-1416
Canton (G-2365)
Dynamic Custom Machining LLC....G....231 853-8648
Ravenna (G-13119)
Engineered Concepts Inc....F....574 333-9110
Cassopolis (G-2530)
Engineered Resources Inc....G....248 399-5500
Oak Park (G-12066)
Epic Equipment & Engrg Inc....D....586 314-0020
Shelby Township (G-14589)
Esys Automation LLC....D....248 754-1900
Auburn Hills (G-856)
Fischell Machinery LLC....G....517 445-2828
Clayton (G-3007)
General Processing Systems Inc....F....630 554-7804
Holland (G-7640)
Genix LLC....F....248 419-0231
Sterling Heights (G-15360)
Geolean USA LLC....F....313 859-9780
Livonia (G-9751)
Green Age Products & Svcs LLC....F....586 207-5724
Washington (G-17304)
Gregory M Boese....F....989 754-2990
Saginaw (G-14052)
Hardy-Reed Tool & Die Co Inc....F....517 547-7107
Manitou Beach (G-10448)
Harmon Sign Inc....G....248 348-8150
Wixom (G-17824)
Holloway Equipment Co Inc....F....810 748-9577
Harsens Island (G-7369)
Huff Machine & Tool Co Inc....F....231 734-3291
Evart (G-4882)
ID Engnring Atmted Systems Inc....F....616 656-0182
Kentwood (G-9012)
Jobs Inc....G....810 714-0522
Allen Park (G-199)
K&W Tool and Machine Inc....F....616 754-7540
Greenville (G-7141)
Kentwater Tool & Mfg Co....G....616 784-7171
Comstock Park (G-3489)
Ketchum Machine Corporated....F....616 765-5101
Freeport (G-5765)
King Tool & Die Inc....F....517 265-2741
Adrian (G-73)
Kotzian Tool Inc....F....231 861-5377
Shelby (G-14530)
Leading Edge Engineering Inc....F....586 786-0382
Shelby Township (G-14625)
Link Mechanical Solutions LLC....F....734 744-5616
Livonia (G-9811)
M & F Machine & Tool Inc....E....734 847-0571
Erie (G-4806)
McDonald Acquisitions LLC....E....616 878-7800
Byron Center (G-2198)
Michigan Rebuild & Automtn Inc....F....517 542-6000
Litchfield (G-9609)
Momentum Industries Inc....E....989 681-5735
Saint Louis (G-14366)
National Bulk Equipment Inc....C....616 399-2220
Holland (G-7752)
Oakland Automation LLC....F....810 874-3061
Novi (G-11961)
P D E Systems Inc....E....586 725-3330
Chesterfield (G-2814)
Panter Master Controls Inc....F....810 687-5600
Flint (G-5478)
Paragon Model and Tool Inc....G....248 960-1223
Wixom (G-17875)
Park Street Machine Inc....E....231 739-9165
Muskegon (G-11399)
Patch Works Farms Inc....G....989 430-3610
Wheeler (G-17617)
Pentier Group Inc....F....810 664-7997
Lapeer (G-9480)
Perfecto Industries Inc....E....989 732-2941
Gaylord (G-5888)
Performance Tool Inc....G....231 943-9338
Traverse City (G-16065)
Pollington Machine Tool Inc....E....231 743-2003
Marion (G-10493)
Quality Eqp Installations....G....616 249-3649
Grandville (G-7068)
R & D Machine and Tool Inc....G....231 798-8500
Norton Shores (G-11789)
R K C Corporation....G....231 627-9131
Cheboygan (G-2692)
Schaller Tool & Die Co....E....586 949-5500
Chesterfield (G-2838)
Schuler Incorporated....D....734 207-7200
Canton (G-2425)
Sebright Machining Inc....F....616 399-0445
Holland (G-7798)
Smoracy LLC....G....989 561-2270
Remus (G-13241)
Steel-Fab Wilson & Machine....G....989 773-6046
Mount Pleasant (G-11230)
Sun Tool Company....G....313 837-2442
Detroit (G-4385)
T S Manufacturing & Design....G....517 543-5368
Charlotte (G-2669)
Trusted Tool Mfg Inc....G....810 750-6000
Fenton (G-5247)
Tuff Automation Inc....E....616 735-3939
Grand Rapids (G-6940)
Turbo-Spray Midwest Inc....F....517 548-9096
Howell (G-8116)
Ultra Fab & Machine Inc....G....248 628-7065
Oxford (G-12380)
United Systems....G....248 583-9670
Troy (G-16664)
Veit Tool & Gage Inc....F....810 658-4949
Davison (G-3665)
Wells Helicopter Service Inc....G....616 874-6255
Greenville (G-7160)

MACHINERY: Deburring

Casalbi Company Inc....F....517 782-0345
Jackson (G-8403)
Clm Vibetech Inc....F....269 344-3878
Kalamazoo (G-8708)
Hammond Machinery Inc....D....269 345-7151
Kalamazoo (G-8759)
Kalamazoo Company....E....269 345-7151
Kalamazoo (G-8786)
Microprecision Cleaning....E....586 997-6960
Sterling Heights (G-15422)
Robert Bosch LLC....E....248 921-9054
Novi (G-11987)
Robert Bosch LLC....A....734 979-3000
Plymouth (G-12741)
Rock Tool & Machine Co Inc....E....734 455-9840
Plymouth (G-12743)

MACHINERY: Die Casting

Advance Products Corporation....E....269 849-1000
Benton Harbor (G-1480)
Buhlerprince Inc....C....616 394-8248
Holland (G-7581)
Die Cast Press Mfg Co Inc....E....269 657-6060
Paw Paw (G-12403)
Diversified Metal Products Inc....E....989 448-7120
Gaylord (G-5856)
Industrial Innovations Inc....F....616 249-1525
Grandville (G-7052)
Selmuro Ltd....E....810 603-2117
Grand Blanc (G-5983)

MACHINERY: Dredging

W & S Development Inc....F....989 724-5463
Greenbush (G-7121)

MACHINERY: Drill Presses

Clausing Industrial Inc....E....269 345-7155
Kalamazoo (G-8706)
Clausing Industrial Inc....D....269 345-7155
Kalamazoo (G-8707)

MACHINERY: Electrical Discharge Erosion

Tarus Products Inc....D....586 977-1400
Sterling Heights (G-15520)

MACHINERY: Electronic Component Making

DAS Technologies Inc....G....269 657-0541
Paw Paw (G-12401)
Environ Manufacturing Inc....G....616 644-6846
Battle Creek (G-1178)
Firstronic LLC....B....616 456-9220
Grand Rapids (G-6408)
Greene Manufacturing Tech LLC....C....810 982-9720
Port Huron (G-12924)
Senstronic Inc....C....586 466-4108
Clinton Township (G-3222)
Toyota Industries Elctc Sys N....G....248 489-7700
Novi (G-12018)

PRODUCT SECTION

MACHINERY: Electronic Teaching Aids
J N B Machinery LLC ....G...... 517 223-0711
 Fowlerville (G-5572)
Realm ....G...... 313 706-4401
 Wayne (G-17441)

MACHINERY: Extruding
Clark Granco Inc ....D...... 616 794-2600
 Belding (G-1407)

MACHINERY: Fiber Optics Strand Coating
Euclid Coating Systems Inc ....F...... 989 922-4789
 Bay City (G-1309)

MACHINERY: Folding
A S R C Inc ....G...... 517 545-7430
 Howell (G-8008)

MACHINERY: Gear Cutting & Finishing
Bmt Aerospace Usa Inc ....D...... 586 285-7700
 Fraser (G-5630)

MACHINERY: General, Industrial, NEC
Conair North America ....E...... 814 437-6861
 Pinconning (G-12507)
Geofabrica Inc ....G...... 810 728-2468
 Bloomfield Hills (G-1767)
Keane Saunders & Associates ....G...... 616 954-7088
 Grand Rapids (G-6571)
Sk Enterprises Inc ....F...... 616 785-1070
 Grand Rapids (G-6867)
SMS Technical Services ....G...... 586 445-0330
 Warren (G-17243)
Smullen Fire App Sales & Svcs ....G...... 517 546-8898
 Howell (G-8100)

MACHINERY: Glass Cutting
Northwods Prperty Holdings LLC ....G...... 231 334-3000
 Glen Arbor (G-5941)

MACHINERY: Glassmaking
Art Glass Inc ....G...... 586 731-8627
 Sterling Heights (G-15264)
Il Enterprises Inc ....F...... 734 285-6030
 Wyandotte (G-17962)

MACHINERY: Grinding
Accurate Machined Service Inc ....G...... 734 421-4660
 Livonia (G-9626)
Berger LLC ....G...... 734 414-0402
 Plymouth (G-12585)
C & B Machinery Company ....E...... 734 462-0600
 Brighton (G-1894)
Diversified Precision Pdts Inc ....E...... 517 750-2310
 Spring Arbor (G-15121)
Emag LLC ....E...... 248 477-7440
 Farmington Hills (G-4983)
Machine Control Technology ....G...... 517 655-3506
 Williamston (G-17734)
New Unison Corporation ....E...... 248 544-9500
 Ferndale (G-5304)
Palfam Industries Inc ....E...... 248 922-0590
 Ortonville (G-12201)
Quality Tool Company Inc ....G...... 517 869-2490
 Allen (G-8007)
Ra Prcsion Grnding Mtlwrks Inc ....F...... 586 783-7776
 Harrison Township (G-7346)
Superabrasives Inc ....E...... 248 348-7670
 Wixom (G-17901)
United Mfg Netwrk Inc ....G...... 586 321-7887
 Warren (G-17274)
Variable Machining & Tool Inc ....G...... 586 778-8030
 Warren (G-17278)

MACHINERY: Ice Cream
Spotted Cow ....E...... 517 265-6188
 Adrian (G-97)
Taylor Freezer Michigan Inc ....F...... 616 453-0531
 Grand Rapids (G-6916)

MACHINERY: Ice Crushers
Nu-Ice Age Inc ....F...... 517 990-0665
 Clarklake (G-2897)

MACHINERY: Ice Making
Acme Tool & Die Co ....G...... 231 938-1260
 Acme (G-1)

MACHINERY: Industrial, NEC
Advanced Electric ....G...... 517 529-9050
 Clarklake (G-2893)
Astraeus Wind Energy Inc ....G...... 517 663-5455
 Eaton Rapids (G-4716)
Bay Tool Inc ....G...... 989 894-2863
 Essexville (G-4871)
Buffoli North America Corp ....G...... 616 610-4362
 Holland (G-7580)
Darrell R Hanson ....G...... 810 364-7892
 Marysville (G-10602)
Equip Consumable Group ....G...... 248 588-9981
 Madison Heights (G-10249)
Koehler Industries Inc ....G...... 269 934-9670
 Benton Harbor (G-1521)
Maxum LLC ....G...... 248 726-7110
 Rochester Hills (G-13469)
Platt Mounts - Usa Inc ....G...... 586 202-2920
 Lake Orion (G-9155)
Trolley Rebuilders Inc ....G...... 810 364-4820
 Marysville (G-10624)
Woodville Heights Enterprises ....F...... 231 629-7750
 Big Rapids (G-1647)

MACHINERY: Kilns
Kiln Kreations ....G...... 989 435-3296
 Beaverton (G-1386)
Lumbertown Portable Sawmill ....G...... 231 206-4600
 Muskegon (G-11369)

MACHINERY: Kilns, Lumber
Black Creek Timber LLC ....G...... 517 202-2169
 Rudyard (G-13983)

MACHINERY: Labeling
Converting Systems Inc ....G...... 616 698-1882
 Nunica (G-12034)
Take-A-Label Inc ....F...... 616 698-1882
 Nunica (G-12044)

MACHINERY: Lapping
Helical Lap & Manufacturing Co ....F...... 586 307-8322
 Mount Clemens (G-11132)

MACHINERY: Marking, Metalworking
Columbia Marking Tools Inc ....E...... 586 949-8400
 Chesterfield (G-2754)
Hanson International Inc ....D...... 269 429-5555
 Saint Joseph (G-14316)
Marking Machine Co ....F...... 517 767-4155
 Tekonsha (G-15820)
SB Investments LLC ....E...... 734 462-9478
 Livonia (G-9921)

MACHINERY: Metalworking
Accu-Rite Industries LLC ....E...... 586 247-0060
 Shelby Township (G-14538)
Advanced Feedlines LLC ....D...... 248 583-9400
 Troy (G-16169)
Aludyne US LLC ....D...... 810 987-1112
 Port Huron (G-12889)
Anderson-Cook Inc ....D...... 586 954-0700
 Clinton Township (G-3053)
Anderson-Cook Inc ....D...... 586 293-0800
 Fraser (G-5620)
Ats Assembly and Test Inc ....D...... 734 266-4713
 Livonia (G-9657)
Automation Specialists Inc ....F...... 616 738-8288
 Holland (G-7562)
Bel-Kur Inc ....E...... 734 847-0651
 Temperance (G-15823)
Boxer Equipment/Morbark Inc ....G...... 989 866-2381
 Winn (G-17746)
Burke E Porter Machinery Co ....C...... 616 234-1200
 Grand Rapids (G-6243)
Burton Press Co Inc ....G...... 248 853-0212
 Rochester Hills (G-13380)
Cardinal Machine Co ....E...... 810 686-1190
 Clio (G-3267)
Carter Products Company Inc ....F...... 616 647-3380
 Grand Rapids (G-6256)
Coleman Machine Inc ....E...... 906 863-1113
 Menominee (G-10728)
D K Products Inc ....E...... 517 263-3025
 Adrian (G-56)
Dake Corporation ....D...... 616 842-7110
 Grand Haven (G-6008)
Experienced Concepts Inc ....F...... 586 752-4200
 Armada (G-719)
Flagler Corporation ....E...... 586 749-6300
 Chesterfield (G-2776)
Fontijne Grotnes Inc ....E...... 269 262-4700
 Niles (G-11611)
Friendship Industries Inc ....E...... 586 323-0033
 Sterling Heights (G-15349)
Friendship Industries Inc ....F...... 586 997-1325
 Sterling Heights (G-15350)
Gatco Incorporated ....F...... 734 453-2295
 Plymouth (G-12626)
Hak Inc ....G...... 231 587-5322
 Mancelona (G-10392)
Harvey S Freeman ....E...... 248 852-2222
 West Bloomfield (G-17479)
HMS Products Co ....D...... 248 689-8120
 Troy (G-16398)
Hti Cybernetics Inc ....E...... 586 826-8346
 Sterling Heights (G-15369)
Impres Engineering Svcs LLC ....G...... 616 283-4112
 Holland (G-7689)
Industrial Automation LLC ....D...... 248 598-5900
 Rochester Hills (G-13449)
Kailing Machine Shop ....G...... 616 677-3629
 Marne (G-10509)
Kapex Manufacturing LLC ....G...... 989 928-4993
 Saginaw (G-14069)
Kuka Robotics Corporation ....E...... 586 795-2000
 Shelby Township (G-14615)
Leonard Machine Tool Systems ....E...... 586 757-8040
 Warren (G-17127)
M & F Machine & Tool Inc ....E...... 734 847-0571
 Erie (G-4806)
Manufacturers / Mch Bldrs Svcs ....G...... 734 748-3706
 Livonia (G-9821)
Manufctring Solutions Tech LLC ....G...... 734 744-5050
 Commerce Township (G-3426)
Mega Screen Corp ....G...... 517 849-7057
 Jonesville (G-8663)
Metal Stmping Spport Group LLC ......F...... 586 777-7440
 Roseville (G-13834)
Milacron LLC ....E...... 517 424-8981
 Tecumseh (G-15802)
Modern Tool and Tapping Inc ....G...... 586 777-5144
 Fraser (G-5694)
Morbark LLC ....B...... 989 866-2381
 Winn (G-17747)
Motion Machine Company ....F...... 810 664-9901
 Lapeer (G-9476)
Naams LLC ....F...... 586 285-5684
 Warren (G-17165)
New Unison Corporation ....E...... 248 544-9500
 Ferndale (G-5304)
Norgren Automtn Solutions LLC ....C...... 586 463-3000
 Rochester Hills (G-13481)
Northwest Tool & Machine Inc ....E...... 517 750-1332
 Jackson (G-8544)
On The Mark Inc ....G...... 989 317-8033
 Mount Pleasant (G-11216)
Precision Plus ....F...... 906 553-7900
 Escanaba (G-4853)
Priority Tool Inc ....G...... 616 847-1337
 Grand Haven (G-6064)
R & S Tool & Die Inc ....E...... 989 673-8511
 Caro (G-2476)
Reger Manufacturing Company ....G...... 586 293-5096
 Fraser (G-5716)
Rod Chomper Inc ....F...... 616 392-9677
 Holland (G-7790)
Savard Corporation ....F...... 313 931-6880
 Detroit (G-4353)
Sharp Die & Mold Co ....F...... 586 293-8660
 Fraser (G-5724)
Signet Machine Inc ....G...... 616 261-2939
 Grandville (G-7071)
Tannewitz Inc ....E...... 616 457-5999
 Jenison (G-8644)
Thielenhaus Microfinish Corp ....E...... 248 349-9450
 Novi (G-12015)
Tri-Mation Industries Inc ....F...... 269 668-4333
 Mattawan (G-10670)
Trinity Tool Co ....E...... 586 296-5900
 Fraser (G-5741)

Employee Codes: A=Over 500 employees, B=251-500
C=101-250, D=51-100, E=20-50, F=10-19, G=3-9

2020 Harris Michigan Industrial Directory

MACHINERY: Metalworking

Veet Industries Inc ....F 586 776-3000
 Warren *(G-17281)*

MACHINERY: Milling

DTe Hankin Inc ....F 734 279-1831
 Petersburg *(G-12435)*
Enagon LLC ....G 269 455-5110
 Saugatuck *(G-14458)*
Enihcam Corp ....G 810 354-0404
 Fenton *(G-5203)*
Extrude Hone LLC ....F 616 647-9050
 Grand Rapids *(G-6395)*
George Kotzian ....G 231 861-6520
 Shelby *(G-14525)*
Manufacturing Associates Inc ....G 248 421-4943
 Livonia *(G-9822)*
Max2 LLC ....F 269 468-3452
 Coloma *(G-3360)*
Riverside Cnc LLC ....G 616 246-6000
 Wyoming *(G-18032)*
SMW Tooling Inc ....F 616 355-9822
 Holland *(G-7808)*

MACHINERY: Mining

Classfcation Flotation Systems ....G 810 714-5200
 Fenton *(G-5194)*
Contract Welding and Fabg Inc ......E 734 699-5561
 Van Buren Twp *(G-16753)*
Cows Locomotive Mfg Co ....E 248 583-7150
 Madison Heights *(G-10221)*
General Machine Services ....G 269 695-2244
 Buchanan *(G-2119)*
Lake Shore Systems Inc ....D 906 774-1500
 Kingsford *(G-9061)*
Lake Shore Systems Inc ....D 906 265-5414
 Iron River *(G-8313)*
Mq Operating Company ....E 906 337-1515
 Calumet *(G-2330)*
Pillar Manufacturing Inc ....F 269 628-5605
 Gobles *(G-5948)*
U P Fabricating Co Inc ....E 906 475-4400
 Negaunee *(G-11478)*
Yerington Brothers Inc ....G 269 695-7669
 Niles *(G-11652)*

MACHINERY: Packaging

A & B Packing Equipment Inc ....G 616 294-3539
 Holland *(G-7544)*
A-OK Precision Prototype Inc ....F 586 758-3430
 Ray *(G-13131)*
Anchor Bay Packaging Corp ....E 586 949-4040
 Chesterfield *(G-2738)*
BP Pack Inc ....G 612 594-0839
 Bellaire *(G-1436)*
British Cnvrtng Sltns Nrth AME .....E 281 764-6651
 Kalamazoo *(G-8701)*
Butcher Engineering Entps ....D 734 246-7700
 Brownstown *(G-2060)*
Camaco LLC ....E 248 442-6800
 Farmington Hills *(G-4954)*
Change Parts Incorporated ....E 231 845-5107
 Ludington *(G-10052)*
Coleman Bowman & Associates ...G 248 642-8221
 Bloomfield Hills *(G-1755)*
D J S Systems Inc ....E 517 568-4444
 Homer *(G-7941)*
Dura-Pack Inc ....E 313 299-9600
 Taylor *(G-15711)*
Gentile Packaging Machinery Co ..G 734 429-1177
 Saline *(G-14393)*
Hot Melt Technologies Inc ....E 248 853-2011
 Rochester Hills *(G-13446)*
Kalamazoo Packaging Systems .....G 616 534-2600
 Grand Rapids *(G-6568)*
Korten Quality Inc ....C 586 752-6255
 Bruce Twp *(G-2086)*
Meca-Systeme Usa Inc ....G 616 843-5566
 Grand Haven *(G-6055)*
Nyx Inc ....B 734 261-7535
 Livonia *(G-9870)*
Nyx LLC ....C 734 462-2385
 Livonia *(G-9871)*
Robert Bosch LLC ....D 616 466-4063
 Bridgman *(G-1873)*
Robert Bosch LLC ....G 734 302-2000
 Ann Arbor *(G-623)*
Robert Bosch LLC ....E 248 921-9054
 Novi *(G-11987)*
Robert Bosch LLC ....A 734 979-3000
 Plymouth *(G-12741)*
Rollstock Inc ....G 616 803-5370
 Grand Rapids *(G-6836)*
Tekkra Systems Inc ....E 517 568-4121
 Homer *(G-7950)*
Tetra Pak Inc ....E 517 629-2163
 Albion *(G-133)*
Tindall Packaging Inc ....G 269 649-1163
 Portage *(G-13050)*

MACHINERY: Paint Making

Peloton Inc ....G 269 694-9702
 Otsego *(G-12252)*
Tzamco Inc ....E 248 624-7710
 Walled Lake *(G-16904)*

MACHINERY: Paper Industry Miscellaneous

Accu-Shape Die Cutting Inc ....E 810 230-2445
 Flint *(G-5368)*
B&P Littleford Day LLC ....D 989 757-1300
 Saginaw *(G-13998)*
Bernal LLC ....D 248 299-3600
 Rochester Hills *(G-13377)*
Paper Machine Service Inds ....F 989 695-2646
 Saginaw *(G-14119)*

MACHINERY: Pharmaciutical

Graminex LLC ....G 989 797-5502
 Saginaw *(G-14051)*
Velesco Phrm Svcs Inc ....G 734 545-0696
 Wixom *(G-17924)*
Velesco Phrm Svcs Inc ....F 734 527-9125
 Plymouth *(G-12787)*

MACHINERY: Photographic Reproduction

Arts Crafts Hardware ....F 586 231-5344
 Mount Clemens *(G-11123)*
Laser Connection LLC ....E 989 662-4022
 Auburn *(G-755)*

MACHINERY: Plastic Working

Applied Instruments Company ......E 810 227-5510
 Brighton *(G-1886)*
Bekum America Corporation ....C 517 655-4331
 Williamston *(G-17727)*
Brown LLC ....C 989 435-7741
 Beaverton *(G-1383)*
C M E Plastic Company ....G 517 456-7722
 Clinton *(G-3015)*
Century Inc ....C 231 947-6400
 Traverse City *(G-15932)*
Ess Tec Inc ....D 616 394-0230
 Holland *(G-7625)*
Fbe Corp ....G 517 333-2605
 East Lansing *(G-4656)*
Gluco Inc ....G 616 457-1212
 Jenison *(G-8627)*
Glycon Corp ....E 517 423-8356
 Tecumseh *(G-15795)*
Innovative Engineering Mich ....G 517 977-0460
 Lansing *(G-9236)*
Kapex Manufacturing LLC ....E 989 928-4993
 Saginaw *(G-14069)*
Lyle Industries ....D 989 435-7717
 Beaverton *(G-1388)*
Mann + Hummel Inc ....G 269 329-3900
 Portage *(G-13013)*
Michigan Roll Form Inc ....E 248 669-3700
 Commerce Township *(G-3433)*
Miller Mold Co ....E 989 793-8881
 Frankenmuth *(G-5594)*
Quantum Mold & Engineering LLC ...F 586 276-0100
 Sterling Heights *(G-15460)*
R & B Plastics Machinery LLC ....E 734 429-9421
 Saline *(G-14410)*
R & S Tool & Die Inc ....C 989 673-8511
 Caro *(G-2476)*
Size Reduction Specialists ....G 517 333-2605
 East Lansing *(G-4675)*
Spirit Industries Inc ....E 517 371-7840
 Lansing *(G-9266)*
Thermfrmer Parts Suppliers LLC ...G 989 435-3800
 Beaverton *(G-1394)*
Thermoforming Tech Group LLC ...G 989 435-7741
 Beaverton *(G-1395)*
Thoreson-Mc Cosh Inc ....E 248 362-0960
 Troy *(G-16638)*
Ube Machinery Inc ....D 734 741-7000
 Ann Arbor *(G-685)*
Uniloy Inc ....D 514 424-8900
 Tecumseh *(G-15815)*
Valley Gear and Machine Inc ....F 989 269-8177
 Bad Axe *(G-1076)*

MACHINERY: Polishing & Buffing

Abrasive Services Incorporated .....G 734 941-2144
 Romulus *(G-13647)*
Changeover Integration LLC ....F 231 845-5320
 Ludington *(G-10053)*
Multifinish-Usa Inc ....G 248 528-1154
 Troy *(G-16516)*

MACHINERY: Printing Presses

Conrad Machine Company ....F 231 893-7455
 Whitehall *(G-17663)*
Eagle Press Repairs & Ser ....F 419 539-7206
 Adrian *(G-60)*
Maple Leaf Press Inc ....G 616 846-8844
 Grand Haven *(G-6054)*
Sunraise Inc ....E 810 359-7301
 Lexington *(G-9560)*
Voxeljet America Inc ....F 734 709-8237
 Canton *(G-2442)*

MACHINERY: Recycling

Air Tight Solutions LLC ....G 248 629-0461
 Detroit *(G-3848)*
Compac Specialties Inc ....F 616 786-9100
 Holland *(G-7595)*
Environmental Products Corp ....G 248 471-4770
 Livonia *(G-9728)*
Geep USA Inc ....E 313 937-5350
 Auburn Hills *(G-880)*
Huron Valley Steel Corporation ....C 734 479-3500
 Trenton *(G-16155)*
Kansmackers Manufacturing Co ...G 248 249-6666
 Lansing *(G-9239)*
Libra Industries Inc Michigan ....G 517 787-5675
 Jackson *(G-8499)*
Loadmaster Corporation ....E 906 563-9226
 Norway *(G-11817)*
Usher Enterprises Inc ....E 313 834-7055
 Detroit *(G-4418)*

MACHINERY: Riveting

Davison Tool Service Inc ....G 810 653-6920
 Davison *(G-3646)*
Orbitform Group LLC ....D 800 957-4838
 Jackson *(G-8545)*

MACHINERY: Road Construction & Maintenance

Spaulding Mfg Inc ....E 989 777-4550
 Saginaw *(G-14154)*

MACHINERY: Robots, Molding & Forming Plastics

Karamon Sales Company ....G 810 984-1750
 Port Huron *(G-12933)*
Pine Needle People LLC ....G 517 242-4752
 Lansing *(G-9256)*

MACHINERY: Rubber Working

Oakley Industries Sub Assembly ..D 586 754-5555
 Warren *(G-17176)*

MACHINERY: Saw & Sawing

B & O Saws Inc ....E 616 794-7297
 Belding *(G-1397)*
Rattunde Corporation ....G 616 940-3340
 Caledonia *(G-2312)*

MACHINERY: Screening Eqpt, Electric

Online Engineering Inc ....F 906 341-0090
 Manistique *(G-10445)*

MACHINERY: Semiconductor Manufacturing

Eaton Aerospace LLC ....B 616 949-1090
 Grand Rapids *(G-6368)*
Minland Machine Inc ....G 269 641-7998
 Edwardsburg *(G-4768)*

PRODUCT SECTION

MAIL-ORDER HOUSES: Computer Software

Myron Zucker Inc ....G....... 586 979-9955
　Sterling Heights *(G-15430)*
Ovshinsky Technologies LLC...............G.... 248 390-3564
　Pontiac *(G-12854)*

MACHINERY: Separation Eqpt, Magnetic

Ep Magnets & Components LLC ....G....... 734 398-7188
　Canton *(G-2372)*
Magnetic Products Inc..........................D.... 248 887-5600
　Highland *(G-7497)*
Puritan Magnetics Inc...........................F.... 248 628-3808
　Oxford *(G-12365)*
Universal Magnetics Inc ....G.... 231 937-5555
　Howard City *(G-8007)*

MACHINERY: Sheet Metal Working

Atlas Technologies LLC ....D.... 810 714-2128
　Fenton *(G-5183)*
Boral Building Products Inc..................C.... 248 668-6400
　Wixom *(G-17777)*
Die-Matic LLC ....E.... 616 531-0060
　Grand Rapids *(G-6349)*
Flagler Corporation ....E.... 586 749-6300
　Chesterfield *(G-2776)*
Impel Industries Inc ....E.... 586 254-5800
　Sterling Heights *(G-15371)*
Tapco Holdings Inc ....C.... 248 668-6400
　Wixom *(G-17905)*
Tox Presso Technik ....G.... 248 374-1877
　Wixom *(G-17913)*

MACHINERY: Snow Making

Snow Machines Incorporated ....E....... 989 631-6091
　Midland *(G-10917)*

MACHINERY: Specialty

Arcon Vernova Inc ....G....... 734 904-1895
　Saline *(G-14378)*
B K Corporation ....G....... 989 777-2111
　Saginaw *(G-13997)*
Brothers Industrials Inc..........................G....... 248 794-5080
　Farmington Hills *(G-4947)*
Lumbee Custom Painting LLC...............G....... 586 296-5083
　Fraser *(G-5685)*

MACHINERY: Tapping

American Gator Tool Company ....G....... 231 347-3222
　Harbor Springs *(G-7272)*
Illinois Tool Works Inc ....D.... 248 589-2500
　Troy *(G-16410)*

MACHINERY: Textile

B&P Littleford Day LLC ....D....... 989 757-1300
　Saginaw *(G-13998)*
Howa USA Holdings Inc ....G.... 248 715-4000
　Novi *(G-11902)*
Star Shade Cutter Co............................G.... 269 983-2403
　Saint Joseph *(G-14341)*

MACHINERY: Thread Rolling

Salvo Tool & Engineering Co ....E....... 810 346-2727
　Brown City *(G-2057)*

MACHINERY: Tire Shredding

Universal Tire Recycling Inc ....F.... 313 429-1212
　Detroit *(G-4416)*

MACHINERY: Wire Drawing

Basis Machining LLC............................G....... 517 542-3818
　Litchfield *(G-9600)*
Demmer Investments Inc ....G....... 517 321-3600
　Lansing *(G-9221)*
Dnl Fabrication LLC..............................F.... 586 872-2656
　Roseville *(G-13796)*
Edgewater Automation LLC ....D.... 269 983-1300
　Saint Joseph *(G-14308)*
I Machine LLC ....G.... 616 532-8020
　Grandville *(G-7049)*
Mark 7 Machine Inc ....G.... 989 922-7335
　Bay City *(G-1327)*
ND Industries Inc ....E.... 248 288-0000
　Troy *(G-16521)*
Weber Electric Mfg Co ....E.... 586 323-9000
　Shelby Township *(G-14721)*

MACHINERY: Woodworking

Alexander Dodds Company ....G....... 616 784-6000
　Grand Rapids *(G-6156)*
Automated Precision Eqp LLC ....G.... 517 481-2414
　Eaton Rapids *(G-4717)*
Boxer Equipment/Morbark Inc ....G.... 989 866-2381
　Winn *(G-17746)*
Carter Products Company Inc ....F.... 616 647-3380
　Grand Rapids *(G-6256)*
Conway-Cleveland Corp.......................G.... 616 458-0056
　Grand Rapids *(G-6309)*
Gudho USA Inc ....F.... 616 682-7814
　Ada *(G-17)*
Homag Machinery North Amer Inc ......F.... 616 254-8181
　Grand Rapids *(G-6515)*
International Fenestration ....G.... 248 735-6880
　Northville *(G-11701)*
Macali Inc ....G.... 616 447-1202
　Grand Rapids *(G-6639)*
Morbark LLC ....B.... 989 866-2381
　Winn *(G-17747)*
Tannewitz Inc ....E.... 616 457-5999
　Jenison *(G-8644)*

MACHINES: Forming, Sheet Metal

Ace Welding & Machine Inc ....F....... 231 941-9664
　Traverse City *(G-15887)*
Fabrilaser Mfg LLC ....E.... 269 789-9490
　Marshall *(G-10567)*
Prototech Laser Inc..............................E.... 586 598-6900
　Chesterfield *(G-2827)*

MACHINISTS' TOOLS & MACHINES: Measuring, Metalworking Type

Arm Tooling Systems Inc ....F....... 586 759-5677
　Warren *(G-16938)*
Buster Mathis Foundation.....................G.... 616 843-4433
　Wyoming *(G-17990)*

MACHINISTS' TOOLS: Measuring, Precision

Accu Products International ....G....... 734 429-9571
　Saline *(G-14372)*
Control Gaging Inc...............................E.... 734 668-6750
　Ann Arbor *(G-404)*
Dme Company LLC ....B.... 248 398-6000
　Madison Heights *(G-10233)*
Fisk Precision Tech LLC ....G.... 616 514-1415
　Wyoming *(G-18002)*
G&G Industries Inc ....E.... 586 726-6000
　Shelby Township *(G-14595)*
Linamar Holding Nevada Inc ....F.... 248 477-6240
　Livonia *(G-9807)*
Measuring Tool Services ....G.... 734 261-1107
　Livonia *(G-9835)*
Sme Holdings LLC................................E.... 586 254-5310
　Sterling Heights *(G-15500)*

MACHINISTS' TOOLS: Precision

Anbo Tool & Manufacturing Inc............G....... 586 465-7610
　Clinton Township *(G-3052)*
Dependable Gage & Tool Co ....F.... 248 545-2100
　Oak Park *(G-12058)*
Fitz Manufacturing Inc.........................F.... 248 589-1780
　Troy *(G-16365)*
Flex Manufacturing Inc........................F.... 586 469-1076
　Clinton Township *(G-3122)*
Gage Rite Products Inc ....F.... 248 588-7796
　Troy *(G-16377)*
Grand Rapids Metaltek Inc..................E.... 616 791-2373
　Grand Rapids *(G-6460)*
Grind-All Precision Tool Co ....F.... 586 954-3430
　Clinton Township *(G-3132)*
Hope Focus Companies Inc................E.... 313 494-5500
　Detroit *(G-4130)*
Image Machine & Tool Inc ....G.... 586 466-3400
　Fraser *(G-5669)*
J & B Precision Inc ....G.... 313 565-3431
　Taylor *(G-15729)*
Jt Manufacturing Inc............................E.... 517 849-2923
　Jonesville *(G-8658)*
Kenrie Inc...F.... 616 494-3200
　Holland *(G-7710)*
Khalsa Metal Products Inc ....G.... 616 791-4794
　Kentwood *(G-9014)*
Kooiker Tool & Die Inc.........................F.... 616 554-3630
　Caledonia *(G-2305)*

Lancer Tool Co ....F....... 248 380-8830
　Wixom *(G-17844)*
Lead Screws International Inc ....E.... 262 786-1500
　Traverse City *(G-16022)*
Line Precision Inc ....E.... 248 474-5280
　Farmington Hills *(G-5044)*
Machining Technologies LLC ....G.... 248 379-4201
　Clarkston *(G-2935)*
Majeske Machine Inc ....F.... 319 273-8905
　Plymouth *(G-12682)*
Maro Precision Tool Company ....F.... 734 261-3100
　West Bloomfield *(G-17483)*
Master Machine & Tool Co Inc ....G.... 586 469-4243
　Clinton Township *(G-3169)*
Micro Form Inc ....G.... 517 750-3660
　Spring Arbor *(G-15126)*
Precise Cnc Routing Inc......................E.... 616 538-8608
　Grand Rapids *(G-6763)*
Precision Devices Inc ....E.... 734 439-2462
　Milan *(G-10950)*
Puritan Automation LLC ....F.... 248 668-1114
　Wixom *(G-17881)*
Rayco Manufacturing Inc ....F.... 586 795-2884
　Sterling Heights *(G-15462)*
Salerno Tool Works Inc ....G.... 586 755-5000
　Warren *(G-17227)*
Selector Spline Products Co................F.... 586 254-4020
　Sterling Heights *(G-15488)*
Steel Craft Technologies Inc................C.... 616 866-4400
　Belmont *(G-1471)*
Witco Inc ....D.... 810 387-4231
　Greenwood *(G-7163)*

MAGNESIUM

Nanomag LLC..G....... 734 261-2800
　Livonia *(G-9858)*

MAGNETIC INK & OPTICAL SCANNING EQPT

LMI Technologies Inc............................G....... 248 298-2839
　Royal Oak *(G-13944)*

MAGNETIC RESONANCE IMAGING DEVICES: Nonmedical

Alliance Hni LLC ....D....... 989 729-2804
　Owosso *(G-12277)*
Authentic 3d ....G.... 248 469-8809
　Bingham Farms *(G-1649)*

MAGNETIC SHIELDS, METAL

Cruux LLC...G....... 248 515-8411
　Troy *(G-16288)*
Fluxtrol Inc..G.... 248 393-2000
　Auburn Hills *(G-877)*

MAGNETIC TAPE, AUDIO: Prerecorded

Brilliance Publishing Inc ....C....... 616 846-5256
　Grand Haven *(G-5998)*

MAGNETS: Ceramic

My Permit Pal Inc ....G....... 248 432-2699
　West Bloomfield *(G-17488)*

MAGNETS: Permanent

Advanced Magnet Source Corp............G....... 734 398-7188
　Canton *(G-2345)*
Bergamot Inc..G.... 586 372-7109
　Lakeville *(G-9177)*
Industrial Magnetics Inc ....D.... 231 582-3100
　Boyne City *(G-1823)*
Magnetic Systems Intl Inc ....F.... 231 582-9600
　Boyne City *(G-1828)*
Tengam Engineering Inc ....E.... 269 694-9466
　Otsego *(G-12256)*
Universal Magnetics Inc ....G.... 231 937-5555
　Howard City *(G-8007)*

MAIL-ORDER HOUSE, NEC

Viking Group Inc ....G....... 616 432-6800
　Caledonia *(G-2322)*

MAIL-ORDER HOUSES: Computer Software

Rutherford & Associates Inc................E....... 616 392-5000
　Holland *(G-7792)*

Employee Codes: A=Over 500 employees, B=251-500
C=101-250, D=51-100, E=20-50, F=10-19, G=3-9

2020 Harris Michigan Industrial Directory

MAIL-ORDER HOUSES: Cosmetics & Perfumes

US Salon Supply LLC .... G 616 365-5790
  Paw Paw *(G-12415)*

MAIL-ORDER HOUSES: Educational Splys & Eqpt

Esl Supplies LLC .... G 517 525-7877
  Mason *(G-10637)*

MAIL-ORDER HOUSES: Fitness & Sporting Goods

Homedics Usa LLC .... B 248 863-3000
  Commerce Township *(G-3414)*

MAIL-ORDER HOUSES: Fruit

Thomas Cooper .... G 231 599-2251
  Ellsworth *(G-4789)*

MAIL-ORDER HOUSES: Record & Tape, Music Or Video Club

Pull Our Own Weight .... G 313 686-4685
  Detroit *(G-4316)*

MAIL-ORDER HOUSES: Tools & Hardware

Accu Products International .... G 734 429-9571
  Saline *(G-14372)*

MAIL-ORDER HOUSES: Women's Apparel

Real Love Printwear .... G 248 327-7181
  Southfield *(G-15011)*

MAILBOX RENTAL & RELATED SVCS

Crk Ltd .... G 586 779-5240
  Eastpointe *(G-4699)*

MAILING & MESSENGER SVCS

Allied Bindery LLC .... E 248 588-5990
  Madison Heights *(G-10188)*

MAILING LIST: Compilers

Kent Communications Inc .... D 616 957-2120
  Grand Rapids *(G-6575)*
Postal Savings Direct Mktg .... F 810 238-8866
  Flint *(G-5480)*

MAILING SVCS, NEC

Aldinger Inc .... E 517 394-2424
  Lansing *(G-9334)*
Brightformat Inc .... E 616 247-1161
  Grand Rapids *(G-6236)*
Bruce Inc .... G 517 371-5205
  Lansing *(G-9352)*
CPM Services Group Inc .... G 248 624-5100
  Wixom *(G-17791)*
Data Mail Services Inc .... E 248 588-2415
  Madison Heights *(G-10228)*
Domart LLC .... G 616 285-9177
  Grand Rapids *(G-6357)*
Generation Press Inc .... G 616 392-4405
  Holland *(G-7642)*
Kimprint Inc .... E 734 459-2960
  Plymouth *(G-12668)*
Kolossos Printing Inc .... F 734 994-5400
  Ann Arbor *(G-517)*
Lake Michigan Mailers Inc .... D 269 383-9333
  Kalamazoo *(G-8804)*
New Echelon Direct Mktg LLC .... G 248 809-2485
  Brighton *(G-1967)*
Print House Inc .... F 248 473-1414
  Farmington Hills *(G-5100)*
Source One Dist Svcs Inc .... G 248 399-5060
  Madison Heights *(G-10355)*
TGI Direct Inc .... F 810 239-5553
  Ann Arbor *(G-667)*
TGI Direct Inc .... E 810 239-5553
  Flint *(G-5509)*
Your Hometown Shopper LLC .... F 586 412-8500
  Shelby Township *(G-14725)*

MANAGEMENT CONSULTING SVCS: Administrative

PM Power Group Inc .... G 906 885-7100
  White Pine *(G-17658)*

MANAGEMENT CONSULTING SVCS: Automation & Robotics

CCS Design LLC .... G 248 313-9178
  Wixom *(G-17781)*
Esys Automation LLC .... D 248 754-1900
  Auburn Hills *(G-856)*
Lorna Icr LLC 586 582-1500
  Warren *(G-17131)*
Recognition Robotics Inc .... G 440 590-0499
  Wixom *(G-17884)*
Strik-Wstfen-Dynarad Frnc Corp .... G 616 355-2327
  Holland *(G-7817)*

MANAGEMENT CONSULTING SVCS: Business

F I D Corporation .... F 248 373-7005
  Rochester Hills *(G-13422)*
Human Synergistics Inc .... E 734 459-1030
  Plymouth *(G-12644)*
Ideation International Inc .... F 248 737-8854
  Farmington Hills *(G-5025)*
Lol Telcom Inc .... B 616 888-6171
  Hudsonville *(G-8162)*
Whiteside Consulting Group LLC .... G 313 288-6598
  Detroit *(G-4440)*

MANAGEMENT CONSULTING SVCS: Construction Project

Curbco Inc .... D 810 232-2121
  Flint *(G-5409)*
Gloria C Williams 313 220-2735
  Southfield *(G-14922)*
Lrh & Associates Inc .... G 517 784-1055
  Jackson *(G-8500)*

MANAGEMENT CONSULTING SVCS: Hospital & Health

Grass Lake Community Pharmacy .... G 517 522-4100
  Grass Lake *(G-7088)*
Medical Infrmtics Slutions LLC .... G 248 851-3124
  Bloomfield Hills *(G-1781)*

MANAGEMENT CONSULTING SVCS: Industrial

Trucent Inc .... G 734 426-9015
  Dexter *(G-4515)*
Trucent Separation Tech LLC .... D 734 426-9015
  Dexter *(G-4516)*

MANAGEMENT CONSULTING SVCS: Industrial & Labor

Probus Technical Services Inc .... F 876 226-5692
  Troy *(G-16563)*

MANAGEMENT CONSULTING SVCS: Industrial Hygiene

Acorn Industries Inc .... D 734 261-2940
  Livonia *(G-9627)*
Wonder Makers Environmental .... F 269 382-4154
  Kalamazoo *(G-8926)*

MANAGEMENT CONSULTING SVCS: Industry Specialist

Busch Industries Inc .... G 616 957-3737
  Grand Rapids *(G-6246)*
Ezbake Technologies LLC .... G 817 430-1621
  Fenton *(G-5206)*
Moldex3d Northern America Inc .... F 248 946-4570
  Farmington Hills *(G-5072)*

MANAGEMENT CONSULTING SVCS: Maintenance

Digital Performance Tech .... F 877 983-4230
  Troy *(G-16320)*

MANAGEMENT CONSULTING SVCS: Management Engineering

Detroit Materials Inc .... G 248 924-5436
  Farmington *(G-4897)*
Metalform Industries LLC .... G 248 462-0056
  Shelby Township *(G-14639)*

MANAGEMENT CONSULTING SVCS: Manufacturing

Tindall Packaging Inc .... G 269 649-1163
  Portage *(G-13050)*

MANAGEMENT CONSULTING SVCS: Quality Assurance

Artcraft Pattern Works Inc .... F 734 729-0022
  Westland *(G-17543)*
Em A Give Break Safety .... F 231 263-6625
  Kingsley *(G-9071)*

MANAGEMENT CONSULTING SVCS: Retail Trade Consultant

Auction Masters .... G 586 576-7777
  Oak Park *(G-12050)*

MANAGEMENT SERVICES

B L Harroun and Son Inc .... E 269 345-8657
  Kalamazoo *(G-8692)*
Berkshire & Associates Inc .... F 734 719-1822
  Canton *(G-2351)*
Covenant Cpitl Investments Inc .... F 248 477-4230
  Farmington Hills *(G-4967)*
Dominos Pizza LLC .... C 734 930-3030
  Ann Arbor *(G-424)*
Gemini Group Inc .... F 989 269-6272
  Bad Axe *(G-1062)*
Grand Rapids Gravel Company .... F 616 538-9000
  Grand Rapids *(G-6454)*
Multiax International Inc 616 534-4530
  Grandville *(G-7060)*
Synod of Great Lakes .... C 616 698-7071
  Grand Rapids *(G-6910)*
Taylor Communications Inc .... F 248 304-4800
  Southfield *(G-15043)*
Yanfeng US Automotive .... G 616 394-1523
  Holland *(G-7866)*

MANAGEMENT SVCS, FACILITIES SUPPORT: Environ Remediation

Birks Works Environmental LLC .... G 313 891-1310
  Detroit *(G-3904)*
North American Aqua Envmtl LLC .... F 269 476-2092
  Vandalia *(G-16802)*
Regency Construction Corp .... E 586 741-8000
  Clinton Township *(G-3208)*
Swat Environmental Inc .... E 517 322-2999
  Lansing *(G-9427)*

MANAGEMENT SVCS: Business

917 Chittock Street LLC .... F 866 945-0269
  Lansing *(G-9331)*
Allegra Print and Imaging .... G 616 784-6699
  Grand Rapids *(G-6160)*
Integrated Program MGT LLC .... G 248 241-9257
  Clarkston *(G-2932)*
Talon LLC .... D 313 392-1000
  Detroit *(G-4395)*

MANAGEMENT SVCS: Construction

Doan Construction Co .... F 734 971-4678
  Ypsilanti *(G-18067)*
Lrh & Associates Inc .... G 517 784-1055
  Jackson *(G-8500)*
Rock Industries Inc .... E 248 338-2800
  Bloomfield Hills *(G-1796)*
Saginaw Asphalt Paving Co .... D 989 755-8147
  Carrollton *(G-2487)*

MANAGEMENT SVCS: Hospital

Hackley Health Ventures Inc .... G 231 728-5720
  Muskegon *(G-11342)*
Mercy Health Partners .... D 231 728-4032
  Muskegon *(G-11373)*

MANAGEMENT SVCS: Restaurant

Veritas Vineyard LLC .... E 517 962-2427
Jackson *(G-8600)*

MANHOLES & COVERS: Metal

City of East Jordan .... G 231 536-2561
East Jordan *(G-4627)*
Ej Americas LLC .... G 231 536-2261
East Jordan *(G-4629)*
Ej Asia-Pacific Inc .... G 231 536-2261
East Jordan *(G-4631)*
Ej Europe LLC .... G 231 536-2261
East Jordan *(G-4633)*
Ej Group Inc .... E 231 536-2261
East Jordan *(G-4634)*
Ej Usa Inc .... E 248 546-2004
Oak Park *(G-12065)*
Ej Usa Inc .... F 616 538-2040
Wyoming *(G-17997)*

MANHOLES COVERS: Concrete

Ej Ardmore Inc .... C 231 536-2261
East Jordan *(G-4630)*

MANICURE PREPARATIONS

Eve Salonspa .... G 269 327-4811
Portage *(G-12994)*

MANIFOLDS: Pipe, Fabricated From Purchased Pipe

Key Gas Components Inc .... E 269 673-2151
Allegan *(G-169)*
Loftis Alumi-TEC Inc .... E 616 846-1990
Grand Haven *(G-6050)*

MANNEQUINS

Denton Atd Inc .... D 734 451-7878
Plymouth *(G-12608)*

MANUFACTURED & MOBILE HOME DEALERS

Advantage Housing Inc .... G 269 792-6291
Wayland *(G-17397)*
Kearsley Lake Terrace LLC .... G 810 736-7000
Flint *(G-5453)*

MANUFACTURING INDUSTRIES, NEC

Abletech Industries LLC .... G 734 677-2420
Dexter *(G-4471)*
Access Manufacturing Techn .... F 224 610-0171
Niles *(G-11593)*
Accurate Mfg Solutions LLC .... G 248 553-2225
Farmington Hills *(G-4918)*
Achieve Industries LLC .... G 586 493-9780
Clinton Township *(G-3034)*
Adapt .... G 989 343-9755
West Branch *(G-17505)*
Allied Support Systems .... G 734 721-4040
Wayne *(G-17421)*
Alta Distribution LLC .... F 313 363-1682
Southfield *(G-14829)*
AME International LLC .... E 586 532-8981
Clinton Township *(G-3044)*
American Battery Solutions Inc .... E 248 462-6364
Lake Orion *(G-9125)*
BEAM Industries Inc .... G 989 799-4044
Saginaw *(G-14002)*
Bentley Industries .... G 810 625-0400
Flint *(G-5387)*
Bloom Industries LLC .... G 616 453-2946
Grand Rapids *(G-6232)*
Bolden Industries Inc .... F 248 387-9489
Detroit *(G-3907)*
Capler Mfg .... G 586 264-7851
Sterling Heights *(G-15281)*
Cmb Mfg LLC .... G 920 915-2079
Menominee *(G-10727)*
Collective Industries Corp .... G 313 879-1080
Allen Park *(G-195)*
Connely Company .... G 586 977-0700
Sterling Heights *(G-15295)*
Danif Industries Inc .... G 248 539-0295
West Bloomfield *(G-17473)*
Dewsbury Manufacturing Company .... G 734 839-6376
Livonia *(G-9709)*
Diverse Manufacturing Soltion .... G 517 423-6691
Tecumseh *(G-15788)*
DMS Manufacturing Solutions .... G 517 423-6691
Tecumseh *(G-15789)*
Dog Brown Manufacturing LLC .... G 313 255-1400
Redford *(G-13159)*
ECM Manufacturing Inc .... G 810 736-0299
Flint *(G-5421)*
Emerald Mfg .... G 269 483-2676
White Pigeon *(G-17647)*
Fusion Strategies LLC .... G 734 776-1734
Livonia *(G-9745)*
G & L Mfg Inc .... G 810 724-4101
Imlay City *(G-8199)*
Ganas LLC .... F 734 748-0434
Detroit *(G-4076)*
Gr X Manufacturing .... G 616 541-7420
Caledonia *(G-2296)*
Haven Sports Manufacturing LLC .... G 269 639-8782
South Haven *(G-14762)*
Hilljack Industries LLC .... G 517 552-3874
Howell *(G-8049)*
Hills Manufacturing LLC .... G 248 536-3307
Farmington Hills *(G-5020)*
Hoosier Tank and Manufacturing .... G 269 683-2550
Niles *(G-11616)*
Industrial Services Group .... E 269 945-5291
Lowell *(G-10031)*
Innovative Fabrication LLC .... E 734 789-9099
Flat Rock *(G-5356)*
International Wood Inds Inc .... G 800 598-9663
Grand Rapids *(G-6542)*
Irene Industries LLC .... G 757 696-3969
Commerce Township *(G-3417)*
J&D Industries LLC .... G 734 430-6582
Newport *(G-11588)*
Jamieson Fabrication Unlimited .... G 269 760-1473
Richland *(G-13250)*
Jennco Industries LLC .... G 269 290-3145
Allegan *(G-167)*
Jupiter Manufacturing .... G 989 551-0519
Harbor Beach *(G-7268)*
Kenny G Mfg & Sls LLC .... G 313 218-6297
Brownstown *(G-2066)*
Kenyon Tj & Associates Inc .... E 231 544-1144
Bellaire *(G-1438)*
Knapp Manufacturing LLC .... G 517 279-9538
Coldwater *(G-3312)*
Kopach Filter LLC .... G 906 863-8611
Wallace *(G-16886)*
Liberty Automotive Tech LLC .... G 269 487-8114
Holland *(G-7723)*
Manufctring Partners Group LLC .... G 517 749-4050
Lapeer *(G-9473)*
Marrone Michigan Manufactoring .... G 269 427-0300
Bangor *(G-1093)*
Mettle Craft Manufacturing LLC .... G 586 306-8962
Sterling Heights *(G-15418)*
Midwest Defense Corp .... G 231 590-6857
Traverse City *(G-16036)*
Mote Industries Inc .... F 248 613-3413
New Haven *(G-11525)*
Mount Mfg LLC .... G 231 487-2118
Boyne City *(G-1830)*
Mr McGooz Products Inc .... G 313 693-4003
Detroit *(G-4258)*
Msmac Designs LLC .... G 313 521-6289
Detroit *(G-4260)*
Nathan Slagter .... G 616 648-7423
Lowell *(G-10038)*
Niemela .... G 906 523-4362
Chassell *(G-2674)*
Oak Mountain Industries .... G 734 941-7000
Romulus *(G-13716)*
Odin Defense Industries Inc .... G 248 434-5072
Troy *(G-16532)*
Palm Industries LLC .... G 248 444-7921
Plymouth *(G-12707)*
Palo Alto Manufacturing LLC .... G 248 266-3669
Auburn Hills *(G-969)*
Pl Optima Manufacturing LLC .... F 616 931-9750
Zeeland *(G-18174)*
Pingree Mfg L3c .... G 313 444-8428
Detroit *(G-4302)*
Precision Mfg Group Inc .... F 616 837-6764
Nunica *(G-12042)*
Pro-Built Mfg .... G 989 354-1321
Alpena *(G-308)*
Production & Prototype Svc LLC .... G 586 924-7479
Lenox *(G-9523)*
Profile EDM LLC .... G 586 949-4586
Chesterfield *(G-2823)*
R J Manufacturing .... G 810 610-0205
Davison *(G-3660)*
Real Steel Manufacturing LLC .... G 231 457-4673
Muskegon *(G-11414)*
Red Rock Industries Inc .... G 734 992-3522
Allen Park *(G-205)*
Rilas & Rogers LLC .... F 937 901-4228
Canton *(G-2422)*
Rottman Manufacturing Group .... G 586 693-5676
Sterling Heights *(G-15480)*
Rpd Manufacturing LLC .... G 248 760-4796
Milford *(G-10983)*
Sampo Company LLC .... G 734 664-9761
Plymouth *(G-12749)*
Seewald Industries .... G 586 322-1042
Almont *(G-265)*
Shoreline Manufacturing LLC .... G 616 834-1503
Holland *(G-7802)*
Speed Industry LLC .... G 248 458-1335
Troy *(G-16616)*
Stansley Industries Inc .... G 810 515-1919
Flint *(G-5505)*
Summit Cutting Tools and Mfg .... G 248 859-2625
Wixom *(G-17899)*
Sustainable Industries LLC .... G 248 213-6599
Detroit *(G-4390)*
Tallman Industries Inc .... G 231 879-4755
Fife Lake *(G-5343)*
Tide Rings LLC .... G 586 206-3142
Allenton *(G-230)*
Tip Top Screw Manufacturi .... G 989 739-5157
Saginaw *(G-14164)*
Tjb Industries .... G 248 690-9608
Oakland *(G-12109)*
Total Repair Express MI LLC .... F 248 690-9410
Lake Orion *(G-9166)*
Triunfar Industries Inc .... G 313 790-5592
South Lyon *(G-14814)*
Uis Industries LLC .... G 734 443-3737
Livonia *(G-9980)*
Winsol Electronics LLC .... G 810 767-2987
Flint *(G-5524)*
Wooley Industries Inc .... G 810 341-8823
Flint *(G-5526)*
World Industries Inc .... G 248 288-0000
Clawson *(G-2990)*
Yukon Manufacturing .... F 989 358-6248
Alpena *(G-321)*
Zoe Health .... G 616 485-1909
Kentwood *(G-9036)*

MAPS

Metro Graphic Arts Inc .... F 616 245-2271
Grand Rapids *(G-6663)*

MAPS & CHARTS, WHOLESALE

Metro Graphic Arts Inc .... F 616 245-2271
Grand Rapids *(G-6663)*

MARBLE, BUILDING: Cut & Shaped

Dura Sill Corporation .... G 248 348-2490
Novi *(G-11873)*
K2 Stoneworks LLC .... G 989 790-3250
Saginaw *(G-14068)*
Lakeshore Marble Company Inc .... E 269 429-8241
Stevensville *(G-15574)*
Marble Deluxe A C .... G 248 668-8200
Commerce Township *(G-3427)*
Tile Craft Inc .... F 231 929-7207
Traverse City *(G-16124)*
Usm Acquisition LLC .... D 989 561-2293
Remus *(G-13243)*
Zimmer Marble Co Inc .... F 517 787-1500
Jackson *(G-8615)*

MARINAS

Eldean Yacht Basin Ltd .... E 616 786-2205
Holland *(G-7620)*
Floatation Docking Inc .... E 906 484-3422
Cedarville *(G-2567)*
Midwest Aquatics Group Inc .... G 734 426-4155
Pinckney *(G-12500)*

MARINE BASIN OPERATIONS

Superior Mar & Envmtl Svcs LLC .... G 906 253-9448
Sault Sainte Marie *(G-14475)*

PRODUCT

Employee Codes: A=Over 500 employees, B=251-500
C=101-250, D=51-100, E=20-50, F=10-19, G=3-9

2020 Harris Michigan
Industrial Directory

1289

MARINE CARGO HANDLING SVCS: Marine Terminal

Nicholson Terminal & Dock Co ....C....... 313 842-4300
  River Rouge *(G-13279)*

MARINE CARGO HANDLING SVCS: Waterfront Terminal Operations

Louis Padnos Iron and Metal Co ....F....... 231 722-6081
  Muskegon *(G-11368)*
Louis Padnos Iron and Metal Co ....F....... 616 301-7900
  Wyoming *(G-18018)*

MARINE ENGINE REPAIR SVCS

Arthur R Sommers ....G....... 586 469-1280
  Harrison Township *(G-7322)*
Creek Diesel Services Inc ....F....... 800 974-4600
  Grand Rapids *(G-6316)*
Marsh Brothers Inc ....F....... 517 869-2653
  Quincy *(G-13096)*
Murleys Marine ....G....... 586 725-7446
  Ira *(G-8264)*

MARINE HARDWARE

A & A Marine & Mfg Inc ....G....... 231 723-8308
  Manistee *(G-10413)*
A & B Tube Benders Inc ....E....... 586 773-0440
  Warren *(G-16905)*
Attwood Corporation ....C....... 616 897-9241
  Lowell *(G-10023)*
Detmar Corporation ....F....... 313 831-1155
  Detroit *(G-3969)*
Fathom Drones Inc ....G....... 586 216-7047
  Grand Rapids *(G-6402)*
HI TEC Stainless Inc ....E....... 269 543-4205
  Fennville *(G-5174)*
Hurley Marine Inc ....G....... 906 553-6249
  Escanaba *(G-4834)*
Jay & Kay Manufacturing LLC ....E....... 810 679-2333
  Croswell *(G-3598)*
Marine Industries Inc ....G....... 989 635-3644
  Marlette *(G-10500)*
T & L Products ....G....... 989 868-4428
  Reese *(G-13234)*
Tecla Company Inc ....E....... 248 624-8200
  Commerce Township *(G-3453)*

MARINE PROPELLER REPAIR SVCS

Allied Welding Incorporated ....G....... 248 360-1122
  Commerce Township *(G-3388)*
Falcon Motorsports Inc ....G....... 248 328-2222
  Holly *(G-7878)*

MARINE RELATED EQPT

Fireboy-Xintex Inc ....F....... 616 735-9380
  Grand Rapids *(G-6406)*
Lsp Inc ....E....... 517 639-3815
  Quincy *(G-13095)*
PSI Marine Inc ....F....... 989 695-2646
  Saginaw *(G-14126)*
Quality Marine Electronics LLC ....G....... 616 566-2101
  Zeeland *(G-18182)*

MARINE SPLY DEALERS

Holiday Distributing Co ....E....... 517 782-7146
  Jackson *(G-8466)*
Kts Enterprises ....G....... 269 624-3435
  Lawton *(G-9512)*

MARINE SPLYS WHOLESALERS

A & A Marine & Mfg Inc ....G....... 231 723-8308
  Manistee *(G-10413)*
Hella Corporate Center USA Inc ....E....... 586 232-4788
  Northville *(G-11697)*
T & L Products ....G....... 989 868-4428
  Reese *(G-13234)*

MARKERS

Carco Inc ....F....... 313 925-1053
  Detroit *(G-3930)*

MARKETS: Meat & fish

Kowalski Companies Inc ....C....... 313 873-8200
  Detroit *(G-4182)*

Smith & Sons Meat Proc Inc ....G....... 989 772-6048
  Mount Pleasant *(G-11227)*

MARKING DEVICES

Argon Tool Inc ....F....... 248 583-1605
  Madison Heights *(G-10195)*
Borries Mkg Systems Partnr ....G....... 734 761-9549
  Ann Arbor *(G-388)*
Carco Inc ....F....... 313 925-1053
  Detroit *(G-3930)*
Carcone Co ....G....... 248 348-2677
  Novi *(G-11843)*
Columbia Marking Tools Inc ....E....... 586 949-8400
  Chesterfield *(G-2754)*
F & A Enterprises of Michigan ....G....... 906 228-3222
  Marquette *(G-10531)*
JL Geisler Sign Company ....F....... 586 574-1800
  Troy *(G-16438)*
Mark-Pack Inc ....E....... 616 837-5400
  Coopersville *(G-3564)*
Michigan Shippers Supply Inc ....F....... 616 935-6680
  Spring Lake *(G-15163)*
Nelson Paint Co of Mich Inc ....G....... 906 774-5566
  Kingsford *(G-9063)*
Rite Mark Stamp Company ....E....... 248 391-7600
  Auburn Hills *(G-992)*
Stamping Grounds Inc ....G....... 248 851-6764
  Bloomfield Hills *(G-1798)*
Volk Corporation ....G....... 616 940-9900
  Farmington Hills *(G-5150)*

MARKING DEVICES: Embossing Seals & Hand Stamps

Detroit Marking Products Corp ....F....... 313 838-9760
  Canton *(G-2364)*
New Method Steel Stamps Inc ....G....... 586 293-0200
  Fraser *(G-5697)*
Rodzina Industries Inc ....G....... 810 235-2341
  Flint *(G-5493)*
Rubber Stamps Unlimited Inc ....F....... 734 451-7300
  Plymouth *(G-12746)*
Stamp-Rite Incorporated ....E....... 517 487-5071
  Lansing *(G-9267)*
West Michigan Stamp & Seal ....E....... 269 323-1913
  Portage *(G-13055)*

MARKING DEVICES: Printing Dies, Marking Mach, Rubber/Plastic

Mark Maker Company Inc ....E....... 616 538-6980
  Grand Rapids *(G-6643)*

MARKING DEVICES: Screens, Textile Printing

All American Embroidery Inc ....F....... 734 421-9292
  Livonia *(G-9634)*

MARKING DEVICES: Seal Presses, Notary & Hand

Mlh Services LLC ....G....... 313 768-4403
  Detroit *(G-4252)*

MASKS: Gas

Avon Protection Systems Inc ....C....... 231 779-6200
  Cadillac *(G-2230)*

MASQUERADE OR THEATRICAL COSTUMES STORES

Excellent Designs Swimwear ....E....... 586 977-9140
  Warren *(G-17025)*

MASSAGE MACHINES, ELECTRIC: Barber & Beauty Shops

Body Contour Ventures LLC ....G....... 248 579-6772
  Farmington Hills *(G-4945)*

MATERIAL GRINDING & PULVERIZING SVCS NEC

Dgh Enterprises Inc ....E....... 269 925-0657
  Benton Harbor *(G-1494)*
Helsels Tree Service Inc ....G....... 231 879-3666
  Manton *(G-10454)*

United Mfg Netwrk Inc ....G....... 586 321-7887
  Warren *(G-17274)*
Williams Diversified Inc ....E....... 734 421-6100
  Livonia *(G-10009)*

MATERIALS HANDLING EQPT WHOLESALERS

Albion Industries LLC ....C....... 800 835-8911
  Albion *(G-113)*
Detroit Wire Rope Splcing Corp ....F....... 248 585-1063
  Madison Heights *(G-10230)*
Dobson Industrial Inc ....E....... 800 298-6063
  Bay City *(G-1304)*
Great Lakes Allied LLC ....G....... 231 924-5794
  White Cloud *(G-17622)*
Material Handling Tech Inc ....D....... 586 725-5546
  Ira *(G-8260)*

MATS, MATTING & PADS: Nonwoven

Apparelmaster-Muskegon Inc ....E....... 231 728-5406
  Muskegon *(G-11271)*
HR Technologies Inc ....C....... 248 284-1170
  Madison Heights *(G-10271)*
N A Visscher-Caravelle Inc ....G....... 248 851-9800
  Bloomfield Hills *(G-1786)*

MEAL DELIVERY PROGRAMS

Goodwill Inds Nthrn Mich Inc ....G....... 231 779-1361
  Cadillac *(G-2251)*
Goodwill Inds Nthrn Mich Inc ....G....... 231 779-1311
  Cadillac *(G-2250)*
Goodwill Inds Nthrn Mich Inc ....G....... 231 922-4890
  Traverse City *(G-15981)*

MEAT & MEAT PRDTS WHOLESALERS

Boars Head Provisions Co Inc ....B....... 941 955-0994
  Holland *(G-7572)*
Kellys Catering ....G....... 231 796-5414
  Big Rapids *(G-1635)*
Protein Procurement Svcs Inc ....G....... 248 738-7970
  Bloomfield Hills *(G-1792)*
T Wigley Inc ....F....... 313 831-6881
  Detroit *(G-4394)*

MEAT CUTTING & PACKING

Alto Meat Processing ....G....... 616 868-6080
  Alto *(G-322)*
Bellinger Packing ....F....... 989 838-2274
  Ashley *(G-726)*
Bernthal Packing Inc ....E....... 989 652-2648
  Frankenmuth *(G-5583)*
Bert Hazekamp & Son Inc ....C....... 231 773-8302
  Muskegon *(G-11279)*
Berthiaume Slaughter House ....G....... 989 879-4921
  Pinconning *(G-12506)*
Boars Head Provisions Co Inc ....B....... 941 955-0994
  Holland *(G-7572)*
Boyers Meat Processing Inc ....G....... 734 495-1342
  Canton *(G-2355)*
C Roy Inc ....E....... 810 387-3975
  Yale *(G-18045)*
Cargill Incorporated ....F....... 608 868-5150
  Owosso *(G-12281)*
Carol Packing House ....G....... 989 673-2688
  Caro *(G-2466)*
Clemens Welcome Center ....G....... 517 278-2500
  Coldwater *(G-3296)*
Cole Carter Inc ....G....... 269 626-8891
  Scotts *(G-14504)*
Cornbelt Beef Corporation ....E....... 313 237-0087
  Oak Park *(G-12054)*
Countryside Quality Meats LLC ....G....... 517 741-4275
  Union City *(G-16732)*
Dan Drummond ....G....... 231 853-6200
  Ravenna *(G-13118)*
Erlas Inc ....D....... 989 872-2191
  Cass City *(G-2514)*
Fillmore Beef Company Inc ....G....... 616 396-6693
  Holland *(G-7631)*
Flemings Meat Processing ....G....... 810 679-3668
  Croswell *(G-3596)*
Gainors Meat Packing Inc ....G....... 989 269-8161
  Bad Axe *(G-1061)*
Garys Custom Meats ....G....... 269 641-5683
  Union *(G-16728)*
Gibbies Deer Processing ....F....... 231 924-6042
  Fremont *(G-5774)*

PRODUCT SECTION

Hormel Foods Corporation ....C...... 616 454-0418
Grand Rapids *(G-6516)*
Kellys Catering ....G...... 231 796-5414
Big Rapids *(G-1635)*
Kent Quality Foods Inc ....C...... 616 459-4595
Hudsonville *(G-8161)*
L&J Packaging ....G...... 269 782-2628
Dowagiac *(G-4546)*
Lake Odessa Meat Processing ....G...... 616 374-8392
Lake Odessa *(G-9116)*
Lloyd Johnson Livestock Inc ....G...... 906 786-4878
Escanaba *(G-4840)*
Makkedah Mt Proc & Bulk Fd Str ....G...... 231 873-2113
Hart *(G-7376)*
Maurer Meat Processors Inc ....E...... 989 658-8185
Ubly *(G-16719)*
Michigan Meat Processing ....F...... 906 786-7010
Escanaba *(G-4845)*
Mmm Meat LLC ....F...... 616 669-6140
Hudsonville *(G-8171)*
Mypac Inc ....G...... 616 896-9359
Hudsonville *(G-8172)*
Nagel Meat Processing ....F...... 517 568-5035
Homer *(G-7947)*
Northwest Market ....G...... 517 787-5005
Jackson *(G-8543)*
Oles Meat Processing ....G...... 989 866-6442
Vestaburg *(G-16827)*
Packerland Packing Co ....G...... 269 685-6886
Plainwell *(G-12533)*
Pooles Meat Processing ....G...... 989 846-6348
Standish *(G-15225)*
Rays Game ....G...... 810 346-2628
Brown City *(G-2056)*
Ricks Meat Processing LLC ....G...... 517 628-2263
Eaton Rapids *(G-4733)*
Smith & Sons Meat Proc Inc ....G...... 989 772-6048
Mount Pleasant *(G-11227)*
Smith - Sons ME ....G...... 989 772-6048
Mount Pleasant *(G-11228)*
Smith Meat Packing Inc ....E...... 810 985-5900
Port Huron *(G-12967)*
Standard Provision LLC ....G...... 989 354-4975
Alpena *(G-313)*
Tyson ....G...... 231 922-3214
Traverse City *(G-16132)*
Tyson Foods Inc ....B...... 231 929-2456
Traverse City *(G-16133)*
Tyson Fresh Meats Inc ....D...... 248 213-1000
Southfield *(G-15051)*
US Guys Deer Processing LLC ....G...... 616 642-0967
Saranac *(G-14456)*
Vin-Lee-Ron Meat Packing LLC ....E...... 574 353-1386
Cassopolis *(G-2538)*

MEAT MARKETS

Bellinger Packing ....F...... 989 838-2274
Ashley *(G-726)*
Bernthal Packing Inc ....E...... 989 652-2648
Frankenmuth *(G-5583)*
Cattlemans Meat Company ....B...... 734 287-8260
Taylor *(G-15699)*
Dan Drummond ....G...... 231 853-6200
Ravenna *(G-13118)*
Flemings Meat Processing ....G...... 810 679-3668
Croswell *(G-3596)*
Ilowski Sausage Company Inc ....G...... 810 329-9117
East China *(G-4622)*
Kerns Sausages Inc ....E...... 989 652-2684
Frankenmuth *(G-5590)*
Marquette Meats In City LLC ....G...... 906 226-8333
Marquette *(G-10545)*
Northwest Market ....G...... 517 787-5005
Jackson *(G-8543)*
Richmond Meat Packers Inc ....G...... 586 727-1450
Richmond *(G-13270)*
Russo Bros Inc ....E...... 906 485-5250
Ishpeming *(G-8353)*
Viaus Super Market ....G...... 906 786-1950
Escanaba *(G-4866)*

MEAT PRDTS: Boxed Beef, From Slaughtered Meat

Jbs Packerland Inc ....E...... 269 685-6886
Plainwell *(G-12526)*
Jbs Plainwell Inc ....C...... 269 685-6886
Plainwell *(G-12527)*

MEAT PRDTS: Canned Exc Baby Food, From Slaughtered Meat

Spillson Ltd ....G...... 734 384-0284
Monroe *(G-11068)*

MEAT PRDTS: Cooked Meats, From Purchased Meat

Great Fresh Foods Co LLC ....F...... 586 846-3521
Taylor *(G-15726)*
Pioneer Meats LLC ....F...... 248 862-1988
Birmingham *(G-1698)*

MEAT PRDTS: Corned Beef, From Purchased Meat

T Wigley Inc ....F...... 313 831-6881
Detroit *(G-4394)*

MEAT PRDTS: Cured, From Slaughtered Meat

A & R Packing Co Inc ....E...... 734 422-2060
Livonia *(G-9618)*
Tolmans Processing ....G...... 616 875-8598
Hudsonville *(G-8183)*

MEAT PRDTS: Frankfurters, From Purchased Meat

Koegel Meats Inc ....C...... 810 238-3685
Flint *(G-5456)*

MEAT PRDTS: Lamb, From Slaughtered Meat

Berry & Sons-Rababeh ....G...... 313 259-6925
Detroit *(G-3901)*
Michigan Veal Inc ....F...... 616 669-6688
Hudsonville *(G-8169)*

MEAT PRDTS: Luncheon Meat, From Purchased Meat

Boars Head Provisions Co Inc ....B...... 941 955-0994
Holland *(G-7572)*

MEAT PRDTS: Meat By-Prdts, From Slaughtered Meat

Prime Cuts of Jackson LLC ....E...... 517 768-8090
Jackson *(G-8557)*
Scotts Hook & Cleaver Inc ....E...... 269 626-6891
Scotts *(G-14507)*

MEAT PRDTS: Pork, From Slaughtered Meat

Clemens Food Group LLC ....G...... 517 278-2500
Coldwater *(G-3295)*

MEAT PRDTS: Prepared Beef Prdts From Purchased Beef

Cattlemans Meat Company ....B...... 734 287-8260
Taylor *(G-15699)*
Smigelski Properties LLC ....G...... 989 255-6252
Alpena *(G-312)*

MEAT PRDTS: Prepared Pork Prdts, From Purchased Meat

Quincy Street Inc ....C...... 616 399-3330
Holland *(G-7781)*

MEAT PRDTS: Sausages & Related Prdts, From Purchased Meat

Louies Meats Inc ....F...... 231 946-4811
Traverse City *(G-16028)*

MEAT PRDTS: Sausages, From Purchased Meat

Detroit Sausage Co Inc ....F...... 313 259-0555
Detroit *(G-4002)*
Kowalski Companies Inc ....C...... 313 873-8200
Detroit *(G-4182)*
Krzysiak Family Restaurant ....D...... 989 894-4531
Bay City *(G-1326)*
Macomb Smoked Meats LLC ....D...... 313 842-2375
Dearborn *(G-3735)*
Mello Meats Inc ....F...... 800 852-5019
Auburn Hills *(G-945)*
Vandco Incorporated ....E...... 906 482-1550
Hancock *(G-7258)*
Viaus Super Market ....G...... 906 786-1950
Escanaba *(G-4866)*
Winter Sausage Mfg Co Inc ....E...... 586 777-9080
Eastpointe *(G-4713)*

MEAT PRDTS: Sausages, From Slaughtered Meat

Bob Evans Farms Inc ....D...... 517 437-3349
Hillsdale *(G-7518)*
Safari Meats Llc ....G...... 313 539-3367
Oak Park *(G-12097)*

MEAT PRDTS: Smoked

A & R Packing Co Inc ....E...... 734 422-2060
Livonia *(G-9618)*
Big O Smokehouse ....F...... 616 891-5555
Caledonia *(G-2289)*

MEAT PRDTS: Snack Sticks, Incl Jerky, From Purchased Meat

Classic Jerky Company ....D...... 313 357-9904
Taylor *(G-15701)*
Deerings Jerky Co LLC ....G...... 231 590-5687
Interlochen *(G-8239)*
Heinzerling Enterprises Inc ....G...... 734 529-9100
Dundee *(G-4586)*
Marquette Meats In City LLC ....G...... 906 226-8333
Marquette *(G-10545)*
Zicks Specialty Meats Inc ....G...... 269 471-7121
Berrien Springs *(G-1602)*

MEAT PRDTS: Veal, From Slaughtered Meat

Wolverine Packing Co ....D...... 313 259-7500
Detroit *(G-4446)*

MEAT PROCESSED FROM PURCHASED CARCASSES

Alexander and Hornung Inc ....D...... 586 771-9880
Saint Clair Shores *(G-14238)*
Bernthal Packing Inc ....E...... 989 652-2648
Frankenmuth *(G-5583)*
Bert Hazekamp & Son Inc ....C...... 231 773-8302
Muskegon *(G-11279)*
Clemens Food Group LLC ....G...... 517 278-2500
Coldwater *(G-3295)*
Darling Ingredients Inc ....E...... 269 751-0560
Hamilton *(G-7231)*
Dina Mia Kitchens Inc ....F...... 906 265-9082
Iron River *(G-8308)*
Erlas Inc ....D...... 989 872-2191
Cass City *(G-2514)*
Hillshire Brands Company ....A...... 616 875-8131
Zeeland *(G-18150)*
Ilowski Sausage Company Inc ....G...... 810 329-9117
East China *(G-4622)*
Johnston Meat Processing ....G...... 810 378-5455
Peck *(G-12419)*
Kellys Catering ....G...... 231 796-5414
Big Rapids *(G-1635)*
Kent Quality Foods Inc ....C...... 616 459-4595
Hudsonville *(G-8161)*
Kerns Sausages Inc ....E...... 989 652-2684
Frankenmuth *(G-5590)*
Kgdh LLC ....G...... 989 652-9041
Frankenmuth *(G-5591)*
L&J Packaging ....G...... 269 782-2628
Dowagiac *(G-4546)*

MEAT PROCESSING MACHINERY

Lowry Joanellen ....G...... 231 873-2323
Hesperia *(G-7478)*
Saa Tech Inc ....G...... 313 933-4960
Detroit *(G-4351)*

MEATS, PACKAGED FROZEN: Wholesalers

Wolverine Packing Co ....D...... 313 259-7500
Detroit *(G-4446)*

MEDIA: Magnetic & Optical Recording

Storch Products Company Inc ....F 734 591-2200
Livonia *(G-9946)*

MEDICAL & HOSPITAL EQPT WHOLESALERS

Alta Distribution LLC ....F 313 363-1682
Southfield *(G-14829)*
Lake Erie Med Surgical Sup Inc ....E 734 847-3847
Temperance *(G-15833)*
Landra Prsthtics Orthotics Inc ....G 586 294-7188
Saint Clair Shores *(G-14259)*
MCS Consultants Inc ....F 810 229-4222
Brighton *(G-1958)*
Northwest Tool & Machine Inc ....E 517 750-1332
Jackson *(G-8544)*
Vets Access LLC ....G 810 639-2222
Flushing *(G-5544)*

MEDICAL & HOSPITAL SPLYS: Radiation Shielding Garments

Radiolgical Fabrication Design ....G 810 632-6000
Howell *(G-8087)*

MEDICAL & SURGICAL SPLYS: Abdominal Support, Braces/Trusses

Bms Great Lakes LLC ....G 248 390-1598
Lake Orion *(G-9126)*

MEDICAL & SURGICAL SPLYS: Absorbent Cotton, Sterilized

Beltone Skoric Hearng Aid Cntr ....G 906 379-0606
Sault Sainte Marie *(G-14461)*
Beltone Skoric Hearng Aid Cntr ....G 906 553-4460
Escanaba *(G-4817)*

MEDICAL & SURGICAL SPLYS: Bandages & Dressings

Shock-Tek LLC ....G 313 886-0530
Grosse Pointe Farms *(G-7188)*

MEDICAL & SURGICAL SPLYS: Belts, Surg, Sanitary & Corrective

Trulife Inc ....E 517 787-1600
Jackson *(G-8596)*

MEDICAL & SURGICAL SPLYS: Braces, Orthopedic

Becker Oregon Inc ....E 248 588-7480
Troy *(G-16235)*
Brenner Orthtic Prsthetic Labs ....G 248 615-0600
Livonia *(G-9670)*
Greater Lansing Orthotic Clini ....G 517 337-0856
Lansing *(G-9377)*
Instep Pedorthics LLC ....G 810 285-9109
Traverse City *(G-16006)*
Oakland Orthopedic Appls Inc ....D 989 893-7544
Bay City *(G-1339)*
Paul W Reed DDS ....F 231 347-4145
Petoskey *(G-12467)*
Twin Cities Orthotic & Prosthe ....G 269 428-2910
Saint Joseph *(G-14345)*

MEDICAL & SURGICAL SPLYS: Clothing, Fire Resistant & Protect

Douglass Safety Systems LLC ....G 989 687-7600
Sanford *(G-14449)*
Sure-Fit Glove & Safety ....G 734 729-4960
Westland *(G-17601)*

MEDICAL & SURGICAL SPLYS: Cosmetic Restorations

Agelessmage Fcial Asthtics LLC ....G 269 998-5547
Farmington Hills *(G-4922)*
Luma Laser and Medi Spa ....G 248 817-5499
Troy *(G-16466)*

MEDICAL & SURGICAL SPLYS: Crutches & Walkers

Hi-Trac Industries Inc ....G 810 625-7193
Linden *(G-9592)*

MEDICAL & SURGICAL SPLYS: Ear Plugs

McKeon Products Inc ....E 586 427-7560
Warren *(G-17146)*

MEDICAL & SURGICAL SPLYS: Foot Appliances, Orthopedic

First Response Med Sups LLC ....F 313 731-2554
Dearborn *(G-3707)*

MEDICAL & SURGICAL SPLYS: Hydrotherapy

Total Health Colon Care ....G 586 268-5444
Sterling Heights *(G-15526)*

MEDICAL & SURGICAL SPLYS: Limbs, Artificial

American Prosthetic Institute ....G 517 349-3130
Okemos *(G-12112)*
Becker Orthopedic Appliance Co ....D 248 588-7480
Troy *(G-16236)*
College Park Industries Inc ....E 586 294-7950
Warren *(G-16987)*
Going Out On A Limb ....G 231 347-4631
Petoskey *(G-12449)*
Landra Prsthtics Orthotics Inc ....G 734 281-8144
Southgate *(G-15080)*
Northern Orthotics Prosthetics ....G 906 353-7161
Baraga *(G-1111)*
Ropp Orthopedic Clinic LLC ....G 248 669-9222
Commerce Township *(G-3451)*
Swanson Orthtic Prsthetics Ctr ....G 734 241-4397
Monroe *(G-11071)*
Ultralight Prosthetics Inc ....G 313 538-8500
Redford *(G-13204)*
Wright Brace & Limb Inc ....G 989 343-0300
West Branch *(G-17530)*

MEDICAL & SURGICAL SPLYS: Models, Anatomical

Studio One Midwest Inc ....F 269 962-3475
Battle Creek *(G-1255)*

MEDICAL & SURGICAL SPLYS: Orthopedic Appliances

Active Brace and Limb LLC ....F 231 932-8702
Traverse City *(G-15889)*
Avasure Holdings Inc ....E 616 301-0129
Belmont *(G-1456)*
Biocorrect Orthotics Lab ....G 616 356-5030
Kentwood *(G-9003)*
Brand Orthopedic & Shoe Svcs ....G 248 352-0000
Southfield *(G-14856)*
David Epstein Inc ....F 248 542-0802
Ferndale *(G-5270)*
Davismade Inc ....F 810 743-5262
Flint *(G-5415)*
Hanger Prsthetcs & Ortho Inc ....G 248 683-5070
Waterford *(G-17348)*
Mount Clemens Orthopedic Appls ......G 586 463-3600
Clinton Township *(G-3181)*
Northwest Orthotics-Prosthetic ....G 248 477-1443
Novi *(G-11955)*
O and P Sparton ....G 517 220-4960
East Lansing *(G-4673)*
Oakland Orthopedic Appls Inc ....G 989 839-9241
Midland *(G-10898)*
Orthotic Insoles LLC ....G 517 641-4166
Bath *(G-1135)*
Orthotic Shop Inc ....G 800 309-0412
Shelby Township *(G-14658)*
Preferred Products Inc ....E 248 255-0200
Commerce Township *(G-3441)*
Strive Orthtics Prsthetics LLC ....G 586 803-4325
Sterling Heights *(G-15514)*
Teter Orthotics & Prosthetics ....G 231 779-8022
Cadillac *(G-2282)*
Tulip US Holdings Inc ....E 517 694-2300
Holt *(G-7931)*

Um Orthotics Pros Cntr ....G 734 764-3100
Ann Arbor *(G-687)*
Wolverine Orthotics Inc ....G 248 360-3736
Commerce Township *(G-3457)*

MEDICAL & SURGICAL SPLYS: Personal Safety Eqpt

Aactus Inc ....G 734 425-1212
Livonia *(G-9623)*
James Glove & Supply ....F 810 733-5780
Flint *(G-5452)*
Joyson Safety Systems ....B 248 373-8040
Auburn Hills *(G-922)*
Se-Kure Controls Inc ....E 269 651-9351
Sturgis *(G-15633)*
Skyline Window Cleaning Inc ....G 616 813-0536
West Olive *(G-17535)*
Stryker Corporation ....E 269 389-3741
Portage *(G-13037)*
Stryker Corporation ....E 269 323-1027
Portage *(G-13042)*

MEDICAL & SURGICAL SPLYS: Prosthetic Appliances

Anew Lf Prsthtics Orthtics LLC ....G 313 870-9610
Detroit *(G-3871)*
Axiobionics ....G 734 327-2946
Ann Arbor *(G-378)*
Binson-Becker Inc ....F 888 246-7667
Center Line *(G-2579)*
Biopro Inc ....E 810 982-7777
Port Huron *(G-12899)*
Bremer Prosthetic Design Inc ....G 810 733-3375
Flint *(G-5394)*
Hackley Health Ventures Inc ....G 231 728-5720
Muskegon *(G-11342)*
Hanger Inc ....D 616 940-0878
Grand Rapids *(G-6493)*
Hanger Prsthetcs & Ortho Inc ....F 517 394-5850
Lansing *(G-9381)*
Hellner & Associates Inc ....G 810 220-3472
Brighton *(G-1938)*
Landra Prsthtics Orthotics Inc ....G 586 294-7188
Saint Clair Shores *(G-14259)*
Metro Medical Eqp Mfg Inc ....D 734 522-8400
Livonia *(G-9840)*
Mobile Prosthetics ....G 989 875-7000
Ithaca *(G-8366)*
P & O Services Inc ....G 248 809-3072
Southfield *(G-14994)*
Precision Gage Inc ....D 517 439-1690
Hillsdale *(G-7534)*
Pros-Tech Inc ....F 248 680-2800
Troy *(G-16568)*
Prosthetic & Implant Dentistry ....G 248 254-3945
Farmington Hills *(G-5103)*
Prosthetic Center Inc ....G 517 372-7007
Dimondale *(G-4519)*
Solus Innovations LLC ....G 231 744-9832
Muskegon *(G-11427)*
Springer Prsthtic Orthtic Svcs ....F 517 337-0300
Lansing *(G-9426)*
Trulife ....E 800 492-1088
Jackson *(G-8595)*
Wright & Filippis Inc ....G 313 832-5020
Detroit *(G-4450)*

MEDICAL & SURGICAL SPLYS: Respiratory Protect Eqpt, Personal

Carlson Technology Inc ....G 248 476-0013
Livonia *(G-9677)*
Rpb Safety LLC ....E 866 494-4599
Royal Oak *(G-13969)*

MEDICAL & SURGICAL SPLYS: Technical Aids, Handicapped

Assistive Technology Mich Inc ....G 248 348-7161
Novi *(G-11832)*
Gresham Driving Aids Inc ....E 248 624-1533
Wixom *(G-17820)*
Lift Aid Inc ....G 248 345-5110
Farmington *(G-4903)*

PRODUCT SECTION — MEMBERSHIP ORGANIZATIONS, RELIGIOUS: Reformed Church

MEDICAL & SURGICAL SPLYS: Traction Apparatus
- Micro Engineering Inc .... E 616 534-9681
  Byron Center (G-2200)

MEDICAL & SURGICAL SPLYS: Trusses, Orthopedic & Surgical
- Troy Orthopedic Associates PLC .... G 248 244-9426
  Troy (G-16651)

MEDICAL & SURGICAL SPLYS: Walkers
- Crescent Corporation .... G 810 982-2784
  Fort Gratiot (G-5548)
- Georgia Walker & Assoc Inc .... G 248 594-6447
  Bloomfield Hills (G-1768)

MEDICAL & SURGICAL SPLYS: Welders' Hoods
- Bold Fusion Fabg & Customs LLC .... G 269 345-0681
  Kalamazoo (G-8699)
- Gipson Fabrications .... G 616 245-7331
  Wyoming (G-18003)

MEDICAL EQPT: Cardiographs
- Eaton Industries Inc .... G 734 428-0000
  Ann Arbor (G-431)

MEDICAL EQPT: Diagnostic
- Bd Diagnostic Systems .... E 313 442-8800
  Detroit (G-3894)
- Becton Dickinson and Company .... E 313 442-8700
  Detroit (G-3898)
- Complete Health System .... G 810 720-3891
  Flint (G-5401)
- Deuwave LLC .... G 888 238-9283
  Northville (G-11688)
- Genesis Innovation Group LLC .... G 616 294-1026
  Holland (G-7643)
- Isensium .... G 517 580-9022
  East Lansing (G-4666)
- Michigan Med Innovations LLC .... G 616 682-4848
  Ada (G-24)
- Pinnacle Technology Group .... D 734 568-6600
  Ottawa Lake (G-12268)
- Pointe Scientific Inc .... E 734 487-8300
  Canton (G-2417)
- Predxion Bio Inc .... G 734 353-0191
  Dexter (G-4504)
- Premier Imaging Center .... G 248 594-3201
  Franklin (G-5608)

MEDICAL EQPT: Dialyzers
- Rockwell Medical Inc .... C 248 960-9009
  Wixom (G-17886)

MEDICAL EQPT: Electromedical Apparatus
- Gelman Sciences Inc .... A 734 665-0651
  Ann Arbor (G-469)
- Heart Sync Inc .... F 734 213-5530
  Ann Arbor (G-488)

MEDICAL EQPT: Electrotherapeutic Apparatus
- Oncofusion Therapeutics Inc .... G 248 361-3441
  Northville (G-11719)

MEDICAL EQPT: Heart-Lung Machines, Exc Iron Lungs
- Accutherm Systems Inc .... G 734 930-0461
  Ann Arbor (G-341)

MEDICAL EQPT: Laser Systems
- American Lazer Centers .... G 248 798-6552
  Clinton Township (G-3048)
- Innovtive Srgcal Solutions LLC .... F 248 595-0420
  Wixom (G-17834)
- Physicians Technology LLC .... F 734 241-5060
  Monroe (G-11061)

MEDICAL EQPT: TENS Units/Transcutaneous Elec Nerve Stimulatr
- Merlin Simulation Inc .... F 703 560-7203
  Dexter (G-4498)

MEDICAL EQPT: Ultrasonic Scanning Devices
- Endra Life Sciences Inc .... G 734 255-0242
  Ann Arbor (G-445)
- Histosonics Inc .... G 734 926-4630
  Ann Arbor (G-493)
- Xoran Holdings LLC .... G 734 418-5108
  Ann Arbor (G-703)
- Xoran Technologies LLC .... D 734 663-7194
  Ann Arbor (G-704)

MEDICAL HELP SVCS
- Liver Transplant/Univ of Mich .... G 734 936-7670
  Ann Arbor (G-531)

MEDICAL SUNDRIES: Rubber
- MCS Consultants Inc .... F 810 229-4222
  Brighton (G-1958)

MEDICAL SVCS ORGANIZATION
- Intrinsic4d LLC .... F 248 469-8811
  Bingham Farms (G-1654)
- Landra Prsthtics Orthotics Inc .... G 586 294-7188
  Saint Clair Shores (G-14259)
- Versant Medical Physics .... E 888 316-3644
  Kalamazoo (G-8918)

MEDICAL, DENTAL & HOSP EQPT, WHOLESALE: X-ray Film & Splys
- Associated Metals Inc .... G 734 369-3851
  Ann Arbor (G-371)
- Radiolgical Fabrication Design .... G 810 632-6000
  Howell (G-8087)

MEDICAL, DENTAL & HOSPITAL EQPT, WHOL: Hospital Eqpt & Splys
- Bmc/Industrial Eductl Svcs Inc .... E 231 733-1206
  Muskegon (G-11280)

MEDICAL, DENTAL & HOSPITAL EQPT, WHOL: Hosptl Eqpt/Furniture
- Bay Home Medical and Rehab Inc .... E 231 933-1200
  Grandville (G-7021)
- Creative Engineering Inc .... G 734 996-5900
  Ann Arbor (G-408)
- E & C Manufacturing LLC .... F 248 330-0400
  Troy (G-16332)
- Industrial Woodworking Corp .... E 616 741-9663
  Zeeland (G-18158)
- Wright & Filippis Inc .... F 517 484-2624
  Lansing (G-9435)

MEDICAL, DENTAL & HOSPITAL EQPT, WHOLESALE: Diagnostic, Med
- Steele Supply Co .... G 269 983-0920
  Saint Joseph (G-14342)

MEDICAL, DENTAL & HOSPITAL EQPT, WHOLESALE: Hosp Furniture
- Custom Components Corporation .... F 616 523-1111
  Ionia (G-8247)

MEDICAL, DENTAL & HOSPITAL EQPT, WHOLESALE: Med Eqpt & Splys
- C2dx Inc .... F 269 409-0068
  Schoolcraft (G-14489)
- Diversfied Prcurement Svcs LLC .... G 248 821-1147
  Ferndale (G-5280)
- Grand River Aseptic Mfg Inc .... F 616 464-5072
  Grand Rapids (G-6467)
- Healthcare Dme LLC .... G 734 975-6668
  Ann Arbor (G-485)
- Homedics Usa LLC .... B 248 863-3000
  Commerce Township (G-3414)
- Kgf Enterprise Inc .... G 586 430-4182
  Columbus (G-3380)
- Midbrook Medical Dist Inc .... G 517 787-3481
  Jackson (G-8526)
- Rankin Biomedical Corporation .... F 248 625-4104
  Holly (G-7893)
- Solaire Medical Storage LLC .... D 888 435-2256
  Marne (G-10513)
- Tri State Optical Inc .... G 517 279-2701
  Coldwater (G-3338)
- Vidatak LLC .... G 877 392-6273
  Ann Arbor (G-692)

MEDICAL, DENTAL & HOSPITAL EQPT, WHOLESALE: Medical Lab
- Marketlab Inc .... D 866 237-3722
  Caledonia (G-2307)
- Tokusen Hytech Inc .... C 269 685-1768
  Plainwell (G-12547)

MEDICAL, DENTAL & HOSPITAL EQPT, WHOLESALE: Orthopedic
- Orthotool LLC .... G 734 455-8103
  Plymouth (G-12704)

MEDICAL, DENTAL & HOSPITAL EQPT, WHOLESALE: Therapy
- Theradapt Products Inc .... G 231 480-4008
  Ludington (G-10082)

MEDICAL, DENTAL/HOSPITAL EQPT, WHOL: Tech Aids, Handicapped
- Assistive Technology Mich Inc .... G 248 348-7161
  Novi (G-11832)

MEMBERSHIP ORGANIZATIONS, BUSINESS: Growers' Association
- Liveroof LLC .... E 616 842-1392
  Nunica (G-12040)

MEMBERSHIP ORGANIZATIONS, NEC: Amateur Sports Promotion
- Michigan Rifle and Pistol Assn .... G 269 781-1223
  Marshall (G-10583)

MEMBERSHIP ORGANIZATIONS, NEC: Automobile Owner Association
- SAE International .... E 248 273-2455
  Troy (G-16589)

MEMBERSHIP ORGANIZATIONS, NEC: Charitable
- Childrens Bible Hour Inc .... F 616 647-4500
  Grand Rapids (G-6274)

MEMBERSHIP ORGANIZATIONS, PROFESSIONAL: Health Association
- Community Mental Health .... D 517 323-9558
  Lansing (G-9210)
- Michigan Acdemy Fmly Physcians .... G 517 347-0098
  Okemos (G-12131)
- Michigan State Medical Society .... E 517 337-1351
  East Lansing (G-4670)

MEMBERSHIP ORGANIZATIONS, REL: Covenant & Evangelical Church
- Living Word International Inc .... E 989 832-7547
  Midland (G-10882)

MEMBERSHIP ORGANIZATIONS, RELIGIOUS: Catholic Church
- Diocese of Lansing .... F 517 484-4449
  Lansing (G-9361)

MEMBERSHIP ORGANIZATIONS, RELIGIOUS: Reformed Church
- Synod of Great Lakes .... C 616 698-7071
  Grand Rapids (G-6910)

Employee Codes: A=Over 500 employees, B=251-500
C=101-250, D=51-100, E=20-50, F=10-19, G=3-9

MEMBERSHIP ORGS, CIVIC, SOCIAL & FRATERNAL: Protection

Meridian Lightweight Tech Inc ....G...... 248 663-8100
  Plymouth *(G-12690)*

MEMBERSHIP SPORTS & RECREATION CLUBS

United Kennel Club Inc ....E...... 269 343-9020
  Portage *(G-13052)*

MEMORIES: Solid State

Viking Technologies Inc ....G...... 586 914-0819
  Madison Heights *(G-10377)*

MEN'S & BOYS' CLOTHING ACCESS STORES

Lighthouse Direct Buy LLC ....G...... 313 340-1850
  Detroit *(G-4204)*

MEN'S & BOYS' CLOTHING STORES

Allie Brothers Inc ....F...... 248 477-4434
  Livonia *(G-9635)*
Reed Sportswear Mfg Co ....G...... 313 963-7980
  Detroit *(G-4337)*

MEN'S & BOYS' CLOTHING WHOLESALERS, NEC

Access Business Group LLC ....B...... 616 787-6000
  Ada *(G-3)*
Alticor Global Holdings Inc ....F...... 616 787-1000
  Ada *(G-5)*
Alticor Inc ....C...... 616 787-1000
  Ada *(G-6)*
Hemp Global Products Inc ....G...... 616 617-6476
  Holland *(G-7661)*

MEN'S & BOYS' SPORTSWEAR CLOTHING STORES

Delux Monogramming Screen Prtg ......G...... 989 288-5321
  Durand *(G-4607)*
Guess Inc ....F...... 517 546-2933
  Howell *(G-8046)*

MEN'S & BOYS' SPORTSWEAR WHOLESALERS

American Silk Screen & EMB ....E...... 248 474-1000
  Farmington Hills *(G-4930)*
Apparel Sales Inc ....G...... 616 842-5650
  Jenison *(G-8617)*
Delta Sports Service & EMB ....G...... 517 482-6565
  Lansing *(G-9215)*
Delux Monogramming Screen Prtg ......G...... 989 288-5321
  Durand *(G-4607)*
Heikkinen Productions Inc ....G...... 734 485-4020
  Ypsilanti *(G-18076)*
R H & Company Inc ....F...... 269 345-7814
  Kalamazoo *(G-8867)*
RPC Company ....F...... 989 752-3618
  Saginaw *(G-14134)*

MEN'S & BOYS' UNDERWEAR WHOLESALERS

Lockett Enterprises LLC ....G...... 810 407-6644
  Flint *(G-5459)*

MEN'S & BOYS' WORK CLOTHING WHOLESALERS

Kaul Glove and Mfg Co ....E...... 313 894-9494
  Detroit *(G-4172)*

MEN'S SUITS STORES

Van Boven Incorporated ....G...... 734 665-7228
  Ann Arbor *(G-690)*

MERCHANDISING MACHINE OPERATORS: Vending

Asw Amerca Inc ....G...... 248 957-9638
  Farmington Hills *(G-4934)*

METAL & STEEL PRDTS: Abrasive

Dryden Steel LLC ....G...... 586 777-7600
  Dryden *(G-4569)*
Heartland Steel Products LLC ....E...... 810 364-7421
  Marysville *(G-10603)*
Nakagawa Special Stl Amer Inc ....G...... 248 449-6050
  Novi *(G-11952)*
Patch Works Farms Inc ....G...... 989 430-3610
  Wheeler *(G-17617)*

METAL COMPONENTS: Prefabricated

Huys Electrodes Inc ....G...... 215 723-4897
  Romulus *(G-13686)*
Laser North Inc ....G...... 906 353-6090
  Baraga *(G-1106)*
Mpi Products Holdings LLC ....G...... 248 237-3007
  Rochester Hills *(G-13477)*
Ridgeview Metals Incorporated ....G...... 850 259-1808
  Casnovia *(G-2508)*
Ross Sheet Metal Inc ....G...... 248 543-1170
  Ferndale *(G-5316)*
Trigon Steel Components Inc ....G...... 616 834-0506
  Holland *(G-7841)*

METAL CUTTING SVCS

Arlington Metals Corporation ....D...... 269 426-3371
  Sawyer *(G-14481)*
B & B Holdings Groesbeck LLC ....F...... 586 554-7600
  Sterling Heights *(G-15269)*
Copeland-Gibson Products Corp ....F...... 248 740-4400
  Troy *(G-16282)*
Die-Verse Solutions LLC ....F...... 616 384-3550
  Coopersville *(G-3557)*
Fabrilaser Mfg LLC ....E...... 269 789-9490
  Marshall *(G-10567)*
Fire-Rite Inc ....E...... 313 273-3730
  Detroit *(G-4060)*
K&W Tool and Machine Inc ....F...... 616 754-7540
  Greenville *(G-7141)*
Kendor Steel Rule Die Inc ....E...... 586 293-7111
  Fraser *(G-5678)*
Laser North Inc ....G...... 906 353-6090
  Baraga *(G-1106)*
Set Enterprises Inc ....E...... 586 573-3600
  Sterling Heights *(G-15493)*
TEC International II ....G...... 248 724-1800
  Auburn Hills *(G-1014)*
Virtec Manufacturing LLC ....F...... 313 590-2367
  Roseville *(G-13889)*

METAL FABRICATORS: Architechtural

A D Johnson Engraving Co Inc ....F...... 269 385-0044
  Kalamazoo *(G-8672)*
Aluminum Architectural Met Co ....F...... 313 895-2555
  Detroit *(G-3862)*
Aluminum Blanking Co Inc ....D...... 248 338-4422
  Pontiac *(G-12802)*
Aluminum Supply Company Inc ....E...... 313 491-5040
  Detroit *(G-3863)*
Blacksmith Shop LLC ....G...... 616 754-4719
  Greenville *(G-7123)*
Britten Inc ....C...... 231 941-8200
  Traverse City *(G-15920)*
CEi Composite Materials LLC ....E...... 734 212-3006
  Manchester *(G-10403)*
Cr Forge LLC ....G...... 231 924-2033
  Fremont *(G-5769)*
Creative Composites Inc ....E...... 906 474-9941
  Rapid River *(G-13111)*
Davis Iron Works Inc ....E...... 248 624-5960
  Commerce Township *(G-3398)*
Grattan Family Enterprises LLC ....G...... 248 547-3870
  Ferndale *(G-5290)*
Guile & Son Inc ....G...... 517 376-2116
  Byron *(G-2172)*
Harlow Sheet Metal LLC ....G...... 734 996-1509
  Ann Arbor *(G-482)*
Iron Capital of America Co ....G...... 586 771-5840
  Warren *(G-17098)*
Iron Fetish Metalworks Inc ....F...... 586 776-8311
  Roseville *(G-13822)*
J D Russell Company ....E...... 586 254-8500
  Utica *(G-16743)*
Jack-Post Corporation ....F...... 269 695-7000
  Buchanan *(G-2121)*
Kern-Liebers Pieron Inc ....E...... 248 427-1100
  Farmington Hills *(G-5037)*

Mayo Welding & Fabricating Co ....G...... 248 435-2730
  Royal Oak *(G-13948)*
Merrill Technologies Group Inc ....C...... 989 462-0330
  Alma *(G-241)*
Minuteman Metal Works Inc ....G...... 989 269-8342
  Bad Axe *(G-1069)*
Mol Belting Systems Inc ....D...... 616 453-2484
  Grand Rapids *(G-6696)*
Niles Aluminum Products Inc ....F...... 269 683-1191
  Niles *(G-11632)*
O I K Industries Inc ....E...... 269 382-1210
  Kalamazoo *(G-8838)*
Phoenix Wire Cloth Inc ....E...... 248 585-6350
  Troy *(G-16547)*
R B Christian Inc ....G...... 269 963-9327
  Battle Creek *(G-1239)*
Symbiote Inc ....E...... 616 772-1790
  Zeeland *(G-18189)*
Syncreonus Inc ....G...... 586 754-4100
  Warren *(G-17259)*
Syncreonus Inc ....D...... 248 377-4700
  Auburn Hills *(G-1010)*
United Lighting Standards Inc ....D...... 586 774-5650
  Warren *(G-17273)*
Valley City Sign Company ....E...... 616 784-5711
  Comstock Park *(G-3519)*
Worthington Armstrong Venture ....F...... 269 934-6200
  Benton Harbor *(G-1572)*

METAL FABRICATORS: Plate

A & B Welding & Fabricating ....G...... 231 733-2661
  Muskegon *(G-11255)*
Admin Industries LLC ....F...... 989 685-3438
  Rose City *(G-13756)*
Alro Riverside LLC ....G...... 517 782-8322
  Jackson *(G-8382)*
Ambassador Steel Corporation ....E...... 517 455-7216
  Lansing *(G-9336)*
American Metal Fab Inc ....D...... 269 279-5108
  Three Rivers *(G-15854)*
Amhawk LLC ....E...... 269 468-4177
  Hartford *(G-7381)*
Anchor Lamina America Inc ....E...... 248 489-9122
  Novi *(G-11826)*
Baker Enterprises Inc ....E...... 989 354-2189
  Alpena *(G-280)*
Berrien Metal Products Inc ....F...... 269 695-5000
  Buchanan *(G-2110)*
Besser Company ....B...... 989 354-4111
  Alpena *(G-282)*
Bills Custom Fab Inc ....F...... 989 772-5817
  Mount Pleasant *(G-11179)*
CAM Fab ....G...... 269 685-1000
  Martin *(G-10595)*
Chicago Blow Pipe Company ....F...... 773 533-6100
  Marquette *(G-10522)*
Conner Steel Products ....G...... 248 852-5110
  Rochester Hills *(G-13394)*
Constructive Sheet Metal Inc ....E...... 616 245-5306
  Allendale *(G-215)*
Contech Engnered Solutions LLC ....G...... 517 676-3000
  Mason *(G-10630)*
Corotech Acquisition Co ....F...... 616 456-5557
  Grand Rapids *(G-6312)*
D-M-E USA Inc ....G...... 616 754-4601
  Greenville *(G-7126)*
Davco Manufacturing LLC ....D...... 734 429-5665
  Saline *(G-14385)*
Delta Iron Works Inc ....F...... 313 579-1445
  Detroit *(G-3967)*
Detroit Boiler Company ....F...... 313 921-7060
  Detroit *(G-3972)*
Detroit Plate Fabricators Inc ....G...... 313 921-7020
  Detroit *(G-3997)*
Die-Mold-Automation Component ....G...... 313 581-6510
  Dearborn *(G-3693)*
Fab-Alloy Company ....G...... 517 787-4313
  Jackson *(G-8447)*
Fabrications Unlimited Inc ....G...... 313 567-9616
  Detroit *(G-4049)*
Fluid Hutchinson Management ....D...... 248 679-1327
  Auburn Hills *(G-876)*
Glycon Corp ....E...... 517 423-8356
  Tecumseh *(G-15795)*
Great Lakes Laser Dynamics Inc ....D...... 616 892-7070
  Allendale *(G-218)*
Greene Metal Products Inc ....E...... 586 465-6800
  Clinton Township *(G-3130)*
Greens Welding & Repair Co ....G...... 734 721-5434
  Westland *(G-17564)*

Grossel Tool Co ..... D 586 294-3660
Fraser (G-5658)
H & M Welding and Fabricating ..... G 517 764-3630
Jackson (G-8461)
Highland Engineering Inc ..... E 517 548-4372
Howell (G-8048)
Hornet Manufacturing Inc ..... G 517 448-8203
Hudson (G-8131)
Hydro-Craft Inc ..... E 248 652-8100
Rochester Hills (G-13448)
Impert Industries Inc ..... G 269 694-2727
Otsego (G-12241)
K & W Manufacturing Co Inc ..... F 517 369-9708
Bronson (G-2031)
Krista Messer ..... G 734 459-1952
Canton (G-2391)
Kurrent Welding Inc ..... G 734 753-9197
New Boston (G-11501)
Liberty Steel Fabricating Inc ..... E 269 556-9792
Saint Joseph (G-14327)
Lochinvar LLC ..... E 734 454-4480
Plymouth (G-12676)
Magnetic Products Inc ..... D 248 887-5600
Highland (G-7497)
Marsh Industrial Services Inc ..... F 231 258-4870
Kalkaska (G-8949)
Massie Mfg Inc ..... E 906 353-6381
Baraga (G-1109)
Matrix North Amercn Cnstr Inc ..... C 734 847-4605
Temperance (G-15836)
Mayo Welding & Fabricating Co ..... G 248 435-2730
Royal Oak (G-13948)
MB Aerospace Warren LLC ..... C 586 772-2500
Warren (G-17144)
Merrill Technologies Group Inc ..... D 989 791-6676
Saginaw (G-14090)
Nelson Steel Products Inc ..... D 616 396-1515
Holland (G-7753)
Nicholson Terminal & Dock Co ..... C 313 842-4300
River Rouge (G-13279)
North Central Welding Co ..... E 989 275-8054
Roscommon (G-13751)
Northern Machining & Repr Inc ..... E 906 786-0526
Escanaba (G-4847)
Northwest Fabrication Inc ..... G 231 536-3229
East Jordan (G-4641)
Parton & Preble Inc ..... E 586 773-6000
Warren (G-17180)
Power Industries Corp ..... G 586 783-3818
Harrison Township (G-7343)
Process Systems Inc ..... D 586 757-5711
Warren (G-17198)
Production Fabricators Inc ..... E 231 777-3822
Muskegon (G-11407)
Quigley Industries Inc ..... D 248 426-8600
Farmington Hills (G-5109)
R W Fernstrum & Company ..... E 906 863-5553
Menominee (G-10756)
Refrigeration Research Inc ..... D 810 227-1151
Brighton (G-1985)
RK Wojan Inc ..... E 231 347-1160
Charlevoix (G-2628)
Schad Boiler Setting Company ..... D 313 273-2235
Detroit (G-4355)
Sloan Valve Company ..... D 248 446-5300
New Hudson (G-11555)
Special Mold Engineering Inc ..... E 248 652-6600
Rochester Hills (G-13516)
SPX Corporation ..... C 586 574-2332
Warren (G-17252)
Steel Tank & Fabricating Co ..... E 231 587-8412
Mancelona (G-10399)
Taylor Controls Inc ..... F 269 637-8521
South Haven (G-14777)
Trimas Corporation ..... E 248 631-5450
Bloomfield Hills (G-1807)
True Fabrications & Machine ..... F 248 288-0140
Troy (G-16653)
Van Loon Industries Inc ..... E 586 532-8530
Shelby Township (G-14716)
Vent-Rite Valve Corp ..... E 269 925-8812
Benton Harbor (G-1560)
W Soule & Co ..... C 269 344-0139
Kalamazoo (G-8920)
Walbro LLC ..... C 989 872-2131
Cass City (G-2524)
Waltz-Holst Blow Pipe Company ..... E 616 676-8119
Ada (G-33)
Welding & Joining Tech LLC ..... G 248 625-3045
Clarkston (G-2965)
Wolverine Metal Stamping Inc ..... D 269 429-6600
Saint Joseph (G-14354)
Yale Steel Inc ..... G 810 387-2567
Brockway (G-2021)

METAL FABRICATORS: Sheet

A & B Welding & Fabricating ..... G 231 733-2661
Muskegon (G-11255)
Access Heating & Cooling Inc ..... G 734 464-0566
Livonia (G-9625)
Accurate Engineering & Mfg LLC ..... F 616 738-1261
Holland (G-7547)
Ackerman Brothers Inc ..... G 989 892-4122
Bay City (G-1270)
Acme Carbide Die Inc ..... E 734 722-2303
Westland (G-17538)
Acme Tool & Die Co ..... G 231 938-1260
Acme (G-1)
Admin Industries LLC ..... F 989 685-3438
Rose City (G-13756)
Advanced Sheet Metal ..... G 616 301-3828
Grand Rapids (G-6149)
Advantage Laser Inc ..... G 734 367-9936
Livonia (G-9629)
Alliance Sheet Metal Inc ..... F 269 795-2954
Middleville (G-10797)
Allied Machine Inc ..... E 231 834-0050
Grant (G-7077)
Allor Manufacturing Inc ..... D 248 486-4500
Brighton (G-1883)
Aluminum Blanking Co Inc ..... D 248 338-4422
Pontiac (G-12802)
American Blower Supply Inc ..... F 586 771-7337
Warren (G-16929)
American Fabricated Pdts Inc ..... F 616 607-8785
Spring Lake (G-15133)
American Tchncal Fbrcators LLC ..... E 989 269-6262
Bad Axe (G-1056)
Amhawk LLC ..... E 269 468-4177
Hartford (G-7381)
Amjs Incorporated ..... G .....
Lawton (G-9510)
Anderson Welding & Mfg Inc ..... F 906 523-4661
Chassell (G-2671)
Arnold & Sautter Co ..... F 989 684-7557
Bay City (G-1276)
Attentive Industries Inc ..... F 810 233-7077
Flint (G-5379)
Attentive Industries Inc ..... G 810 233-7077
Flint (G-5380)
Austin Tube Products Inc ..... E 231 745-2741
Baldwin (G-1082)
B & L Industries Inc ..... F 810 987-9121
Port Huron (G-12896)
Baldauf Enterprises Inc ..... D 989 686-0350
Bay City (G-1279)
Bar Processing Corporation ..... D 734 782-4454
Warren (G-16952)
Bauer Sheet Metal & Fabg Inc ..... E 231 773-3244
Muskegon (G-11276)
Belco Industries Inc ..... C 616 794-0410
Belding (G-1399)
Belco Industries Inc ..... E 616 794-0410
Belding (G-1400)
Benteler Automotive Corp ..... B 616 247-3936
Auburn Hills (G-791)
Bestway Building Supply Co ..... G 810 732-6280
Flint (G-5388)
Beswick Corporation ..... F 248 589-0562
Troy (G-16239)
Bico Michigan Inc ..... E 616 453-2400
Grand Rapids (G-6218)
Blade Welding Service Inc ..... G 734 941-4253
Van Buren Twp (G-16749)
Bmc/Industrial Eductl Svcs Inc ..... E 231 733-1206
Muskegon (G-11280)
Boral Building Products Inc ..... C 248 668-6400
Wixom (G-17777)
Bristol Steel & Conveyor Corp ..... E 810 658-9510
Davison (G-3641)
Britten Inc ..... C 231 941-8200
Traverse City (G-15920)
Burnham & Northern Inc ..... G 517 279-7501
Coldwater (G-3292)
Buy Best Manufacturing LLC ..... F 248 875-2491
Brighton (G-1891)
C & T Fabrication LLC ..... G 616 678-5133
Kent City (G-8988)
C L Rieckhoff Company Inc ..... C 734 946-8220
Taylor (G-15697)
Cdp Environmental Inc ..... E 586 776-7890
Roseville (G-13780)
Certainteed Corporation ..... B 517 787-8898
Jackson (G-8405)
Certainteed Corporation ..... E 517 787-1737
Jackson (G-8406)
Commercial Mfg & Assembly Inc ..... E 616 847-9980
Grand Haven (G-6005)
Conner Steel Products ..... G 248 852-5110
Rochester Hills (G-13394)
Conquest Manufacturing LLC ..... D 586 576-7600
Warren (G-16991)
Consolidated Metal Pdts Inc ..... G 616 538-1000
Grand Rapids (G-6302)
Contractors Sheet Metal Inc ..... G 231 348-0753
Harbor Springs (G-7278)
Corlett-Turner Co ..... G 616 772-9082
Grand Rapids (G-6311)
Custo Arch Shee Meta ..... F 313 571-2277
Detroit (G-3958)
Custom Design & Manufacturing ..... F 989 754-9962
Carrollton (G-2484)
Custom Fab Inc ..... G 586 755-7260
Warren (G-16995)
Customer Metal Fabrication Inc ..... E 906 774-3216
Iron Mountain (G-8282)
Dee Cramer Inc ..... E 517 485-5519
Lansing (G-9286)
Delducas Welding & Co Inc ..... G 810 743-1990
Flint (G-5416)
Delta Iron Works Inc ..... F 313 579-1445
Detroit (G-3967)
Delta Tube & Fabricating Corp ..... C 248 634-8267
Holly (G-7875)
Denlin Industries Inc ..... G 586 303-5209
Milford (G-10960)
Designers Sheet Metal Inc ..... G 269 429-4133
Saint Joseph (G-14306)
Detroit Cornice & Slate Co Inc ..... E 248 398-7690
Ferndale (G-5275)
Dewys Manufacturing Inc ..... C 616 677-5281
Marne (G-10507)
Digital Fabrication Inc ..... F 616 794-2848
Belding (G-1409)
Dorris Company ..... E 586 293-5260
Fraser (G-5644)
Douglas King Industries Inc ..... E 989 642-2865
Hemlock (G-7461)
Dowding Industries Inc ..... E 517 663-5455
Eaton Rapids (G-4720)
Dowding Tool Products LLC ..... F 517 541-2795
Springport (G-15210)
Dubois Production Services Inc ..... E 616 785-0088
Comstock Park (G-3480)
Duo-Gard Industries Inc ..... D 734 207-9700
Canton (G-2367)
E & S Sheet Metal ..... G 989 871-2067
Millington (G-10995)
East Muskegon Roofg Shtmtl Co ..... D 231 744-2461
Muskegon (G-11313)
East Muskegon Roofg Shtmtl Co ..... F 616 791-6900
Grand Rapids (G-6367)
Electrolabs Inc ..... F 586 294-4150
Fraser (G-5650)
Elevated Technologies Inc ..... F 616 288-9817
Grand Rapids (G-6375)
Envirodyne Technologies Inc ..... E 269 342-1918
Kalamazoo (G-8739)
Envision Engineering LLC ..... G 616 897-0599
Lowell (G-10027)
Erbsloeh Alum Solutions Inc ..... B 269 323-2565
Portage (G-12993)
Experi-Metal Inc ..... C 586 977-7800
Sterling Heights (G-15335)
Fab-Alloy Company ..... G 517 787-4313
Jackson (G-8447)
Fabrication Specialties Inc ..... G 313 891-7181
Davisburg (G-3632)
Fabrications Plus Inc ..... G 269 749-3050
Olivet (G-12141)
Fenixx Technologies LLC ..... G 586 254-6000
Sterling Heights (G-15338)
Fhc Holding Company ..... G 616 538-3231
Wyoming (G-18001)
Flex-N-Gate Stamping LLC ..... F 810 772-1514
Warren (G-17040)
Flex-N-Gate Stamping LLC ..... E 586 759-8900
Warren (G-17041)
Frank W Small Met Fabrication ..... G 269 422-2001
Baroda (G-1124)

Employee Codes: A=Over 500 employees, B=251-500
C=101-250, D=51-100, E=20-50, F=10-19, G=3-9
2020 Harris Michigan
Industrial Directory
1295

METAL FABRICATORS: Sheet

Frankenmuth Welding & Fabg ....G..... 989 754-9457
  Saginaw *(G-14038)*
Frenchys Skirting Inc ....G..... 734 721-3013
  Wayne *(G-17430)*
G A Richards Company ....D..... 616 243-2800
  Grand Rapids *(G-6427)*
G A Richards Plant Two ....G..... 616 850-8528
  Spring Lake *(G-15143)*
Gee & Missler Inc ....E..... 734 284-1224
  Wyandotte *(G-17959)*
Geerpres Inc ....E..... 231 773-3211
  Muskegon *(G-11329)*
General Motors LLC ....D..... 810 234-2710
  Flint *(G-5434)*
Gladwin Tank Manufacturing Inc ....F..... 989 426-4768
  Gladwin *(G-5932)*
Gokoh Coldwater Incorporated ....F..... 517 279-1080
  Coldwater *(G-3305)*
Gray Brothers Mfg Inc ....E..... 269 483-7615
  White Pigeon *(G-17650)*
Great Lakes Mechanical Corp ....C..... 313 581-1400
  Dearborn *(G-3717)*
Great Lakes Powder Coating LLC ....F..... 248 522-6222
  Walled Lake *(G-16894)*
Greene Manufacturing Inc ....E..... 734 428-8304
  Chelsea *(G-2712)*
Greene Metal Products Inc ....E..... 586 465-6800
  Clinton Township *(G-3130)*
Greene Metal Products Inc ....F..... 586 465-6800
  Clinton Township *(G-3131)*
Greens Welding & Repair Co ....G..... 734 721-5434
  Westland *(G-17564)*
H & M Welding and Fabricating ....G..... 517 764-3630
  Jackson *(G-8461)*
HPS Fabrications Inc ....F..... 734 282-2285
  Wyandotte *(G-17961)*
Hutchinson Sealing Syst ....D..... 248 375-3721
  Auburn Hills *(G-904)*
Hydro Extrusion North Amer LLC ....B..... 269 349-6626
  Kalamazoo *(G-8772)*
Industrial Ducts Systems Inc ....G..... 586 498-3993
  Roseville *(G-13818)*
Industrial Mtal Fbricators LLC ....F..... 810 765-8960
  Cottrellville *(G-3588)*
Innovate Industries Inc ....C..... 586 558-8990
  Warren *(G-17092)*
Innovative Sheet Metals ....G..... 231 788-5751
  Muskegon *(G-11348)*
J & L Mfg Co ....E..... 586 445-9530
  Warren *(G-17104)*
J & M Machine Products Inc ....D..... 231 755-1622
  Norton Shores *(G-11764)*
J M L Contracting & Sales Inc ....F..... 586 756-4133
  Warren *(G-17108)*
Jackson Architctural Mtl Fabri ....G..... 517 782-8884
  Jackson *(G-8474)*
JC Metal Fabricating Inc ....F..... 231 629-0425
  Reed City *(G-13216)*
Jervis B Webb Company ....D..... 231 582-6558
  Boyne City *(G-1825)*
K & W Manufacturing Co Inc ....F..... 517 369-9708
  Bronson *(G-2031)*
Kalamazoo Mechanical Inc ....F..... 269 343-5351
  Kalamazoo *(G-8790)*
Kolkema Fabricating ....G..... 231 865-6380
  Fruitport *(G-5794)*
Kriewall Enterprises Inc ....E..... 586 336-0600
  Romeo *(G-13631)*
Lanzen-Petoskey LLC ....E..... 231 881-9602
  Petoskey *(G-12454)*
Laser Fab Inc ....G..... 586 415-8090
  Fraser *(G-5683)*
Legacy Metal Fabricating LLC ....E..... 616 258-8406
  Grand Rapids *(G-6625)*
Liberty Steel Fabricating Inc ....E..... 269 556-9792
  Saint Joseph *(G-14327)*
Light Metals Corporation ....B..... 616 538-3030
  Wyoming *(G-18016)*
Llink Technologies LLC ....E..... 586 336-9370
  Brown City *(G-2054)*
Loftis Machine Company ....E..... 616 846-1990
  Grand Haven *(G-6051)*
Lv Metals Inc ....G..... 734 654-8081
  Carleton *(G-2460)*
M J Mechanical Inc ....E..... 989 865-9633
  Saint Charles *(G-14195)*
Magnetic Products Inc ....D..... 248 887-5600
  Highland *(G-7497)*
Manning Enterprises Inc ....E..... 269 657-2346
  Paw Paw *(G-12408)*

Marsh Industrial Services Inc ....F..... 231 258-4870
  Kalkaska *(G-8949)*
Matrix Tool Co ....E..... 586 296-6010
  Clinton Township *(G-3170)*
Mayo Welding & Fabricating Co ....G..... 248 435-2730
  Royal Oak *(G-13948)*
MB Aerospace Warren LLC ....C..... 586 772-2500
  Warren *(G-17144)*
McElroy Metal Mill Inc ....E..... 269 781-8313
  Marshall *(G-10582)*
Mechanical Sheet Metal Co ....F..... 734 284-1006
  Wyandotte *(G-17967)*
Metal Components Employment ....D..... 616 252-1900
  Grand Rapids *(G-6661)*
Metalworks Inc ....C..... 231 845-5136
  Ludington *(G-10073)*
Meter Devices Company Inc ....A..... 330 455-0301
  Farmington Hills *(G-5064)*
Metro Duct Inc ....E..... 517 783-2646
  Jackson *(G-8517)*
Michigan Metal Fabricators ....G..... 586 754-0421
  Warren *(G-17153)*
Midbrook Inc ....D..... 800 966-9274
  Jackson *(G-8525)*
Midwest Wall Company LLC ....F..... 517 881-3701
  Dewitt *(G-4465)*
Monarch Metal Mfg Inc ....G..... 616 247-0412
  Grand Rapids *(G-6699)*
Monarch Welding & Engrg Inc ....F..... 231 733-7222
  Muskegon *(G-11384)*
MSE Fabrication LLC ....F..... 586 991-6138
  Sterling Heights *(G-15429)*
Muskegon Awning & Mfg Co ....E..... 231 759-0911
  Muskegon *(G-11387)*
Nankin Welding Co Inc ....G..... 734 458-3980
  Livonia *(G-9857)*
National Ordnance Auto Mfg LLC ....G..... 248 853-8822
  Auburn Hills *(G-953)*
Nelson Steel Products Inc ....D..... 616 396-1515
  Holland *(G-7753)*
Nicholson Terminal & Dock Co ....C..... 313 842-4300
  River Rouge *(G-13279)*
North Woods Industrial ....G..... 616 784-2840
  Comstock Park *(G-3502)*
Northern Machining & Repr Inc ....E..... 906 786-0526
  Escanaba *(G-4847)*
Northland Corporation ....D..... 616 754-5601
  Greenville *(G-7147)*
Northland Corporation ....F..... 616 754-5601
  Greenville *(G-7148)*
Northwest Fabrication Inc ....G..... 231 536-3229
  East Jordan *(G-4641)*
Pardon Inc ....F..... 906 428-3494
  Gladstone *(G-5918)*
Parton & Preble Inc ....E..... 586 773-6000
  Warren *(G-17180)*
Plesko Sheet Metal Inc ....G..... 989 847-3771
  Ashley *(G-728)*
Portage Wire Systems Inc ....E..... 231 889-4215
  Onekama *(G-12151)*
Precision Prototype & Mfg Inc ....F..... 517 663-4114
  Eaton Rapids *(G-4729)*
Production Fabricators Inc ....E..... 231 777-3822
  Muskegon *(G-11407)*
Production Tube Company Inc ....C..... 313 259-3990
  Detroit *(G-4312)*
Professional Metal Works Inc ....E..... 517 351-7411
  Haslett *(G-7398)*
Quality Alum Acquisition LLC ....F..... 734 783-0990
  Flat Rock *(G-5359)*
Quality Finishing Systems ....F..... 231 834-9131
  Grant *(G-7081)*
Quality Metalcraft Inc ....C..... 734 261-6700
  Livonia *(G-9900)*
R & DS Manufacturing LLC ....G..... 586 716-9900
  New Baltimore *(G-11490)*
R B I Mechanical Inc ....E..... 231 582-2970
  Boyne City *(G-1834)*
Richmond Bros Fabrication LLC ....G..... 989 551-1996
  Bay Port *(G-1374)*
Rochester Welding Company Inc ....E..... 248 628-0801
  Oxford *(G-12369)*
Roth Fabricating Inc ....E..... 517 458-7541
  Morenci *(G-11114)*
S & B Roofing Services Inc ....D..... 248 334-5372
  Pontiac *(G-12863)*
S & N Machine & Fabricating ....F..... 231 894-2658
  Rothbury *(G-13895)*
Saginaw Control & Engrg Inc ....B..... 989 799-6871
  Saginaw *(G-14138)*

Salem/Savard Industries LLC ....E..... 313 931-6880
  Detroit *(G-4352)*
Sandvik Inc ....E..... 269 926-7241
  Benton Harbor *(G-1545)*
Scotten Steel Processing Inc ....F..... 313 897-8837
  Detroit *(G-4356)*
Security Steelcraft Corp ....E..... 231 733-1101
  Muskegon *(G-11420)*
Sequoia Tool Inc ....D..... 586 463-4400
  Clinton Township *(G-3223)*
Servotech Industries Inc ....F..... 734 697-5555
  Taylor *(G-15764)*
Set Duct Manufacturing LLC ....E..... 313 491-4380
  Detroit *(G-4358)*
Sfi Acquisition Inc ....E..... 248 471-1500
  Farmington Hills *(G-5122)*
Sheren Plumbing & Heating Inc ....E..... 231 943-7916
  Traverse City *(G-16101)*
Sparta Sheet Metal Inc ....F..... 616 784-9035
  Grand Rapids *(G-6876)*
Spectrum Metal Products Inc ....G..... 734 595-7600
  Westland *(G-17600)*
Spinform Inc ....G..... 810 767-4660
  Flint *(G-5502)*
Stageright Corporation ....C..... 989 386-7393
  Clare *(G-2890)*
Stainless Fabg & Engrg Inc ....G..... 269 329-6142
  Portage *(G-13034)*
Stewart Steel Specialties ....G..... 248 477-0680
  Farmington Hills *(G-5132)*
Stus Welding & Fabrication ....G..... 616 392-8459
  Holland *(G-7818)*
Tapco Holdings Inc ....C..... 248 668-6400
  Wixom *(G-17905)*
Target Construction Inc ....D..... 616 866-7728
  Cedar Springs *(G-2564)*
TEC International II ....E..... 586 469-9611
  Macomb *(G-10166)*
TEC-3 Prototypes Inc ....E..... 810 678-8909
  Metamora *(G-10782)*
Thermal Designs & Manufacturng ....E..... 586 773-5231
  Roseville *(G-13878)*
Thierica Equipment Corporation ....E..... 616 453-6570
  Grand Rapids *(G-6928)*
Tigmaster Co ....E..... 800 824-4830
  Baroda *(G-1132)*
Town & Country Cedar Homes ....G..... 231 347-4360
  Boyne Falls *(G-1842)*
Tri-Vision Inc ....F..... 313 526-6020
  Detroit *(G-4407)*
Triumph Gear Systems - Macomb ....C..... 586 781-2800
  Macomb *(G-10170)*
Tru Flo Carbide Inc ....D..... 989 658-8515
  Ubly *(G-16724)*
Tubelite Inc ....D..... 800 866-2227
  Walker *(G-16880)*
Turnkey Fabrication LLC ....G..... 616 248-9116
  Grand Rapids *(G-6941)*
Unifab Corporation ....E..... 269 382-2803
  Portage *(G-13051)*
Universal Fabricators Inc ....E..... 248 399-7565
  Madison Heights *(G-10373)*
Van Loon Industries Inc ....E..... 586 532-8530
  Shelby Township *(G-14716)*
Ventcon Inc ....C..... 313 336-4000
  Allen Park *(G-212)*
Versatile Fabrication Co Inc ....E..... 231 739-7115
  Muskegon *(G-11446)*
W Soule & Co ....C..... 269 344-0139
  Kalamazoo *(G-8920)*
Waltz-Holst Blow Pipe Company ....E..... 616 676-8119
  Ada *(G-33)*
Wendling Sheet Metal Inc ....E..... 989 753-5286
  Saginaw *(G-14182)*
West Side Mfg Fabrication Inc ....F..... 248 380-6640
  Wixom *(G-17928)*
Williams Business Services ....G..... 248 280-0073
  Rochester Hills *(G-13547)*
Wm Kloeffler Industries Inc ....E..... 810 765-4068
  Marine City *(G-10487)*
Wolfgang Moneta ....G..... 269 422-2296
  Baroda *(G-1133)*
Worthington Armstrong Venture ....F..... 269 934-6200
  Benton Harbor *(G-1572)*

METAL FABRICATORS: Structural, Ship

Douglas Steel Fabricating Corp ....D..... 517 322-2050
  Lansing *(G-9288)*
Northwoods Manufacturing Inc ....D..... 906 779-2370
  Kingsford *(G-9065)*

PRODUCT SECTION

METAL STAMPING, FOR THE TRADE

PSI Marine Inc ....F...... 989 695-2646
Saginaw *(G-14126)*

METAL FABRICATORS: Structural, Ship

Premier Prototype Inc................................E...... 586 323-6114
Sterling Heights *(G-15450)*

METAL FINISHING SVCS

Accurate Coating Inc ....G...... 616 452-0016
Grand Rapids *(G-6134)*
Alpha Metal Finishing Co ....F...... 734 426-2855
Dexter *(G-4475)*
Bar Processing Corporation ....D...... 734 243-8937
Monroe *(G-11019)*
Bar Processing Corporation ....C...... 734 782-4454
Flat Rock *(G-5349)*
Bar Processing Corporation ....D...... 734 782-4454
Warren *(G-16952)*
Bellevue Proc Met Prep Inc ....E...... 313 921-1931
Detroit *(G-3900)*
Blough Inc ....D...... 616 897-8407
Lowell *(G-10024)*
Bopp-Busch Manufacturing Co ....E...... 989 876-7924
Au Gres *(G-745)*
Chor Industries Inc ....E...... 248 585-3323
Troy *(G-16267)*
Complete Metal Finishing Inc ....F...... 269 343-0500
Kalamazoo *(G-8711)*
Finishing Touch Inc ....E...... 517 542-5581
Litchfield *(G-9601)*
Grand Northern Products.....................G...... 800 968-1811
Grand Rapids *(G-6450)*
High Prfmce Met Finshg Inc ....F...... 269 327-8897
Portage *(G-13000)*
Kalamazoo Stripping Derusting ....F...... 269 323-1340
Portage *(G-13005)*
Kevco Metal Surface Prep ....G...... 616 538-1377
Wyoming *(G-18014)*
Margate Industries Inc..........................G...... 810 387-4300
Yale *(G-18046)*
Matthews Plating Inc ....E...... 517 784-3535
Jackson *(G-8510)*
Metal Prep Technology Inc..................F...... 313 843-2890
Dearborn *(G-3739)*
Midwest II Inc...C...... 734 856-5200
Ottawa Lake *(G-12266)*
Muskegon Industrial Finishng ....G...... 231 733-7663
Muskegon *(G-11389)*
New Lfe Cppr & Brss Maint Free ....G...... 586 725-3286
Casco *(G-2503)*
Oliver Industries Inc..............................E...... 586 977-7750
Sterling Heights *(G-15440)*
Port City Industrial Finishing ....D...... 231 726-4288
Muskegon *(G-11401)*
Precision Finishing Co Inc ....E...... 616 245-2255
Grand Rapids *(G-6765)*
Shields Acquisition Co Inc ....G...... 734 782-4454
Flat Rock *(G-5364)*
South Haven Finishing Inc ....E...... 269 637-2047
South Haven *(G-14772)*
USA Quality Metal Finshg LLC ....F...... 269 427-9000
Lawrence *(G-9509)*
V & V Inc ....F...... 616 842-8611
Grand Haven *(G-6093)*
Zav-Tech Metal Finishing ....G...... 269 422-2559
Stevensville *(G-15587)*

METAL MINING SVCS

Meridian Lightweight Tech Inc............G...... 248 663-8100
Plymouth *(G-12690)*
URS Energy & Construction Inc ....C...... 989 642-4190
Hemlock *(G-7464)*

METAL RESHAPING & REPLATING SVCS

Die-Verse Solutions LLC ....F...... 616 384-3550
Coopersville *(G-3557)*

METAL SERVICE CENTERS & OFFICES

Arlington Metals Corporation ....D...... 269 426-3371
Sawyer *(G-14481)*
Conway Detroit Corporation ....E...... 586 552-8413
Roseville *(G-13786)*
Diez Group LLC ....D...... 734 675-1700
Woodhaven *(G-17939)*
Greens Welding & Repair Co ....G...... 734 721-5434
Westland *(G-17564)*
Greer Industries Inc ....E...... 800 388-2868
Ferndale *(G-5292)*

Lv Metals Inc ....G...... 734 654-8081
Carleton *(G-2460)*
Mann Metal Finishing Inc ....D...... 269 621-6359
Hartford *(G-7385)*
National Galvanizing LP ....A...... 734 243-1882
Monroe *(G-11059)*
Nor-Cote Inc ....E...... 586 756-1200
Warren *(G-17170)*
Preferred Industries Inc........................E...... 810 364-4090
Kimball *(G-9048)*
Sandvik Inc ....E...... 269 926-7241
Benton Harbor *(G-1545)*
Sas Global Corporation ....C...... 248 414-4470
Warren *(G-17229)*
Scotten Steel Processing Inc ....F...... 313 897-8837
Detroit *(G-4356)*
Specialty Steel Treating Inc ....E...... 586 293-5355
Fraser *(G-5730)*
Van Pelt Corporation ....G...... 313 365-3600
Sterling Heights *(G-15538)*
Western International Inc ....E...... 866 814-2470
Troy *(G-16689)*

METAL SLITTING & SHEARING

Lv Metals Inc ....G...... 734 654-8081
Carleton *(G-2460)*
Van S Fabrications Inc..........................G...... 810 679-2115
Croswell *(G-3605)*

METAL SPINNING FOR THE TRADE

Globe Technologies Corporation ....E...... 989 846-9591
Standish *(G-15219)*
Weber Bros & White Metal Works ......G...... 269 751-5193
Hamilton *(G-7242)*

METAL STAMPING, FOR THE TRADE

A-1 Stampings Inc.................................G...... 586 294-7790
Fraser *(G-5611)*
Acemco Incorporated ....C...... 231 799-8612
Norton Shores *(G-11806)*
Acorn Stamping Inc ....F...... 248 628-5216
Oxford *(G-12332)*
Admat Manufacturing Inc.....................F...... 269 641-7453
Union *(G-16727)*
Ajax Spring and Mfg Co ....F...... 248 588-5700
Madison Heights *(G-10184)*
Bayloff Stmped Pdts Dtroit Inc ....D...... 734 397-9116
Van Buren Twp *(G-16747)*
Big Rapids Products Inc ....D...... 231 796-3593
Big Rapids *(G-1622)*
Burkland Inc ....D...... 810 636-2233
Goodrich *(G-5952)*
Burnside Acquisition LLC ....G...... 616 243-2800
Grand Rapids *(G-6245)*
Burnside Acquisition LLC ....D...... 231 798-3394
Norton Shores *(G-11810)*
Co-Dee Stamping Inc...........................G...... 269 948-8631
Hastings *(G-7404)*
Conner Steel Products ....G...... 248 852-5110
Rochester Hills *(G-13394)*
Consolidated Clips Clamps Inc ....D...... 734 455-0880
Plymouth *(G-12601)*
Consolidated Metal Pdts Inc ....G...... 616 538-1000
Grand Rapids *(G-6302)*
Corban Industries Inc ....D...... 248 393-2720
Orion *(G-12177)*
Dajaco Industries Inc............................D...... 586 949-1590
Chesterfield *(G-2760)*
Dgh Enterprises Inc ....E...... 269 925-0657
Benton Harbor *(G-1494)*
Dgh Enterprises Inc ....G...... 269 925-0657
Benton Harbor *(G-1495)*
Dietech Tool & Mfg Inc ....D...... 810 724-0505
Imlay City *(G-8198)*
Douglas Stamping Company ....G...... 248 542-3940
Madison Heights *(G-10234)*
Duggan Manufacturing LLC.................F...... 586 254-7400
Shelby Township *(G-14581)*
Electro Optics Mfg Inc..........................F...... 734 283-3000
Wyandotte *(G-17957)*
Experi-Metal Inc ....C...... 586 977-7800
Sterling Heights *(G-15335)*
Falcon Stamping Inc.............................E...... 517 540-6197
Howell *(G-8040)*
Four Star Tooling & Engrg Inc ....G...... 586 264-4090
Sterling Heights *(G-15346)*
Future Industries Inc.............................E...... 616 844-0772
Grand Haven *(G-6017)*

Gar-V Manufacturing Inc ....G...... 269 279-5134
Three Rivers *(G-15863)*
Gordon Metal Products Inc ....F...... 586 445-0960
Livonia *(G-9754)*
Gray Bros Stamping & Mch Inc ....G...... 269 483-7615
White Pigeon *(G-17649)*
Great Lakes Metal Stamping Inc.........E...... 269 465-4415
Bridgman *(G-1864)*
Highland Engineering Inc ....E...... 517 548-4372
Howell *(G-8048)*
Highwood Die & Engineering Inc ....E...... 248 338-1807
Pontiac *(G-12835)*
Illinois Tool Works Inc ....B...... 616 772-1910
Zeeland *(G-18157)*
Independent Tool and Mfg Co..............E...... 269 521-4811
Allegan *(G-165)*
Industrial Engineering Service ....F...... 616 794-1330
Belding *(G-1419)*
Innovative Tool and Design Inc ....E...... 248 542-1831
Oak Park *(G-12075)*
Jackson Precision Inds Inc ....E...... 517 782-8103
Jackson *(G-8479)*
Jireh Metal Products Inc ....D...... 616 531-7581
Grandville *(G-7053)*
JMS of Holland Inc...............................D...... 616 796-2727
Holland *(G-7694)*
Jsj Corporation ....B...... 616 842-5500
Grand Haven *(G-6041)*
L & W Inc..F...... 517 627-7333
Grand Ledge *(G-6110)*
L & W Inc..C...... 517 486-6321
Blissfield *(G-1717)*
L & W Inc..F...... 734 529-7290
Dundee *(G-4590)*
L & W Inc..D...... 734 397-6300
New Boston *(G-11502)*
Marshall Metal Products Inc ....G...... 269 781-3924
Marshall *(G-10579)*
Mayville Engineering Co Inc ....B...... 616 878-5235
Byron Center *(G-2197)*
Metal Flow Corporation ....C...... 616 392-7976
Holland *(G-7743)*
Mico Industries Inc ....D...... 616 245-6426
Grand Rapids *(G-6679)*
Mico Industries Inc ....F...... 616 245-6426
Grand Rapids *(G-6680)*
Mico Industries Inc ....E...... 616 514-1143
Grand Rapids *(G-6681)*
Mid-Tech Inc ....G...... 734 426-4327
Ann Arbor *(G-557)*
Middleville Tool & Die Co Inc ....D...... 269 795-3646
Middleville *(G-10805)*
Modineer Co ....C...... 269 683-2550
Niles *(G-11627)*
Modineer Co ....C...... 269 684-3138
Niles *(G-11628)*
Nelson Steel Products Inc...................D...... 616 396-1515
Holland *(G-7753)*
New 11 Inc ....E...... 616 494-9370
Holland *(G-7754)*
Nor-Dic Tool Company Inc ....F...... 734 326-3610
Romulus *(G-13715)*
Northern Stampings Inc ....F...... 586 598-6969
Rochester Hills *(G-13483)*
Oakland Stamping LLC ....C...... 734 397-6300
Detroit *(G-4283)*
Oakland Stamping LLC ....E...... 248 340-2520
Lake Orion *(G-9152)*
Pac-Cnc Inc ....E...... 616 288-3389
Grand Rapids *(G-6737)*
Palmer Engineering Inc.......................E...... 517 321-3600
Lansing *(G-9251)*
Permaloc Corporation ....F...... 616 399-9600
Holland *(G-7769)*
Pinconning Metals Inc ....G...... 989 879-3144
Pinconning *(G-12512)*
Precision Resource Inc ....G...... 248 478-3704
Troy *(G-16561)*
Production Spring LLC.........................E...... 248 583-0036
Troy *(G-16566)*
Proos Manufacturing Inc......................D...... 616 454-5622
Grand Rapids *(G-6791)*
Quality Tool & Stamping Co Inc ....C...... 231 733-2538
Muskegon *(G-11410)*
Quigley Industries Inc ....D...... 248 426-8600
Farmington Hills *(G-5109)*
R E D Industries Inc.............................F...... 248 542-2211
Hazel Park *(G-7451)*
Reliant Industries Inc............................E...... 586 275-0479
Sterling Heights *(G-15464)*

Employee Codes: A=Over 500 employees, B=251-500
C=101-250, D=51-100, E=20-50, F=10-19, G=3-9

METAL STAMPING, FOR THE TRADE — PRODUCT SECTION

Rew Industries Inc .... E 586 803-1150
  Shelby Township *(G-14679)*
Riverview Products Inc .... G 616 866-1305
  Rockford *(G-13586)*
Sage International Inc .... D 972 623-2004
  Novi *(G-11989)*
Silver Creek Manufacturing Inc .... F 231 798-3003
  Norton Shores *(G-11793)*
Sintel Inc .... C 616 842-6960
  Spring Lake *(G-15178)*
Stanco Metal Products Inc .... E 616 842-5000
  Grand Haven *(G-6082)*
Standard Die International Inc .... E 800 838-5464
  Livonia *(G-9941)*
Synergy Prototype Stamping LLC ...... E 586 961-6109
  Clinton Township *(G-3242)*
Technical Stamping Inc .... G 586 948-3285
  Chesterfield *(G-2846)*
Tg Manufacturing LLC .... E 616 842-1503
  Grand Rapids *(G-6925)*
Trans-Matic Mfg Co Inc .... C 616 820-2500
  Holland *(G-7834)*
Transfer Tool Systems Inc .... D 616 846-8510
  Grand Haven *(G-6090)*
Universal Stamping Inc .... E 269 925-5300
  Benton Harbor *(G-1558)*
Van S Fabrications Inc .... G 810 679-2115
  Croswell *(G-3605)*
Van-Dies Engineering Inc .... E 586 293-1430
  Fraser *(G-5745)*
Vinewood Metalcraft Inc .... E 734 946-8733
  Taylor *(G-15778)*
Wolverine Metal Stamping Inc .... D 269 429-6600
  Saint Joseph *(G-14354)*
Yarema Die & Engineering Co .... E 248 689-5777
  Troy *(G-16703)*

METAL STAMPINGS: Ornamental

Haerter Stamping LLC .... D 616 871-9400
  Kentwood *(G-9008)*
Schwab Industries Inc .... C 586 566-8090
  Shelby Township *(G-14688)*

METAL STAMPINGS: Patterned

Contour Engineering Inc .... F 989 828-6526
  Shepherd *(G-14727)*
Four Way Industries Inc .... F 248 588-5421
  Clawson *(G-2978)*
KB Stamping Inc .... F 616 866-5917
  Belmont *(G-1464)*
Northwest Pattern Company .... G 248 477-7070
  Farmington Hills *(G-5082)*
Tenibac-Graphion Inc .... D 586 792-0150
  Clinton Township *(G-3245)*
Tenibac-Graphion Inc .... F 616 647-3333
  Grand Rapids *(G-6921)*

METAL STAMPINGS: Perforated

Clark Perforating Company Inc .... F 734 439-1170
  Milan *(G-10935)*
Expan Inc .... E 586 725-0405
  New Baltimore *(G-11484)*
Fisher & Company Incorporated .... D 586 746-2000
  Sterling Heights *(G-15341)*
Gns Holland Inc .... G 616 796-0433
  Holland *(G-7645)*

METAL TREATING COMPOUNDS

Cross Technologies Group Inc .... F 734 895-8084
  Westland *(G-17548)*
General Chemical Corporation .... G 248 587-5600
  Brighton *(G-1929)*
Haas Group International LLC .... G 810 236-0032
  Flint *(G-5444)*
Kolene Corporation .... E 313 273-9220
  Detroit *(G-4180)*
Macdermid Incorporated .... E 248 399-3553
  Ferndale *(G-5298)*
Morning Star Land Company LLC ..... E 734 459-8022
  Canton *(G-2408)*
Ncoc Inc .... E 248 548-5950
  Oak Park *(G-12088)*
Tuocai America LLC .... G 248 346-5910
  Troy *(G-16657)*
V & V Industries Inc .... F 248 624-7943
  Wixom *(G-17923)*

METALS SVC CENTERS & WHOL: Structural Shapes, Iron Or Steel

Eaton Steel Corporation .... D 248 398-3434
  Oak Park *(G-12064)*
Eaton Steel Corporation .... D 248 398-3434
  Livonia *(G-9719)*

METALS SVC CENTERS & WHOLESALERS: Bars, Metal

BR Safety Products Inc .... G 734 582-4499
  Plymouth *(G-12589)*

METALS SVC CENTERS & WHOLESALERS: Casting, Rough, Iron/Steel

Acme Casting Enterprises Inc .... G 586 755-0300
  Warren *(G-16916)*
J J Pattern & Castings Inc .... G 248 543-7119
  Madison Heights *(G-10281)*
Teksid Inc .... F 734 846-5897
  Farmington *(G-4914)*

METALS SVC CENTERS & WHOLESALERS: Copper

Rivore Metals LLC .... D 800 248-1250
  Troy *(G-16581)*

METALS SVC CENTERS & WHOLESALERS: Copper Prdts

New Lfe Cppr & Brss Maint Free .... G 586 725-3286
  Casco *(G-2503)*

METALS SVC CENTERS & WHOLESALERS: Ferroalloys

Howmet Corporation .... E 231 894-5686
  Whitehall *(G-17669)*
Howmet Holdings Corporation .... G 231 894-5686
  Whitehall *(G-17676)*

METALS SVC CENTERS & WHOLESALERS: Ferrous Metals

Mill Steel Co .... D 616 949-6700
  Grand Rapids *(G-6690)*

METALS SVC CENTERS & WHOLESALERS: Flat Prdts, Iron Or Steel

Allied Metals Corp .... E 248 680-2400
  Auburn Hills *(G-765)*
Machine Tool & Gear Inc .... D 989 743-3936
  Corunna *(G-3581)*

METALS SVC CENTERS & WHOLESALERS: Foundry Prdts

Ajf Inc .... E 734 753-4410
  New Boston *(G-11496)*

METALS SVC CENTERS & WHOLESALERS: Iron & Steel Prdt, Ferrous

Georgetown Steel LLC .... G 734 568-6148
  Ottawa Lake *(G-12264)*
Titanium Industries Inc .... G 973 983-1185
  Plymouth *(G-12771)*

METALS SVC CENTERS & WHOLESALERS: Misc Nonferrous Prdts

Allen Tool .... G 517 566-2200
  Sunfield *(G-15644)*
Aluminum Supply Company Inc .... E 313 491-5040
  Detroit *(G-3863)*

METALS SVC CENTERS & WHOLESALERS: Pipe & Tubing, Steel

Energy Steel & Supply Co .... D 810 538-4990
  Lapeer *(G-9458)*
Ferguson Enterprises Inc .... E 989 790-2220
  Saginaw *(G-14037)*
Loonar Stn Two The 2 or 2nd .... G 419 720-1222
  Temperance *(G-15834)*
Mid Michigan Pipe Inc .... G 989 772-5664
  Grand Rapids *(G-6683)*
Midway Strl Pipe & Sup Inc .... G 517 787-1350
  Jackson *(G-8527)*
Piping Components Inc .... G 313 382-6400
  Melvindale *(G-10705)*
Stephens Pipe & Steel LLC .... E 616 248-3433
  Grand Rapids *(G-6892)*
Venture Technology Groups Inc .... F 248 473-8450
  Novi *(G-12025)*

METALS SVC CENTERS & WHOLESALERS: Plates, Metal

Pioneer Steel Corporation .... E 313 933-9400
  Detroit *(G-4303)*

METALS SVC CENTERS & WHOLESALERS: Rope, Wire, Exc Insulated

Commercial Group Inc .... E 313 931-6100
  Taylor *(G-15704)*

METALS SVC CENTERS & WHOLESALERS: Stampings, Metal

Serra Spring & Mfg LLC .... G 586 932-2202
  Sterling Heights *(G-15491)*

METALS SVC CENTERS & WHOLESALERS: Steel

Ace Drill Corporation .... G 517 265-5184
  Adrian *(G-42)*
Actron Steel Inc .... E 231 947-3981
  Traverse City *(G-15890)*
Alro Steel Corporation .... F 989 893-9553
  Bay City *(G-1274)*
Alro Steel Corporation .... D 810 695-7300
  Grand Blanc *(G-5958)*
Alro Steel Corporation .... E 517 371-9600
  Lansing *(G-9335)*
Ameristeel Inc .... F 586 585-5250
  Fraser *(G-5619)*
Bico Michigan Inc .... E 616 453-2400
  Grand Rapids *(G-6218)*
Bills Custom Fab Inc .... F 989 772-5817
  Mount Pleasant *(G-11179)*
Bohley Industries .... G 734 455-3430
  Northville *(G-11680)*
Brown-Campbell Company .... F 586 884-2180
  Shelby Township *(G-14555)*
Campbell & Shaw Steel Inc .... F 810 364-5100
  Marysville *(G-10600)*
Capital Steel & Builders Sup .... F 517 694-0451
  Holt *(G-7905)*
Contractors Steel Company .... E 616 531-4000
  Grand Rapids *(G-6306)*
Delaco Steel Corporation .... D 313 491-1200
  Dearborn *(G-3692)*
Detroit Steel Group Inc .... G 248 298-2900
  Royal Oak *(G-13918)*
Ferro Fab LLC .... F 586 791-3561
  Clinton Township *(G-3115)*
Greenwell Machine Shop Inc .... G 231 347-3346
  Petoskey *(G-12450)*
Harbor Steel and Supply Corp .... F 616 786-0002
  Holland *(G-7657)*
Harrison Steel LLC .... G 586 247-1230
  Shelby Township *(G-14599)*
J B Lunds & Sons Inc .... G 231 627-9070
  Cheboygan *(G-2682)*
JIT Steel Corp .... C 313 491-3212
  Dearborn *(G-3728)*
K & L Sheet Metal LLC .... G 269 965-0027
  Battle Creek *(G-1205)*
King Steel Corporation .... E 800 638-2530
  Grand Blanc *(G-5972)*
Metal Mart USA Inc .... G 586 977-5820
  Warren *(G-17148)*
MNP Corporation .... A 586 254-1320
  Utica *(G-16744)*
Padnos Leitelt Inc .... F 616 363-3817
  Grand Rapids *(G-6739)*
Peerless Steel Company .... E 616 530-6695
  Grandville *(G-7063)*
Rolled Alloys Inc .... D 800 521-0332
  Temperance *(G-15842)*
S & S Parts LLC .... G 517 467-6511
  Onsted *(G-12156)*

PRODUCT SECTION — MILLWORK

Samuel Son & Co (usa) Inc .... D 414 486-1556
  Troy *(G-16592)*
Sas Global Corporation .... E 248 414-4470
  Warren *(G-17230)*
SOO Welding Inc .... F 906 632-8241
  Sault Sainte Marie *(G-14474)*
Spartan Metal Fab LLC .... G 517 322-9050
  Lansing *(G-9263)*
Surplus Steel Inc .... G 248 338-0000
  Auburn Hills *(G-1007)*
Very Best Steel LLC .... G 734 697-8609
  Belleville *(G-1451)*
World Class Steel & Proc Inc .... G 586 585-1734
  Troy *(G-16699)*

METALS SVC CENTERS & WHOLESALERS: Zinc

Metropolitan Alloys Corp .... E 313 366-4443
  Detroit *(G-4233)*

METALS SVC CNTRS & WHOL: Metal Wires, Ties, Cables/Screening

Heidtman Steel Products Inc .... D 734 848-2115
  Erie *(G-4803)*

METALS SVC CTRS & WHOLESALERS: Aluminum Bars, Rods, Etc

Wayne-Craft Inc .... F 734 421-8800
  Livonia *(G-10001)*

METALS: Antifriction Bearing, Lead-Base

Meter of America Inc .... G 810 216-6074
  Port Huron *(G-12940)*

METALS: Precious NEC

Usmfg Inc .... G 269 637-6392
  Southfield *(G-15057)*

METALS: Precious, Secondary

Trelleborg Corporation .... G 269 639-9891
  South Haven *(G-14778)*

METALS: Primary Nonferrous, NEC

Cannon-Muskegon Corporation .... C 231 755-1681
  Norton Shores *(G-11744)*
Eclectic Metal Arts LLC .... G 248 251-5924
  Detroit *(G-4026)*
Expan Inc .... E 586 725-0405
  New Baltimore *(G-11484)*
Materion Brush Inc .... F 586 443-4925
  Warren *(G-17143)*
Metropolitan Alloys Corp .... E 313 366-4443
  Detroit *(G-4233)*
Resource Rcovery Solutions Inc .... G 248 454-3442
  Pontiac *(G-12861)*
Specialty Steel Treating Inc .... E 586 293-5355
  Fraser *(G-5730)*

METALWORK: Miscellaneous

Aarons Fabrication of Steel .... G 586 883-0652
  Clinton Township *(G-3032)*
Ambassador Steel Corporation .... E 517 455-7216
  Lansing *(G-9336)*
Bach Ornamental & Strl Stl Inc .... G 517 694-4311
  Holt *(G-7904)*
Bristol Steel & Conveyor Corp .... E 810 658-9510
  Davison *(G-3641)*
Butler Mill Service Company .... C 313 429-2486
  Detroit *(G-3922)*
Campbell & Shaw Steel Inc .... F 810 364-5100
  Marysville *(G-10600)*
Challenge Mfg Company .... G 616 735-6500
  Lansing *(G-9209)*
Concept Metal Products Inc .... D 231 799-3202
  Spring Lake *(G-15136)*
Depottey Acquisition Inc .... E 616 846-4150
  Grand Haven *(G-6009)*
Die Stampco Inc .... F 989 893-7790
  Bay City *(G-1302)*
Dowding Industries Inc .... E 517 663-5455
  Eaton Rapids *(G-4720)*
F&B Technologies .... F 734 856-2118
  Ottawa Lake *(G-12262)*

Frankenmuth Welding & Fabg .... G 989 754-9457
  Saginaw *(G-14038)*
Great Lakes Wire Packaging LLC ..... G 269 428-7220
  Stevensville *(G-15568)*
Grippe Machining and Mfg Co .... F 586 778-3150
  Roseville *(G-13813)*
Howard Finishing LLC .... C 248 588-9050
  Madison Heights *(G-10269)*
Ideal Shield LLC .... E 866 825-8659
  Detroit *(G-4133)*
Jcr Fabrication LLC .... G 906 235-2683
  Ontonagon *(G-12159)*
JD Metalworks Inc .... D 989 386-3231
  Clare *(G-2873)*
Kenowa Industries Inc .... E 616 392-7080
  Holland *(G-7709)*
Kenowa Industries Inc .... G 517 322-0311
  Lansing *(G-9304)*
Kustom Creations Inc .... G 586 997-4141
  Sterling Heights *(G-15394)*
Llink Technologies LLC .... E 586 336-9370
  Brown City *(G-2054)*
Lor Products Inc .... G 989 382-9020
  Remus *(G-13240)*
M J Day Machine Tool Company ...... G 313 730-1200
  Allen Park *(G-201)*
Netshape International LLC .... C 616 846-8700
  Grand Haven *(G-6059)*
R & S Propeller Inc .... F 616 636-8202
  Sand Lake *(G-14426)*
S & N Machine & Fabricating .... F 231 894-2658
  Rothbury *(G-13895)*
Shape Corp .... B 616 296-6300
  Grand Haven *(G-6076)*
Shape Corp .... B 616 846-8700
  Grand Haven *(G-6077)*
Shape Corp .... G 616 846-8700
  Norton Shores *(G-11815)*
Shape Corp .... E 616 844-3215
  Grand Haven *(G-6078)*
Shape Corp .... C 616 846-8700
  Grand Haven *(G-6079)*
Shape Corp .... C 248 788-8444
  Novi *(G-11995)*
Shape Corp .... D 616 842-2825
  Spring Lake *(G-15177)*
Shape Corp .... C 616 846-8700
  Grand Haven *(G-6080)*
Speedrack Products Group Ltd .... C 517 639-8781
  Quincy *(G-13098)*
Speedrack Products Group Ltd .... E 616 887-0002
  Sparta *(G-15113)*
Standard Coating Inc .... D 248 297-6650
  Madison Heights *(G-10359)*
Tial Products Inc .... E 989 729-8553
  Owosso *(G-12322)*
Tracy Wilk .... G 231 477-5135
  Brethren *(G-1847)*
Tubelite Inc .... D 800 866-2227
  Walker *(G-16880)*
Tubelite Inc .... F 800 866-2227
  Reed City *(G-13224)*
Walther Trowal LLC .... F 616 455-8940
  Grand Rapids *(G-6978)*
Weldaloy Products Company .... D 586 758-5550
  Warren *(G-17290)*
Witzenmann Usa LLC .... C 248 588-6033
  Troy *(G-16692)*
Worthington Armstrong Venture .... F 269 934-6200
  Benton Harbor *(G-1572)*

METALWORK: Ornamental

Delta Tube & Fabricating Corp .... C 810 239-0154
  Flint *(G-5418)*
Michigan Ornamental Ir & Fabg .... F 616 899-2441
  Conklin *(G-3530)*
Southwest Metals Incorporated .... G 313 842-2700
  Detroit *(G-4369)*

METEOROLOGIC TRACKING SYSTEMS

International Met Systems Inc .... F 616 971-1005
  Grand Rapids *(G-6541)*

METERING DEVICES: Water Quality Monitoring & Control Systems

Carlon Meter Company Inc .... G 616 842-0420
  Grand Haven *(G-6000)*
SLC Meter LLC .... F 248 625-0667
  Pontiac *(G-12867)*

METERS: Liquid

Advance Tech Solutions LLC .... G 989 928-1806
  Saginaw *(G-13992)*

METERS: Pyrometers, Indl Process

Pyro Service Company .... G 248 547-2552
  Madison Heights *(G-10340)*

METERS: Solarimeters

Solar Street Lights Usa LLC .... G 616 399-6166
  Holland *(G-7809)*

MGMT CONSULTING SVCS: Matls, Incl Purch, Handle & Invntry

Falcon Consulting Services LLC .... G 989 262-9325
  Alpena *(G-288)*

MICA PRDTS

Neuvokas Corporation .... G 906 934-2661
  Ahmeek *(G-108)*

MICROCIRCUITS, INTEGRATED: Semiconductor

ABB Enterprise Software Inc .... G 313 863-1909
  Detroit *(G-3836)*
Johnson Electric N Amer Inc .... D 734 392-5300
  Plymouth *(G-12658)*
Maxim Integrated Products Inc .... G 408 601-1000
  Brighton *(G-1956)*
Xilinx Inc .... G 248 344-0786
  Wixom *(G-17932)*

MICROFILM SVCS

Pro Search .... G 248 553-7700
  Farmington Hills *(G-5102)*

MICROPHONES

Stedman Corp .... G 269 629-5930
  Richland *(G-13256)*

MICROPROCESSORS

Compunetics Incorporated .... E 248 524-6376
  Troy *(G-16276)*

MICROSCOPES: Electron & Proton

Carl Zeiss Microscopy LLC .... F 248 486-7600
  Brighton *(G-1898)*
Jade Scientific Inc .... F 734 207-3775
  Westland *(G-17572)*

MICROWAVE COMPONENTS

Cobham McRlctrnic Slutions Inc .... G 734 426-1230
  Ann Arbor *(G-403)*
Pribusin Inc .... G 734 677-0459
  Ann Arbor *(G-603)*

MILITARY INSIGNIA

G & R Machine Tool Inc .... G 734 641-6560
  Taylor *(G-15724)*

MILLING: Chemical

Future Mill Inc .... G 586 754-8088
  Warren *(G-17047)*

MILLING: Corn Grits & Flakes, For Brewers' Use

Right Brain Brewery .... G 231 922-9662
  Traverse City *(G-16094)*

MILLWORK

Air Conditioning Products Co .... D 734 326-0050
  Romulus *(G-13649)*
Architectural Elements Inc .... F 616 241-6001
  Grand Rapids *(G-6179)*
Architectural Planners Inc .... E 248 674-1340
  Waterford *(G-17322)*
Architectural Products Inc .... G 248 585-8272
  Royal Oak *(G-13905)*
Audia Woodworking & Fine Furn ...... F 586 296-6330
  Clinton Township *(G-3058)*

Employee Codes: A=Over 500 employees, B=251-500
C=101-250, D=51-100, E=20-50, F=10-19, G=3-9

MILLWORK

Bay Wood Homes Inc .... E 989 245-4156
  Fenton *(G-5187)*
BMC East LLC .... E 313 963-2044
  Detroit *(G-3906)*
Brunt Associates Inc .... E 248 960-8295
  Wixom *(G-17779)*
C & A Wood Products Inc .... E 313 365-8400
  Detroit *(G-3924)*
C & K Hardwoods LLC .... G 269 231-0048
  Three Oaks *(G-15848)*
C & S Millwork Inc .... F 586 465-6470
  Clinton Township *(G-3072)*
Casing Innovations LLC .... G 248 939-0821
  Clinton *(G-3016)*
Chippewa Development Inc .... F 269 685-2646
  Plainwell *(G-12519)*
Classic Woodworks of Michigan ... G 248 628-3356
  Oxford *(G-12343)*
D & D Building Inc .... F 616 248-7908
  Grand Rapids *(G-6328)*
Dads Panels Inc .... G 810 245-1871
  Lapeer *(G-9455)*
Dagenham Millworks LLC .... G 616 698-8883
  Grand Rapids *(G-6332)*
Daniel D Slater .... G 989 833-7135
  Riverdale *(G-13284)*
Decatur Wood Products Inc .... E 269 657-6041
  Decatur *(G-3802)*
Dovetails Inc .... F 248 674-8777
  Waterford *(G-17337)*
Downriver Creative Woodworking .. G 313 274-4090
  Allen Park *(G-197)*
Duane Young & Son Lumber .... G 586 727-1470
  Columbus *(G-3378)*
E Leet Woodworking .... G 269 664-5203
  Plainwell *(G-12524)*
Elan Designs Inc .... G 248 682-3000
  Pontiac *(G-12820)*
Emery Design & Woodwork LLC .. G 734 709-1687
  South Lyon *(G-14790)*
Euclid Industries Inc .... C 989 686-8920
  Bay City *(G-1310)*
Forsyth Millwork and Farms .... F 810 266-4000
  Byron *(G-2171)*
G F Inc .... F 231 946-5330
  Traverse City *(G-15975)*
General Hardwood Company .... F 313 365-7733
  Detroit *(G-4080)*
George Washburn .... G 269 694-2930
  Otsego *(G-12240)*
Goodrich Brothers Inc .... G 989 224-4944
  Saint Johns *(G-14283)*
Goodrich Brothers Inc .... E 989 593-2104
  Pewamo *(G-12479)*
Goodwill Inds Nthrn Mich Inc .... G 231 779-1311
  Cadillac *(G-2250)*
Goodwill Inds Nthrn Mich Inc .... G 231 922-4890
  Traverse City *(G-15981)*
Goodwill Inds Nthrn Mich Inc .... G 231 779-1361
  Cadillac *(G-2251)*
Grand Rapids Carvers Inc .... E 616 538-0022
  Grand Rapids *(G-6452)*
Grand Valley Wood Products Inc .. E 616 475-5890
  Grand Rapids *(G-6471)*
Great Lakes Wood Products .... G 906 228-3737
  Negaunee *(G-11470)*
Heartwood Mills LLC .... F 888 829-5909
  Boyne Falls *(G-1839)*
Innovative Woodworking .... G 269 926-9663
  Benton Harbor *(G-1513)*
J J Wohlferts Custom Furniture .... F 989 593-3283
  Fowler *(G-5553)*
Kent Door & Specialty Inc .... E 616 534-9691
  Grand Rapids *(G-6576)*
Kropp Woodworking Inc .... F 586 463-2300
  Mount Clemens *(G-11138)*
Kropp Woodworking Inc .... G 586 997-3000
  Sterling Heights *(G-15391)*
L E Q Inc .... G 248 257-5466
  Waterford *(G-17356)*
Lakeview Manufacturing .... G 231 348-2596
  Petoskey *(G-12453)*
Legendary Millwork Inc .... G 248 588-5663
  Troy *(G-16460)*
Masters Millwork LLC .... F 248 987-4511
  Farmington Hills *(G-5059)*
McCoy Craftsman LLC .... F 616 634-7455
  Grand Rapids *(G-6654)*
Metrie Inc .... F 313 299-1860
  Taylor *(G-15740)*
Michigan Woodwork .... G 517 204-4394
  Mason *(G-10647)*
Mod Interiors Inc .... E 586 725-8227
  Ira *(G-8261)*
Modern Millwork Inc .... F 248 347-4777
  Wixom *(G-17857)*
Modern Woodsmith LLC .... G 906 387-5577
  Wetmore *(G-17616)*
North American Forest Products ... G 269 663-8500
  Edwardsburg *(G-4770)*
Northern Mich Hardwoods Inc ...... F 231 347-4575
  Petoskey *(G-12460)*
Northern Millwork Co .... F 313 365-7733
  Detroit *(G-4276)*
Northern Woods Finishing LLC .... F 231 536-9640
  East Jordan *(G-4640)*
Oak North Manufacturing Inc .... F 906 475-7992
  Negaunee *(G-11472)*
Odl Incorporated .... B 616 772-9111
  Zeeland *(G-18171)*
Owens Building Co Inc .... E 989 835-1293
  Midland *(G-10901)*
Parkway Drapery & Uphl Co Inc .. G 734 779-1300
  Livonia *(G-9884)*
Phil Elenbaas Millwork Inc .... G 231 526-8399
  Harbor Springs *(G-7291)*
Pine Tech Inc .... E 989 426-0006
  Plymouth *(G-12716)*
Poor Boy Woodworks Inc .... G 989 799-9440
  Saginaw *(G-14125)*
Quality Wood Products Inc .... F 989 658-2160
  Ubly *(G-16722)*
Rekmakker Millwork Inc .... G 616 546-3680
  Holland *(G-7786)*
Richmond Millwork Inc .... F 586 727-6747
  Lenox *(G-9524)*
Sawmill Bill Lumber Inc .... G 231 275-3000
  Interlochen *(G-8245)*
Standale Lumber and Supply Co .. D 616 530-8200
  Grandville *(G-7072)*
Sterling Millwork Inc .... D 248 427-1400
  Farmington Hills *(G-5131)*
Tapco Holdings Inc .... C 248 668-6400
  Wixom *(G-17905)*
Thomas and Milliken Mllwk Inc .... F 231 386-7236
  Northport *(G-11673)*
Town & Country Cedar Homes ..... G 231 347-4360
  Boyne Falls *(G-1842)*
Trend Millwork LLC .... E 313 383-6300
  Lincoln Park *(G-9586)*
Troy Millwork Inc .... G 248 852-8383
  Rochester Hills *(G-13532)*
Uncle Rons Woodworking .... G 248 585-7837
  Madison Heights *(G-10372)*
United Mill & Cabinet Company .... F 734 482-1981
  Willis *(G-17745)*
Van Enk Woodcrafters LLC .... F 616 931-0090
  Zeeland *(G-18191)*
Vander Roest Homes Fine Wdwkg .. G 269 353-3175
  Kalamazoo *(G-8917)*
Virtuoso Custom Creations LLC ... G 313 332-1299
  Detroit *(G-4431)*
Western Reflections LLC .... E 616 772-9111
  Zeeland *(G-18196)*
William S Wixtrom .... G 906 376-8247
  Republic *(G-13247)*
Wood Smiths Inc .... F 269 372-6432
  Kalamazoo *(G-8927)*
Woodworks & Design Company ... F 517 482-6665
  Lansing *(G-9434)*

MINE DEVELOPMENT SVCS: Nonmetallic Minerals

Bourque H James & Assoc Inc .... G 906 635-9191
  Brimley *(G-2013)*

MINERAL MINING: Nonmetallic

Discovery Gold Corp .... G 269 429-7002
  Stevensville *(G-15564)*

MINERAL WOOL

Autoneum North America Inc .... D 248 848-0100
  Farmington Hills *(G-4936)*
Eftec North America LLC .... D 248 585-2200
  Taylor *(G-15713)*
HP Pelzer Auto Systems Inc .... E 810 987-4444
  Port Huron *(G-12926)*
Manta Group LLC .... F 248 325-8264
  Pontiac *(G-12847)*
Mbcd Inc .... E 517 484-4426
  Lansing *(G-9395)*
Owens Corning Sales LLC .... E 248 668-7500
  Novi *(G-11968)*
Ufp Technologies Inc .... D 616 949-8100
  Grand Rapids *(G-6948)*
Unique Fabricating Inc .... E 248 853-2333
  Auburn Hills *(G-1034)*
Unique Fabricating Na Inc .... B 248 853-2333
  Auburn Hills *(G-1035)*

MINERALS: Ground Or Otherwise Treated

Novaceuticals LLC .... G 248 309-3402
  Auburn Hills *(G-962)*
R J Marshall Company .... F 248 353-4100
  Southfield *(G-15009)*

MINERALS: Ground or Treated

Edw C Levy Co .... D 313 843-7200
  Detroit *(G-4028)*
Fritz Enterprises .... G 734 283-7272
  Trenton *(G-16154)*
Imerys Perlite Usa Inc .... F 269 649-1352
  Vicksburg *(G-16836)*
Michigan Metals and Mfg Inc .... E 248 910-7674
  Southfield *(G-14981)*
R J Marshall Company .... E 734 848-5325
  Erie *(G-4810)*
R J Marshall Company .... E 734 379-4044
  Rockwood *(G-13611)*

MINIATURES

Deans Hobby Stop .... G 989 720-2137
  Owosso *(G-12288)*

MINING EXPLORATION & DEVELOPMENT SVCS

Makaveli Cnstr & Assoc Inc .... G 810 892-3412
  Detroit *(G-4217)*
Minerals Processing Corp .... G 906 352-4024
  Menominee *(G-10751)*

MINING MACHINERY & EQPT WHOLESALERS

Superior Equipment & Supply Co .. G 906 774-1789
  Iron Mountain *(G-8302)*

MINING MACHINES & EQPT: Grinders, Stone, Stationary

Centerpoint Tungsten LLC .... G 810 797-5196
  Metamora *(G-10773)*

MINING MACHINES & EQPT: Pellet Mills

Michigan Wood Pellet LLC .... F 989 348-4100
  Grayling *(G-7112)*

MINING MACHINES & EQPT: Rock Crushing, Stationary

Rock-Way LLC .... G 734 357-2112
  Plymouth *(G-12744)*

MINING MACHINES & EQPT: Stamping Mill Machinery

Ring Screw LLC .... D 586 997-5600
  Sterling Heights *(G-15470)*

MIRRORS: Motor Vehicle

Gentex Corporation .... C 616 772-1800
  Zeeland *(G-18138)*
Gentex Corporation .... E 616 772-1800
  Zeeland *(G-18139)*
Gentex Corporation .... C 616 772-1800
  Zeeland *(G-18140)*
Gentex Corporation .... C 616 772-1800
  Zeeland *(G-18141)*
Gentex Corporation .... C 616 772-1800
  Zeeland *(G-18143)*
Magna Mirrors America Inc .... E 616 786-5120
  Grand Rapids *(G-6640)*
Magna Mirrors America Inc .... G 616 786-7000
  Holland *(G-7734)*

PRODUCT SECTION

MOLDING COMPOUNDS

Magna Mirrors America Inc ....D...... 616 786-7300
  Holland *(G-7735)*
Magna Mirrors America Inc ....C...... 616 942-0163
  Newaygo *(G-11573)*
Magna Mirrors America Inc ....E...... 616 786-7000
  Kentwood *(G-9019)*
Magna Mirrors America Inc ....A...... 616 786-7772
  Holland *(G-7738)*
Magna Mirrors America Inc ....B...... 231 652-4450
  Newaygo *(G-11574)*
Magna Mirrors America Inc ....C...... 616 786-7000
  Holland *(G-7737)*
Magna Mirrors North Amer LLC ....A...... 616 868-6122
  Alto *(G-329)*
Narens Associates Inc ....G...... 248 304-0300
  Farmington Hills *(G-5076)*
SMR Automotive Systems USA Inc ......A...... 810 364-4141
  Marysville *(G-10616)*

MISCELLANEOUS FINANCIAL INVEST ACT: Oil/Gas Lease Brokers

Aquila Resources Inc ....G...... 906 352-4024
  Menominee *(G-10724)*

MISSILES: Ballistic, Complete

Bear Creek Ballistics Co ....G...... 269 806-2020
  East Leroy *(G-4684)*

MIXING EQPT

Brawn Mixer Inc ....F....... 616 399-5600
  Holland *(G-7576)*

MIXTURES & BLOCKS: Asphalt Paving

A & M Distributors ....G...... 586 755-9045
  Warren *(G-16907)*
A Plus Asphalt LLC ....E...... 888 754-1125
  Bloomfield Hills *(G-1739)*
Alco Products LLC ....E...... 313 823-7500
  Detroit *(G-3853)*
Aztec Azphalt Technology Inc ....G...... 248 627-2120
  Goodrich *(G-5951)*
Barrett Paving Materials Inc ....E...... 734 985-9480
  Ypsilanti *(G-18055)*
Bdk Group Northern Mich Inc ....E...... 574 875-5183
  Charlevoix *(G-2609)*
Cadillac Asphalt LLC ....E...... 248 215-0416
  Southfield *(G-14862)*
Cadillac Asphalt LLC ....D...... 734 397-2050
  Canton *(G-2356)*
Carlo John Inc ....E...... 586 254-3800
  Shelby Township *(G-14557)*
Celia Deboer ....F....... 269 279-9102
  Three Rivers *(G-15859)*
Central Asphalt Inc ....F....... 989 772-0720
  Mount Pleasant *(G-11183)*
Colorado Pavers & Walls Inc ....G...... 517 881-1704
  Flint *(G-5400)*
D O W Asphalt Paving LLC ....F....... 810 743-2633
  Swartz Creek *(G-15665)*
Dans Concrete LLC ....G...... 517 242-0754
  Grand Ledge *(G-6104)*
Delta Paving Inc ....F....... 810 232-0220
  Flint *(G-5417)*
Edw C Levy Co ....E...... 248 349-8600
  Novi *(G-11880)*
Elmers Crane and Dozer Inc ....C...... 231 943-3443
  Traverse City *(G-15962)*
Fendt Builders Supply Inc ....E...... 248 474-3211
  Farmington Hills *(G-4999)*
H & T Skidmore Asphalt ....G...... 269 468-3530
  Benton Harbor *(G-1506)*
Hd Selcating Pav Solutions LLC ....G...... 248 241-6526
  Clarkston *(G-2925)*
J L Milling Inc ....F....... 269 679-5769
  Schoolcraft *(G-14496)*
Lafarge North America Inc ....F....... 703 480-3600
  Dundee *(G-4591)*
Lakeland Asphalt Corporation ....E...... 269 964-1720
  Springfield *(G-15196)*
Laser Mfg Inc ....G...... 313 292-2299
  Romulus *(G-13699)*
Lite Load Services LLC ....F....... 269 751-6037
  Hamilton *(G-7236)*
Michigan Paving and Mtls Co ....E...... 734 485-1717
  Van Buren Twp *(G-16772)*
Michigan Paving and Mtls Co ....E...... 616 459-9545
  Grand Rapids *(G-6675)*
Michigan Paving and Mtls Co ....F....... 989 463-1323
  Alma *(G-242)*
Michigan Paving and Mtls Co ....D...... 517 787-4200
  Jackson *(G-8520)*
Nagle Paving Company ....C...... 734 591-1484
  Livonia *(G-9856)*
North American Asphalt ....G...... 586 754-0014
  Warren *(G-17172)*
Oldcastle Materials Inc ....E...... 269 343-4659
  Kalamazoo *(G-8839)*
Peake Asphalt Inc ....F....... 586 254-4567
  Shelby Township *(G-14661)*
Pyramid Paving and Contg Co ....E...... 989 895-5861
  Bay City *(G-1343)*
Rieth-Riley Cnstr Co Inc ....F....... 231 263-2100
  Grawn *(G-7100)*
Rieth-Riley Cnstr Co Inc ....E...... 616 248-0920
  Wyoming *(G-18030)*
RWS & Associates LLC ....F....... 517 278-3134
  Coldwater *(G-3328)*
Shooks Asphalt Paving Co Inc ....F....... 989 236-7740
  Perrinton *(G-12432)*
Tri-City Aggregates Inc ....E...... 248 634-8276
  Holly *(G-7900)*

MOBILE COMMUNICATIONS EQPT

Plymouth Computer & ....G...... 734 744-9563
  Livonia *(G-9890)*

MOBILE HOME REPAIR SVCS

Cedar Mobile Home Service Inc ....G...... 616 696-1580
  Cedar Springs *(G-2546)*

MOBILE HOMES

Advantage Housing Inc ....G...... 269 792-6291
  Wayland *(G-17397)*
Arbor Woods Mfg Home Community ..G...... 734 482-4305
  Ypsilanti *(G-18052)*
Cedar Mobile Home Service Inc ....G...... 616 696-1580
  Cedar Springs *(G-2546)*
Continental Communities ....G...... 586 757-7412
  Warren *(G-16992)*
Cross Country Homes ....G...... 517 694-0778
  Potterville *(G-13073)*
Larkhite Development System ....G...... 616 457-6722
  Jenison *(G-8632)*
Montrose Trailers Inc ....G...... 810 639-7431
  Montrose *(G-11105)*
Sun Communities Inc ....C...... 248 208-2500
  Southfield *(G-15036)*
Windsong Mobile Home ....G...... 248 758-2140
  Bloomfield Hills *(G-1811)*

MOBILE HOMES, EXC RECREATIONAL

Champion Home Builders Inc ....D...... 248 614-8200
  Troy *(G-16263)*

MOBILE HOMES: Personal Or Private Use

Hometown America LLC ....G...... 810 686-7020
  Mount Morris *(G-11162)*

MODELS

Hgks Industrial Clay Tool Co I ....G...... 734 340-5500
  Canton *(G-2383)*
Industrial Pattern of Lansing ....G...... 517 482-9835
  Lansing *(G-9298)*
Sika Auto Eaton Rapids Inc ....F....... 248 588-2270
  Madison Heights *(G-10352)*
Zoyes East Inc ....G...... 248 584-3300
  Ferndale *(G-5331)*

MODELS: Airplane, Exc Toy

Palm Industries LLC ....G...... 248 444-7922
  South Lyon *(G-14808)*

MODELS: General, Exc Toy

Active Plastics Inc ....F....... 616 813-5109
  Caledonia *(G-2288)*
D & F Corporation ....D...... 586 254-5300
  Sterling Heights *(G-15306)*
Metro Engrg of Grnd Rapids ....F....... 616 458-2823
  Grand Rapids *(G-6662)*
Paragon Molds Corporation ....E...... 586 294-7630
  Fraser *(G-5704)*
Protojet LLC ....F....... 810 956-8000
  Fraser *(G-5712)*
USF Delta Tooling LLC ....C...... 248 391-6800
  Auburn Hills *(G-1041)*

MODELS: Railroad, Exc Toy

River Raisin Models ....G...... 248 366-9621
  West Bloomfield *(G-17494)*

MODULES: Computer Logic

Compucom Computers Inc ....G...... 989 837-1895
  Midland *(G-10826)*
Tenneco Inc ....F....... 248 354-7700
  Southfield *(G-15044)*

MODULES: Solid State

Pacific Insight Elec Corp ....E...... 248 344-2569
  Southfield *(G-14996)*
Sonima Corp ....G...... 302 450-6452
  Lake Orion *(G-9163)*

MOLDED RUBBER PRDTS

Advanced Rubber & Plastic ....G...... 586 754-7398
  Warren *(G-16920)*
Advanced Rubber Tech Inc ....F....... 231 775-3112
  Cadillac *(G-2222)*
Aerofab Company Inc ....E...... 248 542-0051
  Ferndale *(G-5253)*
Anand Nvh North America Inc ....C...... 810 724-2400
  Imlay City *(G-8196)*
Aptargroup Inc ....C...... 989 631-8030
  Midland *(G-10816)*
Clair Evans-St Inc ....G...... 313 259-2266
  Detroit *(G-3938)*
Dti Molded Products Inc ....F....... 248 647-0400
  Bingham Farms *(G-1652)*
Exotic Rubber & Plastics Corp ....D...... 248 477-2122
  Farmington Hills *(G-4996)*
Giv LLC ....G...... 248 467-6852
  Livonia *(G-9752)*
Great Lakes Rubber Co ....D...... 248 624-5710
  Wixom *(G-17819)*
H A King Co Inc ....G...... 248 280-0006
  Royal Oak *(G-13931)*
HI-Tech Flexible Products Inc ....F....... 517 783-5911
  Jackson *(G-8465)*
Hutchinson Antivibration ....B...... 616 459-4541
  Grand Rapids *(G-6519)*
Hutchinson Antivibration ....C...... 231 775-9737
  Cadillac *(G-2254)*
Hutchinson Corporation ....G...... 616 459-4541
  Grand Rapids *(G-6520)*
Interdyne Inc ....E...... 517 849-2281
  Jonesville *(G-8656)*
Jfp Acquisition LLC ....E...... 517 787-8877
  Jackson *(G-8483)*
Luebke & Vogt Corporation ....G...... 248 449-3232
  Novi *(G-11930)*
Missaukee Molded Rubber Inc ....F....... 231 839-5309
  Lake City *(G-9094)*
Peck Engineering Inc ....F....... 313 534-2950
  Redford *(G-13179)*
Pegasus Tool LLC ....G...... 313 255-5900
  Detroit *(G-4295)*
Power Seal International LLC ....E...... 248 537-1103
  Troy *(G-16555)*
R H M Rubber & Manufacturing ....G...... 248 624-8277
  Novi *(G-11984)*
Rehau Incorporated ....E...... 269 651-7845
  Sturgis *(G-15632)*
Schroth Enterprises Inc ....E...... 586 759-4240
  Grosse Pointe Farms *(G-7187)*
Simolex Rubber Corporation ....F....... 734 453-4500
  Plymouth *(G-12755)*
Tillerman Jfp LLC ....E...... 616 443-8346
  Middleville *(G-10810)*
Uniflex Inc ....G...... 248 486-6000
  Brighton *(G-2002)*
Vte Inc ....E...... 231 539-8000
  Pellston *(G-12426)*
Zhongding Saling Parts USA Inc ....G...... 734 241-8870
  Monroe *(G-11088)*

MOLDING COMPOUNDS

Acp Technologies LLC ....G...... 586 322-3511
  Sterling Heights *(G-15251)*
Bakelite N Sumitomo Amer Inc ....G...... 248 313-7000
  Novi *(G-11837)*
Camryn Industries LLC ....C...... 248 663-5850
  Southfield *(G-14863)*

Employee Codes: A=Over 500 employees, B=251-500
C=101-250, D=51-100, E=20-50, F=10-19, G=3-9

Camryn Industries LLC ......E 248 663-5900
Detroit ***(G-3927)***
Century Plastics Inc ......G 586 566-3900
Shelby Township ***(G-14560)***
CMC Plastyk LLC ......G 989 588-4468
Farwell ***(G-5160)***
Coplas Inc ......G 586 739-8940
Sterling Heights ***(G-15300)***
Csn Manufacturing Inc ......E 616 364-0027
Grand Rapids ***(G-6320)***
Delta Polymers Co ......E 586 795-2900
Sterling Heights ***(G-15309)***
Durez Corporation ......C 248 313-7000
Novi ***(G-11874)***
Grand Traverse Tool Inc ......G 231 929-4743
Traverse City ***(G-15989)***
Heritage Mfg Inc ......G 586 949-7446
Chesterfield ***(G-2784)***
Indelco Plastics Corporation ......G 616 452-7077
Grand Rapids ***(G-6531)***
Innovatec LLC ......G 813 545-6818
Berkley ***(G-1585)***
Lej Investments LLC ......G 616 452-3707
Grandville ***(G-7056)***
Mac Material Acquisition Co ......G 248 685-8393
Highland ***(G-7496)***
MRM Industries Inc ......E 989 723-7443
Owosso ***(G-12306)***
Next Specialty Resins Inc ......F 419 843-4600
Addison ***(G-37)***
Quantum Composites Inc ......F 989 922-3863
Bay City ***(G-1345)***
Total Molding Solutions Inc ......E 517 424-5900
Tecumseh ***(G-15813)***
Universal Consumer Pdts Inc ......G 616 364-6161
Grand Rapids ***(G-6953)***
Xc LLC ......E 586 755-1660
Warren ***(G-17300)***

MOLDING SAND MINING

Atlantic Precision Pdts Inc ......F 586 532-9420
Shelby Township ***(G-14550)***

MOLDINGS & TRIM: Metal, Exc Automobile

Fft Sidney LLC ......F 248 647-0400
Sidney ***(G-14739)***

MOLDINGS & TRIM: Wood

Interntonal Hardwoods Michiana ......G 517 278-8446
Coldwater ***(G-3310)***
Lapeer Plating & Plastics Inc ......C 810 667-4240
Lapeer ***(G-9468)***
Thomas Cheal ......G 906 288-3487
Toivola ***(G-15885)***

MOLDINGS OR TRIM: Automobile, Stamped Metal

D & N Bending Corp ......E 586 752-5511
Romeo ***(G-13626)***
Dti Molded Products Inc ......F 248 647-0400
Bingham Farms ***(G-1652)***
Great Lakes Trim Inc ......D 231 267-3000
Williamsburg ***(G-17713)***
Guardian Automotive Corp ......C 586 757-7800
Sterling Heights ***(G-15365)***
Guardian Automotive Corp ......D 586 757-7800
Warren ***(G-17070)***
Marcus Automotive LLC ......G 616 494-6400
Holland ***(G-7739)***
Qp Acquisition 2 Inc ......E 248 594-7432
Southfield ***(G-15006)***
Sakaiya Company America Ltd ......E 517 521-5633
Webberville ***(G-17454)***
Versatube Corporation ......F 248 524-0299
Troy ***(G-16683)***
Yarema Die & Engineering Co ......D 248 585-2830
Troy ***(G-16702)***

MOLDINGS: Picture Frame

A&Lb Custom Framing LLC ......G 517 783-3810
Jackson ***(G-8370)***
Dko Intl ......F 248 926-9115
Commerce Township ***(G-3401)***
Millworks Engineering Inc ......F 517 741-5511
Union City ***(G-16735)***
Tc Moulding ......G 248 588-2333
Madison Heights ***(G-10366)***

MOLDS: Indl

2k Tool LLC ......G 616 452-4927
Wyoming ***(G-17983)***
A & O Mold and Eng Inc ......E 269 649-0600
Vicksburg ***(G-16830)***
Action Mold & Machining Inc ......E 616 452-1580
Grand Rapids ***(G-6137)***
Adept Tool & Mold Inc ......G 269 461-3765
Eau Claire ***(G-4737)***
Advanced Integ Tooling Solns ......C 586 749-5525
Chesterfield ***(G-2733)***
Advanced Mold Solutions ......G 586 468-6883
Clinton Township ***(G-3038)***
Advantage Industries Inc ......E 616 669-2400
Jenison ***(G-8616)***
Alliance Industries Inc ......E 248 656-3473
Macomb ***(G-10106)***
American Assemblers Inc ......G 248 334-9777
Pontiac ***(G-12803)***
American Die and Mold Inc ......G 231 269-3788
Buckley ***(G-2128)***
Armick Inc ......G 616 481-5882
Grand Rapids ***(G-6182)***
Ascent Aerospace LLC ......A 586 726-0500
Macomb ***(G-10108)***
Axis Mold Works Inc ......F 616 866-2222
Rockford ***(G-13558)***
B & L Pattern Company ......G 269 982-0214
Saint Joseph ***(G-14301)***
Best Tool & Engineering Co ......F 586 792-4119
Clinton Township ***(G-3066)***
Byrnes Tool Co Inc ......G 810 664-3686
Lapeer ***(G-9447)***
Century Tool & Gage LLC ......D 810 629-0784
Fenton ***(G-5193)***
Choice Corporation ......E 586 783-5600
Clinton Township ***(G-3078)***
Choice Mold Components Inc ......E 586 783-5600
Clinton Township ***(G-3079)***
Christensen Fiberglass LLC ......E 616 738-1219
Holland ***(G-7589)***
Circle C Mold & Plastics Group ......F 269 496-5515
Mendon ***(G-10712)***
Class A Tool & Machine LLC ......G 231 788-3822
Muskegon ***(G-11294)***
Colonial Mold Inc ......E 586 469-4944
Clinton Township ***(G-3083)***
Concept Molds Inc ......E 269 679-2100
Schoolcraft ***(G-14493)***
Contour Mold Corporation ......G 810 245-4070
Lapeer ***(G-9451)***
Convex Mold Inc ......G 586 978-0808
Sterling Heights ***(G-15299)***
Cs Tool Engineering Inc ......E 616 696-0940
Cedar Springs ***(G-2552)***
Dehring Mold E-D-M ......G 269 683-5970
Niles ***(G-11607)***
Delta Precision Inc ......G 586 415-9005
Fraser ***(G-5641)***
Deppe Mold & Tooling Inc ......E 616 530-1331
Grandville ***(G-7027)***
Dm Tool & Fab Inc ......D 586 726-8390
Sterling Heights ***(G-15319)***
Dme Company LLC ......B 248 398-6000
Madison Heights ***(G-10233)***
Dr & Hl Mold & Machine In ......G 989 746-9290
Saginaw ***(G-14029)***
Ds Mold LLC ......E 616 794-1639
Belding ***(G-1411)***
Du Val Industries LLC ......E 586 737-2710
Sterling Heights ***(G-15321)***
Dynamic Plastics Inc ......E 586 749-6100
Chesterfield ***(G-2768)***
Eagle Masking Fabrication Inc ......G 586 992-3080
Sterling Heights ***(G-15326)***
Eifel Mold & Engineering Inc ......E 586 296-9640
Fraser ***(G-5648)***
Eimo Technologies Inc ......D 269 649-5031
Vicksburg ***(G-16835)***
Eimo Technologies Inc ......E 269 649-0545
Vicksburg ***(G-16834)***
Everson Tool & Machine Ltd ......F 906 932-3440
Ironwood ***(G-8327)***
Extreme Tool and Engrg Inc ......D 906 229-9100
Wakefield ***(G-16850)***
Franchino Mold & Engrg Co ......D 517 321-5609
Lansing ***(G-9231)***
Inglass Usa Inc ......F 616 228-6900
Byron Center ***(G-2195)***
International Mold Corporation ......D 586 783-6890
Clinton Township ***(G-3143)***
Iq Manufacturing LLC ......G 586 634-7185
Auburn Hills ***(G-915)***
J M Mold Technologies Inc ......F 586 773-6664
Warren ***(G-17109)***
Johnson Precision Mold & Engrg ......G 269 651-2553
Sturgis ***(G-15609)***
Kidder Machine Company ......G 231 775-9271
Cadillac ***(G-2258)***
Krieger Craftsmen Inc ......E 616 735-9200
Grand Rapids ***(G-6591)***
Lakeshore Mold and Die LLC ......G 269 429-6764
Stevensville ***(G-15575)***
Liberty Manufacturing Company ......E 269 327-0997
Portage ***(G-13008)***
Louca Mold Arspc Machining Inc ......C 248 391-1616
Auburn Hills ***(G-930)***
M C Ward Inc ......E 810 982-9720
Port Huron ***(G-12936)***
Mac-Mold Base Inc ......E 586 752-1956
Bruce Twp ***(G-2091)***
Mach Mold Incorporated ......E 269 925-2044
Benton Harbor ***(G-1524)***
Madison Machine Company ......G 517 265-8532
Adrian ***(G-76)***
Marten Models & Molds Inc ......E 586 293-2260
Fraser ***(G-5691)***
Master Model & Fixture Inc ......F 586 532-1153
Shelby Township ***(G-14635)***
MGR Molds Inc ......F 586 254-6020
Sterling Heights ***(G-15419)***
Michigan Manufactured Pdts Inc ......G 586 770-2584
Port Huron ***(G-12941)***
Michigan Metal Tech Inc ......E 586 598-7800
Chesterfield ***(G-2806)***
Michigan Mold Inc ......E 269 468-3346
Coloma ***(G-3362)***
Micro Precision Molds Inc ......D 269 344-2044
Kalamazoo ***(G-8825)***
Midwest Mold Services Inc ......E 586 888-8800
Roseville ***(G-13837)***
Model-Matic Inc ......F 248 528-1680
Troy ***(G-16511)***
Mold Matter ......G 231 933-6653
Traverse City ***(G-16041)***
Mold Specialties Inc ......G 586 247-4660
Shelby Township ***(G-14646)***
Oceans Sands Scuba ......G 616 396-0068
Holland ***(G-7762)***
Omega Plastics Inc ......D 586 954-2100
Clinton Township ***(G-3190)***
Opus Mach LLC ......G 586 270-5170
Warren ***(G-17177)***
Pacific Tool & Engineering Ltd ......G 586 737-2710
Sterling Heights ***(G-15441)***
Par Molds Inc ......F 616 396-5249
Holland ***(G-7766)***
Paragon Molds Corporation ......E 586 294-7630
Fraser ***(G-5704)***
Paramount Tool and Die Inc ......F 616 677-0000
Marne ***(G-10511)***
Pedri Mold Inc ......G 586 598-0882
Chesterfield ***(G-2815)***
Pegasus Industries Inc ......F 313 937-0770
Redford ***(G-13180)***
Pentagon Mold Co ......G 269 496-7072
Mendon ***(G-10717)***
Plas-Tech Mold and Design Inc ......G 269 225-1223
Plainwell ***(G-12538)***
Plastic Engrg Tchncal Svcs Inc ......E 248 373-0800
Auburn Hills ***(G-974)***
Precision Masters Inc ......E 248 853-0308
Rochester Hills ***(G-13497)***
Precision Mold & Engineering ......E 586 774-2421
Warren ***(G-17193)***
Precision Tool & Mold LLC ......F 906 932-3440
Ironwood ***(G-8338)***
Prime Mold LLC ......F 586 221-2512
Clinton Township ***(G-3203)***
Project Die and Mold Inc ......G 616 862-8689
Grand Rapids ***(G-6788)***
Q M E Inc ......E 269 422-2137
Baroda ***(G-1129)***
Qc Tech LLC ......D 248 597-3984
Madison Heights ***(G-10341)***
R & B Plastics Machinery LLC ......E 734 429-9421
Saline ***(G-14410)***
Ravenna Pattern & Mfg ......E 231 853-2264
Ravenna ***(G-13127)***

PRODUCT SECTION

MOTOR VEHICLE ASSEMBLY, COMPLETE: Autos, Incl Specialty

Rm Machine & Mold ....G....... 734 721-8800
  Romulus *(G-13730)*
Romeo Mold Technologies Inc ....F....... 586 336-1245
  Bruce Twp *(G-2094)*
Romeo Technologies Inc ....D....... 586 336-5015
  Bruce Twp *(G-2095)*
Ronningen Research and Dev Co ....C....... 269 649-0520
  Vicksburg *(G-16842)*
Rowland Mold & Machine Inc ....G....... 616 875-5400
  Zeeland *(G-18185)*
Select Tool and Die Inc ....G....... 269 422-2812
  Baroda *(G-1131)*
Sharp Die & Mold Co ....F....... 586 293-8660
  Fraser *(G-5724)*
Simpsons Enterprises Inc ....E....... 269 279-7237
  Three Rivers *(G-15877)*
Special Mold Engineering Inc ....E....... 248 652-6600
  Rochester Hills *(G-13516)*
Special Tool & Engineering Inc ....D....... 586 285-5900
  Fraser *(G-5728)*
Spray Metal Mold Technology ....G....... 269 781-7151
  Marshall *(G-10589)*
Steenson Enterprises ....G....... 248 628-0036
  Leonard *(G-9528)*
Su-Dan Plastics Inc ....B....... 248 651-6035
  Rochester *(G-13354)*
Su-Dan Plastics Inc ....F....... 248 651-6035
  Rochester Hills *(G-13520)*
Summit Services Inc ....E....... 586 977-8300
  Shelby Township *(G-14705)*
Talon LLC ....D....... 313 392-1000
  Detroit *(G-4395)*
Target Mold Corporation ....F....... 231 798-3535
  Norton Shores *(G-11799)*
Tk Mold & Engineering Inc ....E....... 586 752-5840
  Romeo *(G-13640)*
Tony S Die Machine Company ....F....... 586 773-7379
  Warren *(G-17266)*
Tooling Technology LLC ....D....... 937 381-9211
  Macomb *(G-10169)*
Tri-Star Tooling LLC ....F....... 586 978-0435
  Sterling Heights *(G-15529)*
Twin Mold and Engineering LLC ....E....... 586 532-8558
  Shelby Township *(G-14713)*
Unytrex Inc ....F....... 810 796-9074
  Dryden *(G-4572)*
USF Delta Tooling LLC ....C....... 248 391-6800
  Auburn Hills *(G-1041)*
Vanex Mold Inc ....G....... 616 662-4100
  Jenison *(G-8647)*
Vision Global Industries ....G....... 248 390-5805
  Macomb *(G-10173)*
Wolverine Products Inc ....F....... 586 792-3740
  Clinton Township *(G-3261)*
Xcentric Mold & Engrg Inc ....F....... 586 598-4636
  Clinton Township *(G-3262)*
Z Mold & Engineering Inc ....G....... 586 948-5000
  Chesterfield *(G-2857)*

MOLDS: Plastic Working & Foundry

A & D Plastics Inc ....E....... 734 455-2255
  Plymouth *(G-12557)*
Accu Die & Mold Inc ....E....... 269 465-4020
  Stevensville *(G-15551)*
Advanced Special Tools Inc ....C....... 269 962-9697
  Battle Creek *(G-1141)*
Affinity Custom Molding Inc ....E....... 269 496-8423
  Mendon *(G-10711)*
Astar Inc ....E....... 574 234-2137
  Niles *(G-11595)*
Baker Industries Inc ....C....... 586 286-4900
  Macomb *(G-10111)*
Baumann Tool & Die ....G....... 616 772-6768
  Zeeland *(G-18116)*
Custom Design Inc ....E....... 269 323-8561
  Portage *(G-12990)*
D & L Tooling Inc ....G....... 517 369-5655
  Bronson *(G-2022)*
D-M-E USA Inc ....E....... 616 754-4601
  Greenville *(G-7126)*
Envisiontec Inc ....D....... 313 436-4300
  Dearborn *(G-3702)*
Formfab LLC ....E....... 248 844-3676
  Rochester Hills *(G-13427)*
Foust Electro Mold Inc ....G....... 517 439-1062
  Hillsdale *(G-7524)*
H & S Mold Inc ....F....... 989 732-3566
  Gaylord *(G-5864)*
Hi-Craft Engineering Inc ....D....... 586 293-0551
  Fraser *(G-5663)*

Hi-Tech Mold & Engineering Inc ....E....... 248 844-0722
  Rochester Hills *(G-13441)*
Hi-Tech Mold & Engineering Inc ....F....... 248 844-9159
  Rochester Hills *(G-13442)*
Hi-Tech Mold & Engineering Inc ....E....... 248 852-6600
  Rochester Hills *(G-13443)*
Innovative Mold Inc ....E....... 586 752-2996
  Washington *(G-17305)*
Jems of Litchfield Inc ....F....... 517 542-5367
  Litchfield *(G-9605)*
Legacy Precision Molds Inc ....G....... 616 532-6536
  Grandville *(G-7055)*
Leroy Tool & Die Inc ....D....... 231 768-4336
  Leroy *(G-9533)*
Levannes Inc ....F....... 269 327-4484
  Portage *(G-13007)*
Magna Exteriors America Inc ....A....... 248 631-1100
  Troy *(G-16472)*
Magna Exteriors America Inc ....B....... 248 409-1817
  Auburn Hills *(G-936)*
Mark Four CAM Inc ....G....... 586 204-5906
  Saint Clair Shores *(G-14261)*
Master Precision Products Inc ....E....... 616 754-5483
  Greenville *(G-7145)*
Mayer Tool & Engineering Inc ....E....... 269 651-1428
  Sturgis *(G-15616)*
Mesick Mold Co ....E....... 231 885-1304
  Mesick *(G-10771)*
Midland Mold & Machining Inc ....G....... 989 832-9534
  Midland *(G-10890)*
Midwest Plastic Engineering ....D....... 269 651-5223
  Sturgis *(G-15620)*
Mpp Corp ....E....... 810 364-2939
  Kimball *(G-9045)*
Nankin Welding Co Inc ....G....... 734 458-3980
  Livonia *(G-9857)*
Plastic-Plate Inc ....F....... 616 698-2030
  Grand Rapids *(G-6758)*
Proficient Products Inc ....G....... 586 977-8630
  Sterling Heights *(G-15453)*
Pti Engineered Plastics Inc ....B....... 586 263-5100
  Macomb *(G-10159)*
Quasar Industries Inc ....C....... 248 844-7190
  Rochester Hills *(G-13501)*
Quasar Industries Inc ....C....... 248 852-0300
  Rochester Hills *(G-13502)*
Ready Molds Inc ....E....... 248 474-4007
  Farmington Hills *(G-5113)*
Riverside Tool & Mold Inc ....G....... 989 435-9142
  Beaverton *(G-1390)*
S & K Tool & Die Company Inc ....F....... 269 345-2174
  Portage *(G-13029)*
Superior Mold Services Inc ....F....... 586 264-9570
  Sterling Heights *(G-15516)*
TNT-Edm Inc ....E....... 734 459-1700
  Plymouth *(G-12772)*
Trainer Metal Forming Co Inc ....E....... 616 844-9982
  Grand Haven *(G-6089)*
W & W Tool and Die Inc ....G....... 989 835-5522
  Midland *(G-10923)*
Wright Plastic Products Co LLC ....D....... 810 326-3000
  Saint Clair *(G-14237)*

MONASTERIES

Society of Saint John Inc ....G....... 906 289-4484
  Eagle Harbor *(G-4618)*

MONUMENTS & GRAVE MARKERS, EXC TERRAZZO

Signature Cnstr Svcs LLC ....G....... 616 451-0549
  Comstock Park *(G-3516)*
Superior Monuments Co ....G....... 231 728-2211
  Muskegon *(G-11433)*

MONUMENTS & GRAVE MARKERS, WHOLESALE

Fenton Corporation ....G....... 810 629-2858
  Fenton *(G-5209)*
Fenton Memorials & Vaults Inc ....F....... 810 629-2858
  Fenton *(G-5210)*
Patten Monument Company ....D....... 616 785-4141
  Comstock Park *(G-3506)*
Steinbrecher Stone Corp ....G....... 906 563-5852
  Norway *(G-11820)*

MONUMENTS: Cut Stone, Exc Finishing Or Lettering Only

Muskegon Monument & Stone Co ....G....... 231 722-2730
  Muskegon *(G-11390)*
Steinbrecher Stone Corp ....G....... 906 563-5852
  Norway *(G-11820)*

MOPS: Floor & Dust

Tuway American Group Inc ....C....... 248 205-9999
  Troy *(G-16658)*

MOTEL: Franchised

Qp Acquisition 2 Inc ....E....... 248 594-7432
  Southfield *(G-15006)*

MOTION PICTURE & VIDEO PRODUCTION SVCS

Livbig LLC ....G....... 888 519-8290
  Portage *(G-13010)*

MOTOR & GENERATOR PARTS: Electric

Ballard Power Systems Corp ....A....... 313 583-5980
  Dearborn *(G-3680)*
Edwards Industrial Sales Inc ....G....... 517 887-6100
  Lansing *(G-9363)*

MOTOR HOME DEALERS

Cedar Mobile Home Service Inc ....G....... 616 696-1580
  Cedar Springs *(G-2546)*

MOTOR HOMES

Auto-Masters Inc ....E....... 616 455-4510
  Grand Rapids *(G-6190)*

MOTOR REBUILDING SVCS, EXC AUTOMOTIVE

Alpena Electric Motor Service ....G....... 989 354-8780
  Alpena *(G-275)*

MOTOR REPAIR SVCS

Lincoln Service LLC ....G....... 734 793-0083
  Livonia *(G-9808)*
Lorna Icr LLC ....G....... 586 582-1500
  Warren *(G-17131)*
Motown Harley-Davidson Inc ....D....... 734 947-4647
  Taylor *(G-15748)*
Timco Engine Center Inc ....D....... 989 739-2194
  Oscoda *(G-12221)*

MOTOR VEHICLE ASSEMBLY, COMPLETE: Ambulances

Horstman Inc ....E....... 586 737-2100
  Sterling Heights *(G-15368)*

MOTOR VEHICLE ASSEMBLY, COMPLETE: Autos, Incl Specialty

Aapico Detroit LLC ....G....... 313 652-5254
  Detroit *(G-3833)*
Aapico Detroit LLC ....B....... 313 551-6001
  Detroit *(G-3834)*
Aftershock Motorsports ....G....... 586 273-1333
  Casco *(G-2498)*
Ai-Genesee LLC ....D....... 810 720-4848
  Flint *(G-5373)*
Comstar Automotive USA LLC ....F....... 517 266-2445
  Tecumseh *(G-15785)*
Creative Automation Solutions ....G....... 313 790-4848
  Livonia *(G-9692)*
Dakkota Integrated Systems LLC ....B....... 517 694-6500
  Brighton *(G-1908)*
Dakkota Integrated Systems LLC ....D....... 517 321-3064
  Lansing *(G-9213)*
Dakkota Integrated Systems LLC ....E....... 517 694-6500
  Holt *(G-7907)*
FCA North America Holdings LLC ....E....... 248 512-2950
  Auburn Hills *(G-866)*
FCA US LLC ....C....... 248 576-5741
  Auburn Hills *(G-869)*
Federal-Mogul Motorparts LLC ....E....... 248 354-7700
  Southfield *(G-14908)*

Employee Codes: A=Over 500 employees, B=251-500
C=101-250, D=51-100, E=20-50, F=10-19, G=3-9

MOTOR VEHICLE ASSEMBLY, COMPLETE: Autos, Incl Specialty

Finish Line Fabricating LLC .... G 269 686-8400
  Allegan *(G-161)*
Ford Motor Company .... B 313 322-3000
  Dearborn *(G-3709)*
General Motors LLC .... A 313 972-6000
  Detroit *(G-4084)*
General Motors LLC .... C 248 874-1737
  Pontiac *(G-12826)*
Global Impact Group LLC .... G 248 895-9900
  Grand Blanc *(G-5966)*
GM Laam Holdings LLC .... G 313 556-5000
  Detroit *(G-4093)*
Illinois Tool Works Inc .... D 248 589-2500
  Troy *(G-16410)*
Inventev LLC .... G 248 535-0477
  Detroit *(G-4148)*
Jasco International LLC .... F 313 841-5000
  Detroit *(G-4159)*
Mahindra North American .... C 248 268-6600
  Auburn Hills *(G-940)*
Mahindra Vehicle Mfrs Ltd .... C 248 268-6600
  Auburn Hills *(G-941)*
Manufacturing Products & Svcs .... F 734 927-1964
  Plymouth *(G-12683)*
Mico Industries Inc .... D 616 245-6426
  Grand Rapids *(G-6679)*
Midstates Industrial Group Inc .... E 586 307-3414
  Clinton Township *(G-3174)*
Morris Associates Inc .... E 248 355-9055
  Southfield *(G-14987)*
Moser Racing Inc .... F 248 348-6502
  Northville *(G-11712)*
Omaha Automation Inc .... G 313 557-3565
  Detroit *(G-4284)*
Onyx Manufacturing Inc .... G 248 687-8611
  Rochester Hills *(G-13487)*
Osbern Racing .... G 313 538-8933
  Detroit *(G-4285)*
Racers Inc .... G 586 727-4069
  Columbus *(G-3382)*
Redline Fabrications .... G 810 984-5621
  Clyde *(G-3284)*
Rivian Automotive Inc .... D 734 855-4350
  Plymouth *(G-12737)*
Rivian Automotive Inc .... G 408 483-1987
  Plymouth *(G-12738)*
Ruhlman Race Cars .... G 517 529-4661
  Clarklake *(G-2899)*
Sas Automotive Usa Inc .... E 248 606-1152
  Sterling Heights *(G-15485)*
Skinny Kid Race Cars .... G 248 668-1040
  Commerce Township *(G-3452)*
Smart Automation Systems Inc .... G 248 651-5911
  Rochester Hills *(G-13514)*
Tunkers Inc .... E 734 744-5990
  Sterling Heights *(G-15531)*
Turn Key Automotive LLC .... E 248 628-5556
  Oxford *(G-12378)*
Veigel North America LLC .... F 586 843-3816
  Shelby Township *(G-14717)*
Wgs Global Services LC .... D 810 239-4947
  Flint *(G-5523)*
Wgs Global Services LC .... D 810 694-3843
  Grand Blanc *(G-5989)*

MOTOR VEHICLE ASSEMBLY, COMPLETE: Buses, All Types

General Coach America Inc .... G 810 724-6474
  Imlay City *(G-8200)*

MOTOR VEHICLE ASSEMBLY, COMPLETE: Cars, Armored

Armored Group LLC .... E 602 840-2271
  Dearborn Heights *(G-3779)*
CATI Armor LLC .... G 269 788-4322
  Charlotte *(G-2637)*

MOTOR VEHICLE ASSEMBLY, COMPLETE: Fire Department Vehicles

Quality First Fire Alarm .... G 810 736-4911
  Flint *(G-5488)*
Spartan Motors Usa Inc .... D 517 543-6400
  Charlotte *(G-2667)*
Spencer Manufacturing Inc .... F 269 637-9459
  South Haven *(G-14775)*
Township of Saline .... F 734 429-4440
  Saline *(G-14418)*

MOTOR VEHICLE ASSEMBLY, COMPLETE: Hearses

Bennett Funeral Coaches Inc .... G 616 538-8100
  Byron Center *(G-2179)*

MOTOR VEHICLE ASSEMBLY, COMPLETE: Military Motor Vehicle

American Fabricated Pdts Inc .... F 616 607-8785
  Spring Lake *(G-15133)*
Aom Engineering Solutions LLC .... G 313 406-8130
  Dearborn Heights *(G-3778)*
Demmer Corporation .... D 517 323-4504
  Lansing *(G-9220)*
Meritor Heavy Vhcl Systems LLC .... C 248 435-1000
  Troy *(G-16494)*
Onodi Tool & Engineering Co .... E 313 386-6682
  Melvindale *(G-10704)*
Oshkosh Defense LLC .... E 586 576-8301
  Warren *(G-17178)*
P2r Metal Fabrication Inc .... G 888 727-5587
  Macomb *(G-10151)*

MOTOR VEHICLE ASSEMBLY, COMPLETE: Motor Homes, Self Containd

R V Wolverine .... F 989 426-9241
  Gladwin *(G-5934)*

MOTOR VEHICLE ASSEMBLY, COMPLETE: Scout Cars

Famek Inc .... G 734 895-6794
  Southfield *(G-14902)*

MOTOR VEHICLE ASSEMBLY, COMPLETE: Snow Plows

Trynex International LLC .... F 248 586-3500
  Madison Heights *(G-10371)*

MOTOR VEHICLE ASSEMBLY, COMPLETE: Truck & Tractor Trucks

Advance Vehicle Assembly Inc .... F 989 823-3800
  Vassar *(G-16810)*
Meyers John .... G 989 236-5400
  Middleton *(G-10793)*
Valley Truck Parts Inc .... D 616 241-5431
  Wyoming *(G-18040)*

MOTOR VEHICLE ASSEMBLY, COMPLETE: Truck Tractors, Highway

Trailer Tech Repair Inc .... G 734 354-6680
  Plymouth *(G-12777)*

MOTOR VEHICLE ASSEMBLY, COMPLETE: Trucks, Pickup

Mid-West Truck Accessories .... G 313 592-1788
  Detroit *(G-4247)*

MOTOR VEHICLE ASSEMBLY, COMPLETE: Universal Carriers, Mil

Armartis Manufacturing Inc .... E 248 308-9622
  Roseville *(G-13775)*
SGC Industries Inc .... E 586 293-5260
  Fraser *(G-5723)*

MOTOR VEHICLE ASSEMBLY, COMPLETE: Wreckers, Tow Truck

Horizon Global Corporation .... C 248 593-8820
  Troy *(G-16401)*
Junk Man LLC .... G 248 459-7359
  Pontiac *(G-12843)*

MOTOR VEHICLE DEALERS: Automobiles, New & Used

FCA US LLC .... A 800 247-9753
  Auburn Hills *(G-868)*
FCA US LLC .... D 586 978-0067
  Sterling Heights *(G-15337)*
FCA US LLC .... C 248 576-5741
  Auburn Hills *(G-869)*
Ford Motor Company .... A 734 484-8000
  Ypsilanti *(G-18074)*
Ford Motor Company .... A 734 377-4954
  Livonia *(G-9743)*
Ford Motor Company .... A 313 594-4090
  Allen Park *(G-198)*
Ford Motor Company .... E 910 381-7998
  Taylor *(G-15723)*
Ford Motor Company .... A 734 523-3000
  Livonia *(G-9744)*
Ford Motor Company .... A 734 942-6248
  Brownstown *(G-2062)*
General Motors Company .... F 248 249-6347
  Brownstown *(G-2063)*
General Motors Company .... B 586 218-9240
  Warren *(G-17051)*
General Motors Holdings LLC .... E 313 556-5000
  Detroit *(G-4083)*
General Motors LLC .... D 810 234-2710
  Flint *(G-5434)*
General Motors LLC .... B 989 894-7210
  Bay City *(G-1315)*
General Motors LLC .... F 810 234-2710
  Flint *(G-5435)*
General Motors LLC .... A 517 885-6669
  Lansing *(G-9290)*
General Motors LLC .... F 931 486-5049
  Warren *(G-17053)*
General Motors LLC .... C 313 410-2704
  Detroit *(G-4085)*
General Motors LLC .... E 248 456-5000
  Pontiac *(G-12827)*
General Motors LLC .... A 248 857-3500
  Pontiac *(G-12828)*
GM Components Holdings LLC .... C 313 665-4707
  Detroit *(G-4092)*
RSM & Associates Co .... F 517 750-9330
  Jackson *(G-8566)*

MOTOR VEHICLE DEALERS: Cars, Used Only

Kern Auto Sales and Svc LLC .... F 734 475-2722
  Chelsea *(G-2715)*

MOTOR VEHICLE DEALERS: Pickups, New & Used

Detroit Wrecker Sales Llc .... G 313 835-8700
  Detroit *(G-4005)*

MOTOR VEHICLE DEALERS: Trucks, Tractors/Trailers, New & Used

Benlee Inc .... E 586 791-1830
  Romulus *(G-13656)*
Gld Holdings Inc .... F 616 877-4288
  Moline *(G-11010)*
Midwest Tractor & Equipment Co ...... F 231 269-4100
  Buckley *(G-2130)*
Tow-Line Trailers .... G 989 752-0055
  Saginaw *(G-14165)*
UP Truck Center Inc .... E 906 774-0098
  Quinnesec *(G-13103)*
Wells Equipment Sales Inc .... F 517 542-2376
  Litchfield *(G-9613)*

MOTOR VEHICLE PARTS & ACCESS: Air Conditioner Parts

Denso Air Systems Michigan Inc .... D 269 962-9676
  Battle Creek *(G-1171)*
Fluid Hutchinson Management .... D 248 679-1327
  Auburn Hills *(G-876)*
Formfab LLC .... E 248 844-3676
  Rochester Hills *(G-13427)*
Hanon Systems Usa LLC .... B 248 907-8000
  Novi *(G-11893)*
Mahle Behr Mfg MGT Inc .... A 248 735-3623
  Troy *(G-16480)*
Skg International Inc .... F 248 620-4139
  Clarkston *(G-2956)*
Stewart Industries LLC .... D 269 660-9290
  Battle Creek *(G-1253)*

MOTOR VEHICLE PARTS & ACCESS: Axel Housings & Shafts

Angstrom Automotive Group LLC ...... G 313 295-0100
  Taylor *(G-15689)*

PRODUCT SECTION

MOTOR VEHICLE PARTS & ACCESS: Engines & Parts

CCI Driveline LLC ....G....... 586 716-1160
  Casco *(G-2499)*
Horstman Inc ....E....... 586 737-2100
  Sterling Heights *(G-15368)*

MOTOR VEHICLE PARTS & ACCESS: Ball Joints

Federal-Mogul Products US LLC ....A....... 248 354-7700
  Southfield *(G-14911)*

MOTOR VEHICLE PARTS & ACCESS: Bearings

Federal-Mogul Powertrain LLC ....B....... 616 754-5681
  Greenville *(G-7132)*
Mahle Industries Incorporated ....C....... 231 722-1300
  Muskegon *(G-11372)*

MOTOR VEHICLE PARTS & ACCESS: Body Components & Frames

Antolin Interiors Usa Inc ....A....... 810 329-1045
  China *(G-2858)*
Complete Prototype Svcs Inc ....B....... 586 690-8897
  Clinton Township *(G-3085)*
CTA Acoustics Inc ....E....... 248 544-2580
  Madison Heights *(G-10223)*
Design Converting Inc ....F....... 616 942-7780
  Grand Rapids *(G-6344)*
Drake Enterprises Inc ....E....... 586 783-3009
  Clinton Township *(G-3105)*
Grupo Antolin Michigan Inc ....C....... 989 635-5055
  Marlette *(G-10497)*
Grupo Antolin Michigan Inc ....E....... 989 635-5080
  Warren *(G-17069)*
Grupo Antolin Primera Auto Sys ....D....... 734 495-9180
  Canton *(G-2381)*
Johnson Controls Inc ....C....... 586 826-8845
  Sterling Heights *(G-15382)*
Kiekert Usa Inc ....C....... 248 960-4100
  Wixom *(G-17842)*
M S Manufacturing Inc ....F....... 586 463-2788
  Clinton Township *(G-3161)*
Magna Exteriors America Inc ....A....... 248 631-1100
  Troy *(G-16472)*
Magna Modular Systems LLC ....C....... 586 279-2000
  Warren *(G-17137)*
Magneti Marelli North Amer Inc ....G....... 248 418-3000
  Auburn Hills *(G-939)*
Mssc Inc ....E....... 248 502-8000
  Troy *(G-16515)*
Owens Products Inc ....E....... 269 651-2300
  Sturgis *(G-15625)*
Precision Gage Inc ....D....... 517 439-1690
  Hillsdale *(G-7534)*
Rack & Pinion Inc ....G....... 517 563-8872
  Horton *(G-7970)*
Rose-A-Lee Technologies Inc ....G....... 586 799-4555
  Sterling Heights *(G-15479)*
Sliding Systems Inc ....E....... 517 339-1455
  Haslett *(G-7399)*

MOTOR VEHICLE PARTS & ACCESS: Brakes, Air

Akebono Brake Corporation ....C....... 248 489-7400
  Farmington Hills *(G-4925)*
Haldex Brake Products Corp ....C....... 616 827-9641
  Wyoming *(G-18007)*
Seg Automotive North Amer LLC ....F....... 248 465-2602
  Novi *(G-11991)*

MOTOR VEHICLE PARTS & ACCESS: Brakes, Vacuum

Rassini Brakes LLC ....G....... 810 780-4600
  Flint *(G-5490)*

MOTOR VEHICLE PARTS & ACCESS: Clutches

Exedy-Dynax America Corp ....F....... 734 397-6556
  Van Buren Twp *(G-16760)*
Ogura Corporation ....C....... 586 749-1900
  Chesterfield *(G-2812)*
Precision Torque Control Inc ....F....... 989 495-9330
  Midland *(G-10903)*
Valeo Friction Materials Inc ....G....... 248 619-8400
  Troy *(G-16675)*

MOTOR VEHICLE PARTS & ACCESS: Connecting Rods

Baldwin Precision Inc ....E....... 231 237-4515
  Charlevoix *(G-2608)*
TRW Automotive JV LLC ....G....... 734 855-2787
  Livonia *(G-9975)*
ZF Active Safety US Inc ....B....... 734 855-2542
  Livonia *(G-10015)*
ZF Active Safety US Inc ....E....... 734 855-2470
  Livonia *(G-10017)*

MOTOR VEHICLE PARTS & ACCESS: Cylinder Heads

Bleistahl N Amer Ltd Partnr ....E....... 269 719-8585
  Battle Creek *(G-1155)*

MOTOR VEHICLE PARTS & ACCESS: Defrosters

Therma-Tech Engineering Inc ....E....... 313 537-5330
  Redford *(G-13201)*

MOTOR VEHICLE PARTS & ACCESS: Directional Signals

Havis Inc ....E....... 734 414-0699
  Plymouth *(G-12634)*

MOTOR VEHICLE PARTS & ACCESS: Electrical Eqpt

Dura Operating LLC ....C....... 248 299-7500
  Auburn Hills *(G-846)*
Eberspecher Contrls N Amer Inc ....G....... 248 994-7010
  Brighton *(G-1916)*
Gentherm Incorporated ....B....... 248 504-0500
  Northville *(G-11694)*
Grakon LLC ....G....... 734 462-1201
  Livonia *(G-9755)*
Grand Traverse Stamping Co ....F....... 231 929-4215
  Traverse City *(G-15988)*
Henniges Auto Holdings Inc ....B....... 248 340-4100
  Auburn Hills *(G-896)*
Hi-Lex Controls Incorporated ....F....... 517 542-2955
  Litchfield *(G-9604)*
Lear Automotive Mfg LLC ....F....... 248 447-1603
  Detroit *(G-4196)*
Lear Automotive Mfg LLC ....F....... 248 447-1603
  Detroit *(G-4197)*
Lear Corporation ....B....... 989 588-6181
  Farwell *(G-5163)*
Lear Corporation ....C....... 989 275-5794
  Roscommon *(G-13750)*
Lear Corporation ....B....... 248 447-1500
  Southfield *(G-14962)*
Lear Corporation ....A....... 313 731-0833
  Flint *(G-5457)*
Lear Corporation ....B....... 269 496-2215
  Mendon *(G-10715)*
Lear European Operations Corp ....G....... 248 447-1500
  Southfield *(G-14963)*
P3 Product Solutions Inc ....F....... 248 703-7724
  Madison Heights *(G-10320)*
Stoneridge Inc ....G....... 248 489-9300
  Novi *(G-12004)*
Tram Inc ....C....... 734 254-8500
  Plymouth *(G-12778)*
Trmi Inc ....A....... 269 966-0800
  Battle Creek *(G-1261)*
Valeo North America Inc ....D....... 248 619-8300
  Troy *(G-16677)*
Valeo Radar Systems Inc ....F....... 248 619-8300
  Troy *(G-16678)*

MOTOR VEHICLE PARTS & ACCESS: Engines & Parts

Ace Controls Inc ....C....... 248 476-0213
  Farmington Hills *(G-4919)*
American Axle & Mfg Inc ....G....... 586 415-2000
  Fraser *(G-5616)*
Autocam Corporation ....D....... 269 789-4000
  Marshall *(G-10562)*
Autocam Corporation ....C....... 269 782-5186
  Dowagiac *(G-4533)*
Black River Manufacturing Inc ....E....... 810 982-8912
  Port Huron *(G-12900)*
Black River Manufacturing Inc ....D....... 810 982-9812
  Port Huron *(G-12901)*
Cequent Uk Ltd ....G....... 734 656-3000
  Plymouth *(G-12595)*
D M P E ....G....... 269 428-5070
  Stevensville *(G-15561)*
Denso International Amer Inc ....A....... 248 350-7500
  Southfield *(G-14879)*
Detroit Diesel Corporation ....A....... 313 592-5000
  Detroit *(G-3980)*
Detroit Diesel Corporation ....F....... 313 592-8256
  Redford *(G-13157)*
Dolphin Manufacturing Inc ....E....... 734 946-6322
  Taylor *(G-15707)*
Eaton Aerospace LLC ....B....... 616 949-1090
  Grand Rapids *(G-6368)*
FCA Intrntional Operations LLC ....E....... 800 334-9200
  Auburn Hills *(G-865)*
GKN Sinter Metals LLC ....G....... 248 296-7832
  Auburn Hills *(G-888)*
Grupo Antolin North Amer Inc ....C....... 248 373-1749
  Auburn Hills *(G-891)*
Gt Technologies Inc ....E....... 734 467-8371
  Westland *(G-17566)*
Hacker Machine Inc ....F....... 517 569-3348
  Rives Junction *(G-13308)*
Hemco Machine Co Inc ....G....... 586 264-8911
  Warren *(G-17079)*
Ilmor Engineering Inc ....D....... 734 456-3600
  Plymouth *(G-12646)*
Magna Powertrain Usa Inc ....D....... 248 680-4900
  Troy *(G-16476)*
Magna Powertrain Usa Inc ....B....... 248 524-1397
  Troy *(G-16477)*
Mahle Industries Incorporated ....E....... 248 305-8200
  Farmington Hills *(G-5052)*
Mall Tooling & Engineering ....F....... 586 463-6520
  Mount Clemens *(G-11140)*
Marimba Auto LLC ....D....... 734 398-9000
  Canton *(G-2397)*
Millennium Steering LLC ....D....... 989 872-8823
  Cass City *(G-2521)*
Mitsubishi Steel Mfg Co Ltd ....E....... 248 502-8000
  Troy *(G-16509)*
Motor Parts Inc of Michigan ....E....... 248 852-1522
  Rochester Hills *(G-13476)*
Mpt Lansing LLC ....C....... 517 316-1013
  Lansing *(G-9403)*
Oakwood Metal Fabricating Co ....B....... 313 561-7740
  Dearborn *(G-3746)*
Performance Engrg Racg Engs ....G....... 616 669-5800
  Jenison *(G-8636)*
Performance Springs Inc ....F....... 248 486-3372
  New Hudson *(G-11551)*
Pierburg Us LLC ....F....... 864 688-1322
  Auburn Hills *(G-973)*
Prestige Engrg Rsrces Tech Inc ....F....... 586 573-3070
  Clinton Township *(G-3202)*
Prestige Engrg Rsrces Tech Inc ....E....... 586 573-3070
  Madison Heights *(G-10336)*
Quigley Co ....E....... 989 983-3911
  Vanderbilt *(G-16809)*
Ridge & Kramer Motor Supply Co ....G....... 269 685-5838
  Plainwell *(G-12541)*
Robert Bosch LLC ....A....... 734 979-3000
  Plymouth *(G-12741)*
Roush Enterprises Inc ....C....... 734 805-4400
  Farmington *(G-4909)*
Roush Industries Inc ....E....... 734 779-7013
  Livonia *(G-9913)*
Specialty Eng Components LLC ....D....... 734 955-6500
  Taylor *(G-15770)*
Sterling Performance Inc ....E....... 248 685-7811
  Milford *(G-10987)*
Swoboda Inc ....C....... 616 554-6161
  Grand Rapids *(G-6909)*
TAC Manufacturing Inc ....B....... 517 789-7000
  Jackson *(G-8582)*
Tenneco Automotive Oper Co Inc ....G....... 734 243-8039
  Monroe *(G-11072)*
Tenneco Clean Air US Inc ....G....... 734 384-7867
  Lansing *(G-9432)*
Uc Holdings Inc ....D....... 248 728-8642
  Southfield *(G-15052)*
Visteon Corporation ....B....... 800 847-8366
  Van Buren Twp *(G-16790)*
Visteon Systems LLC ....E....... 800 847-8366
  Van Buren Twp *(G-16795)*
Weber Automotive Corporation ....C....... 248 393-5520
  Auburn Hills *(G-1050)*

Employee Codes: A=Over 500 employees, B=251-500
C=101-250, D=51-100, E=20-50, F=10-19, G=3-9

MOTOR VEHICLE PARTS & ACCESS: Engines & Parts

ZF Active Safety US Inc ....F...... 734 812-6979
  Livonia (G-10016)
ZF Active Safety US Inc ....C...... 586 899-2807
  Sterling Heights (G-15548)
Zhongli North America Inc ....D...... 248 733-9300
  Troy (G-16705)

MOTOR VEHICLE PARTS & ACCESS: Engs & Trans, Factory, Rebuilt

Advance Motor Rebuilders Inc ....G...... 586 222-9583
  Warren (G-16919)
Navarre Inc ....E...... 313 892-7300
  Detroit (G-4264)

MOTOR VEHICLE PARTS & ACCESS: Frames

Pritech Corporation ....G...... 248 488-9120
  Canton (G-2420)

MOTOR VEHICLE PARTS & ACCESS: Fuel Pumps

Carter Fuel Systems LLC ....G...... 248 371-8392
  Rochester Hills (G-13386)
Slw Automotive Inc ....C...... 248 464-6200
  Rochester Hills (G-13513)
TI Group Auto Systems LLC ....E...... 248 494-5000
  Troy (G-16642)

MOTOR VEHICLE PARTS & ACCESS: Fuel Systems & Parts

Alfmeier Friedrichs & Rath LLC .....G...... 248 526-1650
  Troy (G-16186)
Alternative Fuel Tech LLC ....G...... 313 417-9212
  Grosse Pointe Park (G-7189)
Continental Auto Systems Inc ....B...... 248 209-4000
  Auburn Hills (G-820)
Continental Auto Systems Inc ....B...... 248 874-1801
  Auburn Hills (G-822)
Cummins Inc ....C...... 906 774-2424
  Iron Mountain (G-8281)
Davco Technology LLC ....D...... 734 429-5665
  Saline (G-14386)
Fluid Routing Solutions Inc ....E...... 231 796-4489
  Big Rapids (G-1629)
GM Components Holdings LLC ....E...... 616 246-2000
  Grand Rapids (G-6444)
Impco Technologies Inc ....E...... 586 264-1200
  Sterling Heights (G-15370)
Nostrum Energy LLC ....F...... 734 548-8677
  Ann Arbor (G-576)
Oscar W Larson Company ....G...... 248 575-0320
  Clarkston (G-2943)
Plastic Omnium Auto Inergy ....B...... 734 753-1350
  New Boston (G-11508)
Plastic Omnium Auto Inergy LLC ..B...... 248 743-5700
  Troy (G-16553)
Robert Bosch Fuel Systems LLC ..C...... 616 554-6500
  Kentwood (G-9030)
Sloan Transportation Pdts Inc ......D...... 616 395-5600
  Holland (G-7806)
TI Group Auto Systems LLC ....B...... 248 296-8000
  Auburn Hills (G-1022)
Veritas USA Corporation ....G...... 248 374-5019
  Novi (G-12026)
Yapp USA Auto Systems Inc ....G...... 248 404-8696
  Romulus (G-13745)

MOTOR VEHICLE PARTS & ACCESS: Gas Tanks

Raval USA Inc ....F...... 248 260-4050
  Rochester Hills (G-13503)

MOTOR VEHICLE PARTS & ACCESS: Gears

AA Gear LLC ....F...... 517 552-3100
  Howell (G-8009)
Anderson-Cook Inc ....D...... 586 954-0700
  Clinton Township (G-3053)
Anderson-Cook Inc ....D...... 586 293-0800
  Fraser (G-5620)
Anderson-Cook Inc ....E...... 586 954-0700
  Clinton Township (G-3054)
Atlas Gear Company ....F...... 248 583-2964
  Madison Heights (G-10198)
Detail Production Company Inc .....F...... 248 544-3390
  Ferndale (G-5272)

Getrag Transmissions Corp ....C...... 586 620-1300
  Troy (G-16383)
Gleason Works ....F...... 248 522-0305
  Farmington Hills (G-5009)
Leedy Manufacturing Co LLC ....D...... 616 245-0517
  Grand Rapids (G-6624)
Libertys High Prfmce Pdts Inc ....F...... 586 469-1140
  Harrison Township (G-7338)
Nexteer Automotive Corporation ...A...... 989 757-5000
  Saginaw (G-14106)
Rochester Gear Inc ....D...... 989 659-2899
  Clifford (G-3011)
Von Weise LLC ....F...... 517 618-9763
  Eaton Rapids (G-4736)

MOTOR VEHICLE PARTS & ACCESS: Heaters

Kongsberg Automotive Inc ....D...... 248 468-1300
  Novi (G-11918)
Kurabe America Corporation ....A...... 248 939-5803
  Farmington Hills (G-5039)

MOTOR VEHICLE PARTS & ACCESS: Horns

Fiamm Technologies LLC ....F...... 231 775-2900
  Cadillac (G-2247)
Fiamm Technologies LLC ....C...... 248 427-3200
  Farmington Hills (G-5000)

MOTOR VEHICLE PARTS & ACCESS: Instrument Board Assemblies

Ese LLc ....G...... 810 538-1000
  Lapeer (G-9459)
Intertec Systems LLC ....D...... 734 254-3268
  Plymouth (G-12649)
Kautex Inc ....A...... 248 616-5100
  Troy (G-16444)

MOTOR VEHICLE PARTS & ACCESS: Manifolds

Benteler Automotive Corp ....C...... 248 364-7190
  Auburn Hills (G-792)
Metaldyne Tblar Components LLC ...C... 248 727-1800
  Southfield (G-14979)

MOTOR VEHICLE PARTS & ACCESS: Mufflers, Exhaust

Bay Alphi Manufacturing Inc ....E...... 517 849-9945
  Jonesville (G-8653)
Faurecia USA Holdings Inc ....G...... 248 724-5100
  Auburn Hills (G-864)
Tenneco Automotive Oper Co Inc ..C...... 269 781-1350
  Marshall (G-10590)
Tenneco Automotive Oper Co Inc ..C...... 517 542-5511
  Litchfield (G-9611)

MOTOR VEHICLE PARTS & ACCESS: Oil Pumps

Highland Manufacturing Inc ....F...... 248 585-8040
  Madison Heights (G-10267)
J & J Industries Inc ....C...... 517 784-3586
  Jackson (G-8473)
Melling Tool Co ....B...... 517 787-8172
  Jackson (G-8514)

MOTOR VEHICLE PARTS & ACCESS: Pickup Truck Bed Liners

Line X of Westbranch ....G...... 989 345-7800
  West Branch (G-17512)
Sports Resorts International ....D...... 989 725-8354
  Owosso (G-12318)
Tectum Holdings Inc ....D...... 734 926-2362
  Ann Arbor (G-656)
Truck Acquisition Inc ....G...... 877 875-4376
  Ann Arbor (G-681)
Truck Hero Inc ....D...... 877 875-4376
  Ann Arbor (G-682)
Truck Holdings Inc ....G...... 877 875-4376
  Ann Arbor (G-683)

MOTOR VEHICLE PARTS & ACCESS: Power Steering Eqpt

Cooper-Standard Automotive Inc ..C...... 989 848-2272
  Fairview (G-4889)

Nexteer Automotive Corporation ...C...... 989 757-5000
  Saginaw (G-14113)

MOTOR VEHICLE PARTS & ACCESS: Pumps, Hydraulic Fluid Power

J Drummond Service Inc ....G...... 248 624-0190
  Livonia (G-9790)
Med-Kas Hydraulics Inc ....F...... 248 585-3220
  Troy (G-16491)
Panagon Systems Inc ....E...... 586 786-3920
  Macomb (G-10152)
Pardon Inc ....E...... 906 428-3494
  Gladstone (G-5918)

MOTOR VEHICLE PARTS & ACCESS: Rear Axel Housings

American Axle & Mfg Inc ....B...... 313 758-3600
  Detroit (G-3865)
Axletech Intl Holdings LLC ....D...... 248 658-7200
  Troy (G-16232)
Dana Off-Hghway Components LLC ..E... 586 467-1600
  Flint (G-5414)
Diversified Mfg & Assembly LLC ...F...... 586 272-2431
  Sterling Heights (G-15318)

MOTOR VEHICLE PARTS & ACCESS: Thermostats

Magnumm Corporation ....F...... 586 427-9420
  Warren (G-17138)

MOTOR VEHICLE PARTS & ACCESS: Tops

D & M Truck Top Co Inc ....G...... 248 792-7972
  Troy (G-16292)
Webasto Convertibles USA Inc .....C...... 734 582-5900
  Plymouth (G-12791)

MOTOR VEHICLE PARTS & ACCESS: Trailer Hitches

Garrisons Hitch Center Inc ....G...... 810 239-5728
  Flint (G-5432)
Horizon Global Americas Inc ....C...... 734 656-3000
  Plymouth (G-12643)
Horizon Global Corporation ....C...... 248 593-8820
  Troy (G-16401)
Lee Industries Inc ....E...... 231 777-2537
  Muskegon (G-11365)
Saf-Holland Inc ....B...... 231 773-3271
  Muskegon (G-11417)

MOTOR VEHICLE PARTS & ACCESS: Transmission Housings Or Parts

Extreme Machine Inc ....D...... 810 231-0521
  Whitmore Lake (G-17699)
Means Industries Inc ....C...... 989 754-1433
  Saginaw (G-14086)
Meritor Specialty Products LLC ....D...... 517 545-5800
  Howell (G-8062)
Neapco Drivelines LLC ....B...... 734 447-1316
  Van Buren Twp (G-16775)
Neapco Drivelines LLC ....C...... 734 447-1300
  Van Buren Twp (G-16776)
Quality Clutches Inc ....G...... 734 782-0783
  Flat Rock (G-5360)
S & W Holdings Ltd ....D...... 248 723-2870
  Birmingham (G-1701)
Torsion Control Products Inc ....F...... 248 537-1900
  Rochester Hills (G-13528)
Trans Parts Plus Inc ....G...... 734 427-6844
  Garden City (G-5844)

MOTOR VEHICLE PARTS & ACCESS: Transmissions

1st Quality LLC ....E...... 313 908-4864
  Dearborn (G-3669)
Aw Transmission Engrg USA Inc ..D...... 734 454-1710
  Plymouth (G-12581)
Borgwarner Emissions ....D...... 248 754-9600
  Auburn Hills (G-796)
Borgwarner Transm Systems Inc ..B...... 248 754-9200
  Auburn Hills (G-804)
Extreme Machine Inc ....D...... 810 231-0521
  Whitmore Lake (G-17700)
Jasper Weller LLC ....C...... 616 724-2000
  Grand Rapids (G-6554)

PRODUCT SECTION

MOTOR VEHICLES & CAR BODIES

R Cushman & Associates Inc ....E 248 477-9900
  Livonia (G-9904)

MOTOR VEHICLE PARTS & ACCESS: Universal Joints

GKN Driveline North Amer Inc ....B 248 296-7000
  Auburn Hills (G-885)

MOTOR VEHICLE PARTS & ACCESS: Water Pumps

Engineered Machined Pdts Inc ....B 906 786-8404
  Escanaba (G-4826)
Kerkstra Mechanical LLC ....G 616 532-6100
  Grand Rapids (G-6581)

MOTOR VEHICLE PARTS & ACCESS: Wheel rims

Fontijne Grotnes Inc ....E 269 262-4700
  Niles (G-11611)

MOTOR VEHICLE PARTS & ACCESS: Wiring Harness Sets

Creative Performance Racg LLC ....G 248 250-6187
  Troy (G-16285)
Dontech Solutions LLC ....E 248 789-3086
  Howell (G-8033)
Howell Engine Developments Inc ....F 810 765-5100
  Cottrellville (G-3587)
Newtech 3 Inc ....E 248 912-0807
  Wixom (G-17864)
Pgf Technology Group Inc ....E 248 852-2800
  Rochester Hills (G-13492)
Precision Race Services Inc ....G 248 634-4010
  Davisburg (G-3638)
Tesca Usa Inc ....E 586 991-0744
  Rochester Hills (G-13524)
Wiric Corporation ....E 248 598-5297
  Rochester Hills (G-13548)

MOTOR VEHICLE RADIOS WHOLESALERS

Alpine Electronics America Inc ....C 248 409-9444
  Auburn Hills (G-766)
Clarion Corporation America ....E 248 991-3100
  Farmington (G-4896)
Robert Bosch LLC ....E 248 921-9054
  Novi (G-11987)
Robert Bosch LLC ....A 734 979-3000
  Plymouth (G-12741)

MOTOR VEHICLE SPLYS & PARTS WHOLESALERS: New

Brembo North America Inc ....D 734 416-1275
  Plymouth (G-12590)
Bridgewater Interiors LLC ....C 313 842-3300
  Detroit (G-3916)
Carter Industries Inc ....E 510 324-6700
  Adrian (G-53)
Continental Auto Systems Inc ....E 248 267-9408
  Troy (G-16277)
Davco Manufacturing LLC ....D 734 429-5665
  Saline (G-14385)
Diversfied Prcurement Svcs LLC ....G 248 821-1147
  Ferndale (G-5280)
Elliott Tape Inc ....E 248 475-2000
  Auburn Hills (G-854)
Gestamp Mason LLC ....B 517 244-8800
  Mason (G-10641)
GKN North America Inc ....A 248 296-7200
  Auburn Hills (G-886)
H R P Motor Sports Inc ....G 616 874-6338
  Rockford (G-13570)
Hydraulic Systems Technology ....G 248 656-5810
  Rochester Hills (G-13447)
L Barge & Associates Inc ....F 248 582-3430
  Ferndale (G-5297)
Lydall Sealing Solutions Inc ....D 248 596-2800
  Northville (G-11706)
Mayser Usa Inc ....D 734 858-1290
  Van Buren Twp (G-16771)
Midwest Bus Corporation ....D 989 723-5241
  Owosso (G-12304)
Muskegon Brake & Distrg Co LLC ....E 231 733-0874
  Norton Shores (G-11776)
Overseas Auto Parts Inc ....E 734 427-4840
  Livonia (G-9877)

P G S Inc ....C 248 526-3800
  Troy (G-16540)
Pittsburgh Glass Works LLC ....C 248 371-1700
  Rochester Hills (G-13494)
Sam Brown Sales LLC ....E 248 358-2626
  Farmington (G-4911)
Southern Auto Wholesalers Inc ....F 248 335-5555
  Pontiac (G-12869)
Teamtech Motorsports Safety ....G 989 792-4880
  Saginaw (G-14163)
Thyssenkrupp Automotive Sales ....F 248 530-2991
  Troy (G-16639)
Thyssenkrupp Automotive Sales ....E 248 530-2902
  Troy (G-16640)
United Foam A Ufp Tech Brnd ....D 616 949-8100
  Grand Rapids (G-6952)
Welk-Ko Fabricators Inc ....G 810 227-7500
  Brighton (G-2008)

MOTOR VEHICLE: Hardware

American Arrow Corp Inc ....G 248 435-6115
  Clawson (G-2971)
Dura Operating LLC ....C 248 299-7500
  Auburn Hills (G-846)
Grupo Antolin Michigan Inc ....E 989 635-5080
  Warren (G-17069)
Miller Industrial Products Inc ....E 517 783-2756
  Jackson (G-8528)
Tubular PDT Solutions NA LLC ....G 248 388-4664
  Troy (G-16656)
Twb of Indiana Inc ....E 734 289-6400
  Monroe (G-11081)

MOTOR VEHICLE: Radiators

Aerospace America Inc ....E 989 684-2121
  Bay City (G-1273)
AM Specialties Inc ....F 586 795-9000
  Sterling Heights (G-15258)
Heatex Warehouse LLC ....G 586 773-0770
  Roseville (G-13815)
Mahle Behr Troy Inc ....C 248 743-3700
  Troy (G-16481)
Mahle Behr USA Inc ....B 248 743-3700
  Troy (G-16483)
United Systems Group LLC ....G 810 227-4567
  Brighton (G-2004)
Valeo North America Inc ....C 313 883-8850
  Detroit (G-4421)

MOTOR VEHICLE: Shock Absorbers

Enertrols Inc ....E 734 595-4500
  Farmington Hills (G-4988)
Marelli Tennessee USA LLC ....G 248 418-3000
  Auburn Hills (G-942)
Marelli Tennessee USA LLC ....A 248 680-8872
  Troy (G-16485)
Ride Control LLC ....D 248 247-7600
  Farmington Hills (G-5115)
Tenneco Automotive Oper Co Inc ....E 734 243-8000
  Lansing (G-9269)
Tenneco Automotive Oper Co Inc ....B 734 243-8000
  Monroe (G-11074)
Thyssenkrupp Bilstein Amer Inc ....F 248 530-2900
  Troy (G-16641)

MOTOR VEHICLE: Steering Mechanisms

Douglas Autotech Corporation ....E 517 369-2315
  Bronson (G-2025)
Letts Industries Inc ....G 313 579-1100
  Detroit (G-4200)
Mason Forge & Die Inc ....F 517 676-2992
  Mason (G-10645)
Nexteer Automotive Corporation ....B 989 757-5000
  Saginaw (G-14104)
NSK Americas Inc ....C 734 913-7500
  Ann Arbor (G-577)
NSK Steering Systems Amer Inc ....C 734 913-7500
  Ann Arbor (G-578)
ZF Chassis Components LLC ....C 810 245-2000
  Lapeer (G-9494)
ZF Chassis Components LLC ....B 810 245-2000
  Lapeer (G-9495)

MOTOR VEHICLE: Wheels

Dicastal North America Inc ....B 616 303-0306
  Greenville (G-7127)
Maxion Fumagalli Auto USA ....D 734 737-5000
  Novi (G-11938)

Maxion Wheels ....D 734 737-5000
  Novi (G-11940)
Maxion Wheels USA LLC ....D 734 737-5000
  Novi (G-11942)

MOTOR VEHICLES & CAR BODIES

Adac Door Components Inc ....G 616 957-0311
  Grand Rapids (G-6139)
Advanced Def Vhcl Systems Corp ....E 248 391-3200
  Clarkston (G-2905)
Android Industries-Sterling ....E 586 486-5616
  Warren (G-16933)
Asp Grede Acquisitionco LLC ....G 248 727-1800
  Southfield (G-14842)
Asp Grede Intrmdate Hldngs LLC ....A 313 758-2000
  Detroit (G-3882)
Asp Hhi Acquisition Co Inc ....G 313 758-2000
  Detroit (G-3883)
Asp Hhi Intermediate Holdings ....G 248 727-1800
  Southfield (G-14843)
Asp Hhi Intrmdate Holdings Inc ....G 248 727-1800
  Southfield (G-14844)
Autoalliance Management Co ....A 734 782-7800
  Flat Rock (G-5348)
Autoform Development Inc ....F 616 392-4909
  Holland (G-7561)
BDS Company Inc ....E 517 279-2135
  Coldwater (G-3291)
Bearing Holdings LLC ....G 313 758-2000
  Detroit (G-3896)
Champion Bus Inc ....B 810 724-1753
  Imlay City (G-8197)
Chrysler Group LLC ....D 586 977-4900
  Sterling Heights (G-15288)
Citation Lost Foam Pttrns LLC ....E 248 727-1800
  Southfield (G-14868)
Cloyes Gear Holdings LLC ....G 313 758-2000
  Detroit (G-3940)
Eagle Assemblies Inc ....E 586 296-4836
  Fraser (G-5646)
FCA US LLC ....C 586 468-2891
  Mount Clemens (G-11130)
FCA US LLC ....D 313 956-6460
  Detroit (G-4055)
FCA US LLC ....B 248 576-5741
  Warren (G-17031)
FCA US LLC ....A 586 497-3630
  Warren (G-17029)
FCA US LLC ....A 800 247-9753
  Auburn Hills (G-868)
FCA US LLC ....D 586 978-0067
  Sterling Heights (G-15337)
Ficosa North America Corp ....E 248 307-2230
  Madison Heights (G-10253)
Ford Global Treasury Inc ....G 313 322-3000
  Dearborn (G-3708)
Ford Motor Company ....A 313 322-7715
  Dearborn (G-3711)
Forging Holdings LLC ....G 313 758-2000
  Detroit (G-4070)
Frank Industries Inc ....E 810 346-3234
  Brown City (G-2051)
G Tech Sales LLC ....G 586 803-9393
  Sterling Heights (G-15353)
Gearing Holdings LLC ....G 313 758-2000
  Detroit (G-4078)
General Motors Company ....B 313 667-1500
  Detroit (G-4082)
General Motors LLC ....A 313 972-6000
  Detroit (G-4086)
General Motors LLC ....C 313 556-5000
  Detroit (G-4087)
General Motors LLC ....A 248 857-3500
  Pontiac (G-12828)
Gestamp Mason LLC ....B 517 244-8800
  Mason (G-10641)
Gibbs Sports Amphibians Inc ....D 248 572-6670
  Oxford (G-12346)
GM Gdls Defense Group LLC ....G 586 825-4000
  Sterling Heights (G-15362)
GM Orion Assembly ....G 248 377-5260
  Lake Orion (G-9137)
Grede Machining LLC ....E 248 727-1800
  Southfield (G-14927)
Grede Omaha LLC ....E 248 727-1800
  Southfield (G-14928)
Grede Radford LLC ....E 248 727-1800
  Southfield (G-14929)
GSC Riii - Grede LLC ....G 248 727-1800
  Southfield (G-14933)

Employee Codes: A=Over 500 employees, B=251-500
C=101-250, D=51-100, E=20-50, F=10-19, G=3-9

2020 Harris Michigan
Industrial Directory

1307

MOTOR VEHICLES & CAR BODIES — PRODUCT SECTION

Hayes-Albion Corporation ....F ... 517 629-2141
  Jackson (G-8463)
Hhi Formtech LLC ....B ... 313 758-2000
  Detroit (G-4121)
Hhi Formtech Holdings LLC ....G ... 313 758-2000
  Detroit (G-4122)
Hhi Funding II LLC ....C ... 313 758-2000
  Detroit (G-4123)
Hhi Holdings LLC ....G ... 313 758-2000
  Detroit (G-4124)
Hme Inc ....C ... 616 534-1463
  Wyoming (G-18011)
Holbrook Racing Engines ....F ... 734 762-4315
  Livonia (G-9772)
Impact Forge Holdings LLC ....G ... 313 758-2000
  Detroit (G-4137)
Jeff Schaller Transport Inc ....G ... 810 724-7640
  Imlay City (G-8205)
Jernberg Holdings LLC ....G ... 313 758-2000
  Detroit (G-4161)
KYB Americas Corporation ....G ... 248 374-0100
  Novi (G-11923)
Kyklos Holdings Inc ....G ... 313 758-2000
  Detroit (G-4186)
Magna Steyr LLC ....C ... 248 740-0214
  Troy (G-16478)
Marrel Corporation ....G ... 616 863-9155
  Rockford (G-13578)
Maven Drive LLC ....D ... 313 667-1541
  Detroit (G-4220)
May Mobility Inc ....F ... 312 869-2711
  Ann Arbor (G-550)
Mobility Innovations LLC ....G ... 586 843-3816
  Shelby Township (G-14643)
Nationwide Design Inc ....F ... 586 254-5493
  Sterling Heights (G-15433)
Nexteer Automotive Corporation ......B ... 989 757-5000
  Saginaw (G-14104)
Pcm US Steering Holding LLC ....G ... 313 556-5000
  Detroit (G-4292)
Pims Co ....G ... 313 665-8837
  Detroit (G-4301)
Rivian Automotive LLC ....D ... 734 855-4350
  Plymouth (G-12739)
Roush Enterprises Inc ....E ... 313 294-8200
  Allen Park (G-207)
Saleen Special Vehicles Inc ....B ... 909 978-6700
  Troy (G-16591)
Shop IV Sbusid Inv Grede LLC ....B ... 248 727-1800
  Southfield (G-15027)
Supreme Gear Co ....E ... 586 775-6325
  Fraser (G-5736)
Tecstar LP ....D ... 734 604-8962
  Grand Blanc (G-5986)
Tesla Inc ....G ... 248 205-3206
  Troy (G-16637)
Think North America Inc ....E ... 313 565-6781
  Dearborn (G-3765)
Transglobal Design & Mfg LLC ....D ... 734 525-2651
  Auburn Hills (G-1030)
United Collision ....G ... 269 792-7274
  Wayland (G-17418)
Visteon Intl Holdings Inc ....F ... 734 710-2000
  Van Buren Twp (G-16794)
Visteon Systems LLC ....C ... 313 755-9500
  Dearborn (G-3768)
ZF TRW Auto Holdings Corp ....A ... 734 855-2600
  Livonia (G-10021)

MOTOR VEHICLES, WHOLESALE: Fire Trucks

Front Line Services Inc ....F ... 989 695-6633
  Freeland (G-5757)

MOTOR VEHICLES, WHOLESALE: Snowmobiles

Micro Engineering Inc ....E ... 616 534-9681
  Byron Center (G-2200)

MOTOR VEHICLES, WHOLESALE: Trailers, Truck, New & Used

Clydes Frame & Wheel Service ....F ... 248 338-0323
  Pontiac (G-12810)

MOTOR VEHICLES, WHOLESALE: Truck bodies

NBC Truck Equipment Inc ....E ... 586 774-4900
  Roseville (G-13845)

MOTOR VEHICLES, WHOLESALE: Trucks, commercial

Valley Truck Parts Inc ....D ... 616 241-5431
  Wyoming (G-18040)

MOTORCYCLE & BICYCLE PARTS: Frames

Assenmacher Lightweight Cycles .....G ... 810 635-7844
  Swartz Creek (G-15661)
Technique Inc ....D ... 517 789-8988
  Jackson (G-8585)

MOTORCYCLE ACCESS

Ron Watkins ....G ... 517 439-5451
  Hillsdale (G-7537)

MOTORCYCLE DEALERS

C & C Sports Inc ....E ... 810 227-7068
  Brighton (G-1895)
Motown Harley-Davidson Inc ....D ... 734 947-4647
  Taylor (G-15748)
Riverfront Cycle Inc ....G ... 517 482-8585
  Lansing (G-9418)

MOTORCYCLE PARTS & ACCESS DEALERS

Aftershock Motorsports ....G ... 586 273-1333
  Casco (G-2498)
Area Cycle Inc ....G ... 989 777-0850
  Bridgeport (G-1849)

MOTORCYCLE REPAIR SHOPS

Area Cycle Inc ....G ... 989 777-0850
  Bridgeport (G-1849)
C & C Sports Inc ....E ... 810 227-7068
  Brighton (G-1895)

MOTORCYCLES & RELATED PARTS

Detriot Choppers Inc ....G ... 586 498-8909
  Roseville (G-13792)
Marlin Corporation ....G ... 248 683-1536
  Orchard Lake (G-12167)
Pritech Corporation ....G ... 248 488-9120
  Canton (G-2420)

MOTORS: Electric

Allied Motion Technologies Inc ....C ... 989 725-5151
  Owosso (G-12278)
American Mitsuba Corporation ....C ... 989 773-0377
  Mount Pleasant (G-11169)
Bay Motor Products Inc ....E ... 231 941-0411
  Traverse City (G-15907)
Continental Auto Systems Inc ....B ... 248 209-4000
  Auburn Hills (G-820)
Denso Manufacturing NC Inc ....A ... 269 441-2040
  Battle Creek (G-1172)
Electric Apparatus Company ....E ... 248 682-7992
  Howell (G-8037)
Motor Products Corportation ....C ... 989 725-5151
  Owosso (G-12305)
Prestolite Electric LLC ....G ... 248 313-3807
  Novi (G-11978)
Prestolite Electric Holding ....G ... 248 313-3807
  Novi (G-11979)
Pro Slot Ltd ....G ... 616 897-6000
  Hartford (G-7386)
Reuland Electric Co ....D ... 517 546-4400
  Howell (G-8091)
Satori E-Technology Inc ....G ... 408 517-9130
  Farmington Hills (G-5120)
Southern Auto Wholesalers Inc ....F ... 248 335-5555
  Pontiac (G-12869)
Vandervest Electric Mtr & Fabg ....G ... 231 843-6196
  Ludington (G-10086)

MOTORS: Generators

ABB Motors and Mechanical Inc ......F ... 586 978-9800
  Sterling Heights (G-15248)
Ametek Inc ....F ... 248 435-7540
  Peck (G-12418)
Continental Auto Systems Inc ....E ... 248 267-9408
  Troy (G-16277)
Controlled Power Tech Inc ....D ... 248 825-0100
  Southfield (G-14873)
Detroit Coil Co ....E ... 248 658-1543
  Ferndale (G-5274)
Diamond Electric Mfg Corp ....F ... 734 995-5525
  Ann Arbor (G-420)
DMS Electric Apparatus Service ......E ... 269 349-7000
  Kalamazoo (G-8729)
Ehc Inc ....G ... 313 259-2266
  Detroit (G-4030)
Energy Products Inc ....G ... 248 866-5622
  Troy (G-16345)
Etx Holdings Inc ....G ... 989 463-1151
  Alma (G-237)
Feed - Lease Corp ....E ... 248 377-0000
  Auburn Hills (G-871)
Flint Hydrostatics Inc ....F ... 901 794-2462
  Chesterfield (G-2777)
Ford Motor Company ....A ... 734 484-8000
  Ypsilanti (G-18074)
Fortis Energy Services Inc ....E ... 231 258-4596
  Bloomfield Hills (G-1766)
Fortis Energy Services Inc ....D ... 248 283-7100
  Troy (G-16370)
Gast Manufacturing Inc ....B ... 269 926-6171
  Benton Harbor (G-1503)
Genco Alliance LLC ....E ... 269 216-5500
  Kalamazoo (G-8748)
H W Jencks Incorporated ....E ... 231 352-4422
  Frankfort (G-5603)
Heco Inc ....D ... 269 381-7200
  Kalamazoo (G-8762)
Hydraulex Intl Holdings Inc ....E ... 914 682-2700
  Chesterfield (G-2786)
Independent Mfg Solutions Corp .....E ... 248 960-3550
  Wixom (G-17833)
Induction Engineering Inc ....F ... 586 716-4700
  New Baltimore (G-11486)
Industrial Computer & Controls ......F ... 734 697-4152
  Van Buren Twp (G-16765)
Magna E-Car USA LLC ....C ... 248 606-0600
  Holly (G-7885)
Magna E-Car USA LLC ....G ... 248 606-0600
  Holly (G-7886)
Maxitrol Company ....E ... 517 486-2820
  Blissfield (G-1719)
Milair LLC ....G ... 513 576-0123
  Sterling Heights (G-15425)
Minowitz Manufacturing Co ....E ... 586 779-5940
  Huntington Woods (G-8190)
Monarch Electric Service Co ....E ... 313 388-7800
  Melvindale (G-10702)
Morrell Incorporated ....D ... 248 373-1600
  Auburn Hills (G-949)
Mtu Onsite Energy Corporation ....G ... 805 879-3499
  Walled Lake (G-16899)
Nidec Motors & Actuators (usa) ......E ... 248 340-9977
  Auburn Hills (G-957)
Patriot Sensors & Contrls Corp ....D ... 248 435-0700
  Clawson (G-2983)
Pontiac Coil Inc ....C ... 248 922-1100
  Clarkston (G-2947)
Power Controllers LLC ....G ... 248 888-9896
  Farmington Hills (G-5098)
Powerthru Inc ....G ... 734 583-5004
  Livonia (G-9892)
Powerthru Inc ....F ... 734 853-5004
  Livonia (G-9893)
Twm Technology LLC ....F ... 989 684-7050
  Bay City (G-1365)
Z & R Electric Service Inc ....F ... 906 774-0468
  Iron Mountain (G-8306)

MOTORS: Pneumatic

Jamco Manufacturing Inc ....G ... 248 852-1988
  Auburn Hills (G-918)
Matt and Dave LLC ....G ... 734 439-1988
  Dundee (G-4595)

MOTORS: Starting, Automotive & Aircraft

Auto Electric International ....F ... 248 354-2082
  Southfield (G-14846)
Kessler USA Inc ....F ... 734 404-0152
  Plymouth (G-12666)
Prestolite Electric LLC ....G ... 248 313-3807
  Novi (G-11978)
Prestolite Electric Holding ....A ... 248 313-3807
  Novi (G-11979)

PRODUCT SECTION

NETTING: Cargo

Robert Bosch LLC .... E 248 921-9054
  Novi *(G-11987)*
Robert Bosch LLC .... A 734 979-3000
  Plymouth *(G-12741)*
Southern Auto Wholesalers Inc .... F 248 335-5555
  Pontiac *(G-12869)*

MOUTHWASHES

Abaco Partners LLC .... C 616 532-1700
  Kentwood *(G-8997)*
Microcide Inc .... G 248 526-9663
  Troy *(G-16506)*

MUCILAGE

Trenton Corporation .... E 734 424-3600
  Ann Arbor *(G-680)*

MUSEUMS

Pewabic Society Inc .... E 313 626-2000
  Detroit *(G-4300)*

MUSIC BOXES

Imagillation Inc .... G 734 481-0140
  Ypsilanti *(G-18079)*

MUSIC BROADCASTING SVCS

Archer Record Pressing Co .... G 313 365-9545
  Detroit *(G-3875)*

MUSIC DISTRIBUTION APPARATUS

American Mus Environments Inc .... F 248 646-2020
  Bloomfield Hills *(G-1744)*

MUSIC RECORDING PRODUCER

Ball Hard Music Group LLC .... G 734 636-0038
  Monroe *(G-11018)*
Developmental Services Inc .... G 313 653-1185
  Detroit *(G-4006)*

MUSICAL INSTRUMENT LESSONS

Mathew Parmelee .... G 248 894-5955
  Rochester Hills *(G-13468)*

MUSICAL INSTRUMENTS & ACCESS: NEC

Farmer Musical Instruments .... G 206 412-5379
  Cedar *(G-2541)*
Ferrees Tools Inc .... E 269 965-0511
  Battle Creek *(G-1187)*

MUSICAL INSTRUMENTS & ACCESS: Pipe Organs

Adams Jerroll Organ Builder .... G 734 439-7203
  Milan *(G-10931)*
Lauck Pipe Organ Co .... G 269 694-4500
  Otsego *(G-12243)*
Wigton Pipe Organs Inc .... G 810 796-3311
  Dryden *(G-4573)*

MUSICAL INSTRUMENTS & PARTS: String

Kyoei Electronics America Inc .... F 248 773-3690
  Novi *(G-11924)*

MUSICAL INSTRUMENTS & SPLYS STORES

Black Swamp Percussion LLC .... G 800 557-0988
  Zeeland *(G-18122)*
Gundry Media Inc .... G 616 734-8977
  Grand Rapids *(G-6486)*
Heritage Guitar Inc .... F 269 385-5721
  Kalamazoo *(G-8768)*
Stedman Corp .... G 269 629-5930
  Richland *(G-13256)*

MUSICAL INSTRUMENTS & SPLYS STORES: String instruments

Alf Enterprises Inc .... G 734 665-2012
  Ann Arbor *(G-351)*

MUSICAL INSTRUMENTS/SPLYS STORE: Drums/Rltd Percussion Instr

Rebeats .... F 989 463-4757
  Alma *(G-248)*

MUSICAL INSTRUMENTS: Autophones/Organs W/Perfrtd Music Rolls

Harman Becker Auto Systems Inc .... B 248 785-2361
  Novi *(G-11896)*

MUSICAL INSTRUMENTS: Fretted Instruments & Parts

Heritage Guitar Inc .... F 269 385-5721
  Kalamazoo *(G-8768)*

MUSICAL INSTRUMENTS: Guitars & Parts, Electric & Acoustic

Black Swamp Percussion LLC .... G 800 557-0988
  Zeeland *(G-18122)*
Fred Kelly Picks LLC .... G 989 348-2938
  Grayling *(G-7106)*
Ghs Corporation .... B 269 968-3351
  Springfield *(G-15192)*
Grip Studios .... G 248 757-0796
  Plymouth *(G-12633)*
Gundry Media Inc .... G 616 734-8977
  Grand Rapids *(G-6486)*

MUSICAL INSTRUMENTS: Organ Parts & Materials

Rt Swanson Inc .... G 517 627-4955
  Grand Ledge *(G-6115)*

MUSICAL INSTRUMENTS: Organs

Brian M Fowler Pipe Organs .... G 517 485-3748
  Eaton Rapids *(G-4719)*

MUSICAL INSTRUMENTS: Saxophones & Parts

Klingler Consulting & Mfg .... F 810 765-3700
  Marine City *(G-10476)*

MUSICAL INSTRUMENTS: Strings, Instrument

GHS Corporation .... E 800 388-4447
  Springfield *(G-15193)*
Guarneri House LLC .... G 616 451-4960
  Hudsonville *(G-8158)*

MUSICAL INSTRUMENTS: Violins & Parts

Alf Enterprises Inc .... G 734 665-2012
  Ann Arbor *(G-351)*

NAILS: Steel, Wire Or Cut

National Nail Corp .... C 616 538-8000
  Wyoming *(G-18021)*

NAME PLATES: Engraved Or Etched

Cushion Lrry Trphies Engrv LLC .... G 517 332-1667
  Lansing *(G-9358)*
Dag Ltd LLC .... F 586 276-9310
  Sterling Heights *(G-15307)*
Detroit Name Plate Etching Inc .... E 248 543-5200
  Ferndale *(G-5278)*
Joseph M Hoffman Inc .... F 586 774-8500
  Roseville *(G-13824)*
Royal Oak Name Plate Company .... F 586 774-8500
  Roseville *(G-13863)*

NAMEPLATES

American Label & Tag Inc .... E 734 454-7600
  Canton *(G-2347)*

NATIONAL SECURITY FORCES

Dla Document Services .... G 269 961-4895
  Battle Creek *(G-1175)*

NATURAL GAS COMPRESSING SVC, On-Site

Riverside Energy Michigan LLC .... E 231 995-4000
  Traverse City *(G-16095)*

NATURAL GAS DISTRIBUTION TO CONSUMERS

Howard Energy Co Inc .... E 231 995-7850
  Traverse City *(G-15999)*
Option Energy LLC .... F 269 329-4317
  Traverse City *(G-16061)*

NATURAL GAS LIQUIDS PRODUCTION

Tronox Incorporated .... G 231 328-4986
  Merritt *(G-10765)*

NATURAL GAS PRODUCTION

A1 Utility Contractor Inc .... D 989 324-8581
  Evart *(G-4877)*
DTE Energy Co .... F 616 632-2663
  Grand Rapids *(G-6362)*
Jackhill Oil Company .... G 734 994-6599
  Ann Arbor *(G-509)*
Linn Energy Inc .... E 231 922-7302
  Traverse City *(G-16026)*
McNic Oil & Gas Properties .... G 313 256-5500
  Detroit *(G-4223)*
Michael R Burzynski .... G 989 732-1820
  Gaylord *(G-5881)*
Option Energy LLC .... F 269 329-4317
  Traverse City *(G-16061)*

NATURAL GAS STORAGE SVCS

Howard Energy Co Inc .... E 231 995-7850
  Traverse City *(G-15999)*

NATURAL GAS TRANSMISSION & DISTRIBUTION

Altagas Marketing (us) Inc .... G 810 887-4105
  Port Huron *(G-12885)*
Altagas Power Holdings US Inc .... G 810 887-4105
  Port Huron *(G-12886)*
DTE Energy Company .... E 313 235-4000
  Detroit *(G-4019)*
DTE Energy Trust II .... G 313 235-8822
  Detroit *(G-4021)*

NATURAL GASOLINE PRODUCTION

Altagas Marketing (us) Inc .... G 810 887-4105
  Port Huron *(G-12885)*
Altagas Power Holdings US Inc .... G 810 887-4105
  Port Huron *(G-12886)*
Everest Energy Fund L L C .... G 586 445-2300
  Warren *(G-17023)*

NATURAL LIQUEFIED PETROLEUM GAS PRODUCTION

Genesee Valley Petroleum .... G 231 946-8630
  Traverse City *(G-15977)*

NATURAL RESOURCE PRESERVATION SVCS

North American Aqua Envmtl LLC .... F 269 476-2092
  Vandalia *(G-16802)*

NAUTICAL REPAIR SVCS

Schwartz Boiler Shop Inc .... G 231 627-2556
  Cheboygan *(G-2694)*

NAVIGATIONAL SYSTEMS & INSTRUMENTS

Applied Analytics Inc .... F 616 285-7810
  Grand Rapids *(G-6173)*
Harman Becker Auto Systems Inc .... B 248 785-2361
  Novi *(G-11896)*

NEIGHBORHOOD DEVELOPMENT GROUP

Hope Focus .... C 313 494-5500
  Detroit *(G-4129)*

NETTING: Cargo

Networks Enterprises Inc .... G 248 446-8590
  New Hudson *(G-11549)*

Employee Codes: A=Over 500 employees, B=251-500
C=101-250, D=51-100, E=20-50, F=10-19, G=3-9

NEW & USED CAR DEALERS • PRODUCT SECTION

NEW & USED CAR DEALERS
General Motors LLC..................F....... 586 731-2743
  Sterling Heights *(G-15358)*
Michigan East Side Sales LLC..............G....... 989 354-6867
  Alpena *(G-299)*

NEWS DEALERS & NEWSSTANDS
Daughtry Nwspapers Investments........F....... 269 683-2100
  Niles *(G-11606)*

NEWSPAPERS & PERIODICALS NEWS REPORTING SVCS
Newark Morning Ledger Co ....E....... 517 487-8888
  Lansing *(G-9406)*

NEWSPAPERS, WHOLESALE
Herald Newspapers Company Inc ....D....... 810 766-6100
  Flint *(G-5446)*

NICKEL ALLOY
David Nickels..............................G....... 248 634-5420
  Holly *(G-7873)*
Dodge West Joe Nickel ....G....... 810 691-2133
  Clio *(G-3270)*
Tom Nickels..................................G....... 248 348-7974
  Northville *(G-11729)*

NONCURRENT CARRYING WIRING DEVICES
Allied Tube & Conduit Corp ....C....... 734 721-4040
  Wayne *(G-17422)*
Apw...G....... 231 922-1863
  Traverse City *(G-15895)*
Ews Legacy LLC ....E....... 248 853-6363
  Rochester Hills *(G-13421)*
Meter Devices Company Inc ....A....... 330 455-0301
  Farmington Hills *(G-5064)*
Riley Enterprises LLC.........................G....... 517 263-9115
  Adrian *(G-90)*
Tesa Tape Inc................................G....... 616 785-6970
  Grand Rapids *(G-6924)*
Tesa Tape Inc................................D....... 616 887-3107
  Sparta *(G-15116)*
Zygot Operations Limited ....F....... 810 736-2900
  Flint *(G-5529)*

NONDAIRY BASED FROZEN DESSERTS
Sugar Kissed Cupcakes LLC..................G....... 231 421-9156
  Traverse City *(G-16115)*

NONFERROUS: Rolling & Drawing, NEC
Anchor Lamina America Inc ....C....... 231 533-8646
  Bellaire *(G-1434)*
Anchor Lamina America Inc ....E....... 248 489-9122
  Novi *(G-11826)*
Autocam-Pax Inc ....E....... 269 782-5186
  Dowagiac *(G-4534)*
Concept Alloys Inc............................G....... 734 449-9680
  Whitmore Lake *(G-17692)*
Dirksen Screw Products Co..................E....... 586 247-5400
  Shelby Township *(G-14579)*
Moheco Products Company ....G....... 734 855-4194
  Livonia *(G-9847)*
Ncoc Inc ....E....... 248 548-5950
  Oak Park *(G-12088)*
Oerlikon Metco (us) Inc ....E....... 248 288-0027
  Troy *(G-16533)*
Radiolgical Fabrication Design ....G....... 810 632-6000
  Howell *(G-8087)*
Traverse City Products Inc..................D....... 231 946-4414
  Traverse City *(G-16128)*
Weldall Corporation ....G....... 989 375-2251
  Elkton *(G-4786)*

NONMETALLIC MINERALS: Support Activities, Exc Fuels
Aquila Resources Inc ....G....... 906 352-4024
  Menominee *(G-10724)*
Detroit Salt Company LC....................E....... 313 554-0456
  Detroit *(G-4001)*

NOTEBOOKS, MADE FROM PURCHASED MATERIALS
Scientific Notebook Company ....F....... 269 429-8285
  Stevensville *(G-15580)*

NOTIONS: Buttons, Collar Or Cuff, Exc Semi & Precious
Schafer Products Co ....G....... 517 238-2266
  Coldwater *(G-3329)*

NOTIONS: Fasteners, Glove
Ebinger Manufacturing Company ....F....... 248 486-8880
  Brighton *(G-1917)*

NOVELTIES
Engineering Graphics Inc ....G....... 517 485-5828
  Lansing *(G-9225)*
Maple Ridge Companies Inc ....E....... 989 356-4807
  Posen *(G-13070)*
McLeod Wood and Christmas Pdts.......G....... 989 777-4800
  Bridgeport *(G-1853)*
Rodco Ltd ....G....... 517 244-0200
  Holt *(G-7923)*

NOVELTIES, DURABLE, WHOLESALE
Rodco Ltd ....G....... 517 244-0200
  Holt *(G-7923)*

NOVELTIES: Plastic
Fitness Finders Inc ....E....... 517 750-1500
  Jackson *(G-8449)*

NOZZLES & SPRINKLERS Lawn Hose
Titan Sprinkler LLC...........................G....... 517 540-1851
  Howell *(G-8111)*

NOZZLES: Fire Fighting
Douglass Safety Systems LLC ....G....... 989 687-7600
  Sanford *(G-14449)*

NOZZLES: Spray, Aerosol, Paint Or Insecticide
Incoe Corporation ....C....... 248 616-0220
  Auburn Hills *(G-910)*
Spraying Systems Co ....F....... 248 473-1331
  Farmington Hills *(G-5128)*

NURSERIES & LAWN & GARDEN SPLY STORE, RET: Lawn/Garden Splys
D & G Equipment Inc ....C....... 517 655-4606
  Williamston *(G-17729)*
Lumberjack Shack Inc ....G....... 810 724-7230
  Imlay City *(G-8207)*

NURSERIES & LAWN & GARDEN SPLY STORES, RETAIL: Fertilizer
Corunna Mills Feed LLC ....G....... 989 743-3110
  Corunna *(G-3580)*

NURSERIES & LAWN/GARDEN SPLY STORE, RET: Lawnmowers/Tractors
Area Cycle Inc ....G....... 989 777-0850
  Bridgeport *(G-1849)*
Bader & Co ....E....... 810 648-2404
  Sandusky *(G-14429)*
C & C Sports Inc...............................E....... 810 227-7068
  Brighton *(G-1895)*
D P Equipment Co.............................F....... 517 368-5266
  Camden *(G-2340)*
Ebels Hardware Inc...........................F....... 231 826-3334
  Falmouth *(G-4892)*

NURSERIES & LAWN/GARDEN SPLY STORES, RET: Garden Splys/Tools
Growgeneration Michigan Corp ....G....... 248 473-0450
  Lansing *(G-9379)*

NURSERIES/LAWN/GRDN SPLY STORE, RET: Nursery Stck, Seed/Bulb
Walters Seed Co LLC ....F....... 616 355-7333
  Holland *(G-7852)*

NURSERY & GARDEN CENTERS
Lake Orion Concrete Orna Pdts ....G....... 248 693-8683
  Lake Orion *(G-9144)*
Wahmhoff Farms LLC........................F....... 269 628-4308
  Gobles *(G-5950)*

NURSERY STOCK, WHOLESALE
Bruning Forest Products......................C....... 989 733-2880
  Onaway *(G-12145)*

NURSING CARE FACILITIES: Skilled
Worthington Armstrong Venture ....F....... 269 934-6200
  Benton Harbor *(G-1572)*

NUTRITION SVCS
Extreme Fitness Gym ....G....... 989 681-8339
  Saint Louis *(G-14363)*
Kemin Industries Inc..........................F....... 248 869-3080
  Plymouth *(G-12663)*

NUTS: Metal
Ankara Industries Incorporated............F....... 586 749-1190
  Chesterfield *(G-2740)*
Fastenetch ....G....... 313 299-8500
  Romulus *(G-13675)*
Federal Screw Works..........................C....... 734 941-4211
  Romulus *(G-13677)*
Hexagon Enterprises Inc ....E....... 248 583-0550
  Troy *(G-16395)*
Lay Manufacturing Inc........................G....... 313 369-1627
  Warren *(G-17125)*
Midwest Acorn Nut Company ....E....... 800 422-6887
  Troy *(G-16508)*
Perigee Manufacturing Co Inc ....F....... 313 933-4420
  Detroit *(G-4298)*
Rippa Products Inc ....E....... 906 337-0010
  Calumet *(G-2333)*
Rush Machining Inc ....F....... 248 583-0550
  Troy *(G-16585)*
Taper-Line Inc..................................G....... 586 775-5960
  Clinton Township *(G-3243)*
Vamp Screw Products Company..........E....... 734 676-8020
  Brownstown Twp *(G-2076)*

OFFICE EQPT WHOLESALERS
Clare Print & Pulp ....G....... 989 386-3497
  Clare *(G-2867)*
Lowry Holding Company Inc ....C....... 810 229-7200
  Brighton *(G-1952)*
Maleports Sault Prtg Co Inc.................E....... 906 632-3369
  Sault Sainte Marie *(G-14468)*
Reyers Company Inc ....F....... 616 414-5530
  Spring Lake *(G-15172)*

OFFICE EQPT, WHOLESALE: Photocopy Machines
Technology Network Svcs Inc ....F....... 586 294-7771
  Saint Clair Shores *(G-14271)*

OFFICE SPLY & STATIONERY STORES
Fedex Office & Print Svcs Inc ....E....... 616 957-7888
  Grand Rapids *(G-6405)*
Horn Corporation ....E....... 248 583-7789
  Troy *(G-16402)*
Office Express Inc.............................E....... 248 307-1850
  Troy *(G-16534)*

OFFICE SPLY & STATIONERY STORES: Office Forms & Splys
Big Rapids Printing............................G....... 231 796-8588
  Grand Rapids *(G-6220)*
Business Helper LLC ....G....... 231 271-4404
  Suttons Bay *(G-15651)*
Cadillac Printing Company ....F....... 231 775-2488
  Cadillac *(G-2239)*
Clare Print & Pulp ....G....... 989 386-3497
  Clare *(G-2867)*

PRODUCT SECTION

OILS & GREASES: Lubricating

Compatible Laser Products Inc ....F 810 629-0459
  Fenton (G-5197)
Fas N Nedschroef Amer Inc ....G 586 795-1220
  Sterling Heights (G-15336)
Garants Office Sups & Prtg Inc ....G 989 356-3930
  Alpena (G-291)
Gazelle Publishing ....G 734 529-2688
  Dundee (G-4584)
Hawk Design Inc ....G 989 781-1152
  Saginaw (G-14055)
Jackpine Press Incorporated ....F 231 723-8344
  Manistee (G-10425)
L D J Inc ....F 906 524-6194
  Lanse (G-9198)
Northland Publishers Inc ....F 906 265-9927
  Iron River (G-8318)
Ontonagon Herald Co Inc ....G 906 884-2826
  Ontonagon (G-12163)
Peterson Publishing Inc ....G 906 387-3282
  Munising (G-11247)
Print n go ....G 989 362-6041
  East Tawas (G-4694)
Rush Stationers Printers Inc ....F 989 891-9305
  Bay City (G-1351)
Specifications Service Company ....F 248 353-0244
  Bloomfield (G-1736)
W B Mason Co Inc ....D 734 947-6370
  Taylor (G-15780)
Wakefield News ....G 906 224-9561
  Wakefield (G-16856)

OFFICE SPLYS, NEC, WHOLESALE

Intra Business LLC ....G 269 262-0863
  Niles (G-11621)
JL Geisler Sign Company ....F 586 574-1800
  Troy (G-16438)
Maleports Sault Prtg Co Inc ....E 906 632-3369
  Sault Sainte Marie (G-14468)
Mis Associates Inc ....G 844 225-8156
  Pontiac (G-12850)
Office Connection Inc ....E 248 871-2003
  Farmington Hills (G-5086)

OFFICES & CLINICS OF DOCTORS OF MEDICINE: Dermatologist

Harper Dermatology PC ....G 586 776-7546
  Grosse Pointe Shores (G-7199)

OFFICES & CLINICS OF DOCTORS OF MEDICINE: Psychiatrist

Therapyline Technologies Inc ....E 734 407-9626
  Brownstown (G-2068)

OFFICES & CLINICS OF DOCTORS OF MEDICINE: Surgeon, Plastic

Luma Laser and Medi Spa ....G 248 817-5499
  Troy (G-16466)

OFFICES & CLINICS OF DRS OF MED: Cardiologist & Vascular

Iha Vsclar Endvsclar Spcalists ....G 734 712-8150
  Ypsilanti (G-18078)

OFFICES & CLINICS OF DRS OF MED: Health Maint Org Or HMO

Hackley Health Ventures Inc ....G 231 728-5720
  Muskegon (G-11342)

OFFICES & CLINICS OF DRS OF MEDICINE: Physician, Orthopedic

Orthopaedic Associates Mich ....D 616 459-7101
  Grand Rapids (G-6734)
Orthoview LLC ....G 800 318-0923
  Plymouth (G-12705)

OFFICES & CLINICS OF HEALTH PRACTITIONERS: Nutrition

Nubreed Nutrition Inc ....G 734 272-7395
  Troy (G-16529)

OFFICES & CLINICS OF HEALTH PRACTITIONERS: Occu Therapist

Hackley Health Ventures Inc ....G 231 728-5720
  Muskegon (G-11342)

OFFICES & CLINICS OF HEALTH PRACTITIONERS: Physical Therapy

Stryker Far East Inc ....E 269 385-2600
  Portage (G-13044)

OFFICES & CLINICS OF OPTOMETRISTS: Specialist, Optometrists

Bad Axe Family Vision Center ....G 989 269-5393
  Bad Axe (G-1058)

OIL & GAS FIELD MACHINERY

Blackmer ....D 616 241-1611
  Grand Rapids (G-6229)
Merrill Technologies Group Inc ....C 989 462-0330
  Alma (G-241)
N G S G I Natural Gas Ser ....G 989 786-3788
  Lewiston (G-9553)
Ranch Production LLC ....F 231 869-2050
  Pentwater (G-12430)
Titan Global Oil Services Inc ....F 248 594-5983
  Birmingham (G-1705)

OIL FIELD MACHINERY & EQPT

Cameron International Corp ....D 248 646-6743
  Beverly Hills (G-1615)
Cameron International Corp ....E 231 788-7020
  Muskegon (G-11290)
General Machine Services ....G 269 695-2244
  Buchanan (G-2119)
Millennium Planet LLC ....G 248 835-2331
  Farmington Hills (G-5068)
United Metal Technology Inc ....F 517 787-7940
  Jackson (G-8599)

OIL FIELD SVCS, NEC

B & H Cementing Services Inc ....G 989 773-5975
  Mount Pleasant (G-11172)
Baker Hghes Olfld Oprtions LLC ....G 989 772-1600
  Mount Pleasant (G-11174)
Baker Hghes Olfld Oprtions LLC ....F 989 773-7992
  Mount Pleasant (G-11175)
Beckman Production Svcs Inc ....D 231 258-9524
  Kalkaska (G-8939)
Beckman Production Svcs Inc ....E 989 539-7126
  Harrison (G-7309)
Beckman Production Svcs Inc ....G 231 885-1665
  Mesick (G-10766)
Beckman Production Svcs Inc ....E 989 732-9341
  Gaylord (G-5850)
Bruno Wojcik ....G 989 785-5555
  Atlanta (G-730)
Coil Drilling Technologies Inc ....G 989 773-6504
  Mount Pleasant (G-11190)
Cross Country Oilfld Svcs Inc ....G 337 366-3840
  Metamora (G-10774)
D & W Flow Testing Inc ....G 231 258-4926
  Kalkaska (G-8940)
Dama Tool & Gauge Company ....F 616 842-9631
  Norton Shores (G-11747)
Double Check Tools Service ....G 231 947-1632
  Williamsburg (G-17711)
Field Tech Services Inc ....G 989 786-7046
  Lewiston (G-9548)
Forsters and Sons Oil Change ....F 248 618-6860
  Waterford (G-17345)
Go Frac LLC ....E 817 731-0301
  Detroit (G-4094)
Great Lakes Compression Inc ....E 989 786-3788
  Lewiston (G-9549)
GTM Steamer Service Inc ....G 989 732-7678
  Gaylord (G-5863)
Jet Subsurface Rod Pumps Corp ....G 989 732-7513
  Gaylord (G-5869)
Lapeer Fuel Ventures Inc ....G 810 664-8770
  Lapeer (G-9466)
Loshaw Bros Inc ....G 989 732-7263
  Gaylord (G-5875)
Maximum Oilfield Service Inc ....E 989 731-0099
  Elmira (G-4791)
McConnell & Scully Inc ....E 517 568-4104
  Homer (G-7945)
Michigan Wireline Service ....F 989 772-5075
  Mount Pleasant (G-11205)
Mid State Oil Tools Inc ....E 989 773-4114
  Mount Pleasant (G-11207)
Mikes Steamer Service Inc ....E 231 258-8500
  Kalkaska (G-8954)
Northern Tank Truck Service ....G 989 732-7531
  Gaylord (G-5885)
Penin Oil & Gas Compan Michiga ....G 616 676-2090
  Ada (G-26)
Phoenix Operating Company Inc ....G 231 929-7171
  Williamsburg (G-17719)
Rcs Services Company LLC ....F 989 732-7999
  Johannesburg (G-8650)
Rowsey Construction & Dev LLC ....G 313 675-2464
  Detroit (G-4348)
Saginaw Valley Inst Mtls Inc ....G 989 496-2307
  Midland (G-10911)
Sappington Henry Machine & Tl ....E 989 345-0711
  West Branch (G-17522)
Schunk Oil Field Service Inc ....G 517 676-8900
  Mason (G-10654)
Seal Right Services Inc ....G 231 357-5595
  Buckley (G-2131)
Soli-Bond Inc ....G 989 684-9611
  Bay City (G-1359)
Srw Inc ....G 989 732-8884
  Traverse City (G-16110)
Srw Inc ....F 989 269-8528
  Bad Axe (G-1071)
Target Oil Tools LLC ....G 231 258-4960
  Kalkaska (G-8960)
Tuscola Energy ....G 989 894-5815
  Bay City (G-1364)
Uncle Eds Oil Shoppes Inc ....G 269 962-0999
  Battle Creek (G-1262)
Woder Construction Inc ....E 989 731-6371
  Gaylord (G-5900)

OILS & ESSENTIAL OILS

Stony Creek Essential Oils ....G 989 227-5500
  Saint Johns (G-14297)

OILS & GREASES: Blended & Compounded

Amcol Corporation ....E 248 414-5700
  Hazel Park (G-7434)
Argent Limited ....G 734 427-5533
  Livonia (G-9652)
Chicago Mfg & Dist Co ....G 989 665-2531
  Gagetown (G-5801)
Condat Corporation ....E 734 944-4994
  Saline (G-14383)
Lord Laboratories ....G 586 447-8955
  Saint Clair Shores (G-14260)
Marand Products Company Inc ....G 313 369-2000
  Detroit (G-4218)
Persons Inc ....G 989 734-3835
  Rogers City (G-13620)
Rap Products Inc ....G 989 893-5583
  Bay City (G-1348)
Sterling Oil & Chemical Co ....G 248 298-2973
  Royal Oak (G-13973)
TMC Group Inc ....F 248 819-6063
  Pleasant Ridge (G-12556)

OILS & GREASES: Lubricating

Apollo Idemitsu Corporation ....G 248 675-4345
  Wixom (G-17761)
BP Lubricants USA Inc ....E 231 689-0002
  White Cloud (G-17620)
Chemtool Incorporated ....G 734 439-7010
  Milan (G-10934)
Chrysan Industries Inc ....E 734 451-5411
  Plymouth (G-12597)
Coxen Enterprises Inc ....D 248 486-3800
  Brighton (G-1906)
Cummings-Moore Graphite Co ....E 313 841-1615
  Detroit (G-3957)
Diversified Chemical Tech Inc ....C 313 867-5444
  Detroit (G-4011)
Eastern Oil Company ....E 248 333-1333
  Pontiac (G-12819)
Excelda Mfg Holdg LLC ....F 517 223-8000
  Fowlerville (G-5563)
Fortech Products Inc ....E 248 446-9500
  Brighton (G-1925)
Fuchs Lubricants Co ....G 708 333-8900
  Grand Rapids (G-6423)

Employee Codes: A=Over 500 employees, B=251-500
C=101-250, D=51-100, E=20-50, F=10-19, G=3-9

2020 Harris Michigan Industrial Directory

1311

OILS & GREASES: Lubricating

Graphtek Inc .... G 810 985-4545
  Port Huron *(G-12923)*
H and M Lube DBA Jlube .... G 231 929-1197
  Traverse City *(G-15995)*
Idemitsu Lubricants Amer Corp .... F 248 355-0666
  Southfield *(G-14943)*
Lub-Tech Inc .... G 616 299-3540
  Grand Rapids *(G-6634)*
Lubecon Systems Inc .... D 231 689-0002
  White Cloud *(G-17625)*
MB Fluid Services LLC .... F 616 392-7036
  Holland *(G-7741)*
Oil Chem Inc .... E 810 235-3040
  Flint *(G-5476)*
Stt Usa Inc .... G 248 522-9655
  Wixom *(G-17898)*
Wilbur Products Inc .... F 231 755-3805
  Muskegon *(G-11451)*

OILS: Cutting

Edrich Products Inc .... F 586 296-3350
  Fraser *(G-5647)*
Houghton International Inc .... D 313 273-7374
  Detroit *(G-4131)*
Metalworking Lubricants Co .... C 248 332-3500
  Pontiac *(G-12849)*
Vaughan Industries Inc .... F 313 935-2040
  Detroit *(G-4423)*

OILS: Essential

Bio Source Naturals LLC .... G 734 335-6798
  Canton *(G-2352)*

OILS: Lubricating

Belding Quicklube Plus .... G 616 794-9548
  Belding *(G-1401)*
Bva Inc .... E 248 348-4920
  New Hudson *(G-11533)*
Joy-Max Inc .... G 616 847-0990
  Grand Haven *(G-6040)*
Lube Zone LLC .... G 313 543-2910
  Redford *(G-13169)*

OILS: Lubricating

A K Oil LLC DBA Speedy Oil and .... G 616 233-9505
  Grand Rapids *(G-6125)*
Big Rays Express Lube 28th St .... G 616 447-9710
  Grand Rapids *(G-6221)*
Cadillac Oil Company .... F 313 365-6200
  Detroit *(G-3926)*
Cobb Robert 3 Rachel .... G 616 374-7420
  Lake Odessa *(G-9113)*
Eastpointe Lube Express .... G 586 775-3234
  Eastpointe *(G-4701)*
Huron Industries Inc .... G 810 984-4213
  Port Huron *(G-12928)*
Khi Coating .... G 248 236-2100
  Oxford *(G-12353)*
Mr Lube Inc .... G 313 615-6161
  Wyandotte *(G-17969)*
Permawick Company Inc .... G 248 433-3500
  Birmingham *(G-1697)*
PMS Products Inc .... G 616 355-6615
  Holland *(G-7772)*
Quality Lube Express Inc .... G 586 421-0600
  Chesterfield *(G-2828)*
Warner Oil Company .... F 517 278-5844
  Coldwater *(G-3341)*
Xaerus Performance Fluids LLC .... E 989 631-7871
  Midland *(G-10927)*

OILS: Magnetic Inspection Or Powder

Toda America Incorporated .... G 269 962-0353
  Battle Creek *(G-1258)*

OPERATOR: Apartment Buildings

Arbor Woods Mfg Home Community .... G 734 482-4305
  Ypsilanti *(G-18052)*
Bahama Souvenirs Inc .... G 269 964-8275
  Battle Creek *(G-1149)*
Edgewater Apartments .... G 517 663-8123
  Eaton Rapids *(G-4722)*

OPERATOR: Nonresidential Buildings

Gehring Corporation .... D 248 478-8060
  Farmington Hills *(G-5008)*

Mercy Health Partners .... D 231 728-4032
  Muskegon *(G-11373)*

OPHTHALMIC GOODS

Diagnostic Instruments Inc .... E 586 731-6000
  Sterling Heights *(G-15316)*
Essilor Laboratories Amer Inc .... E 231 922-0344
  Traverse City *(G-15966)*
Flint Optical Company Inc .... G 810 235-4607
  Flint *(G-5429)*
General Scientific Corporation .... E 734 996-9200
  Ann Arbor *(G-471)*
Inland Diamond Products Co .... E 248 585-1762
  Madison Heights *(G-10276)*
Luxottica of America Inc .... E 517 349-0784
  Okemos *(G-12129)*
McKeon Products Inc .... E 586 427-7560
  Warren *(G-17146)*
Rx Optical Laboratories Inc .... G 269 349-7627
  Kalamazoo *(G-8879)*
Rx Optical Laboratories Inc .... G 269 965-5106
  Battle Creek *(G-1243)*
Rx Optical Laboratories Inc .... G 269 342-5958
  Kalamazoo *(G-8878)*
Tri State Optical Inc .... G 517 279-2701
  Coldwater *(G-3338)*

OPHTHALMIC GOODS WHOLESALERS

Rx Optical Laboratories Inc .... D 269 342-5958
  Kalamazoo *(G-8878)*
Tri State Optical Inc .... G 517 279-2701
  Coldwater *(G-3338)*

OPHTHALMIC GOODS, NEC, WHOLESALE: Frames

Hi-Tech Optical Inc .... E 989 799-9390
  Saginaw *(G-14057)*

OPHTHALMIC GOODS: Frames, Lenses & Parts, Eyeglasses

Cooperative Optical Services .... D 313 366-5100
  Detroit *(G-3948)*

OPHTHALMIC GOODS: Lenses, Ophthalmic

Bad Axe Family Vision Center .... G 989 269-5393
  Bad Axe *(G-1058)*
Fairway Optical Inc .... G 231 744-6168
  Muskegon *(G-11320)*
Vision-Craft Inc .... E 248 669-1130
  Commerce Township *(G-3456)*

OPHTHALMIC GOODS: Protectors, Eye

Noir Laser Company LLC .... E 800 521-9746
  Milford *(G-10977)*

OPTICAL GOODS STORES

Cooperative Optical Services .... D 313 366-5100
  Detroit *(G-3948)*

OPTICAL GOODS STORES: Eyeglasses, Prescription

Luxottica of America Inc .... E 517 349-0784
  Okemos *(G-12129)*

OPTICAL GOODS STORES: Opticians

Flint Optical Company Inc .... G 810 235-4607
  Flint *(G-5429)*
Rx Optical Laboratories Inc .... G 269 342-5958
  Kalamazoo *(G-8878)*
Rx Optical Laboratories Inc .... G 269 349-7627
  Kalamazoo *(G-8879)*
Rx Optical Laboratories Inc .... G 269 965-5106
  Battle Creek *(G-1243)*

OPTICAL INSTRUMENTS & APPARATUS

Berner Scientific Inc .... G 248 253-0077
  Dexter *(G-4477)*
Clark-Mxr Inc .... E 734 426-2803
  Dexter *(G-4481)*
General Dynamics Glbl IMG Tech .... A 248 293-2929
  Rochester Hills *(G-13432)*
General Dynamics Mission .... A 530 271-2500
  Rochester Hills *(G-13434)*

Perform3-D LLC .... G 734 604-4100
  Ann Arbor *(G-591)*
Visotek Inc .... F 734 427-4800
  Livonia *(G-9990)*

OPTICAL INSTRUMENTS & LENSES

Browe Inc .... G 248 877-3800
  Madison Heights *(G-10207)*
Carl Zeiss Indus Metrology LLC .... E 248 486-2670
  Brighton *(G-1897)*
Contour Metrological & Mfg Inc .... F 248 273-1111
  Troy *(G-16279)*
Crl Inc .... E 906 428-3710
  Gladstone *(G-5910)*
Diagnostic Instruments Inc .... E 586 731-6000
  Sterling Heights *(G-15316)*
Electro-Optics Technology Inc .... D 231 935-4044
  Traverse City *(G-15961)*
Eotech Inc .... G 734 741-8868
  Ann Arbor *(G-446)*
Eyewear Detroit Company .... G 248 396-2214
  Clarkston *(G-2920)*
First Optometry Lab .... G 248 546-1300
  Madison Heights *(G-10254)*
Jenoptik Automotive N Amer LLC .... C 248 853-5888
  Rochester Hills *(G-13453)*
Lumenflow Corp .... G 269 795-9007
  Grand Rapids *(G-6636)*
Magna Mirrors America Inc .... E 616 786-5120
  Grand Rapids *(G-6640)*
Magna Mirrors America Inc .... G 616 786-7000
  Holland *(G-7734)*
Magna Mirrors America Inc .... D 616 786-7300
  Holland *(G-7735)*
Magna Mirrors America Inc .... C 616 942-0163
  Newaygo *(G-11573)*
Michigan Development Corp .... C 734 302-4600
  Ann Arbor *(G-554)*
Optec Inc .... F 616 897-9351
  Lowell *(G-10039)*
Perceptron Inc .... C 734 414-6100
  Plymouth *(G-12712)*
Seneca Enterprises LLC .... C 231 943-1171
  Traverse City *(G-16100)*
Visioncraft .... G 586 949-6540
  Chesterfield *(G-2855)*
X-Rite Incorporated .... C 616 803-2100
  Grand Rapids *(G-7006)*

OPTICAL SCANNING SVCS

Software Finesse LLC .... G 248 737-8990
  Farmington Hills *(G-5126)*

OPTOMETRIC EQPT & SPLYS WHOLESALERS

Visioncraft .... G 586 949-6540
  Chesterfield *(G-2855)*

OPTOMETRISTS' OFFICES

Rx-Rite Optical Co .... E 586 294-8500
  Fraser *(G-5719)*

ORDNANCE

Autoneum North America Inc .... D 248 848-0100
  Farmington Hills *(G-4936)*
Camdex Inc .... G 248 528-2300
  Troy *(G-16256)*
Lanzen Incorporated .... D 586 771-7070
  Bruce Twp *(G-2090)*

ORGAN TUNING & REPAIR SVCS

Adams Jerroll Organ Builder .... G 734 439-7203
  Milan *(G-10931)*
Brian M Fowler Pipe Organs .... G 517 485-3748
  Eaton Rapids *(G-4719)*
Wigton Pipe Organs Inc .... G 810 796-3311
  Dryden *(G-4573)*

ORGANIZATIONS & UNIONS: Labor

Amalgamated Uaw .... G 231 734-9286
  Evart *(G-4878)*

ORGANIZATIONS: Medical Research

Imperial Clinical RES Svcs Inc .... C 616 784-0100
  Grand Rapids *(G-6528)*

PRODUCT SECTION

PACKAGING MATERIALS: Plastic Film, Coated Or Laminated

ORGANIZATIONS: Noncommercial Biological Research

Manufacturing & Indus Tech Inc..............E........ 248 814-8544
Lake Orion *(G-9147)*

ORGANIZATIONS: Physical Research, Noncommercial

Suematek...G........ 517 614-2235
Ypsilanti *(G-18103)*

ORGANIZATIONS: Religious

Ifca International Inc..............................G........ 616 531-1840
Grandville *(G-7051)*
Rosary Workshop...................................G........ 906 788-4846
Stephenson *(G-15239)*

ORGANIZATIONS: Research Institute

Kellogg Company ....B........ 269 961-2000
Battle Creek *(G-1210)*

ORGANIZATIONS: Scientific Research Agency

Innovative Weld Solutions LLC ....G........ 937 545-7695
Rochester *(G-13329)*
Teamtech Motorsports Safety................G........ 989 792-4880
Saginaw *(G-14163)*
TMC Group Inc ....F........ 248 819-6063
Pleasant Ridge *(G-12556)*

ORGANIZERS, CLOSET & DRAWER Plastic

Chadko LLC...G........ 616 402-9207
Grand Haven *(G-6002)*

ORNAMENTS: Christmas Tree, Exc Electrical & Glass

Keystone Products LLC ....G........ 248 363-5552
Southfield *(G-14954)*

ORNAMENTS: Lawn

Potteryland Inc......................................G........ 586 781-4425
Washington *(G-17310)*
Rmcs Wings Enterprise.........................G........ 269 426-3559
Sawyer *(G-14488)*

OUTBOARD MOTOR DEALERS

Leaders Inc..G........ 269 372-1072
Kalamazoo *(G-8807)*
Marsh Brothers Inc ....F........ 517 869-2653
Quincy *(G-13096)*

OUTLETS: Electric, Convenience

Dollars Sense...G........ 231 369-3610
Fife Lake *(G-5339)*

OVENS: Infrared

Thermal Designs & Mfg..........................E........ 248 476-2978
Novi *(G-12014)*

OVENS: Paint Baking & Drying

Belco Industries Inc...............................E........ 616 794-0410
Belding *(G-1400)*
Gallagher-Kaiser Corporation................D........ 313 368-3100
Troy *(G-16378)*
R J Manufacturing Incorporated............G........ 906 779-9151
Crystal Falls *(G-3613)*
Rapid Engineering LLC ....D........ 616 784-0500
Comstock Park *(G-3513)*

OVENS: Smelting

Fritz Enterprises....................................E........ 313 841-9460
Detroit *(G-4073)*

PACKAGING & LABELING SVCS

C W A Manufacturing Co Inc..................E........ 810 686-3030
Mount Morris *(G-11159)*
Connection Service Company ....F........ 269 926-2658
Benton Harbor *(G-1491)*
Coxen Enterprises Inc ....D........ 248 486-3800
Brighton *(G-1906)*
Delta Containers Inc..............................E........ 810 742-2730
Bay City *(G-1300)*
Display Pack Inc....................................C........ 616 451-3061
Cedar Springs *(G-2553)*
Domart LLC..G........ 616 285-9177
Grand Rapids *(G-6357)*
Euclid Industries Inc..............................C........ 989 686-8920
Bay City *(G-1310)*
Excelda Mfg Holdg LLC.........................F........ 517 223-8000
Fowlerville *(G-5563)*
Grand Industries Inc..............................E........ 616 846-7120
Grand Haven *(G-6026)*
Grand Rapids Label Company................D........ 616 459-8134
Grand Rapids *(G-6455)*
Helm Incorporated.................................D........ 734 468-3700
Plymouth *(G-12637)*
Inter-Pack Corporation...........................E........ 734 242-7755
Monroe *(G-11042)*
Locpac Inc..E........ 734 453-2300
Plymouth *(G-12677)*
Lotis Technologies Inc ....G........ 248 340-6065
Orion *(G-12182)*
March Coatings Inc................................D........ 810 229-6464
Brighton *(G-1953)*
Mollers North America Inc ....D........ 616 942-6504
Grand Rapids *(G-6698)*
Roskam Baking Company.......................C........ 616 574-5757
Grand Rapids *(G-6839)*
Tamsco Inc...F........ 586 415-1500
Fraser *(G-5737)*
TGI Direct Inc...G........ 810 239-5553
Flint *(G-5509)*
Total Packaging Solutions LLC ....G........ 248 519-2376
Troy *(G-16649)*
Watson Sales..G........ 517 296-4275
Montgomery *(G-11100)*
Zoomer Display LLC...............................G........ 616 734-0300
Grand Rapids *(G-7014)*

PACKAGING MATERIALS, INDL: Wholesalers

Commercial Mfg & Assembly Inc ....E........ 616 847-9980
Grand Haven *(G-6005)*

PACKAGING MATERIALS, WHOLESALE

Bear Packaging and Supply....................G........ 989 772-2268
Mount Pleasant *(G-11177)*
Delta Containers Inc..............................E........ 810 742-2730
Bay City *(G-1300)*
J W Manchester Company Inc ....G........ 810 632-5409
Hartland *(G-7393)*
Metals Preservation Group LLC ....F........ 586 944-2720
Saint Clair Shores *(G-14263)*
Oliver Products Company......................D........ 616 456-7711
Grand Rapids *(G-6728)*
Sekisui Plastics U S A Inc ....F........ 248 308-3000
Wixom *(G-17892)*
Valmec Inc...G........ 810 629-8750
Fenton *(G-5248)*
West Michigan Tag & Label Inc ....E........ 616 235-0120
Grand Rapids *(G-6987)*

PACKAGING MATERIALS: Paper

Advance Engineering Company.............E........ 989 435-3641
Beaverton *(G-1382)*
Allsales Enterprises Inc ....F........ 616 437-0639
Grand Rapids *(G-6164)*
Alpha Data Business Forms Inc............G........ 248 540-5930
Birmingham *(G-1674)*
American Label & Tag Inc ....E........ 734 454-7600
Canton *(G-2347)*
Anchor Bay Packaging Corp ....E........ 586 949-1500
Chesterfield *(G-2739)*
Andex Industries Inc..............................D........ 800 338-9882
Escanaba *(G-4811)*
Andex Industries Inc..............................E........ 906 786-7588
Escanaba *(G-4812)*
Argent Tape & Label Inc ....F........ 734 582-9956
Plymouth *(G-12573)*
CAM Packaging LLC..............................F........ 989 426-1200
Gladwin *(G-5925)*
Cello-Foil Products Inc..........................C........ 229 435-4777
Battle Creek *(G-1164)*
Cherokee Industries Inc ....E........ 248 333-1343
Pontiac *(G-12808)*
Classic Container Corporation..............E........ 734 853-3000
Livonia *(G-9684)*
Creative Foam Corporation...................D........ 810 714-0140
Fenton *(G-5199)*
Cummins Label Company......................E........ 269 345-3386
Kalamazoo *(G-8721)*
Delta Containers Inc..............................C........ 810 742-2730
Bay City *(G-1299)*
Fabricon Products Inc...........................F........ 313 841-8200
River Rouge *(G-13276)*
Fibre Converters Inc..............................E........ 269 279-1700
Constantine *(G-3535)*
General Tape Label Liquidating.............D........ 248 437-5200
Wixom *(G-17817)*
Holo-Source Corporation.......................G........ 734 427-1530
Livonia *(G-9773)*
Impact Label Corporation.......................E........ 269 381-4280
Galesburg *(G-5811)*
International Master Pdts Corp.............C........ 231 894-5651
Montague *(G-11091)*
J W Manchester Company Inc ....G........ 810 632-5409
Hartland *(G-7393)*
Jetco Packaging Solutions LLC ....G........ 616 588-2492
Grand Rapids *(G-6559)*
Loper Corporation..................................G........ 810 620-0202
Mount Morris *(G-11164)*
Macarthur Corp ....E........ 810 606-1777
Grand Blanc *(G-5975)*
MPS Lansing Inc....................................A........ 517 323-9000
Lansing *(G-9248)*
Noble Films Corporation........................G........ 616 977-3770
Ada *(G-25)*
Nyx Inc...B........ 734 261-7535
Livonia *(G-9870)*
Nyx LLC..C........ 734 462-2385
Livonia *(G-9871)*
Packaging Specialties Inc ....E........ 586 473-6703
Romulus *(G-13718)*
Shawmut Corporation............................C........ 810 987-2222
Port Huron *(G-12965)*
Shoreline Container Inc........................C........ 616 399-2088
Holland *(G-7800)*
Siliconature Corporation.......................E........ 312 987-1848
Caledonia *(G-2315)*
Smartstart Medical LLC........................G........ 616 227-4560
Grand Rapids *(G-6869)*
Stamp-Rite Incorporated ....E........ 517 487-5071
Lansing *(G-9267)*
Svrc Industries Inc................................D........ 989 723-8205
Owosso *(G-12320)*
Tesa Tape Inc...G........ 616 785-6970
Grand Rapids *(G-6924)*
Tesa Tape Inc...D........ 616 887-3107
Sparta *(G-15116)*
Timbertech Inc.......................................E........ 231 348-2750
Harbor Springs *(G-7295)*
Ufp Technologies Inc.............................D........ 616 949-8100
Grand Rapids *(G-6948)*
Unique Fabricating Inc ....E........ 248 853-2333
Auburn Hills *(G-1034)*
Unique Fabricating Na Inc....................B........ 248 853-2333
Auburn Hills *(G-1035)*

PACKAGING MATERIALS: Paper, Coated Or Laminated

Central Ohio Paper & Packg Inc............G........ 734 955-9960
Romulus *(G-13662)*
Dunn Paper Inc......................................F........ 810 984-5521
Port Huron *(G-12913)*
Tryco Inc ....F........ 734 953-6800
Farmington Hills *(G-5144)*
Venchurs Inc..E........ 517 263-1206
Adrian *(G-99)*
Venchurs Inc..F........ 517 263-8937
Adrian *(G-100)*
Verso Paper Holding LLC......................F........ 906 779-3200
Quinnesec *(G-13104)*
Verso Paper Holding LLC......................B........ 906 396-2358
Quinnesec *(G-13105)*
Watson Sales..G........ 517 296-4275
Montgomery *(G-11100)*
Zajac Industries Inc...............................F........ 586 489-6746
Clinton Township *(G-3264)*

PACKAGING MATERIALS: Plastic Film, Coated Or Laminated

Filcon Inc...F........ 989 386-2986
Clare *(G-2870)*
Quality Transparent Bag Inc ....F........ 989 893-3561
Bay City *(G-1344)*

Employee Codes: A=Over 500 employees, B=251-500
C=101-250, D=51-100, E=20-50, F=10-19, G=3-9

2020 Harris Michigan Industrial Directory

PACKAGING MATERIALS: Polystyrene Foam

Ameripak Inc	F	248 858-9000
Pontiac (G-12804)		
Barber Packaging Company	E	269 427-7995
Bangor (G-1089)		
Cantrick Kip Co	G	248 644-7622
Birmingham (G-1675)		
Classic Container Corporation	E	734 853-3000
Livonia (G-9684)		
Creative Foam Corporation	C	269 782-3483
Dowagiac (G-4537)		
Creative Foam Corporation	D	810 714-0140
Fenton (G-5199)		
Eagle Industries Inc	E	248 624-4266
Wixom (G-17797)		
Epic Materials Inc	G	586 294-0300
Fraser (G-5652)		
Fapco Inc	G	269 695-6889
Buchanan (G-2115)		
Fxi Inc	F	248 553-1039
Southfield (G-14917)		
Genesis Manufacturing Entps	G	734 243-5302
Monroe (G-11032)		
Global Autopack LLC	G	248 390-2434
New Hudson (G-11541)		
Kalamazoo Plastics Company	E	269 381-0010
Kalamazoo (G-8795)		
Meiki Corporation	G	248 680-4638
Troy (G-16492)		
N Pack Ship Center	G	906 863-4095
Menominee (G-10752)		
Nu-Pak Solutions Inc	F	231 755-1662
Norton Shores (G-11784)		
Ortus Enterprises LLC	G	269 491-1447
Portage (G-13020)		
Packaging Engineering LLC	G	248 437-9444
Brighton (G-1973)		
Pedmic Converting Inc	E	810 679-9600
Croswell (G-3602)		
Pregis LLC	F	616 520-1550
Grand Rapids (G-6767)		
Russell R Peters Co LLC	G	989 732-0660
Gaylord (G-5891)		
Sekisui Plastics US A Inc	F	248 308-3000
Wixom (G-17892)		
Sonoco Prtective Solutions Inc	D	989 723-3720
Owosso (G-12317)		
Superior Surface Protection Co	G	517 206-1541
Jackson (G-8579)		
Westpack Inc	G	231 725-9200
Muskegon (G-11448)		

PACKAGING: Blister Or Bubble Formed, Plastic

Innovative Packg Solutions LLC	G	517 213-3169
Holt (G-7914)		

PACKING & CRATING SVC

Action Wood Technologies Inc	E	586 468-2300
Clinton Township (G-3036)		
Industrial Wood Fab & Packg Co	G	734 284-4808
Riverview (G-13298)		

PACKING & CRATING SVCS: Containerized Goods For Shipping

Delta Containers Inc	C	810 742-2730
Bay City (G-1299)		
Fabricari LLC	G	734 972-2042
Dexter (G-4492)		

PACKING MATERIALS: Mechanical

Crk Ltd	G	586 779-5240
Eastpointe (G-4699)		
Green Polymeric Materials Inc	E	313 933-7390
Detroit (G-4102)		
Oliver Products Company	D	616 456-7711
Grand Rapids (G-6728)		
Package Design & Mfg Inc	E	248 486-4390
Brighton (G-1972)		

PACKING SVCS: Shipping

Ajax Metal Processing Inc	G	313 267-2100
Detroit (G-3850)		
Business Helper LLC	G	231 271-4404
Suttons Bay (G-15651)		
Cal-Chlor Corp	E	231 843-1147
Ludington (G-10051)		
Domart LLC	G	616 285-9177
Grand Rapids (G-6357)		
Donalyn Enterprises Inc	F	517 546-9798
Howell (G-8032)		
Epic Materials Inc	G	586 294-0300
Fraser (G-5652)		
Export Corporation	D	810 227-6153
Brighton (G-1920)		
Lake Michigan Mailers Inc	D	269 383-9333
Kalamazoo (G-8804)		
Mollewood Export Inc	E	248 624-1885
Wixom (G-17859)		
Pak-Rite Industries Inc	D	313 388-6400
Ecorse (G-4744)		

PADDING: Foamed Plastics

Brooklyn Products Intl	E	517 592-2185
Brooklyn (G-2036)		
Carcoustics Usa Inc	D	517 548-6700
Howell (G-8019)		
Nanosystems Inc	F	734 274-0020
Ann Arbor (G-570)		
Schmitz Foam Products LLC	E	517 781-6615
Coldwater (G-3330)		

PADS & PADDING: Insulator, Cordage

Hestia Inc	G	231 747-8157
Norton Shores (G-11760)		
Poly-Green Foam LLC	E	517 279-8019
Coldwater (G-3320)		

PADS: Athletic, Protective

Mike Vaughn Custom Sports Inc	E	248 969-8956
Oxford (G-12361)		

PAILS: Shipping, Metal

Shamrock Fabricating Inc	F	810 744-0677
Burton (G-2165)		

PAINT & PAINTING SPLYS STORE

Nelson Paint Company Mich Inc	G	906 774-5566
Iron Mountain (G-8291)		
Sames Kremlin Inc	C	734 979-0100
Plymouth (G-12747)		
Sames Kremlin Inc		734 979-0100
Plymouth (G-12748)		
Teknicolors Inc	G	734 414-9900
Canton (G-2434)		

PAINT & PAINTING SPLYS STORE: Brushes, Rollers, Sprayers

Mack Andrew & Son Brush Co	G	517 849-9272
Jonesville (G-8660)		

PAINT STORE

Arquette Concrete & Supply	G	989 846-4131
Standish (G-15216)		
Polymer Inc	D	248 353-3035
Southfield (G-15001)		
Port City Paints Mfg Inc	G	231 726-5911
Muskegon (G-11402)		
Repcolite Paints Inc	D	616 396-5213
Holland (G-7787)		

PAINTING SVC: Metal Prdts

Act Test Panels LLC	E	517 439-1485
Hillsdale (G-7515)		
Almond Products Inc	D	616 844-1813
Spring Lake (G-15132)		
Cg Liquidation Incorporated	E	586 575-9800
Warren (G-16978)		
Crm Inc	D	231 947-0304
Traverse City (G-15952)		
Express Coat Corporation	E	586 773-2682
Warren (G-17026)		
Finishers Unlimited Monroe Inc	E	734 243-3502
Monroe (G-11031)		
Finishing Specialties Inc	G	586 954-1338
Clinton Township (G-3118)		
Glw Finishing	E	616 395-0112
Holland (G-7644)		
H & J Mfg Consulting Svcs Corp	G	734 941-8314
Romulus (G-13684)		
Hj Manufacturing Inc	F	906 233-1500
Escanaba (G-4833)		
Knape Industries Inc	E	616 866-1651
Rockford (G-13577)		
Kopacz Industrial Painting	G	734 427-6740
Livonia (G-9799)		
Lincoln Industries	G	989 736-6421
Lincoln (G-9565)		
Locpac Inc	E	734 453-2300
Plymouth (G-12677)		
March Coatings Inc	D	810 229-6464
Brighton (G-1953)		
Material Sciences Corporation	F	734 207-4444
Canton (G-2398)		
Midwest Products Finshg Co Inc	C	734 856-5200
Ottawa Lake (G-12267)		
Paint Work Incorporated	F	586 759-6640
Warren (G-17179)		
PPG Coating Services	D	313 922-8433
Detroit (G-4307)		
Schroth Enterprises Inc	E	586 759-4240
Grosse Pointe Farms (G-7187)		
Seaver Finishing Inc	D	616 844-4360
Grand Haven (G-6073)		
Seaver-Smith Inc	E	616 842-8560
Grand Haven (G-6075)		
Specular LLC	G	248 680-1720
Sterling Heights (G-15505)		

PAINTS & ADDITIVES

Benchmark Coating Systems LLC	G	517 782-4061
Ann Arbor (G-382)		
Michigan Coating Products Inc	G	616 456-8800
Grand Rapids (G-6669)		
Michigan Industrial Finishes	E	248 553-7014
Farmington Hills (G-5065)		
Ncp Coatings Inc	D	269 683-3377
Niles (G-11631)		
Nelson Paint Company Ala Inc	G	906 774-5566
Kingsford (G-9064)		
Nelson Paint Company Mich Inc	G	906 774-5566
Iron Mountain (G-8291)		
Northern Coatings & Chem Co	E	906 863-2641
Menominee (G-10753)		
Peter-Lacke Usa LLC	G	248 588-9400
Troy (G-16545)		
PPG Industries Inc	E	517 394-9093
Lansing (G-9412)		
PPG Industries Inc	E	616 846-4400
Grand Haven (G-6063)		
PPG Industries Inc	E	517 263-7831
Adrian (G-86)		
PPG Industries Inc	F	248 641-2000
Troy (G-16557)		
Pro Coatings Inc	F	616 887-8808
Sparta (G-15107)		
Quantum Chemical LLC	G	734 429-0033
Livonia (G-9901)		
Red Spot Westland Inc	C	734 729-1913
Westland (G-17594)		
Repcolite Paints Inc	D	616 396-5213
Holland (G-7787)		
Vinyl Industrial Paints Inc	G	734 284-3536
Wyandotte (G-17979)		
Z Technologies Corporation	E	313 937-0710
Redford (G-13209)		

PAINTS & ALLIED PRODUCTS

Akzo Nobel Coatings Inc	D	248 451-6231
Pontiac (G-12800)		
Akzo Nobel Coatings Inc	E	248 637-0400
Troy (G-16177)		
Akzo Nobel Coatings Inc	E	248 451-6231
Troy (G-16178)		
Akzo Nobel Coatings Inc	G	248 528-0715
Troy (G-16179)		
Akzo Nobel Coatings Inc	E	312 544-7000
Troy (G-16180)		
All-Cote Coatings Company LLC	G	586 427-0062
Center Line (G-2577)		
Alloying Surfaces Inc	G	248 524-9200
Troy (G-16191)		
Axalta Coating Systems LLC	G	586 846-4160
Clinton Township (G-3061)		
BASF Construction Chem LLC	E	269 668-3371
Mattawan (G-10662)		
Cass Polymers	E	517 543-7510
Charlotte (G-2636)		
Chemetall US Inc	F	517 787-4846
Jackson (G-8408)		

PRODUCT SECTION

PALLETS: Plastic

Dhake Industries Inc..................................E...... 734 420-0101
  Plymouth *(G-12610)*
Douglas Corp..F...... 517 767-4112
  Tekonsha *(G-15818)*
Eco Smart Coatings LLC..........................G...... 574 370-5708
  Cassopolis *(G-2529)*
Eftec North America LLC ....D...... 248 585-2200
  Taylor *(G-15713)*
Flow Coatings LLC ....G...... 248 625-3052
  Clarkston *(G-2922)*
Full Spektrem LLC....................................G...... 313 910-1920
  Saint Clair Shores *(G-14253)*
Greenglow Products LLC.........................G...... 248 827-1451
  Southfield *(G-14931)*
Industrial Finishing Co LLC......................G...... 616 784-5737
  Comstock Park *(G-3485)*
Innovative Solutions Tech Inc ....G...... 734 335-6665
  Canton *(G-2387)*
Instacoat Premium Products LLC............G...... 586 770-1773
  Oscoda *(G-12211)*
Lenawee Industrial Pnt Sup Inc...............G...... 734 729-8080
  Wayne *(G-17436)*
Materials Processing Inc ....D...... 734 282-1888
  Riverview *(G-13301)*
Nb Coatings Inc ....G...... 248 365-1100
  Auburn Hills *(G-954)*
Ncoc Inc ....E...... 248 548-5950
  Oak Park *(G-12088)*
ND Industries Inc ....C...... 248 288-0000
  Clawson *(G-2982)*
North Group Inc ....G...... 517 540-0038
  Howell *(G-8069)*
Ot Dynamics LLC......................................F...... 734 984-7022
  Flat Rock *(G-5358)*
Pacific Epoxy Polymers Inc ....E...... 616 949-1634
  Grand Rapids *(G-6738)*
Pittsburgh Glass Works LLC ....C...... 248 371-1700
  Rochester Hills *(G-13494)*
Portland Plastics Co ....E...... 517 647-4115
  Portland *(G-13065)*
PPG Coating Services ....D...... 734 421-7300
  Livonia *(G-9894)*
PPG Industrial Coatings...........................G...... 616 844-4391
  Grand Haven *(G-6062)*
PPG Industries Inc ....E...... 248 640-4174
  Macomb *(G-10153)*
PPG Industries Inc ....G...... 810 767-8030
  Flint *(G-5481)*
PPG Industries Inc ....E...... 248 625-7282
  Clarkston *(G-2948)*
PPG Industries Inc ....E...... 517 784-6138
  Jackson *(G-8555)*
PPG Industries Inc ....E...... 248 478-1300
  Novi *(G-11977)*
PPG Industries Inc ....G...... 586 566-3789
  Shelby Township *(G-14670)*
PPG Industries Inc ....E...... 248 357-4817
  Southfield *(G-15002)*
PPG Industries Inc ....G...... 734 287-2110
  Taylor *(G-15754)*
PPG Industries Inc ....E...... 248 683-8052
  Waterford *(G-17370)*
PPG Industries Inc ....E...... 586 755-2011
  Warren *(G-17189)*
Richter Precision Inc ....E...... 586 465-0500
  Fraser *(G-5718)*
Riverside Spline & Gear Inc ....E...... 810 765-8302
  Marine City *(G-10481)*
Rolled Alloys Inc.......................................D...... 800 521-0332
  Temperance *(G-15842)*
Rollie Williams Paint Spot........................G...... 616 791-6100
  Grand Rapids *(G-6835)*
S P Kish Industries Inc ....E...... 517 543-2650
  Charlotte *(G-2663)*
Single Source Inc......................................G...... 765 825-4111
  Flat Rock *(G-5365)*
Statistical Processed Products ....E...... 586 792-6900
  Clinton Township *(G-3235)*
Tru Custom Blends Inc............................G...... 810 407-6207
  Flint *(G-5514)*
Ziebart International Corp ....C...... 248 588-4100
  Troy *(G-16706)*

PAINTS, VARNISHES & SPLYS WHOLESALERS

Aactus Inc..G...... 734 425-1212
  Livonia *(G-9623)*

PAINTS, VARNISHES & SPLYS, WHOLESALE: Colors & Pigments

Chromatech Inc..F...... 734 451-1230
  Canton *(G-2361)*

PAINTS, VARNISHES & SPLYS, WHOLESALE: Paints

Ventra Ionia Main LLC ....E...... 616 597-3220
  Ionia *(G-8252)*
Ventra Ionia Main LLC ....C...... 616 597-3220
  Ionia *(G-8253)*

PAINTS: Oil Or Alkyd Vehicle Or Water Thinned

Coat It Inc of Detroit................................G...... 313 869-8500
  Detroit *(G-3941)*
Helen Inc ....F...... 616 698-8102
  Caledonia *(G-2297)*
Palmer Paint Products Inc ....D...... 248 588-4500
  Troy *(G-16541)*
Polymer Inc...D...... 248 353-3035
  Southfield *(G-15001)*
Port City Paints Mfg Inc...........................G...... 231 726-5911
  Muskegon *(G-11402)*
United Paint and Chemical Corp ....D...... 248 353-3035
  Southfield *(G-15054)*

PAINTS: Waterproof

Nelson Paint Co of Mich Inc....................G...... 906 774-5566
  Kingsford *(G-9063)*

PALLET REPAIR SVCS

Mobile Pallet Service Inc ....E...... 269 792-4200
  Wayland *(G-17407)*

PALLETIZERS & DEPALLETIZERS

Automated Machine Systems Inc...........E...... 616 662-1309
  Jenison *(G-8618)*
Mollers North America Inc ....D...... 616 942-6504
  Grand Rapids *(G-6698)*

PALLETS

Anayas Pallets & Transport Inc ....E...... 313 843-6570
  Detroit *(G-3869)*
Artists Pallet...G...... 248 889-2440
  Highland *(G-7486)*
Baby Pallet..G...... 248 210-3851
  Waterford *(G-17324)*
C & J Pallets Inc ....G...... 517 263-7415
  Adrian *(G-52)*
C&D Pallets Inc ....G...... 517 285-5228
  Eagle *(G-4616)*
County Line Pallet....................................G...... 231 834-8416
  Kent City *(G-8989)*
Four Way Pallet Service ....F...... 734 782-5914
  Flat Rock *(G-5354)*
Gonzalez Universal Pallets LLC ....G...... 616 243-5524
  Grand Rapids *(G-6447)*
Grand Rustic Pallet Co ....G...... 231 329-5035
  Grand Rapids *(G-6470)*
Guerreros Pallets......................................G...... 616 808-4721
  Grand Rapids *(G-6484)*
H & M Pallet LLC ....F...... 231 821-8800
  Holton *(G-7932)*
Hillsdale Pallet LLC..................................G...... 517 254-4777
  Hillsdale *(G-7527)*
Hillside Pallets ....G...... 231 824-3761
  Manton *(G-10455)*
J & G Pallets Inc.......................................G...... 313 921-0222
  Detroit *(G-4154)*
J and K Pallet ....G...... 517 648-5974
  North Adams *(G-11655)*
Jerrys Pallets..G...... 734 242-1577
  Monroe *(G-11043)*
Kerry J McNeely ....G...... 734 776-1928
  Livonia *(G-9796)*
Lakeland Pallets Inc.................................G...... 616 997-4441
  Coopersville *(G-3563)*
Marion Pallet..G...... 231 743-6124
  Marion *(G-10491)*
Mid West Pallet..G...... 810 919-3072
  Burton *(G-2158)*
Pallet Man ....G...... 269 274-8825
  Springfield *(G-15199)*
Pallet Pros LLC...G...... 586 864-3353
  Center Line *(G-2581)*
Pink Pallet LLC...G...... 586 873-2982
  Grand Blanc *(G-5977)*
Precision Pallet LLC ....G...... 252 943-5193
  Charlevoix *(G-2627)*
Rochester Pallet.......................................G...... 248 266-1094
  Rochester Hills *(G-13506)*
Rose Acres Pallets LLC............................G...... 989 268-3074
  Vestaburg *(G-16828)*
Spartan Pallet LLC...................................G...... 586 291-8898
  Clinton Township *(G-3232)*
Union Pallet & Cont Co Inc ....G...... 517 279-4888
  Coldwater *(G-3339)*
White Pallet Chair ....G...... 989 424-8771
  Clare *(G-2892)*

PALLETS & SKIDS: Wood

AAR Manufacturing Inc ....E...... 231 779-8800
  Cadillac *(G-2220)*
American Pallet Company LLC................G...... 231 834-5056
  Grant *(G-7078)*
Breiten Box & Packaging Co Inc ....G...... 586 469-0800
  Harrison Township *(G-7324)*
Complete Packaging Inc ....E...... 734 241-2794
  Monroe *(G-11025)*
Curtis Country Connection LLC ....F...... 517 368-5542
  Camden *(G-2339)*
Delta Containers Inc ....C...... 810 742-2730
  Bay City *(G-1299)*
Demeester Wood Products Inc..............F...... 616 677-5995
  Coopersville *(G-3556)*
Diversified Pdts & Svcs LLC ....G...... 616 836-6600
  Holland *(G-7608)*
Donald Gleason..G...... 269 673-6802
  Allegan *(G-158)*
Fair & Square Pallet & Lbr Co ....G...... 989 727-3949
  Hubbard Lake *(G-8125)*
Holland Pallet Repair Inc ....E...... 616 875-8642
  Holland *(G-7673)*
Las Tortugas Pallet Co ....G...... 313 283-3279
  Lincoln Park *(G-9580)*
Lightning Technologies LLC ....F...... 248 977-5566
  Lake Orion *(G-9146)*
Lightning Technologies LLC ....E...... 248 572-6700
  Oxford *(G-12355)*
Luberda Wood Products Inc ....G...... 989 876-4334
  Omer *(G-12144)*
Matthews Mill Inc ....F...... 989 257-3271
  South Branch *(G-14749)*
Michael Chris Storms ....G...... 231 263-7516
  Kingsley *(G-9072)*
Mobile Pallet Service Inc ....E...... 269 792-4200
  Wayland *(G-17407)*
Ottawa Forest Products Inc ....E...... 906 932-9701
  Ironwood *(G-8336)*
Pallet Masters..G...... 313 995-1131
  Livonia *(G-9882)*
Prairie Wood Products Inc ....G...... 269 659-1163
  Sturgis *(G-15630)*
Process Systems Inc ....D...... 586 757-5711
  Warren *(G-17198)*
R Andrews Pallet Co Inc ....F...... 616 677-3270
  Marne *(G-10512)*
Rose Acres Tallets....................................G...... 989 268-3074
  Vestaburg *(G-16829)*
Sfi Acquisition Inc....................................E...... 248 471-1500
  Farmington Hills *(G-5122)*
Vocational Strategies Inc ....E...... 906 482-6142
  Calumet *(G-2335)*
World of Pallets and Trucking ....G...... 313 899-2000
  Detroit *(G-4449)*

PALLETS: Metal

Independent Machine Co Inc ....E...... 906 428-4524
  Escanaba *(G-4836)*
Keller Tool Ltd..D...... 734 425-4500
  Livonia *(G-9794)*
O Keller Tool Engrg Co LLC.....................E...... 734 425-4500
  Livonia *(G-9873)*
Sfi Acquisition Inc....................................E...... 248 471-1500
  Farmington Hills *(G-5122)*

PALLETS: Plastic

Huhtamaki Inc..B...... 989 633-8900
  Coleman *(G-3346)*
Phoenix Packaging Corporation ....G...... 734 944-3916
  Saline *(G-14407)*

Employee Codes: A=Over 500 employees, B=251-500
C=101-250, D=51-100, E=20-50, F=10-19, G=3-9

2020 Harris Michigan Industrial Directory

PALLETS: Plastic

Plastipak Packaging Inc .... C 734 326-6184
  Westland *(G-17589)*

PALLETS: Wood & Metal Combination

Vaive Wood Products Co .... E 586 949-4900
  Macomb *(G-10172)*

PALLETS: Wooden

Acme Pallet Inc .... E 616 738-6452
  Holland *(G-7548)*
Akers Wood Products Inc .... G 269 962-3802
  Battle Creek *(G-1144)*
All American Container Corp .... F 586 949-0000
  Macomb *(G-10105)*
All Size Pallets .... E 810 721-1999
  Imlay City *(G-8195)*
Anbren Inc .... G 269 944-5066
  Benton Harbor *(G-1481)*
Auto Pallets-Boxes Inc .... F 248 559-7744
  Lathrup Village *(G-9498)*
Auto Pallets-Boxes Inc .... G 734 782-1110
  Flat Rock *(G-5347)*
Black River Pallet Company .... E 616 772-6211
  Zeeland *(G-18121)*
Brindley Lumber & Pallet Co .... G 989 345-3497
  Lupton *(G-10091)*
Bunker & Sons Sawmill LLC .... G 989 983-2715
  Vanderbilt *(G-16803)*
Burnrite Pellet Corporation .... G 989 429-1067
  Clare *(G-2865)*
C & K Box Company Inc .... E 517 784-1779
  Jackson *(G-8397)*
Cannonsburg Wood Products Inc .... G 616 866-4459
  Rockford *(G-13563)*
Caveman Pallets LLC .... F 616 675-7270
  Conklin *(G-3529)*
D T Fowler Mfg Co Inc .... G 810 245-9336
  Lapeer *(G-9454)*
Delta Packaging International .... G 517 321-6548
  Lansing *(G-9214)*
Discount Pallets .... G 616 453-5455
  Grand Rapids *(G-6354)*
DRYE Custom Pallets Inc .... D 313 381-2681
  Melvindale *(G-10696)*
Envirnmntal Plllet Slutions Inc .... G 616 283-1784
  Zeeland *(G-18135)*
Fontana Forest Products .... E 313 841-8950
  Detroit *(G-4066)*
General Wood Products Co .... F 248 221-0214
  Big Rapids *(G-1630)*
Golden Eagle Pallets LLC .... F 616 233-0970
  Wyoming *(G-18004)*
Gonzalez Jr Pallets LLC .... G 616 885-0201
  Grand Rapids *(G-6446)*
Great Lakes Pallet Inc .... G 989 883-9220
  Sebewaing *(G-14515)*
Great Northern Lumber Mich LLC ..... E 989 736-6192
  Lincoln *(G-9562)*
Hills Crate Mill Inc .... G 616 761-3555
  Belding *(G-1417)*
Hugo Brothers Pallet Mfg .... G 989 684-5564
  Kawkawlin *(G-8973)*
Industrial Packaging Corp .... F 248 677-0084
  Berkley *(G-1584)*
J & G Pallets Inc .... G 313 921-0222
  Detroit *(G-4155)*
Jarvis Saw Mill Inc .... G 231 861-2078
  Shelby *(G-14526)*
K&P Discount Pallets Inc .... G 616 835-1661
  Belding *(G-1422)*
Kamps Inc .... E 313 381-2681
  Detroit *(G-4170)*
Kamps Inc .... D 616 453-9676
  Grand Rapids *(G-6569)*
Kamps Inc .... F 517 645-2800
  Potterville *(G-13074)*
Kamps Inc .... E 734 281-3300
  Taylor *(G-15732)*
Kamps Inc .... D 517 322-2500
  Lansing *(G-9302)*
Kamps Inc .... E 269 342-8113
  Kalamazoo *(G-8800)*
Krauter Forest Products LLC .... F 815 317-6561
  Reed City *(G-13218)*
Lakeland Pallets Inc .... E 616 949-9515
  Grand Rapids *(G-6615)*
Lanny Bensinger .... G 989 658-2590
  Ubly *(G-16718)*
Lansing Pallet .... G 517 322-2500
  Lansing *(G-9307)*
Maple Valley Pallet Co .... F 231 228-6641
  Maple City *(G-10463)*
Matelski Lumber Company .... E 231 549-2780
  Boyne Falls *(G-1841)*
McPhails Pallets Inc .... F 810 384-6458
  Kenockee *(G-8985)*
Metzger Sawmill .... G 269 963-3022
  Battle Creek *(G-1227)*
Michigan Pallet Inc .... F 517 543-0606
  Charlotte *(G-2660)*
Michigan Pallet Inc .... F 989 865-9915
  Saint Charles *(G-14196)*
Michigan Pallet Inc .... F 269 685-8802
  Plainwell *(G-12530)*
Nelson Company .... G 517 788-6117
  Jackson *(G-8542)*
Northern Pallet .... G 989 386-7556
  Clare *(G-2882)*
Patchwood Products Inc .... G 989 742-2605
  Hillman *(G-7509)*
Patchwood Products Inc .... G 989 742-2605
  Lachine *(G-9077)*
Quality Pallet Inc .... G 231 788-5161
  Muskegon *(G-11409)*
Quality Pallets LLC .... F 231 825-8361
  Mc Bain *(G-10683)*
Ross Pallet Co .... G 810 966-4945
  Port Huron *(G-12963)*
Schmieding Saw Mill Inc .... G 231 861-4189
  Shelby *(G-14535)*
Scotts Enterprises Inc .... G 989 275-5011
  Roscommon *(G-13754)*
Stoutenburg Inc .... E 810 648-4400
  Sandusky *(G-14444)*
Tk Enterprises Inc .... G 989 865-9915
  Saint Charles *(G-14202)*
Tommy Joe Reed .... G 989 291-5768
  Sheridan *(G-14735)*
WB Pallets Inc .... E 616 669-3000
  Hudsonville *(G-8185)*

PANEL & DISTRIBUTION BOARDS & OTHER RELATED APPARATUS

S Main Company LLC .... E 248 960-1540
  Wixom *(G-17888)*

PANEL & DISTRIBUTION BOARDS: Electric

Java Manufacturing Inc .... G 616 784-3873
  Comstock Park *(G-3487)*

PANELS, FLAT: Plastic

Armoured Rsstnce McHanisms Inc ..... F 517 223-7618
  Fowlerville *(G-5558)*
Installations Inc .... F 313 532-9000
  Redford *(G-13166)*

PANELS: Building, Metal

I B P Inc .... E 248 588-4710
  Clarkston *(G-2927)*
Innovate Industries Inc .... E 586 558-8990
  Warren *(G-17092)*
Porter Corp .... D 616 399-1963
  Holland *(G-7773)*

PANELS: Building, Plastic, NEC

Concord Industrial Corporation .... G 248 646-9225
  Bloomfield Hills *(G-1756)*
Reklein Plastics Incorporated .... G 586 739-8850
  Sterling Heights *(G-15463)*

PANELS: Building, Wood

Midwest Panel Systems Inc .... E 517 486-4844
  Blissfield *(G-1720)*

PANELS: Switchboard, Slate

Mis Controls Inc .... F 586 339-3900
  Rochester Hills *(G-13475)*

PANELS: Wood

Precision Framing Systems Inc .... E 704 588-6680
  Taylor *(G-15755)*
Richelieu America Ltd .... E 586 264-1240
  Sterling Heights *(G-15469)*

PAPER & BOARD: Die-cut

Accu-Shape Die Cutting Inc .... E 810 230-2445
  Flint *(G-5368)*
Bradford Company .... C 616 399-3000
  Holland *(G-7575)*
Cadillac Prsentation Solutions .... E 248 288-9777
  Troy *(G-16255)*
Celia Corporation .... D 616 887-7341
  Sparta *(G-15091)*
Classic Container Corporation .... E 734 853-3000
  Livonia *(G-9684)*
Delta Containers Inc .... C 810 742-2730
  Bay City *(G-1299)*
Edgewater Apartments .... G 517 663-8123
  Eaton Rapids *(G-4722)*
Graphic Specialties Inc .... E 616 247-0060
  Grand Rapids *(G-6475)*
Hamblin Company .... E 517 423-7491
  Tecumseh *(G-15796)*
Hexon Corporation .... F 248 585-7585
  Farmington Hills *(G-5018)*
Industrial Imprntng & Die Ctng .... E 586 778-9470
  Eastpointe *(G-4704)*
Jacobsen Industries Inc .... D 734 591-6111
  Livonia *(G-9791)*
Macarthur Corp .... E 810 606-1777
  Grand Blanc *(G-5975)*
Michigan Paper Die Inc .... F 313 873-0404
  Detroit *(G-4242)*
Oliver Packaging and Eqp Co .... D 616 356-2950
  Walker *(G-16872)*
Russell R Peters Co LLC .... G 989 732-0660
  Gaylord *(G-5891)*
Schultz Bindery Inc .... F 586 771-0777
  Warren *(G-17233)*
Trim Pac Inc .... G 269 279-9498
  Three Rivers *(G-15881)*

PAPER CONVERTING

Amaris International LLC .... G 248 427-0472
  Novi *(G-11824)*
Dedicated Converting Group Inc .... F 269 685-8430
  Plainwell *(G-12523)*
Fibers of Kalamazoo Inc .... E 269 344-3122
  Kalamazoo *(G-8743)*
Fineeye Color Solutions Inc .... G 616 988-6119
  Muskegon *(G-11322)*
Progressive Paper Corp .... G 269 279-6320
  Three Rivers *(G-15875)*
Shepherd Speciality Papers Inc .... G 269 629-8001
  Richland *(G-13255)*
Sks Industries Inc .... F 517 546-1117
  Howell *(G-8098)*
Trim Pac Inc .... G 269 279-9498
  Three Rivers *(G-15881)*
Walters Seed Co LLC .... F 616 355-7333
  Holland *(G-7852)*

PAPER MANUFACTURERS: Exc Newsprint

American Twisting Company .... E 269 637-8581
  South Haven *(G-14752)*
Anchor Bay Manufacturing Corp .... G 586 949-4040
  Chesterfield *(G-2737)*
Cadillac Products Inc .... D 989 766-2294
  Rogers City *(G-13613)*
Domtar Industries Inc .... D 810 982-0191
  Port Huron *(G-12912)*
Dunn Paper Holdings Inc .... D 810 984-5521
  Port Huron *(G-12914)*
Handy Wacks Corporation .... E 616 887-8268
  Sparta *(G-15096)*
International Paper Company .... G 269 273-8461
  Three Rivers *(G-15866)*
Menominee Acquisition Corp .... C 906 863-5595
  Menominee *(G-10745)*
Neenah Paper Inc .... B 906 387-2700
  Munising *(G-11246)*
Northstar Sourcing LLC .... G 313 782-4749
  Troy *(G-16527)*
Otsego Paper Inc .... E 269 692-6141
  Otsego *(G-12247)*
Verso Corporation .... A 906 786-1660
  Escanaba *(G-4865)*
Verso Corporation .... B 906 779-3371
  Norway *(G-11821)*
Verso Paper Holding LLC .... F 906 779-3200
  Quinnesec *(G-13104)*
Verso Quinnesec LLC .... G 877 447-2737
  Quinnesec *(G-13106)*

PRODUCT SECTION

PARTITIONS & FIXTURES: Except Wood

Verso Quinnesec Rep LLC .... G 906 779-3200
  Quinnesec (G-13107)

PAPER PRDTS: Book Covers

B & B Entps Prtg Cnvrting Inc .... G 313 891-9840
  Detroit (G-3890)

PAPER PRDTS: Infant & Baby Prdts

Happy Bums .... G 616 987-3159
  Lowell (G-10030)
Kimberly-Clark Corporation .... C 586 949-1649
  Macomb (G-10135)
Kimberly-Clark Corporation .... G 810 985-1830
  Port Huron (G-12934)

PAPER PRDTS: Sanitary

AJM Packaging Corporation .... C 313 842-7530
  Detroit (G-3851)
Chambers Ottawa Inc .... G 231 238-2122
  Cheboygan (G-2676)
Integrated Cmnty Commerce LLC .... G 313 220-2253
  Detroit (G-4142)
Universal Product Mktg LLC .... G 248 585-9959
  Grosse Pointe Park (G-7197)

PAPER PRDTS: Sanitary Tissue Paper

Kimberly-Clark Corporation .... C 586 949-1649
  Macomb (G-10135)
Kimberly-Clark Corporation .... G 810 985-1830
  Port Huron (G-12934)
Thetford Corporation .... C 734 769-6000
  Ann Arbor (G-670)

PAPER PRDTS: Toilet Paper, Made From Purchased Materials

Gadget Locker LLC .... G 702 901-1440
  Detroit (G-4075)

PAPER PRDTS: Toweling Tissue

Ace-Tex Enterprises Inc .... E 313 834-4000
  Detroit (G-3839)
Sanitor Mfg Co .... F 269 327-3001
  Portage (G-13031)

PAPER PRDTS: Towels, Napkins/Tissue Paper, From Purchd Mtrls

Michigan Poly Supplies Inc .... G 734 282-5554
  Taylor (G-15743)

PAPER: Adhesive

Argent Tape & Label Inc .... F 734 582-9956
  Plymouth (G-12573)
Lepages 2000 Inc .... G 416 357-0041
  Romulus (G-13700)
Michigan Shippers Supply Inc .... F 616 935-6680
  Spring Lake (G-15163)
Oliver Packaging and Eqp Co .... D 616 356-2950
  Walker (G-16872)

PAPER: Book

French Paper Company .... D 269 683-1100
  Niles (G-11612)

PAPER: Building, Insulating & Packaging

Everest Manufacturing Inc .... F 313 401-2608
  Farmington Hills (G-4993)

PAPER: Cardboard

M & J Entp Grnd Rapids LLC .... F 616 485-9775
  Comstock Park (G-3494)

PAPER: Coated & Laminated, NEC

Alpha Data Business Forms Inc .... G 248 540-5930
  Birmingham (G-1674)
Celia Corporation .... D 616 887-7341
  Sparta (G-15091)
Cummins Label Company .... E 269 345-3386
  Kalamazoo (G-8721)
Dunn Paper Inc .... F 810 984-5521
  Port Huron (G-12913)
Dunn Paper Holdings Inc .... G 810 984-5521
  Port Huron (G-12914)

Fedex Office & Print Svcs Inc .... E 616 336-1900
  Grand Rapids (G-6404)
Fedex Office & Print Svcs Inc .... F 313 359-3124
  Dearborn (G-3705)
Impact Label Corporation .... D 269 381-4280
  Galesburg (G-5811)
Lawson Printers Inc .... E 269 965-0525
  Battle Creek (G-1222)
Litsenberger Print Shop .... G 906 482-3903
  Houghton (G-7976)
Lowry Holding Company Inc .... C 810 229-7200
  Brighton (G-1952)
Macarthur Corp .... E 810 606-1777
  Grand Blanc (G-5975)
McCray Press .... E 989 792-8681
  Saginaw (G-14084)
Mead Westvaco Paper Div .... G 906 233-2362
  Escanaba (G-4841)
Plasti-Fab Inc .... E 248 543-1415
  Ferndale (G-5311)
Qrp Inc .... G 989 496-2955
  Midland (G-10905)
Ron Rowe .... G 231 652-2642
  Newaygo (G-11577)
Shawmut Corporation .... C 810 987-2222
  Port Huron (G-12965)
Stewart Sutherland Inc .... C 269 649-0530
  Vicksburg (G-16844)
Technology MGT & Budgt Dept .... D 517 322-1897
  Lansing (G-9430)
Witchcraft Tape Products Inc .... D 269 468-3399
  Coloma (G-3368)

PAPER: Corrugated

Allegiance Packaging LLC .... G 586 846-2453
  Clinton Township (G-3042)
Delta Containers Inc .... E 810 742-2730
  Bay City (G-1300)

PAPER: Packaging

E B Eddy Paper Inc .... B 810 982-0191
  Port Huron (G-12915)
Rizzo Packaging Inc .... E 269 685-5808
  Plainwell (G-12542)

PAPER: Printer

Eagle Ridge Paper Ltd .... G 248 376-9503
  Romulus (G-13669)
Vision Solutions Inc .... G 810 695-9569
  Grand Blanc (G-5987)

PAPER: Specialty

Elegus Eps LLC .... G 734 224-9900
  Ann Arbor (G-440)

PAPER: Waxed, Made From Purchased Materials

Stewart Sutherland Inc .... C 269 649-0530
  Vicksburg (G-16844)

PAPER: Wrapping & Packaging

Kolossos Printing Inc .... G 734 741-1600
  Ann Arbor (G-518)
Package Design & Mfg Inc .... E 248 486-4390
  Brighton (G-1972)
Pure Pulp Products Inc .... E 269 385-5050
  Kalamazoo (G-8863)

PAPERBOARD

Anchor Bay Packaging Corp .... E 586 949-1500
  Chesterfield (G-2739)
Classic Container Corporation .... E 734 853-3000
  Livonia (G-9684)
Coveris .... E 269 964-1130
  Battle Creek (G-1169)
Fibre Converters Inc .... E 269 279-1700
  Constantine (G-3535)
Graphic Packaging Intl LLC .... D 269 383-5000
  Kalamazoo (G-8754)
Graphic Packaging Intl LLC .... B 269 343-6104
  Kalamazoo (G-8755)
Kentwood Packaging Corporation .... D 616 698-9000
  Walker (G-16869)
Lydall Performance Mtls US Inc .... G 248 596-2800
  Northville (G-11705)

MRC Industries Inc .... D 269 343-0747
  Kalamazoo (G-8832)
Packaging Specialties Inc .... E 586 473-6703
  Romulus (G-13718)
Rizzo Packaging Inc .... E 269 685-5808
  Plainwell (G-12542)
Sonoco Products Company .... D 269 408-0182
  Saint Joseph (G-14339)
South Park Sales & Mfg Inc .... G 313 381-7579
  Dearborn (G-3762)
Spartan Paperboard Company Inc .... F 269 381-0192
  Kalamazoo (G-8896)

PAPERBOARD CONVERTING

Manchester Industries Inc VA .... E 269 496-2715
  Mendon (G-10716)
Str Company .... G 517 206-6058
  Grass Lake (G-7094)
Tru Blu Industries LLC .... D 269 684-4989
  Niles (G-11650)

PAPERBOARD PRDTS: Coated & Treated Board

Utility Supply and Cnstr Co .... G 231 832-2297
  Reed City (G-13225)

PAPERBOARD PRDTS: Container Board

Graphic Packaging Intl LLC .... C 269 963-6135
  Battle Creek (G-1195)

PAPERBOARD PRDTS: Packaging Board

Cascade Paper Converters LLC .... F 616 974-9165
  Grand Rapids (G-6263)
Display Pack Disc Inc .... G 616 451-3061
  Cedar Springs (G-2554)
Display Pack Disc Vdh Inc .... G 616 451-3061
  Cedar Springs (G-2555)

PAPERBOARD: Boxboard

Artistic Carton Company .... D 269 483-7601
  White Pigeon (G-17644)
Campbell Industrial Force LLC .... E 989 427-0011
  Edmore (G-4749)

PAPERBOARD: Chipboard

Trim Pac Inc .... G 269 279-9498
  Three Rivers (G-15881)

PAPERBOARD: Coated

Handy Wacks Corporation .... E 616 887-8268
  Sparta (G-15097)
Ox Paperboard Michigan LLC .... D 800 345-8881
  Constantine (G-3543)

PARKING LOTS & GARAGES

Cincinnati Time Systems Inc .... F 248 615-8300
  Farmington Hills (G-4963)

PARTICLEBOARD

Rospatch Jessco Corporation .... B 269 782-8661
  Dowagiac (G-4558)

PARTICLEBOARD: Laminated, Plastic

Bourne Industries Inc .... E 989 743-3461
  Corunna (G-3578)

PARTITIONS & FIXTURES: Except Wood

Allen Pattern of Michigan .... F 269 963-4131
  Battle Creek (G-1145)
Borroughs Corporation .... D 800 748-0227
  Kalamazoo (G-8700)
Compact Engineering Corp .... F 231 788-5470
  Muskegon (G-11298)
Creative Solutions Group Inc .... D 248 288-9700
  Clawson (G-2975)
Creative Solutions Group Inc .... G 734 425-2257
  Redford (G-13154)
Dads Panels Inc .... G 810 245-1871
  Lapeer (G-9455)
Dee-Blast Corporation .... F 269 428-2400
  Stevensville (G-15563)
Ferrante Manufacturing Co .... E 313 571-1111
  Detroit (G-4056)

PARTITIONS & FIXTURES: Except Wood

G & W Display Fixtures Inc ....E 517 369-7110
 Bronson *(G-2026)*
Gonzalez Prod Systems Inc ....D 313 297-6682
 Detroit *(G-4097)*
Greenfield Cabinetry Inc ....F 586 759-3300
 Warren *(G-17066)*
Harbor Industries Inc ....B 231 547-3280
 Charlevoix *(G-2617)*
Herman Miller Inc ....B 616 654-3000
 Zeeland *(G-18147)*
JMJ Inc ....E 269 948-2828
 Hastings *(G-7417)*
Loudon Steel Inc ....D 989 871-9353
 Millington *(G-10997)*
Pinnacle Cabinet Company Inc ....E 989 772-3866
 Mount Pleasant *(G-11217)*
Structural Plastics Inc ....E 810 953-9400
 Holly *(G-7898)*

PARTITIONS: Solid Fiber, Made From Purchased Materials

Bradford Company ....C 616 399-3000
 Holland *(G-7575)*

PARTITIONS: Wood & Fixtures

Bay Wood Homes Inc ....E 989 245-4156
 Fenton *(G-5187)*
Bennett Wood Specialties Inc ....F 616 772-6683
 Zeeland *(G-18117)*
Compatico Inc ....E 616 940-1772
 Grand Rapids *(G-6291)*
Design Fabrications Inc ....D 248 597-0988
 Madison Heights *(G-10229)*
European Cabinet Mfg Co ....E 586 445-8909
 Roseville *(G-13802)*
G & G Wood & Supply Inc ....F 586 293-0450
 Roseville *(G-13805)*
G & W Display Fixtures Inc ....E 517 369-7110
 Bronson *(G-2026)*
Gast Cabinet Co ....E 269 422-1587
 Baroda *(G-1125)*
H L F Furniture Incorporated ....E 734 697-3000
 Van Buren Twp *(G-16762)*
Harbor Industries Inc ....D 616 842-5330
 Grand Haven *(G-6033)*
Harbor Industries Inc ....B 231 547-3280
 Charlevoix *(G-2617)*
Herman Miller Inc ....B 616 654-3000
 Zeeland *(G-18147)*
Knape & Vogt Manufacturing Co ....A 616 459-3311
 Grand Rapids *(G-6585)*
Knoll Inc ....C 616 949-1050
 Grand Rapids *(G-6587)*
Kurtis Mfg & Distrg Corp ....E 734 522-7600
 Livonia *(G-9802)*
M and G Laminated Products ....G 517 784-4974
 Jackson *(G-8502)*
Millennm-The Inside Sltion Inc ....E 248 645-9005
 Farmington Hills *(G-5069)*
Owens Building Co Inc ....E 989 835-1293
 Midland *(G-10901)*
Pageant Homes Inc ....G 517 694-0431
 Holt *(G-7921)*
Panel Processing Inc ....E 517 279-8051
 Coldwater *(G-3317)*
PCI Industries Inc ....D 248 542-2570
 Oak Park *(G-12090)*
Programmed Products Corp ....D 248 348-7755
 Novi *(G-11983)*
Sterling Millwork Inc ....D 248 427-1400
 Farmington Hills *(G-5131)*
Van Zee Corporation ....D 616 245-9000
 Grand Rapids *(G-6959)*
W S Townsend Company ....C 269 781-5131
 Marshall *(G-10593)*

PARTS: Metal

B & G Products Inc ....F 616 698-9050
 Grand Rapids *(G-6198)*
Diversfied Prcurement Svcs LLC ....G 248 821-1147
 Ferndale *(G-5280)*
Fabrilaser Mfg LLC ....E 269 789-9490
 Marshall *(G-10567)*
L Barge & Associates Inc ....F 248 582-3430
 Ferndale *(G-5297)*
Marix Specialty Welding Co ....E 586 754-9685
 Warren *(G-17140)*
Rae Manufacturing Company ....F 810 987-9170
 Port Huron *(G-12960)*
RC Metal Products Inc ....G 616 696-1694
 Sand Lake *(G-14427)*
Tower Defense & Aerospace LLC ....C 248 675-6000
 Livonia *(G-9966)*

PATTERNS: Indl

Advanced Technology and Design ....G 248 889-5658
 Highland *(G-7485)*
Advantage Industries Inc ....E 616 669-2400
 Jenison *(G-8616)*
Al-Craft Design & Engrg Inc ....G 248 589-3827
 Troy *(G-16181)*
Allen Pattern of Michigan ....F 269 963-4131
 Battle Creek *(G-1145)*
Arbor Gage & Tooling Inc ....E 616 454-8266
 Grand Rapids *(G-6178)*
Associate Mfg Inc ....G 989 345-0025
 West Branch *(G-17506)*
Astro-Netics Inc ....D 248 585-4890
 Madison Heights *(G-10197)*
Aurora Cad CAM Inc ....F 810 678-2128
 Metamora *(G-10772)*
Azko Pattern Mfg Inc ....G 231 733-0888
 Muskegon *(G-11274)*
B & L Pattern Company ....G 269 982-0214
 Saint Joseph *(G-14301)*
Bespro Pattern Inc ....F 586 268-6970
 Madison Heights *(G-10204)*
Big Dome Holdings Inc ....D 616 735-6228
 Grand Rapids *(G-6219)*
Briggs Industries Inc ....E 586 749-5191
 Chesterfield *(G-2747)*
C & D Enterprises Inc ....F 248 373-0011
 Burton *(G-2147)*
C & D Gage Inc ....G 517 548-7049
 Howell *(G-8018)*
Champion Charter Sls & Svc Inc ....G 906 779-2300
 Iron Mountain *(G-8280)*
Cobra Patterns & Models Inc ....E 248 588-2669
 Madison Heights *(G-10215)*
Complete Prototype Svcs Inc ....B 586 690-8897
 Clinton Township *(G-3085)*
Crescent Pattern Company ....F 248 541-1052
 Oak Park *(G-12056)*
Decca Pattern Co Inc ....G 586 775-8450
 Roseville *(G-13790)*
Dhs Inc ....G 313 724-6566
 Detroit *(G-4007)*
Elmhirst Industries Inc ....E 586 731-8663
 Sterling Heights *(G-15330)*
Gage Pattern & Model Inc ....E 248 361-6609
 Madison Heights *(G-10255)*
Gicmac Industrial Inc ....G 248 308-2743
 Novi *(G-11891)*
GM Bassett Pattern Inc ....G 248 477-6454
 Farmington Hills *(G-5012)*
Grand Rapids Carvers Inc ....E 616 538-0022
 Grand Rapids *(G-6452)*
Holland Pattern Co ....G 616 396-6348
 Holland *(G-7675)*
Homestead Tool and Machine ....E 989 465-6182
 Coleman *(G-3344)*
Husite Engineering Co Inc ....E 248 588-0337
 Clinton Township *(G-3136)*
Industrial Model Inc ....G 586 254-0450
 Auburn Hills *(G-913)*
J J Pattern & Castings Inc ....G 248 543-7119
 Madison Heights *(G-10281)*
Jay/Enn Corporation ....D 248 588-2393
 Troy *(G-16433)*
L & L Pattern Inc ....G 231 733-2646
 Muskegon *(G-11359)*
Logan Pattern & Engrg Co LLC ....G 810 364-9298
 Saint Clair *(G-14226)*
Majestic Pattern Company Inc ....G 313 892-5800
 Detroit *(G-4216)*
Mantissa Industries Inc ....G 517 694-2260
 Holt *(G-7915)*
Marten Models & Molds Inc ....E 586 293-2260
 Fraser *(G-5691)*
Metro Technologies Ltd ....D 248 528-9240
 Troy *(G-16502)*
Michalski Enterprises Inc ....E 517 703-0777
 Lansing *(G-9245)*
Michigan Pattern Works Inc ....E 616 245-9259
 Grand Rapids *(G-6674)*
Model Pattern Company Inc ....E 616 878-9710
 Byron Center *(G-2204)*
Modern Age Pattern Mfg Inc ....G 231 788-1222
 Muskegon *(G-11383)*
National Pattern Inc ....E 989 755-6274
 Saginaw *(G-14101)*
Northern Sierra Corporation ....G 989 777-4784
 Saginaw *(G-14116)*
Paragon Molds Corporation ....E 586 294-7630
 Fraser *(G-5704)*
Parker Pattern Inc ....F 586 466-5900
 Mount Clemens *(G-11143)*
Parker Tooling & Design Inc ....F 616 791-1080
 Grand Rapids *(G-6743)*
Portenga Manufacturing Company ....G 616 846-2691
 Ferrysburg *(G-5337)*
Pre-Cut Patterns Inc ....G 616 392-4415
 Holland *(G-7774)*
Prompt Pattern Inc ....E 586 759-2030
 Warren *(G-17201)*
Proto-Cast Inc ....E 313 565-5400
 Inkster *(G-8233)*
Ravenna Pattern & Mfg ....E 231 853-2264
 Ravenna *(G-13127)*
Rehau Incorporated ....E 269 651-7845
 Sturgis *(G-15632)*
Sbti Company ....D 586 726-5756
 Shelby Township *(G-14685)*
Simpsons Enterprises Inc ....E 269 279-7237
 Three Rivers *(G-15877)*
Tedson Industries Inc ....F 248 588-9230
 Troy *(G-16635)*
Tri-Star Tooling LLC ....F 586 978-0435
 Sterling Heights *(G-15529)*
Vans Pattern Corp ....E 616 364-9483
 Grand Rapids *(G-6961)*
Wing Pattern Inc ....G 248 588-1121
 Sterling Heights *(G-15546)*
Wolverine Products Inc ....F 586 792-3740
 Clinton Township *(G-3261)*

PAVING BREAKERS

Outline Industries LLC ....G 303 632-6782
 Boyne City *(G-1831)*

PAVING MATERIALS: Prefabricated, Concrete

Asphalt Paving Inc ....F 231 733-1409
 Muskegon *(G-11272)*

PAWN SHOPS

Novus Corporation ....E 248 545-8600
 Warren *(G-17175)*

PAYROLL SVCS

Workforce Payhub Inc ....G 517 759-4026
 Adrian *(G-104)*

PEARLS, WHOLESALE

Combine International Inc ....C 248 585-9900
 Troy *(G-16273)*

PEAT GRINDING SVCS

Bay-Houston Towing Company ....E 810 648-2210
 Sandusky *(G-14430)*

PEAT MINING SVCS

Markham Peat Corp ....F 800 851-7230
 Lakeview *(G-9175)*

PERFORMANCE RIGHTS, PUBLISHING & LICENSING

Dillion Renee Entities ....G 989 443-0654
 Lansing *(G-9360)*

PERFUMES

Fragrance Outlet Inc ....G 517 552-9545
 Howell *(G-8042)*
Jogue Inc ....F 248 349-1501
 Northville *(G-11703)*
Jogue Inc ....E 734 207-0100
 Plymouth *(G-12654)*
Rodco Ltd ....G 517 244-0200
 Holt *(G-7923)*
Scentmatchers LLC ....G 800 859-9878
 Gaylord *(G-5892)*
Wellington Fragrance ....G 734 261-5531
 Livonia *(G-10005)*

PRODUCT SECTION

PHARMACEUTICALS

PERLITE: Processed
Montcalm Aggregates Inc ....G....... 989 772-7038
Mount Pleasant *(G-11209)*

PERSONAL & HOUSEHOLD GOODS REPAIR, NEC
J & K Canvas Products ....G....... 810 635-7711
Flint *(G-5451)*

PERSONAL CREDIT INSTITUTIONS: Financing, Autos, Furniture
Ford Motor Company ....B....... 313 322-3000
Dearborn *(G-3709)*
Ford Motor Company ....A....... 734 523-3000
Livonia *(G-9744)*
General Motors LLC ....A....... 313 972-6000
Detroit *(G-4084)*

PESTICIDES
Biobest USA Inc ....G....... 734 626-5693
Romulus *(G-13657)*
Gantec Inc ....G....... 989 631-9300
Midland *(G-10864)*

PESTICIDES WHOLESALERS
Hpi Products Inc ....G....... 248 773-7460
Northville *(G-11698)*

PET & PET SPLYS STORES
Pet Supplies Plus ....F....... 616 554-3600
Grand Rapids *(G-6752)*
Springfield Landscape Mtls ....G....... 269 965-6748
Springfield *(G-15204)*

PET ACCESS: Collars, Leashes, Etc, Exc Leather
Brollytime Inc ....F....... 312 854-7606
Royal Oak *(G-13911)*

PET SPLYS
Best Buy Bones Inc ....G....... 810 631-6971
Mount Morris *(G-11158)*
Fowlerville Feed & Pet Sups ....G....... 517 223-9115
Fowlerville *(G-5565)*
Joshs Frogs ....G....... 517 648-0260
Byron *(G-2173)*
Kitty Condo LLC ....E....... 419 690-9063
Livonia *(G-9797)*
Pet Supplies Plus ....F....... 616 554-3600
Grand Rapids *(G-6752)*
Ruff Life LLC ....G....... 231 347-1214
Petoskey *(G-12474)*
Sk Enterprises Inc ....F....... 616 785-1070
Grand Rapids *(G-6867)*
Studtmans Stuff ....G....... 269 673-3126
Allegan *(G-189)*
Tecla Company Inc ....E....... 248 624-8200
Commerce Township *(G-3453)*
Ultramouse Ltd ....G....... 734 761-1144
Ann Arbor *(G-686)*
Viladon Corporation ....G....... 248 548-0043
Oak Park *(G-12103)*
W M Enterprises ....G....... 810 694-4384
Grand Blanc *(G-5988)*

PETROLEUM & PETROLEUM PRDTS, WHOLESALE Fuel Oil
Lansing Ice and Fuel Company ....F....... 517 372-3850
Lansing *(G-9240)*
Pacific Oil Resources Inc ....E....... 734 397-1120
Van Buren Twp *(G-16777)*

PETROLEUM BULK STATIONS & TERMINALS
BP Lubricants USA Inc ....E....... 231 689-0002
White Cloud *(G-17620)*

PETROLEUM PRDTS WHOLESALERS
M R D Industries ....G....... 269 623-8452
Delton *(G-3818)*

Warner Oil Company ....F....... 517 278-5844
Coldwater *(G-3341)*

PHARMACEUTICAL PREPARATIONS: Adrenal
Atterocor Inc ....G....... 734 845-9300
Ann Arbor *(G-372)*
Corium International Inc ....E....... 616 656-4563
Grand Rapids *(G-6310)*
L Perrigo Company ....G....... 269 673-7962
Allegan *(G-171)*

PHARMACEUTICAL PREPARATIONS: Druggists' Preparations
Abaco Partners LLC ....C....... 616 532-1700
Kentwood *(G-8997)*
Abbott Laboratories ....B....... 269 651-0600
Sturgis *(G-15594)*
Abbott Laboratories ....E....... 734 324-6666
Wyandotte *(G-17944)*
Abbvie Inc ....G....... 734 324-6650
Wyandotte *(G-17945)*
Charles Bowman & Company ....F....... 616 786-4000
Holland *(G-7588)*
Ds Biotech LLC ....G....... 248 894-1474
Bloomfield Hills *(G-1761)*
Grass Lake Community Pharmacy ....G....... 517 522-4100
Grass Lake *(G-7088)*
Physicians Compounding Phrm ....G....... 248 758-9100
Bloomfield Hills *(G-1791)*
Soleo Health Inc ....G....... 248 513-8687
Novi *(G-12000)*
Velesco Phrm Svcs Inc ....G....... 734 545-0696
Wixom *(G-17924)*
Velesco Phrm Svcs Inc ....F....... 734 527-9125
Plymouth *(G-12787)*

PHARMACEUTICAL PREPARATIONS: Emulsions
Tetra Corporation ....F....... 401 529-1630
Eaton Rapids *(G-4734)*

PHARMACEUTICAL PREPARATIONS: Medicines, Capsule Or Ampule
Port Huron Medical Assoc ....G....... 810 982-0100
Fort Gratiot *(G-5551)*

PHARMACEUTICAL PREPARATIONS: Powders
Welchdry Inc ....F....... 616 399-2711
Holland *(G-7853)*

PHARMACEUTICAL PREPARATIONS: Proprietary Drug PRDTS
Ocusano Inc ....G....... 734 730-5407
Grand Rapids *(G-6727)*
Penrose Therapeutix LLC ....G....... 847 370-0303
Plymouth *(G-12711)*
Wandas Barium Cookie LLC ....G....... 906 281-1788
Calumet *(G-2336)*

PHARMACEUTICAL PREPARATIONS: Solutions
Grand River Aseptic Mfg Inc ....F....... 616 464-5072
Grand Rapids *(G-6467)*
Telocyte LLC ....G....... 616 570-4515
Ada *(G-30)*

PHARMACEUTICAL PREPARATIONS: Tablets
H & A Pharmacy II LLC ....G....... 313 995-4552
Westland *(G-17567)*
Tabletting Inc ....G....... 616 957-0281
Grand Rapids *(G-6913)*

PHARMACEUTICALS
Akorn Inc ....E....... 800 579-8327
Ann Arbor *(G-350)*
Aspire Pharmacy ....G....... 989 773-7849
Mount Pleasant *(G-11171)*
Astellas Pharma Us Inc ....G....... 231 947-3630
Traverse City *(G-15897)*

Avomeen LLC ....E....... 734 222-1090
Ann Arbor *(G-377)*
Barclay Pharmacy ....G....... 248 852-4600
Rochester Hills *(G-13375)*
Berkley Pharmacy LLC ....F....... 586 573-8300
Warren *(G-16955)*
Biolyte Laboratories LLC ....G....... 616 350-9055
Grand Rapids *(G-6223)*
Biopolymer Innovations LLC ....E....... 517 432-3044
East Lansing *(G-4652)*
Bristol-Myers Squibb Company ....D....... 248 528-2476
Troy *(G-16247)*
Caraco Pharma Inc ....G....... 313 871-8400
Detroit *(G-3928)*
Cayman Chemical Company Inc ....D....... 734 971-3335
Ann Arbor *(G-395)*
Central Admxture Phrm Svcs Inc ....E....... 734 953-6760
Livonia *(G-9680)*
Cns Inc ....G....... 616 242-7704
Grand Rapids *(G-6283)*
Copagen LLC ....G....... 734 904-0365
Ann Arbor *(G-405)*
Diapin Therapeutics LLC ....G....... 734 764-9123
Ann Arbor *(G-421)*
Diplomat Spclty Phrm Flint LLC ....B....... 810 768-9000
Flint *(G-5419)*
Dow Chemical Company ....C....... 989 636-4406
Midland *(G-10836)*
DSC Laboratories Inc ....E....... 800 492-5988
Muskegon *(G-11307)*
Eastside Pharmacy Inc ....F....... 313 579-1755
Detroit *(G-4024)*
Elba Inc ....E....... 248 288-6098
Troy *(G-16336)*
Emergent Biodef Oper Lnsng LLC ....B....... 517 327-1500
Lansing *(G-9224)*
Esperion Therapeutics Inc ....D....... 734 887-3903
Ann Arbor *(G-448)*
Ferndale Laboratories Inc ....B....... 248 548-0900
Ferndale *(G-5284)*
Ferndale Pharma Group Inc ....B....... 248 548-0900
Ferndale *(G-5285)*
GE Healthcare Inc ....E....... 616 554-5717
Grand Rapids *(G-6432)*
Gemphire Therapeutics Inc ....F....... 734 245-1700
Livonia *(G-9750)*
Genentech Inc ....G....... 650 225-1000
Lake Orion *(G-9136)*
Genoa Healthcare LLC ....G....... 313 989-0536
Detroit *(G-4088)*
Glaxosmithkline LLC ....E....... 989 450-9859
Frankenmuth *(G-5588)*
Glaxosmithkline LLC ....E....... 989 928-6535
Oxford *(G-12347)*
Glaxosmithkline LLC ....E....... 989 280-1225
Midland *(G-10866)*
Glaxosmithkline LLC ....E....... 248 561-3022
Bloomfield Hills *(G-1769)*
Greenmark Biomedical Inc ....G....... 517 336-4665
Lansing *(G-9378)*
Healthplus Spclty Pharma ....G....... 734 769-1300
Ann Arbor *(G-486)*
Hello Life Inc ....F....... 616 808-3290
Grand Rapids *(G-6504)*
Hello Life Inc ....F....... 616 808-3290
Grand Rapids *(G-6505)*
Housey Phrm RES Labs LLC ....G....... 248 663-7000
Southfield *(G-14938)*
Innovative Pharmaceuticals ....G....... 248 789-0999
Brighton *(G-1943)*
Jade Pharmaceuticals Entp LLC ....G....... 248 716-8333
Livonia *(G-9792)*
King Pharmaceuticals LLC ....D....... 248 650-6400
Rochester *(G-13332)*
L Perrigo Company ....A....... 269 673-8451
Allegan *(G-170)*
L Perrigo Company ....G....... 269 673-7962
Allegan *(G-172)*
L Perrigo Company ....D....... 269 673-1608
Allegan *(G-173)*
LLC Ash Stevens ....D....... 734 282-3370
Riverview *(G-13300)*
Lymphogen Inc ....G....... 906 281-7372
Houghton *(G-7977)*
McKesson Corporation ....D....... 734 953-2523
Livonia *(G-9833)*
Med Share Inc ....F....... 888 266-3567
Dearborn *(G-3738)*
Mercury Drugs LLC ....G....... 248 545-3600
Oak Park *(G-12084)*

PHARMACEUTICALS

Meridianrx LLC	D	855 323-4580
Detroit (G-4226)		
Millendo Therapeutics Inc	E	734 845-9000
Ann Arbor (G-559)		
Millendo Transactionsub Inc	G	734 845-9300
Ann Arbor (G-560)		
Mills Phrm & Apothecary LLC	G	248 633-2872
Birmingham (G-1693)		
N F P Inc	G	989 631-0009
Midland (G-10896)		
Nopras Technologies Inc	G	248 486-6684
South Lyon (G-14807)		
Norman A Lewis	G	248 219-5736
Farmington Hills (G-5080)		
Onl Therapeutics LLC	G	734 998-8339
Ann Arbor (G-583)		
Painex Corporation	G	313 863-1200
Detroit (G-4286)		
Painexx Corporation	G	313 863-1200
Detroit (G-4287)		
Pancheck LLC	F	989 288-6886
Durand (G-4611)		
Par Sterile Products LLC	C	248 651-9081
Rochester (G-13344)		
Parkedale Pharmaceuticals Inc	D	248 650-6400
Rochester (G-13345)		
PBM Nutritionals LLC	F	269 673-8451
Allegan (G-180)		
Perrigo Company	F	269 686-1973
Allegan (G-181)		
Perrigo Company	G	616 396-0941
Holland (G-7770)		
Perrigo Company	G	269 673-7962
Allegan (G-183)		
Perrigo Pharmaceuticals Co	F	269 673-8451
Allegan (G-184)		
Pfizer Inc	C	248 867-9067
Clarkston (G-2944)		
Pfizer Inc	F	248 650-6400
Rochester (G-13346)		
Pfizer Inc	G	734 679-7368
Grosse Ile (G-7175)		
Pfizer Inc	G	734 671-9315
Trenton (G-16156)		
Pfizer Inc	C	269 833-5143
Kalamazoo (G-8848)		
Pharmacia & Upjohn Company LLC	D	908 901-8000
Kalamazoo (G-8849)		
Plasma Biolife Services L P	G	616 667-0264
Grandville (G-7064)		
PMI Branded Pharmaceuticals	F	269 673-8451
Allegan (G-185)		
Qsv Pharma LLC	G	269 324-2358
Portage (G-13025)		
Renucell	G	888 400-6032
Grand Haven (G-6071)		
Safe N Simple LLC	F	248 875-0840
Clarkston (G-2953)		
Sun Pharmaceutical Inds Inc	G	248 346-7302
Farmington Hills (G-5135)		
Sun Pharmaceutical Inds Inc	E	609 495-2800
Detroit (G-4384)		
Team Pharma	G	269 344-8326
Kalamazoo (G-8908)		
Uckele Health and Nutrition	E	800 248-0330
Blissfield (G-1729)		
United State Phrm Group	G	734 462-3685
Livonia (G-9981)		
Urban Specialty Apparel Inc	F	248 395-9500
Southfield (G-15056)		
Vectech Pharmaceutical Cons	F	248 478-5820
Brighton (G-2005)		
Vortech Pharmaceutical Ltd	F	313 584-4088
Dearborn (G-3770)		
Zoetis LLC	E	888 963-8471
Kalamazoo (G-8929)		
Zomedica Pharmaceutical Inc	G	734 369-2555
Ann Arbor (G-710)		

PHARMACEUTICALS: Medicinal & Botanical Prdts

Aapharmasyn LLC	F	734 213-2123
Ann Arbor (G-337)		
Hearing Health Science Inc	G	734 476-9490
Ann Arbor (G-487)		
Metabolic Solutions Dev Co LLC	F	269 343-6732
Kalamazoo (G-8822)		

PHARMACIES & DRUG STORES

Jorgensens Inc	E	989 831-8338
Greenville (G-7140)		
Kroger Co	C	586 727-4946
Richmond (G-13265)		
Nopras Technologies Inc	G	248 486-6684
South Lyon (G-14807)		
Soleo Health Inc	G	248 513-8687
Novi (G-12000)		
Spartannash Company	C	517 629-6313
Albion (G-132)		
Spartannash Company	D	517 278-8963
Coldwater (G-3333)		
Walmart Inc	B	517 541-1481
Charlotte (G-2670)		

PHOSPHORIC ACID ESTERS

Metalworking Lubricants Co	C	248 332-3500
Pontiac (G-12849)		

PHOTO RECONNAISSANCE SYSTEMS

Orion Test Systems Inc	D	248 373-9097
Auburn Hills (G-967)		

PHOTOCOPY MACHINE REPAIR SVCS

Nationwide Laser Technologies	G	248 488-0155
Farmington Hills (G-5077)		

PHOTOCOPYING & DUPLICATING SVCS

A 1 Printing and Copy Center	G	269 381-0093
Kalamazoo (G-8671)		
Acadia Group LLC	E	734 944-1404
Saline (G-14371)		
Accelerated Press Inc	G	248 524-1850
Troy (G-16165)		
An Corporate Center LLC	E	248 669-1188
Plymouth (G-12571)		
August Communications Inc	G	313 561-8000
Dearborn Heights (G-3780)		
Elston Enterprises Inc	F	313 561-8000
Dearborn Heights (G-3784)		
Fedex Office & Print Svcs Inc	F	517 347-8656
Okemos (G-12123)		
Fedex Office & Print Svcs Inc	E	616 336-1900
Grand Rapids (G-6404)		
Fedex Office & Print Svcs Inc	F	734 761-4539
Ann Arbor (G-459)		
Fedex Office & Print Svcs Inc	F	313 359-3124
Dearborn (G-3705)		
Fedex Office & Print Svcs Inc	F	248 932-3373
Farmington Hills (G-4998)		
Fedex Office & Print Svcs Inc	G	517 332-5855
East Lansing (G-4657)		
Fedex Office & Print Svcs Inc	F	248 377-2222
Auburn Hills (G-870)		
Fedex Office & Print Svcs Inc	E	616 957-7888
Grand Rapids (G-6405)		
Fedex Office & Print Svcs Inc	E	248 355-5670
Southfield (G-14915)		
Fedex Office & Print Svcs Inc	E	269 344-7445
Portage (G-12995)		
Fedex Office & Print Svcs Inc	E	586 296-4890
Roseville (G-13803)		
Fedex Office & Print Svcs Inc	E	248 443-2679
Lathrup Village (G-9499)		
Fedex Office & Print Svcs Inc	F	734 522-7322
Westland (G-17555)		
Fedex Office & Print Svcs Inc	F	313 271-8877
Dearborn (G-3706)		
Fedex Office & Print Svcs Inc	F	734 996-0050
Ann Arbor (G-460)		
Fedex Office & Print Svcs Inc	F	248 680-0280
Troy (G-16361)		
Fedex Office & Print Svcs Inc	F	734 374-0225
Taylor (G-15722)		
Fedex Office & Print Svcs Inc	G	248 651-2679
Rochester (G-13321)		
Gary Cork Incorporated		231 946-1061
Traverse City (G-15976)		
Insty-Prints West Inc		517 321-7091
Lansing (G-9299)		
J & M Reproductions Corp	E	248 588-8100
Troy (G-16429)		
K & S Printing Centers Inc		734 482-1680
Ann Arbor (G-514)		
Kenewell Group	G	810 714-4290
Fenton (G-5222)		
Kmak Inc	G	517 784-8800
Jackson (G-8489)		
Kolossos Printing Inc	F	734 994-5400
Ann Arbor (G-517)		
Kwikie Inc	G	231 946-9942
Traverse City (G-16019)		
Lightning Litho Inc	F	517 394-2995
Lansing (G-9392)		
Lopez Reproductions Inc		313 386-4526
Detroit (G-4209)		
Mega Printing Inc	G	248 624-6065
Walled Lake (G-16898)		
Megee Printing Inc	F	269 344-3226
Kalamazoo (G-8820)		
Muhleck Enterprises Inc	F	517 333-0713
Okemos (G-12133)		
Print Tech Printing Place Inc	G	989 772-6109
Mount Pleasant (G-11221)		
Printing Centre Inc	F	517 694-2400
Holt (G-7922)		
Quickprint of Adrian Inc	F	517 263-2290
Adrian (G-89)		
Rumler Brothers Inc	G	517 437-2990
Hillsdale (G-7538)		
Specifications Service Company	F	248 353-0244
Bloomfield (G-1736)		
Wholesale Weave Inc	F	800 762-2037
Detroit (G-4441)		

PHOTOENGRAVING SVC

Brophy Engraving Co Inc	E	313 871-2333
Detroit (G-3919)		
Fusion Flexo LLC		269 685-5827
Richland (G-13249)		
Fusion Flexo LLC	E	269 685-5827
Plainwell (G-12525)		
Owosso Graphic Arts Inc	E	989 725-7112
Owosso (G-12309)		
Rob Enterprises Inc	F	269 685-5827
Plainwell (G-12543)		

PHOTOGRAMMATIC MAPPING SVCS

Superior Information Tech LLC	F	734 666-9963
Livonia (G-9948)		

PHOTOGRAPHIC EQPT & SPLYS

Accuform Prtg & Graphics Inc	F	313 271-5600
Detroit (G-3838)		
Compatible Laser Products Inc	F	810 629-0459
Fenton (G-5197)		
General Dynamics Glbl IMG Tech	A	248 293-2929
Rochester Hills (G-13432)		
General Dynamics Mission	A	530 271-2500
Rochester Hills (G-13434)		
Skypersonic LLC	G	248 648-4822
Troy (G-16607)		

PHOTOGRAPHIC EQPT & SPLYS WHOLESALERS

Photo Systems Inc	E	734 424-9625
Dexter (G-4503)		

PHOTOGRAPHIC EQPT & SPLYS, WHOLESALE: Printing Apparatus

Ahearn Signs and Printing	G	734 699-3777
Belleville (G-1440)		

PHOTOGRAPHIC EQPT & SPLYS: Cameras, Aerial

Envirodrone Inc	G	226 344-5614
Detroit (G-4039)		

PHOTOGRAPHIC EQPT & SPLYS: Densitometers

X-Rite Incorporated	C	616 803-2100
Grand Rapids (G-7006)		

PHOTOGRAPHIC EQPT & SPLYS: Printing Eqpt

Douthitt Corporation	E	313 259-1565
Detroit (G-4016)		
Douthitt Corporation	F	313 259-1565
Detroit (G-4017)		

PRODUCT SECTION

PIPE & TUBES: Seamless

PHOTOGRAPHIC EQPT & SPLYS: Printing Frames
Northern Michig .... F 989 340-1272
Lachine *(G-9076)*

PHOTOGRAPHIC EQPT & SPLYS: Toners, Prprd, Not Chem Plnts
Lasers Resource Inc .... E 616 554-5555
Grand Rapids *(G-6620)*
Nationwide Laser Technologies .... G 248 488-0155
Farmington Hills *(G-5077)*
Precision Printer Services Inc .... F 269 384-5725
Portage *(G-13023)*

PHOTOGRAPHY SVCS: Commercial
Appropos LLC .... E 844 462-7776
Grand Rapids *(G-6175)*
Engineering Graphics Inc .... G 517 485-5828
Lansing *(G-9225)*
Graphic Enterprises Inc .... D 248 616-4900
Madison Heights *(G-10258)*
Livbig LLC .... G 888 519-8290
Portage *(G-13010)*

PHOTOGRAPHY SVCS: Portrait Studios
Celebrations .... G 906 482-4946
Hancock *(G-7250)*
Main Street Portraits .... G 269 321-3310
Richland *(G-13251)*

PHOTOGRAPHY SVCS: School
Great Lakes Photo Inc .... G 586 784-5446
Richmond *(G-13264)*

PHOTOGRAPHY SVCS: Still Or Video
Livbig LLC .... G 888 519-8290
Portage *(G-13010)*

PHOTOTYPESETTING SVC
Tweddle Group Inc .... C 586 307-3700
Clinton Township *(G-3252)*

PHOTOVOLTAIC Solid State
Nuvosun Inc .... D 408 514-6200
Midland *(G-10897)*
Suematek .... G 517 614-2235
Ypsilanti *(G-18103)*

PHYSICAL FITNESS CENTERS
Grit Obstacle Training LLP .... G 248 829-0414
Rochester *(G-13323)*
Vanroth LLC .... F 734 929-5268
Ann Arbor *(G-691)*

PHYSICIANS' OFFICES & CLINICS: Medical doctors
Affiliated Troy Dermatologist .... F 248 267-5020
Troy *(G-16171)*
Remnant Publications Inc .... E 517 279-1304
Coldwater *(G-3327)*
Thompson Surgical Instrs Inc .... E 231 922-0177
Traverse City *(G-16122)*
Trulife Inc .... E 517 787-1600
Jackson *(G-8596)*

PICTURE FRAMES: Wood
Art of Custom Framing Inc .... G 248 435-3726
Troy *(G-16218)*
Martin Products Company Inc .... F 269 651-1721
Sturgis *(G-15615)*
Studio of Fine Arts Inc .... G 313 280-1177
Royal Oak *(G-13974)*

PIECE GOODS & NOTIONS WHOLESALERS
Haartz Corporation .... G 248 646-8200
Bloomfield Hills *(G-1771)*
Morris Associates Inc .... E 248 355-9055
Southfield *(G-14987)*
Tennant & Associates Inc .... G 248 643-6140
Troy *(G-16636)*

PIECE GOODS, NOTIONS & DRY GOODS, WHOL: Textile Converters
Acme Mills Company .... C 517 437-8940
Hillsdale *(G-7513)*

PIECE GOODS, NOTIONS & OTHER DRY GOODS, WHOL: Fabric, Coated
Sassy Fabrics Inc .... G 810 694-0440
Grand Blanc *(G-5982)*

PIECE GOODS, NOTIONS & OTHER DRY GOODS, WHOL: Flags/Banners
Signs365com LLC .... G 800 265-8830
Shelby Township *(G-14694)*

PIECE GOODS, NOTIONS & OTHER DRY GOODS, WHOLESALE: Fabrics
Allender & Company .... G 248 398-5776
Ferndale *(G-5258)*

PIECE GOODS, NOTIONS/DRY GOODS, WHOL: Drapery Mtrl, Woven
Parkway Drapery & Uphl Co Inc .... G 734 779-1300
Livonia *(G-9884)*

PIECE GOODS, NOTIONS/DRY GOODS, WHOL: Silk Piece, Woven
J America Licensed Pdts Inc .... G 517 655-8800
Fowlerville *(G-5571)*

PIGMENTS, INORGANIC: Bone Black
Ebonex Corporation .... F 313 388-0063
Melvindale *(G-10697)*

PILLOW FILLING MTRLS: Curled Hair, Cotton Waste, Moss
Airlite Synthetics Mfg Inc .... F 248 335-8131
Pontiac *(G-12799)*
Augustine Innovations LLC .... G 248 686-1822
Commerce Township *(G-3392)*

PINS
Dyer Corporation .... G 231 894-4282
Montague *(G-11090)*
Fred Oswalts Pins Unltd .... G 269 342-1387
Portage *(G-12997)*
Pink Pin Lady LLC .... G 586 731-1532
Shelby Township *(G-14666)*
Shellys Pins N Needles .... G 517 861-7110
Howell *(G-8096)*

PINS: Dowel
Henry Plambeck .... G 586 463-3410
Harrison Township *(G-7332)*
Merchants Automatic Pdts Inc .... E 734 829-0020
Canton *(G-2401)*
Warren Screw Works Inc .... G 734 525-2920
Livonia *(G-9998)*

PIPE & FITTING: Fabrication
A & B Tube Benders Inc .... G 586 773-0440
Warren *(G-16906)*
Austin Tube Products Inc .... E 231 745-2741
Baldwin *(G-1082)*
B L Harroun and Son Inc .... E 269 345-8657
Kalamazoo *(G-8692)*
Baldauf Enterprises Inc .... D 989 686-0350
Bay City *(G-1279)*
Big Foot Manufacturing Co .... F 231 775-5588
Cadillac *(G-2231)*
Blissfield Manufacturing Co .... B 517 486-2121
Blissfield *(G-1713)*
Bundy Corporation .... G 517 439-1132
Hillsdale *(G-7519)*
Burnham & Northern Inc .... G 517 279-7501
Coldwater *(G-3292)*
Cadillac Culvert Inc .... F 231 775-3761
Cadillac *(G-2236)*
Computer Operated Mfg .... E 989 686-1333
Bay City *(G-1297)*
Denso Air Systems Michigan Inc .... D 269 962-9676
Battle Creek *(G-1171)*
Detroit Nipple Works Inc .... F 313 872-6370
Detroit *(G-3996)*
Fernco Inc .... C 810 503-9000
Davison *(G-3648)*
Fhc Holding Company .... G 616 538-3231
Wyoming *(G-18001)*
Flexible Metal Inc .... D 810 231-1300
Hamburg *(G-7225)*
Fluid Routing Solutions Inc .... E 231 592-1700
Big Rapids *(G-1628)*
Formfab LLC .... E 248 844-3676
Rochester Hills *(G-13427)*
Future Industries Inc .... E 616 844-0772
Grand Haven *(G-6017)*
Gonzalez Group Jonesville LLC .... E 517 849-9908
Jonesville *(G-8655)*
Gray Brothers Mfg Inc .... E 269 483-7615
White Pigeon *(G-17650)*
Huron Inc .... E 810 359-5344
Lexington *(G-9558)*
JCs Tool & Mfg Co Inc .... E 989 892-8975
Essexville *(G-4873)*
Manistee Wldg & Piping Svc Inc .... G 231 723-2551
Manistee *(G-10428)*
Marshall Excelsior Co .... E 269 789-6700
Marshall *(G-10577)*
Meccom Corporation .... G 313 895-4900
Detroit *(G-4224)*
Metaldyne Tblar Components LLC .... C 248 727-1800
Southfield *(G-14979)*
Motor City Bending & Rolling .... G 313 368-4400
Detroit *(G-4255)*
Nelson Hardware .... G 269 327-3583
Portage *(G-13018)*
Novi Tool & Machine Company .... D 313 532-0900
Redford *(G-13176)*
Oilpatch Machine Tool Inc .... G 989 772-0637
Mount Pleasant *(G-11215)*
Parma Tube Co Inc .... E 269 651-2351
Sturgis *(G-15626)*
Patton Welding Inc .... F 231 258-9925
Kalkaska *(G-8957)*
Pipe Fabricators Inc .... D 269 345-8657
Kalamazoo *(G-8853)*
Pontiac Coil Inc .... C 248 922-1100
Clarkston *(G-2947)*
Power Process Piping Inc .... C 734 451-0130
Plymouth *(G-12724)*
Pyramid Tubular Tech Inc .... G 810 732-6335
Flint *(G-5486)*
River Valley Machine Inc .... E 269 673-8070
Allegan *(G-187)*
Roman Engineering .... D 231 238-7644
Afton *(G-106)*
S & S Tube Inc .... F 989 656-7211
Bay Port *(G-1375)*
Spiral Industries Inc .... E 810 632-6300
Howell *(G-8101)*
St Regis Culvert Inc .... F 517 543-3430
Charlotte *(G-2668)*
TI Group Auto Systems LLC .... C 859 235-5420
Auburn Hills *(G-1023)*
Unified Industries Inc .... F 517 546-3220
Howell *(G-8118)*
W Soule & Co .... E 616 975-6272
Grand Rapids *(G-6975)*

PIPE & FITTINGS: Cast Iron
Michigan Poly Pipe Inc .... G 517 709-8100
Grand Ledge *(G-6111)*

PIPE & FITTINGS: Pressure, Cast Iron
Threaded Products Co .... E 586 727-3435
Richmond *(G-13272)*

PIPE & TUBES: Copper & Copper Alloy
Mueller Industries Inc .... D 248 446-3720
Brighton *(G-1964)*

PIPE & TUBES: Seamless
Dwm Holdings Inc .... D 586 541-0013
Warren *(G-17011)*
Forged Tubular Products Inc .... G 313 843-6720
Detroit *(G-4069)*
Seadrift Pipeline Corp .... F 989 636-6636
Midland *(G-10913)*

Employee Codes: A=Over 500 employees, B=251-500
C=101-250, D=51-100, E=20-50, F=10-19, G=3-9

2020 Harris Michigan Industrial Directory

PIPE FITTINGS: Plastic

PIPE FITTINGS: Plastic

- Colonial Engineering Inc ....F...... 269 323-2495
  Portage *(G-12989)*
- Conley Composites LLC ....E...... 918 299-5051
  Grand Rapids *(G-6300)*
- Ethylene LLC ....E...... 616 554-3464
  Kentwood *(G-9005)*
- Etx Holdings Inc ....G...... 989 463-1151
  Alma *(G-237)*
- GLS Industries LLC ....G...... 586 255-9221
  Warren *(G-17058)*
- GLS Industries LLC ....E...... 586 255-9221
  Warren *(G-17059)*
- Mueller Industries Inc ....D...... 248 446-3720
  Brighton *(G-1964)*

PIPE JOINT COMPOUNDS

- Bear Cub Holdings Inc ....G...... 231 242-1152
  Harbor Springs *(G-7274)*
- Huhnseal USA Inc ....G...... 248 347-0606
  Novi *(G-11903)*
- Scodeller Construction Inc ....D...... 248 374-1102
  Wixom *(G-17890)*

PIPE SECTIONS, FABRICATED FROM PURCHASED PIPE

- Myco Enterprises Inc ....G...... 248 348-3806
  Northville *(G-11713)*
- Quality Pipe Products Inc ....E...... 734 606-5100
  New Boston *(G-11509)*

PIPE, SEWER: Concrete

- Co-Pipe Products Inc ....E...... 734 287-1000
  Taylor *(G-15702)*
- Upper Peninsula Con Pipe Co ....F...... 906 786-0934
  Escanaba *(G-4863)*

PIPE: Brass & Bronze

- Mueller Brass Co ....D...... 810 987-7770
  Port Huron *(G-12945)*

PIPE: Concrete

- Carlesimo Products Inc ....E...... 248 474-0415
  Farmington Hills *(G-4957)*
- National Concrete Products Co ....E...... 734 453-8448
  Plymouth *(G-12698)*
- Northern Concrete Pipe Inc ....D...... 517 645-2777
  Charlotte *(G-2662)*
- Northern Concrete Pipe Inc ....E...... 989 892-3545
  Bay City *(G-1338)*

PIPE: Plastic

- Advanced Drainage Systems Inc .....G...... 989 761-7610
  Clifford *(G-3009)*
- Advanced Drainage Systems Inc .....D...... 989 723-5208
  Owosso *(G-12275)*
- Conley Composites LLC ....E...... 918 299-5051
  Grand Rapids *(G-6300)*
- Creek Plastics LLC ....F...... 517 423-1003
  Tecumseh *(G-15786)*
- Ethylene LLC ....E...... 616 554-3464
  Kentwood *(G-9005)*
- Genova Products Inc ....D...... 810 744-4500
  Davison *(G-3650)*
- Vidon Plastics Inc ....D...... 810 667-0634
  Lapeer *(G-9490)*

PIPE: Sewer, Cast Iron

- M & E Manufacturing Inc ....G...... 616 241-1509
  Grand Rapids *(G-6638)*

PIPE: Sheet Metal

- Ede Co ....G...... 586 756-7555
  Warren *(G-17016)*

PIPELINE TERMINAL FACILITIES: Independent

- Sadia Enterprises Inc ....G...... 248 854-4666
  Troy *(G-16588)*

PIPES & TUBES

- Creform Corporation ....F...... 248 926-2555
  Novi *(G-11858)*
- Gladiator Quality Sorting LLC ....G...... 734 578-1950
  Canton *(G-2378)*
- WM Tube & Wire Forming Inc ....F...... 231 830-9393
  Muskegon *(G-11454)*

PIPES & TUBES: Steel

- A & B Tube Benders Inc ....E...... 586 773-0440
  Warren *(G-16905)*
- Ace Consulting & MGT Inc ....G...... 989 821-7040
  Roscommon *(G-13747)*
- Advanced Drainage Systems Inc .....D...... 989 723-5208
  Owosso *(G-12275)*
- All Bending & Tubular Pdts LLC ....F...... 616 333-2364
  Grand Rapids *(G-6158)*
- Atlas Tube (plymouth) Inc ....D...... 734 738-5600
  Plymouth *(G-12575)*
- Austin Tube Products Inc ....E...... 231 745-2741
  Baldwin *(G-1082)*
- Benteler Automotive Corp ....A...... 616 245-4607
  Grand Rapids *(G-6212)*
- Benteler Automotive Corp ....B...... 616 247-3936
  Auburn Hills *(G-791)*
- Berkley Industries Inc ....F...... 989 656-2171
  Bay Port *(G-1372)*
- Burgaflex North America Inc ....E...... 810 584-7296
  Grand Blanc *(G-5961)*
- Delta Tube & Fabricating Corp ....E...... 248 634-8267
  Holly *(G-7874)*
- Diversified Tube LLC ....F...... 313 790-7348
  Southfield *(G-14882)*
- Dundee Products Company ....E...... 734 529-2441
  Dundee *(G-4581)*
- Energy Steel & Supply Co ....D...... 810 538-4990
  Lapeer *(G-9458)*
- Exceptional Product Sales LLC ....F...... 586 286-3240
  Clinton Township *(G-3110)*
- Formfab LLC ....E...... 248 844-3676
  Rochester Hills *(G-13427)*
- General Structures Inc ....E...... 586 774-6105
  Warren *(G-17054)*
- Inline Tube ....G...... 586 294-4093
  Fraser *(G-5670)*
- M & W Manufacturing Co LLC ....G...... 586 741-8897
  Chesterfield *(G-2800)*
- Martinrea Industries Inc ....C...... 231 832-5504
  Reed City *(G-13220)*
- Martinrea Industries Inc ....H...... 734 428-2400
  Manchester *(G-10408)*
- Midway Strl Pipe & Sup Inc ....G...... 517 787-1350
  Jackson *(G-8527)*
- New 11 Inc ....E...... 616 494-9370
  Holland *(G-7754)*
- Parma Tube Corp ....E...... 269 651-2351
  Sturgis *(G-15626)*
- Rbc Enterprises Inc ....E...... 313 491-3350
  Detroit *(G-4330)*
- Rock River Fabrications Inc ....E...... 616 281-5769
  Grand Rapids *(G-6832)*
- Rolled Alloys Inc ....D...... 800 521-0332
  Temperance *(G-15842)*
- Roman Engineering ....D...... 231 238-7644
  Afton *(G-106)*
- S & S Tube Inc ....F...... 989 656-7211
  Bay Port *(G-1375)*
- TI Automotive LLC ....F...... 586 948-6036
  New Haven *(G-11528)*
- TI Group Auto Systems LLC ....C...... 859 235-5420
  Auburn Hills *(G-1023)*
- Trans Tube Inc ....F...... 248 334-5720
  Pontiac *(G-12871)*
- Transportation Tech Group Inc ....E...... 810 233-0440
  Flint *(G-5512)*
- Usui International Corporation ....E...... 734 354-3626
  Plymouth *(G-12784)*

PIPES & TUBES: Welded

- Arcelormittal USA LLC ....F...... 313 332-5600
  Detroit *(G-3874)*
- Ernest Industries Acquisition, ...E...... 734 595-9500
  Westland *(G-17554)*
- Grinding Specialists Inc ....E...... 734 729-1775
  Westland *(G-17565)*

PIPES: Steel & Iron

- Hydraulic Tubes & Fittings LLC ....E...... 810 660-8088
  Lapeer *(G-9464)*

PIPES: Tobacco

- Loonar Stn Two The 2 or 2nd ....G...... 419 720-1222
  Temperance *(G-15834)*

PISTONS & PISTON RINGS

- Federal Screw Works ....F...... 734 941-4211
  Romulus *(G-13676)*
- Federal-Mogul Piston Rings Inc ....F...... 248 354-7700
  Southfield *(G-14909)*
- Federal-Mogul Powertrain LLC ....E...... 734 930-1590
  Ann Arbor *(G-458)*
- Kaydon Corporation ....B...... 734 747-7025
  Ann Arbor *(G-516)*
- Mahle Eng Components USA Inc ....F...... 248 305-8200
  Farmington Hills *(G-5051)*

PLANING MILL, NEC

- lll 702 Cedar River Lbr Inc ....E...... 906 497-5365
  Powers *(G-13076)*
- Willsie Lumber Company ....F...... 989 695-5094
  Freeland *(G-5761)*

PLANING MILLS: Millwork

- Canusa Inc ....G...... 906 446-3327
  Gwinn *(G-7217)*

PLANTERS: Plastic

- Blackmore Co Inc ....D...... 734 483-8661
  Belleville *(G-1442)*
- Bloem LLC ....F...... 616 622-6344
  Hudsonville *(G-8148)*

PLANTS: Artificial & Preserved

- US Energy Systems Inc ....G...... 248 765-7995
  Rochester Hills *(G-13538)*

PLAQUES: Clay, Plaster/Papier-Mache, Factory Production

- R L Hume Award Co ....G...... 269 324-3063
  Portage *(G-13026)*

PLAQUES: Picture, Laminated

- M P C Awards ....G...... 586 254-4660
  Shelby Township *(G-14629)*

PLASMAS

- Biolife Plasma Services LP ....G...... 989 773-1500
  Mount Pleasant *(G-11180)*
- Octapharma Plasma Inc ....G...... 248 597-0314
  Madison Heights *(G-10316)*
- Plasma Pros ....G...... 734 354-6737
  Westland *(G-17588)*

PLASTIC COLORING & FINISHING

- Albar Industries Inc ....B...... 810 667-0150
  Lapeer *(G-9440)*
- Tribar Manufacturing LLC ....E...... 248 669-0077
  Wixom *(G-17916)*
- Tribar Manufacturing LLC ....G...... 248 374-5870
  Wixom *(G-17917)*

PLASTIC PRDTS

- ABC Packaging Equipment & Mtls ...F...... 616 784-2330
  Comstock Park *(G-3458)*
- D B International LLC ....G...... 616 796-0679
  Holland *(G-7603)*
- Hubble Enterprises Inc ....G...... 616 676-4485
  Ada *(G-18)*
- John Allen Enterprises ....G...... 734 426-2507
  Ann Arbor *(G-512)*
- Kurt Dubowski ....G...... 231 796-0055
  Big Rapids *(G-1637)*
- Plastipak Packaging Inc ....G...... 734 529-2475
  Dundee *(G-4597)*
- Prompt Plastics ....G...... 586 307-8525
  Warren *(G-17202)*
- Range Cards ....G...... 248 880-8444
  Clarkston *(G-2950)*
- Silikids Inc ....G...... 866 789-7454
  Traverse City *(G-16104)*
- U S Farathane Port Huron LLC ....G...... 248 754-7000
  Auburn Hills *(G-1033)*

PRODUCT SECTION

PLASTICS PROCESSING

USF Westland LLC Auburn Hills (G-1042)	G	248 754-7000

PLASTICS FILM & SHEET

Berry Global Inc Zeeland (G-18118)	B	616 772-4635
Dow Chemical Company Midland (G-10836)	C	989 636-4406
Dow Chemical Company Midland (G-10834)	B	989 636-1000
Dow Chemical Company Midland (G-10848)	D	989 636-5409
Dow Inc Midland (G-10851)	G	989 636-1000
Mpf Acquisitions Inc Martin (G-10596)	E	269 672-5511
Petoskey Plastics Inc Petoskey (G-12469)	E	231 347-2602
Petoskey Plastics Inc Petoskey (G-12470)	C	231 347-2602

PLASTICS FILM & SHEET: Polyethylene

Cadillac Products Inc Troy (G-16253)	B	248 813-8200
Cadillac Products Inc Roseville (G-13779)	D	586 774-1700
Environmental Protection Inc Traverse City (G-15965)	F	231 943-2265
Jsp International LLC Madison Heights (G-10285)	F	248 397-3200
Jsp International LLC Detroit (G-4167)	E	313 834-0612
National Plastek Inc Caledonia (G-2310)	E	616 698-9559
Profile Industrial Packg Corp Grand Rapids (G-6785)	C	616 245-7260

PLASTICS FILM & SHEET: Vinyl

Coral Corporation Alto (G-326)	G	616 868-6295

PLASTICS FINISHED PRDTS: Laminated

H & R Wood Specialties Inc Gobles (G-5947)	E	269 628-2181
Janice Morse Inc West Bloomfield (G-17482)	E	248 624-7300
Key Plastics LLC Plymouth (G-12667)	G	248 449-6100
Noron Composite Technologies Manistee (G-10433)	E	231 723-9277
Paramount Solutions Inc Ray (G-13135)	G	586 914-0708
Tuscarora Inc -Vs Owosso (G-12325)	G	989 729-2780

PLASTICS FOAM, WHOLESALE

Michigan Foam Products Inc Grand Rapids (G-6671)	F	616 452-9611

PLASTICS MATERIAL & RESINS

Advanced Elastomers Corp Livonia (G-9628)	G	734 458-4194
Alumilite Corporation Galesburg (G-5805)	F	269 488-4000
Amplas Compounding LLC Sterling Heights (G-15260)	F	586 795-2555
Anderson Development Company Adrian (G-49)	C	517 263-2121
API Polymers Inc Clinton Township (G-3055)	G	855 274-7659
BASF Corporation Livonia (G-9660)	D	734 591-5560
C & D Enterprises Inc Burton (G-2147)	F	248 373-0011
Cartex Corporation Romulus (G-13660)	D	734 857-5961
Chase Plastic Services Inc Grand Rapids (G-6273)	G	616 246-7190
Chelsea-Megan Holding Inc Troy (G-16265)	F	248 307-9160
Cleanese Americas LLC Auburn Hills (G-814)	G	248 377-2700
Cole Polymer Technologies Inc Buchanan (G-2114)	G	269 695-6275
Covestro LLC Auburn Hills (G-828)	E	248 475-7700
Cytec Industries Inc Kalamazoo (G-8722)	C	269 349-6677
Dart Container Corp Kentucky Mason (G-10632)	B	517 676-3800
Dow Chemical Company Midland (G-10839)	G	989 636-8587
Dow Chemical Company Midland (G-10840)	G	989 636-1000
Dow Chemical Company Midland (G-10845)	D	989 636-0540
E I Du Pont De Nemours & Co Auburn Hills (G-849)	E	302 999-6566
Eagle Design & Technology Inc Zeeland (G-18133)	E	616 748-1022
Eastman Chemical Company Trenton (G-16153)	G	734 672-7823
Envisiontec Inc Dearborn (G-3702)	D	313 436-4300
Florida Production Engrg Inc Troy (G-16368)	F	248 588-4870
FM Research Management LLC Trenary (G-16150)	G	906 360-5833
Foampartner Americas Inc Rochester Hills (G-13426)	G	248 243-3100
Freudenberg N Amer Ltd Partnr Plymouth (G-12623)	G	734 354-5505
Freudenberg-Nok General Partnr Plymouth (G-12624)	C	734 451-0020
Geomembrane Research Traverse City (G-15978)	G	231 943-2266
Georgia-Pacific LLC Grayling (G-7107)	E	989 348-7275
Harbor Green Solutions LLC Benton Harbor (G-1507)	G	269 352-0265
Huntsman Advanced Materials AM East Lansing (G-4662)	C	517 351-5900
Huntsman-Cooper LLC Auburn Hills (G-902)	D	248 322-7300
Interfibe Corporation Schoolcraft (G-14495)	F	269 327-6141
JB Products Inc Troy (G-16434)	G	248 549-1900
Kayler Mold & Engineering Sterling Heights (G-15388)	G	586 739-0699
Kentwood Packaging Corporation Walker (G-16869)	D	616 698-9000
Lakeshore Marble Company Inc Stevensville (G-15574)	E	269 429-8241
Lauren Plastics LLC Spring Lake (G-15158)	E	330 339-3373
McKechnie Vhcl Cmpnnts USA Inc Roseville (G-13832)	E	218 894-1218
Michigan Polymer Reclaim Inc Saint Johns (G-14290)	F	989 227-0497
Midwest Resin Inc Roseville (G-13838)	G	586 803-3417
Mitsubishi Chls Perf Plyrs Inc Warren (G-17157)	E	586 755-1660
Navtech LLC Wixom (G-17862)	G	248 427-1080
New Boston Rtm Inc New Boston (G-11505)	E	734 753-9956
Package Design & Mfg Inc Brighton (G-1972)	E	248 486-4390
Palmer Distributors Inc Fraser (G-5703)	D	586 772-4225
Pier One Polymers Incorporated Saint Clair (G-14231)	F	810 326-1456
Pittsburgh Glass Works LLC Rochester Hills (G-13494)	C	248 371-1700
Plascon Inc Traverse City (G-16070)	E	231 935-1580
Plascon Films Inc Traverse City (G-16071)	F	231 935-1580
Plascon Packaging Inc Traverse City (G-16072)	E	231 935-1580
Plasteel Corporation Inkster (G-8231)	F	313 562-5400
Plastic Flow LLC Hancock (G-7255)	G	906 483-0691
Plasticos Inc Clinton Township (G-3195)	G	586 493-1908
Plastics Plus Inc Auburn Hills (G-975)	E	800 975-8694
PPG Industries Inc Troy (G-16557)	F	248 641-2000
Pro Polymers Inc Stockbridge (G-15592)	G	734 222-8820
Quality Dairy Company Lansing (G-9416)	D	517 319-4302
Reklein Plastics Incorporated Sterling Heights (G-15463)	G	586 739-8850
Resinate Materials Group Inc Plymouth (G-12734)	F	800 891-2955
Revstone Industries LLC Troy (G-16577)	G	248 351-1000
Revstone Industries LLC Southfield (G-15014)	F	248 351-8800
Rhe-Tech LLC Fowlerville (G-5579)	G	517 223-4874
Rohm Haas Dnmark Invstmnts LLC Midland (G-10909)	G	989 636-1463
Rosler Metal Finishing USA LLC Battle Creek (G-1242)	D	269 441-3000
Rubber & Plastics Co Auburn Hills (G-995)	E	248 370-0700
Saint-Gobain Prfmce Plas Corp Beaverton (G-1391)	D	989 435-9533
Sekisui America Corporation Coldwater (G-3331)	C	517 279-7587
Sekisui Polymr Innovations LLC Holland (G-7799)	D	616 392-9004
Shapeshift LLC Lansing (G-9322)	G	517 910-3078
Sigma International Inc Livonia (G-9928)	E	248 230-9681
Solutia Inc Trenton (G-16157)	B	734 676-4400
Specialty Products Us LLC Midland (G-10919)	G	989 636-4341
Stonecrafters Inc Clarklake (G-2901)	F	517 529-4990
Summit Polymers Inc Vicksburg (G-16845)	C	269 649-4900
Toray Resin Company Troy (G-16647)	D	248 269-8800
Trinseo Midland (G-10921)	G	989 636-5409
Ufp Technologies Inc Grand Rapids (G-6948)	D	616 949-8100
United Foam A Ufp Tech Brnd Grand Rapids (G-6952)	D	616 949-8100
Vibracoustic North America L P South Haven (G-14780)	E	269 637-2116
Vibracoustic North America LP Farmington Hills (G-5148)	G	248 410-5066
Wmc LLC Greenville (G-7161)	E	616 560-4142
Woodbridge Sales & Engrg Inc Troy (G-16698)	C	248 288-0100
Xg Sciences Inc Lansing (G-9436)	F	517 316-2038

PLASTICS MATERIALS, BASIC FORMS & SHAPES WHOLESALERS

H & L Advantage Inc Grandville (G-7042)	E	616 532-1012
Harbor Green Solutions LLC Benton Harbor (G-1507)	G	269 352-0265
Idemitsu Chemicals USA Corp Southfield (G-14942)	G	248 355-0666
Idemitsu Lubricants Amer Corp Southfield (G-14943)	F	248 355-0666
Key Plastics LLC Plymouth (G-12667)	G	248 449-6100
Marelli North America Inc Farmington Hills (G-5057)	C	248 848-4800
Mark Schwager Inc Shelby Township (G-14633)	G	248 275-1978
Material Difference Tech LLC Macomb (G-10140)	F	888 818-1283
Recycling Concepts W Mich Inc Grand Rapids (G-6815)	D	616 942-8888

PLASTICS PROCESSING

Active Plastics Inc Caledonia (G-2288)	F	616 813-5109
Advanced Binding Solutions LLC Wallace (G-16885)	E	920 664-1469
AIN Plastics Southfield (G-14824)	F	248 356-4000
Aluminum Textures Inc Grandville (G-7020)	E	616 538-3144
Americo Corporation Dearborn (G-3675)	G	313 565-6550
Amplas Compounding LLC Sterling Heights (G-15260)	F	586 795-2555
Aqpe LLC Saint Clair (G-14204)	G	810 329-9259

Employee Codes: A=Over 500 employees, B=251-500
C=101-250, D=51-100, E=20-50, F=10-19, G=3-9

Automotive Plastics Recycling..............E....... 810 767-3800
Flint *(G-5381)*
Clearform..............G....... 616 656-5359
Caledonia *(G-2295)*
Continental Strl Plas Inc..............C....... 248 237-7800
Auburn Hills *(G-823)*
Continental Strl Plas Inc..............E....... 248 593-9500
Troy *(G-16278)*
Continntal Strl Plas Hldngs Co..............C....... 248 237-7800
Auburn Hills *(G-824)*
CSP Holding Corp..............F....... 248 237-7800
Auburn Hills *(G-831)*
CSP Holding Corp..............G....... 248 724-4410
Auburn Hills *(G-832)*
Dendritic Nanotechnologies Inc..............G....... 989 774-3096
Midland *(G-10831)*
Destiny Plastics Incorporated..............F....... 810 622-0018
Deckerville *(G-3807)*
Display Pack Inc..............C....... 616 451-3061
Cedar Springs *(G-2553)*
Display Pack Inc..............B....... 616 451-3061
Grand Rapids *(G-6356)*
E & D Engineering Systems LLC..............G....... 989 246-0770
Gladwin *(G-5929)*
Echo Engrg & Prod Sups Inc..............D....... 734 241-9622
Monroe *(G-11029)*
Factory Products Inc..............G....... 269 668-3329
Mattawan *(G-10664)*
Filcon Inc..............F....... 989 386-2986
Clare *(G-2870)*
Harbor Green Solutions LLC..............G....... 269 352-0265
Benton Harbor *(G-1507)*
Homestead Products Inc..............F....... 989 465-6182
Coleman *(G-3343)*
Icon Industries Inc..............G....... 616 241-1877
Grand Rapids *(G-6524)*
Ideal Shield LLC..............E....... 866 825-8659
Detroit *(G-4133)*
Jolicor Manufacturing Services..............F....... 586 323-5090
Shelby Township *(G-14612)*
Keltrol Enterprises Inc..............G....... 734 697-3011
Belleville *(G-1447)*
Km and I..............G....... 248 792-2782
Troy *(G-16447)*
Kunststoff Technik Scherer..............D....... 734 944-5080
Troy *(G-16452)*
Lacks Industries Inc..............C....... 616 698-3600
Grand Rapids *(G-6607)*
Lacks Industries Inc..............E....... 616 554-7135
Kentwood *(G-9017)*
Lear Operations Corporation..............G....... 248 447-1500
Southfield *(G-14965)*
Loper Corporation..............G....... 810 620-0202
Mount Morris *(G-11164)*
Maine Plastics Incorporated..............E....... 269 679-3988
Kalamazoo *(G-8815)*
Manufacturers Services Inds..............G....... 906 493-6685
Drummond Island *(G-4565)*
Martinrea Industries Inc..............C....... 231 832-5504
Reed City *(G-13220)*
Mega Screen Corp..............G....... 517 849-7057
Jonesville *(G-8663)*
Montaplast North America Inc..............F....... 248 353-5553
Auburn Hills *(G-947)*
Noack Ventures LLC..............G....... 248 583-0311
Troy *(G-16526)*
Northern Logistics LLC..............E....... 989 386-2389
Clare *(G-2881)*
Northern Plastics Inc..............F....... 586 979-7737
Sterling Heights *(G-15438)*
Paul Murphy Plastics Co..............E....... 586 774-4880
Roseville *(G-13851)*
Plasti-Fab Inc..............E....... 248 543-1415
Ferndale *(G-5311)*
Polyply Composites LLC..............E....... 616 842-6330
Grand Haven *(G-6061)*
Robmar Plastics Inc..............G....... 989 386-9600
Clare *(G-2885)*
Sgp Technologies..............G....... 810 744-1715
Burton *(G-2164)*
Stellar Plastics Corporation..............G....... 313 527-7337
Detroit *(G-4377)*
Stellar Plastics Fabg LLC..............G....... 313 527-7337
Detroit *(G-4378)*
Sumitomo Chemical America Inc..............G....... 248 284-4797
Novi *(G-12008)*
Techniplas LLC..............B....... 517 849-9911
Jonesville *(G-8669)*
Tecla Company Inc..............E....... 248 624-8200
Commerce Township *(G-3453)*
Teijin Advan Compo Ameri Inc..............G....... 248 365-6600
Auburn Hills *(G-1016)*
Tg Fluid Systems USA Corp..............B....... 810 220-6161
Brighton *(G-1997)*
TI Group Auto Systems LLC..............C....... 810 364-3277
Marysville *(G-10623)*
Total Plastics Resources LLC..............F....... 248 299-9500
Rochester Hills *(G-13529)*
Trellborg Sling Sltions US Inc..............G....... 269 639-4217
Benton Harbor *(G-1556)*
Trellborg Sling Sltions US Inc..............G....... 734 354-1250
Northville *(G-11730)*
Willco Extrusion LLC..............G....... 248 817-2373
Troy *(G-16691)*
Yanfeng US Automotive..............F....... 517 721-0179
Novi *(G-12028)*
ZF Active Safety & Elec US LLC..............C....... 734 855-2600
Livonia *(G-10014)*
ZF Passive Safety..............B....... 586 232-7200
Washington *(G-17316)*

PLASTICS SHEET: Packing Materials

A-Pac Manufacturing Company..............E....... 616 791-7222
Grand Rapids *(G-6126)*
Cadillac Products Packaging Co..............C....... 248 879-5000
Troy *(G-16254)*
Link Tech Inc..............G....... 269 427-8297
Bangor *(G-1092)*

PLASTICS: Blow Molded

ABC Group Holdings Inc..............G....... 248 352-3706
Southfield *(G-14823)*
Acm Plastic Products Inc..............D....... 269 651-7888
Sturgis *(G-15595)*
Eaton Inoac Company..............E....... 248 226-6200
Southfield *(G-14895)*
Gt Plastics & Equipment LLC..............F....... 616 678-7445
Kent City *(G-8991)*
Harman Corporation..............E....... 248 651-4477
Rochester *(G-13324)*
M C Molds Inc..............E....... 517 655-5481
Williamston *(G-17733)*
N A Actuaplast Inc..............F....... 734 744-4010
Livonia *(G-9855)*
Penguin LLC..............C....... 269 651-9488
Sturgis *(G-15628)*
Plastic Ominium Auto Inergy..............C....... 517 265-1100
Adrian *(G-85)*
Plastipak Holdings Inc..............F....... 734 455-3600
Plymouth *(G-12718)*
Regency Plastics - Ubly Inc..............D....... 989 658-8504
Ubly *(G-16723)*
Romeo-Rim Inc..............C....... 586 336-5800
Bruce Twp *(G-2096)*
SPI Blow Molding LLC..............E....... 269 849-3200
Coloma *(G-3365)*
Spirit Industries Inc..............G....... 517 371-7840
Lansing *(G-9266)*
Srg Global Coatings Inc..............C....... 248 509-1100
Troy *(G-16618)*
Statistical Processed Products..............E....... 586 792-6900
Clinton Township *(G-3235)*

PLASTICS: Cast

Alumilite Corporation..............F....... 269 488-4000
Galesburg *(G-5805)*
Global Technology Ventures Inc..............G....... 248 324-3707
Farmington Hills *(G-5011)*
Glove Coaters Incorporated..............E....... 517 741-8402
Union City *(G-16734)*
Pace Industries LLC..............A....... 231 777-3941
Muskegon *(G-11396)*
Port City Group Inc..............F....... 231 777-3941
Muskegon *(G-11400)*

PLASTICS: Extruded

Composite Development Corporat..............G....... 269 694-4159
Otsego *(G-12236)*
Delfingen Us Inc..............E....... 716 215-0300
Rochester Hills *(G-13404)*
Delfingen Us- Holding Inc..............G....... 248 519-0534
Rochester Hills *(G-13405)*
Delfingen Us-Central Amer Inc..............G....... 248 230-3500
Rochester Hills *(G-13406)*
Extrusions Division Inc..............G....... 616 247-3611
Grand Rapids *(G-6396)*
Gemini Group Inc..............F....... 989 269-6272
Bad Axe *(G-1062)*
Gemini Plastics De Mexico Inc..............G....... 989 658-8557
Ubly *(G-16717)*
Guardian Automotive Corp..............D....... 586 757-7800
Warren *(G-17070)*
Johnson Walker & Assoc LLC..............G....... 810 688-1600
North Branch *(G-11660)*
Marcon Technologies LLC..............E....... 269 279-1701
Constantine *(G-3538)*
Pepro Enterprises Inc..............D....... 989 658-3200
Ubly *(G-16720)*
Pepro Enterprises Inc..............C....... 989 658-3200
Ubly *(G-16721)*
Plastic Trim Inc..............B....... 937 429-1100
Tawas City *(G-15676)*
Plastic Trim International Inc..............C....... 989 362-4419
East Tawas *(G-4693)*
Polymerica Limited Company..............C....... 248 542-2000
Huntington Woods *(G-8191)*
Riverside Plastic Co..............E....... 231 937-7333
Howard City *(G-8006)*
Ssb Holdings Inc..............E....... 586 755-1660
Rochester Hills *(G-13517)*
Vidon Plastics Inc..............D....... 810 667-0634
Lapeer *(G-9490)*
Vintech Industries Inc..............C....... 810 724-7400
Imlay City *(G-8214)*

PLASTICS: Finished Injection Molded

2255srv Llv..............E....... 616 678-4900
Kent City *(G-8986)*
Advanced Auto Trends Inc..............E....... 248 628-6111
Oxford *(G-12333)*
Advanced Auto Trends Inc..............E....... 810 672-9203
Snover *(G-14741)*
Advanced Auto Trends Inc..............E....... 248 628-4850
Oxford *(G-12334)*
Agape Plastics Inc..............C....... 616 735-4091
Grand Rapids *(G-6152)*
Akwel Cadillac Usa Inc..............B....... 231 876-8020
Cadillac *(G-2223)*
AMP Innovative Tech LLC..............E....... 586 465-2700
Harrison Township *(G-7319)*
Ansco Pattern & Machine Co..............G....... 248 625-1362
Clarkston *(G-2907)*
Arrow Die & Mold Repair..............G....... 231 689-1829
White Cloud *(G-17619)*
B & H Plastic Co Inc..............F....... 586 727-7100
Richmond *(G-13260)*
Bermar Associates Inc..............F....... 248 589-2460
Troy *(G-16238)*
Blade Industrial Products Inc..............G....... 248 773-7400
Wixom *(G-17774)*
Bomaur Quality Plastics Inc..............F....... 810 629-9701
Fenton *(G-5190)*
Cadillac Engineered Plas Inc..............F....... 231 775-2900
Cadillac *(G-2237)*
Cel Plastics Inc..............F....... 231 777-3941
Muskegon *(G-11292)*
Craig Assembly Inc..............C....... 810 326-1374
Saint Clair *(G-14212)*
Creative Foam Corporation..............D....... 810 714-0140
Fenton *(G-5199)*
Creative Foam Corporation..............C....... 810 629-4149
Fenton *(G-5198)*
Creative Techniques Inc..............D....... 248 373-3050
Orion *(G-12178)*
D Find Corporation..............G....... 248 641-2858
Troy *(G-16293)*
Dare Products Inc..............E....... 269 965-2307
Springfield *(G-15190)*
Djw Enterprises Inc..............D....... 262 251-9500
Crystal Falls *(G-3609)*
Dl Engineering & Tech Inc..............G....... 248 852-6900
Rochester Hills *(G-13409)*
Ehc Inc..............G....... 313 259-2266
Detroit *(G-4030)*
Eimo Technologies Inc..............E....... 269 649-0545
Vicksburg *(G-16834)*
Elmet North America Inc..............F....... 517 664-9011
Lansing *(G-9364)*
Enterprise Plastics LLC..............F....... 586 665-1030
Shelby Township *(G-14588)*
Ess Tec Inc..............D....... 616 394-0230
Holland *(G-7625)*
Excel Medical Products Inc..............F....... 810 714-4775
Wixom *(G-17808)*
Exotic Rubber & Plastics Corp..............D....... 248 477-2122
Farmington Hills *(G-4996)*
Fido Enterprises Inc..............G....... 586 790-8200
Clinton Township *(G-3116)*

Future Technologies Group LLC G 810 733-3870
Flushing *(G-5536)*

Ghsp Inc F 231 873-3300
Hart *(G-7371)*

Global Supply Integrator LLC G 586 484-0734
Davisburg *(G-3635)*

Great Lakes Die Cast Corp D 231 726-4002
Muskegon *(G-11337)*

Gt Technologies Inc E 734 467-8371
Westland *(G-17566)*

HMS Mfg Co D 248 689-3232
Troy *(G-16397)*

Iig-Dss Technologies LLC E 586 725-5300
Ira *(G-8258)*

Illinois Tool Works Inc D 248 969-4248
Oxford *(G-12350)*

Imlay City Molded Pdts Corp E 810 721-9100
Imlay City *(G-8204)*

Instaset Plastics Company LLC B 586 725-0229
Anchorville *(G-331)*

Ironwood Plastics Inc C 906 932-5025
Ironwood *(G-8330)*

Jma Tool Company Inc E 586 270-6706
New Haven *(G-11524)*

Jsj Corporation E 616 842-6350
Grand Haven *(G-6042)*

Kamex Molded Products LLC G 616 355-5900
Holland *(G-7706)*

Kem Enterprises Inc G 616 676-0213
Ada *(G-21)*

Kreft Injection Technology LLC G 248 589-9202
Madison Heights *(G-10294)*

Lapeer Plating & Plastics Inc C 810 667-4240
Lapeer *(G-9468)*

Lexamar Corporation B 231 582-3163
Boyne City *(G-1827)*

M-R Products Inc G 231 378-2251
Copemish *(G-3573)*

Mark Schwager Inc G 248 275-1978
Shelby Township *(G-14633)*

Mason Tackle Company E 810 631-4571
Otisville *(G-12233)*

McG Plastics Inc E 989 667-4349
Bay City *(G-1328)*

MGR Molds Inc F 586 254-6020
Sterling Heights *(G-15419)*

Michigan Church Supply Co Inc F 810 686-8877
Mount Morris *(G-11165)*

Midwest Plastic Engineering D 269 651-5223
Sturgis *(G-15620)*

Mohr Engineering Inc E 810 227-4598
Brighton *(G-1963)*

Molding Concepts Inc E 586 264-6990
Sterling Heights *(G-15426)*

Novares US Eng Components Inc D 248 799-8949
Southfield *(G-14992)*

Novares US LLC C 517 546-1900
Howell *(G-8071)*

Novares US LLC B 616 554-3555
Grand Rapids *(G-6723)*

Oakwood Custom Coating Inc F 313 561-7740
Dearborn *(G-3745)*

Oakwood Energy Management Inc C 734 947-7700
Taylor *(G-15750)*

Oakwood Metal Fabricating Co B 313 561-7740
Dearborn *(G-3746)*

Omega Plastics Inc D 586 954-2100
Clinton Township *(G-3190)*

Petersen Products Inc F 248 446-0500
Brighton *(G-1978)*

Phillips-Medisize LLC F 248 592-2144
West Bloomfield *(G-17493)*

Plast-O-Foam LLC D 586 307-3790
Clinton Township *(G-3194)*

Proto-TEC Inc F 616 772-9511
Zeeland *(G-18181)*

Pti Engineered Plastics Inc B 586 263-5100
Macomb *(G-10159)*

R & L Frye G 989 821-6661
Roscommon *(G-13753)*

R B L Plastics Incorporated E 313 873-8800
Detroit *(G-4325)*

R C Plastics Inc F 517 523-2112
Osseo *(G-12228)*

Ray Scott Industries Inc G 248 535-2528
Port Huron *(G-12962)*

RCO Engineering Inc D 586 620-4133
Roseville *(G-13860)*

Reliable Reasonable Tl Svc LLC F 586 630-6016
Clinton Township *(G-3209)*

Robinson Industries Inc C 989 465-6111
Coleman *(G-3350)*

Ronningen Research and Dev Co C 269 649-0520
Vicksburg *(G-16842)*

Royal Technologies Corporation A 616 669-3393
Hudsonville *(G-8178)*

Royal Technologies Corporation C 616 667-4102
Hudsonville *(G-8179)*

Seaway Plastics Corporation E 810 765-8864
Marine City *(G-10482)*

Special Mold Engineering Inc E 248 652-6600
Rochester Hills *(G-13516)*

SPI LLC E 586 566-5870
Shelby Township *(G-14701)*

Systex Products Corporation D 269 964-8800
Battle Creek *(G-1257)*

Th Plastics Inc B 269 496-8495
Mendon *(G-10719)*

Thermoforms Inc F 616 974-0055
Kentwood *(G-9033)*

Thumb Plastics Inc E 989 269-9791
Bad Axe *(G-1074)*

Transnav Technologies Inc C 888 249-9955
New Baltimore *(G-11495)*

Tri-Way Manufacturing Inc E 586 776-0700
Roseville *(G-13880)*

Tribar Manufacturing LLC B 248 516-1600
Howell *(G-8115)*

Triple C Geothermal Inc G 517 282-7249
Muskegon *(G-11442)*

Universal Products Inc E 231 937-5555
Rockford *(G-13595)*

University Plastics Inc G 734 668-8773
Ann Arbor *(G-688)*

Urgent Plastic Services Inc G 248 852-8999
Rochester Hills *(G-13537)*

West Michigan Molding Inc C 616 846-4950
Grand Haven *(G-6097)*

Worswick Mold & Tool Inc F 810 765-1700
Marine City *(G-10488)*

Wright Plastic Products Co LLC D 810 326-3000
Saint Clair *(G-14237)*

Yanfeng US Automotive C 313 259-3226
Detroit *(G-4454)*

PLASTICS: Injection Molded

21st Century Plastics Corp D 517 645-2695
Potterville *(G-13072)*

3d Polymers Inc D 248 588-5562
Orchard Lake *(G-12164)*

A M R Inc G 810 329-9049
East China *(G-4619)*

Accurate Injection Molds Inc F 586 954-2553
Clinton Township *(G-3033)*

Acrylic Specialties G 248 588-4390
Madison Heights *(G-10180)*

Adac Automotive Trim Inc E 616 957-0311
Grand Rapids *(G-6138)*

Adac Door Components Inc G 616 957-0311
Grand Rapids *(G-6139)*

Adac Plastics Inc E 616 957-0311
Grand Rapids *(G-6140)*

Adac Plastics Inc C 231 777-2645
Muskegon *(G-11260)*

Adac Plastics Inc F 616 957-0311
Grand Rapids *(G-6141)*

Adac Plastics Inc C 616 957-0520
Muskegon *(G-11261)*

Adac Plastics Inc B 616 957-0311
Muskegon *(G-11262)*

Adac Plastics Inc E 616 957-0311
Grand Rapids *(G-6142)*

Adept Plastic Finishing Inc F 248 863-5930
Wixom *(G-17753)*

Advanced Rubber & Plastic G 586 754-7398
Warren *(G-16920)*

Aees Power Systems Ltd Partnr F 269 668-4429
Farmington Hills *(G-4921)*

Affinity Custom Molding Inc E 269 496-8423
Mendon *(G-10711)*

Aim Plastics Inc E 586 954-2553
Clinton Township *(G-3040)*

Alco Plastics Inc D 586 752-4527
Romeo *(G-13623)*

Alp Lighting Ceiling Pdts Inc D 231 547-6584
Charlevoix *(G-2606)*

Ameri-Kart(mi) Corp C 269 641-5811
Cassopolis *(G-2527)*

Ann Arbor Plastics Inc G 734 944-0800
Saline *(G-14377)*

Anticipated Plastics Inc F 586 427-9450
Warren *(G-16935)*

Astar Inc E 574 234-2137
Niles *(G-11595)*

Automotive Manufacturing G 517 566-8174
Sunfield *(G-15645)*

Avon Plastic Products Inc D 248 852-1000
Rochester Hills *(G-13374)*

B & N Plastics Inc G 586 758-0030
Warren *(G-16948)*

B C & A Co E 734 429-3129
Saline *(G-14379)*

Bangor Plastics Inc E 269 427-7971
Bangor *(G-1088)*

Belmont Engineered Plas LLC D 616 785-6279
Belmont *(G-1457)*

Bentzer Incorporated E 269 663-3649
Edwardsburg *(G-4759)*

Bridgville Plastics Inc F 269 465-6516
Stevensville *(G-15558)*

Built Rite Tool and Engrg LLC G 810 966-5133
Port Huron *(G-12905)*

Butler Plastics Company E 810 765-8811
Marine City *(G-10471)*

C E B Tooling Inc G 269 489-2251
Burr Oak *(G-2134)*

C-Plastics Inc E 616 837-7396
Nunica *(G-12033)*

Camcar Plastics Inc F 231 726-5000
Muskegon *(G-11289)*

Cascade Engineering Inc A 616 975-4800
Grand Rapids *(G-6260)*

Cascade Engineering Inc C 616 975-4800
Grand Rapids *(G-6261)*

Cascade Engineering Inc C 616 975-4923
Grand Rapids *(G-6262)*

Castano Plastics Inc G 248 624-3724
Wolverine Lake *(G-17935)*

Castino Corporation E 734 941-7200
Romulus *(G-13661)*

Century Plastics LLC G 586 697-5752
Macomb *(G-10115)*

Century Plastics LLC C 586 566-3900
Shelby Township *(G-14559)*

Cg Plastics Inc G 616 785-1900
Comstock Park *(G-3468)*

Chambers Industrial Tech Inc G 616 249-8190
Wyoming *(G-17991)*

Champion Plastics Inc F 248 373-8995
Auburn Hills *(G-812)*

Clarion Technologies Inc C 616 698-7277
Holland *(G-7592)*

Classic Die Inc E 616 454-3760
Grand Rapids *(G-6277)*

Cni Plastics LLC E 517 541-4960
Charlotte *(G-2641)*

Colonial Manufacturing LLC F 269 926-1000
Benton Harbor *(G-1490)*

Colonial Plastics Incorporated E 586 469-4944
Shelby Township *(G-14564)*

Composite Techniques Inc F 616 878-9795
Byron Center *(G-2181)*

Coral Corporation G 616 868-6295
Alto *(G-326)*

Cs Manufacturing Inc C 616 696-2772
Cedar Springs *(G-2551)*

Cup Acquisition LLC C 616 735-4410
Grand Rapids *(G-6322)*

D T M 1 Inc E 248 889-9210
Highland *(G-7491)*

Davalor Mold Company LLC C 586 598-0100
Chesterfield *(G-2762)*

Derby Fabg Solutions LLC D 616 866-1650
Rockford *(G-13566)*

Diversified Engrg & Plas LLC D 517 789-8118
Jackson *(G-8434)*

Dlhbowles Inc F 248 569-0652
Southfield *(G-14883)*

Do-All Plastic Inc F 313 824-6565
Detroit *(G-4014)*

Downriver Plastics Inc G 734 246-3031
Canton *(G-2366)*

Dse Industries LLC G 313 530-6668
Macomb *(G-10118)*

Dunnage Engineering Inc E 810 229-9501
Brighton *(G-1913)*

Eagle Fasteners Inc F 248 577-1441
Troy *(G-16333)*

Eagle Manufacturing Corp F 586 323-0303
Shelby Township *(G-14585)*

PRODUCT

Employee Codes: A-Over 500 employees, B=251-500 C=101-250, D=51-100, E=20-50, F=10-19, G=3-9

2020 Harris Michigan Industrial Directory

1325

Eclipse Mold Incorporated ... C ... 586 792-3320
Chesterfield *(G-2771)*

Elite Plastic Products Inc ... E ... 586 247-5800
Shelby Township *(G-14587)*

Ell Tron Manufacturing Co ... E ... 989 983-3181
Vanderbilt *(G-16804)*

Ell Tron Manufacturing Co ... G ... 989 983-3181
Vanderbilt *(G-16805)*

Engineered Plastic Components ... C ... 810 326-1650
Saint Clair *(G-14217)*

Engineered Plastic Components ... C ... 810 326-3010
Saint Clair *(G-14218)*

Engineered Polymer Products ... E ... 269 461-6955
Eau Claire *(G-4738)*

Enginred Plstic Components Inc ... D ... 248 825-4508
Troy *(G-16347)*

Engtechnik Inc ... G ... 734 667-4237
Canton *(G-2371)*

Enkon LLC ... F ... 937 890-5678
Manchester *(G-10405)*

Epc-Columbia Inc ... D ... 810 326-1650
Saint Clair *(G-14219)*

Erwin Quarder Inc ... D ... 616 575-1600
Grand Rapids *(G-6383)*

Evans Industries Inc ... G ... 313 259-2266
Detroit *(G-4045)*

Exo-S US LLC ... G ... 248 614-9707
Troy *(G-16355)*

Exo-S US LLC ... D ... 517 278-8567
Coldwater *(G-3303)*

Exsto US Inc ... G ... 734 834-7225
Ann Arbor *(G-453)*

Extreme Tool and Engrg Inc ... G ... 906 229-9100
Wakefield *(G-16851)*

Faith Plastics LLC ... E ... 269 646-2294
Marcellus *(G-10465)*

Ferro Industries Inc ... E ... 586 792-6001
Harrison Township *(G-7330)*

Flight Mold & Engineering Inc ... E ... 810 329-2900
Saint Clair *(G-14220)*

Gem Plastics Inc ... G ... 616 538-5966
Grand Rapids *(G-6433)*

Gemini Group Plastic Sales ... G ... 248 435-7991
Auburn Hills *(G-881)*

Gemini Group Services Inc ... G ... 248 435-7271
Bad Axe *(G-1063)*

Glov Enterprises LLC ... D ... 517 423-9700
Tecumseh *(G-15794)*

Grace Production Services LLC ... G ... 810 643-8070
Chesterfield *(G-2783)*

Grand Haven Custom Molding LLC ... E ... 616 935-3160
Grand Haven *(G-6021)*

Green Plastics LLC ... E ... 616 295-2718
Holland *(G-7654)*

Grw Technologies Inc ... C ... 616 575-8119
Grand Rapids *(G-6483)*

Gt Plastics Incorporated ... F ... 989 739-7803
Oscoda *(G-12210)*

Harbor Isle Plastics LLC ... E ... 269 465-6004
Stevensville *(G-15570)*

Heritage Services Company Inc ... G ... 734 282-4566
Riverview *(G-13296)*

Hi-Craft Engineering Inc ... D ... 586 293-0551
Fraser *(G-5663)*

Hicks Plastics Company Inc ... D ... 586 786-5640
Macomb *(G-10129)*

Holland Plastics Corporation ... E ... 616 844-2505
Grand Haven *(G-6037)*

Industries Unlimited Inc ... E ... 586 949-4300
Chesterfield *(G-2788)*

Integra Mold Inc ... G ... 269 327-4337
Portage *(G-13002)*

Inteva Products LLC ... B ... 517 266-8030
Adrian *(G-69)*

Intrepid Plastics Mfg Inc ... F ... 616 901-5718
Lakeview *(G-9174)*

Jac Holding Corporation ... G ... 248 874-1800
Pontiac *(G-12839)*

Jac Products Inc ... D ... 248 874-1800
Pontiac *(G-12840)*

Jer-Den Plastics Inc ... E ... 989 681-4303
Saint Louis *(G-14364)*

Jgr Plastics LLC ... E ... 810 990-1957
Port Huron *(G-12932)*

Jimdi Plastics Inc ... E ... 616 895-7766
Allendale *(G-219)*

JK Machining Inc ... F ... 269 344-0870
Kalamazoo *(G-8779)*

Kam Plastics Corp ... D ... 616 355-5900
Holland *(G-7705)*

Klann ... G ... 313 565-4135
Dearborn *(G-3730)*

Kruger Plastic Products LLC ... G ... 269 465-6404
Bridgman *(G-1869)*

Kruger Plastics Products LLC ... E ... 269 545-3311
Galien *(G-5818)*

Lacks Wheel Trim Systems LLC ... F ... 248 351-0555
Novi *(G-11927)*

Lacks Wheel Trim Systems LLC ... E ... 616 949-6570
Grand Rapids *(G-6613)*

Lawrence Plastics LLC ... D ... 248 475-0186
Clarkston *(G-2934)*

LDB Plastics Inc ... G ... 586 566-9698
Shelby Township *(G-14623)*

Leeann Plastics Inc ... F ... 269 489-5035
Burr Oak *(G-2136)*

Liberty Plastics Inc ... G ... 616 994-7033
Holland *(G-7724)*

Lincoln Industries ... G ... 989 736-6421
Lincoln *(G-9565)*

Luckmarr Plastics Inc ... D ... 586 978-8498
Sterling Heights *(G-15403)*

Luttmann Precision Mold Inc ... E ... 269 651-1193
Sturgis *(G-15614)*

M & E Plastics LLC ... F ... 989 875-4191
Ithaca *(G-8362)*

Mann + Hummel Usa Inc ... F ... 248 857-8500
Bloomfield Hills *(G-1780)*

Mann + Hummel Usa Inc ... E ... 248 857-8501
Kalamazoo *(G-8818)*

Mann + Hummel Usa Inc ... F ... 269 329-3900
Portage *(G-13014)*

Mantissa Industries Inc ... G ... 517 694-2260
Holt *(G-7915)*

Maple Valley Plastics LLC ... E ... 810 346-3040
Brown City *(G-2055)*

Matrix Manufacturing Inc ... G ... 616 532-6000
Grand Rapids *(G-6649)*

Maya Plastics Inc ... E ... 586 997-6000
Shelby Township *(G-14636)*

Mayco International LLC ... C ... 586 803-6000
Clinton Township *(G-3171)*

Mayco International LLC ... E ... 586 803-6000
Auburn Hills *(G-944)*

Mayco International LLC ... A ... 586 803-6000
Sterling Heights *(G-15414)*

Mayfair Plastics Inc ... D ... 989 732-2441
Gaylord *(G-5880)*

Mc Pherson Plastics Inc ... D ... 269 694-9487
Otsego *(G-12244)*

Mecaplast Usa LLC ... G ... 248 594-8082
Livonia *(G-9836)*

Medbio Inc ... D ... 616 245-0214
Grand Rapids *(G-6656)*

Michigan Manufactured Pdts Inc ... G ... 586 770-2584
Port Huron *(G-12941)*

Micro Plastics Mfg & Sls ... G ... 517 320-2488
Hillsdale *(G-7531)*

Miniature Custom Mfg LLC ... F ... 269 998-1277
Vicksburg *(G-16839)*

Mmi Companies LLC ... E ... 248 528-1680
Troy *(G-16510)*

Mmi Engineered Solutions Inc ... D ... 734 429-4664
Saline *(G-14403)*

Mmi Engineered Solutions Inc ... E ... 734 429-5130
Warren *(G-17158)*

Mold Masters Co ... C ... 810 245-4100
Lapeer *(G-9475)*

Mold-Rite LLC ... G ... 586 296-3970
Fraser *(G-5695)*

Molded Plastic Industries Inc ... E ... 517 694-7434
Holt *(G-7916)*

Molded Plastics & Tooling ... G ... 517 268-0849
Holt *(G-7917)*

Moldex3d Northern America Inc ... F ... 248 946-4570
Farmington Hills *(G-5072)*

Molding Solutions Inc ... E ... 616 847-6822
Grand Haven *(G-6056)*

Moller Group North America Inc ... F ... 586 532-0860
Shelby Township *(G-14647)*

Mollertech LLC ... C ... 586 532-0860
Shelby Township *(G-14648)*

Monroe Inc ... G ... 616 284-3358
Grand Rapids *(G-6703)*

Moon Roof Corporation America ... E ... 586 552-1901
Roseville *(G-13840)*

Morren Mold & Machine Inc ... G ... 616 892-7474
Allendale *(G-223)*

Motus LLC ... G ... 734 266-3237
Livonia *(G-9851)*

Mp6 LLC ... G ... 231 409-7530
Traverse City *(G-16045)*

Mpi Plastics ... G ... 201 502-1534
Macomb *(G-10146)*

Msinc ... G ... 248 275-1978
Shelby Township *(G-14650)*

Multi-Form Plastics Inc ... F ... 586 786-4229
Macomb *(G-10147)*

N-K Manufacturing Tech LLC ... E ... 616 248-3200
Grand Rapids *(G-6710)*

Nova Industries Inc ... E ... 586 294-9182
Fraser *(G-5700)*

Nyloncraft of Michigan Inc ... B ... 517 849-9911
Jonesville *(G-8665)*

Nyx Inc ... B ... 734 261-7535
Livonia *(G-9870)*

Nyx LLC ... C ... 734 462-2385
Livonia *(G-9871)*

Nyx LLC ... C ... 734 467-7200
Westland *(G-17585)*

Nyx LLC ... C ... 734 421-3850
Livonia *(G-9872)*

Oakley Industries Inc ... E ... 586 791-3194
Clinton Township *(G-3187)*

Oth Consultants Inc ... C ... 586 598-0100
Chesterfield *(G-2813)*

P & K Technologies Inc ... G ... 586 336-9545
Romeo *(G-13634)*

Park Molded Specialties Inc ... G ... 906 225-0385
Marquette *(G-10551)*

Parousia Plastics Inc ... G ... 989 832-4054
Midland *(G-10902)*

Patton Tool and Die Inc ... F ... 810 359-5336
Lexington *(G-9559)*

Pds Plastics Inc ... F ... 616 896-1109
Dorr *(G-4525)*

Pearce Plastics LLC ... G ... 231 519-5994
Fremont *(G-5781)*

Pegasus Tool LLC ... G ... 313 255-5900
Detroit *(G-4295)*

Phillips-Medisize LLC ... C ... 616 878-5030
Byron Center *(G-2207)*

Pioneer Molded Products Inc ... E ... 616 977-4172
Grand Rapids *(G-6755)*

Plastechs LLC ... G ... 734 429-3129
Saline *(G-14408)*

Plastic Dress-Up Service Inc ... E ... 586 727-7878
Port Huron *(G-12956)*

Plastic Mold Technology Inc ... D ... 616 698-9810
Kentwood *(G-9022)*

Plastic Mold Technology Inc ... G ... 616 698-9810
Grand Rapids *(G-6756)*

Plastic Molding Development ... G ... 586 739-4500
Sterling Heights *(G-15446)*

Plastic Tag & Trade Check Co ... F ... 989 892-7913
Bay City *(G-1340)*

Plastico Industries Inc ... F ... 616 304-6289
Carson City *(G-2496)*

Pliant Plastics Corp ... D ... 616 844-0300
Spring Lake *(G-15169)*

Pliant Plastics Corp ... F ... 616 844-3215
Spring Lake *(G-15170)*

Poly Flex Products Inc ... E ... 734 458-4194
Farmington Hills *(G-5096)*

Polymer Process Dev LLC ... D ... 586 464-6400
Shelby Township *(G-14669)*

Precision Industries Inc ... F ... 810 239-5816
Flint *(G-5482)*

Precision Masters Inc ... E ... 248 648-8071
Auburn Hills *(G-979)*

Precision Mold & Engineering ... E ... 586 774-2421
Warren *(G-17193)*

Precision Polymer Mfg Inc ... E ... 269 344-2044
Kalamazoo *(G-8860)*

Primera Plastics Inc ... D ... 616 748-6248
Zeeland *(G-18177)*

Prism Plastics Inc ... E ... 810 292-6300
Shelby Township *(G-14671)*

Pro Slot Ltd ... G ... 616 897-6000
Hartford *(G-7386)*

Proper Polymers - Anderson LLC ... G ... 586 408-9120
Warren *(G-17206)*

Proper Polymers-Pulaski LLC ... D ... 931 371-3147
Warren *(G-17209)*

Proto Crafts Inc ... D ... 810 376-3665
Deckerville *(G-3810)*

Proto Shapes Inc ... F ... 517 278-3947
Coldwater *(G-3321)*

Purforms Inc ... E ... 616 897-3000
Lowell *(G-10041)*

PRODUCT SECTION

PLASTICS: Polystyrene Foam

Quality Assured Plastics Inc	E	269 674-3888
Lawrence (G-9506)		
Quality Models Intl Inc	G	519 727-4255
Melvindale (G-10706)		
Realbio Technology Inc	G	269 544-1088
Kalamazoo (G-8869)		
Reed City Group LLC	D	231 832-7500
Reed City (G-13222)		
Regal Finishing Co Inc	D	269 849-2963
Coloma (G-3364)		
Revere Plastics Systems LLC	C	586 415-4823
Fraser (G-5717)		
Revere Plastics Systems LLC	B	419 547-6918
Novi (G-11986)		
Rkaa Business LLC	E	231 734-5517
Evart (G-4886)		
Robroy Industries Inc	D	616 794-0700
Belding (G-1429)		
Roto-Plastics Corporation	D	517 263-8981
Adrian (G-92)		
Royal Plastics LLC	G	616 669-3393
Hudsonville (G-8176)		
Royal Technologies Corporation	C	616 667-4102
Hudsonville (G-8177)		
Royal Technologies Corporation	C	616 669-3393
Hudsonville (G-8180)		
RPS Tool and Engineering Inc	E	586 298-6590
Roseville (G-13864)		
Sac Plastics Inc	G	616 846-0820
Spring Lake (G-15174)		
Saginaw Bay Plastics Inc	D	989 686-7860
Kawkawlin (G-8975)		
Seabrook Plastics Inc	E	231 759-8820
Norton Shores (G-11792)		
Seagate Plastics Company	E	517 547-8123
Addison (G-39)		
Sebro Plastics Inc	E	248 348-4121
Wixom (G-17891)		
Soltis Plastics Corp	G	248 698-1440
White Lake (G-17639)		
Speed Cinch Inc	G	269 646-2016
Marcellus (G-10468)		
Spencer Plastics Inc	E	231 942-7100
Cadillac (G-2279)		
Spiratex Company	D	734 289-4800
Monroe (G-11069)		
Sr Injection Molding Inc	C	586 260-2360
Harrison Township (G-7350)		
Stexley-Brake LLC	G	231 421-3092
Traverse City (G-16111)		
Stone Plastics and Mfg Inc	C	616 748-9740
Zeeland (G-18188)		
Sturgis Molded Products Co	G	269 651-9381
Sturgis (G-15636)		
Su-Dan Plastics Inc	B	248 651-6035
Rochester (G-13354)		
Su-Dan Plastics Inc	F	248 651-6035
Rochester Hills (G-13520)		
Summit Polymers Inc	C	269 324-9330
Portage (G-13045)		
Summit Polymers Inc	B	269 324-9330
Kalamazoo (G-8901)		
Summit Polymers Inc	B	269 323-1301
Portage (G-13047)		
Supreme Industries LLC	G	586 725-2500
Ira (G-8273)		
Tech Group Grand Rapids Inc	B	616 643-6001
Walker (G-16879)		
Ten X Plastics LLC	G	616 813-3037
Grand Rapids (G-6920)		
Tesca Inc	E	586 991-0744
Rochester Hills (G-13524)		
Tomas Plastics Inc	F	734 455-4706
Plymouth (G-12774)		
Tooling Cncepts Design Not Inc	F	810 444-9807
Port Huron (G-12972)		
Trans Industries Plastics LLC	E	248 310-0008
Rochester (G-13355)		
Transnav Holdings Inc	C	586 716-5600
New Baltimore (G-11494)		
Travis Creek Tooling	G	269 685-2000
Plainwell (G-12549)		
Trestle Plastic Services LLC	G	616 262-5484
Hamilton (G-7241)		
Tri-Star Molding LLC	E	269 646-0062
Marcellus (G-10469)		
Undercar Products Group Inc	B	616 719-4571
Wyoming (G-18039)		
Uniflex Inc	G	248 486-6000
Brighton (G-2002)		
US Farathane Holdings Corp	C	586 726-1200
Sterling Heights (G-15535)		
US Farathane Holdings Corp	B	586 726-1200
Shelby Township (G-14714)		
US Farathane Holdings Corp	D	586 978-2800
Troy (G-16666)		
US Farathane Holdings Corp	C	248 754-7000
Port Huron (G-12974)		
US Farathane Holdings Corp	F	248 754-7000
Lake Orion (G-9168)		
US Farathane Holdings Corp	E	586 685-4000
Sterling Heights (G-15537)		
US Farathane Holdings Corp	C	248 754-7000
Auburn Hills (G-1040)		
US Farathane Holdings Corp	D	248 754-7000
Orion (G-12191)		
USA Summit Plas Silao 1 LLC	G	269 324-9330
Portage (G-13053)		
Vacuum Orna Metal Company Inc	E	734 941-9100
Romulus (G-13738)		
Valtec LLC	C	810 724-5048
Imlay City (G-8213)		
Vaupell Molding & Tooling Inc	D	269 435-8414
Constantine (G-3545)		
Ventra Evart LLC	G	231 734-9000
Evart (G-4888)		
Vivatar Inc	E	616 928-0750
Holland (G-7849)		
Western Diversified Plas LLC	G	269 668-3393
Mattawan (G-10671)		
Western Michigan Plastics	F	616 394-9269
Holland (G-7857)		
World Class Prototypes Inc	F	616 355-0200
Holland (G-7862)		
Wow Products USA	G	989 672-1300
Caro (G-2483)		
Wright Plastic Products Co LLC	D	989 291-3211
Sheridan (G-14736)		
Yanfeng US Automotive	C	734 254-5000
Plymouth (G-12796)		

PLASTICS: Molded

A S Plus Industries Inc	G	586 741-0400
Clinton Township (G-3030)		
Advanced Plastic Mfg Inc	G	269 962-9697
Battle Creek (G-1140)		
Advanced Special Tools Inc	C	269 962-9697
Battle Creek (G-1141)		
Atlantic Precision Pdts Inc	F	586 532-9420
Shelby Township (G-14550)		
Clarion Technologies Inc	C	616 754-1199
Greenville (G-7125)		
Cusolar Industries Inc	E	586 949-3880
Chesterfield (G-2757)		
Delta Molded Products	G	586 731-9595
Sterling Heights (G-15308)		
Die Stampco Inc	D	989 893-7790
Bay City (G-1302)		
Eco - Composites LLC	G	616 395-8902
Holland (G-7617)		
GMI Composites Inc	D	231 755-1611
Muskegon (G-11331)		
Graflex Inc	F	616 842-3654
Spring Lake (G-15146)		
Grm Corporation	D	989 453-2322
Pigeon (G-12489)		
Hilco Industrial Plastics LLC	G	616 323-1330
Grand Rapids (G-6512)		
Hilco Plastic Products Co	E	616 554-8833
Caledonia (G-2300)		
Humphrey Companies LLC	C	616 530-1717
Grandville (G-7048)		
ICM Enterprises LLC	G	586 415-2567
Fraser (G-5668)		
Innovative Engineering Mich	G	517 977-0460
Lansing (G-9236)		
Lacks Enterprises Inc	D	616 949-6570
Grand Rapids (G-6595)		
Lacks Enterprises Inc	D	616 656-2910
Grand Rapids (G-6596)		
Lacks Enterprises Inc	D	616 698-2030
Grand Rapids (G-6597)		
Lacks Enterprises Inc	D	616 949-6570
Grand Rapids (G-6598)		
Lacks Industries Inc	C	616 698-6890
Grand Rapids (G-6606)		
Lacks Industries Inc	D	616 698-6854
Grand Rapids (G-6608)		
Lacks Industries Inc	D	616 698-2776
Grand Rapids (G-6611)		
Latin American Industries LLC	G	616 301-1878
Grand Rapids (G-6622)		
Leon Interiors Inc	B	616 422-7479
Holland (G-7721)		
McKechnie Vhcl Cmpnnts USA Inc	E	218 894-1218
Roseville (G-13832)		
Mig Molding LLC	G	810 660-8435
Almont (G-264)		
Mold-Msters Injctioneering LLC	F	905 877-0185
Madison Heights (G-10309)		
Monroe LLC	B	616 942-9820
Grand Rapids (G-6702)		
Monroe Mold LLC	G	734 241-6898
Monroe (G-11056)		
Morren Plastic Molding Inc	F	616 997-7474
Allendale (G-224)		
Palmer Distributors Inc	D	586 772-4225
Fraser (G-5703)		
PDM Industries Inc	E	231 943-9601
Traverse City (G-16063)		
Penguin Molding LLC	F	847 297-0560
Sturgis (G-15629)		
Pinconning Metals Inc	E	989 879-3144
Pinconning (G-12512)		
Plastic Solutions LLC	G	231 824-7350
Traverse City (G-16074)		
Plastics Technology Co	G	586 421-0479
Chesterfield (G-2818)		
Reeves Plastics LLC	E	616 997-0777
Coopersville (G-3569)		
Rockford Molding & Trim	G	616 874-8997
Rockford (G-13588)		
Sequoia Molding	G	586 463-4400
Grosse Pointe (G-7183)		
Shape Corp	B	616 846-8700
Grand Haven (G-6077)		
Shape Corp	E	616 844-3215
Grand Haven (G-6078)		
Shoreline Mold & Engrg LLC	G	269 926-2223
Benton Harbor (G-1546)		
Soroc Products Inc	E	810 743-2660
Burton (G-2166)		
Summit Plastic Molding Inc	E	586 262-4500
Shelby Township (G-14703)		
Summit Plastic Molding II Inc	G	586 977-8300
Sterling Heights (G-15515)		
Summit Plastic Molding II Inc	F	586 262-4500
Shelby Township (G-14704)		
Talco Industries	G	989 269-6260
Bad Axe (G-1072)		
TAW Plastics LLC	G	616 302-0954
Greenville (G-7157)		
Three 60 Corporation	F	517 545-3600
Howell (G-8110)		
Ventra Ionia Main LLC	E	616 597-3220
Ionia (G-8252)		
Ventra Ionia Main LLC	C	616 597-3220
Ionia (G-8253)		
WI Molding of Michigan LLC	D	269 327-3075
Portage (G-13057)		

PLASTICS: Polystyrene Foam

Action Fabricators Inc	C	616 957-2032
Grand Rapids (G-6136)		
Advance Engineering Company	E	989 435-3641
Beaverton (G-1382)		
Armaly Sponge Company	E	248 669-2100
Commerce Township (G-3391)		
Aspen Technologies Inc	D	248 446-1485
Brighton (G-1887)		
Bespro Pattern Inc	F	586 268-6970
Madison Heights (G-10204)		
Blue Water Bioproducts LLC	G	586 453-9219
Port Huron (G-12902)		
Bremen Corp	G	574 546-4238
Fenton (G-5191)		
Briggs Industries Inc	E	586 749-5191
Chesterfield (G-2747)		
Creative Foam Corporation	C	810 629-4149
Fenton (G-5198)		
Creatv Foam Cmpsite Systms	E	810 629-4149
Flint (G-5408)		
Dart Container Corporation	A	800 248-5960
Mason (G-10633)		
Derby Fabg Solutions LLC	D	616 866-1650
Rockford (G-13566)		
Dow Chemical Company	D	989 636-5430
Midland (G-10843)		
Dow Chemical Company	C	989 636-4406
Midland (G-10836)		

Employee Codes: A=Over 500 employees, B=251-500
C=101-250, D=51-100, E=20-50, F=10-19, G=3-9

Dow Chemical Company.......................B....... 989 636-1000
Midland *(G-10834)*
Dow Chemical Company.......................D....... 989 636-0540
Midland *(G-10845)*
Dow Chemical Company.......................D....... 989 636-5409
Midland *(G-10848)*
Dow Inc.......................G....... 989 636-1000
Midland *(G-10851)*
Duna USA Inc.......................G....... 231 425-4300
Ludington *(G-10058)*
Envirolite LLC.......................D....... 888 222-2191
Coldwater *(G-3302)*
Envirolite LLC.......................F....... 248 792-3184
Troy *(G-16349)*
Floracraft Corporation.......................C....... 231 845-5127
Ludington *(G-10059)*
Fomcore LLC.......................D....... 231 366-4791
Muskegon *(G-11325)*
Fxi Novi.......................G....... 248 994-0630
Novi *(G-11889)*
Gemini Plastics Inc.......................C....... 989 658-8557
Ubly *(G-16716)*
Green Polymeric Materials Inc.......................E....... 313 933-7390
Detroit *(G-4102)*
Huntington Foam LLC.......................E....... 661 225-9951
Greenville *(G-7139)*
Inter-Pack Corporation.......................E....... 734 242-7755
Monroe *(G-11042)*
Jsj Corporation.......................E....... 616 842-6350
Grand Haven *(G-6042)*
Kent Manufacturing Company.......................D....... 616 454-9495
Grand Rapids *(G-6577)*
Kringer Industrial Corporation.......................F....... 519 818-3509
Warren *(G-17122)*
Leon Interiors Inc.......................B....... 616 422-7479
Holland *(G-7721)*
Light Metal Forming Corp.......................F....... 248 851-3984
Bloomfield Hills *(G-1777)*
Package Design & Mfg Inc.......................E....... 248 486-4390
Brighton *(G-1972)*
Plascore Inc.......................D....... 616 772-1220
Zeeland *(G-18176)*
Pregis LLC.......................D....... 810 320-3005
Marysville *(G-10611)*
Reklein Plastics Incorporated.......................G....... 586 739-8850
Sterling Heights *(G-15463)*
Revstone Industries LLC.......................F....... 248 351-1000
Troy *(G-16577)*
Rogers Foam Automotive Corp.......................E....... 810 820-6323
Flint *(G-5494)*
Sekisui America Corporation.......................C....... 517 279-7587
Coldwater *(G-3331)*
Sekisui Voltek LLC.......................C....... 517 279-7587
Coldwater *(G-3332)*
Simco Automotive Trim Inc.......................E....... 616 608-9818
Grand Rapids *(G-6865)*
Southwestern Foam Tech Inc.......................E....... 616 726-1677
Grand Rapids *(G-6874)*
Special Projects Engineering.......................G....... 517 676-8525
Mason *(G-10659)*
Transpak Inc.......................E....... 586 264-2064
Sterling Heights *(G-15528)*
Ufp Technologies Inc.......................D....... 616 949-8100
Grand Rapids *(G-6948)*
Unique Fabricating Inc.......................E....... 248 853-2333
Auburn Hills *(G-1034)*
Unique Fabricating Inc.......................E....... 248 853-2333
Rochester Hills *(G-13535)*
Unique Fabricating Na Inc.......................B....... 248 853-2333
Auburn Hills *(G-1035)*
Unique Molded Foam Tech Inc.......................C....... 517 524-9010
Concord *(G-3527)*
United Foam A Ufp Tech Brnd.......................D....... 616 949-8100
Grand Rapids *(G-6952)*
Whisper Creative Products Inc.......................G....... 734 529-2734
Dundee *(G-4603)*
Woodbridge Holdings Inc.......................C....... 734 942-0458
Romulus *(G-13742)*
Woodbridge Holdings Inc.......................G....... 248 288-0100
Troy *(G-16697)*

PLASTICS: Thermoformed

Advance Engineering Company.......................E....... 989 435-3641
Beaverton *(G-1382)*
Airpark Plastics LLC.......................F....... 989 846-1029
Standish *(G-15215)*
Cadillac Products Inc.......................B....... 248 813-8200
Troy *(G-16253)*
Contour Engineering Inc.......................F....... 989 828-6526
Shepherd *(G-14727)*
Fabri-Kal Corporation.......................E....... 269 385-5050
Kalamazoo *(G-8740)*
Formed Solutions Inc.......................F....... 616 395-5455
Holland *(G-7635)*
Forming Technologies LLC.......................D....... 231 777-7030
Muskegon *(G-11326)*
Garett Tunison.......................G....... 248 330-9835
Oakland *(G-12106)*
Industrial Pattern of Lansing.......................G....... 517 482-9835
Lansing *(G-9298)*
Plexicase Inc.......................G....... 616 246-6400
Wyoming *(G-18028)*
PRA Company.......................D....... 989 846-1029
Standish *(G-15226)*
Scooters Refuse Service Inc.......................G....... 269 962-2201
Battle Creek *(G-1244)*
Shuert Industries Inc.......................C....... 586 254-4590
Sterling Heights *(G-15497)*
Summit Polymers Inc.......................B....... 269 651-1643
Sturgis *(G-15638)*
Two Mitts Inc.......................G....... 800 888-5054
Kalamazoo *(G-8915)*

PLATE WORK: For Nuclear Industry

Metal Quest Inc.......................D....... 989 733-2011
Onaway *(G-12147)*

PLATE WORK: Metalworking Trade

Moore Flame Cutting Co.......................D....... 586 978-1090
Bloomfield Hills *(G-1784)*

PLATEMAKING SVC: Color Separations, For The Printing Trade

Al Corp.......................F....... 734 475-7357
Chelsea *(G-2701)*
Alpha 21 LLC.......................G....... 248 352-7330
Southfield *(G-14828)*
North American Color Inc.......................E....... 269 323-0552
Portage *(G-13019)*

PLATEMAKING SVC: Embossing, For The Printing Trade

Art In Transit Inc.......................G....... 248 585-5566
Troy *(G-16217)*

PLATEMAKING SVC: Gravure

Diamond Graphics Inc.......................G....... 269 345-1164
Kalamazoo *(G-8726)*

PLATEMAKING SVC: Gravure, Plates Or Cylinders

Trico Incorporated.......................G....... 517 764-1780
Jackson *(G-8592)*

PLATEMAKING SVC: Letterpress

Weighman Enterprises Inc.......................G....... 989 755-2116
Saginaw *(G-14181)*

PLATES

A D Johnson Engraving Co Inc.......................F....... 269 385-0044
Kalamazoo *(G-8672)*
Behrmann Printing Company Inc.......................F....... 248 799-7771
Southfield *(G-14851)*
Breck Graphics Incorporated.......................E....... 616 248-4110
Grand Rapids *(G-6235)*
Britten Inc.......................C....... 231 941-8200
Traverse City *(G-15920)*
Celia Corporation.......................D....... 616 887-7341
Sparta *(G-15091)*
Dearborn Lithograph Inc.......................E....... 734 464-4242
Livonia *(G-9701)*
F & A Enterprises of Michigan.......................G....... 906 228-3222
Marquette *(G-10531)*
Fortis Sltions Group Centl LLC.......................D....... 248 437-5200
Wixom *(G-17812)*
Graphic Enterprises Inc.......................D....... 248 616-4900
Madison Heights *(G-10258)*
Graphic Specialties Inc.......................E....... 616 247-0060
Grand Rapids *(G-6475)*
Hamblin Company.......................E....... 517 423-7491
Tecumseh *(G-15796)*
Industrial Imprntng & Die Ctng.......................G....... 586 778-9470
Eastpointe *(G-4704)*
Kalamazoo Photo Comp Svcs.......................E....... 269 345-3706
Kalamazoo *(G-8794)*
Mark Maker Company Inc.......................E....... 616 538-6980
Grand Rapids *(G-6643)*
Marketing VI Group Inc.......................G....... 989 793-3933
Saginaw *(G-14081)*
Mel Printing Co Inc.......................E....... 313 928-5440
Taylor *(G-15738)*
Microforms Inc.......................D....... 586 939-7900
Beverly Hills *(G-1620)*
North American Graphics Inc.......................E....... 586 486-1110
Warren *(G-17173)*
Qrp Inc.......................G....... 989 496-2955
Midland *(G-10905)*
Safran Printing Company Inc.......................E....... 586 939-7600
Beverly Hills *(G-1621)*
Schawk Inc.......................G....... 269 381-3820
Kalamazoo *(G-8884)*
Sgk LLC.......................D....... 269 381-3820
Battle Creek *(G-1245)*
Stamp-Rite Incorporated.......................E....... 517 487-5071
Lansing *(G-9267)*
Twin City Engraving Company.......................G....... 269 983-0601
Saint Joseph *(G-14346)*

PLATES: Paper, Made From Purchased Materials

AJM Packaging Corporation.......................D....... 248 901-0040
Bloomfield Hills *(G-1743)*
AJM Packaging Corporation.......................C....... 313 842-7530
Detroit *(G-3851)*
SF Holdings Group Inc.......................D....... 800 248-5960
Mason *(G-10656)*

PLATES: Plastic Exc Polystyrene Foam

Alternative Systems Inc.......................F....... 269 384-2008
Kalamazoo *(G-8677)*

PLATES: Sheet & Strip, Exc Coated Prdts

Omega Steel Incorporated.......................G....... 616 877-3782
Wayland *(G-17408)*
Sandvik Inc.......................E....... 269 926-7241
Benton Harbor *(G-1545)*

PLATES: Steel

De Luxe Die Set Inc.......................G....... 810 227-2556
Brighton *(G-1910)*
Industrial Marking Products.......................G....... 517 699-2160
Holt *(G-7913)*
Parton & Preble Inc.......................E....... 586 773-6000
Warren *(G-17180)*
Steel 21 LLC.......................E....... 616 884-2121
Cedar Springs *(G-2562)*

PLATES: Truss, Metal

Superior Steel Components Inc.......................D....... 616 866-4759
Grand Rapids *(G-6904)*

PLATING & FINISHING SVC: Decorative, Formed Prdts

Flexible Controls Corporation.......................D....... 313 368-3630
Detroit *(G-4062)*
Lawrence Surface Tech Inc.......................G....... 248 609-9001
Troy *(G-16459)*

PLATING & POLISHING SVC

Able Welding Inc.......................G....... 989 865-9611
Saint Charles *(G-14189)*
Acorn Industries Inc.......................D....... 734 261-2940
Livonia *(G-9627)*
Aft.......................G....... 313 320-0218
Detroit *(G-3845)*
American Metal Restoration.......................G....... 810 364-4820
Marysville *(G-10598)*
ARC Services of Macomb Inc.......................E....... 586 469-1600
Clinton Township *(G-3056)*
B and L Metal Finishing LLC.......................G....... 269 767-2225
Allegan *(G-151)*
Beacon Park Finishing LLC.......................F....... 248 318-4286
Roseville *(G-13777)*
Cal Grinding Inc.......................E....... 906 786-8749
Escanaba *(G-4821)*
Cds Specialty Coatings LLC.......................G....... 734 244-6708
Westland *(G-17547)*

PRODUCT SECTION — PLEATING & STITCHING FOR THE TRADE: Decorative & Novelty

Cg Liquidation Incorporated ....E...... 586 575-9800
   Warren *(G-16978)*
Cyclone Manufacturing Inc ....G...... 269 782-9670
   Dowagiac *(G-4539)*
DC Byers Co/Grand Rapids Inc ....F...... 616 538-7300
   Grand Rapids *(G-6338)*
Detroit Steel Treating Company ......E...... 248 334-7436
   Pontiac *(G-12816)*
Diamond Tool Manufacturing Inc ......E...... 734 416-1900
   Plymouth *(G-12611)*
Downriver Deburring Inc ....G...... 313 388-2640
   Taylor *(G-15709)*
Eastern Oil Company ....E...... 248 333-1333
   Pontiac *(G-12819)*
ECJ Processing ....G...... 248 540-2336
   Southfield *(G-14896)*
Electro Chemical Finishing Co ....G...... 616 249-7092
   Grandville *(G-7032)*
Elm Plating ....G...... 517 795-1574
   Jackson *(G-8444)*
Fire-Rite Inc ....E...... 313 273-3730
   Detroit *(G-4060)*
Flat Rock Metal Inc ....C...... 734 782-4454
   Flat Rock *(G-5353)*
Gj Prey Coml & Indus Pntg Cov ....G...... 248 250-4792
   Clawson *(G-2980)*
Gokoh Coldwater Incorporated ....F...... 517 279-1080
   Coldwater *(G-3305)*
Hi-Tech Coatings Inc ....E...... 586 759-3559
   Warren *(G-17081)*
Industrial Finishing Co LLC ....G...... 616 784-5737
   Comstock Park *(G-3485)*
Keen Point International Inc ....E...... 248 340-8732
   Auburn Hills *(G-925)*
Kenwal Pickling LLC ....E...... 313 739-1040
   Dearborn *(G-3729)*
Kriseler Welding Inc ....G...... 989 624-9266
   Birch Run *(G-1664)*
Lacks Enterprises Inc ....D...... 616 698-2030
   Grand Rapids *(G-6597)*
Lacks Industries Inc ....C...... 616 698-9852
   Grand Rapids *(G-6609)*
Lee Industries Inc ....E...... 231 777-2537
   Muskegon *(G-11365)*
McGean-Rohco Inc ....E...... 216 441-4900
   Livonia *(G-9832)*
Metal Finishing Technology ....G...... 231 733-9736
   Muskegon *(G-11376)*
Mid-Michigan Industries Inc ....D...... 989 773-6918
   Mount Pleasant *(G-11208)*
Mid-Michigan Industries Inc ....E...... 989 386-7707
   Clare *(G-2877)*
Mvc Holdings LLC ....F...... 586 491-2600
   Roseville *(G-13843)*
National Galvanizing LP ....A...... 734 243-1882
   Monroe *(G-11059)*
National Zinc Processors Inc ....F...... 269 926-1161
   Benton Harbor *(G-1535)*
Non-Ferrous Cast Alloys Inc ....D...... 231 799-0550
   Norton Shores *(G-11782)*
Nor-Cote Inc ....E...... 586 756-1200
   Warren *(G-17170)*
Pioneer Metal Finishing LLC ....C...... 734 384-9000
   Monroe *(G-11062)*
Premier Finishing Inc ....E...... 616 785-3070
   Grand Rapids *(G-6768)*
Production Tube Company Inc ....G...... 313 259-3990
   Detroit *(G-4312)*
Prs Manufacturing Inc ....G...... 616 784-4409
   Grand Rapids *(G-6794)*
Qmi Group Inc ....E...... 248 589-0505
   Madison Heights *(G-10342)*
Quali Tone Corporation ....F...... 269 426-3664
   Sawyer *(G-14487)*
Richcoat LLC ....E...... 586 978-1311
   Sterling Heights *(G-15468)*
Seaver Industrial Finishing Co ......D...... 616 842-8560
   Grand Haven *(G-6074)*
Spectrum Industries Inc ....D...... 616 451-0784
   Grand Rapids *(G-6884)*
Superior Mtal Finshg Rustproof ......F...... 313 893-1050
   Detroit *(G-4388)*

PLATING COMPOUNDS

Plating Systems and Tech Inc ....G...... 517 783-4776
   Jackson *(G-8554)*
Surface Activation Tech LLC ....G...... 248 273-0037
   Troy *(G-16628)*

PLATING SVC: Chromium, Metals Or Formed Prdts

Arted Chrome Plating ....G...... 586 758-0050
   Warren *(G-16939)*
Dmi Automotive Inc ....F...... 517 548-1414
   Howell *(G-8031)*
Empire Hardchrome ....G...... 810 392-3122
   Richmond *(G-13262)*
Jo-Mar Enterprises Inc ....G...... 313 365-9200
   Detroit *(G-4162)*
Sodus Hard Chrome Inc ....F...... 269 925-2077
   Sodus *(G-14747)*

PLATING SVC: Electro

Ace Finishing Inc ....G...... 586 777-1390
   Warren *(G-16914)*
Asp Plating Company ....G...... 616 842-8080
   Grand Haven *(G-5992)*
Cadillac Plating Corporation ....D...... 586 771-9191
   Warren *(G-16975)*
Classic Plating Inc ....G...... 313 532-1440
   Redford *(G-13153)*
Controlled Plating Tech Inc ....E...... 616 243-6622
   Grand Rapids *(G-6307)*
Detroit Chrome Inc ....E...... 313 341-9478
   Detroit *(G-3976)*
Diamond Chrome Plating Inc ....D...... 517 546-0150
   Howell *(G-8030)*
Dyna Plate Inc ....E...... 616 452-6763
   Grand Rapids *(G-6363)*
Electro Chemical Finishing Co ....F...... 616 531-0670
   Grandville *(G-7031)*
Electro Chemical Finishing Co ....F...... 616 531-1250
   Grand Rapids *(G-6373)*
Electro Chemical Finishing Co ....F...... 616 531-0670
   Wyoming *(G-17999)*
Electro-Plating Service Inc ....F...... 248 541-0035
   Madison Heights *(G-10242)*
Electroplating Industries Inc ....F...... 586 469-2390
   Clinton Township *(G-3109)*
Finishing Services Inc ....C...... 734 484-1700
   Ypsilanti *(G-18073)*
Fintex LLC ....E...... 734 946-3100
   Romulus *(G-13678)*
Fitzgerald Finishing LLC ....D...... 313 368-3630
   Detroit *(G-4061)*
Gladwin Metal Processing Inc ....G...... 989 426-9038
   Gladwin *(G-5931)*
Great Lakes Finishing Inc ....F...... 231 733-9566
   Muskegon *(G-11338)*
Highpoint Finshg Solutions Inc ......D...... 616 772-4425
   Zeeland *(G-18148)*
Holly Plating Co Inc ....E...... 810 714-9213
   Fenton *(G-5220)*
Hpc Holdings Inc ....E...... 248 634-9361
   Holly *(G-7883)*
JD Plating Company Inc ....E...... 248 547-5200
   Madison Heights *(G-10283)*
Kalamazoo Metal Finishers Inc ....F...... 269 382-1611
   Kalamazoo *(G-8791)*
KC Jones Plating Co ....E...... 586 755-4900
   Warren *(G-17119)*
KC Jones Plating Co ....E...... 248 399-8500
   Hazel Park *(G-7440)*
Marsh Plating Corporation ....D...... 734 483-5767
   Ypsilanti *(G-18088)*
Material Sciences Corporation ....F...... 734 207-4444
   Canton *(G-2398)*
Mid-State Plating Co Inc ....E...... 810 767-1622
   Flint *(G-5467)*
Perfection Industries Inc ....E...... 313 272-4040
   Detroit *(G-4297)*
Plymouth Plating Works Inc ....F...... 734 453-1560
   Plymouth *(G-12720)*
Robert & Son Black Ox Special ....G...... 586 778-7633
   Roseville *(G-13862)*
Siemens Vai Services LLC ....F...... 269 927-3591
   Benton Harbor *(G-1548)*
SMS Modern Hard Chrome LLC ....D...... 586 445-0330
   Warren *(G-17242)*
Technickel Inc ....F...... 269 926-8505
   Benton Harbor *(G-1553)*
Wolverine Plating Corporation ....E...... 586 771-5000
   Roseville *(G-13892)*

PLATING SVC: NEC

ABC Custom Chrome Inc ....G...... 248 674-4333
   Waterford *(G-17321)*
Acme Plating Inc ....G...... 313 838-3870
   Detroit *(G-3840)*
Ajax Metal Processing Inc ....G...... 313 267-2100
   Detroit *(G-3850)*
All Chrome LLC ....G...... 517 554-1649
   Albion *(G-115)*
Allied Finishing Inc ....C...... 616 698-7550
   Grand Rapids *(G-6163)*
Arted Chrome Plating Inc ....F...... 313 871-3331
   Detroit *(G-3880)*
Auto Anodics Inc ....E...... 810 984-5600
   Port Huron *(G-12895)*
B & L Plating Co Inc ....G...... 586 778-9300
   Warren *(G-16947)*
Cadon Plating & Coatings LLC ....D...... 734 282-8100
   Wyandotte *(G-17950)*
Chemical Process Inds LLC ....F...... 248 547-5200
   Madison Heights *(G-10209)*
Color Coat Plating Company ....F...... 248 744-0445
   Madison Heights *(G-10216)*
D & B Metal Finishing ....G...... 586 725-6056
   Chesterfield *(G-2758)*
Dn-Lawrence Industries Inc ....F...... 269 552-4999
   Kalamazoo *(G-8730)*
Dynamic Finishing LLC ....G...... 231 727-8811
   Muskegon *(G-11308)*
Dynamic Finishing LLC ....G...... 231 737-8130
   Fruitport *(G-5792)*
Expert Coating Company Inc ....F...... 616 453-8261
   Grand Rapids *(G-6393)*
Fini Finish Metal Finishing ....F...... 586 758-0050
   Warren *(G-17033)*
Honhart Mid-Nite Black Co ....E...... 248 588-1515
   Troy *(G-16399)*
Lansing Plating Company ....G...... 517 485-6915
   Lansing *(G-9241)*
Master Finish Co ....C...... 877 590-5819
   Grand Rapids *(G-6648)*
Michigan Plating LLC ....G...... 248 544-3500
   Hazel Park *(G-7444)*
Michner Plating Company ....D...... 517 789-6627
   Jackson *(G-8521)*
Micro Platers Sales Inc ....E...... 313 865-2293
   Detroit *(G-4245)*
Midwest Plating Company Inc ....E...... 616 451-2007
   Grand Rapids *(G-6685)*
Norbrook Plating Inc ....E...... 586 755-4110
   Warren *(G-17171)*
Norbrook Plating Inc ....G...... 313 369-9304
   Detroit *(G-4275)*
Plating Specialties Inc ....F...... 248 547-8660
   Madison Heights *(G-10330)*
Ppi LLC ....E...... 586 772-7736
   Warren *(G-17190)*
Selfridge Plating Inc ....D...... 586 469-3141
   Harrison Township *(G-7348)*
Tawas Plating Company ....D...... 989 362-2011
   Tawas City *(G-15683)*
Thomas Frankini ....G...... 517 783-2400
   Jackson *(G-8589)*
Tri K Cylinder Service Inc ....G...... 269 965-3981
   Springfield *(G-15207)*
Tru-Coat Inc ....G...... 810 785-3331
   Montrose *(G-11106)*
W A Thomas Company ....G...... 734 955-6500
   Taylor *(G-15779)*
Western Engineered Products ....G...... 248 371-9259
   Lake Orion *(G-9170)*
Williams Diversified Inc ....E...... 734 421-6100
   Livonia *(G-10009)*
Williams Finishing Inc ....G...... 734 421-6100
   Livonia *(G-10010)*

PLAYGROUND EQPT

J C Walker & Sons Corp ....G...... 248 752-8165
   Swartz Creek *(G-15668)*
Kennedy Sales Inc ....G...... 586 228-9390
   Clinton Township *(G-3154)*
Penchura LLC ....F...... 810 229-6245
   Brighton *(G-1977)*
Quality Industries Inc ....E...... 517 439-1591
   Hillsdale *(G-7536)*
Shane Group LLC ....G...... 517 439-4316
   Hillsdale *(G-7541)*

PLEATING & STITCHING FOR THE TRADE: Decorative & Novelty

Kountry Keepsakes ....G...... 586 294-4895
   Fraser *(G-5680)*

Employee Codes: A=Over 500 employees, B=251-500
C=101-250, D=51-100, E=20-50, F=10-19, G=3-9

2020 Harris Michigan Industrial Directory

PLEATING & STITCHING SVC

- AP Impressions Inc..............................G...... 734 464-8009
  Livonia *(G-9650)*
- Authority Customwear Ltd...................E...... 248 588-8075
  Madison Heights *(G-10199)*
- Celia Corporation................................D...... 616 887-7341
  Sparta *(G-15091)*
- Impact Label Corporation...................D...... 269 381-4280
  Galesburg *(G-5811)*
- J2 Licensing Inc..................................G...... 586 307-3400
  Troy *(G-16431)*
- Lazer Graphics....................................E...... 269 926-1066
  Benton Harbor *(G-1522)*
- Mackellar Associates Inc....................F...... 248 335-4440
  Rochester Hills *(G-13466)*
- Nobby Inc..E...... 810 984-3300
  Fort Gratiot *(G-5550)*
- Perrin Souvenir Distrs Inc..................B...... 616 785-9700
  Comstock Park *(G-3508)*
- Stahls Inc..D...... 800 478-2457
  Sterling Heights *(G-15508)*
- Twin City Engraving Company............G...... 269 983-0601
  Saint Joseph *(G-14346)*

PLUGS: Electric

- Hug-A-Plug Inc...................................G...... 810 626-1224
  Brighton *(G-1942)*

PLUMBING & HEATING EQPT & SPLY, WHOL: Htg Eqpt/Panels, Solar

- Triangle Product Distributors..............F...... 970 609-9001
  Holland *(G-7839)*

PLUMBING & HEATING EQPT & SPLY, WHOLESALE: Hydronic Htg Eqpt

- Alhern-Martin Indus Frnc Co..............E...... 248 689-6363
  Troy *(G-16187)*
- Moore Brothers Electrical Co..............G...... 810 232-2148
  Flint *(G-5471)*

PLUMBING & HEATING EQPT & SPLYS WHOLESALERS

- Maple Valley Concrete Products........G...... 517 852-1900
  Nashville *(G-11460)*
- Marquis Industries Inc........................F...... 616 842-2810
  Spring Lake *(G-15160)*
- McLaren Inc..G...... 989 720-4328
  Owosso *(G-12302)*
- Spheros North America Inc...............G...... 734 218-7350
  Canton *(G-2427)*
- Walters Plumbing Company...............F...... 269 962-6253
  Battle Creek *(G-1266)*
- Young Supply Company.....................E...... 313 875-3280
  Detroit *(G-4455)*
- Zurn Industries LLC............................F...... 313 864-2800
  Detroit *(G-4458)*

PLUMBING & HEATING EQPT & SPLYS, WHOL: Plumbing Fitting/Sply

- Etna Distributors LLC.........................G...... 906 273-2331
  Marquette *(G-10530)*
- Ferguson Enterprises Inc...................E...... 989 790-2220
  Saginaw *(G-14037)*
- Shane Group LLC..............................G...... 517 439-4316
  Hillsdale *(G-7541)*

PLUMBING & HEATING EQPT & SPLYS, WHOL: Water Purif Eqpt

- Aqua Fine Inc.....................................G...... 616 392-7843
  Holland *(G-7560)*

PLUMBING & HEATING EQPT & SPLYS, WHOLESALE: Brass/Fittings

- American Beverage Equipment Co....E...... 586 773-0094
  Roseville *(G-13772)*

PLUMBING & HEATING EQPT & SPLYS, WHOLESALE: Gas Burners

- Banner Engineering & Sales Inc........F...... 989 755-0584
  Saginaw *(G-14000)*

PLUMBING & HEATING EQPT & SPLYS, WHOLESALE: Sanitary Ware

- Armstrong Hot Water Inc....................E...... 269 278-1413
  Three Rivers *(G-15857)*
- Select Distributors LLC......................F...... 586 510-4647
  Warren *(G-17237)*

PLUMBING & HEATING EQPT/SPLYS, WHOL: Boilers, Hot Water Htg

- Hamilton Engineering Inc...................E...... 734 419-0200
  Livonia *(G-9764)*

PLUMBING FIXTURES

- Barbron Corporation...........................E...... 586 716-3530
  Kalkaska *(G-8937)*
- Decker Manufacturing Corp...............D...... 517 629-3955
  Albion *(G-122)*
- Etna Distributors LLC.........................G...... 906 273-2331
  Marquette *(G-10530)*
- Incoe Corporation...............................C...... 248 616-0220
  Auburn Hills *(G-910)*
- Ingersoll-Rand Company....................E...... 248 398-6200
  Madison Heights *(G-10275)*
- Kerkstra Precast Inc..........................C...... 616 457-4920
  Grandville *(G-7054)*
- Key Gas Components Inc..................E...... 269 673-2151
  Allegan *(G-169)*
- Masco De Puerto Rico Inc.................G...... 313 274-7400
  Taylor *(G-15737)*
- Parker-Hannifin Corporation..............B...... 269 694-9411
  Otsego *(G-12249)*
- Plastic Trends Inc..............................D...... 586 232-4167
  Shelby Township *(G-14668)*
- SH Leggitt Company..........................C...... 269 781-3901
  Marshall *(G-10588)*
- Tops All Clamps Inc...........................G...... 313 533-7500
  Redford *(G-13202)*
- Vic Bond Sales Inc.............................G...... 517 548-0107
  Howell *(G-8121)*

PLUMBING FIXTURES: Brass, Incl Drain Cocks, Faucets/Spigots

- Brasscraft Manufacturing Co.............C...... 248 305-6000
  Novi *(G-11840)*
- Marquis Industries Inc........................F...... 616 842-2810
  Spring Lake *(G-15160)*
- United Brass Manufacturers Inc........D...... 734 941-0700
  Romulus *(G-13736)*
- United Brass Manufacturers Inc........E...... 734 942-9224
  Romulus *(G-13737)*

PLUMBING FIXTURES: Plastic

- Conway Products Corporation...........E...... 616 698-2601
  Grand Rapids *(G-6308)*
- Lakeshore Marble Company Inc.......E...... 269 429-8241
  Stevensville *(G-15574)*
- Lyons Industries Inc...........................G...... 269 782-9516
  Dowagiac *(G-4549)*
- Masco Corporation.............................A...... 313 274-7400
  Livonia *(G-9826)*
- R A Townsend Company...................G...... 989 498-7000
  Saginaw *(G-14129)*
- Rick Owen & Jason Vogel Partnr.......G...... 734 417-3401
  Dexter *(G-4507)*
- Zimmer Marble Co Inc.......................F...... 517 787-1500
  Jackson *(G-8615)*

POINT OF SALE DEVICES

- Marketing Communications Inc.........G...... 616 784-4488
  Comstock Park *(G-3496)*
- PC Complete Inc................................E...... 248 545-4211
  Ferndale *(G-5308)*

POLISHING SVC: Metals Or Formed Prdts

- Coles Polishing..................................G...... 269 625-2542
  Colon *(G-3371)*
- D & D Buffing & Polishing..................G...... 616 866-1015
  Rockford *(G-13565)*
- Detroit Metalcraft Finishing................G...... 586 415-7760
  Fraser *(G-5643)*
- Grand River Polishing Co Corp.........E...... 616 846-1420
  Spring Lake *(G-15147)*
- Jackson Tumble Finish Corp.............E...... 517 787-0368
  Jackson *(G-8481)*
- Kepco Inc...E...... 269 649-5800
  Vicksburg *(G-16838)*
- M&M Polishing Inc.............................F...... 269 468-4407
  Coloma *(G-3359)*
- Mann Metal Finishing Inc...................D...... 269 621-6359
  Hartford *(G-7385)*
- Marble Grinding & Polishing..............G...... 586 321-0543
  Ray *(G-13134)*

POLYMETHYL METHACRYLATE RESINS: Plexiglas

- Lyondellbasell Industries Inc.............F...... 517 336-4800
  Lansing *(G-9393)*

POLYOXYMETHYLENE RESINS

- Sumika Polymers North Amer LLC....E...... 248 284-4797
  Farmington Hills *(G-5134)*

POLYPROPYLENE RESINS

- Concepp Technologies........................F...... 734 324-6750
  Wyandotte *(G-17953)*
- Jsp International LLC.........................D...... 517 748-5200
  Jackson *(G-8485)*

POLYSTYRENE RESINS

- Huntsman Corporation.......................D...... 248 322-8682
  Auburn Hills *(G-901)*

POLYURETHANE RESINS

- Arvron Inc...E...... 616 530-1888
  Grand Rapids *(G-6186)*
- Blue Water Bioproducts LLC.............G...... 586 453-9219
  Port Huron *(G-12902)*
- Innovative Polymers Inc....................F...... 989 224-9500
  Saint Johns *(G-14284)*
- Recycled Polymetric Materials..........G...... 313 957-6373
  Detroit *(G-4335)*

POLYVINYL CHLORIDE RESINS

- Oscoda Plastics Inc...........................E...... 989 739-6900
  Oscoda *(G-12216)*
- Vi-Chem Corp.....................................E...... 616 247-8501
  Grand Rapids *(G-6969)*

PONTOONS: Rubber

- Apex Marine Inc.................................D...... 989 681-4300
  Saint Louis *(G-14359)*

POPULAR MUSIC GROUPS OR ARTISTS

- Pull Our Own Weight..........................G...... 313 686-4685
  Detroit *(G-4316)*

POSTAL EQPT: Locker Boxes, Exc Wood

- Hss Industries Inc..............................E...... 231 946-6101
  Traverse City *(G-16000)*

POSTERS

- Prop Art Studio Inc.............................G...... 313 824-2200
  Detroit *(G-4314)*

POSTERS, WHOLESALE

- Fairfax Prints Ltd................................F...... 517 321-5590
  Lansing *(G-9227)*

POTPOURRI

- Havers Heritage.................................G...... 517 423-3455
  Clinton *(G-3022)*

POTTING SOILS

- Great Lakes Nursery Soils Inc..........F...... 231 788-3123
  Muskegon *(G-11339)*
- Sun Gro Horticulture Dist Inc............D...... 517 639-3115
  Quincy *(G-13100)*
- Trp Enterprises Inc............................G...... 810 329-4027
  East China *(G-4625)*

POULTRY & SMALL GAME SLAUGHTERING & PROCESSING

- Cargill Incorporated...........................F...... 608 868-5150
  Owosso *(G-12281)*

PRODUCT SECTION

Cargill Americas Inc ....D...... 810 989-7689
  New Haven *(G-11522)*
Hillshire Brands Company ....A...... 616 875-8131
  Zeeland *(G-18150)*
Tyson Foods /Hr ....G...... 616 875-2311
  Zeeland *(G-18190)*

POWDER PUFFS & MITTS

Powder It Inc..G...... 586 949-0395
  Chesterfield *(G-2820)*

POWDER: Metal

Advantage Sintered Metals Inc............C...... 269 964-1212
  Battle Creek *(G-1142)*
Century Inc ....C...... 231 947-6400
  Traverse City *(G-15932)*
Century Inc ....D...... 231 941-7800
  Traverse City *(G-15934)*
Coldwter Sintered Met Pdts Inc............E...... 517 278-8750
  Coldwater *(G-3298)*
H & H Powdercoating Inc ....G...... 810 750-1800
  Fenton *(G-5218)*
Lakeshore Custom Powdr Coating ....G...... 616 296-9330
  Grand Haven *(G-6046)*
Paul Tousley Inc ....F...... 313 841-5400
  Detroit *(G-4291)*
Peerless Metal Powders ....F...... 313 841-5400
  Detroit *(G-4293)*
Wall Co Incorporated ....E...... 248 585-6400
  Madison Heights *(G-10379)*
Westside Powder Coat LLC ....G...... 734 729-1667
  Romulus *(G-13739)*

POWDER: Silver

Custom Powder Coating LLC ....G...... 616 454-9730
  Grand Rapids *(G-6325)*

POWER GENERATORS

Kraft Power Corporation ....F...... 989 748-4040
  Gaylord *(G-5872)*

POWER MOWERS WHOLESALERS

Great Lakes Snow & Ice Inc ....G...... 989 584-1211
  Carson City *(G-2490)*

POWER SPLY CONVERTERS: Static, Electronic Applications

Progressive Dynamics Inc ....D...... 269 781-4241
  Marshall *(G-10585)*

POWER SUPPLIES: All Types, Static

Lappans of Gaylord Inc ....G...... 989 732-3274
  Gaylord *(G-5874)*
Practical Power ....G...... 866 385-2961
  Rochester *(G-13347)*

POWER TOOLS, HAND: Chain Saws, Portable

Ebels Hardware Inc ....F...... 231 826-3334
  Falmouth *(G-4892)*

POWER TOOLS, HAND: Drills & Drilling Tools

Ace Drill Corporation ....G...... 517 265-5184
  Adrian *(G-42)*

POWER TOOLS, HAND: Drills, Port, Elec/Pneumatic, Exc Rock

Anchor Lamina America Inc ....E...... 248 489-9122
  Novi *(G-11826)*
Lamina Inc ....C...... 248 489-9122
  Farmington Hills *(G-5042)*

POWER TOOLS, HAND: Grinders, Portable, Electric Or Pneumatic

Gch Tool Group Inc ....E...... 586 777-6250
  Warren *(G-17050)*

POWER TOOLS, HAND: Guns, Pneumatic, Chip Removal

K M S Company......................................G...... 616 994-7000
  Holland *(G-7704)*

POWER TOOLS, HAND: Hammers, Portable, Elec/Pneumatic, Chip

Striker Tools LLC ....G...... 248 990-7767
  Manitou Beach *(G-10449)*

POWER TRANSMISSION EQPT WHOLESALERS

Motion Industries Inc.............................G...... 989 771-0200
  Saginaw *(G-14100)*

POWER TRANSMISSION EQPT: Aircraft

Advance Turning and Mfg Inc................C...... 517 783-2713
  Jackson *(G-8373)*

POWER TRANSMISSION EQPT: Mechanical

Accurate Gauge & Mfg Inc ....D...... 248 853-2400
  Rochester Hills *(G-13362)*
Allor Manufacturing Inc ....D...... 248 486-4500
  Brighton *(G-1883)*
Arthur R Sommers ....G...... 586 469-1280
  Harrison Township *(G-7322)*
Barnes Industries Inc ....E...... 248 541-2333
  Madison Heights *(G-10201)*
BDS Company Inc ....E...... 517 279-2135
  Coldwater *(G-3291)*
Borgwarner Powdered Metals Inc ....E...... 734 261-5322
  Livonia *(G-9668)*
Borgwarner Thermal Systems Inc........E...... 231 779-7500
  Cadillac *(G-2233)*
Colonial Bushings Inc ....F...... 586 954-3880
  Clinton Township *(G-3082)*
Dayco LLC ....G...... 248 404-6500
  Troy *(G-16296)*
Dayco Products LLC ....B...... 248 404-6500
  Troy *(G-16299)*
Equitable Engineering Co Inc ....E...... 248 689-9700
  Troy *(G-16351)*
Federal-Mogul Powertrain LLC ....B...... 616 754-5681
  Greenville *(G-7132)*
Ford Motor Company ....E...... 313 805-5938
  Dearborn *(G-3712)*
Gates Corporation ....D...... 248 260-2300
  Rochester Hills *(G-13431)*
Gateway Engineering Inc ....E...... 616 284-1425
  Grand Rapids *(G-6430)*
Geislinger Corporation ....F...... 269 441-7000
  Battle Creek *(G-1192)*
GKN Sinter Metals LLC ....G...... 248 296-7832
  Auburn Hills *(G-888)*
Hole Industries Incorporated ....G...... 517 548-4229
  Howell *(G-8050)*
Idc Industries Inc ....E...... 586 427-4321
  Clinton Township *(G-3139)*
Jatco Usa Inc..D...... 248 306-9390
  Farmington Hills *(G-5031)*
JD Norman Industries Inc ....D...... 517 589-8241
  Leslie *(G-9542)*
Kaydon Corporation ....C...... 231 755-3741
  Norton Shores *(G-11766)*
M C Carbide Tool Co ....F...... 248 486-9590
  Wixom *(G-17850)*
Melling Tool Co ....B...... 517 787-8172
  Jackson *(G-8514)*
Michigan Auto Comprsr Inc ....B...... 517 796-3200
  Parma *(G-12391)*
Milan Screw Products Inc ....E...... 734 439-2431
  Milan *(G-10949)*
Mq Operating Company ....E...... 906 337-1515
  Calumet *(G-2330)*
Murray Equipment Company Inc ....F...... 313 869-4444
  Warren *(G-17163)*
Neapco Holdings LLC ....C...... 248 699-6500
  Farmington Hills *(G-5079)*
O TP Industrial Solutions ....G...... 248 745-5503
  Pontiac *(G-12853)*
PCI Procal Inc ....F...... 989 358-7070
  Alpena *(G-307)*
Powertrain Integration LLC ....F...... 248 577-0010
  Madison Heights *(G-10333)*
Precision Torque Control Inc ....F...... 989 495-9330
  Midland *(G-10903)*

PRINTED CIRCUIT BOARDS

Quality Steel Products Inc ....E...... 248 684-0555
  Milford *(G-10981)*
Riverside Spline & Gear Inc ....E...... 810 765-8302
  Marine City *(G-10481)*
Saf-Holland Inc ....B...... 231 773-3271
  Muskegon *(G-11417)*
Supreme Gear Co ....E...... 586 775-6325
  Fraser *(G-5736)*
Ton-Tex Corporation ....E...... 616 957-3200
  Greenville *(G-7158)*
Ton-Tex Corporation ....G...... 616 957-3200
  Grand Rapids *(G-6932)*
Tractech Inc ....E...... 248 226-6800
  Southfield *(G-15048)*
U S Graphite Inc ....C...... 989 755-0441
  Saginaw *(G-14172)*
Wilkie Bros Conveyors Inc ....G...... 810 364-4820
  Marysville *(G-10626)*
Wolverine Machine Products Co ....E...... 248 634-9952
  Holly *(G-7902)*

PRECAST TERRAZZO OR CONCRETE PRDTS

Arbor Stone ....G...... 517 750-1340
  Spring Arbor *(G-15119)*
Gibbs Precast Co Inc ....G...... 517 768-9100
  Jackson *(G-8457)*
Lakeshore Cement Products ....G...... 989 739-9341
  Oscoda *(G-12213)*
Quality Precast Inc.................................E...... 269 342-0539
  Kalamazoo *(G-8866)*
Ruth Drain Tile Inc ....G...... 989 864-3406
  Ruth *(G-13989)*
Stress Con Industries Inc ....B...... 269 381-1550
  Kalamazoo *(G-8899)*

PRECIOUS STONE MINING SVCS, NEC

J M Longyear Heirs Inc..........................G...... 906 228-7960
  Marquette *(G-10535)*

PRERECORDED TAPE, COMPACT DISC & RECORD STORES

Spartannash Company ....D...... 517 278-8963
  Coldwater *(G-3333)*

PRERECORDED TAPE, COMPACT DISC & RECORD STORES: Records

Algo Especial Variety Str Inc ....G...... 313 963-9013
  Detroit *(G-3854)*
Archer Record Pressing Co ....G...... 313 365-9545
  Detroit *(G-3875)*

PRESSES

Kasten Machinery Inc ....G...... 269 945-1999
  Hastings *(G-7419)*
Oak Press Solutions Inc ....E...... 269 651-8513
  Sturgis *(G-15624)*

PRIMARY METAL PRODUCTS

Wes Corp ....G...... 231 536-2500
  East Jordan *(G-4647)*

PRIMARY ROLLING MILL EQPT

Mill Assist Services Inc ....F...... 269 692-3211
  Otsego *(G-12245)*

PRINT CARTRIDGES: Laser & Other Computer Printers

Cau Acquisition Company LLC ....D...... 989 875-8133
  Ithaca *(G-8357)*
Compatible Laser Products Inc ....F...... 810 629-0459
  Fenton *(G-5197)*
Lps-2 Inc ....G...... 313 538-0181
  Redford *(G-13168)*
Mikan Corporation ....F...... 734 944-9447
  Saline *(G-14401)*
Visionit Supplies and Svcs Inc ....A...... 313 664-5650
  Detroit *(G-4432)*

PRINTED CIRCUIT BOARDS

3dxtech LLC ....G...... 616 717-3811
  Grand Rapids *(G-6121)*

PRINTED CIRCUIT BOARDS

A and D Design Electronics ....G...... 989 493-1884
  Auburn *(G-748)*
Acromag Incorporated ....D...... 248 624-1541
  Wixom *(G-17751)*
Aero Embedded Technologies Inc ....G...... 586 251-2980
  Sterling Heights *(G-15255)*
Amtech Electrocircuits Inc ....G...... 248 583-1801
  Troy *(G-16200)*
Assem-Tech Inc................................E...... 616 846-3410
  Grand Haven *(G-5993)*
Assembly Alternatives Inc ....G...... 248 362-1616
  Rochester Hills *(G-13371)*
Boyd Manufacturing LLC..................G...... 734 649-9765
  Muskegon *(G-11284)*
Bralyn Inc..F...... 231 865-3186
  Fruitport *(G-5790)*
Burton Industries Inc........................E...... 906 932-5970
  Ironwood *(G-8324)*
Ci Lighting LLC ....G...... 248 997-4415
  Auburn Hills *(G-813)*
Cusolar Industries Inc ....E...... 586 949-3880
  Chesterfield *(G-2757)*
Debron Industrial Elec Inc................E...... 248 588-7220
  Troy *(G-16300)*
Diversified Mfg & Assembly LLC......G...... 313 758-4797
  Sterling Hts *(G-15549)*
Dse Industries LLC..........................G...... 313 530-6668
  Macomb *(G-10118)*
Dupearl Technology LLC..................D...... 248 390-9609
  Bloomfield Hills *(G-1762)*
Excel Circuits LLC ....F...... 248 373-0700
  Auburn Hills *(G-857)*
Flextronics Intl USA Inc...................B...... 616 837-9711
  Coopersville *(G-3558)*
Ghi Electronics LLC.........................F...... 248 397-8856
  Madison Heights *(G-10257)*
Glassmaster Controls Co Inc............E...... 269 382-2010
  Kalamazoo *(G-8753)*
Hewtech Electronics ....G...... 810 765-0820
  China *(G-2860)*
Hgc Westshore LLC ....D...... 616 796-1218
  Holland *(G-7664)*
I Parth Inc......................................G...... 248 548-9722
  Ferndale *(G-5293)*
Jabil Circuit Inc ....A...... 248 292-6000
  Auburn Hills *(G-916)*
Jabil Circuit Michigan Inc................E...... 248 292-6000
  Auburn Hills *(G-917)*
Keska LLC ....G...... 616 283-7056
  Holland *(G-7711)*
M T S Chenault LLC ....G...... 269 861-0053
  Benton Harbor *(G-1523)*
Magna Electronics Inc......................C...... 248 729-2643
  Auburn Hills *(G-933)*
Micro Logic ....G...... 248 432-7209
  West Bloomfield *(G-17486)*
N S International Ltd.......................C...... 248 251-1600
  Troy *(G-16519)*
Northville Circuits Inc......................G...... 248 853-3232
  Rochester Hills *(G-13484)*
Obertron Electronic Mfg Inc ....F...... 734 428-0722
  Manchester *(G-10409)*
Odyssey Electronics Inc ....D...... 734 421-8340
  Livonia *(G-9874)*
P M Z Technology Inc ....G...... 248 471-0447
  Livonia *(G-9879)*
Petra Electronic Mfg Inc..................F...... 616 877-1991
  Holland *(G-7771)*
Pgf Technology Group Inc ....E...... 248 852-2800
  Rochester Hills *(G-13492)*
Plymouth Computer & ....G...... 734 744-9563
  Livonia *(G-9890)*
Protodesign Inc...............................E...... 586 739-4340
  Shelby Township *(G-14673)*
Ram Electronics Inc.........................F...... 231 865-3186
  Fruitport *(G-5799)*
Rockstar Digital Inc.........................F...... 888 808-5868
  Sterling Heights *(G-15477)*
Saline Lectronics Inc.......................C...... 734 944-1972
  Saline *(G-14413)*
Semicndctor Hybrid Assmbly Inc......F...... 248 668-9050
  Wixom *(G-17893)*
Xilinx Inc.......................................G...... 248 344-0786
  Wixom *(G-17932)*

PRINTERS & PLOTTERS

Appliction Spclist Kompany Inc........F...... 517 676-6633
  Lansing *(G-9339)*
Electronics For Imaging Inc ....D...... 734 641-3062
  Ypsilanti *(G-18069)*

PRINTERS' SVCS: Folding, Collating, Etc

Accuform Prtg & Graphics Inc..........F...... 313 271-5600
  Detroit *(G-3838)*
Hexon Corporation ....F...... 248 585-7585
  Farmington Hills *(G-5018)*
Industrial Imprntng & Die Ctng........G...... 586 778-9470
  Eastpointe *(G-4704)*
Logan Marketing Group LLC ....F...... 248 731-7650
  Bloomfield Hills *(G-1778)*
Ray Scott Industries Inc ....G...... 248 535-2528
  Port Huron *(G-12962)*

PRINTERS: Computer

Kingdom Cartridge Inc ....G...... 734 564-1590
  Plymouth *(G-12669)*
Printek Inc......................................C...... 269 925-3200
  Saint Joseph *(G-14336)*
Visionit Supplies and Svcs Inc ....A...... 313 664-5650
  Detroit *(G-4432)*

PRINTERS: Magnetic Ink, Bar Code

Bcc Distribution Inc.........................F...... 734 737-9300
  Canton *(G-2350)*
Compunetics Systems Inc ....G...... 248 531-0015
  Rochester Hills *(G-13393)*
Kace Logistics LLC ....D...... 734 946-8600
  Carleton *(G-2458)*

PRINTING & BINDING: Books

A Time To Remember ....G...... 517 263-1960
  Adrian *(G-41)*
Best Binding LLC............................G...... 734 459-7785
  Plymouth *(G-12586)*
Edwards Brothers Inc......................C...... 800 722-3231
  Ann Arbor *(G-436)*
Great Lakes Photo Inc.....................G...... 586 784-5446
  Richmond *(G-13264)*
Imagemaster Printing LLC................E...... 734 821-2511
  Ann Arbor *(G-502)*
Malloy Incorporated ....A...... 734 665-6113
  Ann Arbor *(G-542)*
McNaughton & Gunn Inc..................C...... 734 429-5411
  Saline *(G-14399)*
Printing Perspectives LLC ....G...... 810 410-8186
  Flint *(G-5485)*
William B Eerdmans Pubg Co...........F...... 616 459-4591
  Grand Rapids *(G-6994)*

PRINTING & BINDING: Pamphlets

Lottery Info ....G...... 734 326-0097
  Wayne *(G-17437)*

PRINTING & BINDING: Textbooks

Superior Text LLC ....F...... 866 482-8762
  Ypsilanti *(G-18104)*

PRINTING & EMBOSSING: Plastic Fabric Articles

Flint Group Packaging Inks ....G...... 513 619-2085
  Livonia *(G-9738)*
Flint Group Packaging Inks ....G...... 734 781-4600
  Livonia *(G-9739)*
Great Lakes Embroidery ....G...... 248 543-5164
  Madison Heights *(G-10260)*
Mayfair Golf Accessories ....F...... 989 732-8400
  Gaylord *(G-5879)*
Real Green Systems Inc ....D...... 888 345-2154
  Commerce Township *(G-3447)*
Rj Corp ....F...... 616 396-0552
  Holland *(G-7788)*

PRINTING & ENGRAVING: Invitation & Stationery

Celebrations ....G...... 906 482-4946
  Hancock *(G-7250)*
Invitations By Design ....G...... 269 342-8551
  Kalamazoo *(G-8775)*
Parkside Printing Inc.......................G...... 810 765-4500
  Marine City *(G-10479)*
Village Printing & Supply Inc ....G...... 810 664-2270
  Lapeer *(G-9491)*

PRINTING & STAMPING: Fabric Articles

Cedar Springs Sales LLC ....G...... 616 696-2111
  Cedar Springs *(G-2548)*
Delux Monogramming Screen Prtg ...G...... 989 288-5321
  Durand *(G-4607)*
East End Sports Awards Inc ....G...... 906 293-8895
  Newberry *(G-11579)*
Loyalty 1977 Ink ....G...... 313 759-1006
  Detroit *(G-4211)*
Sigma International Inc ....E...... 248 230-9681
  Livonia *(G-9928)*
Suite 600 T-Shirts LLC....................G...... 866 712-7749
  Detroit *(G-4382)*

PRINTING & WRITING PAPER WHOLESALERS

Wixom Moving Boxes LLC................G...... 248 613-5078
  Wixom *(G-17931)*

PRINTING INKS WHOLESALERS

Grand Rapids Printing Ink Co...........F...... 616 241-5681
  Grand Rapids *(G-6462)*
Mis Associates Inc..........................G...... 844 225-8156
  Pontiac *(G-12850)*

PRINTING MACHINERY

A C Steel Rule Dies Inc...................G...... 248 588-5600
  Madison Heights *(G-10175)*
Alpine Sign and Prtg Sup Inc ....F...... 517 487-1400
  Lansing *(G-9275)*
Benmar Communications LLC ....F...... 313 593-0690
  Dearborn *(G-3681)*
Brown LLC......................................C...... 989 435-7741
  Beaverton *(G-1383)*
Douthitt Corporation........................E...... 313 259-1565
  Detroit *(G-4016)*
Elk Lake Tool Co ....E...... 231 264-5616
  Elk Rapids *(G-4777)*
Innovative Machines Inc..................E...... 616 669-1649
  Jenison *(G-8630)*
Qmi Group Inc ....E...... 248 589-0505
  Madison Heights *(G-10342)*
Sgk LLC ....D...... 269 381-3820
  Battle Creek *(G-1245)*
Thermoforming Tech Group LLC ......G...... 989 435-7741
  Beaverton *(G-1395)*
Unique-Intasco Usa Inc ....G...... 810 982-3360
  Auburn Hills *(G-1036)*

PRINTING MACHINERY, EQPT & SPLYS: Wholesalers

Graphic Art Service & Supply ....G...... 810 229-4700
  Brighton *(G-1933)*
Graphic Arts Service & Sup Inc ....F...... 616 698-9300
  Grand Rapids *(G-6473)*
Michigan Roller Inc ....G...... 269 651-2304
  Sturgis *(G-15618)*
Village Printing & Supply Inc ....G...... 810 664-2270
  Lapeer *(G-9491)*

PRINTING, COMMERCIAL Newspapers, NEC

Grand Blanc Printing Inc..................E...... 810 694-1155
  Grand Blanc *(G-5968)*
North Country Publishing Corp.........G...... 231 526-2191
  Harbor Springs *(G-7290)*

PRINTING, COMMERCIAL: Business Forms, NEC

Consoldted Dcment Slutions LLC......F...... 586 293-8100
  Fraser *(G-5638)*
Imagemaster LLC............................G...... 734 821-2500
  Ann Arbor *(G-501)*
Imprint House LLC..........................G...... 810 985-8203
  Port Huron *(G-12929)*
Multi Packg Solutions Intl Ltd..........A...... 517 323-9000
  Lansing *(G-9250)*
TGI Direct Inc.................................E...... 810 239-5553
  Flint *(G-5509)*

PRINTING, COMMERCIAL: Calendars, NEC

Moonpeace ....G...... 616 456-1128
  Grand Rapids *(G-6705)*
Ozland Enterprises Inc ....G...... 269 649-0706
  Vicksburg *(G-16840)*

PRINTING, COMMERCIAL: Cards, Visiting, Incl Business, NEC

Main Street Portraits ....G 269 321-3310
 Richland *(G-13251)*

PRINTING, COMMERCIAL: Catalogs, NEC

Adair Printing Company ....E 734 426-2822
 Dexter *(G-4472)*

PRINTING, COMMERCIAL: Coupons, NEC

Save On Everything Inc ....D 248 362-9119
 Troy *(G-16594)*

PRINTING, COMMERCIAL: Envelopes, NEC

The Envelope Printery Inc ....D 734 398-7700
 Van Buren Twp *(G-16787)*

PRINTING, COMMERCIAL: Imprinting

Flying Colors Imprinting Inc ....F 734 641-1300
 Melvindale *(G-10698)*
Impression Center Co ....G 248 989-8080
 Troy *(G-16413)*
Kick It Around Sports ....G 810 232-4986
 Flint *(G-5455)*
Mayfair Accessories Inc ....G 989 732-8400
 Gaylord *(G-5878)*

PRINTING, COMMERCIAL: Invitations, NEC

R S V P Inc ....G 734 455-7229
 Plymouth *(G-12729)*

PRINTING, COMMERCIAL: Labels & Seals, NEC

Amery Tape & Label Co Inc ....G 586 759-3230
 Warren *(G-16932)*
FSI Label Company ....E 586 776-4110
 Holland *(G-7637)*
General Tape Label Liquidating ....D 248 437-5200
 Wixom *(G-17817)*
Great Lakes Label LLC ....E 616 647-9880
 Comstock Park *(G-3483)*
Impact Label Corporation ....D 269 381-4280
 Galesburg *(G-5811)*
Label Tech Inc ....F 586 247-6444
 Shelby Township *(G-14619)*
Northern Label Inc ....G 231 854-6301
 Hesperia *(G-7479)*
Perrin Souvenir Distrs Inc ....B 616 785-9700
 Comstock Park *(G-3508)*
Precision Label Inc ....G 616 534-9935
 Grandville *(G-7066)*
Precision Label Specialist ....G 248 673-5010
 Waterford *(G-17371)*
Stamp-Rite Incorporated ....E 517 487-5071
 Lansing *(G-9267)*
Stylerite Label Corporation ....E 248 853-7977
 Rochester Hills *(G-13519)*

PRINTING, COMMERCIAL: Letterpress & Screen

Cedar Springs Sales LLC ....G 616 696-2111
 Cedar Springs *(G-2548)*
Danmark Graphics LLC ....G 616 675-7499
 Casnovia *(G-2507)*
J2 Licensing Inc ....G 586 307-3400
 Troy *(G-16431)*
Mylockercom LLC ....B 877 898-3366
 Detroit *(G-4261)*
Threadworks Ltd Inc ....G 517 548-9745
 New Boston *(G-11513)*
Total Lee Sports Inc ....G 989 772-6121
 Mount Pleasant *(G-11234)*

PRINTING, COMMERCIAL: Literature, Advertising, NEC

D J Rotunda Associates Inc ....G 586 772-3350
 West Bloomfield *(G-17472)*
Help-U-Sell RE Big Rapids ....F 231 796-3966
 Big Rapids *(G-1634)*
Interntonal Innovative Systems ....G 248 524-2222
 Troy *(G-16421)*
IXL Graphics Inc ....G 313 350-2800
 South Lyon *(G-14796)*

MPS Holdco Inc ....C 517 886-2526
 Lansing *(G-9246)*

PRINTING, COMMERCIAL: Magazines, NEC

Step Into Success Inc ....G 734 426-1075
 Pinckney *(G-12504)*

PRINTING, COMMERCIAL: Menus, NEC

Focus Marketing ....E 616 355-4362
 Holland *(G-7633)*

PRINTING, COMMERCIAL: Music, Sheet, NEC

Gods Children In Unity Intl M ....G 313 528-8285
 Detroit *(G-4095)*

PRINTING, COMMERCIAL: Periodicals, NEC

Bible Doctrines To Live By Inc ....G 616 453-0493
 Comstock Park *(G-3463)*

PRINTING, COMMERCIAL: Post Cards, Picture, NEC

Star Line Commercial Printing ....F 810 733-1152
 Flushing *(G-5542)*

PRINTING, COMMERCIAL: Promotional

Community Mental Health ....D 517 323-9558
 Lansing *(G-9210)*
Fonts About Inc ....G 248 767-7504
 Northville *(G-11692)*
Graphicolor Systems Inc ....G 248 347-0271
 Livonia *(G-9758)*
H E L P Printers Inc ....G 734 847-0554
 Temperance *(G-15830)*
Reynolds Bus Solutions LLC ....G 616 293-6449
 Grand Rapids *(G-6821)*

PRINTING, COMMERCIAL: Publications

Extreme Screenprints ....G 616 889-8305
 Grandville *(G-7034)*
Labor Education and Res Prj ....G 313 842-6262
 Detroit *(G-4189)*
Print Shop 4u LLC ....G 810 721-7500
 Imlay City *(G-8211)*
Rbd Creative ....G 313 259-5507
 Plymouth *(G-12731)*
Solutionsnowbiz ....G 269 321-5062
 Portage *(G-13033)*

PRINTING, COMMERCIAL: Ready

P D Q Press Inc ....G 586 725-1888
 Ira *(G-8265)*

PRINTING, COMMERCIAL: Screen

1365267 Ontario Inc ....G 888 843-5245
 Port Huron *(G-12879)*
A-1 Screenprinting LLC ....D 734 665-2692
 Ann Arbor *(G-335)*
Adams Shirt Shack Inc ....G 269 964-3323
 Battle Creek *(G-1137)*
Adlib Grafix & Apparel ....G 269 964-2810
 Battle Creek *(G-1139)*
Adrians Screen Print ....G 734 994-1367
 Holland *(G-7550)*
ADS Plus Printing ....G 810 659-7190
 Flushing *(G-5530)*
Advanced Screenprinting ....G 586 979-4412
 Sterling Heights *(G-15254)*
Advanced Tex Screen Printing ....E 989 643-7288
 Bay City *(G-1272)*
Allgraphics Corp ....G 248 994-7373
 Farmington Hills *(G-4928)*
Americas Finest Prtg Graphics ....G 586 296-1312
 Fraser *(G-5618)*
AP Impressions Inc ....G 734 464-8009
 Livonia *(G-9650)*
Apparel Printers Limited ....G 517 882-5700
 Lansing *(G-9337)*
Apparel Sales Inc ....G 616 842-5650
 Jenison *(G-8617)*
Applied Graphics & Fabricating ....F 989 662-3334
 Auburn *(G-750)*
Ar2 Engineering LLC ....E 248 735-9999
 Novi *(G-11829)*

Beyond Embroidery ....G 616 726-7000
 Grand Rapids *(G-6216)*
Big D LLC ....G 248 787-2724
 Redford *(G-13149)*
Bivins Graphics ....G 616 453-2211
 Grand Rapids *(G-6227)*
Blts Wearable Art Inc ....G 517 669-9659
 Dewitt *(G-4459)*
Bradford Printing Inc ....G 517 887-0044
 Lansing *(G-9349)*
Celia Corporation ....G 616 887-7387
 Sparta *(G-15090)*
Cobrex Ltd ....G 734 429-9758
 Saline *(G-14382)*
Complete Source Inc ....G 616 285-9110
 Grand Rapids *(G-6293)*
Contractors Printing ....G 517 622-1888
 Grand Ledge *(G-6103)*
Corporate Colors Inc ....G 269 323-2000
 Kalamazoo *(G-8719)*
Creative Awards ....G 586 739-4999
 Sterling Heights *(G-15303)*
Custom Royaltees ....G 586 943-9849
 Clinton Township *(G-3096)*
D & M Silkscreening ....G 517 694-4199
 Holt *(G-7906)*
Darson Corporation ....F 313 875-7781
 Ferndale *(G-5269)*
Delta Sports Service & EMB ....G 517 482-6565
 Lansing *(G-9215)*
Designs By Bean ....G 989 845-4371
 Chesaning *(G-2723)*
Designshirtscom Inc ....G 734 414-7604
 Plymouth *(G-12609)*
Detroit Impression Company Inc ....G 313 921-9077
 Detroit *(G-3986)*
Domer Industries LLC ....F 269 226-4000
 Kalamazoo *(G-8731)*
E X P Screen Printers ....G 586 772-6660
 Eastpointe *(G-4700)*
Earthbound Inc ....G 616 774-0096
 Grand Rapids *(G-6366)*
Eclipse Print Emporium Inc ....G 248 477-8337
 Livonia *(G-9720)*
Edens Political ....G 313 277-0700
 Dearborn *(G-3699)*
Edwards Sign & Screen Printing ....G 989 725-2988
 Owosso *(G-12290)*
Emerald Graphics Inc ....G 616 871-3020
 Grand Rapids *(G-6376)*
Essential Screen Printing LLC ....G 313 300-6411
 Detroit *(G-4042)*
Extreme Fitness Gym ....G 989 681-8339
 Saint Louis *(G-14363)*
Fams T-Shirts and Designs ....G 248 841-1086
 Rochester *(G-13320)*
Faro Screen Process Inc ....F 734 207-8400
 Canton *(G-2375)*
First Imprssons Cstm Printwear ....F 586 783-5210
 Clinton Township *(G-3119)*
Flavored Group LLC ....G 517 775-4371
 Lansing *(G-9289)*
Foresight Group Inc ....E 517 485-5700
 Lansing *(G-9230)*
Fug Inc ....G 269 781-8036
 Marshall *(G-10568)*
Futuristic Artwear Inc ....E 248 680-0200
 Rochester Hills *(G-13429)*
Genesis Graphics Inc ....G 906 786-4913
 Escanaba *(G-4831)*
Globe Printing & Specialties ....F 906 485-1033
 Ishpeming *(G-8345)*
Grafaktri Inc ....G 734 665-0717
 Ann Arbor *(G-476)*
Grand Rapids Graphix ....G 616 359-2383
 Wyoming *(G-18005)*
Grasel Graphics ....G 989 652-5151
 Frankenmuth *(G-5589)*
Hilton Screeners Inc ....G 810 653-0711
 Davison *(G-3654)*
Holland Screen Print Inc ....G 616 396-7630
 Holland *(G-7677)*
Homestead Graphics Design Inc ....G 906 353-6741
 Baraga *(G-1103)*
Industrial Mtal Idntfction Inc ....G 616 847-0060
 Spring Lake *(G-15153)*
Inkorporated ....G 734 261-4657
 Garden City *(G-5827)*
Integrity Marketing Products ....G 734 522-5050
 Garden City *(G-5829)*

Employee Codes: A=Over 500 employees, B=251-500
C=101-250, D=51-100, E=20-50, F=10-19, G=3-9

PRINTING, COMMERCIAL: Screen

JD Group Inc .... E 248 735-9999
  Novi *(G-11911)*
Jentees Custom Screen Prtg LLC ...... F 231 929-3610
  Traverse City *(G-16011)*
K G S Screen Process Inc .... G 313 794-2777
  Detroit *(G-4169)*
Kennedy Acquisition Inc .... G 616 871-3020
  Grand Rapids *(G-6573)*
Kpmf Usa Inc .... F 248 377-4999
  Lake Orion *(G-9142)*
Lansing Athletics .... G 517 327-8828
  Lansing *(G-9305)*
Larsen Graphics Inc .... E 989 823-3000
  Vassar *(G-16812)*
Let Love Rule .... G 734 749-7435
  Rockwood *(G-13607)*
Livonia Trophy & Screen Prtg .... G 734 464-9191
  Livonia *(G-9816)*
M&S Printmedia Inc .... G 248 601-1200
  Rochester Hills *(G-13464)*
Malachi Printing LLC .... G 517 395-4813
  Jackson *(G-8508)*
Mega Screen Corp .... G 517 849-7057
  Jonesville *(G-8663)*
Mettek LLC .... G 616 895-2033
  Allendale *(G-222)*
Michael Anderson .... G 231 652-5717
  Newaygo *(G-11575)*
Michigan Screen Printing .... G 810 687-5550
  Clio *(G-3276)*
Midwest Graphics & Awards Inc .... G 734 424-3700
  Dexter *(G-4500)*
Modzel Screen Printing .... G 231 941-0911
  Traverse City *(G-16040)*
Monograms & More Inc .... E 313 299-3140
  Taylor *(G-15746)*
Monroe Sp Inc .... G 517 374-6544
  Lansing *(G-9313)*
Ninja Tees N More .... G 248 541-2547
  Hazel Park *(G-7448)*
Northern Screen Printing & EMB .... G 906 786-0373
  Escanaba *(G-4848)*
Personal Graphics .... G 231 347-6347
  Petoskey *(G-12468)*
Precision Dial Co .... G 269 375-5601
  Kalamazoo *(G-8857)*
Primo Crafts .... G 248 373-3229
  Pontiac *(G-12858)*
Pro Shop The/P S Graphics .... G 517 448-8490
  Hudson *(G-8139)*
Progress Custom Screen Prtg .... G 248 982-4247
  Ferndale *(G-5314)*
Progressive Graphics .... G 269 945-9249
  Hastings *(G-7423)*
Quantum Graphics Inc .... E 586 566-5656
  Shelby Township *(G-14675)*
R & J Quality Screenprinting .... G 989 345-8614
  West Branch *(G-17518)*
Robert J Lidzan .... G 616 361-6446
  Grand Rapids *(G-6831)*
Rods Prints & Promotions .... G 269 639-8814
  South Haven *(G-14769)*
Royal Stewart Enterprises .... G 734 224-7994
  Temperance *(G-15843)*
Sandlot Sports .... F 989 391-9684
  Bay City *(G-1355)*
Sandlot Sports .... G 989 835-9696
  Saginaw *(G-14145)*
Screen Graphics Co Inc .... G 231 238-4499
  Indian River *(G-8222)*
Screen Ideas Inc .... G 616 458-5119
  Grand Rapids *(G-6855)*
Screen Print Department .... E 616 235-2200
  Grand Rapids *(G-6856)*
Screened Image Graphic Design .... G 906 226-6112
  Marquette *(G-10556)*
Screentek Imaging .... G 586 759-4850
  Warren *(G-17235)*
Screenworks Cstm Scrn Printg & .... G 616 754-7762
  Greenville *(G-7152)*
Serviscreen Inc .... D 616 669-1640
  Jenison *(G-8643)*
Shirt Tails Inc .... G 906 774-3370
  Iron Mountain *(G-8300)*
Sign Screen Inc .... G 810 239-1100
  Flint *(G-5499)*
Signs365com LLC .... G 800 265-8830
  Shelby Township *(G-14694)*
Silk Screenstuff .... G 517 543-7716
  Charlotte *(G-2664)*

Spectrum Graphics Inc .... F 248 589-2795
  Troy *(G-16615)*
Sports Inc .... G 734 728-1313
  Wayne *(G-17443)*
Sports Junction .... G 989 791-5900
  Saginaw *(G-14156)*
Sports Junction .... G 989 835-9696
  Midland *(G-10920)*
Sunrise Screen Printing Inc .... G 734 769-3888
  Ann Arbor *(G-650)*
Swift Printing Co .... F 616 459-4263
  Grand Rapids *(G-6908)*
Sylvesters .... G 989 348-9097
  Grayling *(G-7116)*
Trikala Inc .... G 517 646-8188
  Dimondale *(G-4520)*
Triple Creek Shirts and More .... G 269 273-5154
  Three Rivers *(G-15882)*
Triple Thread .... G 248 321-7757
  Clawson *(G-2987)*
Vector Distribution LLC .... G 616 361-2021
  Grand Rapids *(G-6962)*
Vgkids Inc .... F 734 485-5128
  Ypsilanti *(G-18107)*
Vision Designs Inc .... G 616 994-7054
  Holland *(G-7848)*
Wellard Inc .... G 312 752-0155
  West Olive *(G-17536)*
Zodiac Enterprises LLC .... G 810 640-7146
  Mount Morris *(G-11167)*

PRINTING, COMMERCIAL: Tags, NEC

All Access Name Tags .... G 866 955-8247
  Troy *(G-16188)*

PRINTING, COMMERCIAL: Tickets, NEC

Meteor Web Marketing Inc .... F 734 822-4999
  Ann Arbor *(G-553)*
Tickets Plus Inc .... E 616 222-4000
  Grand Rapids *(G-6931)*

PRINTING, LITHOGRAPHIC: Advertising Posters

Detroit Newspaper Partnr LP .... A 586 826-7187
  Sterling Heights *(G-15314)*
Epi Printers Inc .... D 734 261-9400
  Livonia *(G-9729)*
Paul C Doerr .... G 734 242-2058
  Monroe *(G-11060)*

PRINTING, LITHOGRAPHIC: Catalogs

Business Design Solutions Inc .... G 248 672-8007
  Southfield *(G-14861)*
Npi Wireless .... E 231 922-9273
  Traverse City *(G-16053)*

PRINTING, LITHOGRAPHIC: Decals

Celia Corporation .... D 616 887-7341
  Sparta *(G-15091)*
Commercial Trck Transf Signs .... G 586 754-7100
  Warren *(G-16988)*

PRINTING, LITHOGRAPHIC: Forms & Cards, Business

Daniel Ward .... G 810 965-6535
  Mount Morris *(G-11160)*
Digital Imaging Group Inc .... C 269 686-8744
  Allegan *(G-157)*
Embroidery House Inc .... G 616 669-6400
  Jenison *(G-8625)*
Intelliform Inc .... G 248 541-4000
  Berkley *(G-1586)*
Utley Brothers Inc .... E 248 585-1700
  Troy *(G-16672)*

PRINTING, LITHOGRAPHIC: Forms, Business

Timbertech Inc .... E 231 348-2750
  Harbor Springs *(G-7295)*
Total Business Systems Inc .... F 248 307-1076
  Madison Heights *(G-10368)*
Walker Printery Inc .... F 248 548-5100
  Oak Park *(G-12104)*

PRINTING, LITHOGRAPHIC: Newspapers

Enjoyment Image Publications .... G 269 782-8259
  Dowagiac *(G-4542)*
Graph-ADS Printing Inc .... C 989 779-6000
  Mount Pleasant *(G-11195)*
Mid-State Printing Inc .... F 989 875-4163
  Ithaca *(G-8364)*

PRINTING, LITHOGRAPHIC: Offset & photolithographic printing

Copy Central Inc .... G 231 941-2298
  Traverse City *(G-15947)*
I D Enterprises LLC .... G 734 513-0800
  Livonia *(G-9777)*
Vtec Graphics Inc .... G 734 953-9729
  Livonia *(G-9993)*

PRINTING, LITHOGRAPHIC: On Metal

Bastian Brothers & Company .... E 989 239-5107
  Freeland *(G-5752)*
Clare Print & Pulp .... G 989 386-3497
  Clare *(G-2867)*
Foremost Graphics LLC .... D 616 453-4747
  Grand Rapids *(G-6415)*
Ideal Printing Company .... E 616 454-9224
  Grand Rapids *(G-6525)*
Parkside Speedy Print Inc .... G 810 985-8484
  Port Huron *(G-12955)*
Pellow Printing Co .... G 906 475-9431
  Negaunee *(G-11473)*
Web Litho Inc .... G 586 803-9000
  Rochester Hills *(G-13542)*
West Michigan Printing Inc .... G 616 676-2190
  Ada *(G-34)*

PRINTING, LITHOGRAPHIC: Periodicals

Journal Disposition Corp .... G 269 428-2054
  Saint Joseph *(G-14319)*

PRINTING, LITHOGRAPHIC: Posters

Fairfax Prints Ltd .... G 517 321-5590
  Lansing *(G-9227)*

PRINTING, LITHOGRAPHIC: Posters & Decals

Word Baron Inc .... F 248 471-4080
  Ann Arbor *(G-702)*

PRINTING, LITHOGRAPHIC: Promotional

Avanzado LLC .... E 248 615-0538
  Farmington Hills *(G-4938)*
Quantum Digital Ventures LLC .... E 248 292-5686
  Warren *(G-17212)*
Real Estate One Inc .... G 248 851-2600
  Commerce Township *(G-3446)*
Sinclair Graphics LLC .... G 269 621-3651
  Hartford *(G-7387)*

PRINTING, LITHOGRAPHIC: Tags

International Master Pdts Corp .... C 231 894-5651
  Montague *(G-11091)*

PRINTING, LITHOGRAPHIC: Transfers, Decalcomania Or Dry

Whisper Creative Products Inc .... G 734 529-2734
  Dundee *(G-4603)*

PRINTING, LITHOGRAPHIC: Wrappers & Seals

Unique-Intasco Usa Inc .... G 810 982-3360
  Auburn Hills *(G-1036)*

PRINTING: Books

Creative Graphics Inc .... G 517 784-0391
  Jackson *(G-8424)*
Cushing-Malloy Inc .... E 734 663-8554
  Ann Arbor *(G-409)*
Edwards Brothers Malloy Inc .... B 734 665-6113
  Ann Arbor *(G-437)*
Michigan Brlle Trnscrbing Fund .... G 517 780-5096
  Jackson *(G-8519)*

PRODUCT SECTION

PRINTING: Commercial, NEC

PRINTING: Books

Edward Brothers Malloy	G	734 665-6113
Ann Arbor (G-435)		
Epi Printers Inc	D	734 261-9400
Livonia (G-9729)		
Imperial Clinical RES Svcs Inc	C	616 784-0100
Grand Rapids (G-6528)		
Jenkins Group Inc	F	231 933-4954
Traverse City (G-16010)		
Mel Printing Co Inc	E	313 928-5440
Taylor (G-15738)		
Practical Paper Inc	F	616 887-1723
Cedar Springs (G-2559)		
R W Patterson Printing Co	D	269 925-2177
Benton Harbor (G-1542)		
Rogers Printing Inc	C	231 853-2244
Ravenna (G-13128)		
Sheridan Pubg Grnd Rapids Inc	D	616 957-5100
Grand Rapids (G-6860)		
Success By Design Inc	F	800 327-0057
Wyoming (G-18033)		
Tweddle Group Inc	C	586 307-3700
Clinton Township (G-3252)		

PRINTING: Broadwoven Fabrics. Cotton

Inkpressions LLC	E	248 461-2555
Commerce Township (G-3416)		
Meridian Screen Prtg & Design	G	517 351-2525
Okemos (G-12130)		

PRINTING: Commercial, NEC

Advance Graphic Systems Inc	E	248 656-8000
Rochester Hills (G-13365)		
Advantage Label and Packg Inc	E	616 656-1900
Grand Rapids (G-6150)		
Al Corp	F	734 475-7357
Chelsea (G-2701)		
Aldinger Inc	E	517 394-2424
Lansing (G-9334)		
Allesk Enterprises Inc	G	231 941-5770
Traverse City (G-15894)		
Alpha Data Business Forms Inc	G	248 540-5930
Birmingham (G-1674)		
American Reprographics Co LLC	E	248 299-8900
Clawson (G-2973)		
An Corporate Center LLC	E	248 669-1188
Plymouth (G-12571)		
Apb Inc	G	248 528-2990
Troy (G-16204)		
Applied Visual Concepts LLC	G	866 440-6888
Warren (G-16937)		
ARC Print Solutions LLC	F	248 917-7052
Beverly Hills (G-1613)		
Arrow Printing LLC	G	248 738-2222
Waterford (G-17323)		
Art Craft Display Inc	D	517 485-2221
Lansing (G-9278)		
B C P Printing	G	269 695-3877
Buchanan (G-2109)		
Behrmann Printing Company Inc	F	248 799-7771
Southfield (G-14851)		
Best Impressions	G	313 389-1202
Lincoln Park (G-9574)		
Big Color Printing Center	G	313 933-9290
Detroit (G-3903)		
Big Rapids Printing	G	231 796-8588
Grand Rapids (G-6220)		
Bivins Graphics	G	616 453-2211
Grand Rapids (G-6226)		
Blue Water Printing Co Inc	G	810 664-0643
Lapeer (G-9443)		
Brightformat Inc	E	616 247-1161
Grand Rapids (G-6236)		
Bronco Printing Company	G	248 544-1120
Hazel Park (G-7435)		
Brophy Engraving Co Inc	E	313 871-2333
Detroit (G-3919)		
C2 Imaging LLC	C	248 743-2903
Troy (G-16251)		
Cadillac Prsentation Solutions	E	248 288-9777
Troy (G-16255)		
Christian Unity Press Inc	G	402 362-5133
Flint (G-5397)		
Columbia Marking Tools Inc	E	586 949-8400
Chesterfield (G-2754)		
Commercial Blueprint Inc	E	517 372-8360
Lansing (G-9357)		
Custom Printers Inc	D	616 454-9224
Grand Rapids (G-6326)		
Custom Threads and Sports LLC	G	248 391-0088
Lake Orion (G-9133)		
Data Mail Services Inc	E	248 588-2415
Madison Heights (G-10228)		
Dearborn Imaging Group LLC	G	313 561-1173
Dearborn (G-3689)		
Del Printing Inc	F	586 445-3044
Saint Clair Shores (G-14243)		
Detroit Evrlasting Dezigns Inc	G	248 790-0850
West Bloomfield (G-17475)		
Digital Imaging Group Inc	C	269 686-8744
Allegan (G-157)		
Display Pack Inc	C	616 451-3061
Cedar Springs (G-2553)		
Dobb Printing Inc	E	231 722-1060
Muskegon (G-11306)		
Domart LLC	G	616 285-9177
Grand Rapids (G-6357)		
Donna Jeroy	G	313 554-2722
River Rouge (G-13275)		
Earle Press Inc	E	231 773-2111
Muskegon (G-11312)		
Ecoprint Services LLC	G	616 254-8019
Grand Rapids (G-6369)		
Elite Business Services & Exec	D	734 956-4550
Bloomfield Hills (G-1763)		
Epi Printers Inc	D	734 261-9400
Livonia (G-9729)		
F & A Enterprises of Michigan	G	906 228-3222
Marquette (G-10531)		
F P Horak Company	C	989 892-6505
Bay City (G-1312)		
Fabulous Printing Inc	G	734 422-5555
Livonia (G-9733)		
Fedex Office & Print Svcs Inc	E	734 996-0050
Ann Arbor (G-460)		
Fedex Office & Print Svcs Inc	F	313 359-3124
Dearborn (G-3705)		
Fedex Office & Print Svcs Inc	F	248 932-3373
Farmington Hills (G-4998)		
Fedex Office & Print Svcs Inc	E	248 355-5670
Southfield (G-14915)		
Fedex Office & Print Svcs Inc	F	248 680-0280
Troy (G-16361)		
Fedex Office & Print Svcs Inc	F	734 374-0225
Taylor (G-15722)		
Field Crafts Inc	E	231 325-1122
Honor (G-7952)		
Flint Group US LLC	D	269 279-5161
Three Rivers (G-15862)		
Frye Printing Company Inc	F	517 456-4124
Clinton (G-3021)		
Gemini Sales Org LLC	G	248 765-1118
Sterling Heights (G-15355)		
Genesee County Herald Inc	F	810 686-3840
Clio (G-3272)		
Grand Traverse Continuous Inc	E	231 941-5400
Traverse City (G-15983)		
Graphic Enterprises Inc	D	248 616-4900
Madison Heights (G-10258)		
Graphic Impressions Inc	G	616 455-0303
Grand Rapids (G-6474)		
Graphics & Printing LLC	G	313 942-2022
Dearborn Heights (G-3786)		
Graphix 2 Go Inc	G	269 969-7321
Battle Creek (G-1196)		
Greystone Imaging LLC	G	616 742-3810
Grand Rapids (G-6482)		
Group 7500 Inc	F	313 875-9026
Detroit (G-4107)		
Hamblin Company	E	517 423-7491
Tecumseh (G-15796)		
Herald Newspapers Company Inc	E	989 895-8551
Flint (G-5447)		
Hodges & Irvine Inc	F	810 329-4787
Saint Clair (G-14222)		
Husky Envelope Products Inc	D	248 624-7070
Walled Lake (G-16895)		
IAC Creative LLC	F	248 455-7000
Southfield (G-14940)		
Imperial Clinical RES Svcs Inc	C	616 784-0100
Grand Rapids (G-6528)		
Industrial Imprntng & Die Ctng	G	586 778-9470
Eastpointe (G-4704)		
International Master Pdts Corp	C	231 894-5651
Montague (G-11091)		
Irwin Enterprises Inc	E	810 732-0770
Flint (G-5449)		
J-Ad Graphics Inc	D	800 870-7085
Hastings (G-7416)		
Job Shop Ink Inc	G	517 372-3900
Lansing (G-9300)		
Jomar Inc	F	269 925-2222
Benton Harbor (G-1515)		
Jomark Inc	F	248 478-2600
Farmington Hills (G-5033)		
Just Wing It Inc	G	248 549-9338
Madison Heights (G-10286)		
Kenewell Group	G	810 714-4290
Fenton (G-5222)		
Ktr Printing Inc	F	989 386-9740
Clare (G-2875)		
Lamon Group Inc	E	616 710-3169
Byron Center (G-2196)		
Lawson Printers Inc	E	269 965-0525
Battle Creek (G-1222)		
Lithotech	F	269 471-6027
Berrien Springs (G-1598)		
Lowery Corporation	C	616 554-5200
Grand Rapids (G-6633)		
M & J Graphics Enterprises Inc	E	734 542-8800
Livonia (G-9820)		
Macarthur Corp	E	810 606-1777
Grand Blanc (G-5975)		
Mahoney & Associates Inc	G	517 669-4300
Dewitt (G-4464)		
Main Street Printing	G	517 851-3816
Stockbridge (G-15591)		
Maleports Sault Prtg Co Inc	E	906 632-3369
Sault Sainte Marie (G-14468)		
McKay Press Inc	C	989 631-2360
Midland (G-10883)		
Meta4mat LLC	G	616 214-7418
Comstock Park (G-3500)		
Michael Niederpruem	G	231 935-0241
Kalkaska (G-8951)		
Microforms Inc	D	586 939-7900
Beverly Hills (G-1620)		
Mid-State Printing Inc	F	989 875-4163
Ithaca (G-8364)		
Mogul Minds LLC	G	682 217-9506
Wayne (G-17438)		
Monroe Publishing Company	D	734 242-1100
Monroe (G-11057)		
Moonlight Graphics Inc	G	616 243-3166
Grand Rapids (G-6704)		
Moormann Printing Inc	G	269 423-2411
Decatur (G-3805)		
MPS Hrl LLC	F	800 748-0517
Lansing (G-9247)		
MPS Lansing Inc	A	517 323-9000
Lansing (G-9248)		
Multi Packaging Solutions Inc	E	616 355-6024
Holland (G-7751)		
Munideals LLC	G	248 945-0991
Madison Heights (G-10313)		
Nalcor LLC	D	248 541-1140
Ferndale (G-5303)		
New Echelon Direct Mktg LLC	G	248 809-2485
Brighton (G-1967)		
Nje Enterprises LLC	G	313 963-3600
Detroit (G-4273)		
Nu-Tech North Inc	G	231 347-1992
Petoskey (G-12466)		
Ogemaw County Herald Inc	E	989 345-0044
West Branch (G-17514)		
Pds Plastics Inc	F	616 896-1109
Dorr (G-4525)		
Peg-Master Business Forms Inc	G	586 566-8694
Shelby Township (G-14662)		
Pilgrim Printing	G	586 752-9664
Washington (G-17309)		
Pioneer Press	E	231 723-3592
Manistee (G-10436)		
Premiums Plus More	G	734 485-2423
Ypsilanti (G-18095)		
Presscraft Papers Inc	E	231 882-5505
Benzonia (G-1576)		
Prest Sales Co	G	586 566-6900
Sterling Heights (G-15451)		
Print Tech Printing Place Inc	G	989 772-6109
Mount Pleasant (G-11221)		
Printcomm Inc	D	810 239-5763
Flint (G-5484)		
Printery Inc	E	616 396-4655
Holland (G-7777)		
Printing Consolidation Co LLC	G	616 233-3161
Grand Rapids (G-6776)		
Printlink Short Run	F	269 965-1336
Battle Creek (G-1237)		

Employee Codes: A=Over 500 employees, B=251-500
C=101-250, D=51-100, E=20-50, F=10-19, G=3-9

2020 Harris Michigan Industrial Directory

PRINTING: Commercial, NEC

Printwell Acquisition Co Inc ....D.... 734 941-6300
  Taylor *(G-15758)*
Printxpress Inc ....G.... 313 846-1644
  Dearborn *(G-3751)*
Pro Connections LLC ....G.... 269 962-4219
  Springfield *(G-15201)*
Qrp Inc ....E.... 989 496-2955
  Midland *(G-10906)*
R & R Harwood Inc ....G.... 616 669-6400
  Jenison *(G-8640)*
Regents of The University Mich ....E.... 734 764-6230
  Ann Arbor *(G-615)*
Religious Communications LLC..........G.... 313 822-3361
  Detroit *(G-4340)*
Riegle Press Inc ....E.... 810 653-9631
  Davison *(G-3661)*
River Run Press Inc ....E.... 269 349-7603
  Kalamazoo *(G-8873)*
Riverhill Publications & Prtg...............F.... 586 468-6011
  Ira *(G-8268)*
Rodriguez Printing Services ....G.... 248 651-7774
  Farmington Hills *(G-5116)*
Rogers Printing Inc ....C.... 231 853-2244
  Ravenna *(G-13128)*
RPC Company ....F.... 989 752-3618
  Saginaw *(G-14134)*
Rusas Printing Co Inc ....G.... 313 952-2977
  Redford *(G-13190)*
Safran Printing Company Inc..............E.... 586 939-7600
  Beverly Hills *(G-1621)*
Shannons Innovative Creat LLC.........G.... 313 282-2724
  Harper Woods *(G-7305)*
Slick Shirts Screen Printing...............F.... 517 371-3600
  Lansing *(G-9424)*
Source One Digital LLC ....E.... 231 799-4040
  Norton Shores *(G-11797)*
Spartan Forms Inc ....G.... 313 278-6960
  Dearborn Heights *(G-3797)*
Statewide Printing LLC......................G.... 517 485-4466
  Lansing *(G-9268)*
T J K Inc ....G.... 586 731-9639
  Sterling Heights *(G-15518)*
Techno Urban 3d LLC ....F.... 313 740-8110
  Detroit *(G-4398)*
Tectonics Industries LLC ....G.... 248 597-1600
  Auburn Hills *(G-1015)*
TGI Direct Inc ....F.... 810 239-5553
  Ann Arbor *(G-667)*
Thomas Kenyon Inc ....G.... 248 476-8130
  Saint Clair Shores *(G-14272)*
Thorpe Printing Services Inc ....G.... 810 364-6222
  Marysville *(G-10622)*
Timbertech Inc ....E.... 231 348-2750
  Harbor Springs *(G-7295)*
Travel Information Services ....F.... 989 275-8042
  Roscommon *(G-13755)*
Tribar Manufacturing LLC ....E.... 248 669-0077
  Wixom *(G-17916)*
Troy Haygood ....G.... 313 478-3308
  Ferndale *(G-5322)*
Turner Business Forms Inc ....E.... 989 752-5540
  Saginaw *(G-14171)*
Tuscola County Advertiser Inc ....B.... 517 673-3181
  Caro *(G-2480)*
Tweddle Group Inc ....C.... 586 307-3700
  Clinton Township *(G-3252)*
Ultra-Tech Printing Co ....F.... 616 249-0500
  Wyoming *(G-18038)*
V&R Enterprize ....G.... 313 837-5545
  Detroit *(G-4420)*
Val Valley Inc ....G.... 248 474-7335
  Farmington Hills *(G-5145)*
Valassis International Inc ....B.... 734 591-3000
  Livonia *(G-9987)*
Van Kehrberg Vern.............................G.... 810 364-1066
  Marysville *(G-10625)*
Weighman Enterprises Inc ....G.... 989 755-2116
  Saginaw *(G-14181)*
Whitlock Distribution Svcs LLC.........D.... 248 548-1040
  Madison Heights *(G-10382)*
Your Home Town USA Inc ....E.... 517 529-9421
  Clarklake *(G-2902)*
Zeeland Record Co ....G.... 616 772-2131
  Zeeland *(G-18203)*

PRINTING: Flexographic

Anchor Printing Company ....E.... 248 335-7440
  Novi *(G-11827)*
Converting Systems Inc ....G.... 616 698-1882
  Nunica *(G-12034)*
Cummins Label Company..................E.... 269 345-3386
  Kalamazoo *(G-8721)*
Flint Group US LLC ....A.... 734 781-4600
  Livonia *(G-9741)*
Fortis Sltions Group Centl LLC ....D.... 248 437-5200
  Wixom *(G-17812)*
Grand Rapids Label Company............D.... 616 459-8134
  Grand Rapids *(G-6455)*
Middleton Printing Inc ....G.... 616 247-8742
  Grand Rapids *(G-6684)*
Whitlam Group Inc ....C.... 586 757-5100
  Center Line *(G-2586)*

PRINTING: Gravure, Forms, Business

Aip Group Inc ....G.... 248 828-4400
  Troy *(G-16173)*
Taylor Communications Inc ....F.... 248 304-4800
  Southfield *(G-15043)*

PRINTING: Gravure, Job

Exone Americas LLC ....G.... 248 740-1580
  Troy *(G-16356)*
Hodges & Irvine Inc ....F.... 810 329-4787
  Saint Clair *(G-14222)*

PRINTING: Gravure, Labels

Advantage Label and Packg Inc ....E.... 616 656-1900
  Grand Rapids *(G-6150)*
Eagile Incorporated ....F.... 616 243-1200
  Grand Rapids *(G-6364)*
Norman Industries Inc ....G.... 248 669-6213
  Wixom *(G-17867)*
Rainbow Tape & Label Inc ....E.... 734 941-6090
  Romulus *(G-13726)*

PRINTING: Gravure, Rotogravure

Capital Imaging Inc ....F.... 517 482-2292
  Lansing *(G-9355)*
High Impact Solutions Inc ....G.... 248 473-9804
  Farmington Hills *(G-5019)*
Safran Printing Company Inc.............E.... 586 939-7600
  Beverly Hills *(G-1621)*

PRINTING: Gravure, Stationery & Invitation

Occasions...G.... 517 694-6437
  Holt *(G-7918)*

PRINTING: Gravure, Wrapper & Seal

Rainbow Wrap ....F.... 586 949-3976
  Chesterfield *(G-2830)*

PRINTING: Laser

Ancor Information MGT LLC ....D.... 248 740-8866
  Troy *(G-16201)*
Artistic Printing Inc...........................G.... 248 356-1004
  Southfield *(G-14840)*
Lasertec Inc ....E.... 586 274-4500
  Madison Heights *(G-10298)*
Materialise Usa LLC..........................C.... 734 259-6445
  Plymouth *(G-12686)*
Sage Direct Inc ....F.... 616 940-8311
  Grand Rapids *(G-6850)*
Source One Dist Svcs Inc ....F.... 248 399-5060
  Madison Heights *(G-10355)*

PRINTING: Letterpress

A B C Printing Inc ....G.... 248 887-0010
  Highland *(G-7483)*
Bastian Brothers & Company ....E.... 989 239-5107
  Freeland *(G-5752)*
Bayside Printing Inc ....G.... 231 352-4440
  Frankfort *(G-5598)*
Berci Printing Services Inc ....G.... 248 350-0206
  Southfield *(G-14852)*
City Printing Co of Ypsilanti..............G.... 734 482-8490
  Ypsilanti *(G-18060)*
Clemco Printing Inc ....G.... 989 269-8364
  Bad Axe *(G-1059)*
De Vru Printing Co ....G.... 616 452-5451
  Grand Rapids *(G-6339)*
Dekoff & Sons Inc ....G.... 269 344-5816
  Kalamazoo *(G-8724)*
E & S Graphics Inc............................G.... 989 875-2828
  Ithaca *(G-8359)*
Fletcher Printing ....G.... 517 625-7030
  Morrice *(G-11119)*
Gary Printing Company Inc................G.... 313 383-3222
  Lincoln Park *(G-9578)*
Grand Rapids Letter Service..............G.... 616 459-4711
  Grand Rapids *(G-6457)*
Hadd Enterprises ....G.... 586 773-4260
  Eastpointe *(G-4702)*
Handy Bindery Co Inc........................E.... 586 469-2240
  Clinton Township *(G-3133)*
Houghton Lake Resorter Inc..............E.... 989 366-5341
  Houghton Lake *(G-7993)*
Johnson-Clark Printers Inc ....F.... 231 947-6898
  Traverse City *(G-16014)*
Lamour Printing Co ....G.... 734 241-6006
  Monroe *(G-11050)*
Lesnau Printing Company ....F.... 586 795-9200
  Sterling Heights *(G-15396)*
Micrgraphics Printing Inc ....E.... 231 739-6575
  Norton Shores *(G-11773)*
Pellow Printing Co ....G.... 906 475-9431
  Negaunee *(G-11473)*
Pioneer Press Printing ....G.... 231 864-2404
  Bear Lake *(G-1380)*
Pointe Printing Inc ....G.... 313 821-0030
  Grosse Pointe Park *(G-7195)*
Raenell Press LLC ....G.... 616 534-8890
  Grand Rapids *(G-6806)*
Ray Printing Company Inc ....F.... 517 787-4130
  Jackson *(G-8561)*
Romeo Printing Company Inc............G.... 586 752-9003
  Romeo *(G-13637)*
Signal-Return Inc ....G.... 313 567-8970
  Detroit *(G-4362)*
Standard Printing...............................G.... 734 483-0339
  Ypsilanti *(G-18102)*
Standard Printing of Warren ....G.... 586 771-3770
  Warren *(G-17253)*
Straits Area Printing Corp ....G.... 231 627-5647
  Cheboygan *(G-2696)*
Unique Reproductions Inc ....G.... 248 788-2887
  West Bloomfield *(G-17504)*
Waterman and Sons Prtg Co Inc ....G.... 313 864-5562
  Detroit *(G-4436)*
Whipple Printing Inc ....G.... 313 382-8033
  Allen Park *(G-213)*
Wholesale Ticket Co Inc ....F.... 616 642-9476
  Saranac *(G-14457)*
Zak Brothers Printing LLC ....G.... 313 831-3216
  Detroit *(G-4456)*

PRINTING: Lithographic

A Koppel Color Image Company ....G.... 616 534-3600
  Grandville *(G-7015)*
Aalpha Tinadawn Inc ....G.... 517 351-1200
  East Lansing *(G-4649)*
Adair Printing Company ....E.... 734 426-2822
  Dexter *(G-4472)*
Advance Graphic Systems Inc ....E.... 248 656-8000
  Rochester Hills *(G-13365)*
Ahearn Signs and Printing.................G.... 734 699-3777
  Belleville *(G-1440)*
Aldinger Inc ....E.... 517 394-2424
  Lansing *(G-9334)*
Alpha Data Business Forms Inc.........G.... 248 540-5930
  Birmingham *(G-1674)*
America Ink Print ....G.... 586 790-2555
  Clinton Township *(G-3045)*
Americas Finest Prtg Graphics ....G.... 586 296-1312
  Fraser *(G-5618)*
AP Impressions Inc............................G.... 734 464-8009
  Livonia *(G-9650)*
Apms Incorporated ....G.... 248 268-1477
  Madison Heights *(G-10193)*
Argus Press Company ....D.... 989 725-5136
  Owosso *(G-12280)*
Associated Print & Graphics ....G.... 734 676-8896
  Grosse Ile *(G-7167)*
August Communications Inc ....G.... 313 561-8000
  Dearborn Heights *(G-3780)*
Automotive Media LLC......................C.... 248 537-8500
  Pontiac *(G-12806)*
Bayside Printing Inc ....G.... 231 352-4440
  Frankfort *(G-5598)*
Bizcard Xpress ....G.... 248 288-4800
  Rochester *(G-13315)*
Bowman Printing Inc ....G.... 810 982-8202
  Port Huron *(G-12904)*
Brophy Engraving Co Inc ....E.... 313 871-2333
  Detroit *(G-3919)*
Bruce Inc...G.... 517 371-5205
  Lansing *(G-9352)*

C S L Inc....G....248 549-4434
Royal Oak (G-13912)
Capital City Blue Print Inc....G....517 482-5431
Lansing (G-9207)
Carrigan Graphics Inc....G....734 455-6550
Canton (G-2357)
Celani Printing Co....G....810 395-1609
Capac (G-2447)
Child Evngelism Fellowship Inc....E....269 461-6953
Berrien Center (G-1590)
Colorhub LLC....F....616 333-4411
Grand Rapids (G-6290)
Copies & More Inc....G....231 865-6370
Fruitport (G-5791)
Corporate Electronic Sty Inc....D....248 583-7070
Troy (G-16283)
Cushing-Malloy Inc....E....734 663-8554
Ann Arbor (G-409)
Custom Embroidery Plus LLC....G....517 316-9902
Lansing (G-9211)
Daily Oakland Press....B....248 332-8181
Pontiac (G-12813)
Daily Reporter....E....517 278-2318
Coldwater (G-3300)
David H Bosley & Associates....G....734 261-8390
Livonia (G-9698)
Derk Pieter Co Inc....G....616 554-7777
Grand Rapids (G-6343)
Detroit Litho Inc....G....313 993-6186
Detroit (G-3988)
Detroit News Inc....G....313 222-6400
Sterling Heights (G-15313)
Digital Printing Solutions LLC....G....586 566-4910
Shelby Township (G-14578)
Dla Document Services....G....269 961-4895
Battle Creek (G-1175)
E and J Advertising LLC....G....586 977-3500
Warren (G-17013)
Elston Enterprises Inc....F....313 561-8000
Dearborn Heights (G-3784)
Epi Printers Inc....E....269 964-4600
Battle Creek (G-1182)
Extreme Screen Prints....G....616 889-8305
Grand Rapids (G-6394)
Faubles Prtg & Specialities....G....231 775-4973
Cadillac (G-2246)
Fedex Office & Print Svcs Inc....F....734 522-7322
Westland (G-17555)
Fedex Office & Print Svcs Inc....F....734 374-0225
Taylor (G-15722)
Flashes Shoppers Guide & News....G....517 663-2361
Charlotte (G-2649)
Foltz Screen Printing....G....989 772-3947
Mount Pleasant (G-11193)
Forsons Inc....G....517 787-4562
Jackson (G-8450)
Franklin Press Inc....F....616 538-5320
Grand Rapids (G-6418)
Gannett Co Inc....C....269 964-7161
Battle Creek (G-1191)
Gannett Co Inc....D....517 377-1000
Lansing (G-9371)
Genesee County Herald Inc....F....810 686-3840
Clio (G-3272)
Genesis Service Associates LLC....G....734 994-3900
Dexter (G-4493)
Global Digital Printing....G....734 244-5010
Monroe (G-11036)
Grand Haven Publishing Corp....E....616 842-6400
Grand Haven (G-6024)
Grand Traverse Continuous Inc....E....231 941-5400
Traverse City (G-15983)
Graphic Impressions Inc....G....616 455-0303
Grand Rapids (G-6474)
Graphics Unlimited Inc....G....231 773-2696
Muskegon (G-11336)
Great Lakes Prtg Solutions Inc....F....231 799-6000
Norton Shores (G-11758)
Herald Bi-County Inc....G....517 448-2201
Hudson (G-8129)
Herald Publishing Company....E....517 423-2174
Tecumseh (G-15797)
Hodges & Irvine Inc....F....810 329-4787
Saint Clair (G-14222)
Homestead Graphics Design Inc....G....906 353-6741
Baraga (G-1103)
Horn Corporation....E....248 583-7789
Troy (G-16402)
Huron Publishing Company Inc....D....989 269-6461
Bad Axe (G-1067)
Industrial Imprntng & Die Ctng....G....586 778-9470
Eastpointe (G-4704)
Instant Framer....G....231 947-8908
Traverse City (G-16005)
Insty-Prints West Inc....G....517 321-7091
Lansing (G-9299)
International Master Pdts Corp....G....800 253-0439
Montague (G-11092)
Iris Design & Print Inc....G....313 277-0505
Dearborn (G-3727)
J-Ad Graphics Inc....E....269 965-3955
Battle Creek (G-1202)
Janet Kelly....F....231 775-2313
Cadillac (G-2256)
JMS Printing Svc LLC....G....734 414-6203
Warren (G-17115)
Job Shop Ink Inc....G....517 372-3900
Lansing (G-9300)
Johnnie On Spot Inc....G....248 673-2233
Waterford (G-17352)
Kent Communications Inc....D....616 957-2120
Grand Rapids (G-6575)
Lake Michigan Mailers Inc....D....269 383-9333
Kalamazoo (G-8804)
Larsen Graphics Inc....E....989 823-3000
Vassar (G-16812)
Leader Publications LLC....D....269 683-2100
Niles (G-11623)
Logospot....G....616 785-7170
Belmont (G-1467)
Malloy Incorporated....A....734 665-6113
Ann Arbor (G-542)
Marketing Vl Group Inc....G....989 793-3933
Saginaw (G-14081)
Maslin Corporation....G....586 777-7500
Harper Woods (G-7302)
Mendoza Enterprises....G....248 792-9120
Bloomfield Hills (G-1782)
Menominee Cnty Jurnl Print Sp....F....906 753-2296
Stephenson (G-15237)
Metro Prints Inc....F....586 979-9690
Sterling Heights (G-15417)
Mid-Michigan Screen Printing....G....989 624-9827
Birch Run (G-1666)
Midland Publishing Company....C....989 835-7171
Midland (G-10891)
Minden City Herald....G....989 864-3630
Minden City (G-11000)
Mj Creative Printing LLC....G....248 891-1117
Livonia (G-9846)
Modern Printing Services Inc....G....586 792-9700
Ira (G-8262)
Moormann Printing Inc....G....269 646-2101
Marcellus (G-10466)
Moormann Printing Inc....G....269 423-2411
Decatur (G-3805)
Morris Communications Co LLC....D....616 546-4200
Holland (G-7748)
Morris Communications Corp....C....269 673-2141
Allegan (G-177)
Neetz Printing Inc....G....989 684-4620
Bay City (G-1336)
North American Color Inc....E....269 323-0552
Portage (G-13019)
North American Graphics Inc....E....586 486-1110
Warren (G-17173)
Northwest Graphic Services....G....248 349-9480
Rochester Hills (G-13485)
Nutting Newspapers Inc....E....906 482-1500
Houghton (G-7979)
Ogemaw County Herald Inc....E....989 345-0044
West Branch (G-17514)
On The Side Sign Dsign Grphics....G....810 266-7446
Byron (G-2174)
Page Litho Inc....E....313 885-8555
Grosse Pointe (G-7181)
Performance Print and Mktg....G....517 896-9682
Williamston (G-17736)
Personal Graphics....G....231 347-6347
Petoskey (G-12468)
Pgi Holdings Inc....E....231 796-4831
Big Rapids (G-1640)
Pickle Print & Marketing LLC....G....231 668-4148
Traverse City (G-16069)
Pippa Custom Design Printing....G....734 552-1598
Woodhaven (G-17941)
Prestige Printing Inc....G....616 532-5133
Grand Rapids (G-6771)
Print All....G....586 430-4383
Richmond (G-13268)
Printer Ink Warehousecom LLC....G....269 649-5492
Vicksburg (G-16841)
Printing Buying Service....G....586 907-2011
Saint Clair Shores (G-14269)
Printing By Marc....G....248 355-0848
Southfield (G-15005)
Printing Systems Inc....G....734 946-5111
Taylor (G-15757)
Printwand Inc....G....248 738-7225
Pontiac (G-12859)
Prism Printing....G....586 786-1250
Macomb (G-10157)
Professional Instant Printing....G....248 335-1117
Waterford (G-17372)
Proforma Pltnum Prtg Prmotions....G....248 341-3814
Clawson (G-2985)
Psp Office Solutions LLC....F....517 817-0680
Jackson (G-8558)
Quad/Graphics Inc....G....248 637-9950
Troy (G-16572)
R & L Color Graphics Inc....G....313 345-3838
Detroit (G-4324)
R & R Harwood Inc....G....616 669-6400
Jenison (G-8640)
Real Love Printwear....G....248 327-7181
Southfield (G-15011)
Regents of The University Mich....E....734 764-6230
Ann Arbor (G-615)
Rider Type & Design....G....989 839-0015
Midland (G-10908)
Rite Way Printing....G....734 721-2746
Romulus (G-13729)
Safran Printing Company Inc....E....586 939-7600
Beverly Hills (G-1621)
Spinnaker Forms Systems Corp....G....616 956-7677
Grand Rapids (G-6886)
Sports Ink Screen Prtg EMB LLC....G....231 723-5696
Manistee (G-10437)
Stafford Media Inc....E....616 754-9301
Greenville (G-7154)
Sullivan Reproductions Inc....E....313 965-3666
Detroit (G-4383)
Superior Graphics Studios Ltd....G....906 482-7891
Houghton (G-7985)
Swift Printing Co....F....616 459-4263
Grand Rapids (G-6908)
T J K Inc....G....586 731-9639
Sterling Heights (G-15518)
Tatum Bindery Company....G....616 458-8991
Grand Rapids (G-6915)
Technology MGT & Budgt Dept....D....517 322-1897
Lansing (G-9430)
Tee To Green Print & Promo Pro....G....517 322-3088
Lansing (G-9325)
TGI Direct Inc....F....810 239-5553
Ann Arbor (G-667)
The Envelope Printery Inc....D....734 398-7700
Van Buren Twp (G-16787)
Thomas Kenyon Inc....G....248 476-8130
Saint Clair Shores (G-14272)
Times Herald Company....F....810 985-7171
Port Huron (G-12971)
TLC Printing....G....248 620-3228
Clarkston (G-2961)
Traverse Cy Record- Eagle Inc....G....231 946-2000
Traverse City (G-16129)
Tweddle Group Inc....C....586 307-3700
Clinton Township (G-3252)
Ultra Printing....G....248 352-7238
Southfield (G-15053)
Universal Print....G....989 525-5055
Bay City (G-1367)
Universal Printing Company Inc....F....989 671-9409
Bay City (G-1368)
Valassis International Inc....B....734 591-3000
Livonia (G-9987)
Voila Print Inc....G....866 942-1677
Livonia (G-9991)
W B Mason Co Inc....D....734 947-6370
Taylor (G-15780)
Yale Expositor....G....810 387-2300
Yale (G-18048)

PRINTING: Offset

A 1 Printing and Copy Center....G....269 381-0093
Kalamazoo (G-8671)
A B C Printing Inc....G....248 887-0010
Highland (G-7483)
Acadia Group LLC....E....734 944-1404
Saline (G-14371)

PRODUCT

Accelerated Press Inc....G....248 524-1850
Troy (G-16165)
Action Printech Inc....E....734 207-6000
Plymouth (G-12561)
Admore Inc....D....586 949-8200
Macomb (G-10102)
Advance BCI Inc....D....616 669-5210
Grand Rapids (G-6145)
Advance BCI Inc....D....616 669-1366
Grand Rapids (G-6144)
Advance Print & Graphics Inc....E....734 663-6816
Ann Arbor (G-345)
Aladdin Printing....G....248 360-2842
Commerce Township (G-3386)
Alco Printing Services Inc....G....248 280-1124
Royal Oak (G-13899)
Alcock Printing Inc....G....586 731-4366
Shelby Township (G-14544)
Allagra Print and Imaging....G....586 263-0060
Clinton Township (G-3041)
Allegra Network LLC....F....248 360-1290
West Bloomfield (G-17464)
Allegra Print & Imaging....G....248 354-1313
Southfield (G-14827)
Allegra Print and Imaging....G....616 784-6699
Grand Rapids (G-6160)
Allesk Enterprises Inc....G....231 941-5770
Traverse City (G-15894)
Alliance Franchise Brands LLC....E....248 596-8600
Plymouth (G-12568)
Allied Mailing and Prtg Inc....E....810 750-8291
Fenton (G-5181)
Allied Printing Co Inc....E....248 541-0551
Ferndale (G-5259)
Allied Printing Co Inc....E....248 514-7394
Ferndale (G-5260)
Ameri-Print Inc....E....734 427-2887
Livonia (G-9642)
American Graphics Inc....G....586 774-8880
Saint Clair Shores (G-14240)
American Ink USA Prntg & Grphc....G....586 790-2555
Clinton Township (G-3047)
American Speedy Printing Ctrs....G....989 723-5196
Owosso (G-12279)
American Speedy Printing Ctrs....G....313 928-5820
Taylor (G-15686)
An Corporate Center LLC....E....248 669-1188
Plymouth (G-12571)
Anchor Printing Company....E....248 335-7440
Novi (G-11827)
Andex Industries Inc....E....906 786-7588
Escanaba (G-4812)
Apb Inc....G....248 528-2990
Troy (G-16204)
Arbor Press LLC....D....248 549-0150
Royal Oak (G-13904)
Arrow Printing LLC....G....248 738-2222
Waterford (G-17323)
Artcraft Printing Corporation....G....734 455-8893
Plymouth (G-12574)
Artech Printing Inc....G....248 545-0088
Madison Heights (G-10196)
Artigy Printing....G....269 373-6591
Kalamazoo (G-8684)
Artistic Printing Inc....G....248 356-1004
Southfield (G-14840)
ASAP Printing Inc....G....517 882-3500
Lansing (G-9341)
ASAP Printing Inc....E....517 882-3500
Okemos (G-12114)
Avery Color Studios Inc....G....906 346-3908
Gwinn (G-7216)
B & M Imaging Inc....G....269 968-2403
Battle Creek (G-1148)
B-Quick Instant Printing....G....616 243-6562
Grand Rapids (G-6199)
Bagnall Enterprises Inc....G....734 457-0500
Monroe (G-11017)
Batson Printing Inc....D....269 926-6011
Benton Harbor (G-1484)
BCI Group Inc....E....248 925-2000
Troy (G-16234)
Behrmann Printing Company Inc....F....248 799-7771
Southfield (G-14851)
Benjamin Press....G....269 964-7562
Battle Creek (G-1153)
Berci Printing Services Inc....G....248 350-0206
Southfield (G-14852)
Blue Water Printing Co Inc....G....810 664-0643
Lapeer (G-9443)
Book Concern Printers....G....906 482-1250
Hancock (G-7248)
Brd Printing Inc....E....517 372-0268
Lansing (G-9350)
Breck Graphics Incorporated....E....616 248-4110
Grand Rapids (G-6235)
Bretts Printing Service....G....517 482-2256
Lansing (G-9351)
Bronco Printing Company....G....248 544-1120
Hazel Park (G-7435)
Business Cards Plus Inc....D....269 327-7727
Portage (G-12988)
Business Helper LLC....G....231 271-4404
Suttons Bay (G-15651)
Business Press Inc....G....248 652-8855
Rochester (G-13316)
C H M Graphics & Litho Inc....G....586 777-4550
Saint Clair Shores (G-14241)
C J Graphics Inc....G....906 774-8636
Kingsford (G-9055)
C W Enterprises Inc....G....810 385-9100
Fort Gratiot (G-5547)
Cadillac Printing Company....F....231 775-2488
Cadillac (G-2239)
Capital Imaging Inc....F....517 482-2292
Lansing (G-9355)
Cascade Printing and Graphics....G....616 222-2937
Grand Rapids (G-6264)
Central Michigan Rapid Print....G....989 772-3110
Mount Pleasant (G-11185)
Chiodini & Sons Printing....G....248 548-0064
Hazel Park (G-7436)
Christman Screenprint Inc....F....800 962-9330
Springfield (G-15189)
City Printing Co of Ypsilanti....G....734 482-8490
Ypsilanti (G-18060)
Clark Graphic Service Inc....D....586 772-4900
Warren (G-16981)
Clemco Printing Inc....G....989 269-8364
Bad Axe (G-1059)
Color Connection....G....248 351-0920
Southfield (G-14870)
Color House Graphics Inc....E....616 241-1916
Grand Rapids (G-6289)
Color Source Graphics Inc....G....248 458-2040
Troy (G-16272)
Colortech Graphics Inc....D....586 779-7800
Roseville (G-13783)
Commercial Graphics Company....G....517 278-2159
Coldwater (G-3299)
Commercial Graphics Inc....G....586 726-8150
Sterling Heights (G-15292)
Commercial Graphics of Mich....G....810 744-2102
Burton (G-2150)
Complete Home Adv Media/Promo....G....586 254-9555
Shelby Township (G-14565)
Copies Plus Printing Co LLC....G....616 696-1288
Cedar Springs (G-2549)
Copilot Printing....G....248 398-5301
Madison Heights (G-10220)
Copper Island Prtg Grphic Svcs....G....906 337-1300
Calumet (G-2326)
Copyrite Printing Inc....G....586 774-0006
Roseville (G-13787)
Country Printing....G....734 782-4044
Flat Rock (G-5351)
CPM Services Group Inc....G....248 624-5100
Wixom (G-17791)
Craft Press Printing Inc....G....269 683-9694
Niles (G-11602)
Creative Characters Inc....G....231 544-6084
Central Lake (G-2589)
Creative Print Crew LLC....G....248 629-9404
Troy (G-16286)
Creative Printing & Graphics....G....810 235-8815
Flint (G-5407)
Crop Marks Printing....G....616 356-5555
Grand Rapids (G-6317)
Curtis Printing Inc....G....810 230-6711
Flint (G-5410)
Custom Printers Inc....D....616 454-9224
Grand Rapids (G-6326)
Custom Printing of Michigan....F....248 585-9222
Troy (G-16290)
Custom Service Printers Inc....F....231 726-3297
Muskegon (G-11303)
D & D Printing Co....E....616 454-7710
Grand Rapids (G-6330)
D J Rotunda Associates Inc....G....586 772-3350
West Bloomfield (G-17472)
Data Reproductions Corporation....D....248 371-3700
Auburn Hills (G-837)
De Vru Printing Co....G....616 452-5451
Grand Rapids (G-6339)
Dearborn Lithograph Inc....E....734 464-4242
Livonia (G-9701)
Dearborn Offset Printing Inc....G....313 561-1173
Dearborn (G-3690)
Decka Digital LLC....G....231 347-1253
Harbor Springs (G-7281)
Dekoff & Sons Inc....G....269 344-5816
Kalamazoo (G-8724)
Depex Print Services....G....586 465-6820
Clinton Township (G-3100)
Designotype Printers Inc....G....906 482-2424
Laurium (G-9503)
DGa Printing Inc....G....586 979-2244
Troy (G-16315)
Digital Printing & Graphics....G....586 566-9499
Shelby Township (G-14577)
Dobb Printing Inc....E....231 722-1060
Muskegon (G-11306)
Donalyn Enterprises Inc....F....517 546-9798
Howell (G-8032)
DPrinter Inc....G....517 423-6554
Tecumseh (G-15791)
E & S Graphics Inc....G....989 875-2828
Ithaca (G-8359)
Earle Press Inc....E....231 773-2111
Muskegon (G-11312)
Econo Print Inc....G....734 878-5806
Pinckney (G-12496)
Egt Printing Solutions LLC....C....248 583-2500
Madison Heights (G-10241)
Empire Printing....G....248 547-9223
Royal Oak (G-13924)
Encore Impression LLC....G....248 478-1221
Farmington Hills (G-4987)
Epi Printers Inc....E....800 562-9733
Battle Creek (G-1179)
Epi Printers Inc....C....269 968-2221
Battle Creek (G-1180)
Epi Printers Inc....D....269 968-2221
Battle Creek (G-1181)
Epi Printers Inc....D....269 964-6744
Battle Creek (G-1183)
Excel Graphics....G....248 442-9390
Livonia (G-9731)
Exclusive Imagery Inc....G....248 436-2999
Royal Oak (G-13927)
F P Horak Company....C....989 892-6505
Bay City (G-1312)
Falcon Printing Inc....E....616 676-3737
Ada (G-15)
Fenton Printing Inc....G....810 750-9450
Fenton (G-5211)
Flashes Publishers Inc....C....269 673-2141
Allegan (G-162)
Fletcher Printing....G....517 625-7030
Morrice (G-11119)
Frye Printing Company Inc....F....517 456-4124
Clinton (G-3021)
Future Reproductions Inc....F....248 350-2060
Southfield (G-14916)
G G & D Inc....G....248 623-1212
Clarkston (G-2924)
Gage Company....F....269 965-4279
Springfield (G-15191)
Garants Office Sups & Prtg Inc....G....989 356-3930
Alpena (G-291)
Gary Cork Incorporated....G....231 946-1061
Traverse City (G-15976)
Gary Printing Company Inc....G....313 383-3222
Lincoln Park (G-9578)
Generation Press Inc....G....616 392-4405
Holland (G-7642)
Globe Printing & Specialties....F....906 485-1033
Ishpeming (G-8345)
Goetz Craft Printers Inc....F....734 973-7604
Brooklyn (G-2037)
Gombar Corp....G....989 793-9427
Saginaw (G-14048)
Grahams Printing Company Inc....G....313 925-1188
Detroit (G-4098)
Grand Blanc Printing Inc....E....810 694-1155
Grand Blanc (G-5968)
Grand Rapids Letter Service....G....616 459-4711
Grand Rapids (G-6457)
Grandville Printing Co....C....616 534-8647
Grandville (G-7040)

Graphic Enterprises Inc D 248 616-4900
Madison Heights *(G-10258)*
Graphics & Printing Co Inc G 269 381-1482
Kalamazoo *(G-8756)*
Graphics 3 Inc F 517 278-2159
Coldwater *(G-3306)*
Graphics East Inc E 586 598-1500
Roseville *(G-13810)*
Graphics House Publishing E 231 739-4004
Muskegon *(G-11333)*
Graphics Plus Inc G 989 893-0651
Bay City *(G-1318)*
Greko Print & Imaging Inc F 734 453-0341
Plymouth *(G-12632)*
Grigg Graphic Services Inc F 248 356-5005
Southfield *(G-14932)*
Grondin Printing and Awards G 269 781-5447
Marshall *(G-10570)*
H E L P Printers Inc G 734 847-0554
Temperance *(G-15830)*
Hadd Enterprises G 586 773-4260
Eastpointe *(G-4702)*
Halsan Inc G 734 285-5420
Southgate *(G-15078)*
Hamblin Company E 517 423-7491
Tecumseh *(G-15796)*
Hanon Printing Company G 248 541-9099
Pleasant Ridge *(G-12555)*
Harold K Schultz F 517 279-9764
Coldwater *(G-3308)*
Hatteras Inc E 734 525-5500
Dearborn *(G-3719)*
Hawk Design Inc G 989 781-1152
Saginaw *(G-14055)*
Hess Printing G 734 285-4377
Wyandotte *(G-17960)*
Hi-Lites Graphic Inc E 231 924-0630
Fremont *(G-5775)*
HI-Lites Graphic Inc G 231 924-4540
Fremont *(G-5776)*
Higgins Printing Services LLC G 734 414-6203
Plymouth *(G-12639)*
Holland Litho Service Inc D 616 392-4644
Zeeland *(G-18153)*
Holland Printing Center Inc F 616 786-3101
Holland *(G-7676)*
Houghton Lake Resorter Inc E 989 366-5341
Houghton Lake *(G-7993)*
Image Factory Inc G 989 732-2712
Gaylord *(G-5866)*
Image Printing Inc G 248 585-4080
Royal Oak *(G-13935)*
Imax Printing Co G 248 629-9680
Ferndale *(G-5294)*
Imperial Press Inc G 734 728-5430
Wayne *(G-17432)*
Inco Development Corporation D 517 323-8448
Lansing *(G-9297)*
Irwin Enterprises Inc E 810 732-0770
Flint *(G-5449)*
J & M Reproductions Corp E 248 588-8100
Troy *(G-16429)*
J R C Inc F 810 648-4000
Sandusky *(G-14436)*
J-Ad Graphics Inc D 800 870-7085
Hastings *(G-7416)*
J-Ad Graphics Inc G 517 543-4041
Charlotte *(G-2656)*
Jackpine Press Incorporated F 231 723-8344
Manistee *(G-10425)*
Jackson Printing Company Inc F 517 783-2705
Jackson *(G-8480)*
Janutol Printing Co Inc G 313 526-6196
Detroit *(G-4157)*
Jerrys Quality Quick Print G 248 354-1313
Southfield *(G-14952)*
Jet Speed Printing Company G 989 224-6475
Saint Johns *(G-14285)*
Jiffy Print G 269 692-3128
Otsego *(G-12242)*
Johnson-Clark Printers Inc F 231 947-6898
Traverse City *(G-16014)*
Johnston Printing & Offset G 906 786-1493
Escanaba *(G-4837)*
Jomark Inc F 248 478-2600
Farmington Hills *(G-5033)*
K & S Printing Centers Inc G 734 482-1680
Ann Arbor *(G-514)*
K Printing Public Relations Co G 810 648-4410
Sandusky *(G-14438)*
Kaufman Enterprises Inc G 269 324-0040
Portage *(G-13006)*
Kay Screen Printing Inc C 248 377-4999
Lake Orion *(G-9141)*
Kendall & Company Inc G 810 733-7330
Flint *(G-5454)*
Keystone Printing Inc F 517 627-4078
Grand Ledge *(G-6109)*
Kimprint Inc E 734 459-2960
Plymouth *(G-12668)*
Kmak Inc G 517 784-8800
Jackson *(G-8489)*
Knapp Printing Services Inc G 616 754-9159
Greenville *(G-7143)*
Kolossos Printing Inc F 734 994-5400
Ann Arbor *(G-517)*
Kwikie Inc G 231 946-9942
Traverse City *(G-16019)*
L D J Inc F 906 524-6194
Lanse *(G-9198)*
L&L Printing Inc G 586 263-0060
Clinton Township *(G-3158)*
Lake Superior Press Inc F 906 228-7450
Marquette *(G-10538)*
Lamour Printing Co G 734 241-6006
Monroe *(G-11050)*
Lawson Printers Inc E 269 965-0525
Battle Creek *(G-1222)*
Leader Printing and Design Inc F 313 565-0061
Dearborn Heights *(G-3788)*
Lee Printing Company F 586 463-1564
Clinton Township *(G-3160)*
Lesnau Printing Company F 586 795-9200
Sterling Heights *(G-15396)*
Lightning Litho Inc F 517 394-2995
Lansing *(G-9392)*
Lindy Press Inc G 231 937-6169
Howard City *(G-8003)*
Litho Printers Inc F 269 651-7309
Sturgis *(G-15613)*
Litho Printing Service Inc G 586 772-6067
Eastpointe *(G-4706)*
Litsenberger Print Shop G 906 482-3903
Houghton *(G-7976)*
Lloyd Waters & Associates G 734 525-2777
Livonia *(G-9817)*
Local Printers Inc G 586 795-1290
Sterling Heights *(G-15402)*
Logan Brothers Printing Inc F 517 485-3771
Dewitt *(G-4463)*
Lopez Reproductions Inc G 313 386-4526
Detroit *(G-4209)*
M Beshara Inc G 248 542-9220
Oak Park *(G-12079)*
Macdonald Publications Inc F 989 875-4151
Ithaca *(G-8363)*
Macomb Business Forms Inc F 586 790-8500
Clinton Township *(G-3162)*
Macomb Printing Inc E 586 463-2301
Clinton Township *(G-3163)*
Madden Enterprises Inc G 734 284-5330
Wyandotte *(G-17966)*
Maleports Sault Prtg Co Inc E 906 632-3369
Sault Sainte Marie *(G-14468)*
Mega Printing Inc G 248 624-6065
Walled Lake *(G-16898)*
Megee Printing Inc F 269 344-3226
Kalamazoo *(G-8820)*
Mel Printing Co Inc E 313 928-5440
Taylor *(G-15738)*
Merritt Press Inc F 517 394-0118
Lansing *(G-9396)*
Messenger Printing & Copy Svc G 616 669-5620
Hudsonville *(G-8166)*
Messenger Printing Service E 313 381-0300
Taylor *(G-15739)*
Metro Printing Service Inc G 248 545-4444
Troy *(G-16501)*
Metropolitan Indus Lithography G 269 323-9333
Portage *(G-13016)*
Mettes Printery Inc G 734 261-6262
Livonia *(G-9841)*
Michigan State Medical Society E 517 337-1351
East Lansing *(G-4670)*
Michigan Wholesale Prtg Inc G 248 350-8230
Farmington Hills *(G-5066)*
Micrgraphics Printing Inc E 231 739-6575
Norton Shores *(G-11773)*
Microforms Inc D 586 939-7900
Beverly Hills *(G-1620)*
Mid North Printing Inc G 989 732-1313
Gaylord *(G-5882)*
Millbrook Press Works G 517 323-2111
Lansing *(G-9311)*
Millbrook Printing Co E 517 627-4078
Grand Ledge *(G-6112)*
Mitchell Graphics Inc E 231 347-4635
Petoskey *(G-12459)*
MKP Enterprises Inc G 248 809-2525
Southfield *(G-14985)*
Model Printing Service Inc F 989 356-0834
Alpena *(G-301)*
Monarch Print and Mail LLC G 734 620-8378
Westland *(G-17581)*
Monarch Print Solutions LLC G 517 522-8457
Michigan Center *(G-10788)*
Motivation Ideas Inc G 989 356-1817
Alpena *(G-302)*
MPS/lh LLC G 517 323-9001
Lansing *(G-9249)*
Msw Print and Imaging F 734 544-1626
Ypsilanti *(G-18092)*
Muhleck Enterprises Inc F 517 333-0713
Okemos *(G-12133)*
Munro Printing G 586 773-9579
Eastpointe *(G-4707)*
National Printing Services G 616 813-0758
Wyoming *(G-18022)*
National Wholesale Prtg Corp G 734 416-8400
Plymouth *(G-12699)*
Nationwide Envlope Spclsts Inc F 248 354-5500
Walled Lake *(G-16900)*
Newberry News Inc G 906 293-8401
Newberry *(G-11583)*
Nje Enterprises LLC G 313 963-3600
Detroit *(G-4273)*
Northamerican Reproduction F 734 421-6800
Livonia *(G-9863)*
Northern Specialty Co G 906 376-8165
Republic *(G-13246)*
Ntvb Media Inc E 248 583-4190
Troy *(G-16528)*
Office Connection Inc E 248 871-2003
Farmington Hills *(G-5086)*
Office Express Inc E 248 307-1850
Troy *(G-16534)*
P J Printing G 269 673-3372
Allegan *(G-179)*
Palmer Envelope Co E 269 965-1336
Battle Creek *(G-1235)*
Pariseaus Printing Inc G 810 653-8420
Davison *(G-3657)*
Parkside Printing Inc G 810 765-4500
Marine City *(G-10479)*
Patton Printing Inc G 313 535-9099
Redford *(G-13178)*
PDQ Ink Inc F 810 229-2989
Brighton *(G-1975)*
Peg-Master Business Forms Inc G 586 566-8694
Shelby Township *(G-14662)*
Perfect Impressions Inc G 248 478-2644
Farmington Hills *(G-5091)*
Perrigo Printing Inc G 616 454-6761
Grand Rapids *(G-6751)*
Phase III Graphics Inc G 616 949-9290
Grand Rapids *(G-6753)*
Phoenix Press Incorporated E 248 435-8040
Troy *(G-16546)*
Photo Offset Inc G 906 786-5800
Escanaba *(G-4851)*
Pioneer Press F 231 796-8072
Big Rapids *(G-1642)*
Pioneer Press Printing G 231 864-2404
Bear Lake *(G-1380)*
Pleasant Graphics Inc F 989 773-7777
Mount Pleasant *(G-11219)*
Pointe Printing Inc G 313 821-0030
Grosse Pointe Park *(G-7195)*
Popcorn Press Inc E 248 588-4444
Madison Heights *(G-10332)*
Postal Savings Direct Mktg F 810 238-8866
Flint *(G-5480)*
Preferred Printing Inc F 269 782-5488
Dowagiac *(G-4557)*
Presto Print Inc F 616 364-7132
Grand Rapids *(G-6772)*
Pride Printing Inc G 906 228-8182
Marquette *(G-10554)*
Print Haus G 616 786-4030
Holland *(G-7776)*

Employee Codes: A=Over 500 employees, B=251-500
C=101-250, D=51-100, E=20-50, F=10-19, G=3-9
2020 Harris Michigan
Industrial Directory
1339

PRINTING: Offset

Print House Inc — Farmington Hills (G-5100)	F	248 473-1414
Print Masters Inc — Madison Heights (G-10339)	F	248 548-7100
Print Plus Inc — Saint Clair Shores (G-14268)	G	586 888-8000
Print Shop — Petoskey (G-12471)	G	231 347-2000
Print Tech Printing Place Inc — Mount Pleasant (G-11221)	G	989 772-6109
Print Xpress — Grosse Pointe Woods (G-7208)	G	313 886-6850
Print-Tech Inc — Ann Arbor (G-604)	E	734 996-2345
Printcomm Inc — Flint (G-5484)	D	810 239-5763
Printed Impressions Inc — Farmington Hills (G-5101)	G	248 473-5333
Printery Inc — Holland (G-7777)	E	616 396-4655
Printex Printing & Graphics — Richland (G-13253)	G	269 629-0122
Printing Centre Inc — Holt (G-7922)	F	517 694-2400
Printing Industries of Mich — Novi (G-11982)	G	248 946-5895
Printing Plus Inc — Ypsilanti (G-18096)	G	734 482-1680
Printing Productions Ink — Grand Rapids (G-6777)	G	616 871-9292
Printing Service Inc — Clay (G-3001)	G	586 718-4103
Printing Services — Portage (G-13024)	G	269 321-9826
Printing Services Inc — Saline (G-14409)	E	734 944-1404
Printmill Inc — Kalamazoo (G-8862)	G	269 382-0428
Progress Printers Inc — Traverse City (G-16081)	E	231 947-5311
Progressive Prtg & Graphics — Battle Creek (G-1238)	G	269 965-8909
Pummill Print Services Lc — Comstock Park (G-3510)	G	616 785-7960
Qg LLC — Midland (G-10904)	B	989 496-3333
Qrp Inc — Midland (G-10905)	G	989 496-2955
Qrp Inc — Midland (G-10906)	E	989 496-2955
Quad/Graphics Inc — Midland (G-10907)	F	989 698-5598
Quad/Graphics Inc — Greenville (G-7150)	C	616 754-3672
Quality Printing & Graphics — Grand Rapids (G-6801)	G	616 949-3400
Quick Printing Company Inc — Grand Rapids (G-6802)	G	616 241-0506
Quickprint of Adrian Inc — Adrian (G-89)	F	517 263-2290
R N E Business Enterprises — Detroit (G-4326)	G	313 963-3600
R R Donnelley & Sons Company — Detroit (G-4327)	D	313 964-1330
R W Patterson Printing Co — Benton Harbor (G-1542)	D	269 925-2177
Raenell Press LLC — Grand Rapids (G-6806)	E	616 534-8890
Rapid Graphics Inc — Benton Harbor (G-1543)	G	269 925-7087
Rar Group Inc — Southfield (G-15010)	G	248 353-2266
Ray Printing Company Inc — Jackson (G-8561)	F	517 787-4130
Raze-It Printing — Hazel Park (G-7452)	G	248 543-3813
Reimold Printing Corporation — Saginaw (G-14132)	G	989 799-0784
Rex Printing Company — Sterling Heights (G-15467)	G	586 323-4002
Richard Larabee — Southfield (G-15015)	G	248 827-7755
Richards Printing — Escanaba (G-4856)	G	906 786-3540
Riegle Press Inc — Davison (G-3661)	E	810 653-9631
River Run Press Inc — Kalamazoo (G-8873)	E	269 349-7603
Riverside Prtg of Grnd Rapids — Grand Rapids (G-6828)	G	616 458-8011
Rocket Print Copy Ship Center — Royal Oak (G-13966)	G	248 336-3636
Rogers Printing Inc — Ravenna (G-13128)	C	231 853-2244
Romeo Printing Company Inc — Romeo (G-13637)	G	586 752-9003
Ron Rowe — Newaygo (G-11577)	G	231 652-2642
Rose Business Forms Company — Southfield (G-15017)	E	734 424-5200
Rtr Alpha Inc — Auburn Hills (G-994)	G	248 377-4060
Rumler Brothers Inc — Hillsdale (G-7538)	E	517 437-2990
Rush Stationers Printers Inc — Bay City (G-1351)	F	989 891-9305
S & N Aziza Inc — Troy (G-16586)	G	248 879-9396
S & N Graphic Solutions LLC — Canton (G-2424)	G	734 495-3314
SBR Printing USA Inc — Port Huron (G-12964)	F	810 388-9441
Schepeler Corporation — Brooklyn (G-2042)	F	517 592-6811
Seifert City-Wide Printing Co — Farmington (G-4912)	G	248 477-9525
Shamrock Printing — Bruce Twp (G-2100)	G	586 752-8580
Shayleslie Corporation — Holt (G-7929)	G	517 694-4115
Sheridan Books Inc — Chelsea (G-2719)	C	734 475-9145
Skip Printing and Dup Co — Roseville (G-13870)	G	586 779-2640
Slades Printing Company Inc — Pontiac (G-12866)	F	248 334-6257
Sourceone Imaging LLC — Grand Rapids (G-6872)	G	616 452-2001
Spartan Printing Inc — Lansing (G-9264)	E	517 372-6910
Specifications Service Company — Bloomfield (G-1736)	F	248 353-0244
Spectrum Printers Inc — Tecumseh (G-15809)	E	517 423-5735
Spectrum Printing — Clarkston (G-2957)	G	248 625-5014
Stamp-Rite Incorporated — Lansing (G-9267)	E	517 487-5071
Standard Printing — Ypsilanti (G-18102)	G	734 483-0339
Standard Printing of Warren — Warren (G-17253)	G	586 771-3770
Steketee-Van Huis Inc — Holland (G-7814)	C	616 392-2326
Stewart Printing Company Inc — Wyandotte (G-17976)	G	734 283-8440
Straits Area Printing Corp — Cheboygan (G-2696)	G	231 627-5647
Stylecraft Printing Co — Canton (G-2430)	D	734 455-5500
Sugar Bush Printing Inc — Bloomfield Hills (G-1799)	G	248 373-8888
Summit Printing & Graphics — Bay City (G-1362)	G	989 892-2267
Sunrise Print Cmmnications Inc — West Branch (G-17523)	F	989 345-4475
Superior Imaging Services Inc — Kalamazoo (G-8904)	G	269 382-0428
Superior Typesetting Service — Kalamazoo (G-8905)	G	269 382-0428
Systems Duplicating Co Inc — Troy (G-16629)	F	248 585-7590
T-Print USA — Hamilton (G-7240)	G	269 751-4603
Temperance Printing — Lambertville (G-9186)	G	419 290-6846
Thorpe Printing Services Inc — Marysville (G-10622)	G	810 364-6222
Tigner Printing Inc — Coleman (G-3351)	G	989 465-6916
Triangle Printing Inc — Roseville (G-13881)	G	586 293-7530
Tsunami Inc — Saginaw (G-14168)	G	989 497-5200
Turner Business Forms Inc — Saginaw (G-14171)	E	989 752-5540
Turner Business Forms Inc — Flint (G-5515)	G	810 244-6980
Tuteur Inc — Saint Joseph (G-14344)	G	269 983-1246
Ultra-Tech Printing Co — Wyoming (G-18038)	F	616 249-0500
Unigraphics — East Lansing (G-4681)	G	517 337-9316
US Printers — Daggett (G-3623)	G	906 639-3100
Val Valley Inc — Farmington Hills (G-5145)	G	248 474-7335
Ver Duins Inc — Grand Haven (G-6095)	G	616 842-0730
Village Graphics Inc — Charlevoix (G-2634)	G	231 547-4172
Village Printing & Supply Inc — Lapeer (G-9491)	G	810 664-2270
Village Shop Inc — Traverse City (G-16138)	D	231 946-3712
Washington Street Printers LLC — Monroe (G-11083)	G	734 240-5541
Waterman and Sons Prtg Co Inc — Detroit (G-4436)	G	313 864-5562
Web Printing & Mktg Concepts — Saint Joseph (G-14351)	G	269 983-4646
Weighman Enterprises Inc — Saginaw (G-14181)	G	989 755-2116
West Colony Graphic Inc — Kalamazoo (G-8922)	G	269 375-6625
West Michigan Tag & Label Inc — Grand Rapids (G-6987)	E	616 235-0120
Whipple Printing Inc — Allen Park (G-213)	G	313 382-8033
White Pines Corporation — Ann Arbor (G-699)	E	734 761-2670
Wholesale Ticket Co Inc — Saranac (G-14457)	F	616 642-9476
William C Fox Enterprises Inc — Cadillac (G-2286)	E	231 775-2732
Willoughby Press — Owosso (G-12330)	G	989 723-3360
Wolverine Printing Company LLC — Grand Rapids (G-6999)	E	616 451-2075
Woodhams Enterprises Inc — Climax (G-3014)	G	269 383-0600
Workman Printing Inc — Muskegon (G-11455)	G	231 744-5500
Worten Copy Center Inc — Ludington (G-10089)	G	231 845-7030
Wynalda Litho Inc — Belmont (G-1476)	C	616 866-1561
X-Treme Printing Inc — Flint (G-5528)	G	810 232-3232
Yti Office Express LLC — Troy (G-16704)	G	866 996-8952
Zak Brothers Printing LLC — Detroit (G-4456)	G	313 831-3216
Zeeland Print Shop Co — Zeeland (G-18202)	G	616 772-6636

PRINTING: Photo-Offset

Print Metro Inc — Sparta (G-15106)	G	616 887-1723
Print n go — East Tawas (G-4694)	G	989 362-6041

PRINTING: Photogravure

Axis Digital Inc — Grand Rapids (G-6197)	E	616 698-9890

PRINTING: Photolithographic

Lighthouse Direct Buy LLC — Detroit (G-4204)	G	313 340-1850

PRINTING: Rotary Photogravure

Seeley Inc — Williamston (G-17740)	E	517 655-5631

PRINTING: Screen, Broadwoven Fabrics, Cotton

Advanced Printwear Inc — Madison Heights (G-10182)	G	248 585-4412
Advertising Accents Inc — Redford (G-13142)	E	313 937-3890
Allgraphics Corp — Farmington Hills (G-4928)	G	248 994-7373
Baumans Running Center Inc — Flint (G-5385)	G	810 238-5981
Charlevoix Screen Masters Inc — Charlevoix (G-2612)	G	231 547-5111

PRODUCT SECTION

PRINTING: Screen, Fabric (continued)

Great Put On Inc .... G 810 733-8021
  Flint *(G-5442)*
Hilton Screeners Inc .... G 810 653-0711
  Davison *(G-3654)*
Perrin Screen Printing Inc .... D 616 785-9900
  Comstock Park *(G-3507)*
Pro Shop The/P S Graphics .... G 517 448-8490
  Hudson *(G-8139)*
Prong Horn .... G 616 456-1903
  Grand Rapids *(G-6789)*
Sign of The Loon Gifts Inc .... G 231 436-5155
  Mackinaw City *(G-10101)*
Slick Shirts Screen Printing .... F 517 371-3600
  Lansing *(G-9424)*
Trophy Center West Michigan .... G 231 893-1686
  Whitehall *(G-17678)*

PRINTING: Screen, Fabric

1st Class Embroidery LLC .... G 734 282-7745
  Southgate *(G-15071)*
A Game Apparel .... F 810 564-2600
  Mount Morris *(G-11155)*
American Silk Screen & EMB .... E 248 474-1000
  Farmington Hills *(G-4930)*
Applied Graphics & Fabricating .... F 989 662-3334
  Auburn *(G-750)*
Ascott Corporation .... G 734 663-2023
  Ann Arbor *(G-369)*
Athletic Uniform Lettering .... G 313 533-9071
  Redford *(G-13145)*
Bay Supply & Marketing Inc .... G 231 943-3249
  Traverse City *(G-15908)*
C & C Enterprises Inc .... G 989 772-5095
  Mount Pleasant *(G-11182)*
Chromatic Graphics Inc .... G 616 393-0034
  Holland *(G-7590)*
Crawford Associates Inc .... G 248 549-9494
  Royal Oak *(G-13915)*
Design Tech LLC .... G 616 459-2885
  Grand Rapids *(G-6346)*
Designs By Bean .... G 989 845-4371
  Chesaning *(G-2723)*
Elephant Head LLC .... G 734 256-4555
  Romulus *(G-13670)*
Elite Active Wear Inc .... G 616 396-1229
  Holland *(G-7621)*
Embroidery House Inc .... G 616 669-6400
  Jenison *(G-8625)*
Ethnic Artwork Inc .... F 586 726-1400
  Sterling Heights *(G-15333)*
Exclusive Imagery Inc .... G 248 436-2999
  Royal Oak *(G-13927)*
Field Crafts Inc .... E 231 325-1122
  Honor *(G-7952)*
Flaunt It Sportswear .... G 616 696-9084
  Cedar Springs *(G-2556)*
Gottch-Ya Graphix USA .... G 269 979-7587
  Battle Creek *(G-1193)*
Hankerds Sportswear Basic TS .... G 989 725-2979
  Owosso *(G-12294)*
Imprint House LLC .... G 810 985-8203
  Port Huron *(G-12929)*
Jam Enterprises .... G 313 417-9200
  Detroit *(G-4156)*
Jbl Enterprises .... G 616 530-8647
  Grand Rapids *(G-6555)*
JS Original Silkscreens LLC .... G 586 779-5456
  Eastpointe *(G-4705)*
Kalamazoo Sportswear Inc .... F 269 344-4242
  Kalamazoo *(G-8798)*
M & M Associates .... G 231 845-7034
  Ludington *(G-10070)*
Mvp Sports Store .... G 517 764-5165
  Jackson *(G-8539)*
Perrin Screen Printing Inc .... D 616 785-9900
  Comstock Park *(G-3507)*
Player Prints LLC .... G 844 774-7773
  Clarkston *(G-2946)*
R H & Company Inc .... F 269 345-7814
  Kalamazoo *(G-8867)*
Rsls Corp .... G 248 726-0675
  Shelby Township *(G-14683)*
S & H Trophy & Sports .... G 616 754-0005
  Greenville *(G-7151)*
Saginaw Knitting Mills Inc .... F 989 695-2481
  Freeland *(G-5759)*
Shirts n More Inc .... F 269 963-3266
  Battle Creek *(G-1246)*
Silk Screenstuff .... G 517 543-7716
  Charlotte *(G-2664)*

Sporting Image Inc .... F 269 657-5646
  Paw Paw *(G-12413)*
Sports Stop .... G 517 676-2199
  Mason *(G-10660)*
Sunset Sportswear Inc .... F 248 437-7611
  Wixom *(G-17900)*
Sylvesters .... G 989 348-9097
  Grayling *(G-7116)*
T - Shirt Printing Plus Inc .... F 269 383-3666
  Kalamazoo *(G-8907)*

PRINTING: Screen, Manmade Fiber & Silk, Broadwoven Fabric

Armada Printwear Inc .... G 586 784-5553
  Armada *(G-715)*
Creative Promotions .... G 734 854-2292
  Lambertville *(G-9181)*

PRINTING: Thermography

American Thermographers .... E 248 398-3810
  Madison Heights *(G-10190)*
Corporate Electronic Sty Inc .... D 248 583-7070
  Troy *(G-16283)*
MBA Printing Inc .... G 616 243-1600
  Comstock Park *(G-3498)*
Utley Brothers Inc .... E 248 585-1700
  Troy *(G-16672)*

PRODUCT ENDORSEMENT SVCS

High Impact Solutions Inc .... G 248 473-9804
  Farmington Hills *(G-5019)*

PROFESSIONAL EQPT & SPLYS, WHOLESALE: Analytical Instruments

Jade Scientific Inc .... F 734 207-3775
  Westland *(G-17572)*

PROFESSIONAL EQPT & SPLYS, WHOLESALE: Law Enforcement

Mission Critical Firearms LLC .... G 586 232-5185
  Shelby Township *(G-14641)*

PROFESSIONAL EQPT & SPLYS, WHOLESALE: Optical Goods

Essilor Laboratories Amer Inc .... E 231 922-0344
  Traverse City *(G-15966)*
Fairway Optical Inc .... G 231 744-6168
  Muskegon *(G-11320)*
Hi-Tech Optical Inc .... E 989 799-9390
  Saginaw *(G-14057)*

PROFESSIONAL EQPT & SPLYS, WHOLESALE: Precision Tools

Arch Global Precision LLC .... F 734 266-6900
  Bloomfield Hills *(G-1747)*

PROFESSIONAL EQPT & SPLYS, WHOLESALE: Scientific & Engineerg

Envision Engineering LLC .... G 616 897-0599
  Lowell *(G-10027)*
Inora Technologies Inc .... F 734 302-7488
  Ann Arbor *(G-506)*

PROFESSIONAL INSTRUMENT REPAIR SVCS

Applied Instruments Company .... E 810 227-5510
  Brighton *(G-1886)*
Dixon & Ryan Corporation .... F 248 549-4000
  Royal Oak *(G-13919)*
Envisiontec Inc .... D 313 436-4300
  Dearborn *(G-3702)*
Measuring Tool Services .... G 734 261-1107
  Livonia *(G-9835)*
Midwest Vibro Inc .... G 616 532-7670
  Grandville *(G-7058)*
Mycrona Inc .... F 734 453-9348
  Plymouth *(G-12697)*
Sun-Tec Corp .... G 248 669-3100
  Novi *(G-12009)*

PROFILE SHAPES: Unsupported Plastics

Alloy Exchange Inc .... F 616 863-0640
  Rockford *(G-13557)*
Gazelle Prototype LLC .... G 616 844-1820
  Spring Lake *(G-15145)*
Highland Plastics Inc .... E 989 828-4400
  Shepherd *(G-14728)*
Idemitsu Chemicals USA Corp .... G 248 355-0666
  Southfield *(G-14942)*
Plastic Plaque Inc .... G 810 982-9591
  Port Huron *(G-12957)*
Porex Technologies Corporation .... E 989 865-8200
  Saint Charles *(G-14198)*
Spiratex Company .... D 734 289-4800
  Monroe *(G-11069)*
Tg Fluid Systems USA Corp .... B 810 220-6161
  Brighton *(G-1997)*

PROGRAMMERS: Indl Process

Endlich Studios LLC .... G 248 524-9671
  Troy *(G-16344)*

PROMOTERS OF SHOWS & EXHIBITIONS

Bob Allison Enterprises .... G 248 540-8467
  Bloomfield Hills *(G-1752)*
Graphicolor Systems Inc .... G 248 347-0271
  Livonia *(G-9758)*

PROMOTION SVCS

Valassis International Inc .... B 734 591-3000
  Livonia *(G-9987)*

PROPELLERS: Boat & Ship, Machined

Lorenz Propellers & Engrg Co .... G 231 728-3245
  Muskegon *(G-11366)*

PROPELLERS: Ship, Cast Brass

Michigan Wheel Operations LLC .... E 616 452-6941
  Grand Rapids *(G-6677)*

PROPULSION UNITS: Guided Missiles & Space Vehicles

Northrop Grumman Innovation .... D 313 424-9411
  Shelby Township *(G-14657)*

PUBLIC FINANCE, TAX & MONETARY POLICY OFFICES, GOVT: State

Technology MGT & Budgt Dept .... D 517 322-1897
  Lansing *(G-9430)*

PUBLIC LIBRARY

Elmont District Library .... G 810 798-3100
  Almont *(G-256)*

PUBLIC RELATIONS & PUBLICITY SVCS

All Seasons Agency Inc .... G 586 752-6381
  Bruce Twp *(G-2077)*
Dale Corporation .... E 248 542-2400
  Madison Heights *(G-10227)*
K Printing Public Relations Co .... G 810 648-4410
  Sandusky *(G-14438)*
K S B Promotions Inc .... G 616 676-0758
  Ada *(G-20)*
Pharmacia & Upjohn Company LLC ... D 908 901-8000
  Kalamazoo *(G-8849)*

PUBLIC RELATIONS SVCS

Michigan Banker Magazine .... G 517 484-0775
  Lansing *(G-9397)*

PUBLISHERS: Art Copy & Poster

Amplified Life Network LLC .... G 800 453-7733
  Byron Center *(G-2176)*

PUBLISHERS: Book

American Soc AG Blgcal Engners ..... E 269 429-0300
  Saint Joseph *(G-14300)*
Banggameus .... G 734 904-1916
  Ann Arbor *(G-380)*
Broadblade Press .... G 810 635-3156
  Swartz Creek *(G-15664)*

Employee Codes: A=Over 500 employees, B=251-500
C=101-250, D=51-100, E=20-50, F=10-19, G=3-9

PUBLISHERS: Book

Cbm LLC — Ann Arbor (G-396)	F	800 487-2323
Central Michigan University — Mount Pleasant (G-11187)	F	989 774-3216
Chandler Ricchio Pubg LLC — Battle Creek (G-1166)	G	269 660-0840
Childrens Bible Hour Inc — Grand Rapids (G-6274)	F	616 647-4500
Complete Services LLC — Livonia (G-9686)	F	248 470-8247
Conant Gardeners — Detroit (G-3946)	G	313 863-2624
Dac Inc — Detroit (G-3960)	E	313 388-4342
Dzanc Books Inc — Ann Arbor (G-429)	G	734 756-5701
E D C O Publishing Inc — Clarkston (G-2917)	G	248 690-9184
Elmont District Library — Almont (G-256)	G	810 798-3100
Entertainment Publications Inc — Troy (G-16348)	B	248 404-1000
Foreword Magazine Inc — Traverse City (G-15972)	F	231 933-3699
Harvard Square Editions — Ann Arbor (G-483)	G	734 668-7523
Jenkins Group Inc — Traverse City (G-16010)	F	231 933-4954
Jkr Ventures LLC — Traverse City (G-16013)	G	734 645-2320
K S B Promotions Inc — Ada (G-20)	G	616 676-0758
Living Word International Inc — Midland (G-10882)	E	989 832-7547
Mendenhall Associates Inc — Ann Arbor (G-552)	G	734 741-4710
Michigan State Univ Press — East Lansing (G-4671)	F	517 355-9543
New Issues Poetry and Prose — Kalamazoo (G-8835)	G	269 387-8185
Regents of The University Mich — Ann Arbor (G-615)	G	734 764-6230
Regents of The University Mich — Ann Arbor (G-616)	E	734 764-4388
Roger D Rapoport — Muskegon (G-11416)	G	231 755-6665
Team Breadwinner LLC — Detroit (G-4396)	G	313 460-0152
Watchdog Quarterly Inc — Chelsea (G-2721)	G	734 593-7039
Windword Press — Keego Harbor (G-8982)	G	248 681-7905
XMCO Inc — Warren (G-17301)	D	586 558-8510

PUBLISHERS: Book Clubs, No Printing

Thunder Bay Press Inc — Holt (G-7930)	E	517 694-3205

PUBLISHERS: Books, No Printing

A B Publishing Inc — Ithaca (G-8355)	G	989 875-4985
Avko Eductl Res Foundation — Birch Run (G-1663)	F	810 686-9283
Baker Book House Company — Ada (G-10)	C	616 676-9185
Baker Book House Company — Grand Rapids (G-6201)	E	616 957-3110
Black Cobra Financial Svcs LLC — Bloomfield Hills (G-1751)	G	248 298-9368
Boskage Commerce Publications — Portage (G-12986)	G	269 673-7242
Dalton Armond Publishers Inc — Okemos (G-12118)	G	517 351-8520
Developmental Services Inc — Detroit (G-4006)	G	313 653-1185
Front Porch Press — Bath (G-1134)	G	888 484-1997
Harbor House Publishers Inc — Boyne City (G-1821)	F	231 582-2814
Harper Arrington Pubg LLC — Detroit (G-4117)	G	313 282-6751
HSP Epi Acquisition LLC — Troy (G-16406)	D	248 404-1520
Master Handyman Press Inc — Troy (G-16489)	G	248 616-0810
Mehring Books Inc — Oak Park (G-12083)	G	248 967-2924
Mott Media LLC — Fenton (G-5226)	F	810 714-4280
Pierian Press Inc — Ypsilanti (G-18094)	G	734 434-4074
Quirkroberts Publishing Ltd — Troy (G-16573)	G	248 879-2598
Robbie Dean Press LLC — Ann Arbor (G-622)	G	734 973-9511
Rockman & Sons Publishing LLC — Fenton (G-5235)	F	810 750-6011
Stoney Creek Collection Inc — Grand Rapids (G-6893)	E	616 363-4858
Thomson Reuters Corporation — Ann Arbor (G-672)	D	734 913-3930
William B Eerdmans Pubg Co — Grand Rapids (G-6994)	E	616 459-4591
Zondervan Corporation LLC — Grand Rapids (G-7013)	B	616 698-6900

PUBLISHERS: Catalogs

Ideation Inc — Ann Arbor (G-499)	E	734 761-4360

PUBLISHERS: Directories, NEC

Computer Composition Corp — Madison Heights (G-10218)	F	248 545-4330
Fourth Seacoast Publishing Co — Saint Clair Shores (G-14252)	G	586 779-5570

PUBLISHERS: Directories, Telephone

Adtek Graphics Inc — Eaton Rapids (G-4715)	F	517 663-2460

PUBLISHERS: Guides

Advertiser Publishing Co Inc — Saranac (G-14452)	G	616 642-9411
Shoreline Creations Ltd — Holland (G-7801)	E	616 393-2077
Upper Michigan Newspapers LLC — Gaylord (G-5898)	F	989 732-5125

PUBLISHERS: Magazines, No Printing

A & F Enterprises Inc — Milford (G-10953)	F	248 714-6529
African American Parent Pubg — Ferndale (G-5254)	G	248 398-3400
Agenda 2020 Inc — Grand Rapids (G-6153)	F	616 581-6271
All Dealer Inventory LLC — Lake Ann (G-9083)	G	231 342-9823
All Kids Considered Publishing — Ferndale (G-5257)	F	248 398-3400
All Seasons Agency Inc — Bruce Twp (G-2077)	G	586 752-6381
Ann Arbor Observer Company — Ann Arbor (G-358)	E	734 769-3175
Auto Connection — Bruce Twp (G-2078)	G	586 752-6371
Caribbean Adventure LLC — Battle Creek (G-1163)	F	269 441-5675
Castine Communications Inc — Farmington (G-4895)	G	248 477-1600
Choice Publications Inc — Gaylord (G-5852)	G	989 732-8160
Crain Communications Inc — Detroit (G-3950)	B	313 446-6000
Crain Communications Inc — Detroit (G-3951)	B	313 446-6000
Double Gun Journal — East Jordan (G-4628)	G	231 536-7439
Elsie Publishing Institute — Lansing (G-9365)	F	517 371-5257
Farago & Associates LLC — Southfield (G-14903)	F	248 546-7070
Foreword Magazine Inc — Traverse City (G-15972)	F	231 933-3699
Gemini Corporation — Grand Rapids (G-6434)	E	616 459-4545
Gongwer News Service Inc — Lansing (G-9375)	F	517 482-3500
Grand Traverse Woman Mag — Interlochen (G-8242)	G	231 276-5105
Graphics Hse Spt Prmotions Inc — Muskegon (G-11334)	E	231 739-4004
Harp Column LLC — Zeeland (G-9361)	G	215 564-3232
Hour Media LLC — Troy (G-16403)	E	248 691-1800
Informa Business Media Inc — Southfield (G-14947)	E	248 357-0800
International Smart Tan Netwrk — Jackson (G-8472)	E	517 841-4920
Lexicom Publishing Group — Ann Arbor (G-529)	G	734 994-8600
Michigan Oil and Gas Assn — Lansing (G-9399)	G	517 487-0480
Michigan Vue Magazine — Waterford (G-17357)	G	248 681-2410
Prism Publications Inc — Traverse City (G-16078)	E	231 941-8174
Renaissance Media LLC — Southfield (G-15013)	D	248 354-6060
Revue Holding Company — Grand Rapids (G-6820)	G	616 608-6170
Rider Report Magazine — Auburn Hills (G-990)	G	248 854-8460
Roe LLC — Muskegon (G-11415)	E	231 755-5043
Shoreline Creations Ltd — Holland (G-7801)	E	616 393-2077
Southwest Michigan Living — Kalamazoo (G-8894)	G	269 344-7438
Toastmasters International — Burtchville (G-2141)	F	810 385-5477
Toastmasters International — Laingsburg (G-9081)	E	517 651-6507
Towing & Equipment Magazine — Rochester Hills (G-13530)	G	248 601-1385
United Kennel Club Inc — Portage (G-13052)	E	269 343-9020
Varsity Monthly Thumb — Caro (G-2481)	G	810 404-5297
Verdoni Productions Inc — Saginaw (G-14179)	G	989 790-0845
W W Thayne Advertising Cons — Battle Creek (G-1264)	F	269 979-1411

PUBLISHERS: Miscellaneous

AGS Publishing — Detroit (G-3846)	G	313 494-1000
Ahearn Signs and Printing — Belleville (G-1440)	G	734 699-3777
All Kids Considered Pubg Group — Ferndale (G-5256)	G	248 398-3400
American Mathematical Society — Ann Arbor (G-352)	D	734 996-5250
Avanti Press Inc — Detroit (G-3886)	E	800 228-2684
Avery Color Studios Inc — Gwinn (G-7216)	G	906 346-3908
Ball Hard Music Group LLC — Monroe (G-11018)	G	734 636-6038
Blackberry Publications — Ecorse (G-4742)	E	313 627-1520
Boone Express — Ortonville (G-12196)	G	248 583-7080
Caffeinated Press Inc — Grand Rapids (G-6251)	G	888 809-1686
City Press Inc — Ortonville (G-12197)	G	800 867-2626
Cobblestone Press — Midland (G-10825)	G	989 832-0166
Complete Services LLC — Livonia (G-9686)	F	248 470-8247
Concordant Publishing Concern — Almont (G-254)	G	810 798-3563
Conine Publishing Inc — Manistee (G-10418)	E	231 723-3592
Copyright Traveler S Trunk P — Cedar Springs (G-2550)	G	937 903-9233
Cornell Publications LLC — Brighton (G-1903)	G	810 225-3075
Country Register of Mich Inc — Saginaw (G-14022)	G	989 793-4211
Cs Express Inc — Rochester Hills (G-13399)	G	248 425-1726
Deslatae — Detroit (G-3968)	G	313 820-4321
Diggypod Inc — Tecumseh (G-15787)	G	734 429-3307
Digitalmuni LLC — Wyandotte (G-17955)	G	248 237-4077
Dillion Renee Entities — Lansing (G-9360)	G	989 443-0654
Diocese of Lansing — Lansing (G-9361)	F	517 484-4449
Discovery House Publishers — Grand Rapids (G-6355)	E	616 942-9218
E D C O Publishing Inc — Clarkston (G-2917)	G	248 690-9184

PRODUCT SECTION

PUBLISHERS: Newspaper

Edward G Hinkelman ....F...... 707 778-1124
  Traverse City *(G-15960)*
Encore Publishing Group Inc ....G...... 269 383-4433
  Kalamazoo *(G-8737)*
Engai ....G...... 313 605-8220
  Wixom *(G-17805)*
Flipsnack LLC ....E...... 650 741-1328
  Troy *(G-16367)*
Forensic Press ....G...... 734 997-0256
  Ann Arbor *(G-464)*
Frontlines Publishing ....E...... 616 887-6256
  Grand Rapids *(G-6419)*
Gemini Corporation ....E...... 616 459-4545
  Grand Rapids *(G-6434)*
Graphics Hse Spt Prmotions Inc ....E...... 231 739-4004
  Muskegon *(G-11334)*
Grayton Integrated Pubg LLC ....G...... 313 881-1734
  Grosse Pointe *(G-7180)*
Great Lakes Spt Publications ....G...... 734 507-0241
  Ann Arbor *(G-478)*
Hammond Publishing Company ....G...... 810 686-8879
  Mount Morris *(G-11161)*
Hang On Express ....G...... 231 271-0202
  Suttons Bay *(G-15652)*
Health Enhancement Systems Inc ....F...... 989 839-0852
  Midland *(G-10868)*
House of Hero LLC ....G...... 248 260-8300
  Bloomfield Hills *(G-1774)*
Human Synergistics Inc ....E...... 734 459-1030
  Plymouth *(G-12644)*
Ifca International Inc ....G...... 616 531-1840
  Grandville *(G-7051)*
Leader Publications LLC ....D...... 269 683-2100
  Niles *(G-11623)*
Llomen Inc ....G...... 269 345-3555
  Portage *(G-13011)*
Lucky Press LLC ....G...... 614 309-0048
  Harbor Springs *(G-7288)*
Manistee News Advocate ....F...... 231 723-3592
  Manistee *(G-10427)*
Maple Press LLC ....F...... 248 733-9669
  Madison Heights *(G-10301)*
Michigan Acdemy Fmly Physcians ....G...... 517 347-0098
  Okemos *(G-12131)*
Michigan Legal Publishing Ltd ....G...... 877 525-1990
  Grandville *(G-7057)*
Midwest Press and Automtn LLC ....G...... 586 212-1937
  Clinton Township *(G-3175)*
MJL Publishing LLC ....G...... 734 268-6187
  Pinckney *(G-12501)*
Morning Star ....G...... 989 755-2660
  Saginaw *(G-14099)*
Morning Star Publishing Co ....F...... 989 463-6071
  Alma *(G-243)*
New Genesis Enterprise Inc ....F...... 313 220-0365
  Westland *(G-17583)*
Northern Michigan Publishing ....G...... 231 946-7878
  Traverse City *(G-16052)*
Paine Press LLC ....G...... 231 645-1970
  Boyne City *(G-1832)*
Panda King Express ....G...... 616 796-3286
  Holland *(G-7765)*
Parker & Associates ....G...... 269 694-6709
  Otsego *(G-12248)*
Pierian Press Inc ....G...... 734 434-4074
  Ypsilanti *(G-18094)*
Press On Juice ....G...... 231 409-9971
  Traverse City *(G-16077)*
Press Play LLC ....G...... 248 802-3837
  Auburn Hills *(G-980)*
Proquest Outdoor Solutions Inc ....G...... 734 761-4700
  Ann Arbor *(G-606)*
Quality Guest Publishing Inc ....F...... 616 894-1111
  Cedar Springs *(G-2561)*
R & R Harwood Inc ....G...... 616 669-6400
  Jenison *(G-8640)*
R S C Productions ....G...... 586 532-9200
  Shelby Township *(G-14677)*
Raymond S Ross ....G...... 231 922-0235
  Traverse City *(G-16092)*
Reflective Art Inc ....E...... 616 452-0712
  Grand Rapids *(G-6817)*
Roe Publishing Department ....G...... 517 522-3598
  Jackson *(G-8564)*
Sharedbook Inc ....E...... 734 302-6500
  Ann Arbor *(G-629)*
Source Point Press ....G...... 269 501-3690
  Midland *(G-10918)*
Spry Publishing Llc ....G...... 877 722-2264
  Ann Arbor *(G-643)*
Srose Publishing Company ....G...... 248 208-7073
  Southfield *(G-15032)*
Stafford Media Inc ....E...... 616 754-9301
  Greenville *(G-7154)*
Star Buyers Guide ....G...... 989 366-8341
  Houghton Lake *(G-7998)*
Subterranean Press ....G...... 810 232-1489
  Flint *(G-5507)*
Summit Training Source Inc ....E...... 800 842-0466
  Grand Rapids *(G-6897)*
Thomson-Shore Inc ....C...... 734 426-3939
  Dexter *(G-4514)*
Timothy J Tade Inc ....G...... 248 552-8583
  Troy *(G-16644)*
Tuscola County Advertiser Inc ....F...... 989 823-8651
  Vassar *(G-16815)*
Tuscola County Advertiser Inc ....E...... 989 673-3181
  Caro *(G-2479)*
Valley Publishing ....C...... 989 671-1200
  Bay City *(G-1369)*
Village Press Inc ....G...... 231 946-3712
  Traverse City *(G-16137)*
Visible Ink Press LLC ....G...... 734 667-3211
  Canton *(G-2439)*
Wallace Publishing LLC ....E...... 248 416-7259
  Hazel Park *(G-7458)*
Wicwas Press ....G...... 269 344-8027
  Kalamazoo *(G-8924)*
Yeungs Lotus Express ....G...... 248 380-3820
  Novi *(G-12029)*
Zimbell House Publishing LLC ....G...... 248 909-0143
  Waterford *(G-17388)*
Zoomer Display LLC ....G...... 616 734-0300
  Grand Rapids *(G-7014)*

PUBLISHERS: Music Book & Sheet Music

Ayotte Cstm Mscal Engrvngs LLC ....G...... 734 595-1901
  Westland *(G-17545)*
Live Track Productions Inc ....G...... 313 704-2224
  Detroit *(G-4207)*
Paul F Hester ....F...... 616 302-6039
  Pullman *(G-13087)*

PUBLISHERS: Newsletter

Automotive Info Systems Inc ....G...... 734 332-1970
  Ann Arbor *(G-374)*
Synod of Great Lakes ....C...... 616 698-7071
  Grand Rapids *(G-6910)*
Verdoni Productions Inc ....G...... 989 790-0845
  Saginaw *(G-14179)*

PUBLISHERS: Newspaper

Adrian Team LLC ....G...... 517 264-6148
  Adrian *(G-47)*
Advance BCI Inc ....D...... 616 669-1366
  Grand Rapids *(G-6144)*
Advance BCI Inc ....D...... 616 669-5210
  Grand Rapids *(G-6145)*
Algo Especial Variety Str Inc ....G...... 313 963-9013
  Detroit *(G-3854)*
Angler Strategies LLC ....G...... 248 439-1420
  Royal Oak *(G-13902)*
Ann Arbor Chronicle ....G...... 734 645-2633
  Ann Arbor *(G-356)*
Ann Arbor Journal ....G...... 734 429-7380
  Saline *(G-14376)*
Ann Arbor Observer Company ....E...... 734 769-3175
  Ann Arbor *(G-358)*
Associated Newspapers Michigan ......G...... 734 467-1900
  Wayne *(G-17424)*
Benson Distribution Inc ....G...... 269 344-5529
  Kalamazoo *(G-8696)*
Billie Times Ltd ....G...... 248 813-9114
  Troy *(G-16240)*
Booth Newspaper ....G...... 517 487-8888
  Lansing *(G-9348)*
Buyers Guide ....F...... 616 897-9261
  Lowell *(G-10025)*
Calcomco Inc ....G...... 313 885-9228
  Kalamazoo *(G-8703)*
Chris Faulknor ....G...... 231 645-1970
  Boyne City *(G-1819)*
City of Greenville ....E...... 616 754-0100
  Greenville *(G-7124)*
Cmu ....F...... 989 774-7143
  Mount Pleasant *(G-11189)*
Crain Communications Inc ....B...... 313 446-6000
  Detroit *(G-3951)*
Detroit News Inc ....G...... 313 223-4500
  Detroit *(G-3992)*
Detroit News Inc ....G...... 313 222-6400
  Detroit *(G-3993)*
Detroit Newspaper Partnr LP ....G...... 989 752-3023
  Saginaw *(G-14026)*
Eastern Michigan University ....D...... 734 487-1010
  Ypsilanti *(G-18068)*
El Informador LLC ....G...... 616 272-1092
  Wyoming *(G-17998)*
Evening News ....G...... 734 242-1100
  Monroe *(G-11030)*
Famethis Inc ....G...... 734 645-9100
  Pinckney *(G-12497)*
Fenton Chamber Commerce ....G...... 810 629-5447
  Fenton *(G-5207)*
Gannett Co Inc ....D...... 517 377-1000
  Lansing *(G-9371)*
Gannett Co Inc ....F...... 517 548-2000
  Howell *(G-8043)*
Grand Rapids Press Inc ....F...... 616 459-1400
  Grand Rapids *(G-6461)*
Graphics Hse Spt Prmotions Inc ....E...... 231 739-4004
  Muskegon *(G-11334)*
Harbor Beach Times ....G...... 989 479-3605
  Harbor Beach *(G-7266)*
Harvey Bock Co ....G...... 616 566-1372
  Holland *(G-7658)*
Herald Newspapers Company Inc ....D...... 734 834-6376
  Grand Rapids *(G-6507)*
Herald Newspapers Company Inc ....D...... 269 388-8501
  Kalamazoo *(G-8766)*
Herald Publishing Company ....E...... 517 423-2174
  Tecumseh *(G-15797)*
Hometown Publishing Inc ....G...... 989 834-2264
  Ovid *(G-12272)*
Hydraulic Press Service ....G...... 586 859-7099
  Shelby Township *(G-14602)*
Infoguys Inc ....G...... 517 482-2125
  Lansing *(G-9385)*
Jams Media LLC ....G...... 810 664-0811
  Lapeer *(G-9465)*
Macomb North Clinton Advisor ....E...... 586 731-1000
  Shelby Township *(G-14630)*
Maquet Monthly ....G...... 906 226-6500
  Marquette *(G-10542)*
McComb County Legal News ....G...... 586 463-4300
  Mount Clemens *(G-11141)*
MI News 26 ....G...... 231 577-1844
  Cadillac *(G-2265)*
Monroe Evening News ....G...... 734 242-1100
  Monroe *(G-11055)*
Monroe Success Vlc ....G...... 734 682-3720
  Monroe *(G-11058)*
Morris Communications Co LLC ....D...... 616 546-4200
  Holland *(G-7748)*
Morris Communications Corp ....C...... 269 673-2141
  Allegan *(G-177)*
Neumann Enterprises Inc ....G...... 906 293-8122
  Newberry *(G-11581)*
Newark Morning Ledger Co ....E...... 517 487-8888
  Lansing *(G-9406)*
Old Mission Gazette ....G...... 231 590-4715
  Traverse City *(G-16057)*
Onesian Enterprises Inc ....G...... 313 382-5875
  Allen Park *(G-203)*
Plymouth-Canton Cmnty Crier ....E...... 734 453-6900
  Plymouth *(G-12722)*
Punkin Dsgn Seds Orgnlity LLC ....G...... 313 347-8488
  Detroit *(G-4317)*
Reporter Papers Inc ....F...... 734 429-5428
  Saline *(G-14412)*
River Raisin Publications ....G...... 517 486-2400
  Blissfield *(G-1725)*
Rockman Communications Inc ....E...... 810 433-6800
  Fenton *(G-5236)*
Royal Lux Magazine ....G...... 248 602-6565
  Southfield *(G-15018)*
Treasure Enterprise LLC ....F...... 810 233-7141
  Flint *(G-5513)*
Up Catholic Newspaper ....G...... 906 226-8821
  Marquette *(G-10560)*
Up North Publications Inc ....G...... 231 587-8471
  Mancelona *(G-10400)*
View Newspaper ....G...... 734 697-8255
  Belleville *(G-1452)*
Vintage Views Press ....G...... 616 475-7662
  Grand Rapids *(G-6973)*
West Michigan Medical ....G...... 269 673-2141
  Allegan *(G-191)*

PUBLISHERS: Newspaper

Your Custom Image ....G...... 989 621-2250
  Mount Pleasant *(G-11236)*

PUBLISHERS: Newspapers, No Printing

A B Rusgo Inc ....G...... 586 296-7714
  Fraser *(G-5610)*
Action Ad Newspapers Inc ....G...... 734 740-6966
  Belleville *(G-1439)*
Alcona County Review ....G...... 989 724-6384
  Harrisville *(G-7361)*
Anteebo Publishers Inc ....E...... 313 882-6900
  Grosse Pointe Park *(G-7190)*
Argus Press Company ....D...... 989 725-5136
  Owosso *(G-12280)*
Belleville Area Independent ....G...... 734 699-9020
  Belleville *(G-1441)*
Brown City Banner Inc ....G...... 810 346-2753
  Brown City *(G-2047)*
Budget Europe Travel Service ....G...... 734 668-0529
  Ann Arbor *(G-391)*
Business News Publishing ....B...... 248 362-3700
  Troy *(G-16248)*
C & G Publishing Inc ....D...... 586 498-8000
  Warren *(G-16971)*
Campub Inc ....F...... 517 368-0365
  Camden *(G-2338)*
Cass City Chronicle Inc ....G...... 989 872-2010
  Cass City *(G-2512)*
Cedar Springs Post Inc ....G...... 616 696-3655
  Cedar Springs *(G-2547)*
Clare County Review ....G...... 989 386-4414
  Clare *(G-2866)*
Conine Publishing Company ....G...... 231 832-5566
  Reed City *(G-13212)*
Conine Publishing Inc ....G...... 231 352-9659
  Frankfort *(G-5600)*
Daily Reporter ....E...... 517 278-2318
  Coldwater *(G-3300)*
Daughtry Nwspapers Investments ....F...... 269 683-2100
  Niles *(G-11606)*
Detroit Jewish News Ltd Partnr ....D...... 248 354-6060
  Southfield *(G-14881)*
Detroit Legal News Pubg LLC ....G...... 734 477-0201
  Ann Arbor *(G-418)*
Detroit News Inc ....B...... 313 222-6400
  Detroit *(G-3990)*
Detroit Newspaper Partnr LP ....A...... 313 222-2300
  Detroit *(G-3994)*
El Vocero Hispano Inc ....F...... 616 246-6023
  Grand Rapids *(G-6372)*
Express Publications Inc ....F...... 231 947-8787
  Traverse City *(G-15967)*
Fowlerville News & Views ....G...... 517 223-8760
  Fowlerville *(G-5567)*
Gazette Newspapers Inc ....G...... 248 524-4868
  Troy *(G-16380)*
Gemini Corporation ....E...... 616 459-4545
  Grand Rapids *(G-6434)*
GLS Diocesan Reports ....G...... 989 793-7661
  Saginaw *(G-14046)*
Grand Haven Publishing Corp ....E...... 616 842-6400
  Grand Haven *(G-6024)*
Great Lakes Pilot Pubg Co ....G...... 906 494-2391
  Grand Marais *(G-6118)*
Hamtramck Review Inc ....G...... 313 874-2100
  Detroit *(G-4115)*
Harold K Schultz ....F...... 517 279-9764
  Coldwater *(G-3308)*
Herald Newspapers Company Inc ....D...... 810 766-6100
  Flint *(G-5446)*
Herald Newspapers Company Inc ....G...... 989 895-8551
  Flint *(G-5447)*
Herald Newspapers Company Inc ....E...... 269 373-7100
  Kalamazoo *(G-8765)*
Houghton Lake Resorter Inc ....E...... 989 366-5341
  Houghton Lake *(G-7993)*
Hudson Post Gazette ....G...... 517 448-2611
  Hudson *(G-8132)*
Huron Publishing Company Inc ....D...... 989 269-6461
  Bad Axe *(G-1067)*
Indpndent Advsor Nwsppr Group ....E...... 989 723-1118
  Owosso *(G-12296)*
Kaechele Inc ....G...... 269 857-2570
  Saugatuck *(G-14459)*
Kaechele Publications Inc ....E...... 269 673-5534
  Allegan *(G-168)*
Lansing Labor News Inc ....G...... 517 484-7408
  Lansing *(G-9306)*
Leelanau Enterprise Inc ....F...... 231 256-9827
  Lake Leelanau *(G-9104)*

Local Media Group Inc ....D...... 313 885-2612
  Detroit *(G-4208)*
Michigan Front Page LLC ....G...... 313 963-5522
  Detroit *(G-4241)*
Midland Publishing Company ....C...... 989 835-7171
  Midland *(G-10891)*
Minden City Herald ....G...... 989 864-3630
  Minden City *(G-11000)*
Morenci Observer ....G...... 517 458-6811
  Morenci *(G-11113)*
New Buffalo Times ....G...... 269 469-1100
  New Buffalo *(G-11517)*
Newberry News Inc ....G...... 906 293-8401
  Newberry *(G-11583)*
Northern Michigan Review Inc ....G...... 231 547-6558
  Petoskey *(G-12464)*
Nutting Newspapers Inc ....G...... 906 482-1500
  Houghton *(G-7979)*
Ogden Newspapers Inc ....D...... 906 786-2021
  Escanaba *(G-4849)*
Ogden Newspapers Inc ....G...... 906 497-5652
  Powers *(G-13078)*
Ogden Newspapers Inc ....F...... 906 774-2772
  Iron Mountain *(G-8296)*
Ogden Newspapers Inc ....G...... 906 789-9122
  Escanaba *(G-4850)*
Ogemaw County Herald Inc ....E...... 989 345-0044
  West Branch *(G-17514)*
Otsego County Herald Times ....F...... 989 732-1111
  Gaylord *(G-5886)*
Page One Inc ....E...... 810 724-0254
  Imlay City *(G-8209)*
Pgi Holdings Inc ....G...... 231 723-3592
  Manistee *(G-10435)*
Pgi Holdings Inc ....G...... 231 745-4635
  Baldwin *(G-1085)*
Plymouth-Canton Cmnty Crier ....E...... 734 453-6900
  Plymouth *(G-12721)*
Porcupine Press Inc ....G...... 906 439-5111
  Chatham *(G-2675)*
Schepeler Corporation ....F...... 517 592-6811
  Brooklyn *(G-2042)*
Sherman Publications Inc ....F...... 248 628-4801
  Oxford *(G-12372)*
Sherman Publications Inc ....G...... 248 625-3370
  Clarkston *(G-2955)*
Sherman Publications Inc ....G...... 248 693-8331
  Lake Orion *(G-9161)*
Sherman Publications Inc ....G...... 248 627-4332
  Ortonville *(G-12204)*
South Haven Tribune ....G...... 269 637-1104
  South Haven *(G-14774)*
Springer Publishing Co Inc ....F...... 586 939-6800
  Warren *(G-17250)*
State News Inc ....C...... 517 295-1680
  East Lansing *(G-4676)*
Straitsland Resorter ....G...... 231 238-7362
  Indian River *(G-8223)*
Times Indicator Publications ....G...... 231 924-4400
  Fremont *(G-5784)*
Traverse Cy Record- Eagle Inc ....G...... 231 946-2000
  Traverse City *(G-16129)*
Tuscola County Advertiser Inc ....E...... 989 673-3181
  Caro *(G-2479)*
Vineyard Press Inc ....F...... 269 657-5080
  Paw Paw *(G-12416)*
Voice Communications Corp ....E...... 586 716-8100
  Clinton Township *(G-3257)*
Your Hometown Shopper LLC ....F...... 586 412-8500
  Shelby Township *(G-14725)*

PUBLISHERS: Pamphlets, No Printing

Amplified Life Network LLC ....G...... 800 453-7733
  Byron Center *(G-2176)*

PUBLISHERS: Periodical, With Printing

Crain Communications Inc ....B...... 313 446-6000
  Detroit *(G-3952)*
Detroit Legal News Company ....D...... 313 961-6000
  Detroit *(G-3987)*
Diocese of Lansing ....F...... 517 484-4449
  Lansing *(G-9361)*
Michigan Banker Magazine ....G...... 517 484-0775
  Lansing *(G-9397)*
Upston Associates Inc ....G...... 269 349-2782
  Battle Creek *(G-1263)*
West Michigan Printing Inc ....G...... 616 676-2190
  Ada *(G-34)*

PUBLISHERS: Periodicals, Magazines

Advisor Inc ....G...... 906 341-2424
  Manistique *(G-10438)*
Bob Allison Enterprises ....G...... 248 540-8467
  Bloomfield Hills *(G-1752)*
Effective Schools Products ....G...... 517 349-8841
  Okemos *(G-12121)*
G L Nelson Inc ....G...... 630 682-5958
  Indian River *(G-8218)*
Infoguys Inc ....G...... 517 482-2125
  Lansing *(G-9385)*
Land & Homes Inc ....G...... 616 534-5792
  Grand Rapids *(G-6617)*
Laribits Keaton Publ Group ....G...... 231 537-3330
  Harbor Springs *(G-7286)*
Living Word International Inc ....E...... 989 832-7547
  Midland *(G-10882)*
Logan Marketing Group LLC ....F...... 248 731-7650
  Bloomfield Hills *(G-1778)*
Magazines In Motion Inc ....G...... 248 310-7647
  Farmington Hills *(G-5048)*
Morris Communications Co LLC ....D...... 616 546-4200
  Holland *(G-7748)*
Morris Communications Corp ....C...... 269 673-2141
  Allegan *(G-177)*
Pierian Press Inc ....G...... 734 434-4074
  Ypsilanti *(G-18094)*
Pride Source Corporation ....F...... 734 293-7200
  Livonia *(G-9898)*
Profiles Magazine ....G...... 313 531-9041
  Detroit *(G-4313)*
R J Michaels Inc ....F...... 517 783-2637
  Jackson *(G-8560)*
Reliable Freight Fwdg Inc ....G...... 734 595-6165
  Romulus *(G-13727)*
Resort + Recreation Magazine ....G...... 616 891-5747
  Caledonia *(G-2313)*
Rockman & Sons Publishing LLC ....F...... 810 750-6011
  Fenton *(G-5235)*
Stoney Creek Collection Inc ....E...... 616 363-4858
  Grand Rapids *(G-6893)*
Suburban Hockey LLC ....G...... 248 478-1600
  Farmington Hills *(G-5133)*
Wright Communications Inc ....F...... 248 585-3838
  Troy *(G-16700)*

PUBLISHERS: Periodicals, No Printing

Dale Corporation ....E...... 248 542-2400
  Madison Heights *(G-10227)*
Dynamic Color Publications ....G...... 248 553-3115
  Farmington Hills *(G-4976)*
Faith Alive Christn Resources ....E...... 800 333-8300
  Grand Rapids *(G-6397)*
Karle Pblctions Communications ....G...... 517 351-2791
  East Lansing *(G-4667)*
Nationwide Network Inc ....E...... 989 793-0123
  Saginaw *(G-14103)*
Opensystems Publishing LLC ....F...... 586 415-6500
  Saint Clair Shores *(G-14266)*
Pressure Releases Corporation ....F...... 616 531-8116
  Grand Rapids *(G-6770)*
Your Home Town USA Inc ....E...... 517 529-9421
  Clarklake *(G-2902)*

PUBLISHERS: Shopping News

Buyers Guide ....F...... 616 897-9251
  Lowell *(G-10025)*
Buyers Guide ....F...... 231 722-3784
  Muskegon *(G-11287)*
Flashes Shoppers Guide & News ....G...... 517 663-2361
  Charlotte *(G-2649)*
Herald Bi-County Inc ....G...... 517 448-2201
  Hudson *(G-8129)*
Hi-Lites Graphic Inc ....E...... 231 924-0630
  Fremont *(G-5775)*
Oceanas Herald-Journal Inc ....F...... 231 873-5602
  Hart *(G-7378)*
Pgi Holdings Inc ....G...... 231 937-4740
  Big Rapids *(G-1641)*
Presque Isle Newspapers Inc ....F...... 989 734-2105
  Rogers City *(G-13621)*
Salesman Inc ....F...... 517 563-8860
  Concord *(G-3524)*
Thumb Blanket ....G...... 989 269-9918
  Bad Axe *(G-1073)*
Vanguard Publications Inc ....G...... 517 336-1600
  Okemos *(G-12140)*
Vineyard Press Inc ....F...... 269 657-5080
  Paw Paw *(G-12416)*

PUBLISHERS: Technical Manuals

Technical Illustration Corp....................F....... 313 982-9660
Canton *(G-2432)*

PUBLISHERS: Technical Manuals & Papers

E D P Technical Services Inc.................G....... 734 591-9176
Livonia *(G-9718)*
Helm Incorporated..................................D....... 734 468-3700
Plymouth *(G-12637)*
SAE International....................................E....... 248 273-2455
Troy *(G-16589)*
Tweddle Group Inc..................................C....... 586 307-3700
Clinton Township *(G-3252)*

PUBLISHERS: Telephone & Other Directory

Great Lakes Publishing Inc....................G....... 517 647-4444
Portland *(G-13062)*
Little Blue Book Inc................................F....... 313 469-0052
Grosse Pointe Woods *(G-7206)*
Review Directories Inc...........................F....... 231 347-8606
Petoskey *(G-12472)*
Total Local Acquisitions LLC.................G....... 517 663-2405
Eaton Rapids *(G-4735)*

PUBLISHERS: Textbooks, No Printing

Cooper Publishing Group LLC...............G....... 231 933-9958
Traverse City *(G-15946)*
Hayden - McNeil LLC.............................E....... 734 455-7900
Plymouth *(G-12635)*
Next Level Media Inc...............................G....... 248 762-7043
Southfield *(G-14991)*

PUBLISHERS: Trade journals, No Printing

American Journal Hlth Prom Inc...........G....... 248 682-0707
Troy *(G-16196)*
BNP Media Inc..C....... 248 362-3700
Troy *(G-16242)*
Dental Consultants Inc...........................E....... 734 663-6777
Ann Arbor *(G-415)*
Timothy J Tade Inc..................................G....... 248 552-8583
Troy *(G-16644)*

PUBLISHING & BROADCASTING: Internet Only

Black Cobra Financial Svcs LLC...........G....... 248 298-9368
Bloomfield Hills *(G-1751)*
Bramin Enterprises.................................G....... 313 960-1528
Detroit *(G-3913)*
Curvy LLC..G....... 917 960-3774
Northville *(G-11685)*
Digital Success Network.........................E....... 517 244-0771
Mason *(G-10636)*
Direct Aim Media LLC.............................E....... 800 817-7101
Grand Rapids *(G-6353)*
Fusion Design Group Ltd........................G....... 269 469-8226
New Buffalo *(G-11514)*
Hmg Agency...F....... 989 443-3819
Saginaw *(G-14059)*
Konnections Blog....................................G....... 888 921-1114
Detroit *(G-4181)*
Tapoos LLC..G....... 619 319-4872
Taylor *(G-15776)*
Weyv Inc...F....... 248 614-2400
Troy *(G-16690)*
Zenwolf Technologies Group.................E....... 517 618-2000
Howell *(G-8124)*

PUBLISHING & PRINTING: Art Copy

Campub Inc...F....... 517 368-0365
Camden *(G-2338)*

PUBLISHING & PRINTING: Book Music

Pull Our Own Weight...............................G....... 313 686-4685
Detroit *(G-4316)*
Sheptime Music.......................................F....... 586 806-9058
Warren *(G-17238)*

PUBLISHING & PRINTING: Books

Christian Schools Intl..............................E....... 616 957-1070
Grand Rapids *(G-6275)*
Creative Characters Inc..........................G....... 231 544-6084
Central Lake *(G-2589)*
Diocese of Lansing..................................F....... 517 484-4449
Lansing *(G-9361)*
Evia Learning Inc.....................................G....... 616 393-8803
Holland *(G-7628)*
Faith Alive Christn Resources...............E....... 800 333-8300
Grand Rapids *(G-6397)*
Iris Design & Print Inc.............................G....... 313 277-0505
Dearborn *(G-3727)*
MPS Lansing Inc......................................A....... 517 323-9000
Lansing *(G-9248)*
NA Publishing Inc....................................E....... 734 302-6500
Saline *(G-14405)*

PUBLISHING & PRINTING: Comic Books

Pathway Publishing Corporation...........G....... 269 521-3025
Bloomingdale *(G-1813)*
Wallace Studios LLC...............................G....... 248 917-2459
Southfield *(G-15065)*

PUBLISHING & PRINTING: Directories, NEC

Elm International Inc...............................G....... 517 332-4900
Okemos *(G-12122)*
Ethnicemedia LLC....................................G....... 248 762-8904
Troy *(G-16352)*
EZ Vent LLC..G....... 616 874-2787
Rockford *(G-13568)*

PUBLISHING & PRINTING: Directories, Telephone

Ludington Daily News Inc.......................D....... 231 845-5181
Ludington *(G-10069)*
Npi Wireless...E....... 231 922-9273
Traverse City *(G-16053)*

PUBLISHING & PRINTING: Guides

J-Ad Graphics Inc....................................D....... 800 870-7085
Hastings *(G-7416)*
J-Ad Graphics Inc....................................G....... 269 945-9554
Marshall *(G-10573)*
J-Ad Graphics Inc....................................G....... 517 543-4041
Charlotte *(G-2656)*

PUBLISHING & PRINTING: Magazines: publishing & printing

Adjunct Advocate Corporation...............G....... 734 930-6854
Ann Arbor *(G-344)*
Ambassador Magazine............................G....... 313 965-6789
Detroit *(G-3864)*
Arena Publishing Co Inc.........................G....... 586 296-5369
Fraser *(G-5621)*
Big Money Magazine...............................G....... 810 655-0621
Swartz Creek *(G-15662)*
Bowman Enterprises Inc........................G....... 269 720-1946
Portage *(G-12987)*
Chas Levy Circulating Co.......................G....... 231 779-8940
Cadillac *(G-2241)*
Cte Publishing LLC.................................G....... 313 338-4335
Detroit *(G-3956)*
Faith Publishing Service.........................E....... 517 853-7600
Lansing *(G-9228)*
Greater Lansing Bus Monthly................G....... 517 203-0123
Lansing *(G-9376)*
Halloween Events....................................G....... 248 332-7884
Troy *(G-16389)*
Harbor House Publishers Inc.................F....... 231 582-2814
Boyne City *(G-1821)*
K and A Publishing Co LLC....................G....... 734 743-1541
Detroit *(G-4168)*
Kissman Consulting LLC........................G....... 517 256-1077
Okemos *(G-12128)*
Mary Pantely Associates........................G....... 248 723-8771
Rochester *(G-13333)*
Metra Inc...G....... 248 543-3500
Hazel Park *(G-7443)*
Michigan Movie Magazine LLC..............G....... 734 726-5299
Dexter *(G-4499)*
Planning & Zoning Center Inc................G....... 517 886-0555
Lansing *(G-9258)*
Sway Magazine Publishing....................G....... 517 394-4295
Lansing *(G-9428)*
Vanguard Publications Inc......................G....... 517 336-1600
Okemos *(G-12140)*
Village Shop Inc.......................................D....... 231 946-3712
Traverse City *(G-16138)*
Womens Lifestyle Inc..............................G....... 616 458-2121
Grand Rapids *(G-7001)*

PUBLISHING & PRINTING: Newsletters, Business Svc

Diocesan Publications.............................E....... 616 878-5200
Byron Center *(G-2187)*
Eiklae Products..G....... 734 671-0752
Grosse Ile *(G-7172)*
Forsons Inc...G....... 517 787-4562
Jackson *(G-8450)*

PUBLISHING & PRINTING: Newspapers

21st Century Newspapers Inc................C....... 586 469-4510
Clinton Township *(G-3026)*
21st Century Newspapers Inc................D....... 810 664-0811
Lapeer *(G-9439)*
21st Century Newspapers Inc................D....... 586 469-4510
Pontiac *(G-12797)*
Arab American News Inc.........................G....... 313 582-4888
Dearborn *(G-3678)*
Board For Student Publications.............B....... 734 418-4115
Ann Arbor *(G-385)*
Boyne City Gazette..................................G....... 231 582-2799
Boyne City *(G-1817)*
Bulletin Moon...G....... 734 453-9985
Plymouth *(G-12592)*
Bulletin of Concerned Asi........................G....... 231 228-7116
Cedar *(G-2539)*
Business News...G....... 231 929-7919
Traverse City *(G-15925)*
Central Michigan University...................G....... 989 774-3493
Mount Pleasant *(G-11186)*
Chaldean News LLC................................F....... 248 996-8360
Bingham Farms *(G-1650)*
Clare County Cleaver Inc........................G....... 989 539-7496
Harrison *(G-7310)*
Community Marketing Group LLC.........G....... 810 966-9982
Port Huron *(G-12909)*
Community Shoppers Guide Inc............G....... 269 694-9431
Otsego *(G-12235)*
Coopersville Observer Inc......................G....... 616 997-5049
Coopersville *(G-3554)*
Crain Communications Inc.....................B....... 313 446-6000
Detroit *(G-3950)*
Current...G....... 906 563-5212
Norway *(G-11816)*
Daily Bill..G....... 989 631-2068
Midland *(G-10828)*
Daily Brews Gourmet Coffe....................G....... 269 792-2739
Wayland *(G-17403)*
Daily Contracts LLC................................G....... 734 676-0903
Grosse Ile *(G-7169)*
Daily De-Lish..G....... 616 450-9562
Ada *(G-12)*
Daily Fantasy King..................................G....... 734 238-2622
Southgate *(G-15076)*
Daily Gardener LLC.................................G....... 734 754-6527
Ann Arbor *(G-411)*
Daily Oakland Press................................B....... 248 332-8181
Pontiac *(G-12813)*
Daily Recycling of Michigan...................G....... 734 654-9800
Carleton *(G-2453)*
Deadline Detroit.......................................G....... 248 219-5985
Detroit *(G-3964)*
Detroit Legal News Pubg LLC................E....... 248 577-6100
Troy *(G-16314)*
Detroit News Inc......................................B....... 313 222-2300
Detroit *(G-3991)*
Detroit News Inc......................................G....... 313 222-6400
Sterling Heights *(G-15313)*
Detroit Newspaper Partnr LP.................A....... 313 222-6400
Detroit *(G-3995)*
Eager Beaver Clean & Store..................G....... 231 448-2476
Beaver Island *(G-1381)*
Eldon Publishing LLC.............................G....... 810 648-5282
Sandusky *(G-14433)*
Federated Publications Inc.....................C....... 269 962-5394
Battle Creek *(G-1186)*
Fine Tool Journal LLC............................G....... 269 463-8255
Watervliet *(G-17392)*
Forum and Link Inc..................................G....... 313 945-5465
Dearborn *(G-3713)*
Four Seasons Publishing Inc..................G....... 906 341-5200
Manistique *(G-10440)*
Gannett Co Inc...C....... 269 964-7161
Battle Creek *(G-1191)*
Gannett Stllite Info Ntwrk Inc................C....... 734 229-1150
Detroit *(G-4077)*
Gatehouse Media LLC............................F....... 517 265-5111
Adrian *(G-66)*

PRODUCT

Employee Codes: A=Over 500 employees, B=251-500
C=101-250, D=51-100, E=20-50, F=10-19, G=3-9
2020 Harris Michigan
Industrial Directory
1345

PUBLISHING & PRINTING: Newspapers

Gatehouse Media LLC ....E 269 651-5407
  Sturgis *(G-15604)*
General Media LLC ....E 586 541-0075
  Saint Clair Shores *(G-14254)*
Grand Rapids Legal News ....G 616 454-9293
  Grand Rapids *(G-6456)*
Great American Publishing Co ....E 616 887-9008
  Sparta *(G-15095)*
Great Lakes Post LLC ....G 248 941-1349
  Milford *(G-10965)*
Green Sheet ....G 517 548-2570
  Howell *(G-8045)*
Grosse Pointe News ....G 734 674-0131
  Canton *(G-2380)*
Hamp ....G 989 366-5341
  Houghton Lake *(G-7991)*
Herald Newspapers Company Inc ....C 269 345-3511
  Kalamazoo *(G-8764)*
Herald Newspapers Company Inc ....D 231 722-3161
  Muskegon *(G-11344)*
Herald Newspapers Company Inc ....D 616 222-5400
  Grand Rapids *(G-6506)*
Herald Newspapers Company Inc ....C 734 926-4510
  Ann Arbor *(G-489)*
Herald Newspapers Company Inc ....C 989 752-7171
  Flint *(G-5445)*
Herald Newspapers Company Inc ....C 517 787-2300
  Jackson *(G-8464)*
Herald Publishing Company LLC ....G 616 222-5400
  Grand Rapids *(G-6508)*
Herald Publishing Company LLC ....E 616 222-5400
  Walker *(G-16867)*
Heritage Newspapers ....G 586 783-0300
  Pontiac *(G-12834)*
Homer Index ....G 517 568-4646
  Homer *(G-7944)*
Igan Mich Publishing LLC ....G 248 877-4649
  West Bloomfield *(G-17481)*
Independent Newspapers Inc ....C 586 469-4510
  Mount Clemens *(G-11134)*
Indiana Newspapers LLC ....E 248 680-9905
  Troy *(G-16415)*
Iosco News Press Publishing Co ....F 989 362-3456
  East Tawas *(G-4689)*
Island Sun Times Inc ....F 810 230-1735
  Flint *(G-5450)*
J R C Inc ....F 810 648-4000
  Sandusky *(G-14436)*
J-Ad Graphics Inc ....D 800 870-7085
  Hastings *(G-7416)*
J-Ad Graphics Inc ....E 269 965-3955
  Battle Creek *(G-1202)*
Journal Register Company ....D 586 790-1600
  Mount Clemens *(G-11137)*
L D J Inc ....F 906 524-6194
  Lanse *(G-9198)*
Latino Press Inc ....G 313 361-3000
  Detroit *(G-4194)*
Leader Publications LLC ....D 269 683-2100
  Niles *(G-11623)*
Livonia Observer ....G 734 525-4657
  Livonia *(G-9815)*
Macdonald Publications Inc ....F 989 875-4151
  Ithaca *(G-8363)*
Macomb County Republican Party ....G 586 662-3703
  Sterling Heights *(G-15406)*
Mark Sikorski MD ....G 586 786-1800
  Macomb *(G-10139)*
McClatchy Newspapers Inc ....D 734 525-2224
  Livonia *(G-9830)*
Metro Times Inc ....E 313 961-4060
  Ferndale *(G-5301)*
Michigan Bingo Bugle ....G 616 784-9344
  Grand Rapids *(G-6668)*
Michigan Chronicle Pubg Co ....E 313 963-5522
  Detroit *(G-4240)*
Michigan Live Inc ....F 734 997-7090
  Ann Arbor *(G-555)*
Michigan Maps Inc ....G 231 264-6800
  Elk Rapids *(G-4779)*
Milliman Communications Inc ....G 517 327-8407
  Lansing *(G-9312)*
Mining Jrnl Bsness Offc-Dtrial ....E 906 228-2500
  Marquette *(G-10546)*
Mlive Com ....G 517 768-4984
  Jackson *(G-8533)*
Monroe Publishing Company ....D 734 242-1100
  Monroe *(G-11057)*
Moormann Printing Inc ....G 269 646-2101
  Marcellus *(G-10466)*
Moormann Printing Inc ....G 269 423-2411
  Decatur *(G-3805)*
Morning Star ....G 989 755-2660
  Saginaw *(G-14099)*
Morning Star Publishing Co ....F 989 463-6071
  Alma *(G-243)*
Morning Star Publishing Co ....C 989 779-6000
  Alma *(G-244)*
Morning Star Publishing Co ....C 989 779-6000
  Alma *(G-245)*
Morning Star Publishing Co ....F 989 732-5125
  Pontiac *(G-12851)*
Morris Communications Co LLC ....E 517 437-3253
  Hillsdale *(G-7532)*
Muslim Observer ....G 248 426-7777
  Farmington Hills *(G-5074)*
Ndex ....F 248 432-9000
  Farmington Hills *(G-5078)*
New Monitor ....G 248 439-1863
  Hazel Park *(G-7447)*
News One Inc ....F 231 798-4669
  Norton Shores *(G-11780)*
North Wind Student Newspaper ....E 906 227-2545
  Marquette *(G-10547)*
Northland Publishers Inc ....G 906 265-9927
  Iron River *(G-8318)*
Now Ogden News Pubg of Mich ....F 906 774-3708
  Iron Mountain *(G-8295)*
Npi Wireless ....E 231 922-9273
  Traverse City *(G-16053)*
Oakland Sail Inc ....E 248 370-4268
  Rochester *(G-13338)*
Ogden Newspapers Virginia LLC ....G 906 228-8920
  Marquette *(G-10549)*
Paxton Media Group LLC ....D 269 429-2400
  Saint Joseph *(G-14334)*
Pinconning Journal ....G 989 879-3811
  Pinconning *(G-12511)*
Qp Acquisition 2 Inc ....E 248 594-7432
  Southfield *(G-15006)*
Real Detroit Weekly LLC ....F 248 591-7325
  Ferndale *(G-5315)*
Reminder Shopping Guide Inc ....G 269 427-7474
  Bangor *(G-1094)*
Rockman & Sons Publishing LLC ....F 810 750-6011
  Fenton *(G-5235)*
Sault Tribe News ....F 906 632-6398
  Sault Sainte Marie *(G-14473)*
Silent Observer ....G 616 392-4443
  Holland *(G-7805)*
Silent Observer ....G 269 966-3550
  Battle Creek *(G-1248)*
Sun Daily ....G 248 842-2925
  Orchard Lake *(G-12170)*
Three Rivers Commercial News ....E 269 279-7488
  Three Rivers *(G-15880)*
Times Herald Company ....F 810 985-7171
  Port Huron *(G-12971)*
Univesity Michigan-Dearborn ....F 313 593-5428
  Dearborn *(G-3767)*
USA Today Advertising ....G 248 680-6530
  Troy *(G-16668)*
W News ....G 231 946-4446
  Traverse City *(G-16141)*
W Vbh ....G 269 927-1527
  Benton Harbor *(G-1563)*
Wall Street Journal Gate A 20 ....G 734 941-4139
  Detroit *(G-4435)*
Washtenaw Voice ....G 734 677-5405
  Ann Arbor *(G-697)*
White Lake Beacon Inc ....G 231 894-5356
  Whitehall *(G-17680)*
Wochen-Post ....E 248 641-9944
  Warren *(G-17295)*
Yale Expositor ....G 810 387-2300
  Yale *(G-18048)*
Z & A News ....G 231 747-6232
  Muskegon *(G-11456)*

PUBLISHING & PRINTING: Pamphlets

Rbc Ministries ....C 616 942-6770
  Grand Rapids *(G-6812)*

PUBLISHING & PRINTING: Posters

Star Design Metro Detroit LLC ....E 734 740-0189
  Livonia *(G-9944)*

PUBLISHING & PRINTING: Shopping News

Advance BCI Inc ....D 616 669-1366
  Grand Rapids *(G-6144)*
Flashes Publishers Inc ....C 269 673-2141
  Allegan *(G-162)*
G L Nelson Inc ....G 630 682-5958
  Indian River *(G-8218)*
Great Northern Publishing Inc ....E 810 648-4000
  Sandusky *(G-14434)*
J-Ad Graphics Inc ....E 269 965-3955
  Battle Creek *(G-1202)*
Macdonald Publications Inc ....F 989 875-4151
  Ithaca *(G-8363)*
Morning Star Publishing Co ....G 989 779-6000
  Alma *(G-245)*
Morris Communications Corp ....C 269 673-2141
  Allegan *(G-177)*
S G Publications Inc ....F 517 676-5100
  Mason *(G-10653)*
Saginaw Valley Shopper Inc ....G 989 842-3164
  Breckenridge *(G-1846)*

PUBLISHING & PRINTING: Textbooks

Remnant Publications Inc ....E 517 279-1304
  Coldwater *(G-3327)*
Zonya Health International ....G 517 467-6995
  Onsted *(G-12157)*

PUBLISHING & PRINTING: Trade Journals

Engravers Journal ....G 810 229-5725
  Brighton *(G-1919)*

PUBLISHING & PRINTING: Yearbooks

Walsworth Publishing Co Inc ....B 269 428-2054
  Saint Joseph *(G-14350)*

PULLEYS: Metal

Motion Systems Incorporated ....F 586 774-5666
  Warren *(G-17160)*

PULLEYS: Power Transmission

Auburn Hills Manufacturing Inc ....C 313 758-2000
  Auburn Hills *(G-782)*
Engineered Machined Pdts Inc ....B 906 786-8404
  Escanaba *(G-4826)*

PULP MILLS

Fibrek Inc ....C 906 864-9125
  Menominee *(G-10733)*
Fibrek US Inc ....G 906 864-9125
  Menominee *(G-10735)*
Forest Blake Products Inc ....G 231 879-3913
  Fife Lake *(G-5340)*
Forest Corullo Products Corp ....E 906 667-0275
  Bessemer *(G-1605)*
Friedland Industries Inc ....E 517 482-3000
  Lansing *(G-9232)*
General Mill Supply Company ....E 248 668-0800
  Wixom *(G-17816)*
Great Lakes Paper Stock Corp ....D 586 779-1310
  Roseville *(G-13811)*
Long Lake Forest Products ....G 989 239-6527
  Harrison *(G-7314)*
Louis Padnos Iron and Metal Co ....E 616 459-4208
  Grand Rapids *(G-6631)*
Ronald Bradley ....G 989 422-5609
  Houghton Lake *(G-7996)*
V & M Corporation ....E 248 541-4020
  Royal Oak *(G-13980)*
Verso Paper Holding LLC ....F 906 779-3200
  Quinnesec *(G-13104)*

PULP MILLS: Chemical & Semichemical Processing

Fibrek Recycling US Inc ....C 906 863-8137
  Menominee *(G-10734)*
Upcycle Polymers LLC ....G 248 446-8750
  Howell *(G-8120)*

PULP MILLS: Mechanical & Recycling Processing

Gfl Envronmental Real Property ....E 888 877-4996
  Southfield *(G-14919)*

PRODUCT SECTION

Gfl Envronmental Real Property ....G....... 586 774-1360
  Warren *(G-17057)*
Kevin Butzin Recycling Inc ....G....... 734 587-3710
  Willis *(G-17744)*
Midland Cmpnding Cnsulting Inc ....G....... 989 495-9367
  Midland *(G-10888)*
Recycling Rizzo Services LLC ....D....... 248 541-4020
  Royal Oak *(G-13964)*
United Fr Survl St Joseph Recy ....E....... 269 983-3820
  Saint Joseph *(G-14347)*

PULVERIZED EARTH

D J McQuestion & Sons Inc ....F....... 231 768-4403
  Leroy *(G-9530)*

PUMICE: Abrasives

Acme Holding Company ....E....... 586 759-3332
  Warren *(G-16917)*

PUMP JACKS & OTHER PUMPING EQPT: Indl

Pump Solutions Group ....E....... 616 241-1611
  Grand Rapids *(G-6797)*

PUMPS

AA Anderson & Co Inc ....G....... 734 432-9800
  Livonia *(G-9622)*
Backos Engineering Co ....G....... 734 513-0020
  Livonia *(G-9659)*
Benecor Inc ....F....... 248 437-4437
  Fenton *(G-5188)*
Cpj Company Inc ....E....... 616 784-6355
  Comstock Park *(G-3472)*
Emp Advanced Development LLC ....D....... 906 789-7497
  Escanaba *(G-4824)*
Engineered Machined Pdts Inc ....E....... 906 789-7497
  Escanaba *(G-4827)*
Engineered Machined Pdts Inc ....B....... 906 786-8404
  Escanaba *(G-4826)*
Flowserve US Inc ....G....... 989 496-3897
  Midland *(G-10862)*
Ford Motor Company ....A....... 734 484-8000
  Ypsilanti *(G-18074)*
Gast Manufacturing Inc ....B....... 269 926-6171
  Benton Harbor *(G-1503)*
General Motors LLC ....B....... 989 894-7210
  Bay City *(G-1315)*
H & R Industries Inc ....F....... 616 247-1165
  Grand Rapids *(G-6487)*
Independent Mfg Solutions Corp ....E....... 248 960-3550
  Wixom *(G-17833)*
Ingersoll-Rand Company ....E....... 734 525-6030
  Livonia *(G-9783)*
Jacksons Industrial Mfg ....F....... 616 531-1820
  Wyoming *(G-18012)*
Kerr Pump and Supply Inc ....E....... 248 543-3880
  Oak Park *(G-12076)*
Kristus Inc ....F....... 269 321-3330
  Scotts *(G-14505)*
Ksb Dubric Inc ....E....... 616 784-6355
  Comstock Park *(G-3492)*
M P Pumps Inc ....D....... 586 293-8240
  Fraser *(G-5688)*
Melling Tool Co ....B....... 517 787-8172
  Jackson *(G-8514)*
Nortek Air Solutions LLC ....D....... 616 738-7148
  Holland *(G-7759)*
North America Fuel Systems R ....C....... 616 541-1100
  Grand Rapids *(G-6719)*
Plasma-Tec Inc ....E....... 616 455-2593
  Wayland *(G-17409)*
Pump Solutions Group ....B....... 616 241-1611
  Grand Rapids *(G-6796)*
Ramparts LLC ....C....... 616 656-2250
  Kentwood *(G-9028)*
Sales Driven Ltd Liability Co ....E....... 269 254-8497
  Kalamazoo *(G-8881)*
Sames Kremlin Inc ....F....... 734 979-0100
  Plymouth *(G-12748)*
Sloan Transportation Pdts Inc ....D....... 616 395-5600
  Holland *(G-7806)*
Tramec Sloan LLC ....D....... 616 395-5600
  Holland *(G-7833)*
Vogel Engineering Inc ....G....... 231 821-2125
  Holton *(G-7935)*
Walbro LLC ....C....... 989 872-2131
  Cass City *(G-2524)*
Water Master Inc ....G....... 313 255-3930
  Canton *(G-2443)*

PUMPS & PARTS: Indl

Becktold Enterprises Inc ....G....... 269 349-3656
  Kalamazoo *(G-8694)*
Clyde Union (holdings) Inc ....B....... 269 966-4600
  Battle Creek *(G-1168)*
Fluid Systems Engineering Inc ....E....... 586 790-8880
  Clinton Township *(G-3123)*
Global Pump Company LLC ....G....... 810 653-4828
  Davison *(G-3652)*
Hydra-Tech Inc ....G....... 586 232-4479
  Macomb *(G-10130)*
Jetech Inc ....E....... 269 965-6311
  Battle Creek *(G-1204)*
K and K Machine Tools Inc ....G....... 586 463-1177
  Clinton Township *(G-3152)*
Neptune Chemical Pump Company ....C....... 215 699-8700
  Grand Rapids *(G-6714)*
Process Systems Inc ....D....... 586 757-5711
  Warren *(G-17198)*
QEd Envmtl Systems Inc ....D....... 734 995-2547
  Dexter *(G-4506)*
Thin Line Pump ....G....... 231 258-2692
  Kalkaska *(G-8963)*

PUMPS & PUMPING EQPT REPAIR SVCS

Arrow Motor & Pump Inc ....E....... 734 285-7860
  Wyandotte *(G-17946)*
Core Electric Company Inc ....F....... 313 382-7140
  Melvindale *(G-10694)*
Douglas Corp ....F....... 517 767-4112
  Tekonsha *(G-15818)*
Global Pump Company LLC ....G....... 810 653-4828
  Davison *(G-3652)*
Kennedy Industries Inc ....D....... 248 684-1200
  Wixom *(G-17840)*
North End Electric Company ....G....... 248 398-8187
  Royal Oak *(G-13954)*
Phillips Service Inds Inc ....F....... 734 853-5000
  Plymouth *(G-12714)*
Process Systems Inc ....D....... 586 757-5711
  Warren *(G-17198)*
PSI Hydraulics ....C....... 734 261-4160
  Plymouth *(G-12725)*
PSI Repair Services Inc ....C....... 734 853-5000
  Livonia *(G-9899)*

PUMPS & PUMPING EQPT WHOLESALERS

AA Anderson & Co Inc ....G....... 734 432-9800
  Livonia *(G-9622)*
Arrow Motor & Pump Inc ....E....... 734 285-7860
  Wyandotte *(G-17946)*
Clyde Union (holdings) Inc ....B....... 269 966-4600
  Battle Creek *(G-1168)*
Commercial Welding Company Inc ....G....... 269 782-5252
  Dowagiac *(G-4536)*
Global Pump Company LLC ....G....... 810 653-4828
  Davison *(G-3652)*
North End Electric Company ....G....... 248 398-8187
  Royal Oak *(G-13954)*
Process Systems Inc ....D....... 586 757-5711
  Warren *(G-17198)*
Vic Bond Sales Inc ....G....... 517 548-0107
  Howell *(G-8121)*

PUMPS, HEAT: Electric

Nortek Air Solutions LLC ....D....... 616 738-7148
  Holland *(G-7759)*

PUMPS: Domestic, Water Or Sump

Sales Driven Services LLC ....G....... 586 854-9494
  Rochester *(G-13350)*
Shellback Manufacturing Co ....G....... 248 544-4600
  Hazel Park *(G-7455)*
Vent-Rite Valve Corp ....E....... 269 925-8812
  Benton Harbor *(G-1560)*
Water Department ....E....... 313 943-2307
  Dearborn *(G-3773)*

PUMPS: Fluid Power

Ace Controls Inc ....C....... 248 476-0213
  Farmington Hills *(G-4919)*
Armstrong Fluid Handling Inc ....C....... 269 279-3600
  Three Rivers *(G-15856)*
Kennedy Industries Inc ....D....... 248 684-1200
  Wixom *(G-17840)*
Oilgear Company ....D....... 231 929-1660
  Traverse City *(G-16055)*

RACE CAR OWNERS

Parker-Hannifin Corporation ....A....... 269 384-3400
  Kalamazoo *(G-8844)*

PUMPS: Gasoline, Measuring Or Dispensing

Bennett Commercial Pump Co ....D....... 231 798-1310
  Norton Shores *(G-11808)*
Bpc Acquisition Company ....D....... 231 798-1310
  Norton Shores *(G-11809)*

PUMPS: Hydraulic Power Transfer

Bucher Hydraulics Inc ....C....... 616 458-1306
  Grand Rapids *(G-6238)*
Bucher Hydraulics Inc ....E....... 231 652-2773
  Newaygo *(G-11564)*
Eaton Aerospace LLC ....B....... 616 949-1090
  Grand Rapids *(G-6368)*
Hydraulic Systems Inc ....E....... 517 787-7818
  Jackson *(G-8467)*

PUMPS: Measuring & Dispensing

Accurate Gauge & Mfg Inc ....D....... 248 853-2400
  Rochester Hills *(G-13362)*
Atlas Copco Ias LLC ....D....... 248 377-9722
  Auburn Hills *(G-781)*
Dispense Technologies LLC ....G....... 248 486-6244
  Brighton *(G-1911)*
Neptune Chemical Pump Company ....C....... 215 699-8700
  Grand Rapids *(G-6714)*
Nordson Corporation ....D....... 734 459-8600
  Wixom *(G-17866)*

PUMPS: Vacuum, Exc Laboratory

Gast Manufacturing Inc ....B....... 269 926-6171
  Benton Harbor *(G-1503)*
Gast Manufacturing Inc ....B....... 269 926-6171
  Benton Harbor *(G-1504)*

PUNCHES: Forming & Stamping

Air-Hydraulics Inc ....F....... 517 787-9444
  Jackson *(G-8377)*
Commercial Mfg & Assembly Inc ....E....... 616 847-9980
  Grand Haven *(G-6005)*
M Curry Corporation ....E....... 989 777-7950
  Saginaw *(G-14080)*
Master Precision Tool Corp ....F....... 586 739-3240
  Sterling Heights *(G-15412)*
Metal Punch Corporation ....E....... 231 775-8391
  Cadillac *(G-2264)*

PUPPETS & MARIONETTES

Mannetron ....E....... 269 962-3475
  Battle Creek *(G-1225)*

PURIFICATION & DUST COLLECTION EQPT

Airhug LLC ....G....... 734 262-0431
  Canton *(G-2346)*
Custom Service & Design Inc ....E....... 248 340-9005
  Auburn Hills *(G-833)*
Depierre Industries Inc ....E....... 517 263-5781
  Adrian *(G-59)*
New Way Air Solution Company ....G....... 248 676-9418
  Milford *(G-10976)*
Paul Horn and Associates ....G....... 248 682-8490
  Waterford *(G-17365)*

PURSES: Women's

Sandusky Concrete & Supply ....G....... 810 648-2627
  Sandusky *(G-14442)*

QUILTING SVC

Quilting By Cheryl ....G....... 616 669-5636
  Jenison *(G-8639)*

QUILTING SVC & SPLYS, FOR THE TRADE

All About Quilting and Design ....G....... 269 471-7359
  Berrien Springs *(G-1591)*

RACE CAR OWNERS

Roush Enterprises Inc ....C....... 734 805-4400
  Farmington *(G-4909)*

RACE TRACK OPERATION

RACE TRACK OPERATION
Sports Resorts International..............D....... 989 725-8354
  Owosso (G-12318)

RACETRACKS
Roush Industries Inc..............E....... 734 779-7016
  Livonia (G-9912)

RACEWAYS
Austin Company..............F....... 269 329-1181
  Portage (G-12982)
Merritt Raceway LLC..............G....... 231 590-4431
  Mancelona (G-10396)

RACKS: Display
Associated Rack Corporation..............G....... 616 554-6004
  Grand Rapids (G-6187)
Fmmb LLC..............E....... 313 372-7420
  Detroit (G-4065)
J H P Inc..............G....... 248 588-0110
  Madison Heights (G-10280)
National Intgrated Systems Inc..............F....... 734 927-3030
  Wixom (G-17861)
Royal Design & Manufacturing..............D....... 248 588-0110
  Madison Heights (G-10346)
Tarpon Industries Inc..............C....... 810 364-7421
  Marysville (G-10620)

RACKS: Garment, Exc Wood
L & S Products LLC..............G....... 517 238-4645
  Coldwater (G-3313)

RACKS: Pallet, Exc Wood
F & F Industries Inc..............E....... 313 278-7600
  Taylor (G-15718)
F F Industries..............G....... 313 291-7600
  Taylor (G-15719)
Sfi Acquisition Inc..............E....... 248 471-1500
  Farmington Hills (G-5122)

RACKS: Trash, Metal Rack
Returnable Packaging Corp..............F....... 586 206-8050
  Clinton Township (G-3210)
Saline Manufacturing Inc..............F....... 586 294-4701
  Roseville (G-13865)

RADAR SYSTEMS & EQPT
Micromet Corp..............G....... 231 885-1047
  Bloomfield Hills (G-1783)
Valeo Radar Systems Inc..............E....... 248 340-3126
  Auburn Hills (G-1044)

RADIATORS: Stationary Engine
Dewitts Radiator LLC..............F....... 517 548-0600
  Howell (G-8029)

RADIO & TELEVISION COMMUNICATIONS EQUIPMENT
Bob Allison Enterprises..............G....... 248 540-8467
  Bloomfield Hills (G-1752)
C & A Wholesale Inc..............G....... 248 302-3555
  Detroit (G-3923)
Cco Holdings LLC..............G....... 517 583-4125
  Tekonsha (G-15817)
Cco Holdings LLC..............G....... 616 244-2071
  Belding (G-1406)
Cco Holdings LLC..............G....... 616 384-2060
  Coopersville (G-3551)
Cco Holdings LLC..............G....... 517 639-1060
  Quincy (G-13091)
Cco Holdings LLC..............G....... 734 244-8028
  Monroe (G-11024)
Cco Holdings LLC..............G....... 734 868-5044
  Ida (G-8193)
Cco Holdings LLC..............G....... 810 270-1002
  North Branch (G-11657)
Cco Holdings LLC..............G....... 810 375-7020
  Dryden (G-4568)
Cco Holdings LLC..............G....... 810 545-4020
  Columbiaville (G-3376)
Cco Holdings LLC..............G....... 906 285-6497
  Ironwood (G-8325)
Cco Holdings LLC..............G....... 906 239-3763
  Iron Mountain (G-8279)
Cco Holdings LLC..............G....... 906 346-1000
  Gwinn (G-7218)
Cco Holdings LLC..............G....... 231 720-0688
  Muskegon (G-11291)
Cco Holdings LLC..............G....... 248 494-4550
  Auburn Hills (G-811)
Cco Holdings LLC..............G....... 269 202-3286
  Coloma (G-3355)
Cco Holdings LLC..............G....... 269 216-6680
  Kalamazoo (G-8704)
Cco Holdings LLC..............G....... 269 432-0052
  Colon (G-3370)
Cco Holdings LLC..............G....... 269 464-3454
  White Pigeon (G-17646)
Cco Holdings LLC..............G....... 989 328-4187
  Sidney (G-14738)
Cco Holdings LLC..............G....... 989 567-0151
  Shepherd (G-14726)
Cco Holdings LLC..............G....... 989 863-4023
  Reese (G-13229)
Cco Holdings LLC..............G....... 989 853-2008
  Muir (G-11237)
Emag Technologies Inc..............F....... 734 996-3624
  Ann Arbor (G-442)
Information Stn Specialists..............F....... 616 772-2300
  Zeeland (G-18159)
L3 Technologies Inc..............A....... 231 724-2151
  Muskegon (G-11361)
Lor Manufacturing Co Inc..............G....... 866 644-8622
  Weidman (G-17458)
Mobimogul Inc..............G....... 313 575-2795
  Southfield (G-14986)
Moody Bible Inst of Chicago..............G....... 616 772-7300
  Zeeland (G-18167)
Nht Sales Inc..............G....... 248 623-6114
  Auburn Hills (G-956)
Sound Productions Entrmt..............E....... 989 386-2221
  Clare (G-2889)
Spectrum Wireless (usa) Inc..............F....... 586 693-7525
  Saint Clair Shores (G-14270)

RADIO & TELEVISION RECEIVER INSTALLATION SVCS
Satellite Tracking Systems..............G....... 248 627-3334
  Ortonville (G-12202)

RADIO & TELEVISION REPAIR
Bluewater Tech Group Inc..............G....... 231 885-2600
  Mesick (G-10767)
Bluewater Tech Group Inc..............F....... 616 656-9380
  Grand Rapids (G-6233)

RADIO BROADCASTING & COMMUNICATIONS EQPT
Washtenaw Communications Inc..............G....... 734 662-7138
  Ann Arbor (G-696)

RADIO BROADCASTING STATIONS
Bob Allison Enterprises..............G....... 248 540-8467
  Bloomfield Hills (G-1752)

RADIO PRODUCERS
Childrens Bible Hour Inc..............F....... 616 647-4500
  Grand Rapids (G-6274)
Rbc Ministries..............C....... 616 942-6770
  Grand Rapids (G-6812)

RADIO RECEIVER NETWORKS
Startech-Solutions LLC..............G....... 248 419-0650
  West Bloomfield (G-17499)

RADIO REPAIR & INSTALLATION SVCS
Intaglio LLC..............F....... 616 243-3300
  Grand Rapids (G-6539)
Washtenaw Communications Inc..............G....... 734 662-7138
  Ann Arbor (G-696)

RADIO, TELEVISION & CONSUMER ELECTRONICS STORES: Eqpt, NEC
Stratos Technologies Inc..............G....... 248 808-2117
  Ann Arbor (G-649)
Uv Partners Inc..............G....... 616 204-5416
  Livonia (G-9984)

RADIO, TELEVISION & CONSUMER ELECTRONICS STORES: TV Sets
Northland..............G....... 231 775-3101
  Cadillac (G-2268)

RADIO, TV & CONSUMER ELEC STORES: Automotive Sound Eqpt
Car Audio Outlet LLC..............G....... 810 686-3300
  Clio (G-3266)

RADIO, TV & CONSUMER ELEC STORES: High Fidelity Stereo Eqpt
Rebeats..............F....... 989 463-4757
  Alma (G-248)

RADIO, TV & CONSUMER ELEC STORES: Radios, Receiver Type
Chrouch Communications Inc..............G....... 231 972-0339
  Mecosta (G-10687)

RADIO, TV/CONSUMER ELEC STORES: Antennas, Satellite Dish
Satellite Tracking Systems..............G....... 248 627-3334
  Ortonville (G-12202)

RAIL & STRUCTURAL SHAPES: Aluminum rail & structural shapes
Brooks & Perkins Inc..............D....... 231 775-2229
  Cadillac (G-2234)

RAILINGS: Prefabricated, Metal
Aquarius Recreational Products..............G....... 586 469-4600
  Harrison Township (G-7320)
San Marino Iron Company..............G....... 313 526-9255
  Warren (G-17228)

RAILROAD CAR RENTING & LEASING SVCS
Andersons Inc..............G....... 989 642-5291
  Hemlock (G-7459)

RAILROAD CAR REPAIR SVCS
Escanaba and Lk Superior RR Co..............G....... 906 786-9399
  Escanaba (G-4828)

RAILROAD CARGO LOADING & UNLOADING SVCS
Gb Dynamics Inc..............E....... 313 400-3570
  Port Huron (G-12921)

RAILROAD CROSSINGS: Steel Or Iron
Crown Steel Rail Co..............G....... 248 593-7100
  West Bloomfield (G-17471)

RAILROAD EQPT
Amsted Rail Company Inc..............G....... 517 568-4161
  Homer (G-7936)
Harsco Corporation..............D....... 231 843-3431
  Ludington (G-10062)
Hj Manufacturing Inc..............F....... 906 233-1500
  Escanaba (G-4833)
Mitchell Equipment Corporation..............E....... 734 529-3400
  Dundee (G-4596)
Rescar Inc..............G....... 517 486-3130
  Blissfield (G-1724)
Trinity Equipment Co..............G....... 231 719-1813
  Muskegon (G-11441)

RAILROAD EQPT & SPLYS WHOLESALERS
Crown Steel Rail Co..............G....... 248 593-7100
  West Bloomfield (G-17471)
Hj Manufacturing Inc..............F....... 906 233-1500
  Escanaba (G-4833)

RAILROAD EQPT: Brakes, Air & Vacuum
Braetec Inc..............G....... 269 968-4711
  Battle Creek (G-1156)
Gorang Industries Inc..............G....... 248 651-9010
  Rochester (G-13322)

PRODUCT SECTION

RAILROAD EQPT: Cars & Eqpt, Dining
Arcosa Shoring Products Inc ....E 517 741-4300
  Union City (G-16731)
First Choice of Elkhart Inc ....G 269 483-2010
  White Pigeon (G-17648)
Floss Automotive Group ....G 734 773-2524
  Inkster (G-8227)
Trinity Industries Inc ....G 586 285-1692
  Fraser (G-5740)

RAILROAD EQPT: Cars, Rebuilt
Delta Tube & Fabricating Corp ....E 248 634-8267
  Holly (G-7874)

RAILROAD EQPT: Locomotives & Parts, Indl
S & S Parts LLC ....G 517 467-6511
  Onsted (G-12156)

RAILROAD EQPT: Street Cars & Eqpt
Peaker Services Inc ....D 248 437-4174
  Brighton (G-1976)

RAILROAD MAINTENANCE & REPAIR SVCS
Jackson Pandrol Inc ....B 231 843-3431
  Ludington (G-10068)

RAILROAD RELATED EQPT
Independent Machine Co Inc ....E 906 428-4524
  Escanaba (G-4836)
Jackson Pandrol Inc ....B 231 843-3431
  Ludington (G-10068)

RAILROADS: Long Haul
Straits Corporation ....F 989 684-5088
  Tawas City (G-15679)

RAILS: Steel Or Iron
Champlain Specialty Metals Inc ....E 269 926-7241
  Benton Harbor (G-1489)
Paich Railworks Inc ....G 734 397-2424
  Van Buren Twp (G-16778)

RAMPS: Prefabricated Metal
Alumiramp Inc ....F 517 639-5103
  Quincy (G-13088)
Inner Box Loading Systems Inc ....G 616 241-4330
  Grand Rapids (G-6536)
Tj Rampit Usa Inc ....E 517 278-9015
  Coldwater (G-3337)
Vets Access LLC ....G 810 639-2222
  Flushing (G-5544)

RAZORS, RAZOR BLADES
Art of Shaving - Fl LLC ....G 248 649-5872
  Troy (G-16219)
Edgewell Personal Care Company .....G 866 462-8669
  Taylor (G-15712)

REAL ESTATE AGENCIES & BROKERS
Developmental Services Inc ....G 313 653-1185
  Detroit (G-4006)

REAL ESTATE AGENCIES: Leasing & Rentals
Eggers Excavating LLC ....F 989 695-5205
  Freeland (G-5756)
Melix Services Inc ....G 248 387-9303
  Hamtramck (G-7244)
Michigan East Side Sales LLC ....G 989 354-6867
  Alpena (G-299)

REAL ESTATE AGENTS & MANAGERS
917 Chittock Street LLC ....F 866 945-0269
  Lansing (G-9331)
Gemini Plastics Inc ....C 989 658-8557
  Ubly (G-16716)
Great Lakes Publishing Inc ....G 517 647-4444
  Portland (G-13062)
Help-U-Sell RE Big Rapids ....F 231 796-3966
  Big Rapids (G-1634)
Marshalls Crossing ....G 810 639-4740
  Montrose (G-11104)

Trinity Holding Inc ....F 517 787-3100
  Jackson (G-8593)

REAL ESTATE INVESTMENT TRUSTS
Chain Industries Inc ....E 248 348-7722
  Wixom (G-17783)
Sun Communities Inc ....C 248 208-2500
  Southfield (G-15036)

REAL ESTATE LISTING SVCS
Miller Investment Company LLC ....G 231 933-3233
  Traverse City (G-16038)

REAL ESTATE OPERATORS, EXC DEVELOPERS: Commercial/Indl Bldg
Ace Vending Service Inc ....E 616 243-7983
  Grand Rapids (G-6135)
G & G Wood & Supply Inc ....F 586 293-0450
  Roseville (G-13805)
Honhart Mid-Nite Black Co ....E 248 588-1515
  Troy (G-16399)
Mirkwood Properties Inc ....G 586 727-3363
  Richmond (G-13266)
National Credit Corporation ....F 734 459-8100
  West Bloomfield (G-17491)
Vectech Pharmaceutical Cons ....F 248 478-5820
  Brighton (G-2005)

RECLAIMED RUBBER: Reworked By Manufacturing Process
Cg & D Group ....G 248 310-9166
  Farmington Hills (G-4960)
Green Polymeric Materials Inc ....E 313 933-7390
  Detroit (G-4102)

RECORD BLANKS: Phonographic
Archer Record Pressing Co ....G 313 365-9545
  Detroit (G-3875)

RECORDING & PLAYBACK HEADS: Magnetic
Wmc Lievense Company ....E 231 946-3800
  Traverse City (G-16148)

RECORDING TAPE: Video, Blank
Stans Affordable Videography ....G 734 671-2975
  Trenton (G-16158)

RECORDS & TAPES: Prerecorded
Summit Training Source Inc ....E 800 842-0466
  Grand Rapids (G-6897)

RECORDS OR TAPES: Masters
River City Studios Ltd ....E 616 456-1404
  Grand Rapids (G-6827)
Super Video Service Center ....G 248 358-4794
  Southfield (G-15037)

RECOVERY SVCS: Metal
Total MGT Reclamation Svcs LLC .....G 734 384-3500
  Taylor (G-15777)

RECREATIONAL SPORTING EQPT REPAIR SVCS
Riverfront Cycle Inc ....G 517 482-8585
  Lansing (G-9418)

RECREATIONAL VEHICLE DEALERS
Irish Boat Shop Inc ....E 231 547-9967
  Charlevoix (G-2619)
Stromberg-Carlson Products Inc ....F 231 947-8600
  Traverse City (G-16114)

RECREATIONAL VEHICLE PARTS & ACCESS STORES
Northland ....G 231 775-3101
  Cadillac (G-2268)

RECREATIONAL VEHICLE REPAIRS
Lumberjack Shack Inc ....G 810 724-7230
  Imlay City (G-8207)

RECREATIONAL VEHICLE: Wholesalers
Michigan East Side Sales LLC ....G 989 354-6867
  Alpena (G-299)

RECTIFIERS: Mercury Arc, Electrical
Optimystic Enterprises Inc ....G 269 695-7741
  Buchanan (G-2124)

RECYCLING: Paper
Anchor Recycling Inc ....G 810 984-5545
  Port Huron (G-12891)
Bpv LLC ....E 616 281-4502
  Byron Center (G-2180)
Custom Crushing & Recycle Inc ....G 616 249-3329
  Byron Center (G-2185)
Infinity Recycling LLC ....F 248 939-2563
  Clinton Township (G-3140)
Recycling Concepts W Mich Inc ....D 616 942-8888
  Grand Rapids (G-6815)
Ricks Custom Cycle LLP ....G 734 762-2077
  Garden City (G-5836)
Southast Berrien Cnty Landfill ....F 269 695-2500
  Niles (G-11646)

REELS: Cable, Metal
Zks Sales ....G 810 360-0682
  Brighton (G-2012)

REELS: Fiber, Textile, Made From Purchased Materials
Rokan Corp ....G 810 735-9170
  Linden (G-9595)

REFINERS & SMELTERS: Aluminum
Constellium Automotive USA LLC .....C 734 879-9700
  Van Buren Twp (G-16752)
Continental Aluminum LLC ....E 248 437-1001
  New Hudson (G-11534)
Real Alloy Recycling LLC ....C 517 279-9596
  Coldwater (G-3325)

REFINERS & SMELTERS: Copper
Materion Brush Inc ....F 586 443-4925
  Warren (G-17143)
PM Power Group Inc ....G 906 885-7100
  White Pine (G-17658)
Specialty Steel Treating Inc ....E 586 293-5355
  Fraser (G-5730)

REFINERS & SMELTERS: Copper, Secondary
White Pine Copper Refinery Inc ....G 906 885-7100
  White Pine (G-17659)

REFINERS & SMELTERS: Gold, Secondary
Johnson Matthey North Amer Inc ......G 734 946-9856
  Taylor (G-15731)

REFINERS & SMELTERS: Lead, Secondary
Mayer Metals Corporation ....G 248 742-0077
  Ferndale (G-5300)

REFINERS & SMELTERS: Nonferrous Metal
Allied Metals Corp ....E 248 680-2400
  Auburn Hills (G-765)
Alloying Surfaces Inc ....G 248 524-9200
  Troy (G-16191)
Aluminum Blanking Co Inc ....D 248 338-4422
  Pontiac (G-12802)
Astech Inc ....E 989 823-7211
  Vassar (G-16811)
Benteler Aluminium Systems ....E 616 396-6591
  Holland (G-7568)
Cannon-Muskegon Corporation ....C 231 755-1681
  Norton Shores (G-11744)
Colfran Industrial Sales Inc ....F 734 595-8920
  Romulus (G-13663)
Eutectic Engineering Co Inc ....E 313 892-2248
  Bloomfield Hills (G-1765)

REFINERS & SMELTERS: Nonferrous Metal

Fpt Schlafer .... E 313 925-8200
  Detroit *(G-4071)*
Franklin Iron & Metal Co Inc .... E 269 968-6111
  Battle Creek *(G-1190)*
Franklin Metal Trading Corp .... E 616 374-7171
  Lake Odessa *(G-9114)*
Friedland Industries Inc .... E 517 482-3000
  Lansing *(G-9232)*
Great Lakes Paper Stock Corp .... D 586 779-1310
  Roseville *(G-13811)*
Intern Metals and Energy .... G 248 765-7747
  Jackson *(G-8471)*
Lorbec Metals - Usa Ltd .... E 810 736-0961
  Flint *(G-5462)*
Louis Padnos Iron and Metal Co .... E 616 459-4208
  Grand Rapids *(G-6631)*
Louis Padnos Iron and Metal Co .... E 517 372-6600
  Lansing *(G-9309)*
Louis Padnos Iron and Metal Co .... G 616 452-6037
  Grand Rapids *(G-6632)*
Martin Bros Mill Fndry Sup Co .... E 269 927-1355
  Benton Harbor *(G-1525)*
Materion Brush Inc .... F 586 443-4925
  Warren *(G-17143)*
Metropolitan Alloys Corp .... E 313 366-4443
  Detroit *(G-4233)*
National Galvanizing LP .... A 734 243-1882
  Monroe *(G-11059)*
Oerlikon Metco (us) Inc .... E 248 288-0027
  Troy *(G-16533)*
Real Alloy Recycling LLC .... D 517 279-9596
  Coldwater *(G-3324)*
Revstone Industries LLC .... F 248 351-1000
  Troy *(G-16577)*
Rolled Alloys Inc .... D 800 521-0332
  Temperance *(G-15842)*
Sandvik Inc .... G 989 345-6138
  West Branch *(G-17520)*
Schneider Iron & Metal Inc .... F 906 774-0644
  Iron Mountain *(G-8299)*
Shoreline Recycling & Supply .... E 231 722-6081
  Muskegon *(G-11424)*
Strong Steel Products LLC .... E 313 267-3300
  Detroit *(G-4381)*
V & M Corporation .... E 248 541-4020
  Royal Oak *(G-13980)*

REFINERS & SMELTERS: Zinc, Primary, Including Zinc Residue

Arco Alloys Corp .... E 313 871-2680
  Detroit *(G-3876)*

REFINERS & SMELTERS: Zinc, Secondary

Arco Alloys Corp .... E 313 871-2680
  Detroit *(G-3876)*
Huron Valley Steel Corporation .... C 734 479-3500
  Trenton *(G-16155)*
National Zinc Processors Inc .... F 269 926-1161
  Benton Harbor *(G-1535)*

REFINING LUBRICATING OILS & GREASES, NEC

Fuel Source LLC .... G 313 506-0448
  Grosse Ile *(G-7173)*
Lube-Tech Inc .... G 269 329-1269
  Portage *(G-13012)*

REFINING: Petroleum

Bertoldi Oil Service Inc .... G 906 774-1707
  Iron Mountain *(G-8276)*
Hitachi America Ltd .... E 248 477-5400
  Farmington Hills *(G-5021)*
Marysville Hydrocarbons LLC .... G 586 445-2300
  Warren *(G-17142)*
Miller Exploration Company .... F 231 941-0004
  Traverse City *(G-16037)*
Murphy USA Inc .... F 517 541-0502
  Charlotte *(G-2661)*
Stop & Go Transportation LLC .... G 313 346-7114
  Washington *(G-17311)*

REFLECTIVE ROAD MARKERS, WHOLESALE

Carrier & Gable Inc .... E 248 477-8700
  Farmington Hills *(G-4958)*

REFRACTORIES: Castable, Clay

Mono Ceramics Inc .... E 269 925-0212
  Benton Harbor *(G-1532)*

REFRACTORIES: Cement

Chase Nedrow Manufacturing Inc .... E 248 669-9886
  Wixom *(G-17786)*
Stellar Materials Intl LLC .... E 561 504-3924
  Whitmore Lake *(G-17707)*

REFRACTORIES: Cement, nonclay

Cheminicon Inc .... G 734 439-2478
  Milan *(G-10933)*

REFRACTORIES: Clay

Alco Products LLC .... E 313 823-7500
  Detroit *(G-3853)*
Alpha Resources LLC .... E 269 465-5559
  Stevensville *(G-15553)*
Harbisonwalker Intl Inc .... C 231 689-6641
  White Cloud *(G-17623)*
Marshall-Gruber Company LLC .... F 248 353-4100
  Southfield *(G-14973)*

REFRACTORIES: Graphite, Carbon Or Ceramic Bond

Ajf Inc .... E 734 753-4410
  New Boston *(G-11496)*

REFRACTORIES: Nonclay

Cerco Inc .... E 734 362-8664
  Brownstown Twp *(G-2071)*
Harbisonwalker Intl Inc .... C 231 689-6641
  White Cloud *(G-17623)*
Midwest Product Spc Inc .... G 231 767-9942
  Muskegon *(G-11381)*
Nedrow Refractories Co .... E 248 669-2500
  Wixom *(G-17863)*
Osmi Inc .... F 561 504-3924
  Whitmore Lake *(G-17705)*
Rex Materials Inc .... E 517 223-3787
  Howell *(G-8092)*

REFRACTORIES: Tile & Brick, Exc Plastic

Schad Boiler Setting Company .... D 313 273-2235
  Detroit *(G-4355)*

REFRIGERATION & HEATING EQUIPMENT

Blissfield Manufacturing Co .... B 517 486-2121
  Blissfield *(G-1713)*
Bolhouse LLC .... G 616 209-7543
  Jenison *(G-8619)*
Dimplex Thermal Solutions Inc .... C 269 349-6800
  Kalamazoo *(G-8728)*
Glastender Inc .... C 989 752-4275
  Saginaw *(G-14045)*
Grand Traverse Mech Contg LLC .... G 231 943-7400
  Interlochen *(G-8241)*
Hella Corporate Center USA Inc .... E 586 232-4788
  Northville *(G-11697)*
Hussmann Corporation .... D 248 668-0790
  Wixom *(G-17832)*
Johnson Controls Inc .... C 313 842-3479
  Van Buren Twp *(G-16766)*
Kraftube Inc .... C 231 832-5562
  Reed City *(G-13217)*
Mahle Behr Industy America Lp .... D 616 647-3490
  Belmont *(G-1468)*
Microtemp Fluid Systems LLC .... G 248 703-5056
  Farmington Hills *(G-5067)*
National Aircraft Service Inc .... F 517 423-7589
  Tecumseh *(G-15803)*
Nortek Inc .... G 616 719-5588
  Grand Rapids *(G-6718)*
Opti Temp Inc .... E 231 946-2931
  Traverse City *(G-16060)*
Ostrander Company Inc .... G 248 646-6680
  Madison Heights *(G-10318)*
Riedel USA Inc .... G 734 595-9820
  Kalamazoo *(G-8871)*
Scientemp Corp .... E 517 263-6020
  Adrian *(G-94)*
TI Group Auto Systems LLC .... B 248 296-8000
  Auburn Hills *(G-1022)*
TMI Climate Solutions Inc .... C 810 603-3300
  Holly *(G-7899)*
Trane US Inc .... E 800 245-3964
  Flint *(G-5511)*
Trane US Inc .... G 734 367-0700
  Livonia *(G-9969)*
Trane US Inc .... D 734 452-2000
  Livonia *(G-9970)*

REFRIGERATION EQPT & SPLYS WHOLESALERS

Young Supply Company .... E 313 875-3280
  Detroit *(G-4455)*

REFRIGERATION EQPT & SPLYS, WHOLESALE: Beverage Coolers

Keglove LLC .... E 616 610-7289
  Holland *(G-7708)*
Pepsi-Cola Metro Btlg Co Inc .... D 989 755-1020
  Saginaw *(G-14121)*

REFRIGERATION EQPT & SPLYS, WHOLESALE: Ice Cream Cabinets

Taylor Freezer Michigan Inc .... F 616 453-0531
  Grand Rapids *(G-6916)*

REFRIGERATION EQPT: Complete

Chrysler & Koppin Company .... F 313 491-7100
  Detroit *(G-3936)*
Forma-Kool Manufacturing Inc .... E 586 949-4813
  Chesterfield *(G-2778)*
La Rosa Refrigeration & Eqp Co .... E 313 368-6620
  Detroit *(G-4187)*
Refrigeration Research Inc .... G 989 773-7540
  Mount Pleasant *(G-11223)*
Refrigeration Research Inc .... D 810 227-1151
  Brighton *(G-1985)*
Su-Tec Inc .... F 248 852-4711
  Rochester Hills *(G-13521)*

REFRIGERATION REPAIR SVCS

Refrigeration Concepts Inc .... E 616 785-7335
  Comstock Park *(G-3514)*

REFRIGERATION SVC & REPAIR

Pepsi-Cola Metro Btlg Co Inc .... D 517 272-2800
  Lansing *(G-9410)*

REFUSE SYSTEMS

Automotive Plastics Recycling .... E 810 767-3800
  Flint *(G-5381)*
Daily Recycling of Michigan .... G 734 654-9800
  Carleton *(G-2453)*
Strong Steel Products LLC .... E 313 267-3300
  Detroit *(G-4381)*
URS Energy & Construction Inc .... C 989 642-4190
  Hemlock *(G-7464)*
V & M Corporation .... E 248 541-4020
  Royal Oak *(G-13980)*

REGISTERS: Air, Metal

Hart & Cooley Inc .... C 616 656-8200
  Grand Rapids *(G-6495)*

REGULATORS: Power

H H Barnum Co .... G 248 486-5982
  Brighton *(G-1937)*
Hear Clear Inc .... G 734 525-8467
  Saline *(G-14394)*

REGULATORS: Transmission & Distribution Voltage

D & W Square LLC .... G 313 493-4970
  Detroit *(G-3959)*

REHABILITATION CENTER, OUTPATIENT TREATMENT

Hackley Health Ventures Inc .... G 231 728-5720
  Muskegon *(G-11342)*

PRODUCT SECTION

RELAYS & SWITCHES: Indl, Electric
Bay Electronics Inc .... E 586 296-0900
  Roseville *(G-13776)*
Edon Controls Inc .... G 248 280-0420
  Troy *(G-16335)*
Electromech Service Corp .... G 989 362-6066
  East Tawas *(G-4688)*
Hella Corporate Center USA Inc ... E 586 232-4788
  Northville *(G-11697)*
Hella Lighting Corporation .... E 734 414-0900
  Plymouth *(G-12636)*
Stoneridge Control Devices Inc ... G 248 489-9300
  Novi *(G-12005)*

RELAYS: Control Circuit, Ind
Flextronics Automotive USA Inc ... D 248 853-5724
  Rochester Hills *(G-13425)*
Flextronics Intl USA Inc .... B 616 837-9711
  Coopersville *(G-3558)*
Sine Systems Corporation .... C 586 465-3131
  Clinton Township *(G-3230)*
Wired Technologies LLC .... G 313 800-1611
  Livonia *(G-10011)*

RELAYS: Electronic Usage
Mercury Displacement Inds Inc .... D 269 663-8574
  Edwardsburg *(G-4766)*

RELIGIOUS SPLYS WHOLESALERS
Faith Alive Christn Resources ... E 800 333-8300
  Grand Rapids *(G-6397)*
Michigan Church Supply Co Inc ... F 810 686-8877
  Mount Morris *(G-11165)*
Religious Communications LLC ... G 313 822-3361
  Detroit *(G-4340)*

REMOVERS & CLEANERS
B & G Enterprises .... G 231 348-2705
  Charlevoix *(G-2607)*
Star 10 Inc .... G 231 830-8070
  Muskegon *(G-11430)*

REMOVERS: Paint
General Chemical Corporation ... G 248 587-5600
  Brighton *(G-1929)*
MPS Trading Group LLC .... G 313 841-7588
  Farmington Hills *(G-5073)*
Rap Products Inc .... G 989 893-5583
  Bay City *(G-1348)*

RENT-A-CAR SVCS
Broadmoor Motor Sales Inc ...... G 269 320-6304
  Hastings *(G-7402)*

RENTAL SVCS: Audio-Visual Eqpt & Sply
Bluewater Tech Group Inc .... C 248 356-4399
  Southfield *(G-14854)*
City Animation Co .... E 248 589-0600
  Troy *(G-16268)*
City Animation Co .... F 989 743-3458
  Corunna *(G-3579)*

RENTAL SVCS: Bicycle
Riverfront Cycle Inc .... G 517 482-8585
  Lansing *(G-9418)*

RENTAL SVCS: Business Machine & Electronic Eqpt
M & M Typewriter Service Inc ... G 734 995-4033
  Ann Arbor *(G-536)*
Pitney Bowes Inc .... F 248 591-2800
  Madison Heights *(G-10328)*

RENTAL SVCS: Invalid Splys
Wright & Filippis Inc .... E 248 336-4460
  Detroit *(G-3822)*

RENTAL SVCS: Musical Instrument
Guarneri House LLC .... G 616 451-4960
  Hudsonville *(G-8158)*

RENTAL SVCS: Oil Eqpt
Great Lakes Wellhead Inc .... G 231 943-9100
  Grawn *(G-7098)*

RENTAL SVCS: Personal Items, Exc Recreation & Medical
J & K Canvas Products .... G 810 635-7711
  Flint *(G-5451)*

RENTAL SVCS: Pleasure Boat
Pontoon Rentals .... G 906 387-2685
  Munising *(G-11248)*

RENTAL SVCS: Propane Eqpt
U S Distributing Inc .... E 248 646-0550
  Birmingham *(G-1707)*

RENTAL SVCS: Sign
Amor Sign Studios Inc .... F 231 723-8361
  Manistee *(G-10414)*
Poco Inc .... E 313 220-6752
  Canton *(G-2416)*

RENTAL SVCS: Sound & Lighting Eqpt
Band-Ayd Systems Intl Inc .... F 586 294-8851
  Madison Heights *(G-10200)*

RENTAL SVCS: Tent & Tarpaulin
Ace Canvas & Tent Co .... F 313 842-3011
  Troy *(G-16166)*
Dial Tent & Awning Co .... F 989 793-0741
  Saginaw *(G-14027)*

RENTAL SVCS: Tuxedo
Baryames Tux Shop Inc .... G 517 349-6555
  Okemos *(G-12116)*
Celebrations .... G 906 482-4946
  Hancock *(G-7250)*
Demmem Enterprises LLC .... F 810 564-9500
  Clio *(G-3269)*

RENTAL SVCS: Video Cassette Recorder & Access
Super Video Service Center ...... G 248 358-4794
  Southfield *(G-15037)*

RENTAL: Portable Toilet
Ameriform Acquisition Co LLC ... B 231 733-2725
  Muskegon *(G-11269)*

REPLATING SHOP, EXC SILVERWARE
All Chrome LLC .... G 517 554-1649
  Albion *(G-115)*

RESEARCH, DEV & TESTING SVCS, COMM: Chem Lab, Exc Testing
Advanced Urethanes Inc .... G 313 273-5705
  Detroit *(G-3844)*

RESEARCH, DEVELOPMENT & TEST SVCS, COMM: Research, Exc Lab
Imra America Inc .... E 734 669-7377
  Ann Arbor *(G-503)*
Lenderink Inc .... F 616 887-8257
  Belmont *(G-1466)*
Michigan Development Corp ..... C 734 302-4600
  Ann Arbor *(G-554)*

RESEARCH, DEVELOPMENT & TESTING SVCS, COMM: Natural Resource
Alternative Fuel Tech LLC .... G 313 417-9212
  Grosse Pointe Park *(G-7189)*
Ovshinsky Technologies LLC .... G 248 390-3564
  Pontiac *(G-12854)*

RESEARCH, DEVELOPMENT & TESTING SVCS, COMM: Research Lab
Applied Molecules LLC .... G 810 355-1475
  Whitmore Lake *(G-17688)*
Certainteed Corporation .... E 517 787-1737
  Jackson *(G-8406)*

RESEARCH, DEVELOPMENT & TESTING SVCS, COMMERCIAL: Business
Emag Technologies Inc .... F 734 996-3624
  Ann Arbor *(G-442)*

RESEARCH, DEVELOPMENT & TESTING SVCS, COMMERCIAL: Education
Avko Eductl Res Foundation .... F 810 686-9283
  Birch Run *(G-1663)*
Effective Schools Products .... G 517 349-8841
  Okemos *(G-12121)*

RESEARCH, DEVELOPMENT & TESTING SVCS, COMMERCIAL: Energy
Suematek .... G 517 614-2235
  Ypsilanti *(G-18103)*

RESEARCH, DEVELOPMENT & TESTING SVCS, COMMERCIAL: Food
Sunopta Ingredients Inc .... E 502 587-7999
  Schoolcraft *(G-14502)*

RESEARCH, DEVELOPMENT & TESTING SVCS, COMMERCIAL: Medical
Carlson Technology Inc .... G 248 476-0013
  Livonia *(G-9677)*
Clark-Mxr Inc .... E 734 426-2803
  Dexter *(G-4481)*
Hello Life Inc .... F 616 808-3290
  Grand Rapids *(G-6505)*
Millendo Therapeutics Inc .... E 734 845-9000
  Ann Arbor *(G-559)*
Millendo Transactionsub Inc ... G 734 845-9300
  Ann Arbor *(G-560)*

RESEARCH, DEVELOPMENT & TESTING SVCS, COMMERCIAL: Physical
Hygratek LLC .... G 847 962-6180
  Ann Arbor *(G-498)*
Xg Sciences Inc .... G 517 703-1110
  Lansing *(G-9437)*

RESEARCH, DEVELOPMENT SVCS, COMMERCIAL: Indl Lab
Stm Power Inc .... F 734 214-1448
  Ann Arbor *(G-647)*

RESEARCH, DVLPT & TEST SVCS, COMM: Mkt Analysis or Research
Ampm Inc .... F 989 837-8800
  Midland *(G-10814)*
Ecology Coatings .... G 248 723-2223
  Bloomfield *(G-1733)*
Elm International Inc .... G 517 332-4900
  Okemos *(G-12122)*

RESEARCH, DVLPT & TESTING SVCS, COMM: Survey, Mktg
Nits Solutions Inc .... F 248 231-2267
  Novi *(G-11953)*

RESIDENTIAL REMODELERS
D Michael Services .... G 810 794-2407
  Clay *(G-2996)*
W S Townsend Company .... G 517 393-7300
  Lansing *(G-9433)*

RESINS: Custom Compound Purchased
Aci Plastics Inc .... E 810 767-3800
  Flint *(G-5369)*
Alpha Resins LLC .... G 313 366-9300
  Detroit *(G-3861)*

RESINS: Custom Compound Purchased

Alumilite Corporation ....F...... 269 488-4000
  Galesburg *(G-5805)*
American Commodities Inc................E...... 810 767-3800
  Flint *(G-5376)*
Amplas Compounding LLC ....F...... 586 795-2555
  Sterling Heights *(G-15260)*
Azon Usa Inc ....F...... 269 385-5942
  Kalamazoo *(G-8690)*
Azon Usa Inc ....E...... 269 385-5942
  Kalamazoo *(G-8691)*
Byk USA Inc..................E...... 203 265-2086
  Rochester Hills *(G-13382)*
Cass Polymers ....E...... 517 543-7510
  Charlotte *(G-2636)*
Clean Tech Inc ....E...... 734 455-3600
  Plymouth *(G-12598)*
Clean Tech Inc ....E...... 734 529-2475
  Dundee *(G-4577)*
Eco Bio Plastics Midland Inc ....F...... 989 496-1934
  Midland *(G-10858)*
Georgia-Pacific LLC..................E...... 989 348-7275
  Grayling *(G-7107)*
Material Difference Tech LLC..........F...... 888 818-1283
  Macomb *(G-10140)*
Nano Materials & Processes Inc..........G...... 248 529-3873
  Milford *(G-10974)*
Portland Plastics Co ....E...... 517 647-4115
  Portland *(G-13065)*
Rhe-Tech LLC ....G...... 517 223-4874
  Fowlerville *(G-5579)*
Ssb Holdings Inc ....E...... 586 755-1660
  Rochester Hills *(G-13517)*
Ticona Polymers Inc ....D...... 248 377-6868
  Auburn Hills *(G-1026)*

RESISTORS

Touchstone Systems & Svcs Inc..........G...... 616 532-0060
  Wyoming *(G-18035)*

RESPIRATORS

Air Supply Inc..................G...... 586 773-6600
  Warren *(G-16921)*

RESTAURANT EQPT REPAIR SVCS

Auction Masters ....G...... 586 576-7777
  Oak Park *(G-12050)*

RESTAURANT EQPT: Carts

Effizient LLC..................G...... 616 935-3170
  Grand Haven *(G-6012)*

RESTAURANT EQPT: Food Wagons

Perfect Dish LLC..................G...... 313 784-3976
  Taylor *(G-15753)*

RESTAURANT EQPT: Sheet Metal

Dts Enterprises Inc ....E...... 231 599-3123
  Ellsworth *(G-4787)*
M C M Fixture Company Inc..........E...... 248 547-9280
  Hazel Park *(G-7442)*
Quality Stainless Mfg Co..........F...... 248 546-4141
  Madison Heights *(G-10343)*

RESTAURANTS: Delicatessen

Marshalls Trail Inc..................F...... 231 436-5082
  Mackinaw City *(G-10099)*

RESTAURANTS: Full Svc, American

CHI Co/Tabor Hill Winery..........D...... 269 422-1161
  Buchanan *(G-2113)*
Corner Brewery LLC ....E...... 734 480-2739
  Ypsilanti *(G-18061)*
Detroit Rivertwn Brewing Co LL..........C...... 313 877-9205
  Detroit *(G-4000)*

RESTAURANTS: Full Svc, Family

Sweetheart Bakery of Michigan..........D...... 586 795-1660
  Harper Woods *(G-7306)*

RESTAURANTS: Full Svc, Family, Chain

Big Boy Restaurants Intl LLC..........C...... 586 759-6000
  Warren *(G-16958)*
Big Boy Restaurants Intl LLC..........D...... 586 263-6220
  Clinton Township *(G-3067)*

RESTAURANTS: Full Svc, Family, Independent

Frankenmuth Brewing Company..........D...... 989 262-8300
  Frankenmuth *(G-5586)*
Krzysiak Family Restaurant..........D...... 989 894-5531
  Bay City *(G-1326)*

RESTAURANTS: Full Svc, Steak

Mountain Town Stn Brew Pub LLC..........C...... 989 775-2337
  Mount Pleasant *(G-11211)*

RESTAURANTS: Limited Svc, Coffee Shop

Coffee Beanery Ltd..................E...... 810 733-1020
  Flushing *(G-5533)*
Good Sense Coffee LLC..................G...... 810 355-2349
  Brighton *(G-1932)*

RESTAURANTS: Limited Svc, Drive-In

Deans Ice Cream Inc..................F...... 269 685-6641
  Plainwell *(G-12522)*

RESTAURANTS: Limited Svc, Fast-Food, Independent

MHR Investments Inc..................F...... 989 832-5395
  Midland *(G-10884)*

RESTAURANTS: Limited Svc, Grill

Bells Brewery Inc..................G...... 906 233-5000
  Escanaba *(G-4816)*

RESTAURANTS: Limited Svc, Ice Cream Stands Or Dairy Bars

Calder Bros Dairy Inc..................E...... 313 381-8858
  Lincoln Park *(G-9575)*
Cold Stone Creamery..................G...... 313 886-4020
  Grosse Pointe Park *(G-7192)*
Dairy Queen..................F...... 616 235-0102
  Grand Rapids *(G-6333)*
Moomers Homemade Ice Cream LLC...E...... 231 941-4122
  Traverse City *(G-16043)*
Original Murdicks Fudge Co..........E...... 906 847-3530
  Mackinac Island *(G-10097)*
Rays Ice Cream Co Inc..................E...... 248 549-5256
  Royal Oak *(G-13963)*

RESTAURANTS: Limited Svc, Pizza

Kring Pizza Inc..................G...... 586 792-0049
  Harrison Township *(G-7336)*

RESTAURANTS: Limited Svc, Pizzeria, Chain

Dominos Pizza LLC..................C...... 734 930-3030
  Ann Arbor *(G-424)*

RESTAURANTS: Limited Svc, Pizzeria, Independent

Klaus Nixdorf..................E...... 269 429-3259
  Stevensville *(G-15573)*

RESTAURANTS: Limited Svc, Sandwiches & Submarines Shop

Subway Restaurant..................G...... 248 625-5739
  Clarkston *(G-2960)*

RESTAURANTS: Limited Svc, Snack Shop

Cherry Republic Inc..................D...... 231 334-3150
  Glen Arbor *(G-5940)*

RESTAURANTS: Ltd Svc, Ice Cream, Soft Drink/Fountain Stands

Dunkin Donuts & Baskin-Robbins..........E...... 989 835-8412
  Midland *(G-10856)*
Guernsey Dairy Stores Inc..........C...... 248 349-1466
  Northville *(G-11696)*

RETAIL BAKERY: Bagels

New York Bagel Baking Co..........F...... 248 548-2580
  Ferndale *(G-5305)*

RETAIL BAKERY: Bread

Great Harvest Bread Co..................G...... 586 566-9500
  Shelby Township *(G-14598)*
Julian Brothers Inc..................E...... 248 588-0280
  Clawson *(G-2981)*
Mackenzies Bakery..................E...... 269 343-8440
  Kalamazoo *(G-8814)*
New Yasmeen Detroit Inc..................E...... 313 582-6035
  Dearborn *(G-3744)*
Roma Bakery & Imported Foods..........E...... 517 485-9466
  Lansing *(G-9419)*
Stone House Bread LLC..................E...... 231 933-8864
  Traverse City *(G-16112)*

RETAIL BAKERY: Cakes

Cake Connection Tc LLC..................G...... 231 943-3531
  Traverse City *(G-15928)*
G M Paris Bakery Inc..................E...... 734 425-2060
  Livonia *(G-9746)*
Home Bakery..................E...... 248 651-4830
  Rochester *(G-13326)*
Klaus Nixdorf..................E...... 269 429-3259
  Stevensville *(G-15573)*
Sweet & Sweeter Inc..................G...... 586 977-9338
  Sterling Heights *(G-15517)*

RETAIL BAKERY: Cookies

Carlson Enterprises Inc..................G...... 248 656-1442
  Rochester Hills *(G-13385)*
Looney Baker of Livonia Inc..........E...... 734 425-8569
  Livonia *(G-9818)*

RETAIL BAKERY: Doughnuts

Barneys Bakery..................G...... 989 895-5466
  Bay City *(G-1281)*
Donutville..................G...... 616 396-1160
  Holland *(G-7610)*
Dunkin Donuts & Baskin-Robbins..........E...... 989 835-8412
  Midland *(G-10856)*
Sweetwaters Donut Mill..................F...... 269 979-1944
  Battle Creek *(G-1256)*
Yates Cider Mill Inc..................G...... 248 651-8300
  Rochester Hills *(G-13551)*

RETAIL BAKERY: Pastries

Josefs French Pastry Shop Co..........E...... 313 881-5710
  Grosse Pointe Woods *(G-7204)*

RETAIL BAKERY: Pretzels

American Gourmet Snacks LLC..........G...... 989 892-4856
  Essexville *(G-4867)*
B & B Pretzels Inc..................E...... 248 358-1655
  Southfield *(G-14848)*
Karemor Inc..................G...... 517 323-3042
  Lansing *(G-9303)*

RETAIL FIREPLACE STORES

Hearth-N-Home Inc..................G...... 517 625-5586
  Owosso *(G-12295)*

RETAIL LUMBER YARDS

B & B Heartwoods Inc..................G...... 734 332-9525
  Ann Arbor *(G-379)*
Carson Wood Specialties Inc..........G...... 269 465-6091
  Stevensville *(G-15559)*
Cedar Log Lbr Millersburg Inc..........F...... 989 733-2676
  Millersburg *(G-10991)*
Lumber & Truss Inc..................E...... 810 664-7290
  Lapeer *(G-9472)*
Prells Saw Mill Inc..................E...... 989 734-2939
  Hawks *(G-7430)*
Standale Lumber and Supply Co..........G...... 616 530-8200
  Grandville *(G-7072)*
Thomas J Moyle Jr Incorporated..........E...... 906 482-3000
  Houghton *(G-7986)*

RETAIL STORES: Alarm Signal Systems

George Jensen..................G...... 269 329-1543
  Portage *(G-12998)*

RETAIL STORES: Alcoholic Beverage Making Eqpt & Splys

D C Norris North America LLC..........G...... 231 935-1519
  Traverse City *(G-15955)*

PRODUCT SECTION

RETAIL STORES: Aquarium Splys

Aqua Systems Inc ....G...... 810 346-2525
  Brown City **(G-2044)**

RETAIL STORES: Art & Architectural Splys

Shop Makarios LLC ....G...... 800 479-0032
  Byron Center **(G-2211)**

RETAIL STORES: Artificial Limbs

Springer Prsthtic Orthtic Svcs...............F 517 337-0300
  Lansing **(G-9426)**

RETAIL STORES: Audio-Visual Eqpt & Splys

Corporate AV Services LLC ....G...... 248 939-0900
  Commerce Township **(G-3395)**
Earbyte Inc ....G...... 734 418-8661
  Southfield **(G-14892)**
Silent Call Corporation ....F 248 673-7353
  Waterford **(G-17377)**

RETAIL STORES: Awnings

Advanced Inc....................................G...... 231 938-2233
  Acme **(G-2)**
Patio Land Mfg Inc ....G...... 586 758-6660
  Warren **(G-17184)**

RETAIL STORES: Banners

A-1 Signs ....G...... 269 488-9411
  Portage **(G-12980)**
Bannergalaxycom LLC ....G...... 231 941-8200
  Traverse City **(G-15903)**
Shields & Shields Enterprises ....G...... 269 345-7744
  Kalamazoo **(G-8886)**

RETAIL STORES: Batteries, Non-Automotive

Zeeland Component Sales LLC ....G...... 616 399-8614
  Zeeland **(G-18200)**

RETAIL STORES: Business Machines & Eqpt

3dm Source Inc ....F 616 647-9513
  Grand Rapids **(G-6120)**
Fedex Office & Print Svcs Inc ....F 248 377-2222
  Auburn Hills **(G-870)**
Jackpine Press Incorporated ....F 231 723-8344
  Manistee **(G-10425)**

RETAIL STORES: Canvas Prdts

Belle Isle Awning Co Inc.....................E 586 294-6050
  Warren **(G-16954)**

RETAIL STORES: Christmas Lights & Decorations

Bronner Display Sign Advg Inc ....C....... 989 652-9931
  Frankenmuth **(G-5584)**
McLeod Wood and Christmas Pdts......G...... 989 777-4800
  Bridgeport **(G-1853)**

RETAIL STORES: Cleaning Eqpt & Splys

Great Lakes Allied LLC.......................G...... 231 924-5794
  White Cloud **(G-17622)**
Photodon LLC ....G...... 847 377-1185
  Traverse City **(G-16068)**

RETAIL STORES: Concrete Prdts, Precast

Gildners Concrete..............................G...... 989 356-5156
  Alpena **(G-292)**

RETAIL STORES: Convalescent Eqpt & Splys

Wright & Filippis Inc ....F 586 756-4020
  Warren **(G-17298)**

RETAIL STORES: Cosmetics

Lee Beauty & Gen Mechandise...........G...... 586 294-4400
  Fraser **(G-5684)**
Tetra Corporation..............................F 401 529-1630
  Eaton Rapids **(G-4734)**

RETAIL STORES: Electronic Parts & Eqpt

Ghi Electronics LLC...........................F 248 397-8856
  Madison Heights **(G-10257)**

Static Controls Corp ....E...... 248 926-4400
  Wixom **(G-17896)**
Z & R Electric Service Inc...................F 906 774-0468
  Iron Mountain **(G-8306)**

RETAIL STORES: Engine & Motor Eqpt & Splys

Cummins Inc ....F 989 732-5055
  Gaylord **(G-5854)**

RETAIL STORES: Farm Eqpt & Splys

D & G Equipment Inc ....C....... 517 655-4606
  Williamston **(G-17729)**
Glenn Knochel ....G...... 989 684-7869
  Kawkawlin **(G-8971)**
Wells Equipment Sales Inc ....F 517 542-2376
  Litchfield **(G-9613)**

RETAIL STORES: Farm Machinery, NEC

Gillisons Var Fabrication Inc...............E 231 882-5921
  Benzonia **(G-1575)**

RETAIL STORES: Fire Extinguishers

Con-De Manufacturing Inc ....G...... 269 651-3756
  Sturgis **(G-15601)**
Exquise Inc......................................G...... 248 220-9048
  Detroit **(G-4047)**
Gallagher Fire Equipment Co ....E 248 477-1540
  Livonia **(G-9748)**

RETAIL STORES: Flags

American Flag & Banner Company......G...... 248 288-3010
  Clawson **(G-2972)**
Battle Creek Tent & Awning Co ....G...... 269 964-1824
  Battle Creek **(G-1152)**

RETAIL STORES: Foam & Foam Prdts

Envirolite LLC...................................F 248 792-3184
  Troy **(G-16349)**
Envirolite LLC...................................D...... 888 222-2191
  Coldwater **(G-3302)**

RETAIL STORES: Hair Care Prdts

Art of Shaving - Fl LLC......................G...... 248 649-5872
  Troy **(G-16219)**

RETAIL STORES: Hearing Aids

Bieri Hearing Instruments Inc.............F 989 793-2701
  Saginaw **(G-14007)**

RETAIL STORES: Hospital Eqpt & Splys

Metro Medical Eqp Mfg Inc.................D...... 734 522-8400
  Livonia **(G-9840)**
Wright & Filippis Inc ....E 248 336-8460
  Detroit **(G-3822)**

RETAIL STORES: Maps & Charts

Metro Graphic Arts Inc ....F 616 245-2271
  Grand Rapids **(G-6663)**

RETAIL STORES: Medical Apparatus & Splys

Bay Home Medical and Rehab Inc......E 231 933-1200
  Grandville **(G-7021)**
Prosthetic Center Inc.........................G...... 517 372-7007
  Dimondale **(G-4519)**
Signal Medical Corporation ....F 810 364-7070
  Marysville **(G-10614)**
Sobaks Pharmacy Inc........................F 989 725-2785
  Owosso **(G-12316)**
Wright & Filippis Inc ....E 313 386-3330
  Lincoln Park **(G-9589)**

RETAIL STORES: Mobile Telephones & Eqpt

Elite Business Services & Exec...........D....... 734 956-4550
  Bloomfield Hills **(G-1763)**

RETAIL STORES: Monuments, Finished To Custom Order

Arnets Inc ....F 734 665-3650
  Ann Arbor **(G-367)**
Muskegon Monument & Stone Co.......G...... 231 722-2730
  Muskegon **(G-11390)**

Steinbrecher Stone Corp....................G...... 906 563-5852
  Norway **(G-11820)**
Superior Monuments Co ....G...... 616 844-1700
  Grand Haven **(G-6087)**
Superior Monuments Co ....G...... 231 728-2211
  Muskegon **(G-11433)**

RETAIL STORES: Motors, Electric

Electric Motor Service ....G...... 269 945-5113
  Hastings **(G-7408)**
Kalamazoo Electric Motor Inc.............G...... 269 345-7802
  Kalamazoo **(G-8788)**
Nieboer Electric Inc ....F 231 924-0960
  Fremont **(G-5779)**

RETAIL STORES: Orthopedic & Prosthesis Applications

American Prosthetic Institute ....G...... 517 349-3130
  Okemos **(G-12112)**
Becker Orthopedic Appliance Co ....D...... 248 588-7480
  Troy **(G-16236)**
Binson-Becker Inc ....F 888 246-7667
  Center Line **(G-2579)**
Biopro Inc ....E 810 982-7777
  Port Huron **(G-12899)**
Bremer Prosthetic Design Inc ....G...... 810 733-3375
  Flint **(G-5394)**
Brenner Orthtic Prsthetic Labs...........G...... 248 615-0600
  Livonia **(G-9670)**
Greater Lansing Orthotic Clini............G...... 517 337-0856
  Lansing **(G-9377)**
Hanger Prsthetcs & Ortho Inc............F 517 394-5850
  Lansing **(G-9381)**
Mount Clemens Orthopedic Appls ......G...... 586 463-3600
  Clinton Township **(G-3181)**
Northern Orthotics Prosthetics ....G...... 906 353-7161
  Baraga **(G-1111)**
Northwest Orthotics-Prosthetic..........G...... 248 477-1443
  Novi **(G-11955)**
Oakland Orthopedic Appls Inc ....G...... 989 839-9241
  Midland **(G-10898)**
Oakland Orthopedic Appls Inc ....D...... 989 893-7544
  Bay City **(G-1339)**
Wright & Filippis Inc ....F 517 484-2624
  Lansing **(G-9435)**

RETAIL STORES: Pet Splys

Go Cat Feather Toys ....G...... 517 543-7519
  Charlotte **(G-2652)**
Ruff Life LLC ....G...... 231 347-1214
  Petoskey **(G-12474)**
Studtmans Stuff ....G...... 269 673-3126
  Allegan **(G-189)**
Ultramouse Ltd.................................G...... 734 761-1144
  Ann Arbor **(G-686)**

RETAIL STORES: Posters

Fairfax Prints Ltd ....G...... 517 321-5590
  Lansing **(G-9227)**

RETAIL STORES: Religious Goods

Lighthouse Direct Buy LLC.................G...... 313 340-1850
  Detroit **(G-4204)**

RETAIL STORES: Rock & Stone Specimens

Lewiston Sand & Gravel Inc................G...... 989 786-2742
  Lewiston **(G-9552)**

RETAIL STORES: Rubber Stamps

Bk Mattson Enterprises Inc.................G...... 906 774-0097
  Iron Mountain **(G-8278)**
Rubber Stamps Unlimited Inc.............F 734 451-7300
  Plymouth **(G-12746)**
Rush Stationers Printers Inc...............F 989 891-9305
  Bay City **(G-1351)**
Stamping Grounds Inc ....G...... 248 851-6764
  Bloomfield Hills **(G-1798)**

RETAIL STORES: Safety Splys & Eqpt

Skyline Window Cleaning Inc.............G...... 616 813-0536
  West Olive **(G-17535)**

RETAIL STORES: Sales Barns

K-Mar Structures LLC........................F 231 924-3895
  Fremont **(G-5777)**

RETAIL STORES: Sauna Eqpt & Splys
Ahs LLC .... F 888 355-3050
  Holland *(G-7552)*

RETAIL STORES: Spas & Hot Tubs
Northwoods Hot Sprng Spas Inc .... G 231 347-1134
  Petoskey *(G-12465)*

RETAIL STORES: Swimming Pools, Above Ground
Hotwater Works Inc .... G 517 364-8827
  Lansing *(G-9382)*

RETAIL STORES: Technical Aids For The Handicapped
Assistive Technology Mich Inc .... G 248 348-7161
  Novi *(G-11832)*

RETAIL STORES: Telephone & Communication Eqpt
Lol Telcom Inc .... B 616 888-6171
  Hudsonville *(G-8162)*

RETAIL STORES: Telephone Eqpt & Systems
Huron Valley Telecom .... G 734 995-9780
  Ann Arbor *(G-497)*
Npi Wireless .... E 231 922-9273
  Traverse City *(G-16053)*

RETAIL STORES: Water Purification Eqpt
Douglas Water Conditioning .... E 248 363-8383
  Waterford *(G-17336)*
Michigan Soft Water of Centr .... D 517 339-0722
  East Lansing *(G-4669)*
Reynolds Water Conditioning Co .... F 248 888-5000
  Farmington Hills *(G-5114)*
Village & Country Water Trtmnt .... F 810 632-7880
  Hartland *(G-7395)*

RETAIL STORES: Welding Splys
Andritz Metals Inc .... G 248 305-2969
  Novi *(G-11828)*
Cramblits Welding LLC .... G 906 932-1908
  Ironwood *(G-8326)*
Greenville Trck Wldg Sups LLC .... F 616 754-6120
  Greenville *(G-7136)*
North East Fabrication Co Inc .... F 517 849-8090
  Jonesville *(G-8664)*
Praxair Distribution Inc .... E 313 778-7085
  Detroit *(G-4308)*
Praxair Distribution Inc .... E 616 451-3055
  Grand Rapids *(G-6762)*

RETORTS: Indl, Smelting, Etc
Larsen Service Inc .... G 810 374-6132
  Otisville *(G-12232)*

RETREADING MATERIALS: Tire
Great Lakes Tire LLC .... D 586 939-7000
  Warren *(G-17063)*

REUPHOLSTERY & FURNITURE REPAIR
Hollow Metal Services LLC .... G 248 394-0233
  Clarkston *(G-2926)*
Kindel Furniture Company LLC .... C 616 243-3676
  Grand Rapids *(G-6583)*
Sassy Fabrics Inc .... G 810 694-0440
  Grand Blanc *(G-5982)*

REUPHOLSTERY SVCS
Grand Traverse Canvas Works .... F 231 947-3140
  Traverse City *(G-15982)*
Gustafson Smoked Fish .... G 906 292-5424
  Moran *(G-11107)*
Homespun Furniture Inc .... F 734 284-6277
  Riverview *(G-13297)*
Melco Dctg & Furn Restoration .... G 989 723-3335
  Owosso *(G-12303)*
Parkway Drapery & Uphl Co Inc .... G 734 779-1300
  Livonia *(G-9884)*
Quality Awning Shops Inc .... G 517 882-2491
  Lansing *(G-9415)*

Tamarack Uphl & Interiors .... G 616 866-2922
  Rockford *(G-13592)*

REWINDING SVCS
John V Gedda Jr .... G 906 482-5037
  Hancock *(G-7253)*
Metal-Line Corp .... E 231 723-7041
  Muskegon *(G-11377)*

RHEOSTATS: Electronic
Mark Griessel .... G 810 378-6060
  Melvin *(G-10691)*

RIVETS: Metal
Aero Auto Stud Specialists Inc .... E 248 437-2171
  Whitmore Lake *(G-17685)*
Detroit Tubular Rivet Inc .... D 734 282-7979
  Wyandotte *(G-17954)*
Gage Bilt Inc .... E 586 226-1500
  Clinton Township *(G-3128)*
H & L Tool Company Inc .... D 248 585-7474
  Madison Heights *(G-10263)*
Securit Metal Products Co .... E 269 782-7076
  Dowagiac *(G-4561)*
Smsg LLC .... G 517 787-9447
  Jackson *(G-8574)*

ROBOTS, SERVICES OR NOVELTY, WHOLESALE
Mannetron .... E 269 962-3475
  Battle Creek *(G-1225)*

ROBOTS: Assembly Line
Allfi Robotics Inc .... G 586 248-1198
  Wixom *(G-17757)*
Aoa Productions LLC .... G 517 256-0820
  Williamston *(G-17725)*
Applied & Integrated Mfg Inc .... G 248 370-8950
  Rochester *(G-13313)*
Becker Robotic Equipment Corp .... G 470 249-7880
  Orion *(G-12175)*
Bobier Tool Supply Inc .... F 810 732-4030
  Flint *(G-5392)*
Borneman & Peterson Inc .... F 810 744-1890
  Flint *(G-5393)*
Classic Systems LLC .... C 248 588-2738
  Troy *(G-16270)*
Engineered Automation Systems .... G 616 897-0920
  Belding *(G-1412)*
Fanuc America Corporation .... B 248 377-7000
  Rochester Hills *(G-13423)*
Global Electronics Limited .... E 248 353-0100
  Bloomfield Hills *(G-1770)*
Industrial Atomated Design LLC .... E 810 648-9200
  Sandusky *(G-14435)*
Industrial Service Tech Inc .... F 616 288-3352
  Grand Rapids *(G-6533)*
Jax Services LLC .... G 586 703-3212
  Warren *(G-17112)*
Krush Industries Inc .... G 248 238-2296
  Taylor *(G-15733)*
Light Robotics Automation Inc .... G 586 254-6655
  Sterling Heights *(G-15399)*
Master Robotics LLC .... G 586 484-7710
  Almont *(G-262)*
Motion Industries Inc .... G 269 926-7216
  Benton Harbor *(G-1533)*
Onyx Manufacturing Inc .... G 248 687-8611
  Rochester Hills *(G-13487)*
R Concepts Incorporated .... G 810 632-4857
  Howell *(G-8086)*
Recognition Robotics Inc .... G 440 590-0499
  Wixom *(G-17884)*
Thyssenkrupp System Engrg .... C 248 340-8000
  Auburn Hills *(G-1019)*
Universal TI Eqp & Contrls Inc .... D 586 268-4380
  Sterling Heights *(G-15534)*
Yaskawa America Inc .... G 248 668-8800
  Rochester Hills *(G-13550)*

ROBOTS: Indl Spraying, Painting, Etc
Parker Engineering Amer Co Ltd .... F 734 326-7630
  Westland *(G-17586)*

ROD & BAR Aluminum
Extruded Metals Inc .... C 616 794-4851
  Belding *(G-1414)*
Kaiser Aluminum Fab Pdts LLC .... D 269 250-8400
  Kalamazoo *(G-8784)*
Petschke Manufacturing Company .... F 586 463-0841
  Mount Clemens *(G-11144)*

RODS: Steel & Iron, Made In Steel Mills
Ivan Doverspike .... E 313 579-3000
  Detroit *(G-4153)*
Mueller Industrial Realty Co .... B 810 987-7770
  Port Huron *(G-12947)*

RODS: Welding
Eureka Welding Alloys Inc .... E 248 588-0001
  Madison Heights *(G-10250)*

ROLL FORMED SHAPES: Custom
A & B Welding & Fabricating .... G 231 733-2661
  Muskegon *(G-11255)*
Dlh Rollform LLC .... G 586 231-0507
  New Baltimore *(G-11483)*
Mig Molding LLC .... G 810 724-7400
  Imlay City *(G-8208)*
Porter Steel & Welding Company .... F 231 733-4495
  Muskegon *(G-11404)*
Raq LLC .... F 313 473-7271
  Pontiac *(G-12860)*
Shape Corp .... G 616 846-8700
  Spring Lake *(G-15176)*

ROLLING MACHINERY: Steel
D-N-S Industries Inc .... F 586 465-2444
  Clinton Township *(G-3098)*

ROLLING MILL EQPT: Rod Mills
Mikes Garage .... G 734 779-7383
  Belleville *(G-1448)*

ROLLING MILL MACHINERY
Dalton Industries LLC .... E 248 673-0755
  Waterford *(G-17333)*
Dexter Roll Form Company .... G 586 573-6930
  Warren *(G-17001)*
Feed - Lease Corp .... E 248 377-0000
  Auburn Hills *(G-871)*
Fontijne Grotnes Inc .... E 269 262-4700
  Niles *(G-11611)*
Novi Tool & Machine Company .... D 313 532-0900
  Redford *(G-13176)*
Perfecto Industries Inc .... E 989 732-2941
  Gaylord *(G-5888)*
Rod Chomper Inc .... F 616 392-9677
  Holland *(G-7790)*
Tube Forming and Machine Inc .... E 989 739-3323
  Oscoda *(G-12223)*

ROLLING MILL ROLLS: Cast Iron
Vx-LLC .... G 734 854-8700
  Lambertville *(G-9187)*

ROLLS & BLANKETS, PRINTERS': Rubber Or Rubberized Fabric
Day International Group Inc .... E 734 781-4600
  Plymouth *(G-12606)*
Flint Group US LLC .... D 269 279-5161
  Three Rivers *(G-15862)*
Flint Group US LLC .... A 734 781-4600
  Livonia *(G-9741)*
Michigan Roller Inc .... G 269 651-2304
  Sturgis *(G-15618)*

ROLLS & ROLL COVERINGS: Rubber
Marco Rollo Inc .... F 269 279-5246
  Three Rivers *(G-15869)*
Republic Roller Corporation .... E 269 273-9591
  Three Rivers *(G-15876)*

ROOF DECKS
Metal Sales Manufacturing Corp .... E 989 686-5879
  Bay City *(G-1331)*

PRODUCT SECTION

ROOFING MATERIALS: Asphalt

Green Link Inc .... F 269 216-9229
  Kalamazoo *(G-8758)*
Michigan Steel and Trim Inc .... G 517 647-4555
  Portland *(G-13063)*

ROOFING MATERIALS: Sheet Metal

Hancock Enterprises Inc .... D 734 287-8840
  Taylor *(G-15728)*
Reurink Sales & Service LLC .... G 616 522-9100
  Ionia *(G-8251)*
Sage International Inc .... D 972 623-2004
  Novi *(G-11989)*
Trade Specific Solutions LLC .... G 734 752-7124
  Southgate *(G-15085)*

ROOMING & BOARDING HOUSES: Furnished Room Rental

Rooms of Grand Rapids LLC .... F 616 260-1452
  Spring Lake *(G-15173)*

ROTORS: Motor

Celerity Systems N Amer Inc .... G 248 994-7696
  Novi *(G-11846)*

RUBBER

Aptargroup Inc .... C 989 631-8030
  Midland *(G-10816)*
Armada Rubber Manufacturing Co ..... D 586 784-9135
  Armada *(G-716)*
Covestro LLC .... E 248 475-7700
  Auburn Hills *(G-828)*
Dawson Manufacturing Company .... C 269 925-0100
  Benton Harbor *(G-1493)*
Flexfab Horizons Intl Inc .... E 269 945-4700
  Hastings *(G-7409)*
Flexfab LLC .... G 269 945-2433
  Hastings *(G-7410)*
Mitsubishi Chls Perf Plyrs Inc .... E 586 755-1660
  Warren *(G-17157)*
Mykin Inc .... F 248 667-8030
  South Lyon *(G-14804)*
Saint-Gobain Prfmce Plas Corp .... D 989 435-9533
  Beaverton *(G-1392)*

RUBBER PRDTS: Automotive, Mechanical

Akwel Cadillac Usa Inc .... C 231 775-6571
  Cadillac *(G-2224)*
Dawson Manufacturing Company .... C 269 925-0100
  Benton Harbor *(G-1492)*
HP Pelzer Auto Systems Inc .... E 248 280-1010
  Troy *(G-16405)*
Opeo Inc .... F 248 299-4000
  Auburn Hills *(G-966)*
Pullman Company .... F 734 243-8000
  Monroe *(G-11064)*
Uchiyama Mktg & Dev Amer LLC .... F 248 859-3986
  Novi *(G-12022)*
Vibracoustic Usa Inc .... C 269 637-2116
  South Haven *(G-14781)*
Vibracoustic Usa Inc .... B 810 648-2100
  Sandusky *(G-14446)*

RUBBER PRDTS: Mechanical

Advanced Manufacturing LLC .... G 231 826-3859
  Falmouth *(G-4891)*
Akwel Cadillac Usa Inc .... B 231 876-8020
  Cadillac *(G-2223)*
Akwel Usa Inc .... C 231 775-6571
  Cadillac *(G-2226)*
Anand Nvh North America Inc .... C 810 724-2400
  Imlay City *(G-8196)*
Armada Rubber Manufacturing Co ..... D 586 784-9135
  Armada *(G-716)*
Basic Rubber and Plastics Co .... E 248 360-7400
  Walled Lake *(G-16891)*
Black River Manufacturing Inc .... E 810 982-9810
  Port Huron *(G-12900)*
BRC Rubber & Plastics Inc .... G 248 745-9200
  Auburn Hills *(G-806)*
Contitech North America Inc .... F 248 312-3050
  Rochester Hills *(G-13396)*
Creative Foam Corporation .... C 810 629-4149
  Fenton *(G-5198)*
Dawson Manufacturing Company .... C 269 925-0100
  Benton Harbor *(G-1493)*
Die Stampco Inc .... F 989 893-7790
  Bay City *(G-1302)*
Fluid Hutchinson Management .... D 248 679-1327
  Auburn Hills *(G-876)*
Four Star Rubber Inc .... G 810 632-3335
  Commerce Township *(G-3407)*
Freudenberg N Amer Ltd Partnr .... G 734 354-5505
  Plymouth *(G-12623)*
Freudenberg-Nok General Partnr .... C 734 451-0020
  Plymouth *(G-12624)*
Hutchinson Antivibration .... B 616 459-4541
  Grand Rapids *(G-6519)*
Hutchinson Antivibration .... C 231 775-9737
  Cadillac *(G-2254)*
Midwest Rubber Company .... D 810 376-2085
  Deckerville *(G-3809)*
Polymer Products Group Inc .... G 989 723-9510
  Owosso *(G-12311)*
R & J Manufacturing Company .... E 248 669-2460
  Commerce Township *(G-3445)*
R H M Rubber & Manufacturing .... G 248 624-8277
  Novi *(G-11984)*
Reliance Rubber Industries Inc .... G 734 641-4100
  Westland *(G-17596)*
Rosta USA Corp .... F 269 841-5448
  Benton Harbor *(G-1544)*
Trelleborg Automotive USA Inc .... E 734 254-9140
  Northville *(G-11731)*
Uniflex Inc .... G 248 486-6000
  Brighton *(G-2002)*
Vibracoustic North America L P .... E 269 637-2116
  South Haven *(G-14780)*
Vibracoustic Usa Inc .... G 810 648-2100
  Sandusky *(G-14447)*

RUBBER PRDTS: Reclaimed

First Class Tire Shredders Inc .... F 810 639-5888
  Clio *(G-3271)*

RUBBER PRDTS: Silicone

Dow Corning Corporation .... G 989 839-2808
  Midland *(G-10849)*
Grm Corporation .... D 989 453-2322
  Pigeon *(G-12489)*
ICM Products Inc .... E 269 445-0847
  Cassopolis *(G-2531)*
Specialty Manufacturing Inc .... E 989 790-9011
  Saginaw *(G-14155)*

RUBBER PRDTS: Sponge

Basic Rubber and Plastics Co .... E 248 360-7400
  Walled Lake *(G-16891)*

RUBBER STAMP, WHOLESALE

Classic Stamp & Signs .... G 231 737-0200
  Norton Shores *(G-11746)*
Rubber Stamps Unlimited Inc .... F 734 451-7300
  Plymouth *(G-12746)*

RUBBER, CRUDE, WHOLESALE

Exotic Rubber & Plastics Corp .... D 248 477-2122
  Farmington Hills *(G-4996)*
Innovative Engineering Mich .... G 517 977-0460
  Lansing *(G-9236)*

RUGS : Hand & Machine Made

Classic Designs Cstm Area Rugs .... G 616 530-0740
  Grandville *(G-7026)*

RUST PROOFING SVC: Hot Dipping, Metals & Formed Prdts

Superior Collision Inc .... G 231 946-4983
  Traverse City *(G-16117)*
Volcor Finishing Inc .... E 616 527-5555
  Ionia *(G-8254)*

RUST REMOVERS

Metals Preservation Group LLC .... F 586 944-2720
  Saint Clair Shores *(G-14263)*

RUST RESISTING

A-Line Products Corporation .... F 313 571-8300
  Detroit *(G-3830)*
Emco Chemical Inc .... F 313 894-7650
  Detroit *(G-4036)*

SAND & GRAVEL

Magni Group Inc .... F 248 647-4500
  Birmingham *(G-1690)*
Magni-Industries Inc .... E 313 843-7855
  Detroit *(G-4215)*

SAFES & VAULTS: Metal

A & L Metal Products .... G 734 654-8990
  Carleton *(G-2451)*

SAFETY EQPT & SPLYS WHOLESALERS

James Glove & Supply .... F 810 733-5780
  Flint *(G-5452)*
Midwest Safety Products Inc .... E 616 554-5155
  Grand Rapids *(G-6686)*

SAILBOAT BUILDING & REPAIR

Quantum Sails Design Group LLC ...... F 231 941-1222
  Traverse City *(G-16087)*

SAILS

Kent Sail Co Inc .... G 586 791-2580
  Harrison Township *(G-7335)*
Luker Enterprises Inc .... G 231 894-9702
  Montague *(G-11094)*
North Sails Group LLC .... G 586 776-1330
  Saint Clair Shores *(G-14265)*
Performance Sailing Inc .... F 586 790-7500
  Clinton Township *(G-3193)*

SALES PROMOTION SVCS

Forsons Inc .... G 517 787-4562
  Jackson *(G-8450)*

SALT

Cargill Incorporated .... B 810 329-2736
  Saint Clair *(G-14207)*

SALT & SULFUR MINING

Morton Salt Inc .... F 231 398-0758
  Manistee *(G-10431)*

SAND & GRAVEL

A & E Agg Inc .... F 248 547-4711
  Berkley *(G-1577)*
A Y Sand and Gravel .... G 313 779-4825
  Romulus *(G-13645)*
Afgco Sand & Gravel Co Inc .... G 810 798-3293
  Almont *(G-250)*
Aggregtes Excvtg Logistics LLC .... G 231 737-4949
  Muskegon *(G-11264)*
Bouchey and Sons Inc .... G 989 588-4118
  Farwell *(G-5158)*
Brewer Sand & Gravel Inc .... G 616 393-8990
  Holland *(G-7577)*
Briggs Contracting .... G 989 687-7331
  Sanford *(G-14448)*
Cheboygan Cement Products Inc .... E 231 627-5631
  Cheboygan *(G-2677)*
Downriver Crushed Concrete .... G 734 283-1833
  Taylor *(G-15708)*
Elmers Crane and Dozer Inc .... C 231 943-3443
  Traverse City *(G-15962)*
Fenton Sand & Gravel Inc .... G 810 750-4293
  Fenton *(G-5213)*
Fidelis Contracting LLC .... G 313 361-1000
  Detroit *(G-4057)*
Finch Sand & Gravel LLC .... G 734 439-1044
  Milan *(G-10937)*
Frisbie Sand & Gravel .... G 269 432-3379
  Colon *(G-3372)*
Fritz Enterprises .... G 734 283-7272
  Trenton *(G-16154)*
Fyke Washed Sand Gravel .... G 248 547-4714
  Berkley *(G-1583)*
Genesis Sand and Gravel Inc .... G 313 587-8530
  West Bloomfield *(G-17477)*
Grand Rapids Gravel Company .... F 616 538-9000
  Belmont *(G-1462)*
Grand Rapids Gravel Company .... F 616 538-9000
  Grand Rapids *(G-6454)*
Grifco Inc .... G 989 352-7965
  Lakeview *(G-9173)*
Heritage Resources Inc .... G 616 554-9888
  Caledonia *(G-2298)*
High Grade Materials Company .... E 616 754-5545
  Greenville *(G-7138)*

SAND & GRAVEL

Huizenga Gravel Company Inc ....F 616 772-6241
  Zeeland (G-18156)
J T Express Ltd ....G 810 724-6471
  Brown City (G-2052)
Jeff Brown Sand & Gravel ....G 517 445-2700
  Clayton (G-3008)
Koenig Sand & Gravel LLC ....G 248 628-2711
  Oxford (G-12354)
Lafarge North America Inc ....F 703 480-3600
  Dundee (G-4591)
M-52 Sand & Gravel LLC ....G 734 453-3695
  Plymouth (G-12680)
M-57 Aggregate Company ....G 810 639-7516
  Montrose (G-11103)
Maple Valley Concrete Products ....G 517 852-1900
  Nashville (G-11460)
Marsack Sand & Gravel Inc ....F 586 293-4414
  Roseville (G-13829)
Mbcd Inc ....E 517 484-4426
  Lansing (G-9395)
Michigan Aggr Sand/Gravel Haul ....F 231 258-8237
  Kalkaska (G-8952)
Modern Industries Inc ....E 810 767-3330
  Flint (G-5469)
Nivers Sand Gravel ....F 231 743-6126
  Marion (G-10492)
Nugent Sand Company Inc ....E 231 755-1686
  Norton Shores (G-11785)
R and Js Gravel ....G 906 663-4571
  Bessemer (G-1606)
Saginaw Rock Products Co ....E 989 754-6589
  Saginaw (G-14144)
Schultz Sand Gravel LLC ....G 269 720-7225
  Plainwell (G-12544)
Searles Construction Inc ....G 989 224-3297
  Saint Johns (G-14295)
Sebewa Sand & Gravel LLC ....G 517 647-4296
  Portland (G-13067)
South Kent Gravel Inc ....E 269 795-3500
  Middleville (G-10807)
Stansley Mineral Resources Inc ....G 517 456-6310
  Clinton (G-3025)
Summers Road Gravel & Dev LLC ....G 810 798-8533
  Almont (G-268)
Trillacorpe/Bk LLC ....G 248 433-0585
  Bingham Farms (G-1662)
Trp Enterprises Inc ....G 810 329-4027
  East China (G-4625)
Vermeulen & Associates Inc ....G 616 291-1255
  Grand Rapids (G-6966)
Waanders Concrete Co ....E 269 673-6352
  Allegan (G-190)

SAND LIME PRDTS

Vico Company ....G 734 453-3777
  Plymouth (G-12789)

SAND MINING

American Aggregates Mich Inc ....F 248 348-8511
  Wixom (G-17760)
Bailey Sand & Gravel Co ....F 517 750-4889
  Jackson (G-8387)
Falcon Trucking Company ....G 313 843-7200
  Dearborn (G-3704)
Falcon Trucking Company ....E 989 656-2831
  Bay Port (G-1373)
Falcon Trucking Company ....F 248 634-9471
  Davisburg (G-3633)
Gale Briggs Inc ....G 517 543-1320
  Charlotte (G-2651)
Ken Measel Supply Inc ....G 810 798-3293
  Almont (G-260)
Michiana Aggregate Inc ....G 269 695-7669
  Niles (G-11626)
Mottes Materials Inc ....E 906 265-9955
  Iron River (G-8316)
Sand Products Wisconsin LLC ....G 231 722-6691
  Muskegon (G-11418)
Technisand Inc ....D 269 465-5833
  Benton Harbor (G-1554)
Tri-City Aggregates Inc ....E 248 634-8276
  Holly (G-7900)

SAND: Hygrade

Cabot Corporation ....E 989 495-2113
  Midland (G-10821)
Carrollton Paving Co ....F 989 752-7139
  Saginaw (G-14012)
Eggers Excavating LLC ....F 989 695-5205
  Freeland (G-5756)

SANDBLASTING EQPT

Horizon Bros Painting Corp ....G 810 632-3362
  Howell (G-8051)

SANDBLASTING SVC: Building Exterior

GTM Steamer Service Inc ....G 989 732-7678
  Gaylord (G-5863)

SANDSTONE: Crushed & Broken

American Aggregate Inc ....G 269 683-6160
  Niles (G-11594)

SANITARY SVC, NEC

City of Taylor ....E 734 374-1372
  Taylor (G-15700)

SANITARY SVCS: Refuse Collection & Disposal Svcs

Manistique Rentals Inc ....G 906 341-6955
  Manistique (G-10443)
Scooters Refuse Service Inc ....G 269 962-2201
  Battle Creek (G-1244)

SANITARY SVCS: Sanitary Landfill, Operation Of

K and W Landfill Inc ....F 906 883-3504
  Ontonagon (G-12160)
Southast Berrien Cnty Landfill ....F 269 695-2500
  Niles (G-11646)

SANITARY SVCS: Waste Materials, Recycling

Aci Plastics Inc ....E 810 767-3800
  Flint (G-5369)
American Commodities Inc ....E 810 767-3800
  Flint (G-5369)
Anchor Recycling Inc ....G 810 984-5545
  Port Huron (G-12891)
Applegate Insul Systems Inc ....E 517 521-3545
  Webberville (G-17446)
Clean Tech Inc ....E 734 529-2475
  Dundee (G-4577)
Clean Tech Inc ....E 734 455-3600
  Plymouth (G-12598)
Friedland Industries Inc ....E 517 482-3000
  Lansing (G-9232)
Glass Recyclers Ltd ....D 313 584-3434
  Dearborn (G-3715)
Jolicor Manufacturing Services ....F 586 323-5090
  Shelby Township (G-14612)
Lakestate Industries Inc ....E 906 786-9212
  Escanaba (G-4838)
Louis Padnos Iron and Metal Co ....E 616 452-6037
  Grand Rapids (G-6632)
Louis Padnos Iron and Metal Co ....E 517 372-6600
  Lansing (G-9309)
McM Disposal LLC ....G 616 656-4049
  Byron Center (G-2199)
National Zinc Processors Inc ....F 269 926-1161
  Benton Harbor (G-1535)
Real Alloy Recycling LLC ....D 517 279-9596
  Coldwater (G-3324)
Recycling Rizzo Services LLC ....D 248 541-4020
  Royal Oak (G-13964)
Trucent Inc ....G 734 426-9015
  Dexter (G-4515)

SANITARY WARE: Metal

Lakeshore Marble Company Inc ....E 269 429-8241
  Stevensville (G-15574)
Marbelite Corp ....E 248 348-1900
  Novi (G-11934)
Sloan Valve Company ....D 248 446-5300
  New Hudson (G-11555)
Thetford Corporation ....D 734 769-6000
  Dexter (G-4513)
Thetford Corporation ....C 734 769-6000
  Ann Arbor (G-670)

SANITATION CHEMICALS & CLEANING AGENTS

Access Business Group LLC ....B 616 787-6000
  Ada (G-3)
B W Manufacturing Inc ....G 616 447-9076
  Comstock Park (G-3461)
Bissell Better Life LLC ....G 800 237-7691
  Grand Rapids (G-6224)
Caravan Technologies Inc ....F 313 341-2551
  Detroit (G-3929)
Chemical Company of America ....G 313 272-4310
  Detroit (G-3932)
Coxen Enterprises Inc ....D 248 486-3800
  Brighton (G-1906)
Diversified Chemical Tech Inc ....C 313 867-5444
  Detroit (G-4011)
Formax Manufacturing Corp ....E 616 456-5458
  Grand Rapids (G-6416)
H & J Mfg Consulting Svcs Corp ....G 734 941-8314
  Romulus (G-13684)
Henkel Surface Technologies ....G 248 307-0240
  Madison Heights (G-10265)
Kath Khemicals LLC ....G 586 275-2646
  Sterling Heights (G-15387)
Kmi Cleaning Solutions Inc ....F 269 964-2557
  Battle Creek (G-1220)
McGean-Rohco Inc ....G 216 441-4900
  Livonia (G-9832)
SC Johnson & Son ....G 989 667-0235
  Bay City (G-1356)
Schaffner Manufacturing Co ....G 248 735-8900
  Northville (G-11724)
Tennant Commercial ....B 616 994-4000
  Holland (G-7826)
Thetford Corporation ....D 734 769-6000
  Dexter (G-4513)
Transtar Autobody Tech LLC ....C 810 220-3000
  Brighton (G-1999)
Ziebart International Corp ....C 248 588-4100
  Troy (G-16706)

SASHES: Door Or Window, Metal

George W Trapp Co ....E 313 531-7180
  Redford (G-13163)
Litex Inc ....G 248 852-0661
  Rochester Hills (G-13461)
Vertex Steel Inc ....E 248 684-4177
  Milford (G-10990)

SATCHELS

Tallulahs Satchels ....G 231 775-4082
  Cadillac (G-2281)

SATELLITE COMMUNICATIONS EQPT

Michigan Satellite ....E 989 792-6666
  Saginaw (G-14091)
Signal Group LLC ....E 248 479-1517
  Novi (G-11997)

SATELLITES: Communications

C & V Services Inc ....G 810 632-9677
  Hartland (G-7388)
Change Healthcare Tech LLC ....G 810 985-0029
  Port Huron (G-12906)

SAUNA ROOMS: Prefabricated

Ahs LLC ....F 888 355-3050
  Holland (G-7552)
Northwoods Hot Sprng Spas Inc ....G 231 347-1134
  Petoskey (G-12465)

SAW BLADES

Martin Saw & Tool Inc ....G 906 863-6812
  Menominee (G-10744)
Menominee Saw and Supply Co ....E 906 863-2609
  Menominee (G-10747)
Schott Saw Co ....G 269 782-3203
  Dowagiac (G-4560)
Workblades Inc ....E 586 778-0060
  Warren (G-17297)

SAWING & PLANING MILLS

American Classic Homes Inc ....G 616 594-5900
  Holland (G-7558)

PRODUCT SECTION

SCRAP & WASTE MATERIALS, WHOLESALE: Ferrous Metal

Applegate Insul Systems Inc ....E 517 521-3545
  Webberville *(G-17446)*
Atwood Forest Products Inc ....E 616 696-0081
  Cedar Springs *(G-2545)*
Bennett Sawmill ....G 231 734-5733
  Evart *(G-4879)*
Besse Forest Products Inc ....E 906 353-7193
  Baraga *(G-1098)*
Blough Hardwoods Inc ....G 616 693-2174
  Clarksville *(G-2966)*
Buskirk Lumber Company ....E 616 765-5103
  Freeport *(G-5763)*
Caledonia Cmnty Sawmill LLC ....G 616 891-8561
  Alto *(G-324)*
Casselman Logging ....G 231 885-1040
  Mesick *(G-10768)*
Cedar Mill LLC ....G 906 297-2318
  De Tour Village *(G-3667)*
Coe Creek Portable Sawmill ....G 231 829-3035
  Tustin *(G-16710)*
Collins Brothers Sawmill Inc ....F 906 524-5511
  Lanse *(G-9190)*
Country Side Sawmill ....G 989 352-7198
  Lakeview *(G-9171)*
Creekside Lumber ....G 231 924-1934
  Newaygo *(G-11566)*
Cruse Hardwood Lumber Inc ....G 517 688-4891
  Birmingham *(G-1679)*
Cygeirts Sawmill ....G 231 821-0083
  Brunswick *(G-2107)*
Cyrus Forest Products ....G 269 751-6535
  Allegan *(G-154)*
Daniel D Slater ....G 989 833-7135
  Riverdale *(G-13284)*
Decatur Wood Products Inc ....E 269 657-6041
  Decatur *(G-3802)*
Don Sawmill Inc ....G 989 733-2780
  Onaway *(G-12146)*
Dowd Brothers Forestry ....G 989 345-7459
  Alger *(G-138)*
E H Tulgestka & Sons Inc ....F 989 734-2129
  Rogers City *(G-13615)*
Ecostrat USA Inc ....G 416 968-8884
  Madison Heights *(G-10239)*
Eovations LLC ....G 616 361-7136
  Grand Rapids *(G-6382)*
Fairview Sawmill Inc ....G 989 848-5238
  Fairview *(G-4890)*
Forest Blake Products Inc....................G 231 879-3913
  Fife Lake *(G-5340)*
Forest Corullo Products Corp ....E 906 667-0275
  Bessemer *(G-1605)*
Forte Industries Mill Inc ....F 906 753-6256
  Stephenson *(G-15235)*
Gatien Farm & Forest Pdts LLC ....G 906 497-5541
  Powers *(G-13077)*
Grand Traverse Assembly Inc ....E 231 588-2406
  Ellsworth *(G-4788)*
Green Gables Saw Mill ....G 989 386-7846
  Clare *(G-2871)*
Gyms Sawmill ....G 989 826-8299
  Mio *(G-11003)*
Hmi Hardwoods LLC ....D 517 456-7431
  Clinton *(G-3023)*
Hochstetler Sawmill ....G 269 467-7018
  Centreville *(G-2595)*
Housler Sawmill Inc ....F 231 824-6353
  Mesick *(G-10770)*
Ida D Byler ....G 810 672-9355
  Cass City *(G-2515)*
Integrity Forest Products LLC ....G 513 871-8988
  Kenton *(G-8996)*
Jaroche Brothers Inc ....F 231 525-8100
  Wolverine *(G-17934)*
Jerome Miller Lumber Co ....G 231 745-3694
  Baldwin *(G-1083)*
Jerome Miller Lumber Co ....G 231 745-3694
  Baldwin *(G-1084)*
John A Biewer Lumber Company ....G 231 839-7646
  Lake City *(G-9089)*
John A Biewer Lumber Company ....D 231 825-2855
  Mc Bain *(G-10682)*
Kappen Saw Mill ....G 989 872-4410
  Cass City *(G-2516)*
Kells Sawmill Inc ....G 906 753-2778
  Stephenson *(G-15236)*
Maeder Bros Qlty WD Pllets Inc ....F 989 644-3500
  Weidman *(G-17460)*
Master Woodworks ....G 269 240-3262
  Saint Joseph *(G-14328)*

Matthews Mill Inc ....F 989 257-3271
  South Branch *(G-14749)*
Mc Guire Mill & Lumber ....G 989 735-3851
  Glennie *(G-5945)*
Michigan Lumber & Wood Fiber I ....E 989 848-2100
  Comins *(G-3383)*
Mlc of Wakefield Inc ....F 906 224-1120
  Wakefield *(G-16854)*
North American Forest Products ....G 269 663-8500
  Edwardsburg *(G-4770)*
Northern Hardwoods Oper Co LLC .....D 860 632-3505
  South Range *(G-14818)*
Northern Michigan Sawmill ....G 231 409-1314
  Williamsburg *(G-17716)*
Northern Products of Wisconsin ....G 715 589-4417
  Iron Mountain *(G-8293)*
Northwest Hardwoods Inc ....E 989 786-6100
  Lewiston *(G-9554)*
Northwood Lumber ....G 989 826-1751
  Mio *(G-11007)*
Oceana Forest Products Inc ....G 231 861-6115
  Shelby *(G-14532)*
Old Sawmill Woodworking Co ....G 248 366-6245
  Commerce Township *(G-3434)*
Parks Sawmill Products ....G 231 229-4551
  Lake City *(G-9095)*
Pollums Natural Resources ....G 810 245-7268
  Lapeer *(G-9481)*
Precision Hrdwood Rsources Inc........F 734 475-0144
  Chelsea *(G-2718)*
Prells Saw Mill Inc ....E 989 734-2939
  Hawks *(G-7430)*
Richter Sawmill ....G 231 829-3071
  Leroy *(G-9537)*
Riverbend Timber Framing Inc ....D 517 486-3629
  Blissfield *(G-1726)*
Sabertooth Enterprises LLC ....F 989 539-9842
  Harrison *(G-7316)*
Sagola Hardwoods Inc ....D 906 542-7200
  Sagola *(G-14188)*
Sawing Logz LLC ....G 586 883-5649
  Warren *(G-17231)*
Sawmill Estates ....G 269 792-7500
  Wayland *(G-17414)*
Schleben Forest Products Inc ....G 989 734-2858
  Rogers City *(G-13622)*
Silver Leaf Sawmill ....G 231 584-2003
  Elmira *(G-4793)*
Southwestern Hardwoods LLC ....G 269 795-0004
  Middleville *(G-10808)*
St Charles Hardwood Michigan ....F 989 865-9299
  Saint Charles *(G-14201)*
Superior Lumber Inc ....G 906 786-1638
  Gladstone *(G-5920)*
T Warren Sawmill ....G 989 619-0840
  Grayling *(G-7117)*
Terry Heiden ....G 906 753-6248
  Stephenson *(G-15241)*
Thorn Creek Lumber LLC ....G 231 832-1600
  Reed City *(G-13223)*
Timber Products Co Ltd Partnr ....C 906 452-6221
  Munising *(G-11250)*
Total Chips Company Inc ....F 989 866-2610
  Shepherd *(G-14731)*
Town & Country Cedar Homes ....G 231 347-4360
  Boyne Falls *(G-1842)*
Ufp Atlantic LLC ....G 616 364-6161
  Grand Rapids *(G-6945)*
Ufp Eastern Division Inc ....E 616 364-6161
  Grand Rapids *(G-6946)*
Ufp West Central LLC ....G 616 364-6161
  Grand Rapids *(G-6949)*
Waltons Sawmill ....G 517 841-5241
  Jackson *(G-8604)*
Wheelers Wolf Lake Sawmill ....G 231 745-7078
  Baldwin *(G-1086)*
William S Wixtrom ....G 906 376-8247
  Republic *(G-13247)*

SAWING & PLANING MILLS: Custom

Black Creek Timber LLC ....G 517 202-2169
  Rudyard *(G-13983)*
Great Northern Lumber Mich LLC ......E 989 736-6192
  Lincoln *(G-9562)*
Northern Sawmills Inc ....G 231 547-9452
  Charlevoix *(G-2622)*
Zulski Lumber Inc ....G 231 539-8909
  Pellston *(G-12427)*

SAWS & SAWING EQPT

Area Cycle Inc ....G 989 777-0850
  Bridgeport *(G-1849)*
Coxline Inc ....E 269 345-1132
  Kalamazoo *(G-8720)*
Elmo Manufacturing Co Inc ....G 734 995-5966
  Ann Arbor *(G-441)*
Jones & Hollands Inc ....G 810 364-6400
  Marysville *(G-10605)*
Lumberjack Shack Inc ....G 810 724-7230
  Imlay City *(G-8207)*
Pitchford Bertie ....G 517 627-1151
  Grand Ledge *(G-6113)*

SAWS: Portable

D & D Production Inc ....F 248 334-2112
  Waterford *(G-17332)*

SCAFFOLDS: Mobile Or Stationary, Metal

Swing-Lo Suspended Scaffold Co ....F 269 764-8989
  Covert *(G-3591)*

SCALE REPAIR SVCS

Kanawha Scales & Systems Inc ....F 734 947-4030
  Romulus *(G-13695)*
Standard Scale & Supply Co ....G 313 255-6700
  Detroit *(G-4374)*
Sterling Scale Company ....G 248 358-0590
  Southfield *(G-15035)*

SCALES & BALANCES, EXC LABORATORY

Hanchett Manufacturing Inc ....C 231 796-7678
  Big Rapids *(G-1632)*
Heco Inc ....D 269 381-7200
  Kalamazoo *(G-8762)*
Kanawha Scales & Systems Inc ....F 734 947-4030
  Romulus *(G-13695)*
M2 Scientifics LLC ....G 616 379-9080
  Holland *(G-7728)*

SCALES: Indl

Standard Scale & Supply Co ....G 313 255-6700
  Detroit *(G-4374)*
Sterling Scale Company ....G 248 358-0590
  Southfield *(G-15035)*
Universal Impex Inc ....G 734 306-6684
  Canton *(G-2437)*

SCALES: Truck

Trucksforsalecom ....G 989 883-3382
  Sebewaing *(G-14520)*

SCHOOL SPLYS, EXC BOOKS: Wholesalers

Weaver Instructional Systems ....G 616 942-2891
  Grand Rapids *(G-6981)*

SCHOOLS: Elementary & Secondary

Independent Mfg Solutions Corp ....E 248 960-3550
  Wixom *(G-17833)*

SCHOOLS: Vocational, NEC

Hope Focus ....C 313 494-5500
  Detroit *(G-4129)*
Royal ARC Welding Company ....E 734 789-9099
  Flat Rock *(G-5362)*

SCIENTIFIC EQPT REPAIR SVCS

Kaltec Scientific Inc ....G 248 349-8100
  Novi *(G-11913)*

SCIENTIFIC INSTRUMENTS WHOLESALERS

Instrumented Sensor Tech Inc ....G 517 349-8487
  Okemos *(G-12126)*

SCRAP & WASTE MATERIALS, WHOLESALE: Ferrous Metal

Drayton Iron & Metal Inc ....F 248 673-1269
  Waterford *(G-17339)*
Fpt Schlafer ....E 313 925-8200
  Detroit *(G-4071)*
Franklin Iron & Metal Co Inc ....E 269 968-6111
  Battle Creek *(G-1190)*

Employee Codes: A=Over 500 employees, B=251-500
C=101-250, D=51-100, E=20-50, F=10-19, G=3-9

SCRAP & WASTE MATERIALS, WHOLESALE: Ferrous Metal

Franklin Metal Trading Corp ....E...... 616 374-7171
   Lake Odessa *(G-9114)*
Friedland Industries Inc ....E...... 517 482-3000
   Lansing *(G-9232)*
Lorbec Metals - Usa Ltd ....E...... 810 736-0961
   Flint *(G-5462)*
Louis Padnos Iron and Metal Co ....E...... 616 459-4208
   Grand Rapids *(G-6631)*
Martin Bros Mill Fndry Sup Co ....E...... 269 927-1355
   Benton Harbor *(G-1525)*
Schneider Iron & Metal Inc ....F...... 906 774-0644
   Iron Mountain *(G-8299)*
Strong Steel Products LLC ....E...... 313 267-3300
   Detroit *(G-4381)*

SCRAP & WASTE MATERIALS, WHOLESALE: Metal

General Mill Supply Company ....E...... 248 668-0800
   Wixom *(G-17816)*
Louis Padnos Iron and Metal Co ....E...... 517 372-6600
   Lansing *(G-9309)*
Louis Padnos Iron and Metal Co ....F...... 231 722-6081
   Muskegon *(G-11368)*
Louis Padnos Iron and Metal Co ....F...... 616 301-7900
   Wyoming *(G-18018)*
Recycling Concepts W Mich Inc ....D...... 616 942-8888
   Grand Rapids *(G-6815)*
Shoreline Recycling & Supply ....E...... 231 722-6081
   Muskegon *(G-11424)*

SCRAP & WASTE MATERIALS, WHOLESALE: Nonferrous Metals Scrap

Huron Valley Steel Corporation ....C...... 734 479-3500
   Trenton *(G-16155)*
Resource Rcovery Solutions Inc ....G...... 248 454-3442
   Pontiac *(G-12861)*

SCRAP & WASTE MATERIALS, WHOLESALE: Oil

Usher Enterprises Inc ....E...... 313 834-7055
   Detroit *(G-4418)*

SCRAP & WASTE MATERIALS, WHOLESALE: Paper

Great Lakes Paper Stock Corp ....D...... 586 779-1310
   Roseville *(G-13811)*
V & M Corporation ....E...... 248 541-4020
   Royal Oak *(G-13980)*

SCRAP & WASTE MATERIALS, WHOLESALE: Plastics Scrap

Harbor Green Solutions LLC ....G...... 269 352-0265
   Benton Harbor *(G-1507)*
Upcycle Polymers LLC ....G...... 248 446-8750
   Howell *(G-8120)*

SCRAP STEEL CUTTING

Scotten Steel Processing Inc ....F...... 313 897-8837
   Detroit *(G-4356)*

SCREENS: Woven Wire

PA Products Inc ....G...... 734 421-1060
   Livonia *(G-9880)*

SCREW MACHINE PRDTS

AAA Industries Inc ....E...... 313 255-0420
   Redford *(G-13140)*
Accuspec Grinding Inc ....E...... 269 556-1410
   Stevensville *(G-15552)*
Advance Turning and Mfg Inc ....C...... 517 783-2713
   Jackson *(G-8373)*
Air-Matic Products Company Inc ....E...... 248 356-4200
   Southfield *(G-14825)*
Alco Manufacturing Corp ....E...... 734 426-3941
   Dexter *(G-4474)*
Allan Tool & Machine Co Inc ....D...... 248 585-2910
   Troy *(G-16190)*
American Screw Products Inc ....G...... 248 543-0991
   Madison Heights *(G-10189)*
Amerikam Inc ....D...... 616 243-5833
   Grand Rapids *(G-6167)*
Atf Inc ....E...... 989 685-2468
   Rose City *(G-13760)*

Atg Precision Products LLC ....E...... 586 247-5400
   Canton *(G-2349)*
Autocam-Pax Inc ....E...... 269 782-5186
   Dowagiac *(G-4534)*
B M Industries Inc ....G...... 810 658-0052
   Lapeer *(G-9442)*
Belgian Screw Machine Pdts Inc ....G...... 517 524-8825
   Concord *(G-3523)*
Berkley Screw Machine Pdts Inc ....E...... 248 853-0044
   Rochester Hills *(G-13376)*
Black River Manufacturing Inc ....E...... 810 982-9812
   Port Huron *(G-12900)*
BMC Bil-Mac Corporation ....D...... 616 538-1930
   Grandville *(G-7024)*
Borneman & Peterson Inc ....F...... 810 744-1890
   Flint *(G-5393)*
Brown City Machine Pdts LLC ....E...... 810 346-3070
   Brown City *(G-2048)*
Bulk AG Innovations LLC ....E...... 269 925-0900
   Benton Harbor *(G-1488)*
C S M Manufacturing Corp ....D...... 248 471-0700
   Farmington Hills *(G-4952)*
C Thorrez Industries Inc ....D...... 517 750-3160
   Jackson *(G-8399)*
Cap Collet & Tool Co Inc ....F...... 734 283-4040
   Wyandotte *(G-17951)*
Cardinal Group Industries Corp ....E...... 517 437-6000
   Hillsdale *(G-7521)*
Central Screw Products Company ....F...... 313 893-9100
   Troy *(G-16262)*
Comtronics ....G...... 517 750-3160
   Jackson *(G-8417)*
Condor Manufacturing Inc ....E...... 586 427-4715
   Warren *(G-16990)*
Core Electric Company Inc ....F...... 313 382-7140
   Melvindale *(G-10694)*
Corlett-Turner Co ....D...... 616 772-9082
   Zeeland *(G-18127)*
CPM Acquisition Corp ....D...... 231 947-6400
   Traverse City *(G-15951)*
Davison-Rite Products Co ....F...... 734 513-0505
   Livonia *(G-9699)*
Dennison Automatics LLC ....G...... 616 837-7063
   Nunica *(G-12035)*
Denny Grice Inc ....F...... 269 279-6113
   Three Rivers *(G-15860)*
Dexter Automatic Products Co ....C...... 734 426-8900
   Dexter *(G-4485)*
Dimension Machine Tech LLC ....F...... 586 649-4747
   Bloomfield Hills *(G-1759)*
Dirksen Screw Products Co ....E...... 586 247-5400
   Shelby Township *(G-14579)*
DPM Manufacturing LLC ....F...... 248 349-6375
   Livonia *(G-9715)*
Drews Manufacturing Co ....G...... 616 534-3482
   Grand Rapids *(G-6361)*
Durant and Sons Inc ....E...... 248 548-8646
   Oak Park *(G-12061)*
Dynamic Corporation ....D...... 616 399-9391
   Holland *(G-7613)*
E and P Form Tool Company Inc ....F...... 734 261-3530
   Garden City *(G-5823)*
Eagle Creek Mfg & Sales ....E...... 989 643-7521
   Saint Charles *(G-14192)*
ECM Specialties Inc ....G...... 810 736-0299
   Flint *(G-5422)*
Edmore Tool & Grinding Inc ....E...... 989 427-3790
   Edmore *(G-4750)*
Elkins Machine & Tool Co Inc ....E...... 734 941-0266
   Romulus *(G-13671)*
Elkins Machine & Tool Co Inc ....E...... 734 941-0266
   Romulus *(G-13672)*
Embers Ballscrew Repair ....F...... 586 216-8444
   Detroit *(G-4035)*
Extreme Precision Screw Pdts ....F...... 810 744-1980
   Flint *(G-5427)*
F & H Manufacturing Co Inc ....E...... 517 783-2311
   Jackson *(G-8445)*
Federal Screw Works ....E...... 734 941-4211
   Big Rapids *(G-1626)*
Federal Screw Works ....E...... 810 227-7712
   Brighton *(G-1922)*
Fettes Manufacturing Co ....E...... 586 939-8500
   Sterling Heights *(G-15339)*
Fordsell Machine Products Co ....E...... 586 751-4700
   Warren *(G-17042)*
Form All Tool Company ....F...... 231 894-6303
   Whitehall *(G-17666)*
Fox Mfg Co ....E...... 586 468-1421
   Harrison Township *(G-7331)*

Grace Engineering Corp ....D...... 810 392-2181
   Memphis *(G-10710)*
Grand Haven Steel Products Inc ....G...... 616 842-2740
   Grand Haven *(G-6025)*
Green Industries Inc ....F...... 248 446-8900
   South Lyon *(G-14793)*
Greendale Screw Pdts Co Inc ....E...... 586 759-8100
   Warren *(G-17065)*
H & K Machine Company Inc ....G...... 269 756-7339
   Three Oaks *(G-15849)*
H & L Tool Company Inc ....D...... 248 585-7474
   Madison Heights *(G-10263)*
H G Geiger Manufacturing Co ....F...... 517 369-7357
   Bronson *(G-2028)*
Harbor Screw Machine Products ....G...... 269 925-5855
   Benton Harbor *(G-1508)*
Hemingway Screw Products Inc ....G...... 313 383-7300
   Melvindale *(G-10699)*
Hibshman Screw Mch Pdts Inc ....E...... 269 641-7525
   Union *(G-16730)*
Hil-Man Automation LLC ....F...... 616 741-9099
   Zeeland *(G-18149)*
Hill Screw Machine Products ....G...... 734 427-8237
   Westland *(G-17570)*
Hollander Machine Co Inc ....G...... 810 742-1660
   Burton *(G-2156)*
Holt Products Company ....D...... 517 699-2111
   Holt *(G-7912)*
Hosco Inc ....F...... 248 912-1750
   Wixom *(G-17828)*
Huron Inc ....E...... 810 359-5344
   Lexington *(G-9558)*
Inland Lakes Machine Inc ....E...... 231 775-6543
   Cadillac *(G-2255)*
J & J Industries Inc ....G...... 517 784-3586
   Jackson *(G-8473)*
J C Gibbons Mfg Inc ....E...... 734 266-5544
   Livonia *(G-9789)*
J&J Machine Products Co Inc ....E...... 313 534-8024
   Redford *(G-13167)*
Jamco Manufacturing Inc ....G...... 248 852-1988
   Auburn Hills *(G-918)*
K & Y Manufacturing Inc ....E...... 734 414-7000
   Canton *(G-2390)*
Kalkaska Screw Products Inc ....E...... 231 258-2560
   Kalkaska *(G-8946)*
Kerr Screw Products Co Inc ....G...... 248 589-2200
   Madison Heights *(G-10290)*
L A Martin Company ....E...... 313 581-3444
   Dearborn *(G-3732)*
Lakeshore Automatic Pdts Inc ....G...... 616 846-4005
   Grand Haven *(G-6045)*
Lakeshore Fittings Inc ....D...... 616 846-5090
   Grand Haven *(G-6047)*
Lester Detterbeck Entps Ltd ....E...... 906 265-5121
   Iron River *(G-8314)*
Liberty Research Co Inc ....G...... 734 508-6237
   Milan *(G-10943)*
Liberty Turned Components LLC ....F...... 734 508-6237
   Milan *(G-10944)*
Livonia Automatic Incorporated ....G...... 734 591-0321
   Livonia *(G-9814)*
Lyon Manufacturing Inc ....E...... 734 359-3000
   Canton *(G-2395)*
Lyons Tool and Mfg Corp ....E...... 248 344-9644
   Wixom *(G-17849)*
M & N Machine LLC ....G...... 231 722-7085
   Muskegon *(G-11370)*
Malabar Manufacturing Inc ....F...... 517 448-2155
   Hudson *(G-8135)*
Master Automatic Mch Co Inc ....C...... 734 414-0500
   Plymouth *(G-12685)*
Maynard L Maclean L C ....D...... 586 949-0471
   Chesterfield *(G-2802)*
McNees Manufacturing Inc ....F...... 616 675-7480
   Bailey *(G-1080)*
Melling Tool Co ....B...... 517 787-8172
   Jackson *(G-8514)*
Merchants Automatic Pdts Inc ....E...... 734 829-0020
   Canton *(G-2401)*
Mercury Manufacturing Company ....D...... 734 285-5150
   Wyandotte *(G-17968)*
Michigan Precision Swiss Prts ....E...... 810 329-2270
   Saint Clair *(G-14229)*
Micromatic Screw Products Inc ....F...... 517 787-3666
   Jackson *(G-8522)*
Mid-West Screw Products Co ....F...... 734 591-1800
   Livonia *(G-9843)*
Milan Screw Products Inc ....E...... 734 439-2431
   Milan *(G-10949)*

MK Chambers Company ....E 810 688-3750
North Branch *(G-11663)*
Modern Tech Machining LLC ....G 810 531-7992
Port Huron *(G-12944)*
Mohr Engineering Inc ....E 810 227-4598
Brighton *(G-1963)*
Mountain Machine LLC ....F 734 480-2200
Van Buren Twp *(G-16774)*
Nelms Technologies Inc ....D 734 955-6500
Romulus *(G-13712)*
North Shore Machine Works Inc ....F 616 842-8360
Ferrysburg *(G-5336)*
Northern Precision Pdts Inc ....E 231 768-4435
Leroy *(G-9534)*
Nuko Precision LLC ....F 734 464-6856
Livonia *(G-9868)*
Omlor Enterprises Inc ....F 616 837-6361
Coopersville *(G-3567)*
Petschke Manufacturing Company ....F 586 463-0841
Mount Clemens *(G-11144)*
Phillips Bros Screw Pdts Co ....G 517 882-0279
Lansing *(G-9411)*
Pinckney Automatic & Mfg ....G 734 878-3430
Pinckney *(G-12502)*
Piper Industries Inc ....D 586 771-5100
Roseville *(G-13855)*
Precision Machine Co S Haven ....G 269 637-2372
South Haven *(G-14768)*
Prescott Products Inc ....G 517 787-8172
Jackson *(G-8556)*
Pro Slot Ltd ....G 616 897-6000
Hartford *(G-7386)*
Qualtek Inc ....G 269 781-2835
Marshall *(G-10587)*
R & D Screw Products Inc ....E 517 546-2380
Howell *(G-8084)*
Rae Manufacturing Company ....F 810 987-9170
Port Huron *(G-12960)*
Rempco Acquisition Inc ....E 231 775-0108
Cadillac *(G-2274)*
Rima Manufacturing Company ....D 517 448-8921
Hudson *(G-8141)*
Rite Machine Products Inc ....F 586 465-9393
Clinton Township *(G-3212)*
Riverside Screw Mch Pdts Inc ....F 269 962-5449
Battle Creek *(G-1241)*
Ryan Polishing Corporation ....F 248 548-6832
Oak Park *(G-12096)*
Ryder Automatic & Mfg ....G 586 293-2109
Fraser *(G-5720)*
SH Leggitt Company ....C 269 781-3901
Marshall *(G-10588)*
Sharp Screw Products Inc ....G 586 598-0440
Chesterfield *(G-2840)*
Sigma Machine Inc ....D 269 345-6316
Kalamazoo *(G-8887)*
Slater Tools Inc ....E 586 465-5000
Clinton Township *(G-3231)*
South Park Sales & Mfg Inc ....G 313 381-7579
Dearborn *(G-3762)*
Springdale Automatics Inc ....G 517 523-2424
Osseo *(G-12229)*
St Joe Tool Co ....E 269 426-4300
Bridgman *(G-1874)*
Stagg Machine Products Inc ....G 231 775-2355
Cadillac *(G-2280)*
State Screw Products Corp ....F 586 463-3892
Clinton Township *(G-3234)*
Steadfast Engineered Pdts LLC ....F 616 846-4747
Grand Haven *(G-6085)*
Stockbridge Manufacturing Co ....E 517 851-7865
Stockbridge *(G-15593)*
Stonebridge Industries Inc ....A 586 323-0348
Sterling Heights *(G-15513)*
Supreme Domestic Intl Sls Corp ....G 616 842-6550
Spring Lake *(G-15182)*
Supreme Machined Pdts Co Inc ....C 616 842-6550
Spring Lake *(G-15183)*
Supreme Machined Pdts Co Inc ....E 616 842-6550
Spring Lake *(G-15184)*
Swiss American Screw Pdts Inc ....F 734 397-1600
Canton *(G-2431)*
Swiss Industries Inc ....G 517 437-3682
Hillsdale *(G-7542)*
T & D Machine Inc ....G 517 423-0778
Tecumseh *(G-15810)*
Taylor Machine Products Inc ....C 734 287-3550
Plymouth *(G-12765)*
Taylor Screw Products Company ....G 734 697-8018
Van Buren Twp *(G-16786)*
Terry Tool & Die Co ....F 517 750-1771
Jackson *(G-8587)*
Tompkins Products Inc ....D 313 894-2222
Detroit *(G-4403)*
Topcraft Metal Products Inc ....E 616 669-1790
Hudsonville *(G-8184)*
Tri-Matic Screw Products Co ....E 517 548-6414
Howell *(G-8114)*
Tribal Manufacturing Inc ....E 269 781-3901
Marshall *(G-10591)*
Trinity Holding Inc ....F 517 787-3100
Jackson *(G-8593)*
Tru-Line Screw Products Inc ....E 734 261-8780
Livonia *(G-9972)*
Tru-Line Screw Products Inc ....E 734 261-8780
Livonia *(G-9973)*
United Precision Pdts Co Inc ....E 313 292-0100
Dearborn Heights *(G-3800)*
Victor Screw Products Co ....G 269 489-2760
Burr Oak *(G-2138)*
W A Thomas Company ....G 734 475-8626
Chelsea *(G-2720)*
Warren Screw Products Inc ....C 586 757-1280
Warren *(G-17288)*
Warren Scrw Products Inc ....G 586 994-0342
Rochester Hills *(G-13541)*
Westgood Manufacturing Co ....E 586 771-3970
Roseville *(G-13890)*
Wolverine Machine Products Co ....E 248 634-9952
Holly *(G-7902)*
Wsp Management LLC ....G 586 447-2750
Warren *(G-17299)*
Yankee Screw Products Company ....F 248 634-3011
Holly *(G-7903)*
Yarbrough Precision Screws LLC ....F 586 776-0752
Fraser *(G-5749)*
Zimmermann Engineering Co Inc ....G 248 358-0044
Southfield *(G-15070)*
Zygot Operations Limited ....F 810 736-2900
Flint *(G-5529)*

SCREW MACHINES

Amex Mfg & Distrg Co Inc ....G 734 439-8560
Milan *(G-10932)*
Champion Screw Machine Svcs ....G 248 624-4545
Wixom *(G-17784)*
Champion Screw Mch Engrg Inc ....F 248 624-4545
Wixom *(G-17785)*
Hollander Machine Co Inc ....G 810 742-1660
Burton *(G-2156)*
R E Gallaher Corp ....E 586 725-3333
Ira *(G-8267)*

SCREWS: Metal

Beaver Aerospace & Defense Inc ....D 734 853-5003
Livonia *(G-9662)*
E J M Ball Screw LLC ....F 989 893-7674
Bay City *(G-1307)*
Maynard L Maclean L C ....D 586 949-0471
Chesterfield *(G-2802)*
Modular Systems Inc ....G 231 865-3167
Fruitport *(G-5797)*
SA Industries 2 Inc ....G 248 693-9100
Lake Orion *(G-9158)*
W G Benjey Inc ....G 989 356-0027
Alpena *(G-320)*
Wedin International Inc ....D 231 779-8650
Cadillac *(G-2284)*

SEALANTS

Bars Products Inc ....E 248 634-8278
Holly *(G-7871)*
Connells Restoration & Sealan ....G 269 370-0805
Vandalia *(G-16800)*
Denarco Inc ....G 269 435-8404
Constantine *(G-3533)*
Huntler Industries Inc ....E 586 566-7684
Shelby Township *(G-14601)*
Huron Industries Inc ....G 810 984-4213
Port Huron *(G-12928)*
Lymtal International Inc ....E 248 373-8100
Orion *(G-12183)*
Precision Packing Corporation ....E 586 756-8700
Warren *(G-17194)*
Pro Sealants ....G 616 318-6067
Grand Rapids *(G-6779)*
Royal Adhesives & Sealants LLC ....D 517 764-0334
Michigan Center *(G-10790)*
Wright Sealant Restoration Inc ....G 616 453-5914
Walker *(G-16883)*
Z Technologies Corporation ....E 313 937-0710
Redford *(G-13209)*

SEALING COMPOUNDS: Sealing, synthetic rubber or plastic

Diversified Chemical Tech Inc ....C 313 867-5444
Detroit *(G-4011)*

SEALS: Hermetic

Tecumseh Products Company LLC ....A 734 585-9500
Ann Arbor *(G-661)*
Tecumseh Products Holdings LLC ....F 734 585-9500
Ann Arbor *(G-663)*

SEALS: Oil, Rubber

John Crane Inc ....F 989 496-9292
Midland *(G-10876)*

SEARCH & DETECTION SYSTEMS, EXC RADAR

Charles Walton ....G 517 332-1842
East Lansing *(G-4654)*

SEARCH & NAVIGATION SYSTEMS

A2 Motus LLC ....G 734 780-7334
Ann Arbor *(G-336)*
Aertech Machining & Mfg Inc ....E 517 782-4644
Jackson *(G-8375)*
Eaton Corporation ....F 517 787-8121
Ann Arbor *(G-430)*
Envisics LLC ....G 248 802-4461
Rochester Hills *(G-13419)*
Equitable Engineering Co Inc ....E 248 689-9700
Troy *(G-16351)*
Glassmaster Controls Co Inc ....E 269 382-2010
Kalamazoo *(G-8753)*
Green Bridge Tech Intl Inc ....G 810 410-8177
Linden *(G-9591)*
Honeywell International Inc ....C 231 582-5686
Boyne City *(G-1822)*
Hytrol Manufacturing Inc ....E 734 261-8030
Jackson *(G-8468)*
Instrumented Sensor Tech Inc ....G 517 349-8487
Okemos *(G-12126)*
Kva Engineering Inc ....G 616 745-7483
Grand Rapids *(G-6592)*
L3harris Technologies Inc ....G 517 780-0695
Jackson *(G-8492)*
Mistequay Group Ltd ....F 989 752-7700
Saginaw *(G-14097)*
Niles Precision Company ....C 269 683-0585
Niles *(G-11634)*
Parker-Hannifin Corporation ....B 269 384-3459
Kalamazoo *(G-8843)*
Quanenergy Systems Inc ....G 248 859-5587
Commerce Township *(G-3443)*
Rapp & Son Inc ....C 734 283-1000
Wyandotte *(G-17971)*
Senscomp Inc ....E 734 953-4783
Livonia *(G-9925)*
Sniffer Robotics LLC ....G 855 476-4333
Ann Arbor *(G-637)*
Star Lite International LLC ....G 248 546-4489
Oak Park *(G-12100)*
Swiss Precision Machining Inc ....F 586 677-7558
Macomb *(G-10165)*
Truform Machine Inc ....E 517 782-8523
Jackson *(G-8594)*
Woodward Inc ....B 616 772-9171
Zeeland *(G-18197)*

SEAT BELTS: Automobile & Aircraft

Key Safety Systems Inc ....C 586 726-3800
Auburn Hills *(G-926)*
Key Sfety Rstraint Systems Inc ....A 586 726-3800
Auburn Hills *(G-927)*
Takata Americas ....E 336 547-1600
Auburn Hills *(G-1012)*
Teamtech Motorsports Safety ....G 989 792-4880
Saginaw *(G-14163)*
Tk Holdings Inc ....C 517 545-9535
Howell *(G-8112)*
Wooshin Safety Systems ....G 248 615-4946
Farmington Hills *(G-5153)*

Employee Codes: A=Over 500 employees, B=251-500
C=101-250, D=51-100, E=20-50, F=10-19, G=3-9
2020 Harris Michigan
Industrial Directory
1359
PRODUCT

SEATING: Bleacher, Portable
- American Athletic .... F 231 798-7300
  Muskegon *(G-11266)*
- Stadium Bleachers LLC .... G 810 245-6258
  Lapeer *(G-9488)*

SEATING: Chairs, Table & Arm
- Carson Wood Specialties Inc .... G 269 465-6091
  Stevensville *(G-15559)*

SEATING: Stadium
- Baker Road Upholstery Inc .... G 616 794-3027
  Belding *(G-1398)*
- Interkal LLC .... C 269 349-1521
  Kalamazoo *(G-8773)*
- Kotocorp (usa) Inc .... G 269 349-1521
  Kalamazoo *(G-8802)*
- Midwest Seating Solutions Inc .... F 616 222-0636
  Grand Rapids *(G-6687)*

SEATING: Transportation
- Flint Stool & Chair Co Inc .... G 810 235-7001
  Flint *(G-5430)*

SECRETARIAL & COURT REPORTING
- Americas Finest Prtg Graphics .... G 586 296-1312
  Fraser *(G-5618)*
- Arena Publishing Co Inc .... G 586 296-5369
  Fraser *(G-5621)*
- Derk Pieter Co Inc .... G 616 554-7777
  Grand Rapids *(G-6343)*
- Faubles Prtg & Specialities .... G 231 775-4973
  Cadillac *(G-2246)*
- Fedex Office & Print Svcs Inc .... F 517 347-8656
  Okemos *(G-12123)*
- Fedex Office & Print Svcs Inc .... F 734 374-0225
  Taylor *(G-15722)*
- Fedex Office & Print Svcs Inc .... F 734 761-4539
  Ann Arbor *(G-459)*
- Fedex Office & Print Svcs Inc .... F 313 271-8877
  Dearborn *(G-3706)*
- Fedex Office & Print Svcs Inc .... E 734 996-0050
  Ann Arbor *(G-460)*
- Jomark Inc .... F 248 478-2600
  Farmington Hills *(G-5033)*
- Parkside Printing Inc .... G 810 765-4500
  Marine City *(G-10479)*
- Safran Printing Company Inc .... E 586 939-7600
  Beverly Hills *(G-1621)*
- T J K Inc .... G 586 731-9639
  Sterling Heights *(G-15518)*
- Thomas Kenyon Inc .... G 248 476-8130
  Saint Clair Shores *(G-14272)*

SECURITY CONTROL EQPT & SYSTEMS
- Dice Corporation .... E 989 891-2800
  Bay City *(G-1301)*
- Integrated Security Corp .... F 248 624-0700
  Novi *(G-11906)*
- Se-Kure Controls Inc .... E 269 651-9351
  Sturgis *(G-15633)*
- Securecom Inc .... G 989 837-4005
  Midland *(G-10914)*
- Weber Security Group Inc .... G 586 582-0000
  Mount Clemens *(G-11153)*

SECURITY DEVICES
- Cypress Computer Systems Inc .... F 810 245-2300
  Lapeer *(G-9453)*
- George Jensen .... G 269 329-1543
  Portage *(G-12998)*
- Identify Inc .... F 313 802-2015
  Madison Heights *(G-10273)*
- Pct Security Inc .... G 888 567-3287
  Clinton Township *(G-3192)*
- Picpatch LLC .... G 248 670-2681
  Milford *(G-10979)*
- Secure Crossing RES & Dev Inc .... F 248 535-3800
  Dearborn *(G-3756)*
- Volkswagen Group America Inc .... D 248 754-5000
  Auburn Hills *(G-1048)*

SECURITY EQPT STORES
- Creative Engineering Inc .... G 734 996-5900
  Ann Arbor *(G-408)*

- Intuitive Technology Inc .... G 602 249-5750
  Dexter *(G-4495)*

SECURITY PROTECTIVE DEVICES MAINTENANCE & MONITORING SVCS
- Executive Operations LLC .... E 313 312-0653
  Canton *(G-2373)*

SECURITY SYSTEMS SERVICES
- Cornelius Systems Inc .... E 248 545-5558
  Berkley *(G-1582)*
- Dice Corporation .... E 989 891-2800
  Bay City *(G-1301)*
- Ensure Technologies Inc .... F 734 668-8800
  Ypsilanti *(G-18072)*
- Hacks Key Shop Inc .... F 517 485-9488
  Lansing *(G-9380)*
- Honeywell International Inc .... D 248 926-4800
  Wixom *(G-17827)*
- Pct Security Inc .... G 888 567-3287
  Clinton Township *(G-3192)*
- Se-Kure Domes & Mirrors Inc .... E 269 651-9351
  Sturgis *(G-15634)*
- Traffic Sfety Ctrl Systems Inc .... E 248 348-0570
  Wixom *(G-17914)*

SEMICONDUCTOR & RELATED DEVICES: Read-Only Memory Or ROM
- Star Board Multi Media Inc .... G 616 296-0823
  Grand Haven *(G-6084)*

SEMICONDUCTOR CIRCUIT NETWORKS
- Bay Carbon Inc .... E 989 686-8090
  Bay City *(G-1282)*

SEMICONDUCTORS & RELATED DEVICES
- Advanced Photonix Inc .... G 734 864-5647
  Ann Arbor *(G-346)*
- Allegro Microsystems LLC .... G 248 242-5044
  Auburn Hills *(G-764)*
- American Wind & Solar LLC .... G 734 904-8490
  Woodhaven *(G-17937)*
- AMF-Nano Corporation .... G 734 726-0148
  Ann Arbor *(G-353)*
- API Technologies Corp .... G 301 846-9222
  Ann Arbor *(G-361)*
- Edward D Jones & Co LP .... G 616 583-0387
  Byron Center *(G-2188)*
- Electro-Matic Ventures Inc .... D 248 478-1182
  Farmington Hills *(G-4981)*
- Evjump Solar Inc .... G 734 277-5075
  Saline *(G-14388)*
- Gan Systems Corp .... G 248 609-7643
  Ann Arbor *(G-468)*
- Hemlock Smcndctor Oprtions LLC .... B 989 642-5201
  Hemlock *(G-7463)*
- Infineon Tech Americas Corp .... D 734 464-0891
  Livonia *(G-9782)*
- Instrumented Sensor Tech Inc .... G 517 349-8487
  Okemos *(G-12126)*
- International Bus Mchs Corp .... B 517 391-5248
  East Lansing *(G-4665)*
- Moog Inc .... E 734 738-5862
  Plymouth *(G-12695)*
- Optimems Technology Inc .... G 248 660-0380
  Novi *(G-11966)*
- Powerlase Photonics Inc .... G 248 305-2963
  Novi *(G-11976)*
- Promethient Inc .... G 231 525-0500
  Traverse City *(G-16082)*
- Sand Traxx .... G 616 460-5137
  Wayland *(G-17413)*
- Siemens AG .... G 248 307-3400
  Troy *(G-16599)*
- Teradyne Inc .... C 313 425-3900
  Allen Park *(G-211)*
- Terametrix LLC .... C 540 769-8430
  Ann Arbor *(G-664)*
- Texas Instruments Incorporated .... F 248 305-5718
  Novi *(G-12013)*
- Toshiba America Electronic .... G 248 347-2608
  Wixom *(G-17912)*
- Uusi LLC .... E 231 832-5513
  Reed City *(G-13226)*
- Veoneer Us Inc .... C 248 223-8074
  Southfield *(G-15059)*

SENSORS: Infrared, Solid State
- Piezonix LLC .... G 517 231-9586
  East Lansing *(G-4674)*
- Teslir LLC .... G 248 644-5500
  Bloomfield Hills *(G-1802)*

SENSORS: Radiation
- Lexatronics LLC .... G 734 878-6237
  Pinckney *(G-12499)*
- Tetradyn Ltd .... G 202 415-7295
  Traverse City *(G-16120)*

SENSORS: Temperature For Motor Windings
- Solidica Inc .... F 734 222-4680
  Ann Arbor *(G-639)*

SEPTIC TANK CLEANING SVCS
- Busscher Septic Tank Service .... G 616 392-9653
  Holland *(G-7582)*
- Forbes Sanitation & Excavation .... F 231 723-2311
  Manistee *(G-10422)*
- Franke Salisbury Virginia .... G 231 775-7014
  Cadillac *(G-2248)*

SEPTIC TANKS: Concrete
- Acme Septic Tank Co .... F 989 684-3852
  Kawkawlin *(G-8969)*
- Becker & Scrivens Con Pdts Inc .... E 517 437-4250
  Hillsdale *(G-7517)*
- Busscher Septic Tank Service .... G 616 392-9653
  Holland *(G-7582)*
- Cheboygan Cement Products Inc .... E 231 627-5631
  Cheboygan *(G-2677)*
- Daves Concrete Products Inc .... F 269 624-4100
  Lawton *(G-9511)*
- Deforest & Bloom Septic Tanks .... G 231 544-3599
  Central Lake *(G-2590)*
- Forbes Sanitation & Excavation .... F 231 723-2311
  Manistee *(G-10422)*
- Franke Salisbury Virginia .... G 231 775-7014
  Cadillac *(G-2248)*
- Imlay City Concrete Inc .... F 810 724-3905
  Imlay City *(G-8203)*
- Iron City Enterprises Inc .... G 906 863-2630
  Menominee *(G-10739)*
- Jordan Valley Concrete Service .... F 231 536-7701
  East Jordan *(G-4637)*
- Kerkstra Precast Inc .... C 616 457-4920
  Grandville *(G-7054)*
- Lenox Cement Products Inc .... G 586 727-1488
  Lenox *(G-9521)*
- Lenox Inc .... G 586 727-1488
  Lenox *(G-9522)*
- Maxs Concrete Inc .... G 231 972-7558
  Mecosta *(G-10690)*
- Nears Inc .... G 989 756-2203
  Whittemore *(G-17709)*
- Newberry Redi-Mix Inc .... G 906 293-5178
  Newberry *(G-11584)*
- Rudy Goupille & Sons Inc .... G 906 475-9816
  Negaunee *(G-11476)*
- Sandusky Concrete & Supply .... G 810 648-2627
  Sandusky *(G-14442)*
- Simmons Gravel Co .... G 616 754-7073
  Greenville *(G-7153)*
- Ted Voss & Sons Inc .... G 616 396-8344
  Holland *(G-7825)*
- W L Snow Enterprises Inc .... G 989 732-9501
  Gaylord *(G-5899)*

SEWAGE & WATER TREATMENT EQPT
- Central Lenawee Sewage Plant .... G 517 263-0955
  Adrian *(G-55)*
- Hygratek LLC .... G 847 962-6180
  Ann Arbor *(G-498)*
- Prime Solution Inc .... F 269 694-6666
  Otsego *(G-12253)*
- Sebright Products Inc .... E 269 792-6229
  Wayland *(G-17415)*
- Sludgehammer Group Ltd .... G 231 348-5866
  Petoskey *(G-12476)*
- Wayne County Laboratory .... G 734 285-5215
  Wyandotte *(G-17981)*

PRODUCT SECTION

SEWAGE FACILITIES
Kemin Industries Inc .... F 248 869-3080
  Plymouth *(G-12663)*

SEWER CLEANING EQPT: Power
Great Lakes Service & Supplies .... G 734 854-8542
  Petersburg *(G-12436)*
Hollis Sewer & Plumbing Svc .... G 517 263-8151
  Adrian *(G-67)*
Inland Management Inc .... G 313 899-3014
  Detroit *(G-4140)*
Spartan Tool LLC .... E 815 539-7411
  Niles *(G-11647)*
William Cosgriff Electrc .... G 313 832-6958
  Detroit *(G-4442)*

SEWING CONTRACTORS
Inplast Interior Tech LLC .... G 810 724-3500
  Almont *(G-258)*
Jacquart Fabric Products Inc .... C 906 932-1339
  Ironwood *(G-8332)*

SEWING MACHINE STORES
Fabric Patch Ltd .... G 906 932-5260
  Ironwood *(G-8328)*

SEWING, NEEDLEWORK & PIECE GOODS STORE: Quilting Matls/Splys
Quilters Garden Inc .... G 810 750-8104
  Fenton *(G-5233)*

SEWING, NEEDLEWORK & PIECE GOODS STORES: Sewing & Needlework
Sandlot Sports .... G 989 835-9696
  Saginaw *(G-14145)*

SHADES: Window
McDonald Wholesale Distributor .... G 313 273-2870
  Detroit *(G-4222)*
Royal Crest Inc .... G 248 399-2476
  Oak Park *(G-12095)*

SHAFTS: Flexible
Masterline Design & Mfg .... E 586 463-5888
  Harrison Township *(G-7339)*
Orlandi Gear Company Inc .... E 586 285-9900
  Fraser *(G-5701)*

SHAPES & PILINGS, STRUCTURAL: Steel
Bnb Welding & Fabrication Inc .... G 810 820-1508
  Burton *(G-2145)*
Fab Concepts .... G 586 466-6411
  Clinton Township *(G-3111)*
G & G Steel Fabricating Co .... G 586 979-4112
  Warren *(G-17048)*
Mean Erectors Inc .... E 989 737-3285
  Saginaw *(G-14085)*
Nelson Manufacturing Inc .... G 810 648-0065
  Sandusky *(G-14440)*
Sundown Sheet Metal Inc .... G 616 846-7674
  Spring Lake *(G-15181)*

SHAPES: Extruded, Aluminum, NEC
Sign Cabinets Inc .... G 231 725-7187
  Muskegon *(G-11425)*

SHEET METAL SPECIALTIES, EXC STAMPED
Accuform Industries Inc .... F 616 363-3801
  Grand Rapids *(G-6132)*
Accuform Industries Inc .... F 616 363-3801
  Grand Rapids *(G-6133)*
American Metal Fab Inc .... D 269 279-5108
  Three Rivers *(G-15854)*
Bauer Sheet Metal & Fabg Inc .... G 231 757-4993
  Scottville *(G-14508)*
Carlson Metal Products Inc .... E 248 528-1931
  Troy *(G-16259)*
Cmn Fabrication Inc .... G 586 294-1941
  Roseville *(G-13782)*
CNC Products LLC .... E 269 684-5500
  Niles *(G-11599)*
Cse Morse Inc .... D 269 962-5548
  Battle Creek *(G-1170)*
Custom Metal Products Corp .... G 734 591-2500
  Livonia *(G-9695)*
Custom Products Inc .... F 269 983-9500
  Saint Joseph *(G-14305)*
D&M Metal Products Company .... E 616 784-0601
  Comstock Park *(G-3474)*
Design Metal Inc .... F 248 547-4170
  Oak Park *(G-12059)*
Detronic Industries Inc .... D 586 268-6392
  Sterling Heights *(G-15315)*
Diversified Metal Fabricators .... E 248 541-0500
  Ferndale *(G-5281)*
Douglas West Company Inc .... G 734 676-8882
  Grosse Ile *(G-7171)*
Flat-To-Form Metal Spc Inc .... F 231 924-1288
  Fremont *(G-5771)*
Fortress Manufacturing Inc .... F 269 925-1336
  Benton Harbor *(G-1498)*
Hdn F&A Inc .... E 269 965-3268
  Battle Creek *(G-1197)*
J and N Fabrications Inc .... G 586 751-6350
  Warren *(G-17105)*
Jones Mfg & Sup Co Inc .... E 616 877-4442
  Moline *(G-11011)*
Kimbow Inc .... F 616 774-4680
  Comstock Park *(G-3490)*
Kulick Enterprises Inc .... G 734 283-6999
  Wyandotte *(G-17964)*
Lahti Fabrication Inc .... F 989 343-0420
  West Branch *(G-17510)*
Lanzen Incorporated .... D 586 771-7070
  Bruce Twp *(G-2090)*
Lyndon Fabricators Inc .... G 313 937-3640
  Detroit *(G-4212)*
Metallist Inc .... G 517 437-4476
  Hillsdale *(G-7530)*
Milton Manufacturing Inc .... E 313 366-2450
  Detroit *(G-4250)*
Mlp Mfg Inc .... E 616 842-8767
  Spring Lake *(G-15164)*
Modern Metalcraft Inc .... F 989 835-3716
  Midland *(G-10895)*
Modulated Metals Inc .... F 586 749-8400
  Chesterfield *(G-2807)*
National Roofg & Shtmtl Co Inc .... D 989 964-0557
  Saginaw *(G-14102)*
Professional Fabricating Inc .... E 616 531-1240
  Grand Rapids *(G-6782)*
Protofab Corporation .... G 248 689-3730
  Troy *(G-16569)*
Schuler Incorporated .... D 734 207-7200
  Canton *(G-2425)*
Shouldice Indus Mfrs Cntrs Inc .... D 269 962-5579
  Battle Creek *(G-1247)*
Sintel Inc .... C 616 842-6960
  Spring Lake *(G-15178)*
Steinke-Fenton Fabricators .... F 517 782-8174
  Jackson *(G-8577)*
Stelmatic Industries Inc .... F 586 949-0160
  Chesterfield *(G-2843)*
Sure-Weld & Plating Rack Co .... G 248 304-9430
  Southfield *(G-15040)*
Tel-X Corporation .... E 734 425-2225
  Garden City *(G-5843)*
Trigon Metal Products Inc .... G 734 513-3488
  Livonia *(G-9971)*
Vanmeer Corporation .... F 269 694-6090
  Otsego *(G-12258)*
W Soule & Co .... E 616 975-6272
  Grand Rapids *(G-6975)*
W Soule & Co .... D 269 324-7001
  Portage *(G-13054)*
Welk-Ko Fabricators Inc .... F 734 425-6840
  Livonia *(G-10004)*
Welk-Ko Fabricators Inc .... G 810 227-7500
  Brighton *(G-2008)*
Westco Metalcraft Inc .... F 734 425-0900
  Livonia *(G-10008)*
Zinger Sheet Metal Inc .... F 616 532-3121
  Grand Rapids *(G-7012)*

SHEETING: Laminated Plastic
Mediaform LLC .... E 248 548-0260
  Royal Oak *(G-13950)*

SHEETS & STRIPS: Aluminum
Arconic Inc .... G 231 894-5686
  Whitehall *(G-17662)*
Tech Forms Metal Ltd .... G 616 956-0430
  Grand Rapids *(G-6918)*

SHEETS: Fabric, From Purchased Materials
Spec International Inc .... E 616 248-9116
  Grand Rapids *(G-6878)*

SHEETS: Hard Rubber
Thunder Technologies LLC .... F 248 844-4875
  Rochester Hills *(G-13526)*

SHEETS: Solid Fiber, Made From Purchased Materials
Recycled Paperboard Pdts Corp .... G 313 579-6608
  Detroit *(G-4334)*

SHELLAC
Titan Sales International LLC .... G 313 469-7105
  Detroit *(G-4401)*

SHELTERED WORKSHOPS
ARC Services of Macomb Inc .... E 586 469-1600
  Clinton Township *(G-3056)*
Goodwill Inds Nthrn Mich Inc .... G 231 779-1311
  Cadillac *(G-2250)*
Goodwill Inds Nthrn Mich Inc .... G 231 779-1361
  Cadillac *(G-2251)*
Goodwill Inds Nthrn Mich Inc .... G 231 922-4890
  Traverse City *(G-15981)*
Vocational Strategies Inc .... E 906 482-6142
  Calumet *(G-2335)*

SHELVES & SHELVING: Wood
Modular Systems Inc .... G 231 865-3167
  Fruitport *(G-5797)*

SHELVING, MADE FROM PURCHASED WIRE
Adrian Steel Company .... B 517 265-6194
  Adrian *(G-46)*
Archer Wire International Corp .... D 231 869-6911
  Pentwater *(G-12428)*

SHELVING: Office & Store, Exc Wood
Basc Manufacturing Inc .... G 248 360-2272
  Commerce Township *(G-3393)*
Casper Corporation .... F 248 442-9000
  Farmington Hills *(G-4959)*
Knape & Vogt Manufacturing Co .... A 616 459-3311
  Grand Rapids *(G-6585)*

SHIP BUILDING & REPAIRING: Cargo Vessels
LA East Inc .... D 269 476-7170
  Vandalia *(G-16801)*

SHIP BUILDING & REPAIRING: Rigging, Marine
FD Lake Company .... F 616 241-5639
  Grand Rapids *(G-6403)*

SHIPBUILDING & REPAIR
Beardslee Investments Inc .... F 810 748-9951
  Harsens Island *(G-7368)*
Jag Industrial Services Inc .... G 678 592-6860
  Jonesville *(G-8657)*
Lake Shore Systems Inc .... D 906 265-5414
  Iron River *(G-8313)*
Lake Shore Systems Inc .... D 906 774-1500
  Kingsford *(G-9061)*
Merchant Holdings Inc .... G 906 786-7120
  Escanaba *(G-4844)*
Nicholson Terminal & Dock Co .... C 313 842-4300
  River Rouge *(G-13279)*
Nk Dockside Service & Repair .... G 906 420-0777
  Escanaba *(G-4846)*

SHIPPING AGENTS
N Pack Ship Center .... G 906 863-4095
  Menominee *(G-10752)*

SHIPS WHOLESALERS
Guys Timing Inc .... G 517 404-3746
  Brighton *(G-1936)*

Employee Codes: A=Over 500 employees, B=251-500
C=101-250, D=51-100, E=20-50, F=10-19, G=3-9

SHOE & BOOT ACCESS

Bond Manufacturing LLC ....G....... 313 671-0799
Detroit *(G-3909)*

SHOE MATERIALS: Counters

Bean Counter Inc ....G....... 906 523-5027
Calumet *(G-2325)*
Midwest Cabinet Counters ....G....... 248 586-4260
Madison Heights *(G-10306)*
Security Countermeasures Tech ....G....... 248 237-6263
Livonia *(G-9924)*

SHOE MATERIALS: Quarters

Canusa LLC ....F....... 906 259-0800
Sault Sainte Marie *(G-14462)*
Fresh Strt Transitional Living ....G....... 269 757-5195
Benton Harbor *(G-1499)*
Quarter Mania ....G....... 734 368-2765
Belleville *(G-1450)*
Quarters Vending LLC ....G....... 313 510-5555
Commerce Township *(G-3444)*
Zobl Quarter Horses ....G....... 810 479-9534
Clyde *(G-3285)*

SHOE MATERIALS: Rands

Rand L Industries Inc ....G....... 989 657-5175
Alpena *(G-311)*
Rand Worldwide Subsidiary Inc ....G....... 616 261-8183
Grandville *(G-7069)*

SHOE STORES

Hi-Tech Optical Inc ....E....... 989 799-9390
Saginaw *(G-14057)*

SHOE STORES: Athletic

Baumans Running Center Inc ....G....... 810 238-5981
Flint *(G-5385)*
Skechers USA Inc ....F....... 989 624-9336
Birch Run *(G-1672)*

SHOE STORES: Custom

Fourth Ave Birkenstock ....G....... 734 663-1644
Ann Arbor *(G-466)*

SHOE STORES: Custom & Orthopedic

Kalamazoo Orthotics & Dbtc ....F....... 269 349-2247
Kalamazoo *(G-8793)*

SHOE STORES: Men's

Millers Shoe Parlor Inc ....G....... 517 783-1258
Jackson *(G-8530)*

SHOE STORES: Orthopedic

Celebrations ....G....... 906 482-4946
Hancock *(G-7250)*
First Response Med Sups LLC ....F....... 313 731-2554
Dearborn *(G-3707)*

SHOES & BOOTS WHOLESALERS

Hush Puppies Retail LLC ....E....... 231 937-1004
Howard City *(G-8001)*

SHOES: Athletic, Exc Rubber Or Plastic

Warrior Sports Inc ....D....... 800 968-7845
Warren *(G-17289)*
Wolverine World Wide Inc ....C....... 616 866-5500
Rockford *(G-13600)*

SHOES: Canvas, Rubber Soled

Musical Sneakers Incorporated ....F....... 888 410-7050
Grandville *(G-7061)*

SHOES: Infants' & Children's

Saucony Inc ....G....... 616 866-5500
Rockford *(G-13589)*

SHOES: Men's

Hush Puppies Retail LLC ....E....... 231 937-1004
Howard City *(G-8001)*
Veldheer Tulip Garden Inc ....D....... 616 399-1900
Holland *(G-7844)*

Wolverine Procurement Inc ....E....... 616 866-9521
Rockford *(G-13597)*
Wolverine Procurement Inc ....F....... 616 866-5500
Rockford *(G-13598)*
Wolverine World Wide Inc ....C....... 616 866-5500
Rockford *(G-13600)*
Wolverine World Wide Inc ....G....... 616 863-3983
Rockford *(G-13601)*
Wolverine World Wide Inc ....G....... 616 866-5500
Rockford *(G-13602)*

SHOES: Orthopedic, Children's

Orthotool LLC ....G....... 734 455-8103
Plymouth *(G-12704)*

SHOES: Orthopedic, Men's

Kalamazoo Orthotics & Dbtc ....F....... 269 349-2247
Kalamazoo *(G-8793)*
Millers Shoe Parlor Inc ....G....... 517 783-1258
Jackson *(G-8530)*
Orthotool LLC ....G....... 734 455-8103
Plymouth *(G-12704)*
Shoe Shop ....G....... 231 739-2174
Muskegon *(G-11422)*

SHOES: Orthopedic, Women's

Millers Shoe Parlor Inc ....G....... 517 783-1258
Jackson *(G-8530)*
Orthotool LLC ....G....... 734 455-8103
Plymouth *(G-12704)*

SHOES: Plastic Or Rubber

Nike Retail Services Inc ....E....... 248 858-9291
Auburn Hills *(G-958)*
Original Footwear Company ....B....... 231 796-5828
Big Rapids *(G-1639)*
Wolverine Procurement Inc ....F....... 616 866-5500
Rockford *(G-13598)*

SHOES: Plastic Or Rubber Soles With Fabric Uppers

Atlantic Precision Pdts Inc ....F....... 586 532-9420
Shelby Township *(G-14550)*
Fernand Corporation ....G....... 231 882-9622
Kalamazoo *(G-8742)*

SHOES: Women's

Wolverine Procurement Inc ....E....... 616 866-9521
Rockford *(G-13597)*
Wolverine World Wide Inc ....C....... 616 866-5500
Rockford *(G-13600)*

SHOES: Women's, Dress

Bella Sposa Bridal & Prom ....G....... 616 364-0777
Grand Rapids *(G-6209)*

SHOPPING CART REPAIR SVCS

Effizient LLC ....G....... 616 935-3170
Grand Haven *(G-6012)*

SHOPPING CENTERS & MALLS

Reyers Company Inc ....F....... 616 414-5530
Spring Lake *(G-15172)*

SHOT PEENING SVC

Federal Industrial Svcs Inc ....F....... 586 427-6383
Warren *(G-17032)*
M P D Welding Inc ....E....... 248 340-0330
Orion *(G-12184)*
Metal Improvement Company LLC ......D....... 734 728-8600
Romulus *(G-13705)*
Metal Prep Technology Inc ....F....... 313 843-2890
Dearborn *(G-3739)*
Temp Rite Steel Treating Inc ....E....... 586 469-3071
Harrison Township *(G-7353)*

SHOW CARD & POSTER PAINTING

Pubsof Chicago LLC ....G....... 312 448-8282
Traverse City *(G-16083)*

SHOWCASES & DISPLAY FIXTURES: Office & Store

Arbor Gage & Tooling Inc ....E....... 616 454-8266
Grand Rapids *(G-6178)*
Arlington Display Inds Inc ....G....... 313 837-1212
Detroit *(G-3877)*
Michalski Enterprises Inc ....E....... 517 703-0777
Lansing *(G-9245)*
SC Custom Display Inc ....G....... 616 940-0563
Kentwood *(G-9032)*
Shaw & Slavsky Inc ....E....... 313 834-3990
Detroit *(G-4359)*
Vista Manufacturing Inc ....E....... 616 719-5520
Walker *(G-16881)*

SHOWER STALLS: Plastic & Fiberglass

D and G Glass Inc ....G....... 734 341-0038
Carleton *(G-2452)*
Your Shower Door ....G....... 616 940-0900
Grand Rapids *(G-7010)*

SHREDDERS: Indl & Commercial

Amos Mfg Inc ....E....... 989 358-7187
Alpena *(G-276)*
Chip Systems International ....F....... 269 626-8000
Scotts *(G-14503)*
Getecha Inc ....G....... 269 373-8896
Kalamazoo *(G-8752)*
Max Endura Inc ....E....... 989 356-1593
Alpena *(G-297)*

SHUNTS: Electric

S and S Enterprise LLC ....G....... 989 894-7002
Bay City *(G-1353)*

SHUTTERS, DOOR & WINDOW: Metal

Arnold & Sautter Co ....F....... 989 684-7557
Bay City *(G-1276)*
Atlantic Shutter ....G....... 248 668-6408
Wixom *(G-17762)*
Behind Shutter LLC ....G....... 248 467-7237
Grand Blanc *(G-5960)*
Secure Door LLC ....F....... 586 792-2402
Mount Clemens *(G-11149)*
Shutterbooth ....G....... 734 680-6067
Ann Arbor *(G-630)*
Shutterbooth ....G....... 586 747-4110
West Bloomfield *(G-17496)*
Shutters Chandeliers LLC ....G....... 989 773-0929
Mount Pleasant *(G-11226)*

SHUTTERS, DOOR & WINDOW: Plastic

Boral Building Products Inc ....C....... 248 668-6400
Wixom *(G-17777)*
Tapco Holdings Inc ....C....... 248 668-6400
Wixom *(G-17905)*

SIDING & STRUCTURAL MATERIALS: Wood

Decorative Panels Intl Inc ....E....... 989 354-2121
Alpena *(G-285)*
Nu-Tran LLC ....G....... 616 350-9575
Wyoming *(G-18023)*
Pure Products International In ....G....... 989 471-1104
Ossineke *(G-12231)*
Sensitile Systems LLC ....E....... 313 872-6314
Ypsilanti *(G-18100)*
Ufp Grand Rapids LLC ....F....... 616 464-1650
Grand Rapids *(G-6947)*
Universal Forest Products Inc ....C....... 616 364-6161
Grand Rapids *(G-6954)*
Yard & Home LLC ....G....... 844 927-3466
Grand Rapids *(G-7007)*

SIDING MATERIALS

Pine River Inc ....F....... 231 758-3400
Charlevoix *(G-2626)*

SIDING: Plastic

Certainteed Corporation ....B....... 517 787-8898
Jackson *(G-8405)*

SIDING: Sheet Metal

Dri-Design Inc ....E....... 616 355-2970
Holland *(G-7612)*

PRODUCT SECTION

SIGNS & ADVERTISING SPECIALTIES

Quality Alum Acquisition LLC ....D...... 800 550-1667
  Hastings *(G-7424)*

SIGN LETTERING & PAINTING SVCS

Amor Sign Studios Inc ....F...... 231 723-8361
  Manistee *(G-10414)*
Bill Carr Signs Inc ....F...... 810 232-1569
  Flint *(G-5389)*
Vital Signs Michigan Inc ....G...... 906 632-7602
  Sault Sainte Marie *(G-14478)*

SIGN PAINTING & LETTERING SHOP

Colonial Sign Co ....G...... 616 534-1400
  Newaygo *(G-11565)*
Handicap Sign Inc ....G...... 616 454-9416
  Grand Rapids *(G-6489)*
Kolossos Printing Inc ....F...... 734 994-5400
  Ann Arbor *(G-517)*
Landers Drafting Inc ....G...... 906 228-8690
  Marquette *(G-10539)*
Meiers Signs Inc ....G...... 906 786-3424
  Escanaba *(G-4843)*
Scotts Signs ....G...... 616 532-2034
  Grandville *(G-7070)*
Sun Ray Sign Group Inc ....G...... 616 392-2824
  Holland *(G-7820)*

SIGNALING APPARATUS: Electric

National Time and Signal Corp ....E...... 248 291-5867
  Oak Park *(G-12087)*
R H K Technology Inc ....E...... 248 577-5426
  Troy *(G-16574)*
Tecumseh Signals LLC ....G...... 517 301-2064
  Tecumseh *(G-15812)*

SIGNALS: Traffic Control, Electric

City of Saginaw ....F...... 989 759-1670
  Saginaw *(G-14019)*
Give-Em A Brake Safety LLC ....E...... 616 531-8705
  Grandville *(G-7037)*
National Sign & Signal Co ....E...... 269 963-2817
  Battle Creek *(G-1231)*

SIGNS & ADVERTISING SPECIALTIES

3 D & A Display LLC ....G...... 616 827-3323
  Grand Rapids *(G-6119)*
5 Pyn Inc ....G...... 906 228-2828
  Negaunee *(G-11466)*
A D Johnson Engraving Co Inc ....F...... 269 385-0044
  Kalamazoo *(G-8672)*
A-1 Engraving & Signs Inc ....G...... 810 231-2227
  Brighton *(G-1875)*
A-1 Signs ....G...... 269 488-9411
  Portage *(G-12980)*
Adams Outdoor Advg Ltd Partnr ....E...... 517 321-2121
  Lansing *(G-9201)*
Advantage Sign Supply Inc ....E...... 877 237-4464
  Hudsonville *(G-8143)*
All American Embroidery Inc ....F...... 734 421-9292
  Livonia *(G-9634)*
Allen Pattern of Michigan ....F...... 269 963-4131
  Battle Creek *(G-1145)*
Allied Signs Inc ....F...... 586 791-7900
  Clinton Township *(G-3043)*
Alternative Heating & Fuel ....G...... 231 745-6110
  Baldwin *(G-1081)*
Ar2 Engineering LLC ....E...... 248 735-9999
  Novi *(G-11829)*
Archer Wire International Corp ....D...... 231 869-6911
  Pentwater *(G-12428)*
Armstrong Display Concepts ....F...... 231 652-1675
  Newaygo *(G-11563)*
Art & Image ....G...... 800 566-4162
  Benton Harbor *(G-1483)*
Attitude & Experience Inc ....F...... 231 946-7446
  Traverse City *(G-15900)*
Ausable Woodworking Co Inc ....E...... 989 348-7086
  Frederic *(G-5750)*
Auto Trim Northwest Ohio In ....G...... 517 265-3202
  Adrian *(G-50)*
Auxier & Associates LLC ....G...... 231 486-0641
  Traverse City *(G-15901)*
Barrett Signs ....F...... 989 792-7446
  Saginaw *(G-14001)*
Bauman Engraving & Signs Inc .....G...... 906 774-9460
  Kingsford *(G-9054)*
Bayview Sign & Design ....G...... 231 922-7759
  Traverse City *(G-15910)*

Berline Group Inc ....E...... 248 203-0492
  Royal Oak *(G-13907)*
Bill Daup Signs Inc ....G...... 810 235-4080
  Swartz Creek *(G-15663)*
Blue De-Signs LLC ....G...... 248 808-2583
  Royal Oak *(G-13908)*
Britten Inc ....C...... 231 941-8200
  Traverse City *(G-15920)*
Broadmoor Motor Sales Inc ....G...... 269 320-6304
  Hastings *(G-7402)*
Bronco Printing Company ....G...... 248 544-1120
  Hazel Park *(G-7435)*
Burkett Signs Corp ....G...... 269 746-4285
  Climax *(G-3013)*
C G Witvoet & Sons Company ....E...... 616 534-6677
  Grand Rapids *(G-6249)*
C M S Sales Company Inc ....G...... 248 853-7446
  Rochester Hills *(G-13383)*
C T L Enterprises Inc ....F...... 616 392-1159
  Holland *(G-7583)*
Carrier & Gable Inc ....E...... 248 477-8700
  Farmington Hills *(G-4958)*
Charlies Wood Shop ....F...... 989 845-2632
  Chesaning *(G-2722)*
City Animation Co ....E...... 248 589-0600
  Troy *(G-16268)*
City Animation Co ....F...... 989 743-3458
  Corunna *(G-3579)*
Classic Stamp & Signs ....G...... 231 737-0200
  Norton Shores *(G-11746)*
Clips Coupons of Ann Arbo ....G...... 248 437-9294
  South Lyon *(G-14789)*
Cobrex Ltd ....G...... 734 429-9758
  Saline *(G-14382)*
Company B Graphic Design Inc ....G...... 906 228-5887
  Marquette *(G-10524)*
Consort Corporation ....E...... 269 388-4532
  Kalamazoo *(G-8713)*
Copy Central Inc ....G...... 231 941-2298
  Traverse City *(G-15947)*
Cotton Concepts Printing LLC ....G...... 313 444-3857
  Detroit *(G-3949)*
Creative Promotions ....G...... 734 854-2292
  Lambertville *(G-9181)*
Cronen Signs LLC ....G...... 269 692-2159
  Otsego *(G-12237)*
Custom Vinyl Signs & Designs ....G...... 989 261-7446
  Sheridan *(G-14732)*
D & D Signs Inc ....G...... 231 941-0340
  Traverse City *(G-15954)*
D & G Signs LLC ....G...... 810 230-6445
  Flint *(G-5411)*
D T R Sign Co LLC ....G...... 616 889-8927
  Hastings *(G-7405)*
Dearborn Signs & Awnings ....G...... 313 584-8828
  Dearborn *(G-3691)*
Decor Group International Inc ....F...... 248 307-2430
  Orchard Lake *(G-12165)*
Delux Monogramming Screen Prtg 989 288-5321
  Durand *(G-4607)*
Design Fabrications Inc ....D...... 248 597-0988
  Madison Heights *(G-10229)*
Detroit Marking Products Corp ......F...... 313 838-9760
  Canton *(G-2364)*
Detroit Name Plate Etching Inc ......E...... 248 543-5200
  Ferndale *(G-5278)*
Dicks Signs ....G...... 810 987-9002
  Port Huron *(G-12911)*
Digital Impact Design Inc ....G...... 269 337-4200
  Kalamazoo *(G-8727)*
Digital Information Svcs LLC ....G...... 313 365-7299
  Detroit *(G-4009)*
Dmp Sign Company ....G...... 248 996-9281
  Southfield *(G-14885)*
Donald Francis Strzynski ....G...... 231 929-7443
  Cadillac *(G-2244)*
Dornbos Sign Inc ....F...... 517 543-4000
  Charlotte *(G-2645)*
Douglas E Fulk ....G...... 517 482-2090
  Lansing *(G-9362)*
E and J Advertising LLC ....G...... 586 977-3500
  Warren *(G-17013)*
Edwards Outdoor Science ....G...... 906 353-7375
  Baraga *(G-1102)*
Epi Printers Inc ....D...... 734 261-9400
  Livonia *(G-9729)*
Fantastic Images Signs ....G...... 248 683-5556
  Waterford *(G-17343)*
Fastsigns ....G...... 248 488-9010
  Farmington Hills *(G-4997)*

Fastsigns International Inc ....G...... 231 941-0300
  Traverse City *(G-15968)*
Fedex Office & Print Svcs Inc ....F...... 313 359-3124
  Dearborn *(G-3705)*
Fedex Office & Print Svcs Inc ....E...... 734 996-0050
  Ann Arbor *(G-460)*
Firebolt Group Inc ....F...... 248 624-8880
  Wixom *(G-17810)*
Flairwood Industries Inc ....E...... 231 798-8324
  Norton Shores *(G-11756)*
Fosters Ventures LLC ....F...... 248 519-7446
  Troy *(G-16371)*
Freshwater Dgtal Mdia Prtnrs ....F...... 616 446-1771
  Kentwood *(G-9007)*
Fug Inc ....G...... 269 781-8036
  Marshall *(G-10568)*
G & W Display Fixtures Inc ....E...... 517 369-7110
  Bronson *(G-2026)*
Genesee County Herald Inc ....F...... 810 686-3840
  Clio *(G-3272)*
George P Johnson Company ....D...... 248 475-2500
  Auburn Hills *(G-883)*
Golden Pointe Inc ....G...... 313 581-8284
  Detroit *(G-4096)*
Graphic Cmmnctions Design Svcs 586 566-5200
  Shelby Township *(G-14597)*
Graphic Visions Inc ....F...... 248 347-3355
  Farmington Hills *(G-5013)*
Graphics Hse Spt Prmotions Inc ....E...... 231 733-1877
  Muskegon *(G-11335)*
Graphicus Signs & Designs ....G...... 231 652-9160
  Newaygo *(G-11569)*
Graphix Signs & Embroidery ....G...... 616 396-0009
  Holland *(G-7650)*
Grasshopper Signs Graphics LLC ......F...... 248 946-8475
  Farmington Hills *(G-5014)*
H M Day Signs Inc ....G...... 231 946-7132
  Traverse City *(G-15996)*
Handicap Sign Inc ....G...... 616 454-9416
  Grand Rapids *(G-6489)*
Harbor Industries Inc ....D...... 616 842-5330
  Grand Haven *(G-6032)*
HB Stubbs Company LLC ....F...... 586 574-9700
  Warren *(G-17078)*
Heileman Sons Signs & Ltg Svcs ...G...... 810 364-2900
  Saint Clair *(G-14221)*
Hexon Corporation ....F...... 248 585-7585
  Farmington Hills *(G-5018)*
HI-Lites Graphic Inc ....G...... 231 924-4540
  Fremont *(G-5776)*
Highlander Graphics LLC ....G...... 734 449-9733
  Ann Arbor *(G-491)*
Imagepro Inc ....G...... 231 723-7906
  Manistee *(G-10424)*
Images Unlimited LLC ....G...... 248 608-8685
  Rochester *(G-13328)*
Infonorm Inc ....G...... 248 276-9027
  Lake Orion *(G-9140)*
James D Frisbie ....F...... 616 868-0092
  Alto *(G-327)*
Janet Kelly ....F...... 231 775-2313
  Cadillac *(G-2256)*
JD Group Inc ....E...... 248 735-9999
  Novi *(G-11911)*
JD Hemp Inc ....G...... 248 549-0095
  Royal Oak *(G-13938)*
Jetco Signs ....G...... 269 420-0202
  Battle Creek *(G-1203)*
Johnson Sign Mint Cnslting LLC ....F...... 231 796-8880
  Paris *(G-12386)*
Jordan Advertising Inc ....F...... 989 792-7446
  Saginaw *(G-14067)*
K-Bur Enterprises Inc ....G...... 616 447-7446
  Grand Rapids *(G-6566)*
Kore Group Inc ....G...... 248 449-6500
  Livonia *(G-9800)*
Kore Group Inc ....G...... 734 677-1500
  Ann Arbor *(G-519)*
Lettering Inc of Michigan ....F...... 248 223-9700
  Livonia *(G-9806)*
Lobo Signs Inc ....E...... 231 941-7739
  Traverse City *(G-16027)*
Mackellar Associates Inc ....F...... 248 335-4440
  Rochester Hills *(G-13466)*
Majik Graphics Inc ....G...... 586 792-8055
  Clinton Township *(G-3165)*
Marketplace Signs ....G...... 248 393-1609
  Orion *(G-12185)*
Marygrove Awnings ....F...... 734 422-7110
  Livonia *(G-9824)*

Employee Codes: A=Over 500 employees, B=251-500
C=101-250, D=51-100, E=20-50, F=10-19, G=3-9

2020 Harris Michigan
Industrial Directory

1363

Maw Ventures Inc E 231 798-8324
Norton Shores *(G-11772)*
Mayfair Golf Accessories F 989 732-8400
Gaylord *(G-5879)*
Media Solutions Inc G 313 831-3152
Detroit *(G-4225)*
Meiers Signs Inc G 906 786-3424
Escanaba *(G-4843)*
Metro Sign Fabricators Inc G 586 493-0502
Clinton Township *(G-3173)*
MHR Investments Inc F 989 832-5395
Midland *(G-10884)*
Michigan Graphic Arts G 517 278-4120
Coldwater *(G-3315)*
Midwest Safety Products Inc E 616 554-5155
Grand Rapids *(G-6686)*
Mitchart Inc G 989 835-3964
Midland *(G-10892)*
Mod Signs Inc F 616 455-0260
Grand Rapids *(G-6694)*
Moody Sign Co G 517 626-6404
Portland *(G-13064)*
Moore Signs Investments Inc E 586 783-9339
Shelby Township *(G-14649)*
Motor City Manufacturing Ltd G 586 731-1086
Ferndale *(G-5302)*
Motor City Wraps LLC G 734 812-4580
Howell *(G-8067)*
Mrj Sign Company LLC G 248 521-2431
Ortonville *(G-12200)*
Nalcor LLC D 248 541-1140
Ferndale *(G-5303)*
New Rules Marketing Inc E 800 962-3119
Spring Lake *(G-15166)*
Nicolet Sign & Design G 906 265-5220
Iron River *(G-8317)*
Normic Industries Inc E 231 947-8860
Traverse City *(G-16049)*
Norris Graphics Inc G 586 447-0646
Clinton Township *(G-3184)*
On The Side Sign Dsign Grphics G 810 266-7446
Byron *(G-2174)*
Outfront Media LLC F 616 452-3171
Grand Rapids *(G-6736)*
Pappys Pad LLC G 231 894-0888
Montague *(G-11096)*
Perfect Impressions Inc G 248 478-2644
Farmington Hills *(G-5091)*
Perfect Signs G 231 233-3721
Manistee *(G-10434)*
Phillips Enterprises Inc E 586 615-6208
Shelby Township *(G-14665)*
Poco Inc E 313 220-6752
Canton *(G-2416)*
Praise Sign Company G 616 439-0315
Grandville *(G-7065)*
Printastic LLC F 248 761-5697
Novi *(G-11981)*
Pro-Motion Tech Group LLC D 248 668-3100
Wixom *(G-17880)*
Programmed Products Corp D 248 348-7755
Novi *(G-11983)*
Qmi Group Inc E 248 589-0505
Madison Heights *(G-10342)*
Quicktrophy LLC F 906 228-2604
Marquette *(G-10555)*
R & R Harwood Inc G 616 669-6400
Jenison *(G-8640)*
R L Hume Award Co G 269 324-3063
Portage *(G-13026)*
Revolutions Signs Designs LLC G 248 439-0727
Royal Oak *(G-13965)*
Richman Company Products Inc G 989 686-6251
Bay City *(G-1350)*
Rockstar Digital Inc F 888 808-5868
Sterling Heights *(G-15477)*
Rodzina Industries Inc G 810 235-2341
Flint *(G-5493)*
Route One G 616 455-4883
Grand Rapids *(G-6845)*
Royal Oak Name Plate Company F 586 774-8500
Roseville *(G-13863)*
Scotts Signs G 616 532-2034
Grandville *(G-7070)*
Sgo Corporate Center LLC F 248 596-8626
Plymouth *(G-12752)*
Shaw & Slavsky Inc E 313 834-3990
Detroit *(G-4359)*
Shelby Signarama Township G 586 843-3702
Shelby Township *(G-14693)*
Shields & Shields Enterprises G 269 345-7744
Kalamazoo *(G-8886)*
Shorecrest Enterprises Inc G 586 948-9226
Clinton Township *(G-3225)*
Sign & Art Inc G 734 522-0520
Livonia *(G-9930)*
Sign & Graphics Operations LLC E 248 596-8626
Plymouth *(G-12753)*
Sign A Rama Canton G 734 844-9068
Riverview *(G-13305)*
Sign A Rama Inc G 810 494-7446
Brighton *(G-1990)*
Sign Center of Kalamazoo Inc G 269 381-6869
Kalamazoo *(G-8889)*
Sign City Inc G 269 375-1385
Kalamazoo *(G-8890)*
Sign Fabricators Inc G 586 468-7360
Harrison Township *(G-7349)*
Sign Impressions Inc G 269 382-5152
Kalamazoo *(G-8891)*
Sign On Inc G 269 381-6869
Kalamazoo *(G-8892)*
Sign Screen Inc G 810 239-1100
Flint *(G-5499)*
Sign Stuff Inc G 734 458-1055
Livonia *(G-9931)*
Sign-A-Rama G 586 792-7446
Clinton Township *(G-3228)*
Sign-A-Rama Inc G 734 522-6661
Garden City *(G-5842)*
Signature Signs Inc G 989 777-8701
Bridgeport *(G-1856)*
Signs & Laser Engraving G 248 577-6191
Troy *(G-16602)*
Signs By Tomorrow G 810 225-7446
Brighton *(G-1991)*
Signs By Tomorrow G 734 822-0537
Ann Arbor *(G-633)*
Signs Letters & Graphics Inc G 231 536-7929
East Jordan *(G-4644)*
Signs Now G 248 623-4966
Waterford *(G-17376)*
Signs365com LLC G 800 265-8830
Shelby Township *(G-14694)*
Sky Promotions F 248 613-1637
Ann Arbor *(G-635)*
Spry Sign & Graphics Co LLC G 517 524-7685
Concord *(G-3525)*
Steel Skinz LLC G 517 545-9955
Howell *(G-8103)*
Sunset Enterprises Inc F 269 373-6440
Kalamazoo *(G-8902)*
Superior Graphics Studios Ltd G 906 482-7891
Houghton *(G-7985)*
Sylvesters G 989 348-9097
Grayling *(G-7116)*
T M Shea Products Inc F 800 992-5233
Troy *(G-16630)*
Terrell Assoc Signs & Disp G 517 726-0455
Vermontville *(G-16824)*
Tile By Bill & Sondra G 616 554-5413
Caledonia *(G-2319)*
Tischco Signs G 231 755-5529
Muskegon *(G-11438)*
Toms Sign Service G 248 852-3550
Rochester Hills *(G-13527)*
Tyes Inc F 888 219-6301
Ludington *(G-10083)*
Upper Level Graphics Inc G 734 525-7111
Livonia *(G-9982)*
Valassis International Inc B 734 591-3000
Livonia *(G-9987)*
Vinyl Graphix Inc G 586 774-1188
Saint Clair Shores *(G-14275)*
Visual Productions Inc E 248 356-4399
Southfield *(G-15061)*
Visual Workplace LLC F 616 583-9400
Byron Center *(G-2215)*
Vocational Strategies Inc E 906 482-6142
Calumet *(G-2335)*
Wenz & Gibbens Enterprises G 248 333-7938
Pontiac *(G-12874)*
West Shore Signs Inc G 734 324-7076
Riverview *(G-13306)*
Whitehall Products LLC D 231 894-2688
Whitehall *(G-17682)*
Wilde Signs F 231 727-1200
Muskegon *(G-11452)*
Wilfred Swartz & Swartz G G 989 652-6322
Reese *(G-13236)*
Wooden Moon Studio G 269 329-3229
Portage *(G-13059)*
Woods Graphics F 616 691-8025
Greenville *(G-7162)*

SIGNS & ADVERTISING SPECIALTIES: Artwork, Advertising

Detroit Art Collection LLC G 313 373-7689
Detroit *(G-3970)*
Epic Fine Arts Company Inc G 313 274-7400
Taylor *(G-15716)*
Laughabits LLC G 248 990-3011
Detroit *(G-4195)*

SIGNS & ADVERTISING SPECIALTIES: Displays, Paint Process

Kurth Bayard Co F 586 771-5174
Saint Clair Shores *(G-14258)*

SIGNS & ADVERTISING SPECIALTIES: Letters For Signs, Metal

Fairfield Investment Co G 734 427-4141
Livonia *(G-9734)*
Rsls Corp G 248 726-0675
Shelby Township *(G-14683)*

SIGNS & ADVERTISING SPECIALTIES: Novelties

Advertsing Ntwrk Solutions Inc G 248 475-7881
Rochester *(G-13312)*
Engineering Reproduction Inc F 313 366-3390
Detroit *(G-4038)*
Versatility Inc G 616 957-5555
Grand Rapids *(G-6967)*

SIGNS & ADVERTISING SPECIALTIES: Scoreboards, Electric

General Scoreboard Services G 734 753-5652
Belleville *(G-1445)*

SIGNS & ADVERTISING SPECIALTIES: Signs

Advance Graphic Systems Inc E 248 656-8000
Rochester Hills *(G-13365)*
Advanced Signs Incorporated F 616 846-4667
Ferrysburg *(G-5333)*
Agnew Grphics Signs Promotions G 989 723-4621
Owosso *(G-12276)*
Alex Delvecchio Entps Inc E 248 619-9600
Troy *(G-16184)*
Allstate Sign Company Inc G 989 386-4045
Farwell *(G-5157)*
Arnets Inc F 734 665-3650
Ann Arbor *(G-367)*
Art/Fx Sign Co G 269 465-5706
Bridgman *(G-1860)*
Auxier & Associates LLC G 231 933-7446
Traverse City *(G-15902)*
Banacom Instant Signs G 810 230-0233
Flint *(G-5382)*
Barrys Sign Company G 810 234-9919
Flint *(G-5384)*
Bcs Creative LLC G 248 917-1660
Davisburg *(G-3627)*
Bigsignscom E 800 790-7611
Grand Haven *(G-5996)*
Bill Carr Signs Inc F 810 232-1569
Flint *(G-5389)*
Castleton Village Center Inc G 616 247-8100
Grand Rapids *(G-6266)*
Commercial Graphics of Mich G 810 744-2102
Burton *(G-2150)*
Cook Sign Plus G 586 254-7000
Shelby Township *(G-14568)*
Craigs Signs G 810 667-7446
Lapeer *(G-9452)*
Creative Designs & Signs Inc G 248 334-5580
Pontiac *(G-12811)*
Creative Vinyl G 269 782-2833
Dowagiac *(G-4538)*
Dimension Graphics Inc G 616 245-1447
Grand Rapids *(G-6352)*
Eagle Graphics and Design G 248 618-0000
Waterford *(G-17340)*
Eberhard and Father Signworks G 989 892-5566
Essexville *(G-4872)*

Erie Marking Inc ... F ... 989 754-8360
Saginaw (G-14035)
Expressign Design ... G ... 734 747-7444
Ann Arbor (G-452)
Fairmont Sign Company ... E ... 313 368-4000
Detroit (G-4050)
Griffon Inc ... F ... 231 788-4630
Muskegon (G-11340)
Illusion Signs & Graphics Inc ... G ... 313 581-4376
Dearborn (G-3724)
Jacobs Signs ... G ... 810 659-2149
Flushing (G-5537)
JL Geisler Sign Company ... F ... 586 574-1800
Troy (G-16438)
Johnson Sign Company Inc ... F ... 517 784-3720
Jackson (G-8484)
Lavanway Sign Co Inc ... G ... 248 356-1600
Southfield (G-14959)
Marketing Displays Inc ... C ... 248 553-1900
Farmington Hills (G-5058)
Media Swing LLC ... G ... 313 885-2525
Grosse Pointe Farms (G-7186)
MI Custom Signs LLC ... F ... 734 946-7446
Taylor (G-15741)
Michigan Graphics & Signs ... G ... 989 224-1936
Saint Johns (G-14289)
Michigan Highway Signs Inc ... G ... 810 695-7529
Flint (G-5465)
Michigan Plaques & Awards Inc ... E ... 248 398-6400
Berkley (G-1587)
Miller Designworks LLC ... G ... 313 562-4000
Dearborn (G-3742)
MLS Signs Inc ... F ... 586 948-0200
Macomb (G-10145)
National Sign & Signal Co ... E ... 269 963-2817
Battle Creek (G-1231)
Northwood Signs Inc ... G ... 231 843-3956
Ludington (G-10074)
P D Q Signs Inc ... G ... 248 669-8600
White Lake (G-17637)
Plasticrafts Inc ... G ... 313 532-1900
Redford (G-13183)
Port Cy Archtctral Signage LLC ... G ... 231 739-3463
Muskegon (G-11403)
Rathco Safety Supply Inc ... E ... 269 323-0153
Portage (G-13027)
S S Graphics Inc ... G ... 734 246-4420
Wyandotte (G-17974)
Shop Makarios LLC ... G ... 800 479-0032
Byron Center (G-2211)
Sign and Design ... G ... 231 348-9256
Petoskey (G-12475)
Sign Concepts Corporation ... F ... 248 680-8970
Troy (G-16600)
Sign Specialties Co Inc ... G ... 313 928-4230
Allen Park (G-209)
Sign Up Inc ... G ... 906 789-7446
Escanaba (G-4860)
Signarama Ann Arbor ... G ... 734 221-5141
Ann Arbor (G-632)
Signcrafters Inc ... G ... 231 773-3343
Muskegon (G-11426)
Signplicity Sign Systems Inc ... G ... 231 943-3800
Traverse City (G-16103)
Signproco Inc ... F ... 248 585-6880
Troy (G-16601)
Signs & Designs Inc ... G ... 248 549-4850
Royal Oak (G-13970)
Signs & Designs Inc ... G ... 269 968-8909
Springfield (G-15203)
Signs Etc ... G ... 734 941-6991
Wyandotte (G-17975)
Signs Plus ... F ... 810 987-7446
Port Huron (G-12966)
Signs Unlimited ... G ... 906 226-7446
Marquette (G-10557)
Signtext Incorporated ... E ... 248 442-9080
Farmington Hills (G-5124)
Signworks of Michigan Inc ... G ... 616 954-2554
Grand Rapids (G-6864)
Sporting Image Inc ... F ... 269 657-5646
Paw Paw (G-12413)
Stamp-Rite Incorporated ... E ... 517 487-5071
Lansing (G-9267)
Supersine Company ... E ... 313 892-6200
Lathrup Village (G-9501)
Traffic Displays LLC ... G ... 616 225-8865
Greenville (G-7159)
TSS Inc ... E ... 586 427-0070
Warren (G-17271)
USA Sign Frame & Stake Inc ... G ... 616 662-9100
Jenison (G-8646)
Van Kehrberg Vern ... G ... 810 364-1066
Marysville (G-10625)
Vital Signs Inc ... G ... 313 491-2010
Canton (G-2441)
Wheelhouse Graphix LLC ... F ... 800 732-0815
Bloomfield Hills (G-1810)

SIGNS & ADVERTSG SPECIALTIES: Displays/Cutouts Window/Lobby

Arlington Display Inds Inc ... G ... 313 837-1212
Detroit (G-3877)
Display Structures Inc ... F ... 810 991-0801
Troy (G-16321)
Grafaktri Inc ... G ... 734 665-0717
Ann Arbor (G-476)
Harbor Industries Inc ... B ... 231 547-3280
Charlevoix (G-2617)
Top Deck Systems Inc ... G ... 586 263-1550
Clinton Township (G-3249)
Westcott Displays Inc ... E ... 313 872-1200
Detroit (G-4437)

SIGNS, EXC ELECTRIC, WHOLESALE

Attitude & Experience Inc ... F ... 231 946-7446
Traverse City (G-15900)
Erie Marking Inc ... F ... 989 754-8360
Saginaw (G-14035)
Infonorm Inc ... G ... 248 276-9027
Lake Orion (G-9140)
Screen Ideas Inc ... G ... 616 458-5119
Grand Rapids (G-6855)
Sign-A-Rama Inc ... G ... 734 522-6661
Garden City (G-5842)

SIGNS: Electrical

Amor Sign Studios Inc ... F ... 231 723-8361
Manistee (G-10414)
Earl Daup Signs ... F ... 810 767-2020
Flint (G-5420)
Eco Sign Solutions LLC ... G ... 734 276-8585
Ann Arbor (G-432)
Euko Design-Signs Inc ... G ... 248 478-1330
Farmington Hills (G-4992)
Fire Safety Displays Co ... G ... 313 274-7888
Dearborn Heights (G-3785)
Gardner Signs Inc ... F ... 248 689-9100
Troy (G-16379)
Hardy & Sons Sign Service Inc ... G ... 586 779-8018
Saint Clair Shores (G-14256)
Higgins Electric Sign Co ... G ... 517 351-5255
East Lansing (G-4661)
Huron Advertising Company Inc ... E ... 734 483-2000
Ypsilanti (G-18077)
Icon Sign & Design Inc ... G ... 517 372-1104
Lansing (G-9294)
Identicom Sign Solutions LLC ... G ... 248 344-9590
Farmington Hills (G-5026)
Japhil Inc ... G ... 616 455-0260
Grand Rapids (G-6553)
Jvrf Unified Inc ... G ... 248 973-2006
Sterling Heights (G-15383)
Landers Drafting Inc ... G ... 906 228-8690
Marquette (G-10539)
Michigan Signs Inc ... G ... 734 662-1503
Ann Arbor (G-556)
Pro Image Design ... G ... 231 322-8052
Traverse City (G-16079)
R J Designers Inc ... G ... 517 750-1990
Spring Arbor (G-15127)
Rwl Sign Co LLC ... G ... 269 372-3629
Kalamazoo (G-8877)
Sign Art Inc ... E ... 269 381-3012
Kalamazoo (G-8888)
Sign Image Inc ... F ... 989 781-5229
Saginaw (G-14149)
Sign Works Inc ... G ... 517 546-3620
Howell (G-8097)
Signs By Crannie Inc ... E ... 810 487-0000
Flint (G-5500)
Star Design Metro Detroit LLC ... E ... 734 740-0189
Livonia (G-9944)
Steves Custom Signs Inc ... F ... 734 662-5964
Ann Arbor (G-646)
Sun Ray Sign Group Inc ... G ... 616 392-2824
Holland (G-7820)
System 2/90 Inc ... D ... 616 656-4310
Grand Rapids (G-6911)
Tecart Industries Inc ... E ... 248 624-8880
Wixom (G-17907)
Traffic Signs Inc ... G ... 269 964-7511
Springfield (G-15206)
Transign LLC ... G ... 248 623-6400
Auburn Hills (G-1031)
Ucb Advertising ... G ... 269 808-2411
Plainwell (G-12550)
Universal Sign Inc ... E ... 616 554-9999
Grand Rapids (G-6955)
Valley City Sign Company ... E ... 616 784-5711
Comstock Park (G-3519)
Venture Grafix LLC ... G ... 248 449-1330
Wixom (G-17926)
Vinyl Express ... G ... 269 469-5165
New Buffalo (G-11518)
Vital Signs Michigan Inc ... G ... 906 632-7602
Sault Sainte Marie (G-14478)
Whitcomb and Sons Sign Co Inc ... G ... 586 752-3576
Romeo (G-13641)
Zk Enterprises Inc ... G ... 989 728-4439
Alger (G-140)

SIGNS: Neon

Bright Star Sign Inc ... G ... 313 933-4460
Detroit (G-3917)
Brownie Signs LLC ... G ... 248 437-0800
South Lyon (G-14787)
Colonial Sign Co ... G ... 616 534-1400
Newaygo (G-11565)
D Sign LLC ... G ... 616 392-3841
Holland (G-7604)
Graph-X Signs ... G ... 734 420-0906
Plymouth (G-12631)
Harmon Sign Inc ... G ... 248 348-8150
Wixom (G-17824)
Inter City Neon Inc ... G ... 586 754-6020
Warren (G-17095)
Modern Neon Sign Co Inc ... F ... 269 349-8636
Kalamazoo (G-8830)
Radiant Electric Sign Corp ... G ... 313 835-1400
Detroit (G-4328)
Scott Roberts ... G ... 269 668-5355
Kalamazoo (G-8885)
Signmakers Ltd ... G ... 616 455-4220
Grand Rapids (G-6863)
Signz LLC ... G ... 586 940-9891
Sterling Heights (G-15498)
Spectrum Neon Company ... G ... 313 366-7333
Detroit (G-4371)

SILICON: Pure

Snyder Plastics Inc ... E ... 989 684-8355
Bay City (G-1358)

SILICONE RESINS

Dow Silicones Corporation ... A ... 989 496-4000
Auburn (G-751)
Dow Silicones Corporation ... D ... 989 496-4137
Midland (G-10855)
Zander Colloids Lc ... G ... 810 714-1623
Fenton (G-5249)

SILICONES

Ddp Specialty Electnc ... G ... 989 496-4400
Midland (G-10829)
Dow Corning Corporation ... G ... 989 839-2808
Midland (G-10849)
Dow Silicones Corporation ... C ... 989 496-4000
Midland (G-10854)
Dow Silicones Corporation ... C ... 989 496-1306
Auburn (G-752)
Dow Silicones Corporation ... A ... 989 496-4000
Auburn (G-751)
Dow Silicones Corporation ... D ... 989 496-4137
Midland (G-10855)
Wacker Chemical Corporation ... A ... 517 264-8500
Adrian (G-103)

SILK SCREEN DESIGN SVCS

Authority Customwear Ltd ... E ... 248 588-8075
Madison Heights (G-10199)
Done Right Engraving Inc ... G ... 248 332-3133
Pontiac (G-12818)
East End Sports Awards Inc ... G ... 906 293-8895
Newberry (G-11579)
Engrave & Graphic Inc ... G ... 616 245-8082
Grand Rapids (G-6381)

Employee Codes: A=Over 500 employees, B=251-500
C=101-250, D=51-100, E=20-50, F=10-19, G=3-9
2020 Harris Michigan
Industrial Directory
1365

SILK SCREEN DESIGN SVCS

Exposure Unlimited Inc ....G....... 248 459-9104
  Fenton *(G-5205)*
G T Jerseys LLC ....G....... 248 588-3231
  Troy *(G-16376)*
Hi-Lites Graphic Inc ....E....... 231 924-0630
  Fremont *(G-5775)*
Sign Impressions Inc ....G....... 269 382-5152
  Kalamazoo *(G-8891)*
Sign Screen Inc ....G....... 810 239-1100
  Flint *(G-5499)*

SILLS: Concrete

Dlh World LLC ....G....... 313 915-0274
  Detroit *(G-4013)*

SILVER ORE MINING

Trelleborg Corporation ....G....... 269 639-9891
  South Haven *(G-14778)*

SILVERWARE & PLATED WARE

H M Products Inc ....G....... 313 875-5148
  Detroit *(G-4109)*
Rivore Metals LLC ....E....... 248 397-8724
  Detroit *(G-4346)*
Rivore Metals LLC ....E....... 248 397-8724
  Pontiac *(G-12862)*
Samco Industries LLC ....F....... 586 447-3900
  Roseville *(G-13866)*

SIMULATORS: Flight

Yakkertech Limited ....G....... 734 568-6162
  Ottawa Lake *(G-12270)*

SIRENS: Vehicle, Marine, Indl & Warning

West Shore Services Inc ....E....... 616 895-4347
  Allendale *(G-227)*

SKIDS: Wood

L & M Hardwood & Skids LLC ....G....... 734 281-3043
  Southgate *(G-15079)*

SKILL TRAINING CENTER

Summit Training Source Inc ....E....... 800 842-0466
  Grand Rapids *(G-6897)*

SKIN CARE PRDTS: Suntan Lotions & Oils

Sb3 LLC ....G....... 877 978-6286
  Ada *(G-29)*

SKYLIGHTS

Ceeflow Inc ....G....... 231 526-5579
  Harbor Springs *(G-7276)*

SLABS: Steel

Harrison Steel LLC ....G....... 586 247-1230
  Shelby Township *(G-14599)*

SLAG PRDTS

Edw C Levy Co ....B....... 313 429-2200
  Dearborn *(G-3700)*

SLAG: Crushed Or Ground

Tms International LLC ....F....... 734 241-3007
  Monroe *(G-11078)*

SLATE PRDTS

Moderne Slate Inc ....G....... 231 584-3499
  Mancelona *(G-10397)*

SLAUGHTERING & MEAT PACKING

Rogers Beef Farms ....G....... 906 632-1584
  Sault Sainte Marie *(G-14472)*

SLINGS: Lifting, Made From Purchased Wire

American Indus Training Inc ....G....... 734 752-2451
  Brownstown *(G-2058)*
Center Mass Inc ....G....... 734 207-8934
  Canton *(G-2359)*

SLINGS: Rope

Bundeze LLC ....G....... 248 343-9179
  West Olive *(G-17532)*
Canco Inc ....G....... 810 664-3520
  Lapeer *(G-9449)*
Quickmitt Inc ....G....... 517 849-2141
  Jonesville *(G-8667)*

SLIP RINGS

Kaydon Corporation ....B....... 734 747-7025
  Ann Arbor *(G-516)*

SLIPPERS: House

Wolverine Slipper Group Inc ....G....... 616 866-5500
  Rockford *(G-13599)*

SMOKE DETECTORS

Apollo America Inc ....D....... 248 332-3900
  Auburn Hills *(G-776)*
Gentex Corporation ....C....... 616 772-1800
  Zeeland *(G-18140)*
Gentex Corporation ....C....... 616 772-1800
  Zeeland *(G-18138)*

SNOW PLOWING SVCS

Clydes Frame & Wheel Service ....F....... 248 338-0323
  Pontiac *(G-12810)*
GTM Steamer Service Inc ....G....... 989 732-7678
  Gaylord *(G-5863)*
Mid Michigan Pipe Inc ....G....... 989 772-5664
  Grand Rapids *(G-6683)*
Shais Ldscpg Snow Plowing LLC ....G....... 248 234-3663
  Walled Lake *(G-16903)*
Unlimited Marine Inc ....G....... 248 249-0222
  White Lake *(G-17641)*

SNOW REMOVAL EQPT: Residential

Coffman Electrical Eqp Co ....E....... 616 452-8708
  Grand Rapids *(G-6286)*
Grandville Tractor Svcs LLC ....F....... 616 530-2030
  Grandville *(G-7041)*

SNOWMOBILE DEALERS

C & C Sports Inc ....E....... 810 227-7068
  Brighton *(G-1895)*
Floatation Docking Inc ....E....... 906 484-3422
  Cedarville *(G-2567)*
H R P Motor Sports Inc ....G....... 616 874-6338
  Rockford *(G-13570)*
Leaders Inc ....G....... 269 372-1072
  Kalamazoo *(G-8807)*
Micro Engineering Inc ....E....... 616 534-9681
  Byron Center *(G-2200)*
Spicers Boat Cy of Houghton Lk ....E....... 989 366-8384
  Houghton Lake *(G-7997)*

SNOWMOBILES

K & J Enterprises Inc ....G....... 231 548-5222
  Alanson *(G-111)*
Liberty Products Inc ....G....... 231 853-2323
  Ravenna *(G-13123)*
Pro-Powersports ....G....... 734 457-0829
  Monroe *(G-11063)*

SOAPS & DETERGENTS

Amway International Dev Inc ....F....... 616 787-6000
  Ada *(G-8)*
Aqua-Gel Corporation ....G....... 313 538-9240
  Redford *(G-13143)*
Caravan Technologies Inc ....F....... 313 341-2551
  Detroit *(G-3929)*
Continental Bldg Svs of Cinci ....F....... 313 336-8543
  Grosse Pointe Woods *(G-7202)*
Diversified Chemical Tech Inc ....G....... 313 867-5444
  Detroit *(G-4011)*
DSC Laboratories Inc ....E....... 800 492-5988
  Muskegon *(G-11307)*
Ecolab Inc ....E....... 248 697-0202
  Novi *(G-11879)*
Expert Cleaning Solutions Inc ....G....... 517 545-9095
  Howell *(G-8039)*
Fred Carter ....G....... 989 799-7176
  Saginaw *(G-14039)*
Hydro-Chem Systems Inc ....E....... 616 531-6420
  Caledonia *(G-2301)*
K C M Inc ....F....... 616 245-8599
  Grand Rapids *(G-6565)*
L I S Manufacturing Inc ....F....... 734 525-3070
  Livonia *(G-9803)*
Moon River Soap Co LLC ....G....... 248 930-9467
  Rochester *(G-13335)*
Sanitation Strategies LLC ....F....... 517 268-3303
  Holt *(G-7925)*
Sterling Laboratories Inc ....G....... 248 233-1190
  Southfield *(G-15034)*
Stone Soap Company Inc ....E....... 248 706-1000
  Sylvan Lake *(G-15672)*
Trinity Seven Enterprises Inc ....G....... 216 906-0984
  Canton *(G-2436)*
Vaughan Industries Inc ....F....... 313 935-2040
  Detroit *(G-4423)*

SOAPS & DETERGENTS: Scouring Compounds

Gage Global Services Inc ....E....... 248 541-3824
  Ferndale *(G-5287)*

SOAPS & DETERGENTS: Textile

Ipax Atlantic LLC ....F....... 313 933-4211
  Detroit *(G-4149)*

SOCIAL CLUBS

Great Lakes Fish Decoy Collect ....G....... 734 427-7768
  Livonia *(G-9759)*

SOCIAL SVCS, HANDICAPPED

Grace Extended ....G....... 616 502-2078
  Grand Haven *(G-6020)*

SOCKETS: Electric

Brooks Utility Products Group ....E....... 248 477-0250
  Novi *(G-11841)*
State Tool & Manufacturing Co ....D....... 269 927-3153
  Benton Harbor *(G-1552)*

SOFT DRINKS WHOLESALERS

Coca-Cola Refreshments USA Inc ....E....... 231 347-3242
  Petoskey *(G-12445)*
Mac Material Acquisition Co ....G....... 248 685-8393
  Highland *(G-7496)*
Pepsi-Cola Metro Btlg Co Inc ....D....... 810 232-3925
  Flint *(G-5479)*
South Range Bottling Works Inc ....G....... 906 370-2295
  South Range *(G-14819)*

SOFTWARE PUBLISHERS: Application

AK Rewards LLC ....G....... 734 272-7078
  Ann Arbor *(G-349)*
Alta Vista Technology LLC ....F....... 248 733-4504
  Southfield *(G-14830)*
Apis North America LLC ....G....... 800 470-8970
  Royal Oak *(G-13903)*
Arbormetrix Inc ....F....... 734 661-7944
  Ann Arbor *(G-366)*
Arctuition LLC ....G....... 616 635-9959
  Ada *(G-9)*
Argus Technologies LLC ....G....... 616 538-9895
  Grand Rapids *(G-6180)*
Asset Health Inc ....E....... 248 822-2870
  Troy *(G-16225)*
Automated Media Inc ....D....... 313 662-0185
  Redford *(G-13146)*
Avocadough LLC ....G....... 908 596-1437
  Byron Center *(G-2178)*
Black Ski Weekend LLC ....G....... 313 879-7150
  West Bloomfield *(G-17466)*
Bokhara Pet Care Centers ....F....... 231 264-6667
  Elk Rapids *(G-4775)*
Braiq Inc ....G....... 858 729-4116
  Detroit *(G-3912)*
C S Systems Inc ....G....... 269 962-8434
  Battle Creek *(G-1161)*
Capital Software Inc Michigan ....G....... 517 324-9100
  East Lansing *(G-4653)*
Chalq LLC ....G....... 269 330-1514
  Kalamazoo *(G-8705)*
Change Dynamix Inc ....G....... 248 671-6700
  Royal Oak *(G-13913)*
Collagecom LLC ....G....... 248 971-0538
  White Lake *(G-17631)*

Complete Data Products Inc ....G....... 248 651-8602
Troy *(G-16275)*
Cygnet Financial Planning Inc ....G....... 248 673-2900
Waterford *(G-17331)*
Dassault Systemes Americas ....C....... 248 267-9696
Auburn Hills *(G-836)*
Detroit Art Collection LLC ....G....... 313 373-7689
Detroit *(G-3970)*
Dynatrace LLC ....D....... 313 227-7300
Detroit *(G-4022)*
E Z Logic Data Systems Inc ....E....... 248 817-8800
Farmington Hills *(G-4977)*
Epath Logic Inc ....G....... 313 375-5375
Royal Oak *(G-13926)*
Eview 360 Corp ....E....... 248 306-5191
Farmington Hills *(G-4995)*
Flashplays Live LLC ....G....... 978 888-3935
Ann Arbor *(G-462)*
Gene Codes Forensics Inc ....F....... 734 769-7249
Ann Arbor *(G-470)*
Genesee Free Net ....G....... 810 720-2880
Flint *(G-5438)*
Gentry Services of Alabama ....G....... 248 321-6368
Warren *(G-17056)*
Greenview Data Inc ....E....... 734 426-7500
Ann Arbor *(G-479)*
Grit Obstacle Training LLP ....G....... 248 829-0414
Rochester *(G-13323)*
High Touch Healthcare LLC ....G....... 248 513-2425
Novi *(G-11901)*
Hypertek Corporation ....G....... 248 619-0395
Troy *(G-16407)*
Infor (us) Inc ....C....... 616 258-3311
Grand Rapids *(G-6534)*
Inora Technologies Inc ....F....... 734 302-7488
Ann Arbor *(G-506)*
Inovision Sftwr Solutions Inc ....G....... 586 598-8750
Chesterfield *(G-2791)*
Integrted Database Systems Inc ....F....... 989 546-4512
Mount Pleasant *(G-11197)*
Intellibee Inc ....G....... 313 586-4122
Detroit *(G-4145)*
Interpro Technology Inc ....F....... 248 650-8695
Rochester *(G-13330)*
Intrinsic4d LLC ....F....... 248 469-8811
Bingham Farms *(G-1654)*
Jrop LLC ....F....... 800 404-9494
Royal Oak *(G-13940)*
Kumanu Inc ....F....... 734 822-6673
Ann Arbor *(G-521)*
Life Is Digital LLC ....G....... 734 252-6449
Southfield *(G-14968)*
Local Mobile Services LLC ....G....... 313 963-1917
Plymouth *(G-12675)*
Logic Solutions Inc ....G....... 734 930-0009
Ann Arbor *(G-533)*
Lokol LLC ....G....... 586 615-1727
Walled Lake *(G-16897)*
Luhu LLC ....G....... 320 469-3162
East Lansing *(G-4668)*
Mathworks Inc ....F....... 248 596-7920
Novi *(G-11937)*
Medical Systems Resource Group ....G....... 248 476-5400
Farmington Hills *(G-5061)*
Menu Pulse Inc ....G....... 989 708-1207
Saginaw *(G-14088)*
Method Technology Service LLC ....E....... 312 622-7697
Troy *(G-16500)*
Mighty Legal LLC ....G....... 800 870-4605
Ann Arbor *(G-558)*
National Instruments Corp ....B....... 734 464-2310
Livonia *(G-9860)*
Neurable LLC ....G....... 206 696-4469
Ann Arbor *(G-573)*
Nexiq Technologies Inc ....F....... 248 293-8200
Rochester Hills *(G-13480)*
Nits Solutions Inc ....F....... 248 231-2267
Novi *(G-11953)*
Novation Analytics LLC ....G....... 313 910-3280
Auburn Hills *(G-963)*
Opio LLc ....F....... 313 433-1098
Wayne *(G-17440)*
Ops Solutions LLC ....E....... 248 374-8000
Wixom *(G-17874)*
Orthoview LLC ....G....... 800 318-0923
Plymouth *(G-12705)*
Perception Anlytics Rbtics LLC ....G....... 734 846-5650
Ann Arbor *(G-589)*
Phoenix Data Incorporated ....F....... 248 281-0054
Southfield *(G-14998)*
Pure Virtual Studios LLC ....G....... 248 250-4070
Oak Park *(G-12091)*
Rane Innovation LLC ....G....... 419 577-2126
Bay City *(G-1347)*
Rezoop LLC ....G....... 248 952-8070
Bloomfield *(G-1735)*
Ripple Science Corporation ....G....... 919 451-0241
Ann Arbor *(G-621)*
Rose Mobile Computer Repr LLC ....F....... 248 653-0865
Troy *(G-16583)*
Saagara LLC ....F....... 734 658-4693
Ann Arbor *(G-627)*
Saba Software Inc ....E....... 248 228-7300
Southfield *(G-15019)*
Sbsi Software Inc ....G....... 248 567-3044
Farmington Hills *(G-5121)*
Securitysnares Inc ....G....... 734 308-5106
Maybee *(G-10672)*
Selfies 2 Helpease Inc ....G....... 517 769-6900
Pleasant Lake *(G-12554)*
Simerics Inc ....G....... 248 513-3200
Novi *(G-11998)*
Sizzl LLC ....F....... 201 454-1938
Ann Arbor *(G-634)*
Sodius Corporation ....G....... 720 507-7078
Royal Oak *(G-13971)*
Software Advantage Consulting ....G....... 586 264-5632
Sterling Heights *(G-15503)*
Spindance Inc ....G....... 616 355-7000
Holland *(G-7811)*
Star Board Multi Media Inc ....G....... 616 296-0823
Grand Haven *(G-6084)*
Strider Software Inc ....G....... 906 863-7798
Menominee *(G-10757)*
Sunera Technologies Inc ....E....... 248 524-0222
Troy *(G-16625)*
Superior Information Tech LLC ....F....... 734 666-9963
Livonia *(G-9948)*
Supported Intelligence LLC ....G....... 517 908-4420
East Lansing *(G-4679)*
Thangbom LLC ....G....... 517 862-0144
Flint *(G-5510)*
Therapyline Technologies Inc ....E....... 734 407-9626
Brownstown *(G-2068)*
Totle Inc ....G....... 248 645-1111
Birmingham *(G-1706)*
True Anlytics Mfg Slutions LLC ....G....... 517 902-9700
Ida *(G-8194)*
Vanroth LLC ....F....... 734 929-5268
Ann Arbor *(G-691)*
Ventuor LLC ....G....... 248 790-8700
Flint *(G-5520)*
Virtual Emergency Services LLC ....F....... 734 324-2299
Wyandotte *(G-17980)*
Visiun Inc ....G....... 734 741-0356
Ann Arbor *(G-693)*
Vivian Enterprises LLC ....E....... 248 792-9925
Southfield *(G-15063)*
Weaver Instructional Systems ....G....... 616 942-2891
Grand Rapids *(G-6981)*
Xilinx Inc ....G....... 248 344-0786
Wixom *(G-17932)*

SOFTWARE PUBLISHERS: Business & Professional

313 Certified LLC ....G....... 248 915-8419
Bloomfield Hills *(G-1738)*
Appropos LLC ....E....... 844 462-7776
Grand Rapids *(G-6175)*
Automated Bookkeeping Inc ....G....... 866 617-3122
Detroit *(G-3884)*
Bell and Howell LLC ....G....... 734 421-1727
Livonia *(G-9664)*
Blue Pony LLC ....G....... 616 291-5554
Hudsonville *(G-8149)*
Blujay Solutions Co ....G....... 616 738-6400
Holland *(G-7571)*
Broadsword Solutions Corp ....F....... 248 341-3367
Waterford *(G-17326)*
Coeus LLC ....F....... 248 564-1958
Bloomfield Hills *(G-1754)*
Computer Mail Services Inc ....F....... 248 352-6700
Sterling Heights *(G-15293)*
Consistacom Inc ....G....... 906 482-7653
Houghton *(G-7972)*
Core Technology Corporation ....F....... 517 627-1521
Lansing *(G-9285)*
Cq Simple LLC ....G....... 989 492-7068
Midland *(G-10827)*
Datamatic Processing Inc ....E....... 517 882-4401
Lansing *(G-9359)*
Dna Software Inc ....F....... 734 222-9080
Ann Arbor *(G-422)*
DRae LLC ....G....... 313 923-7230
Oak Park *(G-12060)*
E-Con LLC ....E....... 248 766-9000
Birmingham *(G-1682)*
E-Procurement Services LLC ....E....... 248 630-7200
Auburn Hills *(G-850)*
EMC Corporation ....G....... 248 374-5009
Novi *(G-11883)*
Export Service International ....G....... 248 620-7100
Clarkston *(G-2919)*
Faac Incorporated ....C....... 734 761-5836
Ann Arbor *(G-456)*
Greenback Inc ....G....... 313 443-4272
Birmingham *(G-1685)*
Idv Solutions LLC ....E....... 517 853-3755
Lansing *(G-9295)*
Infotech Imaging Inc ....F....... 616 458-8686
Grand Rapids *(G-6535)*
Lakeside Software Inc ....E....... 248 686-1700
Bloomfield Hills *(G-1776)*
Level Eleven LLC ....E....... 313 662-2000
Detroit *(G-4201)*
Marykay Software Inc ....G....... 989 463-4385
Alma *(G-239)*
Mastery Technologies Inc ....F....... 248 888-8420
Novi *(G-11936)*
Mc Donald Computer Corporation ....F....... 248 350-9290
Southfield *(G-14975)*
Michigan Interactive LLC ....G....... 517 241-4341
Bingham Farms *(G-1657)*
Mscsoftware Corporation ....C....... 734 994-3800
Ann Arbor *(G-567)*
Onestream Software Corp ....G....... 248 841-1356
Rochester *(G-13341)*
Onestream Software LLC ....F....... 248 342-1541
Rochester *(G-13342)*
Optimizerx Corporation ....G....... 248 651-6568
Rochester *(G-13343)*
Oracle Corporation ....B....... 248 393-2498
Orion *(G-12187)*
Orion Bus Accnting Sltions LLC ....G....... 248 893-1060
Wyandotte *(G-17970)*
Parameter Driven Software Inc ....F....... 248 553-6410
Farmington Hills *(G-5088)*
Paramount Technologies Inc ....E....... 248 960-0909
Walled Lake *(G-16901)*
Platformsh Inc ....F....... 734 707-9124
Brooklyn *(G-2041)*
Prehab Technologies LLC ....G....... 734 368-9983
Ann Arbor *(G-602)*
Qe Tools LLC ....G....... 734 330-4707
Ann Arbor *(G-609)*
Quest - IV Incorporated ....F....... 734 847-5487
Lambertville *(G-9184)*
Salespage Technologies LLC ....D....... 269 567-7400
Kalamazoo *(G-8883)*
Siemens Product Life Mgmt Sftw ....E....... 313 317-6100
Allen Park *(G-208)*
Siemens Product Life Mgmt Sftw ....D....... 734 953-2700
Livonia *(G-9926)*
Siemens Product Life Mgmt Sftw ....D....... 734 994-7300
Ann Arbor *(G-631)*
Solid Logic LLC ....F....... 616 738-8922
Holland *(G-7810)*
Talbot & Associates Inc ....F....... 248 723-9700
Franklin *(G-5609)*
Taxtime USA Inc ....G....... 248 642-7070
Bingham Farms *(G-1661)*
Technology Network Svcs Inc ....F....... 586 294-7771
Saint Clair Shores *(G-14271)*
Titania Software LLC ....G....... 734 786-8225
Ann Arbor *(G-676)*
Torenzo Inc ....F....... 313 732-7874
Bloomfield Hills *(G-1804)*
Tru-Syzygy Inc ....G....... 248 622-7211
Lake Orion *(G-9167)*
Truarx Inc ....F....... 248 538-7809
Southfield *(G-15050)*
Ultimate Software Group Inc ....E....... 517 540-9718
Howell *(G-8117)*
Urefer Inc ....G....... 734 585-5684
Ann Arbor *(G-689)*
Valassis Communications Inc ....C....... 734 591-3000
Livonia *(G-9985)*
Valassis Communications Inc ....C....... 734 432-8000
Livonia *(G-9986)*

Employee Codes: A=Over 500 employees, B=251-500
C=101-250, D=51-100, E=20-50, F=10-19, G=3-9

2020 Harris Michigan
Industrial Directory

1367

Wilson Technologies Inc.......G....... 248 655-0005
Clawson *(G-2989)*
Workforce Payhub Inc.......G....... 517 759-4026
Adrian *(G-104)*
Workforce Software LLC.......C....... 734 542-4100
Livonia *(G-10012)*
Zferral Inc.......G....... 248 792-3472
Royal Oak *(G-13982)*

SOFTWARE PUBLISHERS: Computer Utilities

Click Care LLC.......G....... 989 792-1544
Saginaw *(G-14020)*

SOFTWARE PUBLISHERS: Education

Eca Educational Services Inc.......E....... 248 669-7170
Commerce Township *(G-3403)*
Epic 4d LLC.......G....... 800 470-8948
Detroit *(G-4040)*
Expectancy Learning LLC.......G....... 866 829-9533
Grand Rapids *(G-6392)*
Fbe Associates Inc.......G....... 989 894-2785
Bay City *(G-1314)*
Ginkgotree Inc.......G....... 734 707-7191
Detroit *(G-4091)*
Jam-Live LLC.......G....... 517 282-5410
Howell *(G-8054)*
Mejenta Systems Inc.......E....... 248 434-2583
Southfield *(G-14977)*
Possibilities For Change LLC.......G....... 810 333-1347
Ann Arbor *(G-596)*

SOFTWARE PUBLISHERS: NEC

21st Century Graphic Tech LLC.......G....... 586 463-9599
Utica *(G-16740)*
360ofme Inc.......G....... 844 360-6363
Royal Oak *(G-13897)*
3r Info LLC.......F....... 201 221-6133
Canton *(G-2342)*
4d Systems LLC.......E....... 800 380-9165
Flint *(G-5366)*
Accessible Information LLC.......G....... 248 338-4928
Bloomfield Hills *(G-1740)*
Akamai Technologies Inc.......G....... 734 424-1142
Pinckney *(G-12495)*
Altair Engineering Inc.......C....... 248 614-2400
Troy *(G-16192)*
Amicus Software.......G....... 313 417-9550
White Lake *(G-17629)*
Amt Software LLC.......G....... 248 458-0359
Bloomfield Hills *(G-1745)*
Ansys Inc.......G....... 248 613-2677
Ann Arbor *(G-359)*
Applied Computer Technologies.......F....... 248 388-0211
West Bloomfield *(G-17465)*
Atos Syntel Inc.......C....... 248 619-2800
Troy *(G-16228)*
Autodesk Inc.......D....... 248 347-9650
Novi *(G-11833)*
Auvesy Inc.......G....... 616 888-3770
Grand Rapids *(G-6194)*
Biscayne and Associates Inc.......E....... 248 304-0600
Milford *(G-10955)*
BMC Software Inc.......F....... 248 888-4600
Farmington Hills *(G-4944)*
Brinston Acquisition LLC.......E....... 248 269-1000
Troy *(G-16246)*
C R T & Associates Inc.......G....... 231 946-1680
Traverse City *(G-15926)*
Cadfem Americas Inc.......G....... 248 919-8410
Farmington Hills *(G-4953)*
Capital Billing Systems Inc.......G....... 248 478-7298
Farmington Hills *(G-4955)*
Catalina Software.......G....... 734 429-3550
Saline *(G-14381)*
Chain-Sys Corporation.......F....... 517 627-1173
Lansing *(G-9281)*
Comet Information Systems LLC.......F....... 248 686-2600
Grand Blanc *(G-5963)*
Competitive Cmpt Info Tech Inc.......E....... 732 829-9699
Northville *(G-11683)*
Compucare.......G....... 616 245-5371
Grand Rapids *(G-6297)*
Computer Sciences Corporation.......C....... 586 825-5043
Sterling Heights *(G-15294)*
Compuware Corporation.......C....... 313 227-7300
Detroit *(G-3945)*
Covisint Corporation.......D....... 248 483-2000
Southfield *(G-14874)*
Cyberlogic Technologies Inc.......E....... 248 631-2200
Troy *(G-16291)*
Design Safety Engineering Inc.......G....... 734 483-2033
Ypsilanti *(G-18065)*
Driven-4 LLC.......G....... 269 281-7567
Saint Joseph *(G-14307)*
Duo Security Inc.......C....... 734 330-2673
Ann Arbor *(G-427)*
Edi Experts LLC.......G....... 734 844-7016
Canton *(G-2370)*
Ejustice Solutions LLC.......E....... 248 232-0509
Ann Arbor *(G-438)*
EMC Corporation.......C....... 248 957-5800
Farmington Hills *(G-4984)*
Empower Financials Inc.......F....... 734 747-9393
Ann Arbor *(G-443)*
Engineering Tech Assoc Inc.......D....... 248 729-3010
Troy *(G-16346)*
Enterprise Services LLC.......F....... 734 523-6525
Livonia *(G-9727)*
Foresee Session Replay Inc.......G....... 800 621-2850
Ann Arbor *(G-465)*
Freedom Imaging Systems.......E....... 734 327-5600
Ann Arbor *(G-467)*
Global Information Systems.......D....... 248 223-9800
Southfield *(G-14921)*
Gnu Software Development Inc.......G....... 586 778-9182
Warren *(G-17060)*
Great Lakes Infotronics Inc.......E....... 248 476-2500
Northville *(G-11695)*
Harbor Software Intl Inc.......G....... 231 347-8866
Petoskey *(G-12451)*
Herfert Software.......G....... 586 776-2880
Eastpointe *(G-4703)*
Hilgraeve Inc.......G....... 734 243-0576
Monroe *(G-11039)*
Ht Computing Services.......G....... 313 563-0087
Dearborn *(G-3722)*
I-9 Advantage.......G....... 800 724-8546
Troy *(G-16408)*
Ideation International Inc.......F....... 248 737-8854
Farmington Hills *(G-5025)*
Information Builders Inc.......E....... 248 641-8820
Troy *(G-16417)*
Innovative Programming Systems.......G....... 810 695-9332
Grand Blanc *(G-5971)*
Inovision Inc.......E....... 248 299-1915
Rochester Hills *(G-13450)*
Integrated Practice Service.......G....... 248 646-7009
South Lyon *(G-14794)*
Interact Websites Inc.......F....... 800 515-9672
Midland *(G-10871)*
Jda Software Group Inc.......G....... 734 741-4205
Ann Arbor *(G-510)*
Kemari LLC.......G....... 248 348-7407
South Lyon *(G-14797)*
Kingston Educational Software.......G....... 248 895-4803
Farmington Hills *(G-5038)*
Lakeside Software Inc.......F....... 248 686-1700
Ann Arbor *(G-524)*
Laydon Technology Inc.......G....... 906 774-5780
Iron Mountain *(G-8289)*
Linked Live Inc.......G....... 248 345-5993
Madison Heights *(G-10299)*
Lintech Global Inc.......D....... 248 553-8033
Farmington Hills *(G-5045)*
Lspedia LLC.......G....... 248 320-1909
Farmington Hills *(G-5046)*
Magnetic Michigan.......D....... 734 922-7068
Ann Arbor *(G-540)*
Magnus Software Inc.......G....... 517 294-0315
Fowlerville *(G-5574)*
Marc Schrreiber & Company LLC.......F....... 734 222-9930
Ann Arbor *(G-543)*
Marketplus Software Inc.......F....... 269 968-4240
Springfield *(G-15198)*
Master Data Center Inc.......D....... 248 352-5810
Bingham Farms *(G-1656)*
Matthews Software Inc.......G....... 248 593-6999
Birmingham *(G-1692)*
McKesson Pharmacy Systems LLC.......A....... 800 521-1758
Livonia *(G-9834)*
Medimage Inc.......G....... 734 665-5400
Ann Arbor *(G-551)*
Melange Computer Services Inc.......E....... 517 321-8434
Lansing *(G-9310)*
Micro Focus Software Inc.......A....... 248 353-8010
Southfield *(G-14982)*
Mighty Co.......E....... 616 822-1013
Hudsonville *(G-8170)*
New Concepts Software Inc.......G....... 586 776-2855
Roseville *(G-13846)*
Nuance Communications Inc.......G....... 248 919-7700
Farmington Hills *(G-5085)*
Oracle America Inc.......E....... 989 495-0465
Midland *(G-10900)*
Oracle America Inc.......G....... 248 273-1934
Troy *(G-16535)*
Oracle Systems Corporation.......B....... 248 614-5139
Rochester Hills *(G-13488)*
Oracle Systems Corporation.......C....... 248 816-8050
Troy *(G-16536)*
Orbit Technology Inc.......G....... 906 776-7248
Iron Mountain *(G-8297)*
Pace Software Systems Inc.......F....... 586 727-3189
Casco *(G-2504)*
PC Solutions.......F....... 517 787-9934
Jackson *(G-8548)*
Peninsular Technologies LLC.......F....... 616 676-9811
Ada *(G-27)*
Perennial Software.......F....... 734 414-0760
Canton *(G-2415)*
Pitss America LLC.......E....... 248 740-0935
Troy *(G-16549)*
Platform Computing Inc.......G....... 248 359-7825
Southfield *(G-15000)*
Polyhedron LLC.......G....... 313 318-4807
Grosse Pointe *(G-7182)*
Polyworks USA Training Center.......G....... 216 226-1617
Novi *(G-11974)*
Premier Software Inc.......G....... 616 940-8601
Grand Rapids *(G-6769)*
Professional Sftwr Assoc Inc.......G....... 727 724-0000
Lapeer *(G-9482)*
Quantum Compliance Systems.......D....... 734 930-0009
Ypsilanti *(G-18099)*
Radley Corporation.......E....... 616 554-9060
Grand Rapids *(G-6805)*
Rearden Development Corp.......G....... 616 464-4434
Grand Rapids *(G-6813)*
Redtail Software.......G....... 231 587-0720
Mancelona *(G-10398)*
Regents of The University Mich.......F....... 734 936-0435
Ann Arbor *(G-617)*
Reilly & Associates Inc.......F....... 248 605-9393
Clarkston *(G-2952)*
Relative Path LLC.......G....... 217 840-6376
Mount Pleasant *(G-11224)*
Ringmaster Software Corp.......F....... 802 383-1050
Troy *(G-16580)*
Riverside Internet Services.......G....... 231 652-2562
Newaygo *(G-11576)*
Rutherford & Associates Inc.......E....... 616 392-5000
Holland *(G-7792)*
S2 Games LLC.......D....... 269 344-8020
Portage *(G-13030)*
Sales Page Technologies Inc.......G....... 269 567-7401
Kalamazoo *(G-8882)*
Signalx Technologies LLC.......F....... 248 935-4237
Plymouth *(G-12754)*
Signmeupcom Inc.......G....... 312 343-1263
Monroe *(G-11065)*
Silkroute Global Inc.......E....... 248 854-3409
Troy *(G-16603)*
Simna Solutions LLC.......G....... 313 442-7305
Farmington Hills *(G-5125)*
Sims Software II Inc.......G....... 586 491-0058
Clinton Township *(G-3229)*
Skysync Inc.......E....... 734 822-6858
Ann Arbor *(G-636)*
Software Finesse LLC.......G....... 248 737-8990
Farmington Hills *(G-5126)*
Spiders Software Solutions LLC.......E....... 248 305-3225
Northville *(G-11727)*
Stardock Systems Inc.......E....... 734 927-0677
Plymouth *(G-12760)*
Startech Software Systems Inc.......G....... 248 344-2266
Novi *(G-12003)*
Sterling Software Inc.......G....... 248 528-6500
Troy *(G-16622)*
Strategic Computer Solutions.......G....... 248 888-0666
Ann Arbor *(G-648)*
Stunt3 Multimedia LLC.......G....... 313 417-0909
Grosse Pointe *(G-7184)*
Suse LLC.......F....... 248 353-8010
Southfield *(G-15041)*
Tebis America Inc.......E....... 248 524-0430
Troy *(G-16634)*
Tecra Systems Inc.......E....... 248 888-1116
Westland *(G-17602)*

PRODUCT SECTION

SPORTING & ATHLETIC GOODS: Balls, Baseball, Football, Etc

Third Wave Computing ....G...... 616 855-5501
 Grand Rapids *(G-6929)*
Towerline Software LLC ....G...... 517 669-8112
 Dewitt *(G-4469)*
TST Tooling Software Tech LLC ....F...... 248 922-9293
 Clarkston *(G-2962)*
Tweddle Group Inc ....E...... 586 840-3275
 Detroit *(G-4410)*
Tyler Technologies Inc ....F...... 734 677-0550
 Ann Arbor *(G-684)*
Umakanth Consultants Inc ....F...... 517 347-7500
 Okemos *(G-12139)*
Universal Sftwr Solutions Inc ....F...... 810 653-5000
 Davison *(G-3664)*
V E S T Inc ....G...... 248 649-9550
 Troy *(G-16673)*
Varatech Inc ....F...... 616 393-6408
 Holland *(G-7843)*
Vector North America Inc ....D...... 248 449-9290
 Novi *(G-12024)*
Vertigee Corporation ....G...... 313 999-1020
 Saline *(G-14420)*
Virtual Advantage LLc ....G...... 877 772-6886
 Troy *(G-16685)*
Visual Components N Amer Corp ....G...... 855 823-3746
 Orion *(G-12192)*
World of Cd-Rom ....F...... 269 382-3766
 Kalamazoo *(G-8928)*
Wowza ME LLC ....G...... 734 636-4460
 Monroe *(G-11085)*
Zume It Inc ....G...... 248 522-6868
 Farmington Hills *(G-5156)*

SOFTWARE PUBLISHERS: Operating Systems

3dfx Interactive Inc ....E...... 918 938-8967
 Saginaw *(G-13990)*
J H P Inc ....G...... 248 588-0110
 Madison Heights *(G-10280)*
Nemo Capital Partners LLC ....F...... 248 213-9899
 Southfield *(G-14990)*

SOFTWARE PUBLISHERS: Publisher's

Harper Arrington Pubg LLC ....G...... 313 282-6751
 Detroit *(G-4117)*
Thunderhead Enterprises LLC ....G...... 248 210-1146
 Novi *(G-12016)*

SOFTWARE TRAINING, COMPUTER

Apis North America LLC ....G...... 800 470-8970
 Royal Oak *(G-13903)*
Applied Automation Tech Inc ....E...... 248 656-4930
 Rochester Hills *(G-13369)*

SOLAR CELLS

Altronics Energy LLC ....F...... 616 662-7401
 Hudsonville *(G-8145)*
Helios Solar LLC ....G...... 269 343-5581
 Kalamazoo *(G-8763)*
Ovshinsky Technologies LLC ....G...... 248 390-3564
 Pontiac *(G-12854)*
Patriot Solar Group LLC ....E...... 517 629-9292
 Albion *(G-128)*
Seelye Equipment Specialist ....G...... 231 547-9430
 Charlevoix *(G-2630)*

SOLAR HEATING EQPT

Great Lakes Electric LLC ....G...... 269 408-8276
 Saint Joseph *(G-14313)*
Pyrinas LLC ....G...... 810 422-7535
 Traverse City *(G-16084)*
Refrigeration Research Inc ....D...... 810 227-1151
 Brighton *(G-1985)*
Solar Control Systems ....G...... 734 671-6899
 Grosse Ile *(G-7176)*
Solar EZ Inc ....F...... 989 773-3447
 Mount Pleasant *(G-11229)*

SOLDERING EQPT: Electrical, Exc Handheld

Delfab Inc ....E...... 906 428-9570
 Gladstone *(G-5913)*

SOLDERING EQPT: Irons Or Coppers

Assembly Technologies Intl ....F...... 248 280-2810
 Troy *(G-16224)*

SOLENOIDS

Eto Magnetic Corp ....D...... 616 957-2570
 Grand Rapids *(G-6387)*
Fema Corporation of Michigan ....C...... 269 323-1369
 Portage *(G-12996)*
Nass Corporation ....F...... 586 725-6610
 New Baltimore *(G-11489)*

SOLID CONTAINING UNITS: Concrete

K-Mar Structures LLC ....F...... 231 924-3895
 Fremont *(G-5777)*

SOLVENTS

Genova Products Inc ....D...... 810 744-4500
 Davison *(G-3650)*

SOLVENTS: Organic

Eq Resource Recovery Inc ....G...... 734 727-5500
 Romulus *(G-13673)*
Gage Corporation ....F...... 248 541-3824
 Ferndale *(G-5286)*
Kelley Laboratories Inc ....F...... 231 861-6257
 Shelby *(G-14528)*

SONAR SYSTEMS & EQPT

Talkin Tackle LLC ....G...... 517 474-6241
 Jackson *(G-8583)*

SOUND EFFECTS & MUSIC PRODUCTION: Motion Picture

Pull Our Own Weight ....G...... 313 686-4685
 Detroit *(G-4316)*

SOUND EQPT: Electric

Band-Ayd Systems Intl Inc ....F...... 586 294-8851
 Madison Heights *(G-10200)*
Emergency Technology Inc ....D...... 616 896-7100
 Hudsonville *(G-8155)*

SOUND RECORDING STUDIOS

Paul F Hester ....F...... 616 302-6039
 Pullman *(G-13087)*

SOUVENIRS, WHOLESALE

Bahama Souvenirs Inc ....G...... 269 964-8275
 Battle Creek *(G-1149)*

SOYBEAN PRDTS

Ferguson Landscaping ....G...... 248 761-1005
 Oak Park *(G-12067)*
Michigan Soy Products Company ....G...... 248 544-7742
 Royal Oak *(G-13951)*
Zeeland Bio-Based Products LLC ....F...... 616 748-1831
 Zeeland *(G-18199)*
Zeeland Farm Services Inc ....C...... 616 772-9042
 Zeeland *(G-18201)*

SPACE VEHICLE EQPT

Advance Turning and Mfg Inc ....C...... 517 783-2713
 Jackson *(G-8373)*
Dorris Company ....E...... 586 293-5260
 Fraser *(G-5644)*
MB Aerospace Warren LLC ....C...... 586 772-2500
 Warren *(G-17144)*
Mistequay Group Ltd ....D...... 989 846-1000
 Standish *(G-15224)*
Parker-Hannifin Corporation ....B...... 269 384-3459
 Kalamazoo *(G-8843)*
Rapp & Son Inc ....C...... 734 283-1000
 Wyandotte *(G-17971)*
SGC Industries Inc ....E...... 586 293-5260
 Fraser *(G-5723)*
Swiss American Screw Pdts Inc ....F...... 734 397-1600
 Canton *(G-2431)*
Truform Machine Inc ....E...... 517 782-8523
 Jackson *(G-8594)*

SPAS

Body Contour Ventures LLC ....G...... 248 579-6772
 Farmington Hills *(G-4945)*

SPEAKER SYSTEMS

Leon Speakers Inc ....E...... 734 213-2151
 Ann Arbor *(G-528)*
Moss Audio Corporation ....D...... 616 451-9933
 Grand Rapids *(G-6707)*

SPECIAL EVENTS DECORATION SVCS

Perrin Souvenir Distrs Inc ....B...... 616 785-9700
 Comstock Park *(G-3508)*

SPECIALTY FOOD STORES: Coffee

Hermans Boy ....G...... 616 866-2900
 Rockford *(G-13571)*
Royal Accoutrements Inc ....G...... 517 347-7983
 Okemos *(G-12136)*

SPECIALTY FOOD STORES: Dietetic Foods

Hello Life Inc ....F...... 616 808-3290
 Grand Rapids *(G-6504)*

SPECIALTY FOOD STORES: Health & Dietetic Food

Hello Life Inc ....F...... 616 808-3290
 Grand Rapids *(G-6505)*
Ionxhealth Inc ....E...... 616 808-3290
 Grand Rapids *(G-6544)*
N F P Inc ....G...... 989 631-0009
 Midland *(G-10896)*

SPECIALTY OUTPATIENT CLINICS, NEC

Liver Transplant/Univ of Mich ....G...... 734 936-7670
 Ann Arbor *(G-531)*

SPECIALTY SAWMILL PRDTS

Biewer Forest Management LLC ....G...... 231 825-2855
 Mc Bain *(G-10678)*

SPEED CHANGERS

Cone Drive Operations Inc ....C...... 231 946-8410
 Traverse City *(G-15945)*

SPICE & HERB STORES

Country Home Creations Inc ....E...... 810 244-7348
 Flint *(G-5405)*

SPINDLES: Textile

Precision Spindle Service Co ....F...... 248 544-0100
 Ferndale *(G-5313)*

SPONGES, ANIMAL, WHOLESALE

Armaly Sponge Company ....E...... 248 669-2100
 Commerce Township *(G-3391)*

SPONGES: Bleached & Dyed

Technacraft Corp ....G...... 810 227-8281
 Brighton *(G-1995)*

SPONGES: Plastic

Armaly Sponge Company ....E...... 248 669-2100
 Commerce Township *(G-3391)*

SPOOLS: Indl

Faulkner Fabricators Inc ....F...... 269 473-3073
 Berrien Springs *(G-1596)*

SPORTING & ATHLETIC GOODS: Arrows, Archery

Carbon Impact Inc ....E...... 231 929-8152
 Traverse City *(G-15930)*

SPORTING & ATHLETIC GOODS: Balls, Baseball, Football, Etc

B4 Sports Inc ....G...... 248 454-9700
 Bloomfield Hills *(G-1749)*

Employee Codes: A=Over 500 employees, B=251-500
C=101-250, D=51-100, E=20-50, F=10-19, G=3-9

2020 Harris Michigan Industrial Directory

SPORTING & ATHLETIC GOODS: Bowling Alleys & Access

SPORTING & ATHLETIC GOODS: Bowling Alleys & Access

Double Six Sports Complex ....F 989 762-5342
  Stanton *(G-15229)*

SPORTING & ATHLETIC GOODS: Bows, Archery

Container Specialties Inc ....E 989 728-4231
  Hale *(G-7224)*
Lone Wolf Custom Bows ....G 989 735-3358
  Glennie *(G-5944)*

SPORTING & ATHLETIC GOODS: Camping Eqpt & Splys

Delta 6 LLC ....G 248 778-6414
  Livonia *(G-9703)*
My-Can LLC ....G 989 288-7779
  Durand *(G-4610)*
Northern Trading Group LLC ....G 248 885-8750
  Birmingham *(G-1696)*
Perfect Expressions ....G 248 640-1287
  Bloomfield Hills *(G-1790)*

SPORTING & ATHLETIC GOODS: Exercising Cycles

Assenmacher Lightweight Cycles ....G 810 232-2994
  Flint *(G-5378)*

SPORTING & ATHLETIC GOODS: Fishing Bait, Artificial

K & E Tackle Inc ....F 269 945-4496
  Hastings *(G-7418)*

SPORTING & ATHLETIC GOODS: Fishing Eqpt

Dreamweaver Lure Company Inc ....F 231 843-3652
  Ludington *(G-10057)*
Ed Cumings Inc ....E 810 736-0130
  Flint *(G-5423)*
Fish On Sports Inc ....G 231 342-5231
  Interlochen *(G-8240)*
Mitchell Coates ....D 231 582-5878
  Boyne City *(G-1829)*
North Post Inc ....G 906 482-5210
  Hancock *(G-7254)*
Proos Manufacturing Inc ....D 616 454-5622
  Grand Rapids *(G-6791)*
Superior Marine Products LLC ....G 906 370-9908
  Hancock *(G-7257)*

SPORTING & ATHLETIC GOODS: Fishing Tackle, General

Eppinger Mfg Co ....F 313 582-3205
  Dearborn *(G-3703)*
Grapentin Specialties Inc ....G 810 724-0636
  Imlay City *(G-8201)*
HI Outdoors ....G 989 422-3264
  Houghton Lake *(G-7992)*
Northport Manufacturing Inc ....G 616 874-6455
  Rockford *(G-13584)*
Pressweld Manufacturing Co ....G 734 675-8282
  Portland *(G-13066)*

SPORTING & ATHLETIC GOODS: Football Eqpt & Splys, NEC

Rogers Athletic Company Inc ....F 989 386-2950
  Farwell *(G-5165)*

SPORTING & ATHLETIC GOODS: Gymnasium Eqpt

Pull-Buoy Inc ....G 586 997-0900
  Sterling Heights *(G-15456)*
Ripper Ventures LLC ....G 248 808-2325
  Plymouth *(G-12736)*
Spieth Anderson USA Lc ....F 817 536-3366
  Lansing *(G-9265)*
T L V Inc ....F 989 773-4362
  Mount Pleasant *(G-11232)*

SPORTING & ATHLETIC GOODS: Hockey Eqpt & Splys, NEC

BJ Sports Inc ....F 269 342-2415
  Portage *(G-12985)*
Rolston Hockey Academy LLC ....G 248 450-5300
  Oak Park *(G-12093)*
Superior Hockey LLC ....G 906 225-9008
  Marquette *(G-10559)*
Warrior Sports Inc ....D 800 968-7845
  Warren *(G-17289)*

SPORTING & ATHLETIC GOODS: Hooks, Fishing

Randlis Manufacturing Co ....G 313 368-0220
  Detroit *(G-4329)*

SPORTING & ATHLETIC GOODS: Hunting Eqpt

Aerospace America Inc ....E 989 684-2121
  Bay City *(G-1273)*
Buck Stop Lure Company Inc ....G 989 762-5091
  Stanton *(G-15228)*
Family Trdtons Tree Stands LLC ....G 517 543-3926
  Charlotte *(G-2647)*
R and T Sporting Clays Inc ....G 586 215-9861
  Harrison Township *(G-7345)*

SPORTING & ATHLETIC GOODS: Masks, Hockey, Baseball, Etc

Trainingmask LLC ....F 888 407-7555
  Cadillac *(G-2283)*

SPORTING & ATHLETIC GOODS: Protective Sporting Eqpt

Powerplus Mouthguard ....G 231 357-2167
  Traverse City *(G-16075)*
United Shield Intl LLC ....E 231 933-1179
  Traverse City *(G-16135)*

SPORTING & ATHLETIC GOODS: Shafts, Golf Club

Cheboygan Golf and Country CLB ......E 231 627-4264
  Cheboygan *(G-2678)*

SPORTING & ATHLETIC GOODS: Shooting Eqpt & Splys, General

Elite Arms Inc ....F 734 424-9955
  Chelsea *(G-2709)*

SPORTING & ATHLETIC GOODS: Shuffleboards & Shuffleboard Eqpt

McClure Tables Inc ....G 616 662-5974
  Hudsonville *(G-8165)*
McClure Tables Inc ....G 616 662-5974
  Jenison *(G-8633)*

SPORTING & ATHLETIC GOODS: Skateboards

Chiipss ....G 248 345-6112
  Detroit *(G-3935)*
Marhar Snowboards LLC ....G 616 432-3104
  Fruitport *(G-5796)*
Pluskate Boarding Company ....G 248 426-0899
  Farmington *(G-4908)*

SPORTING & ATHLETIC GOODS: Snow Skis

Plastisnow LLC ....G 414 397-1233
  Plainwell *(G-12539)*

SPORTING & ATHLETIC GOODS: Strings, Tennis Racket

Total Tennis LLC ....G 248 594-1749
  Bloomfield Hills *(G-1805)*

SPORTING & ATHLETIC GOODS: Targets, Archery & Rifle Shooting

Arrowmat LLC ....G 800 920-6035
  Howell *(G-8016)*

Assra ....F 906 225-1828
  Marquette *(G-10518)*
U S Target Inc ....G 586 445-3131
  Roseville *(G-13884)*

SPORTING & ATHLETIC GOODS: Team Sports Eqpt

Guys Timing Inc ....G 517 404-3746
  Brighton *(G-1936)*

SPORTING & ATHLETIC GOODS: Trampolines & Eqpt

Supertramp Custom Trampoline ....F 616 634-2010
  Grand Rapids *(G-6905)*

SPORTING & ATHLETIC GOODS: Water Sports Eqpt

Craig C Askins ....G 810 231-4340
  Brighton *(G-1907)*
Soupcan Inc ....F 269 381-2101
  Galesburg *(G-5815)*

SPORTING & RECREATIONAL GOODS & SPLYS WHOLESALERS

Delta Sports Service & EMB ....G 517 482-6565
  Lansing *(G-9215)*
Dunhams Athleisure Corporation ....F 248 658-1382
  Madison Heights *(G-10235)*
J C Walker & Sons Corp ....G 248 752-8165
  Swartz Creek *(G-15668)*
Leapers Inc ....E 734 542-1500
  Livonia *(G-9805)*
Total Lee Sports Inc ....G 989 772-6121
  Mount Pleasant *(G-11234)*

SPORTING & RECREATIONAL GOODS, WHOL: Sharpeners, Sporting

Wilbur Products Inc ....F 231 755-3805
  Muskegon *(G-11451)*

SPORTING & RECREATIONAL GOODS, WHOLESALE: Athletic Goods

Nipguards LLC ....G 734 544-4490
  Ann Arbor *(G-574)*

SPORTING & RECREATIONAL GOODS, WHOLESALE: Boat Access & Part

Canvas Concepts Inc ....G 810 794-3305
  Algonac *(G-142)*

SPORTING & RECREATIONAL GOODS, WHOLESALE: Canoes

Paddlesports Warehouse Inc ....G 231 757-9051
  Scottville *(G-14510)*

SPORTING & RECREATIONAL GOODS, WHOLESALE: Fishing Tackle

Grapentin Specialties Inc ....G 810 724-0636
  Imlay City *(G-8201)*
HI Outdoors ....G 989 422-3264
  Houghton Lake *(G-7992)*

SPORTING & RECREATIONAL GOODS, WHOLESALE: Fitness

Inplast Interior Tech LLC ....G 810 724-3500
  Almont *(G-258)*

SPORTING & RECREATIONAL GOODS, WHOLESALE: Golf

Consumer Advntage Rference Svc .....G 586 783-1806
  Clinton Township *(G-3089)*

SPORTING & RECREATIONAL GOODS, WHOLESALE: Golf & Skiing

King Par, LLC ....D 810 732-2470
  Flushing *(G-5539)*

PRODUCT SECTION

SPORTING & RECREATIONAL GOODS, WHOLESALE: Gymnasium

T L V Inc .... F 989 773-4362
  Mount Pleasant **(G-11232)**

SPORTING & RECREATIONAL GOODS, WHOLESALE: Hunting

Stewart Knives LLC .... E 906 789-1801
  Escanaba **(G-4861)**

SPORTING FIREARMS WHOLESALERS

Elite Arms Inc .... F 734 424-9955
  Chelsea **(G-2709)**

SPORTING GOODS

Baum Sports Inc .... G 231 922-2125
  Traverse City **(G-15904)**
Bill Eldridge Associates .... G 248 698-3705
  White Lake **(G-17630)**
Bronco Connection Inc .... G 616 997-2263
  Coopersville **(G-3549)**
Bucks Sports Products Inc .... G 763 229-1331
  Gladstone **(G-5908)**
Conway Products Corporation .... E 616 698-2601
  Grand Rapids **(G-6308)**
Crl Inc .... E 906 428-3710
  Gladstone **(G-5910)**
Discraft Inc .... E 248 624-2250
  Wixom **(G-17794)**
Dunhams Athleisure Corporation .... F 248 658-1382
  Madison Heights **(G-10235)**
Great Lakes Fish Decoy Collect .... G 734 427-7768
  Livonia **(G-9759)**
Killer Paint Ball .... G 248 491-0088
  South Lyon **(G-14798)**
Kokaly Sports .... G 989 671-7412
  Bay City **(G-1325)**
Liebner Enterprises LLC .... G 231 331-3076
  Cheboygan **(G-2686)**
M B B M Inc .... G 269 344-6361
  Kalamazoo **(G-8813)**
M-22 Challenge .... G 231 392-2212
  Traverse City **(G-16029)**
Mason Tackle Company .... E 810 631-4571
  Otisville **(G-12233)**
McKeon Products Inc .... E 586 427-7560
  Warren **(G-17146)**
Mmp Molded Magnesium Pdts LLC . G 517 789-8505
  Jackson **(G-8534)**
Nelson Technologies Inc .... D 906 774-5566
  Iron Mountain **(G-8292)**
Nipguards LLC .... G 734 544-4490
  Ann Arbor **(G-574)**
Owosso Country Club Pro Shop .... G 989 723-1470
  Owosso **(G-12308)**
Qsr Outdoor Products Inc .... G 989 354-0777
  Alpena **(G-310)**
Rochester Sports LLC .... F 248 608-6000
  Rochester Hills **(G-13507)**
Rogers Athletic .... G 989 386-7393
  Clare **(G-2887)**
Thomson Plastics Inc .... D 517 545-5026
  Howell **(G-8109)**
Thunderdome Media LLC .... G 800 978-0206
  Plymouth **(G-12770)**
Turkey Creek Inc .... F 517 451-5221
  Tecumseh **(G-15814)**
Wellmans Sport Center .... G 989 739-2869
  Oscoda **(G-12224)**
Witchcraft Tape Products Inc .... D 269 468-3399
  Coloma **(G-3368)**

SPORTING GOODS STORES, NEC

Aerospoke Incorporated .... G 248 685-9009
  Brighton **(G-1878)**
Assenmacher Lightweight Cycles ... G 810 232-2994
  Flint **(G-5378)**
Flare Fittings Incorporated .... E 269 344-7600
  Kalamazoo **(G-8744)**
Nelson Paint Co of Mich Inc .... G 906 774-5566
  Kingsford **(G-9063)**
Nobby Inc .... E 810 984-3300
  Fort Gratiot **(G-5550)**
Pro Shop The/P S Graphics .... G 517 448-8490
  Hudson **(G-8139)**
S & H Trophy & Sports .... G 616 754-0005
  Greenville **(G-7151)**

Sports Inc .... G 734 728-1313
  Wayne **(G-17443)**
Sports Junction .... G 989 835-9696
  Midland **(G-10920)**
Total Lee Sports Inc .... G 989 772-6121
  Mount Pleasant **(G-11234)**
Trophy Center West Michigan .... G 231 893-1686
  Whitehall **(G-17678)**
Winn Archery Equipment Co .... G 269 637-2658
  South Haven **(G-14784)**
Wiz Wheelz Inc .... F 616 455-5988
  Grand Rapids **(G-6995)**

SPORTING GOODS STORES: Archery Splys

Bay Archery Sales Co .... G 989 894-5800
  Essexville **(G-4868)**
Container Specialties Inc .... E 989 728-4231
  Hale **(G-7224)**

SPORTING GOODS STORES: Camping & Backpacking Eqpt

Bearcub Outfitters LLC .... F 231 439-9500
  Petoskey **(G-12441)**

SPORTING GOODS STORES: Firearms

Mission Critical Firearms LLC .... G 586 232-5185
  Shelby Township **(G-14641)**
Williams Gun Sight Company .... D 800 530-9028
  Davison **(G-3666)**

SPORTING GOODS STORES: Fishing Eqpt

Grapentin Specialties Inc .... G 810 724-0636
  Imlay City **(G-8201)**

SPORTING GOODS STORES: Playground Eqpt

Penchura LLC .... F 810 229-6245
  Brighton **(G-1977)**
Recycletech Products Inc .... E 517 649-2243
  Mulliken **(G-11240)**

SPORTING GOODS STORES: Skiing Eqpt

R & L Frye .... G 989 821-6661
  Roscommon **(G-13753)**

SPORTING GOODS STORES: Soccer Splys

Kick It Around Sports .... G 810 232-4986
  Flint **(G-5455)**

SPORTING GOODS STORES: Specialty Sport Splys, NEC

Dunhams Athleisure Corporation .... F 248 658-1382
  Madison Heights **(G-10235)**
Marrs Discount Furniture .... G 989 720-5436
  Owosso **(G-12300)**

SPORTING GOODS STORES: Team sports Eqpt

Lansing Athletics .... G 517 327-8828
  Lansing **(G-9305)**
M B B M Inc .... G 269 344-6361
  Kalamazoo **(G-8813)**
Sports Junction .... G 989 791-5900
  Saginaw **(G-14156)**

SPORTING GOODS: Archery

Bitzenburger Machine & Tool .... G 517 627-8433
  Grand Ledge **(G-6102)**
Bohning Company Ltd .... E 231 229-4247
  Lake City **(G-9085)**
Bohning Company Ltd .... E 231 229-4247
  Lake City **(G-9086)**
G5 Outdoors LLC .... G 866 456-8836
  Memphis **(G-10709)**
Overkill Research & Dev Labs .... G 517 768-8155
  Jackson **(G-8546)**
Pro Release Inc .... G 810 512-4120
  Marine City **(G-10480)**
Winn Archery Equipment Co .... G 269 637-2658
  South Haven **(G-14784)**

SPORTING GOODS: Fishing Nets

Ed Cumings Inc .... E 810 736-0130
  Flint **(G-5423)**
Gerry Gostenik .... G 313 319-0100
  Dearborn **(G-3714)**
Randlis Manufacturing Co .... G 313 368-0220
  Detroit **(G-4329)**

SPORTING GOODS: Hammocks, Fabric, Made From Purchased Mat

Flo-Tec Inc .... D 734 455-7655
  Livonia **(G-9742)**

SPORTS APPAREL STORES

Baumans Running Center Inc .... G 810 238-5981
  Flint **(G-5385)**
Bearcub Outfitters LLC .... F 231 439-9500
  Petoskey **(G-12441)**
Delux Monogramming Screen Prtg .. G 989 288-5321
  Durand **(G-4607)**
Dunhams Athleisure Corporation .... F 248 658-1382
  Madison Heights **(G-10235)**
Embroidery & Much More LLC .... F 586 771-3832
  Saint Clair Shores **(G-14246)**
Jans Sport Shop Inc .... F 810 636-2241
  Goodrich **(G-5954)**
Lansing Athletics .... G 517 327-8828
  Lansing **(G-9305)**
R & L Frye .... G 989 821-6661
  Roscommon **(G-13753)**
R H & Company Inc .... F 269 345-7814
  Kalamazoo **(G-8867)**
Sports Junction .... G 989 791-5900
  Saginaw **(G-14156)**
Sports Junction .... G 989 835-9696
  Midland **(G-10920)**
Sports Stop .... G 517 676-2199
  Mason **(G-10660)**

SPORTS PROMOTION SVCS

Buster Mathis Foundation .... G 616 843-4433
  Wyoming **(G-17990)**

SPOUTING: Plastic & Fiberglass Reinforced

E-T-M Enterprises I Inc .... E 517 627-8461
  Grand Ledge **(G-6105)**
Hanwha Azdel Inc .... F 810 629-2496
  Warren **(G-17075)**

SPRAYING & DUSTING EQPT

Precision Masking Inc .... E 734 848-4200
  Erie **(G-4808)**
Spray Foam Fabrication LLC .... G 517 745-7885
  Parma **(G-12394)**

SPRAYING EQPT: Agricultural

Root-Lowell Manufacturing Co .... D 616 897-9211
  Lowell **(G-10042)**
Unist Inc .... E 616 949-0853
  Grand Rapids **(G-6951)**

SPRINGS: Automobile

American MSC Inc .... D 248 589-7770
  Troy **(G-16197)**
American MSC Inc .... E 248 589-7770
  Troy **(G-16198)**
Arvinmeritor Inc .... E 248 435-1000
  Troy **(G-16222)**
Meritor Inc .... C 248 435-1000
  Troy **(G-16493)**

SPRINGS: Clock, Precision

Hilite Industries Inc .... G 248 475-4580
  Lake Orion **(G-9138)**

SPRINGS: Coiled Flat

Jade Mfg Inc .... G 734 942-1462
  Romulus **(G-13691)**
M D Hubbard Spring Co Inc .... E 248 628-2528
  Oxford **(G-12358)**

Employee Codes: A=Over 500 employees, B=251-500
C=101-250, D=51-100, E=20-50, F=10-19, G=3-9

2020 Harris Michigan
Industrial Directory

SPRINGS: Cold Formed

Weiser Metal Products Inc .... G 989 736-8151
Lincoln *(G-9571)*

SPRINGS: Instrument, Precision

M & S Spring Company Inc .... F 586 296-9850
Fraser *(G-5687)*

SPRINGS: Leaf, Automobile, Locomotive, Etc

Eaton Detroit Spring Svc Co .... F 313 963-3839
Detroit *(G-4025)*
Qp Acquisition 2 Inc .... E 248 594-7432
Southfield *(G-15006)*

SPRINGS: Mechanical, Precision

General Automatic Mch Pdts Co .... E 517 437-6000
Hillsdale *(G-7526)*
Hyde Spring and Wire Company .... F 313 272-2201
Detroit *(G-4132)*
Michigan Spring & Stamping LLC .... C 231 755-1691
Muskegon *(G-11379)*
Peterson American Corporation .... E 248 616-3380
Madison Heights *(G-10323)*
Quality Spring/Togo Inc .... C 517 278-2391
Coldwater *(G-3323)*
Serra Spring & Mfg LLC .... G 586 932-2202
Sterling Heights *(G-15491)*

SPRINGS: Precision

De-Sta-Co Cylinders Inc .... B 248 836-6700
Auburn Hills *(G-838)*
Motion Dynamics Corporation .... D 231 865-7400
Fruitport *(G-5798)*

SPRINGS: Steel

A N L Spring Manufacturing .... G 313 837-0200
Detroit *(G-3828)*
Ajax Spring and Mfg Co .... F 248 588-5700
Madison Heights *(G-10184)*
American Ring Manufacturing .... F 734 402-0426
Livonia *(G-9644)*
Gill Corporation .... B 616 453-4491
Grand Rapids *(G-6438)*
Gill Corporation .... C 616 453-4491
Grand Rapids *(G-6439)*
Llink Technologies LLC .... E 586 336-9370
Brown City *(G-2054)*
Mid-West Spring & Stamping Inc .... E 231 777-2707
Muskegon *(G-11380)*
Muskegon Brake & Distrg Co LLC .... E 231 733-0874
Norton Shores *(G-11776)*
Novi Spring Inc .... F 248 486-4220
Brighton *(G-1971)*
P J Wallbank Springs Inc .... D 810 987-2992
Port Huron *(G-12953)*
Peterson American Corporation .... E 248 616-3380
Madison Heights *(G-10323)*
Quality Spring/Togo Inc .... C 517 278-2391
Coldwater *(G-3323)*

SPRINGS: Torsion Bar

Automatic Spring Products Corp .... C 616 842-2284
Grand Haven *(G-5995)*
J & J Spring Co Inc .... F 586 566-7600
Shelby Township *(G-14606)*

SPRINGS: Wire

A N L Spring Manufacturing .... G 313 837-0200
Detroit *(G-3828)*
Apex Spring & Stamping Corp .... D 616 453-5463
Grand Rapids *(G-6171)*
Barnes Group Inc .... G 734 737-0958
Plymouth *(G-12582)*
Barnes Group Inc .... E 734 429-2022
Plymouth *(G-12583)*
Barnes Group Inc .... G 586 415-6677
Fraser *(G-5627)*
Demlow Products Inc .... F 517 436-3529
Clayton *(G-3006)*
Dover Energy Inc .... C 248 836-6750
Auburn Hills *(G-842)*
Dowsett Spring Company .... G 269 782-2138
Dowagiac *(G-4541)*
Gill Corporation .... B 616 453-4491
Grand Rapids *(G-6438)*
Gill Corporation .... C 616 453-4491
Grand Rapids *(G-6439)*
Hz Industries Inc .... B 616 453-4491
Grand Rapids *(G-6521)*
J & J Spring Co Inc .... F 586 566-7600
Shelby Township *(G-14606)*
J & J Spring Enterprises LLC .... G 586 566-7600
Shelby Township *(G-14607)*
Lakeside Spring Products Inc .... G 616 847-2706
Muskegon *(G-11364)*
M D Hubbard Spring Co Inc .... E 248 628-2528
Oxford *(G-12358)*
Magiera Holdings Inc .... D 269 685-1768
Plainwell *(G-12529)*
Mc Guire Spring Corporation .... G 517 546-7311
Brighton *(G-1957)*
Michigan Spring & Stamp .... G 248 344-1459
Novi *(G-11948)*
Michigan Steel Finishing Co .... F 313 838-3925
Detroit *(G-4243)*
Mid-West Spring & Stamping Inc .... E 231 777-2707
Muskegon *(G-11380)*
Peterson American Corp .... D 269 279-7421
Three Rivers *(G-15872)*
Peterson American Corporation .... E 248 799-5400
Southfield *(G-14997)*
Peterson American Corporation .... G 248 799-5400
Madison Heights *(G-10324)*
Peterson American Corporation .... F 269 279-7421
Three Rivers *(G-15873)*
Peterson American Corporation .... G 248 799-5410
Commerce Township *(G-3438)*
Scherdel Sales & Tech Inc .... D 231 777-7774
Muskegon *(G-11419)*
Spring Design and Mfg Inc .... E 586 566-9741
Shelby Township *(G-14702)*
Spring Dynamics Inc .... E 810 798-2622
Almont *(G-267)*
Spring Saginaw Company .... G 989 624-9333
Birch Run *(G-1673)*
Sterling Spring LLC .... E 517 782-2479
Jackson *(G-8578)*
Stump Schlele Somappa Sprng .... E 616 361-2791
Grand Rapids *(G-6895)*
Stumpp Schuele Somappa USA Inc .... F 616 361-2791
Grand Rapids *(G-6896)*
TEC-3 Prototypes Inc .... E 810 678-8909
Metamora *(G-10782)*
Tokusen Hytech Inc .... C 269 685-1768
Plainwell *(G-12547)*
Tokusen Hytech Inc .... D 269 658-1768
Plainwell *(G-12548)*
Wolverine Coil Spring Company .... D 616 459-3504
Grand Rapids *(G-6996)*

SPRINKLER SYSTEMS: Field

SGS Inc .... G 989 239-1726
Birch Run *(G-1671)*
W L Hamilton & Co .... F 269 781-6941
Marshall *(G-10592)*

SPRINKLING SYSTEMS: Fire Control

Fabrication Concepts LLC .... F 517 750-4742
Spring Arbor *(G-15122)*
Gallagher Fire Equipment Co .... E 248 477-1540
Livonia *(G-9748)*
Viking Group Inc .... G 616 432-6800
Caledonia *(G-2322)*

SPROCKETS: Power Transmission

Leedy Manufacturing Co LLC .... D 616 245-0517
Grand Rapids *(G-6624)*

STACKING MACHINES: Automatic

Jervis B Webb Company .... B 248 553-1000
Novi *(G-11912)*

STADIUM EVENT OPERATOR SERVICES

Livespace LLC .... F 616 929-0191
Grand Rapids *(G-6629)*

STAFFING, EMPLOYMENT PLACEMENT

Etcs Inc .... F 586 268-4870
Warren *(G-17022)*

STAGE LIGHTING SYSTEMS

Tls Productions Inc .... E 810 220-8577
Ann Arbor *(G-677)*

STAINLESS STEEL

AK Steel Corporation .... A 800 532-8857
Dearborn *(G-3673)*
Atlantis Tech Corp .... G 989 356-6954
Alpena *(G-277)*
Carry Manufacturing Inc .... G 989 672-2779
Caro *(G-2467)*
Disrupttech LLC .... G 248 225-8383
Saint Clair Shores *(G-14244)*
Dpr Manufacturing & Svcs Inc .... E 586 757-1421
Warren *(G-17006)*

STAINLESS STEEL WARE

Carry Manufacturing Inc .... G 989 672-2779
Caro *(G-2467)*
Infra Corporation .... F 248 623-0400
Waterford *(G-17351)*
McCallum Fabricating LLC .... F 586 784-5555
Allenton *(G-229)*

STAINS: Wood

Akzo Nobel Coatings Inc .... E 248 637-0400
Pontiac *(G-12801)*

STAIRCASES & STAIRS, WOOD

Beaver Stair Company .... F 248 628-0441
Oxford *(G-12340)*
Great Lakes Stair & Case Co .... G 269 465-3777
Bridgman *(G-1865)*
Macomb Stairs Inc .... F 586 226-2800
Shelby Township *(G-14631)*
Northern Staircase Co Inc .... F 248 836-0652
Pontiac *(G-12852)*
Novo Building Products LLC .... G 800 253-9000
Zeeland *(G-18169)*
Stair Specialist Inc .... G 269 964-2351
Battle Creek *(G-1252)*

STAMPINGS: Automotive

3715-11th Street Corp .... G 734 523-1000
Livonia *(G-9615)*
A-1 Stampings Inc .... G 586 294-7790
Fraser *(G-5611)*
Acemco Incorporated .... C 231 799-8612
Norton Shores *(G-11806)*
Advance Engineering Company .... D 313 537-3500
Canton *(G-2344)*
Advanced Auto Trends Inc .... E 248 628-6111
Oxford *(G-12333)*
Advanced Auto Trends Inc .... E 248 628-4850
Oxford *(G-12334)*
Ajax Spring and Mfg Co .... F 248 588-5700
Madison Heights *(G-10184)*
Allied Engineering Inc .... G 616 748-7990
Zeeland *(G-18110)*
AM Specialties Inc .... G 586 795-9000
Sterling Heights *(G-15257)*
AMI Livonia LLC .... D 734 428-3132
Livonia *(G-9646)*
Ankara Industries Incorporated .... F 586 749-1190
Chesterfield *(G-2740)*
Aphase II Inc .... D 586 977-0790
Sterling Heights *(G-15262)*
ARC Metal Stamping LLC .... D 517 448-8954
Hudson *(G-8127)*
ARC-Kecy LLC .... D 517 448-8954
Hudson *(G-8128)*
Arvinmeritor Inc .... E 248 435-1000
Troy *(G-16222)*
Auto Metal Craft Inc .... E 248 398-2240
Oak Park *(G-12051)*
Automatic Spring Products Corp .... C 616 842-2284
Grand Haven *(G-5995)*
Benteler Automotive Corp .... B 616 247-3936
Auburn Hills *(G-791)*
Benteler Automotive Corp .... C 248 364-7190
Auburn Hills *(G-792)*
Bopp-Busch Manufacturing Co .... E 989 876-7924
Au Gres *(G-745)*
Britten Metalworks LLC .... G 231 421-1615
Traverse City *(G-15921)*
Burkland Inc .... D 810 636-2233
Goodrich *(G-5952)*

C & H Stamping Inc E 517 750-3600
Jackson *(G-8396)*
C & M Manufacturing Corp Inc E 586 749-3455
Chesterfield *(G-2750)*
Capital Stamping & Machine Inc E 248 471-0700
Farmington Hills *(G-4956)*
Cg & D Group G 248 310-9166
Farmington Hills *(G-4960)*
Challenge Mfg Company F 616 735-6530
Walker *(G-16862)*
Challenge Mfg Company C 616 735-6500
Grand Rapids *(G-6268)*
Challenge Mfg Company A 616 396-2079
Holland *(G-7587)*
Challenge Mfg Company LLC B 616 735-6500
Walker *(G-16864)*
Crescive Die and Tool Inc B 734 482-0303
Saline *(G-14384)*
Delaco Steel Corporation D 313 491-1200
Dearborn *(G-3692)*
Demmer Corporation C 517 321-3600
Lansing *(G-9217)*
Design Metal Inc F 248 547-4170
Oak Park *(G-12059)*
Dgh Enterprises Inc E 269 925-0657
Benton Harbor *(G-1494)*
Diversfied Prcurement Svcs LLC G 248 821-1147
Ferndale *(G-5280)*
Douglas Stamping Company G 248 542-3940
Madison Heights *(G-10234)*
E & E Manufacturing Co Inc E 734 451-7600
Plymouth *(G-12616)*
E & E Manufacturing Co Inc F 248 616-1300
Clawson *(G-2977)*
Elring Klinger Sealing Systems G 734 542-1522
Livonia *(G-9725)*
Elringklinger Auto Mfg Inc E 248 727-6600
Southfield *(G-14898)*
Elringklinger Auto Mfg Inc G 586 445-3050
Roseville *(G-13800)*
Fab-All Manufacturing Inc D 248 585-6700
Troy *(G-16358)*
FCA US LLC A 248 512-2950
Auburn Hills *(G-867)*
FCA US LLC A 586 497-3630
Warren *(G-17029)*
Fisher & Company Incorporated C 248 280-0808
Troy *(G-16363)*
Forward Metal Craft Inc F 616 459-6051
Grand Rapids *(G-6417)*
Franklin Fastener Company E 313 537-8900
Redford *(G-13162)*
Gedia Michigan Inc E 248 392-9090
Orion *(G-12180)*
General Motors LLC C 517 721-2000
Lansing *(G-9291)*
General Motors LLC D 810 234-2710
Flint *(G-5434)*
General Motors LLC F 810 234-2710
Flint *(G-5435)*
General Motors LLC B 810 236-1970
Flint *(G-5436)*
Gestamp Mason LLC B 517 244-8800
Mason *(G-10641)*
Gfm LLC E 586 777-4542
Roseville *(G-13807)*
Gill Corporation B 616 453-4491
Grand Rapids *(G-6438)*
Gill Holding Company Inc E 616 559-2700
Grand Rapids *(G-6440)*
Gill Industries Inc C 616 559-2700
Grand Rapids *(G-6441)*
Global Fmi LLC D 810 964-5555
Fenton *(G-5216)*
Globe Tech LLC E 734 656-2200
Plymouth *(G-12630)*
Guyoung Tech Usa Inc E 248 746-4261
Southfield *(G-14934)*
Hamlin Tool & Machine Co Inc D 248 651-6302
Rochester Hills *(G-13438)*
Hilltop Manufacturing Co Inc G 248 437-2530
New Hudson *(G-11544)*
Illinois Tool Works Inc D 248 589-2500
Troy *(G-16410)*
Inalfa/Ssi Roof Systems LLC D 586 758-6620
Warren *(G-17086)*
Integrated Program MGT LLC G 248 241-9257
Clarkston *(G-2932)*
Iroquois Industries Inc D 586 771-5734
Warren *(G-17100)*
Iroquois Industries Inc E 586 465-1023
Cottrellville *(G-3589)*
J & J Spring Co Inc F 586 566-7600
Shelby Township *(G-14606)*
J & L Mfg Co E 586 445-9530
Warren *(G-17104)*
Jaytec LLC F 734 713-4500
Milan *(G-10942)*
Jaytec LLC F 734 397-6300
Chelsea *(G-2714)*
Jaytec LLC F 517 451-8272
New Boston *(G-11500)*
Jsj Corporation E 616 842-6350
Grand Haven *(G-6042)*
K & K Mfg Inc G 616 784-4286
Sparta *(G-15100)*
Kadest Industries G 810 614-5362
Brown City *(G-2053)*
Kirchhoff Auto Tecumseh Inc F 517 490-9965
Tecumseh *(G-15799)*
Kirmin Die & Tool Inc E 734 722-9210
Romulus *(G-13697)*
L & W Inc C 734 397-8085
Van Buren Twp *(G-16769)*
L & W Inc C 517 486-6321
Blissfield *(G-1717)*
L & W Inc F 734 529-7290
Dundee *(G-4590)*
L & W Inc D 734 397-6300
New Boston *(G-11502)*
L & W Inc B 734 397-2212
Van Buren Twp *(G-16770)*
L & W Inc C 616 394-9665
Holland *(G-7715)*
L Barge & Associates Inc F 248 582-3430
Ferndale *(G-5297)*
Lacy Tool Company Inc G 248 476-5250
Novi *(G-11928)*
Laser Cutting Co E 586 468-5300
Harrison Township *(G-7337)*
Lgb USA Inc G 586 777-4542
Roseville *(G-13826)*
Llink Technologies LLC E 586 336-9370
Brown City *(G-2054)*
Manufacturing Products & Svcs F 734 927-1964
Plymouth *(G-12683)*
Martinrea Hot Stampings Inc E 859 509-3031
Warren *(G-17141)*
Means Industries Inc C 989 754-1433
Saginaw *(G-14086)*
Meritor Inc C 248 435-1000
Troy *(G-16493)*
Mh Industries Ltd G 734 261-7560
West Bloomfield *(G-17485)*
Middleville Tool & Die Co Inc D 269 795-3646
Middleville *(G-10805)*
Midstates Industrial Group Inc E 586 307-3414
Clinton Township *(G-3174)*
Midway Products Group Inc C 734 241-7242
Monroe *(G-11052)*
Multimatic Michigan LLC E 517 962-7190
Jackson *(G-8538)*
Mvc Holdings LLC F 586 491-2600
Roseville *(G-13843)*
Northern Industrial Mfg Corp E 586 468-2790
Harrison Township *(G-7341)*
Northern Metalcraft Inc F 586 997-9630
Shelby Township *(G-14656)*
Oakland Stamping LLC G 313 867-3700
New Boston *(G-11506)*
Oakley Industries Inc E 586 791-3194
Clinton Township *(G-3187)*
Oakley Industries Inc E 586 792-1261
Clinton Township *(G-3188)*
Oakwood Metal Fabricating Co B 734 947-7740
Taylor *(G-15751)*
Oblut Ltd F 248 645-9130
Clarkston *(G-2941)*
Orion Manufacturing Inc F 616 527-5994
Ionia *(G-8250)*
P & C Group I Inc E 248 442-6800
Farmington Hills *(G-5087)*
Page Components Corporation F 231 922-3600
Traverse City *(G-16062)*
Precision Parts Holdings Inc A 248 853-9010
Rochester Hills *(G-13498)*
Prestige Advanced Inc D 586 868-4000
Madison Heights *(G-10335)*
Prestige Stamping LLC C 586 773-2700
Warren *(G-17196)*
Pridgeon & Clay Inc A 616 241-5675
Grand Rapids *(G-6774)*
Pt Tech Stamping Inc E 586 293-1810
Fraser *(G-5713)*
Quality Metalcraft Inc C 734 261-6700
Livonia *(G-9900)*
Quigley Industries Inc D 248 426-8600
Farmington Hills *(G-5109)*
Quigley Manufacturing Inc C 248 426-8600
Farmington Hills *(G-5110)*
Radar Mexican Investments LLC G 586 779-0300
Warren *(G-17215)*
Ralco Industries Inc E 248 853-3200
Auburn Hills *(G-987)*
Reko International Holdings G 519 737-6974
Bloomfield Hills *(G-1793)*
Reliant Industries Inc E 586 275-0479
Sterling Heights *(G-15464)*
S & G Prototype Inc F 586 716-3600
New Baltimore *(G-11491)*
Set Enterprises Inc E 586 573-3600
Sterling Heights *(G-15493)*
Shiloh Manufacturing LLC F 586 873-2835
Roseville *(G-13868)*
Shiloh Manufacturing LLC D 586 779-0300
Warren *(G-17239)*
Sodecia Auto Detroit Corp C 586 759-2200
Lake Orion *(G-9162)*
Span America Detroit Inc E 734 957-1600
Van Buren Twp *(G-16784)*
Stanco Metal Products Inc E 616 842-5000
Grand Haven *(G-6082)*
Startech Services Inc G 586 752-2460
Romeo *(G-13639)*
Statistical Processed Products E 586 792-6900
Clinton Township *(G-3235)*
Sterling Die & Engineering Inc E 586 677-0707
Macomb *(G-10163)*
Superior Machining Inc F 248 446-9451
New Hudson *(G-11556)*
TEC-3 Prototypes Inc E 810 678-8909
Metamora *(G-10782)*
Technique Inc D 517 789-8988
Jackson *(G-8585)*
Tel-X Corporation E 734 425-2225
Garden City *(G-5843)*
Tesca Usa Inc E 586 991-0744
Rochester Hills *(G-13524)*
Tower Autmtve Oprtns USA III G 248 675-6000
Livonia *(G-9959)*
Tower Auto Holdings I LLC G 248 675-6000
Livonia *(G-9960)*
Tower Auto Holdings II A LLC G 248 675-6000
Livonia *(G-9961)*
Tower Auto Holdings II B LLC G 248 675-6000
Livonia *(G-9962)*
Tower Auto Holdings USA LLC F 248 675-6000
Livonia *(G-9963)*
Tower Automotive Operations D 248 675-6000
Livonia *(G-9964)*
Tower Automotive Operations G 248 675-6000
Livonia *(G-9965)*
Tower Automotive Operations I B 989 375-2201
Elkton *(G-4784)*
Tower Automotive Operations I D 616 802-1600
Grand Rapids *(G-6934)*
Tower Automotive Operations I B 586 465-5158
Clinton Township *(G-3250)*
Tower Automotive Operations I C 734 414-3100
Plymouth *(G-12776)*
Tower Defense & Aerospace LLC C 248 675-6000
Livonia *(G-9966)*
Tower International Inc G 989 623-2174
Elkton *(G-4785)*
Trans-Matic Mfg Co Inc C 616 820-2500
Holland *(G-7834)*
Traverse City Products Inc D 231 946-4414
Traverse City *(G-16128)*
Trianon Industries Corporation A 586 759-2200
Center Line *(G-2585)*
Troy Design & Manufacturing Co C 734 738-2300
Plymouth *(G-12781)*
Twb Company LLC C 734 289-6400
Monroe *(G-11080)*
UNI Vue Inc E 248 545-0810
Ferndale *(G-5325)*
Van-Rob Inc C 517 657-2450
Lansing *(G-9271)*
Variety Die & Stamping Co D 734 426-4488
Dexter *(G-4517)*

STAMPINGS: Automotive

Washers Incorporated ....C...... 734 523-1000
  Livonia *(G-9999)*
Washers Incorporated ....G...... 734 523-1000
  Livonia *(G-10000)*
Webster Cold Forge Co ....F...... 313 554-4500
  Northville *(G-11734)*
Wellington Industries Inc ....E...... 734 403-6112
  Van Buren Twp *(G-16797)*
Wico Metal Products Company ....C...... 586 755-9600
  Warren *(G-17293)*
Wirco Manufacturing LLC ....F...... 810 984-5576
  Port Huron *(G-12976)*

STAMPINGS: Metal

A & A Manufacturing Co ....G...... 616 846-1730
  Spring Lake *(G-15130)*
A & R Specialty Services Corp ....E...... 313 933-8750
  Detroit *(G-3826)*
A & S Reel & Tackle Inc ....G...... 313 928-1667
  Ecorse *(G-4741)*
A Raymond Corp N Amer Inc ....E...... 248 853-2500
  Rochester Hills *(G-13358)*
Acme Tool & Die Co ....G...... 231 938-1260
  Acme *(G-1)*
Actron Steel Inc ....E...... 231 947-3981
  Traverse City *(G-15890)*
Advance Engineering Company ....D...... 313 537-3500
  Canton *(G-2344)*
Advanced Auto Trends Inc ....E...... 248 628-6111
  Oxford *(G-12333)*
Alternate Number Five Inc ....D...... 616 842-2581
  Grand Haven *(G-5991)*
Aluminum Blanking Co Inc ....D...... 248 338-4422
  Pontiac *(G-12802)*
Aluminum Textures Inc ....E...... 616 538-3144
  Grandville *(G-7020)*
American Engnred Cmponents Inc ....C...... 734 428-8301
  Manchester *(G-10402)*
American Fabricated Pdts Inc ....F...... 616 607-8785
  Spring Lake *(G-15133)*
American Metal Fab Inc ....D...... 269 279-5108
  Three Rivers *(G-15854)*
Anand Nvh North America Inc ....C...... 810 724-2400
  Imlay City *(G-8196)*
Anrod Screen Cylinder Company ....E...... 989 872-2101
  Cass City *(G-2511)*
Apex Spring & Stamping Corp ....D...... 616 453-5463
  Grand Rapids *(G-6171)*
Arnold Tool & Die Co ....E...... 586 598-0099
  Chesterfield *(G-2741)*
Automatic Spring Products Corp ....C...... 616 842-2284
  Grand Haven *(G-5995)*
Automotive Prototype Stamping ....G...... 586 445-6792
  Clinton Township *(G-3060)*
Bae Industries Inc ....C...... 586 754-3000
  Warren *(G-16950)*
Bae Industries Inc ....F...... 248 475-9600
  Auburn Hills *(G-790)*
Barnes Group Inc ....G...... 734 737-0958
  Plymouth *(G-12582)*
Barnes Group Inc ....E...... 734 429-2022
  Plymouth *(G-12583)*
Barnes Group Inc ....G...... 586 415-6677
  Fraser *(G-5627)*
Belwith Products LLC ....F...... 616 247-4000
  Grandville *(G-7022)*
Benteler Automotive Corp ....B...... 616 247-3936
  Auburn Hills *(G-791)*
Blue Fire Manufacturing LLC ....E...... 248 714-7166
  Waterford *(G-17325)*
Bopp-Busch Manufacturing Co ....E...... 989 876-7924
  Au Gres *(G-745)*
Broaching Industries Inc ....E...... 586 949-3775
  Chesterfield *(G-2748)*
Cameron Tool Corporation ....D...... 517 487-3671
  Lansing *(G-9353)*
Challenge Mfg Company ....C...... 616 735-6500
  Grand Rapids *(G-6268)*
Challenge Mfg Company ....A...... 616 396-2079
  Holland *(G-7587)*
Commercial Mfg & Assembly Inc ....E...... 616 847-9980
  Grand Haven *(G-6005)*
Complete Metalcraft LLC ....G...... 248 990-0850
  Highland *(G-7489)*
Continental Strctrl Plstc Mch ....D...... 734 428-8301
  Manchester *(G-10404)*
Contract Welding and Fabg Inc ....E...... 734 699-5561
  Van Buren Twp *(G-16753)*
Craft Steel Products Inc ....E...... 616 935-7575
  Spring Lake *(G-15137)*

Dajaco Ind Inc ....G...... 586 949-1590
  Chesterfield *(G-2759)*
Dee-Blast Corporation ....F...... 269 428-2400
  Stevensville *(G-15563)*
Degele Manufacturing Inc ....E...... 586 949-3550
  Chesterfield *(G-2763)*
Demmer Investments Inc ....G...... 517 321-3600
  Lansing *(G-9221)*
Diamond Press Solutions LLC ....G...... 269 945-1997
  Hastings *(G-7406)*
Die-Verse Solutions LLC ....F...... 616 384-3550
  Coopersville *(G-3557)*
Dorr Industries Inc ....F...... 616 681-9440
  Dorr *(G-4523)*
Duggans Limited LLC ....F...... 586 254-7400
  Shelby Township *(G-14582)*
Dynamic Corporation ....D...... 616 399-9391
  Holland *(G-7613)*
E & E Manufacturing Co Inc ....B...... 734 451-7600
  Plymouth *(G-12615)*
E & E Manufacturing Co Inc ....F...... 248 616-1300
  Clawson *(G-2977)*
Edmar Manufacturing Inc ....D...... 616 392-7218
  Holland *(G-7618)*
Elkins Machine & Tool Co Inc ....E...... 734 941-0266
  Romulus *(G-13672)*
Elmhirst Industries Inc ....E...... 586 731-8663
  Sterling Heights *(G-15330)*
Ernest Inds Acquisition LLC ....G...... 734 459-8881
  Plymouth *(G-12618)*
Ernest Industries Acquisition, ...E...... 734 595-9500
  Westland *(G-17554)*
Euclid Manufacturing Co Inc ....E...... 734 397-6300
  Detroit *(G-4043)*
European Cabinet Mfg Co ....E...... 586 445-8909
  Roseville *(G-13802)*
Fisher & Company Incorporated ....C...... 248 280-0808
  Troy *(G-16363)*
Fortress Manufacturing Inc ....F...... 269 925-1336
  Benton Harbor *(G-1498)*
Franklin Fastener Company ....E...... 313 537-8900
  Redford *(G-13162)*
Gill Corporation ....B...... 616 453-4491
  Grand Rapids *(G-6438)*
Global Advanced Products LLC ....D...... 586 749-6800
  Chesterfield *(G-2781)*
Global Automotive Systems LLC ....E...... 248 299-7500
  Auburn Hills *(G-889)*
Global Rollforming Systems LLC ....G...... 586 218-5100
  Roseville *(G-13808)*
Globe Tech LLC ....E...... 734 656-2200
  Plymouth *(G-12630)*
Grant Industries Incorporated ....D...... 586 293-9200
  Fraser *(G-5657)*
Grattan Family Enterprises LLC ....D...... 248 547-3870
  Ferndale *(G-5290)*
Gray Brothers Mfg Inc ....G...... 269 483-7615
  White Pigeon *(G-17650)*
Greenfield Die & Mfg Corp ....C...... 734 454-4000
  Canton *(G-2379)*
Hatch Stamping Company LLC ....D...... 517 223-1293
  Fowlerville *(G-5569)*
Hatch Stamping Company LLC ....C...... 517 540-1021
  Howell *(G-8047)*
Heinzmann D Tool & Die Inc ....F...... 248 363-5115
  Commerce Township *(G-3410)*
Hibshman Screw Mch Pdts Inc ....E...... 269 641-7525
  Union *(G-16730)*
High-Star Corporation ....G...... 734 743-1503
  Westland *(G-17569)*
Hilite Industries Inc ....E...... 248 475-4580
  Lake Orion *(G-9138)*
Hilltop Manufacturing Co Inc ....D...... 248 437-2530
  New Hudson *(G-11544)*
Hope Network West Michigan ....E...... 231 775-3425
  Cadillac *(G-2252)*
Hope Network West Michigan ....C...... 231 796-4801
  Paris *(G-12385)*
Illinois Tool Works Inc ....E...... 734 855-3709
  Livonia *(G-9779)*
Inalfa/Ssi Roof Systems LLC ....D...... 586 758-6620
  Warren *(G-17086)*
Industrial Exprmental Tech LLC ....E...... 248 371-8000
  Auburn Hills *(G-912)*
Industrial Innovations Inc ....F...... 616 249-1525
  Grandville *(G-7052)*
Industrial Machine Pdts Inc ....D...... 248 628-3621
  Oxford *(G-12351)*
Industrial Stamping & Mfg Co ....E...... 586 772-8430
  Roseville *(G-13819)*

Innotec Corp ....D...... 616 772-5959
  Zeeland *(G-18160)*
Iroquois Industries Inc ....E...... 586 756-6922
  Warren *(G-17101)*
J & L Mfg Co ....E...... 586 445-9530
  Warren *(G-17104)*
John Lamantia Corporation ....G...... 269 428-8100
  Stevensville *(G-15572)*
Jordan Manufacturing Company ....E...... 616 794-0900
  Belding *(G-1421)*
Jsj Corporation ....E...... 616 842-6350
  Grand Haven *(G-6042)*
K & K Die Inc ....E...... 586 268-5185
  Sterling Heights *(G-15384)*
K&K Stamping Company ....E...... 586 443-7900
  Saint Clair Shores *(G-14257)*
Kecy Corporation ....E...... 517 448-8954
  Hudson *(G-8133)*
Kecy Products Inc ....D...... 517 448-8954
  Hudson *(G-8134)*
Kendor Steel Rule Die Inc ....E...... 586 293-7111
  Fraser *(G-5678)*
Keyes-Davis Company ....E...... 269 962-7505
  Springfield *(G-15195)*
Kinney Tool and Die Inc ....D...... 616 997-0901
  Coopersville *(G-3562)*
Kriewall Enterprises Inc ....E...... 586 336-0600
  Romeo *(G-13631)*
L & W Inc ....C...... 734 397-8085
  Van Buren Twp *(G-16769)*
L T C Roll & Engineering Co ....E...... 586 465-1023
  Clinton Township *(G-3157)*
Lab Tool and Engineering Corp ....E...... 517 750-4131
  Spring Arbor *(G-15124)*
Lacy Tool Company Inc ....G...... 248 476-5250
  Novi *(G-11928)*
Laser Cutting Co ....E...... 586 468-5300
  Harrison Township *(G-7337)*
Llink Technologies LLC ....E...... 586 336-9370
  Brown City *(G-2054)*
Low Cost Surcing Solutions LLC ....G...... 248 535-7721
  Washington *(G-17306)*
Luckmarr Plastics Inc ....D...... 586 978-8498
  Sterling Heights *(G-15403)*
Lupaul Industries Inc ....F...... 517 783-3223
  Saint Johns *(G-14286)*
M D Hubbard Spring Co Inc ....E...... 248 628-2528
  Oxford *(G-12358)*
M P I International Inc ....D...... 608 764-5416
  Rochester Hills *(G-13463)*
Means Industries Inc ....D...... 989 754-3300
  Saginaw *(G-14087)*
Metro Stamping & Mfg Co ....F...... 313 538-6464
  Redford *(G-13173)*
Michigan Rod Products Inc ....D...... 517 552-9812
  Howell *(G-8065)*
Michigan Scientific Corp ....D...... 231 547-5511
  Charlevoix *(G-2620)*
Mittex Group ....G...... 616 878-4090
  Byron Center *(G-2202)*
Mpi Products LLC ....E...... 248 237-3007
  Rochester Hills *(G-13478)*
Mueller Impacts Company Inc ....C...... 810 364-3700
  Marysville *(G-10608)*
Munn Manufacturing Company ....E...... 616 765-3067
  Freeport *(G-5766)*
New Center Stamping Inc ....C...... 313 872-3500
  Detroit *(G-4267)*
Northern Industrial Mfg Corp ....E...... 586 468-2790
  Harrison Township *(G-7341)*
Os Holdings LLc ....G...... 734 397-6300
  New Boston *(G-11507)*
Ovidon Manufacturing LLC ....D...... 517 548-4005
  Howell *(G-8075)*
Page Components Corporation ....F...... 231 922-3600
  Traverse City *(G-16062)*
Patton Tool and Die Inc ....F...... 810 359-5336
  Lexington *(G-9559)*
Paw Paw Everlast Label Company ....G...... 269 657-4921
  Paw Paw *(G-12411)*
Precision Parts Holdings Inc ....A...... 248 853-9010
  Rochester Hills *(G-13498)*
Precision Prototype & Mfg Inc ....F...... 517 663-4114
  Eaton Rapids *(G-4729)*
Premier Prototype Inc ....E...... 586 323-6114
  Sterling Heights *(G-15450)*
Press-Way Inc ....D...... 586 790-3324
  Clinton Township *(G-3201)*
Pro Stamp Plus LLC ....G...... 616 447-2988
  Grand Rapids *(G-6780)*

PRODUCT SECTION   STEEL FABRICATORS

Production Fabricators Inc ....E 231 777-3822
 Muskegon *(G-11407)*
Profile Inc ....E 517 224-8012
 Potterville *(G-13075)*
Punching Concepts Inc ....F 989 358-7070
 Alpena *(G-309)*
Quality Metalcraft Inc ....C 734 261-6700
 Livonia *(G-9900)*
Quigley Manufacturing Inc ....C 248 426-8600
 Farmington Hills *(G-5110)*
R-Bo Co Inc ....E 616 748-9733
 Zeeland *(G-18184)*
Radar Mexican Investments LLC ....G 586 779-0300
 Warren *(G-17215)*
Ranger Tool & Die Co ....E 989 754-1403
 Saginaw *(G-14130)*
Ridgeview Industries Inc ....B 616 453-8636
 Grand Rapids *(G-6825)*
Ridgeview Industries Inc ....D 616 414-6500
 Nunica *(G-12043)*
Ridgeview Industries Inc ....C 616 453-8636
 Grand Rapids *(G-6826)*
Rose Engraving Company ....G 616 243-3108
 Grand Rapids *(G-6837)*
Rose-A-Lee Technologies Inc ....G 586 799-4555
 Sterling Heights *(G-15479)*
Royal Flex-N-Gate Oak LLC ....B 248 549-3800
 Warren *(G-17225)*
Selective Industries Inc ....D 810 765-4666
 Marine City *(G-10483)*
Set Enterprises of Mi Inc ....C 586 573-3600
 Sterling Heights *(G-15494)*
Shape Corp ....D 616 842-2825
 Spring Lake *(G-15177)*
Shiloh Industries Inc ....D 734 454-4000
 Canton *(G-2426)*
Shiloh Manufacturing LLC ....D 586 779-0300
 Warren *(G-17239)*
Shiloh Manufacturing LLC ....F 586 873-2835
 Roseville *(G-13868)*
SOS Engineering Inc ....F 616 846-5767
 Grand Haven *(G-6081)*
Specialty Tube LLC ....E 616 949-5990
 Grand Rapids *(G-6882)*
Spinform Inc ....G 810 767-4660
 Flint *(G-5502)*
Spirit Industries Inc ....G 517 371-7840
 Lansing *(G-9266)*
Sterling Die & Engineering Inc ....E 586 677-0707
 Macomb *(G-10163)*
Stus Welding & Fabrication ....G 616 392-8459
 Holland *(G-7818)*
Sycron Technologies Inc.......................G 810 694-4007
 Grand Blanc *(G-5985)*
Ta Delaware Inc ....E 248 675-6000
 Novi *(G-12011)*
Technique Inc ....D 517 789-8988
 Jackson *(G-8585)*
Tg Manufacturing LLC ....E 616 935-7575
 Byron Center *(G-2212)*
Thai Summit America Corp ....D 517 548-4900
 Howell *(G-8107)*
Thomas Industrial Rolls Inc ....F 313 584-9696
 Dearborn *(G-3766)*
TI Automotive LLC ....G 248 393-4525
 Auburn Hills *(G-1021)*
Trans-Matic Mfg Co Inc ....G 616 820-2541
 Holland *(G-7835)*
TRW Automotive US LLC ....E 248 426-3901
 Farmington Hills *(G-5143)*
Uei Inc ....E 616 361-6093
 Grand Rapids *(G-6944)*
Ultraform Industries Inc ....D 586 752-4508
 Bruce Twp *(G-2105)*
Unified Brands Inc ....E 989 644-3331
 Weidman *(G-17462)*
United Manufacturing Inc ....E 616 738-8888
 Holland *(G-7842)*
Usher Tool & Die Inc ....F 616 583-9160
 Byron Center *(G-2213)*
Van Loon Industries Inc ....E 586 532-8530
 Shelby Township *(G-14716)*
Variety Die & Stamping Co ....D 734 426-4488
 Dexter *(G-4517)*
Ventra Ionia Main LLC ....E 616 597-3220
 Ionia *(G-8252)*
Ventra Ionia Main LLC ....C 616 597-3220
 Ionia *(G-8253)*
Versatube Corporation ....F 248 524-0299
 Troy *(G-16683)*

Vintech Mexico Holdings LLC ....G 810 387-3224
 Imlay City *(G-8215)*
Wallin Brothers Inc ....G 734 525-7750
 Livonia *(G-9995)*
Webasto Roof Systems Inc ....A 248 299-2000
 Rochester Hills *(G-13544)*
Webasto Roof Systems Inc ....F 248 997-5100
 Rochester Hills *(G-13545)*
Webasto Roof Systems Inc ....C 734 452-2600
 Livonia *(G-10002)*
Webster Cold Forge Co ....F 313 554-4500
 Northville *(G-11734)*
Western Engineered Products..............G 248 371-9259
 Lake Orion *(G-9170)*
Wico Metal Products Company ....C 586 755-9600
 Warren *(G-17293)*
ZF Active Safety & Elec US LLC ....C 734 855-2600
 Livonia *(G-10014)*
ZF North America Inc ....G 248 478-7210
 Farmington Hills *(G-5154)*
ZF Passive Safety ....G 734 855-3631
 Livonia *(G-10018)*
ZF Passive Safety ....B 586 232-7200
 Washington *(G-17316)*
Zygot Operations Limited ....F 810 736-2900
 Flint *(G-5529)*

STANDS & RACKS: Engine, Metal

Steelhead Industries LLC ....F 989 506-7416
 Mount Pleasant *(G-11231)*

STARTERS & CONTROLLERS: Motor, Electric

Dare Auto Inc ....E 734 228-6243
 Plymouth *(G-12605)*
Electrocraft Michigan Inc ....F 603 516-1297
 Saline *(G-14387)*

STARTERS: Electric Motor

Denso International Amer Inc ....G 248 359-4177
 Van Buren Twp *(G-16757)*
Radam Motors LLC ....G 269 365-4982
 Otsego *(G-12254)*

STARTERS: Motor

Car Audio Outlet LLC ....G 810 686-3300
 Clio *(G-3266)*
Precision Power Inc ....G 517 371-4274
 Lansing *(G-9414)*
Prestolite Electric Inc ....F 866 463-7078
 Novi *(G-11980)*

STATIONARY & OFFICE SPLYS, WHOLESALE: Inked Ribbons

Label Tech Inc ....F 586 247-6444
 Shelby Township *(G-14619)*

STATIONARY & OFFICE SPLYS, WHOLESALE: Office Filing Splys

FSI Label Company ....E 586 776-4110
 Holland *(G-7637)*

STATIONERY & OFFICE SPLYS WHOLESALERS

Accuform Prtg & Graphics Inc..............F 313 271-5600
 Detroit *(G-3838)*
Consoldted Dcment Slutions LLC ....F 586 293-8100
 Fraser *(G-5638)*
Imperial Clinical RES Svcs Inc ....C 616 784-0100
 Grand Rapids *(G-6528)*
Mikan Corporation ....F 734 944-9447
 Saline *(G-14401)*
Office Express Inc ....E 248 307-1850
 Troy *(G-16534)*
US Salon Supply LLC ....G 616 365-5790
 Paw Paw *(G-12415)*
Utley Brothers Inc ....E 248 585-1700
 Troy *(G-16672)*
Yti Office Express LLC ....G 866 996-8952
 Troy *(G-16704)*

STATIONERY PRDTS

Presscraft Papers Inc ....E 231 882-5505
 Benzonia *(G-1576)*

STATORS REWINDING SVCS

Warfield Electric Company Inc ....G 734 722-4044
 Westland *(G-17609)*

STEEL & ALLOYS: Tool & Die

Alloy Resources LLC ....E 231 777-3941
 Muskegon *(G-11265)*
Aweba Tool & Die Corp ....F 478 296-2002
 Hastings *(G-7401)*
Blades Enterprises LLC ....F 734 449-4479
 Wixom *(G-17775)*
Fabtronic Inc ....F 586 786-6114
 Macomb *(G-10121)*
Form G Tech Co ....D 248 583-3610
 Troy *(G-16369)*
Gale Tool Co Inc ....G 248 437-4610
 South Lyon *(G-14792)*
Industrial Engineering Service ....F 616 794-1330
 Belding *(G-1419)*
Kena Corporation ....G 586 873-4761
 Chesterfield *(G-2795)*
Major Industries Ltd..............................D 810 985-9372
 Port Huron *(G-12938)*
Proservice Machine Ltd ....E 734 317-7266
 Erie *(G-4809)*
St Johns Computer Machining ....G 989 224-7664
 Saint Johns *(G-14296)*
The Pom Group Inc ....F 248 409-7900
 Auburn Hills *(G-1018)*
W A Thomas Company ....E 734 955-6500
 Taylor *(G-15779)*

STEEL FABRICATORS

A & S Industrial LLC ....G 906 482-8007
 Hancock *(G-7247)*
A N M Products ....G 269 483-1228
 White Pigeon *(G-17643)*
A-1 Fabrication Inc ....G 586 775-8392
 Roseville *(G-13766)*
AB Custom Fabricating LLC ....E 269 663-8100
 Edwardsburg *(G-4756)*
Ability Mfg & Engrg Co ....F 269 227-3292
 Fennville *(G-5169)*
Ace Welding & Machine Inc ....F 231 941-9664
 Traverse City *(G-15887)*
Actron Steel Inc ....E 231 947-3981
 Traverse City *(G-15890)*
Admin Industries LLC ....F 989 685-3438
 Rose City *(G-13756)*
Adrian Tool Corporation ....E 517 263-6530
 Adrian *(G-48)*
ADW Industries Inc ....E 989 466-4742
 Alma *(G-231)*
Aero Inc ....F 248 669-4085
 Walled Lake *(G-16889)*
Alco Products LLC ....E 313 823-7500
 Detroit *(G-3853)*
Allegan Metal Fabricators Inc ....G 269 751-7130
 Hamilton *(G-7229)*
Allor Manufacturing Inc ....D 248 486-4500
 Brighton *(G-1883)*
Alloy Construction Service Inc ....E 989 486-6960
 Midland *(G-10813)*
Alro Steel Corporation ....D 810 695-7300
 Grand Blanc *(G-5958)*
Ambassador Steel Corporation ....E 517 455-7216
 Lansing *(G-9336)*
American Steel Fabricators ....F 248 476-8433
 Farmington *(G-4894)*
American Steel Works Inc ....F 734 282-0300
 Riverview *(G-13290)*
Amerikam Inc ....D 616 243-5833
 Grand Rapids *(G-6167)*
Amhawk LLC ....F 269 468-4141
 Coloma *(G-3353)*
Amhawk LLC ....E 269 468-4177
 Hartford *(G-7381)*
Amigo Mobility Intl Inc ....D 989 777-0910
 Bridgeport *(G-1848)*
Austin Tube Products Inc ....E 231 745-2741
 Baldwin *(G-1082)*
B & G Custom Works Inc ....E 269 686-9420
 Allegan *(G-150)*
Baker Enterprises Inc ....E 989 354-2189
 Alpena *(G-280)*
Bauer Sheet Metal & Fabg Inc ....E 231 773-3244
 Muskegon *(G-11276)*
Bennett Steel LLC ....F 616 401-5271
 Grand Rapids *(G-6211)*

Employee Codes: A=Over 500 employees, B=251-500
C=101-250, D=51-100, E=20-50, F=10-19, G=3-9

2020 Harris Michigan
Industrial Directory

1375

Black River Manufacturing Inc ....E 810 982-9812
Port Huron *(G-12900)*
Boones Welding & Fabricating ....G 517 782-7461
Jackson *(G-8393)*
Bridgeport Manufacturing Inc ....G 989 777-4314
Bridgeport *(G-1850)*
Builders Iron Inc ....E 616 887-9127
Comstock Park *(G-3465)*
Burnham & Northern Inc ....G 517 279-7501
Coldwater *(G-3292)*
C & J Fabrication Inc ....G 586 791-6269
Clinton Township *(G-3071)*
C & M Manufacturing Inc ....E 517 279-0013
Coldwater *(G-3293)*
Cadillac Fabrication Inc ....E 231 775-7386
Cadillac *(G-2238)*
CAM Fab ....G 269 685-1000
Martin *(G-10595)*
Campbell & Shaw Steel Inc ....F 810 364-5100
Marysville *(G-10600)*
Camryn Fabrication LLC ....C 586 949-0818
Chesterfield *(G-2751)*
Capital Steel & Builders Sup ....F 517 694-0451
Holt *(G-7905)*
Cardinal Fabricating Inc ....E 517 655-2155
Williamston *(G-17728)*
Casadei Structural Steel Inc ....E 586 698-2898
Sterling Heights *(G-15283)*
Cbp Fabrication Inc ....E 313 653-4220
Detroit *(G-3931)*
Centerline Indus Fabrication ....G 313 977-9056
Newport *(G-11587)*
Cerco Inc ....E 734 362-8664
Brownstown Twp *(G-2071)*
Chicago Blow Pipe Company ....F 773 533-6100
Marquette *(G-10522)*
Circle S Products Inc ....G 734 675-2960
Woodhaven *(G-17938)*
Clair Sawyer ....G 906 228-8242
Marquette *(G-10523)*
Complex Steel & Wire Corp ....F 734 326-1600
Wayne *(G-17428)*
Cooper & Cooper Sales Inc ....G 810 327-6247
Port Huron *(G-12910)*
Corban Industries Inc ....D 248 393-2720
Orion *(G-12177)*
Cornerstone Fabg & Cnstr Inc ....E 989 642-5241
Hemlock *(G-7460)*
Corsair Engineering Inc ....D 810 234-3664
Flint *(G-5404)*
Cox Brothers Machining Inc ....E 517 796-4662
Jackson *(G-8422)*
Custom Architectural Products ....G 616 748-1905
Zeeland *(G-18129)*
Custom Design & Manufacturing ....F 989 754-9962
Carrollton *(G-2484)*
Custom Welding Service LLC ....F 616 402-6681
Grand Haven *(G-6007)*
Cvm Services LLC ....E 269 521-4811
Allegan *(G-153)*
David A Mohr Jr ....G 517 266-2694
Adrian *(G-58)*
Delducas Welding & Co Inc ....G 810 743-1990
Flint *(G-5416)*
Delta Steel Inc ....G 989 752-5129
Saginaw *(G-14025)*
Demaria Building Company Inc ....G 248 486-2598
New Hudson *(G-11537)*
Demmer Corporation ....C 517 321-3600
Lansing *(G-9217)*
Diversified Fabricators Inc ....F 586 868-1000
Clinton Township *(G-3104)*
Dobson Industrial Inc ....E 800 298-6063
Bay City *(G-1304)*
Douglas King Industries Inc ....E 989 642-2865
Hemlock *(G-7461)*
Dowding Industries Inc ....E 517 663-5455
Eaton Rapids *(G-4720)*
Dunnage Engineering Inc ....E 810 229-9501
Brighton *(G-1913)*
Dunns Welding Inc ....G 248 356-3866
Southfield *(G-14887)*
Eab Fabrication Inc ....E 517 639-7080
Quincy *(G-13094)*
Eastern Michigan Industries ....E 586 757-4140
Warren *(G-17015)*
EMC Welding & Fabrication Inc ....G 231 788-4172
Muskegon *(G-11316)*
Empire Machine & Conveyors Inc ....F 989 541-2060
Durand *(G-4608)*
Engineered Alum Fabricators Co ....G 248 582-3430
Ferndale *(G-5282)*
Ethylene LLC ....E 616 554-3464
Kentwood *(G-9005)*
Fab Masters Company Inc ....D 269 646-5315
Marcellus *(G-10464)*
Fab-Lite Inc ....D 231 398-8280
Manistee *(G-10421)*
Fabricated Components & Assemb ....F 269 673-7100
Allegan *(G-160)*
Ferguson Steel Inc ....F 810 984-3918
Fort Gratiot *(G-5549)*
Ferro Fab LLC ....F 586 791-3561
Clinton Township *(G-3115)*
Frankenmuth Industrial Svcs ....E 989 652-3322
Frankenmuth *(G-5587)*
Fusion Fabricating and Mfg LLC ....G 586 739-1970
Sterling Heights *(G-15351)*
Gen-Oak Fabricators Inc ....G 248 373-1515
Orion *(G-12181)*
Genco Alliance LLC ....E 269 216-5500
Kalamazoo *(G-8748)*
General Motors LLC ....G 517 242-2158
Lansing *(G-9372)*
General Motors LLC ....B 989 894-7210
Bay City *(G-1315)*
Gerref Industries Inc ....E 616 794-3110
Belding *(G-1416)*
Global Strgc Sup Solutions LLC ....D 734 525-9100
Livonia *(G-9753)*
Gosen Tool & Machine Inc ....F 989 777-6493
Saginaw *(G-14049)*
Gray Brothers Mfg Inc ....E 269 483-7615
White Pigeon *(G-17650)*
Great Lakes Contracting Inc ....F 616 846-8888
Grand Haven *(G-6027)*
Great Lakes Metal Works ....G 269 789-2342
Marshall *(G-10569)*
Great Lakes Stainless Inc ....E 231 943-7648
Traverse City *(G-15993)*
Great Lakes Towers LLC ....C 734 682-4000
Monroe *(G-11037)*
Greene Metal Products Inc ....E 586 465-6800
Clinton Township *(G-3130)*
Griptrac Inc ....F 231 853-2284
Ravenna *(G-13120)*
H & M Welding and Fabricating ....G 517 764-3630
Jackson *(G-8461)*
Hamilton Steel Fabrications ....G 269 751-8757
Hamilton *(G-7234)*
Harrington Construction Co ....G 269 543-4251
Fennville *(G-5173)*
HC Starck Inc ....E 517 279-9511
Coldwater *(G-3309)*
Heys Fabrication and Mch Co ....F 616 247-0065
Wyoming *(G-18009)*
Highland Engineering Inc ....E 517 548-4372
Howell *(G-8048)*
Ideal Steel & Bldrs Sups LLC ....E 313 849-0000
Detroit *(G-4134)*
Imm Inc ....E 989 344-7662
Grayling *(G-7108)*
Industrial Fabricating Inc ....F 734 676-2710
Rockwood *(G-13605)*
Industrial Fabrication LLC ....E 269 465-5960
Bridgman *(G-1867)*
Industrial Machine & Tool ....G 231 734-2794
Evart *(G-4883)*
Innovative Iron Inc ....G 616 248-4250
Grand Rapids *(G-6538)*
Inter-Lakes Bases Inc ....E 586 294-8120
Fraser *(G-5671)*
International Extrusions Inc ....C 734 427-8700
Garden City *(G-5830)*
Iron Fetish Metalworks Inc ....F 586 776-8311
Roseville *(G-13822)*
J & B Metal Fabicators LLC ....G 616 837-6764
Nunica *(G-12037)*
J & J Burning Co ....E 586 758-7619
Warren *(G-17103)*
J & J Fabrications Inc ....G 269 673-5488
Allegan *(G-166)*
J & J United Industries LLC ....G 734 443-3737
Livonia *(G-9787)*
J & M Machine Products Inc ....D 231 755-1622
Norton Shores *(G-11764)*
Jay Industries Inc ....G 313 240-7535
Northville *(G-11702)*
Jr Kandler & Sons ....G 734 241-0270
Monroe *(G-11044)*
JS Welding Inc ....G 517 451-2098
Britton *(G-2018)*
K & L Sheet Metal LLC ....G 269 965-0027
Battle Creek *(G-1205)*
K-R Metal Engineers Corp ....F 989 892-1901
Bay City *(G-1324)*
Kalamazoo Metal Muncher Inc ....G 269 492-0268
Plainwell *(G-12528)*
Kehrig Steel Inc ....G 586 716-9700
Ira *(G-8259)*
Ken Gorsline Welding ....G 269 649-0650
Vicksburg *(G-16837)*
Kenowa Industries Inc ....G 517 322-0311
Lansing *(G-9304)*
Kirby Metal Corporation ....E 810 743-3360
Burton *(G-2157)*
Kraftube Inc ....C 231 832-5562
Reed City *(G-13217)*
Kriewall Enterprises Inc ....E 586 336-0600
Romeo *(G-13631)*
L & W Inc ....C 734 397-8085
Van Buren Twp *(G-16769)*
L & W Inc ....D 734 397-6300
New Boston *(G-11502)*
Laduke Corporation ....E 248 414-6600
Oak Park *(G-12077)*
Lake Shore Services Inc ....F 734 285-7007
Wyandotte *(G-17965)*
Laser Craft LLC ....F 248 340-8922
Lake Orion *(G-9145)*
Lasers Unlimited Inc ....F 616 977-2668
Grand Rapids *(G-6621)*
Liberty Fabricators Inc ....F 810 877-7117
Flint *(G-5458)*
Lincoln Welding Company ....G 313 292-2299
Stockbridge *(G-15590)*
Loudon Steel Inc ....D 989 871-9353
Millington *(G-10997)*
Madar Metal Fabricating LLC ....F 517 267-9610
Lansing *(G-9243)*
Magnum Fabricating ....G 734 484-5800
Ypsilanti *(G-18087)*
Manistee Wldg & Piping Svc Inc ....G 231 723-2551
Manistee *(G-10428)*
Marsh Plating Corporation ....D 734 483-5767
Ypsilanti *(G-18088)*
Maslo Fabrication LLC ....G 616 298-7700
Holland *(G-7740)*
Matrix North Amercn Cnstr Inc ....C 734 847-4605
Temperance *(G-15836)*
Mayo Welding & Fabricating Co ....G 248 435-2730
Royal Oak *(G-13948)*
Mbm Fabricators Co Inc ....C 734 941-0100
Romulus *(G-13704)*
MCS Industries Inc ....E 517 568-4161
Homer *(G-7946)*
Men of Steel Inc ....F 989 635-4866
Marlette *(G-10501)*
Merrill Institute Inc ....G 989 462-0330
Alma *(G-240)*
Metal Mart USA Inc ....G 586 977-5820
Warren *(G-17148)*
Metalbuilt LLC ....E 586 786-9106
Chesterfield *(G-2804)*
Metaldyne Tblar Components LLC ....C 248 727-1800
Southfield *(G-14979)*
Metalfab Inc ....G 313 381-7579
Dearborn *(G-3740)*
Metalfab Manufacturing Inc ....E 989 826-2301
Mio *(G-11004)*
Michigan Diversified Metals ....G 517 223-7730
Fowlerville *(G-5576)*
Michigan Indus Met Pdts Inc ....E 616 786-3922
Muskegon *(G-11378)*
Michigan Steel Fabricators Inc ....E 810 785-1478
Flint *(G-5466)*
Mid Michigan Pipe Inc ....G 989 772-5664
Grand Rapids *(G-6683)*
Mid-West Innovators Inc ....F 989 358-7147
Alpena *(G-300)*
Midwest Fabricating Inc ....G 734 921-3914
Taylor *(G-15744)*
Midwest Steel Inc ....E 313 873-2220
Detroit *(G-4248)*
Mike Manufacturing Corporation ....G 586 759-1140
Warren *(G-17156)*
Milton Manufacturing Inc ....E 313 366-2450
Detroit *(G-4250)*
Mitchell Welding Co LLC ....G 517 265-8105
Adrian *(G-82)*

PRODUCT SECTION — STEEL MILLS

Mkr Fabricating Inc — Saginaw (G-14098)	F	989 753-8100
Moore Flame Cutting Co — Bloomfield Hills (G-1784)	D	586 978-1090
Moran Iron Works Inc — Onaway (G-12148)	D	989 733-2011
Morkin and Sowards Inc — Wayne (G-17439)	F	734 729-4242
Mound Steel & Supply Inc — Troy (G-16513)	F	248 852-6630
Mtw Performance & Fab — Mount Pleasant (G-11212)	G	989 317-3301
National Metal Sales Inc — Romulus (G-13711)	G	734 942-3000
National Ordanace Auto Mfg LLC — Auburn Hills (G-952)	G	248 853-8822
NBC Truck Equipment Inc — Roseville (G-13845)	E	586 774-4900
Nelson Iron Works Inc — Detroit (G-4266)	G	313 925-5355
Newco Industries LLC — Litchfield (G-9610)	E	517 542-0105
Nisshinbo Automotive Mfg Inc — Sterling Heights (G-15436)	D	586 997-1000
Northern Chain Specialties — Kaleva (G-8934)	F	231 889-3151
Northern Concrete Pipe Inc — Bay City (G-1338)	E	989 892-3545
Northern Machining & Repr Inc — Escanaba (G-4847)	E	906 786-0526
Northwest Fabrication Inc — East Jordan (G-4641)	G	231 536-3229
Oakwood Custom Coating Inc — Dearborn (G-3745)	F	313 561-7740
Oakwood Energy Management Inc — Taylor (G-15750)	C	734 947-7700
Oakwood Metal Fabricating Co — Dearborn (G-3746)	B	313 561-7740
ONiel Metal Forming Inc — Commerce Township (G-3435)	G	248 960-1804
P I W Corporation — Gaylord (G-5887)	G	989 448-2501
Parton & Preble Inc — Warren (G-17180)	E	586 773-6000
Paul W Marino Gages Inc — Roseville (G-13852)	E	586 772-2400
Pioneer Machine and Tech Inc — Madison Heights (G-10327)	G	248 546-4451
Plutchak Fab — Menominee (G-10755)	G	906 864-4650
Ponder Industrial Incorporated — Bay City (G-1342)	E	989 684-9841
Powell Fabrication & Mfg Inc — Saint Louis (G-14369)	E	989 681-2158
Power Industries Corp — Harrison Township (G-7343)	G	586 783-3818
Precision Metals Plus Inc — Kalamazoo (G-8859)	G	269 342-6330
Precision Mtl Hdlg Eqp LLC — Inkster (G-8232)	D	313 789-8101
Precision Mtl Hdlg Eqp LLC — Romulus (G-13724)	D	734 351-7350
Production Fabricators Inc — Muskegon (G-11407)	E	231 777-3822
Quality Fabg & Erection Co — Durand (G-4613)	G	989 288-5210
Quality Finishing Systems — Grant (G-7081)	F	231 834-9131
R B Machine — Holland (G-7783)	G	616 928-8690
R T C Enviro Fab Inc — Munith (G-11254)	F	517 596-2987
R-Bo Co Inc — Zeeland (G-18184)	E	616 748-9733
Red Iron Strl Consulting Corp — Harbor Springs (G-7292)	G	810 364-5100
Red Laser Inc — Howell (G-8089)	G	517 540-1300
REO Fab LLC — Lapeer (G-9485)	G	810 969-4667
Richard Bennett & Associates — Detroit (G-4345)	G	313 831-4262
Richmonds Steel Inc — Pigeon (G-12492)	F	989 453-7010
Rives Manufacturing Inc — Rives Junction (G-13310)	E	517 569-3380
RKP Consulting Inc — Caledonia (G-2314)	E	616 698-0300
Royal ARC Welding Company — Flat Rock (G-5362)	E	734 789-9099
RSI Global Sourcing LLC — Novi (G-11988)	F	734 604-2448
Rt Manufacturing Inc — Escanaba (G-4858)	F	906 233-9158
Ruess Winchester Inc — Owosso (G-12312)	F	989 725-5809
S & G Erection Company — Howell (G-8095)	F	517 546-9240
S & N Machine & Fabricating — Rothbury (G-13895)	F	231 894-2658
Sales & Engineering Inc — Livonia (G-9919)	E	734 525-9030
Samuel Son & Co (usa) Inc — Troy (G-16592)	D	414 486-1556
Sanilac Steel Inc — Marlette (G-10502)	F	989 635-2992
Sas Global Corporation — Warren (G-17229)	C	248 414-4470
Sas Global Corporation — Warren (G-17230)	E	248 414-4470
Savs Welding Services Inc — Detroit (G-4354)	G	313 841-3430
Schneider Fabrication Inc — Saint Johns (G-14294)	G	989 224-6937
Service Iron Works Inc — South Lyon (G-14812)	E	248 446-9750
Servotech Industries Inc — Taylor (G-15764)	F	734 697-5555
Sexton Enterprize Inc — Ferndale (G-5318)	G	248 545-5880
Sharpe Fabricating Inc — Clinton Township (G-3224)	G	586 465-4468
Sherwood Manufacturing Corp — Northport (G-11671)	E	231 386-5132
Shoreline Mtal Fabricators Inc — Muskegon (G-11423)	E	231 722-4443
SL Holdings Inc — Chesterfield (G-2841)	G	586 949-0818
Smede-Son Steel and Sup Co Inc — Redford (G-13192)	D	313 937-8300
Smede-Son Steel and Sup Co Inc — Pontiac (G-12868)	G	248 332-0300
SMI American Inc — Taylor (G-15767)	G	313 438-0096
Sol-I-Cor Industries — Livonia (G-9935)	F	248 476-0670
South Park Sales & Mfg Inc — Dearborn (G-3762)	G	313 381-7579
Spartan Metal Fab LLC — Lansing (G-9263)	G	517 322-9050
Special Fabricators Inc — Madison Heights (G-10357)	G	248 588-6717
Special Projects Inc — Plymouth (G-12759)	E	734 455-7130
Steel Craft Inc — Alpena (G-314)	E	989 358-7196
Steel Supply & Engineering Co — Grand Rapids (G-6888)	E	616 452-3281
Stevens Custom Fabrication — Alpena (G-315)	G	989 340-1184
Stevens Custom Fabrication — Alpena (G-316)	G	989 340-1184
Stone For You — Rochester (G-13353)	G	248 651-9940
Structural Standards Inc — Sparta (G-15115)	F	616 813-1798
Superior Suppliers Network LLC — Crystal Falls (G-3614)	F	906 284-1561
Surplus Steel Inc — Auburn Hills (G-1007)	G	248 338-0000
Synergy Additive Mfg LLC — Clinton Township (G-3241)	G	248 719-2194
Tartan Industries Inc — Yale (G-18047)	G	810 387-4255
Tfi Inc — Muskegon (G-11436)	E	231 728-2310
Tg Manufacturing LLC — Byron Center (G-2212)	E	616 935-7575
Tower International Inc — Grand Rapids (G-6935)	G	616 802-1600
Tri-County Fab Inc — Roseville (G-13879)	G	586 443-5130
Trimet Industries Inc — Traverse City (G-16130)	E	231 929-9100
U P Fabricating Co Inc — Negaunee (G-11478)	E	906 475-4400
U S Fabrication & Design LLC — Livonia (G-9979)	F	248 919-2910
Uacj Automotive Whitehall Inds — Ludington (G-10085)	C	231 845-5101
Unistrut International Corp — Wayne (G-17445)	C	734 721-4040
United Fabricating Company — Highland (G-7501)	G	248 887-7289
Upnorth Design & Repair Inc — Manton (G-10458)	G	231 824-6025
Utica Steel Inc — Chesterfield (G-2853)	D	586 949-1900
Valley Steel Company — Saginaw (G-14177)	F	989 799-2600
Van Dam Iron Works Inc — Grand Rapids (G-6957)	E	616 452-8627
Van Pelt Corporation — Sterling Heights (G-15538)	G	313 365-3600
Van Pelt Corporation — Detroit (G-4422)	F	313 365-6500
Vanco Steel Inc — North Branch (G-11666)	F	810 688-4333
Varneys Fab & Weld LLC — Nunica (G-12046)	G	231 865-6856
Versatile Fabrication Co Inc — Muskegon (G-11446)	E	231 739-7115
Vochaska Engineering — South Haven (G-14782)	G	269 637-5670
Wagon Automotive Inc — Wixom (G-17927)	D	248 262-2020
Wahmhoff Farms LLC — Gobles (G-5950)	F	269 628-4308
Webasto Roof Systems Inc — Rochester Hills (G-13543)	B	248 997-5100
Webasto Roof Systems Inc — Rochester Hills (G-13545)	F	248 997-5100
West Michigan Metals LLC — Allegan (G-192)	G	269 978-7021
Wisner Machine Works LLC — Akron (G-109)	G	989 274-7690
Wm Kloeffler Industries Inc — Marine City (G-10487)	E	810 765-4068
Wpw Inc — Flint (G-5527)	F	810 785-1478

STEEL MILLS

ABC Coating Company Inc — Grand Rapids (G-6128)	F	616 245-4626
AK Steel Corporation — Dearborn (G-3672)	B	313 317-8900
AK Steel Corporation — Troy (G-16176)	E	513 425-2707
ARC Mit — Ferndale (G-5261)	G	248 399-4800
Arlington Metals Corporation — Sawyer (G-14481)	D	269 426-3371
Autocam-Pax Inc — Dowagiac (G-4534)	E	269 782-5186
Bar Processing Corporation — Warren (G-16952)	D	734 782-4454
Benteler Automotive Corp — Auburn Hills (G-791)	B	616 247-3936
Benteler Defense Corp — Auburn Hills (G-793)	G	248 377-9999
Bjerke Forgings Inc — Taylor (G-15696)	A	313 382-2600
Borneman & Peterson Inc — Flint (G-5393)	F	810 744-1890
Brake Roller Co Inc — Battle Creek (G-1157)	E	269 965-2371
Broaching Industries Inc — Chesterfield (G-2748)	E	586 949-3775
Burnham & Northern Inc — Coldwater (G-3292)	G	517 279-7501
Cannon-Muskegon Corporation — Norton Shores (G-11744)	C	231 755-1681
Coach House Iron Inc — Sparta (G-15092)	G	616 785-8967
Delaco Steel Corporation — Dearborn (G-3692)	D	313 491-1200
Detroit Steel Group Inc — Royal Oak (G-13918)	G	248 298-2900
Die Cast Press Mfg Co Inc — Paw Paw (G-12403)	E	269 657-6060
Frank W Small Met Fabrication — Baroda (G-1124)	G	269 422-2001
Fritz Enterprises Inc — River Rouge (G-13277)	F	734 283-7272
Gill Corporation — Grand Rapids (G-6439)	C	616 453-4491
Grant Industries Incorporated — Fraser (G-5657)	D	586 293-9200
Greer Industries Inc — Ferndale (G-5292)	E	800 388-2868

Employee Codes: A=Over 500 employees, B=251-500, C=101-250, D=51-100, E=20-50, F=10-19, G=3-9

2020 Harris Michigan Industrial Directory

STEEL MILLS — PRODUCT SECTION

JIT Steel Corp..C...... 313 491-3212
  Dearborn *(G-3728)*
Manistee Wldg & Piping Svc Inc............G...... 231 723-2551
  Manistee *(G-10428)*
Meyers Metal Fab Inc.............................G...... 248 620-5411
  Clarkston *(G-2937)*
Michigan Rod Products Inc....................D...... 517 552-9812
  Howell *(G-8065)*
Mill Steel Co...D...... 616 949-6700
  Grand Rapids *(G-6690)*
Peerless Steel Company..........................E...... 616 530-6695
  Grandville *(G-7063)*
Premium Air Systems Inc.......................D...... 248 680-8800
  Troy *(G-16562)*
Repair Industries Michigan Inc..............C...... 313 365-5300
  Detroit *(G-4344)*
Resetar Equipment Inc...........................G...... 313 291-0500
  Dearborn Heights *(G-3794)*
Rod Chomper Inc....................................F...... 616 392-9677
  Holland *(G-7790)*
Samuel Son & Co (usa) Inc....................D...... 414 486-1556
  Troy *(G-16592)*
Service Iron Works Inc...........................G...... 248 446-9750
  South Lyon *(G-14812)*
Set Enterprises Inc..................................E...... 586 573-3600
  Sterling Heights *(G-15493)*
Shoreline Recycling & Supply................E...... 231 722-6081
  Muskegon *(G-11424)*
Steel Mill Components Inc.....................F...... 586 920-2595
  Warren *(G-17255)*
Strong Steel Products LLC.....................E...... 313 267-3300
  Detroit *(G-4381)*
TI Group Auto Systems LLC..................D...... 517 437-7462
  Hillsdale *(G-7543)*
Timkensteel Corporation........................G...... 248 994-4422
  Novi *(G-12017)*
Tms International LLC..........................G...... 734 241-3007
  Monroe *(G-11077)*
Tms International LLC..........................G...... 517 764-5123
  Jackson *(G-8590)*
Tms International LLC..........................G...... 313 378-6502
  Ecorse *(G-4746)*
Universal Hdlg Eqp Owosso LLC...........E...... 989 720-1650
  Owosso *(G-12326)*
Welk-Ko Fabricators Inc........................G...... 248 486-2598
  New Hudson *(G-11559)*
Worthington Steel of Michigan..............E...... 734 374-3260
  Taylor *(G-15783)*

STEEL SHEET: Cold-Rolled

Georgetown Steel LLC............................G...... 734 568-6148
  Ottawa Lake *(G-12264)*

STEEL WOOL

Enkon LLC...F...... 937 890-5678
  Manchester *(G-10405)*
Schwab Industries Inc............................C...... 586 566-8090
  Shelby Township *(G-14688)*

STEEL, COLD-ROLLED: Sheet Or Strip, From Own Hot-Rolled

Georgetown Steel LLC............................G...... 734 568-6148
  Ottawa Lake *(G-12264)*

STEEL, COLD-ROLLED: Strip NEC, From Purchased Hot-Rolled

National Galvanizing LP.........................A...... 734 243-1882
  Monroe *(G-11059)*

STEEL, COLD-ROLLED: Strip Or Wire

Heidtman Steel Products Inc.................D...... 734 848-2115
  Erie *(G-4803)*
Kena Corporation....................................G...... 586 873-4761
  Chesterfield *(G-2795)*
Samuel Son & Co (usa) Inc....................D...... 414 486-1556
  Troy *(G-16592)*

STEEL, HOT-ROLLED: Sheet Or Strip

National Galvanizing LP.........................A...... 734 243-1882
  Monroe *(G-11059)*
United States Steel Corp.........................C...... 313 749-2100
  Ecorse *(G-4747)*

STEEL: Cold-Rolled

Alro Steel Corporation............................E...... 517 371-9600
  Lansing *(G-9335)*
Bar Processing Corporation...................D...... 734 782-4454
  Warren *(G-16952)*
Cold Heading Co.....................................D...... 586 497-7016
  Warren *(G-16986)*
Diez Group LLC......................................D...... 734 675-1700
  Woodhaven *(G-17939)*
Fabtec Enterprises Inc............................F...... 616 878-9288
  Byron Center *(G-2190)*
Flat Rock Metal Inc................................C...... 734 782-4454
  Flat Rock *(G-5353)*
Gerdau Macsteel Inc...............................E...... 517 782-0415
  Jackson *(G-8456)*
Gerdau Macsteel Inc...............................B...... 517 764-3920
  Jackson *(G-8455)*
Gerdau Macsteel Inc...............................B...... 734 243-2446
  Monroe *(G-11034)*
Grant Industries Incorporated...............D...... 586 293-9200
  Fraser *(G-5657)*
Greer Industries Inc................................G...... 800 388-2868
  Ferndale *(G-5292)*
H & L Tool Company Inc.......................D...... 248 585-7474
  Madison Heights *(G-10263)*
Nss Technologies Inc..............................E...... 734 459-9500
  Canton *(G-2412)*
Peerless Steel Company..........................E...... 616 530-6695
  Grandville *(G-7063)*
Sandvik Inc..E...... 269 926-7241
  Benton Harbor *(G-1545)*
Van Emon Bruce......................................G...... 269 467-7803
  Centreville *(G-2598)*
Wolverine Carbide Die Company...........E...... 248 280-0300
  Troy *(G-16695)*
Worthington Industries Inc...................G...... 734 397-6187
  Canton *(G-2444)*
Worthington Steel of Michigan..............E...... 734 374-3260
  Taylor *(G-15783)*

STEERING SYSTEMS & COMPONENTS

Asama Coldwater Mfg Inc......................B...... 517 279-1090
  Coldwater *(G-3289)*
Ididit Inc...E...... 517 424-0577
  Tecumseh *(G-15798)*
Key Safety Systems Inc..........................C...... 586 726-3800
  Auburn Hills *(G-926)*
Nexteer Automotive Corporation..........B...... 989 757-5000
  Saginaw *(G-14114)*
Nexteer Automotive Group Ltd.............A...... 989 757-5000
  Saginaw *(G-14115)*
Sweet Manufacturing Inc.......................E...... 269 344-2086
  Kalamazoo *(G-8906)*
Turn One Inc...G...... 989 652-2778
  Saginaw *(G-14170)*

STENCILS

Collier Enterprise III..............................G...... 269 503-3402
  Sturgis *(G-15600)*
Lakeside Property Services....................G...... 863 455-9038
  Holland *(G-7718)*

STERILIZERS, BARBER & BEAUTY SHOP

Skin Bar VII LLC....................................G...... 313 701-7958
  Detroit *(G-4364)*

STITCHING SVCS

Corporate Colors Inc..............................G...... 269 323-2000
  Kalamazoo *(G-8719)*

STITCHING SVCS: Custom

G T Jerseys LLC......................................G...... 248 588-3231
  Troy *(G-16376)*
Graphix Signs & Embroidery.................G...... 616 396-0009
  Holland *(G-7650)*
Shop Makarios LLC................................G...... 800 479-0032
  Byron Center *(G-2211)*

STOKERS: Mechanical, Domestic Or Indl

D S C Services Inc..................................G...... 734 241-9500
  Monroe *(G-11026)*
Detroit Stoker Company.........................C...... 734 241-9500
  Monroe *(G-11028)*
Messersmith Manufacturing Inc............G...... 906 466-9010
  Bark River *(G-1121)*

STONE: Crushed & Broken, NEC

Sandys Contracting................................G...... 810 629-2259
  Fenton *(G-5237)*

STONE: Dimension, NEC

Michigan Tile and Marble Co.................E...... 313 931-1700
  Detroit *(G-4244)*
TNT Marble and Stone Inc.....................G...... 248 887-8237
  Hartland *(G-7394)*

STONE: Quarrying & Processing, Own Stone Prdts

Lewiston Sand & Gravel Inc...................G...... 989 786-2742
  Lewiston *(G-9552)*
Quarry Ridge Stone Inc..........................F...... 616 827-8244
  Byron Center *(G-2210)*
Rockwood Quarry LLC..........................C...... 734 783-7415
  South Rockwood *(G-14822)*
Rockwood Quarry LLC..........................G...... 734 783-7400
  Newport *(G-11590)*
Stone Shop Inc..F...... 248 852-4700
  Port Huron *(G-12969)*

STOOLS: Factory

Wm Kloeffler Industries Inc..................E...... 810 765-4068
  Marine City *(G-10487)*

STORE FIXTURES: Exc Wood

Construction Retail Svcs Inc..................G...... 586 469-2289
  Clinton Township *(G-3088)*
Mega Wall Inc...F...... 616 647-4190
  Comstock Park *(G-3499)*
T M Shea Products Inc...........................G...... 800 992-5233
  Troy *(G-16630)*

STORE FIXTURES: Wood

Competitive Edge Wood Spc Inc............D...... 616 842-1063
  Muskegon *(G-11299)*
Hilco Fixture Finders LLC.....................E...... 616 453-1300
  Grand Rapids *(G-6511)*
Holsinger Manufacturing Corp..............F...... 989 684-3101
  Kawkawlin *(G-8972)*
Panel Processing Oregon Inc.................E...... 989 356-9007
  Alpena *(G-306)*

STORES: Auto & Home Supply

Hemco Machine Co Inc..........................G...... 586 264-8911
  Warren *(G-17079)*
Monroes Custom Campers Inc...............G...... 231 773-0005
  Muskegon *(G-11385)*
Walmart Inc..B...... 517 541-1481
  Charlotte *(G-2670)*

STORES: Drapery & Upholstery

American Roll Shutter Awng Co............E...... 734 422-7110
  Livonia *(G-9645)*

STOVES: Wood & Coal Burning

Kampers Woodfire Company Inc...........G...... 906 478-7902
  Rudyard *(G-13984)*
Leaders Inc..G...... 269 372-1072
  Kalamazoo *(G-8807)*
Nu-Way Stove Inc...................................G...... 989 733-8792
  Onaway *(G-12149)*

STRAIN GAGES: Solid State

AG Precision Gage Inc...........................G...... 248 374-0063
  Wixom *(G-17755)*
Birdsall Tool & Gage Co.........................E...... 248 474-5150
  Farmington Hills *(G-4941)*
Precision Gage Inc..................................D...... 517 439-1690
  Hillsdale *(G-7534)*
Riverside Cnc LLC..................................G...... 616 246-6000
  Wyoming *(G-18032)*

STRAPS: Cotton Webbing

B Erickson Manufacturing Ltd..............F...... 810 765-1144
  Marine City *(G-10470)*

STRAPS: Spindle Banding

Superior Spindle Services LLC..............F...... 734 946-4646
  Taylor *(G-15774)*

PRODUCT SECTION — SVC ESTABLISHMENT EQPT & SPLYS WHOLESALERS

STRAWS: Drinking, Made From Purchased Materials
Solo Cup Company LLC ....C...... 800 248-5960
  Mason *(G-10657)*

STRINGING BEADS
Sashabaw Bead Co ....G...... 248 969-1353
  Oxford *(G-12371)*

STRUCTURAL SUPPORT & BUILDING MATERIAL: Concrete
Kelder LLC ....G...... 231 757-3000
  Scottville *(G-14509)*
Liberty Transit Mix LLC ....G...... 586 254-2212
  Shelby Township *(G-14627)*
Martin Structural Consult ....G...... 810 633-9111
  Applegate *(G-712)*

STUDIOS: Artists & Artists' Studios
Liedel Power Cleaning ....F...... 734 848-2827
  Erie *(G-4805)*

STUDS & JOISTS: Sheet Metal
B & D Thread Rolling Inc ....D...... 734 728-7070
  Taylor *(G-15693)*
Federal Screw Works ....F...... 734 941-4211
  Romulus *(G-13676)*
State Building Product Inc ....E...... 586 772-8878
  Warren *(G-17254)*

SUBMARINE BUILDING & REPAIR
General Dynamics Corporation ...E...... 586 825-8228
  Macomb *(G-10125)*

SUBPRESSES, METALWORKING
Acg Services Inc ....G...... 586 232-4698
  Shelby Township *(G-14540)*

SUNDRIES & RELATED PRDTS: Medical & Laboratory, Rubber
Kent Manufacturing Company .....D...... 616 454-9495
  Grand Rapids *(G-6577)*
Tissue Seal LLC ....F...... 734 213-5530
  Ann Arbor *(G-675)*

SUNGLASSES, WHOLESALE
Nalcor LLC ....D...... 248 541-1140
  Ferndale *(G-5303)*

SUNROOFS: Motor Vehicle
Inalfa Road System Inc ....B...... 248 371-3060
  Auburn Hills *(G-908)*
Inalfa Roof Systems Inc ....B...... 248 371-3060
  Auburn Hills *(G-909)*
Qp Acquisition 2 Inc ....E...... 248 594-7432
  Southfield *(G-15006)*
Webasto Roof Systems Inc ....C...... 734 452-2600
  Livonia *(G-10002)*
Webasto Roof Systems Inc ....B...... 248 997-5100
  Rochester Hills *(G-13543)*

SUPERMARKETS & OTHER GROCERY STORES
Apple Valley Natural Foods ....C...... 269 471-3234
  Berrien Springs *(G-1592)*
Brownwood Acres Foods Inc ......F...... 231 599-3101
  Eastport *(G-4714)*
Jorgensens Inc ....E...... 989 831-8338
  Greenville *(G-7140)*
Olivo LLC ....G...... 313 573-7202
  Lincoln Park *(G-9582)*
Randall Foods Inc ....F...... 517 767-3247
  Tekonsha *(G-15821)*
Visual Identification Products .....G...... 231 941-7272
  Traverse City *(G-16239)*

SURFACE ACTIVE AGENTS
BASF Corporation ....C...... 734 324-6000
  Wyandotte *(G-17948)*
Ipax Atlantic LLC ....F...... 313 933-4211
  Detroit *(G-4149)*

SURFACE ACTIVE AGENTS: Emulsifiers, Exc Food & Pharmaceutical
Metalworking Lubricants Co ....C...... 248 332-3500
  Pontiac *(G-12849)*

SURFACE ACTIVE AGENTS: Textile Processing Assistants
McCarthy Group Incorporated .....G...... 616 977-2900
  Grand Rapids *(G-6652)*

SURFACERS: Concrete Grinding
CPS LLC ....F...... 517 639-1464
  Quincy *(G-13093)*
Creative Surfaces Inc ....F...... 586 226-2950
  Clinton Township *(G-3092)*
Syncon Inc ....E...... 313 914-4481
  Livonia *(G-9950)*

SURGICAL APPLIANCES & SPLYS
Plasma Biolife Services L P ....G...... 616 667-0264
  Grandville *(G-7064)*

SURGICAL APPLIANCES & SPLYS
3dm Source Inc ....F...... 616 647-9513
  Grand Rapids *(G-6120)*
Auric Enterprises Inc ....G...... 231 882-7251
  Beulah *(G-1608)*
Auto Engineering Lab ....E...... 734 764-4254
  Ann Arbor *(G-373)*
Biomedical Designs ....G...... 517 784-6617
  Jackson *(G-8390)*
Curbell Plastics Inc ....G...... 734 513-0531
  Livonia *(G-9694)*
Dabir Surfaces Inc ....G...... 248 796-0802
  Southfield *(G-14877)*
Danmar Products Inc ....E...... 734 761-1990
  Ann Arbor *(G-412)*
Davis Dental Laboratory ....G...... 616 261-9191
  Wyoming *(G-17995)*
Ever-Flex Inc ....E...... 313 389-2060
  Lincoln Park *(G-9576)*
Hanger Inc ....F...... 616 949-0075
  Grand Rapids *(G-6491)*
Hanger Inc ....E...... 616 458-8080
  Grand Rapids *(G-6492)*
Hanger Inc ....E...... 248 615-0601
  Livonia *(G-9765)*
Hi-Tech Optical Inc ....E...... 989 799-9390
  Saginaw *(G-14057)*
Howmedica Osteonics Corp ....G...... 269 389-8959
  Portage *(G-13001)*
Jacquart Fabric Products Inc .....C...... 906 932-1339
  Ironwood *(G-8332)*
Magnetic Ventures LLC ....E...... 313 670-3036
  Dearborn *(G-3736)*
Medical Cmfort Specialists LLC ..F...... 810 229-4222
  Fowlerville *(G-5575)*
Medtronic Inc ....G...... 616 643-5200
  Grand Rapids *(G-6658)*
Mercy Health Partners ....G...... 231 672-4886
  Muskegon *(G-11374)*
MII Disposition Inc ....E...... 616 554-9696
  Grand Rapids *(G-6689)*
Noir Medical Technologies LLC ...F...... 248 486-3760
  South Lyon *(G-14806)*
Orthopaedic Associates Mich .....D...... 616 459-7101
  Grand Rapids *(G-6734)*
Porex Technologies Corporation .E...... 989 865-8200
  Saint Charles *(G-14198)*
Regents of The University Mich .E...... 734 973-2400
  Ann Arbor *(G-618)*
Signal Medical Corporation ....F...... 810 364-7070
  Marysville *(G-10614)*
Sigvaris Inc ....E...... 616 741-4281
  Holland *(G-7804)*
Steele Supply Co ....G...... 269 983-0920
  Saint Joseph *(G-14342)*
Tesa Tape Inc ....F...... 616 785-6970
  Grand Rapids *(G-6924)*
Tesa Tape Inc ....D...... 616 887-3107
  Sparta *(G-15116)*
Thierica Equipment Corporation .E...... 616 453-6570
  Grand Rapids *(G-6928)*
Warwick Mas & Equipment Co ....F...... 810 966-3431
  Port Huron *(G-12975)*
Wright & Filippis Inc ....F...... 517 484-2624
  Lansing *(G-9435)*
Wright & Filippis Inc ....F...... 586 756-4020
  Warren *(G-17298)*
Wright & Filippis Inc ....E...... 248 336-8460
  Detroit *(G-3822)*
Wright & Filippis Inc ....E...... 313 386-3330
  Lincoln Park *(G-9589)*
XYZ McHine TI Fabrications Inc .G...... 517 482-3668
  Lansing *(G-9329)*

SURGICAL EQPT: See Also Instruments
Berchtold Corporation ....G...... 269 329-2001
  Portage *(G-12984)*
Bio-Vac Inc ....E...... 248 350-2150
  Southfield *(G-14853)*
Gelman Sciences Inc ....A...... 734 665-0651
  Ann Arbor *(G-469)*
Omega Surgical Instruments ......G...... 810 695-9800
  Flint *(G-5477)*
Slaughter Instrument Company ..F...... 269 428-7471
  Stevensville *(G-15581)*
Stryker Australia LLC ....G...... 269 385-2600
  Portage *(G-13036)*
Stryker Corporation ....E...... 269 385-2600
  Portage *(G-13038)*
Stryker Corporation ....B...... 269 329-2100
  Portage *(G-13040)*
Stryker Corporation ....C...... 269 389-2300
  Portage *(G-13041)*
Stryker Far East Inc ....E...... 269 385-2600
  Portage *(G-13044)*
Tambra Investments Inc ....G...... 866 662-7897
  Warren *(G-17261)*

SURGICAL IMPLANTS
Autocam Med DVC Holdings LLC .G...... 616 541-8080
  Kentwood *(G-9002)*
Autocam Medical Devices LLC ...E...... 877 633-8080
  Grand Rapids *(G-6191)*
Berchtold Corporation ....G...... 269 329-2001
  Portage *(G-12984)*
Set Liquidation Inc ....D...... 517 694-2300
  Holt *(G-7928)*
Stryker Australia LLC ....G...... 269 385-2600
  Portage *(G-13036)*
Stryker Corporation ....E...... 269 385-2600
  Portage *(G-13038)*
Stryker Corporation ....B...... 269 329-2100
  Portage *(G-13040)*
Stryker Customs Brokers LLC ....F...... 269 389-2300
  Portage *(G-13043)*
Stryker Far East Inc ....E...... 269 385-2600
  Portage *(G-13044)*

SURVEYING & MAPPING: Land Parcels
Dcr Services & Cnstr Inc ....F...... 313 297-6544
  Detroit *(G-3962)*

SUSPENSION SYSTEMS: Acoustical, Metal
ITT Motion Tech Amer LLC ....F...... 248 863-2161
  Novi *(G-11909)*
St USA Holding Corp ....D...... 517 278-7144
  Coldwater *(G-3334)*
St USA Holding Corp ....C...... 800 637-3303
  Coldwater *(G-3335)*
Vogt Industries Inc ....G...... 616 531-4830
  Grand Rapids *(G-6974)*

SVC ESTABLISH EQPT, WHOLESALE: Carpet/Rug Clean Eqpt & Sply
Creative Products Intl ....F...... 616 335-3333
  Holland *(G-7600)*

SVC ESTABLISHMENT EQPT & SPLYS WHOLESALERS
Bio Kleen Products Inc ....G...... 269 567-9400
  Kalamazoo *(G-8697)*
Eastern Oil Company ....E...... 248 333-1333
  Pontiac *(G-12819)*
Intuitive Technology Inc ....G...... 602 249-5750
  Dexter *(G-4495)*
M & M Typewriter Service Inc ....G...... 734 995-4033
  Ann Arbor *(G-536)*
Weaver Instructional Systems ....G...... 616 942-2891
  Grand Rapids *(G-6981)*

Employee Codes: A=Over 500 employees, B=251-500
C=101-250, D=51-100, E=20-50, F=10-19, G=3-9

SVC ESTABLISHMENT EQPT, WHOL: Cleaning & Maint Eqpt & Splys

Diversified Davitco LLC ....F....... 248 681-9197
Waterford *(G-17334)*
Enviro-Brite Solutions LLC ....G...... 989 387-2758
Oscoda *(G-12209)*
Power Cleaning Systems Inc ....G...... 248 347-7727
Wixom *(G-17878)*

SVC ESTABLISHMENT EQPT, WHOL: Concrete Burial Vaults & Boxes

Superior Vault Co ....G...... 989 643-4200
Merrill *(G-10762)*

SVC ESTABLISHMENT EQPT, WHOLESALE: Cemetery Splys & Eqpt

Superior Monuments Co ....G...... 616 844-1700
Grand Haven *(G-6087)*

SVC ESTABLISHMENT EQPT, WHOLESALE: Firefighting Eqpt

Front Line Services Inc ....F....... 989 695-6633
Freeland *(G-5757)*

SVC ESTABLISHMENT EQPT, WHOLESALE: Shredders, Indl & Comm

Technology Network Svcs Inc ....F....... 586 294-7771
Saint Clair Shores *(G-14271)*

SVC ESTABLISHMENT EQPT, WHOLESALE: Vacuum Cleaning Systems

Wal-Vac Inc ....G...... 616 241-6717
Wyoming *(G-18042)*

SVC ESTABLISHMENT EQPT, WHOLESALE: Vending Machines & Splys

Vendco LLC ....G...... 800 764-8245
Shelby Township *(G-14718)*

SWEEPING COMPOUNDS

Global Wholesale & Marketing ....G...... 248 910-8302
Sterling Heights *(G-15361)*

SWIMMING POOLS, EQPT & SPLYS: Wholesalers

Lochinvar LLC ....E....... 734 454-4480
Plymouth *(G-12676)*

SWITCHBOARDS & PARTS: Power

Tara Industries Inc ....F....... 248 477-6520
Livonia *(G-9953)*

SWITCHES

Panel Pro LLC ....G...... 734 427-1691
Livonia *(G-9883)*
Prestolite Electric LLC ....G...... 248 313-3807
Novi *(G-11978)*
Semtron Inc ....F....... 810 732-9080
Flint *(G-5498)*
Southern Auto Wholesalers Inc ....F....... 248 335-5555
Pontiac *(G-12869)*
Trmi Inc ....A...... 269 966-0800
Battle Creek *(G-1261)*

SWITCHES: Electric Power

Meter Devices Company Inc ....A...... 330 455-0301
Farmington Hills *(G-5064)*
Valeo North America Inc ....C...... 248 619-8300
Troy *(G-16676)*

SWITCHES: Electronic

Aktv8 LLC ....G...... 517 775-1270
South Lyon *(G-14785)*
Cardell Corporation ....F....... 248 371-9700
Auburn Hills *(G-810)*
Detectir Inc ....G...... 724 681-0975
East Lansing *(G-4655)*
Five-Way Switch Music ....G...... 269 425-2843
Battle Creek *(G-1188)*

Ssi Electronics Inc ....E....... 616 866-8880
Belmont *(G-1470)*
ZF Active Safety & Elec US LLC .....C...... 734 855-2600
Livonia *(G-10014)*
ZF Passive Safety ....B...... 586 232-7200
Washington *(G-17316)*

SWITCHES: Electronic Applications

AEL/Span LLC ....E....... 734 957-1600
Van Buren Twp *(G-16746)*
Affordable Mobile Devices LLC ....G...... 313 433-9242
Lathrup Village *(G-9497)*
Patriot Sensors & Contrls Corp ....D...... 248 435-0700
Clawson *(G-2983)*
Safari Circuits Inc ....C...... 269 694-9471
Otsego *(G-12255)*
Winford Engineering LLC ....G...... 989 671-9721
Auburn *(G-758)*

SWITCHES: Solenoid

Detroit Coil Co ....E....... 248 658-1543
Ferndale *(G-5274)*
Eto Magnetic Corp ....D...... 616 957-2570
Grand Rapids *(G-6387)*
Johnson Electric N Amer Inc ....D...... 734 392-5300
Plymouth *(G-12658)*

SWITCHES: Time, Electrical Switchgear Apparatus

Fairchilds Daughters & Son LLC .....G...... 906 239-6061
Iron Mountain *(G-8283)*

SWITCHGEAR & SWITCHBOARD APPARATUS

A & L Metal Products ....G...... 734 654-8990
Carleton *(G-2451)*
Benesh Corporation ....E....... 734 244-4143
Monroe *(G-11023)*
Classic Accents Inc ....G...... 734 284-7661
Southgate *(G-15075)*
Eagle Engineering & Supply Co ......E....... 989 356-4526
Alpena *(G-286)*
Ews Legacy LLC ....E....... 248 853-6363
Rochester Hills *(G-13421)*
Harlo Corporation ....E....... 616 538-0550
Grandville *(G-7046)*
Henshaw Inc ....E....... 586 752-0700
Romeo *(G-13629)*
Hydro-Logic Inc ....E....... 586 757-7477
Warren *(G-17083)*
International Door Inc ....E....... 248 547-7240
Canton *(G-2388)*
Kostal of America Inc ....E....... 248 284-6500
Troy *(G-16450)*
Memcon North America LLC ....F....... 269 281-0478
Stevensville *(G-15578)*
Parker-Hannifin Corporation ....B...... 269 629-5000
Richland *(G-13252)*
Patriot Sensors & Contrls Corp ....D...... 810 378-5511
Peck *(G-12420)*
Patriot Sensors & Contrls Corp ....D...... 248 435-0700
Clawson *(G-2983)*
Schneider Electric Usa Inc ....C...... 810 733-9400
Flint *(G-5497)*
Solarbos ....G...... 616 588-7270
Grand Rapids *(G-6870)*
Ssi Electronics Inc ....E....... 616 866-8880
Belmont *(G-1470)*
X-Rite Incorporated ....C...... 616 803-2100
Grand Rapids *(G-7006)*

SYNTHETIC RESIN FINISHED PRDTS, NEC

Orbis Corporation ....C...... 248 616-3232
Troy *(G-16537)*
Protojet LLC ....F....... 810 956-8000
Fraser *(G-5712)*
Saint-Gobain Prfmce Plas Corp ......D...... 989 435-9533
Beaverton *(G-1392)*

SYRUPS, DRINK

Coca-Cola Refreshments USA Inc ...C...... 517 322-2349
Lansing *(G-9283)*
Contract Flavors Inc ....F....... 616 454-5950
Grand Rapids *(G-6304)*
Leonard Fountain Spc Inc ....D...... 313 891-4141
Detroit *(G-4199)*

Northwoods Soda and Syrup Co ......G...... 231 267-5853
Williamsburg *(G-17717)*

SYSTEMS ENGINEERING: Computer Related

Superior Information Tech LLC ....F....... 734 666-9963
Livonia *(G-9948)*

SYSTEMS INTEGRATION SVCS

Bull Hn Info Systems Inc ....F....... 616 942-7126
Grand Rapids *(G-6240)*
Computer Sciences Corporation .....C...... 586 825-5043
Sterling Heights *(G-15294)*
Corporate AV Services LLC ....G...... 248 939-0900
Commerce Township *(G-3395)*
Fenton Systems Inc ....G...... 810 636-6318
Goodrich *(G-5953)*
Indocomp Systems Inc ....F....... 810 678-3990
Metamora *(G-10776)*
Lowry Holding Company Inc ....C...... 810 229-7200
Brighton *(G-1952)*
Machine Control Technology ....G...... 517 655-3506
Williamston *(G-17734)*
Medical Systems Resource Group ..G...... 248 476-5400
Farmington Hills *(G-5061)*
Smart Label Solutions LLC ....G...... 800 996-7343
Howell *(G-8099)*

SYSTEMS INTEGRATION SVCS: Local Area Network

Parameter Driven Software Inc ....F....... 248 553-6410
Farmington Hills *(G-5088)*
Simna Solutions LLC ....G...... 313 442-7305
Farmington Hills *(G-5125)*

SYSTEMS INTEGRATION SVCS: Office Computer Automation

Whiteside Consulting Group LLC .....G...... 313 288-6598
Detroit *(G-4440)*

SYSTEMS SOFTWARE DEVELOPMENT SVCS

Advanced Integrated Mfg ....F....... 586 439-0300
Fraser *(G-5613)*
Artic Technologies Intl ....G...... 248 689-9884
Troy *(G-16220)*
Click Care LLC ....G...... 989 792-1544
Saginaw *(G-14020)*
Complete Data Products Inc ....G...... 248 651-8602
Troy *(G-16275)*
Lintech Global Inc ....D...... 248 553-8033
Farmington Hills *(G-5045)*
Mejenta Systems Inc ....E....... 248 434-2583
Southfield *(G-14977)*
Tru-Syzygy Inc ....G...... 248 622-7211
Lake Orion *(G-9167)*
Varatech Inc ....F....... 616 393-6408
Holland *(G-7843)*
Wow Plastics LLC ....G...... 760 827-7800
Caro *(G-2482)*

TABLE OR COUNTERTOPS, PLASTIC LAMINATED

Carpenters Cabinets ....G...... 989 777-1070
Saginaw *(G-14010)*
Custom Components Corporation ..F....... 616 523-1111
Ionia *(G-8247)*
Custom Counter Top Company ....G...... 616 534-5894
Grand Rapids *(G-6323)*
Greenfield Cabinetry Inc ....F....... 586 759-3300
Warren *(G-17066)*
Michael Nadeau Cabinet Making .....G...... 989 356-0229
Alpena *(G-298)*
Nu-Tran LLC ....G...... 616 350-9575
Wyoming *(G-18023)*

TABLES: Lift, Hydraulic

Air-Hydraulics Inc ....F....... 517 787-9444
Jackson *(G-8377)*
Columbus McKinnon Corporation ...G...... 800 955-5541
Muskegon *(G-11296)*

PRODUCT SECTION

TABLEWARE OR KITCHEN ARTICLES: Commercial, Fine Earthenware

Mdg Commercial Kitchen LLC...............G....... 269 207-1344
 Portage *(G-13015)*

TAGS & LABELS: Paper

Middleton Printing Inc ....G....... 616 247-8742
 Grand Rapids *(G-6684)*
Richman Company Products Inc............G....... 989 686-6251
 Bay City *(G-1350)*
Watson Sales ....G....... 517 296-4275
 Montgomery *(G-11100)*

TALLOW: Animal

Darling Ingredients Inc ....F....... 989 752-4340
 Carrollton *(G-2485)*
Kellys Recycling Service Inc ....G....... 313 389-7870
 Detroit *(G-4174)*

TANK COMPONENTS: Military, Specialized

Plasan North America Inc ....D....... 616 559-0032
 Walker *(G-16875)*
Ronal Industries Inc............................F....... 248 616-9691
 Sterling Heights *(G-15478)*

TANK REPAIR & CLEANING SVCS

Matrix North Amercn Cnstr Inc..............C....... 734 847-4605
 Temperance *(G-15836)*

TANK REPAIR SVCS

Fischer Tanks LLC ....D....... 231 362-8265
 Kaleva *(G-8932)*
Gld Holdings Inc ....F....... 616 877-4288
 Moline *(G-11010)*
Saranac Tank Inc................................G....... 616 642-9481
 Saranac *(G-14455)*

TANKS & OTHER TRACKED VEHICLE CMPNTS

American Rhnmtall Vehicles LLC..........G....... 703 221-9288
 Sterling Heights *(G-15259)*
Bae Systems Land Armaments LP........F....... 586 596-4123
 Sterling Heights *(G-15270)*
Benteler Defense Corp ....G....... 248 377-9999
 Auburn Hills *(G-793)*
Burch Tank & Truck Inc ....G....... 989 495-0342
 Midland *(G-10820)*
Burch Tank & Truck Inc ....D....... 989 772-6266
 Mount Pleasant *(G-11181)*
Demmer Corporation ....D....... 517 703-3116
 Lansing *(G-9216)*
Demmer Corporation ....C....... 517 321-3600
 Lansing *(G-9217)*
Demmer Corporation ....D....... 517 703-3163
 Lansing *(G-9218)*
Demmer Corporation ....D....... 517 703-3131
 Lansing *(G-9219)*
Demmer Corporation ....E....... 517 321-3600
 Lansing *(G-9287)*
Demmer Corporation ....D....... 517 323-4504
 Lansing *(G-9220)*
Generaleral Dynamics ....G....... 601 877-6436
 Sterling Heights *(G-15359)*
Horstman Inc ....E....... 586 737-2100
 Sterling Heights *(G-15368)*
Odt Systems Inc ....F....... 248 953-9512
 Rochester *(G-13339)*
Reutter LLC ....G....... 248 621-9220
 Bingham Farms *(G-1659)*
Supreme Gear Co ....E....... 586 775-6325
 Fraser *(G-5736)*
Tank Truck Service & Sales Inc ....E....... 586 757-6500
 Warren *(G-17262)*

TANKS: Concrete

Leelanau Redi-Mix Inc ....E....... 231 228-5005
 Maple City *(G-10462)*

TANKS: Cryogenic, Metal

Custom Biogenic Systems Inc ....E....... 586 331-2600
 Bruce Twp *(G-2080)*

TANKS: For Tank Trucks, Metal Plate

Riverside Tank & Mfg Corp ....E....... 810 329-7143
 Saint Clair *(G-14234)*

TANKS: Fuel, Including Oil & Gas, Metal Plate

Fischer Tanks LLC ....D....... 231 362-8265
 Kaleva *(G-8932)*
Western International Inc ....E....... 866 814-2470
 Troy *(G-16689)*

TANKS: Lined, Metal

Gld Holdings Inc ....F....... 616 877-4288
 Moline *(G-11010)*
R T C Enviro Fab Inc ....F....... 517 596-2987
 Munith *(G-11254)*

TANKS: Military, Amphibian

General Dynamics Land ....G....... 586 825-8400
 Sterling Heights *(G-15357)*

TANKS: Plastic & Fiberglass

Denso Manufacturing NC Inc ....A....... 269 441-2040
 Battle Creek *(G-1172)*
Vitec LLC ....B....... 313 633-2254
 Detroit *(G-4433)*

TANKS: Standard Or Custom Fabricated, Metal Plate

A A Tanks Co ....G....... 586 427-7700
 Warren *(G-16908)*
American Tank Fabrication LLC ....F....... 780 663-3552
 Okemos *(G-12113)*
Clawson Tank Company ....E....... 248 625-8700
 Clarkston *(G-2914)*
Commercial Welding Company Inc.......G....... 269 782-5252
 Dowagiac *(G-4536)*
Diversified Mech Svcs Inc ....F....... 616 785-2735
 Comstock Park *(G-3478)*
Fabrications Unlimited Inc ....G....... 313 567-9616
 Shelby Township *(G-14591)*
Gladwin Tank Manufacturing Inc ....F....... 989 426-4768
 Gladwin *(G-5932)*
Ideal Fabricators Inc ....E....... 734 422-5320
 Livonia *(G-9778)*
Merrill Technologies Group Inc ....C....... 989 462-0330
 Alma *(G-241)*
Saranac Tank Inc................................G....... 616 642-9481
 Saranac *(G-14455)*
Steel Tank & Fabricating Co ....D....... 248 625-8700
 Clarkston *(G-2959)*

TANNERIES: Leather

Larrys Taxidermy Inc ....G....... 517 769-6104
 Pleasant Lake *(G-12552)*

TANNING SALONS

Horn Corp ....G....... 248 358-8883
 Brighton *(G-1940)*

TAPE PRINT UNITS: Computer

Quartech Corporation..........................G....... 586 781-0373
 Macomb *(G-10160)*

TAPES: Fabric

Nitto Inc...G....... 248 449-2300
 Novi *(G-11954)*
Permacel Corporation ....G....... 248 347-2843
 Novi *(G-11973)*

TAPES: Plastic Coated

Witchcraft Tape Products Inc ....D....... 269 468-3399
 Coloma *(G-3368)*

TAPES: Pressure Sensitive

Elliott Tape Inc...................................E....... 248 475-2000
 Auburn Hills *(G-854)*
Independent Die Cutting Inc ....F....... 616 452-3197
 Grand Rapids *(G-6532)*
Intertape Polymer Corp ....C....... 810 364-9000
 Marysville *(G-10604)*
Kent Manufacturing Company..............D....... 616 454-9495
 Grand Rapids *(G-6577)*
Michigan Tape Inc..............................G....... 734 582-9800
 Plymouth *(G-12692)*
Tesa Tape Inc....................................G....... 616 785-6970
 Grand Rapids *(G-6924)*
Tesa Tape Inc....................................D....... 616 887-3107
 Sparta *(G-15116)*
Trimas Corporation ....E....... 248 631-5450
 Bloomfield Hills *(G-1807)*
Yamato International Corp ....E....... 734 675-6055
 Woodhaven *(G-17942)*

TAPES: Tie, Woven Or Braided

Global Strapping LLC ....G....... 517 545-4900
 Howell *(G-8044)*

TAPS

Widell Industries Inc ....E....... 989 742-4528
 Hillman *(G-7511)*

TARPAULINS

Detroit Tarpaulin Repr Sp Inc ....E....... 734 955-8200
 Romulus *(G-13666)*
J C Goss Company ....G....... 313 259-3520
 Romulus *(G-13689)*
Larrys Tarpaulin Shop LLC ....G....... 313 563-2292
 Inkster *(G-8229)*
National Case Corporation...................G....... 586 726-1710
 Sterling Heights *(G-15432)*
Quick Draw Tarpaulin Systems ....F....... 313 561-0554
 Inkster *(G-8234)*
Quick Draw Tarpaulin Systems ....F....... 313 945-0766
 Dearborn *(G-3752)*

TARPAULINS, WHOLESALE

Verduyn Tarps Detroit Inc ....G....... 313 270-4890
 Detroit *(G-4425)*

TAX RETURN PREPARATION SVCS

Jax Services LLC ....G....... 586 703-3212
 Warren *(G-17112)*
Mach II Enterprises Inc ....G....... 248 347-8822
 Northville *(G-11708)*

TAXI CABS

Opio LLc ....F....... 313 433-1098
 Wayne *(G-17440)*

TAXIDERMISTS

Larrys Taxidermy Inc ....G....... 517 769-6104
 Pleasant Lake *(G-12552)*

TECHNICAL WRITING SVCS

TMC Group Inc ....F....... 248 819-6063
 Pleasant Ridge *(G-12556)*

TELECOMMUNICATION EQPT REPAIR SVCS, EXC TELEPHONES

Startech-Solutions LLC ....G....... 248 419-0650
 West Bloomfield *(G-17499)*

TELECOMMUNICATION SYSTEMS & EQPT

Balogh...G....... 734 283-3972
 Taylor *(G-15695)*
Central On Line Data Systems.............G....... 586 939-7000
 Sterling Heights *(G-15284)*
Code Blue Corporation........................E....... 616 392-8296
 Holland *(G-7594)*
Nuwave Technology Partners LLC.......F....... 616 942-7520
 Grand Rapids *(G-6725)*
Nuwave Technology Partners LLC.......G....... 269 342-4400
 Saint Joseph *(G-14333)*
Nuwave Technology Partners LLC.......G....... 517 336-9915
 East Lansing *(G-4672)*
Nuwave Technology Partners LLC.......F....... 517 322-2200
 Lansing *(G-9315)*
Nuwave Technology Partners LLC.......F....... 269 342-4400
 Kalamazoo *(G-8837)*
Omnilink Communications Corp ....E....... 517 336-1800
 Lansing *(G-9408)*
Phone Guy LLC ....G....... 248 361-0132
 Oxford *(G-12363)*

Employee Codes: A=Over 500 employees, B=251-500
C=101-250, D=51-100, E=20-50, F=10-19, G=3-9

TELECOMMUNICATION SYSTEMS & EQPT — PRODUCT SECTION

Rti Products LLC .... F 269 684-9960
  Niles *(G-11644)*
Spectra Link .... G 313 417-3723
  Grosse Pointe Woods *(G-7209)*

TELECOMMUNICATIONS CARRIERS & SVCS: Wired

Huron Valley Telecom .... G 734 995-9780
  Ann Arbor *(G-497)*

TELEGRAPH OR TELEPHONE CARRIER & REPEATER EQPT

Clarity Comm Advisors Inc .... E 248 327-4390
  Southfield *(G-14869)*

TELEMARKETING BUREAUS

Nits Solutions Inc .... F 248 231-2267
  Novi *(G-11953)*

TELEMETERING EQPT

L3 Technologies Inc .... C 734 741-8868
  Ann Arbor *(G-523)*

TELEPHONE COUNSELING SVCS

Therapyline Technologies Inc .... E 734 407-9626
  Brownstown *(G-2068)*

TELEPHONE EQPT: Modems

Fox Charlevoix Ford Modem .... G 231 547-4401
  Charlevoix *(G-2614)*
Multiax International Inc .... G 616 534-4530
  Grandville *(G-7060)*

TELEPHONE EQPT: NEC

Semtron Inc .... F 810 732-9080
  Flint *(G-5498)*

TELEPHONE SVCS

Elite Business Services & Exec .... D 734 956-4550
  Bloomfield Hills *(G-1763)*

TELEPHONE: Fiber Optic Systems

Huron Valley Telecom .... G 734 995-9780
  Ann Arbor *(G-497)*
Lol Telcom Inc .... B 616 888-6171
  Hudsonville *(G-8162)*
Safari Circuits Inc .... C 269 694-9471
  Otsego *(G-12255)*

TELEPHONE: Headsets

DB Communications Inc .... F 800 692-8200
  Livonia *(G-9700)*
Wireless 4 Less Inc .... G 313 653-3345
  Detroit *(G-4444)*

TELESCOPES

Meridian Mechatronics LLC .... G 517 447-4587
  Deerfield *(G-3813)*
Planewave Instruments Inc .... G 310 639-1662
  Adrian *(G-84)*

TELEVISION BROADCASTING & COMMUNICATIONS EQPT

Satellite Tracking Systems .... G 248 627-3334
  Ortonville *(G-12202)*

TELEVISION BROADCASTING STATIONS

Detroit News Inc .... B 313 222-2300
  Detroit *(G-3991)*
Paxton Media Group LLC .... D 269 429-2400
  Saint Joseph *(G-14334)*

TELEVISION SETS

Lotus International Company .... A 734 245-0140
  Canton *(G-2394)*

TELEVISION: Closed Circuit Eqpt

Thalner Electronic Labs Inc .... E 734 761-4506
  Ann Arbor *(G-668)*

TEMPERING: Metal

Commercial Steel Treating Corp .... D 248 588-3300
  Madison Heights *(G-10217)*
State Heat Treating Company .... E 616 243-0178
  Grand Rapids *(G-6887)*
Steel Processing Company Inc .... F 586 772-3310
  Warren *(G-17256)*

TEMPORARY HELP SVCS

Manufacturing & Indus Tech Inc .... E 248 814-8544
  Lake Orion *(G-9147)*
Vectech Pharmaceutical Cons .... F 248 478-5820
  Brighton *(G-2005)*

TENT REPAIR SHOP

Ace Canvas & Tent Co .... F 313 842-3011
  Troy *(G-16166)*
Battle Creek Tent & Awning Co .... G 269 964-1824
  Battle Creek *(G-1152)*

TENTS: All Materials

Ace Canvas & Tent Co .... F 313 842-3011
  Troy *(G-16166)*
Holland Awning Co .... D 616 772-2052
  Zeeland *(G-18152)*

TEST BORING, METAL MINING

Battjes Boring Inc .... G 616 363-1969
  Grand Rapids *(G-6205)*

TESTERS: Battery

Electrodynamics Inc .... G 734 422-5420
  Livonia *(G-9723)*

TESTERS: Environmental

Celsee Diagnostics Inc .... E 866 748-1448
  Ann Arbor *(G-397)*
Espec Corp .... E 616 896-6100
  Hudsonville *(G-8156)*
Hanse Environmental Inc .... F 269 673-8638
  Allegan *(G-164)*
Kuka Assembly and Test Corp .... D 810 593-0350
  Fenton *(G-5224)*
Venturedyne Ltd .... B 616 392-6550
  Holland *(G-7847)*
Venturedyne Ltd .... E 616 392-1491
  Holland *(G-7846)*

TESTERS: Hardness

Electro ARC Manufacturing Co .... E 734 483-4233
  Dexter *(G-4491)*
Service Diamond Tool Company .... G 248 669-3100
  Novi *(G-11993)*

TESTERS: Physical Property

Electronic Apps Spec Ists Inc .... G 248 491-4988
  Milford *(G-10963)*
Kemkraft Engineering Inc .... F 734 414-6500
  Plymouth *(G-12664)*
Landis Precision Inc .... G 248 685-8032
  Milford *(G-10968)*
Link Manufacturing Inc .... C 734 453-0800
  Plymouth *(G-12673)*
Link Manufacturing Inc .... F 734 387-1001
  Ottawa Lake *(G-12265)*
Pcb Load & Torque Inc .... E 248 471-0065
  Farmington Hills *(G-5089)*
Precision Devices Inc .... E 734 439-2462
  Milan *(G-10950)*
Rs Technologies Ltd .... E 248 888-8260
  Farmington Hills *(G-5118)*
Sun-Tec Corp .... G 248 669-3100
  Novi *(G-12009)*
Testek LLC .... D 248 573-4980
  Wixom *(G-17909)*
Testron Incorporated .... F 734 513-6820
  Livonia *(G-9955)*

TESTERS: Water, Exc Indl Process

QEd Envmtl Systems Inc .... D 734 995-2547
  Dexter *(G-4506)*

TESTING SVCS

Capsonic Automotive Inc .... G 248 754-1100
  Auburn Hills *(G-809)*
Touchstone Systems & Svcs Inc .... G 616 532-0060
  Wyoming *(G-18035)*

TEXTILE & APPAREL SVCS

Adlib Grafix & Apparel .... G 269 964-2810
  Battle Creek *(G-1139)*
Great Put On Inc .... G 810 733-8021
  Flint *(G-5442)*

TEXTILE FINISHING: Embossing, Cotton, Broadwoven

Adco Specialties Inc .... G 616 452-6882
  Grand Rapids *(G-6143)*

TEXTILE PRDTS: Hand Woven & Crocheted

Silk Reflections .... G 313 292-1150
  Taylor *(G-15766)*

TEXTILE: Finishing, Cotton Broadwoven

Janet Kelly .... F 231 775-2313
  Cadillac *(G-2256)*

TEXTILE: Finishing, Raw Stock NEC

Karms LLC .... G 810 229-0829
  Brighton *(G-1946)*

TEXTILE: Goods, NEC

Thomasine D Jones LLC .... G 773 726-1404
  Union Pier *(G-16739)*

TEXTILES

West Michigan Canvas Company .... G 616 355-7855
  Holland *(G-7855)*

TEXTILES: Linen Fabrics

3-D Designs LLC .... G 313 658-1249
  Detroit *(G-3823)*

TEXTILES: Linings, Carpet, Exc Felt

Gails Carpet Care Repair .... G 248 684-8789
  Milford *(G-10964)*

TEXTILES: Mill Waste & Remnant

Clamp Industries Incorporated .... F 248 335-8131
  Pontiac *(G-12809)*

TEXTILES: Tops, Manmade Fiber

Martak Cultured Marble .... G 313 891-5400
  Detroit *(G-4219)*

THEATRICAL LIGHTING SVCS

Tls Productions Inc .... E 810 220-8577
  Ann Arbor *(G-677)*

THEATRICAL PRODUCERS & SVCS

Metro Times Inc .... E 313 961-4060
  Ferndale *(G-5301)*

THEATRICAL PRODUCTION SVCS

Red Carpet Capital Inc .... G 248 952-8583
  Orchard Lake *(G-12169)*

THERMOCOUPLES

Neptech Inc .... E 810 225-2222
  Highland *(G-7498)*
Temprel Inc .... E 231 582-6585
  Boyne City *(G-1835)*

THERMOCOUPLES: Indl Process

Industrial Temperature Control .... G 734 451-8740
  Canton *(G-2384)*

THERMOELECTRIC DEVICES: Solid State

T E Technology Inc .... E 231 929-3966
  Traverse City *(G-16118)*

PRODUCT SECTION

TOILETRIES, WHOLESALE: Toilet Soap

THERMOMETERS: Indl
Oden Machinery Inc ....G...... 716 874-3000
  Ludington *(G-10076)*

THERMOPLASTIC MATERIALS
Alliance Polymers and Svcs LLC ....G...... 734 710-6700
  Romulus *(G-13650)*
American Compounding Spc LLC........D...... 810 227-3500
  Brighton *(G-1884)*
Asahi Kasei Plas N Amer Inc ....C...... 517 223-2000
  Fowlerville *(G-5559)*
Asahi Kasei Plastics Amer Inc..............E...... 517 223-2000
  Fowlerville *(G-5560)*
D T M 1 Inc ....E...... 248 889-9210
  Highland *(G-7491)*
Dow Chemical Company ....B...... 989 636-1000
  Midland *(G-10834)*
Dow Chemical Company ....D...... 231 845-4285
  Ludington *(G-10056)*
Dow Chemical Company ....D...... 989 636-1000
  Midland *(G-10835)*
Dow Chemical Company ....D...... 810 966-9816
  Clyde *(G-3282)*
Dow Chemical Company ....G...... 989 708-6737
  Midland *(G-10837)*
Dow Chemical Company ....G...... 989 636-1000
  Midland *(G-10838)*
Dow Chemical Company ....C...... 989 832-1000
  Midland *(G-10844)*
Dow Chemical Company ....D...... 989 636-6351
  Midland *(G-10847)*
Dow Chemical Company ....D...... 989 636-5409
  Midland *(G-10848)*
Dow Inc ....G...... 989 636-1000
  Midland *(G-10851)*
Dow International Holdings Co ....G...... 989 636-1000
  Midland *(G-10852)*

THERMOPLASTICS
Hanwha Azdel Inc ....F...... 810 629-2496
  Warren *(G-17075)*

THERMOSETTING MATERIALS
Advanced Polymers Composites ....G...... 248 766-1507
  Clarkston *(G-2906)*

THIN FILM CIRCUITS
Prochimir Inc ....G...... 248 457-4538
  Troy *(G-16564)*

THREAD: Embroidery
RPC Company ....F...... 989 752-3618
  Saginaw *(G-14134)*

THREAD: Hand Knitting
Notions Marketing ....B...... 616 243-8424
  Grand Rapids *(G-6722)*

THREAD: Natural Fiber
American & Efird LLC ....F...... 248 399-1166
  Berkley *(G-1579)*

TIES, FORM: Metal
Michigan Wheel Operations LLC........E...... 616 452-6941
  Grand Rapids *(G-6677)*
Starbuck Machining Inc.......................F...... 616 399-9720
  Holland *(G-7813)*

TILE: Brick & Structural, Clay
Theut Products Inc ....F...... 810 364-7132
  Marysville *(G-10621)*

TILE: Clay Refractory
Pewabic Society Inc............................E...... 313 626-2000
  Detroit *(G-4300)*

TILE: Clay, Drain & Structural
Precision Plumbing - T ....G...... 269 695-2402
  Buchanan *(G-2125)*

TILE: Stamped Metal, Floor Or Wall
Benteler Defense Corp ....G...... 248 377-9999
  Auburn Hills *(G-793)*
Interior Resource Supply Inc ....G...... 313 584-4399
  Dearborn *(G-3726)*

TILE: Wall, Fiberboard
Ox Engineered Products LLC.............F...... 248 289-9950
  Northville *(G-11720)*
Ox Engineered Products LLC.............D...... 269 435-2425
  Constantine *(G-3542)*

TIMBER PRDTS WHOLESALERS
Long Lake Forest Products ....G...... 989 239-6527
  Harrison *(G-7314)*
Plum Creek Timber Company Inc........G...... 715 453-7952
  Escanaba *(G-4852)*

TIMING DEVICES: Cycle & Program Controllers
Midwest Timer Service Inc ....D...... 269 849-2800
  Benton Harbor *(G-1530)*

TIN
Fine Arts ....E...... 269 695-6263
  Buchanan *(G-2116)*
Nolans Top Tin Inc ....G...... 586 899-3421
  Warren *(G-17169)*
Red Tin Boat ....G...... 734 239-3796
  Ann Arbor *(G-613)*

TIRE & INNER TUBE MATERIALS & RELATED PRDTS
Hot Wheels City Inc ....E...... 248 589-8800
  Madison Heights *(G-10268)*

TIRE CORD & FABRIC
Ton-Tex Corporation ....E...... 616 957-3200
  Greenville *(G-7158)*

TIRE CORD & FABRIC: Cord, Rubber, Reinforcing
Takata Americas..................................E...... 336 547-1600
  Auburn Hills *(G-1012)*

TIRE CORD & FABRIC: Steel
Ferro Fab LLC ....F...... 586 791-3561
  Clinton Township *(G-3115)*

TIRE DEALERS
Goodyear Tire & Rubber Company ......G...... 248 336-0135
  Royal Oak *(G-13930)*
Hot Wheels City Inc ....E...... 248 589-8800
  Madison Heights *(G-10268)*
Jam Tire Inc ....D...... 586 772-2900
  Clinton Township *(G-3147)*
Muskegon Brake & Distrg Co LLC ......E...... 231 733-0874
  Norton Shores *(G-11776)*
Tire Wholesalers Company ....D...... 269 349-9401
  Kalamazoo *(G-8913)*

TIRE INNER-TUBES
Goodyear Tire & Rubber Company ......G...... 248 336-0135
  Royal Oak *(G-13930)*

TIRE RECAPPING & RETREADING
Jam Tire Inc ....D...... 586 772-2900
  Clinton Township *(G-3147)*
Northern Tire Inc ....F...... 906 486-4463
  Ishpeming *(G-8350)*

TIRES & INNER TUBES
Jam Tire Inc ....D...... 586 772-2900
  Clinton Township *(G-3147)*
Omni United (usa) Inc ....G...... 231 943-9804
  Interlochen *(G-8244)*
Plastic Omnium Inc ....G...... 248 458-0772
  Troy *(G-16550)*
Tire Wholesalers Company ....D...... 269 349-9401
  Kalamazoo *(G-8913)*

Universal Components LLC.................G...... 517 861-7064
  Howell *(G-8119)*

TIRES & TUBES WHOLESALERS
Jam Tire Inc ....D...... 586 772-2900
  Clinton Township *(G-3147)*
Northern Tire Inc ....F...... 906 486-4463
  Ishpeming *(G-8350)*
Roman Engineering ....D...... 231 238-7644
  Afton *(G-106)*

TIRES: Cushion Or Solid Rubber
Hutchinson Corporation ....G...... 616 459-4541
  Grand Rapids *(G-6520)*

TITANIUM MILL PRDTS
Scitex LLC ....G...... 517 694-7449
  Holt *(G-7926)*
Scitex LLC ....E...... 517 694-7449
  Holt *(G-7927)*
Scitex Trick Titanium LLC ....G...... 517 349-3736
  Okemos *(G-12137)*
Titanium Building Co Inc ....G...... 586 634-8580
  Macomb *(G-10168)*
Titanium Operations LLC ....G...... 616 717-0218
  Ada *(G-32)*
Titanium Sports LLC...........................G...... 734 818-0904
  Dundee *(G-4602)*
Titanium Technologies Inc ....G...... 248 836-2100
  Auburn Hills *(G-1027)*

TITLE ABSTRACT & SETTLEMENT OFFICES
Meridian Energy Corporation ....F...... 517 339-8444
  Haslett *(G-7397)*

TOBACCO & TOBACCO PRDTS WHOLESALERS
R J Reynolds Tobacco Company ....G...... 616 949-3740
  Kentwood *(G-9027)*

TOBACCO STORES & STANDS
Eaton Corporation ....A...... 248 226-6347
  Southfield *(G-14893)*

TOBACCO: Cigarettes
R J Reynolds Tobacco Company ....G...... 616 949-3740
  Kentwood *(G-9027)*

TOBACCO: Smoking
Akston Hughes Intl LLC ....F...... 989 448-2322
  Gaylord *(G-5847)*
D & T Smoke LLC..............................G...... 586 263-6888
  Clinton Township *(G-3097)*
Smoker Butts ....G...... 586 362-2451
  Fraser *(G-5725)*

TOILET SEATS: Wood
Aisin Holdings America Inc ....G...... 734 453-5551
  Northville *(G-11676)*

TOILETRIES, COSMETICS & PERFUME STORES
Cindys Suds LLC ....G...... 616 485-1983
  Lowell *(G-10026)*
Preeminence Inc ....G...... 313 737-7920
  Redford *(G-13185)*
Sun Chemical Corporation..................F...... 513 681-5950
  Muskegon *(G-11431)*

TOILETRIES, WHOLESALE: Razor Blades
Art of Shaving - Fl LLC ....G...... 248 649-5872
  Troy *(G-16219)*

TOILETRIES, WHOLESALE: Toilet Articles
Product Resource Company................G...... 517 484-8400
  Lansing *(G-9261)*

TOILETRIES, WHOLESALE: Toilet Soap
Cindys Suds LLC ....G...... 616 485-1983
  Lowell *(G-10026)*

Employee Codes: A=Over 500 employees, B=251-500
C=101-250, D=51-100, E=20-50, F=10-19, G=3-9

2020 Harris Michigan Industrial Directory

1383

TOILETRIES, WHOLESALE: Toiletries

Amway International Inc .... E 616 787-1000
  Ada *(G-7)*

TOILETRIES, WHOLESALE: Toothbrushes, Exc Electric

Nopras Technologies Inc .... G 248 486-6684
  South Lyon *(G-14807)*

TOILETS: Portable Chemical, Plastics

Five Peaks Technology LLC .... E 231 830-8099
  Muskegon *(G-11323)*
Thetford Corporation .... C 734 769-6000
  Ann Arbor *(G-670)*
Vintech Mexico Holdings LLC .... G 810 387-3224
  Imlay City *(G-8215)*

TOLLS: Caulking

Sulzer Mixpac USA Inc .... F 517 339-3330
  Haslett *(G-7400)*

TOOL & DIE STEEL

Accutek Mold & Engineering .... F 586 978-1335
  Sterling Heights *(G-15250)*
Acme Tool & Die Co .... G 231 938-1260
  Acme *(G-1)*
Bbg North America Ltd Partnr .... F 248 572-6550
  Oxford *(G-12339)*
C & M Manufacturing Corp Inc .... E 586 749-3455
  Chesterfield *(G-2750)*
C P I Inc .... G 810 664-8686
  Lapeer *(G-9448)*
Custom Mold Tool and Die Corp .... G 810 688-3711
  North Branch *(G-11658)*
First Place Manufacturing LLC .... G 231 798-1694
  Norton Shores *(G-11755)*
General Motors LLC .... B 810 236-1970
  Flint *(G-5436)*
Gill Corporation .... B 616 453-4491
  Grand Rapids *(G-6438)*
Marjo Plastics Company Inc .... G 734 455-4130
  Plymouth *(G-12684)*
Pat McArdle .... G 989 375-4321
  Elkton *(G-4782)*
Pdf Mfg Inc .... G 517 522-8431
  Grass Lake *(G-7091)*
Quality Cavity Inc .... F 248 344-9995
  Wixom *(G-17882)*
Ram Die Corp .... F 616 647-2855
  Grand Rapids *(G-6807)*
Sabre Manufacturing .... G 269 945-4120
  Hastings *(G-7425)*
Taylor Tooling Group LLC .... E 616 805-3917
  Grand Rapids *(G-6917)*
Wiesen EDM Inc .... E 616 794-9870
  Belding *(G-1433)*

TOOL REPAIR SVCS

Convex Mold Inc .... G 586 978-0808
  Sterling Heights *(G-15299)*
Davison Tool Service Inc .... G 810 653-6920
  Davison *(G-3646)*
Mac-Tech Tooling Corporation .... G 248 743-1400
  Troy *(G-16468)*

TOOLS: Carpenters', Including Levels & Chisels, Exc Saws

Wranosky & Sons Inc .... G 586 336-9761
  Romeo *(G-13642)*

TOOLS: Hand

Affinity Tool Works LLC .... G 248 588-0395
  Troy *(G-16172)*
Atlas Welding Accessories Inc .... D 248 588-4666
  Troy *(G-16226)*
Aven Inc .... F 734 973-0099
  Ann Arbor *(G-375)*
Balance Technology Inc .... D 734 769-2100
  Whitmore Lake *(G-17689)*
Bartlett Manufacturing Co LLC .... G 989 635-8900
  Marlette *(G-10494)*
Bay-Houston Towing Company .... E 810 648-2210
  Sandusky *(G-14430)*
Boral Building Products Inc .... C 248 668-6400
  Wixom *(G-17777)*
Cobra Maufacturing .... F 248 585-1606
  Troy *(G-16271)*
Cows Locomotive Mfg Co .... E 248 583-7150
  Madison Heights *(G-10221)*
Custom Sockets Inc .... G 616 355-1971
  Holland *(G-7601)*
Detroit Edge Tool Company .... D 313 366-4120
  Detroit *(G-3983)*
Detroit Steel Treating Company .... E 248 334-7436
  Pontiac *(G-12816)*
E M I Construction Products .... D 616 392-7207
  Holland *(G-7615)*
Ferrees Tools Inc .... E 269 965-0511
  Battle Creek *(G-1187)*
Gill Industries Inc .... C 616 559-2700
  Grand Rapids *(G-6442)*
Grace Metal Prods Inc .... G 231 264-8133
  Williamsburg *(G-17712)*
Hanchett Manufacturing Inc .... C 231 796-7678
  Big Rapids *(G-1632)*
Hank Thorn Co .... F 248 348-7800
  Wixom *(G-17823)*
Hansen Machine & Tool Corp .... E 616 361-2842
  Grand Rapids *(G-6494)*
Hastings Fiber Glass Pdts Inc .... D 269 945-9541
  Hastings *(G-7412)*
Hgks Industrial Clay Tool Co I .... G 734 340-5500
  Canton *(G-2383)*
Lach Diamond .... G 616 698-0101
  Grand Rapids *(G-6594)*
Lakeland Mills Inc .... E 989 427-5133
  Edmore *(G-4752)*
Megapro Marketing Usa Inc .... F 866 522-3652
  Niles *(G-11625)*
Mercedes-Benz Extra LLC .... E 205 747-8006
  Farmington Hills *(G-5063)*
Micro Engineering Inc .... E 616 534-9681
  Byron Center *(G-2200)*
Patco Air Tool Inc .... G 248 648-8830
  Orion *(G-12188)*
Port Austin Level & Tl Mfg Co .... F 989 738-5291
  Port Austin *(G-12878)*
R J S Tool & Gage Co .... E 248 642-8620
  Birmingham *(G-1700)*
Rock Tool & Machine Co Inc .... E 734 455-9840
  Plymouth *(G-12743)*
Roesch Maufacturing Co LLC .... G 517 424-6300
  Tecumseh *(G-15808)*
RTS Cutting Tools Inc .... E 586 954-1900
  Clinton Township *(G-3217)*
Safecutters Inc .... G 866 865-7171
  Norton Shores *(G-11791)*
Schenck USA Corp .... E 248 377-2100
  Southfield *(G-15024)*
Schimmelmanns Tool .... G 586 795-0538
  Warren *(G-17232)*
Shaws Enterprises Inc .... E 810 664-2981
  Lapeer *(G-9486)*
Sourcehub LLC .... G 800 246-1844
  Troy *(G-16613)*
Specialty Steel Treating Inc .... E 586 293-5355
  Fraser *(G-5730)*
Steelcraft Tool Co Inc .... E 734 522-7130
  Livonia *(G-9945)*
Summit Tooling & Mfg Inc .... G 231 856-7037
  Morley *(G-11118)*
Tapco Holdings Inc .... C 248 668-6400
  Wixom *(G-17905)*
Tekton Inc .... D 616 243-2443
  Grand Rapids *(G-6919)*
Umix Dissoultion Corp .... E 586 446-9950
  Sterling Heights *(G-15532)*

TOOLS: Hand, Ironworkers'

Eagle Tool Group LLC .... F 586 997-0800
  Sterling Heights *(G-15328)*

TOOLS: Hand, Power

A W B Industries Inc .... E 989 739-1447
  Oscoda *(G-12205)*
Anchor Lamina America Inc .... C 231 533-8646
  Bellaire *(G-1434)*
Avalon Tools Inc .... G 248 269-0001
  Troy *(G-16230)*
Black & Decker (us) Inc .... G 410 716-3900
  Grand Rapids *(G-6228)*
Black & Decker (us) Inc .... G 616 261-0425
  Grandville *(G-7023)*
Carbide Technologies Inc .... E 586 296-5200
  Fraser *(G-5634)*
Clausing Industrial Inc .... E 269 345-7155
  Kalamazoo *(G-8706)*
Clausing Industrial Inc .... D 269 345-7155
  Kalamazoo *(G-8707)*
Conway-Cleveland Corp .... G 616 458-0056
  Grand Rapids *(G-6309)*
Hank Thorn Co .... F 248 348-7800
  Wixom *(G-17823)*
Heck Industries Incorporated .... F 810 632-5400
  Hartland *(G-7390)*
Hme Inc .... C 616 534-1463
  Wyoming *(G-18011)*
Hougen Manufacturing Inc .... C 810 635-7111
  Swartz Creek *(G-15667)*
Jemms-Cascade Inc .... F 248 526-8100
  Troy *(G-16436)*
Lutco Inc .... G 231 972-5566
  Mecosta *(G-10688)*
Menominee Saw and Supply Co .... E 906 863-2609
  Menominee *(G-10747)*
Michigan Deburring Tool LLC .... G 810 227-1000
  Brighton *(G-1959)*
Plum Brothers LLC .... G 734 947-8100
  Romulus *(G-13723)*
Roesch Maufacturing Co LLC .... G 517 424-6300
  Tecumseh *(G-15808)*
RTS Cutting Tools Inc .... E 586 954-1900
  Clinton Township *(G-3217)*
Star Cutter Co .... E 248 474-8200
  Farmington Hills *(G-5129)*
Telco Tools .... F 616 296-0253
  Spring Lake *(G-15185)*
Waber Tool & Engineering Co .... G 269 342-0765
  Kalamazoo *(G-8921)*

TOOLS: Hand, Shovels Or Spades

Sure-Loc Aluminum Edging Inc .... G 616 392-3209
  Holland *(G-7822)*

TOOLS: Soldering

Persico Usa Inc .... D 248 299-5100
  Shelby Township *(G-14664)*

TOOTHBRUSHES: Exc Electric

Ranir LLC .... B 616 698-8880
  Grand Rapids *(G-6808)*

TOUR OPERATORS

Budget Europe Travel Service .... G 734 668-0529
  Ann Arbor *(G-391)*

TOWERS, SECTIONS: Transmission, Radio & Television

Universal Manufacturing Co .... F 586 463-2560
  Clinton Township *(G-3254)*
Vertigo .... G 910 381-8925
  Quinnesec *(G-13108)*

TOWING & TUGBOAT SVC

Central Mich Knwrth Lnsing LLC .... G 517 394-7000
  Lansing *(G-9356)*
Central Mich Knwrth Sginaw LLC ...... G 989 754-4500
  Saginaw *(G-14014)*
Maslo Fabrication LLC .... G 616 298-7700
  Holland *(G-7740)*

TOWING BARS & SYSTEMS

Detroit Wrecker Sales Llc .... G 313 835-8700
  Detroit *(G-4005)*
Hydro King Incorporated .... F 313 835-8700
  Southfield *(G-14939)*
Rapidtek LLC .... G 616 662-0954
  Hudsonville *(G-8175)*

TOWING SVCS: Marine

Superior Mar & Envmtl Svcs LLC ...... G 906 253-9448
  Sault Sainte Marie *(G-14475)*

TOWING SVCS: Mobile Homes

Jrop LLC .... F 800 404-9494
  Royal Oak *(G-13940)*

TOYS

Abbotts Magic Manufacturing Co	G	269 432-3235
Colon (G-3369)		
American Plastic Toys Inc	D	989 685-2455
Rose City (G-13757)		
Ann Williams Group LLC	G	248 731-8588
Bloomfield Hills (G-1746)		
Charlies Wood Shop	F	989 845-2632
Chesaning (G-2722)		
Claybanks Kids LLC	G	231 893-4071
Montague (G-11089)		
Fourth Ave Birkenstock	G	734 663-1644
Ann Arbor (G-466)		
Houseparty	G	616 422-1226
Holland (G-7681)		
Kid By Kid Inc	G	586 781-2345
Macomb (G-10134)		
Merdel Game Manufacturing Co	G	231 845-1263
Ludington (G-10071)		
Poof-Slinky LLC	E	734 454-9552
Plymouth (G-12723)		
Sassy 14 LLC	E	616 243-0767
Kentwood (G-9031)		
Shelti Inc	E	989 893-1739
Bay City (G-1357)		

TOYS & HOBBY GOODS & SPLYS, WHOLESALE: Arts/Crafts Eqpt/Sply

Mac Enterprises Inc	F	313 846-4567
Manchester (G-10407)		

TOYS & HOBBY GOODS & SPLYS, WHOLESALE: Dolls

Dolls By Maurice Inc	G	586 739-5147
Utica (G-16741)		

TOYS & HOBBY GOODS & SPLYS, WHOLESALE: Toys & Games

St Evans Inc	G	269 663-6100
Edwardsburg (G-4772)		

TOYS & HOBBY GOODS & SPLYS, WHOLESALE: Toys, NEC

American Plastic Toys Inc	D	989 685-2455
Rose City (G-13757)		

TOYS, HOBBY GOODS & SPLYS WHOLESALERS

Ideal Wholesale Inc	G	989 873-5850
Prescott (G-13080)		

TOYS: Rubber

Go Cat Feather Toys	G	517 543-7519
Charlotte (G-2652)		

TRADE SHOW ARRANGEMENT SVCS

Sparks Exhbits Envrnments Corp	G	248 291-0007
Royal Oak (G-13972)		

TRAILER PARKS

Denali Seed Co	G	907 344-0347
Pentwater (G-12429)		

TRAILERS & CHASSIS: Camping

County of Muskegon	F	231 744-3580
Muskegon (G-11302)		
Technology Plus Trailers Inc	F	734 928-0001
Canton (G-2433)		

TRAILERS & PARTS: Boat

Boat Customs Trailers LLC	G	517 712-3512
Caledonia (G-2291)		
Phoenix Trailers LLC	G	231 536-9760
East Jordan (G-4642)		
US 223 Inland Marine LLC	G	517 547-2628
Addison (G-40)		

TRAILERS & PARTS: Truck & Semi's

Ajax Trailers Inc	F	586 757-7676
Warren (G-16923)		
Anderson Welding & Mfg Inc	F	906 523-4661
Chassell (G-2671)		
Automotive Service Co	F	517 784-6131
Jackson (G-8385)		
Benlee Inc	E	586 791-1830
Romulus (G-13656)		
Clydes Frame & Wheel Service	F	248 338-0323
Pontiac (G-12810)		
Eddies Quick Stop Inc	F	313 712-1818
Dearborn (G-3698)		
Express Welding Inc	G	906 786-8808
Escanaba (G-4829)		
Intermodal Technologies Inc	G	989 775-3799
Mount Pleasant (G-11198)		
Jbs Transport LLC	G	248 636-5546
Troy (G-16435)		
Joes Trailer Manufacturing	G	734 261-0050
Livonia (G-9793)		
Lupa R A and Sons Repair	G	810 346-3579
Marlette (G-10498)		
Montrose Trailers Inc	G	810 639-7431
Montrose (G-11105)		
Mtm Transport	G	989 709-0475
Alger (G-139)		
Neo Manufacturing Inc	F	269 503-7630
Sturgis (G-15623)		
Oshkosh Defense LLC	E	586 576-8301
Warren (G-17178)		
Saf-Holland Inc	B	231 773-3271
Muskegon (G-11417)		
Scott Enterprises	G	734 279-2078
Dundee (G-4600)		
Superior Synchronized Sys	D	906 863-7824
Wallace (G-16888)		
Technology Plus Trailers Inc	F	734 928-0001
Canton (G-2433)		
Tow-Line Trailers	G	989 752-0055
Saginaw (G-14165)		
Trimas Company LLC	F	248 631-5450
Bloomfield Hills (G-1806)		
Wolverine Trailers Inc	G	517 782-4950
Jackson (G-8610)		
Wolverine Trailers Inc	G	517 782-4950
Jackson (G-8611)		
Woodland Industries	G	989 686-6176
Kawkawlin (G-8976)		
Xpo Cnw Inc	C	734 757-1444
Ann Arbor (G-705)		

TRAILERS & TRAILER EQPT

Bedford Machinery Inc	G	734 848-4980
Erie (G-4801)		
Dexko Global Inc	G	248 533-0029
Novi (G-11867)		
Dragon Acquisition Intermediat	G	248 692-4367
Novi (G-11871)		
Dragon Acquisition Parent Inc	G	248 692-4367
Novi (G-11872)		
Great Lakes Lift Inc	G	989 673-2109
Caro (G-2469)		
Jrm Industries Inc	F	616 837-9758
Nunica (G-12039)		
Midwest Direct Transport Inc	F	616 698-8900
Byron Center (G-2201)		
Montrose Trailers Inc	G	810 639-7431
Montrose (G-11105)		
Nash Car Trailer Corporation	F	269 673-5776
Allegan (G-178)		
P2r Metal Fabrication Inc	G	888 727-5587
Macomb (G-10151)		
Phoenix Trailer & Body Company	F	248 360-7184
Commerce Township (G-3439)		
Quadra Manufacturing Inc	E	269 483-9633
White Pigeon (G-17655)		
Viking Sales Inc	F	810 227-2222
Brighton (G-2007)		
Windsor Mold USA Inc	E	734 944-5080
Saline (G-14421)		

TRAILERS OR VANS: Horse Transportation, Fifth-Wheel Type

Merhow Acquisition LLC	D	269 483-0010
White Pigeon (G-17653)		

TRAILERS: Bodies

Hulet Body Co Inc	E	313 931-6000
Northville (G-11699)		
Pullman Company	F	734 243-8000
Monroe (G-11064)		
Saf-Holland Inc	C	616 396-6501
Holland (G-7795)		
Thumb Truck and Trailer Co	G	989 453-3133
Pigeon (G-12493)		
Transport Trailers Co	G	269 543-4405
Fennville (G-5178)		

TRAILERS: Bus, Tractor Type

Bobbys Mobile Service LLC	G	517 206-6026
Jackson (G-8392)		

TRAILERS: House, Exc Permanent Dwellings

Michigan East Side Sales LLC	G	989 354-6867
Alpena (G-299)		

TRAILERS: Semitrailers, Missile Transportation

Executive Operations LLC	E	313 312-0653
Canton (G-2373)		

TRAILERS: Semitrailers, Truck Tractors

Leonard & Randy Inc	G	734 287-9500
Taylor (G-15735)		
Trailer Tech Holdings LLC	E	248 960-9700
Wixom (G-17915)		

TRAILERS: Truck, Chassis

Arboc Ltd	G	248 684-2895
Commerce Township (G-3390)		
Pratt Industries Inc	D	269 465-7676
Bridgman (G-1872)		

TRANSDUCERS: Electrical Properties

Pcb Piezotronics Inc	F	888 684-0014
Novi (G-11971)		
Sage Acoustics LLC	G	269 861-5593
Bangor (G-1095)		
Sensata Technologies Inc	G	805 523-2000
Northville (G-11725)		

TRANSDUCERS: Pressure

Precision Measurement Co	E	734 995-0041
Ann Arbor (G-601)		

TRANSFORMERS: Control

Marcie Electric Inc	G	248 486-1200
Brighton (G-1954)		

TRANSFORMERS: Distribution

Detroit Renewable Energy LLC	C	313 972-5700
Detroit (G-3999)		

TRANSFORMERS: Distribution, Electric

Meiden America Inc	F	734 459-1781
Northville (G-11709)		

TRANSFORMERS: Doorbell, Electric

Houseart LLC	G	248 651-8124
Rochester (G-13327)		

TRANSFORMERS: Electric

Heyboer Transformers Inc	E	616 842-5830
Grand Haven (G-6036)		
Osborne Transformer Corp	E	586 218-6900
Fraser (G-5702)		

TRANSFORMERS: Electronic

Powertran Corporation	E	248 399-4300
Ferndale (G-5312)		

TRANSFORMERS: Fluorescent Lighting

Tara Industries Inc	F	248 477-6520
Livonia (G-9953)		

TRANSFORMERS: Furnace, Electric

Ajax Tocco Magnethermic Corp	E	248 589-2524
Madison Heights (G-10185)		
Ajax Tocco Magnethermic Corp	F	248 585-1140
Madison Heights (G-10186)		

Employee Codes: A=Over 500 employees, B=251-500
C=101-250, D=51-100, E=20-50, F=10-19, G=3-9

TRANSFORMERS: Power Related

Advance Cylinder Products LLC	G	586 991-2445
Shelby Township *(G-14542)*		
Eastern Power and Lighting	G	248 739-0908
Dearborn Heights *(G-3783)*		
Ebw Electronics Inc	E	616 786-0575
Holland *(G-7616)*		
Gti Liquidating Inc	D	616 842-5430
Grand Haven *(G-6028)*		
Maxitrol Company	D	248 356-1400
Southfield *(G-14974)*		
Parker-Hannifin Corporation	B	269 629-5000
Richland *(G-13252)*		
Rtg Products Inc	G	734 323-8916
Redford *(G-13189)*		
SH Leggitt Company	C	269 781-3901
Marshall *(G-10588)*		
Syndevco Inc	F	248 356-2839
Southfield *(G-15042)*		
US Green Energy Solutions LLC	G	810 955-2992
Livonia *(G-9983)*		

TRANSFORMERS: Rectifier

Controlled Power Company	C	248 528-3700
Troy *(G-16281)*		

TRANSFORMERS: Toy

Sandcastle For Kids Inc	F	616 396-5955
Holland *(G-7796)*		

TRANSFORMERS: Voltage Regulating

Power Control Systems Inc	F	517 339-1442
Okemos *(G-12135)*		

TRANSLATION & INTERPRETATION SVCS

AAA Language Services	F	248 239-1138
Bloomfield *(G-1731)*		
Iris Design & Print Inc	G	313 277-0505
Dearborn *(G-3727)*		
J & M International Corp	G	248 588-8108
Troy *(G-16428)*		

TRANSMISSIONS: Motor Vehicle

Aqueous Orbital Systems LLC	G	269 501-7461
Kalamazoo *(G-8681)*		
Borgwarner Powdered Metals Inc	E	734 261-5322
Livonia *(G-9668)*		
Eaton Corporation	B	269 342-3000
Galesburg *(G-5809)*		
Eaton Corporation	C	269 342-3000
Galesburg *(G-5810)*		
Emergency Services LLC	G	231 727-7400
Muskegon *(G-11317)*		
Fte Automotive USA Inc	C	248 209-8239
Highland Park *(G-7505)*		
GKN North America Inc	A	248 296-7200
Auburn Hills *(G-886)*		
GKN North America Services Inc	F	248 377-1200
Auburn Hills *(G-887)*		
M P I International Inc	D	608 764-5416
Rochester Hills *(G-13463)*		
Metaldyne Prfmce Group Inc	E	248 727-1800
Southfield *(G-14978)*		
Musashi Auto Parts Mich Inc	B	269 965-0057
Battle Creek *(G-1230)*		
Newcor Inc	C	248 537-0014
Corunna *(G-3584)*		
Systrand Manufacturing Corp	C	734 479-8100
Brownstown Twp *(G-2074)*		
Transform Automotive LLC	C	586 826-8500
Sterling Heights *(G-15527)*		

TRANSPORTATION BROKERS: Truck

Foreward Logistics LLC	G	877 488-9724
Oak Park *(G-12068)*		
Kace Logistics LLC	D	734 946-8600
Carleton *(G-2458)*		

TRANSPORTATION EPQT & SPLYS, WHOLESALE: Marine Crafts/Splys

Midwest Aquatics Group Inc	G	734 426-4155
Pinckney *(G-12500)*		

TRANSPORTATION EPQT & SPLYS, WHOLESALE: Tanks & Tank Compnts

Burch Tank & Truck Inc	G	989 495-0342
Midland *(G-10820)*		
Burch Tank & Truck Inc	D	989 772-6266
Mount Pleasant *(G-11181)*		

TRANSPORTATION EQUIPMENT, NEC

Guiding Our Destiny Ministry	G	313 212-9063
Detroit *(G-4108)*		
Xpo Nlm	G	866 251-3651
Southfield *(G-15068)*		

TRANSPORTATION SVCS: Rental, Local

Executive Operations LLC	E	313 312-0653
Canton *(G-2373)*		

TRANSPORTATION: Bus Transit Systems

Dgp Inc	E	989 635-7531
Marlette *(G-10495)*		

TRANSPORTATION: Local Passenger, NEC

May Mobility Inc	F	312 869-2711
Ann Arbor *(G-550)*		

TRANSPORTATION: Transit Systems, NEC

Cooper-Standard Auto OH LLC	G	248 596-5900
Novi *(G-11853)*		
Csa Services Inc	G	248 596-6184
Novi *(G-11859)*		

TRAPS: Animal, Iron Or Steel

Detroit Auto Specialties Inc	G	248 496-3856
West Bloomfield *(G-17474)*		
Shane Group LLC	G	517 439-4316
Hillsdale *(G-7541)*		

TRAPS: Stem

Armstrong International Inc	C	269 273-1415
Three Rivers *(G-15858)*		

TRAVEL AGENCIES

Black Ski Weekend LLC	G	313 879-7150
West Bloomfield *(G-17466)*		
Nationwide Network Inc	E	989 793-0123
Saginaw *(G-14103)*		

TRAVEL TRAILER DEALERS

Technology Plus Trailers Inc	F	734 928-0001
Canton *(G-2433)*		

TRAVEL TRAILERS & CAMPERS

Ajax Trailers Inc	F	586 757-7676
Warren *(G-16923)*		
Bnm Trailers Sales Inc	E	989 862-5252
Elsie *(G-4795)*		
D & W Management Company Inc	E	586 758-2284
Warren *(G-16996)*		
Frank Industries Inc		810 346-3234
Brown City *(G-2051)*		
Gibbys Transport LLC	G	269 838-2794
Hastings *(G-7411)*		
Montrose Trailers Inc		810 639-7431
Montrose *(G-11105)*		
Mvm7 LLC	E	989 317-3901
Mount Pleasant *(G-11213)*		
Steffens Enterprises Inc		616 656-6886
Caledonia *(G-2317)*		

TRAVERTINE: Crushed & Broken

Osborne Materials Company	E	906 493-5211
Drummond Island *(G-4566)*		

TRAYS: Plastic

Peninsula Plastics Company Inc	D	248 852-3731
Auburn Hills *(G-971)*		
R L Adams Plastics Inc	D	616 261-4400
Grand Rapids *(G-6803)*		
Sohner Plastics LLC	F	734 222-4847
Dexter *(G-4511)*		

TROPHIES, NEC

Fun Promotion LLC	G	616 453-4245
Grand Rapids *(G-6424)*		
M P C Awards	G	586 254-4660
Shelby Township *(G-14629)*		
Michigan Plaques & Awards Inc	E	248 398-6400
Berkley *(G-1587)*		
Quicktrophy LLC	F	906 228-2604
Marquette *(G-10555)*		

TROPHIES, PLATED, ALL METALS

American Awards & Engrv LLC	G	810 229-5911
Milford *(G-10954)*		

TROPHIES, WHOLESALE

Lachman Enterprises Inc	G	248 948-9944
Southfield *(G-14958)*		
MJB Concepts Inc	G	616 866-1470
Rockford *(G-13580)*		

TROPHIES: Metal, Exc Silver

Contemporary Industries Inc	G	248 478-8850
Farmington Hills *(G-4966)*		
East End Sports Awards Inc	G	906 293-8895
Newberry *(G-11579)*		
R L Hume Award Co	G	269 324-3063
Portage *(G-13026)*		

TROPHY & PLAQUE STORES

Amazing Engraving	G	989 652-8503
Frankenmuth *(G-5582)*		
American Awards & Engrv LLC	G	810 229-5911
Milford *(G-10954)*		
Creative Awards	G	586 739-4999
Sterling Heights *(G-15303)*		
Cushion Lrry Trphies Engrv LLC	G	517 332-1667
Lansing *(G-9358)*		
Imagecraft	G	517 750-0077
Jackson *(G-8469)*		
Livonia Trophy & Screen Prtg	G	734 464-9191
Livonia *(G-9816)*		
M P C Awards	G	586 254-4660
Shelby Township *(G-14629)*		
Marquee Engraving Inc	G	810 686-7550
Clio *(G-3275)*		
Michael Anderson	G	231 652-5717
Newaygo *(G-11575)*		
Midwest Graphics & Awards Inc	G	734 424-3700
Dexter *(G-4500)*		
Nobby Inc	E	810 984-3300
Fort Gratiot *(G-5550)*		
Pro Shop The/P S Graphics	G	517 448-8490
Hudson *(G-8139)*		
Qmi Group Inc	E	248 589-0505
Madison Heights *(G-10342)*		
Quality Engraving Service		269 781-4822
Marshall *(G-10586)*		
Quicktrophy LLC	F	906 228-2604
Marquette *(G-10555)*		
S & H Trophy & Sports	G	616 754-0005
Greenville *(G-7151)*		
Sports Inc	G	734 728-1313
Wayne *(G-17443)*		
Sylvesters	G	989 348-9097
Grayling *(G-7116)*		
Trophy Center West Michigan	G	231 893-1686
Whitehall *(G-17678)*		

TRUCK & BUS BODIES: Bus Bodies

Transit Bus Rebuilders Inc	E	989 277-3645
Owosso *(G-12324)*		

TRUCK & BUS BODIES: Car Carrier

Weiderman Motorsports	G	269 689-0264
Sturgis *(G-15641)*		

TRUCK & BUS BODIES: Cement Mixer

Bucks Cement Inc	G	810 233-4141
Burton *(G-2146)*		

TRUCK & BUS BODIES: Dump Truck

Mobile Haulaway LLC	G	616 402-7878
Muskegon *(G-11382)*		

PRODUCT SECTION

TRUCKS & TRACTORS: Industrial

TRUCK & BUS BODIES: Garbage Or Refuse Truck

Loadmaster Corporation .... E 906 563-9226
Norway *(G-11817)*

TRUCK & BUS BODIES: Motor Vehicle, Specialty

Hovertechnics LLC .... G 269 461-3934
Benton Harbor *(G-1511)*
Mahindra North American .... C 248 268-6600
Auburn Hills *(G-940)*
Mahindra Vehicle Mfrs Ltd .... C 248 268-6600
Auburn Hills *(G-941)*
Perspective Enterprises Inc .... G 269 327-0869
Portage *(G-13021)*

TRUCK & BUS BODIES: Truck Beds

Precision Laser & Mfg LLC .... G 519 733-8422
Sterling Heights *(G-15449)*

TRUCK & BUS BODIES: Truck, Motor Vehicle

Automotive Service Co .... F 517 784-6131
Jackson *(G-8385)*
Csi Emergency Apparatus LLC .... F 989 348-2877
Grayling *(G-7105)*
Hulet Body Co Inc .... E 313 931-6000
Northville *(G-11699)*
Lodal Inc .... D 906 779-1700
Kingsford *(G-9062)*
Morgan Olson LLC .... A 269 659-0200
Sturgis *(G-15622)*
Velcro USA Inc .... G 248 583-6060
Troy *(G-16682)*

TRUCK & BUS BODIES: Utility Truck

Wolverine Trailers Inc .... F 517 782-4950
Jackson *(G-8612)*

TRUCK & BUS BODIES: Van Bodies

Mobility Trnsp Svcs Inc .... E 734 453-6452
Canton *(G-2406)*
Mobilitytrans LLC .... E 734 453-6452
Canton *(G-2407)*

TRUCK BODIES: Body Parts

Advanced C & T Manufacturers .... G 517 882-2444
Lansing *(G-9333)*
Aeroefficient LLC .... G 847 784-8100
Livonia *(G-9631)*
BDS Company Inc .... E 517 279-2135
Coldwater *(G-3291)*
Central Mich Knwrth Lnsing LLC .... G 517 394-7000
Lansing *(G-9356)*
Central Mich Knwrth Sginaw LLC .... G 989 754-4500
Saginaw *(G-14014)*
Gac .... E 269 639-3010
South Haven *(G-14760)*
Johnson Controls Inc .... B 734 254-5000
Plymouth *(G-12655)*
O E M Parts Supply Inc .... G 313 729-4283
Detroit *(G-4281)*
Off Site Mfg Tech Inc .... D 586 598-3110
Chesterfield *(G-2810)*
Steffens Enterprises Inc .... E 616 656-6886
Caledonia *(G-2317)*
Tectum Holdings Inc .... E 734 677-0444
Ann Arbor *(G-655)*
Worldwide Marketing Services .... G 269 556-2000
Saint Joseph *(G-14355)*

TRUCK BODY SHOP

Hulet Body Co Inc .... E 313 931-6000
Northville *(G-11699)*

TRUCK GENERAL REPAIR SVC

Benlee Inc .... E 586 791-1830
Romulus *(G-13656)*
Circle K Service Corporation .... E 989 496-0511
Midland *(G-10824)*
D & W Management Company Inc ..... E 586 758-2284
Warren *(G-16996)*
Eleven Mile Trck Frme & Ax .... D 248 399-7536
Madison Heights *(G-10244)*
Lupa R A and Sons Repair .... G 810 346-3579
Marlette *(G-10498)*

TRUCK PAINTING & LETTERING SVCS

Dicks Signs .... G 810 987-9002
Port Huron *(G-12911)*
West Shore Signs Inc .... G 734 324-7076
Riverview *(G-13306)*

TRUCK PARTS & ACCESSORIES: Wholesalers

Automotive Service Co .... F 517 784-6131
Jackson *(G-8385)*
Joint Clutch & Gear Svc Inc .... E 734 641-7575
Romulus *(G-13693)*
Monroe Truck Equipment Inc .... E 810 238-4603
Flint *(G-5470)*
NBC Truck Equipment Inc .... E 586 774-4900
Roseville *(G-13845)*
Tectum Holdings Inc .... E 734 677-0444
Ann Arbor *(G-655)*

TRUCKING & HAULING SVCS: Animal & Farm Prdt

F C Simpson Lime Co .... G 810 367-3510
Kimball *(G-9043)*
Keays Family Truckin .... F 231 838-6430
Gaylord *(G-5871)*

TRUCKING & HAULING SVCS: Contract Basis

Xpo Cnw Inc .... C 734 757-1444
Ann Arbor *(G-705)*

TRUCKING & HAULING SVCS: Furniture, Local W/out Storage

Designtec Services Inc .... G 734 216-6051
Howell *(G-8028)*

TRUCKING & HAULING SVCS: Garbage, Collect/Transport Only

Scooters Refuse Service Inc .... G 269 962-2201
Battle Creek *(G-1244)*
Southast Berrien Cnty Landfill .... F 269 695-2500
Niles *(G-11646)*

TRUCKING & HAULING SVCS: Lumber & Log, Local

Nickels Logging .... G 906 563-5880
Norway *(G-11818)*

TRUCKING & HAULING SVCS: Mail Carriers, Contract

Allied Printing Co Inc .... E 248 541-0551
Ferndale *(G-5259)*

TRUCKING & HAULING SVCS: Mobile Homes

Cedar Mobile Home Service Inc .... G 616 696-1580
Cedar Springs *(G-2546)*

TRUCKING & HAULING SVCS: Petroleum, Local

Wara Construction Company LLC .... D 248 299-2410
Rochester Hills *(G-13540)*

TRUCKING & HAULING SVCS: Steel, Local

Leonard & Randy Inc .... G 734 287-9500
Taylor *(G-15735)*

TRUCKING & HAULING SVCS: Timber, Local

Marvin Nelson Forest Products .... F 906 384-6700
Cornell *(G-3575)*
McNamara & Mcnamara .... F 906 293-5281
Newberry *(G-11580)*

TRUCKING, AUTOMOBILE CARRIER

IKEA Chip LLC .... G 877 218-9931
Troy *(G-16409)*

TRUCKING, DUMP

Bouchey and Sons Inc .... G 989 588-4118
Farwell *(G-5158)*
Crandell Bros Trucking Co .... E 517 543-2930
Charlotte *(G-2644)*
Doug Wirt Enterprises Inc .... G 989 684-5777
Bay City *(G-1305)*
Franke Salisbury Virginia .... G 231 775-7014
Cadillac *(G-2248)*
Miller Sand & Gravel Company .... G 269 672-5601
Hopkins *(G-7959)*
Priority Waste LLC .... E 586 228-1200
Clinton Township *(G-3205)*
Yerington Brothers Inc .... G 269 695-7669
Niles *(G-11652)*
Zeeland Farm Services Inc .... C 616 772-9042
Zeeland *(G-18201)*

TRUCKING: Except Local

E H Tulgestka & Sons Inc .... F 989 734-2129
Rogers City *(G-13615)*
Forest Blake Products Inc .... G 231 879-3913
Fife Lake *(G-5340)*
Indian Summer Cooperative Inc .... C 231 845-6248
Ludington *(G-10067)*
Jasco International LLC .... F 313 841-5000
Detroit *(G-4159)*
Koppers Performance Chem Inc .... E 906 296-8271
Hubbell *(G-8126)*
Manigg Enterprises Inc .... F 989 356-4986
Alpena *(G-296)*
Northern Logistics LLC .... E 989 386-2389
Clare *(G-2881)*

TRUCKING: Local, With Storage

Aldez North America LLC .... G 810 577-3891
Almont *(G-251)*
Constine Inc .... E 989 723-6043
Owosso *(G-12284)*
J T Express Ltd .... G 810 724-6471
Brown City *(G-2052)*
Jasco International LLC .... F 313 841-5000
Detroit *(G-4159)*
Trinity Holding Inc .... F 517 787-3100
Jackson *(G-8593)*

TRUCKING: Local, Without Storage

Allied Printing Co Inc .... E 248 514-7394
Ferndale *(G-5260)*
Bay-Houston Towing Company .... E 810 648-2210
Sandusky *(G-14430)*
City of Taylor .... E 734 374-1372
Taylor *(G-15700)*
Darling Ingredients Inc .... F 989 752-4340
Carrollton *(G-2485)*
Decockers Inc .... G 517 447-3635
Deerfield *(G-3811)*
Falcon Trucking Company .... G 313 843-7200
Dearborn *(G-3704)*
Forest Blake Products Inc .... G 231 879-3913
Fife Lake *(G-5340)*
Genoak Materials Inc .... C 248 634-8276
Holly *(G-7880)*
James Spicer Inc .... G 906 265-2385
Iron River *(G-8311)*
Rudy Goupille & Sons Inc .... G 906 475-9816
Negaunee *(G-11476)*
Straits Steel and Wire Company .... D 231 843-3416
Ludington *(G-10080)*
Superior Distribution Svcs LLC .... G 616 453-6358
Grand Rapids *(G-6902)*
Tri-City Aggregates Inc .... E 248 634-8276
Holly *(G-7900)*

TRUCKS & TRACTORS: Industrial

AAR Manufacturing Inc .... E 231 779-8800
Cadillac *(G-2220)*
Alta Equipment Holdings Inc .... E 248 449-6700
Livonia *(G-9638)*
Archer Wire International Corp .... D 231 869-6911
Pentwater *(G-12428)*
Baker Enterprises Inc .... E 989 354-2189
Alpena *(G-280)*
Bay Wood Homes Inc .... E 989 245-4156
Fenton *(G-5187)*
Besser Company USA .... E 616 399-5215
Zeeland *(G-18119)*

Employee Codes: A=Over 500 employees, B=251-500
C=101-250, D=51-100, E=20-50, F=10-19, G=3-9

TRUCKS & TRACTORS: Industrial

Bucher Hydraulics Inc .... E 231 652-2773
  Newaygo (G-11564)
Charles Lange .... G 989 777-0110
  Saginaw (G-14016)
Circle K Service Corporation .... E 989 496-0511
  Midland (G-10824)
Commercial Group Inc .... E 313 931-6100
  Taylor (G-15704)
Delta Tube & Fabricating Corp .... C 248 634-8267
  Holly (G-7875)
Dematic .... G 616 395-8671
  Holland (G-7607)
Egemin Automation Inc .... C 616 393-0101
  Holland (G-7619)
Frost Incorporated .... E 616 453-7781
  Grand Rapids (G-6421)
Harvey S Freeman .... E 248 852-2222
  West Bloomfield (G-17479)
Hme Inc .... C 616 534-1463
  Wyoming (G-18011)
Hobart Brothers Company .... F 231 933-1234
  Traverse City (G-15998)
Humphrey Companies LLC .... C 616 530-1717
  Grandville (G-7048)
Joam Inc .... G 989 828-5749
  Shepherd (G-14729)
L A S Leasing Inc .... F 734 727-5148
  Wayne (G-17435)
Lake Shore Systems Inc .... D 906 774-1500
  Kingsford (G-9061)
Loudon Steel Inc .... D 989 871-9353
  Millington (G-10997)
Marsh Industrial Services Inc .... F 231 258-4870
  Kalkaska (G-8949)
Metzgar Conveyor Co .... E 616 784-0930
  Grand Rapids (G-6664)
Midwest Tractor & Equipment Co .... F 231 269-4100
  Buckley (G-2130)
Milsco LLC .... B 517 787-3650
  Jackson (G-8531)
Montrose Trailers Inc .... G 810 639-7431
  Montrose (G-11105)
Nyx Inc .... B 734 464-0800
  Livonia (G-9869)
PCI Procal Inc .... F 989 358-7070
  Alpena (G-307)
Peninsular Inc .... E 586 775-7211
  Roseville (G-13853)
Perfecto Industries Inc .... E 989 732-2941
  Gaylord (G-5888)
Prophotonix Limited .... E 586 778-1100
  Roseville (G-13856)
Roberts Sinto Corporation .... D 517 371-2471
  Grand Ledge (G-6114)
Saf-Holland Inc .... B 231 773-3271
  Muskegon (G-11417)
Saginaw Products Corporation .... E 989 753-1411
  Saginaw (G-14141)
Systems Unlimited Inc .... E 517 279-8407
  Coldwater (G-3336)
Thoreson-Mc Cosh Inc .... E 248 362-0960
  Troy (G-16638)
Versatile Fabrication Co Inc .... E 231 739-7115
  Muskegon (G-11446)

TRUCKS: Forklift

Bell Fork Lift Inc .... F 313 841-1220
  Detroit (G-3899)
Bell Forklifts .... G 586 469-7979
  Clinton Township (G-3064)
Bristol Manufacturing Inc .... E 810 658-9510
  Davison (G-3640)
Harlo Products Corporation .... E 616 538-0550
  Grandville (G-7047)
Ihs Inc .... G 616 464-4224
  Grand Rapids (G-6527)
West Michigan Forklift Inc .... E 616 262-4949
  Wayland (G-17420)

TRUCKS: Indl

Aimrite LLC .... G 248 693-8925
  Lake Orion (G-9124)
J & J Transport LLC .... G 231 582-6083
  Boyne City (G-1824)
Superior Distribution Svcs LLC .... G 616 453-6358
  Grand Rapids (G-6902)

TRUNKS

Grand Trunk RR .... G 248 452-4881
  Pontiac (G-12830)

TRUSSES & FRAMING: Prefabricated Metal

Progressive Panel Systems .... F 616 748-1384
  Zeeland (G-18180)

TRUSSES: Wood, Floor

Allwood Building Components .... D 586 727-2731
  Richmond (G-13259)
G & G Wood & Supply Inc .... F 586 293-0450
  Roseville (G-13805)
Letherer Truss Inc .... E 989 386-4999
  Clare (G-2876)
Maple Valley Truss Co .... E 989 389-4267
  Prudenville (G-13085)
Marshall Bldg Components Corp .... F 269 781-4236
  Marshall (G-10575)
Superior Country Wood Truss .... G 906 499-3354
  Seney (G-14522)
Wood Tech Inc .... E 616 455-0800
  Byron Center (G-2217)

TRUSSES: Wood, Roof

Century Truss .... G 248 486-4000
  Livonia (G-9682)
Custom Components Truss Co .... E 810 744-0771
  Burton (G-2153)
Heart Truss & Engineering Corp .... D 517 372-0850
  Lansing (G-9234)
Joseph Miller .... G 231 821-2430
  Holton (G-7933)
Ken Luneack Construction Inc .... C 989 681-5774
  Saint Louis (G-14365)
Lumber & Truss Inc .... E 810 664-7290
  Lapeer (G-9472)
Maverick Building Systems LLC .... F 248 366-9410
  Commerce Township (G-3428)
Precision Framing Systems Inc .... E 704 588-6680
  Taylor (G-15755)
Truss Technologies Inc .... E 231 788-6330
  Muskegon (G-11443)
Trussway .... G 713 691-6900
  Jenison (G-8645)
Wendricks Truss Inc .... F 906 635-8822
  Sault Sainte Marie (G-14479)
Wendricks Truss Inc .... E 906 498-7709
  Hermansville (G-7468)

TUBE & PIPE MILL EQPT

Delta Tube & Fabricating Corp .... C 248 634-8267
  Holly (G-7875)

TUBE & TUBING FABRICATORS

A & B Tube Benders Inc .... E 586 773-0440
  Warren (G-16905)
Acme Tube Bending Company .... G 248 545-8500
  Berkley (G-1578)
Allegan Tubular Products Inc .... D 269 673-6636
  Allegan (G-149)
Almarc Tube Co Inc .... G 989 654-2660
  Sterling (G-15242)
Alro Steel Corporation .... F 989 893-9553
  Bay City (G-1274)
Angstrom Automotive Group LLC .... E 248 627-2871
  Ortonville (G-12193)
Berkley Industries Inc .... F 989 656-2171
  Bay Port (G-1372)
Detroit Tube Products LLC .... E 313 841-0300
  Detroit (G-4003)
Erin Industries Inc .... E 248 669-2050
  Walled Lake (G-16893)
Fabricari LLC .... G 734 972-2042
  Dexter (G-4492)
Gray Bros Stamping & Mch Inc .... E 269 483-7615
  White Pigeon (G-17649)
Harbor Steel and Supply Corp .... F 616 786-0002
  Holland (G-7657)
J & L Manufacturing Co Inc .... E 269 789-1507
  Marshall (G-10572)
Jems of Litchfield Inc .... E 517 542-5367
  Litchfield (G-9605)
L & R Machine Inc .... F 517 523-2978
  Osseo (G-12226)
L A Burnhart Inc .... E 810 227-4567
  Brighton (G-1948)
Leggett Platt Components Inc .... D 616 784-7000
  Sparta (G-15101)
Macomb Tube Fabricating Co .... F 586 445-6770
  Warren (G-17135)
Masterbilt Products Corp .... E 269 749-4841
  Olivet (G-12142)
Mayville Engineering Co Inc .... C 989 748-6031
  Vanderbilt (G-16806)
Mayville Engineering Co Inc .... D 616 877-2073
  Wayland (G-17406)
Melling Products North LLC .... D 989 588-6147
  Farwell (G-5164)
Midwest Tube Fabricators Inc .... E 586 264-9898
  Sterling Heights (G-15424)
Paumac Tubing LLC .... D 810 985-9400
  Marysville (G-10610)
Picko Ferrum Fabricating LLC .... G 810 626-7086
  Hamburg (G-7227)
Production Tube Company Inc .... E 313 259-3990
  Detroit (G-4312)
Quality Manufacturing .... G 989 736-8121
  Lincoln (G-9570)
Quigley Manufacturing Inc .... C 248 426-8600
  Farmington Hills (G-5110)
Ridgid Slotting LLC .... F 616 847-0332
  Grand Haven (G-6072)
Rochester Tube Products Ltd .... E 586 726-4816
  Shelby Township (G-14680)
Rock River Fabrications Inc .... E 616 281-5769
  Grand Rapids (G-6832)
Ryson Tube Inc .... F 810 227-4567
  Brighton (G-1987)
Sales & Engineering Inc .... E 734 525-9030
  Livonia (G-9919)
South Park Sales & Mfg Inc .... G 313 381-7579
  Dearborn (G-3762)
Tempro Industries Inc .... F 734 451-5900
  Plymouth (G-12768)
Tg Manufacturing LLC .... E 616 935-7575
  Byron Center (G-2212)
TI Group Auto Systems LLC .... C 248 494-5000
  Auburn Hills (G-1024)
Toolcraft Machine Co Inc .... G 517 223-9265
  Gregory (G-7166)
Troy Tube & Manufacturing Co .... D 586 949-8700
  Chesterfield (G-2851)
Tube Fab/Roman Engrg Co Inc .... C 231 238-9366
  Afton (G-107)
Tube Forming and Machine Inc .... E 989 739-3323
  Oscoda (G-12223)
Tube Wright Inc .... E 810 227-4567
  Brighton (G-2000)
Tube-Co Inc .... G 586 775-0244
  Warren (G-17272)
Tubesource Manufacturing Inc .... F 248 543-4746
  Ferndale (G-5324)
Universal Tube Inc .... C 248 853-5100
  Rochester Hills (G-13536)
Universal Warranty Corpor .... G 248 263-6900
  Southfield (G-15055)
Van Pelt Industries LLC .... G 616 842-1200
  Grand Haven (G-6094)
Volos Tube Form Inc .... E 586 416-3600
  Macomb (G-10174)
West Michigan Fab Corp .... G 616 794-3750
  Belding (G-1432)

TUBES: Extruded Or Drawn, Aluminum

Brazeway Inc .... D 517 265-2121
  Adrian (G-51)

TUBES: Finned, For Heat Transfer

Burr Oak Tool Inc .... C 269 651-9393
  Sturgis (G-15599)

TUBES: Gas Or Vapor

Puff Baby LLC .... G 734 620-9991
  Garden City (G-5835)

TUBES: Paper

Cascade Paper Converters LLC .... F 616 974-9165
  Grand Rapids (G-6263)
Nagel Paper Inc .... E 989 753-4405
  Swartz Creek (G-15669)

TUBES: Steel & Iron

Fluid Routing Solutions Inc .... E 231 592-1700
  Big Rapids (G-1628)

Percor Manufacturing Inc .... F 616 554-1668
  Wyoming *(G-18026)*
River Valley Machine Inc .... E 269 673-8070
  Allegan *(G-187)*
S F R Precision Turning Inc .... G 517 709-3367
  Holt *(G-7924)*
TI Automotive LLC .... C 248 494-5000
  Auburn Hills *(G-1020)*
TI Group Auto Systems LLC .... B 248 296-8000
  Auburn Hills *(G-1022)*

TUBES: Welded, Aluminum

Christianson Industries Inc .... E 269 663-8502
  Edwardsburg *(G-4763)*

TUBES: Wrought, Welded Or Lock Joint

Detroit Tubing Mill Inc .... E 313 491-8823
  Detroit *(G-4004)*
Interntonal Specialty Tube LLC .... C 313 923-2000
  Livonia *(G-9784)*
James Steel & Tube Company .... E 248 547-4200
  Madison Heights *(G-10282)*
Tarpon Industries Inc .... C 810 364-7421
  Marysville *(G-10620)*

TUBING: Copper

Midbrook Medical Dist Inc .... G 517 787-3481
  Jackson *(G-8526)*

TUBING: Flexible, Metallic

Blissfield Manufacturing Co .... B 517 486-2121
  Blissfield *(G-1713)*
Lowing Products LLC .... G 616 530-7440
  Wyoming *(G-18019)*
Versatube Corporation .... F 248 524-0299
  Troy *(G-16683)*

TUBING: Plastic

Belmont Plastics Solutions LLC .... G 616 340-3147
  Belmont *(G-1458)*
Dlhbowles Inc .... F 248 569-0652
  Southfield *(G-14883)*
Trico Products Corporation .... C 248 371-1700
  Rochester Hills *(G-13531)*

TUBING: Rubber

Trico Products Corporation .... C 248 371-1700
  Rochester Hills *(G-13531)*

TUBING: Seamless

Angstrom USA LLC .... E 313 295-0100
  Southfield *(G-14838)*
Burr Oak Tool Inc .... C 269 651-9393
  Sturgis *(G-15599)*
Michigan Seamless Tube LLC .... B 248 486-0100
  South Lyon *(G-14801)*
Perforated Tubes Inc .... E 616 942-4550
  Ada *(G-28)*
TI Automotive LLC .... C 248 494-5000
  Auburn Hills *(G-1020)*
TI Group Auto Systems LLC .... B 248 296-8000
  Auburn Hills *(G-1022)*
TI Group Auto Systems LLC .... B 248 475-4663
  Auburn Hills *(G-1025)*
Van Pelt Corporation .... F 313 365-6500
  Detroit *(G-4422)*

TUMBLING

Automotive Tumbling Co Inc .... G 313 925-7450
  Detroit *(G-3885)*
Crown Industrial Services Inc .... E 734 483-7270
  Ypsilanti *(G-18062)*
DNR Inc .... G 734 722-4000
  Plymouth *(G-12613)*
DNR Inc .... F 734 722-4000
  Westland *(G-17550)*
Liberty Burnishing Co .... G 313 366-7878
  Detroit *(G-4203)*

TUNGSTEN MILL PRDTS

Carbide Technologies Inc .... E 586 296-5200
  Fraser *(G-5634)*

TURBINE GENERATOR SET UNITS: Hydraulic, Complete

Ahd LLC .... G 586 922-6511
  Shelby Township *(G-14543)*
Marsh Plating Corporation .... D 734 483-5767
  Ypsilanti *(G-18088)*

TURBINES & TURBINE GENERATOR SET UNITS, COMPLETE

3dfx Interactive Inc .... E 918 938-8967
  Saginaw *(G-13990)*
Dowding Machining LLC .... F 517 663-5455
  Eaton Rapids *(G-4721)*

TURBINES & TURBINE GENERATOR SETS

Behco Inc .... G 248 478-6336
  Farmington Hills *(G-4940)*
Dynamic Energy Tech LLC .... G 248 212-5904
  Oak Park *(G-12062)*
Ener2 LLC .... F 248 842-2662
  Brighton *(G-1918)*
Horiba Instruments Inc .... D 734 213-6555
  Ann Arbor *(G-495)*
Kinetic Wave Power LLC .... G 989 839-9757
  Midland *(G-10880)*
Metro Machine Works Inc .... D 734 941-4571
  Romulus *(G-13707)*
Multi-Sync Power LLC .... G 734 658-3384
  Canton *(G-2410)*
Nu Con Corporation .... E 734 525-0770
  Livonia *(G-9867)*
Plasma-Tec Inc .... E 616 455-2593
  Wayland *(G-17409)*
Steel Tool & Engineering Co .... D 734 692-8580
  Brownstown Twp *(G-2072)*
Windtronics Inc .... G 231 332-1200
  Muskegon *(G-11453)*
Wmh Fluidpower Inc .... F 269 327-7011
  Portage *(G-13058)*

TURBINES: Hydraulic, Complete

Altronics Energy LLC .... F 616 662-7401
  Hudsonville *(G-8145)*

TURKEY PROCESSING & SLAUGHTERING

Michigan Turkey Producers .... B 616 245-2221
  Wyoming *(G-18020)*
Michigan Turkey Producers .... G 616 875-1838
  Zeeland *(G-18163)*
Michigan Turkey Producers .... F 616 245-2221
  Grand Rapids *(G-6676)*

TURNKEY VENDORS: Computer Systems

3dfx Interactive Inc .... E 918 938-8967
  Saginaw *(G-13990)*
Comptek Inc .... F 248 477-5215
  Farmington Hills *(G-4965)*

TWINE PRDTS

American Twisting Company .... E 269 637-8581
  South Haven *(G-14752)*

TWINE: Binder & Baler

Cascade Paper Converters LLC ...... F 616 974-9165
  Grand Rapids *(G-6263)*

TYPESETTING SVC

A 1 Printing and Copy Center .... G 269 381-0093
  Kalamazoo *(G-8671)*
A Koppel Color Image Company ...... G 616 534-3600
  Grandville *(G-7015)*
AAA Language Services .... F 248 239-1138
  Bloomfield *(G-1731)*
Adgravers Inc .... E 313 259-3780
  Detroit *(G-3842)*
Advance BCI Inc .... D 616 669-5210
  Grand Rapids *(G-6145)*
Advance Graphic Systems Inc .... E 248 656-8000
  Rochester Hills *(G-13365)*
Al Corp .... F 734 475-7357
  Chelsea *(G-2701)*
Aladdin Printing .... G 248 360-2842
  Commerce Township *(G-3386)*
Aldinger Inc .... E 517 394-2424
  Lansing *(G-9334)*
American Reprographics Co LLC .... E 248 299-8900
  Clawson *(G-2973)*
Americas Finest Prtg Graphics .... G 586 296-1312
  Fraser *(G-5618)*
Anteebo Publishers Inc .... E 313 882-6900
  Grosse Pointe Park *(G-7190)*
AP Impressions Inc .... G 734 464-8009
  Livonia *(G-9650)*
Apb Inc .... G 248 528-2990
  Troy *(G-16204)*
Argus Press Company .... D 989 725-5136
  Owosso *(G-12280)*
ASAP Printing Inc .... F 517 882-3500
  Okemos *(G-12114)*
Bastian Brothers & Company .... E 989 239-5107
  Freeland *(G-5752)*
Beljan Ltd Inc .... F 734 426-3503
  Dexter *(G-4476)*
Bookcomp Inc .... F 616 774-9700
  Belmont *(G-1459)*
Breck Graphics Incorporated .... E 616 248-4110
  Grand Rapids *(G-6235)*
Bronco Printing Company .... G 248 544-1120
  Hazel Park *(G-7435)*
Brophy Engraving Co Inc .... E 313 871-2333
  Detroit *(G-3919)*
Bruce Inc .... G 517 371-5205
  Lansing *(G-9352)*
Business Press Inc .... G 248 652-8855
  Rochester *(G-13316)*
Clark Graphic Service Inc .... D 586 772-4900
  Warren *(G-16981)*
Color Connection .... G 248 351-0920
  Southfield *(G-14870)*
Commercial Graphics of Mich .... G 810 744-2102
  Burton *(G-2150)*
Composition Unlimited Inc .... G 616 451-2222
  Grand Rapids *(G-6295)*
Copy Central Inc .... G 231 941-2298
  Traverse City *(G-15947)*
Corporate Electronic Sty Inc .... D 248 583-7070
  Troy *(G-16283)*
Daily Oakland Press .... B 248 332-8181
  Pontiac *(G-12813)*
De Vru Printing Co .... G 616 452-5451
  Grand Rapids *(G-6339)*
Dekoff & Sons Inc .... G 269 344-5816
  Kalamazoo *(G-8724)*
Delmas Typesetting .... G 734 662-8899
  Ann Arbor *(G-414)*
Derk Pieter Co Inc .... G 616 554-7777
  Grand Rapids *(G-6343)*
Detroit Legal News Pubg LLC .... E 248 577-6100
  Troy *(G-16314)*
Different By Design Inc .... E 248 588-4840
  Farmington Hills *(G-4972)*
DPrinter Inc .... G 517 423-6554
  Tecumseh *(G-15791)*
Earle Press Inc .... E 231 773-2111
  Muskegon *(G-11312)*
Econo Print Inc .... G 734 878-5806
  Pinckney *(G-12496)*
F P Horak Company .... C 989 892-6505
  Bay City *(G-1312)*
Fedex Office & Print Svcs Inc .... E 616 336-1900
  Grand Rapids *(G-6404)*
Fedex Office & Print Svcs Inc .... F 734 761-4539
  Ann Arbor *(G-459)*
Fedex Office & Print Svcs Inc .... F 248 932-3373
  Farmington Hills *(G-4998)*
Fedex Office & Print Svcs Inc .... F 517 332-5855
  East Lansing *(G-4657)*
Fedex Office & Print Svcs Inc .... E 248 355-5670
  Southfield *(G-14915)*
Fedex Office & Print Svcs Inc .... E 269 344-7445
  Portage *(G-12995)*
Fedex Office & Print Svcs Inc .... F 734 522-7322
  Westland *(G-17555)*
Fedex Office & Print Svcs Inc .... F 313 271-8877
  Dearborn *(G-3706)*
Fedex Office & Print Svcs Inc .... E 734 996-0050
  Ann Arbor *(G-460)*
Fedex Office & Print Svcs Inc .... F 248 680-0280
  Troy *(G-16361)*
Fedex Office & Print Svcs Inc .... F 517 347-8656
  Okemos *(G-12123)*
Fedex Office & Print Svcs Inc .... F 248 377-2222
  Auburn Hills *(G-870)*

Employee Codes: A=Over 500 employees, B=251-500
C=101-250, D=51-100, E=20-50, F=10-19, G=3-9

TYPESETTING SVC

Fedex Office & Print Svcs Inc ....E 616 957-7888
  Grand Rapids (G-6405)
Fedex Office & Print Svcs Inc ....E 586 296-4890
  Roseville (G-13803)
Fedex Office & Print Svcs Inc ....F 734 374-0225
  Taylor (G-15722)
Foremost Graphics LLC ....D 616 453-4747
  Grand Rapids (G-6415)
Forsons Inc ....G 517 787-4562
  Jackson (G-8450)
Future Reproductions Inc ....F 248 350-2060
  Southfield (G-14916)
GAMS Inc ....G 269 926-6765
  Benton Harbor (G-1502)
Gazette Newspapers Inc ....G 248 524-4868
  Troy (G-16380)
Genesee County Herald Inc ....F 810 686-3840
  Clio (G-3272)
Gombar Corp ....G 989 793-9427
  Saginaw (G-14048)
Grand Blanc Printing Inc ....E 810 694-1155
  Grand Blanc (G-5968)
Graphics Unlimited Inc ....G 231 773-2696
  Muskegon (G-11336)
Halsan Inc ....G 734 285-5420
  Southgate (G-15078)
Hatteras Inc ....E 734 525-5500
  Dearborn (G-3719)
Hi-Lites Graphic Inc ....E 231 924-0630
  Fremont (G-5775)
J & M International Corp ....G 248 588-8108
  Troy (G-16428)
J-Ad Graphics Inc ....D 800 870-7085
  Hastings (G-7416)
Jomark Inc ....F 248 478-2600
  Farmington Hills (G-5033)
Jtc Inc ....E 517 784-0576
  Jackson (G-8486)
Kalamazoo Photo Comp Svcs ....E 269 345-3706
  Kalamazoo (G-8794)
Larsen Graphics Inc ....E 989 823-3000
  Vassar (G-16812)
Lasertec Inc ....E 586 274-4500
  Madison Heights (G-10298)
Litsenberger Print Shop ....G 906 482-3903
  Houghton (G-7976)
Macomb Printing Inc ....E 586 463-2301
  Clinton Township (G-3163)
Marketing VI Group Inc ....G 989 793-3933
  Saginaw (G-14081)
Metropolitan Indus Lithography ....G 269 323-9333
  Portage (G-13016)
Micrgraphics Printing Inc ....E 231 739-6575
  Norton Shores (G-11773)
Microforms Inc ....D 586 939-7900
  Beverly Hills (G-1620)
Mid-State Printing Inc ....F 989 875-4163
  Ithaca (G-8364)
Millbrook Printing Co ....E 517 627-4078
  Grand Ledge (G-6112)
Mitchell Graphics Inc ....E 231 347-4635
  Petoskey (G-12459)
Moormann Printing Inc ....G 269 423-2411
  Decatur (G-3805)
Morris Communications Corp ....C 269 673-2141
  Allegan (G-177)
North American Graphics Inc ....E 586 486-1110
  Warren (G-17173)
Ogemaw County Herald Inc ....E 989 345-0044
  West Branch (G-17514)
Parkside Printing Inc ....G 810 765-4500
  Marine City (G-10479)
Parkside Speedy Print Inc ....G 810 985-8484
  Port Huron (G-12955)
Paul C Doerr ....G 734 242-2058
  Monroe (G-11260)
Peg-Master Business Forms Inc ....G 586 566-8694
  Shelby Township (G-14662)
Phase III Graphics Inc ....G 616 949-9290
  Grand Rapids (G-6753)
Plymouth-Canton Cmnty Crier ....E 734 453-6900
  Plymouth (G-12722)
Print Masters Inc ....F 248 548-7100
  Madison Heights (G-10339)
Print-Tech Inc ....E 734 996-2345
  Ann Arbor (G-604)
Printcomm Inc ....D 810 239-5763
  Flint (G-5484)
Printery Inc ....E 616 396-4655
  Holland (G-7777)

Printing Centre Inc ....F 517 694-2400
  Holt (G-7922)
Progressive Prtg & Graphics ....G 269 965-8909
  Battle Creek (G-1238)
Qrp Inc ....E 989 496-2955
  Midland (G-10906)
Qrp Inc ....G 989 496-2955
  Midland (G-10905)
Quick Printing Company Inc ....G 616 241-0506
  Grand Rapids (G-6802)
R R Donnelley & Sons Company ....D 313 964-1330
  Detroit (G-4327)
Richard Larabee ....G 248 827-7755
  Southfield (G-15015)
Rider Type & Design ....G 989 839-0015
  Midland (G-10908)
River Run Press Inc ....E 269 349-7603
  Kalamazoo (G-8873)
Safran Printing Company Inc ....E 586 939-7600
  Beverly Hills (G-1621)
Sans Serif Inc ....G 734 944-1190
  Saline (G-14414)
Spartan Printing Inc ....E 517 372-6910
  Lansing (G-9264)
Spectrum Printers Inc ....E 517 423-5735
  Tecumseh (G-15809)
Stafford Media Inc ....E 616 754-9301
  Greenville (G-7154)
Stafford Media Inc ....D 616 754-1178
  Greenville (G-7155)
Statewide Printing LLC ....G 517 485-4466
  Lansing (G-9268)
T J K Inc ....G 586 731-9639
  Sterling Heights (G-15518)
Technology MGT & Budgt Dept ....D 517 322-1897
  Lansing (G-9430)
TGI Direct Inc ....F 810 239-5553
  Ann Arbor (G-667)
The Envelope Printery Inc ....D 734 398-7700
  Van Buren Twp (G-16787)
Thomas Kenyon Inc ....G 248 476-8130
  Saint Clair Shores (G-14272)
Times Herald Company ....F 810 985-7171
  Port Huron (G-12971)
Turner Business Forms Inc ....E 989 752-5540
  Saginaw (G-14171)
Val Valley Inc ....G 248 474-7335
  Farmington Hills (G-5145)
Village Shop Inc ....D 231 946-3712
  Traverse City (G-16138)
We Print Everything Inc ....G 989 723-6499
  Owosso (G-12328)
Wolverine Printing Company LLC ....E 616 451-2075
  Grand Rapids (G-6999)
Woodhams Enterprises Inc ....G 269 383-0600
  Climax (G-3014)
Worten Copy Center Inc ....G 231 845-7030
  Ludington (G-10089)

TYPESETTING SVC: Computer

Computer Composition Corp ....F 248 545-4330
  Madison Heights (G-10218)
P D Q Press Inc ....G 586 725-1888
  Ira (G-8265)
Poly Tech Industries Inc ....G 248 589-9950
  Madison Heights (G-10331)
Skip Printing and Dup Co ....G 586 779-2640
  Roseville (G-13870)
Thorpe Printing Services Inc ....G 810 364-6222
  Marysville (G-10622)
Whiteside Consulting Group LLC ....G 313 288-6598
  Detroit (G-4440)

TYPESETTING SVC: Hand Composition

Loc Industries Inc ....G 586 759-8412
  Warren (G-17129)

ULTRASONIC EQPT: Cleaning, Exc Med & Dental

Branson Ultrasonics Corp ....F 586 276-0150
  Sterling Heights (G-15277)
Electro-Matic Visual Inc ....G 248 478-1182
  Farmington Hills (G-4982)
Gvn Group Corp ....E 248 340-0342
  Pontiac (G-12831)
H & R Industries Inc ....F 616 247-1165
  Grand Rapids (G-6487)
Power Cleaning Systems Inc ....G 248 347-7727
  Wixom (G-17878)

Telsonic Ultrasonics Inc ....E 586 802-0033
  Shelby Township (G-14708)
Weber Ultrasonics America LLC ....G 248 620-5142
  Clarkston (G-2964)

UMBRELLAS & CANES

Brollytime Inc ....F 312 854-7606
  Royal Oak (G-13911)

UNDERGROUND IRON ORE MINING

Constine Inc ....E 989 723-6043
  Owosso (G-12284)

UNIFORM STORES

Allie Brothers Inc ....F 248 477-4434
  Livonia (G-9635)
Embroidery Shoppe LLC ....G 734 595-7612
  Westland (G-17552)
G T Jerseys LLC ....G 248 588-3231
  Troy (G-16376)
P & D Uniforms and ACC Inc ....G 313 881-3881
  Eastpointe (G-4708)

UNIVERSITY

Central Michigan University ....F 989 774-3216
  Mount Pleasant (G-11187)
Eastern Michigan University ....D 734 487-1010
  Ypsilanti (G-18068)
Regents of The University Mich ....E 734 764-4388
  Ann Arbor (G-616)
Regents of The University Mich ....F 734 936-0435
  Ann Arbor (G-617)
Regents of The University Mich ....E 734 973-2400
  Ann Arbor (G-618)
Univesity Michigan-Dearborn ....F 313 593-5428
  Dearborn (G-3767)

UNSUPPORTED PLASTICS: Tile

Dow Chemical Company ....G 989 636-1000
  Midland (G-10840)

UPHOLSTERY FILLING MATERIALS

Gabriel North America Inc ....G 616 202-5770
  Grand Rapids (G-6429)
Guilford of Maine Marketing Co ....D 616 554-2250
  Grand Rapids (G-6485)

UPHOLSTERY MATERIAL

La-Z-Boy Casegoods Inc ....E 734 242-1444
  Monroe (G-11047)

URNS: Cut Stone

Eternal Image Inc ....G 248 932-3333
  Farmington Hills (G-4990)

USED CAR DEALERS

Crain Communications Inc ....B 313 446-6000
  Detroit (G-3951)
Floss Automotive Group ....G 734 773-2524
  Inkster (G-8227)
Trucksforsalecom ....G 989 883-3382
  Sebewaing (G-14520)

USED CLOTHING STORES

Goodwill Inds Nthrn Mich Inc ....G 231 779-1311
  Cadillac (G-2250)

USED MERCHANDISE STORES

Goodwill Inds Nthrn Mich Inc ....G 231 779-1361
  Cadillac (G-2251)
Goodwill Inds Nthrn Mich Inc ....G 231 922-4890
  Traverse City (G-15981)
Services To Enhance Potential ....G 313 278-3040
  Dearborn (G-3757)

USED MERCHANDISE STORES: Office Furniture & Store Fixtures

Anso Products ....G 248 357-2300
  Southfield (G-14839)

PRODUCT SECTION   VALVES: Engine

UTENSILS: Household, Cooking & Kitchen, Metal

Seasoned Home LLC .... G 616 392-8350
  Holland *(G-7797)*

UTILITY TRAILER DEALERS

Ajax Trailers Inc .... F 586 757-7676
  Warren *(G-16923)*
Tow-Line Trailers .... G 989 752-0055
  Saginaw *(G-14165)*
Woodland Industries .... G 989 686-6176
  Kawkawlin *(G-8976)*

VACUUM CLEANER REPAIR SVCS

Ameri-Serv Group .... F 734 426-9700
  Troy *(G-16195)*
Wal-Vac Inc .... G 616 241-6717
  Wyoming *(G-18042)*

VACUUM CLEANER STORES

Electrolux Professional Inc .... G 248 338-4320
  Pontiac *(G-12821)*

VACUUM CLEANERS: Household

Bissell Better Life LLC .... G 800 237-7691
  Grand Rapids *(G-6224)*
Bissell Homecare Inc .... C 616 453-4451
  Grand Rapids *(G-6225)*
Electrolux Professional Inc .... G 248 338-4320
  Pontiac *(G-12821)*
Maytag Corporation .... C 269 923-5000
  Benton Harbor *(G-1529)*
Rexair Holdings Inc .... G 248 643-7222
  Troy *(G-16578)*
Rexair LLC .... G 248 643-7222
  Troy *(G-16579)*
Wal-Vac Inc .... G 616 241-6717
  Wyoming *(G-18042)*
Whirlpool Corporation .... A 269 923-5000
  Benton Harbor *(G-1565)*
Whirlpool Corporation .... G 269 923-5000
  Benton Harbor *(G-1566)*
Whirlpool Corporation .... B 269 923-5000
  Benton Harbor *(G-1570)*

VACUUM CLEANERS: Indl Type

Birks Works Environmental LLC .... G 313 891-1310
  Detroit *(G-3904)*
Bissell Better Life LLC .... G 800 237-7691
  Grand Rapids *(G-6224)*
Hydrochem LLC .... C 313 841-5800
  Monroe *(G-11040)*
Vaclovers Inc .... E 616 246-1700
  Grand Rapids *(G-6956)*

VACUUM CLEANERS: Wholesalers

Electrolux Professional Inc .... G 248 338-4320
  Pontiac *(G-12821)*

VALUE-ADDED RESELLERS: Computer Systems

Christopher S Campion .... G 517 414-6796
  Jackson *(G-8409)*
Edi Experts LLC .... G 734 844-7016
  Canton *(G-2370)*

VALVE REPAIR SVCS, INDL

Fcx Performance Inc .... E 734 654-2201
  Carleton *(G-2454)*
Rvm Company of Toledo .... E 734 654-2201
  Carleton *(G-2462)*

VALVES

Air Brake Systems Inc .... G 989 775-8880
  Mount Pleasant *(G-11168)*
Autocam-Pax Inc .... E 269 782-5186
  Dowagiac *(G-4534)*
Bucher Hydraulics Inc .... E 231 652-2773
  Newaygo *(G-11564)*
Flowcor LLC .... G 616 554-1100
  Kentwood *(G-9006)*
Nelms Technologies Inc .... D 734 955-6500
  Romulus *(G-13712)*
Polyvalve LLC .... G 616 656-2264
  Kentwood *(G-9025)*

VALVES & PARTS: Gas, Indl

Key Gas Components Inc .... E 269 673-2151
  Allegan *(G-169)*

VALVES & PIPE FITTINGS

2 Brothers Holdings LLC .... G 517 487-3900
  Lansing *(G-9330)*
Anrod Screen Cylinder Company .... E 989 872-2101
  Cass City *(G-2511)*
Autocam-Pax Inc .... E 269 782-5186
  Dowagiac *(G-4534)*
Automatic Valve Corp .... E 248 474-6761
  Novi *(G-11835)*
Barbron Corporation .... E 586 716-3530
  Kalkaska *(G-8937)*
Beaden Screen Inc .... E 810 679-3119
  Croswell *(G-3595)*
Bucher Hydraulics Inc .... E 231 652-2773
  Newaygo *(G-11564)*
Cal Grinding Inc .... E 906 786-8749
  Escanaba *(G-4821)*
Colonial Engineering Inc .... F 269 323-2495
  Portage *(G-12989)*
Computer Operated Mfg .... E 989 686-1333
  Bay City *(G-1297)*
Conley Composites LLC .... E 918 299-5051
  Grand Rapids *(G-6300)*
Dcl Inc .... C 231 547-5600
  Charlevoix *(G-2613)*
Delta Machining Inc .... D 269 683-7775
  Niles *(G-11608)*
Dexter Automatic Products Co .... C 734 426-8900
  Dexter *(G-4485)*
Dover Energy Inc .... C 248 836-6750
  Auburn Hills *(G-842)*
Dutchman Mfg Co LLC .... G 734 922-5803
  Traverse City *(G-15959)*
Eaton Corporation .... C 517 787-7220
  Jackson *(G-8439)*
Eaton-Aeroquip Llc .... B 949 452-9575
  Jackson *(G-8440)*
Extrusion Punch & Tool Inc .... E 248 689-3300
  Troy *(G-16357)*
Flow-Rite Controls Ltd .... E 616 583-1700
  Byron Center *(G-2191)*
Great Lakes Hydra Corporation .... F 616 949-8844
  Grand Rapids *(G-6479)*
Hill Machinery Co .... D 616 940-2800
  Grand Rapids *(G-6514)*
Jdl Enterprises Inc .... F 586 977-8863
  Sterling Heights *(G-15380)*
Jet Industries Inc .... E 734 641-0900
  Westland *(G-17574)*
Key Gas Components Inc .... E 269 673-2151
  Allegan *(G-169)*
Lennon Fluid Systems LLC .... E 248 474-6624
  Farmington Hills *(G-5043)*
Loftis Alumi-TEC Inc .... E 616 846-1990
  Grand Haven *(G-6050)*
Lpm Supply Inc .... G 248 333-9440
  Pontiac *(G-12846)*
Mac Valve Asia Inc .... G 248 624-7700
  Wixom *(G-17851)*
Mac Valves Inc. .... A 248 624-7700
  Wixom *(G-17852)*
Mac Valves Inc. .... E 734 529-5099
  Dundee *(G-4594)*
Marshall Excelsior Co .... E 269 789-6700
  Marshall *(G-10577)*
Maxitrol Company .... D 248 356-1400
  Southfield *(G-14974)*
Maxitrol Company .... E 517 486-2820
  Blissfield *(G-1719)*
Melling Tool Co .... B 517 787-8172
  Jackson *(G-8514)*
Mueller Industries Inc .... D 248 446-3720
  Brighton *(G-1964)*
Nitz Valve Hardware Inc .... F 989 883-9500
  Sebewaing *(G-14517)*
Nordson Corporation .... D 734 459-8600
  Wixom *(G-17866)*
Novi Tool & Machine Company .... D 313 532-0900
  Redford *(G-13176)*
Npi .... G 248 478-0010
  Farmington Hills *(G-5083)*
Parker-Hannifin Corporation .... B 269 629-5000
  Richland *(G-13252)*
Parker-Hannifin Corporation .... B 269 694-9411
  Otsego *(G-12249)*
Pittsfield Products Inc .... E 734 665-3771
  Ann Arbor *(G-593)*
Power Process Engrg Co Inc .... G 248 473-8450
  Novi *(G-11975)*
Primore Inc .... E 517 263-2220
  Adrian *(G-88)*
Quality Filters Inc .... F 734 668-0211
  Ann Arbor *(G-611)*
Quality Pipe Products Inc .... E 734 606-5100
  New Boston *(G-11509)*
R M Wright Company Inc .... E 248 476-9800
  Farmington Hills *(G-5111)*
River Valley Machine Inc .... E 269 673-8070
  Allegan *(G-187)*
Rosedale Products Inc .... D 734 665-8201
  Ann Arbor *(G-624)*
Scott Machine Inc .... E 517 787-6616
  Jackson *(G-8571)*
Set Liquidation Inc .... D 517 694-2300
  Holt *(G-7928)*
SH Leggitt Company .... C 269 781-3901
  Marshall *(G-10588)*
Sloan Valve Company .... D 248 446-5300
  New Hudson *(G-11555)*
Srg Global Coatings Inc .... C 248 509-1100
  Troy *(G-16618)*
Tops All Clamps Inc .... G 313 533-7500
  Redford *(G-13202)*
Tribal Manufacturing Inc .... E 269 781-3901
  Marshall *(G-10591)*
Unist Inc .... E 616 949-0853
  Grand Rapids *(G-6951)*
Ventura Aerospace LLC .... E 734 357-0114
  Wixom *(G-17925)*
Wayne Wire Cloth Products Inc .... C 989 742-4591
  Hillman *(G-7510)*

VALVES & REGULATORS: Pressure, Indl

Century Instrument Company .... E 734 427-0340
  Livonia *(G-9681)*
Mercury Manufacturing Company .... D 734 285-5150
  Wyandotte *(G-17968)*

VALVES: Aerosol, Metal

Greenville Engineered & Tooled .... G 616 292-0701
  Greenville *(G-7134)*
Metal Standard Corp .... D 616 396-6356
  Holland *(G-7744)*
Mpg Inc .... A 734 207-6200
  Plymouth *(G-12696)*
National Ordnance Auto Mfg LLC ...... G 248 853-8822
  Auburn Hills *(G-953)*
Oronoko Iron Works Inc .... G 269 326-7045
  Baroda *(G-1128)*

VALVES: Aircraft, Control, Hydraulic & Pneumatic

Airman Inc .... E 248 960-1354
  Brighton *(G-1880)*

VALVES: Aircraft, Fluid Power

Eaton-Aeroquip Llc .... B 949 452-9575
  Jackson *(G-8440)*

VALVES: Control, Automatic

Asco LP .... C 248 596-3200
  Novi *(G-11830)*
Honeywell International Inc .... D 248 926-4800
  Wixom *(G-17827)*
Primore Inc .... F 517 263-2220
  Adrian *(G-87)*

VALVES: Engine

Cal Grinding Inc .... E 906 786-8749
  Escanaba *(G-4821)*
Dexter Automatic Products Co .... C 734 426-8900
  Dexter *(G-4485)*
Federal-Mogul Valve Train Inte .... E 248 354-7700
  Southfield *(G-14912)*
L E Jones Company .... B 906 863-1043
  Menominee *(G-10741)*

Employee Codes: A=Over 500 employees, B=251-500
C=101-250, D=51-100, E=20-50, F=10-19, G=3-9

2020 Harris Michigan Industrial Directory

1391

VALVES: Fluid Power, Control, Hydraulic & pneumatic

PRODUCT SECTION

VALVES: Fluid Power, Control, Hydraulic & pneumatic

- Airman Products LLC .... E 248 960-1354
  Brighton *(G-1881)*
- Buhler Technologies LLC .... F 248 652-1546
  Rochester Hills *(G-13379)*
- Humphrey Products Company .... C 269 381-5500
  Kalamazoo *(G-8770)*
- Mac Valve Asia Inc .... G 248 624-7700
  Wixom *(G-17851)*
- Mac Valves Inc .... A 248 624-7700
  Wixom *(G-17852)*
- McLaren Inc .... G 989 720-4328
  Owosso *(G-12302)*
- Oilgear Company .... D 231 929-1660
  Traverse City *(G-16055)*
- Parker-Hannifin Corporation .... D 330 253-5239
  Otsego *(G-12251)*
- Stonebrdge Technical Entps Ltd .... F 810 750-0040
  Fenton *(G-5240)*
- Wmh Fluidpower Inc .... F 269 327-7011
  Portage *(G-13058)*

VALVES: Indl

- Asco LP .... C 810 648-9141
  Sandusky *(G-14428)*
- Automatic Valve Corp .... E 248 474-6761
  Novi *(G-11835)*
- Champion Charter Sls & Svc Inc .... G 906 779-2300
  Iron Mountain *(G-8280)*
- Conley Composites LLC .... E 918 299-5051
  Grand Rapids *(G-6300)*
- Dss Valve Products Inc .... F 269 409-6080
  Niles *(G-11609)*
- Dutchman Mfg Co LLC .... G 734 922-5803
  Traverse City *(G-15959)*
- Fcx Performance Inc .... E 734 654-2201
  Carleton *(G-2454)*
- Flaretite Inc .... G 810 750-4140
  Brighton *(G-1923)*
- Flowtek Inc .... F 231 734-3415
  Evart *(G-4881)*
- Hills-Mccanna LLC .... D 616 554-9308
  Kentwood *(G-9011)*
- Hydronic Components Inc .... F 586 268-1640
  Warren *(G-17084)*
- Instrument and Valve Services .... G 734 459-0375
  Plymouth *(G-12647)*
- Jdl Enterprises Inc .... G 586 977-8863
  Warren *(G-17113)*
- Jdl Enterprises Inc .... F 586 977-8863
  Sterling Heights *(G-15380)*
- Mac Valve Asia Inc .... G 248 624-7700
  Wixom *(G-17851)*
- Mac Valves Inc .... A 248 624-7700
  Wixom *(G-17852)*
- Mac Valves Inc .... E 734 529-5099
  Dundee *(G-4594)*
- Morgold Inc .... G 269 445-3844
  Cassopolis *(G-2534)*
- Nil-Cor LLC .... C 616 554-3100
  Kentwood *(G-9021)*
- Nordson Corporation .... D 734 459-8600
  Wixom *(G-17866)*
- Novi Tool & Machine Company .... D 313 532-0900
  Redford *(G-13176)*
- Primore Inc .... E 517 263-2220
  Adrian *(G-88)*
- Sedco Inc .... E 517 263-2220
  Adrian *(G-95)*
- SH Leggitt Company .... C 269 781-3901
  Marshall *(G-10588)*
- Sloan Transportation Pdts Inc .... D 616 395-5600
  Holland *(G-7806)*
- Triad Process Equipment Inc .... G 248 685-9938
  Milford *(G-10989)*

VALVES: Plumbing & Heating

- Dart Energy Center .... G 248 203-2924
  Birmingham *(G-1680)*
- Genova Products Inc .... D 810 744-4500
  Davison *(G-3650)*
- Metal Forming Technology Inc .... F 586 949-4586
  Chesterfield *(G-2803)*

VALVES: Regulating & Control, Automatic

- Ecorse McHy Sls & Rbldrs Inc .... E 313 383-2100
  Wyandotte *(G-17956)*

- Marshall Gas Controls Inc .... G 269 781-3901
  Marshall *(G-10578)*

VALVES: Regulating, Process Control

- Neptech Inc .... E 810 225-2222
  Highland *(G-7498)*

VALVES: Water Works

- Rocon LLC .... G 248 542-9635
  Hazel Park *(G-7453)*

VAN CONVERSIONS

- Lippert Components Mfg Inc .... C 989 845-3061
  Chesaning *(G-2725)*
- Mid-West Truck Accessories .... G 313 592-1788
  Detroit *(G-4247)*
- Mobility Trnsp Svcs Inc .... E 734 453-6452
  Canton *(G-2406)*
- Mobilitytrans LLC .... E 734 453-6452
  Canton *(G-2407)*

VAN CONVERSIONS

- Frank Industries Inc .... E 810 346-3234
  Brown City *(G-2051)*
- Riverside Vans Inc .... F 269 432-3212
  Colon *(G-3375)*

VEHICLE DRIVING SCHOOL

- Liquid Drive Corporation .... E 248 634-5382
  Mount Clemens *(G-11139)*

VEHICLES: All Terrain

- Power Sports Ann Arbor LLC .... F 734 585-3300
  Ann Arbor *(G-597)*
- Rdz Racing Incorporated .... G 517 468-3254
  Fowlerville *(G-5578)*

VEHICLES: Recreational

- Chassis Shop Prfmce Pdts Inc .... G 231 873-3640
  Mears *(G-10686)*
- Christmas Sports Enterprise .... G 616 895-6238
  Hudsonville *(G-8150)*
- Ds Automotion LLC .... G 248 370-8950
  Rochester *(G-13319)*
- H W Motor Homes Inc .... G 734 394-2000
  Canton *(G-2382)*
- K & K Racing LLC .... F 906 322-1276
  Sault Sainte Marie *(G-14467)*
- Rocky Mountain Rv .... G 435 713-4242
  Grand Rapids *(G-6833)*
- Sled Shed Enterprises LLC .... G 517 783-5136
  Jackson *(G-8573)*

VENDING MACHINE OPERATORS: Sandwich & Hot Food

- Ace Vending Service Inc .... E 616 243-7983
  Grand Rapids *(G-6135)*

VENDING MACHINES & PARTS

- Gail Parker .... G 734 261-3842
  Garden City *(G-5825)*
- Maytag Corporation .... C 269 923-5000
  Benton Harbor *(G-1529)*
- Quarters LLC .... G 313 510-5555
  Plymouth *(G-12727)*

VENETIAN BLINDS & SHADES

- Elsie Inc .... F 734 421-8844
  Livonia *(G-9726)*

VENTILATING EQPT: Metal

- Hmw Contracting LLC .... C 313 531-8477
  Detroit *(G-4125)*
- L D S Sheet Metal Inc .... G 313 892-2624
  Warren *(G-17124)*
- Selkirk Corporation .... E 616 656-8200
  Grand Rapids *(G-6857)*
- Ventilation + Plus Eqp Inc .... G 231 487-1156
  Harbor Springs *(G-7297)*

VENTILATING EQPT: Sheet Metal

- Air Conditioning Products Co .... D 734 326-0050
  Romulus *(G-13649)*

- Commercial Indus A Sltions LLC .... G 269 373-8797
  Kalamazoo *(G-8709)*

VESSELS: Process, Indl, Metal Plate

- Old Xembedded LLC .... G 734 975-0577
  Ann Arbor *(G-582)*

VETERINARY PHARMACEUTICAL PREPARATIONS

- Ionxhealth Inc .... E 616 808-3290
  Grand Rapids *(G-6544)*
- Jice Pharmaceuticals Co Inc .... G 616 897-5910
  Belding *(G-1420)*
- Zomedica Pharmaceuticals Corp .... F 734 369-2555
  Ann Arbor *(G-711)*

VETERINARY PRDTS: Instruments & Apparatus

- Neogen Corporation .... B 517 372-9200
  Lansing *(G-9405)*
- Robert A Nelson .... G 231 597-9225
  Cheboygan *(G-2693)*

VIBRATORS: Concrete Construction

- Midwest Vibro Inc .... G 616 532-7670
  Grandville *(G-7058)*

VIBRATORS: Interrupter

- Aprotech Powertrain LLC .... E 248 649-9200
  Troy *(G-16206)*

VIDEO & AUDIO EQPT, WHOLESALE

- City Animation Co .... E 248 589-0600
  Troy *(G-16268)*
- City Animation Co .... F 989 743-3458
  Corunna *(G-3579)*
- Corporate AV Services LLC .... G 248 939-0900
  Commerce Township *(G-3395)*
- Startech-Solutions LLC .... G 248 419-0650
  West Bloomfield *(G-17499)*
- Startech-Solutions LLC .... G 248 419-0650
  Southfield *(G-15033)*
- Thalner Electronic Labs Inc .... E 734 761-4506
  Ann Arbor *(G-668)*

VIDEO PRODUCTION SVCS

- Freshwater Dgtal Mdia Prtnrs .... F 616 446-1771
  Kentwood *(G-9007)*

VIDEO REPAIR SVCS

- Bluewater Tech Group Inc .... C 248 356-4399
  Southfield *(G-14854)*

VIDEO TAPE PRODUCTION SVCS

- City Animation Co .... E 248 589-0600
  Troy *(G-16268)*
- City Animation Co .... F 989 743-3458
  Corunna *(G-3579)*
- Safari Circuits Inc .... C 269 694-9471
  Otsego *(G-12255)*
- Super Video Service Center .... G 248 358-4794
  Southfield *(G-15037)*

VINYL RESINS, NEC

- Weatherproof Inc .... E 517 764-1330
  Jackson *(G-8606)*

VISES: Machine

- Yost Vises LLC .... G 616 396-2063
  Holland *(G-7867)*

VISUAL COMMUNICATIONS SYSTEMS

- Advanced-Cable LLC .... F 586 491-3073
  Troy *(G-16170)*
- Blackbox Visual Design Inc .... G 734 459-1307
  Plymouth *(G-12588)*
- Bluewater Tech Group Inc .... G 248 356-4399
  Farmington Hills *(G-4943)*
- Nationwide Communications LLC .... G 517 990-1223
  Jackson *(G-8541)*
- Tpk America LLC .... F 616 786-5300
  Holland *(G-7832)*

PRODUCT SECTION

VITAMINS: Natural Or Synthetic, Uncompounded, Bulk

Access Business Group LLC .... B 616 787-6000
  Ada *(G-3)*
Alticor Global Holdings Inc .... F 616 787-1000
  Ada *(G-5)*
Alticor Inc .... C 616 787-1000
  Ada *(G-6)*
Kinder Products Unlimited LLC .... G 586 557-3453
  Sterling Heights *(G-15389)*
Visionary Vitamin Co .... G 734 788-5934
  Melvindale *(G-10708)*

VITAMINS: Pharmaceutical Preparations

Pro Bottle LLC .... G 248 345-9224
  Williamston *(G-17737)*
Supplement Group Inc .... F 248 588-2055
  Madison Heights *(G-10365)*

VOCATIONAL REHABILITATION AGENCY

Crossroads Industries Inc .... D 989 732-1233
  Gaylord *(G-5853)*
Lakestate Industries Inc .... E 906 786-9212
  Escanaba *(G-4838)*
MRC Industries Inc .... D 269 343-0747
  Kalamazoo *(G-8832)*
Peckham Vocational Inds Inc .... A 517 316-4000
  Lansing *(G-9252)*
Peckham Vocational Inds Inc .... C 517 316-4478
  Lansing *(G-9253)*
Svrc Industries Inc .... E 989 280-3038
  Saginaw *(G-14159)*
Svrc Industries Inc .... D 989 723-8205
  Owosso *(G-12320)*

VOCATIONAL TRAINING AGENCY

Mid-Michigan Industries Inc .... D 989 773-6918
  Mount Pleasant *(G-11208)*
Mid-Michigan Industries Inc .... E 989 386-7707
  Clare *(G-2877)*

WALLBOARD, EXC GYPSUM

Holland Panel Products Inc .... E 616 392-1826
  Holland *(G-7674)*

WALLS: Curtain, Metal

Northern Michigan Glass LLC .... E 231 941-0050
  Traverse City *(G-16051)*

WAREHOUSING & STORAGE FACILITIES, NEC

Intern Metals and Energy .... G 248 765-7747
  Jackson *(G-8471)*
Irish Boat Shop Inc .... E 231 547-9967
  Charlevoix *(G-2619)*
Materials Processing Inc .... D 734 282-1888
  Riverview *(G-13301)*
Span America Detroit Inc .... E 734 957-1600
  Van Buren Twp *(G-16784)*
Unlimited Marine Inc .... G 248 249-0222
  White Lake *(G-17641)*

WAREHOUSING & STORAGE, REFRIGERATED: Cold Storage Or Refrig

All American Whse & Cold Stor .... E 313 865-3870
  Detroit *(G-3856)*
Burnette Foods Inc .... E 231 223-4282
  Traverse City *(G-15924)*

WAREHOUSING & STORAGE, REFRIGERATED: Frozen Or Refrig Goods

Hanson Cold Storage Co .... F 269 982-1390
  Saint Joseph *(G-14314)*

WAREHOUSING & STORAGE: Farm Prdts

Chelsea Grain LLC .... G 734 475-1386
  Chelsea *(G-2703)*

WAREHOUSING & STORAGE: General

Alliance Polymers and Svcs LLC .... G 734 710-6700
  Romulus *(G-13650)*
Aptargroup Inc .... C 989 631-8030
  Midland *(G-10816)*
Eberspaecher North America Inc .... E 517 303-1775
  Wixom *(G-17798)*
Greer Industries Inc .... E 800 388-2868
  Ferndale *(G-5292)*
Il Enterprises Inc .... F 734 285-6030
  Wyandotte *(G-17962)*
Iroquois Industries Inc .... E 586 756-6922
  Warren *(G-17101)*
Materion Brush Inc .... F 586 443-4925
  Warren *(G-17143)*
Nicholson Terminal & Dock Co .... C 313 842-4300
  River Rouge *(G-13279)*
Pepsi-Cola Metro Btlg Co Inc .... D 616 285-8200
  Grand Rapids *(G-6747)*
Summit-Reed City Inc .... E 989 433-5716
  Rosebush *(G-13765)*
Twin City Engraving Company .... G 269 983-0601
  Saint Joseph *(G-14346)*

WAREHOUSING & STORAGE: General

ABB Motors and Mechanical Inc .... F 586 978-9800
  Sterling Heights *(G-15248)*
AEL/Span LLC .... E 734 957-1600
  Van Buren Twp *(G-16746)*
Aunt Millies Bakeries Inc .... E 734 528-1475
  Ypsilanti *(G-18053)*
General Mills Inc .... G 269 337-0288
  Kalamazoo *(G-8750)*
Hanson Cold Storage Co .... F 269 982-1390
  Saint Joseph *(G-14314)*
Korten Quality Inc .... C 586 752-6255
  Bruce Twp *(G-2086)*
Manufacturing Products & Svcs .... F 734 927-1964
  Plymouth *(G-12683)*
Materials Processing Inc .... D 734 282-1888
  Riverview *(G-13301)*
Pepsi-Cola Metro Btlg Co Inc .... E 810 987-2181
  Kimball *(G-9047)*
Roger Mix Storage .... G 231 352-9762
  Frankfort *(G-5605)*
Ryder Integrated Logistics Inc .... A 517 492-4446
  Lansing *(G-9321)*
Transpak Inc .... E 586 264-2064
  Sterling Heights *(G-15528)*
West Mich Off Interiors Inc .... G 269 344-0768
  Kalamazoo *(G-8923)*
Western International Inc .... E 866 814-2470
  Troy *(G-16689)*

WAREHOUSING & STORAGE: Liquid

Trelleborg Corporation .... G 269 639-9891
  South Haven *(G-14778)*

WAREHOUSING & STORAGE: Miniwarehouse

Pro Connections LLC .... G 269 962-4219
  Springfield *(G-15201)*
Shady Nook Farms .... G 989 236-7240
  Middleton *(G-10795)*

WAREHOUSING & STORAGE: Self Storage

Sparta Wash & Storage LLC .... G 616 887-1034
  Sparta *(G-15111)*

WAREHOUSING & STORAGE: Textile

McCarthy Group Incorporated .... G 616 977-2900
  Grand Rapids *(G-6652)*

WARM AIR HEATING & AC EQPT & SPLYS, WHOL: Dust Collecting

Beckert & Hiester Inc .... G 989 793-2420
  Saginaw *(G-14003)*
Paul Horn and Associates .... G 248 682-8490
  Waterford *(G-17365)*

WARM AIR HEATING & AC EQPT & SPLYS, WHOLESALE Air Filters

Aero Filter Inc .... E 248 837-4100
  Madison Heights *(G-10183)*
Omega Industries Michigan LLC .... G 616 460-0500
  Grand Rapids *(G-6729)*

WARM AIR HEATING & AC EQPT & SPLYS, WHOLESALE Furnaces, Elec

Phoenix Induction Corporation .... F 248 486-7377
  South Lyon *(G-14809)*

WARM AIR HEATING/AC EQPT/SPLYS, WHOL Dehumidifiers, Exc Port

Compressor Technologies Inc .... F 616 949-7000
  Grand Rapids *(G-6296)*

WARM AIR HEATING/AC EQPT/SPLYS, WHOL Warm Air Htg Eqpt/Splys

Industrial Temperature Control .... G 734 451-8740
  Canton *(G-2384)*
Vic Bond Sales Inc .... G 517 548-0107
  Howell *(G-8121)*

WASHERS

Ecoclean Inc .... C 248 450-2000
  Southfield *(G-14897)*
Michigan Steel Finishing Co .... F 313 838-3925
  Detroit *(G-4243)*
Steel Master LLC .... E 810 771-4943
  Grand Blanc *(G-5984)*
Under Pressure Pwr Washers LLC ...... G 616 292-4289
  Marne *(G-10514)*
Utica Washers .... G 313 571-1568
  Detroit *(G-4419)*

WASHERS: Metal

Prestige Stamping LLC .... C 586 773-2700
  Warren *(G-17196)*
Washers Incorporated .... C 734 523-1000
  Livonia *(G-9999)*
Washers Incorporated .... G 734 523-1000
  Livonia *(G-10000)*

WASHING MACHINES: Household

Whirlpool Corporation .... B 269 923-5000
  Benton Harbor *(G-1570)*

WATCH REPAIR SVCS

Preusser Jewelers .... G 616 458-1425
  Grand Rapids *(G-6773)*

WATER HEATERS

Bradford-White Corporation .... A 269 795-3364
  Middleville *(G-10799)*

WATER HEATERS WHOLESALERS EXCEPT ELECTRIC

Lochinvar LLC .... E 734 454-4480
  Plymouth *(G-12676)*

WATER PURIFICATION EQPT: Household

Business Connect L3c .... G 616 443-8070
  Grandville *(G-7025)*

WATER PURIFICATION PRDTS: Chlorination Tablets & Kits

Kassouni Manufacturing Inc .... E 616 794-0989
  Belding *(G-1423)*

WATER SOFTENER SVCS

Aqua Fine Inc .... G 616 392-7843
  Holland *(G-7560)*
Bauer Soft Water Co .... G 269 695-7900
  Niles *(G-11596)*
Douglas Water Conditioning .... E 248 363-8383
  Waterford *(G-17336)*
Lane Soft Water .... G 269 673-3272
  Allegan *(G-175)*
McIntyre Softwater Service .... E 810 735-5778
  Linden *(G-9593)*
Village & Country Water Trtmnt .... F 810 632-7880
  Hartland *(G-7395)*

WATER SOFTENING WHOLESALERS

Michigan Soft Water of Centr .... D 517 339-0722
  East Lansing *(G-4669)*

WATER SOFTENING WHOLESALERS

Plymouth Technology Inc ....F 248 537-0081
  Rochester Hills (G-13496)

WATER SPLY: Irrigation

Jolman & Jolman Enterprises ....G 231 744-4500
  Muskegon (G-11355)

WATER TREATMENT EQPT: Indl

City of Port Huron ....E 810 984-9775
  Port Huron (G-12908)
D & L Water Control Inc ....F 734 455-6982
  Canton (G-2363)
Dancorp Inc ....F 269 663-5566
  Edwardsburg (G-4764)
Digested Organics LLC ....G 844 934-4378
  Farmington Hills (G-4973)
Dihydro Services Inc ....E 586 978-0900
  Sterling Heights (G-15317)
Douglas Water Conditioning ....E 248 363-8383
  Waterford (G-17336)
Ener-TEC Inc ....F 517 741-5015
  Union City (G-16733)
Evoqua Water Technologies LLC ....D 616 772-9011
  Holland (G-7629)
GCI Water Solutions LLC ....G 312 928-9992
  Midland (G-10865)
H-O-H Water Technology Inc ....F 248 669-6667
  Commerce Township (G-3409)
J Mark Systems Inc ....G 616 784-6005
  Grand Rapids (G-6548)
Mar Cor Purification Inc ....F 248 373-7844
  Lake Orion (G-9148)
Menominee City of Michigan ....G 906 863-3050
  Menominee (G-10746)
Monroe Environmental Corp............E 734 242-2420
  Monroe (G-11054)
North American Aqua Envmtl LLC ....F 269 476-2092
  Vandalia (G-16802)
Reynolds Water Conditioning Co ....F 248 888-5000
  Farmington Hills (G-5114)
Seymour Dehaan............G 269 672-7377
  Martin (G-10597)
Telespector Corporation ....F 248 373-5400
  Auburn Hills (G-1017)
Vanaire Inc ....D 906 428-4656
  Gladstone (G-5921)
Vital Technologies ....G 231 352-9364
  Frankfort (G-5607)

WATER: Distilled

Shay Water Co Inc ....E 989 755-3221
  Saginaw (G-14148)

WATER: Mineral, Carbonated, Canned & Bottled, Etc

Aqua Fine Inc ....G 616 392-7843
  Holland (G-7560)

WATER: Pasteurized & Mineral, Bottled & Canned

Arbor Springs Water Company ....E 734 668-8270
  Ann Arbor (G-365)
Crystal Pure Water Inc............G 989 681-3547
  Saint Louis (G-14362)
Pure Water Tech of Mid-MI ....G 888 310-9848
  Grand Blanc (G-5979)

WATER: Pasteurized, Canned & Bottled, Etc

Absopure Water Company LLC............B 734 459-8000
  Plymouth (G-12560)
Crystal Falls Springs Inc............G 906 875-3191
  Crystal Falls (G-3608)

WATERPROOFING COMPOUNDS

Marshall Ryerson Co ....F 616 299-1751
  Grand Rapids (G-6645)

WAVEGUIDE STRUCTURES: Accelerating

Silent Call Corporation ....F 248 673-7353
  Waterford (G-17377)

WAX Sealing wax

M Argueso & Co Inc............C 231 759-7304
  Norton Shores (G-11771)

WEATHER STRIP: Sponge Rubber

Toyoda Gosei North Amer Corp ....C 248 280-2100
  Troy (G-16650)

WEATHER VANES

Whitehall Products LLC ....D 231 894-2688
  Whitehall (G-17682)

WEDDING CONSULTING SVCS

Sheri Boston............G 248 627-9576
  Ortonville (G-12203)

WELDING & CUTTING APPARATUS & ACCESS, NEC

Atlas Welding Accessories Inc ....D 248 588-4666
  Troy (G-16226)
Bielomatik Inc............E 248 446-9910
  New Hudson (G-11531)
GAL Gage Co ....E 269 465-5750
  Bridgman (G-1863)
Hilltop Manufacturing Co Inc ....G 248 437-2530
  New Hudson (G-11544)
Hmr Fabrication Unlimited Inc............F 586 569-4288
  Fraser (G-5664)
Lloyd Tool & Mfg Corp............E 810 694-3519
  Grand Blanc (G-5973)
Northwoods Manufacturing Inc ....G 906 779-2370
  Kingsford (G-9065)
Nortronic Company ....G 313 893-3730
  Detroit (G-4277)
Sas Global Corporation ....E 248 414-4470
  Warren (G-17230)
Welding Technology Corp ....F 248 477-3900
  Farmington Hills (G-5151)
Wolverine Hydraulics & Mfg Co............G 248 543-5261
  Madison Heights (G-10383)

WELDING EQPT

Airgas Usa LLC ....E 248 545-9353
  Ferndale (G-5255)
Alcotec Wire Corporation............D 800 228-0750
  Traverse City (G-15891)
All-Fab Corporation ....G 269 673-6572
  Allegan (G-147)
Amada Miyachi America Inc ....G 248 313-3078
  Wixom (G-17759)
Anroid Industries Inc............E 248 732-0000
  Auburn Hills (G-774)
Emabond Solutions LLC ....E 201 767-7400
  Auburn Hills (G-855)
Grossel Tool Co ....D 586 294-3660
  Fraser (G-5658)
Hobart Brothers Company ....F 231 933-1234
  Traverse City (G-15998)
Mid Michigan Repair Service ....G 989 835-6014
  Midland (G-10886)
MST Steel Corp ....F 586 359-2648
  Roseville (G-13842)
Nadex of America Corporation............E 248 477-3900
  Farmington Hills (G-5075)
Paslin Company ....E 586 755-3606
  Warren (G-17183)
Peak Industries Co Inc ....D 313 846-8666
  Dearborn (G-3747)
Purity Cylinder Gases Inc ....E 517 321-9555
  Lansing (G-9262)
RSI Global Sourcing LLC ....F 734 604-2448
  Novi (G-11988)
Santanna Tool & Design LLC ....D 248 541-3500
  Madison Heights (G-10348)
Thyssenkrupp System Engrg ....C 248 340-8000
  Auburn Hills (G-1019)
Tupes of Saginaw Inc ....F 989 799-1550
  Saginaw (G-14169)
Utica Enterprises Inc ....C 586 726-4300
  Troy (G-16670)
Welform Electrodes Inc ....D 586 755-1184
  Warren (G-17292)

WELDING EQPT & SPLYS WHOLESALERS

Airgas Usa LLC ....F 517 673-0997
  Blissfield (G-1712)
Assembly Technologies Intl............F 248 280-2810
  Troy (G-16224)
Atlas Welding Accessories Inc............D 248 588-4666
  Troy (G-16226)
Dytron Corporation............E 586 296-9600
  Fraser (G-5645)
Eureka Welding Alloys Inc ....E 248 588-0001
  Madison Heights (G-10250)
Fabrilaser Mfg LLC ....G 269 789-9490
  Marshall (G-10567)
Gnutti Carlo Usa Inc ....B 517 223-1059
  Webberville (G-17450)
K-C Welding Supply Inc ....F 989 893-6509
  Essexville (G-4874)
Marathon Weld Group LLC ....E 517 782-8040
  Jackson (G-8509)
Mid Michigan Repair Service ....G 989 835-6014
  Midland (G-10886)
Nortronic Company ....G 313 893-3730
  Detroit (G-4277)
Praxair Distribution Inc ....E 616 451-3055
  Grand Rapids (G-6762)
Purity Cylinder Gases Inc ....F 517 321-9555
  Lansing (G-9262)
South Park Welding Sups LLC ....F 810 364-6521
  Marysville (G-10618)
Tupes of Saginaw Inc ....F 989 799-1550
  Saginaw (G-14169)

WELDING EQPT & SPLYS: Arc Welders, Transformer-Rectifier

Cobra Truck & Fabrication ....G 734 854-5663
  Ottawa Lake (G-12260)
Saginaw Machine Systems Inc ....D 989 753-8465
  Saginaw (G-14140)

WELDING EQPT & SPLYS: Electrodes

Eureka Welding Alloys Inc ....E 248 588-0001
  Madison Heights (G-10250)
Huebner E W & Son Mfg Co Inc ....G 734 427-2600
  Livonia (G-9775)
Obara Corporation USA ....G 586 755-1250
  Novi (G-11962)
Tipaloy Inc ....F 313 875-5145
  Detroit (G-4400)

WELDING EQPT & SPLYS: Resistance, Electric

1271 Associates Inc ....D 586 948-4300
  Chesterfield (G-2730)
Arplas USA LLC ....G 888 527-5553
  Detroit (G-3878)
Comau LLC ....B 248 353-8888
  Southfield (G-14871)
Comau LLC ....C 248 305-9662
  Novi (G-11851)
Craft Industries Inc ....A 586 726-4300
  Shelby Township (G-14570)
Fair Industries LLC ....C 248 740-7841
  Troy (G-16359)
Great Lakes Laser Services ....G 248 584-1828
  Madison Heights (G-10262)
Hti Cybernetics Inc ....E 586 826-8346
  Sterling Heights (G-15369)
J W Holdings Inc ....E 616 530-9889
  Grand Rapids (G-6549)

WELDING EQPT & SPLYS: Spot, Electric

Knight Kraft Inc ....F 586 726-6821
  Sterling Heights (G-15390)
Mc REA Corporation ....G 734 420-2116
  Plymouth (G-12687)
Resistance Welding Machne & AC ....F 269 428-4770
  Saint Joseph (G-14337)
Sanyo Machine America Corp ....D 248 651-5911
  Rochester Hills (G-13510)

WELDING EQPT & SPLYS: Wire, Bare & Coated

Cor-Met Inc ....E 810 227-0004
  Brighton (G-1902)
D J and G Enterprise Inc ....G 231 258-9925
  Kalkaska (G-8941)
Dytron Corporation ....E 586 296-9600
  Fraser (G-5645)

WELDING EQPT REPAIR SVCS

Assembly Technologies Intl ....F 248 280-2810
  Troy (G-16224)

Mid Michigan Repair Service ....G....... 989 835-6014
Midland (G-10886)
Nortronic Company ....G....... 313 893-3730
Detroit (G-4277)

WELDING EQPT: Electric

Aro Welding Technologies Inc...............D....... 586 949-9353
Chesterfield (G-2742)
Fanuc America Corporation..................B....... 248 377-7000
Rochester Hills (G-13423)
K&S Consultants LLC............................G....... 269 240-7767
Buchanan (G-2122)
KIWOTO Inc...G....... 269 944-1552
Benton Harbor (G-1520)
Lakeland Elec Mtr Svcs Inc...................E....... 616 647-0331
Comstock Park (G-3493)
Owosso Automation Inc.......................G....... 989 725-8804
Owosso (G-12307)
Paslin Company.....................................A....... 586 758-0200
Warren (G-17182)
Paslin Company.....................................C....... 248 953-8419
Shelby Township (G-14660)
Utica International Inc ....C....... 586 726-4330
Troy (G-16671)

WELDING EQPT: Electrical

Welform Electrodes Inc........................D....... 586 755-1184
Warren (G-17292)

WELDING MACHINES & EQPT: Ultrasonic

Changer & Dresser Inc..........................G....... 256 832-4392
Novi (G-11847)
Gnutti Carlo Usa Inc ....B....... 517 223-1059
Webberville (G-17450)
Lastek Industries LLC............................G....... 586 739-6666
Shelby Township (G-14622)
Ms Plastic Welders LLC ....E....... 517 223-1059
Webberville (G-17452)

WELDING REPAIR SVC

A & B Welding & Fabricating ....G....... 231 733-2661
Muskegon (G-11255)
A M T Welding Inc..................................G....... 586 463-7030
Clinton Township (G-3028)
A R C Welding & Repair........................G....... 517 628-2475
Mason (G-10628)
Ability Mfg & Engrg Co..........................F....... 269 227-3292
Fennville (G-5169)
Able Welding Inc....................................G....... 989 865-9611
Saint Charles (G-14189)
Absolute Lser Wldg Sltions LLC ....F....... 586 932-2597
Sterling Heights (G-15249)
Ace Welding & Machine Inc ....F....... 231 941-9664
Traverse City (G-15887)
Achs Metal Products Inc.......................G....... 586 772-2734
Warren (G-16915)
Ackerman Brothers Inc ....G....... 989 892-4122
Bay City (G-1270)
Advanced Special Tools Inc..................C....... 269 962-9697
Battle Creek (G-1141)
Aegis Welding Supply ....G....... 248 475-9860
Auburn Hills (G-761)
Aggressive Tooling Inc..........................E....... 616 754-1404
Greenville (G-7122)
Airway Welding Inc................................F....... 517 789-6125
Jackson (G-8379)
All Phase Welding Service Inc..............G....... 616 235-6100
Grand Rapids (G-6159)
All Welding and Fabg Co Inc ....F....... 248 689-0986
Troy (G-16189)
Allegan Metal Fabricators Inc...............G....... 269 751-7130
Hamilton (G-7229)
Allied Machine Inc..................................E....... 231 834-0050
Grant (G-7077)
Allied Welding Incorporated ....G....... 248 360-1122
Commerce Township (G-3388)
Allynn Corp..G....... 269 383-1199
Kalamazoo (G-8676)
American Welding Inc ....G....... 734 279-1625
Petersburg (G-12434)
American Wldg & Press Repr Inc..........F....... 248 358-2050
Southfield (G-14837)
Amtrade Systems Inc ....G....... 734 522-9500
Livonia (G-9647)
Andritz Metals Inc..................................G....... 248 305-2969
Novi (G-11828)
Anywhere Welding.................................G....... 906 250-7217
Trenary (G-16149)
Austin Engineering.................................G....... 269 659-6335
Sturgis (G-15597)
Autorack Technologies Inc ....E....... 517 437-4800
Hillsdale (G-7516)
B & G Custom Works Inc ....E....... 269 686-9420
Allegan (G-150)
Bach Ornamental & Strl Stl Inc.............G....... 517 694-4311
Holt (G-7904)
Bairds Machine Shop ....G....... 269 795-9524
Middleville (G-10798)
Bakker Welding & Mechanics LLC........G....... 616 828-8664
Coopersville (G-3548)
Bannasch Welding Inc...........................F....... 517 482-2916
Lansing (G-9205)
Beattie Spring & Welding Svc...............G....... 810 239-9151
Flint (G-5386)
Beishlag Welding LLC ....G....... 231 881-5023
Elmira (G-4790)
Bel-Kur Inc..E....... 734 847-0651
Temperance (G-15823)
Blade Welding Service Inc ....G....... 734 941-4253
Van Buren Twp (G-16749)
Bnb Welding & Fabrication Inc..............G....... 810 820-1508
Burton (G-2145)
Bobs Welding & Fabricating ....F....... 810 324-2592
Kenockee (G-8984)
Bond Bailey and Smith Company ....G....... 313 496-0177
Detroit (G-3908)
Bopp-Busch Manufacturing Co.............E....... 989 876-7924
Au Gres (G-745)
Boyne Area Wldg & Fabrication ....F....... 231 582-6078
Boyne City (G-1816)
Brico Welding & Fab Inc.......................E....... 586 948-8881
Chesterfield (G-2746)
Buckeys Contracting & Service.............G....... 989 835-9512
Midland (G-10819)
Buiter Tool & Die Inc..............................E....... 616 455-7410
Grand Rapids (G-6239)
C & R Tool Die ....G....... 231 584-3588
Alba (G-112)
C C Welding...G....... 517 783-2305
Jackson (G-8398)
Cal Manufacturing Company Inc...........G....... 269 649-2942
Vicksburg (G-16832)
Cal Tolliver..G....... 586 790-1610
Clinton Township (G-3073)
Campbell Inc Press Repair....................E....... 517 371-1034
Lansing (G-9354)
Case Welding & Fabrication Inc ....G....... 517 278-2729
Coldwater (G-3294)
Century Tool Welding Inc.......................G....... 586 758-3330
Fraser (G-5637)
Clair Sawyer ....G....... 906 228-8242
Marquette (G-10523)
Cobra Torches Inc..................................G....... 248 499-8122
Lake Orion (G-9128)
Cobra Truck & Fabrication ....G....... 734 854-5663
Ottawa Lake (G-12260)
Colberg Radiator & Welding ....G....... 810 742-0028
Burton (G-2149)
Commercial Mfg & Assembly Inc ....E....... 616 847-9980
Grand Haven (G-6005)
Consolidated Metal Pdts Inc..................G....... 616 538-1000
Grand Rapids (G-6302)
Contract Welding and Fabg Inc ....E....... 734 699-5561
Van Buren Twp (G-16753)
Cooks Blacksmith Welding Inc..............G....... 231 796-6819
Big Rapids (G-1625)
Coppertec Inc...E....... 313 278-0139
Inkster (G-8226)
Corban Industries Inc.............................D....... 248 393-2720
Orion (G-12177)
Cramblits Welding LLC ....G....... 906 932-1908
Ironwood (G-8326)
Custom Design & Manufacturing ....F....... 989 754-9962
Carrollton (G-2484)
Customer Metal Fabrication Inc ....E....... 906 774-3216
Iron Mountain (G-8282)
Cw Champion Welding Alloys LLC ....G....... 906 296-9633
Lake Linden (G-9107)
Cw Creative Welding Inc ....G....... 586 294-1050
Fraser (G-5640)
Delducas Welding & Co Inc ....G....... 810 743-1990
Flint (G-5416)
Deltaic Welding Inc................................G....... 734 207-1080
Plymouth (G-12607)
Dickaren Inc..G....... 517 283-2444
Reading (G-13136)
Diversified Welding & Fabg ....G....... 616 738-0400
Holland (G-7609)
Dons Welding..G....... 989 792-0287
Saginaw (G-14028)
Dubois Production Services Inc............E....... 616 785-0088
Comstock Park (G-3480)
Dunns Welding Inc.................................G....... 248 356-3866
Southfield (G-14887)
Dutchmans Welding & Repair...............G....... 989 584-6861
Carson City (G-2488)
Eagle Welding LLC ....G....... 810 750-0772
Fenton (G-5201)
Envision Machine and Mfg LLC............G....... 616 953-8580
Holland (G-7624)
Erwin Quarder Inc..................................D....... 616 575-1600
Grand Rapids (G-6383)
Escanaba and Lk Superior RR Co.........G....... 906 786-9399
Escanaba (G-4828)
Express Machine & Tool Co..................G....... 586 758-5080
Warren (G-17027)
Express Welding Inc...............................G....... 906 786-8808
Escanaba (G-4829)
Fab-N-Weld Sheetmetal.........................G....... 269 471-7453
Berrien Springs (G-1594)
Figlan Welding ....G....... 586 739-6837
Shelby Township (G-14593)
Frankenmuth Industrial Svcs.................E....... 989 652-3322
Frankenmuth (G-5587)
Frankenmuth Welding & Fabg..............G....... 989 754-9457
Saginaw (G-14038)
Fraser Fab and Machine Inc..................E....... 248 852-9050
Rochester Hills (G-13428)
Gaastra Welding & Supply Inc..............G....... 906 265-4288
Iron River (G-8309)
Garden City Products Inc.......................F....... 269 684-6264
Niles (G-11614)
Gonzalez Welding ....G....... 248 469-3016
Waterford (G-17346)
Grand Rapids Metaltek Inc....................E....... 616 791-2373
Grand Rapids (G-6460)
Great Lakes Weld LLC...........................G....... 231 943-4180
Traverse City (G-15994)
Greens Welding & Repair Co................G....... 734 721-5434
Westland (G-17564)
Griptrac Inc...F....... 231 853-2284
Ravenna (G-13120)
H & H Welding & Repair LLC ....D....... 517 676-1800
Mason (G-10642)
H & M Machining Inc..............................F....... 586 778-5028
Roseville (G-13814)
H & M Welding and Fabricating............G....... 517 764-3630
Jackson (G-8461)
Hanks Welding Service Inc ....G....... 517 568-3804
Homer (G-7943)
Hel Inc..F....... 616 774-9032
Grand Rapids (G-6503)
Innovated Portable Weldin.....................G....... 586 322-4442
Casco (G-2501)
Integrity Fab & Machine Inc ....F....... 989 481-3200
Breckenridge (G-1843)
Iron Fetish Metalworks Inc.....................F....... 586 776-8311
Roseville (G-13822)
Iron Mikes WELding& Fabg ....G....... 810 234-2996
Flint (G-5448)
Ithaca Manufacturing Corp ....G....... 989 875-4949
Ithaca (G-8361)
J G Welding & Maintenance Inc............G....... 586 758-0150
China (G-2861)
Jerrys Welding Inc..................................G....... 231 853-6494
Ravenna (G-13121)
Jerz Machine Tool Corporation ....G....... 269 782-3535
Dowagiac (G-4545)
Jlore Welding ....G....... 989 402-7201
Sparta (G-15099)
JS Welding Inc ....G....... 517 451-2098
Britton (G-2018)
K & S Welding ....G....... 517 629-7842
Albion (G-126)
K-C Welding Supply Inc ....F....... 989 893-6509
Essexville (G-4874)
Kardux Welding & Fabricating...............G....... 231 873-4648
Hart (G-7375)
Kenowa Industries Inc...........................E....... 616 392-7080
Holland (G-7709)
Kent Welding Inc.....................................G....... 616 363-4414
Grand Rapids (G-6578)
Kinross Fab & Machine Inc....................E....... 906 495-1900
Kincheloe (G-9052)
Kk Welding Services Inc ....G....... 810 664-5564
North Branch (G-11662)
Koski Welding Inc...................................G....... 906 353-7588
Baraga (G-1105)

PRODUCT

Employee Codes: A=Over 500 employees, B=251-500
C=101-250, D=51-100, E=20-50, F=10-19, G=3-9
2020 Harris Michigan
Industrial Directory
1395

WELDING REPAIR SVC

Kriseler Welding Inc	Birch Run (G-1664)	G 989 624-9266
Kurrent Welding Inc	New Boston (G-11501)	G 734 753-9197
Lake Shore Services Inc	Wyandotte (G-17965)	F 734 285-7007
Lakeside Mechanical Contrs	Allegan (G-174)	E 616 786-0211
Laser Access Inc	Grand Rapids (G-6618)	C 616 459-5496
Laylin Welding Inc	Dowagiac (G-4547)	G 269 782-2910
Le Forges Pipe & Fab Inc	Ypsilanti (G-18084)	G 734 482-2100
Lewis Welding Inc	Wyoming (G-18015)	E 616 452-9226
Lincolns Welding	Springfield (G-15197)	G 269 964-1858
Loneys Welding & Excvtg Inc	Merritt (G-10764)	G 231 328-4408
Luans Welding LLC	Oak Park (G-12078)	G 248 787-5735
M & B Welding Inc	Marlette (G-10499)	G 989 635-8017
M P D Welding Inc	Orion (G-12184)	E 248 340-0330
Manistee Wldg & Piping Svc Inc	Manistee (G-10428)	G 231 723-2551
Manning Enterprises Inc	Paw Paw (G-12408)	E 269 657-2346
Marsh Industrial Services Inc	Kalkaska (G-8949)	F 231 258-4870
Marshall Welding & Fabrication	Marshall (G-10580)	G 269 781-4010
Material Handling Tech Inc	Ira (G-8260)	D 586 725-5546
Matteson Manufacturing Inc	Cadillac (G-2263)	G 231 779-2898
Matuschek Welding Products Inc	Sterling Heights (G-15413)	G 586 991-2434
Maxable Inc	Brooklyn (G-2039)	E 517 592-5638
Mayo Welding & Fabricating Co	Royal Oak (G-13948)	G 248 435-2730
McCullys Wldg Fabrication LLC	East Jordan (G-4639)	G 231 499-3842
Meccom Corporation	Detroit (G-4224)	C 313 895-4900
Mechanical Supply A Division	Escanaba (G-4842)	E 906 789-0355
Menominee Saw and Supply Co	Menominee (G-10748)	G 906 863-8998
Metal Worxs Inc	Clay (G-2999)	G 586 484-9355
Metal-Line Corp	Muskegon (G-11377)	E 231 723-7041
Metro Machine Works Inc	Romulus (G-13707)	D 734 941-4571
Mid Michigan Repair Service	Midland (G-10886)	G 989 835-6014
Mj-Hick Inc	West Branch (G-17513)	G 989 345-7610
Monarch Welding & Engrg Inc	Muskegon (G-11384)	F 231 733-7222
Morgans Welding	Osseo (G-12227)	G 517 523-3666
Mpd Welding - Grand Rapids Inc	Grand Rapids (G-6708)	G 616 248-9353
Nash Services	Dowagiac (G-4555)	G 269 782-2016
National Tool & Die Welding	Livonia (G-9861)	F 734 522-0072
Nelson Steel Products Inc	Holland (G-7753)	G 616 396-1515
Nicholson Terminal & Dock Co	River Rouge (G-13279)	C 313 842-4300
Northern Design Services Inc	Kalkaska (G-8956)	E 231 258-9900
Northern Machining & Repr Inc	Escanaba (G-4847)	E 906 786-0526
Oilpatch Machine Tool Inc	Mount Pleasant (G-11215)	G 989 772-0637
Olivet Machine Tool Engrg Co	Olivet (G-12143)	F 269 749-2671
Parker Tooling & Design Inc	Grand Rapids (G-6743)	G 616 791-1080
Parma Tube Corp	Sturgis (G-15626)	E 269 651-2351
Phil Brown Welding Corporation	Conklin (G-3531)	F 616 784-3046
Pin Point Welding Inc	Chesterfield (G-2817)	G 586 598-7382
Pinnacle Engineering Co Inc	Manchester (G-10410)	F 734 428-7039
Pipe Fabricators Inc	Kalamazoo (G-8853)	D 269 345-8657
Porter Steel & Welding Company	Muskegon (G-11404)	F 231 733-4495
Precision Polymer Mfg Inc	Kalamazoo (G-8860)	E 269 344-2044
Prima Welding & Experimental	Fraser (G-5709)	G 586 415-8873
Proto Tool & Gage Inc	Ypsilanti (G-18097)	G 734 487-0830
Pushard Welding LLC	Mattawan (G-10668)	G 269 760-9611
Pushman Manufacturing Co Inc	Fenton (G-5232)	E 810 629-9688
Rak Welding	Honor (G-7953)	G 231 651-0732
Ranger Tool & Die Co	Saginaw (G-14130)	E 989 754-1403
Rays Welding Co Inc	Berrien Springs (G-1600)	G 269 473-1140
Ridgeview Industries Inc	Grand Rapids (G-6826)	C 616 453-8636
Ripley Products Company Inc	Hancock (G-7256)	G 906 482-1380
Rise Machine Company Inc	Mount Pleasant (G-11225)	G 989 772-2151
Robotic Welded Parts Inc	Clare (G-2886)	E 989 386-5376
Ryson Tube Inc	Brighton (G-1987)	F 810 227-4567
Salenbien Welding Service Inc	Dundee (G-4599)	F 734 529-3280
Savs Welding Services Inc	Detroit (G-4354)	E 313 841-3430
Senneker Enterprises Inc	Dorr (G-4528)	E 616 877-4440
Set Enterprises of Mi Inc	Sterling Heights (G-15494)	C 586 573-3600
Sexton Enterprize Inc	Ferndale (G-5318)	E 248 545-5880
Sharpco Wldg & Fabrication LLC	Clare (G-2888)	G 989 915-0556
Sherwood Manufacturing Corp	Northport (G-11671)	E 231 386-5132
Smith Welding and Repair LLC	Lake Odessa (G-9119)	G 616 374-1445
SOO Welding Inc	Sault Sainte Marie (G-14474)	F 906 632-8241
Soutec Div of Andritz Bricmont	Novi (G-12001)	G 248 305-2955
Spaulding Machine Co Inc	Saginaw (G-14153)	E 989 777-0694
Specialty Welding	Grand Ledge (G-6116)	G 517 627-5566
Starlite Tool & Die Welding	Detroit (G-4376)	G 313 533-3462
Stus Welding & Fabrication	Holland (G-7818)	E 616 392-8459
Superior Welding & Mfg Inc	Hermansville (G-7467)	E 906 498-7616
Supreme Welding Inc	Clinton Township (G-3240)	G 586 791-8860
Sws - Trimac Inc	Saginaw (G-14162)	E 989 791-4595
Systems Unlimited Inc	Coldwater (G-3336)	E 517 279-8407
Tec-Option Inc	Blissfield (G-1727)	F 517 486-6055
Texas Metal Industries Inc	Warren (G-17265)	G 586 261-0090
Thermal Designs & Manufacturng	Roseville (G-13878)	E 586 773-5231
Tigmaster Co	Baroda (G-1132)	E 800 824-4830
Titanium Products Corp	Saint Clair (G-14235)	G 810 326-4325
Titus Welding Company	Farmington Hills (G-5141)	F 248 476-9366
Todds Welding Service Inc	Kalkaska (G-8964)	F 231 587-9969
Troy Tube & Manufacturing Co	Chesterfield (G-2851)	D 586 949-8700
Tumbleweed Weld/Fab	Dearborn Heights (G-3799)	G 313 277-6860
Tupes of Saginaw Inc	Saginaw (G-14169)	F 989 799-1550
V S America Inc	Troy (G-16674)	G 248 585-6715
Valiant Specialties Inc	Rochester Hills (G-13539)	G 248 656-1001
Van Straten Brothers Inc	Baraga (G-1116)	E 906 353-6490
Vochaska Engineering	South Haven (G-14782)	G 269 637-5670
Vs Products	Stanton (G-15230)	G 989 831-4861
Vulcanmasters Welding Inc	White Lake (G-17642)	F 313 843-5043
Walter Sappington	West Branch (G-17527)	G 989 345-1052
Warren Industrial Welding Co	Warren (G-17287)	F 586 756-0230
Warren Industrial Welding Co	Clinton Township (G-3258)	G 586 463-6600
Weld Tech Unlimited Inc	Cheboygan (G-2697)	G 231 627-7531
Weldcraft Inc	Livonia (G-10003)	G 734 779-1303
Welders & Presses Inc	Chesterfield (G-2856)	G 586 948-4300
Welding & Joining Tech LLC	Clarkston (G-2965)	G 248 625-3045
Welding Fabricating Inc	Wayland (G-17419)	G 616 877-4345
West Side Mfg Fabrication Inc	Wixom (G-17928)	F 248 380-6640
Wheelock & Son Welding Shop	Traverse City (G-16145)	G 231 947-6557
Whites Bridge Tooling Inc	Lowell (G-10045)	E 616 897-4151
Williams Welding and Repair	Jackson (G-8609)	G 517 783-3977
Wm Kloeffler Industries Inc	Marine City (G-10487)	E 810 765-4068
Yonker Welding Service Inc	Grand Rapids (G-7009)	G 616 534-2774

WELDING SPLYS, EXC GASES: Wholesalers

1271 Associates Inc	Chesterfield (G-2730)	D 586 948-4300
Airgas Usa LLC	Blissfield (G-1712)	F 517 673-0997
Eureka Welding Alloys Inc	Madison Heights (G-10250)	E 248 588-0001
SOO Welding Inc	Sault Sainte Marie (G-14474)	F 906 632-8241

WELDING TIPS: Heat Resistant, Metal

North East Fabrication Co Inc	Jonesville (G-8664)	F 517 849-8090
Praxair Distribution Inc	Macomb (G-10155)	F 586 598-9020
Scenario Systems Ltd	Shelby Township (G-14686)	G 586 532-1320
West Mich Auto Stl & Engrg Inc	Belding (G-1431)	E 616 560-8198

WELDMENTS

Anderson Welding & Mfg Inc	Chassell (G-2671)	F 906 523-4661
Metal Tech Products Inc	Detroit (G-4227)	E 313 533-5277
Michigan Metal Fabricators	Warren (G-17153)	G 586 754-0421
Mitchells Fabrication Co	Auburn Hills (G-946)	G 248 373-2199
Northern Fab & Machine LLC	Menominee (G-10754)	F 906 863-8506
Rendon & Sons Machining Inc	Gobles (G-5949)	F 269 628-2200
S N D Steel Fabrication Inc	Shelby Township (G-14684)	F 586 997-1500
Sfi Acquisition Inc	Farmington Hills (G-5122)	E 248 471-1500
Southfield Machining Inc	Detroit (G-4368)	G 313 871-8200

WET CORN MILLING

Darwin Sneller	Sebewaing (G-14514)	G 989 977-3718
Schuette Farms	Elkton (G-4783)	G 989 550-0563

PRODUCT SECTION WINDSHIELD WIPER SYSTEMS

WHEEL BALANCING EQPT: Automotive

AME For Auto Dealers Inc..............G...... 248 720-0245
 Auburn Hills *(G-768)*
International Wheel & Tire Inc............E...... 248 298-0207
 Farmington Hills *(G-5029)*

WHEELCHAIR LIFTS

Bach Mobilities Inc........................G...... 906 789-9490
 Escanaba *(G-4815)*
Bay Home Medical and Rehab Inc......E...... 231 933-1200
 Grandville *(G-7021)*
Wright & Filippis Inc......................F...... 517 484-2624
 Lansing *(G-9435)*

WHEELCHAIRS

Amigo Mobility Intl Inc....................D...... 989 777-0910
 Bridgeport *(G-1848)*
Clinton River Medical Pdts LLC..........G...... 248 289-1825
 Auburn Hills *(G-815)*
Innovative Cargo Systems LLC..........G...... 734 568-6084
 Lambertville *(G-9183)*
Miller Technical Services Inc............F...... 734 207-3159
 Plymouth *(G-12694)*
Reflection Medical Inc...................G...... 734 850-0777
 Temperance *(G-15841)*
Standing Company........................F...... 989 746-9100
 Saginaw *(G-14157)*

WHEELS

Bazzi Tire & Wheels......................G...... 313 846-8888
 Detroit *(G-3893)*
Chrome Wheel Exchange LLC..........G...... 810 360-0298
 Howell *(G-8024)*
Hot Wheels City Inc......................E...... 248 589-8800
 Madison Heights *(G-10268)*
Prime Wheel Corporation................G...... 248 207-4739
 Canton *(G-2418)*
Rucci Forged Wheels Inc................G...... 248 577-3500
 Sterling Heights *(G-15481)*
SL Wheels Inc.............................G...... 734 744-8500
 Livonia *(G-9932)*

WHEELS & GRINDSTONES, EXC ARTIFICIAL: Abrasive

Belanger Abrasives Inc..................D...... 248 735-8900
 Northville *(G-11679)*
Midwest Superior Abrasives.............G...... 248 202-0454
 Novi *(G-11949)*
Vachon Industries Inc....................F...... 517 278-2354
 Coldwater *(G-3340)*

WHEELS & PARTS

Mvc Holdings LLC........................F...... 586 491-2600
 Roseville *(G-13843)*
Oakley Industries Sub Assembly........D...... 586 754-5555
 Warren *(G-17176)*
Oakley Industries Sub Assembly........E...... 810 720-4444
 Flint *(G-5473)*
Oakley Sub Assembly Inc...............E...... 810 720-4444
 Flint *(G-5474)*
Superior Industries Intl Inc..............C...... 248 352-7300
 Southfield *(G-15038)*
Superior Industries N Amer LLC........E...... 248 352-7300
 Southfield *(G-15039)*
Tenneco Automotive Oper Co..........B...... 248 849-1258
 Northville *(G-11728)*

WHEELS, GRINDING: Artificial

Cincinnati Tyrolit Inc.....................C...... 513 458-8121
 Shelby Township *(G-14562)*
Diamondback Corp......................E...... 248 960-8260
 Commerce Township *(G-3399)*
Warren Abrasives Inc...................F...... 586 772-0002
 Warren *(G-17285)*

WHEELS: Abrasive

Dianamic Abrasive Products............F...... 248 280-1185
 Troy *(G-16316)*
Duramic Abrasive Products Inc........E...... 586 755-7220
 Warren *(G-17009)*
Helro Corporation........................G...... 248 650-8500
 Rochester *(G-13325)*
Inland Diamond Products Co..........E...... 248 585-1762
 Madison Heights *(G-10276)*

Krmc LLC..................................G...... 734 955-9311
 Romulus *(G-13698)*
Schaffner Manufacturing Co............G...... 248 735-8900
 Northville *(G-11724)*

WHEELS: Buffing & Polishing

Formax Manufacturing Corp............E...... 616 456-5458
 Grand Rapids *(G-6416)*

WHEELS: Disc, Wheelbarrow, Stroller, Etc, Stamped Metal

Meter USA LLC...........................F...... 810 388-9373
 Marysville *(G-10607)*

WHEELS: Iron & Steel, Locomotive & Car

Hayes Lemmerz Intl-GA LLC............C...... 734 737-5000
 Novi *(G-11898)*

WICKER PRDTS

Flanders Industries Inc..................C...... 906 863-4491
 Menominee *(G-10736)*

WICKING

Louis J Wickings.........................G...... 989 823-8765
 Vassar *(G-16813)*

WIGS & HAIRPIECES

Tru-Fit International Inc.................G...... 248 855-8845
 West Bloomfield *(G-17502)*

WIGS, DOLL: Hair

Wholesale Weave Inc...................F...... 800 762-2037
 Detroit *(G-4441)*

WINCHES

Leedy Manufacturing Co LLC..........D...... 616 245-0517
 Grand Rapids *(G-6624)*

WIND CHIMES

Bay Archery Sales Co...................G...... 989 894-5800
 Essexville *(G-4868)*

WINDINGS: Coil, Electronic

Cusolar Industries Inc...................E...... 586 949-3880
 Chesterfield *(G-2757)*
Pontiac Coil Inc..........................C...... 248 922-1100
 Clarkston *(G-2947)*
Prosys Industries Inc....................E...... 734 207-3710
 Canton *(G-2421)*
South Haven Coil Inc....................E...... 269 637-5201
 South Haven *(G-14771)*

WINDMILLS: Electric Power Generation

3dfx Interactive Inc......................E...... 918 938-8967
 Saginaw *(G-13990)*
Altagas Rnwable Enrgy Colo LLC......G...... 810 987-2200
 Port Huron *(G-12887)*
Mackinaw Power LLC...................G...... 906 264-5025
 Marquette *(G-10541)*
Spina Wind LLC..........................G...... 586 771-8080
 Warren *(G-17248)*

WINDMILLS: Farm Type

Harrison Partners Inv Group............G...... 419 708-8154
 Milan *(G-10940)*

WINDOW & DOOR FRAMES

Architectural Glass & Mtls Inc..........F...... 269 375-6165
 Kalamazoo *(G-8682)*
Lean Factory America LLC..............G...... 513 297-3086
 Buchanan *(G-2123)*
Mt Clemens Glass & Mirror Co........F...... 586 465-1733
 Clinton Township *(G-3182)*
Shure Star LLC...........................G...... 248 365-4382
 Dearborn *(G-3760)*
Shure Star LLC...........................E...... 248 365-4382
 Auburn Hills *(G-998)*
Tubelite Inc...............................D...... 800 866-2227
 Walker *(G-16880)*

WINDOW FRAMES & SASHES: Plastic

D & W Awning and Window Co..........E...... 810 742-0340
 Davison *(G-3645)*
Johns Glass...............................G...... 269 468-4227
 Coloma *(G-3357)*
Sunaire Window Manufacturing........G...... 248 437-5870
 Brighton *(G-1993)*
Vinyl Craft Window LLC.................F...... 231 832-8905
 Hersey *(G-7476)*
Weather King Windows Doors Inc....D...... 313 933-1234
 Farmington *(G-4915)*

WINDOW FRAMES, MOLDING & TRIM: Vinyl

American Standard Windows...........F...... 734 788-2261
 Farmington Hills *(G-4931)*
Antcliff Windows & Doors Inc..........F...... 810 742-5963
 Burton *(G-2144)*
Duo-Gard Industries Inc................D...... 734 207-9700
 Canton *(G-2367)*
Genex Window Inc......................G...... 586 754-2917
 Warren *(G-17055)*
Lites Alternative Inc.....................F...... 989 685-3476
 Rose City *(G-13762)*
May-Day Window Manufacturing.......G...... 989 348-2809
 Grayling *(G-7111)*
Modern Builders Supply Inc............G...... 517 787-3633
 Jackson *(G-8535)*
Overhead Door Company Alpena......G...... 989 354-8316
 Alpena *(G-305)*
Vinyl Tech Window Systems Inc.......F...... 248 634-8900
 Holly *(G-7901)*
Weather King Windows Doors Inc....E...... 248 478-7788
 Farmington *(G-4916)*
Weather Pane Inc.......................G...... 810 798-8695
 Almont *(G-270)*
Weathergard Window Company Inc....D...... 248 967-8822
 Oak Park *(G-12105)*

WINDOW FURNISHINGS WHOLESALERS

McDonald Wholesale Distributor........G...... 313 273-2870
 Detroit *(G-4222)*
Melody Digiglio...........................F...... 586 754-4405
 Warren *(G-17147)*
Triangle Window Fashions Inc..........E...... 616 538-9676
 Wyoming *(G-18036)*

WINDOW SQUEEGEES

Dorden & Company Inc.................G...... 313 834-7910
 Detroit *(G-4015)*

WINDOWS: Frames, Wood

Champion Window & Patio Room......E...... 616 554-1600
 Grand Rapids *(G-6270)*

WINDOWS: Louver, Glass, Wood Framed

Northview Window & Door..............G...... 231 889-4565
 Bear Lake *(G-1379)*

WINDOWS: Storm, Wood

Mlc Window Co Inc......................E...... 586 731-3500
 Shelby Township *(G-14642)*

WINDOWS: Wood

Andersen Corporation...................A...... 734 237-1052
 Livonia *(G-9648)*
Nowaks Window Door & Cab Co......G...... 989 734-2808
 Rogers City *(G-13617)*
Oxbowindo...............................E...... 248 698-9400
 White Lake *(G-17636)*

WINDSHIELD WIPER SYSTEMS

Everblades Inc............................G...... 906 483-0174
 Atlantic Mine *(G-735)*
Hudson Industries Inc...................G...... 800 459-1077
 Warren *(G-17082)*
Trico Products Corporation.............C...... 248 371-1700
 Rochester Hills *(G-13531)*
West/Win Ltd.............................G...... 734 525-9000
 Livonia *(G-10007)*
Wiper Shaker LLC.......................G...... 231 668-2418
 Williamsburg *(G-17724)*

Employee Codes: A=Over 500 employees, B=251-500
C=101-250, D=51-100, E=20-50, F=10-19, G=3-9

WINE CELLARS, BONDED: Wine, Blended

Aurora Cellars 2015 LLC	F	231 994-3188
Lake Leelanau (G-9099)		
Black & Red Inc	G	231 271-8888
Suttons Bay (G-15649)		
Evergreen Winery LLC	G	989 392-2044
Bay City (G-1311)		
Left Foot Charley	F	231 995-0500
Traverse City (G-16025)		
Stoney Acres Winery	G	989 356-1041
Alpena (G-317)		
Vineyard 2121 LLC	F	269 429-0555
Benton Harbor (G-1561)		
Wine Cellar Visions LLC	G	517 332-1026
East Lansing (G-4682)		

WIRE

Dw-National Standard-Niles LLC	C	269 683-8100
Niles (G-11610)		
Elco Enterprises Inc	E	517 782-8040
Jackson (G-8443)		
Marathon Weld Group LLC		517 782-8040
Jackson (G-8509)		
Morstar Inc	F	248 605-3291
Livonia (G-9848)		
National-Standard LLC	C	269 683-9902
Niles (G-11630)		
Whisper Creative Products Inc	G	734 529-2734
Dundee (G-4603)		

WIRE & CABLE: Aluminum

Anwc LLC	G	248 759-1164
Oakland Township (G-12110)		

WIRE & CABLE: Aluminum

Alcotec Wire Corporation	D	800 228-0750
Traverse City (G-15891)		
Madison Electric Company	E	586 294-8300
Fraser (G-5689)		
Turn Key Harness & Wire LLC	G	248 236-9915
Oxford (G-12379)		

WIRE & CABLE: Nonferrous, Automotive, Exc Ignition Sets

AGM Automotive LLC	D	248 776-0600
Farmington Hills (G-4923)		
Gemo Hopkins Usa Inc	G	734 330-1271
Auburn Hills (G-882)		
Kurabe America Corporation	A	248 939-5803
Farmington Hills (G-5039)		
Matrix Engineering and Sls Inc	G	734 981-7321
Canton (G-2399)		
Tsk of America Inc	F	517 542-2955
Litchfield (G-9612)		

WIRE & CABLE: Nonferrous, Building

Federal Screw Works	C	734 941-4211
Romulus (G-13677)		

WIRE & WIRE PRDTS

A A A Wire Rope & Splicing Inc	F	734 283-1765
Riverview (G-13288)		
AB Electrical Wires Inc	E	231 737-9200
Muskegon (G-11258)		
Accra-Wire Controls Inc	F	616 866-3434
Rockford (G-13555)		
Acme Wire & Iron Works LLC	F	313 923-7555
Detroit (G-3841)		
Ajax Spring and Mfg Co	F	248 588-5700
Madison Heights (G-10184)		
Ambassador Steel Corporation	E	517 455-7216
Lansing (G-9336)		
Apex Spring & Stamping Corp	D	616 453-5463
Grand Rapids (G-6171)		
Awcoa Inc	G	313 892-4100
Detroit (G-3887)		
Barbron Corporation	E	586 716-3530
Kalkaska (G-8937)		
Big Foot Manufacturing Co	F	231 775-5588
Cadillac (G-2231)		
Blade Welding Service Inc	G	734 941-4253
Van Buren Twp (G-16749)		
Bopp-Busch Manufacturing Co	E	989 876-7924
Au Gres (G-745)		
Burnside Industries LLC	D	231 798-3394
Norton Shores (G-11811)		
Clark Engineering Co	E	989 723-7930
Owosso (G-12282)		
Clipper Belt Lacer Company	D	616 459-3196
Grand Rapids (G-6281)		
Consolidated Clips Clamps Inc	D	734 455-0880
Plymouth (G-12601)		
Constructive Sheet Metal Inc	E	616 245-5306
Allendale (G-215)		
Cor-Met Inc	E	810 227-0004
Brighton (G-1902)		
Corsair Engineering Inc	D	810 234-3664
Flint (G-5404)		
Corsair Engineering Inc	F	810 233-0440
Flint (G-5403)		
Dare Products Inc	E	269 965-2307
Springfield (G-15190)		
Delta Tube & Fabricating Corp	E	248 634-8267
Holly (G-7874)		
Demlow Products Inc	F	517 436-3529
Clayton (G-3006)		
Deshler Group Inc	C	734 525-9100
Livonia (G-9706)		
E M I Construction Products	D	616 392-7207
Holland (G-7615)		
Essex Weld USA Inc	E	519 776-9153
Warren (G-17021)		
Fab-Jet Services LLC	E	586 463-9622
Clinton Township (G-3112)		
Flex-N-Gate Stamping LLC	F	810 772-1514
Warren (G-17040)		
Flex-N-Gate Stamping LLC	E	586 759-8900
Warren (G-17041)		
Franklin Fastener Company	E	313 537-8900
Redford (G-13162)		
Gill Corporation		616 453-4491
Grand Rapids (G-6439)		
Gill Corporation	B	616 453-4491
Grand Rapids (G-6438)		
Glassmaster Controls Co Inc	E	269 382-2010
Kalamazoo (G-8753)		
Hi-Lex America Incorporated		517 542-2955
Litchfield (G-9603)		
Kentwood Packaging Corporation	D	616 698-9000
Walker (G-16869)		
Leisure Studios Inc	C	269 428-5299
Saint Joseph (G-14326)		
Loudon Steel Inc	D	989 871-9353
Millington (G-10997)		
Lupaul Industries Inc	F	517 783-3223
Saint Johns (G-14286)		
M D Hubbard Spring Co Inc	E	248 628-2528
Oxford (G-12358)		
Maine Ornamental LLC	F	800 556-8449
White Pigeon (G-17652)		
Mason Tackle Company	E	810 631-4571
Otisville (G-12233)		
Mazzella Lifting Tech Inc	G	734 953-7300
Livonia (G-9829)		
Mazzella Lifting Tech Inc	G	248 585-1063
Madison Heights (G-10303)		
Memtech Inc	F	734 455-8550
Plymouth (G-12689)		
Michigan Rod Products Inc	D	517 552-9812
Howell (G-8065)		
Mid-West Spring & Stamping Inc	E	231 777-2707
Muskegon (G-11380)		
Mid-West Wire Products Inc	D	248 548-3200
Rochester Hills (G-13474)		
Milton Manufacturing Inc	E	313 366-2450
Detroit (G-4250)		
National-Standard LLC	C	269 683-9902
Niles (G-11630)		
Northern Cable & Automtn LLC	D	231 937-8000
Howard City (G-8004)		
Petschke Manufacturing Company	F	586 463-0841
Mount Clemens (G-11144)		
Pittsfield Products Inc	E	734 665-3771
Ann Arbor (G-593)		
Plastgage Cstm Fabrication LLC	G	517 817-0719
Jackson (G-8553)		
Precision Wire Forms Inc	E	269 279-0053
Three Rivers (G-15874)		
Production Fabricators Inc	E	231 777-3822
Muskegon (G-11407)		
Quality Filters Inc	F	734 668-0211
Ann Arbor (G-611)		
Quality Manufacturing	G	989 736-8121
Lincoln (G-9570)		
Ranch Life Plastics Inc	F	517 663-2350
Eaton Rapids (G-4731)		
Rapid River Rustic Inc	E	906 474-6404
Rapid River (G-13114)		
Rives Manufacturing Inc	E	517 569-3380
Rives Junction (G-13310)		
Rod Chomper Inc	F	616 392-9677
Holland (G-7790)		
Salco Engineering and Mfg Inc	F	517 789-9010
Jackson (G-8569)		
Ssw Holding Company LLC	G	231 780-0230
Ludington (G-10079)		
Sterling Die & Engineering Inc	E	586 677-0707
Macomb (G-10163)		
Stonebridge Industries Inc	A	586 323-0348
Sterling Heights (G-15513)		
Straits Steel and Wire Company	D	231 843-3416
Ludington (G-10080)		
Strema Sales Corp	G	248 645-0626
Bingham Farms (G-1660)		
TEC-3 Prototypes Inc	E	810 678-8909
Metamora (G-10782)		
Tigmaster Co	E	800 824-4830
Baroda (G-1132)		
Unified Screening and Crushing	F	888 464-9473
Saint Johns (G-14299)		
Wayne Wire A Bag Cmponents Inc	E	231 258-9187
Kalkaska (G-8966)		
Wayne Wire Cloth Products Inc	D	231 258-9187
Kalkaska (G-8967)		
Wayne Wire Cloth Products Inc	C	989 742-4591
Hillman (G-7510)		
West Michigan Wire Co	D	231 845-1281
Ludington (G-10087)		
Wire Fab Inc	F	313 893-8816
Detroit (G-4443)		

WIRE CLOTH & WOVEN WIRE PRDTS, MADE FROM PURCHASED WIRE

Northern Process Systems Inc	G	810 714-5200
Fenton (G-5227)		

WIRE CLOTH: Cylinder, Made From Purchased Wire

Anrod Screen Cylinder Company	E	989 872-2101
Cass City (G-2511)		
Beaden Screen Inc	E	810 679-3119
Croswell (G-3595)		

WIRE FABRIC: Welded Steel

Ernest Industries Acquisition,	E	734 595-9500
Westland (G-17554)		

WIRE FENCING & ACCESS WHOLESALERS

Bradys Fence Company Inc	G	313 492-8804
South Rockwood (G-14820)		
Midway Strl Pipe & Sup Inc	G	517 787-1350
Jackson (G-8527)		
Pro-Soil Site Services Inc	G	517 267-8767
Lansing (G-9260)		

WIRE MATERIALS: Steel

AG Manufacturing Inc	E	989 479-9590
Harbor Beach (G-7263)		
Breasco LLC	G	734 961-9020
Ypsilanti (G-18057)		
Jems of Litchfield Inc	F	517 542-5367
Litchfield (G-9605)		
Kendall Microtech Inc	G	517 565-3802
Stockbridge (G-15589)		
McClure Metals Group Inc	G	616 957-5955
Grand Rapids (G-6653)		
Philips Machining Company	F	616 997-7777
Coopersville (G-3568)		
Stephens Pipe & Steel LLC	E	616 248-3433
Grand Rapids (G-6892)		
Straits Steel and Wire Company	D	231 843-3416
Ludington (G-10080)		
Van Ron Steel Services LLC	F	616 813-6907
Marne (G-10515)		
Ventura Manufacturing Inc	C	616 772-7405
Zeeland (G-18192)		
West Michigan Wire Co	D	231 845-1281
Ludington (G-10087)		

WIRE PRDTS: Steel & Iron

Lake Michigan Wire LLC	F	616 786-9200
Holland (G-7717)		

PRODUCT SECTION

WIRE WHOLESALERS
Phoenix Wire Cloth Inc .... E 248 585-6350
  Troy *(G-16547)*

WIRE: Communication
Cardell Corporation .... F 248 371-9700
  Auburn Hills *(G-810)*

WIRE: Magnet
Weather-Rite LLC .... D 612 338-1401
  Comstock Park *(G-3520)*

WIRE: Mesh
Phoenix Wire Cloth Inc .... E 248 585-6350
  Troy *(G-16547)*
Richfield Industries Inc .... F 810 233-0440
  Flint *(G-5492)*

WIRE: Nonferrous
Active Solutions Group Inc .... G 313 278-4522
  Dearborn *(G-3671)*
Bulls-Eye Wire & Cable Inc .... G 810 245-8600
  Lapeer *(G-9445)*
Coppertec Inc .... E 313 278-0139
  Inkster *(G-8226)*
Engineered Prfmce Mtls Co LLC ...... G 734 904-4023
  Whitmore Lake *(G-17698)*
Ews Legacy LLC .... E 248 853-6363
  Rochester Hills *(G-13421)*
Glassmaster Controls Co Inc .... E 269 382-2010
  Kalamazoo *(G-8753)*
Hi-Lex America Incorporated .... B 269 968-0781
  Battle Creek *(G-1198)*
Madison Electric Company .... E 586 294-8300
  Fraser *(G-5689)*
Morrell Incorporated .... D 248 373-1600
  Auburn Hills *(G-949)*
Quad Electronics Inc .... D 800 969-9220
  Troy *(G-16571)*
Reeling Systems LLC .... G 810 364-3900
  Saint Clair *(G-14233)*
Sanderson Insulation .... G 269 496-7660
  Mendon *(G-10718)*
Sine Systems Corporation .... C 586 465-3131
  Clinton Township *(G-3230)*
Temprel Inc .... E 231 582-6585
  Boyne City *(G-1835)*

WIRE: Wire, Ferrous Or Iron
Wapc Holdings Inc .... F 586 939-0770
  Sterling Heights *(G-15543)*
WM Tube & Wire Forming Inc .... F 231 830-9393
  Muskegon *(G-11454)*

WOMEN'S & CHILDREN'S CLOTHING WHOLESALERS, NEC
Access Business Group LLC .... B 616 787-6000
  Ada *(G-3)*
Alticor Global Holdings Inc .... F 616 787-1000
  Ada *(G-5)*
Alticor Inc .... C 616 787-1000
  Ada *(G-6)*
Brintley Enterprises .... G 248 991-4086
  Detroit *(G-3918)*
Candela Products Inc .... G 248 541-2547
  Warren *(G-16976)*
Hemp Global Products Inc .... G 616 617-6476
  Holland *(G-7661)*

WOMEN'S & GIRLS' SPORTSWEAR WHOLESALERS
American Silk Screen & EMB .... E 248 474-1000
  Farmington Hills *(G-4930)*
Delux Monogramming Screen Prtg ... G 989 288-5321
  Durand *(G-4607)*

WOMEN'S CLOTHING STORES
Recollections Co .... E 989 734-0566
  Hawks *(G-7431)*
Reed Sportswear Mfg Co .... G 313 963-7980
  Detroit *(G-4337)*

WOMEN'S SPORTSWEAR STORES
Guess Inc .... F 517 546-2933
  Howell *(G-8046)*

WOOD CARVINGS, WHOLESALE
Dog Might LLC .... F 734 679-0646
  Ann Arbor *(G-423)*

WOOD CHIPS, PRODUCED AT THE MILL
Elenz Inc .... F 989 732-7233
  Gaylord *(G-5857)*
McPhails Pallets Inc .... F 810 384-6458
  Kenockee *(G-8985)*
Pulpwood & Forestry Products .... F 231 788-3088
  Muskegon *(G-11408)*

WOOD FENCING WHOLESALERS
Cherry Creek Post LLC .... G 231 734-2466
  Evart *(G-4880)*

WOOD PRDTS
Chivis Sportsman Cases .... G 231 834-1162
  Grant *(G-7079)*
Pwgg .... F 989 506-9402
  Weidman *(G-17461)*
Shelfactory LLC .... G 734 709-3615
  Dearborn *(G-3759)*

WOOD PRDTS: Applicators
Larson-Juhl US LLC .... F 734 416-3302
  Plymouth *(G-12671)*

WOOD PRDTS: Barrels & Barrel Parts
Biewer Sawmill Inc .... E 231 825-2855
  Mc Bain *(G-10679)*

WOOD PRDTS: Beekeeping Splys
Jonathan Showalter .... G 269 496-7001
  Mendon *(G-10714)*

WOOD PRDTS: Engraved
Czuk Studio .... G 269 628-2568
  Kendall *(G-8983)*

WOOD PRDTS: Hampers, Laundry
Home Niches Inc .... G 734 330-9189
  Ann Arbor *(G-494)*

WOOD PRDTS: Laundry
Custom Door Parts .... G 616 949-5000
  Byron Center *(G-2186)*
Innovtive Dsplay Solutions LLC .... F 616 896-6080
  Hudsonville *(G-8160)*
Whisper Creative Products Inc .... G 734 529-2734
  Dundee *(G-4603)*

WOOD PRDTS: Mantels
Bourne Specialties .... G 269 663-2187
  Edwardsburg *(G-4760)*
Mendota Mantels LLC .... G 651 271-7544
  Ironwood *(G-8335)*

WOOD PRDTS: Moldings, Unfinished & Prefinished
Doltek Enterprises Inc .... E 616 837-7828
  Nunica *(G-12036)*
Elenbaas Hardwood Incorporated .... G 616 669-3085
  Jenison *(G-8624)*
Elenbaas Hardwood Incorporated .... G 269 343-7791
  Kalamazoo *(G-8733)*
Fiber-Char Corporation .... E 989 356-5501
  Alpena *(G-289)*
Gl Millworks Inc .... F 734 451-1100
  Plymouth *(G-12627)*
Great Lake Woods Inc .... C 616 399-3300
  Holland *(G-7651)*
North Amrcn Mlding Lqdtion LLC .... E 269 663-5300
  Edwardsburg *(G-4771)*
Phil Elenbaas Millwork Inc .... E 616 791-1616
  Grand Rapids *(G-6754)*
Rosati Specialties LLC .... E 586 783-3866
  Clinton Township *(G-3214)*
Specialty Hardwood Moldings .... F 734 847-3997
  Temperance *(G-15844)*
Superior Wood Products Inc .... F 616 453-4100
  Allendale *(G-226)*
Tafcor Inc .... F 269 471-2351
  Berrien Springs *(G-1601)*

WOOD PRDTS: Mulch Or Sawdust
Applegate Insul Systems Inc .... E 517 521-3545
  Webberville *(G-17446)*
Enviro Industries Inc .... G 906 492-3402
  Paradise *(G-12382)*
Michigan Wood Fuels LLC .... F 616 355-4955
  Holland *(G-7747)*

WOOD PRDTS: Mulch, Wood & Bark
Beaver Creek Wood Products LLC .... E 920 680-9663
  Menominee *(G-10725)*
Kamps Inc .... E 313 381-2681
  Detroit *(G-4170)*
Kamps Inc .... D 616 453-9676
  Grand Rapids *(G-6569)*
Michigan Wood Fibers Llc .... G 616 875-2241
  Zeeland *(G-18164)*
Nu-Wool Co Inc .... D 800 748-0128
  Jenison *(G-8635)*
Rhino Seed & Landscape Sup LLC ... E 800 482-3130
  Wayland *(G-17411)*

WOOD PRDTS: Novelties, Fiber
Moonlight Tiffanies LLC .... G 517 372-2795
  Lansing *(G-9402)*

WOOD PRDTS: Oars & Paddles
Paddlesports Warehouse Inc .... G 231 757-9051
  Scottville *(G-14510)*
Paddletek LLC .... F 269 340-5967
  Niles *(G-11635)*

WOOD PRDTS: Outdoor, Structural
Open Air Lifestyles LLC .... F 586 716-2233
  Macomb *(G-10150)*
Ridgewood Stoves LLC .... G 989 488-3397
  Hersey *(G-7475)*

WOOD PRDTS: Paint Sticks
Anthony and Company .... F 906 786-7573
  Escanaba *(G-4813)*

WOOD PRDTS: Poles
Hydrolake Inc .... G 231 825-2233
  Reed City *(G-13215)*
Hydrolake Inc .... G 231 825-2233
  Mc Bain *(G-10681)*

WOOD PRDTS: Shoe & Boot Prdts
Veldheer Tulip Garden Inc .... D 616 399-1900
  Holland *(G-7844)*

WOOD PRDTS: Signboards
Wood Shop Inc .... G 231 582-9835
  Boyne City *(G-1838)*

WOOD PRDTS: Survey Stakes
Astro Wood Stake Inc .... G 616 875-8118
  Zeeland *(G-18114)*
Kells Sawmill Inc .... G 906 753-2778
  Stephenson *(G-15236)*
Klein Bros Fence & Stakes LLC .... G 248 684-6919
  Milford *(G-10967)*
Lakestate Industries Inc .... E 906 786-9212
  Escanaba *(G-4838)*

WOOD PRDTS: Trim
H & R Wood Specialties Inc .... E 269 628-2181
  Gobles *(G-5947)*
True Built Woodworking .... G 517 626-6482
  Eagle *(G-4617)*
True Built Woodworking .... G 989 587-3041
  Fowler *(G-5556)*

Employee Codes: A=Over 500 employees, B=251-500
C=101-250, D=51-100, E=20-50, F=10-19, G=3-9

WOOD PRDTS: Veneer Work, Inlaid

Oakwood Veneer Company .... F 248 720-0288
  Troy *(G-16531)*

WOOD PRODUCTS: Reconstituted

Abcor Industries LLC .... F 616 994-9577
  Holland *(G-7545)*
Alpena Biorefinery .... G 989 340-1190
  Alpena *(G-274)*
Brookfield Inc .... G 616 997-9663
  Coopersville *(G-3550)*
Dorel Home Furnishings Inc .... B 269 782-8661
  Dowagiac *(G-4540)*
Fultz Manufacturing Inc .... G 231 947-5801
  Traverse City *(G-15974)*
Hammond Publishing Company .... G 810 686-8879
  Mount Morris *(G-11161)*
Northeastern Products Corp .... E 906 265-6241
  Caspian *(G-2509)*
Weyerhaeuser Company .... C 989 348-2881
  Grayling *(G-7118)*
Wood-N-Stuff Inc .... G 616 677-0177
  Marne *(G-10516)*

WOOD TREATING: Bridges & Trestles

Midwest Timber Inc .... E 269 663-5315
  Edwardsburg *(G-4767)*

WOOD TREATING: Creosoting

Straits Corporation .... F 989 684-3584
  Bay City *(G-1361)*

WOOD TREATING: Flooring, Block

United Global Sourcing Inc .... F 248 952-5700
  Troy *(G-16663)*

WOOD TREATING: Structural Lumber & Timber

2nd Chance Wood Company .... G 989 472-4488
  Durand *(G-4604)*
Biewer Lumber LLC .... E 810 326-3930
  Saint Clair *(G-14206)*
Biewer Sawmill Inc .... E 231 825-2855
  Mc Bain *(G-10679)*
Charter Inds Extrusions Inc .... G 616 245-3388
  Grand Rapids *(G-6272)*
Hoover Treated Wood Pdts Inc .... E 313 365-4200
  Detroit *(G-4127)*

JKL Hardwoods Inc .... F 906 265-9130
  Iron River *(G-8312)*
John A Biewer Co of Illinois .... E 810 326-3930
  Saint Clair *(G-14224)*
John A Biewer Lumber Company .... B 810 329-4789
  Saint Clair *(G-14225)*
John A Biewer Lumber Company .... D 231 825-2855
  Mc Bain *(G-10682)*

WOODWORK & TRIM: Interior & Ornamental

A & L Woods .... G 616 374-7820
  Lake Odessa *(G-9110)*
Architectural Design Wdwrk Inc .... G 586 726-9050
  Shelby Township *(G-14548)*
Britten Woodworks Inc .... E 231 275-5457
  Interlochen *(G-8237)*
Creative Millwork Corporation .... G 231 526-0201
  Harbor Springs *(G-7280)*
Iannuzzi Millwork Inc .... F 586 285-1000
  Fraser *(G-5667)*
Michael Nadeau Cabinet Making .... G 989 356-0229
  Alpena *(G-298)*
Prime Wood Products Inc .... G 616 399-4700
  Holland *(G-7775)*
Valley Enterprises Ubly Inc .... F 989 269-6272
  Ubly *(G-16725)*

WOODWORK: Carved & Turned

Bainbridge Manufacturing Inc .... G 616 447-7631
  Grand Rapids *(G-6200)*
Chainsaw Man of Michigan .... G 586 977-7856
  Chesterfield *(G-2752)*

WOODWORK: Interior & Ornamental, NEC

Cedar Log Lbr Millersburg Inc .... F 989 733-2676
  Millersburg *(G-10991)*
Flairwood Industries Inc .... E 231 798-8324
  Norton Shores *(G-11756)*
Maw Ventures Inc .... E 231 798-8324
  Norton Shores *(G-11772)*

WOODWORK: Ornamental, Cornices, Mantels, Etc.

Wexford Wood Workings LLC .... G 231 876-9663
  Cadillac *(G-2285)*

WOVEN WIRE PRDTS, NEC

National Industrial Sup Co Inc .... F 248 588-1828
  Troy *(G-16520)*

Schroth Enterprises Inc .... F 586 939-0770
  Sterling Heights *(G-15486)*
Schroth Enterprises Inc .... E 586 759-4240
  Grosse Pointe Farms *(G-7187)*

WREATHS: Artificial

Northwoods Wreathing Company .... G 906 202-2888
  Gwinn *(G-7221)*
Wreaths By Heather RE Nee .... G 810 874-3119
  Swartz Creek *(G-15670)*

WRENCHES

Muskegon Tools LLC .... G 231 788-4633
  Muskegon *(G-11391)*

X-RAY EQPT & TUBES

I D Medical Systems Inc .... G 616 698-0535
  Grand Rapids *(G-6523)*
Kgf Enterprise Inc .... G 586 430-4182
  Columbus *(G-3380)*

YARN : Crochet, Spun

Woolly & Co LLC .... G 248 480-4354
  Birmingham *(G-1709)*

YARN MILLS: Texturizing, Throwing & Twisting

Ophir Crafts LLC .... G 734 794-7777
  Ann Arbor *(G-584)*

YARN WHOLESALERS

Woolly & Co LLC .... G 248 480-4354
  Birmingham *(G-1709)*

YARN: Knitting, Spun

True Teknit Inc .... E 616 656-5111
  Grand Rapids *(G-6938)*

YOGURT WHOLESALERS

General Mills Inc .... G 269 337-0288
  Kalamazoo *(G-8750)*

ZINC ORE MINING

Trelleborg Corporation .... G 269 639-9891
  South Haven *(G-14778)*